rma®

THE RISK MANAGEMENT ASSOCIATION

Serving the Financial Services Industry

# ANNUAL STATEMENT STUDIES

## Financial Ratio Benchmarks

# 2012
# 2013

# TABLE OF CONTENTS

*General Industries Format means that a valid construction NAICS was assigned to the subject companies contained in the sample; however, the financial statements were prepared using a general or traditional manufacturing or service industries presentation of results versus using a percentage-of-completion method of accounting. Industries found in the percentage-of-completion presentation follow the presentation used by RMA in the past.

## About RMA

Founded in 1914, The Risk Management Association is a not-for-profit, member-driven professional association whose sole purpose is to advance the use of sound risk principles in the financial services industry. RMA promotes an enterprise approach to risk management that focuses on credit risk, market risk, and operational risk.

Headquartered in Philadelphia, Pennsylvania, RMA has 2,500 institutional members that include banks of all sizes as well as nonbank financial institutions. They are represented in the association by 16,000 risk management professionals who are chapter members in financial centers throughout North America, Europe, and Asia/Pacific. Visit RMA on the Web at www.rmahq.org.

# RMA ACKNOWLEDGES AND THANKS THE FOLLOWING INSTITUTIONS, CONTRIBUTORS TO THE 2012 STATEMENT STUDIES DATA SUBMISSION PROGRAM.

## Alabama

BBVA Compass
Regions Financial Corp.

## Alaska

Northrim Bank

## Arizona

Arizona Business Bank
Johnson Bank
Simmons First National
    Corporation

## California

Bank of Agriculture & Commerce
Bank of the West
Citizens Business Bank
Farmers & Merchants Bank Of
    Central CA
Grand Point Bank
Pacific Enterprise Bank
Valley Community Bank
Wells Fargo Bank NA
Westamerica Bank

## Colorado

Alpine Bank
ANB Bank
CoBank
Colorado Business Bank
First National Bank of Durango
Sunflower Bank, N.A.

## Connecticut

Chelsea Groton Bank
Dime Bank
Jewett City Savings Bank
The Milford Bank

## Florida

Bank of Tampa
Seacoast National Bank

## Georgia

BrandBank
First American Bank & Trust
    Company

Georgia Bank & Trust Company
HeritageBank of the South
SunTrust Banks, Inc

## Hawaii

American Savings Bank
Central Pacific Bank
Finance Factors, Ltd.
First Hawaiian Bank
Hawaii National Bank

## Illinois

Albany Bank & Trust Company NA
Alpine Bank & Trust Co.
Busey Bank
First Midwest Bank
Glenview State Bank
National Republic Bank of Chicago

## Indiana

1st Source Bank
First Federal Savings Bank
Home Building Savings Bank
Lake City Bank
M & T Bank NA
Old National Bank
STAR Financial Bank

## Iowa

American Trust and Savings Bank
Farmers State Bank
Heartland Financial USA, Inc.
Security National Bank
Wells Fargo Bank NA

## Kansas

Alliance Bank
Emprise Bank
Fidelity Bank
INTRUST Bank, NA
Midland National Bank
Silver Lake Bank
Sunflower Bank, N.A.

## Kentucky

Community Trust Bank, Inc.
M & T Bank NA

## Louisiana

Red River Bank
South Louisiana Bank
Whitney Bank

## Maine

Gorham Savings Bank
Kennebunk Savings Bank
Norway Savings Bank
The First, NA

## Maryland

County First Bank
First United Bank & Trust
Frederick County Bank
New Windsor State Bank
OBA Bank
Sandy Spring Bank
Susquehanna Bank
The Bank of Glen Burnie

## Massachusetts

Bank of Canton
BankFive
Bristol County Savings Bank
Community Bank
Enterprise Bank & Trust Company
Lowell Five Cents Savings Bank
North Middlesex Savings Bank
Peoples Savings Bank
Rockland Trust Company
United Bank

## Michigan

Citizens Bank
Citizens National Bank Of
    Cheboygan
Commercial Bank
Huron Community Bank
Michigan Commerce Bank
The State Bank
United Bank of Michigan

## Minnesota

AgriBank FCB
American Bank of Saint Paul
Anchor Bank, N.A.
Beacon Bank
Citizens Independent Bank

Community Bank Corporation
Fidelity Bank
First Minnetonka City Bank
Home Federal Savings Bank
KleinBank
Merchants Bank, NA
Northeast Bank
StearnsBank, N.A.
Western Bank

## Mississippi

Hancock Bank
The Peoples Bank
Trustmark National Bank

## Missouri

Cass Commercial Bank
Central Bancompany
Commerce Bank NA
First Banks
Missouri Bank
Royal Banks of Missouri
Sunflower Bank, N.A.
Triad Bank

## Montana

First Interstate Bancsystem

## Nebraska

First National Bank & Trust Company
First National Bank North Platte
First National Bank of Omaha
Nebraska Bank of Commerce
Union Bank & Trust Company

## New Hampshire

Bank of New Hampshire
Connecticut River Bank, NA

## New Jersey

Harmony Bank
Peapack-Gladstone Bank
Sun National Bank
TD Banknorth NA
Union Center National Bank

## New York

Adirondack Bank
Alliance Bank, N.A.
Bank of Castile
CIT Group
Community Bank, N.A.
Elmira Savings Bank
HSBC Bank USA N.A.
M & T Bank NA
Mahopac National Bank
NBT Bank, N.A.

Pioneer Bank
Steuben Trust Company
The Adirondack Trust Company
The Bank of New York Mellon
Tioga State Bank
Tompkins Trust Company

## North Carolina

First Citizens Bank
NewBridge Bank

## North Dakota

Bell State Bank & Trust
State Bank & Trust

## Ohio

First Financial Bank, N.A.
FirstMerit Bank, N.A.
Liberty Savings Bank FSB
The Huntington National Bank

## Oklahoma

Stillwater National Bank

## Oregon

Bank of Astoria
Columbia State Bank
People's Bank of Commerce
West Coast Bank

## Pennsylvania

Bryn Mawr Trust
CNB Bank
Community Bank
DNB First, National Association
Dollar Bank, FSB
Ephrata National Bank
Fidelity Bank Pa SB
Fidelity Deposit & Discount Bank
First Columbia Bank & Trust Co.
First Commonwealth Bank
First Liberty Bank and Trust
First National Bank of
    Pennsylvania
Firstrust Bank
Fulton Bank
Luzerne Bank
National Penn Bank
New Tripoli Bank
Orrstown Bank
PennStar Bank, a division of NBT
    Bank, N.A.
PeoplesBank, a Codorus Valley
    Company
S&T Bank
Somerset Trust Company
Susquehanna Bank

The Bank of New York Mellon
Univest National Bank & Trust Co
VIST Financial Corp
Washington Financial
Woodlands Bank
York Traditions Bank

## Rhode Island

The Washington Trust Company

## South Carolina

Conway National Bank
First Citizens Bank
Greer State Bank
Harbor National Bank

## South Dakota

First Interstate Bancsystem
First National Bank in Sioux Falls
First National Bank South Dakota
First Premier Bank
Home Federal Bank

## Tennessee

First Farmers and Merchants Bank
First Tennessee Bank

## Texas

Amarillo National Bank
American Bank of Texas
Bank of America
Broadway Bank
Extraco Banks, N.A.
First State Bank Central Texas
Frost Bank
Southside Bank
Southwest Bank
WestStar Bank

## Utah

Zions Bancorporation

## Vermont

Community National Bank
Merchants Bank
National Bank of Middlebury
The Bank of Bennington

## Virginia

Capital One, N.A.
First Community Bank
Monarch Bank
Stellar One Bank
TowneBank
Virginia Commerce Bank
Virginia National Bank

## Washington

Bank of the Pacific
Banner Bank
Columbia State Bank
Northwest Farm Credit Services
Security State Bank
Sterling Savings Bank
Washington Trust Bank
Whidbey Island Bank

## West Virginia

United Bank

## Wisconsin

Associated Bank
Bank of Sun Prairie
First National Bank and Trust Co
First National Bank - Fox Valley
Horicon Bank
Johnson Bank
M&I Bank
TCF National Bank
The Business Bank

## Wyoming

First Interstate Bancsystem

Washington
Bank of the Pacific
Banner Bank
Columbia State Bank
Northwest Farm Credit Services
Security State Bank
Sterling Savings Bank
Washington Trust Bank
Whidbey Island Bank

West Virginia
United Bank

Wisconsin
Associated Bank
Bank of Sun Prairie
First National Bank and Trust Co
First National Bank - Fox Valley
Horicon Bank
Johnson Bank
M&I Bank
TCF National Bank
The Richland Bank

Wyoming
First Interstate BankSystem

# Introduction to
## *Annual Statement Studies:*
## *Financial Ratio Benchmarks,*
## *2012-2013*
## and
## General Organization of Content

The notes below will explain the presentation of *Annual Statement Studies: Financial Ratio Benchmarks,* describe how the book is organized, and answer most of your questions.

- **The Quality You Expect from RMA:** RMA is the most respected source of objective, unbiased information on issues of importance to credit risk professionals. For over 93 years, RMA's *Annual Statement Studies®* has been the industry standard for comparison financial data. Material contained in today's *Annual Statement Studies* was first published in the March 1919 issue of the *Federal Reserve Bulletin.* In the days before computers, the *Annual Statement Studies* data was recorded in pencil on yellow ledger paper! Today, it features data for over 808 industries derived <u>directly</u> from more than 280,000 statements of financial institutions' borrowers and prospects.

- **Data That Comes Straight from Original Sources:** The more than 280,000 statements used to produce the composites presented here come directly from RMA member institutions and represent the financials from their commercial customers and prospects. RMA does not know the names of the individual entities. In fact, to ensure confidentiality, company names are removed before the data is even delivered to RMA. The raw data making up each composite is not available to any third party.

- **Data Presented in Common Size:** *Annual Statement Studies: Financial Ratio Benchmarks* contains composite financial data. Balance sheet and income statement information is shown in common size format, with each item a percentage of total assets and sales. RMA computes common size statements for each individual statement in an industry group, then aggregates and averages all the figures. In some cases, because of computer rounding, the figures to the right of the decimal point do not balance exactly with the totals shown. A minus sign beside the value indicates credits and losses.

- **Includes the Most Widely Used Ratios:** Nineteen of the most widely used ratios in the financial services industry accompany the balance sheet information, including various types of liquidity, coverage, leverage, and operating ratios.

- **Organized by the NAICS for Ease of Use:** This edition is organized according to the North American Industry Classification System (NAICS), a product of the U.S. Office of Management and Budget. At the top of each page of data, you will find the NAICS.

- **Twenty Sections Outline Major Types of Businesses:** To provide further delineation, the book is divided into 20 sections outlining major lines of businesses. If you know the NAICS number you are looking for, use the NAICS-page guide provided in the front of this book. In general, the book is arranged in ascending NAICS numerical order. For your convenience, full descriptions of each NAICS are presented in this book. In addition, you will find a text-based index near the end of the book.

- **If You Do Not Know the NAICS Code You Are Looking for...** If you do not know the precise industry NAICS you are looking for, contact the Census Bureau at 1-888-75NAICS or naics@census.gov. Describe the activity of the establishment for which you need an industry code and you will receive a reply. Another source to help you assign the correct NAICS industry name and number can be found at www.census.gov/epcd/www/naics.html.

- **Can't Find the Industry You Want?** There are a number of reasons you may not find the industry you are looking for (i.e., you know you need industry xxxxxx but it is not in the product). Many times we have information on an industry, but it is not published because the sample size was too small or there were significant questions concerning the data. (For an industry to be displayed in the *Annual Statement Studies: Financial Ratio Benchmarks,* there must be at least 30 valid statements submitted to RMA.) In other instances, we simply do not have the data. Generally, most of what we receive is published.

- **Composite Data Not Shown?** When there are fewer than 10 financial statements in a particular asset or sales size category, the composite data is not shown because a sample this small is not considered representative and could be misleading. However, all the data for that industry is shown in the All Sizes column. The total number of statements for each size category is shown in bold print at the top of each column. In addition, the number of statements used in a ratio array will differ from the number of statements in a sample because certain elements of data may not be present in all financial statements. In these cases, the number of statements used is shown in parentheses to the left of the array.

- **Presentation of the Data on Each Page-Spread:** For all non-contracting spread statements, the data for a particular industry appears on both the left and right pages. The heading Current Data Sorted by Assets is in the five columns on the left side. The center section of the double-page presentation contains the Comparative Historical Data, with the All Sizes column for the current year shown under the heading 4/1/xx-3/31/xx. Comparable data from past editions of the *Annual Statement Studies: Financial Ratio Benchmarks* also appears in this section. Current Data Sorted by Sales is displayed in the five columns to the far right.

- **Companies with Less than $250 Million in Total Assets:** In our presentation, we used companies having less than $250 million in total assets—except in the case of contractors who use the percentage-of-completion method of accounting. *The section for contractors using the percentage-of-completion method of accounting contains data only sorted by revenue.* There is no upper limit placed on revenue size for any industry. Its information is found on only one page.

- **Page Headers:** The information shown at the top of each page includes the following: 1) the identity of the industry group; 2) its North American Industry Classification System (NAICS); 3) a breakdown by size categories of the types of financial statements reported; 4) the number of statements in each category; 5) the dates of the statements used; and 6) the size categories. For instance, 16 (4/1-9/30/11) means that 16 statements with fiscal dates between April 1 and September 30, 2011 make up part of the sample.

- **Page Footers:** At the bottom of each page, we have included the sum of the sales (or revenues) and total assets for all the financial statements in each size category. This data allows recasting of the common size statements into dollar amounts. To do this, divide the number at the bottom of the page by the number of statements in that size category. Then multiply the result by the percentages in the common size statement.
Please note: The dollar amounts will be an approximation because RMA computes the balance sheet and income statement percentages for each individual statement in an industry group, then aggregates and averages all the figures.

- **Our Thanks to CFMA:** RMA appreciates the cooperation of the Construction Financial Management Association in permitting us to reproduce excerpts from its *Construction Industry Annual Financial Survey*. This data complements the RMA contractor industry data. For more details on this data, please visit www.cfma.org.

- **Recommended for Use as General Guidelines:** RMA recommends you use *Annual Statement Studies: Financial Ratio Benchmarks* data only as general guidelines and not as absolute industry norms. There are several reasons why the data may not be fully representative of a given industry:

1. **Data Not Random**—The financial statements used in the *Annual Statement Studies: Financial Ratio Benchmarks* are not selected by any random or statistically reliable method. RMA member banks voluntarily submit the raw data they have available each year with no limitation on company size.

2. **Categorized by Primary Product Only**—Many companies have varied product lines; however, the *Annual Statement Studies: Financial Ratio Benchmarks* categorizes them by their primary product NAICS number only.

3. **Small Samples**—Some of the industry samples are small in relation to the total number of firms for a given industry. A relatively small sample can increase the chances that some composites do not fully represent an industry.

4. **Extreme Statements**—An extreme or outlier statement can occasionally be present in a sample, causing a disproportionate influence on the industry composite. This is particularly true in a relatively small sample.

5. **Operational Differences**—Companies within the same industry may differ in their method of operations, which in turn can directly influence their financial statements. Since they are included in the sample, these statements can significantly affect the composite calculations.

6. **Additional Considerations**—There are other considerations that can result in variations among different companies engaged in the same general line of business. These include different labor markets, geographical location, different accounting methods, quality of products handled, sources and methods of financing, and terms of sale.

For these reasons, RMA does not recommend using the *Annual Statement Studies: Financial Ratio Benchmarks* figures as absolute norms for a given industry. Rather, you should use the figures only as general guidelines and as a supplement to the other methods of financial analysis. RMA makes no claim regarding how representative the figures printed in this book are.

# DEFINITION OF RATIOS
## INTRODUCTION

On each data page, below the common-size balance sheet and income statement information, you will find a series of ratios computed from the financial statement data.

*Here is how these figures are calculated for any given ratio:*

1. The ratio is computed for each financial statement in the sample.

2. These values are arrayed (listed) in an order from the strongest to the weakest. In interpreting ratios, the "strongest" or "best" value is not always the largest numerical value, nor is the "weakest" always the lowest numerical value. (For certain ratios, there may be differing opinions as to what constitutes a strong or a weak value. RMA follows general banking guidelines consistent with sound credit practice to resolve this problem.)

3. The array of values is divided into four groups of equal size. The description of each ratio appearing in the *Statement Studies* provides details regarding the arraying of the values.

## What Are Quartiles?

Each ratio has three points, or "cut-off values," that divide an array of values into four equal-sized groups called quartiles, as shown below. The quartiles include the upper quartile, upper-middle quartile, lower-middle quartile, and the lower quartile. The upper quartile is the cut-off value where one-quarter of the array of ratios falls between it and the strongest ratio. The median is the midpoint—that is, the middle cut-off value where half of the array falls above it and half below it. The lower quartile is the point where one-quarter of the array falls between it and the weakest ratio. In many cases, the average of two values is used to arrive at the quartile value. You will find the median and quartile values on all *Statement Studies* data pages in the order indicated in the chart below.

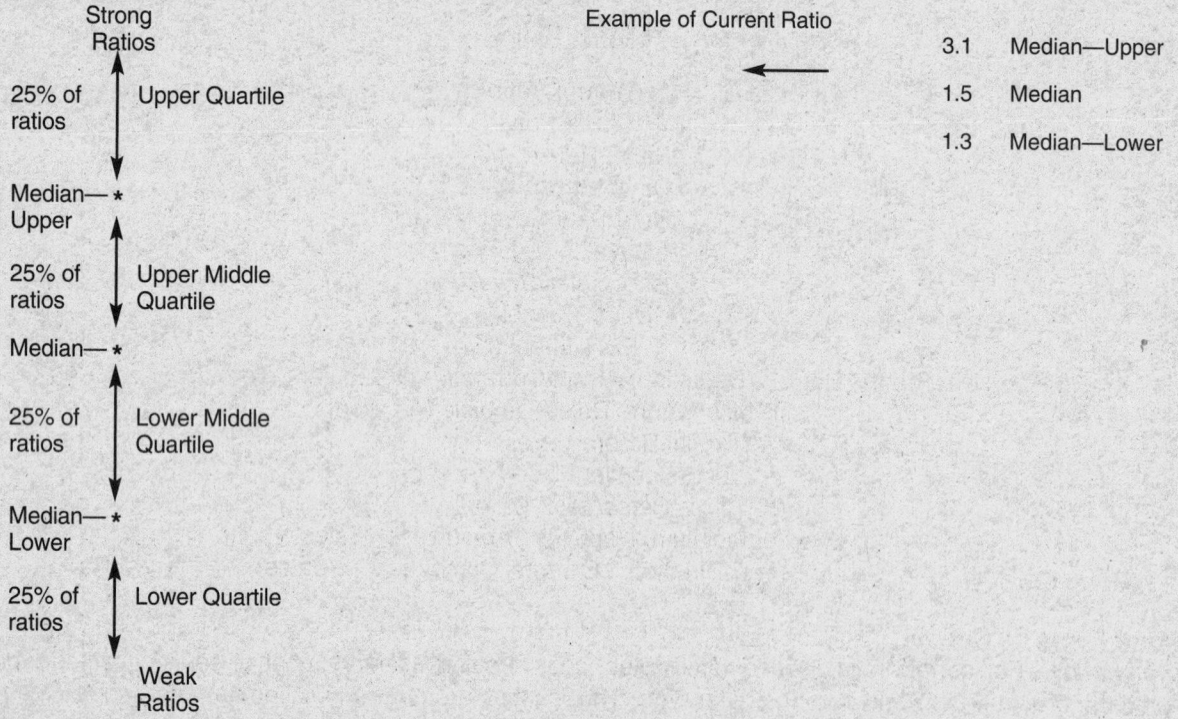

## Why Use Medians/Quartiles Instead of the Average?

There are several reasons medians and quartiles are used instead of an average. Medians and quartiles eliminate the influence an "outlier" (an extremely high or low value compared to the rest of the values). They also more accurately reflect the ranges of ratio values than a straight averaging method would.

It is important to understand that the spread (range) between the upper and lower quartiles represents the middle 50% of all the companies in a sample. Therefore, ratio values greater than the upper quartile or less than the lower quartile may begin to approach "unusual" values.

## Non-Conventional Values:
For some ratio values, you will occasionally see an entry that is other than a conventional number. These entries are defined as follows:

(1) <u>UND</u>—This stands for "undefined," the result of the denominator in a ratio calculation approaching zero.

(2) <u>NM</u>—This may occasionally appear as a quartile or median for the ratios sales/working capital, debt/worth, and fixed/worth. It stands for "no meaning" in cases where the dispersion is so small that any interpretation is meaningless.

(3) <u>999.8</u>—When a ratio value equals 1,000 or more, it also becomes an "unusual" value and is given the "999.8" designation. This is considered to be a close enough approximation to the actual unusually large value.

## Linear versus Nonlinear Ratios:
An array that is ordered in ascending sequence or in descending sequence is linear. An array that deviates from true ascending or true descending when its values change from positive to negative (low to high positive, followed by high to low negative) is nonlinear.

A specific example of a nonlinear ratio would be the Sales/Working Capital ratio. In other words, when the Sales/Working Capital ratio is positive, then the top quartile would be represented by the *lowest positive* ratio. However, if the ratio is negative, the top quartile will be represented by the *highest negative* ratio! In a nonlinear array such as this, the median could be either positive or negative because it is whatever the middle value is in the particular array of numbers.

### Nonlinear Ratios

Sales/Working Capital
Fixed/Worth
Debt/Worth

### Linear Ratios

Current Ratio
Quick Ratio
Sales Receivables
Days' Receivables
Cost of Sales/Inventory
Days' Inventory
Cost of Sales/Payables
Days' Payables
EBIT/Interest
Net Profit + Deprec, Depletion, Amort/Current Maturities Long-Term Debt
% Profits Before Taxes/Tangible Net Worth
% Profits Before Taxes/Total Assets
Sales/Net Fixed Assets
Sales/Total Assets
% Depreciation, Depletion, Amortization/Sales
% Officers', Directors', Owners' Compensation/Sales

## Important Notes on Ratios:
*Turnover Ratios*—For certain ratios (sales/receivables, cost of sales/inventory, cost of sales/payables) you will see two numbers, one in **BOLD** and one in regular type. These ratios are generally called turnover ratios. The number in **BOLD** represents **the number of days** and the number in regular type is the **number of times**. Please see the definition of sales/receivables on the following pages for a more complete description of the two types of calculations and what each means.

*Inventory Presentations*—**Inventory presentations** are based on fiscal year-end point-in-time balances, not averages. In addition, our data capture does not permit us to know what method of inventory accounting (LIFO or FIFO, for instance) was used.

The following ratios contained in the *Statement Studies* are grouped into five principal categories: liquidity, coverage, leverage, operating, and specific expense items.

# LIQUIDITY RATIOS

Liquidity is a measure of the quality and adequacy of current assets to meet current obligations as they come due. In other words, can a firm quickly convert its assets to cash—without a loss in value—in order to meet its immediate and short-term obligations? For firms such as utilities that can readily and accurately predict their cash inflows, liquidity is not nearly as critical as it is for firms like airlines or manufacturing businesses that can have wide fluctuations in demand and revenue streams. These ratios provide a level of comfort to lenders in case of liquidation.

## 1. Current Ratio

**How to Calculate:** Divide total current assets by total current liabilities.

$$\frac{\text{Total Current Assets}}{\text{Total Current Liabilities}}$$

**How to Interpret:** This ratio is a rough indication of a firm's ability to service its current obligations. Generally, the higher the current ratio, the greater the "cushion" between current obligations and a firm's ability to pay them. While a stronger ratio shows that the numbers for current assets exceed those for current liabilities, the composition and quality of current assets are critical factors in the analysis of an individual firm's liquidity.

The ratio values are arrayed from the highest positive to the lowest positive.

## 2. Quick Ratio

**How to Calculate:** Add cash and equivalents to trade receivables. Then, divide by total current liabilities.

$$\frac{\text{Cash \& Equivalents + Trade Receivables (net)}}{\text{Total Current Liabilities}}$$

**How to Interpret:** Also known as the "acid test" ratio, this is a stricter, more conservative measure of liquidity than the current ratio. This ratio reflects the degree to which a company's current liabilities are covered by its most liquid current assets, the kind of assets that can be converted quickly to cash and at amounts close to book value. Inventory and other less liquid current assets are removed from the calculation. Generally, if the ratio produces a value that's less than 1 to 1, it implies a "dependency" on inventory or other "less" current assets to liquidate short-term debt.

The ratio values are arrayed from the highest positive to the lowest positive.

## 3. Sales/Receivables

**How to Calculate:** Divide net sales by trade receivables.

$$\frac{\text{Net Sales}}{\text{Trade Receivables (net)}}$$

*Please note*—In the contractor section, both accounts receivable-progress billings and accounts receivable-current retention are included in the receivables figure used in calculating the revenues/receivables and receivables/payables ratios.

**How to Interpret:** This ratio measures the number of times trade receivables turn over during the year. The higher the turnover of receivables, the shorter the time between sale and cash collection.

For example, a company with sales of $720,000 and receivables of $120,000 would have a sales/receivables ratio of 6.0. This means receivables turn over six times a year. If a company's receivables appear to be turning more slowly than the rest of the industry, further research is needed and the quality of the receivables should be examined closely.

*Cautions*—A problem with this ratio is that it compares one day's receivables, shown at statement date, to total annual sales and does not take into consideration seasonal fluctuations. An additional problem in interpretation may arise when there is a large proportion of cash sales to total sales.

When the receivables figure is zero, the quotient will be undefined (UND) and represents the best possible ratio. The ratio values are therefore arrayed starting with undefined (UND) and then from the numerically highest value to the numerically lowest value. The only time a zero will appear in the array is when the sales figure is low and the quotient rounds off to zero. By definition, this ratio cannot be negative.

## 4. Days' Receivables

The sales/receivables ratio will have a figure printed in bold type directly to the left of the array. This figure is the days' receivables.

**How to Calculate the Days' Receivables:** Divide the sales/receivables ratio into 365 (the number of days in one year).

$$\frac{365}{\text{Sales/Receivable ratio}}$$

**How to Interpret the Days' Receivables:** This figure expresses the average number of days that receivables are outstanding. Generally, the greater the number of days outstanding, the greater the probability of delinquencies in accounts receivable. A comparison of a company's daily receivables may indicate the extent of a company's control over credit and collections.

*Please note*—You should take into consideration the terms offered by a company to its customers because these may differ from terms within the industry.

> For example, using the sales/receivable ratio calculated above, 365 ÷ 6 = 61 (i.e., the average receivable is collected in 61 days).

## 5. Cost of Sales/Inventory

**How to Calculate:** Divide cost of sales by inventory.

$$\frac{\text{Cost of Sales}}{\text{Inventory}}$$

**How to Interpret:** This ratio measures the number of times inventory is turned over during the year.

*High Inventory Turnover*—On the positive side, high inventory turnover can indicate greater liquidity or superior merchandising. Conversely, it can indicate a shortage of needed inventory for sales.

*Low Inventory Turnover*—Low inventory turnover can indicate poor liquidity, possible overstocking, or obsolescence. On the positive side, it could indicate a planned inventory buildup in the case of material shortages.

*Cautions*—A problem with this ratio is that it compares one day's inventory to cost of goods sold and does not take seasonal fluctuations into account. When the inventory figure is zero, the quotient will be undefined (UND) and represents the best possible ratio. The ratio values are arrayed starting with undefined (UND) and then from the numerically highest value to the numerically lowest value. The only time a zero will appear in the array is when the figure for cost of sales is very low and the quotient rounds off to zero.

*Please note*—For service industries, the cost of sales is included in operating expenses. In addition, please note that the data collection process does not differentiate the method of inventory valuation.

## 6. Days' Inventory

The days' inventory is the figure printed in bold directly to the left of the cost of sales/inventory ratio.

**How to Calculate the Days' Inventory:** Divide the cost of sales/inventory ratio into 365 (the number of days in one year).

$$\frac{365}{\text{Cost of Sales/Inventory ratio}}$$

**How to Interpret:** Dividing the inventory turnover ratio into 365 days yields the average length of time units are in inventory.

## 7. Cost of Sales/Payables

**How to Calculate:** Divide cost of sales by trade payables.

$$\frac{\text{Cost of Sales}}{\text{Trade Payables}}$$

*Please note*—In the contractor section, both accounts payable-trade and accounts payable-retention are included in the payables figure used in calculating the cost of revenues/payables and receivables/payables ratios.

**How to Interpret:** This ratio measures the number of times trade payables turn over during the year. The higher the turnover of payables, the shorter the time between purchase and payment. If a company's payables appear to be turning more slowly than the industry, then the company may be experiencing cash shortages, disputing invoices with suppliers, enjoying extended terms, or deliberately expanding its trade credit. The ratio comparison of company to industry suggests the existence of these or other possible causes. If a firm buys on 30-day terms, it is reasonable to expect this ratio to turn over in approximately 30 days.

*Cautions*—A problem with this ratio is that it compares one day's payables to cost of goods sold and does not take seasonal fluctuations into account. When the payables figure is zero, the quotient will be undefined (UND) and represents the best possible ratio. The ratio values are arrayed starting with undefined (UND) and then from the numerically highest to the numerically lowest value. The only time a zero will appear in the array is when the figure for cost of sales is very low and the quotient rounds off to zero.

## 8. Days' Payables

The days' payables is the figure printed in bold type directly to the left of the cost of sales/payables ratio.

**How to Calculate the Days' Payables:** Divide the cost of sales/payables ratio into 365 (the number of days in one year).

$$\frac{365}{\text{Cost of Sales/Payables ratio}}$$

**How to Interpret:** Division of the payables turnover ratio into 365 days yields the average length of time trade debt is outstanding.

## 9. Sales/Working Capital

**How to Calculate:** Divide net sales by net working capital (current assets less current liabilities equals net working capital).

$$\frac{\text{Net Sales}}{\text{Net Working Capital}}$$

**How to Interpret:** Because it reflects the ability to finance current operations, working capital is a measure of the margin of protection for current creditors. When you relate the level of sales resulting from operations to the underlying working capital, you can measure how efficiently working capital is being used.

*Low ratio* (close to zero)—A low ratio may indicate an inefficient use of working capital.

*High ratio* (high positive or high negative)—A very high ratio often signifies overtrading, which is a vulnerable position for creditors.

*Please note*—sales/working capital ratio is a nonlinear array. In other words, an array that is NOT ordered from highest positive to highest negative as is the case for linear arrays. The ratio values are arrayed from the lowest positive to the highest positive, to undefined (UND), and then from the highest negative to the lowest negative. If working capital is zero, the quotient is undefined (UND).

If the sales/working capital ratio is positive, then the top quartile would be represented by the *lowest positive* ratio. However, if the ratio is negative, the top quartile will be represented by the *highest negative* ratio! In a nonlinear array such as the sales/working capital ratio, the median could be either positive or negative because it is whatever the middle value is in the particular array of numbers.

*Cautions*—When analyzing this ratio, you need to focus on working capital, not on the sales figure. Although sales cannot be negative, working capital can be. If you have a large, positive working capital number, the ratio will be small *and* positive—which is good. Because negative working capital is bad, if you have a large, negative working capital number, the sales/working capital ratio will be small *and* negative—which is NOT good. Therefore, the lowest positive ratio is the best and the lowest negative ratio is the worst. If working capital is a small negative number, the ratio will be large, which is the best of the negatives.

# COVERAGE RATIOS

Coverage ratios measure a firm's ability to service its debt. In other words, how well does the flow of a company's funds cover its short-term financial obligations? In contrast to liquidity ratios that focus on the possibility of liquidation, coverage ratios seek to provide lenders a comfort level based on the belief the firm will remain a viable enterprise.

## 1. Earnings Before Interest and Taxes (EBIT)/Interest

**How to Calculate:** Divide earnings (profit) before annual interest expense and taxes by annual interest expense.

$$\frac{\text{Earnings Before Interest \& Taxes}}{\text{Annual Interest Expense}}$$

**How to Interpret:** This ratio measures a firm's ability to meet interest payments. A high ratio may indicate that a borrower can easily meet the interest obligations of a loan. This ratio also indicates a firm's capacity to take on additional debt.

*Please note*—Only statements reporting annual interest expense were used in the calculation of this ratio. The ratio values are arrayed from the highest positive to the lowest positive and then from the lowest negative to the highest negative.

## 2. Net Profit + Depreciation, Depletion, Amortization/Current Maturities Long-Term Debt

**How to Calculate:** Add net profit to depreciation, depletion, and amortization expenses. Then, divide by the current portion of long-term debt.

$$\frac{\text{Net Profit + Depreciation, Depletion, Amortization Expenses}}{\text{Current Portion of Long-Term Debt}}$$

**How to Interpret:** This ratio reflects how well cash flow from operations covers current maturities. Because cash flow is the primary source of debt retirement, the ratio measures a firm's ability to service principal repayment and take on additional debt. Even though it is a mistake to believe all cash flow is available for debt service, this ratio is still a valid measure of the ability to service long-term debt.

*Please note*—Only data for corporations with the following items was used:

    (1) Profit or loss after taxes (positive, negative, or zero).

    (2) A positive figure for depreciation/depletion/amortization expenses.

    (3) A positive figure for current maturities of long-term debt.

Ratio values are arrayed from the highest to the lowest positive and then from the lowest to the highest negative.

# LEVERAGE RATIOS

How much protection do a company's assets provide for the debt held by its creditors? Highly leveraged firms are companies with heavy debt in relation to their net worth. These firms are more vulnerable to business downturns than those with lower debt-to-worth positions. While leverage ratios help measure this vulnerability, keep in mind that these ratios vary greatly depending on the requirements of particular industry groups.

## 1. Fixed/Worth

**How to Calculate:** Divide fixed assets (net of accumulated depreciation) by tangible net worth (net worth minus intangibles).

$$\frac{\text{Net Fixed Assets}}{\text{Tangible Net Worth}}$$

**How to Interpret:** This ratio measures the extent to which owner's equity (capital) has been invested in plant and equipment (fixed assets). A lower ratio indicates a proportionately smaller investment in fixed assets in relation to net worth and a better "cushion" for creditors in case of liquidation. Similarly, a higher ratio would indicate the opposite situation. The presence of a substantial number of fixed assets that are leased—and not appearing on the balance sheet—may result in a deceptively lower ratio.

Fixed assets may be zero, in which case the quotient is zero. If tangible net worth is zero, the quotient is undefined (UND). If tangible net worth is negative, the quotient is negative.

*Please note*—Like the sales/working capital ratio discussed above, this fixed/worth ratio is a nonlinear array. In other words, it is an array that is NOT ordered from highest positive to highest negative as a linear array would be. The ratio values are arrayed from the lowest positive to the highest positive, to undefined (UND), and then from the highest negative to the lowest negative.

If the Fixed/Worth ratio is positive, then the top quartile would be represented by the *lowest positive* ratio. However, if the ratio is negative, the top quartile will be represented by the *highest negative* ratio! In a nonlinear array such as this, the median could be either positive or negative because it is whatever the middle value is in the particular array of numbers.

## 2. Debt/Worth

**How to Calculate:** Divide total liabilities by tangible net worth.

$$\frac{\text{Total Liabilities}}{\text{Tangible Net Worth}}$$

**How to Interpret:** This ratio expresses the relationship between capital contributed by creditors and that contributed by owners. Basically, it shows how much protection the owners are providing creditors. The higher the ratio, the greater the risk being assumed by creditors. A lower ratio generally indicates greater long-term financial safety. Unlike a highly leveraged firm, a firm with a low debt/worth ratio usually has greater flexibility to borrow in the future.

Tangible net worth may be zero, in which case the ratio is undefined (UND). Tangible net worth may also be negative, which results in the quotient being negative. The ratio values are arrayed from the lowest to highest positive, to undefined, and then from the highest to lowest negative.

*Please note*—Like the sales/working capital ratio discussed above, this debt/worth ratio is a nonlinear array. In other words, it is an array that is NOT ordered from highest positive to highest negative as a linear array would be. The ratio values are arrayed from the lowest positive to the highest positive, to undefined (UND), and then from the highest negative to the lowest negative.

If the debt/worth ratio is positive, then the top quartile would be represented by the *lowest positive ratio*. However, if the ratio is negative, the top quartile will be represented by the *highest negative ratio*! In a nonlinear array such as this, the median could be either positive or negative because it is whatever the middle value is in the particular array of numbers.

## OPERATING RATIOS

Operating ratios are designed to assist in the evaluation of management performance.

## 1. % Profits Before Taxes/Tangible Net Worth

**How to Calculate:** Divide profit before taxes by tangible net worth. Then, multiply by 100.

$$\frac{\text{Profit Before Taxes}}{\text{Tangible Net Worth}} \times 100$$

**How to Interpret:** This ratio expresses the rate of return on tangible capital employed. While it can serve as an indicator of management performance, you should always use it in conjunction with other ratios. Normally associated with effective management, a high return could actually point to an undercapitalized firm. Conversely, a low return that's usually viewed as an indicator of inefficient management performance could actually reflect a highly capitalized, conservatively operated business.

This ratio has been multiplied by 100 because it is shown as a percentage.

Profit before taxes may be zero, in which case the ratio is zero. Profits before taxes may be negative, resulting in negative quotients. Firms with negative tangible net worth have been omitted from the ratio arrays. Negative ratios will therefore only result in the case of negative profit before taxes. If the tangible net worth is zero, the quotient is undefined (UND). If there are fewer than 10 ratios for a particular size class, the result is not shown. The ratio values are arrayed starting with undefined (UND), then from the highest to the lowest positive values, and finally from the lowest to the highest negative values.

## 2. % Profits Before Taxes/Total Assets

**How to Calculate:** Divide profit before taxes by total assets and multiply by 100.

$$\frac{\text{Profit Before Taxes}}{\text{Total Assets}} \times 100$$

**How to Interpret:** This ratio expresses the pre-tax return on total assets and measures the effectiveness of management in employing the resources available to it. If a specific ratio varies considerably from the ranges found in this book, the analyst will need to examine the makeup of the assets and take a closer look at the earnings figure. A heavily depreciated plant and a large amount of intangible assets or unusual income or expense items will cause distortions of this ratio.

This ratio has been multiplied by 100 since it is shown as a percentage. If profit before taxes is zero, the quotient is zero. If profit before taxes is negative, the quotient is negative. These ratio values are arrayed from the highest to the lowest positive and then from the lowest to the highest negative.

## 3. Sales/Net Fixed Assets

**How to Calculate:** Divide net sales by net fixed assets (net of accumulated depreciation).

$$\frac{\text{Net Sales}}{\text{Net Fixed Assets}}$$

**How to Interpret:** This ratio is a measure of the productive use of a firm's fixed assets. Largely depreciated fixed assets or a labor-intensive operation may cause a distortion of this ratio.

This ratio is a measure of the productive use of a firm's fixed assets. Largely depreciated fixed assets or a labor-intensive operation may cause a distortion of this ratio.

They are arrayed from undefined (UND) and then from the highest to the lowest positive values.

## 4. Sales/Total Assets

**How to Calculate:** Divide net sales by total assets.

$$\frac{\text{Net Sales}}{\text{Total Assets}}$$

**How to Interpret:** This ratio is a general measure of a firm's ability to generate sales in relation to total assets. It should be used only to compare firms within specific industry groups and in conjunction with other operating ratios to determine the effective employment of assets.

The only time a zero will appear in the array will be when the net sales figure is low and the quotient rounds off to zero. The ratio values cannot be negative. They are arrayed from the highest to the lowest positive values.

## EXPENSE TO SALES RATIOS

The following two ratios relate specific expense items to net sales and express this relationship as a percentage. Comparisons are convenient because the item, net sales, is used as a constant. Variations in these ratios are most pronounced between capital- and labor-intensive industries.

## 1. % Depreciation, Depletion, Amortization/Sales

**How to Calculate:** Divide annual depreciation, amortization, and depletion expenses by net sales and multiply by 100.

$$\frac{\text{Depreciation, Amortization, Depletion Expenses}}{\text{Net Sales}} \times 100$$

## 2. % Officers', Directors', Owners' Compensation/Sales

**How to Calculate:** Divide annual officers', directors', owners' compensation by net sales and multiply by 100. Include total salaries, bonuses, commissions, and other monetary remuneration to all officers, directors, and/or owners of the firm during the year covered by the statement. This includes drawings of partners and proprietors.

$$\frac{\text{Officers', Directors', Owners' Compensation}}{\text{Net Sales}} \times 100$$

Only statements showing a positive figure for each of the expense categories shown above were used. The ratios are arrayed from the lowest to highest positive values.

# Explanation of Noncontractor Balance Sheet and Income Data

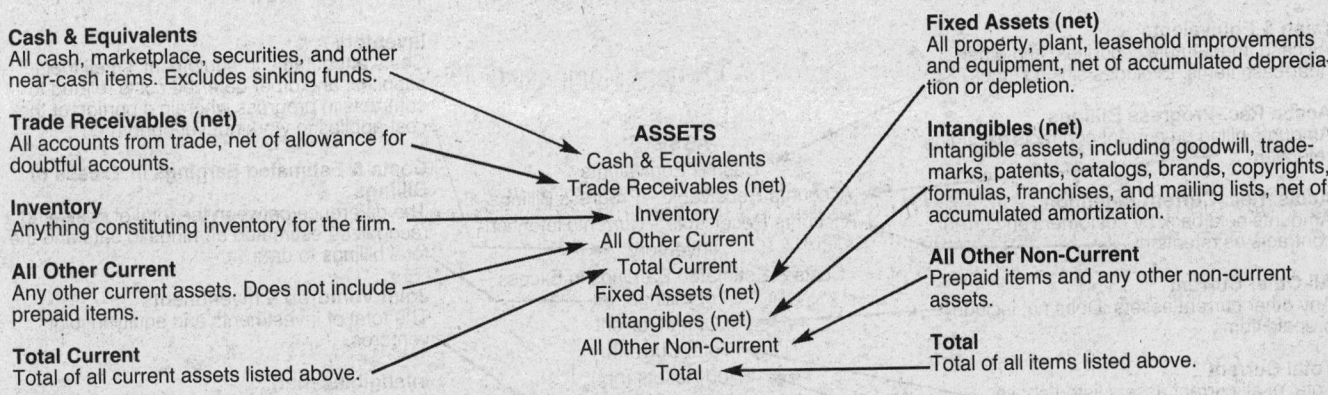

**Cash & Equivalents**
All cash, marketplace, securities, and other near-cash items. Excludes sinking funds.

**Trade Receivables (net)**
All accounts from trade, net of allowance for doubtful accounts.

**Inventory**
Anything constituting inventory for the firm.

**All Other Current**
Any other current assets. Does not include prepaid items.

**Total Current**
Total of all current assets listed above.

**ASSETS**
Cash & Equivalents
Trade Receivables (net)
Inventory
All Other Current
Total Current
Fixed Assets (net)
Intangibles (net)
All Other Non-Current
Total

**Fixed Assets (net)**
All property, plant, leasehold improvements and equipment, net of accumulated depreciation or depletion.

**Intangibles (net)**
Intangible assets, including goodwill, trademarks, patents, catalogs, brands, copyrights, formulas, franchises, and mailing lists, net of accumulated amortization.

**All Other Non-Current**
Prepaid items and any other non-current assets.

**Total**
Total of all items listed above.

**Notes Payable—Short Term**
All short-term note obligations, including bank and commercial paper. Does not include trade notes payable.

**Current Maturities—L/T/D**
That portion of long-term obligations that is due within the next fiscal year.

**Trade Payables**
Open accounts due to the trade.

**Income Taxes Payable**
Income taxes including current portion of deferred taxes.

**All Other Current**
Any other current liabilities, including bank overdrafts and accrued expenses.

**LIABILITIES**
Notes Payable-Short Term
Cur. Mat.-L/T/D
Trade Payables
Income Taxes Payable
All Other Current
Total Current
Long-Term Debt
Deferred Taxes
All Other Non-Current
Net Worth
Total Liabilities & Net Worth

**Total Current**
Total of all current liabilities listed above.

**Long-Term Debt**
All senior debt, including bonds, debentures, bank debt, mortgages, deferred portions of long-term debt, and capital lease obligations.

**Deferred Taxes**
All deferred taxes.

**All Other Non-Current**
Any other non-current liabilities, including subordinated debt, and liability reserves.

**Net Worth**
Difference between Total Liabilities and Total Assets. Minority interest is included here.

**Total Liabilities & Net Worth**
Total of all items listed above.

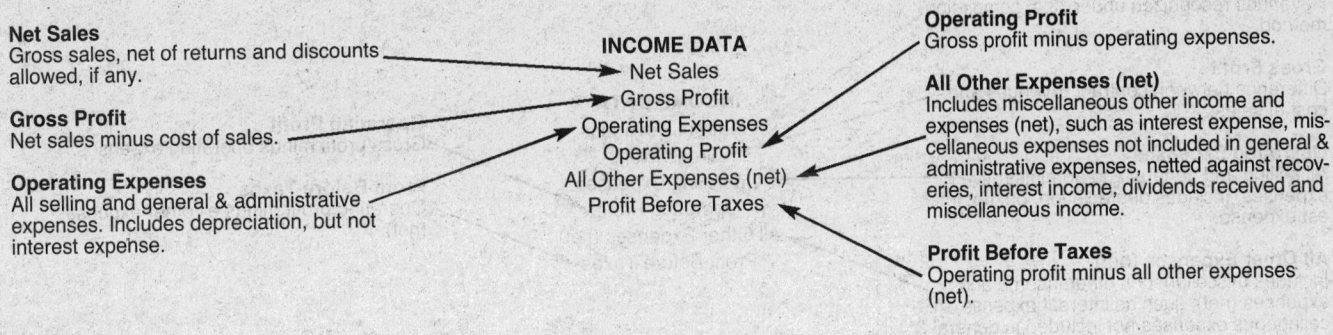

**Net Sales**
Gross sales, net of returns and discounts allowed, if any.

**Gross Profit**
Net sales minus cost of sales.

**Operating Expenses**
All selling and general & administrative expenses. Includes depreciation, but not interest expense.

**INCOME DATA**
Net Sales
Gross Profit
Operating Expenses
Operating Profit
All Other Expenses (net)
Profit Before Taxes

**Operating Profit**
Gross profit minus operating expenses.

**All Other Expenses (net)**
Includes miscellaneous other income and expenses (net), such as interest expense, miscellaneous expenses not included in general & administrative expenses, netted against recoveries, interest income, dividends received and miscellaneous income.

**Profit Before Taxes**
Operating profit minus all other expenses (net).

# Explanation of Contractor Percentage-of-Completion Basis of Accounting Balance Sheet and Income Data

**Cash & Equivalents**
All cash, marketable securities, and other near-cash items. Excludes sinking funds.

**Accts. Rec.-Progress Billings**
Amounts billed on current contracts excluding retention.

**Accts. Rec.-Current Retention**
Amounts held back by customers on current contracts as retention.

**All Other Current**
Any other current assets. Does not include prepaid items.

**Total Current**
Total of all current assets listed above.

**Fixed Assets (net)**
All property, plant, leasehold improvements and equipment, net of accumulated depreciation or depletion.

**All Other Non-Current**
Prepaid items and other non-current assets.

**Inventory**
Costs attributable to equipment, small tools, supplies, and other deferred costs related to contracts in progress wherein a portion of the cost applies to work not yet performed.

**Costs & Estimated Earnings in Excess of Billings**
The difference between the total of costs and recognized estimated earnings to date and the total billings to date.

**Joint Ventures & Investments**
The total of investments and equity in joint ventures.

**Intangibles (net)**
Intangible assets, including goodwill, trademarks, patents, catalogs, brands, copyrights, formulas, franchises, and mailing lists, net of accumulated amortization.

**Total**
Total of all items listed above.

### ASSETS
Cash & Equivalents
Accounts Receivable—Progress Billings
Accounts Receivable—Current Retention
Inventory
Costs & Estimated Earnings in Excess of Billings
All Other Current
Total Current
Fixed Assets (net)
Joint Ventures & Investments
Intangibles (net)
All Other Non-Current
Total

**Notes Payable—Short Term**
All short-term note obligations, including bank and commercial paper. Does not include trade notes payable.

**Accounts Payable—Trade**
Open accounts and note obligations due to the trade.

**Accounts Payable—Retention**
Amounts held back as retention in payments to subcontractors on current contracts.

**Long-Term Debt**
All senior debt, including bonds, debentures, bank debt, mortgages, deferred portions of long-term debt, and capital lease obligations.

**Deferred Taxes**
Total of all deferred taxes.

**All Other Non-Current**
Any other non-current liabilities, including subordinated debt, and liability reserves.

**Billings in Excess of Costs & Est. Earn.**
The difference between the total billings to date and the total of costs and recognized estimated earnings to date.

**Income Taxes Payable**
Income taxes including current portion of deferred taxes.

**Current Maturities—LTD**
That portion of long-term obligations that is due within the next fiscal year.

**All Other Current**
Any other current liabilities, including bank overdrafts and accrued expenses.

**Total Current**
Total of all current liabilities listed above.

**Net Worth**
Difference between total assets and total liabilities. Minority interest is included here.

**Total Liabilities & Net Worth**
Total of all items listed above.

### LIABILITIES
Notes Payable—Short Term
Accounts Payable—Trade
Accounts Payable—Retention
Billings in Excess of Costs & Estimated Earnings
Income Taxes Payable
Current Maturities—LTD
All Other Current
Total Current
Long-Term Debt
Deferred Taxes
All Other Non-Current
Net Worth
Total Liabilities & Net Worth

**Contract Revenues**
Revenues recognized under % of completion method.

**Gross Profit**
Difference between contract revenues and cost of sales.

**Operating Expenses**
All selling and general and administrative expenses. Includes depreciation, but not interest expense.

**All Other Expenses (net)**
Includes miscellaneous other income and expenses (net), such as interest expense, miscellaneous expenses not included in general & administrative expenses, netted against recoveries, interest income, dividends received and miscellaneous income.

**Operating Profit**
Gross profit minus operating expenses.

**Profit Before Taxes**
Operating profit minus all other expenses (net).

### INCOME DATA
Contract Revenues
Gross Profit
Operating Expenses
Operating Profit
All Other Expenses (net)
Profit Before Taxes

**For further analysis, please refer to *Industry Default Probabilities and Cash Flow Measures***

If you think *Financial Ratio Benchmarks* is a valuable resource, wait until you see its companion study. Now in its eleventh year and bigger than ever, *Industry Default Probabilities and Cash Flow Measures* is a major expansion of our *Annual Statement Studies.* It brings together the power of Moody's RiskCalc™ Plus for private companies and the *Statement Studies* database to provide distribution statistics on one-year and five-year probability of default estimates by industry. The new benchmarks add substantial value to the critical analysis of cash flow for private companies.

The latest edition of *Industry Default Probabilities and Cash Flow Measures* includes many new industries, stronger statements, five years of historical data sorted by assets and sales. In short, it is more like our traditional *Statement Studies*.

*Industry Default Probabilities and Cash Flow Measures* includes:

- Probability of default estimates on a percentage scale, mapped to a "dot" EDF bond rating scale.
- Cash flow measures on a common-size percentage scale. Ratios include:
  - Cash from Trading
  - Cash after Operations
  - Net Cash after Operations
  - Cash after Debt Amortization
  - Debt Service P&I Coverage
  - Interest Coverage (Operating Cash)
- Change in position, normalized, year over year, for eight financial statement line items. Ratios include:
  - Change in Inventory
  - Total Current Assets (TCA)
  - Total Assets (TA)
  - Retained Earnings (RE)
  - Net Sales (NS)
  - Cost of Goods Sold (CGS)
  - Profit before Interest & Taxes (PBIT)
  - Depreciation/Depletion/Amortization (DDA)
- Trend data available for the past five years.
- Other ratios.
  - Sustainable Growth Rate
  - Funded Debt/EBITDA
- Data arrayed by asset and sales size.

**Please see the next page for a copy of a sample report. Please see the inside front cover for more information, or upgrade now to eStatement Studies online database by calling 1-800-677-7621.**

# INDUSTRY DEFAULT PROBABILITIES
# AND CASH FLOW MEASURES
# SAMPLE REPORT

## AGRICULTURE—Soybean Farming  NAICS 111110

| Current Data Sorted by Assets | | | | | | Type of Statement | Comparative Historical Data | |
|---|---|---|---|---|---|---|---|---|
| | | 1 | 2 | | 2 | Unqualified | 4 | 6 |
| | 1 | 2 | 3 | | | Reviewed | 5 | 8 |
| | 5 | 3 | 1 | | | Compiled | 2 | |
| 2 | 1 | 2 | 1 | 1 | 2 | Tax Returns | 3 | 3 |
| 2 | | 8 | 4 | | | Other | 3 | 9 |
| | 3 (4/1-9/30/10) | | 40 (10/1/10-3/31/11) | | | | 4/1/06-3/31/07 | 4/1/07-3/31/08 |
| 0-500M | 500M-2MM | 2-10MM | 10-50MM | 50-100MM | 100-250MM | Assets Size | ALL | ALL |
| 4 | 7 | 16 | 11 | 1 | 4 | Number of Statements | 17 | 26 |
| % | % | % | % | % | % | **EXPECTED DEFAULT FREQUENCY** | % | % |
| | | .22 | .15 | | | Risk Calc Plus EDF | .19 | .26 |
| | | .36 | .21 | | | (1 yr) | .29 | .70 |
| | | .67 | .46 | | | | 1.37 | 1.69 |
| | | Baa1 1.72 | A1 .79 | | | **Moodys EDF** Rating (see note) | Baa1 1.37 | Baa2 2.34 |
| | | Baa2 2.80 | Baa1 1.53 | | | Risk Calc Plus | Baa2 2.33 | Baa3 4.02 |
| | | Ba1 4.77 | Baa3 3.12 | | | EDF (5 yr) | Ba2 7.51 | Ba3 8.02 |
| % | % | % | % | % | % | **CASH FLOW MEASURES** | % | % |
| | | | | | | Cash from Trading/Sales | | |
| | | 24.1 | 20.5 | | | Cash after | 10.4 | 19.7 |
| | | 11.3 | 5.8 | | | Operations/Sales | 1.6 | 2.4 |
| | | 6.3 | -5.2 | | | | -9.3 | -1.2 |
| | | 24.2 | 17.6 | | | Net Cash after | 13.6 | 21.2 |
| | | 10.4 | 6.0 | | | Operations/Sales | 2.1 | 2.2 |
| | | 6.0 | 3.0 | | | | -3.2 | -.8 |
| | | 9.2 | 6.0 | | | Net Cash after Debt | 4.6 | 7.2 |
| | | 3.1 | 1.8 | | | Amortization/Sales | -1.3 | .8 |
| | | -1.9 | -3.0 | | | | -13.3 | -5.9 |
| | | 4.3 | 4.3 | | | Debt Service | (16) 5.8 | (24) 3.6 |
| | | 2.0 | 1.5 | | | P&I Coverage | 1.3 | 1.2 |
| | | .8 | .9 | | | | -.4 | .0 |
| | | (15) 10.7 | 11.1 | | | Interest Coverage | (15) 5.6 | (21) 5.2 |
| | | 4.3 | 7.1 | | | (Operating Cash) | 1.5 | 1.1 |
| | | 3.1 | 3.2 | | | | -.6 | -.3 |
| | | (12) 37.2 | | | | Δ Inventory | (12) 92.6 | (14) 20.1 |
| | | 9.0 | | | | | 11.8 | .4 |
| | | -10.5 | | | | | -15.9 | -16.9 |
| | | 29.9 | 24.9 | | | Δ Total Current Assets | 37.0 | 53.6 |
| | | 8.9 | 22.9 | | | | 10.3 | 9.3 |
| | | -21.3 | 16.1 | | | | .5 | -11.6 |
| | | 28.9 | 16.5 | | | Δ Total Assets | 13.8 | 27.2 |
| | | 4.8 | 11.4 | | | | 8.1 | 6.3 |
| | | -1.0 | 6.0 | | | | -2.6 | -5.0 |
| | | (14) 60.9 | (10) 35.2 | | | Δ Retained Earnings | (16) 16.3 | (25) 40.3 |
| | | 33.4 | 27.7 | | | | -1.9 | 6.4 |
| | | 5.0 | 10.8 | | | | -23.6 | -8.2 |
| | | 63.2 | 10.5 | | | Δ Net Sales | 27.9 | 29.5 |
| | | 17.5 | 2.3 | | | | 10.9 | 12.6 |
| | | -.4 | -1.3 | | | | -10.4 | -.2 |
| | | | | | | Δ Cost of Goods Sold | | |
| | | 160.5 | 76.7 | | | Δ Profit before | 103.6 | 78.5 |
| | | 73.8 | 9.8 | | | Int. & Taxes | -.1 | -3.8 |
| | | -3.9 | -9.0 | | | | -66.2 | -47.6 |
| | | 17.3 | 8.1 | | | Δ Depr./Depl./Amort. | (16) 62.9 | (24) 123.4 |
| | | -5.7 | 3.4 | | | | 32.0 | 5.4 |
| | | -19.6 | -12.1 | | | | -39.1 | -33.7 |
| | | 31.0 | 27.0 | | | **RATIOS** | 36.7 | 30.6 |
| | | 11.1 | 10.1 | | | Sustainable | 4.4 | 6.2 |
| | | .4 | -59.0 | | | Growth Rate | -8.0 | -9.4 |
| | | 1.0 | .5 | | | | 1.1 | .5 |
| | | 3.8 | 1.4 | | | Funded Debt/EBITDA | 3.6 | 2.6 |
| | | 5.5 | 2.7 | | | | 30.2 | 7.5 |
| 2692M | 4512M | 146626M | 376639M | 57623M | 814847M | Net Sales ($) | 310277M | 1029126M |
| 1344M | 9688M | 85395M | 196364M | 88829M | 608288M | Total Assets ($) | 368953M | 393681M |

M = $ thousand   MM = $ million

**Note:** The ratings are Moody's.edf rating (e.g. Ba1.edf) and not Moody's Investor Services Long-Term Bond Ratings. If a number of statements appears for the Risk Calc Plus EDF (1 yr), it also applies to the (5 yr).

## AGRICULTURE—Soybean Farming  NAICS 111110

| Comparative Historical Data | | | Type of Statement | Current Data Sorted by Sales | | | | | |
|---|---|---|---|---|---|---|---|---|---|
| | | | | | | | | 4 | |
| 2 | 7 | 5 | Unqualified | 1 | | | | 3 | |
| 11 | | 5 | Reviewed | | | | | | |
| | 4 | 5 | Compiled | 1 | 1 | 1 | 2 | 2 | |
| 3 | 18 | 10 | Tax Returns | 6 | 2 | | 1 | 1 | |
| 3 | 17 | 18 | Other | 1 | 3 | 2 | 2 | 5 | 5 |
| 4/1/08- | 4/1/09- | 4/1/10- | | 3 (4/1-9/30/10) | | | 40 (10/1/10-3/31/11) | | |
| 3/31/09 | 3/31/10 | 3/31/11 | | 0-1MM | 1-3MM | 3-5MM | 5-10MM | 10-25MM | 25MM & OVER |
| ALL | ALL | ALL | Sales Size | | | | | | |
| 19 | 46 | 43 | Number of Statements | 9 | 6 | 3 | 5 | 8 | 12 |
| % | % | % | EXPECTED DEFAULT FREQUENCY | % | % | % | % | % | % |
| .28 | .29 | .21 | | | | | | | .17 |
| .36 (45) | .76 | .33 | Risk Calc Plus EDF | | | | | | .27 |
| 1.28 | 2.02 | 1.00 | (1 yr) | | | | | | 1.21 |
| Baa1 1.76 | Baa2 2.37 | Baa1 1.53 | Moodys EDF | | | | | | A2 .97 |
| Baa2 2.43 | Baa3 4.30 | Baa3 2.99 | Rating (see note)  Risk Calc Plus EDF (5 yr) | | | | | | Baa2 2.21 |
| Ba1 5.52 | Ba3 8.90 | Ba2 6.13 | | | | | | | Ba2 7.35 |
| % | % | % | CASH FLOW MEASURES | % | % | % | % | % | % |
| | | | Cash from Trading/Sales | | | | | | |
| 15.8 | 26.0 | 24.2 | | | | | | | 5.7 |
| 7.2 | 12.8 | 10.7 | Cash after Operations/Sales | | | | | | -.1 |
| 2.3 | 2.6 | 2.7 | | | | | | | -7.3 |
| 16.5 | 21.2 | 25.5 | | | | | | | 5.5 |
| 7.1 | 12.7 | 10.1 | Net Cash after Operations/Sales | | | | | | 2.8 |
| 1.4 | 2.6 | 2.9 | | | | | | | -7.0 |
| 4.3 | 9.8 | 9.5 | | | | | | | 1.3 |
| .4 | 2.7 | 2.9 | Net Cash after Debt Amortization/Sales | | | | | | -1.6 |
| -3.8 | -7.4 | -2.7 | | | | | | | -7.8 |
| 11.9 | 5.5 | 4.3 | | | | | | | 2.3 |
| (16) 3.1 | (40) 1.7 | (42) 1.5 | Debt Service P&I Coverage | | | | | | 1.0 |
| .4 | .3 | .9 | | | | | | | -7.4 |
| 17.8 | 13.5 | 9.6 | | | | | | | 9.5 |
| (15) 8.5 | (37) 5.6 | (41) 5.5 | Interest Coverage (Operating Cash) | | | | | | 2.6 |
| 1.6 | 1.1 | 2.3 | | | | | | | -7.4 |
| | 5.9 | 36.7 | | | | | | | 47.9 |
| | (24) -6.0 | (32) 3.1 | Δ Inventory | | | | | | (10) 7.9 |
| | -16.2 | -12.0 | | | | | | | -6.1 |
| 23.4 | 67.0 | 24.9 | | | | | | | 30.5 |
| 2.7 | 7.7 | 10.8 | Δ Total Current Assets | | | | | | 19.5 |
| -10.3 | -16.9 | -11.7 | | | | | | | 4.2 |
| 14.3 | 29.2 | 24.5 | | | | | | | 26.8 |
| 3.0 | .8 | 8.8 | Δ Total Assets | | | | | | 9.2 |
| -6.4 | -8.0 | .3 | | | | | | | 1.8 |
| 16.0 | 64.8 | 59.0 | | | | | | | 28.3 |
| 8.1 | 2.1 | (40) 27.7 | Δ Retained Earnings | | | | | | (11) 12.3 |
| -17.6 | -7.4 | 7.0 | | | | | | | 6.5 |
| 18.1 | 13.1 | 29.5 | | | | | | | 18.8 |
| 8.3 | 3.3 | 7.0 | Δ Net Sales | | | | | | 6.3 |
| -6.8 | -16.8 | -1.3 | | | | | | | -1.1 |
| | | | Δ Cost of Goods Sold | | | | | | |
| 1.6 | 83.6 | 138.7 | | | | | | | 212.7 |
| -16.2 | (45) 1.8 | 36.7 | Δ Profit before Int. & Taxes | | | | | | 48.5 |
| -80.1 | -68.1 | -17.7 | | | | | | | -4.3 |
| 36.6 | 38.2 | 19.4 | | | | | | | 8.1 |
| (16) 11.8 | (42) -1.0 | (40) -.2 | Δ Depr./Depl./Amort. | | | | | | (11) 2.3 |
| -4.7 | -66.8 | -16.7 | | | | | | | -12.1 |
| 16.4 | 13.2 | 27.0 | RATIOS | | | | | | 22.2 |
| 9.2 | 1.3 | 9.0 | Sustainable Growth Rate | | | | | | 10.8 |
| -15.4 | -9.8 | .0 | | | | | | | 7.3 |
| .1 | .2 | .7 | | | | | | | .5 |
| 1.0 | 1.6 | 3.4 | Funded Debt/EBITDA | | | | | | 2.1 |
| 3.2 | 5.8 | 5.7 | | | | | | | 5.6 |
| 518971M | 419387M | 1402939M | Net Sales ($) | 3721M | 9642M | 11984M | 38242M | 129560M | 1209790M |
| 496803M | 303566M | 989908M | Total Assets ($) | 20361M | 17721M | 9448M | 41212M | 58979M | 842187M |

© RMA 2011
M = $ thousand   MM = $ million
See Pages 00 through 00 for Explanation of Ratios and Data
Note: The ratings are Moody's.edf rating (e.g. Ba1.edf) and not Moody's Investor Services Long-Term Bond Ratings. If a number of statements appears for the Risk Calc Plus EDF (1 yr), it also applies to the (5 yr).

# NAICS CODES APPEARING IN THE STATEMENT STUDIES

| NAICS Codes | Page | NAICS Codes | Page | NAICS Codes | Page |
|---|---|---|---|---|---|
| 111110 | 100-101 | 238120 | 214-215, 1722 | 314999 | 324-325 |
| 111140 | 102-103 | 238130 | 216-217 | 315211 | 326-327 |
| 111150 | 104-105 | 238140 | 218-219, 1723 | 315212 | 328-329 |
| 111199 | 106-107 | 238150 | 220-221, 1724 | 315222 | 330-331 |
| 111211 | 108-109 | 238160 | 222-223, 1725 | 315228 | 332-333 |
| 111219 | 110-111 | 238190 | 224-225 | 315233 | 334-335 |
| 111310 | 112-113 | 238210 | 226-227, 1726 | 315239 | 336-337 |
| 111331 | 114-115 | 238220 | 228-229, 1727 | 315299 | 338-339 |
| 111332 | 116-117 | 238290 | 230-231 | 315999 | 340-341 |
| 111335 | 118-119 | 238310 | 232-233, 1728 | 316110 | 342-343 |
| 111411 | 120-121 | 238320 | 234-235, 1729 | 321113 | 344-345 |
| 111421 | 122-123 | 238330 | 236-237, 1730 | 321114 | 346-347 |
| 111910 | 124-125 | 238340 | 238-239 | 321211 | 348-349 |
| 111920 | 126-127 | 238350 | 240-241 | 321214 | 350-351 |
| 111998 | 128-129 | 238390 | 242-243 | 321911 | 352-353 |
| 112111 | 130-131 | 238910 | 244-245, 1731 | 321912 | 354-355 |
| 112112 | 132-133 | 238990 | 246-247, 1732 | 321918 | 356-357 |
| 112120 | 134-135 | 311119 | 250-251 | 321920 | 358-359 |
| 112210 | 136-137 | 311211 | 252-253 | 321991 | 360-361 |
| 112310 | 138-139 | 311330 | 254-255 | 321992 | 362-363 |
| 112920 | 140-141 | 311411 | 256-257 | 321999 | 364-365 |
| 113110 | 142-143 | 311412 | 258-259 | 322121 | 366-367 |
| 113310 | 144-145 | 311421 | 260-261 | 322211 | 368-369 |
| 114111 | 146-147 | 311423 | 262-263 | 322212 | 370-371 |
| 114112 | 148-149 | 311511 | 264-265 | 322213 | 372-373 |
| 115111 | 150-151 | 311513 | 266-267 | 322221 | 374-375 |
| 115112 | 152-153 | 311520 | 268-269 | 322222 | 376-377 |
| 115114 | 154-155 | 311611 | 270-271 | 322223 | 378-379 |
| 115116 | 156-157 | 311612 | 272-273 | 322232 | 380-381 |
| 115210 | 158-159 | 311613 | 274-275 | 322291 | 382-383 |
| 211111 | 162-163 | 311615 | 276-277 | 322299 | 384-385 |
| 212111 | 164-165 | 311712 | 278-279 | 323110 | 386-387 |
| 212312 | 166-167 | 311811 | 280-281 | 323111 | 388-389 |
| 212319 | 168-169 | 311812 | 282-283 | 323112 | 390-391 |
| 212321 | 170-171 | 311821 | 284-285 | 323113 | 392-393 |
| 213111 | 172-173 | 311911 | 286-287 | 323114 | 394-395 |
| 213112 | 174-175, 1710 | 311919 | 288-289 | 323115 | 396-397 |
| 221111 | 178-179 | 311920 | 290-291 | 323116 | 398-399 |
| 221122 | 180-181 | 311930 | 292-293 | 323117 | 400-401 |
| 221210 | 182-183 | 311941 | 294-295 | 323119 | 402-403 |
| 221310 | 184-185 | 311942 | 296-297 | 323121 | 404-405 |
| 236115 | 188-189, 1711 | 311991 | 298-299 | 323122 | 406-407 |
| 236116 | 190-191, 1712 | 311999 | 300-301 | 324110 | 408-409 |
| 236117 | 192-193, 1713 | 312111 | 302-303 | 324121 | 410-411 |
| 236118 | 194-195, 1714 | 312112 | 304-305 | 324191 | 412-413 |
| 236210 | 196-197, 1715 | 312120 | 306-307 | 324199 | 414-415 |
| 236220 | 198-199, 1716 | 312130 | 308-309 | 325188 | 416-417 |
| 237110 | 200-201, 1717 | 313111 | 310-311 | 325193 | 418-419 |
| 237120 | 202-203 | 313210 | 312-313 | 325199 | 420-421 |
| 237130 | 204-205 | 313311 | 314-315 | 325211 | 422-423 |
| 237210 | 206-207, 1718 | 313320 | 316-317 | 325311 | 424-425 |
| 237310 | 208-209, 1719 | 314110 | 318-319 | 325314 | 426-427 |
| 237990 | 210-211, 1720 | 314129 | 320-321 | 325320 | 428-429 |
| 238110 | 212-213, 1721 | 314912 | 322-323 | 325411 | 430-431 |

# NAICS CODES APPEARING IN THE STATEMENT STUDIES

# NAICS CODES APPEARING IN THE STATEMENT STUDIES

# NAICS CODES APPEARING IN THE STATEMENT STUDIES

# NAICS CODES APPEARING IN THE STATEMENT STUDIES

# DESCRIPTION OF INDUSTRIES INCLUDED IN THE STATEMENT STUDIES

# AGRICULTURE, FORESTRY, FISHING AND HUNTING

# MINING

# MINING

# UTILITIES

# UTILITIES

# CONSTRUCTION—GENERAL

**236115** **New Single-Family Housing Construction (except Operative Builders).** This U.S. industry comprises general contractor establishments primarily responsible for the entire construction of new single-family housing, such as single-family detached houses and town houses or row houses where each housing unit (1) is separated from its neighbors by a ground-to-roof wall and (2) has no housing units constructed above or below. This industry includes general contractors responsible for the on-site assembly of modular and prefabricated houses. Single-family housing design-build firms and single-family construction management firms acting as general contractors are included in this industry. . . . . . . . . . . . . . . . . . . . . . . . . . . . . .   188-189

**236116** **New Multifamily Housing Construction (except Operative Builders).** This U.S. industry comprises general contractor establishments responsible for the construction of new multifamily residential housing units (e.g., high-rise, garden, and town house apartments and condominiums where each unit is not separated from its neighbors by a ground-to-roof wall). Multifamily design-build firms and multifamily housing construction management firms acting as general contractors are included in this industry. . . . . . . . . . . . . . . . . . . . . . . . . . .   190-191

**236117** **New Housing Operative Builders.** This U.S. industry comprises operative builders primarily responsible for the entire construction of new houses and other residential buildings, single-family and multifamily, on their own account for sale. Operative builders are also known as speculative or merchant builders. . . . . . . . . . . . . . . . . . . . . . . . . . . . . . . . . . . . . .   192-193

**236118** **Residential Remodelers.** This U.S. industry comprises establishments primarily responsible for the remodeling construction (including additions, alterations, reconstruction, maintenance and repair work) of houses and other residential buildings, single-family and multifamily. Included in this industry are remodeling general contractors, operative remodelers, remodeling design-build firms, and remodeling project construction management firms. . . . . . . . . . . . . . . . .   194-195

**236210** **Industrial Building Construction.** This industry comprises establishments primarily responsible for the construction (including new work, additions, alterations, maintenance, and repairs) of industrial buildings (except warehouses). The construction of selected additional structures, whose production processes are similar to those for industrial buildings (e.g., incinerators, cement plants, blast furnaces, and similar nonbuilding structures), is included in this industry. Included in this industry are industrial building general contractors, industrial building operative builders, industrial building design-build firms, and industrial building construction management firms. . . . . . . . . . . . . . . . . . . . . . . . . . . . . . . . . . . . . . . . . . . . . . . . . . . . .   196-197

**236220** **Commercial and Institutional Building Construction.** This industry comprises establishments primarily responsible for the construction (including new work, additions, alterations, maintenance, and repairs) of commercial and institutional buildings and related structures, such as stadiums, grain elevators, and indoor swimming pools. This industry includes establishments responsible for the on-site assembly of modular or prefabricated commercial and institutional buildings. Included in this industry are commercial and institutional building general contractors, commercial and institutional building operative builders, commercial and institutional building design-build firms, and commercial and institutional building project construction management firms. . . . . . . . . . . . . . . . . . . . . . . . . . . . . . . . . . . . . . . .   198-199

**237110** **Water and Sewer Line and Related Structures Construction.** This industry comprises establishments primarily engaged in the construction of water and sewer lines, mains, pumping stations, treatment plants and storage tanks. The work performed may include new work, reconstruction, rehabilitation, and repairs. Specialty trade contractors are included in this group if they are engaged in activities primarily related to water and sewer line and related structures construction. All structures (including buildings) that are integral parts of water and sewer networks (e.g., storage tanks, pumping stations, water treatment plants, and sewage treatment plants) are included in this industry. . . . . . . . . . . . . . . . . . . . . . . . . . . . . . . . . . . . . .   200-201

**237120** **Oil and Gas Pipeline and Related Structures Construction.** This industry comprises establishments primarily engaged in the construction of oil and gas lines, mains, refineries, and storage tanks. The work performed may include new work, reconstruction, rehabilitation, and repairs. Specialty trade contractors are included in this group if they are engaged in activities primarily related to oil and gas pipeline and related structures construction. All structures (including buildings) that are integral parts of oil and gas networks (e.g., storage tanks, pumping stations, and refineries) are included in this industry. . . . . . . . . . . . . . . . . . . . . . . . . . .   202-203

# CONSTRUCTION-GENERAL

# CONSTRUCTION-GENERAL

# MANUFACTURING

# MANUFACTURING

# MANUFACTURING

# MANUFACTURING

## MANUFACTURING

# MANUFACTURING

# MANUFACTURING

# MANUFACTURING

# MANUFACTURING

# MANUFACTURING

# MANUFACTURING

# MANUFACTURING

# MANUFACTURING

# MANUFACTURING

# MANUFACTURING

# MANUFACTURING

# WHOLESALE TRADE

# WHOLESALE

# RETAIL

# RETAIL TRADE

# RETAIL

# RETAIL

# RETAIL

# TRANSPORTATION AND WAREHOUSING

# TRANSPORTATION

# INFORMATION

# INFORMATION

# INFORMATION

# FINANCE AND INSURANCE

# FINANCE

# REAL ESTATE AND RENTAL AND LEASING

# REAL ESTATE

# PROFESSIONAL, SCIENTIFIC, AND TECHNICAL SERVICES

**541110** **Offices of Lawyers.** This industry comprises offices of legal practitioners known as lawyers or attorneys (i.e., counselors-at-law) primarily engaged in the practice of law. Establishments in this industry may provide expertise in a range or in specific areas of law, such as criminal law, corporate law, family and estate law, patent law, real estate law, or tax law. . . . . . . . . . . . . 1290-1291

**541191** **Title Abstract and Settlement Offices.** This U.S. industry comprises establishments (except offices of lawyers and attorneys) primarily engaged in one or more of the following activities: (1) researching public land records to gather information relating to real estate titles; (2) preparing documents necessary for the transfer of the title, financing, and settlement; (3) conducting final real estate settlements and closings; and (4) filing legal and other documents relating to the sale of real estate. Real estate settlement offices, title abstract companies, and title search companies are included in this industry. . . . . . . . . . . . . . . . . . . . . . . . . 1292-1293

**541199** **All Other Legal Services.** This U.S. industry comprises establishments of legal practitioners (except offices of lawyers and attorneys, settlement offices, and title abstract offices). These establishments are primarily engaged in providing specialized legal or paralegal services. . . 1294-1295

**541211** **Offices of Certified Public Accountants.** This U.S. industry comprises establishments of accountants that are certified to audit the accounting records of public and private organizations and to attest to compliance with generally accepted accounting practices. Offices of certified public accountants (CPAs) may provide one or more of the following accounting services: (1) auditing financial statements; (2) designing accounting systems; (3) preparing financial statements; (4) developing budgets; and (5) providing advice on matters related to accounting. These establishments may also provide related services, such as bookkeeping, tax return preparation, and payroll processing. . . . . . . . . . . . . . . . . . . . . . . . . . . . . . . . . 1296-1297

**541214** **Payroll Services.** This U.S. industry comprises establishments (except offices of CPAs) engaged in the following without also providing accounting, bookkeeping, or billing services: (1) collecting information on hours worked, pay rates, deductions, and other payroll- related data from their clients and (2) using that information to generate paychecks, payroll reports, and tax filings. These establishments may use data processing and tabulating techniques as part of providing their services. . . . . . . . . . . . . . . . . . . . . . . . . . . . . . . . . . . . . 1298-1299

**541219** **Other Accounting Services.** This U.S. industry comprises establishments (except offices of CPAs) engaged in providing accounting services (except tax return preparation services only or payroll services only). These establishments may also provide tax return preparation or payroll services. Accountant (except CPA) offices, bookkeeper offices, and billing offices are included in this industry. . . . . . . . . . . . . . . . . . . . . . . . . . . . . . . . . . . . . . . . 1300-1301

**541310** **Architectural Services.** This industry comprises establishments primarily engaged in planning and designing residential, institutional, leisure, commercial, and industrial buildings and structures by applying knowledge of design, construction procedures, zoning regulations, building codes, and building materials. . . . . . . . . . . . . . . . . . . . . . . . . . . . . . . . . . 1302-1303

**541320** **Landscape Architectural Services.** This industry comprises establishments primarily engaged in planning and designing the development of land areas for projects, such as parks and other recreational areas; airports; highways; hospitals; schools; land subdivisions; and commercial, industrial, and residential areas, by applying knowledge of land characteristics, location of buildings and structures, use of land areas, and design of landscape projects. . . . . . . . . . . . 1304-1305

**541330** **Engineering Services.** This industry comprises establishments primarily engaged in applying physical laws and principles of engineering in the design, development, and utilization of machines, materials, instruments, structures, processes, and systems. The assignments undertaken by these establishments may involve any of the following activities: provision of advice, preparation of feasibility studies, preparation of preliminary and final plans and designs, provision of technical services during the construction or installation phase, inspection and evaluation of engineering projects, and related services. . . . . . . . . . . . . . . . . . . . . . . . 1306-1307

**541370** **Surveying and Mapping (except Geophysical) Services.** This industry comprises establishments primarily engaged in performing surveying and mapping services of the surface of the earth, including the sea floor. These services may include surveying and mapping of areas above or below the surface of the earth, such as the creation of view easements or segregating rights in parcels of land by creating underground utility easements. . . . . . . . . . . . . . . . 1308-1309

# PROFESSIONAL SERVICES

# PROFESSIONAL SERVICES

# MANAGEMENT

# MANAGEMENT OF COMPANIES AND ENTERPRISES

# ADMINISTRATIVE AND SUPPORT AND WASTE MANAGEMENT AND REMEDIATION SERVICES

# ADMIN & WASTE MANAGEMENT SERVICES

# EDUCATIONAL SERVICES

# HEALTH CARE

# HEALTH CARE AND SOCIAL ASSISTANCE

# HEALTH CARE

# HEALTH CARE

# HEALTH CARE

# ENTERTAINMENT

# ARTS, ENTERTAINMENT, AND RECREATION

# RESTAURANT/LODGING

# ACCOMMODATION AND FOOD SERVICES

# OTHER SERVICES

# OTHER SERVICES (EXCEPT PUBLIC ADMINISTRATION)

# OTHER SERVICES

# PUBLIC ADMINISTRATION

# PUBLIC ADMINISTRATION

# CONSTRUCTION-% OF COMPLETION

# CONSTRUCTION—PERCENTAGE OF COMPLETION

# CONSTRUCTION-% OF COMPLETION

**NAICS #**

# CONSTRUCTION-% OF COMPLETION

# AGRICULTURE, FORESTRY, FISHING AND HUNTING

## Current Data Sorted by Assets        Comparative Historical Data

| 0-500M | 500M-2MM | 2-10MM | 10-50MM | 50-100MM | 100-250MM | Type of Statement | 4/1/07-3/31/08 ALL | 4/1/08-3/31/09 ALL |
|---|---|---|---|---|---|---|---|---|
| | 4 | 4 | 7 | 1 | 4 | Unqualified | 6 | 2 |
| 3 | 4 | 2 | 4 | | | Reviewed | 8 | 12 |
| 5 | 14 | 5 | 1 | | 1 | Compiled | 2 | 1 |
| 6 | 14 | 6 | 1 | | | Tax Returns | 5 | 4 |
| | 14 | 14 | 8 | 2 | | Other | 17 | 7 |
| | 20 (4/1-9/30/11) | | 90 (10/1/11-3/31/12) | | | | | |
| 14 | 36 | 31 | 21 | 3 | 5 | NUMBER OF STATEMENTS | 38 | 26 |
| % | % | % | % | % | % | **ASSETS** | % | % |
| 31.3 | 11.2 | 13.3 | 13.8 | | | Cash & Equivalents | 14.0 | 13.6 |
| 8.9 | 10.3 | 8.7 | 13.4 | | | Trade Receivables (net) | 16.2 | 24.5 |
| 13.5 | 4.9 | 10.0 | 8.4 | | | Inventory | 18.5 | 12.4 |
| 1.0 | 1.1 | 1.5 | 6.8 | | | All Other Current | 5.9 | 7.6 |
| 54.7 | 27.4 | 33.5 | 42.3 | | | Total Current | 54.6 | 58.0 |
| 29.0 | 52.6 | 55.0 | 45.0 | | | Fixed Assets (net) | 36.0 | 34.8 |
| 6.1 | 1.2 | 3.7 | 4.3 | | | Intangibles (net) | 2.4 | 2.7 |
| 10.2 | 18.7 | 7.8 | 8.4 | | | All Other Non-Current | 7.0 | 4.5 |
| 100.0 | 100.0 | 100.0 | 100.0 | | | Total | 100.0 | 100.0 |
| | | | | | | **LIABILITIES** | | |
| 35.5 | 13.6 | 15.9 | 4.1 | | | Notes Payable-Short Term | 12.4 | 4.4 |
| 3.1 | 8.0 | 6.7 | 4.1 | | | Cur. Mat.-L.T.D. | 2.7 | 3.1 |
| 8.4 | 7.3 | 3.9 | 8.9 | | | Trade Payables | 10.1 | 13.0 |
| .0 | .0 | .1 | .1 | | | Income Taxes Payable | .0 | .1 |
| 19.1 | 6.3 | 2.1 | 17.8 | | | All Other Current | 9.2 | 10.3 |
| 66.1 | 35.2 | 28.7 | 35.1 | | | Total Current | 34.4 | 31.0 |
| 65.1 | 36.0 | 35.7 | 25.2 | | | Long-Term Debt | 31.9 | 18.7 |
| .0 | .2 | .0 | .4 | | | Deferred Taxes | .0 | .0 |
| 18.3 | 15.4 | 3.3 | 4.8 | | | All Other Non-Current | 5.7 | 7.0 |
| -49.5 | 13.1 | 32.3 | 34.5 | | | Net Worth | 27.9 | 42.9 |
| 100.0 | 100.0 | 100.0 | 100.0 | | | Total Liabilities & Net Worth | 100.0 | 100.0 |
| | | | | | | **INCOME DATA** | | |
| 100.0 | 100.0 | 100.0 | 100.0 | | | Net Sales | 100.0 | 100.0 |
| | | | | | | Gross Profit | | |
| 95.4 | 84.6 | 78.3 | 86.7 | | | Operating Expenses | 91.2 | 95.1 |
| 4.6 | 15.4 | 21.7 | 13.3 | | | Operating Profit | 8.8 | 4.9 |
| 1.8 | 5.9 | 11.1 | 3.6 | | | All Other Expenses (net) | 8.3 | 3.2 |
| 2.8 | 9.5 | 10.6 | 9.7 | | | Profit Before Taxes | .5 | 1.7 |
| | | | | | | **RATIOS** | | |
| 4.3 | 2.1 | 3.2 | 2.0 | | | | 3.0 | 5.2 |
| .7 | .7 | 1.1 | 1.5 | | | Current | 1.4 | 1.6 |
| .4 | .2 | .5 | .6 | | | | 1.0 | 1.1 |
| 2.5 | 1.7 | 1.7 | 1.7 | | | | 1.4 | 2.1 |
| .6 | .4 | .6 | .7 | | | Quick | .9 | .9 |
| .2 | .1 | .1 | .2 | | | | .2 | .5 |
| 0 UND | 0 UND | 0 UND | 3 108.7 | | | | 0 UND | 8 46.7 |
| 0 UND | 0 UND | 0 999.8 | 25 14.8 | | | Sales/Receivables | 10 36.9 | 45 8.0 |
| 6 59.5 | 17 21.3 | 33 11.2 | 54 6.7 | | | | 42 8.7 | 63 5.8 |
| | | | | | | Cost of Sales/Inventory | | |
| | | | | | | Cost of Sales/Payables | | |
| 13.3 | 12.8 | 3.8 | 5.6 | | | | 5.8 | 3.8 |
| -44.9 | -30.4 | 21.3 | 13.6 | | | Sales/Working Capital | 17.1 | 10.5 |
| -20.5 | -2.7 | -10.4 | -19.5 | | | | UND | 94.0 |
| | 6.0 | 35.6 | 41.5 | | | | 5.7 | 8.8 |
| | (23) 3.2 | (21) 3.5 | (17) 7.7 | | | EBIT/Interest | (25) 2.4 | (20) 4.2 |
| | 1.5 | 1.1 | 2.0 | | | | .9 | .6 |
| | | | | | | Net Profit + Depr., Dep., Amort./Cur. Mat. L/T/D | | |
| .3 | .5 | .4 | .3 | | | | .1 | .1 |
| NM | 2.6 | 1.2 | 1.1 | | | Fixed/Worth | .9 | .8 |
| -.3 | -21.6 | 12.6 | 4.9 | | | | 15.7 | 1.4 |
| 1.9 | .8 | .3 | .5 | | | | .9 | .6 |
| NM | 3.8 | 1.7 | 1.5 | | | Debt/Worth | 2.1 | 1.2 |
| -1.8 | -48.9 | 11.9 | 10.0 | | | | 20.5 | 3.9 |
| | 62.0 | 31.2 | 27.2 | | | | 48.1 | 35.0 |
| | (26) 27.1 | (24) 11.6 | (18) 18.4 | | | % Profit Before Taxes/Tangible Net Worth | (30) 10.4 | (25) 19.1 |
| | 2.5 | 1.2 | 5.5 | | | | -1.2 | -2.0 |
| 42.8 | 16.6 | 9.5 | 13.8 | | | | 16.0 | 13.8 |
| 14.0 | 4.9 | 4.4 | 5.1 | | | % Profit Before Taxes/Total Assets | 3.4 | 7.0 |
| 7.5 | .8 | .3 | 1.2 | | | | -1.0 | -2.4 |
| 102.3 | 15.7 | 11.1 | 25.5 | | | | 83.2 | 44.8 |
| 42.1 | 3.2 | 1.1 | 4.5 | | | Sales/Net Fixed Assets | 9.3 | 11.0 |
| 5.9 | 1.2 | .2 | .2 | | | | .5 | 1.5 |
| 9.6 | 3.0 | 1.7 | 2.7 | | | | 3.0 | 2.5 |
| 5.1 | 1.8 | .6 | 1.3 | | | Sales/Total Assets | 1.6 | 2.0 |
| 3.1 | .7 | .2 | .2 | | | | .3 | .9 |
| | 1.5 | .6 | 1.5 | | | | .6 | .7 |
| | (26) 4.6 | (23) 7.6 | (16) 3.4 | | | % Depr., Dep., Amort./Sales | (25) 1.7 | (23) 2.3 |
| | 18.4 | 15.6 | 7.0 | | | | 6.5 | 8.9 |
| | 2.5 | | | | | | 1.9 | |
| | (13) 4.9 | | | | | % Officers', Directors' Owners' Comp/Sales | (12) 4.6 | |
| | 8.2 | | | | | | 6.2 | |
| 17701M | 96651M | 140238M | 728570M | 287366M | 1452463M | Net Sales ($) | 1065309M | 685004M |
| 2987M | 41389M | 143059M | 442197M | 230560M | 839933M | Total Assets ($) | 473036M | 596750M |

M = $ thousand     MM = $ million
See Pages 9 through 22 for Explanation of Ratios and Data

## Comparative Historical Data / Current Data Sorted by Sales

| Hist 1 | Hist 2 | Hist 3 | Item | 0-1MM | 1-3MM | 3-5MM | 5-10MM | 10-25MM | 25MM & OVER |
|---|---|---|---|---|---|---|---|---|---|
| | | | **Type of Statement** | | | | | | |
| 10 | 5 | 16 | Unqualified | 2 | 3 | 1 | 2 | 1 | 9 |
| 2 | 6 | 10 | Reviewed | | 2 | 1 | 2 | 1 | 3 |
| 8 | 6 | 13 | Compiled | 3 | 5 | 2 | 2 | 1 | |
| 22 | 15 | 27 | Tax Returns | 9 | 9 | 3 | 4 | 1 | 1 |
| 25 | 28 | 44 | Other | 12 | 16 | 3 | 4 | 3 | 6 |
| 4/1/09-3/31/10 ALL | 4/1/10-3/31/11 ALL | 4/1/11-3/31/12 ALL | | 20 (4/1-9/30/11) | | | 90 (10/1/11-3/31/12) | | |
| 67 | 60 | 110 | **NUMBER OF STATEMENTS** | 26 | 35 | 10 | 12 | 8 | 19 |
| % | % | % | **ASSETS** | % | % | % | % | % | % |
| 14.5 | 9.7 | 14.6 | Cash & Equivalents | 9.4 | 16.0 | 11.6 | 26.7 | | 12.2 |
| 12.0 | 12.6 | 11.9 | Trade Receivables (net) | 3.5 | 9.2 | 12.2 | 10.2 | | 22.8 |
| 14.5 | 16.2 | 9.0 | Inventory | 2.9 | 7.4 | 19.5 | 6.3 | | 16.2 |
| 3.8 | 4.5 | 2.5 | All Other Current | 1.1 | .8 | 3.2 | .2 | | 6.6 |
| 44.7 | 43.0 | 37.9 | Total Current | 16.8 | 33.4 | 46.5 | 43.4 | | 57.7 |
| 41.5 | 43.0 | 46.8 | Fixed Assets (net) | 69.0 | 52.0 | 42.2 | 37.1 | | 28.8 |
| 6.5 | 5.5 | 3.7 | Intangibles (net) | .5 | 3.1 | 7.2 | 4.0 | | 8.7 |
| 7.3 | 8.5 | 11.7 | All Other Non-Current | 13.7 | 11.5 | 4.1 | 15.5 | | 4.8 |
| 100.0 | 100.0 | 100.0 | Total | 100.0 | 100.0 | 100.0 | 100.0 | | 100.0 |
| | | | **LIABILITIES** | | | | | | |
| 14.2 | 10.0 | 15.3 | Notes Payable-Short Term | 6.4 | 22.8 | 18.9 | 5.0 | | 6.5 |
| 4.1 | 5.2 | 5.8 | Cur. Mat.-L.T.D. | 4.2 | 7.3 | 4.6 | 8.2 | | 3.8 |
| 7.2 | 8.7 | 6.8 | Trade Payables | .3 | 7.9 | 6.9 | 10.0 | | 12.5 |
| .1 | .4 | .1 | Income Taxes Payable | .0 | .1 | .0 | .0 | | .3 |
| 7.0 | 7.6 | 9.2 | All Other Current | 7.0 | 6.3 | 1.6 | 11.3 | | 23.3 |
| 32.6 | 32.0 | 37.1 | Total Current | 17.9 | 44.4 | 32.0 | 34.5 | | 46.4 |
| 37.7 | 24.7 | 35.9 | Long-Term Debt | 64.9 | 36.0 | 35.4 | 22.5 | | 14.0 |
| .4 | .8 | .2 | Deferred Taxes | .0 | .0 | .8 | .1 | | .7 |
| 2.5 | 3.3 | 9.6 | All Other Non-Current | 14.0 | 7.6 | 2.5 | 22.9 | | 5.9 |
| 26.8 | 39.3 | 17.3 | Net Worth | 3.2 | 11.9 | 29.4 | 20.0 | | 32.9 |
| 100.0 | 100.0 | 100.0 | Total Liabilities & Net Worth | 100.0 | 100.0 | 100.0 | 100.0 | | 100.0 |
| | | | **INCOME DATA** | | | | | | |
| 100.0 | 100.0 | 100.0 | Net Sales | 100.0 | 100.0 | 100.0 | 100.0 | | 100.0 |
| | | | Gross Profit | | | | | | |
| 85.9 | 86.7 | 85.0 | Operating Expenses | 66.3 | 86.5 | 94.6 | 94.3 | | 96.5 |
| 14.1 | 13.3 | 15.0 | Operating Profit | 33.7 | 13.5 | 5.4 | 5.7 | | 3.5 |
| 6.6 | 3.6 | 6.2 | All Other Expenses (net) | 17.2 | 4.1 | 4.2 | .5 | | .9 |
| 7.6 | 9.7 | 8.8 | Profit Before Taxes | 16.6 | 9.4 | 1.1 | 5.2 | | 2.6 |
| | | | **RATIOS** | | | | | | |
| 2.8 | 2.4 | 2.4 | | 2.1 | 2.1 | 5.2 | 3.6 | | 2.0 |
| 1.5 | 1.3 | 1.1 | Current | .6 | .7 | 1.3 | .8 | | 1.6 |
| .8 | .6 | .4 | | .1 | .2 | .5 | .6 | | 1.2 |
| 1.6 | 1.3 | 1.7 | | 2.1 | 1.6 | 2.2 | 2.0 | | 1.7 |
| .9 | .6 | .6 | Quick | .6 | .5 | .5 | .8 | | 1.1 |
| .2 | .2 | .2 | | .1 | .1 | .0 | .4 | | .4 |
| 0 UND | 0 UND | 0 UND | | 0 UND | 0 UND | 0 UND | 0 UND | | 10 36.8 |
| 4 96.2 | 18 20.5 | 4 81.2 | Sales/Receivables | 0 UND | 0 755.0 | 9 41.3 | 14 26.7 | | 41 9.0 |
| 37 9.8 | 48 7.7 | 36 10.0 | | 0 UND | 15 23.9 | 34 10.7 | 34 10.7 | | 61 6.0 |
| | | | Cost of Sales/Inventory | | | | | | |
| | | | Cost of Sales/Payables | | | | | | |
| 6.8 | 5.2 | 5.7 | | 6.6 | 6.1 | 5.5 | 4.7 | | 5.1 |
| 12.3 | 17.2 | 46.8 | Sales/Working Capital | -27.1 | -48.6 | 17.0 | -110.9 | | 13.4 |
| -24.9 | -10.6 | -7.9 | | -2.8 | -6.1 | -12.0 | -26.6 | | 57.0 |
| 8.9 | 10.5 | 13.0 | | 3.3 | 5.8 | | 139.1 | | 25.1 |
| (47) 3.8 | (51) 5.5 | (76) 3.2 | EBIT/Interest | (10) 1.6 | (23) 3.2 | | (10) 8.2 | | 7.7 |
| 1.2 | 1.7 | 1.2 | | 1.3 | 1.1 | | 2.4 | | .8 |
| | 7.8 | 22.8 | Net Profit + Depr., Dep., | | | | | | |
| | (13) 3.9 | (10) 5.1 | Amort./Cur. Mat. L/T/D | | | | | | |
| | 1.9 | 2.4 | | | | | | | |
| .2 | .5 | .3 | | 1.1 | .8 | .4 | .1 | | .3 |
| 1.2 | 1.1 | 1.4 | Fixed/Worth | 2.9 | 2.4 | 1.2 | 1.9 | | .6 |
| 9.9 | 2.9 | NM | | -13.9 | -21.5 | NM | NM | | 2.5 |
| .6 | .7 | .6 | | .4 | .3 | .5 | .7 | | .7 |
| 2.1 | 1.9 | 2.4 | Debt/Worth | 3.8 | 4.1 | 4.3 | 2.8 | | 1.6 |
| 29.7 | 3.8 | NM | | -15.6 | -33.0 | NM | NM | | 5.8 |
| 36.5 | 43.4 | 44.4 | | 42.7 | 49.5 | | | | 32.8 |
| (51) 12.0 | (53) 20.8 | (83) 17.0 | % Profit Before Taxes/Tangible Net Worth | (18) 7.6 | (25) 19.1 | | | | (16) 21.5 |
| 4.3 | 2.4 | 2.4 | | 2.0 | 8.2 | | | | 12.0 |
| 14.9 | 14.8 | 14.2 | | 10.2 | 23.7 | 10.9 | 17.9 | | 14.7 |
| 5.2 | 6.3 | 5.2 | % Profit Before Taxes/Total Assets | 4.4 | 6.1 | 3.7 | 6.1 | | 6.5 |
| .3 | 1.2 | .8 | | .8 | 1.5 | -.7 | 1.5 | | -1.1 |
| 31.1 | 17.7 | 27.8 | | 8.7 | 29.0 | 41.7 | 76.0 | | 27.4 |
| 5.8 | 5.5 | 4.7 | Sales/Net Fixed Assets | .3 | 3.0 | 9.9 | 9.7 | | 10.9 |
| 1.0 | .9 | .8 | | .1 | 1.1 | .7 | 4.0 | | 4.1 |
| 3.2 | 2.4 | 3.1 | | .8 | 3.1 | 3.1 | 4.9 | | 3.5 |
| 1.8 | 1.6 | 1.6 | Sales/Total Assets | .2 | 1.7 | 1.5 | 2.6 | | 1.9 |
| .5 | .4 | .4 | | .1 | .6 | .6 | 1.3 | | 1.3 |
| 1.1 | 1.3 | 1.3 | | 7.6 | 1.3 | | .6 | | .7 |
| (54) 4.2 | (47) 2.8 | (79) 4.0 | % Depr., Dep., Amort./Sales | (16) 17.3 | (28) 6.0 | | (11) 1.3 | | (15) 2.0 |
| 12.5 | 8.3 | 15.0 | | 28.4 | 16.9 | | 4.7 | | 4.0 |
| 2.6 | | 1.1 | | | 1.9 | | | | |
| (21) 5.1 | | (28) 2.8 | % Officers', Directors' Owners' Comp/Sales | | (12) 3.0 | | | | |
| 11.4 | | 6.8 | | | 8.5 | | | | |
| 751059M | 1491565M | 2722989M | Net Sales ($) | 12939M | 60220M | 38583M | 82559M | 131872M | 2396816M |
| 462939M | 1095325M | 1700125M | Total Assets ($) | 88338M | 90560M | 50138M | 48499M | 265857M | 1156733M |

© RMA 2012

M = $ thousand    MM = $ million
See Pages 9 through 22 for Explanation of Ratios and Data

## Current Data Sorted by Assets | Comparative Historical Data

| Type of Statement | | | | | | | | |
|---|---|---|---|---|---|---|---|---|
| 2 | | 1 | 3 | 2 | 5 | Unqualified | 35 | 24 |
| | 2 | 1 | 8 | | | Reviewed | 24 | 21 |
| 1 | 2 | 4 | 1 | | | Compiled | 16 | 15 |
| 5 | 6 | 4 | 2 | | | Tax Returns | 19 | 26 |
| 3 | 5 | 17 | 10 | | 3 | Other | 70 | 53 |
| | 18 (4/1-9/30/11) | | | 69 (10/1/11-3/31/12) | | | 4/1/07-3/31/08 | 4/1/08-3/31/09 |
| 0-500M | 500M-2MM | 2-10MM | 10-50MM | 50-100MM | 100-250MM | | ALL | ALL |
| 11 | 15 | 27 | 24 | 2 | 8 | NUMBER OF STATEMENTS | 164 | 139 |
| % | % | % | % | % | % | ASSETS | % | % |
| 32.7 | 8.5 | 8.3 | 10.0 | | | Cash & Equivalents | 12.3 | 12.3 |
| 2.8 | 18.0 | 10.3 | 23.8 | | | Trade Receivables (net) | 20.5 | 18.0 |
| 9.7 | 6.7 | 12.6 | 16.1 | | | Inventory | 15.4 | 18.3 |
| .9 | 4.8 | 4.4 | 3.3 | | | All Other Current | 4.3 | 3.5 |
| 46.2 | 37.9 | 35.5 | 53.1 | | | Total Current | 52.6 | 52.0 |
| 30.8 | 41.7 | 55.3 | 41.0 | | | Fixed Assets (net) | 35.9 | 35.1 |
| 8.4 | 5.6 | 5.3 | 2.1 | | | Intangibles (net) | 4.4 | 4.7 |
| 14.6 | 14.8 | 3.9 | 3.8 | | | All Other Non-Current | 7.1 | 8.2 |
| 100.0 | 100.0 | 100.0 | 100.0 | | | Total | 100.0 | 100.0 |
| | | | | | | LIABILITIES | | |
| 17.3 | 9.4 | 9.8 | 10.7 | | | Notes Payable-Short Term | 15.6 | 13.9 |
| 10.3 | 14.8 | 7.3 | 2.3 | | | Cur. Mat.-L.T.D. | 3.7 | 2.9 |
| 3.6 | 16.2 | 7.9 | 16.2 | | | Trade Payables | 10.1 | 11.7 |
| .0 | .7 | .0 | .1 | | | Income Taxes Payable | .5 | .4 |
| 3.6 | 7.1 | 4.2 | 6.2 | | | All Other Current | 8.6 | 8.6 |
| 34.8 | 48.1 | 29.2 | 35.6 | | | Total Current | 38.5 | 37.5 |
| 12.0 | 44.9 | 26.2 | 20.6 | | | Long-Term Debt | 25.0 | 21.2 |
| .0 | .0 | 1.2 | .5 | | | Deferred Taxes | .3 | .4 |
| 1.3 | 8.8 | 8.0 | .6 | | | All Other Non-Current | 7.1 | 5.9 |
| 51.9 | -1.9 | 35.3 | 42.7 | | | Net Worth | 29.2 | 35.0 |
| 100.0 | 100.0 | 100.0 | 100.0 | | | Total Liabilities & Net Worth | 100.0 | 100.0 |
| | | | | | | INCOME DATA | | |
| 100.0 | 100.0 | 100.0 | 100.0 | | | Net Sales | 100.0 | 100.0 |
| | | | | | | Gross Profit | | |
| 79.4 | 88.0 | 86.0 | 88.6 | | | Operating Expenses | 86.5 | 88.1 |
| 20.6 | 12.0 | 14.0 | 11.4 | | | Operating Profit | 13.5 | 11.9 |
| 6.4 | 7.6 | 5.5 | 3.1 | | | All Other Expenses (net) | 4.6 | 3.6 |
| 14.2 | 4.4 | 8.5 | 8.3 | | | Profit Before Taxes | 8.9 | 8.4 |
| | | | | | | RATIOS | | |
| 10.0 | 3.5 | 3.0 | 2.9 | | | | 2.4 | 2.3 |
| .7 | .9 | 1.3 | 1.4 | | | Current | 1.4 | 1.4 |
| .3 | .5 | .4 | 1.1 | | | | 1.0 | .9 |
| 10.0 | 1.0 | 1.3 | 2.3 | | | | 1.8 | 1.7 |
| .7 | .6 | .4 | 1.1 | | | Quick | 1.0 | .8 |
| .1 | .3 | .2 | .6 | | | | .4 | .4 |
| 0 UND | 0 UND | 0 UND | 1 255.9 | | | | 0 999.8 | 2 152.3 |
| 0 999.8 | 12 29.2 | 1 258.8 | 30 12.3 | | | Sales/Receivables | 28 13.1 | 28 13.0 |
| 3 130.0 | 42 8.7 | 24 15.1 | 66 5.5 | | | | 53 6.9 | 47 7.8 |
| | | | | | | Cost of Sales/Inventory | | |
| | | | | | | Cost of Sales/Payables | | |
| 16.9 | 6.8 | 3.4 | 7.1 | | | | 4.7 | 5.4 |
| -52.6 | -26.0 | 9.7 | 11.5 | | | Sales/Working Capital | 16.8 | 16.2 |
| -6.7 | -9.3 | -6.6 | 48.4 | | | | -114.5 | -67.8 |
| | | 7.1 | 9.2 | 21.1 | | | 7.6 | 16.0 |
| | (10) 3.7 | (22) 2.8 | (19) 4.6 | | | EBIT/Interest | (133) 3.4 | (111) 4.0 |
| | | -.3 | 1.4 | 2.1 | | | 1.5 | 1.4 |
| | | | | | | Net Profit + Depr., Dep., | 5.9 | 8.6 |
| | | | | | | Amort./Cur. Mat. L/T/D | (25) 2.5 | (22) 3.2 |
| | | | | | | | .8 | 1.6 |
| .0 | .7 | .6 | .4 | | | | .3 | .2 |
| .2 | 3.5 | 1.3 | .8 | | | Fixed/Worth | 1.2 | .8 |
| 8.7 | -.6 | -942.3 | 1.6 | | | | 4.8 | 2.3 |
| .1 | .6 | .5 | .4 | | | | .8 | .7 |
| 3.5 | 2.9 | 1.8 | 1.5 | | | Debt/Worth | 2.5 | 1.9 |
| 8.1 | -3.0 | -999.8 | 4.4 | | | | 11.0 | 6.7 |
| | | 52.9 | 37.7 | | | % Profit Before Taxes/Tangible | 53.1 | 48.5 |
| | (20) 3.2 | (22) 21.8 | | | | Net Worth | (134) 20.3 | (118) 16.6 |
| | | -2.8 | 6.8 | | | | 6.3 | 4.1 |
| 129.2 | 11.1 | 13.2 | 14.2 | | | % Profit Before Taxes/Total | 15.8 | 15.4 |
| 14.3 | 7.2 | 4.6 | 5.0 | | | Assets | 6.6 | 5.6 |
| 2.1 | -.3 | .3 | 1.7 | | | | 2.0 | 1.0 |
| UND | 25.9 | 11.8 | 22.9 | | | | 31.0 | 48.0 |
| 74.0 | 6.2 | 1.1 | 7.7 | | | Sales/Net Fixed Assets | 7.7 | 7.6 |
| 1.9 | .8 | .4 | .9 | | | | 2.5 | 2.3 |
| 13.9 | 3.5 | 1.9 | 3.3 | | | | 3.3 | 3.1 |
| 10.0 | 2.4 | .8 | 1.5 | | | Sales/Total Assets | 1.7 | 2.0 |
| 1.2 | .6 | .3 | .4 | | | | .9 | .8 |
| | .7 | 3.4 | .9 | | | | .8 | .8 |
| | (13) 2.9 | (23) 8.2 | (23) 2.9 | | | % Depr., Dep., Amort./Sales | (126) 2.0 | (109) 2.5 |
| | | 7.1 | 18.8 | 8.9 | | | 5.5 | 6.3 |
| | | | | | | % Officers', Directors' | .8 | 1.3 |
| | | | | | | Owners' Comp/Sales | (42) 3.1 | (29) 3.3 |
| | | | | | | | 7.0 | 5.5 |
| 25360M | 36223M | 194437M | 1572376M | 297407M | 848531M | Net Sales ($) | 5938124M | 8189597M |
| 2978M | 17761M | 140325M | 499791M | 155107M | 1084230M | Total Assets ($) | 3618296M | 3930356M |

M = $ thousand    MM = $ million
See Pages 9 through 22 for Explanation of Ratios and Data

## Comparative Historical Data | Current Data Sorted by Sales

| | | | Type of Statement | | | | | | |
|---|---|---|---|---|---|---|---|---|---|
| | | | Unqualified | 2 | 1 | | 2 | 3 | 8 |
| 21 | 12 | 13 | Reviewed | | | | | 3 | 5 |
| 16 | 17 | 11 | Compiled | 1 | 2 | 4 | 1 | 1 | |
| 17 | 8 | 8 | Tax Returns | 5 | 8 | 2 | 1 | 1 | |
| 22 | 21 | 17 | Other | 6 | 8 | 3 | 7 | 7 | 7 |
| 51 | 35 | 38 | | | 18 (4/1-9/30/11) | | | 69 (10/1/11-3/31/12) | |
| 4/1/09-3/31/10 ALL | 4/1/10-3/31/11 ALL | 4/1/11-3/31/12 ALL | | 0-1MM | 1-3MM | 3-5MM | 5-10MM | 10-25MM | 25MM & OVER |
| 127 | 93 | 87 | NUMBER OF STATEMENTS | 14 | 19 | 9 | 11 | 14 | 20 |
| % | % | % | ASSETS | % | % | % | % | % | % |
| 13.8 | 9.9 | 12.1 | Cash & Equivalents | 10.2 | 15.7 | | 9.6 | 11.6 | 11.0 |
| 14.5 | 15.2 | 15.0 | Trade Receivables (net) | 3.1 | 6.9 | | 8.3 | 20.1 | 31.5 |
| 10.3 | 13.8 | 13.4 | Inventory | 6.7 | 4.1 | | 23.5 | 15.5 | 22.1 |
| 4.8 | 5.3 | 3.5 | All Other Current | 1.5 | 5.9 | | 3.8 | 3.3 | 3.3 |
| 43.4 | 44.2 | 44.0 | Total Current | 21.4 | 32.6 | | 45.2 | 50.5 | 67.9 |
| 46.4 | 45.3 | 42.3 | Fixed Assets (net) | 65.9 | 51.4 | | 34.4 | 35.4 | 19.3 |
| 3.6 | 3.9 | 6.0 | Intangibles (net) | 10.2 | 2.2 | | 6.5 | 5.9 | 9.0 |
| 6.6 | 6.5 | 7.7 | All Other Non-Current | 2.4 | 13.8 | | 13.8 | 8.2 | 3.7 |
| 100.0 | 100.0 | 100.0 | Total | 100.0 | 100.0 | | 100.0 | 100.0 | 100.0 |
| | | | LIABILITIES | | | | | | |
| 12.9 | 14.6 | 10.6 | Notes Payable-Short Term | 3.9 | 9.5 | | 18.1 | 13.2 | 10.8 |
| 4.0 | 5.0 | 7.6 | Cur. Mat.-L.T.D. | 12.4 | 11.0 | | 9.1 | 1.7 | 5.0 |
| 9.3 | 9.2 | 11.1 | Trade Payables | 2.8 | 2.4 | | 10.7 | 16.2 | 18.5 |
| .3 | .3 | .2 | Income Taxes Payable | .0 | .5 | | .0 | .2 | .2 |
| 13.2 | 11.2 | 5.3 | All Other Current | 1.2 | 5.8 | | 3.7 | 5.7 | 7.5 |
| 39.6 | 40.2 | 34.8 | Total Current | 20.3 | 29.2 | | 41.5 | 37.0 | 42.0 |
| 32.6 | 21.0 | 25.6 | Long-Term Debt | 56.5 | 29.6 | | 14.9 | 15.8 | 14.7 |
| .4 | .7 | .5 | Deferred Taxes | .0 | 1.6 | | .0 | .8 | .0 |
| 3.8 | 5.0 | 6.0 | All Other Non-Current | 7.7 | .3 | | 12.8 | 6.2 | 4.8 |
| 23.7 | 33.1 | 33.2 | Net Worth | 15.5 | 39.3 | | 30.8 | 40.2 | 38.4 |
| 100.0 | 100.0 | 100.0 | Total Liabilities & Net Worth | 100.0 | 100.0 | | 100.0 | 100.0 | 100.0 |
| | | | INCOME DATA | | | | | | |
| 100.0 | 100.0 | 100.0 | Net Sales | 100.0 | 100.0 | | 100.0 | 100.0 | 100.0 |
| | | | Gross Profit | | | | | | |
| 89.6 | 88.3 | 87.4 | Operating Expenses | 61.6 | 89.2 | | 91.0 | 91.0 | 95.0 |
| 10.4 | 11.7 | 12.6 | Operating Profit | 38.4 | 10.8 | | 9.0 | 9.0 | 5.0 |
| 3.5 | 4.7 | 4.8 | All Other Expenses (net) | 20.4 | 3.8 | | .6 | .6 | 1.5 |
| 6.9 | 7.0 | 7.8 | Profit Before Taxes | 18.1 | 7.0 | | 8.3 | 8.4 | 3.5 |
| | | | RATIOS | | | | | | |
| 2.6 | 2.0 | 3.1 | Current | 3.2 | 7.5 | | 3.0 | 3.3 | 2.4 |
| 1.3 | 1.1 | 1.3 | | .6 | 2.0 | | 1.3 | 1.6 | 1.4 |
| .7 | .6 | .7 | | .1 | 1.0 | | .5 | 1.0 | 1.2 |
| 1.9 | 1.3 | 1.9 | Quick | .8 | 1.6 | | 3.0 | 3.0 | 1.9 |
| .8 | .6 | .7 | | .4 | .8 | | .4 | 1.0 | 1.1 |
| .2 | .2 | .3 | | .1 | .6 | | .0 | .4 | .5 |
| 0 UND | 0 UND | 0 UND | Sales/Receivables | 0 UND | 0 UND | | 0 UND | 19 18.8 | 27 13.5 |
| 19 19.2 | 15 23.9 | 12 29.2 | | 0 UND | 1 326.6 | | 1 401.9 | 29 12.4 | 53 6.9 |
| 44 8.4 | 53 6.8 | 49 7.4 | | 1 342.3 | 24 15.2 | | 15 23.6 | 83 4.4 | 66 5.5 |
| | | | Cost of Sales/Inventory | | | | | | |
| | | | Cost of Sales/Payables | | | | | | |
| 4.9 | 6.4 | 5.3 | Sales/Working Capital | 5.1 | 2.8 | | 3.4 | 3.8 | 6.8 |
| 16.5 | 35.8 | 14.4 | | -15.3 | 7.3 | | 20.5 | 13.0 | 11.3 |
| -16.2 | -8.2 | -23.9 | | -1.4 | 79.5 | | -26.0 | 79.8 | 48.4 |
| 9.8 | 15.2 | 8.2 | EBIT/Interest | | 11.1 | | | 6.9 | 15.7 |
| (109) 2.6 | (80) 3.7 | (67) 3.4 | | (14) 2.7 | | | | (12) 4.2 | (18) 4.2 |
| .5 | 1.2 | 1.6 | | | -.8 | | | 2.0 | 2.5 |
| 2.3 | 13.4 | 4.4 | Net Profit + Depr., Dep., Amort./Cur. Mat. L/T/D | | | | | | |
| (18) 1.5 | (11) 1.9 | (13) 1.7 | | | | | | | |
| 1.0 | .8 | -.1 | | | | | | | |
| .4 | .6 | .4 | Fixed/Worth | 1.4 | .5 | | .4 | .4 | .2 |
| 1.2 | 1.3 | 1.0 | | 10.7 | 1.0 | | .7 | .7 | .7 |
| 5.4 | 7.3 | 22.3 | | -8.1 | 2.1 | | -3.6 | 1.8 | 1.3 |
| .6 | .6 | .5 | Debt/Worth | .5 | .3 | | .2 | .3 | .9 |
| 2.0 | 2.1 | 1.9 | | 14.1 | 1.0 | | 7.4 | 1.9 | 2.0 |
| 15.2 | 31.6 | 68.0 | | -9.4 | 4.6 | | -22.6 | 24.2 | 4.7 |
| 32.3 | 37.8 | 45.1 | % Profit Before Taxes/Tangible Net Worth | | 70.2 | | | 41.7 | 51.9 |
| (101) 8.7 | (74) 13.3 | (66) 17.8 | | (16) 11.7 | | | | (12) 20.9 | (17) 26.6 |
| -1.1 | 1.0 | 1.6 | | | -1.1 | | | 4.9 | 11.1 |
| 12.0 | 13.6 | 14.3 | % Profit Before Taxes/Total Assets | 10.0 | 19.9 | | 14.3 | 13.5 | 20.7 |
| 2.3 | 4.2 | 6.3 | | 4.6 | 2.8 | | 7.5 | 4.5 | 8.3 |
| -.7 | .0 | 1.0 | | .2 | -1.5 | | 2.1 | 1.8 | 2.6 |
| 20.8 | 23.1 | 28.1 | Sales/Net Fixed Assets | 5.3 | 17.2 | | 30.0 | 24.8 | 57.1 |
| 3.7 | 3.6 | 6.8 | | .7 | 1.7 | | 11.8 | 7.1 | 18.8 |
| .8 | .7 | .8 | | .2 | .4 | | 1.1 | 1.3 | 8.1 |
| 2.7 | 3.0 | 3.2 | Sales/Total Assets | 1.3 | 2.5 | | 4.8 | 2.0 | 3.8 |
| 1.4 | 1.3 | 1.2 | | .4 | .6 | | 1.7 | 1.1 | 2.9 |
| .5 | .5 | .4 | | .2 | .3 | | .6 | .4 | 1.0 |
| 1.9 | 1.0 | 1.0 | % Depr., Dep., Amort./Sales | 4.6 | 2.5 | | | .5 | .4 |
| (99) 5.1 | (75) 4.0 | (71) 3.8 | | (11) 10.5 | (13) 23.1 | | | (13) 2.9 | (19) 1.1 |
| 12.1 | 13.7 | 10.9 | | 18.7 | 45.6 | | | 9.9 | 3.4 |
| 1.6 | 1.1 | .5 | % Officers', Directors' Owners' Comp/Sales | | | | | | |
| (37) 3.9 | (25) 3.4 | (19) 3.9 | | | | | | | |
| 7.1 | 6.3 | 5.8 | | | | | | | |
| 3637165M | 3779093M | 2974334M | Net Sales ($) | 5713M | 40770M | 35788M | 82891M | 231483M | 2577689M |
| 1792627M | 2107477M | 1900192M | Total Assets ($) | 22158M | 94594M | 30859M | 69438M | 388090M | 1295053M |

M = $ thousand    MM = $ million
See Pages 9 through 22 for Explanation of Ratios and Data

## Current Data Sorted by Assets      Comparative Historical Data

| 0-500M | 500M-2MM | 2-10MM | 10-50MM | 50-100MM | 100-250MM | Type of Statement | 4/1/07-3/31/08 ALL | 4/1/08-3/31/09 ALL |
|---|---|---|---|---|---|---|---|---|
| | 1 | 1 | 1 | | | Unqualified | 8 | 4 |
| | 1 | 3 | 3 | | | Reviewed | 7 | 11 |
| | | 5 | 4 | | | Compiled | 6 | 11 |
| 2 | 8 | 11 | 3 | | | Tax Returns | 22 | 29 |
| 1 | 3 | 11 | 4 | 2 | 1 | Other | 7 | 16 |
| | 3 (4/1-9/30/11) | 61 (10/1/11-3/31/12) | | | | | | |
| 3 | 12 | 31 | 15 | 2 | 1 | NUMBER OF STATEMENTS | 50 | 71 |
| % | % | % | % | % | % | **ASSETS** | % | % |
| | 4.5 | 6.1 | 3.2 | | | Cash & Equivalents | 4.9 | 7.1 |
| | 1.0 | 9.2 | 9.7 | | | Trade Receivables (net) | 7.0 | 10.7 |
| | 13.8 | 20.1 | 16.3 | | | Inventory | 16.8 | 16.7 |
| | 7.3 | 5.3 | 4.9 | | | All Other Current | 6.4 | 4.1 |
| | 26.6 | 40.6 | 34.0 | | | Total Current | 35.1 | 38.6 |
| | 61.9 | 52.7 | 59.6 | | | Fixed Assets (net) | 54.0 | 52.3 |
| | 1.3 | .4 | 1.2 | | | Intangibles (net) | 2.0 | 1.9 |
| | 10.2 | 6.3 | 5.2 | | | All Other Non-Current | 9.0 | 7.2 |
| | 100.0 | 100.0 | 100.0 | | | Total | 100.0 | 100.0 |
| | | | | | | **LIABILITIES** | | |
| | 22.9 | 11.6 | 14.9 | | | Notes Payable-Short Term | 17.3 | 21.5 |
| | .6 | 4.6 | 3.7 | | | Cur. Mat.-L.T.D. | 6.4 | 7.3 |
| | 11.6 | 3.6 | 6.7 | | | Trade Payables | 4.7 | 3.8 |
| | .2 | .0 | .3 | | | Income Taxes Payable | .1 | .0 |
| | 3.8 | 9.0 | 2.9 | | | All Other Current | 8.6 | 9.5 |
| | 39.1 | 28.9 | 28.6 | | | Total Current | 37.1 | 42.0 |
| | 25.7 | 28.7 | 25.0 | | | Long-Term Debt | 29.0 | 32.9 |
| | .0 | .7 | 1.1 | | | Deferred Taxes | .4 | .2 |
| | 4.4 | 2.6 | 1.2 | | | All Other Non-Current | 2.5 | 3.3 |
| | 30.8 | 39.1 | 44.1 | | | Net Worth | 31.0 | 21.7 |
| | 100.0 | 100.0 | 100.0 | | | Total Liabilities & Net Worth | 100.0 | 100.0 |
| | | | | | | **INCOME DATA** | | |
| | 100.0 | 100.0 | 100.0 | | | Net Sales | 100.0 | 100.0 |
| | | | | | | Gross Profit | | |
| | 88.1 | 89.5 | 89.8 | | | Operating Expenses | 93.4 | 85.0 |
| | 11.9 | 10.5 | 10.2 | | | Operating Profit | 6.6 | 15.0 |
| | 1.9 | 3.4 | 4.7 | | | All Other Expenses (net) | 2.3 | 3.4 |
| | 10.1 | 7.0 | 5.5 | | | Profit Before Taxes | 4.3 | 11.6 |
| | | | | | | **RATIOS** | | |
| | 1.3 | 3.9 | 1.5 | | | | 2.0 | 1.7 |
| | .9 | 1.6 | 1.3 | | | Current | 1.1 | 1.2 |
| | .1 | 1.1 | 1.1 | | | | .6 | .3 |
| | .7 | 1.2 | .5 | | | | .6 | 1.1 |
| | .0 | .4 | .4 | | | Quick | .2 | .3 |
| | .0 | .2 | .1 | | | | .1 | .1 |
| | 0 UND | 0 UND | 1 566.6 | | | | 0 UND | 0 UND |
| | 0 UND | 3 107.3 | 22 16.4 | | | Sales/Receivables | | 2 217.9 |
| | 0 UND | 42 8.7 | 111 3.3 | | | | 19 18.7 | 40 9.1 |
| | | | | | | Cost of Sales/Inventory | | |
| | | | | | | Cost of Sales/Payables | | |
| | 12.0 | 1.8 | 3.3 | | | | 4.6 | 4.2 |
| | NM | 4.9 | 11.2 | | | Sales/Working Capital | 20.9 | 25.7 |
| | -4.4 | 36.8 | 39.2 | | | | -9.3 | -7.2 |
| | | 7.9 | 3.7 | | | | 4.2 | 7.3 |
| | | (26) 3.9 | (12) 1.8 | | | EBIT/Interest | (46) 2.2 | (66) 3.1 |
| | | 1.1 | -.3 | | | | 1.1 | 1.3 |
| | | | | | | Net Profit + Depr., Dep., Amort./Cur. Mat. L/T/D | | |
| | .2 | .6 | .9 | | | | .8 | .8 |
| | 2.1 | 1.2 | 1.3 | | | Fixed/Worth | 1.3 | 1.8 |
| | 6.6 | 2.3 | 2.1 | | | | NM | 90.5 |
| | .5 | .4 | .4 | | | | .6 | 1.0 |
| | 3.4 | 1.3 | 2.1 | | | Debt/Worth | 1.9 | 2.3 |
| | 28.4 | 4.1 | 3.9 | | | | NM | -739.0 |
| | 72.8 | 22.9 | 15.9 | | | | 24.2 | 50.7 |
| | (10) 23.7 | (25) 7.5 | 6.3 | | | % Profit Before Taxes/Tangible Net Worth | (38) 8.8 | (53) 18.7 |
| | 5.2 | .8 | .5 | | | | 3.0 | 3.5 |
| | 20.0 | 12.6 | 5.6 | | | | 9.9 | 15.4 |
| | 10.3 | 3.9 | 1.9 | | | % Profit Before Taxes/Total Assets | 4.4 | 5.2 |
| | 2.7 | .2 | .2 | | | | .4 | .6 |
| | UND | 3.2 | 3.1 | | | | 6.1 | 7.1 |
| | 2.6 | .9 | .9 | | | Sales/Net Fixed Assets | 1.9 | 2.1 |
| | .7 | .4 | .2 | | | | .5 | .5 |
| | 2.7 | 1.0 | .9 | | | | 2.3 | 2.7 |
| | 1.3 | .6 | .7 | | | Sales/Total Assets | .9 | .9 |
| | .7 | .3 | .2 | | | | .4 | .4 |
| | | 2.8 | 3.2 | | | | 2.1 | 1.6 |
| | | (28) 7.5 | (14) 15.3 | | | % Depr., Dep., Amort./Sales | (47) 5.6 | (58) 6.6 |
| | | 13.6 | 31.3 | | | | 11.7 | 15.0 |
| | | | | | | | 1.5 | 2.2 |
| | | | | | | % Officers', Directors' Owners' Comp/Sales | (13) 4.1 | (20) 3.6 |
| | | | | | | | 6.5 | 5.0 |
| 2655M | 21971M | 139890M | 183013M | 102243M | 90055M | Net Sales ($) | 764427M | 768872M |
| 830M | 14112M | 182542M | 236194M | 152407M | 115087M | Total Assets ($) | 657420M | 820588M |

© RMA 2012

M = $ thousand    MM = $ million

See Pages 9 through 22 for Explanation of Ratios and Data

| Comparative Historical Data | | | | Current Data Sorted by Sales | | | | | |
|---|---|---|---|---|---|---|---|---|---|
| | | | **Type of Statement** | 1 | | | | 1 | 1 |
| 4 | 5 | 3 | Unqualified | | 1 | 1 | 2 | 1 | 1 |
| 7 | 7 | 6 | Reviewed | 1 | | 4 | 2 | 2 | |
| 8 | 9 | 9 | Compiled | 5 | 12 | 4 | 1 | 2 | |
| 27 | 31 | 24 | Tax Returns | 4 | 9 | 2 | 1 | | 2 |
| 15 | 18 | 22 | Other | | | | | | |
| 4/1/09-3/31/10 | 4/1/10-3/31/11 | 4/1/11-3/31/12 | | 3 (4/1-9/30/11) | | | 61 (10/1/11-3/31/12) | | |
| ALL | ALL | ALL | | 0-1MM | 1-3MM | 3-5MM | 5-10MM | 10-25MM | 25MM & OVER |
| 61 | 70 | 64 | **NUMBER OF STATEMENTS** | 11 | 22 | 11 | 6 | 10 | 4 |
| % | % | % | **ASSETS** | % | % | % | % | % | % |
| 8.9 | 8.6 | 5.1 | Cash & Equivalents | 2.7 | 6.5 | 3.4 | | 5.5 | |
| 7.0 | 5.9 | 7.3 | Trade Receivables (net) | .9 | .7 | 8.4 | | 19.3 | |
| 15.8 | 18.8 | 17.8 | Inventory | 5.4 | 15.3 | 16.5 | | 21.4 | |
| 5.2 | 4.9 | 5.6 | All Other Current | 5.3 | 2.5 | 11.9 | | 6.3 | |
| 37.0 | 38.2 | 35.8 | Total Current | 14.2 | 25.0 | 40.2 | | 52.6 | |
| 51.1 | 51.6 | 56.8 | Fixed Assets (net) | 73.9 | 67.5 | 53.6 | | 44.1 | |
| 1.2 | 1.9 | .8 | Intangibles (net) | .6 | .4 | 1.5 | | .7 | |
| 10.7 | 8.2 | 6.6 | All Other Non-Current | 11.3 | 7.2 | 4.7 | | 2.6 | |
| 100.0 | 100.0 | 100.0 | Total | 100.0 | 100.0 | 100.0 | | 100.0 | |
| | | | **LIABILITIES** | | | | | | |
| 21.7 | 28.5 | 19.9 | Notes Payable-Short Term | 4.9 | 32.6 | 8.1 | | 17.8 | |
| 4.3 | 5.5 | 3.3 | Cur. Mat.-L.T.D. | 3.6 | 1.7 | 2.3 | | 2.5 | |
| 4.5 | 3.9 | 5.6 | Trade Payables | .4 | 4.7 | 6.1 | | 13.9 | |
| .1 | .0 | .1 | Income Taxes Payable | .2 | .0 | .1 | | .0 | |
| 4.4 | 4.3 | 6.4 | All Other Current | 3.6 | 9.2 | 8.0 | | 4.7 | |
| 34.9 | 42.3 | 35.4 | Total Current | 12.7 | 48.2 | 24.6 | | 39.0 | |
| 26.6 | 29.3 | 27.2 | Long-Term Debt | 31.9 | 31.8 | 28.3 | | 18.9 | |
| .6 | .6 | .6 | Deferred Taxes | .0 | .0 | .1 | | .3 | |
| 2.7 | 2.6 | 2.6 | All Other Non-Current | 6.5 | 1.8 | .7 | | 4.4 | |
| 35.2 | 25.2 | 34.2 | Net Worth | 49.0 | 18.2 | 46.3 | | 37.4 | |
| 100.0 | 100.0 | 100.0 | Total Liabilties & Net Worth | 100.0 | 100.0 | 100.0 | | 100.0 | |
| | | | **INCOME DATA** | | | | | | |
| 100.0 | 100.0 | 100.0 | Net Sales | 100.0 | 100.0 | 100.0 | | 100.0 | |
| | | | Gross Profit | | | | | | |
| 88.7 | 89.2 | 90.2 | Operating Expenses | 94.1 | 89.4 | 89.9 | | 93.4 | |
| 11.3 | 10.8 | 9.8 | Operating Profit | 5.9 | 10.6 | 10.1 | | 6.6 | |
| 5.0 | 3.9 | 3.3 | All Other Expenses (net) | 5.5 | 3.5 | 2.7 | | 2.2 | |
| 6.3 | 6.9 | 6.6 | Profit Before Taxes | .3 | 7.2 | 7.4 | | 4.4 | |
| | | | **RATIOS** | | | | | | |
| 1.8 | 2.2 | 2.0 | | 10.1 | 1.7 | 6.7 | | 1.6 | |
| 1.1 | 1.3 | 1.4 | Current | 1.3 | 1.0 | 1.4 | | 1.3 | |
| .4 | .4 | .6 | | .0 | .1 | 1.1 | | 1.0 | |
| .8 | .9 | .9 | | 1.1 | 1.0 | .6 | | .9 | |
| .3 | .2 | .3 | Quick | .1 | .2 | .4 | | .4 | |
| .0 | .0 | .1 | | .0 | .0 | .1 | | .3 | |
| 0 UND | 0 UND | 0 UND | | 0 UND | 0 UND | 0 UND | | 2 156.3 | |
| 0 UND | 0 UND | 3 128.0 | Sales/Receivables | 0 UND | 0 UND | 4 103.9 | | 38 9.6 | |
| 31 11.9 | 28 12.8 | 38 9.6 | | 16 23.2 | 4 85.1 | 50 7.3 | | 64 5.7 | |
| | | | Cost of Sales/Inventory | | | | | | |
| | | | Cost of Sales/Payables | | | | | | |
| 5.6 | 3.3 | 3.5 | | .8 | 3.4 | 1.8 | | 7.3 | |
| 20.6 | 8.9 | 11.1 | Sales/Working Capital | 20.6 | NM | 4.3 | | 13.7 | |
| -4.0 | -3.6 | -7.4 | | -1.6 | -4.0 | 25.4 | | NM | |
| 7.0 | 9.4 | 6.3 | | | 7.6 | | | | |
| (54) 2.9 | (62) 3.8 | (53) 3.2 | EBIT/Interest | | (19) 3.2 | | | | |
| 1.0 | .9 | 1.0 | | | -1.6 | | | | |
| | | | Net Profit + Depr., Dep., Amort./Cur. Mat. L/T/D | | | | | | |
| .6 | .6 | .8 | | 1.2 | .8 | .5 | | .7 | |
| 1.3 | 1.2 | 1.2 | Fixed/Worth | 1.6 | 1.4 | 1.2 | | 1.3 | |
| 3.4 | 23.6 | 2.8 | | 3.0 | NM | 1.8 | | 2.0 | |
| .6 | .5 | .4 | | .3 | .4 | .4 | | 1.5 | |
| 1.7 | 1.9 | 1.8 | Debt/Worth | .6 | 3.0 | 1.0 | | 2.0 | |
| 5.6 | 289.4 | 4.4 | | 3.2 | -14.5 | 2.3 | | 2.9 | |
| 26.8 | 30.9 | 23.7 | % Profit Before Taxes/Tangible Net Worth | 17.6 | 20.3 | 12.9 | | 26.4 | |
| (52) 11.2 | (54) 12.2 | (55) 8.8 | | (10) .7 | (16) 8.0 | (10) 7.5 | | 14.0 | |
| .8 | 1.5 | .7 | | -4.4 | 1.3 | -.8 | | 3.0 | |
| 10.8 | 11.6 | 10.9 | % Profit Before Taxes/Total Assets | 8.2 | 12.4 | 9.0 | | 10.5 | |
| 4.1 | 5.2 | 4.1 | | .5 | 3.7 | 4.0 | | 3.6 | |
| .1 | .1 | .3 | | -3.4 | -.1 | .2 | | .6 | |
| 6.6 | 8.8 | 3.4 | | .4 | 1.5 | 3.9 | | 9.0 | |
| 1.9 | 1.7 | 1.0 | Sales/Net Fixed Assets | .2 | .6 | 1.5 | | 3.1 | |
| .4 | .6 | .4 | | .1 | .3 | .6 | | 1.2 | |
| 2.2 | 1.7 | 1.2 | | .3 | 1.1 | 2.8 | | 2.1 | |
| .8 | .7 | .8 | Sales/Total Assets | .1 | .5 | .7 | | 1.3 | |
| .3 | .5 | .3 | | .1 | .3 | .4 | | .8 | |
| 2.7 | 3.6 | 3.6 | | 7.4 | 6.2 | | | 1.1 | |
| (54) 6.8 | (59) 7.7 | (55) 7.9 | % Depr., Dep., Amort./Sales | (10) 28.7 | (17) 11.5 | | | 3.5 | |
| 16.4 | 17.6 | 16.1 | | 48.3 | 14.3 | | | 7.2 | |
| .7 | .3 | 1.8 | | | .7 | | | | |
| (16) 2.1 | (16) 1.5 | (22) 4.5 | % Officers', Directors' Owners' Comp/Sales | | (10) 4.5 | | | | |
| 3.7 | 3.7 | 8.9 | | | 7.0 | | | | |
| 694681M | 633061M | 539827M | Net Sales ($) | 4769M | 41294M | 43198M | 43509M | 165454M | 241603M |
| 580585M | 757356M | 701172M | Total Assets ($) | 41551M | 102479M | 81322M | 45117M | 181132M | 249571M |

M = $ thousand     MM = $ million
See Pages 9 through 22 for Explanation of Ratios and Data

# AGRICULTURE—All Other Grain Farming  NAICS 111199

| Current Data Sorted by Assets | | | | | | | | Comparative Historical Data | |
|---|---|---|---|---|---|---|---|---|---|

| 0-500M | 500M-2MM | 2-10MM | 10-50MM | 50-100MM | 100-250MM | Type of Statement | | 4/1/07-3/31/08 ALL | 4/1/08-3/31/09 ALL |
|---|---|---|---|---|---|---|---|---|---|
| | 1 | 5 | 5 | 2 | 2 | Unqualified | | 10 | 11 |
| 1 | 1 | 14 | 5 | | | Reviewed | | 11 | 11 |
| 1 | 4 | 16 | 2 | | | Compiled | | 12 | 21 |
| 6 | 14 | 11 | 4 | | | Tax Returns | | 25 | 36 |
| | 6 | | 5 | 1 | 3 | Other | | 24 | 19 |
| | 16 (4/1-9/30/11) | | 93 (10/1/11-3/31/12) | | | | | | |
| 8 | 26 | 46 | 21 | 3 | 5 | NUMBER OF STATEMENTS | | 82 | 98 |

| 0-500M | 500M-2MM | 2-10MM | 10-50MM | 50-100MM | 100-250MM | Item | | 4/1/07-3/31/08 ALL | 4/1/08-3/31/09 ALL |
|---|---|---|---|---|---|---|---|---|---|
| % | % | % | % | % | % | **ASSETS** | | % | % |
| | 11.4 | 7.7 | 5.5 | | | Cash & Equivalents | | 7.6 | 5.7 |
| | 4.4 | 5.6 | 15.2 | | | Trade Receivables (net) | | 7.6 | 9.9 |
| | 18.6 | 20.5 | 16.9 | | | Inventory | | 17.5 | 16.4 |
| | 3.5 | 6.6 | 4.0 | | | All Other Current | | 9.8 | 8.2 |
| | 38.0 | 40.4 | 41.6 | | | Total Current | | 42.6 | 40.2 |
| | 44.0 | 51.2 | 39.9 | | | Fixed Assets (net) | | 41.6 | 47.2 |
| | 4.7 | .2 | 5.8 | | | Intangibles (net) | | 1.1 | .6 |
| | 13.3 | 8.2 | 12.7 | | | All Other Non-Current | | 14.7 | 12.0 |
| | 100.0 | 100.0 | 100.0 | | | Total | | 100.0 | 100.0 |
| | | | | | | **LIABILITIES** | | | |
| | 17.1 | 12.7 | 14.8 | | | Notes Payable-Short Term | | 31.4 | 24.2 |
| | 7.0 | 3.7 | 2.2 | | | Cur. Mat.-L.T.D. | | 8.4 | 11.0 |
| | 6.8 | 5.2 | 9.9 | | | Trade Payables | | 7.1 | 5.4 |
| | .1 | .1 | .1 | | | Income Taxes Payable | | .3 | .2 |
| | 2.2 | 3.9 | 4.7 | | | All Other Current | | 7.1 | 8.6 |
| | 33.1 | 25.5 | 31.7 | | | Total Current | | 54.3 | 49.4 |
| | 25.8 | 20.7 | 21.4 | | | Long-Term Debt | | 26.3 | 26.8 |
| | .6 | .2 | .3 | | | Deferred Taxes | | .1 | .2 |
| | 6.0 | 7.3 | .1 | | | All Other Non-Current | | 4.1 | 3.8 |
| | 34.4 | 46.2 | 46.5 | | | Net Worth | | 15.2 | 19.7 |
| | 100.0 | 100.0 | 100.0 | | | Total Liabilities & Net Worth | | 100.0 | 100.0 |
| | | | | | | **INCOME DATA** | | | |
| | 100.0 | 100.0 | 100.0 | | | Net Sales | | 100.0 | 100.0 |
| | | | | | | Gross Profit | | | |
| | 91.6 | 85.9 | 85.0 | | | Operating Expenses | | 86.6 | 88.0 |
| | 8.4 | 14.1 | 15.0 | | | Operating Profit | | 13.4 | 12.0 |
| | .6 | 3.8 | 4.6 | | | All Other Expenses (net) | | 3.8 | 3.2 |
| | 7.7 | 10.3 | 10.3 | | | Profit Before Taxes | | 9.6 | 8.8 |
| | | | | | | **RATIOS** | | | |
| | 2.5 | 2.6 | 2.1 | | | | | 2.1 | 1.6 |
| | 1.2 | 1.8 | 1.3 | | | Current | | 1.1 | 1.1 |
| | .5 | 1.1 | 1.1 | | | | | .4 | .3 |
| | 1.6 | 1.3 | 1.3 | | | | | .9 | .6 |
| | .7 | .3 | .6 | | | Quick | | .3 | (96) .2 |
| | .5 | .1 | .4 | | | | | .1 | .0 |
| | 0 UND | 0 UND | 5 74.2 | | | | | 0 UND | 0 UND |
| | 0 UND | 1 379.2 | 34 10.7 | | | Sales/Receivables | | 1 598.5 | 2 218.7 |
| | 3 139.2 | 17 21.4 | 152 2.4 | | | | | 19 18.9 | 27 13.7 |
| | | | | | | | | | |
| | | | | | | Cost of Sales/Inventory | | | |
| | | | | | | | | | |
| | | | | | | Cost of Sales/Payables | | | |
| | 10.4 | 2.7 | 3.5 | | | | | 4.0 | 6.6 |
| | 45.0 | 4.5 | 9.6 | | | Sales/Working Capital | | 34.8 | 62.3 |
| | -8.6 | 159.2 | 132.0 | | | | | -5.0 | -4.2 |
| | 8.1 | 12.9 | 7.6 | | | | | 5.4 | 5.7 |
| | (22) 3.5 | (43) 3.9 | (19) 3.2 | | | EBIT/Interest | | (71) 2.7 | (92) 3.0 |
| | .3 | 1.6 | 1.9 | | | | | 1.4 | 1.1 |
| | | | | | | Net Profit + Depr., Dep., Amort./Cur. Mat. L/T/D | | | |
| | .5 | .5 | .7 | | | | | .5 | .7 |
| | 1.5 | 1.1 | 1.1 | | | Fixed/Worth | | 1.0 | 1.5 |
| | 22.2 | 1.9 | 2.1 | | | | | 11.7 | 13.1 |
| | .9 | .5 | .6 | | | | | .8 | 1.1 |
| | 2.9 | .9 | 1.5 | | | Debt/Worth | | 3.0 | 2.9 |
| | 36.5 | 2.8 | 2.5 | | | | | 128.6 | 87.4 |
| | 63.7 | 31.6 | 31.1 | | | | | 37.5 | 58.6 |
| | (21) 9.5 | (43) 12.9 | (20) 13.9 | | | % Profit Before Taxes/Tangible Net Worth | | (64) 15.4 | (78) 22.1 |
| | -4.1 | 1.5 | 3.8 | | | | | 2.4 | 6.1 |
| | 12.5 | 13.6 | 9.4 | | | | | 15.3 | 12.0 |
| | 3.6 | 5.3 | 3.0 | | | % Profit Before Taxes/Total Assets | | 4.7 | 5.7 |
| | -1.3 | .9 | 2.2 | | | | | .8 | .5 |
| | 19.4 | 10.6 | 11.2 | | | | | 17.4 | 11.7 |
| | 4.1 | 1.3 | 1.7 | | | Sales/Net Fixed Assets | | 3.9 | 3.1 |
| | 1.8 | .5 | .6 | | | | | 1.0 | .7 |
| | 2.6 | 1.4 | 2.4 | | | | | 2.6 | 2.4 |
| | 1.3 | .7 | .8 | | | Sales/Total Assets | | 1.3 | 1.2 |
| | 1.0 | .3 | .3 | | | | | .6 | .6 |
| | 1.7 | 1.1 | .7 | | | | | 1.6 | 2.2 |
| | (20) 6.0 | (40) 10.9 | (19) 1.8 | | | % Depr., Dep., Amort./Sales | | (61) 5.0 | (83) 6.7 |
| | 15.8 | 20.1 | 10.5 | | | | | 9.8 | 14.4 |
| | 1.7 | 1.1 | | | | | | 1.7 | 1.1 |
| | (14) 2.4 | (13) 3.2 | | | | % Officers', Directors' Owners' Comp/Sales | | (20) 3.8 | (31) 1.6 |
| | 4.5 | 5.3 | | | | | | 6.1 | 3.1 |
| 8861M | 62697M | 266005M | 929834M | 588227M | 1512091M | Net Sales ($) | | 1283224M | 4659895M |
| 2340M | 28410M | 207423M | 475900M | 216948M | 888712M | Total Assets ($) | | 792676M | 1245167M |

M = $ thousand   MM = $ million
See Pages 9 through 22 for Explanation of Ratios and Data

## Comparative Historical Data / Current Data Sorted by Sales

| H1 | H2 | H3 | Type of Statement | C1 0-1MM | C2 1-3MM | C3 3-5MM | C4 5-10MM | C5 10-25MM | C6 25MM & OVER |
|---|---|---|---|---|---|---|---|---|---|
| 17 | 10 | 10 | Unqualified |  |  |  | 1 | 1 | 8 |
| 12 | 8 | 12 | Reviewed | 1 | 1 | 2 |  | 5 | 3 |
| 19 | 19 | 21 | Compiled | 1 | 8 | 7 | 3 | 1 | 1 |
| 35 | 36 | 40 | Tax Returns | 12 | 19 | 4 | 4 | 1 | 1 |
| 23 | 37 | 26 | Other | 5 | 5 | 8 |  | 3 | 5 |
| 4/1/09-3/31/10 ALL | 4/1/10-3/31/11 ALL | 4/1/11-3/31/12 ALL |  | 16 (4/1-9/30/11) | | | 93 (10/1/11-3/31/12) | | |
| 106 | 110 | 109 | NUMBER OF STATEMENTS | 19 | 33 | 21 | 8 | 10 | 18 |
| % | % | % | ASSETS | % | % | % | % | % | % |
| 9.9 | 7.0 | 9.1 | Cash & Equivalents | 7.8 | 7.2 | 10.5 |  | 10.2 | 12.0 |
| 11.1 | 11.0 | 7.1 | Trade Receivables (net) | 1.7 | 2.7 | 6.8 |  | 12.7 | 19.2 |
| 19.1 | 19.7 | 19.6 | Inventory | 12.2 | 16.2 | 24.8 |  | 12.4 | 31.5 |
| 3.8 | 5.3 | 5.7 | All Other Current | 1.3 | 5.7 | 1.0 |  | 19.5 | 8.5 |
| 43.9 | 43.0 | 41.6 | Total Current | 23.0 | 31.8 | 43.0 |  | 54.9 | 71.2 |
| 43.8 | 49.0 | 45.2 | Fixed Assets (net) | 61.9 | 57.1 | 41.1 |  | 37.7 | 17.2 |
| 1.2 | 1.3 | 2.5 | Intangibles (net) | 5.3 | 1.6 | 2.1 |  | .1 | 2.3 |
| 11.0 | 6.8 | 10.7 | All Other Non-Current | 9.7 | 9.5 | 13.8 |  | 7.3 | 9.4 |
| 100.0 | 100.0 | 100.0 | Total | 100.0 | 100.0 | 100.0 |  | 100.0 | 100.0 |
|  |  |  | LIABILITIES |  |  |  |  |  |  |
| 21.1 | 18.3 | 15.7 | Notes Payable-Short Term | 6.1 | 24.0 | 9.7 |  | 11.1 | 18.7 |
| 8.6 | 3.8 | 4.0 | Cur. Mat.-L.T.D. | 3.5 | 3.9 | 3.5 |  | 6.2 | 1.2 |
| 6.7 | 6.9 | 7.1 | Trade Payables | 4.4 | .4 | 10.2 |  | 5.3 | 20.5 |
| .2 | .2 | .1 | Income Taxes Payable | .0 | .1 | .3 |  | .0 | .2 |
| 8.0 | 4.5 | 4.3 | All Other Current | 2.1 | 1.6 | 3.4 |  | 15.2 | 8.2 |
| 44.5 | 33.6 | 31.2 | Total Current | 16.1 | 30.1 | 27.1 |  | 37.9 | 48.7 |
| 24.9 | 26.0 | 23.7 | Long-Term Debt | 20.7 | 35.8 | 23.9 |  | 17.5 | 12.1 |
| .3 | .3 | .3 | Deferred Taxes | .5 | .2 | .1 |  | 1.5 | .1 |
| 1.8 | 9.5 | 4.7 | All Other Non-Current | 7.5 | 3.0 | 11.9 |  | .2 | .7 |
| 28.5 | 30.7 | 40.1 | Net Worth | 55.3 | 30.9 | 37.0 |  | 43.0 | 38.4 |
| 100.0 | 100.0 | 100.0 | Total Liabilities & Net Worth | 100.0 | 100.0 | 100.0 |  | 100.0 | 100.0 |
|  |  |  | INCOME DATA |  |  |  |  |  |  |
| 100.0 | 100.0 | 100.0 | Net Sales | 100.0 | 100.0 | 100.0 |  | 100.0 | 100.0 |
|  |  |  | Gross Profit |  |  |  |  |  |  |
| 90.7 | 88.4 | 88.1 | Operating Expenses | 82.4 | 88.6 | 85.6 |  | 93.5 | 94.4 |
| 9.3 | 11.6 | 11.9 | Operating Profit | 17.6 | 11.4 | 14.4 |  | 6.5 | 5.6 |
| 1.9 | 4.3 | 2.6 | All Other Expenses (net) | 7.9 | 2.3 | 1.2 |  | 2.3 | .2 |
| 7.4 | 7.3 | 9.4 | Profit Before Taxes | 9.7 | 9.1 | 13.2 |  | 4.2 | 5.4 |
|  |  |  | RATIOS |  |  |  |  |  |  |
| 1.8 | 2.3 | 2.3 | Current | 2.5 | 2.2 | 2.4 |  | 1.8 | 2.1 |
| 1.2 | 1.4 | 1.4 |  | 1.9 | 1.1 | 1.8 |  | 1.3 | 1.5 |
| .8 | 1.0 | 1.0 |  | .6 | .4 | 1.2 |  | 1.0 | 1.1 |
| 1.0 | 1.0 | 1.3 | Quick | 1.9 | 1.0 | 1.6 |  | 1.1 | .8 |
| .4 | .4 | .5 |  | 1.1 | .1 | .7 |  | .5 | .6 |
| .1 | .1 | .1 |  | .2 | .0 | .2 |  | .2 | .2 |
| 0 UND | 0 UND | 0 UND | Sales/Receivables | 0 UND | 0 UND | 0 UND |  | 1 354.0 | 6 57.2 |
| 9 40.2 | 5 80.6 | 1 260.6 |  | 0 UND | 0 UND | 12 31.4 |  | 8 48.3 | 15 24.0 |
| 35 10.4 | 36 10.1 | 26 13.8 |  | 0 UND | 2 175.0 | 29 12.5 |  | 126 2.9 | 35 10.4 |
|  |  |  | Cost of Sales/Inventory |  |  |  |  |  |  |
|  |  |  | Cost of Sales/Payables |  |  |  |  |  |  |
| 4.3 | 3.4 | 3.2 | Sales/Working Capital | 2.8 | 3.1 | 2.3 |  | 6.2 | 8.2 |
| 20.4 | 13.7 | 14.0 |  | 8.8 | 43.5 | 4.8 |  | 15.0 | 15.6 |
| -28.6 | 288.1 | 372.3 |  | -11.0 | -8.4 | 35.3 |  | NM | 44.4 |
| 7.1 | 8.6 | 11.2 | EBIT/Interest | 7.1 | 15.5 | 28.5 |  |  | 12.5 |
| (95) 2.8 | (93) 4.4 | (96) 3.8 |  | (13) 3.9 | (31) 3.1 | 4.2 |  |  | (16) 5.8 |
| 1.3 | 1.6 | 1.8 |  | 1.4 | 1.0 | 2.4 |  |  | 3.3 |
| 6.3 | 7.2 | 9.2 | Net Profit + Depr., Dep., Amort./Cur. Mat. L/T/D |  |  |  |  |  |  |
| (13) 3.9 | (15) 3.4 | (10) 4.4 |  |  |  |  |  |  |  |
| 2.2 | 1.9 | 1.9 |  |  |  |  |  |  |  |
| .6 | .7 | .6 | Fixed/Worth | 1.0 | .7 | .6 |  | .4 | .2 |
| 1.1 | 1.2 | 1.1 |  | 1.2 | 1.4 | 1.2 |  | .9 | .6 |
| 3.1 | 2.8 | 2.4 |  | 2.3 | 11.0 | 3.4 |  | 2.0 | .7 |
| .8 | .6 | .6 | Debt/Worth | .3 | .4 | .6 |  | .8 | .7 |
| 2.0 | 1.8 | 1.3 |  | 1.1 | 1.3 | 1.1 |  | 1.5 | 1.6 |
| 7.5 | 6.2 | 4.0 |  | 1.9 | 13.0 | 24.0 |  | 2.5 | 4.0 |
| 34.2 | 43.6 | 34.0 | % Profit Before Taxes/Tangible Net Worth | 25.2 | 42.5 | 35.4 |  | 32.2 | 36.6 |
| (89) 12.9 | (94) 15.9 | (98) 15.6 |  | (18) 2.5 | (27) 12.9 | (18) 11.6 |  | 10.3 | (17) 26.4 |
| 2.4 | 3.4 | 2.4 |  | .5 | .0 | 4.9 |  | 3.5 | 17.0 |
| 13.7 | 11.1 | 12.7 | % Profit Before Taxes/Total Assets | 5.6 | 19.3 | 14.2 |  | 9.8 | 13.2 |
| 4.6 | 4.4 | 5.3 |  | 1.3 | 4.1 | 8.8 |  | 3.8 | 8.7 |
| .9 | 1.4 | 1.1 |  | .2 | .0 | 2.9 |  | 1.3 | 4.7 |
| 13.0 | 9.2 | 14.5 | Sales/Net Fixed Assets | 2.1 | 6.6 | 16.0 |  | 23.8 | 82.9 |
| 3.1 | 2.0 | 2.9 |  | .3 | 1.9 | 2.0 |  | 5.5 | 14.5 |
| .8 | .7 | .8 |  | .1 | .7 | .8 |  | 1.1 | 9.2 |
| 2.7 | 2.2 | 2.5 | Sales/Total Assets | 1.0 | 1.6 | 1.8 |  | 5.2 | 5.3 |
| 1.2 | .9 | 1.0 |  | .2 | .8 | 1.0 |  | 1.5 | 3.1 |
| .5 | .4 | .5 |  | .1 | .5 | .4 |  | .6 | 1.3 |
| 1.3 | 2.4 | 1.2 | % Depr., Dep., Amort./Sales | 10.9 | 4.2 | 1.5 |  |  | .2 |
| (89) 4.2 | (90) 6.9 | (89) 6.6 |  | (13) 19.7 | (28) 9.7 | (17) 5.4 |  | (15) .7 |  |
| 13.0 | 13.1 | 13.7 |  | 31.3 | 23.0 | 12.9 |  |  | 1.5 |
| 1.4 | 1.0 | 1.5 | % Officers', Directors' Owners' Comp/Sales |  |  | 1.9 |  |  |  |
| (37) 3.7 | (27) 2.7 | (33) 3.1 |  |  | (16) 2.9 |  |  |  |  |
| 5.8 | 4.3 | 5.3 |  |  | 4.5 |  |  |  |  |
| 4342060M | 1664563M | 3367715M | Net Sales ($) | 8591M | 58069M | 81184M | 63036M | 196428M | 2960407M |
| 2187837M | 1295142M | 1819733M | Total Assets ($) | 43794M | 100864M | 125177M | 59272M | 175457M | 1315169M |

## Current Data Sorted by Assets                                   Comparative Historical Data

| 0-500M | 500M-2MM | 2-10MM | 10-50MM | 50-100MM | 100-250MM | Type of Statement | 4/1/07-3/31/08 ALL | 4/1/08-3/31/09 ALL |
|---|---|---|---|---|---|---|---|---|
| | | | 2 | 1 | 2 | Unqualified | 6 | 6 |
| | | 3 | 3 | 3 | | Reviewed | 14 | 19 |
| | 4 | 1 | 8 | 3 | 2 | Compiled | 15 | 23 |
| 3 | 4 | 4 | 3 | | | Tax Returns | 7 | 6 |
| 1 | 2 | 5 | 5 | 2 | 2 | Other | 19 | 16 |
| | 12 (4/1-9/30/11) | | 51 (10/1/11-3/31/12) | | | | | |
| 4 | 10 | 13 | 21 | 9 | 6 | **NUMBER OF STATEMENTS** | 61 | 70 |
| % | % | % | % | % | % | **ASSETS** | % | % |
| | 2.0 | 14.1 | 3.1 | | | Cash & Equivalents | 9.4 | 5.5 |
| | 11.6 | 19.7 | 15.0 | | | Trade Receivables (net) | 12.7 | 11.9 |
| | 9.4 | 12.3 | 22.1 | | | Inventory | 13.2 | 17.8 |
| | 8.6 | 4.3 | 8.0 | | | All Other Current | 4.7 | 5.3 |
| | 31.6 | 50.3 | 48.2 | | | Total Current | 40.0 | 40.5 |
| | 64.5 | 39.9 | 41.0 | | | Fixed Assets (net) | 40.0 | 44.4 |
| | .0 | .5 | 1.6 | | | Intangibles (net) | 3.8 | 3.8 |
| | 3.8 | 9.3 | 9.2 | | | All Other Non-Current | 16.1 | 11.4 |
| | 100.0 | 100.0 | 100.0 | | | Total | 100.0 | 100.0 |
| | | | | | | **LIABILITIES** | | |
| | 33.5 | 16.7 | 15.8 | | | Notes Payable-Short Term | 16.2 | 17.4 |
| | 2.0 | 4.6 | 2.6 | | | Cur. Mat.-L.T.D. | 9.7 | 6.2 |
| | 5.5 | 21.3 | 6.2 | | | Trade Payables | 7.0 | 4.3 |
| | .0 | 1.1 | 2.7 | | | Income Taxes Payable | .3 | .6 |
| | 2.8 | 17.4 | 6.7 | | | All Other Current | 7.2 | 8.9 |
| | 43.8 | 61.2 | 34.0 | | | Total Current | 40.4 | 37.4 |
| | 48.2 | 27.8 | 23.2 | | | Long-Term Debt | 27.8 | 26.9 |
| | .0 | .1 | .1 | | | Deferred Taxes | .5 | .5 |
| | .7 | 2.6 | .7 | | | All Other Non-Current | 5.1 | 3.6 |
| | 7.3 | 8.4 | 41.9 | | | Net Worth | 26.2 | 31.7 |
| | 100.0 | 100.0 | 100.0 | | | Total Liabilities & Net Worth | 100.0 | 100.0 |
| | | | | | | **INCOME DATA** | | |
| | 100.0 | 100.0 | 100.0 | | | Net Sales | 100.0 | 100.0 |
| | | | | | | Gross Profit | | |
| | 85.0 | 85.6 | 92.1 | | | Operating Expenses | 86.1 | 86.1 |
| | 15.0 | 14.4 | 7.9 | | | Operating Profit | 13.9 | 13.9 |
| | 5.1 | 1.9 | 2.0 | | | All Other Expenses (net) | 4.3 | 3.7 |
| | 9.9 | 12.5 | 5.9 | | | Profit Before Taxes | 9.6 | 10.2 |
| | | | | | | **RATIOS** | | |
| | 2.5 | 1.4 | 1.9 | | | | 2.9 | 2.4 |
| | 1.2 | 1.1 | 1.6 | | | Current | 1.2 | 1.2 |
| | .1 | .3 | .8 | | | | .9 | .6 |
| | .9 | 1.1 | .8 | | | | 1.8 | 1.2 |
| | .1 | .6 | .3 | | | Quick | .7 | .3 |
| | .0 | .1 | .1 | | | | .1 | .1 |
| 0 UND | 0 UND | 0 UND | | | | | 0 UND | 0 UND |
| 0 UND | 11 31.8 | 20 18.3 | | | | Sales/Receivables | 23 16.1 | 28 12.9 |
| 37 9.8 | 48 7.6 | 72 5.1 | | | | | 49 7.4 | 56 6.5 |
| | | | | | | Cost of Sales/Inventory | | |
| | | | | | | Cost of Sales/Payables | | |
| | 5.7 | 6.2 | 2.9 | | | | 4.6 | 2.9 |
| | 7.9 | 30.8 | 7.4 | | | Sales/Working Capital | 16.1 | 12.9 |
| | -4.9 | -6.7 | -29.7 | | | | -12.9 | -9.8 |
| | | 7.3 | 12.6 | | | | 10.7 | 6.9 |
| | | 5.1 | (20) 4.3 | | | EBIT/Interest | (50) 2.1 | (61) 3.6 |
| | | 1.2 | 3.4 | | | | 1.3 | 1.5 |
| | | | | | | Net Profit + Depr., Dep., | 2.9 | 4.2 |
| | | | | | | Amort./Cur. Mat. L/T/D | (10) 1.5 | (17) 2.7 |
| | | | | | | | -.4 | 1.4 |
| | .9 | .5 | .3 | | | | .3 | .7 |
| | 4.8 | 1.1 | .9 | | | Fixed/Worth | 1.2 | 1.3 |
| | NM | NM | 1.6 | | | | 5.2 | 3.7 |
| | .7 | 1.3 | .8 | | | | .4 | .7 |
| | 7.3 | 4.2 | 1.2 | | | Debt/Worth | 1.8 | 1.8 |
| | NM | NM | 2.5 | | | | 18.7 | 20.4 |
| | | 36.7 | 30.3 | | | % Profit Before Taxes/Tangible | 36.8 | 54.6 |
| | | (10) 22.8 | (20) 17.5 | | | Net Worth | (52) 10.0 | (59) 18.5 |
| | | 2.6 | 5.4 | | | | 5.3 | 4.5 |
| | 18.7 | 14.8 | 10.5 | | | % Profit Before Taxes/Total | 9.0 | 13.9 |
| | 8.1 | 5.7 | 6.3 | | | Assets | 4.5 | 5.6 |
| | .2 | .4 | 1.9 | | | | 1.4 | 1.4 |
| | 8.5 | 50.5 | 8.6 | | | | 7.9 | 5.6 |
| | 3.4 | 3.7 | 4.5 | | | Sales/Net Fixed Assets | 2.9 | 2.2 |
| | 1.2 | .9 | 1.2 | | | | 1.1 | 1.1 |
| | 3.4 | 3.2 | 2.1 | | | | 1.8 | 1.9 |
| | 1.7 | 1.5 | 1.0 | | | Sales/Total Assets | 1.0 | .9 |
| | .6 | .5 | .6 | | | | .5 | .5 |
| | | | 1.9 | | | | 2.7 | 3.2 |
| | | | 4.7 | | | % Depr., Dep., Amort./Sales | (51) 5.0 | (63) 5.0 |
| | | | 8.3 | | | | 7.9 | 7.5 |
| | | | | | | | | 1.1 |
| | | | | | | % Officers', Directors' | | (13) 4.5 |
| | | | | | | Owners' Comp/Sales | | 7.5 |
| 5315M | 31921M | 135390M | 929279M | 312770M | 647534M | Net Sales ($) | 1487510M | 1762945M |
| 1139M | 11739M | 75214M | 418207M | 551431M | 953053M | Total Assets ($) | 1264892M | 1862901M |

## Comparative Historical Data | Current Data Sorted by Sales

| Type of Statement | 4/1/09-3/31/10 ALL | 4/1/10-3/31/11 ALL | 4/1/11-3/31/12 ALL | 0-1MM | 1-3MM | 3-5MM | 5-10MM | 10-25MM | 25MM & OVER |
|---|---|---|---|---|---|---|---|---|---|
| Unqualified | 8 | 7 | 5 | | | | | 1 | 4 |
| Reviewed | 13 | 17 | 9 | | | | 1 | 3 | 5 |
| Compiled | 12 | 21 | 18 | | 2 | 2 | 3 | 9 | 2 |
| Tax Returns | 23 | 12 | 14 | 2 | 4 | 1 | 3 | 4 | |
| Other | 15 | 15 | 17 | 3 | 2 | 2 | | 4 | 6 |
| | 4/1/09-3/31/10 ALL | 4/1/10-3/31/11 ALL | 4/1/11-3/31/12 ALL | 12 (4/1-9/30/11) 0-1MM | 1-3MM | 3-5MM | 51 (10/1/11-3/31/12) 5-10MM | 10-25MM | 25MM & OVER |
| **NUMBER OF STATEMENTS** | 71 | 72 | 63 | 5 | 8 | 5 | 7 | 21 | 17 |
| | % | % | % | % | % | % | % | % | % |
| **ASSETS** | | | | | | | | | |
| Cash & Equivalents | 8.1 | 6.2 | 5.5 | | | | | 4.2 | 1.9 |
| Trade Receivables (net) | 11.3 | 11.9 | 13.8 | | | | | 15.5 | 19.6 |
| Inventory | 13.3 | 15.5 | 16.5 | | | | | 18.9 | 22.5 |
| All Other Current | 5.9 | 6.4 | 6.0 | | | | | 9.5 | 4.6 |
| Total Current | 38.7 | 40.0 | 41.8 | | | | | 48.1 | 48.6 |
| Fixed Assets (net) | 48.6 | 48.3 | 48.7 | | | | | 42.4 | 33.5 |
| Intangibles (net) | 2.1 | 1.9 | 1.7 | | | | | 1.5 | 3.8 |
| All Other Non-Current | 10.6 | 9.8 | 7.8 | | | | | 7.9 | 14.2 |
| Total | 100.0 | 100.0 | 100.0 | | | | | 100.0 | 100.0 |
| **LIABILITIES** | | | | | | | | | |
| Notes Payable-Short Term | 21.4 | 20.2 | 18.5 | | | | | 17.2 | 12.5 |
| Cur. Mat.-L.T.D. | 6.5 | 3.6 | 2.8 | | | | | 2.1 | 2.4 |
| Trade Payables | 5.8 | 5.8 | 8.2 | | | | | 11.9 | 9.7 |
| Income Taxes Payable | .4 | 1.0 | 1.3 | | | | | 3.3 | .6 |
| All Other Current | 6.1 | 5.0 | 7.1 | | | | | 10.5 | 9.9 |
| Total Current | 40.2 | 35.6 | 37.8 | | | | | 45.1 | 35.2 |
| Long-Term Debt | 31.6 | 29.7 | 28.7 | | | | | 20.4 | 16.3 |
| Deferred Taxes | .3 | .5 | .1 | | | | | .1 | .3 |
| All Other Non-Current | 3.2 | 1.6 | 6.1 | | | | | 1.6 | .9 |
| Net Worth | 24.7 | 32.7 | 27.3 | | | | | 32.8 | 47.3 |
| Total Liabilities & Net Worth | 100.0 | 100.0 | 100.0 | | | | | 100.0 | 100.0 |
| **INCOME DATA** | | | | | | | | | |
| Net Sales | 100.0 | 100.0 | 100.0 | | | | | 100.0 | 100.0 |
| Gross Profit | | | | | | | | | |
| Operating Expenses | 90.9 | 90.4 | 87.7 | | | | | 92.9 | 88.7 |
| Operating Profit | 9.1 | 9.6 | 12.3 | | | | | 7.1 | 11.3 |
| All Other Expenses (net) | 2.4 | 1.3 | 1.7 | | | | | -.5 | -.1 |
| Profit Before Taxes | 6.6 | 8.3 | 10.7 | | | | | 7.6 | 11.4 |
| **RATIOS** | | | | | | | | | |
| Current | 2.3 | 2.2 | 1.9 | | | | | 2.0 | 1.9 |
| | 1.2 | 1.3 | 1.3 | | | | | 1.3 | 1.4 |
| | .7 | .8 | .9 | | | | | .7 | 1.0 |
| Quick | 1.5 | 1.1 | .9 | | | | | .9 | .9 |
| | .5 | .4 | .4 | | | | | .2 | .5 |
| | .1 | .2 | .1 | | | | | .1 | .3 |
| Sales/Receivables | 0 UND | 0 UND | 0 UND | | | | | 0 UND | 29 12.5 |
| | 21 17.6 | 28 13.0 | 26 14.3 | | | | | 24 15.3 | 50 7.3 |
| | 58 6.3 | 58 6.3 | 68 5.4 | | | | | 78 4.7 | 68 5.4 |
| Cost of Sales/Inventory | | | | | | | | | |
| Cost of Sales/Payables | | | | | | | | | |
| Sales/Working Capital | 3.5 | 3.5 | 4.4 | | | | | 3.0 | 5.2 |
| | 14.9 | 13.2 | 10.2 | | | | | 10.2 | 12.5 |
| | -6.3 | -13.6 | -83.5 | | | | | -29.7 | 44.0 |
| EBIT/Interest | 9.3 | 7.2 | 9.5 | | | | | 9.6 | 15.8 |
| | (64) 3.3 | (65) 2.8 | (58) 5.5 | | | | | (19) 4.4 | 8.4 |
| | .7 | 1.1 | 3.0 | | | | | 1.2 | 5.4 |
| Net Profit + Depr., Dep., Amort./Cur. Mat. L/T/D | 5.8 | 7.0 | 8.9 | | | | | | |
| | (16) 3.1 | (12) 2.7 | (11) 4.4 | | | | | | |
| | .0 | .6 | 2.4 | | | | | | |
| Fixed/Worth | .7 | .7 | .5 | | | | | .3 | .4 |
| | 1.9 | 1.3 | 1.1 | | | | | 1.1 | .8 |
| | 4.7 | 2.7 | 3.8 | | | | | 2.8 | 1.2 |
| Debt/Worth | 1.1 | .9 | .8 | | | | | .5 | .9 |
| | 2.7 | 1.5 | 1.3 | | | | | 1.1 | 1.1 |
| | 9.3 | 4.5 | 4.2 | | | | | 3.6 | 2.1 |
| % Profit Before Taxes/Tangible Net Worth | 40.8 | 29.3 | 31.2 | | | | | 30.4 | 37.1 |
| | (60) 15.1 | (66) 10.8 | (55) 20.7 | | | | | (19) 15.0 | 29.0 |
| | -2.9 | .9 | 8.7 | | | | | 2.3 | 18.1 |
| % Profit Before Taxes/Total Assets | 11.4 | 10.6 | 12.6 | | | | | 10.7 | 15.5 |
| | 5.9 | 4.9 | 8.9 | | | | | 4.8 | 9.4 |
| | -1.1 | .4 | 2.4 | | | | | .6 | 8.7 |
| Sales/Net Fixed Assets | 4.1 | 4.3 | 6.2 | | | | | 8.7 | 15.9 |
| | 2.2 | 2.0 | 2.6 | | | | | 5.0 | 3.2 |
| | 1.1 | .7 | .9 | | | | | 1.3 | 1.2 |
| Sales/Total Assets | 1.8 | 2.0 | 2.5 | | | | | 2.2 | 2.9 |
| | 1.0 | .7 | .8 | | | | | 1.0 | .8 |
| | .5 | .5 | .5 | | | | | .7 | .6 |
| % Depr., Dep., Amort./Sales | 3.1 | 3.3 | 3.7 | | | | | 3.8 | 1.4 |
| | (65) 5.6 | (66) 5.9 | (54) 5.6 | | | | | (19) 5.7 | (16) 3.3 |
| | 9.3 | 10.1 | 9.0 | | | | | 8.2 | 4.9 |
| % Officers', Directors', Owners' Comp/Sales | 1.1 | .9 | 1.3 | | | | | | |
| | (19) 2.1 | (17) 1.7 | (20) 2.1 | | | | | | |
| | 5.4 | 4.5 | 3.2 | | | | | | |
| Net Sales ($) | 1696471M | 1604983M | 2062209M | 1583M | 11489M | 18440M | 58592M | 382488M | 1589617M |
| Total Assets ($) | 1509619M | 1920070M | 2010783M | 6658M | 18486M | 14426M | 132254M | 522767M | 1316192M |

M = $ thousand    MM = $ million
See Pages 9 through 22 for Explanation of Ratios and Data

## Current Data Sorted by Assets      Comparative Historical Data

| 0-500M | 500M-2MM | 2-10MM | 10-50MM | 50-100MM | 100-250MM | Type of Statement | 4/1/07-3/31/08 ALL | 4/1/08-3/31/09 ALL |
|---|---|---|---|---|---|---|---|---|
|  |  |  | 5 | 5 | 3 | Unqualified | 12 | 13 |
|  |  | 3 | 8 | 3 |  | Reviewed | 11 | 24 |
| 2 | 4 | 15 | 2 |  |  | Compiled | 13 | 20 |
| 5 | 9 | 6 | 2 | 1 |  | Tax Returns | 12 | 15 |
| 3 |  | 17 | 17 | 2 | 3 | Other | 32 | 31 |
|  | 28 (4/1-9/30/11) |  | 87 (10/1/11-3/31/12) |  |  |  |  |  |
| **10** | **13** | **41** | **34** | **11** | **6** | **NUMBER OF STATEMENTS** | **80** | **103** |
| % | % | % | % | % | % | **ASSETS** | % | % |
| 12.0 | 12.8 | 13.0 | 11.5 | 4.2 |  | Cash & Equivalents | 8.8 | 7.8 |
| 15.1 | 23.0 | 18.0 | 15.9 | 15.6 |  | Trade Receivables (net) | 17.4 | 16.9 |
| 8.9 | 10.4 | 12.6 | 17.8 | 18.3 |  | Inventory | 14.5 | 16.2 |
| 5.3 | 7.6 | 4.6 | 4.3 | 3.2 |  | All Other Current | 5.8 | 6.1 |
| 41.4 | 53.9 | 48.2 | 49.4 | 41.3 |  | Total Current | 46.4 | 47.0 |
| 49.4 | 33.5 | 38.4 | 39.4 | 37.3 |  | Fixed Assets (net) | 39.3 | 38.5 |
| .2 | .1 | 4.6 | 3.9 | 6.7 |  | Intangibles (net) | 1.8 | 3.1 |
| 9.0 | 12.5 | 8.7 | 7.2 | 14.6 |  | All Other Non-Current | 12.5 | 11.5 |
| 100.0 | 100.0 | 100.0 | 100.0 | 100.0 |  | Total | 100.0 | 100.0 |
|  |  |  |  |  |  | **LIABILITIES** |  |  |
| 32.1 | 34.5 | 16.4 | 10.6 | 4.9 |  | Notes Payable-Short Term | 17.7 | 15.7 |
| 5.5 | 2.3 | 4.7 | 2.7 | 1.6 |  | Cur. Mat.-L.T.D. | 3.1 | 4.2 |
| 14.3 | 7.6 | 12.5 | 7.8 | 9.1 |  | Trade Payables | 11.7 | 11.6 |
| .0 | .0 | .0 | .1 | .0 |  | Income Taxes Payable | .4 | .5 |
| 4.3 | 7.8 | 6.0 | 6.8 | 6.0 |  | All Other Current | 9.8 | 12.7 |
| 56.1 | 52.2 | 39.7 | 27.9 | 21.5 |  | Total Current | 42.7 | 44.6 |
| 42.9 | 21.5 | 25.1 | 16.6 | 18.8 |  | Long-Term Debt | 16.9 | 20.8 |
| .0 | .0 | .6 | .4 | .1 |  | Deferred Taxes | .7 | .8 |
| 35.5 | 21.2 | 3.0 | 2.8 | 1.6 |  | All Other Non-Current | 5.4 | 5.2 |
| -34.5 | 5.1 | 31.7 | 52.2 | 58.0 |  | Net Worth | 34.3 | 28.6 |
| 100.0 | 100.0 | 100.0 | 100.0 | 100.0 |  | Total Liabilities & Net Worth | 100.0 | 100.0 |
|  |  |  |  |  |  | **INCOME DATA** |  |  |
| 100.0 | 100.0 | 100.0 | 100.0 | 100.0 |  | Net Sales | 100.0 | 100.0 |
|  |  |  |  |  |  | Gross Profit |  |  |
| 98.8 | 92.7 | 97.0 | 93.8 | 93.3 |  | Operating Expenses | 94.2 | 95.0 |
| 1.2 | 7.3 | 3.0 | 6.2 | 6.7 |  | Operating Profit | 5.8 | 5.0 |
| 2.7 | 1.0 | .3 | .1 | .5 |  | All Other Expenses (net) | 1.5 | 1.8 |
| -1.5 | 6.3 | 2.8 | 6.1 | 6.2 |  | Profit Before Taxes | 4.4 | 3.2 |
|  |  |  |  |  |  | **RATIOS** |  |  |
| 2.8 | 14.9 | 3.4 | 3.9 | 4.0 |  | Current | 2.3 | 2.4 |
| .8 | 1.3 | 1.5 | 1.5 | 2.9 |  |  | 1.3 | 1.2 |
| .0 | .3 | .6 | 1.0 | 1.3 |  |  | .8 | .8 |
| 2.2 | 3.4 | 2.8 | 1.9 | 2.0 |  | Quick | 1.4 | 1.2 |
| .3 | 1.1 | .6 | .8 | 1.2 |  |  | .6 | .5 |
| .0 | .2 | .2 | .5 | 1.0 |  |  | .2 | .3 |
| 0 UND | 0 UND | 4 103.0 | 16 22.7 | 25 14.6 |  | Sales/Receivables | 0 999.8 | 1 254.7 |
| 0 UND | 12 29.9 | 24 14.9 | 38 9.7 | 36 10.1 |  |  | 24 15.5 | 29 12.4 |
| 0 UND | 35 10.4 | 47 7.7 | 57 6.4 | 66 5.5 |  |  | 46 7.9 | 51 7.1 |
|  |  |  |  |  |  | Cost of Sales/Inventory |  |  |
|  |  |  |  |  |  |  |  |  |
|  |  |  |  |  |  |  |  |  |
|  |  |  |  |  |  | Cost of Sales/Payables |  |  |
|  |  |  |  |  |  |  |  |  |
|  |  |  |  |  |  |  |  |  |
| 41.1 | 6.7 | 4.7 | 3.0 | 4.4 |  | Sales/Working Capital | 5.7 | 6.0 |
| -92.2 | 39.1 | 21.7 | 8.4 | 8.3 |  |  | 19.7 | 18.9 |
| -13.0 | -10.8 | -8.9 | 148.8 | 10.3 |  |  | -38.1 | -26.4 |
|  | 13.4 | 11.7 | 32.9 | 56.5 |  | EBIT/Interest | 15.5 | 7.6 |
|  | (11) 2.4 | (38) 5.3 | (32) 8.2 | 9.9 |  |  | (70) 5.0 | (90) 3.3 |
|  | 1.7 | .5 | .7 | 4.7 |  |  | 1.2 | .6 |
|  |  |  | 7.1 |  |  | Net Profit + Depr., Dep., Amort./Cur. Mat. L/T/D | 19.0 | 3.9 |
|  |  | (12) | 2.6 |  |  |  | (13) 4.4 | (23) 2.1 |
|  |  |  | .6 |  |  |  | 1.2 | 1.3 |
| .0 | .2 | .3 | .4 | .6 |  | Fixed/Worth | .4 | .4 |
| 1.6 | .5 | .6 | .8 | .7 |  |  | .8 | 1.0 |
| -1.2 | -1.1 | 3.7 | 1.5 | .9 |  |  | 2.6 | 2.6 |
| .9 | .4 | .5 | .2 | .4 |  | Debt/Worth | .6 | .6 |
| 5.5 | 1.9 | 1.4 | 1.2 | .5 |  |  | 1.2 | 1.5 |
| -1.7 | -2.6 | 6.9 | 2.6 | 1.4 |  |  | 3.7 | 10.4 |
|  |  | 29.9 | 28.9 | 21.7 |  | % Profit Before Taxes/Tangible Net Worth | 30.7 | 37.3 |
|  |  | (34) 12.4 | (32) 15.1 | (10) 13.3 |  |  | (69) 15.2 | (81) 10.6 |
|  |  | 3.3 | .5 | 10.6 |  |  | 2.2 | .1 |
| 42.2 | 31.6 | 18.4 | 16.1 | 9.8 |  | % Profit Before Taxes/Total Assets | 14.7 | 13.1 |
| 18.2 | 8.5 | 4.8 | 5.2 | 9.3 |  |  | 5.4 | 3.9 |
| -20.5 | 1.2 | .7 | .0 | 6.8 |  |  | -.5 | -.2 |
| UND | 55.4 | 19.5 | 10.1 | 7.3 |  | Sales/Net Fixed Assets | 12.7 | 13.5 |
| 25.1 | 8.4 | 6.3 | 3.7 | 6.2 |  |  | 4.8 | 7.2 |
| 2.6 | 3.8 | 3.1 | 2.1 | 2.3 |  |  | 2.3 | 3.1 |
| 18.2 | 6.5 | 3.7 | 1.9 | 2.6 |  | Sales/Total Assets | 2.9 | 3.3 |
| 6.6 | 3.1 | 2.3 | 1.4 | 1.6 |  |  | 1.8 | 1.9 |
| 1.8 | 1.6 | 1.1 | .6 | 1.0 |  |  | 1.1 | 1.1 |
|  | 1.1 | 1.1 | 1.5 | 2.2 |  | % Depr., Dep., Amort./Sales | 1.4 | 1.4 |
|  | (11) 2.7 | (36) 2.7 | (28) 2.9 | 2.8 |  |  | (64) 2.9 | (94) 2.6 |
|  | 3.8 | 5.2 | 5.3 | 4.8 |  |  | 4.9 | 4.3 |
|  |  |  | 1.1 |  |  | % Officers', Directors' Owners' Comp/Sales | 1.2 | 1.0 |
|  |  | (11) 2.1 |  |  |  |  | (20) 2.1 | (32) 2.4 |
|  |  | 13.6 |  |  |  |  | 4.6 | 6.3 |
| 19806M | 68352M | 422533M | 1179641M | 1090237M | 926916M | Net Sales ($) | 2953240M | 4110465M |
| 2295M | 17392M | 165559M | 784982M | 729498M | 711555M | Total Assets ($) | 1924935M | 2490137M |

M = $ thousand    MM = $ million
See Pages 9 through 22 for Explanation of Ratios and Data

## Comparative Historical Data — Current Data Sorted by Sales

| 4/1/09-3/31/10 ALL | 4/1/10-3/31/11 ALL | 4/1/11-3/31/12 ALL | Type of Statement | 0-1MM | 1-3MM | 3-5MM | 5-10MM | 10-25MM | 25MM & OVER |
|---|---|---|---|---|---|---|---|---|---|
| 18 | 13 | 13 | Unqualified | | | | | 3 | 10 |
| 19 | 13 | 14 | Reviewed | | | | | 7 | 7 |
| 21 | 14 | 23 | Compiled | 2 | 2 | 5 | 8 | 5 | 1 |
| 19 | 18 | 23 | Tax Returns | 3 | 5 | 4 | 7 | 1 | 3 |
| 41 | 46 | 42 | Other | 1 | 3 | 5 | 5 | 12 | 16 |
| | | | | | 28 (4/1-9/30/11) | | 87 (10/1/11-3/31/12) | | |
| 118 | 104 | 115 | NUMBER OF STATEMENTS | 6 | 10 | 14 | 20 | 28 | 37 |
| % | % | % | **ASSETS** | % | % | % | % | % | % |
| 9.7 | 9.8 | 11.2 | Cash & Equivalents | 13.1 | 3.9 | 14.1 | | 17.2 | 8.0 |
| 17.0 | 17.7 | 17.4 | Trade Receivables (net) | 23.5 | 9.0 | 11.7 | | 23.0 | 19.5 |
| 13.2 | 12.6 | 14.4 | Inventory | .2 | 19.6 | 14.5 | | 12.0 | 18.0 |
| 5.8 | 5.6 | 4.9 | All Other Current | 4.5 | 8.4 | 5.4 | | 4.8 | 4.0 |
| 45.6 | 45.8 | 48.0 | Total Current | 41.3 | 40.9 | 45.8 | | 57.1 | 49.5 |
| 40.5 | 38.1 | 38.9 | Fixed Assets (net) | 43.7 | 49.1 | 41.3 | | 26.5 | 39.7 |
| 1.4 | 1.6 | 3.5 | Intangibles (net) | .1 | .1 | 4.1 | | 8.2 | 2.4 |
| 12.5 | 14.5 | 9.6 | All Other Non-Current | 14.9 | 9.8 | 8.8 | | 8.2 | 8.4 |
| 100.0 | 100.0 | 100.0 | Total | 100.0 | 100.0 | 100.0 | 100.0 | 100.0 | 100.0 |
| | | | **LIABILITIES** | | | | | | |
| 13.8 | 14.3 | 16.5 | Notes Payable-Short Term | 17.1 | 37.1 | 19.5 | | 8.9 | 12.7 |
| 3.0 | 3.9 | 3.5 | Cur. Mat.-L.T.D. | 6.4 | 3.0 | 2.7 | | 4.9 | 2.8 |
| 10.3 | 10.8 | 10.2 | Trade Payables | 14.6 | 8.1 | 9.0 | | 12.1 | 10.7 |
| .3 | .5 | .1 | Income Taxes Payable | .1 | .1 | .0 | | .0 | .3 |
| 16.4 | 9.3 | 6.3 | All Other Current | 5.5 | 4.0 | 7.5 | | 9.5 | 4.8 |
| 43.7 | 38.7 | 36.7 | Total Current | 43.8 | 52.2 | 38.7 | | 35.4 | 31.2 |
| 26.4 | 21.6 | 22.5 | Long-Term Debt | 23.9 | 20.2 | 24.8 | | 22.3 | 14.9 |
| 1.0 | .8 | .4 | Deferred Taxes | .0 | .8 | .0 | | .8 | .5 |
| 8.6 | 10.4 | 8.1 | All Other Non-Current | 20.2 | 19.6 | 2.6 | | 4.2 | 2.8 |
| 20.3 | 28.4 | 32.3 | Net Worth | 12.1 | 7.1 | 33.9 | | 37.4 | 50.7 |
| 100.0 | 100.0 | 100.0 | Total Liabilities & Net Worth | 100.0 | 100.0 | 100.0 | 100.0 | 100.0 | 100.0 |
| | | | **INCOME DATA** | | | | | | |
| 100.0 | 100.0 | 100.0 | Net Sales | 100.0 | 100.0 | 100.0 | 100.0 | 100.0 | 100.0 |
| | | | Gross Profit | | | | | | |
| 93.8 | 93.9 | 95.2 | Operating Expenses | 98.8 | 94.9 | 97.6 | | 96.2 | 93.9 |
| 6.2 | 6.1 | 4.8 | Operating Profit | 1.2 | 5.1 | 2.4 | | 3.8 | 6.1 |
| 1.7 | .5 | .6 | All Other Expenses (net) | .5 | 2.5 | .0 | | .3 | .0 |
| 4.5 | 5.6 | 4.2 | Profit Before Taxes | .7 | 2.7 | 2.4 | | 3.5 | 6.1 |
| | | | **RATIOS** | | | | | | |
| 2.6 | 2.5 | 3.7 | Current | 18.4 | 5.7 | 2.6 | | 4.2 | 3.8 |
| 1.5 | 1.6 | 1.5 | | .8 | .9 | 1.3 | | 1.6 | 2.0 |
| .8 | .8 | .9 | | .2 | .3 | .7 | | 1.1 | 1.2 |
| 1.6 | 1.5 | 2.3 | Quick | 16.0 | 1.4 | 2.0 | | 3.7 | 1.9 |
| .7 | .9 | .8 | | .5 | .2 | .6 | | 1.0 | 1.0 |
| .3 | .4 | .3 | | .2 | .0 | .2 | | .4 | .6 |
| 1 426.3 | 4 99.4 | 3 126.2 | Sales/Receivables | 0 UND | 0 UND | 0 UND | | 13 28.3 | 23 15.7 |
| 28 13.1 | 30 12.2 | 26 13.8 | | 14 26.3 | 0 UND | 11 33.9 | | 25 14.7 | 36 10.1 |
| 49 7.4 | 51 7.1 | 50 7.3 | | 54 6.7 | 61 6.0 | 30 12.0 | | 54 6.8 | 53 6.9 |
| | | | Cost of Sales/Inventory | | | | | | |
| | | | Cost of Sales/Payables | | | | | | |
| 5.0 | 5.5 | 4.5 | Sales/Working Capital | 3.0 | 2.6 | 5.7 | | 6.0 | 4.0 |
| 13.6 | 12.5 | 11.2 | | NM | NM | 27.5 | | 9.8 | 8.9 |
| -25.2 | -43.0 | -80.0 | | -5.4 | -3.6 | -31.2 | | 90.4 | 55.9 |
| 9.6 | 10.2 | 19.0 | EBIT/Interest | | | 12.5 | 7.0 | 20.1 | 33.2 |
| (102) 3.6 | (97) 5.1 | (106) 5.9 | | | | 2.8 | (19) 2.1 | (25) 6.3 | (35) 10.0 |
| .5 | .9 | .9 | | | | -.2 | -.6 | -.6 | 2.8 |
| 11.6 | 11.1 | 8.3 | Net Profit + Depr., Dep., Amort./Cur. Mat. L/T/D | | | | | | 23.9 |
| (27) 3.6 | (26) 2.8 | (28) 2.1 | | | | | | (14) 6.5 |
| 1.5 | .8 | -.8 | | | | | | | 2.1 |
| .5 | .4 | .4 | Fixed/Worth | .3 | .4 | .3 | | .3 | .5 |
| 1.1 | .9 | .7 | | .5 | 1.7 | .9 | | .7 | .7 |
| NM | 2.4 | 2.2 | | NM | NM | 3.9 | | 2.1 | 1.5 |
| .6 | .5 | .5 | Debt/Worth | .2 | .7 | .6 | | .4 | .3 |
| 1.9 | 1.5 | 1.3 | | 1.1 | 1.6 | 1.9 | | 2.2 | 1.0 |
| NM | 6.1 | 4.8 | | -2.8 | NM | 6.2 | | 6.2 | 1.8 |
| 33.2 | 36.6 | 29.9 | % Profit Before Taxes/Tangible Net Worth | | | 8.4 | 22.9 | 34.8 | 29.8 |
| (89) 12.9 | (88) 16.0 | (97) 14.5 | | | | (11) 4.4 | (17) 3.9 | (23) 17.9 | (35) 17.6 |
| 2.3 | 2.4 | 3.0 | | | | 1.1 | -6.6 | 3.6 | 11.0 |
| 15.3 | 13.4 | 17.9 | % Profit Before Taxes/Total Assets | 25.5 | 4.9 | 20.4 | | 20.0 | 16.4 |
| 4.7 | 7.5 | 6.5 | | 10.4 | 2.8 | 2.5 | | 9.9 | 9.4 |
| -.4 | .1 | 1.0 | | -3.8 | -5.8 | -1.4 | | -.7 | 4.4 |
| 14.4 | 13.6 | 13.2 | Sales/Net Fixed Assets | UND | 11.3 | 22.1 | | 23.1 | 8.8 |
| 4.9 | 5.6 | 6.1 | | 3.8 | 3.9 | 7.1 | | 11.1 | 5.6 |
| 2.4 | 2.4 | 2.4 | | 1.5 | 1.6 | 4.8 | | 3.7 | 2.7 |
| 3.3 | 3.3 | 3.2 | Sales/Total Assets | 6.9 | 3.3 | 4.2 | | 4.1 | 2.6 |
| 1.7 | 1.7 | 1.8 | | 1.5 | 1.5 | 2.4 | | 2.2 | 1.6 |
| 1.1 | 1.1 | 1.1 | | .8 | .8 | 1.2 | | 1.3 | 1.2 |
| 1.2 | 1.5 | 1.4 | % Depr., Dep., Amort./Sales | | | 2.7 | .7 | 1.0 | 1.5 |
| (104) 2.4 | (89) 3.1 | (97) 2.7 | | | | (12) 5.0 | (18) 2.7 | (23) 2.1 | (32) 2.3 |
| 5.2 | 4.7 | 5.1 | | | | 6.8 | 6.0 | 5.1 | 4.0 |
| 1.5 | 1.0 | 1.2 | % Officers', Directors' Owners' Comp/Sales | | | | | | |
| (38) 1.9 | (24) 1.5 | (30) 3.1 | | | | | | | |
| 3.8 | 4.3 | 6.4 | | | | | | | |
| 4996250M | 3335279M | 3707485M | Net Sales ($) | 2774M | 22049M | 55308M | 143905M | 423044M | 3060405M |
| 3235705M | 2233915M | 2411281M | Total Assets ($) | 4622M | 18218M | 83141M | 129865M | 273853M | 1901582M |

M = $ thousand   MM = $ million
See Pages 9 through 22 for Explanation of Ratios and Data

## Current Data Sorted by Assets      Comparative Historical Data

| 0-500M | 500M-2MM | 2-10MM | 10-50MM | 50-100MM | 100-250MM | Type of Statement | 4/1/07-3/31/08 ALL | 4/1/08-3/31/09 ALL |
|---|---|---|---|---|---|---|---|---|
| | 1 | | 7 | 2 | 5 | Unqualified | 9 | 14 |
| 1 | | | | | | Reviewed | 6 | 5 |
| 1 | 2 | 6 | 2 | | | Compiled | 10 | 11 |
| 4 | 6 | 4 | 2 | | | Tax Returns | 10 | 11 |
| 2 | 3 | 5 | 1 | 1 | | Other | 6 | 7 |
| | 27 (4/1-9/30/11) | | 32 (10/1/11-3/31/12) | | | | | |
| 8 | 12 | 15 | 16 | 3 | 5 | **NUMBER OF STATEMENTS** | 41 | 48 |
| % | % | % | % | % | % | **ASSETS** | % | % |
| | 4.4 | 12.3 | 16.0 | | | Cash & Equivalents | 18.9 | 12.8 |
| | 7.0 | 5.7 | 9.9 | | | Trade Receivables (net) | 4.3 | 7.3 |
| | 5.4 | 5.1 | 7.3 | | | Inventory | 9.1 | 8.5 |
| | 14.3 | 2.6 | 6.5 | | | All Other Current | 1.3 | 1.6 |
| | 31.1 | 25.8 | 39.7 | | | Total Current | 33.6 | 30.1 |
| | 67.2 | 63.6 | 46.8 | | | Fixed Assets (net) | 50.1 | 53.6 |
| | .3 | .2 | 4.3 | | | Intangibles (net) | 1.2 | .9 |
| | 1.5 | 10.4 | 9.2 | | | All Other Non-Current | 15.2 | 15.3 |
| | 100.0 | 100.0 | 100.0 | | | Total | 100.0 | 100.0 |
| | | | | | | **LIABILITIES** | | |
| | 18.5 | 5.3 | 7.4 | | | Notes Payable-Short Term | 5.9 | 7.3 |
| | 2.2 | 2.7 | 16.7 | | | Cur. Mat.-L.T.D. | 2.8 | 2.9 |
| | 1.2 | 3.1 | 8.2 | | | Trade Payables | 4.7 | 6.1 |
| | .0 | .0 | .3 | | | Income Taxes Payable | .3 | .5 |
| | 17.6 | 12.4 | 8.1 | | | All Other Current | 10.9 | 4.9 |
| | 39.5 | 23.5 | 40.6 | | | Total Current | 24.6 | 21.8 |
| | 33.5 | 41.1 | 13.0 | | | Long-Term Debt | 29.8 | 30.4 |
| | .0 | .1 | .6 | | | Deferred Taxes | 1.1 | 1.6 |
| | .6 | 4.3 | 4.1 | | | All Other Non-Current | 4.9 | 4.1 |
| | 26.4 | 31.0 | 41.7 | | | Net Worth | 39.6 | 42.2 |
| | 100.0 | 100.0 | 100.0 | | | Total Liabilities & Net Worth | 100.0 | 100.0 |
| | | | | | | **INCOME DATA** | | |
| | 100.0 | 100.0 | 100.0 | | | Net Sales | 100.0 | 100.0 |
| | | | | | | Gross Profit | | |
| | 90.6 | 90.1 | 93.4 | | | Operating Expenses | 80.4 | 88.1 |
| | 9.4 | 9.9 | 6.6 | | | Operating Profit | 19.6 | 11.9 |
| | 4.9 | 2.9 | .5 | | | All Other Expenses (net) | 3.4 | 4.3 |
| | 4.5 | 7.0 | 6.1 | | | Profit Before Taxes | 16.2 | 7.6 |
| | | | | | | **RATIOS** | | |
| | 3.6 | 4.5 | 1.8 | | | | 3.4 | 3.2 |
| | .7 | .9 | 1.3 | | | Current | 1.8 | 1.2 |
| | .1 | .2 | 1.0 | | | | 1.0 | .6 |
| | 1.7 | 1.7 | 1.4 | | | | 2.4 | 2.2 |
| | .4 | .3 | .9 | | | Quick | 1.1 | .7 |
| | .0 | .1 | .3 | | | | .4 | .3 |
| 0 UND | 0 UND | 0 UND | 3 124.6 | | | | 0 UND | 0 UND |
| 0 UND | 0 UND | 0 UND | 9 42.1 | | | Sales/Receivables | 0 UND | 4 90.3 |
| 0 UND | 0 UND | 3 115.4 | 35 10.4 | | | | 18 19.7 | 36 10.3 |
| | | | | | | Cost of Sales/Inventory | | |
| | | | | | | Cost of Sales/Payables | | |
| | 3.6 | 4.3 | 9.0 | | | | 3.4 | 2.5 |
| | -32.2 | -35.2 | 15.2 | | | Sales/Working Capital | 12.4 | 18.1 |
| | -1.4 | -6.2 | NM | | | | -512.6 | -11.9 |
| | | 7.0 | 43.6 | | | | 20.7 | 10.5 |
| | (11) | 2.3 | 7.6 | | | EBIT/Interest | (35) 5.6 | (38) 2.6 |
| | | 1.8 | 1.5 | | | | 2.1 | 1.1 |
| | | | | | | | | 17.3 |
| | | | | | | Net Profit + Depr., Dep., Amort./Cur. Mat. L/T/D | | (11) 8.4 |
| | | | | | | | | 1.6 |
| | 1.1 | 1.0 | .5 | | | | .6 | .7 |
| | 11.4 | 1.6 | .8 | | | Fixed/Worth | 1.1 | 1.2 |
| | -9.2 | 88.0 | 2.2 | | | | 5.9 | 4.6 |
| | .4 | .5 | .6 | | | | .3 | .4 |
| | 11.2 | 1.6 | 1.3 | | | Debt/Worth | 1.2 | 1.2 |
| | -10.3 | 543.7 | 2.0 | | | | 8.2 | 5.3 |
| | | 48.2 | 51.7 | | | | 33.8 | 22.2 |
| | (12) | 13.3 | (15) 18.1 | | | % Profit Before Taxes/Tangible Net Worth | (34) 17.5 | (43) 5.8 |
| | | 4.4 | 3.1 | | | | 5.2 | .6 |
| | 14.1 | 13.3 | 23.7 | | | | 16.4 | 12.1 |
| | -.1 | 4.3 | 9.1 | | | % Profit Before Taxes/Total Assets | 9.1 | 2.9 |
| | -5.5 | .3 | .6 | | | | 2.2 | .0 |
| | 4.3 | 3.3 | 9.5 | | | | 6.4 | 3.7 |
| | .7 | 1.4 | 2.6 | | | Sales/Net Fixed Assets | 1.5 | 1.3 |
| | .4 | .5 | .8 | | | | .6 | .5 |
| | .9 | 1.4 | 2.3 | | | | 1.5 | 1.3 |
| | .5 | .9 | 1.4 | | | Sales/Total Assets | .6 | .7 |
| | .4 | .4 | .5 | | | | .4 | .3 |
| | 1.9 | 3.7 | 1.8 | | | | 1.6 | 2.4 |
| | 15.2 | (12) 6.0 | (15) 3.9 | | | % Depr., Dep., Amort./Sales | (37) 5.7 | (44) 6.1 |
| | 22.8 | 9.5 | 8.4 | | | | 9.3 | 12.3 |
| | | | | | | % Officers', Directors' Owners' Comp/Sales | | |
| 7407M | 14200M | 114510M | 404715M | 236409M | 343266M | Net Sales ($) | 947315M | 1503199M |
| 1646M | 14665M | 84265M | 282686M | 214574M | 835589M | Total Assets ($) | 1375214M | 2113556M |

M = $ thousand    MM = $ million
See Pages 9 through 22 for Explanation of Ratios and Data

## Comparative Historical Data | Current Data Sorted by Sales

| 13 | 14 | 15 | Type of Statement | 0-1MM | 1-3MM | 3-5MM | 5-10MM | 10-25MM | 25MM & OVER |
|---|---|---|---|---|---|---|---|---|---|
| 13 | 14 | 15 | Unqualified | | | | 2 | 4 | 9 |
| 6 | 5 | 5 | Reviewed | 1 | | | 2 | 2 | 2 |
| 13 | 21 | 11 | Compiled | 2 | 3 | 1 | 2 | 2 | 1 |
| 16 | 29 | 16 | Tax Returns | 8 | 3 | 3 | | 2 | 2 |
| 19 | 9 | 12 | Other | 3 | 3 | 2 | 1 | 2 | 1 |
| 4/1/09-3/31/10 ALL | 4/1/10-3/31/11 ALL | 4/1/11-3/31/12 ALL | | 27 (4/1-9/30/11) | | | 32 (10/1/11-3/31/12) | | |
| 67 | 78 | 59 | NUMBER OF STATEMENTS | 14 | 9 | 6 | 7 | 10 | 13 |
| % | % | % | ASSETS | % | % | % | % | % | % |
| 13.8 | 9.2 | 12.4 | Cash & Equivalents | 9.2 | | | | 10.5 | 14.1 |
| 9.3 | 7.0 | 6.7 | Trade Receivables (net) | .1 | | | | 13.7 | 11.0 |
| 7.9 | 6.7 | 6.3 | Inventory | 1.0 | | | | 3.8 | 14.6 |
| 6.9 | 3.7 | 5.5 | All Other Current | 8.6 | | | | 10.4 | 1.1 |
| 37.9 | 26.6 | 30.9 | Total Current | 18.9 | | | | 38.5 | 40.7 |
| 46.2 | 53.1 | 55.2 | Fixed Assets (net) | 65.7 | | | | 46.8 | 48.6 |
| 1.1 | 1.4 | 2.2 | Intangibles (net) | 3.9 | | | | 5.8 | 1.0 |
| 14.7 | 18.9 | 11.7 | All Other Non-Current | 11.2 | | | | 9.0 | 9.6 |
| 100.0 | 100.0 | 100.0 | Total | 100.0 | | | | 100.0 | 100.0 |
| | | | LIABILITIES | | | | | | |
| 11.9 | 13.0 | 9.4 | Notes Payable-Short Term | 11.4 | | | | 2.4 | 11.5 |
| 4.1 | 4.8 | 6.4 | Cur. Mat.-L.T.D. | 1.8 | | | | 26.1 | 4.5 |
| 8.0 | 3.7 | 4.3 | Trade Payables | 1.1 | | | | 8.8 | 7.5 |
| .0 | .0 | .1 | Income Taxes Payable | .0 | | | | .2 | .2 |
| 8.1 | 10.2 | 18.9 | All Other Current | 15.0 | | | | 10.0 | 5.6 |
| 32.0 | 31.7 | 39.0 | Total Current | 29.3 | | | | 47.4 | 29.4 |
| 29.8 | 34.9 | 29.0 | Long-Term Debt | 41.2 | | | | 37.1 | 23.1 |
| .8 | .8 | .4 | Deferred Taxes | .0 | | | | .8 | .9 |
| 3.6 | 6.2 | 3.0 | All Other Non-Current | 4.6 | | | | 4.4 | 4.5 |
| 33.7 | 26.4 | 28.6 | Net Worth | 24.9 | | | | 10.3 | 42.2 |
| 100.0 | 100.0 | 100.0 | Total Liabilties & Net Worth | 100.0 | | | | 100.0 | 100.0 |
| | | | INCOME DATA | | | | | | |
| 100.0 | 100.0 | 100.0 | Net Sales | 100.0 | | | | 100.0 | 100.0 |
| | | | Gross Profit | | | | | | |
| 91.1 | 91.1 | 93.4 | Operating Expenses | 97.0 | | | | 92.4 | 90.5 |
| 8.9 | 8.9 | 6.6 | Operating Profit | 3.0 | | | | 7.6 | 9.5 |
| 4.7 | 5.2 | 2.6 | All Other Expenses (net) | 6.8 | | | | 2.8 | 1.9 |
| 4.2 | 3.7 | 4.1 | Profit Before Taxes | -3.9 | | | | 4.8 | 7.6 |
| | | | RATIOS | | | | | | |
| 2.6 | 1.9 | 2.5 | | 3.7 | | | | 2.8 | 2.2 |
| 1.2 | 1.0 | 1.2 | Current | .7 | | | | 1.3 | 1.6 |
| .6 | .2 | .3 | | .0 | | | | .2 | .8 |
| 1.7 | 1.3 | 1.4 | | .8 | | | | 1.3 | 1.4 |
| .7 | .5 | .5 | Quick | .3 | | | | .8 | .5 |
| .2 | .1 | .1 | | .0 | | | | .1 | .3 |
| 0 UND | 0 UND | 0 UND | | 0 UND | | | | 0 UND | 5 67.2 |
| 2 151.2 | 0 UND | 2 200.7 | Sales/Receivables | 0 UND | | | | 7 54.4 | 32 11.5 |
| 41 9.0 | 33 11.2 | 26 14.2 | | 0 UND | | | | 25 14.5 | 48 7.6 |
| | | | Cost of Sales/Inventory | | | | | | |
| | | | Cost of Sales/Payables | | | | | | |
| 2.6 | 6.0 | 4.8 | | 2.2 | | | | 2.3 | 6.6 |
| 19.4 | NM | 46.9 | Sales/Working Capital | -32.2 | | | | 14.5 | 13.2 |
| -13.9 | -3.9 | -7.6 | | -2.3 | | | | -2.9 | -17.6 |
| 10.9 | 8.0 | 8.2 | | 5.1 | | | | | 10.9 |
| (59) 2.6 | (68) 2.1 | (50) 2.4 | EBIT/Interest | (11) -.2 | | | | (12) 4.4 | |
| .5 | .0 | .2 | | -3.2 | | | | | 1.5 |
| | 12.1 | | | | | | | | |
| | (14) 3.0 | | Net Profit + Depr., Dep., Amort./Cur. Mat. L/T/D | | | | | | |
| | 1.5 | | | | | | | | |
| .4 | .7 | .7 | | .9 | | | | .8 | .4 |
| 1.1 | 1.4 | 1.4 | Fixed/Worth | 11.1 | | | | 1.6 | 1.2 |
| 4.4 | 17.2 | 20.3 | | -6.2 | | | | NM | 2.3 |
| .4 | .5 | .5 | | .1 | | | | 1.4 | .7 |
| 1.5 | 1.5 | 1.7 | Debt/Worth | 11.3 | | | | 1.9 | 1.4 |
| 11.6 | 34.6 | 20.8 | | -7.2 | | | | NM | 2.1 |
| 40.6 | 36.2 | 32.3 | | | | | | | 61.9 |
| (52) 5.9 | (61) 6.4 | (46) 10.4 | % Profit Before Taxes/Tangible Net Worth | | | | | (12) 10.4 | |
| -1.8 | -2.5 | .5 | | | | | | | 2.5 |
| 10.8 | 7.2 | 13.3 | | 11.0 | | | | 13.9 | 24.9 |
| 3.2 | 2.6 | 4.1 | % Profit Before Taxes/Total Assets | -2.1 | | | | 9.0 | 6.9 |
| -1.5 | -2.7 | -.8 | | -8.9 | | | | 1.3 | 1.5 |
| 14.6 | 3.2 | 4.3 | | 2.6 | | | | 6.0 | 12.4 |
| 1.8 | 1.2 | 1.3 | Sales/Net Fixed Assets | .5 | | | | 3.1 | 2.3 |
| .8 | .6 | .6 | | .4 | | | | 1.2 | .9 |
| 1.6 | 1.3 | 1.4 | | .8 | | | | 1.4 | 3.3 |
| .8 | .6 | .8 | Sales/Total Assets | .4 | | | | 1.3 | 1.4 |
| .4 | .3 | .4 | | .3 | | | | .7 | .5 |
| 1.9 | 3.0 | 2.5 | | 5.5 | | | | | 1.4 |
| (53) 5.0 | (73) 5.6 | (50) 6.0 | % Depr., Dep., Amort./Sales | (13) 20.8 | | | | (10) 4.4 | |
| 9.5 | 10.3 | 12.8 | | 33.0 | | | | | 7.0 |
| | 1.2 | | | | | | | | |
| | (10) 2.3 | | % Officers', Directors' Owners' Comp/Sales | | | | | | |
| | 7.5 | | | | | | | | |
| 1632191M | 1757725M | 1120507M | Net Sales ($) | 4953M | 15836M | 20671M | 49217M | 161085M | 868745M |
| 2443328M | 2245555M | 1433425M | Total Assets ($) | 15049M | 18286M | 40650M | 65687M | 182750M | 1111003M |

M = $ thousand   MM = $ million
See Pages 9 through 22 for Explanation of Ratios and Data

## Current Data Sorted by Assets        Comparative Historical Data

| 0-500M | 500M-2MM | 2-10MM | 10-50MM | 50-100MM | 100-250MM | Type of Statement | 4/1/07-3/31/08 ALL | 4/1/08-3/31/09 ALL |
|---|---|---|---|---|---|---|---|---|
| | | | 1 | | 1 | Unqualified | 3 | 7 |
| 2 | 1 | 1 | 4 | 2 | | Reviewed | 8 | 5 |
| 2 | 8 | | 2 | 1 | 1 | Compiled | 11 | 15 |
| 4 | 3 | | 1 | | | Tax Returns | 1 | 3 |
| | | | 1 | | | Other | 7 | 5 |
| | 9 (4/1-9/30/11) | | 26 (10/1/11-3/31/12) | | | | | |
| | 8 | 13 | 9 | 3 | 2 | **NUMBER OF STATEMENTS** | 30 | 35 |
| % | % | % | % | % | % | **ASSETS** | % | % |
| | | 13.5 | | | | Cash & Equivalents | 6.4 | 6.8 |
| | | 6.2 | | | | Trade Receivables (net) | 9.8 | 11.8 |
| | | 15.1 | | | | Inventory | 20.4 | 28.1 |
| | | 7.8 | | | | All Other Current | 2.6 | 2.8 |
| | | 42.6 | | | | Total Current | 39.3 | 49.5 |
| | | 43.2 | | | | Fixed Assets (net) | 54.8 | 46.6 |
| | | 1.4 | | | | Intangibles (net) | .2 | .7 |
| | | 12.8 | | | | All Other Non-Current | 5.6 | 3.2 |
| | | 100.0 | | | | Total | 100.0 | 100.0 |
| | | | | | | **LIABILITIES** | | |
| | | 9.4 | | | | Notes Payable-Short Term | 17.1 | 18.9 |
| | | 3.1 | | | | Cur. Mat.-L.T.D. | 4.5 | 2.7 |
| | | 10.9 | | | | Trade Payables | 4.8 | 6.1 |
| | | .0 | | | | Income Taxes Payable | .1 | .0 |
| | | 14.9 | | | | All Other Current | 2.7 | 6.1 |
| | | 38.3 | | | | Total Current | 29.2 | 33.8 |
| | | 10.4 | | | | Long-Term Debt | 26.0 | 25.4 |
| | | .3 | | | | Deferred Taxes | .3 | .3 |
| | | 7.2 | | | | All Other Non-Current | 1.2 | .7 |
| | | 43.7 | | | | Net Worth | 43.3 | 39.8 |
| | | 100.0 | | | | Total Liabilities & Net Worth | 100.0 | 100.0 |
| | | | | | | **INCOME DATA** | | |
| | | 100.0 | | | | Net Sales | 100.0 | 100.0 |
| | | | | | | Gross Profit | | |
| | | 87.8 | | | | Operating Expenses | 88.0 | 86.4 |
| | | 12.2 | | | | Operating Profit | 12.0 | 13.6 |
| | | -.2 | | | | All Other Expenses (net) | 2.5 | 2.5 |
| | | 12.4 | | | | Profit Before Taxes | 9.5 | 11.1 |
| | | | | | | **RATIOS** | | |
| | | 9.8 | | | | | 2.1 | 3.3 |
| | | 1.1 | | | | Current | 1.4 | 1.5 |
| | | 1.0 | | | | | 1.0 | 1.1 |
| | | 1.9 | | | | | 1.2 | 1.1 |
| | | .6 | | | | Quick | .4 | .6 |
| | | .1 | | | | | .0 | .0 |
| | 0 | UND | | | | | 0 UND | 0 UND |
| | 0 | UND | | | | Sales/Receivables | 14 26.3 | 16 23.1 |
| | 29 | 12.6 | | | | | 45 8.2 | 59 6.2 |
| | | | | | | Cost of Sales/Inventory | | |
| | | | | | | Cost of Sales/Payables | | |
| | | 1.5 | | | | | 3.7 | 3.0 |
| | | 44.3 | | | | Sales/Working Capital | 12.5 | 6.4 |
| | | NM | | | | | NM | 38.5 |
| | | 25.2 | | | | | 6.1 | 9.4 |
| | (11) | 2.3 | | | | EBIT/Interest | (29) 3.9 | (32) 3.4 |
| | | -.2 | | | | | 1.1 | 1.6 |
| | | | | | | Net Profit + Depr., Dep., Amort./Cur. Mat. L/T/D | | |
| | | .5 | | | | | 1.1 | .9 |
| | | .9 | | | | Fixed/Worth | 1.3 | 1.2 |
| | | -23.4 | | | | | 2.2 | 3.0 |
| | | .2 | | | | | .4 | .8 |
| | | .6 | | | | Debt/Worth | 1.8 | 1.7 |
| | | -38.0 | | | | | 3.2 | 4.1 |
| | | | | | | | 35.9 | 51.0 |
| | | | | | | % Profit Before Taxes/Tangible Net Worth | 22.1 (34) | 19.2 |
| | | | | | | | .7 | 1.6 |
| | | 14.6 | | | | | 16.7 | 16.4 |
| | | 3.9 | | | | % Profit Before Taxes/Total Assets | 8.5 | 8.1 |
| | | -.4 | | | | | .6 | 1.5 |
| | | 4.6 | | | | | 2.5 | 4.1 |
| | | 2.2 | | | | Sales/Net Fixed Assets | 1.6 | 1.8 |
| | | 1.4 | | | | | 1.1 | 1.2 |
| | | 1.5 | | | | | 1.5 | 1.3 |
| | | .7 | | | | Sales/Total Assets | .9 | .8 |
| | | .6 | | | | | .7 | .6 |
| | | 2.0 | | | | | 3.2 | 3.6 |
| | | 4.1 | | | | % Depr., Dep., Amort./Sales | (25) 5.1 | (29) 4.6 |
| | | 6.4 | | | | | 8.5 | 6.4 |
| | | | | | | % Officers', Directors' Owners' Comp/Sales | | |
| | 13864M | 61987M | 218136M | 113181M | 171081M | Net Sales ($) | 741511M | 726160M |
| | 11138M | 66746M | 281194M | 189593M | 315064M | Total Assets ($) | 830751M | 725391M |

Note: Left columns under "DATA NOT AVAILABLE" (0-500M) contain no data.

## Comparative Historical Data | Current Data Sorted by Sales

| | | | Type of Statement | | | | | | |
|---|---|---|---|---|---|---|---|---|---|
| 2 | 4 | 3 | Unqualified | | | | 1 | | 2 |
| 3 | 8 | 9 | Reviewed | | 1 | | 2 | 2 | 3 |
| 9 | 12 | 12 | Compiled | | 3 | 4 | 2 | 4 | 1 |
| 7 | 7 | 3 | Tax Returns | | 1 | | 1 | 1 | |
| 6 | 9 | 8 | Other | 3 | 1 | 1 | | 1 | |
| 4/1/09- 3/31/10 | 4/1/10- 3/31/11 | 4/1/11- 3/31/12 | | 9 (4/1-9/30/11) | | | 26 (10/1/11-3/31/12) | | |
| ALL | ALL | ALL | | 0-1MM | 1-3MM | 3-5MM | 5-10MM | 10-25MM | 25MM & OVER |
| 27 | 40 | 35 | NUMBER OF STATEMENTS | 4 | 6 | 5 | 6 | 8 | 6 |
| % | % | % | ASSETS | % | % | % | % | % | % |
| 7.7 | 8.3 | 10.7 | Cash & Equivalents | | | | | | |
| 10.4 | 9.5 | 8.2 | Trade Receivables (net) | | | | | | |
| 18.0 | 15.6 | 18.3 | Inventory | | | | | | |
| 2.8 | 3.8 | 4.8 | All Other Current | | | | | | |
| 38.9 | 37.2 | 42.0 | Total Current | | | | | | |
| 55.1 | 52.6 | 45.2 | Fixed Assets (net) | | | | | | |
| .9 | .8 | 1.8 | Intangibles (net) | | | | | | |
| 5.2 | 9.4 | 11.0 | All Other Non-Current | | | | | | |
| 100.0 | 100.0 | 100.0 | Total | | | | | | |
| | | | LIABILITIES | | | | | | |
| 19.9 | 11.3 | 9.4 | Notes Payable-Short Term | | | | | | |
| 2.9 | 5.5 | 2.8 | Cur. Mat.-L.T.D. | | | | | | |
| 4.4 | 5.1 | 5.2 | Trade Payables | | | | | | |
| .0 | .1 | .3 | Income Taxes Payable | | | | | | |
| 5.4 | 3.9 | 10.0 | All Other Current | | | | | | |
| 32.7 | 25.8 | 27.8 | Total Current | | | | | | |
| 29.1 | 32.6 | 28.0 | Long-Term Debt | | | | | | |
| .8 | 1.2 | .9 | Deferred Taxes | | | | | | |
| 9.6 | 7.2 | 3.1 | All Other Non-Current | | | | | | |
| 27.8 | 33.2 | 40.2 | Net Worth | | | | | | |
| 100.0 | 100.0 | 100.0 | Total Liabilities & Net Worth | | | | | | |
| | | | INCOME DATA | | | | | | |
| 100.0 | 100.0 | 100.0 | Net Sales | | | | | | |
| | | | Gross Profit | | | | | | |
| 95.4 | 87.1 | 86.5 | Operating Expenses | | | | | | |
| 4.6 | 12.9 | 13.5 | Operating Profit | | | | | | |
| 2.0 | 4.3 | 2.0 | All Other Expenses (net) | | | | | | |
| 2.7 | 8.6 | 11.5 | Profit Before Taxes | | | | | | |
| | | | RATIOS | | | | | | |
| 1.6 | 2.1 | 11.1 | | | | | | | |
| 1.2 | 1.2 | 1.4 | Current | | | | | | |
| .7 | .9 | 1.1 | | | | | | | |
| 1.1 | .9 | 2.7 | | | | | | | |
| .5 | .7 | .7 | Quick | | | | | | |
| .2 | .3 | .2 | | | | | | | |
| 0 999.8 | 0 UND | 0 UND | | | | | | | |
| 27 13.6 | 32 11.3 | 3 125.6 | Sales/Receivables | | | | | | |
| 52 7.1 | 64 5.7 | 54 6.7 | | | | | | | |
| | | | Cost of Sales/Inventory | | | | | | |
| | | | Cost of Sales/Payables | | | | | | |
| 5.0 | 3.5 | 1.9 | | | | | | | |
| 25.5 | 17.8 | 5.3 | Sales/Working Capital | | | | | | |
| -12.3 | -87.4 | 167.2 | | | | | | | |
| 5.6 | 6.9 | 7.7 | | | | | | | |
| (25) 2.3 | (37) 2.7 | (29) 2.7 | EBIT/Interest | | | | | | |
| .6 | 1.2 | 1.0 | | | | | | | |
| | | | Net Profit + Depr., Dep., Amort./Cur. Mat. L/T/D | | | | | | |
| .8 | .8 | .6 | | | | | | | |
| 1.6 | 1.7 | 1.2 | Fixed/Worth | | | | | | |
| 4.2 | 2.7 | 4.6 | | | | | | | |
| .8 | .7 | .4 | | | | | | | |
| 2.2 | 2.0 | 1.8 | Debt/Worth | | | | | | |
| 4.8 | 5.3 | 8.9 | | | | | | | |
| 28.0 | 26.9 | 29.8 | % Profit Before Taxes/Tangible Net Worth | | | | | | |
| (22) 12.8 | (38) 16.9 | (27) 14.2 | | | | | | | |
| .8 | -.8 | 3.6 | | | | | | | |
| 12.6 | 11.8 | 14.8 | % Profit Before Taxes/Total Assets | | | | | | |
| 3.2 | 5.0 | 5.8 | | | | | | | |
| -1.7 | -.3 | .2 | | | | | | | |
| 3.8 | 4.5 | 3.6 | | | | | | | |
| 2.0 | 1.5 | 1.6 | Sales/Net Fixed Assets | | | | | | |
| 1.2 | .8 | 1.3 | | | | | | | |
| 2.1 | 1.7 | 1.2 | | | | | | | |
| .9 | .7 | .7 | Sales/Total Assets | | | | | | |
| .7 | .5 | .6 | | | | | | | |
| 4.1 | 2.9 | 3.0 | | | | | | | |
| (25) 5.8 | (33) 6.1 | (32) 5.2 | % Depr., Dep., Amort./Sales | | | | | | |
| 7.6 | 8.9 | 8.0 | | | | | | | |
| | | | % Officers', Directors' Owners' Comp/Sales | | | | | | |
| 446648M | 951941M | 578249M | Net Sales ($) | 2539M | 9491M | 20132M | 41714M | 149426M | 354947M |
| 461559M | 1353560M | 863735M | Total Assets ($) | 5490M | 10754M | 30638M | 34909M | 248276M | 533668M |

M = $ thousand   MM = $ million
See Pages 9 through 22 for Explanation of Ratios and Data

# AGRICULTURE—Grape Vineyards  NAICS 111332

| | Current Data Sorted by Assets | | | | | | | Comparative Historical Data | |
|---|---|---|---|---|---|---|---|---|---|
| | 0-500M | 500M-2MM | 2-10MM | 10-50MM | 50-100MM | 100-250MM | **Type of Statement** | 5 | 3 |
| | | | 1 | 4 | 1 | 1 | Unqualified | 5 | 3 |
| | | | 5 | 8 | 2 | 1 | Reviewed | 4 | 17 |
| | | 2 | 4 | 5 | | | Compiled | 15 | 11 |
| | 5 | 13 | 11 | 1 | | | Tax Returns | 21 | 30 |
| | 2 | 12 | 16 | 15 | | 2 | Other | 33 | 32 |
| | | 4 (4/1-9/30/11) | | 111 (10/1/11-3/31/12) | | | | 4/1/07-3/31/08 ALL | 4/1/08-3/31/09 ALL |
| | 7 | 27 | 37 | 33 | 7 | 4 | **NUMBER OF STATEMENTS** | 78 | 93 |
| | % | % | % | % | % | % | **ASSETS** | % | % |
| | | 14.6 | 6.0 | 4.4 | | | Cash & Equivalents | 6.8 | 7.9 |
| | | 8.0 | 10.8 | 16.1 | | | Trade Receivables (net) | 9.4 | 8.8 |
| | | 4.5 | 3.7 | 12.0 | | | Inventory | 9.9 | 9.8 |
| | | 9.8 | 5.9 | 4.2 | | | All Other Current | 4.2 | 7.4 |
| | | 36.8 | 26.3 | 36.7 | | | Total Current | 30.3 | 33.8 |
| | | 56.7 | 64.2 | 53.4 | | | Fixed Assets (net) | 55.9 | 53.5 |
| | | .3 | .4 | 1.7 | | | Intangibles (net) | 2.5 | 1.2 |
| | | 6.2 | 9.1 | 8.2 | | | All Other Non-Current | 11.4 | 11.4 |
| | | 100.0 | 100.0 | 100.0 | | | Total | 100.0 | 100.0 |
| | | | | | | | **LIABILITIES** | | |
| | | 11.8 | 14.0 | 10.6 | | | Notes Payable-Short Term | 14.1 | 13.0 |
| | | 3.8 | 2.3 | 3.3 | | | Cur. Mat.-L.T.D. | 2.7 | 2.7 |
| | | 2.4 | 2.3 | 3.6 | | | Trade Payables | 3.5 | 3.4 |
| | | .0 | .5 | .0 | | | Income Taxes Payable | .1 | .0 |
| | | 2.3 | 8.0 | 3.7 | | | All Other Current | 9.0 | 6.4 |
| | | 20.3 | 27.1 | 21.2 | | | Total Current | 29.4 | 25.6 |
| | | 62.0 | 39.2 | 38.1 | | | Long-Term Debt | 41.7 | 42.3 |
| | | .0 | .0 | .1 | | | Deferred Taxes | .2 | .6 |
| | | 7.0 | 4.3 | 11.0 | | | All Other Non-Current | 7.8 | 8.6 |
| | | 10.7 | 29.4 | 29.6 | | | Net Worth | 20.9 | 22.9 |
| | | 100.0 | 100.0 | 100.0 | | | Total Liabilities & Net Worth | 100.0 | 100.0 |
| | | | | | | | **INCOME DATA** | | |
| | | 100.0 | 100.0 | 100.0 | | | Net Sales | 100.0 | 100.0 |
| | | | | | | | Gross Profit | | |
| | | 80.2 | 83.8 | 84.2 | | | Operating Expenses | 90.4 | 90.8 |
| | | 19.8 | 16.2 | 15.8 | | | Operating Profit | 9.6 | 9.2 |
| | | 9.6 | 12.4 | 7.3 | | | All Other Expenses (net) | 5.2 | 7.2 |
| | | 10.1 | 3.8 | 8.4 | | | Profit Before Taxes | 4.4 | 2.0 |
| | | | | | | | **RATIOS** | | |
| | | 6.2 | 2.9 | 3.3 | | | | 3.3 | 4.3 |
| | | 2.3 | 1.1 | 1.8 | | | Current | 1.6 | 1.5 |
| | | .4 | .2 | 1.1 | | | | .4 | .6 |
| | | 5.4 | 2.0 | 1.7 | | | | 1.8 | 2.2 |
| | | 1.1 | .7 | 1.0 | | | Quick | .6 (92) | .7 |
| | | .1 | .1 | .5 | | | | .1 | .1 |
| | 0 UND | 0 UND | 10 37.5 | | | | | 0 UND | 0 UND |
| | 0 UND | 19 19.0 | 72 5.1 | | | | Sales/Receivables | 11 32.6 | 10 36.2 |
| | 31 11.6 | 94 3.9 | 152 2.4 | | | | | 76 4.8 | 72 5.1 |
| | | | | | | | Cost of Sales/Inventory | | |
| | | | | | | | Cost of Sales/Payables | | |
| | | 1.6 | 3.4 | 1.5 | | | | 2.6 | 2.4 |
| | | 3.8 | 68.1 | 3.6 | | | Sales/Working Capital | 10.1 | 14.2 |
| | | -7.5 | -3.9 | 20.6 | | | | -6.0 | -7.5 |
| | | 8.1 | 9.2 | 7.3 | | | | 3.7 | 4.4 |
| | | (21) 2.7 | (28) 2.4 | (25) 2.9 | | | EBIT/Interest | (61) 1.4 | (68) 1.5 |
| | | 1.7 | .3 | 1.0 | | | | .3 | -.3 |
| | | | | | | | | | 4.3 |
| | | | | | | | Net Profit + Depr., Dep., Amort./Cur. Mat. L/T/D | | (16) 2.1 |
| | | | | | | | | | -.1 |
| | | .7 | .9 | .5 | | | | .8 | .9 |
| | | 2.1 | 2.2 | 1.8 | | | Fixed/Worth | 1.7 | 1.5 |
| | | -7.8 | -61.3 | NM | | | | -14.2 | -8.5 |
| | | .5 | .6 | .5 | | | | .5 | .6 |
| | | 4.9 | 1.8 | 1.9 | | | Debt/Worth | 1.9 | 2.5 |
| | | -3.7 | -75.0 | NM | | | | -19.2 | -12.9 |
| | | 30.5 | 14.6 | 27.5 | | | | 17.3 | 24.7 |
| | | (17) 15.1 | (27) 9.0 | (25) 14.2 | | | % Profit Before Taxes/Tangible Net Worth | (55) 6.5 | (64) 4.0 |
| | | 1.2 | -3.9 | 1.3 | | | | -10.3 | -7.5 |
| | | 24.3 | 6.3 | 9.5 | | | | 9.9 | 7.1 |
| | | 5.7 | 1.0 | 2.7 | | | % Profit Before Taxes/Total Assets | 2.5 | .5 |
| | | .1 | -2.9 | -.4 | | | | -2.7 | -4.8 |
| | | 2.9 | 2.7 | 2.4 | | | | 3.4 | 6.4 |
| | | 1.7 | .8 | .9 | | | Sales/Net Fixed Assets | 1.2 | 1.2 |
| | | .5 | .2 | .3 | | | | .7 | .5 |
| | | 1.1 | 1.0 | .7 | | | | 1.1 | 1.1 |
| | | .6 | .6 | .5 | | | Sales/Total Assets | .6 | .6 |
| | | .4 | .2 | .3 | | | | .4 | .3 |
| | | 2.6 | 3.3 | 3.8 | | | | 3.8 | 3.5 |
| | | (18) 7.2 | (31) 8.9 | (31) 7.7 | | | % Depr., Dep., Amort./Sales | (68) 6.9 | (79) 8.6 |
| | | 21.0 | 18.4 | 13.8 | | | | 13.4 | 14.7 |
| | | | | | | | | 1.8 | 1.3 |
| | | | | | | | % Officers', Directors' Owners' Comp/Sales | (14) 2.9 | (20) 4.0 |
| | | | | | | | | 7.4 | 6.4 |
| | 7612M | 25178M | 115758M | 402221M | 382488M | 551038M | Net Sales ($) | 1155100M | 1028417M |
| | 1813M | 35816M | 152121M | 695261M | 509702M | 545555M | Total Assets ($) | 1346911M | 1190133M |

© RMA 2012

M = $ thousand    MM = $ million
See Pages 9 through 22 for Explanation of Ratios and Data

## Comparative Historical Data | Current Data Sorted by Sales

| | | | Type of Statement | | | | | | |
|---|---|---|---|---|---|---|---|---|---|
| 3 | 6 | 7 | Unqualified | 1 | 1 | | 1 | 1 | 3 |
| 15 | 15 | 16 | Reviewed | | 3 | 2 | 3 | 5 | 3 |
| 18 | 13 | 11 | Compiled | 2 | 3 | 1 | 4 | | 1 |
| 29 | 22 | 30 | Tax Returns | 18 | 8 | 9 | 3 | | 1 |
| 48 | 45 | 51 | Other | 16 | 12 | | 5 | 5 | 4 |
| 4/1/09-3/31/10 ALL | 4/1/10-3/31/11 ALL | 4/1/11-3/31/12 ALL | | 4 (4/1-9/30/11) | | | 111 (10/1/11-3/31/12) | | |
| | | | | 0-1MM | 1-3MM | 3-5MM | 5-10MM | 10-25MM | 25MM & OVER |
| 113 | 101 | 115 | NUMBER OF STATEMENTS | 37 | 27 | 12 | 16 | 11 | 12 |
| % | % | % | ASSETS | % | % | % | % | % | % |
| 8.7 | 8.8 | 9.8 | Cash & Equivalents | 15.5 | 8.2 | 4.6 | 3.9 | 7.6 | 11.0 |
| 7.7 | 10.7 | 12.2 | Trade Receivables (net) | 4.2 | 16.0 | 14.1 | 17.6 | 11.1 | 20.2 |
| 9.3 | 8.7 | 7.6 | Inventory | 5.4 | 1.8 | 2.5 | 7.4 | 21.3 | 20.3 |
| 6.3 | 4.6 | 6.0 | All Other Current | 6.2 | 7.0 | 7.6 | 4.9 | 3.5 | 5.5 |
| 32.1 | 32.8 | 35.7 | Total Current | 31.4 | 33.0 | 28.9 | 33.8 | 43.5 | 56.9 |
| 57.7 | 58.5 | 55.2 | Fixed Assets (net) | 62.1 | 55.8 | 59.7 | 56.1 | 47.3 | 33.8 |
| 1.6 | 1.3 | 1.1 | Intangibles (net) | .3 | .4 | .3 | 3.0 | .1 | 4.4 |
| 8.7 | 7.3 | 8.0 | All Other Non-Current | 6.2 | 10.8 | 11.1 | 7.1 | 9.1 | 4.8 |
| 100.0 | 100.0 | 100.0 | Total | 100.0 | 100.0 | 100.0 | 100.0 | 100.0 | 100.0 |
| | | | LIABILITIES | | | | | | |
| 13.8 | 16.1 | 12.2 | Notes Payable-Short Term | 5.6 | 22.5 | 12.0 | 14.9 | 8.0 | 10.0 |
| 2.9 | 4.8 | 3.4 | Cur. Mat.-L.T.D. | 3.4 | 3.9 | 3.4 | 4.9 | 2.9 | 1.0 |
| 3.0 | 3.7 | 3.0 | Trade Payables | .5 | 2.9 | 3.5 | 1.8 | 3.3 | 11.3 |
| .1 | .1 | .2 | Income Taxes Payable | .0 | .7 | .0 | .0 | .0 | .1 |
| 4.0 | 3.4 | 4.3 | All Other Current | 3.9 | 7.0 | 1.5 | 4.1 | 2.4 | 4.4 |
| 23.8 | 28.2 | 23.1 | Total Current | 13.4 | 37.0 | 20.4 | 25.7 | 16.5 | 26.8 |
| 44.7 | 47.5 | 45.2 | Long-Term Debt | 49.5 | 60.0 | 51.8 | 39.2 | 23.3 | 19.8 |
| .3 | .1 | .1 | Deferred Taxes | .0 | .0 | .3 | .0 | .0 | .5 |
| 6.7 | 7.1 | 6.7 | All Other Non-Current | 8.0 | 4.9 | 6.6 | 5.5 | 7.4 | 7.8 |
| 24.5 | 17.1 | 25.0 | Net Worth | 29.2 | -1.9 | 20.9 | 29.6 | 52.8 | 45.1 |
| 100.0 | 100.0 | 100.0 | Total Liabilities & Net Worth | 100.0 | 100.0 | 100.0 | 100.0 | 100.0 | 100.0 |
| | | | INCOME DATA | | | | | | |
| 100.0 | 100.0 | 100.0 | Net Sales | 100.0 | 100.0 | 100.0 | 100.0 | 100.0 | 100.0 |
| | | | Gross Profit | | | | | | |
| 83.5 | 82.4 | 83.7 | Operating Expenses | 81.0 | 81.4 | 80.1 | 95.6 | 82.1 | 86.0 |
| 16.5 | 17.6 | 16.3 | Operating Profit | 19.0 | 18.6 | 19.9 | 4.4 | 17.9 | 14.0 |
| 8.0 | 8.1 | 8.5 | All Other Expenses (net) | 15.3 | 7.8 | 7.3 | 5.0 | 1.1 | 2.2 |
| 8.6 | 9.5 | 7.8 | Profit Before Taxes | 3.7 | 10.8 | 12.6 | -.6 | 16.9 | 11.8 |
| | | | RATIOS | | | | | | |
| 5.2 | 5.3 | 4.8 | Current | 6.5 | 2.9 | 4.5 | 3.3 | 8.8 | 4.4 |
| 1.9 | 1.8 | 1.8 | | 2.3 | 1.2 | 1.4 | 2.2 | 2.6 | 2.0 |
| .8 | .7 | .8 | | .4 | .2 | 1.1 | .7 | 1.1 | 1.5 |
| 2.7 | 3.4 | 2.6 | Quick | 4.2 | 1.8 | 4.5 | 1.8 | 5.6 | 1.9 |
| .7 | .8 | 1.0 | | 1.2 | .8 | 1.4 | .8 | 1.0 | .9 |
| .1 | .2 | .3 | | .2 | .0 | .3 | .6 | .6 | .4 |
| 0 UND | 0 UND | 0 UND | Sales/Receivables | 0 UND | 0 UND | 0 UND | 11 33.5 | 15 24.8 | 13 29.1 |
| 9 42.5 | 20 18.3 | 19 19.0 | | 0 UND | 3 110.2 | 47 7.8 | 54 6.7 | 39 9.4 | 42 8.7 |
| 73 5.0 | 95 3.8 | 104 3.5 | | 37 9.9 | 114 3.2 | 304 1.2 | 140 2.6 | 135 2.7 | 89 4.1 |
| | | | Cost of Sales/Inventory | | | | | | |
| | | | Cost of Sales/Payables | | | | | | |
| 1.9 | 1.6 | 1.7 | Sales/Working Capital | 1.3 | 3.1 | 3.7 | 1.6 | 2.2 | 1.8 |
| 5.8 | 6.8 | 6.2 | | 3.4 | 57.1 | 6.2 | 10.1 | 3.6 | 3.5 |
| -11.6 | -13.6 | -22.8 | | -7.9 | -6.5 | 14.0 | -13.8 | 17.7 | 9.4 |
| 9.5 | 8.5 | 9.1 | EBIT/Interest | 3.7 | 12.7 | 12.5 | 4.1 | | 24.7 |
| (89) 3.3 | (85) 3.5 | (89) 2.9 | | (21) 2.6 | (23) 3.0 | (10) 3.9 | (14) 2.6 | | 5.8 |
| 1.0 | 1.3 | 1.5 | | 1.3 | 1.7 | .8 | .1 | | 2.1 |
| 9.7 | 4.6 | 12.9 | Net Profit + Depr., Dep., Amort./Cur. Mat. L/T/D | | | | | | |
| (17) 3.4 | (13) 3.4 | (15) 2.4 | | | | | | | |
| 1.8 | 1.6 | 1.0 | | | | | | | |
| .7 | .7 | .7 | Fixed/Worth | .9 | .4 | .8 | .7 | .3 | .2 |
| 1.5 | 1.7 | 1.5 | | 1.8 | 3.5 | 1.6 | 9.3 | 1.1 | 1.0 |
| 41.7 | -17.5 | 51.8 | | 16.4 | -1.8 | NM | -18.1 | 2.7 | 1.5 |
| .5 | .6 | .5 | Debt/Worth | .7 | .3 | .4 | .4 | .1 | .6 |
| 1.7 | 1.9 | 1.6 | | 1.8 | 8.5 | 1.3 | 26.8 | .8 | 1.2 |
| NM | -21.3 | -27.3 | | 50.9 | -3.6 | NM | -23.9 | 2.3 | 2.9 |
| 30.0 | 25.6 | 26.3 | % Profit Before Taxes/Tangible Net Worth | 14.8 | 90.8 | | 20.9 | 28.7 | 32.9 |
| (85) 9.6 | (73) 11.0 | (85) 11.6 | | (29) 4.4 | (16) 26.0 | | (10) 3.0 | (10) 15.7 | (11) 18.1 |
| -.2 | 1.7 | 1.6 | | -5.6 | 3.4 | | -11.5 | 10.0 | 7.1 |
| 11.1 | 11.5 | 11.6 | % Profit Before Taxes/Total Assets | 7.2 | 32.2 | 11.0 | 7.1 | 17.4 | 17.7 |
| 3.6 | 5.2 | 4.4 | | 2.2 | 6.4 | 2.3 | .7 | 7.7 | 9.1 |
| -.5 | -.2 | .0 | | -2.5 | .5 | -.3 | -3.1 | 5.5 | 1.7 |
| 2.6 | 2.3 | 3.3 | Sales/Net Fixed Assets | 2.2 | 3.6 | 1.5 | 3.8 | 2.9 | 6.8 |
| .9 | .9 | 1.2 | | .3 | 2.0 | .7 | 1.3 | 1.6 | 4.6 |
| .4 | .4 | .4 | | .2 | .8 | .4 | .4 | .9 | 1.3 |
| 1.1 | .9 | 1.1 | Sales/Total Assets | .6 | 1.6 | 1.1 | 1.4 | 1.2 | 1.7 |
| .6 | .6 | .6 | | .3 | .8 | .4 | .6 | .8 | .8 |
| .3 | .3 | .3 | | .1 | .6 | .3 | .3 | .4 | .7 |
| 3.5 | 3.9 | 3.3 | % Depr., Dep., Amort./Sales | 4.4 | 2.5 | 8.4 | 2.9 | 3.6 | 1.9 |
| (93) 6.7 | (90) 8.3 | (92) 7.1 | | (28) 14.1 | (19) 7.3 | (10) 10.6 | (15) 6.8 | (10) 5.7 | (10) 3.5 |
| 11.6 | 15.6 | 14.3 | | 31.5 | 10.5 | 12.8 | 17.4 | 7.2 | 7.0 |
| 1.7 | 1.5 | 1.5 | % Officers', Directors' Owners' Comp/Sales | | | | | | |
| (23) 4.9 | (16) 3.5 | (11) 3.2 | | | | | | | |
| 8.7 | 8.8 | 5.0 | | | | | | | |
| 1223504M | 1176009M | 1484295M | Net Sales ($) | 20564M | 51962M | 48461M | 129773M | 192313M | 1041222M |
| 1634792M | 1769898M | 1940268M | Total Assets ($) | 90967M | 114954M | 127415M | 288336M | 325692M | 992904M |

© RMA 2012

M = $ thousand    MM = $ million
See Pages 9 through 22 for Explanation of Ratios and Data

## Current Data Sorted by Assets      Comparative Historical Data

| 0-500M | 500M-2MM | 2-10MM | 10-50MM | 50-100MM | 100-250MM | Type of Statement | 4/1/07-3/31/08 ALL | 4/1/08-3/31/09 ALL |
|---|---|---|---|---|---|---|---|---|
| | | | 1 | 3 | | | Unqualified | 2 | 11 |
| | 1 | 2 | 2 | 2 | 2 | Reviewed | 2 | 11 |
| | | 11 | 2 | 3 | 1 | 1 | Compiled | 6 | 10 |
| 4 | 3 | 12 | 3 | | | Tax Returns | 3 | 8 |
| 2 | 3 | 12 | 6 | 1 | 1 | Other | 5 | 21 |
| | | 8 (4/1-9/30/11) | | 65 (10/1/11-3/31/12) | | | | |
| 6 | 7 | 38 | 14 | 4 | 4 | NUMBER OF STATEMENTS | 18 | 61 |
| % | % | % | % | % | % | **ASSETS** | % | % |
| | | 5.1 | 4.9 | | | Cash & Equivalents | 5.8 | 7.6 |
| | | 14.5 | 8.7 | | | Trade Receivables (net) | 9.8 | 16.3 |
| | | 6.7 | 13.7 | | | Inventory | 19.4 | 9.8 |
| | | 6.6 | 4.3 | | | All Other Current | 6.5 | 5.1 |
| | | 32.9 | 31.6 | | | Total Current | 41.4 | 38.8 |
| | | 53.9 | 56.6 | | | Fixed Assets (net) | 47.6 | 47.7 |
| | | .8 | .1 | | | Intangibles (net) | .2 | .3 |
| | | 12.3 | 11.7 | | | All Other Non-Current | 10.8 | 13.1 |
| | | 100.0 | 100.0 | | | Total | 100.0 | 100.0 |
| | | | | | | **LIABILITIES** | | |
| | | 17.9 | 14.1 | | | Notes Payable-Short Term | 26.6 | 23.6 |
| | | 3.6 | 1.6 | | | Cur. Mat.-L.T.D. | 3.0 | 1.3 |
| | | 2.0 | 5.5 | | | Trade Payables | 5.4 | 4.3 |
| | | .3 | .0 | | | Income Taxes Payable | .6 | .7 |
| | | 8.2 | 4.1 | | | All Other Current | 11.8 | 2.9 |
| | | 31.9 | 25.4 | | | Total Current | 47.5 | 32.7 |
| | | 35.2 | 37.1 | | | Long-Term Debt | 21.4 | 25.3 |
| | | .4 | .9 | | | Deferred Taxes | .7 | 2.2 |
| | | 2.9 | 2.1 | | | All Other Non-Current | 5.0 | 1.8 |
| | | 29.6 | 34.5 | | | Net Worth | 25.4 | 38.0 |
| | | 100.0 | 100.0 | | | Total Liabilities & Net Worth | 100.0 | 100.0 |
| | | | | | | **INCOME DATA** | | |
| | | 100.0 | 100.0 | | | Net Sales | 100.0 | 100.0 |
| | | | | | | Gross Profit | | |
| | | 79.2 | 79.4 | | | Operating Expenses | 91.1 | 84.6 |
| | | 20.8 | 20.6 | | | Operating Profit | 8.9 | 15.4 |
| | | 3.7 | 6.2 | | | All Other Expenses (net) | 6.1 | 3.4 |
| | | 17.1 | 14.4 | | | Profit Before Taxes | 2.7 | 12.1 |
| | | | | | | **RATIOS** | | |
| | | 12.8 | 3.6 | | | | 4.2 | 3.2 |
| | | 1.5 | 1.3 | | | Current | 1.2 | 1.6 |
| | | .4 | .8 | | | | .4 | 1.0 |
| | | 3.8 | 1.6 | | | | 3.7 | 2.9 |
| | | 1.0 | .8 | | | Quick | .3 | 1.0 |
| | | .0 | .3 | | | | .1 | .3 |
| | | 0   UND | 0   UND | | | | 0   UND | 0   UND |
| | | 34   10.8 | 99   3.7 | | | Sales/Receivables | 9   42.7 | 36   10.2 |
| | | 192   1.9 | 174   2.1 | | | | 38   9.6 | 203   1.8 |
| | | | | | | Cost of Sales/Inventory | | |
| | | | | | | Cost of Sales/Payables | | |
| | | 1.7 | 1.7 | | | | 4.6 | 2.2 |
| | | 8.6 | 15.5 | | | Sales/Working Capital | 25.8 | 6.1 |
| | | -3.4 | -6.9 | | | | -1.3 | 369.1 |
| | | 9.7 | 6.9 | | | | 2.0 | 15.9 |
| | | (33) 4.1 | (13) 2.1 | | | EBIT/Interest | (15) 1.2 | (56) 2.9 |
| | | 1.2 | .4 | | | | -.5 | .0 |
| | | | | | | Net Profit + Depr., Dep., | | 12.1 |
| | | | | | | Amort./Cur. Mat. L/T/D | | (12) 5.1 |
| | | | | | | | | 3.5 |
| | | .7 | .8 | | | | .5 | .6 |
| | | 1.5 | 1.6 | | | Fixed/Worth | 1.6 | 1.0 |
| | | NM | 3.1 | | | | -6.3 | 2.7 |
| | | .8 | .9 | | | | .9 | .4 |
| | | 1.8 | 2.1 | | | Debt/Worth | 3.6 | 1.2 |
| | | NM | 9.5 | | | | -10.2 | 7.1 |
| | | 48.4 | 42.8 | | | % Profit Before Taxes/Tangible | 23.5 | 30.7 |
| | | (29) 26.5 | 8.2 | | | Net Worth | (13) 5.5 | (51) 11.6 |
| | | 4.0 | -3.4 | | | | -5.1 | -2.3 |
| | | 18.7 | 7.9 | | | % Profit Before Taxes/Total | 3.6 | 19.9 |
| | | 5.6 | 3.5 | | | Assets | 2.2 | 5.3 |
| | | -.4 | -1.4 | | | | -2.9 | -3.0 |
| | | 1.9 | 1.8 | | | | 9.7 | 5.2 |
| | | 1.2 | .4 | | | Sales/Net Fixed Assets | 2.3 | 1.6 |
| | | .8 | .2 | | | | .8 | .7 |
| | | 1.0 | .5 | | | | 2.5 | 1.8 |
| | | .6 | .3 | | | Sales/Total Assets | 1.1 | .7 |
| | | .4 | .2 | | | | .5 | .4 |
| | | 3.0 | 3.2 | | | | 1.5 | 2.5 |
| | | (34) 6.1 | (12) 8.3 | | | % Depr., Dep., Amort./Sales | (17) 3.1 | (49) 5.2 |
| | | 9.7 | 16.2 | | | | 6.7 | 10.7 |
| | | 1.5 | | | | % Officers', Directors' | | 1.7 |
| | | (10) 2.6 | | | | Owners' Comp/Sales | | (10) 5.1 |
| | | 4.8 | | | | | | 10.2 |
| 5973M | 10783M | 150229M | 109654M | 109517M | 373027M | Net Sales ($) | 571060M | 982100M |
| 1183M | 7793M | 205294M | 319745M | 260615M | 549106M | Total Assets ($) | 353557M | 1146874M |

M = $ thousand    MM = $ million
See Pages 9 through 22 for Explanation of Ratios and Data

## Comparative Historical Data                                    Current Data Sorted by Sales

| | | | Type of Statement | | | | | | |
|---|---|---|---|---|---|---|---|---|---|
| 4 | 4 | 4 | Unqualified | | | | 1 | 3 | |
| 7 | 14 | 9 | Reviewed | | 4 | | 1 | 1 | 3 |
| 10 | 9 | 16 | Compiled | 2 | 2 | 5 | 5 | 1 | 1 |
| 10 | 11 | 19 | Tax Returns | 5 | 5 | 5 | 3 | 1 | |
| 24 | 20 | 25 | Other | 6 | 8 | 5 | 4 | | 2 |
| 4/1/09- | 4/1/10- | 4/1/11- | | | 8 (4/1-9/30/11) | | 65 (10/1/11-3/31/12) | | |
| 3/31/10 | 3/31/11 | 3/31/12 | | | | | | | |
| ALL | ALL | ALL | | 0-1MM | 1-3MM | 3-5MM | 5-10MM | 10-25MM | 25MM & OVER |
| 55 | 58 | 73 | NUMBER OF STATEMENTS | 13 | 19 | 15 | 14 | 6 | 6 |
| % | % | % | ASSETS | % | % | % | % | % | % |
| 7.3 | 9.2 | 7.7 | Cash & Equivalents | 18.6 | 2.6 | 8.7 | 3.5 | | |
| 15.9 | 15.1 | 12.5 | Trade Receivables (net) | 2.9 | 17.5 | 14.7 | 7.9 | | |
| 11.8 | 11.5 | 7.4 | Inventory | .7 | 7.1 | 4.4 | 13.8 | | |
| 5.3 | 5.4 | 6.1 | All Other Current | 6.5 | 4.3 | 7.6 | 4.7 | | |
| 40.3 | 41.1 | 33.6 | Total Current | 28.8 | 31.6 | 35.4 | 29.8 | | |
| 48.7 | 49.0 | 51.9 | Fixed Assets (net) | 66.9 | 48.8 | 52.6 | 49.1 | | |
| .7 | .7 | 1.6 | Intangibles (net) | .1 | 2.3 | .0 | .1 | | |
| 10.2 | 9.3 | 12.8 | All Other Non-Current | 4.2 | 17.3 | 12.0 | 21.0 | | |
| 100.0 | 100.0 | 100.0 | Total | 100.0 | 100.0 | 100.0 | 100.0 | | |
| | | | LIABILITIES | | | | | | |
| 18.3 | 18.1 | 19.1 | Notes Payable-Short Term | 16.9 | 21.0 | 17.9 | 21.6 | | |
| 3.5 | 5.7 | 2.7 | Cur. Mat.-L.T.D. | 1.5 | 2.5 | 2.8 | 5.2 | | |
| 6.3 | 6.6 | 3.4 | Trade Payables | 2.9 | 1.7 | 1.8 | 1.7 | | |
| .2 | .1 | .2 | Income Taxes Payable | .0 | .6 | .0 | .0 | | |
| 6.4 | 7.5 | 6.5 | All Other Current | 3.9 | 11.9 | .8 | 9.7 | | |
| 34.7 | 38.0 | 32.0 | Total Current | 25.2 | 37.7 | 23.3 | 38.2 | | |
| 33.4 | 30.0 | 36.0 | Long-Term Debt | 32.1 | 46.9 | 35.3 | 32.1 | | |
| .3 | .5 | .4 | Deferred Taxes | .0 | .0 | .0 | .0 | | |
| 5.7 | 4.7 | 3.1 | All Other Non-Current | .4 | 4.1 | 1.4 | 7.2 | | |
| 25.9 | 26.7 | 28.6 | Net Worth | 42.2 | 11.3 | 40.0 | 22.4 | | |
| 100.0 | 100.0 | 100.0 | Total Liabilities & Net Worth | 100.0 | 100.0 | 100.0 | 100.0 | | |
| | | | INCOME DATA | | | | | | |
| 100.0 | 100.0 | 100.0 | Net Sales | 100.0 | 100.0 | 100.0 | 100.0 | | |
| | | | Gross Profit | | | | | | |
| 88.7 | 83.7 | 77.5 | Operating Expenses | 78.7 | 81.0 | 71.9 | 84.9 | | |
| 11.3 | 16.3 | 22.5 | Operating Profit | 21.3 | 19.0 | 28.1 | 15.1 | | |
| 3.9 | 2.9 | 4.5 | All Other Expenses (net) | 2.8 | 3.0 | 3.4 | 11.7 | | |
| 7.4 | 13.4 | 17.9 | Profit Before Taxes | 18.5 | 16.0 | 24.7 | 3.4 | | |
| | | | RATIOS | | | | | | |
| 2.6 | 4.7 | 5.7 | | 4.7 | 5.6 | 13.5 | 2.6 | | |
| 1.3 | 1.2 | 1.3 | Current | 1.0 | 1.2 | 1.8 | 1.1 | | |
| .7 | .6 | .5 | | .4 | .3 | .4 | .4 | | |
| 1.8 | 2.4 | 2.5 | | 4.7 | 2.5 | 7.6 | 1.6 | | |
| .7 | .6 | .8 | Quick | .5 | .5 | 1.0 | .3 | | |
| .2 | .2 | .1 | | .2 | .0 | .0 | .1 | | |
| 0 UND | 0 UND | 0 UND | | 0 UND | 0 UND | 0 UND | 0 UND | | |
| 29 12.6 | 24 15.4 | 31 11.6 | Sales/Receivables | 0 UND | 114 3.2 | 31 11.6 | 12 30.9 | | |
| 95 3.8 | 162 2.3 | 182 2.0 | | 69 5.3 | 261 1.4 | 174 2.1 | 140 2.6 | | |
| | | | Cost of Sales/Inventory | | | | | | |
| | | | Cost of Sales/Payables | | | | | | |
| 3.6 | 2.0 | 1.8 | | 2.4 | 1.8 | 1.5 | 2.1 | | |
| 8.9 | 14.4 | 10.9 | Sales/Working Capital | -515.0 | 4.6 | 12.6 | 23.4 | | |
| -21.8 | -10.3 | -4.0 | | -3.4 | -3.3 | -5.6 | -3.1 | | |
| 5.9 | 10.8 | 12.3 | | | 6.4 | 27.5 | 6.9 | | |
| (50) 2.6 | (54) 3.9 | (62) 5.2 | EBIT/Interest | (16) | 4.0 (13) | 6.5 (13) | 3.9 | | |
| .8 | 1.3 | 1.7 | | | .8 | 1.7 | -.1 | | |
| 3.9 | 23.2 | 10.4 | Net Profit + Depr., Dep., | | | | | | |
| (15) 2.9 | (12) 2.4 | (16) 5.6 | Amort./Cur. Mat. L/T/D | | | | | | |
| 1.5 | 1.4 | 2.5 | | | | | | | |
| 1.0 | .6 | .7 | | .8 | 1.0 | .6 | .6 | | |
| 1.2 | 1.3 | 1.4 | Fixed/Worth | 1.3 | 3.0 | 1.7 | 1.3 | | |
| 3.6 | 3.3 | 23.8 | | 4.6 | -2.3 | 13.4 | -29.0 | | |
| 1.2 | .7 | .7 | | .1 | 1.0 | .2 | .9 | | |
| 2.3 | 2.0 | 2.0 | Debt/Worth | 1.1 | 4.8 | 1.7 | 5.0 | | |
| 9.0 | 8.3 | 39.7 | | 4.5 | -5.2 | 19.8 | -39.5 | | |
| 35.0 | 42.3 | 56.9 | % Profit Before Taxes/Tangible | 97.6 | 36.0 | 183.3 | 38.1 | | |
| (46) 7.4 | (50) 16.2 | (58) 26.2 | Net Worth | (12) 14.2 | (12) 10.1 | (14) 71.9 | (10) 6.4 | | |
| .3 | 4.6 | 4.2 | | -3.6 | .2 | 28.5 | -6.1 | | |
| 11.5 | 18.3 | 22.9 | % Profit Before Taxes/Total | 43.3 | 19.9 | 30.9 | 9.4 | | |
| 3.8 | 5.0 | 7.5 | Assets | 4.5 | 6.3 | 18.3 | .5 | | |
| -.5 | 1.1 | .6 | | -2.2 | -1.3 | 4.1 | -2.9 | | |
| 5.3 | 7.1 | 2.2 | | 1.5 | 1.6 | 4.7 | 2.6 | | |
| 2.0 | 1.7 | 1.2 | Sales/Net Fixed Assets | .9 | 1.0 | 1.4 | 1.7 | | |
| .7 | .8 | .7 | | .3 | .6 | .9 | .3 | | |
| 2.0 | 2.0 | 1.0 | | .9 | .8 | 1.0 | 1.1 | | |
| .7 | .8 | .6 | Sales/Total Assets | .6 | .5 | .8 | .5 | | |
| .4 | .4 | .3 | | .2 | .3 | .6 | .2 | | |
| 2.6 | 2.6 | 3.1 | | | 5.1 | 3.3 | 2.4 | | |
| (44) 9.2 | (40) 6.6 | (60) 6.4 | % Depr., Dep., Amort./Sales | (17) 8.0 | (11) 5.3 | (13) 4.7 | | |
| 13.7 | 12.2 | 9.8 | | | 11.2 | 11.8 | 10.2 | | |
| | 2.2 | 1.6 | % Officers', Directors' | | | | | | |
| | (12) 5.2 | (14) 2.2 | Owners' Comp/Sales | | | | | | |
| | 9.1 | 4.8 | | | | | | | |
| 789742M | 1032899M | 759183M | Net Sales ($) | 6889M | 42502M | 60315M | 94160M | 82853M | 472464M |
| 712848M | 990039M | 1343736M | Total Assets ($) | 29128M | 112569M | 79699M | 364166M | 204767M | 553407M |

© RMA 2012

M = $ thousand    MM = $ million
See Pages 9 through 22 for Explanation of Ratios and Data

## Current Data Sorted by Assets | Comparative Historical Data

| | 0-500M | 500M-2MM | 2-10MM | 10-50MM | 50-100MM | 100-250MM | Type of Statement | 4/1/07-3/31/08 ALL | 4/1/08-3/31/09 ALL |
|---|---|---|---|---|---|---|---|---|---|
| | | | 1 | | | | Unqualified | 3 | 1 |
| | | | 2 | 3 | | | Reviewed | 6 | 3 |
| | | | 5 | 3 | 1 | | Compiled | 13 | 12 |
| | 2 | | 1 | | | | Tax Returns | 9 | 2 |
| | 1 | 3 | 8 | 4 | 2 | | Other | 8 | 3 |
| | | | 5 (4/1-9/30/11) | 31 (10/1/11-3/31/12) | | | | | |
| | 3 | 3 | 17 | 10 | 3 | | NUMBER OF STATEMENTS | 39 | 21 |
| | % | % | % | % | % | % | ASSETS | % | % |
| | | | 5.2 | 2.7 | | | Cash & Equivalents | 5.7 | 1.8 |
| | | | 23.6 | 12.6 | | | Trade Receivables (net) | 23.9 | 22.5 |
| | | | 25.0 | 17.2 | | | Inventory | 14.3 | 15.0 |
| | | | .7 | .5 | | | All Other Current | .6 | 1.0 |
| | | | 54.6 | 33.0 | | | Total Current | 44.5 | 40.3 |
| | | | 33.4 | 62.4 | | | Fixed Assets (net) | 43.1 | 51.0 |
| | | | 3.3 | .2 | | | Intangibles (net) | 2.2 | 2.2 |
| | | | 8.7 | 4.3 | | | All Other Non-Current | 10.2 | 6.5 |
| | | | 100.0 | 100.0 | | | Total | 100.0 | 100.0 |
| | | | | | | | LIABILITIES | | |
| | | | 7.9 | 7.0 | | | Notes Payable-Short Term | 13.6 | 11.0 |
| | | | 2.7 | 5.1 | | | Cur. Mat.-L.T.D. | 8.2 | 8.9 |
| | | | 18.8 | 14.3 | | | Trade Payables | 20.8 | 15.7 |
| | | | .6 | .0 | | | Income Taxes Payable | .2 | .3 |
| | | | 8.7 | 2.5 | | | All Other Current | 6.6 | 2.4 |
| | | | 38.7 | 28.9 | | | Total Current | 49.4 | 38.3 |
| | | | 21.4 | 45.9 | | | Long-Term Debt | 37.3 | 37.5 |
| | | | .0 | .0 | | | Deferred Taxes | .4 | .4 |
| | | | 2.9 | 2.7 | | | All Other Non-Current | 1.5 | .1 |
| | | | 37.0 | 22.5 | | | Net Worth | 11.4 | 23.6 |
| | | | 100.0 | 100.0 | | | Total Liabilities & Net Worth | 100.0 | 100.0 |
| | | | | | | | INCOME DATA | | |
| | | | 100.0 | 100.0 | | | Net Sales | 100.0 | 100.0 |
| | | | | | | | Gross Profit | | |
| | | | 89.1 | 92.2 | | | Operating Expenses | 98.2 | 97.8 |
| | | | 10.9 | 7.8 | | | Operating Profit | 1.8 | 2.2 |
| | | | 5.7 | 5.5 | | | All Other Expenses (net) | 1.6 | 1.7 |
| | | | 5.2 | 2.4 | | | Profit Before Taxes | .2 | .5 |
| | | | | | | | RATIOS | | |
| | | | 1.7 | 2.1 | | | | 1.6 | 2.1 |
| | | | 1.4 | .9 | | | Current | 1.1 | 1.1 |
| | | | 1.2 | .4 | | | | .5 | .6 |
| | | | .9 | | | | | 1.0 | 1.0 |
| | | | .7 | | | | Quick | .5 | .7 |
| | | | .3 | | | | | .3 | .3 |
| | | 22 | 16.3 | 0 UND | | | | 2  148.4 | 20  17.8 |
| | | 27 | 13.3 | 24  15.4 | | | Sales/Receivables | 29  12.4 | 33  10.9 |
| | | 38 | 9.6 | 33  11.0 | | | | 37  9.8 | 37  9.9 |
| | | | | | | | Cost of Sales/Inventory | | |
| | | | | | | | Cost of Sales/Payables | | |
| | | | 14.6 | 21.3 | | | | 21.4 | 14.0 |
| | | | 27.5 | NM | | | Sales/Working Capital | 170.0 | 65.0 |
| | | | 49.9 | -8.1 | | | | -22.2 | -12.7 |
| | | | 9.6 | | | | | 6.9 | 8.6 |
| | | (14) | 4.3 | | | | EBIT/Interest | (36)  1.2 | 1.0 |
| | | | 1.6 | | | | | -.1 | -.6 |
| | | | | | | | Net Profit + Depr., Dep., Amort./Cur. Mat. L/T/D | | |
| | | | .3 | 1.2 | | | | .8 | .6 |
| | | | .7 | 4.8 | | | Fixed/Worth | 1.7 | 1.8 |
| | | | 1.5 | -120.2 | | | | 16.6 | -43.6 |
| | | | .6 | 1.7 | | | | 1.4 | 1.1 |
| | | | 1.7 | 6.1 | | | Debt/Worth | 4.8 | 4.0 |
| | | | 5.7 | -125.7 | | | | 247.6 | -59.6 |
| | | | 55.8 | | | | | 47.0 | 26.8 |
| | | (16) | 20.1 | | | | % Profit Before Taxes/Tangible Net Worth | (30)  7.0 | (15)  17.2 |
| | | | 5.9 | | | | | -9.7 | -11.2 |
| | | | 11.9 | 6.6 | | | | 12.1 | 9.1 |
| | | | 5.4 | 2.8 | | | % Profit Before Taxes/Total Assets | .5 | .2 |
| | | | 1.9 | -2.3 | | | | -3.4 | -8.3 |
| | | | 37.1 | 5.5 | | | | 21.0 | 8.6 |
| | | | 9.7 | 2.8 | | | Sales/Net Fixed Assets | 9.0 | 4.4 |
| | | | 4.5 | 1.2 | | | | 4.2 | 2.1 |
| | | | 4.1 | 2.8 | | | | 6.3 | 3.1 |
| | | | 3.2 | 1.5 | | | Sales/Total Assets | 3.7 | 2.3 |
| | | | 1.3 | .8 | | | | 2.1 | 1.4 |
| | | | .9 | | | | | .6 | 1.2 |
| | | (13) | 1.7 | | | | % Depr., Dep., Amort./Sales | (35)  1.8 | (19)  1.7 |
| | | | 4.9 | | | | | 4.0 | 6.1 |
| | | | | | | | % Officers', Directors' Owners' Comp/Sales | .7 | |
| | | (14) | | | | | | 1.5 | |
| | | | | | | | | 2.9 | |
| | 3790M | 8318M | 210328M | 238915M | 385194M | | Net Sales ($) | 615247M | 429662M |
| | 999M | 3076M | 69501M | 143044M | 207483M | | Total Assets ($) | 245030M | 215262M |

*(Center columns marked "DATA NOT AVAILABLE" for asset categories; N/A for 0-500M, 500M-2MM, 50-100MM, and 100-250MM size ranges.)*

M = $ thousand    MM = $ million
See Pages 9 through 22 for Explanation of Ratios and Data

## Comparative Historical Data  &  Current Data Sorted by Sales

### Type of Statement

| Type of Statement | 4/1/09–3/31/10 ALL | 4/1/10–3/31/11 ALL | 4/1/11–3/31/12 ALL | 0-1MM | 1-3MM | 3-5MM | 5-10MM | 10-25MM | 25MM & OVER |
|---|---|---|---|---|---|---|---|---|---|
| Unqualified | 2 | 4 | 1 | | | | | 1 | |
| Reviewed | 7 | 11 | 5 | | | | | 1 | |
| Compiled | 25 | 18 | 9 | 1 | 1 | | | 2 | 2 |
| Tax Returns | 4 | 6 | 3 | 2 | 1 | | 3 | 4 | 3 |
| Other | 13 | 13 | 18 | 1 | 4 | | 2 | 5 | 3 |
| | | | | 5 (4/1-9/30/11) | | | 31 (10/1/11-3/31/12) | | |
| **NUMBER OF STATEMENTS** | 51 | 52 | 36 | 4 | 6 | | 5 | 13 | 8 |

*Note: For the ASSETS, LIABILITIES, and INCOME DATA sections the 0-1MM, 1-3MM, 3-5MM and 5-10MM columns are marked "DATA NOT AVAILABLE."*

| | % | % | % | % | % | % | % | % | % |
|---|---|---|---|---|---|---|---|---|---|
| **ASSETS** | | | | | | | | | |
| Cash & Equivalents | 3.9 | 5.4 | 6.6 | | | | | 2.4 | |
| Trade Receivables (net) | 18.3 | 18.4 | 17.9 | | | | | 15.7 | |
| Inventory | 16.3 | 17.2 | 18.4 | | | | | 25.8 | |
| All Other Current | 1.2 | 1.9 | 1.6 | | | | | .6 | |
| Total Current | 39.7 | 42.9 | 44.5 | | | | | 44.5 | |
| Fixed Assets (net) | 50.5 | 48.1 | 44.3 | | | | | 45.0 | |
| Intangibles (net) | 1.5 | .8 | 3.0 | | | | | .1 | |
| All Other Non-Current | 8.4 | 8.2 | 8.1 | | | | | 10.4 | |
| Total | 100.0 | 100.0 | 100.0 | | | | | 100.0 | |
| **LIABILITIES** | | | | | | | | | |
| Notes Payable-Short Term | 14.3 | 8.9 | 8.4 | | | | | 8.7 | |
| Cur. Mat.-L.T.D. | 4.8 | 4.0 | 3.1 | | | | | 3.9 | |
| Trade Payables | 14.3 | 19.4 | 20.7 | | | | | 12.6 | |
| Income Taxes Payable | .4 | .0 | .4 | | | | | .8 | |
| All Other Current | 6.1 | 4.9 | 8.0 | | | | | 6.2 | |
| Total Current | 39.9 | 37.2 | 40.6 | | | | | 32.3 | |
| Long-Term Debt | 43.2 | 35.6 | 27.9 | | | | | 32.9 | |
| Deferred Taxes | .9 | .2 | .1 | | | | | .0 | |
| All Other Non-Current | 1.6 | 2.2 | 2.2 | | | | | 5.0 | |
| Net Worth | 14.4 | 24.7 | 29.2 | | | | | 29.9 | |
| Total Liabilities & Net Worth | 100.0 | 100.0 | 100.0 | | | | | 100.0 | |
| **INCOME DATA** | | | | | | | | | |
| Net Sales | 100.0 | 100.0 | 100.0 | | | | | 100.0 | |
| Gross Profit | | | | | | | | | |
| Operating Expenses | 93.9 | 94.1 | 91.7 | | | | | 96.6 | |
| Operating Profit | 6.1 | 5.9 | 8.3 | | | | | 3.4 | |
| All Other Expenses (net) | 4.0 | 3.1 | 4.4 | | | | | .9 | |
| Profit Before Taxes | 2.1 | 2.8 | 4.0 | | | | | 2.5 | |

### RATIOS

| Ratio | 4/1/09–3/31/10 ALL | 4/1/10–3/31/11 ALL | 4/1/11–3/31/12 ALL | 10-25MM |
|---|---|---|---|---|
| Current | 1.9 | 2.0 | 1.6 | 1.6 |
| | .9 | 1.2 | 1.2 | 1.3 |
| | .5 | .7 | .5 | .9 |
| Quick | 1.0 | 1.2 | 1.0 | .8 |
| | .5 | .6 | (35) .7 | (12) .7 |
| | .3 | .3 | .3 | .4 |
| Sales/Receivables | 0  UND | 6  60.1 | 13  28.7 | 1  513.1 |
| | 25  14.8 | 25  14.8 | 26  13.8 | 26  14.1 |
| | 42  8.8 | 34  10.8 | 34  10.8 | 27  13.3 |
| Cost of Sales/Inventory | | | | |
| Cost of Sales/Payables | | | | |
| Sales/Working Capital | 11.4 | 11.0 | 15.7 | 18.5 |
| | -247.5 | 46.8 | 42.0 | 30.4 |
| | -14.9 | -18.1 | -9.6 | NM |
| EBIT/Interest | 7.3 | 6.3 | 7.1 | 8.3 |
| | (48) 2.2 | (45) 2.8 | (31) 3.4 | 3.4 |
| | .4 | .8 | 1.3 | .9 |
| Net Profit + Depr., Dep., Amort./Cur. Mat. L/T/D | | | | |
| Fixed/Worth | 1.0 | .6 | .6 | .6 |
| | 3.2 | 1.6 | 1.2 | 1.1 |
| | -6.0 | 7.1 | 7.6 | 4.8 |
| Debt/Worth | 1.7 | 1.0 | 1.2 | 1.5 |
| | 4.6 | 2.6 | 2.0 | 2.7 |
| | -26.9 | 8.7 | 9.8 | 8.0 |
| % Profit Before Taxes/Tangible Net Worth | 33.3 | 42.3 | 30.9 | 35.2 |
| | (35) 16.1 | (43) 21.5 | (30) 19.4 | (12) 15.7 |
| | -6.2 | 2.5 | 9.7 | 5.9 |
| % Profit Before Taxes/Total Assets | 10.7 | 10.2 | 9.4 | 11.2 |
| | 3.3 | 5.0 | 5.4 | 5.1 |
| | -2.1 | -1.1 | .6 | -.2 |
| Sales/Net Fixed Assets | 14.4 | 14.1 | 15.3 | 15.7 |
| | 3.8 | 5.4 | 6.2 | 6.6 |
| | 1.9 | 2.3 | 2.7 | 2.2 |
| Sales/Total Assets | 4.1 | 3.7 | 3.7 | 3.9 |
| | 2.2 | 2.2 | 2.7 | 2.7 |
| | 1.0 | 1.2 | 1.2 | 1.2 |
| % Depr., Dep., Amort./Sales | 1.7 | 1.8 | 1.2 | 1.3 |
| | (50) 2.9 | (45) 2.6 | (28) 2.5 | (12) 2.3 |
| | 6.7 | 6.2 | 6.9 | 4.2 |
| % Officers', Directors' Owners' Comp/Sales | 1.0 | 1.1 | .8 | |
| | (19) 1.3 | (22) 1.5 | (13) 1.4 | |
| | 2.4 | 2.7 | 2.2 | |

| | 4/1/09–3/31/10 ALL | 4/1/10–3/31/11 ALL | 4/1/11–3/31/12 ALL | 0-1MM | 1-3MM | 3-5MM | 5-10MM | 10-25MM | 25MM & OVER |
|---|---|---|---|---|---|---|---|---|---|
| Net Sales ($) | 997478M | 1271029M | 846545M | 2077M | 10597M | | 36903M | 202772M | 594196M |
| Total Assets ($) | 602912M | 714783M | 424103M | 7741M | 19303M | | 12521M | 117288M | 267250M |

© RMA 2012

M = $ thousand    MM = $ million

See Pages 9 through 22 for Explanation of Ratios and Data

## Current Data Sorted by Assets      Comparative Historical Data

| 0-500M | 500M-2MM | 2-10MM | 10-50MM | 50-100MM | 100-250MM | Type of Statement | 4/1/07-3/31/08 ALL | 4/1/08-3/31/09 ALL |
|---|---|---|---|---|---|---|---|---|
| | | 2 | 6 | 6 | 7 | Unqualified | 18 | 22 |
| | 1 | 8 | 13 | 3 | | Reviewed | 27 | 33 |
| 3 | 6 | 23 | 4 | | | Compiled | 28 | 37 |
| 11 | 8 | 4 | 2 | | | Tax Returns | 27 | 23 |
| 7 | 21 | 26 | 17 | 3 | 1 | Other | 58 | 80 |
| | 46 (4/1-9/30/11) | | 136 (10/1/11-3/31/12) | | | | | |
| 21 | 36 | 63 | 42 | 12 | 8 | **NUMBER OF STATEMENTS** | 158 | 195 |
| % | % | % | % | % | % | **ASSETS** | % | % |
| 21.1 | 7.8 | 4.3 | 3.7 | 2.4 | | Cash & Equivalents | 6.8 | 5.7 |
| 8.3 | 14.3 | 15.4 | 7.5 | 12.4 | | Trade Receivables (net) | 12.2 | 13.1 |
| 16.9 | 18.2 | 31.6 | 46.9 | 46.7 | | Inventory | 30.9 | 33.6 |
| 1.5 | 5.9 | 5.5 | 1.7 | 1.0 | | All Other Current | 2.3 | 3.2 |
| 47.8 | 46.2 | 56.7 | 59.8 | 62.5 | | Total Current | 52.2 | 55.6 |
| 35.0 | 31.7 | 37.5 | 34.0 | 26.3 | | Fixed Assets (net) | 39.2 | 34.3 |
| 4.7 | 7.5 | .6 | 2.6 | 2.1 | | Intangibles (net) | 1.6 | 2.1 |
| 12.5 | 14.5 | 5.2 | 3.6 | 9.0 | | All Other Non-Current | 7.0 | 7.9 |
| 100.0 | 100.0 | 100.0 | 100.0 | 100.0 | | Total | 100.0 | 100.0 |
| | | | | | | **LIABILITIES** | | |
| 53.8 | 16.4 | 14.3 | 16.1 | 15.3 | | Notes Payable-Short Term | 16.3 | 20.9 |
| 4.3 | 4.0 | 2.5 | 3.8 | 3.7 | | Cur. Mat.-L.T.D. | 3.7 | 4.0 |
| 4.1 | 11.5 | 13.2 | 10.0 | 7.0 | | Trade Payables | 11.4 | 10.3 |
| .0 | .5 | .6 | 1.2 | 2.0 | | Income Taxes Payable | 1.2 | .8 |
| 12.9 | 18.0 | 6.7 | 4.5 | 13.0 | | All Other Current | 8.9 | 8.9 |
| 75.1 | 50.5 | 37.2 | 35.6 | 40.9 | | Total Current | 41.5 | 45.0 |
| 24.2 | 22.6 | 26.2 | 22.0 | 14.5 | | Long-Term Debt | 28.7 | 22.9 |
| .0 | .2 | 1.2 | 2.2 | 4.9 | | Deferred Taxes | .9 | .9 |
| 15.0 | 9.8 | 4.2 | 5.6 | 3.2 | | All Other Non-Current | 7.7 | 7.0 |
| -14.2 | 17.0 | 31.2 | 34.7 | 36.5 | | Net Worth | 21.2 | 24.2 |
| 100.0 | 100.0 | 100.0 | 100.0 | 100.0 | | Total Liabilities & Net Worth | 100.0 | 100.0 |
| | | | | | | **INCOME DATA** | | |
| 100.0 | 100.0 | 100.0 | 100.0 | 100.0 | | Net Sales | 100.0 | 100.0 |
| 53.4 | 48.5 | 40.1 | 40.7 | 37.2 | | Gross Profit | 38.2 | 39.7 |
| 54.8 | 45.2 | 37.3 | 36.7 | 33.4 | | Operating Expenses | 34.2 | 37.5 |
| -1.3 | 3.3 | 2.9 | 4.0 | 3.8 | | Operating Profit | 4.0 | 2.2 |
| 1.0 | .8 | 1.9 | 2.1 | .5 | | All Other Expenses (net) | 2.3 | 2.4 |
| -2.3 | 2.4 | 1.0 | 1.9 | 3.4 | | Profit Before Taxes | 1.7 | -.2 |
| | | | | | | **RATIOS** | | |
| 3.3 | 2.1 | 4.0 | 2.6 | 1.8 | | | 2.9 | 3.0 |
| 1.2 | 1.0 | 1.5 | 1.6 | 1.4 | | Current | 1.5 | 1.4 |
| .4 | .4 | .8 | 1.2 | 1.1 | | | 1.0 | .8 |
| 1.7 | 1.4 | 1.2 | .5 | .5 | | | 1.0 | 1.0 |
| .7 | .4 | .4 | .2 | .2 | | Quick | .4 (193) | .4 |
| .2 | .1 | .3 | .1 | .1 | | | .2 | .2 |
| 0 UND | 3 116.8 | 16 22.7 | 9 40.7 | 13 28.4 | | | 2 218.0 | 13 29.2 |
| 4 101.9 | 13 27.3 | 29 12.5 | 19 19.4 | 35 10.4 | | Sales/Receivables | 19 18.9 | 27 13.5 |
| 14 26.4 | 49 7.4 | 53 6.9 | 40 9.1 | 72 5.1 | | | 47 7.8 | 49 7.4 |
| 0 UND | 0 UND | 0 UND | 96 3.8 | 182 2.0 | | | 10 36.5 | 28 13.2 |
| 22 16.8 | 20 17.9 | 104 3.5 | 261 1.4 | 365 1.0 | | Cost of Sales/Inventory | 85 4.3 | 112 3.3 |
| 62 5.9 | 140 2.6 | 332 1.1 | 730 .5 | 521 .7 | | | 234 1.6 | 358 1.0 |
| 0 UND | 0 UND | 12 31.6 | 24 15.1 | 22 16.6 | | | 0 999.8 | 7 53.2 |
| 1 396.0 | 25 14.6 | 37 9.9 | 43 8.4 | 34 10.6 | | Cost of Sales/Payables | 25 14.6 | 29 12.5 |
| 18 20.7 | 64 5.7 | 83 4.4 | 79 4.6 | 74 4.9 | | | 55 6.6 | 64 5.7 |
| 15.1 | 7.4 | 2.2 | 1.7 | 2.8 | | | 4.2 | 2.8 |
| 46.6 | UND | 7.9 | 5.0 | 7.6 | | Sales/Working Capital | 11.0 | 9.6 |
| -12.5 | -5.7 | -28.1 | 23.5 | 20.3 | | | -82.7 | -27.3 |
| 4.9 | 8.9 | 6.3 | 5.1 | 7.2 | | | 4.0 | 4.3 |
| (18) 2.1 | (32) 2.4 | (57) 1.4 | 2.0 | 4.3 | | EBIT/Interest | (150) 1.8 | (183) 1.7 |
| -3.2 | -.3 | -1.2 | .8 | 1.0 | | | .4 | -.6 |
| | | 4.3 | 3.8 | | | | 3.7 | 2.7 |
| | (12) 1.0 | (14) 1.4 | | | | Net Profit + Depr., Dep., Amort./Cur. Mat. L/T/D | (41) 1.8 | (42) 1.4 |
| | .1 | .6 | | | | | .7 | -.7 |
| .2 | .4 | .4 | .5 | .4 | | | .5 | .4 |
| 3.1 | 1.8 | 1.0 | 1.1 | .7 | | Fixed/Worth | 1.2 | 1.0 |
| -.4 | -1.8 | 2.3 | 1.8 | 1.9 | | | 4.9 | 3.8 |
| 1.1 | 1.1 | .6 | 1.3 | 1.2 | | | 1.0 | .8 |
| 4.0 | 5.6 | 2.1 | 1.9 | 1.6 | | Debt/Worth | 2.7 | 2.1 |
| -2.6 | -5.3 | 4.9 | 3.5 | 4.9 | | | 9.8 | 10.3 |
| 30.1 | 46.8 | 15.7 | 20.8 | 28.3 | | | 26.4 | 22.3 |
| (14) 11.2 | (24) 12.5 | (54) 4.5 | (38) 5.8 | 13.1 | | % Profit Before Taxes/Tangible Net Worth | (129) 11.6 | (162) 7.6 |
| -22.7 | 1.5 | -7.1 | -.3 | .5 | | | .3 | -4.9 |
| 14.1 | 15.6 | 7.3 | 7.6 | 7.2 | | | 8.8 | 7.4 |
| 5.6 | 2.6 | 1.2 | 2.3 | 3.0 | | % Profit Before Taxes/Total Assets | 3.8 | 1.9 |
| -14.1 | -1.9 | -6.1 | -.6 | .2 | | | -2.1 | -3.9 |
| 64.0 | 59.0 | 9.3 | 8.4 | 5.6 | | | 10.3 | 10.9 |
| 18.2 | 7.3 | 4.6 | 3.8 | 3.7 | | Sales/Net Fixed Assets | 4.6 | 4.6 |
| 4.6 | 3.7 | 2.5 | 1.6 | 2.7 | | | 2.5 | 2.4 |
| 5.8 | 3.6 | 2.4 | | 1.0 | | | 2.7 | 2.3 |
| 3.5 | 2.2 | 1.2 | .9 | .8 | | Sales/Total Assets | 1.6 | 1.3 |
| 2.1 | 1.3 | .7 | .6 | .6 | | | .9 | .7 |
| 1.1 | 1.9 | 1.7 | 2.2 | 1.4 | | | 1.9 | 1.7 |
| (13) 2.8 | (24) 3.9 | (58) 3.2 | 3.6 | (10) 3.0 | | % Depr., Dep., Amort./Sales | (143) 2.9 | (168) 3.2 |
| 4.6 | 6.6 | 4.8 | 5.2 | 4.3 | | | 4.7 | 5.0 |
| 5.9 | 3.4 | 1.8 | | | | | 1.9 | 2.0 |
| (12) 9.4 | (17) 5.6 | (23) 4.9 | | | | % Officers', Directors' Owners' Comp/Sales | (59) 2.8 | (60) 3.5 |
| 17.1 | 7.7 | 8.7 | | | | | 7.9 | 9.3 |
| 21297M | 94668M | 464393M | 974925M | 840602M | 1426814M | Net Sales ($) | 3254239M | 4651251M |
| 5164M | 39127M | 300588M | 908047M | 850923M | 1405173M | Total Assets ($) | 3128917M | 4790815M |

## Comparative Historical Data / Current Data Sorted by Sales

| Type of Statement | | | | | | | | | |
|---|---|---|---|---|---|---|---|---|---|
| | 27 | 19 | 21 | Unqualified | | | 2 | 4 | 15 |
| | 33 | 28 | 25 | Reviewed | | 2 | 2 | 11 | 8 |
| | 44 | 32 | 36 | Compiled | | 10 | 2 | 4 | 1 |
| | 23 | 27 | 25 | Tax Returns | 10 | 7 | 12 | 2 | |
| | 65 | 71 | 75 | Other | 13 | 17 | 3 | 12 | 10 |

| | 4/1/09-3/31/10 ALL | 4/1/10-3/31/11 ALL | 4/1/11-3/31/12 ALL | | 0-1MM | 1-3MM | 3-5MM | 5-10MM | 10-25MM | 25MM & OVER |
|---|---|---|---|---|---|---|---|---|---|---|
| NUMBER OF STATEMENTS | 192 | 177 | 182 | | 23 | 36 | 19 | 37 | 33 | 34 |
| **ASSETS** | % | % | % | | % | % | % | % | % | % |
| Cash & Equivalents | 5.2 | 6.3 | 6.5 | | 9.5 | 9.4 | 3.4 | 8.1 | 4.9 | 3.1 |
| Trade Receivables (net) | 11.2 | 12.7 | 12.2 | | 6.9 | 12.1 | 11.3 | 16.1 | 12.3 | 12.1 |
| Inventory | 33.3 | 30.5 | 31.7 | | 13.1 | 27.3 | 33.0 | 32.2 | 42.4 | 37.4 |
| All Other Current | 2.8 | 3.4 | 3.7 | | 3.7 | 8.0 | 4.8 | 2.5 | 2.5 | 1.1 |
| Total Current | 52.5 | 53.0 | 54.2 | | 33.1 | 56.9 | 52.5 | 58.8 | 62.2 | 53.9 |
| Fixed Assets (net) | 37.4 | 36.7 | 34.6 | | 41.3 | 28.6 | 37.2 | 35.3 | 32.1 | 36.6 |
| Intangibles (net) | 3.1 | 3.4 | 3.5 | | 6.8 | 4.0 | 4.7 | .9 | 1.7 | 4.7 |
| All Other Non-Current | 7.0 | 7.0 | 7.7 | | 18.7 | 10.5 | 5.5 | 5.0 | 4.0 | 4.9 |
| Total | 100.0 | 100.0 | 100.0 | | 100.0 | 100.0 | 100.0 | 100.0 | 100.0 | 100.0 |
| **LIABILITIES** | | | | | | | | | | |
| Notes Payable-Short Term | 19.1 | 17.3 | 19.7 | | 48.7 | 13.5 | 22.3 | 13.7 | 17.4 | 13.7 |
| Cur. Mat.-L.T.D. | 3.8 | 3.9 | 3.4 | | 2.6 | 5.4 | 1.6 | 2.7 | 3.1 | 4.0 |
| Trade Payables | 10.2 | 9.9 | 10.5 | | 3.7 | 9.8 | 6.9 | 12.8 | 12.9 | 13.0 |
| Income Taxes Payable | 1.1 | 1.1 | .7 | | .0 | .5 | .7 | .7 | .9 | 1.2 |
| All Other Current | 7.7 | 5.8 | 9.4 | | 8.2 | 17.7 | 9.0 | 8.2 | 5.4 | 6.5 |
| Total Current | 41.9 | 38.0 | 43.7 | | 63.2 | 46.9 | 40.6 | 38.1 | 39.8 | 38.5 |
| Long-Term Debt | 27.6 | 24.0 | 23.2 | | 32.1 | 26.1 | 13.0 | 26.5 | 19.5 | 19.9 |
| Deferred Taxes | .9 | 1.0 | 1.3 | | .1 | 1.3 | 1.1 | .3 | 2.5 | 2.0 |
| All Other Non-Current | 5.9 | 5.6 | 6.7 | | 12.1 | 11.9 | 6.5 | 2.6 | 4.0 | 4.6 |
| Net Worth | 23.8 | 31.4 | 25.2 | | -7.6 | 13.7 | 38.9 | 32.5 | 34.2* | 35.1 |
| Total Liabilities & Net Worth | 100.0 | 100.0 | 100.0 | | 100.0 | 100.0 | 100.0 | 100.0 | 100.0 | 100.0 |
| **INCOME DATA** | | | | | | | | | | |
| Net Sales | 100.0 | 100.0 | 100.0 | | 100.0 | 100.0 | 100.0 | 100.0 | 100.0 | 100.0 |
| Gross Profit | 40.0 | 41.1 | 42.8 | | 54.8 | 50.7 | 47.7 | 35.0 | 39.7 | 34.9 |
| Operating Expenses | 37.7 | 38.1 | 40.0 | | 54.3 | 47.3 | 46.1 | 33.6 | 34.2 | 31.7 |
| Operating Profit | 2.4 | 3.0 | 2.8 | | .5 | 3.4 | 1.6 | 1.4 | 5.5 | 3.3 |
| All Other Expenses (net) | 3.2 | 2.0 | 1.3 | | 3.9 | 1.5 | -.2 | 2.1 | 1.1 | -.3 |
| Profit Before Taxes | -.8 | 1.0 | 1.5 | | -3.4 | 2.0 | 1.8 | -.6 | 4.4 | 3.5 |
| **RATIOS** | | | | | | | | | | |
| Current | 2.4 | 2.8 | 2.7 | | 1.9 | 4.2 | 3.6 | 3.9 | 2.6 | 1.7 |
| | 1.4 | 1.5 | 1.4 | | 1.1 | 1.8 | 1.1 | 1.7 | 1.5 | 1.4 |
| | .8 | 1.0 | .9 | | .1 | .6 | .7 | 1.1 | 1.1 | 1.1 |
| Quick | .8 | .9 | 1.0 | | .7 | 1.6 | 1.0 | 1.6 | .6 | .6 |
| | .4 | .5 | .4 | | .3 | .4 | .4 | .5 | .3 | .3 |
| | .1 | .1 | .2 | | .1 | .2 | .2 | .3 | .2 | .2 |
| Sales/Receivables | 8  47.5 | 6  61.7 | 7  49.2 | | 0  UND | 4  82.4 | 9  39.5 | 14  25.7 | 12  29.5 | 10  38.2 |
| | 21  17.7 | 22  16.4 | 23  15.6 | | 4  101.9 | 26  14.0 | 24  15.0 | 26  14.3 | 21  17.5 | 26  13.8 |
| | 47  7.7 | 46  7.9 | 47  7.8 | | 25  14.5 | 49  7.4 | 37  9.9 | 47  7.7 | 42  8.7 | 50  7.3 |
| Cost of Sales/Inventory | 28  13.1 | 14  25.7 | 16  23.1 | | 0  UND | 0  UND | 20  18.3 | 0  UND | 76  4.8 | 66  5.5 |
| | 107  3.4 | 82  4.5 | 101  3.6 | | 0  UND | 89  4.1 | 126  2.9 | 87  4.2 | 243  1.5 | 159  2.3 |
| | 297  1.2 | 252  1.4 | 332  1.1 | | 68  5.4 | 215  1.7 | 521  .7 | 332  1.1 | 608  .6 | 332  1.1 |
| Cost of Sales/Payables | -4  86.9 | 6  61.8 | 9  40.6 | | 0  UND | 1  366.8 | 4  100.4 | 9  38.7 | 15  24.9 | 23  15.6 |
| | 28  13.0 | 24  15.1 | 29  12.4 | | 1  471.0 | 33  11.2 | 28  13.0 | 26  13.9 | 40  9.2 | 38  9.7 |
| | 68  5.4 | 55  6.7 | 69  5.3 | | 33  11.1 | 65  5.6 | 70  5.2 | 94  3.9 | 87  4.2 | 63  5.8 |
| Sales/Working Capital | 3.3 | 4.1 | 3.2 | | 6.4 | 3.8 | 1.8 | 3.3 | 2.0 | 3.9 |
| | 10.7 | 10.9 | 11.1 | | 53.2 | 14.3 | 79.9 | 7.3 | 7.1 | 12.0 |
| | -22.4 | -149.8 | -35.3 | | -5.1 | -7.8 | -25.5 | 136.4 | 225.4 | 26.0 |
| EBIT/Interest | 5.3 | 5.2 | 5.9 | | 2.9 | 5.6 | 24.3 | 3.4 | 7.6 | 7.7 |
| | (176) 1.6 | (164) 1.9 | (169) 2.0 | | (20) .7 | (33) 3.3 | (18) 2.9 | (32) 1.3 | (32) 2.0 | 3.9 |
| | -.8 | -.1 | -.4 | | -5.3 | .4 | -1.4 | -1.0 | .0 | 1.2 |
| Net Profit + Depr., Dep., Amort./Cur. Mat. L/T/D | 4.4 | 4.3 | 3.1 | | | | | | 7.8 | 4.3 |
| | (54) 2.4 | (35) 1.7 | (35) 1.3 | | | | | | (10) 1.2 | (12) 1.7 |
| | 1.4 | .5 | .5 | | | | | | .4 | -.3 |
| Fixed/Worth | .4 | .4 | .4 | | 1.0 | .2 | .2 | .3 | .5 | .6 |
| | 1.3 | 1.0 | 1.1 | | 4.0 | 1.0 | 1.2 | .9 | 1.0 | 1.0 |
| | 5.2 | 3.0 | 4.1 | | -2.1 | -1.3 | 12.2 | 2.2 | 1.8 | 1.9 |
| Debt/Worth | .9 | .7 | 1.0 | | 1.8 | .8 | .4 | .6 | 1.1 | 1.2 |
| | 2.3 | 1.8 | 2.1 | | 4.9 | 3.0 | 3.1 | 1.7 | 1.9 | 1.8 |
| | 8.9 | 5.5 | 6.6 | | -5.6 | -5.1 | 16.1 | 4.2 | 3.7 | 2.3 |
| % Profit Before Taxes/Tangible Net Worth | 29.9 | 27.5 | 23.1 | | 28.8 | 37.9 | 16.4 | 10.2 | 20.2 | 31.3 |
| | (159) 7.0 | (150) 7.5 | (150) 6.6 | | (17) 4.7 | (25) 10.3 | (16) 4.0 | (32) 1.6 | (29) 5.5 | (31) 17.3 |
| | -7.9 | -5.1 | -1.6 | | -37.4 | .9 | -18.4 | -4.8 | 1.9 | 2.0 |
| % Profit Before Taxes/Total Assets | 8.7 | 8.9 | 8.9 | | 7.6 | 15.1 | 9.2 | 5.7 | 7.5 | 10.5 |
| | 1.9 | 2.9 | 2.2 | | .6 | 5.1 | 2.3 | .6 | 1.5 | 4.7 |
| | -3.9 | -2.0 | -3.1 | | -14.1 | -1.3 | -7.3 | -2.5 | -1.5 | .5 |
| Sales/Net Fixed Assets | 10.0 | 13.4 | 10.9 | | 21.1 | 31.8 | 9.3 | 12.3 | 11.7 | 6.0 |
| | 4.4 | 5.3 | 5.1 | | 3.6 | 8.6 | 4.8 | 6.3 | 5.3 | 4.1 |
| | 2.1 | 2.2 | 2.4 | | 1.2 | 3.4 | 2.7 | 2.4 | 1.7 | 2.7 |
| Sales/Total Assets | 2.6 | 2.8 | 2.5 | | 3.4 | 3.3 | 3.7 | 2.7 | 1.9 | 2.0 |
| | 1.2 | 1.4 | 1.4 | | 1.5 | 1.8 | 1.1 | 1.6 | 1.0 | 1.1 |
| | .8 | .8 | .8 | | .5 | .7 | .7 | 1.0 | .7 | .8 |
| % Depr., Dep., Amort./Sales | 1.9 | 1.8 | 1.8 | | 3.0 | 1.6 | 2.0 | 1.8 | 1.7 | 1.5 |
| | (173) 3.5 | (150) 3.4 | (153) 3.3 | | (15) 4.6 | (26) 2.2 | (18) 4.2 | (31) 3.5 | 3.7 | (30) 2.8 |
| | 5.5 | 5.1 | 5.0 | | 7.7 | 3.5 | 5.3 | 4.8 | 5.2 | 4.5 |
| % Officers', Directors' Owners' Comp/Sales | 2.1 | 2.2 | 2.9 | | 3.8 | 3.3 | | 2.0 | | |
| | (56) 3.1 | (62) 4.2 | (58) 5.6 | | (12) 8.3 | (16) 6.7 | | (14) 5.0 | | |
| | 8.4 | 8.4 | 9.2 | | 18.2 | 9.7 | | 8.6 | | |
| Net Sales ($) | 4705062M | 3607806M | 3822699M | | 13129M | 70225M | 74021M | 254318M | 500537M | 2910469M |
| Total Assets ($) | 4689088M | 3346617M | 3509022M | | 22031M | 64444M | 80076M | 203945M | 583592M | 2554934M |

Date headers for Current Data columns: 46 (4/1-9/30/11) covers 0-1MM, 1-3MM, 3-5MM; 136 (10/1/11-3/31/12) covers 5-10MM, 10-25MM, 25MM & OVER.

M = $ thousand    MM = $ million
See Pages 9 through 22 for Explanation of Ratios and Data

## Current Data Sorted by Assets     Comparative Historical Data

| | | | | | | Type of Statement | | |
|---|---|---|---|---|---|---|---|---|
| | | | | | | Unqualified | | |
| | | | | 2 | 1 | Reviewed | 1 | 1 |
| 1 | | 1 | | 1 | | Compiled | | |
| 6 | 2 | 3 | | 1 | | Tax Returns | 2 | 5 |
| 3 | 7 | 4 | 1 | 1 | 1 | Other | 1 | 1 |
| | 3 | | | | | | | |
| 0-500M | 2 (4/1-9/30/11) 500M-2MM | 2-10MM | 31 (10/1/11-3/31/12) 10-50MM | 50-100MM | 100-250MM | | 4/1/07-3/31/08 ALL | 4/1/08-3/31/09 ALL |
| 7 | 12 | 8 | 4 | 2 | | NUMBER OF STATEMENTS | 4 | 8 |
| % | % | % | % | % | % | ASSETS | % | % |
| | 14.9 | | | | | Cash & Equivalents | | |
| | 7.4 | | | | D | Trade Receivables (net) | | |
| | 2.7 | | | | A | Inventory | | |
| | .2 | | | | T | All Other Current | | |
| | 25.1 | | | | A | Total Current | | |
| | 46.7 | | | | | Fixed Assets (net) | | |
| | .1 | | | | N | Intangibles (net) | | |
| | 28.2 | | | | O | All Other Non-Current | | |
| | 100.0 | | | | T | Total | | |
| | | | | | A | LIABILITIES | | |
| | 16.0 | | | | V | Notes Payable-Short Term | | |
| | 6.7 | | | | A | Cur. Mat.-L.T.D. | | |
| | 1.8 | | | | I | Trade Payables | | |
| | .0 | | | | L | Income Taxes Payable | | |
| | 18.9 | | | | A | All Other Current | | |
| | 43.3 | | | | B | Total Current | | |
| | 40.0 | | | | L | Long-Term Debt | | |
| | .0 | | | | E | Deferred Taxes | | |
| | .0 | | | | | All Other Non-Current | | |
| | 16.7 | | | | | Net Worth | | |
| | 100.0 | | | | | Total Liabilties & Net Worth | | |
| | | | | | | INCOME DATA | | |
| | 100.0 | | | | | Net Sales | | |
| | | | | | | Gross Profit | | |
| | 96.6 | | | | | Operating Expenses | | |
| | 3.4 | | | | | Operating Profit | | |
| | 2.7 | | | | | All Other Expenses (net) | | |
| | .7 | | | | | Profit Before Taxes | | |
| | | | | | | RATIOS | | |
| | 1.6 | | | | | | | |
| | .7 | | | | | Current | | |
| | .1 | | | | | | | |
| | 1.6 | | | | | | | |
| | .7 | | | | | Quick | | |
| | .0 | | | | | | | |
| 0 | UND | | | | | | | |
| 0 | UND | | | | | Sales/Receivables | | |
| 2 | 183.5 | | | | | | | |
| | | | | | | Cost of Sales/Inventory | | |
| | | | | | | Cost of Sales/Payables | | |
| | 40.9 | | | | | | | |
| | -86.2 | | | | | Sales/Working Capital | | |
| | -1.6 | | | | | | | |
| | 20.2 | | | | | | | |
| (10) | 2.2 | | | | | EBIT/Interest | | |
| | -2.2 | | | | | | | |
| | | | | | | Net Profit + Depr., Dep., Amort./Cur. Mat. L/T/D | | |
| | 1.7 | | | | | | | |
| | 7.3 | | | | | Fixed/Worth | | |
| | -4.8 | | | | | | | |
| | 1.7 | | | | | | | |
| | 60.2 | | | | | Debt/Worth | | |
| | -9.6 | | | | | | | |
| | | | | | | % Profit Before Taxes/Tangible Net Worth | | |
| | 25.7 | | | | | | | |
| | 6.3 | | | | | % Profit Before Taxes/Total Assets | | |
| | -9.6 | | | | | | | |
| | 50.2 | | | | | | | |
| | 10.4 | | | | | Sales/Net Fixed Assets | | |
| | 1.7 | | | | | | | |
| | 6.7 | | | | | | | |
| | 2.0 | | | | | Sales/Total Assets | | |
| | 1.0 | | | | | | | |
| | | | | | | % Depr., Dep., Amort./Sales | | |
| | | | | | | % Officers', Directors' Owners' Comp/Sales | | |
| 6964M | 35891M | 33400M | 151224M | 219023M | | Net Sales ($) | 14949M | 36795M |
| 1230M | 11874M | 35285M | 89199M | 138056M | | Total Assets ($) | 14853M | 43992M |

© RMA 2012

M = $ thousand    MM = $ million

See Pages 9 through 22 for Explanation of Ratios and Data

## Comparative Historical Data        Current Data Sorted by Sales

| | | | Type of Statement | | | | | | |
|---|---|---|---|---|---|---|---|---|---|
| | | | Unqualified | | | | | | |
| | | 1 | Reviewed | | 1 | | | | |
| 3 | 3 | 3 | Compiled | | 1 | 1 | 1 | 1 | 3 |
| 1 | | 4 | Tax Returns | 9 | 6 | 1 | 4 | 1 | |
| 10 | 2 | 16 | Other | 3 | | | 1 | | 1 |
| | 6 | 9 | | | | | | | |
| 4/1/09-3/31/10 ALL | 4/1/10-3/31/11 ALL | 4/1/11-3/31/12 ALL | | 0-1MM | 2 (4/1-9/30/11) 1-3MM | 3-5MM | 31 (10/1/11-3/31/12) 5-10MM | 10-25MM | 25MM & OVER |
| 14 | 11 | 33 | NUMBER OF STATEMENTS | 12 | 8 | 2 | 5 | 2 | 4 |
| % | % | % | ASSETS | % | % | % | % | % | % |
| 12.3 | 3.3 | 14.7 | Cash & Equivalents | 22.6 | | | | | |
| 10.1 | 12.0 | 8.8 | Trade Receivables (net) | .0 | | | | | |
| 11.1 | 14.5 | 8.2 | Inventory | 2.0 | | | | | |
| 11.8 | 3.7 | 2.7 | All Other Current | 5.3 | | | | | |
| 45.3 | 33.5 | 34.3 | Total Current | 29.9 | | | | | |
| 45.5 | 46.8 | 49.8 | Fixed Assets (net) | 59.2 | | | | | |
| 4.9 | .1 | .4 | Intangibles (net) | .2 | | | | | |
| 4.3 | 19.6 | 15.5 | All Other Non-Current | 10.7 | | | | | |
| 100.0 | 100.0 | 100.0 | Total | 100.0 | | | | | |
| | | | LIABILITIES | | | | | | |
| 20.2 | 15.6 | 16.1 | Notes Payable-Short Term | 5.0 | | | | | |
| 5.3 | 2.1 | 13.6 | Cur. Mat.-L.T.D. | 6.6 | | | | | |
| .8 | 2.1 | 4.6 | Trade Payables | .2 | | | | | |
| 1.7 | 2.4 | .0 | Income Taxes Payable | .0 | | | | | |
| 5.9 | 12.4 | 17.1 | All Other Current | 19.8 | | | | | |
| 33.9 | 34.6 | 51.4 | Total Current | 31.6 | | | | | |
| 31.8 | 20.0 | 36.3 | Long-Term Debt | 34.8 | | | | | |
| .2 | .2 | .0 | Deferred Taxes | .0 | | | | | |
| 5.3 | 3.0 | .0 | All Other Non-Current | .0 | | | | | |
| 28.8 | 42.2 | 12.3 | Net Worth | 33.6 | | | | | |
| 100.0 | 100.0 | 100.0 | Total Liabilities & Net Worth | 100.0 | | | | | |
| | | | INCOME DATA | | | | | | |
| 100.0 | 100.0 | 100.0 | Net Sales | 100.0 | | | | | |
| | | | Gross Profit | | | | | | |
| 92.1 | 79.6 | 90.0 | Operating Expenses | 76.3 | | | | | |
| 7.9 | 20.4 | 10.0 | Operating Profit | 23.7 | | | | | |
| 1.3 | 3.0 | 5.3 | All Other Expenses (net) | 13.7 | | | | | |
| 6.7 | 17.4 | 4.8 | Profit Before Taxes | 9.9 | | | | | |
| | | | RATIOS | | | | | | |
| 3.0 | 1.6 | 1.5 | | 9.0 | | | | | |
| 1.5 | .9 | .9 | Current | .6 | | | | | |
| .5 | .3 | .1 | | .1 | | | | | |
| 2.4 | .5 | 1.2 | | 4.3 | | | | | |
| .4 | .2 | .5 | Quick | .2 | | | | | |
| .1 | .1 | .1 | | .0 | | | | | |
| 0 UND | 0 UND | 0 UND | | 0 UND | | | | | |
| 0 UND | 13 27.9 | 0 UND | Sales/Receivables | 0 UND | | | | | |
| 28 13.0 | 33 10.9 | 29 12.6 | | 0 UND | | | | | |
| | | | Cost of Sales/Inventory | | | | | | |
| | | | Cost of Sales/Payables | | | | | | |
| 3.0 | 4.0 | 20.6 | | 4.7 | | | | | |
| 25.3 | -32.1 | -141.2 | Sales/Working Capital | -4.8 | | | | | |
| -27.8 | -4.8 | -2.5 | | -1.5 | | | | | |
| 6.0 | 5.0 | 8.0 | | | | | | | |
| (13) 2.3 | (10) 2.0 | (27) 3.3 | EBIT/Interest | | | | | | |
| .1 | 1.1 | .6 | | | | | | | |
| | | | Net Profit + Depr., Dep., Amort./Cur. Mat. L/T/D | | | | | | |
| .4 | .5 | .7 | | .3 | | | | | |
| 1.8 | .8 | 2.4 | Fixed/Worth | 2.0 | | | | | |
| -10.8 | 2.7 | -9.3 | | 10.1 | | | | | |
| 1.1 | .6 | .9 | | .3 | | | | | |
| 3.9 | 1.4 | 5.6 | Debt/Worth | 1.7 | | | | | |
| -13.2 | 3.6 | -12.4 | | NM | | | | | |
| 22.2 | 27.0 | 62.0 | | | | | | | |
| (10) 9.1 | 7.0 | (22) 16.8 | % Profit Before Taxes/Tangible Net Worth | | | | | | |
| 1.8 | 3.8 | -1.1 | | | | | | | |
| 12.3 | 7.9 | 12.8 | | 8.1 | | | | | |
| 2.4 | 3.6 | 4.3 | % Profit Before Taxes/Total Assets | 1.0 | | | | | |
| -1.0 | 1.4 | -3.6 | | -10.0 | | | | | |
| 44.8 | 5.3 | 27.2 | | 29.6 | | | | | |
| 4.4 | 1.9 | 4.8 | Sales/Net Fixed Assets | .5 | | | | | |
| 1.6 | .4 | .7 | | .2 | | | | | |
| 3.8 | 1.5 | 4.6 | | 3.8 | | | | | |
| 1.6 | .5 | 1.4 | Sales/Total Assets | .4 | | | | | |
| .9 | .3 | .6 | | .2 | | | | | |
| 3.9 | | 3.3 | | | | | | | |
| (12) 5.5 | | (26) 5.2 | % Depr., Dep., Amort./Sales | | | | | | |
| 8.8 | | 13.4 | | | | | | | |
| | | | % Officers', Directors' Owners' Comp/Sales | | | | | | |
| 95535M | 153213M | 446502M | Net Sales ($) | 6719M | 14382M | 8162M | 34461M | 32650M | 350128M |
| 78063M | 130818M | 275644M | Total Assets ($) | 20244M | 8756M | 2919M | 18733M | 19633M | 205359M |

M = $ thousand    MM = $ million
See Pages 9 through 22 for Explanation of Ratios and Data

## AGRICULTURE—Cotton Farming NAICS 111920

### Current Data Sorted by Assets       Comparative Historical Data

| 0-500M | 500M-2MM | 2-10MM | 10-50MM | 50-100MM | 100-250MM | Type of Statement | 4/1/07-3/31/08 ALL | 4/1/08-3/31/09 ALL |
|---|---|---|---|---|---|---|---|---|
| | | | | | | Unqualified | 2 | 2 |
| | | 2 | 1 | 1 | 1 | Reviewed | 7 | 15 |
| 5 | 9 | 9 | 1 | | | Compiled | 10 | 16 |
| 3 | 9 | 2 | 1 | | | Tax Returns | 14 | 17 |
| 3 | 6 | 1 | | | | Other | 13 | 12 |
| | 3 (4/1-9/30/11) | | 51 (10/1/11-3/31/12) | | | | | |
| 11 | 24 | 14 | 3 | 1 | 1 | **NUMBER OF STATEMENTS** | 46 | 62 |
| % | % | % | % | % | % | **ASSETS** | % | % |
| 17.7 | 10.2 | 9.7 | | | | Cash & Equivalents | 12.3 | 12.4 |
| .0 | 2.1 | 17.6 | | | | Trade Receivables (net) | 12.9 | 12.6 |
| .0 | 6.0 | 4.6 | | | | Inventory | 7.4 | 12.0 |
| .0 | 3.1 | 4.8 | | | | All Other Current | 5.6 | 4.0 |
| 17.7 | 21.4 | 36.6 | | | | Total Current | 38.2 | 41.0 |
| 63.9 | 64.2 | 55.9 | | | | Fixed Assets (net) | 53.0 | 50.0 |
| .0 | .1 | .1 | | | | Intangibles (net) | 1.0 | .6 |
| 18.4 | 14.3 | 7.4 | | | | All Other Non-Current | 7.8 | 8.4 |
| 100.0 | 100.0 | 100.0 | | | | Total | 100.0 | 100.0 |
| | | | | | | **LIABILITIES** | | |
| 62.2 | 28.7 | 23.5 | | | | Notes Payable-Short Term | 36.1 | 28.2 |
| 12.9 | 8.4 | 9.5 | | | | Cur. Mat.-L.T.D. | 19.0 | 11.8 |
| .1 | .5 | 1.6 | | | | Trade Payables | 5.3 | 2.0 |
| .0 | .3 | .1 | | | | Income Taxes Payable | .0 | .0 |
| 5.7 | 9.7 | .8 | | | | All Other Current | 5.4 | 5.1 |
| 80.8 | 47.7 | 35.6 | | | | Total Current | 65.8 | 47.1 |
| 47.6 | 40.0 | 35.1 | | | | Long-Term Debt | 30.7 | 28.5 |
| .0 | .0 | .0 | | | | Deferred Taxes | .1 | .0 |
| 3.6 | 1.8 | .9 | | | | All Other Non-Current | 2.1 | 3.5 |
| -32.1 | 10.4 | 28.5 | | | | Net Worth | 1.3 | 20.9 |
| 100.0 | 100.0 | 100.0 | | | | Total Liabilities & Net Worth | 100.0 | 100.0 |
| | | | | | | **INCOME DATA** | | |
| 100.0 | 100.0 | 100.0 | | | | Net Sales | 100.0 | 100.0 |
| | | | | | | Gross Profit | | |
| 96.2 | 85.8 | 84.3 | | | | Operating Expenses | 93.5 | 89.4 |
| 3.8 | 14.2 | 15.7 | | | | Operating Profit | 6.5 | 10.6 |
| -.3 | 7.1 | 3.1 | | | | All Other Expenses (net) | 3.2 | 2.2 |
| 4.1 | 7.0 | 12.6 | | | | Profit Before Taxes | 3.3 | 8.4 |
| | | | | | | **RATIOS** | | |
| 1.0 | 1.0 | 6.5 | | | | | 1.6 | 3.2 |
| .7 | .4 | 1.2 | | | | Current | 1.0 | 1.6 |
| .2 | .1 | .6 | | | | | .4 | .7 |
| 1.0 | .7 | 4.7 | | | | | 1.1 | 2.5 |
| .7 | .2 | .8 | | | | Quick | .5 | .8 |
| .2 | .1 | .3 | | | | | .2 | .2 |
| 0 UND | 0 UND | 0 UND | | | | | 0 UND | 0 UND |
| 0 UND | 0 UND | 85 4.3 | | | | Sales/Receivables | 8 43.9 | 2 222.4 |
| 0 UND | 6 65.9 | 126 2.9 | | | | | 95 3.8 | 87 4.2 |
| | | | | | | Cost of Sales/Inventory | | |
| | | | | | | Cost of Sales/Payables | | |
| UND | -294.5 | 3.4 | | | | | 9.3 | 3.4 |
| -11.5 | -5.9 | 14.8 | | | | Sales/Working Capital | 681.5 | 11.1 |
| -6.8 | -1.6 | -5.5 | | | | | -3.2 | -6.7 |
| | 9.8 | 7.9 | | | | | 4.7 | 7.0 |
| | (19) 2.2 | (13) 3.6 | | | | EBIT/Interest | (40) 1.0 | (60) 3.0 |
| | .4 | 1.1 | | | | | -2.1 | 1.1 |
| | | | | | | Net Profit + Depr., Dep., Amort./Cur. Mat. L/T/D | | |
| .5 | 1.3 | .7 | | | | | .7 | .7 |
| 1.1 | 2.7 | 1.7 | | | | Fixed/Worth | 1.6 | 1.3 |
| -1.1 | -9.2 | -3.4 | | | | | -14.2 | 7.9 |
| .1 | 1.3 | .7 | | | | | .8 | .7 |
| 1.4 | 2.8 | 1.5 | | | | Debt/Worth | 3.1 | 2.1 |
| -2.2 | -12.1 | -8.1 | | | | | -9.7 | UND |
| | 112.1 | | | | | | 22.5 | 34.7 |
| | (17) 7.5 | | | | | % Profit Before Taxes/Tangible Net Worth | (32) 3.5 | (48) 15.8 |
| | -13.9 | | | | | | -6.2 | 2.1 |
| 53.2 | 20.3 | 18.0 | | | | | 12.6 | 15.8 |
| 35.4 | 4.0 | 6.1 | | | | % Profit Before Taxes/Total Assets | .0 | 4.3 |
| -7.0 | -2.9 | .6 | | | | | -4.8 | .2 |
| 30.7 | 5.4 | 2.4 | | | | | 5.2 | 13.6 |
| 9.6 | 2.0 | 1.6 | | | | Sales/Net Fixed Assets | 1.9 | 2.1 |
| 5.3 | .6 | .8 | | | | | .9 | .9 |
| 15.3 | 3.3 | 1.1 | | | | | 1.8 | 1.9 |
| 4.9 | 1.7 | .8 | | | | Sales/Total Assets | 1.1 | 1.1 |
| 2.3 | .4 | .6 | | | | | .5 | .5 |
| | 2.8 | 2.3 | | | | | 2.8 | 3.6 |
| | (18) 5.6 | (12) 4.5 | | | | % Depr., Dep., Amort./Sales | (35) 6.2 | (50) 5.9 |
| | 18.5 | 10.8 | | | | | 9.7 | 14.1 |
| | | | | | | | | 3.5 |
| | | | | | | % Officers', Directors' Owners' Comp/Sales | | (11) 7.2 |
| | | | | | | | | 10.8 |
| 14017M | 49054M | 40927M | 32816M | 64040M | 180028M | Net Sales ($) | 496764M | 637995M |
| 2066M | 27120M | 50172M | 38532M | 64108M | 206068M | Total Assets ($) | 358832M | 630295M |

M = $ thousand    MM = $ million
See Pages 9 through 22 for Explanation of Ratios and Data

## Comparative Historical Data

## Current Data Sorted by Sales

| Type of Statement | 4/1/09-3/31/10 ALL | 4/1/10-3/31/11 ALL | 4/1/11-3/31/12 ALL | 0-1MM | 1-3MM | 3-5MM | 5-10MM | 10-25MM | 25MM & OVER |
|---|---|---|---|---|---|---|---|---|---|
| Unqualified | 3 | 2 | 2 | | | | | | 2 |
| Reviewed | 9 | 8 | 3 | | 2 | | | 1 | 1 |
| Compiled | 15 | 17 | 24 | 10 | 8 | 4 | 1 | 1 | |
| Tax Returns | 20 | 20 | 15 | 3 | 6 | 3 | 3 | | |
| Other | 10 | 11 | 10 | 3 | | 1 | | | |
| | | | | 3 (4/1-9/30/11) | | | 51 (10/1/11-3/31/12) | | |
| **NUMBER OF STATEMENTS** | 57 | 58 | 54 | 16 | 22 | 8 | 4 | 2 | 2 |
| | % | % | % | % | % | % | % | % | % |
| **ASSETS** | | | | | | | | | |
| Cash & Equivalents | 11.8 | 10.9 | 11.0 | 7.6 | 10.1 | | | | |
| Trade Receivables (net) | 7.0 | 6.9 | 7.1 | .8 | 8.0 | | | | |
| Inventory | 9.1 | 6.6 | 6.7 | 3.2 | 5.4 | | | | |
| All Other Current | 3.7 | 6.0 | 3.1 | .7 | 4.7 | | | | |
| Total Current | 31.5 | 30.5 | 27.9 | 12.2 | 28.2 | | | | |
| Fixed Assets (net) | 53.5 | 55.2 | 58.7 | 63.9 | 68.5 | | | | |
| Intangibles (net) | 1.8 | .2 | .2 | .1 | .0 | | | | |
| All Other Non-Current | 13.2 | 14.2 | 13.3 | 23.8 | 3.2 | | | | |
| Total | 100.0 | 100.0 | 100.0 | 100.0 | 100.0 | | | | |
| **LIABILITIES** | | | | | | | | | |
| Notes Payable-Short Term | 21.7 | 34.9 | 33.1 | 24.1 | 43.4 | | | | |
| Cur. Mat.-L.T.D. | 6.9 | 10.0 | 9.0 | 2.9 | 13.4 | | | | |
| Trade Payables | 1.3 | .7 | 1.2 | .3 | 1.1 | | | | |
| Income Taxes Payable | .1 | .0 | .2 | .5 | .1 | | | | |
| All Other Current | 20.4 | 6.0 | 6.3 | 3.3 | 3.6 | | | | |
| Total Current | 50.4 | 51.7 | 49.7 | 31.1 | 61.6 | | | | |
| Long-Term Debt | 26.6 | 35.3 | 38.2 | 27.6 | 48.3 | | | | |
| Deferred Taxes | .0 | .1 | .1 | .0 | .0 | | | | |
| All Other Non-Current | 4.0 | 3.3 | 1.9 | 2.5 | 2.5 | | | | |
| Net Worth | 19.0 | 9.6 | 10.1 | 38.8 | -12.4 | | | | |
| Total Liabilities & Net Worth | 100.0 | 100.0 | 100.0 | 100.0 | 100.0 | | | | |
| **INCOME DATA** | | | | | | | | | |
| Net Sales | 100.0 | 100.0 | 100.0 | 100.0 | 100.0 | | | | |
| Gross Profit | | | | | | | | | |
| Operating Expenses | 85.9 | 90.4 | 86.2 | 83.3 | 89.5 | | | | |
| Operating Profit | 14.1 | 9.6 | 13.8 | 16.7 | 10.5 | | | | |
| All Other Expenses (net) | 4.3 | 4.2 | 5.0 | 11.3 | 2.2 | | | | |
| Profit Before Taxes | 9.8 | 5.4 | 8.8 | 5.4 | 8.3 | | | | |
| **RATIOS** | | | | | | | | | |
| Current | 2.1 / 1.1 / .3 | 1.7 / .7 / .2 | 1.9 / .7 / .2 | .7 / .3 / .1 | 1.5 / .8 / .2 | | | | |
| Quick | 1.3 / .6 / .1 | 1.1 / .3 / .0 | 1.0 / .4 / .2 | .5 / .2 / .1 | 1.0 / .5 / .2 | | | | |
| Sales/Receivables | 0 UND / 0 UND / 43 8.5 | 0 UND / 0 UND / 30 12.2 | 0 UND / 0 UND / 41 8.8 | 0 UND / 0 UND / 5 72.5 | 0 UND / 0 UND / 51 7.1 | | | | |
| Cost of Sales/Inventory | | | | | | | | | |
| Cost of Sales/Payables | | | | | | | | | |
| Sales/Working Capital | 5.2 / 150.5 / -5.5 | 4.4 / -21.0 / -3.2 | 9.2 / -28.8 / -4.1 | -9.3 / -3.7 / -1.2 | 8.5 / -31.5 / -6.4 | | | | |
| EBIT/Interest | 7.8 / (46) 2.2 / .8 | 9.7 / (52) 2.6 / .5 | 10.0 / (45) 3.6 / 1.0 | | 8.1 / (20) 4.1 / 1.4 | | | | |
| Net Profit + Depr., Dep., Amort./Cur. Mat. L/T/D | | | | | | | | | |
| Fixed/Worth | .8 / 1.3 / -11.8 | .8 / 1.7 / NM | .9 / 1.8 / -7.6 | .9 / 1.5 / 3.6 | 1.3 / 2.5 / -2.9 | | | | |
| Debt/Worth | .6 / 1.6 / -11.8 | .6 / 2.3 / -13.9 | .8 / 1.6 / -11.4 | .8 / 1.4 / 4.0 | .7 / 3.2 / -4.6 | | | | |
| % Profit Before Taxes/Tangible Net Worth | 38.5 / (41) 12.0 / 1.8 | 43.0 / (43) 7.7 / -2.4 | 80.3 / (38) 19.2 / 1.2 | 11.2 / (14) 1.8 / -23.4 | 115.9 / (13) 79.9 / 18.6 | | | | |
| % Profit Before Taxes/Total Assets | 16.8 / 5.8 / -.5 | 18.6 / 2.4 / -4.0 | 25.9 / 6.9 / -.2 | 4.4 / 1.2 / -6.5 | 53.0 / 17.6 / 4.1 | | | | |
| Sales/Net Fixed Assets | 9.2 / 2.1 / .9 | 10.3 / 1.6 / .7 | 6.8 / 2.6 / 1.1 | 2.4 / .7 / .2 | 12.9 / 3.9 / 1.9 | | | | |
| Sales/Total Assets | 1.8 / 1.1 / .5 | 1.5 / .9 / .5 | 3.0 / 1.4 / .6 | 1.2 / .4 / .2 | 5.8 / 1.9 / 1.0 | | | | |
| % Depr., Dep., Amort./Sales | 3.1 / (45) 7.4 / 14.9 | 2.5 / (51) 7.3 / 12.3 | 2.5 / (41) 4.6 / 18.0 | 3.8 / (13) 8.1 / 24.0 | 1.9 / (17) 4.1 / 18.1 | | | | |
| % Officers', Directors' Owners' Comp/Sales | | 2.7 / (11) 4.1 / 10.5 | 3.1 / (10) 4.4 / 6.5 | | | | | | |
| Net Sales ($) | 155569M | 579673M | 380882M | 7532M | 43998M | 30100M | 22934M | 32250M | 244068M |
| Total Assets ($) | 226656M | 466863M | 388066M | 25485M | 31851M | 25282M | 7519M | 27753M | 270176M |

© RMA 2012  
**M = $ thousand   MM = $ million**  
See Pages 9 through 22 for Explanation of Ratios and Data

## Current Data Sorted by Assets | Comparative Historical Data

### Type of Statement

| 0-500M | 500M-2MM | 2-10MM | 10-50MM | 50-100MM | 100-250MM | Type of Statement | 4/1/07-3/31/08 ALL | 4/1/08-3/31/09 ALL |
|---|---|---|---|---|---|---|---|---|
|  | 1 | 8 | 9 | 5 |  | Unqualified | 18 | 26 |
| 1 | 4 | 18 | 21 | 5 | 3 | Reviewed | 35 | 46 |
| 2 | 16 | 26 | 16 | 3 | 2 | Compiled | 65 | 68 |
| 24 | 55 |  | 4 |  | 1 | Tax Returns | 82 | 91 |
| 11 | 17 | 32 | 15 | 4 |  | Other | 76 | 81 |
| 38 | 93 | 84 | 65 | 17 | 6 | **NUMBER OF STATEMENTS** | 276 | 312 |

Column header periods: 0-500M, 500M-2MM, 2-10MM | 44 (4/1-9/30/11) | 259 (10/1/11-3/31/12), 10-50MM, 50-100MM, 100-250MM

### Financial Data

| 0-500M | 500M-2MM | 2-10MM | 10-50MM | 50-100MM | 100-250MM | Item | 4/1/07-3/31/08 ALL | 4/1/08-3/31/09 ALL |
|---|---|---|---|---|---|---|---|---|
| % | % | % | % | % | % | **ASSETS** | % | % |
| 20.5 | 15.8 | 8.0 | 5.6 | 1.9 |  | Cash & Equivalents | 8.0 | 8.3 |
| 2.8 | 7.9 | 10.6 | 13.7 | 10.1 |  | Trade Receivables (net) | 9.2 | 8.9 |
| 5.9 | 10.0 | 12.2 | 17.0 | 15.1 |  | Inventory | 13.1 | 13.3 |
| 3.1 | 2.9 | 5.5 | 6.2 | 9.5 |  | All Other Current | 6.4 | 6.7 |
| 32.3 | 36.6 | 36.2 | 42.5 | 36.6 |  | Total Current | 36.8 | 37.2 |
| 51.0 | 47.9 | 50.3 | 48.8 | 37.4 |  | Fixed Assets (net) | 52.1 | 50.9 |
| 3.0 | 2.2 | 2.7 | 1.0 | 9.5 |  | Intangibles (net) | 2.5 | 1.0 |
| 13.8 | 13.3 | 10.8 | 7.7 | 16.5 |  | All Other Non-Current | 8.6 | 11.0 |
| 100.0 | 100.0 | 100.0 | 100.0 | 100.0 |  | Total | 100.0 | 100.0 |
|  |  |  |  |  |  | **LIABILITIES** |  |  |
| 44.3 | 32.1 | 10.8 | 11.5 | 9.8 |  | Notes Payable-Short Term | 24.4 | 22.6 |
| 16.2 | 9.5 | 5.5 | 3.9 | 2.4 |  | Cur. Mat.-L.T.D. | 6.3 | 5.5 |
| 2.9 | 4.8 | 6.5 | 6.3 | 4.7 |  | Trade Payables | 5.5 | 5.0 |
| .0 | .4 | .1 | 1.5 | .4 |  | Income Taxes Payable | .5 | .4 |
| 13.2 | 5.0 | 5.0 | 5.0 | 4.6 |  | All Other Current | 8.7 | 6.9 |
| 76.6 | 51.8 | 27.9 | 28.2 | 21.8 |  | Total Current | 45.3 | 40.4 |
| 45.8 | 35.3 | 26.1 | 22.1 | 23.3 |  | Long-Term Debt | 30.8 | 28.8 |
| .0 | .2 | .2 | 1.2 | 1.7 |  | Deferred Taxes | .5 | .5 |
| 13.7 | 7.6 | 10.6 | 2.9 | 5.2 |  | All Other Non-Current | 4.3 | 4.6 |
| -36.1 | 5.2 | 35.3 | 45.6 | 47.9 |  | Net Worth | 19.1 | 25.7 |
| 100.0 | 100.0 | 100.0 | 100.0 | 100.0 |  | Total Liabilities & Net Worth | 100.0 | 100.0 |
|  |  |  |  |  |  | **INCOME DATA** |  |  |
| 100.0 | 100.0 | 100.0 | 100.0 | 100.0 |  | Net Sales | 100.0 | 100.0 |
|  |  |  |  |  |  | Gross Profit |  |  |
| 88.4 | 89.4 | 88.8 | 91.1 | 82.7 |  | Operating Expenses | 88.9 | 90.4 |
| 11.6 | 10.6 | 11.2 | 8.9 | 17.3 |  | Operating Profit | 11.1 | 9.6 |
| 1.6 | 2.0 | .6 | 1.4 | 3.0 |  | All Other Expenses (net) | 3.2 | 3.1 |
| 9.9 | 8.6 | 10.6 | 7.5 | 14.3 |  | Profit Before Taxes | 7.9 | 6.5 |
|  |  |  |  |  |  | **RATIOS** |  |  |
| 1.7 | 2.1 | 3.9 | 2.8 | 2.8 |  | Current | 1.9 | 2.1 |
| .3 | 1.0 | 1.8 | 1.5 | 1.8 |  | | 1.1 | 1.1 |
| .1 | .2 | .4 | 1.0 | 1.5 |  | | .3 | .4 |
| 1.2 | 1.2 | 1.8 | 1.6 | 1.5 |  | Quick | 1.0 | 1.0 |
| .2 | .4 | .5 | .6 | .5 |  | | .3 | .4 |
| .1 | .1 | .1 | .3 | .2 |  | | .1 | .1 |
| 0 UND | 0 UND | 0 UND | 14 25.4 | 10 34.8 |  | Sales/Receivables | 0 UND | 0 UND |
| 0 UND | 0 UND | 2 178.0 | 32 11.5 | 35 10.5 |  | | 5 75.0 | 8 44.7 |
| 0 UND | 11 34.3 | 51 7.2 | 68 5.4 | 114 3.2 |  | | 35 10.4 | 42 8.7 |
|  |  |  |  |  |  | Cost of Sales/Inventory |  |  |
|  |  |  |  |  |  | Cost of Sales/Payables |  |  |
| 19.5 | 7.0 | 2.5 | 2.9 | 2.2 |  | Sales/Working Capital | 4.5 | 4.4 |
| -15.0 | -205.8 | 8.4 | 6.6 | 2.8 |  | | 51.5 | 27.0 |
| -3.9 | -4.5 | -10.4 | NM | 10.7 |  | | -5.4 | -6.9 |
| 10.9 | 8.6 | 15.6 | 10.6 | 12.3 |  | EBIT/Interest | 6.1 | 7.1 |
| (30) 4.3 | (81) 3.4 | (78) 5.0 | (60) 5.2 | (16) 6.1 |  | | (249) 2.8 | (281) 2.6 |
| .1 | .8 | 1.3 | 1.9 | 2.1 |  | | 1.1 | .9 |
|  |  | 7.0 | 4.3 |  |  | Net Profit + Depr., Dep., Amort./Cur. Mat. L/T/D | 5.2 | 5.5 |
|  |  | (11) 1.3 | (21) 2.0 |  |  | | (39) 2.3 | (56) 2.9 |
|  |  | .4 | 1.2 |  |  | | 1.4 | 1.3 |
| .9 | .7 | .7 | .6 | .6 |  | Fixed/Worth | .7 | .7 |
| 5.4 | 2.2 | 1.3 | 1.0 | 1.0 |  | | 1.5 | 1.3 |
| -1.6 | -6.1 | 7.6 | 1.6 | 1.4 |  | | 17.6 | 4.5 |
| .7 | .8 | .5 | .6 | .8 |  | Debt/Worth | .7 | .7 |
| UND | 4.8 | 1.4 | 1.3 | 1.5 |  | | 2.2 | 1.7 |
| -2.6 | -12.8 | 10.4 | 2.3 | 2.1 |  | | 34.1 | 7.3 |
| 170.4 | 66.5 | 44.2 | 36.2 | 30.3 |  | % Profit Before Taxes/Tangible Net Worth | 41.0 | 34.3 |
| (20) 73.3 | (61) 24.9 | (70) 21.9 | (62) 16.3 | (15) 19.9 |  | | (221) 17.4 | (259) 12.1 |
| 17.7 | 4.0 | 3.1 | 2.9 | 6.8 |  | | 4.3 | 1.0 |
| 40.0 | 24.7 | 16.3 | 14.3 | 11.4 |  | % Profit Before Taxes/Total Assets | 15.0 | 12.1 |
| 16.4 | 6.6 | 8.4 | 5.8 | 9.3 |  | | 5.8 | 4.2 |
| .6 | -.1 | 1.1 | 1.4 | 2.8 |  | | .4 | -.3 |
| 63.5 | 11.7 | 8.8 | 5.4 | 8.4 |  | Sales/Net Fixed Assets | 7.1 | 6.9 |
| 8.5 | 4.6 | 2.3 | 2.0 | 1.8 |  | | 2.6 | 2.2 |
| 2.0 | 2.1 | 1.0 | .9 | .9 |  | | 1.0 | .9 |
| 6.2 | 3.2 | 2.1 | 1.5 | .7 |  | Sales/Total Assets | 2.2 | 2.1 |
| 2.2 | 1.9 | .9 | .9 | .5 |  | | 1.3 | 1.0 |
| 1.1 | .9 | .5 | .6 | .3 |  | | .5 | .5 |
| 1.2 | 2.2 | 2.4 | 2.1 | 3.3 |  | % Depr., Dep., Amort./Sales | 2.5 | 3.1 |
| (26) 3.0 | (73) 5.2 | (64) 5.6 | (59) 5.0 | (16) 4.5 |  | | (241) 5.7 | (269) 6.2 |
| 8.8 | 12.9 | 10.4 | 8.7 | 9.0 |  | | 11.1 | 11.2 |
|  | 1.6 | 1.4 | .6 |  |  | % Officers', Directors' Owners' Comp/Sales | 1.6 | 2.0 |
|  | (36) 2.3 | (20) 2.7 | (11) 1.5 |  |  | | (58) 3.3 | (83) 3.3 |
|  | 7.2 | 6.3 | 2.2 |  |  | | 7.2 | 6.4 |
| 36308M | 244230M | 610492M | 1714264M | 776864M | 194126M | Net Sales ($) | 3275098M | 3863180M |
| 10843M | 106921M | 379016M | 1440225M | 1135687M | 894631M | Total Assets ($) | 3026334M | 3928484M |

M = $ thousand    MM = $ million
See Pages 9 through 22 for Explanation of Ratios and Data

## Comparative Historical Data

## Current Data Sorted by Sales

| | | | Type of Statement | | | | | | |
|---|---|---|---|---|---|---|---|---|---|
| 21 | 19 | 15 | Unqualified | | 1 | | 1 | 4 | 9 |
| 41 | 39 | 42 | Reviewed | 3 | 4 | 5 | 1 | 16 | 13 |
| 65 | 65 | 57 | Compiled | 5 | 17 | 4 | 17 | 6 | 8 |
| 107 | 82 | 110 | Tax Returns | 35 | 42 | 16 | 10 | 5 | 2 |
| 76 | 90 | 79 | Other | 22 | 11 | 6 | 15 | 15 | 10 |
| 4/1/09-3/31/10 ALL | 4/1/10-3/31/11 ALL | 4/1/11-3/31/12 ALL | | 44 (4/1-9/30/11) | | | 259 (10/1/11-3/31/12) | | |
| | | | | 0-1MM | 1-3MM | 3-5MM | 5-10MM | 10-25MM | 25MM & OVER |
| 310 | 295 | 303 | NUMBER OF STATEMENTS | 65 | 75 | 31 | 44 | 46 | 42 |
| % | % | % | **ASSETS** | % | % | % | % | % | % |
| 9.8 | 10.1 | 11.0 | Cash & Equivalents | 15.3 | 13.7 | 13.4 | 12.0 | 4.3 | 3.9 |
| 8.8 | 8.8 | 9.3 | Trade Receivables (net) | 4.4 | 4.9 | 8.3 | 12.6 | 16.7 | 13.6 |
| 12.1 | 14.3 | 11.9 | Inventory | 6.5 | 10.2 | 11.5 | 13.7 | 15.6 | 17.3 |
| 5.0 | 5.8 | 5.1 | All Other Current | 1.2 | 4.7 | 5.2 | 5.1 | 7.3 | 9.4 |
| 35.7 | 38.9 | 37.2 | Total Current | 27.4 | 33.5 | 38.4 | 43.4 | 44.0 | 44.2 |
| 52.9 | 48.9 | 48.4 | Fixed Assets (net) | 61.2 | 48.2 | 47.2 | 45.6 | 38.8 | 43.1 |
| 1.5 | 1.8 | 2.6 | Intangibles (net) | 1.4 | 4.0 | .7 | .5 | 5.6 | 2.2 |
| 10.0 | 10.3 | 11.9 | All Other Non-Current | 10.0 | 14.4 | 13.7 | 10.6 | 11.6 | 10.6 |
| 100.0 | 100.0 | 100.0 | Total | 100.0 | 100.0 | 100.0 | 100.0 | 100.0 | 100.0 |
| | | | **LIABILITIES** | | | | | | |
| 21.3 | 23.6 | 21.6 | Notes Payable-Short Term | 15.6 | 36.8 | 30.2 | 10.1 | 19.2 | 11.9 |
| 4.7 | 5.9 | 7.5 | Cur. Mat.-L.T.D. | 14.8 | 7.4 | 6.0 | 4.9 | 3.6 | 4.4 |
| 4.0 | 4.6 | 5.3 | Trade Payables | 3.4 | 3.3 | 2.6 | 5.5 | 8.7 | 9.7 |
| .5 | .4 | .5 | Income Taxes Payable | .0 | .3 | .7 | .2 | 1.7 | .5 |
| 8.1 | 6.2 | 6.1 | All Other Current | 6.4 | 7.0 | 4.3 | 7.2 | 3.0 | 7.7 |
| 38.6 | 40.6 | 41.0 | Total Current | 40.2 | 54.8 | 43.8 | 27.9 | 36.3 | 34.2 |
| 30.8 | 32.6 | 30.1 | Long-Term Debt | 39.4 | 30.6 | 44.6 | 30.6 | 18.1 | 16.4 |
| .5 | .6 | .5 | Deferred Taxes | .0 | .1 | .2 | .4 | .9 | 1.8 |
| 6.4 | 6.9 | 8.3 | All Other Non-Current | 14.2 | 7.8 | 8.2 | 11.0 | 4.7 | 1.6 |
| 23.7 | 19.3 | 20.1 | Net Worth | 6.1 | 6.7 | 3.1 | 30.0 | 40.0 | 46.1 |
| 100.0 | 100.0 | 100.0 | Total Liabilities & Net Worth | 100.0 | 100.0 | 100.0 | 100.0 | 100.0 | 100.0 |
| | | | **INCOME DATA** | | | | | | |
| 100.0 | 100.0 | 100.0 | Net Sales | 100.0 | 100.0 | 100.0 | 100.0 | 100.0 | 100.0 |
| | | | Gross Profit | | | | | | |
| 88.9 | 90.0 | 88.9 | Operating Expenses | 81.4 | 91.7 | 88.8 | 91.3 | 90.6 | 91.3 |
| 11.1 | 10.0 | 11.1 | Operating Profit | 18.6 | 8.3 | 11.2 | 8.7 | 9.4 | 8.7 |
| 3.3 | 2.8 | 1.6 | All Other Expenses (net) | 3.0 | 2.1 | 1.6 | .3 | 1.1 | .6 |
| 7.8 | 7.2 | 9.5 | Profit Before Taxes | 15.7 | 6.2 | 9.6 | 8.4 | 8.3 | 8.2 |
| | | | **RATIOS** | | | | | | |
| 2.3 | 2.7 | 2.8 | Current | 3.3 | 1.9 | 3.5 | 4.1 | 2.9 | 2.0 |
| 1.1 | 1.3 | 1.4 | | 1.0 | .8 | 1.1 | 1.8 | 1.8 | 1.4 |
| .4 | .6 | .3 | | .2 | .1 | .2 | .9 | .8 | 1.0 |
| 1.3 | 1.3 | 1.6 | Quick | 2.5 | 1.0 | 1.6 | 2.0 | 1.8 | 1.0 |
| (309) .4 | (294) .5 | .4 | | .4 | .2 | .6 | .6 | .6 | .5 |
| .1 | .1 | .1 | | .1 | .1 | .1 | .2 | .2 | .3 |
| 0 UND | 0 UND | 0 UND | Sales/Receivables | 0 UND | 0 UND | 0 UND | 0 UND | 5 78.1 | 15 24.1 |
| 3 132.0 | 2 176.6 | 2 229.9 | | 0 UND | 0 UND | 0 UND | 20 18.3 | 27 13.6 | 31 11.8 |
| 40 9.2 | 46 7.9 | 38 9.5 | | 2 207.4 | 9 42.1 | 62 5.9 | 63 5.8 | 76 4.8 | 39 9.3 |
| | | | Cost of Sales/Inventory | | | | | | |
| | | | Cost of Sales/Payables | | | | | | |
| 4.7 | 4.0 | 3.4 | Sales/Working Capital | 2.7 | 6.6 | 2.2 | 2.7 | 2.7 | 4.0 |
| 32.7 | 16.1 | 15.1 | | 143.8 | -20.5 | 10.8 | 9.9 | 4.8 | 9.7 |
| -8.8 | -11.4 | -9.0 | | -3.6 | -3.6 | -18.0 | -50.3 | -22.5 | NM |
| 9.4 | 9.0 | 12.1 | EBIT/Interest | 10.1 | 7.5 | 12.9 | 14.4 | 19.3 | 18.7 |
| (273) 3.1 | (270) 3.3 | (270) 4.5 | | (52) 3.5 | (65) 3.5 | (28) 4.4 | (41) 4.3 | (43) 5.0 | (41) 6.8 |
| .9 | 1.2 | 1.4 | | 1.1 | .8 | -.1 | 1.5 | 1.8 | 2.3 |
| 6.0 | 5.9 | 7.6 | Net Profit + Depr., Dep., Amort./Cur. Mat. L/T/D | | | | | 7.8 | 6.2 |
| (55) 2.3 | (50) 2.7 | (42) 2.4 | | | | | | (15) 1.7 | (15) 3.1 |
| .9 | 1.2 | 1.2 | | | | | | 1.0 | 2.0 |
| .7 | .6 | .7 | Fixed/Worth | 1.1 | .7 | .8 | .5 | .5 | .6 |
| 1.3 | 1.3 | 1.3 | | 2.0 | 1.8 | 3.1 | 1.3 | .9 | 1.0 |
| 4.3 | 4.4 | 9.1 | | -8.8 | -8.0 | -2.8 | 3.9 | 1.9 | 1.4 |
| .6 | .6 | .6 | Debt/Worth | .5 | .8 | 1.1 | .6 | .4 | .8 |
| 1.7 | 1.7 | 1.9 | | 3.2 | 5.2 | 4.8 | 1.3 | 1.3 | 1.3 |
| 6.8 | 8.1 | 34.2 | | -10.5 | -13.4 | -5.2 | 8.4 | 2.9 | 2.2 |
| 33.8 | 33.0 | 48.6 | % Profit Before Taxes/Tangible Net Worth | 56.9 | 131.6 | 107.1 | 40.3 | 37.4 | 37.9 |
| (257) 13.5 | (238) 12.5 | (234) 21.3 | | (45) 13.2 | (51) 24.9 | (20) 30.2 | (37) 16.4 | (40) 15.5 | (41) 27.1 |
| .6 | 2.7 | 3.5 | | 3.5 | 1.4 | 7.7 | 3.6 | 2.9 | 9.1 |
| 14.2 | 14.1 | 18.0 | % Profit Before Taxes/Total Assets | 19.1 | 19.1 | 34.0 | 15.8 | 15.0 | 20.4 |
| 4.9 | 4.9 | 7.6 | | 5.0 | 6.8 | 13.3 | 6.9 | 5.9 | 10.2 |
| -.4 | .5 | 1.1 | | .8 | -.4 | 1.6 | 1.9 | 1.4 | -3.7 |
| 7.7 | 9.0 | 10.6 | Sales/Net Fixed Assets | 8.5 | 8.3 | 13.6 | 11.4 | 14.7 | 10.1 |
| 2.1 | 2.7 | 2.9 | | 1.4 | 3.6 | 4.4 | 4.1 | 3.4 | 4.2 |
| .9 | .9 | 1.1 | | .4 | 1.4 | 2.2 | 1.1 | 1.5 | 1.6 |
| 2.2 | 2.3 | 2.6 | Sales/Total Assets | 1.4 | 2.6 | 2.9 | 3.4 | 2.2 | 3.0 |
| 1.1 | 1.0 | 1.1 | | .7 | 1.3 | 1.5 | 1.4 | .9 | 1.8 |
| .5 | .5 | .6 | | .3 | .7 | .9 | .6 | .6 | .7 |
| 2.8 | 2.7 | 2.2 | % Depr., Dep., Amort./Sales | 1.3 | 2.8 | 2.7 | 1.9 | 3.3 | 1.6 |
| (243) 6.6 | (237) 6.3 | (244) 5.0 | | (48) 4.7 | (62) 6.4 | (26) 4.7 | (34) 5.1 | (36) 4.9 | (38) 3.3 |
| 10.7 | 11.7 | 9.7 | | 17.9 | 13.1 | 9.4 | 8.1 | 7.3 | 7.7 |
| 1.5 | 1.8 | 1.5 | % Officers', Directors' Owners' Comp/Sales | 5.2 | 2.0 | | 1.1 | 1.0 | |
| (87) 3.1 | (67) 4.2 | (78) 2.4 | | (14) 8.4 | (23) 3.0 | | (14) 1.6 | (12) 1.4 | |
| 6.3 | 8.5 | 7.1 | | 9.4 | 6.5 | | 6.6 | 2.1 | |
| 4030350M | 3846466M | 3576284M | Net Sales ($) | 32111M | 142198M | 120113M | 296564M | 743391M | 2241907M |
| 3238317M | 3612951M | 3967323M | Total Assets ($) | 71339M | 187966M | 146445M | 452083M | 1225064M | 1884426M |

© RMA 2012

M = $ thousand    MM = $ million
See Pages 9 through 22 for Explanation of Ratios and Data

## Current Data Sorted by Assets  |  Comparative Historical Data

| 0-500M | 500M-2MM | 2-10MM | 10-50MM | 50-100MM | 100-250MM | Type of Statement | 4/1/07-3/31/08 ALL | 4/1/08-3/31/09 ALL |
|---|---|---|---|---|---|---|---|---|
| | | 2 | 5 | | | Unqualified | 7 | 6 |
| | 2 | 12 | 12 | 2 | 1 | Reviewed | 15 | 17 |
| 2 | 4 | 5 | 5 | | | Compiled | 32 | 33 |
| 11 | 15 | 19 | 3 | | | Tax Returns | 36 | 44 |
| 2 | 6 | 14 | 18 | 2 | 1 | Other | 39 | 47 |
| | 14 (4/1-9/30/11) | | 129 (10/1/11-3/31/12) | | | | | |
| 15 | 27 | 52 | 43 | 4 | 2 | **NUMBER OF STATEMENTS** | 129 | 147 |
| % | % | % | % | % | % | **ASSETS** | % | % |
| 23.9 | 3.2 | 8.2 | 2.0 | | | Cash & Equivalents | 10.1 | 7.0 |
| 6.4 | 4.6 | 3.5 | 4.8 | | | Trade Receivables (net) | 5.7 | 7.1 |
| 7.4 | 30.5 | 31.1 | 38.9 | | | Inventory | 25.1 | 27.0 |
| 3.5 | 5.9 | 6.3 | 4.0 | | | All Other Current | 4.5 | 6.4 |
| 41.1 | 44.2 | 49.1 | 49.7 | | | Total Current | 45.4 | 47.5 |
| 54.1 | 47.0 | 46.4 | 39.6 | | | Fixed Assets (net) | 46.7 | 44.9 |
| .8 | .5 | .1 | 1.0 | | | Intangibles (net) | .8 | .1 |
| 3.9 | 8.3 | 4.4 | 9.7 | | | All Other Non-Current | 7.0 | 7.5 |
| 100.0 | 100.0 | 100.0 | 100.0 | | | Total | 100.0 | 100.0 |
| | | | | | | **LIABILITIES** | | |
| 10.7 | 29.7 | 29.0 | 25.9 | | | Notes Payable-Short Term | 28.7 | 25.8 |
| 7.3 | 2.9 | 5.8 | 1.6 | | | Cur. Mat.-L.T.D. | 4.0 | 4.9 |
| .1 | 1.7 | 3.6 | 4.1 | | | Trade Payables | 4.1 | 2.5 |
| .1 | .0 | .3 | .7 | | | Income Taxes Payable | .3 | .7 |
| 4.4 | 9.4 | 5.7 | 6.8 | | | All Other Current | 4.5 | 7.2 |
| 22.7 | 43.7 | 44.4 | 38.9 | | | Total Current | 41.8 | 41.1 |
| 50.0 | 22.6 | 12.2 | 19.2 | | | Long-Term Debt | 20.2 | 21.0 |
| .0 | .0 | .3 | .1 | | | Deferred Taxes | .2 | .4 |
| 3.5 | 5.8 | 6.1 | .8 | | | All Other Non-Current | 4.4 | 5.4 |
| 23.8 | 28.0 | 37.1 | 41.0 | | | Net Worth | 33.5 | 32.1 |
| 100.0 | 100.0 | 100.0 | 100.0 | | | Total Liabilities & Net Worth | 100.0 | 100.0 |
| | | | | | | **INCOME DATA** | | |
| 100.0 | 100.0 | 100.0 | 100.0 | | | Net Sales | 100.0 | 100.0 |
| | | | | | | Gross Profit | | |
| 97.0 | 86.8 | 92.5 | 83.5 | | | Operating Expenses | 91.0 | 94.4 |
| 3.0 | 13.2 | 7.5 | 16.5 | | | Operating Profit | 9.0 | 5.6 |
| 3.0 | 7.1 | 2.5 | 2.3 | | | All Other Expenses (net) | 4.0 | 2.9 |
| .0 | 6.1 | 5.0 | 14.2 | | | Profit Before Taxes | 5.0 | 2.8 |
| | | | | | | **RATIOS** | | |
| 4.2 | 2.3 | 2.8 | 1.8 | | | Current | 2.3 | 2.2 |
| 2.0 | 1.0 | 1.2 | 1.4 | | | | 1.2 | 1.1 |
| .1 | .3 | .6 | 1.2 | | | | .7 | .7 |
| 4.2 | 1.0 | .6 | .3 | | | Quick | .8 | .7 |
| .7 | (26) .0 | .1 | .1 | | | | (128) .2 | .2 |
| .1 | .0 | .0 | .0 | | | | .0 | .0 |
| 0 UND | 0 UND | 0 UND | 0 UND | | | Sales/Receivables | 0 UND | 0 UND |
| 0 UND | 0 UND | 0 UND | 3 114.4 | | | | 0 UND | 0 UND |
| 0 UND | 7 50.0 | 7 54.8 | 15 24.1 | | | | 15 24.3 | 18 20.2 |
| | | | | | | Cost of Sales/Inventory | | |
| | | | | | | Cost of Sales/Payables | | |
| 2.0 | 2.6 | 2.2 | 2.4 | | | Sales/Working Capital | 4.0 | 4.1 |
| 61.6 | 53.6 | 11.9 | 6.2 | | | | 21.9 | 27.1 |
| -5.3 | -3.3 | -10.5 | 20.4 | | | | -12.2 | -6.2 |
| | 5.3 | 9.1 | 15.6 | | | EBIT/Interest | 4.6 | 3.2 |
| | (21) 2.6 | (46) 2.8 | (39) 6.9 | | | | (112) 1.8 | (124) 1.7 |
| | .2 | .9 | 1.6 | | | | .9 | .0 |
| | | | | | | Net Profit + Depr., Dep., Amort./Cur. Mat. L/T/D | 6.6 | 5.2 |
| | | | | | | | (11) 3.6 | (16) 1.0 |
| | | | | | | | 1.0 | -2.6 |
| .1 | .3 | .3 | .4 | | | Fixed/Worth | .5 | .5 |
| 1.7 | 1.2 | 1.0 | .8 | | | | 1.3 | 1.1 |
| 4.7 | 2.2 | 2.6 | 1.3 | | | | 4.2 | 2.9 |
| .5 | .6 | .4 | .7 | | | Debt/Worth | .6 | .6 |
| 1.9 | 2.2 | 1.7 | 1.3 | | | | 1.5 | 1.7 |
| 8.5 | 29.4 | 5.6 | 2.6 | | | | 9.1 | 6.4 |
| 35.6 | 36.3 | 26.0 | 34.0 | | | % Profit Before Taxes/Tangible Net Worth | 20.7 | 16.4 |
| (12) 10.2 | (22) 10.2 | (44) 6.7 | (40) 18.2 | | | | (107) 7.4 | (121) 3.8 |
| -1.9 | -1.2 | -1.4 | 2.6 | | | | 1.0 | -3.5 |
| 5.6 | 8.3 | 9.0 | 12.7 | | | % Profit Before Taxes/Total Assets | 7.3 | 5.9 |
| .7 | 2.4 | 3.2 | 7.1 | | | | 2.6 | 1.5 |
| -6.1 | -1.9 | -.7 | .9 | | | | -.3 | -3.0 |
| 58.9 | 23.8 | 11.4 | 8.5 | | | Sales/Net Fixed Assets | 14.2 | 12.5 |
| 1.3 | 1.2 | 1.6 | 2.8 | | | | 2.1 | 2.7 |
| .4 | .5 | .6 | .6 | | | | .7 | .7 |
| 1.4 | 1.9 | 1.8 | 1.2 | | | Sales/Total Assets | 1.9 | 1.9 |
| 1.1 | .6 | .8 | .7 | | | | 1.0 | .8 |
| .3 | .2 | .4 | .3 | | | | .5 | .4 |
| | 2.5 | 2.4 | 1.1 | | | % Depr., Dep., Amort./Sales | 1.0 | 1.0 |
| | (19) 9.7 | (42) 7.0 | (34) 3.5 | | | | (104) 3.7 | (122) 4.7 |
| | 23.3 | 14.7 | 7.9 | | | | 10.6 | 11.1 |
| | | .3 | | | | % Officers', Directors' Owners' Comp/Sales | .9 | .7 |
| | (11) | .9 | | | | | (32) 1.9 | (39) 2.1 |
| | | 2.3 | | | | | 6.4 | 5.5 |
| 20013M | 29671M | 438171M | 810390M | 346194M | 253723M | Net Sales ($) | 2505764M | 1588660M |
| 5644M | 30924M | 231131M | 892522M | 257807M | 226597M | Total Assets ($) | 1790535M | 1307862M |

© RMA 2012

M = $ thousand    MM = $ million
See Pages 9 through 22 for Explanation of Ratios and Data

## Comparative Historical Data

## Current Data Sorted by Sales

| | | | Type of Statement | | | | | | |
|---|---|---|---|---|---|---|---|---|---|
| 6 | 6 | 8 | Unqualified | 1 | 1 | | 2 | | 4 |
| 13 | 23 | 28 | Reviewed | 3 | 1 | 4 | 4 | 10 | 6 |
| 28 | 24 | 16 | Compiled | 4 | 2 | 4 | 3 | 2 | 1 |
| 56 | 58 | 48 | Tax Returns | 25 | 11 | 4 | 3 | 8 | 1 |
| 31 | 49 | 43 | Other | 8 | 12 | 8 | 3 | 8 | 4 |
| 4/1/09-3/31/10 ALL | 4/1/10-3/31/11 ALL | 4/1/11-3/31/12 ALL | | 14 (4/1-9/30/11) | | | 129 (10/1/11-3/31/12) | | |
| | | | | 0-1MM | 1-3MM | 3-5MM | 5-10MM | 10-25MM | 25MM & OVER |
| 134 | 160 | 143 | NUMBER OF STATEMENTS | 41 | 27 | 20 | 15 | 24 | 16 |
| % | % | % | ASSETS | % | % | % | % | % | % |
| 8.3 | 6.4 | 6.8 | Cash & Equivalents | 10.6 | 4.3 | 5.7 | 4.7 | 6.1 | 5.3 |
| 5.6 | 4.3 | 4.7 | Trade Receivables (net) | 2.5 | 4.6 | 1.1 | 8.3 | 4.3 | 12.1 |
| 26.7 | 25.6 | 31.3 | Inventory | 7.7 | 33.5 | 30.9 | 52.0 | 47.3 | 45.0 |
| 5.6 | 4.3 | 5.2 | All Other Current | 4.8 | 3.6 | 8.2 | 5.6 | 5.2 | 4.4 |
| 46.1 | 40.6 | 47.9 | Total Current | 25.6 | 46.0 | 45.9 | 70.7 | 62.9 | 66.8 |
| 42.3 | 50.1 | 44.8 | Fixed Assets (net) | 67.0 | 46.1 | 49.1 | 21.3 | 30.1 | 24.1 |
| 1.7 | .5 | .5 | Intangibles (net) | .5 | .2 | .2 | .1 | .8 | 1.2 |
| 9.9 | 8.7 | 6.8 | All Other Non-Current | 6.9 | 7.6 | 4.7 | 7.9 | 6.1 | 7.9 |
| 100.0 | 100.0 | 100.0 | Total | 100.0 | 100.0 | 100.0 | 100.0 | 100.0 | 100.0 |
| | | | LIABILITIES | | | | | | |
| 41.7 | 34.5 | 26.4 | Notes Payable-Short Term | 10.1 | 35.2 | 30.5 | 38.9 | 28.1 | 33.4 |
| 4.0 | 2.4 | 3.9 | Cur. Mat.-L.T.D. | 3.5 | 5.2 | 3.8 | 9.1 | 2.2 | .7 |
| 2.2 | 3.4 | 3.1 | Trade Payables | 1.0 | .8 | 1.3 | 6.7 | 3.1 | 11.4 |
| .1 | .3 | .4 | Income Taxes Payable | .1 | .0 | .5 | 1.2 | .3 | .9 |
| 5.7 | 7.9 | 6.7 | All Other Current | 7.5 | 1.5 | 6.9 | 6.8 | 8.3 | 10.3 |
| 53.6 | 48.4 | 40.4 | Total Current | 22.2 | 42.7 | 43.1 | 62.7 | 42.1 | 56.6 |
| 19.5 | 21.7 | 20.2 | Long-Term Debt | 33.5 | 11.7 | 19.5 | 12.6 | 18.0 | 11.7 |
| .5 | .2 | .1 | Deferred Taxes | .0 | .2 | .5 | .2 | .0 | .1 |
| 4.5 | 5.3 | 4.0 | All Other Non-Current | 3.9 | 8.7 | 3.3 | 4.1 | .5 | 1.9 |
| 21.7 | 24.3 | 35.3 | Net Worth | 40.4 | 36.7 | 33.6 | 20.4 | 39.4 | 29.7 |
| 100.0 | 100.0 | 100.0 | Total Liabilties & Net Worth | 100.0 | 100.0 | 100.0 | 100.0 | 100.0 | 100.0 |
| | | | INCOME DATA | | | | | | |
| 100.0 | 100.0 | 100.0 | Net Sales | 100.0 | 100.0 | 100.0 | 100.0 | 100.0 | 100.0 |
| | | | Gross Profit | | | | | | |
| 95.4 | 90.3 | 89.1 | Operating Expenses | 84.9 | 89.8 | 91.8 | 92.5 | 86.4 | 96.0 |
| 4.6 | 9.7 | 10.9 | Operating Profit | 15.1 | 10.2 | 8.2 | 7.5 | 13.6 | 4.0 |
| 2.2 | 2.0 | 3.2 | All Other Expenses (net) | 10.3 | .6 | 1.4 | 1.1 | .0 | -1.7 |
| 2.4 | 7.7 | 7.7 | Profit Before Taxes | 4.9 | 9.6 | 6.8 | 6.4 | 13.6 | 5.7 |
| | | | RATIOS | | | | | | |
| 1.8 | 2.0 | 2.3 | | 3.8 | 2.4 | 2.6 | 1.4 | 2.2 | 1.6 |
| 1.1 | 1.2 | 1.3 | Current | 1.0 | 1.3 | 1.2 | 1.0 | 1.5 | 1.3 |
| .7 | .6 | .8 | | .1 | .5 | .6 | .9 | 1.2 | 1.1 |
| .7 | .5 | .6 | | 2.1 | .5 | .3 | .6 | .4 | .7 |
| (132) .2 | (158) .2 | (142) .1 | Quick | .3 (26) .1 | .1 | .1 | .1 | .1 | .1 |
| .0 | .0 | .0 | | .0 | .0 | .0 | .0 | .0 | .1 |
| | | | | 0 UND | 0 UND | 0 UND | 0 UND | 0 UND | 2 189.4 |
| 0 UND | 0 UND | 0 UND | Sales/Receivables | 0 UND | 0 UND | 0 999.8 | 4 87.5 | 2 189.6 | 6 58.4 |
| 0 UND | 0 UND | 0 UND | | 0 UND | 2 174.8 | 8 45.6 | 76 4.8 | 11 34.5 | 14 25.7 |
| 19 19.3 | 11 33.5 | 8 45.1 | Cost of Sales/Inventory | | | | | | |
| | | | Cost of Sales/Payables | | | | | | |
| 4.3 | 3.5 | 2.6 | | 1.5 | 2.4 | 1.9 | 6.0 | 3.4 | 6.2 |
| 40.3 | 16.1 | 9.6 | Sales/Working Capital | 123.2 | 9.6 | 8.2 | -107.6 | 7.3 | 8.7 |
| -8.3 | -7.1 | -14.0 | | -1.5 | -4.9 | -6.2 | -18.1 | 15.5 | 801.2 |
| 4.5 | 5.9 | 10.7 | | 5.7 | 7.3 | 9.0 | 7.3 | 16.6 | 17.0 |
| (122) 1.1 | (140) 2.5 | (120) 3.6 | EBIT/Interest | (25) 2.3 | (24) 3.5 | (19) 3.3 | 2.9 | (22) 8.9 | (15) 11.0 |
| -1.2 | 1.1 | 1.2 | | .7 | .8 | 1.6 | 1.8 | 1.5 | 1.6 |
| 8.0 | 6.7 | 8.2 | Net Profit + Depr., Dep., | | | | | | |
| (15) 2.3 | (14) 2.5 | (12) 4.2 | Amort./Cur. Mat. L/T/D | | | | | | |
| .8 | .9 | 1.7 | | | | | | | |
| .4 | .5 | .3 | | .8 | .4 | .7 | .1 | .3 | .1 |
| 1.1 | 1.2 | .9 | Fixed/Worth | 1.4 | .9 | 1.5 | .5 | .5 | .5 |
| 3.4 | 4.0 | 2.1 | | 2.8 | 1.7 | 4.1 | 1.3 | 1.0 | 1.4 |
| .7 | .6 | .6 | | .4 | .3 | .3 | 1.3 | .7 | .9 |
| 1.7 | 1.6 | 1.5 | Debt/Worth | 1.0 | 1.4 | 1.7 | 3.4 | 1.4 | 1.6 |
| 8.9 | 5.9 | 4.4 | | 3.2 | 8.2 | 5.7 | 25.2 | 2.2 | 9.7 |
| 18.3 | 25.4 | 33.1 | % Profit Before Taxes/Tangible | 15.4 | 45.1 | 15.8 | 44.5 | 34.8 | 67.5 |
| (105) 2.7 | (132) 7.5 | (124) 12.1 | Net Worth | (35) 3.3 | (23) 4.6 | (17) 8.2 | (12) 20.1 | (22) 21.8 | (15) 30.0 |
| -6.4 | 1.0 | 1.1 | | -2.1 | -2.0 | 2.3 | 2.3 | 4.3 | 14.9 |
| 5.9 | 10.2 | 10.5 | % Profit Before Taxes/Total | 5.4 | 9.3 | 9.0 | 8.9 | 19.7 | 15.8 |
| .7 | 3.0 | 4.0 | Assets | .7 | 2.8 | 4.5 | 6.0 | 9.1 | 10.8 |
| -5.1 | .1 | -.6 | | -2.4 | -1.5 | .5 | 1.1 | .7 | 3.1 |
| 16.4 | 6.3 | 10.8 | | 1.3 | 10.5 | 4.3 | 145.0 | 12.2 | 99.9 |
| 2.6 | 1.5 | 1.8 | Sales/Net Fixed Assets | .5 | 1.1 | 1.4 | 5.2 | 5.7 | 11.3 |
| .8 | .6 | .6 | | .2 | .6 | .6 | 1.8 | 2.5 | 7.0 |
| 1.9 | 1.5 | 1.6 | | .8 | 1.8 | 1.3 | 1.8 | 2.3 | 2.8 |
| 1.0 | .7 | .8 | Sales/Total Assets | .3 | .6 | .7 | .8 | 1.1 | 1.7 |
| .4 | .4 | .3 | | .1 | .3 | .4 | .6 | .7 | 1.0 |
| 1.0 | 1.6 | 1.6 | | 8.8 | 2.4 | 2.1 | | .6 | .4 |
| (113) 4.5 | (129) 5.4 | (108) 5.5 | % Depr., Dep., Amort./Sales | (31) 20.0 | (17) 11.1 | (18) 7.5 | | (20) 2.2 | (13) .6 |
| 13.0 | 12.7 | 15.4 | | 30.7 | 19.5 | 12.9 | | 3.8 | 1.0 |
| .8 | 1.6 | .6 | % Officers', Directors' | | | | | | |
| (42) 2.0 | (31) 3.1 | (28) 1.3 | Owners' Comp/Sales | | | | | | |
| 4.6 | 7.5 | 3.4 | | | | | | | |
| 1211848M | 2419362M | 1898162M | Net Sales ($) | 16904M | 52419M | 76499M | 107753M | 395874M | 1248713M |
| 1243164M | 1868687M | 1644625M | Total Assets ($) | 101654M | 149287M | 139591M | 170422M | 362910M | 720761M |

M = $ thousand    MM = $ million
See Pages 9 through 22 for Explanation of Ratios and Data

## Current Data Sorted by Assets / Comparative Historical Data

| 0-500M | 500M-2MM | 2-10MM | 10-50MM | 50-100MM | 100-250MM | Type of Statement | 4/1/07-3/31/08 ALL | 4/1/08-3/31/09 ALL |
|---|---|---|---|---|---|---|---|---|
|  | 1 | 4 | 14 | 8 | 10 | Unqualified | 34 | 38 |
| 1 | 2 | 15 | 22 | 6 | 2 | Reviewed | 49 | 47 |
| 1 | 3 | 18 | 5 | 1 | 2 | Compiled | 27 | 39 |
| 5 | 10 | 8 | 2 |  | 2 | Tax Returns | 15 | 16 |
|  | 6 | 20 | 25 | 8 | 5 | Other | 72 | 80 |
|  | 47 (4/1-9/30/11) |  | 157 (10/1/11-3/31/12) |  |  |  |  |  |
| 7 | 22 | 65 | 68 | 23 | 19 | **NUMBER OF STATEMENTS** | 197 | 220 |
| % | % | % | % | % | % | **ASSETS** | % | % |
|  | 4.1 | 4.9 | 5.0 | 3.9 | 1.4 | Cash & Equivalents | 4.3 | 5.4 |
|  | 8.2 | 18.9 | 21.6 | 13.3 | 10.4 | Trade Receivables (net) | 16.5 | 16.6 |
|  | 47.5 | 35.6 | 44.3 | 50.3 | 58.1 | Inventory | 43.6 | 41.3 |
|  | 7.5 | 6.6 | 9.1 | 9.3 | 9.2 | All Other Current | 6.5 | 6.6 |
|  | 67.2 | 66.1 | 80.1 | 76.8 | 79.1 | Total Current | 70.9 | 69.9 |
|  | 26.9 | 26.1 | 14.0 | 20.5 | 14.7 | Fixed Assets (net) | 21.0 | 21.8 |
|  | 1.1 | 2.5 | .8 | .1 | .4 | Intangibles (net) | .3 | .3 |
|  | 4.8 | 5.3 | 5.2 | 2.6 | 5.8 | All Other Non-Current | 7.8 | 8.0 |
|  | 100.0 | 100.0 | 100.0 | 100.0 | 100.0 | Total | 100.0 | 100.0 |
|  |  |  |  |  |  | **LIABILITIES** |  |  |
|  | 48.7 | 32.4 | 39.4 | 36.2 | 36.9 | Notes Payable-Short Term | 39.8 | 36.2 |
|  | 7.0 | 1.4 | 1.1 | 1.0 | .8 | Cur. Mat.-L.T.D. | 1.4 | 1.4 |
|  | 7.7 | 8.9 | 8.8 | 7.1 | 4.3 | Trade Payables | 5.8 | 5.8 |
|  | .5 | .2 | .6 | .0 | .3 | Income Taxes Payable | .3 | .2 |
|  | 2.1 | 8.4 | 8.1 | 8.9 | 6.2 | All Other Current | 6.8 | 6.4 |
|  | 66.0 | 51.3 | 58.0 | 53.2 | 48.5 | Total Current | 54.0 | 50.0 |
|  | 21.9 | 14.0 | 7.3 | 11.0 | 7.0 | Long-Term Debt | 12.1 | 13.5 |
|  | .2 | .3 | .4 | .2 | .5 | Deferred Taxes | .5 | .4 |
|  | 3.7 | 4.0 | 2.7 | 1.4 | 2.0 | All Other Non-Current | 4.2 | 3.1 |
|  | 8.2 | 30.4 | 31.7 | 34.2 | 42.0 | Net Worth | 29.4 | 33.0 |
|  | 100.0 | 100.0 | 100.0 | 100.0 | 100.0 | Total Liabilities & Net Worth | 100.0 | 100.0 |
|  |  |  |  |  |  | **INCOME DATA** |  |  |
|  | 100.0 | 100.0 | 100.0 | 100.0 | 100.0 | Net Sales | 100.0 | 100.0 |
|  |  |  |  |  |  | Gross Profit |  |  |
|  | 92.0 | 91.9 | 94.2 | 95.4 | 92.1 | Operating Expenses | 94.8 | 95.7 |
|  | 8.0 | 8.1 | 5.8 | 4.6 | 7.9 | Operating Profit | 5.2 | 4.3 |
|  | .8 | 2.2 | .9 | .6 | -.3 | All Other Expenses (net) | 3.3 | 2.4 |
|  | 7.2 | 5.9 | 4.9 | 4.0 | 8.2 | Profit Before Taxes | 2.0 | 1.9 |
|  |  |  |  |  |  | **RATIOS** |  |  |
|  | 2.4 | 1.5 | 1.7 | 1.7 | 1.7 |  | 1.9 | 2.0 |
|  | 1.5 | 1.3 | 1.3 | 1.3 | 1.5 | Current | 1.3 | 1.3 |
|  | 1.0 | 1.0 | 1.1 | 1.2 | 1.4 |  | 1.1 | 1.1 |
|  | .9 | .8 | .9 | .6 | .3 |  | .7 | .8 |
|  | .2 | .3 | .3 | .3 | .2 | Quick | .3 (216) | .3 |
|  | .0 | .1 | .1 | .2 | .1 |  | .1 | .1 |
| 0 UND | 0 UND | 6 60.3 | 3 105.4 | 10 35.2 |  |  | 2 188.8 | 1 282.6 |
| 4 89.5 | 14 25.9 | 25 14.8 | 16 22.2 | 23 15.8 |  | Sales/Receivables | 19 18.8 | 16 22.7 |
| 29 12.5 | 49 7.5 | 74 4.9 | 46 8.0 | 60 6.1 |  | 50 7.3 | 53 6.9 |
|  |  |  |  |  |  | Cost of Sales/Inventory |  |  |
|  |  |  |  |  |  | Cost of Sales/Payables |  |  |
|  | 4.4 | 8.2 | 4.4 | 6.6 | 3.3 |  | 4.2 | 4.0 |
|  | 16.5 | 16.2 | 9.5 | 10.0 | 5.3 | Sales/Working Capital | 10.1 | 10.5 |
|  | -217.2 | 401.8 | 24.4 | 19.0 | 6.7 |  | 43.2 | 27.7 |
|  | 8.8 | 8.0 | 10.2 | 11.8 | 12.2 |  | 3.7 | 4.5 |
| (17) 1.4 | (59) 3.1 | (65) 4.7 | (22) 4.9 | 7.3 |  | EBIT/Interest | (185) 1.6 | (205) 1.5 |
|  | .6 | 1.5 | 2.4 | 1.1 | 4.5 |  | .6 | -.1 |
|  |  | 23.6 |  |  |  |  | 11.3 | 11.7 |
|  | (14) 7.8 |  |  |  |  | Net Profit + Depr., Dep., Amort./Cur. Mat. L/T/D | (30) 2.4 | (20) 3.3 |
|  | 3.4 |  |  |  |  |  | .8 | -.5 |
|  | .2 | .1 | .1 | .2 | .1 |  | .2 | .1 |
|  | .7 | .6 | .4 | .7 | .3 | Fixed/Worth | .5 | .6 |
|  | -2.1 | 2.0 | .7 | 1.1 | .6 |  | 1.4 | 1.3 |
|  | 1.0 | 1.1 | 1.4 | 1.0 | 1.3 |  | 1.0 | .8 |
|  | 2.3 | 2.9 | 3.2 | 2.8 | 1.6 | Debt/Worth | 2.6 | 2.3 |
|  | -4.4 | 5.8 | 5.5 | 5.7 | 2.3 |  | 5.5 | 5.8 |
|  | 17.6 | 30.4 | 40.6 | 37.5 | 37.3 |  | 20.0 | 25.9 |
| (15) 8.2 | (55) 13.1 | (66) 23.4 | 18.4 | 21.3 |  | % Profit Before Taxes/Tangible Net Worth | (178) 7.9 | (197) 5.8 |
|  | -.1 | 4.4 | 10.8 | 3.0 | 12.9 |  | -3.2 | -5.4 |
|  | 12.7 | 9.4 | 10.5 | 10.9 | 11.6 |  | 6.3 | 9.1 |
|  | 2.6 | 4.4 | 6.4 | 7.4 | 9.0 | % Profit Before Taxes/Total Assets | 2.3 | 1.7 |
|  | -.1 | .8 | 3.1 | .7 | 5.1 |  | -1.3 | -3.3 |
|  | 20.3 | 90.2 | 56.0 | 21.2 | 25.1 |  | 29.6 | 36.3 |
|  | 12.3 | 12.0 | 16.1 | 13.3 | 14.1 | Sales/Net Fixed Assets | 9.9 | 10.7 |
|  | 8.0 | 4.0 | 7.6 | 7.7 | 6.9 |  | 5.2 | 4.8 |
|  | 3.5 | 3.0 | 2.2 | 2.2 | 1.9 |  | 2.2 | 2.3 |
|  | 2.4 | 2.1 | 1.5 | 1.9 | 1.3 | Sales/Total Assets | 1.5 | 1.6 |
|  | 1.0 | 1.3 | 1.1 | 1.3 | 1.0 |  | 1.0 | 1.0 |
|  | 1.2 | .6 | .6 | .6 | .5 |  | .7 | .7 |
| (13) 1.5 | (53) 1.4 | (56) 1.0 | (18) 1.0 | (17) .7 |  | % Depr., Dep., Amort./Sales | (164) 1.4 | (175) 1.4 |
|  | 3.3 | 2.6 | 1.5 | 1.5 | 1.2 |  | 2.5 | 2.4 |
|  |  | .2 | .3 |  |  |  | .4 | .3 |
|  | (12) 1.0 | (16) .6 |  |  |  | % Officers', Directors' Owners' Comp/Sales | (45) 1.3 | (46) .8 |
|  | 1.7 | 1.9 |  |  |  |  | 3.7 | 2.2 |
| 32509M | 75851M | 1176126M | 3048543M | 3094730M | 3578361M | Net Sales ($) | 8389083M | 10754155M |
| 2243M | 27408M | 386173M | 1669423M | 1632163M | 2679437M | Total Assets ($) | 5536584M | 6575425M |

M = $ thousand    MM = $ million
See Pages 9 through 22 for Explanation of Ratios and Data

## Comparative Historical Data / Current Data Sorted by Sales

| 4/1/09-3/31/10 ALL | 4/1/10-3/31/11 ALL | 4/1/11-3/31/12 ALL | Type of Statement | 0-1MM | 1-3MM | 3-5MM | 5-10MM | 10-25MM | 25MM & OVER |
|---|---|---|---|---|---|---|---|---|---|
| 40 | 40 | 37 | Unqualified | | | | 1 | 4 | 32 |
| 51 | 52 | 48 | Reviewed | | | 4 | 2 | 14 | 26 |
| 32 | 33 | 30 | Compiled | 2 | 3 | 1 | 6 | 10 | 10 |
| 18 | 23 | 25 | Tax Returns | 7 | 6 | 4 | 2 | 4 | 2 |
| 57 | 70 | 64 | Other | 5 | 4 | 2 | 7 | 20 | 26 |
| | | | | 47 (4/1-9/30/11) | | | 157 (10/1/11-3/31/12) | | |
| 198 | 218 | 204 | **NUMBER OF STATEMENTS** | 14 | 13 | 11 | 18 | 52 | 96 |
| % | % | % | **ASSETS** | % | % | % | % | % | % |
| 4.8 | 4.4 | 4.6 | Cash & Equivalents | 6.2 | 3.8 | 3.8 | 6.1 | 4.3 | 4.4 |
| 15.7 | 14.5 | 17.2 | Trade Receivables (net) | 4.3 | 10.7 | 15.3 | 16.4 | 22.9 | 17.2 |
| 40.5 | 42.5 | 43.4 | Inventory | 29.3 | 35.9 | 44.2 | 34.9 | 41.9 | 48.8 |
| 6.0 | 7.4 | 8.0 | All Other Current | 7.5 | 3.0 | 2.6 | 5.7 | 7.0 | 10.3 |
| 67.0 | 68.8 | 73.1 | Total Current | 47.3 | 53.4 | 65.9 | 63.1 | 76.1 | 80.7 |
| 24.2 | 23.8 | 20.3 | Fixed Assets (net) | 41.6 | 40.0 | 33.7 | 28.1 | 16.3 | 13.7 |
| .2 | .6 | 1.2 | Intangibles (net) | 3.2 | 2.4 | .0 | .5 | 2.1 | .6 |
| 8.6 | 6.8 | 5.2 | All Other Non-Current | 7.3 | 4.3 | .3 | 8.2 | 5.4 | 4.9 |
| 100.0 | 100.0 | 100.0 | Total | 100.0 | 100.0 | 100.0 | 100.0 | 100.0 | 100.0 |
| | | | **LIABILITIES** | | | | | | |
| 38.8 | 36.7 | 37.0 | Notes Payable-Short Term | 12.4 | 29.4 | 33.2 | 54.1 | 37.1 | 38.7 |
| 2.0 | 2.5 | 2.0 | Cur. Mat.-L.T.D. | 3.6 | 5.5 | 6.7 | 3.6 | .8 | 1.0 |
| 6.3 | 7.2 | 8.0 | Trade Payables | 4.8 | 3.4 | 9.3 | 8.8 | 8.2 | 8.6 |
| .2 | .2 | .4 | Income Taxes Payable | .7 | .0 | .5 | .0 | .1 | .5 |
| 6.9 | 7.1 | 7.5 | All Other Current | 4.5 | 4.1 | 1.9 | 6.1 | 9.1 | 8.5 |
| 54.1 | 53.7 | 54.8 | Total Current | 26.0 | 42.5 | 51.5 | 72.6 | 55.3 | 57.4 |
| 14.9 | 17.8 | 12.1 | Long-Term Debt | 24.6 | 40.8 | 18.4 | 16.7 | 7.4 | 7.3 |
| .4 | .3 | .3 | Deferred Taxes | .0 | .0 | .0 | .2 | .3 | .4 |
| 4.4 | 4.4 | 2.9 | All Other Non-Current | 3.9 | 1.5 | 6.4 | 2.8 | 2.0 | 3.1 |
| 26.1 | 23.9 | 29.9 | Net Worth | 44.9 | 15.3 | 23.7 | 7.7 | 35.0 | 31.8 |
| 100.0 | 100.0 | 100.0 | Total Liabilities & Net Worth | 100.0 | 100.0 | 100.0 | 100.0 | 100.0 | 100.0 |
| | | | **INCOME DATA** | | | | | | |
| 100.0 | 100.0 | 100.0 | Net Sales | 100.0 | 100.0 | 100.0 | 100.0 | 100.0 | 100.0 |
| | | | Gross Profit | | | | | | |
| 97.1 | 92.5 | 93.1 | Operating Expenses | 73.6 | 88.2 | 91.2 | 97.2 | 95.2 | 95.1 |
| 2.9 | 7.5 | 6.9 | Operating Profit | 26.4 | 11.8 | 8.8 | 2.8 | 4.8 | 4.9 |
| 1.6 | 1.9 | 1.2 | All Other Expenses (net) | 9.4 | 5.0 | -.4 | 1.2 | .2 | .3 |
| 1.3 | 5.5 | 5.6 | Profit Before Taxes | 17.0 | 6.9 | 9.2 | 1.6 | 4.6 | 4.6 |
| | | | **RATIOS** | | | | | | |
| 1.7 | 2.0 | 1.7 | Current | 12.3 | 2.5 | 1.8 | 1.5 | 1.9 | 1.7 |
| 1.2 | 1.3 | 1.3 | | 1.5 | 1.6 | 1.4 | 1.3 | 1.2 | 1.3 |
| 1.0 | 1.1 | 1.1 | | .9 | .8 | .8 | .9 | 1.1 | 1.2 |
| .7 | .7 | .8 | Quick | 7.2 | .7 | .8 | .8 | .9 | .7 |
| (196) .2 | (217) .3 | .3 | | .8 | .2 | .2 | .2 | .5 | .3 |
| .1 | .1 | .1 | | .0 | .0 | .0 | .1 | .1 | .1 |
| 4 102.4 | 1 359.2 | 3 132.9 | Sales/Receivables | 0 UND | 0 UND | 0 UND | 3 116.7 | 2 185.5 | 5 69.2 |
| 17 21.0 | 16 22.8 | 18 20.3 | | 0 UND | 0 UND | 20 18.5 | 28 13.2 | 20 18.7 | 17 21.7 |
| 45 8.2 | 45 8.1 | 48 7.6 | | 32 11.4 | 33 11.2 | 40 9.2 | 66 5.5 | 72 5.1 | 46 7.9 |
| | | | Cost of Sales/Inventory | | | | | | |
| | | | Cost of Sales/Payables | | | | | | |
| 5.2 | 3.4 | 5.1 | Sales/Working Capital | 2.0 | 4.6 | 7.6 | 7.7 | 4.3 | 5.6 |
| 11.3 | 9.1 | 10.6 | | 14.1 | 7.1 | 11.8 | 12.9 | 11.4 | 10.1 |
| 156.8 | 52.4 | 39.8 | | UND | -10.3 | -10.2 | NM | 28.1 | 27.7 |
| 5.5 | 7.5 | 9.9 | EBIT/Interest | | | 4.9 | 5.0 | 9.9 | 11.1 |
| (190) 1.6 | (201) 3.5 | (186) 4.3 | | | | 1.6 | 2.9 | (50) 4.6 | (92) 5.0 |
| -.5 | 1.4 | 1.7 | | | | 1.0 | .9 | 2.2 | 2.1 |
| 6.5 | 10.0 | 12.1 | Net Profit + Depr., Dep., Amort./Cur. Mat. L/T/D | | | | | | 19.1 |
| (19) 1.8 | (27) 6.8 | (30) 5.7 | | | | | | (20) 7.2 | |
| .2 | 1.7 | 2.6 | | | | | | | 3.6 |
| .2 | .2 | .1 | Fixed/Worth | .1 | .4 | .2 | .5 | .1 | .1 |
| .6 | .5 | .5 | | .7 | 1.4 | 1.1 | .8 | .4 | .4 |
| 1.4 | 1.3 | 1.1 | | NM | -1.6 | 2.8 | -8.9 | .8 | .7 |
| 1.0 | .9 | 1.0 | Debt/Worth | .2 | .5 | 1.2 | 1.0 | .8 | 1.4 |
| 2.5 | 2.5 | 2.5 | | 1.2 | 3.3 | 2.7 | 2.6 | 2.5 | 2.7 |
| 5.4 | 6.3 | 5.4 | | NM | -10.0 | 4.6 | -12.8 | 4.7 | 5.2 |
| 22.4 | 29.1 | 36.5 | % Profit Before Taxes/Tangible Net Worth | 14.8 | 25.3 | | 23.6 | 37.9 | 39.3 |
| (176) 5.8 | (191) 15.9 | (183) 18.5 | | (11) 6.3 | (10) 8.4 | | (13) 7.0 | (49) 20.0 | (92) 22.6 |
| -7.0 | 5.2 | 6.0 | | -2.7 | -.7 | | 2.3 | 9.1 | 10.9 |
| 6.8 | 8.9 | 10.5 | % Profit Before Taxes/Total Assets | 10.6 | 19.7 | 6.2 | 6.1 | 11.0 | 11.0 |
| 1.5 | 4.9 | 5.9 | | 7.3 | 2.0 | 2.0 | 2.7 | 5.6 | 7.4 |
| -3.2 | .7 | 1.6 | | .9 | -.2 | .0 | -.2 | 1.9 | 2.6 |
| 29.0 | 38.9 | 38.6 | Sales/Net Fixed Assets | 27.4 | 17.7 | 51.4 | 11.8 | 44.5 | 67.6 |
| 10.5 | 10.9 | 14.0 | | 5.2 | 3.3 | 9.2 | 8.5 | 13.6 | 18.3 |
| 3.8 | 3.9 | 6.8 | | .2 | 1.1 | 2.0 | 3.8 | 7.6 | 9.7 |
| 2.3 | 2.1 | 2.6 | Sales/Total Assets | 1.6 | 3.0 | 2.6 | 2.6 | 2.7 | 2.9 |
| 1.6 | 1.4 | 1.8 | | .6 | 1.2 | 2.1 | 1.8 | 1.8 | 1.9 |
| .9 | .8 | 1.1 | | .2 | .4 | .6 | 1.0 | 1.2 | 1.3 |
| .7 | .8 | .6 | % Depr., Dep., Amort./Sales | 2.6 | 1.5 | | .7 | .7 | .5 |
| (167) 1.5 | (174) 1.4 | (163) 1.1 | | (10) 17.6 | (10) 5.2 | | (17) 1.5 | (41) 1.2 | (78) .9 |
| 3.1 | 3.3 | 1.9 | | 35.3 | 15.5 | | 2.6 | 1.9 | 1.3 |
| .4 | .4 | .3 | % Officers', Directors' Owners' Comp/Sales | | | | | .5 | .2 |
| (44) 1.0 | (39) 1.2 | (44) 2.0 | | | | | | (10) 1.0 | (20) .5 |
| 3.7 | 3.6 | 2.0 | | | | | | 2.0 | 2.9 |
| 9641184M | 8607918M | 11006120M | Net Sales ($) | 7608M | 27325M | 43409M | 130779M | 889697M | 9907302M |
| 5784216M | 6227457M | 6396847M | Total Assets ($) | 24595M | 52356M | 38635M | 121371M | 595671M | 5564219M |

© RMA 2012

M = $ thousand    MM = $ million
See Pages 9 through 22 for Explanation of Ratios and Data

## Current Data Sorted by Assets

## Comparative Historical Data

### Type of Statement

| | 0-500M | 500M-2MM | 2-10MM | 10-50MM | 50-100MM | 100-250MM | Type of Statement | 4/1/07-3/31/08 ALL | 4/1/08-3/31/09 ALL |
|---|---|---|---|---|---|---|---|---|---|
| | | | | | | | Unqualified | 6 | 13 |
| | | 9 | 119 | 257 | 2 | 4 | Reviewed | 257 | 365 |
| | 1 | 11 | 57 | 36 | 19 | 9 | Compiled | 80 | 106 |
| | 5 | 20 | 15 | 6 | 3 | | Tax Returns | 51 | 47 |
| | 1 | 6 | 24 | 26 | 6 | 1 | Other | 52 | 61 |
| | | 35 (4/1-9/30/11) | 610 (10/1/11-3/31/12) | | | | | | |
| | 7 | 46 | 217 | 331 | 30 | 14 | **NUMBER OF STATEMENTS** | 446 | 592 |

### Main Data

| 0-500M | 500M-2MM | 2-10MM | 10-50MM | 50-100MM | 100-250MM | | 4/1/07-3/31/08 ALL | 4/1/08-3/31/09 ALL |
|---|---|---|---|---|---|---|---|---|
| % | % | % | % | % | % | **ASSETS** | % | % |
| | 3.9 | 1.7 | .9 | .6 | 2.4 | Cash & Equivalents | 1.9 | 1.4 |
| | 5.5 | 7.6 | 8.4 | 7.5 | 12.5 | Trade Receivables (net) | 8.6 | 7.0 |
| | 8.3 | 13.7 | 13.9 | 15.1 | 11.8 | Inventory | 14.1 | 15.4 |
| | 4.8 | 3.5 | 2.8 | 1.0 | 1.0 | All Other Current | 4.0 | 3.0 |
| | 22.5 | 26.6 | 26.0 | 24.3 | 27.7 | Total Current | 28.6 | 26.9 |
| | 60.9 | 62.0 | 63.6 | 67.9 | 59.6 | Fixed Assets (net) | 60.3 | 61.1 |
| | 5.0 | .9 | .4 | .4 | 1.7 | Intangibles (net) | 1.5 | .6 |
| | 11.6 | 10.5 | 10.0 | 7.4 | 11.1 | All Other Non-Current | 9.6 | 11.5 |
| | 100.0 | 100.0 | 100.0 | 100.0 | 100.0 | Total | 100.0 | 100.0 |
| | | | | | | **LIABILITIES** | | |
| | 10.1 | 12.7 | 13.8 | 12.1 | 9.4 | Notes Payable-Short Term | 14.5 | 15.8 |
| | 10.9 | 6.0 | 5.9 | 5.9 | 3.9 | Cur. Mat.-L.T.D. | 4.9 | 5.0 |
| | 6.3 | 6.3 | 4.2 | 4.4 | 5.0 | Trade Payables | 3.5 | 4.4 |
| | .0 | .0 | .0 | .0 | .0 | Income Taxes Payable | .1 | .0 |
| | 1.6 | 2.8 | 3.0 | 2.0 | 6.7 | All Other Current | 3.4 | 3.1 |
| | 28.8 | 27.9 | 26.9 | 24.5 | 25.0 | Total Current | 26.4 | 28.4 |
| | 89.3 | 39.6 | 37.3 | 43.5 | 41.4 | Long-Term Debt | 40.6 | 38.8 |
| | .0 | .3 | .1 | .0 | .3 | Deferred Taxes | .2 | .2 |
| | 15.1 | 5.2 | 4.0 | 3.3 | 4.0 | All Other Non-Current | 5.2 | 3.9 |
| | -33.2 | 27.0 | 31.8 | 28.7 | 29.2 | Net Worth | 27.7 | 28.8 |
| | 100.0 | 100.0 | 100.0 | 100.0 | 100.0 | Total Liabilities & Net Worth | 100.0 | 100.0 |
| | | | | | | **INCOME DATA** | | |
| | 100.0 | 100.0 | 100.0 | 100.0 | 100.0 | Net Sales | 100.0 | 100.0 |
| | | | | | | Gross Profit | | |
| | 88.8 | 86.3 | 84.4 | 84.3 | 86.5 | Operating Expenses | 81.8 | 92.1 |
| | 11.2 | 13.7 | 15.6 | 15.7 | 13.5 | Operating Profit | 18.2 | 7.9 |
| | 6.4 | 4.5 | 3.9 | 5.4 | 3.8 | All Other Expenses (net) | 6.6 | 5.1 |
| | 4.8 | 9.2 | 11.6 | 10.3 | 9.7 | Profit Before Taxes | 11.5 | 2.8 |
| | | | | | | **RATIOS** | | |
| | 2.7 | 1.4 | 1.5 | 1.6 | 1.5 | | 1.7 | 1.5 |
| | .8 | 1.0 | 1.0 | 1.0 | 1.2 | Current | 1.1 | 1.0 |
| | .2 | .6 | .7 | .7 | .7 | | .8 | .7 |
| | 1.1 | .5 | .6 | .6 | .9 | | .7 | .5 |
| | (45) .4 | (216) .3 | .3 | .3 | .5 | Quick | (444) .3 | (588) .2 |
| | .1 | .1 | .2 | .2 | .3 | | .2 | .1 |
| 0 UND | 10 35.7 | 16 22.2 | 24 15.1 | 27 13.6 | | | 17 21.2 | 13 27.2 |
| 0 UND | 19 19.3 | 29 12.8 | 31 11.7 | 42 8.7 | | Sales/Receivables | 30 12.3 | 22 16.4 |
| 18 20.2 | 31 11.6 | 56 6.5 | 45 8.1 | 78 4.7 | | 47 7.7 | 37 10.0 |
| | | | | | | Cost of Sales/Inventory | | |
| | | | | | | Cost of Sales/Payables | | |
| | 10.5 | 11.6 | 7.9 | 6.9 | 9.8 | | 6.9 | 7.8 |
| | -27.8 | -140.3 | 311.9 | 53.3 | 15.5 | Sales/Working Capital | 49.9 | -210.0 |
| | -8.6 | -10.1 | -10.2 | -7.2 | -10.1 | | -13.5 | -8.4 |
| | 8.0 | 6.9 | 8.5 | 6.2 | 8.8 | | 5.3 | 3.5 |
| | (36) 2.1 | (206) 3.6 | (324) 4.9 | 3.6 (13) | 3.1 | EBIT/Interest | (426) 3.4 | (573) 1.6 |
| | -.6 | 1.8 | 2.9 | 2.2 | 1.6 | | 1.8 | .2 |
| | | 14.2 | 5.7 | | | | 3.9 | 3.0 |
| | (11) 2.7 | (14) 2.8 | | | | Net Profit + Depr., Dep., Amort./Cur. Mat. L/T/D | (17) 2.1 | (29) 1.3 |
| | .9 | 1.0 | | | | | .4 | .6 |
| | 1.1 | 1.3 | 1.3 | 1.6 | 1.4 | | 1.2 | 1.2 |
| | 5.0 | 2.2 | 2.0 | 2.3 | 2.2 | Fixed/Worth | 2.1 | 2.0 |
| | -.6 | 5.1 | 3.5 | 5.0 | 4.9 | | 4.8 | 3.9 |
| | .9 | 1.2 | 1.1 | 1.3 | 1.3 | | 1.2 | 1.2 |
| | 10.0 | 2.3 | 2.1 | 2.5 | 1.9 | Debt/Worth | 2.3 | 2.2 |
| | -2.3 | 5.8 | 4.4 | 5.8 | 6.4 | | 5.8 | 5.0 |
| | 48.1 | 43.4 | 39.9 | 32.2 | 43.0 | | 51.2 | 17.2 |
| | (26) 12.2 | (185) 20.2 | (307) 26.7 | (27) 24.0 | (13) 26.9 | % Profit Before Taxes/Tangible Net Worth | (400) 30.7 | (536) 6.9 |
| | -4.9 | 6.7 | 14.5 | 14.6 | 13.2 | | 12.8 | -5.0 |
| | 13.3 | 12.3 | 12.9 | 8.9 | 11.1 | | 15.3 | 6.2 |
| | 1.9 | 6.1 | 8.7 | 6.9 | 6.3 | % Profit Before Taxes/Total Assets | 9.0 | 1.8 |
| | -2.8 | 2.0 | 4.9 | 4.1 | 2.6 | | 2.4 | -2.1 |
| | 6.7 | 2.3 | 1.7 | 1.1 | 2.8 | | 2.1 | 1.9 |
| | 2.6 | 1.5 | 1.1 | .9 | 1.1 | Sales/Net Fixed Assets | 1.2 | 1.2 |
| | 1.0 | 1.0 | .9 | .7 | .9 | | .9 | .8 |
| | 2.8 | 1.2 | .9 | .8 | 1.6 | | 1.0 | 1.0 |
| | 1.4 | .9 | .7 | .6 | .7 | Sales/Total Assets | .8 | .7 |
| | .7 | .7 | .6 | .5 | .5 | | .6 | .5 |
| | 4.0 | 5.5 | 6.0 | 6.5 | 2.3 | | 5.9 | 6.5 |
| | (40) 6.1 | (208) 7.7 | (315) 8.5 | (28) 8.1 | (11) 5.7 | % Depr., Dep., Amort./Sales | (422) 8.5 | (559) 8.9 |
| | 8.9 | 10.4 | 10.4 | 12.0 | 8.9 | | 11.6 | 12.2 |
| | 1.3 | .8 | .4 | | | | .5 | .6 |
| | (13) 2.2 | (51) 1.5 | (82) .6 | | | % Officers', Directors' Owners' Comp/Sales | (113) 1.0 | (153) 1.2 |
| | 3.3 | 2.9 | 1.1 | | | | 2.5 | 2.6 |
| 9497M | 91953M | 1336097M | 5531130M | 1435184M | 2581737M | Net Sales ($) | 5023836M | 10964876M |
| 1805M | 54417M | 1311515M | 7128139M | 2015287M | 2085074M | Total Assets ($) | 7351873M | 11314558M |

## Comparative Historical Data

## Current Data Sorted by Sales

| Type of Statement | | | | 0-1MM | 1-3MM | 3-5MM | 5-10MM | 10-25MM | 25MM & OVER |
|---|---|---|---|---|---|---|---|---|---|
| 17 | 13 | 14 | Unqualified | 9 | 18 | 30 | 115 | 176 | 65 |
| 354 | 448 | 413 | Reviewed | 8 | 13 | 19 | 42 | 22 | 4 |
| 103 | 102 | 108 | Compiled | 12 | 19 | 7 | 2 | 5 | 1 |
| 44 | 42 | 46 | Tax Returns | 2 | 9 | 8 | 14 | 20 | 11 |
| 68 | 80 | 64 | Other | | | 2 | | | 12 |

Periods: 4/1/09-3/31/10 ALL | 4/1/10-3/31/11 ALL | 4/1/11-3/31/12 ALL  —  35 (4/1-9/30/11) · 610 (10/1/11-3/31/12)

| 586 | 685 | 645 | NUMBER OF STATEMENTS | 31 | 59 | 66 | 173 | 223 | 93 |
|---|---|---|---|---|---|---|---|---|---|
| % | % | % | **ASSETS** | % | % | % | % | % | % |
| 1.6 | 1.5 | 1.6 | Cash & Equivalents | 5.7 | 3.0 | 2.4 | 1.2 | .7 | 1.8 |
| 5.5 | 6.2 | 8.0 | Trade Receivables (net) | 2.6 | 4.9 | 6.8 | 8.1 | 9.0 | 9.8 |
| 11.1 | 11.4 | 13.3 | Inventory | .6 | 10.1 | 11.8 | 14.1 | 15.4 | 14.4 |
| 2.6 | 2.8 | 3.0 | All Other Current | 5.5 | 2.8 | 4.2 | 3.0 | 2.7 | 2.3 |
| 20.8 | 21.9 | 26.0 | Total Current | 14.4 | 20.9 | 25.2 | 26.4 | 27.8 | 28.3 |
| 67.0 | 65.9 | 63.0 | Fixed Assets (net) | 76.3 | 67.6 | 64.3 | 60.6 | 61.2 | 63.8 |
| 1.0 | 1.2 | .9 | Intangibles (net) | .2 | 3.8 | 1.6 | .7 | .4 | .5 |
| 11.2 | 11.0 | 10.1 | All Other Non-Current | 9.1 | 7.7 | 8.9 | 12.3 | 10.6 | 7.3 |
| 100.0 | 100.0 | 100.0 | Total | 100.0 | 100.0 | 100.0 | 100.0 | 100.0 | 100.0 |
| | | | **LIABILITIES** | | | | | | |
| 14.8 | 13.8 | 12.9 | Notes Payable-Short Term | 2.2 | 10.2 | 14.2 | 12.8 | 13.9 | 15.3 |
| 6.1 | 7.0 | 6.3 | Cur. Mat.-L.T.D. | 4.0 | 8.7 | 5.8 | 6.5 | 6.3 | 5.6 |
| 4.4 | 4.4 | 5.0 | Trade Payables | 1.5 | 3.9 | 5.4 | 6.2 | 4.3 | 6.4 |
| .0 | .0 | .0 | Income Taxes Payable | .2 | .0 | .0 | .0 | .0 | .0 |
| 3.1 | 3.6 | 3.0 | All Other Current | 4.3 | 1.9 | 2.8 | 2.8 | 3.0 | 4.1 |
| 28.5 | 28.9 | 27.4 | Total Current | 12.2 | 24.8 | 28.3 | 28.3 | 27.6 | 31.3 |
| 48.7 | 45.2 | 42.4 | Long-Term Debt | 79.4 | 56.2 | 45.2 | 41.0 | 36.3 | 36.5 |
| .2 | .1 | .2 | Deferred Taxes | 1.4 | .0 | .2 | .1 | .1 | .1 |
| 4.4 | 5.6 | 5.1 | All Other Non-Current | 4.2 | 10.6 | 6.4 | 4.2 | 4.7 | 3.8 |
| 18.2 | 20.1 | 24.9 | Net Worth | 2.8 | 8.5 | 20.0 | 26.4 | 31.3 | 28.3 |
| 100.0 | 100.0 | 100.0 | Total Liabilities & Net Worth | 100.0 | 100.0 | 100.0 | 100.0 | 100.0 | 100.0 |
| | | | **INCOME DATA** | | | | | | |
| 100.0 | 100.0 | 100.0 | Net Sales | 100.0 | 100.0 | 100.0 | 100.0 | 100.0 | 100.0 |
| | | | Gross Profit | | | | | | |
| 110.1 | 88.7 | 85.5 | Operating Expenses | 63.0 | 91.5 | 90.1 | 87.6 | 84.1 | 85.4 |
| -10.1 | 11.3 | 14.5 | Operating Profit | 37.0 | 8.5 | 9.9 | 12.4 | 15.9 | 14.6 |
| 7.3 | 5.8 | 4.3 | All Other Expenses (net) | 19.9 | 4.4 | 1.9 | 3.8 | 3.3 | 4.4 |
| -17.4 | 5.4 | 10.2 | Profit Before Taxes | 17.1 | 4.1 | 8.0 | 8.6 | 12.6 | 10.2 |
| | | | **RATIOS** | | | | | | |
| 1.2 | 1.2 | 1.5 | Current | 3.9 | 2.2 | 1.6 | 1.3 | 1.5 | 1.5 |
| .8 | .8 | 1.0 | | .6 | 1.3 | .9 | .9 | 1.1 | .9 |
| .5 | .5 | .7 | | .1 | .4 | .5 | .7 | .8 | .7 |
| .4 | .4 | .6 | Quick | 3.1 | .6 | .7 | .5 | .7 | .6 |
| .2 | .2 (643) | .3 | | .3 (58) | .3 | .2 (172) | .3 | .3 | .3 |
| .1 | .1 | .2 | | .0 | .1 | .1 | .2 | .2 | .2 |
| 18  20.1 | 16  23.0 | 15  24.2 | Sales/Receivables | 0  UND | 0  UND | 0  UND | 16  23.0 | 17  22.1 | 18  20.8 |
| 24  14.9 | 23  16.0 | 26  14.2 | | 0  UND | 2  162.1 | 20  18.0 | 27  13.4 | 28  13.0 | 28  12.9 |
| 40  9.1 | 33  11.2 | 39  9.3 | | 0  UND | 30  12.2 | 33  11.2 | 35  10.4 | 56  6.5 | 44  8.3 |
| | | | Cost of Sales/Inventory | | | | | | |
| | | | Cost of Sales/Payables | | | | | | |
| 19.4 | 20.0 | 9.5 | Sales/Working Capital | 14.9 | 5.2 | 11.2 | 11.7 | 7.8 | 10.1 |
| -11.4 | -19.5 | 999.8 | | -6.6 | 18.2 | -44.4 | -48.9 | 40.2 | -60.2 |
| -4.1 | -5.6 | -10.1 | | -2.0 | -12.0 | -7.3 | -10.8 | -14.8 | -8.2 |
| -.4 | 4.4 | 7.7 | EBIT/Interest | 9.8 | 5.7 | 6.7 | 6.5 | 9.4 | 7.4 |
| (555) -2.5 | (648) 2.3 | (612) 4.2 | | (13) 2.8 | (53) 2.1 | (64) 3.0 | (171) 3.6 | (219) 5.4 | (92) 4.6 |
| -5.8 | 1.2 | 2.1 | | .7 | -.1 | 1.1 | 1.9 | 3.3 | 2.2 |
| 2.6 | 3.2 | 5.9 | Net Profit + Depr., Dep., Amort./Cur. Mat. L/T/D | | | | 13.8 | | 4.8 |
| (26) .2 | (28) 1.9 | (32) 3.0 | | | | (10) 3.4 | | (10) 3.2 | |
| -1.0 | .9 | 1.1 | | | | 1.0 | | 1.4 | |
| 1.5 | 1.5 | 1.3 | Fixed/Worth | 1.9 | 1.4 | 1.1 | 1.2 | 1.2 | 1.5 |
| 2.9 | 2.7 | 2.1 | | 5.1 | 2.2 | 2.2 | 2.2 | 1.9 | 2.1 |
| 9.8 | 7.6 | 4.7 | | -6.0 | 9.3 | 15.2 | 4.9 | 3.2 | 4.2 |
| 1.5 | 1.3 | 1.2 | Debt/Worth | 1.3 | .8 | 1.1 | 1.2 | 1.1 | 1.4 |
| 3.3 | 2.9 | 2.3 | | 5.6 | 2.1 | 2.2 | 2.3 | 2.0 | 2.3 |
| 13.5 | 11.1 | 5.6 | | -11.6 | 10.2 | 20.4 | 5.7 | 4.1 | 5.5 |
| -6.0 | 27.6 | 40.3 | % Profit Before Taxes/Tangible Net Worth | 17.8 | 33.8 | 37.6 | 39.0 | 42.3 | 43.9 |
| (474) -29.1 | (561) 13.3 | (562) 24.5 | | (21) 6.9 | (46) 8.4 | (51) 16.4 | (153) 20.4 | (206) 30.4 | (85) 27.5 |
| -71.1 | 3.7 | 10.9 | | 2.9 | -7.2 | 2.3 | 9.0 | 19.5 | 15.1 |
| -3.1 | 7.8 | 12.5 | % Profit Before Taxes/Total Assets | 5.7 | 12.5 | 12.2 | 10.8 | 14.0 | 12.6 |
| -10.0 | 3.5 | 7.7 | | 2.4 | 2.5 | 5.1 | 6.5 | 10.0 | 7.5 |
| -16.4 | .4 | 2.9 | | -.3 | -3.0 | .1 | 2.7 | 6.2 | 4.5 |
| 1.3 | 1.6 | 2.0 | Sales/Net Fixed Assets | 1.5 | 2.6 | 2.9 | 2.0 | 1.9 | 2.1 |
| .8 | 1.0 | 1.2 | | .2 | 1.3 | 1.5 | 1.3 | 1.3 | 1.2 |
| .6 | .7 | .9 | | .1 | .5 | .9 | .9 | 1.0 | .9 |
| .7 | .9 | 1.1 | Sales/Total Assets | .5 | 1.4 | 1.5 | 1.0 | 1.0 | 1.1 |
| .5 | .7 | .8 | | .1 | .9 | .9 | .8 | .8 | .8 |
| .4 | .5 | .6 | | .1 | .5 | .6 | .6 | .6 | .6 |
| 9.0 | 6.9 | 5.6 | % Depr., Dep., Amort./Sales | 5.3 | 5.0 | 5.0 | 6.1 | 5.6 | 4.3 |
| (555) 12.5 | (644) 10.1 | (607) 8.1 | | (26) 21.1 | (56) 7.6 | (64) 8.1 | (163) 7.9 | (212) 8.2 | (86) 8.1 |
| 16.4 | 12.9 | 10.4 | | 41.9 | 11.6 | 10.4 | 10.4 | 9.7 | 10.4 |
| .7 | .6 | .5 | % Officers', Directors' Owners' Comp/Sales | | 1.2 | 1.4 | .7 | .4 | .3 |
| (137) 1.5 | (146) 1.3 | (151) .9 | | (15) 3.4 | (17) 1.6 | (35) 1.1 | (62) .6 | (18) .5 | |
| 2.9 | 2.3 | 1.8 | | 5.4 | 2.5 | 1.8 | .9 | .9 | |
| 8143166M | 9943738M | 10985598M | Net Sales ($) | 14648M | 114103M | 267351M | 1271397M | 3411670M | 5906429M |
| 11505553M | 13611475M | 12596237M | Total Assets ($) | 85772M | 211112M | 355126M | 1723092M | 4516150M | 5704985M |

M = $ thousand    MM = $ million

See Pages 9 through 22 for Explanation of Ratios and Data

## Current Data Sorted by Assets

## Comparative Historical Data

| 0-500M | 500M-2MM | 2-10MM | 10-50MM | 50-100MM | 100-250MM | Type of Statement | 4/1/07-3/31/08 ALL | 4/1/08-3/31/09 ALL |
|---|---|---|---|---|---|---|---|---|
|  |  | 1 | 4 | 5 | 2 | Unqualified | 9 | 13 |
|  |  | 1 | 5 | 1 |  | Reviewed | 9 | 12 |
|  |  | 6 | 7 |  |  | Compiled | 11 | 4 |
| 3 | 8 | 6 |  | 5 |  | Tax Returns | 20 | 23 |
| 2 | 1 | 10 | 13 |  | 2 | Other | 36 | 28 |
|  |  | 11 (4/1-9/30/11) |  | 71 (10/1/11-3/31/12) |  |  |  |  |
| 5 | 9 | 24 | 29 | 11 | 4 | **NUMBER OF STATEMENTS** | 85 | 80 |
| % | % | % | % | % | % | **ASSETS** | % | % |
|  |  | 4.4 | 2.4 | 3.5 |  | Cash & Equivalents | 2.8 | 4.9 |
|  |  | 4.4 | 7.0 | 6.3 |  | Trade Receivables (net) | 9.1 | 3.2 |
|  |  | 33.1 | 40.8 | 43.2 |  | Inventory | 29.3 | 27.4 |
|  |  | 2.2 | 1.3 | 5.3 |  | All Other Current | 3.7 | 3.3 |
|  |  | 44.1 | 51.4 | 58.3 |  | Total Current | 44.8 | 38.8 |
|  |  | 43.5 | 39.1 | 34.4 |  | Fixed Assets (net) | 44.2 | 49.5 |
|  |  | .1 | 4.2 | 2.3 |  | Intangibles (net) | .4 | .3 |
|  |  | 12.2 | 5.3 | 5.0 |  | All Other Non-Current | 10.5 | 11.5 |
|  |  | 100.0 | 100.0 | 100.0 |  | Total | 100.0 | 100.0 |
|  |  |  |  |  |  | **LIABILITIES** |  |  |
|  |  | 26.9 | 18.5 | 23.5 |  | Notes Payable-Short Term | 17.6 | 16.9 |
|  |  | 7.1 | 3.7 | 3.1 |  | Cur. Mat.-L.T.D. | 5.0 | 4.0 |
|  |  | 7.3 | 6.2 | 7.0 |  | Trade Payables | 5.8 | 3.8 |
|  |  | .8 | .2 | .0 |  | Income Taxes Payable | .1 | .1 |
|  |  | 4.9 | 6.1 | 4.6 |  | All Other Current | 4.6 | 6.6 |
|  |  | 47.1 | 34.6 | 38.1 |  | Total Current | 33.2 | 31.3 |
|  |  | 30.6 | 23.3 | 19.1 |  | Long-Term Debt | 35.6 | 40.0 |
|  |  | .2 | .1 | .1 |  | Deferred Taxes | .4 | .1 |
|  |  | 5.1 | 1.6 | .5 |  | All Other Non-Current | 4.5 | 4.2 |
|  |  | 17.0 | 40.3 | 42.2 |  | Net Worth | 26.2 | 24.4 |
|  |  | 100.0 | 100.0 | 100.0 |  | Total Liabilities & Net Worth | 100.0 | 100.0 |
|  |  |  |  |  |  | **INCOME DATA** |  |  |
|  |  | 100.0 | 100.0 | 100.0 |  | Net Sales | 100.0 | 100.0 |
|  |  |  |  |  |  | Gross Profit |  |  |
|  |  | 88.9 | 91.9 | 90.9 |  | Operating Expenses | 97.2 | 97.0 |
|  |  | 11.1 | 8.1 | 9.1 |  | Operating Profit | 2.8 | 3.0 |
|  |  | 1.6 | .2 | -.8 |  | All Other Expenses (net) | 2.1 | 3.4 |
|  |  | 9.5 | 7.9 | 9.9 |  | Profit Before Taxes | .7 | -.4 |
|  |  |  |  |  |  | **RATIOS** |  |  |
|  |  | 2.1 | 2.6 | 2.5 |  |  | 2.3 | 2.1 |
|  |  | 1.1 | 1.5 | 1.3 |  | Current | 1.3 | 1.3 |
|  |  | .9 | 1.1 | 1.2 |  |  | .8 | .8 |
|  |  | .6 | .6 | .8 |  |  | .6 | .6 |
|  |  | .2 | .2 | .2 |  | Quick | (83) .2 | (79) .2 |
|  |  | .1 | .1 | .1 |  |  | .1 | .1 |
| 0 UND | 4 87.2 | 4 84.0 |  |  |  |  | 0 UND | 0 UND |
| 5 74.1 | 8 46.0 | 5 70.7 |  |  |  | Sales/Receivables | 7 49.0 | 4 100.2 |
| 21 17.8 | 16 23.5 | 21 17.7 |  |  |  |  | 26 13.9 | 18 20.5 |
|  |  |  |  |  |  | Cost of Sales/Inventory |  |  |
|  |  |  |  |  |  | Cost of Sales/Payables |  |  |
|  |  | 7.4 | 4.7 | 4.4 |  |  | 4.6 | 4.8 |
|  |  | 28.7 | 9.2 | 10.5 |  | Sales/Working Capital | 15.8 | 15.5 |
|  |  | -42.8 | 339.7 | 30.4 |  |  | -19.2 | -21.6 |
|  |  | 11.4 | 8.2 | 13.8 |  |  | 5.6 | 3.6 |
|  | (22) | 4.4 | 5.2 | 9.2 |  | EBIT/Interest | (80) 1.3 | (72) .4 |
|  |  | 2.1 | 2.5 | 5.4 |  |  | -1.2 | -3.6 |
|  |  |  |  |  |  | Net Profit + Depr., Dep., Amort./Cur. Mat. L/T/D |  |  |
|  |  | .4 | .6 | .5 |  |  | .5 | .8 |
|  |  | 1.2 | 1.3 | .9 |  | Fixed/Worth | 1.1 | 1.4 |
|  |  | NM | 3.6 | 1.1 |  |  | 3.3 | 5.0 |
|  |  | .8 | .5 | 1.0 |  |  | .9 | .8 |
|  |  | 1.7 | 1.2 | 1.4 |  | Debt/Worth | 1.7 | 2.2 |
|  |  | -11.9 | 7.0 | 3.0 |  |  | 6.6 | 12.4 |
|  |  | 43.8 | 43.3 | 68.8 |  |  | 21.1 | 15.2 |
|  | (17) | 26.4 | (23) 18.0 | 37.4 |  | % Profit Before Taxes/Tangible Net Worth | (76) 6.6 | (68) .0 |
|  |  | 16.7 | 8.6 | 16.2 |  |  | -15.5 | -35.8 |
|  |  | 18.9 | 15.7 | 19.1 |  |  | 8.6 | 5.6 |
|  |  | 9.6 | 6.8 | 14.1 |  | % Profit Before Taxes/Total Assets | 1.0 | -.6 |
|  |  | 4.9 | 4.0 | 5.8 |  |  | -6.6 | -12.4 |
|  |  | 15.0 | 19.5 | 9.5 |  |  | 13.0 | 6.5 |
|  |  | 3.6 | 3.8 | 5.9 |  | Sales/Net Fixed Assets | 3.1 | 2.3 |
|  |  | 1.3 | 1.3 | 2.1 |  |  | 1.6 | 1.1 |
|  |  | 2.7 | 2.2 | 2.5 |  |  | 2.0 | 1.7 |
|  |  | 1.3 | 1.4 | 1.1 |  | Sales/Total Assets | 1.2 | 1.2 |
|  |  | .9 | .8 | 1.1 |  |  | .8 | .8 |
|  |  | 2.2 | 1.8 | 1.0 |  |  | 1.8 | 2.6 |
|  | (19) | 5.3 | (25) 4.3 | 1.4 |  | % Depr., Dep., Amort./Sales | (62) 4.1 | (64) 6.0 |
|  |  | 10.4 | 6.1 | 3.7 |  |  | 11.2 | 18.8 |
|  |  |  |  |  |  | % Officers', Directors' Owners' Comp/Sales | .5 | .7 |
|  |  |  |  |  |  |  | (17) 1.3 | (14) 1.7 |
|  |  |  |  |  |  |  | 4.5 | 5.0 |
| 3154M | 15777M | 199359M | 1179394M | 1476552M | 575691M | Net Sales ($) | 2739630M | 2029348M |
| 1440M | 8653M | 107807M | 616184M | 828748M | 642150M | Total Assets ($) | 1961762M | 1808970M |

M = $ thousand    MM = $ million
See Pages 9 through 22 for Explanation of Ratios and Data

## Comparative Historical Data | Current Data Sorted by Sales

| Type of Statement | | | | | | | | | |
|---|---|---|---|---|---|---|---|---|---|
| Unqualified | 9 | 10 | 12 | | | | 1 | | 11 |
| Reviewed | 8 | 9 | 7 | | | 1 | 1 | | 5 |
| Compiled | 13 | 9 | 13 | | 1 | 1 | 6 | 4 | 1 |
| Tax Returns | 18 | 18 | 17 | 4 | 10 | 1 | 2 | | |
| Other | 23 | 25 | 33 | 2 | 3 | 1 | 3 | 6 | 18 |
| | 4/1/09-3/31/10 ALL | 4/1/10-3/31/11 ALL | 4/1/11-3/31/12 ALL | 0-1MM | 1-3MM | 3-5MM | 5-10MM | 10-25MM | 25MM & OVER |
| | | | | | 11 (4/1-9/30/11) | | 71 (10/1/11-3/31/12) | | |
| NUMBER OF STATEMENTS | 71 | 71 | 82 | 6 | 14 | 4 | 13 | 10 | 35 |
| | % | % | % | % | % | % | % | % | % |
| **ASSETS** | | | | | | | | | |
| Cash & Equivalents | 3.8 | 3.7 | 3.4 | | 3.1 | | 3.9 | .8 | 3.3 |
| Trade Receivables (net) | 6.1 | 5.3 | 5.6 | | 1.1 | | 4.7 | 3.8 | 8.6 |
| Inventory | 30.3 | 32.1 | 32.2 | | 6.1 | | 26.0 | 56.1 | 45.2 |
| All Other Current | 2.5 | 3.7 | 2.3 | | .7 | | .8 | 2.9 | 3.6 |
| Total Current | 42.8 | 44.9 | 43.4 | | 11.0 | | 35.4 | 63.7 | 60.6 |
| Fixed Assets (net) | 48.8 | 47.2 | 45.7 | | 72.6 | | 58.6 | 29.7 | 28.1 |
| Intangibles (net) | 2.1 | 1.1 | 1.9 | | .6 | | .1 | .1 | 4.2 |
| All Other Non-Current | 6.3 | 6.9 | 9.0 | | 15.9 | | 5.9 | 6.6 | 7.2 |
| Total | 100.0 | 100.0 | 100.0 | | 100.0 | | 100.0 | 100.0 | 100.0 |
| **LIABILITIES** | | | | | | | | | |
| Notes Payable-Short Term | 28.4 | 25.7 | 21.6 | | 35.9 | | 8.6 | 36.6 | 21.4 |
| Cur. Mat.-L.T.D. | 5.2 | 5.1 | 5.5 | | 4.3 | | 9.0 | 5.8 | 3.5 |
| Trade Payables | 8.0 | 5.1 | 6.1 | | 1.0 | | 7.2 | 11.7 | 7.1 |
| Income Taxes Payable | .2 | .1 | .3 | | .0 | | .0 | .4 | .0 |
| All Other Current | 4.3 | 4.1 | 8.1 | | 2.2 | | 6.9 | 3.8 | 6.4 |
| Total Current | 46.2 | 40.1 | 41.7 | | 43.4 | | 31.7 | 58.3 | 38.4 |
| Long-Term Debt | 40.8 | 34.9 | 30.0 | | 56.6 | | 28.9 | 24.4 | 18.4 |
| Deferred Taxes | .4 | .2 | .1 | | .0 | | .0 | .4 | .0 |
| All Other Non-Current | 4.7 | 4.6 | 3.1 | | 5.0 | | .0 | 13.2 | 1.6 |
| Net Worth | 8.0 | 20.2 | 25.1 | | -5.0 | | 39.4 | 3.7 | 41.6 |
| Total Liabilities & Net Worth | 100.0 | 100.0 | 100.0 | | 100.0 | | 100.0 | 100.0 | 100.0 |
| **INCOME DATA** | | | | | | | | | |
| Net Sales | 100.0 | 100.0 | 100.0 | | 100.0 | | 100.0 | 100.0 | 100.0 |
| Gross Profit | | | | | | | | | |
| Operating Expenses | 102.9 | 91.4 | 90.9 | | 90.0 | | 90.1 | 93.9 | 91.9 |
| Operating Profit | -2.9 | 8.6 | 9.1 | | 10.0 | | 9.9 | 6.1 | 8.1 |
| All Other Expenses (net) | 2.4 | 1.6 | .5 | | 1.5 | | 1.3 | .3 | -1.1 |
| Profit Before Taxes | -5.3 | 7.0 | 8.6 | | 8.5 | | 8.6 | 5.7 | 9.3 |
| **RATIOS** | | | | | | | | | |
| Current | 1.6 | 2.1 | 2.3 | | 1.4 | | 4.0 | 1.7 | 2.6 |
| | 1.2 | 1.3 | 1.3 | | .7 | | 1.3 | 1.3 | 1.5 |
| | .6 | .8 | .8 | | .0 | | .7 | .7 | 1.2 |
| Quick | .5 | .4 | .5 | | .5 | | .4 | .1 | .7 |
| | .2 | .1 | .2 | | .1 | | .3 | .1 | .3 |
| | .1 | .0 | .1 | | .0 | | .1 | .0 | .1 |
| Sales/Receivables | 0 UND | 0 UND | 0 UND | | 0 UND | | 0 UND | 0 UND | 5 70.7 |
| | 7 53.8 | 4 92.8 | 6 64.9 | | 0 UND | | 13 28.9 | 5 74.1 | 8 46.0 |
| | 19 19.4 | 18 20.5 | 18 20.1 | | 0 772.3 | | 22 16.4 | 6 58.4 | 26 13.8 |
| Cost of Sales/Inventory | | | | | | | | | |
| | | | | | | | | | |
| | | | | | | | | | |
| Cost of Sales/Payables | | | | | | | | | |
| | | | | | | | | | |
| | | | | | | | | | |
| Sales/Working Capital | 7.6 | 5.5 | 5.4 | | 16.1 | | 5.8 | 6.5 | 4.4 |
| | 27.8 | 13.8 | 11.7 | | -59.8 | | 10.3 | 19.8 | 7.7 |
| | -13.6 | -16.7 | -28.4 | | -4.5 | | -21.8 | -11.2 | 29.8 |
| EBIT/Interest | 1.9 | 8.2 | 11.6 | | 7.5 | | 11.9 | 13.0 | 13.8 |
| | (63) -.1 | (67) 3.5 | (79) 5.2 | | (13) 3.8 | | 4.6 | 4.0 | 6.8 |
| | -6.4 | 1.2 | 2.5 | | .1 | | 1.9 | 2.1 | 3.5 |
| Net Profit + Depr., Dep., Amort./Cur. Mat. L/T/D | | | (12) 6.6 | | | | | | |
| | | | 3.9 | | | | | | |
| | | | 1.2 | | | | | | |
| Fixed/Worth | .9 | .7 | .5 | | 2.1 | | .8 | .0 | .4 |
| | 1.8 | 1.3 | 1.3 | | NM | | 1.2 | 1.0 | .8 |
| | -7.1 | -7.4 | NM | | -2.0 | | 1.9 | -320.9 | 2.2 |
| Debt/Worth | 1.3 | 1.0 | .7 | | 1.2 | | .6 | 1.5 | .5 |
| | 3.6 | 2.3 | 1.6 | | NM | | 1.0 | 17.0 | 1.2 |
| | -18.3 | -10.7 | -360.3 | | -4.8 | | 1.7 | -3.4 | 3.8 |
| % Profit Before Taxes/Tangible Net Worth | 16.1 | 39.4 | 43.0 | | | | 25.3 | | 54.8 |
| | (51) -1.0 | (50) 18.7 | (61) 22.0 | | | | (11) 14.1 | | (30) 37.4 |
| | -55.9 | 5.6 | 12.1 | | | | 5.6 | | 15.9 |
| % Profit Before Taxes/Total Assets | 3.0 | 14.5 | 18.9 | | 12.4 | | 15.2 | 19.4 | 19.1 |
| | -1.5 | 7.1 | 9.5 | | 7.4 | | 9.6 | 11.4 | 11.3 |
| | -20.5 | .1 | 4.3 | | -.7 | | 2.9 | 3.6 | 4.7 |
| Sales/Net Fixed Assets | 8.6 | 7.3 | 10.5 | | 3.4 | | 5.3 | UND | 18.4 |
| | 3.1 | 2.9 | 3.6 | | 2.5 | | 1.3 | 14.6 | 7.0 |
| | 1.2 | 1.0 | 1.4 | | .9 | | .9 | 1.7 | 2.9 |
| Sales/Total Assets | 2.1 | 2.0 | 2.5 | | 2.1 | | 2.6 | 3.6 | 2.2 |
| | 1.3 | 1.2 | 1.4 | | 1.2 | | 1.2 | 2.8 | 1.7 |
| | .7 | .7 | .9 | | .7 | | .6 | 1.4 | 1.1 |
| % Depr., Dep., Amort./Sales | 2.2 | 2.6 | 2.0 | | 5.6 | | 2.7 | | 1.1 |
| | (59) 5.0 | (60) 5.2 | (70) 4.4 | | (12) 8.3 | | 6.5 | | (30) 2.5 |
| | 11.9 | 8.7 | 8.8 | | 18.1 | | 9.7 | | 4.3 |
| % Officers', Directors' Owners' Comp/Sales | .6 | .5 | .7 | | | | | | |
| | (15) 1.5 | (15) 2.1 | (14) 3.5 | | | | | | |
| | 5.5 | 4.3 | 6.1 | | | | | | |
| Net Sales ($) | 2009538M | 1780641M | 3449927M | 3194M | 25956M | 14414M | 94127M | 180285M | 3131951M |
| Total Assets ($) | 1549897M | 1473391M | 2204982M | 3125M | 32493M | 16355M | 108924M | 99774M | 1944311M |

M = $ thousand    MM = $ million
See Pages 9 through 22 for Explanation of Ratios and Data

# AGRICULTURE—Chicken Egg Production  NAICS 112310

| Current Data Sorted by Assets | | | | | | | Comparative Historical Data | |
|---|---|---|---|---|---|---|---|---|
| | | | | | | **Type of Statement** | | |
| 1 | | | 1 | 9 | 3 | Unqualified | 10 | 14 |
| | | | 5 | 1 | | Reviewed | 4 | 6 |
| 1 | 1 | 4 | 1 | | | Compiled | 5 | 5 |
| 2 | 5 | 2 | 1 | | | Tax Returns | 7 | 11 |
| | | 3 | 8 | | | Other | 15 | 8 |
| | 10 (4/1-9/30/11) | | | 38 (10/1/11-3/31/12) | | | 4/1/07-3/31/08 | 4/1/08-3/31/09 |
| 0-500M | 500M-2MM | 2-10MM | 10-50MM | 50-100MM | 100-250MM | | ALL | ALL |
| 4 | 6 | 9 | 16 | 10 | 3 | **NUMBER OF STATEMENTS** | 41 | 44 |
| % | % | % | % | % | % | **ASSETS** | % | % |
| | | | 9.5 | 5.0 | | Cash & Equivalents | 12.6 | 17.5 |
| | | | 17.8 | 14.9 | | Trade Receivables (net) | 17.2 | 14.0 |
| | | | 14.1 | 25.1 | | Inventory | 17.3 | 16.7 |
| | | | 3.9 | .8 | | All Other Current | 3.3 | 2.7 |
| | | | 45.4 | 45.7 | | Total Current | 50.3 | 51.0 |
| | | | 44.9 | 48.3 | | Fixed Assets (net) | 42.6 | 43.0 |
| | | | .6 | .8 | | Intangibles (net) | 2.6 | 1.3 |
| | | | 9.1 | 5.2 | | All Other Non-Current | 4.5 | 4.8 |
| | | | 100.0 | 100.0 | | Total | 100.0 | 100.0 |
| | | | | | | **LIABILITIES** | | |
| | | | 9.4 | 7.6 | | Notes Payable-Short Term | 8.2 | 6.9 |
| | | | 2.0 | 3.6 | | Cur. Mat.-L.T.D. | 4.3 | 5.6 |
| | | | 10.4 | 7.9 | | Trade Payables | 11.2 | 10.5 |
| | | | .0 | 1.3 | | Income Taxes Payable | .8 | .7 |
| | | | 6.3 | 4.6 | | All Other Current | 10.9 | 10.2 |
| | | | 28.1 | 25.1 | | Total Current | 35.5 | 33.9 |
| | | | 13.7 | 19.1 | | Long-Term Debt | 21.6 | 23.7 |
| | | | 1.0 | 4.5 | | Deferred Taxes | .4 | 1.0 |
| | | | 1.5 | 2.6 | | All Other Non-Current | 1.4 | 2.0 |
| | | | 55.7 | 48.8 | | Net Worth | 41.1 | 39.5 |
| | | | 100.0 | 100.0 | | Total Liabilities & Net Worth | 100.0 | 100.0 |
| | | | | | | **INCOME DATA** | | |
| | | | 100.0 | 100.0 | | Net Sales | 100.0 | 100.0 |
| | | | | | | Gross Profit | | |
| | | | 93.8 | 98.1 | | Operating Expenses | 88.0 | 86.8 |
| | | | 6.2 | 1.9 | | Operating Profit | 12.0 | 13.2 |
| | | | .6 | 1.0 | | All Other Expenses (net) | 1.8 | 2.5 |
| | | | 5.6 | 1.0 | | Profit Before Taxes | 10.2 | 10.7 |
| | | | | | | **RATIOS** | | |
| | | | 3.7 | 3.0 | | | 3.3 | 3.8 |
| | | | 2.1 | 1.7 | | Current | 1.3 | 1.8 |
| | | | .9 | 1.3 | | | .8 | 1.1 |
| | | | 2.4 | 1.6 | | | 1.9 | 2.0 |
| | | | 1.1 | .8 | | Quick | .7 | 1.0 |
| | | | .3 | .4 | | | .4 | .5 |
| | | 19 | 19.6 | 22 16.8 | | | 22 16.8 | 0 UND |
| | | 28 | 13.0 | 29 12.7 | | Sales/Receivables | 30 12.4 | 21 17.6 |
| | | 51 | 7.2 | 35 10.3 | | | 36 10.1 | 26 13.8 |
| | | | | | | Cost of Sales/Inventory | | |
| | | | | | | Cost of Sales/Payables | | |
| | | | 4.7 | 4.5 | | | 5.4 | 5.0 |
| | | | 8.6 | 9.5 | | Sales/Working Capital | 14.2 | 10.1 |
| | | | -51.7 | 26.7 | | | -23.2 | 168.2 |
| | | | 22.7 | 6.8 | | | 14.1 | 32.7 |
| | | (13) | 6.4 | 3.4 | | EBIT/Interest | (33) 5.7 | (35) 10.2 |
| | | | 1.0 | .1 | | | 2.4 | 1.9 |
| | | | | | | Net Profit + Depr., Dep., Amort./Cur. Mat. L/T/D | | |
| | | | .4 | .6 | | | .5 | .4 |
| | | | .7 | 1.0 | | Fixed/Worth | .9 | .8 |
| | | | 1.0 | 1.9 | | | 3.5 | 2.0 |
| | | | .2 | .4 | | | .7 | .3 |
| | | | .9 | 1.3 | | Debt/Worth | 2.4 | 1.1 |
| | | | 1.5 | 2.5 | | | 5.0 | 4.5 |
| | | | 25.1 | 12.9 | | % Profit Before Taxes/Tangible | 69.6 | 65.0 |
| | | | 8.7 | 5.0 | | Net Worth | (38) 45.2 | (40) 41.0 |
| | | | -1.6 | -4.1 | | | 16.6 | 10.5 |
| | | | 16.9 | 7.0 | | % Profit Before Taxes/Total | 31.5 | 41.4 |
| | | | 5.9 | 2.3 | | Assets | 12.3 | 14.7 |
| | | | -.5 | -1.4 | | | 4.5 | 1.8 |
| | | | 10.3 | 5.5 | | | 13.3 | 14.5 |
| | | | 3.0 | 3.8 | | Sales/Net Fixed Assets | 4.6 | 5.0 |
| | | | 2.1 | 2.7 | | | 2.7 | 2.3 |
| | | | 2.8 | 2.0 | | | 2.5 | 2.9 |
| | | | 1.5 | 1.7 | | Sales/Total Assets | 1.8 | 1.8 |
| | | | 1.1 | 1.4 | | | 1.4 | 1.2 |
| | | | .8 | | | | 1.5 | 1.5 |
| | | (11) | 5.7 | | | % Depr., Dep., Amort./Sales | (35) 2.7 | (34) 3.6 |
| | | | 13.3 | | | | 6.1 | 8.8 |
| | | | | | | % Officers', Directors' Owners' Comp/Sales | | |
| 904M | 16156M | 179240M | 693694M | 1376893M | 1055761M | Net Sales ($) | 2306692M | 3274193M |
| 554M | 6682M | 43001M | 380986M | 785779M | 519540M | Total Assets ($) | 1330454M | 1773839M |

M = $ thousand    MM = $ million
See Pages 9 through 22 for Explanation of Ratios and Data

## Comparative Historical Data | Current Data Sorted by Sales

| 4/1/09-3/31/10 ALL | 4/1/10-3/31/11 ALL | 4/1/11-3/31/12 ALL | Type of Statement | 0-1MM | 1-3MM | 3-5MM | 5-10MM | 10-25MM | 25MM & OVER |
|---|---|---|---|---|---|---|---|---|---|
| 14 | 14 | 14 | Unqualified |  |  |  | 1 | 1 | 12 |
| 7 | 6 | 6 | Reviewed |  |  |  | 2 | 2 | 4 |
| 5 | 7 | 6 | Compiled |  | 1 | 1 | 2 | 3 | 2 |
| 12 | 12 | 9 | Tax Returns | 5 |  |  |  | 3 | 1 |
| 15 | 16 | 13 | Other | 2 |  |  |  | 3 | 8 |
|  |  |  | 10 (4/1-9/30/11) | | | | 38 (10/1/11-3/31/12) | | |
| 53 | 55 | 48 | **NUMBER OF STATEMENTS** | 8 | 1 | 1 | 2 | 9 | 27 |
| % | % | % | **ASSETS** | % | % | % | % | % | % |
| 9.8 | 10.6 | 7.8 | Cash & Equivalents |  |  |  |  |  | 7.6 |
| 14.1 | 14.5 | 15.3 | Trade Receivables (net) |  |  |  |  |  | 20.9 |
| 16.9 | 15.8 | 17.3 | Inventory |  |  |  |  |  | 20.3 |
| 1.9 | 1.2 | 2.0 | All Other Current |  |  |  |  |  | 2.5 |
| 42.6 | 42.1 | 42.3 | Total Current |  |  |  |  |  | 51.4 |
| 48.8 | 51.0 | 50.2 | Fixed Assets (net) |  |  |  |  |  | 42.5 |
| 1.5 | 1.8 | 1.4 | Intangibles (net) |  |  |  |  |  | .8 |
| 7.1 | 5.1 | 6.0 | All Other Non-Current |  |  |  |  |  | 5.2 |
| 100.0 | 100.0 | 100.0 | Total |  |  |  |  |  | 100.0 |
|  |  |  | **LIABILITIES** |  |  |  |  |  |  |
| 5.1 | 6.0 | 8.7 | Notes Payable-Short Term |  |  |  |  |  | 6.0 |
| 3.9 | 3.6 | 2.4 | Cur. Mat.-L.T.D. |  |  |  |  |  | 2.0 |
| 10.3 | 8.1 | 10.3 | Trade Payables |  |  |  |  |  | 16.0 |
| .6 | .7 | .3 | Income Taxes Payable |  |  |  |  |  | .5 |
| 5.3 | 7.3 | 6.9 | All Other Current |  |  |  |  |  | 8.1 |
| 25.1 | 25.8 | 28.6 | Total Current |  |  |  |  |  | 32.6 |
| 25.0 | 25.1 | 25.8 | Long-Term Debt |  |  |  |  |  | 11.8 |
| 1.3 | .7 | 1.3 | Deferred Taxes |  |  |  |  |  | 1.7 |
| 7.8 | 3.1 | 1.3 | All Other Non-Current |  |  |  |  |  | 1.8 |
| 40.8 | 45.4 | 42.9 | Net Worth |  |  |  |  |  | 52.0 |
| 100.0 | 100.0 | 100.0 | Total Liabilities & Net Worth |  |  |  |  |  | 100.0 |
|  |  |  | **INCOME DATA** |  |  |  |  |  |  |
| 100.0 | 100.0 | 100.0 | Net Sales |  |  |  |  |  | 100.0 |
|  |  |  | Gross Profit |  |  |  |  |  | 96.8 |
| 93.0 | 92.4 | 95.4 | Operating Expenses |  |  |  |  |  | 3.2 |
| 7.0 | 7.6 | 4.6 | Operating Profit |  |  |  |  |  | .5 |
| 1.5 | 2.0 | 2.6 | All Other Expenses (net) |  |  |  |  |  | 2.7 |
| 5.5 | 5.6 | 1.9 | Profit Before Taxes |  |  |  |  |  |  |
|  |  |  | **RATIOS** |  |  |  |  |  |  |
| 3.0 | 4.2 | 3.0 | | | | | | | 3.1 |
| 2.0 | 1.9 | 2.0 | Current | | | | | | 2.1 |
| .9 | .9 | .8 | | | | | | | 1.3 |
| 1.5 | 2.2 | 1.9 | | | | | | | 1.9 |
| .9 | .9 | .9 | Quick | | | | | | .9 |
| .4 | .4 | .3 | | | | | | | .5 |
| 0 UND | 1 297.1 | 7 49.8 | | | | | | 21 | 17.5 |
| 23 15.9 | 22 16.8 | 23 15.8 | Sales/Receivables | | | | | 28 | 13.0 |
| 31 11.9 | 36 10.1 | 34 10.8 | | | | | | 35 | 10.4 |
|  |  |  | Cost of Sales/Inventory |  |  |  |  |  |  |
|  |  |  | Cost of Sales/Payables |  |  |  |  |  |  |
| 5.6 | 6.0 | 5.6 | | | | | | | 6.6 |
| 9.1 | 10.4 | 11.5 | Sales/Working Capital | | | | | | 9.4 |
| -120.6 | -42.8 | -45.1 | | | | | | | 14.4 |
|  |  |  | | | | | | | 19.6 |
| 29.0 | 12.6 | 17.3 | EBIT/Interest | | | | | (23) | 6.2 |
| (41) 4.2 | (43) 5.6 | (38) 5.3 | | | | | | | .8 |
| 1.8 | 1.1 | .7 | | | | | | | |
| 5.0 |  |  | Net Profit + Depr., Dep., | | | | | | |
| (10) 1.9 |  |  | Amort./Cur. Mat. L/T/D | | | | | | |
| 1.1 |  |  | | | | | | | .5 |
| .5 | .6 | .6 | | | | | | | .7 |
| 1.0 | 1.0 | .9 | Fixed/Worth | | | | | | 1.7 |
| 2.5 | 2.9 | 3.0 | | | | | | | .2 |
| .3 | .3 | .3 | | | | | | | .7 |
| 1.2 | 1.2 | 1.2 | Debt/Worth | | | | | | 2.5 |
| 2.9 | 3.1 | 4.1 | | | | | | | 24.2 |
| 24.3 | 34.6 | 28.3 | % Profit Before Taxes/Tangible | | | | | (26) | 8.7 |
| (48) 13.3 | (49) 16.9 | (42) 12.9 | Net Worth | | | | | | -2.8 |
| 5.5 | 4.6 | -1.6 | | | | | | | 15.0 |
| 13.9 | 15.3 | 14.7 | % Profit Before Taxes/Total | | | | | | 4.6 |
| 6.5 | 8.1 | 5.4 | Assets | | | | | | -.7 |
| 1.3 | 1.4 | -1.3 | | | | | | | 11.3 |
| 10.4 | 7.6 | 7.7 | | | | | | | 4.2 |
| 3.5 | 3.8 | 3.7 | Sales/Net Fixed Assets | | | | | | 3.0 |
| 1.6 | 1.9 | 2.2 | | | | | | | 3.3 |
| 3.1 | 3.0 | 3.1 | | | | | | | 2.0 |
| 1.6 | 1.6 | 1.8 | Sales/Total Assets | | | | | | 1.5 |
| 1.0 | 1.0 | 1.3 | | | | | | | .9 |
| 1.9 | 2.2 | 1.0 | | | | | | (17) | 3.1 |
| (44) 4.5 | (43) 4.5 | (35) 3.7 | % Depr., Dep., Amort./Sales | | | | | | 5.3 |
| 10.1 | 8.6 | 9.9 | | | | | | | |
| .8 |  |  | % Officers', Directors' | | | | | | |
| (10) 1.5 |  |  | Owners' Comp/Sales | | | | | | |
| 2.5 |  |  | | | | | | | |
| 2978291M | 3258831M | 3322648M | Net Sales ($) | 2218M | 1459M | 4476M | 12518M | 154829M | 3147148M |
| 1784788M | 1992773M | 1736542M | Total Assets ($) | 4518M | 1883M | 2485M | 4331M | 126141M | 1597184M |

© RMA 2012

M = $ thousand    MM = $ million
See Pages 9 through 22 for Explanation of Ratios and Data

## Current Data Sorted by Assets     Comparative Historical Data

**Type of Statement**

| | 0-500M | 500M-2MM | 2-10MM | 10-50MM | 50-100MM | 100-250MM | | 4/1/07-3/31/08 ALL | 4/1/08-3/31/09 ALL |
|---|---|---|---|---|---|---|---|---|---|
| Unqualified | | | | | | | | 1 | |
| Reviewed | | | | | | | | 1 | 1 |
| Compiled | 1 | 1 | 2 | | | | | 4 | 3 |
| Tax Returns | 4 | 5 | 4 | 1 | 1 | | | 10 | 8 |
| Other | 1 | 5 | 11 | 5 | 1 | | | 5 | 11 |
| | | 2 (4/1-9/30/11) | | 40 (10/1/11-3/31/12) | | | | | |
| NUMBER OF STATEMENTS | 6 | 11 | 17 | 6 | 2 | | | 21 | 23 |

*(Columns 10-50MM, 50-100MM, 100-250MM: DATA NOT AVAILABLE for Assets, Liabilities, Income Data and upper Ratios)*

| | 0-500M % | 500M-2MM % | 2-10MM % | 10-50MM % | 50-100MM % | 100-250MM % | | 4/1/07-3/31/08 ALL % | 4/1/08-3/31/09 ALL % |
|---|---|---|---|---|---|---|---|---|---|
| **ASSETS** | | | | | | | | | |
| Cash & Equivalents | | 15.5 | 8.2 | | | | | 18.5 | 12.9 |
| Trade Receivables (net) | | 11.0 | 12.3 | | | | | 15.5 | 17.8 |
| Inventory | | 11.5 | 7.5 | | | | | 7.1 | 2.0 |
| All Other Current | | 21.1 | 12.7 | | | | | 2.1 | 2.0 |
| Total Current | | 59.1 | 40.7 | | | | | 43.1 | 34.7 |
| Fixed Assets (net) | | 29.3 | 38.6 | | | | | 41.0 | 49.2 |
| Intangibles (net) | | 1.2 | 10.9 | | | | | 3.3 | .1 |
| All Other Non-Current | | 10.5 | 9.9 | | | | | 12.7 | 16.1 |
| Total | | 100.0 | 100.0 | | | | | 100.0 | 100.0 |
| **LIABILITIES** | | | | | | | | | |
| Notes Payable-Short Term | | 28.7 | 17.4 | | | | | 9.2 | 30.3 |
| Cur. Mat.-L.T.D. | | 10.9 | 3.7 | | | | | 13.0 | 4.4 |
| Trade Payables | | 8.0 | 8.7 | | | | | 7.7 | 21.5 |
| Income Taxes Payable | | .0 | .0 | | | | | .0 | .1 |
| All Other Current | | 23.3 | 12.8 | | | | | 20.5 | 35.4 |
| Total Current | | 70.9 | 42.7 | | | | | 50.4 | 91.7 |
| Long-Term Debt | | 33.6 | 37.7 | | | | | 34.7 | 25.7 |
| Deferred Taxes | | .0 | .0 | | | | | .0 | .2 |
| All Other Non-Current | | 8.8 | 18.8 | | | | | 15.0 | 12.8 |
| Net Worth | | -13.2 | .8 | | | | | -.1 | -30.4 |
| Total Liabilties & Net Worth | | 100.0 | 100.0 | | | | | 100.0 | 100.0 |
| **INCOME DATA** | | | | | | | | | |
| Net Sales | | 100.0 | 100.0 | | | | | 100.0 | 100.0 |
| Gross Profit | | | | | | | | | |
| Operating Expenses | | 87.5 | 90.6 | | | | | 91.0 | 103.2 |
| Operating Profit | | 12.5 | 9.4 | | | | | 9.0 | -3.2 |
| All Other Expenses (net) | | .5 | 3.9 | | | | | 3.6 | 3.4 |
| Profit Before Taxes | | 12.0 | 5.5 | | | | | 5.4 | -6.7 |
| **RATIOS** | | | | | | | | | |
| Current | | 2.5 / 1.5 / .3 | 1.8 / 1.2 / .4 | | | | | 5.4 / 1.2 / .3 | 1.2 / .4 / .1 |
| Quick | | 1.1 / .3 / .1 | 1.1 / .4 / .1 | | | | | 5.4 / .5 / .1 | 1.1 / .3 / .1 |
| Sales/Receivables | 0 UND / 11 34.2 / 45 8.1 | | 0 UND / 14 26.1 / 40 9.1 | | | | | 0 UND / 17 20.9 / 67 5.5 | 0 UND / 23 16.1 / 89 4.1 |
| Cost of Sales/Inventory | | | | | | | | | |
| Cost of Sales/Payables | | | | | | | | | |
| Sales/Working Capital | | 1.5 / 4.7 / -3.1 | 3.6 / 51.0 / -4.8 | | | | | 5.6 / 45.0 / -3.5 | 13.2 / -15.4 / -1.9 |
| EBIT/Interest | | | 12.1 / (14) 3.7 / -14.2 | | | | | 11.3 / (15) 1.6 / .9 | 3.1 / (21) 1.0 / -6.2 |
| Net Profit + Depr., Dep., Amort./Cur. Mat. L/T/D | | | | | | | | | |
| Fixed/Worth | | .0 / .9 / 12.0 | .6 / -276.0 / -1.0 | | | | | .1 / 1.8 / -1.2 | .6 / 2.8 / -.5 |
| Debt/Worth | | .8 / 1.9 / -10.2 | 1.0 / -999.8 / -2.4 | | | | | .2 / 2.6 / -6.0 | 1.1 / 3.5 / -2.3 |
| % Profit Before Taxes/Tangible Net Worth | | | | | | | | 45.6 / (15) 3.2 / -1.0 | 18.0 / (14) -.8 / -30.7 |
| % Profit Before Taxes/Total Assets | | 25.1 / 7.3 / 1.5 | 13.1 / 2.5 / -3.0 | | | | | 14.7 / 1.7 / -1.4 | 8.5 / .2 / -11.9 |
| Sales/Net Fixed Assets | | 41.2 / 4.6 / 1.4 | 10.5 / 3.8 / 1.0 | | | | | 42.0 / 4.0 / 1.5 | 14.4 / 4.8 / 1.3 |
| Sales/Total Assets | | 1.1 / .8 / .5 | 1.1 / .8 / .3 | | | | | 2.4 / 1.2 / .6 | 3.0 / 1.4 / .5 |
| % Depr., Dep., Amort./Sales | | | 2.9 / (11) 5.7 / 10.0 | | | | | 1.1 / (15) 4.8 / 21.4 | 3.7 / (15) 5.8 / 24.2 |
| % Officers', Directors' Owners' Comp/Sales | | | | | | | | | |
| Net Sales ($) | 2530M | 10819M | 76802M | 47060M | 37690M | | | 110004M | 134532M |
| Total Assets ($) | 1293M | 14057M | 79481M | 130899M | 161068M | | | 132623M | 169222M |

M = $ thousand     MM = $ million
See Pages 9 through 22 for Explanation of Ratios and Data

## Comparative Historical Data | Current Data Sorted by Sales

| 1 (4/1/09-3/31/10) ALL | 3 (4/1/10-3/31/11) ALL | 2 (4/1/11-3/31/12) ALL | Type of Statement | 0-1MM | 1-3MM | 3-5MM | 5-10MM | 10-25MM | 25MM & OVER |
|---|---|---|---|---|---|---|---|---|---|
| 1 | 3 | 2 | Unqualified | | 1 | | 1 | 1 | 1 |
| 2 | 2 | 4 | Reviewed | 2 | | | 2 | | |
| 5 | 12 | 13 | Compiled | | | | | | |
| 7 | | | Tax Returns | 7 | 4 | | 1 | | |
| 12 | 12 | 23 | Other | 7 | 5 | 3 | 5 | 3 | |
| | | | | 2 (4/1-9/30/11) | | 3 | 40 (10/1/11-3/31/12) | | 1 |
| 27 | 29 | 42 | **NUMBER OF STATEMENTS** | 16 | 10 | 3 | 8 | 4 | 1 |
| % | % | % | **ASSETS** | % | % | % | % | % | % |
| 16.3 | 17.7 | 13.5 | Cash & Equivalents | 21.0 | 9.0 | | | | |
| 7.3 | 6.8 | 9.5 | Trade Receivables (net) | 5.9 | 12.6 | | | | |
| 5.2 | 5.2 | 6.7 | Inventory | 5.2 | 11.6 | | | | |
| 5.4 | 7.8 | 12.7 | All Other Current | 16.2 | 15.1 | | | | |
| 34.2 | 37.4 | 42.3 | Total Current | 48.3 | 48.4 | | | | |
| 48.7 | 50.1 | 41.7 | Fixed Assets (net) | 37.0 | 41.0 | | | | |
| 2.3 | .4 | 5.4 | Intangibles (net) | 5.0 | 1.3 | | | | |
| 14.8 | 12.0 | 10.6 | All Other Non-Current | 9.7 | 9.2 | | | | |
| 100.0 | 100.0 | 100.0 | Total | 100.0 | 100.0 | | | | |
| | | | **LIABILITIES** | | | | | | |
| 16.4 | 18.4 | 22.9 | Notes Payable-Short Term | 22.2 | 23.7 | | | | |
| 7.1 | 3.4 | 5.0 | Cur. Mat.-L.T.D. | 7.9 | 7.2 | | | | |
| 8.0 | 9.7 | 6.2 | Trade Payables | 2.4 | 12.0 | | | | |
| .0 | .0 | .0 | Income Taxes Payable | .0 | .0 | | | | |
| 15.5 | 21.2 | 15.9 | All Other Current | 11.2 | 30.3 | | | | |
| 47.0 | 52.7 | 50.0 | Total Current | 43.7 | 73.2 | | | | |
| 43.7 | 38.8 | 36.0 | Long-Term Debt | 45.5 | 37.1 | | | | |
| .0 | .0 | .0 | Deferred Taxes | .0 | .0 | | | | |
| 4.9 | 11.7 | 14.8 | All Other Non-Current | 11.5 | 12.6 | | | | |
| 4.5 | -3.1 | -.8 | Net Worth | -.7 | -22.9 | | | | |
| 100.0 | 100.0 | 100.0 | Total Liabilties & Net Worth | 100.0 | 100.0 | | | | |
| | | | **INCOME DATA** | | | | | | |
| 100.0 | 100.0 | 100.0 | Net Sales | 100.0 | 100.0 | | | | |
| | | | Gross Profit | | | | | | |
| 93.0 | 93.0 | 91.7 | Operating Expenses | 87.9 | 85.7 | | | | |
| 7.0 | 7.0 | 8.3 | Operating Profit | 12.1 | 14.3 | | | | |
| 2.2 | 3.5 | 3.4 | All Other Expenses (net) | 3.0 | 3.8 | | | | |
| 4.8 | 3.5 | 4.8 | Profit Before Taxes | 9.1 | 10.5 | | | | |
| | | | **RATIOS** | | | | | | |
| 3.0 | 2.1 | 2.3 | | 2.5 | 4.1 | | | | |
| .7 | .5 | 1.2 | Current | 1.4 | 1.6 | | | | |
| .2 | .2 | .4 | | .4 | .2 | | | | |
| 1.6 | 1.2 | 1.4 | | 1.9 | 1.5 | | | | |
| .5 | .4 | .3 | Quick | .5 | .2 | | | | |
| .2 | .2 | .1 | | .2 | .0 | | | | |
| 0 UND | 0 UND | 0 UND | | 0 UND | 0 UND | | | | |
| 1 725.0 | 3 109.6 | 9 38.5 | Sales/Receivables | 0 UND | 12 31.4 | | | | |
| 43 8.4 | 47 7.7 | 43 8.5 | | 0 UND | 43 8.5 | | | | |
| | | | Cost of Sales/Inventory | | | | | | |
| | | | Cost of Sales/Payables | | | | | | |
| 4.4 | 15.9 | 2.4 | | 2.1 | 1.7 | | | | |
| -73.8 | -29.0 | 51.0 | Sales/Working Capital | 40.8 | 7.9 | | | | |
| -1.6 | -4.5 | -2.8 | | -4.0 | -3.1 | | | | |
| 4.8 | 16.9 | 11.0 | | 13.9 | | | | | |
| (25) 1.3 | (20) 2.7 | (32) 3.9 | EBIT/Interest | (10) 5.7 | | | | | |
| -4.0 | -1.7 | -8.9 | | -10.1 | | | | | |
| | | | Net Profit + Depr., Dep., Amort./Cur. Mat. L/T/D | | | | | | |
| .5 | .4 | .4 | | .1 | .2 | | | | |
| 4.0 | 1.4 | 1.3 | Fixed/Worth | 1.0 | 1.2 | | | | |
| -1.7 | -1.1 | -1.3 | | -70.4 | -.4 | | | | |
| .8 | .4 | .6 | | .6 | .3 | | | | |
| 16.3 | 3.3 | 1.9 | Debt/Worth | 5.5 | 1.7 | | | | |
| -4.1 | -3.4 | -2.7 | | -13.7 | -2.1 | | | | |
| 71.8 | 159.0 | 26.5 | % Profit Before Taxes/Tangible Net Worth | 54.2 | | | | | |
| (16) 3.0 | (19) 12.5 | (26) 6.5 | | (10) 20.2 | | | | | |
| -29.7 | -4.2 | -4.7 | | -.5 | | | | | |
| 17.6 | 22.8 | 13.1 | % Profit Before Taxes/Total Assets | 14.2 | 27.2 | | | | |
| 1.6 | 5.3 | 3.4 | | 4.5 | 5.4 | | | | |
| -10.7 | -4.0 | -6.1 | | -5.8 | 1.0 | | | | |
| 36.2 | 38.6 | 11.1 | Sales/Net Fixed Assets | 26.9 | 11.0 | | | | |
| 2.1 | 3.1 | 2.2 | | 2.2 | 5.3 | | | | |
| .7 | .8 | .8 | | 1.5 | .3 | | | | |
| 2.5 | 3.8 | 1.3 | Sales/Total Assets | 1.6 | 1.6 | | | | |
| 1.0 | 1.1 | .8 | | .8 | .8 | | | | |
| .5 | .5 | .3 | | .2 | .2 | | | | |
| 3.0 | 2.1 | 4.1 | % Depr., Dep., Amort./Sales | 3.1 | | | | | |
| (15) 7.1 | (17) 6.6 | (28) 6.1 | | (10) 15.1 | | | | | |
| 22.8 | 27.3 | 22.2 | | 32.4 | | | | | |
| 1.7 | .8 | 2.4 | % Officers', Directors' Owners' Comp/Sales | | | | | | |
| (12) 5.4 | (14) 3.5 | (13) 10.0 | | | | | | | |
| 10.6 | 8.3 | 18.7 | | | | | | | |
| 130833M | 183138M | 174901M | Net Sales ($) | 8728M | 18039M | 11974M | 52717M | 55470M | 27973M |
| 148793M | 309322M | 386798M | Total Assets ($) | 18454M | 59686M | 23094M | 117367M | 70354M | 97843M |

M = $ thousand     MM = $ million
See Pages 9 through 22 for Explanation of Ratios and Data

## Current Data Sorted by Assets | Comparative Historical Data

| | Current Data Sorted by Assets | | | | | Type of Statement | Comparative Historical Data | |
|---|---|---|---|---|---|---|---|---|
| | | | | | | Unqualified | 15 | 15 |
| | | | | | | Reviewed | 11 | 17 |
| | | | | | | Compiled | 12 | 23 |
| | | | | | | Tax Returns | 18 | 18 |
| | | | | | | Other | 27 | 32 |
| | 12 (4/1-9/30/11) | | 86 (10/1/11-3/31/12) | | | | 4/1/07-3/31/08 | 4/1/08-3/31/09 |
| 0-500M | 500M-2MM | 2-10MM | 10-50MM | 50-100MM | 100-250MM | | ALL | ALL |
| 8 | 19 | 33 | 21 | 8 | 9 | NUMBER OF STATEMENTS | 83 | 105 |
| % | % | % | % | % | % | **ASSETS** | % | % |
| | 8.7 | 7.4 | 6.2 | | | Cash & Equivalents | 6.4 | 8.3 |
| | 9.9 | 10.9 | 7.5 | | | Trade Receivables (net) | 8.8 | 7.5 |
| | 26.3 | 22.0 | 9.1 | | | Inventory | 18.4 | 17.0 |
| | 6.2 | 5.4 | 4.7 | | | All Other Current | 4.4 | 3.8 |
| | 51.1 | 45.7 | 27.5 | | | Total Current | 37.9 | 36.5 |
| | 24.6 | 34.6 | 47.1 | | | Fixed Assets (net) | 46.8 | 45.5 |
| | 4.0 | 1.3 | 1.1 | | | Intangibles (net) | 1.2 | 1.1 |
| | 20.4 | 18.4 | 24.2 | | | All Other Non-Current | 14.1 | 16.9 |
| | 100.0 | 100.0 | 100.0 | | | Total | 100.0 | 100.0 |
| | | | | | | **LIABILITIES** | | |
| | 20.0 | 11.6 | 12.6 | | | Notes Payable-Short Term | 16.4 | 20.5 |
| | 2.4 | 8.3 | 5.0 | | | Cur. Mat.-L.T.D. | 6.8 | 4.8 |
| | 4.4 | 4.4 | 3.4 | | | Trade Payables | 5.3 | 4.3 |
| | .0 | .1 | .2 | | | Income Taxes Payable | .3 | .0 |
| | 31.9 | 6.3 | 7.9 | | | All Other Current | 5.6 | 8.3 |
| | 58.6 | 30.7 | 29.0 | | | Total Current | 34.4 | 38.0 |
| | 24.7 | 14.9 | 26.9 | | | Long-Term Debt | 30.0 | 33.3 |
| | .0 | .2 | .6 | | | Deferred Taxes | .6 | .4 |
| | 8.3 | 3.5 | 2.2 | | | All Other Non-Current | 7.3 | 3.7 |
| | 8.4 | 50.8 | 41.3 | | | Net Worth | 27.7 | 24.7 |
| | 100.0 | 100.0 | 100.0 | | | Total Liabilties & Net Worth | 100.0 | 100.0 |
| | | | | | | **INCOME DATA** | | |
| | 100.0 | 100.0 | 100.0 | | | Net Sales | 100.0 | 100.0 |
| | | | | | | Gross Profit | | |
| | 99.7 | 89.1 | 81.7 | | | Operating Expenses | 88.4 | 89.6 |
| | .3 | 10.9 | 18.3 | | | Operating Profit | 11.6 | 10.4 |
| | .0 | 1.4 | 4.2 | | | All Other Expenses (net) | 4.0 | 6.0 |
| | .3 | 9.5 | 14.1 | | | Profit Before Taxes | 7.7 | 4.5 |
| | | | | | | **RATIOS** | | |
| | 2.3 | 4.3 | 2.0 | | | | 2.9 | 2.9 |
| | 1.0 | 1.9 | .7 | | | Current | 1.1 | 1.2 |
| | .3 | .7 | .4 | | | | .6 | .5 |
| | .8 | 2.2 | .8 | | | | 1.3 | 1.5 |
| | .3 | .4 | .2 | | | Quick | .4 | .4 |
| | .1 | .2 | .1 | | | | .1 | .1 |
| 0 UND | 3 113.9 | 1 452.2 | | | | | 0 UND | 1 384.6 |
| 5 75.9 | 9 40.9 | 13 28.1 | | | | Sales/Receivables | 10 37.3 | 9 41.3 |
| 16 23.3 | 21 17.8 | 22 16.7 | | | | | 22 16.7 | 22 16.9 |
| | | | | | | Cost of Sales/Inventory | | |
| | | | | | | Cost of Sales/Payables | | |
| | 10.8 | 5.0 | 11.5 | | | | 6.5 | 4.7 |
| | 547.6 | 13.0 | -31.7 | | | Sales/Working Capital | 52.7 | 63.8 |
| | -11.8 | -37.6 | -2.6 | | | | -11.5 | -11.5 |
| | 5.5 | 10.5 | 9.0 | | | | 4.3 | 3.3 |
| (17) 1.0 | (28) 2.0 | (20) 3.9 | | | | EBIT/Interest | (69) 2.0 | (86) 1.2 |
| -2.5 | .6 | 1.1 | | | | 1.0 | -.6 |
| | | | | | | Net Profit + Depr., Dep., | 4.7 | 6.1 |
| | | | | | | Amort./Cur. Mat. L/T/D | (16) 1.3 | (16) 1.2 |
| | | | | | | | .4 | .4 |
| | .1 | .3 | .4 | | | | .6 | .4 |
| | .7 | .6 | .8 | | | Fixed/Worth | 1.4 | 1.4 |
| | -1.0 | 1.5 | 3.3 | | | | 3.9 | 4.8 |
| | .4 | .2 | .8 | | | | 1.0 | .9 |
| | 3.0 | 1.1 | 1.1 | | | Debt/Worth | 2.2 | 2.2 |
| | -3.3 | 3.2 | 5.0 | | | | 10.5 | 11.0 |
| | 11.6 | 20.6 | 23.7 | | | % Profit Before Taxes/Tangible | 35.5 | 25.6 |
| (13) -5.3 | (31) 6.0 | 8.7 | | | | Net Worth | (74) 13.2 | (88) 5.5 |
| | -16.4 | -.2 | 1.3 | | | | .5 | -4.5 |
| | 8.8 | 10.5 | 10.1 | | | % Profit Before Taxes/Total | 6.7 | 7.0 |
| | .0 | 3.8 | 6.3 | | | Assets | 3.4 | 1.1 |
| | -6.1 | -.1 | .4 | | | | .0 | -3.5 |
| | 191.8 | 35.4 | 5.8 | | | | 23.3 | 18.2 |
| | 32.0 | 9.1 | 1.4 | | | Sales/Net Fixed Assets | 3.0 | 3.3 |
| | 13.8 | 2.8 | .5 | | | | .7 | .4 |
| | 6.2 | 5.0 | 1.6 | | | | 3.5 | 3.6 |
| | 3.8 | 1.9 | .7 | | | Sales/Total Assets | 1.0 | 1.0 |
| | 1.9 | .5 | .3 | | | | .3 | .3 |
| | .1 | .3 | 2.5 | | | | 1.2 | .8 |
| (12) 1.2 | (26) 2.2 | (18) 4.9 | | | | % Depr., Dep., Amort./Sales | (74) 4.4 | (93) 3.5 |
| | 5.6 | 4.8 | 7.7 | | | | 10.4 | 10.1 |
| | | 1.0 | | | | | 1.2 | 1.0 |
| | (10) 1.4 | | | | | % Officers', Directors' | (18) 2.0 | (24) 1.7 |
| | 3.7 | | | | | Owners' Comp/Sales | 5.2 | 2.9 |
| 9627M | 94465M | 403146M | 743488M | 397574M | 1080518M | Net Sales ($) | 1527490M | 2148210M |
| 2011M | 23070M | 176526M | 520682M | 546852M | 1483459M | Total Assets ($) | 1957947M | 2586946M |

M = $ thousand     MM = $ million
See Pages 9 through 22 for Explanation of Ratios and Data

## Comparative Historical Data / Current Data Sorted by Sales

| 4/1/09-3/31/10 ALL | 4/1/10-3/31/11 ALL | 4/1/11-3/31/12 ALL | Type of Statement | 0-1MM | 1-3MM | 3-5MM | 5-10MM | 10-25MM | 25MM & OVER |
|---|---|---|---|---|---|---|---|---|---|
| 18 | 14 | 12 | Unqualified | | 1 | | 1 | 2 | 8 |
| 15 | 18 | 17 | Reviewed | | 1 | 5 | 1 | 5 | 5 |
| 19 | 22 | 17 | Compiled | 4 | 2 | 5 | | 5 | 1 |
| 24 | 15 | 15 | Tax Returns | 3 | 3 | 3 | 3 | 2 | 1 |
| 38 | 43 | 37 | Other | 3 | 8 | 3 | 4 | 8 | 11 |
| | | | | 12 (4/1-9/30/11) | | | 86 (10/1/11-3/31/12) | | |
| 114 | 112 | 98 | **NUMBER OF STATEMENTS** | 10 | 15 | 16 | 9 | 22 | 26 |
| % | % | % | **ASSETS** | % | % | % | % | % | % |
| 6.7 | 8.1 | 8.1 | Cash & Equivalents | 12.8 | 12.3 | 5.5 | | 4.6 | 7.4 |
| 9.5 | 10.3 | 9.6 | Trade Receivables (net) | 2.3 | 8.7 | 8.6 | | 8.0 | 14.2 |
| 18.0 | 12.7 | 16.4 | Inventory | 3.0 | 6.3 | 11.7 | | 27.0 | 14.0 |
| 3.5 | 4.3 | 4.4 | All Other Current | 2.6 | 6.4 | 2.6 | | 4.2 | 5.2 |
| 37.7 | 35.4 | 38.6 | Total Current | 20.7 | 33.8 | 28.3 | | 43.8 | 40.8 |
| 45.0 | 45.3 | 41.0 | Fixed Assets (net) | 37.2 | 39.6 | 48.6 | | 39.7 | 45.5 |
| 1.6 | 1.2 | 1.8 | Intangibles (net) | 3.2 | 7.4 | .0 | | 1.0 | .4 |
| 15.6 | 18.1 | 18.6 | All Other Non-Current | 38.9 | 19.2 | 23.0 | | 15.5 | 13.3 |
| 100.0 | 100.0 | 100.0 | Total | 100.0 | 100.0 | 100.0 | | 100.0 | 100.0 |
| | | | **LIABILITIES** | | | | | | |
| 15.7 | 14.3 | 12.8 | Notes Payable-Short Term | 11.4 | 11.3 | 7.8 | | 20.1 | 11.7 |
| 7.5 | 6.8 | 5.9 | Cur. Mat.-L.T.D. | 5.5 | 5.2 | 8.3 | | 8.6 | 4.1 |
| 3.9 | 4.2 | 4.1 | Trade Payables | 5.5 | 2.6 | 2.4 | | 5.3 | 3.7 |
| .1 | .2 | .1 | Income Taxes Payable | .0 | .0 | .0 | | .2 | .2 |
| 8.5 | 8.5 | 11.8 | All Other Current | 18.8 | 16.9 | 17.8 | | 4.7 | 7.5 |
| 35.7 | 34.0 | 34.7 | Total Current | 41.3 | 36.0 | 36.3 | | 38.9 | 27.2 |
| 31.6 | 26.2 | 26.0 | Long-Term Debt | 29.2 | 23.5 | 27.3 | | 19.3 | 34.6 |
| .6 | .4 | .3 | Deferred Taxes | .0 | .0 | .0 | | .5 | .5 |
| 5.7 | 5.7 | 7.4 | All Other Non-Current | 4.7 | 31.8 | 4.3 | | 1.6 | 3.6 |
| 26.5 | 33.7 | 31.5 | Net Worth | 24.8 | 8.6 | 32.1 | | 39.7 | 34.1 |
| 100.0 | 100.0 | 100.0 | Total Liabilities & Net Worth | 100.0 | 100.0 | 100.0 | | 100.0 | 100.0 |
| | | | **INCOME DATA** | | | | | | |
| 100.0 | 100.0 | 100.0 | Net Sales | 100.0 | 100.0 | 100.0 | | 100.0 | 100.0 |
| | | | Gross Profit | | | | | | |
| 94.1 | 90.5 | 89.9 | Operating Expenses | 72.0 | 85.9 | 85.5 | | 98.2 | 93.8 |
| 5.9 | 9.5 | 10.1 | Operating Profit | 28.0 | 14.1 | 14.5 | | 1.8 | 6.2 |
| 3.0 | 2.8 | 2.7 | All Other Expenses (net) | 3.8 | 6.1 | .2 | | 3.6 | 2.1 |
| 2.9 | 6.7 | 7.4 | Profit Before Taxes | 24.2 | 7.9 | 14.3 | | -1.8 | 4.1 |
| | | | **RATIOS** | | | | | | |
| 2.8 | 2.0 | 2.6 | Current | 2.3 | 1.9 | 2.3 | | 3.0 | 2.2 |
| 1.1 | 1.2 | 1.2 | | .3 | .8 | .6 | | 1.3 | 1.5 |
| .5 | .6 | .4 | | .1 | .3 | .3 | | .8 | .9 |
| 1.3 | 1.1 | 1.3 | Quick | 2.3 | 1.2 | .9 | | .9 | 1.4 |
| .4 | .5 | .4 | | .2 | .3 | .4 | | .3 | .7 |
| .2 | .2 | .2 | | .0 | .1 | .0 | | .2 | .4 |
| 0 UND | 2 194.7 | 0 UND | Sales/Receivables | 0 UND | 0 UND | 0 UND | | 3 107.7 | 13 28.4 |
| 11 33.4 | 11 34.1 | 10 35.1 | | 0 UND | 0 UND | 6 59.4 | | 10 38.3 | 20 18.0 |
| 24 15.2 | 26 14.3 | 24 15.5 | | 15 24.9 | 12 29.9 | 15 24.2 | | 23 15.9 | 29 12.5 |
| | | | Cost of Sales/Inventory | | | | | | |
| | | | Cost of Sales/Payables | | | | | | |
| 5.8 | 9.7 | 7.1 | Sales/Working Capital | 2.1 | 37.0 | 10.4 | | 5.9 | 7.7 |
| 35.0 | 37.5 | 38.2 | | -9.5 | -112.4 | -70.5 | | 11.8 | 14.2 |
| -8.3 | -13.2 | -12.5 | | -.2 | -4.9 | -1.4 | | -31.3 | -71.2 |
| 4.5 | 7.7 | 9.0 | EBIT/Interest | | 5.1 | 16.8 | | 7.4 | 5.5 |
| (99) 1.3 | (92) 3.1 | (84) 2.8 | | | (11) 1.6 | (15) 3.1 | | (19) 1.0 | (24) 3.5 |
| -.9 | 1.1 | .7 | | | -6.9 | 1.2 | | .3 | .6 |
| 4.7 | 6.5 | 2.0 | Net Profit + Depr., Dep., | | | | | | |
| (15) 1.2 | (16) 1.7 | (11) 1.1 | Amort./Cur. Mat. L/T/D | | | | | | |
| -.7 | .5 | .1 | | | | | | | |
| .5 | .5 | .3 | Fixed/Worth | .0 | .1 | .3 | | .4 | .4 |
| 1.7 | 1.3 | .8 | | .7 | 1.2 | .8 | | .7 | 1.3 |
| 5.3 | 3.7 | 3.2 | | -1.7 | -1.0 | 2.9 | | 2.0 | 2.3 |
| 1.0 | .6 | .6 | Debt/Worth | .2 | .3 | .5 | | .8 | 1.1 |
| 2.3 | 1.8 | 1.5 | | 1.8 | 2.4 | 1.8 | | 1.3 | 1.4 |
| 8.4 | 6.6 | 6.0 | | -12.9 | -3.0 | 3.4 | | 4.4 | 3.7 |
| 26.5 | 34.4 | 19.7 | % Profit Before Taxes/Tangible | | | 24.3 | | 6.9 | 23.9 |
| (98) 2.6 | (99) 9.6 | (85) 6.5 | Net Worth | | (15) 9.9 | | | (21) -.1 | (25) 13.8 |
| -8.4 | 1.6 | -2.5 | | | 2.6 | | | -8.7 | -.9 |
| 7.3 | 9.6 | 10.4 | % Profit Before Taxes/Total | 12.2 | 20.1 | 19.0 | | 4.2 | 10.5 |
| .6 | 2.4 | 3.9 | Assets | 5.4 | 1.4 | 5.9 | | .0 | 5.6 |
| -3.0 | -.4 | -1.2 | | -.2 | -9.3 | .9 | | -2.4 | -1.2 |
| 15.6 | 15.7 | 33.9 | Sales/Net Fixed Assets | 40.2 | 45.3 | 57.9 | | 15.7 | 28.3 |
| 3.6 | 4.2 | 4.4 | | 3.9 | 11.8 | 2.0 | | 7.6 | 3.3 |
| .8 | .9 | 1.5 | | 1.5 | .6 | .5 | | 2.3 | 1.5 |
| 3.2 | 3.6 | 4.0 | Sales/Total Assets | 2.1 | 4.3 | 3.6 | | 5.0 | 3.3 |
| 1.2 | 1.4 | 1.5 | | .2 | 1.5 | 1.0 | | 2.2 | 1.5 |
| .4 | .5 | .4 | | .1 | .5 | .3 | | .7 | .9 |
| 1.0 | .7 | .6 | % Depr., Dep., Amort./Sales | | .6 | .5 | | .6 | 1.3 |
| (93) 4.3 | (90) 3.6 | (74) 2.8 | | (12) 1.5 | (14) 4.9 | | | (19) 2.6 | (17) 4.4 |
| 11.4 | 9.4 | 7.6 | | | 5.4 | 15.8 | | 5.4 | 8.0 |
| 1.2 | 1.1 | 1.1 | % Officers', Directors' | | | | | | |
| (23) 1.7 | (22) 2.0 | (25) 1.9 | Owners' Comp/Sales | | | | | | |
| 4.3 | 5.0 | 6.6 | | | | | | | |
| 1822116M | 2322256M | 2728818M | Net Sales ($) | 5686M | 30797M | 65112M | 76351M | 346430M | 2204442M |
| 2183243M | 2724187M | 2752600M | Total Assets ($) | 34165M | 102817M | 189797M | 47914M | 539468M | 1838439M |

© RMA 2012

M = $ thousand    MM = $ million
See Pages 9 through 22 for Explanation of Ratios and Data

## Current Data Sorted by Assets                                   Comparative Historical Data

**Type of Statement**

| Type | 0-500M | 500M-2MM | 2-10MM | 10-50MM | 50-100MM | 100-250MM | | 4/1/07-3/31/08 ALL | 4/1/08-3/31/09 ALL |
|---|---|---|---|---|---|---|---|---|---|
| Unqualified | | | | | | | | | |
| Reviewed | | 1 | 6 | 3 | | | | 7 | 5 |
| Compiled | 5 | 9 | 8 | 2 | 1 | | | 19 | 16 |
| Tax Returns | 14 | 30 | 11 | | | | | 32 | 17 |
| Other | | 7 | 13 | | 2 | | | 37 | 36 |
| | | | | | | | | 32 | 28 |
| | 23 (4/1-9/30/11) | | | 89 (10/1/11-3/31/12) | | | | | |
| **NUMBER OF STATEMENTS** | 19 | 47 | 38 | 5 | 3 | | | 127 | 102 |

*(Current data for the 100-250MM column: DATA NOT AVAILABLE)*

| 0-500M | 500M-2MM | 2-10MM | 10-50MM | 50-100MM | 100-250MM | | 4/1/07-3/31/08 ALL | 4/1/08-3/31/09 ALL |
|---|---|---|---|---|---|---|---|---|
| % | % | % | % | % | % | **ASSETS** | % | % |
| 21.8 | 11.9 | 5.4 | | | | Cash & Equivalents | 9.7 | 10.5 |
| 5.9 | 9.8 | 13.1 | | | | Trade Receivables (net) | 8.3 | 9.7 |
| 6.7 | 9.4 | 16.6 | | | | Inventory | 14.3 | 13.4 |
| 2.0 | 3.2 | 3.5 | | | | All Other Current | 3.9 | 3.3 |
| 36.5 | 34.2 | 38.5 | | | | Total Current | 36.1 | 36.9 |
| 54.1 | 45.7 | 52.1 | | | | Fixed Assets (net) | 53.1 | 51.7 |
| 1.9 | 1.3 | 2.4 | | | | Intangibles (net) | 1.6 | 3.2 |
| 7.3 | 18.8 | 7.0 | | | | All Other Non-Current | 9.1 | 8.1 |
| 100.0 | 100.0 | 100.0 | | | | Total | 100.0 | 100.0 |
| | | | | | | **LIABILITIES** | | |
| 22.6 | 12.7 | 15.6 | | | | Notes Payable-Short Term | 12.9 | 14.1 |
| 13.1 | 10.2 | 7.1 | | | | Cur. Mat.-L.T.D. | 11.5 | 10.3 |
| 4.0 | 7.4 | 8.8 | | | | Trade Payables | 6.7 | 5.1 |
| .0 | .2 | .1 | | | | Income Taxes Payable | .2 | .0 |
| 21.4 | 5.2 | 5.5 | | | | All Other Current | 3.8 | 7.6 |
| 61.1 | 35.8 | 37.1 | | | | Total Current | 35.1 | 37.2 |
| 78.7 | 42.6 | 26.0 | | | | Long-Term Debt | 38.3 | 32.9 |
| .0 | .0 | 1.5 | | | | Deferred Taxes | .6 | .5 |
| 6.8 | 1.7 | 7.2 | | | | All Other Non-Current | 3.6 | 4.6 |
| -46.6 | 19.9 | 28.2 | | | | Net Worth | 22.4 | 24.8 |
| 100.0 | 100.0 | 100.0 | | | | Total Liabilities & Net Worth | 100.0 | 100.0 |
| | | | | | | **INCOME DATA** | | |
| 100.0 | 100.0 | 100.0 | | | | Net Sales | 100.0 | 100.0 |
| 51.7 | 46.3 | 33.2 | | | | Gross Profit | 37.0 | 36.0 |
| 49.4 | 45.2 | 30.9 | | | | Operating Expenses | 34.5 | 34.5 |
| 2.3 | 1.1 | 2.2 | | | | Operating Profit | 2.5 | 1.5 |
| .2 | .0 | -.1 | | | | All Other Expenses (net) | 1.0 | .7 |
| 2.0 | 1.1 | 2.3 | | | | Profit Before Taxes | 1.5 | .7 |
| | | | | | | **RATIOS** | | |
| 3.1 | 2.4 | 1.5 | | | | | 2.1 | 2.5 |
| .4 | 1.1 | 1.0 | | | | Current | 1.0 | 1.1 |
| .2 | .5 | .5 | | | | | .4 | .5 |
| 1.6 | 2.3 | 1.0 | | | | | 1.3 | 1.5 |
| .3 (45) | .7 | .4 | | | (126) | Quick | .5 (100) | .5 |
| .1 | .2 | .2 | | | | | .2 | .2 |
| 0 UND | 0 UND | 5 68.6 | | | | | 0 UND | 0 UND |
| 0 UND | 6 61.7 | 14 25.7 | | | | Sales/Receivables | 8 48.0 | 6 56.3 |
| 3 119.4 | 17 21.0 | 30 12.0 | | | | | 20 18.1 | 15 23.9 |
| 0 UND | 0 UND | 0 UND | | | | | 0 UND | 0 UND |
| 0 UND | 0 UND | 17 21.6 | | | | Cost of Sales/Inventory | 8 43.4 | 5 76.1 |
| 2 167.0 | 26 14.3 | 74 4.9 | | | | | 58 6.3 | 43 8.5 |
| 0 UND | 0 UND | 5 70.3 | | | | | 0 849.0 | 0 940.2 |
| 0 UND | 4 103.8 | 14 25.9 | | | | Cost of Sales/Payables | 8 47.9 | 6 56.4 |
| 4 81.4 | 26 14.0 | 36 10.2 | | | | | 26 14.1 | 19 19.6 |
| 13.3 | 22.1 | 17.4 | | | | | 12.9 | 10.8 |
| -21.8 | 56.3 | NM | | | | Sales/Working Capital | 295.8 | 83.4 |
| -8.2 | -17.7 | -15.1 | | | | | -13.9 | -13.0 |
| 4.7 | 5.8 | 5.9 | | | | | 4.2 | 5.4 |
| (16) 2.5 | 1.9 | (37) 1.6 | | | (119) | EBIT/Interest | 1.7 (96) | 1.9 |
| .8 | -1.1 | .8 | | | | | -.2 | -.9 |
| | | | | | | Net Profit + Depr., Dep., | 3.2 | 4.2 |
| | | | | | (23) | Amort./Cur. Mat. L/T/D | 1.7 (13) | 1.9 |
| | | | | | | | .8 | .9 |
| 50.0 | .4 | 1.0 | | | | | .8 | .7 |
| -1.6 | 2.3 | 1.6 | | | | Fixed/Worth | 3.0 | 1.7 |
| -.4 | -8.4 | 4.5 | | | | | 21.0 | NM |
| 84.4 | 1.0 | 1.1 | | | | | 1.1 | .7 |
| -4.6 | 4.2 | 2.4 | | | | Debt/Worth | 3.9 | 2.1 |
| -1.9 | -13.5 | 10.4 | | | | | 39.3 | NM |
| | 73.7 | 44.4 | | | | % Profit Before Taxes/Tangible | 33.3 | 32.0 |
| (34) 19.7 | (33) 12.6 | | | | (98) | Net Worth | 12.8 (77) | 10.8 |
| -.6 | -.3 | | | | | | .6 | -3.7 |
| 28.9 | 15.0 | 8.6 | | | | % Profit Before Taxes/Total | 10.0 | 11.4 |
| 9.6 | 2.7 | 2.3 | | | | Assets | 3.7 | 3.6 |
| -4.9 | -9.6 | -.3 | | | | | -5.7 | -7.4 |
| 42.8 | 23.8 | 6.5 | | | | | 10.8 | 8.9 |
| 10.1 | 7.5 | 2.9 | | | | Sales/Net Fixed Assets | 4.4 | 5.1 |
| 4.8 | 3.5 | 2.0 | | | | | 2.4 | 2.6 |
| 10.1 | 5.2 | 3.1 | | | | | 3.3 | 3.5 |
| 4.5 | 3.4 | 1.8 | | | | Sales/Total Assets | 2.3 | 2.4 |
| 3.1 | 2.2 | 1.0 | | | | | 1.6 | 1.6 |
| 6.3 | 3.5 | 1.3 | | | | | 2.7 | 2.4 |
| (11) 7.5 | (37) 5.4 | (32) 5.4 | | | (112) | % Depr., Dep., Amort./Sales | 8.3 (82) | 7.1 |
| 18.0 | 10.9 | 11.0 | | | | | 11.8 | 12.7 |
| 2.0 | 1.6 | .7 | | | | | 1.8 | 1.5 |
| (13) 8.8 | (36) 3.7 | (20) 1.5 | | | (63) | % Officers', Directors' | 3.5 (51) | 2.1 |
| 11.7 | 5.3 | 3.7 | | | | Owners' Comp/Sales | 5.4 | 4.0 |
| 25485M | 192487M | 405550M | 73328M | 371713M | | Net Sales ($) | 1687253M | 1119120M |
| 4501M | 52468M | 176346M | 101053M | 249562M | | Total Assets ($) | 865255M | 564898M |

M = $ thousand     MM = $ million
See Pages 9 through 22 for Explanation of Ratios and Data

# AGRICULTURE—Logging  NAICS 113310

**Comparative Historical Data**       **Current Data Sorted by Sales**

| 4/1/09-3/31/10 ALL | 4/1/10-3/31/11 ALL | 4/1/11-3/31/12 ALL | Type of Statement | 0-1MM | 1-3MM | 3-5MM | 5-10MM | 10-25MM | 25MM & OVER |
|---|---|---|---|---|---|---|---|---|---|
| | | | | | | | | | |
| 2 | 3 | | Unqualified | 4 | 1 | 2 | 1 | 4 | 2 |
| 19 | 14 | 10 | Reviewed | | 4 | 5 | 7 | 4 | 1 |
| 37 | 28 | 25 | Compiled | | 19 | 10 | 8 | 6 | 2 |
| 39 | 34 | 55 | Tax Returns | | | | | 2 | 3 |
| 25 | 23 | 22 | Other | 10 | 5 | 6 | 6 | | |
| | | | | 23 (4/1-9/30/11) | | | 89 (10/1/11-3/31/12) | | |
| 122 | 102 | 112 | **NUMBER OF STATEMENTS** | 14 | 29 | 23 | 22 | 16 | 8 |
| % | % | % | **ASSETS** | % | % | % | % | % | % |
| 14.3 | 10.8 | 11.0 | Cash & Equivalents | 15.7 | 15.6 | 7.3 | 10.4 | 8.2 | |
| 9.8 | 11.4 | 10.1 | Trade Receivables (net) | 1.4 | 9.6 | 12.7 | 9.0 | 7.9 | |
| 12.6 | 12.1 | 11.5 | Inventory | 7.6 | 8.3 | 9.1 | 12.0 | 17.5 | |
| 4.7 | 3.4 | 3.1 | All Other Current | 1.8 | 1.5 | 1.7 | 8.3 | 2.7 | |
| 41.4 | 37.7 | 35.7 | Total Current | 26.5 | 34.9 | 30.8 | 39.7 | 36.4 | |
| 48.1 | 50.0 | 50.0 | Fixed Assets (net) | 63.7 | 45.3 | 57.1 | 46.9 | 50.9 | |
| 1.9 | 2.1 | 1.7 | Intangibles (net) | 2.3 | 3.2 | 1.0 | 1.5 | .5 | |
| 8.5 | 10.2 | 12.6 | All Other Non-Current | 7.4 | 16.5 | 11.1 | 11.9 | 12.3 | |
| 100.0 | 100.0 | 100.0 | Total | 100.0 | 100.0 | 100.0 | 100.0 | 100.0 | |
| | | | **LIABILITIES** | | | | | | |
| 11.4 | 12.2 | 15.4 | Notes Payable-Short Term | 16.3 | 14.0 | 13.4 | 16.2 | 15.4 | |
| 8.7 | 10.6 | 9.2 | Cur. Mat.-L.T.D. | 12.0 | 6.7 | 11.4 | 12.4 | 6.8 | |
| 5.5 | 6.5 | 7.1 | Trade Payables | 2.1 | 7.1 | 7.0 | 6.3 | 8.9 | |
| .1 | .2 | .1 | Income Taxes Payable | .0 | .1 | .0 | .2 | .4 | |
| 7.7 | 5.8 | 7.9 | All Other Current | 15.2 | 5.0 | 11.6 | 7.4 | 4.0 | |
| 33.4 | 35.3 | 39.6 | Total Current | 45.6 | 32.9 | 43.4 | 42.5 | 35.6 | |
| 34.5 | 30.8 | 41.5 | Long-Term Debt | 92.4 | 39.8 | 51.7 | 23.4 | 23.8 | |
| .7 | .9 | .5 | Deferred Taxes | .0 | .1 | .5 | 1.0 | 1.4 | |
| 4.2 | 8.1 | 4.6 | All Other Non-Current | 3.1 | 6.7 | 1.4 | 5.5 | 3.6 | |
| 27.2 | 25.0 | 13.8 | Net Worth | -41.2 | 20.5 | 2.9 | 27.6 | 35.6 | |
| 100.0 | 100.0 | 100.0 | Total Liabilities & Net Worth | 100.0 | 100.0 | 100.0 | 100.0 | 100.0 | |
| | | | **INCOME DATA** | | | | | | |
| 100.0 | 100.0 | 100.0 | Net Sales | 100.0 | 100.0 | 100.0 | 100.0 | 100.0 | |
| 39.2 | 40.6 | 41.8 | Gross Profit | 56.4 | 52.7 | 46.3 | 29.1 | 31.7 | |
| 36.8 | 38.0 | 39.4 | Operating Expenses | 53.6 | 51.3 | 45.2 | 26.0 | 28.4 | |
| 2.5 | 2.6 | 2.3 | Operating Profit | 2.9 | 1.4 | 1.1 | 3.1 | 3.3 | |
| .5 | .1 | .1 | All Other Expenses (net) | 2.0 | -1.0 | .1 | -.1 | .1 | |
| 2.0 | 2.5 | 2.3 | Profit Before Taxes | .9 | 2.3 | 1.0 | 3.1 | 3.2 | |
| | | | **RATIOS** | | | | | | |
| 2.5 | 2.0 | 2.0 | Current | 3.4 | 4.0 | 1.8 | 1.8 | 1.6 | |
| 1.3 | 1.1 | 1.0 | | .3 | 1.2 | .6 | 1.1 | .9 | |
| .5 | .6 | .5 | | .1 | .5 | .5 | .6 | .5 | |
| 1.8 | 1.4 | 1.2 | Quick | .9 | 4.0 | 1.3 | 1.0 | .6 | |
| (121) .6 | (101) .6 | (110) .5 | | .3 | .8 | (22) .6 | (21) .6 | .3 | |
| .2 | .2 | .2 | | .1 | .1 | .2 | .3 | .2 | |
| 0 UND | 0 UND | 0 UND | Sales/Receivables | 0 UND | 0 UND | 0 UND | 0 UND | 6 65.5 | |
| 9 39.3 | 10 36.3 | 7 53.9 | | 0 UND | 6 63.6 | 6 61.7 | 10 35.3 | 8 47.0 | |
| 25 14.9 | 28 13.2 | 19 18.8 | | 0 UND | 33 11.0 | 24 15.0 | 20 18.6 | 16 22.3 | |
| 0 UND | 0 UND | 0 UND | Cost of Sales/Inventory | 0 UND | 0 UND | 0 UND | 0 UND | 1 427.0 | |
| 6 57.3 | 2 162.5 | 1 305.9 | | 0 UND | 0 UND | 3 130.5 | 0 UND | 7 50.7 | |
| 43 8.6 | 48 7.6 | 41 9.0 | | 3 128.8 | 87 4.2 | 31 11.8 | 33 10.9 | 45 8.1 | |
| 0 UND | 0 UND | 0 UND | Cost of Sales/Payables | 0 UND | 0 UND | 0 UND | 0 UND | 2 157.9 | |
| 7 55.2 | 9 41.7 | 8 46.0 | | 0 UND | 4 81.4 | 8 45.5 | 11 33.3 | 10 36.5 | |
| 23 15.8 | 33 11.0 | 29 12.5 | | 0 UND | 79 4.6 | 41 8.9 | 28 13.1 | 18 20.6 | |
| 7.0 | 9.6 | 18.2 | Sales/Working Capital | 22.9 | 10.6 | 29.7 | 17.4 | 30.4 | |
| 41.6 | 55.7 | NM | | -19.4 | 39.5 | -42.9 | 72.4 | -286.5 | |
| -14.4 | -18.1 | -13.3 | | -7.0 | -11.5 | -8.2 | -23.5 | -20.7 | |
| 4.3 | 6.4 | 6.3 | EBIT/Interest | 4.7 | 6.5 | 4.8 | 11.0 | 9.1 | |
| (111) 1.7 | (95) 2.7 | (108) 2.2 | | (11) 2.4 | 2.2 | 1.6 | 2.1 | (15) 2.8 | |
| .1 | .3 | .4 | | .2 | -1.9 | -1.1 | 1.0 | 1.2 | |
| 2.9 | 1.1 | | Net Profit + Depr., Dep., Amort./Cur. Mat. L/T/D | | | | | | |
| (17) 1.7 | (15) .7 | | | | | | | | |
| .7 | .4 | | | | | | | | |
| .6 | .8 | .9 | Fixed/Worth | 11.4 | .8 | 1.5 | .6 | .8 | |
| 1.9 | 1.6 | 2.5 | | -3.2 | 2.8 | 6.4 | 1.6 | 1.3 | |
| 13.5 | 101.4 | -5.0 | | -.7 | 77.3 | -1.9 | 4.0 | 6.9 | |
| .6 | .9 | 1.1 | Debt/Worth | 21.9 | .8 | 2.0 | 1.0 | .3 | |
| 2.7 | 1.8 | 3.7 | | -4.7 | 3.5 | 8.8 | 2.4 | 1.6 | |
| 22.2 | 170.1 | -10.4 | | -2.0 | 103.5 | -3.8 | 11.0 | 30.9 | |
| 29.8 | 32.9 | 54.7 | % Profit Before Taxes/Tangible Net Worth | | 51.7 | 63.3 | 42.0 | 55.0 | |
| (98) 9.6 | (78) 11.5 | (80) 17.8 | | | (23) 11.5 | (12) 22.5 | (19) 14.2 | (14) 12.4 | |
| -2.3 | -.7 | 1.1 | | | -13.3 | 3.3 | 2.5 | 7.3 | |
| 11.5 | 12.5 | 13.4 | % Profit Before Taxes/Total Assets | 28.0 | 16.5 | 7.8 | 10.6 | 7.8 | |
| 2.7 | 4.7 | 3.7 | | 11.9 | 3.7 | 1.0 | 3.3 | 4.4 | |
| -1.8 | -2.9 | -1.5 | | -30.8 | -7.7 | -11.7 | .0 | 1.5 | |
| 17.6 | 11.3 | 16.6 | Sales/Net Fixed Assets | 33.8 | 9.5 | 10.4 | 40.9 | 16.1 | |
| 4.9 | 4.7 | 5.3 | | 5.2 | 5.5 | 3.4 | 7.4 | 4.8 | |
| 2.7 | 2.3 | 2.7 | | 3.1 | 2.5 | 2.2 | 2.7 | 2.9 | |
| 3.1 | 3.7 | 4.7 | Sales/Total Assets | 10.7 | 3.7 | 3.5 | 5.7 | 4.9 | |
| 2.2 | 2.1 | 2.7 | | 4.4 | 2.2 | 2.3 | 3.0 | 2.8 | |
| 1.6 | 1.3 | 1.6 | | 2.3 | 1.1 | 1.5 | 1.6 | 1.8 | |
| 2.1 | 2.4 | 2.8 | % Depr., Dep., Amort./Sales | | 5.8 | 3.7 | 1.0 | 1.0 | |
| (108) 5.8 | (87) 6.3 | (88) 6.1 | | | (22) 8.1 | (20) 8.2 | (15) 4.9 | (15) 5.1 | |
| 11.3 | 10.4 | 10.7 | | | 11.1 | 11.7 | 6.2 | 9.2 | |
| 1.7 | 1.9 | 1.4 | % Officers', Directors' Owners' Comp/Sales | | 2.1 | 1.7 | 1.3 | | |
| (57) 3.2 | (54) 2.9 | (72) 2.9 | | | (21) 3.6 | (16) 3.7 | (15) 2.4 | | |
| 6.4 | 6.6 | 5.4 | | | 7.4 | 4.2 | 3.8 | | |
| 1110257M | 1585646M | 1068563M | Net Sales ($) | 9975M | 62261M | 88758M | 153427M | 205106M | 549036M |
| 711237M | 866562M | 583930M | Total Assets ($) | 3064M | 43587M | 45317M | 70923M | 118684M | 302355M |

M = $ thousand     MM = $ million
See Pages 9 through 22 for Explanation of Ratios and Data

## Current Data Sorted by Assets

## Comparative Historical Data

| | 0-500M | 500M-2MM | 2-10MM | 10-50MM | 50-100MM | 100-250MM | Type of Statement | 4/1/07-3/31/08 ALL | 4/1/08-3/31/09 ALL |
|---|---|---|---|---|---|---|---|---|---|
| | | 1 | 2 | 4 | 3 | 1 | Unqualified | 9 | 6 |
| | | 1 | 3 | 1 | | 1 | Reviewed | 6 | 2 |
| | | | | | | | Compiled | 4 | 6 |
| | 15 | 8 | 1 | | | | Tax Returns | 5 | 10 |
| | 1 | 2 | 5 | 7 | 4 | 2 | Other | 21 | 33 |
| | | 4 (4/1-9/30/11) | | 58 (10/1/11-3/31/12) | | | | 4/1/07-3/31/08 | 4/1/08-3/31/09 |
| NUMBER OF STATEMENTS | 16 | 12 | 11 | 12 | 7 | 4 | | 45 | 57 |
| | % | % | % | % | % | % | ASSETS | % | % |
| Cash & Equivalents | 22.3 | 7.6 | 8.6 | 8.6 | | | | 14.7 | 14.8 |
| Trade Receivables (net) | .5 | 6.7 | 6.3 | 8.0 | | | | 10.7 | 8.7 |
| Inventory | 5.6 | 1.7 | 11.3 | 16.6 | | | | 10.8 | 8.8 |
| All Other Current | .7 | .2 | 11.0 | 2.6 | | | | 3.4 | 5.8 |
| Total Current | 29.1 | 16.3 | 37.1 | 35.8 | | | | 39.5 | 38.0 |
| Fixed Assets (net) | 34.0 | 18.3 | 37.9 | 40.8 | | | | 34.5 | 35.7 |
| Intangibles (net) | 13.1 | 16.1 | 11.3 | 17.0 | | | | 12.9 | 15.4 |
| All Other Non-Current | 23.7 | 49.4 | 13.7 | 6.4 | | | | 13.1 | 10.9 |
| Total | 100.0 | 100.0 | 100.0 | 100.0 | | | | 100.0 | 100.0 |
| | | | | | | | LIABILITIES | | |
| Notes Payable-Short Term | 41.8 | 10.6 | 11.6 | 7.4 | | | | 6.0 | 10.4 |
| Cur. Mat.-L.T.D. | 10.5 | 4.7 | 2.7 | 3.3 | | | | 4.2 | 13.5 |
| Trade Payables | .8 | 7.3 | 10.1 | 8.4 | | | | 4.7 | 5.9 |
| Income Taxes Payable | .0 | .0 | .4 | .1 | | | | .2 | .2 |
| All Other Current | 17.5 | 21.3 | 5.6 | 6.5 | | | | 4.8 | 14.5 |
| Total Current | 70.6 | 43.9 | 30.4 | 25.7 | | | | 19.9 | 44.5 |
| Long-Term Debt | 49.9 | 56.4 | 15.0 | 25.8 | | | | 34.5 | 46.1 |
| Deferred Taxes | .0 | .0 | .9 | .9 | | | | .4 | .5 |
| All Other Non-Current | 9.8 | 6.7 | 1.1 | 2.6 | | | | 5.3 | 2.2 |
| Net Worth | -30.4 | -7.0 | 52.6 | 45.0 | | | | 39.9 | 6.7 |
| Total Liabilities & Net Worth | 100.0 | 100.0 | 100.0 | 100.0 | | | | 100.0 | 100.0 |
| | | | | | | | INCOME DATA | | |
| Net Sales | 100.0 | 100.0 | 100.0 | 100.0 | | | | 100.0 | 100.0 |
| Gross Profit | | | | | | | | | |
| Operating Expenses | 88.8 | 89.9 | 77.9 | 85.8 | | | | 85.9 | 86.4 |
| Operating Profit | 11.2 | 10.1 | 22.1 | 14.2 | | | | 14.1 | 13.6 |
| All Other Expenses (net) | 2.6 | 2.8 | 4.3 | 3.0 | | | | 2.2 | 3.6 |
| Profit Before Taxes | 8.5 | 7.3 | 17.8 | 11.1 | | | | 11.9 | 10.0 |
| | | | | | | | RATIOS | | |
| Current | 11.7 | 1.6 | 2.1 | 2.2 | | | | 4.8 / 3.3 | |
| | .3 | .4 | 1.1 | 1.6 | | | | 1.9 / 1.7 | |
| | .1 | .0 | .1 | .5 | | | | 1.1 / 1.0 | |
| Quick | 8.6 | 1.0 | 1.5 | 1.9 | | | | 2.4 / 2.4 | |
| | .2 | .4 | .4 | .4 | | | | 1.3 / 1.1 | |
| | .0 | .0 | .0 | .2 | | | | .7 / .3 | |
| Sales/Receivables | 0 UND | 0 UND | 0 UND | 2 206.8 | | | | 0 UND / 0 UND | |
| | 0 UND | 0 UND | 0 UND | 9 38.8 | | | | 14 27.0 / 13 28.2 | |
| | 0 UND | 2 150.9 | 25 14.8 | 28 12.9 | | | | 37 9.8 / 39 9.5 | |
| Cost of Sales/Inventory | | | | | | | | | |
| Cost of Sales/Payables | | | | | | | | | |
| Sales/Working Capital | 22.9 | 259.7 | 9.3 | 4.5 | | | | 4.7 / 4.2 | |
| | -59.4 | -14.3 | 137.6 | 10.9 | | | | 9.1 / 10.5 | |
| | -6.7 | -3.4 | -23.0 | NM | | | | 30.9 / -650.6 | |
| EBIT/Interest | 14.6 | 14.2 | | 15.7 | | | | (43) 11.3 / (51) 10.8 | |
| | (14) 5.8 | (11) 7.2 | | (10) 4.1 | | | | 4.2 / 5.6 | |
| | -.1 | .6 | | 2.7 | | | | 2.3 / 2.0 | |
| Net Profit + Depr., Dep., Amort./Cur. Mat. L/T/D | | | | | | | | | |
| Fixed/Worth | .1 | .0 | .2 | .3 | | | | .5 / .5 | |
| | 5.5 | -1.4 | .7 | 1.2 | | | | 1.4 / 1.5 | |
| | -.7 | -.3 | 2.4 | NM | | | | 3.7 / -1.5 | |
| Debt/Worth | 2.7 | 2.0 | .5 | .6 | | | | .7 / .7 | |
| | UND | -9.2 | 1.4 | 1.3 | | | | 2.2 / 2.1 | |
| | -1.7 | -2.5 | 3.0 | NM | | | | 21.6 / -5.9 | |
| % Profit Before Taxes/Tangible Net Worth | 109.4 | 31.1 | 61.8 | 19.4 | | | | 80.6 / 60.9 | |
| | 43.1 | 10.3 | 23.0 | 9.3 | | | | (36) 40.2 / (39) 31.1 | |
| | -4.4 | -4.8 | 2.8 | 3.7 | | | | 15.2 / 8.0 | |
| % Profit Before Taxes/Total Assets | 215.1 | 395.5 | 23.8 | 11.7 | | | | 26.4 / 28.7 | |
| | 22.2 | 22.7 | 5.3 | 4.4 | | | | 9.3 / 9.2 | |
| | 6.5 | 4.8 | 2.0 | 1.8 | | | | 2.8 / 1.6 | |
| Sales/Net Fixed Assets | 5.6 | 2.7 | 3.1 | 1.9 | | | | 10.0 / 10.7 | |
| | 4.0 | 1.7 | 1.5 | 1.2 | | | | 4.3 / 4.4 | |
| | 2.1 | 1.1 | .6 | .8 | | | | 2.0 / 2.1 | |
| Sales/Total Assets | .7 | .3 | | 1.7 | | | | 2.3 / 2.6 | |
| | (12) 5.0 | (10) 2.5 | | 3.7 | | | | 1.2 / 1.2 | |
| | 11.2 | 5.6 | | 9.1 | | | | .8 / .7 | |
| % Depr., Dep., Amort./Sales | | | | | | | | 2.8 / 1.8 | |
| | | | | | | | | (37) 4.3 / (47) 4.6 | |
| | | | | | | | | 9.0 / 7.5 | |
| % Officers', Directors' Owners' Comp/Sales | | | | | | | | 1.3 / 2.0 | |
| | | | | | | | | (16) 2.6 / (11) 4.4 | |
| | | | | | | | | 5.7 / 7.7 | |
| Net Sales ($) | 14979M | 43647M | 124518M | 371115M | 387740M | 415848M | | 1236803M | 1439570M |
| Total Assets ($) | 3645M | 11524M | 58332M | 273365M | 494727M | 590639M | | 978190M | 1213677M |

M = $ thousand　　MM = $ million
See Pages 9 through 22 for Explanation of Ratios and Data

# AGRICULTURE—Finfish Fishing   NAICS 114111

| Comparative Historical Data | | | Current Data Sorted by Sales | | | | | |
|---|---|---|---|---|---|---|---|---|
| **Type of Statement** | | | | | | | | |

**Type of Statement**

| | 4/1/09-3/31/10 ALL | 4/1/10-3/31/11 ALL | 4/1/11-3/31/12 ALL | 0-1MM | 1-3MM | 3-5MM | 5-10MM | 10-25MM | 25MM & OVER |
|---|---|---|---|---|---|---|---|---|---|
| Unqualified | 9 | 8 | 11 | 2 | | | 1 | 2 | 6 |
| Reviewed | 4 | 3 | 6 | | | | 1 | 2 | 2 |
| Compiled | 8 | 4 | 24 | | | 1 | | | |
| Tax Returns | 14 | 10 | 21 | 12 | 12 | | | 2 | |
| Other | 24 | 20 | 24 | | 4 | | 2 | 5 | 10 |
| | | | | | 4 (4/1-9/30/11) | | 58 (10/1/11-3/31/12) | | |
| **NUMBER OF STATEMENTS** | 59 | 45 | 62 | 14 | 16 | 1 | 4 | 9 | 18 |
| **ASSETS** | % | % | % | % | % | | % | % | % |
| Cash & Equivalents | 13.6 | 17.6 | 11.6 | 8.5 | 21.7 | | | | 7.6 |
| Trade Receivables (net) | 4.5 | 6.8 | 5.2 | 1.4 | 1.4 | | | | 8.5 |
| Inventory | 7.6 | 9.1 | 9.4 | 7.4 | .5 | | | | 18.2 |
| All Other Current | 1.9 | 2.8 | 3.9 | 8.1 | .2 | | | | 4.9 |
| Total Current | 27.6 | 36.2 | 30.0 | 25.3 | 23.8 | | | | 39.1 |
| Fixed Assets (net) | 36.0 | 32.9 | 32.5 | 31.9 | 21.2 | | | | 37.6 |
| Intangibles (net) | 20.2 | 20.3 | 15.6 | 17.2 | 10.6 | | | | 14.1 |
| All Other Non-Current | 16.2 | 10.6 | 21.9 | 25.6 | 44.5 | | | | 9.2 |
| Total | 100.0 | 100.0 | 100.0 | 100.0 | 100.0 | | | | 100.0 |
| **LIABILITIES** | | | | | | | | | |
| Notes Payable-Short Term | 27.7 | 43.3 | 17.3 | 60.1 | 3.4 | | | | 7.2 |
| Cur. Mat.-L.T.D. | 6.6 | 5.9 | 5.2 | 7.6 | 6.4 | | | | 2.7 |
| Trade Payables | 3.5 | 6.1 | 5.8 | 1.8 | 1.0 | | | | 7.7 |
| Income Taxes Payable | .1 | .0 | .2 | .0 | .0 | | | | .5 |
| All Other Current | 6.7 | 8.4 | 12.4 | 12.8 | 22.1 | | | | 10.5 |
| Total Current | 44.5 | 63.7 | 41.0 | 82.3 | 32.9 | | | | 28.7 |
| Long-Term Debt | 42.5 | 33.3 | 37.3 | 55.1 | 38.1 | | | | 29.0 |
| Deferred Taxes | .4 | .5 | .5 | .0 | .0 | | | | 1.1 |
| All Other Non-Current | 2.7 | 6.2 | 5.4 | 12.3 | .0 | | | | 4.1 |
| Net Worth | 9.7 | -3.8 | 15.8 | -49.8 | 28.9 | | | | 37.1 |
| Total Liabilities & Net Worth | 100.0 | 100.0 | 100.0 | 100.0 | 100.0 | | | | 100.0 |
| **INCOME DATA** | | | | | | | | | |
| Net Sales | 100.0 | 100.0 | 100.0 | 100.0 | 100.0 | | | | 100.0 |
| Gross Profit | | | | | | | | | 86.0 |
| Operating Expenses | 86.4 | 88.6 | 86.2 | 91.7 | 80.7 | | | | 86.0 |
| Operating Profit | 13.6 | 11.4 | 13.8 | 8.3 | 19.3 | | | | 14.0 |
| All Other Expenses (net) | 3.9 | 3.0 | 2.8 | 6.6 | 1.1 | | | | 2.6 |
| Profit Before Taxes | 9.6 | 8.3 | 11.0 | 1.7 | 18.2 | | | | 11.4 |
| **RATIOS** | | | | | | | | | |
| Current | 2.3 | 1.9 | 2.1 | 1.6 | 7.4 | | | | 3.8 |
| | 1.3 | 1.3 | 1.1 | .3 | .5 | | | | 1.5 |
| | .3 | .4 | .2 | .0 | .0 | | | | .7 |
| Quick | 1.8 | 1.4 | 1.5 | .9 | 7.3 | | | | 2.6 |
| | .5 | .8 | .4 | .1 | .5 | | | | .4 |
| | .2 | .2 | .1 | .0 | .0 | | | | .2 |
| Sales/Receivables | 0 UND | 0 UND | 0 UND | 0 UND | 0 UND | | | | 6 62.6 |
| | 0 UND | 1 387.1 | 1 581.7 | 0 UND | 0 UND | | | | 23 15.8 |
| | 20 18.0 | 25 14.9 | 21 17.2 | 1 535.2 | 0 UND | | | | 35 10.5 |
| Cost of Sales/Inventory | | | | | | | | | |
| Cost of Sales/Payables | | | | | | | | | |
| Sales/Working Capital | 5.9 | 8.0 | 7.4 | 36.9 | 10.2 | | | | 3.0 |
| | 20.9 | 45.1 | 93.4 | -12.3 | -54.1 | | | | 8.6 |
| | -4.9 | -10.6 | -8.4 | -4.0 | -5.8 | | | | -18.6 |
| EBIT/Interest | 11.7 | 12.7 | 14.2 | 9.6 | 20.9 | | | | 16.0 |
| | (54) 4.0 | (40) 4.0 | (55) 5.7 | (13) 1.1 | (13) 14.2 | | | | (17) 6.3 |
| | .7 | .6 | 1.4 | -.7 | 4.9 | | | | 2.5 |
| Net Profit + Depr., Dep., Amort./Cur. Mat. L/T/D | | | | | | | | | |
| Fixed/Worth | .5 | .4 | .2 | .0 | .1 | | | | .4 |
| | 1.7 | 1.8 | 1.5 | NM | .7 | | | | 1.0 |
| | -1.2 | -1.1 | -1.8 | -.3 | -1.2 | | | | -16.8 |
| Debt/Worth | .8 | 2.0 | .9 | 3.9 | .4 | | | | .7 |
| | 9.2 | 7.0 | 3.0 | -5.7 | 3.0 | | | | 1.8 |
| | -2.4 | -2.7 | -5.3 | -1.7 | -7.7 | | | | -22.1 |
| % Profit Before Taxes/Tangible Net Worth | 55.6 | 109.5 | 138.4 | | 200.0 | | | | 61.6 |
| | (33) 26.9 | (26) 37.1 | (38) 49.6 | | (11) 97.3 | | | | (12) 38.7 |
| | 1.7 | 4.9 | 16.3 | | 42.7 | | | | 16.2 |
| % Profit Before Taxes/Total Assets | 18.5 | 21.0 | 36.8 | 29.0 | 74.4 | | | | 20.9 |
| | 5.9 | 6.2 | 14.6 | .5 | 41.4 | | | | 12.6 |
| | -.9 | -4.1 | 1.9 | -7.2 | 18.7 | | | | 2.9 |
| Sales/Net Fixed Assets | 19.6 | 22.7 | 29.2 | UND | 236.4 | | | | 5.2 |
| | 3.8 | 6.7 | 6.0 | 18.7 | 24.9 | | | | 3.7 |
| | 1.6 | 2.9 | 2.9 | 3.5 | 5.9 | | | | 2.9 |
| Sales/Total Assets | 2.2 | 3.4 | 3.2 | 3.9 | 4.6 | | | | 1.9 |
| | 1.1 | 1.3 | 1.6 | 2.0 | 2.3 | | | | 1.1 |
| | .7 | .7 | .9 | 1.0 | 1.1 | | | | .7 |
| % Depr., Dep., Amort./Sales | 2.4 | 2.9 | 1.9 | | .3 | | | | 2.2 |
| | (44) 5.6 | (34) 6.0 | (52) 3.9 | | (14) 2.4 | | | | (17) 3.6 |
| | 11.7 | 12.8 | 7.3 | | 5.4 | | | | 4.7 |
| % Officers', Directors' Owners' Comp/Sales | | | 5.2 | | | | | | |
| | | | (11) 8.5 | | | | | | |
| | | | 15.0 | | | | | | |
| Net Sales ($) | 1439716M | 1383760M | 1357847M | 8181M | 27759M | 4332M | 25530M | 165300M | 1126745M |
| Total Assets ($) | 1121023M | 1064440M | 1432232M | 7131M | 18226M | 1465M | 45973M | 149662M | 1209775M |

M = $ thousand    MM = $ million
See Pages 9 through 22 for Explanation of Ratios and Data

# AGRICULTURE—Shellfish Fishing  NAICS 114112

| Current Data Sorted by Assets | | | | | | | Comparative Historical Data | |

### Type of Statement

| | 0-500M | 500M-2MM | 2-10MM | 10-50MM | 50-100MM | 100-250MM | | 4/1/07-3/31/08 ALL | 4/1/08-3/31/09 ALL |
|---|---|---|---|---|---|---|---|---|---|
| Unqualified | | | | 1 | | | | 1 | 1 |
| Reviewed | 1 | 1 | 3 | 4 | 1 | | | 4 | 6 |
| Compiled | 7 | 11 | 4 | 1 | 1 | | | 12 | 5 |
| Tax Returns | 6 | 8 | 1 | 3 | 1 | | | 20 | 21 |
| Other | 1 | | 4 | | | | | 11 | 10 |
| | | 8 (4/1-9/30/11) | | 51 (10/1/11-3/31/12) | | | | | |
| NUMBER OF STATEMENTS | 15 | 20 | 12 | 9 | 3 | | | 48 | 43 |

| 0-500M % | 500M-2MM % | 2-10MM % | 10-50MM % | 50-100MM % | 100-250MM % | | | 4/1/07-3/31/08 ALL % | 4/1/08-3/31/09 ALL % |
|---|---|---|---|---|---|---|---|---|---|
| | | | | | | **ASSETS** | | | |
| 34.9 | 14.9 | 9.7 | | | | Cash & Equivalents | | 14.7 | 13.6 |
| .8 | 3.9 | 11.9 | | | | Trade Receivables (net) | | 7.2 | 5.3 |
| 6.7 | 4.7 | 8.2 | | | | Inventory | | 5.4 | 6.4 |
| .0 | 1.4 | 3.1 | | | | All Other Current | | 4.5 | 1.4 |
| 42.3 | 24.9 | 32.8 | | | | Total Current | | 31.8 | 26.8 |
| 34.5 | 28.9 | 34.6 | | | | Fixed Assets (net) | | 42.5 | 44.7 |
| 8.9 | 30.5 | 15.1 | | | | Intangibles (net) | | 15.2 | 18.7 |
| 14.3 | 15.7 | 17.5 | | | | All Other Non-Current | | 10.5 | 9.8 |
| 100.0 | 100.0 | 100.0 | | | | Total | | 100.0 | 100.0 |
| | | | | | | **LIABILITIES** | | | |
| 9.0 | 3.8 | 9.0 | | | | Notes Payable-Short Term | | 7.4 | 8.4 |
| 6.8 | 5.6 | 5.4 | | | | Cur. Mat.-L.T.D. | | 17.2 | 4.2 |
| 6.8 | 4.6 | 3.7 | | | | Trade Payables | | 5.1 | 4.3 |
| .0 | .0 | .0 | | | | Income Taxes Payable | | .0 | .3 |
| 30.1 | 5.5 | 6.5 | | | | All Other Current | | 21.8 | 6.6 |
| 52.6 | 19.5 | 24.7 | | | | Total Current | | 51.5 | 23.8 |
| 21.0 | 52.1 | 35.8 | | | | Long-Term Debt | | 36.4 | 38.8 |
| .0 | .0 | .0 | | | | Deferred Taxes | | 2.0 | .3 |
| 13.1 | 8.7 | 3.7 | | | | All Other Non-Current | | 10.9 | 11.3 |
| 13.2 | 19.7 | 35.9 | | | | Net Worth | | -.8 | 25.8 |
| 100.0 | 100.0 | 100.0 | | | | Total Liabilities & Net Worth | | 100.0 | 100.0 |
| | | | | | | **INCOME DATA** | | | |
| 100.0 | 100.0 | 100.0 | | | | Net Sales | | 100.0 | 100.0 |
| | | | | | | Gross Profit | | | |
| 89.8 | 81.2 | 82.5 | | | | Operating Expenses | | 86.2 | 91.2 |
| 10.2 | 18.8 | 17.5 | | | | Operating Profit | | 13.8 | 8.8 |
| 1.3 | 4.0 | 1.0 | | | | All Other Expenses (net) | | 3.4 | 2.3 |
| 8.9 | 14.8 | 16.5 | | | | Profit Before Taxes | | 10.4 | 6.5 |
| | | | | | | **RATIOS** | | | |
| 2.0 | 4.9 | 2.1 | | | | | | 3.6 | 2.4 |
| 1.1 | 1.1 | 1.5 | | | | Current | | 1.4 | 1.1 |
| .0 | .2 | .4 | | | | | | .2 | .2 |
| 2.0 | 4.8 | 1.4 | | | | | | 2.2 | 1.4 |
| .9 | .9 | .8 | | | | Quick | | 1.1 | .6 |
| .0 | .2 | .4 | | | | | | .1 | .1 |
| 0 UND | 0 UND | 0 UND | | | | | | 0 UND | 0 UND |
| 0 UND | 0 UND | 7 54.3 | | | | Sales/Receivables | | 0 UND | 0 UND |
| 0 UND | 9 39.6 | 50 7.3 | | | | | | 20 18.0 | 25 14.5 |
| | | | | | | Cost of Sales/Inventory | | | |
| | | | | | | Cost of Sales/Payables | | | |
| 26.3 | 9.1 | 6.0 | | | | | | 8.4 | 7.9 |
| 409.0 | 267.5 | 14.0 | | | | Sales/Working Capital | | 24.1 | 172.8 |
| -8.6 | -15.9 | -17.0 | | | | | | -25.6 | -11.2 |
| | 16.8 | 43.1 | | | | | | 8.5 | 7.2 |
| (15) 7.1 | 9.3 | | | | | EBIT/Interest | (43) 3.0 | (38) 2.6 |
| 1.2 | 2.3 | | | | | | | .7 | .5 |
| | | | | | | Net Profit + Depr., Dep., Amort./Cur. Mat. L/T/D | | | |
| .1 | .0 | .2 | | | | | | | |
| .8 | .7 | .9 | | | | Fixed/Worth | | .7 | .9 |
| -1.8 | 3.4 | 35.5 | | | | | | 1.5 | 1.7 |
| .7 | .5 | .7 | | | | | | 49.7 | -5.6 |
| 3.5 | 3.3 | 2.5 | | | | Debt/Worth | | 1.0 | .5 |
| -2.8 | -1.2 | 41.3 | | | | | | 4.2 | 3.9 |
| 404.8 | 94.9 | 114.8 | | | | | | -2.8 | -2.7 |
| (10) 94.8 | (13) 36.3 | (10) 37.7 | | | | % Profit Before Taxes/Tangible Net Worth | (31) 95.7 | (29) 49.4 |
| 28.1 | 22.1 | 23.4 | | | | | | 38.0 | 11.1 |
| 73.0 | 31.5 | 23.7 | | | | | | 8.4 | -5.4 |
| 22.8 | 17.4 | 14.8 | | | | % Profit Before Taxes/Total Assets | | 25.8 | 18.9 |
| -2.4 | 4.5 | 6.2 | | | | | | 7.3 | 4.7 |
| 124.9 | 269.2 | 18.7 | | | | | | .8 | -1.4 |
| 12.1 | 8.7 | 8.1 | | | | Sales/Net Fixed Assets | | 26.6 | 9.5 |
| 5.0 | 2.5 | 1.9 | | | | | | 7.2 | 2.9 |
| 6.8 | 2.1 | 2.1 | | | | | | 2.3 | 1.5 |
| 4.3 | 1.3 | 1.2 | | | | Sales/Total Assets | | 3.6 | 2.3 |
| 2.3 | .9 | .9 | | | | | | 1.8 | 1.1 |
| .9 | 3.2 | 1.6 | | | | | | .9 | .7 |
| (12) 4.6 | (12) 6.6 | (11) 2.9 | | | | % Depr., Dep., Amort./Sales | (39) 4.9 | (33) 8.0 |
| 8.5 | 12.6 | 9.2 | | | | | | 8.4 | 12.9 |
| | | | | | | | | .5 | 2.9 |
| | | | | | | % Officers', Directors' Owners' Comp/Sales | (12) 1.9 | (16) 4.6 |
| | | | | | | | | 8.4 | 10.5 |
| 11654M | 34890M | 96508M | 177743M | 170474M | | Net Sales ($) | | 401652M | 203517M |
| 2719M | 23507M | 58489M | 203351M | 195496M | | Total Assets ($) | | 148873M | 188036M |

*(Note: the columns 10-50MM, 50-100MM and 100-250MM display the notation "DATA NOT AVAILABLE" across the Assets, Liabilities, Income Data and Ratios sections.)*

M = $ thousand   MM = $ million
See Pages 9 through 22 for Explanation of Ratios and Data

## Comparative Historical Data  &  Current Data Sorted by Sales

| 4/1/09-3/31/10 ALL | 4/1/10-3/31/11 ALL | 4/1/11-3/31/12 ALL | Type of Statement | 0-1MM | 1-3MM | 3-5MM | 5-10MM | 10-25MM | 25MM & OVER |
|---|---|---|---|---|---|---|---|---|---|
| 1 | 2 | 1 | Unqualified | | | | | | |
| 5 | 5 | 9 | Reviewed | | 1 | | 2 | 1 | 3 |
| 8 | 10 | 14 | Compiled | 6 | 4 | 1 | 2 | 2 | 2 |
| 20 | 14 | 18 | Tax Returns | 8 | 10 | | 2 | 3 | 2 |
| 10 | 19 | 17 | Other | 5 | 5 | | | | |
| | | | *8 (4/1-9/30/11)* | | | | | *51 (10/1/11-3/31/12)* | |
| **44** | **50** | **59** | **NUMBER OF STATEMENTS** | 19 | 20 | 1 | 6 | 6 | 7 |
| % | % | % | **ASSETS** | % | % | % | % | % | % |
| 14.2 | 10.5 | 17.2 | Cash & Equivalents | 26.8 | 15.2 | | | | |
| 7.6 | 6.3 | 4.7 | Trade Receivables (net) | .6 | 3.4 | | | | |
| 4.8 | 5.4 | 7.2 | Inventory | 5.3 | 3.8 | | | | |
| 1.8 | 3.3 | 1.5 | All Other Current | 1.1 | .4 | | | | |
| 28.4 | 25.4 | 30.6 | Total Current | 33.8 | 22.8 | | | | |
| 32.8 | 34.7 | 32.7 | Fixed Assets (net) | 32.8 | 30.8 | | | | |
| 23.4 | 24.8 | 20.7 | Intangibles (net) | 21.4 | 31.1 | | | | |
| 15.5 | 15.0 | 16.0 | All Other Non-Current | 12.0 | 15.3 | | | | |
| 100.0 | 100.0 | 100.0 | Total | 100.0 | 100.0 | | | | |
| | | | **LIABILITIES** | | | | | | |
| 9.8 | 9.7 | 6.1 | Notes Payable-Short Term | 7.3 | 3.7 | | | | |
| 4.6 | 3.5 | 5.5 | Cur. Mat.-L.T.D. | 5.3 | 7.4 | | | | |
| 5.9 | 7.2 | 4.6 | Trade Payables | 6.8 | 2.0 | | | | |
| .0 | 1.4 | .1 | Income Taxes Payable | .0 | .0 | | | | |
| 6.0 | 7.9 | 11.0 | All Other Current | 16.1 | 12.8 | | | | |
| 26.4 | 29.7 | 27.3 | Total Current | 35.5 | 26.0 | | | | |
| 50.4 | 37.1 | 37.6 | Long-Term Debt | 23.4 | 61.7 | | | | |
| .4 | .3 | .2 | Deferred Taxes | .0 | .0 | | | | |
| 8.6 | 7.0 | 7.8 | All Other Non-Current | 11.0 | 10.0 | | | | |
| 14.2 | 26.0 | 27.0 | Net Worth | 30.1 | 2.4 | | | | |
| 100.0 | 100.0 | 100.0 | Total Liabilities & Net Worth | 100.0 | 100.0 | | | | |
| | | | **INCOME DATA** | | | | | | |
| 100.0 | 100.0 | 100.0 | Net Sales | 100.0 | 100.0 | | | | |
| | | | Gross Profit | | | | | | |
| 84.7 | 86.7 | 82.2 | Operating Expenses | 79.0 | 82.5 | | | | |
| 15.3 | 13.3 | 17.8 | Operating Profit | 21.0 | 17.5 | | | | |
| 4.7 | 5.1 | 3.1 | All Other Expenses (net) | 5.0 | 4.1 | | | | |
| 10.7 | 8.2 | 14.6 | Profit Before Taxes | 16.0 | 13.5 | | | | |
| | | | **RATIOS** | | | | | | |
| 2.2 | 2.6 | 2.2 | | 2.2 | 1.3 | | | | |
| 1.2 | .9 | 1.3 | Current | 1.2 | .7 | | | | |
| .3 | .1 | .3 | | .1 | .1 | | | | |
| 1.9 | 1.6 | 1.5 | | 2.2 | 1.1 | | | | |
| .7 | .5 | .7 | Quick | .9 | .4 | | | | |
| .3 | .1 | .2 | | .0 | .1 | | | | |
| 0 UND | 0 UND | 0 UND | | 0 UND | 0 UND | | | | |
| 0 UND | 0 UND | 0 UND | Sales/Receivables | 0 UND | 0 UND | | | | |
| 18 20.6 | 31 11.8 | 11 32.0 | | 0 UND | 18 20.6 | | | | |
| | | | Cost of Sales/Inventory | | | | | | |
| | | | Cost of Sales/Payables | | | | | | |
| 9.0 | 6.7 | 8.5 | | 13.2 | 16.6 | | | | |
| 46.4 | -538.7 | 40.0 | Sales/Working Capital | 224.3 | -166.1 | | | | |
| -10.4 | -4.1 | -17.7 | | -3.1 | -8.1 | | | | |
| 12.1 | 16.5 | 16.8 | | | 12.9 | | | | |
| (38) 3.6 | (41) 4.0 | (44) 6.1 | EBIT/Interest | | (17) 6.5 | | | | |
| .9 | .5 | 2.3 | | | 1.9 | | | | |
| | | | Net Profit + Depr., Dep., Amort./Cur. Mat. L/T/D | | | | | | |
| .3 | .4 | .2 | | .0 | .1 | | | | |
| 1.0 | .9 | .8 | Fixed/Worth | .6 | 1.4 | | | | |
| -2.8 | -6.4 | 7.4 | | 18.0 | -2.0 | | | | |
| .7 | .5 | .7 | | .4 | 1.8 | | | | |
| 4.0 | 3.5 | 3.4 | Debt/Worth | 3.5 | 29.0 | | | | |
| -2.2 | -2.0 | -2.2 | | -2.2 | -1.2 | | | | |
| 77.0 | 47.1 | 88.4 | | 260.7 | 200.0 | | | | |
| (26) 29.9 | (33) 20.3 | (42) 31.2 | % Profit Before Taxes/Tangible Net Worth | (13) 50.0 | (11) 75.4 | | | | |
| 7.2 | -1.5 | 20.9 | | 18.4 | 30.9 | | | | |
| 32.6 | 23.6 | 25.2 | | 35.8 | 31.5 | | | | |
| 8.0 | 7.0 | 14.4 | % Profit Before Taxes/Total Assets | 12.4 | 16.3 | | | | |
| .9 | -2.3 | 4.7 | | -2.4 | 4.1 | | | | |
| 50.6 | 19.1 | 34.9 | | 194.5 | 138.2 | | | | |
| 8.7 | 4.9 | 7.9 | Sales/Net Fixed Assets | 12.1 | 8.1 | | | | |
| 1.9 | 1.9 | 2.6 | | 3.7 | 2.7 | | | | |
| 2.7 | 1.9 | 2.3 | | 6.0 | 2.2 | | | | |
| 1.1 | 1.1 | 1.3 | Sales/Total Assets | 2.3 | 1.4 | | | | |
| .6 | .7 | .8 | | .7 | 1.0 | | | | |
| 2.0 | 2.7 | 1.6 | | 1.0 | 2.7 | | | | |
| (32) 4.3 | (37) 7.2 | (45) 4.4 | % Depr., Dep., Amort./Sales | (12) 4.8 | (14) 5.0 | | | | |
| 10.6 | 12.6 | 8.3 | | 9.7 | 11.5 | | | | |
| 1.6 | 1.9 | 1.6 | | 1.4 | | | | | |
| (17) 3.6 | (15) 3.7 | (21) 3.4 | % Officers', Directors' Owners' Comp/Sales | (10) 1.9 | | | | | |
| 8.6 | 10.1 | 8.4 | | 8.9 | | | | | |
| 280397M | 459602M | 491269M | Net Sales ($) | 11025M | 37287M | 3145M | 46374M | 99849M | 293589M |
| 276781M | 434333M | 483562M | Total Assets ($) | 17228M | 36851M | 6208M | 29547M | 110145M | 283583M |

© RMA 2012

M = $ thousand   MM = $ million
See Pages 9 through 22 for Explanation of Ratios and Data

## Current Data Sorted by Assets      Comparative Historical Data

| 0-500M | 500M-2MM | 2-10MM | 10-50MM | 50-100MM | 100-250MM | Type of Statement | 4/1/07-3/31/08 ALL | 4/1/08-3/31/09 ALL |
|---|---|---|---|---|---|---|---|---|
| 1 | 5 | 9 | 1 | 1 | 1 | Unqualified | 22 | 20 |
| | 1 | 7 | 2 | | | Reviewed | 7 | 8 |
| | 3 | 5 | 2 | | | Compiled | 7 | 7 |
| 6 | 10 | 2 | 1 | | | Tax Returns | 7 | 7 |
| | 9 | 7 | 2 | | | Other | 2 | 4 |
| 31 (4/1-9/30/11) | | | 44 (10/1/11-3/31/12) | | | | | |
| 7 | 28 | 30 | 8 | 1 | 1 | **NUMBER OF STATEMENTS** | 45 | 46 |
| % | % | % | % | % | % | **ASSETS** | % | % |
| | 14.2 | 16.9 | | | | Cash & Equivalents | 8.9 | 11.3 |
| | 14.4 | 24.0 | | | | Trade Receivables (net) | 14.6 | 16.1 |
| | 12.6 | 13.0 | | | | Inventory | 11.4 | 12.7 |
| | 8.6 | 4.0 | | | | All Other Current | 4.9 | 3.8 |
| | 49.9 | 57.8 | | | | Total Current | 39.8 | 43.9 |
| | 39.3 | 33.5 | | | | Fixed Assets (net) | 50.0 | 44.1 |
| | .6 | .7 | | | | Intangibles (net) | .3 | .1 |
| | 10.2 | 8.1 | | | | All Other Non-Current | 9.9 | 11.9 |
| | 100.0 | 100.0 | | | | Total | 100.0 | 100.0 |
| | | | | | | **LIABILITIES** | | |
| | 10.7 | 7.9 | | | | Notes Payable-Short Term | 10.5 | 9.9 |
| | 6.2 | 3.6 | | | | Cur. Mat.-L.T.D. | 5.2 | 6.0 |
| | 8.1 | 11.6 | | | | Trade Payables | 5.0 | 8.5 |
| | .1 | .1 | | | | Income Taxes Payable | .2 | .1 |
| | 14.7 | 16.0 | | | | All Other Current | 9.2 | 9.8 |
| | 39.8 | 39.2 | | | | Total Current | 30.2 | 34.4 |
| | 22.6 | 11.5 | | | | Long-Term Debt | 22.9 | 19.1 |
| | .0 | .6 | | | | Deferred Taxes | .2 | .1 |
| | .7 | 2.3 | | | | All Other Non-Current | 1.3 | 2.1 |
| | 36.9 | 46.5 | | | | Net Worth | 45.4 | 44.3 |
| | 100.0 | 100.0 | | | | Total Liabilities & Net Worth | 100.0 | 100.0 |
| | | | | | | **INCOME DATA** | | |
| | 100.0 | 100.0 | | | | Net Sales | 100.0 | 100.0 |
| | | | | | | Gross Profit | | |
| | 88.6 | 84.0 | | | | Operating Expenses | 86.2 | 87.8 |
| | 11.4 | 16.0 | | | | Operating Profit | 13.8 | 12.2 |
| | 1.2 | .3 | | | | All Other Expenses (net) | .7 | -.6 |
| | 10.1 | 15.7 | | | | Profit Before Taxes | 13.0 | 12.8 |
| | | | | | | **RATIOS** | | |
| | 2.5 | 2.3 | | | | | 2.4 | 2.3 |
| | 1.7 | 1.4 | | | | Current | 1.2 | 1.3 |
| | .9 | 1.2 | | | | | 1.0 | 1.0 |
| | 1.9 | 1.8 | | | | | 1.7 | 1.5 |
| | .8 | 1.0 | | | | Quick | 1.0 | .9 |
| | .3 | .6 | | | | | .3 | .6 |
| | 0 UND | 11 32.5 | | | | | 7 52.5 | 2 208.6 |
| | 12 29.2 | 52 7.0 | | | | Sales/Receivables | 21 17.4 | 23 15.9 |
| | 33 11.2 | 101 3.6 | | | | | 56 6.5 | 69 5.3 |
| | | | | | | | | |
| | | | | | | Cost of Sales/Inventory | | |
| | | | | | | | | |
| | | | | | | Cost of Sales/Payables | | |
| | 8.2 | 5.2 | | | | | 4.3 | 4.8 |
| | 19.1 | 9.8 | | | | Sales/Working Capital | 12.0 | 13.9 |
| | NM | 20.2 | | | | | -179.6 | -412.2 |
| | 37.4 | 43.8 | | | | | 29.4 | 22.7 |
| | (23) 4.1 | (22) 11.1 | | | | EBIT/Interest | (39) 3.5 | (38) 4.6 |
| | .9 | 2.4 | | | | | 1.4 | -.6 |
| | | | | | | Net Profit + Depr., Dep., Amort./Cur. Mat. L/T/D | 12.4 | |
| | | | | | | | (13) 3.6 | |
| | | | | | | | 1.7 | |
| | .3 | .5 | | | | | .5 | .4 |
| | .9 | .8 | | | | Fixed/Worth | 1.0 | .9 |
| | 2.3 | 1.4 | | | | | 1.4 | 1.3 |
| | .4 | .5 | | | | | .4 | .4 |
| | 2.0 | .9 | | | | Debt/Worth | 1.0 | .9 |
| | 4.6 | 4.1 | | | | | 2.0 | 3.2 |
| | 83.2 | 57.1 | | | | | 56.9 | 49.3 |
| | (25) 28.9 | (27) 26.4 | | | | % Profit Before Taxes/Tangible Net Worth | (42) 15.6 | (43) 14.4 |
| | 7.5 | 12.0 | | | | | 2.8 | 1.1 |
| | 25.2 | 27.3 | | | | | 25.1 | 29.2 |
| | 6.7 | 13.4 | | | | % Profit Before Taxes/Total Assets | 6.1 | 6.2 |
| | 2.4 | 3.1 | | | | | 1.4 | -4.5 |
| | 20.4 | 18.2 | | | | | 8.6 | 7.7 |
| | 7.2 | 3.4 | | | | Sales/Net Fixed Assets | 2.0 | 2.8 |
| | 2.6 | 2.1 | | | | | 1.4 | 1.2 |
| | 3.9 | 2.4 | | | | | 1.9 | 1.9 |
| | 1.9 | 1.3 | | | | Sales/Total Assets | 1.1 | 1.1 |
| | 1.3 | .8 | | | | | .7 | .7 |
| | .8 | 2.3 | | | | | 2.3 | 2.2 |
| | (21) 1.9 | (25) 4.3 | | | | % Depr., Dep., Amort./Sales | (44) 5.3 | (45) 4.2 |
| | 5.0 | 6.8 | | | | | 10.1 | 9.2 |
| | 1.2 | | | | | | | |
| | (10) 3.1 | | | | | % Officers', Directors' Owners' Comp/Sales | | |
| | 6.8 | | | | | | | |
| 13543M | 105694M | 249859M | 175391M | 3823M | 359653M | Net Sales ($) | 230058M | 337202M |
| 1882M | 33511M | 152341M | 136676M | 78644M | 133251M | Total Assets ($) | 299748M | 301384M |

M = $ thousand    MM = $ million
See Pages 9 through 22 for Explanation of Ratios and Data

## Comparative Historical Data

## Current Data Sorted by Sales

| | Type of Statement | 0-1MM | 1-3MM | 3-5MM | 5-10MM | 10-25MM | 25MM & OVER |
|---|---|---|---|---|---|---|---|
| 25  23  18 | Unqualified | | 4 | 4 | 6 | 2 | 2 |
| 15  13  10 | Reviewed | | 4 | 2 | 1 | 2 | 1 |
| 7  13  10 | Compiled | 1 | 2 | 3 | 3 | 2 | 1 |
| 15  21  19 | Tax Returns | 3 | 9 | 4 | 2 | 2 | 2 |
| 18  14  18 | Other | 1 | 6 | 2 | 2 | 5 | 2 |
| 4/1/09-3/31/10 ALL   4/1/10-3/31/11 ALL   4/1/11-3/31/12 ALL | | | 31 (4/1-9/30/11) | | 44 (10/1/11-3/31/12) | | |
| 80  84  75 | NUMBER OF STATEMENTS | 5 | 25 | 15 | 14 | 10 | 6 |

| Hist 1 % | Hist 2 % | Hist 3 % | | 0-1MM | 1-3MM % | 3-5MM % | 5-10MM % | 10-25MM % | 25MM& OVER % |
|---|---|---|---|---|---|---|---|---|---|
| | | | **ASSETS** | | | | | | |
| 12.7 | 12.9 | 16.4 | Cash & Equivalents | | 20.3 | 12.2 | 21.4 | 12.8 | |
| 14.5 | 15.2 | 19.4 | Trade Receivables (net) | | 7.0 | 28.6 | 21.8 | 35.7 | |
| 12.6 | 15.0 | 13.5 | Inventory | | 9.6 | 9.5 | 17.8 | 16.8 | |
| 2.5 | 4.3 | 5.5 | All Other Current | | 6.2 | .9 | 3.2 | 8.9 | |
| 42.3 | 47.4 | 54.7 | Total Current | | 43.2 | 51.1 | 64.2 | 74.2 | |
| 45.9 | 40.9 | 35.5 | Fixed Assets (net) | | 45.7 | 33.5 | 31.1 | 17.7 | |
| .7 | 1.2 | 1.6 | Intangibles (net) | | .7 | 6.4 | .0 | .6 | |
| 11.0 | 10.5 | 8.1 | All Other Non-Current | | 10.4 | 9.0 | 4.7 | 7.5 | |
| 100.0 | 100.0 | 100.0 | Total | | 100.0 | 100.0 | 100.0 | 100.0 | |
| | | | **LIABILITIES** | | | | | | |
| 9.0 | 12.0 | 11.2 | Notes Payable-Short Term | | 9.0 | 8.6 | 9.1 | 10.0 | |
| 6.3 | 6.0 | 4.3 | Cur. Mat.-L.T.D. | | 4.7 | 9.1 | 1.8 | 1.1 | |
| 7.3 | 7.9 | 10.4 | Trade Payables | | 7.3 | 6.0 | 8.7 | 30.6 | |
| .1 | .2 | .2 | Income Taxes Payable | | .0 | .0 | .0 | .6 | |
| 15.9 | 10.9 | 13.9 | All Other Current | | 14.1 | 10.7 | 21.1 | 5.3 | |
| 38.5 | 37.1 | 40.0 | Total Current | | 35.0 | 34.3 | 40.7 | 47.5 | |
| 21.0 | 23.8 | 15.8 | Long-Term Debt | | 19.9 | 20.1 | 9.5 | 3.0 | |
| .1 | .3 | .3 | Deferred Taxes | | .0 | .2 | .2 | 1.2 | |
| 5.3 | 4.5 | 2.6 | All Other Non-Current | | 3.4 | .1 | .0 | 6.9 | |
| 35.2 | 34.3 | 41.3 | Net Worth | | 41.7 | 45.3 | 49.5 | 41.4 | |
| 100.0 | 100.0 | 100.0 | Total Liabilties & Net Worth | | 100.0 | 100.0 | 100.0 | 100.0 | |
| | | | **INCOME DATA** | | | | | | |
| 100.0 | 100.0 | 100.0 | Net Sales | | 100.0 | 100.0 | 100.0 | 100.0 | |
| | | | Gross Profit | | | | | | |
| 89.0 | 90.3 | 87.2 | Operating Expenses | | 81.6 | 86.8 | 90.4 | 90.6 | |
| 11.0 | 9.7 | 12.8 | Operating Profit | | 18.4 | 13.2 | 9.6 | 9.4 | |
| 1.5 | .2 | .6 | All Other Expenses (net) | | 1.6 | -.2 | -1.5 | .2 | |
| 9.4 | 9.5 | 12.2 | Profit Before Taxes | | 16.8 | 13.4 | 11.0 | 9.2 | |
| | | | **RATIOS** | | | | | | |
| 2.5 / 1.3 / .7 | 2.7 / 1.4 / .9 | 2.3 / 1.4 / 1.1 | Current | | 2.3 / 1.7 / .4 | 2.4 / 1.4 / 1.1 | 2.7 / 1.5 / 1.0 | 3.1 / 1.4 / 1.2 | |
| 1.9 / .8 / .2 | 1.5 / .8 / .3 | 1.8 / .9 / .4 | Quick | | 1.7 / .7 / .1 | 1.8 / 1.2 / .5 | 2.0 / 1.1 / .6 | 1.9 / 1.0 / .6 | |
| 1 249.4 / 20 18.5 / 44 8.3 | 3 114.2 / 18 20.8 / 65 5.6 | 3 107.9 / 18 20.8 / 57 6.4 | Sales/Receivables | | 0 UND / 7 48.7 / 36 10.2 | 13 27.3 / 30 12.2 / 126 2.9 | 9 40.1 / 46 8.0 / 122 3.0 | 12 29.4 / 42 8.6 / 78 4.7 | |
| | | | Cost of Sales/Inventory | | | | | | |
| | | | Cost of Sales/Payables | | | | | | |
| 5.2 / 13.2 / -23.4 | 5.2 / 14.7 / -39.1 | 6.4 / 13.6 / 66.2 | Sales/Working Capital | | 3.0 / 24.7 / -6.9 | 3.8 / 9.5 / 88.2 | 5.1 / 11.6 / NM | 8.5 / 11.2 / 15.0 | |
| 16.6 / (61) 3.0 / .5 | 30.1 / (69) 5.8 / 1.2 | 28.3 / (59) 6.6 / 2.4 | EBIT/Interest | | 19.4 / (22) 4.4 / 1.2 | 16.3 / (10) 10.8 / 3.7 | 123.0 / (11) 18.3 / 2.4 | | |
| 4.7 / (10) 1.8 / .4 | 3.7 / (10) 3.1 / 1.8 | 17.3 / (11) 5.5 / 1.7 | Net Profit + Depr., Dep., Amort./Cur. Mat. L/T/D | | | | | | |
| .5 / .9 / 2.3 | .4 / .8 / 2.7 | .3 / .8 / 2.1 | Fixed/Worth | | .3 / .9 / 2.8 | .6 / .8 / 2.3 | .4 / .8 / 1.8 | .2 / .4 / .8 | |
| .4 / 1.1 / 5.1 | .5 / 1.8 / 5.0 | .5 / 1.8 / 4.1 | Debt/Worth | | .5 / 1.3 / 4.7 | .5 / 1.7 / 3.5 | .2 / 1.1 / 3.6 | .4 / 2.1 / 4.1 | |
| 38.5 / (69) 15.8 / -.8 | 40.4 / (71) 16.3 / 4.4 | 57.6 / (68) 27.0 / 8.9 | % Profit Before Taxes/Tangible Net Worth | | 88.4 / (23) 26.4 / 3.2 | 54.9 / (12) 28.1 / 11.2 | 52.4 / 21.1 / 2.2 | | |
| 16.8 / 6.7 / -1.9 | 15.6 / 5.4 / .3 | 23.5 / 10.9 / 1.9 | % Profit Before Taxes/Total Assets | | 27.4 / 6.9 / 1.3 | 23.5 / 13.0 / 4.0 | 23.2 / 6.4 / 1.1 | 35.6 / 9.0 / .3 | |
| 8.7 / 3.0 / 1.2 | 15.9 / 3.9 / 1.7 | 23.5 / 5.8 / 2.4 | Sales/Net Fixed Assets | | 9.9 / 2.8 / 1.9 | 38.6 / 4.6 / 2.5 | 14.6 / 5.7 / 3.3 | 56.0 / 22.7 / 6.4 | |
| 2.8 / 1.3 / .6 | 2.7 / 1.2 / .7 | 3.3 / 1.6 / 1.0 | Sales/Total Assets | | 2.3 / 1.4 / .9 | 3.7 / 1.3 / .9 | 3.0 / 1.6 / .8 | 4.4 / 2.5 / 1.7 | |
| 2.4 / (67) 5.0 / 10.0 | 1.5 / (72) 4.9 / 8.7 | 1.1 / (59) 2.9 / 5.7 | % Depr., Dep., Amort./Sales | | 1.3 / (20) 3.8 / 9.9 | 1.4 / (12) 3.9 / 6.3 | 1.1 / (13) 2.4 / 4.5 | | |
| .8 / (13) 2.3 / 7.8 | 2.3 / (23) 5.0 / 10.3 | 1.3 / (22) 4.2 / 6.8 | % Officers', Directors' Owners' Comp/Sales | | | | | | |
| 1589947M / 614038M | 1643765M / 714482M | 907963M / 536305M | Net Sales ($) / Total Assets ($) | 2931M / 3035M | 45610M / 58625M | 60388M / 115396M | 100695M / 85128M | 156896M / 67716M | 541443M / 206405M |

© RMA 2012

M = $ thousand     MM = $ million

See Pages 9 through 22 for Explanation of Ratios and Data

## Current Data Sorted by Assets

## Comparative Historical Data

| Type of Statement | 0-500M | 500M-2MM | 2-10MM | 10-50MM | 50-100MM | 100-250MM | | 4/1/07-3/31/08 ALL | 4/1/08-3/31/09 ALL |
|---|---|---|---|---|---|---|---|---|---|
| Unqualified | | | 1 | | 1 | 1 | | 7 | 7 |
| Reviewed | | 6 | 5 | 4 | | | | 7 | 7 |
| Compiled | 2 | 15 | 2 | 3 | | 2 | | 21 | 16 |
| Tax Returns | 7 | 8 | 9 | 1 | | | | 22 | 12 |
| Other | 6 | | | 2 | | | | 14 | 10 |
| | 13 (4/1-9/30/11) | | | 65 (10/1/11-3/31/12) | | | | | |
| **NUMBER OF STATEMENTS** | 15 | 30 | 17 | 10 | 3 | 3 | | 71 | 52 |
| | % | % | % | % | % | % | | % | % |
| **ASSETS** | | | | | | | | | |
| Cash & Equivalents | 24.0 | 16.0 | 7.4 | 7.3 | | | | 12.3 | 13.6 |
| Trade Receivables (net) | 7.1 | 12.7 | 15.7 | 16.6 | | | | 14.9 | 18.8 |
| Inventory | 7.8 | 12.1 | 14.9 | 23.3 | | | | 12.7 | 18.5 |
| All Other Current | 6.6 | 2.3 | 12.3 | 2.5 | | | | 4.0 | 4.7 |
| Total Current | 45.5 | 43.1 | 50.3 | 49.6 | | | | 43.8 | 55.7 |
| Fixed Assets (net) | 47.9 | 47.8 | 33.8 | 42.5 | | | | 46.3 | 35.3 |
| Intangibles (net) | .0 | .7 | 1.2 | .8 | | | | 2.8 | 1.1 |
| All Other Non-Current | 6.7 | 8.4 | 14.8 | 7.1 | | | | 7.1 | 7.9 |
| Total | 100.0 | 100.0 | 100.0 | 100.0 | | | | 100.0 | 100.0 |
| **LIABILITIES** | | | | | | | | | |
| Notes Payable-Short Term | 9.0 | 6.7 | 10.6 | 11.3 | | | | 17.8 | 12.2 |
| Cur. Mat.-L.T.D. | 5.7 | 7.3 | 3.9 | 3.4 | | | | 6.9 | 5.2 |
| Trade Payables | 5.9 | 15.8 | 10.6 | 13.5 | | | | 9.1 | 9.9 |
| Income Taxes Payable | .0 | .0 | .0 | .2 | | | | .2 | .2 |
| All Other Current | 6.1 | 10.0 | 12.9 | 7.5 | | | | 8.4 | 10.2 |
| Total Current | 26.7 | 39.8 | 38.0 | 35.9 | | | | 42.5 | 37.7 |
| Long-Term Debt | 31.7 | 41.4 | 19.6 | 16.1 | | | | 29.0 | 24.9 |
| Deferred Taxes | .2 | .1 | .0 | .1 | | | | .1 | .5 |
| All Other Non-Current | 27.0 | 5.4 | 2.1 | 2.2 | | | | 3.8 | 2.1 |
| Net Worth | 14.5 | 13.4 | 40.3 | 45.8 | | | | 24.6 | 34.8 |
| Total Liabilities & Net Worth | 100.0 | 100.0 | 100.0 | 100.0 | | | | 100.0 | 100.0 |
| **INCOME DATA** | | | | | | | | | |
| Net Sales | 100.0 | 100.0 | 100.0 | 100.0 | | | | 100.0 | 100.0 |
| Gross Profit | | | | | | | | | |
| Operating Expenses | 99.2 | 91.9 | 87.4 | 88.6 | | | | 95.0 | 92.8 |
| Operating Profit | .8 | 8.1 | 12.6 | 11.4 | | | | 5.0 | 7.2 |
| All Other Expenses (net) | .8 | 1.7 | 2.3 | .7 | | | | .9 | -.1 |
| Profit Before Taxes | .0 | 6.4 | 10.2 | 10.8 | | | | 4.0 | 7.4 |
| **RATIOS** | | | | | | | | | |
| | 3.0 | 2.4 | 2.3 | 2.8 | | | | 2.2 | 3.0 |
| Current | 2.2 | 1.3 | 1.2 | 1.3 | | | | 1.2 | 1.6 |
| | .7 | .4 | .9 | 1.0 | | | | .6 | 1.0 |
| | 3.0 | 2.1 | 1.3 | 1.3 | | | | 1.7 | 1.6 |
| Quick | 1.0 | .6 | .8 | .5 | | | | .6 | .8 |
| | .2 | .2 | .2 | .4 | | | | .3 | .3 |
| | 0 UND | 0 UND | 10 35.4 | 19 18.8 | | | | 0 732.8 | 4 89.8 |
| Sales/Receivables | 0 UND | 14 26.7 | 19 18.9 | 27 13.4 | | | | 19 19.2 | 27 13.5 |
| | 13 27.4 | 27 13.5 | 34 10.8 | 52 7.0 | | | | 45 8.1 | 62 5.9 |
| Cost of Sales/Inventory | | | | | | | | | |
| Cost of Sales/Payables | | | | | | | | | |
| | 8.2 | 7.7 | 6.3 | 5.6 | | | | 8.3 | 4.7 |
| Sales/Working Capital | 19.2 | 35.9 | 18.3 | 13.6 | | | | 37.8 | 13.1 |
| | -75.7 | -8.5 | -107.8 | 254.8 | | | | -17.9 | 426.9 |
| | 6.9 | 6.4 | 6.5 | 20.2 | | | | 9.0 | 11.0 |
| EBIT/Interest | (12) 2.1 | (26) 2.4 | (13) 3.3 | 10.7 | | | | (66) 2.7 | (47) 4.5 |
| | -3.2 | .5 | 2.3 | 4.4 | | | | .7 | 2.0 |
| Net Profit + Depr., Dep., Amort./Cur. Mat. L/T/D | | | | | | | | 11.0 | |
| | | | | | | | | (15) 2.0 | |
| | | | | | | | | .8 | |
| | .7 | .9 | .3 | .5 | | | | .6 | .4 |
| Fixed/Worth | 1.6 | 2.6 | .8 | .9 | | | | 1.8 | .8 |
| | -13.1 | NM | 1.4 | 1.4 | | | | 90.0 | 2.2 |
| | .5 | 1.7 | .5 | .8 | | | | .6 | .7 |
| Debt/Worth | 3.3 | 3.9 | 1.8 | 1.5 | | | | 4.4 | 2.0 |
| | -32.5 | NM | 4.6 | 3.0 | | | | 140.5 | 5.2 |
| % Profit Before Taxes/Tangible Net Worth | 36.4 | 75.5 | 40.9 | 54.6 | | | | 69.8 | 62.3 |
| | (11) 5.1 | (23) 29.3 | 22.4 | 28.9 | | | | (55) 16.8 | (49) 29.9 |
| | -22.1 | 7.0 | 8.2 | 12.5 | | | | 1.3 | 10.5 |
| % Profit Before Taxes/Total Assets | 9.9 | 16.6 | 15.7 | 22.7 | | | | 13.0 | 22.7 |
| | 2.4 | 4.6 | 6.9 | 9.8 | | | | 5.0 | 8.8 |
| | -1.3 | -.5 | 3.5 | 6.5 | | | | -1.3 | 2.5 |
| Sales/Net Fixed Assets | 18.6 | 9.7 | 34.7 | 14.6 | | | | 13.2 | 18.4 |
| | 9.4 | 4.7 | 6.2 | 4.4 | | | | 4.9 | 6.8 |
| | 2.9 | 1.9 | 1.9 | 1.6 | | | | 2.4 | 3.5 |
| Sales/Total Assets | 7.5 | 3.3 | 2.4 | 2.3 | | | | 3.6 | 3.1 |
| | 3.1 | 1.9 | 1.7 | 1.7 | | | | 1.9 | 1.9 |
| | 1.5 | 1.2 | 1.0 | .9 | | | | 1.2 | 1.4 |
| % Depr., Dep., Amort./Sales | | 2.6 | 1.2 | | | | | 1.8 | 1.5 |
| | (21) 6.5 | (13) 4.8 | | | | | | (68) 4.9 | (44) 3.6 |
| | 14.7 | 9.7 | | | | | | 11.1 | 10.2 |
| % Officers', Directors' Owners' Comp/Sales | | 1.4 | | | | | | 1.6 | .9 |
| | (14) 2.4 | | | | | | | (27) 4.9 | (21) 1.7 |
| | 9.7 | | | | | | | 9.4 | 6.8 |
| Net Sales ($) | 14630M | 81134M | 160296M | 332423M | 281166M | 737020M | | 684447M | 1384893M |
| Total Assets ($) | 3429M | 34018M | 89231M | 220864M | 191739M | 433706M | | 395444M | 771715M |

© RMA 2012

M = $ thousand    MM = $ million
See Pages 9 through 22 for Explanation of Ratios and Data

## Comparative Historical Data      Current Data Sorted by Sales

**Type of Statement**

| | | | | 0-1MM | 1-3MM | 3-5MM | 5-10MM | 10-25MM | 25MM & OVER |
|---|---|---|---|---|---|---|---|---|---|
| | | | Unqualified | | 1 | | | 2 | 3 |
| | | | Reviewed | | | | 1 | 1 | 3 |
| | | | Compiled | | 7 | 3 | 1 | 3 | 1 |
| 7 | 8 | 6 | Tax Returns | 7 | 11 | 2 | 2 | 4 | 5 |
| 10 | 11 | 5 | Other | 6 | 7 | | | 5 | 5 |
| 18 | 14 | 14 | | | | | | | |
| 18 | 19 | 24 | | | | | | | |
| 16 | 25 | 29 | | | 13 (4/1-9/30/11) | | | 65 (10/1/11-3/31/12) | |
| 4/1/09-3/31/10 ALL | 4/1/10-3/31/11 ALL | 4/1/11-3/31/12 ALL | | | | | | | |

| 4/1/09-3/31/10 ALL | 4/1/10-3/31/11 ALL | 4/1/11-3/31/12 ALL | | 0-1MM | 1-3MM | 3-5MM | 5-10MM | 10-25MM | 25MM & OVER |
|---|---|---|---|---|---|---|---|---|---|
| 69 | 77 | 78 | **NUMBER OF STATEMENTS** | 13 | 26 | 7 | 9 | 12 | 11 |
| % | % | % | **ASSETS** | % | % | % | % | % | % |
| 16.1 | 9.5 | 14.8 | Cash & Equivalents | 11.6 | 19.7 | | | 10.3 | 14.7 |
| 11.3 | 16.3 | 12.6 | Trade Receivables (net) | 2.2 | 9.5 | | | 17.6 | 17.1 |
| 13.7 | 15.6 | 13.5 | Inventory | 9.0 | 6.6 | | | 18.9 | 22.4 |
| 3.3 | 4.7 | 5.5 | All Other Current | 3.7 | 6.0 | | | 7.5 | 2.9 |
| 44.4 | 46.1 | 46.4 | Total Current | 26.5 | 41.8 | | | 54.3 | 57.1 |
| 39.8 | 40.4 | 42.8 | Fixed Assets (net) | 52.2 | 52.7 | | | 38.0 | 27.7 |
| 2.1 | 3.3 | 1.3 | Intangibles (net) | .1 | .8 | | | .4 | 5.5 |
| 13.7 | 10.2 | 9.5 | All Other Non-Current | 21.4 | 4.7 | | | 7.3 | 9.8 |
| 100.0 | 100.0 | 100.0 | Total | 100.0 | 100.0 | | | 100.0 | 100.0 |
| | | | **LIABILITIES** | | | | | | |
| 15.5 | 16.0 | 8.5 | Notes Payable-Short Term | 15.2 | 5.5 | | | 13.9 | 11.2 |
| 5.3 | 5.8 | 5.6 | Cur. Mat.-L.T.D. | 6.4 | 7.7 | | | 3.9 | 4.6 |
| 4.5 | 9.0 | 11.6 | Trade Payables | 3.4 | 10.4 | | | 14.3 | 12.5 |
| .4 | .3 | .1 | Income Taxes Payable | .0 | .0 | | | .1 | .3 |
| 8.5 | 9.7 | 10.2 | All Other Current | 6.0 | 6.8 | | | 12.5 | 13.4 |
| 34.1 | 40.7 | 36.0 | Total Current | 31.1 | 30.4 | | | 44.6 | 42.0 |
| 28.8 | 26.1 | 29.9 | Long-Term Debt | 37.8 | 46.1 | | | 12.8 | 15.7 |
| .2 | .4 | .1 | Deferred Taxes | .2 | .1 | | | .0 | .5 |
| 2.2 | 5.8 | 8.3 | All Other Non-Current | 25.9 | 3.2 | | | .6 | 4.1 |
| 34.7 | 27.0 | 25.6 | Net Worth | 5.2 | 20.2 | | | 41.9 | 37.7 |
| 100.0 | 100.0 | 100.0 | Total Liabilities & Net Worth | 100.0 | 100.0 | | | 100.0 | 100.0 |
| | | | **INCOME DATA** | | | | | | |
| 100.0 | 100.0 | 100.0 | Net Sales | 100.0 | 100.0 | | | 100.0 | 100.0 |
| | | | Gross Profit | | | | | 95.2 | 82.7 |
| 90.2 | 91.8 | 90.9 | Operating Expenses | 81.6 | 95.5 | | | | |
| 9.8 | 8.2 | 9.1 | Operating Profit | 18.4 | 4.5 | | | 4.8 | 17.3 |
| 2.0 | 1.3 | 1.6 | All Other Expenses (net) | 6.0 | .7 | | | -.6 | 1.8 |
| 7.7 | 6.8 | 7.4 | Profit Before Taxes | 12.4 | 3.8 | | | 5.4 | 15.5 |
| | | | **RATIOS** | | | | | | |
| 2.6 | 2.7 | 2.4 | Current | 2.3 | 3.4 | | | 2.3 | 2.7 |
| 1.4 | 1.3 | 1.3 | | 1.3 | 1.5 | | | 1.3 | 1.2 |
| .6 | .8 | .7 | | .1 | .5 | | | 1.0 | 1.0 |
| 2.2 | 1.8 | 2.0 | Quick | 1.8 | 2.6 | | | 1.1 | 2.0 |
| .7 | .6 | .7 | | .3 | .9 | | | .5 | .8 |
| .2 | .3 | .3 | | .0 | .2 | | | .4 | .4 |
| 0 UND | 1 384.7 | 0 UND | Sales/Receivables | 0 UND | 0 UND | | | 11 32.6 | 20 18.7 |
| 15 23.9 | 24 15.4 | 16 23.2 | | 0 UND | 3 130.5 | | | 21 17.4 | 29 12.5 |
| 41 8.9 | 49 7.5 | 27 13.5 | | 12 30.0 | 27 13.5 | | | 31 11.7 | 52 7.0 |
| | | | Cost of Sales/Inventory | | | | | | |
| | | | Cost of Sales/Payables | | | | | | |
| 4.8 | 5.6 | 7.2 | Sales/Working Capital | 7.8 | 7.2 | | | 11.2 | 5.9 |
| 15.6 | 19.0 | 18.9 | | 41.5 | 31.3 | | | 18.1 | 17.7 |
| -38.7 | -24.8 | -23.4 | | -1.8 | -11.9 | | | NM | 228.6 |
| 21.4 | 12.7 | 8.8 | EBIT/Interest | 8.1 | 4.0 | | | 9.2 | 30.1 |
| (62) 4.6 | (68) 4.3 | (67) 4.1 | | (10) 3.8 | (22) 2.0 | | | (11) 4.2 | 11.7 |
| 1.7 | 1.9 | 1.6 | | .0 | .5 | | | 2.9 | 8.5 |
| 6.6 | 17.5 | 8.0 | Net Profit + Depr., Dep., Amort./Cur. Mat. L/T/D | | | | | | |
| (16) 3.3 | (13) 3.5 | (11) 2.9 | | | | | | | |
| 1.7 | .6 | 1.1 | | | | | | | |
| .3 | .4 | .7 | Fixed/Worth | .5 | 1.3 | | | .5 | .3 |
| .7 | 1.1 | 1.3 | | 1.9 | 2.5 | | | .8 | .9 |
| 2.7 | 3.2 | 3.3 | | -8.0 | 16.6 | | | 1.3 | 1.4 |
| .4 | .7 | .9 | Debt/Worth | .9 | 1.6 | | | .9 | .7 |
| 1.6 | 2.0 | 2.9 | | 3.8 | 3.3 | | | 1.5 | 1.7 |
| 3.8 | 5.7 | 7.4 | | -9.7 | 25.7 | | | 5.1 | 3.3 |
| 42.5 | 50.2 | 58.8 | % Profit Before Taxes/Tangible Net Worth | | 55.9 | | | 41.9 | 115.9 |
| (62) 21.1 | (67) 20.1 | (66) 25.8 | | | (21) 9.7 | | | 26.4 | (10) 43.9 |
| 6.4 | 8.7 | 8.3 | | | -4.6 | | | 10.0 | 32.6 |
| 16.8 | 19.7 | 17.8 | % Profit Before Taxes/Total Assets | 12.1 | 11.2 | | | 16.8 | 33.9 |
| 8.1 | 6.7 | 6.9 | | 2.4 | 4.9 | | | 7.4 | 18.4 |
| 1.7 | 2.0 | 1.8 | | .8 | -1.4 | | | 4.8 | 9.1 |
| 14.4 | 11.8 | 14.2 | Sales/Net Fixed Assets | 5.6 | 9.6 | | | 35.0 | 15.1 |
| 8.6 | 5.1 | 5.8 | | 1.7 | 5.3 | | | 8.2 | 11.4 |
| 2.6 | 2.3 | 2.1 | | .8 | 2.0 | | | 2.1 | 3.5 |
| 2.8 | 2.5 | 3.0 | Sales/Total Assets | 2.4 | 3.3 | | | 4.1 | 2.3 |
| 1.7 | 1.5 | 1.9 | | .7 | 1.8 | | | 2.1 | 1.8 |
| 1.1 | 1.1 | 1.1 | | .3 | 1.2 | | | 1.3 | 1.1 |
| 1.6 | 2.4 | 1.7 | % Depr., Dep., Amort./Sales | | 3.5 | | | .7 | |
| (54) 4.8 | (61) 5.2 | (54) 4.5 | | | (17) 9.0 | | | (11) 2.8 | |
| 10.4 | 10.1 | 12.2 | | | 15.3 | | | 4.8 | |
| 1.3 | 1.8 | 2.1 | % Officers', Directors', Owners' Comp/Sales | | 2.4 | | | | |
| (22) 4.6 | (28) 3.4 | (28) 3.8 | | | (13) 5.6 | | | | |
| 10.5 | 6.5 | 8.8 | | | 10.0 | | | | |
| 1600354M | 992565M | 1606669M | Net Sales ($) | 4215M | 46728M | 27101M | 67877M | 200180M | 1260568M |
| 1071308M | 735106M | 972987M | Total Assets ($) | 7968M | 30587M | 11931M | 37812M | 130785M | 753904M |

© RMA 2012     **M = $ thousand   MM = $ million**
See Pages 9 through 22 for Explanation of Ratios and Data

# AGRICULTURE—Postharvest Crop Activities (except Cotton Ginning) NAICS 115114

| Current Data Sorted by Assets | | | | | | | Comparative Historical Data | |
|---|---|---|---|---|---|---|---|---|
| 2 | 1 | 6<br>23<br>17<br>10<br>23 | 20<br>24<br>15<br>2<br>12 | 7<br>6<br>1 | 5<br>1 | **Type of Statement**<br>Unqualified<br>Reviewed<br>Compiled<br>Tax Returns<br>Other | 47<br>55<br>49<br>11<br>58 | 48<br>55<br>42<br>18<br>73 |
| 5<br>6 | 6<br>10<br>9 | | | | | | | |
| | 90 (4/1-9/30/11) | | 128 (10/1/11-3/31/12) | | | | 4/1/07-<br>3/31/08 | 4/1/08-<br>3/31/09 |
| 0-500M | 500M-2MM | 2-10MM | 10-50MM | 50-100MM | 100-250MM | | ALL | ALL |
| 13 | 26 | 79 | 73 | 20 | 7 | **NUMBER OF STATEMENTS** | 220 | 236 |
| % | % | % | % | % | % | | % | % |
| 25.1 | 17.9 | 11.5 | 8.3 | 9.7 | | **ASSETS**<br>Cash & Equivalents | 8.8 | 8.6 |
| 12.6 | 17.0 | 25.0 | 22.7 | 14.1 | | Trade Receivables (net) | 19.0 | 20.3 |
| 16.9 | 6.0 | 16.3 | 18.7 | 25.6 | | Inventory | 20.5 | 19.8 |
| 1.1 | 3.5 | 3.9 | 5.0 | 4.3 | | All Other Current | 6.1 | 5.8 |
| 55.7 | 44.4 | 56.6 | 54.8 | 53.7 | | Total Current | 54.3 | 54.5 |
| 23.9 | 45.1 | 36.9 | 35.9 | 32.1 | | Fixed Assets (net) | 36.7 | 36.7 |
| .0 | .8 | 1.1 | 1.9 | 6.0 | | Intangibles (net) | 1.1 | 1.3 |
| 20.2 | 9.7 | 5.3 | 7.5 | 8.1 | | All Other Non-Current | 7.8 | 7.4 |
| 100.0 | 100.0 | 100.0 | 100.0 | 100.0 | | Total | 100.0 | 100.0 |
| | | | | | | **LIABILITIES** | | |
| 23.5 | 12.1 | 9.8 | 8.0 | 8.9 | | Notes Payable-Short Term | 14.5 | 12.4 |
| 8.2 | 7.8 | 3.5 | 3.0 | 2.7 | | Cur. Mat.-L.T.D. | 3.6 | 4.3 |
| 2.5 | 5.1 | 16.4 | 15.4 | 13.0 | | Trade Payables | 13.4 | 14.5 |
| .0 | .0 | .1 | .1 | .2 | | Income Taxes Payable | .2 | .3 |
| 24.6 | 19.0 | 12.7 | 14.8 | 12.1 | | All Other Current | 11.3 | 10.6 |
| 58.9 | 44.1 | 42.5 | 41.3 | 36.8 | | Total Current | 43.0 | 42.0 |
| 24.3 | 33.4 | 19.0 | 16.0 | 19.8 | | Long-Term Debt | 18.9 | 17.7 |
| .0 | .0 | .5 | 1.4 | .8 | | Deferred Taxes | .7 | .6 |
| 10.7 | 2.8 | 3.0 | 4.6 | 5.8 | | All Other Non-Current | 2.8 | 3.6 |
| 5.9 | 19.7 | 34.9 | 36.7 | 36.8 | | Net Worth | 34.6 | 36.0 |
| 100.0 | 100.0 | 100.0 | 100.0 | 100.0 | | Total Liabilities & Net Worth | 100.0 | 100.0 |
| | | | | | | **INCOME DATA** | | |
| 100.0 | 100.0 | 100.0 | 100.0 | 100.0 | | Net Sales | 100.0 | 100.0 |
| 88.0 | 90.7 | 92.2 | 90.7 | 85.1 | | Gross Profit | | |
| 12.0 | 9.3 | 7.8 | 9.3 | 14.9 | | Operating Expenses | 92.6 | 91.0 |
| -.2 | 2.6 | 1.5 | 1.1 | 1.6 | | Operating Profit | 7.4 | 9.0 |
| 12.2 | 6.7 | 6.3 | 8.2 | 13.3 | | All Other Expenses (net) | 1.8 | 1.4 |
| | | | | | | Profit Before Taxes | 5.6 | 7.6 |
| | | | | | | **RATIOS** | | |
| 4.8 | 4.5 | 2.1 | 1.9 | 2.1 | | | 1.8 | 1.8 |
| 1.3 | 1.2 | 1.4 | 1.4 | 1.8 | | Current | 1.2 | 1.3 |
| .2 | .5 | .9 | 1.0 | 1.1 | | | 1.0 | 1.0 |
| 4.1 | 3.8 | 1.5 | 1.2 | 1.1 | | | 1.1 | 1.1 |
| .9 | 1.0 | .9 | .7 | .7 | | Quick | .6 (235) | .6 |
| .1 | .3 | .5 | .4 | .4 | | | .3 | .3 |
| 0 UND | 0 UND | 21 17.2 | 21 17.6 | 24 15.4 | | | 12 31.5 | 12 31.4 |
| 0 UND | 1 574.5 | 35 10.4 | 35 10.5 | 38 9.5 | | Sales/Receivables | 30 12.2 | 30 12.0 |
| 17 21.8 | 36 10.2 | 64 5.7 | 81 4.5 | 54 6.7 | | | 52 7.1 | 60 6.1 |
| | | | | | | Cost of Sales/Inventory | | |
| | | | | | | Cost of Sales/Payables | | |
| 9.8 | 11.1 | 7.4 | 4.5 | 4.4 | | | 6.4 | 6.7 |
| 15.0 | 36.5 | 16.8 | 10.9 | 9.9 | | Sales/Working Capital | 19.1 | 19.1 |
| -14.6 | -6.1 | -96.9 | NM | 26.7 | | | -499.5 | -228.5 |
| | 11.4 | 19.8 | 17.8 | 24.2 | | | 7.0 | 12.5 |
| (23) | 4.8 (72) | 6.0 (70) | 6.7 (19) | 8.7 | | EBIT/Interest | (209) 3.1 (225) | 3.5 |
| | 1.7 | 1.6 | 3.0 | 4.8 | | | 1.3 | 1.7 |
| | | 3.4 | 11.0 | | | | 7.8 | 8.8 |
| | (20) | 2.0 (28) | 5.9 | | | Net Profit + Depr., Dep.,<br>Amort./Cur. Mat. L/T/D | (75) 3.7 (82) | 3.6 |
| | | 1.2 | 2.2 | | | | 1.3 | |
| .2 | .3 | .4 | .4 | .5 | | | 1.1 | 1.3 |
| .4 | 1.4 | .9 | .9 | 1.1 | | Fixed/Worth | .5 | .5 |
| -1.8 | -12.2 | 3.4 | 1.8 | 1.7 | | | 1.0 | .9 |
| .3 | .4 | .9 | 1.0 | .9 | | | 2.0 | 1.8 |
| 1.0 | 1.4 | 1.6 | 1.8 | 1.4 | | Debt/Worth | .9 | .9 |
| -10.9 | -15.8 | 6.9 | 3.3 | 7.9 | | | 2.0 | 1.8 |
| | 36.1 | 50.0 | 49.0 | 35.8 | | | 4.8 | 4.6 |
| (18) | 17.1 (70) | 18.1 (69) | 25.3 (18) | 27.0 | | % Profit Before Taxes/Tangible<br>Net Worth | 36.4 | 40.8 |
| | 9.2 | 5.0 | 8.4 | 20.4 | | | (201) 18.5 (215) | 20.1 |
| 33.9 | 17.8 | 18.1 | 15.7 | 17.3 | | | 5.3 | 7.9 |
| 10.8 | 6.6 | 6.2 | 7.6 | 10.8 | | % Profit Before Taxes/Total<br>Assets | 11.9 | 13.4 |
| -10.3 | .9 | 1.1 | 2.7 | 4.8 | | | 5.5 | 6.3 |
| 141.3 | 33.9 | 21.2 | 10.1 | 20.1 | | | 1.0 | 1.4 |
| 22.0 | 10.9 | 7.4 | 5.4 | 6.3 | | Sales/Net Fixed Assets | 14.5 | 17.3 |
| 9.5 | 2.2 | 2.5 | 1.9 | 1.4 | | | 6.5 | 6.3 |
| 7.7 | 4.8 | 2.8 | 2.7 | 1.9 | | | 2.3 | 2.2 |
| 4.8 | 2.7 | 1.8 | 1.3 | 1.2 | | Sales/Total Assets | 2.9 | 3.0 |
| 2.5 | .9 | 1.1 | .8 | .7 | | | 1.7 | 1.7 |
| | 1.1 | 1.1 | 1.1 | .9 | | | 1.0 | .9 |
| (22) | 3.1 (72) | 2.7 (69) | 2.9 (16) | 3.7 | | % Depr., Dep., Amort./Sales | 1.1 | .9 |
| | 12.3 | 7.2 | 6.3 | 7.6 | | | (200) 2.1 (208) | 2.0 |
| | | 1.1 | .8 | | | | 4.7 | 6.1 |
| | (16) | 1.9 (19) | 1.1 | | | % Officers', Directors'<br>Owners' Comp/Sales | .8 | 1.0 |
| | | 3.8 | 2.1 | | | | (41) 1.2 (43) | 1.3 |
| | | | | | | | 3.0 | 3.1 |
| 16447M | 113870M | 863961M | 7249810M | 1977520M | 2027804M | Net Sales ($) | 8374995M | 11506260M |
| 2903M | 32166M | 399687M | 1671558M | 1433126M | 1261944M | Total Assets ($) | 5006363M | 5797190M |

© RMA 2012

M = $ thousand    MM = $ million
See Pages 9 through 22 for Explanation of Ratios and Data

## Comparative Historical Data | Current Data Sorted by Sales

| 4/1/09-3/31/10 ALL | 4/1/10-3/31/11 ALL | 4/1/11-3/31/12 ALL | Type of Statement | 0-1MM | 1-3MM | 3-5MM | 5-10MM | 10-25MM | 25MM & OVER |
|---|---|---|---|---|---|---|---|---|---|
| 55 | 46 | 39 | Unqualified | 2 | 2 | 2 | 3 | 8 | 24 |
| 51 | 60 | 56 | Reviewed | 2 | 2 | 1 | 11 | 17 | 23 |
| 33 | 35 | 39 | Compiled | 1 | 3 | 4 | 11 | 11 | 9 |
| 19 | 24 | 27 | Tax Returns | 4 | 6 | 7 | 3 | 6 | 1 |
| 72 | 60 | 57 | Other | 5 | 10 | 5 | 13 | 7 | 17 |
| | | | | 90 (4/1-9/30/11) | | | 128 (10/1/11-3/31/12) | | |
| 230 | 225 | 218 | NUMBER OF STATEMENTS | 14 | 21 | 19 | 41 | 49 | 74 |
| % | % | % | **ASSETS** | % | % | % | % | % | % |
| 9.3 | 10.0 | 11.9 | Cash & Equivalents | 16.7 | 10.7 | 8.8 | 16.0 | 11.7 | 9.9 |
| 19.2 | 20.1 | 21.2 | Trade Receivables (net) | 9.4 | 17.2 | 14.7 | 21.1 | 24.0 | 24.4 |
| 18.9 | 17.4 | 17.7 | Inventory | 12.8 | 8.5 | 8.7 | 17.9 | 15.6 | 24.8 |
| 5.5 | 5.2 | 4.1 | All Other Current | .7 | 1.6 | 2.4 | 5.2 | 6.0 | 4.1 |
| 52.8 | 52.7 | 54.9 | Total Current | 39.6 | 38.0 | 34.6 | 60.2 | 57.3 | 63.2 |
| 38.1 | 37.6 | 35.8 | Fixed Assets (net) | 45.3 | 49.2 | 60.6 | 27.8 | 35.0 | 28.8 |
| 1.6 | 1.7 | 1.7 | Intangibles (net) | .5 | .1 | 1.4 | 1.0 | 1.3 | 3.1 |
| 7.5 | 8.0 | 7.6 | All Other Non-Current | 14.4 | 12.7 | 3.4 | 11.0 | 6.5 | 4.9 |
| 100.0 | 100.0 | 100.0 | Total | 100.0 | 100.0 | 100.0 | 100.0 | 100.0 | 100.0 |
| | | | **LIABILITIES** | | | | | | |
| 11.5 | 11.3 | 10.3 | Notes Payable-Short Term | 7.5 | 14.4 | 5.7 | 13.4 | 9.9 | 9.4 |
| 4.1 | 3.6 | 4.0 | Cur. Mat.-L.T.D. | 6.3 | 7.4 | 3.3 | 4.0 | 3.6 | 3.0 |
| 14.1 | 13.8 | 13.6 | Trade Payables | 2.8 | 7.4 | 5.7 | 14.6 | 12.6 | 19.4 |
| .2 | .3 | .1 | Income Taxes Payable | .0 | .0 | .0 | .1 | .2 | .1 |
| 10.0 | 11.6 | 14.9 | All Other Current | 9.9 | 24.6 | 12.9 | 18.4 | 12.2 | 13.3 |
| 39.8 | 40.6 | 42.8 | Total Current | 26.6 | 53.8 | 27.7 | 50.5 | 38.5 | 45.3 |
| 20.3 | 18.3 | 19.7 | Long-Term Debt | 32.1 | 19.5 | 36.7 | 18.4 | 20.9 | 12.9 |
| .6 | .7 | .7 | Deferred Taxes | .0 | .2 | .0 | .7 | 1.2 | .9 |
| 3.0 | 3.4 | 4.6 | All Other Non-Current | 8.2 | 2.9 | 3.0 | 5.6 | 3.3 | 5.1 |
| 36.3 | 37.0 | 32.2 | Net Worth | 32.9 | 23.6 | 32.7 | 24.7 | 36.1 | 35.8 |
| 100.0 | 100.0 | 100.0 | Total Liabilities & Net Worth | 100.0 | 100.0 | 100.0 | 100.0 | 100.0 | 100.0 |
| | | | **INCOME DATA** | | | | | | |
| 100.0 | 100.0 | 100.0 | Net Sales | 100.0 | 100.0 | 100.0 | 100.0 | 100.0 | 100.0 |
| | | | Gross Profit | | | | | | |
| 91.8 | 89.9 | 90.6 | Operating Expenses | 71.9 | 89.2 | 96.5 | 92.1 | 91.6 | 91.5 |
| 8.2 | 10.1 | 9.4 | Operating Profit | 28.1 | 10.8 | 3.5 | 7.9 | 8.4 | 8.5 |
| 1.6 | 1.9 | 1.4 | All Other Expenses (net) | 7.9 | 1.4 | 2.6 | .3 | 1.2 | .5 |
| 6.6 | 8.2 | 8.0 | Profit Before Taxes | 20.2 | 9.4 | .9 | 7.5 | 7.2 | 8.0 |
| | | | **RATIOS** | | | | | | |
| 1.8 | 1.8 | 2.2 | Current | 2.5 | 3.9 | 2.2 | 2.4 | 2.3 | 1.9 |
| 1.3 | 1.3 | 1.4 | | 1.0 | .9 | 1.5 | 1.3 | 1.5 | 1.4 |
| 1.0 | 1.0 | 1.0 | | .2 | .3 | .9 | 1.0 | 1.0 | 1.1 |
| 1.2 | 1.3 | 1.4 | Quick | 1.5 | 2.4 | 1.8 | 1.7 | 1.6 | 1.1 |
| (229) .6 | (224) .7 | .8 | | .6 | .6 | 1.0 | .9 | .9 | .7 |
| .3 | .3 | .4 | | .1 | .2 | .5 | .4 | .5 | .5 |
| 11 32.4 | 9 39.4 | 15 23.7 | Sales/Receivables | 0 UND | 0 UND | 0 UND | 16 22.9 | 17 21.7 | 22 16.3 |
| 32 11.3 | 34 10.7 | 33 11.2 | | 0 UND | 18 19.8 | 28 13.2 | 46 8.0 | 33 11.0 | 34 10.7 |
| 50 7.2 | 63 5.8 | 62 5.9 | | 60 6.1 | 57 6.4 | 66 5.5 | 104 3.5 | 64 5.7 | 49 7.4 |
| | | | Cost of Sales/Inventory | | | | | | |
| | | | Cost of Sales/Payables | | | | | | |
| 5.9 | 6.9 | 5.8 | Sales/Working Capital | 11.3 | 5.8 | 8.7 | 4.9 | 6.2 | 5.0 |
| 15.7 | 13.6 | 14.7 | | NM | -77.6 | 16.8 | 10.4 | 15.1 | 12.1 |
| -174.6 | -114.1 | -131.7 | | -3.0 | -3.6 | -36.5 | -88.8 | NM | 37.0 |
| 11.4 | 14.1 | 18.5 | EBIT/Interest | | 12.0 | 3.1 | 16.5 | 33.0 | 29.8 |
| (219) 4.1 | (210) 5.7 | (200) 6.3 | | (18) 5.0 | (18) 1.1 | (38) 4.3 | (48) 7.4 | (70) 9.1 | |
| 1.4 | 2.1 | 2.2 | | -2.3 | .0 | 1.7 | 2.9 | 3.8 | |
| 9.5 | 7.3 | 7.7 | Net Profit + Depr., Dep., Amort./Cur. Mat. L/T/D | | | | 6.9 | 7.5 | 8.4 |
| (73) 3.4 | (65) 3.7 | (61) 3.6 | | | | | (13) 1.8 | (15) 4.3 | (24) 4.5 |
| 1.4 | 2.0 | 1.7 | | | | | 1.0 | 2.6 | 2.3 |
| .5 | .4 | .4 | Fixed/Worth | .2 | .7 | 1.2 | .3 | .4 | .4 |
| 1.0 | .9 | .9 | | .9 | 1.5 | 1.9 | .7 | .8 | .8 |
| 2.0 | 1.7 | 2.2 | | NM | NM | 7.0 | 1.9 | 2.3 | 1.5 |
| .9 | .8 | .9 | Debt/Worth | .5 | .4 | .6 | 1.0 | .9 | 1.0 |
| 1.7 | 1.7 | 1.6 | | 1.2 | 1.5 | 3.6 | 1.9 | 1.3 | 1.6 |
| 3.6 | 3.8 | 5.6 | | NM | NM | 8.7 | 5.8 | 7.0 | 3.6 |
| 35.6 | 39.5 | 48.6 | % Profit Before Taxes/Tangible Net Worth | 59.5 | 30.3 | 16.2 | 49.5 | 55.2 | 48.5 |
| (208) 16.7 | (207) 20.5 | (191) 23.4 | | (11) 32.2 | (16) 15.0 | (16) 2.0 | (36) 17.6 | (44) 26.7 | (68) 27.8 |
| 4.6 | 7.3 | 8.3 | | 17.0 | 4.6 | -13.0 | 5.2 | 10.9 | 12.9 |
| 12.2 | 12.9 | 17.7 | % Profit Before Taxes/Total Assets | 29.5 | 19.4 | 4.7 | 13.8 | 20.5 | 18.0 |
| 5.8 | 7.0 | 7.9 | | 9.6 | 5.4 | .0 | 4.9 | 10.4 | 10.1 |
| .9 | 1.8 | 1.8 | | 1.1 | -3.0 | -4.7 | 1.2 | 4.1 | 4.3 |
| 14.2 | 14.8 | 21.0 | Sales/Net Fixed Assets | 24.5 | 26.0 | 5.2 | 18.5 | 29.0 | 20.9 |
| 6.1 | 6.0 | 6.7 | | 7.4 | 8.3 | 1.3 | 5.4 | 8.2 | 7.7 |
| 1.9 | 1.9 | 2.4 | | .5 | .9 | .8 | 2.9 | 2.0 | 4.7 |
| 2.7 | 2.7 | 3.1 | Sales/Total Assets | 3.1 | 4.0 | 1.9 | 2.0 | 4.0 | 3.3 |
| 1.6 | 1.6 | 1.7 | | .7 | 1.8 | 1.1 | 1.5 | 2.0 | 2.0 |
| .9 | .8 | .9 | | .3 | .8 | .6 | .7 | .9 | 1.2 |
| 1.2 | 1.2 | 1.0 | % Depr., Dep., Amort./Sales | | 1.3 | 3.5 | 1.1 | 1.1 | .7 |
| (204) 2.3 | (203) 2.7 | (191) 2.7 | | | (18) 5.6 | (17) 7.3 | (40) 2.8 | (42) 2.6 | (66) 1.3 |
| 5.8 | 6.8 | 6.6 | | | 18.6 | 13.7 | 5.9 | 6.3 | 3.4 |
| .9 | .8 | 1.0 | % Officers', Directors' Owners' Comp/Sales | | | | | .8 | .5 |
| (44) 1.5 | (57) 1.8 | (46) 1.4 | | | | | | (15) 2.7 | (14) 1.1 |
| 4.1 | 5.2 | 3.5 | | | | | | 5.9 | 2.1 |
| 11802094M | 8400474M | 12249412M | Net Sales ($) | 5991M | 36618M | 78068M | 293935M | 799734M | 11035066M |
| 6712774M | 5196828M | 4801384M | Total Assets ($) | 14056M | 38434M | 93248M | 296402M | 613886M | 3745358M |

M = $ thousand     MM = $ million
See Pages 9 through 22 for Explanation of Ratios and Data

## Current Data Sorted by Assets

## Comparative Historical Data

| | 0-500M | 500M-2MM | 2-10MM | 10-50MM | 50-100MM | 100-250MM | Type of Statement | 4/1/07-3/31/08 | 4/1/08-3/31/09 |
|---|---|---|---|---|---|---|---|---|---|
| | | | | | | 1 | Unqualified | 3 | 3 |
| | | 1 | 2 | 1 | 1 | | Reviewed | 2 | 5 |
| | | 2 | 2 | 1 | 2 | | Compiled | 4 | 6 |
| | 4 | 2 | 2 | 1 | | | Tax Returns | 2 | 1 |
| | 1 | 2 | 1 | 2 | 2 | 1 | Other | 3 | 5 |
| | | 7 (4/1-9/30/11) | | 21 (10/1/11-3/31/12) | | | | ALL | ALL |
| NUMBER OF STATEMENTS | 5 | 9 | 7 | 5 | 1 | 1 | | 14 | 20 |
| | % | % | % | % | % | % | ASSETS | % | % |
| | | | | | | | Cash & Equivalents | 21.3 | 24.4 |
| | | | | | | | Trade Receivables (net) | 5.9 | 7.9 |
| | | | | | | | Inventory | 10.1 | 4.4 |
| | | | | | | | All Other Current | 3.3 | 9.7 |
| | | | | | | | Total Current | 40.5 | 46.4 |
| | | | | | | | Fixed Assets (net) | 42.4 | 40.7 |
| | | | | | | | Intangibles (net) | .4 | 5.9 |
| | | | | | | | All Other Non-Current | 16.7 | 7.0 |
| | | | | | | | Total | 100.0 | 100.0 |
| | | | | | | | LIABILITIES | | |
| | | | | | | | Notes Payable-Short Term | 6.0 | 10.8 |
| | | | | | | | Cur. Mat.-L.T.D. | 5.1 | 5.3 |
| | | | | | | | Trade Payables | 9.7 | 9.7 |
| | | | | | | | Income Taxes Payable | .0 | .0 |
| | | | | | | | All Other Current | 6.2 | 12.1 |
| | | | | | | | Total Current | 27.0 | 37.8 |
| | | | | | | | Long-Term Debt | 25.9 | 18.6 |
| | | | | | | | Deferred Taxes | .0 | .0 |
| | | | | | | | All Other Non-Current | 5.9 | 6.0 |
| | | | | | | | Net Worth | 41.2 | 37.7 |
| | | | | | | | Total Liabilities & Net Worth | 100.0 | 100.0 |
| | | | | | | | INCOME DATA | | |
| | | | | | | | Net Sales | 100.0 | 100.0 |
| | | | | | | | Gross Profit | | |
| | | | | | | | Operating Expenses | 92.5 | 93.4 |
| | | | | | | | Operating Profit | 7.5 | 6.6 |
| | | | | | | | All Other Expenses (net) | 1.3 | 1.3 |
| | | | | | | | Profit Before Taxes | 6.2 | 5.3 |
| | | | | | | | RATIOS | | |
| | | | | | | | Current | 3.3 | 2.4 |
| | | | | | | | | 1.5 | 1.1 |
| | | | | | | | | .5 | .6 |
| | | | | | | | Quick | 2.5 | 1.8 |
| | | | | | | | | .8 | .9 |
| | | | | | | | | .0 | .1 |
| | | | | | | | Sales/Receivables | 0  UND | 0  UND |
| | | | | | | | | 0  UND | 0  UND |
| | | | | | | | | 10  36.1 | 31  11.8 |
| | | | | | | | Cost of Sales/Inventory | | |
| | | | | | | | Cost of Sales/Payables | | |
| | | | | | | | Sales/Working Capital | 5.0 | 4.4 |
| | | | | | | | | 24.4 | 24.7 |
| | | | | | | | | -21.3 | -12.3 |
| | | | | | | | EBIT/Interest | 25.1 | 17.0 |
| | | | | | | | | (12)  11.6 | (15)  2.9 |
| | | | | | | | | 1.7 | -.3 |
| | | | | | | | Net Profit + Depr., Dep., Amort./Cur. Mat. L/T/D | | |
| | | | | | | | Fixed/Worth | .2 | .3 |
| | | | | | | | | .6 | 1.1 |
| | | | | | | | | 1.7 | 3.2 |
| | | | | | | | Debt/Worth | .5 | .6 |
| | | | | | | | | 1.2 | 2.0 |
| | | | | | | | | 2.3 | 7.8 |
| | | | | | | | % Profit Before Taxes/Tangible Net Worth | 68.5 | 24.8 |
| | | | | | | | | (12)  24.7 | (17)  8.5 |
| | | | | | | | | 2.6 | -5.7 |
| | | | | | | | % Profit Before Taxes/Total Assets | 32.8 | 10.8 |
| | | | | | | | | 6.6 | 1.0 |
| | | | | | | | | 1.2 | -2.4 |
| | | | | | | | Sales/Net Fixed Assets | 24.6 | 20.3 |
| | | | | | | | | 6.8 | 4.7 |
| | | | | | | | | 3.1 | 2.7 |
| | | | | | | | Sales/Total Assets | 3.6 | 2.5 |
| | | | | | | | | 1.8 | 1.7 |
| | | | | | | | | .3 | .8 |
| | | | | | | | % Depr., Dep., Amort./Sales | 1.3 | 1.7 |
| | | | | | | | | (11)  2.2 | (18)  4.1 |
| | | | | | | | | 7.1 | 8.2 |
| | | | | | | | % Officers', Directors' Owners' Comp/Sales | | |
| 7862M | 20651M | 88397M | 116635M | 73133M | 47937M | | Net Sales ($) | 113190M | 226803M |
| 1284M | 8118M | 26621M | 80899M | 52512M | 130173M | | Total Assets ($) | 170610M | 341424M |

M = $ thousand    MM = $ million
See Pages 9 through 22 for Explanation of Ratios and Data

# AGRICULTURE—Farm Management Services  NAICS 115116

| Comparative Historical Data | | | | Current Data Sorted by Sales | | | | | |
|---|---|---|---|---|---|---|---|---|---|
| 4/1/09-3/31/10 ALL | 4/1/10-3/31/11 ALL | 4/1/11-3/31/12 ALL | **Type of Statement** | 0-1MM | 1-3MM | 3-5MM | 5-10MM | 10-25MM | 25MM & OVER |
| 3 | 5 | 4 | Unqualified | | | | 1 | 1 | 2 |
| 5 | 5 | 6 | Reviewed | | 2 | 2 | | 1 | 1 |
| 6 | 8 | 3 | Compiled | | 2 | | | | 1 |
| 3 | 7 | 8 | Tax Returns | 3 | | | 1 | 3 | 1 |
| 2 | 6 | 7 | Other | | 6 | 1 | | | |
| | | | | | 7 (4/1-9/30/11) | | | 21 (10/1/11-3/31/12) | |
| 19 | 31 | 28 | **NUMBER OF STATEMENTS** | 3 | 10 | 3 | 2 | 5 | 5 |
| % | % | % | **ASSETS** | % | % | % | % | % | % |
| 24.7 | 21.1 | 26.1 | Cash & Equivalents | | 34.2 | | | | |
| 7.3 | 13.8 | 13.5 | Trade Receivables (net) | | 5.4 | | | | |
| 3.5 | 8.1 | 4.8 | Inventory | | .8 | | | | |
| 6.6 | 6.6 | 6.3 | All Other Current | | 9.9 | | | | |
| 42.1 | 49.6 | 50.6 | Total Current | | 50.4 | | | | |
| 45.1 | 35.4 | 39.6 | Fixed Assets (net) | | 40.5 | | | | |
| .3 | 1.1 | 2.6 | Intangibles (net) | | 4.3 | | | | |
| 12.6 | 13.9 | 7.2 | All Other Non-Current | | 4.8 | | | | |
| 100.0 | 100.0 | 100.0 | Total | | 100.0 | | | | |
| | | | **LIABILITIES** | | | | | | |
| 6.0 | 11.2 | 12.1 | Notes Payable-Short Term | | 9.7 | | | | |
| 6.1 | 3.3 | 4.2 | Cur. Mat.-L.T.D. | | 5.2 | | | | |
| 7.8 | 9.2 | 8.4 | Trade Payables | | 2.2 | | | | |
| .0 | .3 | .4 | Income Taxes Payable | | .0 | | | | |
| 9.3 | 10.0 | 10.9 | All Other Current | | 16.3 | | | | |
| 29.2 | 34.0 | 36.0 | Total Current | | 33.4 | | | | |
| 20.9 | 17.7 | 27.2 | Long-Term Debt | | 31.5 | | | | |
| 1.0 | .1 | .3 | Deferred Taxes | | .0 | | | | |
| .2 | 2.9 | 5.4 | All Other Non-Current | | 11.7 | | | | |
| 48.9 | 45.3 | 31.0 | Net Worth | | 23.5 | | | | |
| 100.0 | 100.0 | 100.0 | Total Liabilities & Net Worth | | 100.0 | | | | |
| | | | **INCOME DATA** | | | | | | |
| 100.0 | 100.0 | 100.0 | Net Sales | | 100.0 | | | | |
| | | | Gross Profit | | 94.6 | | | | |
| 87.1 | 90.7 | 89.3 | Operating Expenses | | 5.4 | | | | |
| 12.9 | 9.3 | 10.7 | Operating Profit | | .5 | | | | |
| 1.7 | -.1 | 2.2 | All Other Expenses (net) | | 4.9 | | | | |
| 11.2 | 9.4 | 8.4 | Profit Before Taxes | | | | | | |
| | | | **RATIOS** | | | | | | |
| 3.3 | 4.8 | 3.6 | | | 7.4 | | | | |
| 1.3 | 1.5 | 1.6 | Current | | 3.7 | | | | |
| .4 | .8 | .7 | | | 1.0 | | | | |
| 2.9 | 4.4 | 3.5 | | | 7.2 | | | | |
| .7 | 1.3 | 1.2 | Quick | | 3.2 | | | | |
| .0 | .4 | .4 | | | .2 | | | | |
| 0 UND | 0 UND | 0 UND | | | 0 UND | | | | |
| 0 UND | 15 24.6 | 19 18.9 | Sales/Receivables | | 0 UND | | | | |
| 23 15.7 | 34 10.7 | 43 8.5 | | | 0 UND | | | | |
| | | | Cost of Sales/Inventory | | | | | | |
| | | | Cost of Sales/Payables | | | | | | |
| 4.3 | 5.2 | 6.5 | | | 8.7 | | | | |
| 39.8 | 13.0 | 18.1 | Sales/Working Capital | | 18.1 | | | | |
| -4.5 | -16.9 | -25.9 | | | NM | | | | |
| 14.0 | 18.6 | 25.2 | | | | | | | |
| (15) 6.6 | (22) 4.7 | (21) 5.3 | EBIT/Interest | | | | | | |
| 4.1 | 2.6 | 2.6 | | | | | | | |
| | | | Net Profit + Depr., Dep., Amort./Cur. Mat. L/T/D | | | | | | |
| .3 | .2 | .2 | | | .2 | | | | |
| 1.1 | .6 | .7 | Fixed/Worth | | .9 | | | | |
| 1.6 | 1.9 | 5.2 | | | NM | | | | |
| .4 | .5 | .7 | | | .3 | | | | |
| .9 | 1.2 | 1.6 | Debt/Worth | | 2.0 | | | | |
| 3.8 | 3.0 | 8.8 | | | NM | | | | |
| 52.7 | 50.7 | 95.7 | % Profit Before Taxes/Tangible Net Worth | | | | | | |
| (18) 28.4 | (30) 28.4 | (25) 48.8 | | | | | | | |
| 12.4 | 8.5 | 10.1 | | | | | | | |
| 21.8 | 19.2 | 25.5 | % Profit Before Taxes/Total Assets | | 26.6 | | | | |
| 11.6 | 8.0 | 9.8 | | | 12.6 | | | | |
| 3.3 | 2.1 | 3.2 | | | .9 | | | | |
| 17.2 | 28.0 | 27.9 | Sales/Net Fixed Assets | | 34.6 | | | | |
| 3.9 | 6.1 | 7.8 | | | 9.1 | | | | |
| 1.6 | 2.3 | 3.4 | | | 3.7 | | | | |
| 3.0 | 3.2 | 3.9 | Sales/Total Assets | | 5.2 | | | | |
| 1.7 | 1.8 | 2.4 | | | 3.0 | | | | |
| .6 | 1.2 | 1.4 | | | 2.3 | | | | |
| 2.1 | 1.9 | 1.1 | % Depr., Dep., Amort./Sales | | | | | | |
| (17) 5.5 | (21) 4.7 | (24) 2.4 | | | | | | | |
| 9.2 | 9.0 | 4.9 | | | | | | | |
| | .5 | .9 | % Officers', Directors' Owners' Comp/Sales | | | | | | |
| | (10) 3.6 | (11) 5.0 | | | | | | | |
| | 6.3 | 6.2 | | | | | | | |
| 150428M | 594759M | 354615M | Net Sales ($) | 1504M | 20340M | 11269M | 16010M | 78358M | 227134M |
| 220297M | 444401M | 299607M | Total Assets ($) | 3386M | 6710M | 4367M | 5642M | 49080M | 230422M |

M = $ thousand   MM = $ million
See Pages 9 through 22 for Explanation of Ratios and Data

## Current Data Sorted by Assets
## Comparative Historical Data

| 0-500M | 500M-2MM | 2-10MM | 10-50MM | 50-100MM | 100-250MM | Type of Statement | 4/1/07-3/31/08 ALL | 4/1/08-3/31/09 ALL |
|---|---|---|---|---|---|---|---|---|
|  |  | 2 | 5 | 3 | 1 | Unqualified | 14 | 13 |
| 1 |  | 2 | 2 |  |  | Reviewed | 9 | 9 |
| 4 | 5 | 3 |  |  |  | Compiled | 13 | 11 |
| 15 | 10 | 5 |  |  |  | Tax Returns | 22 | 24 |
| 4 | 8 | 8 | 2 | 1 | 2 | Other | 22 | 28 |
|  | 13 (4/1-9/30/11) |  | 70 (10/1/11-3/31/12) |  |  |  |  |  |
| 24 | 23 | 20 | 9 | 4 | 3 | NUMBER OF STATEMENTS | 80 | 85 |
| % | % | % | % | % | % | ASSETS | % | % |
| 28.2 | 5.2 | 5.1 |  |  |  | Cash & Equivalents | 11.8 | 9.5 |
| 12.8 | 15.7 | 28.6 |  |  |  | Trade Receivables (net) | 19.6 | 16.0 |
| 9.6 | 15.2 | 14.2 |  |  |  | Inventory | 14.7 | 17.8 |
| 4.0 | 1.5 | 3.8 |  |  |  | All Other Current | 3.5 | 3.3 |
| 54.6 | 37.6 | 51.7 |  |  |  | Total Current | 49.6 | 46.7 |
| 32.7 | 56.9 | 31.2 |  |  |  | Fixed Assets (net) | 37.6 | 39.3 |
| 3.4 | 3.5 | 4.9 |  |  |  | Intangibles (net) | 3.1 | 5.9 |
| 9.4 | 2.0 | 12.2 |  |  |  | All Other Non-Current | 9.6 | 8.1 |
| 100.0 | 100.0 | 100.0 |  |  |  | Total | 100.0 | 100.0 |
|  |  |  |  |  |  | LIABILITIES |  |  |
| 31.0 | 9.9 | 12.2 |  |  |  | Notes Payable-Short Term | 11.4 | 12.5 |
| 5.7 | 2.0 | 3.3 |  |  |  | Cur. Mat.-L.T.D. | 2.2 | 3.9 |
| 9.2 | 7.4 | 14.3 |  |  |  | Trade Payables | 13.1 | 11.0 |
| .0 | .0 | .2 |  |  |  | Income Taxes Payable | .2 | .2 |
| 15.7 | 8.4 | 8.5 |  |  |  | All Other Current | 11.3 | 11.7 |
| 61.6 | 27.8 | 38.5 |  |  |  | Total Current | 38.1 | 39.2 |
| 35.5 | 33.8 | 13.9 |  |  |  | Long-Term Debt | 21.6 | 28.3 |
| .0 | .0 | .6 |  |  |  | Deferred Taxes | .4 | .4 |
| 18.2 | 12.3 | 1.0 |  |  |  | All Other Non-Current | 4.3 | 3.8 |
| -15.4 | 26.2 | 46.1 |  |  |  | Net Worth | 35.6 | 28.2 |
| 100.0 | 100.0 | 100.0 |  |  |  | Total Liabilities & Net Worth | 100.0 | 100.0 |
|  |  |  |  |  |  | INCOME DATA |  |  |
| 100.0 | 100.0 | 100.0 |  |  |  | Net Sales | 100.0 | 100.0 |
|  |  |  |  |  |  | Gross Profit |  |  |
| 95.5 | 91.7 | 91.1 |  |  |  | Operating Expenses | 89.7 | 90.7 |
| 4.5 | 8.3 | 8.9 |  |  |  | Operating Profit | 10.3 | 9.3 |
| 2.2 | 4.3 | 2.0 |  |  |  | All Other Expenses (net) | 2.2 | 3.7 |
| 2.3 | 4.1 | 6.9 |  |  |  | Profit Before Taxes | 8.1 | 5.6 |
|  |  |  |  |  |  | RATIOS |  |  |
| 8.5 | 3.8 | 2.6 |  |  |  |  | 2.8 | 2.2 |
| 1.4 | 1.4 | 1.4 |  |  |  | Current | 1.5 | 1.3 |
| .6 | .6 | 1.3 |  |  |  |  | 1.0 | .7 |
| 3.3 | 2.3 | 1.6 |  |  |  |  | 1.6 | 1.3 |
| 1.3 | .7 | 1.1 |  |  |  | Quick | .9 | .7 |
| .2 | .3 | .4 |  |  |  |  | .4 | .3 |
| 0 UND | 0 UND | 10 36.9 |  |  |  |  | 7 53.5 | 1 275.2 |
| 0 UND | 13 27.4 | 26 14.2 |  |  |  | Sales/Receivables | 26 13.9 | 21 17.4 |
| 32 11.4 | 41 8.8 | 54 6.7 |  |  |  |  | 47 7.7 | 41 8.9 |
|  |  |  |  |  |  | Cost of Sales/Inventory |  |  |
|  |  |  |  |  |  | Cost of Sales/Payables |  |  |
| 5.5 | 4.2 | 6.7 |  |  |  |  | 4.7 | 5.9 |
| 64.6 | 21.2 | 14.1 |  |  |  | Sales/Working Capital | 15.2 | 27.5 |
| -32.8 | -17.0 | 62.2 |  |  |  |  | -160.1 | -18.8 |
| 8.5 | 7.3 | 66.9 |  |  |  |  | 12.1 | 16.8 |
| (16) 2.3 | (22) 1.7 | (19) 3.6 |  |  |  | EBIT/Interest | (62) 3.6 | (69) 3.1 |
| -.7 | .3 | 1.8 |  |  |  |  | 1.3 | .9 |
| .1 | .4 | .3 |  |  |  |  |  | 10.7 |
| UND | 1.8 | .7 |  |  |  | Net Profit + Depr., Dep., Amort./Cur. Mat. L/T/D |  | (10) 4.8 |
| -.8 | -24.3 | 1.1 |  |  |  |  |  | .8 |
| .3 | 1.0 | .6 |  |  |  |  | .3 | .3 |
| UND | 2.8 | 1.6 |  |  |  | Fixed/Worth | .8 | .9 |
| -2.5 | -29.3 | 3.6 |  |  |  |  | 2.0 | 6.4 |
| 113.3 | 42.9 | 36.8 |  |  |  |  | .5 | .7 |
| (13) 58.9 | (16) 6.9 | (19) 10.8 |  |  |  | Debt/Worth | 1.4 | 1.9 |
| 1.0 | 1.8 | 6.2 |  |  |  |  | 4.4 | 12.0 |
| 46.0 | 11.5 | 8.1 |  |  |  |  | 35.3 | 49.2 |
| 12.9 | 1.6 | 3.9 |  |  |  | % Profit Before Taxes/Tangible Net Worth | (71) 14.8 | (70) 13.1 |
| -6.1 | -4.0 | 2.3 |  |  |  |  | 4.8 | .5 |
| 61.3 | 11.6 | 115.3 |  |  |  |  | 14.7 | 18.7 |
| 24.6 | 2.6 | 11.5 |  |  |  | % Profit Before Taxes/Total Assets | 5.7 | 4.3 |
| 8.2 | .5 | 1.1 |  |  |  |  | 1.0 | -.3 |
| 10.9 | 2.5 | 3.8 |  |  |  |  | 16.4 | 21.5 |
| 4.6 | 1.4 | 1.7 |  |  |  | Sales/Net Fixed Assets | 5.4 | 6.0 |
| 2.7 | .4 | .6 |  |  |  |  | 2.5 | 1.7 |
|  |  |  |  |  |  |  | 2.7 | 3.2 |
|  |  |  |  |  |  | Sales/Total Assets | 1.7 | 1.7 |
|  |  |  |  |  |  |  | .7 | .6 |
| 1.2 | 1.3 | 1.5 |  |  |  |  | 1.4 | 1.4 |
| (16) 1.8 | (16) 2.8 | (13) 2.1 |  |  |  | % Depr., Dep., Amort./Sales | (63) 2.9 | (71) 3.0 |
| 5.1 | 6.1 | 10.3 |  |  |  |  | 6.2 | 6.3 |
| 3.0 | 3.0 |  |  |  |  |  | 1.0 | 1.5 |
| (10) 8.7 | (13) 4.7 |  |  |  |  | % Officers', Directors' Owners' Comp/Sales | (27) 3.6 | (31) 3.1 |
| 15.4 | 12.6 |  |  |  |  |  | 13.4 | 8.0 |
| 30688M | 51463M | 306249M | 317395M | 799555M | 734005M | Net Sales ($) | 2130115M | 2571115M |
| 4296M | 28812M | 91703M | 191923M | 312155M | 481261M | Total Assets ($) | 1580938M | 1344095M |

## Comparative Historical Data / Current Data Sorted by Sales

### Type of Statement

| | | | | | | | | | |
|---|---|---|---|---|---|---|---|---|---|
| 12 | 15 | 12 | Unqualified | 1 | | | | 5 | 6 |
| 8 | 10 | 4 | Reviewed | | | | | 3 | 1 |
| 23 | 11 | 12 | Compiled | 3 | 6 | 2 | 2 | | 2 |
| 31 | 35 | 30 | Tax Returns | 14 | 10 | 4 | | 3 | 5 |
| 32 | 24 | 25 | Other | 9 | 4 | | 3 | | |
| 4/1/09-3/31/10 ALL | 4/1/10-3/31/11 ALL | 4/1/11-3/31/12 ALL | | 0-1MM | 1-3MM | 3-5MM | 5-10MM | 10-25MM | 25MM & OVER |

Period counts: 13 (4/1-9/30/11); 70 (10/1/11-3/31/12)

| 4/1/09-3/31/10 | 4/1/10-3/31/11 | 4/1/11-3/31/12 | | 0-1MM | 1-3MM | 3-5MM | 5-10MM | 10-25MM | 25MM & OVER |
|---|---|---|---|---|---|---|---|---|---|
| 106 | 95 | 83 | NUMBER OF STATEMENTS | 27 | 20 | 6 | 5 | 11 | 14 |
| % | % | % | | % | % | % | % | % | % |
| | | | **ASSETS** | | | | | | |
| 10.6 | 12.0 | 12.3 | Cash & Equivalents | 17.1 | 16.7 | | | 11.8 | 2.8 |
| 18.9 | 13.5 | 18.4 | Trade Receivables (net) | 10.8 | 13.9 | | | 27.0 | 29.7 |
| 17.0 | 17.7 | 13.9 | Inventory | 6.1 | 14.5 | | | 12.4 | 23.3 |
| 2.8 | 3.8 | 3.3 | All Other Current | 3.3 | 4.2 | | | 2.0 | 4.6 |
| 49.3 | 47.0 | 47.9 | Total Current | 37.3 | 49.3 | | | 53.1 | 60.4 |
| 34.9 | 40.7 | 38.1 | Fixed Assets (net) | 52.1 | 37.6 | | | 24.8 | 21.2 |
| 5.9 | 4.9 | 4.9 | Intangibles (net) | 7.4 | 1.5 | | | 3.2 | 8.5 |
| 9.9 | 7.4 | 9.1 | All Other Non-Current | 3.4 | 11.6 | | | 18.9 | 9.9 |
| 100.0 | 100.0 | 100.0 | Total | 100.0 | 100.0 | | | 100.0 | 100.0 |
| | | | **LIABILITIES** | | | | | | |
| 19.9 | 13.3 | 16.0 | Notes Payable-Short Term | 12.2 | 19.7 | | | 10.3 | 9.0 |
| 4.8 | 3.7 | 3.5 | Cur. Mat.-L.T.D. | 2.8 | 5.9 | | | 1.9 | 3.4 |
| 13.5 | 9.6 | 9.8 | Trade Payables | 7.6 | 6.6 | | | 7.5 | 17.8 |
| .2 | .2 | .1 | Income Taxes Payable | .0 | .1 | | | .4 | .2 |
| 9.7 | 9.5 | 10.7 | All Other Current | 6.6 | 15.9 | | | 9.2 | 12.0 |
| 48.0 | 36.3 | 40.1 | Total Current | 29.2 | 48.1 | | | 29.2 | 42.3 |
| 28.1 | 26.0 | 25.0 | Long-Term Debt | 42.2 | 23.4 | | | 7.2 | 9.6 |
| .4 | .3 | .3 | Deferred Taxes | .0 | .0 | | | .9 | 1.1 |
| 3.4 | 10.3 | 10.1 | All Other Non-Current | 14.8 | 10.6 | | | 3.6 | 4.2 |
| 20.1 | 27.0 | 24.4 | Net Worth | 13.7 | 17.9 | | | 59.1 | 42.8 |
| 100.0 | 100.0 | 100.0 | Total Liabilities & Net Worth | 100.0 | 100.0 | | | 100.0 | 100.0 |
| | | | **INCOME DATA** | | | | | | |
| 100.0 | 100.0 | 100.0 | Net Sales | 100.0 | 100.0 | | | 100.0 | 100.0 |
| | | | Gross Profit | | | | | | |
| 94.2 | 93.8 | 93.0 | Operating Expenses | 92.8 | 89.4 | | | 95.6 | 94.8 |
| 5.8 | 6.2 | 7.0 | Operating Profit | 7.2 | 10.6 | | | 4.4 | 5.2 |
| .8 | 2.6 | 2.2 | All Other Expenses (net) | 5.6 | 1.5 | | | -.5 | -.1 |
| 5.0 | 3.6 | 4.8 | Profit Before Taxes | 1.6 | 9.1 | | | 5.0 | 5.3 |
| | | | **RATIOS** | | | | | | |
| 2.0 | 2.3 | 3.3 | Current | 9.8 | 3.2 | | | 3.5 | 1.9 |
| 1.4 | 1.4 | 1.5 | | 1.5 | 1.5 | | | 1.8 | 1.4 |
| .4 | .7 | 1.0 | | .6 | .9 | | | 1.3 | 1.2 |
| 1.4 | 1.3 | 2.1 | Quick | 3.0 | 2.5 | | | 2.1 | 1.1 |
| .7 (94) | .6 | 1.0 | | 1.3 | .9 | | | 1.6 | .7 |
| .2 | .3 | .3 | | .2 | .2 | | | .7 | .4 |
| 3  120.9 | 0  UND | 0  UND | Sales/Receivables | 0  UND | 0  UND | | | 21  17.8 | 10  36.4 |
| 19  19.0 | 17  21.9 | 17  21.7 | | 0  UND | 2  164.7 | | | 40  9.2 | 27  13.4 |
| 40  9.2 | 33  11.1 | 43  8.5 | | 39  9.3 | 41  8.8 | | | 43  8.4 | 72  5.1 |
| | | | Cost of Sales/Inventory | | | | | | |
| | | | Cost of Sales/Payables | | | | | | |
| 7.2 | 7.7 | 5.2 | Sales/Working Capital | 3.5 | 8.5 | | | 5.2 | 6.1 |
| 34.2 | 30.9 | 18.5 | | 19.2 | 53.6 | | | 12.4 | 22.1 |
| -17.5 | -49.5 | 181.3 | | -12.4 | -80.9 | | | 18.5 | 68.8 |
| 12.5 | 12.2 | 14.7 | EBIT/Interest | 5.4 | 26.2 | | | | 28.2 |
| (88) 3.3 | (80) 3.6 | (70) 3.4 | | (18) .9 | (19) 2.6 | | | | 10.6 |
| .8 | 1.5 | 1.4 | | -1.5 | 1.7 | | | | 4.3 |
| | 15.9 | | Net Profit + Depr., Dep., Amort./Cur. Mat. L/T/D | | | | | | |
| | (12) 4.7 | | | | | | | | |
| | 2.3 | | | | | | | | |
| .3 | .3 | .3 | Fixed/Worth | .4 | .4 | | | .1 | .3 |
| .7 | 1.1 | 1.0 | | 3.8 | 1.0 | | | .5 | .6 |
| 3.5 | 3.6 | UND | | -1.0 | -27.2 | | | .7 | 1.1 |
| .7 | .7 | .6 | Debt/Worth | .4 | .7 | | | .3 | .8 |
| 2.1 | 2.0 | 1.8 | | 3.0 | 3.1 | | | .7 | 1.6 |
| 11.7 | 5.7 | UND | | -2.9 | -31.5 | | | 1.4 | 3.8 |
| 48.5 | 44.9 | 48.3 | % Profit Before Taxes/Tangible Net Worth | 52.7 | 107.6 | | | 28.9 | 35.8 |
| (84) 10.7 | (76) 15.5 | (63) 15.8 | | (17) 6.5 | (14) 46.6 | | | 10.9 | (13) 18.5 |
| .4 | 5.1 | 5.3 | | .0 | 2.6 | | | 3.6 | 10.0 |
| 17.8 | 22.0 | 18.1 | % Profit Before Taxes/Total Assets | 20.5 | 34.9 | | | 16.2 | 13.7 |
| 4.4 | 7.7 | 5.6 | | 1.6 | 11.9 | | | 3.6 | 8.4 |
| -.4 | 1.4 | .9 | | -7.7 | .6 | | | 2.3 | 5.2 |
| 44.1 | 22.3 | 30.1 | Sales/Net Fixed Assets | 14.7 | 38.8 | | | 19.3 | 136.3 |
| 10.3 | 8.3 | 9.7 | | 4.6 | 16.9 | | | 12.4 | 10.1 |
| 4.2 | 2.3 | 2.6 | | .4 | 2.6 | | | 2.9 | 4.7 |
| 4.7 | 3.9 | 4.4 | Sales/Total Assets | 3.4 | 10.5 | | | 2.7 | 6.3 |
| 2.5 | 2.4 | 2.2 | | 1.4 | 2.3 | | | 2.0 | 2.2 |
| 1.4 | 1.1 | 1.0 | | .4 | 1.0 | | | 1.3 | 1.4 |
| .7 | 1.4 | 1.4 | % Depr., Dep., Amort./Sales | 2.3 | 1.2 | | | | .4 |
| (78) 1.9 | (71) 2.9 | (60) 2.3 | | (17) 4.0 | (15) 1.5 | | | | (12) 2.0 |
| 4.5 | 6.7 | 6.1 | | 10.2 | 3.0 | | | | 3.4 |
| 1.8 | 1.2 | 1.9 | % Officers', Directors' Owners' Comp/Sales | | | | | 2.9 | |
| (47) 4.8 | (35) 2.5 | (31) 4.7 | | | | | | (13) 8.5 | |
| 9.1 | 7.8 | 10.8 | | | | | | 15.0 | |
| 2585266M | 2251271M | 2239355M | Net Sales ($) | 13195M | 42433M | 23316M | 35821M | 209137M | 1915453M |
| 1339829M | 1101523M | 1110150M | Total Assets ($) | 26303M | 27497M | 16612M | 6198M | 117482M | 916058M |

M = $ thousand   MM = $ million
See Pages 9 through 22 for Explanation of Ratios and Data

© RMA 2012

# MINING

## Current Data Sorted by Assets

## Comparative Historical Data

### Type of Statement

| | 0-500M | 500M-2MM | 2-10MM | 10-50MM | 50-100MM | 100-250MM | Type of Statement | 4/1/07-3/31/08 ALL | 4/1/08-3/31/09 ALL |
|---|---|---|---|---|---|---|---|---|---|
| Unqualified | | 2 | 4 | 26 | 10 | 29 | | 57 | 59 |
| Reviewed | | 2 | 4 | 7 | 2 | | | 7 | 12 |
| Compiled | | 2 | 8 | 3 | 2 | 1 | | 14 | 16 |
| Tax Returns | 4 | 1 | 5 | 1 | | 1 | | 14 | 16 |
| Other | 4 | 10 | 24 | 23 | 8 | 13 | | 105 | 112 |

Sub-period totals: 21 (4/1-9/30/11) · 175 (10/1/11-3/31/12)

### Main Data

| 0-500M | 500M-2MM | 2-10MM | 10-50MM | 50-100MM | 100-250MM | | 4/1/07-3/31/08 ALL | 4/1/08-3/31/09 ALL |
|---|---|---|---|---|---|---|---|---|
| 8 | 17 | 45 | 60 | 22 | 44 | **NUMBER OF STATEMENTS** | 197 | 215 |
| % | % | % | % | % | % | **ASSETS** | % | % |
| | 14.4 | 19.4 | 11.5 | 12.9 | 4.1 | Cash & Equivalents | 10.2 | 10.3 |
| | 26.4 | 17.4 | 12.4 | 8.2 | 7.8 | Trade Receivables (net) | 15.4 | 12.3 |
| | 2.6 | 2.2 | 2.2 | 1.2 | .9 | Inventory | 1.8 | 2.2 |
| | 4.9 | 3.5 | 4.6 | 3.8 | 3.4 | All Other Current | 4.0 | 5.5 |
| | 48.4 | 42.5 | 30.6 | 26.1 | 16.1 | Total Current | 31.3 | 30.3 |
| | 40.8 | 34.7 | 59.9 | 68.4 | 76.5 | Fixed Assets (net) | 56.2 | 59.1 |
| | 2.5 | 4.5 | 1.8 | .8 | 3.5 | Intangibles (net) | 2.0 | 1.8 |
| | 8.4 | 18.3 | 7.7 | 4.7 | 3.9 | All Other Non-Current | 10.5 | 8.8 |
| | 100.0 | 100.0 | 100.0 | 100.0 | 100.0 | Total | 100.0 | 100.0 |
| | | | | | | **LIABILITIES** | | |
| | 17.0 | 5.9 | 5.0 | .8 | .6 | Notes Payable-Short Term | 6.8 | 6.3 |
| | 1.0 | .6 | 2.6 | 2.8 | 1.8 | Cur. Mat.-L.T.D. | 3.2 | 3.4 |
| | 8.1 | 8.0 | 9.1 | 10.5 | 8.2 | Trade Payables | 10.7 | 10.0 |
| | .4 | .0 | .1 | .0 | .0 | Income Taxes Payable | .4 | .1 |
| | 11.3 | 10.0 | 6.6 | 7.1 | 4.4 | All Other Current | 7.4 | 6.9 |
| | 37.9 | 24.5 | 23.4 | 21.2 | 15.0 | Total Current | 28.4 | 26.8 |
| | 32.7 | 15.6 | 20.0 | 13.8 | 30.4 | Long-Term Debt | 25.0 | 23.6 |
| | .0 | .2 | 1.4 | 1.7 | 1.1 | Deferred Taxes | .9 | .9 |
| | 3.4 | 6.3 | 5.5 | 4.1 | 4.0 | All Other Non-Current | 7.6 | 4.9 |
| | 26.0 | 53.4 | 49.7 | 59.3 | 49.5 | Net Worth | 38.1 | 43.8 |
| | 100.0 | 100.0 | 100.0 | 100.0 | 100.0 | Total Liabilities & Net Worth | 100.0 | 100.0 |
| | | | | | | **INCOME DATA** | | |
| | 100.0 | 100.0 | 100.0 | 100.0 | 100.0 | Net Sales | 100.0 | 100.0 |
| | 64.6 | 49.7 | 50.2 | 67.5 | 59.9 | Gross Profit | 57.0 | 59.7 |
| | 50.6 | 34.2 | 35.8 | 44.5 | 42.1 | Operating Expenses | 33.4 | 35.1 |
| | 14.0 | 15.5 | 14.4 | 23.0 | 17.8 | Operating Profit | 23.6 | 24.7 |
| | 2.2 | 2.0 | 2.2 | 2.7 | 5.7 | All Other Expenses (net) | 4.4 | 4.6 |
| | 11.8 | 13.5 | 12.2 | 20.3 | 12.1 | Profit Before Taxes | 19.2 | 20.1 |
| | | | | | | **RATIOS** | | |
| | 2.5 | 4.5 | 3.9 | 4.0 | 2.4 | | 2.7 | 3.0 |
| | 1.5 | 2.4 | 1.4 | 1.0 | 1.2 | Current | 1.2 | 1.4 |
| | 1.0 | 1.5 | .7 | .6 | .7 | | .7 | .6 |
| | 2.3 | 3.9 | 2.8 | 2.2 | 1.7 | | 1.9 | 2.2 |
| | 1.5 | 1.7 | 1.1 | .7 | .8 | Quick | 1.0 | .9 |
| | .7 | .7 | .4 | .4 | .4 | | .5 | .4 |
| | 0 UND | 0 UND | 18 20.1 | 35 10.4 | 32 11.4 | | 13 27.5 | 7 50.6 |
| | 29 12.7 | 21 17.3 | 34 10.6 | 59 6.2 | 54 6.7 | Sales/Receivables | 42 8.8 | 23 15.7 |
| | 89 4.1 | 64 5.7 | 68 5.4 | 81 4.5 | 70 5.2 | | 76 4.8 | 47 7.8 |
| | 0 UND | 0 UND | 0 UND | 0 UND | 0 UND | | 0 UND | 0 UND |
| | 0 UND | 0 UND | 0 UND | 0 UND | 0 UND | Cost of Sales/Inventory | 0 UND | 0 UND |
| | 0 UND | 1 394.0 | 4 88.2 | 17 21.6 | 5 78.6 | | 3 146.0 | 2 241.5 |
| | 0 UND | 4 85.8 | 12 29.6 | 34 10.8 | 49 7.5 | | 12 30.5 | 9 39.0 |
| | 23 16.0 | 30 12.0 | 42 8.7 | 159 2.3 | 152 2.4 | Cost of Sales/Payables | 56 6.5 | 46 8.0 |
| | 78 4.7 | 69 5.3 | 91 4.0 | 456 .8 | 281 1.3 | | 184 2.0 | 211 1.7 |
| | 5.1 | 3.7 | 4.5 | 4.4 | 3.3 | | 6.6 | 5.8 |
| | 9.9 | 7.9 | 13.5 | 95.9 | 59.3 | Sales/Working Capital | 22.1 | 22.7 |
| | NM | 25.7 | -10.1 | -2.8 | -6.4 | | -9.6 | -15.7 |
| | 11.3 | 39.1 | 19.9 | 613.2 | 6.8 | | 21.3 | 29.7 |
| | (13) 2.6 | (29) 18.7 | (49) 4.4 | (18) 6.6 | (39) 3.6 | EBIT/Interest | (161) 4.8 | (174) 7.7 |
| | -5.4 | 2.4 | .9 | -.3 | 1.4 | | 1.5 | 1.8 |
| | | | 4.9 | | | | 82.2 | 107.4 |
| | | (11) 4.1 | | | | Net Profit + Depr., Dep., Amort./Cur. Mat. L/T/D | (21) 8.3 | (12) 11.5 |
| | | | 1.3 | | | | 3.0 | 3.5 |
| | .3 | .2 | .7 | .7 | 1.1 | | .7 | .7 |
| | 1.0 | .6 | 1.2 | 1.2 | 1.6 | Fixed/Worth | 1.2 | 1.4 |
| | NM | 2.2 | 3.5 | 1.9 | 3.7 | | 3.3 | 3.0 |
| | .5 | .2 | .3 | .3 | .4 | | .4 | .4 |
| | 1.6 | .6 | 1.0 | .7 | 1.0 | Debt/Worth | 1.3 | 1.1 |
| | NM | 2.3 | 3.4 | 1.4 | 3.8 | | 5.3 | 4.7 |
| | 24.1 | 48.9 | 32.9 | 52.4 | 27.2 | | 55.6 | 58.0 |
| | (13) 10.5 | (40) 17.5 | (55) 11.4 | (21) 16.9 | (42) 7.7 | % Profit Before Taxes/Tangible Net Worth | (172) 22.9 | (189) 23.2 |
| | -12.8 | 4.1 | -3.9 | -3.7 | -.1 | | 8.1 | 6.5 |
| | 22.5 | 27.3 | 18.0 | 35.5 | 7.6 | | 22.1 | 25.1 |
| | 9.7 | 12.8 | 6.8 | 7.5 | 3.3 | % Profit Before Taxes/Total Assets | 8.1 | 10.3 |
| | -4.2 | 3.5 | .0 | -3.5 | -.2 | | 1.9 | 2.4 |
| | 17.8 | 32.2 | 4.8 | 1.4 | .7 | | 4.3 | 6.5 |
| | 4.0 | 4.7 | 1.2 | .6 | .4 | Sales/Net Fixed Assets | 1.3 | 1.3 |
| | 1.0 | 1.1 | .4 | .4 | .2 | | .4 | .4 |
| | 4.9 | 2.3 | 1.3 | .7 | .5 | | 1.5 | 1.8 |
| | 1.0 | .9 | .6 | .4 | .3 | Sales/Total Assets | .6 | .7 |
| | .5 | .4 | .3 | .3 | .2 | | .3 | .3 |
| | | 1.0 | 5.2 | 12.9 | 7.4 | | 2.6 | 3.1 |
| | | (31) 7.2 | (52) 13.1 | (13) 17.5 | (18) 21.0 | % Depr., Dep., Amort./Sales | (135) 8.9 | (142) 9.9 |
| | | 21.9 | 23.2 | 34.7 | 27.3 | | 19.8 | 20.6 |
| | | 1.8 | | | | | 1.4 | 1.1 |
| | | (11) 3.9 | | | | % Officers', Directors', Owners' Comp/Sales | (23) 4.4 | (32) 4.3 |
| | | 6.8 | | | | | 7.5 | 8.9 |
| 6849M | 46236M | 422742M | 2519409M | 811397M | 6753624M | Net Sales ($) | 12816137M | 9792082M |
| 2526M | 20494M | 226988M | 1548602M | 1528960M | 7240269M | Total Assets ($) | 10808083M | 11145386M |

© RMA 2012

M = $ thousand    MM = $ million
See Pages 9 through 22 for Explanation of Ratios and Data

## Comparative Historical Data | Current Data Sorted by Sales

| | | | Type of Statement | | | | | | |
|---|---|---|---|---|---|---|---|---|---|
| 61 | 70 | 71 | Unqualified | 2 | 4 | 4 | 9 | 17 | 35 |
| 9 | 14 | 15 | Reviewed | 1 | 1 | 1 | 3 | 2 | 7 |
| 15 | 18 | 16 | Compiled | 1 | 4 | 2 | 3 | 4 | 2 |
| 16 | 23 | 12 | Tax Returns | | | | 1 | 1 | 2 |
| 107 | 99 | 82 | Other | 3 | 5 | | 8 | 8 | 33 |
| | | | | 11 | 11 | 11 | | | |
| 4/1/09- 3/31/10 ALL | 4/1/10- 3/31/11 ALL | 4/1/11- 3/31/12 ALL | | 21 (4/1-9/30/11) | | | 175 (10/1/11-3/31/12) | | |
| | | | | 0-1MM | 1-3MM | 3-5MM | 5-10MM | 10-25MM | 25MM & OVER |
| 208 | 224 | 196 | NUMBER OF STATEMENTS | 18 | 25 | 18 | 24 | 32 | 79 |
| % | % | % | ASSETS | % | % | % | % | % | % |
| 10.5 | 9.5 | 12.3 | Cash & Equivalents | 20.6 | 12.3 | 17.5 | 11.4 | 12.9 | 9.4 |
| 11.2 | 14.7 | 13.6 | Trade Receivables (net) | 14.3 | 11.0 | 8.7 | 18.0 | 10.6 | 15.3 |
| 2.6 | 3.0 | 2.0 | Inventory | 2.5 | 1.3 | .5 | 3.6 | .8 | 2.4 |
| 6.0 | 4.1 | 4.4 | All Other Current | 8.0 | 5.2 | 3.7 | 1.8 | 2.2 | 5.0 |
| 30.2 | 31.4 | 32.3 | Total Current | 45.4 | 29.8 | 30.4 | 34.9 | 26.6 | 32.0 |
| 56.3 | 55.5 | 56.0 | Fixed Assets (net) | 42.7 | 49.7 | 44.0 | 55.6 | 63.7 | 60.7 |
| 2.4 | 3.3 | 2.7 | Intangibles (net) | 2.3 | 6.3 | 3.3 | .4 | 2.7 | 2.2 |
| 11.1 | 9.9 | 9.0 | All Other Non-Current | 9.7 | 14.2 | 22.4 | 9.1 | 7.0 | 5.0 |
| 100.0 | 100.0 | 100.0 | Total | 100.0 | 100.0 | 100.0 | 100.0 | 100.0 | 100.0 |
| | | | LIABILITIES | | | | | | |
| 5.0 | 5.1 | 5.4 | Notes Payable-Short Term | 20.1 | 5.5 | 8.5 | 4.0 | 2.4 | 2.9 |
| 3.5 | 4.0 | 1.8 | Cur. Mat.-L.T.D. | .5 | 1.4 | 1.1 | 1.3 | 3.5 | 2.0 |
| 7.6 | 7.8 | 8.7 | Trade Payables | 3.4 | 7.1 | 5.1 | 8.6 | 9.6 | 10.9 |
| .1 | .1 | .1 | Income Taxes Payable | .4 | .0 | .0 | .0 | .0 | .1 |
| 7.4 | 7.1 | 7.5 | All Other Current | 9.6 | 6.0 | 4.9 | 8.9 | 3.7 | 9.3 |
| 23.6 | 24.1 | 23.5 | Total Current | 34.1 | 19.9 | 19.5 | 22.9 | 19.2 | 25.2 |
| 29.8 | 20.1 | 21.4 | Long-Term Debt | 14.7 | 32.2 | 20.0 | 23.5 | 20.3 | 19.7 |
| .8 | .8 | .9 | Deferred Taxes | .0 | .0 | .0 | .8 | 2.2 | 1.1 |
| 6.6 | 5.6 | 4.8 | All Other Non-Current | .2 | 8.7 | 8.6 | 3.7 | 5.0 | 4.0 |
| 39.2 | 49.5 | 49.4 | Net Worth | 51.1 | 39.2 | 51.9 | 49.2 | 53.3 | 50.1 |
| 100.0 | 100.0 | 100.0 | Total Liabilities & Net Worth | 100.0 | 100.0 | 100.0 | 100.0 | 100.0 | 100.0 |
| | | | INCOME DATA | | | | | | |
| 100.0 | 100.0 | 100.0 | Net Sales | 100.0 | 100.0 | 100.0 | 100.0 | 100.0 | 100.0 |
| 54.8 | 55.1 | 55.7 | Gross Profit | 68.0 | 56.1 | 61.4 | 54.8 | 60.4 | 49.9 |
| 43.5 | 37.8 | 39.3 | Operating Expenses | 44.9 | 37.8 | 50.0 | 40.2 | 44.3 | 33.7 |
| 11.3 | 17.3 | 16.4 | Operating Profit | 23.1 | 18.4 | 11.3 | 14.6 | 16.0 | 16.1 |
| 4.8 | 3.3 | 2.9 | All Other Expenses (net) | 3.4 | 5.5 | 2.8 | 1.9 | .7 | 3.2 |
| 6.5 | 14.0 | 13.5 | Profit Before Taxes | 19.7 | 12.8 | 8.6 | 12.8 | 15.3 | 12.9 |
| | | | RATIOS | | | | | | |
| 3.0 | 3.4 | 3.5 | | 7.9 | 5.0 | 8.7 | 3.1 | 2.9 | 2.9 |
| 1.3 | 1.5 | 1.5 | Current | 1.5 | 2.3 | 1.6 | 1.7 | 1.3 | 1.4 |
| .8 | .8 | .7 | | .2 | .8 | .4 | .5 | .8 | .7 |
| 2.1 | 2.3 | 2.8 | | 6.7 | 4.1 | 8.6 | 2.5 | 2.7 | 1.9 |
| .9 | 1.1 | 1.1 | Quick | 1.2 | 1.8 | 1.4 | 1.4 | 1.0 | 1.0 |
| .4 | .6 | .5 | | .2 | .3 | .4 | .5 | .5 | .5 |
| 11 32.7 | 18 20.5 | 9 41.8 | | 0 UND | 0 UND | 0 UND | 10 37.7 | 31 11.8 | 19 19.7 |
| 40 9.2 | 45 8.2 | 41 8.8 | Sales/Receivables | 9 41.4 | 21 17.8 | 39 9.3 | 47 7.7 | 59 6.2 | 41 8.9 |
| 63 5.8 | 73 5.0 | 69 5.3 | | 79 4.6 | 68 5.4 | 68 5.4 | 74 4.9 | 89 4.1 | 65 5.6 |
| 0 UND | 0 UND | 0 UND | | 0 UND | 0 UND | 0 UND | 0 UND | 0 UND | 0 UND |
| 0 UND | 0 UND | 0 UND | Cost of Sales/Inventory | 0 UND | 0 UND | 0 UND | 0 UND | 0 UND | 0 UND |
| 18 20.2 | 19 19.7 | 4 88.2 | | 0 UND | 0 UND | 3 110.1 | 0 UND | 4 103.3 | 8 45.3 |
| 7 53.9 | 11 34.5 | 12 29.6 | | 0 UND | 0 UND | 0 UND | 21 17.8 | 30 12.2 | 16 22.2 |
| 36 10.1 | 47 7.8 | 51 7.2 | Cost of Sales/Payables | 13 28.0 | 53 6.9 | 52 7.0 | 41 9.0 | 107 3.4 | 51 7.1 |
| 100 3.7 | 136 2.7 | 174 2.1 | | 54 6.8 | 87 4.2 | 89 4.1 | 107 3.4 | 365 1.0 | 215 1.7 |
| 4.5 | 4.0 | 4.1 | | 1.2 | 3.7 | 3.3 | 3.6 | 4.3 | 4.8 |
| 14.7 | 14.3 | 11.9 | Sales/Working Capital | 6.3 | 9.9 | 8.0 | 10.3 | 12.4 | 18.0 |
| -15.2 | -20.9 | -12.4 | | -2.9 | -28.6 | -6.7 | -20.4 | -15.4 | -11.8 |
| 9.7 | 25.6 | 24.8 | | 13.3 | 9.9 | 15.4 | 14.7 | 26.9 | 37.4 |
| (174) 2.5 | (182) 5.3 | (154) 4.7 | EBIT/Interest | (11) 4.8 | (19) 2.4 | (13) 4.6 | (17) 3.8 | (28) 9.8 | (66) 4.8 |
| -.6 | 1.2 | 1.2 | | -4.8 | -4.8 | -.2 | .2 | 3.0 | 1.6 |
| 37.0 | 35.7 | 41.9 | Net Profit + Depr., Dep., | | | | | | 41.9 |
| (20) 2.0 | (18) 4.2 | (19) 4.2 | Amort./Cur. Mat. L/T/D | | | | | (11) | 4.7 |
| .3 | 2.2 | 1.4 | | | | | | | 1.4 |
| .6 | .7 | .6 | | .3 | .5 | .1 | .4 | .8 | .7 |
| 1.4 | 1.2 | 1.2 | Fixed/Worth | .8 | 1.4 | .8 | 1.2 | 1.5 | 1.1 |
| 2.6 | 2.0 | 2.4 | | 3.1 | 80.3 | 6.1 | 2.3 | 2.0 | 2.2 |
| .4 | .3 | .3 | | .1 | .3 | .1 | .4 | .4 | .4 |
| 1.2 | .9 | .9 | Debt/Worth | .8 | 1.6 | .5 | .8 | 1.1 | .9 |
| 3.6 | 2.5 | 2.6 | | 3.3 | 80.9 | 12.9 | 3.0 | 1.8 | 2.6 |
| 22.9 | 39.2 | 34.5 | % Profit Before Taxes/Tangible | 33.2 | 15.0 | 45.5 | 43.4 | 44.2 | 41.6 |
| (188) 6.2 | (200) 17.0 | (178) 13.5 | Net Worth | (15) 14.1 | (20) 2.2 | (15) 11.0 | (23) 10.5 | (31) 15.1 | (74) 18.5 |
| -4.0 | .3 | .3 | | 8.0 | -11.4 | -3.9 | -2.4 | 4.0 | .4 |
| 12.0 | 18.0 | 18.0 | % Profit Before Taxes/Total | 16.5 | 9.4 | 20.5 | 22.2 | 17.4 | 23.0 |
| 2.8 | 6.8 | 6.4 | Assets | 9.7 | 3.3 | 11.4 | 6.0 | 7.5 | 5.4 |
| -2.4 | .5 | .2 | | 5.7 | -2.0 | -.9 | .0 | 2.8 | .3 |
| 5.9 | 4.0 | 6.0 | | 6.6 | 11.5 | 18.6 | 7.7 | 1.8 | 7.8 |
| 1.1 | 1.3 | 1.2 | Sales/Net Fixed Assets | 1.5 | 1.3 | 3.2 | 1.6 | .7 | 1.2 |
| .4 | .4 | .4 | | .6 | .4 | .4 | .4 | .4 | .4 |
| 1.4 | 1.5 | 1.5 | | 1.3 | .9 | 1.6 | 2.3 | .9 | 2.4 |
| .5 | .6 | .5 | Sales/Total Assets | .5 | .5 | .5 | .9 | .5 | .7 |
| .3 | .3 | .3 | | .4 | .2 | .3 | .3 | .3 | .3 |
| 4.8 | 4.2 | 2.7 | | 2.2 | 4.5 | 8.0 | 3.0 | 7.7 | .6 |
| (135) 14.1 | (155) 11.1 | (126) 13.0 | % Depr., Dep., Amort./Sales | (10) 15.1 | (15) 24.0 | (12) 12.5 | (18) 15.2 | (27) 16.7 | (44) 6.7 |
| 27.5 | 19.8 | 24.1 | | 24.9 | 39.1 | 18.0 | 22.6 | 30.1 | 17.9 |
| 2.5 | 2.0 | 1.2 | % Officers', Directors' | | | | | | .2 |
| (24) 5.9 | (23) 4.1 | (28) 3.1 | Owners' Comp/Sales | | | | | (11) | 2.5 |
| 12.2 | 8.5 | 5.0 | | | | | | | 3.8 |
| 7145647M | 7389944M | 10560257M | Net Sales ($) | 10917M | 53044M | 73314M | 177515M | 540416M | 9705051M |
| 11651379M | 11906842M | 10567839M | Total Assets ($) | 22735M | 286318M | 238338M | 338361M | 1489739M | 8192348M |

M = $ thousand   MM = $ million

See Pages 9 through 22 for Explanation of Ratios and Data

## Current Data Sorted by Assets
## Comparative Historical Data

| 0-500M | 500M-2MM | 2-10MM | 10-50MM | 50-100MM | 100-250MM | Type of Statement | 4/1/07-3/31/08 ALL | 4/1/08-3/31/09 ALL |
|---|---|---|---|---|---|---|---|---|
| 1 | | 1 | 5 | 4 | 9 | Unqualified | 20 | 28 |
| | | 1 | 5 | | | Reviewed | 5 | 9 |
| | 1 | 2 | 1 | | | Compiled | 11 | 4 |
| 2 | 1 | 4 | | | 1 | Tax Returns | 4 | 11 |
| | 3 | 4 | 13 | 10 | 7 | Other | 28 | 43 |
| | 6 (4/1-9/30/11) | | 69 (10/1/11-3/31/12) | | | | | |
| 3 | 5 | 12 | 24 | 14 | 17 | NUMBER OF STATEMENTS | 68 | 95 |
| % | % | % | % | % | % | ASSETS | % | % |
| | | 21.9 | 9.2 | 18.3 | 2.7 | Cash & Equivalents | 10.9 | 11.6 |
| | | 24.8 | 21.4 | 11.0 | 7.4 | Trade Receivables (net) | 16.7 | 19.8 |
| | | 3.4 | 6.8 | 5.9 | 4.1 | Inventory | 3.9 | 6.4 |
| | | 2.9 | 2.8 | 3.4 | .9 | All Other Current | 4.5 | 2.3 |
| | | 53.0 | 40.3 | 38.5 | 15.1 | Total Current | 36.0 | 40.1 |
| | | 29.5 | 43.7 | 46.4 | 59.3 | Fixed Assets (net) | 44.3 | 45.1 |
| | | 3.3 | 3.5 | 2.8 | 12.6 | Intangibles (net) | 3.9 | 3.4 |
| | | 14.2 | 12.6 | 12.3 | 13.0 | All Other Non-Current | 15.9 | 11.4 |
| | | 100.0 | 100.0 | 100.0 | 100.0 | Total | 100.0 | 100.0 |
| | | | | | | LIABILITIES | | |
| | | 2.3 | 2.7 | 1.9 | 1.5 | Notes Payable-Short Term | 5.3 | 4.3 |
| | | 7.2 | 8.4 | 3.4 | 7.0 | Cur. Mat.-L.T.D. | 6.0 | 6.1 |
| | | 23.9 | 17.1 | 8.1 | 7.9 | Trade Payables | 14.3 | 15.8 |
| | | .0 | .2 | .0 | .3 | Income Taxes Payable | .1 | .1 |
| | | 16.2 | 7.5 | 9.3 | 8.0 | All Other Current | 12.7 | 16.1 |
| | | 49.6 | 35.9 | 22.7 | 24.7 | Total Current | 38.4 | 42.4 |
| | | 18.9 | 16.3 | 19.3 | 16.6 | Long-Term Debt | 26.5 | 22.6 |
| | | .0 | .4 | 1.2 | 2.1 | Deferred Taxes | .6 | .4 |
| | | 9.7 | 8.0 | 12.5 | 10.6 | All Other Non-Current | 7.8 | 7.8 |
| | | 21.8 | 39.5 | 44.3 | 46.0 | Net Worth | 26.7 | 26.7 |
| | | 100.0 | 100.0 | 100.0 | 100.0 | Total Liabilities & Net Worth | 100.0 | 100.0 |
| | | | | | | INCOME DATA | | |
| | | 100.0 | 100.0 | 100.0 | 100.0 | Net Sales | 100.0 | 100.0 |
| | | 30.9 | 23.6 | 29.0 | 18.7 | Gross Profit | 24.3 | 25.7 |
| | | 26.7 | 17.0 | 20.6 | 8.6 | Operating Expenses | 19.3 | 18.7 |
| | | 4.2 | 6.6 | 8.4 | 10.1 | Operating Profit | 5.0 | 7.0 |
| | | -1.6 | -.8 | .4 | .9 | All Other Expenses (net) | 1.1 | .7 |
| | | 5.8 | 7.5 | 8.0 | 9.2 | Profit Before Taxes | 3.9 | 6.4 |
| | | | | | | RATIOS | | |
| | | 2.4 | 2.1 | 3.6 | .9 | | 1.8 | 1.7 |
| | | 1.3 | 1.2 | 1.4 | .8 | Current | 1.0 | 1.2 |
| | | .5 | .4 | .5 | .4 | | .6 | .6 |
| | | 2.1 | 1.5 | 3.0 | .6 | | 1.4 | 1.5 |
| | | 1.1 | .9 | .8 | .5 | Quick | .8 | .8 |
| | | .4 | .4 | .3 | .2 | | .3 | .4 |
| | | 14 26.5 | 19 19.0 | 14 27.0 | 16 23.2 | | 10 37.1 | 14 25.7 |
| | | 24 15.5 | 33 11.1 | 36 10.1 | 26 14.3 | Sales/Receivables | 22 16.8 | 27 13.4 |
| | | 35 10.5 | 54 6.8 | 45 8.2 | 41 9.0 | | 37 9.8 | 40 9.0 |
| | | 0 UND | 4 91.0 | 8 43.2 | 7 49.0 | | 0 UND | 0 UND |
| | | 0 UND | 8 45.4 | 20 18.2 | 13 28.3 | Cost of Sales/Inventory | 3 117.7 | 6 56.2 |
| | | 2 151.7 | 31 11.7 | 43 8.4 | 23 15.9 | | 20 18.4 | 23 15.8 |
| | | 20 18.3 | 25 14.5 | 22 16.6 | 20 17.9 | | 15 25.1 | 14 26.3 |
| | | 29 12.6 | 32 11.3 | 30 12.3 | 31 11.8 | Cost of Sales/Payables | 26 14.2 | 26 14.2 |
| | | 35 10.5 | 68 5.4 | 43 8.5 | 51 7.2 | | 43 8.4 | 48 7.6 |
| | | 7.8 | 6.5 | 3.7 | NM | | 9.6 | 8.7 |
| | | 78.9 | 42.6 | 10.7 | -22.7 | Sales/Working Capital | 195.3 | 40.1 |
| | | -16.3 | -10.1 | -10.4 | -4.6 | | -21.9 | -12.5 |
| | | 39.2 | 25.9 | 19.7 | 39.8 | | 13.3 | 13.6 |
| | | (11) 11.3 | (22) 10.4 | (12) 3.7 | 4.9 | EBIT/Interest | (60) 2.2 | (83) 5.2 |
| | | 1.4 | 1.6 | 1.4 | 1.8 | | .3 | 1.0 |
| | | | | | | Net Profit + Depr., Dep., | 2.9 | 8.6 |
| | | | | | | Amort./Cur. Mat. L/T/D | (12) 1.6 | (17) 2.3 |
| | | | | | | | .9 | .8 |
| | | .5 | .5 | .7 | 1.1 | | .6 | .7 |
| | | 1.0 | 1.0 | 1.2 | 1.9 | Fixed/Worth | 1.8 | 1.6 |
| | | 20.3 | 6.4 | 2.8 | 4.4 | | 8.0 | 6.3 |
| | | 1.3 | .8 | .3 | .4 | | .6 | .9 |
| | | 6.5 | 1.2 | 1.5 | 1.9 | Debt/Worth | 2.5 | 2.4 |
| | | 48.8 | 7.4 | 3.8 | 5.2 | | 91.5 | 12.2 |
| | | 750.0 | 60.5 | 20.7 | 33.6 | | 66.6 | 64.1 |
| | | (11) 115.9 | (20) 30.9 | (13) 10.3 | (15) 20.4 | % Profit Before Taxes/Tangible Net Worth | (55) 20.5 | (77) 32.5 |
| | | 8.3 | 9.1 | 3.6 | 9.8 | | -7.2 | 3.3 |
| | | 55.3 | 26.3 | 10.2 | 19.2 | | 14.9 | 25.9 |
| | | 9.4 | 10.7 | 3.8 | 5.9 | % Profit Before Taxes/Total Assets | 3.6 | 8.7 |
| | | 1.4 | 2.6 | .9 | 3.2 | | -3.2 | .1 |
| | | 53.9 | 7.8 | 4.0 | 3.1 | | 9.6 | 11.0 |
| | | 9.0 | 3.8 | 2.3 | 1.3 | Sales/Net Fixed Assets | 3.4 | 3.7 |
| | | 5.7 | 2.3 | 1.6 | 1.1 | | 1.9 | 1.9 |
| | | 5.4 | 2.8 | 1.5 | 1.1 | | 3.2 | 2.8 |
| | | 3.5 | 1.7 | 1.0 | .9 | Sales/Total Assets | 1.6 | 1.6 |
| | | 2.4 | 1.1 | .8 | .8 | | .9 | 1.0 |
| | | 1.0 | 3.9 | 4.0 | | | 2.0 | 1.6 |
| | | (11) 3.4 | (19) 6.5 | (12) 5.6 | | % Depr., Dep., Amort./Sales | (52) 4.8 | (75) 4.6 |
| | | 5.0 | 8.8 | 6.6 | | | 7.8 | 7.5 |
| | | | | | | | | .6 |
| | | | | | | % Officers', Directors' Owners' Comp/Sales | (11) 1.5 | 1.5 |
| | | | | | | | 5.9 | |
| 9525M | 47286M | 228453M | 1173774M | 1102864M | 2855074M | Net Sales ($) | 4657346M | 8426836M |
| 873M | 7931M | 56501M | 598712M | 924905M | 2995754M | Total Assets ($) | 3161034M | 5129130M |

## Comparative Historical Data | Current Data Sorted by Sales

| | 4/1/09-3/31/10 ALL | 4/1/10-3/31/11 ALL | 4/1/11-3/31/12 ALL | Type of Statement | 0-1MM | 1-3MM | 3-5MM | 5-10MM | 10-25MM | 25MM & OVER |
|---|---|---|---|---|---|---|---|---|---|---|
| | 30 | 29 | 20 | Unqualified | 1 | | | | 3 | 16 |
| | 4 | 7 | 6 | Reviewed | | | | 1 | 2 | 3 |
| | 5 | 8 | 5 | Compiled | | 1 | | | 2 | 3 |
| | 7 | 6 | 7 | Tax Returns | | 2 | 2 | 2 | 2 | 1 |
| | 41 | 37 | 37 | Other | | 1 | 1 | 4 | 4 | 28 |
| | | | | | 6 (4/1-9/30/11) | | | 69 (10/1/11-3/31/12) | | |
| **NUMBER OF STATEMENTS** | 87 | 87 | 75 | | 1 | | 4 | 7 | 12 | 51 |
| | % | % | % | **ASSETS** | % | % | % | % | % | % |
| Cash & Equivalents | 12.8 | 10.6 | 12.8 | | | | | | 14.5 | 10.1 |
| Trade Receivables (net) | 14.1 | 13.2 | 16.8 | | | | | | 24.4 | 15.1 |
| Inventory | 6.5 | 8.6 | 4.9 | | | | | | 7.0 | 4.4 |
| All Other Current | 2.5 | 3.4 | 2.3 | | | | | | 1.1 | 2.4 |
| Total Current | 35.9 | 35.7 | 36.8 | | | | | | 47.0 | 31.9 |
| Fixed Assets (net) | 46.9 | 45.5 | 43.9 | | | | | | 35.9 | 49.3 |
| Intangibles (net) | 3.5 | 2.5 | 5.2 | | | | | | 3.5 | 6.6 |
| All Other Non-Current | 13.7 | 16.3 | 14.0 | | | | | | 13.6 | 12.2 |
| Total | 100.0 | 100.0 | 100.0 | | | | | | 100.0 | 100.0 |
| | | | | **LIABILITIES** | | | | | | |
| Notes Payable-Short Term | 4.3 | 2.9 | 3.7 | | | | | | 9.4 | 1.8 |
| Cur. Mat.-L.T.D. | 6.1 | 6.1 | 7.6 | | | | | | 6.4 | 6.7 |
| Trade Payables | 9.9 | 11.5 | 15.7 | | | | | | 22.0 | 13.4 |
| Income Taxes Payable | .3 | .2 | .1 | | | | | | .1 | .2 |
| All Other Current | 9.8 | 9.8 | 9.6 | | | | | | 4.1 | 11.2 |
| Total Current | 30.4 | 30.5 | 36.7 | | | | | | 42.0 | 33.3 |
| Long-Term Debt | 20.8 | 17.1 | 17.8 | | | | | | 21.4 | 16.5 |
| Deferred Taxes | .7 | 1.0 | .8 | | | | | | .5 | 1.1 |
| All Other Non-Current | 14.4 | 17.3 | 10.3 | | | | | | 4.7 | 10.5 |
| Net Worth | 33.8 | 34.1 | 34.3 | | | | | | 31.4 | 38.7 |
| Total Liabilities & Net Worth | 100.0 | 100.0 | 100.0 | | | | | | 100.0 | 100.0 |
| | | | | **INCOME DATA** | | | | | | |
| Net Sales | 100.0 | 100.0 | 100.0 | | | | | | 100.0 | 100.0 |
| Gross Profit | 26.4 | 30.4 | 25.6 | | | | | | 31.1 | 21.7 |
| Operating Expenses | 14.2 | 19.8 | 17.5 | | | | | | 24.0 | 14.4 |
| Operating Profit | 12.2 | 10.5 | 8.0 | | | | | | 7.1 | 7.3 |
| All Other Expenses (net) | 2.1 | .5 | -.3 | | | | | | -.9 | -.1 |
| Profit Before Taxes | 10.2 | 10.0 | 8.4 | | | | | | 8.0 | 7.4 |
| | | | | **RATIOS** | | | | | | |
| Current | 2.0 | 2.0 | 1.8 | | | | | | 2.5 | 1.5 |
| | 1.1 | 1.2 | 1.0 | | | | | | 1.7 | .9 |
| | .8 | .7 | .4 | | | | | | .9 | .4 |
| Quick | 1.5 | 1.6 | 1.3 | | | | | | 2.1 | 1.1 |
| | .8 | .7 | .7 | | | | | | 1.1 | .6 |
| | .4 | .3 | .3 | | | | | | .6 | .3 |
| Sales/Receivables | 16 22.8 | 15 23.9 | 15 24.1 | | | | | | 19 19.4 | 14 25.4 |
| | 26 13.9 | 29 12.5 | 28 13.1 | | | | | | 30 12.3 | 30 12.0 |
| | 40 9.2 | 38 9.7 | 42 8.7 | | | | | | 65 5.6 | 43 8.5 |
| Cost of Sales/Inventory | 2 187.6 | 2 176.6 | 0 UND | | | | | | 0 UND | 5 67.6 |
| | 14 26.1 | 12 31.0 | 8 45.7 | | | | | | 4 104.1 | 9 38.9 |
| | 35 10.5 | 51 7.1 | 28 13.2 | | | | | | 44 8.3 | 26 14.0 |
| Cost of Sales/Payables | 16 22.4 | 17 21.9 | 22 16.9 | | | | | | 29 12.5 | 22 16.5 |
| | 23 16.2 | 26 13.9 | 31 11.8 | | | | | | 35 10.3 | 31 11.8 |
| | 38 9.5 | 37 9.8 | 46 8.0 | | | | | | 91 4.0 | 46 8.0 |
| Sales/Working Capital | 7.9 | 6.9 | 8.2 | | | | | | 4.6 | 13.1 |
| | 47.0 | 35.1 | 367.8 | | | | | | 16.1 | -61.1 |
| | -25.4 | -20.6 | -9.4 | | | | | | NM | -7.7 |
| EBIT/Interest | 30.2 | 25.4 | 27.5 | | | | | | 20.9 | 35.1 |
| | (81) 10.6 | (81) 9.0 | (69) 7.8 | | | | | | (11) 10.2 | (47) 5.7 |
| | 1.8 | 2.3 | 1.8 | | | | | | 2.0 | 1.8 |
| Net Profit + Depr., Dep., Amort./Cur. Mat. L/T/D | 8.7 | | | | | | | | | |
| | (15) 2.3 | | | | | | | | | |
| | .8 | | | | | | | | | |
| Fixed/Worth | .7 | .6 | .6 | | | | | | .4 | .8 |
| | 1.5 | 1.2 | 1.2 | | | | | | 1.1 | 1.4 |
| | 4.3 | 2.4 | 3.8 | | | | | | 68.6 | 3.6 |
| Debt/Worth | .9 | .7 | .6 | | | | | | 1.0 | .8 |
| | 2.3 | 1.5 | 1.6 | | | | | | 1.4 | 1.9 |
| | 10.9 | 4.4 | 8.3 | | | | | | 169.1 | 6.1 |
| % Profit Before Taxes/Tangible Net Worth | 79.4 | 53.4 | 61.1 | | | | | | 200.9 | 54.1 |
| | (73) 33.5 | (78) 28.8 | (63) 21.4 | | | | | | (10) 46.7 | (44) 22.0 |
| | 12.6 | 18.4 | 8.3 | | | | | | 5.7 | 9.9 |
| % Profit Before Taxes/Total Assets | 23.5 | 22.0 | 22.0 | | | | | | 37.5 | 21.4 |
| | 13.9 | 10.6 | 6.3 | | | | | | 5.5 | 7.3 |
| | 1.5 | 3.2 | 1.9 | | | | | | 2.5 | 2.8 |
| Sales/Net Fixed Assets | 5.5 | 6.7 | 8.7 | | | | | | 13.2 | 6.8 |
| | 3.0 | 3.6 | 3.8 | | | | | | 6.5 | 2.7 |
| | 1.6 | 1.9 | 1.6 | | | | | | 2.8 | 1.3 |
| Sales/Total Assets | 2.1 | 2.3 | 3.0 | | | | | | 3.5 | 2.3 |
| | 1.3 | 1.4 | 1.4 | | | | | | 2.0 | 1.3 |
| | .9 | .9 | .9 | | | | | | 1.0 | .9 |
| % Depr., Dep., Amort./Sales | 2.7 | 2.5 | 3.4 | | | | | | 3.4 | 3.2 |
| | (62) 5.7 | (65) 5.2 | (51) 5.0 | | | | | | (11) 4.4 | (31) 5.5 |
| | 8.4 | 8.8 | 7.3 | | | | | | 8.8 | 6.9 |
| % Officers', Directors' Owners' Comp/Sales | | | | | | | | | | |
| Net Sales ($) | 7820633M | 7318026M | 5416976M | | 207M | | 15856M | 53890M | 218398M | 5128625M |
| Total Assets ($) | 5922641M | 5456304M | 4584676M | | 239M | | 6707M | 78110M | 134231M | 4365389M |

Note: For the 0-1MM, 1-3MM, 3-5MM and 5-10MM columns the ASSETS, LIABILITIES and INCOME DATA sections read "DATA NOT AVAILABLE".

M = $ thousand    MM = $ million
See Pages 9 through 22 for Explanation of Ratios and Data

## Current Data Sorted by Assets        Comparative Historical Data

| 0-500M | 500M-2MM | 2-10MM | 10-50MM | 50-100MM | 100-250MM | | 4/1/07-3/31/08 ALL | 4/1/08-3/31/09 ALL |
|---|---|---|---|---|---|---|---|---|
| | | | | | | **Type of Statement** | | |
| | | 6 | 8 | 2 | 4 | Unqualified | 23 | 14 |
| 2 | | 5 | 4 | 1 | | Reviewed | 10 | 7 |
| 1 | 4 | 4 | 1 | | | Compiled | 7 | 11 |
| | | | 1 | | | Tax Returns | 9 | 9 |
| | | 9 | 14 | | 6 | Other | 29 | 26 |
| 3 | 4 | 24 | 28 | 7 | 10 | **NUMBER OF STATEMENTS** | 78 | 67 |
| % | % | % | % | % | % | **ASSETS** | % | % |
| | | 12.4 | 7.6 | | 6.2 | Cash & Equivalents | 9.0 | 10.7 |
| | | 15.1 | 10.3 | | 9.2 | Trade Receivables (net) | 12.9 | 14.8 |
| | | 12.3 | 15.4 | | 8.7 | Inventory | 13.8 | 14.9 |
| | | 2.2 | 2.1 | | 1.1 | All Other Current | 2.2 | 2.2 |
| | | 42.1 | 35.4 | | 25.2 | Total Current | 37.9 | 42.5 |
| | | 52.5 | 51.0 | | 47.3 | Fixed Assets (net) | 52.4 | 48.4 |
| | | .5 | 7.3 | | 15.8 | Intangibles (net) | 3.6 | 3.1 |
| | | 4.9 | 6.3 | | 11.8 | All Other Non-Current | 6.1 | 6.0 |
| | | 100.0 | 100.0 | | 100.0 | Total | 100.0 | 100.0 |
| | | | | | | **LIABILITIES** | | |
| | | 4.6 | 2.7 | | 1.3 | Notes Payable-Short Term | 5.0 | 6.3 |
| | | 4.1 | 8.7 | | 2.6 | Cur. Mat.-L.T.D. | 4.4 | 5.8 |
| | | 9.5 | 4.9 | | 4.3 | Trade Payables | 7.8 | 6.5 |
| | | .2 | .2 | | .1 | Income Taxes Payable | .2 | .0 |
| | | 7.5 | 5.5 | | 3.3 | All Other Current | 5.1 | 7.5 |
| | | 25.9 | 21.9 | | 11.6 | Total Current | 22.6 | 26.2 |
| | | 17.2 | 17.2 | | 22.7 | Long-Term Debt | 25.5 | 28.2 |
| | | .8 | 1.0 | | 2.8 | Deferred Taxes | 1.4 | .9 |
| | | 2.1 | .8 | | 5.3 | All Other Non-Current | 4.8 | 3.4 |
| | | 53.9 | 59.2 | | 57.6 | Net Worth | 45.7 | 41.4 |
| | | 100.0 | 100.0 | | 100.0 | Total Liabilities & Net Worth | 100.0 | 100.0 |
| | | | | | | **INCOME DATA** | | |
| | | 100.0 | 100.0 | | 100.0 | Net Sales | 100.0 | 100.0 |
| | | 30.8 | 27.2 | | 33.5 | Gross Profit | 34.2 | 29.6 |
| | | 28.3 | 18.8 | | 25.4 | Operating Expenses | 23.8 | 23.8 |
| | | 2.5 | 8.4 | | 8.1 | Operating Profit | 10.4 | 5.9 |
| | | .2 | .7 | | 1.7 | All Other Expenses (net) | 2.9 | 1.0 |
| | | 2.3 | 7.7 | | 6.4 | Profit Before Taxes | 7.5 | 4.8 |
| | | | | | | **RATIOS** | | |
| | | 4.7 | 4.3 | | 3.7 | | 3.4 | 3.6 |
| | | 2.3 | 2.4 | | 2.5 | Current | 2.1 | 1.9 |
| | | 1.1 | 1.5 | | 1.9 | | 1.2 | 1.1 |
| | | 3.0 | 2.8 | | 2.4 | | 2.1 | 2.4 |
| | | 1.1 | 1.0 | | 1.2 | Quick | 1.0 | 1.0 |
| | | .7 | .5 | | .7 | | .5 | .5 |
| | | 25 14.5 | 30 12.3 | | 32 11.3 | | 24 15.4 | 21 17.7 |
| | | 31 11.6 | 32 11.3 | | 43 8.5 | Sales/Receivables | 35 10.4 | 30 12.2 |
| | | 47 7.8 | 38 9.5 | | 61 6.0 | | 44 8.2 | 44 8.3 |
| | | 0 UND | 38 9.7 | | 32 11.3 | | 22 16.9 | 7 50.7 |
| | | 24 15.4 | 85 4.3 | | 49 7.5 | Cost of Sales/Inventory | 50 7.3 | 40 9.0 |
| | | 96 3.8 | 130 2.8 | | 111 3.3 | | 96 3.8 | 82 4.4 |
| | | 15 23.9 | 13 27.7 | | 20 18.5 | | 17 22.0 | 14 26.4 |
| | | 24 15.1 | 22 16.7 | | 26 14.2 | Cost of Sales/Payables | 26 13.8 | 21 17.4 |
| | | 64 5.7 | 33 11.0 | | 48 7.6 | | 43 8.4 | 33 11.2 |
| | | 4.7 | 3.6 | | 3.0 | | 4.0 | 4.1 |
| | | 11.0 | 4.9 | | 5.7 | Sales/Working Capital | 6.9 | 9.5 |
| | | 572.4 | 13.2 | | 13.1 | | 72.5 | 51.9 |
| | | 10.2 | 23.8 | | 9.5 | | 9.5 | 8.8 |
| | | (20) 3.7 | (25) 6.4 | | 6.2 | EBIT/Interest | (68) 4.0 | (60) 2.8 |
| | | 1.0 | 1.7 | | 2.6 | | 1.8 | .9 |
| | | | | | | | 6.8 | 15.2 |
| | | | | | | Net Profit + Depr., Dep., Amort./Cur. Mat. L/T/D | (15) 3.7 | (16) 4.1 |
| | | | | | | | 1.5 | 2.1 |
| | | .6 | .7 | | .7 | | .8 | .7 |
| | | 1.1 | .9 | | 1.2 | Fixed/Worth | 1.3 | 1.1 |
| | | 1.7 | 1.3 | | 117.7 | | 2.2 | 2.8 |
| | | .3 | .2 | | .6 | | .5 | .6 |
| | | .7 | .7 | | 1.0 | Debt/Worth | 1.3 | 1.5 |
| | | 1.8 | 1.6 | | 203.8 | | 3.3 | 3.8 |
| | | 34.7 | 23.2 | | | % Profit Before Taxes/Tangible Net Worth | 38.9 | 34.8 |
| | | (22) 9.8 | (26) 13.9 | | | | (71) 17.0 | (59) 13.1 |
| | | .4 | 4.3 | | | | 8.7 | 2.0 |
| | | 12.4 | 13.8 | | 7.2 | % Profit Before Taxes/Total Assets | 13.1 | 14.4 |
| | | 5.3 | 9.1 | | 5.8 | | 7.7 | 6.1 |
| | | .0 | 1.4 | | 3.2 | | 2.7 | .4 |
| | | 4.3 | 3.0 | | 2.1 | | 3.7 | 5.2 |
| | | 2.4 | 1.7 | | 1.8 | Sales/Net Fixed Assets | 2.1 | 2.7 |
| | | 1.6 | .9 | | 1.2 | | 1.3 | 1.5 |
| | | 2.1 | 1.3 | | .9 | | 1.6 | 2.0 |
| | | 1.3 | .8 | | .8 | Sales/Total Assets | 1.1 | 1.2 |
| | | 1.0 | .5 | | .5 | | .8 | .8 |
| | | 3.5 | 4.2 | | | | 3.9 | 4.0 |
| | | 5.3 | (25) 8.1 | | | % Depr., Dep., Amort./Sales | (68) 6.5 | (60) 6.2 |
| | | 9.4 | 11.0 | | | | 10.7 | 9.6 |
| | | 1.4 | | | | | 1.1 | 1.6 |
| | | (12) 4.4 | | | | % Officers', Directors' Owners' Comp/Sales | (16) 1.5 | (22) 3.1 |
| | | 6.4 | | | | | 7.3 | 8.7 |
| 2489M | 10029M | 161032M | 659083M | 513894M | 911470M | Net Sales ($) | 3066362M | 1738397M |
| 724M | 5771M | 106391M | 683952M | 553922M | 1285025M | Total Assets ($) | 3134426M | 1667753M |

Date ranges: 10 (4/1-9/30/11) · 66 (10/1/11-3/31/12)

## Comparative Historical Data | Current Data Sorted by Sales

| 4/1/09-3/31/10 ALL | 4/1/10-3/31/11 ALL | 4/1/11-3/31/12 ALL | Type of Statement | 0-1MM | 1-3MM | 3-5MM | 5-10MM | 10-25MM | 25MM & OVER |
|---|---|---|---|---|---|---|---|---|---|
| 15 | 15 | 14 | Unqualified |  |  |  | 1 | 4 | 9 |
| 13 | 6 | 11 | Reviewed |  | 2 |  | 2 | 4 | 1 |
| 8 | 7 | 8 | Compiled |  | 1 |  | 2 | 2 | 1 |
| 9 | 3 | 10 | Tax Returns |  | 6 |  | 2 |  |  |
| 32 | 33 | 33 | Other | 2 | 2 |  | 6 | 4 | 17 |
|  |  |  |  | 10 (4/1-9/30/11) | | | 66 (10/1/11-3/31/12) | | |
| 77 | 64 | 76 | NUMBER OF STATEMENTS | 2 | 11 | 8 | 13 | 14 | 28 |
| % | % | % | **ASSETS** | % | % | % | % | % | % |
| 8.2 | 9.1 | 8.6 | Cash & Equivalents |  | 9.3 |  | 7.1 | 11.5 | 6.0 |
| 12.1 | 12.5 | 14.2 | Trade Receivables (net) |  | 18.4 |  | 13.4 | 9.7 | 12.7 |
| 15.2 | 13.7 | 12.6 | Inventory |  | 15.1 |  | 15.7 | 10.5 | 12.4 |
| 1.8 | 5.7 | 2.4 | All Other Current |  | 3.8 |  | 1.4 | 2.7 | 2.1 |
| 37.3 | 41.1 | 37.7 | Total Current |  | 46.5 |  | 37.6 | 34.4 | 33.2 |
| 52.6 | 47.2 | 49.1 | Fixed Assets (net) |  | 48.9 |  | 53.9 | 52.8 | 46.8 |
| 3.3 | 5.2 | 6.6 | Intangibles (net) |  | 1.0 |  | .5 | 8.8 | 11.4 |
| 6.8 | 6.5 | 6.6 | All Other Non-Current |  | 3.6 |  | 8.1 | 3.9 | 8.6 |
| 100.0 | 100.0 | 100.0 | Total |  | 100.0 |  | 100.0 | 100.0 | 100.0 |
|  |  |  | **LIABILITIES** |  |  |  |  |  |  |
| 12.7 | 4.7 | 4.0 | Notes Payable-Short Term |  | .2 |  | 3.9 | 5.2 | 3.6 |
| 4.4 | 6.0 | 6.5 | Cur. Mat.-L.T.D. |  | 7.6 |  | 4.2 | 14.9 | 2.8 |
| 6.7 | 8.1 | 8.6 | Trade Payables |  | 10.9 |  | 5.8 | 7.1 | 6.2 |
| .1 | .2 | .1 | Income Taxes Payable |  | .0 |  | .0 | .0 | .2 |
| 4.1 | 4.8 | 5.4 | All Other Current |  | 9.4 |  | 3.5 | 6.4 | 3.8 |
| 28.0 | 23.8 | 24.6 | Total Current |  | 28.1 |  | 17.4 | 33.6 | 16.6 |
| 24.4 | 22.5 | 21.5 | Long-Term Debt |  | 40.0 |  | 18.5 | 13.5 | 22.8 |
| 1.0 | 1.1 | 1.2 | Deferred Taxes |  | .1 |  | .6 | .7 | 2.3 |
| 5.2 | 4.8 | 2.8 | All Other Non-Current |  | 9.9 |  | .8 | .7 | 2.9 |
| 41.3 | 47.8 | 49.9 | Net Worth |  | 21.8 |  | 62.7 | 51.4 | 55.4 |
| 100.0 | 100.0 | 100.0 | Total Liabilities & Net Worth |  | 100.0 |  | 100.0 | 100.0 | 100.0 |
|  |  |  | **INCOME DATA** |  |  |  |  |  |  |
| 100.0 | 100.0 | 100.0 | Net Sales |  | 100.0 |  | 100.0 | 100.0 | 100.0 |
| 33.0 | 30.9 | 29.6 | Gross Profit |  | 32.8 |  | 39.5 | 21.4 | 23.7 |
| 23.7 | 22.8 | 23.8 | Operating Expenses |  | 32.8 |  | 30.0 | 16.6 | 16.2 |
| 9.3 | 8.1 | 5.8 | Operating Profit |  | -.1 |  | 9.5 | 4.8 | 7.5 |
| 2.1 | 1.6 | 1.2 | All Other Expenses (net) |  | .1 |  | .9 | .5 | 1.9 |
| 7.2 | 6.5 | 4.6 | Profit Before Taxes |  | -.2 |  | 8.7 | 4.3 | 5.6 |
|  |  |  | **RATIOS** |  |  |  |  |  |  |
| 4.3 | 3.9 | 3.6 | Current |  | 5.1 |  | 4.4 | 3.7 | 3.3 |
| 2.2 | 2.2 | 2.1 |  |  | 2.4 |  | 2.7 | 1.5 | 2.3 |
| 1.1 | 1.1 | 1.2 |  |  | 1.3 |  | 1.4 | .8 | 1.4 |
| 2.1 | 2.3 | 2.1 | Quick |  | 5.0 |  | 2.9 | 2.7 | 2.0 |
| 1.1 | 1.0 | 1.0 |  |  | 1.4 |  | 1.9 | .8 | 1.0 |
| .4 | .4 | .5 |  |  | .9 |  | .4 | .2 | .6 |
| 27 13.7 | 26 13.8 | 29 12.5 | Sales/Receivables | 31 11.6 |  |  | 21 17.3 | 18 20.1 | 31 11.9 |
| 38 9.5 | 39 9.5 | 33 10.9 |  | 42 8.7 |  |  | 33 11.2 | 30 12.0 | 36 10.0 |
| 46 7.9 | 50 7.3 | 46 7.9 |  | 63 5.8 |  |  | 46 7.9 | 35 10.3 | 50 7.3 |
| 16 22.7 | 11 32.9 | 8 43.3 | Cost of Sales/Inventory | 0 UND |  |  | 0 UND | 15 24.8 | 26 13.8 |
| 61 6.0 | 42 8.7 | 56 6.5 |  | 41 8.9 |  |  | 54 6.7 | 59 6.2 | 63 5.8 |
| 118 3.1 | 123 3.0 | 118 3.1 |  | 192 1.9 |  |  | 130 2.8 | 118 3.1 | 87 4.2 |
| 14 25.3 | 16 22.5 | 16 22.4 | Cost of Sales/Payables | 16 23.2 |  |  | 13 27.1 | 19 19.2 | 17 20.9 |
| 27 13.4 | 25 14.8 | 24 15.1 |  | 25 14.7 |  |  | 20 18.2 | 29 12.7 | 26 14.2 |
| 46 7.9 | 47 7.8 | 39 9.3 |  | 74 4.9 |  |  | 38 9.6 | 34 10.8 | 37 9.9 |
| 3.2 | 2.6 | 3.9 | Sales/Working Capital |  | 2.0 |  | 3.2 | 3.3 | 4.0 |
| 6.7 | 6.8 | 7.8 |  |  | 8.7 |  | 7.0 | 377.9 | 6.1 |
| 54.5 | 31.9 | 28.5 |  |  | 15.1 |  | 34.5 | -22.5 | 10.6 |
| 11.1 | 8.0 | 11.9 | EBIT/Interest |  | 4.1 |  | 13.7 | 24.0 | 22.0 |
| (70) 3.6 | (57) 3.2 | (67) 3.7 |  | (10) 1.5 |  |  | (11) 6.8 | (13) 3.7 | (25) 6.3 |
| 1.7 | 1.5 | 1.2 |  |  | -5.0 |  | 4.0 | .2 | 1.6 |
| 11.4 | 3.2 | 7.2 | Net Profit + Depr., Dep., Amort./Cur. Mat. L/T/D |  |  |  |  |  |  |
| (14) 3.3 | (12) 1.4 | (16) 2.5 |  |  |  |  |  |  |  |
| 1.4 | .1 | .7 |  |  |  |  |  |  |  |
| .7 | .7 | .7 | Fixed/Worth |  | .7 |  | .5 | .9 | .7 |
| 1.1 | 1.0 | 1.1 |  |  | 1.5 |  | 1.1 | 1.2 | 1.0 |
| 2.0 | 1.6 | 2.2 |  |  | -9.5 |  | 1.6 | 1.9 | 3.0 |
| .4 | .5 | .3 | Debt/Worth |  | .7 |  | .1 | .3 | .3 |
| 1.1 | 1.0 | .9 |  |  | 1.2 |  | .4 | .8 | 1.1 |
| 2.7 | 3.4 | 2.9 |  |  | -13.6 |  | 1.1 | 2.0 | 2.9 |
| 30.7 | 19.7 | 23.3 | % Profit Before Taxes/Tangible Net Worth |  |  |  | 21.4 | 30.5 | 23.3 |
| (71) 13.3 | (57) 10.3 | (67) 13.6 |  |  |  |  | (12) 13.9 | (13) 10.3 | (25) 17.5 |
| 3.9 | 2.7 | 2.9 |  |  |  |  | 8.8 | 2.5 | 9.7 |
| 10.8 | 9.3 | 10.7 | % Profit Before Taxes/Total Assets |  | 7.1 |  | 12.8 | 16.0 | 10.7 |
| 5.2 | 4.9 | 5.6 |  |  | .9 |  | 7.5 | 2.9 | 7.7 |
| 1.9 | 1.2 | .6 |  |  | -3.3 |  | 5.2 | -.8 | 2.7 |
| 3.1 | 3.7 | 4.2 | Sales/Net Fixed Assets |  | 5.1 |  | 3.3 | 3.2 | 2.7 |
| 1.8 | 2.2 | 2.1 |  |  | 2.1 |  | 2.1 | 1.7 | 2.1 |
| 1.0 | 1.2 | 1.2 |  |  | 1.1 |  | 1.5 | .9 | 1.3 |
| 1.4 | 1.3 | 1.6 | Sales/Total Assets |  | 1.6 |  | 1.7 | 1.6 | 1.4 |
| .9 | .9 | 1.0 |  |  | 1.0 |  | 1.2 | .8 | .9 |
| .6 | .7 | .7 |  |  | .7 |  | .8 | .5 | .7 |
| 4.5 | 5.1 | 4.4 | % Depr., Dep., Amort./Sales |  | 4.4 |  | 2.8 | 6.4 | 4.1 |
| (68) 8.0 | (57) 8.8 | (69) 6.9 |  |  | 6.7 |  | 4.4 | 9.4 | (24) 8.3 |
| 11.8 | 11.4 | 10.3 |  |  | 13.4 |  | 7.9 | 12.4 | 10.7 |
| 2.2 | 1.9 | 1.9 | % Officers', Directors' Owners' Comp/Sales |  |  |  |  |  |  |
| (21) 4.7 | (15) 5.0 | (22) 5.1 |  |  |  |  |  |  |  |
| 9.4 | 7.1 | 7.1 |  |  |  |  |  |  |  |
| 1953770M | 2414517M | 2257997M | Net Sales ($) | 719M | 25598M | 34821M | 100696M | 222382M | 1873781M |
| 2214606M | 2364939M | 2635785M | Total Assets ($) | 229M | 30435M | 64213M | 96411M | 288628M | 2155869M |

M = $ thousand    MM = $ million
See Pages 9 through 22 for Explanation of Ratios and Data

## Current Data Sorted by Assets      Comparative Historical Data

| | 0-500M | 500M-2MM | 2-10MM | 10-50MM | 50-100MM | 100-250MM | Type of Statement | 4/1/07-3/31/08 ALL | 4/1/08-3/31/09 ALL |
|---|---|---|---|---|---|---|---|---|---|
| | | 2 | 2 | 5 | 1 | 5 | Unqualified | 10 | 12 |
| | | 2 | 4 | 8 | 1 | 1 | Reviewed | 13 | 10 |
| | | 2 | 6 | 3 | | | Compiled | 8 | 10 |
| | | 6 | 3 | 9 | | | Tax Returns | 4 | 2 |
| | 2 | 5 | | 8 | | 1 | Other | 28 | 30 |
| | | 6 (4/1-9/30/11) | | 67 (10/1/11-3/31/12) | | 2 | | | |
| NUMBER OF STATEMENTS | 2 | 15 | 24 | 22 | 3 | 7 | | 63 | 64 |
| | % | % | % | % | % | % | **ASSETS** | % | % |
| | | 9.9 | 8.8 | 7.1 | | | Cash & Equivalents | 6.8 | 7.2 |
| | | 13.4 | 16.8 | 12.5 | | | Trade Receivables (net) | 13.4 | 14.5 |
| | | 23.7 | 9.2 | 14.3 | | | Inventory | 9.9 | 13.9 |
| | | 1.0 | 5.3 | 4.1 | | | All Other Current | 5.2 | 1.2 |
| | | 48.0 | 40.0 | 38.0 | | | Total Current | 35.3 | 36.9 |
| | | 45.4 | 49.6 | 50.5 | | | Fixed Assets (net) | 48.8 | 48.6 |
| | | 2.3 | 3.2 | 5.5 | | | Intangibles (net) | 6.7 | 6.7 |
| | | 4.4 | 7.1 | 6.0 | | | All Other Non-Current | 9.2 | 7.8 |
| | | 100.0 | 100.0 | 100.0 | | | Total | 100.0 | 100.0 |
| | | | | | | | **LIABILITIES** | | |
| | | 7.6 | 3.1 | 3.2 | | | Notes Payable-Short Term | 5.3 | 5.5 |
| | | 9.3 | 5.4 | 5.6 | | | Cur. Mat.-L.T.D. | 7.2 | 5.2 |
| | | 13.0 | 8.9 | 4.5 | | | Trade Payables | 8.2 | 7.4 |
| | | .0 | .0 | .0 | | | Income Taxes Payable | .3 | .2 |
| | | 24.3 | 10.8 | 10.7 | | | All Other Current | 5.4 | 4.7 |
| | | 54.2 | 28.2 | 24.0 | | | Total Current | 26.4 | 22.9 |
| | | 37.4 | 20.9 | 15.5 | | | Long-Term Debt | 30.8 | 28.1 |
| | | .4 | .1 | .3 | | | Deferred Taxes | .8 | .7 |
| | | 11.6 | 5.8 | 7.8 | | | All Other Non-Current | 5.5 | 7.7 |
| | | -3.6 | 45.1 | 52.4 | | | Net Worth | 36.4 | 40.6 |
| | | 100.0 | 100.0 | 100.0 | | | Total Liabilities & Net Worth | 100.0 | 100.0 |
| | | | | | | | **INCOME DATA** | | |
| | | 100.0 | 100.0 | 100.0 | | | Net Sales | 100.0 | 100.0 |
| | | 44.8 | 38.5 | 30.4 | | | Gross Profit | 29.4 | 25.6 |
| | | 43.7 | 31.1 | 25.2 | | | Operating Expenses | 18.1 | 18.8 |
| | | 1.1 | 7.3 | 5.2 | | | Operating Profit | 11.3 | 6.8 |
| | | .4 | 1.0 | 1.8 | | | All Other Expenses (net) | 3.3 | 2.1 |
| | | .7 | 6.3 | 3.4 | | | Profit Before Taxes | 8.1 | 4.7 |
| | | | | | | | **RATIOS** | | |
| | | 4.7 | 3.1 | 4.1 | | | Current | 3.1 | 4.1 |
| | | .9 | 1.6 | 1.7 | | | | 1.5 | 1.7 |
| | | .3 | .7 | .8 | | | | .8 | .9 |
| | | 1.9 | 2.0 | 2.4 | | | Quick | 1.6 | 1.8 |
| | | .4 | 1.1 | .8 | | | | .9 | .9 |
| | | .1 | .5 | .4 | | | | .4 | .4 |
| | | 10   37.9 | 34   10.7 | 39   9.4 | | | Sales/Receivables | 22   16.7 | 21   17.0 |
| | | 28   13.1 | 47   7.8 | 46   7.9 | | | | 38   9.5 | 37   9.9 |
| | | 34   10.6 | 58   6.3 | 70   5.2 | | | | 51   7.2 | 51   7.2 |
| | | 0   UND | 10   35.2 | 34   10.7 | | | Cost of Sales/Inventory | 13   28.0 | 14   25.4 |
| | | 85   4.3 | 37   9.9 | 101   3.6 | | | | 47   7.8 | 51   7.2 |
| | | 304   1.2 | 91   4.0 | 166   2.2 | | | | 75   4.8 | 89   4.1 |
| | | 8   44.3 | 19   19.4 | 15   24.9 | | | Cost of Sales/Payables | 14   26.5 | 10   36.8 |
| | | 32   11.5 | 42   8.7 | 26   14.0 | | | | 22   16.8 | 19   19.3 |
| | | 87   4.2 | 79   4.6 | 45   8.2 | | | | 40   9.0 | 33   11.2 |
| | | 2.5 | 4.6 | 2.6 | | | Sales/Working Capital | 5.1 | 4.4 |
| | | -98.8 | 8.4 | 4.1 | | | | 8.5 | 10.0 |
| | | -2.0 | -11.4 | -32.6 | | | | -14.2 | -73.7 |
| | | 8.4 | 12.9 | 20.1 | | | EBIT/Interest | 7.2 | 6.6 |
| | | (11) 2.1 | (21) 2.2 | (21) 3.7 | | | | (57) 3.1 | (55) 2.7 |
| | | -3.9 | .8 | -.2 | | | | 1.0 | -.6 |
| | | | | | | | Net Profit + Depr., Dep., Amort./Cur. Mat. L/T/D | 9.0 | 8.6 |
| | | | | | | | | (21) 3.1 | (12) 2.4 |
| | | | | | | | | 1.3 | .7 |
| | | .4 | .6 | .6 | | | Fixed/Worth | .7 | .7 |
| | | 6.4 | 1.3 | 1.1 | | | | 1.5 | 1.3 |
| | | -.9 | 2.9 | 2.1 | | | | 8.8 | 4.8 |
| | | 1.3 | .6 | .2 | | | Debt/Worth | .5 | .4 |
| | | -18.4 | 1.3 | 1.1 | | | | 1.9 | 1.5 |
| | | -2.7 | 4.8 | 2.8 | | | | 21.6 | 6.5 |
| | | | 65.7 | 23.2 | | | % Profit Before Taxes/Tangible Net Worth | 37.2 | 30.7 |
| | | (23) 16.7 | (21) 8.0 | | | | | (51) 22.0 | (55) 16.3 |
| | | | -8.2 | -6.9 | | | | 12.3 | -6.0 |
| | | 4.7 | 14.1 | 11.6 | | | % Profit Before Taxes/Total Assets | 11.5 | 14.2 |
| | | 1.5 | 7.8 | 4.3 | | | | 7.8 | 6.6 |
| | | -11.5 | -.6 | -3.3 | | | | .3 | -3.8 |
| | | 12.0 | 4.7 | 4.0 | | | Sales/Net Fixed Assets | 3.9 | 4.1 |
| | | 3.3 | 2.3 | 1.4 | | | | 2.2 | 2.5 |
| | | 1.4 | 1.0 | 1.0 | | | | 1.3 | 1.5 |
| | | 2.3 | 1.6 | 1.0 | | | Sales/Total Assets | 1.6 | 1.6 |
| | | 1.4 | 1.0 | .8 | | | | 1.0 | 1.2 |
| | | .9 | .7 | .6 | | | | .7 | .7 |
| | | 2.6 | 4.3 | 5.8 | | | % Depr., Dep., Amort./Sales | 4.1 | 3.7 |
| | | (13) 9.5 | (22) 8.4 | (21) 10.8 | | | | (59) 6.8 | (56) 7.4 |
| | | 18.7 | 12.7 | 18.1 | | | | 10.9 | 10.8 |
| | | | | | | | % Officers', Directors', Owners' Comp/Sales | 1.3 | 1.5 |
| | | | | | | | | (10) 2.0 | (10) 2.1 |
| | | | | | | | | 3.4 | 4.2 |
| | 789M | 27448M | 160143M | 317188M | 201028M | 845376M | Net Sales ($) | 1595412M | 1937836M |
| | 696M | 17406M | 138591M | 414151M | 192895M | 942863M | Total Assets ($) | 1707801M | 1668728M |

M = $ thousand    MM = $ million
See Pages 9 through 22 for Explanation of Ratios and Data

## Comparative Historical Data | Current Data Sorted by Sales

### Type of Statement

| Type of Statement | 4/1/09-3/31/10 ALL | 4/1/10-3/31/11 ALL | 4/1/11-3/31/12 ALL | 0-1MM | 1-3MM | 3-5MM | 5-10MM | 10-25MM | 25MM & OVER |
|---|---|---|---|---|---|---|---|---|---|
| Unqualified | 11 | 14 | 13 |  | 4 | 2 |  | 4 | 7 |
| Reviewed | 10 | 8 | 15 | 1 | 1 |  | 4 | 7 | 2 |
| Compiled | 9 | 7 | 9 |  | 4 |  | 4 | 1 |  |
| Tax Returns | 4 | 5 | 9 | 2 | 3 | 2 | 2 |  |  |
| Other | 23 | 25 | 27 | 3 | 3 | 3 | 4 | 7 | 3 |
| | 57 | 59 | 73 | 6 (4/1-9/30/11) | | | 67 (10/1/11-3/31/12) | | |
| **NUMBER OF STATEMENTS** | 57 | 59 | 73 | 6 | 15 | 7 | 14 | 19 | 12 |

### ASSETS (%)

| | 4/1/09-3/31/10 ALL | 4/1/10-3/31/11 ALL | 4/1/11-3/31/12 ALL | 1-3MM | 5-10MM | 10-25MM | 25MM & OVER |
|---|---|---|---|---|---|---|---|
| Cash & Equivalents | 8.5 | 7.7 | 8.4 | 8.1 | 12.6 | 6.3 | 7.3 |
| Trade Receivables (net) | 15.3 | 11.1 | 14.0 | 7.9 | 11.8 | 20.3 | 14.2 |
| Inventory | 14.2 | 16.2 | 14.6 | 16.8 | 12.9 | 15.6 | 15.8 |
| All Other Current | 2.4 | 3.9 | 3.9 | 2.8 | 1.2 | 2.6 | 7.9 |
| Total Current | 40.4 | 38.9 | 40.9 | 35.5 | 38.5 | 44.8 | 45.2 |
| Fixed Assets (net) | 48.4 | 47.9 | 48.9 | 53.6 | 53.2 | 43.4 | 42.6 |
| Intangibles (net) | 4.8 | 4.6 | 3.8 | 4.8 | 1.5 | 5.3 | 3.5 |
| All Other Non-Current | 6.4 | 8.6 | 6.5 | 6.1 | 6.8 | 6.5 | 8.8 |
| Total | 100.0 | 100.0 | 100.0 | 100.0 | 100.0 | 100.0 | 100.0 |

### LIABILITIES (%)

| | 4/1/09-3/31/10 ALL | 4/1/10-3/31/11 ALL | 4/1/11-3/31/12 ALL | 1-3MM | 5-10MM | 10-25MM | 25MM & OVER |
|---|---|---|---|---|---|---|---|
| Notes Payable-Short Term | 4.9 | 5.8 | 4.2 | 5.8 | 3.2 | 3.8 | 4.3 |
| Cur. Mat.-L.T.D. | 5.1 | 5.6 | 5.8 | 9.9 | 4.3 | 6.7 | 2.5 |
| Trade Payables | 9.8 | 6.5 | 8.0 | 7.0 | 5.2 | 8.7 | 6.4 |
| Income Taxes Payable | .1 | .0 | .0 | .0 | .0 | .0 | .0 |
| All Other Current | 5.4 | 6.3 | 12.6 | 23.8 | 8.0 | 8.8 | 4.9 |
| Total Current | 25.3 | 24.2 | 30.6 | 46.4 | 20.7 | 28.0 | 18.2 |
| Long-Term Debt | 28.2 | 24.7 | 27.3 | 37.4 | 13.9 | 20.0 | 35.2 |
| Deferred Taxes | .9 | 1.0 | .3 | .4 | .3 | .0 | .5 |
| All Other Non-Current | 8.1 | 10.1 | 7.6 | 16.3 | 4.3 | 4.6 | 4.7 |
| Net Worth | 37.5 | 40.0 | 34.2 | -.4 | 60.8 | 47.4 | 41.5 |
| Total Liabilties & Net Worth | 100.0 | 100.0 | 100.0 | 100.0 | 100.0 | 100.0 | 100.0 |

### INCOME DATA (%)

| | 4/1/09-3/31/10 ALL | 4/1/10-3/31/11 ALL | 4/1/11-3/31/12 ALL | 1-3MM | 5-10MM | 10-25MM | 25MM & OVER |
|---|---|---|---|---|---|---|---|
| Net Sales | 100.0 | 100.0 | 100.0 | 100.0 | 100.0 | 100.0 | 100.0 |
| Gross Profit | 31.9 | 37.6 | 35.5 | 36.4 | 39.8 | 30.6 | 22.1 |
| Operating Expenses | 24.6 | 29.1 | 29.4 | 32.7 | 38.1 | 21.7 | 11.5 |
| Operating Profit | 7.3 | 8.4 | 6.0 | 3.7 | 1.7 | 8.9 | 10.5 |
| All Other Expenses (net) | 2.3 | 3.4 | 1.5 | 4.2 | 1.0 | 1.2 | 3.1 |
| Profit Before Taxes | 5.0 | 5.0 | 4.5 | -.5 | .6 | 7.7 | 7.4 |

### RATIOS

Values shown as upper quartile / median / lower quartile. Day-ratios shown as days/times.

| | 4/1/09-3/31/10 ALL | 4/1/10-3/31/11 ALL | 4/1/11-3/31/12 ALL | 1-3MM | 5-10MM | 10-25MM | 25MM & OVER |
|---|---|---|---|---|---|---|---|
| Current | 4.4 / 2.1 / 1.0 | 4.6 / 1.8 / 1.0 | 3.4 / 1.8 / .8 | 4.7 / .4 / .3 | 3.9 / 1.9 / 1.4 | 3.1 / 1.7 / 1.0 | 5.3 / 2.2 / 2.0 |
| Quick | 2.0 / .9 / .6 | 1.8 / .9 / .4 | 1.9 / .8 / .4 | 1.9 / .3 / .1 | 2.3 / 1.3 / .7 | 1.6 / 1.0 / .5 | 3.6 / 1.0 / .7 |
| Sales/Receivables | 26/13.9 / 39/9.4 / 52/7.1 | 22/16.7 / 37/9.8 / 57/6.4 | 29/12.8 / 43/8.5 / 65/5.6 | 14/26.8 / 29/12.6 / 36/10.1 | 31/11.8 / 45/8.2 / 50/7.3 | 40/9.2 / 47/7.8 / 87/4.2 | 33/11.1 / 54/6.8 / 83/4.4 |
| Cost of Sales/Inventory | 20/18.6 / 71/5.2 / 115/3.2 | 23/15.8 / 87/4.2 / 167/2.2 | 21/17.4 / 74/4.9 / 135/2.7 | 24/15.5 / 87/4.2 / 182/2.0 | 6/63.8 / 61/6.0 / 104/3.5 | 25/14.5 / 73/5.0 / 152/2.4 | 50/7.3 / 73/5.0 / 118/3.1 |
| Cost of Sales/Payables | 14/26.8 / 23/15.9 / 47/7.7 | 10/38.2 / 24/15.3 / 65/5.6 | 15/24.4 / 32/11.5 / 61/6.0 | 12/29.9 / 32/11.5 / 83/4.4 | 9/40.5 / 17/22.1 / 47/7.8 | 21/17.4 / 34/10.7 / 58/6.3 | 21/17.3 / 32/10.4 / 36/10.1 |
| Sales/Working Capital | 2.9 / 6.7 / NM | 2.9 / 6.1 / -54.5 | 3.0 / 6.2 / -16.9 | 3.0 / -6.7 / -2.0 | 4.0 / 5.9 / NM | 2.9 / 6.2 / -108.6 | 2.4 / 3.5 / 6.8 |
| EBIT/Interest | 11.5 / (51) 2.1 / -.3 | 7.2 / (53) 3.1 / .8 | 12.6 / (65) 2.7 / .2 | 2.0 / (12) .4 / -.5 | 16.2 / (13) 4.5 / .1 | 17.7 / (18) 3.9 / 1.1 | 9.5 / 4.2 / 1.6 |
| Net Profit + Depr., Dep., Amort./Cur. Mat. L/T/D | 15.1 / (16) 4.7 / 1.4 | 11.1 / (12) 2.0 / 1.0 | 3.3 / (12) 1.7 / -.1 |  |  |  |  |
| Fixed/Worth | .6 / 1.1 / 4.0 | .5 / 1.2 / 15.0 | .6 / 1.1 / 3.4 | 1.9 / -4.8 / -1.7 | .6 / .9 / 1.5 | .7 / 1.1 / 1.9 | .6 / .7 / 1.2 |
| Debt/Worth | .3 / 1.0 / 12.2 | .3 / 1.1 / 41.8 | .5 / 1.6 / 6.5 | 1.3 / -7.0 / -5.1 | .3 / .5 / 2.1 | .7 / 1.6 / 2.6 | .2 / .6 / 1.8 |
| % Profit Before Taxes/Tangible Net Worth | 23.5 / (47) 12.3 / 1.6 | 20.8 / (47) 7.2 / .3 | 26.0 / (61) 12.8 / .5 |  | 24.3 / 8.6 / -14.2 | 26.2 / 21.2 / .8 | 15.7 / (11) 7.6 / .2 |
| % Profit Before Taxes/Total Assets | 14.7 / 3.2 / -2.5 | 12.0 / 3.3 / -.4 | 11.0 / 3.5 / -3.4 | 3.5 / -.9 / -8.5 | 13.2 / 4.0 / -9.1 | 13.8 / 8.4 / .3 | 11.0 / 5.0 / .8 |
| Sales/Net Fixed Assets | 3.8 / 2.4 / 1.2 | 5.1 / 2.3 / 1.2 | 4.3 / 2.0 / 1.1 | 5.1 / 2.0 / .9 | 2.9 / 2.3 / 1.2 | 6.0 / 2.6 / 1.2 | 4.0 / 2.2 / 1.1 |
| Sales/Total Assets | 1.4 / 1.0 / .7 | 1.4 / .9 / .5 | 1.4 / .9 / .6 | 1.4 / 1.0 / .6 | 1.5 / 1.1 / .7 | 1.4 / .9 / .7 | 1.3 / .9 / .6 |
| % Depr., Dep., Amort./Sales | 4.0 / (48) 7.7 / 12.2 | 4.9 / (53) 8.6 / 12.9 | 4.0 / (67) 8.7 / 14.5 | 4.8 / (14) 10.9 / 15.8 | 7.8 / (13) 9.0 / 16.2 | 4.0 / (18) 7.9 / 14.2 | 2.6 / (11) 4.0 / 9.7 |
| % Officers', Directors' Owners' Comp/Sales |  | (11) 2.0 / 4.1 / 5.9 | 2.4 / 5.2 / 7.4 |  |  |  |  |

### Net Sales / Total Assets ($)

| | 4/1/09-3/31/10 ALL | 4/1/10-3/31/11 ALL | 4/1/11-3/31/12 ALL | 0-1MM | 1-3MM | 3-5MM | 5-10MM | 10-25MM | 25MM & OVER |
|---|---|---|---|---|---|---|---|---|---|
| Net Sales ($) | 1582390M | 955043M | 1551972M | 3277M | 28789M | 26554M | 101185M | 290063M | 1102104M |
| Total Assets ($) | 1581474M | 1101097M | 1706602M | 4755M | 42210M | 41716M | 108995M | 320272M | 1188654M |

M = $ thousand    MM = $ million
See Pages 9 through 22 for Explanation of Ratios and Data

## Current Data Sorted by Assets | Comparative Historical Data

| 0-500M | 500M-2MM | 2-10MM | 10-50MM | 50-100MM | 100-250MM | Type of Statement | 4/1/07-3/31/08 ALL | 4/1/08-3/31/09 ALL |
|---|---|---|---|---|---|---|---|---|
| 1 | 2 | 4 | 15 | 4 | 4 | Unqualified | 33 | 29 |
| 2 | 9 | 26 | 17 | 2 | 1 | Reviewed | 47 | 41 |
| 4 | 12 | 7 | 6 | 1 | | Compiled | 28 | 27 |
| 2 | 8 | 5 | 2 | | | Tax Returns | 26 | 28 |
| | | 32 | 14 | 4 | 3 | Other | 69 | 61 |
| 29 (4/1-9/30/11) | | | 155 (10/1/11-3/31/12) | | | | | |

| 0-500M | 500M-2MM | 2-10MM | 10-50MM | 50-100MM | 100-250MM | | 4/1/07-3/31/08 ALL | 4/1/08-3/31/09 ALL |
|---|---|---|---|---|---|---|---|---|
| 9 | 31 | 74 | 54 | 9 | 7 | NUMBER OF STATEMENTS | 203 | 186 |
| % | % | % | % | % | % | | % | % |
| | | | | | | **ASSETS** | | |
| | 10.3 | 8.9 | 6.7 | | | Cash & Equivalents | 10.7 | 9.2 |
| | 21.7 | 20.1 | 14.5 | | | Trade Receivables (net) | 16.2 | 16.4 |
| | 16.1 | 11.6 | 8.5 | | | Inventory | 8.5 | 9.3 |
| | 2.3 | 3.8 | 1.2 | | | All Other Current | 3.0 | 2.4 |
| | 50.3 | 44.4 | 30.8 | | | Total Current | 38.4 | 37.3 |
| | 43.6 | 45.5 | 56.5 | | | Fixed Assets (net) | 50.6 | 50.6 |
| | 1.0 | 3.5 | 4.4 | | | Intangibles (net) | 2.6 | 3.4 |
| | 5.1 | 6.6 | 8.2 | | | All Other Non-Current | 8.5 | 8.6 |
| | 100.0 | 100.0 | 100.0 | | | Total | 100.0 | 100.0 |
| | | | | | | **LIABILITIES** | | |
| | 9.0 | 6.8 | 4.0 | | | Notes Payable-Short Term | 5.8 | 6.3 |
| | 8.4 | 5.7 | 6.6 | | | Cur. Mat.-L.T.D. | 7.0 | 7.4 |
| | 12.6 | 10.3 | 8.7 | | | Trade Payables | 6.6 | 7.5 |
| | .3 | .4 | .3 | | | Income Taxes Payable | .6 | .3 |
| | 9.1 | 9.2 | 3.9 | | | All Other Current | 6.3 | 7.7 |
| | 39.3 | 32.5 | 23.5 | | | Total Current | 26.3 | 29.3 |
| | 37.0 | 23.6 | 21.7 | | | Long-Term Debt | 25.7 | 31.0 |
| | .8 | .4 | 1.2 | | | Deferred Taxes | 1.0 | .5 |
| | 4.9 | 9.2 | 7.5 | | | All Other Non-Current | 5.4 | 5.3 |
| | 18.0 | 34.3 | 46.2 | | | Net Worth | 41.6 | 33.9 |
| | 100.0 | 100.0 | 100.0 | | | Total Liabilities & Net Worth | 100.0 | 100.0 |
| | | | | | | **INCOME DATA** | | |
| | 100.0 | 100.0 | 100.0 | | | Net Sales | 100.0 | 100.0 |
| | 50.9 | 33.6 | 26.6 | | | Gross Profit | 34.3 | 30.7 |
| | 43.9 | 29.8 | 21.5 | | | Operating Expenses | 24.9 | 27.0 |
| | 7.0 | 3.8 | 5.1 | | | Operating Profit | 9.4 | 3.8 |
| | 2.3 | .9 | .4 | | | All Other Expenses (net) | 2.2 | 2.3 |
| | 4.7 | 2.9 | 4.7 | | | Profit Before Taxes | 7.3 | 1.5 |
| | | | | | | **RATIOS** | | |
| | 2.6 | 2.9 | 2.7 | | | | 2.9 | 2.6 |
| | 1.7 | 1.4 | 1.5 | | | Current | 1.7 | 1.4 |
| | .9 | 1.0 | .9 | | | | .9 | .8 |
| | 1.6 | 1.6 | 1.7 | | | | 2.1 | 1.8 |
| | 1.0 | .7 | 1.0 | | | Quick | 1.0 (185) | 1.0 |
| | .5 | .5 | .6 | | | | .5 | .5 |
| | 26 14.1 | 31 11.9 | 34 10.7 | | | | 25 14.5 | 25 14.8 |
| | 38 9.6 | 49 7.4 | 48 7.6 | | | Sales/Receivables | 40 9.2 | 40 9.1 |
| | 60 6.1 | 76 4.8 | 65 5.6 | | | | 55 6.7 | 60 6.1 |
| | 0 UND | 0 UND | 7 49.8 | | | | 0 UND | 0 UND |
| | 74 4.9 | 44 8.3 | 22 16.8 | | | Cost of Sales/Inventory | 20 18.1 | 19 18.9 |
| | 140 2.6 | 99 3.7 | 72 5.1 | | | | 60 6.1 | 67 5.5 |
| | 2 219.7 | 14 26.5 | 16 22.6 | | | | 12 31.6 | 40 40.4 |
| | 27 13.4 | 38 9.7 | 27 13.6 | | | Cost of Sales/Payables | 20 18.2 | 19 18.8 |
| | 72 5.1 | 83 4.4 | 70 5.2 | | | | 37 9.9 | 43 8.5 |
| | 2.7 | 4.7 | 4.2 | | | | 4.6 | 4.8 |
| | 9.7 | 11.9 | 12.4 | | | Sales/Working Capital | 11.1 | 13.1 |
| | -59.1 | -67.8 | -44.2 | | | | -75.3 | -19.6 |
| | 8.2 | 4.8 | 10.8 | | | | 11.2 | 6.2 |
| | (26) 3.5 | (62) 2.1 | (52) 3.8 | | | EBIT/Interest | (177) 3.0 | (169) 2.0 |
| | .5 | -.2 | .7 | | | | 1.2 | .1 |
| | | 11.3 | 5.9 | | | | 3.4 | 3.0 |
| | | (10) 3.6 | (17) 1.7 | | | Net Profit + Depr., Dep., Amort./Cur. Mat. L/T/D | (36) 2.0 | (28) 1.9 |
| | | .9 | 1.0 | | | | 1.0 | .4 |
| | 1.0 | .6 | .9 | | | | .7 | .8 |
| | 2.8 | 1.3 | 1.2 | | | Fixed/Worth | 1.2 | 1.5 |
| | -11.2 | 5.4 | 2.5 | | | | 2.8 | 4.9 |
| | .8 | .6 | .5 | | | | .5 | .7 |
| | 4.3 | 1.9 | 1.3 | | | Debt/Worth | 1.1 | 1.7 |
| | -66.2 | 7.0 | 2.3 | | | | 4.3 | 8.8 |
| | 50.3 | 26.1 | 27.3 | | | | 37.8 | 29.0 |
| | (23) 26.1 | (62) 5.9 | (50) 9.6 | | | % Profit Before Taxes/Tangible Net Worth | (175) 16.7 | (152) 9.6 |
| | 3.0 | -5.5 | .8 | | | | 3.4 | -2.2 |
| | 15.8 | 8.3 | 12.2 | | | | 16.5 | 11.8 |
| | 4.7 | 2.3 | 4.6 | | | % Profit Before Taxes/Total Assets | 6.4 | 2.9 |
| | .1 | -2.1 | -.3 | | | | .3 | -2.4 |
| | 9.1 | 5.1 | 3.2 | | | | 4.7 | 5.2 |
| | 5.0 | 2.5 | 1.4 | | | Sales/Net Fixed Assets | 2.7 | 2.6 |
| | 1.1 | 1.2 | .8 | | | | 1.4 | 1.2 |
| | 2.9 | 1.6 | 1.5 | | | | 1.9 | 1.9 |
| | 1.7 | 1.2 | .8 | | | Sales/Total Assets | 1.2 | 1.3 |
| | .8 | .7 | .5 | | | | .8 | .7 |
| | 3.7 | 3.4 | 5.4 | | | | 4.3 | 4.0 |
| | (27) 7.2 | (70) 7.4 | 8.0 | | | % Depr., Dep., Amort./Sales | (181) 7.4 | (167) 7.7 |
| | 11.3 | 13.5 | 14.9 | | | | 12.6 | 13.1 |
| | 1.2 | 1.4 | | | | | 1.9 | 1.4 |
| | (14) 2.1 | (18) 2.4 | | | | % Officers', Directors' Owners' Comp/Sales | (62) 3.4 | (57) 3.5 |
| | 4.2 | 6.5 | | | | | 6.7 | 6.6 |
| 4953M | 65900M | 437874M | 1221169M | 562600M | 854583M | Net Sales ($) | 4411726M | 3706324M |
| 2197M | 37108M | 376786M | 1169216M | 562225M | 972032M | Total Assets ($) | 3710540M | 3312624M |

M = $ thousand   MM = $ million
See Pages 9 through 22 for Explanation of Ratios and Data

## Comparative Historical Data

## Current Data Sorted by Sales

### Type of Statement

| | | | | | | | | | | |
|---|---|---|---|---|---|---|---|---|---|---|
| 30 | 31 | 27 | Unqualified | | 1 | 2 | 2 | 7 | 15 |
| 30 | 30 | 48 | Reviewed | 2 | 7 | 10 | 11 | 12 | 6 |
| 28 | 28 | 25 | Compiled | 1 | 9 | 1 | 7 | 6 | 1 |
| 31 | 22 | 23 | Tax Returns | 6 | 8 | 6 | 3 | | |
| 57 | 68 | 61 | Other | 9 | 6 | 11 | 13 | 14 | 8 |

| 4/1/09-3/31/10 ALL | 4/1/10-3/31/11 ALL | 4/1/11-3/31/12 ALL | | 29 (4/1-9/30/11) | | | 155 (10/1/11-3/31/12) | | |
|---|---|---|---|---|---|---|---|---|---|
| | | | | 0-1MM | 1-3MM | 3-5MM | 5-10MM | 10-25MM | 25MM & OVER |
| 176 | 179 | 184 | NUMBER OF STATEMENTS | 18 | 31 | 30 | 36 | 39 | 30 |
| % | % | % | ASSETS | % | % | % | % | % | % |
| 11.7 | 10.6 | 8.3 | Cash & Equivalents | 6.9 | 13.7 | 2.8 | 8.0 | 9.7 | 7.4 |
| 13.7 | 15.2 | 18.2 | Trade Receivables (net) | 8.2 | 16.8 | 17.5 | 24.5 | 17.2 | 19.9 |
| 9.5 | 9.5 | 11.5 | Inventory | 20.3 | 13.1 | 15.1 | 7.3 | 7.3 | 11.2 |
| 3.4 | 2.8 | 2.6 | All Other Current | 5.4 | 1.8 | .7 | 4.8 | 1.4 | 2.2 |
| 38.3 | 38.1 | 40.5 | Total Current | 40.8 | 45.4 | 36.1 | 44.7 | 35.6 | 40.7 |
| 48.1 | 48.8 | 47.0 | Fixed Assets (net) | 35.4 | 47.1 | 52.2 | 48.1 | 50.9 | 42.4 |
| 4.0 | 3.0 | 3.3 | Intangibles (net) | .6 | 3.8 | 6.8 | .6 | 4.8 | 2.2 |
| 9.5 | 10.2 | 9.2 | All Other Non-Current | 23.3 | 3.6 | 4.9 | 6.6 | 8.7 | 14.8 |
| 100.0 | 100.0 | 100.0 | Total | 100.0 | 100.0 | 100.0 | 100.0 | 100.0 | 100.0 |
| | | | **LIABILITIES** | | | | | | |
| 5.1 | 6.6 | 5.9 | Notes Payable-Short Term | 5.1 | 7.4 | 7.8 | 6.8 | 4.8 | 3.5 |
| 6.9 | 7.1 | 6.6 | Cur. Mat.-L.T.D. | 9.6 | 5.1 | 7.6 | 6.6 | 6.6 | 5.1 |
| 6.7 | 8.6 | 10.0 | Trade Payables | 8.7 | 9.1 | 14.0 | 10.3 | 9.0 | 8.8 |
| .2 | .2 | .3 | Income Taxes Payable | .0 | .2 | .3 | .7 | .4 | .0 |
| 6.8 | 6.6 | 7.9 | All Other Current | 13.5 | 9.5 | 7.6 | 8.6 | 6.1 | 4.9 |
| 25.7 | 29.2 | 30.8 | Total Current | 36.7 | 31.4 | 37.2 | 33.0 | 26.9 | 22.3 |
| 27.4 | 32.2 | 24.6 | Long-Term Debt | 28.0 | 32.0 | 30.6 | 21.7 | 20.9 | 17.0 |
| .5 | .6 | .7 | Deferred Taxes | .0 | 1.0 | .8 | .8 | .6 | .6 |
| 5.7 | 5.1 | 9.1 | All Other Non-Current | 19.0 | 8.2 | 10.4 | 3.7 | 8.6 | 9.6 |
| 40.7 | 32.9 | 34.9 | Net Worth | 16.2 | 27.4 | 21.0 | 40.8 | 42.9 | 50.4 |
| 100.0 | 100.0 | 100.0 | Total Liabilties & Net Worth | 100.0 | 100.0 | 100.0 | 100.0 | 100.0 | 100.0 |
| | | | **INCOME DATA** | | | | | | |
| 100.0 | 100.0 | 100.0 | Net Sales | 100.0 | 100.0 | 100.0 | 100.0 | 100.0 | 100.0 |
| 34.2 | 34.3 | 34.1 | Gross Profit | 49.8 | 48.0 | 35.3 | 32.6 | 27.9 | 19.3 |
| 30.8 | 30.3 | 28.8 | Operating Expenses | 41.7 | 40.9 | 34.4 | 30.6 | 19.9 | 12.6 |
| 3.4 | 4.0 | 5.3 | Operating Profit | 8.1 | 7.1 | .9 | 2.0 | 8.0 | 6.7 |
| 2.1 | 1.7 | .9 | All Other Expenses (net) | 3.2 | 2.4 | 1.3 | -.7 | .4 | .4 |
| 1.3 | 2.3 | 4.4 | Profit Before Taxes | 4.9 | 4.7 | -.4 | 2.7 | 7.6 | 6.2 |
| | | | **RATIOS** | | | | | | |
| 3.6 | 2.9 | 2.7 | Current | 5.8 | 2.8 | 1.7 | 2.5 | 3.0 | 3.3 |
| 1.7 | 1.5 | 1.4 | | 2.2 | 1.4 | 1.2 | 1.3 | 1.5 | 2.2 |
| .9 | .8 | .9 | | .4 | 1.0 | .7 | 1.0 | .7 | 1.4 |
| 2.1 | 1.8 | 1.7 | Quick | 3.5 | 1.6 | .9 | 1.6 | 1.9 | 2.1 |
| 1.0 | 1.0 | .9 | | .4 | 1.0 | .6 | .9 | .9 | 1.4 |
| .5 | .5 | .5 | | .1 | .3 | .3 | .6 | .6 | .8 |
| 26 13.8 | 23 15.8 | 31 11.8 | Sales/Receivables | 0 UND | 28 13.1 | 30 12.3 | 32 11.5 | 31 11.6 | 36 10.1 |
| 41 8.9 | 40 9.1 | 46 7.9 | | 24 15.2 | 49 7.5 | 42 8.7 | 48 7.6 | 51 7.2 | 50 7.3 |
| 59 6.1 | 67 5.5 | 73 5.0 | | 39 9.3 | 76 4.8 | 79 4.6 | 74 4.9 | 78 4.7 | 66 5.5 |
| 0 UND | 3 145.2 | 5 75.0 | Cost of Sales/Inventory | 0 UND | 0 UND | 23 15.9 | 0 UND | 3 136.5 | 12 30.6 |
| 31 11.9 | 26 13.8 | 35 10.4 | | 73 5.0 | 78 4.7 | 66 5.5 | 18 19.9 | 25 14.7 | 30 12.2 |
| 89 4.1 | 80 4.6 | 96 3.8 | | 456 .8 | 192 1.9 | 114 3.2 | 65 5.6 | 68 5.4 | 61 6.0 |
| 11 34.2 | 11 34.4 | 12 30.0 | Cost of Sales/Payables | 0 UND | 4 91.2 | 14 26.5 | 15 24.9 | 17 21.4 | 17 22.0 |
| 24 15.5 | 24 15.3 | 28 13.1 | | 13 27.3 | 23 15.6 | 63 5.8 | 27 13.3 | 28 13.1 | 24 15.3 |
| 51 7.1 | 55 6.6 | 66 5.5 | | 57 6.4 | 104 3.5 | 130 2.8 | 55 6.6 | 60 6.1 | 38 9.5 |
| 3.1 | 3.8 | 4.2 | Sales/Working Capital | 1.5 | 2.5 | 6.7 | 5.0 | 4.4 | 3.1 |
| 8.5 | 11.3 | 11.6 | | 10.8 | 7.2 | 21.6 | 13.0 | 13.7 | 7.7 |
| -39.8 | -20.2 | -50.3 | | -12.6 | 197.8 | -6.5 | -175.8 | -28.8 | 18.7 |
| 9.9 | 5.5 | 8.2 | EBIT/Interest | 8.5 | 8.2 | 4.2 | 7.3 | 10.8 | 23.7 |
| (152) 1.9 | (158) 2.1 | (163) 3.2 | | (13) 2.9 | (26) 3.2 | (28) .7 | (30) 3.1 | (36) 3.9 | 6.6 |
| -.3 | .0 | .7 | | .9 | .2 | -1.9 | .4 | 1.6 | 2.0 |
| 3.9 | 4.8 | 6.1 | Net Profit + Depr., Dep., Amort./Cur. Mat. L/T/D | | | | | 7.7 | 6.5 |
| (33) 1.9 | (36) 1.8 | (35) 2.4 | | | | | | (12) 1.6 | (10) 2.9 |
| 1.0 | 1.1 | 1.1 | | | | | | 1.0 | 1.7 |
| .6 | .7 | .7 | Fixed/Worth | .3 | .9 | 1.1 | .8 | .6 | .6 |
| 1.2 | 1.3 | 1.2 | | 2.2 | 2.0 | 3.3 | 1.2 | 1.2 | .8 |
| 3.0 | 5.3 | 4.0 | | -10.2 | -5.7 | NM | 2.6 | 3.3 | 1.2 |
| .5 | .6 | .6 | Debt/Worth | .4 | .6 | 1.7 | .5 | .5 | .4 |
| 1.3 | 1.6 | 1.7 | | 3.3 | 1.9 | 4.7 | 1.7 | 1.4 | .8 |
| 4.3 | 11.8 | 6.5 | | -57.1 | -10.3 | NM | 3.1 | 3.1 | 1.6 |
| 20.6 | 23.1 | 30.6 | % Profit Before Taxes/Tangible Net Worth | 40.4 | 42.0 | 25.5 | 28.3 | 25.5 | 34.5 |
| (149) 3.8 | (144) 7.0 | (155) 9.5 | | (13) 15.3 | (22) 10.0 | (23) -3.3 | (33) 8.0 | (36) 11.8 | (28) 14.5 |
| -7.8 | -5.6 | -.3 | | 2.3 | -2.8 | -48.1 | -3.9 | 3.9 | 4.0 |
| 9.7 | 9.6 | 10.8 | % Profit Before Taxes/Total Assets | 11.1 | 14.7 | 7.3 | 11.1 | 9.3 | 12.9 |
| 1.9 | 2.8 | 3.7 | | 3.0 | 4.7 | -.7 | 2.0 | 3.9 | 6.2 |
| -3.4 | -2.5 | -1.5 | | -1.6 | -1.9 | -3.7 | -1.7 | 1.4 | 1.8 |
| 4.5 | 4.1 | 5.1 | Sales/Net Fixed Assets | 9.9 | 5.3 | 3.8 | 8.1 | 3.4 | 4.3 |
| 2.3 | 2.2 | 2.4 | | 2.3 | 2.4 | 2.2 | 2.9 | 1.5 | 3.2 |
| 1.0 | 1.2 | 1.1 | | .8 | .9 | .9 | 1.1 | 1.0 | 2.2 |
| 1.6 | 1.6 | 1.6 | Sales/Total Assets | 1.8 | 1.9 | 1.5 | 1.9 | 1.6 | 1.7 |
| 1.0 | 1.0 | 1.0 | | .7 | 1.0 | 1.1 | 1.3 | .9 | 1.3 |
| .6 | .6 | .6 | | .5 | .5 | .7 | .7 | .6 | .9 |
| 4.5 | 4.7 | 3.8 | % Depr., Dep., Amort./Sales | 4.2 | 4.5 | 3.6 | 3.7 | 3.6 | 3.4 |
| (155) 8.4 | (152) 8.7 | (169) 7.3 | | (11) 8.2 | (29) 9.1 | (29) 7.4 | (34) 8.2 | (38) 7.7 | (28) 5.6 |
| 16.4 | 14.5 | 12.4 | | 12.5 | 14.8 | 13.5 | 14.9 | 13.1 | 7.0 |
| 1.5 | 1.5 | 1.4 | % Officers', Directors', Owners' Comp/Sales | | 1.6 | | | 1.4 | |
| (45) 3.2 | (56) 2.7 | (42) 2.5 | | | (12) 2.8 | | | (13) 2.4 | |
| 8.2 | 7.4 | 6.1 | | | 7.3 | | | 5.2 | |
| 3433877M | 3187715M | 3147079M | Net Sales ($) | 10645M | 55646M | 120052M | 253420M | 591726M | 2115590M |
| 3224234M | 3444222M | 3119564M | Total Assets ($) | 18412M | 91590M | 133117M | 244452M | 741186M | 1890807M |

© RMA 2012

M = $ thousand    MM = $ million
See Pages 9 through 22 for Explanation of Ratios and Data

## Current Data Sorted by Assets  /  Comparative Historical Data

| | 0-500M | 500M-2MM | 2-10MM | 10-50MM | 50-100MM | 100-250MM | Type of Statement | 4/1/07-3/31/08 ALL | 4/1/08-3/31/09 ALL |
|---|---|---|---|---|---|---|---|---|---|
| | | 1 | 1 | 7 | 5 | 7 | Unqualified | 19 | 18 |
| | | 2 | 10 | 9 | 1 | 1 | Reviewed | 12 | 13 |
| | | 4 | 6 | 1 | | 1 | Compiled | 18 | 8 |
| | 7 | 7 | 7 | 1 | | | Tax Returns | 7 | 16 |
| | 4 | 13 | 23 | 20 | 9 | 10 | Other | 51 | 72 |
| | | 14 (4/1-9/30/11) | | 143 (10/1/11-3/31/12) | | | | | |
| NUMBER OF STATEMENTS | 11 | 27 | 47 | 38 | 15 | 19 | | 107 | 127 |
| | % | % | % | % | % | % | | % | % |
| **ASSETS** | | | | | | | | | |
| Cash & Equivalents | 25.1 | 13.8 | 9.4 | 11.4 | 6.3 | 6.0 | | 12.0 | 9.8 |
| Trade Receivables (net) | 18.8 | 29.3 | 24.1 | 24.1 | 19.4 | 10.7 | | 17.7 | 17.5 |
| Inventory | 9.7 | 3.4 | 5.1 | 3.6 | 2.0 | 6.1 | | 3.7 | 4.3 |
| All Other Current | 7.4 | 1.1 | 2.3 | 5.5 | 3.0 | 2.9 | | 3.5 | 3.1 |
| Total Current | 61.0 | 47.6 | 40.8 | 44.6 | 30.7 | 25.7 | | 36.9 | 34.6 |
| Fixed Assets (net) | 27.7 | 41.7 | 48.0 | 44.7 | 60.7 | 62.0 | | 52.0 | 53.0 |
| Intangibles (net) | 6.4 | 1.2 | 1.1 | 1.7 | 5.8 | 5.3 | | 4.9 | 4.0 |
| All Other Non-Current | 4.9 | 9.6 | 10.0 | 9.1 | 2.7 | 7.1 | | 6.2 | 8.4 |
| Total | 100.0 | 100.0 | 100.0 | 100.0 | 100.0 | 100.0 | | 100.0 | 100.0 |
| **LIABILITIES** | | | | | | | | | |
| Notes Payable-Short Term | 11.2 | 7.5 | 6.9 | 7.7 | 5.1 | 1.2 | | 6.5 | 7.5 |
| Cur. Mat.-L.T.D. | 5.5 | 6.4 | 5.5 | 5.2 | 3.8 | 2.7 | | 5.7 | 6.1 |
| Trade Payables | 9.6 | 7.3 | 10.6 | 9.8 | 6.6 | 6.8 | | 7.9 | 9.7 |
| Income Taxes Payable | .0 | .8 | .2 | .6 | .1 | .1 | | .3 | .2 |
| All Other Current | 7.5 | 8.3 | 7.4 | 10.1 | 7.1 | 4.0 | | 8.8 | 8.3 |
| Total Current | 33.8 | 30.4 | 30.7 | 33.4 | 22.6 | 14.8 | | 29.2 | 31.8 |
| Long-Term Debt | 44.1 | 30.1 | 20.8 | 14.5 | 20.7 | 25.2 | | 22.5 | 25.5 |
| Deferred Taxes | .0 | .2 | .4 | 1.2 | 4.4 | 3.0 | | .9 | .7 |
| All Other Non-Current | 1.5 | 6.6 | 5.3 | 2.8 | 2.4 | 5.5 | | 5.9 | 4.2 |
| Net Worth | 20.8 | 32.8 | 42.7 | 48.1 | 49.8 | 51.5 | | 41.6 | 37.8 |
| Total Liabilities & Net Worth | 100.0 | 100.0 | 100.0 | 100.0 | 100.0 | 100.0 | | 100.0 | 100.0 |
| **INCOME DATA** | | | | | | | | | |
| Net Sales | 100.0 | 100.0 | 100.0 | 100.0 | 100.0 | 100.0 | | 100.0 | 100.0 |
| Gross Profit | | | | | | | | | |
| Operating Expenses | 87.4 | 94.0 | 84.0 | 86.0 | 90.0 | 82.3 | | 84.9 | 85.1 |
| Operating Profit | 12.6 | 6.0 | 16.0 | 14.0 | 10.0 | 17.7 | | 15.1 | 14.9 |
| All Other Expenses (net) | .9 | 2.7 | .8 | .6 | 2.7 | 3.4 | | 1.9 | 3.2 |
| Profit Before Taxes | 11.7 | 3.2 | 15.2 | 13.4 | 7.4 | 14.3 | | 13.2 | 11.8 |

### RATIOS

| | 0-500M | 500M-2MM | 2-10MM | 10-50MM | 50-100MM | 100-250MM | | 4/1/07-3/31/08 ALL | 4/1/08-3/31/09 ALL |
|---|---|---|---|---|---|---|---|---|---|
| Current | 3.8 | 4.4 | 2.4 | 4.7 | 2.2 | 4.2 | | 2.2 | 2.0 |
| | 2.2 | 1.9 | 1.5 | 1.5 | 1.4 | 1.7 | | 1.3 | 1.1 |
| | .9 | .7 | .8 | .9 | .8 | .9 | | .7 | .6 |
| Quick | 2.8 | 4.2 | 2.1 | 3.9 | 1.8 | 3.0 | | 1.9 | 1.7 |
| | 1.3 | 1.2 | 1.3 | 1.2 | 1.2 | 1.1 | | 1.1 | .8 |
| | .2 | .7 | .6 | .7 | .7 | .7 | | .6 | .5 |
| Sales/Receivables | 0 UND | 23  15.7 | 25  14.4 | 34  10.8 | 54  6.7 | 47  7.8 | | 19  19.3 | 12  31.1 |
| | 0 UND | 43  8.4 | 47  7.8 | 59  6.2 | 64  5.7 | 59  6.2 | | 49  7.4 | 38  9.7 |
| | 49  7.5 | 68  5.4 | 72  5.1 | 85  4.3 | 85  4.3 | 76  4.8 | | 71  5.1 | 63  5.8 |
| Cost of Sales/Inventory | | | | | | | | | |
| Cost of Sales/Payables | | | | | | | | | |
| Sales/Working Capital | 8.3 | 4.6 | 5.7 | 4.0 | 5.1 | 3.2 | | 5.6 | 6.1 |
| | 13.4 | 20.0 | 17.2 | 11.2 | 9.1 | 6.4 | | 17.7 | 86.8 |
| | -143.2 | -16.9 | -17.0 | -401.5 | -13.4 | -22.1 | | -11.5 | -8.7 |
| EBIT/Interest | | 29.1 | 51.2 | 30.3 | 15.3 | 23.2 | | 17.3 | 19.0 |
| | (23) 3.4 | (44) 17.2 | (33) 11.6 | | 10.0 | (15) 9.3 | | (93) 6.8 | (113) 5.2 |
| | | -4.3 | 2.9 | 4.5 | 2.9 | 5.1 | | 2.2 | 1.7 |
| Net Profit + Depr., Dep., Amort./Cur. Mat. L/T/D | | | | | | | | 18.6 | 6.1 |
| | | | | | | | | (19) 9.3 | (22) 2.6 |
| | | | | | | | | 2.1 | 2.0 |
| Fixed/Worth | .0 | .3 | .5 | .5 | 1.0 | .8 | | .8 | .7 |
| | .5 | .8 | 1.0 | 1.0 | 1.3 | 1.4 | | 1.3 | 1.4 |
| | 8.0 | 6.5 | 2.4 | 1.7 | 2.5 | 2.0 | | 3.4 | 4.0 |
| Debt/Worth | 1.5 | .3 | .5 | .5 | .5 | .6 | | .6 | .6 |
| | 2.0 | 1.8 | 1.1 | 1.2 | 1.6 | .8 | | 1.7 | 1.4 |
| | -8.9 | 10.2 | 3.0 | 1.6 | 2.5 | 2.2 | | 6.7 | 4.8 |
| % Profit Before Taxes/Tangible Net Worth | | 82.5 | 96.8 | 67.7 | 44.6 | 26.7 | | 77.8 | 65.8 |
| | (22) 25.1 | (43) 38.1 | (35) 37.1 | | 37.7 | (17) 18.5 | | (90) 42.0 | (109) 30.5 |
| | | -23.1 | 11.8 | 15.0 | 3.5 | 10.9 | | 18.5 | 6.4 |
| % Profit Before Taxes/Total Assets | 136.4 | 58.7 | 34.6 | 27.3 | 17.1 | 12.3 | | 25.6 | 25.0 |
| | 27.1 | 5.4 | 18.2 | 14.8 | 10.9 | 8.2 | | 12.5 | 10.4 |
| | 10.0 | -10.5 | 5.5 | 7.4 | 2.3 | 4.5 | | 3.9 | .6 |
| Sales/Net Fixed Assets | UND | 31.1 | 6.0 | 5.5 | 2.5 | 1.9 | | 5.4 | 6.8 |
| | 25.7 | 5.0 | 3.5 | 2.8 | 1.8 | .8 | | 2.4 | 2.7 |
| | 12.4 | 2.3 | 1.8 | 1.6 | .8 | .5 | | 1.2 | 1.2 |
| Sales/Total Assets | 7.3 | 3.1 | 2.2 | 1.5 | 1.3 | .8 | | 2.0 | 2.1 |
| | 4.3 | 2.2 | 1.5 | 1.2 | .9 | .5 | | 1.3 | 1.4 |
| | 2.7 | 1.2 | 1.0 | 1.0 | .6 | .4 | | .6 | .7 |
| % Depr., Dep., Amort./Sales | | 3.0 | 3.9 | 4.0 | 6.0 | | | 3.0 | 3.9 |
| | | (10) 5.7 | (32) 6.8 | (32) 7.2 | (14) 11.6 | | | (86) 7.0 | (103) 8.0 |
| | | 10.3 | 9.0 | 13.1 | 16.0 | | | 11.8 | 14.3 |
| % Officers', Directors', Owners' Comp/Sales | | 3.8 | .8 | | | | | 1.4 | 1.4 |
| | | (10) 6.2 | (19) 1.4 | | | | | (25) 2.8 | (30) 4.3 |
| | | 9.7 | 4.9 | | | | | 5.9 | 8.7 |
| Net Sales ($) | 15847M | 70944M | 422505M | 1103043M | 1294436M | 1953940M | | 3104123M | 3264442M |
| Total Assets ($) | 3047M | 31239M | 220613M | 800592M | 973558M | 3260276M | | 3036347M | 3181116M |

M = $ thousand   MM = $ million
See Pages 9 through 22 for Explanation of Ratios and Data

## Comparative Historical Data | | | Type of Statement | Current Data Sorted by Sales

| | | | | | | Type of Statement | | | | | | |
|---|---|---|---|---|---|---|---|---|---|---|---|---|
| | 18 | | 15 | | 21 | Unqualified | | 1 | 2 | | 4 | 14 |
| | 13 | | 13 | | 23 | Reviewed | | 3 | 4 | 6 | 6 | 4 |
| | 11 | | 14 | | 12 | Compiled | | 1 | 3 | 3 | 3 | 2 |
| | 19 | | 26 | | 22 | Tax Returns | 3 | 10 | 2 | 3 | 4 | |
| | 64 | | 67 | | 79 | Other | 6 | 12 | 10 | 8 | 12 | 31 |
| | 4/1/09-3/31/10 | | 4/1/10-3/31/11 | | 4/1/11-3/31/12 | | | 14 (4/1-9/30/11) | | 143 (10/1/11-3/31/12) | | |
| | ALL | | ALL | | ALL | | 0-1MM | 1-3MM | 3-5MM | 5-10MM | 10-25MM | 25MM & OVER |
| | 125 | | 135 | | 157 | NUMBER OF STATEMENTS | 9 | 27 | 21 | 20 | 29 | 51 |
| | % | | % | | % | | % | % | % | % | % | % |
| | | | | | | ASSETS | | | | | | |
| | 10.5 | | 12.0 | | 11.0 | Cash & Equivalents | | 11.4 | 15.6 | 10.0 | 11.0 | 7.9 |
| | 18.5 | | 19.8 | | 22.5 | Trade Receivables (net) | | 18.4 | 22.5 | 30.8 | 25.4 | 20.9 |
| | 7.6 | | 5.2 | | 4.6 | Inventory | | 6.2 | .3 | 5.7 | 5.5 | 4.1 |
| | 3.7 | | 4.6 | | 3.4 | All Other Current | | 5.0 | 3.7 | 2.3 | 3.0 | 3.6 |
| | 40.3 | | 41.5 | | 41.5 | Total Current | | 41.0 | 42.0 | 48.8 | 44.9 | 36.4 |
| | 48.2 | | 49.2 | | 47.6 | Fixed Assets (net) | | 46.9 | 44.7 | 45.8 | 47.0 | 53.6 |
| | 5.0 | | 3.2 | | 2.6 | Intangibles (net) | | 1.5 | .4 | 1.1 | 2.2 | 3.9 |
| | 6.5 | | 6.1 | | 8.3 | All Other Non-Current | | 10.6 | 12.9 | 4.3 | 5.9 | 6.1 |
| | 100.0 | | 100.0 | | 100.0 | Total | | 100.0 | 100.0 | 100.0 | 100.0 | 100.0 |
| | | | | | | LIABILITIES | | | | | | |
| | 5.2 | | 5.8 | | 6.7 | Notes Payable-Short Term | | 6.0 | 16.7 | 6.4 | 3.6 | 4.3 |
| | 8.2 | | 8.3 | | 5.1 | Cur. Mat.-L.T.D. | | 3.6 | 5.0 | 9.5 | 5.1 | 3.6 |
| | 8.7 | | 10.2 | | 8.9 | Trade Payables | | 6.2 | 7.7 | 11.0 | 8.3 | 10.3 |
| | .1 | | .2 | | .4 | Income Taxes Payable | | .3 | .1 | .2 | .8 | .0 |
| | 7.6 | | 8.0 | | 7.8 | All Other Current | | 10.6 | 12.7 | 5.3 | 5.0 | 7.3 |
| | 29.8 | | 32.6 | | 28.8 | Total Current | | 26.7 | 42.2 | 32.4 | 22.8 | 25.5 |
| | 26.7 | | 29.8 | | 23.0 | Long-Term Debt | | 28.0 | 20.3 | 31.5 | 13.9 | 20.2 |
| | 1.1 | | 1.0 | | 1.2 | Deferred Taxes | | .4 | .3 | .8 | 1.1 | 2.6 |
| | 8.1 | | 4.4 | | 4.4 | All Other Non-Current | | 6.3 | 9.9 | 3.5 | 2.0 | 3.7 |
| | 34.4 | | 32.2 | | 42.5 | Net Worth | | 38.7 | 27.3 | 31.7 | 60.2 | 48.0 |
| | 100.0 | | 100.0 | | 100.0 | Total Liabilities & Net Worth | | 100.0 | 100.0 | 100.0 | 100.0 | 100.0 |
| | | | | | | INCOME DATA | | | | | | |
| | 100.0 | | 100.0 | | 100.0 | Net Sales | | 100.0 | 100.0 | 100.0 | 100.0 | 100.0 |
| | | | | | | Gross Profit | | | | | | |
| | 92.5 | | 88.7 | | 86.8 | Operating Expenses | | 90.2 | 90.1 | 92.4 | 79.4 | 85.8 |
| | 7.5 | | 11.3 | | 13.2 | Operating Profit | | 9.8 | 9.9 | 7.6 | 20.6 | 14.2 |
| | 2.2 | | 2.6 | | 1.6 | All Other Expenses (net) | | 2.1 | .7 | 1.1 | .4 | 1.8 |
| | 5.3 | | 8.7 | | 11.6 | Profit Before Taxes | | 7.7 | 9.3 | 6.4 | 20.2 | 12.4 |
| | | | | | | RATIOS | | | | | | |
| | 2.8 | | 2.5 | | 3.4 | | | 6.1 | 2.1 | 2.4 | 6.3 | 3.2 |
| | 1.3 | | 1.4 | | 1.5 | Current | | 1.8 | 1.2 | 1.4 | 2.8 | 1.4 |
| | .8 | | .7 | | .8 | | | .8 | .6 | .8 | .9 | 1.0 |
| | 2.1 | | 1.9 | | 2.5 | | | 4.2 | 2.1 | 2.0 | 5.6 | 1.8 |
| | .9 | | 1.0 | | 1.2 | Quick | | 1.0 | 1.0 | 1.3 | 2.1 | 1.2 |
| | .5 | | .4 | | .7 | | | .3 | .5 | .7 | .7 | .8 |
| 25 | 14.8 | 22 | 16.6 | 31 | 11.7 | | 1 | 298.8 | 0 UND | 31 | 11.8 | 34 | 10.7 | 43 | 8.4 |
| 44 | 8.3 | 48 | 7.6 | 54 | 6.7 | Sales/Receivables | 42 | 8.7 | 41 | 8.8 | 54 | 6.7 | 60 | 6.1 | 60 | 6.1 |
| 70 | 5.2 | 70 | 5.2 | 74 | 4.9 | | 66 | 5.5 | 85 | 4.3 | 83 | 4.4 | 81 | 4.5 | 81 | 4.5 |
| | | | | | | Cost of Sales/Inventory | | | | | | |
| | | | | | | Cost of Sales/Payables | | | | | | |
| | 5.1 | | 5.0 | | 4.7 | | | 7.3 | 6.8 | 5.5 | 3.2 | 4.5 |
| | 15.5 | | 16.1 | | 12.3 | Sales/Working Capital | | 20.0 | 17.2 | 15.3 | 5.6 | 12.3 |
| | -18.6 | | -9.5 | | -25.0 | | | -16.9 | -8.7 | -20.8 | NM | -526.7 |
| | 9.6 | | 13.0 | | 31.6 | | | 26.2 | 30.6 | 34.0 | 74.4 | 27.2 |
| (106) | 2.1 | (119) | 4.3 | (138) | 9.8 | EBIT/Interest | (24) | 4.4 | (18) | 13.4 | (19) | 4.4 | (27) | 17.0 | (45) | 10.0 |
| | -.5 | | .8 | | 2.5 | | | -2.0 | 1.6 | .7 | 7.6 | 5.4 |
| | 4.6 | | 4.8 | | 13.3 | Net Profit + Depr., Dep., | | | | | | |
| (21) | 2.4 | (21) | 1.8 | (20) | 3.2 | Amort./Cur. Mat. L/T/D | | | | | | |
| | 1.4 | | .9 | | 1.4 | | | | | | | |
| | .6 | | .8 | | .5 | | | .5 | .4 | .6 | .4 | .8 |
| | 1.4 | | 1.4 | | 1.1 | Fixed/Worth | | .9 | 1.3 | 1.6 | .9 | 1.2 |
| | 3.4 | | 2.9 | | 2.2 | | | 4.0 | 15.4 | 4.1 | 1.6 | 1.8 |
| | .6 | | .7 | | .5 | | | .3 | .6 | .9 | .2 | .6 |
| | 1.4 | | 1.5 | | 1.2 | Debt/Worth | | 1.8 | 2.1 | 1.5 | 1.0 | 1.3 |
| | 5.8 | | 6.4 | | 3.0 | | | 5.2 | 23.4 | 14.0 | 1.4 | 2.2 |
| | 47.8 | | 58.0 | | 76.7 | % Profit Before Taxes/Tangible | | 85.7 | 123.6 | 85.4 | 78.2 | 47.9 |
| (107) | 10.7 | (119) | 18.1 | (140) | 33.0 | Net Worth | (23) | 32.8 | (17) | 44.4 | (17) | 20.0 | 38.1 | (48) | 26.7 |
| | -5.1 | | -1.2 | | 11.4 | | | .1 | 10.7 | 7.2 | 18.0 | 10.6 |
| | 14.6 | | 22.0 | | 27.1 | % Profit Before Taxes/Total | | 35.5 | 35.2 | 25.4 | 57.7 | 17.6 |
| | 5.4 | | 6.7 | | 13.5 | Assets | | 10.0 | 19.2 | 9.7 | 19.2 | 12.3 |
| | -4.4 | | -1.1 | | 3.0 | | | -7.3 | 2.6 | -.7 | 8.5 | 4.7 |
| | 8.1 | | 9.5 | | 6.6 | | | 12.4 | 11.5 | 7.7 | 5.4 | 4.2 |
| | 2.7 | | 2.7 | | 2.9 | Sales/Net Fixed Assets | | 4.7 | 2.2 | 4.7 | 2.6 | 2.0 |
| | 1.1 | | 1.1 | | 1.6 | | | 2.0 | 1.5 | 1.9 | 1.8 | .8 |
| | 2.2 | | 2.1 | | 2.2 | | | 2.8 | 2.8 | 2.3 | 2.2 | 1.5 |
| | 1.1 | | 1.3 | | 1.3 | Sales/Total Assets | | 1.6 | 1.4 | 1.8 | 1.3 | 1.0 |
| | .6 | | .6 | | .8 | | | 1.0 | .7 | 1.3 | 1.0 | .5 |
| | 3.7 | | 4.2 | | 3.5 | | | 3.1 | 3.6 | 3.4 | 5.4 | 1.5 |
| (89) | 9.1 | (98) | 7.9 | (94) | 7.0 | % Depr., Dep., Amort./Sales | (15) | 6.7 | (13) | 9.0 | (15) | 7.0 | (21) | 7.1 | (30) | 6.2 |
| | 13.6 | | 14.7 | | 12.3 | | | 10.3 | 28.5 | 8.8 | 12.8 | 12.7 |
| | 1.1 | | 1.1 | | 1.3 | | | 2.5 | | | | |
| (30) | 4.6 | (33) | 4.1 | (43) | 4.0 | % Officers', Directors' Owners' Comp/Sales | (10) | 5.7 | | | | |
| | 10.6 | | 8.6 | | 6.7 | | | 10.4 | | | | |
| | 3106694M | | 3697273M | | 4860715M | Net Sales ($) | 4909M | 54035M | 88498M | 144640M | 458473M | 4110160M |
| | 3491082M | | 3993849M | | 5289325M | Total Assets ($) | 9046M | 41324M | 144873M | 88452M | 389393M | 4616237M |

M = $ thousand   MM = $ million
See Pages 9 through 22 for Explanation of Ratios and Data

## Current Data Sorted by Assets

## Comparative Historical Data

| | | | | | | Type of Statement | | |
|---|---|---|---|---|---|---|---|---|
| | 1 | 10 | 45 | 28 | 33 | Unqualified | 79 | 86 |
| | 4 | 11 | 19 | 2 | 1 | Reviewed | 27 | 34 |
| 6 | 16 | 29 | 11 | 3 | 2 | Compiled | 40 | 45 |
| 2 | 33 | 16 | 2 | | | Tax Returns | 27 | 19 |
| 9 | 46 | 97 | 106 | 48 | 38 | Other | 177 | 195 |
| | 76 (4/1-9/30/11) | | 542 (10/1/11-3/31/12) | | | | 4/1/07-3/31/08 | 4/1/08-3/31/09 |
| 0-500M | 500M-2MM | 2-10MM | 10-50MM | 50-100MM | 100-250MM | | ALL | ALL |
| 17 | 100 | 163 | 183 | 81 | 74 | NUMBER OF STATEMENTS | 350 | 379 |
| % | % | % | % | % | % | ASSETS | % | % |
| 18.6 | 18.7 | 12.8 | 7.7 | 7.1 | 6.9 | Cash & Equivalents | 10.1 | 8.6 |
| 22.4 | 29.2 | 36.8 | 27.2 | 20.6 | 22.9 | Trade Receivables (net) | 28.1 | 27.3 |
| 1.6 | 5.0 | 6.3 | 6.8 | 10.7 | 9.3 | Inventory | 7.2 | 7.7 |
| 7.3 | 4.7 | 2.8 | 4.0 | 4.1 | 2.9 | All Other Current | 5.5 | 5.1 |
| 49.8 | 57.6 | 58.6 | 45.8 | 42.4 | 41.9 | Total Current | 50.9 | 48.7 |
| 40.5 | 31.9 | 32.7 | 42.3 | 38.6 | 43.6 | Fixed Assets (net) | 39.2 | 40.0 |
| .8 | 1.8 | 2.9 | 6.6 | 13.0 | 9.9 | Intangibles (net) | 4.7 | 5.2 |
| 8.9 | 8.7 | 5.8 | 5.4 | 5.9 | 4.6 | All Other Non-Current | 5.2 | 6.1 |
| 100.0 | 100.0 | 100.0 | 100.0 | 100.0 | 100.0 | Total | 100.0 | 100.0 |
| | | | | | | LIABILITIES | | |
| .6 | 8.5 | 7.0 | 5.5 | 4.8 | 5.5 | Notes Payable-Short Term | 8.2 | 7.6 |
| 37.6 | 4.9 | 5.7 | 5.7 | 4.3 | 3.3 | Cur. Mat.-L.T.D. | 4.8 | 4.8 |
| 9.7 | 11.9 | 13.4 | 11.1 | 9.3 | 13.1 | Trade Payables | 10.7 | 11.4 |
| .9 | .3 | .1 | .3 | .5 | .3 | Income Taxes Payable | .7 | .6 |
| 29.0 | 6.8 | 8.2 | 9.3 | 8.6 | 5.5 | All Other Current | 10.0 | 8.5 |
| 77.8 | 32.3 | 34.5 | 31.9 | 27.4 | 27.7 | Total Current | 34.3 | 32.9 |
| 27.1 | 24.8 | 16.9 | 17.1 | 16.7 | 18.5 | Long-Term Debt | 20.6 | 20.0 |
| .0 | .1 | .2 | 1.3 | 2.2 | 1.5 | Deferred Taxes | 1.0 | 1.0 |
| 11.0 | 6.5 | 5.7 | 4.4 | 5.5 | 4.8 | All Other Non-Current | 4.5 | 4.2 |
| -15.9 | 36.3 | 42.8 | 45.3 | 48.2 | 47.4 | Net Worth | 39.6 | 41.9 |
| 100.0 | 100.0 | 100.0 | 100.0 | 100.0 | 100.0 | Total Liabilties & Net Worth | 100.0 | 100.0 |
| | | | | | | INCOME DATA | | |
| 100.0 | 100.0 | 100.0 | 100.0 | 100.0 | 100.0 | Net Sales | 100.0 | 100.0 |
| | | | | | | Gross Profit | | |
| 92.8 | 89.5 | 90.3 | 83.9 | 88.8 | 83.2 | Operating Expenses | 86.7 | 87.4 |
| 7.2 | 10.5 | 9.7 | 16.1 | 11.2 | 16.8 | Operating Profit | 13.3 | 12.6 |
| .6 | 1.0 | 1.6 | 2.5 | 2.9 | 2.9 | All Other Expenses (net) | 1.7 | 1.8 |
| 6.6 | 9.5 | 8.1 | 13.7 | 8.3 | 13.8 | Profit Before Taxes | 11.6 | 10.8 |
| | | | | | | RATIOS | | |
| 2.3 | 4.8 | 3.3 | 2.3 | 2.5 | 2.7 | | 2.7 | 2.6 |
| 1.1 | 2.3 | 1.8 | 1.5 | 1.5 | 1.6 | Current | 1.5 | 1.6 |
| .2 | 1.2 | 1.2 | 1.0 | 1.0 | 1.1 | | 1.0 | 1.0 |
| 2.3 | 4.1 | 2.7 | 1.8 | 1.7 | 1.8 | | 2.1 | 1.9 |
| 1.0 | 1.7 | 1.5 | 1.1 | 1.0 | 1.2 | Quick | 1.1 (378) | 1.1 |
| .1 | .8 | .9 | .7 | .6 | .7 | | .6 | .7 |
| 0 UND | 3 108.5 | 41 9.0 | 47 7.8 | 44 8.3 | 45 8.1 | | 34 10.7 | 31 11.8 |
| 13 28.2 | 36 10.1 | 59 6.2 | 68 5.4 | 64 5.7 | 69 5.3 | Sales/Receivables | 56 6.6 | 54 6.8 |
| 73 5.0 | 68 5.4 | 83 4.4 | 87 4.2 | 79 4.6 | 83 4.4 | | 72 5.1 | 79 4.6 |
| | | | | | | Cost of Sales/Inventory | | |
| | | | | | | Cost of Sales/Payables | | |
| 8.5 | 4.9 | 5.1 | 5.0 | 4.1 | 4.0 | | 5.2 | 5.1 |
| 182.7 | 10.0 | 9.9 | 12.2 | 8.2 | 8.6 | Sales/Working Capital | 13.5 | 11.3 |
| -8.9 | 83.6 | 26.8 | -955.2 | -342.0 | 35.0 | | -272.5 | -363.3 |
| 21.3 | 32.4 | 36.9 | 30.0 | 15.7 | 25.9 | | 24.6 | 23.9 |
| (10) 5.0 | (80) 6.8 | (143) 13.9 | (162) 11.6 | (78) 5.7 | (63) 6.8 | EBIT/Interest | (313) 8.1 | (332) 7.7 |
| -2.5 | 1.4 | 1.1 | 3.7 | 1.3 | 3.5 | | 2.9 | 2.5 |
| | | 10.9 | 6.3 | 9.5 | 12.2 | | 13.2 | 10.2 |
| | (14) 2.3 | (46) 2.5 | (25) 4.0 | (15) 3.9 | | Net Profit + Depr., Dep., Amort./Cur. Mat. L/T/D | (77) 4.2 | (88) 3.4 |
| | .5 | 1.1 | 2.5 | 2.2 | | | 1.4 | 1.6 |
| .4 | .2 | .2 | .5 | .6 | .7 | | .4 | .4 |
| 1.3 | .7 | .7 | 1.0 | 1.2 | 1.2 | Fixed/Worth | 1.1 | 1.1 |
| -2.5 | 2.3 | 1.5 | 2.2 | 2.8 | 2.4 | | 2.3 | 2.9 |
| 1.8 | .4 | .5 | .6 | .7 | .7 | | .7 | .7 |
| UND | 1.4 | 1.3 | 1.3 | 1.7 | 1.6 | Debt/Worth | 1.6 | 1.7 |
| -5.5 | 6.5 | 3.4 | 3.8 | 3.3 | 4.0 | | 4.3 | 4.2 |
| | 95.8 | 82.1 | 76.3 | 55.1 | 63.7 | | 78.7 | 69.8 |
| (85) 49.3 | (146) 37.9 | (169) 42.9 | (71) 26.5 | (70) 25.8 | % Profit Before Taxes/Tangible Net Worth | (311) 44.7 | (341) 36.2 |
| | 13.4 | 9.5 | 17.3 | 9.0 | 12.2 | | 22.4 | 12.8 |
| 46.0 | 37.8 | 33.7 | 28.4 | 19.9 | 19.9 | | 28.6 | 26.7 |
| 28.9 | 12.0 | 15.5 | 14.8 | 10.8 | 9.7 | % Profit Before Taxes/Total Assets | 15.5 | 12.4 |
| -8.5 | 3.7 | 1.5 | 4.6 | 1.2 | 3.8 | | 5.2 | 3.5 |
| 54.5 | 42.6 | 44.3 | 9.1 | 6.8 | 9.0 | | 17.3 | 16.7 |
| 6.6 | 12.1 | 8.7 | 3.5 | 3.4 | 2.0 | Sales/Net Fixed Assets | 5.1 | 4.2 |
| 3.4 | 4.0 | 3.4 | 1.7 | 1.8 | .9 | | 2.1 | 1.8 |
| 5.5 | 4.0 | 3.3 | 2.0 | 1.7 | 1.5 | | 2.7 | 2.6 |
| 3.2 | 2.5 | 2.0 | 1.3 | 1.1 | .9 | Sales/Total Assets | 1.7 | 1.6 |
| 1.4 | 1.4 | 1.3 | .9 | .7 | .5 | | 1.0 | .9 |
| | 1.1 | 1.0 | 2.4 | -2.1 | .6 | | 1.1 | 1.1 |
| (45) 4.4 | (107) 3.6 | (164) 5.7 | (68) 5.7 | (42) 3.6 | % Depr., Dep., Amort./Sales | (276) 3.4 | (297) 3.9 |
| | 10.4 | 6.6 | 9.9 | 10.1 | 6.7 | | 7.3 | 8.0 |
| | 2.5 | 1.4 | 1.1 | | | | 1.0 | 1.6 |
| (35) 3.7 | (52) 3.1 | (17) 2.3 | | | % Officers', Directors' Owners' Comp/Sales | (77) 2.4 | (66) 3.1 |
| | 7.8 | 6.0 | 3.2 | | | | 6.5 | 7.0 |
| 18025M | 399810M | 2443038M | 7157784M | 7546318M | 15348202M | Net Sales ($) | 19467672M | 22856599M |
| 4928M | 114236M | 803196M | 4490691M | 5826445M | 11700369M | Total Assets ($) | 11894206M | 14725459M |

M = $ thousand    MM = $ million
See Pages 9 through 22 for Explanation of Ratios and Data

## Comparative Historical Data | Current Data Sorted by Sales

| | 4/1/09-3/31/10 ALL | 4/1/10-3/31/11 ALL | 4/1/11-3/31/12 ALL | 0-1MM | 1-3MM | 3-5MM | 5-10MM | 10-25MM | 25MM & OVER |
|---|---|---|---|---|---|---|---|---|---|
| **Type of Statement** | | | | | | | | | |
| Unqualified | 80 | 85 | 117 | | 3 | 2 | 8 | 19 | 85 |
| Reviewed | 36 | 44 | 37 | 2 | 3 | 2 | 3 | 14 | 13 |
| Compiled | 36 | 38 | 67 | 4 | 16 | 7 | 14 | 12 | 14 |
| Tax Returns | 32 | 42 | 53 | 4 | 13 | 14 | 11 | 10 | 1 |
| Other | 226 | 292 | 344 | 19 | 27 | 25 | 45 | 61 | 167 |
| | | | | 76 (4/1-9/30/11) | | 542 (10/1/11-3/31/12) | | | |
| **NUMBER OF STATEMENTS** | 410 | 501 | 618 | 29 | 62 | 50 | 81 | 116 | 280 |
| | % | % | % | % | % | % | % | % | % |
| **ASSETS** | | | | | | | | | |
| Cash & Equivalents | 10.8 | 10.8 | 11.0 | 11.3 | 19.1 | 12.5 | 14.5 | 10.0 | 8.2 |
| Trade Receivables (net) | 20.7 | 25.9 | 28.5 | 22.0 | 22.1 | 28.2 | 31.0 | 32.6 | 28.3 |
| Inventory | 6.7 | 8.0 | 7.0 | 1.7 | 3.9 | 6.6 | 4.8 | 6.2 | 9.4 |
| All Other Current | 3.5 | 3.8 | 3.8 | 8.5 | 3.7 | 3.4 | 1.9 | 3.4 | 4.0 |
| Total Current | 41.7 | 48.4 | 50.3 | 43.5 | 48.9 | 50.7 | 52.3 | 52.2 | 49.8 |
| Fixed Assets (net) | 43.7 | 39.0 | 37.7 | 43.2 | 43.5 | 37.3 | 39.4 | 35.2 | 36.4 |
| Intangibles (net) | 7.5 | 6.8 | 5.9 | 3.0 | 1.0 | 2.4 | 1.9 | 6.8 | 8.8 |
| All Other Non-Current | 7.1 | 5.8 | 6.1 | 10.2 | 6.7 | 9.6 | 6.4 | 5.8 | 4.9 |
| Total | 100.0 | 100.0 | 100.0 | 100.0 | 100.0 | 100.0 | 100.0 | 100.0 | 100.0 |
| **LIABILITIES** | | | | | | | | | |
| Notes Payable-Short Term | 7.1 | 7.2 | 6.1 | 4.6 | 8.6 | 6.6 | 4.4 | 5.5 | 6.4 |
| Cur. Mat.-L.T.D. | 5.2 | 5.5 | 6.0 | 20.2 | 7.7 | 6.0 | 5.7 | 6.1 | 4.1 |
| Trade Payables | 9.6 | 11.1 | 11.8 | 18.7 | 7.6 | 9.2 | 9.0 | 12.9 | 12.8 |
| Income Taxes Payable | .3 | .4 | .3 | .6 | .2 | .1 | .3 | .2 | .4 |
| All Other Current | 8.9 | 8.9 | 8.6 | 17.6 | 9.0 | 10.3 | 7.6 | 5.1 | 9.0 |
| Total Current | 31.1 | 33.0 | 32.8 | 61.7 | 33.1 | 32.1 | 27.1 | 29.9 | 32.8 |
| Long-Term Debt | 21.5 | 17.8 | 18.7 | 18.4 | 37.3 | 18.6 | 21.8 | 16.1 | 14.7 |
| Deferred Taxes | 1.2 | 1.1 | .9 | .0 | .2 | .1 | .3 | .8 | 1.5 |
| All Other Non-Current | 6.7 | 5.8 | 5.5 | 9.3 | 8.9 | 5.2 | 4.7 | 3.1 | 5.6 |
| Net Worth | 39.5 | 42.4 | 42.1 | 10.6 | 20.5 | 43.9 | 46.1 | 50.1 | 45.4 |
| Total Liabilities & Net Worth | 100.0 | 100.0 | 100.0 | 100.0 | 100.0 | 100.0 | 100.0 | 100.0 | 100.0 |
| **INCOME DATA** | | | | | | | | | |
| Net Sales | 100.0 | 100.0 | 100.0 | 100.0 | 100.0 | 100.0 | 100.0 | 100.0 | 100.0 |
| Gross Profit | | | | | | | | | |
| Operating Expenses | 92.0 | 90.0 | 87.3 | 82.9 | 88.8 | 88.9 | 89.5 | 85.6 | 87.2 |
| Operating Profit | 8.0 | 10.0 | 12.7 | 17.1 | 11.2 | 11.1 | 10.5 | 14.4 | 12.8 |
| All Other Expenses (net) | 2.8 | 2.6 | 2.1 | 3.4 | 2.1 | 3.9 | 1.9 | 1.6 | 1.9 |
| Profit Before Taxes | 5.2 | 7.4 | 10.6 | 13.8 | 9.1 | 7.2 | 8.6 | 12.8 | 10.9 |
| **RATIOS** | | | | | | | | | |
| Current | 2.6 | 3.0 | 2.8 | 2.5 | 3.7 | 4.1 | 3.8 | 2.7 | 2.4 |
| | 1.4 | 1.6 | 1.7 | 1.1 | 1.7 | 2.0 | 2.0 | 1.7 | 1.6 |
| | .8 | 1.0 | 1.1 | .2 | .8 | 1.2 | 1.1 | 1.2 | 1.1 |
| Quick | 2.0 | 2.3 | 2.3 | 2.1 | 3.1 | 3.9 | 3.7 | 2.3 | 1.8 |
| | 1.1 | 1.1 | 1.3 | .6 | 1.4 | 1.5 | 1.7 | 1.4 | 1.2 |
| | .5 | .7 | .7 | .2 | .6 | .5 | .9 | .9 | .7 |
| Sales/Receivables | 28  13.2 | 33  11.0 | 38  9.7 | 0  UND | 2  220.0 | 20  18.7 | 39  9.3 | 42  8.6 | 44  8.3 |
| | 49  7.4 | 57  6.4 | 61  6.0 | 78  4.7 | 31  11.7 | 53  6.9 | 60  6.1 | 65  5.6 | 63  5.8 |
| | 69  5.3 | 78  4.7 | 81  4.5 | 174  2.1 | 68  5.4 | 83  4.4 | 85  4.3 | 89  4.1 | 78  4.7 |
| Cost of Sales/Inventory | | | | | | | | | |
| Cost of Sales/Payables | | | | | | | | | |
| Sales/Working Capital | 5.3 | 4.4 | 4.8 | 3.1 | 4.6 | 5.0 | 4.8 | 4.9 | 4.9 |
| | 13.8 | 10.7 | 10.3 | 15.0 | 11.0 | 7.8 | 11.0 | 10.1 | 10.6 |
| | -18.7 | -166.3 | 90.4 | -4.2 | -16.8 | 28.4 | 34.6 | 38.3 | 102.1 |
| EBIT/Interest | 12.7 | 20.4 | 29.3 | 19.2 | 11.4 | 25.0 | 27.2 | 45.8 | 28.4 |
| | (354) 3.3 | (427) 5.2 | (536) 8.7 | (20) 4.4 | (50) 3.8 | (40) 5.4 | (72) 9.6 | (100) 21.7 | (254) 9.5 |
| | .1 | 1.4 | 2.3 | .8 | .5 | .4 | 1.5 | 4.1 | 2.9 |
| Net Profit + Depr., Dep., Amort./Cur. Mat. L/T/D | 4.9 | 5.1 | 9.0 | | | | | 3.6 | 11.0 |
| | (84) 2.3 | (92) 2.0 | (103) 3.1 | | | | | (21) 2.4 | (74) 3.9 |
| | 1.2 | 1.0 | 1.5 | | | | | 1.0 | 1.9 |
| Fixed/Worth | .5 | .4 | .4 | .2 | .4 | .3 | .4 | .3 | .4 |
| | 1.4 | 1.0 | .9 | 1.1 | 1.6 | .7 | .9 | .7 | 1.0 |
| | 4.0 | 2.6 | 2.3 | UND | NM | 1.3 | 1.8 | 1.5 | 2.3 |
| Debt/Worth | .7 | .5 | .6 | .6 | 1.3 | .3 | .4 | .5 | .7 |
| | 1.8 | 1.6 | 1.5 | 1.9 | 3.3 | 1.0 | 1.2 | 1.0 | 1.5 |
| | 6.1 | 4.1 | 4.0 | UND | NM | 4.3 | 2.9 | 2.6 | 3.4 |
| % Profit Before Taxes/Tangible Net Worth | 45.5 | 55.5 | 79.6 | 81.2 | 96.4 | 96.0 | 77.1 | 74.6 | 77.8 |
| | (346) 15.8 | (439) 25.5 | (550) 38.1 | (22) 15.0 | (47) 49.3 | (44) 22.9 | (76) 30.3 | (107) 40.8 | (254) 41.6 |
| | -2.3 | 6.7 | 13.1 | 1.5 | 13.2 | 7.6 | 5.0 | 16.4 | 17.3 |
| % Profit Before Taxes/Total Assets | 16.4 | 22.9 | 28.3 | 22.7 | 27.4 | 25.6 | 32.5 | 33.3 | 25.9 |
| | 4.7 | 8.3 | 12.9 | 3.7 | 9.8 | 8.8 | 12.1 | 17.6 | 14.2 |
| | -1.9 | 1.2 | 3.2 | .0 | -.4 | .4 | 1.5 | 4.1 | 4.4 |
| Sales/Net Fixed Assets | 12.6 | 18.1 | 18.4 | 6.1 | 24.0 | 30.1 | 18.9 | 17.0 | 18.4 |
| | 3.0 | 4.4 | 4.8 | 3.1 | 5.5 | 7.1 | 5.9 | 5.1 | 4.2 |
| | 1.4 | 1.8 | 2.0 | 1.0 | 1.7 | 1.9 | 1.9 | 1.9 | 2.0 |
| Sales/Total Assets | 2.3 | 2.5 | 2.7 | 1.4 | 3.0 | 2.9 | 2.9 | 2.9 | 2.4 |
| | 1.3 | 1.5 | 1.6 | .8 | 1.8 | 1.6 | 1.9 | 1.6 | 1.4 |
| | .7 | .8 | .9 | .3 | 1.0 | 1.0 | 1.0 | 1.0 | .9 |
| % Depr., Dep., Amort./Sales | 2.0 | 1.8 | 1.7 | 4.3 | 2.1 | 2.3 | 1.7 | 2.3 | 1.0 |
| | (303) 5.7 | (366) 5.3 | (433) 4.9 | (14) 6.7 | (33) 6.3 | (29) 6.1 | (52) 5.1 | (95) 5.2 | (210) 4.1 |
| | 12.5 | 10.8 | 9.0 | 14.6 | 12.4 | 14.7 | 11.1 | 9.3 | 7.6 |
| % Officers', Directors', Owners' Comp/Sales | 1.3 | 1.2 | 1.4 | | 2.8 | 2.5 | 2.0 | 1.0 | .7 |
| | (88) 3.4 | (109) 2.9 | (118) 2.8 | (19) 3.9 | (19) 4.3 | (27) 3.5 | (22) 2.1 | (27) 1.3 | |
| | 8.5 | 5.8 | 5.9 | | 8.2 | 7.8 | 6.0 | 4.1 | 2.9 |
| Net Sales ($) | 17491067M | 24593546M | 32913177M | 15494M | 121332M | 193369M | 595646M | 1913171M | 30074165M |
| Total Assets ($) | 17354542M | 17627278M | 22939865M | 38225M | 99115M | 302066M | 577534M | 1880519M | 20042406M |

© RMA 2012

M = $ thousand    MM = $ million
See Pages 9 through 22 for Explanation of Ratios and Data

# UTILITIES

## Current Data Sorted by Assets

## Comparative Historical Data

| 0-500M | 500M-2MM | 2-10MM | 10-50MM | 50-100MM | 100-250MM | Type of Statement | 4/1/07-3/31/08 ALL | 4/1/08-3/31/09 ALL |
|---|---|---|---|---|---|---|---|---|
| 1 | 5 | 13 | 6 | 3 | 10 | Unqualified | 14 | 6 |
|  |  |  | 1 |  |  | Reviewed | 2 |  |
|  | 1 |  |  |  |  | Compiled | 1 |  |
| 1 | 1 |  |  |  |  | Tax Returns | 1 |  |
| 1 | 1 | 1 | 2 | 1 | 2 | Other | 12 | 9 |
|  | 10 (4/1-9/30/11) |  | 40 (10/1/11-3/31/12) |  |  |  |  |  |
| 3 | 8 | 14 | 9 | 4 | 12 | NUMBER OF STATEMENTS | 30 | 15 |
| % | % | % | % | % | % | | % | % |
| | | | | | | **ASSETS** | | |
| | | 6.2 | | | 5.6 | Cash & Equivalents | 11.1 | 7.1 |
| | | 11.1 | | | 5.6 | Trade Receivables (net) | 10.9 | 13.9 |
| | | .9 | | | 1.9 | Inventory | 5.4 | 6.8 |
| | | 1.4 | | | 2.0 | All Other Current | 3.8 | 3.0 |
| | | 19.6 | | | 15.1 | Total Current | 31.2 | 30.7 |
| | | 46.4 | | | 66.1 | Fixed Assets (net) | 57.5 | 58.0 |
| | | 11.1 | | | 5.0 | Intangibles (net) | 2.0 | 4.7 |
| | | 22.9 | | | 13.8 | All Other Non-Current | 9.2 | 6.6 |
| | | 100.0 | | | 100.0 | Total | 100.0 | 100.0 |
| | | | | | | **LIABILITIES** | | |
| | | 2.7 | | | .6 | Notes Payable-Short Term | 3.5 | 6.0 |
| | | 1.7 | | | 1.9 | Cur. Mat.-L.T.D. | 4.9 | 6.1 |
| | | 5.0 | | | 2.2 | Trade Payables | 4.4 | 6.9 |
| | | .6 | | | .0 | Income Taxes Payable | .0 | .1 |
| | | 5.8 | | | 3.7 | All Other Current | 10.1 | 5.6 |
| | | 15.9 | | | 8.4 | Total Current | 23.0 | 24.7 |
| | | 24.8 | | | 50.2 | Long-Term Debt | 31.5 | 26.3 |
| | | 1.1 | | | .1 | Deferred Taxes | 1.3 | .7 |
| | | 25.8 | | | 4.0 | All Other Non-Current | 5.8 | 5.5 |
| | | 32.4 | | | 37.2 | Net Worth | 38.3 | 42.9 |
| | | 100.0 | | | 100.0 | Total Liabilties & Net Worth | 100.0 | 100.0 |
| | | | | | | **INCOME DATA** | | |
| | | 100.0 | | | 100.0 | Net Sales | 100.0 | 100.0 |
| | | | | | | Gross Profit | | |
| | | 91.9 | | | 87.5 | Operating Expenses | 81.7 | 77.5 |
| | | 8.1 | | | 12.5 | Operating Profit | 18.3 | 22.5 |
| | | 2.9 | | | 7.1 | All Other Expenses (net) | 6.1 | 6.2 |
| | | 5.3 | | | 5.4 | Profit Before Taxes | 12.2 | 16.4 |
| | | | | | | **RATIOS** | | |
| | | 1.4 | | | 2.4 | | 1.9 | 2.0 |
| | | 1.2 | | | 1.7 | Current | 1.4 | 1.0 |
| | | .8 | | | 1.0 | | .8 | .3 |
| | | 1.3 | | | 1.8 | | 1.3 | 1.4 |
| | | .8 | | | 1.0 | Quick | .9 | .6 |
| | | .7 | | | .7 | | .5 | .3 |
| | 27 | 13.3 | 21 | | 17.5 | | 23  15.5 | 27  13.6 |
| | 52 | 7.0 | 29 | | 12.4 | Sales/Receivables | 35  10.5 | 35  10.4 |
| | 78 | 4.7 | 32 | | 11.4 | | 52  7.0 | 43  8.4 |
| | | | | | | Cost of Sales/Inventory | | |
| | | | | | | Cost of Sales/Payables | | |
| | | 9.3 | | | 2.9 | | 4.5 | 8.0 |
| | | 31.8 | | | 9.3 | Sales/Working Capital | 15.3 | 88.3 |
| | | -22.4 | | | NM | | -13.2 | -3.1 |
| | | 4.0 | | | | | 6.0 | 13.7 |
| | (13) | 2.3 | | | | EBIT/Interest | (26)  3.2 | (13)  3.5 |
| | | 1.2 | | | | | 2.1 | 2.5 |
| | | | | | | Net Profit + Depr., Dep., Amort./Cur. Mat. L/T/D | | |
| | | 2.1 | | | 1.4 | | .7 | .7 |
| | | 3.3 | | | 2.3 | Fixed/Worth | 2.0 | 1.7 |
| | | 7.8 | | | 3.2 | | 2.6 | 2.4 |
| | | 2.5 | | | .9 | | 1.3 | .9 |
| | | 3.9 | | | 1.9 | Debt/Worth | 2.0 | 1.7 |
| | | 9.5 | | | 3.3 | | 2.6 | 2.0 |
| | | 53.3 | | | 12.6 | % Profit Before Taxes/Tangible Net Worth | 23.7 | 68.1 |
| | (13) | 12.7 | (10) | | 8.7 | | (29)  14.0 | (14)  16.7 |
| | | 5.4 | | | 2.5 | | 6.4 | 12.2 |
| | | 5.8 | | | 4.3 | % Profit Before Taxes/Total Assets | 10.0 | 28.5 |
| | | 3.0 | | | 2.8 | | 5.1 | 6.5 |
| | | .5 | | | -.1 | | 1.7 | 3.7 |
| | | 2.8 | | | 1.1 | | 2.6 | 11.5 |
| | | .7 | | | .6 | Sales/Net Fixed Assets | .7 | .7 |
| | | .5 | | | .5 | | .5 | .5 |
| | | .8 | | | .6 | | .8 | 2.7 |
| | | .4 | | | .4 | Sales/Total Assets | .5 | .5 |
| | | .3 | | | .3 | | .4 | .4 |
| | | 5.1 | | | 4.9 | % Depr., Dep., Amort./Sales | 2.9 | 3.0 |
| | (13) | 8.2 | | | 6.3 | | (28)  7.7 | (14)  7.0 |
| | | 13.0 | | | 16.7 | | 11.7 | 10.0 |
| | | | | | | % Officers', Directors' Owners' Comp/Sales | | |
| 579M | 15454M | 60836M | 219500M | 282359M | 927421M | Net Sales ($) | 1096988M | 1050115M |
| 658M | 11248M | 64587M | 254744M | 314977M | 1953830M | Total Assets ($) | 1554707M | 1147285M |

M = $ thousand    MM = $ million
See Pages 9 through 22 for Explanation of Ratios and Data

## Comparative Historical Data / Current Data Sorted by Sales

| | 4/1/09-3/31/10 ALL | 4/1/10-3/31/11 ALL | 4/1/11-3/31/12 ALL | Type of Statement | 0-1MM | 1-3MM | 3-5MM | 5-10MM | 10-25MM | 25MM & OVER |
|---|---|---|---|---|---|---|---|---|---|---|
| | 8 | 9 | 38 | Unqualified | 5 | 12 | 1 | 2 | 7 | 11 |
| | 2 | 1 | 1 | Reviewed | | | | | | 1 |
| | 3 | 1 | 1 | Compiled | | | | 1 | | |
| | 2 | | 2 | Tax Returns | 1 | | 1 | | 1 | |
| | 9 | 4 | 8 | Other | 1 | 2 | 1 | | 1 | 3 |
| | | | | | 10 (4/1-9/30/11) | | | 40 (10/1/11-3/31/12) | | |
| NUMBER OF STATEMENTS | 24 | 15 | 50 | | 7 | 12 | 4 | 4 | 8 | 15 |
| | % | % | % | ASSETS | % | % | % | % | % | % |
| Cash & Equivalents | 14.3 | 5.8 | 5.4 | | | 4.3 | | | | 4.8 |
| Trade Receivables (net) | 15.2 | 11.8 | 13.2 | | | 5.7 | | | | 14.6 |
| Inventory | 5.5 | 5.5 | 4.1 | | | 1.1 | | | | 5.3 |
| All Other Current | 3.3 | 4.8 | 3.3 | | | 2.2 | | | | 4.1 |
| Total Current | 38.4 | 27.9 | 26.0 | | | 13.3 | | | | 28.8 |
| Fixed Assets (net) | 45.6 | 57.0 | 52.3 | | | 59.7 | | | | 54.0 |
| Intangibles (net) | 3.2 | 3.9 | 5.5 | | | 9.4 | | | | 4.1 |
| All Other Non-Current | 12.8 | 11.0 | 16.2 | | | 17.7 | | | | 13.2 |
| Total | 100.0 | 100.0 | 100.0 | | | 100.0 | | | | 100.0 |
| | | | | LIABILITIES | | | | | | |
| Notes Payable-Short Term | 3.0 | 4.5 | 3.5 | | | 1.6 | | | | 4.6 |
| Cur. Mat.-L.T.D. | 3.6 | 4.5 | 2.1 | | | 2.0 | | | | 1.6 |
| Trade Payables | 6.5 | 4.8 | 5.7 | | | 2.0 | | | | 7.1 |
| Income Taxes Payable | .8 | .0 | .4 | | | .6 | | | | .1 |
| All Other Current | 14.2 | 5.5 | 6.0 | | | 5.2 | | | | 5.6 |
| Total Current | 28.1 | 19.3 | 17.8 | | | 11.5 | | | | 18.9 |
| Long-Term Debt | 16.8 | 29.1 | 34.2 | | | 29.7 | | | | 36.8 |
| Deferred Taxes | .5 | .9 | .6 | | | .2 | | | | .1 |
| All Other Non-Current | 17.0 | 7.7 | 13.5 | | | 31.3 | | | | 3.5 |
| Net Worth | 37.6 | 43.0 | 33.8 | | | 27.2 | | | | 40.8 |
| Total Liabilties & Net Worth | 100.0 | 100.0 | 100.0 | | | 100.0 | | | | 100.0 |
| | | | | INCOME DATA | | | | | | |
| Net Sales | 100.0 | 100.0 | 100.0 | | | 100.0 | | | | 100.0 |
| Gross Profit | | | | | | | | | | |
| Operating Expenses | 86.5 | 80.1 | 86.8 | | | 92.3 | | | | 91.9 |
| Operating Profit | 13.5 | 19.9 | 13.2 | | | 7.7 | | | | 8.1 |
| All Other Expenses (net) | 2.6 | 6.8 | 6.3 | | | 2.7 | | | | 3.0 |
| Profit Before Taxes | 10.9 | 13.1 | 6.9 | | | 5.0 | | | | 5.1 |
| | | | | RATIOS | | | | | | |
| Current | 2.1 | 2.1 | 2.1 | | | 1.4 | | | | 2.1 |
| | 1.5 | 1.4 | 1.4 | | | 1.2 | | | | 1.5 |
| | .6 | 1.0 | .9 | | | .8 | | | | .8 |
| Quick | 1.8 | 1.8 | 1.7 | | | 1.0 | | | | 1.7 |
| | 1.0 | .9 | .9 | | | .8 | | | | .9 |
| | .4 | .5 | .7 | | | .7 | | | | .6 |
| Sales/Receivables | 28  12.8 | 32  11.4 | 30  12.3 | | | 32  11.3 | | | | 25  14.8 |
| | 37  9.8 | 39  9.5 | 45  8.1 | | | 48  7.6 | | | | 31  11.6 |
| | 46  7.9 | 43  8.4 | 62  5.9 | | | 69  5.3 | | | | 51  7.2 |
| Cost of Sales/Inventory | | | | | | | | | | |
| Cost of Sales/Payables | | | | | | | | | | |
| Sales/Working Capital | 5.5 | 6.3 | 4.6 | | | 6.3 | | | | 6.9 |
| | 13.5 | 14.1 | 12.6 | | | 31.8 | | | | 13.8 |
| | -10.4 | UND | -36.9 | | | -22.2 | | | | -38.1 |
| EBIT/Interest | 17.4 | 5.4 | 4.7 | | | 3.3 | | | | 4.7 |
| | (20)  5.7 | 2.7 | (44)  2.8 | | | 2.2 | | | (12) | 2.7 |
| | 1.7 | 1.3 | 1.7 | | | 1.1 | | | | 1.9 |
| Net Profit + Depr., Dep., Amort./Cur. Mat. L/T/D | | | 30.9 | | | | | | | |
| | | (17) | 5.4 | | | | | | | |
| | | | 1.2 | | | | | | | |
| Fixed/Worth | .2 | .7 | 1.0 | | | 2.7 | | | | .6 |
| | 1.1 | 1.5 | 2.2 | | | 3.3 | | | | 1.6 |
| | 2.0 | 2.3 | 3.3 | | | 6.1 | | | | 2.5 |
| Debt/Worth | .6 | 1.0 | 1.4 | | | 2.5 | | | | 1.2 |
| | 1.3 | 1.4 | 2.4 | | | 3.7 | | | | 1.8 |
| | 2.1 | 2.6 | 4.2 | | | 7.4 | | | | 2.6 |
| % Profit Before Taxes/Tangible Net Worth | 49.1 | 15.3 | 18.2 | | | 46.6 | | | | 12.6 |
| | (22)  12.6 | 10.3 | (44)  10.7 | | | 14.3 | | | (14) | 9.2 |
| | 1.3 | 4.3 | 4.5 | | | 3.3 | | | | 4.3 |
| % Profit Before Taxes/Total Assets | 16.9 | 8.6 | 5.5 | | | 4.0 | | | | 4.5 |
| | 6.5 | 4.2 | 3.1 | | | 2.8 | | | | 3.0 |
| | .3 | .5 | .5 | | | .2 | | | | 1.9 |
| Sales/Net Fixed Assets | 23.7 | 1.5 | 2.9 | | | .8 | | | | 3.6 |
| | 1.7 | .8 | .7 | | | .7 | | | | 1.0 |
| | .6 | .3 | .5 | | | .5 | | | | .6 |
| Sales/Total Assets | 2.5 | 1.0 | .9 | | | .5 | | | | .9 |
| | .6 | .5 | .5 | | | .4 | | | | .6 |
| | .4 | .2 | .3 | | | .3 | | | | .4 |
| % Depr., Dep., Amort./Sales | 1.0 | 3.4 | 3.7 | | | 6.6 | | | | 2.7 |
| | (22)  5.2 | 6.9 | (46)  6.8 | | | 7.8 | | | | 4.8 |
| | 9.8 | 13.7 | 11.6 | | | 12.4 | | | | 7.0 |
| % Officers', Directors' Owners' Comp/Sales | | | | | | | | | | |
| Net Sales ($) | 753508M | 471217M | 1506149M | | 3018M | 18153M | 14545M | 24306M | 146326M | 1299801M |
| Total Assets ($) | 862016M | 837958M | 2600044M | | 9077M | 48687M | 114579M | 49979M | 443164M | 1934558M |

© RMA 2012

M = $ thousand     MM = $ million
See Pages 9 through 22 for Explanation of Ratios and Data

## Current Data Sorted by Assets      Comparative Historical Data

| | 0-500M | 500M-2MM | 2-10MM | 10-50MM | 50-100MM | 100-250MM | Type of Statement | 4/1/07-3/31/08 ALL | 4/1/08-3/31/09 ALL |
|---|---|---|---|---|---|---|---|---|---|
| | 2 | 2 | 25 | 149 | 163 | 149 | Unqualified | 308 | 158 |
| | | 3 | 11 | 5 | | | Reviewed | 12 | 11 |
| | | 2 | 3 | 1 | | | Compiled | 9 | 5 |
| | 1 | 4 | | 1 | | | Tax Returns | 4 | 4 |
| | 4 | 4 | 16 | 18 | 10 | 13 | Other | 58 | 54 |
| | | 139 (4/1-9/30/11) | | 447 (10/1/11-3/31/12) | | | | | |
| NUMBER OF STATEMENTS | 7 | 15 | 55 | 174 | 173 | 162 | | 391 | 232 |
| | % | % | % | % | % | % | **ASSETS** | % | % |
| | | 14.8 | 14.9 | 6.6 | 4.5 | 4.2 | Cash & Equivalents | 6.9 | 9.0 |
| | | 23.9 | 21.5 | 8.4 | 5.4 | 4.8 | Trade Receivables (net) | 9.7 | 13.5 |
| | | 9.9 | 3.0 | 3.0 | 1.5 | 1.2 | Inventory | 2.6 | 3.0 |
| | | 2.6 | 3.8 | 1.6 | 1.4 | 1.7 | All Other Current | 2.2 | 4.0 |
| | | 51.2 | 43.2 | 19.5 | 12.9 | 11.9 | Total Current | 21.3 | 29.5 |
| | | 32.4 | 40.8 | 65.3 | 71.4 | 73.1 | Fixed Assets (net) | 64.7 | 55.7 |
| | | 2.3 | 5.4 | 1.5 | .6 | 2.1 | Intangibles (net) | 2.2 | 2.1 |
| | | 14.1 | 10.6 | 13.6 | 15.1 | 12.9 | All Other Non-Current | 11.8 | 12.6 |
| | | 100.0 | 100.0 | 100.0 | 100.0 | 100.0 | Total | 100.0 | 100.0 |
| | | | | | | | **LIABILITIES** | | |
| | | 13.5 | 4.8 | 2.7 | .9 | 1.4 | Notes Payable-Short Term | 2.5 | 3.1 |
| | | 7.4 | 2.1 | 1.9 | 1.9 | 2.1 | Cur. Mat.-L.T.D. | 2.9 | 4.1 |
| | | 13.5 | 12.4 | 5.3 | 4.2 | 4.0 | Trade Payables | 6.6 | 8.3 |
| | | .0 | .4 | .3 | .3 | .3 | Income Taxes Payable | .4 | .4 |
| | | 14.1 | 10.2 | 4.7 | 3.0 | 3.7 | All Other Current | 5.2 | 6.8 |
| | | 48.6 | 29.9 | 14.9 | 10.3 | 11.4 | Total Current | 17.6 | 22.6 |
| | | 80.8 | 24.4 | 35.4 | 40.5 | 43.1 | Long-Term Debt | 37.1 | 33.4 |
| | | .5 | 1.9 | .4 | .1 | .3 | Deferred Taxes | .7 | 1.3 |
| | | 5.6 | 4.7 | 3.9 | 3.7 | 5.2 | All Other Non-Current | 5.2 | 7.4 |
| | | -35.4 | 39.2 | 45.4 | 45.5 | 40.0 | Net Worth | 39.4 | 35.4 |
| | | 100.0 | 100.0 | 100.0 | 100.0 | 100.0 | Total Liabilities & Net Worth | 100.0 | 100.0 |
| | | | | | | | **INCOME DATA** | | |
| | | 100.0 | 100.0 | 100.0 | 100.0 | 100.0 | Net Sales | 100.0 | 100.0 |
| | | | | | | | Gross Profit | | |
| | | 77.7 | 88.8 | 91.1 | 92.2 | 90.2 | Operating Expenses | 89.1 | 89.2 |
| | | 22.3 | 11.2 | 8.9 | 7.8 | 9.8 | Operating Profit | 10.9 | 10.8 |
| | | 6.1 | 3.9 | 2.2 | 1.5 | 3.6 | All Other Expenses (net) | 2.8 | 3.2 |
| | | 16.2 | 7.3 | 6.7 | 6.2 | 6.2 | Profit Before Taxes | 8.1 | 7.6 |
| | | | | | | | **RATIOS** | | |
| | | 2.4 | 2.1 | 2.0 | 1.7 | 1.5 | | 1.7 | 1.9 |
| | | 1.5 | 1.4 | 1.4 | 1.2 | 1.0 | Current | 1.1 | 1.3 |
| | | .3 | 1.0 | 1.0 | .9 | .8 | | .8 | .9 |
| | | 2.4 | 2.1 | 1.5 | 1.4 | 1.2 | | 1.3 | 1.5 |
| | | 1.1 | 1.0 | 1.1 | .9 | .8 | Quick | .8 | .9 |
| | | .3 | .5 | .7 | .6 | .5 | | .5 | .6 |
| | | 18  20.6 | 20  18.6 | 30  12.2 | 27  13.6 | 23  15.8 | | 26  14.3 | 26  14.0 |
| | | 35  10.4 | 39  9.4 | 40  9.2 | 35  10.5 | 33  11.1 | Sales/Receivables | 36  10.2 | 36  10.2 |
| | | 59  6.2 | 63  5.8 | 56  6.5 | 42  8.6 | 42  8.7 | | 46  7.9 | 53  6.9 |
| | | | | | | | Cost of Sales/Inventory | | |
| | | | | | | | Cost of Sales/Payables | | |
| | | 3.9 | 4.9 | 6.0 | 9.9 | 12.4 | | 8.9 | 7.6 |
| | | 14.4 | 12.5 | 12.2 | 30.4 | 132.1 | Sales/Working Capital | 46.0 | 20.1 |
| | | -3.4 | -64.5 | -73.0 | -46.7 | -19.2 | | -18.4 | -31.4 |
| | | 16.1 | 5.5 | 4.0 | 3.7 | 3.2 | | 4.0 | 5.4 |
| | | (12) 5.8 | (41) 2.4 | (161) 2.5 | (169) 2.5 | (156) 2.4 | EBIT/Interest | (358) 2.4 | (205) 3.0 |
| | | 1.4 | 1.3 | 1.8 | 2.0 | 1.8 | | 1.7 | 1.9 |
| | | | 3.3 | 7.4 | 6.7 | 7.3 | Net Profit + Depr., Dep., | 7.0 | 7.3 |
| | | | (11) 1.7 | (16) 4.2 | (13) 3.2 | (11) 3.6 | Amort./Cur. Mat. L/T/D | (52) 3.7 | (47) 2.7 |
| | | | .4 | 1.9 | 2.4 | 2.7 | | 1.5 | 1.4 |
| | | .7 | .2 | 1.1 | 1.3 | 1.5 | | 1.1 | .8 |
| | | 6.8 | .9 | 1.7 | 1.7 | 1.9 | Fixed/Worth | 1.8 | 1.5 |
| | | -.1 | 2.2 | 2.2 | 2.1 | 2.4 | | 2.5 | 2.5 |
| | | 1.4 | .7 | .8 | .8 | 1.2 | | .9 | .7 |
| | | 6.3 | 2.0 | 1.4 | 1.3 | 1.6 | Debt/Worth | 1.6 | 1.6 |
| | | -2.0 | 3.7 | 2.0 | 1.7 | 2.1 | | 2.4 | 3.1 |
| | | | 35.5 | 9.8 | 9.4 | 11.5 | % Profit Before Taxes/Tangible | 13.0 | 23.2 |
| | | | (50) 9.6 | (170) 6.6 | (171) 6.8 | (161) 8.2 | Net Worth | (372) 8.3 | (213) 8.8 |
| | | | 1.8 | 3.9 | 5.3 | 5.4 | | 5.1 | 4.4 |
| | | 25.0 | 7.7 | 4.3 | 4.5 | 4.3 | % Profit Before Taxes/Total | 5.1 | 7.2 |
| | | 9.7 | 3.2 | 2.9 | 3.1 | 3.1 | Assets | 3.4 | 3.5 |
| | | 3.2 | .7 | 1.6 | 2.2 | 1.9 | | 1.8 | 1.3 |
| | | 44.5 | 34.7 | .9 | .8 | .8 | | 1.1 | 4.4 |
| | | 11.7 | 3.0 | .6 | .6 | .7 | Sales/Net Fixed Assets | .7 | 1.0 |
| | | 2.2 | .6 | .5 | .5 | .5 | | .5 | .6 |
| | | 2.9 | 2.5 | .6 | .6 | .6 | | .8 | 1.3 |
| | | 1.6 | .7 | .4 | .5 | .5 | Sales/Total Assets | .5 | .7 |
| | | .8 | .4 | .4 | .4 | .4 | | .4 | .4 |
| | | .5 | 1.7 | 5.9 | 5.6 | 5.5 | | 4.7 | 3.0 |
| | | (13) 2.0 | (46) 7.8 | (170) 7.5 | (172) 7.0 | (155) 6.9 | % Depr., Dep., Amort./Sales | (372) 6.4 | (212) 5.8 |
| | | 6.9 | 11.6 | 9.5 | 8.9 | 8.8 | | 8.3 | 8.3 |
| | | | | | | | % Officers', Directors' | 2.6 | 3.6 |
| | | | | | | | Owners' Comp/Sales | (20) 4.2 | (20) 5.1 |
| | | | | | | | | 5.4 | 9.1 |
| | 3200M | 31849M | 664997M | 3100564M | 7255129M | 12770997M | Net Sales ($) | 18663848M | 14267877M |
| | 1739M | 16528M | 319840M | 5362433M | 12578664M | 24961970M | Total Assets ($) | 28108211M | 15783151M |

© RMA 2012

M = $ thousand    MM = $ million
See Pages 9 through 22 for Explanation of Ratios and Data

## Comparative Historical Data | Current Data Sorted by Sales

| Hist 1 | Hist 2 | Hist 3 | Type of Statement | 0-1MM | 1-3MM | 3-5MM | 5-10MM | 10-25MM | 25MM & OVER |
|---|---|---|---|---|---|---|---|---|---|
| 461 | 151 | 490 | Unqualified | 6 | 10 | 11 | 35 | 135 | 293 |
| 11 | 14 | 19 | Reviewed | 1 | 6 | | 4 | 5 | 3 |
| 6 | 5 | 6 | Compiled | 1 | | | 1 | 4 | |
| 4 | 12 | 6 | Tax Returns | 1 | 2 | 1 | 1 | | 1 |
| 73 | 72 | 65 | Other | 9 | 8 | 4 | 4 | 15 | 25 |
| 4/1/09-3/31/10 ALL | 4/1/10-3/31/11 ALL | 4/1/11-3/31/12 ALL | | 139 (4/1-9/30/11) | | | 447 (10/1/11-3/31/12) | | |
| 555 | 254 | 586 | **NUMBER OF STATEMENTS** | 18 | 26 | 16 | 45 | 159 | 322 |
| % | % | % | **ASSETS** | % | % | % | % | % | % |
| 6.5 | 9.6 | 6.5 | Cash & Equivalents | 10.8 | 8.4 | 11.5 | 6.9 | 5.5 | 6.2 |
| 8.7 | 12.0 | 8.2 | Trade Receivables (net) | 4.7 | 15.3 | 19.0 | 11.1 | 7.7 | 7.2 |
| 2.5 | 4.0 | 2.2 | Inventory | 4.7 | 2.1 | 4.5 | 3.1 | 2.2 | 1.8 |
| 2.5 | 2.6 | 1.8 | All Other Current | .7 | 3.0 | 1.8 | 1.9 | 1.8 | 1.7 |
| 20.1 | 28.3 | 18.7 | Total Current | 20.9 | 28.8 | 36.8 | 23.0 | 17.2 | 16.9 |
| 65.1 | 55.5 | 65.8 | Fixed Assets (net) | 52.8 | 49.6 | 46.4 | 62.3 | 68.8 | 67.7 |
| 2.3 | 3.1 | 1.8 | Intangibles (net) | 2.9 | 11.5 | 2.4 | 2.4 | .8 | 1.4 |
| 12.5 | 13.1 | 13.7 | All Other Non-Current | 23.3 | 10.1 | 14.4 | 12.3 | 13.2 | 13.9 |
| 100.0 | 100.0 | 100.0 | Total | 100.0 | 100.0 | 100.0 | 100.0 | 100.0 | 100.0 |
| | | | **LIABILITIES** | | | | | | |
| 3.2 | 4.3 | 2.4 | Notes Payable-Short Term | 4.8 | 8.7 | 2.4 | 3.9 | 2.8 | 1.3 |
| 3.0 | 2.4 | 2.1 | Cur. Mat.-L.T.D. | 7.4 | 2.4 | 1.6 | 2.5 | 1.9 | 1.9 |
| 5.5 | 8.4 | 5.5 | Trade Payables | 2.3 | 6.5 | 14.4 | 6.6 | 4.2 | 5.6 |
| .3 | .2 | .3 | Income Taxes Payable | .6 | .2 | .3 | .3 | .2 | .3 |
| 5.0 | 9.8 | 4.7 | All Other Current | 4.2 | 6.8 | 8.4 | 5.0 | 3.1 | 5.1 |
| 17.1 | 25.1 | 15.0 | Total Current | 19.3 | 24.6 | 27.2 | 18.3 | 12.3 | 14.2 |
| 38.3 | 32.7 | 39.5 | Long-Term Debt | 71.8 | 46.4 | 36.3 | 39.0 | 39.1 | 37.6 |
| .4 | 1.3 | .4 | Deferred Taxes | .5 | 3.5 | .7 | .2 | .4 | .2 |
| 4.5 | 7.8 | 4.7 | All Other Non-Current | 16.1 | 10.8 | 4.2 | 1.9 | 4.0 | 4.3 |
| 39.7 | 33.1 | 40.4 | Net Worth | -7.5 | 14.7 | 31.7 | 40.5 | 44.2 | 43.6 |
| 100.0 | 100.0 | 100.0 | Total Liabilties & Net Worth | 100.0 | 100.0 | 100.0 | 100.0 | 100.0 | 100.0 |
| | | | **INCOME DATA** | | | | | | |
| 100.0 | 100.0 | 100.0 | Net Sales | 100.0 | 100.0 | 100.0 | 100.0 | 100.0 | 100.0 |
| | | | Gross Profit | | | | | | |
| 90.9 | 88.4 | 90.5 | Operating Expenses | 65.7 | 86.2 | 96.9 | 92.2 | 90.3 | 91.7 |
| 9.1 | 11.6 | 9.5 | Operating Profit | 34.3 | 13.8 | 3.1 | 7.8 | 9.7 | 8.3 |
| 2.4 | 3.2 | 2.7 | All Other Expenses (net) | 11.2 | 7.3 | 6.0 | 2.8 | 3.0 | 1.6 |
| 6.7 | 8.4 | 6.8 | Profit Before Taxes | 23.1 | 6.5 | -2.9 | 5.1 | 6.7 | 6.7 |
| | | | **RATIOS** | | | | | | |
| 1.7 | 2.0 | 1.8 | | 1.8 | 2.2 | 3.0 | 2.5 | 2.0 | 1.6 |
| 1.2 | 1.2 | 1.2 | Current | .9 | 1.4 | 1.6 | 1.4 | 1.3 | 1.1 |
| .8 | .8 | .8 | | .2 | 1.1 | 1.1 | .9 | 1.0 | .8 |
| 1.3 | 1.5 | 1.4 | | 1.5 | 2.1 | 2.4 | 2.0 | 1.5 | 1.2 |
| .8 | .9 | .9 | Quick | .5 | 1.0 | 1.2 | 1.2 | 1.0 | .9 |
| .5 | .5 | .6 | | .2 | .5 | .5 | .6 | .6 | .6 |
| 26  14.3 | 25  14.9 | 27  13.7 | | 0  UND | 26  13.9 | 29  12.4 | 33  11.1 | 29  12.5 | 26  14.2 |
| 35  10.3 | 37  9.9 | 36  10.2 | Sales/Receivables | 22  16.9 | 37  9.9 | 60  6.1 | 41  8.9 | 39  9.3 | 34  10.7 |
| 47  7.8 | 50  7.2 | 46  7.9 | | 37  9.9 | 63  5.8 | 192  1.9 | 60  6.1 | 52  7.0 | 42  8.6 |
| | | | Cost of Sales/Inventory | | | | | | |
| | | | Cost of Sales/Payables | | | | | | |
| 8.7 | 6.1 | 7.9 | | 5.5 | 5.5 | 1.4 | 4.3 | 6.4 | 10.3 |
| 37.1 | 24.5 | 23.3 | Sales/Working Capital | UND | 11.2 | 7.0 | 10.0 | 17.2 | 41.6 |
| -20.0 | -17.2 | -33.2 | | -1.5 | NM | 25.5 | -29.1 | -160.3 | -24.4 |
| 3.5 | 6.0 | 3.8 | | 5.7 | 5.8 | 4.4 | 3.3 | 3.3 | 3.8 |
| (523)  2.3 | (228)  3.1 | (543)  2.5 | EBIT/Interest | (11)  3.3 | (23)  2.4 | (10)  1.8 | (42)  2.3 | (149)  2.3 | (308)  2.6 |
| 1.8 | 2.0 | 1.8 | | 1.9 | 1.3 | -3.0 | 1.5 | 1.8 | 1.9 |
| 5.8 | 16.3 | 6.5 | Net Profit + Depr., Dep., | | | | | 6.8 | 7.7 |
| (62)  2.9 | (48)  3.7 | (51)  3.3 | Amort./Cur. Mat. L/T/D | | | | | (17)  3.2 | (21)  3.6 |
| 1.6 | 1.7 | 2.0 | | | | | | 1.8 | 2.8 |
| 1.2 | 1.0 | 1.2 | | .2 | 1.0 | .7 | 1.0 | 1.2 | 1.2 |
| 1.8 | 1.6 | 1.7 | Fixed/Worth | 1.7 | 2.2 | 1.4 | 1.7 | 1.8 | 1.7 |
| 2.5 | 2.6 | 2.3 | | 9.2 | -.9 | 2.3 | 2.4 | 2.2 | 2.2 |
| 1.0 | .8 | .9 | | .4 | 1.7 | .6 | .9 | .9 | 1.0 |
| 1.5 | 1.4 | 1.5 | Debt/Worth | 1.5 | 2.3 | 2.1 | 1.6 | 1.5 | 1.4 |
| 2.4 | 3.0 | 2.1 | | NM | -3.9 | 4.5 | 2.5 | 1.9 | 1.9 |
| 12.0 | 16.7 | 11.1 | % Profit Before Taxes/Tangible | 48.2 | 13.6 | 16.9 | 8.8 | 9.5 | 11.4 |
| (531)  7.7 | (223)  9.2 | (564)  7.3 | Net Worth | (14)  22.8 | (19)  9.9 | (14)  3.1 | (43)  6.8 | (156)  6.6 | (318)  7.6 |
| 5.0 | 5.8 | 4.9 | | 4.0 | 2.9 | -1.2 | 3.5 | 4.2 | 5.5 |
| 4.6 | 7.4 | 4.6 | % Profit Before Taxes/Total | 21.6 | 5.9 | 3.7 | 3.8 | 4.3 | 4.6 |
| 3.1 | 3.9 | 3.0 | Assets | 7.1 | 3.2 | 1.3 | 2.6 | 2.8 | 3.2 |
| 1.9 | 1.9 | 1.9 | | 1.5 | .7 | -2.4 | 1.2 | 1.7 | 2.1 |
| 1.1 | 4.0 | .9 | | 8.1 | 15.8 | 6.4 | .9 | .8 | 1.0 |
| .7 | .8 | .7 | Sales/Net Fixed Assets | .7 | .6 | .7 | .6 | .6 | .7 |
| .5 | .5 | .5 | | .2 | .5 | .5 | .4 | .5 | .6 |
| .7 | 1.3 | .7 | | 1.0 | 1.4 | .7 | .5 | .5 | .7 |
| .5 | .6 | .5 | Sales/Total Assets | .6 | .4 | .5 | .4 | .4 | .5 |
| .4 | .4 | .4 | | .1 | .3 | .3 | .3 | .4 | .4 |
| 5.1 | 3.6 | 5.5 | % Depr., Dep., Amort./Sales | 7.0 | 2.4 | 5.7 | 6.7 | 6.1 | 5.2 |
| (531)  6.7 | (229)  6.1 | (561)  7.0 | | (14)  14.3 | (25)  9.0 | (13)  8.5 | 8.8 | (155)  7.7 | (309)  6.5 |
| 8.7 | 9.1 | 9.1 | | 34.0 | 13.7 | 11.1 | 10.8 | 9.9 | 7.9 |
| 1.7 | 1.0 | 1.2 | % Officers', Directors' | | | | | | |
| (17)  4.4 | (25)  4.0 | (18)  2.8 | Owners' Comp/Sales | | | | | | |
| 6.8 | 6.5 | 5.6 | | | | | | | |
| 24178816M | 11943868M | 23826736M | Net Sales ($) | 8891M | 51065M | 67239M | 334451M | 2734808M | 20630282M |
| 40692192M | 14703407M | 43241174M | Total Assets ($) | 31398M | 135708M | 298783M | 995598M | 6675982M | 35103705M |

## Current Data Sorted by Assets      Comparative Historical Data

| 0-500M | 500M-2MM | 2-10MM | 10-50MM | 50-100MM | 100-250MM | Type of Statement | 4/1/07-3/31/08 ALL | 4/1/08-3/31/09 ALL |
|---|---|---|---|---|---|---|---|---|
|  | 3 | 5 | 22 | 12 | 18 | Unqualified | 62 | 50 |
|  | 2 | 6 | 5 | 1 |  | Reviewed | 16 | 17 |
| 4 | 3 | 6 |  |  |  | Compiled | 17 | 10 |
| 3 | 4 | 3 | 2 |  |  | Tax Returns | 6 | 7 |
| 2 | 8 | 13 | 13 | 8 | 12 | Other | 50 | 58 |
|  | 44 (4/1-9/30/11) |  | 110 (10/1/11-3/31/12) |  |  |  |  |  |
| 9 | 20 | 32 | 42 | 21 | 30 | NUMBER OF STATEMENTS | 151 | 142 |
| % | % | % | % | % | % | ASSETS | % | % |
|  | 8.1 | 15.6 | 13.8 | 12.9 | 5.7 | Cash & Equivalents | 10.9 | 9.7 |
|  | 21.8 | 27.2 | 24.1 | 20.6 | 13.9 | Trade Receivables (net) | 22.5 | 22.4 |
|  | 9.4 | 7.3 | 4.7 | 6.2 | 4.2 | Inventory | 7.9 | 7.9 |
|  | 2.2 | 1.7 | 4.1 | 4.5 | 3.1 | All Other Current | 3.8 | 3.8 |
|  | 41.4 | 51.8 | 46.7 | 44.1 | 27.0 | Total Current | 45.0 | 43.8 |
|  | 39.1 | 35.7 | 39.2 | 47.1 | 63.1 | Fixed Assets (net) | 44.3 | 43.5 |
|  | 6.5 | 4.1 | 3.8 | 1.8 | 3.3 | Intangibles (net) | 4.3 | 4.0 |
|  | 13.1 | 8.5 | 10.3 | 6.9 | 6.7 | All Other Non-Current | 6.3 | 8.7 |
|  | 100.0 | 100.0 | 100.0 | 100.0 | 100.0 | Total | 100.0 | 100.0 |
|  |  |  |  |  |  | **LIABILITIES** |  |  |
|  | 7.8 | 6.4 | 5.3 | 7.6 | 2.4 | Notes Payable-Short Term | 8.0 | 7.4 |
|  | 3.2 | 2.9 | 2.8 | 6.7 | 2.3 | Cur. Mat.-L.T.D. | 1.9 | 3.5 |
|  | 22.4 | 19.5 | 20.4 | 13.1 | 8.6 | Trade Payables | 16.2 | 17.7 |
|  | .2 | .2 | .2 | .0 | .7 | Income Taxes Payable | .3 | .4 |
|  | 6.3 | 7.7 | 7.1 | 6.8 | 5.2 | All Other Current | 7.5 | 8.3 |
|  | 39.8 | 36.7 | 35.7 | 34.2 | 19.2 | Total Current | 34.0 | 37.3 |
|  | 18.1 | 13.2 | 11.8 | 17.6 | 21.7 | Long-Term Debt | 23.4 | 19.2 |
|  | .6 | 2.5 | 2.5 | .9 | 2.5 | Deferred Taxes | 1.7 | 1.8 |
|  | 22.1 | 3.9 | 3.7 | 3.7 | 5.9 | All Other Non-Current | 4.1 | 4.0 |
|  | 19.3 | 43.7 | 46.4 | 43.6 | 50.7 | Net Worth | 36.8 | 37.8 |
|  | 100.0 | 100.0 | 100.0 | 100.0 | 100.0 | Total Liabilities & Net Worth | 100.0 | 100.0 |
|  |  |  |  |  |  | **INCOME DATA** |  |  |
|  | 100.0 | 100.0 | 100.0 | 100.0 | 100.0 | Net Sales | 100.0 | 100.0 |
|  |  |  |  |  |  | Gross Profit |  |  |
|  | 95.9 | 90.0 | 92.6 | 86.6 | 85.1 | Operating Expenses | 89.4 | 89.9 |
|  | 4.1 | 10.0 | 7.4 | 13.4 | 14.9 | Operating Profit | 10.6 | 10.1 |
|  | .6 | 1.4 | 1.0 | 1.1 | 4.2 | All Other Expenses (net) | 3.0 | 2.1 |
|  | 3.5 | 8.6 | 6.4 | 12.3 | 10.7 | Profit Before Taxes | 7.6 | 8.0 |
|  |  |  |  |  |  | **RATIOS** |  |  |
|  | 1.8 | 2.1 | 2.0 | 2.3 | 2.9 | Current | 2.0 | 1.7 |
|  | 1.2 | 1.3 | 1.3 | 1.6 | 1.2 |  | 1.3 | 1.2 |
|  | .6 | .9 | .9 | 1.0 | .9 |  | 1.0 | .9 |
|  | 1.4 | 1.7 | 1.6 | 1.7 | 1.8 | Quick | 1.5 | 1.2 |
|  | .8 | 1.1 | 1.0 | 1.0 | .7 |  | (150) 1.0 | .9 |
|  | .3 | .6 | .6 | .7 | .4 |  | .6 | .5 |
| 10 | 37.6 | 18 19.8 | 16 22.2 | 23 15.6 | 19 19.1 | Sales/Receivables | 15 23.9 | 14 25.2 |
| 23 | 15.6 | 28 13.0 | 26 14.2 | 37 9.8 | 35 10.4 |  | 31 11.9 | 29 12.8 |
| 41 | 8.8 | 46 8.0 | 35 10.3 | 65 5.6 | 46 8.0 |  | 50 7.3 | 47 7.8 |
|  |  |  |  |  |  | Cost of Sales/Inventory |  |  |
|  |  |  |  |  |  | Cost of Sales/Payables |  |  |
|  | 11.3 | 6.6 | 7.6 | 4.5 | 4.2 | Sales/Working Capital | 7.3 | 13.1 |
|  | NM | 33.4 | 36.2 | 14.8 | 45.3 |  | 23.5 | 43.9 |
|  | -14.9 | NM | -44.3 | NM | -12.7 |  | 999.8 | -48.7 |
|  | 11.6 | 20.5 | 37.9 | 14.3 | 10.3 | EBIT/Interest | 7.0 | 7.0 |
|  | (16) 2.8 | (24) 8.4 | (35) 7.2 | (18) 6.0 | (25) 4.9 |  | (129) 4.0 | (119) 4.2 |
|  | -.1 | 2.9 | 3.3 | 2.8 | 2.6 |  | 1.9 | 2.3 |
|  |  |  | 10.6 |  | 9.9 | Net Profit + Depr., Dep., Amort./Cur. Mat. L/T/D | 9.5 | 8.6 |
|  |  |  | (10) 2.6 |  | (11) 2.0 |  | (43) 3.5 | (28) 3.1 |
|  |  |  | 1.9 |  | .6 |  | 1.6 | 1.9 |
|  | .9 | .1 | .1 | .7 | .9 | Fixed/Worth | .7 | .7 |
|  | 2.2 | .9 | 1.0 | 1.4 | 1.6 |  | 1.3 | 1.2 |
|  | NM | 1.6 | 1.8 | 2.4 | 2.1 |  | 2.8 | 2.6 |
|  | .9 | .7 | .5 | .5 | .6 | Debt/Worth | .9 | 1.0 |
|  | 4.7 | 1.6 | 1.5 | 1.5 | 1.6 |  | 2.3 | 2.0 |
|  | -17.4 | 2.6 | 4.6 | 4.3 | 2.3 |  | 5.3 | 4.0 |
|  | 28.1 | 37.3 | 31.6 | 21.8 | 18.1 | % Profit Before Taxes/Tangible Net Worth | 39.4 | 35.5 |
|  | (14) 12.3 | (30) 15.4 | (40) 12.6 | (20) 12.0 | 13.6 |  | (137) 16.0 | (132) 17.7 |
|  | -13.5 | 8.5 | 6.3 | 7.0 | 3.7 |  | 7.4 | 8.1 |
|  | 22.1 | 13.6 | 12.2 | 8.3 | 7.4 | % Profit Before Taxes/Total Assets | 11.9 | 8.9 |
|  | 5.9 | 6.6 | 4.7 | 6.0 | 5.5 |  | 5.2 | 5.2 |
|  | -.2 | 4.7 | 1.6 | 3.0 | 2.0 |  | 2.1 | 2.8 |
|  | 63.0 | 215.9 | 188.5 | 74.1 | 1.9 | Sales/Net Fixed Assets | 32.6 | 40.4 |
|  | 5.6 | 14.8 | 5.9 | 1.8 | .7 |  | 2.9 | 3.4 |
|  | 2.4 | 1.0 | .9 | .5 | .5 |  | 1.0 | 1.0 |
|  | 7.5 | 5.8 | 5.0 | 3.9 | 1.2 | Sales/Total Assets | 4.2 | 4.6 |
|  | 2.0 | 2.3 | 1.4 | 1.0 | .5 |  | 1.5 | 1.6 |
|  | 1.3 | .8 | .6 | .3 | .3 |  | .6 | .7 |
|  | 1.7 | .4 | .1 | .3 | 3.7 | % Depr., Dep., Amort./Sales | .9 | .7 |
|  | (17) 3.4 | (25) 3.5 | (37) 4.3 | (18) 4.3 | (22) 6.5 |  | (129) 3.7 | (123) 3.0 |
|  | 4.9 | 6.2 | 6.6 | 17.0 | 11.3 |  | 6.4 | 5.2 |
|  |  |  |  |  |  | % Officers', Directors' Owners' Comp/Sales | .6 | .4 |
|  |  |  |  |  |  |  | (20) 1.5 | (26) 1.4 |
|  |  |  |  |  |  |  | 2.5 | 3.5 |
| 24474M | 119283M | 815274M | 2682096M | 4930932M | 6835972M | Net Sales ($) | 20177920M | 19888544M |
| 2779M | 24267M | 177732M | 970608M | 1493319M | 4916740M | Total Assets ($) | 6681617M | 6714545M |

© RMA 2012

M = $ thousand    MM = $ million
See Pages 9 through 22 for Explanation of Ratios and Data

## Comparative Historical Data / Current Data Sorted by Sales

| | | | Type of Statement | 0-1MM | 1-3MM | 3-5MM | 5-10MM | 10-25MM | 25MM & OVER |
|---|---|---|---|---|---|---|---|---|---|
| 47 | 54 | 60 | Unqualified | 1 | 2 | 4 | 3 | 13 | 37 |
| 15 | 20 | 13 | Reviewed | | 3 | 1 | 1 | 2 | 6 |
| 14 | 13 | 13 | Compiled | 1 | | 4 | 6 | | 2 |
| 6 | 9 | 12 | Tax Returns | | 4 | | 3 | 3 | 2 |
| 57 | 49 | 56 | Other | 4 | 4 | 2 | 5 | 15 | 26 |
| 4/1/09-3/31/10 ALL | 4/1/10-3/31/11 ALL | 4/1/11-3/31/12 ALL | | | 44 (4/1-9/30/11) | | 110 (10/1/11-3/31/12) | | |
| 139 | 145 | 154 | **NUMBER OF STATEMENTS** | 6 | 13 | 11 | 18 | 33 | 73 |
| % | % | % | **ASSETS** | % | % | % | % | % | % |
| 13.0 | 12.1 | 12.1 | Cash & Equivalents | | 8.2 | 13.9 | 11.1 | 11.0 | 13.4 |
| 19.6 | 19.9 | 21.7 | Trade Receivables (net) | | 22.8 | 11.8 | 20.8 | 15.0 | 27.8 |
| 6.6 | 6.5 | 7.0 | Inventory | | 6.4 | 10.3 | 4.0 | 5.3 | 7.6 |
| 3.1 | 3.2 | 3.0 | All Other Current | | .9 | 2.5 | 2.1 | 4.1 | 3.3 |
| 42.4 | 41.7 | 43.8 | Total Current | | 38.3 | 38.6 | 38.1 | 35.4 | 52.1 |
| 46.2 | 46.0 | 43.9 | Fixed Assets (net) | | 51.7 | 49.9 | 46.8 | 51.8 | 36.2 |
| 4.3 | 3.8 | 3.6 | Intangibles (net) | | 2.9 | 4.9 | 5.8 | 4.7 | 2.5 |
| 7.1 | 8.5 | 8.7 | All Other Non-Current | | 7.1 | 6.6 | 9.4 | 8.1 | 9.3 |
| 100.0 | 100.0 | 100.0 | Total | | 100.0 | 100.0 | 100.0 | 100.0 | 100.0 |
| | | | **LIABILITIES** | | | | | | |
| 5.8 | 5.8 | 6.3 | Notes Payable-Short Term | | 15.0 | .3 | 9.4 | 3.5 | 6.5 |
| 2.8 | 2.5 | 3.7 | Cur. Mat.-L.T.D. | | 4.0 | 11.6 | 2.6 | 5.8 | 2.0 |
| 16.6 | 16.7 | 16.3 | Trade Payables | | 11.9 | 7.1 | 13.3 | 11.6 | 22.2 |
| .4 | .3 | .3 | Income Taxes Payable | | .0 | .0 | .4 | .0 | .4 |
| 8.8 | 7.8 | 8.0 | All Other Current | | 11.4 | 16.0 | 4.9 | 6.9 | 7.3 |
| 34.4 | 33.1 | 34.5 | Total Current | | 42.3 | 35.0 | 30.6 | 27.7 | 38.5 |
| 17.8 | 19.4 | 16.6 | Long-Term Debt | | 21.3 | 28.3 | 15.0 | 13.2 | 15.4 |
| 2.2 | 2.5 | 1.9 | Deferred Taxes | | .9 | .9 | 3.8 | 1.9 | 1.6 |
| 4.8 | 4.0 | 7.0 | All Other Non-Current | | 12.8 | 2.8 | 17.1 | 5.0 | 4.1 |
| 40.8 | 41.0 | 40.0 | Net Worth | | 22.7 | 33.0 | 33.6 | 52.2 | 40.5 |
| 100.0 | 100.0 | 100.0 | Total Liabilities & Net Worth | | 100.0 | 100.0 | 100.0 | 100.0 | 100.0 |
| | | | **INCOME DATA** | | | | | | |
| 100.0 | 100.0 | 100.0 | Net Sales | | 100.0 | 100.0 | 100.0 | 100.0 | 100.0 |
| | | | Gross Profit | | | | | | |
| 89.4 | 90.2 | 90.5 | Operating Expenses | | 90.9 | 89.9 | 85.4 | 87.1 | 93.0 |
| 10.6 | 9.8 | 9.5 | Operating Profit | | 9.1 | 10.1 | 14.6 | 12.9 | 7.0 |
| 2.6 | 2.2 | 1.5 | All Other Expenses (net) | | 3.1 | -.6 | 1.5 | 1.5 | 1.5 |
| 7.9 | 7.6 | 8.0 | Profit Before Taxes | | 6.0 | 10.7 | 13.0 | 11.4 | 5.5 |
| | | | **RATIOS** | | | | | | |
| 1.8 | 1.9 | 2.1 | Current | | 1.8 | 3.8 | 2.1 | 2.1 | 2.0 |
| 1.2 | 1.3 | 1.3 | | | .8 | 1.5 | 1.0 | 1.4 | 1.3 |
| .8 | .8 | .8 | | | .5 | .8 | .8 | .8 | 1.0 |
| 1.3 | 1.5 | 1.6 | Quick | | 1.4 | 3.4 | 1.6 | 1.6 | 1.6 |
| .9 | 1.0 | .9 | | | .8 | 1.5 | 1.0 | .8 | .9 |
| .5 | .5 | .5 | | | .4 | .4 | .6 | .3 | .7 |
| 13  28.4 | 14  25.7 | 17  21.0 | Sales/Receivables | | 5  76.7 | 1  474.9 | 20  18.7 | 15  24.2 | 18  20.5 |
| 26  13.9 | 28  12.9 | 29  12.5 | | | 41  8.8 | 22  16.3 | 39  9.4 | 27  13.6 | 29  12.4 |
| 45  8.1 | 45  8.1 | 43  8.4 | | | 49  7.4 | 52  7.0 | 78  4.7 | 46  7.9 | 38  9.7 |
| | | | Cost of Sales/Inventory | | | | | | |
| | | | Cost of Sales/Payables | | | | | | |
| 8.8 | 8.2 | 7.5 | Sales/Working Capital | | 9.9 | 3.7 | 7.8 | 4.2 | 10.3 |
| 44.3 | 32.3 | 36.2 | | | -31.5 | 11.4 | 95.7 | 44.9 | 32.7 |
| -40.0 | -45.3 | -45.6 | | | -4.8 | -101.3 | -18.2 | -12.9 | NM |
| 12.0 | 13.0 | 13.7 | EBIT/Interest | | | | 9.5 | 37.5 | 12.7 |
| (112)  5.3 | (123)  4.9 | (124)  5.7 | | | | | (15)  3.1 | (29)  6.7 | (60)  6.3 |
| 2.0 | 2.4 | 2.5 | | | | | 1.3 | 2.8 | 3.6 |
| 8.3 | 11.0 | 7.9 | Net Profit + Depr., Dep., Amort./Cur. Mat. L/T/D | | | | | | 7.6 |
| (27)  3.4 | (39)  4.3 | (30)  2.3 | | | | | | | (15)  2.1 |
| 1.6 | 2.3 | 1.1 | | | | | | | .6 |
| .5 | .5 | .5 | Fixed/Worth | | .9 | 1.0 | 1.0 | .7 | .1 |
| 1.1 | 1.1 | 1.2 | | | 3.0 | 1.4 | 1.6 | 1.1 | 1.0 |
| 2.3 | 2.2 | 2.3 | | | -5.7 | 15.0 | NM | 2.4 | 1.7 |
| .7 | .7 | .6 | Debt/Worth | | .5 | .4 | .3 | .4 | 1.0 |
| 1.7 | 1.8 | 1.7 | | | 3.3 | 1.8 | 2.0 | .9 | 1.7 |
| 3.4 | 2.8 | 3.9 | | | -11.0 | 16.6 | NM | 2.3 | 3.2 |
| 37.8 | 31.6 | 25.1 | % Profit Before Taxes/Tangible Net Worth | | | | 15.2 | 19.2 | 26.2 |
| (129)  17.8 | (136)  15.5 | (138)  13.0 | | | | | (14)  8.5 | (30)  11.4 | (71)  15.5 |
| 5.8 | 6.3 | 6.4 | | | | | 4.7 | 5.5 | 9.2 |
| 12.2 | 10.0 | 10.2 | % Profit Before Taxes/Total Assets | | 12.7 | 21.9 | 7.7 | 12.4 | 9.0 |
| 6.4 | 5.6 | 5.7 | | | 6.6 | 7.6 | 5.2 | 5.5 | 5.9 |
| 1.8 | 2.1 | 2.0 | | | -7.2 | .6 | 1.5 | 2.4 | 2.8 |
| 52.7 | 43.5 | 89.1 | Sales/Net Fixed Assets | | 8.5 | 24.0 | 25.7 | 31.5 | 329.3 |
| 2.9 | 2.4 | 3.2 | | | 3.0 | 7.4 | 5.0 | 1.0 | 13.5 |
| .8 | .8 | .8 | | | 1.8 | .9 | .9 | .6 | 1.0 |
| 3.7 | 4.3 | 4.7 | Sales/Total Assets | | 3.6 | 8.3 | 3.8 | 2.7 | 7.1 |
| 1.6 | 1.3 | 1.5 | | | 1.6 | 1.8 | 1.3 | .8 | 2.7 |
| .5 | .5 | .6 | | | 1.0 | .5 | .6 | .4 | .6 |
| .6 | .5 | .5 | % Depr., Dep., Amort./Sales | | 3.1 | 2.0 | 3.0 | 4.1 | .1 |
| (114)  4.2 | (128)  4.5 | (125)  4.2 | | | (12)  4.7 | (10)  3.3 | (15)  5.7 | (27)  6.5 | (56)  .7 |
| 7.1 | 7.9 | 7.0 | | | 15.6 | 14.1 | 7.0 | 12.9 | 5.6 |
| .9 | .8 | .7 | % Officers', Directors' Owners' Comp/Sales | | | | | | .7 |
| (24)  2.1 | (23)  2.1 | (28)  1.6 | | | | | | | (11)  1.0 |
| 2.9 | 3.7 | 5.4 | | | | | | | 1.9 |
| 11249834M | 12521125M | 15408031M | Net Sales ($) | 2917M | 24684M | 43456M | 132421M | 549383M | 14655170M |
| 6835692M | 6697057M | 7585445M | Total Assets ($) | 8579M | 30840M | 252781M | 237286M | 1043864M | 6012095M |

M = $ thousand   MM = $ million
See Pages 9 through 22 for Explanation of Ratios and Data

## Current Data Sorted by Assets      Comparative Historical Data

| | | | | | | Type of Statement | | |
|---|---|---|---|---|---|---|---|---|
| 1 | 6 | 30 | 62 | 13 | 18 | Unqualified | 99 | 92 |
| | 3 | 9 | 3 | | | Reviewed | 11 | 17 |
| 2 | 6 | 9 | 2 | | 1 | Compiled | 11 | 17 |
| 12 | 4 | 7 | 2 | | 1 | Tax Returns | 21 | 30 |
| 7 | 13 | 16 | 24 | 3 | | Other | 55 | 57 |
| | 81 (4/1-9/30/11) | | 173 (10/1/11-3/31/12) | | | | 4/1/07-3/31/08 | 4/1/08-3/31/09 |
| 0-500M | 500M-2MM | 2-10MM | 10-50MM | 50-100MM | 100-250MM | | ALL | ALL |
| 22 | 32 | 71 | 93 | 16 | 20 | NUMBER OF STATEMENTS | 197 | 213 |
| % | % | % | % | % | % | ASSETS | % | % |
| 27.1 | 18.3 | 14.0 | 8.4 | 7.5 | 5.5 | Cash & Equivalents | 9.6 | 8.3 |
| 8.1 | 9.0 | 12.7 | 4.6 | 4.8 | 1.6 | Trade Receivables (net) | 10.7 | 10.0 |
| 7.9 | 10.3 | 5.8 | 2.6 | .4 | .4 | Inventory | 5.0 | 4.5 |
| 5.9 | 1.4 | 1.6 | 1.2 | 1.2 | 2.1 | All Other Current | 3.2 | 2.2 |
| 49.1 | 38.9 | 34.1 | 16.8 | 13.9 | 9.5 | Total Current | 28.5 | 25.0 |
| 40.5 | 54.0 | 51.5 | 73.5 | 78.9 | 80.5 | Fixed Assets (net) | 62.6 | 63.3 |
| 2.8 | 2.7 | 2.5 | 2.5 | .7 | 1.6 | Intangibles (net) | 2.3 | 2.2 |
| 7.3 | 4.4 | 11.9 | 7.3 | 6.5 | 8.3 | All Other Non-Current | 6.5 | 9.6 |
| 100.0 | 100.0 | 100.0 | 100.0 | 100.0 | 100.0 | Total | 100.0 | 100.0 |
| | | | | | | LIABILITIES | | |
| 10.3 | 7.9 | 3.6 | 1.5 | .3 | .7 | Notes Payable-Short Term | 3.8 | 4.0 |
| 12.2 | 2.8 | 2.3 | 2.2 | 1.8 | 1.7 | Cur. Mat.-L.T.D. | 3.4 | 3.8 |
| 7.8 | 5.4 | 6.4 | 2.9 | 3.9 | 1.0 | Trade Payables | 5.9 | 5.7 |
| .4 | .1 | .1 | .1 | .1 | .2 | Income Taxes Payable | .1 | .3 |
| 26.2 | 3.5 | 6.2 | 3.0 | 2.3 | 2.4 | All Other Current | 6.7 | 8.3 |
| 56.9 | 19.7 | 18.7 | 9.7 | 8.3 | 6.1 | Total Current | 19.9 | 22.1 |
| 58.7 | 22.1 | 24.8 | 31.6 | 40.9 | 33.2 | Long-Term Debt | 34.2 | 29.7 |
| .0 | .0 | .1 | .5 | .1 | 3.1 | Deferred Taxes | .6 | .8 |
| 3.0 | 11.1 | 4.7 | 6.8 | 5.7 | 18.9 | All Other Non-Current | 8.6 | 7.3 |
| -18.6 | 47.1 | 51.7 | 51.4 | 45.0 | 38.8 | Net Worth | 36.6 | 40.1 |
| 100.0 | 100.0 | 100.0 | 100.0 | 100.0 | 100.0 | Total Liabilities & Net Worth | 100.0 | 100.0 |
| | | | | | | INCOME DATA | | |
| 100.0 | 100.0 | 100.0 | 100.0 | 100.0 | 100.0 | Net Sales | 100.0 | 100.0 |
| | | | | | | Gross Profit | | |
| 84.5 | 85.9 | 84.4 | 83.3 | 82.8 | 79.5 | Operating Expenses | 86.0 | 85.6 |
| 15.5 | 14.1 | 15.6 | 16.7 | 17.2 | 20.5 | Operating Profit | 14.0 | 14.4 |
| 2.7 | 4.9 | 6.6 | 7.3 | 6.6 | 7.3 | All Other Expenses (net) | 4.7 | 6.2 |
| 12.8 | 9.2 | 8.9 | 9.5 | 10.6 | 13.2 | Profit Before Taxes | 9.3 | 8.2 |
| | | | | | | RATIOS | | |
| 2.3 | 3.9 | 5.1 | 4.1 | 4.4 | 2.7 | | 2.9 | 3.0 |
| .8 | 1.8 | 2.3 | 2.2 | 2.1 | 1.6 | Current | 1.5 | 1.3 |
| .5 | 1.0 | 1.4 | 1.1 | 1.5 | .7 | | .9 | .7 |
| 1.2 | 3.8 | 4.1 | 3.5 | 4.1 | 2.0 | | 2.3 | 2.4 |
| .7 | 1.5 | 2.0 | 1.8 | 1.6 | .9 | Quick | 1.1 | 1.1 |
| .3 | .4 | .9 | .8 | 1.2 | .4 | | .6 | .4 |
| 0 UND | 1 422.8 | 16 22.6 | 24 15.0 | 22 16.4 | 20 18.4 | | 23 15.7 | 17 21.1 |
| 0 UND | 21 17.1 | 31 11.6 | 35 10.5 | 32 11.3 | 34 10.7 | Sales/Receivables | 34 10.6 | 32 11.2 |
| 17 21.7 | 34 10.8 | 54 6.8 | 45 8.2 | 59 6.2 | 41 8.8 | | 52 7.1 | 48 7.6 |
| | | | | | | Cost of Sales/Inventory | | |
| | | | | | | Cost of Sales/Payables | | |
| 4.6 | 2.1 | 2.1 | 2.0 | 1.8 | 3.2 | | 2.8 | 3.8 |
| -95.7 | 9.3 | 4.6 | 4.6 | 5.2 | 6.3 | Sales/Working Capital | 9.6 | 12.1 |
| -12.7 | NM | 25.1 | 28.0 | 7.2 | -25.8 | | -51.9 | -11.2 |
| 9.0 | 14.4 | 10.9 | 6.1 | 3.5 | 3.7 | | 5.0 | 6.9 |
| (14) 3.9 | (23) 4.4 | (56) 3.2 | (79) 3.1 | (12) 2.4 | (19) 2.9 | EBIT/Interest | (159) 2.5 | (175) 2.8 |
| 2.4 | 1.7 | 1.3 | 1.7 | 1.0 | 1.7 | | 1.2 | 1.5 |
| | | | 12.7 | | | | 5.7 | 8.8 |
| | | | (15) 2.1 | | | Net Profit + Depr., Dep., Amort./Cur. Mat. L/T/D | (29) 3.1 | (35) 4.5 |
| | | | 1.5 | | | | 1.2 | 1.8 |
| .3 | .7 | .6 | 1.0 | 1.2 | 1.4 | | 1.0 | .9 |
| 9.2 | 1.1 | 1.1 | 1.5 | 1.6 | 2.4 | Fixed/Worth | 1.7 | 1.4 |
| -.7 | 6.7 | 2.5 | 2.2 | 3.2 | 3.2 | | 4.6 | 3.1 |
| .7 | .2 | .3 | .5 | .5 | .8 | | .6 | .5 |
| 36.1 | .8 | .9 | .9 | 1.2 | 2.1 | Debt/Worth | 1.9 | 1.2 |
| -2.5 | 7.9 | 2.9 | 2.0 | 3.0 | 2.7 | | 5.8 | 3.9 |
| 78.4 | 28.2 | 16.9 | 12.2 | 7.9 | 14.8 | | 17.4 | 17.5 |
| (13) 43.9 | (29) 11.8 | (64) 5.8 | (90) 4.1 | (15) 3.3 | (19) 8.4 | % Profit Before Taxes/Tangible Net Worth | (171) 6.7 | (185) 5.4 |
| 15.7 | 2.3 | 1.4 | 1.4 | -.3 | 2.9 | | .6 | .8 |
| 39.0 | 11.0 | 8.2 | 4.4 | 4.4 | 4.2 | | 6.2 | 6.7 |
| 20.3 | 3.7 | 3.2 | 2.1 | 1.7 | 2.7 | % Profit Before Taxes/Total Assets | 2.5 | 2.2 |
| 2.7 | .7 | -.2 | .5 | -.1 | 1.7 | | .2 | .3 |
| 134.6 | 15.8 | 9.8 | .5 | .3 | .3 | | 4.1 | 4.2 |
| 14.7 | 1.3 | .5 | .2 | .2 | .2 | Sales/Net Fixed Assets | .4 | .4 |
| 1.9 | .3 | .3 | .2 | .1 | .1 | | .2 | .2 |
| 9.2 | 2.2 | 1.6 | .3 | .2 | .2 | | 1.5 | 1.6 |
| 2.0 | .8 | .4 | .2 | .2 | .2 | Sales/Total Assets | .3 | .3 |
| 1.1 | .2 | .2 | .1 | .1 | .1 | | .2 | .2 |
| .7 | 3.0 | 3.5 | 10.0 | 13.6 | 11.1 | | 4.1 | 5.1 |
| (13) 4.5 | (22) 6.9 | (61) 11.6 | (91) 17.0 | 18.7 | (19) 15.3 | % Depr., Dep., Amort./Sales | (181) 12.4 | (199) 12.6 |
| 12.7 | 13.4 | 18.1 | 23.3 | 27.1 | 21.5 | | 18.6 | 19.5 |
| | | | 2.4 | | | | 1.2 | 1.6 |
| | | (14) 4.8 | | | | % Officers', Directors' Owners' Comp/Sales | (32) 2.6 | (39) 3.3 |
| | | | 7.4 | | | | 6.1 | 5.7 |
| 29506M | 54148M | 283952M | 767213M | 252920M | 1361916M | Net Sales ($) | 2487855M | 4606446M |
| 4886M | 39157M | 334846M | 2158125M | 993602M | 3430885M | Total Assets ($) | 5937739M | 6585724M |

© RMA 2012

M = $ thousand    MM = $ million
See Pages 9 through 22 for Explanation of Ratios and Data

## Comparative Historical Data | | | | Current Data Sorted by Sales

| | | | Type of Statement | | | | | | |
|---|---|---|---|---|---|---|---|---|---|
| 113 | 111 | 130 | Unqualified | 11 | 47 | 16 | 26 | 17 | 13 |
| 14 | 15 | 15 | Reviewed | 2 | 1 | 2 | 5 | 4 | 1 |
| 12 | 22 | 20 | Compiled | 5 | 4 | 2 | 3 | 4 | 2 |
| 24 | 32 | 26 | Tax Returns | 10 | 6 | 3 | 5 | 1 | 1 |
| 55 | 58 | 63 | Other | 22 | 17 | 8 | 8 | 5 | 3 |
| 4/1/09-3/31/10 ALL | 4/1/10-3/31/11 ALL | 4/1/11-3/31/12 ALL | | 81 (4/1-9/30/11) | | | 173 (10/1/11-3/31/12) | | |
| | | | | 0-1MM | 1-3MM | 3-5MM | 5-10MM | 10-25MM | 25MM & OVER |
| 218 | 238 | 254 | NUMBER OF STATEMENTS | 50 | 75 | 31 | 47 | 31 | 20 |
| % | % | % | **ASSETS** | % | % | % | % | % | % |
| 9.3 | 11.1 | 12.5 | Cash & Equivalents | 16.8 | 11.4 | 14.7 | 12.5 | 11.3 | 4.8 |
| 8.5 | 10.2 | 7.5 | Trade Receivables (net) | 3.5 | 5.3 | 5.2 | 10.6 | 13.3 | 13.1 |
| 3.5 | 4.4 | 4.6 | Inventory | 3.6 | 2.6 | 5.3 | 5.3 | 6.9 | 8.4 |
| 1.6 | 2.5 | 1.8 | All Other Current | 2.3 | .9 | 2.1 | 2.1 | 1.7 | 3.3 |
| 22.9 | 28.2 | 26.5 | Total Current | 26.3 | 20.1 | 27.3 | 30.5 | 33.2 | 29.7 |
| 66.7 | 59.8 | 62.9 | Fixed Assets (net) | 60.7 | 71.0 | 57.1 | 60.8 | 59.4 | 57.6 |
| 2.6 | 3.5 | 2.4 | Intangibles (net) | 1.4 | 2.0 | 4.3 | 2.2 | 2.0 | 4.0 |
| 7.8 | 8.5 | 8.2 | All Other Non-Current | 11.6 | 6.9 | 11.3 | 6.5 | 5.4 | 8.7 |
| 100.0 | 100.0 | 100.0 | Total | 100.0 | 100.0 | 100.0 | 100.0 | 100.0 | 100.0 |
| | | | **LIABILITIES** | | | | | | |
| 3.5 | 5.5 | 3.5 | Notes Payable-Short Term | 5.6 | 2.4 | 5.8 | 1.5 | 2.2 | 6.3 |
| 3.2 | 3.2 | 3.1 | Cur. Mat.-L.T.D. | 3.1 | 2.5 | 6.6 | 2.8 | 1.9 | 2.7 |
| 4.6 | 6.0 | 4.6 | Trade Payables | 2.4 | 3.5 | 2.0 | 8.3 | 5.6 | 7.3 |
| .1 | .1 | .1 | Income Taxes Payable | .1 | .1 | .2 | .1 | .0 | .4 |
| 7.8 | 11.7 | 5.9 | All Other Current | 5.6 | 3.7 | 13.5 | 5.4 | 6.1 | 4.0 |
| 19.2 | 26.4 | 17.2 | Total Current | 16.8 | 12.1 | 28.1 | 18.0 | 15.8 | 20.7 |
| 29.4 | 26.8 | 31.6 | Long-Term Debt | 39.5 | 30.7 | 32.7 | 29.1 | 27.7 | 24.9 |
| .6 | .6 | .4 | Deferred Taxes | .0 | .0 | .7 | .2 | .7 | 2.9 |
| 7.0 | 9.1 | 7.3 | All Other Non-Current | 3.7 | 7.0 | 9.0 | 7.1 | 7.7 | 15.2 |
| 43.8 | 37.0 | 43.5 | Net Worth | 40.0 | 50.2 | 29.5 | 45.7 | 48.1 | 36.3 |
| 100.0 | 100.0 | 100.0 | Total Liabilties & Net Worth | 100.0 | 100.0 | 100.0 | 100.0 | 100.0 | 100.0 |
| | | | **INCOME DATA** | | | | | | |
| 100.0 | 100.0 | 100.0 | Net Sales | 100.0 | 100.0 | 100.0 | 100.0 | 100.0 | 100.0 |
| | | | Gross Profit | | | | | | |
| 87.4 | 87.0 | 83.7 | Operating Expenses | 73.4 | 86.6 | 83.2 | 88.0 | 87.7 | 83.1 |
| 12.6 | 13.0 | 16.3 | Operating Profit | 26.6 | 13.4 | 16.8 | 12.0 | 12.3 | 16.9 |
| 5.0 | 5.4 | 6.4 | All Other Expenses (net) | 11.6 | 5.5 | 5.9 | 5.0 | 2.8 | 5.8 |
| 7.6 | 7.6 | 9.9 | Profit Before Taxes | 15.0 | 7.9 | 10.9 | 7.0 | 9.5 | 11.1 |
| | | | **RATIOS** | | | | | | |
| 3.5 | 3.2 | 4.0 | Current | 4.2 | 4.3 | 3.9 | 4.4 | 4.5 | 2.3 |
| 1.5 | 1.5 | 2.0 | | 1.9 | 2.2 | 2.2 | 2.2 | 1.7 | 1.8 |
| .7 | .9 | 1.0 | | .8 | 1.2 | .9 | 1.0 | 1.2 | .7 |
| 2.7 | 2.8 | 3.4 | Quick | 4.2 | 3.9 | 3.4 | 3.4 | 3.8 | 1.2 |
| 1.1 | 1.2 | 1.6 | | 1.5 | 1.9 | 1.6 | 1.6 | 1.6 | .8 |
| .5 | .5 | .7 | | .5 | 1.0 | .7 | .8 | .9 | .4 |
| 16  22.6 | 17  22.1 | 15  24.5 | Sales/Receivables | 0  UND | 17  21.0 | 12  31.3 | 24  15.2 | 26  14.1 | 16  23.4 |
| 31  12.0 | 34  10.8 | 31  11.6 | | 17  21.3 | 31  11.8 | 28  13.0 | 39  9.3 | 35  10.5 | 33  10.9 |
| 44  8.4 | 49  7.4 | 44  8.3 | | 42  8.6 | 39  9.4 | 39  9.3 | 54  6.8 | 54  6.8 | 60  6.1 |
| | | | Cost of Sales/Inventory | | | | | | |
| | | | Cost of Sales/Payables | | | | | | |
| 3.0 | 3.2 | 2.2 | Sales/Working Capital | 1.8 | 1.8 | 1.7 | 2.4 | 3.5 | 5.3 |
| 10.5 | 9.3 | 5.1 | | 4.1 | 4.0 | 4.9 | 4.6 | 6.2 | 8.6 |
| -19.0 | -40.5 | 76.4 | | -14.7 | 25.1 | -107.0 | 447.9 | 13.3 | -34.2 |
| 5.7 | 6.3 | 6.7 | EBIT/Interest | 10.4 | 5.4 | 4.8 | 9.5 | 18.5 | 6.7 |
| (188) 2.4 | (190) 2.5 | (203) 3.1 | | (29) 3.0 | (61) 2.6 | (27) 2.7 | (38) 3.9 | (29) 3.7 | (19) 3.6 |
| 1.0 | 1.0 | 1.7 | | 1.5 | .9 | 1.7 | 1.5 | 2.4 | 2.9 |
| 8.4 | 10.1 | 13.2 | Net Profit + Depr., Dep., Amort./Cur. Mat. L/T/D | | | | | | 32.8 |
| (38) 2.8 | (32) 3.6 | (34) 2.7 | | | | | | | (10) 6.9 |
| 1.3 | 1.0 | 1.5 | | | | | | | 1.3 |
| 1.0 | .9 | .9 | Fixed/Worth | .7 | 1.0 | 1.2 | .8 | .8 | .9 |
| 1.4 | 1.4 | 1.4 | | 1.2 | 1.5 | 1.5 | 1.4 | 1.2 | 2.1 |
| 3.0 | 4.7 | 2.9 | | 4.8 | 2.3 | 13.6 | 3.3 | 2.8 | 3.0 |
| .5 | .5 | .5 | Debt/Worth | .3 | .3 | .6 | .5 | .4 | 1.0 |
| 1.1 | 1.2 | 1.0 | | .8 | .8 | 1.2 | 1.3 | .9 | 2.3 |
| 3.1 | 6.4 | 3.2 | | 5.0 | 2.1 | 19.2 | 4.9 | 3.4 | 2.7 |
| 13.4 | 15.5 | 16.4 | % Profit Before Taxes/Tangible Net Worth | 36.3 | 11.6 | 15.4 | 20.6 | 21.3 | 26.7 |
| (197) 4.4 | (201) 4.7 | (230) 5.8 | | (43) 6.2 | (70) 3.3 | (25) 4.9 | (44) 5.8 | (29) 7.9 | (19) 14.8 |
| .0 | .2 | 1.7 | | 2.2 | .7 | 1.4 | .8 | 3.1 | 7.4 |
| 6.0 | 6.6 | 7.5 | % Profit Before Taxes/Total Assets | 11.4 | 5.8 | 8.6 | 6.9 | 8.7 | 8.9 |
| 2.1 | 2.1 | 2.6 | | 3.0 | 2.0 | 2.3 | 1.8 | 2.9 | 4.0 |
| .0 | .0 | .5 | | .5 | -.2 | .3 | .2 | 1.7 | 2.3 |
| 3.1 | 5.6 | 4.1 | Sales/Net Fixed Assets | 3.0 | .8 | 7.1 | 12.7 | 7.5 | 10.3 |
| .3 | .5 | .3 | | .4 | .3 | .4 | .5 | .4 | .4 |
| .2 | .2 | .2 | | .2 | .2 | .2 | .2 | .2 | .3 |
| 1.0 | 1.7 | 1.0 | Sales/Total Assets | .8 | .5 | .8 | 1.6 | 2.2 | 1.9 |
| .3 | .3 | .3 | | .2 | .2 | .3 | .3 | .3 | .3 |
| .2 | .2 | .2 | | .1 | .1 | .2 | .2 | .2 | .2 |
| 8.2 | 5.3 | 6.4 | % Depr., Dep., Amort./Sales | 7.0 | 9.2 | 3.1 | 4.1 | 4.6 | 2.0 |
| (197) 14.1 | (204) 12.3 | (222) 14.3 | | (31) 12.9 | (70) 17.8 | 12.4 | (43) 14.9 | (29) 12.9 | (18) 10.8 |
| 21.4 | 20.2 | 21.6 | | 22.4 | 27.8 | 17.9 | 21.1 | 19.2 | 14.9 |
| 2.7 | 1.7 | 2.1 | % Officers', Directors' Owners' Comp/Sales | | 1.0 | | | | |
| (28) 7.5 | (29) 6.7 | (37) 4.8 | | | (12) 5.2 | | | | |
| 10.1 | 12.0 | 8.4 | | | 8.3 | | | | |
| 2132768M | 2657332M | 2749655M | Net Sales ($) | 22961M | 139083M | 120836M | 345689M | 481139M | 1639947M |
| 6318440M | 6318167M | 6961501M | Total Assets ($) | 113356M | 763729M | 462162M | 1301328M | 1827173M | 2493753M |

M = $ thousand    MM = $ million
See Pages 9 through 22 for Explanation of Ratios and Data

# CONSTRUCTION—GENERAL INDUSTRIES FORMAT*

CONSTRUCTION—GENERAL INDUSTRIES FORMAT*

## Current Data Sorted by Assets        Comparative Historical Data

| | | | | | | Type of Statement | | |
|---|---|---|---|---|---|---|---|---|
| 1 | 4 | 15 | 27 | 13 | 6 | Unqualified | 108 | 101 |
| 8 | 24 | 81 | 48 | 11 | | Reviewed | 196 | 179 |
| 17 | 53 | 62 | 19 | 2 | | Compiled | 352 | 279 |
| 169 | 255 | 194 | 16 | 1 | 4 | Tax Returns | 1050 | 969 |
| 54 | 155 | 247 | 92 | 17 | 9 | Other | 1061 | 897 |
| | 124 (4/1-9/30/11) | | 1,480 (10/1/11-3/31/12) | | | | 4/1/07-3/31/08 ALL | 4/1/08-3/31/09 ALL |
| 0-500M | 500M-2MM | 2-10MM | 10-50MM | 50-100MM | 100-250MM | NUMBER OF STATEMENTS | 2767 | 2425 |
| % | % | % | % | % | % | ASSETS | % | % |
| 21.8 | 11.1 | 9.8 | 7.9 | 7.7 | 8.3 | Cash & Equivalents | 9.1 | 9.0 |
| 12.4 | 12.3 | 11.5 | 6.3 | 6.1 | 8.2 | Trade Receivables (net) | 6.6 | 7.7 |
| 21.2 | 41.9 | 49.7 | 62.2 | 60.9 | 40.7 | Inventory | 58.3 | 55.6 |
| 6.1 | 3.9 | 5.3 | 3.5 | 2.7 | 2.3 | All Other Current | 5.9 | 4.3 |
| 61.5 | 69.2 | 76.4 | 79.9 | 77.3 | 59.5 | Total Current | 80.0 | 76.6 |
| 24.0 | 17.6 | 14.2 | 10.8 | 6.9 | 29.5 | Fixed Assets (net) | 12.2 | 14.0 |
| 3.1 | 1.1 | .8 | .2 | 1.9 | 1.8 | Intangibles (net) | .8 | .7 |
| 11.3 | 12.0 | 8.7 | 9.1 | 13.9 | 9.2 | All Other Non-Current | 7.1 | 8.7 |
| 100.0 | 100.0 | 100.0 | 100.0 | 100.0 | 100.0 | Total | 100.0 | 100.0 |
| | | | | | | LIABILITIES | | |
| 29.0 | 26.8 | 28.3 | 32.1 | 27.5 | 22.0 | Notes Payable-Short Term | 40.0 | 37.3 |
| 2.7 | 3.7 | 2.7 | 3.7 | 4.1 | 3.4 | Cur. Mat.-L.T.D. | 5.6 | 5.4 |
| 9.6 | 9.9 | 10.9 | 9.3 | 8.5 | 5.9 | Trade Payables | 7.6 | 7.4 |
| .1 | .1 | .1 | .1 | .0 | .0 | Income Taxes Payable | .2 | .1 |
| 23.8 | 13.3 | 13.5 | 13.7 | 10.9 | 7.2 | All Other Current | 12.3 | 12.7 |
| 65.2 | 53.8 | 55.5 | 58.9 | 51.0 | 38.5 | Total Current | 65.6 | 63.0 |
| 21.0 | 16.7 | 13.4 | 13.1 | 13.6 | 13.8 | Long-Term Debt | 13.9 | 15.7 |
| .0 | .1 | .0 | .0 | .0 | .4 | Deferred Taxes | .0 | .0 |
| 13.4 | 5.9 | 4.0 | 2.8 | 2.0 | 1.6 | All Other Non-Current | 3.6 | 3.3 |
| .3 | 23.6 | 27.0 | 25.0 | 33.4 | 45.7 | Net Worth | 16.8 | 18.0 |
| 100.0 | 100.0 | 100.0 | 100.0 | 100.0 | 100.0 | Total Liabilities & Net Worth | 100.0 | 100.0 |
| | | | | | | INCOME DATA | | |
| 100.0 | 100.0 | 100.0 | 100.0 | 100.0 | 100.0 | Net Sales | 100.0 | 100.0 |
| 25.6 | 20.1 | 17.3 | 15.6 | 16.7 | 23.2 | Gross Profit | 17.7 | 17.9 |
| 22.7 | 17.2 | 13.9 | 12.8 | 14.6 | 18.5 | Operating Expenses | 13.8 | 15.9 |
| 2.9 | 2.9 | 3.4 | 2.8 | 2.1 | 4.6 | Operating Profit | 3.9 | 2.0 |
| .7 | 1.5 | 1.6 | 1.9 | 1.0 | 1.3 | All Other Expenses (net) | 1.7 | 2.0 |
| 2.2 | 1.5 | 1.8 | .9 | 1.1 | 3.3 | Profit Before Taxes | 2.2 | .0 |
| | | | | | | RATIOS | | |
| 2.9 | 2.7 | 2.2 | 1.8 | 2.1 | 3.0 | | 1.7 | 1.8 |
| 1.1 | 1.3 | 1.3 | 1.3 | 1.4 | 1.6 | Current | 1.2 | 1.2 |
| .4 | .9 | 1.0 | 1.1 | 1.1 | 1.1 | | 1.0 | 1.0 |
| 1.8 | 1.2 | .9 | .5 | .5 | 1.2 | | .5 | .6 |
| .4 | (490) .3 | (596) .2 | (200) .1 | .1 | .2 | Quick | (2750) .1 | (2414) .1 |
| .1 | .1 | .0 | .0 | .1 | .1 | | .0 | .0 |
| 0 UND | 0 UND | 0 UND | 0 UND | 0 UND | 0 UND | | 0 UND | 0 UND |
| 0 UND | 0 UND | 0 999.8 | 0 999.8 | 2 200.7 | 1 376.7 | Sales/Receivables | 0 UND | 0 UND |
| 10 35.0 | 20 18.3 | 28 13.0 | 10 35.7 | 12 29.7 | 15 23.7 | | 5 69.6 | 9 40.2 |
| 0 UND | 0 UND | 0 999.8 | 126 2.9 | 114 3.2 | 0 UND | | 3 117.1 | 3 145.5 |
| 0 UND | 85 4.3 | 174 2.1 | 243 1.5 | 261 1.4 | 192 1.9 | Cost of Sales/Inventory | 211 1.7 | 206 1.8 |
| 51 7.2 | 243 1.5 | 406 .9 | 521 .7 | 521 .7 | 521 .7 | | 426 .9 | 488 .7 |
| 0 UND | 0 UND | 1 682.5 | 10 36.8 | 9 41.0 | 4 86.3 | | 0 UND | 0 UND |
| 0 UND | 7 53.1 | 15 24.6 | 19 19.5 | 17 21.4 | 24 15.5 | Cost of Sales/Payables | 8 46.2 | 7 50.9 |
| 13 29.1 | 26 14.0 | 36 10.2 | 37 9.8 | 30 12.0 | 40 9.2 | | 24 15.2 | 24 15.2 |
| 10.8 | 3.4 | 2.8 | 2.6 | 2.2 | 2.2 | | 4.2 | 3.6 |
| 123.7 | 12.9 | 8.7 | 7.2 | 4.9 | 4.5 | Sales/Working Capital | 12.7 | 12.0 |
| -19.6 | -25.3 | 72.9 | 29.5 | 31.9 | 78.3 | | -563.9 | -54.1 |
| 14.9 | 9.5 | 10.6 | 7.5 | 9.5 | 9.9 | | 9.7 | 7.5 |
| (162) 3.1 | (363) 2.3 | (462) 3.2 | (159) 2.5 | (36) 2.3 | (17) 3.6 | EBIT/Interest | (2020) 2.4 | (1791) 1.8 |
| -.5 | -.5 | .7 | .4 | .9 | 1.4 | | .6 | -.5 |
| | 8.3 | 12.6 | 3.0 | | | Net Profit + Depr., Dep., | 5.3 | 8.4 |
| | (13) 2.3 | (30) 2.2 | (14) .8 | | | Amort./Cur. Mat. L/T/D | (111) 1.7 | (126) 2.0 |
| | -2.7 | .1 | -1.7 | | | | .0 | .0 |
| .0 | .0 | .0 | .0 | .0 | .1 | | .0 | .0 |
| .9 | .2 | .1 | .1 | .1 | .3 | Fixed/Worth | .2 | .2 |
| -3.3 | 2.5 | 1.1 | .7 | .4 | 1.0 | | 1.6 | 2.3 |
| 1.2 | 1.1 | 1.3 | 1.5 | 1.0 | .3 | | 2.3 | 1.9 |
| 8.9 | 3.3 | 3.4 | 3.0 | 1.7 | 1.9 | Debt/Worth | 6.1 | 5.3 |
| -4.4 | 30.5 | 11.4 | 6.8 | 5.3 | 3.2 | | 29.0 | 33.0 |
| 114.9 | 57.1 | 42.0 | 31.6 | 26.4 | 16.9 | | 59.7 | 41.5 |
| (155) 45.0 | (400) 17.0 | (518) 13.0 | (180) 10.4 | (42) 8.5 | (18) 8.9 | % Profit Before Taxes/Tangible Net Worth | (2324) 21.2 | (1962) 10.1 |
| .0 | -1.9 | .6 | -.9 | 2.2 | .2 | | .9 | -7.7 |
| 34.2 | 11.8 | 8.7 | 7.2 | 9.1 | 6.0 | | 9.3 | 7.5 |
| 10.8 | 3.5 | 2.6 | 2.2 | 3.0 | 2.6 | % Profit Before Taxes/Total Assets | 2.8 | 1.2 |
| -3.2 | -2.4 | -.3 | -.9 | .3 | .2 | | -.8 | -2.8 |
| UND | 675.5 | 620.3 | 325.9 | 196.5 | 97.1 | | 515.9 | 412.6 |
| 76.0 | 42.0 | 59.7 | 68.0 | 55.8 | 8.9 | Sales/Net Fixed Assets | 72.2 | 56.7 |
| 11.9 | 7.9 | 9.8 | 9.5 | 17.3 | 2.3 | | 16.7 | 10.5 |
| 9.7 | 3.0 | 2.3 | 1.9 | 1.8 | 1.9 | | 2.4 | 2.3 |
| 4.9 | 1.8 | 1.3 | 1.2 | 1.2 | 1.1 | Sales/Total Assets | 1.3 | 1.2 |
| 2.1 | .9 | .6 | .5 | .7 | .6 | | .7 | .6 |
| .4 | .3 | .2 | .2 | .2 | .3 | | .2 | .3 |
| (116) 1.0 | (270) .8 | (316) .5 | (120) .3 | (29) .3 | (11) .8 | % Depr., Dep., Amort./Sales | (1498) .5 | (1364) .6 |
| 2.6 | 1.9 | 1.5 | .9 | .9 | 3.5 | | 1.1 | 1.3 |
| 2.5 | 2.1 | 1.1 | .6 | | | | 1.3 | 1.3 |
| (133) 5.5 | (227) 3.5 | (219) 2.2 | (46) 1.3 | | | % Officers', Directors' Owners' Comp/Sales | (1210) 2.7 | (1021) 2.8 |
| 8.0 | 5.6 | 4.6 | 2.2 | | | | 5.2 | 5.4 |
| 326197M | 1198759M | 4350558M | 5812157M | 4171671M | 3969293M | Net Sales ($) | 54946332M | 32153669M |
| 56668M | 552713M | 2728335M | 4488961M | 2980862M | 3152833M | Total Assets ($) | 38704255M | 26028273M |

M = $ thousand    MM = $ million
See Pages 9 through 22 for Explanation of Ratios and Data

## Comparative Historical Data     Current Data Sorted by Sales

| Type of Statement | | | | | | | | | |
|---|---:|---:|---:|---:|---:|---:|---:|---:|---:|
| Unqualified | 78 | 67 | 66 | | 5 | 3 | 8 | 13 | 37 |
| Reviewed | 192 | 149 | 172 | 10 | 16 | 17 | 34 | 56 | 39 |
| Compiled | 233 | 179 | 153 | 17 | 48 | 30 | 32 | 20 | 6 |
| Tax Returns | 904 | 698 | 639 | 206 | 243 | 87 | 60 | 34 | 9 |
| Other | 734 | 717 | 574 | 96 | 149 | 70 | 107 | 86 | 66 |
| | 4/1/09-3/31/10 ALL | 4/1/10-3/31/11 ALL | 4/1/11-3/31/12 ALL | 124 (4/1-9/30/11) | | | 1,480 (10/1/11-3/31/12) | | |
| | | | | 0-1MM | 1-3MM | 3-5MM | 5-10MM | 10-25MM | 25MM & OVER |
| NUMBER OF STATEMENTS | 2141 | 1810 | 1604 | 329 | 461 | 207 | 241 | 209 | 157 |
| **ASSETS** | % | % | % | % | % | % | % | % | % |
| Cash & Equivalents | 10.4 | 10.9 | 11.7 | 11.5 | 12.4 | 11.4 | 11.2 | 12.2 | 11.0 |
| Trade Receivables (net) | 9.5 | 9.4 | 11.1 | 6.0 | 8.5 | 11.8 | 15.4 | 16.4 | 14.8 |
| Inventory | 50.4 | 48.6 | 44.7 | 42.1 | 42.8 | 46.8 | 46.0 | 44.6 | 51.1 |
| All Other Current | 4.3 | 4.7 | 4.7 | 4.3 | 4.5 | 4.7 | 4.7 | 5.8 | 4.3 |
| Total Current | 74.6 | 73.6 | 72.2 | 63.8 | 68.1 | 74.7 | 77.3 | 79.0 | 81.2 |
| Fixed Assets (net) | 15.6 | 15.5 | 16.3 | 24.8 | 19.0 | 13.0 | 11.7 | 10.3 | 10.1 |
| Intangibles (net) | .8 | .8 | 1.2 | 1.2 | 1.3 | 1.6 | 1.1 | 1.1 | 1.0 |
| All Other Non-Current | 9.0 | 10.1 | 10.3 | 10.1 | 11.6 | 10.7 | 10.0 | 9.6 | 7.7 |
| Total | 100.0 | 100.0 | 100.0 | 100.0 | 100.0 | 100.0 | 100.0 | 100.0 | 100.0 |
| **LIABILITIES** | | | | | | | | | |
| Notes Payable-Short Term | 34.5 | 32.2 | 28.3 | 27.2 | 29.7 | 30.4 | 26.3 | 27.8 | 27.7 |
| Cur. Mat.-L.T.D. | 4.8 | 3.3 | 3.2 | 2.4 | 3.7 | 4.1 | 2.6 | 3.1 | 3.1 |
| Trade Payables | 8.1 | 8.7 | 10.1 | 4.6 | 7.5 | 11.2 | 13.0 | 14.7 | 17.0 |
| Income Taxes Payable | .1 | .1 | .1 | .0 | .1 | .2 | .2 | .2 | .0 |
| All Other Current | 14.1 | 15.4 | 14.9 | 18.8 | 16.0 | 12.3 | 12.3 | 12.9 | 13.8 |
| Total Current | 61.6 | 59.7 | 56.6 | 53.0 | 56.9 | 58.2 | 54.3 | 58.7 | 61.7 |
| Long-Term Debt | 15.1 | 14.8 | 15.6 | 22.3 | 17.9 | 12.9 | 13.7 | 9.6 | 9.0 |
| Deferred Taxes | .1 | .1 | .1 | .0 | .0 | .0 | .1 | .2 | .2 |
| All Other Non-Current | 5.3 | 4.8 | 5.8 | 10.7 | 5.8 | 7.1 | 3.5 | 2.7 | 1.8 |
| Net Worth | 18.0 | 20.5 | 21.9 | 14.0 | 19.4 | 21.7 | 28.3 | 28.9 | 27.3 |
| Total Liabilities & Net Worth | 100.0 | 100.0 | 100.0 | 100.0 | 100.0 | 100.0 | 100.0 | 100.0 | 100.0 |
| **INCOME DATA** | | | | | | | | | |
| Net Sales | 100.0 | 100.0 | 100.0 | 100.0 | 100.0 | 100.0 | 100.0 | 100.0 | 100.0 |
| Gross Profit | 18.1 | 18.9 | 19.3 | 25.7 | 20.0 | 17.2 | 17.2 | 14.8 | 15.9 |
| Operating Expenses | 17.5 | 15.8 | 16.2 | 22.7 | 17.4 | 13.5 | 13.8 | 12.1 | 11.7 |
| Operating Profit | .6 | 3.1 | 3.1 | 2.9 | 2.5 | 3.7 | 3.4 | 2.6 | 4.3 |
| All Other Expenses (net) | 2.0 | 1.8 | 1.4 | 3.5 | 1.2 | .7 | .7 | .7 | .7 |
| Profit Before Taxes | -1.4 | 1.4 | 1.7 | -.5 | 1.3 | 2.9 | 2.7 | 2.0 | 3.6 |
| **RATIOS** | | | | | | | | | |
| Current | 2.1 | 2.2 | 2.3 | 4.0 | 2.5 | 2.3 | 2.2 | 2.0 | 1.7 |
| | 1.2 | 1.3 | 1.3 | 1.3 | 1.2 | 1.3 | 1.4 | 1.3 | 1.3 |
| | 1.0 | .9 | .9 | .7 | .8 | 1.0 | 1.1 | 1.1 | 1.1 |
| Quick | .8 | .8 | 1.0 | .9 | .9 | 1.0 | 1.1 | 1.2 | .9 |
| | (2138) .1 | (1803) .2 | (1598) .2 | (328) .2 | .2 | (206) .2 | (238) .3 | .3 | (156) .2 |
| | .0 | .0 | .1 | .0 | .0 | .0 | .1 | .1 | .1 |
| Sales/Receivables | 0 UND | 0 UND | 0 UND | 0 UND | 0 UND | 0 UND | 0 UND | 0 UND | 0 UND |
| | 0 999.8 | 0 UND | 0 999.8 | 0 UND | 0 UND | 0 999.8 | 2 165.0 | 3 123.2 | 2 233.5 |
| | 17 21.7 | 15 23.6 | 20 18.3 | 7 54.1 | 12 30.1 | 20 18.7 | 34 10.8 | 33 11.0 | 29 12.7 |
| Cost of Sales/Inventory | 0 UND | 0 UND | 0 UND | 0 UND | 0 UND | 0 UND | 0 UND | 0 UND | 1 725.3 |
| | 165 2.2 | 140 2.6 | 122 3.0 | 130 2.8 | 111 3.3 | 101 3.6 | 126 2.9 | 104 3.5 | 135 2.7 |
| | 441 .8 | 368 1.0 | 304 1.2 | 730 .5 | 365 1.0 | 243 1.5 | 261 1.4 | 228 1.6 | 261 1.4 |
| Cost of Sales/Payables | 0 UND | 0 UND | 0 UND | 0 UND | 0 UND | 0 UND | 5 78.8 | 9 39.0 | 11 33.0 |
| | 9 40.5 | 9 39.2 | 11 32.4 | 0 UND | 5 70.6 | 10 34.9 | 17 21.7 | 18 19.8 | 22 16.6 |
| | 27 13.3 | 27 13.7 | 30 12.0 | 17 21.2 | 25 14.6 | 31 11.9 | 33 10.9 | 36 10.2 | 41 8.8 |
| Sales/Working Capital | 3.2 | 3.5 | 3.4 | 1.4 | 3.1 | 3.9 | 3.8 | 5.0 | 4.5 |
| | 11.5 | 11.4 | 11.4 | 12.7 | 14.5 | 12.6 | 8.6 | 11.7 | 10.8 |
| | -45.5 | -55.0 | -64.6 | -10.4 | -20.4 | -101.0 | 31.2 | 39.2 | 59.4 |
| EBIT/Interest | 6.5 | 9.9 | 10.0 | 4.3 | 7.5 | 16.0 | 10.7 | 19.0 | 14.2 |
| | (1602) 1.5 | (1324) 2.3 | (1199) 2.8 | (209) 1.2 | (351) 1.6 | (163) 4.6 | (179) 3.3 | (168) 4.5 | (129) 4.4 |
| | -1.7 | -.2 | .3 | -.9 | -.8 | 1.6 | 1.2 | 1.0 | 1.8 |
| Net Profit + Depr., Dep., Amort./Cur. Mat. L/T/D | 5.2 | 8.7 | 6.1 | | 3.5 | 25.5 | 7.3 | 4.2 | 13.8 |
| | (76) 1.1 | (68) 1.8 | (62) 2.3 | (10) 1.1 | (10) 1.9 | (12) 2.0 | (16) .1 | (13) 3.0 | |
| | -.1 | .3 | -.1 | | -1.4 | .2 | .3 | -3.6 | 1.7 |
| Fixed/Worth | .0 | .0 | .0 | .0 | .0 | .0 | .0 | .0 | .0 |
| | .2 | .2 | .2 | .3 | .3 | .3 | .1 | .1 | .1 |
| | 3.0 | 2.3 | 1.8 | 7.7 | 4.6 | 2.0 | .8 | .6 | .5 |
| Debt/Worth | 1.5 | 1.3 | 1.2 | 1.1 | 1.2 | 1.3 | 1.2 | 1.1 | 1.4 |
| | 4.5 | 3.9 | 3.4 | 4.5 | 4.0 | 4.4 | 3.0 | 2.7 | 2.4 |
| | 42.3 | 24.4 | 19.3 | -687.9 | UND | 23.1 | 9.3 | 5.9 | 5.2 |
| % Profit Before Taxes/Tangible Net Worth | 34.1 | 46.6 | 49.6 | 41.2 | 50.8 | 54.9 | 48.9 | 50.2 | 46.1 |
| | (1698) 7.5 | (1473) 13.7 | (1313) 14.4 | (246) 4.8 | (346) 8.5 | (170) 18.8 | (219) 16.2 | (191) 20.2 | (141) 18.8 |
| | -10.0 | -1.9 | -.2 | -7.6 | -4.5 | 4.0 | 1.2 | 1.9 | 6.5 |
| % Profit Before Taxes/Total Assets | 7.5 | 10.4 | 11.6 | 7.7 | 11.7 | 14.1 | 12.1 | 12.5 | 13.3 |
| | 1.0 | 2.6 | 3.2 | .6 | 1.9 | 6.2 | 4.1 | 4.6 | 4.8 |
| | -4.2 | -1.9 | -1.0 | -4.5 | -2.8 | .9 | .2 | .2 | 2.0 |
| Sales/Net Fixed Assets | 316.6 | 407.2 | 574.0 | UND | 540.5 | 538.6 | 666.1 | 463.5 | 329.0 |
| | 49.0 | 54.8 | 55.3 | 24.1 | 42.3 | 58.8 | 56.2 | 104.8 | 90.6 |
| | 7.6 | 9.0 | 9.2 | 2.5 | 6.6 | 14.5 | 14.1 | 15.8 | 21.5 |
| Sales/Total Assets | 2.7 | 2.9 | 3.0 | 2.2 | 2.8 | 3.6 | 3.0 | 3.1 | 3.1 |
| | 1.3 | 1.5 | 1.6 | .8 | 1.5 | 1.8 | 1.8 | 2.2 | 1.8 |
| | .6 | .7 | .7 | .3 | .7 | 1.1 | 1.1 | 1.3 | 1.3 |
| % Depr., Dep., Amort./Sales | .3 | .2 | .2 | .8 | .3 | .1 | .2 | .2 | .1 |
| | (1229) .7 | (956) .6 | (862) .6 | (151) 1.9 | (247) .7 | (113) .5 | (130) .5 | (126) .3 | (95) .3 |
| | 1.7 | 1.7 | 1.7 | 4.3 | 1.7 | 1.4 | 1.1 | .8 | .6 |
| % Officers', Directors' Owners' Comp/Sales | 1.4 | 1.4 | 1.5 | 3.2 | 2.2 | 1.5 | 1.4 | .8 | .5 |
| | (914) 2.8 | (726) 2.9 | (631) 3.1 | (108) 6.5 | (217) 3.8 | (97) 2.7 | (101) 2.4 | (81) 1.4 | (27) 1.0 |
| | 5.3 | 5.8 | 5.6 | 13.6 | 6.4 | 5.0 | 3.9 | 2.3 | 1.5 |
| Net Sales ($) | 27531598M | 25547164M | 19828635M | 168973M | 851921M | 808485M | 1678130M | 3309053M | 13012073M |
| Total Assets ($) | 20723665M | 16747518M | 13960372M | 385419M | 1019810M | 717740M | 1449256M | 2563324M | 7824823M |

M = $ thousand     MM = $ million
See Pages 9 through 22 for Explanation of Ratios and Data

## Current Data Sorted by Assets     Comparative Historical Data

| 0-500M | 500M-2MM | 2-10MM | 10-50MM | 50-100MM | 100-250MM | Type of Statement | 4/1/07-3/31/08 ALL | 4/1/08-3/31/09 ALL |
|---|---|---|---|---|---|---|---|---|
| | | 8 | 9 | 4 | 5 | Unqualified | 28 | 19 |
| 4 | 5 | 17 | 6 | | 1 | Reviewed | 45 | 30 |
| 2 | 3 | 2 | 2 | | | Compiled | 30 | 17 |
| 5 | 12 | 11 | 2 | | | Tax Returns | 64 | 47 |
| 5 | | 17 | 12 | 5 | 1 | Other | 90 | 78 |
| | 20 (4/1-9/30/11) | | 126 (10/1/11-3/31/12) | | | | | |
| 16 | 28 | 55 | 31 | 9 | 7 | **NUMBER OF STATEMENTS** | 257 | 191 |
| % | % | % | % | % | % | **ASSETS** | % | % |
| 24.1 | 15.7 | 15.8 | 17.9 | | | Cash & Equivalents | 13.8 | 14.3 |
| 22.6 | 31.3 | 33.4 | 32.7 | | | Trade Receivables (net) | 22.5 | 22.4 |
| 19.8 | 17.5 | 20.4 | 16.3 | | | Inventory | 28.0 | 26.4 |
| 4.5 | 12.7 | 7.3 | 12.7 | | | All Other Current | 7.9 | 7.2 |
| 71.1 | 77.1 | 76.9 | 79.7 | | | Total Current | 72.1 | 70.3 |
| 19.6 | 9.0 | 8.5 | 4.3 | | | Fixed Assets (net) | 17.2 | 18.3 |
| .0 | 1.7 | 3.3 | 3.8 | | | Intangibles (net) | 1.3 | 1.8 |
| 9.3 | 12.2 | 11.3 | 12.2 | | | All Other Non-Current | 9.5 | 9.6 |
| 100.0 | 100.0 | 100.0 | 100.0 | | | Total | 100.0 | 100.0 |
| | | | | | | **LIABILITIES** | | |
| 30.7 | 20.8 | 13.0 | 8.0 | | | Notes Payable-Short Term | 20.2 | 20.0 |
| 6.6 | 1.6 | 2.6 | 1.8 | | | Cur. Mat.-L.T.D. | 6.8 | 2.5 |
| 10.4 | 14.4 | 26.5 | 27.7 | | | Trade Payables | 16.7 | 18.4 |
| .1 | .1 | .3 | .0 | | | Income Taxes Payable | .6 | .2 |
| 4.2 | 11.3 | 11.8 | 14.1 | | | All Other Current | 13.4 | 14.7 |
| 52.0 | 48.3 | 54.1 | 51.6 | | | Total Current | 57.6 | 55.8 |
| 6.0 | 5.6 | 7.1 | 6.7 | | | Long-Term Debt | 14.8 | 16.8 |
| .0 | .0 | .4 | .1 | | | Deferred Taxes | .1 | .1 |
| 5.0 | 5.9 | 3.0 | 2.3 | | | All Other Non-Current | 2.6 | 3.4 |
| 37.1 | 40.2 | 35.5 | 39.2 | | | Net Worth | 24.9 | 23.9 |
| 100.0 | 100.0 | 100.0 | 100.0 | | | Total Liabilities & Net Worth | 100.0 | 100.0 |
| | | | | | | **INCOME DATA** | | |
| 100.0 | 100.0 | 100.0 | 100.0 | | | Net Sales | 100.0 | 100.0 |
| 27.9 | 20.7 | 12.4 | 14.2 | | | Gross Profit | 18.9 | 20.6 |
| 18.8 | 20.0 | 11.8 | 10.3 | | | Operating Expenses | 14.6 | 17.2 |
| 9.1 | .8 | .7 | 3.9 | | | Operating Profit | 4.3 | 3.4 |
| .4 | -.6 | .7 | .4 | | | All Other Expenses (net) | .5 | 1.3 |
| 8.7 | 1.3 | .0 | 3.5 | | | Profit Before Taxes | 3.8 | 2.1 |
| | | | | | | **RATIOS** | | |
| 2.7 / 1.5 / .8 | 3.5 / 1.5 / 1.0 | 2.5 / 1.4 / 1.1 | 1.9 / 1.5 / 1.2 | | | Current | 2.0 / 1.3 / 1.0 | 1.9 / 1.3 / 1.0 |
| 1.5 / (15) 1.2 / .4 | 2.0 / 1.0 / .2 | 1.7 / 1.1 / .2 | 1.4 / 1.1 / .6 | | | Quick | 1.3 / .8 / .1 | 1.2 / .7 / .1 |
| 0 UND / 0 UND / 57 6.4 | 0 UND / 34 10.8 / 68 5.4 | 0 UND / 43 8.5 / 64 5.7 | 17 21.4 / 39 9.4 / 81 4.5 | | | Sales/Receivables | 0 UND / 16 23.5 / 55 6.6 | 0 UND / 19 18.9 / 49 7.5 |
| 0 UND / 0 UND / 53 6.9 | 0 UND / 0 UND / 27 13.5 | 0 UND / 0 UND / 43 8.5 | 0 UND / 0 UND / 4 93.6 | | | Cost of Sales/Inventory | 0 UND / 0 999.8 / 228 1.6 | 0 UND / 0 UND / 308 1.2 |
| 0 UND / 0 761.4 / 9 40.0 | 0 UND / 22 16.7 / 41 9.0 | 19 19.2 / 37 9.9 / 65 5.6 | 32 11.5 / 49 7.5 / 68 5.4 | | | Cost of Sales/Payables | 2 185.6 / 17 21.9 / 40 9.2 | 2 154.7 / 24 15.0 / 48 7.6 |
| 8.0 / 25.1 / -109.4 | 3.7 / 10.7 / 404.9 | 5.5 / 11.8 / 323.1 | 3.0 / 9.7 / 21.4 | | | Sales/Working Capital | 5.7 / 18.9 / -144.9 | 5.6 / 16.0 / -999.8 |
| 51.0 / (10) 7.2 / 3.4 | 19.5 / (22) 2.6 / -1.7 | 58.0 / (43) 9.0 / -.9 | 142.9 / (18) 6.0 / -.6 | | | EBIT/Interest | 15.2 / (184) 3.4 / .8 | 31.1 / (134) 5.6 / .0 |
| | | | | | | Net Profit + Depr., Dep., Amort./Cur. Mat. L/T/D | 22.1 / (20) 4.1 / .7 | 14.8 / (16) 5.0 / .6 |
| .0 / .4 / 1.4 | .0 / .2 / .6 | .0 / .1 / .4 | .0 / .1 / .2 | | | Fixed/Worth | .1 / .3 / 2.0 | .0 / .2 / 1.1 |
| 1.0 / 1.5 / 2.7 | .5 / 2.1 / 4.9 | .9 / 1.8 / 5.8 | .9 / 1.9 / 3.5 | | | Debt/Worth | 1.2 / 3.4 / 14.4 | 1.4 / 3.4 / 11.5 |
| 147.9 / (14) 56.3 / 8.0 | 50.3 / (26) 14.5 / -6.5 | 49.5 / (50) 20.7 / 3.8 | 39.8 / (30) 22.6 / -.1 | | | % Profit Before Taxes/Tangible Net Worth | 68.0 / (220) 26.5 / 1.7 | 51.7 / (171) 22.7 / -2.3 |
| 88.1 / 19.7 / 5.3 | 17.6 / 4.6 / -2.2 | 13.8 / 3.7 / -.4 | 16.9 / 5.2 / .2 | | | % Profit Before Taxes/Total Assets | 16.9 / 5.1 / -.1 | 12.8 / 4.0 / -1.7 |
| 196.1 / 88.3 / 15.2 | 191.7 / 37.4 / 11.0 | 999.8 / 81.1 / 35.8 | 310.6 / 115.7 / 43.4 | | | Sales/Net Fixed Assets | 258.3 / 52.6 / 8.2 | 395.1 / 52.5 / 5.5 |
| 8.7 / 4.0 / 3.2 | 4.1 / 2.8 / 1.5 | 3.4 / 2.5 / 1.4 | 3.3 / 2.3 / .6 | | | Sales/Total Assets | 3.7 / 2.0 / .9 | 3.7 / 1.8 / .6 |
| | (17) .3 / .4 / 1.6 | (36) .2 / .4 / .7 | (25) .1 / .2 / 1.1 | | | % Depr., Dep., Amort./Sales | .2 / (164) .5 / 1.2 | .2 / (117) .6 / 1.7 |
| | (14) 2.3 / 4.9 / 8.0 | (13) .4 / 2.2 / 3.5 | | | | % Officers', Directors' Owners' Comp/Sales | 1.3 / (92) 2.5 / 4.8 | 1.1 / (64) 2.5 / 7.6 |
| 22833M | 88152M | 775292M | 1574617M | 1590088M | 829339M | Net Sales ($) | 6650354M | 4877904M |
| 3950M | 31949M | 296907M | 729873M | 679387M | 1047484M | Total Assets ($) | 3995736M | 2899208M |

M = $ thousand    MM = $ million
See Pages 9 through 22 for Explanation of Ratios and Data

## Comparative Historical Data

## Current Data Sorted by Sales

| | | | Type of Statement | | | | | 3 | 23 |
|---|---|---|---|---|---|---|---|---|---|
| 33 | 27 | 26 | Unqualified | 2 | 5 | 2 | 4 | 13 | 7 |
| 33 | 21 | 33 | Reviewed | | 1 | | | | 2 |
| 13 | 9 | 9 | Compiled | 2 | 1 | 2 | 2 | | 1 |
| 45 | 25 | 30 | Tax Returns | 11 | 9 | 3 | 3 | 3 | 1 |
| 64 | 44 | 48 | Other | 1 | 8 | 6 | 10 | 10 | 13 |
| 4/1/09-3/31/10 ALL | 4/1/10-3/31/11 ALL | 4/1/11-3/31/12 ALL | | 0-1MM | 20 (4/1-9/30/11) 1-3MM | 3-5MM | 5-10MM | 126 (10/1/11-3/31/12) 10-25MM | 25MM & OVER |
| 188 | 126 | 146 | NUMBER OF STATEMENTS | 16 | 23 | 13 | 19 | 29 | 46 |
| % | % | % | ASSETS | % | % | % | % | % | % |
| 17.8 | 15.6 | 17.5 | Cash & Equivalents | 9.7 | 13.5 | 21.4 | 19.5 | 16.0 | 21.2 |
| 25.5 | 26.9 | 30.8 | Trade Receivables (net) | 16.4 | 26.4 | 16.9 | 28.3 | 40.1 | 37.1 |
| 22.6 | 19.7 | 18.6 | Inventory | 40.1 | 29.0 | 18.6 | 27.0 | 12.5 | 6.3 |
| 9.0 | 9.4 | 8.9 | All Other Current | 2.5 | 4.5 | 15.0 | 13.4 | 7.1 | 10.9 |
| 75.0 | 71.5 | 75.8 | Total Current | 68.7 | 73.3 | 71.9 | 88.2 | 75.7 | 75.5 |
| 13.3 | 16.8 | 9.8 | Fixed Assets (net) | 21.7 | 15.0 | 6.0 | 6.4 | 4.8 | 8.7 |
| 1.1 | 2.8 | 2.4 | Intangibles (net) | .0 | .0 | 3.6 | .1 | 5.9 | 3.0 |
| 10.6 | 8.9 | 11.9 | All Other Non-Current | 9.5 | 11.7 | 18.6 | 5.3 | 13.7 | 12.7 |
| 100.0 | 100.0 | 100.0 | Total | 100.0 | 100.0 | 100.0 | 100.0 | 100.0 | 100.0 |
| | | | LIABILITIES | | | | | | |
| 17.6 | 14.7 | 14.7 | Notes Payable-Short Term | 30.3 | 27.2 | 21.7 | 19.3 | 7.0 | 4.0 |
| 2.6 | 1.2 | 2.5 | Cur. Mat.-L.T.D. | 4.3 | 3.3 | 1.0 | 3.4 | 3.7 | .9 |
| 20.1 | 18.9 | 22.4 | Trade Payables | 4.9 | 13.0 | 14.8 | 20.7 | 29.3 | 31.8 |
| .3 | .1 | .2 | Income Taxes Payable | .1 | .1 | .0 | .4 | .3 | .1 |
| 14.1 | 15.7 | 11.7 | All Other Current | 1.5 | 4.8 | 14.9 | 9.8 | 13.2 | 17.6 |
| 54.8 | 50.6 | 51.5 | Total Current | 41.1 | 48.4 | 52.4 | 53.6 | 53.5 | 54.3 |
| 11.0 | 12.4 | 7.7 | Long-Term Debt | 19.5 | 5.7 | 17.0 | 3.4 | 3.4 | 6.5 |
| .2 | .0 | .2 | Deferred Taxes | .0 | .0 | .0 | .5 | .3 | .1 |
| 3.8 | 2.5 | 3.8 | All Other Non-Current | 8.1 | 4.9 | .6 | .7 | 4.4 | 3.4 |
| 30.3 | 34.4 | 36.9 | Net Worth | 31.5 | 41.0 | 30.0 | 41.8 | 38.4 | 35.7 |
| 100.0 | 100.0 | 100.0 | Total Liabilties & Net Worth | 100.0 | 100.0 | 100.0 | 100.0 | 100.0 | 100.0 |
| | | | INCOME DATA | | | | | | |
| 100.0 | 100.0 | 100.0 | Net Sales | 100.0 | 100.0 | 100.0 | 100.0 | 100.0 | 100.0 |
| 19.6 | 17.9 | 16.8 | Gross Profit | 24.6 | 16.3 | 21.9 | 15.4 | 16.6 | 13.6 |
| 15.9 | 16.3 | 13.9 | Operating Expenses | 25.6 | 16.2 | 21.0 | 9.8 | 12.4 | 9.4 |
| 3.7 | 1.6 | 2.9 | Operating Profit | -1.1 | .2 | 1.0 | 5.6 | 4.2 | 4.2 |
| 1.1 | 2.0 | .5 | All Other Expenses (net) | 1.5 | .3 | .3 | .8 | .0 | .6 |
| 2.6 | -.4 | 2.3 | Profit Before Taxes | -2.6 | -.1 | .7 | 4.8 | 4.2 | 3.6 |
| | | | RATIOS | | | | | | |
| 2.2 | 2.1 | 2.1 | | 9.6 | 3.1 | 5.4 | 2.7 | 2.5 | 1.7 |
| 1.4 | 1.3 | 1.4 | Current | 1.9 | 1.4 | 1.3 | 1.6 | 1.5 | 1.3 |
| 1.1 | 1.1 | 1.1 | | 1.1 | .9 | .8 | 1.3 | 1.2 | 1.1 |
| 1.4 | 1.5 | 1.6 | | 1.9 | 1.8 | 2.0 | 1.8 | 1.9 | 1.4 |
| (186) 1.0 | 1.0 (145) 1.1 | | Quick | (15) .5 | .9 | .9 | 1.0 | 1.4 | 1.1 |
| .2 | .2 | .4 | | .1 | .2 | .1 | .1 | .8 | .8 |
| 0 930.5 | 0 UND | 0 UND | | 0 UND | 0 UND | 0 UND | 0 UND | 15 24.5 | 27 13.5 |
| 33 11.1 | 33 11.0 | 40 9.1 | Sales/Receivables | 0 UND | 5 79.5 | 29 12.7 | 24 15.0 | 46 8.0 | 47 7.8 |
| 62 5.9 | 63 5.8 | 68 5.4 | | 30 12.2 | 69 5.3 | 62 5.9 | 55 6.6 | 99 3.7 | 73 5.0 |
| 0 UND | 0 UND | 0 UND | | 0 UND | 0 UND | 0 UND | 0 UND | 0 UND | 0 UND |
| 0 UND | 0 UND | 0 UND | Cost of Sales/Inventory | 78 4.7 | 0 UND | 0 UND | 0 UND | 0 UND | 0 UND |
| 161 2.3 | 53 6.8 | 21 17.4 | | 608 .6 | 215 1.7 | 46 7.9 | 152 2.4 | 0 UND | 0 UND |
| 8 45.3 | 7 50.6 | 11 34.7 | | 0 UND | 0 UND | 0 UND | 7 51.0 | 26 13.8 | 28 13.1 |
| 31 11.8 | 25 14.4 | 37 9.9 | Cost of Sales/Payables | 0 UND | 8 45.0 | 24 15.2 | 28 13.0 | 50 7.3 | 51 7.2 |
| 58 6.3 | 57 6.5 | 64 5.7 | | 11 33.0 | 39 9.3 | 44 8.3 | 59 6.2 | 76 4.8 | 69 5.3 |
| 5.0 | 5.0 | 5.2 | | 1.9 | 3.7 | 2.5 | 5.5 | 5.0 | 8.0 |
| 12.1 | 12.1 | 11.8 | Sales/Working Capital | 6.0 | 10.5 | 40.1 | 9.7 | 8.0 | 14.9 |
| 71.1 | 50.1 | 41.5 | | 34.0 | -303.3 | -35.9 | 18.4 | 20.5 | 48.6 |
| 27.6 | 36.1 | 42.7 | | 8.3 | 18.4 | 25.7 | 29.6 | 84.8 | 192.6 |
| (135) 3.9 | (86) 4.0 (106) 5.7 | | EBIT/Interest | (11) -.9 | (17) 2.3 | (12) 2.6 | (14) 6.8 | (23) 22.9 | (29) 22.4 |
| .2 | -.8 | .2 | | -5.1 | -1.8 | -3.4 | -.3 | 2.5 | 1.5 |
| 32.6 | 28.5 | 17.5 | | | | | | | |
| (21) 5.7 | (14) .9 | (13) 4.2 | Net Profit + Depr., Dep., Amort./Cur. Mat. L/T/D | | | | | | |
| 2.4 | -2.3 | 1.4 | | | | | | | |
| .0 | .0 | .0 | | .0 | .0 | .0 | .0 | .0 | .0 |
| .1 | .1 | .1 | Fixed/Worth | .4 | .2 | .1 | .1 | .1 | .1 |
| .8 | 1.1 | .6 | | 1.8 | .7 | .6 | .3 | .3 | .4 |
| 1.0 | 1.0 | .9 | | 1.0 | .5 | 1.2 | .6 | .7 | 1.1 |
| 2.1 | 2.3 | 1.9 | Debt/Worth | 2.0 | 1.3 | 3.5 | 1.6 | 1.3 | 2.1 |
| 9.4 | 4.4 | 3.9 | | 12.0 | 3.0 | NM | 3.4 | 5.7 | 3.8 |
| 38.8 | 46.8 | 49.3 | % Profit Before Taxes/Tangible Net Worth | 64.8 | 50.0 | 66.7 | 54.8 | 46.4 | 42.5 |
| (162) 14.8 | (112) 10.0 (135) 21.7 | | | (14) 12.2 | (21) 4.4 | (10) -1.6 | 36.6 | (27) 22.3 | (44) 25.1 |
| 1.8 | -6.0 | 1.6 | | -21.3 | -4.7 | -13.7 | .7 | 6.1 | 8.8 |
| 10.2 | 11.8 | 17.0 | % Profit Before Taxes/Total Assets | 27.2 | 13.0 | 23.6 | 22.2 | 13.2 | 15.2 |
| 3.8 | 2.0 | 5.4 | | 5.3 | 1.4 | 2.3 | 14.7 | 5.3 | 6.1 |
| -.4 | -3.6 | .2 | | -6.3 | -5.7 | -4.8 | .4 | .4 | 1.5 |
| 305.9 | 289.8 | 299.3 | | 164.8 | 999.8 | UND | 999.8 | 229.6 | 353.6 |
| 60.2 | 64.8 | 73.7 | Sales/Net Fixed Assets | 27.4 | 32.6 | 109.2 | 77.9 | 83.6 | 79.6 |
| 13.4 | 9.0 | 19.5 | | 4.9 | 10.2 | 12.6 | 23.3 | 44.7 | 38.0 |
| 3.4 | 3.7 | 3.7 | | 3.7 | 3.7 | 4.3 | 4.0 | 3.3 | 3.7 |
| 2.0 | 2.3 | 2.6 | Sales/Total Assets | 1.5 | 1.7 | 3.0 | 2.9 | 2.3 | 3.0 |
| .9 | .4 | 1.4 | | .3 | .9 | 1.3 | 2.3 | 1.6 | 1.8 |
| .2 | .3 | .2 | | .5 | .4 | | .3 | .2 | .1 |
| (111) .6 | (77) .5 (99) .4 | | % Depr., Dep., Amort./Sales | (11) 2.8 | (12) .8 | | (12) .4 | (20) .3 | (38) .3 |
| 1.4 | 1.8 | 1.2 | | 5.3 | 1.5 | | .8 | .6 | .9 |
| 1.3 | 1.1 | 1.7 | % Officers', Directors' Owners' Comp/Sales | | | | | | |
| (60) 2.7 | (30) 2.0 (42) 2.6 | | | | | | | | |
| 6.0 | 5.0 | 5.0 | | | | | | | |
| 6868698M | 3145290M | 4880321M | Net Sales ($) | 9510M | 45087M | 53072M | 124800M | 519015M | 4128837M |
| 2499353M | 1903792M | 2789550M | Total Assets ($) | 16475M | 46314M | 49311M | 82421M | 316299M | 2278730M |

© RMA 2012

M = $ thousand    MM = $ million
See Pages 9 through 22 for Explanation of Ratios and Data

## Current Data Sorted by Assets            Comparative Historical Data

| 0-500M | 500M-2MM | 2-10MM | 10-50MM | 50-100MM | 100-250MM | Type of Statement | 4/1/07-3/31/08 ALL | 4/1/08-3/31/09 ALL |
|---|---|---|---|---|---|---|---|---|
| 1 | 3 | 5 | 12 | 4 | 2 | Unqualified | 29 | 25 |
| 3 | 7 | 11 | 22 | 2 | 1 | Reviewed | 36 | 38 |
| 10 | 18 | 21 | 7 | 5 |  | Compiled | 49 | 26 |
| 7 | 33 | 42 | 35 |  | 6 | Tax Returns | 126 | 97 |
|  |  | 24 | 5 | 1 |  | Other | 144 | 133 |
|  | 12 (4/1-9/30/11) |  | 275 (10/1/11-3/31/12) |  |  |  |  |  |
| 21 | 61 | 103 | 81 | 12 | 9 | **NUMBER OF STATEMENTS** | 384 | 319 |
| % | % | % | % | % | % | **ASSETS** | % | % |
| 25.2 | 10.4 | 7.0 | 9.5 | 9.0 |  | Cash & Equivalents | 6.9 | 9.5 |
| 2.2 | 7.3 | 5.2 | 7.0 | 12.5 |  | Trade Receivables (net) | 7.3 | 6.3 |
| 44.2 | 53.3 | 55.3 | 58.8 | 57.5 |  | Inventory | 61.3 | 57.4 |
| 7.1 | 5.8 | 3.8 | 3.7 | 2.0 |  | All Other Current | 4.6 | 3.7 |
| 78.8 | 76.8 | 71.3 | 79.0 | 81.1 |  | Total Current | 80.2 | 76.9 |
| 14.4 | 18.1 | 17.8 | 10.0 | 14.3 |  | Fixed Assets (net) | 12.2 | 14.6 |
| .0 | 1.4 | .7 | .8 | .4 |  | Intangibles (net) | .6 | .3 |
| 6.8 | 3.8 | 10.2 | 10.2 | 4.2 |  | All Other Non-Current | 7.0 | 8.2 |
| 100.0 | 100.0 | 100.0 | 100.0 | 100.0 |  | Total | 100.0 | 100.0 |
|  |  |  |  |  |  | **LIABILITIES** |  |  |
| 53.5 | 32.4 | 29.2 | 29.2 | 20.0 |  | Notes Payable-Short Term | 42.4 | 39.3 |
| 1.6 | 1.8 | 3.3 | 4.3 | 1.7 |  | Cur. Mat.-L.T.D. | 3.6 | 4.1 |
| 3.4 | 8.2 | 7.5 | 8.7 | 10.1 |  | Trade Payables | 6.8 | 6.4 |
| .0 | .0 | .1 | .1 | .0 |  | Income Taxes Payable | .1 | .0 |
| 15.4 | 23.8 | 13.8 | 8.9 | 7.3 |  | All Other Current | 9.8 | 10.8 |
| 74.0 | 66.1 | 53.8 | 51.3 | 39.2 |  | Total Current | 62.8 | 60.7 |
| 11.4 | 9.5 | 16.5 | 10.7 | 22.3 |  | Long-Term Debt | 12.6 | 13.2 |
| .0 | .0 | .1 | .0 | .0 |  | Deferred Taxes | .0 | .1 |
| 6.7 | 6.6 | 7.1 | 5.8 | 3.3 |  | All Other Non-Current | 4.3 | 4.9 |
| 8.0 | 17.7 | 22.5 | 32.2 | 35.2 |  | Net Worth | 20.2 | 21.1 |
| 100.0 | 100.0 | 100.0 | 100.0 | 100.0 |  | Total Liabilities & Net Worth | 100.0 | 100.0 |
|  |  |  |  |  |  | **INCOME DATA** |  |  |
| 100.0 | 100.0 | 100.0 | 100.0 | 100.0 |  | Net Sales | 100.0 | 100.0 |
| 18.9 | 16.4 | 18.4 | 18.5 | 23.5 |  | Gross Profit | 18.9 | 16.8 |
| 16.3 | 16.5 | 15.1 | 15.0 | 14.7 |  | Operating Expenses | 13.4 | 15.3 |
| 2.6 | -.1 | 3.2 | 3.6 | 8.8 |  | Operating Profit | 5.5 | 1.4 |
| .5 | .4 | 2.5 | .6 | 2.6 |  | All Other Expenses (net) | 1.7 | 2.3 |
| 2.1 | -.5 | .7 | 3.0 | 6.2 |  | Profit Before Taxes | 3.7 | -.8 |
|  |  |  |  |  |  | **RATIOS** |  |  |
| 2.4 | 2.1 | 2.3 | 2.3 | 5.1 |  | Current | 1.7 | 1.9 |
| 1.2 | 1.2 | 1.4 | 1.4 | 2.0 |  |  | 1.2 | 1.2 |
| .7 | .9 | 1.0 | 1.1 | 1.4 |  |  | 1.0 | 1.0 |
| .8 | .5 | .6 | .7 | 1.5 |  | Quick | .4 | .5 |
| .1 | .2 | .1 | .2 | .2 |  |  | .1 (316) | .1 |
| .0 | .0 | .0 | .1 | .1 |  |  | .0 | .0 |
| 0 UND | 0 UND | 0 UND | 0 UND | 0 UND |  | Sales/Receivables | 0 UND | 0 UND |
| 0 UND | 0 UND | 0 999.8 | 1 573.3 | 9 39.3 |  |  | 0 999.8 | 0 999.8 |
| 0 UND | 17 22.1 | 15 23.7 | 11 34.6 | 46 7.9 |  |  | 10 36.2 | 8 47.5 |
| 0 UND | 0 UND | 40 9.1 | 101 3.6 | 7 53.3 |  | Cost of Sales/Inventory | 33 11.1 | 2 176.5 |
| 29 12.8 | 114 3.2 | 215 1.7 | 228 1.6 | 261 1.4 |  |  | 235 1.6 | 245 1.5 |
| 215 1.7 | 365 1.0 | 608 .6 | 365 1.0 | 521 .7 |  |  | 466 .8 | 525 .7 |
| 0 UND | 0 UND | 2 231.6 | 12 31.0 | 9 40.9 |  | Cost of Sales/Payables | 0 996.0 | 1 350.2 |
| 0 999.8 | 4 91.5 | 13 28.8 | 22 16.6 | 24 15.3 |  |  | 10 37.4 | 9 39.7 |
| 3 120.3 | 17 21.4 | 34 10.8 | 36 10.1 | 47 7.7 |  |  | 27 13.5 | 26 14.0 |
| 7.0 | 3.9 | 2.1 | 2.3 | 1.4 |  | Sales/Working Capital | 3.6 | 2.5 |
| 35.2 | 15.1 | 6.5 | 5.4 | 3.3 |  |  | 9.7 | 8.8 |
| -25.3 | -23.2 | 999.8 | 20.3 | 10.6 |  |  | 71.1 | 440.2 |
| 20.0 | 13.7 | 7.9 | 10.3 | 12.2 |  | EBIT/Interest | 11.2 | 5.1 |
| (14) 7.2 | (41) 3.9 | (77) 2.9 | (68) 3.7 | (11) 7.2 |  |  | (287) 2.8 | (235) 1.5 |
| .3 | -3.1 | .5 | .0 | 1.4 |  |  | .7 | -1.0 |
|  |  |  |  |  |  | Net Profit + Depr., Dep., Amort./Cur. Mat. L/T/D | 17.9 | 22.5 |
|  |  |  |  |  |  |  | (22) 3.1 / (12) 4.5 | |
|  |  |  |  |  |  |  | .0 | .4 |
| .0 | .0 | .0 | .0 | .0 |  | Fixed/Worth | .0 | .0 |
| .6 | .4 | .2 | .1 | .0 |  |  | .1 | .2 |
| -3.0 | 6.7 | 2.6 | .4 | .6 |  |  | 1.2 | 1.9 |
| .8 | 1.6 | 1.5 | 1.0 | 1.2 |  | Debt/Worth | 2.3 | 1.6 |
| 4.7 | 3.9 | 3.7 | 2.1 | 2.0 |  |  | 5.6 | 4.3 |
| -17.1 | -52.7 | 16.3 | 4.8 | 2.5 |  |  | 18.2 | 15.8 |
| 100.0 | 74.4 | 46.6 | 31.8 | 54.5 |  | % Profit Before Taxes/Tangible Net Worth | 52.4 | 30.0 |
| (15) 48.7 | (43) 20.3 | (88) 10.5 | (73) 12.9 | 22.5 |  |  | (332) 20.6 | (269) 7.6 |
| .0 | -18.3 | -3.7 | 1.6 | 2.2 |  |  | 2.4 | -6.5 |
| 35.5 | 16.9 | 7.0 | 8.2 | 12.5 |  | % Profit Before Taxes/Total Assets | 8.7 | 5.7 |
| 5.7 | 4.4 | 2.9 | 3.8 | 10.1 |  |  | 2.9 | 1.0 |
| -1.5 | -6.3 | -1.7 | -.2 | .9 |  |  | -.4 | -3.1 |
| UND | UND | 301.8 | 460.8 | 352.1 |  | Sales/Net Fixed Assets | 289.2 | 314.8 |
| 100.1 | 27.8 | 42.9 | 91.4 | 91.7 |  |  | 77.3 | 58.8 |
| 22.3 | 10.2 | 7.1 | 12.6 | 10.1 |  |  | 14.8 | 9.6 |
| 8.4 | 2.9 | 1.9 | 1.9 | 2.3 |  | Sales/Total Assets | 2.1 | 2.0 |
| 4.8 | 1.4 | 1.2 | 1.2 | 1.3 |  |  | 1.2 | 1.1 |
| 1.5 | .8 | .5 | .8 | .6 |  |  | .7 | .6 |
|  | .4 | .2 | .1 |  |  | % Depr., Dep., Amort./Sales | .2 | .2 |
|  | (27) .7 | (54) .6 | (52) .3 |  |  |  | (221) .5 | (172) .5 |
|  | 1.7 | 1.5 | .7 |  |  |  | 1.1 | 1.6 |
|  | 1.8 | .9 | .5 |  |  | % Officers', Directors' Owners' Comp/Sales | 1.1 | 1.1 |
|  | (25) 2.9 | (27) 1.9 | (14) .8 |  |  |  | (162) 2.1 | (103) 2.2 |
|  | 5.5 | 3.7 | 2.8 |  |  |  | 4.3 | 3.9 |
| 30528M | 153201M | 737503M | 2447992M | 1218169M | 1998853M | Net Sales ($) | 8061190M | 5965667M |
| 5238M | 73975M | 530999M | 1803783M | 861237M | 1316077M | Total Assets ($) | 6884569M | 5457664M |

M = $ thousand    MM = $ million
See Pages 9 through 22 for Explanation of Ratios and Data

## Comparative Historical Data | Current Data Sorted by Sales

| | Comparative Historical Data | | | Current Data Sorted by Sales | | | | | |
|---|---|---|---|---|---|---|---|---|---|
| **Type of Statement** | | | | | 12 (4/1-9/30/11) | | | 275 (10/1/11-3/31/12) | | |
| Unqualified | 26 | 25 | 23 | | 2 | 2 | 2 | 4 | 13 |
| Reviewed | 30 | 29 | 40 | | 3 | 1 | 8 | 14 | 14 |
| Compiled | 29 | 17 | 38 | 5 | 9 | 3 | 10 | 9 | 2 |
| Tax Returns | 96 | 72 | 58 | 15 | 22 | 5 | 5 | 8 | 3 |
| Other | 108 | 94 | 128 | 18 | 25 | 12 | 22 | 23 | 28 |
| | 4/1/09-3/31/10 ALL | 4/1/10-3/31/11 ALL | 4/1/11-3/31/12 ALL | 0-1MM | 1-3MM | 3-5MM | 5-10MM | 10-25MM | 25MM & OVER |
| **NUMBER OF STATEMENTS** | 289 | 237 | 287 | 38 | 61 | 23 | 47 | 58 | 60 |
| | % | % | % | % | % | % | % | % | % |
| **ASSETS** | | | | | | | | | |
| Cash & Equivalents | 8.4 | 11.2 | 9.9 | 11.9 | 9.9 | 7.5 | 7.2 | 10.3 | 11.6 |
| Trade Receivables (net) | 7.5 | 7.3 | 6.5 | 1.9 | 3.7 | 9.5 | 6.5 | 5.7 | 11.9 |
| Inventory | 52.4 | 48.4 | 54.5 | 55.9 | 56.6 | 49.3 | 52.6 | 56.5 | 53.2 |
| All Other Current | 4.3 | 5.0 | 4.4 | 4.8 | 3.3 | 5.8 | 4.6 | 4.4 | 4.6 |
| Total Current | 72.7 | 72.0 | 75.4 | 74.4 | 73.5 | 72.0 | 70.9 | 77.0 | 81.2 |
| Fixed Assets (net) | 15.8 | 17.9 | 15.0 | 19.6 | 20.2 | 12.5 | 16.2 | 12.4 | 9.5 |
| Intangibles (net) | 1.0 | .5 | .8 | 2.4 | .1 | .4 | 1.2 | .7 | .4 |
| All Other Non-Current | 10.4 | 9.6 | 8.8 | 3.6 | 6.1 | 15.1 | 11.7 | 9.9 | 8.9 |
| Total | 100.0 | 100.0 | 100.0 | 100.0 | 100.0 | 100.0 | 100.0 | 100.0 | 100.0 |
| **LIABILITIES** | | | | | | | | | |
| Notes Payable-Short Term | 33.2 | 26.5 | 30.6 | 40.1 | 37.1 | 30.5 | 23.5 | 29.1 | 25.1 |
| Cur. Mat.-L.T.D. | 3.8 | 1.9 | 3.3 | 2.5 | 2.6 | .9 | 5.1 | 4.1 | 3.1 |
| Trade Payables | 7.8 | 7.1 | 8.1 | 1.9 | 5.5 | 7.8 | 9.6 | 8.0 | 13.5 |
| Income Taxes Payable | .1 | .1 | .1 | .0 | .2 | .0 | .0 | .1 | .1 |
| All Other Current | 13.0 | 13.4 | 14.2 | 16.0 | 22.2 | 12.1 | 16.0 | 7.6 | 10.4 |
| Total Current | 57.9 | 49.0 | 56.2 | 60.5 | 67.6 | 51.3 | 54.3 | 48.9 | 52.2 |
| Long-Term Debt | 16.6 | 17.7 | 13.2 | 12.5 | 16.9 | 13.3 | 16.0 | 11.8 | 9.2 |
| Deferred Taxes | .1 | .1 | .0 | .1 | .0 | .0 | .1 | .1 | .0 |
| All Other Non-Current | 6.1 | 6.3 | 6.4 | 6.9 | 5.5 | 8.6 | 7.9 | 7.7 | 3.5 |
| Net Worth | 19.3 | 26.9 | 24.2 | 20.1 | 10.1 | 26.7 | 21.6 | 31.6 | 35.2 |
| Total Liabilities & Net Worth | 100.0 | 100.0 | 100.0 | 100.0 | 100.0 | 100.0 | 100.0 | 100.0 | 100.0 |
| **INCOME DATA** | | | | | | | | | |
| Net Sales | 100.0 | 100.0 | 100.0 | 100.0 | 100.0 | 100.0 | 100.0 | 100.0 | 100.0 |
| Gross Profit | 15.6 | 19.4 | 18.2 | 18.8 | 20.5 | 20.0 | 17.0 | 17.7 | 16.2 |
| Operating Expenses | 15.8 | 17.1 | 15.5 | 17.5 | 20.3 | 16.4 | 15.2 | 13.1 | 11.3 |
| Operating Profit | -.2 | 2.2 | 2.7 | 1.3 | .1 | 3.6 | 1.9 | 4.6 | 4.9 |
| All Other Expenses (net) | 2.3 | 2.5 | 1.4 | 3.6 | 1.5 | 1.0 | .9 | .7 | .9 |
| Profit Before Taxes | -2.5 | -.2 | 1.4 | -2.3 | -1.4 | 2.5 | .9 | 3.9 | 4.0 |
| **RATIOS** | | | | | | | | | |
| Current | 2.0 | 2.7 | 2.3 | 3.5 | 2.1 | 2.3 | 2.4 | 2.3 | 2.1 |
| | 1.3 | 1.4 | 1.3 | 1.4 | 1.2 | 1.3 | 1.3 | 1.5 | 1.4 |
| | .9 | 1.0 | 1.1 | .6 | .7 | 1.2 | .9 | 1.1 | 1.2 |
| Quick | .7 | .9 | .6 | .3 | .5 | .6 | .8 | .9 | 1.0 |
| | (286) .1 | (235) .2 | .2 | .1 | .1 | .2 | .1 | .2 | .2 |
| | .0 | .0 | .0 | .0 | .0 | .0 | .0 | .1 | .1 |
| Sales/Receivables | 0 UND | 0 UND | 0 UND | 0 UND | 0 UND | 0 UND | 0 UND | 0 UND | 0 UND |
| | 0 999.8 | 0 920.7 | 0 999.8 | 0 UND | 0 UND | 1 346.9 | 1 301.2 | 0 999.8 | 1 293.9 |
| | 12 30.5 | 17 20.9 | 14 25.3 | 12 31.4 | 5 69.8 | 16 22.6 | 15 24.2 | 12 29.3 | 19 19.0 |
| Cost of Sales/Inventory | 4 99.2 | 1 407.2 | 21 17.0 | 0 UND | 34 10.8 | 23 15.6 | 33 10.9 | 19 19.6 | 0 767.4 |
| | 209 1.7 | 200 1.8 | 192 1.9 | 365 1.0 | 281 1.3 | 140 2.6 | 166 2.2 | 182 2.0 | 182 2.0 |
| | 494 .7 | 453 .8 | 456 .8 | 912 .4 | 608 .6 | 365 1.0 | 456 .8 | 304 1.2 | 281 1.3 |
| Cost of Sales/Payables | 0 999.8 | 0 UND | 1 306.4 | 0 UND | 0 UND | 6 65.5 | 4 98.9 | 9 39.2 | 10 38.3 |
| | 10 37.3 | 11 32.6 | 15 24.8 | 0 UND | 9 38.7 | 10 36.9 | 19 19.7 | 17 21.2 | 21 17.2 |
| | 29 12.7 | 33 10.9 | 30 12.1 | 8 45.0 | 27 13.4 | 32 11.5 | 35 10.3 | 36 10.1 | 35 10.5 |
| Sales/Working Capital | 2.3 | 2.1 | 2.4 | 1.0 | 1.8 | 4.3 | 2.5 | 2.8 | 3.1 |
| | 9.4 | 5.9 | 7.3 | 5.4 | 20.8 | 7.7 | 9.4 | 5.7 | 6.7 |
| | -40.9 | NM | 77.6 | -5.2 | -17.7 | 23.7 | -133.9 | 21.8 | 20.2 |
| EBIT/Interest | 5.1 | 9.3 | 12.3 | 6.3 | 10.0 | 14.0 | 11.9 | 8.6 | 17.4 |
| | (221) .8 | (181) 2.4 | (218) 3.7 | (22) .7 | (43) 2.0 | (18) 5.0 | (37) 2.9 | (48) 4.4 | (50) 5.6 |
| | -1.8 | -.2 | .3 | -2.4 | -.3 | 1.9 | -2.3 | .6 | 2.5 |
| Net Profit + Depr., Dep., Amort./Cur. Mat. L/T/D | 5.6 | 7.1 | | | | | | | |
| | (16) 1.2 | (10) 1.9 | | | | | | | |
| | -.1 | .0 | | | | | | | |
| Fixed/Worth | .0 | .0 | .0 | .0 | .0 | .0 | .0 | .0 | .0 |
| | .2 | .1 | .1 | .1 | .6 | .3 | .2 | .1 | .1 |
| | 2.8 | 1.6 | 1.7 | 4.6 | NM | 1.7 | 1.1 | .7 | .3 |
| Debt/Worth | 1.4 | 1.0 | 1.3 | 1.5 | 2.0 | 1.1 | 1.5 | 1.0 | 1.2 |
| | 3.9 | 2.4 | 3.0 | 3.2 | 11.8 | 2.5 | 3.6 | 1.9 | 2.1 |
| | 83.4 | 11.0 | 12.4 | 32.9 | -17.4 | -999.8 | 21.1 | 6.5 | 3.9 |
| % Profit Before Taxes/Tangible Net Worth | 28.0 | 31.7 | 44.4 | 23.5 | 50.9 | 32.6 | 71.0 | 47.2 | 38.0 |
| | (226) 5.3 | (204) 8.4 | (240) 14.6 | (31) .0 | (41) 6.6 | (17) 15.6 | (41) 16.5 | (51) 13.8 | (59) 18.6 |
| | -12.5 | -5.1 | .0 | -18.3 | -16.3 | 4.4 | -6.9 | 2.5 | 6.7 |
| % Profit Before Taxes/Total Assets | 5.4 | 8.6 | 9.8 | 5.0 | 8.8 | 9.6 | 7.1 | 10.8 | 13.5 |
| | .3 | 2.3 | 3.7 | -.4 | 1.9 | 6.2 | 3.3 | 4.2 | 5.9 |
| | -5.0 | -2.3 | -1.5 | -6.1 | -4.3 | 1.5 | -2.4 | .0 | 2.5 |
| Sales/Net Fixed Assets | 220.3 | 625.0 | 403.5 | UND | 346.0 | 204.1 | 293.8 | 523.6 | 290.7 |
| | 47.3 | 45.1 | 65.0 | 25.9 | 42.6 | 48.3 | 46.0 | 121.1 | 97.6 |
| | 6.2 | 6.7 | 11.2 | 5.0 | 7.2 | 12.9 | 10.2 | 11.7 | 26.9 |
| Sales/Total Assets | 2.2 | 2.2 | 2.3 | 1.3 | 2.2 | 2.5 | 3.0 | 2.1 | 2.7 |
| | 1.0 | 1.2 | 1.3 | .7 | .9 | 1.7 | 1.4 | 1.4 | 1.8 |
| | .5 | .5 | .7 | .4 | .4 | .8 | .7 | .9 | 1.2 |
| % Depr., Dep., Amort./Sales | .3 | .2 | .2 | .4 | .4 | .2 | .2 | .1 | .1 |
| | (167) .7 | (124) .6 | (154) .5 | (12) 1.2 | (29) .7 | (12) 1.0 | (25) .7 | (36) .2 | (40) .3 |
| | 1.5 | 1.9 | 1.2 | 3.5 | 1.8 | 1.6 | 1.3 | 1.1 | .5 |
| % Officers', Directors' Owners' Comp/Sales | .9 | 1.3 | .9 | 3.1 | 1.4 | | .9 | .7 | |
| | (92) 2.4 | (75) 2.3 | (76) 2.6 | (13) 7.0 | (19) 2.8 | | (14) 1.7 | (14) 1.4 | |
| | 5.1 | 5.0 | 4.6 | 10.1 | 7.1 | | 3.3 | 3.7 | |
| Net Sales ($) | 6700173M | 5007047M | 6586246M | 23298M | 108933M | 87529M | 333403M | 909149M | 5123934M |
| Total Assets ($) | 5848096M | 4025699M | 4591309M | 60684M | 175546M | 77625M | 336471M | 950343M | 2990640M |

© RMA 2012

M = $ thousand     MM = $ million
See Pages 9 through 22 for Explanation of Ratios and Data

## Current Data Sorted by Assets | Comparative Historical Data

| 0-500M | 500M-2MM | 2-10MM | 10-50MM | 50-100MM | 100-250MM | Type of Statement | 4/1/07-3/31/08 ALL | 4/1/08-3/31/09 ALL |
|---|---|---|---|---|---|---|---|---|
| | 1 | 3 | 4 | 1 | 1 | Unqualified | | |
| 2 | 5 | 9 | 1 | | | Reviewed | 10 | 18 |
| 2 | 11 | 9 | 1 | | | Compiled | 9 | 17 |
| 33 | 17 | 9 | | | 1 | Tax Returns | 39 | 48 |
| 17 | 21 | 11 | 8 | | | Other | 28 | 32 |
| | 14 (4/1-9/30/11) | | 153 (10/1/11-3/31/12) | | | | | |
| **54** | **55** | **41** | **14** | **1** | **2** | **NUMBER OF STATEMENTS** | **86** | **117** |
| % | % | % | % | % | % | **ASSETS** | % | % |
| 18.5 | 17.9 | 13.5 | 16.2 | | | Cash & Equivalents | 15.7 | 14.9 |
| 19.2 | 35.9 | 40.2 | 36.0 | | | Trade Receivables (net) | 26.5 | 28.5 |
| 6.3 | 6.3 | 10.8 | 8.2 | | | Inventory | 14.6 | 10.7 |
| 9.0 | 7.2 | 8.7 | 5.4 | | | All Other Current | 10.1 | 6.8 |
| 53.0 | 67.3 | 73.2 | 65.8 | | | Total Current | 66.8 | 60.9 |
| 31.7 | 17.5 | 18.8 | 9.3 | | | Fixed Assets (net) | 21.6 | 26.4 |
| 4.5 | 4.9 | 3.5 | 13.4 | | | Intangibles (net) | 3.4 | 2.6 |
| 10.8 | 10.3 | 4.4 | 11.5 | | | All Other Non-Current | 8.3 | 10.1 |
| 100.0 | 100.0 | 100.0 | 100.0 | | | Total | 100.0 | 100.0 |
| | | | | | | **LIABILITIES** | | |
| 34.4 | 13.6 | 11.7 | 8.5 | | | Notes Payable-Short Term | 17.4 | 19.5 |
| 11.7 | 3.0 | 4.5 | 1.1 | | | Cur. Mat.-L.T.D. | 6.1 | 4.4 |
| 17.1 | 15.4 | 19.8 | 17.1 | | | Trade Payables | 16.1 | 24.8 |
| .2 | .1 | .0 | .3 | | | Income Taxes Payable | .4 | .3 |
| 36.2 | 13.7 | 16.5 | 21.6 | | | All Other Current | 16.4 | 20.3 |
| 99.5 | 45.7 | 52.6 | 48.5 | | | Total Current | 56.4 | 69.3 |
| 22.9 | 14.2 | 13.3 | 6.8 | | | Long-Term Debt | 18.7 | 23.7 |
| .1 | .0 | .0 | .2 | | | Deferred Taxes | .1 | .1 |
| 18.9 | 4.3 | 2.6 | 8.9 | | | All Other Non-Current | 7.0 | 7.2 |
| -41.2 | 35.8 | 31.4 | 35.5 | | | Net Worth | 17.9 | -.2 |
| 100.0 | 100.0 | 100.0 | 100.0 | | | Total Liabilties & Net Worth | 100.0 | 100.0 |
| | | | | | | **INCOME DATA** | | |
| 100.0 | 100.0 | 100.0 | 100.0 | | | Net Sales | 100.0 | 100.0 |
| 35.6 | 35.4 | 29.1 | 27.8 | | | Gross Profit | 28.8 | 29.5 |
| 31.5 | 30.8 | 24.2 | 23.5 | | | Operating Expenses | 23.7 | 25.5 |
| 4.2 | 4.7 | 4.9 | 4.3 | | | Operating Profit | 5.0 | 4.0 |
| .6 | .8 | .8 | .4 | | | All Other Expenses (net) | 1.1 | 1.2 |
| 3.6 | 3.8 | 4.1 | 3.9 | | | Profit Before Taxes | 3.9 | 2.8 |
| | | | | | | **RATIOS** | | |
| 1.6 | 2.5 | 1.9 | 2.0 | | | | 2.2 | 2.0 |
| .7 | 1.3 | 1.3 | 1.2 | | | Current | 1.3 | 1.2 |
| .3 | .9 | 1.0 | 1.1 | | | | .9 | .8 |
| .9 | 2.2 | 1.6 | 1.4 | | | | 1.6 | 1.8 |
| .5 | (54) 1.0 | 1.0 | 1.0 | | | Quick | .9 | .9 |
| .2 | .7 | .5 | .7 | | | | .4 | .3 |
| 0 UND | 5 77.5 | 28 13.1 | 25 14.7 | | | | 0 UND | 0 UND |
| 6 57.6 | 35 10.4 | 46 7.9 | 52 7.0 | | | Sales/Receivables | 17 21.4 | 19 19.4 |
| 25 14.6 | 54 6.7 | 74 4.9 | 73 5.0 | | | | 46 7.9 | 47 7.7 |
| 0 UND | 0 UND | 0 UND | 0 UND | | | | 0 UND | 0 UND |
| 0 UND | 0 UND | 0 UND | 1 387.3 | | | Cost of Sales/Inventory | 0 UND | 0 UND |
| 4 103.3 | 3 110.3 | 6 59.7 | 26 13.8 | | | | 18 20.7 | 9 38.6 |
| 0 UND | 4 89.3 | 14 25.9 | 18 20.2 | | | | 0 UND | 1 365.8 |
| 7 53.9 | 19 19.3 | 26 13.9 | 33 11.0 | | | Cost of Sales/Payables | 16 23.0 | 15 25.0 |
| 25 14.4 | 38 9.5 | 54 6.8 | 45 8.1 | | | | 36 10.2 | 35 10.4 |
| 55.2 | 7.2 | 6.5 | 6.1 | | | | 8.3 | 9.4 |
| -30.1 | 24.5 | 15.7 | 28.0 | | | Sales/Working Capital | 27.1 | 30.4 |
| -8.1 | -92.1 | NM | 114.9 | | | | -47.5 | -40.4 |
| 20.7 | 27.3 | 25.9 | 39.0 | | | | 18.5 | 13.0 |
| (43) 3.2 | (47) 8.7 | (38) 8.9 | (11) 7.0 | | | EBIT/Interest | (69) 5.9 | (97) 4.4 |
| .6 | 1.5 | 2.5 | 1.1 | | | | 1.1 | 1.4 |
| | | | | | | Net Profit + Depr., Dep., Amort./Cur. Mat. L/T/D | 8.6 | 16.2 |
| | | | | | | | (10) 2.7 | (16) 2.7 |
| | | | | | | | .2 | .6 |
| .5 | .1 | .1 | .1 | | | | .2 | .1 |
| UND | .4 | .3 | .7 | | | Fixed/Worth | .5 | .8 |
| -.5 | 2.2 | 2.5 | NM | | | | 12.8 | UND |
| 2.5 | .9 | .7 | 1.0 | | | | .9 | 1.2 |
| UND | 2.4 | 2.4 | 3.7 | | | Debt/Worth | 3.8 | 3.4 |
| -2.4 | 19.4 | 9.0 | NM | | | | 60.7 | -37.9 |
| 211.8 | 77.0 | 73.7 | 95.7 | | | | 86.8 | 68.0 |
| (27) 68.4 | (48) 44.1 | (36) 31.5 | (11) 24.5 | | | % Profit Before Taxes/Tangible Net Worth | (67) 31.6 | (85) 29.5 |
| .0 | 7.7 | 7.2 | 2.5 | | | | 8.8 | 4.7 |
| 37.0 | 28.1 | 13.3 | 26.4 | | | | 26.6 | 22.6 |
| 9.0 | 12.6 | 7.0 | 9.5 | | | % Profit Before Taxes/Total Assets | 7.5 | 7.2 |
| -1.8 | 1.4 | 2.2 | 1.0 | | | | 1.3 | .8 |
| 95.8 | 122.5 | 65.0 | 64.6 | | | | 124.4 | 98.2 |
| 29.3 | 37.6 | 31.7 | 33.1 | | | Sales/Net Fixed Assets | 32.1 | 25.7 |
| 11.6 | 12.1 | 10.2 | 13.2 | | | | 10.9 | 8.0 |
| 9.3 | 5.7 | 3.8 | 3.0 | | | | 5.5 | 6.9 |
| 5.6 | 3.4 | 2.7 | 2.2 | | | Sales/Total Assets | 3.5 | 3.3 |
| 4.1 | 2.3 | 2.0 | 1.8 | | | | 1.5 | 2.0 |
| .8 | .4 | .4 | .3 | | | | .5 | .5 |
| (40) 1.3 | (38) .7 | (32) 1.1 | (12) .7 | | | % Depr., Dep., Amort./Sales | (58) 1.1 | (86) 1.1 |
| 3.0 | 2.0 | 2.2 | 1.5 | | | | 2.0 | 2.3 |
| 3.2 | 2.1 | 2.3 | | | | | 2.3 | 2.3 |
| (28) 5.5 | (34) 4.1 | (17) 3.8 | | | | % Officers', Directors', Owners' Comp/Sales | (52) 3.5 | (69) 3.9 |
| 9.5 | 6.0 | 5.8 | | | | | 9.0 | 6.2 |
| 78773M | 226921M | 510902M | 626407M | 80578M | 1410395M | Net Sales ($) | 871204M | 1885023M |
| 11610M | 56124M | 171484M | 244082M | 58769M | 409483M | Total Assets ($) | 426249M | 488971M |

M = $ thousand      MM = $ million
See Pages 9 through 22 for Explanation of Ratios and Data

## Comparative Historical Data        Current Data Sorted by Sales

| 4/1/09-3/31/10 ALL | 4/1/10-3/31/11 ALL | 4/1/11-3/31/12 ALL | Type of Statement | 0-1MM | 1-3MM | 3-5MM | 5-10MM | 10-25MM | 25MM & OVER |
|---|---|---|---|---|---|---|---|---|---|
| | | | Unqualified | | 1 | | 1 | 2 | 6 |
| 7 | 6 | 10 | Reviewed | 1 | 2 | 2 | 6 | 6 | |
| 13 | 8 | 17 | Compiled | 4 | 4 | 5 | 7 | 2 | 1 |
| 15 | 19 | 23 | Tax Returns | 15 | 21 | 10 | 8 | 5 | 1 |
| 34 | 48 | 60 | Other | 11 | 13 | 10 | 10 | 4 | 9 |
| 37 | 49 | 57 | | | 14 (4/1-9/30/11) | | 153 (10/1/11-3/31/12) | | |
| 106 | 130 | 167 | **NUMBER OF STATEMENTS** | 31 | 41 | 27 | 32 | 19 | 17 |
| % | % | % | **ASSETS** | % | % | % | % | % | % |
| 16.5 | 16.6 | 16.6 | Cash & Equivalents | 13.9 | 16.8 | 17.9 | 16.8 | 19.3 | 15.3 |
| 28.5 | 28.6 | 31.4 | Trade Receivables (net) | 23.4 | 18.2 | 39.6 | 38.9 | 41.8 | 39.2 |
| 9.5 | 8.4 | 8.1 | Inventory | 8.9 | 10.3 | 2.9 | 9.5 | 1.8 | 13.7 |
| 10.4 | 6.7 | 7.9 | All Other Current | 12.1 | 4.5 | 9.2 | 6.4 | 12.7 | 4.2 |
| 65.0 | 60.3 | 64.0 | Total Current | 58.3 | 49.9 | 69.7 | 71.6 | 75.6 | 72.3 |
| 21.4 | 23.4 | 21.5 | Fixed Assets (net) | 27.8 | 31.3 | 16.4 | 15.6 | 19.8 | 7.4 |
| 6.1 | 8.2 | 5.3 | Intangibles (net) | 7.0 | 3.8 | 4.0 | 5.0 | 1.2 | 12.7 |
| 7.5 | 8.1 | 9.2 | All Other Non-Current | 7.0 | 15.0 | 9.9 | 7.8 | 3.3 | 7.6 |
| 100.0 | 100.0 | 100.0 | Total | 100.0 | 100.0 | 100.0 | 100.0 | 100.0 | 100.0 |
| | | | **LIABILITIES** | | | | | | |
| 17.3 | 21.5 | 19.2 | Notes Payable-Short Term | 30.4 | 31.3 | 13.9 | 8.9 | 11.0 | 6.9 |
| 4.2 | 7.0 | 6.0 | Cur. Mat.-L.T.D. | 15.3 | 5.2 | 2.6 | 3.9 | 4.8 | 1.4 |
| 14.6 | 21.0 | 16.9 | Trade Payables | 18.7 | 14.1 | 14.9 | 15.9 | 22.9 | 19.0 |
| .2 | .2 | .1 | Income Taxes Payable | .0 | .3 | .1 | .1 | .2 | .1 |
| 21.4 | 15.2 | 22.4 | All Other Current | 34.8 | 13.2 | 17.2 | 29.8 | 18.4 | 20.6 |
| 57.7 | 64.8 | 64.7 | Total Current | 99.1 | 64.1 | 48.7 | 58.6 | 57.4 | 48.0 |
| 20.0 | 28.3 | 16.3 | Long-Term Debt | 22.2 | 23.3 | 12.1 | 11.4 | 12.3 | 9.5 |
| .1 | .2 | .1 | Deferred Taxes | .0 | .1 | .0 | .0 | .1 | .3 |
| 11.5 | 9.1 | 8.9 | All Other Non-Current | 25.0 | 9.0 | 3.8 | 4.2 | 2.2 | 3.6 |
| 10.7 | -2.5 | 10.1 | Net Worth | -46.1 | 3.5 | 35.4 | 25.8 | 28.1 | 38.6 |
| 100.0 | 100.0 | 100.0 | Total Liabilities & Net Worth | 100.0 | 100.0 | 100.0 | 100.0 | 100.0 | 100.0 |
| | | | **INCOME DATA** | | | | | | |
| 100.0 | 100.0 | 100.0 | Net Sales | 100.0 | 100.0 | 100.0 | 100.0 | 100.0 | 100.0 |
| 32.1 | 34.4 | 33.2 | Gross Profit | 42.5 | 35.2 | 30.2 | 29.7 | 26.1 | 30.8 |
| 29.4 | 29.7 | 28.7 | Operating Expenses | 35.7 | 31.4 | 25.8 | 25.9 | 24.2 | 24.7 |
| 2.7 | 4.8 | 4.5 | Operating Profit | 6.8 | 3.8 | 4.4 | 3.9 | 1.9 | 6.1 |
| .6 | 1.2 | .7 | All Other Expenses (net) | 2.2 | .9 | .2 | .2 | -.4 | .5 |
| 2.1 | 3.6 | 3.8 | Profit Before Taxes | 4.6 | 2.9 | 4.2 | 3.6 | 2.2 | 5.6 |
| | | | **RATIOS** | | | | | | |
| 2.6 | 2.2 | 1.9 | | 1.6 | 1.7 | 2.7 | 2.8 | 2.1 | 2.0 |
| 1.4 | 1.1 | 1.2 | Current | .9 | .9 | 1.4 | 1.4 | 1.1 | 1.2 |
| .8 | .6 | .7 | | .3 | .4 | .9 | 1.0 | .9 | 1.1 |
| 1.8 | 1.6 | 1.5 | | .9 | 1.2 | 2.5 | 2.1 | 1.8 | 1.4 |
| .9 | .9 (166) | .9 | Quick | .4 | .6 | 1.2 | (31) 1.2 | 1.0 | 1.0 |
| .4 | .3 | .4 | | .2 | .3 | .7 | .7 | .6 | .8 |
| 0 UND | 0 UND | 1 490.2 | | 0 UND | 0 UND | 13 28.6 | 7 51.9 | 30 12.3 | 17 21.4 |
| 25 14.7 | 22 16.4 | 28 13.0 | Sales/Receivables | 19 19.5 | 4 96.1 | 38 9.5 | 33 11.1 | 46 7.9 | 47 7.8 |
| 51 7.1 | 45 8.0 | 54 6.8 | | 29 12.6 | 25 14.8 | 62 5.9 | 68 5.4 | 65 5.6 | 78 4.7 |
| 0 UND | 0 UND | 0 UND | | 0 UND | 0 UND | 0 UND | 0 UND | 0 UND | 0 UND |
| 0 UND | 0 UND | 0 UND | Cost of Sales/Inventory | 0 UND | 0 UND | 0 UND | 0 UND | 0 UND | 1 364.6 |
| 9 40.8 | 3 116.1 | 5 80.9 | | 13 28.0 | 5 68.9 | 0 999.8 | 2 153.5 | 5 80.9 | 26 14.0 |
| 1 546.5 | 1 308.6 | 3 120.2 | | 0 UND | 0 UND | 4 103.8 | 6 62.5 | 14 26.6 | 10 36.9 |
| 14 25.5 | 16 22.6 | 18 20.2 | Cost of Sales/Payables | 11 33.8 | 13 29.1 | 21 17.9 | 17 21.9 | 30 12.2 | 29 12.4 |
| 32 11.2 | 33 11.1 | 41 9.0 | | 68 5.4 | 29 12.4 | 35 10.5 | 38 9.6 | 72 5.1 | 45 8.1 |
| 7.8 | 9.7 | 7.7 | | 7.1 | 22.9 | 7.2 | 6.7 | 10.2 | 7.5 |
| 20.4 | 59.3 | 46.6 | Sales/Working Capital | -61.0 | -92.1 | 21.7 | 15.2 | 29.4 | 28.6 |
| -41.0 | -19.7 | -29.9 | | -4.3 | -15.6 | -53.7 | NM | -65.4 | 70.3 |
| 10.9 | 17.8 | 27.2 | | 16.3 | 34.8 | 23.4 | 35.6 | 20.6 | 56.4 |
| (81) 2.9 | (110) 4.2 | (141) 6.8 | EBIT/Interest | (21) 2.7 | (38) 2.9 | (23) 6.6 | (28) 16.2 | (18) 5.7 | (13) 14.8 |
| -1.2 | .7 | 1.5 | | .5 | .7 | 2.4 | 6.7 | 2.4 | 2.2 |
| | | 7.3 | Net Profit + Depr., Dep., | | | | | | |
| | (11) 2.5 | 2.5 | Amort./Cur. Mat. L/T/D | | | | | | |
| | | -4.0 | | | | | | | |
| .2 | .2 | .1 | | .0 | .5 | .1 | .1 | .1 | .1 |
| .8 | 1.0 | .7 | Fixed/Worth | 1.8 | 2.4 | .4 | .2 | .3 | .1 |
| -2.4 | -1.1 | UND | | -.6 | -2.5 | 3.4 | 2.6 | 3.0 | 2.0 |
| .8 | 1.1 | 1.1 | | 1.6 | 1.5 | .6 | .5 | .7 | 1.0 |
| 3.4 | 3.9 | 3.8 | Debt/Worth | 6.5 | 19.4 | 1.7 | 2.8 | 2.9 | 3.3 |
| -7.7 | -4.4 | -164.4 | | -2.1 | -5.5 | 24.4 | 20.5 | 7.5 | 7.5 |
| 81.9 | 95.6 | 94.1 | % Profit Before Taxes/Tangible | 151.0 | 85.6 | 69.6 | 101.0 | 68.8 | 133.0 |
| (69) 34.6 | (87) 35.4 | (125) 35.1 | Net Worth | (18) 68.4 | (26) 44.5 | (22) 35.9 | (28) 48.9 | (17) 33.9 | (14) 36.7 |
| 4.3 | 5.5 | 6.9 | | .0 | -33.4 | 7.9 | 7.3 | 18.3 | 3.8 |
| 22.6 | 28.3 | 27.6 | % Profit Before Taxes/Total | 34.3 | 33.4 | 21.6 | 26.5 | 12.9 | 30.7 |
| 6.7 | 12.4 | 8.4 | Assets | 14.3 | 6.5 | 6.2 | 11.0 | 8.4 | 10.0 |
| -2.5 | -.4 | .8 | | -.7 | -3.3 | 2.7 | 2.6 | 2.0 | 1.6 |
| 81.1 | 117.6 | 91.9 | | 437.0 | 57.6 | 115.1 | 116.0 | 64.7 | 186.5 |
| 28.3 | 32.6 | 32.6 | Sales/Net Fixed Assets | 15.0 | 22.8 | 35.8 | 47.7 | 20.3 | 44.2 |
| 12.0 | 10.7 | 11.7 | | 5.7 | 11.4 | 16.0 | 18.2 | 9.2 | 27.2 |
| 5.6 | 7.2 | 5.8 | | 6.3 | 6.8 | 5.8 | 6.4 | 4.2 | 3.8 |
| 3.5 | 3.7 | 3.5 | Sales/Total Assets | 3.2 | 4.6 | 3.6 | 3.6 | 3.4 | 2.5 |
| 2.1 | 2.1 | 2.3 | | 1.6 | 2.9 | 2.4 | 2.5 | 2.2 | 1.9 |
| .6 | .3 | .4 | | .9 | .4 | .4 | .3 | .2 | .4 |
| (73) 1.2 | (79) 1.1 | (124) 1.1 | % Depr., Dep., Amort./Sales | (18) 2.9 | (35) 1.1 | (21) .9 | (23) .9 | (14) .9 | (13) .6 |
| 2.1 | 2.3 | 2.2 | | 5.7 | 2.1 | 1.7 | 2.2 | 1.9 | 1.4 |
| 3.0 | 2.0 | 2.4 | % Officers', Directors' | 3.2 | 3.1 | 2.0 | 2.0 | | |
| (53) 5.5 | (69) 3.8 | (83) 4.4 | Owners' Comp/Sales | (11) 8.9 | (26) 5.2 | (16) 4.5 | (20) 3.0 | | |
| 8.5 | 7.3 | 6.9 | | 10.3 | 9.0 | 6.2 | 5.1 | | |
| 3148923M | 3004428M | 2933976M | Net Sales ($) | 14474M | 76349M | 106054M | 247826M | 308755M | 2180518M |
| 853858M | 1097109M | 951552M | Total Assets ($) | 10741M | 24744M | 31432M | 87000M | 107769M | 689866M |

© RMA 2012      M = $ thousand     MM = $ million
See Pages 9 through 22 for Explanation of Ratios and Data

**Current Data Sorted by Assets**      **Comparative Historical Data**

| 0-500M | 500M-2MM | 2-10MM | 10-50MM | 50-100MM | 100-250MM | Type of Statement | 4/1/07-3/31/08 ALL | 4/1/08-3/31/09 ALL |
|---|---|---|---|---|---|---|---|---|
|  | 7 | 42 | 59 | 19 | 9 | Unqualified | 172 | 129 |
| 6 | 39 | 124 | 30 | 2 | 2 | Reviewed | 170 | 175 |
| 4 | 10 | 16 | 5 |  | 2 | Compiled | 24 | 39 |
| 37 | 41 | 24 | 5 |  |  | Tax Returns | 84 | 98 |
| 12 | 43 | 51 | 38 | 8 | 7 | Other | 147 | 139 |
|  | 115 (4/1-9/30/11) | | | 525 (10/1/11-3/31/12) | | | | |
| 59 | 140 | 257 | 137 | 29 | 18 | **NUMBER OF STATEMENTS** | 597 | 580 |
| % | % | % | % | % | % | **ASSETS** | % | % |
| 20.2 | 19.2 | 21.9 | 22.4 | 20.4 | 19.9 | Cash & Equivalents | 18.7 | 19.9 |
| 31.2 | 38.2 | 42.3 | 42.1 | 35.5 | 38.1 | Trade Receivables (net) | 40.3 | 39.0 |
| 5.5 | 4.5 | 3.5 | 3.5 | 2.7 | 3.0 | Inventory | 6.7 | 5.5 |
| 7.0 | 7.3 | 8.6 | 7.0 | 9.0 | 8.4 | All Other Current | 9.6 | 8.0 |
| 63.9 | 69.2 | 76.3 | 75.0 | 67.5 | 69.4 | Total Current | 75.3 | 72.4 |
| 23.9 | 16.1 | 14.4 | 14.1 | 20.7 | 22.7 | Fixed Assets (net) | 16.9 | 18.8 |
| 2.7 | 2.6 | 1.5 | 2.6 | 5.1 | 2.0 | Intangibles (net) | 1.1 | 1.0 |
| 9.5 | 12.1 | 7.8 | 8.3 | 6.6 | 5.9 | All Other Non-Current | 6.7 | 7.8 |
| 100.0 | 100.0 | 100.0 | 100.0 | 100.0 | 100.0 | Total | 100.0 | 100.0 |
|  |  |  |  |  |  | **LIABILITIES** | | |
| 14.6 | 7.8 | 4.8 | 3.0 | 2.9 | .7 | Notes Payable-Short Term | 7.2 | 7.3 |
| 6.5 | 2.9 | 2.1 | 1.2 | 1.6 | 4.5 | Cur. Mat.-L.T.D. | 3.1 | 3.3 |
| 27.1 | 26.0 | 29.0 | 28.5 | 28.3 | 24.5 | Trade Payables | 27.4 | 26.6 |
| .0 | .5 | .5 | .2 | .2 | .2 | Income Taxes Payable | .5 | .5 |
| 36.1 | 14.3 | 13.8 | 17.0 | 18.0 | 20.3 | All Other Current | 17.9 | 18.1 |
| 84.4 | 51.4 | 50.1 | 49.9 | 50.9 | 50.2 | Total Current | 56.2 | 55.8 |
| 8.6 | 12.3 | 6.5 | 7.5 | 8.6 | 10.4 | Long-Term Debt | 8.7 | 11.0 |
| .0 | .3 | .4 | .2 | .1 | .0 | Deferred Taxes | .4 | .2 |
| 8.5 | 2.3 | 1.1 | 2.8 | 3.2 | 4.2 | All Other Non-Current | 3.1 | 2.0 |
| -1.5 | 33.6 | 42.0 | 39.6 | 37.1 | 35.2 | Net Worth | 31.6 | 31.0 |
| 100.0 | 100.0 | 100.0 | 100.0 | 100.0 | 100.0 | Total Liabilities & Net Worth | 100.0 | 100.0 |
|  |  |  |  |  |  | **INCOME DATA** | | |
| 100.0 | 100.0 | 100.0 | 100.0 | 100.0 | 100.0 | Net Sales | 100.0 | 100.0 |
| 28.9 | 25.6 | 15.8 | 13.5 | 14.4 | 14.5 | Gross Profit | 17.6 | 18.7 |
| 28.1 | 21.6 | 12.7 | 10.8 | 11.7 | 8.4 | Operating Expenses | 13.5 | 15.1 |
| .7 | 4.0 | 3.1 | 2.6 | 2.7 | 6.1 | Operating Profit | 4.2 | 3.6 |
| .2 | .5 | .5 | .3 | -.2 | 1.4 | All Other Expenses (net) | .0 | .5 |
| .5 | 3.5 | 2.6 | 2.3 | 2.9 | 4.7 | Profit Before Taxes | 4.2 | 3.1 |
|  |  |  |  |  |  | **RATIOS** | | |
| 2.0 | 2.4 | 2.3 | 2.1 | 2.0 | 1.5 | | 1.9 | 1.9 |
| 1.1 | 1.4 | 1.5 | 1.5 | 1.3 | 1.3 | Current | 1.3 | 1.3 |
| .3 | 1.0 | 1.2 | 1.2 | 1.1 | 1.2 | | 1.1 | 1.1 |
| 1.6 | 1.9 | 1.9 | 1.8 | 1.4 | 1.3 | | 1.5 | 1.6 |
| .8 | 1.2 | 1.3 | 1.3 | 1.1 | 1.1 | Quick | (596) 1.1 | 1.1 |
| .3 | .7 | 1.0 | 1.0 | .9 | .8 | | .8 | .8 |
| 0 UND | 18 20.1 | 36 10.0 | 45 8.1 | 43 8.4 | 45 8.1 | | 28 13.0 | 27 13.5 |
| 14 25.6 | 38 9.6 | 54 6.8 | 65 5.6 | 62 5.9 | 55 6.6 | Sales/Receivables | 50 7.2 | 48 7.7 |
| 52 7.0 | 69 5.3 | 78 4.7 | 83 4.4 | 78 4.7 | 68 5.4 | | 72 5.1 | 71 5.2 |
| 0 UND | 0 UND | 0 UND | 0 UND | 0 UND | 0 UND | | 0 UND | 0 UND |
| 0 UND | 0 UND | 0 UND | 0 UND | 0 UND | 0 UND | Cost of Sales/Inventory | 0 UND | 0 UND |
| 0 UND | 0 864.7 | 0 999.8 | 2 156.7 | 6 60.5 | 5 75.6 | | 1 357.3 | 1 305.2 |
| 0 UND | 12 30.8 | 23 16.2 | 25 14.6 | 23 15.7 | 19 19.0 | | 16 22.6 | 17 21.7 |
| 13 28.4 | 35 10.3 | 41 8.9 | 42 8.6 | 47 7.8 | 38 9.6 | Cost of Sales/Payables | 37 9.9 | 34 10.8 |
| 38 9.5 | 61 6.0 | 65 5.6 | 64 5.7 | 70 5.2 | 50 7.3 | | 59 6.2 | 55 6.7 |
| 11.2 | 7.9 | 5.8 | 5.2 | 7.6 | 8.2 | | 7.5 | 7.9 |
| 72.6 | 20.5 | 11.4 | 11.2 | 12.6 | 13.3 | Sales/Working Capital | 16.2 | 17.0 |
| -24.8 | 385.8 | 24.4 | 21.9 | 33.8 | 27.6 | | 48.2 | 75.3 |
| 12.9 | 27.9 | 24.6 | 35.8 | 51.0 | 52.9 | | 49.8 | 35.4 |
| (37) 3.7 | (105) 6.5 | (191) 9.6 | (102) 12.5 | (24) 8.4 | (15) 7.8 | EBIT/Interest | (476) 11.5 | (463) 8.0 |
| -2.2 | .1 | 2.0 | 3.5 | 3.7 | 3.0 | | 3.2 | 1.6 |
|  | 9.6 | 13.7 | 9.8 |  |  | | 14.4 | 13.5 |
|  | (12) 2.3 | (50) 4.8 | (31) 3.3 |  |  | Net Profit + Depr., Dep., Amort./Cur. Mat. L/T/D | (125) 5.2 | (114) 4.3 |
|  | .4 | 2.5 | 1.2 |  |  | | 2.1 | 1.4 |
| .1 | .1 | .1 | .1 | .2 | .2 | | .1 | .1 |
| 1.3 | .3 | .2 | .2 | .5 | .4 | Fixed/Worth | .3 | .4 |
| -.8 | 1.7 | .5 | .5 | .9 | .9 | | .8 | .9 |
| .6 | .7 | .7 | .9 | .8 | 1.7 | | 1.1 | 1.1 |
| 2.8 | 2.2 | 1.6 | 1.7 | 2.6 | 2.2 | Debt/Worth | 2.3 | 2.4 |
| -4.7 | 9.0 | 3.0 | 3.6 | 6.1 | 2.8 | | 4.9 | 5.4 |
| 67.9 | 56.4 | 30.4 | 22.7 | 31.0 | 32.2 | | 60.5 | 52.8 |
| (41) 20.0 | (117) 20.2 | (247) 13.4 | (131) 12.0 | (28) 19.5 | (17) 15.2 | % Profit Before Taxes/Tangible Net Worth | (558) 32.3 | (525) 23.0 |
| 1.7 | -.6 | 1.0 | 2.6 | 3.4 | 8.9 | | 12.9 | 6.2 |
| 23.8 | 20.7 | 11.7 | 8.9 | 8.0 | 8.3 | | 18.9 | 17.4 |
| 11.3 | 6.9 | 5.0 | 3.6 | 4.4 | 4.9 | % Profit Before Taxes/Total Assets | 9.7 | 6.8 |
| -10.6 | -.6 | .3 | .6 | .9 | 2.8 | | 3.0 | .9 |
| 411.7 | 143.7 | 119.7 | 94.5 | 61.9 | 58.8 | | 94.4 | 105.9 |
| 53.8 | 46.7 | 40.5 | 38.6 | 15.9 | 14.1 | Sales/Net Fixed Assets | 35.1 | 35.6 |
| 15.7 | 11.3 | 11.2 | 13.3 | 4.3 | 3.7 | | 12.2 | 9.5 |
| 10.1 | 4.5 | 3.6 | 3.1 | 3.4 | 3.1 | | 4.0 | 3.9 |
| 5.4 | 3.3 | 2.7 | 2.5 | 1.7 | 2.5 | Sales/Total Assets | 3.0 | 2.9 |
| 3.0 | 2.2 | 1.8 | 1.7 | 1.3 | 1.4 | | 2.1 | 1.9 |
| .3 | .3 | .3 | .2 | .3 | .2 | | .3 | .3 |
| (35) .8 | (96) .8 | (213) .7 | (126) .5 | (28) .9 | (14) 1.1 | % Depr., Dep., Amort./Sales | (496) .7 | (473) .7 |
| 2.3 | 1.8 | 1.6 | 1.5 | 4.2 | 1.4 | | 1.7 | 2.0 |
| 3.9 | 1.7 | 1.1 | .6 |  |  | | 1.0 | 1.0 |
| (31) 5.7 | (74) 3.0 | (99) 2.2 | (35) 3.6 | 2.1 |  | % Officers', Directors' Owners' Comp/Sales | (221) 2.1 | (211) 2.7 |
| 9.2 | 6.1 | 3.6 | 2.1 |  |  | | 4.0 | 4.5 |
| 101582M | 582712M | 3309817M | 7425324M | 4265679M | 6175195M | Net Sales ($) | 30603987M | 23063911M |
| 15742M | 165265M | 1223776M | 3134816M | 2006931M | 2821628M | Total Assets ($) | 10619952M | 8899647M |

M = $ thousand    MM = $ million
See Pages 9 through 22 for Explanation of Ratios and Data

## Comparative Historical Data | | | Current Data Sorted by Sales

| | | | Type of Statement | | | | | | |
|---|---|---|---|---|---|---|---|---|---|
| 188 | 156 | 136 | Unqualified | | 3 | 5 | 6 | 35 | 87 |
| 238 | 218 | 203 | Reviewed | 3 | 19 | 27 | 45 | 70 | 39 |
| 51 | 27 | 35 | Compiled | 4 | 7 | 4 | 11 | 5 | 4 |
| 131 | 90 | 107 | Tax Returns | 18 | 40 | 18 | 17 | 8 | 6 |
| 196 | 163 | 159 | Other | 13 | 24 | 16 | 28 | 38 | 40 |
| 4/1/09-3/31/10 ALL | 4/1/10-3/31/11 ALL | 4/1/11-3/31/12 ALL | | 115 (4/1-9/30/11) | | | 525 (10/1/11-3/31/12) | | |
| | | | | 0-1MM | 1-3MM | 3-5MM | 5-10MM | 10-25MM | 25MM & OVER |
| 804 | 654 | 640 | **NUMBER OF STATEMENTS** | 38 | 93 | 70 | 107 | 156 | 176 |
| % | % | % | **ASSETS** | % | % | % | % | % | % |
| 22.8 | 21.7 | 21.2 | Cash & Equivalents | 14.3 | 17.4 | 23.7 | 21.7 | 21.4 | 23.2 |
| 36.1 | 40.1 | 39.9 | Trade Receivables (net) | 18.0 | 32.4 | 35.8 | 42.0 | 43.5 | 45.6 |
| 5.3 | 3.4 | 3.9 | Inventory | 10.6 | 7.0 | 4.6 | 3.2 | 3.2 | 1.4 |
| 7.1 | 7.5 | 7.8 | All Other Current | 7.0 | 7.2 | 5.7 | 8.4 | 8.3 | 8.5 |
| 71.3 | 72.7 | 72.7 | Total Current | 49.9 | 63.9 | 69.7 | 75.3 | 76.5 | 78.7 |
| 18.5 | 17.1 | 16.1 | Fixed Assets (net) | 30.6 | 21.4 | 18.4 | 14.3 | 13.6 | 12.6 |
| 1.2 | 2.1 | 2.3 | Intangibles (net) | 3.8 | 4.3 | .5 | .9 | 2.0 | 2.6 |
| 9.0 | 8.1 | 8.9 | All Other Non-Current | 15.6 | 10.3 | 11.5 | 9.5 | 7.9 | 6.1 |
| 100.0 | 100.0 | 100.0 | Total | 100.0 | 100.0 | 100.0 | 100.0 | 100.0 | 100.0 |
| | | | **LIABILITIES** | | | | | | |
| 8.9 | 8.0 | 5.8 | Notes Payable-Short Term | 4.4 | 14.2 | 9.6 | 4.0 | 5.0 | 1.8 |
| 2.9 | 2.4 | 2.5 | Cur. Mat.-L.T.D. | 3.6 | 6.4 | 2.0 | 1.7 | 2.0 | 1.3 |
| 24.1 | 25.6 | 27.9 | Trade Payables | 9.1 | 19.7 | 27.7 | 30.6 | 30.1 | 32.7 |
| .4 | .5 | .4 | Income Taxes Payable | .0 | .3 | .9 | .6 | .3 | .2 |
| 16.4 | 15.2 | 17.0 | All Other Current | 43.9 | 13.9 | 14.6 | 15.4 | 13.1 | 18.2 |
| 52.8 | 51.6 | 53.5 | Total Current | 61.0 | 54.5 | 54.8 | 52.5 | 50.5 | 54.3 |
| 10.2 | 8.1 | 8.3 | Long-Term Debt | 27.7 | 11.9 | 5.8 | 8.5 | 6.2 | 5.1 |
| .3 | .3 | .3 | Deferred Taxes | .1 | .2 | .3 | .5 | .3 | .2 |
| 3.2 | 3.1 | 2.6 | All Other Non-Current | 4.4 | 4.2 | 4.3 | 1.3 | 1.7 | 2.2 |
| 33.5 | 36.9 | 35.3 | Net Worth | 6.7 | 29.2 | 34.8 | 37.3 | 41.4 | 38.2 |
| 100.0 | 100.0 | 100.0 | Total Liabilities & Net Worth | 100.0 | 100.0 | 100.0 | 100.0 | 100.0 | 100.0 |
| | | | **INCOME DATA** | | | | | | |
| 100.0 | 100.0 | 100.0 | Net Sales | 100.0 | 100.0 | 100.0 | 100.0 | 100.0 | 100.0 |
| 19.6 | 19.3 | 18.5 | Gross Profit | 40.6 | 29.3 | 20.8 | 18.0 | 14.4 | 11.1 |
| 17.3 | 17.1 | 15.5 | Operating Expenses | 33.5 | 24.7 | 18.4 | 14.8 | 12.3 | 8.9 |
| 2.2 | 2.2 | 3.0 | Operating Profit | 7.1 | 4.6 | 2.3 | 3.3 | 2.1 | 2.3 |
| .4 | .3 | .4 | All Other Expenses (net) | 6.6 | .9 | .0 | .1 | -.4 | .0 |
| 1.8 | 1.8 | 2.6 | Profit Before Taxes | .5 | 3.7 | 2.4 | 3.1 | 2.5 | 2.3 |
| | | | **RATIOS** | | | | | | |
| 2.1 | 2.1 | 2.2 | Current | 3.6 | 2.7 | 2.7 | 2.2 | 2.2 | 1.8 |
| 1.4 | 1.5 | 1.4 | | 1.3 | 1.2 | 1.5 | 1.4 | 1.5 | 1.4 |
| 1.1 | 1.1 | 1.1 | | .4 | .8 | 1.0 | 1.1 | 1.2 | 1.2 |
| 1.7 | 1.8 | 1.8 | Quick | 1.8 | 2.2 | 2.5 | 1.8 | 1.9 | 1.6 |
| 1.2 | 1.3 | 1.2 | | .5 | 1.0 | 1.4 | 1.2 | 1.3 | 1.2 |
| .8 | .9 | .9 | | .1 | .4 | .8 | 1.0 | 1.0 | 1.0 |
| 25  14.6 | 33  10.9 | 32  11.5 | Sales/Receivables | 0  UND | 1  526.7 | 19  19.2 | 33  10.9 | 38  9.5 | 45  8.1 |
| 45  8.1 | 56  6.6 | 52  7.0 | | 10  35.7 | 37  9.9 | 51  7.1 | 47  7.8 | 54  6.8 | 62  5.9 |
| 68  5.4 | 78  4.7 | 76  4.8 | | 46  7.9 | 72  5.1 | 74  4.9 | 72  5.1 | 78  4.7 | 78  4.7 |
| 0  UND | 0  UND | 0  UND | Cost of Sales/Inventory | 0  UND | 0  UND | 0  UND | 0  UND | 0  UND | 0  UND |
| 0  UND | 0  UND | 0  UND | | 0  UND | 0  UND | 0  UND | 0  UND | 0  UND | 0  UND |
| 1  484.9 | 1  333.1 | 1  422.1 | | 27  13.5 | 1  364.3 | 0  954.8 | 0  UND | 2  237.5 | 1  437.4 |
| 16  23.1 | 19  19.7 | 18  20.2 | Cost of Sales/Payables | 0  UND | 9  39.1 | 11  32.3 | 21  17.1 | 23  16.1 | 25  14.8 |
| 32  11.4 | 37  9.9 | 38  9.5 | | 0  UND | 29  12.8 | 35  10.4 | 40  9.1 | 38  9.7 | 43  8.5 |
| 56  6.5 | 62  5.9 | 64  5.7 | | 64  5.7 | 59  6.2 | 64  5.7 | 68  5.4 | 60  6.1 | 64  5.7 |
| 7.0 | 6.0 | 6.3 | Sales/Working Capital | 5.3 | 6.6 | 6.6 | 6.0 | 6.3 | 7.4 |
| 13.6 | 12.2 | 13.2 | | 23.8 | 20.7 | 13.8 | 14.1 | 11.6 | 12.8 |
| 52.2 | 38.9 | 38.4 | | -4.1 | -26.9 | 345.0 | 38.6 | 23.9 | 27.4 |
| 38.3 | 29.0 | 27.6 | EBIT/Interest | 6.3 | 15.2 | 25.4 | 40.0 | 23.0 | 61.1 |
| (612)  6.3 | (500)  6.2 | (474)  8.6 | | (20)  2.4 | (63)  4.1 | (53)  3.8 | (82)  11.5 | (122)  9.7 | (134)  15.3 |
| .6 | .4 | 1.6 | | -.7 | .5 | -2.6 | 1.7 | 1.9 | 4.1 |
| 10.8 | 10.6 | 10.2 | Net Profit + Depr., Dep., Amort./Cur. Mat. L/T/D | | | | 15.8 | 10.8 | 9.0 |
| (152)  3.1 | (111)  3.6 | (104)  3.5 | | | | | (23)  4.9 | (27)  3.8 | (41)  3.3 |
| .8 | 1.0 | 1.6 | | | | | 3.0 | 1.8 | 1.8 |
| .1 | .1 | .1 | Fixed/Worth | .1 | .1 | .1 | .1 | .1 | .1 |
| .3 | .3 | .3 | | 2.2 | .7 | .2 | .2 | .2 | .2 |
| .9 | .8 | .8 | | -2.4 | 15.4 | 1.0 | .6 | .5 | .5 |
| .9 | .7 | .8 | Debt/Worth | .5 | .6 | .5 | .7 | .8 | 1.1 |
| 1.8 | 1.7 | 1.8 | | 13.3 | 3.1 | 1.5 | 1.5 | 1.6 | 1.9 |
| 4.2 | 3.6 | 4.0 | | -4.6 | 24.4 | 3.0 | 3.3 | 2.7 | 3.7 |
| 39.5 | 30.2 | 34.0 | % Profit Before Taxes/Tangible Net Worth | 41.7 | 53.2 | 49.7 | 41.8 | 28.9 | 27.2 |
| (723)  14.3 | (596)  10.7 | (581)  14.2 | | (26)  15.1 | (73)  9.6 | (64)  14.1 | (98)  17.4 | (150)  11.6 | (170)  14.4 |
| .3 | -1.7 | 1.3 | | -8.3 | -1.2 | -1.1 | 3.1 | .9 | 4.3 |
| 13.3 | 11.0 | 12.3 | % Profit Before Taxes/Total Assets | 14.7 | 17.1 | 21.0 | 13.9 | 11.9 | 9.0 |
| 4.4 | 3.8 | 4.7 | | 1.4 | 3.3 | 7.1 | 7.5 | 4.1 | 4.5 |
| -.7 | -1.8 | .3 | | -5.3 | -2.1 | -1.8 | .8 | .5 | 1.2 |
| 92.8 | 80.7 | 120.5 | Sales/Net Fixed Assets | 122.8 | 202.3 | 86.8 | 110.2 | 121.8 | 112.1 |
| 30.6 | 29.2 | 40.4 | | 13.0 | 20.6 | 34.5 | 48.3 | 46.1 | 46.9 |
| 9.6 | 10.5 | 11.9 | | 1.0 | 8.5 | 10.1 | 14.8 | 15.7 | 15.4 |
| 3.9 | 3.6 | 3.8 | Sales/Total Assets | 3.8 | 3.8 | 4.3 | 4.0 | 4.0 | 3.5 |
| 2.7 | 2.7 | 2.7 | | 1.3 | 2.5 | 2.8 | 3.1 | 2.9 | 2.7 |
| 1.8 | 1.8 | 1.8 | | .4 | 1.5 | 1.6 | 1.9 | 2.1 | 2.0 |
| .4 | .3 | .3 | % Depr., Dep., Amort./Sales | 1.5 | .5 | .3 | .3 | .3 | .2 |
| (650)  .8 | (541)  .8 | (512)  .7 | | (17)  2.5 | (62)  1.3 | (52)  .7 | (85)  .8 | (134)  .6 | (162)  .5 |
| 2.3 | 1.9 | 1.6 | | 16.3 | 3.4 | 1.5 | 1.5 | 1.6 | 1.9 |
| 1.5 | 1.3 | 1.2 | % Officers', Directors' Owners' Comp/Sales | 4.8 | 2.4 | 2.4 | 1.4 | .9 | .5 |
| (315)  3.1 | (241)  2.7 | (246)  2.5 | | (15)  8.1 | (43)  4.9 | (33)  4.0 | (62)  2.0 | (57)  1.9 | (36)  .8 |
| 5.5 | 5.1 | 4.9 | | 18.0 | 7.7 | 6.5 | 3.8 | 3.1 | 1.8 |
| 31546146M | 24363799M | 21860309M | Net Sales ($) | 19201M | 181944M | 279883M | 791278M | 2524922M | 18063081M |
| 12009036M | 10098092M | 9368158M | Total Assets ($) | 51182M | 150109M | 131339M | 340498M | 1130072M | 7564958M |

**M = $ thousand    MM = $ million**
See Pages 9 through 22 for Explanation of Ratios and Data

## Current Data Sorted by Assets     Comparative Historical Data

### Type of Statement

| Type of Statement | 0-500M | 500M-2MM | 2-10MM | 10-50MM | 50-100MM | 100-250MM | 4/1/07-3/31/08 ALL | 4/1/08-3/31/09 ALL |
|---|---|---|---|---|---|---|---|---|
| Unqualified | 1 | 10 | 134 | 193 | 44 | 49 | 419 | 510 |
| Reviewed | 10 | 138 | 357 | 72 | 3 | 1 | 527 | 682 |
| Compiled | 19 | 23 | 34 | 2 | 1 | 1 | 81 | 83 |
| Tax Returns | 53 | 68 | 57 | 7 | | | 142 | 215 |
| Other | 28 | 92 | 155 | 74 | 22 | 21 | 339 | 436 |
| | 284 (4/1-9/30/11) | | 1,384 (10/1/11-3/31/12) | | | | | |
| NUMBER OF STATEMENTS | 111 | 331 | 737 | 348 | 70 | 71 | 1508 | 1926 |

### ASSETS (%)

| ASSETS | 0-500M | 500M-2MM | 2-10MM | 10-50MM | 50-100MM | 100-250MM | Hist 07-08 | Hist 08-09 |
|---|---|---|---|---|---|---|---|---|
| Cash & Equivalents | 25.7 | 22.6 | 23.8 | 26.3 | 23.8 | 26.5 | 20.9 | 23.4 |
| Trade Receivables (net) | 26.1 | 40.5 | 45.0 | 45.5 | 41.7 | 47.4 | 45.8 | 43.9 |
| Inventory | 4.4 | 2.6 | 2.0 | 1.7 | 1.5 | .8 | 3.9 | 3.3 |
| All Other Current | 6.6 | 9.0 | 9.6 | 8.1 | 8.5 | 9.7 | 9.0 | 9.0 |
| Total Current | 62.7 | 74.8 | 80.4 | 81.6 | 75.4 | 84.5 | 79.6 | 79.6 |
| Fixed Assets (net) | 23.2 | 14.7 | 11.7 | 10.8 | 16.6 | 7.8 | 13.8 | 13.1 |
| Intangibles (net) | 4.2 | 2.0 | 2.0 | 2.1 | 3.7 | 1.7 | 1.1 | .8 |
| All Other Non-Current | 10.0 | 8.6 | 5.9 | 5.4 | 4.3 | 6.0 | 5.5 | 6.4 |
| Total | 100.0 | 100.0 | 100.0 | 100.0 | 100.0 | 100.0 | 100.0 | 100.0 |

### LIABILITIES

| LIABILITIES | 0-500M | 500M-2MM | 2-10MM | 10-50MM | 50-100MM | 100-250MM | Hist 07-08 | Hist 08-09 |
|---|---|---|---|---|---|---|---|---|
| Notes Payable-Short Term | 25.1 | 8.4 | 4.1 | 2.6 | 2.5 | .8 | 6.0 | 6.0 |
| Cur. Mat.-L.T.D. | 5.5 | 1.9 | 1.4 | 2.8 | 1.2 | .6 | 2.1 | 2.0 |
| Trade Payables | 21.4 | 27.6 | 33.6 | 38.6 | 35.6 | 43.9 | 32.2 | 32.3 |
| Income Taxes Payable | .3 | .4 | .5 | .3 | .2 | .1 | .6 | .5 |
| All Other Current | 19.0 | 13.2 | 13.6 | 16.4 | 18.0 | 23.4 | 18.6 | 17.7 |
| Total Current | 71.3 | 51.5 | 53.2 | 60.6 | 57.5 | 68.7 | 59.5 | 58.5 |
| Long-Term Debt | 18.2 | 6.4 | 5.0 | 6.4 | 6.7 | 4.4 | 7.2 | 6.6 |
| Deferred Taxes | .0 | .5 | .3 | .1 | .6 | .1 | .3 | .3 |
| All Other Non-Current | 3.8 | 3.7 | 2.4 | 1.7 | 2.3 | 2.0 | 2.2 | 2.9 |
| Net Worth | 6.6 | 37.9 | 39.1 | 31.2 | 32.8 | 24.8 | 30.8 | 31.7 |
| Total Liabilities & Net Worth | 100.0 | 100.0 | 100.0 | 100.0 | 100.0 | 100.0 | 100.0 | 100.0 |

### INCOME DATA

| INCOME DATA | 0-500M | 500M-2MM | 2-10MM | 10-50MM | 50-100MM | 100-250MM | Hist 07-08 | Hist 08-09 |
|---|---|---|---|---|---|---|---|---|
| Net Sales | 100.0 | 100.0 | 100.0 | 100.0 | 100.0 | 100.0 | 100.0 | 100.0 |
| Gross Profit | 29.2 | 19.5 | 14.5 | 11.5 | 11.3 | 6.5 | 16.2 | 16.5 |
| Operating Expenses | 27.2 | 16.8 | 12.4 | 9.5 | 8.9 | 5.1 | 12.2 | 13.0 |
| Operating Profit | 2.0 | 2.7 | 2.1 | 2.0 | 2.5 | 1.4 | 4.0 | 3.5 |
| All Other Expenses (net) | .4 | .2 | .1 | .1 | .0 | -.1 | .2 | .3 |
| Profit Before Taxes | 1.5 | 2.5 | 2.0 | 1.8 | 2.4 | 1.5 | 3.8 | 3.2 |

### RATIOS

| RATIOS | 0-500M | 500M-2MM | 2-10MM | 10-50MM | 50-100MM | 100-250MM | Hist 07-08 | Hist 08-09 |
|---|---|---|---|---|---|---|---|---|
| Current | 2.1 | 2.6 | 2.1 | 1.6 | 1.5 | 1.3 | 1.7 | 1.8 |
| | 1.1 | 1.6 | 1.5 | 1.4 | 1.3 | 1.2 | 1.3 | 1.3 |
| | .5 | 1.1 | 1.2 | 1.2 | 1.2 | 1.1 | 1.1 | 1.1 |
| Quick | 1.8 | 2.3 | 1.8 | 1.5 | 1.4 | 1.2 | 1.5 | 1.6 |
| | .8 | 1.3 | 1.3 | 1.2 | 1.2 | 1.1 | (1506) 1.2 | 1.2 |
| | .3 | .8 | 1.0 | 1.0 | 1.0 | 1.0 | .9 | .9 |
| Sales/Receivables | 0 UND | 20 17.9 | 36 10.2 | 47 7.7 | 51 7.1 | 53 6.9 | 35 10.5 | 32 11.4 |
| | 12 29.7 | 41 8.9 | 57 6.4 | 61 6.0 | 65 5.6 | 60 6.1 | 53 6.9 | 50 7.2 |
| | 54 6.8 | 65 5.6 | 79 4.6 | 76 4.8 | 79 4.6 | 69 5.3 | 72 5.0 | 70 5.2 |
| Cost of Sales/Inventory | 0 UND | 0 UND | 0 UND | 0 UND | 0 UND | 0 UND | 0 UND | 0 UND |
| | 0 UND | 0 UND | 0 UND | 0 UND | 0 UND | 0 UND | 0 UND | 0 UND |
| | 0 UND | 0 UND | 0 UND | 0 UND | 0 999.8 | 0 827.4 | 0 999.8 | 0 UND |
| Cost of Sales/Payables | 0 UND | 14 25.8 | 28 13.1 | 40 9.1 | 38 9.5 | 43 8.5 | 22 16.8 | 21 17.3 |
| | 12 31.6 | 31 11.7 | 45 8.2 | 57 6.4 | 61 6.0 | 60 6.1 | 42 8.8 | 41 9.0 |
| | 43 8.4 | 51 7.1 | 66 5.5 | 78 4.7 | 81 4.5 | 73 5.0 | 62 5.9 | 61 6.0 |
| Sales/Working Capital | 11.5 | 6.6 | 6.1 | 7.7 | 8.0 | 11.9 | 9.0 | 8.5 |
| | 414.1 | 13.7 | 11.8 | 13.3 | 11.8 | 20.2 | 17.2 | 17.1 |
| | -12.9 | 63.8 | 26.9 | 24.8 | 23.9 | 30.0 | 36.8 | 41.3 |
| EBIT/Interest | 14.4 | 30.6 | 38.1 | 70.7 | 41.0 | 51.9 | 58.4 | 61.0 |
| | (74) 3.5 | (244) 6.0 | (549) 8.5 | (248) 13.3 | (57) 12.6 | (54) 13.0 | (1169) 13.9 | (1449) 12.3 |
| | -.7 | 1.4 | 1.4 | 2.4 | 2.5 | 3.7 | 3.4 | 2.2 |
| Net Profit + Depr., Dep., Amort./Cur. Mat. L/T/D | | 6.3 | 14.5 | 43.3 | 19.0 | 8.2 | 18.1 | 17.8 |
| | | (45) 2.5 | (164) 4.4 | (75) 6.3 | (15) 6.9 | (18) 3.9 | (319) 5.5 | (380) 6.3 |
| | | -.5 | .7 | 1.6 | 1.8 | 1.9 | 2.2 | 2.0 |
| Fixed/Worth | .2 | .1 | .1 | .1 | .1 | .1 | .1 | .1 |
| | 1.6 | .3 | .2 | .2 | .2 | .2 | .3 | .2 |
| | -1.2 | 1.0 | .5 | .4 | .6 | .4 | .7 | .6 |
| Debt/Worth | .8 | .5 | .8 | 1.3 | 1.5 | 2.3 | 1.3 | 1.1 |
| | 11.1 | 1.4 | 1.8 | 2.2 | 2.4 | 3.4 | 2.6 | 2.3 |
| | -7.7 | 5.3 | 3.6 | 4.2 | 4.2 | 5.1 | 5.3 | 4.8 |
| % Profit Before Taxes/Tangible Net Worth | 107.1 | 51.4 | 31.9 | 29.4 | 20.6 | 32.3 | 61.6 | 53.1 |
| | (65) 33.3 | (288) 16.5 | (706) 11.9 | (333) 12.2 | (68) 10.7 | (70) 15.3 | (1415) 33.0 | (1801) 26.4 |
| | -9.3 | 1.5 | 1.6 | 2.8 | 3.2 | 6.0 | 12.1 | 7.0 |
| % Profit Before Taxes/Total Assets | 38.8 | 18.5 | 11.2 | 8.1 | 5.5 | 7.6 | 17.3 | 16.4 |
| | 7.1 | 6.4 | 4.1 | 3.2 | 3.1 | 3.5 | 8.8 | 7.2 |
| | -5.8 | .4 | .4 | .7 | .7 | 1.3 | 2.6 | 1.8 |
| Sales/Net Fixed Assets | 193.3 | 143.5 | 128.5 | 188.8 | 119.5 | 121.9 | 131.4 | 138.1 |
| | 40.7 | 45.8 | 45.5 | 66.0 | 45.6 | 64.5 | 49.4 | 55.7 |
| | 15.1 | 14.7 | 18.0 | 20.5 | 8.0 | 36.4 | 18.7 | 19.2 |
| Sales/Total Assets | 11.3 | 4.8 | 3.7 | 3.5 | 2.9 | 3.5 | 4.1 | 4.3 |
| | 5.2 | 3.4 | 2.9 | 2.8 | 2.2 | 2.8 | 3.2 | 3.3 |
| | 3.1 | 2.2 | 2.1 | 2.0 | 1.8 | 2.3 | 2.4 | 2.3 |
| % Depr., Dep., Amort./Sales | .4 | .3 | .2 | .2 | .2 | .2 | .2 | .2 |
| | (67) .9 | (238) .7 | (632) .5 | (310) .3 | (65) .4 | (63) .3 | (1295) .4 | (1610) .5 |
| | 2.2 | 1.5 | 1.2 | .8 | 1.7 | .5 | 1.0 | 1.1 |
| % Officers', Directors' Owners' Comp/Sales | 2.7 | 1.8 | 1.0 | .6 | .4 | | 1.1 | 1.0 |
| | (64) 5.3 | (168) 3.1 | (326) 1.7 | (83) 1.0 | (11) .8 | | (570) 2.1 | (722) 2.2 |
| | 10.0 | 5.0 | 3.1 | 1.2 | | | 3.8 | 4.1 |
| Net Sales ($) | 201049M | 1462408M | 10428138M | 21133172M | 11091351M | 31070435M | 92185632M | 102254767M |
| Total Assets ($) | 27982M | 400581M | 3549033M | 7466076M | 4819631M | 10994814M | 26275257M | 33527574M |

M = $ thousand    MM = $ million
See Pages 9 through 22 for Explanation of Ratios and Data

## Comparative Historical Data

| | | | | | | | |
|---|---|---|---|---|---|---|---|
| 437 | 424 | 431 | **Type of Statement** | | | | |
| 617 | 579 | 580 | Unqualified | | | | |
| 86 | 83 | 80 | Reviewed | | | | |
| 154 | 146 | 185 | Compiled | | | | |
| 390 | 367 | 392 | Tax Returns | | | | |
| | | | Other | | | | |

### Current Data Sorted by Sales

| Comparative Historical Data | | | | Current Data Sorted by Sales | | | | | |
|---|---|---|---|---|---|---|---|---|---|
| | | | **Type of Statement** | | 2 | 7 | 31 | 97 | 294 |
| 437 | 424 | 431 | Unqualified | 6 | 58 | 66 | 161 | 194 | 95 |
| 617 | 579 | 580 | Reviewed | 13 | 15 | 10 | 24 | 14 | 4 |
| 86 | 83 | 80 | Compiled | 25 | 55 | 29 | 34 | 32 | 10 |
| 154 | 146 | 185 | Tax Returns | 21 | 52 | 38 | 80 | 83 | 118 |
| 390 | 367 | 392 | Other | | | | | | |
| 4/1/09- 3/31/10 | 4/1/10- 3/31/11 | 4/1/11- 3/31/12 | | | 284 (4/1-9/30/11) | | 1,384 (10/1/11-3/31/12) | | |
| ALL | ALL | ALL | | 0-1MM | 1-3MM | 3-5MM | 5-10MM | 10-25MM | 25MM & OVER |
| 1684 | 1599 | 1668 | **NUMBER OF STATEMENTS** | 65 | 182 | 150 | 330 | 420 | 521 |
| % | % | % | **ASSETS** | % | % | % | % | % | % |
| 25.9 | 24.7 | 24.3 | Cash & Equivalents | 23.9 | 21.9 | 23.8 | 21.9 | 25.5 | 26.0 |
| 40.2 | 41.3 | 42.9 | Trade Receivables (net) | 22.9 | 31.0 | 35.2 | 44.5 | 46.0 | 48.3 |
| 2.7 | 2.4 | 2.1 | Inventory | 7.1 | 2.3 | 4.2 | 3.0 | 1.3 | 1.1 |
| 8.5 | 9.7 | 8.9 | All Other Current | 8.8 | 8.5 | 8.3 | 8.3 | 9.4 | 9.4 |
| 77.2 | 78.1 | 78.3 | Total Current | 62.8 | 63.6 | 71.4 | 77.7 | 82.0 | 84.8 |
| 14.7 | 13.4 | 12.9 | Fixed Assets (net) | 26.0 | 21.8 | 16.7 | 13.4 | 10.6 | 8.6 |
| 1.5 | 1.5 | 2.2 | Intangibles (net) | 3.5 | 2.8 | 3.0 | 2.4 | 1.7 | 2.0 |
| 6.6 | 7.1 | 6.6 | All Other Non-Current | 7.7 | 11.8 | 8.9 | 6.6 | 5.7 | 4.6 |
| 100.0 | 100.0 | 100.0 | Total | 100.0 | 100.0 | 100.0 | 100.0 | 100.0 | 100.0 |
| | | | **LIABILITIES** | | | | | | |
| 6.2 | 6.5 | 5.8 | Notes Payable-Short Term | 15.0 | 16.1 | 7.4 | 5.9 | 3.9 | 2.1 |
| 2.0 | 1.9 | 2.0 | Cur. Mat.-L.T.D. | 4.3 | 3.0 | 2.8 | 1.9 | 1.2 | 1.9 |
| 29.7 | 30.9 | 33.2 | Trade Payables | 15.5 | 20.4 | 25.5 | 29.7 | 36.1 | 41.9 |
| .5 | .4 | .4 | Income Taxes Payable | .1 | .3 | .7 | .5 | .5 | .2 |
| 15.1 | 15.4 | 15.1 | All Other Current | 13.6 | 12.9 | 14.1 | 13.3 | 14.6 | 17.8 |
| 53.5 | 55.1 | 56.5 | Total Current | 48.4 | 52.7 | 50.5 | 51.3 | 56.2 | 64.0 |
| 6.9 | 6.5 | 6.5 | Long-Term Debt | 17.4 | 15.0 | 6.5 | 5.7 | 4.5 | 4.2 |
| .3 | .3 | .3 | Deferred Taxes | .2 | .5 | .3 | .3 | .3 | .2 |
| 2.2 | 2.7 | 2.6 | All Other Non-Current | 3.7 | 4.4 | 3.7 | 3.3 | 1.7 | 1.7 |
| 37.0 | 35.3 | 34.2 | Net Worth | 30.2 | 27.4 | 39.1 | 39.3 | 37.2 | 29.9 |
| 100.0 | 100.0 | 100.0 | Total Liabilities & Net Worth | 100.0 | 100.0 | 100.0 | 100.0 | 100.0 | 100.0 |
| | | | **INCOME DATA** | | | | | | |
| 100.0 | 100.0 | 100.0 | Net Sales | 100.0 | 100.0 | 100.0 | 100.0 | 100.0 | 100.0 |
| 16.8 | 16.4 | 15.3 | Gross Profit | 37.7 | 25.8 | 18.8 | 17.3 | 12.6 | 8.9 |
| 14.6 | 14.4 | 13.2 | Operating Expenses | 32.7 | 23.4 | 17.3 | 14.9 | 10.4 | 7.1 |
| 2.2 | 2.0 | 2.2 | Operating Profit | 5.0 | 2.5 | 1.6 | 2.3 | 2.2 | 1.7 |
| .3 | .3 | .1 | All Other Expenses (net) | 2.7 | .9 | -.1 | -.1 | .0 | -.1 |
| 1.9 | 1.7 | 2.0 | Profit Before Taxes | 2.3 | 1.6 | 1.7 | 2.4 | 2.2 | 1.8 |
| | | | **RATIOS** | | | | | | |
| 2.1 | 2.0 | 1.9 | | 4.1 | 2.9 | 2.9 | 2.3 | 1.9 | 1.6 |
| 1.5 | 1.4 | 1.4 | Current | 1.5 | 1.5 | 1.6 | 1.6 | 1.4 | 1.3 |
| 1.2 | 1.2 | 1.2 | | .7 | .7 | 1.1 | 1.2 | 1.2 | 1.2 |
| 1.8 | 1.8 | 1.7 | | 2.7 | 2.6 | 2.5 | 2.0 | 1.7 | 1.4 |
| 1.3 (1598) | 1.3 | 1.2 | Quick | 1.1 | 1.1 | 1.3 | 1.4 | 1.3 | 1.2 |
| 1.0 | .9 | 1.0 | | .3 | .5 | .8 | 1.0 | 1.0 | 1.0 |

| | | | | | | | | | | | | | | | | | | |
|---|---|---|---|---|---|---|---|---|---|---|---|---|---|---|---|---|---|---|
| 29 | 12.5 | 34 | 10.8 | 34 | 10.8 | Sales/Receivables | 0 | UND | 8 | 45.4 | 21 | 17.6 | 31 | 11.6 | 35 | 10.3 | 46 | 7.9 |
| 48 | 7.6 | 53 | 6.9 | 54 | 6.7 | | 20 | 18.5 | 41 | 9.0 | 43 | 8.5 | 51 | 7.2 | 56 | 6.5 | 59 | 6.2 |
| 68 | 5.4 | 75 | 4.9 | 74 | 4.9 | | 76 | 4.8 | 79 | 4.6 | 70 | 5.2 | 78 | 4.7 | 76 | 4.8 | 72 | 5.1 |
| 0 | UND | 0 | UND | 0 | UND | Cost of Sales/Inventory | 0 | UND | 0 | UND | 0 | UND | 0 | UND | 0 | UND | 0 | UND |
| 0 | UND | 0 | UND | 0 | UND | | 0 | UND | 0 | UND | 0 | UND | 0 | UND | 0 | UND | 0 | UND |
| 0 | UND | 0 | UND | 0 | UND | | 5 | 67.5 | 0 | UND | 0 | 999.8 | 0 | 999.8 | 0 | UND | 0 | UND |
| 21 | 17.6 | 24 | 15.1 | 25 | 14.4 | Cost of Sales/Payables | 0 | UND | 8 | 44.5 | 14 | 26.1 | 21 | 17.7 | 29 | 12.5 | 38 | 9.5 |
| 39 | 9.3 | 44 | 8.3 | 45 | 8.1 | | 31 | 11.6 | 31 | 11.9 | 32 | 11.3 | 37 | 9.8 | 46 | 7.9 | 54 | 6.7 |
| 59 | 6.2 | 67 | 5.4 | 68 | 5.4 | | 74 | 4.9 | 59 | 6.2 | 54 | 6.8 | 66 | 5.5 | 68 | 5.4 | 72 | 5.1 |
| | 6.7 | | 6.4 | | 7.0 | Sales/Working Capital | | 2.2 | | 3.7 | | 5.1 | | 6.4 | | 7.4 | | 9.2 |
| | 13.2 | | 11.9 | | 13.5 | | | 10.6 | | 13.8 | | 12.8 | | 11.6 | | 12.9 | | 15.0 |
| | 32.2 | | 29.7 | | 32.6 | | | -12.4 | | -13.3 | | 74.5 | | 29.8 | | 26.7 | | 27.5 |
| | 39.6 | | 36.0 | | 39.0 | EBIT/Interest | | 4.5 | | 17.5 | | 29.6 | | 32.9 | | 42.9 | | 61.4 |
| (1235) | 7.8 | (1181) | 5.8 | (1226) | 8.4 | | (34) 1.8 | | (139) 5.3 | | (107) 5.8 | | (249) 6.9 | | (315) 9.0 | | (382) 16.6 | |
| | .5 | | -1.1 | | 1.6 | | | -.7 | | -.1 | | -.9 | | .9 | | 1.8 | | 3.6 |
| | 12.6 | | 13.5 | | 15.9 | Net Profit + Depr., Dep., Amort./Cur. Mat. L/T/D | | | | 4.1 | | 3.4 | | 12.8 | | 17.1 | | 21.5 |
| (333) | 4.4 | (316) | 3.7 | (320) | 4.1 | | | | (15) 2.6 | | (19) 1.6 | | (70) 3.2 | | (98) 4.9 | | (116) 5.6 | |
| | .9 | | .9 | | .7 | | | | | | .1 | | -2.2 | | -1.1 | | 1.0 | | 1.8 |
| | .1 | | .1 | | .1 | Fixed/Worth | | .0 | | .1 | | .1 | | .1 | | .1 | | .1 |
| | .2 | | .2 | | .2 | | | .7 | | .5 | | .3 | | .2 | | .2 | | .2 |
| | .6 | | .6 | | .6 | | | -5.5 | | 5.7 | | 1.1 | | .7 | | .5 | | .4 |
| | .8 | | .8 | | .9 | Debt/Worth | | .4 | | .5 | | .5 | | .7 | | .9 | | 1.5 |
| | 1.8 | | 1.8 | | 2.0 | | | 2.5 | | 2.1 | | 1.2 | | 1.5 | | 1.8 | | 2.5 |
| | 3.8 | | 3.8 | | 4.5 | | | -15.5 | | 147.6 | | 5.2 | | 3.7 | | 4.0 | | 4.2 |
| | 38.3 | | 33.2 | | 34.0 | % Profit Before Taxes/Tangible Net Worth | | 19.3 | | 43.1 | | 42.3 | | 38.4 | | 35.5 | | 31.7 |
| (1573) | 14.3 | (1482) | 11.7 | (1530) | 12.6 | | (46) 1.3 | | (140) 9.7 | | (128) 15.2 | | (302) 13.8 | | (405) 12.1 | | (509) 14.3 | |
| | 1.2 | | | | 1.9 | | | -6.7 | | -1.1 | | .0 | | 1.6 | | 1.9 | | 4.3 |
| | 12.9 | | 11.2 | | 11.3 | % Profit Before Taxes/Total Assets | | 14.0 | | 15.9 | | 16.6 | | 15.7 | | 11.8 | | 8.3 |
| | 4.6 | | 3.9 | | 4.1 | | | 1.0 | | 4.3 | | 4.7 | | 5.4 | | 4.0 | | 3.7 |
| | .1 | | -1.0 | | .5 | | | -2.7 | | -2.7 | | -1.4 | | .3 | | .6 | | 1.2 |
| | 116.5 | | 125.1 | | 142.7 | Sales/Net Fixed Assets | | 401.5 | | 85.9 | | 98.8 | | 122.5 | | 140.2 | | 190.2 |
| | 44.2 | | 43.7 | | 50.4 | | | 13.1 | | 23.4 | | 35.8 | | 42.6 | | 54.8 | | 73.7 |
| | 15.4 | | 15.8 | | 17.2 | | | 4.2 | | 8.2 | | 10.7 | | 16.0 | | 23.1 | | 29.8 |
| | 4.1 | | 3.7 | | 3.8 | Sales/Total Assets | | 4.0 | | 3.8 | | 4.3 | | 4.0 | | 3.9 | | 3.6 |
| | 3.0 | | 2.8 | | 2.9 | | | 1.5 | | 2.4 | | 3.0 | | 3.0 | | 3.0 | | 3.0 |
| | 2.1 | | 2.0 | | 2.1 | | | .7 | | 1.4 | | 1.8 | | 2.2 | | 2.3 | | 2.4 |
| | .3 | | .3 | | .2 | % Depr., Dep., Amort./Sales | | .8 | | .6 | | .4 | | .3 | | .2 | | .2 |
| (1423) | .6 | (1308) | .6 | (1375) | .5 | | (33) 2.8 | | (128) 1.1 | | (113) .9 | | (273) .6 | | (364) .5 | | (464) .3 | |
| | 1.4 | | 1.5 | | 1.2 | | | 6.1 | | 2.7 | | 1.8 | | 1.3 | | 1.0 | | .6 |
| | 1.2 | | 1.2 | | 1.1 | % Officers', Directors' Owners' Comp/Sales | | 4.5 | | 2.4 | | 1.7 | | 1.4 | | 1.0 | | .5 |
| (629) | 2.5 | (617) | 2.2 | (660) | 2.1 | | (28) 9.4 | | (102) 4.2 | | (73) 2.6 | | (158) 2.3 | | (177) 1.4 | | (122) .9 | |
| | 4.7 | | 4.3 | | 4.0 | | | 14.3 | | 7.0 | | 5.1 | | 4.0 | | 2.9 | | 1.6 |
| 80513771M | | 62800428M | | 75386553M | | Net Sales ($) | 34557M | | 365831M | | 587875M | | 2400648M | | 6832233M | | 65165409M | |
| 25080585M | | 23347521M | | 27258117M | | Total Assets ($) | 41823M | | 263149M | | 289546M | | 1051355M | | 2613961M | | 22998283M | |

M = $ thousand    MM = $ million
See Pages 9 through 22 for Explanation of Ratios and Data

## Current Data Sorted by Assets      Comparative Historical Data

| 0-500M | 500M-2MM | 2-10MM | 10-50MM | 50-100MM | 100-250MM | Type of Statement | 4/1/07-3/31/08 ALL | 4/1/08-3/31/09 ALL |
|---|---|---|---|---|---|---|---|---|
| | 3 | 31 | 42 | 9 | 4 | Unqualified | 117 | 115 |
| | 25 | 85 | 23 | | | Reviewed | 151 | 168 |
| 5 | 16 | 7 | 2 | | | Compiled | 22 | 34 |
| 17 | 12 | 10 | 2 | 1 | | Tax Returns | 36 | 37 |
| 6 | 18 | 46 | 27 | 5 | 5 | Other | 110 | 111 |
| | 86 (4/1-9/30/11) | | 315 (10/1/11-3/31/12) | | | | | |
| 28 | 74 | 179 | 96 | 15 | 9 | NUMBER OF STATEMENTS | 436 | 465 |
| % | % | % | % | % | % | ASSETS | % | % |
| 17.5 | 14.9 | 15.8 | 12.4 | 18.7 | | Cash & Equivalents | 13.4 | 15.3 |
| 26.0 | 33.5 | 34.2 | 37.9 | 34.2 | | Trade Receivables (net) | 35.6 | 32.8 |
| 4.7 | 4.2 | 3.4 | 2.0 | 2.5 | | Inventory | 3.0 | 3.9 |
| .4 | 4.8 | 8.3 | 11.9 | 11.6 | | All Other Current | 8.5 | 7.6 |
| 48.5 | 57.5 | 61.8 | 64.3 | 67.0 | | Total Current | 60.6 | 59.6 |
| 38.0 | 34.9 | 29.3 | 25.6 | 23.4 | | Fixed Assets (net) | 31.7 | 32.3 |
| 2.7 | 3.4 | 1.1 | 4.1 | 1.5 | | Intangibles (net) | 1.7 | 1.7 |
| 10.8 | 4.2 | 7.9 | 6.0 | 8.1 | | All Other Non-Current | 6.0 | 6.4 |
| 100.0 | 100.0 | 100.0 | 100.0 | 100.0 | | Total | 100.0 | 100.0 |
| | | | | | | LIABILITIES | | |
| 22.9 | 8.8 | 6.8 | 4.2 | 7.9 | | Notes Payable-Short Term | 6.7 | 5.3 |
| 7.6 | 5.6 | 4.2 | 3.9 | 2.7 | | Cur. Mat.-L.T.D. | 5.8 | 5.5 |
| 13.8 | 15.7 | 17.9 | 20.5 | 16.8 | | Trade Payables | 16.4 | 15.6 |
| .0 | .2 | .7 | .2 | .0 | | Income Taxes Payable | 1.0 | .8 |
| 13.7 | 6.7 | 9.7 | 10.3 | 14.9 | | All Other Current | 12.4 | 10.7 |
| 57.9 | 37.1 | 39.4 | 39.1 | 42.3 | | Total Current | 42.3 | 38.0 |
| 33.5 | 14.3 | 10.2 | 9.3 | 12.1 | | Long-Term Debt | 15.6 | 14.9 |
| .0 | .4 | 1.1 | .6 | .7 | | Deferred Taxes | .8 | .9 |
| 23.2 | 5.2 | 1.9 | 3.5 | 1.1 | | All Other Non-Current | 2.9 | 3.0 |
| -14.6 | 43.1 | 47.5 | 47.5 | 43.7 | | Net Worth | 38.5 | 43.3 |
| 100.0 | 100.0 | 100.0 | 100.0 | 100.0 | | Total Liabilties & Net Worth | 100.0 | 100.0 |
| | | | | | | INCOME DATA | | |
| 100.0 | 100.0 | 100.0 | 100.0 | 100.0 | | Net Sales | 100.0 | 100.0 |
| 52.7 | 34.1 | 19.4 | 15.0 | 18.6 | | Gross Profit | 24.1 | 24.0 |
| 50.3 | 31.0 | 17.5 | 11.9 | 14.9 | | Operating Expenses | 18.9 | 20.5 |
| 2.4 | 3.0 | 2.0 | 3.1 | 3.7 | | Operating Profit | 5.2 | 3.5 |
| 1.0 | .4 | .0 | .2 | -.5 | | All Other Expenses (net) | .3 | .4 |
| 1.4 | 2.6 | 1.9 | 2.9 | 4.3 | | Profit Before Taxes | 4.8 | 3.1 |
| | | | | | | RATIOS | | |
| 2.0 | 4.0 | 2.5 | 2.5 | 2.6 | | Current | 2.0 | 2.4 |
| 1.0 | 1.9 | 1.7 | 1.6 | 1.5 | | | 1.5 | 1.6 |
| .3 | 1.1 | 1.1 | 1.2 | 1.1 | | | 1.1 | 1.2 |
| 1.5 | 3.1 | 2.1 | 2.0 | 2.0 | | Quick | 1.7 | 2.0 |
| (27) .9 | 1.6 | 1.3 | 1.2 | 1.1 | | | 1.2 | 1.3 |
| .2 | .8 | .9 | .9 | .9 | | | .9 | .9 |
| 0 UND | 24 15.4 | 41 9.0 | 52 7.0 | 61 6.0 | | Sales/Receivables | 41 8.9 | 36 10.0 |
| 14 25.7 | 55 6.6 | 61 6.0 | 69 5.3 | 81 4.5 | | | 58 6.3 | 54 6.8 |
| 33 11.2 | 85 4.3 | 83 4.4 | 85 4.3 | 96 3.8 | | | 80 4.6 | 75 4.9 |
| 0 UND | 0 UND | 0 UND | 0 UND | 0 UND | | Cost of Sales/Inventory | 0 UND | 0 UND |
| 0 UND | 0 UND | 0 UND | 0 UND | 0 UND | | | 0 UND | 0 UND |
| 9 41.7 | 7 51.9 | 5 80.9 | 5 78.6 | 10 38.1 | | | 4 95.3 | 6 64.9 |
| 0 UND | 11 33.2 | 20 18.5 | 28 13.1 | 20 18.4 | | Cost of Sales/Payables | 18 19.8 | 16 22.2 |
| 0 UND | 26 14.2 | 35 10.3 | 38 9.5 | 42 8.7 | | | 33 11.2 | 27 13.5 |
| 51 7.2 | 54 6.7 | 51 7.2 | 61 6.0 | 68 5.4 | | | 51 7.2 | 47 7.7 |
| 16.4 | 5.5 | 5.0 | 4.4 | 3.0 | | Sales/Working Capital | 6.5 | 5.9 |
| NM | 9.6 | 10.2 | 8.1 | 5.5 | | | 11.6 | 11.0 |
| -10.4 | 77.5 | 38.2 | 16.5 | 27.5 | | | 36.0 | 28.5 |
| 4.7 | 9.4 | 15.3 | 28.6 | 10.6 | | EBIT/Interest | 19.4 | 23.5 |
| (23) 1.9 | (66) 2.8 | (158) 4.2 | (86) 5.8 | (13) 3.5 | | | (396) 6.2 | (428) 4.8 |
| .0 | -1.8 | 1.1 | .9 | .9 | | | 1.6 | .5 |
| | 6.8 | 5.9 | 5.6 | | | Net Profit + Depr., Dep., Amort./Cur. Mat. L/T/D | 4.9 | 5.7 |
| | (10) 1.8 | (57) 1.8 | (28) 2.5 | | | | (144) 2.5 | (153) 2.5 |
| | -2.1 | .6 | 1.7 | | | | 1.2 | 1.2 |
| .6 | .4 | .3 | .3 | .2 | | Fixed/Worth | .4 | .3 |
| 1.6 | .7 | .6 | .6 | .4 | | | .7 | .7 |
| -1.9 | 3.9 | 1.1 | 1.0 | 1.0 | | | 1.5 | 1.4 |
| 2.5 | .4 | .5 | .5 | .7 | | Debt/Worth | .8 | .7 |
| 12.8 | 1.2 | 1.1 | 1.4 | 1.8 | | | 1.4 | 1.3 |
| -3.2 | 7.3 | 1.9 | 2.4 | 2.9 | | | 2.8 | 2.4 |
| 259.7 | 32.3 | 22.3 | 23.2 | 40.0 | | % Profit Before Taxes/Tangible Net Worth | 45.0 | 36.9 |
| (16) 57.4 | (60) 16.1 | (172) 9.0 | (89) 9.0 | 6.7 | | | (410) 21.2 | (440) 14.8 |
| 2.8 | -2.1 | .2 | .2 | .5 | | | 6.2 | -1.2 |
| 25.0 | 14.1 | 10.3 | 9.4 | 12.1 | | % Profit Before Taxes/Total Assets | 16.9 | 15.8 |
| 4.3 | 3.5 | 3.8 | 3.4 | 2.9 | | | 8.6 | 6.2 |
| -5.0 | -3.6 | .1 | .0 | .1 | | | 2.1 | -.9 |
| 67.3 | 15.8 | 15.3 | 18.4 | 18.3 | | Sales/Net Fixed Assets | 15.2 | 15.7 |
| 17.5 | 6.6 | 8.1 | 7.8 | 11.6 | | | 7.7 | 7.4 |
| 5.8 | 3.6 | 4.1 | 4.8 | 5.3 | | | 4.6 | 3.9 |
| 7.0 | 2.9 | 2.6 | 2.4 | 1.9 | | Sales/Total Assets | 2.7 | 2.8 |
| 4.0 | 2.1 | 2.1 | 1.8 | 1.6 | | | 2.2 | 2.1 |
| 2.6 | 1.7 | 1.5 | 1.5 | 1.4 | | | 1.6 | 1.5 |
| .9 | 2.4 | 1.8 | 1.9 | 1.2 | | % Depr., Dep., Amort./Sales | 1.8 | 1.9 |
| (21) 2.8 | (62) 4.2 | (166) 3.3 | (91) 3.2 | (12) 2.2 | | | (382) 3.3 | (423) 3.6 |
| 7.1 | 6.4 | 5.3 | 5.0 | 3.3 | | | 5.1 | 5.7 |
| 5.8 | 3.2 | 1.0 | .8 | | | % Officers', Directors' Owners' Comp/Sales | 1.5 | 1.3 |
| (17) 9.5 | (42) 4.6 | (78) 2.3 | (21) 1.4 | | | | (188) 3.2 | (195) 2.9 |
| 16.0 | 6.1 | 4.7 | 2.6 | | | | 5.9 | 5.6 |
| 26051M | 247068M | 1971882M | 3960297M | 1936620M | 2609941M | Net Sales ($) | 13900791M | 13785628M |
| 6380M | 95834M | 923156M | 2111161M | 1121041M | 1451536M | Total Assets ($) | 6839536M | 6528201M |

M = $ thousand    MM = $ million
See Pages 9 through 22 for Explanation of Ratios and Data

## Comparative Historical Data | Current Data Sorted by Sales

| | | | Type of Statement | | | | | | |
|---|---|---|---|---|---|---|---|---|---|
| 119 | 112 | 89 | Unqualified | | 1 | 3 | 12 | 23 | 50 |
| 162 | 141 | 133 | Reviewed | 2 | 13 | 24 | 32 | 48 | 14 |
| 22 | 21 | 30 | Compiled | 3 | 14 | 5 | 3 | 4 | 1 |
| 42 | 42 | 42 | Tax Returns | 11 | 14 | 5 | 6 | 4 | 2 |
| 133 | 114 | 107 | Other | 6 | 10 | 18 | 15 | 23 | 35 |
| 4/1/09-3/31/10 ALL | 4/1/10-3/31/11 ALL | 4/1/11-3/31/12 ALL | | 86 (4/1-9/30/11) | | 315 (10/1/11-3/31/12) | | | |
| | | | | 0-1MM | 1-3MM | 3-5MM | 5-10MM | 10-25MM | 25MM & OVER |
| 478 | 430 | 401 | NUMBER OF STATEMENTS | 22 | 52 | 55 | 68 | 102 | 102 |
| % | % | % | **ASSETS** | % | % | % | % | % | % |
| 17.1 | 16.2 | 15.1 | Cash & Equivalents | 17.0 | 14.7 | 15.0 | 13.3 | 17.3 | 13.8 |
| 31.2 | 32.5 | 34.4 | Trade Receivables (net) | 15.6 | 28.4 | 33.7 | 35.0 | 35.4 | 40.4 |
| 3.9 | 3.5 | 3.3 | Inventory | 3.3 | 3.5 | 5.4 | 3.3 | 3.5 | 1.7 |
| 7.3 | 8.3 | 8.2 | All Other Current | 1.3 | 3.4 | 4.3 | 8.5 | 10.0 | 12.0 |
| 59.6 | 60.5 | 60.8 | Total Current | 37.2 | 50.0 | 58.5 | 60.0 | 66.2 | 67.9 |
| 31.0 | 30.2 | 29.7 | Fixed Assets (net) | 49.8 | 34.2 | 35.0 | 30.0 | 26.1 | 23.6 |
| 1.9 | 2.0 | 2.6 | Intangibles (net) | 2.0 | 4.7 | 1.4 | 2.5 | 1.6 | 3.3 |
| 7.6 | 7.2 | 6.9 | All Other Non-Current | 11.0 | 11.0 | 5.0 | 7.4 | 6.1 | 5.2 |
| 100.0 | 100.0 | 100.0 | Total | 100.0 | 100.0 | 100.0 | 100.0 | 100.0 | 100.0 |
| | | | **LIABILITIES** | | | | | | |
| 5.7 | 7.0 | 7.7 | Notes Payable-Short Term | 15.9 | 14.2 | 8.8 | 6.4 | 5.6 | 4.8 |
| 5.8 | 4.7 | 4.6 | Cur. Mat.-L.T.D. | 10.9 | 4.3 | 4.4 | 5.9 | 3.8 | 3.3 |
| 15.9 | 18.2 | 17.8 | Trade Payables | 12.3 | 12.3 | 16.0 | 17.3 | 18.9 | 21.8 |
| .6 | .5 | .4 | Income Taxes Payable | .0 | .5 | .3 | 1.1 | .2 | .2 |
| 9.8 | 8.6 | 9.9 | All Other Current | 12.4 | 7.7 | 6.5 | 7.1 | 12.2 | 11.8 |
| 37.7 | 39.0 | 40.3 | Total Current | 51.6 | 39.0 | 35.9 | 37.8 | 40.8 | 42.0 |
| 15.9 | 14.3 | 12.4 | Long-Term Debt | 28.8 | 18.8 | 13.4 | 11.2 | 10.5 | 7.8 |
| .9 | .9 | .8 | Deferred Taxes | .0 | .3 | .9 | 1.6 | .6 | .7 |
| 2.8 | 3.9 | 4.4 | All Other Non-Current | 24.2 | 5.7 | 4.3 | 2.5 | 1.9 | 3.1 |
| 42.8 | 41.9 | 42.2 | Net Worth | -4.7 | 36.2 | 45.5 | 47.0 | 46.3 | 46.4 |
| 100.0 | 100.0 | 100.0 | Total Liabilities & Net Worth | 100.0 | 100.0 | 100.0 | 100.0 | 100.0 | 100.0 |
| | | | **INCOME DATA** | | | | | | |
| 100.0 | 100.0 | 100.0 | Net Sales | 100.0 | 100.0 | 100.0 | 100.0 | 100.0 | 100.0 |
| 24.3 | 22.3 | 23.1 | Gross Profit | 56.3 | 34.4 | 26.7 | 21.0 | 20.2 | 12.5 |
| 21.6 | 19.7 | 20.6 | Operating Expenses | 50.9 | 34.4 | 24.7 | 18.5 | 16.5 | 10.5 |
| 2.8 | 2.7 | 2.5 | Operating Profit | 5.4 | .0 | 2.0 | 2.5 | 3.7 | 2.1 |
| .2 | .1 | .2 | All Other Expenses (net) | 1.9 | .7 | -.1 | .1 | .1 | -.2 |
| 2.6 | 2.5 | 2.3 | Profit Before Taxes | 3.5 | -.8 | 2.1 | 2.4 | 3.6 | 2.2 |
| | | | **RATIOS** | | | | | | |
| 2.5 | 2.6 | 2.6 | Current | 1.5 | 3.3 | 4.2 | 2.3 | 2.5 | 2.4 |
| 1.6 | 1.7 | 1.6 | | .9 | 1.5 | 2.2 | 1.7 | 1.7 | 1.5 |
| 1.1 | 1.2 | 1.1 | | .2 | .9 | 1.1 | 1.1 | 1.3 | 1.3 |
| 2.1 | 2.1 | 2.2 | Quick | 1.3 | 3.0 | 2.9 | 2.0 | 2.1 | 1.8 |
| 1.3 | 1.3 (400) | 1.3 | | .6 | (51) 1.3 | 1.9 | 1.3 | 1.4 | 1.2 |
| .8 | .8 | .9 | | .2 | .7 | .9 | .8 | 1.0 | .9 |
| 35  10.5 | 36  10.1 | 36  10.0 | Sales/Receivables | 0  UND | 22  16.7 | 28  13.0 | 39  9.4 | 41  9.0 | 51  7.2 |
| 55  6.7 | 56  6.5 | 62  5.9 | | 0  UND | 48  7.6 | 61  6.0 | 62  5.9 | 57  6.4 | 70  5.2 |
| 74  4.9 | 76  4.8 | 83  4.4 | | 89  4.1 | 85  4.3 | 89  4.1 | 89  4.1 | 74  4.9 | 85  4.3 |
| 0  UND | 0  UND | 0  UND | Cost of Sales/Inventory | 0  UND | 0  UND | 0  UND | 0  UND | 0  UND | 0  UND |
| 0  UND | 0  UND | 0  UND | | 0  UND | 0  UND | 0  UND | 0  UND | 0  UND | 0  UND |
| 6  59.6 | 5  66.5 | 6  59.1 | | 0  UND | 7  51.6 | 7  53.5 | 9  40.1 | 8  45.0 | 3  104.9 |
| 16  22.8 | 19  19.3 | 19  19.2 | Cost of Sales/Payables | 0  UND | 10  36.4 | 10  34.8 | 19  19.1 | 22  16.5 | 28  13.0 |
| 31  11.8 | 35  10.4 | 35  10.3 | | 0  UND | 30  12.2 | 28  13.1 | 35  10.5 | 35  10.5 | 38  9.5 |
| 51  7.2 | 54  6.7 | 54  6.8 | | 96  3.8 | 51  7.2 | 57  6.4 | 51  7.1 | 51  7.1 | 57  6.4 |
| 5.6 | 5.1 | 5.1 | Sales/Working Capital | 12.0 | 5.5 | 5.0 | 4.9 | 4.9 | 4.9 |
| 10.0 | 9.0 | 9.7 | | -307.7 | 15.8 | 9.6 | 10.0 | 9.1 | 8.7 |
| 37.6 | 36.3 | 41.0 | | -4.6 | -19.5 | 27.8 | 50.5 | 18.8 | 15.8 |
| 18.3 | 21.5 | 14.4 | EBIT/Interest | 7.9 | 5.5 | 7.9 | 9.6 | 39.5 | 30.4 |
| (428) 4.4 | (377) 4.3 | (354) 3.9 | | (17) 2.0 | (45) 1.1 | (50) 2.3 | (62) 4.0 | (91) 7.4 | (89) 5.6 |
| .4 | -.2 | .5 | | -.6 | -2.1 | -4.2 | .2 | 1.5 | 1.0 |
| 6.7 | 7.2 | 5.9 | Net Profit + Depr., Dep., Amort./Cur. Mat. L/T/D | | 6.5 | 2.7 | 3.2 | 9.8 | 5.9 |
| (137) 2.2 | (118) 2.5 | (105) 2.1 | | | (11) 1.6 | (12) 1.0 | (21) 1.6 | (28) 2.4 | (32) 2.6 |
| 1.2 | 1.1 | 1.0 | | | -1.6 | -11.2 | .5 | 1.5 | 1.7 |
| .3 | .3 | .3 | Fixed/Worth | .8 | .3 | .5 | .3 | .2 | .3 |
| .7 | .6 | .6 | | 1.8 | .8 | .8 | .7 | .6 | .5 |
| 1.4 | 1.4 | 1.2 | | -.8 | 4.0 | 1.4 | 1.2 | .9 | .9 |
| .6 | .6 | .5 | Debt/Worth | 1.2 | .5 | .5 | .5 | .5 | .6 |
| 1.2 | 1.2 | 1.3 | | 8.1 | 1.3 | 1.0 | 1.2 | 1.2 | 1.3 |
| 2.7 | 2.7 | 2.7 | | -5.3 | 21.7 | 6.3 | 2.5 | 2.0 | 2.3 |
| 30.7 | 30.5 | 25.6 | % Profit Before Taxes/Tangible Net Worth | 144.9 | 17.2 | 24.1 | 22.7 | 27.6 | 25.9 |
| (441) 11.8 | (396) 9.5 | (360) 10.6 | | (14) 26.3 | (40) 3.9 | (48) 9.8 | (63) 8.5 | (97) 14.8 | (98) 9.3 |
| .1 | -2.0 | .1 | | 12.9 | -4.8 | -8.5 | -2.3 | .9 | .6 |
| 13.8 | 13.3 | 10.9 | % Profit Before Taxes/Total Assets | 22.9 | 6.5 | 11.2 | 10.7 | 12.1 | 9.8 |
| 4.7 | 4.0 | 3.7 | | 6.1 | .2 | 3.7 | 3.4 | 5.2 | 3.6 |
| -.6 | -1.9 | -1.0 | | -.4 | -5.5 | -6.0 | -.7 | .2 | .1 |
| 17.0 | 17.9 | 17.2 | Sales/Net Fixed Assets | 23.8 | 14.9 | 13.9 | 15.4 | 18.4 | 20.2 |
| 7.9 | 8.0 | 8.1 | | 4.5 | 6.3 | 5.9 | 7.3 | 10.1 | 10.9 |
| 4.2 | 4.4 | 4.3 | | 1.5 | 3.5 | 3.6 | 4.0 | 5.3 | 5.5 |
| 2.8 | 2.8 | 2.6 | Sales/Total Assets | 4.5 | 2.6 | 2.5 | 2.5 | 2.8 | 2.6 |
| 2.0 | 2.1 | 2.0 | | 1.9 | 1.9 | 2.0 | 2.0 | 2.2 | 2.0 |
| 1.5 | 1.5 | 1.6 | | 1.1 | 1.2 | 1.5 | 1.5 | 1.7 | 1.7 |
| 1.8 | 1.6 | 1.8 | % Depr., Dep., Amort./Sales | 1.1 | 1.8 | 3.1 | 1.9 | 1.5 | 1.6 |
| (414) 3.6 | (385) 3.3 | (357) 3.3 | | (17) 7.0 | (45) 4.1 | (48) 4.3 | (63) 3.7 | (94) 2.9 | (90) 2.8 |
| 5.9 | 5.7 | 5.4 | | 11.5 | 7.3 | 6.5 | 5.5 | 4.6 | 3.8 |
| 1.4 | 1.8 | 1.3 | % Officers', Directors', Owners' Comp/Sales | | 4.6 | 2.3 | 1.6 | .8 | .5 |
| (212) 2.9 | (174) 3.1 | (161) 3.1 | | | (34) 5.8 | (26) 3.4 | (32) 2.6 | (41) 1.8 | (19) .8 |
| 6.1 | 6.1 | 5.8 | | | 7.8 | 5.2 | 5.1 | 3.2 | 1.3 |
| 11964460M | 11305837M | 10751859M | Net Sales ($) | 12200M | 97919M | 214224M | 495199M | 1613307M | 8319010M |
| 6530784M | 6412005M | 5709108M | Total Assets ($) | 9843M | 71030M | 124138M | 302441M | 822917M | 4378739M |

© RMA 2012

M = $ thousand   MM = $ million
See Pages 9 through 22 for Explanation of Ratios and Data

## Current Data Sorted by Assets        Comparative Historical Data

| | | | 12 | 6 | 7 | Type of Statement | | |
|---|---|---|---|---|---|---|---|---|
| | 2 | 9 | 4 | 1 | | Unqualified | 32 | 21 |
| 2 | 2 | 7 | 4 | | | Reviewed | 15 | 12 |
| 3 | 3 | 2 | | | | Compiled | 9 | 10 |
| 5 | 5 | 10 | 16 | 7 | 5 | Tax Returns | 6 | 8 |
| | 16 (4/1-9/30/11) | | 96 (10/1/11-3/31/12) | | | Other | 37 | 32 |
| 0-500M | 500M-2MM | 2-10MM | 10-50MM | 50-100MM | 100-250MM | | 4/1/07-3/31/08 ALL | 4/1/08-3/31/09 ALL |
| 10 | 12 | 28 | 36 | 14 | 12 | NUMBER OF STATEMENTS | 99 | 83 |
| % | % | % | % | % | % | ASSETS | % | % |
| 12.0 | 28.5 | 11.6 | 13.9 | 11.0 | 8.0 | Cash & Equivalents | 12.3 | 15.5 |
| 23.4 | 22.9 | 33.8 | 33.9 | 26.2 | 28.3 | Trade Receivables (net) | 32.5 | 30.8 |
| 19.8 | 4.3 | 3.6 | 4.6 | 1.4 | 1.5 | Inventory | 5.3 | 3.6 |
| .5 | 3.2 | 2.2 | 5.2 | 4.0 | 9.7 | All Other Current | 6.6 | 5.9 |
| 55.7 | 58.8 | 51.2 | 57.7 | 42.6 | 47.5 | Total Current | 56.7 | 55.8 |
| 40.9 | 37.1 | 33.4 | 27.2 | 49.4 | 23.6 | Fixed Assets (net) | 34.5 | 35.5 |
| .5 | 2.3 | 3.0 | 9.8 | 4.4 | 23.4 | Intangibles (net) | 3.6 | 3.4 |
| 2.8 | 1.7 | 12.4 | 5.2 | 3.6 | 5.5 | All Other Non-Current | 5.2 | 5.3 |
| 100.0 | 100.0 | 100.0 | 100.0 | 100.0 | 100.0 | Total | 100.0 | 100.0 |
| | | | | | | LIABILITIES | | |
| 7.9 | 6.0 | 6.5 | 4.4 | 4.2 | 3.8 | Notes Payable-Short Term | 8.2 | 6.6 |
| 7.5 | 7.0 | 5.7 | 5.5 | 4.0 | 3.2 | Cur. Mat.-L.T.D. | 6.3 | 5.4 |
| 7.0 | 15.6 | 15.1 | 14.1 | 8.4 | 11.3 | Trade Payables | 11.4 | 12.0 |
| .0 | .2 | .3 | .3 | .2 | .0 | Income Taxes Payable | .5 | .7 |
| 15.6 | 7.4 | 10.3 | 10.5 | 5.6 | 9.9 | All Other Current | 11.0 | 12.1 |
| 37.9 | 36.2 | 37.8 | 34.8 | 22.4 | 28.2 | Total Current | 37.5 | 36.7 |
| 29.0 | 24.3 | 15.7 | 12.7 | 16.1 | 16.4 | Long-Term Debt | 18.4 | 18.6 |
| .0 | .0 | .8 | 1.0 | 4.4 | 4.3 | Deferred Taxes | 1.2 | 1.0 |
| 8.3 | 1.2 | 1.9 | 2.8 | 1.1 | 4.7 | All Other Non-Current | 2.2 | 3.6 |
| 24.8 | 38.2 | 43.8 | 48.6 | 56.0 | 46.4 | Net Worth | 40.8 | 40.1 |
| 100.0 | 100.0 | 100.0 | 100.0 | 100.0 | 100.0 | Total Liabilities & Net Worth | 100.0 | 100.0 |
| | | | | | | INCOME DATA | | |
| 100.0 | 100.0 | 100.0 | 100.0 | 100.0 | 100.0 | Net Sales | 100.0 | 100.0 |
| | | | | | | Gross Profit | | |
| 93.4 | 91.9 | 94.2 | 89.5 | 89.5 | 93.7 | Operating Expenses | 87.4 | 90.5 |
| 6.6 | 8.1 | 5.8 | 10.5 | 10.5 | 6.3 | Operating Profit | 12.6 | 9.5 |
| .9 | -.3 | .6 | 1.1 | 1.1 | 3.2 | All Other Expenses (net) | 1.6 | 1.3 |
| 5.8 | 8.4 | 5.1 | 9.4 | 9.3 | 3.2 | Profit Before Taxes | 11.0 | 8.2 |
| | | | | | | RATIOS | | |
| 3.1 | 3.7 | 2.4 | 3.2 | 2.6 | 1.9 | | 2.6 | 2.4 |
| 1.9 | 1.7 | 1.4 | 1.8 | 1.5 | 1.6 | Current | 1.5 | 1.5 |
| .3 | 1.0 | .9 | 1.2 | 1.3 | 1.3 | | 1.1 | .9 |
| 2.1 | 3.0 | 2.4 | 2.1 | 2.5 | 1.6 | | 2.3 | 2.1 |
| .3 | 1.4 | 1.2 | 1.4 | 1.4 | 1.1 | Quick | 1.2 | 1.3 |
| .2 | .7 | .6 | .9 | 1.0 | .9 | | .8 | .8 |
| 0 UND | 0 UND | 28 13.1 | 46 8.0 | 55 6.6 | 43 8.4 | | 34 10.8 | 26 14.1 |
| 29 12.6 | 27 13.6 | 48 7.6 | 59 6.2 | 81 4.5 | 58 6.3 | Sales/Receivables | 52 7.0 | 47 7.8 |
| 43 8.4 | 51 7.1 | 60 6.1 | 89 4.1 | 101 3.6 | 74 4.9 | | 68 5.3 | 66 5.5 |
| | | | | | | Cost of Sales/Inventory | | |
| | | | | | | Cost of Sales/Payables | | |
| 5.4 | 7.3 | 8.0 | 4.4 | 5.8 | 5.2 | | 6.4 | 6.8 |
| 14.0 | 15.6 | 19.1 | 9.5 | 7.1 | 10.9 | Sales/Working Capital | 10.4 | 12.5 |
| -18.5 | NM | -65.2 | 24.6 | 23.1 | 13.1 | | 47.4 | -47.6 |
| | 22.7 | 31.1 | 59.9 | 40.9 | 41.0 | | 32.4 | 41.1 |
| (11) 3.9 | (26) 6.9 | (31) 12.4 | (13) 12.3 | 4.9 | | EBIT/Interest | (89) 9.7 | (78) 10.3 |
| | -2.8 | 2.3 | 7.3 | 1.3 | .4 | | 3.4 | 2.3 |
| | | | 9.0 | | | | 4.5 | 7.0 |
| | | (13) 4.3 | | | | Net Profit + Depr., Dep., Amort./Cur. Mat. L/T/D | (26) 2.4 | (23) 3.2 |
| | | 2.9 | | | | | 1.3 | 1.7 |
| .1 | .2 | .4 | .4 | .7 | .3 | | .4 | .2 |
| 1.0 | 1.1 | .6 | .8 | 1.0 | 1.3 | Fixed/Worth | .8 | .9 |
| -4.3 | 2.1 | 1.5 | 1.5 | 1.5 | 2.0 | | 2.1 | 2.0 |
| .9 | .6 | .7 | .4 | .4 | 1.2 | | .6 | .6 |
| 2.3 | 1.6 | 1.4 | 1.2 | .7 | 2.0 | Debt/Worth | 1.5 | 1.5 |
| -7.2 | 5.1 | 3.5 | 3.8 | 2.1 | 5.0 | | 3.7 | 3.1 |
| | 220.4 | 58.1 | 72.8 | 19.1 | 58.9 | | 76.4 | 79.9 |
| (11) 48.6 | (26) 31.7 | (31) 36.9 | (13) 9.8 | (11) 37.7 | | % Profit Before Taxes/Tangible Net Worth | (87) 41.7 | (74) 40.7 |
| | -5.3 | 4.7 | 20.9 | 3.6 | 17.4 | | 18.1 | 13.1 |
| 54.3 | 58.4 | 26.4 | 24.3 | 13.1 | 16.5 | | 31.5 | 33.7 |
| 17.4 | 17.8 | 11.8 | 12.8 | 5.1 | 12.0 | % Profit Before Taxes/Total Assets | 13.7 | 14.1 |
| -19.0 | -14.1 | 2.8 | 6.5 | .9 | 1.0 | | 5.8 | 4.2 |
| 57.7 | 32.0 | 17.1 | 10.8 | 5.1 | 30.6 | | 21.3 | 28.4 |
| 10.5 | 9.6 | 8.4 | 8.3 | 3.3 | 7.5 | Sales/Net Fixed Assets | 7.7 | 7.7 |
| 3.0 | 3.9 | 4.2 | 5.8 | 1.0 | 3.7 | | 3.8 | 3.5 |
| 5.9 | 4.2 | 3.0 | 2.8 | 1.8 | 2.1 | | 2.9 | 3.3 |
| 2.8 | 2.5 | 2.3 | 2.3 | 1.0 | 1.5 | Sales/Total Assets | 2.3 | 2.5 |
| 1.7 | 2.0 | 2.0 | 1.4 | .6 | 1.1 | | 1.4 | 1.6 |
| | | 1.5 | 1.7 | 5.6 | | | .7 | .7 |
| | (22) 2.9 | (34) 2.9 | (11) 7.6 | | | % Depr., Dep., Amort./Sales | (86) 1.7 | (65) 2.5 |
| | | 7.1 | 5.4 | 11.4 | | | 4.3 | 6.7 |
| | | 1.9 | | | | | .9 | 1.1 |
| | (12) 2.8 | | | | | % Officers', Directors' Owners' Comp/Sales | (29) 2.3 | (23) 2.2 |
| | | 3.8 | | | | | 4.9 | 5.5 |
| 14259M | 40625M | 317436M | 1773132M | 1161071M | 2751770M | Net Sales ($) | 7356188M | 4550801M |
| 2995M | 12352M | 129994M | 888745M | 995697M | 1745295M | Total Assets ($) | 3572069M | 2306040M |

M = $ thousand    MM = $ million
See Pages 9 through 22 for Explanation of Ratios and Data

## Comparative Historical Data | | | | ## Current Data Sorted by Sales

| | | | Type of Statement | 0-1MM | 1-3MM | 3-5MM | 5-10MM | 10-25MM | 25MM & OVER |
|---|---|---|---|---|---|---|---|---|---|
| 25 | 18 | 25 | Unqualified | | | | 2 | | 23 |
| 14 | 13 | 16 | Reviewed | | | 2 | 2 | 6 | 6 |
| 12 | 10 | 15 | Compiled | 1 | 3 | 1 | 4 | 3 | 3 |
| 4 | 8 | 8 | Tax Returns | | 2 | 3 | 2 | 1 | |
| 39 | 38 | 48 | Other | 5 | 7 | | 5 | 6 | 25 |
| 4/1/09-3/31/10 ALL | 4/1/10-3/31/11 ALL | 4/1/11-3/31/12 ALL | | 16 (4/1-9/30/11) | | | 96 (10/1/11-3/31/12) | | |
| 94 | 87 | 112 | NUMBER OF STATEMENTS | 6 | 12 | 6 | 15 | 16 | 57 |
| % | % | % | ASSETS | % | % | % | % | % | % |
| 15.0 | 14.6 | 13.7 | Cash & Equivalents | | 10.1 | | 14.8 | 14.4 | 12.4 |
| 24.5 | 28.3 | 30.2 | Trade Receivables (net) | | 18.1 | | 33.7 | 32.7 | 33.0 |
| 4.5 | 3.4 | 4.9 | Inventory | | 4.0 | | 4.4 | 5.0 | 2.8 |
| 5.9 | 4.5 | 4.1 | All Other Current | | 2.7 | | 3.1 | 1.8 | 6.2 |
| 49.9 | 50.8 | 53.1 | Total Current | | 34.8 | | 56.0 | 53.9 | 54.4 |
| 35.9 | 36.8 | 33.4 | Fixed Assets (net) | | 49.5 | | 27.2 | 33.1 | 30.8 |
| 7.3 | 7.6 | 7.3 | Intangibles (net) | | 1.9 | | 9.7 | 4.9 | 9.7 |
| 6.8 | 4.8 | 6.3 | All Other Non-Current | | 13.9 | | 7.0 | 8.1 | 5.1 |
| 100.0 | 100.0 | 100.0 | Total | | 100.0 | | 100.0 | 100.0 | 100.0 |
| | | | LIABILITIES | | | | | | |
| 6.0 | 8.2 | 5.3 | Notes Payable-Short Term | | 6.3 | | 6.3 | 5.5 | 4.6 |
| 4.3 | 5.4 | 5.4 | Cur. Mat.-L.T.D. | | 7.9 | | 5.1 | 4.9 | 4.9 |
| 11.8 | 10.3 | 12.8 | Trade Payables | | 14.3 | | 14.9 | 15.1 | 12.8 |
| .8 | .4 | .2 | Income Taxes Payable | | .0 | | .7 | .1 | .3 |
| 10.1 | 8.9 | 9.9 | All Other Current | | 15.2 | | 6.2 | 11.3 | 8.9 |
| 33.1 | 33.1 | 33.7 | Total Current | | 43.8 | | 33.2 | 36.8 | 31.5 |
| 19.4 | 14.7 | 17.0 | Long-Term Debt | | 35.9 | | 13.7 | 11.7 | 14.7 |
| 2.0 | 2.4 | 1.5 | Deferred Taxes | | .0 | | 1.5 | .4 | 2.5 |
| 3.4 | 3.5 | 2.9 | All Other Non-Current | | 1.2 | | 2.8 | 1.4 | 2.8 |
| 42.1 | 46.2 | 44.8 | Net Worth | | 19.1 | | 48.7 | 49.7 | 48.4 |
| 100.0 | 100.0 | 100.0 | Total Liabilities & Net Worth | | 100.0 | | 100.0 | 100.0 | 100.0 |
| | | | INCOME DATA | | | | | | |
| 100.0 | 100.0 | 100.0 | Net Sales | | 100.0 | | 100.0 | 100.0 | 100.0 |
| | | | Gross Profit | | | | | | |
| 93.5 | 88.9 | 91.7 | Operating Expenses | | 99.8 | | 90.1 | 93.4 | 91.0 |
| 6.5 | 11.1 | 8.3 | Operating Profit | | .2 | | 9.9 | 6.6 | 9.0 |
| 2.9 | 2.5 | 1.0 | All Other Expenses (net) | | 2.2 | | .0 | -.9 | 1.8 |
| 3.6 | 8.5 | 7.2 | Profit Before Taxes | | -2.0 | | 9.9 | 7.5 | 7.2 |
| | | | RATIOS | | | | | | |
| 2.5 | 2.8 | 2.5 | | | 2.0 | | 2.4 | 2.3 | 2.8 |
| 1.5 | 1.5 | 1.6 | Current | | .9 | | 1.7 | 1.4 | 1.6 |
| 1.0 | 1.0 | 1.1 | | | .2 | | 1.0 | 1.0 | 1.3 |
| 2.1 | 2.4 | 2.1 | | | 1.9 | | 2.4 | 2.3 | 2.1 |
| 1.1 | 1.3 | 1.3 | Quick | | .4 | | 1.4 | 1.3 | 1.4 |
| .7 | .8 | .8 | | | .2 | | 1.0 | .8 | .9 |
| 28  13.2 | 34  10.6 | 33  11.0 | | 0  UND | | 26  13.9 | 27  13.7 | | 45  8.1 |
| 42  8.6 | 55  6.7 | 51  7.1 | Sales/Receivables | 29  12.8 | | 51  7.2 | 51  7.2 | | 63  5.8 |
| 57  6.4 | 76  4.8 | 74  4.9 | | 40  9.2 | | 64  5.7 | 72  5.1 | | 87  4.2 |
| | | | Cost of Sales/Inventory | | | | | | |
| | | | Cost of Sales/Payables | | | | | | |
| 5.4 | 4.8 | 6.1 | | | 10.5 | | 7.8 | 6.5 | 5.2 |
| 13.1 | 12.3 | 10.2 | Sales/Working Capital | | NM | | 10.0 | 17.9 | 9.3 |
| NM | -160.0 | 72.9 | | | -5.3 | | 99.2 | NM | 13.0 |
| 22.5 | 26.9 | 35.9 | | | 10.1 | | 31.0 | 41.0 | 48.9 |
| (86)  5.5 | (76)  9.0 | (101)  8.7 | EBIT/Interest | (11)  1.1 | | (13)  7.4 | (15)  14.1 | (53)  9.3 | |
| .6 | 2.0 | 2.0 | | | -4.5 | | 3.6 | 4.5 | 3.5 |
| 9.1 | 7.9 | 9.3 | | | | | | | 8.1 |
| (29)  2.8 | (21)  2.2 | (26)  4.0 | Net Profit + Depr., Dep., Amort./Cur. Mat. L/T/D | | | | | (20) | 3.3 |
| 1.1 | .6 | 2.1 | | | | | | | 2.0 |
| .4 | .5 | .4 | | | .4 | | .2 | .4 | .4 |
| 1.0 | 1.1 | .8 | Fixed/Worth | | 1.5 | | .8 | .6 | .9 |
| 2.7 | 1.9 | 1.6 | | | NM | | 1.7 | 1.1 | 1.5 |
| .6 | .5 | .5 | | | 1.2 | | .6 | .5 | .4 |
| 1.9 | 1.3 | 1.4 | Debt/Worth | | 3.2 | | 1.7 | .9 | 1.4 |
| 4.5 | 4.0 | 3.3 | | | NM | | 3.8 | 2.2 | 2.9 |
| 44.7 | 65.5 | 71.3 | % Profit Before Taxes/Tangible Net Worth | | | | 105.1 | 53.8 | 58.9 |
| (81)  15.7 | (75)  25.6 | (99)  33.9 | | | | (13)  31.5 | (15)  27.7 | (51)  33.9 | |
| .2 | 7.5 | 9.1 | | | | | 10.6 | 4.7 | 12.0 |
| 18.9 | 19.5 | 24.6 | % Profit Before Taxes/Total Assets | | 28.3 | | 31.6 | 25.3 | 20.3 |
| 5.5 | 9.7 | 11.7 | | | 2.7 | | 12.3 | 9.2 | 12.2 |
| -1.3 | 3.8 | 2.3 | | | -18.0 | | 3.2 | 2.5 | 2.7 |
| 13.5 | 13.2 | 12.5 | | | 10.7 | | 100.5 | 12.5 | 10.5 |
| 6.6 | 5.9 | 7.2 | Sales/Net Fixed Assets | | 4.7 | | 10.3 | 8.3 | 6.7 |
| 3.0 | 3.4 | 3.8 | | | 2.3 | | 5.4 | 4.5 | 4.0 |
| 3.1 | 2.5 | 2.9 | | | 3.7 | | 3.0 | 3.4 | 2.6 |
| 1.7 | 1.7 | 2.1 | Sales/Total Assets | | 2.5 | | 2.6 | 2.1 | 1.9 |
| 1.1 | 1.2 | 1.3 | | | .8 | | 2.0 | 1.6 | 1.2 |
| 1.1 | 2.2 | 1.9 | | | 2.7 | | .6 | 1.5 | 1.9 |
| (78)  3.5 | (67)  4.2 | (91)  3.2 | % Depr., Dep., Amort./Sales | (10)  6.7 | | (11)  2.2 | (14)  3.2 | (47)  3.6 | |
| 6.1 | 7.4 | 6.7 | | | 14.1 | | 5.3 | 6.7 | 6.1 |
| .7 | 1.3 | .9 | % Officers', Directors' Owners' Comp/Sales | | | | | | |
| (23)  1.9 | (17)  2.1 | (25)  1.9 | | | | | | | |
| 10.8 | 5.6 | 3.5 | | | | | | | |
| 6162375M | 5009040M | 6058293M | Net Sales ($) | 2438M | 24673M | 23088M | 123520M | 245882M | 5638692M |
| 4165268M | 3125865M | 3775078M | Total Assets ($) | 1776M | 21093M | 8455M | 177392M | 133393M | 3432969M |

M = $ thousand    MM = $ million
See Pages 9 through 22 for Explanation of Ratios and Data

## Current Data Sorted by Assets

## Comparative Historical Data

| | | | | | | | Type of Statement | | |
|---|---|---|---|---|---|---|---|---|---|
| 1 | 1 | 9 | 15 | 4 | 9 | | Unqualified | 16 | 18 |
| | 9 | 30 | 9 | | | | Reviewed | 19 | 20 |
| 1 | 6 | 6 | 1 | 1 | | | Compiled | 3 | 4 |
| 7 | 8 | 2 | | | | | Tax Returns | 6 | 12 |
| 2 | 11 | 24 | 10 | 4 | 4 | | Other | 27 | 32 |
| | 22 (4/1-9/30/11) | | 152 (10/1/11-3/31/12) | | | | | 4/1/07-3/31/08 | 4/1/08-3/31/09 |
| 0-500M | 500M-2MM | 2-10MM | 10-50MM | 50-100MM | 100-250MM | | | ALL | ALL |
| 11 | 35 | 71 | 35 | 9 | 13 | NUMBER OF STATEMENTS | | 71 | 86 |
| % | % | % | % | % | % | ASSETS | | % | % |
| 24.3 | 14.0 | 13.7 | 8.5 | | 13.5 | Cash & Equivalents | | 9.7 | 12.0 |
| 16.9 | 37.8 | 44.5 | 36.5 | | 28.0 | Trade Receivables (net) | | 40.5 | 40.9 |
| 1.4 | 5.1 | 3.7 | 4.6 | | 2.8 | Inventory | | 3.3 | 2.6 |
| 16.7 | 6.2 | 6.9 | 17.3 | | 10.7 | All Other Current | | 9.6 | 8.8 |
| 59.3 | 63.1 | 68.8 | 66.8 | | 55.0 | Total Current | | 63.2 | 64.3 |
| 34.4 | 29.9 | 22.4 | 21.8 | | 25.8 | Fixed Assets (net) | | 28.8 | 26.0 |
| 1.5 | .2 | 1.9 | 5.3 | | 10.8 | Intangibles (net) | | 1.2 | 3.2 |
| 4.9 | 6.8 | 7.0 | 6.1 | | 8.4 | All Other Non-Current | | 6.8 | 6.5 |
| 100.0 | 100.0 | 100.0 | 100.0 | | 100.0 | Total | | 100.0 | 100.0 |
| | | | | | | LIABILITIES | | | |
| 18.9 | 11.2 | 8.6 | 6.0 | | 2.2 | Notes Payable-Short Term | | 11.0 | 7.9 |
| 8.9 | 8.8 | 3.1 | 4.1 | | 8.2 | Cur. Mat.-L.T.D. | | 4.0 | 7.4 |
| 4.6 | 18.7 | 15.1 | 17.8 | | 13.8 | Trade Payables | | 15.7 | 17.3 |
| .0 | .3 | .3 | .4 | | .7 | Income Taxes Payable | | .5 | .3 |
| 13.5 | 13.5 | 13.5 | 10.5 | | 14.7 | All Other Current | | 12.5 | 10.0 |
| 45.8 | 52.4 | 40.6 | 38.8 | | 39.7 | Total Current | | 43.6 | 42.9 |
| 25.9 | 16.5 | 7.0 | 10.3 | | 13.4 | Long-Term Debt | | 11.5 | 14.1 |
| .0 | .0 | .7 | .2 | | .4 | Deferred Taxes | | .5 | .6 |
| 15.4 | 5.1 | 3.3 | 3.5 | | 4.8 | All Other Non-Current | | 5.6 | 5.3 |
| 12.9 | 26.0 | 48.5 | 47.1 | | 41.7 | Net Worth | | 38.8 | 37.2 |
| 100.0 | 100.0 | 100.0 | 100.0 | | 100.0 | Total Liabilties & Net Worth | | 100.0 | 100.0 |
| | | | | | | INCOME DATA | | | |
| 100.0 | 100.0 | 100.0 | 100.0 | | 100.0 | Net Sales | | 100.0 | 100.0 |
| 62.0 | 34.1 | 28.3 | 19.2 | | 17.4 | Gross Profit | | 25.1 | 26.8 |
| 56.7 | 31.2 | 24.2 | 14.9 | | 13.6 | Operating Expenses | | 19.2 | 20.4 |
| 5.3 | 2.9 | 4.1 | 4.3 | | 3.8 | Operating Profit | | 5.9 | 6.4 |
| -.6 | .6 | .3 | .2 | | 1.7 | All Other Expenses (net) | | .7 | .6 |
| 5.9 | 2.3 | 3.8 | 4.1 | | 2.2 | Profit Before Taxes | | 5.1 | 5.8 |
| | | | | | | RATIOS | | | |
| 7.3 | 2.1 | 2.9 | 2.5 | | 2.1 | | | 2.3 | 2.5 |
| 1.5 | 1.4 | 1.7 | 1.8 | | 1.6 | Current | | 1.5 | 1.5 |
| .5 | 1.0 | 1.2 | 1.4 | | 1.2 | | | 1.2 | 1.2 |
| 4.5 | 1.8 | 2.4 | 1.9 | | 1.6 | | | 1.9 | 2.0 |
| .8 | 1.0 | 1.5 | 1.2 | | 1.2 | Quick | | 1.2 | 1.3 |
| .3 | .6 | 1.1 | .9 | | 1.0 | | | .8 | .9 |

| | | | | | | | | | | | | | | | |
|---|---|---|---|---|---|---|---|---|---|---|---|---|---|---|---|
| 0 | UND | 21 | 17.8 | 49 | 7.5 | 42 | 8.7 | | | 48 | 7.6 | | 45 | 8.1 | 37 | 9.9 |
| 0 | UND | 50 | 7.3 | 65 | 5.6 | 60 | 6.1 | | | 61 | 6.0 | Sales/Receivables | 62 | 5.9 | 55 | 6.7 |
| 32 | 11.5 | 78 | 4.7 | 83 | 4.4 | 78 | 4.7 | | | 79 | 4.6 | | 83 | 4.4 | 73 | 5.0 |
| 0 | UND | 0 | UND | 0 | UND | 0 | UND | | | 0 | UND | | 0 | UND | 0 | UND |
| 0 | UND | 0 | UND | 0 | UND | 5 | 72.5 | | | 1 | 394.7 | Cost of Sales/Inventory | 0 | 913.5 | 0 | UND |
| 0 | UND | 4 | 92.0 | 6 | 57.5 | 18 | 20.0 | | | 10 | 35.8 | | 7 | 54.7 | 5 | 76.8 |
| 0 | UND | 1 | 283.0 | 12 | 30.0 | 19 | 19.1 | | | 20 | 17.9 | | 15 | 23.6 | 12 | 30.6 |
| 0 | UND | 21 | 17.8 | 30 | 12.0 | 27 | 13.6 | | | 37 | 9.8 | Cost of Sales/Payables | 31 | 11.6 | 22 | 16.4 |
| 8 | 46.8 | 44 | 8.3 | 46 | 8.0 | 46 | 7.9 | | | 54 | 6.8 | | 43 | 8.5 | 52 | 7.1 |

| | | | | | | | | | | | | |
|---|---|---|---|---|---|---|---|---|---|---|---|---|
| 10.1 | | 9.3 | | 4.7 | | 5.4 | | 5.5 | | | 6.1 | | 7.5 |
| 17.8 | | 14.4 | | 8.7 | | 8.3 | | 9.1 | Sales/Working Capital | | 12.4 | | 12.8 |
| -20.5 | | -268.4 | | 20.1 | | 12.1 | | 21.9 | | | 36.9 | | 24.8 |

| | | | | | | | | | | | | | |
|---|---|---|---|---|---|---|---|---|---|---|---|---|---|
| | | | 13.7 | | 35.7 | | 26.3 | | 49.2 | | | 9.6 | | 31.3 |
| | (32) | | 3.8 | (63) | 8.2 | (33) | 8.3 | | 4.8 | EBIT/Interest | (61) | 5.1 | (75) | 7.8 |
| | | | -3.7 | | 1.5 | | 3.9 | | 1.1 | | | 2.0 | | 2.9 |

| | | | | | | | | | | | |
|---|---|---|---|---|---|---|---|---|---|---|---|
| | | | 15.2 | | 12.4 | | | | | 5.4 | | 15.4 |
| | (15) | 8.3 | (10) | 3.8 | | | Net Profit + Depr., Dep., Amort./Cur. Mat. L/T/D | (16) | 2.9 | (27) | 3.1 |
| | | 3.0 | | 1.3 | | | | | 1.5 | | 2.0 |

| | | | | | | | | | | |
|---|---|---|---|---|---|---|---|---|---|---|
| .4 | .3 | .2 | .1 | | .5 | | | .4 | | .3 |
| 8.0 | .7 | .4 | .5 | | .9 | Fixed/Worth | | .7 | | .6 |
| -2.2 | 5.5 | 1.0 | .8 | | 1.3 | | | 1.1 | | 1.6 |
| .7 | .6 | .5 | .7 | | 1.1 | | | .8 | | .8 |
| 15.0 | 1.4 | .9 | 1.2 | | 1.6 | Debt/Worth | | 1.5 | | 1.4 |
| -6.6 | 63.8 | 1.9 | 2.9 | | 2.9 | | | 4.3 | | 3.2 |

| | | | | | | | | | | | | |
|---|---|---|---|---|---|---|---|---|---|---|---|---|
| | | 51.0 | | 42.3 | | 38.5 | | | 30.4 | | 48.2 | | 78.1 |
| (27) | 15.1 | (63) | 21.2 | (33) | 18.6 | | (11) | 21.9 | % Profit Before Taxes/Tangible Net Worth | (68) | 27.5 | (78) | 42.4 |
| | -1.3 | | 7.6 | | 8.5 | | | 9.8 | | | 10.0 | | 14.7 |

| | | | | | | | | | |
|---|---|---|---|---|---|---|---|---|---|
| 46.4 | 19.7 | 18.9 | 13.6 | | 13.0 | | | 16.5 | 26.7 |
| 26.5 | 6.0 | 9.5 | 7.8 | | 5.9 | % Profit Before Taxes/Total Assets | | 11.8 | 13.5 |
| -15.4 | -9.0 | .9 | 3.0 | | .1 | | | 2.7 | 4.4 |
| 60.5 | 31.9 | 39.8 | 39.6 | | 12.4 | | | 19.6 | 33.1 |
| 17.9 | 14.4 | 15.2 | 11.3 | | 7.0 | Sales/Net Fixed Assets | | 8.4 | 15.5 |
| 7.4 | 6.1 | 6.4 | 4.5 | | 4.2 | | | 5.1 | 5.6 |
| 8.5 | 4.1 | 3.1 | 2.8 | | 2.1 | | | 2.9 | 3.6 |
| 4.7 | 2.9 | 2.3 | 2.3 | | 1.5 | Sales/Total Assets | | 2.2 | 2.5 |
| 3.4 | 2.1 | 1.8 | 1.5 | | 1.3 | | | 1.7 | 2.0 |

| | | | | | | | | | | | |
|---|---|---|---|---|---|---|---|---|---|---|---|
| | | .9 | | 1.0 | | 1.2 | | | | 1.2 | | .9 |
| | (27) | 2.0 | (58) | 2.1 | (31) | 2.3 | | % Depr., Dep., Amort./Sales | (61) | 2.2 | (72) | 1.9 |
| | | 4.6 | | 4.3 | | 5.4 | | | | 3.9 | | 3.9 |

| | | | | | | | | | | | |
|---|---|---|---|---|---|---|---|---|---|---|---|
| | | 1.7 | | 1.6 | | | | | | 1.5 | | 2.6 |
| | (21) | 3.1 | (18) | 2.9 | | | | % Officers', Directors' Owners' Comp/Sales | (23) | 3.0 | (27) | 5.4 |
| | | 8.4 | | 6.0 | | | | | | 6.1 | | 9.5 |

| | | | | | | | | | |
|---|---|---|---|---|---|---|---|---|---|
| 12279M | 132274M | 857590M | 1631953M | 1080750M | 3254051M | Net Sales ($) | | 1967284M | 2883814M |
| 2466M | 41236M | 345930M | 798007M | 628034M | 2078708M | Total Assets ($) | | 1113720M | 1314575M |

M = $ thousand    MM = $ million
See Pages 9 through 22 for Explanation of Ratios and Data

## Comparative Historical Data | Current Data Sorted by Sales

| 4/1/09-3/31/10 ALL | 4/1/10-3/31/11 ALL | 4/1/11-3/31/12 ALL | Type of Statement | 0-1MM | 1-3MM | 3-5MM | 5-10MM | 10-25MM | 25MM & OVER |
|---|---|---|---|---|---|---|---|---|---|
| 26 | 29 | 39 | Unqualified | | 2 | 1 | 2 | 7 | 27 |
| 31 | 37 | 48 | Reviewed | | 4 | 4 | 14 | 19 | 7 |
| 17 | 10 | 15 | Compiled | 1 | 4 | 3 | 5 | 2 | |
| 8 | 17 | 17 | Tax Returns | 4 | 4 | 4 | 4 | 1 | |
| 37 | 33 | 55 | Other | 2 | 6 | 7 | 17 | 6 | 17 |
| | | | | | 22 (4/1-9/30/11) | | 152 (10/1/11-3/31/12) | | |
| 119 | 126 | 174 | **NUMBER OF STATEMENTS** | 7 | 20 | 16 | 40 | 38 | 53 |
| % | % | % | **ASSETS** | % | % | % | % | % | % |
| 12.8 | 13.3 | 13.2 | Cash & Equivalents | | 7.6 | 13.4 | 16.3 | 13.2 | 10.5 |
| 37.3 | 35.7 | 37.8 | Trade Receivables (net) | | 35.8 | 36.0 | 39.6 | 43.7 | 36.6 |
| 4.0 | 6.5 | 3.9 | Inventory | | 5.2 | 4.5 | 4.6 | 2.6 | 3.7 |
| 8.4 | 9.6 | 9.9 | All Other Current | | 12.1 | 8.6 | 7.2 | 10.5 | 12.4 |
| 62.5 | 65.1 | 64.8 | Total Current | | 60.8 | 62.6 | 67.7 | 69.9 | 63.3 |
| 30.3 | 26.1 | 25.2 | Fixed Assets (net) | | 26.0 | 32.2 | 25.2 | 21.3 | 23.2 |
| 2.7 | 2.1 | 2.9 | Intangibles (net) | | .4 | .2 | 1.5 | 3.1 | 5.8 |
| 4.5 | 6.7 | 7.1 | All Other Non-Current | | 12.8 | 5.0 | 5.6 | 5.7 | 7.7 |
| 100.0 | 100.0 | 100.0 | Total | | 100.0 | 100.0 | 100.0 | 100.0 | 100.0 |
| | | | **LIABILITIES** | | | | | | |
| 9.2 | 9.7 | 8.6 | Notes Payable-Short Term | | 10.5 | 12.3 | 6.9 | 8.1 | 6.0 |
| 5.6 | 6.8 | 5.1 | Cur. Mat.-L.T.D. | | 7.5 | 4.8 | 4.2 | 4.0 | 4.8 |
| 15.6 | 17.1 | 15.3 | Trade Payables | | 12.1 | 16.6 | 17.7 | 15.1 | 15.8 |
| .5 | .3 | .3 | Income Taxes Payable | | .0 | .4 | .3 | .3 | .4 |
| 11.3 | 13.2 | 13.0 | All Other Current | | 18.7 | 10.2 | 11.6 | 13.0 | 13.0 |
| 42.1 | 47.1 | 42.4 | Total Current | | 48.7 | 44.3 | 40.9 | 40.5 | 40.0 |
| 14.0 | 13.5 | 11.6 | Long-Term Debt | | 19.2 | 18.4 | 7.7 | 6.4 | 12.0 |
| .5 | .4 | .4 | Deferred Taxes | | .0 | .0 | .8 | .4 | .5 |
| 7.3 | 4.4 | 4.5 | All Other Non-Current | | 13.7 | 9.3 | 2.1 | 1.9 | 3.3 |
| 36.1 | 34.5 | 41.1 | Net Worth | | 18.3 | 27.9 | 48.4 | 50.9 | 44.2 |
| 100.0 | 100.0 | 100.0 | Total Liabilities & Net Worth | | 100.0 | 100.0 | 100.0 | 100.0 | 100.0 |
| | | | **INCOME DATA** | | | | | | |
| 100.0 | 100.0 | 100.0 | Net Sales | | 100.0 | 100.0 | 100.0 | 100.0 | 100.0 |
| 27.5 | 26.8 | 28.5 | Gross Profit | | 36.4 | 42.6 | 28.8 | 25.7 | 17.7 |
| 23.1 | 23.1 | 24.5 | Operating Expenses | | 36.5 | 36.8 | 26.6 | 20.3 | 13.1 |
| 4.3 | 3.7 | 4.0 | Operating Profit | | -.1 | 5.8 | 2.2 | 5.4 | 4.5 |
| .8 | .6 | .4 | All Other Expenses (net) | | .0 | .7 | -.1 | .4 | .9 |
| 3.5 | 3.1 | 3.6 | Profit Before Taxes | | -.1 | 5.1 | 2.3 | 5.0 | 3.6 |
| | | | **RATIOS** | | | | | | |
| 2.2 | 2.3 | 2.5 | Current | | 2.5 | 5.9 | 3.5 | 2.9 | 2.2 |
| 1.6 | 1.5 | 1.7 | | | 1.1 | 1.7 | 2.1 | 1.6 | 1.7 |
| 1.1 | 1.1 | 1.2 | | | .9 | 1.3 | 1.2 | 1.3 | 1.2 |
| 2.0 | 1.7 | 2.0 | Quick | | 1.7 | 3.1 | 2.5 | 2.3 | 1.7 |
| 1.2 | 1.1 | 1.3 | | | .9 | 1.4 | 1.7 | 1.4 | 1.2 |
| .8 | .8 | .9 | | | .6 | .8 | .9 | 1.1 | .9 |
| 38  9.6 | 34  10.9 | 39  9.3 | Sales/Receivables | | 12  30.0 | 0  UND | 45  8.2 | 43  8.4 | 45  8.2 |
| 58  6.3 | 54  6.8 | 59  6.2 | | | 48  7.6 | 47  7.8 | 65  5.6 | 60  6.1 | 61  6.0 |
| 72  5.1 | 74  4.9 | 76  4.8 | | | 74  4.9 | 87  4.2 | 78  4.7 | 78  4.7 | 74  4.9 |
| 0  UND | 0  UND | 0  UND | Cost of Sales/Inventory | | 0  UND | 0  UND | 0  UND | 0  UND | 0  UND |
| 0  UND | 1  481.7 | 0  UND | | | 0  UND | 3  127.6 | 0  UND | 0  UND | 2  173.5 |
| 9  39.4 | 17  21.8 | 9  39.1 | | | 0  UND | 14  25.8 | 6  57.6 | 7  52.4 | 11  32.4 |
| 12  31.1 | 15  25.1 | 11  33.6 | Cost of Sales/Payables | | 0  UND | 0  UND | 12  30.8 | 13  28.9 | 19  18.8 |
| 27  13.6 | 27  13.4 | 26  14.3 | | | 12  31.7 | 14  25.3 | 32  11.5 | 26  14.2 | 26  14.1 |
| 47  7.7 | 54  6.7 | 46  8.0 | | | 47  7.7 | 61  6.0 | 54  6.7 | 39  9.3 | 45  8.1 |
| 5.6 | 6.0 | 5.7 | Sales/Working Capital | | 10.1 | 6.4 | 4.2 | 5.4 | 6.1 |
| 12.0 | 11.5 | 9.6 | | | 43.1 | 10.8 | 8.4 | 8.0 | 9.1 |
| 62.2 | 52.5 | 24.2 | | | -100.0 | 15.7 | 21.2 | 19.0 | 18.3 |
| 20.4 | 22.3 | 32.5 | EBIT/Interest | | 6.1 | 32.0 | 36.1 | 36.8 | 34.4 |
| (108)  6.5 | (117)  7.2 | (158)  6.9 | | | (18)  2.0 | (15)  6.2 | (33)  10.8 | (35)  7.6 | (51)  8.1 |
| 1.1 | 1.9 | 1.4 | | | -3.5 | -3.9 | -7.4 | 2.1 | 3.0 |
| 7.3 | 7.3 | 13.8 | Net Profit + Depr., Dep., Amort./Cur. Mat. L/T/D | | | | | | 17.6 |
| (25)  2.6 | (31)  2.4 | (37)  3.9 | | | | | | | (17)  3.7 |
| 1.4 | .6 | 1.6 | | | | | | | 1.4 |
| .3 | .2 | .3 | Fixed/Worth | | .1 | .4 | .2 | .2 | .2 |
| .7 | .6 | .6 | | | 1.1 | .8 | .4 | .4 | .6 |
| 1.7 | 1.3 | 1.2 | | | -.8 | NM | 1.2 | .8 | .9 |
| .8 | .7 | .5 | Debt/Worth | | .9 | .5 | .4 | .5 | .7 |
| 1.6 | 1.7 | 1.3 | | | 1.9 | 2.0 | .8 | 1.0 | 1.5 |
| 5.1 | 4.0 | 3.3 | | | -3.8 | NM | 1.6 | 2.1 | 2.8 |
| 59.0 | 50.7 | 41.6 | % Profit Before Taxes/Tangible Net Worth | | 32.1 | 63.2 | 37.0 | 48.2 | 38.4 |
| (104)  23.9 | (114)  24.4 | (149)  21.0 | | | (14)  7.3 | (12)  15.4 | (34)  22.3 | (36)  18.0 | (49)  22.8 |
| .8 | 3.5 | 7.6 | | | -31.2 | 12.5 | 5.8 | 6.9 | 10.2 |
| 22.5 | 18.0 | 18.2 | % Profit Before Taxes/Total Assets | | 10.1 | 25.2 | 19.4 | 20.2 | 15.0 |
| 9.3 | 7.7 | 7.9 | | | 3.1 | 9.3 | 8.6 | 9.0 | 8.7 |
| -.4 | 1.1 | .8 | | | -7.8 | -6.8 | -9.2 | 3.1 | 3.0 |
| 26.0 | 36.8 | 33.2 | Sales/Net Fixed Assets | | 56.0 | 25.5 | 31.9 | 38.7 | 28.9 |
| 9.5 | 10.5 | 11.6 | | | 18.1 | 10.0 | 10.0 | 19.7 | 9.4 |
| 4.4 | 5.1 | 6.0 | | | 5.3 | 5.3 | 6.4 | 6.4 | 5.3 |
| 3.3 | 3.2 | 3.3 | Sales/Total Assets | | 4.1 | 5.1 | 3.1 | 3.5 | 2.8 |
| 2.3 | 2.4 | 2.3 | | | 2.3 | 2.8 | 2.3 | 2.4 | 2.1 |
| 1.6 | 1.6 | 1.7 | | | 1.8 | 1.9 | 1.8 | 1.9 | 1.5 |
| 1.4 | 1.4 | 1.1 | % Depr., Dep., Amort./Sales | | .8 | | .9 | 1.1 | 1.2 |
| (96)  2.6 | (100)  2.7 | (140)  2.4 | | | (14)  1.8 | | (37)  2.2 | (33)  2.0 | (44)  2.7 |
| 5.3 | 6.3 | 4.2 | | | 8.8 | | 4.5 | 4.7 | 4.0 |
| 1.1 | 1.4 | 1.6 | % Officers', Directors' Owners' Comp/Sales | | 4.6 | | 1.3 | | |
| (27)  2.5 | (42)  3.4 | (52)  3.0 | | | (10)  7.8 | | (16)  6.2 | | |
| 4.3 | 7.8 | 7.5 | | | 10.8 | | 6.2 | | |
| 4043366M | 3517304M | 6968897M | Net Sales ($) | 4035M | 39324M | 63834M | 292293M | 630637M | 5938774M |
| 2168586M | 1911460M | 3894381M | Total Assets ($) | 2039M | 18782M | 27222M | 147622M | 304029M | 3394687M |

M = $ thousand    MM = $ million
See Pages 9 through 22 for Explanation of Ratios and Data

## Current Data Sorted by Assets      Comparative Historical Data

| | | | | | | Type of Statement | | |
|---|---|---|---|---|---|---|---|---|
| | 1 | 6 | 12 | 3 | 8 | Unqualified | 76 | 60 |
| 1 | 4 | 15 | 13 | 4 | 1 | Reviewed | 51 | 60 |
| 3 | 12 | 27 | 10 | 3 | | Compiled | 105 | 94 |
| 24 | 50 | 94 | 20 | | | Tax Returns | 352 | 293 |
| 10 | 44 | 106 | 55 | 13 | 7 | Other | 384 | 398 |
| | 48 (4/1-9/30/11) | | | 498 (10/1/11-3/31/12) | | | 4/1/07-3/31/08 | 4/1/08-3/31/09 |
| 0-500M | 500M-2MM | 2-10MM | 10-50MM | 50-100MM | 100-250MM | | ALL | ALL |
| 38 | 111 | 248 | 110 | 23 | 16 | NUMBER OF STATEMENTS | 968 | 905 |
| % | % | % | % | % | % | ASSETS | % | % |
| 15.2 | 6.9 | 4.8 | 7.9 | 6.0 | 10.5 | Cash & Equivalents | 6.7 | 6.9 |
| 5.4 | 3.5 | 4.6 | 2.7 | 2.6 | 2.6 | Trade Receivables (net) | 4.5 | 4.5 |
| 32.0 | 33.0 | 37.3 | 26.7 | 25.5 | 22.1 | Inventory | 38.7 | 36.9 |
| 1.7 | 3.3 | 3.5 | 2.1 | 3.4 | 1.5 | All Other Current | 5.1 | 3.7 |
| 54.3 | 46.7 | 50.2 | 39.4 | 37.5 | 36.8 | Total Current | 55.0 | 52.1 |
| 22.3 | 37.9 | 36.3 | 39.5 | 38.9 | 37.7 | Fixed Assets (net) | 30.2 | 34.1 |
| 2.8 | 1.2 | 1.5 | 1.7 | 1.8 | 1.2 | Intangibles (net) | 1.1 | 1.2 |
| 20.4 | 14.2 | 12.0 | 19.4 | 21.7 | 24.4 | All Other Non-Current | 13.6 | 12.6 |
| 100.0 | 100.0 | 100.0 | 100.0 | 100.0 | 100.0 | Total | 100.0 | 100.0 |
| | | | | | | LIABILITIES | | |
| 36.8 | 19.3 | 17.3 | 15.0 | 10.5 | 12.0 | Notes Payable-Short Term | 19.8 | 18.0 |
| 3.4 | 2.7 | 2.3 | 3.3 | 5.0 | 13.6 | Cur. Mat.-L.T.D. | 4.7 | 3.4 |
| 4.1 | 2.1 | 3.8 | 2.9 | 2.5 | 3.3 | Trade Payables | 3.5 | 4.6 |
| .0 | .0 | .1 | .0 | .0 | .0 | Income Taxes Payable | .1 | .1 |
| 23.9 | 15.5 | 11.7 | 10.9 | 5.4 | 13.0 | All Other Current | 10.3 | 11.8 |
| 68.3 | 39.6 | 35.2 | 32.1 | 23.3 | 42.0 | Total Current | 38.4 | 37.8 |
| 17.7 | 29.1 | 32.8 | 24.7 | 31.0 | 21.9 | Long-Term Debt | 31.4 | 35.1 |
| .0 | .0 | .1 | .0 | 2.1 | .1 | Deferred Taxes | .1 | .1 |
| 3.8 | 9.2 | 3.3 | 6.6 | 5.7 | 5.3 | All Other Non-Current | 4.4 | 3.5 |
| 10.2 | 22.0 | 28.7 | 36.5 | 37.9 | 30.7 | Net Worth | 25.8 | 23.5 |
| 100.0 | 100.0 | 100.0 | 100.0 | 100.0 | 100.0 | Total Liabilities & Net Worth | 100.0 | 100.0 |
| | | | | | | INCOME DATA | | |
| 100.0 | 100.0 | 100.0 | 100.0 | 100.0 | 100.0 | Net Sales | 100.0 | 100.0 |
| | | | | | | Gross Profit | | |
| 85.9 | 80.8 | 82.2 | 83.0 | 86.0 | 91.3 | Operating Expenses | 82.4 | 83.9 |
| 14.1 | 19.2 | 17.8 | 17.0 | 14.0 | 8.7 | Operating Profit | 17.6 | 16.1 |
| 4.4 | 12.7 | 11.6 | 10.2 | 13.3 | 7.2 | All Other Expenses (net) | 8.3 | 10.3 |
| 9.7 | 6.6 | 6.1 | 6.8 | .7 | 1.5 | Profit Before Taxes | 9.3 | 5.8 |
| | | | | | | RATIOS | | |
| 2.2 | 3.0 | 3.2 | 2.7 | 6.1 | 1.7 | | 4.0 | 3.6 |
| 1.2 | 1.1 | 1.3 | 1.3 | 1.3 | 1.1 | Current | 1.3 | 1.3 |
| .4 | .4 | .6 | .4 | .2 | .4 | | .7 | .6 |
| 1.1 | 1.0 | .9 | 1.2 | 1.6 | 1.3 | | 1.0 | .9 |
| .2 | .2 | .2 | .2 | .1 | .5 | Quick | (963) .2 | (904) .2 |
| .0 | .0 | .0 | .0 | .0 | .1 | | .0 | .0 |
| 0 UND | 0 UND | 0 UND | 0 UND | 0 UND | 0 UND | | 0 UND | 0 UND |
| 0 UND | 0 UND | 0 UND | 0 999.8 | 1 508.1 | 5 73.0 | Sales/Receivables | 0 UND | 0 UND |
| 0 UND | 0 UND | 13 28.3 | 9 40.4 | 16 22.8 | 36 10.1 | | 10 37.2 | 12 31.4 |
| | | | | | | Cost of Sales/Inventory | | |
| | | | | | | Cost of Sales/Payables | | |
| 6.7 | 1.7 | .7 | .6 | .4 | 1.8 | | 1.3 | .9 |
| 64.3 | 25.5 | 6.1 | 7.2 | 5.7 | 18.5 | Sales/Working Capital | 7.2 | 8.5 |
| -4.6 | -3.2 | -7.2 | -2.4 | -4.1 | -3.3 | | -8.1 | -5.6 |
| 6.9 | 3.2 | 5.7 | 5.2 | 7.0 | 6.1 | | 8.2 | 6.2 |
| (21) 1.9 | (54) 1.5 | (142) 2.0 | (75) 2.0 | (11) 2.5 | (13) 2.6 | EBIT/Interest | (565) 2.5 | (480) 2.1 |
| -2.2 | -1.2 | -.6 | -1.0 | -7.3 | .3 | | .6 | -.1 |
| | | | | | | | 3.8 | 4.3 |
| | | | | | | Net Profit + Depr., Dep., | (25) 1.0 | (22) 1.2 |
| | | | | | | Amort./Cur. Mat. L/T/D | -.1 | .2 |
| .0 | .0 | .0 | .0 | .1 | .0 | | .0 | .0 |
| .0 | 1.1 | .8 | .9 | 1.7 | 1.1 | Fixed/Worth | .4 | .7 |
| -13.8 | 12.0 | 4.3 | 3.2 | 2.6 | 2.8 | | 3.6 | 4.9 |
| .5 | .9 | .8 | .7 | .7 | .7 | | 1.1 | 1.2 |
| 1.9 | 3.1 | 3.2 | 2.3 | 2.2 | 2.3 | Debt/Worth | 3.8 | 3.7 |
| -9.2 | -104.6 | 30.9 | 8.8 | 5.8 | 7.0 | | 19.7 | 30.2 |
| 81.9 | 32.1 | 26.0 | 16.5 | 22.6 | 10.6 | | 43.9 | 25.1 |
| (24) 14.1 | (81) 6.1 | (201) 3.9 | (97) 2.3 | (21) 2.5 | (15) 2.8 | % Profit Before Taxes/Tangible Net Worth | (806) 11.8 | (733) 5.6 |
| -4.1 | -4.5 | -4.0 | -3.6 | -3.1 | -7.8 | | -.2 | -4.6 |
| 50.1 | 7.4 | 5.6 | 4.7 | 6.0 | 3.1 | | 8.8 | 5.4 |
| 4.7 | 1.4 | 1.4 | .9 | 1.2 | 1.7 | % Profit Before Taxes/Total Assets | 2.2 | 1.0 |
| -4.9 | -2.4 | -1.1 | -1.3 | -1.3 | -3.2 | | -.9 | -1.6 |
| UND | UND | 883.0 | 50.0 | 74.8 | 257.5 | | 999.8 | 999.8 |
| 299.2 | 6.8 | 3.8 | 1.7 | 1.3 | 2.2 | Sales/Net Fixed Assets | 10.0 | 6.6 |
| 8.2 | .2 | .2 | .2 | .1 | .3 | | .6 | .4 |
| 3.1 | .9 | .6 | .5 | .4 | .7 | | 1.0 | .8 |
| 1.3 | .4 | .2 | .2 | .2 | .3 | Sales/Total Assets | .4 | .3 |
| .5 | .1 | .1 | .1 | .1 | .2 | | .2 | .1 |
| .8 | 2.0 | .6 | .8 | 2.3 | .7 | | .5 | .7 |
| (11) 1.7 | (44) 13.3 | (117) 4.6 | (74) 5.9 | (14) 9.3 | (11) 6.8 | % Depr., Dep., Amort./Sales | (503) 2.4 | (446) 4.6 |
| 5.2 | 25.5 | 17.7 | 19.0 | 20.5 | 14.8 | | 11.9 | 15.6 |
| | 1.9 | 1.6 | 1.2 | | | | 1.5 | 1.6 |
| | (10) 3.7 | (30) 5.5 | (16) 3.6 | | | % Officers', Directors' Owners' Comp/Sales | (164) 4.1 | (152) 3.8 |
| | 5.8 | 13.4 | 6.4 | | | | 9.0 | 8.2 |
| 27744M | 91988M | 693124M | 1008530M | 638529M | 1055093M | Net Sales ($) | 10960909M | 10713760M |
| 9781M | 131832M | 1110430M | 2151757M | 1628003M | 2446996M | Total Assets ($) | 18481255M | 14235730M |

M = $ thousand    MM = $ million
See Pages 9 through 22 for Explanation of Ratios and Data

## Comparative Historical Data | Current Data Sorted by Sales

| | Hist 1 | Hist 2 | Hist 3 | Label / Type of Statement | 0-1MM | 1-3MM | 3-5MM | 5-10MM | 10-25MM | 25MM & OVER |
|---|---|---|---|---|---|---|---|---|---|---|
| | 49 | 31 | 30 | Unqualified | 3 | 4 | 5 | 6 | 5 | 7 |
| | 51 | 36 | 38 | Reviewed | 6 | 6 | 4 | 12 | 7 | 3 |
| | 69 | 58 | 55 | Compiled | 21 | 21 | 4 | 1 | 6 | 2 |
| | 263 | 170 | 188 | Tax Returns | 115 | 45 | 13 | 10 | 5 | |
| | 313 | 311 | 235 | Other | 105 | 50 | 22 | 21 | 22 | 15 |
| | 4/1/09-3/31/10 ALL | 4/1/10-3/31/11 ALL | 4/1/11-3/31/12 ALL | | 48 (4/1-9/30/11) | | | 498 (10/1/11-3/31/12) | | |
| | 745 | 606 | 546 | **NUMBER OF STATEMENTS** | 250 | 126 | 48 | 50 | 45 | 27 |
| | % | % | % | **ASSETS** | % | % | % | % | % | % |
| | 7.5 | 7.2 | 6.8 | Cash & Equivalents | 4.6 | 6.1 | 9.6 | 8.3 | 12.1 | 13.8 |
| | 4.5 | 3.4 | 3.9 | Trade Receivables (net) | 1.4 | 4.0 | 2.7 | 7.5 | 10.4 | 10.9 |
| | 31.5 | 34.0 | 33.0 | Inventory | 31.4 | 41.9 | 33.1 | 21.0 | 35.5 | 24.3 |
| | 4.3 | 4.2 | 3.0 | All Other Current | 3.2 | 2.0 | 2.4 | 2.8 | 3.2 | 6.2 |
| | 47.8 | 48.7 | 46.7 | Total Current | 40.6 | 54.0 | 47.9 | 39.5 | 61.2 | 55.3 |
| | 36.4 | 38.9 | 36.5 | Fixed Assets (net) | 43.5 | 28.8 | 37.1 | 39.6 | 22.9 | 22.5 |
| | 1.8 | 1.6 | 1.6 | Intangibles (net) | 1.7 | 1.2 | 1.9 | 1.9 | 1.8 | .9 |
| | 14.0 | 10.7 | 15.3 | All Other Non-Current | 14.2 | 16.0 | 13.2 | 18.9 | 14.1 | 21.3 |
| | 100.0 | 100.0 | 100.0 | Total | 100.0 | 100.0 | 100.0 | 100.0 | 100.0 | 100.0 |
| | | | | **LIABILITIES** | | | | | | |
| | 18.0 | 16.4 | 18.2 | Notes Payable-Short Term | 19.2 | 19.8 | 16.6 | 10.4 | 19.4 | 16.0 |
| | 4.4 | 4.6 | 3.1 | Cur. Mat.-L.T.D. | 2.4 | 2.8 | 3.5 | 4.3 | 2.6 | 9.5 |
| | 3.5 | 2.5 | 3.2 | Trade Payables | 1.0 | 2.7 | 2.0 | 5.4 | 11.2 | 10.8 |
| | .1 | .0 | .1 | Income Taxes Payable | .0 | .0 | .0 | .1 | .4 | .0 |
| | 12.1 | 11.8 | 13.0 | All Other Current | 13.0 | 15.0 | 13.0 | 9.9 | 12.5 | 9.2 |
| | 38.1 | 35.4 | 37.5 | Total Current | 35.5 | 40.3 | 35.1 | 30.1 | 46.1 | 45.5 |
| | 34.3 | 34.3 | 29.0 | Long-Term Debt | 35.9 | 26.9 | 22.9 | 23.9 | 17.2 | 14.4 |
| | .0 | .0 | .1 | Deferred Taxes | .0 | .0 | .8 | .5 | .0 | .0 |
| | 3.8 | 4.7 | 5.3 | All Other Non-Current | 5.4 | 4.4 | 4.1 | 8.2 | 6.1 | 4.3 |
| | 23.8 | 25.5 | 28.1 | Net Worth | 23.1 | 28.4 | 37.1 | 37.2 | 30.6 | 35.7 |
| | 100.0 | 100.0 | 100.0 | Total Liabilties & Net Worth | 100.0 | 100.0 | 100.0 | 100.0 | 100.0 | 100.0 |
| | | | | **INCOME DATA** | | | | | | |
| | 100.0 | 100.0 | 100.0 | Net Sales | 100.0 | 100.0 | 100.0 | 100.0 | 100.0 | 100.0 |
| | | | | Gross Profit | | | | | | |
| | 82.4 | 81.6 | 82.8 | Operating Expenses | 76.6 | 83.8 | 89.8 | 88.7 | 93.0 | 94.6 |
| | 17.6 | 18.4 | 17.2 | Operating Profit | 23.4 | 16.2 | 10.2 | 11.3 | 7.0 | 5.4 |
| | 11.8 | 11.3 | 11.0 | All Other Expenses (net) | 16.3 | 9.3 | 5.1 | 5.3 | 3.9 | 2.3 |
| | 5.8 | 7.1 | 6.2 | Profit Before Taxes | 7.0 | 6.9 | 5.1 | 6.0 | 3.1 | 3.1 |
| | | | | **RATIOS** | | | | | | |
| | 3.0 | 3.9 | 2.9 | Current | 3.3 | 2.5 | 4.4 | 2.4 | 1.9 | 3.2 |
| | 1.3 | 1.4 | 1.2 | | 1.2 | 1.3 | 1.3 | 1.2 | 1.3 | 1.5 |
| | .5 | .6 | .5 | | .3 | .6 | .6 | .4 | .9 | 1.0 |
| | 1.1 | 1.2 | 1.0 | Quick | .9 | .8 | 1.1 | 1.0 | 1.3 | 1.7 |
| | (744) .2 | (605) .2 | .2 | | .1 | .2 | .2 | .3 | .3 | .8 |
| | .0 | .0 | .0 | | .0 | .0 | .0 | .1 | .1 | .1 |
| | 0 UND | 0 UND | 0 UND | Sales/Receivables | 0 UND | 0 UND | 0 UND | 0 UND | 0 UND | 0 999.8 |
| | 0 UND | 0 UND | 0 UND | | 0 UND | 0 UND | 0 UND | 1 452.0 | 3 110.1 | 29 12.4 |
| | 13 27.6 | 8 45.9 | 8 47.7 | | 0 UND | 11 33.3 | 9 39.6 | 21 17.2 | 25 14.8 | 47 7.8 |
| | | | | Cost of Sales/Inventory | | | | | | |
| | | | | Cost of Sales/Payables | | | | | | |
| | 1.0 | .8 | .9 | Sales/Working Capital | .6 | .8 | .6 | 2.4 | 3.8 | 3.6 |
| | 8.5 | 6.0 | 10.6 | | 16.2 | 7.1 | 8.2 | 22.9 | 10.6 | 6.1 |
| | -3.6 | -4.9 | -4.1 | | -2.0 | -5.9 | -7.4 | -3.1 | -14.8 | -999.8 |
| | 5.2 | 5.4 | 5.2 | EBIT/Interest | 3.3 | 4.7 | 6.7 | 12.4 | 7.8 | 6.9 |
| | (401) 1.7 | (321) 1.8 | (316) 1.9 | | (101) 1.1 | (88) 2.0 | (37) 2.5 | (32) 2.0 | (35) 3.2 | (23) 2.8 |
| | -.9 | -.3 | -.8 | | -1.3 | -.7 | -1.5 | -1.6 | -.8 | .6 |
| | 8.7 | 6.5 | 5.3 | Net Profit + Depr., Dep., Amort./Cur. Mat. L/T/D | | | | | | |
| | (24) 1.8 | (26) 2.1 | (20) 1.5 | | | | | | | |
| | .7 | 1.0 | .5 | | | | | | | |
| | .0 | .0 | .0 | Fixed/Worth | .0 | .0 | .1 | .1 | .1 | .0 |
| | .9 | .8 | .9 | | 1.5 | .2 | .9 | 1.1 | .6 | .6 |
| | 6.3 | 4.9 | 4.4 | | 11.1 | 3.0 | 4.0 | 3.2 | 1.8 | 1.9 |
| | 1.2 | .8 | .8 | Debt/Worth | .8 | .9 | .5 | .8 | 1.1 | .7 |
| | 3.4 | 2.7 | 2.9 | | 3.1 | 3.0 | 2.3 | 2.1 | 3.2 | 2.1 |
| | 35.2 | 32.0 | 24.9 | | -209.4 | 41.0 | 17.9 | 6.4 | 6.9 | 4.8 |
| | 22.3 | 23.8 | 22.1 | % Profit Before Taxes/Tangible Net Worth | 14.0 | 36.1 | 25.5 | 28.1 | 36.1 | 18.4 |
| | (594) 3.7 | (488) 5.0 | (439) 4.6 | | (186) 2.3 | (101) 8.2 | (41) 4.8 | (46) 6.0 | (40) 13.8 | (25) 10.5 |
| | -5.4 | -2.5 | -3.6 | | -4.3 | -4.2 | -5.0 | -4.5 | 1.8 | -.7 |
| | 4.5 | 5.5 | 5.9 | % Profit Before Taxes/Total Assets | 4.1 | 7.1 | 6.8 | 10.9 | 9.3 | 6.1 |
| | .8 | 1.1 | 1.4 | | .5 | 1.6 | 2.7 | 2.7 | 3.5 | 2.4 |
| | -2.1 | -1.5 | -1.8 | | -1.9 | -1.8 | -1.4 | -2.1 | .0 | -1.3 |
| | 265.7 | UND | 999.8 | Sales/Net Fixed Assets | UND | UND | 66.5 | 65.0 | 160.3 | 284.9 |
| | 2.9 | 2.8 | 4.0 | | .5 | 26.1 | 2.8 | 3.2 | 20.7 | 13.3 |
| | .2 | .2 | .2 | | .2 | .3 | .5 | .5 | 2.5 | 2.0 |
| | .6 | .7 | .7 | Sales/Total Assets | .3 | .7 | 1.3 | 1.3 | 2.6 | 2.1 |
| | .2 | .2 | .3 | | .2 | .3 | .5 | .5 | 1.2 | 1.0 |
| | .1 | .1 | .1 | | .1 | .2 | .2 | .2 | .4 | .3 |
| | 1.2 | 1.7 | .9 | % Depr., Dep., Amort./Sales | 3.1 | .7 | .6 | .6 | .4 | .3 |
| | (404) 5.7 | (295) 7.9 | (271) 6.3 | | (107) 15.7 | (56) 6.5 | (27) 5.5 | (39) 1.6 | (25) 1.8 | (17) 3.1 |
| | 16.4 | 19.8 | 18.7 | | 23.9 | 19.0 | 18.9 | 7.3 | 6.5 | 7.2 |
| | 1.4 | 1.8 | 1.6 | % Officers', Directors' Owners' Comp/Sales | 5.0 | 1.6 | | 1.7 | | |
| | (91) 3.0 | (52) 3.7 | (65) 4.5 | | (15) 12.4 | (20) 5.0 | | (12) 2.6 | | |
| | 6.8 | 6.3 | 9.2 | | 21.4 | 8.7 | | 4.9 | | |
| | 5060144M | 4284649M | 3515008M | Net Sales ($) | 105293M | 218472M | 181612M | 353379M | 712045M | 1944207M |
| | 10918647M | 9305336M | 7478799M | Total Assets ($) | 705678M | 957671M | 754766M | 1209034M | 1195753M | 2655897M |

© RMA 2012

M = $ thousand    MM = $ million
See Pages 9 through 22 for Explanation of Ratios and Data

## Current Data Sorted by Assets  /  Comparative Historical Data

| Type of Statement | 0-500M | 500M-2MM | 2-10MM | 10-50MM | 50-100MM | 100-250MM | | 4/1/07-3/31/08 ALL | 4/1/08-3/31/09 ALL |
|---|---|---|---|---|---|---|---|---|---|
| Unqualified | 6 | 12 | 94 | 179 | 62 | 28 | | 380 | 418 |
| Reviewed | 6 | 36 | 133 | 53 | 3 | 1 | | 207 | 223 |
| Compiled | 5 | 17 | 13 | 8 | | 1 | | 35 | 40 |
| Tax Returns | 15 | 13 | 14 | 4 | | | | 43 | 41 |
| Other | 11 | 32 | 71 | 77 | 26 | 20 | | 197 | 241 |
| | 153 (4/1-9/30/11) | | | 781 (10/1/11-3/31/12) | | | | | |
| NUMBER OF STATEMENTS | 37 | 110 | 325 | 321 | 91 | 50 | | 862 | 963 |
| **ASSETS** | % | % | % | % | % | % | | % | % |
| Cash & Equivalents | 29.0 | 13.6 | 16.9 | 17.9 | 23.8 | 19.8 | | 17.9 | 18.6 |
| Trade Receivables (net) | 19.2 | 32.9 | 34.7 | 29.3 | 25.9 | 20.9 | | 30.5 | 30.0 |
| Inventory | 2.1 | 5.0 | 3.8 | 5.0 | 3.6 | 4.8 | | 3.5 | 3.9 |
| All Other Current | 4.6 | 6.2 | 6.4 | 7.8 | 8.3 | 7.4 | | 6.7 | 7.6 |
| Total Current | 54.9 | 57.6 | 61.8 | 60.0 | 61.6 | 52.9 | | 58.7 | 60.0 |
| Fixed Assets (net) | 37.5 | 33.5 | 31.8 | 31.3 | 28.6 | 33.2 | | 34.3 | 33.1 |
| Intangibles (net) | 1.7 | 1.4 | 1.8 | 1.7 | 3.1 | 5.2 | | .9 | 1.2 |
| All Other Non-Current | 5.9 | 7.4 | 4.5 | 7.1 | 6.7 | 8.7 | | 6.1 | 5.6 |
| Total | 100.0 | 100.0 | 100.0 | 100.0 | 100.0 | 100.0 | | 100.0 | 100.0 |
| **LIABILITIES** | | | | | | | | | |
| Notes Payable-Short Term | 26.1 | 6.7 | 6.1 | 3.8 | 2.7 | 2.9 | | 4.3 | 4.7 |
| Cur. Mat.-L.T.D. | 6.5 | 6.0 | 4.2 | 4.2 | 2.9 | 2.4 | | 5.4 | 5.0 |
| Trade Payables | 11.7 | 15.3 | 18.5 | 17.7 | 17.9 | 13.6 | | 15.2 | 15.7 |
| Income Taxes Payable | .1 | .2 | .4 | .4 | .2 | .2 | | .6 | .4 |
| All Other Current | 30.4 | 8.5 | 8.9 | 10.8 | 12.7 | 13.5 | | 12.0 | 11.3 |
| Total Current | 74.8 | 36.8 | 38.0 | 36.9 | 36.5 | 32.7 | | 37.5 | 36.9 |
| Long-Term Debt | 25.3 | 16.8 | 11.6 | 12.5 | 9.8 | 12.1 | | 16.0 | 14.9 |
| Deferred Taxes | .2 | 1.0 | 1.2 | 1.1 | 1.2 | 1.2 | | 1.1 | 1.1 |
| All Other Non-Current | 9.2 | 5.7 | 1.8 | 2.7 | 2.3 | 2.6 | | 2.3 | 2.6 |
| Net Worth | -9.4 | 39.7 | 47.4 | 46.8 | 50.2 | 51.4 | | 43.1 | 44.4 |
| Total Liabilities & Net Worth | 100.0 | 100.0 | 100.0 | 100.0 | 100.0 | 100.0 | | 100.0 | 100.0 |
| **INCOME DATA** | | | | | | | | | |
| Net Sales | 100.0 | 100.0 | 100.0 | 100.0 | 100.0 | 100.0 | | 100.0 | 100.0 |
| Gross Profit | 34.8 | 24.9 | 19.1 | 12.6 | 11.4 | 11.0 | | 20.5 | 18.0 |
| Operating Expenses | 30.6 | 21.4 | 16.2 | 10.7 | 8.0 | 8.4 | | 14.1 | 13.6 |
| Operating Profit | 4.3 | 3.5 | 2.9 | 1.9 | 3.4 | 2.6 | | 6.4 | 4.4 |
| All Other Expenses (net) | 1.1 | .5 | .0 | -.2 | .6 | -.4 | | .3 | .3 |
| Profit Before Taxes | 3.2 | 3.0 | 2.8 | 2.1 | 2.9 | 2.9 | | 6.1 | 4.1 |
| **RATIOS** | | | | | | | | | |
| Current | 4.1 | 3.3 | 2.6 | 2.2 | 2.3 | 2.0 | | 2.2 | 2.4 |
| | 1.1 | 1.6 | 1.7 | 1.6 | 1.7 | 1.6 | | 1.6 | 1.6 |
| | .4 | 1.0 | 1.2 | 1.2 | 1.3 | 1.2 | | 1.2 | 1.2 |
| Quick | 3.1 | 2.4 | 2.2 | 1.8 | 1.7 | 1.6 | | 1.8 | 2.0 |
| | 1.0 | 1.3 | 1.5 | 1.2 | 1.3 | 1.2 | | 1.3 | 1.3 |
| | .3 | .9 | .9 | .9 | 1.1 | .8 | | .9 | .9 |
| Sales/Receivables | 0 UND | 16 22.2 | 36 10.2 | 35 10.4 | 35 10.3 | 34 10.8 | | 32 11.3 | 28 13.0 |
| | 11 33.8 | 36 10.0 | 53 6.9 | 51 7.1 | 47 7.8 | 46 8.0 | | 49 7.5 | 47 7.8 |
| | 33 11.1 | 68 5.4 | 78 4.7 | 74 4.9 | 63 5.8 | 68 5.4 | | 70 5.2 | 68 5.4 |
| Cost of Sales/Inventory | 0 UND | 0 UND | 0 UND | 0 UND | 0 UND | 4 96.5 | | 0 UND | 0 UND |
| | 0 UND | 0 UND | 0 UND | 2 147.3 | 4 98.2 | 11 33.6 | | 0 784.4 | 1 661.9 |
| | 0 UND | 5 67.6 | 8 44.4 | 14 25.2 | 14 25.6 | 20 18.3 | | 8 47.2 | 9 41.3 |
| Cost of Sales/Payables | 0 UND | 5 78.2 | 15 23.8 | 21 17.4 | 25 14.6 | 22 16.6 | | 15 23.6 | 14 25.3 |
| | 2 206.0 | 19 19.7 | 32 11.4 | 34 10.6 | 35 10.5 | 35 10.5 | | 29 12.7 | 28 13.1 |
| | 28 12.9 | 41 8.9 | 52 7.0 | 50 7.3 | 52 7.0 | 47 7.8 | | 43 8.5 | 44 8.3 |
| Sales/Working Capital | 11.6 | 5.8 | 5.2 | 5.4 | 4.9 | 5.3 | | 6.1 | 5.8 |
| | 208.7 | 13.7 | 9.6 | 9.7 | 7.3 | 10.0 | | 10.7 | 10.1 |
| | -10.7 | -999.8 | 26.3 | 22.1 | 12.0 | 20.8 | | 24.3 | 23.3 |
| EBIT/Interest | 13.5 | 10.7 | 18.6 | 13.4 | 25.3 | 31.6 | | 21.2 | 22.5 |
| | (27) 3.3 | (93) 3.5 | (292) 4.7 | (287) 3.6 | (79) 6.7 | (49) 3.6 | | (780) 7.2 | (881) 6.1 |
| | .4 | .7 | 1.1 | .8 | 1.9 | 1.9 | | 2.9 | 1.8 |
| Net Profit + Depr., Dep., Amort./Cur. Mat. L/T/D | | 4.1 | 4.6 | 4.9 | 6.3 | 8.9 | | 6.0 | 5.5 |
| | | (18) 2.0 | (89) 2.3 | (122) 2.2 | (45) 2.7 | (18) 2.2 | | (288) 2.6 | (316) 2.4 |
| | | .5 | 1.4 | 1.2 | 1.4 | 1.6 | | 1.6 | 1.4 |
| Fixed/Worth | .3 | .3 | .3 | .4 | .3 | .5 | | .4 | .4 |
| | 1.2 | .8 | .7 | .7 | .6 | .7 | | .8 | .7 |
| | -1.3 | 1.8 | 1.2 | 1.1 | .9 | 1.4 | | 1.3 | 1.3 |
| Debt/Worth | .6 | .6 | .5 | .7 | .7 | .8 | | .7 | .6 |
| | 7.5 | 1.2 | 1.2 | 1.3 | 1.2 | 1.1 | | 1.3 | 1.3 |
| | -2.5 | 5.1 | 2.4 | 2.1 | 1.8 | 1.7 | | 2.5 | 2.4 |
| % Profit Before Taxes/Tangible Net Worth | 108.6 | 45.3 | 27.4 | 20.4 | 20.7 | 23.6 | | 46.1 | 36.4 |
| | (23) 29.4 | (94) 13.7 | (312) 10.6 | (315) 7.8 | 10.6 | 8.0 | | (840) 26.3 | (926) 17.2 |
| | 7.4 | .3 | .4 | .1 | 2.6 | .7 | | 11.3 | 5.1 |
| % Profit Before Taxes/Total Assets | 37.8 | 15.5 | 12.1 | 8.8 | 8.6 | 8.3 | | 19.1 | 15.4 |
| | 9.0 | 4.9 | 4.5 | 3.1 | 4.3 | 3.5 | | 10.1 | 7.2 |
| | -3.7 | -1.8 | .3 | .0 | .9 | .5 | | 4.3 | 1.7 |
| Sales/Net Fixed Assets | 70.1 | 22.5 | 16.2 | 12.4 | 13.0 | 7.7 | | 12.0 | 14.4 |
| | 12.8 | 9.8 | 7.9 | 6.9 | 6.1 | 4.6 | | 6.9 | 7.5 |
| | 6.0 | 4.8 | 4.3 | 4.1 | 4.2 | 3.5 | | 4.1 | 4.1 |
| Sales/Total Assets | 9.8 | 3.7 | 2.8 | 2.5 | 2.1 | 2.0 | | 2.8 | 2.9 |
| | 4.9 | 2.5 | 2.2 | 1.9 | 1.8 | 1.5 | | 2.1 | 2.2 |
| | 2.7 | 1.7 | 1.6 | 1.5 | 1.4 | 1.2 | | 1.6 | 1.7 |
| % Depr., Dep., Amort./Sales | 1.8 | 1.8 | 1.7 | 2.1 | 2.1 | 1.9 | | 1.9 | 1.8 |
| | (24) 4.2 | (87) 3.0 | (289) 2.8 | (311) 3.3 | (89) 3.1 | (37) 3.1 | | (774) 3.2 | (870) 3.0 |
| | 6.8 | 5.4 | 4.9 | 4.8 | 4.9 | 4.0 | | 4.8 | 4.8 |
| % Officers', Directors' Owners' Comp/Sales | 1.2 | 1.7 | 1.5 | .8 | .4 | | | 1.3 | 1.0 |
| | (20) 3.1 | (54) 3.0 | (140) 2.7 | (78) 1.4 | (19) .9 | | | (254) 2.6 | (306) 2.1 |
| | 6.2 | 5.4 | 4.4 | 2.6 | 1.2 | | | 5.0 | |
| Net Sales ($) | 59138M | 384717M | 3658859M | 15364478M | 11699073M | 12680204M | | 42180404M | 51292388M |
| Total Assets ($) | 9836M | 140484M | 1640960M | 7629527M | 6534232M | 7872216M | | 22228306M | 25842125M |

M = $ thousand   MM = $ million
See Pages 9 through 22 for Explanation of Ratios and Data

## Comparative Historical Data | Current Data Sorted by Sales

| Hist 1 | Hist 2 | Hist 3 | Type of Statement | 0-1MM | 1-3MM | 3-5MM | 5-10MM | 10-25MM | 25MM & OVER |
|---|---|---|---|---|---|---|---|---|---|
| 408 | 387 | 375 | Unqualified | | 7 | 11 | 34 | 80 | 243 |
| 237 | 215 | 232 | Reviewed | 6 | 20 | 23 | 71 | 69 | 43 |
| 45 | 44 | 44 | Compiled | 4 | 6 | 10 | 13 | 6 | 5 |
| 46 | 43 | 46 | Tax Returns | 7 | 9 | 12 | 9 | 6 | 3 |
| 272 | 223 | 237 | Other | 10 | 20 | 23 | 29 | 50 | 105 |
| 4/1/09-3/31/10 ALL | 4/1/10-3/31/11 ALL | 4/1/11-3/31/12 ALL | | 153 (4/1-9/30/11) | | | 781 (10/1/11-3/31/12) | | |
| 1008 | 912 | 934 | NUMBER OF STATEMENTS | 27 | 62 | 79 | 156 | 211 | 399 |
| % | % | % | **ASSETS** | % | % | % | % | % | % |
| 20.1 | 18.6 | 18.2 | Cash & Equivalents | 16.0 | 16.1 | 16.3 | 17.7 | 18.5 | 19.0 |
| 27.3 | 28.7 | 30.4 | Trade Receivables (net) | 20.8 | 21.9 | 31.2 | 34.3 | 33.5 | 29.1 |
| 3.9 | 3.9 | 4.3 | Inventory | 8.1 | 3.4 | 3.9 | 3.5 | 4.1 | 4.8 |
| 7.2 | 6.6 | 7.0 | All Other Current | 7.6 | 7.4 | 5.6 | 5.5 | 6.8 | 7.9 |
| 58.4 | 57.8 | 59.9 | Total Current | 52.5 | 48.7 | 56.9 | 61.0 | 63.0 | 60.7 |
| 33.5 | 33.4 | 31.8 | Fixed Assets (net) | 36.4 | 42.1 | 36.9 | 30.4 | 30.5 | 30.2 |
| 1.3 | 1.9 | 2.0 | Intangibles (net) | 2.1 | 2.8 | .7 | 2.5 | 1.4 | 2.3 |
| 6.7 | 7.0 | 6.2 | All Other Non-Current | 8.9 | 6.4 | 5.5 | 6.1 | 5.1 | 6.8 |
| 100.0 | 100.0 | 100.0 | Total | 100.0 | 100.0 | 100.0 | 100.0 | 100.0 | 100.0 |
| | | | **LIABILITIES** | | | | | | |
| 4.9 | 5.0 | 5.7 | Notes Payable-Short Term | 11.0 | 10.3 | 5.6 | 8.6 | 5.3 | 3.7 |
| 5.1 | 5.1 | 4.3 | Cur. Mat.-L.T.D. | 7.8 | 5.1 | 6.2 | 4.1 | 4.4 | 3.5 |
| 14.9 | 15.6 | 17.3 | Trade Payables | 12.9 | 10.7 | 13.9 | 16.5 | 19.6 | 18.3 |
| .5 | .4 | .3 | Income Taxes Payable | .0 | .1 | .3 | .5 | .2 | .3 |
| 10.8 | 10.4 | 11.0 | All Other Current | 35.5 | 7.9 | 7.8 | 9.0 | 8.8 | 12.4 |
| 36.1 | 36.5 | 38.5 | Total Current | 67.3 | 34.2 | 33.8 | 38.8 | 38.3 | 38.2 |
| 14.7 | 14.8 | 12.9 | Long-Term Debt | 19.1 | 17.5 | 20.4 | 10.9 | 12.1 | 11.5 |
| 1.2 | 1.2 | 1.1 | Deferred Taxes | .7 | 1.1 | 1.3 | 1.0 | 1.1 | 1.2 |
| 2.7 | 3.0 | 2.9 | All Other Non-Current | 12.6 | 9.8 | 2.1 | 2.1 | 1.7 | 2.4 |
| 45.4 | 44.5 | 44.5 | Net Worth | .4 | 37.4 | 42.4 | 47.3 | 46.8 | 46.7 |
| 100.0 | 100.0 | 100.0 | Total Liabilities & Net Worth | 100.0 | 100.0 | 100.0 | 100.0 | 100.0 | 100.0 |
| | | | **INCOME DATA** | | | | | | |
| 100.0 | 100.0 | 100.0 | Net Sales | 100.0 | 100.0 | 100.0 | 100.0 | 100.0 | 100.0 |
| 18.8 | 18.2 | 17.0 | Gross Profit | 38.6 | 30.7 | 22.6 | 21.7 | 15.2 | 11.4 |
| 15.1 | 15.5 | 14.3 | Operating Expenses | 32.9 | 27.0 | 20.4 | 18.2 | 12.7 | 9.1 |
| 3.8 | 2.7 | 2.7 | Operating Profit | 5.7 | 3.7 | 2.2 | 3.5 | 2.4 | 2.3 |
| .3 | .1 | .1 | All Other Expenses (net) | 1.5 | .6 | .4 | -.2 | .1 | .0 |
| 3.5 | 2.6 | 2.6 | Profit Before Taxes | 4.2 | 3.0 | 1.8 | 3.7 | 2.4 | 2.3 |
| | | | **RATIOS** | | | | | | |
| 2.5 | 2.5 | 2.4 | Current | 2.5 | 3.3 | 3.7 | 2.7 | 2.6 | 2.1 |
| 1.7 | 1.6 | 1.6 | | 1.1 | 1.5 | 1.9 | 1.7 | 1.7 | 1.6 |
| 1.2 | 1.2 | 1.2 | | .4 | .8 | 1.1 | 1.2 | 1.2 | 1.3 |
| 2.1 | 2.1 | 2.0 | Quick | 1.6 | 2.2 | 2.6 | 2.5 | 2.2 | 1.7 |
| 1.3 | 1.3 | 1.3 | | .5 | 1.2 | 1.5 | 1.5 | 1.3 | 1.2 |
| .9 | .9 | .9 | | .1 | .5 | .9 | 1.0 | .9 | .9 |
| 28  13.1 | 30  12.3 | 33  11.2 | Sales/Receivables | 0  UND | 4  101.8 | 21  17.2 | 35  10.4 | 36  10.0 | 33  10.9 |
| 46  8.0 | 47  7.7 | 48  7.6 | | 20  18.3 | 35  10.4 | 40  9.2 | 49  7.4 | 54  6.7 | 47  7.7 |
| 67  5.5 | 68  5.4 | 73  5.0 | | 70  5.2 | 79  4.6 | 76  4.8 | 76  4.8 | 76  4.8 | 69  5.3 |
| 0  UND | 0  UND | 0  UND | Cost of Sales/Inventory | 0  UND | 0  UND | 0  UND | 0  UND | 0  UND | 0  UND |
| 0  755.6 | 1  673.4 | 1  395.5 | | 0  UND | 0  UND | 0  UND | 0  UND | 0  842.7 | 0  97.3 |
| 10  38.0 | 11  34.5 | 12  29.4 | | 62  5.9 | 2  240.0 | 9  40.0 | 8  44.9 | 11  32.7 | 14  25.6 |
| 14  25.3 | 14  25.9 | 16  22.2 | Cost of Sales/Payables | 0  UND | 4  92.5 | 5  68.2 | 13  27.7 | 20  18.4 | 22  16.7 |
| 28  13.2 | 28  12.9 | 31  11.6 | | 6  66.3 | 24  15.2 | 20  18.7 | 29  12.7 | 33  11.0 | 34  10.6 |
| 44  8.3 | 45  8.1 | 51  7.2 | | 69  5.3 | 55  6.6 | 42  8.6 | 50  7.3 | 55  6.6 | 49  7.4 |
| 5.3 | 5.6 | 5.3 | Sales/Working Capital | 2.8 | 4.7 | 4.9 | 5.3 | 4.8 | 5.9 |
| 9.5 | 9.6 | 9.9 | | 208.7 | 11.1 | 11.4 | 10.4 | 9.0 | 10.0 |
| 24.5 | 26.3 | 27.9 | | -4.0 | -27.5 | 88.8 | 29.3 | 25.5 | 19.8 |
| 22.6 | 17.1 | 15.2 | EBIT/Interest | 11.0 | 7.7 | 12.2 | 24.7 | 13.9 | 17.7 |
| (907)  5.8 | (822)  5.0 | (827)  4.2 | | (15)  1.7 | (50)  3.3 | (71)  2.4 | (139)  5.5 | (190)  4.2 | (362)  4.4 |
| 1.4 | 1.1 | 1.0 | | -4.2 | -1.4 | 1.0 | 1.2 | .9 | 1.2 |
| 5.9 | 4.8 | 5.2 | Net Profit + Depr., Dep., Amort./Cur. Mat. L/T/D | | | 5.9 | 6.5 | 4.5 | 5.7 |
| (339)  2.5 | (285)  2.3 | (293)  2.3 | | | | (15)  2.4 | (38)  2.5 | (75)  2.2 | (158)  2.4 |
| 1.2 | 1.1 | 1.3 | | | | 1.1 | 1.1 | 1.4 | 1.3 |
| .4 | .4 | .4 | Fixed/Worth | .1 | .5 | .3 | .3 | .3 | .4 |
| .7 | .7 | .7 | | .9 | 1.0 | 1.0 | .6 | .7 | .7 |
| 1.2 | 1.2 | 1.2 | | -3.8 | 5.9 | 2.0 | 1.1 | 1.2 | 1.1 |
| .6 | .6 | .6 | Debt/Worth | .5 | .3 | .5 | .5 | .5 | .8 |
| 1.1 | 1.2 | 1.2 | | 2.0 | 1.2 | 1.1 | 1.1 | 1.2 | 1.3 |
| 2.2 | 2.3 | 2.3 | | -5.6 | 22.1 | 3.9 | 2.2 | 2.3 | 2.0 |
| 30.1 | 27.7 | 25.5 | % Profit Before Taxes/Tangible Net Worth | 18.7 | 46.6 | 36.9 | 36.3 | 22.8 | 21.6 |
| (963)  14.8 | (855)  11.6 | (885)  9.4 | | (19)  7.9 | (50)  11.8 | (70)  10.8 | (146)  13.2 | (203)  9.1 | (397)  8.8 |
| 2.4 | 1.2 | .4 | | -4.1 | -.4 | -3.0 | 1.9 | .3 | .7 |
| 14.3 | 13.3 | 11.0 | % Profit Before Taxes/Total Assets | 14.9 | 11.0 | 21.2 | 14.3 | 10.6 | 8.9 |
| 6.2 | 5.1 | 3.8 | | 2.0 | 4.2 | 3.7 | 5.9 | 3.9 | 3.5 |
| .9 | .2 | .1 | | -7.7 | -3.6 | -1.5 | 1.0 | .1 | .3 |
| 12.9 | 13.3 | 14.6 | Sales/Net Fixed Assets | 16.0 | 10.8 | 19.8 | 21.2 | 14.2 | 12.9 |
| 6.8 | 6.8 | 7.2 | | 9.8 | 5.1 | 8.3 | 8.5 | 7.9 | 6.9 |
| 3.9 | 3.9 | 4.3 | | 2.0 | 2.5 | 3.5 | 4.7 | 4.3 | 4.5 |
| 2.7 | 2.7 | 2.7 | Sales/Total Assets | 4.3 | 2.5 | 3.4 | 3.0 | 2.7 | 2.6 |
| 2.0 | 2.0 | 2.0 | | 1.5 | 1.8 | 2.3 | 2.2 | 2.1 | 2.0 |
| 1.5 | 1.5 | 1.5 | | .4 | 1.3 | 1.5 | 1.5 | 1.5 | 1.6 |
| 1.9 | 2.1 | 1.9 | % Depr., Dep., Amort./Sales | 2.4 | 2.1 | 2.1 | 1.7 | 1.9 | 2.0 |
| (889)  3.4 | (811)  3.4 | (837)  3.0 | | (19)  5.3 | (47)  3.7 | (63)  3.6 | (133)  2.9 | (199)  2.9 | (376)  3.0 |
| 5.2 | 5.4 | 4.8 | | 10.2 | 7.3 | 6.4 | 5.0 | 4.6 | 4.3 |
| 1.3 | 1.2 | 1.1 | % Officers', Directors' Owners' Comp/Sales | | 2.0 | 1.8 | 1.7 | 1.0 | .6 |
| (332)  2.5 | (296)  2.6 | (315)  2.2 | | | (26)  4.0 | (45)  3.3 | (75)  2.7 | (73)  1.8 | (88)  1.2 |
| 4.5 | 4.2 | 4.2 | | | 8.6 | 5.4 | 4.2 | 3.2 | 2.4 |
| 46904068M | 39637237M | 43846469M | Net Sales ($) | 13225M | 122157M | 320255M | 1124523M | 3488647M | 38777662M |
| 26038659M | 21938550M | 23827255M | Total Assets ($) | 15999M | 98603M | 183882M | 590107M | 1891420M | 21047244M |

M = $ thousand     MM = $ million
See Pages 9 through 22 for Explanation of Ratios and Data

## Current Data Sorted by Assets     Comparative Historical Data

| | | | | | | Type of Statement | | |
|---|---|---|---|---|---|---|---|---|
| 2 | 9 | 34 | 45 | 12 | 12 | Unqualified | 87 | 90 |
| 6 | 29 | 64 | 20 | 2 | 2 | Reviewed | 119 | 115 |
| 2 | 14 | 11 | 2 | 1 | | Compiled | 22 | 25 |
| 20 | 19 | 20 | 2 | 2 | | Tax Returns | 27 | 44 |
| 7 | 23 | 43 | 30 | 13 | 7 | Other | 91 | 114 |
| | 76 (4/1-9/30/11) | | 373 (10/1/11-3/31/12) | | | | 4/1/07-3/31/08 | 4/1/08-3/31/09 |
| 0-500M | 500M-2MM | 2-10MM | 10-50MM | 50-100MM | 100-250MM | | ALL | ALL |
| 37 | 94 | 172 | 99 | 28 | 19 | NUMBER OF STATEMENTS | 346 | 388 |
| % | % | % | % | % | % | ASSETS | % | % |
| 15.7 | 16.3 | 17.8 | 17.5 | 18.6 | 17.2 | Cash & Equivalents | 14.6 | 15.8 |
| 23.0 | 30.4 | 33.6 | 32.0 | 31.2 | 31.8 | Trade Receivables (net) | 33.6 | 33.2 |
| 7.2 | 4.0 | 3.7 | 2.7 | 7.6 | 2.0 | Inventory | 4.2 | 4.0 |
| 3.2 | 6.6 | 5.6 | 8.3 | 9.6 | 10.3 | All Other Current | 7.2 | 7.1 |
| 49.2 | 57.3 | 60.6 | 60.5 | 67.0 | 61.2 | Total Current | 59.6 | 60.0 |
| 39.1 | 33.4 | 30.8 | 31.0 | 23.4 | 21.3 | Fixed Assets (net) | 34.1 | 32.0 |
| .7 | 2.5 | 2.8 | 2.1 | 1.9 | 5.4 | Intangibles (net) | 1.3 | 1.6 |
| 11.0 | 6.8 | 5.8 | 6.3 | 7.7 | 12.1 | All Other Non-Current | 5.1 | 6.4 |
| 100.0 | 100.0 | 100.0 | 100.0 | 100.0 | 100.0 | Total | 100.0 | 100.0 |
| | | | | | | LIABILITIES | | |
| 18.6 | 7.6 | 6.7 | 3.5 | 5.0 | 1.7 | Notes Payable-Short Term | 6.6 | 6.4 |
| 10.2 | 6.5 | 4.4 | 5.5 | 3.1 | 1.1 | Cur. Mat.-L.T.D. | 5.4 | 6.6 |
| 12.2 | 13.0 | 16.1 | 16.9 | 16.6 | 17.1 | Trade Payables | 16.1 | 16.0 |
| .0 | .1 | .5 | .4 | .5 | .7 | Income Taxes Payable | 1.1 | .6 |
| 9.5 | 11.5 | 7.7 | 13.5 | 22.3 | 21.1 | All Other Current | 12.7 | 12.6 |
| 50.5 | 38.8 | 35.3 | 39.7 | 47.5 | 41.7 | Total Current | 41.8 | 42.2 |
| 26.0 | 22.8 | 13.2 | 13.9 | 9.9 | 7.5 | Long-Term Debt | 17.3 | 16.3 |
| .1 | .5 | .8 | 1.3 | .8 | 1.3 | Deferred Taxes | .8 | .8 |
| 19.6 | 2.9 | 2.7 | 2.1 | 1.8 | 3.3 | All Other Non-Current | 2.1 | 2.2 |
| 4.2 | 35.0 | 48.0 | 43.1 | 40.0 | 46.2 | Net Worth | 38.0 | 38.6 |
| 100.0 | 100.0 | 100.0 | 100.0 | 100.0 | 100.0 | Total Liabilties & Net Worth | 100.0 | 100.0 |
| | | | | | | INCOME DATA | | |
| 100.0 | 100.0 | 100.0 | 100.0 | 100.0 | 100.0 | Net Sales | 100.0 | 100.0 |
| 41.8 | 30.2 | 24.1 | 18.8 | 12.1 | 14.0 | Gross Profit | 26.8 | 24.6 |
| 38.0 | 24.8 | 20.2 | 13.2 | 8.9 | 9.6 | Operating Expenses | 20.8 | 20.1 |
| 3.8 | 5.4 | 3.8 | 5.6 | 3.2 | 4.4 | Operating Profit | 6.0 | 4.4 |
| .7 | .3 | .1 | .3 | .3 | -.1 | All Other Expenses (net) | .7 | .6 |
| 3.1 | 5.1 | 3.8 | 5.3 | 2.9 | 4.5 | Profit Before Taxes | 5.4 | 3.8 |
| | | | | | | RATIOS | | |
| 4.2 | 3.1 | 2.6 | 2.1 | 1.8 | 1.7 | | 2.0 | 2.0 |
| 1.2 | 1.8 | 1.7 | 1.5 | 1.5 | 1.5 | Current | 1.4 | 1.5 |
| .3 | .9 | 1.2 | 1.2 | 1.2 | 1.3 | | 1.1 | 1.1 |
| 3.7 | 2.8 | 2.4 | 1.7 | 1.5 | 1.4 | | 1.7 | 1.8 |
| 1.1 | 1.4 | 1.4 | 1.2 | 1.1 | 1.2 | Quick | 1.2 | 1.2 |
| .2 | .5 | .9 | .8 | .7 | 1.0 | | .8 | .8 |
| 0   UND | 16   22.6 | 35   10.3 | 43   8.5 | 40   9.2 | 45   8.1 | | 37   9.9 | 37   9.9 |
| 9   39.8 | 45   8.1 | 61   6.0 | 64   5.7 | 64   5.7 | 68   5.4 | Sales/Receivables | 60   6.1 | 54   6.8 |
| 60   6.1 | 78   4.7 | 81   4.5 | 89   4.1 | 76   4.8 | 87   4.2 | | 82   4.5 | 73   5.0 |
| 0   UND | 0   UND | 0   UND | 0   UND | 0   UND | 0   UND | | 0   UND | 0   UND |
| 0   UND | 0   UND | 0   UND | 0   UND | 2   167.3 | 2   233.2 | Cost of Sales/Inventory | 0   UND | 0   UND |
| 0   UND | 3   111.1 | 4   95.6 | 6   57.8 | 14   25.9 | 6   71.8 | | 5   75.0 | 6   60.8 |
| 0   UND | 4   92.9 | 15   24.1 | 26   14.1 | 22   16.6 | 33   11.0 | | 16   23.4 | 14   26.2 |
| 12   31.0 | 20   18.4 | 30   12.0 | 41   8.8 | 35   10.4 | 39   9.4 | Cost of Sales/Payables | 33   11.0 | 30   12.3 |
| 25   14.6 | 38   9.5 | 50   7.3 | 58   6.3 | 54   6.8 | 47   7.7 | | 54   6.8 | 48   7.5 |
| 8.6 | 5.1 | 4.6 | 4.8 | 6.3 | 7.1 | | 6.5 | 6.5 |
| 62.2 | 11.9 | 8.9 | 8.9 | 8.7 | 10.8 | Sales/Working Capital | 12.1 | 12.1 |
| -17.2 | -40.7 | 26.4 | 21.7 | 19.1 | 13.6 | | 52.2 | 71.5 |
| 10.8 | 14.1 | 24.4 | 32.4 | 17.2 | 84.8 | | 20.6 | 18.3 |
| (28)   3.0 | (75)   4.6 | (146)   5.6 | (92)   5.6 | (25)   5.0 | (17)   15.1 | EBIT/Interest | (321)   5.7 | (347)   4.8 |
| 1.0 | .5 | 1.3 | 1.0 | 2.0 | 3.7 | | 2.1 | 1.4 |
| | 12.9 | 8.0 | 6.9 | 7.0 | | | 5.7 | 5.9 |
| (11) | 4.1 | (41)   2.6 | (35)   2.0 | (14)   3.9 | | Net Profit + Depr., Dep., Amort./Cur. Mat. L/T/D | (115)   2.6 | (120)   2.3 |
| | 2.5 | .6 | .8 | 1.0 | | | 1.2 | 1.1 |
| .4 | .3 | .3 | .2 | .3 | .3 | | .4 | .4 |
| .7 | .8 | .6 | .7 | .5 | .4 | Fixed/Worth | .7 | .8 |
| -.9 | 2.9 | 1.4 | 1.3 | .7 | .8 | | 1.7 | 1.7 |
| .5 | .5 | .5 | .8 | 1.2 | .9 | | .9 | .8 |
| 2.9 | 1.3 | 1.1 | 1.5 | 1.7 | 1.3 | Debt/Worth | 1.7 | 1.7 |
| -2.9 | 7.7 | 2.7 | 2.8 | 2.6 | 2.0 | | 3.4 | 3.5 |
| 65.2 | 49.9 | 34.1 | 33.6 | 20.9 | 38.0 | | 51.7 | 43.7 |
| (23)   21.2 | (80)   18.2 | (163)   12.6 | (95)   15.2 | 11.0 | 15.8 | % Profit Before Taxes/Tangible Net Worth | (330)   26.7 | (360)   23.9 |
| 8.3 | 2.5 | -2.4 | 2.1 | 6.3 | 1.5 | | 8.2 | 2.4 |
| 39.2 | 22.0 | 14.7 | 14.6 | 8.4 | 11.8 | | 17.8 | 17.7 |
| 13.3 | 6.6 | 5.0 | 5.4 | 3.9 | 5.5 | % Profit Before Taxes/Total Assets | 9.2 | 7.8 |
| .0 | -2.0 | -.9 | .3 | 1.9 | .8 | | 2.4 | .7 |
| 54.5 | 24.1 | 17.8 | 18.7 | 23.4 | 20.1 | | 18.5 | 19.9 |
| 19.8 | 8.7 | 7.8 | 8.4 | 8.7 | 10.0 | Sales/Net Fixed Assets | 7.3 | 7.8 |
| 6.9 | 3.8 | 3.9 | 3.1 | 5.6 | 4.2 | | 3.5 | 3.9 |
| 8.0 | 3.5 | 2.5 | 2.3 | 2.1 | 2.6 | | 2.8 | 2.9 |
| 3.7 | 2.3 | 1.9 | 1.7 | 1.8 | 1.6 | Sales/Total Assets | 2.0 | 2.1 |
| 2.3 | 1.6 | 1.3 | 1.3 | 1.5 | 1.2 | | 1.4 | 1.5 |
| 2.4 | 1.3 | 1.5 | 1.3 | 1.1 | 1.1 | | 1.3 | 1.2 |
| (19)   3.2 | (68)   3.5 | (155)   3.3 | (86)   3.0 | 2.0 | (16)   1.7 | % Depr., Dep., Amort./Sales | (314)   2.9 | (331)   2.9 |
| 6.7 | 5.8 | 5.8 | 5.6 | 3.2 | 3.9 | | 5.5 | 6.3 |
| 2.8 | 2.4 | 1.0 | .7 | | | | 1.2 | 1.3 |
| (20)   5.3 | (41)   4.0 | (69)   2.5 | (29)   1.6 | | | % Officers', Directors' Owners' Comp/Sales | (118)   2.5 | (126)   3.0 |
| 7.7 | 5.7 | 4.5 | 2.7 | | | | 5.1 | 6.0 |
| 44941M | 366456M | 1747310M | 4026135M | 3981826M | 5669276M | Net Sales ($) | 12918545M | 16171289M |
| 8548M | 119106M | 839720M | 2271661M | 2032482M | 3132763M | Total Assets ($) | 6687852M | 8089219M |

## Comparative Historical Data | Current Data Sorted by Sales

| Type of Statement | | | | | | | | | |
|---|---|---|---|---|---|---|---|---|---|
| | 100 | 107 | 114 | Unqualified | 3 | 7 | 5 | 15 | 30 | 54 |
| | 122 | 108 | 121 | Reviewed | 5 | 24 | 14 | 34 | 25 | 19 |
| | 24 | 24 | 30 | Compiled | 3 | 9 | 3 | 8 | 4 | 3 |
| | 41 | 50 | 61 | Tax Returns | 15 | 13 | 16 | 8 | 8 | 1 |
| | 100 | 83 | 123 | Other | 6 | 20 | 8 | 20 | 25 | 44 |

| | 4/1/09-3/31/10 ALL | 4/1/10-3/31/11 ALL | 4/1/11-3/31/12 ALL | | 76 (4/1-9/30/11) | | | 373 (10/1/11-3/31/12) | | |
|---|---|---|---|---|---|---|---|---|---|---|
| | | | | | 0-1MM | 1-3MM | 3-5MM | 5-10MM | 10-25MM | 25MM & OVER |
| NUMBER OF STATEMENTS | 387 | 372 | 449 | | 32 | 73 | 46 | 85 | 92 | 121 |
| | % | % | % | **ASSETS** | % | % | % | % | % | % |
| | 17.9 | 17.1 | 17.3 | Cash & Equivalents | 11.3 | 15.5 | 21.4 | 16.0 | 19.2 | 17.7 |
| | 30.2 | 30.5 | 31.5 | Trade Receivables (net) | 18.7 | 27.2 | 25.3 | 34.6 | 33.3 | 36.2 |
| | 3.9 | 4.1 | 4.0 | Inventory | 7.3 | 4.7 | 5.7 | 4.2 | 1.3 | 4.0 |
| | 7.2 | 6.7 | 6.6 | All Other Current | 2.1 | 4.6 | 4.2 | 6.8 | 6.9 | 9.7 |
| | 59.2 | 58.4 | 59.4 | Total Current | 39.5 | 52.0 | 56.7 | 61.5 | 60.6 | 67.7 |
| | 32.3 | 33.0 | 31.2 | Fixed Assets (net) | 48.3 | 36.2 | 32.7 | 30.8 | 31.0 | 23.6 |
| | 1.9 | 1.9 | 2.5 | Intangibles (net) | 3.0 | 3.3 | 2.8 | 1.6 | 2.2 | 2.6 |
| | 6.6 | 6.7 | 6.9 | All Other Non-Current | 9.3 | 8.5 | 7.8 | 6.1 | 6.3 | 6.1 |
| | 100.0 | 100.0 | 100.0 | Total | 100.0 | 100.0 | 100.0 | 100.0 | 100.0 | 100.0 |
| | | | | **LIABILITIES** | | | | | | |
| | 6.8 | 6.1 | 6.8 | Notes Payable-Short Term | 8.4 | 11.6 | 8.2 | 7.5 | 5.8 | 3.4 |
| | 5.2 | 5.4 | 5.3 | Cur. Mat.-L.T.D. | 10.2 | 6.3 | 6.4 | 5.4 | 5.0 | 3.2 |
| | 15.3 | 15.1 | 15.4 | Trade Payables | 6.3 | 12.5 | 11.2 | 16.3 | 16.4 | 19.7 |
| | .5 | .3 | .4 | Income Taxes Payable | .0 | .1 | .2 | .8 | .3 | .5 |
| | 12.8 | 12.7 | 11.4 | All Other Current | 7.4 | 11.3 | 7.5 | 7.1 | 9.9 | 18.2 |
| | 40.6 | 39.5 | 39.3 | Total Current | 32.4 | 41.8 | 33.5 | 37.0 | 37.3 | 45.0 |
| | 14.9 | 15.9 | 16.0 | Long-Term Debt | 37.8 | 21.9 | 15.2 | 13.8 | 14.1 | 9.7 |
| | .9 | 1.1 | .8 | Deferred Taxes | .6 | .3 | .8 | .6 | 1.4 | .8 |
| | 3.8 | 5.0 | 4.0 | All Other Non-Current | 10.4 | 4.3 | 10.1 | 2.6 | 1.6 | 2.5 |
| | 39.8 | 38.5 | 40.0 | Net Worth | 19.1 | 31.7 | 40.4 | 46.0 | 45.5 | 42.0 |
| | 100.0 | 100.0 | 100.0 | Total Liabilities & Net Worth | 100.0 | 100.0 | 100.0 | 100.0 | 100.0 | 100.0 |
| | | | | **INCOME DATA** | | | | | | |
| | 100.0 | 100.0 | 100.0 | Net Sales | 100.0 | 100.0 | 100.0 | 100.0 | 100.0 | 100.0 |
| | 23.0 | 24.4 | 24.5 | Gross Profit | 46.8 | 34.1 | 26.7 | 26.2 | 19.1 | 14.9 |
| | 20.7 | 20.8 | 20.0 | Operating Expenses | 40.8 | 31.1 | 22.2 | 20.6 | 14.2 | 10.8 |
| | 2.3 | 3.6 | 4.5 | Operating Profit | 6.0 | 3.0 | 4.5 | 5.6 | 4.8 | 4.1 |
| | .5 | .6 | .2 | All Other Expenses (net) | 1.4 | .8 | .1 | -.2 | -.1 | .2 |
| | 1.8 | 3.0 | 4.3 | Profit Before Taxes | 4.6 | 2.2 | 4.4 | 5.7 | 4.9 | 3.9 |
| | | | | **RATIOS** | | | | | | |
| | 2.2 | 2.3 | 2.5 | | 3.9 | 3.5 | 4.0 | 3.0 | 2.3 | 2.0 |
| | 1.5 | 1.6 | 1.6 | Current | 1.2 | 1.8 | 1.8 | 1.7 | 1.6 | 1.5 |
| | 1.1 | 1.1 | 1.1 | | .2 | .9 | 1.1 | 1.1 | 1.1 | 1.3 |
| | 1.9 | 1.9 | 2.2 | | 3.3 | 2.9 | 3.1 | 2.5 | 2.1 | 1.6 |
| | (386) 1.2 | (371) 1.3 | 1.3 | Quick | .9 | 1.3 | 1.6 | 1.2 | 1.3 | 1.2 |
| | .7 | .8 | .8 | | .2 | .6 | .8 | .9 | .9 | .9 |
| | 35 10.5 | 30 12.3 | 31 11.8 | | 0 UND | 13 27.9 | 8 44.7 | 35 10.3 | 38 9.5 | 43 8.5 |
| | 54 6.8 | 54 6.8 | 57 6.4 | Sales/Receivables | 16 23.1 | 47 7.7 | 46 7.9 | 61 6.0 | 62 5.9 | 63 5.8 |
| | 75 4.9 | 79 4.6 | 81 4.5 | | 76 4.8 | 85 4.3 | 64 5.7 | 81 4.5 | 79 4.6 | 87 4.2 |
| | 0 UND | 0 UND | 0 UND | | 0 UND | 0 UND | 0 UND | 0 UND | 0 UND | 0 UND |
| | 0 UND | 0 UND | 0 UND | Cost of Sales/Inventory | 0 UND | 0 UND | 0 UND | 0 UND | 0 UND | 0 999.8 |
| | 8 45.4 | 8 43.7 | 5 71.8 | | 0 UND | 7 50.7 | 5 79.1 | 8 48.2 | 2 160.0 | 7 53.7 |
| | 14 25.6 | 15 24.0 | 14 26.4 | | 0 UND | 7 55.3 | 6 59.5 | 16 23.5 | 20 18.5 | 26 14.2 |
| | 27 13.3 | 29 12.6 | 31 11.9 | Cost of Sales/Payables | 8 45.6 | 20 18.2 | 14 26.2 | 28 12.9 | 37 9.8 | 37 9.8 |
| | 47 7.8 | 50 7.3 | 49 7.4 | | 46 7.9 | 41 8.9 | 38 9.7 | 54 6.7 | 51 7.2 | 51 7.1 |
| | 5.2 | 5.8 | 5.1 | | 3.3 | 4.1 | 3.3 | 5.0 | 5.5 | 6.0 |
| | 10.5 | 10.6 | 10.0 | Sales/Working Capital | 51.0 | 9.5 | 9.2 | 10.5 | 10.0 | 9.3 |
| | 51.9 | 64.6 | 40.8 | | -11.0 | -35.1 | 73.3 | 60.6 | 26.4 | 17.9 |
| | 20.6 | 18.6 | 20.3 | | 6.9 | 8.3 | 15.2 | 34.8 | 18.6 | 38.5 |
| | (358) 4.0 | (337) 3.9 | (383) 5.4 | EBIT/Interest | (23) 2.1 | (60) 2.9 | (40) 5.4 | (69) 6.6 | (80) 6.5 | (111) 6.7 |
| | .6 | .4 | 1.2 | | -.7 | -.2 | .8 | 1.8 | 1.8 | 1.8 |
| | 8.4 | 6.4 | 7.7 | | | | | 3.9 | 10.5 | 7.9 |
| | (123) 2.4 | (113) 2.6 | (108) 2.9 | Net Profit + Depr., Dep., Amort./Cur. Mat. L/T/D | | | | (24) 2.4 | (26) 1.6 | (47) 3.9 |
| | 1.1 | .9 | 1.0 | | | | | .4 | .8 | 1.6 |
| | .3 | .3 | .3 | | .6 | .3 | .3 | .3 | .3 | .3 |
| | .7 | .7 | .7 | Fixed/Worth | 2.2 | .9 | .7 | .6 | .7 | .5 |
| | 1.6 | 1.6 | 1.4 | | NM | 4.0 | 1.7 | 1.5 | 1.3 | .9 |
| | .7 | .6 | .6 | | .4 | .5 | .4 | .4 | .6 | .9 |
| | 1.5 | 1.4 | 1.3 | Debt/Worth | 3.0 | 1.1 | 1.1 | 1.2 | 1.3 | 1.5 |
| | 2.9 | 3.0 | 3.2 | | NM | 12.8 | 3.4 | 4.1 | 2.5 | 2.7 |
| | 34.4 | 34.1 | 38.8 | | 62.5 | 39.0 | 42.8 | 46.1 | 32.6 | 34.2 |
| | (353) 13.4 | (338) 12.7 | (408) 15.2 | % Profit Before Taxes/Tangible Net Worth | (24) 17.2 | (59) 7.5 | (40) 18.2 | (80) 22.1 | (87) 15.8 | (118) 13.5 |
| | .2 | .2 | 1.6 | | 1.0 | -11.9 | 1.6 | 2.4 | 2.9 | 2.1 |
| | 13.4 | 14.6 | 16.3 | | 24.4 | 20.8 | 16.6 | 19.2 | 14.5 | 13.3 |
| | 4.8 | 4.5 | 5.7 | % Profit Before Taxes/Total Assets | 4.4 | 3.3 | 6.2 | 8.5 | 7.6 | 4.6 |
| | -1.5 | -1.2 | .0 | | -.3 | -4.8 | -1.5 | .6 | 1.3 | .8 |
| | 18.2 | 18.0 | 20.7 | | 24.2 | 25.6 | 15.8 | 17.4 | 21.1 | 24.9 |
| | 7.4 | 8.0 | 8.7 | Sales/Net Fixed Assets | 4.1 | 6.8 | 7.2 | 7.9 | 9.2 | 12.4 |
| | 3.8 | 3.8 | 3.8 | | 1.6 | 3.2 | 4.6 | 4.3 | 3.5 | 5.3 |
| | 2.6 | 2.9 | 2.7 | | 3.1 | 3.0 | 2.7 | 2.8 | 2.9 | 2.7 |
| | 2.0 | 2.0 | 2.0 | Sales/Total Assets | 1.6 | 1.7 | 2.1 | 2.0 | 1.9 | 2.0 |
| | 1.4 | 1.4 | 1.4 | | .7 | 1.2 | 1.4 | 1.5 | 1.3 | 1.6 |
| | 1.3 | 1.7 | 1.3 | | 1.4 | 1.3 | 2.6 | 1.6 | 1.0 | 1.0 |
| | (342) 3.2 | (323) 3.6 | (372) 3.0 | % Depr., Dep., Amort./Sales | (19) 8.9 | (52) 4.5 | (36) 3.5 | (76) 3.3 | (80) 2.9 | (109) 2.0 |
| | 6.3 | 6.6 | 5.6 | | 13.7 | 8.5 | 5.7 | 6.0 | 5.5 | 3.6 |
| | 1.6 | 1.4 | 1.4 | | 2.8 | 2.9 | 2.2 | 1.7 | .8 | .6 |
| | (141) 3.6 | (129) 3.6 | (161) 2.9 | % Officers', Directors' Owners' Comp/Sales | (11) 4.8 | (32) 5.3 | (32) 3.8 | (31) 2.5 | (28) 1.3 | (27) 1.1 |
| | 6.3 | 6.2 | 5.2 | | 6.4 | 6.4 | 5.4 | 4.7 | 3.4 | 2.4 |
| | 15655505M | 12500507M | 15835944M | Net Sales ($) | 16273M | 149807M | 176978M | 609374M | 1440400M | 13443112M |
| | 8215238M | 6945310M | 8404280M | Total Assets ($) | 19328M | 119087M | 99929M | 326751M | 987878M | 6851307M |

## Current Data Sorted by Assets | Comparative Historical Data

| 0-500M | 500M-2MM | 2-10MM | 10-50MM | 50-100MM | 100-250MM | Type of Statement | 4/1/07-3/31/08 ALL | 4/1/08-3/31/09 ALL |
|---|---|---|---|---|---|---|---|---|
| | 3 | 17 | 17 | 4 | 2 | Unqualified | 57 | 69 |
| 3 | 25 | 78 | 11 | | | Reviewed | 112 | 122 |
| 8 | 25 | 9 | 2 | | | Compiled | 45 | 53 |
| 46 | 24 | 11 | 2 | | 2 | Tax Returns | 75 | 90 |
| 25 | 43 | 44 | 13 | 1 | 5 | Other | 132 | 157 |
| | 51 (4/1-9/30/11) | | 369 (10/1/11-3/31/12) | | | | | |
| 82 | 120 | 159 | 45 | 5 | 9 | **NUMBER OF STATEMENTS** | 421 | 491 |
| % | % | % | % | % | % | **ASSETS** | % | % |
| 20.3 | 12.5 | 13.7 | 17.1 | | | Cash & Equivalents | 12.3 | 12.6 |
| 27.8 | 39.8 | 44.3 | 38.0 | | | Trade Receivables (net) | 39.6 | 37.4 |
| 3.7 | 4.5 | 3.3 | 2.1 | | | Inventory | 2.6 | 3.0 |
| 3.8 | 5.6 | 7.3 | 8.0 | | | All Other Current | 5.2 | 6.3 |
| 55.7 | 62.4 | 68.6 | 65.3 | | | Total Current | 59.7 | 59.3 |
| 34.2 | 28.2 | 22.9 | 25.5 | | | Fixed Assets (net) | 32.8 | 32.1 |
| 3.4 | 2.1 | 2.3 | 2.1 | | | Intangibles (net) | 2.0 | 2.4 |
| 6.8 | 7.3 | 6.1 | 7.2 | | | All Other Non-Current | 5.5 | 6.2 |
| 100.0 | 100.0 | 100.0 | 100.0 | | | Total | 100.0 | 100.0 |
| | | | | | | **LIABILITIES** | | |
| 34.5 | 11.9 | 8.4 | 5.4 | | | Notes Payable-Short Term | 7.4 | 8.9 |
| 6.1 | 6.2 | 3.2 | 4.3 | | | Cur. Mat.-L.T.D. | 5.5 | 5.2 |
| 15.0 | 20.0 | 21.6 | 19.0 | | | Trade Payables | 17.0 | 17.2 |
| .1 | .0 | .4 | .4 | | | Income Taxes Payable | .4 | .5 |
| 16.6 | 11.5 | 10.6 | 11.3 | | | All Other Current | 10.0 | 11.4 |
| 72.2 | 49.5 | 44.1 | 40.5 | | | Total Current | 40.4 | 43.2 |
| 29.0 | 18.1 | 12.3 | 9.9 | | | Long-Term Debt | 19.6 | 20.8 |
| .2 | .2 | .7 | .9 | | | Deferred Taxes | .6 | .7 |
| 20.9 | 3.5 | 3.1 | 3.1 | | | All Other Non-Current | 3.0 | 5.2 |
| -22.3 | 28.7 | 39.8 | 45.6 | | | Net Worth | 36.5 | 30.0 |
| 100.0 | 100.0 | 100.0 | 100.0 | | | Total Liabilties & Net Worth | 100.0 | 100.0 |
| | | | | | | **INCOME DATA** | | |
| 100.0 | 100.0 | 100.0 | 100.0 | | | Net Sales | 100.0 | 100.0 |
| 39.5 | 27.7 | 20.5 | 17.2 | | | Gross Profit | 27.1 | 25.4 |
| 36.6 | 24.7 | 18.9 | 17.5 | | | Operating Expenses | 21.6 | 22.6 |
| 2.9 | 3.0 | 1.6 | -.3 | | | Operating Profit | 5.5 | 2.8 |
| .4 | .3 | .0 | -.1 | | | All Other Expenses (net) | .5 | .7 |
| 2.5 | 2.7 | 1.6 | -.1 | | | Profit Before Taxes | 5.0 | 2.1 |
| | | | | | | **RATIOS** | | |
| 3.0 | 2.2 | 2.5 | 2.9 | | | Current | 2.5 | 2.5 |
| 1.0 | 1.4 | 1.6 | 1.7 | | | | 1.5 | 1.5 |
| .5 | 1.0 | 1.2 | 1.1 | | | | 1.0 | 1.0 |
| 2.5 | 1.9 | 2.2 | 2.6 | | | Quick | 2.2 | 2.2 |
| .8 | 1.2 | 1.4 | 1.5 | | | (420) | 1.3 | 1.3 |
| .4 | .7 | .9 | .8 | | | | .8 | .7 |
| 0 UND | 24 15.4 | 51 7.2 | 47 7.7 | | | Sales/Receivables | 34 10.9 | 29 12.4 |
| 11 34.5 | 47 7.7 | 68 5.4 | 68 5.4 | | | | 53 6.9 | 50 7.3 |
| 35 10.3 | 72 5.1 | 89 4.1 | 99 3.7 | | | | 75 4.9 | 73 5.0 |
| 0 UND | 0 UND | 0 UND | 0 UND | | | Cost of Sales/Inventory | 0 UND | 0 UND |
| 0 UND | 0 UND | 0 UND | 2 162.2 | | | | 0 UND | 0 UND |
| 0 UND | 2 158.8 | 8 46.2 | 13 28.3 | | | | 3 119.6 | 5 70.4 |
| 0 UND | 9 39.9 | 17 20.9 | 24 15.5 | | | Cost of Sales/Payables | 11 33.8 | 12 31.2 |
| 4 88.6 | 26 14.0 | 35 10.5 | 38 9.7 | | | | 25 14.8 | 25 14.8 |
| 20 18.0 | 47 7.8 | 52 7.0 | 57 6.4 | | | | 44 8.2 | 47 7.8 |
| 15.6 | 8.5 | 5.4 | 3.8 | | | Sales/Working Capital | 6.9 | 7.0 |
| 290.5 | 18.1 | 10.0 | 7.3 | | | | 13.9 | 14.7 |
| -18.4 | -223.8 | 27.5 | 35.3 | | | | 230.4 | -188.6 |
| 9.4 | 10.9 | 16.8 | 10.8 | | | EBIT/Interest | 20.2 | 13.1 |
| (64) 2.2 | (106) 4.7 | (136) 4.8 | (37) 1.8 | | | | (366) 5.4 | (437) 3.3 |
| -2.2 | .3 | .0 | -2.5 | | | | 1.4 | -.5 |
| | 8.1 | 5.5 | 11.7 | | | Net Profit + Depr., Dep., | 5.3 | 5.3 |
| | (16) 3.1 | (30) 1.6 | (16) 3.4 | | | Amort./Cur. Mat. L/T/D | (91) 2.5 | (107) 1.9 |
| | 1.0 | .7 | 1.8 | | | | 1.2 | 1.0 |
| .3 | .3 | .2 | .2 | | | Fixed/Worth | .3 | .3 |
| 3.0 | .8 | .5 | .5 | | | | .7 | .8 |
| -.7 | 1.9 | 1.3 | .9 | | | | 2.0 | 3.0 |
| .5 | .9 | .7 | .5 | | | Debt/Worth | .7 | .8 |
| 74.3 | 1.7 | 1.5 | 1.6 | | | | 1.7 | 1.9 |
| -2.3 | 6.8 | 3.1 | 3.1 | | | | 4.0 | 6.2 |
| 131.3 | 70.2 | 37.9 | -18.8 | | | % Profit Before Taxes/Tangible | 61.3 | 46.4 |
| (42) 36.4 | (101) 22.4 | (144) 9.7 | (41) 4.3 | | | Net Worth | (379) 31.8 | (415) 17.5 |
| -5.1 | 2.6 | -3.9 | -11.1 | | | | 8.8 | .1 |
| 38.1 | 19.8 | 12.3 | 9.0 | | | % Profit Before Taxes/Total | 24.2 | 17.1 |
| 7.5 | 7.2 | 3.4 | .7 | | | Assets | 10.8 | 5.1 |
| -5.4 | -.8 | -2.9 | -4.6 | | | | 2.3 | -2.5 |
| 55.0 | 36.8 | 31.5 | 29.5 | | | Sales/Net Fixed Assets | 27.2 | 27.0 |
| 16.8 | 13.4 | 11.7 | 10.3 | | | | 11.2 | 12.0 |
| 7.6 | 5.9 | 5.8 | 4.8 | | | | 5.3 | 4.9 |
| 9.6 | 4.0 | 3.2 | 2.5 | | | Sales/Total Assets | 3.8 | 3.9 |
| 5.0 | 2.9 | 2.3 | 1.9 | | | | 2.7 | 2.6 |
| 3.2 | 1.9 | 1.7 | 1.3 | | | | 2.0 | 1.8 |
| .9 | .9 | .9 | 1.2 | | | % Depr., Dep., Amort./Sales | 1.0 | 1.1 |
| (45) 3.4 | (90) 2.0 | (132) 2.1 | (44) 2.8 | | | | (352) 2.3 | (409) 2.5 |
| 4.4 | 3.7 | 3.9 | 3.8 | | | | 4.8 | 4.6 |
| 3.3 | 1.9 | 1.4 | 1.3 | | | % Officers', Directors' | 1.5 | 1.5 |
| (59) 5.9 | (56) 3.7 | (65) 2.7 | (16) 1.8 | | | Owners' Comp/Sales | (189) 3.0 | (212) 3.3 |
| 10.0 | 6.3 | 4.4 | 3.5 | | | | 5.4 | 5.7 |
| 107288M | 459847M | 1727268M | 1599864M | 527153M | 5574896M | Net Sales ($) | 9276272M | 11330601M |
| 18058M | 141204M | 718145M | 896481M | 305163M | 1569076M | Total Assets ($) | 3922963M | 4635720M |

M = $ thousand   MM = $ million
See Pages 9 through 22 for Explanation of Ratios and Data

## Comparative Historical Data / Current Data Sorted by Sales

| | Comparative Historical Data | | | Type of Statement | 0-1MM | 1-3MM | 3-5MM | 5-10MM | 10-25MM | 25MM & OVER |
|---|---|---|---|---|---|---|---|---|---|---|
| | 42 | 39 | 43 | Unqualified | 3 | 3 | 1 | 3 | 17 | 19 |
| | 111 | 103 | 117 | Reviewed | 3 | 14 | 16 | 39 | 40 | 5 |
| | 53 | 38 | 44 | Compiled | 7 | 15 | 11 | 8 | 1 | 2 |
| | 88 | 93 | 85 | Tax Returns | 25 | 25 | 16 | 8 | 8 | 3 |
| | 152 | 132 | 131 | Other | 12 | 34 | 17 | 31 | 19 | 18 |
| | 4/1/09-3/31/10 ALL | 4/1/10-3/31/11 ALL | 4/1/11-3/31/12 ALL | | 51 (4/1-9/30/11) | | 369 (10/1/11-3/31/12) | | | |
| NUMBER OF STATEMENTS | 446 | 405 | 420 | | 47 | 91 | 61 | 89 | 85 | 47 |
| | % | % | % | **ASSETS** | % | % | % | % | % | % |
| | 15.6 | 14.9 | 15.1 | Cash & Equivalents | 18.2 | 14.3 | 21.1 | 11.9 | 13.8 | 14.1 |
| | 34.9 | 36.5 | 38.7 | Trade Receivables (net) | 24.4 | 33.0 | 33.8 | 46.8 | 45.0 | 44.0 |
| | 3.8 | 3.8 | 3.5 | Inventory | 7.8 | 2.4 | 4.0 | 3.4 | 3.2 | 1.8 |
| | 6.5 | 6.0 | 6.3 | All Other Current | 3.8 | 5.4 | 5.5 | 6.1 | 7.6 | 9.5 |
| | 60.8 | 61.1 | 63.6 | Total Current | 54.2 | 55.1 | 64.4 | 68.2 | 69.5 | 69.4 |
| | 29.5 | 29.1 | 27.1 | Fixed Assets (net) | 34.5 | 35.0 | 25.0 | 24.0 | 22.5 | 21.5 |
| | 2.5 | 2.3 | 2.6 | Intangibles (net) | 4.6 | 1.5 | 3.1 | 2.3 | 2.1 | 3.2 |
| | 7.2 | 7.5 | 6.7 | All Other Non-Current | 6.7 | 8.4 | 7.6 | 5.5 | 5.9 | 5.8 |
| | 100.0 | 100.0 | 100.0 | Total | 100.0 | 100.0 | 100.0 | 100.0 | 100.0 | 100.0 |
| | | | | **LIABILITIES** | | | | | | |
| | 13.0 | 13.2 | 14.3 | Notes Payable-Short Term | 27.0 | 19.3 | 17.1 | 8.3 | 8.3 | 10.6 |
| | 5.2 | 4.4 | 4.7 | Cur. Mat.-L.T.D. | 5.4 | 5.6 | 5.6 | 3.9 | 4.7 | 2.7 |
| | 16.0 | 18.3 | 19.2 | Trade Payables | 11.7 | 16.9 | 16.4 | 22.6 | 23.6 | 20.4 |
| | .4 | .3 | .2 | Income Taxes Payable | .0 | .1 | .0 | .5 | .4 | .2 |
| | 11.3 | 11.7 | 12.3 | All Other Current | 10.8 | 11.8 | 20.8 | 10.3 | 7.8 | 15.4 |
| | 46.0 | 47.8 | 50.7 | Total Current | 54.9 | 53.7 | 60.0 | 45.5 | 44.8 | 49.4 |
| | 18.4 | 19.4 | 17.0 | Long-Term Debt | 31.3 | 23.9 | 16.0 | 13.8 | 9.4 | 10.2 |
| | .5 | .6 | .5 | Deferred Taxes | .1 | .3 | .3 | .8 | .5 | 1.1 |
| | 4.9 | 6.9 | 6.7 | All Other Non-Current | 13.4 | 9.8 | 10.6 | 1.7 | 4.0 | 3.0 |
| | 30.2 | 25.4 | 25.1 | Net Worth | .2 | 12.3 | 13.0 | 38.2 | 41.3 | 36.3 |
| | 100.0 | 100.0 | 100.0 | Total Liabilities & Net Worth | 100.0 | 100.0 | 100.0 | 100.0 | 100.0 | 100.0 |
| | | | | **INCOME DATA** | | | | | | |
| | 100.0 | 100.0 | 100.0 | Net Sales | 100.0 | 100.0 | 100.0 | 100.0 | 100.0 | 100.0 |
| | 26.4 | 26.2 | 25.9 | Gross Profit | 47.5 | 32.1 | 26.8 | 20.7 | 17.5 | 16.3 |
| | 25.9 | 26.3 | 23.9 | Operating Expenses | 41.9 | 29.2 | 25.6 | 19.9 | 15.9 | 15.6 |
| | .5 | -.2 | 2.0 | Operating Profit | 5.6 | 2.9 | 1.2 | .8 | 1.6 | .7 |
| | .7 | .4 | .2 | All Other Expenses (net) | 1.2 | .3 | -.2 | -.1 | .3 | .0 |
| | -.2 | -.6 | 1.8 | Profit Before Taxes | 4.4 | 2.6 | 1.5 | .9 | 1.3 | .8 |
| | | | | **RATIOS** | | | | | | |
| | 2.4 | 2.6 | 2.5 | Current | 4.0 | 2.3 | 2.4 | 2.5 | 2.8 | 1.9 |
| | 1.4 | 1.4 | 1.5 | | 1.3 | 1.2 | 1.7 | 1.5 | 1.5 | 1.4 |
| | .9 | .9 | 1.0 | | .6 | .6 | 1.1 | 1.1 | 1.2 | 1.1 |
| | 2.1 | 2.2 | 2.1 | Quick | 2.6 | 2.1 | 2.2 | 2.2 | 2.3 | 1.8 |
| | 1.2 | 1.2 | 1.3 | | 1.0 | .9 | 1.4 | 1.4 | 1.4 | 1.3 |
| | .7 | .7 | .7 | | .5 | .4 | .9 | .9 | 1.0 | .8 |
| | 30  12.1 | 28  13.2 | 27  13.7 | Sales/Receivables | 0  UND | 11  32.7 | 21  17.4 | 47  7.8 | 46  7.9 | 49  7.4 |
| | 52  7.0 | 51  7.1 | 54  6.7 | | 12  29.7 | 35  10.5 | 50  7.3 | 69  5.3 | 59  6.2 | 76  4.8 |
| | 73  5.0 | 81  4.5 | 79  4.6 | | 45  8.1 | 66  5.5 | 72  5.1 | 89  4.1 | 83  4.4 | 96  3.8 |
| | 0  UND | 0  UND | 0  UND | Cost of Sales/Inventory | 0  UND | 0  UND | 0  UND | 0  UND | 0  UND | 0  UND |
| | 0  UND | 0  UND | 0  UND | | 0  UND | 0  UND | 0  UND | 0  UND | 0  UND | 1  494.8 |
| | 5  71.6 | 5  69.1 | 5  75.1 | | 1  359.0 | 1  407.0 | 3  111.0 | 6  56.2 | 6  56.7 | 7  54.1 |
| | 10  36.4 | 11  31.7 | 10  35.7 | Cost of Sales/Payables | 0  UND | 4  95.9 | 5  69.2 | 16  22.7 | 21  17.7 | 23  15.9 |
| | 25  14.5 | 29  12.7 | 27  13.7 | | 8  43.6 | 20  18.7 | 19  18.8 | 33  11.0 | 34  10.8 | 33  10.9 |
| | 45  8.1 | 50  7.2 | 49  7.5 | | 35  10.5 | 43  8.5 | 43  8.5 | 52  7.0 | 51  7.2 | 54  6.8 |
| | 6.3 | 5.5 | 6.8 | Sales/Working Capital | 7.4 | 9.4 | 8.0 | 6.3 | 5.1 | 6.0 |
| | 13.3 | 14.0 | 14.9 | | 26.0 | 47.7 | 13.9 | 12.3 | 11.9 | 12.2 |
| | -68.2 | -83.1 | -482.1 | | -19.6 | -12.9 | 53.7 | 56.1 | 24.5 | 46.9 |
| | 9.7 | 9.6 | 12.0 | EBIT/Interest | 12.3 | 8.6 | 11.1 | 14.9 | 20.8 | 7.4 |
| | (386)  1.6 | (351)  2.3 | (356)  4.1 | | (34)  3.4 | (78)  2.9 | (51)  3.2 | (77)  5.6 | (74)  4.8 | (42)  1.4 |
| | -2.9 | -2.7 | -1.4 | | .4 | -1.2 | -1.9 | -2.5 | -.7 | -3.3 |
| | 6.7 | 5.2 | 5.9 | Net Profit + Depr., Dep., Amort./Cur. Mat. L/T/D | | | | 5.8 | 5.9 | 9.8 |
| | (76)  2.1 | (79)  2.1 | (71)  2.0 | | | | | (22)  2.1 | (15)  2.7 | (17)  2.6 |
| | .7 | -.1 | .7 | | | | | .8 | .9 | .0 |
| | .2 | .3 | .2 | Fixed/Worth | .3 | .3 | .3 | .3 | .1 | .2 |
| | .7 | .6 | .7 | | 1.4 | 1.2 | .7 | .6 | .5 | .4 |
| | 2.5 | 3.1 | 2.3 | | -1.6 | -2.5 | 4.7 | 1.3 | .9 | 1.0 |
| | .7 | .7 | .7 | Debt/Worth | .4 | .7 | .7 | .7 | .7 | .8 |
| | 1.6 | 1.7 | 1.7 | | 4.1 | 2.0 | 1.8 | 1.4 | 1.5 | 1.8 |
| | 8.7 | 8.8 | 7.1 | | -2.8 | -7.6 | 37.4 | 3.5 | 2.7 | 3.4 |
| | 34.9 | 27.4 | 45.8 | % Profit Before Taxes/Tangible Net Worth | 132.5 | 58.6 | 58.6 | 40.5 | 38.4 | 23.2 |
| | (370)  10.2 | (327)  8.6 | (340)  12.5 | | (29)  10.9 | (63)  21.7 | (48)  14.7 | (81)  16.8 | (78)  8.4 | (41)  6.5 |
| | -11.6 | -7.5 | -4.6 | | -6.4 | .0 | -10.8 | -5.1 | -1.5 | -9.0 |
| | 12.2 | 11.3 | 16.1 | % Profit Before Taxes/Total Assets | 31.8 | 21.5 | 18.4 | 14.2 | 13.8 | 8.7 |
| | 1.6 | 2.4 | 4.2 | | 6.0 | 7.1 | 4.0 | 4.3 | 3.8 | 1.3 |
| | -9.1 | -7.2 | -3.5 | | -3.0 | -3.1 | -9.2 | -4.4 | -1.7 | -4.7 |
| | 33.8 | 31.1 | 36.8 | Sales/Net Fixed Assets | 26.1 | 46.7 | 47.7 | 27.4 | 68.3 | 33.8 |
| | 11.4 | 12.5 | 13.2 | | 10.5 | 8.4 | 16.2 | 11.5 | 17.3 | 20.2 |
| | 5.1 | 5.7 | 5.9 | | 5.2 | 4.9 | 7.2 | 5.8 | 6.7 | 6.6 |
| | 3.6 | 3.8 | 3.9 | Sales/Total Assets | 4.9 | 4.9 | 4.2 | 3.6 | 3.6 | 3.2 |
| | 2.5 | 2.5 | 2.6 | | 3.1 | 3.0 | 2.9 | 2.5 | 2.6 | 2.4 |
| | 1.7 | 1.7 | 1.8 | | 1.8 | 1.8 | 1.7 | 1.8 | 2.0 | 1.5 |
| | 1.1 | 1.1 | .9 | % Depr., Dep., Amort./Sales | 1.9 | 1.2 | .9 | 1.1 | .6 | .6 |
| | (354)  2.4 | (313)  2.6 | (323)  2.2 | | (29)  4.3 | (58)  2.8 | (46)  1.9 | (74)  2.1 | (72)  2.1 | (44)  2.0 |
| | 4.9 | 5.0 | 4.1 | | 5.7 | 4.7 | 3.8 | 3.9 | 3.5 | 3.4 |
| | 2.2 | 2.0 | 1.7 | % Officers', Directors', Owners' Comp/Sales | 5.7 | 3.0 | 2.1 | 1.5 | 1.4 | .9 |
| | (201)  4.1 | (194)  4.1 | (198)  3.7 | | (28)  8.7 | (53)  4.8 | (31)  3.3 | (44)  3.3 | (30)  2.0 | (12)  1.5 |
| | 7.2 | 7.6 | 6.5 | | 13.7 | 6.8 | 5.0 | 5.6 | 3.6 | 2.8 |
| | 8409892M | 8589221M | 9996316M | Net Sales ($) | 26121M | 176176M | 242006M | 630033M | 1347468M | 7574512M |
| | 3447673M | 3148753M | 3648127M | Total Assets ($) | 13059M | 79085M | 107554M | 297449M | 582220M | 2568760M |

M = $ thousand   MM = $ million
See Pages 9 through 22 for Explanation of Ratios and Data

## Current Data Sorted by Assets      Comparative Historical Data

| 0-500M | 500M-2MM | 2-10MM | 10-50MM | 50-100MM | 100-250MM | Type of Statement | 4/1/07-3/31/08 ALL | 4/1/08-3/31/09 ALL |
|---|---|---|---|---|---|---|---|---|
| 1 | | 13 | 13 | 1 | 4 | Unqualified | 35 | 39 |
| | 9 | 29 | 14 | | | Reviewed | 50 | 57 |
| 1 | 11 | 7 | 1 | | | Compiled | 15 | 16 |
| 7 | 11 | 6 | | | | Tax Returns | 18 | 24 |
| 4 | 19 | 18 | 16 | | 1 | Other | 43 | 42 |
| | 31 (4/1-9/30/11) | | 155 (10/1/11-3/31/12) | | | | 161 | 178 |
| 13 | 50 | 73 | 44 | 1 | 5 | **NUMBER OF STATEMENTS** | 161 | 178 |
| % | % | % | % | % | % | **ASSETS** | % | % |
| 19.7 | 10.8 | 12.2 | 12.7 | | | Cash & Equivalents | 11.0 | 12.6 |
| 40.4 | 46.6 | 47.0 | 38.2 | | | Trade Receivables (net) | 49.9 | 43.9 |
| 6.7 | 4.7 | 5.5 | 7.6 | | | Inventory | 6.2 | 7.2 |
| 5.1 | 3.3 | 11.0 | 8.6 | | | All Other Current | 8.8 | 8.5 |
| 71.9 | 65.3 | 75.6 | 67.1 | | | Total Current | 75.9 | 72.3 |
| 22.4 | 23.1 | 17.9 | 27.1 | | | Fixed Assets (net) | 18.9 | 21.5 |
| 1.0 | 3.5 | 1.4 | 2.2 | | | Intangibles (net) | 1.2 | 1.3 |
| 4.6 | 8.1 | 5.1 | 3.6 | | | All Other Non-Current | 4.0 | 4.9 |
| 100.0 | 100.0 | 100.0 | 100.0 | | | Total | 100.0 | 100.0 |
| | | | | | | **LIABILITIES** | | |
| 30.2 | 13.6 | 11.0 | 6.7 | | | Notes Payable-Short Term | 8.0 | 11.3 |
| 14.1 | 4.3 | 2.0 | 2.9 | | | Cur. Mat.-L.T.D. | 2.5 | 2.9 |
| 32.7 | 14.2 | 21.4 | 14.7 | | | Trade Payables | 18.6 | 15.3 |
| .2 | .3 | .4 | .3 | | | Income Taxes Payable | .7 | .6 |
| 10.1 | 13.1 | 12.2 | 11.8 | | | All Other Current | 18.0 | 14.6 |
| 87.3 | 45.4 | 47.0 | 36.3 | | | Total Current | 47.8 | 44.6 |
| 20.4 | 14.8 | 10.3 | 10.7 | | | Long-Term Debt | 9.9 | 10.4 |
| .0 | .3 | .3 | 1.4 | | | Deferred Taxes | .4 | .7 |
| 37.5 | 5.5 | 2.5 | 3.8 | | | All Other Non-Current | 2.5 | 5.3 |
| -45.2 | 34.0 | 39.8 | 47.8 | | | Net Worth | 39.4 | 39.0 |
| 100.0 | 100.0 | 100.0 | 100.0 | | | Total Liabilities & Net Worth | 100.0 | 100.0 |
| | | | | | | **INCOME DATA** | | |
| 100.0 | 100.0 | 100.0 | 100.0 | | | Net Sales | 100.0 | 100.0 |
| 38.0 | 33.4 | 18.5 | 17.0 | | | Gross Profit | 23.6 | 23.4 |
| 36.9 | 31.7 | 18.3 | 15.3 | | | Operating Expenses | 16.9 | 17.6 |
| 1.1 | 1.6 | .2 | 1.7 | | | Operating Profit | 6.7 | 5.9 |
| .6 | .1 | .1 | -.6 | | | All Other Expenses (net) | .5 | .4 |
| .5 | 1.5 | .1 | 2.4 | | | Profit Before Taxes | 6.2 | 5.4 |
| | | | | | | **RATIOS** | | |
| 3.0 | 2.3 | 2.4 | 2.5 | | | | 2.5 | 2.5 |
| 1.1 | 1.5 | 1.6 | 1.7 | | | Current | 1.6 | 1.6 |
| .4 | .9 | 1.2 | 1.4 | | | | 1.2 | 1.3 |
| 1.8 | 2.2 | 1.9 | 2.0 | | | | 1.9 | 2.0 |
| 1.1 | 1.1 | 1.3 | 1.3 | | | Quick | (160) 1.3 | 1.4 |
| .4 | .7 | 1.0 | 1.0 | | | | 1.0 | 1.0 |
| 8 48.0 | 37 9.9 | 58 6.3 | 61 6.0 | | | | 46 7.9 | 43 8.5 |
| 33 11.2 | 68 5.4 | 81 4.5 | 78 4.7 | | | Sales/Receivables | 69 5.3 | 66 5.5 |
| 52 7.0 | 83 4.4 | 99 3.7 | 87 4.2 | | | | 88 4.1 | 87 4.2 |
| 0 UND | 0 UND | 0 UND | 0 UND | | | | 0 UND | 0 UND |
| 0 UND | 0 UND | 0 UND | 2 240.7 | | | Cost of Sales/Inventory | 1 367.5 | 0 999.8 |
| 0 UND | 8 44.6 | 16 22.9 | 26 13.9 | | | | 15 24.9 | 14 25.7 |
| 1 618.4 | 4 101.5 | 21 17.8 | 20 18.0 | | | | 14 26.0 | 9 39.4 |
| 17 20.9 | 19 19.4 | 36 10.0 | 29 12.6 | | | Cost of Sales/Payables | 27 13.5 | 23 16.2 |
| 40 9.2 | 47 7.8 | 61 6.0 | 47 7.7 | | | | 45 8.2 | 40 9.2 |
| 8.5 | 7.6 | 4.5 | 3.9 | | | | 5.3 | 5.4 |
| 108.4 | 15.4 | 7.8 | 7.8 | | | Sales/Working Capital | 10.0 | 8.6 |
| -15.1 | -73.0 | 19.4 | 11.6 | | | | 25.4 | 19.5 |
| 8.6 | 13.9 | 14.4 | 13.8 | | | | 28.6 | 36.5 |
| (11) .2 | (44) 4.1 | (66) 2.9 | (40) 4.5 | | | EBIT/Interest | (149) 8.3 | (162) 9.4 |
| -3.5 | -2.3 | -2.6 | .3 | | | | 3.3 | 2.3 |
| | | 2.6 | 7.6 | | | Net Profit + Depr., Dep., | 12.6 | 11.9 |
| | (14) .5 | (20) 3.2 | | | | Amort./Cur. Mat. L/T/D | (42) 5.4 | (50) 4.7 |
| | | -6.5 | .3 | | | | 2.8 | 1.8 |
| .7 | .3 | .1 | .2 | | | | .2 | .1 |
| -1.9 | .9 | .3 | .5 | | | Fixed/Worth | .4 | .4 |
| -.2 | 5.0 | .7 | 1.1 | | | | .8 | 1.0 |
| 3.7 | .7 | .7 | .7 | | | | .7 | .6 |
| -7.5 | 2.7 | 1.4 | 1.2 | | | Debt/Worth | 1.7 | 1.4 |
| -1.9 | 19.0 | 3.1 | 2.2 | | | | 3.5 | 3.0 |
| | 53.6 | 21.7 | 25.5 | | | % Profit Before Taxes/Tangible | 64.1 | 61.1 |
| (42) 15.0 | (67) 3.0 | (42) 7.6 | | | Net Worth | (153) 33.2 | (165) 30.1 |
| | -32.4 | -13.3 | .2 | | | | 16.8 | 10.7 |
| 15.5 | 20.3 | 7.9 | 10.0 | | | % Profit Before Taxes/Total | 25.6 | 22.6 |
| 9.8 | 7.0 | 2.7 | 2.7 | | | Assets | 12.2 | 11.3 |
| -26.2 | -8.6 | -4.2 | -.6 | | | | 5.1 | 2.9 |
| 164.9 | 58.0 | 48.6 | 15.7 | | | | 44.0 | 43.3 |
| 31.3 | 17.5 | 16.4 | 8.0 | | | Sales/Net Fixed Assets | 22.8 | 20.4 |
| 17.3 | 7.4 | 7.8 | 4.2 | | | | 9.8 | 7.6 |
| 8.8 | 3.6 | 2.6 | 2.4 | | | | 3.5 | 3.4 |
| 6.3 | 2.9 | 2.0 | 1.6 | | | Sales/Total Assets | 2.7 | 2.6 |
| 3.1 | 2.1 | 1.7 | 1.2 | | | | 2.1 | 1.9 |
| .5 | .6 | .6 | 1.0 | | | | .5 | .6 |
| (11) .9 | (29) 2.3 | (60) 1.3 | (41) 2.2 | | | % Depr., Dep., Amort./Sales | (140) 1.0 | (154) 1.1 |
| 2.3 | 4.3 | 2.4 | 3.8 | | | | 2.0 | 2.4 |
| 2.7 | 2.9 | 1.3 | | | | % Officers', Directors' | 1.5 | 1.3 |
| (10) 4.9 | (23) 4.8 | (30) 2.5 | | | Owners' Comp/Sales | (63) 2.9 | (73) 2.4 |
| 11.0 | 8.4 | 4.0 | | | | | 6.1 | 5.0 |
| 37615M | 170203M | 796763M | 1716324M | 64826M | 916693M | Net Sales ($) | 5766299M | 6655704M |
| 4693M | 54553M | 376265M | 971964M | 61014M | 675145M | Total Assets ($) | 2259480M | 3051311M |

© RMA 2012

M = $ thousand    MM = $ million
See Pages 9 through 22 for Explanation of Ratios and Data

## Comparative Historical Data        Current Data Sorted by Sales

| | | | | | Type of Statement | | | | | | |
|---|---|---|---|---|---|---|---|---|---|---|---|
| | 32 | | 28 | 32 | Unqualified | | 1 | 1 | 3 | 13 | 14 |
| | 63 | | 61 | 52 | Reviewed | | 4 | 6 | 15 | 20 | 7 |
| | 23 | | 26 | 20 | Compiled | 3 | 5 | 4 | 3 | 5 | |
| | 33 | | 29 | 24 | Tax Returns | 1 | 7 | 8 | 4 | 4 | |
| | 56 | | 62 | 58 | Other | 3 | 9 | 9 | 9 | 15 | 13 |
| | 4/1/09- 3/31/10 ALL | | 4/1/10- 3/31/11 ALL | 4/1/11- 3/31/12 ALL | | | 31 (4/1-9/30/11) | | 155 (10/1/11-3/31/12) | | |
| | | | | | | 0-1MM | 1-3MM | 3-5MM | 5-10MM | 10-25MM | 25MM & OVER |
| | 207 | | 206 | 186 | NUMBER OF STATEMENTS | 7 | 26 | 28 | 34 | 57 | 34 |
| | % | | % | % | ASSETS | % | % | % | % | % | % |
| | 16.0 | | 13.1 | 12.6 | Cash & Equivalents | | 9.0 | 14.5 | 15.7 | 13.3 | 11.0 |
| | 37.0 | | 39.4 | 43.6 | Trade Receivables (net) | | 51.3 | 42.9 | 42.2 | 44.1 | 42.4 |
| | 5.9 | | 6.1 | 5.8 | Inventory | | 6.3 | 1.8 | 5.2 | 6.4 | 7.4 |
| | 8.7 | | 8.7 | 7.7 | All Other Current | | 2.7 | 8.3 | 7.1 | 9.8 | 8.8 |
| | 67.6 | | 67.4 | 69.7 | Total Current | | 69.2 | 67.5 | 70.2 | 73.6 | 69.7 |
| | 24.0 | | 24.0 | 22.3 | Fixed Assets (net) | | 19.1 | 23.9 | 23.1 | 20.2 | 23.7 |
| | 2.2 | | 1.7 | 2.2 | Intangibles (net) | | 4.8 | 2.6 | 1.3 | 1.8 | 2.0 |
| | 6.2 | | 6.9 | 5.7 | All Other Non-Current | | 6.9 | 6.0 | 5.5 | 4.4 | 4.6 |
| | 100.0 | | 100.0 | 100.0 | Total | | 100.0 | 100.0 | 100.0 | 100.0 | 100.0 |
| | | | | | LIABILITIES | | | | | | |
| | 11.4 | | 13.3 | 11.7 | Notes Payable-Short Term | | 21.4 | 11.7 | 8.4 | 11.3 | 6.4 |
| | 3.5 | | 3.4 | 4.1 | Cur. Mat.-L.T.D. | | 8.2 | 4.7 | 3.2 | 1.9 | 4.2 |
| | 15.3 | | 15.5 | 18.2 | Trade Payables | | 21.3 | 16.2 | 18.2 | 19.6 | 16.5 |
| | .5 | | .4 | .3 | Income Taxes Payable | | .5 | .5 | .5 | .2 | .2 |
| | 16.7 | | 12.4 | 12.3 | All Other Current | | 8.8 | 18.7 | 9.1 | 11.7 | 15.4 |
| | 47.4 | | 45.0 | 46.6 | Total Current | | 60.1 | 51.8 | 39.3 | 44.6 | 42.8 |
| | 12.0 | | 12.8 | 12.4 | Long-Term Debt | | 15.5 | 12.4 | 16.1 | 9.4 | 9.0 |
| | .6 | | .6 | .6 | Deferred Taxes | | .0 | .4 | .6 | .9 | 1.0 |
| | 6.1 | | 5.3 | 6.0 | All Other Non-Current | | 18.2 | 2.5 | 2.7 | 2.5 | 3.2 |
| | 33.9 | | 36.3 | 34.4 | Net Worth | | 6.2 | 32.9 | 41.3 | 42.5 | 44.1 |
| | 100.0 | | 100.0 | 100.0 | Total Liabilties & Net Worth | | 100.0 | 100.0 | 100.0 | 100.0 | 100.0 |
| | | | | | INCOME DATA | | | | | | |
| | 100.0 | | 100.0 | 100.0 | Net Sales | | 100.0 | 100.0 | 100.0 | 100.0 | 100.0 |
| | 26.5 | | 26.0 | 23.6 | Gross Profit | | 35.7 | 28.1 | 20.0 | 18.6 | 16.8 |
| | 24.7 | | 26.4 | 22.4 | Operating Expenses | | 35.7 | 29.3 | 19.5 | 17.6 | 13.4 |
| | 1.8 | | -.3 | 1.2 | Operating Profit | | .0 | -1.2 | .5 | .9 | 3.4 |
| | .3 | | .4 | .0 | All Other Expenses (net) | | .8 | -.4 | .1 | -.2 | -.1 |
| | 1.5 | | -.8 | 1.3 | Profit Before Taxes | | -.8 | -.8 | .4 | 1.2 | 3.6 |
| | | | | | RATIOS | | | | | | |
| | 2.5 | | 2.8 | 2.4 | | | 2.5 | 2.3 | 2.7 | 2.5 | 2.1 |
| | 1.7 | | 1.6 | 1.6 | Current | | 1.5 | 1.2 | 1.8 | 1.7 | 1.6 |
| | 1.2 | | 1.1 | 1.1 | | | .9 | .8 | 1.2 | 1.2 | 1.3 |
| | 2.1 | | 2.2 | 2.0 | | | 1.8 | 2.2 | 2.1 | 2.2 | 1.8 |
| | 1.3 | | 1.2 | 1.3 | Quick | | 1.2 | 1.1 | 1.3 | 1.3 | 1.3 |
| | .8 | | .8 | .9 | | | .7 | .6 | 1.0 | .9 | 1.0 |
| 38 | 9.6 | 42 | 8.6 | 51  7.1 | Sales/Receivables | 47  7.7 | 14  25.4 | 51  7.1 | 58  6.3 | 59  6.2 |
| 62 | 5.9 | 67 | 5.4 | 74  4.9 | | 70  5.2 | 64  5.7 | 76  4.8 | 78  4.7 | 76  4.8 |
| 84 | 4.3 | 101 | 3.6 | 91  4.0 | | 96  3.8 | 74  4.9 | 99  3.7 | 91  4.0 | 91  4.0 |
| 0 | UND | 0 | UND | 0  UND | Cost of Sales/Inventory | 0  UND | 0  UND | 0  UND | 0  UND | 0  UND |
| 1 | 365.4 | 1 | 268.1 | 0  UND | | 0  UND | 0  UND | 1  354.7 | 0  UND | 2  150.4 |
| 19 | 19.6 | 20 | 18.1 | 13  27.6 | | 24  15.2 | 0  UND | 17  21.8 | 14  26.3 | 23  16.1 |
| 10 | 36.4 | 14 | 26.7 | 15  23.6 | Cost of Sales/Payables | 4  101.5 | 1  493.2 | 17  21.8 | 19  19.5 | 22  16.8 |
| 23 | 15.6 | 33 | 11.1 | 29  12.8 | | 23  15.7 | 16  22.7 | 34  10.8 | 29  12.8 | 30  12.1 |
| 44 | 8.3 | 50 | 7.4 | 48  7.6 | | 47  7.7 | 44  8.3 | 45  8.2 | 57  6.4 | 42  8.6 |
| | 4.8 | | 4.2 | 4.9 | Sales/Working Capital | | 7.6 | 5.4 | 4.6 | 4.4 | 4.9 |
| | 8.8 | | 8.2 | 9.0 | | | 15.1 | 26.7 | 8.2 | 7.5 | 8.4 |
| | 33.5 | | 56.8 | 30.2 | | | -40.8 | -25.5 | 22.3 | 20.4 | 11.7 |
| | 18.4 | | 7.0 | 14.6 | EBIT/Interest | | 9.1 | 65.0 | 15.3 | 9.3 | 33.1 |
| (185) | 4.0 | (181) | 2.0 | (167)  3.5 | | (22)  1.7 | (25)  4.3 | (32)  2.7 | (50)  3.3 | (32)  7.2 |
| | -.3 | | -4.1 | -1.1 | | | -2.8 | -2.6 | -3.2 | -1.4 | 1.3 |
| | 9.0 | | 2.9 | 7.4 | Net Profit + Depr., Dep., Amort./Cur. Mat. L/T/D | | | | | 6.2 | 11.3 |
| (59) | 4.1 | (46) | 1.1 | (42)  1.6 | | | | | (16)  1.0 | (16)  4.0 |
| | 1.1 | | -1.1 | .0 | | | | | | -.3 | 1.1 |
| | .2 | | .2 | .2 | Fixed/Worth | | .3 | .1 | .2 | .1 | .2 |
| | .5 | | .6 | .5 | | | 1.0 | .9 | .5 | .3 | .5 |
| | 1.2 | | 1.4 | 1.5 | | | -2.0 | 4.0 | 1.5 | .7 | .8 |
| | .6 | | .5 | .8 | Debt/Worth | | 1.4 | .6 | .7 | .7 | .8 |
| | 1.3 | | 1.4 | 1.7 | | | 6.5 | 3.4 | 1.6 | 1.2 | 1.2 |
| | 4.2 | | 4.6 | 5.1 | | | -6.3 | 21.2 | 3.1 | 2.3 | 2.2 |
| | 39.2 | | 22.7 | 26.4 | % Profit Before Taxes/Tangible Net Worth | | 50.3 | 51.9 | 25.1 | 22.0 | 27.0 |
| (182) | 13.1 | (179) | 3.6 | (161)  6.4 | | (16)  11.1 | (23)  6.3 | (33)  4.2 | (53)  2.7 | (31)  15.9 |
| | .1 | | -10.3 | -7.6 | | | -92.7 | -23.0 | -22.0 | -7.5 | .5 |
| | 13.6 | | 9.3 | 11.1 | % Profit Before Taxes/Total Assets | | 14.2 | 16.7 | 7.8 | 10.2 | 14.2 |
| | 5.1 | | 1.6 | 3.3 | | | 2.6 | 3.9 | 2.7 | 2.0 | 3.6 |
| | -2.7 | | -8.8 | -3.5 | | | -19.7 | -5.5 | -8.1 | -3.1 | .2 |
| | 35.9 | | 29.9 | 34.5 | Sales/Net Fixed Assets | | 71.1 | 227.1 | 33.9 | 57.0 | 18.1 |
| | 14.5 | | 12.6 | 13.5 | | | 20.8 | 14.6 | 17.6 | 14.6 | 10.4 |
| | 5.8 | | 5.3 | 5.7 | | | 7.6 | 9.1 | 5.7 | 5.1 | 5.4 |
| | 3.2 | | 2.8 | 3.2 | Sales/Total Assets | | 4.2 | 3.6 | 3.0 | 3.0 | 2.7 |
| | 2.2 | | 2.0 | 2.1 | | | 2.7 | 2.9 | 2.0 | 2.0 | 1.8 |
| | 1.6 | | 1.5 | 1.5 | | | 2.1 | 1.9 | 1.3 | 1.5 | 1.5 |
| | .8 | | 1.0 | .7 | % Depr., Dep., Amort./Sales | | .3 | .6 | .7 | .9 | .7 |
| (179) | 1.8 | (172) | 2.0 | (146)  1.7 | | (19)  1.1 | (16)  1.8 | (28)  1.6 | (49)  1.7 | (30)  2.0 |
| | 3.7 | | 3.7 | 3.4 | | | 2.7 | 4.2 | 3.4 | 3.3 | 3.3 |
| | 2.3 | | 2.3 | 1.6 | % Officers', Directors' Owners' Comp/Sales | | 4.0 | 1.8 | 1.9 | .8 | |
| (81) | 4.0 | (93) | 4.2 | (72)  3.6 | | (17)  4.9 | (14)  2.7 | (15)  3.0 | (17)  2.0 | |
| | 8.0 | | 7.3 | 5.5 | | | 8.5 | 6.0 | 4.8 | 4.7 | |
| | 6258262M | | 4103876M | 3702424M | Net Sales ($) | 3968M | 52367M | 108314M | 242411M | 880356M | 2415008M |
| | 2487838M | | 2357295M | 2143634M | Total Assets ($) | 4679M | 19099M | 49790M | 137801M | 521642M | 1410623M |

© RMA 2012

M = $ thousand    MM = $ million
See Pages 9 through 22 for Explanation of Ratios and Data

## Current Data Sorted by Assets

## Comparative Historical Data

| | | | | | | | Type of Statement | | |
|---|---|---|---|---|---|---|---|---|---|
| | | | 1 | 2 | | 1 | Unqualified | 4 | 2 |
| | 5 | | 9 | 1 | | | Reviewed | 11 | 24 |
| 1 | 6 | | 3 | 1 | | | Compiled | 6 | 19 |
| 5 | 3 | | 1 | | | | Tax Returns | 18 | 26 |
| 7 | 5 | | 4 | 3 | | | Other | 31 | 27 |
| | 9 (4/1-9/30/11) | | | 49 (10/1/11-3/31/12) | | | | 4/1/07-3/31/08 | 4/1/08-3/31/09 |
| 0-500M | 500M-2MM | 2-10MM | 10-50MM | 50-100MM | 100-250MM | | | ALL | ALL |
| 13 | 19 | 18 | 7 | | 1 | | NUMBER OF STATEMENTS | 70 | 98 |
| % | % | % | % | % | % | | ASSETS | % | % |
| 15.9 | 10.3 | 18.8 | | | | D | Cash & Equivalents | 12.2 | 16.3 |
| 27.9 | 50.0 | 39.2 | | | | A | Trade Receivables (net) | 38.7 | 37.2 |
| 12.7 | 10.1 | 6.1 | | | | T | Inventory | 13.1 | 9.6 |
| 4.2 | 7.6 | 11.9 | | | | A | All Other Current | 8.6 | 7.7 |
| 60.8 | 78.1 | 76.0 | | | | | Total Current | 72.6 | 70.8 |
| 24.5 | 10.7 | 12.8 | | | | N | Fixed Assets (net) | 18.4 | 18.3 |
| 4.8 | 1.1 | 4.6 | | | | O | Intangibles (net) | 4.2 | 2.9 |
| 10.1 | 10.1 | 6.6 | | | | T | All Other Non-Current | 4.7 | 8.1 |
| 100.0 | 100.0 | 100.0 | | | | | Total | 100.0 | 100.0 |
| | | | | | | A | LIABILITIES | | |
| 43.0 | 22.4 | 9.7 | | | | V | Notes Payable-Short Term | 11.7 | 10.6 |
| 2.9 | 3.9 | 1.1 | | | | A | Cur. Mat.-L.T.D. | 3.9 | 3.0 |
| 12.3 | 21.1 | 16.1 | | | | I | Trade Payables | 21.1 | 22.0 |
| .0 | .7 | .1 | | | | L | Income Taxes Payable | .2 | .2 |
| 15.3 | 8.3 | 11.2 | | | | A | All Other Current | 14.8 | 21.2 |
| 73.5 | 56.5 | 38.1 | | | | B | Total Current | 51.7 | 57.0 |
| 10.8 | 14.4 | 2.5 | | | | L | Long-Term Debt | 14.4 | 15.0 |
| .0 | .3 | .1 | | | | E | Deferred Taxes | .1 | .2 |
| 15.2 | 4.1 | 4.2 | | | | | All Other Non-Current | 5.8 | 4.3 |
| .5 | 24.7 | 55.2 | | | | | Net Worth | 28.0 | 23.5 |
| 100.0 | 100.0 | 100.0 | | | | | Total Liabilities & Net Worth | 100.0 | 100.0 |
| | | | | | | | INCOME DATA | | |
| 100.0 | 100.0 | 100.0 | | | | | Net Sales | 100.0 | 100.0 |
| 43.7 | 29.5 | 24.7 | | | | | Gross Profit | 29.7 | 28.0 |
| 39.0 | 28.6 | 25.0 | | | | | Operating Expenses | 25.1 | 25.9 |
| 4.7 | .9 | -.4 | | | | | Operating Profit | 4.5 | 2.1 |
| 1.1 | .8 | -.7 | | | | | All Other Expenses (net) | .9 | .0 |
| 3.6 | .1 | .3 | | | | | Profit Before Taxes | 3.7 | 2.0 |
| | | | | | | | RATIOS | | |
| 2.3 | 2.5 | 3.7 | | | | | | 2.3 | 2.5 |
| 1.1 | 1.4 | 2.0 | | | | | Current | 1.6 | 1.6 |
| .6 | 1.1 | 1.5 | | | | | | 1.1 | .9 |
| 1.4 | 2.1 | 3.0 | | | | | | 1.8 | 2.0 |
| .6 | 1.3 | 1.3 | | | | | Quick | 1.1 | 1.2 |
| .3 | .8 | 1.0 | | | | | | .6 | .5 |
| 0 UND | 34 10.6 | 41 8.9 | | | | | | 21 17.5 | 16 23.0 |
| 19 18.9 | 51 7.1 | 61 6.0 | | | | | Sales/Receivables | 47 7.7 | 33 11.2 |
| 33 10.9 | 69 5.3 | 73 5.0 | | | | | | 66 5.6 | 64 5.7 |
| 0 UND | 0 UND | 0 UND | | | | | | 0 UND | 0 UND |
| 0 UND | 0 UND | 0 UND | | | | | Cost of Sales/Inventory | 0 780.5 | 0 UND |
| 25 14.5 | 26 13.8 | 3 121.4 | | | | | | 28 13.0 | 15 23.8 |
| 0 UND | 15 24.9 | 13 28.6 | | | | | | 13 28.6 | 9 39.6 |
| 4 95.0 | 23 16.1 | 23 15.7 | | | | | Cost of Sales/Payables | 29 12.4 | 19 19.1 |
| 21 17.4 | 52 7.0 | 37 9.8 | | | | | | 54 6.8 | 38 9.7 |
| 44.8 | 6.7 | 2.8 | | | | | | 7.3 | 7.1 |
| 541.6 | 14.0 | 6.2 | | | | | Sales/Working Capital | 11.4 | 13.5 |
| -10.5 | 60.8 | 15.5 | | | | | | 53.5 | -57.7 |
| 10.0 | 10.9 | 22.7 | | | | | | 12.6 | 18.7 |
| (10) 7.5 | (18) 5.5 | (16) 4.7 | | | | | EBIT/Interest | (67) 4.5 | (85) 5.6 |
| -.2 | -.4 | -.8 | | | | | | 1.4 | .7 |
| | | | | | | | | 22.6 | |
| | | | | | | | Net Profit + Depr., Dep., Amort./Cur. Mat. L/T/D | (12) 2.4 | |
| | | | | | | | | .3 | |
| .1 | .1 | .1 | | | | | | .1 | .1 |
| .6 | .3 | .2 | | | | | Fixed/Worth | .4 | .3 |
| -2.0 | 3.4 | .7 | | | | | | UND | 6.5 |
| 2.0 | .8 | .4 | | | | | | .8 | .7 |
| 9.2 | 3.4 | 1.0 | | | | | Debt/Worth | 2.1 | 1.5 |
| -5.1 | 9.3 | 1.3 | | | | | | -264.1 | NM |
| | 49.5 | 20.6 | | | | | | 57.0 | 58.6 |
| (16) 15.4 | (16) 6.6 | | | | | | % Profit Before Taxes/Tangible Net Worth | (52) 24.8 | (74) 19.9 |
| | -3.6 | -1.4 | | | | | | 9.2 | 1.6 |
| 33.3 | 10.6 | 7.8 | | | | | | 21.2 | 21.4 |
| 24.3 | 5.0 | 3.3 | | | | | % Profit Before Taxes/Total Assets | 9.2 | 7.1 |
| -10.1 | -3.4 | -1.5 | | | | | | 2.4 | -2.0 |
| 197.3 | 169.3 | 62.7 | | | | | | 70.1 | 90.0 |
| 41.7 | 51.1 | 26.8 | | | | | Sales/Net Fixed Assets | 30.8 | 31.5 |
| 11.2 | 15.9 | 10.8 | | | | | | 12.2 | 14.7 |
| 14.0 | 4.3 | 3.6 | | | | | | 4.4 | 5.4 |
| 5.7 | 3.7 | 2.9 | | | | | Sales/Total Assets | 3.2 | 3.4 |
| 2.7 | 2.5 | 1.5 | | | | | | 2.1 | 2.2 |
| | .5 | .7 | | | | | | .4 | .7 |
| (13) | 1.2 (14) | .9 | | | | | % Depr., Dep., Amort./Sales | (49) .8 | (73) 1.1 |
| | 2.6 | 2.2 | | | | | | 1.6 | 1.9 |
| 2.6 | 3.7 | 1.5 | | | | | | 1.8 | 2.2 |
| (10) 4.4 | (11) 4.5 | (12) 2.8 | | | | | % Officers', Directors' Owners' Comp/Sales | (35) 3.5 | (50) 4.7 |
| 10.2 | 8.5 | 7.0 | | | | | | 5.9 | 6.7 |
| 21954M | 84716M | 215210M | 240128M | | 188234M | | Net Sales ($) | 2117209M | 984730M |
| 3079M | 22950M | 87555M | 115906M | | 164736M | | Total Assets ($) | 684479M | 373768M |

M = $ thousand    MM = $ million
See Pages 9 through 22 for Explanation of Ratios and Data

## Comparative Historical Data | Current Data Sorted by Sales

Period headers — left columns: **ALL** for 4/1/09-3/31/10, 4/1/10-3/31/11, 4/1/11-3/31/12.
Right columns: **9 (4/1-9/30/11)** covers 0-1MM & 1-3MM; **49 (10/1/11-3/31/12)** covers 3-5MM, 5-10MM, 10-25MM, 25MM & OVER.

| | 4/1/09-3/31/10 ALL | 4/1/10-3/31/11 ALL | 4/1/11-3/31/12 ALL | | 0-1MM | 1-3MM | 3-5MM | 5-10MM | 10-25MM | 25MM & OVER |
|---|---|---|---|---|---|---|---|---|---|---|
| **Type of Statement** | | | | | | | | | | |
| Unqualified | | | 4 | | | 1 | 4 | 3 | 5 | 3 |
| Reviewed | 22 | 15 | 15 | | | 2 | 1 | 5 | 2 | 2 |
| Compiled | 11 | 10 | 11 | | 1 | 3 | 2 | 2 | 1 | |
| Tax Returns | 21 | 14 | 9 | | 2 | | | | | |
| Other | 18 | 18 | 19 | | 3 | 6 | 3 | 1 | 5 | 1 |
| **NUMBER OF STATEMENTS** | 72 | 57 | 58 | | 6 | 12 | 10 | 11 | 13 | 6 |
| | % | % | % | | % | % | % | % | % | % |
| **ASSETS** | | | | | | | | | | |
| Cash & Equivalents | 19.2 | 16.2 | 13.7 | | | 21.6 | 7.4 | 12.6 | 16.5 | |
| Trade Receivables (net) | 38.7 | 37.4 | 39.5 | | | 19.7 | 64.5 | 44.4 | 34.6 | |
| Inventory | 6.5 | 8.6 | 9.7 | | | 9.9 | 12.2 | 11.7 | 6.0 | |
| All Other Current | 7.6 | 6.3 | 8.8 | | | 9.9 | 2.4 | 8.5 | 10.9 | |
| Total Current | 72.0 | 68.5 | 71.7 | | | 61.0 | 86.4 | 77.2 | 68.1 | |
| Fixed Assets (net) | 15.7 | 18.4 | 16.2 | | | 23.4 | 7.4 | 14.0 | 17.6 | |
| Intangibles (net) | 4.3 | 2.5 | 4.1 | | | .0 | 2.0 | .6 | 10.6 | |
| All Other Non-Current | 8.0 | 10.6 | 8.0 | | | 15.7 | 4.1 | 8.2 | 3.8 | |
| Total | 100.0 | 100.0 | 100.0 | | | 100.0 | 100.0 | 100.0 | 100.0 | |
| **LIABILITIES** | | | | | | | | | | |
| Notes Payable-Short Term | 15.4 | 14.8 | 20.8 | | | 29.8 | 19.4 | 6.0 | 10.7 | |
| Cur. Mat.-L.T.D. | 4.5 | 2.9 | 2.6 | | | 3.6 | .3 | 6.4 | .5 | |
| Trade Payables | 20.4 | 16.2 | 17.5 | | | 10.7 | 25.3 | 16.1 | 18.8 | |
| Income Taxes Payable | .3 | .1 | .3 | | | .1 | .1 | 1.1 | .0 | |
| All Other Current | 17.9 | 13.1 | 10.9 | | | 9.5 | 6.2 | 9.2 | 9.7 | |
| Total Current | 58.5 | 47.1 | 52.1 | | | 53.8 | 51.3 | 38.8 | 39.7 | |
| Long-Term Debt | 14.6 | 17.3 | 10.6 | | | 18.8 | 8.2 | 8.8 | 5.4 | |
| Deferred Taxes | .3 | .3 | .1 | | | .2 | .0 | .3 | .0 | |
| All Other Non-Current | 5.3 | 6.4 | 6.7 | | | 5.0 | 4.7 | 10.6 | 4.6 | |
| Net Worth | 21.3 | 28.9 | 30.5 | | | 22.3 | 35.9 | 41.5 | 50.3 | |
| Total Liabilities & Net Worth | 100.0 | 100.0 | 100.0 | | | 100.0 | 100.0 | 100.0 | 100.0 | |
| **INCOME DATA** | | | | | | | | | | |
| Net Sales | 100.0 | 100.0 | 100.0 | | | 100.0 | 100.0 | 100.0 | 100.0 | |
| Gross Profit | 27.8 | 28.1 | 29.7 | | | 36.5 | 30.3 | 19.9 | 28.8 | |
| Operating Expenses | 25.8 | 27.1 | 27.8 | | | 35.0 | 27.0 | 20.0 | 26.1 | |
| Operating Profit | 2.0 | 1.0 | 1.8 | | | 1.5 | 3.3 | -.2 | 2.6 | |
| All Other Expenses (net) | .3 | .0 | .5 | | | .3 | .5 | -.2 | .3 | |
| Profit Before Taxes | 1.7 | 1.1 | 1.3 | | | 1.2 | 2.8 | .1 | 2.4 | |
| **RATIOS** | | | | | | | | | | |
| Current | 3.0 | 2.4 | 2.5 | | | 2.3 | 2.9 | 3.3 | 3.4 | |
| | 1.4 | 1.9 | 1.5 | | | 1.2 | 1.4 | 2.2 | 1.5 | |
| | .9 | 1.2 | 1.1 | | | .7 | 1.2 | 1.5 | 1.1 | |
| Quick | 2.3 | 1.9 | 1.9 | | | 1.7 | 2.4 | 3.2 | 1.9 | |
| | 1.1 | 1.2 (57) | 1.1 | | | .8 | 1.4 (10) | 1.7 | 1.1 | |
| | .7 | .8 | .8 | | | .3 | 1.2 | 1.2 | .9 | |
| Sales/Receivables | 16  22.8 | 17  21.5 | 23  15.6 | | 0  UND | 31  11.8 | 41  9.0 | 17  21.1 | | |
| | 47  7.8 | 52  7.1 | 52  7.0 | | 18  19.8 | 65  5.6 | 61  6.0 | 34  10.6 | | |
| | 62  5.8 | 74  4.9 | 72  5.1 | | 41  9.0 | 87  4.2 | 72  5.1 | 68  5.4 | | |
| Cost of Sales/Inventory | 0  UND | 0  UND | 0  UND | | 0  UND | 0  UND | 0  UND | 0  UND | | |
| | 0  UND | 3  145.1 | 0  UND | | 0  UND | 0  UND | 1  520.1 | 0  UND | | |
| | 19  19.1 | 21  17.0 | 27  13.7 | | 31  11.8 | 27  13.6 | 26  13.8 | 49  7.4 | | |
| Cost of Sales/Payables | 5  77.8 | 8  44.6 | 8  43.2 | | 0  UND | 7  53.0 | 11  33.4 | 14  25.8 | | |
| | 20  18.1 | 18  20.6 | 22  16.7 | | 18  19.8 | 20  18.6 | 23  16.1 | 26  14.3 | | |
| | 34  10.8 | 44  8.3 | 41  8.8 | | 27  13.3 | 54  6.7 | 37  9.8 | 45  8.2 | | |
| Sales/Working Capital | 5.1 | 5.7 | 5.1 | | | 9.6 | 5.1 | 2.8 | 5.4 | |
| | 15.6 | 8.2 | 11.3 | | | 69.8 | 11.9 | 7.0 | 11.6 | |
| | -43.5 | 202.2 | 79.7 | | | -178.4 | 30.3 | 11.4 | 54.2 | |
| EBIT/Interest | 7.8 | 6.1 | 9.6 | | | 9.3 | 13.9 | | 31.2 | |
| | (58) 1.4 | (48) 2.7 | (51) 4.0 | | | 4.8 | 8.2 | | (11) 5.8 | |
| | -3.6 | -2.6 | .2 | | | -1.2 | 2.2 | | -2.2 | |
| Net Profit + Depr., Dep., Amort./Cur. Mat. L/T/D | | | | | | | | | | |
| Fixed/Worth | .1 | .1 | .1 | | | .1 | .0 | .1 | .1 | |
| | .4 | .4 | .3 | | | .4 | .1 | .2 | .4 | |
| | 4.4 | 4.1 | 1.9 | | | 3.8 | .3 | .5 | 1.3 | |
| Debt/Worth | .7 | .6 | .8 | | | .9 | .7 | .4 | .7 | |
| | 2.0 | 1.2 | 2.2 | | | 5.5 | 2.9 | 1.0 | 1.2 | |
| | 25.0 | 21.2 | 9.6 | | | 10.0 | 6.9 | 5.2 | 2.4 | |
| % Profit Before Taxes/Tangible Net Worth | 45.0 | 29.3 | 42.3 | | | 160.6 | | | 25.9 | |
| | (56) 10.7 | (46) 12.7 | (47) 11.0 | | | (10) 13.9 | | | (11) 19.8 | |
| | -10.8 | -6.5 | -3.1 | | | -96.9 | | | 6.5 | |
| % Profit Before Taxes/Total Assets | 22.6 | 11.6 | 13.8 | | | 47.6 | 17.8 | 5.3 | 9.6 | |
| | 3.8 | 4.6 | 4.5 | | | 5.1 | 7.1 | .4 | 5.0 | |
| | -7.6 | -5.0 | -2.5 | | | -13.3 | 4.0 | -12.6 | -.4 | |
| Sales/Net Fixed Assets | 76.5 | 76.8 | 94.6 | | | 177.6 | 500.5 | 92.0 | 88.9 | |
| | 33.4 | 31.6 | 34.4 | | | 44.5 | 74.1 | 31.1 | 37.0 | |
| | 15.8 | 10.2 | 11.6 | | | 7.4 | 27.9 | 26.1 | 8.8 | |
| Sales/Total Assets | 4.9 | 3.8 | 4.3 | | | 7.6 | 4.7 | 4.1 | 4.3 | |
| | 3.2 | 2.7 | 3.1 | | | 4.3 | 3.8 | 2.8 | 3.3 | |
| | 2.3 | 2.0 | 2.0 | | | 2.4 | 2.3 | 1.4 | 1.5 | |
| % Depr., Dep., Amort./Sales | .5 | .5 | .5 | | | | | | | |
| | (54) 1.0 | (45) 1.0 | (36) .9 | | | | | | | |
| | 2.0 | 2.1 | 2.2 | | | | | | | |
| % Officers', Directors', Owners' Comp/Sales | 2.0 | 2.0 | 2.3 | | | 3.7 | | | | |
| | (42) 5.0 | (30) 3.9 | (34) 4.0 | | | (10) 7.6 | | | | |
| | 8.7 | 7.6 | 8.7 | | | 14.4 | | | | |
| Net Sales ($) | 502281M | 420561M | 750242M | | 2789M | 24894M | 39305M | 81155M | 192060M | 410039M |
| Total Assets ($) | 184743M | 167121M | 394226M | | 1722M | 9686M | 12593M | 37047M | 86263M | 246915M |

**Current Data Sorted by Assets**       **Comparative Historical Data**

### Type of Statement

| Type of Statement | 0-500M | 500M-2MM | 2-10MM | 10-50MM | 50-100MM | 100-250MM | | 4/1/07-3/31/08 ALL | 4/1/08-3/31/09 ALL |
|---|---|---|---|---|---|---|---|---|---|
| Unqualified | | | 6 | 2 | | | | 31 | 27 |
| Reviewed | 2 | 22 | 52 | 1 | 1 | 1 | | 85 | 88 |
| Compiled | 6 | 11 | 4 | | | | | 32 | 21 |
| Tax Returns | 21 | 10 | 7 | | | | | 38 | 35 |
| Other | 7 | 22 | 24 | 9 | | | | 72 | 67 |
| | 25 (4/1-9/30/11) | | | 182 (10/1/11-3/31/12) | | | | | |
| NUMBER OF STATEMENTS | 36 | 65 | 93 | 12 | 1 | | | 258 | 238 |

*(For columns 50-100MM and 100-250MM: DATA NOT AVAILABLE)*

| | 0-500M % | 500M-2MM % | 2-10MM % | 10-50MM % | 50-100MM % | 100-250MM % | | ALL % | ALL % |
|---|---|---|---|---|---|---|---|---|---|
| | | | | | | | **ASSETS** | | |
| | 21.7 | 13.7 | 13.5 | 13.8 | | | Cash & Equivalents | 14.2 | 13.7 |
| | 26.6 | 48.6 | 49.5 | 50.8 | | | Trade Receivables (net) | 47.0 | 46.2 |
| | 5.3 | 5.1 | 3.1 | 2.4 | | | Inventory | 4.3 | 4.9 |
| | 6.6 | 5.1 | 10.2 | 13.0 | | | All Other Current | 7.1 | 7.5 |
| | 60.3 | 72.5 | 76.2 | 80.1 | | | Total Current | 72.7 | 72.4 |
| | 26.7 | 16.5 | 16.1 | 16.6 | | | Fixed Assets (net) | 18.6 | 18.3 |
| | .7 | 2.2 | 2.3 | .6 | | | Intangibles (net) | .9 | 1.8 |
| | 12.3 | 8.8 | 5.5 | 2.7 | | | All Other Non-Current | 7.9 | 7.5 |
| | 100.0 | 100.0 | 100.0 | 100.0 | | | Total | 100.0 | 100.0 |
| | | | | | | | **LIABILITIES** | | |
| | 22.5 | 15.4 | 11.8 | 9.9 | | | Notes Payable-Short Term | 10.0 | 11.0 |
| | 5.3 | 2.7 | 2.0 | 1.7 | | | Cur. Mat.-L.T.D. | 3.0 | 3.0 |
| | 11.1 | 14.9 | 18.0 | 16.4 | | | Trade Payables | 16.6 | 16.3 |
| | .4 | .3 | .7 | .3 | | | Income Taxes Payable | 1.1 | .7 |
| | 35.6 | 10.4 | 14.4 | 23.5 | | | All Other Current | 15.2 | 15.8 |
| | 74.8 | 43.7 | 46.9 | 51.8 | | | Total Current | 45.8 | 46.9 |
| | 27.8 | 5.4 | 7.0 | 5.6 | | | Long-Term Debt | 11.3 | 11.7 |
| | .0 | .2 | .8 | 2.0 | | | Deferred Taxes | .4 | .3 |
| | 3.3 | 4.9 | 3.2 | 4.4 | | | All Other Non-Current | 4.4 | 4.9 |
| | -5.9 | 45.7 | 42.1 | 36.2 | | | Net Worth | 38.2 | 36.3 |
| | 100.0 | 100.0 | 100.0 | 100.0 | | | Total Liabilities & Net Worth | 100.0 | 100.0 |
| | | | | | | | **INCOME DATA** | | |
| | 100.0 | 100.0 | 100.0 | 100.0 | | | Net Sales | 100.0 | 100.0 |
| | 40.5 | 23.7 | 17.2 | 22.9 | | | Gross Profit | 26.3 | 23.4 |
| | 36.5 | 24.2 | 17.3 | 18.5 | | | Operating Expenses | 20.5 | 20.4 |
| | 3.9 | -.5 | -.1 | 4.4 | | | Operating Profit | 5.8 | 3.0 |
| | -.1 | -.1 | .2 | .7 | | | All Other Expenses (net) | .4 | .6 |
| | 4.0 | -.4 | -.3 | 3.7 | | | Profit Before Taxes | 5.4 | 2.4 |
| | | | | | | | **RATIOS** | | |
| | 3.4 | 3.0 | 2.5 | 2.2 | | | | 2.6 | 2.7 |
| | 1.4 | 1.9 | 1.6 | 1.6 | | | Current | 1.6 | 1.7 |
| | .8 | 1.2 | 1.2 | 1.3 | | | | 1.2 | 1.2 |
| | 2.3 | 2.7 | 2.2 | 2.0 | | | | 2.3 | 2.3 |
| | 1.3 | 1.5 | 1.3 | 1.2 | | | Quick | (257) 1.4 | 1.3 |
| | .3 | .9 | 1.0 | .7 | | | | 1.0 | 1.0 |
| | 0 UND | 44 8.3 | 60 6.1 | 56 6.5 | | | | 40 9.1 | 41 9.0 |
| | 21 17.8 | 69 5.3 | 79 4.6 | 79 4.6 | | | Sales/Receivables | 64 5.7 | 64 5.7 |
| | 53 6.9 | 91 4.0 | 101 3.6 | 99 3.7 | | | | 88 4.2 | 92 4.0 |
| | 0 UND | 0 UND | 0 UND | 0 UND | | | | 0 UND | 0 UND |
| | 0 UND | 0 UND | 0 UND | 0 UND | | | Cost of Sales/Inventory | 0 UND | 0 UND |
| | 4 91.5 | 7 55.8 | 4 82.9 | 8 48.2 | | | | 4 95.3 | 3 138.3 |
| | 0 UND | 10 36.3 | 17 21.0 | 18 20.1 | | | | 11 32.4 | 9 42.2 |
| | 2 170.0 | 23 16.2 | 29 12.8 | 25 14.4 | | | Cost of Sales/Payables | 20 18.5 | 22 17.0 |
| | 30 12.1 | 36 10.0 | 46 7.9 | 43 8.4 | | | | 39 9.3 | 37 9.8 |
| | 8.9 | 4.7 | 4.1 | 4.9 | | | | 5.6 | 5.1 |
| | 37.4 | 9.1 | 7.5 | 9.5 | | | Sales/Working Capital | 10.8 | 10.2 |
| | -29.1 | 25.9 | 20.0 | 16.0 | | | | 33.7 | 25.8 |
| | 23.8 | 10.6 | 7.3 | 20.6 | | | | 30.9 | 21.7 |
| | (30) 10.5 | (53) 3.4 | (77) 2.7 | (10) 4.3 | | | EBIT/Interest | (219) 6.4 | (211) 5.1 |
| | 1.0 | -4.0 | -2.1 | 3.2 | | | | 1.9 | -.2 |
| | | 11.8 | 10.1 | | | | Net Profit + Depr., Dep., | 8.9 | 7.8 |
| | | (10) 1.6 | (23) 2.3 | | | | Amort./Cur. Mat. L/T/D | (50) 3.8 | (39) 4.0 |
| | | -5.6 | -.4 | | | | | 1.7 | 1.3 |
| | .2 | .1 | .1 | .2 | | | | .2 | .2 |
| | .9 | .3 | .3 | .3 | | | Fixed/Worth | .3 | .3 |
| | -1.0 | .7 | .9 | 1.0 | | | | 1.0 | .9 |
| | .4 | .4 | .6 | 1.0 | | | | .6 | .6 |
| | 2.5 | 1.0 | 1.6 | 1.9 | | | Debt/Worth | 1.4 | 1.4 |
| | -4.3 | 2.9 | 2.6 | 2.9 | | | | 4.0 | 4.1 |
| | 82.4 | 25.1 | 12.6 | 36.1 | | | % Profit Before Taxes/Tangible | 64.5 | 51.5 |
| | (24) 33.2 | (59) 4.4 | (85) 3.1 | 14.7 | | | Net Worth | (238) 29.4 | (211) 15.2 |
| | 3.9 | -12.8 | -12.0 | 5.4 | | | | 10.0 | .4 |
| | 35.5 | 9.6 | 5.8 | 8.1 | | | % Profit Before Taxes/Total | 23.6 | 19.0 |
| | 22.6 | 2.2 | 1.5 | 3.5 | | | Assets | 10.5 | 6.9 |
| | .6 | -7.5 | -5.2 | 1.9 | | | | 2.6 | -1.6 |
| | 104.4 | 57.4 | 41.4 | 82.1 | | | | 45.0 | 41.9 |
| | 25.7 | 19.7 | 20.1 | 42.5 | | | Sales/Net Fixed Assets | 20.9 | 21.7 |
| | 13.3 | 8.9 | 11.0 | 16.3 | | | | 11.1 | 12.3 |
| | 11.1 | 3.2 | 3.0 | 3.1 | | | | 3.6 | 3.7 |
| | 4.6 | 2.7 | 2.3 | 2.2 | | | Sales/Total Assets | 2.7 | 2.7 |
| | 2.7 | 1.8 | 1.7 | 1.9 | | | | 2.2 | 2.1 |
| | .6 | .4 | .7 | .6 | | | | .7 | .6 |
| | (23) 1.2 | (49) 1.0 | (83) 1.2 | (11) 1.2 | | | % Depr., Dep., Amort./Sales | (212) 1.3 | (192) 1.3 |
| | 2.6 | 2.2 | 2.4 | 3.2 | | | | 2.3 | 2.1 |
| | 2.6 | 2.7 | 1.3 | | | | | 1.8 | 2.0 |
| | (24) 5.3 | (35) 4.8 | (39) 3.1 | | | | % Officers', Directors' Owners' Comp/Sales | (138) 3.6 | (120) 3.9 |
| | 9.3 | 7.4 | 4.7 | | | | | 6.7 | 6.3 |
| | 54720M | 196638M | 1002873M | 588206M | 83633M | | Net Sales ($) | 4099025M | 4830181M |
| | 10153M | 73578M | 419658M | 246224M | 76526M | | Total Assets ($) | 1664492M | 1964403M |

M = $ thousand    MM = $ million
See Pages 9 through 22 for Explanation of Ratios and Data

## Comparative Historical Data / Current Data Sorted by Sales

| | Comparative Historical Data | | | Type of Statement | Current Data Sorted by Sales | | | | | |
|---|---|---|---|---|---|---|---|---|---|---|
| | 19 | 11 | 8 | Unqualified | | | | 3 | 2 | 3 |
| | 73 | 65 | 78 | Reviewed | 2 | 13 | 11 | 31 | 18 | 3 |
| | 20 | 22 | 21 | Compiled | 2 | 11 | 4 | 2 | 2 | |
| | 44 | 34 | 38 | Tax Returns | 13 | 13 | 5 | 5 | 2 | |
| | 50 | 43 | 62 | Other | 5 | 18 | 8 | 9 | 15 | 7 |
| | 4/1/09-3/31/10 ALL | 4/1/10-3/31/11 ALL | 4/1/11-3/31/12 ALL | | 25 (4/1-9/30/11) | | 182 (10/1/11-3/31/12) | | | |
| | | | | | 0-1MM | 1-3MM | 3-5MM | 5-10MM | 10-25MM | 25MM & OVER |
| NUMBER OF STATEMENTS | 206 | 175 | 207 | | 22 | 55 | 28 | 50 | 39 | 13 |
| | % | % | % | ASSETS | % | % | % | % | % | % |
| Cash & Equivalents | 16.8 | 17.1 | 15.0 | | 20.3 | 15.2 | 13.6 | 15.6 | 13.3 | 11.1 |
| Trade Receivables (net) | 40.2 | 37.4 | 45.3 | | 27.7 | 39.8 | 48.6 | 48.4 | 54.5 | 52.0 |
| Inventory | 4.7 | 5.0 | 4.1 | | 2.2 | 7.0 | 4.1 | 3.0 | 2.4 | 4.2 |
| All Other Current | 8.0 | 8.6 | 8.2 | | 7.1 | 5.1 | 6.7 | 10.3 | 9.1 | 14.7 |
| Total Current | 69.7 | 68.2 | 72.5 | | 57.3 | 67.0 | 73.0 | 77.3 | 79.3 | 82.0 |
| Fixed Assets (net) | 19.7 | 20.0 | 18.0 | | 24.0 | 21.1 | 19.8 | 16.5 | 13.0 | 12.1 |
| Intangibles (net) | 2.5 | 2.2 | 1.9 | | 3.8 | 1.5 | 2.4 | 2.0 | 1.1 | 2.1 |
| All Other Non-Current | 8.0 | 9.6 | 7.5 | | 14.8 | 10.4 | 4.8 | 4.2 | 6.6 | 3.9 |
| Total | 100.0 | 100.0 | 100.0 | | 100.0 | 100.0 | 100.0 | 100.0 | 100.0 | 100.0 |
| | | | | LIABILITIES | | | | | | |
| Notes Payable-Short Term | 11.6 | 12.0 | 14.7 | | 18.1 | 19.4 | 15.1 | 12.8 | 9.6 | 10.5 |
| Cur. Mat.-L.T.D. | 3.1 | 3.0 | 2.8 | | 1.7 | 4.1 | 3.0 | 2.4 | 2.0 | 2.1 |
| Trade Payables | 12.3 | 14.8 | 15.7 | | 10.1 | 13.6 | 15.6 | 15.6 | 20.6 | 20.4 |
| Income Taxes Payable | .7 | .6 | .5 | | .0 | .4 | .3 | 1.1 | .2 | .6 |
| All Other Current | 11.8 | 13.1 | 17.4 | | 41.7 | 11.3 | 14.3 | 13.1 | 18.2 | 23.0 |
| Total Current | 39.6 | 43.6 | 51.1 | | 71.7 | 48.8 | 48.3 | 44.9 | 50.7 | 56.6 |
| Long-Term Debt | 12.1 | 11.9 | 10.0 | | 17.8 | 15.3 | 8.0 | 6.0 | 6.8 | 4.1 |
| Deferred Taxes | .4 | .4 | .5 | | .0 | .3 | .9 | .8 | .5 | 1.0 |
| All Other Non-Current | 4.8 | 4.1 | 3.8 | | 3.7 | 5.1 | 4.6 | 1.0 | 4.3 | 6.1 |
| Net Worth | 43.1 | 40.1 | 34.5 | | 6.7 | 30.5 | 38.2 | 47.2 | 37.8 | 32.2 |
| Total Liabilties & Net Worth | 100.0 | 100.0 | 100.0 | | 100.0 | 100.0 | 100.0 | 100.0 | 100.0 | 100.0 |
| | | | | INCOME DATA | | | | | | |
| Net Sales | 100.0 | 100.0 | 100.0 | | 100.0 | 100.0 | 100.0 | 100.0 | 100.0 | 100.0 |
| Gross Profit | 26.9 | 26.4 | 23.6 | | 44.6 | 28.7 | 21.5 | 17.8 | 15.7 | 16.4 |
| Operating Expenses | 25.3 | 26.4 | 22.8 | | 44.5 | 28.1 | 19.5 | 17.5 | 15.4 | 13.8 |
| Operating Profit | 1.6 | .0 | .7 | | .0 | .7 | 2.0 | .3 | .3 | 2.6 |
| All Other Expenses (net) | .3 | .3 | .1 | | -.1 | -.1 | .5 | .1 | .1 | .2 |
| Profit Before Taxes | 1.3 | -.3 | .7 | | .2 | .8 | 1.5 | .3 | .2 | 2.4 |
| | | | | RATIOS | | | | | | |
| Current | 3.6 | 2.7 | 2.8 | | 3.5 | 2.8 | 3.0 | 2.7 | 2.5 | 1.8 |
| | 1.8 | 1.6 | 1.6 | | 1.5 | 1.6 | 1.9 | 1.8 | 1.5 | 1.4 |
| | 1.2 | 1.1 | 1.2 | | .8 | 1.0 | 1.1 | 1.3 | 1.1 | 1.2 |
| Quick | 3.1 | 2.4 | 2.3 | | 3.0 | 2.5 | 2.5 | 2.3 | 2.3 | 1.8 |
| | 1.6 | 1.3 | 1.3 | | 1.3 | 1.3 | 1.5 | 1.4 | 1.2 | 1.2 |
| | 1.0 | .8 | .9 | | .4 | .6 | .9 | 1.1 | 1.0 | .7 |
| Sales/Receivables | 33  10.9 | 33  11.1 | 42  8.6 | | 0  UND | 26  14.1 | 52  7.0 | 45  8.2 | 60  6.1 | 49  7.5 |
| | 61  5.9 | 60  6.1 | 70  5.2 | | 35  10.5 | 53  6.9 | 66  5.5 | 83  4.4 | 76  4.8 | 73  5.0 |
| | 84  4.3 | 89  4.1 | 94  3.9 | | 94  3.9 | 87  4.2 | 99  3.7 | 111  3.3 | 91  4.0 | 91  4.0 |
| Cost of Sales/Inventory | 0  UND | 0  UND | 0  UND | | 0  UND | 0  UND | 0  UND | 0  UND | 0  UND | 0  UND |
| | 0  UND | 0  UND | 0  UND | | 0  UND | 0  UND | 0  UND | 0  999.8 | 0  UND | 0  801.7 |
| | 3  111.2 | 4  86.5 | 4  82.0 | | 5  77.6 | 4  101.1 | 7  53.3 | 5  73.4 | 1  493.4 | 10  37.7 |
| Cost of Sales/Payables | 7  49.2 | 9  40.5 | 10  35.8 | | 0  UND | 8  45.9 | 9  41.3 | 13  27.2 | 18  20.1 | 18  20.1 |
| | 17  22.0 | 23  16.0 | 24  15.4 | | 24  15.2 | 20  17.9 | 20  18.2 | 26  14.1 | 28  13.0 | 22  16.9 |
| | 33  11.1 | 45  8.0 | 40  9.1 | | 39  9.4 | 38  9.6 | 41  8.8 | 41  8.9 | 45  8.2 | 42  8.7 |
| Sales/Working Capital | 4.9 | 4.9 | 4.7 | | 3.0 | 5.3 | 4.9 | 4.3 | 4.5 | 6.9 |
| | 8.5 | 10.5 | 9.3 | | 28.9 | 9.1 | 12.5 | 7.5 | 13.3 | 12.5 |
| | 31.1 | 108.0 | 30.8 | | -32.1 | 71.2 | 41.9 | -16.0 | 25.7 | 17.4 |
| EBIT/Interest | 17.8 | 9.4 | 11.4 | | 13.6 | 11.8 | 11.6 | 17.0 | 7.3 | 25.6 |
| | (176)  4.5 | (149)  1.9 | (171)  3.8 | | (16)  2.6 | (46)  3.3 | (23)  3.2 | (42)  3.8 | (32)  3.7 | (12)  5.4 |
| | -1.4 | -2.9 | -.9 | | -7.3 | -1.3 | .6 | -6.2 | -.4 | 3.7 |
| Net Profit + Depr., Dep., Amort./Cur. Mat. L/T/D | 8.1 | 4.2 | 10.4 | | | | | 7.1 | | |
| | (42)  3.8 | (31)  1.4 | (41)  2.3 | | | | | (10)  1.0 | | |
| | 1.4 | -1.7 | .2 | | | | | -5.7 | | |
| Fixed/Worth | .2 | .1 | .1 | | .1 | .1 | .1 | .1 | .1 | .2 |
| | .3 | .3 | .3 | | .5 | .4 | .4 | .2 | .3 | .3 |
| | 1.0 | 1.1 | 1.1 | | NM | 1.3 | 4.9 | .7 | .9 | .8 |
| Debt/Worth | .4 | .5 | .5 | | .4 | .5 | .5 | .5 | 1.0 | 1.5 |
| | 1.1 | 1.2 | 1.4 | | 1.4 | 1.1 | 1.5 | 1.2 | 1.7 | 2.5 |
| | 3.0 | 4.9 | 3.3 | | -11.0 | 3.4 | 21.5 | 2.2 | 3.3 | 3.6 |
| % Profit Before Taxes/Tangible Net Worth | 38.9 | 21.8 | 24.9 | | 46.3 | 25.1 | 50.5 | 23.3 | 10.8 | 41.9 |
| | (180)  11.0 | (148)  3.9 | (181)  5.5 | | (16)  25.0 | (47)  5.5 | (22)  3.2 | (48)  4.8 | (35)  3.5 | 16.2 |
| | -2.9 | -10.7 | -7.1 | | -26.8 | -8.6 | -.6 | -13.7 | -4.8 | 6.2 |
| % Profit Before Taxes/Total Assets | 14.6 | 12.1 | 11.3 | | 26.6 | 19.7 | 21.3 | 10.4 | 6.9 | 7.5 |
| | 4.3 | 1.6 | 2.9 | | 4.5 | 3.4 | 2.4 | 2.1 | 1.5 | 4.3 |
| | -3.8 | -5.4 | -4.7 | | -20.3 | -5.0 | -.7 | -5.6 | -5.6 | 1.8 |
| Sales/Net Fixed Assets | 37.4 | 42.8 | 53.8 | | 114.7 | 52.8 | 51.3 | 45.1 | 75.6 | 74.7 |
| | 20.3 | 17.4 | 22.5 | | 17.7 | 17.5 | 27.1 | 20.1 | 35.7 | 47.5 |
| | 9.9 | 8.1 | 11.5 | | 3.5 | 9.3 | 8.4 | 12.3 | 14.2 | 21.2 |
| Sales/Total Assets | 3.5 | 3.3 | 3.4 | | 5.9 | 3.6 | 3.4 | 3.0 | 3.4 | 3.8 |
| | 2.5 | 2.4 | 2.6 | | 2.2 | 2.7 | 2.4 | 2.4 | 2.6 | 2.7 |
| | 1.9 | 1.6 | 1.8 | | 1.3 | 1.7 | 1.9 | 1.8 | 2.1 | 2.0 |
| % Depr., Dep., Amort./Sales | .8 | 1.0 | .6 | | 1.0 | .5 | .4 | .6 | .7 | .5 |
| | (174)  1.5 | (139)  2.0 | (167)  1.2 | | (15)  2.0 | (38)  1.4 | (24)  1.0 | (45)  1.4 | (32)  1.1 | .9 |
| | 2.9 | 3.7 | 2.2 | | 4.2 | 2.5 | 2.4 | 2.4 | 1.6 | 1.2 |
| % Officers', Directors' Owners' Comp/Sales | 3.2 | 2.6 | 1.9 | | 3.1 | 2.8 | 1.8 | 1.8 | 1.0 | |
| | (121)  5.8 | (89)  4.5 | (102)  3.7 | | (13)  7.1 | (33)  6.6 | (14)  3.7 | (25)  3.4 | (13)  2.8 | |
| | 10.3 | 9.4 | 7.1 | | 9.3 | 10.9 | 5.7 | 4.4 | 5.6 | |
| Net Sales ($) | 2709288M | 1485977M | 1926070M | | 13653M | 116453M | 110952M | 364549M | 589255M | 731208M |
| Total Assets ($) | 1113575M | 668363M | 826139M | | 6890M | 60468M | 49707M | 163905M | 231579M | 313590M |

© RMA 2012

M = $ thousand    MM = $ million
See Pages 9 through 22 for Explanation of Ratios and Data

**Current Data Sorted by Assets**                                        **Comparative Historical Data**

| Type of Statement | 0-500M | 500M-2MM | 2-10MM | 10-50MM | 50-100MM | 100-250MM | 4/1/07-3/31/08 ALL | 4/1/08-3/31/09 ALL |
|---|---|---|---|---|---|---|---|---|
| Unqualified | | | 5 | 3 | 1 | 1 | 7 | 12 |
| Reviewed | 1 | 13 | 34 | 5 | | | 48 | 69 |
| Compiled | 2 | 14 | 9 | | | | 13 | 14 |
| Tax Returns | 15 | 14 | 3 | | | | 24 | 23 |
| Other | 2 | 16 | 12 | 4 | | | 34 | 44 |
| | 24 (4/1-9/30/11) | | 130 (10/1/11-3/31/12) | | | | | |
| **NUMBER OF STATEMENTS** | 20 | 57 | 63 | 12 | 1 | 1 | 126 | 162 |
| | % | % | % | % | % | % | % | % |
| **ASSETS** | | | | | | | | |
| Cash & Equivalents | 14.5 | 11.1 | 15.3 | 14.0 | | | 12.2 | 15.0 |
| Trade Receivables (net) | 29.9 | 51.9 | 45.0 | 41.8 | | | 50.3 | 47.9 |
| Inventory | 9.3 | 9.2 | 7.3 | 10.0 | | | 11.0 | 7.8 |
| All Other Current | .9 | 6.1 | 11.2 | 12.8 | | | 5.9 | 7.3 |
| Total Current | 54.5 | 78.2 | 78.9 | 78.5 | | | 79.4 | 78.1 |
| Fixed Assets (net) | 25.9 | 13.8 | 14.2 | 17.5 | | | 15.2 | 15.9 |
| Intangibles (net) | 11.4 | 2.9 | 2.8 | 2.0 | | | 1.5 | 2.5 |
| All Other Non-Current | 8.3 | 5.1 | 4.2 | 2.0 | | | 3.9 | 3.6 |
| Total | 100.0 | 100.0 | 100.0 | 100.0 | | | 100.0 | 100.0 |
| **LIABILITIES** | | | | | | | | |
| Notes Payable-Short Term | 22.1 | 14.4 | 10.2 | 11.3 | | | 9.7 | 11.4 |
| Cur. Mat.-L.T.D. | 31.4 | 3.6 | 1.6 | 1.6 | | | 2.7 | 3.8 |
| Trade Payables | 16.3 | 24.4 | 19.8 | 19.5 | | | 19.7 | 18.5 |
| Income Taxes Payable | .0 | .1 | .5 | .0 | | | .9 | 1.0 |
| All Other Current | 9.3 | 10.1 | 12.3 | 15.5 | | | 18.2 | 18.6 |
| Total Current | 79.0 | 52.6 | 44.4 | 48.0 | | | 51.2 | 53.3 |
| Long-Term Debt | 30.5 | 11.7 | 5.9 | 7.5 | | | 10.7 | 8.9 |
| Deferred Taxes | .0 | .2 | .3 | .0 | | | .2 | .3 |
| All Other Non-Current | 10.7 | 3.3 | 2.8 | 5.2 | | | 4.3 | 4.8 |
| Net Worth | -20.2 | 32.2 | 46.6 | 39.3 | | | 33.7 | 32.7 |
| Total Liabilities & Net Worth | 100.0 | 100.0 | 100.0 | 100.0 | | | 100.0 | 100.0 |
| **INCOME DATA** | | | | | | | | |
| Net Sales | 100.0 | 100.0 | 100.0 | 100.0 | | | 100.0 | 100.0 |
| Gross Profit | 51.9 | 30.7 | 23.2 | 20.8 | | | 29.9 | 31.0 |
| Operating Expenses | 49.8 | 30.6 | 23.7 | 20.2 | | | 24.5 | 24.7 |
| Operating Profit | 2.1 | .1 | -.5 | .6 | | | 5.4 | 6.2 |
| All Other Expenses (net) | .7 | .1 | .0 | .6 | | | .6 | .5 |
| Profit Before Taxes | 1.4 | -.1 | -.5 | .1 | | | 4.8 | 5.7 |
| **RATIOS** | | | | | | | | |
| Current | 2.1 | 2.3 | 3.0 | 3.0 | | | 2.3 | 2.4 |
| | 1.0 | 1.6 | 1.7 | 1.9 | | | 1.6 | 1.5 |
| | .3 | 1.1 | 1.3 | 1.2 | | | 1.2 | 1.2 |
| Quick | 1.8 | 2.1 | 2.1 | 1.7 | | | 2.0 | 2.1 |
| | .7 | 1.3 | 1.3 | 1.3 | | | 1.3 | 1.3 |
| | .2 | .8 | .9 | .8 | | | .8 | .9 |
| Sales/Receivables | 0 UND | 41 8.8 | 62 5.9 | 61 6.0 | | | 39 9.5 | 42 8.7 |
| | 24 15.3 | 64 5.7 | 74 4.9 | 74 4.9 | | | 64 5.7 | 64 5.7 |
| | 45 8.2 | 85 4.3 | 101 3.6 | 91 4.0 | | | 89 4.1 | 86 4.2 |
| Cost of Sales/Inventory | 0 UND | 0 UND | 0 UND | 0 UND | | | 0 999.8 | 0 UND |
| | 9 41.7 | 4 91.8 | 1 446.3 | 10 35.7 | | | 8 44.4 | 3 110.8 |
| | 21 17.3 | 20 18.2 | 15 23.6 | 32 11.3 | | | 31 11.8 | 16 23.3 |
| Cost of Sales/Payables | 0 UND | 21 17.3 | 25 14.5 | 23 16.2 | | | 18 20.4 | 16 23.0 |
| | 2 147.8 | 35 10.5 | 37 9.9 | 45 8.1 | | | 33 11.0 | 29 12.6 |
| | 39 9.4 | 54 6.7 | 61 6.0 | 54 6.8 | | | 47 7.8 | 44 8.4 |
| Sales/Working Capital | 12.6 | 5.9 | 4.0 | 4.2 | | | 6.1 | 5.4 |
| | 605.5 | 9.6 | 6.3 | 8.4 | | | 9.4 | 10.6 |
| | -14.3 | 63.1 | 14.1 | 15.4 | | | 25.4 | 20.5 |
| EBIT/Interest | 7.6 | 11.4 | 9.3 | 46.9 | | | 24.9 | 41.9 |
| | (18) 3.0 | (52) 2.2 | (46) 2.6 | (11) 9.4 | | | (114) 7.3 | (146) 12.9 |
| | -1.9 | -3.7 | -4.2 | 1.0 | | | 3.1 | 2.1 |
| Net Profit + Depr., Dep., Amort./Cur. Mat. L/T/D | | | 12.1 | | | | 19.9 | 18.4 |
| | | (16) 1.3 | | | | | (35) 6.0 | (45) 6.9 |
| | | -7.9 | | | | | 2.5 | 2.1 |
| Fixed/Worth | .2 | .2 | .1 | .2 | | | .1 | .1 |
| | 2.3 | .4 | .3 | .4 | | | .3 | .3 |
| | -1.0 | 1.7 | .8 | .6 | | | .8 | .8 |
| Debt/Worth | 3.4 | .9 | .6 | .4 | | | .9 | .7 |
| | NM | 2.1 | 1.4 | 1.3 | | | 2.0 | 1.8 |
| | -3.0 | 10.5 | 2.5 | 6.6 | | | 4.3 | 3.7 |
| % Profit Before Taxes/Tangible Net Worth | 139.4 | 31.9 | 28.0 | 30.7 | | | 61.2 | 77.6 |
| | (10) 77.4 | (48) 4.9 | (60) 5.2 | (11) 14.0 | | | (115) 33.5 | (146) 35.6 |
| | 14.5 | -24.7 | -6.2 | 2.4 | | | 14.2 | 12.1 |
| % Profit Before Taxes/Total Assets | 26.2 | 11.8 | 9.7 | 10.1 | | | 20.1 | 28.3 |
| | 7.3 | 2.3 | 1.6 | 6.4 | | | 9.1 | 12.8 |
| | -8.1 | -11.5 | -4.4 | .0 | | | 4.2 | 2.5 |
| Sales/Net Fixed Assets | 318.3 | 65.1 | 44.0 | 34.9 | | | 63.7 | 67.0 |
| | 46.7 | 30.0 | 24.8 | 16.7 | | | 31.8 | 32.4 |
| | 20.6 | 16.7 | 9.1 | 4.6 | | | 14.4 | 16.2 |
| Sales/Total Assets | 9.8 | 3.6 | 2.9 | 2.5 | | | 3.7 | 4.0 |
| | 5.8 | 3.0 | 2.1 | 2.2 | | | 2.8 | 2.9 |
| | 4.5 | 2.2 | 1.7 | 1.7 | | | 2.2 | 2.2 |
| % Depr., Dep., Amort./Sales | .5 | .5 | .7 | .7 | | | .4 | .4 |
| | (11) 1.0 | (45) .9 | (55) 1.1 | 1.2 | | | (102) .7 | (139) .7 |
| | 2.6 | 1.4 | 1.6 | 2.0 | | | 1.3 | 1.2 |
| % Officers', Directors' Owners' Comp/Sales | 5.7 | 2.7 | 1.5 | | | | 2.2 | 1.7 |
| | (14) 7.1 | (40) 3.8 | (31) 4.1 | | | | (72) 3.6 | (87) 2.9 |
| | 8.2 | 6.3 | 6.1 | | | | 6.2 | 5.0 |
| Net Sales ($) | 29800M | 213237M | 633565M | 458562M | 95895M | 257084M | 4162631M | 3571529M |
| Total Assets ($) | 4082M | 68592M | 293122M | 204410M | 54970M | 202468M | 1359390M | 1308931M |

## Comparative Historical Data | Current Data Sorted by Sales

| 4/1/09-3/31/10 ALL | 4/1/10-3/31/11 ALL | 4/1/11-3/31/12 ALL | Type of Statement | 0-1MM | 1-3MM | 3-5MM | 5-10MM | 10-25MM | 25MM & OVER |
|---|---|---|---|---|---|---|---|---|---|
| 10 | 9 | 10 | Unqualified | | | | 2 | 3 | 5 |
| 64 | 51 | 53 | Reviewed | | 3 | 6 | 24 | 18 | 2 |
| 20 | 18 | 25 | Compiled | 2 | 8 | 5 | 8 | 2 | |
| 19 | 25 | 32 | Tax Returns | 7 | 10 | 11 | 4 | | |
| 27 | 26 | 34 | Other | 2 | 10 | 6 | 6 | 7 | 3 |
| | | | | 24 (4/1-9/30/11) | | | 130 (10/1/11-3/31/12) | | |
| 140 | 129 | 154 | NUMBER OF STATEMENTS | 11 | 31 | 28 | 44 | 30 | 10 |
| % | % | % | **ASSETS** | % | % | % | % | % | % |
| 17.5 | 14.9 | 13.4 | Cash & Equivalents | 4.3 | 13.3 | 11.9 | 16.0 | 14.1 | 14.7 |
| 43.1 | 41.9 | 45.3 | Trade Receivables (net) | 40.1 | 36.1 | 47.8 | 51.0 | 47.5 | 40.4 |
| 8.6 | 11.0 | 8.4 | Inventory | 12.8 | 9.9 | 10.7 | 6.8 | 5.7 | 7.4 |
| 7.4 | 7.9 | 8.4 | All Other Current | .9 | 3.3 | 8.7 | 9.3 | 11.4 | 17.9 |
| 76.6 | 75.7 | 75.5 | Total Current | 58.0 | 62.7 | 79.1 | 83.1 | 78.7 | 80.5 |
| 16.0 | 16.1 | 15.7 | Fixed Assets (net) | 31.4 | 19.2 | 16.9 | 9.5 | 15.2 | 13.6 |
| 2.2 | 3.3 | 3.9 | Intangibles (net) | 1.2 | 10.9 | 2.1 | 2.6 | 1.4 | 3.4 |
| 5.3 | 4.9 | 4.9 | All Other Non-Current | 9.4 | 7.3 | 1.9 | 4.8 | 4.7 | 2.4 |
| 100.0 | 100.0 | 100.0 | Total | 100.0 | 100.0 | 100.0 | 100.0 | 100.0 | 100.0 |
| | | | **LIABILITIES** | | | | | | |
| 13.7 | 11.7 | 13.3 | Notes Payable-Short Term | 15.7 | 21.0 | 18.3 | 9.0 | 9.5 | 3.2 |
| 2.4 | 3.6 | 6.2 | Cur. Mat.-L.T.D. | 4.6 | 4.6 | 20.8 | 2.6 | 1.8 | 1.2 |
| 16.6 | 18.6 | 21.0 | Trade Payables | 26.2 | 14.7 | 22.5 | 23.1 | 22.1 | 17.6 |
| .4 | .4 | .2 | Income Taxes Payable | .1 | .0 | .3 | .5 | .1 | .1 |
| 16.5 | 13.6 | 11.7 | All Other Current | 7.1 | 9.0 | 10.3 | 10.5 | 14.9 | 25.1 |
| 49.6 | 47.8 | 52.4 | Total Current | 53.7 | 49.3 | 72.1 | 45.6 | 48.4 | 47.2 |
| 9.2 | 9.6 | 11.3 | Long-Term Debt | 21.4 | 21.8 | 13.7 | 4.2 | 7.2 | 4.5 |
| .3 | .2 | .2 | Deferred Taxes | .0 | .0 | .5 | .1 | .2 | .0 |
| 6.3 | 4.3 | 4.2 | All Other Non-Current | 12.9 | 7.6 | 1.0 | 4.0 | 1.7 | 1.2 |
| 34.5 | 38.1 | 31.9 | Net Worth | 12.0 | 21.3 | 12.6 | 46.0 | 42.5 | 47.1 |
| 100.0 | 100.0 | 100.0 | Total Liabilities & Net Worth | 100.0 | 100.0 | 100.0 | 100.0 | 100.0 | 100.0 |
| | | | **INCOME DATA** | | | | | | |
| 100.0 | 100.0 | 100.0 | Net Sales | 100.0 | 100.0 | 100.0 | 100.0 | 100.0 | 100.0 |
| 30.6 | 29.4 | 29.4 | Gross Profit | 56.4 | 39.7 | 29.0 | 21.9 | 23.7 | 19.7 |
| 26.5 | 29.2 | 29.2 | Operating Expenses | 55.5 | 39.2 | 30.7 | 21.9 | 23.0 | 15.3 |
| 4.1 | .2 | .3 | Operating Profit | .9 | .5 | -1.7 | .0 | .6 | 4.4 |
| .5 | .1 | .2 | All Other Expenses (net) | .5 | .1 | .6 | -.2 | .4 | .1 |
| 3.7 | .1 | .1 | Profit Before Taxes | .4 | .3 | -2.3 | .2 | .2 | 4.3 |
| | | | **RATIOS** | | | | | | |
| 2.6 | 2.5 | 2.4 | | 1.6 | 2.4 | 1.8 | 3.2 | 2.4 | 2.5 |
| 1.6 | 1.7 | 1.6 | Current | 1.1 | 1.7 | 1.5 | 1.9 | 1.7 | 1.9 |
| 1.3 | 1.3 | 1.1 | | .6 | .8 | 1.0 | 1.3 | 1.3 | 1.3 |
| 2.1 | 2.0 | 2.0 | | 1.3 | 2.4 | 1.4 | 2.6 | 1.8 | 1.8 |
| 1.3 | 1.3 | 1.3 | Quick | .8 | 1.4 | 1.0 | 1.6 | 1.3 | 1.2 |
| .9 | .9 | .8 | | .3 | .4 | .7 | 1.0 | .8 | .8 |
| 36 10.2 | 43 8.4 | 43 8.4 | | 35 10.3 | 0 750.5 | 45 8.2 | 61 6.0 | 49 7.5 | 45 8.2 |
| 54 6.7 | 68 5.4 | 68 5.4 | Sales/Receivables | 36 10.2 | 53 6.9 | 64 5.7 | 73 5.0 | 76 4.8 | 66 5.5 |
| 78 4.7 | 94 3.9 | 91 4.0 | | 45 8.1 | 87 4.2 | 83 4.4 | 91 4.0 | 101 3.6 | 85 4.3 |
| 0 UND | 0 UND | 0 UND | | 10 35.8 | 0 UND | 0 UND | 0 UND | 0 UND | 0 UND |
| 3 104.7 | 8 43.9 | 3 113.9 | Cost of Sales/Inventory | 35 10.4 | 4 90.8 | 15 24.8 | 0 730.6 | 1 363.2 | 0 UND |
| 18 20.1 | 29 12.4 | 18 20.0 | | 49 7.5 | 13 27.2 | 45 8.1 | 13 28.7 | 10 37.7 | 19 19.1 |
| 12 29.4 | 20 18.0 | 21 17.0 | | 25 14.6 | 0 908.0 | 26 14.0 | 28 13.2 | 22 16.3 | 21 17.3 |
| 24 15.0 | 33 10.9 | 34 10.8 | Cost of Sales/Payables | 45 | 18 20.1 | 35 10.4 | 38 9.6 | 38 9.5 | 30 12.2 |
| 44 8.3 | 50 7.3 | 54 6.7 | | 135 2.7 | 54 6.7 | 54 6.8 | 54 6.7 | 55 6.6 | 47 7.7 |
| 5.5 | 4.2 | 5.1 | | 12.0 | 5.6 | 6.1 | 3.9 | 4.5 | 4.9 |
| 10.0 | 8.3 | 9.0 | Sales/Working Capital | 140.0 | 9.6 | 10.2 | 6.6 | 7.2 | 8.4 |
| 21.6 | 18.4 | 37.6 | | -12.7 | -58.3 | 174.5 | 22.0 | 15.1 | 15.8 |
| 32.3 | 10.3 | 11.8 | | 4.6 | 6.9 | 8.1 | 24.7 | 14.4 | |
| (123) 6.5 | (111) 1.8 | (128) 2.7 | EBIT/Interest | (10) 1.5 | (26) 3.3 | (26) .1 | (35) 3.8 | (24) 3.7 | |
| 1.4 | -5.5 | -3.7 | | -4.6 | -1.4 | -7.8 | -3.7 | 1.0 | |
| 13.8 | 8.2 | 10.5 | Net Profit + Depr., Dep., | | | | | 13.0 | |
| (30) 3.6 | (31) 1.4 | (29) 2.7 | Amort./Cur. Mat. L/T/D | | | | | (12) 1.7 | |
| 1.6 | -5.5 | -3.8 | | | | | | -7.9 | |
| .1 | .1 | .1 | | .5 | .2 | .2 | .1 | .1 | .1 |
| .3 | .3 | .4 | Fixed/Worth | 2.4 | .6 | .7 | .3 | .4 | .2 |
| .7 | 1.0 | 1.0 | | -3.1 | -.7 | 2.4 | .4 | .8 | .6 |
| .7 | .6 | .7 | | 5.0 | 1.0 | 1.3 | .4 | .7 | .6 |
| 1.6 | 1.5 | 1.9 | Debt/Worth | 6.2 | 2.7 | 3.0 | 1.0 | 1.4 | 1.2 |
| 3.7 | 4.0 | 6.0 | | -23.5 | -3.7 | 10.5 | 3.0 | 2.3 | 3.2 |
| 44.8 | 17.7 | 33.1 | % Profit Before Taxes/Tangible | | 51.8 | 22.7 | 24.4 | 30.5 | 61.5 |
| (121) 17.3 | (115) 4.1 | (131) 10.3 | Net Worth | | (20) 21.6 | (25) -3.5 | (39) 4.5 | (29) 10.3 | 25.7 |
| 4.0 | -22.2 | -6.2 | | | -11.3 | -74.1 | -6.2 | 1.9 | 12.1 |
| 19.2 | 7.5 | 11.5 | % Profit Before Taxes/Total | 11.5 | 18.3 | 8.1 | 10.3 | 10.4 | 21.4 |
| 7.2 | 1.5 | 3.7 | Assets | 5.0 | 5.9 | -1.6 | 1.5 | 4.3 | 10.2 |
| 1.3 | -6.1 | -7.6 | | -11.9 | -5.4 | -16.3 | -7.4 | .1 | 6.4 |
| 62.8 | 44.6 | 58.4 | | 129.0 | 58.5 | 59.0 | 94.8 | 45.5 | 51.2 |
| 32.8 | 22.9 | 29.6 | Sales/Net Fixed Assets | 10.9 | 30.0 | 24.5 | 34.1 | 29.8 | 25.9 |
| 15.8 | 10.3 | 12.1 | | 6.9 | 13.1 | 10.4 | 19.9 | 7.9 | 13.2 |
| 3.9 | 3.3 | 3.7 | | 5.8 | 5.4 | 3.6 | 3.5 | 3.0 | 2.8 |
| 2.9 | 2.4 | 2.5 | Sales/Total Assets | 4.3 | 2.9 | 2.8 | 2.4 | 2.3 | 2.3 |
| 2.2 | 1.5 | 1.9 | | 2.3 | 1.7 | 1.9 | 1.8 | 1.9 | 1.7 |
| .5 | .6 | .5 | | | .6 | .6 | .6 | .7 | .5 |
| (124) 1.0 | (115) 1.1 | (125) 1.0 | % Depr., Dep., Amort./Sales | | (21) 1.0 | (22) 1.0 | (35) 1.1 | (29) .9 | .7 |
| 1.6 | 2.1 | 1.6 | | | 1.8 | 1.8 | 1.4 | 1.8 | 1.3 |
| 2.5 | 2.7 | 2.5 | % Officers', Directors' | | 2.5 | 3.2 | 2.3 | 1.5 | |
| (80) 3.8 | (73) 5.4 | (87) 4.1 | Owners' Comp/Sales | | (20) 6.4 | (19) 4.4 | (24) 3.7 | (16) 3.3 | |
| 7.8 | 7.8 | 6.8 | | | 8.2 | 6.1 | 6.0 | 4.9 | |
| 1752771M | 1683187M | 1688143M | Net Sales ($) | 8496M | 57859M | 116645M | 297339M | 453217M | 754587M |
| 708745M | 916796M | 827644M | Total Assets ($) | 2961M | 23224M | 49517M | 137002M | 198394M | 416546M |

© RMA 2012

M = $ thousand     MM = $ million
See Pages 9 through 22 for Explanation of Ratios and Data

## Current Data Sorted by Assets      Comparative Historical Data

| | | | | | | Type of Statement | | |
|---|---|---|---|---|---|---|---|---|
| 1 | 2 | 14 | 9 | 4 | 1 | Unqualified | 30 | 34 |
| | 37 | 90 | 10 | | 1 | Reviewed | 140 | 141 |
| 5 | 20 | 9 | 2 | | | Compiled | 33 | 46 |
| 28 | 26 | 16 | | | 1 | Tax Returns | 51 | 52 |
| 16 | 52 | 33 | 10 | | | Other | 90 | 116 |
| | 49 (4/1-9/30/11) | | 338 (10/1/11-3/31/12) | | | | 4/1/07-3/31/08 | 4/1/08-3/31/09 |
| 0-500M | 500M-2MM | 2-10MM | 10-50MM | 50-100MM | 100-250MM | | ALL | ALL |
| 50 | 137 | 162 | 31 | 5 | 2 | NUMBER OF STATEMENTS | 344 | 389 |
| % | % | % | % | % | % | ASSETS | % | % |
| 25.2 | 15.7 | 14.8 | 12.3 | | | Cash & Equivalents | 13.9 | 13.5 |
| 26.8 | 42.0 | 48.0 | 47.6 | | | Trade Receivables (net) | 44.8 | 43.9 |
| 6.1 | 6.6 | 4.9 | 6.8 | | | Inventory | 7.0 | 7.0 |
| 2.5 | 7.5 | 10.2 | 11.2 | | | All Other Current | 8.9 | 8.4 |
| 60.6 | 71.8 | 77.9 | 78.0 | | | Total Current | 74.6 | 72.7 |
| 28.1 | 19.2 | 13.8 | 8.0 | | | Fixed Assets (net) | 16.1 | 17.8 |
| 3.4 | 2.4 | 1.6 | 7.4 | | | Intangibles (net) | 2.1 | 2.4 |
| 7.9 | 6.6 | 6.8 | 6.5 | | | All Other Non-Current | 7.2 | 7.1 |
| 100.0 | 100.0 | 100.0 | 100.0 | | | Total | 100.0 | 100.0 |
| | | | | | | LIABILITIES | | |
| 24.7 | 12.0 | 6.4 | 13.4 | | | Notes Payable-Short Term | 9.8 | 10.1 |
| 8.4 | 2.5 | 1.9 | .7 | | | Cur. Mat.-L.T.D. | 3.1 | 4.1 |
| 23.6 | 21.8 | 20.5 | 20.3 | | | Trade Payables | 19.4 | 19.5 |
| .1 | .3 | .2 | .3 | | | Income Taxes Payable | .5 | .5 |
| 18.7 | 10.7 | 12.5 | 17.4 | | | All Other Current | 15.6 | 16.7 |
| 75.5 | 47.3 | 41.6 | 52.1 | | | Total Current | 48.3 | 50.9 |
| 28.0 | 9.9 | 6.2 | 1.4 | | | Long-Term Debt | 11.7 | 11.1 |
| .0 | .3 | .3 | .1 | | | Deferred Taxes | .4 | .3 |
| 10.5 | 4.1 | 3.5 | 3.8 | | | All Other Non-Current | 4.7 | 5.3 |
| -14.1 | 38.4 | 48.5 | 42.6 | | | Net Worth | 34.9 | 32.4 |
| 100.0 | 100.0 | 100.0 | 100.0 | | | Total Liabilties & Net Worth | 100.0 | 100.0 |
| | | | | | | INCOME DATA | | |
| 100.0 | 100.0 | 100.0 | 100.0 | | | Net Sales | 100.0 | 100.0 |
| 37.1 | 27.3 | 23.6 | 20.2 | | | Gross Profit | 28.3 | 26.9 |
| 35.1 | 25.5 | 19.9 | 17.9 | | | Operating Expenses | 23.5 | 22.9 |
| 1.9 | 1.8 | 3.7 | 2.3 | | | Operating Profit | 4.8 | 4.0 |
| .1 | .1 | .0 | .0 | | | All Other Expenses (net) | .4 | .4 |
| 1.8 | 1.7 | 3.6 | 2.3 | | | Profit Before Taxes | 4.4 | 3.6 |
| | | | | | | RATIOS | | |
| 2.4 | 2.6 | 2.8 | 2.3 | | | | 2.4 | 2.2 |
| .9 | 1.6 | 1.8 | 1.6 | | | Current | 1.6 | 1.5 |
| .4 | 1.2 | 1.5 | 1.2 | | | | 1.2 | 1.1 |
| 1.8 | 2.1 | 2.4 | 1.8 | | | | 1.9 | 1.8 |
| .8 | 1.3 | 1.6 | 1.3 | | | Quick | 1.3 | 1.2 |
| .3 | .8 | 1.1 | .8 | | | | .9 | .8 |
| 0 UND | 24 15.2 | 45 8.1 | 41 9.0 | | | | 31 11.7 | 30 12.2 |
| 10 35.6 | 47 7.8 | 62 5.9 | 72 5.1 | | | Sales/Receivables | 52 7.1 | 51 7.1 |
| 35 10.3 | 66 5.5 | 81 4.5 | 85 4.3 | | | | 73 5.0 | 73 5.0 |
| 0 UND | 0 UND | 0 UND | 1 309.5 | | | | 0 UND | 0 UND |
| 0 UND | 2 157.8 | 4 101.0 | 4 92.5 | | | Cost of Sales/Inventory | 5 81.0 | 4 82.2 |
| 2 206.3 | 11 33.3 | 10 36.5 | 17 21.2 | | | | 14 25.7 | 14 26.0 |
| 0 UND | 14 27.0 | 19 19.4 | 22 16.6 | | | | 13 28.7 | 14 27.0 |
| 11 32.6 | 25 14.7 | 31 11.9 | 27 13.3 | | | Cost of Sales/Payables | 25 14.6 | 26 14.2 |
| 45 8.1 | 42 8.7 | 47 7.8 | 42 8.6 | | | | 40 9.1 | 40 9.1 |
| 37.5 | 6.1 | 5.2 | 4.7 | | | | 6.9 | 7.3 |
| -192.0 | 13.0 | 7.6 | 11.1 | | | Sales/Working Capital | 12.2 | 12.9 |
| -27.5 | 34.9 | 12.6 | 20.7 | | | | 30.7 | 42.1 |
| 11.9 | 19.8 | 37.7 | 34.2 | | | | 28.8 | 22.6 |
| (42) 5.0 | (121) 7.0 | (143) 7.7 | (27) 8.3 | | | EBIT/Interest | (317) 7.0 | (354) 7.0 |
| -.6 | -1.7 | 2.0 | 3.9 | | | | 2.2 | 2.1 |
| | 7.2 | 15.2 | 12.5 | | | | 6.7 | 8.4 |
| | (25) .9 | (47) 4.3 | (10) 6.1 | | | Net Profit + Depr., Dep., Amort./Cur. Mat. L/T/D | (75) 3.0 | (77) 3.2 |
| | .1 | 1.3 | 4.2 | | | | 1.7 | 1.4 |
| .6 | .2 | .1 | .1 | | | | .2 | .2 |
| 6.4 | .4 | .2 | .3 | | | Fixed/Worth | .4 | .4 |
| -.7 | .9 | .5 | .4 | | | | 1.0 | 1.1 |
| 2.4 | .6 | .5 | .7 | | | | .8 | .7 |
| UND | 1.3 | 1.1 | 1.5 | | | Debt/Worth | 1.6 | 1.6 |
| -3.0 | 5.0 | 2.1 | 3.5 | | | | 4.0 | 3.8 |
| 157.0 | 43.6 | 43.7 | 27.9 | | | | 58.3 | 50.2 |
| (26) 46.2 | (117) 13.3 | (156) 15.9 | (29) 15.8 | | | % Profit Before Taxes/Tangible Net Worth | (307) 30.4 | (337) 21.3 |
| -.2 | .1 | 5.1 | -7.2 | | | | 9.3 | 6.3 |
| 39.1 | 17.9 | 18.1 | 11.6 | | | | 24.0 | 21.0 |
| 16.5 | 5.5 | 6.0 | 5.0 | | | % Profit Before Taxes/Total Assets | 10.7 | 7.9 |
| -11.6 | -2.0 | 1.7 | -1.8 | | | | 2.6 | 1.8 |
| 90.8 | 54.9 | 57.2 | 55.2 | | | | 53.6 | 56.8 |
| 38.5 | 26.4 | 31.2 | 33.6 | | | Sales/Net Fixed Assets | 27.7 | 26.1 |
| 21.1 | 15.1 | 14.6 | 22.4 | | | | 15.1 | 14.6 |
| 17.4 | 4.9 | 3.6 | 3.2 | | | | 4.2 | 4.1 |
| 7.4 | 3.4 | 2.7 | 2.6 | | | Sales/Total Assets | 3.2 | 3.2 |
| 4.1 | 2.4 | 2.1 | 2.0 | | | | 2.4 | 2.4 |
| .7 | .5 | .5 | .5 | | | | .6 | .6 |
| (34) 1.2 | (113) 1.2 | (141) .9 | (28) .9 | | | % Depr., Dep., Amort./Sales | (281) 1.1 | (326) 1.1 |
| 1.8 | 1.9 | 1.3 | 1.2 | | | | 1.7 | 1.7 |
| 3.5 | 2.0 | 1.7 | .6 | | | | 2.0 | 2.0 |
| (32) 5.5 | (76) 3.5 | (89) 2.8 | (10) 1.6 | | | % Officers', Directors' Owners' Comp/Sales | (173) 3.3 | (190) 3.3 |
| 8.6 | 5.6 | 5.6 | 7.5 | | | | 6.9 | 6.0 |
| 87893M | 597118M | 1989450M | 1517069M | 890461M | 2022194M | Net Sales ($) | 4524187M | 5839019M |
| 10868M | 161780M | 692927M | 582153M | 380718M | 453729M | Total Assets ($) | 1686472M | 2250632M |

M = $ thousand    MM = $ million
See Pages 9 through 22 for Explanation of Ratios and Data

## Comparative Historical Data | Current Data Sorted by Sales

| Hist 1 | Hist 2 | Hist 3 | Type of Statement | 0-1MM | 1-3MM | 3-5MM | 5-10MM | 10-25MM | 25MM & OVER |
|---|---|---|---|---|---|---|---|---|---|
| 28 | 31 | 31 | Unqualified | 1 |  | 2 | 2 | 13 | 13 |
| 142 | 142 | 138 | Reviewed |  | 16 | 21 | 45 | 38 | 18 |
| 37 | 38 | 36 | Compiled | 1 | 8 | 11 | 11 | 4 | 1 |
| 62 | 67 | 71 | Tax Returns | 10 | 17 | 15 | 20 | 7 | 2 |
| 102 | 97 | 111 | Other | 7 | 30 | 17 | 28 | 17 | 12 |
| 4/1/09-3/31/10 ALL | 4/1/10-3/31/11 ALL | 4/1/11-3/31/12 ALL |  | 49 (4/1-9/30/11) | | | 338 (10/1/11-3/31/12) | | |
| 371 | 375 | 387 | **NUMBER OF STATEMENTS** | 19 | 71 | 66 | 106 | 79 | 46 |
| % | % | % | **ASSETS** | % | % | % | % | % | % |
| 16.1 | 16.4 | 16.3 | Cash & Equivalents | 27.9 | 17.5 | 17.2 | 18.0 | 13.3 | 9.6 |
| 39.8 | 41.4 | 42.9 | Trade Receivables (net) | 29.8 | 33.5 | 40.7 | 43.4 | 50.6 | 51.3 |
| 7.6 | 6.7 | 5.9 | Inventory | 4.2 | 5.7 | 7.9 | 4.6 | 5.4 | 7.7 |
| 7.8 | 8.4 | 8.4 | All Other Current | 4.8 | 4.4 | 9.0 | 8.4 | 10.6 | 11.2 |
| 71.3 | 72.8 | 73.5 | Total Current | 66.7 | 61.2 | 74.8 | 74.4 | 80.0 | 79.8 |
| 18.2 | 17.1 | 17.1 | Fixed Assets (net) | 21.6 | 25.8 | 16.3 | 17.9 | 12.3 | 9.0 |
| 2.4 | 2.9 | 2.6 | Intangibles (net) | 3.6 | 2.4 | 2.7 | 2.1 | 1.5 | 5.7 |
| 8.0 | 7.2 | 6.9 | All Other Non-Current | 8.1 | 10.6 | 6.2 | 5.6 | 6.1 | 5.5 |
| 100.0 | 100.0 | 100.0 | Total | 100.0 | 100.0 | 100.0 | 100.0 | 100.0 | 100.0 |
|  |  |  | **LIABILITIES** |  |  |  |  |  |  |
| 11.3 | 12.0 | 11.5 | Notes Payable-Short Term | 26.4 | 11.2 | 16.0 | 8.7 | 7.4 | 12.9 |
| 3.8 | 2.6 | 2.9 | Cur. Mat.-L.T.D. | .3 | 6.2 | 2.6 | 2.5 | 1.6 | 2.4 |
| 18.8 | 20.4 | 21.4 | Trade Payables | 20.2 | 21.5 | 20.6 | 21.2 | 20.5 | 24.8 |
| .4 | .4 | .3 | Income Taxes Payable | .0 | .4 | .4 | .1 | .3 | .2 |
| 14.0 | 12.7 | 13.0 | All Other Current | 28.1 | 10.8 | 9.5 | 11.6 | 14.8 | 15.5 |
| 48.2 | 48.1 | 49.1 | Total Current | 75.0 | 50.1 | 49.1 | 44.2 | 44.6 | 55.8 |
| 11.2 | 10.3 | 9.9 | Long-Term Debt | 33.3 | 13.7 | 10.9 | 8.9 | 5.8 | 2.2 |
| .4 | .3 | .3 | Deferred Taxes | .0 | .4 | .2 | .4 | .2 | .3 |
| 3.5 | 3.9 | 4.9 | All Other Non-Current | 7.6 | 8.6 | 4.4 | 2.6 | 3.3 | 7.0 |
| 36.7 | 37.4 | 35.9 | Net Worth | -15.8 | 27.2 | 35.5 | 43.9 | 46.2 | 34.8 |
| 100.0 | 100.0 | 100.0 | Total Liabilities & Net Worth | 100.0 | 100.0 | 100.0 | 100.0 | 100.0 | 100.0 |
|  |  |  | **INCOME DATA** |  |  |  |  |  |  |
| 100.0 | 100.0 | 100.0 | Net Sales | 100.0 | 100.0 | 100.0 | 100.0 | 100.0 | 100.0 |
| 27.9 | 27.0 | 26.4 | Gross Profit | 37.8 | 34.6 | 24.7 | 25.4 | 22.3 | 20.6 |
| 25.8 | 24.4 | 23.7 | Operating Expenses | 37.7 | 32.0 | 22.5 | 22.4 | 18.6 | 18.7 |
| 2.1 | 2.7 | 2.7 | Operating Profit | .1 | 2.6 | 2.2 | 3.0 | 3.7 | 1.9 |
| .2 | .0 | .1 | All Other Expenses (net) | .2 | .0 | .2 | .0 | .1 | .1 |
| 1.9 | 2.6 | 2.6 | Profit Before Taxes | -.1 | 2.6 | 2.0 | 2.9 | 3.6 | 1.9 |
|  |  |  | **RATIOS** |  |  |  |  |  |  |
| 2.7 | 2.6 | 2.6 | Current | 3.1 | 3.2 | 2.6 | 2.8 | 2.6 | 2.0 |
| 1.6 | 1.7 | 1.7 |  | 1.1 | 1.5 | 1.7 | 1.7 | 1.8 | 1.5 |
| 1.2 | 1.1 | 1.2 |  | .7 | .9 | 1.2 | 1.3 | 1.3 | 1.1 |
| 1.9 | 2.1 | 2.1 | Quick | 3.0 | 2.7 | 2.0 | 2.2 | 2.2 | 1.7 |
| 1.3 | 1.3 | 1.4 |  | 1.1 | 1.2 | 1.2 | 1.6 | 1.4 | 1.2 |
| .8 | .8 | .8 |  | .4 | .8 | .8 | .9 | 1.0 | .7 |
| 25  14.6 | 27  13.4 | 30  12.2 | Sales/Receivables | 0  UND | 10  35.8 | 27  13.5 | 36  10.0 | 47  7.7 | 40  9.2 |
| 49  7.4 | 50  7.3 | 53  6.9 |  | 28  13.0 | 39  9.3 | 46  7.9 | 54  6.8 | 60  6.1 | 65  5.6 |
| 71  5.1 | 76  4.8 | 74  4.9 |  | 57  6.4 | 64  5.7 | 68  5.4 | 73  5.0 | 79  4.6 | 81  4.5 |
| 0  UND | 0  UND | 0  UND | Cost of Sales/Inventory | 0  UND | 0  UND | 0  UND | 0  UND | 0  UND | 1  322.5 |
| 5  67.9 | 4  98.8 | 2  158.5 |  | 0  UND | 0  UND | 4  98.7 | 3  123.7 | 4  84.4 | 5  78.1 |
| 17  22.0 | 13  27.5 | 11  34.4 |  | 2  216.0 | 12  29.2 | 12  31.3 | 8  43.5 | 12  31.2 | 17  21.0 |
| 14  26.6 | 14  26.3 | 14  25.3 | Cost of Sales/Payables | 0  UND | 6  62.2 | 12  30.3 | 16  23.1 | 19  19.5 | 21  17.4 |
| 26  14.1 | 28  12.9 | 27  13.4 |  | 6  63.0 | 27  13.3 | 25  14.7 | 29  12.8 | 29  12.5 | 27  13.4 |
| 42  8.8 | 45  8.2 | 45  8.2 |  | 51  7.1 | 56  6.5 | 42  8.6 | 43  8.4 | 43  8.4 | 45  8.2 |
| 6.0 | 6.1 | 5.8 | Sales/Working Capital | 12.0 | 6.1 | 5.5 | 5.6 | 5.6 | 6.4 |
| 11.9 | 11.2 | 11.1 |  | 94.3 | 14.9 | 10.4 | 9.5 | 8.7 | 11.9 |
| 48.2 | 44.1 | 45.0 |  | -19.4 | -70.4 | 50.8 | 26.6 | 15.8 | 33.8 |
| 21.4 | 19.8 | 24.5 | EBIT/Interest | 16.5 | 20.5 | 17.6 | 27.2 | 28.7 | 36.8 |
| (330) 3.7 | (318) 5.0 | (340) 7.1 |  | (14) 3.2 | (59) 3.6 | (61) 5.5 | (94) 8.2 | (68) 10.5 | (44) 7.3 |
| -1.3 | .1 | 1.0 |  | -1.2 | -3.3 | 1.0 | 1.5 | 2.4 | 1.4 |
| 6.3 | 6.7 | 8.7 | Net Profit + Depr., Dep., Amort./Cur. Mat. L/T/D |  |  | 10.0 | -7.4 | 14.8 | 15.7 |
| (85) 2.3 | (90) 2.7 | (88) 3.6 |  |  |  | (13) 2.4 | (30) 3.0 | (20) 5.9 | (16) 5.2 |
| -.4 | .6 | .6 |  |  |  | .3 | .4 | 1.8 | 2.8 |
| .2 | .1 | .1 | Fixed/Worth | .3 | .2 | .2 | .2 | .1 | .2 |
| .4 | .3 | .3 |  | 5.5 | .6 | .4 | .3 | .2 | .3 |
| .9 | 1.0 | .9 |  | -.6 | UND | .9 | .6 | .5 | .7 |
| .6 | .6 | .6 | Debt/Worth | 1.3 | .5 | .7 | .6 | .6 | .9 |
| 1.4 | 1.3 | 1.4 |  | -146.0 | 1.7 | 1.4 | 1.1 | 1.3 | 1.8 |
| 3.4 | 4.4 | 5.0 |  | -2.2 | -11.7 | 7.4 | 2.5 | 2.5 | 6.9 |
| 48.6 | 40.4 | 43.9 | % Profit Before Taxes/Tangible Net Worth |  | 51.2 | 42.6 | 40.9 | 49.1 | 31.6 |
| (324) 13.6 | (320) 14.3 | (334) 16.2 |  | (52) 20.2 | (56) 9.9 | (98) 14.9 | (77) 23.4 | (42) 16.1 | |
| -.5 | -.6 | 2.6 |  |  | -3.6 | 1.3 | 4.5 | 7.1 | .4 |
| 19.8 | 18.6 | 18.9 | % Profit Before Taxes/Total Assets | 28.8 | 30.6 | 17.2 | 16.9 | 22.1 | 12.9 |
| 4.5 | 5.6 | 5.9 |  | -.6 | 5.5 | 4.7 | 6.2 | 10.3 | 5.1 |
| -2.3 | -.7 | .1 |  | -17.2 | -6.8 | .1 | 1.4 | 2.2 | -.3 |
| 45.5 | 53.0 | 57.1 | Sales/Net Fixed Assets | 55.0 | 53.2 | 57.9 | 46.0 | 94.7 | 57.1 |
| 23.9 | 26.7 | 29.7 |  | 26.2 | 22.9 | 29.3 | 26.7 | 39.0 | 38.9 |
| 12.9 | 14.3 | 16.5 |  | 9.9 | 9.7 | 16.8 | 14.9 | 21.6 | 23.7 |
| 4.2 | 4.5 | 4.5 | Sales/Total Assets | 7.1 | 5.4 | 5.3 | 4.3 | 4.1 | 3.9 |
| 3.0 | 3.1 | 3.1 |  | 5.2 | 3.1 | 3.3 | 2.9 | 3.1 | 2.7 |
| 2.3 | 2.3 | 2.3 |  | 2.9 | 2.1 | 2.2 | 2.3 | 2.4 | 2.3 |
| .7 | .7 | .5 | % Depr., Dep., Amort./Sales | 1.1 | .6 | .5 | .6 | .5 | .4 |
| (319) 1.4 | (310) 1.1 | (322) 1.0 |  | (13) 1.5 | (51) 1.4 | (58) 1.2 | (87) 1.0 | (70) .9 | (43) .9 |
| 2.0 | 1.9 | 1.6 |  | 2.8 | 2.2 | 1.8 | 1.6 | 1.2 | 1.2 |
| 2.2 | 1.9 | 1.9 | % Officers', Directors' Owners' Comp/Sales |  | 3.5 | 2.3 | 1.9 | 1.3 | 1.1 |
| (194) 4.0 | (198) 3.5 | (208) 3.6 |  | (36) 5.4 | (40) 3.5 | (70) 3.6 | (36) 2.2 | (18) 2.2 | |
| 7.0 | 7.0 | 6.1 |  |  | 7.5 | 5.1 | 6.9 | 5.5 | 6.2 |
| 5311728M | 7097060M | 7104185M | Net Sales ($) | 12520M | 148757M | 261660M | 770301M | 1185440M | 4725507M |
| 2099059M | 2384783M | 2282175M | Total Assets ($) | 3832M | 56883M | 94482M | 264616M | 407098M | 1455264M |

© RMA 2012

M = $ thousand     MM = $ million
See Pages 9 through 22 for Explanation of Ratios and Data

## Current Data Sorted by Assets        Comparative Historical Data

| Type of Statement | 0-500M | 500M-2MM | 2-10MM | 10-50MM | 50-100MM | 100-250MM | | 4/1/07-3/31/08 ALL | 4/1/08-3/31/09 ALL |
|---|---|---|---|---|---|---|---|---|---|
| Unqualified | | 1 | 2 | 3 | | 1 | | 6 | 10 |
| Reviewed | 2 | 6 | 20 | 3 | | | | 11 | 14 |
| Compiled | 5 | 1 | 3 | | | | | 8 | 12 |
| Tax Returns | 17 | 8 | 5 | | | 1 | | 15 | 23 |
| Other | 10 | 13 | 14 | | | | | 13 | 14 |
| | 9 (4/1-9/30/11) | | 112 (10/1/11-3/31/12) | | | | | | |
| NUMBER OF STATEMENTS | 34 | 29 | 44 | 11 | 1 | 2 | | 53 | 73 |
| **ASSETS** | % | % | % | % | % | % | | % | % |
| Cash & Equivalents | 25.7 | 11.8 | 11.1 | 11.8 | | | | 11.3 | 15.0 |
| Trade Receivables (net) | 20.7 | 37.7 | 42.5 | 45.1 | | | | 39.0 | 37.7 |
| Inventory | 4.4 | 9.6 | 7.6 | 4.9 | | | | 8.9 | 7.0 |
| All Other Current | 3.9 | 4.0 | 7.6 | 9.2 | | | | 4.3 | 7.6 |
| Total Current | 54.7 | 63.2 | 68.7 | 71.0 | | | | 63.5 | 67.4 |
| Fixed Assets (net) | 31.5 | 24.2 | 19.9 | 22.7 | | | | 24.0 | 22.9 |
| Intangibles (net) | 3.2 | .6 | 1.7 | .7 | | | | 3.6 | 3.5 |
| All Other Non-Current | 10.5 | 12.1 | 9.7 | 5.6 | | | | 8.8 | 6.2 |
| Total | 100.0 | 100.0 | 100.0 | 100.0 | | | | 100.0 | 100.0 |
| **LIABILITIES** | | | | | | | | | |
| Notes Payable-Short Term | 31.3 | 11.7 | 11.4 | 4.7 | | | | 7.3 | 9.6 |
| Cur. Mat.-L.T.D. | 11.9 | 1.7 | 2.4 | 2.2 | | | | 4.3 | 8.0 |
| Trade Payables | 19.0 | 20.2 | 18.8 | 23.8 | | | | 15.2 | 18.3 |
| Income Taxes Payable | .1 | .0 | .1 | .1 | | | | .7 | .5 |
| All Other Current | 10.3 | 17.5 | 10.6 | 8.8 | | | | 18.8 | 12.9 |
| Total Current | 72.5 | 51.0 | 43.3 | 39.6 | | | | 46.4 | 49.2 |
| Long-Term Debt | 26.6 | 13.8 | 9.6 | 5.0 | | | | 17.8 | 17.5 |
| Deferred Taxes | .0 | .2 | .4 | .0 | | | | .2 | .3 |
| All Other Non-Current | 5.0 | 6.5 | 4.5 | 3.6 | | | | 5.9 | 8.1 |
| Net Worth | -4.2 | 28.6 | 42.3 | 51.8 | | | | 29.8 | 24.9 |
| Total Liabilities & Net Worth | 100.0 | 100.0 | 100.0 | 100.0 | | | | 100.0 | 100.0 |
| **INCOME DATA** | | | | | | | | | |
| Net Sales | 100.0 | 100.0 | 100.0 | 100.0 | | | | 100.0 | 100.0 |
| Gross Profit | 52.3 | 26.8 | 24.7 | 17.4 | | | | 35.4 | 31.9 |
| Operating Expenses | 46.9 | 26.2 | 22.5 | 12.8 | | | | 30.2 | 27.7 |
| Operating Profit | 5.4 | .6 | 2.3 | 4.6 | | | | 5.2 | 4.2 |
| All Other Expenses (net) | .8 | .4 | .2 | .0 | | | | .4 | .3 |
| Profit Before Taxes | 4.5 | .2 | 2.1 | 4.7 | | | | 4.8 | 3.9 |
| **RATIOS** | | | | | | | | | |
| Current | 4.0 | 2.5 | 2.7 | 2.7 | | | | 2.3 | 2.1 |
| | 1.2 | 1.4 | 1.5 | 1.6 | | | | 1.3 | 1.4 |
| | .5 | .8 | 1.2 | 1.2 | | | | 1.0 | 1.0 |
| Quick | 3.7 | 2.0 | 2.4 | 2.0 | | | | 1.6 | 1.7 |
| | (33) .8 | .9 | 1.2 | 1.4 | | | | 1.1 | 1.2 |
| | .3 | .6 | .8 | 1.0 | | | | .7 | .7 |
| Sales/Receivables | 0 UND | 21 17.4 | 43 8.5 | 58 6.3 | | | | 28 13.1 | 23 16.0 |
| | 9 40.4 | 40 9.1 | 64 5.7 | 68 5.4 | | | | 51 7.2 | 44 8.3 |
| | 34 10.7 | 59 6.2 | 94 3.9 | 91 4.0 | | | | 80 4.5 | 72 5.1 |
| Cost of Sales/Inventory | 0 UND | 0 UND | 0 UND | 0 UND | | | | 0 UND | 0 UND |
| | 0 UND | 0 UND | 1 578.8 | 0 UND | | | | 1 461.0 | 0 UND |
| | 5 71.6 | 19 19.3 | 28 13.0 | 3 118.9 | | | | 28 13.2 | 13 27.6 |
| Cost of Sales/Payables | 0 UND | 6 66.2 | 20 18.4 | 33 11.0 | | | | 10 36.7 | 8 47.6 |
| | 0 UND | 27 13.3 | 33 11.1 | 46 8.0 | | | | 26 14.1 | 19 18.8 |
| | 50 7.3 | 45 8.1 | 54 6.7 | 69 5.3 | | | | 52 7.1 | 48 7.6 |
| Sales/Working Capital | 10.1 | 7.2 | 5.7 | 3.6 | | | | 5.9 | 7.4 |
| | 104.8 | 42.7 | 11.5 | 7.6 | | | | 18.9 | 18.5 |
| | -8.6 | -105.5 | 31.2 | 21.8 | | | | 121.0 | 173.8 |
| EBIT/Interest | 8.7 | 10.6 | 15.2 | | | | | 39.7 | 11.5 |
| | (23) 3.8 | (23) 1.3 | (38) 3.9 | | | | | (47) 7.0 | (63) 5.9 |
| | -.2 | -3.4 | -.8 | | | | | 1.5 | 1.6 |
| Net Profit + Depr., Dep., Amort./Cur. Mat. L/T/D | | | 8.7 | | | | | 5.5 | 6.4 |
| | | (12) | 3.3 | | | | | (11) 1.9 | (17) 3.8 |
| | | | -.9 | | | | | 1.8 | 1.7 |
| Fixed/Worth | .5 | .1 | .2 | .1 | | | | .3 | .2 |
| | 2.3 | .6 | .5 | .4 | | | | .9 | .6 |
| | -.6 | 3.2 | 1.1 | .9 | | | | 6.0 | 1.6 |
| Debt/Worth | .6 | .6 | .7 | .6 | | | | 1.1 | 1.0 |
| | 3.0 | 2.9 | 1.4 | .9 | | | | 2.3 | 2.2 |
| | -3.9 | NM | 3.1 | 1.1 | | | | 10.0 | 10.1 |
| % Profit Before Taxes/Tangible Net Worth | 136.6 | 46.9 | 45.8 | 21.5 | | | | 72.4 | 79.8 |
| | (22) 56.8 | (22) 14.2 | (43) 14.8 | 13.8 | | | | (44) 41.6 | (61) 30.5 |
| | -13.7 | -9.5 | -2.6 | 6.5 | | | | 20.9 | 5.7 |
| % Profit Before Taxes/Total Assets | 56.2 | 18.5 | 19.0 | 12.5 | | | | 26.0 | 20.7 |
| | 16.9 | 3.3 | 4.9 | 6.7 | | | | 14.1 | 9.4 |
| | -6.7 | -2.3 | -.5 | 3.4 | | | | 1.6 | 1.3 |
| Sales/Net Fixed Assets | 113.2 | 77.3 | 37.0 | 35.4 | | | | 48.3 | 38.6 |
| | 30.5 | 24.2 | 14.1 | 12.9 | | | | 13.9 | 20.3 |
| | 9.8 | 8.0 | 9.3 | 3.1 | | | | 8.5 | 9.2 |
| Sales/Total Assets | 10.1 | 5.2 | 3.0 | 2.5 | | | | 3.7 | 4.7 |
| | 5.1 | 3.7 | 2.3 | 2.1 | | | | 2.8 | 3.1 |
| | 2.9 | 2.1 | 1.9 | 1.6 | | | | 1.9 | 2.1 |
| % Depr., Dep., Amort./Sales | .6 | .6 | .6 | | | | | .8 | .7 |
| | (20) 1.8 | (18) 1.1 | (37) 1.3 | | | | | (45) 1.9 | (56) 1.9 |
| | 2.9 | 3.3 | 3.2 | | | | | 3.3 | 3.1 |
| % Officers', Directors', Owners' Comp/Sales | 6.3 | 2.2 | 1.3 | | | | | 1.9 | 2.0 |
| | (22) 7.2 | (15) 3.4 | (18) 2.4 | | | | | (23) 4.5 | (40) 3.3 |
| | 9.7 | 5.1 | 4.1 | | | | | 11.9 | 6.3 |
| Net Sales ($) | 46875M | 115846M | 442884M | 651914M | 119015M | 847175M | | 1050839M | 1352128M |
| Total Assets ($) | 7443M | 31304M | 185158M | 272491M | 76653M | 307238M | | 626142M | 637650M |

## Comparative Historical Data        Current Data Sorted by Sales

### Type of Statement

| Type of Statement | 4/1/09-3/31/10 ALL | 4/1/10-3/31/11 ALL | 4/1/11-3/31/12 ALL | 0-1MM | 1-3MM | 3-5MM | 5-10MM | 10-25MM | 25MM & OVER |
|---|---|---|---|---|---|---|---|---|---|
| Unqualified | 9 | 11 | 7 |  | 1 |  | 13 | 9 | 4 |
| Reviewed | 21 | 29 | 31 | 1 | 4 | 2 |  | 2 | 2 |
| Compiled | 12 | 9 | 9 | 2 | 3 |  | 2 | 2 |  |
| Tax Returns | 20 | 22 | 31 | 10 | 11 | 3 | 5 | 1 | 1 |
| Other | 23 | 33 | 43 | 5 | 9 | 6 | 10 | 9 | 4 |
|  | 4/1/09-3/31/10 | 4/1/10-3/31/11 | 4/1/11-3/31/12 | 9 (4/1-9/30/11) |  |  | 112 (10/1/11-3/31/12) |  |  |
| **Number of Statements** | 85 | 104 | 121 | 18 | 28 | 11 | 30 | 23 | 11 |

### ASSETS (%)

| Item | 09-10 ALL | 10-11 ALL | 11-12 ALL | 0-1MM | 1-3MM | 3-5MM | 5-10MM | 10-25MM | 25MM & OVER |
|---|---|---|---|---|---|---|---|---|---|
| Cash & Equivalents | 13.6 | 13.4 | 15.4 | 27.8 | 13.8 | 8.0 | 12.2 | 16.2 | 13.4 |
| Trade Receivables (net) | 34.4 | 36.2 | 35.2 | 16.0 | 33.7 | 36.3 | 39.1 | 40.8 | 47.1 |
| Inventory | 4.3 | 10.1 | 7.1 | 2.4 | 5.9 | 14.9 | 10.5 | 3.3 | 8.5 |
| All Other Current | 7.6 | 5.9 | 5.9 | 5.0 | 3.8 | 5.4 | 3.8 | 10.7 | 9.7 |
| Total Current | 59.9 | 65.6 | 63.6 | 51.1 | 57.3 | 64.5 | 65.6 | 71.0 | 78.7 |
| Fixed Assets (net) | 29.2 | 22.5 | 24.2 | 30.4 | 29.4 | 31.3 | 21.4 | 19.7 | 10.9 |
| Intangibles (net) | 2.0 | 2.3 | 2.2 | 6.0 | .2 | 1.5 | 2.1 | .6 | 5.8 |
| All Other Non-Current | 8.9 | 9.6 | 9.9 | 12.5 | 13.2 | 2.6 | 10.9 | 8.7 | 4.6 |
| Total | 100.0 | 100.0 | 100.0 | 100.0 | 100.0 | 100.0 | 100.0 | 100.0 | 100.0 |

### LIABILITIES

| Item | 09-10 ALL | 10-11 ALL | 11-12 ALL | 0-1MM | 1-3MM | 3-5MM | 5-10MM | 10-25MM | 25MM & OVER |
|---|---|---|---|---|---|---|---|---|---|
| Notes Payable-Short Term | 12.0 | 11.5 | 16.3 | 15.0 | 34.8 | 13.0 | 8.9 | 11.6 | 4.3 |
| Cur. Mat.-L.T.D. | 6.7 | 4.0 | 4.8 | 3.2 | 12.5 | 1.7 | 3.6 | 1.6 | 1.2 |
| Trade Payables | 16.0 | 20.5 | 19.6 | 19.8 | 16.5 | 17.4 | 19.2 | 22.1 | 25.0 |
| Income Taxes Payable | .1 | .2 | .1 | .0 | .1 | .0 | .0 | .1 | .1 |
| All Other Current | 15.1 | 9.8 | 11.9 | 11.5 | 9.4 | 22.3 | 10.2 | 13.8 | 8.9 |
| Total Current | 50.0 | 46.0 | 52.6 | 49.5 | 73.3 | 54.4 | 41.9 | 49.3 | 39.5 |
| Long-Term Debt | 21.4 | 14.2 | 14.9 | 28.8 | 21.9 | 20.2 | 8.6 | 6.6 | 3.6 |
| Deferred Taxes | .5 | .6 | .3 | .0 | .1 | .0 | .5 | .1 | .9 |
| All Other Non-Current | 13.0 | 5.1 | 4.9 | 7.5 | 7.8 | 2.6 | 3.5 | 3.0 | 3.6 |
| Net Worth | 15.1 | 34.1 | 27.3 | 14.2 | -3.2 | 22.7 | 45.6 | 41.0 | 52.4 |
| Total Liabilities & Net Worth | 100.0 | 100.0 | 100.0 | 100.0 | 100.0 | 100.0 | 100.0 | 100.0 | 100.0 |

### INCOME DATA

| Item | 09-10 ALL | 10-11 ALL | 11-12 ALL | 0-1MM | 1-3MM | 3-5MM | 5-10MM | 10-25MM | 25MM & OVER |
|---|---|---|---|---|---|---|---|---|---|
| Net Sales | 100.0 | 100.0 | 100.0 | 100.0 | 100.0 | 100.0 | 100.0 | 100.0 | 100.0 |
| Gross Profit | 31.8 | 30.9 | 32.6 | 58.0 | 36.2 | 26.0 | 29.6 | 20.8 | 21.1 |
| Operating Expenses | 28.6 | 28.1 | 29.4 | 51.4 | 34.5 | 27.8 | 26.5 | 17.2 | 15.7 |
| Operating Profit | 3.2 | 2.8 | 3.1 | 6.6 | 1.7 | -1.8 | 3.0 | 3.6 | 5.3 |
| All Other Expenses (net) | .6 | .5 | .4 | .8 | .5 | 1.4 | .1 | .1 | .1 |
| Profit Before Taxes | 2.6 | 2.3 | 2.7 | 5.8 | 1.1 | -3.2 | 2.9 | 3.5 | 5.2 |

### RATIOS

| Ratio | 09-10 ALL | 10-11 ALL | 11-12 ALL | 0-1MM | 1-3MM | 3-5MM | 5-10MM | 10-25MM | 25MM & OVER |
|---|---|---|---|---|---|---|---|---|---|
| Current | 2.1 | 2.3 | 2.7 | 3.5 | 3.2 | 2.1 | 3.1 | 2.6 | 4.3 |
|  | 1.4 | 1.5 | 1.5 | 1.3 | 1.4 | 1.5 | 1.5 | 1.4 | 1.7 |
|  | .9 | 1.1 | 1.0 | .9 | .5 | 1.1 | 1.0 | 1.1 | 1.4 |
| Quick | 2.0 | 1.8 | 2.2 | 3.5 | 2.5 | 1.6 | 2.3 | 2.5 | 3.6 |
|  | 1.1 | 1.1 (120) | 1.1 | (17) 1.0 | .9 | .9 | 1.3 | 1.1 | 1.5 |
|  | .6 | .7 | .7 | .4 | .4 | .6 | .8 | .9 | 1.0 |
| Sales/Receivables | 17  21.8 | 27  13.6 | 18  20.8 | 0  UND | 0  UND | 27  13.6 | 30  12.2 | 43  8.5 | 51  7.1 |
|  | 46  7.9 | 46  7.9 | 46  8.0 | 4  101.9 | 27  13.6 | 52  7.0 | 46  8.0 | 61  6.0 | 61  6.0 |
|  | 67  5.5 | 65  5.6 | 73  5.0 | 46  7.9 | 64  5.7 | 89  4.1 | 87  4.2 | 74  4.9 | 91  4.0 |
| Cost of Sales/Inventory | 0  UND | 0  UND | 0  UND | 0  UND | 0  UND | 0  UND | 0  UND | 0  UND | 0  UND |
|  | 1  435.0 | 1  434.1 | 0  UND | 0  UND | 0  UND | 4  93.3 | 0  UND | 0  UND | 2  156.0 |
|  | 10  35.6 | 29  12.8 | 18  20.5 | 21  17.2 | 0  UND | 64  5.7 | 27  13.3 | 3  107.9 | 36  10.1 |
| Cost of Sales/Payables | 5  70.6 | 15  25.0 | 6  66.2 | 0  UND | 0  UND | 11  32.2 | 6  62.0 | 22  16.4 | 13  29.1 |
|  | 19  18.8 | 27  13.6 | 28  12.9 | 21  17.2 | 9  40.0 | 20  18.3 | 28  12.9 | 40  9.2 | 50  7.3 |
|  | 41  8.8 | 51  7.2 | 51  7.1 | 101  3.6 | 36  10.0 | 53  6.9 | 45  8.1 | 46  8.0 | 69  5.3 |
| Sales/Working Capital | 5.8 | 6.2 | 6.2 | 6.3 | 5.9 | 7.8 | 7.3 | 6.1 | 2.9 |
|  | 20.8 | 13.5 | 15.8 | 52.7 | 34.8 | 13.5 | 16.0 | 14.1 | 7.6 |
|  | -90.9 | 49.4 | -456.0 | -6.7 | -41.1 | 99.4 | -560.0 | 60.8 | 16.7 |
| EBIT/Interest | 11.1 | 16.0 | 13.0 | 8.3 | 8.7 | 9.7 | 32.6 | 12.2 |  |
|  | (75) 2.7 | (86) 4.5 | (96) 4.5 | (13) 3.8 | (21) 1.0 | (10) 2.1 | (25) 4.0 | (18) 4.8 |  |
|  | -.9 | 1.1 | .3 | -.7 | -6.9 | -24.0 | 1.5 | 1.0 |  |
| Net Profit + Depr., Dep., Amort./Cur. Mat. L/T/D | 7.2 | 6.1 | 7.6 |  |  |  | 6.1 |  |  |
|  | (18) 3.1 | (22) 2.9 | (21) 3.8 |  |  |  | (10) 1.5 |  |  |
|  | 1.1 | 1.6 | .3 |  |  |  | -.6 |  |  |
| Fixed/Worth | .3 | .2 | .2 | .5 | .1 | .5 | .2 | .2 | .1 |
|  | .8 | .5 | .6 | 2.6 | 1.5 | .9 | .5 | .5 | .1 |
|  | 25.3 | 1.5 | 2.8 | -.2 | 6.2 | -10.4 | 1.2 | .9 | .4 |
| Debt/Worth | 1.1 | .7 | .6 | .6 | .9 | 1.2 | .4 | .7 | .5 |
|  | 2.6 | 1.8 | 1.9 | 3.0 | 3.5 | 1.3 | 1.3 | 1.5 | 1.1 |
|  | 78.0 | 3.5 | 8.5 | -3.5 | NM | -29.0 | 5.2 | 2.2 | 2.0 |
| % Profit Before Taxes/Tangible Net Worth | 48.1 | 43.2 | 55.1 | 79.3 | 88.1 |  | 40.6 | 46.6 | 31.3 |
|  | (65) 12.1 | (92) 17.3 | (100) 15.5 | (10) 16.4 | (21) 50.0 | (28) 15.5 | 11.2 |  | (10) 17.6 |
|  | .3 | 1.8 | -1.5 | -12.9 | -26.5 | 3.9 | 1.8 |  | 6.6 |
| % Profit Before Taxes/Total Assets | 15.9 | 19.9 | 24.5 | 51.7 | 32.6 | 18.3 | 25.6 | 14.4 | 13.1 |
|  | 3.7 | 5.9 | 6.8 | 16.9 | 9.3 | 3.4 | 8.7 | 4.8 | 10.7 |
|  | -3.0 | .4 | -2.3 | -6.3 | -8.6 | -35.8 | .4 | .3 | 3.9 |
| Sales/Net Fixed Assets | 27.0 | 46.6 | 52.5 | 145.1 | 55.9 | 25.7 | 47.2 | 53.8 | 42.7 |
|  | 12.8 | 18.6 | 19.8 | 15.1 | 25.1 | 18.3 | 24.5 | 16.7 | 26.0 |
|  | 6.6 | 8.5 | 9.1 | 3.4 | 8.4 | 3.8 | 10.8 | 6.6 | 12.9 |
| Sales/Total Assets | 4.0 | 4.3 | 4.4 | 4.7 | 7.2 | 3.9 | 4.9 | 3.4 | 3.1 |
|  | 2.8 | 2.9 | 2.9 | 2.8 | 3.8 | 2.3 | 2.9 | 2.5 | 2.0 |
|  | 1.9 | 1.7 | 2.1 | 1.5 | 2.3 | 1.4 | 2.1 | 1.9 | 2.0 |
| % Depr., Dep., Amort./Sales | .9 | .7 | .6 | 1.7 | .4 |  | .6 | .5 |  |
|  | (67) 2.4 | (83) 1.8 | (87) 1.4 | (10) 2.3 | (18) 1.5 |  | (23) 1.2 | (19) 1.0 |  |
|  | 4.0 | 3.6 | 3.0 | 13.3 | 3.6 |  | 2.4 | 2.1 |  |
| % Officers', Directors' Owners' Comp/Sales | 2.2 | 1.5 | 2.3 | 6.7 | 3.6 |  | 1.9 |  |  |
|  | (36) 5.7 | (50) 3.1 | (60) 3.8 | (12) 8.3 | (17) 6.3 |  | (17) 2.4 |  |  |
|  | 9.6 | 7.2 | 7.0 | 13.6 | 7.8 |  | 4.1 |  |  |
| Net Sales ($) | 1518228M | 2641745M | 2223709M | 10316M | 51981M | 45201M | 214823M | 326630M | 1574758M |
| Total Assets ($) | 537577M | 1213838M | 880287M | 5979M | 15770M | 21792M | 74604M | 137756M | 624386M |

M = $ thousand     MM = $ million
See Pages 9 through 22 for Explanation of Ratios and Data

### Current Data Sorted by Assets | Comparative Historical Data

| | 0-500M | 500M-2MM | 2-10MM | 10-50MM | 50-100MM | 100-250MM | | 4/1/07-3/31/08 ALL | 4/1/08-3/31/09 ALL |
|---|---|---|---|---|---|---|---|---|---|
| **Type of Statement** | | | | | | | | | |
| Unqualified | 1 | 6 | 68 | 75 | 17 | 7 | | 166 | 193 |
| Reviewed | 3 | 115 | 267 | 67 | | 1 | | 391 | 462 |
| Compiled | 22 | 56 | 37 | 4 | | | | 105 | 109 |
| Tax Returns | 112 | 113 | 37 | 4 | | 2 | | 175 | 191 |
| Other | 52 | 120 | 105 | 71 | 14 | 4 | | 283 | 337 |
| | | 255 (4/1-9/30/11) | | 1,125 (10/1/11-3/31/12) | | | | | |
| **NUMBER OF STATEMENTS** | 190 | 410 | 514 | 221 | 32 | 13 | | 1120 | 1292 |
| | % | % | % | % | % | % | | % | % |
| **ASSETS** | | | | | | | | | |
| Cash & Equivalents | 26.3 | 15.3 | 14.5 | 16.0 | 16.1 | 11.3 | | 13.9 | 15.3 |
| Trade Receivables (net) | 28.7 | 48.7 | 51.8 | 51.0 | 51.4 | 36.1 | | 50.9 | 49.2 |
| Inventory | 6.2 | 6.2 | 4.9 | 2.9 | 1.2 | 6.9 | | 5.4 | 5.4 |
| All Other Current | 4.0 | 5.9 | 9.1 | 11.2 | 11.6 | 12.1 | | 8.1 | 7.8 |
| Total Current | 65.1 | 76.2 | 80.2 | 81.0 | 80.4 | 66.4 | | 78.4 | 77.7 |
| Fixed Assets (net) | 21.5 | 14.5 | 13.0 | 11.1 | 10.8 | 15.7 | | 14.8 | 15.1 |
| Intangibles (net) | 4.3 | 2.3 | 1.8 | 2.6 | 6.7 | 10.7 | | 1.6 | 1.9 |
| All Other Non-Current | 9.1 | 7.0 | 4.9 | 5.3 | 2.1 | 7.2 | | 5.1 | 5.3 |
| Total | 100.0 | 100.0 | 100.0 | 100.0 | 100.0 | 100.0 | | 100.0 | 100.0 |
| **LIABILITIES** | | | | | | | | | |
| Notes Payable-Short Term | 23.9 | 12.3 | 8.0 | 6.7 | 5.2 | 20.0 | | 10.6 | 10.2 |
| Cur. Mat.-L.T.D. | 8.6 | 2.5 | 2.0 | 1.6 | 3.2 | 2.7 | | 3.0 | 3.3 |
| Trade Payables | 18.8 | 20.4 | 20.7 | 19.3 | 15.4 | 18.2 | | 19.1 | 18.0 |
| Income Taxes Payable | .2 | .5 | .5 | .3 | .0 | .2 | | .7 | .6 |
| All Other Current | 12.2 | 11.6 | 14.8 | 21.0 | 23.6 | 19.8 | | 17.7 | 18.0 |
| Total Current | 63.7 | 47.4 | 46.0 | 49.0 | 47.5 | 60.9 | | 51.1 | 50.1 |
| Long-Term Debt | 28.5 | 9.2 | 6.3 | 4.7 | 7.3 | 7.4 | | 10.1 | 9.7 |
| Deferred Taxes | .2 | .4 | .4 | .4 | .8 | .6 | | .4 | .4 |
| All Other Non-Current | 16.5 | 4.4 | 3.1 | 3.2 | 3.1 | 6.0 | | 3.9 | 3.7 |
| Net Worth | -8.9 | 38.6 | 44.1 | 42.8 | 41.3 | 25.1 | | 34.5 | 36.1 |
| Total Liabilities & Net Worth | 100.0 | 100.0 | 100.0 | 100.0 | 100.0 | 100.0 | | 100.0 | 100.0 |
| **INCOME DATA** | | | | | | | | | |
| Net Sales | 100.0 | 100.0 | 100.0 | 100.0 | 100.0 | 100.0 | | 100.0 | 100.0 |
| Gross Profit | 43.4 | 29.6 | 21.3 | 16.7 | 15.7 | 20.6 | | 26.7 | 26.6 |
| Operating Expenses | 39.4 | 27.2 | 18.2 | 13.5 | 11.3 | 17.6 | | 21.8 | 22.2 |
| Operating Profit | 4.0 | 2.4 | 3.1 | 3.2 | 4.4 | 2.9 | | 4.9 | 4.3 |
| All Other Expenses (net) | .4 | .2 | .4 | .1 | .3 | -.6 | | .4 | .5 |
| Profit Before Taxes | 3.6 | 2.2 | 2.7 | 3.1 | 4.1 | 3.6 | | 4.5 | 3.8 |
| **RATIOS** | | | | | | | | | |
| Current | 3.3 | 3.1 | 2.6 | 2.0 | 2.0 | 1.8 | | 2.3 | 2.4 |
| | 1.3 | 1.7 | 1.7 | 1.7 | 1.7 | 1.2 | | 1.6 | 1.6 |
| | .6 | 1.1 | 1.3 | 1.3 | 1.3 | 1.0 | | 1.2 | 1.2 |
| Quick | 2.8 | 2.5 | 2.3 | 1.8 | 1.8 | 1.6 | | 2.0 | 2.0 |
| | 1.0 | 1.4 | 1.4 | 1.4 | 1.3 | .9 | | 1.3 (1291) | 1.4 |
| | .5 | .9 | 1.0 | 1.1 | 1.1 | .6 | | 1.0 | 1.0 |
| Sales/Receivables | 0 UND | 40 9.2 | 51 7.2 | 63 5.8 | 65 5.6 | 27 13.3 | | 44 8.4 | 41 8.8 |
| | 23 16.0 | 58 6.3 | 70 5.2 | 76 4.8 | 81 4.5 | 79 4.6 | | 64 5.7 | 61 6.0 |
| | 51 7.1 | 78 4.7 | 89 4.1 | 91 4.0 | 94 3.9 | 83 4.4 | | 82 4.4 | 81 4.5 |
| Cost of Sales/Inventory | 0 UND | 0 UND | 0 UND | 0 UND | 0 UND | 0 UND | | 0 UND | 0 UND |
| | 0 UND | 2 166.6 | 2 230.7 | 1 494.0 | 0 841.4 | 2 222.4 | | 2 229.7 | 1 322.8 |
| | 10 35.9 | 17 21.5 | 10 35.9 | 4 85.7 | 1 261.4 | 15 24.3 | | 10 35.1 | 8 43.0 |
| Cost of Sales/Payables | 0 UND | 13 27.3 | 18 20.1 | 22 16.6 | 21 17.5 | 22 16.4 | | 15 23.9 | 13 27.4 |
| | 16 22.4 | 28 13.0 | 29 12.4 | 33 10.9 | 28 12.9 | 29 12.8 | | 27 13.5 | 24 15.0 |
| | 49 7.4 | 47 7.8 | 47 7.7 | 46 8.0 | 35 10.3 | 54 6.8 | | 41 8.9 | 40 9.1 |
| Sales/Working Capital | 11.1 | 5.5 | 5.1 | 5.2 | 5.5 | 7.4 | | 6.4 | 6.5 |
| | 46.5 | 9.6 | 8.4 | 7.6 | 8.0 | 21.5 | | 10.7 | 10.6 |
| | -20.1 | 37.4 | 15.7 | 14.8 | 16.8 | NM | | 21.8 | 22.1 |
| EBIT/Interest | 11.2 | 16.3 | 28.5 | 37.0 | 50.9 | 25.3 | | 27.3 | 32.0 |
| | (147) 3.9 | (343) 4.1 | (422) 6.5 | (185) 7.9 | (27) 11.6 | (10) 10.8 | | (979) 8.1 | (1123) 7.8 |
| | -1.0 | .6 | 1.4 | 2.6 | 1.7 | 3.6 | | 2.5 | 2.0 |
| Net Profit + Depr., Dep., Amort./Cur. Mat. L/T/D | | 4.6 | 8.6 | 10.3 | 514.7 | | | 13.2 | 11.4 |
| | | (56) 1.7 | (122) 3.4 | (63) 5.0 | (12) 4.0 | | | (269) 4.6 | (317) 4.2 |
| | | -.5 | .4 | 1.6 | 1.4 | | | 1.9 | 1.4 |
| Fixed/Worth | .2 | .1 | .1 | .1 | .1 | .3 | | .1 | .1 |
| | 1.0 | .3 | .2 | .2 | .3 | .5 | | .3 | .3 |
| | -1.1 | 1.0 | .6 | .4 | .5 | 8.3 | | .8 | .7 |
| Debt/Worth | .8 | .6 | .6 | .8 | .9 | 1.4 | | .9 | .8 |
| | 8.1 | 1.5 | 1.3 | 1.4 | 1.7 | 2.0 | | 1.7 | 1.6 |
| | -3.5 | 5.9 | 2.7 | 2.4 | 3.4 | 26.7 | | 3.7 | 3.7 |
| % Profit Before Taxes/Tangible Net Worth | 155.3 | 45.2 | 37.9 | 32.6 | 35.1 | 102.5 | | 60.3 | 55.2 |
| | (117) 56.2 | (351) 16.3 | (488) 13.4 | (214) 14.7 | (29) 21.0 | (11) 20.9 | | (1005) 29.9 | (1154) 26.0 |
| | 8.7 | .5 | 2.4 | 4.7 | 4.1 | 10.2 | | 11.4 | 8.6 |
| % Profit Before Taxes/Total Assets | 42.5 | 16.4 | 15.2 | 11.9 | 12.7 | 11.1 | | 22.4 | 21.0 |
| | 16.8 | 5.4 | 5.2 | 6.1 | 7.2 | 4.8 | | 10.4 | 9.5 |
| | -3.9 | -.9 | .6 | 1.5 | .9 | 2.4 | | 3.5 | 2.1 |
| Sales/Net Fixed Assets | 200.3 | 77.9 | 73.4 | 72.8 | 84.0 | 53.5 | | 67.2 | 67.3 |
| | 39.9 | 30.5 | 32.5 | 37.2 | 27.6 | 22.2 | | 32.8 | 32.1 |
| | 15.8 | 15.3 | 15.4 | 15.3 | 15.9 | 12.8 | | 16.0 | 16.1 |
| Sales/Total Assets | 7.8 | 3.8 | 3.4 | 2.9 | 3.0 | 3.5 | | 3.9 | 3.9 |
| | 4.7 | 3.0 | 2.7 | 2.4 | 2.3 | 2.6 | | 3.0 | 3.1 |
| | 3.0 | 2.3 | 2.1 | 1.9 | 1.8 | 1.8 | | 2.4 | 2.4 |
| % Depr., Dep., Amort./Sales | .5 | .5 | .5 | .4 | .4 | .3 | | .5 | .5 |
| | (107) 1.2 | (288) 1.0 | (450) .9 | (202) .6 | (29) .6 | (10) .8 | | (920) .8 | (1059) .9 |
| | 3.0 | 1.8 | 1.5 | 1.1 | 1.3 | 2.3 | | 1.6 | 1.7 |
| % Officers', Directors' Owners' Comp/Sales | 4.2 | 2.7 | 1.5 | .9 | | | | 1.9 | 2.1 |
| | (132) 6.9 | (239) 4.2 | (233) 2.6 | (60) 1.6 | | | | (548) 3.5 | (629) 4.0 |
| | 10.6 | 6.5 | 4.3 | 3.6 | | | | 6.9 | 7.2 |
| Net Sales ($) | 260775M | 1506892M | 6862170M | 11717082M | 5367404M | 8360514M | | 27003138M | 30381016M |
| Total Assets ($) | 45999M | 476843M | 2441889M | 4728970M | 2196628M | 1784347M | | 9919711M | 11552286M |

M = $ thousand    MM = $ million
See Pages 9 through 22 for Explanation of Ratios and Data

## Comparative Historical Data

## Current Data Sorted by Sales

| Type of Statement | ALL 4/1/09-3/31/10 | ALL 4/1/10-3/31/11 | ALL 4/1/11-3/31/12 | 0-1MM | 1-3MM | 3-5MM | 5-10MM | 10-25MM | 25MM & OVER |
|---|---|---|---|---|---|---|---|---|---|
| Unqualified | 194 | 164 | 174 | 2 | 2 | 5 | 16 | 48 | 101 |
| Reviewed | 467 | 447 | 453 | 6 | 40 | 64 | 115 | 147 | 81 |
| Compiled | 115 | 120 | 119 | 9 | 45 | 23 | 23 | 15 | 4 |
| Tax Returns | 210 | 243 | 268 | 54 | 92 | 53 | 51 | 10 | 8 |
| Other | 352 | 313 | 366 | 28 | 86 | 51 | 52 | 61 | 88 |
| | | | | 255 (4/1-9/30/11) | | | 1,125 (10/1/11-3/31/12) | | |
| **NUMBER OF STATEMENTS** | 1338 | 1287 | 1380 | 99 | 265 | 196 | 257 | 281 | 282 |
| **ASSETS** | % | % | % | % | % | % | % | % | % |
| Cash & Equivalents | 18.2 | 16.7 | 16.6 | 24.4 | 18.6 | 17.7 | 14.7 | 15.4 | 14.1 |
| Trade Receivables (net) | 44.2 | 45.7 | 47.4 | 25.6 | 40.7 | 47.1 | 49.0 | 54.4 | 53.4 |
| Inventory | 5.8 | 5.7 | 5.1 | 6.1 | 6.7 | 6.0 | 6.1 | 3.6 | 2.9 |
| All Other Current | 7.8 | 8.2 | 7.9 | 4.4 | 4.8 | 6.1 | 7.5 | 10.2 | 11.1 |
| Total Current | 76.1 | 76.3 | 76.9 | 60.5 | 70.9 | 76.9 | 77.3 | 83.6 | 81.5 |
| Fixed Assets (net) | 16.1 | 15.0 | 14.3 | 23.0 | 18.1 | 14.6 | 14.2 | 11.0 | 10.8 |
| Intangibles (net) | 2.3 | 2.5 | 2.6 | 3.0 | 4.2 | 2.1 | 1.9 | 1.2 | 3.3 |
| All Other Non-Current | 5.5 | 6.2 | 6.2 | 13.4 | 6.8 | 6.4 | 6.5 | 4.2 | 4.4 |
| Total | 100.0 | 100.0 | 100.0 | 100.0 | 100.0 | 100.0 | 100.0 | 100.0 | 100.0 |
| **LIABILITIES** | | | | | | | | | |
| Notes Payable-Short Term | 10.5 | 12.1 | 11.3 | 18.9 | 17.4 | 11.8 | 9.9 | 8.0 | 7.1 |
| Cur. Mat.-L.T.D. | 3.5 | 3.0 | 3.0 | 4.4 | 3.9 | 2.5 | 4.9 | 1.7 | 1.8 |
| Trade Payables | 16.9 | 18.9 | 20.0 | 16.5 | 19.9 | 18.6 | 19.9 | 22.7 | 19.7 |
| Income Taxes Payable | .5 | .4 | .4 | .4 | .4 | .5 | .7 | .2 | .3 |
| All Other Current | 17.0 | 15.2 | 14.8 | 10.4 | 10.3 | 12.0 | 13.7 | 17.0 | 21.0 |
| Total Current | 48.5 | 49.6 | 49.5 | 50.5 | 51.9 | 45.4 | 49.1 | 49.6 | 50.1 |
| Long-Term Debt | 9.3 | 10.4 | 10.0 | 25.4 | 16.1 | 9.3 | 8.6 | 5.3 | 5.4 |
| Deferred Taxes | .5 | .4 | .4 | .1 | .4 | .4 | .5 | .3 | .4 |
| All Other Non-Current | 3.9 | 5.1 | 5.4 | 22.4 | 7.2 | 4.1 | 3.5 | 2.2 | 3.6 |
| Net Worth | 37.9 | 34.4 | 34.7 | 1.5 | 24.4 | 40.9 | 38.3 | 42.6 | 40.6 |
| Total Liabilties & Net Worth | 100.0 | 100.0 | 100.0 | 100.0 | 100.0 | 100.0 | 100.0 | 100.0 | 100.0 |
| **INCOME DATA** | | | | | | | | | |
| Net Sales | 100.0 | 100.0 | 100.0 | 100.0 | 100.0 | 100.0 | 100.0 | 100.0 | 100.0 |
| Gross Profit | 27.6 | 26.6 | 26.0 | 49.2 | 34.9 | 28.2 | 24.2 | 18.7 | 16.7 |
| Operating Expenses | 24.5 | 24.3 | 22.9 | 42.5 | 33.1 | 25.4 | 21.0 | 15.9 | 13.4 |
| Operating Profit | 3.1 | 2.4 | 3.1 | 6.8 | 1.8 | 2.8 | 3.2 | 2.8 | 3.4 |
| All Other Expenses (net) | .4 | .4 | .3 | 1.2 | .3 | .3 | .3 | .2 | .1 |
| Profit Before Taxes | 2.7 | 2.0 | 2.8 | 5.5 | 1.5 | 2.4 | 2.9 | 2.6 | 3.3 |
| **RATIOS** | | | | | | | | | |
| Current | 2.9 | 2.6 | 2.6 | 3.9 | 3.2 | 3.2 | 2.7 | 2.6 | 2.1 |
| | 1.7 | 1.7 | 1.7 | 1.5 | 1.6 | 1.8 | 1.7 | 1.7 | 1.7 |
| | 1.2 | 1.2 | 1.2 | .6 | 1.0 | 1.2 | 1.2 | 1.4 | 1.3 |
| Quick | 2.4 | 2.2 | 2.2 | 3.3 | 2.6 | 2.7 | 2.3 | 2.2 | 1.8 |
| | 1.4 | (1286) 1.4 | 1.4 | 1.1 | 1.3 | 1.5 | 1.4 | 1.4 | 1.4 |
| | 1.0 | .9 | 1.0 | .5 | .8 | 1.0 | 1.0 | 1.1 | 1.1 |
| Sales/Receivables | 37 9.8 | 42 8.6 | 42 8.6 | 0 UND | 29 12.4 | 38 9.7 | 45 8.2 | 53 6.9 | 55 6.6 |
| | 59 6.2 | 63 5.8 | 63 5.8 | 29 12.8 | 54 6.8 | 56 6.5 | 63 5.8 | 72 5.1 | 73 5.0 |
| | 79 4.6 | 84 4.3 | 85 4.3 | 56 6.5 | 79 4.6 | 81 4.5 | 81 4.5 | 89 4.1 | 89 4.1 |
| Cost of Sales/Inventory | 0 UND | 0 UND | 0 UND | 0 UND | 0 UND | 0 UND | 0 UND | 0 UND | 0 UND |
| | 1 248.9 | 1 293.0 | 1 383.2 | 0 UND | 1 263.8 | 2 159.8 | 2 206.8 | 1 361.0 | 1 486.7 |
| | 10 35.5 | 12 31.2 | 10 36.7 | 16 23.2 | 20 18.4 | 14 25.9 | 12 31.0 | 6 59.3 | 5 78.4 |
| Cost of Sales/Payables | 12 29.5 | 14 25.3 | 16 23.2 | 0 UND | 8 48.0 | 14 26.9 | 15 25.0 | 19 18.8 | 20 17.9 |
| | 24 15.5 | 29 12.7 | 29 12.7 | 17 22.1 | 30 12.3 | 28 12.9 | 26 14.1 | 31 11.8 | 30 12.2 |
| | 40 9.2 | 48 7.7 | 46 7.9 | 64 5.7 | 56 6.5 | 48 7.6 | 46 8.0 | 43 8.4 | 40 9.2 |
| Sales/Working Capital | 5.4 | 5.2 | 5.5 | 5.7 | 5.8 | 5.0 | 5.7 | 5.3 | 5.8 |
| | 9.5 | 9.4 | 9.5 | 29.4 | 11.7 | 8.6 | 9.9 | 9.0 | 8.4 |
| | 24.3 | 25.2 | 27.3 | -18.1 | -357.2 | 32.0 | 22.3 | 16.2 | 16.3 |
| EBIT/Interest | 30.1 | 21.9 | 24.1 | 8.5 | 10.7 | 28.0 | 24.0 | 28.6 | 40.4 |
| | (1107) 6.1 | (1087) 3.9 | (1134) 5.5 | (71) 4.5 | (214) 3.4 | (163) 4.8 | (218) 4.6 | (229) 8.1 | (239) 9.8 |
| | .3 | -.8 | 1.1 | .4 | -1.6 | .3 | 1.3 | 1.6 | 3.4 |
| Net Profit + Depr., Dep., Amort./Cur. Mat. L/T/D | 8.5 | 7.5 | 8.5 | | 2.5 | 8.0 | 8.5 | 8.0 | 16.4 |
| | (310) 2.8 | (232) 2.5 | (261) 3.0 | | (23) .8 | (32) 3.1 | (55) 1.9 | (65) 2.7 | (85) 5.2 |
| | .9 | .1 | .5 | | -1.8 | 1.7 | -.7 | .7 | 1.6 |
| Fixed/Worth | .1 | .1 | .1 | .1 | .1 | .1 | .1 | .1 | .1 |
| | .3 | .3 | .3 | .8 | .5 | .3 | .3 | .2 | .2 |
| | .8 | .9 | .8 | -25.3 | -62.8 | .7 | .7 | .5 | .4 |
| Debt/Worth | .6 | .7 | .7 | .6 | .6 | .5 | .6 | .6 | .9 |
| | 1.3 | 1.4 | 1.5 | 4.1 | 2.1 | 1.2 | 1.4 | 1.4 | 1.5 |
| | 3.4 | 4.0 | 4.1 | -4.7 | -52.7 | 3.5 | 3.6 | 2.3 | 2.7 |
| % Profit Before Taxes/Tangible Net Worth | 43.4 | 35.4 | 43.5 | 145.4 | 58.2 | 44.4 | 37.9 | 33.8 | 41.2 |
| | (1197) 16.6 | (1119) 12.1 | (1210) 16.4 | (69) 44.0 | (195) 20.1 | (178) 15.0 | (233) 15.6 | (266) 12.2 | (269) 20.4 |
| | 2.1 | -.4 | 2.7 | -.2 | -5.4 | 1.1 | 3.8 | 2.4 | 6.5 |
| % Profit Before Taxes/Total Assets | 18.4 | 14.3 | 17.1 | 38.9 | 20.5 | 17.7 | 15.3 | 14.4 | 14.1 |
| | 5.6 | 4.0 | 6.2 | 14.3 | 6.2 | 5.0 | 6.0 | 4.7 | 7.6 |
| | -.7 | -2.6 | .4 | -2.3 | -6.4 | -.3 | 1.0 | .6 | 1.8 |
| Sales/Net Fixed Assets | 63.4 | 65.4 | 81.9 | 111.7 | 86.9 | 79.2 | 74.2 | 84.5 | 79.7 |
| | 29.0 | 32.1 | 32.6 | 24.4 | 27.3 | 30.7 | 31.2 | 37.5 | 38.8 |
| | 14.2 | 14.7 | 15.5 | 7.6 | 11.9 | 15.8 | 16.0 | 17.9 | 17.7 |
| Sales/Total Assets | 3.7 | 3.6 | 3.7 | 5.4 | 4.1 | 3.9 | 3.7 | 3.5 | 3.3 |
| | 2.9 | 2.7 | 2.8 | 2.8 | 2.8 | 3.0 | 2.8 | 2.8 | 2.7 |
| | 2.2 | 2.1 | 2.1 | 1.5 | 2.1 | 2.1 | 2.1 | 2.2 | 2.2 |
| % Depr., Dep., Amort./Sales | .5 | .5 | .4 | .9 | .6 | .5 | .5 | .4 | .3 |
| | (1087) 1.0 | (1050) 1.0 | (1086) .9 | (55) 1.8 | (172) 1.2 | (150) 1.0 | (209) 1.0 | (245) .8 | (255) .6 |
| | 1.8 | 1.8 | 1.6 | 4.6 | 2.3 | 1.7 | 1.0 | 1.3 | 1.1 |
| % Officers', Directors' Owners' Comp/Sales | 2.4 | 2.2 | 1.9 | 5.3 | 3.4 | 2.8 | 1.8 | 1.4 | .9 |
| | (631) 4.5 | (627) 4.1 | (671) 3.7 | (59) 10.1 | (159) 5.1 | (126) 4.2 | (130) 2.9 | (121) 2.2 | (76) 1.6 |
| | 7.9 | 7.2 | 6.2 | 14.7 | 7.7 | 5.6 | 4.6 | 3.4 | 3.0 |
| Net Sales ($) | 29257198M | 26258502M | 34074837M | 54363M | 524614M | 784564M | 1837150M | 4512014M | 26362132M |
| Total Assets ($) | 11313277M | 10603473M | 11674676M | 33576M | 205571M | 297366M | 737552M | 1718882M | 8681729M |

M = $ thousand    MM = $ million
See Pages 9 through 22 for Explanation of Ratios and Data

## Current Data Sorted by Assets      Comparative Historical Data

| | | | | | | Type of Statement | | |
|---|---|---|---|---|---|---|---|---|
| | 1 | 47 | 62 | 10 | 3 | Unqualified | 139 | 143 |
| 13 | 89 | 245 | 61 | | | Reviewed | 344 | 407 |
| 18 | 54 | 34 | 2 | | 1 | Compiled | 109 | 121 |
| 148 | 115 | 42 | 7 | | 1 | Tax Returns | 235 | 277 |
| 65 | 141 | 136 | 59 | 4 | 8 | Other | 275 | 296 |
| | 239 (4/1-9/30/11) | | 1,127 (10/1/11-3/31/12) | | | | 4/1/07- 3/31/08 | 4/1/08- 3/31/09 |
| 0-500M | 500M-2MM | 2-10MM | 10-50MM | 50-100MM | 100-250MM | | ALL | ALL |
| 244 | 400 | 504 | 191 | 14* | 13 | NUMBER OF STATEMENTS | 1102 | 1244 |
| % | % | % | % | % | % | ASSETS | % | % |
| 22.4 | 14.9 | 14.0 | 16.8 | 12.4 | 12.7 | Cash & Equivalents | 14.6 | 15.6 |
| 27.5 | 42.2 | 50.5 | 48.0 | 46.3 | 35.2 | Trade Receivables (net) | 45.5 | 44.7 |
| 12.3 | 10.2 | 6.1 | 4.5 | 3.7 | 10.8 | Inventory | 7.3 | 7.0 |
| 2.8 | 5.1 | 8.3 | 9.2 | 14.1 | 6.7 | All Other Current | 6.8 | 6.9 |
| 65.0 | 72.4 | 78.9 | 78.4 | 76.5 | 65.3 | Total Current | 74.2 | 74.2 |
| 25.4 | 17.3 | 13.0 | 12.4 | 13.4 | 13.4 | Fixed Assets (net) | 18.0 | 16.6 |
| 2.4 | 3.7 | 2.3 | 5.1 | 7.0 | 10.5 | Intangibles (net) | 2.2 | 2.7 |
| 7.2 | 6.7 | 5.7 | 4.2 | 3.1 | 10.7 | All Other Non-Current | 5.6 | 6.5 |
| 100.0 | 100.0 | 100.0 | 100.0 | 100.0 | 100.0 | Total | 100.0 | 100.0 |
| | | | | | | LIABILITIES | | |
| 23.8 | 11.5 | 8.2 | 6.0 | 7.7 | 4.7 | Notes Payable-Short Term | 9.3 | 10.0 |
| 4.0 | 3.1 | 1.9 | 4.0 | .7 | 3.5 | Cur. Mat.-L.T.D. | 3.4 | 3.4 |
| 19.0 | 21.5 | 24.2 | 20.8 | 25.2 | 14.7 | Trade Payables | 21.0 | 21.0 |
| .2 | .5 | .4 | .4 | .2 | .0 | Income Taxes Payable | .7 | .6 |
| 12.6 | 11.6 | 15.3 | 20.0 | 22.4 | 15.0 | All Other Current | 17.6 | 17.1 |
| 59.8 | 48.1 | 49.9 | 51.1 | 56.2 | 37.9 | Total Current | 52.0 | 52.1 |
| 28.7 | 14.2 | 6.9 | 8.9 | 8.3 | 16.6 | Long-Term Debt | 14.0 | 12.7 |
| .0 | .2 | .3 | .3 | 1.1 | .0 | Deferred Taxes | .3 | .3 |
| 14.7 | 5.9 | 3.4 | 4.0 | .9 | 3.0 | All Other Non-Current | 4.3 | 4.6 |
| -3.2 | 31.6 | 39.5 | 35.6 | 33.6 | 42.4 | Net Worth | 29.3 | 30.3 |
| 100.0 | 100.0 | 100.0 | 100.0 | 100.0 | 100.0 | Total Liabilities & Net Worth | 100.0 | 100.0 |
| | | | | | | INCOME DATA | | |
| 100.0 | 100.0 | 100.0 | 100.0 | 100.0 | 100.0 | Net Sales | 100.0 | 100.0 |
| 45.8 | 33.7 | 22.7 | 20.1 | 15.9 | 29.9 | Gross Profit | 29.1 | 28.0 |
| 42.5 | 30.8 | 20.3 | 16.9 | 12.5 | 25.9 | Operating Expenses | 24.8 | 24.1 |
| 3.2 | 2.9 | 2.3 | 3.2 | 3.4 | 4.0 | Operating Profit | 4.3 | 3.9 |
| .8 | .6 | .3 | .3 | .5 | -.1 | All Other Expenses (net) | .4 | .4 |
| 2.4 | 2.3 | 2.1 | 2.9 | 2.9 | 4.1 | Profit Before Taxes | 4.0 | 3.6 |
| | | | | | | RATIOS | | |
| 2.9 | 2.5 | 2.2 | 2.1 | 1.7 | 3.8 | | 2.1 | 2.2 |
| 1.3 | 1.6 | 1.5 | 1.5 | 1.3 | 2.0 | Current | 1.5 | 1.5 |
| .7 | 1.1 | 1.2 | 1.2 | 1.1 | 1.1 | | 1.2 | 1.2 |
| 2.4 | 2.0 | 1.9 | 1.8 | 1.3 | 3.2 | | 1.8 | 1.8 |
| 1.0 | 1.3 | 1.3 | 1.3 | 1.0 | (12) 1.6 | Quick | (1101) 1.2 | 1.2 |
| .4 | .9 | .9 | 1.0 | .7 | .9 | | .9 | .9 |
| 0 UND | 27 13.7 | 46 7.9 | 57 6.4 | 47 7.8 | 14 25.6 | | 30 12.0 | 30 12.1 |
| 16 22.4 | 47 7.8 | 65 5.6 | 74 4.9 | 63 5.8 | 58 6.3 | Sales/Receivables | 54 6.8 | 53 6.9 |
| 40 9.1 | 66 5.5 | 85 4.3 | 91 4.0 | 87 4.2 | 65 5.6 | | 77 4.7 | 76 4.8 |
| 0 UND | 0 UND | 0 UND | 0 999.8 | 0 UND | 1 625.9 | | 0 UND | 0 UND |
| 4 83.1 | 8 43.8 | 4 95.4 | 3 143.6 | 1 290.9 | 6 64.0 | Cost of Sales/Inventory | 4 102.8 | 3 108.6 |
| 24 15.2 | 23 15.8 | 15 24.2 | 10 35.7 | 10 37.2 | 25 14.4 | | 16 22.7 | 14 25.5 |
| 0 UND | 17 21.7 | 20 18.2 | 24 15.5 | 31 11.8 | 15 24.5 | | 16 22.6 | 14 25.3 |
| 18 19.8 | 29 12.5 | 33 11.0 | 34 10.7 | 40 9.1 | 19 18.9 | Cost of Sales/Payables | 29 12.6 | 28 13.0 |
| 41 9.0 | 46 7.9 | 54 6.7 | 54 6.7 | 54 6.7 | 38 9.5 | | 46 7.9 | 45 8.1 |
| 10.8 | 6.6 | 6.3 | 5.3 | 6.7 | 4.4 | | 7.3 | 7.2 |
| 42.5 | 12.7 | 10.8 | 9.4 | 14.0 | 13.7 | Sales/Working Capital | 13.1 | 13.1 |
| -28.7 | 61.9 | 21.2 | 18.7 | 36.9 | 43.5 | | 37.2 | 42.0 |
| 15.0 | 14.6 | 24.1 | 30.6 | 285.3 | 10.6 | | 26.6 | 27.7 |
| (195) 3.4 | (345) 4.0 | (420) 4.7 | (161) 8.4 | (13) 5.5 | (12) 2.7 | EBIT/Interest | (971) 7.7 | (1102) 6.4 |
| -1.4 | .7 | .8 | 1.7 | 2.1 | 1.6 | | 2.1 | 1.6 |
| | 3.9 | 8.7 | 17.2 | | | | 8.6 | 9.6 |
| | (41) 2.0 | (113) 2.7 | (68) 4.4 | | | Net Profit + Depr., Dep., Amort./Cur. Mat. L/T/D | (228) 4.3 | (265) 3.5 |
| | 1.0 | .9 | 1.3 | | | | 2.1 | 1.2 |
| .2 | .2 | .1 | .1 | .1 | .1 | | .2 | .2 |
| 1.2 | .4 | .3 | .2 | .4 | .4 | Fixed/Worth | .4 | .4 |
| -1.0 | 1.9 | .7 | .6 | .7 | NM | | 1.2 | 1.2 |
| 1.0 | .8 | .8 | .9 | 1.3 | .5 | | .9 | .9 |
| 9.6 | 1.9 | 1.6 | 1.8 | 2.1 | 2.8 | Debt/Worth | 2.1 | 1.9 |
| -3.7 | 8.6 | 3.8 | 3.5 | 5.6 | NM | | 5.3 | 5.0 |
| 128.3 | 46.5 | 38.1 | 35.8 | 41.9 | 30.7 | | 62.0 | 56.2 |
| (146) 55.6 | (327) 18.4 | (472) 13.5 | (173) 14.4 | (13) 15.9 | (10) 14.0 | % Profit Before Taxes/Tangible Net Worth | (950) 30.2 | (1069) 27.3 |
| 6.9 | 2.6 | 1.9 | 3.1 | 3.1 | 2.3 | | 12.0 | 7.5 |
| 39.6 | 17.2 | 13.1 | 12.9 | 11.0 | 14.0 | | 21.3 | 21.0 |
| 11.9 | 5.7 | 4.6 | 5.7 | 4.0 | 3.8 | % Profit Before Taxes/Total Assets | 9.7 | 8.7 |
| -4.6 | -.4 | .2 | 1.1 | .9 | .3 | | 3.0 | 1.6 |
| 140.8 | 65.7 | 61.6 | 72.4 | 109.7 | 71.2 | | 56.9 | 58.9 |
| 32.2 | 27.3 | 33.0 | 30.1 | 28.1 | 20.9 | Sales/Net Fixed Assets | 28.5 | 30.6 |
| 13.9 | 13.5 | 17.1 | 16.0 | 8.1 | 13.6 | | 15.3 | 16.7 |
| 8.1 | 4.5 | 3.6 | 3.1 | 3.5 | 5.7 | | 4.3 | 4.3 |
| 5.2 | 3.3 | 2.9 | 2.4 | 2.9 | 2.7 | Sales/Total Assets | 3.2 | 3.1 |
| 3.4 | 2.5 | 2.3 | 1.8 | 1.6 | 1.2 | | 2.5 | 2.5 |
| .7 | .6 | .5 | .4 | .2 | | | .4 | .5 |
| (130) 1.3 | (287) 1.1 | (434) .9 | (177) .7 | .7 | | % Depr., Dep., Amort./Sales | (905) 1.0 | (1041) .9 |
| 3.0 | 1.8 | 1.4 | 1.3 | 1.8 | | | 1.7 | 1.7 |
| 4.1 | 2.9 | 2.7 | 1.0 | | | | 2.1 | 2.0 |
| (172) 7.1 | (249) 4.3 | (251) 2.7 | (69) 1.5 | | | % Officers', Directors' Owners' Comp/Sales | (569) 4.1 | (685) 3.8 |
| 11.6 | 7.1 | 5.2 | 3.4 | | | | 7.2 | 6.7 |
| 378756M | 1617339M | 7102702M | 11118184M | 2411371M | 6791191M | Net Sales ($) | 30744019M | 28993465M |
| 62665M | 454024M | 2417492M | 3610758M | 945660M | 1905051M | Total Assets ($) | 8777716M | 10095051M |

## Comparative Historical Data  |  Current Data Sorted by Sales

### Type of Statement

| Type of Statement | 4/1/09-3/31/10 ALL | 4/1/10-3/31/11 ALL | 4/1/11-3/31/12 ALL | 0-1MM | 1-3MM | 3-5MM | 5-10MM | 10-25MM | 25MM & OVER |
|---|---|---|---|---|---|---|---|---|---|
| Unqualified | 121 | 117 | 123 | 5 | 32 | 1 | 10 | 36 | 76 |
| Reviewed | 407 | 386 | 408 | 6 | 29 | 49 | 91 | 162 | 69 |
| Compiled | 121 | 135 | 109 | 67 | 115 | 27 | 28 | 16 | 3 |
| Tax Returns | 251 | 251 | 313 |  |  | 49 | 49 | 24 | 9 |
| Other | 350 | 333 | 413 | 30 | 89 | 69 | 74 | 82 | 69 |
|  |  |  |  | 239 (4/1-9/30/11) | | 1,127 (10/1/11-3/31/12) | | | |
| NUMBER OF STATEMENTS | 1250 | 1222 | 1366 | 108 | 265 | 195 | 252 | 320 | 226 |

### ASSETS

| ASSETS | % | % | % | % | % | % | % | % | % |
|---|---|---|---|---|---|---|---|---|---|
| Cash & Equivalents | 17.7 | 16.2 | 16.1 | 20.2 | 18.0 | 15.9 | 15.9 | 15.0 | 14.0 |
| Trade Receivables (net) | 41.4 | 42.4 | 43.4 | 22.8 | 35.8 | 40.0 | 45.6 | 51.4 | 51.3 |
| Inventory | 7.2 | 8.1 | 8.2 | 13.2 | 11.1 | 10.6 | 7.1 | 5.6 | 5.4 |
| All Other Current | 6.7 | 6.9 | 6.6 | 2.2 | 4.2 | 5.5 | 7.0 | 8.0 | 9.8 |
| Total Current | 73.1 | 73.5 | 74.3 | 58.4 | 69.1 | 72.0 | 75.5 | 79.9 | 80.5 |
| Fixed Assets (net) | 17.6 | 17.3 | 16.4 | 31.3 | 19.8 | 17.4 | 14.6 | 12.4 | 12.0 |
| Intangibles (net) | 3.0 | 2.9 | 3.2 | 2.3 | 3.3 | 3.6 | 3.9 | 2.8 | 3.3 |
| All Other Non-Current | 6.3 | 6.3 | 6.1 | 8.0 | 7.8 | 6.9 | 6.0 | 4.9 | 4.2 |
| Total | 100.0 | 100.0 | 100.0 | 100.0 | 100.0 | 100.0 | 100.0 | 100.0 | 100.0 |

### LIABILITIES

| LIABILITIES | | | | | | | | | |
|---|---|---|---|---|---|---|---|---|---|
| Notes Payable-Short Term | 10.2 | 12.0 | 11.6 | 26.1 | 14.0 | 16.0 | 9.3 | 7.7 | 6.1 |
| Cur. Mat.-L.T.D. | 3.3 | 3.1 | 2.9 | 5.0 | 2.8 | 2.7 | 3.1 | 1.5 | 3.9 |
| Trade Payables | 19.8 | 21.6 | 21.9 | 15.0 | 19.5 | 20.2 | 22.9 | 25.5 | 23.4 |
| Income Taxes Payable | .4 | .4 | .4 | .5 | .1 | .6 | .6 | .3 | .3 |
| All Other Current | 17.0 | 14.7 | 14.4 | 12.0 | 10.8 | 11.3 | 15.0 | 15.2 | 20.9 |
| Total Current | 50.7 | 51.8 | 51.3 | 58.6 | 47.3 | 50.9 | 50.9 | 50.2 | 54.6 |
| Long-Term Debt | 12.5 | 12.4 | 13.3 | 38.6 | 19.0 | 12.3 | 11.1 | 5.6 | 8.7 |
| Deferred Taxes | .3 | .3 | .2 | .0 | .2 | .3 | .3 | .3 | .3 |
| All Other Non-Current | 5.9 | 6.4 | 6.2 | 17.2 | 10.1 | 4.7 | 4.9 | 3.3 | 3.2 |
| Net Worth | 30.7 | 29.1 | 29.0 | -14.3 | 23.4 | 31.8 | 32.8 | 40.6 | 33.2 |
| Total Liabilties & Net Worth | 100.0 | 100.0 | 100.0 | 100.0 | 100.0 | 100.0 | 100.0 | 100.0 | 100.0 |

### INCOME DATA

| INCOME DATA | | | | | | | | | |
|---|---|---|---|---|---|---|---|---|---|
| Net Sales | 100.0 | 100.0 | 100.0 | 100.0 | 100.0 | 100.0 | 100.0 | 100.0 | 100.0 |
| Gross Profit | 28.9 | 29.1 | 29.7 | 50.4 | 39.8 | 33.1 | 26.7 | 21.5 | 19.7 |
| Operating Expenses | 25.9 | 27.0 | 26.9 | 48.4 | 36.1 | 30.4 | 24.7 | 18.6 | 16.7 |
| Operating Profit | 3.1 | 2.2 | 2.8 | 2.0 | 3.6 | 2.7 | 2.0 | 2.9 | 3.1 |
| All Other Expenses (net) | .4 | .3 | .5 | 1.5 | .9 | .4 | .3 | .2 | .1 |
| Profit Before Taxes | 2.7 | 1.9 | 2.4 | .6 | 2.8 | 2.4 | 1.7 | 2.6 | 3.0 |

### RATIOS

| RATIOS | | | | | | | | | |
|---|---|---|---|---|---|---|---|---|---|
| Current | 2.4 | 2.5 | 2.3 | 2.9 | 3.1 | 2.4 | 2.4 | 2.2 | 2.0 |
|  | 1.6 | 1.6 | 1.5 | 1.1 | 1.6 | 1.6 | 1.5 | 1.6 | 1.5 |
|  | 1.2 | 1.1 | 1.1 | .6 | 1.1 | 1.2 | 1.1 | 1.2 | 1.2 |
| Quick | 2.0 | 2.0 | 1.9 | 2.0 | 2.7 | 1.9 | 2.0 | 1.9 | 1.7 |
|  | 1.3 | 1.2 (1365) | 1.2 | .8 | 1.3 | 1.3 | 1.2 | 1.3 (225) | 1.2 |
|  | .9 | .8 | .9 | .3 | .7 | .8 | .9 | 1.0 | 1.0 |
| Sales/Receivables | 30  12.1 | 30  12.0 | 29  12.5 | 0 UND | 14  25.9 | 22  16.6 | 33  11.2 | 45  8.1 | 50  7.3 |
|  | 50  7.3 | 56  6.6 | 53  6.9 | 18  20.6 | 41  9.0 | 49  7.5 | 52  7.0 | 66  5.5 | 68  5.4 |
|  | 72  5.1 | 78  4.7 | 76  4.8 | 40  9.1 | 63  5.8 | 72  5.1 | 72  5.1 | 87  4.2 | 87  4.2 |
| Cost of Sales/Inventory | 0 UND | 0 UND | 0 UND | 0 UND | 0 UND | 0 UND | 0 UND | 0 UND | 0 999.8 |
|  | 4  88.7 | 5  73.0 | 4  81.3 | 4  83.1 | 9  41.6 | 7  52.7 | 7  55.8 | 3  129.8 | 3  134.5 |
|  | 16  22.8 | 18  20.2 | 17  20.9 | 30  12.3 | 31  11.6 | 24  15.2 | 16  23.2 | 13  28.8 | 10  37.9 |
| Cost of Sales/Payables | 15  25.1 | 17  21.1 | 16  22.4 | 0 UND | 11  34.7 | 15  24.2 | 17  21.5 | 22  16.6 | 22  16.8 |
|  | 27  13.7 | 31  11.8 | 30  12.0 | 23  15.7 | 24  15.1 | 28  12.9 | 29  12.5 | 36  10.1 | 32  11.5 |
|  | 43  8.4 | 48  7.6 | 50  7.3 | 51  7.1 | 47  7.7 | 49  7.4 | 43  8.4 | 57  6.4 | 49  7.5 |
| Sales/Working Capital | 6.1 | 6.0 | 6.6 | 10.8 | 5.9 | 6.4 | 7.2 | 6.2 | 7.0 |
|  | 11.9 | 11.8 | 12.6 | 92.4 | 13.3 | 12.1 | 12.1 | 10.9 | 12.0 |
|  | 34.3 | 41.4 | 43.0 | -13.7 | 148.7 | 41.1 | 44.2 | 23.0 | 23.1 |
| EBIT/Interest | 24.4 | 18.2 | 19.4 | 5.2 | 14.8 | 16.2 | 17.8 | 25.0 | 39.3 |
|  | (1057) 5.3 | (1034) 4.4 | (1146) 4.6 | (85) 1.4 | (219) 3.8 | (170) 4.9 | (215) 3.3 | (260) 6.0 | (197) 8.9 |
|  | .8 | .3 | .7 | -3.0 | -.1 | .8 | -.1 | 1.5 | 2.6 |
| Net Profit + Depr., Dep., Amort./Cur. Mat. L/T/D | 10.6 | 9.9 | 8.9 |  | 2.6 | 5.5 | 4.4 | 12.1 | 17.2 |
|  | (258) 3.7 | (230) 2.7 | (237) 2.9 |  | (15) 1.0 | (21) 2.3 | (50) 1.8 | (70) 4.1 | (80) 4.0 |
|  | 1.0 | .8 | 1.0 |  | -3.8 | 1.4 | .3 | 1.6 | 1.3 |
| Fixed/Worth | .1 | .1 | .1 | .2 | .2 | .2 | .1 | .1 | .1 |
|  | .4 | .4 | .4 | 1.7 | .6 | .4 | .3 | .3 | .3 |
|  | 1.2 | 1.3 | 1.3 | -1.5 | 29.8 | 1.1 | 1.6 | .6 | .7 |
| Debt/Worth | .8 | .8 | .8 | 1.3 | .6 | .7 | .8 | .8 | 1.1 |
|  | 1.7 | 1.8 | 1.9 | 21.1 | 2.7 | 1.7 | 1.7 | 1.6 | 2.0 |
|  | 4.7 | 5.7 | 6.6 | -3.3 | -23.7 | 6.3 | 6.8 | 3.8 | 3.8 |
| % Profit Before Taxes/Tangible Net Worth | 47.2 | 41.4 | 45.7 | 113.8 | 65.1 | 47.8 | 40.2 | 42.1 | 37.5 |
|  | (1048) 19.0 | (1033) 13.5 | (1141) 17.6 | (58) 25.0 | (196) 26.0 | (165) 16.3 | (212) 13.2 | (304) 14.6 | (206) 17.7 |
|  | 2.7 | 1.1 | 2.7 | -13.1 | 3.8 | 1.7 | -.5 | 3.3 | 6.0 |
| % Profit Before Taxes/Total Assets | 18.1 | 15.5 | 16.6 | 27.9 | 22.6 | 17.5 | 14.2 | 14.3 | 13.5 |
|  | 6.4 | 4.7 | 5.7 | 2.6 | 9.0 | 5.7 | 3.5 | 5.3 | 6.4 |
|  | .0 | -.7 | .0 | -12.4 | -1.3 | -.3 | -1.4 | .8 | 1.6 |
| Sales/Net Fixed Assets | 57.8 | 56.2 | 70.3 | 104.6 | 60.0 | 68.9 | 75.3 | 64.3 | 77.6 |
|  | 28.7 | 27.2 | 31.1 | 18.3 | 23.7 | 27.8 | 36.1 | 34.9 | 34.4 |
|  | 14.2 | 14.2 | 14.9 | 7.6 | 11.7 | 14.4 | 16.5 | 17.9 | 19.3 |
| Sales/Total Assets | 4.1 | 4.0 | 4.3 | 7.1 | 4.8 | 4.7 | 4.4 | 3.6 | 3.7 |
|  | 3.1 | 3.0 | 3.1 | 3.6 | 3.2 | 3.3 | 3.3 | 2.9 | 2.9 |
|  | 2.3 | 2.2 | 2.3 | 2.3 | 2.4 | 2.4 | 2.5 | 2.3 | 2.3 |
| % Depr., Dep., Amort./Sales | .5 | .6 | .5 | .8 | .7 | .5 | .6 | .5 | .4 |
|  | (1016) 1.1 | (990) 1.0 | (1048) .9 | (57) 2.4 | (161) 1.4 | (151) 1.1 | (200) .9 | (275) .8 | (204) .7 |
|  | 1.8 | 1.8 | 1.6 | 3.7 | 2.7 | 1.7 | 1.6 | 1.3 | 1.2 |
| % Officers', Directors', Owners' Comp/Sales | 2.0 | 2.1 | 2.0 | 6.0 | 3.7 | 2.9 | 2.0 | 1.2 | .8 |
|  | (645) 3.9 | (657) 4.2 | (746) 4.0 | (72) 11.1 | (172) 5.8 | (116) 4.1 | (154) 3.7 | (159) 2.0 | (73) 1.8 |
|  | 7.4 | 7.4 | 7.2 | 14.8 | 8.8 | 6.1 | 5.8 | 4.2 | 4.1 |
| Net Sales ($) | 29011800M | 23449906M | 29419543M | 63043M | 503951M | 760812M | 1859136M | 5099628M | 21132973M |
| Total Assets ($) | 9908455M | 8365311M | 9395650M | 22693M | 183941M | 269247M | 768738M | 1951830M | 6199201M |

M = $ thousand     MM = $ million
See Pages 9 through 22 for Explanation of Ratios and Data

**Current Data Sorted by Assets**     **Comparative Historical Data**

### Type of Statement

| 0-500M | 500M-2MM | 2-10MM | 10-50MM | 50-100MM | 100-250MM | Type of Statement | 4/1/07-3/31/08 ALL | 4/1/08-3/31/09 ALL |
|---|---|---|---|---|---|---|---|---|
|  | 2 | 5 | 9 | 1 | 1 | Unqualified | 23 | 21 |
| 2 | 11 | 40 | 10 |  |  | Reviewed | 51 | 61 |
| 6 | 15 | 13 | 2 |  |  | Compiled | 34 | 23 |
| 29 | 33 | 6 |  |  |  | Tax Returns | 36 | 34 |
| 10 | 29 | 32 | 10 |  |  | Other | 55 | 58 |
| 40 (4/1-9/30/11) |  |  | 226 (10/1/11-3/31/12) |  |  |  |  |  |
| 47 | 90 | 96 | 31 | 1 | 1 | NUMBER OF STATEMENTS | 199 | 197 |

### Assets (%)

| 0-500M | 500M-2MM | 2-10MM | 10-50MM | 50-100MM | 100-250MM | ASSETS | 4/1/07-3/31/08 ALL | 4/1/08-3/31/09 ALL |
|---|---|---|---|---|---|---|---|---|
| 19.4 | 13.5 | 13.2 | 16.7 |  |  | Cash & Equivalents | 13.2 | 12.2 |
| 27.5 | 42.0 | 42.8 | 37.5 |  |  | Trade Receivables (net) | 39.9 | 41.8 |
| 12.3 | 12.4 | 7.8 | 7.3 |  |  | Inventory | 10.5 | 10.3 |
| 2.3 | 3.9 | 5.2 | 9.1 |  |  | All Other Current | 5.1 | 6.5 |
| 61.5 | 71.8 | 69.1 | 70.6 |  |  | Total Current | 68.7 | 70.9 |
| 22.6 | 17.1 | 19.1 | 18.3 |  |  | Fixed Assets (net) | 21.3 | 19.3 |
| 4.3 | 3.4 | 3.3 | 4.8 |  |  | Intangibles (net) | 3.0 | 2.9 |
| 11.6 | 7.7 | 8.5 | 6.3 |  |  | All Other Non-Current | 7.1 | 6.9 |
| 100.0 | 100.0 | 100.0 | 100.0 |  |  | Total | 100.0 | 100.0 |

### Liabilities (%)

| 0-500M | 500M-2MM | 2-10MM | 10-50MM | 50-100MM | 100-250MM | LIABILITIES | 4/1/07-3/31/08 ALL | 4/1/08-3/31/09 ALL |
|---|---|---|---|---|---|---|---|---|
| 25.4 | 13.9 | 8.4 | 4.6 |  |  | Notes Payable-Short Term | 11.4 | 13.1 |
| 3.0 | 3.7 | 3.3 | 2.7 |  |  | Cur. Mat.-L.T.D. | 3.4 | 3.1 |
| 21.3 | 16.1 | 18.3 | 17.9 |  |  | Trade Payables | 15.5 | 17.9 |
| .0 | .2 | .3 | .1 |  |  | Income Taxes Payable | .7 | .3 |
| 17.8 | 11.8 | 11.4 | 19.5 |  |  | All Other Current | 12.8 | 16.6 |
| 67.6 | 45.7 | 41.7 | 44.8 |  |  | Total Current | 43.9 | 51.0 |
| 24.0 | 16.0 | 10.1 | 6.4 |  |  | Long-Term Debt | 15.8 | 12.6 |
| .0 | .0 | .4 | 1.4 |  |  | Deferred Taxes | .7 | .5 |
| 30.9 | 5.8 | 6.2 | 12.9 |  |  | All Other Non-Current | 5.7 | 5.4 |
| -22.6 | 32.5 | 41.6 | 34.5 |  |  | Net Worth | 34.0 | 30.5 |
| 100.0 | 100.0 | 100.0 | 100.0 |  |  | Total Liabilities & Net Worth | 100.0 | 100.0 |

### Income Data (%)

| 0-500M | 500M-2MM | 2-10MM | 10-50MM | 50-100MM | 100-250MM | INCOME DATA | 4/1/07-3/31/08 ALL | 4/1/08-3/31/09 ALL |
|---|---|---|---|---|---|---|---|---|
| 100.0 | 100.0 | 100.0 | 100.0 |  |  | Net Sales | 100.0 | 100.0 |
| 42.4 | 34.6 | 28.3 | 22.4 |  |  | Gross Profit | 31.4 | 31.9 |
| 38.7 | 30.2 | 24.6 | 17.3 |  |  | Operating Expenses | 26.2 | 26.9 |
| 3.7 | 4.4 | 3.8 | 5.1 |  |  | Operating Profit | 5.2 | 5.0 |
| .3 | .7 | .8 | 1.0 |  |  | All Other Expenses (net) | .8 | .5 |
| 3.4 | 3.7 | 3.0 | 4.1 |  |  | Profit Before Taxes | 4.4 | 4.5 |

### Ratios

| 0-500M | 500M-2MM | 2-10MM | 10-50MM | 50-100MM | 100-250MM | RATIOS | 4/1/07-3/31/08 ALL | 4/1/08-3/31/09 ALL |
|---|---|---|---|---|---|---|---|---|
| 3.8 | 3.4 | 3.1 | 2.1 |  |  |  | 2.5 | 2.4 |
| 1.4 | 1.6 | 1.7 | 1.5 |  |  | Current | 1.6 | 1.6 |
| .6 | 1.0 | 1.1 | 1.2 |  |  |  | 1.2 | 1.2 |
| 2.7 | 3.1 | 2.1 | 1.7 |  |  |  | 2.0 | 1.9 |
| 1.0 | 1.1 | 1.4 | 1.2 |  |  | Quick | (198) 1.3 | 1.2 |
| .6 | .7 | .9 | .8 |  |  |  | .9 | .8 |
| 0 UND | 30 12.1 | 41 8.8 | 40 9.1 |  |  |  | 32 11.4 | 31 11.8 |
| 19 19.7 | 50 7.3 | 61 6.0 | 64 5.7 |  |  | Sales/Receivables | 53 7.0 | 52 7.1 |
| 36 10.1 | 83 4.4 | 85 4.3 | 78 4.7 |  |  |  | 69 5.3 | 74 5.0 |
| 0 UND | 0 UND | 0 UND | 0 UND |  |  |  | 0 UND | 0 UND |
| 0 UND | 2 178.2 | 4 91.5 | 1 251.9 |  |  | Cost of Sales/Inventory | 5 67.0 | 3 109.8 |
| 19 19.6 | 43 8.4 | 19 18.9 | 18 20.1 |  |  |  | 26 14.0 | 31 11.8 |
| 0 UND | 9 41.8 | 14 26.5 | 17 21.8 |  |  |  | 11 33.8 | 11 32.0 |
| 15 24.9 | 22 16.8 | 32 11.3 | 29 12.6 |  |  | Cost of Sales/Payables | 21 17.6 | 25 14.7 |
| 40 9.2 | 49 7.5 | 58 6.3 | 48 7.6 |  |  |  | 35 10.4 | 44 8.4 |
| 11.4 | 4.8 | 5.1 | 5.5 |  |  |  | 5.7 | 6.1 |
| 31.9 | 11.5 | 9.3 | 10.7 |  |  | Sales/Working Capital | 11.2 | 10.2 |
| -33.4 | 223.1 | 38.5 | 23.2 |  |  |  | 39.9 | 44.8 |
| 10.0 | 21.8 | 15.7 | 78.3 |  |  |  | 15.2 | 23.7 |
| (34) 5.4 | (81) 5.1 | (80) 5.0 | (27) 7.9 |  |  | EBIT/Interest | (166) 4.9 | (172) 6.0 |
| .7 | .8 | 1.5 | 1.3 |  |  |  | 1.9 | 1.8 |
|  |  | 5.4 |  |  |  |  | 8.7 | 17.7 |
|  | (18) | 2.5 |  |  |  | Net Profit + Depr., Dep., Amort./Cur. Mat. L/T/D | (42) 4.1 | (37) 4.4 |
|  |  | .7 |  |  |  |  | 1.8 | 1.7 |
| .0 | .1 | .1 | .1 |  |  |  | .2 | .1 |
| 1.2 | .4 | .3 | .4 |  |  | Fixed/Worth | .4 | .4 |
| -.6 | 1.9 | 1.1 | 1.2 |  |  |  | 1.4 | 1.5 |
| .9 | .6 | .6 | .8 |  |  |  | .9 | .9 |
| 9.6 | 2.1 | 1.6 | 1.8 |  |  | Debt/Worth | 1.9 | 1.7 |
| -4.2 | 12.8 | 3.2 | 3.8 |  |  |  | 4.9 | 5.0 |
| 121.0 | 77.8 | 35.0 | 48.7 |  |  |  | 55.9 | 53.6 |
| (29) 63.4 | (75) 22.2 | (90) 13.4 | (27) 20.0 |  |  | % Profit Before Taxes/Tangible Net Worth | (179) 23.6 | (172) 26.9 |
| 2.8 | 2.2 | 2.1 | 9.0 |  |  |  | 11.9 | 11.1 |
| 43.5 | 21.2 | 12.9 | 15.5 |  |  |  | 19.8 | 20.3 |
| 8.7 | 6.9 | 4.1 | 7.1 |  |  | % Profit Before Taxes/Total Assets | 8.2 | 9.3 |
| .7 | .5 | .5 | .5 |  |  |  | 2.9 | 2.7 |
| 999.8 | 79.5 | 75.0 | 57.6 |  |  |  | 58.0 | 64.3 |
| 40.8 | 33.6 | 24.6 | 28.3 |  |  | Sales/Net Fixed Assets | 21.8 | 28.1 |
| 17.8 | 12.4 | 8.6 | 7.1 |  |  |  | 8.0 | 10.4 |
| 8.4 | 4.3 | 3.3 | 3.1 |  |  |  | 4.1 | 3.9 |
| 4.5 | 2.9 | 2.4 | 2.4 |  |  | Sales/Total Assets | 2.9 | 3.0 |
| 3.3 | 2.0 | 1.7 | 1.6 |  |  |  | 2.0 | 2.2 |
| .6 | .6 | .4 | .7 |  |  |  | .6 | .5 |
| (23) 1.9 | (67) 1.1 | (79) 1.1 | (28) 1.2 |  |  | % Depr., Dep., Amort./Sales | (163) 1.4 | (158) 1.1 |
| 3.1 | 2.5 | 2.3 | 2.8 |  |  |  | 2.7 | 2.3 |
| 2.1 | 2.7 | 1.7 |  |  |  |  | 2.5 | 2.0 |
| (28) 4.5 | (45) 4.6 | (38) 3.4 |  |  |  | % Officers', Directors' Owners' Comp/Sales | (95) 4.5 | (92) 4.0 |
| 9.2 | 6.2 | 5.7 |  |  |  |  | 7.7 | 7.2 |
| 70531M | 314120M | 1044791M | 1491933M | 191216M | 171381M | Net Sales ($) | 4440884M | 3546219M |
| 11657M | 101384M | 430630M | 611965M | 58871M | 229349M | Total Assets ($) | 1637261M | 1571294M |

© RMA 2012

M = $ thousand    MM = $ million
See Pages 9 through 22 for Explanation of Ratios and Data

## Comparative Historical Data | Current Data Sorted by Sales

| | | | Type of Statement | | | | | | |
|---|---|---|---|---|---|---|---|---|---|
| 31 | 16 | 18 | Unqualified | 1 | 1 | | | 5 | 11 |
| 69 | 70 | 63 | Reviewed | 2 | 4 | 8 | 21 | 23 | 5 |
| 27 | 23 | 36 | Compiled | 2 | 11 | 7 | 9 | 4 | 3 |
| 46 | 61 | 68 | Tax Returns | 14 | 28 | 12 | 9 | 4 | 1 |
| 57 | 81 | 81 | Other | 9 | 15 | 17 | 20 | 10 | 10 |
| 4/1/09-3/31/10 ALL | 4/1/10-3/31/11 ALL | 4/1/11-3/31/12 ALL | | 40 (4/1-9/30/11) | | | 226 (10/1/11-3/31/12) | | |
| | | | | 0-1MM | 1-3MM | 3-5MM | 5-10MM | 10-25MM | 25MM & OVER |
| 230 | 251 | 266 | NUMBER OF STATEMENTS | 28 | 59 | 44 | 59 | 46 | 30 |
| % | % | % | ASSETS | % | % | % | % | % | % |
| 14.2 | 15.4 | 14.8 | Cash & Equivalents | 17.4 | 16.2 | 13.9 | 11.9 | 15.1 | 15.8 |
| 36.6 | 38.4 | 39.1 | Trade Receivables (net) | 21.8 | 34.6 | 44.7 | 41.7 | 47.9 | 37.5 |
| 10.3 | 9.4 | 10.1 | Inventory | 15.7 | 13.5 | 9.6 | 8.4 | 5.9 | 8.6 |
| 5.2 | 5.2 | 4.7 | All Other Current | 1.1 | 3.2 | 5.0 | 3.6 | 8.0 | 8.1 |
| 66.4 | 68.5 | 68.7 | Total Current | 56.0 | 67.5 | 73.1 | 65.6 | 77.0 | 70.0 |
| 22.8 | 20.9 | 19.1 | Fixed Assets (net) | 19.5 | 22.9 | 15.0 | 20.1 | 17.5 | 17.7 |
| 3.7 | 3.1 | 3.7 | Intangibles (net) | 6.4 | 3.6 | 2.7 | 3.9 | 2.1 | 5.1 |
| 7.1 | 7.6 | 8.5 | All Other Non-Current | 18.1 | 5.9 | 9.2 | 10.3 | 3.5 | 7.3 |
| 100.0 | 100.0 | 100.0 | Total | 100.0 | 100.0 | 100.0 | 100.0 | 100.0 | 100.0 |
| | | | LIABILITIES | | | | | | |
| 13.8 | 11.9 | 12.8 | Notes Payable-Short Term | 18.2 | 15.0 | 13.3 | 15.7 | 7.4 | 4.9 |
| 6.1 | 4.0 | 3.3 | Cur. Mat.-L.T.D. | 3.3 | 3.9 | 3.3 | 3.9 | 2.2 | 2.6 |
| 16.8 | 17.1 | 17.9 | Trade Payables | 21.9 | 16.3 | 15.5 | 17.0 | 21.9 | 16.9 |
| .4 | .4 | .2 | Income Taxes Payable | .0 | .0 | .3 | .4 | .1 | .1 |
| 14.1 | 12.8 | 13.7 | All Other Current | 20.4 | 12.2 | 10.4 | 9.7 | 16.3 | 19.3 |
| 51.2 | 46.2 | 47.9 | Total Current | 63.8 | 47.5 | 42.8 | 46.8 | 47.9 | 43.8 |
| 15.1 | 16.1 | 14.2 | Long-Term Debt | 28.5 | 20.7 | 9.9 | 11.2 | 9.0 | 8.1 |
| .4 | .3 | .3 | Deferred Taxes | .0 | .0 | .1 | .2 | .9 | .9 |
| 5.4 | 6.5 | 11.2 | All Other Non-Current | 41.2 | 7.4 | 9.2 | 6.9 | 4.4 | 12.3 |
| 27.9 | 30.8 | 26.4 | Net Worth | -33.5 | 24.4 | 37.9 | 34.8 | 37.9 | 35.0 |
| 100.0 | 100.0 | 100.0 | Total Liabilties & Net Worth | 100.0 | 100.0 | 100.0 | 100.0 | 100.0 | 100.0 |
| | | | INCOME DATA | | | | | | |
| 100.0 | 100.0 | 100.0 | Net Sales | 100.0 | 100.0 | 100.0 | 100.0 | 100.0 | 100.0 |
| 32.0 | 32.2 | 32.1 | Gross Profit | 47.0 | 39.0 | 29.6 | 32.5 | 22.3 | 22.8 |
| 29.8 | 29.7 | 28.0 | Operating Expenses | 41.7 | 35.4 | 26.1 | 28.6 | 19.2 | 16.0 |
| 2.2 | 2.5 | 4.1 | Operating Profit | 5.3 | 3.7 | 3.5 | 3.9 | 3.1 | 6.8 |
| .5 | .4 | .7 | All Other Expenses (net) | 1.2 | .3 | .9 | .4 | .3 | 1.8 |
| 1.7 | 2.1 | 3.4 | Profit Before Taxes | 4.2 | 3.4 | 2.6 | 3.5 | 2.8 | 5.0 |
| | | | RATIOS | | | | | | |
| 2.7 | 2.9 | 3.1 | Current | 4.3 | 3.3 | 4.4 | 2.8 | 2.1 | 2.2 |
| 1.7 | 1.7 | 1.6 | | 1.6 | 1.5 | 1.7 | 1.7 | 1.6 | 1.5 |
| 1.1 | 1.2 | 1.1 | | .6 | .9 | 1.0 | 1.1 | 1.2 | 1.2 |
| 2.2 | 2.5 | 2.5 | Quick | 4.3 | 2.5 | 3.8 | 2.6 | 1.7 | 1.6 |
| 1.2 | 1.3 | 1.2 | | .9 | 1.0 | 1.3 | 1.4 | 1.3 | 1.2 |
| .7 | .8 | .7 | | .4 | .6 | .9 | .7 | 1.0 | 1.0 |
| 30 12.1 | 31 11.8 | 27 13.6 | Sales/Receivables | 0 UND | 19 19.7 | 27 13.3 | 39 9.4 | 46 7.9 | 34 10.7 |
| 51 7.1 | 53 6.9 | 50 7.3 | | 29 12.7 | 38 9.6 | 47 7.7 | 59 6.2 | 63 5.8 | 53 6.9 |
| 70 5.2 | 75 4.8 | 78 4.7 | | 50 7.3 | 74 4.9 | 94 3.9 | 81 4.5 | 81 4.5 | 76 4.8 |
| 0 UND | 0 UND | 0 UND | Cost of Sales/Inventory | 0 UND | 0 UND | 0 UND | 0 UND | 0 UND | 0 UND |
| 6 65.2 | 2 232.9 | 2 206.7 | | 0 UND | 5 77.3 | 0 UND | 4 82.0 | 2 243.3 | 2 146.9 |
| 33 11.2 | 25 14.6 | 24 15.1 | | 57 6.4 | 43 8.5 | 33 10.9 | 25 14.4 | 15 24.3 | 24 15.0 |
| 10 37.2 | 12 31.7 | 11 32.2 | Cost of Sales/Payables | 6 65.4 | 7 53.0 | 7 54.3 | 13 28.2 | 15 23.7 | 13 28.9 |
| 24 15.3 | 24 15.1 | 24 15.2 | | 26 14.0 | 17 20.9 | 18 19.8 | 32 11.3 | 33 11.2 | 24 15.4 |
| 41 8.8 | 43 8.5 | 53 6.9 | | 78 4.7 | 55 6.6 | 42 8.7 | 61 6.0 | 49 7.4 | 42 8.6 |
| 5.4 | 5.3 | 5.4 | Sales/Working Capital | 2.3 | 6.0 | 4.6 | 5.3 | 5.8 | 6.3 |
| 10.6 | 10.8 | 11.6 | | 18.7 | 20.3 | 12.0 | 10.8 | 9.5 | 10.9 |
| 332.1 | 34.7 | 131.9 | | -18.9 | -150.0 | 228.2 | 198.9 | 25.9 | 23.2 |
| 17.9 | 18.4 | 19.2 | EBIT/Interest | 7.4 | 14.3 | 22.9 | 22.0 | 16.1 | 86.0 |
| (200) 3.7 | (208) 3.8 | (224) 5.2 | | (17) 2.6 | (53) 5.1 | (36) 4.7 | (56) 5.4 | (36) 4.6 | (26) 9.9 |
| -.4 | -.1 | 1.3 | | -3.6 | .9 | 1.1 | 1.4 | 1.5 | 1.8 |
| 9.8 | 7.0 | 5.2 | Net Profit + Depr., Dep., Amort./Cur. Mat. L/T/D | | | | | 4.5 | |
| (34) 3.0 | (33) 2.7 | (33) 2.4 | | | | | | (12) 2.0 | |
| 1.3 | .5 | .8 | | | | | | .2 | |
| .2 | .1 | .1 | Fixed/Worth | .0 | .2 | .1 | .2 | .1 | .1 |
| .4 | .4 | .4 | | 1.4 | .7 | .2 | .4 | .2 | .4 |
| 2.1 | 2.4 | 1.6 | | -.7 | 4.0 | 1.1 | 1.2 | 1.0 | .9 |
| .6 | .7 | .7 | Debt/Worth | 1.2 | .7 | .3 | .7 | 1.0 | .7 |
| 1.6 | 1.6 | 1.9 | | 8.3 | 1.9 | 1.9 | 1.7 | 1.9 | 1.7 |
| 5.9 | 5.5 | 7.9 | | -2.9 | 51.0 | 11.5 | 4.5 | 3.0 | 4.8 |
| 35.7 | 45.6 | 57.5 | % Profit Before Taxes/Tangible Net Worth | 98.4 | 78.0 | 72.3 | 72.7 | 33.4 | 56.3 |
| (188) 12.0 | (211) 13.1 | (223) 17.0 | | (16) 20.9 | (47) 31.9 | (36) 16.2 | (54) 15.1 | (45) 15.4 | (25) 20.5 |
| -3.3 | -1.8 | 2.7 | | 1.5 | -.4 | 3.0 | 2.4 | 2.1 | 13.5 |
| 14.7 | 19.1 | 20.4 | % Profit Before Taxes/Total Assets | 33.9 | 30.6 | 24.8 | 17.3 | 13.1 | 21.0 |
| 4.8 | 4.6 | 6.1 | | 4.4 | 9.6 | 6.5 | 5.2 | 3.9 | 6.9 |
| -3.2 | -2.1 | .5 | | .7 | .2 | .8 | .3 | .5 | 2.6 |
| 46.6 | 59.9 | 81.5 | Sales/Net Fixed Assets | 328.1 | 85.0 | 95.8 | 70.0 | 85.3 | 68.1 |
| 19.9 | 22.9 | 29.4 | | 27.8 | 25.4 | 35.6 | 29.3 | 40.8 | 27.9 |
| 8.5 | 8.9 | 10.8 | | 8.4 | 10.9 | 15.2 | 9.1 | 10.4 | 8.4 |
| 3.7 | 3.6 | 4.0 | Sales/Total Assets | 4.4 | 4.4 | 5.1 | 3.4 | 3.7 | 3.3 |
| 2.8 | 2.6 | 2.8 | | 2.0 | 3.2 | 3.0 | 2.5 | 2.9 | 2.8 |
| 1.9 | 1.8 | 1.9 | | 1.1 | 2.0 | 2.3 | 1.7 | 2.0 | 2.0 |
| .7 | .6 | .6 | % Depr., Dep., Amort./Sales | 1.0 | .9 | .6 | .5 | .3 | .4 |
| (189) 1.5 | (183) 1.5 | (198) 1.2 | | (13) 3.5 | (39) 1.5 | (31) 1.2 | (49) 1.0 | (39) 1.0 | (27) 1.1 |
| 2.9 | 2.7 | 2.7 | | 8.5 | 2.6 | 3.5 | 2.5 | 2.3 | 1.6 |
| 2.2 | 2.6 | 1.8 | % Officers', Directors' Owners' Comp/Sales | 3.6 | 2.3 | 2.8 | 1.6 | 1.7 | |
| (105) 4.7 | (111) 5.3 | (120) 3.8 | | (10) 7.2 | (34) 4.7 | (23) 4.6 | (27) 3.4 | (19) 3.3 | |
| 7.7 | 8.2 | 6.4 | | 17.4 | 7.2 | 5.9 | 7.1 | 5.0 | |
| 3862510M | 3611445M | 3283972M | Net Sales ($) | 14791M | 121013M | 180433M | 415446M | 724159M | 1828130M |
| 2061419M | 1905667M | 1443856M | Total Assets ($) | 9874M | 44320M | 68535M | 185230M | 300942M | 834955M |

## Current Data Sorted by Assets | Comparative Historical Data

| Type of Statement | 0-500M | 500M-2MM | 2-10MM | 10-50MM | 50-100MM | 100-250MM | | 4/1/07-3/31/08 ALL | 4/1/08-3/31/09 ALL |
|---|---|---|---|---|---|---|---|---|---|
| Unqualified | | 6 | 6 | 12 | 6 | 2 | | 38 | 41 |
| Reviewed | | 28 | 68 | 10 | 1 | | | 90 | 123 |
| Compiled | 7 | 24 | 9 | 3 | | | | 45 | 41 |
| Tax Returns | 33 | 24 | 9 | 2 | | | | 47 | 67 |
| Other | 14 | 39 | 29 | 11 | 2 | 1 | | 87 | 101 |
| | | 63 (4/1-9/30/11) | | 283 (10/1/11-3/31/12) | | | | | |
| NUMBER OF STATEMENTS | 54 | 121 | 121 | 38 | 9 | 3 | | 307 | 373 |
| **ASSETS** | % | % | % | % | % | % | | % | % |
| Cash & Equivalents | 20.7 | 13.2 | 13.7 | 12.3 | | | | 13.0 | 14.1 |
| Trade Receivables (net) | 32.8 | 50.6 | 51.3 | 50.4 | | | | 54.2 | 51.5 |
| Inventory | 6.9 | 5.6 | 4.7 | 3.2 | | | | 5.1 | 6.0 |
| All Other Current | 3.6 | 4.8 | 9.9 | 12.3 | | | | 7.7 | 6.8 |
| Total Current | 64.0 | 74.2 | 79.6 | 78.1 | | | | 80.1 | 78.4 |
| Fixed Assets (net) | 21.5 | 15.0 | 9.4 | 13.2 | | | | 12.5 | 12.7 |
| Intangibles (net) | 3.2 | 2.0 | 2.0 | 1.4 | | | | 1.4 | 1.4 |
| All Other Non-Current | 11.3 | 8.8 | 8.9 | 7.3 | | | | 6.0 | 7.5 |
| Total | 100.0 | 100.0 | 100.0 | 100.0 | | | | 100.0 | 100.0 |
| **LIABILITIES** | | | | | | | | | |
| Notes Payable-Short Term | 29.8 | 13.5 | 10.7 | 6.9 | | | | 12.3 | 14.2 |
| Cur. Mat.-L.T.D. | 5.5 | 2.0 | 1.6 | 1.1 | | | | 2.5 | 3.0 |
| Trade Payables | 21.0 | 17.1 | 16.1 | 14.1 | | | | 14.1 | 14.9 |
| Income Taxes Payable | .0 | .3 | .4 | .1 | | | | .6 | .5 |
| All Other Current | 14.0 | 12.4 | 14.5 | 19.0 | | | | 18.2 | 18.5 |
| Total Current | 70.3 | 45.3 | 43.2 | 41.2 | | | | 47.8 | 51.1 |
| Long-Term Debt | 24.5 | 10.2 | 5.0 | 4.2 | | | | 7.8 | 7.7 |
| Deferred Taxes | .0 | .4 | .2 | .0 | | | | .3 | .2 |
| All Other Non-Current | 8.7 | 5.6 | 3.6 | 4.4 | | | | 4.3 | 4.2 |
| Net Worth | -3.7 | 38.4 | 47.9 | 50.2 | | | | 39.8 | 36.8 |
| Total Liabilties & Net Worth | 100.0 | 100.0 | 100.0 | 100.0 | | | | 100.0 | 100.0 |
| **INCOME DATA** | | | | | | | | | |
| Net Sales | 100.0 | 100.0 | 100.0 | 100.0 | | | | 100.0 | 100.0 |
| Gross Profit | 33.0 | 26.5 | 19.2 | 13.5 | | | | 25.7 | 26.1 |
| Operating Expenses | 30.3 | 26.6 | 18.0 | 13.1 | | | | 19.9 | 22.4 |
| Operating Profit | 2.7 | .0 | 1.2 | .4 | | | | 5.8 | 3.7 |
| All Other Expenses (net) | .8 | .2 | .5 | -.2 | | | | .2 | .4 |
| Profit Before Taxes | 1.9 | -.2 | .8 | .6 | | | | 5.6 | 3.3 |
| **RATIOS** | | | | | | | | | |
| Current | 2.3 | 3.2 | 3.4 | 2.7 | | | | 2.8 | 2.5 |
| | 1.2 | 1.8 | 1.9 | 2.0 | | | | 1.8 | 1.7 |
| | .6 | 1.1 | 1.3 | 1.5 | | | | 1.3 | 1.2 |
| Quick | 2.1 | 2.8 | 2.9 | 2.0 | | | | 2.3 | 2.3 |
| | 1.0 | 1.5 | 1.6 | 1.6 | | | | 1.5 | 1.4 |
| | .3 | 1.0 | 1.0 | 1.2 | | | | 1.0 | .9 |
| Sales/Receivables | 0 UND | 39   9.3 | 58   6.3 | 60   6.1 | | | | 43   8.5 | 41   8.9 |
| | 20   18.2 | 61   6.0 | 78   4.7 | 78   4.7 | | | | 66   5.5 | 62   5.9 |
| | 58   6.3 | 81   4.5 | 96   3.8 | 96   3.8 | | | | 84   4.3 | 82   4.4 |
| Cost of Sales/Inventory | 0 UND | 0 UND | 0 UND | 0 UND | | | | 0 UND | 0 UND |
| | 0 UND | 2   218.6 | 2   181.3 | 2   202.6 | | | | 1   298.2 | 1   398.5 |
| | 5   72.3 | 14   26.2 | 14   26.9 | 6   56.5 | | | | 9   40.0 | 10   38.2 |
| Cost of Sales/Payables | 0 UND | 11   34.4 | 14   26.1 | 18   19.9 | | | | 9   41.9 | 9   41.9 |
| | 9   38.9 | 21   17.2 | 21   17.2 | 23   16.0 | | | | 18   20.7 | 18   20.6 |
| | 31   11.6 | 40   9.1 | 40   9.2 | 30   12.2 | | | | 29   12.8 | 32   11.5 |
| Sales/Working Capital | 12.5 | 5.8 | 4.3 | 4.7 | | | | 5.8 | 6.1 |
| | 51.9 | 8.9 | 6.8 | 6.3 | | | | 9.1 | 9.7 |
| | -19.4 | 35.3 | 13.5 | 9.9 | | | | 19.5 | 32.3 |
| EBIT/Interest | 7.8 | 13.4 | 13.0 | 21.9 | | | | 27.8 | 25.5 |
| | (41) 3.7 | (101) 2.3 | (95) 2.0 | (27) 2.8 | | | | (267) 8.4 | (324) 6.7 |
| | -.6 | -5.3 | -4.1 | -6.2 | | | | 2.0 | 1.3 |
| Net Profit + Depr., Dep., Amort./Cur. Mat. L/T/D | | 2.5 | 9.2 | 126.2 | | | | 17.6 | 17.8 |
| | | (11) -2.3 | (28) .9 | (10) 10.2 | | | | (69) 5.4 | (72) 4.4 |
| | | -7.4 | -5.2 | -5.1 | | | | 1.2 | .9 |
| Fixed/Worth | .1 | .1 | .0 | .0 | | | | .1 | .1 |
| | .9 | .2 | .1 | .2 | | | | .2 | .2 |
| | -.9 | 1.1 | .4 | .3 | | | | .6 | .6 |
| Debt/Worth | .7 | .5 | .4 | .5 | | | | .6 | .7 |
| | 7.3 | 1.2 | 1.2 | 1.0 | | | | 1.4 | 1.5 |
| | -3.0 | 5.4 | 2.5 | 1.9 | | | | 3.1 | 3.8 |
| % Profit Before Taxes/Tangible Net Worth | 90.6 | 44.1 | 22.3 | 23.7 | | | | 63.9 | 51.3 |
| | (31) 24.1 | (101) 4.6 | (114) 6.0 | 4.8 | | | | (287) 33.0 | (334) 23.7 |
| | .6 | -13.5 | -6.5 | -4.4 | | | | 9.8 | 4.8 |
| % Profit Before Taxes/Total Assets | 25.7 | 13.7 | 11.8 | 11.7 | | | | 27.2 | 19.7 |
| | 11.8 | 1.3 | 2.8 | 1.6 | | | | 13.2 | 8.6 |
| | -14.9 | -8.7 | -4.3 | -2.2 | | | | 3.8 | .7 |
| Sales/Net Fixed Assets | 471.6 | 87.9 | 99.6 | 111.2 | | | | 99.5 | 109.8 |
| | 50.5 | 33.1 | 43.4 | 50.0 | | | | 46.4 | 40.8 |
| | 19.9 | 13.0 | 23.3 | 17.1 | | | | 21.7 | 19.4 |
| Sales/Total Assets | 8.1 | 4.0 | 3.0 | 3.0 | | | | 4.0 | 4.2 |
| | 4.8 | 3.0 | 2.5 | 2.7 | | | | 3.2 | 3.1 |
| | 3.5 | 2.3 | 1.9 | 1.7 | | | | 2.5 | 2.4 |
| % Depr., Dep., Amort./Sales | .5 | .5 | .3 | .3 | | | | .3 | .3 |
| | (30) .9 | (88) .8 | (101) .6 | (32) .5 | | | | (241) .6 | (297) .7 |
| | 2.3 | 1.3 | 1.1 | .8 | | | | 1.1 | 1.4 |
| % Officers', Directors' Owners' Comp/Sales | 2.9 | 1.9 | 1.9 | | | | | 1.9 | 2.1 |
| | (32) 4.7 | (70) 4.0 | (58) 2.8 | | | | | (157) 3.2 | (203) 4.1 |
| | 6.7 | 5.7 | 5.1 | | | | | 7.0 | 7.3 |
| Net Sales ($) | 76290M | 423367M | 1338650M | 1644288M | 1193244M | 592405M | | 5783832M | 7181181M |
| Total Assets ($) | 13252M | 134726M | 548704M | 685652M | 720300M | 352641M | | 2048015M | 2891712M |

© RMA 2012

M = $ thousand    MM = $ million

See Pages 9 through 22 for Explanation of Ratios and Data

## Comparative Historical Data | Current Data Sorted by Sales

| | | | Type of Statement | | | | | | |
|---|---|---|---|---|---|---|---|---|---|
| 48 | 43 | 32 | Unqualified | | | 6 | | 7 | 19 |
| 131 | 104 | 107 | Reviewed | 1 | 12 | 11 | 43 | 30 | 10 |
| 33 | 44 | 43 | Compiled | 2 | 14 | 14 | 8 | 3 | 2 |
| 62 | 68 | 68 | Tax Returns | 14 | 30 | 12 | 8 | 3 | 1 |
| 91 | 104 | 96 | Other | 7 | 29 | 12 | 20 | 14 | 14 |
| 4/1/09-3/31/10 ALL | 4/1/10-3/31/11 ALL | 4/1/11-3/31/12 ALL | | 63 (4/1-9/30/11) | | | 283 (10/1/11-3/31/12) | | |
| | | | | 0-1MM | 1-3MM | 3-5MM | 5-10MM | 10-25MM | 25MM & OVER |
| 365 | 363 | 346 | NUMBER OF STATEMENTS | 24 | 85 | 55 | 79 | 57 | 46 |
| % | % | % | **ASSETS** | % | % | % | % | % | % |
| 16.4 | 15.2 | 15.1 | Cash & Equivalents | 21.2 | 16.2 | 13.3 | 15.5 | 9.9 | 17.9 |
| 45.6 | 45.7 | 47.6 | Trade Receivables (net) | 28.3 | 38.4 | 55.1 | 50.1 | 56.3 | 50.6 |
| 5.4 | 4.9 | 5.1 | Inventory | 6.0 | 7.8 | 3.4 | 4.9 | 4.2 | 3.2 |
| 8.1 | 7.7 | 7.4 | All Other Current | 5.5 | 3.7 | 5.2 | 8.3 | 9.8 | 13.7 |
| 75.4 | 73.4 | 75.3 | Total Current | 61.0 | 66.1 | 77.0 | 78.9 | 80.1 | 85.4 |
| 14.4 | 16.0 | 13.5 | Fixed Assets (net) | 24.1 | 20.0 | 14.1 | 8.8 | 11.0 | 6.7 |
| 3.1 | 2.7 | 2.2 | Intangibles (net) | 1.0 | 3.3 | 1.6 | 3.0 | 1.4 | 1.6 |
| 7.0 | 7.8 | 9.0 | All Other Non-Current | 13.9 | 10.6 | 7.4 | 9.4 | 7.5 | 6.2 |
| 100.0 | 100.0 | 100.0 | Total | 100.0 | 100.0 | 100.0 | 100.0 | 100.0 | 100.0 |
| | | | **LIABILITIES** | | | | | | |
| 17.4 | 17.1 | 14.1 | Notes Payable-Short Term | 32.5 | 14.6 | 17.1 | 12.2 | 10.6 | 7.5 |
| 2.2 | 2.2 | 2.3 | Cur. Mat.-L.T.D. | 2.4 | 3.8 | 1.5 | 2.4 | 1.8 | .6 |
| 14.1 | 15.7 | 16.8 | Trade Payables | 25.6 | 13.6 | 19.4 | 15.6 | 19.2 | 14.1 |
| .4 | .4 | .3 | Income Taxes Payable | .0 | .3 | .2 | .4 | .3 | .1 |
| 16.3 | 15.5 | 14.4 | All Other Current | 6.6 | 14.7 | 12.7 | 13.2 | 15.4 | 20.6 |
| 50.4 | 50.8 | 47.8 | Total Current | 67.1 | 47.1 | 50.8 | 43.7 | 47.3 | 43.0 |
| 11.1 | 10.4 | 9.8 | Long-Term Debt | 27.2 | 14.6 | 12.6 | 4.9 | 5.1 | 3.0 |
| .4 | .3 | .2 | Deferred Taxes | .0 | .1 | .7 | .3 | .1 | .1 |
| 4.3 | 7.1 | 5.2 | All Other Non-Current | 12.4 | 5.5 | 5.1 | 6.0 | 2.5 | 2.8 |
| 33.8 | 31.4 | 37.0 | Net Worth | -7.0 | 32.7 | 30.7 | 45.2 | 45.1 | 51.1 |
| 100.0 | 100.0 | 100.0 | Total Liabilities & Net Worth | 100.0 | 100.0 | 100.0 | 100.0 | 100.0 | 100.0 |
| | | | **INCOME DATA** | | | | | | |
| 100.0 | 100.0 | 100.0 | Net Sales | 100.0 | 100.0 | 100.0 | 100.0 | 100.0 | 100.0 |
| 25.5 | 25.3 | 23.2 | Gross Profit | 34.5 | 34.0 | 21.6 | 19.3 | 16.7 | 14.3 |
| 23.7 | 24.7 | 22.3 | Operating Expenses | 31.6 | 33.8 | 22.0 | 17.1 | 16.1 | 13.3 |
| 1.8 | .7 | .9 | Operating Profit | 2.9 | .2 | -.5 | 2.2 | .6 | 1.0 |
| .6 | .4 | .3 | All Other Expenses (net) | 1.1 | .6 | -.1 | .4 | .4 | -.4 |
| 1.2 | .2 | .6 | Profit Before Taxes | 1.8 | -.5 | -.3 | 1.8 | .2 | 1.4 |
| | | | **RATIOS** | | | | | | |
| 3.1 | 3.0 | 3.0 | Current | 3.6 | 2.8 | 3.2 | 3.8 | 2.7 | 2.8 |
| 1.8 | 1.8 | 1.8 | | 1.1 | 1.6 | 1.8 | 1.9 | 1.8 | 2.2 |
| 1.2 | 1.1 | 1.1 | | .2 | .9 | 1.1 | 1.3 | 1.2 | 1.6 |
| 2.5 | 2.7 | 2.6 | Quick | 3.2 | 2.5 | 2.8 | 3.1 | 2.3 | 2.1 |
| 1.5 | 1.4 | 1.5 | | .8 | 1.3 | 1.5 | 1.6 | 1.4 | 1.8 |
| .9 | .9 | 1.0 | | .1 | .7 | 1.0 | 1.0 | 1.0 | 1.3 |
| 39 9.3 | 40 9.0 | 41 8.8 | Sales/Receivables | 0 UND | 23 15.6 | 46 8.0 | 42 8.6 | 60 6.1 | 60 6.1 |
| 60 6.1 | 62 5.9 | 68 5.4 | | 11 34.5 | 51 7.1 | 69 5.3 | 68 5.4 | 74 4.9 | 79 4.6 |
| 78 4.7 | 83 4.4 | 89 4.1 | | 94 3.9 | 74 4.9 | 91 4.0 | 91 4.0 | 91 4.0 | 96 3.8 |
| 0 UND | 0 UND | 0 UND | Cost of Sales/Inventory | 0 UND | 0 UND | 0 UND | 0 UND | 0 UND | 0 UND |
| 1 345.3 | 1 333.5 | 2 223.8 | | 0 UND | 2 155.3 | 0 917.3 | 1 647.0 | 3 133.5 | 2 220.4 |
| 9 39.1 | 9 38.5 | 12 30.7 | | 13 27.6 | 19 18.9 | 7 51.4 | 11 34.0 | 10 38.0 | 5 67.1 |
| 9 40.9 | 10 38.1 | 11 32.3 | Cost of Sales/Payables | 0 UND | 4 82.6 | 13 27.5 | 12 30.8 | 13 27.3 | 17 22.0 |
| 17 21.3 | 19 19.2 | 21 17.3 | | 23 16.0 | 17 21.7 | 21 17.3 | 21 17.5 | 24 15.3 | 22 16.6 |
| 32 11.5 | 33 10.9 | 38 9.6 | | 57 6.4 | 38 9.7 | 46 8.0 | 38 9.7 | 40 9.2 | 29 12.7 |
| 5.3 | 5.0 | 5.1 | Sales/Working Capital | 3.7 | 6.4 | 5.0 | 4.7 | 5.7 | 4.2 |
| 8.7 | 8.8 | 8.1 | | UND | 13.3 | 7.5 | 8.0 | 7.5 | 5.7 |
| 29.0 | 88.9 | 29.9 | | -9.1 | -91.6 | 29.6 | 18.5 | 18.9 | 8.4 |
| 20.9 | 12.9 | 13.1 | EBIT/Interest | 5.1 | 13.1 | 11.4 | 15.4 | 13.0 | 26.8 |
| (317) 5.1 | (312) 3.1 | (274) 2.6 | | (15) 3.7 | (72) 2.0 | (46) .1 | (61) 3.2 | (46) 2.2 | (34) 4.9 |
| -.4 | -5.0 | -3.4 | | -.4 | -2.5 | -12.7 | -2.2 | -4.2 | -2.3 |
| 15.4 | 8.6 | 9.4 | Net Profit + Depr., Dep., Amort./Cur. Mat. L/T/D | | | .0 | 9.2 | 10.1 | 48.7 |
| (66) 3.0 | (66) 3.1 | (57) 1.1 | | | (10) -5.4 | | (11) 1.1 | (16) 5.3 | (14) 5.0 |
| .5 | -.7 | -5.4 | | | -25.3 | | -1.9 | -1.8 | .2 |
| .1 | .1 | .1 | Fixed/Worth | .0 | .1 | .1 | .1 | .1 | .0 |
| .2 | .3 | .2 | | .9 | .5 | .2 | .1 | .1 | .1 |
| .9 | .9 | .8 | | -.9 | 2.4 | 1.1 | .4 | .5 | .2 |
| .6 | .6 | .5 | Debt/Worth | .4 | .6 | .5 | .4 | .5 | .5 |
| 1.3 | 1.3 | 1.3 | | -26.0 | 2.3 | 1.4 | 1.0 | 1.3 | .9 |
| 5.5 | 4.4 | 4.5 | | -2.5 | 9.0 | 3.7 | 3.2 | 2.1 | 1.8 |
| 38.5 | 34.5 | 27.8 | % Profit Before Taxes/Tangible Net Worth | 46.8 | 45.6 | 47.8 | 29.3 | 22.0 | 23.7 |
| (310) 13.4 | (300) 7.2 | (296) 7.0 | | (11) 11.6 | (68) 9.3 | (46) 3.4 | (70) 11.7 | (55) 3.8 | 8.9 |
| .1 | -5.6 | -6.6 | | -13.5 | -24.8 | -14.2 | -2.8 | -3.9 | -1.1 |
| 17.7 | 12.7 | 14.0 | % Profit Before Taxes/Total Assets | 21.1 | 15.1 | 17.6 | 13.3 | 9.3 | 10.8 |
| 4.8 | 2.6 | 2.8 | | 9.0 | 1.9 | .6 | 4.6 | 1.5 | 3.6 |
| -2.8 | -7.4 | -5.6 | | -14.3 | -8.8 | -9.7 | -2.6 | -2.5 | -.6 |
| 77.8 | 75.2 | 101.8 | Sales/Net Fixed Assets | UND | 66.5 | 80.9 | 116.0 | 108.4 | 173.1 |
| 37.2 | 31.0 | 43.3 | | 38.7 | 27.6 | 33.1 | 52.0 | 46.7 | 59.9 |
| 17.2 | 16.8 | 17.7 | | 6.2 | 9.6 | 18.4 | 25.8 | 19.5 | 27.4 |
| 3.8 | 3.8 | 3.7 | Sales/Total Assets | 5.4 | 4.4 | 3.7 | 3.6 | 3.2 | 3.0 |
| 2.9 | 2.8 | 2.8 | | 3.3 | 3.2 | 3.0 | 2.8 | 2.7 | 2.7 |
| 2.2 | 2.1 | 2.1 | | 1.5 | 2.1 | 2.3 | 2.0 | 2.1 | 1.6 |
| .4 | .4 | .3 | % Depr., Dep., Amort./Sales | .5 | .6 | .3 | .3 | .3 | .3 |
| (300) .8 | (294) .9 | (262) .7 | | (13) 1.4 | (51) 1.2 | (47) .8 | (64) .7 | (49) .6 | (38) .4 |
| 1.4 | 1.5 | 1.2 | | 3.1 | 2.6 | 1.2 | 1.2 | .9 | .6 |
| 2.2 | 2.0 | 1.9 | % Officers', Directors' Owners' Comp/Sales | 4.1 | 2.7 | 2.0 | 1.9 | .8 | |
| (184) 4.4 | (208) 4.1 | (170) 3.6 | | (11) 6.7 | (50) 5.3 | (35) 4.1 | (37) 3.1 | (28) 2.3 | |
| 8.0 | 7.9 | 5.7 | | 15.0 | 7.6 | 5.3 | 4.3 | 3.7 | |
| 6602220M | 6570339M | 5268244M | Net Sales ($) | 10799M | 169125M | 213692M | 553852M | 924490M | 3396286M |
| 3060904M | 2534927M | 2455275M | Total Assets ($) | 5307M | 73159M | 81681M | 223462M | 381102M | 1690564M |

© RMA 2012

M = $ thousand    MM = $ million
See Pages 9 through 22 for Explanation of Ratios and Data

## Current Data Sorted by Assets     Comparative Historical Data

| Type of Statement | 0-500M | 500M-2MM | 2-10MM | 10-50MM | 50-100MM | 100-250MM | | 4/1/07-3/31/08 ALL | 4/1/08-3/31/09 ALL |
|---|---|---|---|---|---|---|---|---|---|
| Unqualified | | 4 | 11 | 1 | | | | 21 | 22 |
| Reviewed | 3 | 27 | 38 | 3 | | | | 37 | 73 |
| Compiled | 6 | 10 | 5 | | | | | 27 | 31 |
| Tax Returns | 27 | 12 | 2 | 5 | | | | 34 | 42 |
| Other | 15 | 19 | 17 | | | | | 47 | 43 |
| | 38 (4/1-9/30/11) | | | 167 (10/1/11-3/31/12) | | | | | |
| NUMBER OF STATEMENTS | 51 | 72 | 73 | 9 | | | | 166 | 211 |
| | % | % | % | % | % | % | ASSETS | % | % |
| Cash & Equivalents | 25.4 | 16.2 | 18.7 | | DATA | DATA | | 12.5 | 14.1 |
| Trade Receivables (net) | 19.2 | 46.5 | 48.2 | | NOT | NOT | | 44.8 | 45.7 |
| Inventory | 1.0 | 4.1 | 1.3 | | AVAILABLE | AVAILABLE | | 2.3 | 3.1 |
| All Other Current | 9.7 | 7.8 | 8.7 | | | | | 9.3 | 10.0 |
| Total Current | 55.3 | 74.6 | 76.9 | | | | | 68.9 | 73.0 |
| Fixed Assets (net) | 30.4 | 17.9 | 15.2 | | | | | 22.6 | 18.6 |
| Intangibles (net) | 2.7 | 2.2 | 1.5 | | | | | 2.2 | 2.0 |
| All Other Non-Current | 11.7 | 5.3 | 6.4 | | | | | 6.3 | 6.4 |
| Total | 100.0 | 100.0 | 100.0 | | | | | 100.0 | 100.0 |
| | | | | | | | LIABILITIES | | |
| Notes Payable-Short Term | 33.1 | 14.6 | 7.3 | | | | | 17.2 | 13.7 |
| Cur. Mat.-L.T.D. | 10.2 | 2.3 | 1.3 | | | | | 4.0 | 4.8 |
| Trade Payables | 12.6 | 12.0 | 14.8 | | | | | 13.9 | 13.1 |
| Income Taxes Payable | .3 | .3 | .7 | | | | | .6 | .7 |
| All Other Current | 16.6 | 10.9 | 13.3 | | | | | 12.4 | 16.8 |
| Total Current | 72.7 | 40.2 | 37.3 | | | | | 48.2 | 49.2 |
| Long-Term Debt | 18.2 | 8.0 | 5.1 | | | | | 16.1 | 11.2 |
| Deferred Taxes | .9 | .5 | .6 | | | | | .5 | .4 |
| All Other Non-Current | 7.7 | 6.5 | 2.0 | | | | | 7.7 | 5.3 |
| Net Worth | .4 | 44.8 | 54.9 | | | | | 27.5 | 33.9 |
| Total Liabilities & Net Worth | 100.0 | 100.0 | 100.0 | | | | | 100.0 | 100.0 |
| | | | | | | | INCOME DATA | | |
| Net Sales | 100.0 | 100.0 | 100.0 | | | | | 100.0 | 100.0 |
| Gross Profit | 39.9 | 29.2 | 24.8 | | | | | 31.3 | 31.9 |
| Operating Expenses | 36.9 | 27.1 | 20.2 | | | | | 26.0 | 26.8 |
| Operating Profit | 3.1 | 2.2 | 4.6 | | | | | 5.4 | 5.1 |
| All Other Expenses (net) | .2 | .5 | .2 | | | | | .4 | .6 |
| Profit Before Taxes | 2.9 | 1.6 | 4.4 | | | | | 4.9 | 4.5 |
| | | | | | | | RATIOS | | |
| Current | 4.3 | 3.9 | 4.4 | | | | | 2.7 | 2.9 |
| | .9 | 2.0 | 2.5 | | | | | 1.8 | 1.8 |
| | .4 | 1.3 | 1.4 | | | | | 1.1 | 1.2 |
| Quick | 3.8 | 3.3 | 3.8 | | | | | 2.2 | 2.6 |
| | .7 | 1.6 | 2.2 | | | | | 1.5 | 1.4 |
| | .2 | .9 | 1.2 | | | | | .9 | .9 |
| Sales/Receivables | 0 UND | 38 9.7 | 51 7.1 | | | | | 25 14.4 | 32 11.4 |
| | 3 140.3 | 58 6.3 | 70 5.2 | | | | | 58 6.3 | 57 6.4 |
| | 30 12.1 | 79 4.6 | 87 4.2 | | | | | 77 4.7 | 80 4.6 |
| Cost of Sales/Inventory | 0 UND | 0 UND | 0 UND | | | | | 0 UND | 0 UND |
| | 0 UND | 0 UND | 0 UND | | | | | 0 UND | 0 UND |
| | 0 UND | 3 137.4 | 1 345.6 | | | | | 3 133.4 | 1 336.0 |
| Cost of Sales/Payables | 0 UND | 3 112.1 | 10 36.2 | | | | | 6 57.7 | 7 51.4 |
| | 2 165.5 | 18 20.6 | 18 20.1 | | | | | 19 19.7 | 15 24.9 |
| | 19 19.1 | 28 13.2 | 38 9.7 | | | | | 35 10.4 | 30 12.1 |
| Sales/Working Capital | 11.1 | 4.3 | 3.9 | | | | | 6.0 | 5.6 |
| | -71.1 | 8.9 | 6.1 | | | | | 10.6 | 10.3 |
| | -7.8 | 17.5 | 11.7 | | | | | 51.3 | 34.3 |
| EBIT/Interest | 11.0 | 15.6 | 43.0 | | | | | 26.4 | 25.5 |
| | (41) 3.4 | (63) 5.0 | (61) 7.5 | | | | | (149) 7.8 | (184) 8.0 |
| | -.9 | -1.7 | .0 | | | | | 2.3 | 2.0 |
| Net Profit + Depr., Dep., Amort./Cur. Mat. L/T/D | | | 31.0 | | | | | 8.6 | 8.3 |
| | | (11) | 7.6 | | | | | (28) 5.0 | (44) 3.5 |
| | | | 3.2 | | | | | 1.1 | 1.7 |
| Fixed/Worth | .1 | .1 | .1 | | | | | .1 | .1 |
| | 2.5 | .4 | .2 | | | | | .4 | .4 |
| | -1.0 | .8 | .5 | | | | | 1.1 | 1.0 |
| Debt/Worth | .5 | .4 | .3 | | | | | .6 | .6 |
| | 6.0 | .9 | .7 | | | | | 1.4 | 1.4 |
| | -3.8 | 3.1 | 2.3 | | | | | 4.0 | 4.2 |
| % Profit Before Taxes/Tangible Net Worth | 132.1 | 44.5 | 27.5 | | | | | 58.7 | 60.0 |
| | (29) 53.0 | (64) 12.8 | (70) 13.0 | | | | | (141) 26.3 | (188) 25.0 |
| | -1.7 | -8.8 | 1.2 | | | | | 10.0 | 9.0 |
| % Profit Before Taxes/Total Assets | 50.0 | 20.6 | 16.3 | | | | | 31.1 | 27.7 |
| | 14.4 | 6.1 | 5.0 | | | | | 12.2 | 9.0 |
| | -9.8 | -4.8 | .8 | | | | | 3.7 | 2.8 |
| Sales/Net Fixed Assets | 65.6 | 50.0 | 58.6 | | | | | 64.1 | 79.2 |
| | 29.8 | 21.4 | 25.3 | | | | | 23.9 | 27.6 |
| | 14.3 | 10.7 | 11.2 | | | | | 11.8 | 13.3 |
| Sales/Total Assets | 9.3 | 3.6 | 3.2 | | | | | 4.2 | 4.4 |
| | 5.4 | 2.9 | 2.5 | | | | | 3.3 | 3.3 |
| | 3.2 | 2.0 | 1.5 | | | | | 2.4 | 2.4 |
| % Depr., Dep., Amort./Sales | .6 | 1.0 | .6 | | | | | .6 | .5 |
| | (35) 1.2 | (51) 1.8 | (62) 1.1 | | | | | (140) 1.0 | (167) .9 |
| | 1.6 | 2.3 | 1.7 | | | | | 1.9 | 1.7 |
| % Officers', Directors' Owners' Comp/Sales | 3.2 | 3.6 | 1.9 | | | | | 2.6 | 2.3 |
| | (29) 6.2 | (40) 5.4 | (38) 3.7 | | | | | (99) 4.8 | (105) 4.6 |
| | 12.0 | 8.3 | 6.0 | | | | | 8.5 | 8.8 |
| Net Sales ($) | 67445M | 253784M | 710896M | 250116M | | | | 1615756M | 2593286M |
| Total Assets ($) | 11657M | 83553M | 289864M | 148443M | | | | 548628M | 724646M |

M = $ thousand    MM = $ million

See Pages 9 through 22 for Explanation of Ratios and Data

## Comparative Historical Data | Current Data Sorted by Sales

| | 4/1/09-3/31/10 ALL | 4/1/10-3/31/11 ALL | 4/1/11-3/31/12 ALL | Type of Statement | 0-1MM | 1-3MM | 3-5MM | 5-10MM | 10-25MM | 25MM & OVER |
|---|---|---|---|---|---|---|---|---|---|---|
| | 19 | 16 | 16 | Unqualified | | 2 | 13 | 24 | 15 | 1 |
| | 65 | 60 | 71 | Reviewed | 1 | 16 | 5 | 5 | 1 | 2 |
| | 31 | 24 | 21 | Compiled | 5 | 5 | 5 | 2 | 1 | |
| | 33 | 45 | 41 | Tax Returns | 12 | 20 | 4 | 4 | 6 | 3 |
| | 52 | 50 | 56 | Other | 9 | 16 | 10 | 9 | 9 | |
| | | | | | 38 (4/1-9/30/11) | | | 167 (10/1/11-3/31/12) | | |
| NUMBER OF STATEMENTS | 200 | 195 | 205 | | 27 | 59 | 37 | 44 | 32 | 6 |
| | % | % | % | **ASSETS** | % | % | % | % | % | % |
| | 16.5 | 17.9 | 19.9 | Cash & Equivalents | 28.3 | 20.5 | 16.2 | 16.3 | 20.2 | |
| | 44.0 | 41.2 | 39.8 | Trade Receivables (net) | 15.4 | 32.5 | 46.3 | 50.0 | 52.1 | |
| | 2.6 | 2.6 | 2.2 | Inventory | 3.9 | 2.6 | 2.5 | 2.0 | .2 | |
| | 8.4 | 9.5 | 8.7 | All Other Current | 8.8 | 10.4 | 5.9 | 6.9 | 9.8 | |
| | 71.5 | 71.1 | 70.5 | Total Current | 56.4 | 66.1 | 70.9 | 75.1 | 82.3 | |
| | 19.7 | 19.1 | 20.2 | Fixed Assets (net) | 29.2 | 22.3 | 20.2 | 18.3 | 11.2 | |
| | 1.8 | 2.8 | 2.2 | Intangibles (net) | 2.5 | 2.7 | 1.7 | 1.3 | 3.2 | |
| | 7.1 | 7.0 | 7.1 | All Other Non-Current | 11.9 | 8.9 | 7.2 | 5.3 | 3.3 | |
| | 100.0 | 100.0 | 100.0 | Total | 100.0 | 100.0 | 100.0 | 100.0 | 100.0 | |
| | | | | **LIABILITIES** | | | | | | |
| | 16.3 | 18.3 | 16.2 | Notes Payable-Short Term | 24.2 | 24.9 | 8.0 | 13.9 | 8.2 | |
| | 3.5 | 2.5 | 3.9 | Cur. Mat.-L.T.D. | 10.4 | 4.4 | 2.4 | 2.9 | 1.2 | |
| | 12.4 | 12.9 | 13.3 | Trade Payables | 11.1 | 9.9 | 13.4 | 16.9 | 16.3 | |
| | .6 | .8 | .4 | Income Taxes Payable | .0 | .3 | .5 | .2 | 1.2 | |
| | 14.7 | 15.6 | 13.3 | All Other Current | 15.2 | 13.9 | 12.3 | 12.8 | 10.8 | |
| | 47.4 | 50.2 | 47.1 | Total Current | 60.8 | 53.3 | 36.6 | 46.7 | 37.6 | |
| | 9.4 | 11.4 | 9.5 | Long-Term Debt | 13.6 | 12.9 | 9.8 | 7.8 | 3.1 | |
| | .5 | .3 | .6 | Deferred Taxes | .0 | .1 | 1.3 | 1.4 | .2 | |
| | 7.5 | 7.1 | 4.9 | All Other Non-Current | 8.0 | 8.2 | 4.1 | 1.9 | 2.4 | |
| | 35.2 | 31.1 | 37.8 | Net Worth | 17.6 | 25.5 | 48.2 | 42.2 | 56.6 | |
| | 100.0 | 100.0 | 100.0 | Total Liabilities & Net Worth | 100.0 | 100.0 | 100.0 | 100.0 | 100.0 | |
| | | | | **INCOME DATA** | | | | | | |
| | 100.0 | 100.0 | 100.0 | Net Sales | 100.0 | 100.0 | 100.0 | 100.0 | 100.0 | |
| | 32.2 | 32.4 | 29.9 | Gross Profit | 41.4 | 35.5 | 27.5 | 23.6 | 23.6 | |
| | 29.5 | 29.0 | 26.4 | Operating Expenses | 37.9 | 33.0 | 24.3 | 20.7 | 16.9 | |
| | 2.7 | 3.4 | 3.6 | Operating Profit | 3.5 | 2.5 | 3.2 | 2.9 | 6.7 | |
| | .4 | .3 | .3 | All Other Expenses (net) | 1.2 | .0 | .1 | .6 | .0 | |
| | 2.2 | 3.1 | 3.2 | Profit Before Taxes | 2.3 | 2.5 | 3.1 | 2.3 | 6.6 | |
| | | | | **RATIOS** | | | | | | |
| | 3.6 | 3.9 | 3.9 | Current | 7.5 | 4.4 | 3.9 | 3.9 | 4.1 | |
| | 1.9 | 1.9 | 1.9 | | 1.2 | 1.6 | 2.0 | 2.0 | 2.6 | |
| | 1.2 | 1.1 | 1.1 | | .4 | .8 | 1.3 | 1.3 | 1.5 | |
| | 3.1 | 3.3 | 3.4 | Quick | 5.0 | 3.5 | 3.5 | 3.4 | 3.3 | |
| | 1.5 | 1.5 | 1.6 | | .7 | 1.3 | 1.8 | 1.7 | 2.3 | |
| | .9 | .8 | .8 | | .2 | .6 | 1.1 | 1.1 | 1.3 | |
| | 28  12.9 | 27  13.8 | 25  14.4 | Sales/Receivables | 0  UND | 4  104.1 | 45  8.1 | 36  10.2 | 40  9.2 | |
| | 55  6.6 | 53  6.8 | 51  7.1 | | 0  UND | 41  9.0 | 64  5.7 | 69  5.3 | 72  5.1 | |
| | 81  4.5 | 84  4.4 | 78  4.7 | | 40  9.1 | 72  5.1 | 85  4.3 | 89  4.1 | 83  4.4 | |
| | 0  UND | 0  UND | 0  UND | Cost of Sales/Inventory | 0  UND | 0  UND | 0  UND | 0  UND | 0  UND | |
| | 0  UND | 0  UND | 0  UND | | 0  UND | 0  UND | 0  UND | 0  UND | 0  UND | |
| | 1  248.5 | 2  199.9 | 1  413.5 | | 0  UND | 2  189.0 | 2  151.0 | 3  130.4 | 0  UND | |
| | 6  61.1 | 6  64.6 | 4  98.9 | Cost of Sales/Payables | 0  UND | 0  UND | 3  117.6 | 9  39.5 | 13  29.0 | |
| | 14  25.3 | 16  23.3 | 16  22.2 | | 2  165.5 | 13  27.5 | 18  20.8 | 20  18.1 | 19  19.5 | |
| | 28  13.1 | 32  11.4 | 32  11.4 | | 20  18.4 | 27  13.5 | 27  13.4 | 45  8.1 | 35  10.3 | |
| | 5.0 | 4.6 | 4.6 | Sales/Working Capital | 6.4 | 4.3 | 5.1 | 4.7 | 4.1 | |
| | 9.0 | 9.0 | 8.9 | | 226.7 | 13.5 | 8.9 | 7.6 | 6.0 | |
| | 39.9 | 44.5 | 50.9 | | -7.8 | -68.7 | 19.0 | 20.7 | 11.7 | |
| | (168)  23.7 | (161)  19.5 | (174)  28.8 | EBIT/Interest | (19)  10.0 | (52)  15.5 | (30)  19.0 | (39)  26.6 | (28)  102.7 | |
| | 4.4 | 4.1 | 5.5 | | 5.4 | 4.4 | 4.4 | 8.4 | 20.1 | |
| | -1.8 | .0 | -.1 | | .5 | -2.3 | 1.6 | .1 | 1.7 | |
| | (37)  13.4 | (34)  9.9 | (22)  15.4 | Net Profit + Depr., Dep., Amort./Cur. Mat. L/T/D | | | | | | |
| | 2.9 | 3.4 | 7.2 | | | | | | | |
| | .6 | .4 | 1.2 | | | | | | | |
| | .1 | .1 | .1 | Fixed/Worth | .0 | .1 | .1 | .1 | .1 | |
| | .3 | .3 | .3 | | .5 | .8 | .4 | .3 | .2 | |
| | 1.0 | 1.1 | 1.2 | | -1.4 | -7.0 | .7 | 1.0 | .3 | |
| | .4 | .4 | .4 | Debt/Worth | .9 | .4 | .4 | .4 | .3 | |
| | 1.0 | 1.1 | 1.0 | | 2.7 | 2.3 | .8 | .9 | .7 | |
| | 3.1 | 4.0 | 3.9 | | -4.4 | -13.0 | 2.3 | 2.8 | 1.9 | |
| | (172)  35.7 | (165)  45.8 | (172)  40.5 | % Profit Before Taxes/Tangible Net Worth | (18)  149.2 | (43)  53.0 | (34)  26.5 | (39)  32.3 | 39.8 | |
| | 14.1 | 15.1 | 15.8 | | 62.0 | 24.5 | 7.6 | 9.8 | 15.9 | |
| | -2.5 | 1.4 | .0 | | .1 | -5.6 | 1.5 | -6.9 | 2.9 | |
| | 19.8 | 21.7 | 22.1 | % Profit Before Taxes/Total Assets | 50.8 | 22.9 | 10.5 | 15.2 | 25.6 | |
| | 5.4 | 6.1 | 7.1 | | 15.5 | 7.6 | 2.8 | 4.7 | 6.6 | |
| | -4.7 | -.9 | -2.3 | | -2.1 | -6.5 | -1.9 | -2.7 | 1.1 | |
| | 58.2 | 66.3 | 56.8 | Sales/Net Fixed Assets | 172.8 | 43.9 | 39.9 | 63.0 | 65.8 | |
| | 24.0 | 24.8 | 23.3 | | 25.2 | 23.3 | 17.1 | 23.2 | 35.1 | |
| | 12.2 | 11.8 | 10.7 | | 6.3 | 11.0 | 8.5 | 10.8 | 18.2 | |
| | 4.4 | 4.4 | 4.3 | Sales/Total Assets | 9.1 | 5.4 | 3.6 | 3.6 | 4.3 | |
| | 3.0 | 2.9 | 2.9 | | 3.4 | 3.2 | 2.8 | 2.9 | 2.8 | |
| | 2.1 | 2.1 | 2.0 | | 2.0 | 2.0 | 1.7 | 2.1 | 1.8 | |
| | (166)  .8 | (149)  .7 | (156)  .7 | % Depr., Dep., Amort./Sales | (16)  .9 | (44)  .6 | (26)  .9 | (40)  .6 | (24)  .6 | |
| | 1.3 | 1.3 | 1.2 | | 1.2 | 1.3 | 1.7 | 1.1 | 1.0 | |
| | 2.3 | 2.3 | 1.9 | | 2.5 | 2.7 | 2.3 | 1.8 | 1.4 | |
| | (113)  3.1 | (108)  2.9 | (111)  2.8 | % Officers', Directors' Owners' Comp/Sales | (12)  6.8 | (37)  3.8 | (17)  2.6 | (26)  3.0 | (18)  1.1 | |
| | 5.8 | 4.5 | 4.3 | | 10.0 | 5.2 | 5.0 | 3.6 | 2.8 | |
| | 10.7 | 8.4 | 7.9 | | 12.9 | 8.5 | | 5.7 | 4.8 | |
| | 3022234M | 1121715M | 1282241M | Net Sales ($) | 15167M | 116993M | 149826M | 328144M | 470887M | 201224M |
| | 888566M | 460905M | 533517M | Total Assets ($) | 5588M | 41391M | 65766M | 126078M | 195180M | 99514M |

M = $ thousand    MM = $ million
See Pages 9 through 22 for Explanation of Ratios and Data

# CONSTRUCTION-GENERAL—Flooring Contractors   NAICS 238330

|  | Current Data Sorted by Assets | | | | | | | Comparative Historical Data | |
|---|---|---|---|---|---|---|---|---|---|
| | | | | | | | **Type of Statement** | | |
| | | | | | | | Unqualified | 11 | 7 |
| 1 | 17 | 4 34 | 3 5 | | | | Reviewed | 50 | 59 |
| 5 | 7 | 7 | 5 | | | | Compiled | 25 | 26 |
| 16 | 20 | 15 | | | | | Tax Returns | 30 | 40 |
| 10 | 23 | 27 | 7 | | | | Other | 64 | 52 |
| | 24 (4/1-9/30/11) | | 177 (10/1/11-3/31/12) | | | | | 4/1/07-3/31/08 | 4/1/08-3/31/09 |
| 0-500M | 500M-2MM | 2-10MM | 10-50MM | 50-100MM | 100-250MM | | ALL | ALL |
| 32 | 67 | 87 | 15 | | | **NUMBER OF STATEMENTS** | 180 | 184 |
| % | % | % | % | % | % | **ASSETS** | % | % |
| 12.6 | 8.9 | 6.8 | 5.4 | | | Cash & Equivalents | 10.3 | 10.7 |
| 29.5 | 48.9 | 50.8 | 49.9 | D | D | Trade Receivables (net) | 49.5 | 48.7 |
| 17.2 | 11.9 | 15.4 | 10.0 | A | A | Inventory | 12.8 | 13.3 |
| 5.1 | 6.3 | 8.7 | 8.9 | T | T | All Other Current | 6.9 | 6.6 |
| 64.3 | 76.0 | 81.7 | 74.2 | A | A | Total Current | 79.4 | 79.3 |
| 22.9 | 14.3 | 10.5 | 8.8 | | | Fixed Assets (net) | 14.1 | 14.1 |
| 2.0 | 2.3 | 2.4 | 6.9 | N | N | Intangibles (net) | 1.9 | 3.2 |
| 10.8 | 7.4 | 5.4 | 10.0 | O | O | All Other Non-Current | 4.5 | 3.4 |
| 100.0 | 100.0 | 100.0 | 100.0 | T | T | Total | 100.0 | 100.0 |
| | | | | A | A | **LIABILITIES** | | |
| 18.6 | 18.3 | 16.4 | 18.3 | V | V | Notes Payable-Short Term | 18.4 | 19.5 |
| 7.8 | 1.9 | 2.1 | 1.3 | A | A | Cur. Mat.-L.T.D. | 3.4 | 2.4 |
| 18.5 | 21.0 | 21.0 | 13.7 | I | I | Trade Payables | 18.2 | 18.1 |
| .3 | .4 | .3 | .3 | L | L | Income Taxes Payable | .3 | .3 |
| 10.5 | 9.3 | 12.3 | 13.1 | A | A | All Other Current | 13.9 | 13.1 |
| 55.7 | 51.0 | 52.0 | 46.7 | B | B | Total Current | 54.3 | 53.4 |
| 24.2 | 9.6 | 7.8 | 5.7 | L | L | Long-Term Debt | 10.5 | 11.4 |
| .0 | .2 | .1 | .3 | E | E | Deferred Taxes | .2 | .4 |
| 14.2 | 5.3 | 8.2 | 8.4 | | | All Other Non-Current | 3.8 | 4.1 |
| 6.1 | 34.0 | 31.9 | 38.9 | | | Net Worth | 31.1 | 30.7 |
| 100.0 | 100.0 | 100.0 | 100.0 | | | Total Liabilities & Net Worth | 100.0 | 100.0 |
| | | | | | | **INCOME DATA** | | |
| 100.0 | 100.0 | 100.0 | 100.0 | | | Net Sales | 100.0 | 100.0 |
| 36.8 | 26.0 | 23.2 | 23.6 | | | Gross Profit | 27.3 | 26.3 |
| 34.7 | 24.5 | 20.4 | 20.9 | | | Operating Expenses | 22.8 | 24.2 |
| 2.2 | 1.5 | 2.8 | 2.7 | | | Operating Profit | 4.5 | 2.1 |
| .3 | .0 | .8 | .8 | | | All Other Expenses (net) | .6 | .6 |
| 1.8 | 1.4 | 2.0 | 1.8 | | | Profit Before Taxes | 3.9 | 1.5 |
| | | | | | | **RATIOS** | | |
| 4.4 | 2.4 | 2.3 | 2.5 | | | | 2.2 | 2.4 |
| 1.4 | 1.6 | 1.6 | 1.6 | | | Current | 1.6 | 1.6 |
| .9 | 1.1 | 1.2 | 1.1 | | | | 1.2 | 1.1 |
| 3.5 | 2.0 | 1.6 | 1.9 | | | | 1.9 | 1.8 |
| .7 | 1.2 | 1.1 | 1.2 | | | Quick | 1.2 (183) | 1.1 |
| .4 | .8 | .8 | .8 | | | | .8 | .8 |
| 0 UND | 30 12.0 | 47 7.7 | 60 6.1 | | | | 30 12.2 | 33 10.9 |
| 20 18.0 | 56 6.5 | 65 5.6 | 83 4.4 | | | Sales/Receivables | 55 6.6 | 52 7.0 |
| 36 10.2 | 79 4.6 | 85 4.3 | 89 4.1 | | | | 81 4.5 | 76 4.8 |
| 0 UND | 0 999.8 | 3 136.5 | 1 463.9 | | | | 0 UND | 1 658.2 |
| 4 101.8 | 7 53.1 | 14 25.6 | 12 29.3 | | | Cost of Sales/Inventory | 7 52.2 | 10 35.9 |
| 49 7.4 | 26 14.1 | 33 10.9 | 29 12.8 | | | | 24 15.2 | 28 13.3 |
| 0 UND | 14 26.5 | 15 24.6 | 19 19.1 | | | | 12 30.8 | 12 30.2 |
| 15 24.2 | 26 13.9 | 30 12.3 | 23 15.7 | | | Cost of Sales/Payables | 22 16.8 | 21 17.6 |
| 30 12.1 | 39 9.3 | 54 6.7 | 42 8.6 | | | | 35 10.5 | 33 11.2 |
| 12.5 | 7.2 | 6.6 | 5.8 | | | | 7.6 | 7.1 |
| 34.0 | 11.3 | 10.3 | 9.3 | | | Sales/Working Capital | 13.8 | 11.2 |
| UND | 47.9 | 20.0 | 32.9 | | | | 34.6 | 33.8 |
| 5.5 | 14.7 | 20.0 | 26.3 | | | | 15.1 | 12.8 |
| (20) 3.2 | (60) 3.1 | (80) 4.4 | 4.3 | | | EBIT/Interest | (160) 4.5 | (166) 2.9 |
| -2.1 | .0 | 1.8 | 1.3 | | | | 2.2 | .4 |
| | | 18.9 | | | | | 21.6 | 9.3 |
| | | (18) 4.2 | | | | Net Profit + Depr., Dep., Amort./Cur. Mat. L/T/D | (29) 6.1 | (25) 3.8 |
| | | 1.2 | | | | | 2.6 | 1.3 |
| .1 | .1 | .1 | .1 | | | | .1 | .1 |
| 1.3 | .3 | .2 | .2 | | | Fixed/Worth | .3 | .3 |
| -.7 | 1.7 | .7 | .5 | | | | .8 | 1.0 |
| .4 | .6 | .9 | .7 | | | | .9 | .9 |
| 8.5 | 2.2 | 2.0 | 2.2 | | | Debt/Worth | 1.8 | 2.0 |
| -4.9 | 7.9 | 5.3 | 6.3 | | | | 4.7 | 5.8 |
| 52.2 | 43.7 | 32.4 | 26.0 | | | % Profit Before Taxes/Tangible Net Worth | 66.4 | 47.2 |
| (21) 22.0 | (57) 14.7 | (75) 17.0 | (14) 16.7 | | | | (160) 33.6 | (156) 19.4 |
| -10.0 | -1.0 | 5.4 | 2.7 | | | | 12.6 | .8 |
| 28.7 | 15.9 | 12.3 | 6.6 | | | % Profit Before Taxes/Total Assets | 21.1 | 15.1 |
| 8.7 | 3.8 | 5.5 | 5.2 | | | | 10.2 | 4.7 |
| -4.6 | -2.3 | 1.3 | .2 | | | | 3.9 | -1.3 |
| 112.5 | 87.1 | 129.2 | 92.4 | | | | 100.7 | 151.9 |
| 51.0 | 35.9 | 63.0 | 58.7 | | | Sales/Net Fixed Assets | 43.5 | 44.2 |
| 16.8 | 15.9 | 23.2 | 37.9 | | | | 18.4 | 19.2 |
| 6.2 | 4.0 | 3.7 | 3.2 | | | | 4.9 | 4.7 |
| 5.0 | 3.4 | 3.0 | 2.5 | | | Sales/Total Assets | 3.4 | 3.4 |
| 3.3 | 2.7 | 2.3 | 1.9 | | | | 2.7 | 2.7 |
| .5 | .3 | .3 | .3 | | | | .3 | .3 |
| (15) .9 | (47) .9 | (70) .5 | (14) .5 | | | % Depr., Dep., Amort./Sales | (135) .6 | (147) .6 |
| 1.5 | 1.4 | 1.0 | .8 | | | | 1.3 | 1.3 |
| 3.9 | 1.9 | 1.5 | | | | | 2.2 | 1.9 |
| (19) 6.1 | (35) 4.1 | (43) 2.3 | | | | % Officers', Directors' Owners' Comp/Sales | (87) 3.9 | (90) 3.1 |
| 11.1 | 6.7 | 4.1 | | | | | 6.1 | 5.7 |
| 50544M | 257194M | 1185860M | 745430M | | | Net Sales ($) | 4147738M | 2238505M |
| 9631M | 75249M | 374094M | 290016M | | | Total Assets ($) | 1007376M | 729133M |

M = $ thousand    MM = $ million
See Pages 9 through 22 for Explanation of Ratios and Data

## Comparative Historical Data      Current Data Sorted by Sales

| | 4/1/09-3/31/10 ALL | 4/1/10-3/31/11 ALL | 4/1/11-3/31/12 ALL | Type of Statement | 0-1MM | 1-3MM | 3-5MM | 5-10MM | 10-25MM | 25MM & OVER |
|---|---|---|---|---|---|---|---|---|---|---|
| | 3 | 8 | 7 | Unqualified | 1 | 3 | 13 | 18 | 16 | 6 |
| | 60 | 45 | 57 | Reviewed | 3 | 5 | 3 | 4 | 3 | 1 |
| | 27 | 24 | 19 | Compiled | 4 | 18 | 3 | 13 | 6 | 1 |
| | 42 | 30 | 51 | Tax Returns | 1 | 18 | 9 | 13 | 6 | 1 |
| | 60 | 73 | 67 | Other | | | 9 | 17 | 12 | 10 |
| | | | | | | 24 (4/1-9/30/11) | | 177 (10/1-3/31/12) | | |
| NUMBER OF STATEMENTS | 192 | 180 | 201 | | 9 | 44 | 34 | 53 | 40 | 21 |
| | % | % | % | **ASSETS** | % | % | % | % | % | % |
| Cash & Equivalents | 11.5 | 10.4 | 8.3 | | | 10.7 | 9.9 | 6.5 | 9.2 | 4.3 |
| Trade Receivables (net) | 46.2 | 45.9 | 46.7 | | | 37.7 | 47.0 | 47.1 | 56.3 | 51.3 |
| Inventory | 13.1 | 14.4 | 14.1 | | | 15.7 | 9.9 | 17.0 | 12.0 | 14.9 |
| All Other Current | 7.1 | 5.1 | 7.4 | | | 5.5 | 7.9 | 9.0 | 6.3 | 9.8 |
| Total Current | 77.9 | 75.7 | 76.5 | | | 69.7 | 74.6 | 79.6 | 83.9 | 80.4 |
| Fixed Assets (net) | 14.3 | 13.5 | 13.6 | | | 16.9 | 17.5 | 12.0 | 8.2 | 7.0 |
| Intangibles (net) | 2.6 | 2.5 | 2.6 | | | 3.3 | 1.9 | 2.6 | 2.0 | 5.1 |
| All Other Non-Current | 5.2 | 8.2 | 7.3 | | | 10.1 | 6.0 | 5.8 | 6.0 | 7.5 |
| Total | 100.0 | 100.0 | 100.0 | | | 100.0 | 100.0 | 100.0 | 100.0 | 100.0 |
| | | | | **LIABILITIES** | | | | | | |
| Notes Payable-Short Term | 20.7 | 18.8 | 17.5 | | | 19.2 | 17.5 | 15.5 | 16.8 | 20.4 |
| Cur. Mat.-L.T.D. | 2.4 | 2.3 | 2.9 | | | 4.0 | 1.0 | 1.9 | 1.7 | 2.4 |
| Trade Payables | 18.4 | 18.6 | 20.1 | | | 18.7 | 18.5 | 23.2 | 18.3 | 22.4 |
| Income Taxes Payable | .3 | .4 | .3 | | | .1 | .8 | .3 | .4 | .1 |
| All Other Current | 16.8 | 14.3 | 11.1 | | | 9.3 | 9.2 | 12.1 | 12.1 | 12.6 |
| Total Current | 58.7 | 54.3 | 51.9 | | | 51.2 | 46.9 | 53.0 | 49.3 | 57.9 |
| Long-Term Debt | 11.5 | 11.5 | 10.8 | | | 21.3 | 11.2 | 8.7 | 4.9 | 2.6 |
| Deferred Taxes | .1 | .2 | .1 | | | .0 | .4 | .1 | .1 | .3 |
| All Other Non-Current | 6.1 | 6.8 | 8.2 | | | 4.4 | 3.9 | 9.3 | 7.2 | 4.8 |
| Net Worth | 23.6 | 27.2 | 29.0 | | | 23.1 | 37.6 | 28.9 | 38.6 | 34.4 |
| Total Liabilties & Net Worth | 100.0 | 100.0 | 100.0 | | | 100.0 | 100.0 | 100.0 | 100.0 | 100.0 |
| | | | | **INCOME DATA** | | | | | | |
| Net Sales | 100.0 | 100.0 | 100.0 | | | 100.0 | 100.0 | 100.0 | 100.0 | 100.0 |
| Gross Profit | 29.1 | 28.4 | 26.3 | | | 34.8 | 26.8 | 22.0 | 22.1 | 24.4 |
| Operating Expenses | 27.7 | 25.7 | 24.1 | | | 31.8 | 25.5 | 19.1 | 19.3 | 23.2 |
| Operating Profit | 1.4 | 2.7 | 2.2 | | | 3.1 | 1.4 | 2.9 | 2.8 | 1.2 |
| All Other Expenses (net) | .1 | .4 | .5 | | | .1 | .3 | .7 | 1.0 | .1 |
| Profit Before Taxes | 1.3 | 2.3 | 1.8 | | | 3.0 | 1.1 | 2.2 | 1.8 | 1.1 |
| | | | | **RATIOS** | | | | | | |
| Current | 2.8 / 1.6 / 1.1 | 2.8 / 1.5 / 1.1 | 2.4 / 1.6 / 1.1 | | | 2.5 / 1.6 / 1.0 | 3.1 / 1.7 / 1.1 | 2.2 / 1.5 / 1.3 | 2.5 / 1.7 / 1.4 | 2.3 / 1.3 / 1.1 |
| Quick | 2.1 / 1.3 / .8 | 2.1 / 1.2 / .7 | 1.9 / 1.1 / .7 | | | 2.3 / 1.0 / .5 | 2.4 / 1.5 / .9 | 1.6 / 1.0 / .8 | 1.9 / 1.4 / .9 | 1.9 / 1.0 / .7 |
| Sales/Receivables | 31 11.8 / 54 6.8 / 78 4.7 | 28 12.8 / 54 6.8 / 76 4.8 | 31 11.7 / 54 6.7 / 79 4.6 | | | 14 26.8 / 35 10.4 / 74 4.9 | 37 9.8 / 54 6.7 / 78 4.7 | 36 10.0 / 63 5.8 / 87 4.2 | 47 7.8 / 61 6.0 / 78 4.7 | 42 8.6 / 66 5.5 / 91 4.0 |
| Cost of Sales/Inventory | 0 999.8 / 10 37.5 / 28 13.1 | 1 463.1 / 11 32.1 / 34 10.8 | 1 599.1 / 12 29.5 / 31 11.8 | | | 0 UND / 16 23.2 / 47 7.7 | 0 UND / 4 89.2 / 18 19.9 | 1 473.8 / 11 34.3 / 50 7.3 | 3 134.7 / 13 28.3 / 26 13.9 | 1 246.9 / 20 18.6 / 29 12.4 |
| Cost of Sales/Payables | 9 39.6 / 20 18.3 / 34 10.8 | 11 34.0 / 21 17.3 / 37 9.9 | 13 27.6 / 25 14.4 / 44 8.3 | | | 6 59.9 / 21 17.6 / 41 8.9 | 14 25.8 / 29 12.6 / 42 8.6 | 20 18.1 / 34 10.7 / 50 7.3 | 12 29.4 / 21 17.7 / 38 9.6 | 15 24.8 / 23 15.7 / 48 7.6 |
| Sales/Working Capital | 5.8 / 11.5 / 55.5 | 6.2 / 12.3 / 51.9 | 7.3 / 11.6 / 37.0 | | | 7.4 / 16.4 / UND | 7.5 / 13.3 / 52.3 | 7.5 / 9.8 / 24.6 | 6.9 / 10.9 / 19.0 | 5.9 / 13.6 / 128.4 |
| EBIT/Interest | (166) 12.0 / 2.4 / -.8 | (157) 12.2 / 2.9 / .9 | (175) 15.0 / 4.0 / 1.2 | | | (33) 12.3 / 3.5 / -4.7 | 11.3 / 2.9 / .3 | (49) 18.4 / 3.9 / 1.2 | (35) 35.0 / 7.0 / 2.1 | (20) 22.2 / 4.6 / 1.5 |
| Net Profit + Depr., Dep., Amort./Cur. Mat. L/T/D | (28) 11.7 / 2.3 / .4 | (29) 3.9 / 1.3 / .6 | (29) 11.5 / 4.8 / 1.1 | | | | | | | |
| Fixed/Worth | .1 / .3 / .8 | .1 / .3 / 1.0 | .1 / .2 / 1.6 | | | .2 / 1.0 / -1.4 | .1 / .4 / 2.1 | .0 / .2 / 1.6 | .1 / .1 / .4 | .1 / .2 / .6 |
| Debt/Worth | .6 / 1.7 / 5.9 | .7 / 2.2 / 7.9 | .7 / 2.2 / 7.9 | | | .7 / 3.0 / -11.8 | .5 / 2.2 / 8.1 | 1.1 / 2.4 / 5.9 | .6 / 1.3 / 2.9 | .9 / 3.6 / 6.1 |
| % Profit Before Taxes/Tangible Net Worth | (166) 40.2 / 13.3 / -.3 | (147) 41.9 / 13.4 / .3 | (167) 35.1 / 16.8 / 2.1 | | | (31) 69.9 / 20.1 / -18.4 | (30) 41.9 / 13.7 / -.9 | (45) 31.1 / 14.2 / 2.2 | (35) 35.1 / 19.7 / 13.9 | (20) 32.0 / 17.5 / 1.8 |
| % Profit Before Taxes/Total Assets | 16.7 / 3.6 / -3.5 | 19.9 / 4.3 / -.7 | 13.5 / 5.2 / .3 | | | 25.8 / 9.1 / -13.7 | 12.3 / 3.5 / -.7 | 14.2 / 4.4 / .7 | 16.6 / 9.6 / 2.0 | 9.4 / 5.3 / .3 |
| Sales/Net Fixed Assets | 113.6 / 44.1 / 17.9 | 100.3 / 46.0 / 19.6 | 117.4 / 50.2 / 18.8 | | | 63.5 / 32.1 / 14.9 | 66.0 / 29.7 / 14.7 | 169.1 / 66.2 / 19.7 | 118.7 / 72.7 / 30.6 | 94.8 / 62.8 / 33.8 |
| Sales/Total Assets | 4.3 / 3.2 / 2.5 | 4.2 / 3.1 / 2.4 | 4.1 / 3.3 / 2.4 | | | 4.7 / 3.4 / 2.6 | 4.1 / 3.3 / 2.6 | 3.9 / 3.0 / 2.1 | 4.3 / 3.5 / 2.8 | 3.6 / 3.1 / 2.4 |
| % Depr., Dep., Amort./Sales | (144) .3 / .7 / 1.6 | (140) .3 / .7 / 1.3 | (146) .3 / .6 / 1.2 | | | (24) .5 / 1.0 / 1.5 | (25) .4 / 1.3 / 1.9 | (41) .2 / .5 / 1.1 | (33) .3 / .4 / .9 | (18) .3 / .5 / .8 |
| % Officers', Directors' Owners' Comp/Sales | (96) 2.0 / 4.6 / 7.6 | (87) 2.1 / 3.5 / 6.7 | (101) 1.7 / 3.4 / 6.7 | | | (26) 3.5 / 6.0 / 9.0 | (19) 2.4 / 4.1 / 7.3 | (28) 1.4 / 2.5 / 4.0 | (17) 1.5 / 2.1 / 3.4 | |
| Net Sales ($) | 2941922M | 1729676M | 2239028M | | 5295M | 78478M | 137044M | 385772M | 617873M | 1014566M |
| Total Assets ($) | 689913M | 550205M | 748990M | | 2832M | 26278M | 44471M | 157678M | 192148M | 325583M |

M = $ thousand    MM = $ million
See Pages 9 through 22 for Explanation of Ratios and Data

## Current Data Sorted by Assets      Comparative Historical Data

| Type of Statement | 0-500M | 500M-2MM | 2-10MM | 10-50MM | | | | 4/1/07-3/31/08 ALL | 4/1/08-3/31/09 ALL |
|---|---|---|---|---|---|---|---|---|---|
| Unqualified | | 2 | 5 | | | | | 2 | 2 |
| Reviewed | | 7 | 9 | 4 | | | | 27 | 26 |
| Compiled | 1 | 4 | 5 | | | | | 7 | 13 |
| Tax Returns | 15 | 10 | 3 | 1 | | | | 25 | 21 |
| Other | 6 | 10 | 3 | 3 | | | | 28 | 22 |

Periods: 10 (4/1-9/30/11); 83 (10/1/11-3/31/12)

| | 0-500M | 500M-2MM | 2-10MM | 10-50MM | 50-100MM | 100-250MM | | 4/1/07-3/31/08 ALL | 4/1/08-3/31/09 ALL |
|---|---|---|---|---|---|---|---|---|---|
| **NUMBER OF STATEMENTS** | 22 | 33 | 30 | 8 | | | | 89 | 84 |
| | % | % | % | % | % | % | | % | % |
| **ASSETS** | | | | | | | | | |
| Cash & Equivalents | 13.2 | 9.2 | 7.2 | | DATA | DATA | | 9.5 | 13.0 |
| Trade Receivables (net) | 25.5 | 43.6 | 39.2 | | NOT | NOT | | 40.3 | 42.9 |
| Inventory | 17.1 | 8.8 | 20.4 | | AVAILABLE | AVAILABLE | | 15.0 | 14.6 |
| All Other Current | 6.0 | 5.9 | 5.7 | | | | | 6.4 | 5.0 |
| Total Current | 61.7 | 67.5 | 72.5 | | | | | 71.3 | 75.5 |
| Fixed Assets (net) | 22.7 | 17.1 | 15.3 | | | | | 21.2 | 18.4 |
| Intangibles (net) | 3.5 | 4.9 | 2.4 | | | | | .7 | .3 |
| All Other Non-Current | 12.1 | 10.4 | 9.7 | | | | | 6.9 | 5.8 |
| Total | 100.0 | 100.0 | 100.0 | | | | | 100.0 | 100.0 |
| **LIABILITIES** | | | | | | | | | |
| Notes Payable-Short Term | 32.3 | 15.1 | 11.6 | | | | | 18.4 | 19.0 |
| Cur. Mat.-L.T.D. | 4.7 | 1.2 | 1.7 | | | | | 2.7 | 4.2 |
| Trade Payables | 37.8 | 21.8 | 14.1 | | | | | 19.9 | 16.2 |
| Income Taxes Payable | .0 | .1 | .4 | | | | | .2 | .9 |
| All Other Current | 18.6 | 19.7 | 8.8 | | | | | 10.4 | 12.4 |
| Total Current | 93.5 | 58.0 | 36.5 | | | | | 51.6 | 52.7 |
| Long-Term Debt | 28.6 | 8.2 | 9.7 | | | | | 16.8 | 15.8 |
| Deferred Taxes | .0 | .1 | .2 | | | | | .1 | .1 |
| All Other Non-Current | 5.0 | 7.2 | 7.4 | | | | | 7.5 | 4.7 |
| Net Worth | -27.0 | 26.6 | 46.2 | | | | | 24.0 | 26.7 |
| Total Liabilities & Net Worth | 100.0 | 100.0 | 100.0 | | | | | 100.0 | 100.0 |
| **INCOME DATA** | | | | | | | | | |
| Net Sales | 100.0 | 100.0 | 100.0 | | | | | 100.0 | 100.0 |
| Gross Profit | 46.2 | 32.2 | 25.7 | | | | | 32.4 | 33.3 |
| Operating Expenses | 43.7 | 32.6 | 22.1 | | | | | 27.9 | 30.8 |
| Operating Profit | 2.6 | -.4 | 3.6 | | | | | 4.5 | 2.5 |
| All Other Expenses (net) | 1.0 | .8 | .5 | | | | | .5 | .7 |
| Profit Before Taxes | 1.6 | -1.2 | 3.2 | | | | | 4.0 | 1.8 |
| **RATIOS** | | | | | | | | | |
| Current | 2.3 | 1.9 | 2.6 | | | | | 2.5 | 2.4 |
| | .7 | 1.4 | 2.1 | | | | | 1.5 | 1.7 |
| | .3 | .8 | 1.5 | | | | | 1.1 | 1.1 |
| Quick | 1.2 | 1.5 | 2.0 | | | | | 2.1 | 1.9 |
| | .5 | 1.1 | 1.3 | | | | | 1.0 | 1.2 |
| | .2 | .5 | .8 | | | | | .5 | .7 |
| Sales/Receivables | 0 UND | 27 13.6 | 40 9.1 | | | | | 20 18.2 | 28 12.9 |
| | 16 22.9 | 54 6.8 | 70 5.2 | | | | | 49 7.4 | 51 7.2 |
| | 30 12.0 | 87 4.2 | 91 4.0 | | | | | 74 5.0 | 80 4.6 |
| Cost of Sales/Inventory | 0 UND | 0 UND | 4 89.6 | | | | | 0 UND | 0 UND |
| | 7 52.0 | 9 39.8 | 22 16.4 | | | | | 8 47.8 | 9 42.4 |
| | 34 10.8 | 23 16.0 | 85 4.3 | | | | | 44 8.3 | 51 7.1 |
| Cost of Sales/Payables | 0 UND | 16 22.3 | 14 25.3 | | | | | 10 35.6 | 9 38.5 |
| | 31 11.9 | 33 10.9 | 21 17.7 | | | | | 26 14.0 | 27 13.4 |
| | 65 5.6 | 59 6.2 | 59 6.2 | | | | | 55 6.6 | 45 8.2 |
| Sales/Working Capital | 21.5 | 6.2 | 3.4 | | | | | 5.6 | 5.9 |
| | -74.3 | 20.5 | 6.1 | | | | | 12.8 | 10.9 |
| | -10.2 | -11.2 | 8.4 | | | | | 64.4 | 93.9 |
| EBIT/Interest | 8.2 | 7.5 | 16.3 | | | | | 20.0 | 14.2 |
| | (16) 2.3 | (32) 3.1 | (26) 3.7 | | | | | (78) 4.0 | (73) 3.4 |
| | -1.5 | -22.2 | 1.2 | | | | | 1.5 | -.3 |
| Net Profit + Depr., Dep., Amort./Cur. Mat. L/T/D | | | | | | | | | 4.5 |
| | | | | | | | | (15) 2.4 |
| | | | | | | | | 1.0 |
| Fixed/Worth | .1 | .1 | .1 | | | | | .1 | .1 |
| | 3.5 | .9 | .3 | | | | | .6 | .3 |
| | -.3 | 2.9 | .5 | | | | | 2.1 | 1.3 |
| Debt/Worth | .9 | .8 | .7 | | | | | .7 | .6 |
| | 16.5 | 3.8 | 1.1 | | | | | 2.2 | 1.3 |
| | -2.7 | 55.0 | 2.1 | | | | | 7.2 | 10.1 |
| % Profit Before Taxes/Tangible Net Worth | 168.8 | 40.8 | 33.7 | | | | | 54.1 | 40.6 |
| | (13) 96.4 | (26) 16.9 | (29) 9.2 | | | | | (74) 25.6 | (69) 22.4 |
| | 3.6 | -27.2 | 1.9 | | | | | 8.0 | 4.3 |
| % Profit Before Taxes/Total Assets | 36.2 | 11.7 | 9.2 | | | | | 21.6 | 23.9 |
| | 6.7 | 5.1 | 4.1 | | | | | 7.4 | 7.3 |
| | -9.8 | -18.6 | .6 | | | | | .8 | -2.5 |
| Sales/Net Fixed Assets | 186.2 | 69.2 | 46.6 | | | | | 53.6 | 51.5 |
| | 48.7 | 32.7 | 19.6 | | | | | 22.1 | 28.9 |
| | 23.3 | 8.5 | 9.4 | | | | | 8.6 | 11.6 |
| Sales/Total Assets | 9.3 | 3.4 | 2.7 | | | | | 3.9 | 4.1 |
| | 5.0 | 2.8 | 2.0 | | | | | 2.8 | 3.0 |
| | 3.7 | 1.6 | 1.5 | | | | | 2.1 | 2.4 |
| % Depr., Dep., Amort./Sales | .1 | .6 | .3 | | | | | .6 | .5 |
| | (14) .8 | (24) 1.0 | (27) .9 | | | | | (67) 1.1 | (70) 1.0 |
| | 1.3 | 2.3 | 2.1 | | | | | 2.3 | 1.7 |
| % Officers', Directors' Owners' Comp/Sales | 1.8 | 3.3 | 1.8 | | | | | 1.6 | 2.4 |
| | (18) 4.6 | (17) 5.4 | (11) 3.6 | | | | | (45) 3.0 | (38) 4.3 |
| | 6.2 | 10.6 | 5.0 | | | | | 5.8 | 7.2 |
| Net Sales ($) | 31711M | 107303M | 244963M | 714552M | | | | 695582M | 1219897M |
| Total Assets ($) | 5053M | 39289M | 125829M | 135873M | | | | 268752M | 310646M |

M = $ thousand    MM = $ million
See Pages 9 through 22 for Explanation of Ratios and Data

## Comparative Historical Data · Current Data Sorted by Sales

| 4/1/09-3/31/10 ALL | 4/1/10-3/31/11 ALL | 4/1/11-3/31/12 ALL | Type of Statement | 0-1MM | 1-3MM | 3-5MM | 5-10MM | 10-25MM | 25MM & OVER |
|---|---|---|---|---|---|---|---|---|---|
| | | | | | | 10 (4/1-9/30/11) | | 83 (10/1/11-3/31/12) | |
| 5 | 3 | 7 | Unqualified | | 1 | 1 | 4 | 1 | |
| 16 | 26 | 20 | Reviewed | | 4 | 4 | 6 | 4 | 2 |
| 8 | 9 | 10 | Compiled | | | 6 | 2 | 2 | |
| 25 | 19 | 29 | Tax Returns | 9 | 12 | 4 | 1 | 2 | 1 |
| 32 | 28 | 27 | Other | 4 | 9 | 4 | 7 | 2 | 1 |
| 86 | 85 | 93 | **NUMBER OF STATEMENTS** | 13 | 26 | 19 | 20 | 11 | 4 |
| % | % | % | **ASSETS** | % | % | % | % | % | % |
| 13.4 | 12.6 | 9.2 | Cash & Equivalents | 11.3 | 10.7 | 8.3 | 8.7 | 6.3 | |
| 29.5 | 30.1 | 36.9 | Trade Receivables (net) | 23.4 | 32.4 | 44.7 | 39.5 | 42.5 | |
| 15.6 | 14.3 | 15.6 | Inventory | 14.8 | 14.0 | 15.2 | 16.3 | 20.8 | |
| 4.8 | 5.5 | 6.3 | All Other Current | 6.9 | 5.8 | 3.9 | 6.7 | 7.4 | |
| 63.3 | 62.4 | 67.9 | Total Current | 56.3 | 63.0 | 72.1 | 71.2 | 77.0 | |
| 23.7 | 24.3 | 18.2 | Fixed Assets (net) | 19.7 | 23.6 | 15.1 | 14.9 | 14.1 | |
| 1.6 | 1.2 | 3.8 | Intangibles (net) | 2.2 | 5.0 | 4.3 | 2.9 | 5.3 | |
| 11.3 | 12.1 | 10.0 | All Other Non-Current | 21.8 | 8.5 | 8.6 | 11.0 | 3.7 | |
| 100.0 | 100.0 | 100.0 | Total | 100.0 | 100.0 | 100.0 | 100.0 | 100.0 | |
| | | | **LIABILITIES** | | | | | | |
| 16.1 | 16.1 | 17.4 | Notes Payable-Short Term | 44.3 | 15.6 | 10.1 | 12.1 | 17.2 | |
| 2.9 | 4.4 | 2.3 | Cur. Mat.-L.T.D. | 4.5 | 2.6 | 1.4 | 1.3 | 2.1 | |
| 17.7 | 19.6 | 22.2 | Trade Payables | 20.9 | 34.7 | 19.2 | 16.4 | 13.9 | |
| .3 | .3 | .2 | Income Taxes Payable | .0 | .1 | .6 | .1 | .0 | |
| 13.2 | 10.0 | 15.1 | All Other Current | 24.9 | 15.0 | 18.0 | 10.1 | 7.0 | |
| 50.2 | 50.4 | 57.2 | Total Current | 94.6 | 67.9 | 49.2 | 39.9 | 40.2 | |
| 18.7 | 20.1 | 14.3 | Long-Term Debt | 32.7 | 13.1 | 10.4 | 9.1 | 14.3 | |
| .1 | .1 | .1 | Deferred Taxes | .0 | .1 | .0 | .3 | .0 | |
| 5.4 | 4.2 | 6.4 | All Other Non-Current | .2 | 10.0 | 5.0 | 9.8 | 2.3 | |
| 25.6 | 25.2 | 22.1 | Net Worth | -27.4 | 8.9 | 35.3 | 40.9 | 43.2 | |
| 100.0 | 100.0 | 100.0 | Total Liabilities & Net Worth | 100.0 | 100.0 | 100.0 | 100.0 | 100.0 | |
| | | | **INCOME DATA** | | | | | | |
| 100.0 | 100.0 | 100.0 | Net Sales | 100.0 | 100.0 | 100.0 | 100.0 | 100.0 | |
| 34.2 | 34.4 | 33.4 | Gross Profit | 53.3 | 37.0 | 27.1 | 25.6 | 27.5 | |
| 32.3 | 32.3 | 31.4 | Operating Expenses | 53.4 | 35.5 | 25.6 | 22.9 | 22.5 | |
| 1.8 | 2.1 | 2.0 | Operating Profit | -.1 | 1.5 | 1.5 | 2.8 | 5.0 | |
| .8 | .8 | .8 | All Other Expenses (net) | 1.3 | 1.4 | .1 | .2 | .5 | |
| 1.0 | 1.3 | 1.3 | Profit Before Taxes | -1.5 | .1 | 1.4 | 2.5 | 4.4 | |
| | | | **RATIOS** | | | | | | |
| 2.9 | 3.1 | 2.4 | Current | 1.1 | 2.0 | 2.6 | 2.5 | 2.7 | |
| 1.5 | 1.6 | 1.6 | | .7 | 1.1 | 2.1 | 1.7 | 2.0 | |
| .7 | .8 | .9 | | .3 | .5 | 1.4 | 1.2 | 1.3 | |
| 2.3 | 2.1 | 1.6 | Quick | 1.1 | 1.5 | 1.7 | 1.9 | 2.1 | |
| 1.0 | 1.0 | 1.1 | | .4 | .7 | 1.4 | 1.4 | 1.0 | |
| .4 | .4 | .4 | | .1 | .4 | .8 | .6 | .9 | |
| 10 37.0 | 18 20.4 | 17 21.1 | Sales/Receivables | 0 UND | 17 21.6 | 36 10.1 | 33 10.9 | 45 8.1 | |
| 42 8.8 | 46 8.0 | 47 7.7 | | 16 22.3 | 34 10.8 | 73 5.0 | 61 6.0 | 72 5.1 | |
| 69 5.3 | 79 4.6 | 76 4.8 | | 26 13.8 | 60 6.1 | 94 3.9 | 76 4.8 | 81 4.5 | |
| 0 UND | 0 UND | 0 UND | Cost of Sales/Inventory | 0 UND | 0 UND | 0 UND | 1 546.7 | 4 93.1 | |
| 9 39.7 | 9 38.7 | 14 25.3 | | 0 UND | 13 28.3 | 13 28.6 | 15 24.4 | 42 8.6 | |
| 46 7.9 | 57 6.4 | 43 8.5 | | 60 6.1 | 45 8.2 | 37 9.8 | 43 8.5 | 87 4.2 | |
| 14 27.0 | 15 24.9 | 15 24.7 | Cost of Sales/Payables | 0 UND | 17 21.9 | 13 29.0 | 19 19.2 | 13 27.5 | |
| 27 13.4 | 34 10.6 | 30 12.1 | | 23 16.1 | 37 9.8 | 27 13.4 | 30 12.1 | 21 17.6 | |
| 54 6.7 | 61 6.0 | 59 6.2 | | 64 5.7 | 68 5.4 | 65 5.6 | 49 7.4 | 57 6.4 | |
| 5.4 | 4.7 | 5.6 | Sales/Working Capital | 119.7 | 6.1 | 3.4 | 5.0 | 3.9 | |
| 12.7 | 9.5 | 12.1 | | -10.5 | 130.8 | 8.2 | 7.5 | 6.7 | |
| -24.3 | -34.0 | -144.7 | | -3.3 | -8.5 | 22.6 | 40.1 | 12.4 | |
| 8.0 | 5.1 | 8.9 | EBIT/Interest | 7.1 | 5.6 | 26.7 | 10.3 | | |
| (71) 1.9 | (69) 1.4 | (81) 3.3 | | (10) .4 | (23) 3.0 | (18) 3.4 | (17) 3.8 | | |
| -4.3 | -3.7 | -.2 | | -11.0 | -1.5 | .7 | -.1 | | |
| 6.9 | 5.2 | | Net Profit + Depr., Dep., Amort./Cur. Mat. L/T/D | | | | | | |
| (11) 3.2 | (12) 1.6 | | | | | | | | |
| .5 | .1 | | | | | | | | |
| .2 | .2 | .1 | Fixed/Worth | .1 | .5 | .0 | .1 | .1 | |
| .5 | .6 | .5 | | .9 | 2.5 | .3 | .3 | .2 | |
| 4.4 | 3.3 | 2.9 | | -.5 | -6.3 | 1.7 | .8 | 1.1 | |
| .5 | .6 | .8 | Debt/Worth | 2.5 | -1.2 | .5 | .7 | .9 | |
| 1.7 | 1.8 | 1.9 | | 7.0 | 5.8 | 1.3 | 1.4 | 1.4 | |
| 12.6 | 11.2 | 16.5 | | -2.4 | -8.3 | 3.8 | 4.3 | 2.4 | |
| 32.8 | 26.1 | 43.5 | % Profit Before Taxes/Tangible Net Worth | | 48.6 | 27.4 | 36.6 | 36.2 | |
| (70) 10.6 | (70) 5.6 | (76) 16.4 | | (18) 16.9 | (17) 12.4 | (19) 16.1 | (10) 14.1 | | |
| -9.1 | -11.0 | 2.0 | | -11.8 | 1.7 | 2.1 | 4.9 | | |
| 12.6 | 11.9 | 13.8 | % Profit Before Taxes/Total Assets | 24.9 | 13.9 | 12.3 | 8.8 | 18.1 | |
| 1.8 | 2.0 | 5.1 | | .7 | 5.0 | 5.1 | 3.8 | 5.3 | |
| -7.0 | -6.5 | -1.5 | | -33.5 | -9.3 | .9 | -2.3 | 2.3 | |
| 47.5 | 40.1 | 72.6 | Sales/Net Fixed Assets | 133.8 | 101.3 | 184.4 | 52.6 | 47.0 | |
| 15.9 | 16.6 | 31.1 | | 49.8 | 28.1 | 32.7 | 25.7 | 26.6 | |
| 7.2 | 6.3 | 9.5 | | 9.3 | 8.6 | 10.1 | 10.7 | 7.6 | |
| 3.8 | 3.4 | 3.8 | Sales/Total Assets | 5.9 | 4.7 | 3.3 | 3.0 | 2.8 | |
| 2.6 | 2.3 | 2.7 | | 4.0 | 3.4 | 2.8 | 2.6 | 2.0 | |
| 1.8 | 1.5 | 1.7 | | 1.6 | 1.6 | 1.6 | 1.9 | 1.4 | |
| .8 | .5 | .5 | % Depr., Dep., Amort./Sales | | .4 | .5 | .3 | .7 | |
| (68) 1.7 | (69) 1.2 | (73) 1.0 | | (17) 1.0 | (15) 1.0 | (19) .7 | (10) 1.0 | | |
| 2.9 | 2.3 | 2.0 | | 2.8 | 2.1 | 1.8 | 1.3 | | |
| 2.3 | 2.4 | 2.2 | % Officers', Directors' Owners' Comp/Sales | 2.0 | 3.4 | | | | |
| (45) 6.0 | (46) 4.6 | (49) 4.5 | | (10) 5.0 | (14) 4.9 | | | | |
| 8.8 | 8.7 | 7.3 | | 14.4 | 9.5 | | | | |
| 1195107M | 679414M | 1098529M | Net Sales ($) | 7777M | 49577M | 72465M | 149638M | 172519M | 646553M |
| 440539M | 338748M | 306044M | Total Assets ($) | 3347M | 23572M | 29833M | 74964M | 89795M | 84533M |

M = $ thousand    MM = $ million
See Pages 9 through 22 for Explanation of Ratios and Data

## Current Data Sorted by Assets

| | | | 1 | 1 | 2 |
|---|---|---|---|---|---|
| 2 | 4 | 19 | | | |
| 3 | 10 | 4 | | | |
| 28 | 10 | 4 | | | |
| 4 | 17 | 5 | | 1 | |
| | 15 (4/1-9/30/11) | | 100 (10/1/11-3/31/12) | | |
| 0-500M | 500M-2MM | 2-10MM | 10-50MM | 50-100MM | 100-250MM |
| 37 | 41 | 33 | 2 | 2 | |

## Comparative Historical Data

### Type of Statement

| | 8 | 8 |
|---|---|---|
| Unqualified | | |
| Reviewed | 39 | 17 |
| Compiled | 14 | 13 |
| Tax Returns | 26 | 27 |
| Other | 32 | 29 |
| | 4/1/07-3/31/08 ALL | 4/1/08-3/31/09 ALL |
| NUMBER OF STATEMENTS | 119 | 94 |

For columns 10-50MM, 50-100MM, 100-250MM the percentage-composition sections are marked **DATA NOT AVAILABLE**.

| | 0-500M % | 500M-2MM % | 2-10MM % | Hist 4/1/07-3/31/08 % | Hist 4/1/08-3/31/09 % |
|---|---|---|---|---|---|
| **ASSETS** | | | | | |
| Cash & Equivalents | 16.3 | 11.4 | 15.9 | 15.0 | 16.1 |
| Trade Receivables (net) | 26.4 | 41.4 | 43.4 | 35.5 | 38.1 |
| Inventory | 10.9 | 7.3 | 7.9 | 11.6 | 8.7 |
| All Other Current | 3.0 | 5.2 | 10.0 | 6.1 | 5.4 |
| Total Current | 56.6 | 65.3 | 77.2 | 68.2 | 68.3 |
| Fixed Assets (net) | 24.1 | 22.1 | 15.6 | 21.1 | 24.2 |
| Intangibles (net) | 9.1 | 6.2 | 2.4 | 3.2 | 3.1 |
| All Other Non-Current | 10.3 | 6.4 | 4.8 | 7.5 | 4.4 |
| Total | 100.0 | 100.0 | 100.0 | 100.0 | 100.0 |
| **LIABILITIES** | | | | | |
| Notes Payable-Short Term | 20.7 | 10.6 | 7.7 | 12.2 | 16.8 |
| Cur. Mat.-L.T.D. | 1.9 | 3.1 | 1.0 | 4.3 | 3.9 |
| Trade Payables | 19.0 | 23.5 | 16.3 | 16.7 | 17.8 |
| Income Taxes Payable | .6 | .2 | .1 | .2 | .1 |
| All Other Current | 14.7 | 13.4 | 18.2 | 15.4 | 20.0 |
| Total Current | 56.8 | 50.8 | 43.4 | 48.8 | 58.8 |
| Long-Term Debt | 34.2 | 14.4 | 9.1 | 18.3 | 16.6 |
| Deferred Taxes | .0 | .6 | .1 | .1 | .0 |
| All Other Non-Current | 33.0 | 2.9 | 4.7 | 6.3 | 12.3 |
| Net Worth | -24.2 | 31.3 | 42.8 | 26.4 | 12.3 |
| Total Liabilities & Net Worth | 100.0 | 100.0 | 100.0 | 100.0 | 100.0 |
| **INCOME DATA** | | | | | |
| Net Sales | 100.0 | 100.0 | 100.0 | 100.0 | 100.0 |
| Gross Profit | 45.0 | 35.5 | 25.0 | 32.9 | 32.1 |
| Operating Expenses | 40.3 | 33.4 | 24.0 | 28.5 | 29.7 |
| Operating Profit | 4.6 | 2.0 | 1.0 | 4.4 | 2.5 |
| All Other Expenses (net) | 1.3 | 1.2 | .3 | 1.0 | .7 |
| Profit Before Taxes | 3.3 | .8 | .7 | 3.4 | 1.8 |

### RATIOS

| | 0-500M | 500M-2MM | 2-10MM | Hist 4/1/07-3/31/08 | Hist 4/1/08-3/31/09 |
|---|---|---|---|---|---|
| Current | 3.1 | 2.5 | 2.9 | 2.5 | 2.1 |
| | .9 | 1.3 | 2.1 | 1.5 | 1.3 |
| | .4 | .9 | 1.5 | 1.0 | .9 |
| Quick | 1.6 | 1.8 | 2.6 | 1.8 | 1.7 |
| | .6 | 1.1 | 1.5 | 1.1 | 1.1 |
| | .3 | .6 | 1.0 | .7 | .6 |
| Sales/Receivables | 0 UND | 21 17.1 | 42 8.6 | 22 16.5 | 22 16.8 |
| | 10 38.2 | 41 8.9 | 62 5.9 | 44 8.3 | 43 8.5 |
| | 30 12.2 | 66 5.5 | 99 3.7 | 61 6.0 | 72 5.1 |
| Cost of Sales/Inventory | 0 UND | 0 UND | 0 UND | 0 UND | 0 UND |
| | 1 468.0 | 0 999.8 | 3 125.9 | 8 44.3 | 1 297.5 |
| | 21 17.3 | 27 13.3 | 20 18.1 | 41 9.0 | 21 17.1 |
| Cost of Sales/Payables | 0 UND | 15 23.8 | 17 21.2 | 8 48.5 | 8 47.9 |
| | 15 24.6 | 38 9.6 | 26 14.0 | 23 16.0 | 24 15.0 |
| | 36 10.1 | 54 6.8 | 54 6.7 | 48 7.6 | 43 8.5 |
| Sales/Working Capital | 16.5 | 7.5 | 4.3 | 7.7 | 7.6 |
| | -182.4 | 36.4 | 6.4 | 16.0 | 23.5 |
| | -19.3 | -42.2 | 12.2 | 320.7 | -30.5 |
| EBIT/Interest | 13.9 | 9.8 | 5.1 | 17.8 | 23.7 |
| | (32) 4.0 | (34) 3.9 | (27) 2.4 | (109) 4.1 | (84) 5.4 |
| | -.9 | -2.4 | -2.6 | 1.3 | .1 |
| Net Profit + Depr., Dep., Amort./Cur. Mat. L/T/D | | | | 9.7 | 34.9 |
| | | | | (22) 1.8 | (12) 4.5 |
| | | | | .7 | 1.7 |
| Fixed/Worth | .2 | .2 | .1 | .2 | .3 |
| | 11.0 | .7 | .2 | .6 | .7 |
| | -.3 | 3.8 | .5 | 5.1 | UND |
| Debt/Worth | 3.0 | 1.0 | .6 | .9 | 1.1 |
| | -24.1 | 3.5 | 1.1 | 2.2 | 3.9 |
| | -2.0 | 15.1 | 2.4 | 94.4 | UND |
| % Profit Before Taxes/Tangible Net Worth | 203.2 | 73.4 | 14.2 | 78.7 | 83.2 |
| | (17) 91.5 | (35) 21.2 | (30) 3.0 | (95) 24.9 | (71) 24.6 |
| | -2.8 | -27.7 | -5.9 | 8.0 | 1.7 |
| % Profit Before Taxes/Total Assets | 41.3 | 17.0 | 8.2 | 20.3 | 19.5 |
| | 17.2 | 3.2 | 1.3 | 7.0 | 7.2 |
| | -11.4 | -5.4 | -3.6 | .6 | -1.9 |
| Sales/Net Fixed Assets | 144.6 | 100.7 | 64.2 | 63.1 | 65.4 |
| | 37.3 | 20.8 | 24.1 | 19.9 | 20.7 |
| | 18.2 | 8.8 | 11.4 | 8.9 | 9.5 |
| Sales/Total Assets | 8.5 | 4.7 | 3.1 | 4.8 | 4.7 |
| | 5.4 | 3.3 | 2.2 | 3.1 | 3.0 |
| | 3.1 | 2.5 | 1.6 | 2.2 | 2.5 |
| % Depr., Dep., Amort./Sales | .7 | .5 | .5 | .6 | .6 |
| | (22) .9 | (21) 1.3 | (26) .8 | (92) 1.2 | (76) 1.1 |
| | 2.3 | 2.6 | 1.3 | 2.4 | 2.3 |
| % Officers', Directors' Owners' Comp/Sales | 2.8 | 2.9 | 2.5 | 2.4 | 2.7 |
| | (26) 5.6 | (23) 3.9 | (15) 4.4 | (56) 4.1 | (48) 4.3 |
| | 8.4 | 7.4 | 8.0 | 6.4 | 6.7 |

| | 0-500M | 500M-2MM | 2-10MM | 10-50MM | 50-100MM | Hist 4/1/07-3/31/08 | Hist 4/1/08-3/31/09 |
|---|---|---|---|---|---|---|---|
| Net Sales ($) | 36921M | 154119M | 335585M | 184280M | 362555M | 2053904M | 1427638M |
| Total Assets ($) | 7389M | 44193M | 141636M | 53200M | 169302M | 891497M | 475566M |

M = $ thousand   MM = $ million
See Pages 9 through 22 for Explanation of Ratios and Data

## Comparative Historical Data

## Current Data Sorted by Sales

| | | | | | Type of Statement | | | | | | |
|---|---|---|---|---|---|---|---|---|---|---|---|
| | 6 | | 5 | | 4 | Unqualified | | | | | 1 | 3 |
| | 34 | | 30 | | 25 | Reviewed | 1 | 1 | 5 | 10 | 7 | 1 |
| | 15 | | 9 | | 17 | Compiled | 2 | 4 | 7 | 4 | | |
| | 22 | | 29 | | 42 | Tax Returns | 18 | 14 | 4 | 5 | 1 | |
| | 25 | | 40 | | 27 | Other | 4 | 8 | 8 | 4 | 2 | 1 |
| | 4/1/09- | | 4/1/10- | | 4/1/11- | | | 15 (4/1-9/30/11) | | 100 (10/1/11-3/31/12) | | |
| | 3/31/10 | | 3/31/11 | | 3/31/12 | | | | | | | |
| | ALL | | ALL | | ALL | | 0-1MM | 1-3MM | 3-5MM | 5-10MM | 10-25MM | 25MM & OVER |
| | 102 | | 113 | | 115 | **NUMBER OF STATEMENTS** | 25 | 27 | 24 | 23 | 11 | 5 |
| | % | | % | | % | | % | % | % | % | % | % |
| | | | | | | **ASSETS** | | | | | | |
| | 17.0 | | 15.8 | | 14.5 | Cash & Equivalents | 19.5 | 9.7 | 8.7 | 20.3 | 13.1 | |
| | 35.7 | | 32.7 | | 36.9 | Trade Receivables (net) | 18.8 | 33.7 | 46.4 | 47.4 | 39.5 | |
| | 9.3 | | 10.1 | | 8.7 | Inventory | 11.6 | 8.9 | 5.0 | 5.4 | 17.9 | |
| | 6.2 | | 7.0 | | 6.1 | All Other Current | 4.4 | 1.1 | 9.1 | 7.7 | 8.2 | |
| | 68.3 | | 65.7 | | 66.2 | Total Current | 54.3 | 53.5 | 69.3 | 80.8 | 78.8 | |
| | 23.3 | | 22.4 | | 20.6 | Fixed Assets (net) | 25.5 | 29.1 | 18.1 | 13.3 | 16.1 | |
| | 3.9 | | 3.5 | | 6.2 | Intangibles (net) | 10.1 | 7.5 | 5.6 | 2.4 | 2.3 | |
| | 4.6 | | 8.4 | | 7.0 | All Other Non-Current | 10.1 | 9.9 | 7.0 | 3.6 | 2.9 | |
| | 100.0 | | 100.0 | | 100.0 | Total | 100.0 | 100.0 | 100.0 | 100.0 | 100.0 | |
| | | | | | | **LIABILITIES** | | | | | | |
| | 16.1 | | 21.1 | | 12.7 | Notes Payable-Short Term | 18.6 | 17.6 | 9.4 | 10.6 | 2.1 | |
| | 2.9 | | 3.3 | | 2.1 | Cur. Mat.-L.T.D. | .9 | 3.0 | 3.5 | 1.6 | .4 | |
| | 17.2 | | 17.1 | | 19.9 | Trade Payables | 16.9 | 22.5 | 19.6 | 21.7 | 16.3 | |
| | .2 | | .3 | | .3 | Income Taxes Payable | .9 | .2 | .1 | .1 | .1 | |
| | 13.3 | | 16.2 | | 15.4 | All Other Current | 16.4 | 9.1 | 15.4 | 19.3 | 17.9 | |
| | 49.6 | | 58.0 | | 50.4 | Total Current | 53.7 | 52.4 | 48.0 | 53.3 | 36.8 | |
| | 15.1 | | 17.6 | | 19.0 | Long-Term Debt | 21.2 | 39.5 | 14.8 | 6.6 | 4.2 | |
| | .2 | | .3 | | .3 | Deferred Taxes | .0 | .1 | 1.0 | .1 | .3 | |
| | 10.3 | | 5.1 | | 13.1 | All Other Non-Current | 38.8 | 10.1 | 6.4 | 4.2 | 1.6 | |
| | 24.8 | | 18.9 | | 17.2 | Net Worth | -14.1 | -2.1 | 29.9 | 35.8 | 57.1 | |
| | 100.0 | | 100.0 | | 100.0 | Total Liabilities & Net Worth | 100.0 | 100.0 | 100.0 | 100.0 | 100.0 | |
| | | | | | | **INCOME DATA** | | | | | | |
| | 100.0 | | 100.0 | | 100.0 | Net Sales | 100.0 | 100.0 | 100.0 | 100.0 | 100.0 | |
| | 32.5 | | 32.4 | | 34.8 | Gross Profit | 48.6 | 36.9 | 33.7 | 26.6 | 27.3 | |
| | 30.2 | | 31.2 | | 32.2 | Operating Expenses | 44.5 | 34.1 | 31.6 | 24.1 | 26.5 | |
| | 2.4 | | 1.2 | | 2.6 | Operating Profit | 4.1 | 2.8 | 2.0 | 2.5 | .8 | |
| | .5 | | .7 | | 1.0 | All Other Expenses (net) | 1.6 | 1.3 | 1.2 | .4 | -.4 | |
| | 1.9 | | .5 | | 1.7 | Profit Before Taxes | 2.6 | 1.5 | .9 | 2.2 | 1.3 | |
| | | | | | | **RATIOS** | | | | | | |
| | 3.4 | | 3.1 | | 2.7 | | 5.1 | 1.9 | 4.0 | 2.9 | 3.1 | |
| | 1.6 | | 1.6 | | 1.5 | Current | .9 | 1.1 | 1.7 | 1.6 | 2.5 | |
| | .8 | | .9 | | .9 | | .4 | .8 | 1.0 | 1.0 | 1.8 | |
| | 2.6 | | 2.3 | | 2.1 | | 3.1 | 1.5 | 3.3 | 2.9 | 2.1 | |
| | 1.1 | | .8 | | 1.1 | Quick | .6 | .7 | 1.4 | 1.5 | 1.5 | |
| | .6 | | .4 | | .6 | | .1 | .5 | .8 | .7 | 1.0 | |
| 20 | 18.5 | 16 | 22.4 | 15 | 25.0 | | 0 UND | 9 38.5 | 36 10.2 | 30 12.0 | 21 17.2 | |
| 45 | 8.1 | 35 | 10.6 | 39 | 9.4 | Sales/Receivables | 7 49.1 | 32 11.5 | 49 7.4 | 62 5.9 | 43 8.4 | |
| 75 | 4.9 | 61 | 6.0 | 68 | 5.4 | | 24 14.9 | 68 5.4 | 68 5.4 | 89 4.1 | 60 6.1 | |
| 0 | UND | 0 | UND | 0 | UND | | 0 UND | 0 UND | 0 UND | 0 UND | 0 UND | |
| 7 | 55.7 | 4 | 81.3 | 1 | 299.7 | Cost of Sales/Inventory | 0 UND | 6 62.4 | 0 UND | 3 125.9 | 30 12.3 | |
| 28 | 13.0 | 29 | 12.5 | 23 | 15.8 | | 26 14.3 | 30 12.0 | 0 UND | 18 20.3 | 76 4.8 | |
| 6 | 56.5 | 8 | 48.3 | 9 | 40.7 | | 0 UND | 10 37.0 | 10 36.7 | 16 23.0 | 16 23.2 | |
| 24 | 15.0 | 18 | 19.8 | 26 | 14.2 | Cost of Sales/Payables | 8 44.5 | 30 12.0 | 27 13.6 | 38 9.6 | 23 15.6 | |
| 44 | 8.3 | 38 | 9.6 | 48 | 7.6 | | 53 6.9 | 53 6.9 | 47 7.8 | 54 6.7 | 28 12.9 | |
| | 5.3 | | 5.5 | | 6.4 | | 14.0 | 16.1 | 6.6 | 4.3 | 4.1 | |
| | 9.9 | | 15.2 | | 16.1 | Sales/Working Capital | -103.6 | 70.2 | 9.5 | 6.2 | 7.0 | |
| | -40.0 | | -50.8 | | -60.1 | | -9.6 | -45.9 | NM | 715.0 | 12.3 | |
| | 12.6 | | 11.8 | | 12.3 | | 14.3 | 8.5 | 8.0 | 68.2 | | |
| (86) | 2.2 | (97) | 2.5 | (96) | 3.6 | EBIT/Interest | (22) 4.7 | (24) 1.8 | (19) 3.7 | (19) 2.5 | | |
| | -2.3 | | -4.4 | | -1.8 | | -1.2 | -3.6 | -2.4 | -2.8 | | |
| | 5.9 | | 30.4 | | 7.3 | Net Profit + Depr., Dep., | | | | | | |
| (22) | 2.2 | (14) | 2.7 | (11) | 1.4 | Amort./Cur. Mat. L/T/D | | | | | | |
| | -.1 | | .3 | | -.9 | | | | | | | |
| | .2 | | .1 | | .1 | | .1 | .3 | .0 | .1 | .1 | |
| | .6 | | .6 | | .5 | Fixed/Worth | 7.8 | 2.0 | .4 | .5 | .2 | |
| | 8.4 | | -5.3 | | 11.0 | | -.5 | -.4 | 2.2 | .7 | .5 | |
| | .8 | | .6 | | .9 | | 2.7 | 1.2 | 1.1 | .6 | .5 | |
| | 2.0 | | 2.0 | | 2.7 | Debt/Worth | -24.1 | 9.1 | 3.7 | 1.4 | .6 | |
| | 165.8 | | -18.5 | | -37.5 | | -2.3 | -2.5 | 7.8 | 5.8 | 1.1 | |
| | 50.7 | | 43.4 | | 62.3 | % Profit Before Taxes/Tangible | 183.3 | 81.3 | 70.2 | 68.2 | 13.9 | |
| (78) | 10.1 | (83) | 13.9 | (85) | 8.9 | Net Worth | (11) 64.6 | (19) 3.6 | (20) 6.4 | (20) 4.6 | 8.9 | |
| | -5.8 | | -10.4 | | -6.7 | | 3.1 | -45.2 | -10.6 | -2.0 | .0 | |
| | 12.4 | | 16.4 | | 18.7 | % Profit Before Taxes/Total | 41.3 | 16.8 | 10.4 | 25.8 | 7.4 | |
| | 1.2 | | 4.5 | | 4.1 | Assets | 18.7 | 3.2 | 1.6 | 1.9 | 3.6 | |
| | -4.9 | | -7.2 | | -4.0 | | -12.9 | -7.5 | -7.8 | -1.3 | .0 | |
| | 52.2 | | 74.5 | | 107.8 | | 108.5 | 59.6 | 288.6 | 93.5 | 47.3 | |
| | 19.5 | | 25.0 | | 29.3 | Sales/Net Fixed Assets | 31.6 | 18.6 | 27.3 | 39.0 | 32.6 | |
| | 7.7 | | 9.5 | | 13.7 | | 14.8 | 9.1 | 16.7 | 13.1 | 14.6 | |
| | 4.2 | | 4.6 | | 5.2 | | 8.9 | 6.0 | 4.7 | 3.9 | 4.7 | |
| | 2.7 | | 3.0 | | 3.1 | Sales/Total Assets | 4.0 | 3.1 | 3.1 | 2.5 | 2.9 | |
| | 1.9 | | 2.0 | | 1.9 | | 1.8 | 2.1 | 2.4 | 1.9 | 1.9 | |
| | .7 | | .7 | | .5 | | .7 | .7 | .7 | .5 | .4 | |
| (84) | 1.2 | (81) | 1.2 | (72) | .9 | % Depr., Dep., Amort./Sales | (15) .8 | (15) 2.0 | (13) 1.2 | (14) .7 | .8 | |
| | 2.5 | | 2.5 | | 1.7 | | 2.2 | 2.8 | 1.8 | 1.0 | 1.4 | |
| | 2.4 | | 2.3 | | 2.8 | | 3.2 | 2.9 | 2.3 | 2.5 | | |
| (54) | 5.0 | (59) | 4.8 | (64) | 4.4 | % Officers', Directors' | (15) 7.1 | (19) 4.7 | (15) 3.8 | (10) 4.1 | | |
| | 8.5 | | 7.7 | | 7.6 | Owners' Comp/Sales | 12.4 | 7.6 | 6.0 | 8.3 | | |
| | 1270319M | | 1588537M | | 1073460M | Net Sales ($) | 13966M | 52272M | 91839M | 168424M | 172749M | 574210M |
| | 695967M | | 468320M | | 415720M | Total Assets ($) | 4449M | 19534M | 32909M | 66776M | 65656M | 226396M |

M = $ thousand     MM = $ million
See Pages 9 through 22 for Explanation of Ratios and Data

## Current Data Sorted by Assets      Comparative Historical Data

| Type of Statement | 0-500M | 500M-2MM | 2-10MM | 10-50MM | 50-100MM | 100-250MM | | 4/1/07-3/31/08 ALL | 4/1/08-3/31/09 ALL |
|---|---|---|---|---|---|---|---|---|---|
| Unqualified | 1 | 13 | 4 | 6 | 2 | | | 4 | 5 |
| Reviewed | | | 28 | 3 | | | | 16 | 23 |
| Compiled | 1 | 11 | 3 | 1 | | | | 10 | 11 |
| Tax Returns | 17 | 9 | 6 | | | | | 12 | 25 |
| Other | 12 | 11 | 14 | 3 | 3 | | | 17 | 25 |
| | | 25 (4/1-9/30/11) | | 123 (10/1/11-3/31/12) | | | | | |
| **NUMBER OF STATEMENTS** | 31 | 44 | 55 | 13 | 5 | | | 59 | 89 |
| | % | % | % | % | % | % | | % | % |
| **ASSETS** | | | | | | | | | |
| Cash & Equivalents | 21.8 | 18.1 | 11.0 | 9.0 | | | | 9.0 | 10.5 |
| Trade Receivables (net) | 28.1 | 46.1 | 51.7 | 42.3 | | | | 40.5 | 44.8 |
| Inventory | 5.5 | 11.3 | 5.1 | 20.4 | | | | 9.9 | 8.7 |
| All Other Current | 1.5 | 6.8 | 10.7 | 2.7 | | | | 9.7 | 9.3 |
| Total Current | 56.9 | 82.3 | 78.4 | 74.3 | | | | 69.0 | 73.4 |
| Fixed Assets (net) | 31.9 | 13.3 | 12.2 | 13.3 | | | | 20.8 | 17.6 |
| Intangibles (net) | 5.0 | .6 | 3.7 | 8.6 | | | | 2.6 | 4.2 |
| All Other Non-Current | 6.2 | 3.8 | 5.7 | 3.7 | | | | 7.5 | 4.8 |
| Total | 100.0 | 100.0 | 100.0 | 100.0 | | | | 100.0 | 100.0 |
| **LIABILITIES** | | | | | | | | | |
| Notes Payable-Short Term | 21.0 | 10.7 | 10.9 | 11.1 | | | | 13.9 | 13.9 |
| Cur. Mat.-L.T.D. | 1.9 | 1.2 | 2.3 | 3.2 | | | | 3.4 | 3.6 |
| Trade Payables | 14.6 | 21.9 | 25.3 | 19.6 | | | | 23.3 | 21.8 |
| Income Taxes Payable | .2 | .5 | .4 | .6 | | | | .3 | .5 |
| All Other Current | 39.3 | 15.8 | 13.8 | 15.9 | | | | 14.0 | 13.6 |
| Total Current | 76.9 | 50.1 | 52.7 | 50.5 | | | | 55.0 | 53.4 |
| Long-Term Debt | 22.2 | 6.1 | 5.9 | 9.0 | | | | 26.0 | 14.9 |
| Deferred Taxes | .1 | .5 | .2 | .0 | | | | .1 | .1 |
| All Other Non-Current | 26.9 | 4.3 | 3.8 | 4.5 | | | | 1.7 | 5.1 |
| Net Worth | -26.1 | 38.9 | 37.4 | 36.1 | | | | 17.2 | 26.4 |
| Total Liabilties & Net Worth | 100.0 | 100.0 | 100.0 | 100.0 | | | | 100.0 | 100.0 |
| **INCOME DATA** | | | | | | | | | |
| Net Sales | 100.0 | 100.0 | 100.0 | 100.0 | | | | 100.0 | 100.0 |
| Gross Profit | 41.7 | 34.3 | 24.6 | 24.2 | | | | 28.7 | 30.5 |
| Operating Expenses | 40.5 | 29.9 | 22.0 | 19.7 | | | | 25.1 | 27.2 |
| Operating Profit | 1.2 | 4.4 | 2.7 | 4.5 | | | | 3.5 | 3.3 |
| All Other Expenses (net) | 1.4 | .3 | .1 | .6 | | | | .7 | .9 |
| Profit Before Taxes | -.2 | 4.1 | 2.5 | 3.9 | | | | 2.9 | 2.4 |
| **RATIOS** | | | | | | | | | |
| Current | 2.0 | 3.1 | 2.1 | 2.7 | | | | 1.9 | 2.1 |
| | .9 | 1.6 | 1.5 | 1.3 | | | | 1.4 | 1.5 |
| | .4 | 1.1 | 1.1 | 1.1 | | | | 1.1 | 1.1 |
| Quick | 1.8 | 2.7 | 1.8 | 2.0 | | | | 1.5 | 1.7 |
| | .7 | 1.2 | 1.2 | 1.0 | | | | 1.1 | (88) 1.1 |
| | .3 | .8 | .8 | .5 | | | | .6 | .7 |
| Sales/Receivables | 0 UND | 24 15.2 | 44 8.3 | 33 11.0 | | | | 23 16.1 | 19 19.1 |
| | 24 15.1 | 51 7.1 | 66 5.5 | 46 7.9 | | | | 48 7.7 | 52 7.0 |
| | 45 8.2 | 85 4.3 | 89 4.1 | 68 5.4 | | | | 81 4.5 | 95 3.9 |
| Cost of Sales/Inventory | 0 UND | 0 UND | 0 UND | 0 UND | | | | 0 UND | 0 UND |
| | 0 UND | 2 178.1 | 0 UND | 28 13.0 | | | | 3 120.3 | 2 206.3 |
| | 7 52.2 | 24 15.3 | 10 36.3 | 54 6.8 | | | | 27 13.4 | 16 22.6 |
| Cost of Sales/Payables | 0 UND | 13 28.7 | 25 14.7 | 14 25.8 | | | | 14 25.5 | 12 29.3 |
| | 10 36.0 | 28 13.0 | 41 9.0 | 26 13.9 | | | | 31 11.9 | 33 11.0 |
| | 46 7.9 | 64 5.7 | 62 5.9 | 54 6.7 | | | | 54 6.7 | 55 6.6 |
| Sales/Working Capital | 15.6 | 6.2 | 6.3 | 6.1 | | | | 8.1 | 6.2 |
| | -166.5 | 10.2 | 11.4 | 14.8 | | | | 14.3 | 10.7 |
| | -12.4 | 26.7 | 53.7 | 40.9 | | | | 57.6 | 59.7 |
| EBIT/Interest | 8.6 | 33.7 | 21.7 | 42.5 | | | | 11.8 | 19.2 |
| | (20) 1.3 | (32) 4.5 | (52) 5.9 | 14.6 | | | | (56) 3.6 | (73) 4.8 |
| | -4.2 | 1.8 | -.6 | 4.2 | | | | .6 | 1.7 |
| Net Profit + Depr., Dep., Amort./Cur. Mat. L/T/D | | | 6.4 | | | | | | 17.2 |
| | | | (14) 1.5 | | | | | | (15) 10.9 |
| | | | -5.7 | | | | | | 4.0 |
| Fixed/Worth | .2 | .1 | .1 | .1 | | | | .2 | .1 |
| | 2.0 | .3 | .3 | .6 | | | | .6 | .4 |
| | -2.2 | 1.0 | .7 | 1.1 | | | | 2.7 | 2.1 |
| Debt/Worth | .9 | .5 | 1.0 | .9 | | | | 1.2 | 1.2 |
| | 6.6 | 1.7 | 1.6 | 2.3 | | | | 2.6 | 2.8 |
| | -3.1 | 5.7 | 5.2 | 4.4 | | | | 13.9 | 8.4 |
| % Profit Before Taxes/Tangible Net Worth | 125.1 | 57.8 | 34.3 | 52.4 | | | | 48.7 | 52.6 |
| | (18) 48.3 | (40) 39.3 | (51) 8.4 | (12) 26.0 | | | | (50) 24.4 | (72) 29.1 |
| | -27.2 | 7.1 | -7.7 | 14.7 | | | | 11.4 | 3.9 |
| % Profit Before Taxes/Total Assets | 28.3 | 25.3 | 11.9 | 15.7 | | | | 18.6 | 19.7 |
| | 10.2 | 11.1 | 3.2 | 10.2 | | | | 6.8 | 7.3 |
| | -12.3 | 1.7 | -.7 | 2.2 | | | | -.3 | .7 |
| Sales/Net Fixed Assets | 89.7 | 111.8 | 94.0 | 66.0 | | | | 52.4 | 100.2 |
| | 16.6 | 31.7 | 29.4 | 33.8 | | | | 20.8 | 32.4 |
| | 7.3 | 14.9 | 15.8 | 10.8 | | | | 8.9 | 13.0 |
| Sales/Total Assets | 8.2 | 4.6 | 3.6 | 3.7 | | | | 4.4 | 4.3 |
| | 4.4 | 3.0 | 2.7 | 2.3 | | | | 2.8 | 3.0 |
| | 2.2 | 2.2 | 2.1 | 2.1 | | | | 2.2 | 2.0 |
| % Depr., Dep., Amort./Sales | .3 | .5 | .4 | .4 | | | | .7 | .4 |
| | (17) 1.7 | (29) 1.3 | (46) .9 | (12) .7 | | | | (43) 1.1 | (67) 1.0 |
| | 2.7 | 2.5 | 1.7 | 1.5 | | | | 2.6 | 2.3 |
| % Officers', Directors' Owners' Comp/Sales | 1.9 | 3.3 | 1.7 | | | | | 2.1 | 2.1 |
| | (15) 6.0 | (21) 5.2 | (22) 2.9 | | | | | (35) 3.1 | (51) 3.4 |
| | 8.5 | 6.8 | 5.2 | | | | | 6.0 | 7.7 |
| Net Sales ($) | 35497M | 175653M | 783672M | 715748M | 909066M | | | 858498M | 1852524M |
| Total Assets ($) | 7678M | 53215M | 266927M | 241999M | 345768M | | | 272958M | 695198M |

Note: For the 50-100MM and 100-250MM current-data columns, the ratio section is marked "DATA NOT AVAILABLE."

M = $ thousand    MM = $ million
See Pages 9 through 22 for Explanation of Ratios and Data

## Comparative Historical Data

## Current Data Sorted by Sales

| Comparative Historical Data | | | Type of Statement | Current Data Sorted by Sales | | | | | |
|---|---|---|---|---|---|---|---|---|---|
| 4 | 11 | 12 | Unqualified | 1 | 5 | 7 | 12 | 3 | 9 |
| 31 | 32 | 45 | Reviewed | | | | | 16 | 4 |
| 8 | 12 | 16 | Compiled | | 7 | 2 | 4 | 2 | 1 |
| 16 | 28 | 32 | Tax Returns | 10 | 12 | 1 | 8 | 1 | |
| 24 | 31 | 43 | Other | 10 | 5 | 5 | 8 | 8 | 7 |
| 4/1/09-3/31/10 ALL | 4/1/10-3/31/11 ALL | 4/1/11-3/31/12 ALL | | 25 (4/1-9/30/11) | | | 123 (10/1/11-3/31/12) | | |
| | | | | 0-1MM | 1-3MM | 3-5MM | 5-10MM | 10-25MM | 25MM & OVER |
| 83 | 114 | 148 | NUMBER OF STATEMENTS | 21 | 29 | 15 | 32 | 30 | 21 |
| % | % | % | ASSETS | % | % | % | % | % | % |
| 14.0 | 15.6 | 15.2 | Cash & Equivalents | 23.9 | 22.5 | 8.0 | 15.9 | 9.1 | 9.2 |
| 39.9 | 41.4 | 43.5 | Trade Receivables (net) | 27.2 | 33.3 | 55.5 | 43.3 | 58.7 | 43.6 |
| 7.7 | 10.0 | 8.5 | Inventory | 5.7 | 10.8 | 6.6 | 8.3 | 5.1 | 14.7 |
| 5.7 | 5.7 | 6.8 | All Other Current | 1.0 | 5.1 | 8.1 | 10.3 | 9.9 | 4.1 |
| 67.3 | 72.7 | 73.9 | Total Current | 57.8 | 71.7 | 78.3 | 77.8 | 82.8 | 71.6 |
| 18.9 | 19.2 | 17.3 | Fixed Assets (net) | 30.2 | 22.3 | 15.8 | 13.4 | 9.7 | 15.2 |
| 5.6 | 2.9 | 3.3 | Intangibles (net) | 6.5 | 1.1 | .4 | 4.2 | 2.0 | 6.0 |
| 8.3 | 5.2 | 5.5 | All Other Non-Current | 5.5 | 4.9 | 5.5 | 4.6 | 5.5 | 7.2 |
| 100.0 | 100.0 | 100.0 | Total | 100.0 | 100.0 | 100.0 | 100.0 | 100.0 | 100.0 |
| | | | LIABILITIES | | | | | | |
| 10.8 | 12.4 | 12.7 | Notes Payable-Short Term | 25.3 | 7.6 | 25.7 | 8.4 | 10.3 | 7.6 |
| 4.4 | 2.3 | 2.0 | Cur. Mat.-L.T.D. | 2.2 | .9 | .9 | 2.2 | 2.6 | 2.7 |
| 16.8 | 20.3 | 21.1 | Trade Payables | 8.6 | 22.5 | 18.3 | 25.1 | 24.0 | 23.5 |
| .4 | .3 | .4 | Income Taxes Payable | .0 | .4 | 1.2 | .1 | .5 | .4 |
| 13.0 | 15.1 | 19.9 | All Other Current | 52.3 | 14.3 | 14.2 | 13.9 | 17.2 | 12.3 |
| 45.3 | 50.4 | 56.0 | Total Current | 88.4 | 45.6 | 60.3 | 49.7 | 54.6 | 46.5 |
| 15.1 | 13.3 | 10.9 | Long-Term Debt | 28.8 | 6.7 | 8.4 | 7.3 | 3.2 | 16.8 |
| .4 | .2 | .3 | Deferred Taxes | .0 | .2 | 1.3 | .2 | .2 | .2 |
| 12.0 | 8.9 | 8.9 | All Other Non-Current | 37.2 | 5.6 | 4.4 | 2.8 | 4.2 | 4.1 |
| 27.2 | 27.2 | 24.0 | Net Worth | -54.4 | 41.8 | 25.5 | 40.1 | 37.8 | 32.4 |
| 100.0 | 100.0 | 100.0 | Total Liabilities & Net Worth | 100.0 | 100.0 | 100.0 | 100.0 | 100.0 | 100.0 |
| | | | INCOME DATA | | | | | | |
| 100.0 | 100.0 | 100.0 | Net Sales | 100.0 | 100.0 | 100.0 | 100.0 | 100.0 | 100.0 |
| 31.2 | 31.8 | 31.0 | Gross Profit | 46.6 | 38.7 | 30.4 | 28.3 | 22.6 | 21.3 |
| 26.9 | 29.0 | 28.0 | Operating Expenses | 48.6 | 31.2 | 28.8 | 26.2 | 18.9 | 18.0 |
| 4.3 | 2.8 | 3.0 | Operating Profit | -1.9 | 7.5 | 1.6 | 2.1 | 3.7 | 3.3 |
| .5 | .5 | .5 | All Other Expenses (net) | 1.7 | .4 | .6 | .0 | .1 | .8 |
| 3.8 | 2.3 | 2.5 | Profit Before Taxes | -3.7 | 7.1 | 1.0 | 2.1 | 3.5 | 2.5 |
| | | | RATIOS | | | | | | |
| 2.2 | 2.6 | 2.3 | Current | 1.1 | 3.8 | 2.0 | 2.4 | 2.3 | 2.5 |
| 1.6 | 1.6 | 1.5 | | .7 | 1.9 | 1.5 | 1.7 | 1.5 | 1.4 |
| 1.1 | 1.0 | 1.0 | | .4 | 1.1 | 1.0 | 1.1 | 1.1 | 1.1 |
| 1.8 | 2.1 | 2.0 | Quick | 1.1 | 3.2 | 1.7 | 2.3 | 2.2 | 1.7 |
| 1.2 | 1.3 | 1.1 | | .7 | 1.4 | 1.2 | 1.3 | 1.3 | 1.1 |
| .8 | .7 | .7 | | .2 | .7 | .9 | .8 | .8 | .6 |
| 27 13.5 | 21 17.5 | 26 14.2 | Sales/Receivables | 0 UND | 12 31.6 | 40 9.2 | 25 14.7 | 49 7.4 | 33 11.1 |
| 50 7.3 | 47 7.8 | 50 7.3 | | 24 15.1 | 35 10.3 | 83 4.4 | 51 7.1 | 68 5.4 | 46 8.0 |
| 74 5.0 | 79 4.6 | 79 4.6 | | 52 7.0 | 64 5.7 | 126 2.9 | 73 5.0 | 96 3.8 | 76 4.8 |
| 0 UND | 0 UND | 0 UND | Cost of Sales/Inventory | 0 UND | 0 UND | 0 UND | 0 UND | 0 UND | 0 UND |
| 4 101.9 | 3 134.0 | 0 905.2 | | 0 UND | 0 UND | 0 UND | 2 178.1 | 0 UND | 12 30.5 |
| 16 22.6 | 20 17.9 | 20 18.6 | | 7 48.8 | 29 12.4 | 25 14.8 | 20 18.6 | 9 38.7 | 38 9.6 |
| 7 54.4 | 10 37.9 | 13 28.8 | Cost of Sales/Payables | 0 UND | 14 26.1 | 2 159.6 | 14 26.2 | 18 20.5 | 17 22.1 |
| 24 14.9 | 28 12.9 | 32 11.3 | | 7 49.1 | 35 10.4 | 31 11.6 | 33 11.0 | 37 9.8 | 38 9.7 |
| 42 8.7 | 56 6.5 | 57 6.4 | | 54 6.7 | 62 5.9 | 65 5.6 | 61 6.0 | 57 6.4 | 53 6.9 |
| 6.0 | 6.1 | 6.8 | Sales/Working Capital | 26.1 | 6.4 | 6.2 | 7.2 | 6.3 | 6.1 |
| 10.6 | 10.8 | 13.1 | | -57.7 | 13.5 | 9.7 | 10.3 | 11.3 | 14.8 |
| 156.8 | 517.7 | 812.0 | | -5.4 | 26.9 | 53.7 | 46.0 | 80.2 | 42.9 |
| 17.4 | 13.8 | 22.7 | EBIT/Interest | 4.8 | 19.4 | 12.9 | 32.5 | 31.3 | 34.6 |
| (73) 6.5 | (98) 5.1 | (121) 4.8 | | (13) -.3 | (20) 3.7 | (13) 3.1 | (28) 4.2 | (27) 9.7 | (20) 7.3 |
| .6 | 1.6 | .5 | | -4.8 | 1.6 | .5 | -1.7 | .4 | 1.4 |
| 32.7 | 8.4 | 8.9 | Net Profit + Depr., Dep., Amort./Cur. Mat. L/T/D | | | | | | |
| (16) 2.4 | (24) 3.9 | (26) 2.7 | | | | | | | |
| .9 | .1 | .6 | | | | | | | |
| .2 | .2 | .1 | Fixed/Worth | .2 | .1 | .1 | .2 | .1 | .1 |
| .4 | .4 | .4 | | 2.3 | .5 | .3 | .4 | .3 | .3 |
| 2.8 | 1.7 | 1.3 | | -4.7 | 1.1 | 1.3 | 1.0 | .7 | 1.0 |
| 1.0 | 1.0 | .9 | Debt/Worth | 3.4 | .4 | 1.1 | .8 | .8 | 1.4 |
| 2.6 | 2.0 | 2.0 | | 9.8 | 1.2 | 2.1 | 1.4 | 1.6 | 2.3 |
| 10.8 | 16.8 | 8.3 | | -2.3 | 6.7 | 4.5 | 5.9 | 4.5 | 5.0 |
| 65.2 | 44.3 | 53.6 | % Profit Before Taxes/Tangible Net Worth | 51.2 | 106.1 | 49.0 | 52.0 | 50.3 | 33.4 |
| (66) 24.8 | (92) 21.1 | (125) 20.8 | | (11) 24.4 | (26) 45.9 | (13) 7.9 | (28) 8.1 | (28) 28.0 | (19) 18.1 |
| 4.8 | 3.5 | 3.8 | | -73.1 | 8.8 | -4.9 | -9.0 | 5.7 | 6.1 |
| 20.2 | 18.3 | 19.0 | % Profit Before Taxes/Total Assets | 17.0 | 37.6 | 15.9 | 18.0 | 21.5 | 12.3 |
| 8.7 | 6.6 | 6.3 | | 3.8 | 15.4 | 3.2 | 2.7 | 7.9 | 6.5 |
| -1.7 | .4 | -.5 | | -16.2 | 2.3 | -5.3 | -6.0 | 1.6 | .7 |
| 53.8 | 73.5 | 87.8 | Sales/Net Fixed Assets | 363.1 | 248.1 | 89.7 | 81.4 | 186.0 | 66.0 |
| 18.8 | 22.4 | 28.9 | | 16.6 | 26.1 | 31.8 | 28.9 | 34.0 | 33.8 |
| 10.3 | 12.3 | 13.5 | | 3.7 | 10.7 | 11.1 | 19.0 | 17.3 | 14.7 |
| 4.2 | 4.4 | 4.2 | Sales/Total Assets | 7.4 | 4.5 | 3.5 | 4.7 | 3.8 | 4.0 |
| 2.9 | 3.2 | 3.0 | | 2.3 | 3.5 | 2.5 | 3.3 | 3.0 | 3.0 |
| 1.9 | 2.0 | 2.1 | | 1.5 | 1.8 | 2.2 | 2.2 | 2.2 | 2.1 |
| .7 | .4 | .4 | % Depr., Dep., Amort./Sales | | .5 | .4 | .6 | .3 | .5 |
| (62) 1.2 | (87) 1.1 | (107) 1.1 | | (20) 2.2 | (11) 1.3 | (25) 1.1 | (24) .7 | (18) .7 | |
| 2.4 | 2.1 | 1.9 | | | 3.0 | 3.2 | 1.5 | 1.3 | 1.3 |
| 2.8 | 1.9 | 2.0 | % Officers', Directors' Owners' Comp/Sales | | 2.3 | | 2.0 | .9 | |
| (38) 4.2 | (53) 3.4 | (61) 4.3 | | (20) 5.4 | | (15) 2.9 | (10) 2.3 | | |
| 7.2 | 6.2 | 6.4 | | | 7.1 | | 5.9 | 5.1 | |
| 1183660M | 2146532M | 2619636M | Net Sales ($) | 11849M | 61044M | 56685M | 232782M | 499122M | 1758154M |
| 514719M | 824010M | 915587M | Total Assets ($) | 4980M | 22710M | 22242M | 77359M | 175456M | 612840M |

M = $ thousand   MM = $ million
See Pages 9 through 22 for Explanation of Ratios and Data

# CONSTRUCTION-GENERAL—Site Preparation Contractors  NAICS 238910

## Current Data Sorted by Assets | Comparative Historical Data

| | | | | | | | Type of Statement | | |
|---|---|---|---|---|---|---|---|---|---|
| | | 3 | 49 | 76 | 15 | 8 | Unqualified | 140 | 153 |
| 7 | 83 | 184 | 44 | | | 1 | Reviewed | 281 | 281 |
| 17 | 55 | 43 | 7 | | | | Compiled | 79 | 72 |
| 103 | 83 | 27 | 2 | | 1 | | Tax Returns | 114 | 175 |
| 42 | 73 | 135 | 70 | | 10 | 5 | Other | 209 | 268 |
| | 169 (4/1-9/30/11) | | | 974 (10/1/11-3/31/12) | | | | 4/1/07-3/31/08 ALL | 4/1/08-3/31/09 ALL |
| 0-500M | 500M-2MM | 2-10MM | 10-50MM | 50-100MM | 100-250MM | | NUMBER OF STATEMENTS | | |
| 169 | 297 | 438 | 199 | 26 | 14 | | | 823 | 949 |
| % | % | % | % | % | % | | ASSETS | % | % |
| 22.7 | 12.4 | 10.9 | 12.6 | 13.0 | 11.0 | | Cash & Equivalents | 11.8 | 13.1 |
| 19.2 | 34.9 | 38.0 | 35.0 | 31.2 | 23.1 | | Trade Receivables (net) | 30.1 | 30.4 |
| 3.9 | 4.1 | 3.1 | 3.9 | 2.1 | 4.2 | | Inventory | 3.5 | 4.1 |
| 4.8 | 4.6 | 6.9 | 6.8 | 9.0 | 6.1 | | All Other Current | 6.4 | 5.2 |
| 50.6 | 56.0 | 58.9 | 58.3 | 55.3 | 44.4 | | Total Current | 51.9 | 52.9 |
| 31.5 | 35.1 | 32.3 | 32.7 | 34.6 | 31.2 | | Fixed Assets (net) | 41.6 | 39.5 |
| 3.8 | 1.8 | 2.0 | 2.5 | 5.6 | 14.1 | | Intangibles (net) | 1.0 | 1.5 |
| 14.1 | 7.2 | 6.8 | 6.4 | 4.4 | 10.3 | | All Other Non-Current | 5.6 | 6.1 |
| 100.0 | 100.0 | 100.0 | 100.0 | 100.0 | 100.0 | | Total | 100.0 | 100.0 |
| | | | | | | | LIABILITIES | | |
| 25.3 | 11.7 | 7.9 | 5.7 | 4.4 | 4.0 | | Notes Payable-Short Term | 7.5 | 8.5 |
| 12.1 | 6.7 | 5.9 | 5.3 | 4.8 | 3.7 | | Cur. Mat.-L.T.D. | 7.2 | 6.9 |
| 15.8 | 16.7 | 17.4 | 16.6 | 14.6 | 13.9 | | Trade Payables | 15.0 | 13.5 |
| .0 | .1 | .6 | .5 | .9 | .5 | | Income Taxes Payable | .6 | .5 |
| 17.7 | 8.9 | 9.8 | 10.7 | 12.0 | 13.2 | | All Other Current | 9.9 | 10.0 |
| 71.0 | 44.2 | 41.6 | 38.8 | 36.7 | 35.2 | | Total Current | 40.2 | 39.4 |
| 34.1 | 20.0 | 13.6 | 14.6 | 15.2 | 20.8 | | Long-Term Debt | 24.0 | 22.2 |
| .0 | .3 | 1.2 | 1.0 | 1.2 | 3.5 | | Deferred Taxes | 1.0 | .7 |
| 8.1 | 5.2 | 3.0 | 2.2 | 15.9 | 1.5 | | All Other Non-Current | 2.4 | 3.1 |
| -13.2 | 30.3 | 40.7 | 43.5 | 31.1 | 39.0 | | Net Worth | 32.3 | 34.6 |
| 100.0 | 100.0 | 100.0 | 100.0 | 100.0 | 100.0 | | Total Liabilities & Net Worth | 100.0 | 100.0 |
| | | | | | | | INCOME DATA | | |
| 100.0 | 100.0 | 100.0 | 100.0 | 100.0 | 100.0 | | Net Sales | 100.0 | 100.0 |
| 48.7 | 33.0 | 24.2 | 18.0 | 22.7 | 21.7 | | Gross Profit | 28.6 | 28.2 |
| 43.9 | 30.6 | 20.6 | 13.9 | 12.7 | 18.2 | | Operating Expenses | 23.2 | 24.8 |
| 4.8 | 2.4 | 3.6 | 4.1 | 10.0 | 3.5 | | Operating Profit | 5.4 | 3.3 |
| .9 | .3 | .5 | .3 | .9 | -.1 | | All Other Expenses (net) | .9 | .8 |
| 3.9 | 2.0 | 3.1 | 3.8 | 9.1 | 3.6 | | Profit Before Taxes | 4.5 | 2.5 |
| | | | | | | | RATIOS | | |
| 2.1 | 2.5 | 2.5 | 2.0 | 2.4 | 2.0 | | Current | 2.0 | 2.3 |
| .9 | 1.5 | 1.5 | 1.5 | 1.7 | 1.4 | | | 1.3 | 1.4 |
| .3 | .9 | 1.1 | 1.1 | 1.1 | 1.1 | | | 1.0 | 1.0 |
| 1.9 | 2.1 | 2.1 | 1.7 | 1.7 | 1.6 | | Quick | 1.7 | 2.0 |
| (168) .7 | 1.2 | 1.2 | 1.3 | 1.2 | 1.2 | | | (821) 1.1 / (948) 1.2 | |
| .2 | .6 | .8 | .9 | .8 | .6 | | | .7 | .7 |
| 0 UND | 24 15.0 | 46 7.9 | 48 7.6 | 63 5.8 | 51 7.2 | | Sales/Receivables | 30 12.0 | 27 13.3 |
| 4 89.6 | 46 8.0 | 63 5.8 | 68 5.4 | 70 5.2 | 66 5.5 | | | 53 6.9 | 52 7.1 |
| 32 11.5 | 72 5.1 | 85 4.3 | 91 4.0 | 91 4.0 | 91 4.0 | | | 78 4.7 | 76 4.8 |
| 0 UND | 0 UND | 0 UND | 0 UND | 0 UND | 0 UND | | Cost of Sales/Inventory | 0 UND | 0 UND |
| 0 UND | 0 UND | 0 UND | 1 400.8 | 1 308.8 | 5 70.2 | | | 0 UND | 0 UND |
| 2 207.3 | 5 79.6 | 6 65.7 | 10 36.6 | 8 47.3 | 45 8.2 | | | 3 120.0 | 5 78.1 |
| 0 UND | 10 37.1 | 17 21.4 | 23 15.6 | 15 23.7 | 26 14.2 | | Cost of Sales/Payables | 12 31.1 | 9 39.5 |
| 6 65.0 | 25 14.4 | 31 11.8 | 36 10.1 | 32 11.3 | 32 11.5 | | | 29 12.6 | 25 14.6 |
| 35 10.5 | 49 7.4 | 55 6.6 | 52 7.0 | 46 7.9 | 81 4.5 | | | 51 7.2 | 45 8.1 |
| 13.1 | 6.4 | 5.3 | 5.7 | 5.0 | 6.6 | | Sales/Working Capital | 7.5 | 6.6 |
| -74.3 | 17.0 | 11.9 | 10.7 | 6.8 | 13.4 | | | 19.0 | 15.2 |
| -11.1 | -49.7 | 63.9 | 26.9 | 44.6 | 269.4 | | | -135.8 | -376.3 |
| 12.0 | 12.1 | 14.2 | 17.0 | 25.0 | 7.6 | | EBIT/Interest | 11.7 | 11.1 |
| (133) 3.8 | (262) 2.7 | (393) 4.3 | (189) 4.7 | (23) 6.2 | 2.8 | | | (747) 4.1 | (854) 3.1 |
| .9 | -.9 | 1.0 | .8 | 4.7 | 1.4 | | | 1.3 | -.1 |
| | 3.4 | 3.5 | 4.8 | | | | Net Profit + Depr., Dep., Amort./Cur. Mat. L/T/D | 4.4 | 3.6 |
| | (24) 1.5 | (114) 2.2 | (64) 2.1 | | | | | (211) 2.2 | (232) 1.8 |
| | .4 | .9 | 1.3 | | | | | 1.2 | .8 |
| .3 | .4 | .3 | .4 | .3 | .9 | | Fixed/Worth | .6 | .5 |
| 1.8 | 1.0 | .8 | .7 | 1.0 | 1.2 | | | 1.2 | 1.0 |
| -1.2 | 3.6 | 1.5 | 1.5 | 2.8 | 2.7 | | | 2.4 | 2.3 |
| 1.1 | .6 | .6 | .8 | .8 | .9 | | Debt/Worth | .9 | .7 |
| 10.5 | 1.7 | 1.4 | 1.4 | 1.7 | 2.1 | | | 1.9 | 1.6 |
| -3.7 | 7.6 | 3.1 | 2.5 | 4.2 | 5.9 | | | 4.1 | 3.9 |
| 96.8 | 43.9 | 34.6 | 31.2 | 48.4 | 14.0 | | % Profit Before Taxes/Tangible Net Worth | 48.9 | 37.7 |
| (97) 34.1 | (240) 15.5 | (402) 11.9 | (192) 13.4 | (23) 22.5 | (12) 9.7 | | | (738) 23.4 | (841) 15.2 |
| 1.2 | -4.6 | 1.0 | .6 | 10.5 | 2.2 | | | 7.5 | .3 |
| 33.7 | 16.6 | 12.7 | 12.9 | 13.8 | 6.7 | | % Profit Before Taxes/Total Assets | 17.1 | 14.7 |
| 11.2 | 5.6 | 4.4 | 5.2 | 6.8 | 3.3 | | | 7.9 | 5.0 |
| -.3 | -3.8 | .1 | .0 | 2.5 | .5 | | | 1.5 | -2.4 |
| 121.4 | 20.5 | 16.3 | 11.6 | 15.7 | 8.2 | | Sales/Net Fixed Assets | 10.5 | 14.0 |
| 22.2 | 8.1 | 6.7 | 5.7 | 5.5 | 4.4 | | | 5.0 | 5.7 |
| 7.0 | 3.8 | 3.5 | 3.2 | 1.9 | 2.7 | | | 2.9 | 3.0 |
| 7.3 | 3.7 | 2.7 | 2.2 | 2.1 | 1.6 | | Sales/Total Assets | 2.6 | 2.9 |
| 4.0 | 2.5 | 2.0 | 1.7 | 1.4 | 1.2 | | | 1.9 | 2.1 |
| 2.6 | 1.7 | 1.5 | 1.3 | 1.0 | .8 | | | 1.5 | 1.4 |
| .7 | 1.9 | 1.7 | 2.3 | 2.0 | | | % Depr., Dep., Amort./Sales | 2.4 | 2.2 |
| (106) 2.9 | (233) 4.3 | (372) 3.9 | (182) 4.0 | (23) 4.2 | | | | (724) 4.9 | (808) 4.5 |
| 6.5 | 7.1 | 6.1 | 6.6 | 7.7 | | | | 8.4 | 8.3 |
| 3.1 | 2.4 | 1.6 | .9 | | | | % Officers', Directors' Owners' Comp/Sales | 1.5 | 1.8 |
| (89) 6.2 | (159) 3.9 | (160) 2.7 | (55) 1.5 | | | | | (317) 3.1 | (394) 3.6 |
| 9.3 | 7.0 | 4.2 | 3.9 | | | | | 6.1 | 6.6 |
| 205857M | 977954M | 4281870M | 7411954M | 2834419M | 2441125M | | Net Sales ($) | 16860067M | 18204788M |
| 42278M | 345081M | 2054748M | 4170587M | 1791513M | 1939840M | | Total Assets ($) | 9149097M | 10069535M |

© RMA 2012

M = $ thousand   MM = $ million
See Pages 9 through 22 for Explanation of Ratios and Data

## Comparative Historical Data                                    Current Data Sorted by Sales

| | | | Type of Statement | | | | | | |
|---|---|---|---|---|---|---|---|---|---|
| 158 | 126 | 151 | Unqualified | | 2 | 4 | 23 | 42 | 80 |
| 333 | 313 | 319 | Reviewed | 10 | 55 | 48 | 91 | 84 | 31 |
| 96 | 86 | 122 | Compiled | 17 | 45 | 17 | 26 | 13 | 4 |
| 229 | 203 | 216 | Tax Returns | 61 | 76 | 40 | 29 | 6 | 4 |
| 298 | 288 | 335 | Other | 26 | 64 | 39 | 62 | 86 | 58 |
| 4/1/09-3/31/10 ALL | 4/1/10-3/31/11 ALL | 4/1/11-3/31/12 ALL | | | 169 (4/1-9/30/11) | | 974 (10/1/11-3/31/12) | | |
| | | | | 0-1MM | 1-3MM | 3-5MM | 5-10MM | 10-25MM | 25MM & OVER |
| 1114 | 1016 | 1143 | NUMBER OF STATEMENTS | 114 | 242 | 148 | 231 | 231 | 177 |
| % | % | % | ASSETS | % | % | % | % | % | % |
| 13.0 | 13.0 | 13.4 | Cash & Equivalents | 17.6 | 15.9 | 12.1 | 11.3 | 12.3 | 12.3 |
| 29.6 | 31.0 | 33.6 | Trade Receivables (net) | 19.5 | 24.9 | 35.8 | 38.4 | 40.2 | 37.6 |
| 5.0 | 4.4 | 3.6 | Inventory | 4.3 | 4.1 | 3.4 | 2.9 | 4.0 | 3.0 |
| 6.1 | 6.1 | 6.0 | All Other Current | 4.9 | 4.5 | 5.5 | 6.1 | 7.0 | 7.8 |
| 53.7 | 54.6 | 56.6 | Total Current | 46.2 | 49.4 | 56.8 | 58.8 | 63.6 | 60.7 |
| 36.2 | 35.7 | 33.0 | Fixed Assets (net) | 36.0 | 38.4 | 33.6 | 32.6 | 28.5 | 29.7 |
| 2.2 | 2.0 | 2.5 | Intangibles (net) | 3.2 | 2.8 | 2.1 | 2.1 | 1.8 | 3.7 |
| 7.9 | 7.7 | 7.9 | All Other Non-Current | 14.6 | 9.4 | 7.5 | 6.5 | 6.1 | 5.9 |
| 100.0 | 100.0 | 100.0 | Total | 100.0 | 100.0 | 100.0 | 100.0 | 100.0 | 100.0 |
| | | | LIABILITIES | | | | | | |
| 10.3 | 10.7 | 11.0 | Notes Payable-Short Term | 19.0 | 17.6 | 8.5 | 9.8 | 7.3 | 5.1 |
| 7.1 | 6.3 | 6.8 | Cur. Mat.-L.T.D. | 10.0 | 8.3 | 6.9 | 6.5 | 5.7 | 4.7 |
| 14.7 | 15.7 | 16.7 | Trade Payables | 14.8 | 13.4 | 16.9 | 18.1 | 18.6 | 18.0 |
| .3 | .3 | .4 | Income Taxes Payable | .1 | .2 | .5 | .4 | .6 | .5 |
| 12.7 | 10.9 | 11.0 | All Other Current | 16.0 | 10.0 | 10.8 | 9.5 | 10.8 | 11.6 |
| 45.2 | 44.0 | 45.9 | Total Current | 59.8 | 49.5 | 43.6 | 44.2 | 43.0 | 39.9 |
| 19.8 | 21.6 | 18.6 | Long-Term Debt | 38.3 | 22.0 | 19.2 | 15.1 | 12.7 | 12.8 |
| .7 | .8 | .8 | Deferred Taxes | .0 | .4 | 1.2 | .9 | .9 | 1.0 |
| 4.2 | 4.6 | 4.5 | All Other Non-Current | 9.8 | 5.1 | 3.0 | 4.4 | 2.1 | 4.6 |
| 30.0 | 29.0 | 30.3 | Net Worth | -8.0 | 22.9 | 33.0 | 35.4 | 41.2 | 41.7 |
| 100.0 | 100.0 | 100.0 | Total Liabilities & Net Worth | 100.0 | 100.0 | 100.0 | 100.0 | 100.0 | 100.0 |
| | | | INCOME DATA | | | | | | |
| 100.0 | 100.0 | 100.0 | Net Sales | 100.0 | 100.0 | 100.0 | 100.0 | 100.0 | 100.0 |
| 29.0 | 30.3 | 29.0 | Gross Profit | 49.8 | 39.7 | 28.8 | 25.1 | 21.3 | 16.0 |
| 27.2 | 27.6 | 25.3 | Operating Expenses | 45.0 | 36.2 | 25.9 | 21.7 | 17.2 | 12.2 |
| 1.8 | 2.7 | 3.7 | Operating Profit | 4.8 | 3.4 | 3.0 | 3.4 | 4.1 | 3.7 |
| .8 | .5 | .5 | All Other Expenses (net) | 1.3 | .5 | .5 | .5 | .4 | .1 |
| 1.0 | 2.2 | 3.2 | Profit Before Taxes | 3.5 | 3.0 | 2.5 | 2.9 | 3.8 | 3.7 |
| | | | RATIOS | | | | | | |
| 2.2 | 2.3 | 2.4 | Current | 3.1 | 2.4 | 2.4 | 2.5 | 2.4 | 2.0 |
| 1.4 | 1.4 | 1.4 | | 1.0 | 1.3 | 1.4 | 1.5 | 1.5 | 1.5 |
| .9 | .9 | 1.0 | | .4 | .7 | .9 | 1.0 | 1.1 | 1.2 |
| 1.8 | 2.0 | 2.0 | Quick | 2.5 | 2.0 | 2.1 | 2.1 | 2.1 | 1.6 |
| (1111) 1.1 | 1.1 (1142) | 1.2 | | (113) .6 | 1.1 | 1.1 | 1.2 | 1.3 | 1.3 |
| .6 | .7 | .7 | | .3 | .4 | .7 | .8 | .9 | .9 |
| 28 12.9 | 26 14.2 | 30 12.1 | Sales/Receivables | 0 UND | 4 92.5 | 38 9.6 | 37 9.9 | 43 8.5 | 52 7.0 |
| 53 7.0 | 54 6.8 | 55 6.6 | | 16 22.2 | 38 9.5 | 57 6.4 | 59 6.2 | 63 5.8 | 69 5.3 |
| 77 4.7 | 79 4.6 | 81 4.5 | | 47 7.7 | 69 5.3 | 81 4.4 | 83 4.4 | 85 4.3 | 89 4.1 |
| 0 UND | 0 UND | 0 UND | Cost of Sales/Inventory | 0 UND | 0 UND | 0 UND | 0 UND | 0 UND | 0 UND |
| 0 UND | 0 UND | 0 UND | | 0 UND | 0 UND | 0 UND | 0 UND | 0 UND | 0 UND |
| 11 33.9 | 8 47.4 | 6 61.6 | | 3 120.6 | 5 72.3 | 5 76.6 | 5 78.4 | 8 47.7 | 1 244.7 |
| 12 31.2 | 11 32.5 | 13 28.2 | Cost of Sales/Payables | 0 UND | 3 107.2 | 13 28.2 | 15 24.1 | 21 17.2 | 22 16.4 |
| 25 14.4 | 28 12.8 | 29 12.7 | | 9 41.5 | 19 19.3 | 31 11.6 | 29 12.7 | 33 10.9 | 34 10.7 |
| 49 7.4 | 51 7.2 | 51 7.1 | | 42 8.7 | 50 7.3 | 51 7.1 | 55 6.6 | 52 7.0 | 51 7.2 |
| 6.1 | 6.1 | 5.9 | Sales/Working Capital | 5.9 | 6.5 | 5.2 | 6.4 | 5.6 | 6.1 |
| 16.2 | 15.2 | 14.0 | | NM | 24.9 | 18.5 | 14.1 | 11.6 | 10.7 |
| -37.3 | -51.8 | -127.0 | | -8.9 | -16.9 | -50.9 | 185.1 | 53.6 | 21.5 |
| 8.5 | 11.0 | 13.9 | EBIT/Interest | 9.5 | 9.3 | 13.9 | 14.2 | 21.7 | 17.8 |
| (981) 2.2 | (912) 3.2 | (1014) 4.0 | | (82) 1.9 | (210) 3.3 | (136) 2.9 | (210) 4.1 | (205) 5.0 | (171) 5.4 |
| -1.0 | -.4 | .6 | | .1 | .0 | -.8 | .4 | 1.6 | 1.1 |
| 3.6 | 6.3 | 3.7 | Net Profit + Depr., Dep., Amort./Cur. Mat. L/T/D | | 3.3 | 2.9 | 3.6 | 5.9 | 4.5 |
| (248) 1.7 | (214) 2.2 | (217) 2.0 | | | (17) 1.5 | (25) 1.3 | (45) 2.2 | (72) 2.2 | (56) 2.1 |
| .7 | 1.0 | 1.0 | | | 1.2 | .5 | .5 | 1.3 | 1.3 |
| .4 | .4 | .4 | Fixed/Worth | .4 | .6 | .3 | .4 | .3 | .4 |
| 1.0 | .9 | .9 | | 1.5 | 1.1 | 1.1 | .8 | .7 | .7 |
| 2.4 | 2.9 | 2.1 | | -1.4 | 6.3 | 2.6 | 1.7 | 1.5 | 1.3 |
| .7 | .7 | .7 | Debt/Worth | .7 | .7 | .6 | .7 | .7 | .8 |
| 1.7 | 1.6 | 1.7 | | 4.1 | 1.9 | 1.8 | 1.4 | 1.4 | 1.4 |
| 5.2 | 6.7 | 4.7 | | -3.9 | 24.3 | 5.9 | 4.1 | 3.3 | 2.6 |
| 29.6 | 35.6 | 40.0 | % Profit Before Taxes/Tangible Net Worth | 56.6 | 49.3 | 39.9 | 45.5 | 37.1 | 30.3 |
| (943) 8.9 | (855) 12.5 | (966) 14.7 | | (69) 17.7 | (187) 15.0 | (124) 14.0 | (203) 16.9 | (213) 14.1 | (170) 13.9 |
| -4.2 | -3.3 | .4 | | -1.2 | -.7 | -7.8 | .4 | 3.9 | 1.0 |
| 11.5 | 15.0 | 15.6 | % Profit Before Taxes/Total Assets | 23.0 | 17.7 | 15.9 | 14.9 | 14.4 | 12.4 |
| 3.1 | 4.7 | 5.3 | | 4.7 | 6.9 | 4.6 | 4.6 | 5.5 | 4.6 |
| -4.3 | -3.0 | -.6 | | -4.1 | -1.9 | -3.6 | -.7 | .7 | .2 |
| 18.4 | 17.3 | 21.3 | Sales/Net Fixed Assets | 44.7 | 21.4 | 22.0 | 20.4 | 21.7 | 16.7 |
| 6.0 | 6.6 | 7.5 | | 9.5 | 7.4 | 6.7 | 7.8 | 8.6 | 6.9 |
| 3.1 | 3.4 | 3.8 | | 3.1 | 3.1 | 3.1 | 3.8 | 4.8 | 3.8 |
| 2.9 | 3.0 | 3.2 | Sales/Total Assets | 3.9 | 4.0 | 3.3 | 3.2 | 2.9 | 2.6 |
| 2.0 | 2.0 | 2.2 | | 2.3 | 2.5 | 2.1 | 2.2 | 2.2 | 2.0 |
| 1.3 | 1.4 | 1.5 | | 1.2 | 1.4 | 1.5 | 1.6 | 1.7 | 1.4 |
| 1.9 | 2.0 | 1.8 | % Depr., Dep., Amort./Sales | 1.8 | 2.0 | 2.1 | 1.6 | 1.4 | 1.9 |
| (933) 4.7 | (828) 4.5 | (924) 4.0 | | (78) 4.3 | (190) 4.8 | (114) 3.9 | (186) 4.1 | (201) 3.4 | (155) 3.5 |
| 8.5 | 7.9 | 6.5 | | 9.6 | 7.8 | 6.4 | 6.7 | 5.7 | 5.4 |
| 2.0 | 1.8 | 1.9 | % Officers', Directors' Owners' Comp/Sales | 4.5 | 3.3 | 2.2 | 1.8 | 1.1 | .5 |
| (472) 3.5 | (425) 3.7 | (469) 3.4 | | (52) 7.9 | (124) 5.0 | (76) 2.9 | (87) 2.7 | (94) 2.1 | (36) 1.2 |
| 7.1 | 6.9 | 6.1 | | 11.2 | 8.3 | 4.2 | 3.8 | 4.0 | 3.5 |
| 17516180M | 13694838M | 18153179M | Net Sales ($) | 67770M | 457007M | 583268M | 1638270M | 3602518M | 11804346M |
| 9656220M | 8565860M | 10344047M | Total Assets ($) | 41205M | 269047M | 356358M | 901533M | 1847416M | 6928488M |

M = $ thousand   MM = $ million
See Pages 9 through 22 for Explanation of Ratios and Data

# CONSTRUCTION-GENERAL—All Other Specialty Trade Contractors NAICS 238990

| Current Data Sorted by Assets | | | | | | | Comparative Historical Data | |
|---|---|---|---|---|---|---|---|---|
| | | | | | | **Type of Statement** | | |
| 4 | 6 | 40 | 40 | 12 | 9 | Unqualified | 103 | 113 |
| 9 | 77 | 179 | 37 | | | Reviewed | 255 | 275 |
| 35 | 82 | 53 | 4 | | 2 | Compiled | 135 | 132 |
| 166 | 116 | 50 | 3 | 34 | | Tax Returns | 225 | 241 |
| 67 | 132 | 142 | 34 | 1 | 9 | Other | 303 | 320 |
| | 174 (4/1-9/30/11) | | | 1,135 (10/1/11-3/31/12) | | | 4/1/07-3/31/08 ALL | 4/1/08-3/31/09 ALL |
| 0-500M | 500M-2MM | 2-10MM | 10-50MM | 50-100MM | 100-250MM | **NUMBER OF STATEMENTS** | 1021 | 1081 |
| 281 | 413 | 464 | 118 | 13 | 20 | | | |
| % | % | % | % | % | % | **ASSETS** | % | % |
| 22.8 | 12.9 | 12.5 | 15.9 | 20.4 | 13.3 | Cash & Equivalents | 12.4 | 13.9 |
| 21.6 | 38.2 | 43.2 | 35.8 | 37.7 | 32.5 | Trade Receivables (net) | 35.6 | 34.2 |
| 7.5 | 8.2 | 6.8 | 5.4 | 3.6 | 3.1 | Inventory | 8.3 | 8.4 |
| 2.8 | 5.0 | 7.4 | 7.9 | 8.2 | 5.3 | All Other Current | 6.4 | 6.4 |
| 54.7 | 64.3 | 69.8 | 64.9 | 69.9 | 54.2 | Total Current | 62.7 | 62.9 |
| 26.7 | 24.1 | 21.1 | 26.0 | 19.2 | 28.1 | Fixed Assets (net) | 26.9 | 26.9 |
| 5.1 | 3.3 | 2.7 | 2.7 | 3.8 | 11.5 | Intangibles (net) | 2.8 | 2.8 |
| 13.4 | 8.3 | 6.3 | 6.4 | 7.1 | 6.2 | All Other Non-Current | 7.6 | 7.4 |
| 100.0 | 100.0 | 100.0 | 100.0 | 100.0 | 100.0 | Total | 100.0 | 100.0 |
| | | | | | | **LIABILITIES** | | |
| 24.3 | 13.6 | 8.3 | 5.7 | 4.5 | 2.3 | Notes Payable-Short Term | 11.6 | 12.0 |
| 6.5 | 3.8 | 3.8 | 4.5 | 2.6 | 2.5 | Cur. Mat.-L.T.D. | 5.0 | 4.6 |
| 16.6 | 18.3 | 18.7 | 16.6 | 18.0 | 14.4 | Trade Payables | 15.6 | 15.5 |
| .2 | .4 | .5 | .3 | 1.5 | .1 | Income Taxes Payable | .6 | .6 |
| 18.9 | 10.1 | 11.1 | 12.3 | 18.8 | 14.6 | All Other Current | 13.6 | 13.5 |
| 66.5 | 46.2 | 42.2 | 39.4 | 45.4 | 33.8 | Total Current | 46.5 | 46.1 |
| 31.8 | 16.3 | 11.3 | 12.6 | 11.4 | 17.9 | Long-Term Debt | 17.9 | 17.3 |
| .1 | .4 | .6 | .7 | .4 | 3.1 | Deferred Taxes | .3 | .4 |
| 16.1 | 6.4 | 3.7 | 3.3 | 7.5 | 6.6 | All Other Non-Current | 4.5 | 3.9 |
| -14.4 | 30.7 | 42.2 | 44.1 | 35.3 | 38.6 | Net Worth | 30.8 | 32.2 |
| 100.0 | 100.0 | 100.0 | 100.0 | 100.0 | 100.0 | Total Liabilities & Net Worth | 100.0 | 100.0 |
| | | | | | | **INCOME DATA** | | |
| 100.0 | 100.0 | 100.0 | 100.0 | 100.0 | 100.0 | Net Sales | 100.0 | 100.0 |
| 44.6 | 34.1 | 26.4 | 20.5 | 16.6 | 25.3 | Gross Profit | 33.4 | 33.1 |
| 41.1 | 31.4 | 22.3 | 15.1 | 11.6 | 19.6 | Operating Expenses | 27.6 | 28.4 |
| 3.5 | 2.7 | 4.1 | 5.4 | 5.0 | 5.7 | Operating Profit | 5.8 | 4.7 |
| .4 | .5 | .3 | .5 | .6 | 2.9 | All Other Expenses (net) | .8 | .6 |
| 3.1 | 2.3 | 3.8 | 4.9 | 4.4 | 2.9 | Profit Before Taxes | 5.0 | 4.1 |
| | | | | | | **RATIOS** | | |
| 2.6 | 2.5 | 2.5 | 2.6 | 2.0 | 1.8 | Current | 2.4 | 2.5 |
| 1.1 | 1.5 | 1.6 | 1.6 | 1.7 | 1.5 | | 1.5 | 1.5 |
| .4 | .9 | 1.2 | 1.2 | 1.3 | 1.3 | | 1.0 | 1.0 |
| 2.3 | 2.0 | 2.1 | 2.0 | 1.9 | 1.6 | Quick | 1.9 | 2.0 |
| .8 | 1.1 | 1.3 | 1.3 | 1.5 | 1.3 | | (1020) 1.2 | (1080) 1.2 |
| .3 | .7 | .9 | .9 | 1.1 | 1.1 | | .7 | .7 |
| 0 UND | 23 16.0 | 41 8.8 | 42 8.7 | 49 7.5 | 56 6.5 | Sales/Receivables | 20 18.1 | 19 18.9 |
| 10 37.6 | 44 8.3 | 64 5.7 | 63 5.8 | 68 5.4 | 69 5.3 | | 47 7.8 | 43 8.4 |
| 33 11.0 | 72 5.1 | 85 4.3 | 89 4.1 | 79 4.6 | 85 4.3 | | 72 5.1 | 71 5.2 |
| 0 UND | 0 UND | 0 UND | 0 UND | 0 UND | 0 UND | Cost of Sales/Inventory | 0 UND | 0 UND |
| 0 UND | 2 178.7 | 1 476.7 | 1 496.6 | 0 844.2 | 1 337.0 | | 0 999.8 | 1 325.3 |
| 7 55.4 | 19 19.5 | 15 23.8 | 13 28.3 | 15 24.7 | 13 27.5 | | 17 21.1 | 21 17.1 |
| 0 UND | 10 36.2 | 16 22.9 | 16 23.3 | 16 22.8 | 14 25.2 | Cost of Sales/Payables | 8 44.7 | 8 44.1 |
| 9 38.6 | 27 13.6 | 30 12.0 | 31 11.9 | 25 14.7 | 29 12.4 | | 23 16.1 | 22 16.5 |
| 33 11.2 | 47 7.7 | 51 7.1 | 47 7.8 | 40 9.1 | 62 5.9 | | 43 8.6 | 40 9.1 |
| 14.5 | 6.8 | 5.7 | 4.3 | 5.2 | 7.1 | Sales/Working Capital | 6.8 | 6.6 |
| 198.0 | 16.5 | 10.1 | 8.5 | 8.9 | 9.0 | | 14.2 | 14.1 |
| -16.1 | -86.0 | 24.0 | 27.7 | 16.4 | 17.1 | | 750.2 | 158.7 |
| 13.8 | 16.3 | 18.1 | 41.9 | 10.6 | 34.1 | EBIT/Interest | 19.6 | 18.5 |
| (220) 4.4 | (360) 3.7 | (398) 5.5 | (100) 8.7 | (11) 5.9 | (19) 8.0 | | (902) 5.2 | (936) 5.0 |
| .3 | -1.3 | 1.7 | 1.8 | 1.4 | 1.2 | | 1.6 | 1.1 |
| | 3.8 | 9.0 | 4.8 | | | Net Profit + Depr., Dep., Amort./Cur. Mat. L/T/D | 12.2 | 9.2 |
| | (43) 1.7 | (116) 2.6 | (28) 1.8 | | | | (189) 3.5 | (222) 3.1 |
| | .1 | 1.3 | 1.1 | | | | 1.4 | 1.4 |
| .2 | .2 | .2 | .2 | .2 | .2 | Fixed/Worth | .2 | .2 |
| 1.6 | .6 | .4 | .4 | .7 | .7 | | .6 | .6 |
| -.9 | 3.4 | 1.0 | 1.5 | 1.4 | 2.8 | | 2.2 | 2.0 |
| .9 | .7 | .7 | .6 | 1.2 | 1.2 | Debt/Worth | .8 | .7 |
| 6.3 | 1.9 | 1.5 | 1.3 | 1.8 | 1.9 | | 1.8 | 1.7 |
| -3.2 | 11.9 | 3.0 | 3.0 | 3.4 | 7.9 | | 6.0 | 5.7 |
| 190.3 | 58.7 | 43.5 | 45.9 | 45.3 | 30.6 | % Profit Before Taxes/Tangible Net Worth | 70.2 | 58.7 |
| (170) 67.1 | (331) 19.0 | (430) 18.1 | (114) 18.5 | (12) 18.9 | (17) 11.7 | | (870) 34.5 | (915) 27.0 |
| 17.5 | -2.4 | 3.4 | 2.8 | 4.3 | 3.4 | | 10.3 | 6.5 |
| 37.8 | 20.8 | 17.0 | 16.5 | 11.0 | 12.6 | % Profit Before Taxes/Total Assets | 26.0 | 23.0 |
| 15.2 | 6.0 | 6.9 | 8.1 | 4.6 | 3.9 | | 10.3 | 8.5 |
| -1.8 | -4.0 | 1.2 | 1.1 | 1.1 | -.9 | | 2.1 | .7 |
| 127.3 | 52.0 | 44.5 | 31.5 | 70.6 | 32.7 | Sales/Net Fixed Assets | 41.5 | 44.8 |
| 30.5 | 20.5 | 17.1 | 10.1 | 16.0 | 15.9 | | 16.8 | 17.0 |
| 12.5 | 7.8 | 7.0 | 3.6 | 7.0 | 3.8 | | 6.6 | 6.1 |
| 9.5 | 4.1 | 3.3 | 2.7 | 3.2 | 2.2 | Sales/Total Assets | 4.2 | 4.1 |
| 5.1 | 2.9 | 2.4 | 1.8 | 1.8 | 1.7 | | 2.8 | 2.8 |
| 3.1 | 2.0 | 1.8 | 1.2 | 1.5 | 1.0 | | 1.9 | 1.9 |
| .8 | .7 | .7 | .7 | .4 | .8 | % Depr., Dep., Amort./Sales | .7 | .7 |
| (141) 1.7 | (308) 1.5 | (390) 1.4 | (108) 2.4 | (13) 1.2 | 2.5 | | (816) 1.7 | (869) 1.8 |
| 3.4 | 3.1 | 3.1 | 5.0 | 4.0 | 4.5 | | 3.7 | 3.9 |
| 3.5 | 2.4 | 1.7 | .5 | | | % Officers', Directors' Owners' Comp/Sales | 2.0 | 2.1 |
| (149) 6.2 | (231) 4.2 | (211) 2.7 | (25) 1.4 | | | | (496) 4.0 | (524) 4.1 |
| 11.5 | 7.0 | 4.6 | 3.0 | | | | 7.1 | 6.9 |
| 400768M | 1607907M | 5302632M | 4646619M | 2122011M | 5492498M | Net Sales ($) | 15704369M | 17198724M |
| 66847M | 475665M | 2063484M | 2465899M | 929872M | 3188895M | Total Assets ($) | 6451664M | 7943967M |

M = $ thousand    MM = $ million

© RMA 2012

See Pages 9 through 22 for Explanation of Ratios and Data

## Comparative Historical Data | Current Data Sorted by Sales

| 4/1/09-3/31/10 ALL | 4/1/10-3/31/11 ALL | 4/1/11-3/31/12 ALL | Type of Statement | 0-1MM | 1-3MM | 3-5MM | 5-10MM | 10-25MM | 25MM & OVER |
|---|---|---|---|---|---|---|---|---|---|
| | | | | 174 (4/1-9/30/11) | | | 1,135 (10/1/11-3/31/12) | | |
| 112 | 103 | 111 | Unqualified | 3 | 4 | 5 | 15 | 29 | 55 |
| 264 | 303 | 302 | Reviewed | 6 | 32 | 39 | 90 | 107 | 28 |
| 118 | 111 | 174 | Compiled | 19 | 52 | 37 | 47 | 14 | 5 |
| 283 | 274 | 337 | Tax Returns | 83 | 113 | 61 | 48 | 25 | 7 |
| 332 | 362 | 385 | Other | 46 | 94 | 55 | 93 | 60 | 37 |
| 1109 | 1153 | 1309 | NUMBER OF STATEMENTS | 157 | 295 | 197 | 293 | 235 | 132 |
| % | % | % | **ASSETS** | % | % | % | % | % | % |
| 15.2 | 14.7 | 15.2 | Cash & Equivalents | 21.5 | 15.5 | 15.0 | 12.9 | 12.7 | 17.1 |
| 33.0 | 36.0 | 36.1 | Trade Receivables (net) | 18.2 | 31.9 | 34.6 | 42.2 | 43.3 | 42.6 |
| 7.6 | 7.5 | 7.2 | Inventory | 6.5 | 9.0 | 7.7 | 7.1 | 6.5 | 4.5 |
| 6.1 | 5.9 | 5.7 | All Other Current | 3.1 | 3.6 | 5.2 | 6.2 | 8.4 | 8.2 |
| 61.9 | 64.1 | 64.2 | Total Current | 49.3 | 59.9 | 62.5 | 68.4 | 70.9 | 72.5 |
| 27.6 | 24.7 | 23.8 | Fixed Assets (net) | 31.3 | 26.1 | 24.2 | 21.8 | 21.3 | 18.2 |
| 3.1 | 3.0 | 3.5 | Intangibles (net) | 5.5 | 4.6 | 3.2 | 2.6 | 2.0 | 4.1 |
| 7.5 | 8.2 | 8.5 | All Other Non-Current | 13.9 | 9.4 | 10.1 | 7.2 | 5.8 | 5.2 |
| 100.0 | 100.0 | 100.0 | Total | 100.0 | 100.0 | 100.0 | 100.0 | 100.0 | 100.0 |
| | | | **LIABILITIES** | | | | | | |
| 11.6 | 13.1 | 13.0 | Notes Payable-Short Term | 21.2 | 19.4 | 11.4 | 10.5 | 8.9 | 4.5 |
| 5.2 | 4.7 | 4.4 | Cur. Mat.-L.T.D. | 5.9 | 5.6 | 4.0 | 3.9 | 3.6 | 2.9 |
| 16.4 | 17.6 | 17.9 | Trade Payables | 9.7 | 17.2 | 20.0 | 18.1 | 19.8 | 21.9 |
| .3 | .4 | .4 | Income Taxes Payable | .4 | .2 | .5 | .6 | .2 | .4 |
| 13.3 | 12.8 | 12.7 | All Other Current | 19.1 | 10.9 | 11.7 | 10.6 | 12.0 | 16.1 |
| 46.8 | 48.5 | 48.3 | Total Current | 56.3 | 53.3 | 47.6 | 43.6 | 44.6 | 45.8 |
| 17.5 | 16.1 | 17.5 | Long-Term Debt | 37.8 | 22.0 | 16.0 | 12.3 | 10.2 | 10.0 |
| .5 | .5 | .5 | Deferred Taxes | .2 | .2 | .5 | .6 | .6 | .6 |
| 4.2 | 6.2 | 7.3 | All Other Non-Current | 13.5 | 11.0 | 8.6 | 4.5 | 2.7 | 3.7 |
| 31.0 | 28.7 | 26.5 | Net Worth | -7.8 | 13.4 | 27.3 | 38.9 | 42.0 | 39.8 |
| 100.0 | 100.0 | 100.0 | Total Liabilities & Net Worth | 100.0 | 100.0 | 100.0 | 100.0 | 100.0 | 100.0 |
| | | | **INCOME DATA** | | | | | | |
| 100.0 | 100.0 | 100.0 | Net Sales | 100.0 | 100.0 | 100.0 | 100.0 | 100.0 | 100.0 |
| 32.6 | 32.7 | 32.1 | Gross Profit | 50.3 | 39.0 | 32.5 | 27.5 | 23.6 | 19.5 |
| 29.2 | 29.3 | 28.4 | Operating Expenses | 46.2 | 36.5 | 28.3 | 23.9 | 19.4 | 15.0 |
| 3.4 | 3.5 | 3.7 | Operating Profit | 4.1 | 2.5 | 4.3 | 3.6 | 4.2 | 4.5 |
| .8 | .5 | .4 | All Other Expenses (net) | .8 | .6 | .3 | .3 | .5 | .3 |
| 2.7 | 3.0 | 3.3 | Profit Before Taxes | 3.3 | 1.9 | 4.0 | 3.3 | 3.7 | 4.2 |
| | | | **RATIOS** | | | | | | |
| 2.6 | 2.6 | 2.5 | Current | 2.3 | 2.7 | 2.4 | 2.6 | 2.6 | 2.2 |
| 1.5 | 1.5 | 1.5 | | 1.0 | 1.3 | 1.5 | 1.6 | 1.6 | 1.6 |
| 1.0 | 1.0 | 1.0 | | .4 | .8 | 1.1 | 1.1 | 1.2 | 1.2 |
| 2.1 | 2.2 | 2.0 | Quick | 2.0 | 2.2 | 2.1 | 2.2 | 2.1 | 1.8 |
| 1.2 | 1.2 | 1.2 | | .8 | 1.0 | 1.2 | 1.2 | 1.3 | 1.3 |
| .6 | .7 | .7 | | .3 | .6 | .8 | .9 | .8 | 1.0 |
| 21 17.6 | 23 15.8 | 21 17.0 | Sales/Receivables | 0 UND | 13 27.1 | 16 22.9 | 34 10.8 | 38 9.6 | 41 8.8 |
| 44 8.3 | 50 7.4 | 48 7.6 | | 11 33.6 | 38 9.6 | 42 8.7 | 57 6.4 | 59 6.2 | 63 5.8 |
| 70 5.2 | 77 4.7 | 74 4.9 | | 44 8.3 | 66 5.5 | 73 5.0 | 83 4.4 | 83 4.4 | 81 4.5 |
| 0 UND | 0 UND | 0 UND | Cost of Sales/Inventory | 0 UND | 0 UND | 0 UND | 0 UND | 0 UND | 0 UND |
| 0 844.0 | 1 479.3 | 0 UND | | 0 UND | 0 UND | 2 208.5 | 2 190.3 | 0 999.8 | 1 552.8 |
| 17 21.2 | 19 18.8 | 15 25.1 | | 5 73.7 | 23 16.2 | 14 25.2 | 18 20.0 | 11 33.7 | 8 47.5 |
| 9 39.8 | 10 35.9 | 10 37.8 | Cost of Sales/Payables | 0 UND | 6 63.5 | 6 57.7 | 13 27.3 | 17 22.0 | 16 22.9 |
| 23 15.7 | 26 14.2 | 26 14.1 | | 7 50.3 | 26 14.2 | 24 15.0 | 28 13.2 | 27 13.3 | 31 11.6 |
| 44 8.3 | 50 7.3 | 46 7.9 | | 35 10.4 | 49 7.4 | 46 8.0 | 48 7.6 | 45 8.2 | 51 7.2 |
| 6.5 | 6.0 | 6.6 | Sales/Working Capital | 11.4 | 6.8 | 6.8 | 6.3 | 5.8 | 5.9 |
| 14.1 | 13.4 | 14.2 | | 215.3 | 20.5 | 15.5 | 11.3 | 11.9 | 9.5 |
| -148.5 | 999.8 | 753.5 | | -10.5 | -24.8 | 122.3 | 41.1 | 29.3 | 27.3 |
| 14.8 | 16.4 | 17.0 | EBIT/Interest | 11.3 | 9.9 | 23.6 | 14.7 | 25.8 | 78.4 |
| (961) 3.7 | (961) 4.0 | (1108) 4.8 | | (116) 2.6 | (256) 2.7 | (169) 6.2 | (251) 4.6 | (201) 7.7 | (115) 8.7 |
| .0 | .6 | 1.0 | | -1.5 | -1.0 | 1.3 | 1.3 | 1.9 | 2.1 |
| 4.9 | 6.1 | 6.6 | Net Profit + Depr., Dep., Amort./Cur. Mat. L/T/D | | 5.8 | 7.1 | 4.7 | 7.9 | 11.5 |
| (217) 1.9 | (177) 2.1 | (205) 2.5 | | | (22) 1.9 | (28) 2.9 | (67) 2.2 | (56) 2.3 | (31) 3.1 |
| .7 | .7 | 1.1 | | | -.4 | 1.0 | 1.1 | 1.2 | 1.6 |
| .2 | .2 | .2 | Fixed/Worth | .2 | .2 | .2 | .2 | .2 | .1 |
| .6 | .5 | .6 | | 1.8 | 1.0 | .6 | .4 | .4 | .3 |
| 2.3 | 2.1 | 2.2 | | -1.4 | -4.1 | 2.0 | 1.2 | .9 | 1.0 |
| .7 | .7 | .7 | Debt/Worth | 1.1 | .8 | .7 | .7 | .6 | .9 |
| 1.7 | 1.7 | 1.8 | | 6.2 | 2.5 | 1.6 | 1.7 | 1.4 | 1.6 |
| 6.7 | 6.5 | 7.3 | | -3.5 | -13.4 | 7.0 | 3.5 | 3.2 | 3.3 |
| 49.0 | 51.1 | 56.3 | % Profit Before Taxes/Tangible Net Worth | 119.3 | 66.2 | 66.9 | 46.2 | 49.6 | 53.7 |
| (936) 16.1 | (960) 18.2 | (1074) 21.6 | | (93) 50.0 | (209) 21.3 | (160) 21.4 | (265) 18.6 | (223) 21.1 | (124) 22.9 |
| -.1 | .7 | 2.6 | | -3.3 | -2.5 | 2.8 | 2.6 | 4.0 | 5.5 |
| 19.3 | 18.2 | 20.8 | % Profit Before Taxes/Total Assets | 35.8 | 21.8 | 25.2 | 17.5 | 20.0 | 18.0 |
| 5.3 | 6.3 | 7.7 | | 9.4 | 6.8 | 8.3 | 6.8 | 7.6 | 8.9 |
| -1.6 | -.8 | .1 | | -7.7 | -4.6 | .1 | .7 | 1.4 | 1.2 |
| 38.7 | 45.8 | 53.0 | Sales/Net Fixed Assets | 64.1 | 47.1 | 51.5 | 50.5 | 55.8 | 60.3 |
| 15.0 | 16.9 | 20.2 | | 16.1 | 19.0 | 20.8 | 19.1 | 20.6 | 22.4 |
| 5.8 | 6.7 | 7.7 | | 5.0 | 7.4 | 8.1 | 8.0 | 7.6 | 9.5 |
| 3.8 | 3.9 | 4.1 | Sales/Total Assets | 6.4 | 4.9 | 4.6 | 3.7 | 3.8 | 3.5 |
| 2.6 | 2.6 | 2.8 | | 3.1 | 3.0 | 3.0 | 2.7 | 2.7 | 2.6 |
| 1.8 | 1.8 | 1.9 | | 1.4 | 1.9 | 2.1 | 1.9 | 1.9 | 1.8 |
| .8 | .7 | .7 | % Depr., Dep., Amort./Sales | 1.5 | .8 | .8 | .6 | .6 | .4 |
| (907) 2.0 | (870) 1.7 | (973) 1.5 | | (75) 2.8 | (199) 1.9 | (142) 1.8 | (242) 1.3 | (206) 1.2 | (109) 1.2 |
| 4.2 | 4.0 | 3.3 | | 8.0 | 3.7 | 3.4 | 3.1 | 2.6 | 2.8 |
| 2.2 | 2.1 | 2.0 | % Officers', Directors' Owners' Comp/Sales | 5.3 | 3.0 | 2.2 | 1.9 | 1.4 | 1.0 |
| (567) 4.1 | (575) 4.0 | (621) 3.9 | | (77) 5.3 | (164) 5.3 | (103) 3.6 | (148) 3.1 | (101) 2.3 | (28) 1.6 |
| 7.5 | 7.0 | 7.2 | | 14.4 | 8.0 | 6.1 | 4.7 | 4.1 | 4.7 |
| 17112415M | 20718826M | 19572435M | Net Sales ($) | 86706M | 563884M | 767649M | 2073720M | 3695027M | 12385449M |
| 8864694M | 8693236M | 9190662M | Total Assets ($) | 42065M | 235874M | 316604M | 915391M | 1744711M | 5936017M |

© RMA 2012

M = $ thousand    MM = $ million
See Pages 9 through 22 for Explanation of Ratios and Data

# MANUFACTURING

## Current Data Sorted by Assets      Comparative Historical Data

| 0-500M | 500M-2MM | 2-10MM | 10-50MM | 50-100MM | 100-250MM | Type of Statement | 4/1/07-3/31/08 ALL | 4/1/08-3/31/09 ALL |
|---|---|---|---|---|---|---|---|---|
| 1 | 3 | 4 | 22 | 11 | 4 | Unqualified | 47 | 45 |
|  | 4 | 6 | 6 |  |  | Reviewed | 18 | 19 |
|  | 4 | 6 | 3 |  |  | Compiled | 19 | 19 |
|  | 9 | 5 | 2 |  |  | Tax Returns | 11 | 11 |
| 4 | 6 | 20 | 15 | 2 | 4 | Other | 42 | 61 |
|  | 47 (4/1-9/30/11) |  | 94 (10/1/11-3/31/12) |  |  |  |  |  |
| 5 | 26 | 41 | 48 | 13 | 8 | **NUMBER OF STATEMENTS** | 137 | 155 |
| % | % | % | % | % | % | **ASSETS** | % | % |
|  | 10.0 | 8.3 | 9.1 | 6.4 |  | Cash & Equivalents | 7.7 | 7.2 |
|  | 26.5 | 25.0 | 23.3 | 23.7 |  | Trade Receivables (net) | 25.9 | 26.1 |
|  | 25.9 | 23.2 | 25.4 | 23.7 |  | Inventory | 23.8 | 25.1 |
|  | 3.1 | 2.5 | 3.5 | 2.5 |  | All Other Current | 2.8 | 3.4 |
|  | 65.6 | 59.0 | 61.4 | 56.3 |  | Total Current | 60.2 | 61.8 |
|  | 27.3 | 29.0 | 28.2 | 23.9 |  | Fixed Assets (net) | 30.9 | 28.0 |
|  | 2.2 | 4.3 | 6.9 | 11.6 |  | Intangibles (net) | 2.2 | 2.8 |
|  | 4.9 | 7.7 | 3.6 | 8.1 |  | All Other Non-Current | 6.7 | 7.4 |
|  | 100.0 | 100.0 | 100.0 | 100.0 |  | Total | 100.0 | 100.0 |
|  |  |  |  |  |  | **LIABILITIES** |  |  |
|  | 13.0 | 6.8 | 9.2 | 16.7 |  | Notes Payable-Short Term | 11.9 | 13.7 |
|  | 2.6 | 4.2 | 2.5 | 2.2 |  | Cur. Mat.-L.T.D. | 2.6 | 3.5 |
|  | 17.3 | 16.1 | 16.5 | 14.8 |  | Trade Payables | 17.4 | 18.3 |
|  | .1 | .2 | .1 | .0 |  | Income Taxes Payable | .2 | .2 |
|  | 9.8 | 11.5 | 9.1 | 8.5 |  | All Other Current | 9.5 | 9.4 |
|  | 42.9 | 38.7 | 37.4 | 42.1 |  | Total Current | 41.6 | 45.0 |
|  | 17.2 | 14.2 | 11.1 | 13.8 |  | Long-Term Debt | 16.0 | 13.9 |
|  | .0 | .2 | .3 | .5 |  | Deferred Taxes | .6 | .4 |
|  | 4.2 | 4.7 | 6.6 | 2.8 |  | All Other Non-Current | 5.7 | 4.1 |
|  | 35.7 | 42.2 | 44.6 | 40.9 |  | Net Worth | 36.1 | 36.5 |
|  | 100.0 | 100.0 | 100.0 | 100.0 |  | Total Liabilities & Net Worth | 100.0 | 100.0 |
|  |  |  |  |  |  | **INCOME DATA** |  |  |
|  | 100.0 | 100.0 | 100.0 | 100.0 |  | Net Sales | 100.0 | 100.0 |
|  | 28.8 | 27.1 | 17.7 | 22.0 |  | Gross Profit | 21.1 | 18.7 |
|  | 27.7 | 20.0 | 11.2 | 14.7 |  | Operating Expenses | 16.9 | 15.2 |
|  | 1.1 | 7.1 | 6.4 | 7.3 |  | Operating Profit | 4.2 | 3.5 |
|  | -.1 | .8 | .1 | .4 |  | All Other Expenses (net) | .4 | .3 |
|  | 1.3 | 6.3 | 6.3 | 6.9 |  | Profit Before Taxes | 3.8 | 3.2 |
|  |  |  |  |  |  | **RATIOS** |  |  |
|  | 2.5 | 2.5 | 2.9 | 1.8 |  | Current | 2.1 | 2.0 |
|  | 1.5 | 1.7 | 1.8 | 1.2 |  |  | 1.4 | 1.4 |
|  | 1.1 | 1.1 | 1.2 | 1.1 |  |  | 1.1 | 1.1 |
|  | 1.8 | 1.7 | 1.5 | 1.3 |  | Quick | 1.1 | 1.1 |
|  | .8 | .8 | .8 | .8 |  |  | .7 | .7 |
|  | .5 | .5 | .6 | .5 |  |  | .5 | .4 |
|  | 15 24.2 | 15 24.4 | 19 18.9 | 20 17.9 |  | Sales/Receivables | 21 17.8 | 17 21.9 |
|  | 25 14.5 | 27 13.7 | 27 13.3 | 29 12.7 |  |  | 26 14.1 | 26 14.1 |
|  | 34 10.8 | 40 9.2 | 41 8.9 | 45 8.2 |  |  | 39 9.3 | 35 10.5 |
|  | 17 21.3 | 12 31.3 | 20 18.4 | 14 26.5 |  | Cost of Sales/Inventory | 16 22.4 | 13 28.2 |
|  | 33 10.9 | 31 11.7 | 36 10.0 | 47 7.7 |  |  | 35 10.4 | 30 12.1 |
|  | 78 4.7 | 65 5.6 | 64 5.7 | 57 6.4 |  |  | 59 6.2 | 50 7.3 |
|  | 6 57.8 | 10 35.6 | 11 32.5 | 17 21.7 |  | Cost of Sales/Payables | 13 27.6 | 12 29.6 |
|  | 16 22.3 | 22 16.5 | 19 19.0 | 23 16.1 |  |  | 23 15.8 | 20 18.1 |
|  | 41 9.0 | 41 8.8 | 33 11.1 | 29 12.5 |  |  | 34 10.8 | 33 11.2 |
|  | 8.7 | 8.4 | 8.2 | 8.0 |  | Sales/Working Capital | 9.5 | 11.3 |
|  | 20.2 | 17.7 | 12.0 | 29.3 |  |  | 19.0 | 23.7 |
|  | 127.9 | 229.7 | 24.9 | 55.7 |  |  | 63.4 | 134.2 |
|  | 11.3 | 21.4 | 16.8 | 47.7 |  | EBIT/Interest | 12.0 | 13.8 |
|  | (25) 2.5 | (39) 8.9 | (43) 5.1 | (12) 7.1 |  |  | (128) 3.2 | (147) 4.8 |
|  | -2.1 | 2.8 | 1.4 | 2.5 |  |  | 1.1 | 2.3 |
|  |  |  | 9.6 |  |  | Net Profit + Depr., Dep., | 13.1 | 9.2 |
|  |  |  | (10) 3.9 |  |  | Amort./Cur. Mat. L/T/D | (35) 2.6 | (39) 3.2 |
|  |  |  | 1.8 |  |  |  | 1.3 | 1.2 |
|  | .3 | .4 | .4 | .5 |  | Fixed/Worth | .4 | .3 |
|  | .9 | .8 | .7 | .8 |  |  | .8 | .8 |
|  | 1.8 | 1.6 | 1.5 | 1.7 |  |  | 1.5 | 1.5 |
|  | .5 | .7 | .6 | .8 |  | Debt/Worth | .6 | .9 |
|  | 2.6 | 1.2 | 1.8 | 3.0 |  |  | 1.6 | 1.9 |
|  | 25.7 | 3.5 | 3.4 | 8.5 |  |  | 3.8 | 5.6 |
|  | 38.2 | 39.2 | 38.9 | 58.3 |  | % Profit Before Taxes/Tangible | 35.3 | 52.7 |
|  | (23) 12.3 | (35) 25.6 | (43) 23.1 | (12) 26.9 |  | Net Worth | (127) 17.6 | (145) 25.1 |
|  | -9.5 | 11.9 | 9.4 | 21.6 |  |  | 4.4 | 8.4 |
|  | 17.3 | 18.8 | 18.2 | 18.2 |  | % Profit Before Taxes/Total | 15.6 | 14.9 |
|  | 6.2 | 11.9 | 7.2 | 8.6 |  | Assets | 6.6 | 8.8 |
|  | -3.1 | 5.4 | 1.4 | 4.3 |  |  | .7 | 3.6 |
|  | 40.4 | 34.0 | 22.6 | 22.5 |  | Sales/Net Fixed Assets | 29.2 | 33.7 |
|  | 19.6 | 10.9 | 11.7 | 14.6 |  |  | 11.4 | 15.5 |
|  | 7.5 | 5.4 | 6.7 | 5.6 |  |  | 5.1 | 6.9 |
|  | 5.0 | 4.8 | 4.1 | 4.1 |  | Sales/Total Assets | 3.9 | 4.7 |
|  | 3.4 | 3.1 | 3.0 | 3.0 |  |  | 2.9 | 3.2 |
|  | 2.5 | 1.9 | 1.9 | 1.1 |  |  | 2.0 | 2.4 |
|  | .6 | .8 | .7 | .7 |  | % Depr., Dep., Amort./Sales | .7 | .6 |
|  | (18) 1.5 | (33) 1.3 | (46) 1.5 | (11) 1.0 |  |  | (127) 1.5 | (139) 1.2 |
|  | 2.3 | 2.4 | 2.1 | 4.1 |  |  | 2.3 | 2.1 |
|  |  | .6 |  |  |  | % Officers', Directors' | .6 | .4 |
|  |  | (12) 1.0 |  |  |  | Owners' Comp/Sales | (31) 1.4 | (36) 1.1 |
|  |  | 1.7 |  |  |  |  | 2.8 | 2.5 |
| 5705M | 140427M | 748466M | 3463381M | 2629482M | 3488370M | Net Sales ($) | 8678475M | 15008980M |
| 1921M | 32915M | 219266M | 1058034M | 930524M | 1241677M | Total Assets ($) | 3583113M | 4158198M |

M = $ thousand    MM = $ million
See Pages 9 through 22 for Explanation of Ratios and Data

## Comparative Historical Data / Current Data Sorted by Sales

| | Comp Hist | | | Type of Statement | 0-1MM | 1-3MM | 3-5MM | 5-10MM | 10-25MM | 25MM & OVER |
|---|---|---|---|---|---|---|---|---|---|---|
| | 41 | 45 | 45 | Unqualified | 1 | | 1 | 2 | 5 | 36 |
| | 22 | 28 | 16 | Reviewed | | | 2 | 3 | 2 | 9 |
| | 13 | 12 | 13 | Compiled | 1 | 1 | 2 | 2 | 4 | 3 |
| | 16 | 14 | 16 | Tax Returns | | 3 | 4 | 2 | 4 | 3 |
| | 47 | 43 | 51 | Other | 3 | 4 | 5 | 10 | 7 | 22 |
| | 4/1/09-3/31/10 ALL | 4/1/10-3/31/11 ALL | 4/1/11-3/31/12 ALL | | 47 (4/1-9/30/11) | | 94 (10/1/11-3/31/12) | | | |
| **NUMBER OF STATEMENTS** | 139 | 142 | 141 | | 5 | 8 | 14 | 19 | 22 | 73 |
| | % | % | % | **ASSETS** | % | % | % | % | % | % |
| Cash & Equivalents | 7.7 | 7.2 | 8.8 | | | | 11.4 | 7.0 | 14.4 | 7.4 |
| Trade Receivables (net) | 26.4 | 24.5 | 24.9 | | | | 20.9 | 25.0 | 25.9 | 25.8 |
| Inventory | 23.3 | 23.9 | 24.2 | | | | 24.7 | 23.9 | 21.6 | 25.3 |
| All Other Current | 3.8 | 3.6 | 3.2 | | | | 2.8 | .9 | 1.6 | 3.8 |
| Total Current | 61.2 | 59.3 | 61.0 | | | | 59.9 | 56.8 | 63.6 | 62.2 |
| Fixed Assets (net) | 29.0 | 28.2 | 27.9 | | | | 20.9 | 35.3 | 27.4 | 26.2 |
| Intangibles (net) | 2.9 | 5.6 | 5.6 | | | | 8.4 | 3.5 | 4.9 | 6.6 |
| All Other Non-Current | 6.8 | 7.0 | 5.6 | | | | 10.8 | 4.4 | 4.2 | 5.0 |
| Total | 100.0 | 100.0 | 100.0 | | | | 100.0 | 100.0 | 100.0 | 100.0 |
| | | | | **LIABILITIES** | | | | | | |
| Notes Payable-Short Term | 12.0 | 11.4 | 9.9 | | | | 14.2 | 8.8 | 6.8 | 10.4 |
| Cur. Mat.-L.T.D. | 3.1 | 2.9 | 3.1 | | | | 3.1 | 4.8 | 2.2 | 2.5 |
| Trade Payables | 16.3 | 14.4 | 16.3 | | | | 12.4 | 18.9 | 17.9 | 16.5 |
| Income Taxes Payable | .1 | .2 | .1 | | | | .1 | .0 | .3 | .1 |
| All Other Current | 10.0 | 10.4 | 9.9 | | | | 13.6 | 14.4 | 8.5 | 8.6 |
| Total Current | 41.5 | 39.3 | 39.4 | | | | 43.4 | 46.8 | 35.7 | 38.1 |
| Long-Term Debt | 16.6 | 13.9 | 14.5 | | | | 13.0 | 18.2 | 11.8 | 11.6 |
| Deferred Taxes | .2 | .4 | .4 | | | | .1 | .0 | .3 | .6 |
| All Other Non-Current | 3.8 | 3.5 | 6.0 | | | | 9.2 | 2.2 | 5.4 | 5.5 |
| Net Worth | 37.9 | 42.8 | 39.8 | | | | 34.3 | 32.8 | 46.8 | 44.2 |
| Total Liabilities & Net Worth | 100.0 | 100.0 | 100.0 | | | | 100.0 | 100.0 | 100.0 | 100.0 |
| | | | | **INCOME DATA** | | | | | | |
| Net Sales | 100.0 | 100.0 | 100.0 | | | | 100.0 | 100.0 | 100.0 | 100.0 |
| Gross Profit | 21.7 | 23.5 | 23.2 | | | | 41.2 | 24.5 | 25.2 | 16.1 |
| Operating Expenses | 16.3 | 17.7 | 17.6 | | | | 32.2 | 19.4 | 16.3 | 11.7 |
| Operating Profit | 5.4 | 5.8 | 5.6 | | | | 8.9 | 5.0 | 8.9 | 4.4 |
| All Other Expenses (net) | .5 | .6 | .4 | | | | 1.2 | 1.1 | .2 | .0 |
| Profit Before Taxes | 5.0 | 5.2 | 5.2 | | | | 7.8 | 3.9 | 8.7 | 4.4 |
| | | | | **RATIOS** | | | | | | |
| Current | 2.5 | 2.5 | 2.5 | | | | 2.4 | 1.9 | 2.8 | 2.6 |
| | 1.4 | 1.4 | 1.7 | | | | 1.5 | 1.1 | 2.1 | 1.7 |
| | 1.1 | 1.1 | 1.1 | | | | 1.0 | .9 | 1.2 | 1.2 |
| Quick | 1.3 | 1.2 | 1.5 | | | | 1.7 | .9 | 2.0 | 1.5 |
| | .7 | .8 | .8 | | | | .7 | .6 | 1.5 | .8 |
| | .5 | .5 | .5 | | | | .3 | .3 | .7 | .6 |
| Sales/Receivables | 19 / 19.6 | 19 / 19.6 | 18 / 20.7 | | | | 16 / 22.4 | 20 / 18.5 | 14 / 26.1 | 18 / 20.4 |
| | 30 / 12.1 | 29 / 12.6 | 27 / 13.3 | | | | 32 / 11.5 | 31 / 11.9 | 27 / 13.7 | 27 / 13.3 |
| | 41 / 8.9 | 42 / 8.7 | 41 / 9.0 | | | | 72 / 5.1 | 38 / 9.7 | 49 / 7.5 | 42 / 8.7 |
| Cost of Sales/Inventory | 14 / 26.8 | 19 / 19.7 | 17 / 21.9 | | | | 33 / 11.1 | 19 / 19.0 | 15 / 24.5 | 15 / 25.1 |
| | 32 / 11.5 | 39 / 9.4 | 36 / 10.1 | | | | 68 / 5.4 | 30 / 12.0 | 33 / 10.9 | 31 / 11.6 |
| | 61 / 6.0 | 59 / 6.1 | 63 / 5.8 | | | | 182 / 2.0 | 58 / 6.3 | 65 / 5.6 | 51 / 7.2 |
| Cost of Sales/Payables | 13 / 28.6 | 13 / 28.4 | 11 / 32.4 | | | | 14 / 26.0 | 10 / 36.0 | 9 / 40.9 | 11 / 32.4 |
| | 22 / 16.9 | 20 / 18.5 | 22 / 16.6 | | | | 40 / 9.2 | 25 / 14.6 | 21 / 17.3 | 19 / 19.2 |
| | 34 / 10.8 | 30 / 12.2 | 36 / 10.1 | | | | 56 / 6.5 | 47 / 7.7 | 39 / 9.3 | 30 / 12.2 |
| Sales/Working Capital | 7.9 | 8.2 | 8.3 | | | | 4.3 | 10.2 | 4.9 | 8.3 |
| | 19.6 | 17.8 | 15.6 | | | | 16.5 | 53.0 | 10.9 | 14.8 |
| | 83.1 | 60.5 | 60.3 | | | | NM | -32.3 | 31.9 | 44.4 |
| EBIT/Interest | 18.7 | 22.1 | 16.3 | | | | 13.9 | 18.1 | 18.1 | 23.6 |
| | (126) 5.5 | (131) 6.8 | (128) 5.2 | | (13) 2.6 | | 5.8 | (21) 8.9 | (65) 5.2 | |
| | 1.8 | 2.2 | 1.8 | | | | 1.4 | 1.1 | 3.1 | 2.1 |
| Net Profit + Depr., Dep., Amort./Cur. Mat. L/T/D | 8.3 | 12.9 | 8.9 | | | | | | | 8.9 |
| | (30) 2.9 | (27) 5.2 | (25) 3.9 | | | | | | (17) | 5.9 |
| | .6 | 2.5 | 1.7 | | | | | | | 3.3 |
| Fixed/Worth | .4 | .4 | .4 | | | | .3 | .4 | .3 | .4 |
| | .8 | .7 | .8 | | | | .9 | 1.3 | .7 | .7 |
| | 1.9 | 1.4 | 1.6 | | | | 3.8 | 16.1 | 1.3 | 1.3 |
| Debt/Worth | .6 | .6 | .7 | | | | 1.2 | 1.0 | .8 | .6 |
| | 2.0 | 1.5 | 1.5 | | | | 2.7 | 2.9 | 1.2 | 1.3 |
| | 5.4 | 4.2 | 5.0 | | | | 35.1 | 78.4 | 3.1 | 3.5 |
| % Profit Before Taxes/Tangible Net Worth | 59.2 | 47.4 | 41.0 | | | | 49.9 | 73.1 | 43.2 | 38.0 |
| | (128) 25.9 | (132) 24.3 | (124) 22.9 | | (12) 20.4 | | (15) 12.3 | (20) 25.8 | (68) 23.6 | |
| | 9.3 | 9.2 | 11.3 | | | | 7.4 | 3.3 | 11.3 | 14.8 |
| % Profit Before Taxes/Total Assets | 20.7 | 16.6 | 17.6 | | | | 21.7 | 24.1 | 17.5 | 16.8 |
| | 10.0 | 8.7 | 8.3 | | | | 7.9 | 6.0 | 11.8 | 8.5 |
| | 2.2 | 2.6 | 2.5 | | | | 1.2 | .5 | 6.3 | 3.4 |
| Sales/Net Fixed Assets | 28.4 | 23.8 | 28.4 | | | | 45.5 | 35.4 | 48.2 | 23.5 |
| | 12.9 | 11.6 | 12.6 | | | | 10.8 | 13.3 | 10.1 | 15.0 |
| | 6.2 | 5.6 | 6.8 | | | | 5.1 | 3.9 | 6.2 | 7.8 |
| Sales/Total Assets | 4.1 | 3.8 | 4.2 | | | | 3.0 | 4.5 | 4.3 | 4.5 |
| | 2.9 | 2.8 | 3.0 | | | | 2.5 | 3.2 | 2.7 | 3.3 |
| | 2.1 | 2.1 | 2.1 | | | | 1.1 | 2.0 | 2.1 | 2.3 |
| % Depr., Dep., Amort./Sales | .8 | .7 | .7 | | | | | 1.1 | .7 | .6 |
| | (116) 1.2 | (124) 1.3 | (118) 1.2 | | | | (13) 1.6 | (20) 1.3 | (66) 1.0 | |
| | 2.6 | 2.6 | 2.2 | | | | | 3.7 | 2.4 | 1.8 |
| % Officers', Directors' Owners' Comp/Sales | .7 | .8 | .8 | | | | | | | .8 |
| | (28) 1.7 | (32) 1.7 | (29) 1.7 | | | | | | (11) | 1.4 |
| | 4.5 | 3.1 | 2.9 | | | | | | | 2.3 |
| Net Sales ($) | 9605336M | 11327653M | 10475831M | | 3957M | 14978M | 54834M | 146915M | 361984M | 9893163M |
| Total Assets ($) | 3672779M | 4187378M | 3484337M | | 9261M | 5701M | 39694M | 67156M | 143789M | 3218736M |

M = $ thousand    MM = $ million
See Pages 9 through 22 for Explanation of Ratios and Data

## Current Data Sorted by Assets                                   Comparative Historical Data

| 0-500M | 500M-2MM | 2-10MM | 10-50MM | 50-100MM | 100-250MM | | 4/1/07-3/31/08 ALL | 4/1/08-3/31/09 ALL |
|---|---|---|---|---|---|---|---|---|
| | | | | | | **Type of Statement** | 19 | 22 |
| | | 1 | 8 | 2 | 7 | Unqualified | 19 | 22 |
| | 1 | 5 | 4 | | | Reviewed | 5 | 6 |
| 1 | | 3 | 1 | | | Compiled | 4 | 5 |
| | 1 | 1 | | | | Tax Returns | 3 | 4 |
| 1 | 2 | 2 | 2 | 3 | 4 | Other | 15 | 20 |
| 2 | 4 | 12 | 15 | 5 | 11 | **NUMBER OF STATEMENTS** | 46 | 57 |
| % | % | % | % | % | % | **ASSETS** | % | % |
| | | 7.3 | 6.1 | | 3.8 | Cash & Equivalents | 5.8 | 4.9 |
| | | 24.7 | 16.6 | | 21.5 | Trade Receivables (net) | 19.5 | 20.7 |
| | | 26.4 | 32.2 | | 31.4 | Inventory | 25.8 | 29.9 |
| | | 3.6 | 1.0 | | 6.2 | All Other Current | 4.4 | 3.3 |
| | | 62.0 | 56.0 | | 62.9 | Total Current | 55.5 | 58.8 |
| | | 32.8 | 32.1 | | 30.5 | Fixed Assets (net) | 37.7 | 32.2 |
| | | 3.3 | 4.5 | | .5 | Intangibles (net) | 2.1 | 3.2 |
| | | 1.9 | 7.5 | | 6.1 | All Other Non-Current | 4.7 | 5.9 |
| | | 100.0 | 100.0 | | 100.0 | Total | 100.0 | 100.0 |
| | | | | | | **LIABILITIES** | | |
| | | 9.6 | 16.3 | | 18.3 | Notes Payable-Short Term | 13.7 | 15.6 |
| | | 7.2 | 5.3 | | 1.3 | Cur. Mat.-L.T.D. | 3.0 | 3.5 |
| | | 18.0 | 11.4 | | 13.4 | Trade Payables | 12.8 | 14.1 |
| | | .1 | .1 | | .4 | Income Taxes Payable | .2 | .3 |
| | | 6.7 | 9.8 | | 4.6 | All Other Current | 6.0 | 7.4 |
| | | 41.6 | 42.9 | | 38.1 | Total Current | 35.8 | 40.8 |
| | | 26.9 | 13.4 | | 15.2 | Long-Term Debt | 18.8 | 19.1 |
| | | .1 | 1.1 | | 2.0 | Deferred Taxes | 1.6 | 1.3 |
| | | 3.0 | 5.6 | | 2.6 | All Other Non-Current | 3.8 | 4.4 |
| | | 28.3 | 37.0 | | 42.1 | Net Worth | 40.1 | 34.4 |
| | | 100.0 | 100.0 | | 100.0 | Total Liabilties & Net Worth | 100.0 | 100.0 |
| | | | | | | **INCOME DATA** | | |
| | | 100.0 | 100.0 | | 100.0 | Net Sales | 100.0 | 100.0 |
| | | 24.0 | 21.5 | | 11.0 | Gross Profit | 20.0 | 20.0 |
| | | 22.2 | 14.7 | | 6.4 | Operating Expenses | 14.6 | 15.6 |
| | | 1.8 | 6.9 | | 4.7 | Operating Profit | 5.4 | 4.5 |
| | | 1.3 | 1.2 | | .8 | All Other Expenses (net) | 1.2 | 1.0 |
| | | .4 | 5.7 | | 3.8 | Profit Before Taxes | 4.2 | 3.4 |
| | | | | | | **RATIOS** | | |
| | | 1.9 | 1.8 | | 2.3 | | 2.1 | 1.8 |
| | | 1.4 | 1.6 | | 1.5 | Current | 1.5 | 1.4 |
| | | 1.1 | .8 | | 1.3 | | 1.2 | 1.2 |
| | | 1.3 | 1.0 | | 1.0 | | 1.1 | .9 |
| | | .7 | .6 | | .6 | Quick | .7 | .6 |
| | | .6 | .1 | | .4 | | .4 | .4 |
| | | 25  14.6 | 19  19.7 | | 32  11.5 | | 26  14.2 | 25  14.9 |
| | | 29  12.6 | 33  11.1 | | 35  10.3 | Sales/Receivables | 35  10.4 | 31  11.7 |
| | | 38  9.6 | 46  7.9 | | 42  8.6 | | 44  8.3 | 38  9.7 |
| | | 21  17.4 | 36  10.0 | | 42  8.6 | | 36  10.2 | 34  10.8 |
| | | 29  12.6 | 76  4.8 | | 66  5.5 | Cost of Sales/Inventory | 57  6.4 | 52  7.0 |
| | | 63  5.8 | 101  3.6 | | 72  5.1 | | 77  4.7 | 88  4.1 |
| | | 11  34.4 | 14  25.4 | | 12  30.4 | | 11  34.6 | 9  41.9 |
| | | 34  10.8 | 26  14.2 | | 16  22.6 | Cost of Sales/Payables | 22  16.5 | 23  16.1 |
| | | 68  5.4 | 41  8.9 | | 42  8.7 | | 38  9.6 | 34  10.8 |
| | | 9.9 | 6.6 | | 6.3 | | 7.0 | 9.1 |
| | | 11.3 | 10.3 | | 9.3 | Sales/Working Capital | 12.2 | 13.1 |
| | | 118.6 | -23.9 | | 19.0 | | 23.4 | 36.7 |
| | | 10.2 | 13.1 | | 13.2 | | 11.4 | 7.4 |
| | | 2.5 | 9.4 | | (10)  5.9 | EBIT/Interest | 3.7 | (56)  3.7 |
| | | 1.6 | 2.7 | | 2.4 | | 1.8 | 1.1 |
| | | | | | | Net Profit + Depr., Dep., | 7.6 | 10.9 |
| | | | | | | Amort./Cur. Mat. L/T/D | (12)  2.5 | (21)  4.2 |
| | | | | | | | 1.6 | 1.9 |
| | | .4 | .4 | | .5 | | .5 | .5 |
| | | 1.1 | .8 | | .8 | Fixed/Worth | 1.1 | 1.0 |
| | | 5.1 | 3.0 | | 1.3 | | 1.8 | 1.8 |
| | | .8 | .9 | | .8 | | .9 | 1.1 |
| | | 4.0 | 1.5 | | 1.6 | Debt/Worth | 1.6 | 2.2 |
| | | 12.8 | 7.5 | | 2.5 | | 3.6 | 4.0 |
| | | 31.7 | 41.3 | | 29.8 | % Profit Before Taxes/Tangible | 29.1 | 39.2 |
| | | (11)  17.1 | (13)  23.3 | | 28.2 | Net Worth | 18.7 | (53)  22.7 |
| | | 4.4 | 19.0 | | 16.6 | | 8.2 | 6.2 |
| | | 17.0 | 13.6 | | 11.9 | % Profit Before Taxes/Total | 12.3 | 13.7 |
| | | 5.4 | 10.5 | | 9.6 | Assets | 6.3 | 8.6 |
| | | 1.9 | 3.5 | | 6.3 | | 2.5 | .8 |
| | | 21.7 | 11.8 | | 13.1 | | 11.5 | 15.3 |
| | | 9.6 | 5.1 | | 5.8 | Sales/Net Fixed Assets | 6.8 | 8.3 |
| | | 4.8 | 3.3 | | 5.2 | | 3.0 | 3.9 |
| | | 4.0 | 2.6 | | 2.7 | | 2.9 | 2.9 |
| | | 2.5 | 1.7 | | 2.0 | Sales/Total Assets | 1.8 | 2.2 |
| | | 1.9 | 1.5 | | 1.7 | | 1.5 | 1.7 |
| | | 1.2 | | | | | 1.0 | 1.2 |
| | | 2.1 | | | | % Depr., Dep., Amort./Sales | (41)  2.2 | (53)  2.0 |
| | | 2.7 | | | | | 3.3 | 2.8 |
| | | | | | | % Officers', Directors' Owners' Comp/Sales | | |
| 40M | 21467M | 135377M | 750938M | 845516M | 3982138M | Net Sales ($) | 5007981M | 7591347M |
| 17M | 5842M | 49880M | 390306M | 400839M | 1841843M | Total Assets ($) | 2784036M | 3724441M |

**Note for Comparative Historical Data columns:** 4/1/07-3/31/08 ALL (22 (4/1-9/30/11)); 4/1/08-3/31/09 ALL (27 (10/1/11-3/31/12)).

M = $ thousand    MM = $ million

## Comparative Historical Data / Current Data Sorted by Sales

**Type of Statement**

| 4/1/09-3/31/10 ALL | 4/1/10-3/31/11 ALL | 4/1/11-3/31/12 ALL | Type of Statement | 0-1MM | 1-3MM | 3-5MM | 5-10MM | 10-25MM | 25MM & OVER |
|---|---|---|---|---|---|---|---|---|---|
| 18 | 21 | 18 | Unqualified | | | 1 | | 1 | 17 |
| 5 | 3 | 10 | Reviewed | | | | 1 | 2 | 4 |
| 6 | 6 | 5 | Compiled | 1 | | | 2 | 2 | 1 |
| 4 | 3 | 2 | Tax Returns | | | | 1 | | |
| 16 | 8 | 14 | Other | 1 | 2 | 1 | 2 | 2 | 8 |

Current Data date groups: 22 (4/1-9/30/11) ; 27 (10/1/11-3/31/12)

| 4/1/09-3/31/10 ALL | 4/1/10-3/31/11 ALL | 4/1/11-3/31/12 ALL | | 0-1MM | 1-3MM | 3-5MM | 5-10MM | 10-25MM | 25MM & OVER |
|---|---|---|---|---|---|---|---|---|---|
| 49 | 41 | 49 | **NUMBER OF STATEMENTS** | 2 | 2 | 2 | 6 | 7 | 30 |
| % | % | % | | % | % | % | % | % | % |
| | | | **ASSETS** | | | | | | |
| 7.5 | 6.1 | 6.5 | Cash & Equivalents | | | | | | 5.9 |
| 20.1 | 20.9 | 22.2 | Trade Receivables (net) | | | | | | 19.5 |
| 26.9 | 26.1 | 28.9 | Inventory | | | | | | 31.5 |
| 3.1 | 4.9 | 2.7 | All Other Current | | | | | | 2.9 |
| 57.6 | 58.0 | 60.3 | Total Current | | | | | | 59.9 |
| 33.2 | 32.4 | 31.8 | Fixed Assets (net) | | | | | | 30.6 |
| 2.6 | 1.9 | 3.1 | Intangibles (net) | | | | | | 3.4 |
| 6.7 | 7.7 | 5.1 | All Other Non-Current | | | | | | 6.0 |
| 100.0 | 100.0 | 100.0 | Total | | | | | | 100.0 |
| | | | **LIABILITIES** | | | | | | |
| 13.3 | 11.5 | 14.2 | Notes Payable-Short Term | | | | | | 16.3 |
| 3.5 | 2.6 | 4.4 | Cur. Mat.-L.T.D. | | | | | | 3.6 |
| 11.1 | 11.5 | 15.1 | Trade Payables | | | | | | 11.0 |
| .3 | .4 | .1 | Income Taxes Payable | | | | | | .2 |
| 7.0 | 6.9 | 6.9 | All Other Current | | | | | | 8.4 |
| 35.2 | 32.9 | 40.7 | Total Current | | | | | | 39.4 |
| 17.5 | 17.2 | 20.0 | Long-Term Debt | | | | | | 12.6 |
| 1.2 | .8 | .8 | Deferred Taxes | | | | | | 1.3 |
| 3.9 | 6.6 | 3.6 | All Other Non-Current | | | | | | 3.4 |
| 42.2 | 42.5 | 35.0 | Net Worth | | | | | | 43.3 |
| 100.0 | 100.0 | 100.0 | Total Liabilties & Net Worth | | | | | | 100.0 |
| | | | **INCOME DATA** | | | | | | |
| 100.0 | 100.0 | 100.0 | Net Sales | | | | | | 100.0 |
| 22.3 | 20.8 | 20.8 | Gross Profit | | | | | | 17.2 |
| 15.9 | 14.9 | 16.0 | Operating Expenses | | | | | | 11.0 |
| 6.4 | 5.9 | 4.9 | Operating Profit | | | | | | 6.2 |
| 1.6 | 1.2 | 1.0 | All Other Expenses (net) | | | | | | .8 |
| 4.8 | 4.7 | 3.9 | Profit Before Taxes | | | | | | 5.4 |
| | | | **RATIOS** | | | | | | |
| 2.5 | 3.3 | 2.2 | Current | | | | | | 2.3 |
| 1.6 | 1.9 | 1.5 | | | | | | | 1.6 |
| 1.2 | 1.3 | 1.1 | | | | | | | 1.2 |
| 1.4 | 1.4 | 1.0 | Quick | | | | | | 1.0 |
| .7 | .9 | .7 | | | | | | | .7 |
| .5 | .5 | .5 | | | | | | | .4 |
| 22  16.5 | 22  16.6 | 25  14.6 | Sales/Receivables | | | | | | 25  14.7 |
| 28  12.9 | 30  12.1 | 33  11.1 | | | | | | | 33  10.9 |
| 36  10.2 | 47  7.7 | 42  8.7 | | | | | | | 43  8.5 |
| 33  11.2 | 33  11.1 | 29  12.6 | Cost of Sales/Inventory | | | | | | 41  9.0 |
| 47  7.8 | 52  7.0 | 58  6.3 | | | | | | | 66  5.5 |
| 65  5.6 | 78  4.7 | 76  4.8 | | | | | | | 83  4.4 |
| 9  39.1 | 10  36.2 | 14  27.0 | Cost of Sales/Payables | | | | | | 12  30.4 |
| 16  23.0 | 21  17.6 | 26  14.2 | | | | | | | 18  20.7 |
| 32  11.5 | 30  12.1 | 45  8.1 | | | | | | | 35  10.5 |
| 7.3 | 6.2 | 6.9 | Sales/Working Capital | | | | | | 6.5 |
| 12.1 | 8.5 | 10.3 | | | | | | | 10.1 |
| 19.0 | 18.3 | 62.7 | | | | | | | 24.8 |
| 25.6 | 25.9 | 11.7 | EBIT/Interest | | | | | | 13.0 |
| (37)  5.6 | (45)  6.8 | 5.1 | | | | | | (28) | 7.8 |
| 1.7 | 2.1 | 2.1 | | | | | | | 3.2 |
| 8.4 | 17.0 | 7.4 | Net Profit + Depr., Dep., Amort./Cur. Mat. L/T/D | | | | | | 7.6 |
| (19)  4.7 | (12)  6.0 | (18)  4.2 | | | | | | (15) | 4.8 |
| 1.9 | 1.9 | 1.8 | | | | | | | 2.5 |
| .3 | .3 | .4 | Fixed/Worth | | | | | | .4 |
| .9 | .7 | .8 | | | | | | | .8 |
| 1.6 | 1.4 | 1.4 | | | | | | | 1.3 |
| .8 | .7 | .8 | Debt/Worth | | | | | | .9 |
| 1.7 | 1.5 | 1.7 | | | | | | | 1.5 |
| 3.1 | 3.2 | 5.6 | | | | | | | 3.0 |
| 45.0 | 40.7 | 41.3 | % Profit Before Taxes/Tangible Net Worth | | | | | | 41.3 |
| (48)  30.0 | (39)  32.3 | (45)  25.8 | | | | | | (29) | 28.2 |
| 13.5 | 15.3 | 15.9 | | | | | | | 18.4 |
| 22.4 | 20.1 | 14.5 | % Profit Before Taxes/Total Assets | | | | | | 14.5 |
| 11.8 | 12.1 | 8.8 | | | | | | | 9.8 |
| 2.6 | 3.3 | 2.2 | | | | | | | 7.2 |
| 13.0 | 19.7 | 13.4 | Sales/Net Fixed Assets | | | | | | 13.2 |
| 8.7 | 8.6 | 6.7 | | | | | | | 6.2 |
| 4.5 | 3.8 | 4.8 | | | | | | | 4.9 |
| 3.1 | 2.7 | 2.7 | Sales/Total Assets | | | | | | 2.7 |
| 2.4 | 2.1 | 2.2 | | | | | | | 2.1 |
| 1.9 | 1.6 | 1.7 | | | | | | | 1.6 |
| 1.1 | 1.3 | 1.2 | % Depr., Dep., Amort./Sales | | | | | | .9 |
| (43)  1.8 | (34)  1.9 | (40)  1.9 | | | | | | (27) | 1.5 |
| 2.6 | 3.2 | 2.7 | | | | | | | 2.1 |
| | | .4 | % Officers', Directors' Owners' Comp/Sales | | | | | | |
| | (10)  1.2 | 1.2 | | | | | | | |
| | | 2.6 | | | | | | | |
| 6269175M | 3876283M | 5735476M | Net Sales ($) | 40M | 4758M | 9247M | 45596M | 104819M | 5571016M |
| 2653058M | 1910207M | 2688727M | Total Assets ($) | 17M | 5621M | 4084M | 16014M | 45403M | 2617588M |

M = $ thousand    MM = $ million
See Pages 9 through 22 for Explanation of Ratios and Data

## Current Data Sorted by Assets      Comparative Historical Data

| 0-500M | 500M-2MM | 2-10MM | 10-50MM | 50-100MM | 100-250MM | Type of Statement | 4/1/07-3/31/08 ALL | 4/1/08-3/31/09 ALL |
|---|---|---|---|---|---|---|---|---|
|  |  | 2 | 10 | 1 | 1 | Unqualified | 16 | 14 |
|  | 2 | 11 | 5 |  |  | Reviewed | 13 | 17 |
| 1 | 2 | 2 |  |  |  | Compiled | 12 | 11 |
| 3 | 5 | 2 | 1 |  |  | Tax Returns | 7 | 6 |
| 3 | 5 | 4 | 6 | 4 |  | Other | 28 | 31 |
|  | 28 (4/1-9/30/11) |  | 42 (10/1/11-3/31/12) |  |  |  |  |  |
| 7 | 14 | 21 | 22 | 5 | 1 | **NUMBER OF STATEMENTS** | 76 | 79 |
| % | % | % | % | % | % | **ASSETS** | % | % |
|  | 12.5 | 20.0 | 6.6 |  |  | Cash & Equivalents | 9.5 | 10.2 |
|  | 11.0 | 15.8 | 18.3 |  |  | Trade Receivables (net) | 15.0 | 14.7 |
|  | 33.5 | 25.2 | 28.5 |  |  | Inventory | 31.8 | 30.7 |
|  | 3.3 | 1.9 | 1.9 |  |  | All Other Current | 2.6 | 2.3 |
|  | 60.3 | 62.9 | 55.3 |  |  | Total Current | 58.9 | 57.9 |
|  | 20.9 | 29.1 | 35.6 |  |  | Fixed Assets (net) | 29.0 | 31.7 |
|  | 7.5 | 2.4 | 2.0 |  |  | Intangibles (net) | 5.9 | 5.4 |
|  | 11.2 | 5.6 | 7.1 |  |  | All Other Non-Current | 6.2 | 5.0 |
|  | 100.0 | 100.0 | 100.0 |  |  | Total | 100.0 | 100.0 |
|  |  |  |  |  |  | **LIABILITIES** |  |  |
|  | 15.5 | 4.8 | 10.1 |  |  | Notes Payable-Short Term | 15.3 | 9.6 |
|  | 5.3 | 2.7 | 1.9 |  |  | Cur. Mat.-L.T.D. | 3.5 | 3.0 |
|  | 10.6 | 10.6 | 11.6 |  |  | Trade Payables | 11.0 | 11.8 |
|  | .2 | .5 | .2 |  |  | Income Taxes Payable | .3 | .2 |
|  | 8.3 | 7.6 | 6.5 |  |  | All Other Current | 7.4 | 8.5 |
|  | 39.9 | 26.2 | 30.2 |  |  | Total Current | 37.5 | 33.3 |
|  | 34.9 | 11.8 | 8.1 |  |  | Long-Term Debt | 18.2 | 18.2 |
|  | .1 | 1.0 | 1.3 |  |  | Deferred Taxes | .6 | .5 |
|  | 11.5 | 7.7 | 5.0 |  |  | All Other Non-Current | 6.1 | 4.7 |
|  | 13.5 | 53.3 | 55.5 |  |  | Net Worth | 37.6 | 43.3 |
|  | 100.0 | 100.0 | 100.0 |  |  | Total Liabilities & Net Worth | 100.0 | 100.0 |
|  |  |  |  |  |  | **INCOME DATA** |  |  |
|  | 100.0 | 100.0 | 100.0 |  |  | Net Sales | 100.0 | 100.0 |
|  | 45.5 | 41.1 | 25.1 |  |  | Gross Profit | 34.8 | 36.1 |
|  | 41.4 | 33.6 | 20.6 |  |  | Operating Expenses | 30.1 | 33.4 |
|  | 4.1 | 7.4 | 4.6 |  |  | Operating Profit | 4.7 | 2.7 |
|  | 1.8 | .6 | .4 |  |  | All Other Expenses (net) | 2.3 | 1.9 |
|  | 2.4 | 6.8 | 4.1 |  |  | Profit Before Taxes | 2.4 | .9 |
|  |  |  |  |  |  | **RATIOS** |  |  |
|  | 2.6 | 4.5 | 3.9 |  |  | Current | 3.3 | 3.3 |
|  | 1.8 | 2.4 | 2.0 |  |  |  | 1.7 | 1.8 |
|  | .9 | 1.6 | 1.3 |  |  |  | 1.2 | 1.2 |
|  | 1.9 | 3.0 | 1.6 |  |  | Quick | 1.4 | 1.7 |
|  | .8 | 1.6 | .8 |  |  |  | .7 | .8 |
|  | .2 | .7 | .5 |  |  |  | .4 | .3 |
|  | 4   90.5 | 10   36.7 | 21   17.7 |  |  | Sales/Receivables | 10   35.3 | 11   33.3 |
|  | 13   27.4 | 26   14.2 | 29   12.4 |  |  |  | 21   17.2 | 24   15.0 |
|  | 20   18.7 | 35   10.4 | 45   8.2 |  |  |  | 36   10.2 | 32   11.5 |
|  | 47   7.8 | 46   8.0 | 46   7.9 |  |  | Cost of Sales/Inventory | 44   8.3 | 47   7.8 |
|  | 104   3.5 | 61   6.0 | 62   5.9 |  |  |  | 65   5.6 | 69   5.3 |
|  | 174   2.1 | 87   4.2 | 87   4.2 |  |  |  | 108   3.4 | 102   3.6 |
|  | 6   57.2 | 12   30.2 | 14   25.5 |  |  | Cost of Sales/Payables | 13   28.3 | 11   34.5 |
|  | 15   24.2 | 17   21.6 | 20   18.3 |  |  |  | 24   15.2 | 26   14.3 |
|  | 42   8.6 | 40   9.2 | 30   12.1 |  |  |  | 39   9.4 | 40   9.0 |
|  | 4.7 | 4.3 | 4.9 |  |  | Sales/Working Capital | 5.7 | 5.1 |
|  | 10.3 | 8.4 | 9.1 |  |  |  | 10.7 | 9.0 |
|  | -34.9 | 13.5 | 16.8 |  |  |  | 21.9 | 26.5 |
|  | 10.5 | 44.8 | 24.1 |  |  | EBIT/Interest | 9.3 | 6.7 |
|  | (13) 1.3 | (17) 9.0 | (21) 7.4 |  |  |  | (70) 2.4 | (72) 1.6 |
|  | -1.0 | 2.8 | 2.3 |  |  |  | .7 | -.6 |
|  |  |  | 14.6 |  |  | Net Profit + Depr., Dep., Amort./Cur. Mat. L/T/D | 11.6 | 3.9 |
|  |  |  | (10) 4.9 |  |  |  | (20) 3.4 | (20) 1.5 |
|  |  |  | 2.3 |  |  |  | 1.3 | .5 |
|  | .2 | .2 | .5 |  |  | Fixed/Worth | .4 | .4 |
|  | 1.5 | .5 | .6 |  |  |  | .8 | .8 |
|  | -.5 | 1.2 | .9 |  |  |  | 1.9 | 3.3 |
|  | .4 | .3 | .4 |  |  | Debt/Worth | .7 | .4 |
|  | 4.5 | .8 | .7 |  |  |  | 1.7 | 1.6 |
|  | -2.8 | 2.4 | 1.7 |  |  |  | 11.4 | 7.6 |
|  |  | 50.5 | 24.0 |  |  | % Profit Before Taxes/Tangible Net Worth | 46.5 | 25.8 |
|  |  | (18) 28.0 | (21) 13.6 |  |  |  | (63) 16.0 | (68) 9.0 |
|  |  | 12.9 | 4.8 |  |  |  | 2.6 | -4.1 |
|  | 11.4 | 24.8 | 14.3 |  |  | % Profit Before Taxes/Total Assets | 13.1 | 9.9 |
|  | 1.8 | 13.2 | 6.5 |  |  |  | 5.5 | 2.9 |
|  | -4.1 | 2.6 | 2.3 |  |  |  | -1.4 | -4.4 |
|  | 16.5 | 15.7 | 10.3 |  |  | Sales/Net Fixed Assets | 15.5 | 12.9 |
|  | 11.3 | 7.4 | 6.0 |  |  |  | 8.2 | 7.5 |
|  | 8.6 | 6.3 | 3.8 |  |  |  | 4.5 | 4.6 |
|  | 2.7 | 3.2 | 2.7 |  |  | Sales/Total Assets | 2.8 | 3.0 |
|  | 2.4 | 2.6 | 2.1 |  |  |  | 2.0 | 2.1 |
|  | 1.7 | 2.1 | 1.4 |  |  |  | 1.5 | 1.5 |
|  | 1.1 | 1.0 | 1.8 |  |  | % Depr., Dep., Amort./Sales | 1.6 | 1.2 |
|  | (13) 1.6 | (18) 2.5 | 3.0 |  |  |  | (67) 2.2 | (71) 2.3 |
|  | 2.5 | 3.4 | 3.6 |  |  |  | 3.4 | 3.6 |
|  |  |  |  |  |  | % Officers', Directors', Owners' Comp/Sales | 3.0 | 2.0 |
|  |  |  |  |  |  |  | (19) 6.4 | (24) 4.1 |
|  |  |  |  |  |  |  | 8.8 | 7.2 |
| 7680M | 31936M | 261479M | 1121792M | 809947M | 308249M | Net Sales ($) | 2237951M | 2285137M |
| 1760M | 15106M | 103931M | 525853M | 393548M | 129143M | Total Assets ($) | 1365568M | 1230427M |

M = $ thousand     MM = $ million
See Pages 9 through 22 for Explanation of Ratios and Data

## Comparative Historical Data | Current Data Sorted by Sales

**Type of Statement**

| 4/1/09-3/31/10 | 4/1/10-3/31/11 | 4/1/11-3/31/12 | Type of Statement | 0-1MM | 1-3MM | 3-5MM | 5-10MM | 10-25MM | 25MM & OVER |
|---|---|---|---|---|---|---|---|---|---|
| 17 | 12 | 14 | Unqualified | | 2 | 1 | 4 | 6 | 12 |
| 14 | 16 | 19 | Reviewed | | 2 | | 1 | 1 | 6 |
| 9 | 9 | 7 | Compiled | 3 | 2 | | 1 | 1 | |
| 9 | 7 | 11 | Tax Returns | 3 | 3 | 2 | 2 | 1 | |
| 19 | 27 | 19 | Other | | 2 | 1 | 1 | 4 | 9 |
| ALL | ALL | ALL | | | 28 (4/1-9/30/11) | | | 42 (10/1/11-3/31/12) | |

| 4/1/09-3/31/10 ALL | 4/1/10-3/31/11 ALL | 4/1/11-3/31/12 ALL | | 0-1MM | 1-3MM | 3-5MM | 5-10MM | 10-25MM | 25MM & OVER |
|---|---|---|---|---|---|---|---|---|---|
| 68 | 71 | 70 | **NUMBER OF STATEMENTS** | 6 | 11 | 4 | 9 | 13 | 27 |
| % | % | % | **ASSETS** | % | % | % | % | % | % |
| 9.3 | 10.2 | 12.2 | Cash & Equivalents | | 7.6 | | | 9.7 | 9.4 |
| 15.5 | 16.4 | 15.1 | Trade Receivables (net) | | 9.8 | | | 14.7 | 21.0 |
| 29.2 | 28.4 | 28.8 | Inventory | | 39.3 | | | 28.8 | 25.4 |
| 2.4 | 4.2 | 2.9 | All Other Current | | 6.7 | | | 1.9 | 2.6 |
| 56.5 | 59.2 | 58.9 | Total Current | | 63.4 | | | 55.1 | 58.4 |
| 33.0 | 30.0 | 28.5 | Fixed Assets (net) | | 17.4 | | | 36.7 | 31.8 |
| 5.0 | 6.0 | 4.4 | Intangibles (net) | | 9.3 | | | 1.1 | 3.6 |
| 5.5 | 4.8 | 8.1 | All Other Non-Current | | 9.9 | | | 7.1 | 6.2 |
| 100.0 | 100.0 | 100.0 | Total | | 100.0 | | | 100.0 | 100.0 |
| | | | **LIABILITIES** | | | | | | |
| 12.1 | 13.5 | 10.0 | Notes Payable-Short Term | | 23.1 | | | 8.2 | 7.1 |
| 4.5 | 3.2 | 3.0 | Cur. Mat.-L.T.D. | | 3.9 | | | 3.2 | 1.4 |
| 11.1 | 14.1 | 11.8 | Trade Payables | | 8.8 | | | 12.2 | 10.4 |
| .3 | .2 | .3 | Income Taxes Payable | | .1 | | | .5 | .2 |
| 8.1 | 9.1 | 9.2 | All Other Current | | 13.3 | | | 7.1 | 9.1 |
| 36.1 | 40.1 | 34.2 | Total Current | | 49.2 | | | 31.2 | 28.2 |
| 18.5 | 20.4 | 16.7 | Long-Term Debt | | 25.0 | | | 13.8 | 10.4 |
| .7 | .9 | .8 | Deferred Taxes | | .2 | | | 2.2 | .8 |
| 8.4 | 9.5 | 9.8 | All Other Non-Current | | 15.3 | | | 9.3 | 4.7 |
| 36.3 | 29.1 | 38.6 | Net Worth | | 10.4 | | | 43.5 | 55.8 |
| 100.0 | 100.0 | 100.0 | Total Liabilities & Net Worth | | 100.0 | | | 100.0 | 100.0 |
| | | | **INCOME DATA** | | | | | | |
| 100.0 | 100.0 | 100.0 | Net Sales | | 100.0 | | | 100.0 | 100.0 |
| 35.8 | 35.5 | 36.0 | Gross Profit | | 40.8 | | | 31.9 | 26.9 |
| 33.9 | 31.3 | 30.5 | Operating Expenses | | 36.3 | | | 25.8 | 19.8 |
| 2.0 | 4.2 | 5.5 | Operating Profit | | 4.5 | | | 6.1 | 7.1 |
| 1.0 | 1.0 | .9 | All Other Expenses (net) | | 1.9 | | | 1.1 | .7 |
| 1.0 | 3.2 | 4.6 | Profit Before Taxes | | 2.6 | | | 5.0 | 6.4 |
| | | | **RATIOS** | | | | | | |
| 2.6 | 3.3 | 3.7 | Current | | 2.2 | | | 3.8 | 4.0 |
| 1.6 | 1.6 | 1.8 | | | 1.5 | | | 1.8 | 2.3 |
| 1.1 | 1.0 | 1.3 | | | .9 | | | 1.2 | 1.4 |
| 1.4 | 1.4 | 1.9 | Quick | | | | | 1.8 | 2.3 |
| .7 (70) | .7 (68) | .9 | | | | | | .9 | 1.0 |
| .3 | .4 | .5 | | | | | | .4 | .6 |
| 12  30.9 | 12  29.4 | 9  42.9 | Sales/Receivables | 1  432.0 | | | | 6  58.0 | 24  14.9 |
| 20  18.5 | 24  15.1 | 24  15.2 | | 7  49.9 | | | | 26  14.2 | 31  11.9 |
| 32  11.4 | 36  10.1 | 38  9.6 | | 17  21.1 | | | | 36  10.1 | 43  8.4 |
| 39  9.3 | 35  10.6 | 46  7.9 | Cost of Sales/Inventory | 66  5.5 | | | | 48  7.6 | 41  8.8 |
| 63  5.8 | 66  5.5 | 61  6.0 | | 104  3.5 | | | | 61  6.0 | 55  6.6 |
| 109  3.4 | 99  3.7 | 91  4.0 | | 166  2.2 | | | | 74  4.9 | 74  4.9 |
| 13  27.7 | 11  31.9 | 11  31.8 | Cost of Sales/Payables | 6  60.5 | | | | 11  33.0 | 15  24.8 |
| 24  15.1 | 26  13.9 | 19  19.1 | | 9  39.0 | | | | 17  21.6 | 20  18.4 |
| 39  9.3 | 40  9.2 | 37  9.9 | | 42  8.6 | | | | 42  8.7 | 29  12.5 |
| 6.6 | 6.1 | 5.2 | Sales/Working Capital | | 6.4 | | | 7.4 | 3.9 |
| 12.2 | 12.9 | 9.9 | | | 28.2 | | | 12.6 | 7.9 |
| 29.1 | 180.4 | 28.5 | | | -30.4 | | | 17.1 | 14.4 |
| 12.6 | 10.6 | 20.0 | EBIT/Interest | | 7.4 | | | 18.8 | 30.1 |
| (64) 1.8 | (63) 3.8 | (63) 4.9 | | (10) 1.6 | | | (12) 5.0 | | (25) 10.6 |
| .0 | 1.1 | 1.3 | | | .7 | | | 1.8 | 3.2 |
| 7.1 | 5.3 | 6.7 | Net Profit + Depr., Dep., Amort./Cur. Mat. L/T/D | | | | | | 10.9 |
| (20) 2.8 | (23) 3.5 | (18) 3.5 | | | | | | (11) | 5.9 |
| 1.1 | 2.2 | .8 | | | | | | | 3.3 |
| .4 | .4 | .4 | Fixed/Worth | | .1 | | | .5 | .5 |
| 1.1 | 1.0 | .6 | | | .6 | | | .9 | .6 |
| 4.8 | 9.7 | 2.2 | | | -.6 | | | 1.8 | 1.1 |
| .5 | .5 | .4 | Debt/Worth | | 1.4 | | | .6 | .3 |
| 1.9 | 2.2 | .8 | | | 6.4 | | | 1.0 | .7 |
| UND | -107.0 | 5.0 | | | -2.8 | | | 2.6 | 1.8 |
| 27.7 | 28.4 | 37.1 | % Profit Before Taxes/Tangible Net Worth | | | | | 47.5 | 34.2 |
| (52) 11.7 | (53) 15.5 | (57) 17.4 | | | | | (11) | 25.1 | (25) 18.4 |
| -5.3 | 4.0 | 5.7 | | | | | | 3.3 | 8.2 |
| 12.1 | 13.6 | 16.2 | % Profit Before Taxes/Total Assets | | 10.9 | | | 22.0 | 19.1 |
| 2.6 | 7.4 | 6.5 | | | 1.9 | | | 11.1 | 7.6 |
| -3.6 | .2 | 1.6 | | | -3.6 | | | 1.7 | 3.8 |
| 12.4 | 15.2 | 15.4 | Sales/Net Fixed Assets | | 129.5 | | | 13.2 | 14.0 |
| 7.4 | 9.4 | 9.4 | | | 14.3 | | | 5.4 | 6.6 |
| 4.1 | 5.1 | 5.4 | | | 6.4 | | | 4.4 | 3.9 |
| 3.0 | 3.2 | 2.9 | Sales/Total Assets | | 3.9 | | | 2.8 | 2.8 |
| 2.1 | 2.6 | 2.4 | | | 2.5 | | | 2.4 | 2.3 |
| 1.6 | 1.7 | 1.7 | | | 2.0 | | | 1.8 | 1.6 |
| 1.8 | 1.4 | 1.3 | % Depr., Dep., Amort./Sales | | | | | 1.7 | 1.7 |
| (58) 2.7 | (65) 2.2 | (64) 2.3 | | | | | | 2.9 | (25) 2.4 |
| 4.3 | 3.4 | 3.4 | | | | | | 3.5 | 3.8 |
| 2.1 | 1.8 | 2.1 | % Officers', Directors' Owners' Comp/Sales | | | | | | |
| (21) 4.4 | (24) 3.8 | (29) 4.8 | | | | | | | |
| 7.2 | 7.2 | 6.6 | | | | | | | |
| 1894995M | 2178954M | 2541083M | Net Sales ($) | 5047M | 19330M | 15239M | 73859M | 194326M | 2233282M |
| 1025902M | 1107593M | 1169341M | Total Assets ($) | 2157M | 8992M | 5717M | 32203M | 95927M | 1024345M |

M = $ thousand    MM = $ million
See Pages 9 through 22 for Explanation of Ratios and Data

## Current Data Sorted by Assets / Comparative Historical Data

| 0-500M | 500M-2MM | 2-10MM | 10-50MM | 50-100MM | 100-250MM | Type of Statement | 4/1/07-3/31/08 ALL | 4/1/08-3/31/09 ALL |
|---|---|---|---|---|---|---|---|---|
| 1 | | | 8 | 3 | 8 | Unqualified | 24 | 31 |
| | | 5 | 9 | 5 | | Reviewed | 10 | 16 |
| | | 1 | 1 | | | Compiled | 2 | 2 |
| | 3 | 6 | 1 | | | Tax Returns | 1 | 4 |
| 1 | 2 | 4 | 12 | 1 | 4 | Other | 17 | 14 |
| | 20 (4/1-9/30/11) | | 55 (10/1/11-3/31/12) | | | | | |
| 2 | 5 | 16 | 31 | 9 | 12 | **NUMBER OF STATEMENTS** | 54 | 67 |
| % | % | % | % | % | % | **ASSETS** | % | % |
| | | 5.0 | 4.9 | | 7.0 | Cash & Equivalents | 4.3 | 3.3 |
| | | 24.7 | 20.6 | | 15.0 | Trade Receivables (net) | 18.1 | 16.5 |
| | | 31.0 | 37.1 | | 33.3 | Inventory | 38.8 | 39.2 |
| | | 2.0 | 1.6 | | 1.9 | All Other Current | 3.4 | 3.6 |
| | | 62.6 | 64.2 | | 57.2 | Total Current | 64.6 | 62.5 |
| | | 29.2 | 26.5 | | 31.3 | Fixed Assets (net) | 30.4 | 29.6 |
| | | 3.5 | 3.3 | | 4.7 | Intangibles (net) | 1.8 | 4.2 |
| | | 4.7 | 6.1 | | 6.8 | All Other Non-Current | 3.2 | 3.7 |
| | | 100.0 | 100.0 | | 100.0 | Total | 100.0 | 100.0 |
| | | | | | | **LIABILITIES** | | |
| | | 13.3 | 15.3 | | 9.0 | Notes Payable-Short Term | 19.2 | 19.4 |
| | | 2.6 | 3.2 | | 2.3 | Cur. Mat.-L.T.D. | 2.6 | 2.7 |
| | | 23.3 | 17.2 | | 11.9 | Trade Payables | 13.0 | 15.9 |
| | | .0 | .6 | | .1 | Income Taxes Payable | .3 | .2 |
| | | 6.8 | 8.8 | | 14.2 | All Other Current | 9.3 | 8.8 |
| | | 46.0 | 45.1 | | 37.5 | Total Current | 44.3 | 47.0 |
| | | 14.4 | 15.1 | | 15.5 | Long-Term Debt | 15.5 | 15.8 |
| | | .4 | .6 | | 3.2 | Deferred Taxes | 1.1 | .6 |
| | | 18.1 | 3.2 | | 2.7 | All Other Non-Current | 4.7 | 7.6 |
| | | 21.2 | 36.0 | | 41.2 | Net Worth | 34.3 | 29.0 |
| | | 100.0 | 100.0 | | 100.0 | Total Liabilities & Net Worth | 100.0 | 100.0 |
| | | | | | | **INCOME DATA** | | |
| | | 100.0 | 100.0 | | 100.0 | Net Sales | 100.0 | 100.0 |
| | | 25.3 | 19.2 | | 14.2 | Gross Profit | 18.7 | 20.7 |
| | | 22.1 | 14.6 | | 10.6 | Operating Expenses | 12.5 | 14.7 |
| | | 3.3 | 4.7 | | 3.7 | Operating Profit | 6.2 | 6.1 |
| | | .8 | .2 | | .1 | All Other Expenses (net) | 1.7 | 1.9 |
| | | 2.5 | 4.5 | | 3.5 | Profit Before Taxes | 4.5 | 4.2 |
| | | | | | | **RATIOS** | | |
| | | 2.1 | 2.0 | | 2.1 | | 2.1 | 1.7 |
| | | 1.7 | 1.3 | | 1.5 | Current | 1.4 | 1.3 |
| | | .8 | 1.0 | | 1.1 | | 1.1 | 1.1 |
| | | 1.2 | .9 | | 1.0 | | .8 | .6 |
| | | .7 | .4 | | .5 | Quick | .4 | .4 |
| | | .4 | .4 | | .4 | | .3 | .2 |
| | | 22  16.5 | 24  15.3 | | 20  18.5 | | 25  14.9 | 26  13.8 |
| | | 27  13.5 | 31  11.8 | | 30  12.3 | Sales/Receivables | 32  11.4 | 34  10.7 |
| | | 31  11.6 | 40  9.1 | | 36  10.1 | | 51  7.2 | 43  8.4 |
| | | 15  24.7 | 25  14.6 | | 42  8.6 | | 64  5.7 | 50  7.3 |
| | | 51  7.2 | 81  4.5 | | 73  5.0 | Cost of Sales/Inventory | 99  3.7 | 107  3.4 |
| | | 94  3.9 | 182  2.0 | | 228  1.6 | | 154  2.4 | 167  2.2 |
| | | 28  12.9 | 24  15.5 | | 16  23.0 | | 20  18.3 | 20  18.2 |
| | | 35  10.5 | 33  10.9 | | 31  11.9 | Cost of Sales/Payables | 27  13.5 | 38  9.7 |
| | | 50  7.3 | 46  7.9 | | 60  6.1 | | 47  7.7 | 56  6.6 |
| | | 7.9 | 3.4 | | 3.9 | | 5.5 | 5.2 |
| | | 18.3 | 22.2 | | 9.6 | Sales/Working Capital | 10.3 | 12.2 |
| | | -29.6 | 66.0 | | 16.8 | | 21.5 | 61.3 |
| | | 15.3 | 17.8 | | 13.2 | | 8.2 | 8.0 |
| | | 3.8 | (30) 4.4 | | 5.4 | EBIT/Interest | (53) 2.5 | (65) 2.4 |
| | | 1.2 | 2.5 | | 1.2 | | 1.3 | 1.3 |
| | | | | | | Net Profit + Depr., Dep., | 9.1 | 4.6 |
| | | | | | | Amort./Cur. Mat. L/T/D | (19) 5.0 | (18) 2.1 |
| | | | | | | | 1.5 | 1.4 |
| | | .5 | .2 | | .4 | | .5 | .6 |
| | | 1.4 | .7 | | .6 | Fixed/Worth | 1.0 | 1.1 |
| | | 3.4 | 1.9 | | 1.8 | | 1.8 | 2.3 |
| | | 1.2 | .9 | | .8 | | 1.0 | 1.4 |
| | | 3.4 | 2.1 | | 1.3 | Debt/Worth | 2.2 | 2.7 |
| | | 15.0 | 7.2 | | 2.8 | | 5.1 | 5.3 |
| | | 63.7 | 34.0 | | 19.9 | % Profit Before Taxes/Tangible | 41.2 | 41.6 |
| | (13) 15.0 | | (30) 17.0 | | (10) 15.6 | Net Worth | (50) 24.4 | (57) 16.2 |
| | | 6.9 | 9.3 | | 5.6 | | 9.6 | 5.9 |
| | | 26.8 | 11.6 | | 7.2 | % Profit Before Taxes/Total | 15.3 | 11.2 |
| | | 3.0 | 4.6 | | 5.3 | Assets | 4.8 | 4.6 |
| | | .3 | 2.7 | | .3 | | 1.2 | .8 |
| | | 46.9 | 20.4 | | 8.4 | | 12.1 | 9.8 |
| | | 9.9 | 8.8 | | 5.5 | Sales/Net Fixed Assets | 5.1 | 5.4 |
| | | 5.5 | 4.0 | | 4.8 | | 3.6 | 3.3 |
| | | 4.5 | 2.6 | | 2.3 | | 2.2 | 2.1 |
| | | 3.4 | 1.8 | | 1.6 | Sales/Total Assets | 1.7 | 1.5 |
| | | 1.6 | 1.2 | | 1.1 | | 1.3 | 1.1 |
| | | .5 | 1.1 | | | | 1.2 | 1.6 |
| | (15) | 1.5 | (29) 1.9 | | | % Depr., Dep., Amort./Sales | (50) 2.3 | (62) 2.4 |
| | | 2.5 | 3.0 | | | | 3.1 | 3.6 |
| | | | | | | % Officers', Directors' | | |
| | | | | | | Owners' Comp/Sales | | |
| 809M | 24216M | 232264M | 1743140M | 906203M | 3675464M | Net Sales ($) | 5443186M | 4954708M |
| 429M | 6742M | 73323M | 813008M | 608522M | 2124912M | Total Assets ($) | 3190763M | 3360152M |

M = $ thousand    MM = $ million
See Pages 9 through 22 for Explanation of Ratios and Data

## Comparative Historical Data | Current Data Sorted by Sales

| Type of Statement | | | | | 0-1MM | 1-3MM | 3-5MM | 5-10MM | 10-25MM | 25MM & OVER |
|---|---|---|---|---|---|---|---|---|---|---|
| 23 | 19 | 20 | Unqualified | | 1 | | | | 1 | 18 |
| 17 | 12 | 19 | Reviewed | | | 1 | | | 5 | 13 |
| 3 | 6 | 2 | Compiled | | | | | | 1 | 1 |
| 8 | 8 | 10 | Tax Returns | | | 1 | 1 | 4 | 3 | 1 |
| 16 | 27 | 24 | Other | | 1 | 1 | 2 | | 5 | 15 |
| 4/1/09-3/31/10 ALL | 4/1/10-3/31/11 ALL | 4/1/11-3/31/12 ALL | | | 20 (4/1-9/30/11) | | | 55 (10/1/11-3/31/12) | | |
| 67 | 72 | 75 | **NUMBER OF STATEMENTS** | | 2 | 2 | 4 | 4 | 15 | 48 |
| % | % | % | **ASSETS** | | % | % | % | % | % | % |
| 4.8 | 6.0 | 4.9 | Cash & Equivalents | | | | | | 4.9 | 4.4 |
| 17.5 | 18.3 | 20.8 | Trade Receivables (net) | | | | | | 19.2 | 21.0 |
| 35.9 | 34.3 | 34.5 | Inventory | | | | | | 36.9 | 34.1 |
| 2.7 | 1.8 | 2.1 | All Other Current | | | | | | 1.5 | 2.5 |
| 61.0 | 60.4 | 62.3 | Total Current | | | | | | 62.4 | 62.1 |
| 30.8 | 29.5 | 27.3 | Fixed Assets (net) | | | | | | 26.6 | 27.6 |
| 3.1 | 4.6 | 4.8 | Intangibles (net) | | | | | | 4.2 | 5.7 |
| 5.1 | 5.5 | 5.6 | All Other Non-Current | | | | | | 6.7 | 4.7 |
| 100.0 | 100.0 | 100.0 | Total | | | | | | 100.0 | 100.0 |
| | | | **LIABILITIES** | | | | | | | |
| 16.0 | 14.0 | 13.9 | Notes Payable-Short Term | | | | | | 7.3 | 15.3 |
| 4.9 | 3.1 | 2.9 | Cur. Mat.-L.T.D. | | | | | | 2.0 | 3.1 |
| 14.2 | 15.1 | 18.4 | Trade Payables | | | | | | 15.1 | 17.0 |
| .3 | .1 | .3 | Income Taxes Payable | | | | | | .2 | .4 |
| 7.1 | 10.1 | 9.1 | All Other Current | | | | | | 12.5 | 8.1 |
| 42.6 | 42.4 | 44.5 | Total Current | | | | | | 37.0 | 43.9 |
| 18.2 | 16.6 | 16.1 | Long-Term Debt | | | | | | 15.5 | 14.9 |
| .7 | .9 | 1.1 | Deferred Taxes | | | | | | .5 | 1.4 |
| 7.8 | 9.8 | 8.7 | All Other Non-Current | | | | | | 15.7 | 6.7 |
| 30.7 | 30.3 | 29.7 | Net Worth | | | | | | 31.3 | 33.2 |
| 100.0 | 100.0 | 100.0 | Total Liabilities & Net Worth | | | | | | 100.0 | 100.0 |
| | | | **INCOME DATA** | | | | | | | |
| 100.0 | 100.0 | 100.0 | Net Sales | | | | | | 100.0 | 100.0 |
| 20.1 | 19.2 | 21.0 | Gross Profit | | | | | | 24.3 | 16.5 |
| 14.9 | 16.9 | 16.9 | Operating Expenses | | | | | | 19.2 | 12.5 |
| 5.2 | 2.4 | 4.1 | Operating Profit | | | | | | 5.1 | 4.1 |
| 1.4 | 1.0 | .5 | All Other Expenses (net) | | | | | | .3 | .6 |
| 3.9 | 1.3 | 3.6 | Profit Before Taxes | | | | | | 4.8 | 3.5 |
| | | | **RATIOS** | | | | | | | |
| 2.0 | 2.0 | 2.0 | Current | | | | | | 3.3 | 1.9 |
| 1.4 | 1.5 | 1.4 | | | | | | | 1.9 | 1.4 |
| 1.1 | 1.1 | 1.1 | | | | | | | .9 | 1.1 |
| 1.0 | 1.0 | .9 | Quick | | | | | | 1.1 | .9 |
| .5 | .5 | .5 | | | | | | | .6 | .5 |
| .3 | .3 | .4 | | | | | | | .4 | .4 |
| 23  16.1 | 23  15.6 | 23  15.6 | Sales/Receivables | | | | | | 23  15.8 | 24  15.3 |
| 32  11.4 | 32  11.4 | 30  12.1 | | | | | | | 30  12.1 | 30  12.1 |
| 42  8.6 | 43  8.5 | 40  9.2 | | | | | | | 40  9.2 | 39  9.3 |
| 37  9.8 | 33  11.0 | 26  14.3 | Cost of Sales/Inventory | | | | | | 51  7.2 | 25  14.5 |
| 89  4.1 | 79  4.6 | 79  4.6 | | | | | | | 79  4.6 | 73  5.0 |
| 164  2.2 | 165  2.2 | 152  2.4 | | | | | | | 166  2.2 | 152  2.4 |
| 15  25.1 | 18  20.5 | 23  15.8 | Cost of Sales/Payables | | | | | | 25  14.8 | 23  16.0 |
| 31  11.7 | 29  12.5 | 35  10.5 | | | | | | | 31  11.6 | 34  10.8 |
| 47  7.8 | 48  7.7 | 48  7.6 | | | | | | | 47  7.8 | 43  8.5 |
| 5.7 | 5.2 | 5.3 | Sales/Working Capital | | | | | | 3.4 | 5.2 |
| 10.6 | 13.2 | 16.8 | | | | | | | 9.0 | 16.7 |
| 47.3 | 88.1 | 66.0 | | | | | | | -26.0 | 38.3 |
| 10.6 | 9.8 | 11.1 | EBIT/Interest | | | | | | 42.3 | 11.4 |
| (66)  3.2 | (69)  3.2 | (73)  4.7 | | | | | | | (14)  4.9 | 4.6 |
| 1.5 | .1 | 2.0 | | | | | | | 2.1 | 1.9 |
| 3.6 | 7.4 | 5.6 | Net Profit + Depr., Dep., Amort./Cur. Mat. L/T/D | | | | | | | 4.7 |
| (21)  1.6 | (27)  2.5 | (20)  3.2 | | | | | | | | (16)  3.2 |
| 1.2 | .5 | 1.2 | | | | | | | | 1.2 |
| .5 | .5 | .5 | Fixed/Worth | | | | | | .1 | .5 |
| 1.0 | 1.0 | 1.0 | | | | | | | 1.0 | .9 |
| 2.0 | 3.0 | 2.5 | | | | | | | 2.2 | 2.0 |
| 1.0 | 1.0 | 1.2 | Debt/Worth | | | | | | .6 | 1.2 |
| 2.4 | 2.2 | 2.6 | | | | | | | 1.6 | 2.5 |
| 9.7 | 7.9 | 10.8 | | | | | | | 10.8 | 7.3 |
| 55.7 | 36.1 | 32.4 | % Profit Before Taxes/Tangible Net Worth | | | | | | 49.8 | 28.2 |
| (58)  16.6 | (60)  12.3 | (64)  17.2 | | | | | | | (13)  25.8 | (41)  17.1 |
| 6.6 | -.8 | 9.1 | | | | | | | 9.2 | 8.4 |
| 13.8 | 9.8 | 10.8 | % Profit Before Taxes/Total Assets | | | | | | 31.8 | 9.7 |
| 5.3 | 3.9 | 4.6 | | | | | | | 4.6 | 5.5 |
| 1.5 | -2.3 | 1.6 | | | | | | | .8 | 1.8 |
| 10.7 | 13.2 | 20.2 | Sales/Net Fixed Assets | | | | | | 20.4 | 15.0 |
| 6.3 | 6.8 | 8.5 | | | | | | | 8.0 | 8.4 |
| 2.8 | 3.9 | 4.6 | | | | | | | 4.6 | 4.6 |
| 2.9 | 3.0 | 3.2 | Sales/Total Assets | | | | | | 3.6 | 3.0 |
| 1.5 | 1.7 | 1.8 | | | | | | | 1.8 | 1.8 |
| 1.1 | 1.1 | 1.2 | | | | | | | 1.3 | 1.2 |
| 1.6 | 1.4 | 1.0 | % Depr., Dep., Amort./Sales | | | | | | .2 | 1.1 |
| (59)  2.5 | (64)  2.5 | (67)  1.9 | | | | | | | (13)  1.5 | (43)  1.9 |
| 3.8 | 4.1 | 3.1 | | | | | | | 3.5 | 3.4 |
| | | 1.3 | % Officers', Directors' Owners' Comp/Sales | | | | | | | |
| | (11)  2.3 | | | | | | | | | |
| | 2.6 | | | | | | | | | |
| 5433830M | 5175738M | 6582096M | Net Sales ($) | | 809M | 3734M | 13452M | 32627M | 236599M | 6294875M |
| 3349830M | 3475145M | 3626936M | Total Assets ($) | | 429M | 3136M | 10357M | 6890M | 134389M | 3471735M |

M = $ thousand     MM = $ million
See Pages 9 through 22 for Explanation of Ratios and Data

## Current Data Sorted by Assets      Comparative Historical Data

| 0-500M | 500M-2MM | 2-10MM | 10-50MM | 50-100MM | 100-250MM | Type of Statement | 27 4/1/07-3/31/08 ALL | 33 4/1/08-3/31/09 ALL |
|---|---|---|---|---|---|---|---|---|
| | | 1 | 8 | 4 | 3 | Unqualified | 20 | 21 |
| | | 3 | 8 | 2 | 1 | Reviewed | 11 | 14 |
| | 2 | 4 | 1 | | | Compiled | 4 | 6 |
| | 3 | 3 | | | | Tax Returns | 4 | 3 |
| | 5 | 10 | 13 | 3 | 1 | Other | 27 | 33 |
| | 20 (4/1-9/30/11) | | 55 (10/1/11-3/31/12) | | | | | |
| | 10 | 21 | 30 | 9 | 5 | **NUMBER OF STATEMENTS** | 66 | 77 |
| % | % | % | % | % | % | **ASSETS** | % | % |
| | 9.8 | 5.0 | 7.7 | | | Cash & Equivalents | 6.2 | 6.4 |
| | 33.1 | 23.2 | 19.8 | | | Trade Receivables (net) | 17.6 | 18.7 |
| | 14.4 | 24.6 | 15.1 | | | Inventory | 20.5 | 18.8 |
| | .7 | 1.9 | 2.0 | | | All Other Current | 2.6 | 1.8 |
| | 58.1 | 54.6 | 44.6 | | | Total Current | 46.9 | 45.7 |
| | 29.0 | 38.2 | 39.0 | | | Fixed Assets (net) | 40.9 | 40.8 |
| | 10.3 | 5.1 | 8.7 | | | Intangibles (net) | 8.0 | 9.0 |
| | 2.6 | 2.1 | 7.7 | | | All Other Non-Current | 4.1 | 4.5 |
| | 100.0 | 100.0 | 100.0 | | | Total | 100.0 | 100.0 |
| | | | | | | **LIABILITIES** | | |
| | 9.4 | 12.3 | 4.7 | | | Notes Payable-Short Term | 10.3 | 10.8 |
| | 5.2 | 4.2 | 3.9 | | | Cur. Mat.-L.T.D. | 3.7 | 4.9 |
| | 30.8 | 17.7 | 11.5 | | | Trade Payables | 16.0 | 14.7 |
| | .4 | .0 | .1 | | | Income Taxes Payable | .2 | .2 |
| | 7.8 | 5.3 | 8.7 | | | All Other Current | 8.9 | 7.9 |
| | 53.6 | 39.5 | 28.8 | | | Total Current | 39.1 | 38.5 |
| | 13.0 | 15.2 | 15.3 | | | Long-Term Debt | 23.7 | 21.0 |
| | .0 | .0 | 1.2 | | | Deferred Taxes | .8 | .8 |
| | 12.2 | 2.4 | 3.5 | | | All Other Non-Current | 9.2 | 8.9 |
| | 21.3 | 42.9 | 51.3 | | | Net Worth | 27.3 | 30.9 |
| | 100.0 | 100.0 | 100.0 | | | Total Liabilties & Net Worth | 100.0 | 100.0 |
| | | | | | | **INCOME DATA** | | |
| | 100.0 | 100.0 | 100.0 | | | Net Sales | 100.0 | 100.0 |
| | 42.9 | 26.2 | 24.7 | | | Gross Profit | 26.8 | 24.9 |
| | 43.1 | 21.9 | 19.8 | | | Operating Expenses | 23.2 | 21.8 |
| | -.2 | 4.4 | 4.9 | | | Operating Profit | 3.6 | 3.1 |
| | 1.0 | .8 | .7 | | | All Other Expenses (net) | 1.5 | 1.2 |
| | -1.2 | 3.5 | 4.2 | | | Profit Before Taxes | 2.1 | 1.9 |
| | | | | | | **RATIOS** | | |
| | 1.6 | 2.5 | 2.5 | | | Current | 2.1 | 2.0 |
| | 1.2 | 1.6 | 1.7 | | | | 1.2 | 1.1 |
| | .8 | .9 | 1.1 | | | | .8 | .8 |
| | 1.3 | 1.4 | 1.4 | | | Quick | 1.2 | 1.0 |
| | .8 | .7 | 1.0 | | | | .5 | .6 |
| | .6 | .4 | .6 | | | | .4 | .4 |
| | 20 18.3 | 21 17.1 | 22 16.8 | | | Sales/Receivables | 19 19.3 | 21 17.4 |
| | 23 16.2 | 29 12.4 | 26 14.0 | | | | 24 15.5 | 25 14.6 |
| | 31 11.6 | 39 9.3 | 34 10.8 | | | | 32 11.3 | 32 11.3 |
| | 7 49.6 | 28 13.0 | 21 17.0 | | | Cost of Sales/Inventory | 23 15.9 | 22 16.8 |
| | 25 14.6 | 38 9.6 | 26 13.8 | | | | 37 9.9 | 35 10.5 |
| | 41 8.8 | 60 6.1 | 42 8.6 | | | | 63 5.8 | 45 8.1 |
| | 24 15.4 | 18 19.8 | 14 25.6 | | | Cost of Sales/Payables | 18 19.8 | 17 21.9 |
| | 33 11.1 | 29 12.6 | 20 18.2 | | | | 28 12.9 | 24 15.0 |
| | 60 6.1 | 41 9.0 | 29 12.8 | | | | 41 8.9 | 37 10.0 |
| | 26.2 | 8.4 | 7.4 | | | Sales/Working Capital | 9.4 | 10.6 |
| | 62.6 | 13.8 | 15.2 | | | | 33.3 | 46.8 |
| | -39.6 | -74.9 | 125.6 | | | | -29.4 | -37.5 |
| | | 24.2 | 18.6 | | | EBIT/Interest | 7.5 | 6.1 |
| | | (20) 2.4 | (29) 3.4 | | | | (63) 2.9 | (71) 3.0 |
| | | .1 | .8 | | | | 1.0 | 1.0 |
| | | | 2.7 | | | Net Profit + Depr., Dep., Amort./Cur. Mat. L/T/D | 9.0 | 5.2 |
| | | | (14) 1.1 | | | | (20) 4.0 | (23) 3.2 |
| | | | .5 | | | | 1.3 | 1.4 |
| | .8 | .5 | .4 | | | Fixed/Worth | .7 | .8 |
| | 1.9 | 1.2 | .8 | | | | 2.0 | 1.8 |
| | -13.3 | 2.6 | 1.7 | | | | 279.6 | 3.6 |
| | 3.3 | .6 | .6 | | | Debt/Worth | .9 | .9 |
| | 6.1 | 1.6 | 1.0 | | | | 3.2 | 2.7 |
| | -35.6 | 4.6 | 2.7 | | | | 296.8 | 8.5 |
| | | 46.3 | 30.4 | | | % Profit Before Taxes/Tangible Net Worth | 40.4 | 36.4 |
| | | (19) 18.0 | (28) 12.6 | | | | (51) 18.0 | (62) 22.2 |
| | | -14.4 | .5 | | | | 5.3 | 6.7 |
| | 10.0 | 22.1 | 17.7 | | | % Profit Before Taxes/Total Assets | 10.7 | 9.6 |
| | 1.2 | 5.7 | 3.6 | | | | 5.7 | 4.6 |
| | -8.9 | -2.8 | -.4 | | | | .1 | .3 |
| | 54.5 | 13.1 | 10.2 | | | Sales/Net Fixed Assets | 11.8 | 12.7 |
| | 13.0 | 6.5 | 5.2 | | | | 6.2 | 6.4 |
| | 8.4 | 4.3 | 3.7 | | | | 3.4 | 3.3 |
| | 6.2 | 3.6 | 3.2 | | | Sales/Total Assets | 3.1 | 3.3 |
| | 4.5 | 2.6 | 2.0 | | | | 2.5 | 2.3 |
| | 2.3 | 1.9 | 1.4 | | | | 1.7 | 1.7 |
| | | 1.2 | 1.7 | | | % Depr., Dep., Amort./Sales | 1.4 | 1.4 |
| | | (20) 2.0 | (28) 3.2 | | | | (56) 2.4 | (65) 2.3 |
| | | 3.3 | 4.0 | | | | 3.4 | 3.5 |
| | | | | | | % Officers', Directors' Owners' Comp/Sales | .9 | |
| | | | | | | | (14) 2.5 | |
| | | | | | | | 5.0 | |
| | 58511M | 329094M | 1673244M | 1135251M | 1656833M | Net Sales ($) | 3971702M | 5300375M |
| | 11653M | 114775M | 755261M | 613707M | 622450M | Total Assets ($) | 1792125M | 2403785M |

*(The 0-500M column and portions of the 50-100MM and 100-250MM columns are marked "DATA NOT AVAILABLE".)*

M = $ thousand    MM = $ million
See Pages 9 through 22 for Explanation of Ratios and Data

## Comparative Historical Data

## Current Data Sorted by Sales

| 20 / 15 / 6 / 5 / 34 (4/1/09-3/31/10 ALL) | 19 / 10 / 7 / 6 / 26 (4/1/10-3/31/11 ALL) | 16 / 14 / 7 / 6 / 32 (4/1/11-3/31/12 ALL) | Type of Statement | 0-1MM | 1-3MM | 3-5MM | 5-10MM | 10-25MM | 25MM & OVER |
|---|---|---|---|---|---|---|---|---|---|
| | | | | | | | 20 (4/1-9/30/11) | | 55 (10/1/11-3/31/12) |
| 20 | 19 | 16 | Unqualified | | | | | 1 | 15 |
| 15 | 10 | 14 | Reviewed | | | 1 | | 2 | 11 |
| 6 | 7 | 7 | Compiled | | 1 | 2 | | 3 | 1 |
| 5 | 6 | 6 | Tax Returns | 2 | 1 | 3 | | | |
| 34 | 26 | 32 | Other | | 3 | 3 | | 7 | 19 |
| **80** | **68** | **75** | **NUMBER OF STATEMENTS** | 2 | 5 | 9 | | 13 | 46 |
| % | % | % | **ASSETS** | % | % | % | % | % | % |
| 7.1 | 5.8 | 6.2 | Cash & Equivalents | | | | | 10.6 | 5.7 |
| 19.4 | 21.0 | 22.5 | Trade Receivables (net) | | | | | 26.0 | 21.3 |
| 19.8 | 18.4 | 18.7 | Inventory | | | | | 20.8 | 17.7 |
| 1.6 | 2.1 | 2.0 | All Other Current | | | | | 1.7 | 2.1 |
| 47.9 | 47.4 | 49.4 | Total Current | | | | | 59.1 | 46.8 |
| 37.2 | 36.7 | 36.8 | Fixed Assets (net) | | | | | 27.9 | 38.7 |
| 10.1 | 11.2 | 9.1 | Intangibles (net) | | | | | 9.1 | 8.8 |
| 4.9 | 4.7 | 4.7 | All Other Non-Current | | | | | 3.9 | 5.7 |
| 100.0 | 100.0 | 100.0 | Total | | | | | 100.0 | 100.0 |
| | | | **LIABILITIES** | | | | | | |
| 7.6 | 5.5 | 8.5 | Notes Payable-Short Term | | | | | 7.1 | 7.6 |
| 3.5 | 2.8 | 4.1 | Cur. Mat.-L.T.D. | | | | | 1.3 | 4.1 |
| 14.1 | 14.7 | 15.8 | Trade Payables | | | | | 25.4 | 12.8 |
| .2 | .3 | .1 | Income Taxes Payable | | | | | .3 | .1 |
| 11.6 | 8.1 | 7.9 | All Other Current | | | | | 5.4 | 9.1 |
| 37.1 | 31.5 | 36.4 | Total Current | | | | | 39.5 | 33.7 |
| 22.1 | 22.1 | 15.4 | Long-Term Debt | | | | | 5.9 | 16.5 |
| .8 | 1.1 | .5 | Deferred Taxes | | | | | .6 | .7 |
| 3.8 | 11.9 | 5.0 | All Other Non-Current | | | | | 1.0 | 4.4 |
| 36.2 | 33.4 | 42.7 | Net Worth | | | | | 53.0 | 44.7 |
| 100.0 | 100.0 | 100.0 | Total Liabilities & Net Worth | | | | | 100.0 | 100.0 |
| | | | **INCOME DATA** | | | | | | |
| 100.0 | 100.0 | 100.0 | Net Sales | | | | | 100.0 | 100.0 |
| 25.4 | 27.1 | 27.1 | Gross Profit | | | | | 27.2 | 22.9 |
| 20.2 | 21.4 | 23.1 | Operating Expenses | | | | | 21.3 | 18.9 |
| 5.2 | 5.7 | 4.0 | Operating Profit | | | | | 5.8 | 3.9 |
| 1.2 | 1.0 | 1.0 | All Other Expenses (net) | | | | | .6 | 1.0 |
| 4.0 | 4.8 | 3.0 | Profit Before Taxes | | | | | 5.2 | 2.9 |
| | | | **RATIOS** | | | | | | |
| 2.2 | 2.4 | 2.3 | Current | | | | | 2.6 | 2.0 |
| 1.5 | 1.6 | 1.4 | | | | | | 1.9 | 1.4 |
| .9 | 1.2 | 1.0 | | | | | | 1.0 | 1.0 |
| 1.2 | 1.3 | 1.3 | Quick | | | | | 1.5 | 1.3 |
| .7 | .8 | .7 | | | | | | 1.0 | .7 |
| .5 | .6 | .5 | | | | | | .7 | .5 |
| 19  19.6 | 22  16.5 | 22  16.8 | Sales/Receivables | | | | | 21  17.3 | 24  15.0 |
| 25  14.8 | 27  13.7 | 28  12.9 | | | | | | 23  15.7 | 29  12.7 |
| 34  10.7 | 34  10.7 | 36  10.2 | | | | | | 29  12.5 | 35  10.3 |
| 24  15.0 | 23  15.9 | 23  15.9 | Cost of Sales/Inventory | | | | | 23  16.2 | 22  16.7 |
| 35  10.3 | 32  11.5 | 33  11.2 | | | | | | 37  9.9 | 31  11.7 |
| 54  6.7 | 57  6.4 | 51  7.1 | | | | | | 59  6.2 | 47  7.7 |
| 16  23.3 | 15  23.8 | 18  20.6 | Cost of Sales/Payables | | | | | 19  18.9 | 16  23.4 |
| 23  16.1 | 22  16.6 | 25  14.8 | | | | | | 30  12.3 | 22  16.6 |
| 33  11.1 | 35  10.4 | 36  10.0 | | | | | | 41  8.8 | 35  10.5 |
| 8.7 | 8.3 | 9.1 | Sales/Working Capital | | | | | 7.7 | 9.7 |
| 16.7 | 15.5 | 16.7 | | | | | | 10.7 | 16.6 |
| -69.6 | 54.8 | -999.8 | | | | | | NM | 371.0 |
| 15.3 | 14.5 | 16.4 | EBIT/Interest | | | | | 21.7 | 20.5 |
| (75) 5.0 | (66) 6.6 | (72) 3.6 | | | | | (10) | 6.0 | 5.0 |
| 1.7 | 1.2 | .5 | | | | | | -3.7 | 1.3 |
| 5.4 | 6.5 | 6.1 | Net Profit + Depr., Dep., Amort./Cur. Mat. L/T/D | | | | | | 6.1 |
| (23) 2.4 | (27) 3.6 | (24) 2.0 | | | | | | (22) | 2.0 |
| 1.7 | 2.0 | .7 | | | | | | | .7 |
| .6 | .6 | .6 | Fixed/Worth | | | | | .4 | .5 |
| 1.2 | 1.1 | 1.1 | | | | | | .6 | 1.1 |
| 2.8 | 3.9 | 2.1 | | | | | | 1.1 | 1.7 |
| .9 | .6 | .7 | Debt/Worth | | | | | .3 | .7 |
| 2.0 | 1.6 | 1.6 | | | | | | .8 | 1.4 |
| 7.7 | 8.5 | 4.6 | | | | | | 4.3 | 3.0 |
| 57.9 | 55.1 | 31.9 | % Profit Before Taxes/Tangible Net Worth | | | | | 51.1 | 29.7 |
| (67) 32.9 | (54) 25.1 | (65) 18.0 | | | | | | 30.1 | (40) 14.1 |
| 12.4 | 8.0 | -.8 | | | | | | 1.9 | 3.6 |
| 17.8 | 18.2 | 13.4 | % Profit Before Taxes/Total Assets | | | | | 23.4 | 11.7 |
| 8.1 | 8.1 | 4.0 | | | | | | 14.1 | 4.1 |
| 2.5 | 1.4 | -.7 | | | | | | -.7 | 1.0 |
| 14.2 | 11.7 | 12.9 | Sales/Net Fixed Assets | | | | | 40.4 | 11.4 |
| 7.1 | 6.1 | 5.5 | | | | | | 7.5 | 5.1 |
| 3.8 | 4.0 | 4.0 | | | | | | 5.4 | 3.8 |
| 3.3 | 3.1 | 3.6 | Sales/Total Assets | | | | | 4.6 | 3.2 |
| 2.5 | 2.3 | 2.3 | | | | | | 2.8 | 2.1 |
| 1.6 | 1.7 | 1.6 | | | | | | 2.4 | 1.5 |
| 1.4 | 1.7 | 1.4 | % Depr., Dep., Amort./Sales | | | | | 1.2 | 1.8 |
| (63) 2.3 | (65) 2.5 | (69) 2.5 | | | | | | (12) 2.1 | (43) 2.8 |
| 4.0 | 4.0 | 3.7 | | | | | | 4.0 | 3.9 |
| 1.7 | 1.6 | 1.1 | % Officers', Directors' Owners' Comp/Sales | | | | | | |
| (16) 3.2 | (15) 3.2 | (16) 2.9 | | | | | | | |
| 3.8 | 9.2 | 5.6 | | | | | | | |
| 5440240M | 4167097M | 4852933M | Net Sales ($) | 3678M | 17569M | 57420M | | 235626M | 4538640M |
| 2472449M | 2028724M | 2117846M | Total Assets ($) | 2473M | 6147M | 28019M | | 96563M | 1984644M |

*Note: In the Current Data columns 0-1MM through 5-10MM the ASSETS and LIABILITIES percentage figures are marked* **DATA NOT AVAILABLE**.

M = $ thousand    MM = $ million
See Pages 9 through 22 for Explanation of Ratios and Data

## Current Data Sorted by Assets      Comparative Historical Data

| 0-500M | 500M-2MM | 2-10MM | 10-50MM | 50-100MM | 100-250MM | Type of Statement | 4/1/07-3/31/08 ALL | 4/1/08-3/31/09 ALL |
|---|---|---|---|---|---|---|---|---|
| | | | 1 | 7 | 4 | 13 Unqualified | 30 | 40 |
| | 3 | 7 | 3 | 2 | 1 | Reviewed | 14 | 15 |
| 2 | 2 | 2 | 2 | | | Compiled | 6 | 6 |
| | 2 | 1 | | | | Tax Returns | 8 | 6 |
| 4 | 4 | 6 | 17 | 4 | 5 | Other | 22 | 39 |
| 32 (4/1-9/30/11) | | | 54 (10/1/11-3/31/12) | | | | | |
| 2 | 9 | 17 | 29 | 11 | 18 | **NUMBER OF STATEMENTS** | 80 | 106 |
| % | % | % | % | % | % | **ASSETS** | % | % |
| | | 5.5 | 4.6 | 7.6 | 1.3 | Cash & Equivalents | 4.8 | 5.0 |
| | | 19.8 | 16.4 | 15.8 | 11.4 | Trade Receivables (net) | 18.4 | 16.4 |
| | | 27.1 | 32.9 | 28.3 | 35.2 | Inventory | 38.1 | 36.2 |
| | | 3.5 | 2.5 | 4.5 | 4.4 | All Other Current | 2.9 | 3.0 |
| | | 55.9 | 56.3 | 56.2 | 52.3 | Total Current | 64.2 | 60.6 |
| | | 36.7 | 37.7 | 32.3 | 29.9 | Fixed Assets (net) | 30.3 | 31.5 |
| | | 4.2 | .9 | 6.4 | 13.0 | Intangibles (net) | 2.1 | 3.6 |
| | | 3.1 | 5.1 | 5.1 | 4.7 | All Other Non-Current | 3.4 | 4.4 |
| | | 100.0 | 100.0 | 100.0 | 100.0 | Total | 100.0 | 100.0 |
| | | | | | | **LIABILITIES** | | |
| | | 12.8 | 11.2 | 6.6 | 11.7 | Notes Payable-Short Term | 16.9 | 14.2 |
| | | 4.0 | 2.8 | 2.2 | 2.6 | Cur. Mat.-L.T.D. | 3.6 | 3.2 |
| | | 19.3 | 12.3 | 12.4 | 10.5 | Trade Payables | 15.9 | 14.4 |
| | | .5 | .4 | .3 | .1 | Income Taxes Payable | .1 | .1 |
| | | 3.0 | 7.6 | 8.5 | 6.9 | All Other Current | 6.4 | 6.8 |
| | | 39.6 | 34.2 | 29.9 | 31.7 | Total Current | 42.9 | 38.6 |
| | | 27.1 | 23.2 | 24.0 | 20.3 | Long-Term Debt | 17.2 | 16.3 |
| | | 1.0 | .7 | .4 | 2.5 | Deferred Taxes | .4 | .7 |
| | | 2.7 | 1.9 | 5.5 | 3.7 | All Other Non-Current | 11.4 | 6.9 |
| | | 29.6 | 40.0 | 40.1 | 41.8 | Net Worth | 28.1 | 37.5 |
| | | 100.0 | 100.0 | 100.0 | 100.0 | Total Liabilities & Net Worth | 100.0 | 100.0 |
| | | | | | | **INCOME DATA** | | |
| | | 100.0 | 100.0 | 100.0 | 100.0 | Net Sales | 100.0 | 100.0 |
| | | 26.5 | 19.9 | 23.2 | 15.0 | Gross Profit | 22.8 | 23.4 |
| | | 23.9 | 14.5 | 19.8 | 9.5 | Operating Expenses | 17.3 | 18.1 |
| | | 2.6 | 5.5 | 3.4 | 5.5 | Operating Profit | 5.5 | 5.3 |
| | | 1.1 | 1.1 | -.5 | 1.8 | All Other Expenses (net) | 1.5 | 1.4 |
| | | 1.5 | 4.3 | 3.9 | 3.7 | Profit Before Taxes | 4.1 | 3.9 |
| | | | | | | **RATIOS** | | |
| | | 2.4 | 2.0 | 3.5 | 2.3 | | 2.1 | 2.4 |
| | | 1.4 | 1.5 | 1.9 | 1.6 | Current | 1.5 | 1.6 |
| | | 1.0 | 1.3 | 1.4 | 1.3 | | 1.1 | 1.1 |
| | | .9 | .8 | 1.1 | .7 | | .9 | .8 |
| | | .5 | .6 | .6 | .4 | Quick | .5 | .5 |
| | | .4 | .4 | .6 | .3 | | .3 | .4 |
| 21 | 17.6 | 24  15.3 | 21  17.4 | 22  16.4 | | Sales/Receivables | 22  16.3 | 20  18.3 |
| 26 | 14.2 | 31  11.6 | 26  14.0 | 25  14.6 | | | 28  12.9 | 28  13.0 |
| 33 | 11.2 | 37  9.8 | 39  9.3 | 30  12.2 | | | 38  9.7 | 34  10.7 |
| 13 | 27.5 | 52  7.0 | 35  10.5 | 46  7.9 | | Cost of Sales/Inventory | 43  8.6 | 47  7.7 |
| 51 | 7.1 | 68  5.4 | 94  3.9 | 94  3.9 | | | 84  4.4 | 84  4.4 |
| 76 | 4.8 | 130  2.8 | 122  3.0 | 159  2.3 | | | 144  2.5 | 122  3.0 |
| 18 | 20.3 | 13  28.4 | 26  14.2 | 17  21.2 | | Cost of Sales/Payables | 18  20.5 | 15  23.9 |
| 27 | 13.3 | 31  11.7 | 31  11.9 | 28  12.9 | | | 30  12.1 | 28  12.8 |
| 47 | 7.7 | 48  7.6 | 57  6.4 | 34  10.8 | | | 45  8.2 | 40  9.0 |
| | | 8.9 | 5.4 | 4.0 | 3.7 | Sales/Working Capital | 5.6 | 5.6 |
| | | 12.9 | 9.4 | 7.6 | 8.5 | | 11.3 | 10.6 |
| | | 547.0 | 20.3 | 13.9 | NM | | 42.1 | 40.0 |
| | | 4.6 | 11.2 | 15.9 | 19.4 | EBIT/Interest | 8.9 | 9.7 |
| | | (16) 2.8 | (28) 5.0 | 7.1 | 3.0 | | (76) 2.9 | (100) 3.3 |
| | | .6 | 1.7 | .9 | 1.6 | | 1.4 | 1.7 |
| | | | 5.8 | | | Net Profit + Depr., Dep., | 9.8 | 8.5 |
| | | | (17) 4.1 | | | Amort./Cur. Mat. L/T/D | (36) 3.5 | (43) 4.2 |
| | | | 2.5 | | | | 1.3 | 1.1 |
| | | .8 | .6 | .6 | .5 | Fixed/Worth | .4 | .4 |
| | | 1.7 | .9 | 1.1 | .9 | | .9 | .9 |
| | | 3.4 | 1.6 | 3.7 | NM | | 1.6 | 1.9 |
| | | 1.3 | .8 | 1.1 | .8 | Debt/Worth | 1.1 | .8 |
| | | 3.3 | 1.5 | 1.9 | 1.6 | | 2.1 | 1.7 |
| | | 12.0 | 3.1 | 9.3 | NM | | 3.6 | 5.1 |
| | | 30.1 | 30.4 | 40.5 | 34.8 | % Profit Before Taxes/Tangible Net Worth | 33.4 | 35.6 |
| | | (15) 11.9 | (28) 18.5 | (14) 20.6 | 15.0 | | (68) 20.1 | (93) 22.1 |
| | | 2.0 | 5.5 | -.6 | 7.6 | | 8.7 | 10.6 |
| | | 8.3 | 14.1 | 10.5 | 9.5 | % Profit Before Taxes/Total Assets | 13.2 | 13.6 |
| | | 3.1 | 7.3 | 8.8 | 5.0 | | 5.9 | 7.3 |
| | | -.3 | 2.4 | -.2 | 1.9 | | 1.5 | 1.7 |
| | | 14.4 | 5.8 | 9.3 | 6.8 | Sales/Net Fixed Assets | 14.4 | 14.0 |
| | | 8.5 | 4.4 | 5.0 | 5.1 | | 7.4 | 7.4 |
| | | 3.5 | 3.5 | 4.1 | 4.2 | | 4.6 | 4.1 |
| | | 3.3 | 2.5 | 2.0 | 2.0 | Sales/Total Assets | 3.2 | 2.7 |
| | | 2.4 | 1.7 | 1.6 | 1.3 | | 2.1 | 1.9 |
| | | 2.0 | 1.4 | 1.4 | 1.1 | | 1.5 | 1.5 |
| | | 1.1 | 1.6 | | 1.9 | % Depr., Dep., Amort./Sales | .9 | 1.1 |
| | | 1.5 | (26) 2.3 | | (13) 2.4 | | (72) 1.9 | (91) 2.0 |
| | | 2.6 | 3.3 | | 2.9 | | 3.2 | 3.2 |
| | | | | | | % Officers', Directors' Owners' Comp/Sales | .8 | 1.2 |
| | | | | | | | (16) 2.2 | (25) 2.1 |
| | | | | | | | 3.9 | 5.0 |
| 1853M | 57903M | 210542M | 1423156M | 1301682M | 4368667M | Net Sales ($) | 6516618M | 10249819M |
| 146M | 10858M | 80335M | 758440M | 754289M | 2771617M | Total Assets ($) | 3646516M | 5234612M |

M = $ thousand     MM = $ million
See Pages 9 through 22 for Explanation of Ratios and Data

## Comparative Historical Data

## Current Data Sorted by Sales

| | | | Type of Statement | 0-1MM | 1-3MM | 3-5MM | 5-10MM | 10-25MM | 25MM & OVER |
|---|---|---|---|---|---|---|---|---|---|
| 26 | 31 | 25 | Unqualified | | | | | 3 | 21 |
| 13 | 11 | 12 | Reviewed | | 1 | | 1 | 4 | 6 |
| 5 | 9 | 8 | Compiled | 1 | | | | 4 | 3 |
| 6 | 7 | 5 | Tax Returns | 1 | | 1 | 1 | | |
| 35 | 38 | 36 | Other | | 2 | | 1 | 3 | 24 |
| 4/1/09-3/31/10 ALL | 4/1/10-3/31/11 ALL | 4/1/11-3/31/12 ALL | | | 32 (4/1-9/30/11) | | | 54 (10/1/11-3/31/12) | |
| 85 | 96 | 86 | **NUMBER OF STATEMENTS** | 2 | 3 | 5 | 6 | 16 | 54 |
| % | % | % | **ASSETS** | % | % | % | % | % | % |
| 5.5 | 5.2 | 4.3 | Cash & Equivalents | | | | | 7.8 | 3.9 |
| 17.2 | 15.6 | 18.2 | Trade Receivables (net) | | | | | 26.4 | 15.0 |
| 36.4 | 34.3 | 30.9 | Inventory | | | | | 27.2 | 32.6 |
| 2.7 | 3.1 | 4.2 | All Other Current | | | | | 1.9 | 3.7 |
| 61.8 | 58.2 | 57.5 | Total Current | | | | | 63.4 | 55.2 |
| 30.7 | 31.3 | 32.8 | Fixed Assets (net) | | | | | 28.4 | 34.0 |
| 3.1 | 5.6 | 4.8 | Intangibles (net) | | | | | 4.0 | 6.1 |
| 4.4 | 4.9 | 4.9 | All Other Non-Current | | | | | 4.2 | 4.8 |
| 100.0 | 100.0 | 100.0 | Total | | | | | 100.0 | 100.0 |
| | | | **LIABILITIES** | | | | | | |
| 13.3 | 14.2 | 12.9 | Notes Payable-Short Term | | | | | 7.8 | 10.3 |
| 2.3 | 2.6 | 2.6 | Cur. Mat.-L.T.D. | | | | | 2.7 | 2.5 |
| 13.3 | 12.8 | 16.1 | Trade Payables | | | | | 24.8 | 11.9 |
| .3 | .3 | .3 | Income Taxes Payable | | | | | .5 | .2 |
| 8.3 | 6.9 | 8.8 | All Other Current | | | | | 2.6 | 7.7 |
| 37.6 | 36.7 | 40.6 | Total Current | | | | | 38.4 | 32.6 |
| 16.7 | 16.6 | 24.3 | Long-Term Debt | | | | | 24.1 | 22.2 |
| .6 | .5 | 1.0 | Deferred Taxes | | | | | 1.1 | 1.2 |
| 5.4 | 5.6 | 5.7 | All Other Non-Current | | | | | 2.5 | 3.3 |
| 39.6 | 40.5 | 28.4 | Net Worth | | | | | 33.9 | 40.7 |
| 100.0 | 100.0 | 100.0 | Total Liabilities & Net Worth | | | | | 100.0 | 100.0 |
| | | | **INCOME DATA** | | | | | | |
| 100.0 | 100.0 | 100.0 | Net Sales | | | | | 100.0 | 100.0 |
| 22.6 | 25.1 | 22.2 | Gross Profit | | | | | 19.0 | 19.2 |
| 15.2 | 18.3 | 18.0 | Operating Expenses | | | | | 16.8 | 14.1 |
| 7.4 | 6.7 | 4.3 | Operating Profit | | | | | 2.2 | 5.1 |
| 1.2 | 1.3 | 1.0 | All Other Expenses (net) | | | | | .6 | 1.0 |
| 6.2 | 5.5 | 3.3 | Profit Before Taxes | | | | | 1.6 | 4.1 |
| | | | **RATIOS** | | | | | | |
| 2.4 | 2.3 | 2.3 | Current | | | | | 2.5 | 2.4 |
| 1.7 | 1.6 | 1.5 | | | | | | 1.6 | 1.6 |
| 1.2 | 1.2 | 1.1 | | | | | | 1.1 | 1.4 |
| .9 | .9 | .8 | Quick | | | | | 1.7 | .8 |
| .5 | .5 | .6 | | | | | | .8 | .6 |
| .4 | .3 | .4 | | | | | | .5 | .4 |
| 22  16.3 | 20  17.9 | 21  17.1 | Sales/Receivables | | | | 24  14.9 | 22  16.9 | |
| 28  12.9 | 29  12.8 | 26  13.9 | | | | | 26  14.1 | 27  13.4 | |
| 37  9.7 | 35  10.6 | 35  10.5 | | | | | 32  11.5 | 36  10.2 | |
| 51  7.2 | 45  8.2 | 35  10.5 | Cost of Sales/Inventory | | | | 15  24.6 | 49  7.5 | |
| 82  4.4 | 68  5.3 | 63  5.8 | | | | | 52  7.0 | 76  4.8 | |
| 156  2.3 | 138  2.6 | 118  3.1 | | | | | 70  5.2 | 122  3.0 | |
| 16  22.4 | 16  23.4 | 17  21.8 | Cost of Sales/Payables | | | | 20  18.7 | 16  22.9 | |
| 24  15.5 | 24  15.4 | 29  12.7 | | | | | 28  12.9 | 29  12.8 | |
| 38  9.6 | 42  8.7 | 47  7.8 | | | | | 43  8.4 | 41  9.0 | |
| 5.1 | 5.5 | 5.8 | Sales/Working Capital | | | | | 7.1 | 4.3 |
| 8.2 | 9.5 | 10.3 | | | | | | 10.9 | 8.5 |
| 27.5 | 25.6 | 49.7 | | | | | | 84.6 | 15.8 |
| 15.9 | 18.3 | 9.9 | EBIT/Interest | | | | | 5.1 | 11.9 |
| (80)  4.8 | (88)  5.6 | (83)  4.1 | | | | | (15)  2.6 | (53)  5.5 | |
| 2.5 | 2.4 | 1.4 | | | | | | 1.3 | 1.6 |
| 9.7 | 8.0 | 5.6 | Net Profit + Depr., Dep., Amort./Cur. Mat. L/T/D | | | | | | 5.7 |
| (32)  4.6 | (42)  4.9 | (40)  3.7 | | | | | | (31)  4.1 | |
| 2.6 | 2.4 | 1.7 | | | | | | | 2.5 |
| .5 | .5 | .6 | Fixed/Worth | | | | | .4 | .6 |
| .8 | .9 | 1.1 | | | | | | 1.5 | .9 |
| 1.5 | 2.2 | 3.5 | | | | | | 2.3 | 1.8 |
| .8 | .7 | 1.0 | Debt/Worth | | | | | 1.6 | .8 |
| 1.3 | 1.8 | 2.0 | | | | | | 3.0 | 1.4 |
| 3.0 | 4.3 | 8.2 | | | | | | 3.8 | 4.5 |
| 37.6 | 42.6 | 33.6 | % Profit Before Taxes/Tangible Net Worth | | | | | 27.1 | 34.1 |
| (76)  24.2 | (83)  25.0 | (73)  18.0 | | | | | (15)  14.2 | (49)  18.0 | |
| 15.4 | 9.4 | 4.8 | | | | | | 2.0 | 4.8 |
| 17.3 | 17.7 | 10.4 | % Profit Before Taxes/Total Assets | | | | | 7.6 | 11.7 |
| 9.9 | 7.8 | 5.7 | | | | | | 3.9 | 6.5 |
| 3.7 | 2.6 | .7 | | | | | | .6 | 1.1 |
| 13.2 | 11.9 | 10.1 | Sales/Net Fixed Assets | | | | | 29.0 | 6.5 |
| 5.8 | 6.0 | 5.3 | | | | | | 10.8 | 5.0 |
| 3.6 | 3.6 | 4.0 | | | | | | 5.1 | 4.0 |
| 2.8 | 2.6 | 2.6 | Sales/Total Assets | | | | | 4.0 | 2.1 |
| 1.9 | 1.9 | 1.9 | | | | | | 2.8 | 1.6 |
| 1.4 | 1.3 | 1.3 | | | | | | 1.9 | 1.3 |
| 1.1 | 1.5 | 1.4 | % Depr., Dep., Amort./Sales | | | | | 1.1 | 1.7 |
| (73)  2.0 | (88)  2.2 | (73)  2.3 | | | | | (15)  1.6 | (44)  2.4 | |
| 3.1 | 3.3 | 3.0 | | | | | | 2.7 | 3.0 |
| .7 | 1.4 | .9 | % Officers', Directors' Owners' Comp/Sales | | | | | | |
| (20)  2.0 | (16)  3.0 | (16)  1.6 | | | | | | | |
| 3.8 | 5.5 | 3.3 | | | | | | | |
| 7247976M | 7407839M | 7363803M | Net Sales ($) | 974M | 6778M | 18843M | 40648M | 257723M | 7038837M |
| 3918140M | 4149461M | 4375685M | Total Assets ($) | 899M | 3726M | 9067M | 24650M | 104658M | 4232685M |

© RMA 2012

**M = $ thousand     MM = $ million**
See Pages 9 through 22 for Explanation of Ratios and Data

## Current Data Sorted by Assets     Comparative Historical Data

| 0-500M | 500M-2MM | 2-10MM | 10-50MM | 50-100MM | 100-250MM | | 4/1/07-3/31/08 ALL | 4/1/08-3/31/09 ALL |
|---|---|---|---|---|---|---|---|---|
| | | | | | | **Type of Statement** | | |
| | | 2 | 4 | 7 | 5 | Unqualified | 13 | 14 |
| | 5 | 2 | | | | Reviewed | 4 | 7 |
| | 1 | 1 | 1 | | | Compiled | 6 | 4 |
| | 1 | | 1 | | | Tax Returns | 1 | 2 |
| | 2 | 2 | 4 | 1 | 1 | Other | 17 | 19 |
| | 12 (4/1-9/30/11) | 29 (10/1/11-3/31/12) | | | | | | |
| 5 | 5 | 10 | 12 | 8 | 6 | **NUMBER OF STATEMENTS** | 41 | 46 |
| % | % | % | % | % | % | **ASSETS** | % | % |
| | | 2.2 | 7.5 | | | Cash & Equivalents | 6.3 | 4.4 |
| | | 26.5 | 20.3 | | | Trade Receivables (net) | 20.7 | 20.2 |
| | | 41.0 | 31.8 | | | Inventory | 36.4 | 34.8 |
| | | .9 | .9 | | | All Other Current | 3.1 | 3.0 |
| | | 70.6 | 60.6 | | | Total Current | 66.5 | 62.4 |
| | | 16.4 | 31.6 | | | Fixed Assets (net) | 23.0 | 23.5 |
| | | 2.7 | 5.0 | | | Intangibles (net) | 4.0 | 5.7 |
| | | 10.3 | 2.7 | | | All Other Non-Current | 6.5 | 8.3 |
| | | 100.0 | 100.0 | | | Total | 100.0 | 100.0 |
| | | | | | | **LIABILITIES** | | |
| | | 11.5 | 11.3 | | | Notes Payable-Short Term | 17.5 | 16.3 |
| | | 2.2 | 2.0 | | | Cur. Mat.-L.T.D. | 2.9 | 2.8 |
| | | 22.6 | 8.9 | | | Trade Payables | 17.6 | 14.3 |
| | | .0 | .8 | | | Income Taxes Payable | .2 | .4 |
| | | 5.6 | 8.2 | | | All Other Current | 7.4 | 5.7 |
| | | 41.9 | 31.2 | | | Total Current | 45.6 | 39.5 |
| | | 12.4 | 17.2 | | | Long-Term Debt | 12.6 | 14.6 |
| | | .8 | .2 | | | Deferred Taxes | .5 | .4 |
| | | 2.0 | 12.1 | | | All Other Non-Current | 6.6 | 4.8 |
| | | 42.9 | 39.3 | | | Net Worth | 34.7 | 40.8 |
| | | 100.0 | 100.0 | | | Total Liabilities & Net Worth | 100.0 | 100.0 |
| | | | | | | **INCOME DATA** | | |
| | | 100.0 | 100.0 | | | Net Sales | 100.0 | 100.0 |
| | | 35.0 | 21.3 | | | Gross Profit | 28.8 | 28.3 |
| | | 24.4 | 14.1 | | | Operating Expenses | 21.9 | 20.6 |
| | | 10.6 | 7.2 | | | Operating Profit | 6.9 | 7.7 |
| | | .2 | 1.0 | | | All Other Expenses (net) | 1.5 | .3 |
| | | 10.4 | 6.2 | | | Profit Before Taxes | 5.3 | 7.4 |
| | | | | | | **RATIOS** | | |
| | | 3.1 | 3.6 | | | | 2.3 | 2.8 |
| | | 1.3 | 2.1 | | | Current | 1.5 | 1.5 |
| | | 1.2 | 1.3 | | | | 1.2 | 1.2 |
| | | 1.5 | 1.9 | | | | 1.0 | 1.1 |
| | | .6 | .9 | | | Quick | .5 | .6 |
| | | .4 | .4 | | | | .3 | .4 |
| | | 20   18.0 | 32   11.3 | | | | 22   16.9 | 24   15.4 |
| | | 34   10.6 | 43   8.5 | | | Sales/Receivables | 36   10.1 | 34   10.6 |
| | | 63   5.8 | 60   6.1 | | | | 47   7.8 | 44   8.3 |
| | | 36   10.1 | 24   15.1 | | | | 54   6.7 | 46   7.9 |
| | | 76   4.8 | 81   4.5 | | | Cost of Sales/Inventory | 90   4.1 | 86   4.2 |
| | | 111   3.3 | 130   2.8 | | | | 209   1.7 | 123   3.0 |
| | | 16   23.3 | 12   31.2 | | | | 20   18.5 | 15   25.0 |
| | | 30   12.0 | 21   17.0 | | | Cost of Sales/Payables | 29   12.7 | 22   16.3 |
| | | 62   5.9 | 35   10.4 | | | | 62   5.9 | 51   7.2 |
| | | 7.6 | 3.1 | | | | 5.0 | 5.1 |
| | | 15.2 | 8.5 | | | Sales/Working Capital | 7.4 | 8.9 |
| | | 36.8 | 11.8 | | | | 18.5 | 34.4 |
| | | | 52.9 | | | | 10.8 | 14.0 |
| | | | 5.3 | | | EBIT/Interest | (39) 3.3 | (43) 6.4 |
| | | | 2.2 | | | | 1.2 | 3.0 |
| | | | | | | Net Profit + Depr., Dep., | 16.3 | 30.2 |
| | | | | | | Amort./Cur. Mat. L/T/D | (12) 3.9 | (14) 6.6 |
| | | | | | | | 1.7 | 3.1 |
| | | .1 | .3 | | | | .4 | .3 |
| | | .4 | .7 | | | Fixed/Worth | .7 | .7 |
| | | .8 | 2.5 | | | | 1.4 | 1.2 |
| | | .6 | .6 | | | | 1.1 | .7 |
| | | 1.8 | 2.5 | | | Debt/Worth | 2.4 | 1.9 |
| | | 4.2 | 8.2 | | | | 4.1 | 3.4 |
| | | 125.7 | 75.5 | | | % Profit Before Taxes/Tangible | 53.2 | 46.0 |
| | | 62.0 | 29.1 | | | Net Worth | (37) 20.8 | (42) 28.7 |
| | | 6.8 | 25.0 | | | | 1.3 | 14.3 |
| | | 63.9 | 17.0 | | | % Profit Before Taxes/Total | 15.0 | 20.6 |
| | | 25.1 | 8.0 | | | Assets | 7.2 | 9.4 |
| | | 2.6 | 3.4 | | | | .5 | 5.3 |
| | | 108.9 | 12.2 | | | | 23.8 | 26.0 |
| | | 25.2 | 5.4 | | | Sales/Net Fixed Assets | 8.7 | 8.7 |
| | | 11.3 | 3.2 | | | | 5.9 | 5.5 |
| | | 4.0 | 2.6 | | | | 2.7 | 2.9 |
| | | 2.6 | 1.5 | | | Sales/Total Assets | 1.7 | 1.9 |
| | | 2.2 | 1.1 | | | | 1.4 | 1.4 |
| | | | 1.1 | | | | 1.0 | .9 |
| | | | 2.4 | | | % Depr., Dep., Amort./Sales | (35) 1.6 | (41) 1.6 |
| | | | 2.7 | | | | 2.2 | 2.5 |
| | | | | | | % Officers', Directors' | | .9 |
| | | | | | | Owners' Comp/Sales | (10) | 2.9 |
| | | | | | | | | 7.8 |
| | 20312M | 179721M | 434047M | 1099942M | 1570041M | Net Sales ($) | 2885947M | 3898603M |
| | 5442M | 56350M | 275211M | 576922M | 1020630M | Total Assets ($) | 1703587M | 1997420M |

*(Note: In the printed page, the 0-500M and 500M-2MM columns of the percentage/ratio rows are overlaid with the vertical legend "DATA NOT AVAILABLE".)*

M = $ thousand    MM = $ million
See Pages 9 through 22 for Explanation of Ratios and Data

## Comparative Historical Data | Current Data Sorted by Sales

Type of Statement dating: 12 (4/1-9/30/11) — 29 (10/1/11-3/31/12)

Note: The 0-1MM current column is marked "DATA NOT AVAILABLE."

| 4/1/09-3/31/10 ALL | 4/1/10-3/31/11 ALL | 4/1/11-3/31/12 ALL | Item | 0-1MM | 1-3MM | 3-5MM | 5-10MM | 10-25MM | 25MM & OVER |
|---|---|---|---|---|---|---|---|---|---|
| | | | **Type of Statement** | | | | | | |
| 14 | 15 | 18 | Unqualified | | | | 1 | 3 | 14 |
| 8 | 6 | 7 | Reviewed | | | 1 | | 2 | 4 |
| 3 | 3 | 4 | Compiled | | 1 | | 2 | 1 | |
| 3 | 1 | 2 | Tax Returns | | | | 1 | | 1 |
| 16 | 15 | 10 | Other | | 2 | | | 3 | 5 |
| 44 | 40 | 41 | **NUMBER OF STATEMENTS** | | 3 | 1 | 4 | 9 | 24 |
| % | % | % | **ASSETS** | % | % | % | % | % | % |
| 5.3 | 6.0 | 5.4 | Cash & Equivalents | | | | | | 4.9 |
| 19.3 | 17.9 | 21.5 | Trade Receivables (net) | | | | | | 19.2 |
| 41.7 | 33.2 | 33.8 | Inventory | | | | | | 31.6 |
| 2.0 | 3.3 | 1.4 | All Other Current | | | | | | 1.7 |
| 68.2 | 60.4 | 62.1 | Total Current | | | | | | 57.5 |
| 21.2 | 27.1 | 26.0 | Fixed Assets (net) | | | | | | 31.0 |
| 3.1 | 4.8 | 5.2 | Intangibles (net) | | | | | | 5.7 |
| 7.5 | 7.7 | 6.7 | All Other Non-Current | | | | | | 5.8 |
| 100.0 | 100.0 | 100.0 | Total | | | | | | 100.0 |
| | | | **LIABILITIES** | | | | | | |
| 15.3 | 17.5 | 10.2 | Notes Payable-Short Term | | | | | | 10.5 |
| 2.6 | 2.2 | 2.4 | Cur. Mat.-L.T.D. | | | | | | 3.1 |
| 16.6 | 14.7 | 16.2 | Trade Payables | | | | | | 15.2 |
| .5 | .6 | .3 | Income Taxes Payable | | | | | | .2 |
| 6.0 | 5.9 | 6.1 | All Other Current | | | | | | 7.7 |
| 41.0 | 40.9 | 35.2 | Total Current | | | | | | 36.7 |
| 14.2 | 10.6 | 17.2 | Long-Term Debt | | | | | | 19.6 |
| .4 | .5 | .3 | Deferred Taxes | | | | | | .1 |
| 4.6 | 8.0 | 8.5 | All Other Non-Current | | | | | | 9.2 |
| 39.8 | 40.0 | 38.9 | Net Worth | | | | | | 34.5 |
| 100.0 | 100.0 | 100.0 | Total Liabilities & Net Worth | | | | | | 100.0 |
| | | | **INCOME DATA** | | | | | | |
| 100.0 | 100.0 | 100.0 | Net Sales | | | | | | 100.0 |
| 26.4 | 27.4 | 26.6 | Gross Profit | | | | | | 19.9 |
| 20.7 | 20.5 | 19.2 | Operating Expenses | | | | | | 12.7 |
| 5.8 | 6.9 | 7.4 | Operating Profit | | | | | | 7.3 |
| 1.3 | .7 | .8 | All Other Expenses (net) | | | | | | 1.0 |
| 4.5 | 6.2 | 6.6 | Profit Before Taxes | | | | | | 6.3 |
| | | | **RATIOS** | | | | | | |
| 2.3 | 2.3 | 2.5 | | | | | | | 2.2 |
| 1.5 | 1.4 | 1.8 | Current | | | | | | 1.6 |
| 1.2 | 1.2 | 1.2 | | | | | | | 1.2 |
| 1.0 | 1.1 | 1.5 | | | | | | | 1.2 |
| .5 | .6 | .7 | Quick | | | | | | .6 |
| .3 | .3 | .4 | | | | | | | .4 |
| 28  12.9 | 19  19.1 | 29  12.8 | | | | | | | 27  13.3 |
| 36  10.0 | 38  9.6 | 38  9.6 | Sales/Receivables | | | | | | 35  10.4 |
| 42  8.7 | 48  7.6 | 51  7.1 | | | | | | | 49  7.5 |
| 58  6.3 | 40  9.1 | 36  10.1 | | | | | | | 36  10.2 |
| 129  2.8 | 97  3.7 | 79  4.6 | Cost of Sales/Inventory | | | | | | 55  6.6 |
| 177  2.1 | 131  2.8 | 135  2.7 | | | | | | | 118  3.1 |
| 17  21.9 | 16  22.3 | 17  21.3 | | | | | | | 19  19.7 |
| 28  13.0 | 30  12.2 | 26  13.8 | Cost of Sales/Payables | | | | | | 33  10.9 |
| 83  4.4 | 51  7.2 | 55  6.6 | | | | | | | 54  6.8 |
| 4.5 | 5.0 | 5.1 | | | | | | | 7.0 |
| 8.8 | 9.7 | 9.3 | Sales/Working Capital | | | | | | 9.2 |
| 16.9 | 30.1 | 22.8 | | | | | | | 28.7 |
| 33.1 | 35.6 | 29.6 | | | | | | | 28.9 |
| (43) 5.5 | 5.5 | (39) 6.4 | EBIT/Interest | | | | | | 6.6 |
| 1.7 | 1.3 | 1.9 | | | | | | | 2.5 |
| 10.6 | 5.3 | 24.2 | | | | | | | |
| (15) 3.2 | (13) 2.2 | (12) 2.5 | Net Profit + Depr., Dep., Amort./Cur. Mat. L/T/D | | | | | | |
| 1.8 | -.4 | 1.1 | | | | | | | |
| .2 | .4 | .3 | | | | | | | .4 |
| .5 | .8 | .7 | Fixed/Worth | | | | | | 1.2 |
| 1.0 | 1.7 | 1.5 | | | | | | | 2.6 |
| .8 | .8 | .8 | | | | | | | .8 |
| 2.1 | 2.3 | 2.2 | Debt/Worth | | | | | | 2.3 |
| 2.9 | 4.3 | 5.9 | | | | | | | 6.5 |
| 51.3 | 72.4 | 76.8 | | | | | | | 97.7 |
| (42) 17.8 | (37) 22.1 | (39) 27.7 | % Profit Before Taxes/Tangible Net Worth | | | | | | (23) 31.4 |
| 5.1 | 5.2 | 10.3 | | | | | | | 17.1 |
| 27.5 | 17.2 | 18.7 | | | | | | | 17.4 |
| 8.2 | 9.2 | 7.7 | % Profit Before Taxes/Total Assets | | | | | | 7.5 |
| 1.4 | 1.3 | 2.1 | | | | | | | 3.6 |
| 28.3 | 18.6 | 25.2 | | | | | | | 10.3 |
| 10.9 | 6.9 | 8.6 | Sales/Net Fixed Assets | | | | | | 5.1 |
| 4.1 | 3.8 | 4.1 | | | | | | | 3.9 |
| 2.3 | 2.4 | 2.9 | | | | | | | 2.9 |
| 1.9 | 1.7 | 1.8 | Sales/Total Assets | | | | | | 1.7 |
| 1.2 | 1.2 | 1.4 | | | | | | | 1.3 |
| .8 | .7 | .9 | | | | | | | 1.2 |
| (38) 1.6 | (34) 2.2 | (36) 2.0 | % Depr., Dep., Amort./Sales | | | | | | (21) 2.3 |
| 2.9 | 2.9 | 2.7 | | | | | | | 2.8 |
| | | | % Officers', Directors' Owners' Comp/Sales | | | | | | |
| 3003602M | 2547497M | 3304063M | Net Sales ($) | | 5260M | 4941M | 31537M | 169937M | 3092388M |
| 1808109M | 1789015M | 1934555M | Total Assets ($) | | 3013M | 2140M | 9748M | 116133M | 1803521M |

© RMA 2012

M = $ thousand    MM = $ million
See Pages 9 through 22 for Explanation of Ratios and Data

## Current Data Sorted by Assets        Comparative Historical Data

### Type of Statement

| | 0-500M | 500M-2MM | 2-10MM | 10-50MM | 50-100MM | 100-250MM | Type of Statement | 4/1/07-3/31/08 ALL | 4/1/08-3/31/09 ALL |
|---|---|---|---|---|---|---|---|---|---|
| Unqualified | | | 2 | 10 | 4 | 9 | | 26 | 19 |
| Reviewed | | | 4 | 2 | 1 | | | 5 | 4 |
| Compiled | | | | | | | | 6 | 4 |
| Tax Returns | 1 | | 1 | | | | | 2 | 1 |
| Other | 2 | 3 | 3 | 10 | 4 | 4 | | 21 | 29 |

14 (4/1-9/30/11)     46 (10/1/11-3/31/12)

### Ratios and Data

| 0-500M | 500M-2MM | 2-10MM | 10-50MM | 50-100MM | 100-250MM | Item | 4/1/07-3/31/08 ALL | 4/1/08-3/31/09 ALL |
|---|---|---|---|---|---|---|---|---|
| 3 | 3 | 10 | 22 | 9 | 13 | NUMBER OF STATEMENTS | 60 | 57 |
| % | % | % | % | % | % | ASSETS | % | % |
| | | 15.3 | 10.3 | | 6.5 | Cash & Equivalents | 4.9 | 7.3 |
| | | 30.7 | 31.1 | | 25.8 | Trade Receivables (net) | 30.4 | 27.6 |
| | | 16.7 | 12.7 | | 12.5 | Inventory | 13.1 | 12.7 |
| | | .7 | 2.1 | | .9 | All Other Current | 3.4 | 2.9 |
| | | 63.3 | 56.2 | | 45.7 | Total Current | 51.8 | 50.5 |
| | | 28.3 | 37.8 | | 43.0 | Fixed Assets (net) | 39.3 | 42.1 |
| | | 5.0 | 1.4 | | 5.1 | Intangibles (net) | 1.9 | 1.8 |
| | | 3.4 | 4.5 | | 6.2 | All Other Non-Current | 7.0 | 5.6 |
| | | 100.0 | 100.0 | | 100.0 | Total | 100.0 | 100.0 |
| | | | | | | LIABILITIES | | |
| | | 4.8 | 4.6 | | 7.2 | Notes Payable-Short Term | 7.9 | 7.4 |
| | | 2.1 | 2.6 | | 4.2 | Cur. Mat.-L.T.D. | 3.4 | 3.0 |
| | | 18.3 | 25.1 | | 20.4 | Trade Payables | 24.9 | 20.1 |
| | | .0 | .1 | | .1 | Income Taxes Payable | .1 | .1 |
| | | 3.3 | 9.0 | | 14.7 | All Other Current | 10.6 | 9.3 |
| | | 28.6 | 41.4 | | 46.5 | Total Current | 46.9 | 39.9 |
| | | 13.5 | 12.2 | | 12.6 | Long-Term Debt | 16.1 | 15.7 |
| | | .9 | 1.2 | | 1.2 | Deferred Taxes | .6 | .8 |
| | | 6.0 | 4.1 | | 2.5 | All Other Non-Current | 3.0 | 4.7 |
| | | 51.0 | 41.1 | | 37.1 | Net Worth | 33.5 | 39.0 |
| | | 100.0 | 100.0 | | 100.0 | Total Liabilties & Net Worth | 100.0 | 100.0 |
| | | | | | | INCOME DATA | | |
| | | 100.0 | 100.0 | | 100.0 | Net Sales | 100.0 | 100.0 |
| | | 26.3 | 19.1 | | 17.2 | Gross Profit | 20.6 | 23.5 |
| | | 26.2 | 17.5 | | 13.4 | Operating Expenses | 19.0 | 20.4 |
| | | .1 | 1.7 | | 3.8 | Operating Profit | 1.5 | 3.1 |
| | | .1 | .4 | | .3 | All Other Expenses (net) | .8 | .5 |
| | | .0 | 1.2 | | 3.5 | Profit Before Taxes | .7 | 2.7 |
| | | | | | | RATIOS | | |
| | | 3.9 | 1.9 | | 1.4 | | 1.6 | 1.9 |
| | | 2.5 | 1.5 | | 1.0 | Current | 1.1 | 1.2 |
| | | 1.2 | 1.1 | | .7 | | 1.0 | 1.0 |
| | | 2.7 | 1.5 | | 1.0 | | 1.1 | 1.3 |
| | | 1.6 | 1.0 | | .7 | Quick | .8 | .9 |
| | | 1.0 | .6 | | .4 | | .6 | .6 |
| | | 22  16.7 | 17  21.0 | | 17  21.8 | | 22  16.4 | 18  19.8 |
| | | 26  14.1 | 27  13.7 | | 23  16.1 | Sales/Receivables | 28  13.2 | 24  15.5 |
| | | 29  12.7 | 36  10.2 | | 29  12.5 | | 35  10.3 | 29  12.4 |
| | | 7  53.1 | 8  46.4 | | 10  37.5 | | 10  37.7 | 8  47.3 |
| | | 21  17.2 | 14  25.2 | | 17  21.8 | Cost of Sales/Inventory | 13  28.6 | 12  30.1 |
| | | 44  8.3 | 19  19.6 | | 25  14.7 | | 22  16.6 | 21  17.6 |
| | | 13  28.4 | 19  19.6 | | 5  69.5 | | 21  17.2 | 13  27.3 |
| | | 23  15.6 | 24  15.5 | | 21  17.1 | Cost of Sales/Payables | 26  14.2 | 21  17.3 |
| | | 26  14.2 | 29  12.7 | | 32  11.3 | | 35  10.5 | 27  13.4 |
| | | 6.5 | 15.5 | | 32.6 | | 23.5 | 14.0 |
| | | 9.4 | 24.0 | | -405.4 | Sales/Working Capital | 50.4 | 57.5 |
| | | 58.8 | 162.4 | | -15.1 | | -220.0 | NM |
| | | | 24.0 | | 26.6 | | 7.7 | 15.0 |
| | | | (19) 9.2 | | 7.7 | EBIT/Interest | (55) 1.6 | (53) 7.3 |
| | | | .6 | | 2.6 | | -.2 | 1.7 |
| | | | | | | | 5.3 | 10.8 |
| | | | | | | Net Profit + Depr., Dep., Amort./Cur. Mat. L/T/D | (17) 1.8 | (18) 2.8 |
| | | | | | | | 1.2 | 1.6 |
| | | .2 | .6 | | .8 | | .6 | .6 |
| | | .5 | .8 | | 1.3 | Fixed/Worth | 1.2 | .8 |
| | | 1.3 | 1.4 | | 2.3 | | 2.7 | 2.2 |
| | | .4 | .8 | | 1.0 | | 1.1 | .8 |
| | | .7 | 1.5 | | 2.5 | Debt/Worth | 1.8 | 1.5 |
| | | 2.0 | 3.1 | | 3.8 | | 5.7 | 5.3 |
| | | | 21.7 | | 47.6 | | 32.0 | 37.1 |
| | | | (21) 9.6 | | 18.5 | % Profit Before Taxes/Tangible Net Worth | (56) 8.7 | (55) 17.1 |
| | | | -2.1 | | 13.3 | | -6.7 | 5.8 |
| | | 10.7 | 10.5 | | 14.0 | | 8.2 | 12.5 |
| | | 4.2 | 3.5 | | 7.9 | % Profit Before Taxes/Total Assets | 1.8 | 7.3 |
| | | -12.2 | -2.1 | | 3.7 | | -2.2 | 1.5 |
| | | 61.4 | 34.4 | | 26.3 | | 21.5 | 18.7 |
| | | 10.2 | 9.4 | | 6.9 | Sales/Net Fixed Assets | 8.0 | 8.3 |
| | | 7.1 | 5.5 | | 2.7 | | 5.2 | 5.0 |
| | | 5.6 | 6.1 | | 7.1 | | 4.9 | 5.0 |
| | | 3.3 | 3.9 | | 3.3 | Sales/Total Assets | 3.6 | 3.4 |
| | | 2.7 | 2.8 | | 1.7 | | 2.6 | 2.6 |
| | | | .4 | | | | .9 | .9 |
| | | | (19) 1.7 | | | % Depr., Dep., Amort./Sales | (57) 1.7 | (49) 1.5 |
| | | | 2.4 | | | | 2.7 | 2.5 |
| | | | | | | % Officers', Directors' Owners' Comp/Sales | | |
| 3174M | 19935M | 235233M | 3233098M | 2600874M | 8292010M | Net Sales ($) | 10208956M | 11186658M |
| 756M | 2340M | 52731M | 664023M | 749420M | 2112941M | Total Assets ($) | 2956734M | 2969915M |

## Comparative Historical Data | Current Data Sorted by Sales

| Type of Statement | | | | 0-1MM | 1-3MM | 3-5MM | 5-10MM | 10-25MM | 25MM & OVER |
|---|---|---|---|---|---|---|---|---|---|
| 22 | 21 | 27 | Unqualified | 1 | 1 | | | 2 | 23 |
| 9 | 5 | 7 | Reviewed | | 3 | | | | 4 |
| 3 | 3 | | Compiled | | | | | | |
| 6 | | 4 | Tax Returns | | | | 1 | 1 | 1 |
| 28 | 23 | 22 | Other | 2 | 1 | | | 3 | 17 |
| 4/1/09-3/31/10 ALL | 4/1/10-3/31/11 ALL | 4/1/11-3/31/12 ALL | | 14 (4/1-9/30/11) | | | 46 (10/1/11-3/31/12) | | |
| 68 | 52 | 60 | NUMBER OF STATEMENTS | 1 | 4 | | 1 | 9 | 45 |
| % | % | % | ASSETS | % | % | % | % | % | % |
| 8.6 | 7.9 | 9.4 | Cash & Equivalents | | | | | | 9.9 |
| 24.5 | 30.0 | 28.3 | Trade Receivables (net) | | D | | | | 29.7 |
| 13.5 | 13.1 | 13.3 | Inventory | | A | | | | 12.4 |
| 2.7 | 1.8 | 1.3 | All Other Current | | T | | | | 1.5 |
| 49.2 | 52.8 | 52.3 | Total Current | | A | | | | 53.5 |
| 38.7 | 34.8 | 38.2 | Fixed Assets (net) | | | | | | 36.9 |
| 3.3 | 7.9 | 4.7 | Intangibles (net) | | N | | | | 4.7 |
| 8.8 | 4.5 | 4.8 | All Other Non-Current | | O | | | | 5.0 |
| 100.0 | 100.0 | 100.0 | Total | | T | | | | 100.0 |
| | | | LIABILITIES | | A | | | | |
| 5.5 | 5.4 | 6.0 | Notes Payable-Short Term | | V | | | | 5.7 |
| 3.0 | 3.1 | 3.0 | Cur. Mat.-L.T.D. | | A | | | | 3.1 |
| 20.4 | 22.5 | 20.7 | Trade Payables | | I | | | | 23.2 |
| .1 | .1 | .1 | Income Taxes Payable | | L | | | | .1 |
| 7.8 | 10.2 | 10.3 | All Other Current | | A | | | | 11.6 |
| 36.8 | 41.4 | 40.0 | Total Current | | B | | | | 43.7 |
| 18.1 | 13.1 | 14.7 | Long-Term Debt | | L | | | | 9.8 |
| 1.0 | 1.1 | 1.3 | Deferred Taxes | | E | | | | 1.4 |
| 3.6 | 3.8 | 4.0 | All Other Non-Current | | | | | | 3.4 |
| 40.4 | 40.6 | 40.0 | Net Worth | | | | | | 41.7 |
| 100.0 | 100.0 | 100.0 | Total Liabilities & Net Worth | | | | | | 100.0 |
| | | | INCOME DATA | | | | | | |
| 100.0 | 100.0 | 100.0 | Net Sales | | | | | | 100.0 |
| 26.0 | 20.7 | 21.1 | Gross Profit | | | | | | 17.3 |
| 23.5 | 18.0 | 18.9 | Operating Expenses | | | | | | 15.1 |
| 2.4 | 2.7 | 2.2 | Operating Profit | | | | | | 2.1 |
| .2 | .6 | .5 | All Other Expenses (net) | | | | | | .5 |
| 2.3 | 2.1 | 1.7 | Profit Before Taxes | | | | | | 1.7 |
| | | | RATIOS | | | | | | |
| 1.8 | 1.8 | 1.9 | | | | | | | 1.7 |
| 1.3 | 1.3 | 1.3 | Current | | | | | | 1.2 |
| 1.0 | .9 | .9 | | | | | | | .8 |
| 1.2 | 1.3 | 1.4 | | | | | | | 1.2 |
| .9 | .9 | .9 | Quick | | | | | | .9 |
| .6 | .6 | .6 | | | | | | | .6 |
| 21  17.5 | 20  17.9 | 19  19.7 | Sales/Receivables | | | | | | 18  20.1 |
| 26  14.2 | 24  15.0 | 24  15.4 | | | | | | | 23  15.9 |
| 32  11.3 | 31  11.8 | 31  11.7 | | | | | | | 30  12.0 |
| 9  39.1 | 9  39.7 | 10  38.0 | Cost of Sales/Inventory | | | | | | 8  45.4 |
| 15  25.1 | 16  22.7 | 16  23.2 | | | | | | | 14  25.3 |
| 30  12.1 | 23  15.8 | 28  12.9 | | | | | | | 23  16.2 |
| 18  20.6 | 18  20.4 | 14  26.4 | Cost of Sales/Payables | | | | | | 17  21.8 |
| 27  13.7 | 23  15.6 | 23  15.6 | | | | | | | 23  15.6 |
| 38  9.6 | 34  10.6 | 29  12.5 | | | | | | | 32  11.5 |
| 11.8 | 14.0 | 15.4 | Sales/Working Capital | | | | | | 21.5 |
| 28.7 | 52.2 | 42.5 | | | | | | | 49.3 |
| 501.6 | -90.0 | -114.0 | | | | | | | -56.6 |
| 21.1 | 19.8 | 18.4 | EBIT/Interest | | | | | | 25.9 |
| (63) 5.5 | (47) 5.4 | (56) 4.8 | | | | | | (41) | 5.7 |
| 2.0 | 1.2 | 1.2 | | | | | | | 2.1 |
| 9.8 | 8.9 | 7.7 | Net Profit + Depr., Dep., Amort./Cur. Mat. L/T/D | | | | | | 8.1 |
| (26) 3.8 | (20) 3.2 | (24) 3.2 | | | | | | (18) | 4.4 |
| 2.6 | 1.9 | .3 | | | | | | | 1.0 |
| .6 | .6 | .6 | Fixed/Worth | | | | | | .6 |
| .9 | .9 | 1.0 | | | | | | | .9 |
| 1.7 | 2.0 | 2.2 | | | | | | | 1.9 |
| .7 | .8 | .8 | Debt/Worth | | | | | | .8 |
| 1.3 | 1.3 | 1.8 | | | | | | | 1.7 |
| 3.9 | 4.8 | 3.8 | | | | | | | 3.3 |
| 34.3 | 29.3 | 26.8 | % Profit Before Taxes/Tangible Net Worth | | | | | | 25.7 |
| (64) 19.9 | (48) 14.7 | (55) 13.7 | | | | | | (43) | 13.4 |
| 6.9 | -1.4 | 4.6 | | | | | | | 5.4 |
| 14.1 | 12.1 | 11.3 | % Profit Before Taxes/Total Assets | | | | | | 10.3 |
| 7.2 | 5.3 | 4.3 | | | | | | | 4.0 |
| 2.3 | -.5 | .3 | | | | | | | 2.3 |
| 16.7 | 29.0 | 27.1 | Sales/Net Fixed Assets | | | | | | 34.5 |
| 6.7 | 10.0 | 9.0 | | | | | | | 9.3 |
| 5.2 | 5.6 | 4.7 | | | | | | | 5.3 |
| 4.3 | 5.3 | 5.8 | Sales/Total Assets | | | | | | 6.5 |
| 3.1 | 3.6 | 3.5 | | | | | | | 3.7 |
| 2.4 | 2.7 | 2.2 | | | | | | | 2.2 |
| 1.1 | .7 | .5 | % Depr., Dep., Amort./Sales | | | | | | .5 |
| (61) 1.9 | (47) 1.5 | (50) 1.7 | | | | | | (38) | 1.6 |
| 3.0 | 2.6 | 2.6 | | | | | | | 2.4 |
| .6 | | | % Officers', Directors' Owners' Comp/Sales | | | | | | |
| (14) 1.6 | | | | | | | | | |
| 2.8 | | | | | | | | | |
| 9894416M | 12402166M | 14384324M | Net Sales ($) | 131M | 7930M | | 7791M | 129925M | 14238547M |
| 2957395M | 3069811M | 3582211M | Total Assets ($) | 72M | 1959M | | 2478M | 81429M | 3496273M |

© RMA 2012

M = $ thousand   MM = $ million
See Pages 9 through 22 for Explanation of Ratios and Data

## Current Data Sorted by Assets | Comparative Historical Data

| | | | | | | Type of Statement | | |
|---|---|---|---|---|---|---|---|---|
| | | 2 | 13 | 3 | 4 | Unqualified | 33 | 26 |
| | | 7 | 8 | | 1 | Reviewed | 11 | 10 |
| | | 3 | 1 | | | Compiled | 4 | 5 |
| | | 3 | | | | Tax Returns | 4 | 7 |
| | 1 | 5 | 12 | 2 | 2 | Other | 23 | 39 |
| | 18 (4/1-9/30/11) | | 49 (10/1/11-3/31/12) | | | | 4/1/07-3/31/08 | 4/1/08-3/31/09 |
| 0-500M | 500M-2MM | 2-10MM | 10-50MM | 50-100MM | 100-250MM | | ALL | ALL |
| | 1 | 20 | 34 | 5 | 7 | NUMBER OF STATEMENTS | 75 | 87 |
| % | % | % | % | % | % | ASSETS | % | % |
| | | 7.4 | 7.1 | | | Cash & Equivalents | 5.7 | 7.7 |
| | | 26.9 | 23.1 | | | Trade Receivables (net) | 23.5 | 21.7 |
| | | 27.3 | 23.8 | | | Inventory | 25.6 | 23.6 |
| | | 2.7 | .9 | | | All Other Current | 1.7 | 1.7 |
| | | 64.3 | 54.9 | | | Total Current | 56.5 | 54.7 |
| | | 30.8 | 38.1 | | | Fixed Assets (net) | 37.0 | 36.6 |
| | | .3 | 1.1 | | | Intangibles (net) | 2.4 | 3.3 |
| | | 4.5 | 6.0 | | | All Other Non-Current | 4.1 | 5.4 |
| | | 100.0 | 100.0 | | | Total | 100.0 | 100.0 |
| | | | | | | LIABILITIES | | |
| | | 10.1 | 13.3 | | | Notes Payable-Short Term | 13.1 | 9.3 |
| | | 2.7 | 3.5 | | | Cur. Mat.-L.T.D. | 2.9 | 2.9 |
| | | 23.0 | 16.3 | | | Trade Payables | 18.1 | 18.1 |
| | | .0 | .1 | | | Income Taxes Payable | .2 | .2 |
| | | 6.0 | 6.5 | | | All Other Current | 9.4 | 5.9 |
| | | 41.8 | 39.5 | | | Total Current | 43.6 | 36.4 |
| | | 14.9 | 17.0 | | | Long-Term Debt | 18.4 | 19.5 |
| | | .2 | .3 | | | Deferred Taxes | .8 | .8 |
| | | 6.8 | 4.0 | | | All Other Non-Current | 3.7 | 3.8 |
| | | 36.2 | 39.1 | | | Net Worth | 33.6 | 39.5 |
| | | 100.0 | 100.0 | | | Total Liabilties & Net Worth | 100.0 | 100.0 |
| | | | | | | INCOME DATA | | |
| | | 100.0 | 100.0 | | | Net Sales | 100.0 | 100.0 |
| | | 16.5 | 15.3 | | | Gross Profit | 14.5 | 17.5 |
| | | 15.1 | 11.2 | | | Operating Expenses | 11.9 | 12.9 |
| | | 1.4 | 4.0 | | | Operating Profit | 2.6 | 4.6 |
| | | .3 | .7 | | | All Other Expenses (net) | .6 | 1.0 |
| | | 1.1 | 3.3 | | | Profit Before Taxes | 2.0 | 3.6 |
| | | | | | | RATIOS | | |
| | | 2.5 | 1.8 | | | | 2.1 | 2.3 |
| | | 1.8 | 1.3 | | | Current | 1.4 | 1.6 |
| | | 1.1 | 1.0 | | | | 1.0 | 1.1 |
| | | 1.4 | 1.0 | | | | 1.2 | 1.4 |
| | | .9 | .7 | | | Quick | .7 | .7 |
| | | .5 | .4 | | | | .4 | .4 |
| | 23 | 16.2 | 22 16.7 | | | | 20 18.0 | 19 19.6 |
| | 26 | 13.8 | 27 13.4 | | | Sales/Receivables | 26 13.9 | 25 14.4 |
| | 38 | 9.6 | 35 10.3 | | | | 35 10.5 | 33 10.9 |
| | 10 | 35.0 | 17 20.9 | | | | 18 20.5 | 15 23.7 |
| | 21 | 17.0 | 25 14.7 | | | Cost of Sales/Inventory | 30 12.1 | 27 13.3 |
| | 68 | 5.4 | 62 5.9 | | | | 59 6.1 | 62 5.9 |
| | 17 | 20.9 | 16 22.6 | | | | 19 19.4 | 15 24.4 |
| | 22 | 16.8 | 22 16.4 | | | Cost of Sales/Payables | 24 15.0 | 21 17.6 |
| | 43 | 8.5 | 33 11.2 | | | | 31 11.6 | 33 11.2 |
| | | 8.8 | 10.3 | | | | 9.6 | 9.1 |
| | | 19.0 | 22.6 | | | Sales/Working Capital | 19.8 | 17.5 |
| | | 81.6 | NM | | | | 653.8 | 74.9 |
| | | 46.8 | 24.1 | | | | 7.2 | 15.3 |
| | | (19) 2.7 | (32) 7.5 | | | EBIT/Interest | (70) 3.0 | (80) 5.0 |
| | | -.4 | 1.6 | | | | 1.5 | 1.8 |
| | | | 19.8 | | | | 9.4 | 8.7 |
| | | | (12) 6.4 | | | Net Profit + Depr., Dep., Amort./Cur. Mat. L/T/D | (25) 3.7 | (31) 2.7 |
| | | | 4.0 | | | | 1.4 | 1.4 |
| | | .4 | .6 | | | | .7 | .6 |
| | | .7 | .8 | | | Fixed/Worth | 1.0 | 1.0 |
| | | 1.4 | 2.1 | | | | 1.9 | 2.0 |
| | | .7 | 1.0 | | | | .9 | .7 |
| | | 1.6 | 1.8 | | | Debt/Worth | 1.9 | 1.7 |
| | | 2.6 | 3.0 | | | | 3.5 | 3.2 |
| | | 22.6 | 32.7 | | | | 32.6 | 45.7 |
| | | (18) 15.4 | (33) 17.5 | | | % Profit Before Taxes/Tangible Net Worth | (68) 19.3 | (82) 20.4 |
| | | -2.8 | 5.9 | | | | 4.1 | 9.1 |
| | | 13.1 | 12.9 | | | | 9.0 | 15.9 |
| | | 4.9 | 7.2 | | | % Profit Before Taxes/Total Assets | 4.9 | 7.6 |
| | | -.6 | 3.0 | | | | 1.0 | 1.9 |
| | | 19.4 | 13.2 | | | | 13.9 | 14.5 |
| | | 11.6 | 7.4 | | | Sales/Net Fixed Assets | 8.9 | 7.8 |
| | | 6.0 | 4.3 | | | | 4.3 | 4.6 |
| | | 5.1 | 3.6 | | | | 3.9 | 4.0 |
| | | 3.3 | 2.7 | | | Sales/Total Assets | 3.0 | 2.9 |
| | | 2.1 | 1.9 | | | | 2.0 | 2.0 |
| | | 1.1 | 1.4 | | | | 1.2 | 1.0 |
| | | (19) 1.7 | (33) 1.9 | | | % Depr., Dep., Amort./Sales | (65) 1.5 | (77) 1.5 |
| | | 3.3 | 3.2 | | | | 2.5 | 2.6 |
| | | | | | | | .6 | .4 |
| | | | | | | % Officers', Directors' Owners' Comp/Sales | (23) 1.7 | (23) 1.4 |
| | | | | | | | 3.0 | 2.6 |
| | 5541M | 436949M | 2317005M | 999037M | 2256838M | Net Sales ($) | 9494272M | 10976140M |
| | 1820M | 118516M | 837800M | 346889M | 1016780M | Total Assets ($) | 3437821M | 3767444M |

*(DATA NOT AVAILABLE — columns 0-500M and 500M-2MM)*

M = $ thousand    MM = $ million
See Pages 9 through 22 for Explanation of Ratios and Data

## Comparative Historical Data | Current Data Sorted by Sales

| 4/1/09-3/31/10 ALL | 4/1/10-3/31/11 ALL | 4/1/11-3/31/12 ALL | Type of Statement | 0-1MM | 1-3MM | 3-5MM | 5-10MM | 10-25MM | 25MM & OVER |
|---|---|---|---|---|---|---|---|---|---|
|  |  |  |  |  | 18 (4/1-9/30/11) |  | 49 (10/1/11-3/31/12) |  |  |
| 26 | 21 | 22 | Unqualified |  | 1 |  |  | 2 | 20 |
| 11 | 15 | 16 | Reviewed |  |  |  | 2 | 4 | 10 |
| 7 | 4 | 4 | Compiled |  |  |  | 1 | 1 | 2 |
| 5 | 4 | 3 | Tax Returns |  |  |  | 1 | 1 | 1 |
| 32 | 31 | 22 | Other |  |  |  | 4 | 1 | 17 |
| 81 | 75 | 67 | NUMBER OF STATEMENTS |  | 1 |  | 7 | 9 | 50 |
| % | % | % | ASSETS | % | % | % | % | % | % |
| 7.7 | 6.8 | 7.0 | Cash & Equivalents | — | — | — | — | — | 7.3 |
| 20.0 | 22.5 | 23.1 | Trade Receivables (net) | — | — | — | — | — | 24.2 |
| 24.7 | 24.7 | 25.8 | Inventory | — | — | — | — | — | 23.4 |
| 2.3 | 3.0 | 1.7 | All Other Current | — | — | — | — | — | 1.7 |
| 54.8 | 57.0 | 57.7 | Total Current | — | — | — | — | — | 56.6 |
| 35.1 | 36.8 | 36.4 | Fixed Assets (net) | — | — | — | — | — | 37.6 |
| 3.0 | 2.4 | .8 | Intangibles (net) | — | — | — | — | — | 1.0 |
| 7.1 | 3.8 | 5.0 | All Other Non-Current | — | — | — | — | — | 4.8 |
| 100.0 | 100.0 | 100.0 | Total | — | — | — | — | — | 100.0 |
|  |  |  | LIABILITIES |  |  |  |  |  |  |
| 10.3 | 11.8 | 11.5 | Notes Payable-Short Term | — | — | — | — | — | 11.8 |
| 3.2 | 2.3 | 2.8 | Cur. Mat.-L.T.D. | — | — | — | — | — | 3.0 |
| 16.5 | 17.6 | 17.3 | Trade Payables | — | — | — | — | — | 17.3 |
| .2 | .1 | .0 | Income Taxes Payable | — | — | — | — | — | .0 |
| 7.9 | 5.9 | 6.3 | All Other Current | — | — | — | — | — | 6.2 |
| 38.0 | 37.7 | 38.0 | Total Current | — | — | — | — | — | 38.2 |
| 18.6 | 17.3 | 15.9 | Long-Term Debt | — | — | — | — | — | 14.9 |
| .9 | 1.1 | .5 | Deferred Taxes | — | — | — | — | — | .5 |
| 4.8 | 4.1 | 4.6 | All Other Non-Current | — | — | — | — | — | 3.6 |
| 37.7 | 39.8 | 41.0 | Net Worth | — | — | — | — | — | 42.7 |
| 100.0 | 100.0 | 100.0 | Total Liabilities & Net Worth | — | — | — | — | — | 100.0 |
|  |  |  | INCOME DATA |  |  |  |  |  |  |
| 100.0 | 100.0 | 100.0 | Net Sales | — | — | — | — | — | 100.0 |
| 18.9 | 16.5 | 15.2 | Gross Profit | — | — | — | — | — | 13.7 |
| 13.3 | 11.9 | 11.9 | Operating Expenses | — | — | — | — | — | 10.0 |
| 5.6 | 4.5 | 3.3 | Operating Profit | — | — | — | — | — | 3.6 |
| 1.0 | .9 | .3 | All Other Expenses (net) | — | — | — | — | — | .1 |
| 4.7 | 3.6 | 2.9 | Profit Before Taxes | — | — | — | — | — | 3.5 |
|  |  |  | RATIOS |  |  |  |  |  |  |
| 2.4 | 2.4 | 2.1 | Current |  |  |  |  |  | 2.1 |
| 1.6 | 1.5 | 1.5 |  |  |  |  |  |  | 1.5 |
| 1.1 | 1.1 | 1.1 |  |  |  |  |  |  | 1.1 |
| 1.3 | 1.5 | 1.3 | Quick |  |  |  |  |  | 1.3 |
| .7 | .7 | .7 |  |  |  |  |  |  | .8 |
| .4 | .5 | .4 |  |  |  |  |  |  | .5 |
| 21  17.3 | 22  16.5 | 22  16.5 | Sales/Receivables |  |  |  |  |  | 21  17.2 |
| 27  13.4 | 27  13.4 | 27  13.5 |  |  |  |  |  |  | 26  14.2 |
| 31  11.7 | 33  10.9 | 33  10.9 |  |  |  |  |  |  | 32  11.4 |
| 16  23.5 | 16  22.6 | 14  26.7 | Cost of Sales/Inventory |  |  |  |  |  | 13  27.7 |
| 36  10.2 | 28  13.0 | 28  13.0 |  |  |  |  |  |  | 24  15.2 |
| 64  5.7 | 62  5.9 | 65  5.6 |  |  |  |  |  |  | 63  5.8 |
| 17  21.6 | 17  21.9 | 16  22.4 | Cost of Sales/Payables |  |  |  |  |  | 16  22.6 |
| 26  14.0 | 25  14.7 | 22  16.3 |  |  |  |  |  |  | 21  17.3 |
| 37  9.9 | 34  10.8 | 33  11.0 |  |  |  |  |  |  | 32  11.5 |
| 7.1 | 8.8 | 9.0 | Sales/Working Capital |  |  |  |  |  | 9.7 |
| 15.6 | 15.2 | 16.0 |  |  |  |  |  |  | 17.5 |
| 100.4 | 57.3 | 68.6 |  |  |  |  |  |  | 70.5 |
| 22.9 | 21.1 | 24.8 | EBIT/Interest |  |  |  |  |  | 26.9 |
| (78) 6.6 | (71) 7.4 | (63) 5.5 |  |  |  |  |  | (47) | 8.8 |
| 2.3 | 2.5 | .9 |  |  |  |  |  |  | 1.9 |
| 8.9 | 8.0 | 8.8 | Net Profit + Depr., Dep., Amort./Cur. Mat. L/T/D |  |  |  |  |  | 10.6 |
| (24) 3.6 | (23) 3.9 | (22) 4.4 |  |  |  |  |  | (15) | 5.4 |
| 1.5 | 2.8 | 1.7 |  |  |  |  |  |  | 2.2 |
| .4 | .6 | .5 | Fixed/Worth |  |  |  |  |  | .6 |
| .9 | 1.0 | .8 |  |  |  |  |  |  | .8 |
| 1.9 | 2.0 | 1.5 |  |  |  |  |  |  | 1.5 |
| .7 | .6 | .9 | Debt/Worth |  |  |  |  |  | .9 |
| 1.6 | 1.4 | 1.4 |  |  |  |  |  |  | 1.3 |
| 3.6 | 3.1 | 2.6 |  |  |  |  |  |  | 2.4 |
| 47.4 | 37.7 | 26.2 | % Profit Before Taxes/Tangible Net Worth |  |  |  |  |  | 29.2 |
| (74) 27.5 | (68) 23.1 | (64) 17.5 |  |  |  |  |  | (48) | 18.6 |
| 11.3 | 11.9 | .5 |  |  |  |  |  |  | 9.8 |
| 19.5 | 16.9 | 13.2 | % Profit Before Taxes/Total Assets |  |  |  |  |  | 13.9 |
| 10.9 | 8.8 | 7.3 |  |  |  |  |  |  | 8.3 |
| 3.5 | 3.8 | .6 |  |  |  |  |  |  | 3.8 |
| 14.8 | 13.7 | 13.3 | Sales/Net Fixed Assets |  |  |  |  |  | 13.3 |
| 6.5 | 7.1 | 7.4 |  |  |  |  |  |  | 7.4 |
| 4.3 | 4.7 | 4.8 |  |  |  |  |  |  | 5.5 |
| 3.7 | 3.8 | 3.7 | Sales/Total Assets |  |  |  |  |  | 4.1 |
| 2.6 | 2.8 | 2.8 |  |  |  |  |  |  | 3.1 |
| 1.8 | 2.1 | 1.9 |  |  |  |  |  |  | 2.0 |
| 1.2 | 1.3 | 1.3 | % Depr., Dep., Amort./Sales |  |  |  |  |  | 1.3 |
| (72) 1.8 | (69) 1.8 | (62) 1.7 |  |  |  |  |  | (46) | 1.5 |
| 2.6 | 2.6 | 3.1 |  |  |  |  |  |  | 2.3 |
| .7 | .7 | .6 | % Officers', Directors' Owners' Comp/Sales |  |  |  |  |  | .6 |
| (21) 1.4 | (23) 1.4 | (20) 1.0 |  |  |  |  |  | (13) | 1.0 |
| 2.2 | 2.7 | 2.2 |  |  |  |  |  |  | 2.1 |
| 7379129M | 6665542M | 6015370M | Net Sales ($) |  | 2097M |  | 52414M | 186606M | 5774253M |
| 3040483M | 2669482M | 2321805M | Total Assets ($) |  | 3576M |  | 25376M | 88742M | 2204111M |

Note: In the Current Data columns for Assets, Liabilities, Income Data, and the first ratio groups, the source prints "DATA NOT AVAILABLE" for the 0-1MM, 1-3MM, 3-5MM, 5-10MM, and 10-25MM columns (shown as vertical text).

© RMA 2012

M = $ thousand    MM = $ million
See Pages 9 through 22 for Explanation of Ratios and Data

## Current Data Sorted by Assets      Comparative Historical Data

| 0-500M | 500M-2MM | 2-10MM | 10-50MM | 50-100MM | 100-250MM | Type of Statement | 4/1/07-3/31/08 ALL | 4/1/08-3/31/09 ALL |
|---|---|---|---|---|---|---|---|---|
| | | | 4 | | 2 | Unqualified | 8 | 8 |
| | 1 | 5 | 2 | | | Reviewed | 2 | 3 |
| | | 1 | | | | Compiled | 3 | 5 |
| 1 | | | 1 | | | Tax Returns | 3 | 2 |
| 1 | 2 | 3 | 7 | 2 | | Other | 13 | 11 |
| | 7 (4/1-9/30/11) | | 25 (10/1/11-3/31/12) | | | | | |
| 2 | 3 | 9 | 14 | 2 | 2 | NUMBER OF STATEMENTS | 29 | 29 |
| % | % | % | % | % | % | **ASSETS** | % | % |
| | | | 3.3 | | | Cash & Equivalents | 5.9 | 7.1 |
| | | | 13.9 | | | Trade Receivables (net) | 11.4 | 11.6 |
| | | | 22.3 | | | Inventory | 21.1 | 23.2 |
| | | | .9 | | | All Other Current | 3.5 | 1.5 |
| | | | 40.3 | | | Total Current | 41.9 | 43.4 |
| | | | 50.9 | | | Fixed Assets (net) | 38.4 | 37.9 |
| | | | 4.3 | | | Intangibles (net) | 13.8 | 11.9 |
| | | | 4.6 | | | All Other Non-Current | 5.9 | 6.8 |
| | | | 100.0 | | | Total | 100.0 | 100.0 |
| | | | | | | **LIABILITIES** | | |
| | | | 14.6 | | | Notes Payable-Short Term | 18.5 | 14.9 |
| | | | 8.5 | | | Cur. Mat.-L.T.D. | 3.7 | 3.5 |
| | | | 12.4 | | | Trade Payables | 13.7 | 10.7 |
| | | | .1 | | | Income Taxes Payable | .0 | .1 |
| | | | 7.8 | | | All Other Current | 3.5 | 20.4 |
| | | | 43.3 | | | Total Current | 39.4 | 49.6 |
| | | | 25.3 | | | Long-Term Debt | 22.4 | 22.2 |
| | | | 1.0 | | | Deferred Taxes | 1.0 | .8 |
| | | | 4.9 | | | All Other Non-Current | 7.2 | 7.0 |
| | | | 25.5 | | | Net Worth | 30.0 | 20.4 |
| | | | 100.0 | | | Total Liabilties & Net Worth | 100.0 | 100.0 |
| | | | | | | **INCOME DATA** | | |
| | | | 100.0 | | | Net Sales | 100.0 | 100.0 |
| | | | 29.7 | | | Gross Profit | 36.7 | 38.6 |
| | | | 28.5 | | | Operating Expenses | 35.4 | 36.2 |
| | | | 1.2 | | | Operating Profit | 1.4 | 2.4 |
| | | | 1.5 | | | All Other Expenses (net) | 2.5 | 1.5 |
| | | | -.3 | | | Profit Before Taxes | -1.2 | .9 |
| | | | | | | **RATIOS** | | |
| | | | 1.6 | | | | 1.9 | 2.2 |
| | | | .9 | | | Current | 1.4 | 1.2 |
| | | | .7 | | | | .6 | .8 |
| | | | .5 | | | | .8 | 1.1 |
| | | | .4 | | | Quick | .4 | .5 |
| | | | .2 | | | | .2 | .3 |
| | | | (15) 24.6 | | | | (10) 36.7 | (14) 25.9 |
| | | | (25) 14.7 | | | Sales/Receivables | (20) 17.9 | (20) 18.7 |
| | | | (30) 12.0 | | | | (27) 13.5 | (30) 12.3 |
| | | | (46) 7.9 | | | | (30) 12.2 | (37) 9.8 |
| | | | (56) 6.5 | | | Cost of Sales/Inventory | (50) 7.3 | (65) 5.6 |
| | | | (85) 4.3 | | | | (77) 4.8 | (90) 4.1 |
| | | | (17) 22.0 | | | | (18) 20.5 | (17) 21.9 |
| | | | (34) 10.8 | | | Cost of Sales/Payables | (29) 12.7 | (25) 14.5 |
| | | | (38) 9.6 | | | | (43) 8.4 | (35) 10.5 |
| | | | 12.8 | | | | 11.0 | 8.4 |
| | | | -45.0 | | | Sales/Working Capital | 18.0 | 28.9 |
| | | | -13.9 | | | | -11.3 | -17.8 |
| | | | 2.1 | | | | 3.1 | 12.8 |
| | | | (13) 1.1 | | | EBIT/Interest | (28) .4 | (27) 1.5 |
| | | | .5 | | | | -1.4 | -.4 |
| | | | | | | Net Profit + Depr., Dep., | 2.7 | 7.6 |
| | | | | | | Amort./Cur. Mat. L/T/D | (11) .8 | (10) 1.8 |
| | | | | | | | -1.7 | -.5 |
| | | | 1.2 | | | | .7 | .6 |
| | | | 2.5 | | | Fixed/Worth | 2.1 | 1.5 |
| | | | -66.0 | | | | -1.4 | NM |
| | | | 1.4 | | | | 1.4 | .8 |
| | | | 4.3 | | | Debt/Worth | 2.3 | 1.6 |
| | | | -99.7 | | | | -6.9 | NM |
| | | | | | | % Profit Before Taxes/Tangible | 30.1 | 44.9 |
| | | | | | | Net Worth | (19) 9.6 | (22) 12.8 |
| | | | | | | | -15.5 | -4.9 |
| | | | 2.3 | | | % Profit Before Taxes/Total | 6.3 | 15.8 |
| | | | -.2 | | | Assets | -2.8 | 2.1 |
| | | | -1.9 | | | | -9.0 | -5.0 |
| | | | 6.0 | | | | 15.2 | 10.2 |
| | | | 3.5 | | | Sales/Net Fixed Assets | 9.4 | 6.5 |
| | | | 2.1 | | | | 3.0 | 3.5 |
| | | | 3.0 | | | | 3.0 | 3.0 |
| | | | 1.9 | | | Sales/Total Assets | 1.9 | 2.0 |
| | | | 1.2 | | | | 1.4 | 1.2 |
| | | | 2.8 | | | | 1.2 | 1.5 |
| | | | 3.9 | | | % Depr., Dep., Amort./Sales | (24) 2.0 | (24) 2.0 |
| | | | 6.3 | | | | 4.8 | 3.6 |
| | | | | | | % Officers', Directors' Owners' Comp/Sales | | |
| 1687M | 7961M | 161406M | 671094M | 226512M | 739837M | Net Sales ($) | 1131306M | 1168840M |
| 811M | 3980M | 54529M | 331803M | 144955M | 378761M | Total Assets ($) | 738061M | 663460M |

© RMA 2012

M = $ thousand    MM = $ million
See Pages 9 through 22 for Explanation of Ratios and Data

## Comparative Historical Data | Current Data Sorted by Sales

| | | | Type of Statement | 0-1MM | 1-3MM | 3-5MM | 5-10MM | 10-25MM | 25MM & OVER |
|---|---|---|---|---|---|---|---|---|---|
| 5 | 6 | 6 | Unqualified | | | | | 2 | 4 |
| 3 | 7 | 8 | Reviewed | | 1 | | 1 | 4 | 2 |
| 1 | 2 | 1 | Compiled | | 1 | | | 1 | |
| 3 | 5 | 2 | Tax Returns | | 1 | | | | 1 |
| 12 | 12 | 15 | Other | 1 | 1 | 1 | | 3 | 9 |
| 4/1/09-3/31/10 ALL | 4/1/10-3/31/11 ALL | 4/1/11-3/31/12 ALL | | | 7 (4/1-9/30/11) | | | 25 (10/1/11-3/31/12) | |
| 24 | 32 | 32 | NUMBER OF STATEMENTS | 1 | 3 | 1 | 1 | 10 | 16 |
| % | % | % | ASSETS | % | % | % | % | % | % |
| 9.4 | 7.0 | 3.9 | Cash & Equivalents | | | | | 5.5 | 3.5 |
| 12.1 | 13.3 | 12.8 | Trade Receivables (net) | | | | | 15.0 | 14.4 |
| 21.5 | 23.6 | 23.0 | Inventory | | | | | 21.1 | 24.2 |
| 2.6 | 1.4 | 1.2 | All Other Current | | | | | .3 | 1.0 |
| 45.7 | 45.3 | 40.9 | Total Current | | | | | 41.9 | 43.1 |
| 32.2 | 38.7 | 44.5 | Fixed Assets (net) | | | | | 48.1 | 38.6 |
| 15.6 | 12.2 | 8.6 | Intangibles (net) | | | | | 3.9 | 13.3 |
| 6.6 | 3.8 | 6.0 | All Other Non-Current | | | | | 6.1 | 5.0 |
| 100.0 | 100.0 | 100.0 | Total | | | | | 100.0 | 100.0 |
| | | | LIABILITIES | | | | | | |
| 8.4 | 13.3 | 12.8 | Notes Payable-Short Term | | | | | 8.5 | 14.5 |
| 2.9 | 4.9 | 7.1 | Cur. Mat.-L.T.D. | | | | | 5.5 | 8.6 |
| 12.0 | 12.1 | 11.9 | Trade Payables | | | | | 13.0 | 13.1 |
| .0 | .0 | .1 | Income Taxes Payable | | | | | .0 | .1 |
| 7.1 | 4.5 | 7.9 | All Other Current | | | | | 4.0 | 10.2 |
| 30.3 | 34.9 | 39.8 | Total Current | | | | | 31.0 | 46.5 |
| 28.4 | 37.0 | 26.0 | Long-Term Debt | | | | | 26.2 | 21.1 |
| .6 | 1.2 | 1.5 | Deferred Taxes | | | | | 1.4 | 2.1 |
| 7.4 | 5.2 | 9.1 | All Other Non-Current | | | | | 10.0 | 4.7 |
| 33.3 | 21.7 | 23.7 | Net Worth | | | | | 31.4 | 25.5 |
| 100.0 | 100.0 | 100.0 | Total Liabilities & Net Worth | | | | | 100.0 | 100.0 |
| | | | INCOME DATA | | | | | | |
| 100.0 | 100.0 | 100.0 | Net Sales | | | | | 100.0 | 100.0 |
| 42.4 | 39.5 | 36.0 | Gross Profit | | | | | 33.1 | 28.8 |
| 36.3 | 34.7 | 33.1 | Operating Expenses | | | | | 29.5 | 26.7 |
| 6.1 | 4.9 | 2.9 | Operating Profit | | | | | 3.6 | 2.1 |
| 3.0 | 1.9 | 1.3 | All Other Expenses (net) | | | | | .8 | 1.7 |
| 3.1 | 2.9 | 1.6 | Profit Before Taxes | | | | | 2.7 | .4 |
| | | | RATIOS | | | | | | |
| 2.7 | 2.1 | 1.5 | | | | | | 2.7 | 1.3 |
| 1.4 | 1.2 | 1.0 | Current | | | | | 1.4 | .9 |
| .8 | .8 | .7 | | | | | | .8 | .7 |
| 1.3 | .9 | .5 | | | | | | 1.2 | .4 |
| .6 | .5 | .4 | Quick | | | | | .6 | .4 |
| .4 | .3 | .2 | | | | | | .5 | .2 |
| 13 28.3 | 12 29.6 | 14 25.6 | | | | | | 11 33.2 | 17 22.1 |
| 19 19.4 | 19 19.6 | 19 19.5 | Sales/Receivables | | | | | 17 21.7 | 22 16.3 |
| 29 12.7 | 26 13.9 | 28 13.1 | | | | | | 39 9.4 | 29 12.5 |
| 36 10.2 | 29 12.5 | 38 9.5 | | | | | | 30 12.1 | 47 7.8 |
| 57 6.4 | 50 7.2 | 54 6.7 | Cost of Sales/Inventory | | | | | 38 9.5 | 55 6.6 |
| 90 4.0 | 87 4.2 | 81 4.5 | | | | | | 87 4.2 | 66 5.5 |
| 16 22.3 | 15 25.0 | 18 20.8 | | | | | | 14 25.9 | 23 16.1 |
| 24 15.2 | 24 15.2 | 30 12.0 | Cost of Sales/Payables | | | | | 24 15.3 | 33 11.2 |
| 37 9.8 | 36 10.0 | 38 9.6 | | | | | | 40 9.1 | 38 9.7 |
| 5.0 | 9.5 | 16.0 | | | | | | 10.7 | 20.7 |
| 17.8 | 27.9 | NM | Sales/Working Capital | | | | | 18.0 | -46.5 |
| -50.7 | -16.7 | -17.3 | | | | | | -76.1 | -16.0 |
| 8.9 | 7.4 | 4.8 | | | | | | 6.2 | 3.0 |
| (23) 3.2 | (31) 2.1 | (31) 2.1 | EBIT/Interest | | | | | 3.3 | (15) 1.1 |
| .7 | 1.0 | .7 | | | | | | 1.4 | .1 |
| | 11.0 | 7.8 | | | | | | | |
| (10) 4.5 | (13) 2.5 | | Net Profit + Depr., Dep., Amort./Cur. Mat. L/T/D | | | | | | |
| | 1.5 | 1.4 | | | | | | | |
| .5 | .9 | 1.2 | | | | | | 1.2 | 1.2 |
| 1.3 | 2.7 | 1.8 | Fixed/Worth | | | | | 1.7 | 3.3 |
| -5.4 | -4.3 | -90.9 | | | | | | 18.8 | -3.9 |
| .7 | 1.3 | 1.7 | | | | | | 1.4 | 1.8 |
| 1.6 | 4.7 | 3.2 | Debt/Worth | | | | | 2.7 | 5.1 |
| -15.8 | -16.0 | -135.3 | | | | | | 32.4 | -9.5 |
| 47.0 | 42.5 | 57.9 | | | | | | | |
| (17) 27.4 | (20) 22.7 | (22) 26.6 | % Profit Before Taxes/Tangible Net Worth | | | | | | |
| 2.6 | .6 | -5.6 | | | | | | | |
| 22.1 | 15.9 | 13.2 | | | | | | 10.9 | 6.4 |
| 4.5 | 3.6 | 2.6 | % Profit Before Taxes/Total Assets | | | | | 6.3 | -.2 |
| -1.3 | .2 | -1.7 | | | | | | .7 | -3.6 |
| 19.5 | 18.1 | 8.8 | | | | | | 10.1 | 14.2 |
| 11.1 | 8.9 | 5.0 | Sales/Net Fixed Assets | | | | | 5.1 | 5.0 |
| 4.9 | 2.6 | 2.9 | | | | | | 2.4 | 3.4 |
| 3.2 | 3.4 | 3.0 | | | | | | 2.8 | 3.2 |
| 2.0 | 2.3 | 2.2 | Sales/Total Assets | | | | | 2.3 | 2.0 |
| 1.1 | 1.3 | 1.5 | | | | | | 1.5 | 1.3 |
| 1.2 | 1.4 | 1.6 | | | | | | | 1.8 |
| (20) 2.0 | (29) 2.2 | (29) 3.4 | % Depr., Dep., Amort./Sales | | | | | | (14) 3.4 |
| 5.3 | 5.2 | 5.6 | | | | | | | 4.5 |
| | | | % Officers', Directors' Owners' Comp/Sales | | | | | | |
| 915194M | 945491M | 1808497M | Net Sales ($) | 606M | 5199M | 3843M | 7723M | 192896M | 1598230M |
| 495742M | 564117M | 914839M | Total Assets ($) | 424M | 3326M | 1041M | 2546M | 97785M | 809717M |

© RMA 2012

M = $ thousand    MM = $ million
See Pages 9 through 22 for Explanation of Ratios and Data

## Current Data Sorted by Assets      Comparative Historical Data

| 0-500M | 500M-2MM | 2-10MM | 10-50MM | 50-100MM | 100-250MM | Type of Statement | 4/1/07-3/31/08 ALL | 4/1/08-3/31/09 ALL |
|---|---|---|---|---|---|---|---|---|
| | | 3 | 1 | 5 | 3 | Unqualified | 23 | 24 |
| 1 | 3 | 9 | 7 | 1 | | Reviewed | 12 | 16 |
| 3 | 5 | 4 | 2 | | | Compiled | 11 | 9 |
| 3 | 3 | 2 | 1 | | | Tax Returns | 7 | 4 |
| 2 | 2 | 6 | 6 | 4 | | Other | 35 | 30 |
| | 11 (4/1-9/30/11) | | 65 (10/1/11-3/31/12) | | | | | |
| 9 | 13 | 24 | 17 | 10 | 3 | **NUMBER OF STATEMENTS** | 88 | 83 |
| % | % | % | % | % | % | **ASSETS** | % | % |
| | 9.0 | 4.8 | 4.4 | 12.1 | | Cash & Equivalents | 7.3 | 6.7 |
| | 39.1 | 25.7 | 25.3 | 26.3 | | Trade Receivables (net) | 22.9 | 26.2 |
| | 11.6 | 23.6 | 20.6 | 20.2 | | Inventory | 23.1 | 23.6 |
| | 1.2 | 1.3 | 1.4 | 2.4 | | All Other Current | 2.2 | 2.1 |
| | 60.9 | 55.4 | 51.7 | 61.0 | | Total Current | 55.5 | 58.5 |
| | 31.5 | 33.1 | 34.3 | 37.2 | | Fixed Assets (net) | 33.0 | 33.7 |
| | 1.8 | 2.0 | 8.0 | .5 | | Intangibles (net) | 4.2 | 3.5 |
| | 5.8 | 9.4 | 6.1 | 1.3 | | All Other Non-Current | 7.3 | 4.2 |
| | 100.0 | 100.0 | 100.0 | 100.0 | | Total | 100.0 | 100.0 |
| | | | | | | **LIABILITIES** | | |
| | 15.9 | 8.7 | 10.8 | 14.2 | | Notes Payable-Short Term | 12.7 | 10.3 |
| | 3.7 | 2.9 | 1.8 | 2.0 | | Cur. Mat.-L.T.D. | 3.0 | 4.0 |
| | 21.7 | 21.2 | 15.5 | 10.3 | | Trade Payables | 12.3 | 13.3 |
| | .0 | .4 | .3 | 1.6 | | Income Taxes Payable | .2 | .2 |
| | 2.6 | 12.7 | 7.9 | 8.9 | | All Other Current | 7.2 | 8.4 |
| | 44.0 | 45.8 | 36.2 | 37.0 | | Total Current | 35.3 | 36.4 |
| | 25.4 | 20.4 | 16.3 | 13.6 | | Long-Term Debt | 20.3 | 19.2 |
| | .1 | 1.1 | .8 | .0 | | Deferred Taxes | .4 | .3 |
| | 2.6 | 4.6 | 2.1 | 3.0 | | All Other Non-Current | 7.7 | 8.4 |
| | 28.0 | 28.1 | 44.6 | 46.4 | | Net Worth | 36.3 | 35.7 |
| | 100.0 | 100.0 | 100.0 | 100.0 | | Total Liabilities & Net Worth | 100.0 | 100.0 |
| | | | | | | **INCOME DATA** | | |
| | 100.0 | 100.0 | 100.0 | 100.0 | | Net Sales | 100.0 | 100.0 |
| | 21.7 | 16.5 | 11.2 | 12.5 | | Gross Profit | 19.1 | 16.1 |
| | 22.3 | 16.3 | 9.8 | 8.9 | | Operating Expenses | 16.6 | 14.0 |
| | -.6 | .2 | 1.5 | 3.7 | | Operating Profit | 2.5 | 2.2 |
| | -.9 | .2 | .2 | .3 | | All Other Expenses (net) | .8 | .5 |
| | .4 | .0 | 1.3 | 3.4 | | Profit Before Taxes | 1.7 | 1.7 |
| | | | | | | **RATIOS** | | |
| | 2.7 | 1.9 | 1.7 | 3.9 | | | 2.4 | 2.3 |
| | 1.1 | 1.3 | 1.4 | 1.5 | | Current | 1.6 | 1.7 |
| | 1.0 | 1.0 | 1.2 | 1.1 | | | 1.1 | 1.1 |
| | 1.4 | 1.1 | 1.2 | 3.2 | | | 1.5 | 1.5 |
| | .9 | .7 | .9 | 1.0 | | Quick | .8 | .9 |
| | .5 | .5 | .5 | .7 | | | .5 | .6 |
| 9 39.0 | 13 27.4 | 16 23.3 | 16 22.7 | | | Sales/Receivables | 15 24.5 | 15 24.2 |
| 26 14.1 | 20 18.5 | 23 16.0 | 20 18.7 | | | | 19 18.9 | 20 18.2 |
| 33 11.2 | 29 12.4 | 25 14.4 | 28 12.9 | | | | 26 14.2 | 25 14.3 |
| 0 UND | 9 38.5 | 8 45.4 | 8 43.1 | | | Cost of Sales/Inventory | 13 27.9 | 12 29.6 |
| 10 36.8 | 23 15.7 | 18 20.7 | 12 31.3 | | | | 25 14.7 | 22 16.8 |
| 26 13.8 | 39 9.3 | 31 11.7 | 29 12.8 | | | | 40 9.1 | 40 9.1 |
| 3 109.8 | 5 76.6 | 5 70.1 | 5 79.9 | | | Cost of Sales/Payables | 6 65.6 | 6 62.5 |
| 15 25.1 | 12 29.8 | 13 28.2 | 7 51.1 | | | | 11 33.1 | 10 35.6 |
| 29 12.6 | 35 10.5 | 33 11.2 | 14 25.3 | | | | 19 19.7 | 17 21.7 |
| | 15.2 | 21.9 | 24.4 | 7.5 | | Sales/Working Capital | 11.0 | 11.6 |
| | 85.0 | 39.1 | 33.7 | 24.1 | | | 23.1 | 24.2 |
| | NM | NM | 46.3 | 60.3 | | | 66.5 | 93.9 |
| | 7.2 | 8.3 | 10.9 | 91.6 | | | 6.2 | 12.1 |
| | (12) 2.1 | (22) 2.7 | 4.5 | 12.3 | | EBIT/Interest | (79) 2.7 | (77) 4.4 |
| | 1.0 | 1.6 | 2.0 | 1.3 | | | 1.0 | 1.0 |
| | | 11.2 | | | | Net Profit + Depr., Dep., | 4.0 | 8.5 |
| | (10) 5.5 | | | | | Amort./Cur. Mat. L/T/D | (15) 2.9 | (18) 2.0 |
| | 2.8 | | | | | | 1.6 | .6 |
| | .0 | .4 | .4 | .5 | | | .3 | .4 |
| | .6 | .8 | .9 | 1.1 | | Fixed/Worth | 1.0 | .9 |
| | 3.5 | 4.1 | 2.8 | 1.6 | | | 6.4 | 2.1 |
| | 1.1 | 1.0 | .7 | .3 | | | .8 | .6 |
| | 3.7 | 2.5 | 2.1 | 1.4 | | Debt/Worth | 1.8 | 1.4 |
| | 25.2 | 6.6 | 3.7 | 3.5 | | | 11.6 | 4.5 |
| | 95.9 | 36.6 | 19.6 | 39.2 | | % Profit Before Taxes/Tangible | 45.1 | 44.3 |
| | (12) 13.1 | (22) 12.8 | (15) 11.3 | 21.3 | | Net Worth | (74) 18.8 | (73) 15.4 |
| | .2 | 4.4 | 1.6 | 6.2 | | | 4.4 | 3.4 |
| | 9.8 | 9.4 | 9.5 | 22.3 | | % Profit Before Taxes/Total | 11.5 | 16.4 |
| | 1.4 | 3.6 | 4.2 | 11.2 | | Assets | 5.8 | 5.9 |
| | -1.3 | .3 | .7 | .8 | | | .5 | .5 |
| | 775.2 | 40.7 | 36.1 | 19.5 | | Sales/Net Fixed Assets | 43.4 | 35.5 |
| | 11.0 | 17.9 | 13.7 | 13.1 | | | 12.8 | 12.1 |
| | 5.2 | 11.4 | 6.6 | 10.1 | | | 5.8 | 6.3 |
| | 8.1 | 6.5 | 5.8 | 7.8 | | Sales/Total Assets | 5.7 | 5.8 |
| | 4.1 | 4.7 | 4.7 | 4.2 | | | 3.7 | 3.8 |
| | 2.7 | 3.0 | 2.7 | 2.6 | | | 2.3 | 2.6 |
| | .3 | .4 | .6 | | | % Depr., Dep., Amort./Sales | .4 | .5 |
| | (10) 1.2 | (21) .9 | (16) 1.3 | | | | (76) 1.2 | (77) 1.1 |
| | 4.2 | 1.8 | 2.0 | | | | 2.2 | 1.9 |
| | | 1.3 | | | | % Officers', Directors' | 1.0 | .9 |
| | (11) 2.4 | | | | | Owners' Comp/Sales | (26) 1.9 | (26) 1.7 |
| | 3.0 | | | | | | 3.6 | 4.2 |
| 7657M | 88932M | 626357M | 1852391M | 3500102M | 1063180M | Net Sales ($) | 8975077M | 8487439M |
| 1227M | 17144M | 128601M | 434013M | 755226M | 443530M | Total Assets ($) | 2708863M | 2324899M |

M = $ thousand    MM = $ million
See Pages 9 through 22 for Explanation of Ratios and Data

## Comparative Historical Data

## Current Data Sorted by Sales

| | | | | | | Type of Statement | | | | | | | |
|---|---|---|---|---|---|---|---|---|---|---|---|---|---|
| | 19 | | 16 | | 12 | Unqualified | | | | | | 2 | 10 |
| | 18 | | 12 | | 21 | Reviewed | 1 | | 1 | 2 | | 2 | 15 |
| | 15 | | 10 | | 14 | Compiled | 2 | 2 | 3 | 2 | | 2 | 3 |
| | 5 | | 15 | | 9 | Tax Returns | 2 | 1 | 2 | 1 | | 2 | 1 |
| | 29 | | 22 | | 20 | Other | 2 | 1 | | 1 | | 4 | 12 |
| | 4/1/09-3/31/10 | | 4/1/10-3/31/11 | | 4/1/11-3/31/12 | | | 11 (4/1-9/30/11) | | | 65 (10/1/11-3/31/12) | | |
| | ALL | | ALL | | ALL | | 0-1MM | 1-3MM | 3-5MM | 5-10MM | | 10-25MM | 25MM & OVER |
| | 86 | | 75 | | 76 | NUMBER OF STATEMENTS | 7 | 4 | 6 | 6 | | 12 | 41 |
| | % | | % | | % | ASSETS | % | % | % | % | | % | % |
| | 10.1 | | 9.9 | | 5.5 | Cash & Equivalents | | | | | | 4.3 | 5.6 |
| | 23.4 | | 24.8 | | 26.4 | Trade Receivables (net) | | | | | | 33.6 | 26.9 |
| | 19.1 | | 20.4 | | 21.2 | Inventory | | | | | | 24.1 | 20.8 |
| | 2.7 | | 1.7 | | 1.4 | All Other Current | | | | | | 1.6 | 1.6 |
| | 55.3 | | 56.8 | | 54.5 | Total Current | | | | | | 63.6 | 54.8 |
| | 36.8 | | 34.6 | | 35.6 | Fixed Assets (net) | | | | | | 27.6 | 35.8 |
| | 3.3 | | 2.6 | | 4.0 | Intangibles (net) | | | | | | 3.4 | 5.2 |
| | 4.5 | | 6.1 | | 5.8 | All Other Non-Current | | | | | | 5.3 | 4.1 |
| | 100.0 | | 100.0 | | 100.0 | Total | | | | | | 100.0 | 100.0 |
| | | | | | | LIABILITIES | | | | | | | |
| | 10.7 | | 8.2 | | 10.8 | Notes Payable-Short Term | | | | | | 12.4 | 11.3 |
| | 3.0 | | 3.1 | | 2.5 | Cur. Mat.-L.T.D. | | | | | | 1.4 | 2.2 |
| | 10.4 | | 15.5 | | 17.1 | Trade Payables | | | | | | 26.6 | 16.6 |
| | .1 | | .3 | | .4 | Income Taxes Payable | | | | | | .1 | .7 |
| | 7.8 | | 7.7 | | 8.3 | All Other Current | | | | | | 5.0 | 9.9 |
| | 32.0 | | 34.8 | | 39.1 | Total Current | | | | | | 45.6 | 40.7 |
| | 19.5 | | 20.4 | | 21.6 | Long-Term Debt | | | | | | 14.6 | 15.2 |
| | .3 | | .4 | | .7 | Deferred Taxes | | | | | | .8 | .8 |
| | 6.3 | | 5.8 | | 7.9 | All Other Non-Current | | | | | | 3.3 | 3.9 |
| | 41.9 | | 38.5 | | 30.6 | Net Worth | | | | | | 35.7 | 39.4 |
| | 100.0 | | 100.0 | | 100.0 | Total Liabilties & Net Worth | | | | | | 100.0 | 100.0 |
| | | | | | | INCOME DATA | | | | | | | |
| | 100.0 | | 100.0 | | 100.0 | Net Sales | | | | | | 100.0 | 100.0 |
| | 22.5 | | 18.4 | | 18.7 | Gross Profit | | | | | | 17.1 | 11.8 |
| | 20.3 | | 15.9 | | 17.6 | Operating Expenses | | | | | | 15.7 | 9.7 |
| | 2.2 | | 2.4 | | 1.1 | Operating Profit | | | | | | 1.4 | 2.1 |
| | .1 | | .4 | | .1 | All Other Expenses (net) | | | | | | .3 | .2 |
| | 2.1 | | 2.0 | | 1.1 | Profit Before Taxes | | | | | | 1.1 | 1.9 |
| | | | | | | RATIOS | | | | | | | |
| | 3.3 | | 3.0 | | 2.1 | | | | | | | 1.8 | 2.1 |
| | 1.7 | | 1.7 | | 1.4 | Current | | | | | | 1.4 | 1.4 |
| | 1.1 | | 1.2 | | 1.1 | | | | | | | 1.0 | 1.1 |
| | 2.0 | | 1.7 | | 1.3 | | | | | | | 1.2 | 1.3 |
| | 1.0 | | 1.0 | (74) | .8 | Quick | | | | | | .7 | .8 |
| | .5 | | .6 | | .5 | | | | | | | .4 | .5 |
| 14 | 25.8 | 15 | 24.5 | 13 | 27.4 | | | | | | 9 | 39.4 | 16 | 22.7 |
| 21 | 17.8 | 19 | 18.9 | 20 | 18.2 | Sales/Receivables | | | | | 19 | 19.3 | 21 | 17.2 |
| 29 | 12.7 | 29 | 12.6 | 27 | 13.5 | | | | | | 32 | 11.4 | 26 | 14.1 |
| 10 | 36.6 | 11 | 32.2 | 9 | 42.1 | | | | | | 7 | 55.0 | 9 | 41.5 |
| 19 | 19.1 | 20 | 18.4 | 19 | 19.2 | Cost of Sales/Inventory | | | | | 20 | 18.0 | 15 | 24.1 |
| 38 | 9.5 | 36 | 10.2 | 36 | 10.0 | | | | | | 37 | 9.9 | 31 | 11.8 |
| 5 | 76.5 | 6 | 62.4 | 5 | 76.1 | | | | | | 8 | 47.2 | 5 | 75.2 |
| 10 | 37.7 | 12 | 29.8 | 12 | 29.8 | Cost of Sales/Payables | | | | | 15 | 24.8 | 10 | 37.4 |
| 20 | 18.1 | 23 | 15.7 | 28 | 13.2 | | | | | | 35 | 10.4 | 22 | 16.7 |
| | 9.1 | | 10.4 | | 15.8 | | | | | | | 16.2 | 19.4 |
| | 23.6 | | 20.4 | | 32.9 | Sales/Working Capital | | | | | | 33.2 | 29.4 |
| | 113.6 | | 54.6 | | 235.6 | | | | | | | NM | 49.5 |
| | 13.0 | | 13.3 | | 10.5 | | | | | | | 9.7 | 17.7 |
| (79) | 3.4 | (72) | 3.7 | (70) | 3.1 | EBIT/Interest | | | | | | 3.9 | 4.5 |
| | .0 | | 1.0 | | 1.5 | | | | | | | 2.2 | 1.6 |
| | 4.9 | | 6.7 | | 11.2 | Net Profit + Depr., Dep., | | | | | | | 7.0 |
| (17) | 2.4 | (22) | 3.9 | (21) | 6.0 | Amort./Cur. Mat. L/T/D | | | | | (15) | 5.0 |
| | 1.7 | | 1.1 | | 2.2 | | | | | | | | 3.0 |
| | .4 | | .4 | | .4 | | | | | | | .2 | .6 |
| | .9 | | .9 | | 1.0 | Fixed/Worth | | | | | | .5 | 1.0 |
| | 2.9 | | 2.1 | | 3.3 | | | | | | | 1.2 | 2.1 |
| | .5 | | .6 | | .8 | | | | | | | .9 | .6 |
| | 1.7 | | 1.5 | | 2.5 | Debt/Worth | | | | | | 2.4 | 2.1 |
| | 4.9 | | 4.2 | | 7.3 | | | | | | | 6.5 | 3.5 |
| | 32.6 | | 38.5 | | 32.9 | % Profit Before Taxes/Tangible | | | | | | 36.5 | 29.3 |
| (76) | 14.3 | (70) | 13.4 | (67) | 15.4 | Net Worth | | | | | (11) | 9.1 | (38) | 16.8 |
| | 1.7 | | .5 | | 1.7 | | | | | | | 6.4 | 2.7 |
| | 13.7 | | 13.4 | | 10.5 | % Profit Before Taxes/Total | | | | | | 10.9 | 13.8 |
| | 5.4 | | 4.7 | | 3.6 | Assets | | | | | | 3.6 | 4.9 |
| | -1.1 | | .1 | | .2 | | | | | | | .8 | .7 |
| | 28.2 | | 32.8 | | 37.4 | | | | | | | 96.1 | 21.3 |
| | 10.4 | | 12.0 | | 14.0 | Sales/Net Fixed Assets | | | | | | 40.7 | 13.7 |
| | 4.4 | | 5.3 | | 7.1 | | | | | | | 11.4 | 7.1 |
| | 5.7 | | 5.6 | | 6.4 | | | | | | | 8.0 | 6.3 |
| | 3.4 | | 3.9 | | 4.4 | Sales/Total Assets | | | | | | 6.0 | 4.5 |
| | 2.0 | | 2.4 | | 2.8 | | | | | | | 3.2 | 2.8 |
| | .5 | | .5 | | .5 | | | | | | | .3 | .7 |
| (78) | 1.5 | (71) | 1.1 | (66) | 1.3 | % Depr., Dep., Amort./Sales | | | | | (10) | .7 | (37) | 1.1 |
| | 2.6 | | 2.2 | | 2.2 | | | | | | | 1.9 | 2.0 |
| | 1.0 | | .8 | | .5 | % Officers', Directors' | | | | | | | .3 |
| (29) | 1.9 | (33) | 2.0 | (29) | 1.2 | Owners' Comp/Sales | | | | | | (15) | .8 |
| | 4.8 | | 4.0 | | 2.7 | | | | | | | | 1.4 |
| | 6551663M | | 7072444M | | 7138619M | Net Sales ($) | 3122M | 6654M | 24677M | 42762M | | 189989M | 6871415M |
| | 1720329M | | 1933298M | | 1779741M | Total Assets ($) | 739M | 3001M | 8751M | 12406M | | 42304M | 1712540M |

M = $ thousand   MM = $ million
See Pages 9 through 22 for Explanation of Ratios and Data

## Current Data Sorted by Assets      Comparative Historical Data

| | 0-500M | 500M-2MM | 2-10MM | 10-50MM | 50-100MM | 100-250MM | Type of Statement | 4/1/07-3/31/08 ALL | 4/1/08-3/31/09 ALL |
|---|---|---|---|---|---|---|---|---|---|
| | | | 5 | 11 | 8 | 3 | Unqualified | 36 | 30 |
| | | 1 | 18 | 14 | 1 | | Reviewed | 25 | 30 |
| | 1 | 2 | 11 | 3 | | | Compiled | 17 | 27 |
| | 2 | 8 | 9 | | | | Tax Returns | 10 | 9 |
| | 4 | 4 | 20 | 22 | 13 | 5 | Other | 65 | 57 |
| | | 23 (4/1-9/30/11) | | 142 (10/1/11-3/31/12) | | | | | |
| NUMBER OF STATEMENTS | 7 | 15 | 63 | 50 | 22 | 8 | | 153 | 153 |
| | % | % | % | % | % | % | ASSETS | % | % |
| | | 18.2 | 9.1 | 5.7 | 3.6 | | Cash & Equivalents | 8.1 | 8.5 |
| | | 32.5 | 27.1 | 25.6 | 23.4 | | Trade Receivables (net) | 24.2 | 22.4 |
| | | 21.8 | 21.5 | 21.6 | 30.7 | | Inventory | 22.2 | 24.4 |
| | | 1.7 | 1.8 | 4.1 | .8 | | All Other Current | 3.3 | 2.6 |
| | | 74.1 | 59.5 | 56.9 | 58.5 | | Total Current | 57.8 | 57.9 |
| | | 19.3 | 30.0 | 34.4 | 29.1 | | Fixed Assets (net) | 33.9 | 33.3 |
| | | 3.4 | 5.0 | 3.1 | 10.2 | | Intangibles (net) | 3.4 | 3.6 |
| | | 3.2 | 5.5 | 5.5 | 2.2 | | All Other Non-Current | 5.0 | 5.2 |
| | | 100.0 | 100.0 | 100.0 | 100.0 | | Total | 100.0 | 100.0 |
| | | | | | | | LIABILITIES | | |
| | | 25.2 | 7.5 | 11.1 | 16.6 | | Notes Payable-Short Term | 10.9 | 10.7 |
| | | .9 | 1.9 | 2.5 | 2.6 | | Cur. Mat.-L.T.D. | 3.1 | 3.9 |
| | | 18.1 | 16.5 | 14.7 | 11.6 | | Trade Payables | 13.8 | 12.3 |
| | | .0 | .1 | .0 | .0 | | Income Taxes Payable | .1 | .1 |
| | | 7.7 | 9.4 | 8.3 | 6.6 | | All Other Current | 8.3 | 7.4 |
| | | 51.9 | 35.4 | 36.6 | 37.5 | | Total Current | 36.3 | 34.3 |
| | | 16.0 | 13.6 | 17.5 | 16.2 | | Long-Term Debt | 17.8 | 18.3 |
| | | .0 | .5 | .5 | .8 | | Deferred Taxes | .4 | .3 |
| | | 2.9 | 5.2 | 8.0 | 6.2 | | All Other Non-Current | 6.9 | 6.2 |
| | | 29.3 | 45.3 | 37.4 | 39.3 | | Net Worth | 38.6 | 40.8 |
| | | 100.0 | 100.0 | 100.0 | 100.0 | | Total Liabilities & Net Worth | 100.0 | 100.0 |
| | | | | | | | INCOME DATA | | |
| | | 100.0 | 100.0 | 100.0 | 100.0 | | Net Sales | 100.0 | 100.0 |
| | | 20.0 | 22.6 | 17.4 | 15.7 | | Gross Profit | 19.4 | 21.4 |
| | | 17.3 | 20.1 | 14.9 | 11.8 | | Operating Expenses | 16.6 | 18.1 |
| | | 2.7 | 2.5 | 2.5 | 3.9 | | Operating Profit | 2.7 | 3.3 |
| | | .6 | .3 | .1 | 1.2 | | All Other Expenses (net) | .7 | .7 |
| | | 2.2 | 2.2 | 2.4 | 2.7 | | Profit Before Taxes | 2.1 | 2.6 |
| | | | | | | | RATIOS | | |
| | | 2.9 | 3.3 | 2.9 | 2.5 | | | 2.9 | 2.9 |
| | | 1.7 | 2.0 | 1.8 | 1.4 | | Current | 1.6 | 1.8 |
| | | .8 | 1.1 | 1.0 | 1.2 | | | 1.1 | 1.2 |
| | | 2.4 | 2.0 | 1.7 | 1.2 | | | 1.6 | 1.6 |
| | | 1.3 | 1.0 | .8 | .8 | | Quick | .9 | 1.0 |
| | | .5 | .6 | .5 | .5 | | | .6 | .6 |
| | 13   27.2 | 16   22.5 | 17   21.2 | 17   21.8 | | | | 15   24.6 | 14   25.3 |
| | 19   18.8 | 21   17.4 | 22   16.7 | 28   13.1 | | Sales/Receivables | | 19   19.0 | 20   18.5 |
| | 25   14.4 | 29   12.5 | 27   13.3 | 35   10.5 | | | | 27   13.4 | 26   14.0 |
| | 4   87.8 | 15   24.6 | 14   26.4 | 26   14.2 | | | | 12   29.4 | 15   23.9 |
| | 13   27.4 | 24   15.0 | 23   16.0 | 44   8.3 | | Cost of Sales/Inventory | | 20   17.9 | 29   12.8 |
| | 23   16.1 | 43   8.5 | 40   9.1 | 65   5.6 | | | | 41   8.9 | 51   7.2 |
| | 2   156.0 | 9   38.5 | 8   48.2 | 9   39.1 | | | | 8   47.3 | 7   52.8 |
| | 12   30.3 | 14   25.7 | 13   27.2 | 14   26.9 | | Cost of Sales/Payables | | 13   28.3 | 12   31.5 |
| | 17   21.0 | 25   14.7 | 26   14.3 | 22   16.8 | | | | 21   17.7 | 21   17.8 |
| | | 13.2 | 8.2 | 7.9 | 8.9 | | | 10.4 | 7.9 |
| | | 19.9 | 16.1 | 21.1 | 20.2 | | Sales/Working Capital | 20.6 | 16.7 |
| | | -61.6 | 72.8 | 206.9 | 42.2 | | | 63.6 | 52.0 |
| | | 20.7 | 15.6 | 18.1 | 9.1 | | | 7.6 | 9.8 |
| | | (13) 3.4 | (58) 3.3 | (49) 6.6 | (21) 4.6 | | EBIT/Interest | (139) 3.5 | (146) 3.4 |
| | | .7 | .8 | 2.0 | 1.9 | | | 1.3 | .8 |
| | | | 10.4 | 7.6 | 12.3 | | | 6.6 | 6.6 |
| | | | (13) 1.9 | (14) 3.1 | (10) 3.0 | | Net Profit + Depr., Dep., Amort./Cur. Mat. L/T/D | (37) 3.5 | (38) 2.4 |
| | | | .0 | 1.3 | 2.0 | | | 1.7 | 1.0 |
| | | .0 | .2 | .6 | .5 | | | .4 | .5 |
| | | .4 | .6 | .9 | 1.0 | | Fixed/Worth | .9 | .8 |
| | | 1.9 | 1.3 | 1.6 | -3.6 | | | 2.2 | 2.0 |
| | | .8 | .3 | .9 | .7 | | | .8 | .8 |
| | | 2.0 | 1.1 | 1.5 | 2.2 | | Debt/Worth | 1.7 | 1.7 |
| | | -136.8 | 4.2 | 4.3 | -13.2 | | | 4.8 | 4.2 |
| | | 70.1 | 33.6 | 37.8 | 32.8 | | | 35.0 | 37.7 |
| | | (11) 22.9 | (57) 10.5 | (44) 19.2 | (16) 23.1 | | % Profit Before Taxes/Tangible Net Worth | (142) 14.4 | (140) 14.3 |
| | | .8 | -1.6 | 9.8 | 14.8 | | | 5.5 | 1.2 |
| | | 20.5 | 13.3 | 14.4 | 12.2 | | | 11.5 | 13.2 |
| | | 7.1 | 6.8 | 6.8 | 7.8 | | % Profit Before Taxes/Total Assets | 5.3 | 5.3 |
| | | -4.0 | -.6 | 1.4 | 3.5 | | | 1.6 | -.2 |
| | | 999.8 | 31.7 | 21.6 | 22.5 | | | 31.9 | 23.3 |
| | | 23.1 | 13.5 | 11.7 | 10.6 | | Sales/Net Fixed Assets | 11.5 | 10.6 |
| | | 13.3 | 5.8 | 5.1 | 5.1 | | | 4.9 | 5.6 |
| | | 9.9 | 5.4 | 5.5 | 4.8 | | | 5.7 | 5.2 |
| | | 5.9 | 3.4 | 3.5 | 3.2 | | Sales/Total Assets | 3.4 | 3.3 |
| | | 3.5 | 2.4 | 2.2 | 1.9 | | | 2.2 | 2.2 |
| | | .0 | .7 | .6 | 1.0 | | | .6 | .8 |
| | | (11) .6 | (57) 1.2 | (49) 1.2 | (21) 1.5 | | % Depr., Dep., Amort./Sales | (139) 1.3 | (137) 1.5 |
| | | 1.2 | 2.1 | 1.7 | 2.6 | | | 2.5 | 2.2 |
| | | 1.4 | .8 | .5 | | | | .6 | 1.0 |
| | | (12) 1.8 | (24) 1.5 | (15) 1.0 | | | % Officers', Directors' Owners' Comp/Sales | (53) 1.8 | (44) 2.1 |
| | | 7.0 | 3.9 | 3.0 | | | | 4.2 | 4.8 |
| Net Sales ($) | 11774M | 149833M | 1545107M | 4874102M | 5269222M | 4110834M | | 16838085M | 14382364M |
| Total Assets ($) | 2213M | 17076M | 341236M | 1204636M | 1493379M | 1248973M | | 4771745M | 4237719M |

© RMA 2012

M = $ thousand    MM = $ million
See Pages 9 through 22 for Explanation of Ratios and Data

## Comparative Historical Data | | Current Data Sorted by Sales

| | | | Type of Statement | 0-1MM | 1-3MM | 3-5MM | 5-10MM | 10-25MM | 25MM & OVER |
|---|---|---|---|---|---|---|---|---|---|
| 33 | 29 | 27 | Unqualified | | | | 2 | 3 | 22 |
| 29 | 43 | 34 | Reviewed | | | | 6 | 8 | 20 |
| 25 | 19 | 17 | Compiled | | 1 | 1 | 2 | 4 | 9 |
| 10 | 19 | 19 | Tax Returns | 1 | 4 | 3 | 3 | 7 | 1 |
| 53 | 57 | 68 | Other | | 4 | 2 | 4 | 15 | 44 |
| 4/1/09-3/31/10 ALL | 4/1/10-3/31/11 ALL | 4/1/11-3/31/12 ALL | | 23 (4/1-9/30/11) | | | 142 (10/1/11-3/31/12) | | |
| 150 | 167 | 165 | NUMBER OF STATEMENTS | 1 | 9 | 6 | 16 | 37 | 96 |
| % | % | % | **ASSETS** | % | % | % | % | % | % |
| 9.7 | 8.8 | 7.6 | Cash & Equivalents | | | | 15.4 | 11.8 | 4.2 |
| 20.5 | 23.3 | 25.8 | Trade Receivables (net) | | | | 21.4 | 22.7 | 28.2 |
| 23.7 | 22.7 | 23.0 | Inventory | | | | 18.9 | 18.6 | 26.4 |
| 2.7 | 2.3 | 2.4 | All Other Current | | | | 6.2 | 2.5 | 1.7 |
| 56.6 | 57.2 | 58.8 | Total Current | | | | 62.0 | 55.6 | 60.5 |
| 33.7 | 33.7 | 30.8 | Fixed Assets (net) | | | | 25.6 | 31.9 | 29.9 |
| 4.0 | 4.0 | 5.4 | Intangibles (net) | | | | 6.9 | 5.7 | 5.5 |
| 5.7 | 5.2 | 4.9 | All Other Non-Current | | | | 5.5 | 6.8 | 4.1 |
| 100.0 | 100.0 | 100.0 | Total | | | | 100.0 | 100.0 | 100.0 |
| | | | **LIABILITIES** | | | | | | |
| 10.2 | 9.3 | 11.7 | Notes Payable-Short Term | | | | 10.1 | 6.9 | 13.5 |
| 3.4 | 3.1 | 2.2 | Cur. Mat.-L.T.D. | | | | 1.7 | 2.1 | 2.2 |
| 13.2 | 13.2 | 16.0 | Trade Payables | | | | 14.1 | 15.1 | 15.9 |
| .1 | .1 | .1 | Income Taxes Payable | | | | .0 | .1 | .1 |
| 8.3 | 9.0 | 8.2 | All Other Current | | | | 11.3 | 6.9 | 8.8 |
| 35.2 | 34.8 | 38.2 | Total Current | | | | 37.2 | 31.1 | 40.5 |
| 18.1 | 20.2 | 16.8 | Long-Term Debt | | | | 8.3 | 14.5 | 16.2 |
| .6 | .5 | .5 | Deferred Taxes | | | | .2 | .7 | .6 |
| 6.3 | 7.4 | 7.2 | All Other Non-Current | | | | 8.3 | 7.3 | 5.5 |
| 39.8 | 37.1 | 37.3 | Net Worth | | | | 45.9 | 46.4 | 37.2 |
| 100.0 | 100.0 | 100.0 | Total Liabilities & Net Worth | | | | 100.0 | 100.0 | 100.0 |
| | | | **INCOME DATA** | | | | | | |
| 100.0 | 100.0 | 100.0 | Net Sales | | | | 100.0 | 100.0 | 100.0 |
| 22.6 | 20.4 | 19.6 | Gross Profit | | | | 26.9 | 23.7 | 14.9 |
| 18.8 | 17.6 | 17.0 | Operating Expenses | | | | 23.4 | 21.0 | 12.4 |
| 3.9 | 2.8 | 2.6 | Operating Profit | | | | 3.5 | 2.8 | 2.5 |
| .7 | .7 | .4 | All Other Expenses (net) | | | | .2 | .0 | .5 |
| 3.2 | 2.1 | 2.1 | Profit Before Taxes | | | | 3.2 | 2.7 | 2.0 |
| | | | **RATIOS** | | | | | | |
| 2.8 | 2.9 | 2.8 | | | | | 3.5 | 3.7 | 2.6 |
| 1.6 | 1.8 | 1.7 | Current | | | | 2.5 | 2.0 | 1.6 |
| 1.2 | 1.2 | 1.0 | | | | | 1.3 | 1.1 | 1.1 |
| 1.6 | 1.7 | 1.7 | | | | | 2.8 | 2.0 | 1.3 |
| .9 | .9 | .9 | Quick | | | | 1.4 | 1.0 | .8 |
| .5 | .6 | .5 | | | | | .6 | .6 | .5 |
| 15  23.9 | 16  23.5 | 16  22.6 | | | | | 14  26.5 | 17  21.3 | 17  21.8 |
| 20  18.1 | 21  17.4 | 21  17.2 | Sales/Receivables | | | | 18  20.3 | 21  17.6 | 22  16.6 |
| 26  14.1 | 26  13.8 | 28  13.1 | | | | | 26  14.1 | 30  12.2 | 28  13.1 |
| 16  22.7 | 17  20.9 | 15  25.1 | | | | | 15  24.5 | 16  23.4 | 15  24.7 |
| 29  12.5 | 25  14.8 | 25  14.5 | Cost of Sales/Inventory | | | | 27  13.7 | 24  15.1 | 26  14.3 |
| 50  7.3 | 43  8.4 | 41  8.8 | | | | | 58  6.3 | 35  10.5 | 42  8.6 |
| 8  44.2 | 8  45.9 | 9  39.5 | | | | | 5  81.1 | 10  36.1 | 8  45.2 |
| 14  26.2 | 13  27.9 | 14  26.2 | Cost of Sales/Payables | | | | 13  29.1 | 14  26.8 | 14  26.5 |
| 27  13.6 | 21  17.3 | 24  15.0 | | | | | 21  17.1 | 26  13.8 | 21  17.1 |
| 8.1 | 8.8 | 10.1 | | | | | 4.0 | 7.2 | 12.1 |
| 18.6 | 17.6 | 20.7 | Sales/Working Capital | | | | 9.6 | 14.4 | 23.5 |
| 58.0 | 49.9 | 180.6 | | | | | 36.4 | 172.8 | 114.8 |
| 13.7 | 10.7 | 14.0 | | | | | 11.3 | 19.4 | 13.1 |
| (139)  5.3 | (158)  4.0 | (156)  4.0 | EBIT/Interest | | | | (14)  4.2 | (34)  3.4 | (92)  5.4 |
| 1.9 | 1.2 | 1.5 | | | | | -3.9 | 1.0 | 1.7 |
| 6.0 | 9.8 | 10.2 | Net Profit + Depr., Dep., | | | | | | 10.0 |
| (41)  2.9 | (43)  3.6 | (40)  2.6 | Amort./Cur. Mat. L/T/D | | | | | (29)  2.6 | |
| 1.8 | 1.8 | 1.4 | | | | | | | 1.4 |
| .4 | .4 | .4 | | | | | .2 | .2 | .5 |
| .9 | .9 | .9 | Fixed/Worth | | | | .5 | .9 | .9 |
| 2.1 | 1.9 | 1.8 | | | | | 1.1 | 1.4 | 1.7 |
| .6 | .7 | .8 | | | | | .2 | .6 | .8 |
| 1.7 | 1.6 | 1.6 | Debt/Worth | | | | .9 | 1.3 | 1.8 |
| 4.7 | 3.8 | 5.8 | | | | | NM | 3.7 | 5.0 |
| 42.2 | 39.5 | 36.7 | % Profit Before Taxes/Tangible | | | | 35.5 | 36.7 | 36.0 |
| (136)  22.5 | (148)  19.4 | (137)  19.1 | Net Worth | | | | (12)  7.9 | (34)  21.3 | (80)  18.8 |
| 9.8 | 4.0 | 4.4 | | | | | -6.8 | 1.1 | 9.8 |
| 17.4 | 12.3 | 13.6 | % Profit Before Taxes/Total | | | | 15.4 | 14.1 | 13.6 |
| 9.1 | 6.4 | 6.2 | Assets | | | | 3.8 | 5.2 | 6.6 |
| 2.6 | .3 | 1.0 | | | | | -4.8 | -.1 | 1.6 |
| 22.5 | 20.8 | 27.7 | | | | | 63.3 | 24.4 | 31.2 |
| 10.0 | 10.4 | 13.3 | Sales/Net Fixed Assets | | | | 9.4 | 11.2 | 14.5 |
| 5.8 | 5.6 | 5.8 | | | | | 5.6 | 4.7 | 6.3 |
| 4.6 | 5.1 | 5.6 | | | | | 4.7 | 4.5 | 6.4 |
| 3.1 | 3.5 | 3.7 | Sales/Total Assets | | | | 2.7 | 3.1 | 4.1 |
| 2.2 | 2.2 | 2.4 | | | | | 1.9 | 2.4 | 2.6 |
| .8 | .9 | .7 | | | | | 1.0 | .9 | .6 |
| (135)  1.5 | (149)  1.6 | (150)  1.2 | % Depr., Dep., Amort./Sales | | | | (14)  1.5 | (33)  1.3 | (88)  1.2 |
| 2.4 | 2.6 | 2.2 | | | | | 3.0 | 2.3 | 1.9 |
| .9 | .9 | .8 | | | | | | .9 | .6 |
| (50)  2.3 | (66)  2.0 | (55)  1.7 | % Officers', Directors' Owners' Comp/Sales | | | | | (14)  1.6 | (25)  .9 |
| 3.7 | 4.4 | 3.7 | | | | | | 3.4 | 3.5 |
| 16301591M | 14532540M | 15960872M | Net Sales ($) | 596M | 16612M | 22998M | 116978M | 631624M | 15172064M |
| 4947888M | 4369529M | 4307513M | Total Assets ($) | 154M | 6735M | 9083M | 59245M | 222429M | 4009867M |

M = $ thousand    MM = $ million
See Pages 9 through 22 for Explanation of Ratios and Data

**Current Data Sorted by Assets**                    **Comparative Historical Data**

| 0-500M | 500M-2MM | 2-10MM | 10-50MM | 50-100MM | 100-250MM | Type of Statement | 4/1/07-3/31/08 ALL | 4/1/08-3/31/09 ALL |
|---|---|---|---|---|---|---|---|---|
| | | | 1 | | 3 | Unqualified | 7 | 7 |
| | | | | | 1 | Reviewed | 1 | 1 |
| | 1 | 2 | | | | Compiled | 5 | 2 |
| | | 2 | 1 | | | Tax Returns | 3 | 3 |
| 1 | | 1 | 1 | 1 | | Other | 13 | 10 |
| | | 1 (4/1-9/30/11) | 19 (10/1/11-3/31/12) | | | | | |
| 1 | 1 | 7 | 6 | 1 | 4 | NUMBER OF STATEMENTS | 29 | 23 |
| % | % | % | % | % | % | | % | % |
| | | | | | | **ASSETS** | | |
| | | | | | | Cash & Equivalents | 12.0 | 9.7 |
| | | | | | | Trade Receivables (net) | 20.2 | 21.0 |
| | | | | | | Inventory | 13.2 | 16.2 |
| | | | | | | All Other Current | 2.4 | 1.8 |
| | | | | | | Total Current | 47.9 | 48.6 |
| | | | | | | Fixed Assets (net) | 43.4 | 43.4 |
| | | | | | | Intangibles (net) | 3.3 | 2.4 |
| | | | | | | All Other Non-Current | 5.5 | 5.5 |
| | | | | | | Total | 100.0 | 100.0 |
| | | | | | | **LIABILITIES** | | |
| | | | | | | Notes Payable-Short Term | 6.7 | 8.5 |
| | | | | | | Cur. Mat.-L.T.D. | 2.9 | 2.1 |
| | | | | | | Trade Payables | 5.8 | 8.3 |
| | | | | | | Income Taxes Payable | .4 | .0 |
| | | | | | | All Other Current | 7.9 | 9.8 |
| | | | | | | Total Current | 23.7 | 28.7 |
| | | | | | | Long-Term Debt | 15.8 | 16.5 |
| | | | | | | Deferred Taxes | 1.0 | .1 |
| | | | | | | All Other Non-Current | 7.5 | 4.9 |
| | | | | | | Net Worth | 52.0 | 49.8 |
| | | | | | | Total Liabilities & Net Worth | 100.0 | 100.0 |
| | | | | | | **INCOME DATA** | | |
| | | | | | | Net Sales | 100.0 | 100.0 |
| | | | | | | Gross Profit | 31.0 | 24.5 |
| | | | | | | Operating Expenses | 22.1 | 16.1 |
| | | | | | | Operating Profit | 8.9 | 8.4 |
| | | | | | | All Other Expenses (net) | .9 | .5 |
| | | | | | | Profit Before Taxes | 8.0 | 7.8 |
| | | | | | | **RATIOS** | | |
| | | | | | | Current | 3.2 / 2.0 / 1.5 | 4.0 / 2.0 / 1.1 |
| | | | | | | Quick | 1.7 / 1.4 / 1.0 | 3.2 / 1.5 / .5 |
| | | | | | | Sales/Receivables | 19  19.1 / 31  11.7 / 38  9.5 | 16  23.5 / 24  15.4 / 29  12.6 |
| | | | | | | Cost of Sales/Inventory | 13  28.2 / 20  18.3 / 47  7.8 | 12  30.0 / 22  16.6 / 33  11.2 |
| | | | | | | Cost of Sales/Payables | 5  69.5 / 10  36.7 / 18  20.8 | 6  56.9 / 13  29.1 / 15  23.8 |
| | | | | | | Sales/Working Capital | 7.9 / 11.4 / 15.1 | 6.8 / 14.2 / 60.6 |
| | | | | | | EBIT/Interest | 19.4 / (26) 6.2 / 2.7 | 61.0 / (22) 19.0 / 2.6 |
| | | | | | | Net Profit + Depr., Dep., Amort./Cur. Mat. L/T/D | 17.6 / (10) 7.9 / 1.2 | |
| | | | | | | Fixed/Worth | .6 / .9 / 1.5 | .6 / 1.0 / 1.5 |
| | | | | | | Debt/Worth | .5 / 1.0 / 1.6 | .6 / 1.1 / 2.1 |
| | | | | | | % Profit Before Taxes/Tangible Net Worth | 47.2 / (28) 29.4 / 11.8 | 62.0 / 37.1 / 14.6 |
| | | | | | | % Profit Before Taxes/Total Assets | 22.9 / 11.8 / 5.0 | 34.2 / 16.7 / 2.3 |
| | | | | | | Sales/Net Fixed Assets | 15.8 / 5.5 / 2.7 | 12.6 / 6.5 / 3.6 |
| | | | | | | Sales/Total Assets | 3.3 / 2.7 / 1.4 | 3.7 / 2.9 / 2.0 |
| | | | | | | % Depr., Dep., Amort./Sales | 1.1 / (25) 1.9 / 4.4 | 1.4 / (17) 1.8 / 3.5 |
| | | | | | | % Officers', Directors' Owners' Comp/Sales | | |
| 1241M | 3879M | 110173M | 340110M | 402612M | 1323280M | Net Sales ($) | 2972362M | 3970055M |
| 183M | 940M | 38329M | 134997M | 96432M | 656632M | Total Assets ($) | 1597521M | 1614437M |

## Comparative Historical Data | Current Data Sorted by Sales

| | | | | | | Type of Statement | | | | | | |
|---|---|---|---|---|---|---|---|---|---|---|---|---|
| | 8 | | 8 | | 8 | Unqualified | | | 1 | | | 7 |
| | | | 4 | | 3 | Reviewed | | | | | | 2 |
| | 4 | | 4 | | 3 | Compiled | 1 | | | | 1 | 1 |
| | 2 | | | | 2 | Tax Returns | | 1 | | | 1 | 1 |
| | 9 | | 4 | | 4 | Other | 1 | | | | 1 | 3 |
| | 4/1/09-<br>3/31/10<br>ALL | | 4/1/10-<br>3/31/11<br>ALL | | 4/1/11-<br>3/31/12<br>ALL | | 0-1MM | 1 (4/1-9/30/11)<br>1-3MM | 3-5MM | 19 (10/1/11-3/31/12)<br>5-10MM | 10-25MM | 25MM & OVER |
| | 23 | | 20 | | 20 | NUMBER OF STATEMENTS | 2 | 1 | | 1 | 3 | 13 |
| | % | | % | | % | ASSETS | % | % | % | % | % | % |
| | 11.7 | | 10.5 | | 5.6 | Cash & Equivalents | | | | | | 5.5 |
| | 18.7 | | 19.8 | | 17.7 | Trade Receivables (net) | | | | | | 19.7 |
| | 13.6 | | 14.2 | | 19.6 | Inventory | | | | | | 19.8 |
| | 3.1 | | 2.7 | | 3.6 | All Other Current | | | | | | 4.5 |
| | 47.1 | | 47.3 | | 46.5 | Total Current | | | | | | 49.6 |
| | 47.2 | | 45.9 | | 47.1 | Fixed Assets (net) | | | | | | 43.4 |
| | 2.5 | | 1.8 | | 1.1 | Intangibles (net) | | | | | | 1.4 |
| | 3.2 | | 5.0 | | 5.3 | All Other Non-Current | | | | | | 5.7 |
| | 100.0 | | 100.0 | | 100.0 | Total | | | | | | 100.0 |
| | | | | | | LIABILITIES | | | | | | |
| | 3.9 | | 3.6 | | 8.0 | Notes Payable-Short Term | | | | | | 6.5 |
| | 3.0 | | 1.8 | | 4.5 | Cur. Mat.-L.T.D. | | | | | | 1.5 |
| | 10.6 | | 9.8 | | 9.8 | Trade Payables | | | | | | 8.3 |
| | .0 | | .0 | | .0 | Income Taxes Payable | | | | | | .0 |
| | 9.8 | | 7.0 | | 6.4 | All Other Current | | | | | | 8.3 |
| | 27.4 | | 22.2 | | 28.6 | Total Current | | | | | | 24.6 |
| | 17.0 | | 17.2 | | 22.4 | Long-Term Debt | | | | | | 15.9 |
| | .5 | | .6 | | .9 | Deferred Taxes | | | | | | 1.3 |
| | 8.2 | | 10.7 | | 8.6 | All Other Non-Current | | | | | | 9.7 |
| | 46.8 | | 49.3 | | 39.5 | Net Worth | | | | | | 48.5 |
| | 100.0 | | 100.0 | | 100.0 | Total Liabilities & Net Worth | | | | | | 100.0 |
| | | | | | | INCOME DATA | | | | | | |
| | 100.0 | | 100.0 | | 100.0 | Net Sales | | | | | | 100.0 |
| | 28.3 | | 20.6 | | 22.6 | Gross Profit | | | | | | 22.4 |
| | 21.0 | | 14.9 | | 18.2 | Operating Expenses | | | | | | 16.5 |
| | 7.3 | | 5.7 | | 4.4 | Operating Profit | | | | | | 5.8 |
| | 1.0 | | 1.0 | | .9 | All Other Expenses (net) | | | | | | .5 |
| | 6.3 | | 4.7 | | 3.5 | Profit Before Taxes | | | | | | 5.3 |
| | | | | | | RATIOS | | | | | | |
| | 3.4 | | 3.3 | | 3.1 | | | | | | | 3.6 |
| | 2.1 | | 2.1 | | 1.8 | Current | | | | | | 2.0 |
| | 1.2 | | 1.5 | | 1.0 | | | | | | | 1.4 |
| | 2.2 | | 2.5 | | 1.5 | | | | | | | 1.7 |
| | 1.3 | | 1.5 | | .8 | Quick | | | | | | 1.2 |
| | .6 | | .8 | | .6 | | | | | | | .7 |
| 17 | 20.9 | 19 | 19.3 | 13 | 28.0 | Sales/Receivables | | | | | 16 | 23.5 |
| 24 | 15.1 | 27 | 13.5 | 22 | 16.7 | | | | | | 31 | 11.8 |
| 36 | 10.1 | 35 | 10.3 | 34 | 10.8 | | | | | | 34 | 10.6 |
| 11 | 34.1 | 12 | 30.3 | 20 | 18.7 | Cost of Sales/Inventory | | | | | 23 | 15.9 |
| 27 | 13.3 | 22 | 16.9 | 26 | 13.8 | | | | | | 26 | 14.0 |
| 37 | 9.9 | 34 | 10.8 | 47 | 7.8 | | | | | | 54 | 6.8 |
| 11 | 34.7 | 7 | 52.2 | 10 | 36.6 | Cost of Sales/Payables | | | | | 10 | 37.9 |
| 16 | 22.5 | 13 | 27.6 | 15 | 23.6 | | | | | | 14 | 26.1 |
| 24 | 15.0 | 26 | 14.1 | 19 | 19.4 | | | | | | 17 | 21.5 |
| | 5.7 | | 5.5 | | 6.7 | Sales/Working Capital | | | | | | 6.4 |
| | 10.5 | | 9.9 | | 15.1 | | | | | | | 9.0 |
| | 55.7 | | 26.8 | | NM | | | | | | | 24.9 |
| | 22.4 | | 16.4 | | 19.1 | EBIT/Interest | | | | | | 26.5 |
| (20) | 9.3 | (18) | 6.8 | (19) | 4.4 | | | | | | (12) | 11.3 |
| | 1.9 | | 2.7 | | 1.1 | | | | | | | 1.3 |
| | | | | | | Net Profit + Depr., Dep.,<br>Amort./Cur. Mat. L/T/D | | | | | | |
| | .6 | | .6 | | .7 | Fixed/Worth | | | | | | .6 |
| | 1.2 | | 1.0 | | 1.0 | | | | | | | .9 |
| | 1.4 | | 1.5 | | 2.2 | | | | | | | 2.2 |
| | .6 | | .6 | | .6 | Debt/Worth | | | | | | .4 |
| | 1.0 | | 1.0 | | 1.2 | | | | | | | 1.1 |
| | 1.7 | | 1.8 | | 2.8 | | | | | | | 2.4 |
| | 44.6 | | 39.4 | | 35.9 | % Profit Before Taxes/Tangible<br>Net Worth | | | | | | 34.3 |
| (22) | 29.7 | | 18.9 | (18) | 19.3 | | | | | | | 19.7 |
| | 8.6 | | 9.8 | | 3.3 | | | | | | | 2.3 |
| | 27.3 | | 15.6 | | 16.2 | % Profit Before Taxes/Total<br>Assets | | | | | | 15.5 |
| | 11.1 | | 7.2 | | 10.1 | | | | | | | 10.8 |
| | 2.0 | | 3.3 | | .6 | | | | | | | 1.7 |
| | 13.5 | | 11.6 | | 13.4 | Sales/Net Fixed Assets | | | | | | 16.5 |
| | 6.3 | | 6.5 | | 6.0 | | | | | | | 5.1 |
| | 2.2 | | 2.6 | | 2.8 | | | | | | | 2.9 |
| | 3.8 | | 4.1 | | 4.2 | Sales/Total Assets | | | | | | 4.2 |
| | 2.6 | | 2.8 | | 3.2 | | | | | | | 2.6 |
| | 1.5 | | 1.2 | | 1.4 | | | | | | | 1.4 |
| | 1.4 | | 1.6 | | 1.3 | % Depr., Dep., Amort./Sales | | | | | | 1.2 |
| (18) | 2.3 | (16) | 2.7 | (18) | 2.6 | | | | | | (11) | 2.5 |
| | 4.2 | | 5.3 | | 4.4 | | | | | | | 4.3 |
| | | | | | | % Officers', Directors'<br>Owners' Comp/Sales | | | | | | |
| | 3320555M | | 2482362M | | 2181295M | Net Sales ($) | | 3044M | 3879M | 7487M | 39796M | 2127089M |
| | 1560225M | | 1103635M | | 927513M | Total Assets ($) | | 3472M | 940M | 9171M | 11419M | 902511M |

Note: For the 0-1MM column under ASSETS through RATIOS sections, the text reads vertically: "DATA NOT AVAILABLE"

M = $ thousand     MM = $ million
See Pages 9 through 22 for Explanation of Ratios and Data

## Current Data Sorted by Assets　　　　　　　　　　Comparative Historical Data

### Type of Statement

| 0-500M | 500M-2MM | 2-10MM | 10-50MM | 50-100MM | 100-250MM | Type of Statement | 4/1/07-3/31/08 ALL | 4/1/08-3/31/09 ALL |
|---|---|---|---|---|---|---|---|---|
| 1 |  | 2 | 2 | 7 | 6 | Unqualified | 20 | 20 |
|  | 1 | 6 | 3 |  |  | Reviewed | 6 | 13 |
|  | 1 | 1 |  |  |  | Compiled | 1 | 1 |
| 1 | 1 | 1 |  |  |  | Tax Returns | 1 | 2 |
|  |  | 3 | 2 | 3 | 2 | Other | 32 | 24 |
|  | 9 (4/1-9/30/11) |  |  | 34 (10/1/11-3/31/12) |  |  |  |  |

### Financial Data

| 0-500M | 500M-2MM | 2-10MM | 10-50MM | 50-100MM | 100-250MM |  | 4/1/07-3/31/08 ALL | 4/1/08-3/31/09 ALL |
|---|---|---|---|---|---|---|---|---|
| 2 | 3 | 13 | 7 | 10 | 8 | NUMBER OF STATEMENTS | 60 | 60 |
| % | % | % | % | % | % | **ASSETS** | % | % |
|  |  | 9.4 |  | 3.1 |  | Cash & Equivalents | 5.1 | 6.7 |
|  |  | 18.7 |  | 14.9 |  | Trade Receivables (net) | 15.6 | 17.1 |
|  |  | 19.7 |  | 23.5 |  | Inventory | 24.0 | 23.7 |
|  |  | 6.4 |  | .9 |  | All Other Current | 1.4 | 1.8 |
|  |  | 54.2 |  | 42.4 |  | Total Current | 46.0 | 49.4 |
|  |  | 36.9 |  | 43.7 |  | Fixed Assets (net) | 46.2 | 42.6 |
|  |  | .4 |  | 1.5 |  | Intangibles (net) | 3.0 | 2.3 |
|  |  | 8.5 |  | 12.4 |  | All Other Non-Current | 4.8 | 5.6 |
|  |  | 100.0 |  | 100.0 |  | Total | 100.0 | 100.0 |
|  |  |  |  |  |  | **LIABILITIES** |  |  |
|  |  | 15.9 |  | 6.9 |  | Notes Payable-Short Term | 11.8 | 7.4 |
|  |  | 4.2 |  | 4.6 |  | Cur. Mat.-L.T.D. | 3.1 | 6.6 |
|  |  | 15.1 |  | 10.6 |  | Trade Payables | 10.5 | 12.2 |
|  |  | .2 |  | .3 |  | Income Taxes Payable | .3 | .4 |
|  |  | 3.5 |  | 6.6 |  | All Other Current | 9.3 | 7.3 |
|  |  | 38.8 |  | 28.9 |  | Total Current | 34.9 | 33.9 |
|  |  | 8.3 |  | 17.4 |  | Long-Term Debt | 23.9 | 22.0 |
|  |  | .3 |  | 2.0 |  | Deferred Taxes | 1.0 | 1.3 |
|  |  | 5.3 |  | 2.8 |  | All Other Non-Current | 3.8 | 2.8 |
|  |  | 47.3 |  | 48.9 |  | Net Worth | 36.3 | 40.0 |
|  |  | 100.0 |  | 100.0 |  | Total Liabilities & Net Worth | 100.0 | 100.0 |
|  |  |  |  |  |  | **INCOME DATA** |  |  |
|  |  | 100.0 |  | 100.0 |  | Net Sales | 100.0 | 100.0 |
|  |  | 23.9 |  | 13.8 |  | Gross Profit | 19.4 | 16.2 |
|  |  | 22.7 |  | 10.3 |  | Operating Expenses | 15.7 | 13.8 |
|  |  | 1.2 |  | 3.5 |  | Operating Profit | 3.7 | 2.4 |
|  |  | .1 |  | .5 |  | All Other Expenses (net) | .9 | .8 |
|  |  | 1.0 |  | 3.1 |  | Profit Before Taxes | 2.8 | 1.6 |
|  |  |  |  |  |  | **RATIOS** |  |  |
|  |  | 2.2 |  | 2.0 |  |  | 2.1 | 2.3 |
|  |  | 1.5 |  | 1.4 |  | Current | 1.5 | 1.6 |
|  |  | 1.2 |  | 1.2 |  |  | 1.0 | 1.1 |
|  |  | 1.0 |  | 1.0 |  |  | .9 | 1.0 |
|  |  | .9 |  | .6 |  | Quick | .6 | .7 |
|  |  | .4 |  | .4 |  |  | .4 | .5 |
|  |  | 10　34.9 |  | 18　20.0 |  |  | 16　22.4 | 15　24.9 |
|  |  | 19　19.2 |  | 25　14.8 |  | Sales/Receivables | 20　18.4 | 19　19.2 |
|  |  | 23　16.2 |  | 27　13.4 |  |  | 28　12.9 | 24　14.9 |
|  |  | 15　24.5 |  | 24　14.9 |  |  | 24　15.4 | 20　18.4 |
|  |  | 22　16.6 |  | 33　11.1 |  | Cost of Sales/Inventory | 36　10.1 | 36　10.1 |
|  |  | 39　9.3 |  | 58　6.3 |  |  | 59　6.2 | 50　7.3 |
|  |  | 8　46.3 |  | 11　34.2 |  |  | 14　26.8 | 9　39.0 |
|  |  | 14　26.4 |  | 16　22.5 |  | Cost of Sales/Payables | 17　21.0 | 16　23.1 |
|  |  | 33　10.9 |  | 24　15.4 |  |  | 21　17.2 | 20　17.8 |
|  |  | 13.1 |  | 8.6 |  |  | 9.7 | 9.4 |
|  |  | 25.3 |  | 23.0 |  | Sales/Working Capital | 19.9 | 19.7 |
|  |  | 57.9 |  | 56.3 |  |  | NM | 130.6 |
|  |  | 8.4 |  | 14.5 |  |  | 10.3 | 7.9 |
|  |  | 6.0 |  | 3.3 |  | EBIT/Interest | (57) 2.8 | (57) 2.3 |
|  |  | 2.6 |  | .7 |  |  | .5 | -3.4 |
|  |  |  |  |  |  | Net Profit + Depr., Dep., | 3.1 | 5.4 |
|  |  |  |  |  |  | Amort./Cur. Mat. L/T/D | (16) 2.0 | (21) 2.4 |
|  |  |  |  |  |  |  | 1.5 | .7 |
|  |  | .4 |  | .6 |  |  | .8 | .8 |
|  |  | .7 |  | .9 |  | Fixed/Worth | 1.4 | 1.4 |
|  |  | 1.4 |  | 1.8 |  |  | 2.5 | 2.5 |
|  |  | .3 |  | .5 |  |  | .8 | .7 |
|  |  | 1.5 |  | 1.4 |  | Debt/Worth | 1.9 | 1.5 |
|  |  | 2.4 |  | 2.1 |  |  | 3.8 | 4.4 |
|  |  | 42.1 |  | 24.3 |  | % Profit Before Taxes/Tangible | 34.7 | 40.4 |
|  | (12) | 8.7 |  | 7.9 |  | Net Worth | (55) 15.4 | (56) 12.2 |
|  |  | 5.4 |  | -2.2 |  |  | -1.3 | -13.1 |
|  |  | 12.5 |  | 8.3 |  | % Profit Before Taxes/Total | 12.0 | 15.2 |
|  |  | 4.1 |  | 4.7 |  | Assets | 5.4 | 3.1 |
|  |  | 2.5 |  | -.6 |  |  | -.9 | -8.2 |
|  |  | 17.5 |  | 9.9 |  |  | 8.4 | 10.4 |
|  |  | 10.3 |  | 4.6 |  | Sales/Net Fixed Assets | 5.7 | 6.1 |
|  |  | 6.3 |  | 3.1 |  |  | 4.1 | 4.4 |
|  |  | 5.3 |  | 3.3 |  |  | 3.1 | 3.6 |
|  |  | 3.5 |  | 2.3 |  | Sales/Total Assets | 2.5 | 2.6 |
|  |  | 2.3 |  | 1.5 |  |  | 2.0 | 2.1 |
|  |  | 1.2 |  |  |  |  | 1.3 | 1.3 |
|  | (12) | 1.8 |  |  |  | % Depr., Dep., Amort./Sales | (52) 2.4 | (48) 2.2 |
|  |  | 3.4 |  |  |  |  | 3.9 | 3.1 |
|  |  |  |  |  |  | % Officers', Directors' Owners' Comp/Sales |  |  |
| 797M | 15898M | 279678M | 446501M | 1649929M | 3091632M | Net Sales ($) | 11038751M | 12315398M |
| 357M | 3363M | 77230M | 183924M | 714182M | 1241131M | Total Assets ($) | 4302317M | 4581310M |

© RMA 2012

M = $ thousand　　MM = $ million
See Pages 9 through 22 for Explanation of Ratios and Data

## Comparative Historical Data | Current Data Sorted by Sales

| | | | Type of Statement | 0-1MM | 1-3MM | 3-5MM | 5-10MM | 10-25MM | 25MM & OVER |
|---|---|---|---|---|---|---|---|---|---|
| 27 | 23 | 18 | Unqualified | 1 | | | | 3 | 14 |
| 13 | 8 | 10 | Reviewed | | | | 2 | 3 | 5 |
| 1 | 3 | 2 | Compiled | | | | 1 | | 1 |
| 3 | 2 | 3 | Tax Returns | 1 | 1 | | | 1 | |
| 13 | 24 | 10 | Other | | | | | 1 | 9 |
| 4/1/09-3/31/10 ALL | 4/1/10-3/31/11 ALL | 4/1/11-3/31/12 ALL | | | 9 (4/1-9/30/11) | | 34 (10/1/11-3/31/12) | | |
| 57 | 60 | 43 | NUMBER OF STATEMENTS | 2 | 1 | | 3 | 8 | 29 |
| % | % | % | **ASSETS** | % | % | % | % | % | % |
| 5.2 | 6.9 | 6.4 | Cash & Equivalents | | | | | | 6.1 |
| 19.1 | 19.0 | 16.7 | Trade Receivables (net) | | | | | | 17.4 |
| 22.5 | 21.3 | 21.0 | Inventory | | D | | | | 23.4 |
| 2.1 | 2.4 | 2.9 | All Other Current | | A | | | | 1.5 |
| 48.9 | 49.7 | 47.1 | Total Current | | T | | | | 48.5 |
| 42.4 | 41.5 | 44.7 | Fixed Assets (net) | | A | | | | 42.8 |
| 2.5 | 2.2 | .8 | Intangibles (net) | | | | | | .8 |
| 6.2 | 6.7 | 7.4 | All Other Non-Current | | N | | | | 7.9 |
| 100.0 | 100.0 | 100.0 | Total | | O | | | | 100.0 |
| | | | **LIABILITIES** | | T | | | | |
| 10.7 | 6.8 | 8.9 | Notes Payable-Short Term | | | | | | 9.9 |
| 4.4 | 3.6 | 4.0 | Cur. Mat.-L.T.D. | | A | | | | 3.2 |
| 13.1 | 13.0 | 11.6 | Trade Payables | | V | | | | 12.8 |
| .5 | .6 | .3 | Income Taxes Payable | | A | | | | .4 |
| 8.1 | 6.7 | 4.8 | All Other Current | | I | | | | 6.0 |
| 36.8 | 30.7 | 29.6 | Total Current | | L | | | | 32.2 |
| 17.8 | 15.3 | 18.0 | Long-Term Debt | | A | | | | 18.4 |
| 1.0 | 1.3 | .8 | Deferred Taxes | | B | | | | 1.1 |
| 3.5 | 4.4 | 3.6 | All Other Non-Current | | L | | | | 4.0 |
| 40.9 | 48.3 | 48.2 | Net Worth | | E | | | | 44.2 |
| 100.0 | 100.0 | 100.0 | Total Liabilities & Net Worth | | | | | | 100.0 |
| | | | **INCOME DATA** | | | | | | |
| 100.0 | 100.0 | 100.0 | Net Sales | | | | | | 100.0 |
| 16.0 | 18.7 | 18.1 | Gross Profit | | | | | | 14.9 |
| 11.2 | 14.5 | 15.6 | Operating Expenses | | | | | | 12.1 |
| 4.8 | 4.2 | 2.5 | Operating Profit | | | | | | 2.9 |
| .5 | .4 | .4 | All Other Expenses (net) | | | | | | .5 |
| 4.3 | 3.7 | 2.1 | Profit Before Taxes | | | | | | 2.4 |
| | | | **RATIOS** | | | | | | |
| 2.1 | 2.5 | 2.3 | | | | | | | 2.1 |
| 1.4 | 1.8 | 1.5 | Current | | | | | | 1.4 |
| 1.0 | 1.4 | 1.3 | | | | | | | 1.2 |
| 1.1 | 1.3 | 1.0 | | | | | | | 1.0 |
| .7 | .8 | .7 | Quick | | | | | | .7 |
| .4 | .6 | .4 | | | | | | | .4 |
| 15  24.0 | 14  26.0 | 16  23.3 | | | | | | | 16  22.2 |
| 19  18.9 | 19  18.9 | 20  18.1 | Sales/Receivables | | | | | | 20  17.9 |
| 28  13.3 | 28  13.2 | 26  14.1 | | | | | | | 26  14.1 |
| 15  24.0 | 20  18.6 | 15  23.6 | | | | | | | 20  18.3 |
| 30  12.0 | 33  11.1 | 30  12.0 | Cost of Sales/Inventory | | | | | | 33  11.1 |
| 55  6.7 | 47  7.8 | 54  6.7 | | | | | | | 53  6.9 |
| 10  36.8 | 11  33.9 | 9  38.7 | | | | | | | 9  38.7 |
| 17  22.0 | 16  23.4 | 15  24.0 | Cost of Sales/Payables | | | | | | 15  24.0 |
| 25  14.7 | 23  16.1 | 27  13.5 | | | | | | | 22  16.3 |
| 10.9 | 8.7 | 9.4 | | | | | | | 9.8 |
| 24.5 | 16.2 | 22.4 | Sales/Working Capital | | | | | | 27.2 |
| 847.5 | 29.4 | 40.9 | | | | | | | 45.1 |
| 13.2 | 20.2 | 10.2 | | | | | | | 14.2 |
| (53)  4.0 | (58)  5.3 | (42)  3.3 | EBIT/Interest | | | | | | 3.4 |
| 1.8 | 2.4 | 1.2 | | | | | | | 1.3 |
| 19.2 | 8.9 | | Net Profit + Depr., Dep., | | | | | | |
| (14)  2.8 | (17)  4.4 | | Amort./Cur. Mat. L/T/D | | | | | | |
| 2.3 | 2.4 | | | | | | | | |
| .7 | .5 | .6 | | | | | | | .6 |
| 1.3 | .9 | 1.0 | Fixed/Worth | | | | | | 1.0 |
| 2.0 | 1.9 | 1.8 | | | | | | | 1.8 |
| .6 | .5 | .4 | | | | | | | .5 |
| 1.5 | 1.4 | 1.5 | Debt/Worth | | | | | | 1.6 |
| 3.4 | 2.5 | 2.3 | | | | | | | 2.6 |
| 46.9 | 36.7 | 25.3 | | | | | | | 26.3 |
| (54)  18.3 | 18.7 | (42)  8.2 | % Profit Before Taxes/Tangible Net Worth | | | | | (28)  9.7 | |
| 6.2 | 10.3 | 3.6 | | | | | | | 4.6 |
| 16.8 | 17.4 | 8.1 | | | | | | | 7.8 |
| 8.0 | 7.1 | 4.3 | % Profit Before Taxes/Total Assets | | | | | | 4.5 |
| 2.5 | 2.5 | .3 | | | | | | | .7 |
| 10.7 | 12.6 | 11.2 | | | | | | | 11.0 |
| 6.7 | 7.4 | 6.7 | Sales/Net Fixed Assets | | | | | | 6.7 |
| 4.6 | 4.6 | 3.5 | | | | | | | 3.5 |
| 4.6 | 4.1 | 4.7 | | | | | | | 4.2 |
| 2.7 | 2.9 | 2.6 | Sales/Total Assets | | | | | | 2.6 |
| 2.1 | 2.1 | 1.8 | | | | | | | 1.8 |
| 1.2 | 1.3 | 1.3 | | | | | | | 1.4 |
| (48)  2.1 | (51)  1.9 | (37)  2.1 | % Depr., Dep., Amort./Sales | | | | | (23)  1.9 | |
| 2.9 | 3.1 | 3.5 | | | | | | | 2.9 |
| | | | % Officers', Directors' Owners' Comp/Sales | | | | | | |
| 9997169M | 9045581M | 5484435M | Net Sales ($) | 797M | 2678M | | 21291M | 131694M | 5327975M |
| 3568712M | 3488075M | 2220187M | Total Assets ($) | 357M | 1378M | | 11925M | 84589M | 2121938M |

© RMA 2012

M = $ thousand    MM = $ million
See Pages 9 through 22 for Explanation of Ratios and Data

## Current Data Sorted by Assets      Comparative Historical Data

### Type of Statement

| | 0-500M | 500M-2MM | 2-10MM | 10-50MM | 50-100MM | 100-250MM | Type of Statement | 4/1/07-3/31/08 ALL | 4/1/08-3/31/09 ALL |
|---|---|---|---|---|---|---|---|---|---|
| | | 1 | 1 | 2 | 2 | 5 | Unqualified | 20 | 22 |
| | | 1 | 7 | 5 | | | Reviewed | 13 | 15 |
| | | 2 | 2 | | | | Compiled | 6 | 5 |
| | 1 | 5 | 5 | | | | Tax Returns | 3 | 7 |
| | | 2 | 7 | 13 | 4 | 3 | Other | 39 | 31 |
| | | 9 (4/1-9/30/11) | | 59 (10/1/11-3/31/12) | | | | | |
| NUMBER OF STATEMENTS | 1 | 11 | 22 | 20 | 6 | 8 | | 81 | 80 |

### Data (%)

| | 0-500M | 500M-2MM | 2-10MM | 10-50MM | 50-100MM | 100-250MM | | 4/1/07-3/31/08 ALL | 4/1/08-3/31/09 ALL |
|---|---|---|---|---|---|---|---|---|---|
| | % | % | % | % | % | % | **ASSETS** | % | % |
| | | 24.1 | 11.4 | 6.2 | | | Cash & Equivalents | 7.6 | 7.3 |
| | | 18.1 | 25.0 | 21.4 | | | Trade Receivables (net) | 22.0 | 23.1 |
| | | 14.2 | 29.5 | 33.6 | | | Inventory | 27.4 | 35.4 |
| | | 6.0 | .8 | 1.7 | | | All Other Current | 4.1 | 2.2 |
| | | 62.4 | 66.8 | 62.9 | | | Total Current | 61.1 | 67.9 |
| | | 22.2 | 23.4 | 28.4 | | | Fixed Assets (net) | 29.3 | 25.7 |
| | | .7 | 2.1 | 3.5 | | | Intangibles (net) | 2.6 | 1.1 |
| | | 14.8 | 7.7 | 5.3 | | | All Other Non-Current | 7.0 | 5.3 |
| | | 100.0 | 100.0 | 100.0 | | | Total | 100.0 | 100.0 |
| | | | | | | | **LIABILITIES** | | |
| | | 27.1 | 20.7 | 20.1 | | | Notes Payable-Short Term | 18.6 | 23.1 |
| | | 4.1 | 3.8 | 1.8 | | | Cur. Mat.-L.T.D. | 3.9 | 2.9 |
| | | 15.8 | 17.3 | 12.9 | | | Trade Payables | 13.1 | 16.5 |
| | | .0 | .0 | .0 | | | Income Taxes Payable | .1 | .2 |
| | | 5.2 | 7.4 | 8.1 | | | All Other Current | 7.5 | 8.8 |
| | | 52.2 | 49.2 | 42.9 | | | Total Current | 43.3 | 51.5 |
| | | 15.3 | 12.0 | 16.2 | | | Long-Term Debt | 13.6 | 11.1 |
| | | .0 | .1 | .5 | | | Deferred Taxes | .2 | .4 |
| | | 1.9 | 4.9 | 3.3 | | | All Other Non-Current | 4.8 | 4.5 |
| | | 30.6 | 33.7 | 37.2 | | | Net Worth | 38.1 | 32.6 |
| | | 100.0 | 100.0 | 100.0 | | | Total Liabilities & Net Worth | 100.0 | 100.0 |
| | | | | | | | **INCOME DATA** | | |
| | | 100.0 | 100.0 | 100.0 | | | Net Sales | 100.0 | 100.0 |
| | | 23.5 | 15.8 | 16.8 | | | Gross Profit | 22.4 | 18.7 |
| | | 22.9 | 13.7 | 11.0 | | | Operating Expenses | 17.6 | 15.3 |
| | | .6 | 2.1 | 5.8 | | | Operating Profit | 4.8 | 3.4 |
| | | -.3 | .0 | .6 | | | All Other Expenses (net) | .2 | .9 |
| | | .9 | 2.0 | 5.2 | | | Profit Before Taxes | 4.6 | 2.5 |
| | | | | | | | **RATIOS** | | |
| | | 3.7 | 1.9 | 2.3 | | | | 2.1 | 1.9 |
| | | 1.3 | 1.2 | 1.4 | | | Current | 1.4 | 1.3 |
| | | .7 | 1.0 | 1.1 | | | | 1.1 | 1.0 |
| | | 3.3 | 1.0 | 1.2 | | | | 1.1 | 1.0 |
| | | .8 | .7 | .6 | | | Quick | .6 | .5 |
| | | .2 | .4 | .4 | | | | .4 | .3 |
| | 0 UND | | 12 31.4 | 27 13.4 | | | | 17 21.9 | 18 20.7 |
| | 21 17.8 | | 28 13.0 | 34 10.7 | | | Sales/Receivables | 29 12.5 | 30 12.4 |
| | 24 15.3 | | 39 9.4 | 46 7.9 | | | | 36 10.3 | 37 9.8 |
| | 0 UND | | 16 23.0 | 22 16.4 | | | | 21 17.7 | 28 13.0 |
| | 2 203.2 | | 33 11.0 | 63 5.8 | | | Cost of Sales/Inventory | 46 8.0 | 58 6.3 |
| | 42 8.6 | | 73 5.0 | 85 4.3 | | | | 80 4.6 | 95 3.8 |
| | 0 UND | | 5 72.1 | 10 36.1 | | | | 10 37.7 | 10 37.4 |
| | 14 26.1 | | 17 21.9 | 16 22.7 | | | Cost of Sales/Payables | 18 20.6 | 20 18.5 |
| | 38 9.7 | | 31 11.6 | 34 10.6 | | | | 30 12.3 | 33 11.2 |
| | | 4.8 | 5.3 | 7.7 | | | | 7.9 | 8.7 |
| | | 57.5 | 34.2 | 13.3 | | | Sales/Working Capital | 15.3 | 19.6 |
| | | -21.9 | -116.6 | 35.5 | | | | 68.9 | 256.3 |
| | | 9.6 | 8.1 | 8.0 | | | | 6.4 | 5.8 |
| | | (10) 1.0 | 3.0 | 4.2 | | | EBIT/Interest | (79) 3.0 | (76) 2.5 |
| | | -5.6 | 1.2 | 2.2 | | | | 1.8 | 1.1 |
| | | | | | | | | 12.4 | 9.1 |
| | | | | | | | Net Profit + Depr., Dep., Amort./Cur. Mat. L/T/D | (20) 4.2 | (24) 4.8 |
| | | | | | | | | 1.8 | 2.5 |
| | | .0 | .4 | .2 | | | | .3 | .2 |
| | | .7 | .6 | .8 | | | Fixed/Worth | .7 | .7 |
| | | 653.0 | 2.2 | 1.6 | | | | 1.5 | 1.8 |
| | | .4 | .9 | 1.4 | | | | .9 | .9 |
| | | 1.2 | 2.3 | 2.0 | | | Debt/Worth | 1.7 | 2.1 |
| | | 999.8 | 11.1 | 3.2 | | | | 4.8 | 6.4 |
| | | | 33.7 | 39.7 | | | | 35.7 | 36.3 |
| | | | (20) 15.0 | 26.8 | | | % Profit Before Taxes/Tangible Net Worth | (76) 19.2 | (70) 20.2 |
| | | | 5.8 | 10.6 | | | | 6.6 | 4.0 |
| | | 25.3 | 9.9 | 13.1 | | | | 11.4 | 11.0 |
| | | 1.0 | 3.3 | 9.9 | | | % Profit Before Taxes/Total Assets | 6.2 | 4.4 |
| | | -9.1 | .5 | 2.4 | | | | 2.2 | .6 |
| | | UND | 47.4 | 35.8 | | | | 44.2 | 69.8 |
| | | 22.1 | 15.4 | 10.6 | | | Sales/Net Fixed Assets | 9.0 | 14.7 |
| | | 6.6 | 8.6 | 4.6 | | | | 4.6 | 5.5 |
| | | 4.7 | 5.1 | 3.1 | | | | 3.7 | 3.8 |
| | | 3.1 | 3.8 | 2.2 | | | Sales/Total Assets | 2.5 | 2.8 |
| | | 2.3 | 2.4 | 1.6 | | | | 1.8 | 2.0 |
| | | | .4 | .6 | | | | .7 | .4 |
| | | | (19) 1.6 | (19) .9 | | | % Depr., Dep., Amort./Sales | (70) 1.3 | (69) 1.1 |
| | | | 2.1 | 2.7 | | | | 2.3 | 2.0 |
| | | | .4 | | | | | .5 | 1.0 |
| | | | (12) .8 | | | | % Officers', Directors', Owners' Comp/Sales | (21) 1.8 | (21) 2.9 |
| | | | 2.8 | | | | | 3.1 | 4.0 |
| | 1802M | 54305M | 476865M | 1045823M | 888317M | 2981182M | Net Sales ($) | 6270274M | 6301777M |
| | 261M | 14947M | 136494M | 458519M | 360382M | 1297159M | Total Assets ($) | 3038572M | 2882641M |

## Comparative Historical Data | Current Data Sorted by Sales

Type of Statement counts and number of statements. Right-side grouping: **9 (4/1-9/30/11)** covers the 0-1MM / 1-3MM columns; **59 (10/1/11-3/31/12)** covers the remaining columns. Percentage distribution DATA NOT AVAILABLE for the 0-1MM, 1-3MM, 3-5MM and 5-10MM columns (only 10-25MM and 25MM & OVER columns carry percentage detail).

| | 4/1/09-3/31/10 ALL | 4/1/10-3/31/11 ALL | 4/1/11-3/31/12 ALL | 0-1MM | 1-3MM | 3-5MM | 5-10MM | 10-25MM | 25MM & OVER |
|---|---|---|---|---|---|---|---|---|---|
| **Type of Statement** | | | | | | | | | |
| Unqualified | 22 | 13 | 11 | | 1 | | | | 10 |
| Reviewed | 19 | 17 | 13 | | | | | 5 | 8 |
| Compiled | 5 | 3 | 4 | | | 1 | 3 | | |
| Tax Returns | 9 | 12 | 11 | | | | 3 | 8 | |
| Other | 35 | 32 | 29 | | 4 | 1 | 1 | | 23 |
| **NUMBER OF STATEMENTS** | 90 | 77 | 68 | | 5 | 2 | 7 | 13 | 41 |
| | % | % | % | | % | % | % | % | % |
| **ASSETS** | | | | | | | | | |
| Cash & Equivalents | 7.8 | 9.4 | 11.9 | | | | | 14.2 | 7.7 |
| Trade Receivables (net) | 21.0 | 21.0 | 21.3 | | | | | 26.7 | 22.3 |
| Inventory | 28.8 | 29.1 | 28.7 | | | | | 22.9 | 33.3 |
| All Other Current | 3.7 | 3.2 | 3.1 | | | | | .6 | 3.2 |
| Total Current | 61.1 | 62.7 | 65.0 | | | | | 64.3 | 66.6 |
| Fixed Assets (net) | 30.0 | 29.7 | 24.2 | | | | | 22.2 | 24.1 |
| Intangibles (net) | 3.5 | 3.1 | 2.7 | | | | | 2.8 | 3.3 |
| All Other Non-Current | 5.3 | 4.5 | 8.0 | | | | | 10.7 | 6.0 |
| Total | 100.0 | 100.0 | 100.0 | | | | | 100.0 | 100.0 |
| **LIABILITIES** | | | | | | | | | |
| Notes Payable-Short Term | 16.5 | 16.4 | 21.0 | | | | | 11.6 | 23.0 |
| Cur. Mat.-L.T.D. | 4.4 | 2.3 | 3.2 | | | | | 4.1 | 2.8 |
| Trade Payables | 13.4 | 14.7 | 14.7 | | | | | 22.0 | 13.4 |
| Income Taxes Payable | .2 | .2 | .1 | | | | | .0 | .1 |
| All Other Current | 7.9 | 9.5 | 8.5 | | | | | 7.4 | 9.9 |
| Total Current | 42.4 | 43.1 | 47.4 | | | | | 45.1 | 49.2 |
| Long-Term Debt | 12.9 | 12.6 | 13.0 | | | | | 12.0 | 13.1 |
| Deferred Taxes | .9 | 1.0 | .4 | | | | | .1 | .5 |
| All Other Non-Current | 5.5 | 8.7 | 4.9 | | | | | 3.0 | 5.5 |
| Net Worth | 38.2 | 34.6 | 34.4 | | | | | 39.9 | 31.7 |
| Total Liabilities & Net Worth | 100.0 | 100.0 | 100.0 | | | | | 100.0 | 100.0 |
| **INCOME DATA** | | | | | | | | | |
| Net Sales | 100.0 | 100.0 | 100.0 | | | | | 100.0 | 100.0 |
| Gross Profit | 18.9 | 18.7 | 16.7 | | | | | 15.2 | 14.8 |
| Operating Expenses | 16.6 | 14.1 | 13.3 | | | | | 13.3 | 10.5 |
| Operating Profit | 2.3 | 4.6 | 3.4 | | | | | 1.9 | 4.3 |
| All Other Expenses (net) | .1 | .2 | .3 | | | | | -.3 | .5 |
| Profit Before Taxes | 2.2 | 4.4 | 3.1 | | | | | 2.2 | 3.7 |
| **RATIOS** | | | | | | | | | |
| Current | 2.3 | 2.1 | 2.1 | | | | | 2.6 | 1.6 |
| | 1.5 | 1.4 | 1.4 | | | | | 1.2 | 1.4 |
| | 1.1 | 1.1 | 1.0 | | | | | 1.0 | 1.1 |
| Quick | 1.0 | 1.1 | 1.2 | | | | | 1.2 | .9 |
| | .7 | .7 | .6 | | | | | .8 | .5 |
| | .4 | .4 | .4 | | | | | .5 | .4 |
| Sales/Receivables | 20  17.8 | 19  19.3 | 12  30.7 | | | | | 10  37.7 | 19  19.2 |
| | 30  12.3 | 31  11.9 | 28  12.9 | | | | | 21  17.3 | 34  10.6 |
| | 37  9.9 | 39  9.4 | 40  9.2 | | | | | 34  10.7 | 41  8.9 |
| Cost of Sales/Inventory | 20  18.6 | 19  19.7 | 14  26.3 | | | | | 16  23.4 | 25  14.8 |
| | 46  7.9 | 47  7.7 | 47  7.7 | | | | | 20  18.4 | 59  6.2 |
| | 92  4.0 | 83  4.4 | 85  4.3 | | | | | 54  6.7 | 85  4.3 |
| Cost of Sales/Payables | 9  42.5 | 8  47.2 | 7  49.8 | | | | | 5  78.9 | 8  45.5 |
| | 17  21.4 | 17  22.0 | 15  23.6 | | | | | 21  17.5 | 15  24.6 |
| | 31  11.7 | 35  10.5 | 33  11.2 | | | | | 27  13.7 | 32  11.4 |
| Sales/Working Capital | 6.5 | 7.3 | 7.2 | | | | | 9.6 | 8.7 |
| | 14.2 | 16.8 | 17.8 | | | | | 57.5 | 14.7 |
| | 69.7 | 74.4 | 456.0 | | | | | -106.1 | 48.3 |
| EBIT/Interest | 8.0 | 11.6 | 8.0 | | | | | 6.5 | 8.3 |
| | (88)  3.0 | (74)  4.9 | (67)  3.9 | | | | | (12)  3.0 | 3.9 |
| | 1.1 | 2.1 | 1.7 | | | | | 1.9 | 2.1 |
| Net Profit + Depr., Dep., Amort./Cur. Mat. L/T/D | 17.0 | 22.4 | 8.2 | | | | | | 10.4 |
| | (27)  4.4 | (24)  3.4 | (13)  4.3 | | | | | | (10)  2.7 |
| | 1.3 | 2.0 | 1.9 | | | | | | 1.5 |
| Fixed/Worth | .4 | .3 | .3 | | | | | .1 | .3 |
| | .8 | .7 | .6 | | | | | .5 | .7 |
| | 2.1 | 1.4 | 1.4 | | | | | 1.3 | 1.6 |
| Debt/Worth | .8 | 1.0 | 1.0 | | | | | .7 | 1.4 |
| | 1.6 | 2.0 | 2.1 | | | | | 2.1 | 2.4 |
| | 4.4 | 3.7 | 6.1 | | | | | 8.8 | 4.6 |
| % Profit Before Taxes/Tangible Net Worth | 38.9 | 43.8 | 37.4 | | | | | 40.7 | 38.9 |
| | (79)  16.9 | (70)  26.5 | (62)  19.9 | | | | | (12)  18.5 | (38)  22.7 |
| | 1.0 | 9.3 | 8.6 | | | | | 7.2 | 12.3 |
| % Profit Before Taxes/Total Assets | 10.4 | 16.6 | 11.6 | | | | | 11.4 | 11.3 |
| | 4.2 | 6.4 | 5.4 | | | | | 7.4 | 5.7 |
| | .3 | 2.7 | 1.7 | | | | | 1.9 | 2.1 |
| Sales/Net Fixed Assets | 44.3 | 27.9 | 44.6 | | | | | 77.8 | 40.2 |
| | 10.6 | 11.1 | 13.3 | | | | | 21.6 | 11.1 |
| | 3.8 | 4.2 | 6.2 | | | | | 8.0 | 6.0 |
| Sales/Total Assets | 3.5 | 3.6 | 3.9 | | | | | 5.1 | 3.5 |
| | 2.4 | 2.4 | 2.8 | | | | | 3.9 | 2.7 |
| | 1.5 | 1.7 | 1.9 | | | | | 2.5 | 1.8 |
| % Depr., Dep., Amort./Sales | .7 | .6 | .5 | | | | | .4 | .5 |
| | (80)  1.5 | (68)  1.4 | (59)  1.1 | | | | | (11)  2.0 | (36)  1.1 |
| | 2.7 | 2.6 | 2.7 | | | | | 2.7 | 2.7 |
| % Officers', Directors' Owners' Comp/Sales | .8 | .8 | .6 | | | | | | |
| | (25)  2.0 | (26)  1.8 | (22)  1.1 | | | | | | |
| | 3.5 | 2.8 | 3.2 | | | | | | |
| Net Sales ($) | 6699831M | 3644940M | 5448294M | | 10497M | 8307M | 45863M | 236979M | 5146648M |
| Total Assets ($) | 3475089M | 1847610M | 2267762M | | 4748M | 4294M | 20677M | 71068M | 2166975M |

M = $ thousand    MM = $ million
See Pages 9 through 22 for Explanation of Ratios and Data

## Current Data Sorted by Assets

## Comparative Historical Data

**Type of Statement**

| | 0-500M | 500M-2MM | 2-10MM | 10-50MM | 50-100MM | 100-250MM | | 4/1/07-3/31/08 ALL | 4/1/08-3/31/09 ALL |
|---|---|---|---|---|---|---|---|---|---|
| Unqualified | | | | | | 1 | | 7 | 5 |
| Reviewed | 8 | 16 | 3 | 3 | | | | 15 | 8 |
| Compiled | 21 | 10 | 11 | 6 | | | | 118 | 101 |
| Tax Returns | 9 | 13 | 6 | 6 | | | | 41 | 43 |
| Other | | | 6 | 6 | 2 | | | 45 | 31 |
| | 0-500M | 500M-2MM | 11 (4/1-9/30/11) 2-10MM | 110 (10/1/11-3/31/12) 10-50MM | 50-100MM | 100-250MM | | | |
| **NUMBER OF STATEMENTS** | 38 | 39 | 26 | 15 | 3 | | | 226 | 188 |
| | % | % | % | % | % | % | | % | % |
| **ASSETS** | | | | | | | | | |
| Cash & Equivalents | 13.8 | 8.8 | 8.9 | 8.8 | | | | 9.0 | 9.8 |
| Trade Receivables (net) | 6.1 | 11.0 | 10.9 | 4.1 | | | | 3.6 | 5.3 |
| Inventory | 8.0 | 6.3 | 7.5 | 6.5 | | | | 2.7 | 4.3 |
| All Other Current | 1.2 | 4.3 | 2.9 | .9 | | | | 2.2 | 2.3 |
| Total Current | 29.1 | 30.5 | 30.3 | 20.2 | | | | 17.4 | 21.6 |
| Fixed Assets (net) | 49.8 | 44.1 | 42.8 | 48.6 | | | | 45.5 | 45.0 |
| Intangibles (net) | 12.3 | 10.0 | 17.2 | 22.1 | | | | 24.3 | 21.3 |
| All Other Non-Current | 8.7 | 15.4 | 9.7 | 9.1 | | | | 12.7 | 12.1 |
| Total | 100.0 | 100.0 | 100.0 | 100.0 | | | | 100.0 | 100.0 |
| **LIABILITIES** | | | | | | | | | |
| Notes Payable-Short Term | 12.3 | 4.1 | 2.6 | 1.9 | | | | 1.8 | 3.1 |
| Cur. Mat.-L.T.D. | 6.7 | 4.6 | 6.1 | 8.3 | | | | 6.7 | 6.1 |
| Trade Payables | 10.0 | 8.2 | 10.4 | 5.2 | | | | 5.0 | 6.5 |
| Income Taxes Payable | .0 | .0 | .3 | .0 | | | | .1 | .1 |
| All Other Current | 44.0 | 10.1 | 3.9 | 6.0 | | | | 12.6 | 18.7 |
| Total Current | 73.0 | 27.1 | 23.3 | 21.4 | | | | 26.2 | 34.5 |
| Long-Term Debt | 27.1 | 27.3 | 32.4 | 44.5 | | | | 46.1 | 35.8 |
| Deferred Taxes | .0 | .1 | .0 | .0 | | | | .1 | .0 |
| All Other Non-Current | 26.8 | 5.7 | 14.5 | 4.8 | | | | 14.5 | 14.4 |
| Net Worth | -26.9 | 39.8 | 29.8 | 29.2 | | | | 13.1 | 15.2 |
| Total Liabilities & Net Worth | 100.0 | 100.0 | 100.0 | 100.0 | | | | 100.0 | 100.0 |
| **INCOME DATA** | | | | | | | | | |
| Net Sales | 100.0 | 100.0 | 100.0 | 100.0 | | | | 100.0 | 100.0 |
| Gross Profit | 56.7 | 50.2 | 42.3 | 47.7 | | | | 40.1 | 43.9 |
| Operating Expenses | 53.0 | 45.7 | 35.4 | 39.2 | | | | 35.1 | 39.6 |
| Operating Profit | 3.6 | 4.6 | 6.9 | 8.5 | | | | 5.0 | 4.4 |
| All Other Expenses (net) | .2 | .4 | .5 | 2.4 | | | | 1.9 | 1.5 |
| Profit Before Taxes | 3.4 | 4.2 | 6.4 | 6.1 | | | | 3.0 | 2.9 |
| **RATIOS** | | | | | | | | | |
| Current | 2.1 | 2.3 | 2.1 | 1.8 | | | | 1.5 | 1.6 |
| | .4 | 1.3 | 1.2 | .7 | | | | .6 | .6 |
| | .2 | .5 | .6 | .4 | | | | .3 | .2 |
| Quick | 1.4 | 1.4 | 1.3 | .9 | | | | 1.2 | 1.3 |
| | .3 | .8 | .8 | .4 | | | (225) | .4  (187) | .4 |
| | .1 | .3 | .5 | .3 | | | | .1 | .1 |
| Sales/Receivables | 0 UND | 0 UND | 0 UND | 0 968.7 | | | | 0 UND | 0 UND |
| | 0 UND | 1 272.7 | 6 59.1 | 1 267.9 | | | | 1 521.4 | 1 675.0 |
| | 3 115.7 | 24 15.1 | 26 14.2 | 24 15.3 | | | | 5 77.9 | 8 47.6 |
| Cost of Sales/Inventory | 3 109.7 | 2 151.0 | 3 110.1 | 4 85.6 | | | | 2 171.9 | 2 160.8 |
| | 7 49.5 | 5 73.3 | 8 48.0 | 11 33.8 | | | | 3 104.6 | 4 89.2 |
| | 13 29.1 | 20 17.9 | 30 12.2 | 28 13.1 | | | | 6 62.1 | 10 36.8 |
| Cost of Sales/Payables | 0 UND | 0 755.0 | 6 57.3 | 7 54.3 | | | | 1 260.7 | 1 571.6 |
| | 4 85.8 | 10 37.3 | 19 19.5 | 14 26.0 | | | | 6 58.3 | 7 54.2 |
| | 19 19.2 | 25 14.8 | 35 10.3 | 36 10.0 | | | | 18 20.1 | 16 23.1 |
| Sales/Working Capital | 27.5 | 16.2 | 13.3 | 16.9 | | | | 42.0 | 40.2 |
| | -31.5 | 157.0 | 65.3 | -35.9 | | | | -34.1 | -36.8 |
| | -7.6 | -28.9 | -37.5 | -13.6 | | | | -10.0 | -9.2 |
| EBIT/Interest | 6.0 | 17.8 | 36.8 | 9.6 | | | | 7.0 | 7.3 |
| | (23) 3.4 | (33) 4.1 | 4.7 | (14) 5.8 | | | (205) | 2.6  (168) | 2.6 |
| | -.5 | 1.6 | 1.7 | 1.0 | | | | .7 | .5 |
| Net Profit + Depr., Dep., Amort./Cur. Mat. L/T/D | | | | | | | | 4.3 | |
| | | | | | | | (12) | 1.2 | |
| | | | | | | | | .8 | |
| Fixed/Worth | .4 | .5 | .9 | 1.6 | | | | 1.8 | 1.2 |
| | 6.3 | 1.3 | 1.5 | 12.7 | | | | -11.1 | 7.4 |
| | -.5 | -30.4 | -11.9 | -2.4 | | | | -.8 | -1.4 |
| Debt/Worth | .4 | .5 | .6 | 1.5 | | | | 2.1 | 1.7 |
| | 14.9 | 1.3 | 1.7 | 35.6 | | | | -17.0 | 17.9 |
| | -1.8 | -41.9 | -15.3 | -5.5 | | | | -2.3 | -2.9 |
| % Profit Before Taxes/Tangible Net Worth | 63.9 | 84.4 | 76.3 | | | | | 102.4 | 91.6 |
| | (20) 25.0 | (29) 31.7 | (19) 28.9 | | | | (101) | 54.8  (103) | 43.8 |
| | .8 | 5.7 | 16.1 | | | | | 16.9 | 10.0 |
| % Profit Before Taxes/Total Assets | 25.9 | 22.3 | 23.9 | 20.7 | | | | 19.8 | 18.8 |
| | 9.7 | 11.5 | 7.8 | 11.1 | | | | 6.5 | 6.8 |
| | 1.6 | 2.1 | 3.3 | .3 | | | | -1.5 | -2.6 |
| Sales/Net Fixed Assets | 37.1 | 14.8 | 11.7 | 8.6 | | | | 8.8 | 10.5 |
| | 10.1 | 6.8 | 5.5 | 4.0 | | | | 5.4 | 6.1 |
| | 4.7 | 4.2 | 3.5 | 2.7 | | | | 3.0 | 3.3 |
| Sales/Total Assets | 5.7 | 4.3 | 3.2 | 2.4 | | | | 3.3 | 3.5 |
| | 4.4 | 3.3 | 2.5 | 1.9 | | | | 2.1 | 2.4 |
| | 3.3 | 2.1 | 1.6 | 1.5 | | | | 1.4 | 1.6 |
| % Depr., Dep., Amort./Sales | 1.2 | 1.3 | 1.5 | 2.9 | | | | 2.3 | 2.0 |
| | (29) 2.0 | (30) 2.2 | (25) 3.1 | (14) 3.4 | | | (212) | 3.9  (164) | 3.7 |
| | 4.3 | 4.1 | 5.5 | 4.6 | | | | 5.7 | 5.6 |
| % Officers', Directors' Owners' Comp/Sales | 1.4 | 1.6 | 2.9 | | | | | 1.8 | 1.7 |
| | (21) 3.7 | (16) 4.0 | (13) 3.9 | | | | (112) | 3.5  (106) | 3.4 |
| | 5.5 | 8.3 | 5.4 | | | | | 6.7 | 5.5 |
| Net Sales ($) | 48987M | 147325M | 279216M | 548403M | 312515M | | | 2565633M | 2097482M |
| Total Assets ($) | 10150M | 42745M | 105768M | 292972M | 182242M | | | 1535478M | 936112M |

M = $ thousand    MM = $ million
See Pages 9 through 22 for Explanation of Ratios and Data

## Comparative Historical Data

## Current Data Sorted by Sales

| | | | Type of Statement | | | | | | |
|---|---|---|---|---|---|---|---|---|---|
| 8 | 4 | 1 | Unqualified | | | | | 4 | 1 |
| 9 | 6 | 6 | Reviewed | | | | | 5 | 2 |
| 69 | 36 | 41 | Compiled | 5 | 11 | 6 | 10 | 2 | 4 |
| 35 | 33 | 37 | Tax Returns | 9 | 18 | 4 | 3 | 2 | 1 |
| 41 | 32 | 36 | Other | 7 | 5 | 7 | 5 | 4 | 8 |
| 4/1/09-3/31/10 ALL | 4/1/10-3/31/11 ALL | 4/1/11-3/31/12 ALL | | 11 (4/1-9/30/11) | | | 110 (10/1/11-3/31/12) | | |
| | | | | 0-1MM | 1-3MM | 3-5MM | 5-10MM | 10-25MM | 25MM & OVER |
| 162 | 111 | 121 | NUMBER OF STATEMENTS | 21 | 34 | 17 | 18 | 15 | 16 |
| % | % | % | ASSETS | % | % | % | % | % | % |
| 12.8 | 11.8 | 10.4 | Cash & Equivalents | 16.9 | 8.4 | 7.8 | 9.1 | 13.2 | 7.9 |
| 6.6 | 8.6 | 8.6 | Trade Receivables (net) | 6.0 | 5.7 | 11.0 | 11.8 | 14.2 | 6.8 |
| 5.3 | 6.0 | 7.3 | Inventory | 4.9 | 8.1 | 5.7 | 7.4 | 9.5 | 8.2 |
| 2.2 | 1.9 | 2.6 | All Other Current | .2 | 4.2 | .7 | 2.4 | 6.0 | 1.2 |
| 26.9 | 28.3 | 28.9 | Total Current | 28.1 | 26.3 | 25.2 | 30.7 | 42.9 | 24.1 |
| 43.9 | 46.5 | 45.9 | Fixed Assets (net) | 50.1 | 45.6 | 46.4 | 48.4 | 37.7 | 45.5 |
| 18.7 | 14.2 | 14.1 | Intangibles (net) | 11.2 | 17.1 | 7.6 | 11.6 | 14.6 | 21.0 |
| 10.5 | 11.0 | 11.1 | All Other Non-Current | 10.7 | 11.0 | 20.8 | 9.3 | 4.8 | 9.5 |
| 100.0 | 100.0 | 100.0 | Total | 100.0 | 100.0 | 100.0 | 100.0 | 100.0 | 100.0 |
| | | | LIABILITIES | | | | | | |
| 4.2 | 5.5 | 6.0 | Notes Payable-Short Term | 17.7 | 5.5 | 3.4 | 3.8 | 2.0 | .6 |
| 7.3 | 6.0 | 6.0 | Cur. Mat.-L.T.D. | 6.1 | 6.1 | 4.0 | 6.0 | 6.3 | 7.5 |
| 7.3 | 10.0 | 8.9 | Trade Payables | 10.6 | 6.6 | 6.4 | 9.0 | 13.9 | 9.7 |
| .1 | .2 | .1 | Income Taxes Payable | .1 | .0 | .1 | .0 | .1 | .5 |
| 19.7 | 8.1 | 18.9 | All Other Current | 44.6 | 25.1 | 12.4 | 5.3 | 6.4 | 6.2 |
| 38.6 | 29.8 | 39.9 | Total Current | 79.0 | 43.2 | 26.3 | 24.1 | 28.6 | 24.4 |
| 35.2 | 32.6 | 30.2 | Long-Term Debt | 21.7 | 37.5 | 23.2 | 29.4 | 22.4 | 41.1 |
| .0 | .2 | .0 | Deferred Taxes | .0 | .1 | .0 | .0 | .0 | .1 |
| 11.4 | 10.5 | 14.6 | All Other Non-Current | 34.8 | 10.8 | 9.9 | 2.8 | 3.1 | 25.1 |
| 14.7 | 26.9 | 15.3 | Net Worth | -35.6 | 8.4 | 40.7 | 43.7 | 45.9 | 9.3 |
| 100.0 | 100.0 | 100.0 | Total Liabilities & Net Worth | 100.0 | 100.0 | 100.0 | 100.0 | 100.0 | 100.0 |
| | | | INCOME DATA | | | | | | |
| 100.0 | 100.0 | 100.0 | Net Sales | 100.0 | 100.0 | 100.0 | 100.0 | 100.0 | 100.0 |
| 45.3 | 45.7 | 49.7 | Gross Profit | 61.8 | 54.0 | 50.0 | 43.4 | 38.6 | 41.7 |
| 38.7 | 41.1 | 44.5 | Operating Expenses | 56.9 | 49.6 | 45.3 | 39.7 | 30.5 | 35.2 |
| 6.6 | 4.6 | 5.2 | Operating Profit | 4.9 | 4.5 | 4.8 | 3.7 | 8.1 | 6.5 |
| 1.5 | 1.0 | .6 | All Other Expenses (net) | .4 | .5 | .5 | .5 | -.1 | 2.3 |
| 5.1 | 3.6 | 4.6 | Profit Before Taxes | 4.5 | 4.0 | 4.3 | 3.2 | 8.2 | 4.2 |
| | | | RATIOS | | | | | | |
| 1.6 | 1.8 | 2.1 | | 1.8 | 2.5 | 1.9 | 2.2 | 2.6 | 1.7 |
| .8 | 1.0 | .9 | Current | .3 | .8 | 1.3 | 1.4 | 1.3 | .7 |
| .3 | .4 | .3 | | .2 | .2 | .8 | .7 | .8 | .3 |
| 1.1 | 1.4 | 1.3 | | 1.3 | 1.6 | 1.2 | 1.5 | 1.5 | .9 |
| .5 (110) | .7 | .6 | Quick | .3 | .4 | .8 | .9 | .8 | .5 |
| .1 | .2 | .2 | | .1 | .1 | .5 | .6 | .4 | .3 |
| 0 UND | 0 999.8 | 0 UND | | 0 UND | 0 UND | 0 UND | 1 411.7 | 0 UND | 1 531.3 |
| 1 468.9 | 2 172.3 | 1 279.4 | Sales/Receivables | 0 UND | 0 UND | 2 196.8 | 7 53.5 | 10 38.0 | 4 86.8 |
| 13 27.2 | 17 21.0 | 20 18.6 | | 2 232.6 | 6 65.9 | 24 15.3 | 26 14.1 | 26 14.2 | 26 14.0 |
| 2 154.4 | 3 114.4 | 3 104.5 | | 5 79.7 | 2 189.4 | 2 177.1 | 3 139.5 | 4 90.2 | 5 80.2 |
| 4 81.5 | 8 47.1 | 7 50.5 | Cost of Sales/Inventory | 10 34.9 | 5 78.7 | 6 59.4 | 6 63.0 | 8 45.1 | 13 27.5 |
| 12 31.4 | 20 18.3 | 19 19.7 | | 13 27.7 | 19 19.0 | 20 18.6 | 29 12.8 | 30 12.0 | 28 13.0 |
| 1 258.9 | 5 74.3 | 0 877.4 | | 0 UND | 0 UND | 0 792.6 | 1 427.4 | 9 41.7 | 7 49.2 |
| 9 42.4 | 13 28.4 | 12 29.5 | Cost of Sales/Payables | 5 77.5 | 9 41.1 | 10 37.3 | 14 25.2 | 19 19.0 | 33 11.2 |
| 23 15.8 | 35 10.5 | 30 12.0 | | 30 12.2 | 18 20.2 | 25 14.4 | 29 12.5 | 32 11.5 | 46 7.9 |
| 22.5 | 21.2 | 18.4 | | 67.9 | 13.4 | 47.0 | 14.8 | 12.6 | 32.0 |
| -38.1 | 999.8 | -179.3 | Sales/Working Capital | -28.4 | -159.1 | 158.9 | 40.0 | 20.1 | -29.2 |
| -11.3 | -14.7 | -15.2 | | -5.4 | -11.6 | -49.1 | -34.5 | -75.1 | -14.1 |
| 11.9 | 13.2 | 14.2 | | 7.0 | 7.0 | 18.7 | 11.7 | 65.0 | 6.9 |
| (153) 4.4 | (102) 5.4 | (98) 4.3 | EBIT/Interest | (11) 3.8 | (27) 2.8 | (14) 7.5 | (17) 3.5 | 10.4 | (14) 4.7 |
| 1.7 | 1.4 | 1.5 | | 1.5 | 1.4 | 1.8 | 1.1 | 5.8 | 1.0 |
| 6.0 | 3.5 | | Net Profit + Depr., Dep., Amort./Cur. Mat. L/T/D | | | | | | |
| (23) 2.5 | (13) 1.5 | | | | | | | | |
| 1.4 | .1 | | | | | | | | |
| 1.1 | 1.0 | .8 | | .7 | .6 | .5 | .9 | .4 | 1.2 |
| 7.6 | 2.3 | 1.7 | Fixed/Worth | -8.5 | 5.0 | 1.3 | 1.3 | 1.6 | 22.3 |
| -1.4 | -4.1 | -2.4 | | -.6 | -1.5 | 28.1 | 5.9 | 12.7 | -1.0 |
| 1.4 | 1.0 | .6 | | .5 | .5 | .5 | .5 | .5 | 1.6 |
| 19.7 | 3.1 | 2.3 | Debt/Worth | -21.0 | 6.4 | 1.2 | 1.4 | 1.8 | 27.8 |
| -3.4 | -7.1 | -4.7 | | -1.8 | -2.9 | 41.1 | 14.5 | 35.6 | -3.1 |
| 122.3 | 89.7 | 74.6 | | | 66.3 | 98.3 | 44.4 | 150.8 | |
| (92) 54.3 | (78) 43.8 | (79) 28.2 | % Profit Before Taxes/Tangible Net Worth | (20) 27.1 | (14) 32.2 | (15) 16.1 | (12) 56.7 | | |
| 20.7 | 8.4 | 4.8 | | -.4 | 16.9 | 1.9 | 23.9 | | |
| 25.3 | 23.1 | 22.7 | | 24.6 | 23.9 | 21.3 | 18.3 | 34.3 | 19.5 |
| 11.4 | 9.9 | 8.8 | % Profit Before Taxes/Total Assets | 13.0 | 7.2 | 11.8 | 7.7 | 17.1 | 3.9 |
| 2.5 | .5 | 1.8 | | 5.6 | -1.2 | 2.9 | .7 | 4.7 | -.9 |
| 13.5 | 11.7 | 15.2 | | 30.3 | 20.8 | 17.2 | 10.4 | 22.0 | 8.9 |
| 6.8 | 6.2 | 6.3 | Sales/Net Fixed Assets | 6.6 | 6.7 | 6.6 | 5.8 | 6.3 | 5.7 |
| 3.7 | 3.5 | 3.9 | | 3.5 | 4.4 | 4.2 | 3.8 | 4.1 | 2.9 |
| 4.0 | 3.6 | 4.4 | | 4.6 | 4.4 | 6.4 | 4.2 | 5.5 | 2.5 |
| 2.6 | 2.6 | 2.9 | Sales/Total Assets | 4.3 | 3.0 | 4.2 | 3.0 | 2.6 | 2.0 |
| 1.7 | 1.8 | 2.0 | | 2.5 | 2.1 | 2.0 | 2.2 | 1.8 | 1.6 |
| 2.2 | 1.8 | 1.5 | | 1.3 | 1.6 | 1.0 | 1.4 | 1.0 | 3.3 |
| (142) 3.6 | (95) 3.1 | (101) 2.6 | % Depr., Dep., Amort./Sales | (15) 2.0 | (29) 3.0 | (14) 2.0 | (14) 2.5 | (14) 2.6 | (15) 4.4 |
| 4.6 | 5.0 | 4.4 | | 4.2 | 5.0 | 3.0 | 4.6 | 3.6 | 5.3 |
| 1.7 | 1.3 | 1.8 | | | 1.5 | | | | |
| (65) 3.5 | (49) 3.9 | (57) 3.9 | % Officers', Directors' Owners' Comp/Sales | (20) 3.5 | | | | | |
| 5.7 | 6.5 | 5.7 | | | 5.8 | | | | |
| 1839260M | 2681588M | 1336446M | Net Sales ($) | 14207M | 59986M | 69030M | 116189M | 244989M | 832045M |
| 803097M | 1016464M | 633877M | Total Assets ($) | 5458M | 23834M | 23413M | 41131M | 97341M | 442700M |

M = $ thousand     MM = $ million
See Pages 9 through 22 for Explanation of Ratios and Data

**Current Data Sorted by Assets**     **Comparative Historical Data**

| | 0-500M | 500M-2MM | 2-10MM | 10-50MM | 50-100MM | 100-250MM | Type of Statement | 4/1/07-3/31/08 ALL | 4/1/08-3/31/09 ALL |
|---|---|---|---|---|---|---|---|---|---|
| | | | 6 | 17 | 6 | 3 | Unqualified | 42 | 49 |
| | | 5 | 17 | 22 | | | Reviewed | 34 | 35 |
| | 4 | 9 | 13 | 2 | | | Compiled | 23 | 25 |
| | 9 | 10 | 10 | | | | Tax Returns | 27 | 23 |
| | 3 | 9 | 23 | | 8 | 11 | Other | 67 | 70 |
| | | 32 (4/1-9/30/11) | | 175 (10/1/11-3/31/12) | | | | | |
| **NUMBER OF STATEMENTS** | 16 | 33 | 69 | 61 | 14 | 14 | | 193 | 202 |
| | % | % | % | % | % | % | **ASSETS** | % | % |
| | 11.1 | 10.6 | 7.3 | 8.9 | 8.3 | 6.9 | Cash & Equivalents | 9.8 | 7.5 |
| | 18.2 | 21.7 | 22.8 | 15.7 | 14.8 | 11.4 | Trade Receivables (net) | 17.0 | 18.3 |
| | 9.0 | 13.4 | 14.8 | 9.8 | 12.3 | 7.0 | Inventory | 10.2 | 11.6 |
| | 1.8 | 3.5 | 2.3 | 1.0 | 1.9 | 13.8 | All Other Current | 2.2 | 2.5 |
| | 40.1 | 49.2 | 47.1 | 35.3 | 37.3 | 39.1 | Total Current | 39.3 | 39.8 |
| | 42.7 | 40.4 | 42.1 | 50.4 | 47.3 | 35.9 | Fixed Assets (net) | 48.4 | 48.2 |
| | 11.7 | 5.7 | 3.4 | 5.9 | 8.7 | 14.0 | Intangibles (net) | 4.3 | 4.6 |
| | 5.4 | 4.7 | 7.4 | 8.5 | 6.7 | 11.0 | All Other Non-Current | 8.0 | 7.4 |
| | 100.0 | 100.0 | 100.0 | 100.0 | 100.0 | 100.0 | Total | 100.0 | 100.0 |
| | | | | | | | **LIABILITIES** | | |
| | 6.5 | 6.4 | 7.1 | 7.6 | 5.0 | 3.2 | Notes Payable-Short Term | 5.1 | 8.3 |
| | .0 | 5.8 | 5.3 | 5.9 | 2.1 | 3.0 | Cur. Mat.-L.T.D. | 5.7 | 4.2 |
| | 25.9 | 17.5 | 18.3 | 12.6 | 9.2 | 7.4 | Trade Payables | 14.8 | 14.5 |
| | .0 | .1 | .1 | .1 | .0 | .1 | Income Taxes Payable | .2 | .1 |
| | 12.1 | 18.6 | 8.5 | 6.1 | 11.7 | 10.3 | All Other Current | 8.6 | 8.7 |
| | 44.5 | 48.4 | 39.4 | 32.3 | 28.1 | 24.0 | Total Current | 34.4 | 35.8 |
| | 29.7 | 26.7 | 25.5 | 23.0 | 23.2 | 16.8 | Long-Term Debt | 28.0 | 27.6 |
| | .0 | .4 | .2 | .9 | 2.4 | 1.0 | Deferred Taxes | .7 | .6 |
| | 14.4 | 3.0 | 7.4 | 5.8 | 9.9 | 9.1 | All Other Non-Current | 10.2 | 8.6 |
| | 11.3 | 21.4 | 27.5 | 38.0 | 36.5 | 49.1 | Net Worth | 26.7 | 27.4 |
| | 100.0 | 100.0 | 100.0 | 100.0 | 100.0 | 100.0 | Total Liabilities & Net Worth | 100.0 | 100.0 |
| | | | | | | | **INCOME DATA** | | |
| | 100.0 | 100.0 | 100.0 | 100.0 | 100.0 | 100.0 | Net Sales | 100.0 | 100.0 |
| | 54.8 | 42.3 | 30.6 | 27.2 | 28.6 | 28.2 | Gross Profit | 36.5 | 31.8 |
| | 53.7 | 39.2 | 26.6 | 22.8 | 25.6 | 24.4 | Operating Expenses | 32.1 | 28.7 |
| | 1.1 | 3.1 | 4.0 | 4.3 | 3.0 | 3.8 | Operating Profit | 4.5 | 3.0 |
| | .1 | .9 | .4 | 1.2 | 1.4 | .1 | All Other Expenses (net) | 1.2 | 1.1 |
| | .9 | 2.2 | 3.5 | 3.1 | 1.6 | 3.7 | Profit Before Taxes | 3.3 | 1.9 |
| | | | | | | | **RATIOS** | | |
| | 2.2 | 2.1 | 2.0 | 1.9 | 1.7 | 3.1 | Current | 2.0 | 1.9 |
| | .7 | 1.2 | 1.2 | 1.2 | 1.2 | 1.5 | | 1.2 | 1.2 |
| | .5 | .8 | .9 | .8 | .9 | .8 | | .9 | .7 |
| | 1.8 | 1.7 | 1.2 | 1.5 | 1.1 | 1.4 | Quick | 1.3 | 1.2 |
| | .5 | .7 | .8 | .8 | .7 | .9 | | .8 | .7 |
| | .3 | .5 | .5 | .4 | .4 | .4 | | .5 | .4 |
| | 1  484.5 | 9  39.8 | 19  19.3 | 21  17.6 | 19  19.5 | 21  17.2 | Sales/Receivables | 16  22.7 | 16  22.2 |
| | 8  43.9 | 20  18.0 | 24  15.0 | 27  13.5 | 24  15.4 | 28  13.2 | | 25  14.9 | 24  15.3 |
| | 21  17.4 | 27  13.3 | 34  10.7 | 33  10.9 | 28  13.2 | 43  8.5 | | 34  10.6 | 31  11.9 |
| | 4  87.2 | 9  39.4 | 8  43.7 | 12  29.8 | 18  20.1 | 11  33.9 | Cost of Sales/Inventory | 10  37.7 | 9  42.0 |
| | 14  25.4 | 17  22.1 | 20  18.2 | 19  19.4 | 20  18.1 | 17  21.2 | | 19  19.7 | 18  19.8 |
| | 19  18.8 | 30  12.1 | 32  11.4 | 30  12.3 | 40  9.1 | 39  9.3 | | 31  11.6 | 30  12.2 |
| | 14  25.7 | 13  27.1 | 16  22.5 | 17  21.7 | 14  25.6 | 22  16.9 | Cost of Sales/Payables | 16  23.2 | 14  25.5 |
| | 37  9.8 | 23  15.7 | 24  15.5 | 28  13.2 | 24  15.3 | 28  13.1 | | 27  13.3 | 25  14.7 |
| | 65  5.6 | 39  9.3 | 41  8.9 | 42  8.7 | 34  10.7 | 37  9.9 | | 43  8.0 | 38  9.6 |
| | 29.2 | 13.5 | 11.7 | 13.0 | 10.0 | 3.9 | Sales/Working Capital | 12.0 | 14.0 |
| | -95.4 | 42.6 | 41.1 | 58.1 | 39.2 | 19.9 | | 38.4 | 60.3 |
| | -20.0 | -34.1 | -121.5 | -29.5 | -184.2 | -17.0 | | -49.6 | -24.2 |
| | 10.2 | 11.1 | 10.6 | 13.9 | 21.1 | 36.0 | EBIT/Interest | 8.7 | 6.9 |
| | (10) 2.7 | (31) 3.5 | (65) 5.0 | (58) 4.1 | .3 | (13) 6.7 | | (177) 2.9 | (190) 2.4 |
| | +6.4 | .3 | 1.8 | 1.3 | -.3 | 2.4 | | .9 | .3 |
| | | | 4.6 | 5.1 | | | Net Profit + Depr., Dep., | 5.6 | 3.5 |
| | | | (14) 2.9 | (26) 2.3 | | | Amort./Cur. Mat. L/T/D | (53) 2.4 | (58) 2.2 |
| | | | 1.0 | 1.4 | | | | 1.2 | .7 |
| | .7 | .6 | .8 | .9 | .8 | .6 | Fixed/Worth | .8 | .9 |
| | 1.9 | 1.6 | 1.5 | 1.6 | 1.9 | 1.2 | | 1.7 | 1.8 |
| | -1.5 | NM | 5.0 | 4.5 | 2.5 | NM | | 6.6 | 16.3 |
| | 1.3 | .9 | .8 | 1.0 | .7 | .5 | Debt/Worth | 1.1 | 1.1 |
| | 4.0 | 4.4 | 2.1 | 1.9 | 2.1 | 1.1 | | 2.1 | 2.3 |
| | -5.9 | NM | 8.1 | 4.6 | 3.5 | NM | | 12.4 | 24.7 |
| | 296.1 | 63.2 | 51.6 | 40.1 | 23.0 | 22.3 | % Profit Before Taxes/Tangible | 43.5 | 43.0 |
| | (10) 43.9 | (25) 17.9 | (54) 26.5 | (54) 17.7 | (12) .2 | (11) 15.0 | Net Worth | (155) 20.1 | (159) 15.7 |
| | 5.6 | -6.6 | 5.0 | 7.5 | -10.6 | 9.6 | | 3.7 | 4.4 |
| | 25.1 | 20.0 | 16.8 | 12.8 | 11.7 | 10.1 | % Profit Before Taxes/Total | 14.2 | 11.8 |
| | 6.0 | 3.6 | 8.3 | 6.9 | -1.9 | 6.1 | Assets | 5.4 | 4.6 |
| | -4.6 | -1.8 | 1.7 | .9 | -3.2 | -1.0 | | .2 | -1.9 |
| | 133.5 | 31.2 | 15.4 | 8.5 | 6.4 | 4.9 | Sales/Net Fixed Assets | 10.4 | 10.5 |
| | 16.9 | 13.2 | 7.5 | 4.2 | 4.7 | 3.5 | | 5.3 | 5.2 |
| | 5.3 | 5.4 | 4.2 | 2.6 | 3.2 | 2.7 | | 2.9 | 3.2 |
| | 7.9 | 5.9 | 4.1 | 2.7 | 2.9 | 1.7 | Sales/Total Assets | 3.6 | 3.9 |
| | 5.3 | 4.0 | 2.9 | 2.0 | 2.0 | 1.1 | | 2.5 | 2.6 |
| | 3.5 | 2.7 | 2.2 | 1.5 | 1.7 | .7 | | 1.6 | 1.8 |
| | .3 | .8 | 1.0 | 1.9 | 2.5 | 2.7 | % Depr., Dep., Amort./Sales | 1.9 | 1.6 |
| | (10) 1.3 | (22) 1.9 | (61) 2.3 | (59) 3.2 | (13) 2.5 | (12) 3.6 | | (170) 2.7 | (179) 2.9 |
| | 3.0 | 3.9 | 4.1 | 4.1 | 4.3 | 5.2 | | 4.8 | 4.4 |
| | | 1.3 | 1.5 | 1.4 | | | % Officers', Directors' | 1.4 | 1.1 |
| | (16) | 2.8 | (31) 2.6 | (13) 2.7 | | | Owners' Comp/Sales | (63) 3.5 | (67) 2.8 |
| | | 5.7 | 4.6 | 4.7 | | | | 5.7 | 5.0 |
| | 23690M | 176160M | 1069145M | 2879534M | 2480981M | 2703596M | Net Sales ($) | 7751334M | 9704262M |
| | 3931M | 39308M | 317269M | 1368556M | 1163898M | 2132199M | Total Assets ($) | 3794262M | 4459660M |

M = $ thousand     MM = $ million
See Pages 9 through 22 for Explanation of Ratios and Data

## Comparative Historical Data | Current Data Sorted by Sales

| | | | Type of Statement | | | | | | |
|---|---|---|---|---|---|---|---|---|---|
| 41 | 32 | 32 | Unqualified | | | | 1 | 4 | 27 |
| 51 | 42 | 44 | Reviewed | | 1 | 1 | 11 | 13 | 18 |
| 22 | 23 | 28 | Compiled | 1 | 3 | 7 | 6 | 8 | 3 |
| 24 | 17 | 29 | Tax Returns | 7 | 7 | 2 | 9 | 3 | 1 |
| 62 | 73 | 74 | Other | 2 | 4 | 1 | 17 | 13 | 37 |
| 4/1/09-3/31/10 ALL | 4/1/10-3/31/11 ALL | 4/1/11-3/31/12 ALL | | 0-1MM | 1-3MM | 3-5MM | 5-10MM | 10-25MM | 25MM & OVER |
| | | | | | 32 (4/1-9/30/11) | | 175 (10/1/11-3/31/12) | | |
| 200 | 187 | 207 | **NUMBER OF STATEMENTS** | 10 | 15 | 11 | 44 | 41 | 86 |
| % | % | % | **ASSETS** | % | % | % | % | % | % |
| 10.8 | 8.8 | 8.6 | Cash & Equivalents | 10.4 | 7.6 | 10.6 | 8.1 | 9.5 | 8.2 |
| 17.8 | 18.7 | 18.9 | Trade Receivables (net) | 7.5 | 22.2 | 22.6 | 21.2 | 21.2 | 16.9 |
| 10.7 | 11.5 | 11.9 | Inventory | 6.2 | 8.9 | 13.2 | 13.1 | 13.5 | 11.7 |
| 3.0 | 2.6 | 2.8 | All Other Current | .0 | 2.0 | .9 | 4.3 | 1.2 | 3.5 |
| 42.4 | 41.6 | 42.2 | Total Current | 24.2 | 40.8 | 47.4 | 46.7 | 45.3 | 40.2 |
| 44.6 | 44.1 | 44.2 | Fixed Assets (net) | 66.3 | 43.0 | 38.1 | 41.7 | 44.0 | 44.1 |
| 6.1 | 6.3 | 6.2 | Intangibles (net) | 7.9 | 11.2 | 9.3 | 3.7 | 3.9 | 7.2 |
| 7.0 | 8.0 | 7.3 | All Other Non-Current | 1.7 | 5.1 | 5.3 | 7.8 | 6.9 | 8.6 |
| 100.0 | 100.0 | 100.0 | Total | 100.0 | 100.0 | 100.0 | 100.0 | 100.0 | 100.0 |
| | | | **LIABILITIES** | | | | | | |
| 6.2 | 5.6 | 6.7 | Notes Payable-Short Term | 5.2 | 4.2 | 11.3 | 6.2 | 7.2 | 6.7 |
| 5.1 | 4.5 | 4.8 | Cur. Mat.-L.T.D. | .0 | 2.4 | 3.5 | 6.8 | 5.0 | 4.8 |
| 13.0 | 14.3 | 15.7 | Trade Payables | 18.6 | 18.3 | 13.5 | 14.8 | 19.3 | 14.0 |
| .2 | .3 | .1 | Income Taxes Payable | .0 | .0 | .2 | .1 | .2 | .1 |
| 7.5 | 10.0 | 10.0 | All Other Current | 8.3 | 6.1 | 15.8 | 16.6 | 7.7 | 7.9 |
| 31.9 | 34.8 | 37.3 | Total Current | 32.2 | 31.0 | 44.3 | 44.3 | 39.4 | 33.6 |
| 25.6 | 22.2 | 24.6 | Long-Term Debt | 42.8 | 47.4 | 20.5 | 23.3 | 21.6 | 21.0 |
| .6 | .6 | .6 | Deferred Taxes | .0 | .9 | .0 | .0 | .1 | 1.3 |
| 7.4 | 7.3 | 7.1 | All Other Non-Current | 23.1 | 1.8 | 4.7 | 2.6 | 9.7 | 7.5 |
| 34.4 | 35.2 | 30.4 | Net Worth | 1.9 | 18.9 | 30.4 | 29.7 | 29.2 | 36.6 |
| 100.0 | 100.0 | 100.0 | Total Liabilities & Net Worth | 100.0 | 100.0 | 100.0 | 100.0 | 100.0 | 100.0 |
| | | | **INCOME DATA** | | | | | | |
| 100.0 | 100.0 | 100.0 | Net Sales | 100.0 | 100.0 | 100.0 | 100.0 | 100.0 | 100.0 |
| 36.8 | 34.5 | 33.0 | Gross Profit | 59.9 | 44.6 | 45.6 | 33.1 | 31.3 | 27.0 |
| 30.7 | 29.5 | 29.4 | Operating Expenses | 62.7 | 40.4 | 44.6 | 29.8 | 26.5 | 22.8 |
| 6.1 | 5.1 | 3.6 | Operating Profit | -2.8 | 4.2 | 1.0 | 3.3 | 4.8 | 4.3 |
| .9 | .8 | .8 | All Other Expenses (net) | .9 | .5 | .8 | .7 | .6 | .9 |
| 5.3 | 4.2 | 2.9 | Profit Before Taxes | -3.7 | 3.7 | .1 | 2.5 | 4.2 | 3.4 |
| | | | **RATIOS** | | | | | | |
| 2.3 | 1.9 | 2.0 | Current | 1.6 | 2.8 | 2.5 | 2.2 | 1.7 | 1.8 |
| 1.4 | 1.3 | 1.2 | | .8 | 1.7 | 1.2 | 1.2 | 1.2 | 1.2 |
| 1.0 | .9 | .8 | | .4 | 1.1 | .6 | .8 | .9 | .8 |
| 1.5 | 1.3 | 1.3 | Quick | 1.3 | 1.9 | 1.5 | 1.2 | 1.2 | 1.4 |
| .9 | .8 | .8 | | .6 | 1.3 | .8 | .7 | .8 | .7 |
| .5 | .5 | .5 | | .3 | .6 | .5 | .5 | .5 | .4 |
| 16  22.1 | 18  20.4 | 16  22.6 | Sales/Receivables | 0  UND | 13  28.6 | 16  23.5 | 12  31.0 | 21  17.4 | 19  18.9 |
| 23  15.7 | 25  14.5 | 24  15.1 | | 4  85.7 | 16  23.2 | 21  17.1 | 24  15.1 | 26  14.3 | 25  14.4 |
| 32  11.5 | 34  10.6 | 32  11.5 | | 24  14.9 | 30  12.0 | 47  7.7 | 34  10.6 | 33  11.2 | 32  11.5 |
| 10  36.9 | 11  33.7 | 10  35.5 | Cost of Sales/Inventory | 9  42.6 | 3  119.0 | 15  24.8 | 6  59.6 | 10  37.1 | 13  28.4 |
| 19  19.6 | 20  18.2 | 18  20.2 | | 14  25.4 | 17  21.4 | 30  12.1 | 15  23.9 | 17  21.5 | 20  18.6 |
| 30  12.4 | 30  12.0 | 30  12.1 | | 19  19.0 | 26  14.3 | 47  7.8 | 31  11.6 | 30  12.2 | 30  12.1 |
| 15  24.2 | 15  24.0 | 16  22.3 | Cost of Sales/Payables | 21  17.5 | 16  22.3 | 5  73.8 | 12  30.2 | 21  17.1 | 17  21.9 |
| 25  14.7 | 27  13.5 | 27  13.7 | | 51  7.1 | 25  14.7 | 25  14.5 | 19  19.4 | 31  11.8 | 27  13.7 |
| 34  10.7 | 38  9.5 | 40  9.1 | | 73  5.0 | 40  9.1 | 54  6.8 | 35  10.4 | 45  8.2 | 37  9.8 |
| 10.9 | 11.8 | 12.4 | Sales/Working Capital | 29.7 | 15.8 | 7.1 | 11.7 | 16.9 | 11.7 |
| 30.8 | 34.8 | 46.3 | | -76.5 | 36.2 | 81.2 | 31.9 | 42.6 | 47.5 |
| -164.8 | -65.7 | -44.5 | | -22.7 | 134.5 | -16.0 | -64.2 | -54.1 | -32.1 |
| 13.6 | 13.6 | 11.2 | EBIT/Interest | | 11.5 | 11.1 | 8.0 | 18.8 | 18.4 |
| (183) 4.9 | (170) 4.4 | (191) 4.5 | | (13) 7.7 | 2.1 | (41) 3.6 | (37) 5.8 | (83) 5.1 | |
| 2.1 | 1.6 | .9 | | 1.1 | -.4 | .8 | 1.9 | 1.1 | |
| 4.9 | 4.9 | 4.7 | Net Profit + Depr., Dep., Amort./Cur. Mat. L/T/D | | | | | | 3.7 |
| (61) 2.9 | (59) 2.8 | (56) 2.2 | | | | | | | (34) 2.1 |
| 2.0 | 1.3 | 1.0 | | | | | | | 1.0 |
| .7 | .7 | .8 | Fixed/Worth | 1.1 | .9 | .5 | .6 | .8 | .8 |
| 1.6 | 1.4 | 1.5 | | 6.6 | 9.6 | 1.0 | 1.3 | 1.8 | 1.5 |
| 4.6 | 5.2 | 5.5 | | -1.5 | -1.6 | 5.5 | 3.9 | 4.9 | 3.6 |
| .9 | .9 | .9 | Debt/Worth | .2 | 2.2 | .4 | .8 | .9 | .8 |
| 1.9 | 1.8 | 2.1 | | 8.0 | 11.1 | 4.4 | 2.0 | 2.2 | 1.7 |
| 7.6 | 7.7 | 8.5 | | -5.3 | -5.4 | 6.7 | 6.0 | 5.3 | 7.5 |
| 66.5 | 48.8 | 46.5 | % Profit Before Taxes/Tangible Net Worth | | | | 44.0 | 70.5 | 38.6 |
| (170) 31.3 | (158) 24.5 | (166) 19.3 | | | | | (37) 19.2 | (34) 22.2 | (71) 18.2 |
| 10.1 | 7.0 | 5.2 | | | | | .9 | 9.4 | 7.3 |
| 20.5 | 17.9 | 15.4 | % Profit Before Taxes/Total Assets | 8.9 | 22.0 | 6.4 | 16.3 | 18.9 | 12.5 |
| 9.1 | 7.4 | 6.5 | | -4.4 | 10.9 | 3.4 | 5.7 | 8.3 | 7.0 |
| 3.1 | 1.6 | .0 | | -20.2 | .1 | -3.3 | .2 | 1.9 | .1 |
| 11.4 | 10.8 | 13.0 | Sales/Net Fixed Assets | 14.0 | 78.0 | 18.2 | 15.8 | 13.2 | 9.3 |
| 5.4 | 5.8 | 5.7 | | 4.3 | 8.1 | 5.7 | 10.0 | 6.7 | 5.0 |
| 3.4 | 3.5 | 3.4 | | 1.6 | 3.6 | 4.7 | 4.0 | 3.4 | 3.2 |
| 3.6 | 3.6 | 3.9 | Sales/Total Assets | 5.0 | 5.7 | 4.0 | 4.5 | 4.3 | 3.0 |
| 2.5 | 2.5 | 2.7 | | 2.7 | 3.9 | 2.7 | 2.9 | 2.8 | 2.2 |
| 1.7 | 1.6 | 1.8 | | 1.3 | 2.0 | 1.8 | 2.2 | 1.9 | 1.6 |
| 1.7 | 1.8 | 1.3 | % Depr., Dep., Amort./Sales | | .8 | | 1.1 | .9 | 1.8 |
| (177) 2.9 | (169) 2.9 | (177) 2.5 | | | (10) 2.4 | | (35) 2.5 | (38) 2.3 | (79) 2.8 |
| 4.3 | 4.3 | 4.1 | | | 5.0 | | 4.5 | 4.0 | 4.0 |
| 1.2 | 2.0 | 1.4 | % Officers', Directors' Owners' Comp/Sales | | | | 2.0 | 1.1 | 1.3 |
| (74) 3.2 | (67) 3.5 | (70) 2.7 | | | | | (19) 4.4 | (13) 1.7 | (16) 2.4 |
| 5.5 | 6.6 | 5.1 | | | | | 6.2 | 2.8 | 4.0 |
| 9790312M | 9173462M | 9333106M | Net Sales ($) | 6887M | 27858M | 39662M | 332157M | 712525M | 8214017M |
| 4669417M | 4837616M | 5025161M | Total Assets ($) | 3060M | 10725M | 15674M | 136506M | 324906M | 4534290M |

## Current Data Sorted by Assets

## Comparative Historical Data

| 0-500M | 500M-2MM | 2-10MM | 10-50MM | 50-100MM | 100-250MM | Type of Statement | 4/1/07-3/31/08 ALL | 4/1/08-3/31/09 ALL |
|---|---|---|---|---|---|---|---|---|
| | | | 5 | 1 | | Unqualified | 5 | 8 |
| | | 3 | 1 | | | Reviewed | 4 | 1 |
| | 1 | | 1 | | | Compiled | 3 | 6 |
| | | 1 | | | | Tax Returns | | 3 |
| 1 | 1 | 2 | 2 | 1 | 1 | Other | 9 | 12 |
| | | 2 (4/1-9/30/11) | | 19 (10/1/11-3/31/12) | | | | |
| 1 | 2 | 6 | 9 | 2 | 1 | **NUMBER OF STATEMENTS** | 21 | 30 |
| % | % | % | % | % | % | **ASSETS** | % | % |
| | | | | | | Cash & Equivalents | 6.6 | 13.6 |
| | | | | | | Trade Receivables (net) | 19.8 | 18.5 |
| | | | | | | Inventory | 17.3 | 18.9 |
| | | | | | | All Other Current | 1.1 | 3.5 |
| | | | | | | Total Current | 44.8 | 54.6 |
| | | | | | | Fixed Assets (net) | 38.4 | 36.5 |
| | | | | | | Intangibles (net) | 12.3 | 4.2 |
| | | | | | | All Other Non-Current | 4.5 | 4.6 |
| | | | | | | Total | 100.0 | 100.0 |
| | | | | | | **LIABILITIES** | | |
| | | | | | | Notes Payable-Short Term | 10.8 | 3.7 |
| | | | | | | Cur. Mat.-L.T.D. | 2.8 | 5.6 |
| | | | | | | Trade Payables | 13.7 | 16.3 |
| | | | | | | Income Taxes Payable | .1 | .0 |
| | | | | | | All Other Current | 7.9 | 10.7 |
| | | | | | | Total Current | 35.4 | 36.3 |
| | | | | | | Long-Term Debt | 18.9 | 22.0 |
| | | | | | | Deferred Taxes | .8 | .8 |
| | | | | | | All Other Non-Current | 10.7 | 4.1 |
| | | | | | | Net Worth | 34.2 | 37.0 |
| | | | | | | Total Liabilties & Net Worth | 100.0 | 100.0 |
| | | | | | | **INCOME DATA** | | |
| | | | | | | Net Sales | 100.0 | 100.0 |
| | | | | | | Gross Profit | 28.6 | 33.5 |
| | | | | | | Operating Expenses | 22.3 | 27.1 |
| | | | | | | Operating Profit | 6.2 | 6.5 |
| | | | | | | All Other Expenses (net) | .9 | 1.0 |
| | | | | | | Profit Before Taxes | 5.4 | 5.5 |
| | | | | | | **RATIOS** | | |
| | | | | | | Current | 1.8 | 3.8 |
| | | | | | | | 1.3 | 1.9 |
| | | | | | | | .9 | .9 |
| | | | | | | Quick | 1.2 | 2.1 |
| | | | | | | | .7 | 1.2 |
| | | | | | | | .4 | .4 |
| | | | | | | Sales/Receivables | 24   14.9 | 18   20.4 |
| | | | | | | | 29   12.4 | 25   14.6 |
| | | | | | | | 38   9.6 | 33   11.2 |
| | | | | | | Cost of Sales/Inventory | 23   16.2 | 18   20.0 |
| | | | | | | | 42   8.6 | 30   12.0 |
| | | | | | | | 55   6.6 | 59   6.2 |
| | | | | | | Cost of Sales/Payables | 17   21.8 | 17   22.0 |
| | | | | | | | 30   12.3 | 22   16.7 |
| | | | | | | | 38   9.5 | 37   9.8 |
| | | | | | | Sales/Working Capital | 8.7 | 7.1 |
| | | | | | | | 23.4 | 13.8 |
| | | | | | | | -39.0 | -182.5 |
| | | | | | | EBIT/Interest | 14.3 | 17.3 |
| | | | | | | | (20) 4.0 | (23) 4.4 |
| | | | | | | | 1.4 | 2.0 |
| | | | | | | Net Profit + Depr., Dep., Amort./Cur. Mat. L/T/D | | |
| | | | | | | Fixed/Worth | .5 | .4 |
| | | | | | | | 1.1 | .7 |
| | | | | | | | 2.0 | 3.7 |
| | | | | | | Debt/Worth | .8 | .5 |
| | | | | | | | 1.4 | 1.1 |
| | | | | | | | NM | 5.0 |
| | | | | | | % Profit Before Taxes/Tangible Net Worth | 47.2 | 62.0 |
| | | | | | | | (16) 25.5 | (24) 29.1 |
| | | | | | | | 7.0 | 8.6 |
| | | | | | | % Profit Before Taxes/Total Assets | 15.8 | 27.0 |
| | | | | | | | 9.5 | 14.8 |
| | | | | | | | 2.0 | 1.7 |
| | | | | | | Sales/Net Fixed Assets | 12.3 | 23.8 |
| | | | | | | | 6.7 | 7.5 |
| | | | | | | | 3.0 | 3.9 |
| | | | | | | Sales/Total Assets | 3.0 | 4.0 |
| | | | | | | | 2.4 | 2.8 |
| | | | | | | | 1.4 | 1.8 |
| | | | | | | % Depr., Dep., Amort./Sales | 1.5 | 1.0 |
| | | | | | | | (19) 2.6 | (26) 2.1 |
| | | | | | | | 4.3 | 3.5 |
| | | | | | | % Officers', Directors' Owners' Comp/Sales | | |
| 1520M | 13687M | 74497M | 353152M | 180443M | 459019M | Net Sales ($) | 1517108M | 1311106M |
| 334M | 2369M | 28685M | 202380M | 159714M | 117221M | Total Assets ($) | 681787M | 443329M |

M = $ thousand    MM = $ million
See Pages 9 through 22 for Explanation of Ratios and Data

## Comparative Historical Data        Current Data Sorted by Sales

| Type of Statement | | | | | | | | | |
|---|---|---|---|---|---|---|---|---|---|
| | 3 | 7 | 6 | | | | | | 3 |
| Unqualified | | | | | | | | 3 | |
| Reviewed | 2 | 3 | 4 | | | 2 | | | 2 |
| | | | | | 2 | | | | 2 |
| Compiled | 4 | 5 | 3 | | | | | 2 | 1 |
| Tax Returns | 3 | 3 | | | | | | | |
| Other | 14 | 14 | 8 | | 2 | 1 | 1 | | 4 |

| | 4/1/09-3/31/10 ALL | 4/1/10-3/31/11 ALL | 4/1/11-3/31/12 ALL | 0-1MM | 1-3MM | 3-5MM | 5-10MM | 10-25MM | 25MM & OVER |
|---|---|---|---|---|---|---|---|---|---|
| NUMBER OF STATEMENTS | 26 | 32 | 21 | | 2 | 3 | 1 | 5 | 10 |
| | % | % | % | % | % | % | % | % | % |
| **ASSETS** | | | | | | | | | |
| Cash & Equivalents | 10.7 | 12.5 | 9.2 | | | | | | 10.9 |
| Trade Receivables (net) | 18.0 | 19.0 | 21.1 | | | | | | 21.1 |
| Inventory | 16.5 | 16.4 | 20.2 | | | | | | 21.2 |
| All Other Current | .8 | 1.6 | 2.4 | | | | | | 2.2 |
| Total Current | 45.9 | 49.5 | 52.8 | | | | | | 55.5 |
| Fixed Assets (net) | 40.7 | 40.6 | 38.1 | | | | | | 38.7 |
| Intangibles (net) | 9.9 | 4.3 | 6.1 | | | | | | 3.2 |
| All Other Non-Current | 3.5 | 5.6 | 3.0 | | | | | | 2.6 |
| Total | 100.0 | 100.0 | 100.0 | | | | | | 100.0 |
| **LIABILITIES** | | | | | | | | | |
| Notes Payable-Short Term | 4.2 | 7.3 | 4.5 | | | | | | 1.1 |
| Cur. Mat.-L.T.D. | 3.5 | 3.5 | 3.4 | | | | | | 3.8 |
| Trade Payables | 13.6 | 12.5 | 17.1 | | | | | | 17.8 |
| Income Taxes Payable | .0 | .1 | .0 | | | | | | .0 |
| All Other Current | 7.7 | 6.5 | 10.1 | | | | | | 7.6 |
| Total Current | 29.0 | 29.9 | 35.1 | | | | | | 30.4 |
| Long-Term Debt | 19.4 | 22.6 | 18.7 | | | | | | 9.3 |
| Deferred Taxes | .3 | .9 | .7 | | | | | | 1.4 |
| All Other Non-Current | 3.5 | 2.6 | 4.1 | | | | | | 7.9 |
| Net Worth | 47.8 | 44.0 | 41.4 | | | | | | 51.0 |
| Total Liabilties & Net Worth | 100.0 | 100.0 | 100.0 | | | | | | 100.0 |
| **INCOME DATA** | | | | | | | | | |
| Net Sales | 100.0 | 100.0 | 100.0 | | | | | | 100.0 |
| Gross Profit | 34.2 | 34.5 | 29.2 | | | | | | 31.1 |
| Operating Expenses | 25.8 | 31.1 | 24.1 | | | | | | 20.5 |
| Operating Profit | 8.4 | 3.4 | 5.2 | | | | | | 10.6 |
| All Other Expenses (net) | .3 | .7 | .8 | | | | | | .5 |
| Profit Before Taxes | 8.1 | 2.7 | 4.4 | | | | | | 10.1 |
| **RATIOS** | | | | | | | | | |
| Current | 2.2 | 3.0 | 1.9 | | | | | | 2.3 |
| | 1.6 | 1.6 | 1.5 | | | | | | 1.6 |
| | 1.2 | 1.1 | 1.2 | | | | | | 1.5 |
| Quick | 1.6 | 2.0 | 1.3 | | | | | | 1.5 |
| | 1.0 | 1.1 | .8 | | | | | | .9 |
| | .6 | .4 | .6 | | | | | | .7 |
| Sales/Receivables | 18  20.0 | 19  19.2 | 26  14.2 | | | | | | 26  13.9 |
| | 26  14.0 | 29  12.7 | 30  12.2 | | | | | | 30  12.3 |
| | 31  11.7 | 45  8.1 | 46  8.0 | | | | | | 43  8.5 |
| Cost of Sales/Inventory | 20  18.6 | 29  12.7 | 22  16.3 | | | | | | 32  11.4 |
| | 34  10.8 | 42  8.6 | 51  7.2 | | | | | | 52  7.0 |
| | 52  7.0 | 61  6.0 | 64  5.7 | | | | | | 70  5.2 |
| Cost of Sales/Payables | 20  17.9 | 16  22.6 | 24  15.1 | | | | | | 26  14.3 |
| | 26  14.0 | 28  12.9 | 39  9.3 | | | | | | 35  10.5 |
| | 34  10.7 | 44  8.4 | 51  7.1 | | | | | | 54  6.7 |
| Sales/Working Capital | 8.4 | 5.4 | 7.7 | | | | | | 7.4 |
| | 19.3 | 15.0 | 12.1 | | | | | | 11.1 |
| | 36.3 | 62.3 | 45.9 | | | | | | 17.8 |
| EBIT/Interest | 17.7 | 14.4 | 12.5 | | | | | | |
| | (24)  7.8 | (28)  5.1 | (18)  9.5 | | | | | | |
| | 1.7 | -.5 | -1.6 | | | | | | |
| Net Profit + Depr., Dep., Amort./Cur. Mat. L/T/D | | | | | | | | | |
| Fixed/Worth | .6 | .3 | .6 | | | | | | .2 |
| | 1.1 | 1.3 | 1.0 | | | | | | .8 |
| | 2.7 | 2.0 | 1.9 | | | | | | 1.4 |
| Debt/Worth | .8 | .7 | .9 | | | | | | .7 |
| | 1.4 | 1.4 | 1.4 | | | | | | 1.0 |
| | 4.0 | 2.7 | 2.7 | | | | | | 1.7 |
| % Profit Before Taxes/Tangible Net Worth | 77.1 | 47.4 | 55.2 | | | | | | 68.8 |
| | (23)  24.4 | (28)  21.8 | (19)  23.6 | | | | | | 34.8 |
| | 2.6 | 3.0 | -16.0 | | | | | | 21.9 |
| % Profit Before Taxes/Total Assets | 28.0 | 17.8 | 24.3 | | | | | | 34.1 |
| | 11.3 | 9.7 | 13.0 | | | | | | 18.3 |
| | 1.3 | .1 | -5.5 | | | | | | 12.7 |
| Sales/Net Fixed Assets | 12.3 | 16.2 | 29.7 | | | | | | 35.7 |
| | 6.7 | 5.5 | 5.5 | | | | | | 5.2 |
| | 4.2 | 1.8 | 2.1 | | | | | | 1.7 |
| Sales/Total Assets | 3.6 | 2.9 | 3.3 | | | | | | 3.3 |
| | 2.5 | 1.9 | 2.0 | | | | | | 2.5 |
| | 1.6 | 1.1 | 1.2 | | | | | | 1.2 |
| % Depr., Dep., Amort./Sales | 1.9 | 1.1 | .6 | | | | | | .5 |
| | (22)  2.4 | (31)  2.9 | (20)  2.2 | | | | | | 2.2 |
| | 4.6 | 5.9 | 4.5 | | | | | | 5.2 |
| % Officers', Directors' Owners' Comp/Sales | 2.2 | | | | | | | | |
| | (12)  3.5 | | | | | | | | |
| | 14.9 | | | | | | | | |
| Net Sales ($) | 1593332M | 774759M | 1082318M | | 4314M | 12388M | 6005M | 86779M | 972832M |
| Total Assets ($) | 627932M | 482995M | 510703M | | 1121M | 7765M | 2384M | 61124M | 438309M |

Note: For the current-data columns 0-1MM through 10-25MM, the assets, liabilities, income, and most ratio figures are marked **DATA NOT AVAILABLE**.

Period headers (current data): 2 (4/1-9/30/11) covers 0-1MM and 1-3MM; 19 (10/1/11-3/31/12) covers 3-5MM, 5-10MM, 10-25MM, and 25MM & OVER.

M = $ thousand    MM = $ million
See Pages 9 through 22 for Explanation of Ratios and Data

## Current Data Sorted by Assets  |  Comparative Historical Data

| 0-500M | 500M-2MM | 2-10MM | 10-50MM | 50-100MM | 100-250MM | | 4/1/07-3/31/08 ALL | 4/1/08-3/31/09 ALL |
|---|---|---|---|---|---|---|---|---|
| | | | | | | **Type of Statement** | | |
| | | | 1 | 3 | 4 | Unqualified | 4 | 5 |
| | 1 | 5 | 7 | | 1 | Reviewed | 6 | 5 |
| 1 | 1 | 1 | 1 | | | Compiled | 4 | 3 |
| 2 | 5 | 2 | 2 | | | Tax Returns | | 1 |
| 1 | 1 | 6 | 10 | 5 | 3 | Other | 4 | 10 |
| | 11 (4/1-9/30/11) | | 55 (10/1/11-3/31/12) | | | | | |
| | | | | | | | 4/1/07-3/31/08 | 4/1/08-3/31/09 |
| 4 | 8 | 15 | 23 | 8 | 8 | **NUMBER OF STATEMENTS** | 18 | 24 |
| % | % | % | % | % | % | **ASSETS** | % | % |
| | | 10.4 | 4.0 | | | Cash & Equivalents | 6.6 | 5.0 |
| | | 23.4 | 27.6 | | | Trade Receivables (net) | 24.2 | 30.6 |
| | | 32.2 | 26.4 | | | Inventory | 34.9 | 33.4 |
| | | 2.3 | 4.2 | | | All Other Current | 4.2 | 1.4 |
| | | 68.3 | 62.3 | | | Total Current | 69.8 | 70.5 |
| | | 24.7 | 28.9 | | | Fixed Assets (net) | 21.6 | 18.4 |
| | | .4 | 4.2 | | | Intangibles (net) | 1.0 | 3.9 |
| | | 6.6 | 4.5 | | | All Other Non-Current | 7.5 | 7.2 |
| | | 100.0 | 100.0 | | | Total | 100.0 | 100.0 |
| | | | | | | **LIABILITIES** | | |
| | | 9.1 | 16.7 | | | Notes Payable-Short Term | 14.6 | 19.8 |
| | | 3.4 | 4.7 | | | Cur. Mat.-L.T.D. | 1.1 | 1.8 |
| | | 23.0 | 17.0 | | | Trade Payables | 22.0 | 21.4 |
| | | .0 | .3 | | | Income Taxes Payable | .0 | .2 |
| | | 14.0 | 6.0 | | | All Other Current | 10.1 | 9.4 |
| | | 49.5 | 44.7 | | | Total Current | 47.8 | 52.7 |
| | | 7.0 | 16.5 | | | Long-Term Debt | 7.4 | 8.1 |
| | | .1 | 1.1 | | | Deferred Taxes | .1 | .1 |
| | | 4.9 | 10.0 | | | All Other Non-Current | 3.6 | 3.5 |
| | | 38.6 | 27.7 | | | Net Worth | 41.1 | 35.7 |
| | | 100.0 | 100.0 | | | Total Liabilities & Net Worth | 100.0 | 100.0 |
| | | | | | | **INCOME DATA** | | |
| | | 100.0 | 100.0 | | | Net Sales | 100.0 | 100.0 |
| | | 22.8 | 27.1 | | | Gross Profit | 23.0 | 25.0 |
| | | 20.0 | 18.3 | | | Operating Expenses | 15.1 | 17.0 |
| | | 2.8 | 8.7 | | | Operating Profit | 7.9 | 8.0 |
| | | .2 | 1.8 | | | All Other Expenses (net) | .9 | .9 |
| | | 2.6 | 6.9 | | | Profit Before Taxes | 7.0 | 7.1 |
| | | | | | | **RATIOS** | | |
| | | 2.6 | 2.2 | | | | 2.1 | 1.8 |
| | | 1.5 | 1.4 | | | Current | 1.4 | 1.5 |
| | | 1.2 | 1.0 | | | | 1.2 | 1.0 |
| | | 1.1 | 1.0 | | | | .7 | 1.3 |
| | | .7 | .7 | | | Quick | .6 | .6 |
| | | .5 | .6 | | | | .5 | .5 |
| | | 18  20.6 | 31  11.6 | | | | 24  15.4 | 27  13.7 |
| | | 26  14.3 | 43  8.4 | | | Sales/Receivables | 35  10.4 | 37  9.8 |
| | | 33  11.0 | 64  5.7 | | | | 41  8.8 | 53  6.9 |
| | | 31  11.9 | 33  11.2 | | | | 32  11.4 | 27  13.5 |
| | | 43  8.4 | 43  8.4 | | | Cost of Sales/Inventory | 58  6.3 | 47  7.8 |
| | | 49  7.4 | 73  5.0 | | | | 117  3.1 | 85  4.3 |
| | | 22  16.4 | 17  21.8 | | | | 16  22.2 | 15  24.7 |
| | | 36  10.0 | 35  10.4 | | | Cost of Sales/Payables | 30  12.2 | 28  13.1 |
| | | 45  8.1 | 66  5.5 | | | | 58  6.2 | 60  6.1 |
| | | 9.9 | 5.5 | | | | 5.5 | 6.6 |
| | | 18.7 | 13.1 | | | Sales/Working Capital | 12.1 | 10.9 |
| | | 29.5 | 152.3 | | | | 36.9 | 183.2 |
| | | 9.4 | 14.0 | | | | 11.1 | 38.1 |
| | | 3.0 (22) | 4.6 | | | EBIT/Interest | 5.9 (23) | 5.7 |
| | | 1.1 | 2.0 | | | | 2.3 | 2.1 |
| | | | | | | Net Profit + Depr., Dep., Amort./Cur. Mat. L/T/D | | |
| | | .3 | .7 | | | | .3 | .3 |
| | | .5 | .9 | | | Fixed/Worth | .5 | .5 |
| | | 1.0 | 3.6 | | | | .9 | 1.2 |
| | | .7 | 1.4 | | | | .9 | 1.1 |
| | | 1.2 | 3.8 | | | Debt/Worth | 1.4 | 1.8 |
| | | 3.8 | 11.7 | | | | 2.8 | 8.5 |
| | | 24.5 | 76.6 | | | | 64.3 | 61.9 |
| | | 11.1 (14) | 37.1 (21) | | | % Profit Before Taxes/Tangible Net Worth | 19.8 (20) | 39.8 |
| | | 1.5 | 17.5 | | | | 3.9 | 12.4 |
| | | 11.2 | 14.8 | | | | 14.6 | 25.6 |
| | | 3.6 | 8.0 | | | % Profit Before Taxes/Total Assets | 5.3 | 7.4 |
| | | .5 | 2.6 | | | | 2.2 | 1.7 |
| | | 61.3 | 30.5 | | | | 23.8 | 36.5 |
| | | 17.7 | 8.3 | | | Sales/Net Fixed Assets | 18.0 | 20.2 |
| | | 6.9 | 4.0 | | | | 8.0 | 10.2 |
| | | 4.7 | 3.2 | | | | 3.8 | 4.2 |
| | | 3.4 | 2.0 | | | Sales/Total Assets | 2.6 | 3.0 |
| | | 2.3 | 1.5 | | | | 1.8 | 1.8 |
| | | .8 | 1.0 | | | | .9 | 1.1 |
| | | 1.0 (13) | 1.6 (21) | | | % Depr., Dep., Amort./Sales | 1.2 (15) | 1.4 (20) |
| | | 1.7 | 4.5 | | | | 1.8 | 1.9 |
| | | | | | | % Officers', Directors', Owners' Comp/Sales | | .5 |
| | | | | | | | (11) | 1.4 |
| | | | | | | | | 3.4 |
| 6588M | 35592M | 283546M | 1302893M | 912288M | 2062792M | Net Sales ($) | 1745480M | 1142073M |
| 927M | 10021M | 82411M | 601434M | 487819M | 1160638M | Total Assets ($) | 837947M | 545620M |

© RMA 2012

M = $ thousand    MM = $ million
See Pages 9 through 22 for Explanation of Ratios and Data

## Comparative Historical Data    ·    Current Data Sorted by Sales

| | 4/1/09-3/31/10 ALL | 4/1/10-3/31/11 ALL | 4/1/11-3/31/12 ALL | Type of Statement | 0-1MM | 1-3MM | 3-5MM | 5-10MM | 10-25MM | 25MM & OVER |
|---|---|---|---|---|---|---|---|---|---|---|
| | 7 | 10 | 13 | Unqualified | | | | | 1 | 12 |
| | 7 | 9 | 14 | Reviewed | | 1 | | | 6 | 7 |
| | 7 | 2 | 4 | Compiled | | | 1 | 1 | 1 | 1 |
| | 1 | 3 | 9 | Tax Returns | 1 | 1 | 4 | 1 | 2 | |
| | 14 | 13 | 26 | Other | | 1 | 1 | 2 | 4 | 18 |
| | | | | | 11 (4/1-9/30/11) | | | 55 (10/1/11-3/31/12) | | |
| NUMBER OF STATEMENTS | 36 | 37 | 66 | | 1 | 3 | 6 | 4 | 14 | 38 |
| | % | % | % | **ASSETS** | % | % | % | % | % | % |
| Cash & Equivalents | 6.4 | 9.6 | 8.8 | | | | | | 6.7 | 7.4 |
| Trade Receivables (net) | 23.4 | 22.4 | 24.1 | | | | | | 20.5 | 24.3 |
| Inventory | 27.6 | 29.9 | 27.8 | | | | | | 22.7 | 31.1 |
| All Other Current | 5.3 | 1.8 | 5.4 | | | | | | 2.4 | 7.0 |
| Total Current | 62.7 | 63.7 | 66.1 | | | | | | 52.3 | 69.8 |
| Fixed Assets (net) | 27.7 | 25.6 | 25.3 | | | | | | 35.7 | 22.7 |
| Intangibles (net) | 4.8 | 4.7 | 3.6 | | | | | | 2.7 | 4.8 |
| All Other Non-Current | 4.8 | 5.9 | 4.9 | | | | | | 9.3 | 2.6 |
| Total | 100.0 | 100.0 | 100.0 | | | | | | 100.0 | 100.0 |
| | | | | **LIABILITIES** | | | | | | |
| Notes Payable-Short Term | 17.6 | 15.1 | 13.5 | | | | | | 9.9 | 13.1 |
| Cur. Mat.-L.T.D. | 1.8 | 2.4 | 3.1 | | | | | | 3.3 | 2.6 |
| Trade Payables | 17.2 | 17.9 | 20.2 | | | | | | 16.3 | 19.0 |
| Income Taxes Payable | .6 | .2 | .2 | | | | | | .3 | .2 |
| All Other Current | 9.5 | 9.4 | 10.3 | | | | | | 12.5 | 10.9 |
| Total Current | 46.7 | 45.0 | 47.3 | | | | | | 42.3 | 45.8 |
| Long-Term Debt | 14.1 | 20.2 | 13.3 | | | | | | 14.6 | 12.6 |
| Deferred Taxes | .4 | .2 | .6 | | | | | | .9 | .7 |
| All Other Non-Current | 5.6 | 5.8 | 10.4 | | | | | | 6.0 | 8.5 |
| Net Worth | 33.2 | 28.8 | 28.4 | | | | | | 36.2 | 32.3 |
| Total Liabilities & Net Worth | 100.0 | 100.0 | 100.0 | | | | | | 100.0 | 100.0 |
| | | | | **INCOME DATA** | | | | | | |
| Net Sales | 100.0 | 100.0 | 100.0 | | | | | | 100.0 | 100.0 |
| Gross Profit | 28.3 | 25.1 | 31.1 | | | | | | 35.1 | 27.1 |
| Operating Expenses | 20.6 | 20.3 | 25.1 | | | | | | 24.3 | 21.4 |
| Operating Profit | 7.7 | 4.8 | 5.9 | | | | | | 10.7 | 5.8 |
| All Other Expenses (net) | .6 | .8 | 1.0 | | | | | | 1.7 | .9 |
| Profit Before Taxes | 7.1 | 4.0 | 5.0 | | | | | | 9.1 | 4.8 |
| | | | | **RATIOS** | | | | | | |
| Current | 2.1 | 2.2 | 2.4 | | | | | | 3.0 | 2.4 |
| | 1.4 | 1.3 | 1.5 | | | | | | 1.5 | 1.6 |
| | 1.1 | 1.0 | 1.2 | | | | | | 1.0 | 1.1 |
| Quick | 1.1 | 1.1 | 1.1 | | | | | | 1.7 | 1.0 |
| | .6 | .7 | .7 | | | | | | .7 | .7 |
| | .5 | .4 | .5 | | | | | | .4 | .5 |
| Sales/Receivables | 22  16.8 | 25  14.4 | 18  20.3 | | | | | | 23  15.9 | 24  15.1 |
| | 35  10.4 | 31  11.7 | 31  11.6 | | | | | | 29  12.5 | 37  9.9 |
| | 50  7.2 | 46  8.0 | 49  7.5 | | | | | | 54  6.7 | 52  7.0 |
| Cost of Sales/Inventory | 24  15.1 | 29  12.4 | 29  12.8 | | | | | | 30  12.0 | 37  9.9 |
| | 52  7.0 | 54  6.7 | 46  7.9 | | | | | | 47  7.7 | 54  6.7 |
| | 83  4.4 | 87  4.2 | 96  3.8 | | | | | | 81  4.5 | 99  3.7 |
| Cost of Sales/Payables | 17  22.0 | 16  22.7 | 21  17.7 | | | | | | 24  15.1 | 17  21.4 |
| | 28  13.1 | 26  14.1 | 37  9.8 | | | | | | 36  10.1 | 38  9.6 |
| | 43  8.5 | 49  7.5 | 49  7.4 | | | | | | 46  7.9 | 58  6.3 |
| Sales/Working Capital | 8.3 | 7.2 | 6.7 | | | | | | 4.3 | 6.6 |
| | 16.4 | 20.4 | 13.0 | | | | | | 10.3 | 12.0 |
| | 57.1 | 246.1 | 53.8 | | | | | | NM | 38.8 |
| EBIT/Interest | 10.1 | 7.9 | 14.4 | | | | | | 11.8 | 14.7 |
| | (31) 5.3 | (35) 4.5 | (64) 4.5 | | | | | | (37) 3.5 | 5.6 |
| | 3.6 | 2.9 | 1.3 | | | | | | .5 | 2.3 |
| Net Profit + Depr., Dep., Amort./Cur. Mat. L/T/D | | 5.5 | 21.3 | | | | | | | 36.9 |
| | | (10) 2.5 | (20) 5.8 | | | | | | | (16) 8.8 |
| | | .3 | 2.6 | | | | | | | 2.9 |
| Fixed/Worth | .4 | .4 | .3 | | | | | | .3 | .4 |
| | .7 | 1.1 | .8 | | | | | | .9 | .8 |
| | 3.2 | 4.5 | 2.1 | | | | | | 3.5 | 2.3 |
| Debt/Worth | 1.2 | 2.1 | 1.0 | | | | | | .7 | 1.2 |
| | 2.5 | 3.7 | 2.2 | | | | | | 1.3 | 3.0 |
| | 8.6 | 10.9 | 8.6 | | | | | | 11.2 | 10.1 |
| % Profit Before Taxes/Tangible Net Worth | 62.7 | 48.4 | 47.4 | | | | | | 27.9 | 69.1 |
| | (31) 36.3 | (31) 33.1 | (60) 27.2 | | | | | | (12) 23.3 | (36) 37.7 |
| | 16.6 | 17.7 | 8.4 | | | | | | 4.7 | 10.9 |
| % Profit Before Taxes/Total Assets | 20.0 | 11.6 | 16.6 | | | | | | 16.2 | 20.0 |
| | 8.2 | 7.9 | 6.5 | | | | | | 6.6 | 6.9 |
| | 4.7 | 2.7 | .6 | | | | | | .3 | 2.6 |
| Sales/Net Fixed Assets | 23.6 | 25.7 | 32.6 | | | | | | 28.9 | 27.7 |
| | 13.0 | 11.4 | 13.1 | | | | | | 4.5 | 13.1 |
| | 4.2 | 5.1 | 6.2 | | | | | | 1.8 | 6.3 |
| Sales/Total Assets | 3.4 | 3.4 | 3.8 | | | | | | 3.2 | 3.5 |
| | 2.5 | 2.2 | 2.6 | | | | | | 2.0 | 2.1 |
| | 1.6 | 1.5 | 1.6 | | | | | | 1.0 | 1.6 |
| % Depr., Dep., Amort./Sales | 1.0 | 1.1 | .9 | | | | | | 1.1 | .7 |
| | (31) 1.4 | (32) 1.6 | (57) 1.6 | | | | | | (12) 2.6 | (36) 1.4 |
| | 2.3 | 2.5 | 2.8 | | | | | | 5.7 | 2.4 |
| % Officers', Directors' Owners' Comp/Sales | | | .9 | | | | | | | |
| | | | (14) 1.6 | | | | | | | |
| | | | 7.3 | | | | | | | |
| Net Sales ($) | 1623723M | 1795125M | 4603699M | | 116M | 6472M | 23547M | 28146M | 219663M | 4325755M |
| Total Assets ($) | 821941M | 947430M | 2343250M | | 11M | 916M | 6906M | 8828M | 204678M | 2121911M |

M = $ thousand    MM = $ million
See Pages 9 through 22 for Explanation of Ratios and Data

## Current Data Sorted by Assets      Comparative Historical Data

| 0-500M | 500M-2MM | 2-10MM | 10-50MM | 50-100MM | 100-250MM | Type of Statement | 4/1/07-3/31/08 ALL | 4/1/08-3/31/09 ALL |
|---|---|---|---|---|---|---|---|---|
| 1 |  | 3 | 7 | 4 | 3 | Unqualified | 14 | 13 |
|  | 1 | 8 | 4 |  |  | Reviewed | 10 | 14 |
| 1 | 2 | 5 |  |  |  | Compiled | 5 | 5 |
| 2 | 1 | 7 | 1 |  |  | Tax Returns | 4 | 10 |
| 2 | 10 | 11 | 13 | 6 | 2 | Other | 23 | 39 |
|  | 23 (4/1-9/30/11) |  | 71 (10/1/11-3/31/12) |  |  | | | |
| 6 | 14 | 34 | 25 | 10 | 5 | NUMBER OF STATEMENTS | 56 | 81 |
| % | % | % | % | % | % | ASSETS | % | % |
|  | 8.7 | 8.0 | 7.6 | 1.3 |  | Cash & Equivalents | 4.3 | 6.2 |
|  | 27.5 | 28.3 | 22.3 | 20.0 |  | Trade Receivables (net) | 20.1 | 21.4 |
|  | 26.1 | 23.3 | 23.8 | 23.8 |  | Inventory | 18.4 | 21.6 |
|  | 2.4 | 3.7 | 3.3 | 1.7 |  | All Other Current | 1.9 | 3.0 |
|  | 64.6 | 63.3 | 57.1 | 46.7 |  | Total Current | 44.7 | 52.1 |
|  | 27.8 | 26.4 | 36.0 | 34.9 |  | Fixed Assets (net) | 40.1 | 36.5 |
|  | 1.6 | 3.0 | 4.0 | 12.9 |  | Intangibles (net) | 6.4 | 6.1 |
|  | 6.0 | 7.3 | 3.0 | 5.5 |  | All Other Non-Current | 8.8 | 5.3 |
|  | 100.0 | 100.0 | 100.0 | 100.0 |  | Total | 100.0 | 100.0 |
|  |  |  |  |  |  | **LIABILITIES** | | |
|  | 11.3 | 5.9 | 7.9 | 10.2 |  | Notes Payable-Short Term | 10.9 | 10.0 |
|  | 2.3 | 3.3 | 4.7 | 3.6 |  | Cur. Mat.-L.T.D. | 5.7 | 4.8 |
|  | 16.8 | 22.8 | 15.3 | 12.9 |  | Trade Payables | 16.1 | 18.2 |
|  | .2 | .0 | .1 | .0 |  | Income Taxes Payable | .2 | .1 |
|  | 2.3 | 13.3 | 9.0 | 9.1 |  | All Other Current | 6.2 | 10.2 |
|  | 32.8 | 45.3 | 37.0 | 35.8 |  | Total Current | 39.1 | 43.3 |
|  | 18.0 | 15.0 | 21.0 | 15.7 |  | Long-Term Debt | 27.3 | 20.4 |
|  | .0 | 1.0 | 2.0 | 1.3 |  | Deferred Taxes | 1.1 | .7 |
|  | 19.8 | 8.0 | 6.9 | 4.5 |  | All Other Non-Current | 7.1 | 8.3 |
|  | 29.4 | 30.7 | 33.1 | 42.7 |  | Net Worth | 25.4 | 27.3 |
|  | 100.0 | 100.0 | 100.0 | 100.0 |  | Total Liabilities & Net Worth | 100.0 | 100.0 |
|  |  |  |  |  |  | **INCOME DATA** | | |
|  | 100.0 | 100.0 | 100.0 | 100.0 |  | Net Sales | 100.0 | 100.0 |
|  | 34.7 | 27.4 | 28.7 | 22.3 |  | Gross Profit | 31.9 | 27.4 |
|  | 30.8 | 24.2 | 22.4 | 16.7 |  | Operating Expenses | 29.1 | 24.7 |
|  | 3.9 | 3.3 | 6.3 | 5.5 |  | Operating Profit | 2.8 | 2.7 |
|  | .3 | .4 | 1.2 | .9 |  | All Other Expenses (net) | 1.9 | 1.1 |
|  | 3.7 | 2.9 | 5.1 | 4.6 |  | Profit Before Taxes | .9 | 1.6 |
|  |  |  |  |  |  | **RATIOS** | | |
|  | 8.1 | 2.4 | 2.2 | 1.6 |  |  | 1.7 | 2.1 |
|  | 2.3 | 1.4 | 1.4 | 1.3 |  | Current | 1.1 | 1.3 |
|  | 1.2 | 1.0 | 1.2 | .9 |  |  | .9 | .9 |
|  | 4.1 | 1.2 | 1.1 | .8 |  |  | 1.1 | 1.1 |
|  | 1.3 | .8 | .8 | .6 |  | Quick | .6 | .7 |
|  | .5 | .6 | .6 | .5 |  |  | .4 | .4 |
|  | 21 17.6 | 20 18.7 | 23 15.8 | 25 14.6 |  |  | 25 14.7 | 21 17.1 |
|  | 29 12.7 | 29 12.7 | 32 11.4 | 36 10.0 |  | Sales/Receivables | 32 11.3 | 31 11.9 |
|  | 35 10.5 | 41 9.0 | 39 9.3 | 42 8.6 |  |  | 39 9.4 | 37 10.0 |
|  | 21 17.2 | 22 16.3 | 28 12.9 | 41 9.0 |  |  | 23 16.1 | 19 18.8 |
|  | 51 7.2 | 36 10.2 | 38 9.5 | 47 7.7 |  | Cost of Sales/Inventory | 36 10.1 | 34 10.9 |
|  | 114 3.2 | 69 5.3 | 60 6.1 | 79 4.6 |  |  | 59 6.1 | 48 7.6 |
|  | 11 31.8 | 13 28.1 | 18 19.9 | 22 16.9 |  |  | 22 16.6 | 16 22.7 |
|  | 29 12.6 | 33 11.1 | 30 12.2 | 30 12.2 |  | Cost of Sales/Payables | 35 10.5 | 29 12.4 |
|  | 54 6.7 | 69 5.3 | 38 9.5 | 42 8.7 |  |  | 50 7.3 | 39 9.4 |
|  | 5.4 | 7.4 | 6.9 | 11.3 |  |  | 9.5 | 10.4 |
|  | 11.3 | 15.7 | 19.5 | 20.0 |  | Sales/Working Capital | 51.2 | 36.8 |
|  | 23.4 | NM | 42.8 | -102.5 |  |  | -34.1 | -40.9 |
|  | 31.5 | 19.2 | 14.7 | 37.6 |  |  | 4.4 | 6.2 |
|  | (11) 5.1 | (33) 5.4 | (21) 8.3 | 6.8 |  | EBIT/Interest | (52) 1.9 | (71) 2.6 |
|  | 1.5 | 1.1 | 3.4 | 2.7 |  |  | .4 | .5 |
|  |  | 12.4 | 3.9 |  |  |  | 5.1 | 6.6 |
|  |  | (15) 2.4 | (12) 2.5 |  |  | Net Profit + Depr., Dep., Amort./Cur. Mat. L/T/D | (24) 2.4 | (31) 3.2 |
|  |  | .6 | 1.1 |  |  |  | 1.1 | .9 |
|  | .1 | .4 | .7 | .8 |  |  | .7 | .7 |
|  | .6 | .7 | 1.1 | 1.1 |  | Fixed/Worth | 2.1 | 1.3 |
|  | NM | 5.0 | 2.2 | NM |  |  | -231.6 | -17.8 |
|  | .3 | .6 | 1.0 | .9 |  |  | 1.2 | 1.0 |
|  | 2.4 | 2.1 | 1.4 | 1.8 |  | Debt/Worth | 3.0 | 2.4 |
|  | NM | 24.3 | 6.5 | NM |  |  | -262.1 | -24.6 |
|  | 61.3 | 50.1 | 53.7 |  |  |  | 37.3 | 51.9 |
|  | (11) 32.7 | (27) 15.6 | (22) 30.3 |  |  | % Profit Before Taxes/Tangible Net Worth | (41) 15.6 | (59) 20.1 |
|  | 10.6 | 3.3 | 15.6 |  |  |  | .5 | 3.3 |
|  | 23.8 | 14.6 | 24.9 | 11.9 |  |  | 9.3 | 12.3 |
|  | 10.9 | 4.3 | 9.6 | 6.6 |  | % Profit Before Taxes/Total Assets | 3.3 | 4.3 |
|  | 2.5 | .3 | 4.3 | 4.2 |  |  | -2.1 | -1.0 |
|  | 47.5 | 43.5 | 18.9 | 16.5 |  |  | 10.3 | 16.6 |
|  | 13.3 | 11.6 | 6.6 | 4.9 |  | Sales/Net Fixed Assets | 5.1 | 7.5 |
|  | 5.7 | 7.0 | 4.0 | 4.1 |  |  | 3.3 | 3.9 |
|  | 4.0 | 3.6 | 3.3 | 2.3 |  |  | 2.8 | 3.6 |
|  | 3.1 | 2.7 | 2.3 | 2.0 |  | Sales/Total Assets | 2.2 | 2.4 |
|  | 1.9 | 2.0 | 1.8 | 1.5 |  |  | 1.6 | 1.8 |
|  | .5 | .9 | 1.2 | 1.4 |  |  | 1.5 | 1.4 |
|  | (12) 1.3 | (27) 1.7 | (24) 2.4 | 2.5 |  | % Depr., Dep., Amort./Sales | (52) 2.6 | (69) 2.3 |
|  | 2.7 | 2.6 | 3.3 | 3.5 |  |  | 4.1 | 3.4 |
|  |  | 1.2 |  |  |  |  | 1.8 | 1.6 |
|  |  | (10) 1.9 |  |  |  | % Officers', Directors' Owners' Comp/Sales | (16) 3.3 | (19) 3.5 |
|  |  | 4.3 |  |  |  |  | 7.3 | 4.6 |
| 10265M | 56791M | 540128M | 1652385M | 1484756M | 1789185M | Net Sales ($) | 2677418M | 4561088M |
| 1822M | 18915M | 172455M | 639651M | 752755M | 746546M | Total Assets ($) | 1343476M | 2017545M |

© RMA 2012

M = $ thousand    MM = $ million
See Pages 9 through 22 for Explanation of Ratios and Data

## Comparative Historical Data · Current Data Sorted by Sales

| | | | Type of Statement | 0-1MM | 1-3MM | 3-5MM | 5-10MM | 10-25MM | 25MM & OVER |
|---|---|---|---|---|---|---|---|---|---|
| 20 | 18 | 18 | Unqualified | | 1 | | | 4 | 13 |
| 15 | 13 | 13 | Reviewed | | 1 | 1 | 3 | 2 | 6 |
| 12 | 9 | 8 | Compiled | 1 | | | 3 | 3 | 1 |
| 9 | 17 | 11 | Tax Returns | | 2 | 1 | 2 | 6 | |
| 31 | 33 | 44 | Other | | 7 | 5 | 7 | 5 | 22 |
| 4/1/09-3/31/10 ALL | 4/1/10-3/31/11 ALL | 4/1/11-3/31/12 ALL | | | 23 (4/1-9/30/11) | | 71 (10/1/11-3/31/12) | | |
| 87 | 90 | 94 | NUMBER OF STATEMENTS | 1 | 11 | 7 | 13 | 20 | 42 |
| % | % | % | ASSETS | % | % | % | % | % | % |
| 7.6 | 9.6 | 7.5 | Cash & Equivalents | | 12.8 | | 11.0 | 10.5 | 4.3 |
| 20.3 | 20.6 | 26.1 | Trade Receivables (net) | | 31.4 | | 28.9 | 24.3 | 24.8 |
| 20.2 | 20.4 | 22.8 | Inventory | | 24.8 | | 19.1 | 22.2 | 23.7 |
| 1.8 | 2.0 | 2.8 | All Other Current | | 2.2 | | 5.2 | 3.6 | 2.2 |
| 49.9 | 52.6 | 59.2 | Total Current | | 71.2 | | 64.2 | 60.5 | 55.0 |
| 36.2 | 35.7 | 31.3 | Fixed Assets (net) | | 21.4 | | 26.5 | 30.1 | 35.5 |
| 7.4 | 6.4 | 4.0 | Intangibles (net) | | .2 | | 2.2 | 2.5 | 5.8 |
| 6.5 | 5.2 | 5.4 | All Other Non-Current | | 7.3 | | 7.1 | 6.9 | 3.7 |
| 100.0 | 100.0 | 100.0 | Total | | 100.0 | | 100.0 | 100.0 | 100.0 |
| | | | LIABILITIES | | | | | | |
| 9.3 | 7.7 | 7.7 | Notes Payable-Short Term | | 10.0 | | 7.4 | 6.7 | 7.6 |
| 3.6 | 3.8 | 3.5 | Cur. Mat.-L.T.D. | | .1 | | 3.2 | 4.5 | 4.0 |
| 14.8 | 16.4 | 18.4 | Trade Payables | | 22.9 | | 17.5 | 19.7 | 16.4 |
| .6 | .1 | .1 | Income Taxes Payable | | .2 | | .0 | .2 | .1 |
| 8.8 | 11.8 | 10.5 | All Other Current | | 11.3 | | 15.0 | 6.9 | 11.6 |
| 37.1 | 39.8 | 40.2 | Total Current | | 44.5 | | 43.0 | 38.0 | 39.6 |
| 25.1 | 23.9 | 19.5 | Long-Term Debt | | 13.4 | | 15.6 | 19.2 | 20.2 |
| 1.1 | .9 | 1.2 | Deferred Taxes | | .0 | | .4 | 1.4 | 1.8 |
| 10.6 | 7.4 | 8.7 | All Other Non-Current | | 26.2 | | 3.9 | 4.5 | 8.7 |
| 26.1 | 27.9 | 30.4 | Net Worth | | 15.9 | | 37.0 | 36.9 | 29.7 |
| 100.0 | 100.0 | 100.0 | Total Liabilities & Net Worth | | 100.0 | | 100.0 | 100.0 | 100.0 |
| | | | INCOME DATA | | | | | | |
| 100.0 | 100.0 | 100.0 | Net Sales | | 100.0 | | 100.0 | 100.0 | 100.0 |
| 29.8 | 30.9 | 28.9 | Gross Profit | | 37.4 | | 25.3 | 29.0 | 26.8 |
| 24.6 | 27.7 | 24.2 | Operating Expenses | | 31.2 | | 21.3 | 23.3 | 21.8 |
| 5.2 | 3.2 | 4.7 | Operating Profit | | 6.2 | | 4.0 | 5.8 | 5.0 |
| 1.2 | 1.1 | .7 | All Other Expenses (net) | | .6 | | .5 | .5 | 1.0 |
| 4.0 | 2.1 | 4.1 | Profit Before Taxes | | 5.6 | | 3.5 | 5.2 | 4.0 |
| | | | RATIOS | | | | | | |
| 2.4 | 2.3 | 2.3 | | | 6.4 | | 2.8 | 2.9 | 1.7 |
| 1.3 | 1.4 | 1.4 | Current | | 1.4 | | 1.6 | 1.7 | 1.3 |
| 1.0 | 1.0 | 1.1 | | | 1.1 | | 1.0 | 1.1 | 1.0 |
| 1.4 | 1.4 | 1.2 | | | 5.5 | | 2.1 | 1.8 | .9 |
| .7 | .8 | .8 | Quick | | 1.0 | | .8 | 1.0 | .7 |
| .5 | .5 | .5 | | | .5 | | .5 | .5 | .5 |
| 22 16.3 | 18 20.0 | 21 17.1 | | | 21 17.1 | | 18 19.8 | 20 18.3 | 25 14.7 |
| 30 12.3 | 27 13.3 | 30 12.3 | Sales/Receivables | | 33 11.0 | | 27 13.3 | 35 10.4 | 30 12.3 |
| 37 9.8 | 36 10.1 | 39 9.4 | | | 39 9.4 | | 37 9.8 | 41 8.8 | 38 9.7 |
| 25 14.3 | 20 18.4 | 22 16.3 | | | 9 42.6 | | 22 16.7 | 16 22.4 | 27 13.3 |
| 37 9.9 | 40 9.2 | 39 9.4 | Cost of Sales/Inventory | | 41 8.9 | | 29 12.8 | 42 8.7 | 38 9.7 |
| 58 6.3 | 64 5.7 | 66 5.5 | | | 130 2.8 | | 59 6.2 | 76 4.8 | 54 6.7 |
| 15 24.2 | 17 22.0 | 17 21.8 | | | 8 46.9 | | 10 36.3 | 22 16.8 | 18 20.6 |
| 25 14.6 | 24 14.9 | 28 13.1 | Cost of Sales/Payables | | 17 21.8 | | 20 18.7 | 34 10.6 | 28 13.2 |
| 39 9.3 | 36 10.2 | 44 8.3 | | | 58 6.3 | | 42 8.7 | 53 6.9 | 40 9.2 |
| 8.0 | 8.9 | 8.1 | | | 2.8 | | 8.5 | 6.2 | 11.7 |
| 26.7 | 19.0 | 18.7 | Sales/Working Capital | | 21.8 | | 13.2 | 10.8 | 27.5 |
| -207.4 | -825.6 | 140.5 | | | 47.0 | | NM | 102.3 | NM |
| 11.6 | 19.0 | 15.9 | | | | | 76.0 | 19.2 | 14.5 |
| (79) 3.8 | (78) 3.0 | (83) 6.1 | EBIT/Interest | | | | 5.1 | 13.4 | (37) 6.1 |
| 1.5 | 1.1 | 1.8 | | | | | .3 | 1.9 | 2.3 |
| 11.0 | 13.2 | 7.2 | Net Profit + Depr., Dep., | | | | | | 5.2 |
| (35) 4.5 | (27) 3.6 | (39) 2.5 | Amort./Cur. Mat. L/T/D | | | | | | (24) 2.3 |
| 1.9 | 1.3 | 1.3 | | | | | | | 1.3 |
| .6 | .5 | .4 | | | .1 | | .1 | .5 | .7 |
| 1.3 | 1.1 | .9 | Fixed/Worth | | .2 | | .5 | .8 | 1.2 |
| -60.9 | NM | 2.8 | | | -2.7 | | 3.4 | 4.9 | 2.8 |
| 1.1 | .8 | .8 | | | .1 | | .4 | .6 | 1.0 |
| 2.3 | 1.7 | 2.0 | Debt/Worth | | 2.9 | | 5.0 | 2.1 | 1.8 |
| -56.1 | NM | 10.6 | | | -4.7 | | 17.9 | 10.7 | 6.1 |
| 50.0 | 37.1 | 49.9 | % Profit Before Taxes/Tangible | | | | 78.2 | 53.5 | 45.1 |
| (63) 25.8 | (68) 18.1 | (76) 22.4 | Net Worth | | | | (11) 47.6 | (16) 22.8 | (36) 21.7 |
| 11.7 | 3.2 | 7.6 | | | | | 3.3 | 6.9 | 15.5 |
| 19.7 | 12.6 | 17.9 | % Profit Before Taxes/Total | | | | 26.4 | 23.8 | 15.9 |
| 7.9 | 5.6 | 7.6 | Assets | | | | 11.9 | 5.7 | 9.9 |
| 1.7 | .1 | 2.7 | | | | | 4.0 | .4 | 2.9 |
| 13.5 | 18.4 | 26.6 | | | 156.2 | | 544.1 | 21.6 | 27.4 |
| 6.3 | 7.4 | 8.6 | Sales/Net Fixed Assets | | 23.5 | | 16.1 | 8.2 | 6.8 |
| 4.0 | 4.4 | 4.5 | | | 8.3 | | 8.9 | 4.5 | 4.3 |
| 3.2 | 3.5 | 3.7 | | | 5.9 | | 3.9 | 3.2 | 3.7 |
| 2.3 | 2.5 | 2.5 | Sales/Total Assets | | 4.2 | | 2.9 | 2.4 | 2.4 |
| 1.6 | 1.8 | 1.9 | | | 1.5 | | 2.1 | 2.1 | 1.9 |
| 1.3 | 1.2 | 1.0 | | | | | | 1.1 | 1.2 |
| (75) 2.2 | (77) 1.9 | (78) 2.0 | % Depr., Dep., Amort./Sales | | | | | (18) 2.2 | (38) 2.2 |
| 3.0 | 3.4 | 2.8 | | | | | | 2.8 | 2.8 |
| 1.9 | 1.5 | 1.2 | % Officers', Directors' | | | | | 1.3 | |
| (21) 3.1 | (27) 2.6 | (23) 2.3 | Owners' Comp/Sales | | | | | (10) 2.1 | |
| 5.2 | 5.3 | 4.3 | | | | | | 3.8 | |
| 5084536M | 4596239M | 5533510M | Net Sales ($) | 535M | 24197M | 26312M | 91134M | 321062M | 5070270M |
| 2580963M | 2215817M | 2332144M | Total Assets ($) | 150M | 10251M | 13177M | 39243M | 137383M | 2131940M |

M = $ thousand    MM = $ million
See Pages 9 through 22 for Explanation of Ratios and Data

## Current Data Sorted by Assets       Comparative Historical Data

| | | | 1 | | 3 | | 3 | | 2 | Type of Statement | | 9 | | 6 |
|---|---|---|---|---|---|---|---|---|---|---|---|---|---|---|
| | | | 5 | | 2 | | | | | Unqualified | | 9 | | 6 |
| | 1 | | 3 | | 3 | | | | | Reviewed | | 3 | | 6 |
| | 4 | | 1 | | | | | | | Compiled | | 7 | | 10 |
| | 7 | | | | | | | | | Tax Returns | | 6 | | 7 |
| 1 | 5 | | 9 | | 5 | | 3 | | 3 | Other | | 15 | | 19 |
| 5 | 9 (4/1-9/30/11) | | | | 56 (10/1/11-3/31/12) | | | | | | | 4/1/07-3/31/08 | | 4/1/08-3/31/09 |
| 0-500M | 500M-2MM | | 2-10MM | | 10-50MM | | 50-100MM | | 100-250MM | | | ALL | | ALL |
| 6 | 16 | | 19 | | 13 | | 6 | | 5 | NUMBER OF STATEMENTS | | 40 | | 48 |
| % | % | | % | | % | | % | | % | ASSETS | | % | | % |
| | 14.1 | | 4.8 | | 6.3 | | | | | Cash & Equivalents | | 7.3 | | 5.5 |
| | 22.4 | | 23.1 | | 19.1 | | | | | Trade Receivables (net) | | 21.7 | | 20.4 |
| | 30.3 | | 26.3 | | 28.5 | | | | | Inventory | | 22.3 | | 24.9 |
| | .9 | | 2.8 | | 3.3 | | | | | All Other Current | | 2.4 | | 3.7 |
| | 67.7 | | 57.0 | | 57.2 | | | | | Total Current | | 53.7 | | 54.5 |
| | 23.4 | | 31.9 | | 24.2 | | | | | Fixed Assets (net) | | 30.3 | | 30.8 |
| | 5.3 | | 2.2 | | 14.5 | | | | | Intangibles (net) | | 6.3 | | 7.5 |
| | 3.6 | | 9.0 | | 4.1 | | | | | All Other Non-Current | | 9.7 | | 7.2 |
| | 100.0 | | 100.0 | | 100.0 | | | | | Total | | 100.0 | | 100.0 |
| | | | | | | | | | | LIABILITIES | | | | |
| | 16.4 | | 11.7 | | 8.7 | | | | | Notes Payable-Short Term | | 17.3 | | 10.0 |
| | 2.6 | | 4.3 | | 3.0 | | | | | Cur. Mat.-L.T.D. | | 5.4 | | 3.9 |
| | 22.8 | | 21.2 | | 11.9 | | | | | Trade Payables | | 19.1 | | 18.2 |
| | .0 | | .0 | | .0 | | | | | Income Taxes Payable | | .1 | | .1 |
| | 8.9 | | 8.0 | | 5.4 | | | | | All Other Current | | 7.5 | | 6.1 |
| | 50.8 | | 45.3 | | 29.0 | | | | | Total Current | | 49.5 | | 38.4 |
| | 24.5 | | 8.2 | | 7.5 | | | | | Long-Term Debt | | 20.1 | | 25.7 |
| | .0 | | 1.3 | | .4 | | | | | Deferred Taxes | | .5 | | .6 |
| | 22.2 | | 5.2 | | 6.9 | | | | | All Other Non-Current | | 3.5 | | 5.5 |
| | 2.5 | | 40.1 | | 56.3 | | | | | Net Worth | | 26.4 | | 29.8 |
| | 100.0 | | 100.0 | | 100.0 | | | | | Total Liabilities & Net Worth | | 100.0 | | 100.0 |
| | | | | | | | | | | INCOME DATA | | | | |
| | 100.0 | | 100.0 | | 100.0 | | | | | Net Sales | | 100.0 | | 100.0 |
| | 38.9 | | 35.0 | | 28.4 | | | | | Gross Profit | | 39.9 | | 39.6 |
| | 36.9 | | 31.5 | | 24.8 | | | | | Operating Expenses | | 36.0 | | 38.3 |
| | 2.0 | | 3.5 | | 3.6 | | | | | Operating Profit | | 3.9 | | 1.3 |
| | .8 | | .7 | | 2.0 | | | | | All Other Expenses (net) | | 1.2 | | .8 |
| | 1.2 | | 2.8 | | 1.6 | | | | | Profit Before Taxes | | 2.7 | | .4 |
| | | | | | | | | | | RATIOS | | | | |
| | 2.1 | | 1.8 | | 2.7 | | | | | | | 2.0 | | 2.2 |
| | 1.5 | | 1.2 | | 1.9 | | | | | Current | | 1.2 | | 1.4 |
| | .7 | | .8 | | 1.8 | | | | | | | .8 | | .9 |
| | 1.2 | | .9 | | 1.6 | | | | | | | 1.1 | | 1.0 |
| | .6 | | .6 | | 1.0 | | | | | Quick | | .6 | | .6 |
| | .4 | | .5 | | .5 | | | | | | | .4 | | .4 |
| 18 | 20.3 | 25 | 14.8 | 24 | 15.5 | | | | | | 23 | 15.9 | 19 | 18.7 |
| 23 | 15.9 | 37 | 9.8 | 25 | 14.4 | | | | | Sales/Receivables | 29 | 12.4 | 28 | 13.2 |
| 27 | 13.7 | 54 | 6.7 | 41 | 9.0 | | | | | | 37 | 9.8 | 34 | 10.9 |
| 18 | 20.0 | 36 | 10.0 | 36 | 10.1 | | | | | | 31 | 11.9 | 33 | 11.2 |
| 47 | 7.8 | 49 | 7.4 | 49 | 7.4 | | | | | Cost of Sales/Inventory | 50 | 7.3 | 51 | 7.2 |
| 79 | 4.6 | 70 | 5.2 | 96 | 3.8 | | | | | | 90 | 4.1 | 72 | 5.1 |
| 7 | 50.1 | 40 | 9.2 | 20 | 18.3 | | | | | | 23 | 15.7 | 21 | 17.8 |
| 42 | 8.6 | 49 | 7.4 | 25 | 14.5 | | | | | Cost of Sales/Payables | 36 | 10.0 | 32 | 11.6 |
| 60 | 6.1 | 63 | 5.8 | 28 | 13.1 | | | | | | 64 | 5.7 | 56 | 6.5 |
| | 6.7 | | 7.0 | | 6.4 | | | | | | | 8.3 | | 7.5 |
| | 14.3 | | 34.0 | | 8.3 | | | | | Sales/Working Capital | | 22.1 | | 14.8 |
| | NM | | -30.4 | | 11.4 | | | | | | | -21.9 | | -49.2 |
| | 9.8 | | 7.7 | | 9.7 | | | | | | | 6.0 | | 5.9 |
| (14) | 3.0 | | 4.0 | (12) | 2.9 | | | | | EBIT/Interest | (34) | 2.8 | (44) | 2.1 |
| | -.5 | | -.2 | | .1 | | | | | | | .1 | | .1 |
| | | | | | | | | | | | | | | 8.0 |
| | | | | | | | | | | Net Profit + Depr., Dep., Amort./Cur. Mat. L/T/D | | | (11) | 1.9 |
| | | | | | | | | | | | | | | 1.3 |
| | .2 | | .5 | | .3 | | | | | | | .3 | | .4 |
| | 1.1 | | .9 | | .5 | | | | | Fixed/Worth | | 1.3 | | 1.2 |
| | -1.0 | | 1.4 | | .9 | | | | | | | NM | | 3.9 |
| | 1.5 | | .9 | | .5 | | | | | | | 1.0 | | 1.2 |
| | 3.9 | | 2.3 | | 1.0 | | | | | Debt/Worth | | 3.2 | | 2.6 |
| | -5.7 | | 3.1 | | 1.9 | | | | | | | NM | | 9.9 |
| | 62.0 | | 25.7 | | 21.6 | | | | | % Profit Before Taxes/Tangible Net Worth | | 43.7 | | 25.1 |
| (10) | 17.1 | | 16.3 | (12) | 12.5 | | | | | | (30) | 21.9 | (41) | 15.3 |
| | 6.9 | | -1.6 | | 3.0 | | | | | | | 7.9 | | -6.6 |
| | 15.7 | | 11.0 | | 9.1 | | | | | % Profit Before Taxes/Total Assets | | 13.6 | | 10.3 |
| | 4.8 | | 4.9 | | 5.4 | | | | | | | 6.0 | | 4.2 |
| | -1.3 | | -.9 | | -.6 | | | | | | | -3.9 | | -1.2 |
| | 81.6 | | 10.6 | | 21.6 | | | | | | | 24.9 | | 25.9 |
| | 44.1 | | 8.4 | | 10.8 | | | | | Sales/Net Fixed Assets | | 10.3 | | 9.0 |
| | 7.5 | | 5.0 | | 5.4 | | | | | | | 5.5 | | 5.1 |
| | 5.6 | | 3.0 | | 3.2 | | | | | | | 3.3 | | 3.4 |
| | 3.4 | | 2.4 | | 1.9 | | | | | Sales/Total Assets | | 2.5 | | 2.6 |
| | 2.8 | | 1.9 | | 1.3 | | | | | | | 1.7 | | 2.1 |
| | .8 | | 1.3 | | 1.9 | | | | | | | 1.4 | | 1.1 |
| (13) | 1.6 | (18) | 1.8 | (12) | 3.0 | | | | | % Depr., Dep., Amort./Sales | (27) | 2.6 | (36) | 2.5 |
| | 3.2 | | 4.1 | | 3.9 | | | | | | | 4.4 | | 3.3 |
| | 1.5 | | | | | | | | | % Officers', Directors' Owners' Comp/Sales | | 2.6 | | 1.8 |
| (13) | 3.6 | | | | | | | | | | (16) | 3.4 | (17) | 5.0 |
| | 10.6 | | | | | | | | | | | 11.9 | | 9.6 |
| 1819M | 68286M | | 257499M | | 657921M | | 775406M | | 2022129M | Net Sales ($) | | 1756113M | | 2481365M |
| 1324M | 17246M | | 106922M | | 308194M | | 441806M | | 843304M | Total Assets ($) | | 874716M | | 1053172M |

M = $ thousand     MM = $ million
See Pages 9 through 22 for Explanation of Ratios and Data

## Comparative Historical Data | Current Data Sorted by Sales

### Type of Statement

| 4/1/09-3/31/10 | 4/1/10-3/31/11 | 4/1/11-3/31/12 | Type of Statement | 0-1MM | 1-3MM | 3-5MM | 5-10MM | 10-25MM | 25MM & OVER |
|---|---|---|---|---|---|---|---|---|---|
| 10 | 12 | 9 | Unqualified | | | | | 4 | 5 |
| 8 | 11 | 7 | Reviewed | | | | 1 | 4 | 2 |
| 8 | 5 | 11 | Compiled | 1 | 3 | 1 | | 4 | 2 |
| 9 | 12 | 8 | Tax Returns | | | 3 | 3 | 2 | |
| 24 | 21 | 30 | Other | 5 | 3 | 4 | 1 | 5 | 12 |
| ALL | ALL | ALL | | 9 (4/1-9/30/11) | | | 56 (10/1/11-3/31/12) | | |
| 59 | 61 | 65 | **NUMBER OF STATEMENTS** | 6 | 6 | 8 | 5 | 19 | 21 |

### ASSETS (%)

| 4/1/09-3/31/10 | 4/1/10-3/31/11 | 4/1/11-3/31/12 | ASSETS | 0-1MM | 1-3MM | 3-5MM | 5-10MM | 10-25MM | 25MM & OVER |
|---|---|---|---|---|---|---|---|---|---|
| 7.7 | 6.3 | 8.0 | Cash & Equivalents | | | | | 6.3 | 6.8 |
| 21.1 | 21.6 | 20.1 | Trade Receivables (net) | | | | | 21.2 | 21.1 |
| 25.2 | 27.5 | 27.5 | Inventory | | | | | 19.9 | 28.4 |
| 2.3 | 2.5 | 2.5 | All Other Current | | | | | 2.5 | 4.1 |
| 56.3 | 57.8 | 58.0 | Total Current | | | | | 49.9 | 60.4 |
| 30.6 | 30.2 | 29.3 | Fixed Assets (net) | | | | | 31.7 | 26.7 |
| 8.1 | 5.0 | 5.9 | Intangibles (net) | | | | | 5.9 | 6.7 |
| 4.9 | 7.0 | 6.9 | All Other Non-Current | | | | | 12.6 | 6.2 |
| 100.0 | 100.0 | 100.0 | Total | | | | | 100.0 | 100.0 |

### LIABILITIES

| 4/1/09-3/31/10 | 4/1/10-3/31/11 | 4/1/11-3/31/12 | LIABILITIES | 0-1MM | 1-3MM | 3-5MM | 5-10MM | 10-25MM | 25MM & OVER |
|---|---|---|---|---|---|---|---|---|---|
| 7.0 | 12.4 | 13.2 | Notes Payable-Short Term | | | | | 10.8 | 7.7 |
| 5.1 | 3.8 | 2.8 | Cur. Mat.-L.T.D. | | | | | 4.0 | 2.8 |
| 15.0 | 17.9 | 16.2 | Trade Payables | | | | | 17.6 | 12.0 |
| .1 | .1 | .0 | Income Taxes Payable | | | | | .0 | .0 |
| 10.4 | 8.0 | 7.6 | All Other Current | | | | | 6.9 | 8.6 |
| 37.6 | 42.2 | 39.9 | Total Current | | | | | 39.4 | 31.0 |
| 21.2 | 16.7 | 14.8 | Long-Term Debt | | | | | 9.2 | 11.3 |
| .4 | .5 | .9 | Deferred Taxes | | | | | 1.2 | 1.5 |
| 6.4 | 7.8 | 10.0 | All Other Non-Current | | | | | 3.4 | 6.0 |
| 34.4 | 32.9 | 34.5 | Net Worth | | | | | 46.8 | 50.2 |
| 100.0 | 100.0 | 100.0 | Total Liabilities & Net Worth | | | | | 100.0 | 100.0 |

### INCOME DATA

| 4/1/09-3/31/10 | 4/1/10-3/31/11 | 4/1/11-3/31/12 | INCOME DATA | 0-1MM | 1-3MM | 3-5MM | 5-10MM | 10-25MM | 25MM & OVER |
|---|---|---|---|---|---|---|---|---|---|
| 100.0 | 100.0 | 100.0 | Net Sales | | | | | 100.0 | 100.0 |
| 39.0 | 37.5 | 34.2 | Gross Profit | | | | | 35.9 | 28.7 |
| 35.7 | 33.9 | 31.1 | Operating Expenses | | | | | 32.5 | 24.8 |
| 3.3 | 3.6 | 3.0 | Operating Profit | | | | | 3.4 | 3.9 |
| .7 | .7 | .9 | All Other Expenses (net) | | | | | .3 | 1.2 |
| 2.6 | 2.9 | 2.2 | Profit Before Taxes | | | | | 3.1 | 2.7 |

### RATIOS

| 4/1/09-3/31/10 | 4/1/10-3/31/11 | 4/1/11-3/31/12 | RATIOS | 0-1MM | 1-3MM | 3-5MM | 5-10MM | 10-25MM | 25MM & OVER |
|---|---|---|---|---|---|---|---|---|---|
| 2.9 / 2.1 / 1.1 | 2.1 / 1.4 / 1.0 | 2.2 / 1.5 / 1.1 | Current | | | | | 1.8 / 1.3 / .8 | 2.8 / 1.8 / 1.6 |
| 1.5 / 1.0 / .5 | .9 / .7 / .4 | 1.1 / .7 / .5 | Quick | | | | | 1.0 / .7 / .5 | 1.3 / 1.0 / .6 |
| 22 16.5 / 27 13.6 / 36 10.2 | 20 18.1 / 32 11.5 / 41 8.9 | 20 18.4 / 29 12.8 / 38 9.5 | Sales/Receivables | | | | | 25 14.8 / 34 10.6 / 49 7.5 | 24 15.5 / 31 11.7 / 36 10.1 |
| 37 10.0 / 53 6.9 / 79 4.6 | 40 9.0 / 56 6.5 / 82 4.4 | 36 10.2 / 54 6.8 / 94 3.9 | Cost of Sales/Inventory | | | | | 36 10.2 / 46 7.9 / 70 5.2 | 36 10.2 / 56 6.5 / 89 4.1 |
| 20 18.5 / 31 11.6 / 48 7.6 | 20 18.3 / 32 11.3 / 58 6.3 | 21 17.6 / 31 11.7 / 50 7.3 | Cost of Sales/Payables | | | | | 29 12.8 / 46 8.0 / 60 6.1 | 17 21.9 / 21 17.0 / 26 13.9 |
| 5.6 / 11.7 / 83.9 | 7.0 / 17.7 / 556.0 | 6.7 / 10.6 / 71.7 | Sales/Working Capital | | | | | 7.0 / 34.0 / -30.4 | 6.7 / 8.3 / 13.6 |
| 15.6 / (50) 4.6 / 1.8 | 13.0 / (53) 4.2 / 1.4 | 9.2 / (58) 3.4 / -.2 | EBIT/Interest | | | | | 11.6 / 2.6 / -.3 | 9.8 / (18) 7.1 / 2.6 |
| 7.4 / (10) 4.1 / 2.7 | 15.0 / (17) 5.8 / 1.7 | 7.2 / (16) 2.8 / 1.7 | Net Profit + Depr., Dep., Amort./Cur. Mat. L/T/D | | | | | | |
| .3 / 1.0 / 6.4 | .3 / .9 / 4.3 | .4 / .8 / 1.5 | Fixed/Worth | | | | | .5 / .9 / 1.5 | .4 / .7 / .9 |
| .7 / 1.2 / 17.9 | .8 / 2.4 / 8.3 | .8 / 1.6 / 3.8 | Debt/Worth | | | | | .6 / 1.2 / 3.1 | .6 / 1.2 / 2.2 |
| 47.2 / (46) 25.1 / 13.1 | 33.3 / (50) 17.2 / 10.2 | 23.1 / (56) 12.6 / 4.9 | % Profit Before Taxes/Tangible Net Worth | | | | | 27.9 / 8.4 / -2.3 | 18.8 / (20) 14.2 / 11.8 |
| 14.4 / 8.4 / 3.1 | 16.7 / 6.5 / 1.2 | 9.8 / 4.9 / .7 | % Profit Before Taxes/Total Assets | | | | | 11.4 / 4.8 / -1.3 | 9.0 / 5.4 / 4.1 |
| 24.2 / 8.5 / 5.0 | 25.6 / 9.1 / 4.8 | 21.6 / 9.2 / 5.6 | Sales/Net Fixed Assets | | | | | 14.6 / 8.6 / 5.0 | 16.0 / 9.3 / 5.9 |
| 3.6 / 2.4 / 1.6 | 3.1 / 2.4 / 1.9 | 3.1 / 2.4 / 1.7 | Sales/Total Assets | | | | | 2.9 / 2.3 / 1.7 | 3.1 / 2.3 / 1.8 |
| 1.3 / (46) 2.5 / 3.7 | 1.4 / (44) 1.9 / 3.6 | 1.3 / (51) 2.1 / 3.8 | % Depr., Dep., Amort./Sales | | | | | (18) 1.3 / 2.1 / 4.3 | (14) 1.0 / 2.2 / 3.6 |
| 2.4 / (19) 3.6 / 6.4 | 2.6 / (26) 4.6 / 7.1 | 1.9 / (24) 3.3 / 4.6 | % Officers', Directors' Owners' Comp/Sales | | | | | | |
| 3179131M | 2833879M | 3783060M | Net Sales ($) | 1819M | 12032M | 31246M | 32790M | 288742M | 3416431M |
| 1675040M | 1437226M | 1718796M | Total Assets ($) | 1324M | 10587M | 8463M | 11147M | 186856M | 1500419M |

M = $ thousand    MM = $ million
See Pages 9 through 22 for Explanation of Ratios and Data

## Current Data Sorted by Assets     Comparative Historical Data

| 0-500M | 500M-2MM | 2-10MM | 10-50MM | 50-100MM | 100-250MM | Type of Statement | 4/1/07-3/31/08 ALL | 4/1/08-3/31/09 ALL |
|---|---|---|---|---|---|---|---|---|
| | | | | | | Unqualified | 7 | 7 |
| | | 1 | 4 | 2 | 1 | Reviewed | 9 | 11 |
| 1 | 1 | 1 | | | | Compiled | 7 | 5 |
| 1 | 1 | | | | | Tax Returns | 1 | |
| 1 | 1 | 3 | 12 | 1 | 2 | Other | 20 | 12 |
| | | | 27 (10/1/11-3/31/12) | | | | | |
| | 7 (4/1-9/30/11) | | | | | | | |
| 3 | 3 | 5 | 20 | 3 | 3 | **NUMBER OF STATEMENTS** | 44 | 35 |
| % | % | % | % | % | % | **ASSETS** | % | % |
| | | | 9.8 | | | Cash & Equivalents | 6.6 | 8.1 |
| | | | 21.4 | | | Trade Receivables (net) | 18.6 | 20.7 |
| | | | 28.1 | | | Inventory | 24.9 | 27.8 |
| | | | 1.7 | | | All Other Current | 3.7 | 2.6 |
| | | | 60.9 | | | Total Current | 53.9 | 59.2 |
| | | | 29.3 | | | Fixed Assets (net) | 31.2 | 29.5 |
| | | | 2.7 | | | Intangibles (net) | 8.5 | 5.0 |
| | | | 7.0 | | | All Other Non-Current | 6.4 | 6.2 |
| | | | 100.0 | | | Total | 100.0 | 100.0 |
| | | | | | | **LIABILITIES** | | |
| | | | 7.9 | | | Notes Payable-Short Term | 8.9 | 10.9 |
| | | | 2.3 | | | Cur. Mat.-L.T.D. | 3.6 | 3.2 |
| | | | 11.4 | | | Trade Payables | 15.0 | 15.4 |
| | | | .4 | | | Income Taxes Payable | .3 | .4 |
| | | | 9.0 | | | All Other Current | 6.7 | 6.5 |
| | | | 30.9 | | | Total Current | 34.5 | 36.4 |
| | | | 10.4 | | | Long-Term Debt | 17.7 | 11.1 |
| | | | 1.7 | | | Deferred Taxes | 1.3 | .9 |
| | | | 2.2 | | | All Other Non-Current | 5.9 | 3.6 |
| | | | 54.8 | | | Net Worth | 40.6 | 48.1 |
| | | | 100.0 | | | Total Liabilities & Net Worth | 100.0 | 100.0 |
| | | | | | | **INCOME DATA** | | |
| | | | 100.0 | | | Net Sales | 100.0 | 100.0 |
| | | | 32.3 | | | Gross Profit | 34.5 | 31.4 |
| | | | 23.2 | | | Operating Expenses | 28.0 | 24.3 |
| | | | 9.0 | | | Operating Profit | 6.6 | 7.2 |
| | | | .6 | | | All Other Expenses (net) | 1.3 | .9 |
| | | | 8.5 | | | Profit Before Taxes | 5.3 | 6.3 |
| | | | | | | **RATIOS** | | |
| | | | 3.4 | | | | 2.9 | 2.7 |
| | | | 2.1 | | | Current | 1.4 | 1.6 |
| | | | 1.3 | | | | 1.1 | 1.3 |
| | | | 1.7 | | | | 1.3 | 1.7 |
| | | | 1.1 | | | Quick | .7 | .9 |
| | | | .6 | | | | .4 | .5 |
| | | 29 | 12.6 | | | | 25   14.8 | 26   14.3 |
| | | 35 | 10.3 | | | Sales/Receivables | 33   11.1 | 36   10.1 |
| | | 46 | 8.0 | | | | 44   8.3 | 48   7.6 |
| | | 46 | 8.0 | | | | 43   8.6 | 39   9.3 |
| | | 59 | 6.2 | | | Cost of Sales/Inventory | 61   5.9 | 70   5.2 |
| | | 104 | 3.5 | | | | 100   3.6 | 107   3.4 |
| | | 13 | 28.1 | | | | 24   15.0 | 20   17.9 |
| | | 24 | 15.1 | | | Cost of Sales/Payables | 40   9.0 | 31   11.8 |
| | | 45 | 8.1 | | | | 54   6.8 | 47   7.8 |
| | | | 4.6 | | | | 4.7 | 5.4 |
| | | | 7.4 | | | Sales/Working Capital | 16.4 | 10.3 |
| | | | 16.3 | | | | 61.1 | 24.6 |
| | | | 65.8 | | | | 12.4 | 14.6 |
| | | (18) | 16.1 | | | EBIT/Interest | (41)   3.6 | (32)   6.2 |
| | | | 8.7 | | | | 1.8 | 2.8 |
| | | | | | | Net Profit + Depr., Dep., Amort./Cur. Mat. L/T/D | (19)   5.8   2.7   1.3 | (12)   8.2   4.2   2.7 |
| | | | .3 | | | | .4 | .3 |
| | | | .5 | | | Fixed/Worth | .7 | .7 |
| | | | 1.3 | | | | 2.7 | 1.3 |
| | | | .4 | | | | .8 | .6 |
| | | | .8 | | | Debt/Worth | 1.6 | 1.3 |
| | | | 1.3 | | | | 4.9 | 2.6 |
| | | | 38.3 | | | % Profit Before Taxes/Tangible Net Worth | 56.2 | 54.3 |
| | | (19) | 27.7 | | | | (40)   21.0 | 27.3 |
| | | | 14.8 | | | | 7.3 | 13.8 |
| | | | 21.9 | | | % Profit Before Taxes/Total Assets | 17.8 | 18.1 |
| | | | 15.0 | | | | 8.2 | 10.2 |
| | | | 6.1 | | | | 3.2 | 6.6 |
| | | | 10.2 | | | | 14.6 | 21.5 |
| | | | 7.5 | | | Sales/Net Fixed Assets | 6.6 | 8.7 |
| | | | 5.7 | | | | 4.0 | 4.3 |
| | | | 2.7 | | | | 2.9 | 2.8 |
| | | | 1.9 | | | Sales/Total Assets | 1.8 | 2.1 |
| | | | 1.6 | | | | 1.4 | 1.6 |
| | | | 1.4 | | | | 1.2 | 1.3 |
| | | (19) | 1.7 | | | % Depr., Dep., Amort./Sales | (41)   1.9 | (31)   1.7 |
| | | | 2.1 | | | | 3.5 | 3.3 |
| | | | | | | % Officers', Directors' Owners' Comp/Sales | | |
| | 19864M | 59056M | 927973M | 364404M | 522253M | Net Sales ($) | 1621104M | 1139553M |
| | 3767M | 20011M | 435558M | 230716M | 378457M | Total Assets ($) | 1015134M | 655016M |

## Comparative Historical Data

## Current Data Sorted by Sales

| | | | | | Type of Statement | | | | | | | |
|---|---|---|---|---|---|---|---|---|---|---|---|---|
| | 9 | | 8 | | 7 | Unqualified | | | | | | 7 |
| | 8 | | 8 | | 5 | Reviewed | | | | | 2 | 3 |
| | 6 | | 6 | | 2 | Compiled | | | 1 | 1 | | |
| | 1 | | 1 | | 1 | Tax Returns | | | 1 | | | |
| | 15 | | 14 | | 19 | Other | | 1 | 2 | 3 | | 13 |
| | 4/1/09-3/31/10 ALL | | 4/1/10-3/31/11 ALL | | 4/1/11-3/31/12 ALL | | 0-1MM | 7 (4/1-9/30/11) 1-3MM | 3-5MM | 27 (10/1/11-3/31/12) 5-10MM | 10-25MM | 25MM & OVER |
| | 39 | | 37 | | 34 | NUMBER OF STATEMENTS | | | 1 | 4 | 6 | 23 |
| | % | | % | | % | ASSETS | % | % | % | % | % | % |
| | 12.1 | | 9.9 | | 8.0 | Cash & Equivalents | | | | | | 9.4 |
| | 22.2 | | 22.6 | | 21.8 | Trade Receivables (net) | D | D | | | | 19.8 |
| | 26.8 | | 28.9 | | 27.2 | Inventory | A | A | | | | 27.0 |
| | 3.6 | | 2.7 | | 2.6 | All Other Current | T | T | | | | 2.2 |
| | 64.8 | | 64.1 | | 59.6 | Total Current | A | A | | | | 58.3 |
| | 26.9 | | 28.2 | | 26.6 | Fixed Assets (net) | | | | | | 26.2 |
| | 4.5 | | 5.3 | | 8.9 | Intangibles (net) | N | N | | | | 9.0 |
| | 3.8 | | 2.4 | | 4.9 | All Other Non-Current | O | O | | | | 6.4 |
| | 100.0 | | 100.0 | | 100.0 | Total | T | T | | | | 100.0 |
| | | | | | | LIABILITIES | A | A | | | | |
| | 7.0 | | 7.9 | | 8.9 | Notes Payable-Short Term | V | V | | | | 8.2 |
| | 3.2 | | 2.7 | | 2.4 | Cur. Mat.-L.T.D. | A | A | | | | 2.6 |
| | 11.7 | | 13.6 | | 11.2 | Trade Payables | I | I | | | | 10.1 |
| | .5 | | .4 | | .3 | Income Taxes Payable | L | L | | | | .4 |
| | 7.4 | | 5.7 | | 7.1 | All Other Current | A | A | | | | 8.6 |
| | 29.7 | | 30.4 | | 29.9 | Total Current | B | B | | | | 29.8 |
| | 8.4 | | 13.6 | | 13.1 | Long-Term Debt | L | L | | | | 12.3 |
| | .5 | | .7 | | 2.2 | Deferred Taxes | E | E | | | | 3.2 |
| | 3.1 | | 3.3 | | 4.1 | All Other Non-Current | | | | | | 2.7 |
| | 58.3 | | 52.1 | | 50.6 | Net Worth | | | | | | 52.0 |
| | 100.0 | | 100.0 | | 100.0 | Total Liabilities & Net Worth | | | | | | 100.0 |
| | | | | | | INCOME DATA | | | | | | |
| | 100.0 | | 100.0 | | 100.0 | Net Sales | | | | | | 100.0 |
| | 35.5 | | 36.1 | | 36.0 | Gross Profit | | | | | | 30.4 |
| | 26.1 | | 26.8 | | 26.5 | Operating Expenses | | | | | | 19.5 |
| | 9.4 | | 9.3 | | 9.5 | Operating Profit | | | | | | 10.9 |
| | .5 | | .5 | | 1.0 | All Other Expenses (net) | | | | | | 1.4 |
| | 8.9 | | 8.8 | | 8.4 | Profit Before Taxes | | | | | | 9.5 |
| | | | | | | RATIOS | | | | | | |
| | 3.1 | | 3.9 | | 3.7 | | | | | | | 3.7 |
| | 2.4 | | 2.5 | | 1.9 | Current | | | | | | 2.4 |
| | 1.7 | | 1.6 | | 1.4 | | | | | | | 1.3 |
| | 1.9 | | 2.2 | | 1.7 | | | | | | | 2.0 |
| | 1.3 | | 1.2 | | 1.0 | Quick | | | | | | 1.2 |
| | .7 | | .7 | | .6 | | | | | | | .6 |
| 28 | 12.8 | 27 | 13.5 | 28 | 13.2 | | | | | | 29 | 12.8 |
| 38 | 9.6 | 33 | 11.2 | 36 | 10.0 | Sales/Receivables | | | | | 39 | 9.3 |
| 44 | 8.3 | 44 | 8.3 | 44 | 8.3 | | | | | | 45 | 8.2 |
| 43 | 8.4 | 48 | 7.6 | 46 | 7.9 | | | | | | 46 | 7.9 |
| 66 | 5.6 | 73 | 5.0 | 63 | 5.8 | Cost of Sales/Inventory | | | | | 68 | 5.4 |
| 116 | 3.2 | 104 | 3.5 | 104 | 3.5 | | | | | | 104 | 3.5 |
| 21 | 17.3 | 16 | 23.2 | 16 | 23.2 | | | | | | 15 | 24.5 |
| 28 | 12.9 | 26 | 13.8 | 24 | 15.1 | Cost of Sales/Payables | | | | | 22 | 16.8 |
| 36 | 10.2 | 44 | 8.2 | 38 | 9.5 | | | | | | 37 | 9.9 |
| | 4.0 | | 3.9 | | 4.7 | | | | | | | 3.7 |
| | 6.5 | | 6.9 | | 8.4 | Sales/Working Capital | | | | | | 7.4 |
| | 10.6 | | 12.6 | | 16.8 | | | | | | | 16.7 |
| | 43.5 | | 67.6 | | 42.8 | | | | | | | 114.2 |
| (35) | 13.1 | (36) | 12.0 | (31) | 15.9 | EBIT/Interest | | | | | (21) | 15.9 |
| | 7.4 | | 5.8 | | 3.3 | | | | | | | 6.2 |
| | 11.9 | | 16.3 | | 7.3 | | | | | | | 6.8 |
| (16) | 4.9 | (14) | 4.2 | (14) | 3.0 | Net Profit + Depr., Dep., Amort./Cur. Mat. L/T/D | | | | | (11) | 3.3 |
| | 2.6 | | 2.3 | | 1.7 | | | | | | | 1.8 |
| | .3 | | .3 | | .3 | | | | | | | .3 |
| | .5 | | .6 | | .6 | Fixed/Worth | | | | | | .5 |
| | .8 | | 1.0 | | 1.4 | | | | | | | 1.4 |
| | .4 | | .5 | | .5 | | | | | | | .4 |
| | .7 | | .9 | | 1.0 | Debt/Worth | | | | | | .9 |
| | 1.3 | | 1.9 | | 2.1 | | | | | | | 2.0 |
| | 38.7 | | 44.7 | | 38.3 | | | | | | | 38.3 |
| (37) | 24.0 | (35) | 29.4 | (29) | 24.6 | % Profit Before Taxes/Tangible Net Worth | | | | | (19) | 29.8 |
| | 15.6 | | 11.1 | | 10.6 | | | | | | | 14.8 |
| | 24.6 | | 24.0 | | 22.3 | | | | | | | 22.1 |
| | 14.4 | | 15.4 | | 13.0 | % Profit Before Taxes/Total Assets | | | | | | 16.7 |
| | 8.5 | | 5.7 | | 4.2 | | | | | | | 5.5 |
| | 14.3 | | 19.0 | | 21.5 | | | | | | | 18.8 |
| | 8.7 | | 7.9 | | 8.4 | Sales/Net Fixed Assets | | | | | | 7.4 |
| | 5.8 | | 5.1 | | 5.5 | | | | | | | 5.6 |
| | 3.0 | | 2.8 | | 2.8 | | | | | | | 2.7 |
| | 2.0 | | 2.1 | | 2.1 | Sales/Total Assets | | | | | | 1.9 |
| | 1.4 | | 1.5 | | 1.6 | | | | | | | 1.6 |
| | 1.3 | | 1.0 | | 1.3 | | | | | | | 1.4 |
| (36) | 1.9 | (35) | 1.9 | (32) | 1.7 | % Depr., Dep., Amort./Sales | | | | | (22) | 1.8 |
| | 3.3 | | 3.0 | | 2.8 | | | | | | | 2.4 |
| | 1.1 | | 1.6 | | | | | | | | | |
| (10) | 2.0 | (10) | 2.8 | | | % Officers', Directors' Owners' Comp/Sales | | | | | | |
| | 3.9 | | 13.7 | | | | | | | | | |
| | 1620797M | | 1785904M | | 1893550M | Net Sales ($) | | | 4046M | 31336M | 104882M | 1753286M |
| | 1075065M | | 911587M | | 1068509M | Total Assets ($) | | | 787M | 11352M | 47630M | 1008740M |

M = $ thousand    MM = $ million
See Pages 9 through 22 for Explanation of Ratios and Data

## Current Data Sorted by Assets      Comparative Historical Data

| 0-500M | 500M-2MM | 2-10MM | 10-50MM | 50-100MM | 100-250MM | Type of Statement | 4/1/07-3/31/08 ALL | 4/1/08-3/31/09 ALL |
|---|---|---|---|---|---|---|---|---|
|  |  | 2 | 4 | 1 | 2 | Unqualified | 4 | 8 |
| 1 |  | 3 | 1 |  | 1 | Reviewed | 9 | 10 |
|  |  |  | 2 | 1 |  | Compiled | 2 | 5 |
| 1 | 1 |  |  |  |  | Tax Returns | 2 | 2 |
| 1 | 3 | 5 | 4 |  | 1 | Other | 10 | 11 |
|  |  | 5 (4/1-9/30/11) |  | 27 (10/1/11-3/31/12) |  |  |  |  |
| 2 | 4 | 10 | 11 | 2 | 3 | **NUMBER OF STATEMENTS** | 27 | 36 |
| % | % | % | % | % | % | **ASSETS** | % | % |
|  |  | 5.7 | 7.5 |  |  | Cash & Equivalents | 8.6 | 6.8 |
|  |  | 20.3 | 21.8 |  |  | Trade Receivables (net) | 16.8 | 21.3 |
|  |  | 32.6 | 24.4 |  |  | Inventory | 23.8 | 22.6 |
|  |  | 2.0 | 3.0 |  |  | All Other Current | 2.1 | 1.0 |
|  |  | 60.6 | 56.7 |  |  | Total Current | 51.4 | 51.8 |
|  |  | 29.4 | 37.3 |  |  | Fixed Assets (net) | 36.2 | 36.8 |
|  |  | 6.3 | 2.5 |  |  | Intangibles (net) | 5.9 | 4.3 |
|  |  | 3.6 | 3.4 |  |  | All Other Non-Current | 6.6 | 7.1 |
|  |  | 100.0 | 100.0 |  |  | Total | 100.0 | 100.0 |
|  |  |  |  |  |  | **LIABILITIES** |  |  |
|  |  | 12.7 | 12.9 |  |  | Notes Payable-Short Term | 12.3 | 13.7 |
|  |  | 4.7 | 4.4 |  |  | Cur. Mat.-L.T.D. | 3.7 | 4.2 |
|  |  | 28.5 | 15.4 |  |  | Trade Payables | 12.5 | 15.0 |
|  |  | .0 | .0 |  |  | Income Taxes Payable | .9 | .5 |
|  |  | 5.8 | 5.0 |  |  | All Other Current | 5.9 | 8.2 |
|  |  | 51.7 | 37.7 |  |  | Total Current | 35.2 | 41.5 |
|  |  | 16.1 | 20.2 |  |  | Long-Term Debt | 19.4 | 19.0 |
|  |  | .5 | .6 |  |  | Deferred Taxes | .5 | .4 |
|  |  | 10.5 | 3.2 |  |  | All Other Non-Current | 3.9 | 10.4 |
|  |  | 21.2 | 38.3 |  |  | Net Worth | 41.0 | 28.7 |
|  |  | 100.0 | 100.0 |  |  | Total Liabilities & Net Worth | 100.0 | 100.0 |
|  |  |  |  |  |  | **INCOME DATA** |  |  |
|  |  | 100.0 | 100.0 |  |  | Net Sales | 100.0 | 100.0 |
|  |  | 23.5 | 15.2 |  |  | Gross Profit | 25.6 | 27.5 |
|  |  | 21.0 | 14.7 |  |  | Operating Expenses | 20.0 | 23.0 |
|  |  | 2.5 | .5 |  |  | Operating Profit | 5.6 | 4.5 |
|  |  | 1.3 | 2.3 |  |  | All Other Expenses (net) | 1.2 | 1.3 |
|  |  | 1.2 | -1.7 |  |  | Profit Before Taxes | 4.4 | 3.2 |
|  |  |  |  |  |  | **RATIOS** |  |  |
|  |  | 2.2 | 2.8 |  |  |  | 2.1 | 1.9 |
|  |  | 1.1 | 1.4 |  |  | Current | 1.5 | 1.3 |
|  |  | 1.0 | 1.0 |  |  |  | 1.1 | 1.0 |
|  |  | 1.0 | 2.0 |  |  |  | 1.1 | 1.1 |
|  |  | .5 | .7 |  |  | Quick | .7 | .6 |
|  |  | .4 | .4 |  |  |  | .4 | .4 |
|  |  | 16   22.5 | 22   16.4 |  |  |  | 23   15.8 | 24   15.3 |
|  |  | 27   13.7 | 31   11.7 |  |  | Sales/Receivables | 30   12.1 | 30   12.4 |
|  |  | 33   10.9 | 40   9.2 |  |  |  | 36   10.2 | 38   9.5 |
|  |  | 26   14.1 | 31   11.9 |  |  |  | 33   11.1 | 31   12.0 |
|  |  | 62   5.9 | 36   10.0 |  |  | Cost of Sales/Inventory | 49   7.5 | 43   8.6 |
|  |  | 70   5.2 | 54   6.8 |  |  |  | 90   4.0 | 61   6.0 |
|  |  | 27   13.6 | 21   17.6 |  |  |  | 18   19.9 | 16   23.0 |
|  |  | 37   9.9 | 24   15.2 |  |  | Cost of Sales/Payables | 25   14.6 | 29   12.5 |
|  |  | 50   7.3 | 32   11.3 |  |  |  | 32   11.3 | 35   10.4 |
|  |  | 7.2 | 6.9 |  |  |  | 6.8 | 9.2 |
|  |  | 75.8 | 18.7 |  |  | Sales/Working Capital | 14.5 | 26.8 |
|  |  | -427.7 | 747.5 |  |  |  | 50.2 | 282.0 |
|  |  |  | 8.7 |  |  |  | 6.0 | 5.9 |
|  |  |  | 2.6 |  |  | EBIT/Interest | 3.6 | (35) 3.1 |
|  |  |  | -1.9 |  |  |  | 1.6 | 1.8 |
|  |  |  |  |  |  |  | 4.7 | 5.5 |
|  |  |  |  |  |  | Net Profit + Depr., Dep., Amort./Cur. Mat. L/T/D | (14) 2.3 | (13) 1.6 |
|  |  |  |  |  |  |  | 1.1 | 1.2 |
|  |  | .9 | .5 |  |  |  | .6 | .8 |
|  |  | 2.6 | 1.3 |  |  | Fixed/Worth | 1.2 | 1.3 |
|  |  | NM | 2.1 |  |  |  | 3.4 | 5.4 |
|  |  | 2.2 | 1.0 |  |  |  | .8 | 1.1 |
|  |  | 7.1 | 2.8 |  |  | Debt/Worth | 1.5 | 2.2 |
|  |  | NM | 3.7 |  |  |  | 5.7 | 12.5 |
|  |  |  | 27.8 |  |  |  | 41.3 | 66.9 |
|  |  |  | 13.3 |  |  | % Profit Before Taxes/Tangible Net Worth | (24) 14.8 | (30) 18.0 |
|  |  |  | -39.4 |  |  |  | 2.6 | 6.6 |
|  |  | 7.2 | 10.6 |  |  |  | 8.6 | 11.6 |
|  |  | 3.1 | 3.5 |  |  | % Profit Before Taxes/Total Assets | 5.5 | 5.4 |
|  |  | -9.2 | -6.5 |  |  |  | 2.7 | 2.7 |
|  |  | 17.0 | 9.5 |  |  |  | 9.8 | 11.4 |
|  |  | 10.2 | 7.0 |  |  | Sales/Net Fixed Assets | 6.8 | 7.7 |
|  |  | 6.4 | 5.6 |  |  |  | 3.3 | 3.4 |
|  |  | 4.4 | 3.1 |  |  |  | 2.8 | 3.5 |
|  |  | 2.9 | 2.4 |  |  | Sales/Total Assets | 2.1 | 2.5 |
|  |  | 2.0 | 1.9 |  |  |  | 1.2 | 1.6 |
|  |  |  | 1.3 |  |  |  | 1.9 | 1.1 |
|  |  |  | 2.2 |  |  | % Depr., Dep., Amort./Sales | (25) 3.1 | (33) 2.7 |
|  |  |  | 3.6 |  |  |  | 4.3 | 3.6 |
|  |  |  |  |  |  | % Officers', Directors' Owners' Comp/Sales |  |  |
| 2408M | 17147M | 192938M | 814724M | 270710M | 589101M | Net Sales ($) | 1694387M | 1963688M |
| 446M | 5246M | 58508M | 293165M | 137458M | 422890M | Total Assets ($) | 918695M | 867253M |

## Comparative Historical Data / Current Data Sorted by Sales

| Hist 1 | Hist 2 | Hist 3 | Type of Statement | 0-1MM | 1-3MM | 3-5MM | 5-10MM | 10-25MM | 25MM & OVER |
|---|---|---|---|---|---|---|---|---|---|
| 7 | 6 | 9 | Unqualified | | | | | 3 | 6 |
| 6 | 11 | 5 | Reviewed | 1 | | | | 3 | 1 |
| 6 | 4 | 3 | Compiled | | | | | 1 | 2 |
| 4 | 3 | 2 | Tax Returns | | | 1 | 1 | | |
| 11 | 15 | 13 | Other | 1 | 1 | 1 | 1 | 3 | 6 |
| 4/1/09-3/31/10 ALL | 4/1/10-3/31/11 ALL | 4/1/11-3/31/12 ALL | | | 5 (4/1-9/30/11) | | | 27 (10/1/11-3/31/12) | |
| 34 | 39 | 32 | NUMBER OF STATEMENTS | 2 | 1 | 2 | 2 | 10 | 15 |
| % | % | % | **ASSETS** | % | % | % | % | % | % |
| 10.3 | 10.9 | 6.8 | Cash & Equivalents | | | | | 6.5 | 6.1 |
| 20.0 | 20.6 | 20.5 | Trade Receivables (net) | | | | | 18.3 | 21.6 |
| 29.3 | 24.3 | 27.1 | Inventory | | | | | 30.5 | 26.9 |
| 1.2 | 1.5 | 2.7 | All Other Current | | | | | 2.1 | 3.1 |
| 60.7 | 57.3 | 57.0 | Total Current | | | | | 57.4 | 57.7 |
| 28.8 | 35.5 | 35.5 | Fixed Assets (net) | | | | | 32.8 | 36.3 |
| 6.2 | 4.1 | 4.7 | Intangibles (net) | | | | | 6.5 | 3.2 |
| 4.3 | 3.0 | 2.8 | All Other Non-Current | | | | | 3.3 | 2.7 |
| 100.0 | 100.0 | 100.0 | Total | | | | | 100.0 | 100.0 |
| | | | **LIABILITIES** | | | | | | |
| 10.6 | 9.2 | 13.3 | Notes Payable-Short Term | | | | | 11.8 | 13.6 |
| 2.6 | 4.2 | 4.2 | Cur. Mat.-L.T.D. | | | | | 4.6 | 4.0 |
| 16.2 | 16.5 | 18.2 | Trade Payables | | | | | 23.6 | 18.8 |
| .7 | .3 | .0 | Income Taxes Payable | | | | | .0 | .0 |
| 19.5 | 7.6 | 4.7 | All Other Current | | | | | 5.0 | 4.6 |
| 49.6 | 37.7 | 40.3 | Total Current | | | | | 45.0 | 41.1 |
| 15.0 | 16.8 | 20.5 | Long-Term Debt | | | | | 19.2 | 17.6 |
| .3 | .2 | .4 | Deferred Taxes | | | | | .7 | .4 |
| 6.1 | 4.9 | 8.1 | All Other Non-Current | | | | | 11.5 | 5.3 |
| 29.0 | 40.3 | 30.6 | Net Worth | | | | | 23.7 | 35.6 |
| 100.0 | 100.0 | 100.0 | Total Liabilities & Net Worth | | | | | 100.0 | 100.0 |
| | | | **INCOME DATA** | | | | | | |
| 100.0 | 100.0 | 100.0 | Net Sales | | | | | 100.0 | 100.0 |
| 30.2 | 26.4 | 22.9 | Gross Profit | | | | | 24.6 | 15.3 |
| 25.9 | 21.2 | 21.2 | Operating Expenses | | | | | 21.4 | 14.1 |
| 4.3 | 5.3 | 1.7 | Operating Profit | | | | | 3.2 | 1.2 |
| .5 | 1.0 | 1.5 | All Other Expenses (net) | | | | | 1.4 | 1.9 |
| 3.8 | 4.3 | .2 | Profit Before Taxes | | | | | 1.9 | -.7 |
| | | | **RATIOS** | | | | | | |
| 2.6 | 2.8 | 2.2 | Current | | | | | 2.4 | 2.2 |
| 1.7 | 1.5 | 1.4 | | | | | | 1.1 | 1.4 |
| 1.0 | 1.1 | 1.0 | | | | | | 1.0 | 1.0 |
| 1.7 | 1.7 | 1.5 | Quick | | | | | 1.1 | 1.5 |
| .8 | .7 | .7 | | | | | | .5 | .7 |
| .4 | .5 | .4 | | | | | | .4 | .4 |
| 21  17.8 | 23  15.9 | 22  16.4 | Sales/Receivables | | | | | 20  18.4 | 22  16.4 |
| 28  13.0 | 32  11.5 | 30  12.2 | | | | | | 27  13.7 | 32  11.5 |
| 35  10.4 | 36  10.0 | 38  9.6 | | | | | | 32  11.4 | 39  9.3 |
| 30  12.0 | 35  10.5 | 30  12.2 | Cost of Sales/Inventory | | | | | 41  9.0 | 31  11.9 |
| 47  7.7 | 44  8.4 | 43  8.4 | | | | | | 62  5.9 | 36  10.0 |
| 76  4.8 | 64  5.7 | 66  5.5 | | | | | | 70  5.2 | 51  7.1 |
| 16  23.0 | 17  20.9 | 20  18.0 | Cost of Sales/Payables | | | | | 27  13.5 | 21  17.6 |
| 24  15.2 | 25  14.7 | 30  12.3 | | | | | | 41  9.0 | 24  15.2 |
| 41  8.9 | 42  8.7 | 38  9.7 | | | | | | 50  7.3 | 32  11.3 |
| 7.5 | 6.7 | 7.0 | Sales/Working Capital | | | | | 7.2 | 6.9 |
| 13.0 | 12.1 | 16.8 | | | | | | 75.8 | 13.8 |
| -761.3 | 49.6 | 609.2 | | | | | | -886.1 | 747.5 |
| 24.4 | 13.5 | 5.3 | EBIT/Interest | | | | | | 5.6 |
| (33)  10.2 | (35)  6.1 | (30)  2.5 | | | | | | | 3.9 |
| 4.1 | 2.6 | -1.5 | | | | | | | -1.9 |
| 9.5 | 9.1 | 4.6 | Net Profit + Depr., Dep., Amort./Cur. Mat. L/T/D | | | | | | 4.4 |
| (14)  3.5 | (21)  2.7 | (16)  1.8 | | | | | | | (10)  1.8 |
| 2.2 | 1.5 | .4 | | | | | | | -.2 |
| .5 | .6 | .7 | Fixed/Worth | | | | | .9 | .7 |
| 1.0 | 1.1 | 1.7 | | | | | | 2.1 | 1.6 |
| 2.2 | 2.4 | 3.2 | | | | | | 13.8 | 2.1 |
| .6 | .7 | 1.1 | Debt/Worth | | | | | 2.3 | 1.0 |
| 2.1 | 1.4 | 3.3 | | | | | | 4.1 | 2.8 |
| 3.8 | 3.8 | 5.4 | | | | | | 29.8 | 3.7 |
| 70.6 | 32.8 | 32.2 | % Profit Before Taxes/Tangible Net Worth | | | | | | 34.5 |
| (30)  27.2 | (37)  18.5 | (29)  7.0 | | | | | | | (14)  8.8 |
| 13.4 | 8.8 | -15.2 | | | | | | | -30.7 |
| 20.9 | 13.4 | 8.0 | % Profit Before Taxes/Total Assets | | | | | 9.4 | 8.8 |
| 9.7 | 6.3 | 2.9 | | | | | | 5.6 | 2.4 |
| 4.3 | 3.4 | -4.6 | | | | | | -2.1 | -6.5 |
| 25.5 | 12.4 | 12.4 | Sales/Net Fixed Assets | | | | | 13.6 | 9.3 |
| 8.9 | 7.5 | 6.9 | | | | | | 9.2 | 6.0 |
| 5.1 | 3.1 | 3.9 | | | | | | 6.4 | 3.6 |
| 3.7 | 3.2 | 3.3 | Sales/Total Assets | | | | | 3.6 | 3.1 |
| 2.7 | 2.4 | 2.5 | | | | | | 2.6 | 2.3 |
| 1.6 | 1.5 | 1.7 | | | | | | 2.0 | 1.5 |
| .8 | 1.2 | 1.2 | % Depr., Dep., Amort./Sales | | | | | 1.3 | 1.0 |
| (29)  1.5 | (37)  2.2 | (28)  2.1 | | | | | | 1.9 | (14)  2.0 |
| 3.3 | 3.9 | 3.5 | | | | | | 2.4 | 3.7 |
| | 1.5 | | % Officers', Directors' Owners' Comp/Sales | | | | | | |
| | (10)  2.7 | | | | | | | | |
| | 4.9 | | | | | | | | |
| 1828367M | 1981910M | 1887028M | Net Sales ($) | 893M | 2371M | 9528M | 16546M | 171566M | 1686124M |
| 844840M | 1031704M | 917713M | Total Assets ($) | 982M | 410M | 2613M | 9342M | 66670M | 837696M |

**M = $ thousand    MM = $ million**
See Pages 9 through 22 for Explanation of Ratios and Data

## Current Data Sorted by Assets

## Comparative Historical Data

| | | | | | | Type of Statement | | |
|---|---|---|---|---|---|---|---|---|
| | 1 | 5 | | | 1 | Unqualified | 7 | 6 |
| | 1 | 3 | | | | Reviewed | 5 | 3 |
| | 4 | 2 | | | | Compiled | 5 | 3 |
| | 2 | | | | | Tax Returns | | 3 |
| | 6 | | | | | Other | 14 | 11 |
| | 1 | | 6 | | | | 4/1/07- | 4/1/08- |
| | 8 (4/1-9/30/11) | | 28 (10/1/11-3/31/12) | | | | 3/31/08 | 3/31/09 |
| 0-500M | 500M-2MM | 2-10MM | 10-50MM | 50-100MM | 100-250MM | | ALL | ALL |
| | 1 | 14 | 16 | 2 | 3 | NUMBER OF STATEMENTS | 31 | 26 |
| % | % | % | % | % | % | ASSETS | % | % |
| | | 11.0 | 10.3 | | | Cash & Equivalents | 6.1 | 6.6 |
| | | 24.5 | 18.9 | | | Trade Receivables (net) | 18.9 | 17.6 |
| | | 33.4 | 34.8 | | | Inventory | 26.0 | 32.9 |
| | | 1.7 | 2.2 | | | All Other Current | 4.8 | 1.5 |
| | | 70.5 | 66.2 | | | Total Current | 55.9 | 58.6 |
| | | 24.8 | 29.4 | | | Fixed Assets (net) | 37.1 | 33.0 |
| | | 3.3 | .8 | | | Intangibles (net) | 3.0 | 3.2 |
| | | 1.3 | 3.6 | | | All Other Non-Current | 4.0 | 5.2 |
| | | 100.0 | 100.0 | | | Total | 100.0 | 100.0 |
| | | | | | | LIABILITIES | | |
| | | 6.7 | 7.9 | | | Notes Payable-Short Term | 8.1 | 11.3 |
| | | 3.9 | 2.6 | | | Cur. Mat.-L.T.D. | 4.6 | 1.5 |
| | | 16.0 | 13.4 | | | Trade Payables | 12.2 | 15.0 |
| | | .7 | 1.4 | | | Income Taxes Payable | .1 | .4 |
| | | 6.5 | 5.0 | | | All Other Current | 9.6 | 7.8 |
| | | 33.9 | 30.3 | | | Total Current | 34.6 | 36.0 |
| | | 8.1 | 11.8 | | | Long-Term Debt | 18.5 | 15.6 |
| | | .4 | .4 | | | Deferred Taxes | .4 | .6 |
| | | 10.7 | 1.4 | | | All Other Non-Current | 4.8 | 13.9 |
| | | 46.9 | 56.2 | | | Net Worth | 41.8 | 33.9 |
| | | 100.0 | 100.0 | | | Total Liabilties & Net Worth | 100.0 | 100.0 |
| | | | | | | INCOME DATA | | |
| | | 100.0 | 100.0 | | | Net Sales | 100.0 | 100.0 |
| | | 35.3 | 31.0 | | | Gross Profit | 30.8 | 26.7 |
| | | 27.4 | 21.0 | | | Operating Expenses | 23.1 | 23.4 |
| | | 7.9 | 10.0 | | | Operating Profit | 7.6 | 3.3 |
| | | .7 | .7 | | | All Other Expenses (net) | 1.3 | 1.6 |
| | | 7.2 | 9.3 | | | Profit Before Taxes | 6.3 | 1.7 |
| | | | | | | RATIOS | | |
| | | 3.7 | 4.8 | | | | 2.4 | 2.8 |
| | | 2.3 | 2.5 | | | Current | 1.5 | 1.5 |
| | | 1.5 | 1.8 | | | | 1.2 | 1.2 |
| | | 2.0 | 2.2 | | | | 1.1 | 1.1 |
| | | 1.2 | 1.2 | | | Quick | .8 | .7 |
| | | .6 | .6 | | | | .5 | .5 |
| | | 24  14.9 | 26  13.9 | | | | 23  15.7 | 22  16.7 |
| | | 38  9.6 | 32  11.3 | | | Sales/Receivables | 33  10.9 | 33  11.0 |
| | | 43  8.5 | 38  9.5 | | | | 44  8.3 | 39  9.3 |
| | | 59  6.2 | 63  5.8 | | | | 36  10.2 | 53  6.9 |
| | | 76  4.8 | 73  5.0 | | | Cost of Sales/Inventory | 55  6.6 | 79  4.6 |
| | | 107  3.4 | 130  2.8 | | | | 93  3.9 | 100  3.7 |
| | | 26  13.9 | 18  20.2 | | | | 18  20.0 | 25  14.6 |
| | | 37  9.8 | 32  11.4 | | | Cost of Sales/Payables | 28  12.9 | 35  10.3 |
| | | 45  8.1 | 49  7.4 | | | | 52  7.0 | 44  8.3 |
| | | 4.0 | 3.4 | | | | 5.4 | 5.0 |
| | | 6.7 | 5.3 | | | Sales/Working Capital | 11.5 | 8.6 |
| | | 14.2 | 8.4 | | | | 23.4 | 19.7 |
| | | 41.9 | 135.0 | | | | 8.8 | 10.1 |
| | | (13)  13.4 | (15)  16.3 | | | EBIT/Interest | 3.6 | (25)  2.2 |
| | | 2.7 | 4.4 | | | | 1.5 | .5 |
| | | | | | | Net Profit + Depr., Dep., Amort./Cur. Mat. L/T/D | | |
| | | .3 | .2 | | | | .3 | .4 |
| | | .4 | .5 | | | Fixed/Worth | .9 | .8 |
| | | 1.4 | 1.0 | | | | 2.2 | 1.6 |
| | | .4 | .2 | | | | .7 | .9 |
| | | .9 | 1.0 | | | Debt/Worth | 1.2 | 1.6 |
| | | 2.9 | 1.5 | | | | 2.9 | 3.4 |
| | | 53.2 | 38.8 | | | | 50.2 | 46.8 |
| | | (13)  33.1 | (15)  22.5 | | | % Profit Before Taxes/Tangible Net Worth | (28)  21.8 | (22)  12.0 |
| | | 23.3 | 14.8 | | | | 3.3 | -2.2 |
| | | 26.5 | 25.7 | | | | 16.7 | 9.5 |
| | | 16.9 | 15.5 | | | % Profit Before Taxes/Total Assets | 7.6 | 3.0 |
| | | 3.6 | 5.1 | | | | 1.7 | -1.0 |
| | | 22.4 | 22.6 | | | | 13.7 | 11.5 |
| | | 17.7 | 8.6 | | | Sales/Net Fixed Assets | 3.6 | 6.1 |
| | | 4.8 | 3.6 | | | | 2.5 | 3.4 |
| | | 3.2 | 2.7 | | | | 2.7 | 2.5 |
| | | 2.6 | 2.0 | | | Sales/Total Assets | 1.7 | 1.6 |
| | | 1.9 | 1.5 | | | | 1.3 | 1.3 |
| | | .9 | 1.0 | | | | 1.0 | 1.3 |
| | | 1.7 | 1.5 | | | % Depr., Dep., Amort./Sales | (27)  3.0 | (24)  2.2 |
| | | 2.9 | 2.4 | | | | 3.8 | 3.5 |
| | | | | | | % Officers', Directors' Owners' Comp/Sales | | |
| | 16132M | 204897M | 702352M | 283260M | 644400M | Net Sales ($) | 1121823M | 929724M |
| | 1732M | 80582M | 342776M | 142705M | 436842M | Total Assets ($) | 820683M | 689274M |

The leftmost column (0-500M) is marked **DATA NOT AVAILABLE**.

M = $ thousand    MM = $ million
See Pages 9 through 22 for Explanation of Ratios and Data

## Comparative Historical Data / Current Data Sorted by Sales

| 5 / 4 / 3 / 3 / 13 | 5 / 4 / 5 / 2 / 11 | 7 / 4 / 6 / 2 / 17 | Type of Statement | 0-1MM | 1-3MM | 3-5MM | 5-10MM | 10-25MM | 25MM & OVER |
|---|---|---|---|---|---|---|---|---|---|
| | | | Unqualified | | | | 1 | 1 | 5 |
| | | | Reviewed | | 1 | | | 1 | 2 |
| | | | Compiled | 1 | | | | 4 | 1 |
| | | | Tax Returns | | | | | 1 | 1 |
| | | | Other | | | | 2 | 4 | 11 |
| 4/1/09-3/31/10 ALL | 4/1/10-3/31/11 ALL | 4/1/11-3/31/12 ALL | | | 8 (4/1-9/30/11) | | | 28 (10/1/11-3/31/12) | |
| 28 | 27 | 36 | NUMBER OF STATEMENTS | | | 2 | 3 | 11 | 20 |
| % | % | % | ASSETS | % | % | % | % | % | % |
| 8.6 | 7.4 | 10.4 | Cash & Equivalents | D | D | | | 13.8 | 8.0 |
| 19.4 | 21.7 | 21.0 | Trade Receivables (net) | A | A | | | 27.2 | 19.3 |
| 33.8 | 31.8 | 34.8 | Inventory | T | T | | | 29.0 | 41.5 |
| 2.5 | 1.5 | 1.9 | All Other Current | A | A | | | .6 | 2.5 |
| 64.4 | 62.5 | 68.0 | Total Current | | | | | 70.7 | 71.2 |
| 28.4 | 30.6 | 24.9 | Fixed Assets (net) | N | N | | | 21.3 | 22.7 |
| 2.5 | 2.2 | 3.0 | Intangibles (net) | O | O | | | .8 | 3.0 |
| 4.7 | 4.7 | 4.1 | All Other Non-Current | T | T | | | 7.2 | 3.1 |
| 100.0 | 100.0 | 100.0 | Total | | | | | 100.0 | 100.0 |
| | | | LIABILITIES | A | A | | | | |
| 9.7 | 8.2 | 7.0 | Notes Payable-Short Term | V | V | | | 6.2 | 7.4 |
| 4.3 | 4.8 | 2.9 | Cur. Mat.-L.T.D. | A | A | | | 4.9 | 1.5 |
| 12.6 | 16.1 | 14.7 | Trade Payables | I | I | | | 18.9 | 13.7 |
| 1.0 | .7 | .9 | Income Taxes Payable | L | L | | | 1.4 | .5 |
| 6.3 | 7.0 | 5.8 | All Other Current | A | A | | | 7.3 | 5.6 |
| 33.9 | 36.7 | 31.3 | Total Current | B | B | | | 38.7 | 28.7 |
| 13.7 | 11.7 | 10.7 | Long-Term Debt | L | L | | | 6.1 | 11.7 |
| .4 | .3 | .3 | Deferred Taxes | E | E | | | .2 | .3 |
| 7.8 | 4.6 | 5.6 | All Other Non-Current | | | | | 10.1 | 2.2 |
| 44.3 | 46.7 | 52.1 | Net Worth | | | | | 44.9 | 57.1 |
| 100.0 | 100.0 | 100.0 | Total Liabilities & Net Worth | | | | | 100.0 | 100.0 |
| | | | INCOME DATA | | | | | | |
| 100.0 | 100.0 | 100.0 | Net Sales | | | | | 100.0 | 100.0 |
| 30.3 | 32.2 | 31.5 | Gross Profit | | | | | 37.4 | 28.0 |
| 25.1 | 24.7 | 22.9 | Operating Expenses | | | | | 26.3 | 20.7 |
| 5.2 | 7.5 | 8.6 | Operating Profit | | | | | 11.2 | 7.3 |
| .6 | 1.5 | .7 | All Other Expenses (net) | | | | | .7 | .5 |
| 4.6 | 6.0 | 8.0 | Profit Before Taxes | | | | | 10.5 | 6.8 |
| | | | RATIOS | | | | | | |
| 3.7 | 3.3 | 4.1 | Current | | | | | 2.7 | 5.0 |
| 2.2 | 1.9 | 2.6 | Current | | | | | 1.9 | 3.0 |
| 1.5 | 1.1 | 1.6 | Current | | | | | 1.2 | 2.0 |
| 1.7 | 1.6 | 2.0 | Quick | | | | | 1.7 | 2.3 |
| .9 | 1.0 | 1.1 | Quick | | | | | 1.1 | 1.0 |
| .5 | .5 | .6 | Quick | | | | | .8 | .6 |
| 21  17.5 | 26  14.0 | 26  13.9 | Sales/Receivables | | | | | 25  14.7 | 28  13.0 |
| 29  12.4 | 30  12.0 | 35  10.5 | Sales/Receivables | | | | | 39  9.3 | 33  11.0 |
| 42  8.6 | 37  9.9 | 41  9.0 | Sales/Receivables | | | | | 41  9.0 | 38  9.5 |
| 55  6.7 | 54  6.8 | 63  5.8 | Cost of Sales/Inventory | | | | | 33  11.0 | 64  5.7 |
| 85  4.3 | 70  5.2 | 78  4.7 | Cost of Sales/Inventory | | | | | 73  5.0 | 87  4.2 |
| 106  3.5 | 115  3.2 | 130  2.8 | Cost of Sales/Inventory | | | | | 107  3.4 | 146  2.5 |
| 21  17.1 | 20  18.1 | 21  17.2 | Cost of Sales/Payables | | | | | 29  12.6 | 17  22.1 |
| 29  12.5 | 32  11.4 | 34  10.8 | Cost of Sales/Payables | | | | | 40  9.2 | 27  13.3 |
| 37  9.7 | 49  7.5 | 46  8.0 | Cost of Sales/Payables | | | | | 49  7.4 | 46  8.0 |
| 4.2 | 3.6 | 3.4 | Sales/Working Capital | | | | | 5.0 | 3.4 |
| 6.9 | 8.7 | 5.6 | Sales/Working Capital | | | | | 8.3 | 4.6 |
| 13.8 | 44.6 | 9.2 | Sales/Working Capital | | | | | 14.0 | 6.7 |
| 20.4 | 88.7 | 58.7 | EBIT/Interest | | | | | 47.1 | 125.1 |
| (26) 7.0 | (32) 12.6 | 15.4 | EBIT/Interest | | | | | (16) 20.0 | 18.5 |
| 2.2 | 3.1 | 3.7 | EBIT/Interest | | | | | 6.3 | 3.3 |
| | | 7.3 | Net Profit + Depr., Dep., Amort./Cur. Mat. L/T/D | | | | | | |
| | (13) | 2.6 | Net Profit + Depr., Dep., Amort./Cur. Mat. L/T/D | | | | | | |
| | | 1.8 | Net Profit + Depr., Dep., Amort./Cur. Mat. L/T/D | | | | | | |
| .4 | .3 | .2 | Fixed/Worth | | | | | .2 | .2 |
| .6 | .5 | .4 | Fixed/Worth | | | | | .4 | .3 |
| 1.0 | 1.0 | 1.0 | Fixed/Worth | | | | | .8 | .7 |
| .6 | .4 | .3 | Debt/Worth | | | | | .4 | .3 |
| 1.3 | 1.3 | 1.0 | Debt/Worth | | | | | 1.2 | .7 |
| 3.8 | 4.0 | 1.8 | Debt/Worth | | | | | 1.7 | 1.5 |
| 44.9 | 54.4 | 39.0 | % Profit Before Taxes/Tangible Net Worth | | | | | 103.5 | 34.6 |
| (26) 18.5 | (34) 28.9 | 27.4 | % Profit Before Taxes/Tangible Net Worth | | | | (10) | 44.8 | (19) 19.5 |
| 10.1 | 9.4 | 16.2 | % Profit Before Taxes/Tangible Net Worth | | | | | 17.8 | 13.7 |
| 23.1 | 28.0 | 25.8 | % Profit Before Taxes/Total Assets | | | | | 37.9 | 24.7 |
| 9.5 | 12.3 | 14.5 | % Profit Before Taxes/Total Assets | | | | | 22.7 | 10.9 |
| 2.9 | 3.3 | 4.8 | % Profit Before Taxes/Total Assets | | | | | 3.4 | 5.1 |
| 17.3 | 20.4 | 23.5 | Sales/Net Fixed Assets | | | | | 25.9 | 24.4 |
| 10.1 | 9.7 | 10.2 | Sales/Net Fixed Assets | | | | | 19.1 | 10.2 |
| 5.2 | 4.0 | 5.4 | Sales/Net Fixed Assets | | | | | 9.2 | 6.5 |
| 2.8 | 2.8 | 3.0 | Sales/Total Assets | | | | | 3.7 | 3.0 |
| 2.1 | 2.1 | 2.1 | Sales/Total Assets | | | | | 2.6 | 2.2 |
| 1.3 | 1.6 | 1.5 | Sales/Total Assets | | | | | 2.0 | 1.6 |
| 1.2 | .9 | .8 | % Depr., Dep., Amort./Sales | | | | | .5 | .8 |
| (23) 2.0 | (24) 1.5 | (35) 1.4 | % Depr., Dep., Amort./Sales | | | | | 1.2 | (19) 1.3 |
| 3.1 | 2.4 | 2.5 | % Depr., Dep., Amort./Sales | | | | | 2.0 | 1.9 |
| | | | % Officers', Directors' Owners' Comp/Sales | | | | | | |
| 1211136M | 1105425M | 1851041M | Net Sales ($) | | | 8204M | 20343M | 199923M | 1622571M |
| 647382M | 518587M | 1004637M | Total Assets ($) | | | 9699M | 10804M | 103854M | 880280M |

M = $ thousand    MM = $ million
See Pages 9 through 22 for Explanation of Ratios and Data

## Current Data Sorted by Assets      Comparative Historical Data

| 0-500M | 500M-2MM | 2-10MM | 10-50MM | 50-100MM | 100-250MM | | 4/1/07-3/31/08 ALL | 4/1/08-3/31/09 ALL |
|---|---|---|---|---|---|---|---|---|
| | | | | | | **Type of Statement** | | |
| | | 1 | 4 | 1 | 2 | Unqualified | 5 | 7 |
| | | 4 | 1 | | | Reviewed | 3 | 5 |
| | | 4 | | | | Compiled | 2 | 4 |
| | 2 | 1 | | | | Tax Returns | | 2 |
| 3 | 2 | 8 | 6 | 2 | 1 | Other | 10 | 9 |
| | | 4 (4/1-9/30/11) | 40 (10/1/11-3/31/12) | | | | 10 | 9 |
| 3 | 6 | 18 | 11 | 3 | 3 | **NUMBER OF STATEMENTS** | 20 | 27 |
| % | % | % | % | % | % | **ASSETS** | % | % |
| | | 10.7 | 9.8 | | | Cash & Equivalents | 11.0 | 6.2 |
| | | 19.7 | 15.2 | | | Trade Receivables (net) | 17.4 | 18.4 |
| | | 21.6 | 13.6 | | | Inventory | 14.0 | 17.5 |
| | | 4.0 | 1.8 | | | All Other Current | 3.2 | 1.5 |
| | | 55.9 | 40.4 | | | Total Current | 45.7 | 43.6 |
| | | 27.6 | 47.5 | | | Fixed Assets (net) | 35.5 | 40.8 |
| | | 14.3 | 2.7 | | | Intangibles (net) | 14.5 | 9.9 |
| | | 2.2 | 9.4 | | | All Other Non-Current | 4.3 | 5.7 |
| | | 100.0 | 100.0 | | | Total | 100.0 | 100.0 |
| | | | | | | **LIABILITIES** | | |
| | | 5.9 | 3.8 | | | Notes Payable-Short Term | 5.4 | 8.0 |
| | | 3.3 | 3.1 | | | Cur. Mat.-L.T.D. | 3.1 | 3.6 |
| | | 20.0 | 11.0 | | | Trade Payables | 19.4 | 20.6 |
| | | .0 | .0 | | | Income Taxes Payable | .0 | .1 |
| | | 6.2 | 13.4 | | | All Other Current | 15.8 | 9.7 |
| | | 35.4 | 31.3 | | | Total Current | 43.8 | 42.0 |
| | | 15.7 | 26.6 | | | Long-Term Debt | 23.0 | 29.4 |
| | | .0 | .6 | | | Deferred Taxes | .1 | .9 |
| | | 13.7 | 10.7 | | | All Other Non-Current | 2.9 | 3.1 |
| | | 35.2 | 30.8 | | | Net Worth | 30.1 | 24.6 |
| | | 100.0 | 100.0 | | | Total Liabilties & Net Worth | 100.0 | 100.0 |
| | | | | | | **INCOME DATA** | | |
| | | 100.0 | 100.0 | | | Net Sales | 100.0 | 100.0 |
| | | 30.6 | 23.1 | | | Gross Profit | 25.7 | 27.9 |
| | | 26.8 | 21.8 | | | Operating Expenses | 24.4 | 26.9 |
| | | 3.8 | 1.3 | | | Operating Profit | 1.3 | 1.0 |
| | | .5 | 1.7 | | | All Other Expenses (net) | 1.3 | 1.3 |
| | | 3.3 | -.4 | | | Profit Before Taxes | .1 | -.4 |
| | | | | | | **RATIOS** | | |
| | | 2.3 | 2.3 | | | | 2.1 | 2.4 |
| | | 1.4 | 1.3 | | | Current | 1.0 | .9 |
| | | 1.0 | .8 | | | | .7 | .8 |
| | | 1.8 | 1.4 | | | | 1.3 | 1.0 |
| | | .7 | .8 | | | Quick | .6 | .6 |
| | | .5 | .4 | | | | .4 | .4 |
| | | 13   28.4 | 21   17.2 | | | | 20   18.1 | 19   19.4 |
| | | 19   19.3 | 24   15.3 | | | Sales/Receivables | 24   15.0 | 23   15.8 |
| | | 30   12.3 | 40   9.1 | | | | 31   11.7 | 29   12.4 |
| | | 6   59.4 | 19   18.9 | | | | 17   21.8 | 15   24.8 |
| | | 24   14.9 | 34   10.6 | | | Cost of Sales/Inventory | 24   15.2 | 31   11.9 |
| | | 68   5.4 | 40   9.2 | | | | 43   8.4 | 57   6.4 |
| | | 16   22.3 | 12   29.4 | | | | 23   15.8 | 20   18.1 |
| | | 36   10.1 | 24   15.1 | | | Cost of Sales/Payables | 30   12.3 | 32   11.5 |
| | | 55   6.6 | 28   13.0 | | | | 43   8.5 | 45   8.2 |
| | | 9.2 | 6.2 | | | | 14.0 | 11.4 |
| | | 20.2 | 32.8 | | | Sales/Working Capital | NM | -46.2 |
| | | -789.4 | -25.8 | | | | -17.6 | -23.4 |
| | | 36.5 | 9.4 | | | | 5.0 | 5.2 |
| | | (17) 6.1 | 4.3 | | | EBIT/Interest | (16) 1.4 | 2.4 |
| | | 2.9 | -4.0 | | | | -.8 | * .6 |
| | | | | | | | | 8.2 |
| | | | | | | Net Profit + Depr., Dep., Amort./Cur. Mat. L/T/D | | (13) 4.1 |
| | | | | | | | | 1.5 |
| | | .3 | .9 | | | | 1.0 | 1.3 |
| | | 1.2 | 1.6 | | | Fixed/Worth | 1.9 | 2.9 |
| | | -37.8 | 6.2 | | | | NM | -4.6 |
| | | .7 | 1.1 | | | | 1.3 | 1.4 |
| | | 2.5 | 1.7 | | | Debt/Worth | 3.3 | 5.3 |
| | | -309.3 | 11.6 | | | | NM | -20.6 |
| | | 32.8 | 35.1 | | | | 58.0 | 31.7 |
| | | (13) 25.7 | (10) 20.8 | | | % Profit Before Taxes/Tangible Net Worth | (15) 7.0 | (18) 15.7 |
| | | 8.5 | -18.0 | | | | -10.1 | 2.6 |
| | | 13.8 | 10.4 | | | | 5.5 | 8.7 |
| | | 5.0 | 6.6 | | | % Profit Before Taxes/Total Assets | 2.7 | 4.4 |
| | | 3.3 | -2.9 | | | | -13.6 | -2.0 |
| | | 40.5 | 7.8 | | | | 13.1 | 10.6 |
| | | 8.9 | 4.5 | | | Sales/Net Fixed Assets | 6.5 | 6.1 |
| | | 5.9 | 1.6 | | | | 4.4 | 4.0 |
| | | 4.7 | 2.7 | | | | 3.2 | 3.5 |
| | | 2.4 | 2.3 | | | Sales/Total Assets | 2.3 | 2.3 |
| | | 1.5 | 1.0 | | | | 2.1 | 1.9 |
| | | 1.1 | 1.3 | | | | 1.4 | 1.3 |
| | | (15) 2.0 | 2.4 | | | % Depr., Dep., Amort./Sales | (15) 2.5 | (23) 2.7 |
| | | 3.4 | 3.3 | | | | 3.8 | 4.4 |
| | | | | | | % Officers', Directors' Owners' Comp/Sales | | |
| 3954M | 24531M | 336040M | 604819M | 466711M | 1004999M | Net Sales ($) | 2767852M | 3218909M |
| 468M | 6909M | 106750M | 294066M | 232610M | 553476M | Total Assets ($) | 1050667M | 1256857M |

M = $ thousand    MM = $ million
See Pages 9 through 22 for Explanation of Ratios and Data

**Comparative Historical Data** | **Current Data Sorted by Sales**

| 4/1/09-3/31/10 ALL | 4/1/10-3/31/11 ALL | 4/1/11-3/31/12 ALL | Type of Statement | 0-1MM | 1-3MM | 3-5MM | 5-10MM | 10-25MM | 25MM & OVER |
|---|---|---|---|---|---|---|---|---|---|
| 9 | 9 | 8 | Unqualified | | | | | 2 | 6 |
| 2 | 6 | 5 | Reviewed | | | | 1 | 2 | 2 |
| 6 | 5 | 6 | Compiled | | | | 1 | 3 | 1 |
| 3 | 4 | 6 | Tax Returns | 1 | 3 | 1 | 1 | | |
| 13 | 12 | 19 | Other | | 1 | 1 | | 6 | 10 |
| | | | | 4 (4/1-9/30/11) | | | 40 (10/1/11-3/31/12) | | |
| ALL | ALL | ALL | | | | | | | |
| 33 | 36 | 44 | **NUMBER OF STATEMENTS** | 1 | 5 | 2 | 4 | 13 | 19 |
| % | % | % | **ASSETS** | % | % | % | % | % | % |
| 10.6 | 12.1 | 10.7 | Cash & Equivalents | | | | | 11.3 | 7.3 |
| 18.9 | 17.1 | 17.6 | Trade Receivables (net) | | | | | 19.4 | 19.8 |
| 15.0 | 18.3 | 17.3 | Inventory | | | | | 22.1 | 17.8 |
| 1.4 | 1.3 | 3.7 | All Other Current | | | | | 3.4 | 2.7 |
| 45.8 | 48.8 | 49.2 | Total Current | | | | | 56.2 | 47.7 |
| 40.0 | 37.8 | 35.1 | Fixed Assets (net) | | | | | 34.4 | 35.6 |
| 8.8 | 9.2 | 10.2 | Intangibles (net) | | | | | 7.9 | 8.2 |
| 5.4 | 4.2 | 5.5 | All Other Non-Current | | | | | 1.5 | 8.6 |
| 100.0 * | 100.0 | 100.0 | Total | | | | | 100.0 | 100.0 |
| | | | **LIABILITIES** | | | | | | |
| 6.6 | 7.4 | 5.6 | Notes Payable-Short Term | | | | | 7.7 | 4.2 |
| 3.1 | 2.6 | 2.4 | Cur. Mat.-L.T.D. | | | | | 4.0 | 2.4 |
| 20.0 | 19.7 | 15.2 | Trade Payables | | | | | 20.3 | 14.4 |
| .2 | .1 | .1 | Income Taxes Payable | | | | | .0 | .0 |
| 9.0 | 9.2 | 7.9 | All Other Current | | | | | 11.2 | 6.3 |
| 39.0 | 38.8 | 31.2 | Total Current | | | | | 43.2 | 27.3 |
| 23.7 | 24.4 | 28.0 | Long-Term Debt | | | | | 19.2 | 19.5 |
| .6 | .1 | .2 | Deferred Taxes | | | | | .1 | .3 |
| 9.4 | 10.1 | 12.5 | All Other Non-Current | | | | | 13.0 | 10.4 |
| 27.4 | 26.6 | 28.1 | Net Worth | | | | | 24.4 | 42.5 |
| 100.0 | 100.0 | 100.0 | Total Liabilties & Net Worth | | | | | 100.0 | 100.0 |
| | | | **INCOME DATA** | | | | | | |
| 100.0 | 100.0 | 100.0 | Net Sales | | | | | 100.0 | 100.0 |
| 26.0 | 26.1 | 28.6 | Gross Profit | | | | | 27.0 | 23.2 |
| 22.9 | 22.2 | 24.9 | Operating Expenses | | | | | 26.9 | 18.7 |
| 3.1 | 3.9 | 3.7 | Operating Profit | | | | | .1 | 4.5 |
| 1.4 | .9 | 1.3 | All Other Expenses (net) | | | | | .9 | .8 |
| 1.7 | 3.1 | 2.4 | Profit Before Taxes | | | | | -.9 | 3.7 |
| | | | **RATIOS** | | | | | | |
| 2.5 | 2.6 | 2.5 | | | | | | 2.3 | 2.6 |
| 1.1 | 1.2 | 1.7 | Current | | | | | 1.2 | 1.9 |
| .8 | .9 | 1.0 | | | | | | .8 | 1.0 |
| 1.6 | 1.7 | 1.9 | | | | | | 1.5 | 1.5 |
| .6 | .7 | .8 | Quick | | | | | .6 | .9 |
| .4 | .5 | .4 | | | | | | .3 | .6 |
| 19   19.3 | 16   22.1 | 13   27.3 | | | | | | 14   26.4 | 21   17.2 |
| 25   14.6 | 22   16.8 | 23   16.2 | Sales/Receivables | | | | | 20   17.9 | 24   15.2 |
| 31   11.8 | 29   12.6 | 33   10.9 | | | | | | 41   8.8 | 36   10.1 |
| 10   35.9 | 12   29.7 | 12   29.4 | | | | | | 9   40.0 | 19   19.6 |
| 17   21.0 | 23   15.7 | 26   14.1 | Cost of Sales/Inventory | | | | | 34   10.6 | 30   12.0 |
| 42   8.7 | 49   7.5 | 54   6.7 | | | | | | 69   5.3 | 47   7.7 |
| 20   18.7 | 16   22.7 | 13   28.2 | | | | | | 19   19.2 | 13   27.4 |
| 30   12.1 | 30   12.2 | 26   14.1 | Cost of Sales/Payables | | | | | 36   10.0 | 25   14.8 |
| 49   7.5 | 43   8.5 | 41   8.9 | | | | | | 65   5.6 | 35   10.3 |
| 11.9 | 10.0 | 9.2 | | | | | | 9.2 | 8.1 |
| 93.5 | 42.1 | 19.9 | Sales/Working Capital | | | | | 56.0 | 12.6 |
| -32.4 | -47.2 | NM | | | | | | -62.6 | 264.8 |
| 13.2 | 24.2 | 8.9 | | | | | | 7.6 | 41.6 |
| (30)   4.7 | (33)   3.0 | (39)   4.3 | EBIT/Interest | | | | | 3.1   (17) | 6.9 |
| 1.3 | 1.4 | 1.5 | | | | | | -1.4 | 2.1 |
| 12.1 | | | | | | | | | |
| (10)   6.2 | | | Net Profit + Depr., Dep., Amort./Cur. Mat. L/T/D | | | | | | |
| 1.2 | | | | | | | | | |
| .7 | .6 | .5 | | | | | | .4 | .3 |
| 1.7 | 1.4 | 1.5 | Fixed/Worth | | | | | 1.6 | 1.2 |
| -9.0 | -4.6 | -19.6 | | | | | | -27.2 | 1.8 |
| 1.2 | .9 | .9 | | | | | | .9 | .9 |
| 3.2 | 2.7 | 1.7 | Debt/Worth | | | | | 2.6 | 1.3 |
| -20.7 | -13.0 | -118.0 | | | | | | -209.5 | 8.8 |
| 74.4 | 49.6 | 32.9 | | | | | | | 29.4 |
| (23)   52.8 | (25)   35.0 | (32)   20.4 | % Profit Before Taxes/Tangible Net Worth | | | | | (16)   17.6 | |
| 11.0 | 11.4 | 5.4 | | | | | | | 7.8 |
| 14.3 | 17.0 | 12.5 | | | | | | 6.0 | 13.0 |
| 9.5 | 6.7 | 6.0 | % Profit Before Taxes/Total Assets | | | | | 4.6 | 8.1 |
| 2.6 | 2.4 | 2.8 | | | | | | -2.0 | 3.4 |
| 10.3 | 12.8 | 16.9 | | | | | | 24.2 | 17.2 |
| 6.9 | 7.1 | 8.4 | Sales/Net Fixed Assets | | | | | 6.7 | 7.8 |
| 4.4 | 3.9 | 4.1 | | | | | | 2.9 | 4.5 |
| 3.6 | 3.8 | 4.4 | | | | | | 4.5 | 3.2 |
| 2.6 | 2.5 | 2.4 | Sales/Total Assets | | | | | 2.4 | 2.5 |
| 2.1 | 1.8 | 1.6 | | | | | | 1.5 | 1.9 |
| 1.2 | 1.2 | 1.3 | | | | | | 1.1 | 1.3 |
| (27)   2.6 | (30)   2.1 | (35)   2.3 | % Depr., Dep., Amort./Sales | | | | | 2.4   (15) | 2.3 |
| 3.4 | 3.2 | 3.2 | | | | | | 3.7 | 3.0 |
| | 1.8 | 1.4 | | | | | | | |
| | (12)   4.9 | (12)   2.1 | % Officers', Directors' Owners' Comp/Sales | | | | | | |
| | 6.0 | 4.3 | | | | | | | |
| 4059778M | 4751433M | 2441054M | Net Sales ($) | 258M | 8391M | 8953M | 26658M | 195635M | 2201159M |
| 1448473M | 1851831M | 1194279M | Total Assets ($) | 45M | 3195M | 10884M | 9183M | 101624M | 1069348M |

M = $ thousand     MM = $ million
See Pages 9 through 22 for Explanation of Ratios and Data

# MANUFACTURING—All Other Miscellaneous Food Manufacturing  NAICS 311999

**Current Data Sorted by Assets** | **Comparative Historical Data**

| | 0-500M | 500M-2MM | 2-10MM | 10-50MM | 50-100MM | 100-250MM | | 4/1/07-3/31/08 ALL | 4/1/08-3/31/09 ALL |
|---|---|---|---|---|---|---|---|---|---|
| **Type of Statement** | | | | | | | | | |
| Unqualified | | 2 | 6 | 17 | 11 | 6 | | 42 | 56 |
| Reviewed | 1 | 1 | 21 | 16 | 3 | 1 | | 42 | 44 |
| Compiled | 3 | 7 | 12 | 1 | | | | 16 | 29 |
| Tax Returns | 6 | 15 | 10 | 2 | | 1 | | 21 | 23 |
| Other | 5 | 23 | 29 | 30 | 8 | 5 | | 86 | 93 |
| | | 49 (4/1-9/30/11) | | | 193 (10/1/11-3/31/12) | | | | |
| **NUMBER OF STATEMENTS** | 15 | 48 | 78 | 66 | 22 | 13 | | 207 | 245 |
| | % | % | % | % | % | % | | % | % |
| **ASSETS** | | | | | | | | | |
| Cash & Equivalents | 24.1 | 9.0 | 8.9 | 5.5 | 3.5 | 6.0 | | 7.8 | 7.6 |
| Trade Receivables (net) | 17.5 | 29.8 | 24.1 | 20.8 | 16.9 | 15.8 | | 21.9 | 22.3 |
| Inventory | 15.4 | 23.7 | 26.7 | 26.8 | 30.4 | 26.2 | | 24.5 | 24.6 |
| All Other Current | .5 | .7 | 1.8 | 1.5 | 2.1 | 5.0 | | 3.0 | 2.5 |
| Total Current | 57.5 | 63.3 | 61.5 | 54.6 | 53.0 | 53.0 | | 57.2 | 57.0 |
| Fixed Assets (net) | 30.7 | 21.8 | 29.4 | 32.2 | 37.0 | 30.6 | | 31.0 | 31.9 |
| Intangibles (net) | 2.5 | 8.6 | 4.3 | 6.9 | 7.8 | 14.6 | | 5.6 | 4.7 |
| All Other Non-Current | 9.3 | 6.4 | 4.8 | 6.3 | 2.2 | 1.9 | | 6.2 | 6.4 |
| Total | 100.0 | 100.0 | 100.0 | 100.0 | 100.0 | 100.0 | | 100.0 | 100.0 * |
| **LIABILITIES** | | | | | | | | | |
| Notes Payable-Short Term | 18.5 | 10.5 | 11.6 | 13.0 | 13.9 | 7.7 | | 10.4 | 12.1 |
| Cur. Mat.-L.T.D. | .3 | 2.2 | 2.9 | 3.2 | 3.4 | 1.2 | | 4.7 | 4.0 |
| Trade Payables | 17.5 | 24.7 | 18.3 | 14.4 | 13.8 | 12.5 | | 18.2 | 17.6 |
| Income Taxes Payable | .0 | .1 | .2 | .4 | .1 | .1 | | .3 | .3 |
| All Other Current | 6.1 | 7.9 | 8.2 | 7.1 | 5.3 | 9.1 | | 8.3 | 7.9 |
| Total Current | 42.5 | 45.4 | 41.2 | 38.0 | 36.5 | 30.6 | | 41.9 | 41.9 |
| Long-Term Debt | 30.7 | 17.0 | 14.9 | 16.4 | 16.1 | 17.7 | | 24.1 | 19.5 |
| Deferred Taxes | .0 | .6 | .3 | .3 | 1.7 | .4 | | .5 | .4 |
| All Other Non-Current | 6.8 | 10.1 | 6.2 | 5.3 | 12.7 | 2.3 | | 7.6 | 8.7 |
| Net Worth | 20.0 | 26.9 | 37.5 | 40.1 | 33.1 | 49.0 | | 25.9 | 29.5 |
| Total Liabilities & Net Worth | 100.0 | 100.0 | 100.0 | 100.0 | 100.0 | 100.0 | | 100.0 | 100.0 |
| **INCOME DATA** | | | | | | | | | |
| Net Sales | 100.0 | 100.0 | 100.0 | 100.0 | 100.0 | 100.0 | | 100.0 | 100.0 |
| Gross Profit | 49.4 | 35.2 | 29.7 | 24.3 | 25.2 | 27.6 | | 28.5 | 28.5 |
| Operating Expenses | 42.7 | 30.8 | 23.4 | 18.8 | 14.4 | 18.9 | | 24.1 | 23.7 |
| Operating Profit | 6.7 | 4.3 | 6.2 | 5.5 | 10.8 | 8.8 | | 4.4 | 4.8 |
| All Other Expenses (net) | 1.1 | .6 | .8 | 1.0 | 1.3 | 1.2 | | 1.6 | 1.2 |
| Profit Before Taxes | 5.7 | 3.7 | 5.4 | 4.5 | 9.5 | 7.5 | | 2.8 | 3.6 |
| **RATIOS** | | | | | | | | | |
| Current | 3.3 | 3.0 | 2.5 | 2.0 | 2.0 | 3.0 | | 2.1 | 2.1 |
| | 1.1 | 1.6 | 1.5 | 1.5 | 1.4 | 1.7 | | 1.4 | 1.4 |
| | 1.0 | 1.0 | 1.0 | 1.0 | 1.2 | 1.5 | | 1.0 | 1.1 |
| Quick | 2.9 | 2.0 | 1.7 | .9 | .8 | 1.2 | | 1.1 | 1.3 |
| | .9 | .9 | .7 | .6 | .6 | .9 | | .7 | .7 |
| | .3 | .5 | .5 | .5 | .3 | .5 | | .5 | .4 |
| Sales/Receivables | 1 294.3 | 19 19.1 | 23 15.6 | 25 14.6 | 26 14.1 | 21 17.4 | | 21 17.0 | 20 18.3 |
| | 17 22.0 | 24 15.1 | 33 11.1 | 33 11.0 | 34 10.8 | 26 14.3 | | 29 12.4 | 28 12.9 |
| | 25 14.4 | 45 8.2 | 42 8.6 | 41 8.8 | 37 9.9 | 51 7.2 | | 37 9.8 | 37 9.8 |
| Cost of Sales/Inventory | 0 UND | 8 44.8 | 15 24.5 | 29 12.6 | 44 8.3 | 44 8.3 | | 23 15.8 | 23 16.0 |
| | 14 26.4 | 32 11.4 | 45 8.2 | 53 6.9 | 62 5.9 | 74 4.9 | | 45 8.1 | 42 8.6 |
| | 126 2.9 | 76 4.8 | 81 4.5 | 94 3.9 | 111 3.3 | 99 3.7 | | 82 4.4 | 78 4.7 |
| Cost of Sales/Payables | 3 110.2 | 15 24.8 | 16 22.8 | 16 23.0 | 17 21.4 | 15 24.4 | | 17 21.1 | 15 24.1 |
| | 24 15.4 | 24 14.9 | 25 14.5 | 25 14.4 | 32 11.4 | 37 9.9 | | 32 11.5 | 27 13.6 |
| | 41 8.9 | 53 6.9 | 42 8.7 | 42 8.7 | 53 6.9 | 56 6.5 | | 51 7.2 | 40 9.2 |
| Sales/Working Capital | 16.2 | 6.7 | 5.6 | 7.2 | 7.7 | 5.0 | | 8.4 | 8.3 |
| | 131.4 | 21.2 | 16.4 | 13.1 | 15.2 | 7.3 | | 17.9 | 18.2 |
| | -39.0 | NM | 85.0 | NM | 27.0 | 23.7 | | 227.0 | 127.1 |
| EBIT/Interest | 14.2 | | 21.6 | 12.6 | 16.1 | 50.5 | | 8.6 | 9.8 |
| | | (41) 6.3 | (69) 5.2 | (64) 5.0 | (21) 6.0 | 10.7 | | (189) 2.8 | (224) 3.6 |
| | 1.0 | | 1.1 | 2.0 | 3.3 | 1.9 | | 1.1 | 1.1 |
| Net Profit + Depr., Dep., Amort./Cur. Mat. L/T/D | | | 15.2 | 4.1 | 7.9 | | | 8.8 | 8.1 |
| | | | (17) 4.1 | (29) 2.5 | (10) 2.6 | | | (63) 4.4 | (71) 3.0 |
| | | | 1.2 | 1.4 | 1.8 | | | 1.5 | 1.3 |
| Fixed/Worth | .3 | .3 | .3 | .4 | .9 | .4 | | .5 | .5 |
| | 1.8 | .9 | .8 | .9 | 1.4 | .8 | | 1.2 | 1.1 |
| | -1.4 | -3.0 | 2.0 | 2.2 | 2.3 | 2.4 | | 3.3 | 3.2 |
| Debt/Worth | .3 | .8 | .8 | .9 | 1.3 | .6 | | 1.0 | .9 |
| | 2.0 | 3.3 | 1.8 | 1.9 | 2.4 | 1.3 | | 2.8 | 2.3 |
| | -4.9 | -9.3 | 5.9 | 7.4 | 4.6 | 4.3 | | 9.7 | 7.6 |
| % Profit Before Taxes/Tangible Net Worth | 209.6 | 88.5 | 53.8 | 38.3 | 41.0 | 123.9 | | 51.3 | 53.6 |
| | (10) 54.1 | (34) 31.5 | (72) 23.7 | (60) 24.8 | (19) 23.5 | (12) 33.4 | | (166) 29.4 | (208) 22.7 |
| | 2.9 | 13.7 | .8 | 11.3 | 14.4 | 15.1 | | 7.9 | 7.1 |
| % Profit Before Taxes/Total Assets | 70.3 | 15.7 | 18.2 | 13.4 | 21.7 | 16.3 | | 16.4 | 15.6 |
| | 10.9 | 8.4 | 7.6 | 7.1 | 7.8 | 9.0 | | 7.1 | 6.4 |
| | .0 | 3.4 | .3 | 2.3 | 4.3 | 2.7 | | .2 | .7 |
| Sales/Net Fixed Assets | 53.2 | 58.5 | 46.2 | 15.9 | 9.1 | 18.3 | | 19.8 | 24.9 |
| | 13.0 | 19.9 | 10.5 | 7.4 | 4.8 | 6.5 | | 9.3 | 10.2 |
| | 8.5 | 9.2 | 5.6 | 4.4 | 3.2 | 3.3 | | 4.8 | 4.6 |
| Sales/Total Assets | 7.2 | 5.2 | 3.7 | 2.9 | 2.2 | 2.7 | | 3.4 | 3.8 |
| | 5.0 | 2.9 | 2.8 | 2.0 | 1.8 | 1.7 | | 2.5 | 2.6 |
| | 2.5 | 2.1 | 1.8 | 1.5 | 1.6 | 1.2 | | 1.7 | 1.8 |
| % Depr., Dep., Amort./Sales | | .4 | .7 | 1.2 | 1.2 | .7 | | .9 | .8 |
| | | (32) 1.3 | (64) 1.6 | (61) 1.9 | (20) 1.9 | (12) 2.0 | | (171) 1.8 | (204) 1.7 |
| | | 3.0 | 2.6 | 1.9 | 3.8 | 4.6 | | 3.3 | 2.9 |
| % Officers', Directors' Owners' Comp/Sales | | 2.3 | 1.7 | | | | | 1.6 | 1.2 |
| | | (23) 5.3 | (32) 3.4 | | | | | (57) 2.6 | (61) 2.3 |
| | | 6.7 | 5.7 | | | | | 5.9 | 4.6 |
| Net Sales ($) | 17709M | 210547M | 1076848M | 3795813M | 3037486M | 5205669M | | 10977839M | 16767927M |
| Total Assets ($) | 3867M | 57782M | 388757M | 1732650M | 1587309M | 2209222M | | 4560094M | 7383356M |

© RMA 2012

**M = $ thousand    MM = $ million**
See Pages 9 through 22 for Explanation of Ratios and Data

## Comparative Historical Data                                   Current Data Sorted by Sales

| Hist 1 | Hist 2 | Hist 3 | Type of Statement | 0-1MM | 1-3MM | 3-5MM | 5-10MM | 10-25MM | 25MM & OVER |
|---|---|---|---|---|---|---|---|---|---|
| 56 | 40 | 42 | Unqualified | 2 | | 1 | 1 | 7 | 32 |
| 37 | 38 | 43 | Reviewed | 1 | | 1 | 4 | 18 | 19 |
| 20 | 19 | 23 | Compiled | 1 | 3 | 4 | 5 | 8 | 2 |
| 34 | 33 | 34 | Tax Returns | 2 | 8 | 10 | 7 | 4 | 3 |
| 97 | 90 | 100 | Other | 5 | 11 | 9 | 11 | 24 | 40 |
| 4/1/09-3/31/10 ALL | 4/1/10-3/31/11 ALL | 4/1/11-3/31/12 ALL | | 49 (4/1-9/30/11) | | | 193 (10/1/11-3/31/12) | | |
| 244 | 220 | 242 | NUMBER OF STATEMENTS | 11 | 22 | 24 | 28 | 61 | 96 |
| % | % | % | ASSETS | % | % | % | % | % | % |
| 7.2 | 8.4 | 8.3 | Cash & Equivalents | 5.3 | 24.9 | 12.2 | 8.5 | 6.8 | 4.7 |
| 21.3 | 22.7 | 22.8 | Trade Receivables (net) | 9.7 | 22.7 | 26.9 | 25.8 | 25.3 | 21.0 |
| 26.6 | 25.2 | 25.8 | Inventory | 16.9 | 17.9 | 19.2 | 24.8 | 29.3 | 28.3 |
| 2.5 | 2.3 | 1.6 | All Other Current | .9 | .6 | .8 | .9 | 2.2 | 2.0 |
| 57.7 | 58.6 | 58.5 | Total Current | 32.9 | 66.0 | 59.1 | 60.0 | 63.5 | 55.9 |
| 30.8 | 31.6 | 29.5 | Fixed Assets (net) | 41.9 | 20.9 | 26.7 | 29.5 | 29.0 | 31.0 |
| 5.4 | 5.7 | 6.6 | Intangibles (net) | 18.4 | 4.8 | 8.2 | 2.8 | 3.9 | 8.1 |
| 6.1 | 4.2 | 5.4 | All Other Non-Current | 6.8 | 8.3 | 6.0 | 7.8 | 3.5 | 5.0 |
| 100.0 | 100.0 | 100.0 | Total | 100.0 | 100.0 | 100.0 | 100.0 | 100.0 | 100.0 |
| | | | LIABILITIES | | | | | | |
| 10.2 | 11.4 | 12.2 | Notes Payable-Short Term | 14.6 | 14.1 | 7.1 | 10.6 | 12.1 | 13.2 |
| 4.3 | 3.6 | 2.6 | Cur. Mat.-L.T.D. | 1.5 | 1.1 | 1.4 | 2.2 | 3.5 | 3.0 |
| 15.9 | 17.3 | 17.7 | Trade Payables | 10.8 | 12.8 | 21.4 | 24.2 | 20.5 | 15.1 |
| .4 | .3 | .2 | Income Taxes Payable | .0 | .0 | .2 | .1 | .3 | .3 |
| 9.5 | 8.4 | 7.5 | All Other Current | 5.2 | 7.8 | 4.3 | 4.9 | 10.7 | 7.1 |
| 40.4 | 41.1 | 40.2 | Total Current | 32.1 | 35.8 | 34.5 | 42.0 | 47.1 | 38.7 |
| 19.8 | 15.8 | 17.0 | Long-Term Debt | 36.4 | 22.0 | 19.1 | 13.6 | 14.0 | 15.9 |
| .6 | .6 | .4 | Deferred Taxes | 1.7 | .0 | .0 | .6 | .2 | .6 |
| 8.0 | 7.7 | 7.1 | All Other Non-Current | 3.0 | 20.8 | 3.3 | 4.5 | 7.6 | 5.9 |
| 31.3 | 34.8 | 35.2 | Net Worth | 26.7 | 21.4 | 43.1 | 39.3 | 30.9 | 39.0 |
| 100.0 | 100.0 | 100.0 | Total Liabilities & Net Worth | 100.0 | 100.0 | 100.0 | 100.0 | 100.0 | 100.0 |
| | | | INCOME DATA | | | | | | |
| 100.0 | 100.0 | 100.0 | Net Sales | 100.0 | 100.0 | 100.0 | 100.0 | 100.0 | 100.0 |
| 30.7 | 30.0 | 30.0 | Gross Profit | 54.1 | 41.0 | 37.0 | 29.7 | 28.7 | 23.9 |
| 24.5 | 24.4 | 23.8 | Operating Expenses | 41.8 | 34.5 | 31.0 | 25.7 | 23.5 | 17.0 |
| 6.1 | 5.6 | 6.2 | Operating Profit | 12.3 | 6.5 | 6.0 | 4.0 | 5.1 | 6.9 |
| .8 | 1.0 | .9 | All Other Expenses (net) | 4.1 | .7 | .5 | .5 | .7 | 1.0 |
| 5.3 | 4.6 | 5.3 | Profit Before Taxes | 8.2 | 5.8 | 5.5 | 3.5 | 4.4 | 5.9 |
| | | | RATIOS | | | | | | |
| 2.2 | 2.2 | 2.3 | | 2.4 | 6.1 | 3.3 | 2.8 | 2.0 | 2.1 |
| 1.5 | 1.4 | 1.5 | Current | 1.1 | 2.5 | 1.7 | 1.6 | 1.4 | 1.5 |
| 1.1 | 1.1 | 1.0 | | .6 | 1.0 | 1.3 | 1.0 | 1.0 | 1.1 |
| 1.2 | 1.3 | 1.3 | | .8 | 5.3 | 2.4 | 1.8 | 1.0 | 1.0 |
| .7 | .7 | .7 | Quick | .5 | 1.8 | 1.1 | .9 | .6 | .7 |
| .4 | .4 | .5 | | .1 | .6 | .7 | .4 | .4 | .4 |
| 20  18.1 | 22  16.9 | 21  17.4 | | 0  UND | 8  44.0 | 22  16.5 | 24  14.9 | 24  15.3 | 22  16.6 |
| 27  13.4 | 31  11.9 | 31  11.9 | Sales/Receivables | 17  21.0 | 19  19.7 | 30  12.0 | 32  11.4 | 33  11.2 | 31  11.7 |
| 38  9.7 | 42  8.6 | 41  9.0 | | 26  13.9 | 46  8.0 | 45  8.2 | 47  7.8 | 41  8.9 | 39  9.3 |
| 26  13.9 | 23  16.2 | 20  18.0 | | 0  UND | 0  UND | 6  59.5 | 12  29.3 | 24  15.4 | 35  10.5 |
| 46  8.0 | 47  7.8 | 49  7.5 | Cost of Sales/Inventory | 85  4.3 | 16  22.5 | 45  8.2 | 33  11.1 | 54  6.7 | 53  6.9 |
| 78  4.7 | 80  4.5 | 85  4.3 | | 140  2.6 | 107  3.4 | 62  5.9 | 68  5.4 | 83  4.4 | 96  3.8 |
| 15  24.2 | 15  23.6 | 16  23.0 | | 7  52.4 | 0  UND | 17  20.9 | 17  22.0 | 17  21.5 | 16  23.5 |
| 27  13.5 | 28  12.9 | 26  14.2 | Cost of Sales/Payables | 30  12.0 | 17  21.2 | 29  12.8 | 25  14.5 | 30  12.2 | 26  14.2 |
| 43  8.5 | 48  7.6 | 45  8.2 | | 39  9.4 | 27  13.6 | 52  7.0 | 59  6.2 | 49  7.5 | 42  8.7 |
| 7.0 | 6.7 | 6.7 | | 6.9 | 4.7 | 4.9 | 5.3 | 7.9 | 6.9 |
| 18.0 | 15.8 | 16.2 | Sales/Working Capital | 91.3 | 13.3 | 14.8 | 13.9 | 20.1 | 14.0 |
| 116.0 | 103.0 | 131.0 | | -9.8 | NM | 29.8 | 132.6 | NM | 42.6 |
| 14.7 | 15.0 | 16.9 | | | 9.4 | 28.3 | 9.3 | 21.4 | 18.1 |
| (224)  5.1 | (198)  6.0 | (216)  5.7 | EBIT/Interest | | (15)  3.6 | (21)  9.2 | (22)  4.3 | (60)  6.0 | (92)  5.9 |
| 2.2 | 2.2 | 1.8 | | | -1.2 | 4.0 | -.3 | 1.4 | 2.1 |
| 10.9 | 8.4 | 7.4 | | | | | | 10.1 | 5.8 |
| (80)  4.5 | (59)  3.1 | (71)  3.2 | Net Profit + Depr., Dep., Amort./Cur. Mat. L/T/D | | | | | (17)  4.1 | (44)  2.7 |
| 2.2 | 1.9 | 1.6 | | | | | | 1.9 | 1.6 |
| .4 | .4 | .4 | | 1.8 | .1 | .3 | .3 | .4 | .5 |
| .9 | .9 | .9 | Fixed/Worth | 3.0 | .4 | .8 | .8 | .9 | 1.1 |
| 3.2 | 2.2 | 2.6 | | -1.4 | -4.6 | 2.0 | 2.0 | 2.3 | 2.2 |
| .9 | .8 | .9 | | 1.8 | .3 | .5 | .6 | 1.2 | 1.0 |
| 2.1 | 1.8 | 2.0 | Debt/Worth | 21.0 | 2.8 | 1.4 | 1.1 | 2.2 | 2.2 |
| 7.6 | 6.1 | 8.2 | | -4.0 | -5.6 | 6.9 | 5.0 | 7.1 | 6.6 |
| 60.0 | 57.7 | 51.7 | | | 188.9 | 71.9 | 41.1 | 62.7 | 41.4 |
| (207)  29.5 | (190)  28.8 | (207)  25.0 | % Profit Before Taxes/Tangible Net Worth | (15)  20.7 | (20)  28.5 | (25)  23.8 | (55)  32.0 | (86)  24.9 | |
| 11.5 | 10.2 | 10.4 | | | 10.4 | 16.2 | -2.3 | 8.7 | 14.3 |
| 18.4 | 20.4 | 16.7 | | 6.9 | 21.9 | 34.3 | 15.7 | 18.2 | 15.0 |
| 9.8 | 9.2 | 7.9 | % Profit Before Taxes/Total Assets | 4.0 | 10.6 | 11.6 | 7.8 | 8.8 | 7.7 |
| 3.4 | 2.9 | 2.1 | | .0 | 3.4 | 2.5 | -1.3 | 1.5 | 2.6 |
| 25.5 | 21.8 | 27.2 | | 16.0 | 153.2 | 60.2 | 30.8 | 64.5 | 16.6 |
| 10.2 | 9.1 | 10.3 | Sales/Net Fixed Assets | 8.5 | 18.6 | 15.9 | 16.5 | 11.4 | 7.2 |
| 4.9 | 4.7 | 5.1 | | 1.7 | 9.9 | 4.6 | 5.9 | 5.6 | 4.1 |
| 3.9 | 3.6 | 3.6 | | 3.1 | 5.6 | 5.3 | 3.9 | 4.1 | 3.0 |
| 2.6 | 2.4 | 2.4 | Sales/Total Assets | 1.3 | 2.6 | 2.5 | 2.9 | 3.1 | 2.1 |
| 1.7 | 1.7 | 1.7 | | .5 | 1.9 | 1.8 | 1.3 | 1.9 | 1.6 |
| .9 | 1.0 | 1.0 | | | .3 | .4 | .7 | .8 | 1.0 |
| (206)  1.5 | (186)  2.0 | (195)  1.8 | % Depr., Dep., Amort./Sales | | (11)  1.2 | (17)  1.6 | (21)  1.3 | (51)  1.9 | (88)  1.9 |
| 2.8 | 3.8 | 3.0 | | | 3.4 | 3.0 | 2.7 | 2.9 | 3.1 |
| 1.4 | 1.3 | 1.6 | | | 1.7 | 2.5 | 1.5 | | .9 |
| (77)  2.7 | (64)  2.8 | (74)  3.1 | % Officers', Directors' Owners' Comp/Sales | | (12)  3.5 | (15)  5.3 | (22)  3.3 | | (14)  1.2 |
| 5.8 | 6.6 | 6.0 | | | 6.1 | 5.2 | | | 2.3 |
| 15563089M | 12565106M | 13344072M | Net Sales ($) | 6301M | 40543M | 93169M | 197070M | 958572M | 12048417M |
| 6499468M | 5280339M | 5979587M | Total Assets ($) | 10463M | 16818M | 39185M | 110886M | 420866M | 5381369M |

© RMA 2012                     M = $ thousand     MM = $ million
See Pages 9 through 22 for Explanation of Ratios and Data

## Current Data Sorted by Assets     Comparative Historical Data

Column period notes: 0-500M, 500M-2MM, 2-10MM grouped under **16 (4/1-9/30/11)**; 10-50MM, 50-100MM, 100-250MM grouped under **82 (10/1/11-3/31/12)**. Comparative Historical columns: **42 (4/1/07-3/31/08) ALL** and **35 (4/1/08-3/31/09) ALL**. (0-500M column: DATA NOT AVAILABLE)

| 0-500M | 500M-2MM | 2-10MM | 10-50MM | 50-100MM | 100-250MM | | 4/1/07-3/31/08 ALL | 4/1/08-3/31/09 ALL |
|---|---|---|---|---|---|---|---|---|
| | | | | | | **Type of Statement** | | |
| | | 4 | 12 | 5 | 10 | Unqualified | 25 | 41 |
| | | 3 | 4 | | | Reviewed | 8 | 8 |
| | 1 | 4 | 2 | | | Compiled | 1 | 4 |
| | 2 | 3 | 1 | | | Tax Returns | | 6 |
| | 3 | 11 | 11 | 7 | 15 | Other | 42 | 35 |
| | 6 | 25 | 30 | 12 | 25 | **NUMBER OF STATEMENTS** | 76 | 94 |
| % | % | % | % | % | % | **ASSETS** | % | % |
| | | 8.3 | 10.0 | 6.7 | 4.3 | Cash & Equivalents | 7.8 | 7.3 |
| | | 18.8 | 15.3 | 11.6 | 13.8 | Trade Receivables (net) | 18.4 | 16.1 |
| | | 13.5 | 18.2 | 9.2 | 11.7 | Inventory | 15.2 | 15.8 |
| | | 5.8 | 2.4 | 2.8 | 3.3 | All Other Current | 2.8 | 3.3 |
| | | 46.5 | 45.9 | 30.3 | 33.1 | Total Current | 44.3 | 42.5 |
| | | 31.6 | 32.3 | 33.3 | 27.1 | Fixed Assets (net) | 32.1 | 33.4 |
| | | 12.1 | 13.4 | 20.9 | 28.9 | Intangibles (net) | 14.4 | 13.1 |
| | | 9.8 | 8.4 | 15.5 | 10.9 | All Other Non-Current | 9.3 | 10.9 |
| | | 100.0 | 100.0 | 100.0 | 100.0 | Total | 100.0 | 100.0 |
| | | | | | | **LIABILITIES** | | |
| | | 5.8 | 5.6 | 3.2 | 1.8 | Notes Payable-Short Term | 5.7 | 6.2 |
| | | 3.8 | 2.8 | 1.6 | 2.5 | Cur. Mat.-L.T.D. | 2.3 | 3.5 |
| | | 16.6 | 12.7 | 8.1 | 11.1 | Trade Payables | 13.7 | 13.2 |
| | | .0 | .1 | .7 | .4 | Income Taxes Payable | .1 | .3 |
| | | 9.7 | 7.8 | 15.4 | 9.4 | All Other Current | 6.6 | 10.0 |
| | | 35.9 | 29.0 | 28.9 | 25.2 | Total Current | 28.4 | 33.1 |
| | | 20.1 | 22.8 | 17.2 | 25.2 | Long-Term Debt | 22.2 | 21.1 |
| | | .5 | 1.0 | 1.6 | 4.1 | Deferred Taxes | 1.3 | 1.0 |
| | | 14.1 | 4.8 | 3.8 | 6.6 | All Other Non-Current | 5.9 | 6.9 |
| | | 29.4 | 42.3 | 48.6 | 38.9 | Net Worth | 42.3 | 38.0 |
| | | 100.0 | 100.0 | 100.0 | 100.0 | Total Liabilities & Net Worth | 100.0 | 100.0 |
| | | | | | | **INCOME DATA** | | |
| | | 100.0 | 100.0 | 100.0 | 100.0 | Net Sales | 100.0 | 100.0 |
| | | 29.7 | 29.0 | 35.9 | 33.7 | Gross Profit | 35.4 | 33.3 |
| | | 27.6 | 22.5 | 29.4 | 24.2 | Operating Expenses | 29.3 | 29.1 |
| | | 2.1 | 6.5 | 6.5 | 9.5 | Operating Profit | 6.1 | 4.2 |
| | | .3 | .5 | 1.2 | 2.3 | All Other Expenses (net) | 1.2 | .8 |
| | | 1.8 | 6.0 | 5.3 | 7.3 | Profit Before Taxes | 4.9 | 3.4 |
| | | | | | | **RATIOS** | | |
| | | 3.2 | 2.7 | 2.4 | 1.7 | | 2.6 | 2.4 |
| | | 1.2 | 2.0 | 1.4 | 1.1 | Current | 1.5 | 1.4 |
| | | .7 | 1.3 | .6 | .8 | | 1.1 | .9 |
| | | 2.1 | 1.6 | 1.8 | 1.0 | | 1.5 | 1.4 |
| | | .7 | 1.0 | .6 | .7 | Quick | 1.0 | .8 |
| | | .5 | .6 | .2 | .3 | | .6 | .4 |
| | | 22 · 16.5 | 24 · 15.5 | 22 · 16.6 | 16 · 22.3 | | 23 · 15.8 | 20 · 18.0 |
| | | 31 · 11.8 | 29 · 12.5 | 26 · 14.1 | 28 · 13.2 | Sales/Receivables | 28 · 13.1 | 26 · 14.0 |
| | | 43 · 8.4 | 33 · 11.1 | 28 · 12.9 | 35 · 10.5 | | 35 · 10.6 | 32 · 11.3 |
| | | 15 · 25.1 | 21 · 17.5 | 17 · 21.9 | 21 · 17.3 | | 19 · 19.2 | 20 · 18.2 |
| | | 27 · 13.3 | 33 · 11.2 | 23 · 15.8 | 27 · 13.5 | Cost of Sales/Inventory | 28 · 13.2 | 26 · 12.9 |
| | | 47 · 7.8 | 70 · 5.2 | 36 · 10.1 | 49 · 7.4 | | 46 · 7.9 | 50 · 7.4 |
| | | 17 · 21.3 | 19 · 18.8 | 7 · 53.0 | 19 · 19.2 | | 15 · 25.0 | 14 · 25.5 |
| | | 32 · 11.5 | 28 · 13.2 | 20 · 18.1 | 35 · 10.3 | Cost of Sales/Payables | 30 · 12.1 | 23 · 15.9 |
| | | 54 · 6.8 | 49 · 7.5 | 33 · 10.9 | 45 · 8.2 | | 50 · 7.3 | 42 · 8.7 |
| | | 5.4 | 6.5 | 11.2 | 15.2 | | 6.7 | 7.7 |
| | | 40.7 | 11.5 | 18.2 | 85.1 | Sales/Working Capital | 15.1 | 22.8 |
| | | -17.0 | 27.3 | -15.6 | -39.9 | | 63.7 | -38.8 |
| | | 9.5 | 23.7 | 27.9 | 15.7 | | 14.8 | 17.4 |
| | | (24) 3.0 | (27) 7.5 | (10) 8.4 | (24) 2.6 | EBIT/Interest | (70) 4.5 | (83) 3.6 |
| | | -1.4 | 1.6 | 4.2 | 1.3 | | 1.4 | 1.0 |
| | | | | | | Net Profit + Depr., Dep., | 13.5 | 9.0 |
| | | | | | | Amort./Cur. Mat. L/T/D | (17) 2.1 | (28) 2.9 |
| | | | | | | | 1.2 | 1.3 |
| | | .3 | .5 | .8 | .8 | | .4 | .4 |
| | | 1.2 | .9 | 1.2 | 32.4 | Fixed/Worth | 1.0 | 1.3 |
| | | 6.4 | NM | NM | -.9 | | 6.7 | 11.2 |
| | | .6 | .5 | .6 | 1.1 | | .6 | .7 |
| | | 2.2 | 1.1 | 1.4 | 76.9 | Debt/Worth | 1.5 | 2.2 |
| | | 12.9 | NM | NM | -3.0 | | 21.0 | 18.5 |
| | | 57.2 | 48.8 | | 85.7 | % Profit Before Taxes/Tangible | 48.4 | 45.6 |
| | | (21) 12.3 | (23) 21.4 | | (13) 18.2 | Net Worth | (59) 27.2 | (72) 17.3 |
| | | -1.5 | 6.0 | | 6.4 | | 8.1 | 1.1 |
| | | 12.6 | 19.1 | 12.5 | 9.4 | % Profit Before Taxes/Total | 13.3 | 14.6 |
| | | 5.3 | 7.1 | 6.5 | 2.3 | Assets | 7.3 | 5.5 |
| | | -3.2 | 2.1 | 3.2 | 1.3 | | 1.0 | -.1 |
| | | 15.1 | 11.8 | 12.4 | 11.0 | | 14.7 | 12.4 |
| | | 5.9 | 6.9 | 6.2 | 7.0 | Sales/Net Fixed Assets | 8.1 | 7.5 |
| | | 3.8 | 4.6 | 3.3 | 4.7 | | 4.7 | 4.7 |
| | | 2.5 | 2.5 | 2.5 | 3.0 | | 3.0 | 3.0 |
| | | 1.8 | 2.1 | 1.8 | 1.6 | Sales/Total Assets | 2.0 | 2.2 |
| | | 1.4 | 1.4 | .8 | 1.1 | | 1.4 | 1.4 |
| | | 1.4 | 1.8 | 1.7 | 1.7 | | 1.5 | 1.7 |
| | | (21) 2.1 | (28) 3.2 | (16) 2.9 | 2.6 | % Depr., Dep., Amort./Sales | (60) 2.7 | (82) 2.8 |
| | | 6.2 | 4.7 | 4.1 | 4.2 | | 4.6 | 4.3 |
| | | | | | | | | 1.1 |
| | | | | | | % Officers', Directors' | | (13) 2.4 |
| | | | | | | Owners' Comp/Sales | | 8.1 |
| | 19117M | 271159M | 1556281M | 1494805M | 7500435M | Net Sales ($) | 8855232M | 8086978M |
| | 8290M | 130686M | 745261M | 833338M | 3964940M | Total Assets ($) | 4300349M | 4004243M |

## Comparative Historical Data / Current Data Sorted by Sales

| | 4/1/09-3/31/10 ALL | 4/1/10-3/31/11 ALL | 4/1/11-3/31/12 ALL | Type of Statement | 0-1MM | 1-3MM 16 (4/1-9/30/11) | 3-5MM | 5-10MM | 10-25MM 82 (10/1/11-3/31/12) | 25MM & OVER |
|---|---|---|---|---|---|---|---|---|---|---|
| | 36 | 37 | 31 | Unqualified | | | | 3 | 2 | 26 |
| | 8 | 6 | 7 | Reviewed | | | | | 4 | 3 |
| | 8 | 6 | 7 | Compiled | | | 1 | 2 | 1 | 3 |
| | 5 | 6 | 6 | Tax Returns | | 3 | | 1 | 2 | |
| | 41 | 34 | 47 | Other | | 3 | 3 | 1 | 8 | 32 |
| | 98 | 89 | 98 | NUMBER OF STATEMENTS | | 6 | 4 | 7 | 17 | 64 |
| | % | % | % | ASSETS | % | % | % | % | % | % |
| | 8.8 | 9.6 | 8.2 | Cash & Equivalents | | | | | 7.5 | 7.7 |
| | 16.4 | 16.1 | 15.6 | Trade Receivables (net) | | | | | 17.9 | 14.8 |
| | 15.4 | 13.4 | 14.3 | Inventory | | | | | 17.5 | 13.4 |
| | 2.7 | 3.8 | 3.6 | All Other Current | | | | | 1.4 | 2.9 |
| | 43.2 | 42.8 | 41.8 | Total Current | | | | | 44.3 | 38.8 |
| | 31.8 | 32.7 | 30.9 | Fixed Assets (net) | | | | | 39.9 | 30.3 |
| | 14.0 | 15.3 | 17.2 | Intangibles (net) | | | | | 6.3 | 20.8 |
| | 10.9 | 9.2 | 10.1 | All Other Non-Current | | | | | 9.5 | 10.2 |
| | 100.0 | 100.0 | 100.0 | Total | | | | | 100.0 | 100.0 |
| | | | | LIABILITIES | | | | | | |
| | 4.6 | 2.3 | 4.1 | Notes Payable-Short Term | | | | | 8.6 | 3.5 |
| | 4.4 | 3.7 | 2.8 | Cur. Mat.-L.T.D. | | | | | 5.5 | 2.3 |
| | 14.2 | 12.7 | 12.9 | Trade Payables | | | | | 18.7 | 11.7 |
| | .2 | .2 | .2 | Income Taxes Payable | | | | | .1 | .3 |
| | 9.6 | 10.3 | 9.2 | All Other Current | | | | | 10.1 | 9.1 |
| | 33.0 | 29.2 | 29.2 | Total Current | | | | | 42.9 | 26.8 |
| | 18.1 | 16.9 | 23.4 | Long-Term Debt | | | | | 17.5 | 22.8 |
| | 1.1 | 1.1 | 1.7 | Deferred Taxes | | | | | .0 | 2.4 |
| | 6.0 | 4.0 | 9.0 | All Other Non-Current | | | | | 20.6 | 5.0 |
| | 41.8 | 48.8 | 36.7 | Net Worth | | | | | 19.0 | 43.0 |
| | 100.0 | 100.0 | 100.0 | Total Liabilities & Net Worth | | | | | 100.0 | 100.0 |
| | | | | INCOME DATA | | | | | | |
| | 100.0 | 100.0 | 100.0 | Net Sales | | | | | 100.0 | 100.0 |
| | 29.4 | 32.5 | 32.4 | Gross Profit | | | | | 26.8 | 31.9 |
| | 24.3 | 26.4 | 26.5 | Operating Expenses | | | | | 25.8 | 24.0 |
| | 5.1 | 6.1 | 6.0 | Operating Profit | | | | | 1.1 | 7.9 |
| | .8 | .8 | 1.1 | All Other Expenses (net) | | | | | .1 | 1.4 |
| | 4.4 | 5.3 | 4.8 | Profit Before Taxes | | | | | .9 | 6.5 |
| | | | | RATIOS | | | | | | |
| | 2.7 | 2.8 | 2.5 | Current | | | | | 2.0 | 2.3 |
| | 1.5 | 1.6 | 1.5 | | | | | | 1.1 | 1.5 |
| | .9 | 1.1 | .9 | | | | | | .7 | 1.0 |
| | 1.8 | 1.7 | 1.4 | Quick | | | | | 1.1 | 1.2 |
| | (97) 1.0 | .9 | .8 | | | | | | .6 | .7 |
| | .4 | .5 | .4 | | | | | | .4 | .4 |
| | 19  19.5 | 19  19.5 | 20  18.5 | Sales/Receivables | | | | | 22  16.9 | 21  17.5 |
| | 25  14.3 | 27  13.6 | 29  12.8 | | | | | | 31  11.8 | 27  13.3 |
| | 30  12.0 | 34  10.9 | 34  10.6 | | | | | | 37  9.8 | 33  11.1 |
| | 18  20.8 | 19  19.6 | 20  18.3 | Cost of Sales/Inventory | | | | | 15  25.1 | 20  18.5 |
| | 26  14.0 | 27  13.3 | 30  12.3 | | | | | | 27  13.3 | 28  13.1 |
| | 44  8.3 | 46  8.0 | 51  7.1 | | | | | | 61  6.0 | 43  8.5 |
| | 13  27.8 | 17  21.5 | 17  21.0 | Cost of Sales/Payables | | | | | 20  18.3 | 17  21.4 |
| | 24  15.2 | 26  14.1 | 30  12.2 | | | | | | 33  11.2 | 30  12.2 |
| | 37  9.9 | 41  8.9 | 46  7.9 | | | | | | 62  5.9 | 42  8.7 |
| | 7.9 | 5.7 | 6.7 | Sales/Working Capital | | | | | 6.6 | 8.9 |
| | 17.6 | 16.0 | 18.2 | | | | | | 140.1 | 19.2 |
| | -122.0 | 93.8 | -65.5 | | | | | | -16.2 | 303.5 |
| | 22.9 | 18.6 | 15.5 | EBIT/Interest | | | | | 10.0 | 22.4 |
| | (87) 5.1 | (77) 5.8 | (90) 3.7 | | | | | | 2.7 | (57) 5.3 |
| | 1.4 | 2.0 | 1.4 | | | | | | -2.5 | 1.7 |
| | 10.8 | 9.7 | 3.5 | Net Profit + Depr., Dep., Amort./Cur. Mat. L/T/D | | | | | | 3.6 |
| | (28) 3.8 | (24) 3.3 | (20) 2.4 | | | | | | | (14) 2.9 |
| | 1.6 | .8 | 1.3 | | | | | | | 1.6 |
| | .5 | .5 | .7 | Fixed/Worth | | | | | .7 | .7 |
| | 1.0 | .9 | 1.0 | | | | | | 1.2 | 1.0 |
| | 16.3 | 2.2 | -1.8 | | | | | | 6.4 | -1.3 |
| | .5 | .6 | .7 | Debt/Worth | | | | | .6 | .7 |
| | 1.3 | 1.0 | 1.7 | | | | | | 2.3 | 1.6 |
| | 91.0 | 4.6 | -4.8 | | | | | | 12.9 | -4.0 |
| | 41.8 | 36.9 | 45.0 | % Profit Before Taxes/Tangible Net Worth | | | | | 65.8 | 53.6 |
| | (75) 19.5 | (72) 16.0 | (69) 16.2 | | | | | | (14) 11.1 | (43) 18.5 |
| | 4.7 | 3.2 | 6.5 | | | | | | -17.7 | 8.8 |
| | 14.0 | 11.9 | 12.0 | % Profit Before Taxes/Total Assets | | | | | 13.9 | 12.8 |
| | 6.7 | 5.0 | 4.9 | | | | | | 4.5 | 5.8 |
| | 1.1 | 2.0 | 1.2 | | | | | | -5.9 | 1.9 |
| | 13.5 | 12.3 | 11.2 | Sales/Net Fixed Assets | | | | | 10.1 | 11.3 |
| | 7.8 | 6.6 | 6.3 | | | | | | 4.9 | 6.5 |
| | 5.2 | 4.5 | 4.2 | | | | | | 3.1 | 4.7 |
| | 3.0 | 2.9 | 2.7 | Sales/Total Assets | | | | | 2.5 | 2.9 |
| | 2.2 | 1.9 | 1.8 | | | | | | 1.9 | 1.9 |
| | 1.6 | 1.3 | 1.3 | | | | | | 1.4 | 1.3 |
| | 1.8 | 1.9 | 1.6 | % Depr., Dep., Amort./Sales | | | | | 1.5 | 1.7 |
| | (82) 2.9 | (77) 2.7 | (82) 2.8 | | | | | | (15) 3.2 | (53) 2.8 |
| | 4.1 | 3.9 | 4.9 | | | | | | 6.5 | 4.4 |
| | .8 | .8 | 1.9 | % Officers', Directors' Owners' Comp/Sales | | | | | | |
| | (15) .9 | (14) 2.1 | (15) 3.1 | | | | | | | |
| | 2.2 | 5.7 | 6.6 | | | | | | | |
| | 9022397M | 9558947M | 10841797M | Net Sales ($) | | 12088M | 14708M | 56729M | 237095M | 10521177M |
| | 4448167M | 4927901M | 5682515M | Total Assets ($) | | 11574M | 9992M | 36510M | 129482M | 5494957M |

M = $ thousand    MM = $ million
See Pages 9 through 22 for Explanation of Ratios and Data

## Current Data Sorted by Assets　　　　　　Comparative Historical Data

| Type of Statement | 0-500M | 500M-2MM | 2-10MM | 10-50MM | 50-100MM | 100-250MM | | 4/1/07-3/31/08 ALL | 4/1/08-3/31/09 ALL |
|---|---|---|---|---|---|---|---|---|---|
| Unqualified | | | 2 | 1 | 2 | 1 | | 9 | 9 |
| Reviewed | | | 3 | 3 | | | | 9 | 7 |
| Compiled | 2 | 1 | 2 | 1 | | | | 4 | 8 |
| Tax Returns | 1 | 2 | 1 | | | | | 3 | 7 |
| Other | | 3 | 2 | 5 | 2 | 3 | | 13 | 14 |
| | | | 1 (4/1-9/30/11) | 36 (10/1/11-3/31/12) | | | | | |
| **NUMBER OF STATEMENTS** | 3 | 6 | 10 | 10 | 4 | 4 | | 38 | 45 |
| | % | % | % | % | % | % | | % | % |
| **ASSETS** | | | | | | | | | |
| Cash & Equivalents | | | 1.7 | 6.0 | | | | 7.4 | 5.9 |
| Trade Receivables (net) | | | 14.3 | 16.3 | | | | 16.9 | 15.9 |
| Inventory | | | 10.5 | 12.0 | | | | 18.3 | 14.9 |
| All Other Current | | | 1.0 | 2.3 | | | | 3.1 | 1.3 |
| Total Current | | | 27.5 | 36.6 | | | | 45.8 | 38.0 |
| Fixed Assets (net) | | | 50.3 | 54.0 | | | | 44.1 | 49.0 |
| Intangibles (net) | | | 15.5 | 3.5 | | | | 5.3 | 7.6 |
| All Other Non-Current | | | 6.7 | 5.9 | | | | 4.8 | 5.4 |
| Total | | | 100.0 | 100.0 | | | | 100.0 | 100.0 |
| **LIABILITIES** | | | | | | | | | |
| Notes Payable-Short Term | | | 6.4 | 10.5 | | | | 8.9 | 6.8 |
| Cur. Mat.-L.T.D. | | | 6.3 | 5.2 | | | | 8.8 | 6.8 |
| Trade Payables | | | 9.6 | 7.1 | | | | 12.8 | 10.0 |
| Income Taxes Payable | | | .0 | .0 | | | | .7 | .1 |
| All Other Current | | | 10.1 | 6.3 | | | | 9.1 | 15.9 |
| Total Current | | | 32.4 | 29.2 | | | | 40.2 | 39.6 |
| Long-Term Debt | | | 25.9 | 24.2 | | | | 27.9 | 32.4 |
| Deferred Taxes | | | 3.1 | .6 | | | | .5 | .4 |
| All Other Non-Current | | | 14.7 | 2.1 | | | | 7.4 | 11.1 |
| Net Worth | | | 24.0 | 43.9 | | | | 24.1 | 16.5 |
| Total Liabilties & Net Worth | | | 100.0 | 100.0 | | | | 100.0 | 100.0 |
| **INCOME DATA** | | | | | | | | | |
| Net Sales | | | 100.0 | 100.0 | | | | 100.0 | 100.0 |
| Gross Profit | | | 43.0 | 39.6 | | | | 38.5 | 40.9 |
| Operating Expenses | | | 41.0 | 30.6 | | | | 31.4 | 36.1 |
| Operating Profit | | | 2.0 | 9.0 | | | | 7.1 | 4.9 |
| All Other Expenses (net) | | | 1.1 | .1 | | | | 2.1 | 2.4 |
| Profit Before Taxes | | | .9 | 8.9 | | | | 5.0 | 2.5 |
| **RATIOS** | | | | | | | | | |
| Current | | | 1.5 | 2.7 | | | | 2.5 | 2.1 |
| | | | .7 | 1.4 | | | | 1.1 | 1.2 |
| | | | .4 | 1.0 | | | | .6 | .6 |
| Quick | | | .9 | 1.7 | | | | 1.1 | 1.1 |
| | | | .5 | .8 | | | | .6 | .6 |
| | | | .3 | .4 | | | | .4 | .4 |
| Sales/Receivables | | | 27 13.6 | 34 10.7 | | | | 20 18.1 | 23 16.2 |
| | | | 35 10.3 | 39 9.4 | | | | 29 12.4 | 27 13.7 |
| | | | 48 7.6 | 51 7.1 | | | | 35 10.4 | 39 9.3 |
| Cost of Sales/Inventory | | | 29 12.5 | 24 14.9 | | | | 25 14.9 | 21 17.7 |
| | | | 35 10.5 | 45 8.2 | | | | 44 8.3 | 40 9.2 |
| | | | 41 8.9 | 69 5.3 | | | | 58 6.3 | 55 6.6 |
| Cost of Sales/Payables | | | 14 25.6 | 23 15.9 | | | | 14 25.8 | 14 26.7 |
| | | | 51 7.1 | 33 11.0 | | | | 30 12.2 | 31 11.6 |
| | | | 66 5.5 | 59 6.2 | | | | 50 7.3 | 43 8.6 |
| Sales/Working Capital | | | 10.1 | 3.2 | | | | 9.7 | 9.7 |
| | | | -16.0 | 15.4 | | | | 46.0 | 30.1 |
| | | | -5.2 | NM | | | | -16.1 | -11.4 |
| EBIT/Interest | | | 16.8 | 8.3 | | | | 4.4 | 3.9 |
| | | | 3.6 | 3.8 | | | | (34) 1.7 | (43) 2.2 |
| | | | 1.8 | 1.1 | | | | .4 | -.2 |
| Net Profit + Depr., Dep., Amort./Cur. Mat. L/T/D | | | | | | | | 2.4 | |
| | | | | | | | | (10) 1.4 | |
| | | | | | | | | .7 | |
| Fixed/Worth | | | .8 | .8 | | | | .6 | 1.1 |
| | | | 3.3 | 1.3 | | | | 1.8 | 3.9 |
| | | | -45.7 | 2.8 | | | | -4.9 | -9.5 |
| Debt/Worth | | | 1.5 | .6 | | | | .6 | 1.8 |
| | | | 3.6 | 1.8 | | | | 2.2 | 4.3 |
| | | | -72.1 | 4.0 | | | | -8.2 | -23.1 |
| % Profit Before Taxes/Tangible Net Worth | | | | 36.7 | | | | 31.0 | 39.3 |
| | | | | 17.9 | | | | (27) 16.0 | (32) 15.3 |
| | | | | .3 | | | | 7.6 | -11.7 |
| % Profit Before Taxes/Total Assets | | | 8.7 | 12.6 | | | | 11.6 | 8.2 |
| | | | 5.3 | 4.9 | | | | 3.5 | 3.2 |
| | | | 2.6 | .2 | | | | -2.4 | -4.4 |
| Sales/Net Fixed Assets | | | 4.5 | 3.1 | | | | 9.4 | 7.6 |
| | | | 3.3 | 1.7 | | | | 4.8 | 3.1 |
| | | | 1.5 | 1.1 | | | | 2.6 | 1.3 |
| Sales/Total Assets | | | 1.6 | 1.7 | | | | 3.3 | 2.4 |
| | | | 1.4 | 1.1 | | | | 2.2 | 1.4 |
| | | | 1.2 | .5 | | | | 1.0 | .9 |
| % Depr., Dep., Amort./Sales | | | | 4.5 | | | | 1.7 | 3.3 |
| | | | | 8.2 | | | | (32) 5.1 | (40) 5.7 |
| | | | | 9.1 | | | | 7.2 | 9.3 |
| % Officers', Directors' Owners' Comp/Sales | | | | | | | | | |
| Net Sales ($) | 1681M | 9843M | 84208M | 313233M | 225838M | 898946M | | 1458772M | 1596643M |
| Total Assets ($) | 669M | 5425M | 62034M | 257979M | 223296M | 667962M | | 945395M | 1119287M |

M = $ thousand　　MM = $ million
See Pages 9 through 22 for Explanation of Ratios and Data

## Comparative Historical Data / Current Data Sorted by Sales

| | | | Type of Statement | 0-1MM | 1-3MM | 3-5MM | 5-10MM | 10-25MM | 25MM & OVER |
|---|---|---|---|---|---|---|---|---|---|
| 14 | 7 | 6 | Unqualified | | | | 1 | 2 | 3 |
| 4 | 7 | 6 | Reviewed | | | | 2 | 3 | 1 |
| 5 | 7 | 6 | Compiled | | 3 | | 2 | 1 | |
| 9 | 5 | 4 | Tax Returns | 3 | | | 1 | | |
| 14 | 13 | 15 | Other | 3 | | 1 | 1 | 2 | 8 |
| 4/1/09-3/31/10 ALL | 4/1/10-3/31/11 ALL | 4/1/11-3/31/12 ALL | | | 1 (4/1-9/30/11) | | 36 (10/1/11-3/31/12) | | |
| 46 | 39 | 37 | NUMBER OF STATEMENTS | 6 | 3 | 1 | 7 | 8 | 12 |
| % | % | % | ASSETS | % | % | % | % | % | % |
| 6.4 | 5.4 | 7.3 | Cash & Equivalents | | | | | | 4.0 |
| 17.5 | 14.2 | 14.6 | Trade Receivables (net) | | | | | | 18.3 |
| 15.0 | 15.0 | 8.9 | Inventory | | | | | | 13.3 |
| 2.4 | 2.5 | 1.6 | All Other Current | | | | | | 2.5 |
| 41.3 | 37.2 | 32.4 | Total Current | | | | | | 38.1 |
| 44.7 | 50.5 | 49.9 | Fixed Assets (net) | | | | | | 42.0 |
| 10.6 | 7.9 | 13.1 | Intangibles (net) | | | | | | 17.6 |
| 3.4 | 4.5 | 4.6 | All Other Non-Current | | | | | | 2.3 |
| 100.0 | 100.0 | 100.0 | Total | | | | | | 100.0 |
| | | | LIABILITIES | | | | | | |
| 7.5 | 6.0 | 5.9 | Notes Payable-Short Term | | | | | | 9.0 |
| 5.5 | 4.3 | 4.8 | Cur. Mat.-L.T.D. | | | | | | 3.3 |
| 10.5 | 10.0 | 9.4 | Trade Payables | | | | | | 8.0 |
| .1 | .0 | .3 | Income Taxes Payable | | | | | | .0 |
| 14.3 | 7.1 | 13.5 | All Other Current | | | | | | 7.4 |
| 37.8 | 27.4 | 33.9 | Total Current | | | | | | 27.7 |
| 27.5 | 21.9 | 22.0 | Long-Term Debt | | | | | | 21.1 |
| .6 | 1.2 | 1.7 | Deferred Taxes | | | | | | 2.1 |
| 14.6 | 19.9 | 7.9 | All Other Non-Current | | | | | | 9.8 |
| 19.6 | 29.6 | 34.5 | Net Worth | | | | | | 39.4 |
| 100.0 | 100.0 | 100.0 | Total Liabilities & Net Worth | | | | | | 100.0 |
| | | | INCOME DATA | | | | | | |
| 100.0 | 100.0 | 100.0 | Net Sales | | | | | | 100.0 |
| 40.9 | 42.0 | 42.8 | Gross Profit | | | | | | 26.2 |
| 34.8 | 38.2 | 38.0 | Operating Expenses | | | | | | 23.4 |
| 6.1 | 3.8 | 4.8 | Operating Profit | | | | | | 2.8 |
| 2.9 | 2.5 | 1.4 | All Other Expenses (net) | | | | | | 1.7 |
| 3.2 | 1.3 | 3.3 | Profit Before Taxes | | | | | | 1.0 |
| | | | RATIOS | | | | | | |
| 2.2 | 2.5 | 2.0 | | | | | | | 2.0 |
| 1.4 | 1.4 | 1.3 | Current | | | | | | 1.4 |
| .6 | .9 | .6 | | | | | | | 1.1 |
| 1.2 | 1.3 | 1.2 | | | | | | | 1.1 |
| .8 | .9 | .8 | Quick | | | | | | .8 |
| .4 | .4 | .3 | | | | | | | .5 |
| (23) 15.6 | (21) 17.4 | (26) 14.2 | | | | | | | (35) 10.3 |
| (29) 12.6 | (27) 13.3 | (36) 10.0 | Sales/Receivables | | | | | | (39) 9.4 |
| (39) 9.4 | (39) 9.3 | (42) 8.6 | | | | | | | (46) 7.9 |
| (23) 15.6 | (26) 13.8 | (27) 13.6 | | | | | | | (29) 12.8 |
| (38) 9.5 | (36) 10.1 | (37) 9.8 | Cost of Sales/Inventory | | | | | | (41) 9.0 |
| (57) 6.4 | (66) 5.6 | (54) 6.8 | | | | | | | (54) 6.7 |
| (12) 30.3 | (11) 34.8 | (17) 21.5 | | | | | | | (15) 25.1 |
| (28) 13.1 | (25) 14.8 | (30) 12.3 | Cost of Sales/Payables | | | | | | (23) 15.8 |
| (43) 8.5 | (48) 7.6 | (58) 6.3 | | | | | | | (49) 7.5 |
| 7.4 | 7.2 | 9.8 | | | | | | | 9.2 |
| 17.1 | 21.4 | 37.3 | Sales/Working Capital | | | | | | 15.4 |
| -10.7 | -30.4 | -10.6 | | | | | | | 44.8 |
| 7.6 | 4.7 | 7.5 | | | | | | | 5.1 |
| (42) 2.7 | (35) 2.0 | (35) 2.0 | EBIT/Interest | | | | | | (11) 2.0 |
| 1.4 | -.9 | .8 | | | | | | | .8 |
| 2.3 | | | | | | | | | |
| (10) 2.0 | | | Net Profit + Depr., Dep., Amort./Cur. Mat. L/T/D | | | | | | |
| 1.8 | | | | | | | | | |
| 1.0 | .9 | 1.0 | | | | | | | 1.0 |
| 2.8 | 1.6 | 2.4 | Fixed/Worth | | | | | | 1.8 |
| -4.9 | 4.6 | UND | | | | | | | 31.7 |
| 1.4 | 1.0 | 1.1 | | | | | | | 1.3 |
| 3.3 | 1.9 | 2.7 | Debt/Worth | | | | | | 2.5 |
| -9.6 | 4.8 | UND | | | | | | | 97.5 |
| 52.8 | 28.8 | 43.7 | | | | | | | 92.8 |
| (31) 29.5 | (32) 8.6 | (28) 18.8 | % Profit Before Taxes/Tangible Net Worth | | | | | | (10) 23.9 |
| 5.8 | -8.6 | .2 | | | | | | | -9.2 |
| 10.2 | 9.0 | 9.5 | | | | | | | 11.9 |
| 5.6 | 3.4 | 3.8 | % Profit Before Taxes/Total Assets | | | | | | 3.7 |
| -.1 | -5.7 | -1.0 | | | | | | | -.3 |
| 7.6 | 6.0 | 5.2 | | | | | | | 8.9 |
| 3.6 | 2.9 | 2.7 | Sales/Net Fixed Assets | | | | | | 3.3 |
| 1.9 | 1.9 | 1.5 | | | | | | | 1.6 |
| 2.4 | 2.3 | 2.0 | | | | | | | 2.5 |
| 1.5 | 1.6 | 1.3 | Sales/Total Assets | | | | | | 1.2 |
| 1.1 | 1.1 | .9 | | | | | | | 1.0 |
| 3.0 | 3.1 | 5.2 | | | | | | | |
| (37) 6.2 | (32) 5.5 | (31) 8.1 | % Depr., Dep., Amort./Sales | | | | | | |
| 8.9 | 8.5 | 10.7 | | | | | | | |
| | | | % Officers', Directors' Owners' Comp/Sales | | | | | | |
| 1769423M | 1555569M | 1533749M | Net Sales ($) | 3700M | 5973M | 4510M | 57815M | 125812M | 1335939M |
| 1369300M | 1209866M | 1217365M | Total Assets ($) | 2494M | 5930M | 1750M | 39852M | 205271M | 962068M |

© RMA 2012

M = $ thousand    MM = $ million
See Pages 9 through 22 for Explanation of Ratios and Data

## Current Data Sorted by Assets      Comparative Historical Data

| 0-500M | 500M-2MM | 2-10MM | 10-50MM | 50-100MM | 100-250MM | Type of Statement | 4/1/07-3/31/08 ALL | 4/1/08-3/31/09 ALL |
|---|---|---|---|---|---|---|---|---|
| | 1 | 4 | 8 | 2 | 4 | Unqualified | 12 | 13 |
| 1 | 1 | 5 | 5 | | | Reviewed | 4 | 6 |
| | 1 | 4 | | | | Compiled | 4 | 6 |
| 3 | 11 | 1 | | | | Tax Returns | 7 | 12 |
| 4 | 6 | 14 | 11 | | 5 | Other | 19 | 31 |
| | 3 (4/1-9/30/11) | | 89 (10/1/11-3/31/12) | | | | | |
| 8 | 19 | 28 | 24 | 4 | 9 | NUMBER OF STATEMENTS | 46 | 68 |
| % | % | % | % | % | % | **ASSETS** | % | % |
| | 9.3 | 11.0 | 10.3 | | | Cash & Equivalents | 9.5 | 6.7 |
| | 14.9 | 8.6 | 11.3 | | | Trade Receivables (net) | 9.6 | 12.5 |
| | 17.1 | 13.0 | 11.9 | | | Inventory | 14.2 | 16.2 |
| | 1.8 | 2.2 | 2.4 | | | All Other Current | 4.1 | 4.2 |
| | 43.1 | 34.8 | 36.0 | | | Total Current | 37.4 | 39.6 |
| | 53.5 | 55.5 | 52.6 | | | Fixed Assets (net) | 51.6 | 50.9 |
| | 1.7 | 2.2 | 6.8 | | | Intangibles (net) | 6.2 | 5.9 |
| | 1.7 | 7.5 | 4.6 | | | All Other Non-Current | 4.7 | 3.5 |
| | 100.0 | 100.0 | 100.0 | | | Total | 100.0 | 100.0 |
| | | | | | | **LIABILITIES** | | |
| | 4.4 | 2.5 | 1.2 | | | Notes Payable-Short Term | 5.0 | 5.6 |
| | 2.6 | 4.5 | 3.3 | | | Cur. Mat.-L.T.D. | 5.0 | 3.8 |
| | 14.3 | 11.0 | 9.9 | | | Trade Payables | 12.2 | 11.3 |
| | .0 | .1 | .1 | | | Income Taxes Payable | .2 | .1 |
| | 8.9 | 5.1 | 7.3 | | | All Other Current | 13.5 | 12.5 |
| | 30.2 | 23.1 | 21.8 | | | Total Current | 35.9 | 33.2 |
| | 42.1 | 28.5 | 18.6 | | | Long-Term Debt | 32.8 | 29.8 |
| | .0 | 1.3 | 2.3 | | | Deferred Taxes | 1.0 | 1.1 |
| | 7.1 | 3.5 | 7.0 | | | All Other Non-Current | 3.1 | 6.4 |
| | 20.7 | 43.5 | 50.3 | | | Net Worth | 27.2 | 29.5 |
| | 100.0 | 100.0 | 100.0 | | | Total Liabilities & Net Worth | 100.0 | 100.0 |
| | | | | | | **INCOME DATA** | | |
| | 100.0 | 100.0 | 100.0 | | | Net Sales | 100.0 | 100.0 |
| | 53.6 | 54.0 | 35.0 | | | Gross Profit | 39.9 | 39.6 |
| | 44.1 | 40.7 | 22.6 | | | Operating Expenses | 31.2 | 33.4 |
| | 9.4 | 13.2 | 12.4 | | | Operating Profit | 8.6 | 6.2 |
| | .4 | .3 | .7 | | | All Other Expenses (net) | 1.5 | 1.5 |
| | 9.0 | 13.0 | 11.7 | | | Profit Before Taxes | 7.1 | 4.7 |
| | | | | | | **RATIOS** | | |
| | 2.0 | 2.6 | 2.4 | | | | 1.7 | 2.1 |
| | 1.2 | 1.4 | 1.6 | | | Current | 1.1 | 1.1 |
| | .8 | 1.0 | 1.0 | | | | .8 | .8 |
| | 1.0 | 1.6 | 1.4 | | | | 1.0 | 1.1 |
| | .5 | .8 | .8 | | | Quick | .7 | .5 |
| | .1 | .4 | .4 | | | | .3 | .3 |
| | 3  120.4 | 5  75.4 | 10  37.0 | | | | 5  72.0 | 9  39.7 |
| | 6  64.1 | 19  19.5 | 22  16.3 | | | Sales/Receivables | 21  17.6 | 23  15.7 |
| | 24  15.2 | 26  14.0 | 27  13.4 | | | | 29  12.6 | 35  10.4 |
| | 12  30.7 | 33  11.0 | 39  9.3 | | | | 25  14.7 | 32  11.3 |
| | 45  8.2 | 57  6.4 | 46  7.9 | | | Cost of Sales/Inventory | 48  7.6 | 51  7.1 |
| | 65  5.6 | 81  4.5 | 53  6.9 | | | | 71  5.2 | 84  4.3 |
| | 13  29.0 | 28  13.2 | 21  17.6 | | | | 16  23.2 | 18  20.1 |
| | 49  7.5 | 42  8.6 | 32  11.4 | | | Cost of Sales/Payables | 34  10.6 | 34  10.7 |
| | 57  6.4 | 59  6.2 | 46  7.9 | | | | 53  6.8 | 51  7.1 |
| | 15.2 | 7.8 | 6.8 | | | | 10.9 | 8.5 |
| | 55.1 | 34.1 | 12.1 | | | Sales/Working Capital | 57.9 | 41.7 |
| | -43.3 | -397.6 | NM | | | | -23.1 | -27.9 |
| | 14.8 | 24.0 | 58.4 | | | | 15.2 | 11.3 |
| | (17)  5.8 | (26)  10.6 | (22)  12.2 | | | EBIT/Interest | (41)  5.8 | (61)  3.0 |
| | 1.4 | 5.8 | 5.5 | | | | 1.3 | 1.3 |
| | | | | | | | 7.3 | 6.7 |
| | | | | | | Net Profit + Depr., Dep., Amort./Cur. Mat. L/T/D | (11)  3.1 | (18)  3.5 |
| | | | | | | | 2.0 | 1.5 |
| | .6 | .9 | .8 | | | | 1.0 | .9 |
| | 1.9 | 1.4 | 1.3 | | | Fixed/Worth | 1.7 | 1.9 |
| | 13.5 | 1.9 | 2.1 | | | | 5.0 | 4.4 |
| | 1.2 | .9 | .6 | | | | .9 | 1.0 |
| | 2.2 | 1.4 | 1.1 | | | Debt/Worth | 2.4 | 2.1 |
| | 21.9 | 1.9 | 2.4 | | | | 6.6 | 5.4 |
| | 76.5 | 78.6 | 64.3 | | | | 66.2 | 44.0 |
| | (17)  40.7 | (27)  53.7 | (23)  34.1 | | | % Profit Before Taxes/Tangible Net Worth | (36)  36.3 | (55)  18.1 |
| | 11.3 | 24.0 | 17.4 | | | | 11.5 | 3.2 |
| | 41.4 | 39.8 | 24.4 | | | | 22.5 | 15.3 |
| | 13.6 | 20.5 | 12.4 | | | % Profit Before Taxes/Total Assets | 11.2 | 5.4 |
| | 1.8 | 7.2 | 7.8 | | | | 2.5 | .7 |
| | 10.3 | 4.9 | 10.3 | | | | 9.7 | 7.3 |
| | 4.3 | 3.0 | 2.3 | | | Sales/Net Fixed Assets | 3.5 | 3.2 |
| | 3.1 | 2.0 | 1.4 | | | | 1.6 | 1.7 |
| | 3.6 | 2.3 | 2.0 | | | | 2.3 | 2.6 |
| | 2.9 | 1.7 | 1.4 | | | Sales/Total Assets | 1.4 | 1.7 |
| | 1.6 | 1.2 | 1.0 | | | | 1.0 | 1.2 |
| | 1.8 | 2.9 | 2.5 | | | | 2.7 | 2.4 |
| | (15)  2.7 | (23)  3.4 | (22)  4.5 | | | % Depr., Dep., Amort./Sales | (39)  4.1 | (61)  4.3 |
| | 5.5 | 4.9 | 6.3 | | | | 5.8 | 6.2 |
| | 2.0 | | | | | | .4 | 1.7 |
| | (11)  4.9 | | | | | % Officers', Directors', Owners' Comp/Sales | (10)  2.3 | (16)  2.6 |
| | 6.1 | | | | | | 5.6 | 3.6 |
| 7067M | 71818M | 244948M | 1168799M | 431287M | 2471418M | Net Sales ($) | 1789978M | 2628678M |
| 1732M | 21800M | 140201M | 694206M | 316269M | 1660659M | Total Assets ($) | 1266627M | 1894533M |

© RMA 2012

M = $ thousand     MM = $ million
See Pages 9 through 22 for Explanation of Ratios and Data

## Comparative Historical Data          Current Data Sorted by Sales

| Type of Statement | | | | | | | | | |
|---|---|---|---|---|---|---|---|---|---|
| 16 | 12 | 18 | Unqualified | | | | 2 | 4 | 12 |
| 9 | 7 | 12 | Reviewed | | 1 | 1 | 3 | 3 | 4 |
| 6 | 8 | 5 | Compiled | | 1 | 1 | 1 | 1 | 2 |
| 7 | 19 | 15 | Tax Returns | 2 | 8 | 3 | 1 | 1 | |
| 36 | 35 | 42 | Other | 3 | 6 | 4 | 6 | 9 | 15 |
| 4/1/09-3/31/10 ALL | 4/1/10-3/31/11 ALL | 4/1/11-3/31/12 ALL | | 0-1MM | 3 (4/1-9/30/11) 1-3MM | 3-5MM | 89 (10/1/11-3/31/12) 5-10MM | 10-25MM | 25MM & OVER |
| 74 | 81 | 92 | **NUMBER OF STATEMENTS** | 5 | 15 | 9 | 13 | 19 | 31 |
| % | % | % | **ASSETS** | % | % | % | % | % | % |
| 8.7 | 9.2 | 9.6 | Cash & Equivalents | | 8.8 | | 15.1 | 9.8 | 7.8 |
| 10.6 | 8.6 | 10.5 | Trade Receivables (net) | | 4.7 | | 14.9 | 9.7 | 11.1 |
| 16.0 | 16.8 | 13.3 | Inventory | | 19.5 | | 13.0 | 14.3 | 9.7 |
| 4.0 | 1.6 | 3.1 | All Other Current | | 3.2 | | .6 | 3.2 | 4.5 |
| 39.3 | 36.2 | 36.6 | Total Current | | 36.2 | | 43.7 | 37.0 | 33.2 |
| 49.1 | 51.6 | 50.2 | Fixed Assets (net) | | 59.2 | | 53.8 | 49.9 | 43.8 |
| 8.2 | 8.9 | 8.1 | Intangibles (net) | | 1.5 | | .4 | 7.0 | 17.9 |
| 3.4 | 3.3 | 5.0 | All Other Non-Current | | 3.1 | | 2.1 | 6.1 | 5.1 |
| 100.0 | 100.0 | 100.0 | Total | | 100.0 | | 100.0 | 100.0 | 100.0 |
| | | | **LIABILITIES** | | | | | | |
| 3.8 | 5.4 | 3.2 | Notes Payable-Short Term | | 2.3 | | 1.8 | 3.0 | 1.3 |
| 5.6 | 2.9 | 3.6 | Cur. Mat.-L.T.D. | | 2.9 | | 5.9 | 3.0 | 3.1 |
| 9.7 | 9.6 | 10.6 | Trade Payables | | 9.2 | | 14.3 | 9.9 | 9.8 |
| .2 | .0 | .2 | Income Taxes Payable | | .0 | | .1 | .0 | .5 |
| 10.3 | 6.8 | 7.0 | All Other Current | | 7.4 | | 6.3 | 5.5 | 7.4 |
| 29.5 | 24.7 | 24.6 | Total Current | | 21.8 | | 28.5 | 21.4 | 22.1 |
| 33.3 | 39.1 | 29.0 | Long-Term Debt | | 32.6 | | 23.1 | 24.8 | 23.3 |
| .8 | 1.2 | 1.3 | Deferred Taxes | | .0 | | 1.4 | 2.1 | 1.9 |
| 6.3 | 6.8 | 4.9 | All Other Non-Current | | 4.0 | | 1.2 | 6.2 | 6.2 |
| 30.0 | 28.2 | 40.2 | Net Worth | | 41.6 | | 45.8 | 45.5 | 46.6 |
| 100.0 | 100.0 | 100.0 | Total Liabilities & Net Worth | | 100.0 | | 100.0 | 100.0 | 100.0 |
| | | | **INCOME DATA** | | | | | | |
| 100.0 | 100.0 | 100.0 | Net Sales | | 100.0 | | 100.0 | 100.0 | 100.0 |
| 39.3 | 44.8 | 46.4 | Gross Profit | | 57.1 | | 54.4 | 46.8 | 33.2 |
| 30.3 | 35.3 | 35.5 | Operating Expenses | | 48.1 | | 37.0 | 35.0 | 21.3 |
| 9.0 | 9.5 | 10.9 | Operating Profit | | 9.0 | | 17.5 | 11.8 | 12.0 |
| 1.3 | .7 | .7 | All Other Expenses (net) | | 1.5 | | -.3 | .0 | 1.2 |
| 7.8 | 8.7 | 10.2 | Profit Before Taxes | | 7.5 | | 17.7 | 11.8 | 10.7 |
| | | | **RATIOS** | | | | | | |
| 1.9 | 2.3 | 2.3 | Current | | 3.4 | | 2.8 | 2.4 | 2.4 |
| 1.4 | 1.5 | 1.4 | | | 1.7 | | 1.4 | 1.4 | 1.5 |
| .9 | .9 | .9 | | | .8 | | 1.0 | 1.1 | .8 |
| 1.1 | 1.3 | 1.3 | Quick | | 1.0 | | 2.1 | 1.1 | 1.3 |
| .5 | .6 | .7 | | | .4 | | .8 | .9 | .6 |
| .3 | .3 | .4 | | | .1 | | .5 | .6 | .4 |
| 4  82.6 | 7  55.7 | 5  78.8 | Sales/Receivables | 0  999.8 | | 20  18.4 | 4  88.8 | 15  24.8 | |
| 21  17.3 | 17  21.7 | 17  20.9 | | 5  80.3 | | 25  14.8 | 13  28.2 | 22  16.5 | |
| 30  12.2 | 28  13.2 | 26  14.2 | | 17  21.2 | | 31  11.6 | 25  14.7 | 33  11.2 | |
| 24  15.3 | 35  10.5 | 23  16.1 | Cost of Sales/Inventory | 26  13.8 | | 27  13.4 | 24  15.3 | 20  18.6 | |
| 47  7.7 | 53  6.9 | 47  7.7 | | 70  5.2 | | 61  6.0 | 46  7.9 | 40  9.1 | |
| 67  5.5 | 79  4.6 | 62  5.9 | | 101  3.6 | | 99  3.7 | 51  7.2 | 54  6.8 | |
| 15  23.8 | 16  23.4 | 19  19.5 | Cost of Sales/Payables | 12  29.2 | | 30  12.0 | 24  15.0 | 20  18.1 | |
| 25  14.6 | 34  10.8 | 33  11.2 | | 28  12.9 | | 51  7.1 | 32  11.3 | 31  11.7 | |
| 44  8.3 | 49  7.4 | 54  6.8 | | 51  7.1 | | 74  4.9 | 56  6.5 | 40  9.2 | |
| 9.0 | 6.7 | 8.3 | Sales/Working Capital | | 8.6 | | 11.7 | 7.0 | 6.6 |
| 19.7 | 27.7 | 31.7 | | | 37.4 | | 16.1 | 21.1 | 18.6 |
| -51.5 | -65.3 | -101.3 | | | -17.8 | | -271.0 | 202.2 | -22.0 |
| 13.1 | 17.9 | 23.6 | EBIT/Interest | | 12.9 | | 46.3 | 24.0 | 45.1 |
| (69)  5.5 | (78)  6.6 | (82)  7.8 | | (13)  2.1 | | (11)  11.3 | (18)  9.9 | (28)  9.4 | |
| 2.4 | 2.1 | 2.6 | | | -.6 | | 4.5 | 6.7 | 3.2 |
| 5.8 | 6.1 | 4.7 | Net Profit + Depr., Dep., Amort./Cur. Mat. L/T/D | | | | | | |
| (19)  3.2 | (15)  3.4 | (17)  3.6 | | | | | | | |
| 1.8 | 1.7 | 2.3 | | | | | | | |
| .9 | 1.0 | .8 | Fixed/Worth | | .5 | | .8 | .8 | .8 |
| 1.8 | 1.6 | 1.3 | | | 2.2 | | 1.2 | 1.3 | 1.3 |
| 3.2 | 7.4 | 2.6 | | | 3.8 | | 1.7 | 2.2 | -2.1 |
| 1.0 | .9 | .7 | Debt/Worth | | .9 | | .8 | .9 | .6 |
| 1.7 | 1.6 | 1.4 | | | 1.5 | | 1.4 | 1.3 | .9 |
| 3.6 | 9.7 | 3.1 | | | 3.1 | | 1.7 | 2.6 | -4.3 |
| 70.3 | 88.1 | 71.6 | % Profit Before Taxes/Tangible Net Worth | | 93.2 | | 104.3 | 77.0 | 50.0 |
| (59)  37.0 | (64)  36.9 | (79)  40.7 | | 42.0 | | (18)  54.6 | (23)  61.7 | 27.1 | |
| 11.1 | 10.8 | 16.8 | | | -2.8 | | 15.5 | 35.0 | 15.0 |
| 22.2 | 27.7 | 29.5 | % Profit Before Taxes/Total Assets | | 41.3 | | 59.9 | 38.0 | 21.8 |
| 12.8 | 12.8 | 13.8 | | | 8.6 | | 21.8 | 18.0 | 10.8 |
| 4.2 | 2.2 | 5.2 | | | -2.7 | | 6.4 | 11.7 | 5.0 |
| 9.0 | 8.2 | 9.1 | Sales/Net Fixed Assets | | 4.1 | | 6.8 | 25.3 | 11.4 |
| 3.8 | 3.4 | 3.4 | | | 3.1 | | 3.1 | 4.0 | 2.8 |
| 2.1 | 1.7 | 1.9 | | | 1.5 | | 2.3 | 2.2 | 1.5 |
| 2.7 | 2.8 | 2.9 | Sales/Total Assets | | 3.6 | | 2.5 | 2.7 | 2.0 |
| 1.8 | 1.5 | 1.7 | | | 1.6 | | 1.7 | 2.0 | 1.4 |
| 1.3 | 1.1 | 1.2 | | | 1.2 | | 1.2 | 1.4 | 1.0 |
| 2.0 | 2.2 | 2.5 | % Depr., Dep., Amort./Sales | | 1.7 | | 3.4 | 2.3 | 1.8 |
| (65)  3.7 | (65)  4.3 | (72)  3.9 | | (10)  3.7 | | (10)  4.6 | (17)  2.9 | (25)  4.2 | |
| 7.0 | 7.0 | 6.2 | | | 11.8 | | 8.1 | 3.9 | 6.1 |
| .8 | 2.2 | 2.1 | % Officers', Directors' Owners' Comp/Sales | | | | | | |
| (16)  2.8 | (21)  3.5 | (25)  4.9 | | | | | | | |
| 5.2 | 5.6 | 7.3 | | | | | | | |
| 4000064M | 3418090M | 4395337M | Net Sales ($) | 3156M | 28916M | 32892M | 87752M | 277007M | 3965614M |
| 2189696M | 2388832M | 2834867M | Total Assets ($) | 1016M | 22835M | 15461M | 53705M | 151801M | 2590049M |

M = $ thousand     MM = $ million
See Pages 9 through 22 for Explanation of Ratios and Data

## Current Data Sorted by Assets      Comparative Historical Data

| 0-500M | 500M-2MM | 2-10MM | 10-50MM | 50-100MM | 100-250MM | Type of Statement | 4/1/07-3/31/08 ALL | 4/1/08-3/31/09 ALL |
|---|---|---|---|---|---|---|---|---|
| 1 |  | 4 | 10 | 6 | 10 | Unqualified | 23 | 22 |
|  | 1 | 14 | 23 | 6 | 1 | Reviewed | 28 | 51 |
|  | 7 | 11 | 5 | 1 |  | Compiled | 4 | 14 |
| 5 | 10 | 10 | 1 |  |  | Tax Returns | 17 | 23 |
| 3 | 17 | 41 | 31 | 9 | 4 | Other | 63 | 90 |
| | 28 (4/1-9/30/11) | | 203 (10/1/11-3/31/12) | | | | | |
| 9 | 35 | 80 | 70 | 22 | 15 | **NUMBER OF STATEMENTS** | 135 | 200 |
| % | % | % | % | % | % | **ASSETS** | % | % |
|  | 6.8 | 5.0 | 2.1 | 2.5 | 3.8 | Cash & Equivalents | 3.5 | 2.8 |
|  | 8.2 | 8.3 | 7.6 | 7.5 | 9.3 | Trade Receivables (net) | 7.4 | 8.4 |
|  | 51.5 | 47.5 | 41.1 | 36.5 | 33.0 | Inventory | 39.9 | 45.2 |
|  | 4.5 | 2.1 | 3.2 | 2.8 | 1.9 | All Other Current | 2.9 | 2.4 |
|  | 71.1 | 63.0 | 53.9 | 49.2 | 48.0 | Total Current | 53.7 | 58.8 |
|  | 23.3 | 31.3 | 39.5 | 41.4 | 32.3 | Fixed Assets (net) | 38.1 | 34.1 |
|  | 4.9 | 2.8 | 3.0 | 2.7 | 13.9 | Intangibles (net) | 3.9 | 2.9 |
|  | .7 | 2.9 | 3.5 | 6.7 | 5.8 | All Other Non-Current | 4.3 | 4.3 |
|  | 100.0 | 100.0 | 100.0 | 100.0 | 100.0 | Total | 100.0 | 100.0 |
|  |  |  |  |  |  | **LIABILITIES** |  |  |
|  | 10.9 | 15.5 | 12.7 | 10.3 | 5.2 | Notes Payable-Short Term | 13.4 | 15.4 |
|  | 2.5 | 2.6 | 2.8 | 2.7 | 1.5 | Cur. Mat.-L.T.D. | 2.6 | 2.5 |
|  | 12.9 | 7.7 | 6.0 | 6.1 | 6.8 | Trade Payables | 7.0 | 8.7 |
|  | .1 | .1 | .3 | .2 | .0 | Income Taxes Payable | .2 | .1 |
|  | 12.1 | 4.5 | 5.1 | 9.1 | 5.4 | All Other Current | 6.6 | 7.2 |
|  | 38.5 | 30.4 | 26.9 | 28.3 | 18.9 | Total Current | 29.9 | 33.9 |
|  | 14.2 | 24.5 | 22.6 | 21.1 | 18.7 | Long-Term Debt | 23.3 | 22.3 |
|  | .0 | .2 | .7 | 1.6 | .4 | Deferred Taxes | .5 | .3 |
|  | 9.2 | 9.7 | 5.2 | 1.8 | 6.4 | All Other Non-Current | 4.1 | 6.7 |
|  | 38.1 | 35.3 | 44.6 | 47.2 | 55.6 | Net Worth | 42.2 | 36.8 |
|  | 100.0 | 100.0 | 100.0 | 100.0 | 100.0 | Total Liabilties & Net Worth | 100.0 | 100.0 |
|  |  |  |  |  |  | **INCOME DATA** |  |  |
|  | 100.0 | 100.0 | 100.0 | 100.0 | 100.0 | Net Sales | 100.0 | 100.0 |
|  | 52.8 | 50.0 | 46.6 | 37.5 | 37.9 | Gross Profit | 50.4 | 51.1 |
|  | 47.3 | 41.1 | 35.6 | 22.0 | 25.8 | Operating Expenses | 36.6 | 38.6 |
|  | 5.5 | 8.9 | 10.9 | 15.6 | 12.1 | Operating Profit | 13.8 | 12.5 |
|  | 1.2 | 3.7 | 5.5 | 3.5 | 2.2 | All Other Expenses (net) | 3.6 | 4.6 |
|  | 4.3 | 5.1 | 5.4 | 12.0 | 9.9 | Profit Before Taxes | 10.1 | 8.0 |
|  |  |  |  |  |  | **RATIOS** |  |  |
|  | 4.3 | 4.3 | 3.9 | 2.7 | 8.4 | | 3.6 | 3.2 |
|  | 2.4 | 2.0 | 2.0 | 2.0 | 3.2 | Current | 1.9 | 1.9 |
|  | 1.3 | 1.4 | 1.4 | 1.3 | 1.5 | | 1.4 | 1.3 |
|  | 1.0 | .8 | .6 | .8 | 1.8 | | .7 | .7 |
|  | .4 | .4 | .3 | .3 | .7 | Quick | .3 | .3 |
|  | .1 | .1 | .2 | .2 | .5 | | .2 | .1 |
|  | 4 90.8 | 7 50.8 | 22 16.3 | 25 14.8 | 35 10.3 | | 16 22.9 | 12 29.9 |
|  | 16 23.1 | 29 12.7 | 36 10.2 | 33 10.9 | 46 7.9 | Sales/Receivables | 32 11.5 | 33 11.1 |
|  | 30 12.1 | 56 6.5 | 53 6.9 | 41 9.0 | 68 5.4 | | 49 7.5 | 51 7.1 |
|  | 85 4.3 | 304 1.2 | 304 1.2 | 228 1.6 | 281 1.3 | | 254 1.4 | 272 1.3 |
|  | 406 .9 | 521 .7 | 521 .7 | 332 1.1 | 456 .8 | Cost of Sales/Inventory | 384 1.0 | 490 .7 |
|  | 730 .5 | 730 .5 | 730 .5 | 406 .5 | 521 .7 | | 693 .5 | 830 .4 |
|  | 2 233.4 | 17 21.4 | 24 15.4 | 20 18.7 | 27 13.7 | | 16 23.3 | 19 19.3 |
|  | 44 8.3 | 41 8.9 | 42 8.6 | 34 10.7 | 56 6.5 | Cost of Sales/Payables | 40 9.2 | 55 6.6 |
|  | 104 3.5 | 126 2.9 | 78 4.7 | 68 5.4 | 87 4.2 | | 94 3.9 | 97 3.8 |
|  | 1.8 | 1.6 | 1.4 | 1.7 | 1.2 | | 1.7 | 1.6 |
|  | 2.5 | 2.6 | 2.1 | 3.2 | 1.4 | Sales/Working Capital | 3.2 | 2.9 |
|  | 19.1 | 4.3 | 4.4 | 5.3 | 6.5 | | 6.9 | 7.3 |
|  | 6.7 | 7.1 | 7.6 | 9.9 | 38.5 | | 8.7 | 8.9 |
|  | (30) 2.5 | (73) 2.5 | (66) 2.3 | (21) 6.0 | (14) 7.9 | EBIT/Interest | (125) 3.7 | (182) 3.0 |
|  | .2 | .6 | .9 | 2.5 | 2.2 | | 1.4 | 1.2 |
|  |  |  | 12.4 | 7.7 |  | Net Profit + Depr., Dep., | 11.7 | 13.6 |
|  |  |  | (21) 4.4 | (13) 6.1 |  | Amort./Cur. Mat. L/T/D | (43) 6.2 | (56) 4.5 |
|  |  |  | 2.3 | 2.4 |  | | 1.8 | 1.7 |
|  | .1 | .3 | .5 | .7 | .4 | | .5 | .3 |
|  | .5 | .8 | 1.0 | 1.0 | .8 | Fixed/Worth | .9 | .9 |
|  | 2.4 | 2.3 | 2.1 | 1.3 | 1.6 | | 2.1 | 2.0 |
|  | .5 | .7 | .5 | .7 | .4 | | .7 | .7 |
|  | 1.5 | 2.2 | 1.3 | 1.3 | .9 | Debt/Worth | 1.3 | 1.7 |
|  | 12.8 | 7.5 | 3.4 | 1.7 | 2.5 | | 3.9 | 4.3 |
|  | 49.8 | 25.1 | 19.2 | 27.6 | 32.8 | % Profit Before Taxes/Tangible | 34.6 | 34.4 |
|  | (28) 7.8 | (69) 10.9 | (66) 10.1 | (14) 19.0 | 14.3 | Net Worth | (122) 19.4 | (178) 14.6 |
|  | -.3 | -1.6 | 2.1 | 10.3 | 5.5 | | 5.3 | 2.6 |
|  | 9.3 | 8.9 | 8.4 | 9.7 | 11.7 | % Profit Before Taxes/Total | 14.8 | 13.2 |
|  | 4.3 | 2.8 | 2.9 | 7.9 | 6.8 | Assets | 7.1 | 3.9 |
|  | -1.1 | -1.1 | -.4 | 4.0 | 1.5 | | 1.1 | .3 |
|  | 32.0 | 9.0 | 4.3 | 2.9 | 4.2 | | 4.9 | 8.7 |
|  | 7.1 | 3.5 | 1.6 | 1.7 | 1.6 | Sales/Net Fixed Assets | 2.1 | 2.1 |
|  | 3.3 | 1.0 | .8 | 1.1 | 1.1 | | 1.0 | 1.1 |
|  | 1.4 | 1.1 | .9 | .8 | .8 | | 1.1 | 1.0 |
|  | 1.1 | .7 | .6 | .7 | .7 | Sales/Total Assets | .7 | .7 |
|  | .7 | .4 | .4 | .4 | .3 | | .5 | .4 |
|  | 2.1 | 2.4 | 3.2 | 2.1 | 4.0 | | 3.1 | 2.3 |
|  | (21) 5.1 | (63) 5.1 | (64) 6.4 | 4.8 | (13) 6.0 | % Depr., Dep., Amort./Sales | (113) 5.3 | (158) 4.4 |
|  | 6.8 | 8.7 | 10.3 | 10.4 | 7.9 | | 7.4 | 8.1 |
|  | 2.8 |  |  |  |  | % Officers', Directors' | 3.8 | 2.2 |
|  | (13) 4.3 |  |  |  |  | Owners' Comp/Sales | (24) 7.4 | (32) 7.7 |
|  | 5.3 |  |  |  |  | | 11.8 | 10.2 |
| 7069M | 53159M | 307636M | 1126807M | 1218181M | 1534444M | Net Sales ($) | 3566142M | 4015482M |
| 2943M | 41298M | 402346M | 1710810M | 1709100M | 2228651M | Total Assets ($) | 4160761M | 5212880M |

M = $ thousand     MM = $ million
See Pages 9 through 22 for Explanation of Ratios and Data

## Comparative Historical Data | Current Data Sorted by Sales

| | | | Type of Statement | | | | | | |
|---|---|---|---|---|---|---|---|---|---|
| 24 | 34 | 31 | Unqualified | | 2 | | 9 | 1 | 19 |
| 43 | 46 | 45 | Reviewed | | 6 | 7 | 8 | 16 | 8 |
| 16 | 17 | 24 | Compiled | 3 | 6 | 9 | 2 | 4 | |
| 22 | 21 | 26 | Tax Returns | 10 | 12 | 2 | 2 | | |
| 91 | 100 | 105 | Other | 12 | 25 | 19 | 14 | 18 | 17 |
| 4/1/09- | 4/1/10- | 4/1/11- | | | | 28 (4/1-9/30/11) | 203 (10/1/11-3/31/12) | | |
| 3/31/10 | 3/31/11 | 3/31/12 | | | | | | | |
| ALL | ALL | ALL | | 0-1MM | 1-3MM | 3-5MM | 5-10MM | 10-25MM | 25MM & OVER |
| 196 | 218 | 231 | **NUMBER OF STATEMENTS** | 25 | 51 | 37 | 35 | 39 | 44 |
| % | % | % | **ASSETS** | % | % | % | % | % | % |
| 3.6 | 3.9 | 4.8 | Cash & Equivalents | 6.9 | 6.7 | 5.8 | 4.5 | 2.5 | 3.0 |
| 8.4 | 9.5 | 8.0 | Trade Receivables (net) | 4.1 | 6.3 | 8.6 | 10.7 | 6.9 | 10.6 |
| 46.8 | 43.9 | 44.0 | Inventory | 47.9 | 47.9 | 47.3 | 40.7 | 40.5 | 40.3 |
| 2.1 | 2.3 | 3.1 | All Other Current | 4.1 | 2.8 | 1.1 | 5.4 | 2.6 | 3.0 |
| 60.9 | 59.6 | 59.9 | Total Current | 62.9 | 63.7 | 62.9 | 61.4 | 52.4 | 56.9 |
| 33.4 | 33.4 | 32.9 | Fixed Assets (net) | 29.6 | 31.3 | 31.0 | 33.0 | 38.3 | 33.4 |
| 2.5 | 3.5 | 3.9 | Intangibles (net) | 6.3 | 2.7 | 3.3 | 1.6 | 6.2 | 4.2 |
| 3.1 | 3.4 | 3.3 | All Other Non-Current | 1.1 | 2.3 | 2.8 | 4.0 | 3.1 | 5.6 |
| 100.0 | 100.0 | 100.0 | Total | 100.0 | 100.0 | 100.0 | 100.0 | 100.0 | 100.0 |
| | | | **LIABILITIES** | | | | | | |
| 16.1 | 14.2 | 12.4 | Notes Payable-Short Term | 11.7 | 13.2 | 14.4 | 13.6 | 10.9 | 10.5 |
| 1.8 | 2.4 | 2.5 | Cur. Mat.-L.T.D. | 3.5 | 1.4 | 3.3 | 3.0 | 2.3 | 2.1 |
| 8.6 | 7.9 | 8.4 | Trade Payables | 5.1 | 11.7 | 9.4 | 7.8 | 5.8 | 8.5 |
| .1 | .2 | .1 | Income Taxes Payable | .0 | .1 | .1 | .4 | .1 | .1 |
| 6.2 | 6.3 | 6.3 | All Other Current | 13.7 | 3.8 | 4.5 | 5.2 | 4.2 | 9.1 |
| 32.8 | 31.1 | 29.7 | Total Current | 34.1 | 30.2 | 31.6 | 30.1 | 23.2 | 30.3 |
| 21.9 | 22.3 | 21.2 | Long-Term Debt | 19.0 | 22.9 | 24.7 | 17.6 | 24.9 | 16.9 |
| .4 | .6 | .5 | Deferred Taxes | .0 | .0 | .1 | 1.2 | .9 | .6 |
| 8.5 | 8.5 | 8.0 | All Other Non-Current | 11.4 | 15.1 | 7.8 | 3.3 | 5.5 | 4.0 |
| 36.4 | 37.6 | 40.7 | Net Worth | 35.5 | 31.7 | 35.8 | 47.8 | 45.4 | 48.2 |
| 100.0 | 100.0 | 100.0 | Total Liabilities & Net Worth | 100.0 | 100.0 | 100.0 | 100.0 | 100.0 | 100.0 |
| | | | **INCOME DATA** | | | | | | |
| 100.0 | 100.0 | 100.0 | Net Sales | 100.0 | 100.0 | 100.0 | 100.0 | 100.0 | 100.0 |
| 46.4 | 46.3 | 47.4 | Gross Profit | 59.4 | 50.9 | 47.0 | 46.1 | 46.7 | 38.3 |
| 38.0 | 36.6 | 37.8 | Operating Expenses | 54.0 | 43.7 | 41.4 | 32.4 | 34.9 | 25.4 |
| 8.4 | 9.7 | 9.6 | Operating Profit | 5.4 | 7.3 | 5.6 | 13.7 | 11.7 | 12.9 |
| 5.0 | 4.8 | 3.7 | All Other Expenses (net) | 4.2 | 3.0 | 4.3 | 5.1 | 5.0 | 1.4 |
| 3.4 | 4.9 | 5.9 | Profit Before Taxes | 1.2 | 4.3 | 1.4 | 8.7 | 6.8 | 11.5 |
| | | | **RATIOS** | | | | | | |
| 3.6 | 3.8 | 4.0 | | 5.5 | 4.9 | 3.8 | 3.9 | 4.1 | 3.1 |
| 2.0 | 2.1 | 2.1 | Current | 3.1 | 2.4 | 1.7 | 2.0 | 2.6 | 1.9 |
| 1.3 | 1.4 | 1.4 | | 1.1 | 1.5 | 1.4 | 1.4 | 1.5 | 1.3 |
| .7 | .8 | .8 | | 1.2 | 1.0 | .7 | 1.1 | .8 | .8 |
| .3 | .4 | .4 | Quick | .3 | .4 | .4 | .4 | .5 | .4 |
| .1 | .2 | .2 | | .1 | .1 | .2 | .1 | .2 | .2 |
| 15  25.0 | 19  19.3 | 14  26.6 | | 0  UND | 5  66.4 | 13  28.7 | 18  20.5 | 22  16.6 | 31  11.6 |
| 34  10.8 | 36  10.0 | 30  12.1 | Sales/Receivables | 8  46.4 | 19  19.7 | 30  12.1 | 37  9.9 | 36  10.2 | 39  9.4 |
| 52  7.0 | 55  6.7 | 50  7.3 | | 22  16.5 | 36  10.1 | 56  6.5 | 49  7.4 | 51  7.1 | 52  7.0 |
| 292  1.3 | 260  1.4 | 243  1.5 | | 192  1.9 | 332  1.1 | 243  1.5 | 243  1.5 | 304  1.2 | 228  1.6 |
| 510  .7 | 446  .8 | 456  .8 | Cost of Sales/Inventory | 730  .5 | 456  .8 | 521  .7 | 365  1.0 | 521  .7 | 332  1.1 |
| 894  .4 | 741  .5 | 730  .5 | | 1217  .3 | 912  .4 | 730  .5 | 608  .6 | 608  .6 | 456  .8 |
| 18  20.6 | 18  20.3 | 18  20.2 | | 0  UND | 15  24.8 | 19  18.9 | 21  17.2 | 24  15.0 | 27  13.5 |
| 54  6.7 | 43  8.4 | 41  8.8 | Cost of Sales/Payables | 9  39.1 | 42  8.7 | 51  7.2 | 35  10.5 | 44  8.3 | 52  7.0 |
| 111  3.3 | 86  4.2 | 87  4.2 | | 104  3.5 | 118  3.1 | 111  3.3 | 104  3.5 | 74  4.9 | 72  5.1 |
| 1.4 | 1.6 | 1.5 | | 1.7 | 1.5 | 1.6 | 1.3 | 1.3 | 1.5 |
| 2.5 | 2.5 | 2.5 | Sales/Working Capital | 2.4 | 2.3 | 2.7 | 2.5 | 2.1 | 3.5 |
| 6.0 | 5.6 | 4.8 | | NM | 3.9 | 5.6 | 4.5 | 3.6 | 7.2 |
| 7.6 | 7.8 | 7.7 | | 6.5 | 5.8 | 6.5 | 7.2 | 5.3 | 22.8 |
| (174)  2.4 | (195)  2.1 | (209)  2.8 | EBIT/Interest | (19)  1.4 | (44)  1.9 | (35)  1.9 | (31)  2.3 | (37)  2.3 | (43)  7.8 |
| .5 | .8 | .9 | | .2 | .1 | .6 | .9 | .6 | 3.3 |
| 10.0 | 9.6 | 8.6 | Net Profit + Depr., Dep., | | | | | 9.8 | 11.5 |
| (41)  2.5 | (53)  3.1 | (52)  4.2 | Amort./Cur. Mat. L/T/D | | | | (13)  3.6 | (21)  6.6 |
| .6 | .9 | 1.9 | | | | | | 2.1 | 3.6 |
| .3 | .3 | .3 | | .1 | .3 | .3 | .2 | .5 | .3 |
| .9 | .9 | .9 | Fixed/Worth | .7 | .8 | 1.0 | .9 | 1.0 | .8 |
| 2.3 | 2.0 | 1.9 | | 4.1 | 2.7 | 3.5 | 1.7 | 3.5 | 1.3 |
| .7 | .7 | .6 | | .4 | .7 | .6 | .4 | .5 | .6 |
| 1.8 | 1.5 | 1.4 | Debt/Worth | 2.0 | 2.6 | 2.3 | 1.0 | 1.4 | 1.2 |
| 3.9 | 4.4 | 4.7 | | NM | 11.5 | 13.0 | 3.4 | 4.7 | 1.9 |
| 21.8 | 27.1 | 25.1 | % Profit Before Taxes/Tangible | 27.1 | 20.2 | 34.6 | 25.2 | 20.1 | 33.5 |
| (175)  8.9 | (195)  9.1 | (206)  11.4 | Net Worth | (19)  3.2 | (44)  6.4 | (32)  8.6 | (33)  10.7 | (34)  10.2 | 19.0 |
| -3.1 | -.2 | .8 | | -5.1 | -2.6 | -.5 | 3.0 | .0 | 11.5 |
| 8.5 | 9.8 | 9.6 | % Profit Before Taxes/Total | 7.2 | 7.8 | 9.1 | 12.1 | 6.8 | 12.5 |
| 2.8 | 3.3 | 3.9 | Assets | .5 | 2.4 | 2.7 | 3.6 | 2.6 | 7.9 |
| -1.5 | -.4 | -.3 | | -2.5 | -1.1 | -1.5 | .7 | -1.2 | 4.1 |
| 7.8 | 7.4 | 7.4 | | 25.5 | 10.7 | 9.6 | 7.2 | 4.2 | 5.0 |
| 2.5 | 2.4 | 2.5 | Sales/Net Fixed Assets | 4.1 | 3.8 | 2.6 | 2.3 | 1.6 | 2.5 |
| .9 | 1.0 | 1.0 | | 1.2 | 1.0 | .8 | .9 | .8 | 1.4 |
| 1.1 | 1.0 | 1.1 | | 1.1 | 1.2 | 1.2 | 1.2 | .9 | 1.1 |
| .6 | .7 | .7 | Sales/Total Assets | .7 | .6 | .8 | .7 | .6 | .8 |
| .4 | .4 | .4 | | .5 | .4 | .4 | .4 | .4 | .6 |
| 2.1 | 2.0 | 2.6 | | 4.0 | 2.5 | 1.1 | 2.9 | 3.4 | 1.9 |
| (156)  5.3 | (190)  5.0 | (187)  5.4 | % Depr., Dep., Amort./Sales | (14)  6.1 | (36)  6.0 | (28)  5.2 | (31)  5.3 | (38)  7.0 | (40)  4.3 |
| 10.4 | 9.3 | 8.7 | | 8.9 | 7.8 | 10.3 | 9.5 | 10.6 | 6.2 |
| 2.2 | 2.1 | 1.5 | % Officers', Directors' | | 2.4 | | | | |
| (26)  5.3 | (32)  4.9 | (31)  4.3 | Owners' Comp/Sales | | (11)  4.3 | | | | |
| 11.0 | 8.4 | 8.5 | | | 7.0 | | | | |
| 3921819M | 5301649M | 4247296M | Net Sales ($) | 15336M | 98114M | 145585M | 259805M | 595678M | 3132778M |
| 5229794M | 7057861M | 6095148M | Total Assets ($) | 38996M | 162639M | 227929M | 533332M | 1250873M | 3881379M |

M = $ thousand    MM = $ million
See Pages 9 through 22 for Explanation of Ratios and Data

## Current Data Sorted by Assets  /  Comparative Historical Data

| 0-500M | 500M-2MM | 2-10MM | 10-50MM | 50-100MM | 100-250MM | Type of Statement | 4/1/07-3/31/08 ALL | 4/1/08-3/31/09 ALL |
|---|---|---|---|---|---|---|---|---|
| | | 2 | 6 | 1 | 3 | Unqualified | 9 | 13 |
| | 2 | 4 | 3 | | | Reviewed | 6 | 9 |
| | 3 | | 1 | | | Compiled | 1 | 6 |
| | | | 3 | | | Tax Returns | 2 | 2 |
| 1 | 1 | 3 | 7 | 3 | 5 | Other | 13 | 15 |
| | 8 (4/1-9/30/11) | | 40 (10/1/11-3/31/12) | | | | 31 | 45 |
| 1 | 6 | 9 | 20 | 4 | 8 | NUMBER OF STATEMENTS | 31 | 45 |
| % | % | % | % | % | % | | % | % |
| | | | | | | **ASSETS** | | |
| | | | 9.9 | | | Cash & Equivalents | 6.7 | 5.3 |
| | | | 23.4 | | | Trade Receivables (net) | 27.9 | 23.1 |
| | | | 22.9 | | | Inventory | 30.8 | 31.7 |
| | | | 3.0 | | | All Other Current | 2.9 | 1.9 |
| | | | 59.2 | | | Total Current | 68.2 | 61.9 |
| | | | 31.8 | | | Fixed Assets (net) | 23.7 | 28.0 |
| | | | 1.7 | | | Intangibles (net) | 2.3 | .8 |
| | | | 7.3 | | | All Other Non-Current | 5.7 | 9.4 |
| | | | 100.0 | | | Total | 100.0 | 100.0 |
| | | | | | | **LIABILITIES** | | |
| | | | 3.2 | | | Notes Payable-Short Term | 8.6 | 8.2 |
| | | | 3.4 | | | Cur. Mat.-L.T.D. | 2.6 | 4.6 |
| | | | 11.3 | | | Trade Payables | 14.4 | 10.9 |
| | | | .1 | | | Income Taxes Payable | .2 | .1 |
| | | | 6.0 | | | All Other Current | 5.6 | 12.6 |
| | | | 23.9 | | | Total Current | 31.4 | 36.4 |
| | | | 11.9 | | | Long-Term Debt | 12.4 | 14.7 |
| | | | .3 | | | Deferred Taxes | .8 | 1.4 |
| | | | 3.8 | | | All Other Non-Current | 6.8 | 5.4 |
| | | | 60.1 | | | Net Worth | 48.6 | 42.0 |
| | | | 100.0 | | | Total Liabilities & Net Worth | 100.0 | 100.0 |
| | | | | | | **INCOME DATA** | | |
| | | | 100.0 | | | Net Sales | 100.0 | 100.0 |
| | | | 15.7 | | | Gross Profit | 17.6 | 16.7 |
| | | | 12.6 | | | Operating Expenses | 14.8 | 16.0 |
| | | | 3.1 | | | Operating Profit | 2.8 | .7 |
| | | | .5 | | | All Other Expenses (net) | -.1 | .2 |
| | | | 2.6 | | | Profit Before Taxes | 2.9 | .6 |
| | | | | | | **RATIOS** | | |
| | | | 4.3 | | | Current | 4.1 | 3.3 |
| | | | 2.7 | | | | 2.1 | 2.1 |
| | | | 1.7 | | | | 1.5 | 1.4 |
| | | | 2.0 | | | Quick | 1.8 | 1.6 |
| | | | 1.5 | | | | 1.3 | 1.0 |
| | | | .9 | | | | .7 | .5 |
| | | 33 | 10.9 | | | Sales/Receivables | 36 10.2 | 32 11.2 |
| | | 39 | 9.3 | | | | 50 7.3 | 41 8.9 |
| | | 48 | 7.6 | | | | 67 5.5 | 55 6.7 |
| | | 33 | 11.2 | | | Cost of Sales/Inventory | 38 9.7 | 38 9.5 |
| | | 51 | 7.2 | | | | 57 6.3 | 66 5.5 |
| | | 60 | 6.1 | | | | 96 3.8 | 102 3.6 |
| | | 12 | 30.0 | | | Cost of Sales/Payables | 17 21.5 | 14 25.7 |
| | | 21 | 17.0 | | | | 26 14.1 | 21 17.8 |
| | | 30 | 12.1 | | | | 38 9.5 | 30 12.0 |
| | | | 3.7 | | | Sales/Working Capital | 3.7 | 4.2 |
| | | | 6.4 | | | | 6.6 | 6.9 |
| | | | 17.2 | | | | 10.4 | 20.8 |
| | | | 22.8 | | | EBIT/Interest | 9.0 | 5.2 |
| | | (17) | 4.7 | | | | (28) 2.8 | (41) 2.3 |
| | | | 1.1 | | | | 1.0 | .5 |
| | | | | | | Net Profit + Depr., Dep., Amort./Cur. Mat. L/T/D | 5.4 | 6.9 |
| | | | | | | | (10) 3.0 | (16) 2.0 |
| | | | | | | | 1.1 | .5 |
| | | | .4 | | | Fixed/Worth | .2 | .3 |
| | | | .5 | | | | .5 | .5 |
| | | | .7 | | | | .9 | 1.5 |
| | | | .3 | | | Debt/Worth | .4 | .5 |
| | | | .6 | | | | .9 | 1.2 |
| | | | 1.5 | | | | 3.8 | 3.3 |
| | | | 24.0 | | | % Profit Before Taxes/Tangible Net Worth | 29.0 | 22.3 |
| | | | 5.2 | | | | (28) 8.0 | (41) 3.7 |
| | | | -.6 | | | | .0 | -2.0 |
| | | | 10.2 | | | % Profit Before Taxes/Total Assets | 12.2 | 7.5 |
| | | | 3.1 | | | | 6.2 | 2.1 |
| | | | -.1 | | | | .0 | -3.2 |
| | | | 31.9 | | | Sales/Net Fixed Assets | 24.8 | 19.6 |
| | | | 6.7 | | | | 10.6 | 6.8 |
| | | | 3.4 | | | | 4.7 | 4.1 |
| | | | 2.7 | | | Sales/Total Assets | 2.7 | 2.6 |
| | | | 1.8 | | | | 2.1 | 1.9 |
| | | | 1.5 | | | | 1.7 | 1.3 |
| | | | .8 | | | % Depr., Dep., Amort./Sales | .7 | 1.0 |
| | | (19) | 2.8 | | | | (26) 1.4 | (41) 2.3 |
| | | | 3.8 | | | | 2.8 | 4.1 |
| | | | | | | % Officers', Directors' Owners' Comp/Sales | | 1.7 |
| | | | | | | | | (13) 4.0 |
| | | | | | | | | 7.9 |
| 2975M | 32063M | 106824M | 953154M | 583288M | 3093584M | Net Sales ($) | 2565520M | 3595307M |
| 373M | 8346M | 48483M | 444505M | 299740M | 1429922M | Total Assets ($) | 1269797M | 1738984M |

## Comparative Historical Data | Current Data Sorted by Sales

| | 4/1/09-3/31/10 ALL | 4/1/10-3/31/11 ALL | 4/1/11-3/31/12 ALL | | Type of Statement | 0-1MM | 1-3MM | 3-5MM | 5-10MM | 10-25MM | 25MM & OVER |
|---|---|---|---|---|---|---|---|---|---|---|---|
| | 11 | 10 | 12 | | Unqualified | | | | | 2 | 10 |
| | 11 | 9 | 9 | | Reviewed | | | 3 | | 4 | 2 |
| | 4 | 3 | 4 | | Compiled | | 1 | | 1 | 1 | 1 |
| | 3 | 1 | 3 | | Tax Returns | | | | | 1 | 2 |
| | 13 | 13 | 20 | | Other | | | 3 | | 3 | 13 |
| | | | | | | | 8 (4/1-9/30/11) | | | 40 (10/1/11-3/31/12) | |
| NUMBER OF STATEMENTS | 42 | 36 | 48 | | | | 2 | 3 | 4 | 11 | 28 |
| | % | % | % | | ASSETS | % | % | % | % | % | % |
| Cash & Equivalents | 7.3 | 6.5 | 10.6 | | | | | | | 12.5 | 9.4 |
| Trade Receivables (net) | 24.2 | 28.3 | 22.1 | | | | | | | 20.0 | 22.7 |
| Inventory | 29.4 | 31.2 | 31.4 | | | | | | | 36.0 | 27.5 |
| All Other Current | 2.6 | 3.8 | 1.6 | | | | | | | 1.9 | 2.0 |
| Total Current | 63.5 | 69.8 | 65.7 | | | | | | | 70.4 | 61.5 |
| Fixed Assets (net) | 25.3 | 22.3 | 23.4 | | | | | | | 18.8 | 28.5 |
| Intangibles (net) | 3.2 | 1.0 | 2.3 | | | | | | | .0 | 3.2 |
| All Other Non-Current | 8.0 | 6.9 | 8.6 | | | | | | | 10.7 | 6.8 |
| Total | 100.0 | 100.0 | 100.0 | | | | | | | 100.0 | 100.0 |
| | | | | | LIABILITIES | | | | | | |
| Notes Payable-Short Term | 6.9 | 7.8 | 5.3 | | | | | | | 3.1 | 5.6 |
| Cur. Mat.-L.T.D. | 1.8 | 2.8 | 2.3 | | | | | | | .3 | 3.3 |
| Trade Payables | 12.9 | 16.2 | 14.4 | | | | | | | 15.9 | 13.1 |
| Income Taxes Payable | .3 | .3 | .2 | | | | | | | .0 | .4 |
| All Other Current | 9.1 | 8.2 | 8.7 | | | | | | | 5.7 | 7.8 |
| Total Current | 31.1 | 35.2 | 30.9 | | | | | | | 25.0 | 30.2 |
| Long-Term Debt | 13.9 | 14.3 | 10.1 | | | | | | | 2.2 | 13.5 |
| Deferred Taxes | 1.2 | 1.0 | .6 | | | | | | | .4 | .8 |
| All Other Non-Current | 4.8 | 5.3 | 2.9 | | | | | | | .2 | 3.8 |
| Net Worth | 49.0 | 44.3 | 55.6 | | | | | | | 72.1 | 51.7 |
| Total Liabilities & Net Worth | 100.0 | 100.0 | 100.0 | | | | | | | 100.0 | 100.0 |
| | | | | | INCOME DATA | | | | | | |
| Net Sales | 100.0 | 100.0 | 100.0 | | | | | | | 100.0 | 100.0 |
| Gross Profit | 17.3 | 19.9 | 18.0 | | | | | | | 17.8 | 14.8 |
| Operating Expenses | 15.0 | 14.4 | 14.7 | | | | | | | 15.3 | 10.9 |
| Operating Profit | 2.2 | 5.5 | 3.3 | | | | | | | 2.5 | 3.9 |
| All Other Expenses (net) | 1.0 | .1 | .1 | | | | | | | .3 | .4 |
| Profit Before Taxes | 1.2 | 5.4 | 3.2 | | | | | | | 2.2 | 3.5 |
| | | | | | RATIOS | | | | | | |
| Current | 3.7 | 3.8 | 4.4 | | | | | | | 5.6 | 3.0 |
| | 2.4 | 2.1 | 2.6 | | | | | | | 4.5 | 2.4 |
| | 1.5 | 1.4 | 1.4 | | | | | | | 2.1 | 1.3 |
| Quick | 1.8 | 1.9 | 2.0 | | | | | | | 4.2 | 2.0 |
| | 1.1 | 1.1 | 1.2 | | | | | | | 2.0 | 1.3 |
| | .6 | .6 | .6 | | | | | | | .9 | .6 |
| Sales/Receivables | 32 11.3 | 32 11.5 | 28 13.2 | | | | | | | 18 20.5 | 35 10.3 |
| | 46 7.9 | 41 8.9 | 37 9.8 | | | | | | | 33 10.9 | 42 8.7 |
| | 57 6.4 | 59 6.2 | 44 8.3 | | | | | | | 44 8.3 | 47 7.8 |
| Cost of Sales/Inventory | 39 9.5 | 40 9.1 | 39 9.4 | | | | | | | 40 9.2 | 40 9.1 |
| | 64 5.7 | 57 6.4 | 59 6.2 | | | | | | | 79 4.6 | 56 6.5 |
| | 95 3.8 | 83 4.4 | 91 4.0 | | | | | | | 96 3.8 | 72 5.1 |
| Cost of Sales/Payables | 14 25.2 | 14 25.6 | 14 25.6 | | | | | | | 11 33.0 | 20 18.5 |
| | 28 13.2 | 23 16.1 | 24 14.9 | | | | | | | 23 15.9 | 26 14.2 |
| | 36 10.2 | 40 9.2 | 33 11.1 | | | | | | | 31 11.6 | 30 12.0 |
| Sales/Working Capital | 3.5 | 4.1 | 4.0 | | | | | | | 3.0 | 4.3 |
| | 5.5 | 6.7 | 6.1 | | | | | | | 3.6 | 6.6 |
| | 11.2 | 15.3 | 15.6 | | | | | | | 12.3 | 20.5 |
| EBIT/Interest | 6.9 | 19.8 | 43.1 | | | | | | | | 31.0 |
| | (36) 1.8 | (31) 6.6 | (41) 4.7 | | | | | | | | 4.0 |
| | .6 | 2.9 | 2.5 | | | | | | | | 2.4 |
| Net Profit + Depr., Dep., Amort./Cur. Mat. L/T/D | 7.5 | 27.3 | | | | | | | | | |
| | (12) 3.4 | (12) 8.4 | | | | | | | | | |
| | .9 | 2.9 | | | | | | | | | |
| Fixed/Worth | .2 | .2 | .1 | | | | | | | .0 | .4 |
| | .4 | .4 | .5 | | | | | | | .3 | .5 |
| | 1.0 | 1.0 | .7 | | | | | | | .4 | .8 |
| Debt/Worth | .4 | .6 | .4 | | | | | | | .1 | .5 |
| | .9 | .9 | .6 | | | | | | | .4 | 1.1 |
| | 2.0 | 3.3 | 1.7 | | | | | | | .6 | 2.0 |
| % Profit Before Taxes/Tangible Net Worth | 11.5 | 55.8 | 25.1 | | | | | | | 13.1 | 37.8 |
| | (38) 2.9 | (33) 25.1 | (46) 10.2 | | | | | | | 10.2 | 9.6 |
| | -2.4 | 7.9 | 3.2 | | | | | | | 1.7 | 3.5 |
| % Profit Before Taxes/Total Assets | 5.8 | 17.2 | 10.2 | | | | | | | 10.1 | 11.5 |
| | 1.2 | 7.7 | 5.7 | | | | | | | 6.8 | 3.7 |
| | -.8 | 3.6 | 2.0 | | | | | | | 1.2 | 1.8 |
| Sales/Net Fixed Assets | 22.3 | 47.1 | 42.0 | | | | | | | 143.9 | 21.9 |
| | 8.2 | 16.0 | 9.7 | | | | | | | 10.1 | 8.4 |
| | 3.9 | 5.9 | 5.1 | | | | | | | 5.1 | 4.3 |
| Sales/Total Assets | 2.4 | 3.0 | 3.0 | | | | | | | 2.4 | 2.7 |
| | 1.8 | 2.3 | 2.1 | | | | | | | 2.1 | 1.9 |
| | 1.3 | 1.8 | 1.6 | | | | | | | 1.3 | 1.6 |
| % Depr., Dep., Amort./Sales | 1.0 | .6 | .6 | | | | | | | .4 | .8 |
| | (36) 2.4 | (32) 1.2 | (40) 1.7 | | | | | | | (10) 1.5 | (24) 2.1 |
| | 4.1 | 2.9 | 3.0 | | | | | | | 3.1 | 3.6 |
| % Officers', Directors' Owners' Comp/Sales | 1.8 | | 1.0 | | | | | | | | |
| | (14) 3.6 | | (14) 3.3 | | | | | | | | |
| | 6.0 | | 6.0 | | | | | | | | |
| Net Sales ($) | 2258640M | 2828937M | 4771888M | | | | 5133M | 10851M | 24226M | 171695M | 4559983M |
| Total Assets ($) | 1246892M | 1260546M | 2231369M | | | | 1003M | 5894M | 8656M | 93757M | 2122059M |

*(Columns 0-1MM through 5-10MM marked "DATA NOT AVAILABLE.")*

© RMA 2012

M = $ thousand    MM = $ million
See Pages 9 through 22 for Explanation of Ratios and Data

## Current Data Sorted by Assets       Comparative Historical Data

| 0-500M | 500M-2MM | 2-10MM | 10-50MM | 50-100MM | 100-250MM | | 4/1/07-3/31/08 ALL | 4/1/08-3/31/09 ALL |
|---|---|---|---|---|---|---|---|---|
| | | | | | | **Type of Statement** | | |
| | 1 | 4 | 7 | 3 | 1 | Unqualified | 16 | 21 |
| | 2 | 10 | 6 | | | Reviewed | 17 | 18 |
| 1 | 2 | 3 | 1 | | | Compiled | 5 | 8 |
| 2 | 1 | 3 | | | | Tax Returns | 11 | 9 |
| 2 | 4 | 12 | 12 | 2 | 2 | Other | 26 | 28 |
| | 15 (4/1-9/30/11) | | 66 (10/1/11-3/31/12) | | | | | |
| 5 | 10 | 32 | 26 | 5 | 3 | **NUMBER OF STATEMENTS** | 75 | 84 |
| % | % | % | % | % | % | **ASSETS** | % | % |
| | 10.0 | 8.1 | 6.5 | | | Cash & Equivalents | 7.5 | 6.9 |
| | 32.6 | 21.5 | 27.4 | | | Trade Receivables (net) | 26.7 | 23.9 |
| | 33.1 | 34.4 | 30.8 | | | Inventory | 29.7 | 31.1 |
| | 1.7 | 1.7 | 1.4 | | | All Other Current | 2.6 | 1.8 |
| | 77.5 | 65.7 | 66.0 | | | Total Current | 66.5 | 63.7 |
| | 18.7 | 25.5 | 24.8 | | | Fixed Assets (net) | 22.5 | 22.8 |
| | 1.9 | 2.1 | 3.7 | | | Intangibles (net) | 4.6 | 5.3 |
| | 1.9 | 6.8 | 5.5 | | | All Other Non-Current | 6.5 | 8.2 |
| | 100.0 | 100.0 | 100.0 | | | Total | 100.0 | 100.0 |
| | | | | | | **LIABILITIES** | | |
| | 4.9 | 10.8 | 10.6 | | | Notes Payable-Short Term | 11.3 | 11.5 |
| | 1.1 | 3.3 | 3.0 | | | Cur. Mat.-L.T.D. | 4.4 | 5.2 |
| | 32.1 | 15.4 | 16.5 | | | Trade Payables | 17.3 | 14.2 |
| | .0 | .3 | .0 | | | Income Taxes Payable | .2 | .3 |
| | 13.4 | 7.0 | 9.6 | | | All Other Current | 9.1 | 9.9 |
| | 51.5 | 36.8 | 39.8 | | | Total Current | 42.3 | 41.1 |
| | 12.6 | 18.0 | 25.5 | | | Long-Term Debt | 16.7 | 14.0 |
| | .0 | .6 | .1 | | | Deferred Taxes | .7 | .5 |
| | 22.9 | 3.2 | 8.1 | | | All Other Non-Current | 9.2 | 6.6 |
| | 13.0 | 41.5 | 26.5 | | | Net Worth | 31.2 | 37.9 |
| | 100.0 | 100.0 | 100.0 | | | Total Liabilties & Net Worth | 100.0 | 100.0 |
| | | | | | | **INCOME DATA** | | |
| | 100.0 | 100.0 | 100.0 | | | Net Sales | 100.0 | 100.0 |
| | 31.9 | 26.4 | 18.8 | | | Gross Profit | 24.2 | 22.8 |
| | 35.1 | 22.7 | 14.1 | | | Operating Expenses | 20.5 | 21.3 |
| | -3.3 | 3.6 | 4.7 | | | Operating Profit | 3.7 | 1.5 |
| | .1 | .7 | 1.4 | | | All Other Expenses (net) | 1.0 | 1.3 |
| | -3.4 | 2.9 | 3.3 | | | Profit Before Taxes | 2.7 | .3 |
| | | | | | | **RATIOS** | | |
| | 3.5 | 2.7 | 3.2 | | | | 3.4 | 3.0 |
| | 2.2 | 2.0 | 1.9 | | | Current | 1.8 | 1.7 |
| | .9 | 1.2 | 1.1 | | | | 1.3 | 1.2 |
| | 1.7 | 1.5 | 1.4 | | | | 1.8 | 1.6 |
| | .8 | 1.0 | 1.0 | | | Quick | 1.0 | .8 |
| | .3 | .4 | .6 | | | | .5 | .5 |
| 15 | 25.0   28 | 13.0   34 | 10.8 | | | | 31   11.9 | 26   13.9 |
| 35 | 10.5   40 | 9.2   46 | 7.9 | | | Sales/Receivables | 44   8.3 | 42   8.7 |
| 53 | 6.9   50 | 7.3   63 | 5.8 | | | | 57   6.4 | 58   6.3 |
| 0 | UND   49 | 7.5   38 | 9.6 | | | | 42   8.7 | 40   9.1 |
| 78 | 4.7   78 | 4.7   56 | 6.5 | | | Cost of Sales/Inventory | 65   5.6 | 61   6.0 |
| 130 | 2.8   118 | 3.1   89 | 4.1 | | | | 99   3.7 | 96   3.8 |
| 21 | 17.8   16 | 23.5   22 | 16.5 | | | | 19   19.2 | 16   23.3 |
| 36 | 10.0   31 | 11.6   34 | 10.8 | | | Cost of Sales/Payables | 29   12.5 | 24   15.4 |
| 159 | 2.3   48 | 7.6   38 | 9.5 | | | | 43   8.4 | 38   9.6 |
| | 6.1 | 5.0 | 4.6 | | | | 4.8 | 5.3 |
| | 7.3 | 6.9 | 7.4 | | | Sales/Working Capital | 7.5 | 8.4 |
| | -40.8 | 16.8 | 28.8 | | | | 18.2 | 23.4 |
| | | 16.3 | 16.1 | | | | 11.4 | 11.2 |
| | (30) | 2.6 | (22) 4.3 | | | EBIT/Interest | (66) 2.3 | (79) 2.4 |
| | | .9 | 1.1 | | | | .8 | .0 |
| | | 12.3 | | | | | 5.6 | 5.2 |
| | (10) | 2.6 | | | | Net Profit + Depr., Dep., Amort./Cur. Mat. L/T/D | (19) 1.5 | (24) 1.1 |
| | | 1.6 | | | | | .8 | -.2 |
| | .1 | .2 | .2 | | | | .3 | .2 |
| | 1.2 | .3 | .5 | | | Fixed/Worth | .5 | .5 |
| | -2.9 | 1.6 | 1.3 | | | | 1.6 | 1.4 |
| | .6 | .6 | .5 | | | | .7 | .8 |
| | 92.7 | 1.4 | 1.3 | | | Debt/Worth | 1.7 | 1.5 |
| | -17.4 | 3.1 | 3.9 | | | | 7.9 | 3.9 |
| | | 21.5 | 36.6 | | | | 42.8 | 32.1 |
| | (29) | 6.3 | (22) 18.7 | | | % Profit Before Taxes/Tangible Net Worth | (61) 12.9 | (74) 9.4 |
| | | .7 | 5.1 | | | | -.9 | -9.1 |
| | 28.7 | 13.1 | 15.0 | | | | 15.1 | 10.0 |
| | 11.1 | 2.0 | 7.1 | | | % Profit Before Taxes/Total Assets | 4.6 | 3.6 |
| | -44.8 | .0 | 1.4 | | | | -.7 | -4.0 |
| | 170.2 | 32.3 | 15.1 | | | | 32.7 | 26.1 |
| | 22.2 | 12.8 | 10.0 | | | Sales/Net Fixed Assets | 12.0 | 12.0 |
| | 6.9 | 3.9 | 6.3 | | | | 5.0 | 5.5 |
| | 4.1 | 2.8 | 2.5 | | | | 2.7 | 2.8 |
| | 2.6 | 1.9 | 2.2 | | | Sales/Total Assets | 2.1 | 2.0 |
| | 2.1 | 1.4 | 1.8 | | | | 1.6 | 1.4 |
| | | .9 | 1.2 | | | | .9 | .7 |
| | (29) | 1.2 | (25) 2.3 | | | % Depr., Dep., Amort./Sales | (64) 2.1 | (72) 1.7 |
| | | 4.1 | 3.2 | | | | 3.0 | 3.3 |
| | | | | | | | 1.6 | 1.4 |
| | | | | | | % Officers', Directors' Owners' Comp/Sales | (20) 3.6 | (21) 3.9 |
| | | | | | | | 6.6 | 6.9 |
| 5040M | 35044M | 386068M | 1361795M | 800493M | 633557M | Net Sales ($) | 3944848M | 3431212M |
| 1333M | 12149M | 181238M | 604633M | 389551M | 498670M | Total Assets ($) | 1957269M | 1962002M |

M = $ thousand    MM = $ million
See Pages 9 through 22 for Explanation of Ratios and Data

## Comparative Historical Data / Current Data Sorted by Sales

| Type of Statement | | | | | | | | | |
|---|---|---|---|---|---|---|---|---|---|
| 15 | 25 | 16 | Unqualified | | | | 1 | 2 | 12 |
| 13 | 12 | 18 | Reviewed | | 1 | | 1 | 7 | 7 |
| 15 | 11 | 7 | Compiled | 1 | | 2 | 3 | 1 | 1 |
| 10 | 5 | 6 | Tax Returns | 2 | | 1 | 1 | | |
| 27 | 31 | 34 | Other | | 4 | 2 | 6 | 7 | 15 |
| 4/1/09-3/31/10 | 4/1/10-3/31/11 | 4/1/11-3/31/12 | | 15 (4/1-9/30/11) | | | 66 (10/1/11-3/31/12) | | |
| ALL | ALL | ALL | | 0-1MM | 1-3MM | 3-5MM | 5-10MM | 10-25MM | 25MM & OVER |
| 80 | 84 | 81 | **NUMBER OF STATEMENTS** | 3 | 6 | 8 | 12 | 17 | 35 |
| % | % | % | **ASSETS** | % | % | % | % | % | % |
| 9.9 | 7.3 | 7.9 | Cash & Equivalents | | | | 8.1 | 6.9 | 6.7 |
| 25.1 | 23.9 | 24.9 | Trade Receivables (net) | | | | 19.3 | 26.3 | 26.3 |
| 29.5 | 30.0 | 32.2 | Inventory | | | | 23.3 | 40.8 | 31.3 |
| 1.9 | 2.5 | 1.4 | All Other Current | | | | 1.4 | 1.7 | 1.3 |
| 66.4 | 63.7 | 66.4 | Total Current | | | | 52.1 | 75.7 | 65.6 |
| 22.2 | 23.4 | 24.1 | Fixed Assets (net) | | | | 37.6 | 17.2 | 23.4 |
| 5.6 | 6.2 | 3.6 | Intangibles (net) | | | | 2.0 | .5 | 5.5 |
| 5.8 | 6.8 | 5.9 | All Other Non-Current | | | | 8.3 | 6.6 | 5.5 |
| 100.0 | 100.0 | 100.0 | Total | | | | 100.0 | 100.0 | 100.0 |
| | | | **LIABILITIES** | | | | | | |
| 8.2 | 10.2 | 12.8 | Notes Payable-Short Term | | | | 10.7 | 10.4 | 10.4 |
| 5.2 | 3.5 | 2.7 | Cur. Mat.-L.T.D. | | | | 3.7 | 2.4 | 3.0 |
| 15.0 | 14.9 | 18.0 | Trade Payables | | | | 11.9 | 17.5 | 16.5 |
| 1.4 | .2 | .2 | Income Taxes Payable | | | | .4 | .4 | .1 |
| 7.3 | 10.0 | 11.3 | All Other Current | | | | 5.8 | 6.5 | 9.6 |
| 37.0 | 38.7 | 45.0 | Total Current | | | | 32.4 | 37.3 | 39.5 |
| 17.0 | 22.2 | 19.3 | Long-Term Debt | | | | 20.9 | 13.7 | 22.7 |
| .6 | .4 | .5 | Deferred Taxes | | | | .6 | .5 | .6 |
| 7.1 | 8.2 | 7.9 | All Other Non-Current | | | | 8.2 | .1 | 8.0 |
| 38.3 | 30.5 | 27.3 | Net Worth | | | | 37.9 | 48.4 | 29.3 |
| 100.0 | 100.0 | 100.0 | Total Liabilities & Net Worth | | | | 100.0 | 100.0 | 100.0 |
| | | | **INCOME DATA** | | | | | | |
| 100.0 | 100.0 | 100.0 | Net Sales | | | | 100.0 | 100.0 | 100.0 |
| 24.5 | 25.3 | 24.6 | Gross Profit | | | | 28.3 | 21.9 | 18.5 |
| 21.6 | 22.4 | 21.3 | Operating Expenses | | | | 26.3 | 18.7 | 13.7 |
| 3.0 | 2.9 | 3.3 | Operating Profit | | | | 1.9 | 3.2 | 4.8 |
| 1.2 | 1.3 | .8 | All Other Expenses (net) | | | | 1.1 | .3 | 1.3 |
| 1.8 | 1.6 | 2.5 | Profit Before Taxes | | | | .9 | 2.9 | 3.5 |
| | | | **RATIOS** | | | | | | |
| 3.7 | 2.9 | 2.8 | | | | | 4.3 | 3.6 | 2.6 |
| 2.0 | 2.0 | 2.0 | Current | | | | 1.9 | 2.0 | 2.0 |
| 1.3 | 1.2 | 1.1 | | | | | .9 | 1.4 | 1.2 |
| 2.0 | 1.5 | 1.5 | | | | | 2.3 | 2.1 | 1.4 |
| 1.0 | .9 | 1.0 | Quick | | | | .6 | 1.0 | 1.1 |
| .5 | .4 | .5 | | | | | .4 | .5 | .5 |
| 29  12.8 | 24  14.9 | 29  12.6 | | | | | 23  16.2 | 30  12.0 | 31  11.6 |
| 45  8.2 | 43  8.5 | 41  8.9 | Sales/Receivables | | | | 38  9.6 | 49  7.4 | 42  8.7 |
| 56  6.5 | 57  6.4 | 51  7.1 | | | | | 44  8.3 | 59  6.2 | 59  6.2 |
| 32  11.3 | 41  9.0 | 40  9.1 | | | | | 21  17.0 | 54  6.7 | 45  8.1 |
| 65  5.6 | 73  5.0 | 66  5.5 | Cost of Sales/Inventory | | | | 57  6.4 | 79  4.6 | 60  6.1 |
| 114  3.2 | 106  3.4 | 104  3.5 | | | | | 130  2.8 | 104  3.5 | 81  4.5 |
| 18  20.0 | 19  18.8 | 20  18.7 | | | | | 14  26.1 | 19  19.1 | 23  15.9 |
| 31  11.8 | 33  11.1 | 34  10.8 | Cost of Sales/Payables | | | | 27  13.3 | 35  10.5 | 34  10.8 |
| 42  8.6 | 49  7.5 | 45  8.1 | | | | | 44  8.3 | 47  7.7 | 41  9.0 |
| 4.2 | 4.5 | 4.9 | | | | | 5.7 | 4.3 | 4.9 |
| 7.2 | 6.9 | 7.4 | Sales/Working Capital | | | | 9.1 | 6.0 | 7.4 |
| 15.2 | 25.1 | 25.1 | | | | | NM | 15.2 | 24.6 |
| 12.3 | 16.4 | 17.8 | | | | | 14.9 | 16.3 | 17.9 |
| (73)  3.5 | (77)  5.2 | (73)  3.3 | EBIT/Interest | | | | 1.6 | (14)  3.3 | (32)  5.7 |
| .5 | 1.0 | 1.1 | | | | | -.7 | 1.3 | 1.4 |
| 5.1 | 4.9 | 18.2 | Net Profit + Depr., Dep., | | | | | | 17.4 |
| (19)  2.6 | (19)  3.3 | (22)  3.2 | Amort./Cur. Mat. L/T/D | | | | | | (12)  5.5 |
| .4 | .6 | 1.5 | | | | | | | .7 |
| .2 | .2 | .2 | | | | | .2 | .1 | .3 |
| .5 | .5 | .6 | Fixed/Worth | | | | 1.4 | .3 | .6 |
| 1.5 | 1.7 | 1.9 | | | | | 5.3 | .6 | 1.7 |
| .6 | .6 | .6 | | | | | .3 | .6 | .5 |
| 1.3 | 1.1 | 1.5 | Debt/Worth | | | | 1.6 | .8 | 1.5 |
| 4.3 | 3.2 | 8.2 | | | | | 7.1 | 2.0 | 4.8 |
| 32.3 | 29.3 | 35.8 | | | | | 20.0 | 21.3 | 36.6 |
| (66)  10.3 | (69)  15.4 | (67)  17.0 | % Profit Before Taxes/Tangible Net Worth | | | | (11)  2.6 | (15)  5.5 | (30)  20.6 |
| -.5 | 2.6 | 2.8 | | | | | -8.1 | 1.3 | 6.5 |
| 12.7 | 13.0 | 15.1 | | | | | 10.5 | 12.1 | 15.6 |
| 4.3 | 6.5 | 6.0 | % Profit Before Taxes/Total Assets | | | | .9 | 4.4 | 8.1 |
| -1.5 | .2 | .2 | | | | | -2.6 | .6 | 1.6 |
| 32.5 | 29.4 | 26.5 | | | | | 27.7 | 36.4 | 15.5 |
| 11.7 | 11.5 | 10.9 | Sales/Net Fixed Assets | | | | 4.0 | 16.7 | 9.9 |
| 5.4 | 5.4 | 5.8 | | | | | 2.0 | 6.7 | 6.4 |
| 2.7 | 3.0 | 2.9 | | | | | 2.4 | 3.2 | 2.9 |
| 2.0 | 2.0 | 2.1 | Sales/Total Assets | | | | 1.8 | 2.1 | 2.2 |
| 1.4 | 1.4 | 1.7 | | | | | 1.1 | 1.8 | 1.8 |
| .8 | 1.1 | 1.0 | | | | | .7 | .9 | 1.1 |
| (64)  2.3 | (72)  2.5 | (72)  2.1 | % Depr., Dep., Amort./Sales | | | | (11)  3.0 | (15)  1.1 | (33)  2.1 |
| 4.3 | 3.8 | 3.0 | | | | | 9.0 | 2.2 | 2.6 |
| 1.6 | .7 | .7 | | | | | | | |
| (19)  4.2 | (14)  2.5 | (14)  1.9 | % Officers', Directors' Owners' Comp/Sales | | | | | | |
| 7.0 | 6.9 | 5.4 | | | | | | | |
| 3718881M | 4242587M | 3221997M | Net Sales ($) | 1811M | 11305M | 30097M | 80359M | 250457M | 2847968M |
| 1975096M | 2088030M | 1687574M | Total Assets ($) | 627M | 4792M | 18534M | 52136M | 116100M | 1495385M |

M = $ thousand    MM = $ million
See Pages 9 through 22 for Explanation of Ratios and Data

## Current Data Sorted by Assets     Comparative Historical Data

| | | | | | | Type of Statement | | |
|---|---|---|---|---|---|---|---|---|
| | | | 1 | 1 | 1 | 1 | Unqualified | 12 | 8 |
| | 1 | 1 8 | 1 | | | | Reviewed | 14 | 10 |
| | 1 | 3 | | | | Compiled | 10 | 7 |
| 1 | 1 | 1 | | | | Tax Returns | 4 | 4 |
| 1 | 2 | 4 | 5 | 2 | | Other | 11 | 15 |
| | 8 (4/1-9/30/11) | | 27 (10/1/11-3/31/12) | | | | 4/1/07-3/31/08 | 4/1/08-3/31/09 |
| 0-500M | 500M-2MM | 2-10MM | 10-50MM | 50-100MM | 100-250MM | | ALL | ALL |
| 2 | 5 | 17 | 7 | 3 | 1 | NUMBER OF STATEMENTS | 51 | 44 |
| % | % | % | % | % | % | ASSETS | % | % |
| | | 9.9 | | | | Cash & Equivalents | 5.8 | 7.2 |
| | | 22.0 | | | | Trade Receivables (net) | 24.5 | 24.6 |
| | | 32.2 | | | | Inventory | 36.3 | 33.2 |
| | | 1.3 | | | | All Other Current | 2.8 | 2.2 |
| | | 65.4 | | | | Total Current | 69.3 | 67.2 |
| | | 23.7 | | | | Fixed Assets (net) | 22.4 | 22.3 |
| | | 4.7 | | | | Intangibles (net) | 1.1 | 4.0 |
| | | 6.1 | | | | All Other Non-Current | 7.3 | 6.6 |
| | | 100.0 | | | | Total | 100.0 | 100.0 |
| | | | | | | LIABILITIES | | |
| | | 10.7 | | | | Notes Payable-Short Term | 26.1 | 20.0 |
| | | 1.9 | | | | Cur. Mat.-L.T.D. | 4.7 | 5.9 |
| | | 18.2 | | | | Trade Payables | 18.4 | 16.6 |
| | | .1 | | | | Income Taxes Payable | .3 | .4 |
| | | 12.9 | | | | All Other Current | 12.4 | 7.5 |
| | | 43.8 | | | | Total Current | 61.9 | 50.4 |
| | | 9.1 | | | | Long-Term Debt | 8.0 | 9.6 |
| | | .0 | | | | Deferred Taxes | .6 | .1 |
| | | 1.9 | | | | All Other Non-Current | 9.6 | 3.5 |
| | | 45.1 | | | | Net Worth | 19.9 | 36.5 |
| | | 100.0 | | | | Total Liabilities & Net Worth | 100.0 | 100.0 |
| | | | | | | INCOME DATA | | |
| | | 100.0 | | | | Net Sales | 100.0 | 100.0 |
| | | 27.6 | | | | Gross Profit | 25.9 | 24.6 |
| | | 22.5 | | | | Operating Expenses | 24.1 | 22.5 |
| | | 5.2 | | | | Operating Profit | 1.8 | 2.2 |
| | | .4 | | | | All Other Expenses (net) | 1.8 | 1.3 |
| | | 4.8 | | | | Profit Before Taxes | .0 | .9 |
| | | | | | | RATIOS | | |
| | | 2.5 | | | | | 2.6 | 2.4 |
| | | 1.5 | | | | Current | 1.4 | 1.5 |
| | | 1.3 | | | | | 1.1 | 1.1 |
| | | 1.6 | | | | | 1.2 | 1.2 |
| | | .8 | | | | Quick | .6 | .7 |
| | | .6 | | | | | .3 | .3 |
| | | 7 50.8 | | | | | 24 15.0 | 25 14.6 |
| | | 34 10.6 | | | | Sales/Receivables | 40 9.2 | 36 10.1 |
| | | 52 7.0 | | | | | 58 6.3 | 56 6.5 |
| | | 27 13.7 | | | | | 45 8.1 | 27 13.5 |
| | | 72 5.1 | | | | Cost of Sales/Inventory | 77 4.7 | 63 5.8 |
| | | 104 3.5 | | | | | 113 3.2 | 117 3.1 |
| | | 15 23.8 | | | | | 16 22.9 | 18 19.9 |
| | | 27 13.4 | | | | Cost of Sales/Payables | 31 11.6 | 29 12.6 |
| | | 41 8.8 | | | | | 43 8.5 | 50 7.3 |
| | | 7.0 | | | | | 5.2 | 5.5 |
| | | 10.8 | | | | Sales/Working Capital | 10.5 | 9.9 |
| | | 16.6 | | | | | 35.0 | 48.8 |
| | | 7.8 | | | | | 4.8 | 7.7 |
| | | (12) 5.3 | | | | EBIT/Interest | (50) 1.6 | (42) 1.8 |
| | | 1.9 | | | | | -.9 | .9 |
| | | | | | | Net Profit + Depr., Dep., | 1.9 | 7.5 |
| | | | | | | Amort./Cur. Mat. L/T/D | (12) .9 | (11) 1.0 |
| | | | | | | | -10.6 | -.3 |
| | | .2 | | | | | .2 | .1 |
| | | .4 | | | | Fixed/Worth | .5 | .5 |
| | | 1.1 | | | | | 1.5 | 1.4 |
| | | .4 | | | | | .7 | .9 |
| | | 1.6 | | | | Debt/Worth | 2.1 | 1.8 |
| | | 3.3 | | | | | 6.5 | 4.0 |
| | | 53.5 | | | | % Profit Before Taxes/Tangible | 25.4 | 20.8 |
| | | (15) 12.9 | | | | Net Worth | (42) 6.4 | (41) 5.1 |
| | | 7.1 | | | | | -2.3 | -4.8 |
| | | 16.7 | | | | % Profit Before Taxes/Total | 9.3 | 8.0 |
| | | 9.8 | | | | Assets | 2.0 | 1.7 |
| | | 2.4 | | | | | -4.7 | -.5 |
| | | 47.9 | | | | | 52.3 | 270.5 |
| | | 12.3 | | | | Sales/Net Fixed Assets | 16.2 | 19.6 |
| | | 4.4 | | | | | 7.8 | 5.9 |
| | | 3.1 | | | | | 3.1 | 3.5 |
| | | 2.4 | | | | Sales/Total Assets | 2.3 | 2.0 |
| | | 1.9 | | | | | 1.7 | 1.6 |
| | | .6 | | | | | .4 | .3 |
| | | (11) 1.2 | | | | % Depr., Dep., Amort./Sales | (43) 1.0 | (33) 1.2 |
| | | 2.1 | | | | | 2.1 | 3.0 |
| | | | | | | | 1.3 | 1.3 |
| | | | | | | % Officers', Directors' | (21) 2.8 | (18) 3.4 |
| | | | | | | Owners' Comp/Sales | 7.6 | 5.4 |
| 1148M | 23065M | 181213M | 317836M | 380356M | 260134M | Net Sales ($) | 2069198M | 1458822M |
| 213M | 6946M | 77497M | 172046M | 218063M | 149951M | Total Assets ($) | 1002626M | 755675M |

© RMA 2012

M = $ thousand    MM = $ million
See Pages 9 through 22 for Explanation of Ratios and Data

## Comparative Historical Data | Current Data Sorted by Sales

| | Comparative Historical Data | | | Type of Statement | 0-1MM | 1-3MM | 3-5MM | 5-10MM | 10-25MM | 25MM & OVER |
|---|---|---|---|---|---|---|---|---|---|---|
| | 9 | 8 | 4 | Unqualified | | | | | 1 | 3 |
| | 10 | 13 | 10 | Reviewed | | | | 4 | 6 | |
| | 5 | 5 | 4 | Compiled | | | | 2 | 2 | |
| | 2 | 5 | 3 | Tax Returns | 1 | | 1 | 1 | 1 | |
| | 16 | 15 | 14 | Other | 1 | 2 | | 3 | 2 | 6 |
| | 4/1/09-3/31/10 | 4/1/10-3/31/11 | 4/1/11-3/31/12 | | | 8 (4/1-9/30/11) | | 27 (10/1/11-3/31/12) | | |
| | ALL | ALL | ALL | | | | | | | |
| | 42 | 46 | 35 | NUMBER OF STATEMENTS | 2 | 3 | | 10 | 11 | 9 |
| | % | % | % | ASSETS | % | % | % | % | % | % |
| | 6.8 | 5.2 | 7.9 | Cash & Equivalents | | | | 14.4 | 5.2 | |
| | 25.7 | 30.7 | 24.3 | Trade Receivables (net) | D | | | 23.5 | 23.8 | |
| | 33.1 | 34.3 | 32.6 | Inventory | A | | | 20.5 | 38.8 | |
| | .7 | 1.8 | 1.5 | All Other Current | T | | | 2.0 | .2 | |
| | 66.3 | 72.0 | 66.3 | Total Current | A | | | 60.4 | 68.0 | |
| | 21.8 | 19.5 | 22.5 | Fixed Assets (net) | | | | 23.1 | 24.3 | |
| | 3.0 | 2.9 | 2.6 | Intangibles (net) | N | | | 5.7 | 2.2 | |
| | 8.9 | 5.5 | 8.7 | All Other Non-Current | O | | | 10.8 | 5.6 | |
| | 100.0 | 100.0 | 100.0 | Total | T | | | 100.0 | 100.0 | |
| | | | | LIABILITIES | A | | | | | |
| | 11.9 | 14.3 | 12.7 | Notes Payable-Short Term | V | | | 6.4 | 14.1 | |
| | 4.6 | 1.5 | 1.8 | Cur. Mat.-L.T.D. | A | | | 1.5 | 2.9 | |
| | 17.2 | 21.0 | 20.0 | Trade Payables | I | | | 18.1 | 20.6 | |
| | .3 | .2 | .1 | Income Taxes Payable | L | | | .1 | .0 | |
| | 9.9 | 10.6 | 12.6 | All Other Current | A | | | 7.2 | 7.6 | |
| | 43.9 | 47.6 | 47.2 | Total Current | B | | | 33.3 | 45.3 | |
| | 8.6 | 9.9 | 13.3 | Long-Term Debt | L | | | 3.6 | 12.1 | |
| | .2 | .1 | .0 | Deferred Taxes | E | | | .0 | .0 | |
| | 2.7 | 5.5 | 5.4 | All Other Non-Current | | | | 1.0 | 3.2 | |
| | 44.6 | 36.9 | 34.2 | Net Worth | | | | 62.1 | 39.4 | |
| | 100.0 | 100.0 | 100.0 | Total Liabilities & Net Worth | | | | 100.0 | 100.0 | |
| | | | | INCOME DATA | | | | | | |
| | 100.0 | 100.0 | 100.0 | Net Sales | | | | 100.0 | 100.0 | |
| | 25.7 | 24.9 | 25.4 | Gross Profit | | | | 27.9 | 25.5 | |
| | 22.7 | 21.6 | 22.1 | Operating Expenses | | | | 23.6 | 21.6 | |
| | 3.0 | 3.3 | 3.3 | Operating Profit | | | | 4.3 | 3.9 | |
| | 1.0 | .9 | .5 | All Other Expenses (net) | | | | .1 | .1 | |
| | 2.0 | 2.5 | 2.9 | Profit Before Taxes | | | | 4.2 | 3.9 | |
| | | | | RATIOS | | | | | | |
| | 2.5 | 2.3 | 2.9 | | | | | 3.6 | 2.1 | |
| | 1.6 | 1.6 | 1.4 | Current | | | | 2.3 | 1.4 | |
| | 1.2 | 1.2 | 1.2 | | | | | 1.5 | 1.2 | |
| | 1.5 | 1.4 | 1.8 | | | | | 2.4 | 1.1 | |
| | .6 | .6 | .8 | Quick | | | | 1.1 | .8 | |
| | .4 | .5 | .5 | | | | | .7 | .5 | |
| 26 | 14.2 | 36 10.3 | 25 14.4 | Sales/Receivables | | | | 8 45.0 | 25 14.4 | |
| 45 | 8.1 | 47 7.7 | 39 9.3 | | | | | 46 8.0 | 32 11.5 | |
| 57 | 6.5 | 59 6.2 | 51 7.1 | | | | | 58 6.3 | 45 8.2 | |
| 43 | 8.6 | 46 8.0 | 33 11.2 | Cost of Sales/Inventory | | | | 11 32.8 | 42 8.6 | |
| 69 | 5.3 | 76 4.8 | 72 5.1 | | | | | 38 9.6 | 76 4.8 | |
| 125 | 2.9 | 103 3.5 | 111 3.3 | | | | | 72 5.1 | 118 3.1 | |
| 16 | 22.5 | 19 18.8 | 22 16.7 | Cost of Sales/Payables | | | | 12 31.7 | 14 26.1 | |
| 33 | 11.0 | 37 9.8 | 33 11.2 | | | | | 26 14.3 | 33 11.0 | |
| 50 | 7.4 | 58 6.2 | 46 8.0 | | | | | 42 8.7 | 74 4.9 | |
| | 5.8 | 7.3 | 6.6 | Sales/Working Capital | | | | 6.2 | 7.4 | |
| | 11.4 | 10.4 | 11.0 | | | | | 10.3 | 12.4 | |
| | 25.6 | 25.0 | 46.2 | | | | | 14.2 | 24.1 | |
| | 10.3 | 11.0 | 7.8 | EBIT/Interest | | | | | | |
| (38) | 3.3 | (40) 3.7 | (28) 3.3 | | | | | | | |
| | 1.2 | 1.6 | .9 | | | | | | | |
| | 14.7 | | | Net Profit + Depr., Dep., | | | | | | |
| (10) | 2.6 | | | Amort./Cur. Mat. L/T/D | | | | | | |
| | -.3 | | | | | | | | | |
| | .1 | .1 | .2 | Fixed/Worth | | | | .0 | .3 | |
| | .5 | .4 | .4 | | | | | .3 | .6 | |
| | .9 | 1.4 | 1.5 | | | | | .7 | 1.5 | |
| | .6 | .8 | .5 | Debt/Worth | | | | .2 | .9 | |
| | 1.6 | 1.8 | 1.9 | | | | | .5 | 2.0 | |
| | 3.0 | 4.3 | 5.5 | | | | | 2.0 | 4.4 | |
| | 23.2 | 33.8 | 34.1 | % Profit Before Taxes/Tangible | | | | 35.6 | 39.0 | |
| (41) | 8.2 | (42) 15.9 | (29) 11.7 | Net Worth | | | | 10.0 | (10) 12.2 | |
| | 1.4 | 7.7 | 2.4 | | | | | 3.1 | 5.8 | |
| | 9.5 | 10.6 | 12.5 | % Profit Before Taxes/Total | | | | 16.0 | 14.9 | |
| | 3.9 | 4.7 | 4.8 | Assets | | | | 7.8 | 4.8 | |
| | .9 | 1.3 | .4 | | | | | 2.7 | 2.4 | |
| | 54.1 | 74.6 | 40.7 | Sales/Net Fixed Assets | | | | 405.6 | 64.7 | |
| | 16.8 | 20.1 | 17.2 | | | | | 12.6 | 24.2 | |
| | 4.9 | 5.0 | 6.0 | | | | | 5.6 | 4.5 | |
| | 3.1 | 3.1 | 3.1 | Sales/Total Assets | | | | 3.3 | 3.4 | |
| | 1.9 | 2.5 | 2.3 | | | | | 2.7 | 2.4 | |
| | 1.6 | 1.7 | 1.7 | | | | | 1.5 | 1.9 | |
| | .5 | .5 | .6 | % Depr., Dep., Amort./Sales | | | | | .4 | |
| (35) | 1.2 | (34) 1.2 | (27) 1.3 | | | | | | 1.6 | |
| | 2.8 | 2.3 | 2.2 | | | | | | 2.2 | |
| | 1.2 | 1.0 | | % Officers', Directors' | | | | | | |
| (14) | 2.6 | (11) 1.9 | | Owners' Comp/Sales | | | | | | |
| | 4.6 | 5.9 | | | | | | | | |
| | 1570781M | 1833643M | 1163752M | Net Sales ($) | 1148M | | 11190M | 69310M | 161514M | 920590M |
| | 763000M | 893069M | 624716M | Total Assets ($) | 213M | | 4523M | 31998M | 69513M | 518469M |

M = $ thousand     MM = $ million
See Pages 9 through 22 for Explanation of Ratios and Data

# MANUFACTURING—Fabric Coating Mills  NAICS 313320

## Current Data Sorted by Assets | Comparative Historical Data

| 0-500M | 500M-2MM | 2-10MM | 10-50MM | 50-100MM | 100-250MM | Type of Statement | 4/1/07-3/31/08 ALL | 4/1/08-3/31/09 ALL |
|---|---|---|---|---|---|---|---|---|
| | 2 | 4 | 1 | 2 | 1 | Unqualified | 12 | 13 |
| | | | 3 | | | Reviewed | 6 | 7 |
| | 1 | | | | | Compiled | 3 | 1 |
| | 1 | | | | | Tax Returns | | |
| 1 | 1 | 6 | 5 | 3 | | Other | 14 | 13 |
| 9 (4/1-9/30/11) | | | 22 (10/1/11-3/31/12) | | | | | |
| 1 | 5 | 10 | 9 | 5 | 1 | NUMBER OF STATEMENTS | 35 | 34 |
| % | % | % | % | % | % | | % | % |
| | | 9.3 | | | | ASSETS — Cash & Equivalents | 4.6 | 7.4 |
| | | 32.4 | | | | Trade Receivables (net) | 25.4 | 21.9 |
| | | 27.4 | | | | Inventory | 31.4 | 28.2 |
| | | 2.1 | | | | All Other Current | 2.8 | 2.4 |
| | | 71.3 | | | | Total Current | 64.2 | 60.0 |
| | | 20.9 | | | | Fixed Assets (net) | 23.9 | 24.5 |
| | | 4.0 | | | | Intangibles (net) | 6.6 | 8.0 |
| | | 3.7 | | | | All Other Non-Current | 5.3 | 7.5 |
| | | 100.0 | | | | Total | 100.0 | 100.0 |
| | | 5.7 | | | | LIABILITIES — Notes Payable-Short Term | 8.8 | 14.1 |
| | | 2.0 | | | | Cur. Mat.-L.T.D. | 4.1 | 4.2 |
| | | 16.3 | | | | Trade Payables | 17.7 | 15.1 |
| | | .3 | | | | Income Taxes Payable | .3 | .2 |
| | | 7.4 | | | | All Other Current | 6.8 | 5.8 |
| | | 31.7 | | | | Total Current | 37.7 | 39.4 |
| | | 7.8 | | | | Long-Term Debt | 13.6 | 12.5 |
| | | .0 | | | | Deferred Taxes | 1.0 | 1.0 |
| | | 11.5 | | | | All Other Non-Current | 3.8 | 6.7 |
| | | 48.9 | | | | Net Worth | 43.9 | 40.3 |
| | | 100.0 | | | | Total Liabilities & Net Worth | 100.0 | 100.0 |
| | | 100.0 | | | | INCOME DATA — Net Sales | 100.0 | 100.0 |
| | | 36.8 | | | | Gross Profit | 22.8 | 22.4 |
| | | 29.9 | | | | Operating Expenses | 17.9 | 18.8 |
| | | 6.9 | | | | Operating Profit | 4.9 | 3.6 |
| | | .0 | | | | All Other Expenses (net) | 1.4 | 1.3 |
| | | 6.8 | | | | Profit Before Taxes | 3.5 | 2.3 |
| | | 3.0 | | | | RATIOS — Current | 2.8 | 2.5 |
| | | 2.5 | | | | | 1.7 | 1.6 |
| | | 1.8 | | | | | 1.2 | 1.0 |
| | | 1.9 | | | | Quick | 1.5 | 1.2 |
| | | 1.6 | | | | | .7 | .7 |
| | | .9 | | | | | .5 | .5 |
| | | 40 9.2 | | | | Sales/Receivables | 35 10.5 | 31 11.6 |
| | | 43 8.5 | | | | | 48 7.6 | 41 9.0 |
| | | 53 6.9 | | | | | 55 6.7 | 49 7.4 |
| | | 34 10.7 | | | | Cost of Sales/Inventory | 48 7.5 | 41 8.9 |
| | | 68 5.4 | | | | | 71 5.1 | 62 5.8 |
| | | 104 3.5 | | | | | 107 3.4 | 89 4.1 |
| | | 26 14.3 | | | | Cost of Sales/Payables | 21 17.7 | 17 21.6 |
| | | 29 12.7 | | | | | 35 10.4 | 30 12.1 |
| | | 59 6.2 | | | | | 48 7.6 | 41 8.9 |
| | | 4.4 | | | | Sales/Working Capital | 4.3 | 5.4 |
| | | 6.8 | | | | | 7.1 | 10.2 |
| | | 10.5 | | | | | 20.3 | NM |
| | | | | | | EBIT/Interest | 11.8 | 9.3 |
| | | | | | | | (32) 3.4 | (30) 3.5 |
| | | | | | | | 1.6 | 1.1 |
| | | | | | | Net Profit + Depr., Dep., Amort./Cur. Mat. L/T/D | 13.2 | 8.4 |
| | | | | | | | (13) 2.8 | (12) 2.7 |
| | | | | | | | 1.3 | 1.7 |
| | | .1 | | | | Fixed/Worth | .2 | .4 |
| | | .5 | | | | | .6 | .8 |
| | | .8 | | | | | 2.2 | 2.7 |
| | | .6 | | | | Debt/Worth | .6 | .7 |
| | | .9 | | | | | 1.5 | 1.6 |
| | | 2.1 | | | | | 5.0 | 7.0 |
| | | | | | | % Profit Before Taxes/Tangible Net Worth | 27.6 | 22.4 |
| | | | | | | | (32) 14.8 | (29) 11.5 |
| | | | | | | | 6.9 | 2.6 |
| | | 30.6 | | | | % Profit Before Taxes/Total Assets | 12.6 | 10.4 |
| | | 12.1 | | | | | 6.3 | 3.1 |
| | | 3.1 | | | | | 1.8 | -1.6 |
| | | 27.0 | | | | Sales/Net Fixed Assets | 17.0 | 13.7 |
| | | 13.2 | | | | | 9.2 | 7.3 |
| | | 6.3 | | | | | 5.2 | 4.7 |
| | | 3.2 | | | | Sales/Total Assets | 2.6 | 2.5 |
| | | 2.6 | | | | | 2.0 | 2.0 |
| | | 2.2 | | | | | 1.5 | 1.5 |
| | | | | | | % Depr., Dep., Amort./Sales | .9 | 1.4 |
| | | | | | | | (31) 1.6 | (28) 2.5 |
| | | | | | | | 3.2 | 3.9 |
| | | | | | | % Officers', Directors' Owners' Comp/Sales | 1.3 | |
| | | | | | | | (11) 1.8 | |
| | | | | | | | 4.7 | |
| 816M | 14326M | 120430M | 543146M | 712408M | 127204M | Net Sales ($) | 1649704M | 1868814M |
| 391M | 6720M | 47001M | 248775M | 398530M | 104592M | Total Assets ($) | 833553M | 937999M |

M = $ thousand   MM = $ million
See Pages 9 through 22 for Explanation of Ratios and Data

## Comparative Historical Data | Current Data Sorted by Sales

### Type of Statement

| | | | | 0-1MM | 1-3MM | 3-5MM | 5-10MM | 10-25MM | 25MM & OVER |
|---|---|---|---|---|---|---|---|---|---|
| 9 | 7 | 4 | Unqualified | | | | | | 4 |
| 12 | 8 | 9 | Reviewed | | | | 2 | 5 | 1 |
| 2 | 1 | 1 | Compiled | | 1 | | | | |
| | 3 | 1 | Tax Returns | | | 1 | | | |
| 15 | 14 | 16 | Other | 1 | 2 | 2 | | 5 | 7 |
| | | | | 4/1-9/30/11 | | | 10/1/11-3/31/12 | | |
| 15 4/1/09-3/31/10 ALL | 14 4/1/10-3/31/11 ALL | 16 4/1/11-3/31/12 ALL | | 1 | 9 | | | 5 22 | 7 |
| 38 | 33 | 31 | **NUMBER OF STATEMENTS** | 1 | 3 | 3 | 2 | 10 | 12 |

### Main Data

| Hist 1 | Hist 2 | Hist 3 | | 0-1MM | 1-3MM | 3-5MM | 5-10MM | 10-25MM | 25MM & OVER |
|---|---|---|---|---|---|---|---|---|---|
| % | % | % | **ASSETS** | % | % | % | % | % | % |
| 10.1 | 7.7 | 11.5 | Cash & Equivalents | | | | | 14.6 | 11.3 |
| 25.5 | 23.2 | 25.0 | Trade Receivables (net) | | | | | 28.8 | 25.3 |
| 24.2 | 30.1 | 27.9 | Inventory | | | | | 26.3 | 28.0 |
| 2.4 | 1.5 | 1.4 | All Other Current | | | | | 2.1 | .9 |
| 62.2 | 62.5 | 65.8 | Total Current | | | | | 71.7 | 65.5 |
| 28.2 | 26.4 | 25.9 | Fixed Assets (net) | | | | | 21.4 | 25.9 |
| 4.4 | 5.9 | 3.2 | Intangibles (net) | | | | | 4.0 | 3.9 |
| 5.1 | 5.2 | 5.2 | All Other Non-Current | | | | | 2.9 | 4.7 |
| 100.0 | 100.0 | 100.0 | Total | | | | | 100.0 | 100.0 |
| | | | **LIABILITIES** | | | | | | |
| 9.6 | 8.9 | 8.0 | Notes Payable-Short Term | | | | | 7.5 | 6.3 |
| 5.5 | 3.1 | 2.5 | Cur. Mat.-L.T.D. | | | | | 1.4 | 2.9 |
| 13.6 | 14.2 | 18.3 | Trade Payables | | | | | 17.7 | 18.5 |
| .2 | .1 | .1 | Income Taxes Payable | | | | | .3 | .1 |
| 9.0 | 7.6 | 6.3 | All Other Current | | | | | 6.5 | 6.4 |
| 37.9 | 33.8 | 35.2 | Total Current | | | | | 33.5 | 34.1 |
| 16.3 | 17.4 | 13.2 | Long-Term Debt | | | | | 6.9 | 22.8 |
| .6 | .5 | .1 | Deferred Taxes | | | | | .0 | .4 |
| 4.7 | 8.4 | 11.2 | All Other Non-Current | | | | | 12.0 | 11.2 |
| 40.5 | 39.9 | 40.3 | Net Worth | | | | | 47.5 | 31.4 |
| 100.0 | 100.0 | 100.0 | Total Liabilities & Net Worth | | | | | 100.0 | 100.0 |
| | | | **INCOME DATA** | | | | | | |
| 100.0 | 100.0 | 100.0 | Net Sales | | | | | 100.0 | 100.0 |
| 28.1 | 24.7 | 26.9 | Gross Profit | | | | | 24.9 | 20.2 |
| 24.1 | 20.2 | 21.6 | Operating Expenses | | | | | 20.2 | 13.2 |
| 4.0 | 4.5 | 5.3 | Operating Profit | | | | | 4.7 | 7.0 |
| 1.0 | .1 | -.1 | All Other Expenses (net) | | | | | -1.1 | .8 |
| 3.0 | 4.4 | 5.4 | Profit Before Taxes | | | | | 5.8 | 6.2 |
| | | | **RATIOS** | | | | | | |
| 2.7 | 3.2 | 3.1 | | | | | | 2.7 | 3.5 |
| 1.8 | 2.5 | 2.4 | Current | | | | | 2.0 | 2.5 |
| 1.1 | 1.3 | 1.5 | | | | | | 1.7 | 1.2 |
| 1.8 | 1.6 | 2.0 | | | | | | 1.8 | 2.1 |
| .9 | 1.2 | 1.6 | Quick | | | | | 1.3 | 1.7 |
| .6 | .6 | .7 | | | | | | .7 | .6 |
| 29  12.5 | 28  13.1 | 34  10.8 | | | | | | 39  9.3 | 33  11.2 |
| 47  7.7 | 45  8.1 | 43  8.4 | Sales/Receivables | | | | | 43  8.5 | 49  7.4 |
| 55  6.6 | 52  7.0 | 52  7.0 | | | | | | 49  7.4 | 55  6.6 |
| 36  10.2 | 41  8.9 | 41  8.8 | | | | | | 34  10.7 | 44  8.3 |
| 53  6.9 | 63  5.8 | 56  6.5 | Cost of Sales/Inventory | | | | | 68  5.4 | 55  6.6 |
| 85  4.3 | 104  3.5 | 83  4.4 | | | | | | 78  4.7 | 76  4.8 |
| 13  27.7 | 23  15.8 | 26  14.1 | | | | | | 25  14.4 | 20  17.9 |
| 32  11.5 | 31  11.6 | 34  10.7 | Cost of Sales/Payables | | | | | 28  13.0 | 33  11.2 |
| 45  8.1 | 37  10.0 | 49  7.5 | | | | | | 45  8.2 | 47  7.8 |
| 4.6 | 4.7 | 3.9 | | | | | | 5.4 | 3.5 |
| 8.7 | 6.2 | 6.1 | Sales/Working Capital | | | | | 7.8 | 4.9 |
| 43.7 | 17.2 | 14.3 | | | | | | 10.5 | 14.8 |
| 12.3 | 33.0 | 64.4 | | | | | | | 59.2 |
| (36) 5.4 | (30) 7.8 | (29) 8.3 | EBIT/Interest | | | | | | 8.0 |
| 2.3 | 2.5 | 4.6 | | | | | | | 5.1 |
| 3.5 | | 9.4 | Net Profit + Depr., Dep., | | | | | | |
| (11) 2.6 | | (10) 4.9 | Amort./Cur. Mat. L/T/D | | | | | | |
| 2.0 | | 3.5 | | | | | | | |
| .3 | .4 | .3 | | | | | | .1 | .4 |
| .7 | .7 | .7 | Fixed/Worth | | | | | .5 | .8 |
| 2.2 | 1.8 | 1.0 | | | | | | 1.0 | 1.2 |
| .6 | .6 | .6 | | | | | | .6 | .8 |
| 1.1 | 1.3 | 1.2 | Debt/Worth | | | | | 1.0 | 1.6 |
| 5.4 | 4.7 | 3.1 | | | | | | 2.1 | 4.2 |
| 45.4 | 42.1 | 43.6 | % Profit Before Taxes/Tangible | | | | | | 43.2 |
| (33) 23.7 | (28) 25.6 | (27) 19.4 | Net Worth | | | | | | (10) 24.9 |
| 9.8 | 7.5 | 11.9 | | | | | | | 14.0 |
| 16.9 | 19.3 | 19.9 | % Profit Before Taxes/Total | | | | | 26.2 | 18.6 |
| 8.2 | 9.0 | 7.6 | Assets | | | | | 10.1 | 9.0 |
| 3.3 | 2.7 | 3.2 | | | | | | 3.1 | 6.7 |
| 18.6 | 13.0 | 13.7 | | | | | | 21.6 | 11.7 |
| 7.3 | 7.6 | 8.8 | Sales/Net Fixed Assets | | | | | 13.2 | 7.6 |
| 4.2 | 5.1 | 4.7 | | | | | | 8.1 | 4.9 |
| 2.8 | 2.5 | 2.8 | | | | | | 3.2 | 2.4 |
| 1.9 | 2.0 | 2.1 | Sales/Total Assets | | | | | 2.4 | 1.9 |
| 1.5 | 1.7 | 1.8 | | | | | | 2.0 | 1.8 |
| .9 | 1.4 | 1.1 | | | | | | 1.1 | 1.6 |
| (30) 2.3 | (28) 2.5 | (29) 1.6 | % Depr., Dep., Amort./Sales | | | | | 1.5 | 2.5 |
| 4.0 | 3.7 | 2.5 | | | | | | 1.7 | 3.4 |
| 1.2 | | | % Officers', Directors' | | | | | | |
| (12) 4.6 | | | Owners' Comp/Sales | | | | | | |
| 13.8 | | | | | | | | | |
| 1391270M | 1351902M | 1518330M | Net Sales ($) | 816M | 4850M | 10528M | 17217M | 164701M | 1320218M |
| 824858M | 751467M | 806009M | Total Assets ($) | 391M | 4333M | 4760M | 6843M | 77286M | 712396M |

M = $ thousand    MM = $ million
See Pages 9 through 22 for Explanation of Ratios and Data

## Current Data Sorted by Assets | Comparative Historical Data

| 0-500M | 500M-2MM | 2-10MM | 10-50MM | 50-100MM | 100-250MM | | 4/1/07-3/31/08 ALL | 4/1/08-3/31/09 ALL |
|---|---|---|---|---|---|---|---|---|
| | | | | | | **Type of Statement** | | |
| | | 1 | 4 | 1 | 1 | Unqualified | 13 | 11 |
| | 1 | 3 | 4 | | 1 | Reviewed | 10 | 12 |
| | 1 | 3 | 1 | | 1 | Compiled | 10 | 5 |
| | 1 | | | | | Tax Returns | 5 | 6 |
| 1 | 4 | 4 | 4 | 5 | 1 | Other | 17 | 25 |
| | 6 (4/1-9/30/11) | | 36 (10/1/11-3/31/12) | | | | | |
| 1 | 7 | 11 | 13 | 6 | 4 | **NUMBER OF STATEMENTS** | 55 | 59 |
| % | % | % | % | % | % | | % | % |
| | | | | | | **ASSETS** | | |
| | | 10.9 | 6.0 | | | Cash & Equivalents | 3.6 | 4.8 |
| | | 27.9 | 20.3 | | | Trade Receivables (net) | 24.2 | 23.2 |
| | | 26.9 | 39.4 | | | Inventory | 33.4 | 34.6 |
| | | 1.1 | 4.3 | | | All Other Current | 1.8 | 2.6 |
| | | 66.8 | 69.9 | | | Total Current | 62.9 | 65.2 |
| | | 24.8 | 21.2 | | | Fixed Assets (net) | 27.0 | 24.9 |
| | | 4.4 | 4.2 | | | Intangibles (net) | 3.8 | 3.5 |
| | | 3.9 | 4.6 | | | All Other Non-Current | 6.3 | 6.5 |
| | | 100.0 | 100.0 | | | Total | 100.0 | 100.0 |
| | | | | | | **LIABILITIES** | | |
| | | 6.0 | 11.1 | | | Notes Payable-Short Term | 11.6 | 11.4 |
| | | 2.9 | 4.1 | | | Cur. Mat.-L.T.D. | 3.4 | 4.0 |
| | | 17.2 | 19.1 | | | Trade Payables | 25.1 | 24.4 |
| | | .0 | .3 | | | Income Taxes Payable | .0 | .1 |
| | | 9.5 | 8.2 | | | All Other Current | 11.8 | 11.9 |
| | | 35.6 | 42.8 | | | Total Current | 51.9 | 51.8 |
| | | 15.0 | 6.2 | | | Long-Term Debt | 19.9 | 19.2 |
| | | .0 | .0 | | | Deferred Taxes | .5 | .2 |
| | | 2.1 | 2.0 | | | All Other Non-Current | 1.0 | 4.3 |
| | | 47.2 | 49.0 | | | Net Worth | 26.6 | 24.5 |
| | | 100.0 | 100.0 | | | Total Liabilities & Net Worth | 100.0 | 100.0 |
| | | | | | | **INCOME DATA** | | |
| | | 100.0 | 100.0 | | | Net Sales | 100.0 | 100.0 |
| | | 33.1 | 21.6 | | | Gross Profit | 28.9 | 28.1 |
| | | 26.4 | 18.4 | | | Operating Expenses | 25.3 | 25.2 |
| | | 6.7 | 3.3 | | | Operating Profit | 3.5 | 3.0 |
| | | .9 | .4 | | | All Other Expenses (net) | 1.4 | 1.9 |
| | | 5.8 | 2.9 | | | Profit Before Taxes | 2.2 | 1.1 |
| | | | | | | **RATIOS** | | |
| | | 2.6 | 2.7 | | | Current | 1.9 | 2.3 |
| | | 2.0 | 1.7 | | | | 1.4 | 1.7 |
| | | 1.4 | 1.2 | | | | 1.0 | 1.2 |
| | | 1.8 | 1.1 | | | Quick | .9 | 1.2 |
| | | 1.3 | .5 | | | | .6 | .6 |
| | | .9 | .3 | | | | .3 | .3 |
| | | 33  11.2 | 26  13.9 | | | Sales/Receivables | 20  18.6 | 23  15.9 |
| | | 42  8.6 | 34  10.7 | | | | 35  10.4 | 34  10.6 |
| | | 54  6.8 | 51  7.2 | | | | 49  7.5 | 48  7.6 |
| | | 26  14.0 | 62  5.9 | | | Cost of Sales/Inventory | 29  12.7 | 42  8.7 |
| | | 42  8.6 | 111  3.3 | | | | 77  4.7 | 92  4.0 |
| | | 66  5.5 | 174  2.1 | | | | 130  2.8 | 135  2.7 |
| | | 17  21.2 | 30  12.0 | | | Cost of Sales/Payables | 26  14.0 | 21  17.5 |
| | | 34  10.8 | 42  8.6 | | | | 43  8.6 | 33  11.1 |
| | | 45  8.2 | 54  6.8 | | | | 61  6.0 | 68  5.4 |
| | | 6.1 | 4.4 | | | Sales/Working Capital | 7.8 | 5.9 |
| | | 10.6 | 6.1 | | | | 12.1 | 8.4 |
| | | 12.5 | 32.6 | | | | 304.2 | 21.3 |
| | | | 23.9 | | | EBIT/Interest | 4.7 | 7.7 |
| | | | (12) 11.2 | | | | (53) 2.5 | (56) 2.0 |
| | | | .5 | | | | 1.1 | -.4 |
| | | | | | | Net Profit + Depr., Dep., | 3.5 | 15.5 |
| | | | | | | Amort./Cur. Mat. L/T/D | (11) 2.7 | (11) 5.7 |
| | | | | | | | .9 | 2.2 |
| | | .1 | .1 | | | Fixed/Worth | .4 | .2 |
| | | .5 | .5 | | | | .8 | .7 |
| | | 1.3 | 1.0 | | | | 2.1 | 1.8 |
| | | .7 | .4 | | | Debt/Worth | 1.0 | .8 |
| | | .9 | 1.4 | | | | 2.6 | 1.8 |
| | | 1.8 | 2.5 | | | | 6.4 | 5.9 |
| | | | 28.3 | | | % Profit Before Taxes/Tangible | 34.6 | 26.6 |
| | | | 19.9 | | | Net Worth | (45) 11.7 | (50) 11.7 |
| | | | -.7 | | | | 1.5 | 3.3 |
| | | 31.3 | 13.6 | | | % Profit Before Taxes/Total | 9.1 | 9.4 |
| | | 9.6 | 5.6 | | | Assets | 4.5 | 3.0 |
| | | 3.0 | -.4 | | | | .2 | -1.9 |
| | | 26.5 | 53.5 | | | Sales/Net Fixed Assets | 19.9 | 34.7 |
| | | 16.5 | 9.7 | | | | 8.8 | 10.8 |
| | | 5.6 | 4.2 | | | | 4.6 | 4.3 |
| | | 2.9 | 2.7 | | | Sales/Total Assets | 3.3 | 3.1 |
| | | 2.7 | 1.6 | | | | 2.2 | 1.9 |
| | | 2.3 | 1.4 | | | | 1.6 | 1.5 |
| | | | .5 | | | % Depr., Dep., Amort./Sales | .8 | 1.1 |
| | | | 2.8 | | | | (50) 1.7 | (53) 2.4 |
| | | | 3.5 | | | | 3.3 | 3.8 |
| | | | | | | % Officers', Directors' | .3 | 1.0 |
| | | | | | | Owners' Comp/Sales | (15) 2.2 | (16) 2.1 |
| | | | | | | | 3.4 | 2.6 |
| 445M | 19305M | 191313M | 527585M | 515520M | 769107M | Net Sales ($) | 1760213M | 2469296M |
| 481M | 7577M | 68512M | 293224M | 371720M | 622863M | Total Assets ($) | 969152M | 1421178M |

© RMA 2012

M = $ thousand    MM = $ million
See Pages 9 through 22 for Explanation of Ratios and Data

## Comparative Historical Data | Current Data Sorted by Sales

| 15 / 11 / 10 / 4 / 22 | 11 / 9 / 10 / 5 / 18 | 7 / 9 / 6 / 1 / 19 | Type of Statement | 0-1MM | 1-3MM | 3-5MM | 5-10MM | 10-25MM | 25MM & OVER |
|---|---|---|---|---|---|---|---|---|---|
| 15 | 11 | 7 | Unqualified | | | | | 1 | 6 |
| 11 | 9 | 9 | Reviewed | | 2 | | 1 | 3 | 3 |
| 10 | 10 | 6 | Compiled | | 1 | | 1 | 2 | 3 |
| 4 | 5 | 1 | Tax Returns | | 1 | | | | |
| 22 | 18 | 19 | Other | 2 | 1 | 2 | 1 | 2 | 10 |
| 4/1/09-3/31/10 ALL | 4/1/10-3/31/11 ALL | 4/1/11-3/31/12 ALL | | | 6 (4/1-9/30/11) | | | 36 (10/1/11-3/31/12) | |
| 62 | 53 | 42 | NUMBER OF STATEMENTS | 2 | 5 | 2 | 3 | 8 | 22 |
| % | % | % | ASSETS | % | % | % | % | % | % |
| 8.7 | 9.9 | 8.1 | Cash & Equivalents | | | | | | 4.1 |
| 19.7 | 21.4 | 20.7 | Trade Receivables (net) | | | | | | 21.3 |
| 33.2 | 35.7 | 35.2 | Inventory | | | | | | 35.9 |
| 2.8 | 3.9 | 2.3 | All Other Current | | | | | | 3.7 |
| 64.5 | 70.9 | 66.3 | Total Current | | | | | | 65.0 |
| 24.8 | 22.1 | 24.1 | Fixed Assets (net) | | | | | | 26.0 |
| 2.5 | 1.5 | 3.1 | Intangibles (net) | | | | | | 3.0 |
| 8.1 | 5.5 | 6.6 | All Other Non-Current | | | | | | 6.0 |
| 100.0 | 100.0 | 100.0 | Total | | | | | | 100.0 |
| | | | LIABILITIES | | | | | | |
| 7.1 | 7.5 | 6.3 | Notes Payable-Short Term | | | | | | 5.3 |
| 2.5 | 3.3 | 2.4 | Cur. Mat.-L.T.D. | | | | | | 1.2 |
| 19.2 | 21.2 | 19.7 | Trade Payables | | | | | | 18.0 |
| .2 | .0 | .1 | Income Taxes Payable | | | | | | .2 |
| 11.0 | 12.5 | 11.2 | All Other Current | | | | | | 8.0 |
| 40.1 | 44.6 | 39.7 | Total Current | | | | | | 32.6 |
| 19.4 | 18.3 | 13.9 | Long-Term Debt | | | | | | 14.0 |
| .4 | .4 | .4 | Deferred Taxes | | | | | | .8 |
| 4.9 | 1.0 | 2.0 | All Other Non-Current | | | | | | 2.8 |
| 35.2 | 35.8 | 43.9 | Net Worth | | | | | | 49.9 |
| 100.0 | 100.0 | 100.0 | Total Liabilities & Net Worth | | | | | | 100.0 |
| | | | INCOME DATA | | | | | | |
| 100.0 | 100.0 | 100.0 | Net Sales | | | | | | 100.0 |
| 30.4 | 29.7 | 27.7 | Gross Profit | | | | | | 22.3 |
| 26.4 | 26.8 | 22.5 | Operating Expenses | | | | | | 19.8 |
| 4.0 | 2.9 | 5.2 | Operating Profit | | | | | | 2.5 |
| .7 | .6 | 2.2 | All Other Expenses (net) | | | | | | 1.2 |
| 3.3 | 2.3 | 3.0 | Profit Before Taxes | | | | | | 1.3 |
| | | | RATIOS | | | | | | |
| 2.5 | 3.0 | 2.6 | | | | | | | 2.6 |
| 1.8 | 1.7 | 1.9 | Current | | | | | | 1.9 |
| 1.3 | 1.2 | 1.1 | | | | | | | 1.4 |
| 1.3 | 1.6 | 1.3 | | | | | | | 1.2 |
| .7 | .8 | .8 | Quick | | | | | | .6 |
| .4 | .4 | .4 | | | | | | | .5 |
| 21 / 17.4 | 25 / 14.8 | 26 / 14.2 | | | | | | 30 | 12.3 |
| 37 / 9.9 | 35 / 10.4 | 37 / 9.9 | Sales/Receivables | | | | | 42 | 8.7 |
| 48 / 7.7 | 49 / 7.4 | 52 / 7.0 | | | | | | 50 | 7.3 |
| 41 / 8.9 | 51 / 7.2 | 41 / 8.9 | | | | | | 53 | 6.9 |
| 83 / 4.4 | 92 / 4.0 | 83 / 4.4 | Cost of Sales/Inventory | | | | | 111 | 3.3 |
| 137 / 2.7 | 122 / 3.0 | 146 / 2.5 | | | | | | 166 | 2.2 |
| 23 / 15.8 | 24 / 14.9 | 26 / 14.1 | | | | | | 31 | 11.9 |
| 37 / 9.7 | 41 / 9.0 | 43 / 8.5 | Cost of Sales/Payables | | | | | 45 | 8.2 |
| 56 / 6.5 | 60 / 6.1 | 58 / 6.3 | | | | | | 52 | 7.0 |
| 4.3 | 4.2 | 4.3 | | | | | | | 3.7 |
| 6.6 | 6.1 | 6.9 | Sales/Working Capital | | | | | | 5.6 |
| 13.6 | 21.8 | 25.7 | | | | | | | 10.7 |
| 15.6 | 19.5 | 19.9 | | | | | | | 18.9 |
| (56) 4.0 | (45) 4.7 | (34) 3.9 | EBIT/Interest | | | | | | (19) 1.9 |
| .8 | -1.1 | .3 | | | | | | | .0 |
| 7.3 | | | Net Profit + Depr., Dep., | | | | | | |
| (12) 2.7 | | | Amort./Cur. Mat. L/T/D | | | | | | |
| .6 | | | | | | | | | |
| .2 | .1 | .1 | | | | | | | .1 |
| .5 | .4 | .6 | Fixed/Worth | | | | | | .6 |
| 1.2 | 1.0 | 1.1 | | | | | | | 1.0 |
| .6 | .4 | .6 | | | | | | | .5 |
| 1.3 | 1.0 | 1.4 | Debt/Worth | | | | | | 1.3 |
| 2.7 | 2.6 | 2.5 | | | | | | | 1.9 |
| 25.8 | 30.6 | 28.1 | % Profit Before Taxes/Tangible | | | | | | 24.7 |
| (56) 12.6 | (48) 12.0 | (39) 6.5 | Net Worth | | | | | | 3.1 |
| 2.0 | -1.5 | -2.4 | | | | | | | -3.0 |
| 13.9 | 10.6 | 9.8 | % Profit Before Taxes/Total | | | | | | 9.6 |
| 5.9 | 4.9 | 3.1 | Assets | | | | | | 1.7 |
| .1 | -2.5 | -1.3 | | | | | | | -1.7 |
| 27.5 | 60.1 | 45.4 | | | | | | | 45.4 |
| 8.9 | 18.1 | 10.4 | Sales/Net Fixed Assets | | | | | | 8.1 |
| 4.1 | 3.9 | 4.0 | | | | | | | 3.4 |
| 2.8 | 2.7 | 2.7 | | | | | | | 2.6 |
| 1.9 | 1.8 | 1.9 | Sales/Total Assets | | | | | | 1.6 |
| 1.3 | 1.3 | 1.3 | | | | | | | 1.2 |
| 1.1 | 1.0 | .7 | | | | | | | .6 |
| (49) 2.4 | (41) 1.8 | (34) 1.7 | % Depr., Dep., Amort./Sales | | | | | | (17) 2.1 |
| 3.5 | 4.4 | 3.2 | | | | | | | 3.5 |
| 2.1 | 2.0 | | % Officers', Directors' | | | | | | |
| (13) 3.0 | (17) 2.7 | | Owners' Comp/Sales | | | | | | |
| 4.4 | 6.0 | | | | | | | | |
| 3120075M | 1909754M | 2023275M | Net Sales ($) | 573M | 10719M | 8695M | 21604M | 163408M | 1818276M |
| 1799781M | 1253406M | 1364377M | Total Assets ($) | 1584M | 6712M | 4309M | 7244M | 78386M | 1266142M |

M = $ thousand    MM = $ million
See Pages 9 through 22 for Explanation of Ratios and Data

## Current Data Sorted by Assets                                                         Comparative Historical Data

| 0-500M | 500M-2MM | 2-10MM | 10-50MM | 50-100MM | 100-250MM | Type of Statement | 4/1/07-3/31/08 ALL | 4/1/08-3/31/09 ALL |
|---|---|---|---|---|---|---|---|---|
| | | 2 | 3 | 1 | 1 | Unqualified | 11 | 9 |
| | 1 | 7 | 4 | 1 | | Reviewed | 17 | 10 |
| | 1 | 3 | 1 | | | Compiled | 2 | 3 |
| 2 | 2 | 1 | 1 | | | Tax Returns | 5 | 6 |
| 1 | 1 | 3 | 5 | 2 | 1 | Other | 13 | 13 |
| 2 | 4 | 16 | 14 | 4 | 2 | **NUMBER OF STATEMENTS** | 48 | 41 |
| % | % | % | % | % | % | **ASSETS** | % | % |
| | | 5.2 | 6.1 | | | Cash & Equivalents | 8.3 | 9.2 |
| | | 31.5 | 32.1 | | | Trade Receivables (net) | 25.2 | 20.2 |
| | | 35.5 | 35.8 | | | Inventory | 42.1 | 35.6 |
| | | 2.3 | 2.3 | | | All Other Current | 1.7 | 1.9 |
| | | 74.5 | 76.4 | | | Total Current | 77.2 | 66.9 |
| | | 18.5 | 15.2 | | | Fixed Assets (net) | 15.7 | 22.1 |
| | | 3.3 | 2.4 | | | Intangibles (net) | 2.2 | 3.9 |
| | | 3.7 | 6.1 | | | All Other Non-Current | 4.9 | 7.1 |
| | | 100.0 | 100.0 | | | Total | 100.0 | 100.0 |
| | | | | | | **LIABILITIES** | | |
| | | 10.3 | 19.1 | | | Notes Payable-Short Term | 16.4 | 14.6 |
| | | 4.8 | 1.7 | | | Cur. Mat.-L.T.D. | 2.5 | 7.6 |
| | | 18.3 | 21.8 | | | Trade Payables | 16.2 | 17.1 |
| | | .4 | .2 | | | Income Taxes Payable | .2 | .8 |
| | | 6.4 | 10.0 | | | All Other Current | 10.0 | 10.1 |
| | | 40.0 | 52.8 | | | Total Current | 45.4 | 50.2 |
| | | 9.1 | 15.6 | | | Long-Term Debt | 7.9 | 11.7 |
| | | .0 | .0 | | | Deferred Taxes | .4 | .3 |
| | | 7.0 | 2.9 | | | All Other Non-Current | 3.6 | 4.8 |
| | | 43.8 | 28.7 | | | Net Worth | 42.7 | 33.1 |
| | | 100.0 | 100.0 | | | Total Liabilities & Net Worth | 100.0 | 100.0 |
| | | | | | | **INCOME DATA** | | |
| | | 100.0 | 100.0 | | | Net Sales | 100.0 | 100.0 |
| | | 25.3 | 25.3 | | | Gross Profit | 31.2 | 33.8 |
| | | 22.3 | 21.1 | | | Operating Expenses | 28.6 | 33.2 |
| | | 2.9 | 4.3 | | | Operating Profit | 2.6 | .6 |
| | | .3 | 1.3 | | | All Other Expenses (net) | .6 | 1.4 |
| | | 2.6 | 3.0 | | | Profit Before Taxes | 2.0 | -.8 |
| | | | | | | **RATIOS** | | |
| | | 3.1 | 1.7 | | | | 2.9 | 2.9 |
| | | 1.6 | 1.3 | | | Current | 1.6 | 1.4 |
| | | 1.2 | 1.0 | | | | 1.2 | 1.0 |
| | | 1.4 | 1.0 | | | | 1.3 | 1.2 |
| | | .9 | .6 | | | Quick | .7 | .6 |
| | | .6 | .4 | | | | .5 | .3 |
| | | 36  10.2 | 29  12.8 | | | | 31  11.7 | 16  22.4 |
| | | 43  8.4 | 56  6.5 | | | Sales/Receivables | 42  8.7 | 31  11.7 |
| | | 69  5.3 | 81  4.5 | | | | 49  7.5 | 47  7.8 |
| | | 42  8.6 | 48  7.6 | | | | 56  6.5 | 37  10.0 |
| | | 68  5.4 | 73  5.0 | | | Cost of Sales/Inventory | 94  3.9 | 80  4.5 |
| | | 114  3.2 | 126  2.9 | | | | 136  2.7 | 152  2.4 |
| | | 19  19.0 | 31  11.7 | | | | 15  24.3 | 16  23.4 |
| | | 29  12.8 | 41  8.9 | | | Cost of Sales/Payables | 31  11.6 | 28  13.0 |
| | | 51  7.1 | 62  5.9 | | | | 53  6.9 | 49  7.4 |
| | | 5.0 | 6.2 | | | | 4.7 | 4.6 |
| | | 7.0 | 10.3 | | | Sales/Working Capital | 7.3 | 10.8 |
| | | 25.3 | NM | | | | 15.7 | NM |
| | | 15.5 | 8.5 | | | | 7.2 | 8.3 |
| | | (14) 3.2 | 3.4 | | | EBIT/Interest | (43) 2.7 | (40) 1.6 |
| | | 1.8 | 1.6 | | | | 1.1 | -1.1 |
| | | | | | | Net Profit + Depr., Dep., Amort./Cur. Mat. L/T/D | | |
| | | .0 | .2 | | | | .1 | .1 |
| | | .2 | .4 | | | Fixed/Worth | .3 | .6 |
| | | 2.5 | 1.7 | | | | .8 | 1.7 |
| | | .5 | 1.4 | | | | .5 | .6 |
| | | 1.9 | 2.6 | | | Debt/Worth | 1.8 | 1.6 |
| | | 4.2 | 6.8 | | | | 4.1 | 3.6 |
| | | 20.9 | 27.1 | | | | 37.3 | 35.3 |
| | | (15) 14.7 | (12) 17.6 | | | % Profit Before Taxes/Tangible Net Worth | (46) 11.0 | (35) 11.5 |
| | | 9.9 | 7.5 | | | | .2 | -5.3 |
| | | 12.1 | 10.0 | | | | 12.3 | 9.9 |
| | | 5.6 | 3.6 | | | % Profit Before Taxes/Total Assets | 4.2 | 1.5 |
| | | 1.8 | 1.9 | | | | .3 | -9.9 |
| | | 81.3 | 118.6 | | | | 82.9 | 71.9 |
| | | 36.0 | 27.5 | | | Sales/Net Fixed Assets | 15.2 | 16.2 |
| | | 5.7 | 6.2 | | | | 7.4 | 5.7 |
| | | 3.1 | 2.7 | | | | 2.8 | 2.8 |
| | | 2.3 | 2.1 | | | Sales/Total Assets | 2.0 | 2.1 |
| | | 1.8 | 1.6 | | | | 1.6 | 1.7 |
| | | .3 | .4 | | | | .4 | .7 |
| | | (13) 1.1 | (13) 1.0 | | | % Depr., Dep., Amort./Sales | (40) 1.0 | (29) 1.5 |
| | | 2.2 | 2.9 | | | | 2.0 | 3.1 |
| | | | | | | | 1.4 | 1.6 |
| | | | | | | % Officers', Directors' Owners' Comp/Sales | (19) 2.6 | (17) 3.9 |
| | | | | | | | 4.4 | 8.5 |
| 1769M | 19099M | 216512M | 644466M | 524866M | 667468M | Net Sales ($) | 2308432M | 1606865M |
| 543M | 5070M | 90066M | 324651M | 281134M | 353694M | Total Assets ($) | 1216139M | 751359M |

M = $ thousand    MM = $ million
See Pages 9 through 22 for Explanation of Ratios and Data

**Comparative Historical Data** | **Current Data Sorted by Sales**

### Type of Statement

| | | | | | 0-1MM | 1-3MM | 3-5MM | 5-10MM | 10-25MM | 25MM & OVER |
|---|---|---|---|---|---|---|---|---|---|---|
| | | | Unqualified | | | | | | 2 | 5 |
| | | | Reviewed | | | | 1 | 2 | 7 | 3 |
| | | | Compiled | | | | | 2 | 1 | |
| | | | Tax Returns | | 1 | 2 | 2 | | | 1 |
| | | | Other | | | | | 3 | | 9 |

| 6 | 12 | 7 | | | | | | | | |
| 13 | 14 | 13 | | | | | | | | |
| 4 | 3 | 4 | | | | | | | | |
| 3 | 6 | 6 | | | | | | | | |
| 21 | 19 | 12 | | | | | | | | |

| 4/1/09- 3/31/10 ALL | 4/1/10- 3/31/11 ALL | 4/1/11- 3/31/12 ALL | | | 0-1MM | 1-3MM | 3-5MM | 4 (4/1-9/30/11) 5-10MM | 38 (10/1/11-3/31/12) 10-25MM | 25MM & OVER |
|---|---|---|---|---|---|---|---|---|---|---|
| 47 | 54 | 42 | **NUMBER OF STATEMENTS** | | 1 | 2 | 3 | 7 | 10 | 19 |
| % | % | % | **ASSETS** | | % | % | % | % | % | % |
| 9.6 | 8.1 | 6.8 | Cash & Equivalents | | | | | | 3.5 | 6.4 |
| 28.8 | 29.3 | 29.7 | Trade Receivables (net) | | | | | | 29.7 | 31.1 |
| 31.3 | 34.7 | 35.2 | Inventory | | | | | | 27.4 | 38.6 |
| 2.3 | 4.0 | 2.2 | All Other Current | | | | | | 1.3 | 2.7 |
| 72.0 | 76.2 | 73.8 | Total Current | | | | | | 61.9 | 78.9 |
| 16.2 | 11.4 | 15.9 | Fixed Assets (net) | | | | | | 30.9 | 10.6 |
| 5.7 | 4.6 | 3.8 | Intangibles (net) | | | | | | 2.7 | 4.7 |
| 6.1 | 7.8 | 6.4 | All Other Non-Current | | | | | | 4.5 | 5.7 |
| 100.0 | 100.0 | 100.0 | Total | | | | | | 100.0 | 100.0 |
| | | | **LIABILITIES** | | | | | | | |
| 12.7 | 11.7 | 13.8 | Notes Payable-Short Term | | | | | | 7.4 | 16.7 |
| 2.5 | 3.1 | 3.3 | Cur. Mat.-L.T.D. | | | | | | 7.8 | 2.6 |
| 16.2 | 18.0 | 20.1 | Trade Payables | | | | | | 17.1 | 21.8 |
| .1 | .7 | .3 | Income Taxes Payable | | | | | | .0 | .4 |
| 13.1 | 8.3 | 7.4 | All Other Current | | | | | | 7.6 | 10.7 |
| 44.6 | 41.8 | 45.0 | Total Current | | | | | | 39.9 | 52.1 |
| 12.2 | 10.0 | 12.6 | Long-Term Debt | | | | | | 15.6 | 13.6 |
| .1 | .0 | .0 | Deferred Taxes | | | | | | .0 | .0 |
| 8.4 | 4.9 | 6.7 | All Other Non-Current | | | | | | .8 | 4.9 |
| 34.7 | 43.2 | 35.7 | Net Worth | | | | | | 43.7 | 29.3 |
| 100.0 | 100.0 | 100.0 | Total Liabilities & Net Worth | | | | | | 100.0 | 100.0 |
| | | | **INCOME DATA** | | | | | | | |
| 100.0 | 100.0 | 100.0 | Net Sales | | | | | | 100.0 | 100.0 |
| 32.3 | 30.3 | 27.3 | Gross Profit | | | | | | 24.0 | 24.3 |
| 30.6 | 27.0 | 24.1 | Operating Expenses | | | | | | 19.9 | 21.5 |
| 1.7 | 3.3 | 3.2 | Operating Profit | | | | | | 4.1 | 2.9 |
| .6 | .6 | .8 | All Other Expenses (net) | | | | | | .9 | .9 |
| 1.1 | 2.7 | 2.5 | Profit Before Taxes | | | | | | 3.2 | 2.0 |
| | | | **RATIOS** | | | | | | | |
| 2.5 | 3.3 | 2.3 | | | | | | | 2.5 | 2.0 |
| 1.5 | 2.1 | 1.5 | Current | | | | | | 1.3 | 1.5 |
| 1.2 | 1.2 | 1.2 | | | | | | | 1.2 | 1.2 |
| 1.4 | 1.6 | 1.1 | | | | | | | 1.1 | 1.1 |
| .8 | .9 | .8 | Quick | | | | | | .7 | .6 |
| .5 | .5 | .5 | | | | | | | .5 | .4 |
| 28  12.8 | 25  14.6 | 32  11.3 | | | | | | | 34  10.8 | 36  10.2 |
| 41  8.8 | 44  8.4 | 48  7.6 | Sales/Receivables | | | | | | 43  8.4 | 50  7.3 |
| 66  5.5 | 62  5.9 | 69  5.3 | | | | | | | 61  6.0 | 79  4.6 |
| 43  8.4 | 48  7.6 | 42  8.6 | | | | | | | 37  9.8 | 50  7.3 |
| 69  5.3 | 68  5.3 | 72  5.1 | Cost of Sales/Inventory | | | | | | 55  6.6 | 78  4.7 |
| 112  3.3 | 117  3.1 | 126  2.9 | | | | | | | 76  4.8 | 135  2.7 |
| 16  23.5 | 16  22.8 | 20  18.1 | | | | | | | 18  20.1 | 29  12.7 |
| 25  14.4 | 33  11.2 | 37  9.9 | Cost of Sales/Payables | | | | | | 34  10.8 | 41  8.8 |
| 59  6.2 | 49  7.4 | 57  6.4 | | | | | | | 47  7.7 | 58  6.3 |
| 5.0 | 4.2 | 4.9 | | | | | | | 6.9 | 4.6 |
| 8.7 | 6.8 | 8.5 | Sales/Working Capital | | | | | | 13.1 | 8.8 |
| 14.9 | 19.2 | 25.8 | | | | | | | NM | 26.1 |
| 8.2 | 11.5 | 7.9 | | | | | | | 22.7 | 8.1 |
| (37)  3.1 | (45)  4.4 | (40)  3.1 | EBIT/Interest | | | | | | 3.4 | 3.2 |
| .8 | .7 | 1.7 | | | | | | | 1.8 | 1.7 |
| 4.6 | 5.5 | 23.2 | | | | | | | | |
| (13)  2.6 | (17)  3.1 | (15)  2.4 | Net Profit + Depr., Dep., Amort./Cur. Mat. L/T/D | | | | | | | |
| .2 | .7 | .3 | | | | | | | | |
| .1 | .1 | .1 | | | | | | | .1 | .2 |
| .3 | .2 | .3 | Fixed/Worth | | | | | | .7 | .4 |
| 1.5 | .8 | 2.0 | | | | | | | 1.9 | 2.4 |
| 1.0 | .5 | .8 | | | | | | | .7 | 1.4 |
| 1.7 | 1.3 | 2.2 | Debt/Worth | | | | | | 1.4 | 2.5 |
| 14.6 | 6.1 | 5.4 | | | | | | | 3.7 | 10.1 |
| 28.7 | 38.2 | 22.8 | | | | | | | 22.1 | 28.3 |
| (38)  9.4 | (45)  11.8 | (36)  16.0 | % Profit Before Taxes/Tangible Net Worth | | | | | | 15.7 | (15)  16.6 |
| .7 | 3.7 | 6.6 | | | | | | | 3.4 | 7.3 |
| 8.1 | 11.5 | 10.0 | | | | | | | 13.3 | 10.0 |
| 3.8 | 4.5 | 4.1 | % Profit Before Taxes/Total Assets | | | | | | 5.2 | 3.5 |
| -1.0 | -.2 | 1.7 | | | | | | | 1.3 | 1.9 |
| 110.9 | 88.0 | 70.8 | | | | | | | 131.4 | 58.8 |
| 30.8 | 38.5 | 30.2 | Sales/Net Fixed Assets | | | | | | 6.2 | 29.8 |
| 7.2 | 11.2 | 6.3 | | | | | | | 3.7 | 7.2 |
| 2.9 | 3.0 | 2.8 | | | | | | | 2.9 | 2.6 |
| 2.1 | 2.2 | 2.2 | Sales/Total Assets | | | | | | 2.2 | 2.0 |
| 1.6 | 1.8 | 1.7 | | | | | | | 2.1 | 1.7 |
| .5 | .3 | .3 | | | | | | | .3 | .3 |
| (31)  1.2 | (39)  1.0 | (36)  1.0 | % Depr., Dep., Amort./Sales | | | | | | 1.0 | (17)  1.0 |
| 2.9 | 1.9 | 2.1 | | | | | | | 6.1 | 1.7 |
| 2.3 | 2.0 | 1.7 | | | | | | | | |
| (16)  4.0 | (21)  3.9 | (16)  2.8 | % Officers', Directors' Owners' Comp/Sales | | | | | | | |
| 8.2 | 7.5 | 4.0 | | | | | | | | |
| 1464156M | 3168184M | 2074180M | Net Sales ($) | | 761M | 3571M | 12397M | 50899M | 175930M | 1830622M |
| 748485M | 1565513M | 1055158M | Total Assets ($) | | 351M | 1230M | 9452M | 21515M | 86909M | 935701M |

M = $ thousand    MM = $ million
See Pages 9 through 22 for Explanation of Ratios and Data

## Current Data Sorted by Assets

## Comparative Historical Data

| 0-500M | 500M-2MM | 2-10MM | 10-50MM | 50-100MM | 100-250MM | Type of Statement | 4/1/07-3/31/08 ALL | 4/1/08-3/31/09 ALL |
|---|---|---|---|---|---|---|---|---|
|  |  | 1 | 3 |  | 2 | Unqualified | 9 | 5 |
| 1 |  | 9 | 5 |  |  | Reviewed | 10 | 9 |
|  |  | 2 |  |  |  | Compiled | 13 | 11 |
| 2 | 5 | 2 |  |  |  | Tax Returns | 8 | 12 |
| 2 | 3 | 3 | 6 | 1 |  | Other | 10 | 12 |
| 9 (4/1-9/30/11) |  |  | 38 (10/1/11-3/31/12) |  |  |  |  |  |
| 5 | 8 | 17 | 14 | 1 | 2 | **NUMBER OF STATEMENTS** | 50 | 49 |
| % | % | % | % | % | % | **ASSETS** | % | % |
|  |  | 6.7 | 7.4 |  |  | Cash & Equivalents | 6.2 | 7.8 |
|  |  | 22.5 | 25.7 |  |  | Trade Receivables (net) | 24.2 | 22.6 |
|  |  | 36.2 | 38.0 |  |  | Inventory | 30.9 | 32.3 |
|  |  | 1.7 | .9 |  |  | All Other Current | 4.4 | 3.3 |
|  |  | 67.1 | 72.0 |  |  | Total Current | 65.8 | 66.1 |
|  |  | 21.8 | 11.8 |  |  | Fixed Assets (net) | 21.4 | 21.3 |
|  |  | 2.4 | 6.4 |  |  | Intangibles (net) | 5.0 | 2.4 |
|  |  | 8.7 | 9.8 |  |  | All Other Non-Current | 7.8 | 10.2 |
|  |  | 100.0 | 100.0 |  |  | Total | 100.0 | 100.0 |
|  |  |  |  |  |  | **LIABILITIES** |  |  |
|  |  | 11.7 | 12.6 |  |  | Notes Payable-Short Term | 11.4 | 11.9 |
|  |  | 1.2 | 1.8 |  |  | Cur. Mat.-L.T.D. | 2.3 | 2.6 |
|  |  | 12.7 | 12.5 |  |  | Trade Payables | 14.0 | 12.2 |
|  |  | .4 | .2 |  |  | Income Taxes Payable | .1 | .3 |
|  |  | 4.2 | 11.9 |  |  | All Other Current | 10.5 | 9.9 |
|  |  | 30.1 | 39.1 |  |  | Total Current | 38.3 | 36.9 |
|  |  | 7.0 | 12.5 |  |  | Long-Term Debt | 12.8 | 14.6 |
|  |  | .4 | 1.3 |  |  | Deferred Taxes | .1 | .2 |
|  |  | 5.1 | 3.6 |  |  | All Other Non-Current | 12.4 | 8.8 |
|  |  | 57.4 | 43.5 |  |  | Net Worth | 36.3 | 39.4 |
|  |  | 100.0 | 100.0 |  |  | Total Liabilities & Net Worth | 100.0 | 100.0 |
|  |  |  |  |  |  | **INCOME DATA** |  |  |
|  |  | 100.0 | 100.0 |  |  | Net Sales | 100.0 | 100.0 |
|  |  | 30.0 | 23.8 |  |  | Gross Profit | 32.9 | 36.1 |
|  |  | 25.9 | 18.6 |  |  | Operating Expenses | 29.3 | 31.3 |
|  |  | 4.1 | 5.2 |  |  | Operating Profit | 3.7 | 4.8 |
|  |  | .5 | .2 |  |  | All Other Expenses (net) | .9 | 1.3 |
|  |  | 3.6 | 5.0 |  |  | Profit Before Taxes | 2.8 | 3.5 |
|  |  |  |  |  |  | **RATIOS** |  |  |
|  |  | 3.0 | 4.0 |  |  |  | 3.7 | 3.7 |
|  |  | 2.4 | 2.3 |  |  | Current | 1.7 | 2.0 |
|  |  | 1.7 | 1.1 |  |  |  | 1.3 | 1.2 |
|  |  | 1.6 | 2.3 |  |  |  | 1.5 | 1.6 |
|  |  | 1.0 | .9 |  |  | Quick | .7 | .9 |
|  |  | .5 | .4 |  |  |  | .5 | .5 |
|  |  | 19　18.9 | 43　8.5 |  |  |  | 26　13.8 | 19　19.5 |
|  |  | 46　7.9 | 53　6.9 |  |  | Sales/Receivables | 34　10.6 | 32　11.3 |
|  |  | 54　6.7 | 68　5.4 |  |  |  | 41　8.9 | 49　7.5 |
|  |  | 59　6.2 | 69　5.3 |  |  |  | 40　9.1 | 49　7.5 |
|  |  | 78　4.7 | 83　4.4 |  |  | Cost of Sales/Inventory | 63　5.8 | 79　4.6 |
|  |  | 174　2.1 | 192　1.9 |  |  |  | 110　3.3 | 115　3.2 |
|  |  | 14　27.0 | 12　30.7 |  |  |  | 14　25.3 | 12　31.6 |
|  |  | 24　15.3 | 36　10.2 |  |  | Cost of Sales/Payables | 23　15.6 | 20　18.1 |
|  |  | 38　9.7 | 48　7.6 |  |  |  | 34　10.6 | 41　8.9 |
|  |  | 3.8 | 3.5 |  |  |  | 5.2 | 4.6 |
|  |  | 5.6 | 5.0 |  |  | Sales/Working Capital | 10.7 | 9.6 |
|  |  | 7.8 | 90.5 |  |  |  | 24.3 | 21.1 |
|  |  | 8.0 | 66.3 |  |  |  | 8.2 | 11.7 |
|  |  | (13)　2.2 | 7.4 |  |  | EBIT/Interest | (46)　2.5 | (46)　3.6 |
|  |  | 1.7 | 2.5 |  |  |  | 1.3 | 1.3 |
|  |  |  |  |  |  | Net Profit + Depr., Dep., | 5.1 | 7.2 |
|  |  |  |  |  |  | Amort./Cur. Mat. L/T/D | (10)　2.2 | (11)　3.4 |
|  |  |  |  |  |  |  | 1.1 | 1.1 |
|  |  | .1 | .1 |  |  |  | .2 | .1 |
|  |  | .3 | .2 |  |  | Fixed/Worth | .6 | .4 |
|  |  | .7 | .9 |  |  |  | 1.5 | 1.0 |
|  |  | .4 | .4 |  |  |  | .6 | .5 |
|  |  | .6 | 1.4 |  |  | Debt/Worth | 1.8 | 1.5 |
|  |  | 1.5 | 5.3 |  |  |  | 6.1 | 3.8 |
|  |  | 12.6 | 39.7 |  |  |  | 46.3 | 42.0 |
|  |  | 6.3 | (13)　24.6 |  |  | % Profit Before Taxes/Tangible Net Worth | (44)　10.1 | (45)　13.5 |
|  |  | 2.4 | 9.2 |  |  |  | -2.6 | 2.3 |
|  |  | 6.7 | 15.3 |  |  |  | 12.8 | 13.5 |
|  |  | 2.5 | 6.8 |  |  | % Profit Before Taxes/Total Assets | 4.7 | 7.8 |
|  |  | 1.3 | 2.5 |  |  |  | .2 | .5 |
|  |  | 35.4 | 39.8 |  |  |  | 34.1 | 38.0 |
|  |  | 11.1 | 20.1 |  |  | Sales/Net Fixed Assets | 13.4 | 15.0 |
|  |  | 5.7 | 9.9 |  |  |  | 8.4 | 8.5 |
|  |  | 2.3 | 2.3 |  |  |  | 3.3 | 3.2 |
|  |  | 2.0 | 1.8 |  |  | Sales/Total Assets | 2.4 | 2.4 |
|  |  | 1.5 | 1.5 |  |  |  | 1.9 | 1.8 |
|  |  | .7 | 1.0 |  |  |  | .7 | .8 |
|  |  | (16)　1.1 | (12)　1.5 |  |  | % Depr., Dep., Amort./Sales | (43)　1.4 | (37)　1.3 |
|  |  | 2.0 | 2.8 |  |  |  | 2.4 | 2.8 |
|  |  |  |  |  |  |  | 2.8 | 2.0 |
|  |  |  |  |  |  | % Officers', Directors' Owners' Comp/Sales | (23)　3.9 | (28)　4.4 |
|  |  |  |  |  |  |  | 9.1 | 6.1 |
| 3115M | 21704M | 145204M | 453726M | 65133M | 301914M | Net Sales ($) | 797005M | 898968M |
| 1079M | 7955M | 77536M | 260822M | 67464M | 266957M | Total Assets ($) | 423914M | 488411M |

M = $ thousand　　　MM = $ million
See Pages 9 through 22 for Explanation of Ratios and Data

## Comparative Historical Data | Current Data Sorted by Sales

| Type of Statement | 4/1/09-3/31/10 ALL | 4/1/10-3/31/11 ALL | 4/1/11-3/31/12 ALL | 0-1MM | 1-3MM | 3-5MM | 5-10MM | 10-25MM | 25MM & OVER |
|---|---|---|---|---|---|---|---|---|---|
| Unqualified | 5 | 6 | 6 | | | | 1 | 2 | 3 |
| Reviewed | 11 | 14 | 15 | 1 | | | 4 | 7 | 2 |
| Compiled | 7 | 8 | 2 | | | 1 | 1 | 1 | |
| Tax Returns | 8 | 9 | 9 | 2 | 3 | 2 | 2 | | |
| Other | 16 | 18 | 15 | 2 | 3 | 2 | 3 | 1 | 6 |
| | | | | | 9 (4/1-9/30/11) | | | 38 (10/1/11-3/31/12) | |
| **NUMBER OF STATEMENTS** | 47 | 55 | 47 | 5 | 4 | 6 | 10 | 11 | 11 |
| **ASSETS** | % | % | % | % | % | % | % | % | % |
| Cash & Equivalents | 8.2 | 9.6 | 6.9 | | | | 10.2 | 4.9 | 6.6 |
| Trade Receivables (net) | 21.7 | 22.9 | 22.1 | | | | 22.7 | 19.8 | 25.7 |
| Inventory | 31.3 | 33.0 | 34.4 | | | | 35.1 | 32.5 | 38.0 |
| All Other Current | 3.0 | 2.5 | 1.6 | | | | 1.8 | .5 | 2.3 |
| Total Current | 64.1 | 68.0 | 65.0 | | | | 69.8 | 57.7 | 72.6 |
| Fixed Assets (net) | 23.6 | 22.1 | 20.2 | | | | 21.2 | 22.5 | 10.6 |
| Intangibles (net) | 2.2 | 4.3 | 6.3 | | | | .1 | 9.7 | 11.6 |
| All Other Non-Current | 10.0 | 5.4 | 8.3 | | | | 8.9 | 10.1 | 5.1 |
| Total | 100.0 | 100.0 | 100.0 | | | | 100.0 | 100.0 | 100.0 |
| **LIABILITIES** | | | | | | | | | |
| Notes Payable-Short Term | 11.2 | 11.9 | 11.5 | | | | 14.9 | 14.4 | 8.8 |
| Cur. Mat.-L.T.D. | 2.2 | 3.4 | 1.7 | | | | .7 | 2.6 | 1.9 |
| Trade Payables | 12.0 | 12.3 | 11.2 | | | | 8.7 | 12.6 | 10.4 |
| Income Taxes Payable | .1 | .5 | .2 | | | | .6 | .2 | .0 |
| All Other Current | 10.3 | 10.4 | 9.4 | | | | 5.7 | 11.5 | 8.7 |
| Total Current | 35.8 | 38.5 | 34.2 | | | | 30.6 | 41.4 | 29.8 |
| Long-Term Debt | 10.6 | 11.9 | 14.4 | | | | .8 | 19.0 | 11.7 |
| Deferred Taxes | .1 | .6 | .7 | | | | .6 | 1.6 | .6 |
| All Other Non-Current | 7.7 | 7.9 | 6.3 | | | | 6.8 | .4 | 6.8 |
| Net Worth | 46.0 | 41.3 | 44.3 | | | | 61.2 | 37.6 | 51.1 |
| Total Liabilities & Net Worth | 100.0 | 100.0 | 100.0 | | | | 100.0 | 100.0 | 100.0 |
| **INCOME DATA** | | | | | | | | | |
| Net Sales | 100.0 | 100.0 | 100.0 | | | | 100.0 | 100.0 | 100.0 |
| Gross Profit | 34.6 | 34.3 | 33.0 | | | | 32.4 | 26.9 | 23.8 |
| Operating Expenses | 31.8 | 29.8 | 27.6 | | | | 27.6 | 24.3 | 16.9 |
| Operating Profit | 2.8 | 4.5 | 5.3 | | | | 4.8 | 2.6 | 6.9 |
| All Other Expenses (net) | 1.1 | .6 | .9 | | | | .2 | 1.2 | 1.3 |
| Profit Before Taxes | 1.7 | 3.9 | 4.4 | | | | 4.6 | 1.4 | 5.6 |
| **RATIOS** | | | | | | | | | |
| Current | 2.9 | 3.3 | 3.3 | | | | 3.1 | 2.5 | 4.0 |
| | 1.8 | 2.0 | 1.9 | | | | 2.2 | 1.1 | 2.5 |
| | 1.3 | 1.1 | 1.2 | | | | 1.8 | 1.0 | 1.5 |
| Quick | 1.7 | 1.5 | 1.7 | | | | 1.4 | 1.4 | 2.3 |
| | .9 | .8 | .9 | | | | 1.1 | .4 | 1.2 |
| | .5 | .5 | .5 | | | | .7 | .4 | .6 |
| Sales/Receivables | 27  13.6 | 25  14.7 | 26  14.3 | | | | 10  36.2 | 26  14.3 | 40  9.1 |
| | 34  10.7 | 37  9.9 | 45  8.2 | | | | 41  8.9 | 47  7.8 | 53  6.9 |
| | 50  7.3 | 58  6.3 | 54  6.8 | | | | 49  7.4 | 61  6.0 | 57  6.4 |
| Cost of Sales/Inventory | 48  7.6 | 54  6.7 | 66  5.5 | | | | 49  7.4 | 70  5.2 | 66  5.5 |
| | 82  4.4 | 80  4.5 | 81  4.5 | | | | 74  4.9 | 81  4.5 | 83  4.4 |
| | 140  2.6 | 140  2.6 | 146  2.5 | | | | 107  3.4 | 159  2.3 | 135  2.7 |
| Cost of Sales/Payables | 12  29.3 | 16  22.4 | 13  27.3 | | | | 10  37.2 | 27  13.6 | 9  40.9 |
| | 24  15.2 | 25  14.6 | 24  15.3 | | | | 14  27.0 | 33  11.2 | 24  14.9 |
| | 39  9.4 | 46  8.0 | 43  8.4 | | | | 22  16.5 | 50  7.3 | 43  8.4 |
| Sales/Working Capital | 4.8 | 4.0 | 4.4 | | | | 4.5 | 5.4 | 3.7 |
| | 7.6 | 7.6 | 6.6 | | | | 7.1 | 34.5 | 4.4 |
| | 18.4 | 80.5 | 28.1 | | | | 9.6 | 216.2 | 6.1 |
| EBIT/Interest | 12.9 | 15.6 | 9.4 | | | | | 5.4 | 58.0 |
| | (40) 2.7 | (47) 4.0 | (40) 4.6 | | | | | 2.2 | 8.1 |
| | -1.8 | 1.3 | 1.9 | | | | | 1.8 | 2.7 |
| Net Profit + Depr., Dep., Amort./Cur. Mat. L/T/D | | 1.9 | | | | | | | |
| | | (10) 1.1 | | | | | | | |
| | | .2 | | | | | | | |
| Fixed/Worth | .1 | .1 | .1 | | | | .1 | .2 | .1 |
| | .3 | .4 | .3 | | | | .4 | .7 | .3 |
| | 1.2 | 1.5 | 1.1 | | | | .6 | 1.4 | .9 |
| Debt/Worth | .5 | .5 | .5 | | | | .4 | 1.0 | .5 |
| | .9 | 1.3 | 1.2 | | | | .5 | 1.8 | 1.2 |
| | 2.3 | 4.3 | 4.8 | | | | 1.0 | 5.0 | 6.3 |
| % Profit Before Taxes/Tangible Net Worth | 27.7 | 37.6 | 28.0 | | | | 12.6 | 29.3 | |
| | (45) 12.9 | (47) 11.4 | (40) 10.5 | | | | 6.8 | (10) 7.3 | |
| | -3.8 | 1.8 | 6.1 | | | | 2.0 | 4.8 | |
| % Profit Before Taxes/Total Assets | 11.2 | 14.6 | 10.0 | | | | 8.1 | 7.3 | 24.1 |
| | 5.2 | 5.0 | 4.6 | | | | 2.5 | 2.2 | 6.3 |
| | -2.9 | .6 | 2.0 | | | | .8 | .8 | 4.0 |
| Sales/Net Fixed Assets | 31.3 | 29.2 | 38.4 | | | | 30.9 | 19.3 | 38.4 |
| | 12.7 | 13.1 | 11.1 | | | | 11.1 | 6.5 | 20.9 |
| | 5.4 | 5.7 | 6.4 | | | | 7.4 | 3.9 | 9.8 |
| Sales/Total Assets | 2.7 | 2.6 | 2.4 | | | | 2.5 | 2.0 | 2.3 |
| | 2.1 | 2.1 | 2.0 | | | | 2.3 | 1.5 | 2.0 |
| | 1.7 | 1.5 | 1.5 | | | | 2.2 | 1.4 | 1.0 |
| % Depr., Dep., Amort./Sales | .9 | .5 | .9 | | | | | | 1.3 |
| | (39) 1.8 | (45) 1.4 | (39) 1.4 | | | | | (10) | 1.6 |
| | 3.6 | 2.8 | 2.7 | | | | | | 2.3 |
| % Officers', Directors' Owners' Comp/Sales | 1.7 | 3.3 | 2.3 | | | | | | |
| | (20) 3.0 | (23) 4.4 | (20) 3.3 | | | | | | |
| | 5.6 | 5.7 | 5.4 | | | | | | |
| Net Sales ($) | 648107M | 885840M | 990796M | 2517M | 6916M | 21169M | 75722M | 181612M | 702860M |
| Total Assets ($) | 407080M | 545515M | 681813M | 1232M | 3031M | 13877M | 33320M | 123353M | 507000M |

M = $ thousand    MM = $ million
See Pages 9 through 22 for Explanation of Ratios and Data

## Current Data Sorted by Assets | Comparative Historical Data

| 0-500M | 500M-2MM | 2-10MM | 10-50MM | 50-100MM | 100-250MM | Type of Statement | ALL 4/1/07-3/31/08 | ALL 4/1/08-3/31/09 |
|---|---|---|---|---|---|---|---|---|
| | | 2 | 9 | 4 | 2 | Unqualified | 26 | 23 |
| | 2 | 19 | 6 | | | Reviewed | 23 | 26 |
| 3 | 5 | 6 | 2 | | | Compiled | 20 | 15 |
| 3 | 10 | 4 | 1 | | | Tax Returns | 12 | 14 |
| 3 | 8 | 23 | 11 | 3 | 3 | Other | 57 | 47 |
| | 24 (4/1-9/30/11) | | 105 (10/1/11-3/31/12) | | | | | |
| 9 | 25 | 54 | 29 | 7 | 5 | **NUMBER OF STATEMENTS** | 138 | 125 |
| % | % | % | % | % | % | **ASSETS** | % | % |
| | 10.4 | 8.1 | 8.8 | | | Cash & Equivalents | 6.2 | 7.3 |
| | 24.4 | 27.2 | 21.0 | | | Trade Receivables (net) | 24.6 | 22.7 |
| | 31.6 | 34.7 | 32.8 | | | Inventory | 32.8 | 33.7 |
| | 1.9 | 2.1 | 2.1 | | | All Other Current | 2.0 | 2.3 |
| | 68.3 | 72.1 | 64.6 | | | Total Current | 65.6 | 66.0 |
| | 20.4 | 18.3 | 22.0 | | | Fixed Assets (net) | 22.6 | 23.4 |
| | 2.3 | 2.0 | 6.7 | | | Intangibles (net) | 4.8 | 5.3 |
| | 9.0 | 7.6 | 6.7 | | | All Other Non-Current | 7.1 | 5.2 |
| | 100.0 | 100.0 | 100.0 | | | Total | 100.0 | 100.0 |
| | | | | | | **LIABILITIES** | | |
| | 10.0 | 12.7 | 7.4 | | | Notes Payable-Short Term | 13.7 | 12.9 |
| | 3.7 | 1.8 | 2.4 | | | Cur. Mat.-L.T.D. | 3.6 | 3.7 |
| | 15.5 | 15.9 | 14.1 | | | Trade Payables | 14.5 | 14.7 |
| | .0 | .1 | .1 | | | Income Taxes Payable | .3 | .2 |
| | 11.1 | 10.3 | 5.9 | | | All Other Current | 11.6 | 9.5 |
| | 40.3 | 40.8 | 29.9 | | | Total Current | 43.7 | 41.0 |
| | 23.8 | 8.4 | 11.8 | | | Long-Term Debt | 14.6 | 14.8 |
| | .2 | .0 | .8 | | | Deferred Taxes | .3 | .5 |
| | 5.4 | 7.8 | 11.8 | | | All Other Non-Current | 6.7 | 7.8 |
| | 30.3 | 43.0 | 45.6 | | | Net Worth | 34.7 | 35.9 |
| | 100.0 | 100.0 | 100.0 | | | Total Liabilities & Net Worth | 100.0 | 100.0 |
| | | | | | | **INCOME DATA** | | |
| | 100.0 | 100.0 | 100.0 | | | Net Sales | 100.0 | 100.0 |
| | 40.8 | 28.9 | 27.1 | | | Gross Profit | 30.5 | 28.5 |
| | 36.6 | 24.7 | 19.7 | | | Operating Expenses | 25.2 | 25.1 |
| | 4.2 | 4.2 | 7.4 | | | Operating Profit | 5.4 | 3.3 |
| | .1 | .6 | .1 | | | All Other Expenses (net) | 1.5 | 1.6 |
| | 4.0 | 3.6 | 7.3 | | | Profit Before Taxes | 3.8 | 1.7 |
| | | | | | | **RATIOS** | | |
| | 3.9 | 3.2 | 4.1 | | | | 2.5 | 2.7 |
| | 2.4 | 2.0 | 2.3 | | | Current | 1.7 | 1.7 |
| | 1.1 | 1.2 | 1.7 | | | | 1.3 | 1.2 |
| | 1.9 | 1.3 | 2.7 | | | | 1.2 | 1.2 |
| | 1.1 | .8 | 1.2 | | | Quick | .9 | .7 |
| | .4 | .6 | .6 | | | | .5 | .5 |
| | 13 27.3 | 29 12.4 | 29 12.5 | | | | 30 12.1 | 26 13.9 |
| | 37 9.9 | 41 9.0 | 40 9.2 | | | Sales/Receivables | 40 9.1 | 37 9.9 |
| | 46 8.0 | 54 6.8 | 59 6.2 | | | | 57 6.4 | 50 7.3 |
| | 29 12.6 | 45 8.1 | 49 7.5 | | | | 46 7.9 | 46 7.9 |
| | 56 6.5 | 66 5.5 | 76 4.8 | | | Cost of Sales/Inventory | 77 4.8 | 86 4.3 |
| | 122 3.0 | 118 3.1 | 126 2.9 | | | | 120 3.0 | 131 2.8 |
| | 16 22.4 | 17 21.1 | 14 26.5 | | | | 17 22.0 | 16 23.1 |
| | 32 11.5 | 31 11.6 | 28 13.1 | | | Cost of Sales/Payables | 32 11.5 | 32 11.5 |
| | 49 7.5 | 43 8.4 | 63 5.8 | | | | 47 7.8 | 47 7.8 |
| | 4.5 | 4.0 | 3.8 | | | | 4.8 | 4.6 |
| | 9.5 | 7.2 | 5.0 | | | Sales/Working Capital | 8.3 | 7.2 |
| | NM | 20.0 | 7.5 | | | | 17.1 | 34.9 |
| | 28.0 | 12.3 | 160.7 | | | | 8.0 | 7.2 |
| | (47) 4.7 | (28) 4.4 | 19.3 | | | EBIT/Interest | (123) 2.7 | (114) 2.3 |
| | 1.7 | 1.7 | 1.8 | | | | 1.3 | .7 |
| | | | | | | | 10.7 | 4.5 |
| | | | | | | Net Profit + Depr., Dep., Amort./Cur. Mat. L/T/D | (31) 2.4 | (31) 1.5 |
| | | | | | | | 1.1 | .3 |
| | .1 | .2 | .2 | | | | .2 | .2 |
| | .4 | .4 | .5 | | | Fixed/Worth | .6 | .7 |
| | 2.6 | 1.0 | 1.1 | | | | 1.7 | 1.4 |
| | .5 | .6 | .3 | | | | .7 | .7 |
| | 3.3 | 1.5 | 1.2 | | | Debt/Worth | 1.8 | 1.6 |
| | 10.8 | 3.4 | 4.6 | | | | 5.6 | 4.8 |
| | 59.3 | 49.7 | 46.0 | | | | 45.9 | 27.5 |
| | (21) 18.3 | (53) 24.6 | (26) 24.8 | | | % Profit Before Taxes/Tangible Net Worth | (117) 18.1 | (108) 9.1 |
| | 2.7 | 7.1 | 6.8 | | | | 5.6 | .1 |
| | 19.0 | 17.4 | 17.8 | | | | 15.5 | 10.3 |
| | 8.8 | 7.6 | 10.0 | | | % Profit Before Taxes/Total Assets | 6.2 | 3.9 |
| | 1.5 | 2.4 | 1.0 | | | | .8 | -.9 |
| | 288.1 | 42.1 | 20.9 | | | | 29.4 | 29.2 |
| | 18.9 | 20.6 | 12.3 | | | Sales/Net Fixed Assets | 12.7 | 12.2 |
| | 6.4 | 9.5 | 5.3 | | | | 6.1 | 5.1 |
| | 3.6 | 2.8 | 2.6 | | | | 2.8 | 2.8 |
| | 2.8 | 2.4 | 1.8 | | | Sales/Total Assets | 2.1 | 2.1 |
| | 1.6 | 1.7 | 1.3 | | | | 1.5 | 1.5 |
| | .4 | .6 | .7 | | | | .8 | 1.0 |
| | (18) 1.3 | (43) 1.1 | (25) 1.4 | | | % Depr., Dep., Amort./Sales | (122) 1.6 | (103) 1.7 |
| | 2.2 | 2.6 | 3.9 | | | | 2.7 | 2.7 |
| | 2.9 | 1.6 | | | | | 2.7 | 1.5 |
| | (14) 6.2 | (16) 2.9 | | | | % Officers', Directors' Owners' Comp/Sales | (39) 3.7 | (34) 3.3 |
| | 8.0 | 5.9 | | | | | 6.1 | 5.7 |
| 13749M | 73346M | 677531M | 1266975M | 767232M | 1296759M | Net Sales ($) | 5854754M | 4273886M |
| 2272M | 26707M | 290386M | 665263M | 416278M | 918524M | Total Assets ($) | 3175787M | 2389455M |

© RMA 2012

M = $ thousand    MM = $ million
See Pages 9 through 22 for Explanation of Ratios and Data

## Comparative Historical Data      Current Data Sorted by Sales

| | | | Type of Statement | 0-1MM | 1-3MM | 3-5MM | 5-10MM | 10-25MM | 25MM & OVER |
|---|---|---|---|---|---|---|---|---|---|
| 21 | 20 | 17 | Unqualified | | | 2 | | | 15 |
| 19 | 36 | 27 | Reviewed | | 1 | 1 | 5 | 17 | 3 |
| 17 | 20 | 16 | Compiled | 2 | 4 | 2 | 3 | 3 | 2 |
| 16 | 18 | 18 | Tax Returns | | 9 | 3 | 3 | 2 | 1 |
| 52 | 38 | 51 | Other | 3 | 4 | 9 | 3 | 5 | 16 |
| 4/1/09-3/31/10 ALL | 4/1/10-3/31/11 ALL | 4/1/11-3/31/12 ALL | | | 24 (4/1-9/30/11) | | | 105 (10/1/11-3/31/12) | |
| 125 | 132 | 129 | **NUMBER OF STATEMENTS** | 5 | 18 | 15 | 18 | 36 | 37 |
| % | % | % | **ASSETS** | % | % | % | % | % | % |
| 7.1 | 11.0 | 9.5 | Cash & Equivalents | | 12.0 | 11.4 | 11.8 | 6.4 | 9.0 |
| 24.3 | 24.7 | 24.3 | Trade Receivables (net) | | 20.1 | 23.9 | 25.5 | 29.4 | 21.6 |
| 33.0 | 32.2 | 33.1 | Inventory | | 35.3 | 31.1 | 29.4 | 36.0 | 32.3 |
| 2.3 | 3.8 | 2.6 | All Other Current | | 2.7 | .4 | 1.6 | 2.6 | 3.4 |
| 66.6 | 71.7 | 69.4 | Total Current | | 70.0 | 66.8 | 68.2 | 74.5 | 66.3 |
| 23.1 | 17.9 | 19.0 | Fixed Assets (net) | | 17.3 | 29.0 | 21.1 | 15.9 | 17.8 |
| 4.6 | 4.0 | 4.4 | Intangibles (net) | | 1.5 | 2.6 | 2.4 | 3.0 | 9.3 |
| 5.6 | 6.4 | 7.2 | All Other Non-Current | | 11.2 | 1.6 | 8.3 | 6.5 | 6.6 |
| 100.0 | 100.0 | 100.0 | Total | | 100.0 | 100.0 | 100.0 | 100.0 | 100.0 |
| | | | **LIABILITIES** | | | | | | |
| 13.3 | 10.6 | 9.8 | Notes Payable-Short Term | | 9.0 | 10.1 | 10.4 | 13.5 | 5.3 |
| 4.4 | 3.9 | 2.4 | Cur. Mat.-L.T.D. | | 3.0 | 5.1 | 2.0 | 1.6 | 2.2 |
| 17.9 | 18.2 | 16.0 | Trade Payables | | 15.0 | 20.0 | 13.8 | 17.8 | 14.5 |
| .3 | .2 | .1 | Income Taxes Payable | | .2 | .0 | .0 | .1 | .1 |
| 8.2 | 9.5 | 9.7 | All Other Current | | 9.1 | 13.0 | 6.9 | 12.6 | 7.3 |
| 44.1 | 42.4 | 38.0 | Total Current | | 36.2 | 48.2 | 33.1 | 45.6 | 29.6 |
| 16.5 | 15.6 | 15.5 | Long-Term Debt | | 27.6 | 20.7 | 14.7 | 7.1 | 17.5 |
| .6 | .4 | .6 | Deferred Taxes | | .0 | .0 | .0 | .1 | 2.0 |
| 8.3 | 8.2 | 8.1 | All Other Non-Current | | 8.3 | 11.3 | 9.6 | 4.1 | 9.4 |
| 30.5 | 33.4 | 37.7 | Net Worth | | 27.9 | 19.8 | 42.5 | 43.0 | 41.4 |
| 100.0 | 100.0 | 100.0 | Total Liabilities & Net Worth | | 100.0 | 100.0 | 100.0 | 100.0 | 100.0 |
| | | | **INCOME DATA** | | | | | | |
| 100.0 | 100.0 | 100.0 | Net Sales | | 100.0 | 100.0 | 100.0 | 100.0 | 100.0 |
| 28.4 | 30.9 | 31.3 | Gross Profit | | 41.0 | 39.6 | 28.8 | 26.9 | 26.7 |
| 25.3 | 25.4 | 26.4 | Operating Expenses | | 38.7 | 33.8 | 23.8 | 22.8 | 19.7 |
| 3.0 | 5.4 | 4.9 | Operating Profit | | 2.4 | 5.8 | 5.0 | 4.1 | 7.0 |
| 1.0 | 1.0 | .6 | All Other Expenses (net) | | .5 | .1 | .6 | -.2 | 1.1 |
| 2.1 | 4.5 | 4.3 | Profit Before Taxes | | 1.8 | 5.7 | 4.4 | 4.3 | 5.9 |
| | | | **RATIOS** | | | | | | |
| 2.7 | 3.4 | 3.5 | | | 3.8 | 3.4 | 5.1 | 2.5 | 4.1 |
| 1.6 | 1.9 | 2.0 | Current | | 2.8 | 1.5 | 2.5 | 1.7 | 2.4 |
| 1.1 | 1.3 | 1.3 | | | 1.4 | 1.2 | 1.4 | 1.2 | 1.7 |
| 1.3 | 1.6 | 1.7 | | | 1.8 | 1.4 | 2.9 | 1.0 | 2.4 |
| .7 | .9 | .9 | Quick | | 1.3 | .6 | 1.2 | .7 | 1.2 |
| .5 | .5 | .5 | | | .6 | .3 | .6 | .6 | .5 |
| 24  15.2 | 23  16.0 | 25  14.7 | | | 13  27.7 | 10  35.8 | 31  11.6 | 31  11.9 | 27  13.5 |
| 39  9.4 | 37  9.8 | 39  9.3 | Sales/Receivables | | 29  12.4 | 21  17.5 | 40  9.1 | 41  8.9 | 40  9.2 |
| 54  6.7 | 50  7.3 | 52  7.0 | | | 47  7.8 | 48  7.6 | 54  6.8 | 56  6.5 | 53  6.9 |
| 36  10.2 | 41  8.9 | 41  8.8 | | | 38  9.5 | 30  12.1 | 38  9.6 | 42  8.7 | 51  7.1 |
| 67  5.4 | 66  5.5 | 65  5.6 | Cost of Sales/Inventory | | 61  6.0 | 57  6.4 | 58  6.3 | 70  5.2 | 65  5.6 |
| 120  3.0 | 114  3.2 | 118  3.1 | | | 152  2.4 | 140  2.6 | 107  3.4 | 114  3.2 | 111  3.3 |
| 17  21.4 | 18  20.0 | 17  21.1 | | | 13  27.2 | 13  27.8 | 15  23.9 | 26  14.0 | 15  23.7 |
| 30  12.3 | 32  11.5 | 32  11.3 | Cost of Sales/Payables | | 27  13.6 | 32  11.5 | 27  13.7 | 33  11.0 | 34  10.6 |
| 49  7.5 | 45  8.0 | 47  7.8 | | | 45  8.1 | 57  6.4 | 47  7.7 | 42  8.7 | 49  7.5 |
| 4.7 | 4.1 | 4.1 | | | 3.5 | 3.7 | 3.8 | 5.5 | 4.3 |
| 7.8 | 7.2 | 6.8 | Sales/Working Capital | | 7.3 | 13.2 | 6.2 | 8.2 | 5.8 |
| 86.6 | 23.2 | 18.0 | | | 19.7 | 122.5 | 19.1 | 20.3 | 7.5 |
| 8.3 | 13.4 | 23.4 | | | 9.4 | 20.5 | 55.0 | 12.3 | 68.4 |
| (116)  3.0 | (123)  4.3 | (117)  4.6 | EBIT/Interest | | 2.8 | (13)  7.2 | (15)  11.5 | (32)  4.2 | (35)  10.2 |
| -.2 | 1.8 | 1.5 | | | .3 | 2.5 | 2.6 | 1.6 | 1.6 |
| 5.2 | 8.4 | 11.9 | Net Profit + Depr., Dep., | | | | | | 29.3 |
| (32)  2.1 | (30)  2.6 | (23)  1.9 | Amort./Cur. Mat. L/T/D | | | | | (10)  3.8 | |
| .0 | 1.3 | .4 | | | | | | | .6 |
| .2 | .1 | .2 | | | .0 | .2 | .1 | .2 | .2 |
| .6 | .4 | .4 | Fixed/Worth | | .5 | .8 | .5 | .4 | .4 |
| 1.8 | 1.8 | 1.4 | | | 2.6 | 74.3 | 1.9 | .9 | 1.9 |
| .7 | .7 | .5 | | | .4 | .8 | .6 | .8 | .4 |
| 1.8 | 1.8 | 1.5 | Debt/Worth | | 1.5 | 3.4 | 1.7 | 1.4 | 1.2 |
| 7.2 | 6.6 | 5.0 | | | 14.2 | 113.8 | 4.1 | 3.3 | 30.1 |
| 39.6 | 45.8 | 49.1 | % Profit Before Taxes/Tangible | | 48.8 | 62.2 | 68.1 | 43.7 | 47.3 |
| (105)  14.8 | (112)  22.0 | (114)  23.2 | Net Worth | | (15)  9.1 | (12)  28.2 | (17)  24.8 | 24.0 | (29)  22.9 |
| 1.0 | 7.0 | 6.9 | | | -1.6 | 5.1 | 11.2 | 5.0 | 15.7 |
| 13.0 | 14.9 | 17.1 | % Profit Before Taxes/Total | | 15.4 | 23.3 | 21.3 | 17.2 | 16.9 |
| 3.9 | 6.3 | 8.8 | Assets | | 5.0 | 11.1 | 9.0 | 6.6 | 9.3 |
| -1.6 | 2.2 | 1.8 | | | -1.2 | 3.2 | 5.0 | 2.1 | 3.7 |
| 37.5 | 56.1 | 40.5 | | | 579.9 | 30.4 | 32.8 | 53.9 | 24.7 |
| 13.1 | 21.3 | 17.2 | Sales/Net Fixed Assets | | 24.3 | 16.7 | 14.7 | 22.9 | 13.2 |
| 7.0 | 9.2 | 7.6 | | | 6.8 | 4.7 | 7.8 | 11.1 | 7.6 |
| 3.1 | 3.2 | 2.9 | | | 4.8 | 5.0 | 2.6 | 2.9 | 2.7 |
| 2.2 | 2.3 | 2.3 | Sales/Total Assets | | 2.2 | 3.3 | 2.1 | 2.4 | 2.0 |
| 1.6 | 1.6 | 1.6 | | | 1.4 | 1.7 | 1.7 | 1.8 | 1.5 |
| .7 | .6 | .7 | | | 1.0 | .3 | .4 | .6 | .7 |
| (104)  1.5 | (108)  1.3 | (97)  1.2 | % Depr., Dep., Amort./Sales | | (12)  1.7 | (11)  1.0 | (12)  1.3 | (32)  1.0 | (28)  1.4 |
| 2.8 | 2.7 | 2.7 | | | 3.4 | 2.0 | 3.5 | 1.5 | 3.1 |
| 1.5 | 1.5 | 1.9 | % Officers', Directors' | | 3.2 | | | 1.7 | |
| (44)  3.6 | (50)  2.5 | (45)  3.4 | Owners' Comp/Sales | | (10)  6.4 | | | (10)  2.8 | |
| 5.6 | 5.5 | 6.4 | | | 8.2 | | | 4.4 | |
| 4049995M | 3448608M | 4095592M | Net Sales ($) | 3293M | 33237M | 58801M | 124441M | 574448M | 3301372M |
| 2281048M | 1775095M | 2319430M | Total Assets ($) | 10269M | 16791M | 36148M | 63461M | 253494M | 1939267M |

M = $ thousand     MM = $ million
See Pages 9 through 22 for Explanation of Ratios and Data

### Current Data Sorted by Assets | Comparative Historical Data

| 0-500M | 500M-2MM | 2-10MM | 10-50MM | 50-100MM | 100-250MM | Type of Statement | 4/1/07-3/31/08 ALL | 4/1/08-3/31/09 ALL |
|---|---|---|---|---|---|---|---|---|
| | | 1 | 3 | 2 | | Unqualified | 17 | 18 |
| | 1 | 3 | 6 | | | Reviewed | 14 | 16 |
| | | 2 | 1 | | | Compiled | 6 | 2 |
| 2 | 2 | 2 | | | | Tax Returns | 2 | 1 |
| | 2 | 4 | 5 | 3 | 3 | Other | 16 | 17 |
| 9 (4/1-9/30/11) | | | 33 (10/1/11-3/31/12) | | | | | |
| 2 | 5 | 12 | 15 | 5 | 3 | **NUMBER OF STATEMENTS** | 55 | 54 |
| % | % | % | % | % | % | **ASSETS** | % | % |
| | | 7.1 | 15.3 | | | Cash & Equivalents | 10.5 | 9.8 |
| | | 35.6 | 18.4 | | | Trade Receivables (net) | 25.9 | 32.6 |
| | | 39.0 | 40.5 | | | Inventory | 35.9 | 34.7 |
| | | .8 | 1.9 | | | All Other Current | 4.9 | 3.8 |
| | | 82.6 | 76.1 | | | Total Current | 77.2 | 80.9 |
| | | 10.3 | 15.5 | | | Fixed Assets (net) | 12.7 | 10.7 |
| | | 1.2 | 4.2 | | | Intangibles (net) | 4.3 | 1.9 |
| | | 6.0 | 4.2 | | | All Other Non-Current | 5.9 | 6.5 |
| | | 100.0 | 100.0 | | | Total | 100.0 | 100.0 |
| | | | | | | **LIABILITIES** | | |
| | | 12.9 | 5.8 | | | Notes Payable-Short Term | 13.8 | 15.8 |
| | | 2.2 | 1.1 | | | Cur. Mat.-L.T.D. | 2.8 | 4.1 |
| | | 12.0 | 18.8 | | | Trade Payables | 14.5 | 16.4 |
| | | .0 | .1 | | | Income Taxes Payable | .6 | .2 |
| | | 5.9 | 7.3 | | | All Other Current | 8.3 | 9.5 |
| | | 33.0 | 33.0 | | | Total Current | 39.9 | 46.0 |
| | | 5.1 | 14.2 | | | Long-Term Debt | 11.1 | 6.7 |
| | | .3 | .1 | | | Deferred Taxes | .2 | .1 |
| | | 20.0 | 4.5 | | | All Other Non-Current | 3.5 | 5.1 |
| | | 41.5 | 48.2 | | | Net Worth | 45.3 | 41.9 |
| | | 100.0 | 100.0 | | | Total Liabilities & Net Worth | 100.0 | 100.0 |
| | | | | | | **INCOME DATA** | | |
| | | 100.0 | 100.0 | | | Net Sales | 100.0 | 100.0 |
| | | 31.2 | 30.4 | | | Gross Profit | 31.8 | 32.5 |
| | | 27.2 | 20.3 | | | Operating Expenses | 29.2 | 28.0 |
| | | 4.1 | 10.1 | | | Operating Profit | 2.5 | 4.5 |
| | | 1.4 | 2.8 | | | All Other Expenses (net) | .4 | .4 |
| | | 2.7 | 7.2 | | | Profit Before Taxes | 2.1 | 4.1 |
| | | | | | | **RATIOS** | | |
| | | 12.3 | 4.3 | | | | 4.6 | 2.6 |
| | | 2.1 | 2.4 | | | Current | 1.9 | 1.9 |
| | | 1.6 | 1.4 | | | | 1.5 | 1.4 |
| | | 6.4 | 1.7 | | | | 1.9 | 1.5 |
| | | 1.1 | .9 | | | Quick | 1.0 | .9 |
| | | .5 | .4 | | | | .5 | .5 |
| | | 42  8.7 | 13  28.5 | | | | 19  19.0 | 28  13.2 |
| | | 54  6.7 | 32  11.5 | | | Sales/Receivables | 38  9.6 | 48  7.6 |
| | | 81  4.5 | 53  6.9 | | | | 54  6.7 | 74  5.0 |
| | | 44  8.3 | 42  8.7 | | | | 40  9.2 | 49  7.4 |
| | | 104  3.5 | 81  4.5 | | | Cost of Sales/Inventory | 89  4.1 | 89  4.1 |
| | | 166  2.2 | 243  1.5 | | | | 188  1.9 | 133  2.8 |
| | | 17  21.9 | 13  28.8 | | | | 16  23.2 | 18  20.7 |
| | | 29  12.7 | 31  11.6 | | | Cost of Sales/Payables | 25  14.7 | 29  12.4 |
| | | 41  8.9 | 83  4.4 | | | | 42  8.6 | 52  7.0 |
| | | 2.5 | 3.3 | | | | 3.2 | 3.9 |
| | | 4.0 | 5.3 | | | Sales/Working Capital | 4.8 | 6.1 |
| | | 6.9 | 10.4 | | | | 15.4 | 11.5 |
| | | | 14.3 | | | | 9.0 | 12.5 |
| | | (11) | 3.7 | | | EBIT/Interest | (47) 2.7 | (48) 3.5 |
| | | | 1.6 | | | | -.2 | 1.3 |
| | | | | | | | | 14.8 |
| | | | | | | Net Profit + Depr., Dep., | (14) | 3.9 |
| | | | | | | Amort./Cur. Mat. L/T/D | | .7 |
| | | .1 | .0 | | | | .1 | .0 |
| | | .2 | .2 | | | Fixed/Worth | .2 | .1 |
| | | .8 | .4 | | | | .7 | .5 |
| | | .7 | .4 | | | | .4 | .6 |
| | | 1.6 | 1.2 | | | Debt/Worth | 1.4 | 1.4 |
| | | 7.7 | 1.9 | | | | 3.7 | 3.4 |
| | | 40.6 | 29.9 | | | | 34.9 | 36.5 |
| | | 20.6 | (14) 10.1 | | | % Profit Before Taxes/Tangible Net Worth | (49) 10.8 | (51) 16.8 |
| | | 2.6 | 2.9 | | | | -8.5 | 3.7 |
| | | 7.9 | 8.4 | | | | 16.3 | 16.4 |
| | | 5.7 | 4.6 | | | % Profit Before Taxes/Total Assets | 5.2 | 5.8 |
| | | .6 | 1.0 | | | | -2.4 | 1.3 |
| | | 63.8 | 95.8 | | | | 101.6 | 183.1 |
| | | 21.3 | 26.9 | | | Sales/Net Fixed Assets | 26.2 | 39.1 |
| | | 11.0 | 11.3 | | | | 14.1 | 14.2 |
| | | 2.6 | 2.6 | | | | 3.0 | 2.9 |
| | | 2.0 | 2.0 | | | Sales/Total Assets | 2.2 | 2.2 |
| | | 1.5 | 1.4 | | | | 1.5 | 1.7 |
| | | .2 | .8 | | | | .4 | .3 |
| | | .7 | (13) 1.0 | | | % Depr., Dep., Amort./Sales | (41) .9 | (46) .7 |
| | | 1.3 | 1.9 | | | | 1.7 | 1.0 |
| | | | | | | | 2.0 | 2.5 |
| | | | | | | % Officers', Directors' Owners' Comp/Sales | (20) 5.0 | (18) 4.0 |
| | | | | | | | 11.3 | 5.9 |
| 2734M | 15907M | 161319M | 726727M | 401992M | 804927M | Net Sales ($) | 2223090M | 3108503M |
| 642M | 5354M | 72406M | 336834M | 343371M | 566554M | Total Assets ($) | 1086770M | 1452377M |

M = $ thousand     MM = $ million
See Pages 9 through 22 for Explanation of Ratios and Data

## Comparative Historical Data — Current Data Sorted by Sales

| Hist 1 | Hist 2 | Hist 3 | Type of Statement | 0-1MM | 1-3MM | 3-5MM | 5-10MM | 10-25MM | 25MM & OVER |
|---|---|---|---|---|---|---|---|---|---|
| 14 | 8 | 6 | Unqualified | | | | | 1 | 5 |
| 16 | 16 | 10 | Reviewed | | | 2 | | 4 | 4 |
| 7 | 4 | 3 | Compiled | | | | 1 | 1 | 1 |
| 7 | 8 | 6 | Tax Returns | | | 2 | 2 | | |
| 17 | 23 | 17 | Other | 1 | 3 | 2 | 2 | 3 | 10 |
| 4/1/09-3/31/10 ALL | 4/1/10-3/31/11 ALL | 4/1/11-3/31/12 ALL | | | 9 (4/1-9/30/11) | | | 33 (10/1/11-3/31/12) | |
| | | | | 0-1MM | 1-3MM | 3-5MM | 5-10MM | 10-25MM | 25MM & OVER |
| 61 | 59 | 42 | **NUMBER OF STATEMENTS** | 1 | 5 | 4 | 3 | 9 | 20 |
| % | % | % | **ASSETS** | % | % | % | % | % | % |
| 13.0 | 7.8 | 10.5 | Cash & Equivalents | | | | | | 13.7 |
| 31.3 | 27.8 | 23.7 | Trade Receivables (net) | | | | | | 22.7 |
| 33.3 | 37.8 | 39.7 | Inventory | | | | | | 37.0 |
| 2.0 | 3.4 | 3.5 | All Other Current | | | | | | 2.1 |
| 79.6 | 76.8 | 77.4 | Total Current | | | | | | 75.4 |
| 10.5 | 9.0 | 12.3 | Fixed Assets (net) | | | | | | 11.8 |
| 1.9 | 5.2 | 5.0 | Intangibles (net) | | | | | | 7.0 |
| 8.1 | 9.0 | 5.3 | All Other Non-Current | | | | | | 5.7 |
| 100.0 | 100.0 | 100.0 | Total | | | | | | 100.0 |
| | | | **LIABILITIES** | | | | | | |
| 12.2 | 15.5 | 10.1 | Notes Payable-Short Term | | | | | | 7.3 |
| 3.8 | 4.1 | 3.5 | Cur. Mat.-L.T.D. | | | | | | .8 |
| 17.6 | 13.4 | 13.6 | Trade Payables | | | | | | 14.2 |
| .1 | .2 | .2 | Income Taxes Payable | | | | | | .3 |
| 9.3 | 12.8 | 8.5 | All Other Current | | | | | | 9.6 |
| 43.1 | 46.1 | 35.9 | Total Current | | | | | | 32.2 |
| 6.3 | 6.0 | 9.9 | Long-Term Debt | | | | | | 8.9 |
| .2 | .3 | .8 | Deferred Taxes | | | | | | 1.3 |
| 3.9 | 5.5 | 10.9 | All Other Non-Current | | | | | | 4.1 |
| 46.6 | 42.1 | 42.4 | Net Worth | | | | | | 53.4 |
| 100.0 | 100.0 | 100.0 | Total Liabilities & Net Worth | | | | | | 100.0 |
| | | | **INCOME DATA** | | | | | | |
| 100.0 | 100.0 | 100.0 | Net Sales | | | | | | 100.0 |
| 32.8 | 33.5 | 33.3 | Gross Profit | | | | | | 28.1 |
| 28.3 | 26.5 | 26.5 | Operating Expenses | | | | | | 20.2 |
| 4.5 | 7.0 | 6.8 | Operating Profit | | | | | | 7.9 |
| .7 | 1.4 | 1.9 | All Other Expenses (net) | | | | | | 1.0 |
| 3.8 | 5.7 | 4.9 | Profit Before Taxes | | | | | | 6.9 |
| | | | **RATIOS** | | | | | | |
| 4.2 | 3.0 | 4.8 | | | | | | | 4.9 |
| 2.0 | 1.7 | 2.3 | Current | | | | | | 2.8 |
| 1.3 | 1.3 | 1.6 | | | | | | | 1.7 |
| 2.6 | 1.6 | 2.2 | | | | | | | 2.4 |
| 1.0 | .8 | .9 | Quick | | | | | | 1.1 |
| .6 | .5 | .4 | | | | | | | .6 |
| 29  12.6 | 26  13.9 | 22  16.4 | | | | | | | 23  15.6 |
| 46  8.0 | 46  8.0 | 46  8.0 | Sales/Receivables | | | | | | 49  7.5 |
| 67  5.5 | 63  5.8 | 64  5.7 | | | | | | | 58  6.3 |
| 43  8.4 | 50  7.3 | 54  6.8 | | | | | | | 52  7.0 |
| 84  4.3 | 89  4.1 | 118  3.1 | Cost of Sales/Inventory | | | | | | 91  4.0 |
| 132  2.8 | 165  2.2 | 166  2.2 | | | | | | | 166  2.2 |
| 12  31.4 | 9  42.0 | 10  36.4 | | | | | | | 9  40.1 |
| 33  11.0 | 31  11.9 | 30  12.2 | Cost of Sales/Payables | | | | | | 28  13.0 |
| 66  5.5 | 45  8.1 | 47  7.7 | | | | | | | 41  9.0 |
| 3.2 | 4.0 | 2.8 | | | | | | | 2.6 |
| 5.5 | 6.9 | 4.6 | Sales/Working Capital | | | | | | 3.9 |
| 12.9 | 15.6 | 10.5 | | | | | | | 10.2 |
| 24.3 | 31.2 | 14.2 | | | | | | | 27.2 |
| (52)  5.0 | (52)  6.8 | (32)  2.8 | EBIT/Interest | | | | | | (16)  4.7 |
| 1.3 | 1.5 | 1.4 | | | | | | | 1.3 |
| | | | Net Profit + Depr., Dep., Amort./Cur. Mat. L/T/D | | | | | | |
| .0 | .0 | .1 | | | | | | | .0 |
| .1 | .2 | .2 | Fixed/Worth | | | | | | .2 |
| .4 | .6 | .7 | | | | | | | .6 |
| .4 | .6 | .4 | | | | | | | .3 |
| 1.0 | 1.3 | 1.4 | Debt/Worth | | | | | | .8 |
| 2.3 | 3.0 | 6.0 | | | | | | | 2.6 |
| 35.9 | 42.4 | 35.8 | | | | | | | 24.0 |
| (56)  16.2 | (51)  22.1 | (36)  14.3 | % Profit Before Taxes/Tangible Net Worth | | | | | | (18)  12.7 |
| .9 | 3.3 | 2.4 | | | | | | | 4.6 |
| 15.0 | 18.7 | 11.7 | | | | | | | 15.8 |
| 6.6 | 9.0 | 5.9 | % Profit Before Taxes/Total Assets | | | | | | 6.7 |
| .1 | 1.7 | 1.0 | | | | | | | 1.0 |
| 257.3 | 159.3 | 72.9 | | | | | | | 55.3 |
| 35.8 | 34.6 | 19.7 | Sales/Net Fixed Assets | | | | | | 15.4 |
| 12.8 | 13.7 | 10.8 | | | | | | | 10.2 |
| 3.1 | 2.8 | 2.6 | | | | | | | 2.6 |
| 2.3 | 2.2 | 1.9 | Sales/Total Assets | | | | | | 1.9 |
| 1.6 | 1.6 | 1.4 | | | | | | | 1.3 |
| .3 | .4 | .4 | | | | | | | .7 |
| (51)  .7 | (43)  .8 | (36)  .9 | % Depr., Dep., Amort./Sales | | | | | | (18)  .9 |
| 1.3 | 1.4 | 1.7 | | | | | | | 1.8 |
| 2.6 | 2.3 | 2.7 | | | | | | | |
| (23)  4.6 | (19)  3.4 | (10)  4.0 | % Officers', Directors' Owners' Comp/Sales | | | | | | |
| 7.2 | 6.1 | 8.7 | | | | | | | |
| 2366539M | 2439047M | 2113606M | Net Sales ($) | 879M | 10389M | 16742M | 23170M | 155439M | 1906987M |
| 1198601M | 1499208M | 1325161M | Total Assets ($) | 325M | 16108M | 10941M | 10955M | 94652M | 1192180M |

© RMA 2012

M = $ thousand    MM = $ million
See Pages 9 through 22 for Explanation of Ratios and Data

## Current Data Sorted by Assets | Comparative Historical Data

| 0-500M | 500M-2MM | 2-10MM | 10-50MM | 50-100MM | 100-250MM | Type of Statement | 4/1/07-3/31/08 ALL | 4/1/08-3/31/09 ALL |
|---|---|---|---|---|---|---|---|---|
| | | | 2 | 1 | 4 | Unqualified | 14 | 18 |
| | 3 | 8 | 3 | | 1 | Reviewed | 2 | 6 |
| | | | 1 | | | Compiled | 1 | 1 |
| 1 | 1 | 1 | | | | Tax Returns | 1 | 2 |
| 1 | | 2 | 6 | 1 | 2 | Other | 11 | 11 |
| | 4 (4/1-9/30/11) | | 34 (10/1/11-3/31/12) | | | | | |
| 2 | 4 | 11 | 12 | 2 | 7 | **NUMBER OF STATEMENTS** | 29 | 38 |
| % | % | % | % | % | % | **ASSETS** | % | % |
| | | 8.4 | 9.9 | | | Cash & Equivalents | 11.1 | 10.2 |
| | | 43.7 | 32.9 | | | Trade Receivables (net) | 29.5 | 27.7 |
| | | 28.8 | 42.3 | | | Inventory | 34.8 | 36.5 |
| | | 2.3 | 2.3 | | | All Other Current | 4.5 | 5.4 |
| | | 83.2 | 87.4 | | | Total Current | 79.9 | 79.8 |
| | | 6.7 | 5.8 | | | Fixed Assets (net) | 9.7 | 9.4 |
| | | 2.5 | 3.2 | | | Intangibles (net) | 5.9 | 5.0 |
| | | 7.7 | 3.7 | | | All Other Non-Current | 4.5 | 5.7 |
| | | 100.0 | 100.0 | | | Total | 100.0 | 100.0 |
| | | | | | | **LIABILITIES** | | |
| | | 21.2 | 13.0 | | | Notes Payable-Short Term | 13.1 | 15.5 |
| | | .7 | .1 | | | Cur. Mat.-L.T.D. | 5.7 | 1.9 |
| | | 24.9 | 21.5 | | | Trade Payables | 12.3 | 19.0 |
| | | .1 | .1 | | | Income Taxes Payable | .6 | .4 |
| | | 4.0 | 15.1 | | | All Other Current | 10.7 | 12.9 |
| | | 50.9 | 49.8 | | | Total Current | 42.4 | 49.7 |
| | | 1.2 | .3 | | | Long-Term Debt | 9.5 | 5.8 |
| | | .0 | .0 | | | Deferred Taxes | .3 | .2 |
| | | 5.5 | 31.7 | | | All Other Non-Current | 13.7 | 16.6 |
| | | 42.5 | 18.2 | | | Net Worth | 34.1 | 27.6 |
| | | 100.0 | 100.0 | | | Total Liabilities & Net Worth | 100.0 | 100.0 |
| | | | | | | **INCOME DATA** | | |
| | | 100.0 | 100.0 | | | Net Sales | 100.0 | 100.0 |
| | | 29.7 | 37.9 | | | Gross Profit | 36.8 | 34.9 |
| | | 27.3 | 25.6 | | | Operating Expenses | 30.2 | 30.8 |
| | | 2.4 | 12.3 | | | Operating Profit | 6.6 | 4.1 |
| | | .5 | .7 | | | All Other Expenses (net) | 1.2 | 1.2 |
| | | 1.9 | 11.6 | | | Profit Before Taxes | 5.4 | 2.9 |
| | | | | | | **RATIOS** | | |
| | | 2.6 | 4.4 | | | | 3.4 | 3.9 |
| | | 1.6 | 2.0 | | | Current | 2.1 | 1.9 |
| | | 1.5 | 1.2 | | | | 1.4 | 1.2 |
| | | 1.4 | 1.5 | | | | 1.8 | 1.6 |
| | | 1.0 | .8 | | | Quick | 1.0 | .8 |
| | | .8 | .6 | | | | .5 | .3 |
| | | 37  9.8 | 25  14.6 | | | | 21  17.2 | 7  50.8 |
| | | 66  5.5 | 44  8.3 | | | Sales/Receivables | 47  7.8 | 36  10.1 |
| | | 76  4.8 | 69  5.3 | | | | 65  5.6 | 53  6.8 |
| | | 27  13.5 | 53  6.9 | | | | 52  7.0 | 43  8.5 |
| | | 63  5.8 | 94  3.9 | | | Cost of Sales/Inventory | 66  5.5 | 58  6.3 |
| | | 74  4.9 | 140  2.6 | | | | 133  2.7 | 120  3.0 |
| | | 12  29.3 | 17  21.0 | | | | 16  22.9 | 15  24.3 |
| | | 41  9.0 | 33  10.9 | | | Cost of Sales/Payables | 27  13.6 | 22  16.8 |
| | | 51  7.1 | 87  4.2 | | | | 37  9.8 | 42  8.8 |
| | | 4.6 | 3.4 | | | | 3.8 | 4.1 |
| | | 8.7 | 6.3 | | | Sales/Working Capital | 6.3 | 9.9 |
| | | 12.8 | 21.3 | | | | 15.6 | 36.7 |
| | | 4.8 | 49.2 | | | | 7.5 | 7.7 |
| | | (10)  3.2 | (11)  20.3 | | | EBIT/Interest | (27)  4.3 | (33)  3.5 |
| | | 1.7 | 9.0 | | | | 1.9 | .8 |
| | | | | | | Net Profit + Depr., Dep., Amort./Cur. Mat. L/T/D | | |
| | | .0 | .1 | | | | .1 | .1 |
| | | .1 | .2 | | | Fixed/Worth | .1 | .1 |
| | | .2 | .3 | | | | NM | -7.5 |
| | | .6 | .7 | | | | .5 | .5 |
| | | 1.4 | 2.6 | | | Debt/Worth | 1.7 | 1.8 |
| | | 4.0 | 5.7 | | | | NM | -8.4 |
| | | 27.5 | 103.4 | | | | 54.3 | 53.8 |
| | | 10.5 | (10)  74.2 | | | % Profit Before Taxes/Tangible Net Worth | (22)  30.3 | (27)  31.3 |
| | | 2.8 | 27.7 | | | | 6.4 | 14.0 |
| | | 9.7 | 40.2 | | | | 21.7 | 21.6 |
| | | 2.8 | 22.1 | | | % Profit Before Taxes/Total Assets | 11.6 | 9.0 |
| | | 1.1 | 9.8 | | | | 3.6 | -.7 |
| | | 166.2 | 144.3 | | | | 152.5 | 176.5 |
| | | 61.3 | 65.5 | | | Sales/Net Fixed Assets | 38.9 | 53.5 |
| | | 23.2 | 25.1 | | | | 12.1 | 19.6 |
| | | 3.7 | 3.8 | | | | 3.0 | 4.2 |
| | | 2.8 | 2.9 | | | Sales/Total Assets | 2.4 | 2.8 |
| | | 1.6 | 1.7 | | | | 2.0 | 2.1 |
| | | | .3 | | | | .3 | .2 |
| | | (11) | .5 | | | % Depr., Dep., Amort./Sales | (23)  .5 | (31)  .7 |
| | | | .9 | | | | .9 | 1.0 |
| | | | | | | | | 1.8 |
| | | | | | | % Officers', Directors' Owners' Comp/Sales | | (12)  3.8 |
| | | | | | | | | 6.2 |
| 2273M | 20775M | 151204M | 955525M | 264654M | 1796281M | Net Sales ($) | 4323863M | 4350563M |
| 649M | 5262M | 60638M | 336671M | 146503M | 982341M | Total Assets ($) | 2081015M | 1839155M |

M = $ thousand    MM = $ million
See Pages 9 through 22 for Explanation of Ratios and Data

## Comparative Historical Data

## Current Data Sorted by Sales

| | | | Type of Statement | 0-1MM | 1-3MM | 3-5MM | 5-10MM | 10-25MM | 25MM & OVER |
|---|---|---|---|---|---|---|---|---|---|
| 18 | 14 | 7 | Unqualified | 1 | | 2 | 2 | 6 | 7 |
| 6 | 12 | 15 | Reviewed | | | | | | 4 |
| 2 | | 1 | Compiled | | | | | | 1 |
| 3 | 3 | 3 | Tax Returns | | 1 | | 1 | 1 | 2 |
| 12 | 19 | 12 | Other | 1 | | | 1 | | 8 |
| 4/1/09-3/31/10 ALL | 4/1/10-3/31/11 ALL | 4/1/11-3/31/12 ALL | | | 4 (4/1-9/30/11) | | 34 (10/1/11-3/31/12) | | |
| 41 | 48 | 38 | NUMBER OF STATEMENTS | 2 | 1 | 2 | 4 | 9 | 20 |
| % | % | % | ASSETS | % | % | % | % | % | % |
| 15.3 | 10.6 | 7.8 | Cash & Equivalents | | | | | | 9.0 |
| 29.9 | 32.0 | 34.6 | Trade Receivables (net) | | | | | | 31.0 |
| 28.7 | 32.5 | 35.3 | Inventory | | | | | | 37.2 |
| 3.3 | 3.5 | 4.7 | All Other Current | | | | | | 5.3 |
| 77.1 | 78.5 | 82.4 | Total Current | | | | | | 82.5 |
| 11.0 | 9.6 | 7.5 | Fixed Assets (net) | | | | | | 7.6 |
| 6.9 | 6.4 | 4.1 | Intangibles (net) | | | | | | 6.4 |
| 5.0 | 5.4 | 6.0 | All Other Non-Current | | | | | | 3.5 |
| 100.0 | 100.0 | 100.0 | Total | | | | | | 100.0 |
| | | | LIABILITIES | | | | | | |
| 18.1 | 17.2 | 16.0 | Notes Payable-Short Term | | | | | | 18.7 |
| 2.5 | 3.2 | 1.3 | Cur. Mat.-L.T.D. | | | | | | .7 |
| 17.7 | 17.4 | 20.8 | Trade Payables | | | | | | 15.8 |
| .1 | .2 | .1 | Income Taxes Payable | | | | | | .1 |
| 20.6 | 9.1 | 8.5 | All Other Current | | | | | | 12.4 |
| 59.1 | 47.2 | 46.6 | Total Current | | | | | | 47.8 |
| 4.8 | 8.6 | 8.5 | Long-Term Debt | | | | | | 5.7 |
| .2 | .0 | .0 | Deferred Taxes | | | | | | .0 |
| 16.9 | 22.4 | 15.3 | All Other Non-Current | | | | | | 22.4 |
| 18.9 | 21.9 | 29.5 | Net Worth | | | | | | 24.2 |
| 100.0 | 100.0 | 100.0 | Total Liabilities & Net Worth | | | | | | 100.0 |
| | | | INCOME DATA | | | | | | |
| 100.0 | 100.0 | 100.0 | Net Sales | | | | | | 100.0 |
| 32.8 | 36.5 | 34.3 | Gross Profit | | | | | | 33.1 |
| 28.8 | 31.3 | 28.4 | Operating Expenses | | | | | | 24.0 |
| 4.0 | 5.2 | 6.0 | Operating Profit | | | | | | 9.1 |
| 1.7 | .6 | 1.5 | All Other Expenses (net) | | | | | | 2.7 |
| 2.3 | 4.6 | 4.5 | Profit Before Taxes | | | | | | 6.4 |
| | | | RATIOS | | | | | | |
| 2.8 | 3.1 | 3.2 | | | | | | | 4.4 |
| 1.8 | 1.8 | 1.8 | Current | | | | | | 1.9 |
| 1.1 | 1.2 | 1.3 | | | | | | | 1.2 |
| 1.7 | 1.5 | 1.5 | | | | | | | 1.3 |
| 1.0 | .8 | .9 | Quick | | | | | | .8 |
| .5 | .6 | .5 | | | | | | | .5 |
| 22  16.6 | 18  19.7 | 27  13.4 | | | | | | 31 | 11.9 |
| 41  8.9 | 41  8.8 | 57  6.4 | Sales/Receivables | | | | | 50 | 7.3 |
| 64  5.7 | 64  5.7 | 73  5.0 | | | | | | 72 | 5.1 |
| 29  12.5 | 34  10.8 | 46  7.9 | | | | | | 51 | 7.1 |
| 43  8.4 | 62  5.9 | 74  4.9 | Cost of Sales/Inventory | | | | | 83 | 4.4 |
| 88  4.1 | 99  3.7 | 130  2.8 | | | | | | 126 | 2.9 |
| 17  21.4 | 17  21.2 | 16  22.6 | | | | | | 17 | 21.4 |
| 28  13.3 | 28  13.2 | 33  11.0 | Cost of Sales/Payables | | | | | 24 | 15.0 |
| 47  7.8 | 46  7.9 | 57  6.4 | | | | | | 56 | 6.5 |
| 4.6 | 5.0 | 4.3 | | | | | | | 3.7 |
| 9.5 | 10.4 | 7.0 | Sales/Working Capital | | | | | | 6.9 |
| 38.0 | 27.3 | 13.5 | | | | | | | 21.3 |
| 10.4 | 14.2 | 20.3 | | | | | | | 43.6 |
| (37)  2.1 | (44)  4.5 | (35)  4.4 | EBIT/Interest | | | | | (18) | 10.9 |
| 1.0 | 1.0 | 1.8 | | | | | | | 1.9 |
| 47.9 | | | Net Profit + Depr., Dep., | | | | | | |
| (10)  2.5 | | | Amort./Cur. Mat. L/T/D | | | | | | |
| -24.6 | | | | | | | | | |
| .1 | .1 | .0 | | | | | | | .1 |
| .2 | .2 | .2 | Fixed/Worth | | | | | | .2 |
| NM | 2.1 | .9 | | | | | | | 1.1 |
| .7 | 1.0 | .7 | | | | | | | .7 |
| 2.1 | 2.5 | 2.4 | Debt/Worth | | | | | | 3.8 |
| -20.5 | 11.4 | 6.5 | | | | | | | 18.2 |
| 70.0 | 74.5 | 69.4 | % Profit Before Taxes/Tangible | | | | | | 83.9 |
| (30)  32.0 | (38)  26.9 | (33)  16.6 | Net Worth | | | | | (16) | 42.7 |
| 6.8 | 6.5 | 4.1 | | | | | | | 9.3 |
| 12.6 | 20.6 | 18.5 | % Profit Before Taxes/Total | | | | | | 32.2 |
| 5.8 | 10.8 | 7.4 | Assets | | | | | | 12.4 |
| .3 | .7 | 2.4 | | | | | | | 4.0 |
| 149.3 | 169.6 | 154.7 | | | | | | | 118.8 |
| 51.6 | 61.8 | 56.3 | Sales/Net Fixed Assets | | | | | | 56.3 |
| 13.7 | 17.6 | 19.9 | | | | | | | 23.6 |
| 3.6 | 3.6 | 3.5 | | | | | | | 3.1 |
| 2.7 | 2.6 | 2.7 | Sales/Total Assets | | | | | | 2.4 |
| 2.0 | 2.1 | 1.6 | | | | | | | 1.6 |
| .2 | .2 | .3 | | | | | | | .3 |
| (32)  .5 | (37)  .5 | (28)  .7 | % Depr., Dep., Amort./Sales | | | | | (16) | .7 |
| 1.5 | 1.4 | .9 | | | | | | | 1.3 |
| .9 | 1.5 | 1.1 | % Officers', Directors' | | | | | | |
| (15)  2.7 | (22)  3.7 | (16)  3.3 | Owners' Comp/Sales | | | | | | |
| 5.0 | 6.2 | 5.0 | | | | | | | |
| 3469632M | 4514737M | 3190712M | Net Sales ($) | 1796M | 1458M | 8300M | 33553M | 153683M | 2991922M |
| 1682373M | 1928583M | 1532064M | Total Assets ($) | 785M | 428M | 7740M | 13523M | 60413M | 1449175M |

© RMA 2012

M = $ thousand     MM = $ million
See Pages 9 through 22 for Explanation of Ratios and Data

## Current Data Sorted by Assets  —  Comparative Historical Data

| 0-500M | 500M-2MM | 2-10MM | 10-50MM | 50-100MM | 100-250MM | | 4/1/07-3/31/08 ALL | 4/1/08-3/31/09 ALL |
|---|---|---|---|---|---|---|---|---|
| | | | | | | **Type of Statement** | | |
| | | 1 | | | 2 | Unqualified | 11 | 9 |
| | 1 | 3 | 1 | | | Reviewed | 6 | 4 |
| | 1 | | | | | Compiled | 2 | 1 |
| 2 | | 2 | | | 2 | Tax Returns | 2 | 2 |
| 1 | | 4 | 1 | 3 | | Other | 5 | 6 |
| 3 | 2 | 10 | 2 | 3 | 4 | **NUMBER OF STATEMENTS** | 26 | 22 |
| % | % | % | % | % | % | | % | % |
| | | | | | | **ASSETS** | | |
| | | 9.0 | | | | Cash & Equivalents | 8.2 | 4.7 |
| | | 21.8 | | | | Trade Receivables (net) | 28.1 | 25.9 |
| | | 47.2 | | | | Inventory | 40.0 | 44.7 |
| | | 7.5 | | | | All Other Current | 4.6 | 2.8 |
| | | 85.5 | | | | Total Current | 80.9 | 78.2 |
| | | 10.5 | | | | Fixed Assets (net) | 8.4 | 10.3 |
| | | .6 | | | | Intangibles (net) | 3.8 | 3.9 |
| | | 3.4 | | | | All Other Non-Current | 6.9 | 7.6 |
| | | 100.0 | | | | Total | 100.0 | 100.0 |
| | | | | | | **LIABILITIES** | | |
| | | 20.5 | | | | Notes Payable-Short Term | 11.0 | 15.2 |
| | | 6.3 | | | | Cur. Mat.-L.T.D. | 4.1 | 2.7 |
| | | 22.1 | | | | Trade Payables | 14.4 | 14.8 |
| | | .1 | | | | Income Taxes Payable | .2 | .3 |
| | | 4.7 | | | | All Other Current | 12.5 | 9.3 |
| | | 53.8 | | | | Total Current | 42.2 | 42.3 |
| | | 4.7 | | | | Long-Term Debt | 7.1 | 13.4 |
| | | .1 | | | | Deferred Taxes | .4 | .5 |
| | | 3.8 | | | | All Other Non-Current | 1.4 | 1.5 |
| | | 37.6 | | | | Net Worth | 48.9 | 42.3 |
| | | 100.0 | | | | Total Liabilities & Net Worth | 100.0 | 100.0 |
| | | | | | | **INCOME DATA** | | |
| | | 100.0 | | | | Net Sales | 100.0 | 100.0 |
| | | 28.6 | | | | Gross Profit | 33.9 | 34.0 |
| | | 24.6 | | | | Operating Expenses | 29.2 | 29.7 |
| | | 4.0 | | | | Operating Profit | 4.7 | 4.2 |
| | | .8 | | | | All Other Expenses (net) | .9 | 1.3 |
| | | 3.2 | | | | Profit Before Taxes | 3.8 | 3.0 |
| | | | | | | **RATIOS** | | |
| | | 3.0 | | | | | 2.8 | 2.6 |
| | | 1.8 | | | | Current | 2.2 | 1.9 |
| | | 1.3 | | | | | 1.3 | 1.3 |
| | | .8 | | | | | 1.3 | 1.1 |
| | | .6 | | | | Quick | 1.0 | .7 |
| | | .2 | | | | | .4 | .5 |
| | | 6    63.7 | | | | | 21    17.1 | 18    19.9 |
| | | 18    20.3 | | | | Sales/Receivables | 38    9.5 | 39    9.4 |
| | | 73    5.0 | | | | | 49    7.5 | 67    5.5 |
| | | 24    15.3 | | | | | 54    6.7 | 76    4.8 |
| | | 89    4.1 | | | | Cost of Sales/Inventory | 75    4.8 | 106    3.4 |
| | | 159    2.3 | | | | | 117    3.1 | 147    2.5 |
| | | 17    21.7 | | | | | 14    26.8 | 14    26.7 |
| | | 36    10.2 | | | | Cost of Sales/Payables | 26    13.8 | 30    12.0 |
| | | 74    4.9 | | | | | 43    8.5 | 61    5.9 |
| | | 3.6 | | | | | 4.7 | 4.6 |
| | | 6.9 | | | | Sales/Working Capital | 6.6 | 6.6 |
| | | NM | | | | | 11.8 | 15.8 |
| | | 8.4 | | | | | 16.9 | 7.3 |
| | | 4.4 | | | | EBIT/Interest | (23)    2.6 | (20)    2.0 |
| | | 1.7 | | | | | 1.3 | 1.2 |
| | | | | | | Net Profit + Depr., Dep., Amort./Cur. Mat. L/T/D | | |
| | | .0 | | | | | .1 | .1 |
| | | .1 | | | | Fixed/Worth | .2 | .2 |
| | | .6 | | | | | .3 | .3 |
| | | .6 | | | | | .5 | .9 |
| | | 1.9 | | | | Debt/Worth | 1.0 | 1.5 |
| | | 3.2 | | | | | 2.6 | 2.2 |
| | | | | | | | 29.0 | 32.5 |
| | | | | | | % Profit Before Taxes/Tangible Net Worth | (25)    15.9 | (20)    10.3 |
| | | | | | | | 4.0 | 3.5 |
| | | 15.2 | | | | | 15.5 | 12.1 |
| | | 6.3 | | | | % Profit Before Taxes/Total Assets | 6.6 | 2.7 |
| | | 2.1 | | | | | 1.8 | .9 |
| | | 273.6 | | | | | 100.9 | 62.5 |
| | | 33.0 | | | | Sales/Net Fixed Assets | 35.4 | 33.7 |
| | | 12.4 | | | | | 19.1 | 19.4 |
| | | 4.3 | | | | | 3.4 | 3.1 |
| | | 2.6 | | | | Sales/Total Assets | 2.6 | 2.6 |
| | | 2.0 | | | | | 2.0 | 1.8 |
| | | | | | | | .2 | .6 |
| | | | | | | % Depr., Dep., Amort./Sales | (24)    .8 | (19)    1.0 |
| | | | | | | | 1.3 | 1.1 |
| | | | | | | % Officers', Directors' Owners' Comp/Sales | | |
| 13606M | 7748M | 168052M | 46225M | 323319M | 851703M | Net Sales ($) | 2945119M | 2913883M |
| 664M | 2448M | 52401M | 31704M | 242716M | 567941M | Total Assets ($) | 1463784M | 1250094M |

## Comparative Historical Data  |  Current Data Sorted by Sales

| 4/1/09-3/31/10 ALL | 4/1/10-3/31/11 ALL | 4/1/11-3/31/12 ALL | Type of Statement | 0-1MM | 1-3MM | 3-5MM | 5-10MM | 10-25MM | 25MM & OVER |
|---|---|---|---|---|---|---|---|---|---|
| 5 | 4 | 3 | Unqualified | | | | 1 | | 2 |
| 2 | 5 | 5 | Reviewed | | | | 1 | 2 | 2 |
| 1 | 1 | 1 | Compiled | | 1 | | | | |
| 2 | 3 | 4 | Tax Returns | | | | 1 | 2 | |
| 11 | 9 | 11 | Other | 1 | 1 | 1 | 1 | 2 | 6 |
| | | | | | 6 (4/1-9/30/11) | | 18 (10/1/11-3/31/12) | | |
| 21 | 22 | 24 | NUMBER OF STATEMENTS | 2 | 2 | 1 | 3 | 6 | 10 |
| % | % | % | **ASSETS** | % | % | % | % | % | % |
| 5.5 | 4.7 | 15.4 | Cash & Equivalents | | | | | | 11.9 |
| 26.8 | 25.7 | 19.2 | Trade Receivables (net) | | | | | | 18.6 |
| 38.1 | 36.4 | 33.8 | Inventory | | | | | | 30.7 |
| 3.1 | 5.8 | 7.0 | All Other Current | | | | | | 3.9 |
| 73.6 | 72.5 | 75.3 | Total Current | | | | | | 65.0 |
| 9.1 | 10.1 | 12.5 | Fixed Assets (net) | | | | | | 13.2 |
| 5.7 | 4.2 | 2.9 | Intangibles (net) | | | | | | 5.3 |
| 11.6 | 13.2 | 9.2 | All Other Non-Current | | | | | | 16.4 |
| 100.0 | 100.0 | 100.0 | Total | | | | | | 100.0 |
| | | | **LIABILITIES** | | | | | | |
| 15.6 | 15.1 | 23.9 | Notes Payable-Short Term | | | | | | 17.7 |
| 11.0 | 3.2 | 4.8 | Cur. Mat.-L.T.D. | | | | | | 5.6 |
| 15.4 | 16.4 | 15.3 | Trade Payables | | | | | | 12.2 |
| .8 | .6 | .1 | Income Taxes Payable | | | | | | .3 |
| 13.6 | 10.7 | 9.8 | All Other Current | | | | | | 7.9 |
| 56.4 | 46.0 | 54.1 | Total Current | | | | | | 43.7 |
| 10.7 | 10.3 | 7.0 | Long-Term Debt | | | | | | 13.3 |
| .1 | 1.0 | .7 | Deferred Taxes | | | | | | 1.5 |
| 3.4 | 8.9 | 6.1 | All Other Non-Current | | | | | | 7.3 |
| 29.4 | 33.9 | 32.1 | Net Worth | | | | | | 34.3 |
| 100.0 | 100.0 | 100.0 | Total Liabilities & Net Worth | | | | | | 100.0 |
| | | | **INCOME DATA** | | | | | | |
| 100.0 | 100.0 | 100.0 | Net Sales | | | | | | 100.0 |
| 31.7 | 30.8 | 33.1 | Gross Profit | | | | | | 24.1 |
| 27.6 | 28.9 | 28.4 | Operating Expenses | | | | | | 24.2 |
| 4.1 | 1.9 | 4.7 | Operating Profit | | | | | | -.1 |
| 1.9 | .7 | .2 | All Other Expenses (net) | | | | | | -.5 |
| 2.2 | 1.1 | 4.5 | Profit Before Taxes | | | | | | .4 |
| | | | **RATIOS** | | | | | | |
| 2.7 | 2.6 | 3.2 | Current | | | | | | 2.4 |
| 1.7 | 1.7 | 1.7 | | | | | | | 1.3 |
| .8 | 1.2 | 1.1 | | | | | | | 1.0 |
| 1.4 | 1.3 | 1.0 | Quick | | | | | | 1.2 |
| 1.0 | .9 | .7 | | | | | | | .7 |
| .3 | .2 | .3 | | | | | | | .3 |
| 12 · 31.6 | 17 · 21.3 | 6 · 56.3 | Sales/Receivables | | | | | | 16 · 22.4 |
| 36 · 10.2 | 45 · 8.1 | 45 · 8.1 | | | | | | | 45 · 8.1 |
| 84 · 4.4 | 63 · 5.8 | 65 · 5.6 | | | | | | | 52 · 7.0 |
| 43 · 8.6 | 46 · 7.9 | 30 · 12.0 | Cost of Sales/Inventory | | | | | | 40 · 9.1 |
| 92 · 4.0 | 77 · 4.7 | 81 · 4.5 | | | | | | | 76 · 4.8 |
| 144 · 2.5 | 142 · 2.6 | 135 · 2.7 | | | | | | | 118 · 3.1 |
| 19 · 18.7 | 14 · 25.9 | 15 · 24.1 | Cost of Sales/Payables | | | | | | 19 · 19.6 |
| 24 · 15.1 | 27 · 13.5 | 32 · 11.4 | | | | | | | 25 · 14.7 |
| 57 · 6.4 | 56 · 6.6 | 50 · 7.3 | | | | | | | 42 · 8.7 |
| 4.6 | 4.5 | 2.9 | Sales/Working Capital | | | | | | 4.8 |
| 6.5 | 6.4 | 8.8 | | | | | | | 18.1 |
| -30.7 | 23.7 | 66.6 | | | | | | | NM |
| 6.1 | 6.7 | 7.2 | EBIT/Interest | | | | | | |
| (19) 3.4 | (21) 3.8 | (22) 3.4 | | | | | | | |
| .9 | 1.9 | 1.7 | | | | | | | |
| | | | Net Profit + Depr., Dep., Amort./Cur. Mat. L/T/D | | | | | | |
| .0 | .0 | .0 | Fixed/Worth | | | | | | .0 |
| .1 | .1 | .2 | | | | | | | .6 |
| 1.7 | 1.4 | 2.8 | | | | | | | 5.3 |
| .8 | .7 | .7 | Debt/Worth | | | | | | 1.1 |
| 1.6 | 1.6 | 2.2 | | | | | | | 3.0 |
| 165.3 | 7.6 | 10.1 | | | | | | | 18.1 |
| 29.3 | 30.8 | 46.7 | % Profit Before Taxes/Tangible Net Worth | | | | | | 50.4 |
| (17) 18.5 | (19) 14.0 | (22) 14.1 | | | | | | | 11.6 |
| 3.3 | 1.6 | 3.9 | | | | | | | -70.5 |
| 10.8 | 12.0 | 11.6 | % Profit Before Taxes/Total Assets | | | | | | 7.5 |
| 3.3 | 6.5 | 6.3 | | | | | | | 4.5 |
| -1.1 | 2.1 | 1.4 | | | | | | | -3.1 |
| 156.7 | 130.6 | 225.9 | Sales/Net Fixed Assets | | | | | | 177.1 |
| 34.5 | 46.8 | 28.4 | | | | | | | 10.2 |
| 12.0 | 11.8 | 10.2 | | | | | | | 6.4 |
| 3.0 | 3.1 | 3.8 | Sales/Total Assets | | | | | | 3.1 |
| 2.3 | 2.5 | 2.3 | | | | | | | 1.6 |
| 2.0 | 1.3 | 1.2 | | | | | | | 1.2 |
| .2 | .2 | .1 | % Depr., Dep., Amort./Sales | | | | | | |
| (16) .8 | (14) .6 | (16) 1.1 | | | | | | | |
| 1.3 | 1.1 | 2.3 | | | | | | | |
| | | | % Officers', Directors' Owners' Comp/Sales | | | | | | |
| 2202590M | 2515352M | 1410653M | Net Sales ($) | 874M | 3935M | 3184M | 23816M | 86863M | 1291981M |
| 960675M | 1263295M | 897874M | Total Assets ($) | 328M | 4585M | 2578M | 7874M | 42010M | 840499M |

M = $ thousand   MM = $ million
See Pages 9 through 22 for Explanation of Ratios and Data

## Current Data Sorted by Assets      Comparative Historical Data

### Type of Statement

| 0-500M | 500M-2MM | 2-10MM | 10-50MM | 50-100MM | 100-250MM | Type of Statement | 4/1/07-3/31/08 ALL | 4/1/08-3/31/09 ALL |
|---|---|---|---|---|---|---|---|---|
| | | 1 | | 2 | | Unqualified | 10 | 9 |
| | 1 | 5 | 5 | | | Reviewed | 9 | 11 |
| | | | | | | Compiled | 3 | 2 |
| 2 | | | | | | Tax Returns | 2 | 1 |
| | 1 | 7 | 4 | | 3 | Other | 13 | 15 |
| | | 6 (4/1-9/30/11) | 25 (10/1/11-3/31/12) | | | | | |
| 2 | 2 | 13 | 9 | 2 | 3 | **NUMBER OF STATEMENTS** | 37 | 38 |

### Data

| 0-500M % | 500M-2MM % | 2-10MM % | 10-50MM % | 50-100MM % | 100-250MM % | | 4/1/07-3/31/08 ALL % | 4/1/08-3/31/09 ALL % |
|---|---|---|---|---|---|---|---|---|
| | | | | | | **ASSETS** | | |
| | | 7.4 | | | | Cash & Equivalents | 5.0 | 4.6 |
| | | 25.3 | | | | Trade Receivables (net) | 26.3 | 26.1 |
| | | 45.6 | | | | Inventory | 44.6 | 43.4 |
| | | 5.1 | | | | All Other Current | 4.3 | 3.9 |
| | | 83.4 | | | | Total Current | 80.2 | 78.0 |
| | | 7.5 | | | | Fixed Assets (net) | 9.3 | 10.6 |
| | | 6.3 | | | | Intangibles (net) | 6.3 | 5.7 |
| | | 2.8 | | | | All Other Non-Current | 4.3 | 5.7 |
| | | 100.0 | | | | Total | 100.0 | 100.0 |
| | | | | | | **LIABILITIES** | | |
| | | 28.2 | | | | Notes Payable-Short Term | 21.5 | 24.6 |
| | | .7 | | | | Cur. Mat.-L.T.D. | 2.0 | .6 |
| | | 11.4 | | | | Trade Payables | 12.8 | 11.2 |
| | | .1 | | | | Income Taxes Payable | .6 | .1 |
| | | 4.8 | | | | All Other Current | 7.1 | 8.9 |
| | | 45.3 | | | | Total Current | 43.9 | 45.4 |
| | | 6.1 | | | | Long-Term Debt | 10.3 | 10.7 |
| | | .0 | | | | Deferred Taxes | .4 | .4 |
| | | 4.8 | | | | All Other Non-Current | 8.8 | 5.4 |
| | | 43.8 | | | | Net Worth | 36.6 | 38.1 |
| | | 100.0 | | | | Total Liabilities & Net Worth | 100.0 | 100.0 |
| | | | | | | **INCOME DATA** | | |
| | | 100.0 | | | | Net Sales | 100.0 | 100.0 |
| | | 29.4 | | | | Gross Profit | 30.8 | 31.8 |
| | | 29.5 | | | | Operating Expenses | 28.4 | 31.0 |
| | | -.1 | | | | Operating Profit | 2.4 | .8 |
| | | .8 | | | | All Other Expenses (net) | 2.1 | 2.4 |
| | | -.9 | | | | Profit Before Taxes | .4 | -1.6 |
| | | | | | | **RATIOS** | | |
| | | 3.1 | | | | Current | 2.8 | 3.0 |
| | | 1.8 | | | | | 2.1 | 1.7 |
| | | 1.4 | | | | | 1.4 | 1.3 |
| | | 1.4 | | | | Quick | 1.1 | 1.1 |
| | | .7 | | | | | .8 | .8 |
| | | .4 | | | | | .4 | .4 |
| | | 23  15.9 | | | | Sales/Receivables | 31  11.7 | 30  12.2 |
| | | 58  6.3 | | | | | 49  7.5 | 39  9.3 |
| | | 66  5.5 | | | | | 70  5.2 | 67  5.4 |
| | | 81  4.5 | | | | Cost of Sales/Inventory | 85  4.3 | 81  4.5 |
| | | 126  2.9 | | | | | 138  2.6 | 124  3.0 |
| | | 192  1.9 | | | | | 164  2.2 | 191  1.9 |
| | | 6  62.8 | | | | Cost of Sales/Payables | 17  21.6 | 15  24.8 |
| | | 20  18.2 | | | | | 29  12.4 | 26  14.1 |
| | | 43  8.5 | | | | | 42  8.7 | 41  9.0 |
| | | 3.4 | | | | Sales/Working Capital | 3.5 | 3.6 |
| | | 4.7 | | | | | 4.7 | 5.0 |
| | | 10.3 | | | | | 7.8 | 12.0 |
| | | 14.8 | | | | EBIT/Interest | 5.4 | 4.7 |
| | | (12)  .7 | | | | | (34)  2.4 | (36)  1.5 |
| | | -2.8 | | | | | -.3 | -1.7 |
| | | | | | | Net Profit + Depr., Dep., Amort./Cur. Mat. L/T/D | | |
| | | .1 | | | | Fixed/Worth | .1 | .1 |
| | | .1 | | | | | .2 | .3 |
| | | NM | | | | | .6 | .7 |
| | | .8 | | | | Debt/Worth | .6 | .9 |
| | | 1.3 | | | | | 1.4 | 2.2 |
| | | NM | | | | | 3.4 | 4.4 |
| | | 26.1 | | | | % Profit Before Taxes/Tangible Net Worth | 30.3 | 24.1 |
| | | (10)  4.5 | | | | | (32)  5.4 | (34)  3.7 |
| | | -7.0 | | | | | -4.9 | -34.6 |
| | | 7.7 | | | | % Profit Before Taxes/Total Assets | 7.0 | 7.5 |
| | | .6 | | | | | 3.1 | 1.0 |
| | | -6.1 | | | | | -3.8 | -9.1 |
| | | 108.2 | | | | Sales/Net Fixed Assets | 84.9 | 51.8 |
| | | 55.9 | | | | | 25.9 | 24.3 |
| | | 20.5 | | | | | 13.3 | 14.0 |
| | | 2.3 | | | | Sales/Total Assets | 2.4 | 2.3 |
| | | 1.9 | | | | | 1.9 | 1.9 |
| | | 1.6 | | | | | 1.4 | 1.3 |
| | | | | | | % Depr., Dep., Amort./Sales | .4 | .5 |
| | | | | | | | (34)  .8 | (31)  .7 |
| | | | | | | | 1.9 | 1.7 |
| | | | | | | % Officers', Directors', Owners' Comp/Sales | 1.7 | 2.1 |
| | | | | | | | (12)  3.4 | (15)  5.7 |
| | | | | | | | 5.2 | 7.0 |
| 1573M | 10380M | 117318M | 334132M | 243089M | 559537M | Net Sales ($) | 2141627M | 1726394M |
| 699M | 3078M | 60594M | 173643M | 106152M | 453774M | Total Assets ($) | 1425075M | 1073779M |

M = $ thousand    MM = $ million
See Pages 9 through 22 for Explanation of Ratios and Data

## Comparative Historical Data                                   ## Current Data Sorted by Sales

| 4/1/09-3/31/10 ALL | 4/1/10-3/31/11 ALL | 4/1/11-3/31/12 ALL | Type of Statement | 0-1MM | 1-3MM | 3-5MM | 5-10MM | 10-25MM | 25MM & OVER |
|---|---|---|---|---|---|---|---|---|---|
| 9 | 7 | 3 | Unqualified | | | | | | 2 |
| 7 | 12 | 11 | Reviewed | | | | 1 | 3 | 5 |
| 1 | 2 | 2 | Compiled | | | | | 1 | 2 |
| 2 | 2 | 2 | Tax Returns | 2 | | | | 2 | 5 |
| 9 | 11 | 15 | Other | | 1 | 3 | | 2 | 5 |
| | | | | | | 6 (4/1-9/30/11) | | 25 (10/1/11-3/31/12) | |
| 28 | 34 | 31 | **NUMBER OF STATEMENTS** | 2 | 1 | 3 | 5 | 8 | 12 |
| % | % | % | **ASSETS** | % | % | % | % | % | % |
| 4.2 | 4.1 | 7.2 | Cash & Equivalents | | | | | | 5.7 |
| 24.5 | 20.8 | 22.1 | Trade Receivables (net) | | | | | | 20.4 |
| 44.0 | 49.6 | 46.9 | Inventory | | | | | | 42.2 |
| 3.5 | 6.5 | 3.6 | All Other Current | | | | | | 3.2 |
| 76.2 | 81.1 | 79.7 | Total Current | | | | | | 71.6 |
| 10.2 | 6.6 | 8.3 | Fixed Assets (net) | | | | | | 10.8 |
| 8.3 | 5.6 | 8.1 | Intangibles (net) | | | | | | 13.4 |
| 5.3 | 6.7 | 3.9 | All Other Non-Current | | | | | | 4.2 |
| 100.0 | 100.0 | 100.0 | Total | | | | | | 100.0 |
| | | | **LIABILITIES** | | | | | | |
| 15.6 | 24.4 | 19.7 | Notes Payable-Short Term | | | | | | 9.8 |
| 1.7 | 1.9 | .5 | Cur. Mat.-L.T.D. | | | | | | .3 |
| 17.9 | 20.1 | 12.3 | Trade Payables | | | | | | 15.0 |
| .7 | .1 | .1 | Income Taxes Payable | | | | | | .0 |
| 8.2 | 6.2 | 5.2 | All Other Current | | | | | | 6.8 |
| 44.1 | 52.7 | 37.8 | Total Current | | | | | | 31.9 |
| 17.1 | 5.7 | 6.9 | Long-Term Debt | | | | | | 8.5 |
| .5 | .5 | .5 | Deferred Taxes | | | | | | 1.3 |
| 8.4 | 3.8 | 8.6 | All Other Non-Current | | | | | | 7.7 |
| 29.9 | 37.3 | 46.1 | Net Worth | | | | | | 50.6 |
| 100.0 | 100.0 | 100.0 | Total Liabilities & Net Worth | | | | | | 100.0 |
| | | | **INCOME DATA** | | | | | | |
| 100.0 | 100.0 | 100.0 | Net Sales | | | | | | 100.0 |
| 32.3 | 33.5 | 32.1 | Gross Profit | | | | | | 31.3 |
| 30.4 | 30.5 | 28.7 | Operating Expenses | | | | | | 25.3 |
| 2.0 | 3.1 | 3.5 | Operating Profit | | | | | | 6.1 |
| 2.7 | .9 | .8 | All Other Expenses (net) | | | | | | 1.0 |
| -.8 | 2.2 | 2.7 | Profit Before Taxes | | | | | | 5.1 |
| | | | **RATIOS** | | | | | | |
| 3.1 | 2.8 | 4.5 | | | | | | | 4.6 |
| 2.1 | 1.5 | 2.2 | Current | | | | | | 3.0 |
| 1.4 | 1.2 | 1.6 | | | | | | | 1.7 |
| 1.4 | 1.3 | 1.7 | | | | | | | 3.1 |
| .8 | .4 | .8 | Quick | | | | | | 1.3 |
| .3 | .2 | .5 | | | | | | | .5 |
| 16  23.1 | 9  40.2 | 20  18.5 | | | | | | | 10  38.0 |
| 42  8.8 | 28  12.9 | 39  9.4 | Sales/Receivables | | | | | | 35  10.3 |
| 54  6.7 | 57  6.4 | 63  5.8 | | | | | | | 70  5.2 |
| 62  5.9 | 73  5.0 | 78  4.7 | | | | | | | 61  6.0 |
| 115  3.2 | 131  2.8 | 130  2.8 | Cost of Sales/Inventory | | | | | | 122  3.0 |
| 193  1.9 | 188  1.9 | 215  1.7 | | | | | | | 203  1.8 |
| 19  18.9 | 13  28.8 | 9  38.8 | | | | | | | 5  75.2 |
| 32  11.3 | 31  11.6 | 21  17.5 | Cost of Sales/Payables | | | | | | 26  14.1 |
| 44  8.4 | 65  5.6 | 43  8.4 | | | | | | | 49  7.4 |
| 4.5 | 5.0 | 3.0 | | | | | | | 2.6 |
| 5.8 | 8.1 | 4.7 | Sales/Working Capital | | | | | | 4.7 |
| 11.7 | 24.8 | 6.6 | | | | | | | 6.5 |
| 7.5 | 9.2 | 16.3 | | | | | | | 32.5 |
| 1.3  (33) | 3.1  (28) | 5.6 | EBIT/Interest | | | | | | 7.6 |
| -2.0 | .8 | 1.1 | | | | | | | 2.3 |
| | | | Net Profit + Depr., Dep., Amort./Cur. Mat. L/T/D | | | | | | |
| .1 | .0 | .1 | | | | | | | .2 |
| .3 | .1 | .2 | Fixed/Worth | | | | | | .4 |
| 1.8 | 1.1 | .7 | | | | | | | 1.6 |
| .9 | 1.0 | .4 | | | | | | | .4 |
| 2.1 | 1.9 | 1.5 | Debt/Worth | | | | | | 1.9 |
| 13.4 | 6.6 | 5.0 | | | | | | | 8.0 |
| 36.5 | 63.5 | 46.8 | | | | | | | 54.1 |
| (23)  4.8 | (29)  16.5 | (25)  16.2 | % Profit Before Taxes/Tangible Net Worth | | | | | (10) | 18.7 |
| -18.2 | 2.7 | 3.8 | | | | | | | 5.7 |
| 13.5 | 16.0 | 16.4 | | | | | | | 17.3 |
| 1.4 | 4.9 | 5.7 | % Profit Before Taxes/Total Assets | | | | | | 9.5 |
| -8.6 | -.4 | .0 | | | | | | | 2.3 |
| 87.2 | 178.2 | 114.8 | | | | | | | 50.0 |
| 29.9 | 59.5 | 50.7 | Sales/Net Fixed Assets | | | | | | 15.1 |
| 11.8 | 24.2 | 14.2 | | | | | | | 11.2 |
| 3.0 | 3.0 | 2.3 | | | | | | | 2.4 |
| 2.0 | 2.2 | 1.9 | Sales/Total Assets | | | | | | 1.8 |
| 1.6 | 1.5 | 1.5 | | | | | | | 1.3 |
| .4 | .3 | .3 | | | | | | | .4 |
| (21)  1.0 | (24)  .6 | (21)  1.2 | % Depr., Dep., Amort./Sales | | | | | (11) | 1.2 |
| 2.0 | 1.4 | 1.8 | | | | | | | 2.4 |
| | | | % Officers', Directors', Owners' Comp/Sales | | | | | | |
| 2143362M | 1097091M | 1266029M | Net Sales ($) | 1573M | 2239M | 11557M | 34979M | 114273M | 1101408M |
| 1075084M | 558096M | 797940M | Total Assets ($) | 699M | 3777M | 6565M | 16302M | 62576M | 708021M |

M = $ thousand   MM = $ million
See Pages 9 through 22 for Explanation of Ratios and Data

## Current Data Sorted by Assets

## Comparative Historical Data

| 0-500M | 500M-2MM | 2-10MM | 10-50MM | 50-100MM | 100-250MM | Type of Statement | 4/1/07-3/31/08 ALL | 4/1/08-3/31/09 ALL |
|---|---|---|---|---|---|---|---|---|
| | | 1 | 3 | | | Unqualified | 4 | 2 |
| | 2 | 10 | 4 | 1 | | Reviewed | 9 | 9 |
| | | 2 | | | | Compiled | | |
| 1 | 1 | 1 | | | | Tax Returns | 1 | 1 |
| 2 | 4 | 1 | 2 | 2 | 2 | Other | 11 | 12 |
| | 7 (4/1-9/30/11) | | 32 (10/1/11-3/31/12) | | | | | |
| 0-500M | 500M-2MM | 2-10MM | 10-50MM | 50-100MM | 100-250MM | NUMBER OF STATEMENTS | 25 | 24 |
| 3 | 7 | 15 | 9 | 3 | 2 | | | |
| % | % | % | % | % | % | ASSETS | % | % |
| | | 14.1 | | | | Cash & Equivalents | 6.0 | 11.7 |
| | | 27.8 | | | | Trade Receivables (net) | 28.6 | 22.7 |
| | | 36.7 | | | | Inventory | 35.3 | 37.2 |
| | | 6.1 | | | | All Other Current | 2.6 | 4.6 |
| | | 84.6 | | | | Total Current | 72.5 | 76.2 |
| | | 10.7 | | | | Fixed Assets (net) | 15.2 | 16.1 |
| | | 1.3 | | | | Intangibles (net) | 4.8 | 2.7 |
| | | 3.4 | | | | All Other Non-Current | 7.5 | 5.0 |
| | | 100.0 | | | | Total | 100.0 | 100.0 |
| | | | | | | LIABILITIES | | |
| | | 2.3 | | | | Notes Payable-Short Term | 27.2 | 16.5 |
| | | .7 | | | | Cur. Mat.-L.T.D. | 3.3 | 3.2 |
| | | 38.5 | | | | Trade Payables | 16.4 | 21.1 |
| | | .2 | | | | Income Taxes Payable | .4 | .6 |
| | | 13.4 | | | | All Other Current | 9.6 | 12.3 |
| | | 55.2 | | | | Total Current | 56.9 | 53.7 |
| | | 6.0 | | | | Long-Term Debt | 4.8 | 8.8 |
| | | .0 | | | | Deferred Taxes | .0 | .0 |
| | | 14.5 | | | | All Other Non-Current | 3.9 | 9.1 |
| | | 24.2 | | | | Net Worth | 34.3 | 28.4 |
| | | 100.0 | | | | Total Liabilties & Net Worth | 100.0 | 100.0 |
| | | | | | | INCOME DATA | | |
| | | 100.0 | | | | Net Sales | 100.0 | 100.0 |
| | | 35.8 | | | | Gross Profit | 40.2 | 39.4 |
| | | 31.7 | | | | Operating Expenses | 35.8 | 36.2 |
| | | 4.1 | | | | Operating Profit | 4.4 | 3.2 |
| | | .4 | | | | All Other Expenses (net) | 1.1 | 1.2 |
| | | 3.7 | | | | Profit Before Taxes | 3.3 | 2.0 |
| | | | | | | RATIOS | | |
| | | 1.9 | | | | Current | 1.9 | 2.0 |
| | | 1.6 | | | | | 1.4 | 1.5 |
| | | 1.2 | | | | | 1.2 | 1.2 |
| | | .9 | | | | Quick | 1.1 | 1.0 |
| | | .9 | | | | | .7 | .7 |
| | | .6 | | | | | .2 | .2 |
| | | 9   41.3 | | | | Sales/Receivables | 20   18.5 | 6   63.9 |
| | | 17   21.8 | | | | | 35   10.4 | 25   14.3 |
| | | 30   12.3 | | | | | 55   6.6 | 35   10.3 |
| | | 18   20.7 | | | | Cost of Sales/Inventory | 48   7.6 | 35   10.4 |
| | | 46   8.0 | | | | | 75   4.9 | 74   5.0 |
| | | 73   5.0 | | | | | 116   3.2 | 93   3.9 |
| | | 19   19.5 | | | | Cost of Sales/Payables | 23   16.0 | 13   28.6 |
| | | 37   9.8 | | | | | 30   12.1 | 35   10.6 |
| | | 99   3.7 | | | | | 40   9.1 | 59   6.2 |
| | | 6.6 | | | | Sales/Working Capital | 8.0 | 7.8 |
| | | 20.6 | | | | | 12.5 | 13.0 |
| | | 31.4 | | | | | 24.6 | 37.8 |
| | | 8.5 | | | | EBIT/Interest | 7.4 | 11.4 |
| | | (13)   5.3 | | | | | (23)   2.2 | (22)   2.9 |
| | | 1.7 | | | | | 1.3 | .3 |
| | | | | | | Net Profit + Depr., Dep., Amort./Cur. Mat. L/T/D | | |
| | | .1 | | | | Fixed/Worth | .1 | .1 |
| | | .2 | | | | | .3 | .4 |
| | | .5 | | | | | 1.1 | 2.0 |
| | | 1.4 | | | | Debt/Worth | .8 | 1.0 |
| | | 2.9 | | | | | 1.8 | 2.8 |
| | | 4.8 | | | | | 6.0 | 7.1 |
| | | 85.9 | | | | % Profit Before Taxes/Tangible Net Worth | 38.8 | 58.8 |
| | | (14)   41.9 | | | | | (22)   28.6 | (20)   24.1 |
| | | 5.1 | | | | | 8.0 | 4.0 |
| | | 34.2 | | | | % Profit Before Taxes/Total Assets | 16.6 | 12.6 |
| | | 11.5 | | | | | 7.3 | 8.2 |
| | | 2.0 | | | | | 2.0 | -5.5 |
| | | 198.1 | | | | Sales/Net Fixed Assets | 77.8 | 169.9 |
| | | 78.3 | | | | | 29.7 | 21.9 |
| | | 32.2 | | | | | 12.8 | 12.6 |
| | | 7.3 | | | | Sales/Total Assets | 3.7 | 4.5 |
| | | 4.5 | | | | | 2.9 | 3.0 |
| | | 3.0 | | | | | 2.1 | 2.5 |
| | | .1 | | | | % Depr., Dep., Amort./Sales | .2 | .2 |
| | | (14)   .3 | | | | | (22)   .6 | (21)   .7 |
| | | .8 | | | | | 1.4 | 1.9 |
| | | | | | | % Officers', Directors' Owners' Comp/Sales | | |
| 2490M | 60218M | 456030M | 600112M | 132543M | 620379M | Net Sales ($) | 1774475M | 1095148M |
| 907M | 9605M | 75756M | 178598M | 172350M | 235829M | Total Assets ($) | 658449M | 417247M |

© RMA 2012

M = $ thousand     MM = $ million
See Pages 9 through 22 for Explanation of Ratios and Data

## Comparative Historical Data | Current Data Sorted by Sales

| | Comparative Historical Data | | | Type of Statement | 0-1MM | 1-3MM | 3-5MM | 5-10MM | 10-25MM | 25MM & OVER |
|---|---|---|---|---|---|---|---|---|---|---|
| | 4 | 10 | 4 | Unqualified | | | | 1 | | 3 |
| | 7 | 29 | 17 | Reviewed | | | | 1 | 6 | 10 |
| | 2 | 1 | 2 | Compiled | | | | | 2 | |
| | 1 | 5 | 3 | Tax Returns | 1 | | | 2 | | |
| | 6 | 14 | 13 | Other | 1 | | | 3 | | 6 |
| | 4/1/09-3/31/10 ALL | 4/1/10-3/31/11 ALL | 4/1/11-3/31/12 ALL | | | 7 (4/1-9/30/11) | | 32 (10/1/11-3/31/12) | | |
| | 20 | 59 | 39 | **NUMBER OF STATEMENTS** | 2 | 2 | 1 | 7 | 8 | 19 |
| | % | % | % | | % | % | % | % | % | % |
| | | | | **ASSETS** | | | | | | |
| | 14.7 | 12.3 | 15.3 | Cash & Equivalents | | | | | | 13.0 |
| | 30.8 | 23.6 | 26.2 | Trade Receivables (net) | | | | | | 25.7 |
| | 32.8 | 38.4 | 32.9 | Inventory | | | | | | 29.9 |
| | 2.9 | 5.9 | 6.8 | All Other Current | | | | | | 8.8 |
| | 81.3 | 80.3 | 81.2 | Total Current | | | | | | 77.5 |
| | 11.4 | 8.5 | 7.0 | Fixed Assets (net) | | | | | | 7.3 |
| | 3.2 | 5.2 | 6.3 | Intangibles (net) | | | | | | 10.6 |
| | 4.1 | 6.2 | 5.4 | All Other Non-Current | | | | | | 4.6 |
| | 100.0 | 100.0 | 100.0 | Total | | | | | | 100.0 |
| | | | | **LIABILITIES** | | | | | | |
| | 14.5 | 10.2 | 4.4 | Notes Payable-Short Term | | | | | | 7.2 |
| | 1.7 | 2.2 | .5 | Cur. Mat.-L.T.D. | | | | | | .7 |
| | 20.4 | 26.6 | 28.8 | Trade Payables | | | | | | 23.9 |
| | .2 | .2 | .2 | Income Taxes Payable | | | | | | .3 |
| | 10.8 | 13.3 | 11.5 | All Other Current | | | | | | 16.2 |
| | 47.6 | 52.5 | 45.4 | Total Current | | | | | | 48.2 |
| | 12.4 | 3.5 | 4.4 | Long-Term Debt | | | | | | 4.1 |
| | .0 | .0 | .2 | Deferred Taxes | | | | | | .5 |
| | 8.4 | 5.2 | 11.6 | All Other Non-Current | | | | | | 10.2 |
| | 31.5 | 38.8 | 38.3 | Net Worth | | | | | | 37.1 |
| | 100.0 | 100.0 | 100.0 | Total Liabilities & Net Worth | | | | | | 100.0 |
| | | | | **INCOME DATA** | | | | | | |
| | 100.0 | 100.0 | 100.0 | Net Sales | | | | | | 100.0 |
| | 36.4 | 35.4 | 36.8 | Gross Profit | | | | | | 34.3 |
| | 31.8 | 30.4 | 32.3 | Operating Expenses | | | | | | 28.9 |
| | 4.7 | 5.0 | 4.5 | Operating Profit | | | | | | 5.4 |
| | .8 | .8 | .3 | All Other Expenses (net) | | | | | | .1 |
| | 3.8 | 4.3 | 4.2 | Profit Before Taxes | | | | | | 5.2 |
| | | | | **RATIOS** | | | | | | |
| | 3.1 | 2.6 | 3.5 | | | | | | | 3.5 |
| | 1.5 | 1.5 | 1.7 | Current | | | | | | 1.4 |
| | 1.3 | 1.2 | 1.3 | | | | | | | 1.3 |
| | 2.1 | 1.0 | 1.3 | | | | | | | 1.1 |
| | .9 | .6 | .9 | Quick | | | | | | .8 |
| | .6 | .3 | .6 | | | | | | | .5 |
| | 15 · 24.4 | 5 · 74.8 | 10 · 35.0 | | | | | | | 10 · 35.0 |
| | 38 · 9.6 | 22 · 16.8 | 24 · 15.3 | Sales/Receivables | | | | | | 20 · 17.9 |
| | 64 · 5.7 | 41 · 8.8 | 41 · 8.9 | | | | | | | 45 · 8.1 |
| | 37 · 9.8 | 27 · 13.4 | 24 · 15.3 | | | | | | | 24 · 15.3 |
| | 74 · 4.9 | 62 · 5.9 | 48 · 7.6 | Cost of Sales/Inventory | | | | | | 49 · 7.4 |
| | 117 · 3.1 | 100 · 3.6 | 73 · 5.0 | | | | | | | 63 · 5.8 |
| | 21 · 17.5 | 21 · 17.4 | 24 · 15.2 | | | | | | | 24 · 15.2 |
| | 29 · 12.5 | 35 · 10.3 | 34 · 10.6 | Cost of Sales/Payables | | | | | | 32 · 11.3 |
| | 55 · 6.6 | 50 · 7.3 | 48 · 7.6 | | | | | | | 40 · 9.1 |
| | 4.7 | 6.8 | 3.9 | | | | | | | 5.2 |
| | 8.5 | 17.1 | 15.5 | Sales/Working Capital | | | | | | 17.4 |
| | 19.0 | 45.4 | 28.5 | | | | | | | 28.5 |
| | 16.9 | 13.2 | 18.2 | | | | | | | 19.8 |
| | (16) 3.1 | (53) 4.8 | (31) 5.6 | EBIT/Interest | | | | | | (17) 6.1 |
| | 1.4 | 1.7 | 2.2 | | | | | | | 2.1 |
| | | 17.2 | | Net Profit + Depr., Dep., | | | | | | |
| | | (12) 1.9 | | Amort./Cur. Mat. L/T/D | | | | | | |
| | | .3 | | | | | | | | |
| | .0 | .0 | .0 | | | | | | | .1 |
| | .2 | .2 | .1 | Fixed/Worth | | | | | | .3 |
| | 1.8 | .6 | .5 | | | | | | | 1.0 |
| | .6 | 1.0 | .7 | | | | | | | .8 |
| | 2.8 | 1.8 | 2.1 | Debt/Worth | | | | | | 2.2 |
| | 6.9 | 5.3 | 4.5 | | | | | | | 5.3 |
| | 50.8 | 99.5 | 76.1 | % Profit Before Taxes/Tangible | | | | | | 77.8 |
| | (16) 20.5 | (54) 33.5 | (36) 41.9 | Net Worth | | | | | | (17) 45.0 |
| | 6.0 | 6.1 | 7.3 | | | | | | | 22.1 |
| | 17.1 | 24.6 | 22.4 | % Profit Before Taxes/Total | | | | | | 22.4 |
| | 9.0 | 12.1 | 12.2 | Assets | | | | | | 11.5 |
| | 2.5 | 1.5 | 3.0 | | | | | | | 5.3 |
| | 284.5 | 239.4 | 293.0 | | | | | | | 277.3 |
| | 27.7 | 75.2 | 105.5 | Sales/Net Fixed Assets | | | | | | 78.7 |
| | 13.1 | 25.9 | 34.6 | | | | | | | 32.2 |
| | 3.8 | 5.9 | 6.4 | | | | | | | 5.7 |
| | 2.7 | 3.3 | 3.8 | Sales/Total Assets | | | | | | 3.4 |
| | 1.8 | 2.4 | 2.5 | | | | | | | 2.5 |
| | .2 | .1 | .1 | | | | | | | .1 |
| | (16) .8 | (45) .3 | (28) .3 | % Depr., Dep., Amort./Sales | | | | | | (17) .1 |
| | 1.6 | .8 | .7 | | | | | | | .7 |
| | | 1.7 | 2.3 | % Officers', Directors' | | | | | | 1.2 |
| | (20) | 2.9 | (19) 3.1 | Owners' Comp/Sales | | | | | | (10) 2.4 |
| | | 5.3 | 6.3 | | | | | | | 4.6 |
| | 1636232M | 2296293M | 1871772M | Net Sales ($) | 877M | 3227M | 4781M | 49502M | 141039M | 1672346M |
| | 648515M | 732160M | 673045M | Total Assets ($) | 488M | 1496M | 1934M | 16998M | 30741M | 621388M |

© RMA 2012

M = $ thousand     MM = $ million
See Pages 9 through 22 for Explanation of Ratios and Data

**Current Data Sorted by Assets**      **Comparative Historical Data**

| 0-500M | 500M-2MM | 2-10MM | 10-50MM | 50-100MM | 100-250MM | Type of Statement | 4/1/07-3/31/08 ALL | 4/1/08-3/31/09 ALL |
|---|---|---|---|---|---|---|---|---|
| 1 | 6 | 1 | 6 | 3 | 5 | Unqualified | 9 | 13 |
|  |  | 5 | 6 | 1 |  | Reviewed | 9 | 9 |
|  | 3 | 3 |  |  |  | Compiled | 3 | 1 |
| 1 | 3 | 3 | 4 | 2 | 2 | Tax Returns | 1 | 6 |
|  |  |  |  |  |  | Other | 11 | 12 |
|  | 16 (4/1-9/30/11) |  | 39 (10/1/11-3/31/12) |  |  |  | 11 | 12 |
| 2 | 12 | 12 | 16 | 6 | 7 | NUMBER OF STATEMENTS | 33 | 41 |
| % | % | % | % | % | % | **ASSETS** | % | % |
|  | 9.7 | 10.6 | 8.0 |  |  | Cash & Equivalents | 11.5 | 9.3 |
|  | 33.7 | 37.2 | 25.9 |  |  | Trade Receivables (net) | 30.3 | 29.9 |
|  | 41.0 | 25.4 | 44.8 |  |  | Inventory | 37.1 | 38.4 |
|  | 4.4 | 6.4 | 2.5 |  |  | All Other Current | 4.1 | 4.9 |
|  | 88.7 | 79.5 | 81.2 |  |  | Total Current | 83.0 | 82.5 |
|  | 5.8 | 7.9 | 8.6 |  |  | Fixed Assets (net) | 10.7 | 8.0 |
|  | .3 | 7.0 | 3.5 |  |  | Intangibles (net) | 1.6 | 5.4 |
|  | 5.2 | 5.5 | 6.7 |  |  | All Other Non-Current | 4.7 | 4.1 |
|  | 100.0 | 100.0 | 100.0 |  |  | Total | 100.0 | 100.0 |
|  |  |  |  |  |  | **LIABILITIES** |  |  |
|  | 10.6 | 17.3 | 14.4 |  |  | Notes Payable-Short Term | 18.9 | 21.7 |
|  | .6 | .7 | 2.6 |  |  | Cur. Mat.-L.T.D. | 1.9 | 2.3 |
|  | 39.4 | 22.5 | 22.0 |  |  | Trade Payables | 10.6 | 12.0 |
|  | .1 | .1 | .3 |  |  | Income Taxes Payable | .1 | .0 |
|  | 13.5 | 10.4 | 10.3 |  |  | All Other Current | 11.1 | 8.3 |
|  | 64.1 | 51.0 | 49.6 |  |  | Total Current | 42.6 | 44.4 |
|  | .6 | 3.3 | -4.8 |  |  | Long-Term Debt | 7.3 | 10.6 |
|  | .0 | .0 | .0 |  |  | Deferred Taxes | .2 | .0 |
|  | 8.8 | 13.9 | 11.9 |  |  | All Other Non-Current | 7.8 | 6.2 |
|  | 26.5 | 31.8 | 33.7 |  |  | Net Worth | 42.1 | 38.8 |
|  | 100.0 | 100.0 | 100.0 |  |  | Total Liabilities & Net Worth | 100.0 | 100.0 |
|  |  |  |  |  |  | **INCOME DATA** |  |  |
|  | 100.0 | 100.0 | 100.0 |  |  | Net Sales | 100.0 | 100.0 |
|  | 36.1 | 29.4 | 31.2 |  |  | Gross Profit | 38.7 | 37.7 |
|  | 35.2 | 22.6 | 25.3 |  |  | Operating Expenses | 35.8 | 32.7 |
|  | .9 | 6.8 | 5.9 |  |  | Operating Profit | 2.8 | 5.0 |
|  | .6 | .4 | 1.0 |  |  | All Other Expenses (net) | .9 | 2.0 |
|  | .3 | 6.4 | 4.9 |  |  | Profit Before Taxes | 1.9 | 3.0 |
|  |  |  |  |  |  | **RATIOS** |  |  |
|  | 2.0 | 3.8 | 2.7 |  |  | Current | 2.7 | 2.7 |
|  | 1.8 | 1.6 | 1.6 |  |  |  | 1.7 | 2.0 |
|  | 1.0 | 1.2 | 1.3 |  |  |  | 1.5 | 1.5 |
|  | 1.2 | 2.7 | 1.2 |  |  | Quick | 1.4 | 1.9 |
|  | .9 | 1.2 | .9 |  |  |  | .9 | .7 |
|  | .3 | .4 | .5 |  |  |  | .5 | .3 |
|  | 11   32.9 | 24   14.9 | 5   67.7 |  |  | Sales/Receivables | 14   26.6 | 11   34.3 |
|  | 20   18.5 | 36   10.2 | 32   11.3 |  |  |  | 36   10.1 | 37   9.8 |
|  | 43   8.4 | 49   7.4 | 57   6.4 |  |  |  | 65   5.6 | 69   5.3 |
|  | 28   12.9 | 18   20.0 | 36   10.0 |  |  | Cost of Sales/Inventory | 41   8.8 | 48   7.6 |
|  | 47   7.7 | 27   13.5 | 89   4.1 |  |  |  | 77   4.7 | 74   4.9 |
|  | 61   6.0 | 91   4.0 | 152   2.4 |  |  |  | 146   2.5 | 153   2.4 |
|  | 31   11.8 | 14   25.4 | 20   18.2 |  |  | Cost of Sales/Payables | 13   27.9 | 9   41.2 |
|  | 40   9.1 | 26   13.9 | 37   9.8 |  |  |  | 23   15.6 | 26   13.8 |
|  | 61   6.0 | 45   8.1 | 51   7.1 |  |  |  | 43   8.5 | 49   7.5 |
|  | 7.4 | 5.7 | 5.6 |  |  | Sales/Working Capital | 4.3 | 4.4 |
|  | 13.6 | 7.3 | 7.2 |  |  |  | 6.5 | 6.3 |
|  | NM | 80.7 | 20.7 |  |  |  | 12.2 | 12.1 |
|  | 8.5 |  | 16.1 |  |  | EBIT/Interest | 10.0 | 15.6 |
|  | 4.4 | (15) | 8.7 |  |  |  | (29) 2.3 | (37) 2.8 |
|  | .5 |  | 2.9 |  |  |  | 1.1 | 1.3 |
|  |  |  |  |  |  | Net Profit + Depr., Dep., Amort./Cur. Mat. L/T/D |  |  |
|  | .0 | .0 | .0 |  |  | Fixed/Worth | .1 | .0 |
|  | .0 | .1 | .1 |  |  |  | .2 | .1 |
|  | 8.1 | .4 | 1.0 |  |  |  | .6 | 1.0 |
|  | 1.0 | .4 | 1.1 |  |  | Debt/Worth | .6 | .7 |
|  | 2.0 | 1.5 | 2.8 |  |  |  | 1.4 | 1.3 |
|  | 22.5 | 2.6 | 5.7 |  |  |  | 3.1 | 11.0 |
|  | 62.3 | 84.9 | 102.0 |  |  | % Profit Before Taxes/Tangible Net Worth | 40.6 | 36.9 |
| (10) | 23.3 | (11) 34.0 | (14) 47.5 |  |  |  | (30) 9.2 | (34) 13.9 |
|  | 6.8 | 6.4 | 10.3 |  |  |  | .8 | 4.2 |
|  | 23.3 | 36.9 | 26.8 |  |  | % Profit Before Taxes/Total Assets | 17.2 | 16.3 |
|  | 5.2 | 8.3 | 12.2 |  |  |  | 3.5 | 5.5 |
|  | -4.7 | 2.3 | 3.5 |  |  |  | .2 | .7 |
|  | UND | 909.2 | 194.5 |  |  | Sales/Net Fixed Assets | 67.5 | 283.9 |
|  | 484.5 | 94.2 | 88.8 |  |  |  | 32.8 | 52.7 |
|  | 160.2 | 23.4 | 18.4 |  |  |  | 16.7 | 22.5 |
|  | 7.0 | 4.7 | 3.8 |  |  | Sales/Total Assets | 3.3 | 3.4 |
|  | 5.5 | 3.7 | 2.9 |  |  |  | 2.7 | 2.6 |
|  | 3.2 | 2.3 | 2.4 |  |  |  | 1.8 | 2.0 |
|  |  |  | .2 |  |  | % Depr., Dep., Amort./Sales | .3 | .2 |
|  |  | (15) | .3 |  |  |  | (29) .6 | (29) .5 |
|  |  |  | .6 |  |  |  | 1.4 | 1.3 |
|  |  |  |  |  |  | % Officers', Directors' Owners' Comp/Sales | .9 | 1.1 |
|  |  |  |  |  |  |  | (14) 2.2 | (20) 1.9 |
|  |  |  |  |  |  |  | 7.1 | 5.3 |
| 2579M | 72560M | 219996M | 970997M | 643210M | 1327902M | Net Sales ($) | 1852577M | 2178863M |
| 357M | 14315M | 63300M | 349368M | 446359M | 1029511M | Total Assets ($) | 797386M | 952776M |

M = $ thousand    MM = $ million
See Pages 9 through 22 for Explanation of Ratios and Data

## Comparative Historical Data | Current Data Sorted by Sales

| | | | | | | | | 16 (4/1-9/30/11) | | 39 (10/1/11-3/31/12) | | |
|---|---|---|---|---|---|---|---|---|---|---|---|---|
| 16 | 23 | 15 | **Type of Statement** / Unqualified | | | 1 | | | | | | 14 |
| 14 | 32 | 19 | Reviewed | | 2 | 1 | | 3 | 6 | 7 |
| 1 | 3 | | Compiled | | | | | | | |
| 1 | 4 | 6 | Tax Returns | | 1 | 1 | | 1 | 3 | |
| 19 | 17 | 15 | Other | 1 | | | 1 | 3 | 1 | 10 |
| 4/1/09-3/31/10 ALL | 4/1/10-3/31/11 ALL | 4/1/11-3/31/12 ALL | | 0-1MM | 1-3MM | 3-5MM | 5-10MM | 10-25MM | 25MM & OVER |
| 51 | 79 | 55 | **NUMBER OF STATEMENTS** | 1 | 3 | 3 | 7 | 10 | 31 |
| % | % | % | **ASSETS** | % | % | % | % | % | % |
| 16.0 | 9.8 | 10.4 | Cash & Equivalents | | | | | 8.8 | 8.0 |
| 28.2 | 22.1 | 28.5 | Trade Receivables (net) | | | | | 32.5 | 24.4 |
| 30.4 | 38.6 | 32.8 | Inventory | | | | | 28.0 | 33.7 |
| 5.0 | 7.7 | 4.6 | All Other Current | | | | | 7.5 | 4.0 |
| 79.6 | 78.2 | 76.3 | Total Current | | | | | 76.7 | 70.1 |
| 7.2 | 7.1 | 6.6 | Fixed Assets (net) | | | | | 8.7 | 6.3 |
| 6.9 | 9.0 | 12.1 | Intangibles (net) | | | | | 8.0 | 18.8 |
| 6.2 | 5.8 | 5.0 | All Other Non-Current | | | | | 6.5 | 4.9 |
| 100.0 | 100.0 | 100.0 | Total | | | | | 100.0 | 100.0 |
| | | | **LIABILITIES** | | | | | | |
| 12.0 | 12.9 | 13.5 | Notes Payable-Short Term | | | | | 12.9 | 14.2 |
| 3.4 | 1.9 | 1.6 | Cur. Mat.-L.T.D. | | | | | .9 | 2.4 |
| 19.7 | 26.9 | 21.9 | Trade Payables | | | | | 25.3 | 15.6 |
| .7 | .6 | .2 | Income Taxes Payable | | | | | .0 | .3 |
| 10.5 | 12.1 | 10.2 | All Other Current | | | | | 11.4 | 9.0 |
| 46.2 | 54.4 | 47.4 | Total Current | | | | | 50.6 | 41.6 |
| 7.6 | 4.7 | 5.5 | Long-Term Debt | | | | | 4.0 | 8.3 |
| .1 | .4 | .6 | Deferred Taxes | | | | | .0 | 1.0 |
| 11.2 | 10.9 | 10.2 | All Other Non-Current | | | | | 16.7 | 7.0 |
| 35.0 | 29.5 | 36.3 | Net Worth | | | | | 28.8 | 42.1 |
| 100.0 | 100.0 | 100.0 | Total Liabilities & Net Worth | | | | | 100.0 | 100.0 |
| | | | **INCOME DATA** | | | | | | |
| 100.0 | 100.0 | 100.0 | Net Sales | | | | | 100.0 | 100.0 |
| 35.4 | 33.1 | 34.9 | Gross Profit | | | | | 29.7 | 36.3 |
| 30.3 | 29.6 | 29.2 | Operating Expenses | | | | | 21.5 | 29.8 |
| 5.1 | 3.5 | 5.7 | Operating Profit | | | | | 8.2 | 6.6 |
| 1.3 | 1.1 | 1.1 | All Other Expenses (net) | | | | | .5 | 1.5 |
| 3.8 | 2.4 | 4.6 | Profit Before Taxes | | | | | 7.7 | 5.0 |
| | | | **RATIOS** | | | | | | |
| 2.8 | 2.4 | 2.8 | | | | | | 4.1 | 2.8 |
| 1.9 | 1.6 | 1.9 | Current | | | | | 1.6 | 1.9 |
| 1.5 | 1.2 | 1.3 | | | | | | 1.0 | 1.3 |
| 1.6 | 1.2 | 1.4 | | | | | | 3.3 | 1.4 |
| .9 | .6 | 1.0 | Quick | | | | | .7 | 1.0 |
| .7 | .3 | .5 | | | | | | .3 | .5 |
| 17 21.1 | 6 57.0 | 12 30.8 | | | | | | 22 16.4 | 6 61.9 |
| 41 9.0 | 23 16.0 | 36 10.0 | Sales/Receivables | | | | | 30 12.1 | 46 7.9 |
| 61 6.0 | 49 7.5 | 55 6.6 | | | | | | 45 8.2 | 61 6.0 |
| 33 11.0 | 32 11.3 | 34 10.7 | | | | | | 19 19.5 | 51 7.1 |
| 55 6.6 | 60 6.1 | 61 6.0 | Cost of Sales/Inventory | | | | | 25 14.6 | 96 3.8 |
| 87 4.2 | 88 4.1 | 111 3.3 | | | | | | 101 3.6 | 135 2.7 |
| 17 21.2 | 18 20.6 | 20 18.4 | | | | | | 16 23.4 | 21 17.5 |
| 32 11.5 | 32 11.5 | 35 10.4 | Cost of Sales/Payables | | | | | 26 13.9 | 37 9.9 |
| 48 7.6 | 54 6.8 | 51 7.1 | | | | | | 37 9.8 | 47 7.8 |
| 4.0 | 5.4 | 5.1 | | | | | | 5.3 | 5.1 |
| 7.7 | 10.0 | 7.2 | Sales/Working Capital | | | | | 10.8 | 6.3 |
| 14.7 | 34.3 | 19.2 | | | | | | NM | 14.3 |
| 12.4 | 10.0 | 14.5 | | | | | | | 13.1 |
| (42) 3.0 | (67) 2.8 | (50) 5.5 | EBIT/Interest | | | | | | (29) 4.7 |
| 1.5 | 1.3 | 1.7 | | | | | | | 1.6 |
| 291.3 | 60.4 | | Net Profit + Depr., Dep., | | | | | | |
| (11) 12.2 | (13) 3.6 | | Amort./Cur. Mat. L/T/D | | | | | | |
| .4 | 1.2 | | | | | | | | |
| .0 | .0 | .0 | | | | | | .0 | .1 |
| .1 | .2 | .1 | Fixed/Worth | | | | | .1 | .2 |
| .6 | 1.5 | .6 | | | | | | .7 | 1.2 |
| .7 | 1.0 | 1.0 | | | | | | .4 | 1.0 |
| 1.5 | 2.2 | 2.0 | Debt/Worth | | | | | 1.5 | 2.8 |
| 6.3 | 13.5 | 6.5 | | | | | | 2.1 | 22.6 |
| 53.1 | 60.6 | 67.6 | | | | | | | 67.7 |
| (44) 21.8 | (61) 21.5 | (45) 31.5 | % Profit Before Taxes/Tangible Net Worth | | | | | | (24) 31.3 |
| 1.5 | 5.4 | 4.9 | | | | | | | 1.8 |
| 18.4 | 17.2 | 23.1 | | | | | | 40.6 | 18.2 |
| 6.4 | 4.2 | 8.0 | % Profit Before Taxes/Total Assets | | | | | 20.1 | 8.5 |
| 1.2 | 1.1 | 1.9 | | | | | | 4.6 | 1.2 |
| 209.7 | 238.9 | 456.5 | | | | | | 999.8 | 129.2 |
| 63.4 | 84.1 | 81.9 | Sales/Net Fixed Assets | | | | | 121.2 | 59.1 |
| 27.4 | 36.4 | 25.2 | | | | | | 19.2 | 17.7 |
| 3.7 | 4.7 | 4.6 | | | | | | 4.8 | 3.1 |
| 2.6 | 3.3 | 2.8 | Sales/Total Assets | | | | | 3.8 | 2.3 |
| 1.8 | 2.3 | 1.8 | | | | | | 2.4 | 1.3 |
| .2 | .1 | .2 | | | | | | | .2 |
| (34) .4 | (57) .4 | (38) .4 | % Depr., Dep., Amort./Sales | | | | | | (23) .4 |
| .7 | .7 | 1.4 | | | | | | | 1.9 |
| .8 | 1.2 | 1.0 | | | | | | | 1.0 |
| (21) 2.4 | (34) 2.0 | (22) 2.0 | % Officers', Directors' Owners' Comp/Sales | | | | | | (10) 1.9 |
| 4.1 | 4.2 | 5.1 | | | | | | | 3.0 |
| 2874165M | 4311701M | 3237244M | Net Sales ($) | 123M | 6392M | 13021M | 47778M | 161385M | 3008545M |
| 1401373M | 2028825M | 1903210M | Total Assets ($) | 71M | 2352M | 4885M | 8361M | 47753M | 1839788M |

M = $ thousand   MM = $ million
See Pages 9 through 22 for Explanation of Ratios and Data

**Current Data Sorted by Assets**       **Comparative Historical Data**

Date ranges: 500M-2MM & 2-10MM = **7 (4/1-9/30/11)**; 10-50MM, 50-100MM, 100-250MM = **71 (10/1/11-3/31/12)**; Historical columns = **4/1/07-3/31/08 ALL** and **4/1/08-3/31/09 ALL**.

| | 0-500M | 500M-2MM | 2-10MM | 10-50MM | 50-100MM | 100-250MM | | 4/1/07-3/31/08 ALL | 4/1/08-3/31/09 ALL |
|---|---|---|---|---|---|---|---|---|---|
| **Type of Statement** | | | | | | | | | |
| Unqualified | | 1 | 8 | 8 | 2 | 1 | | 10 | 13 |
| Reviewed | | 3 | | 7 | | | | 11 | 17 |
| Compiled | | 2 | 3 | | | | | 5 | 5 |
| Tax Returns | 2 | 5 | 5 | | | | | 5 | 11 |
| Other | 4 | 7 | 12 | 6 | | 2 | | 15 | 18 |
| NUMBER OF STATEMENTS | 6 | 18 | 28 | 21 | 2 | 3 | | 46 | 64 |
| | % | % | % | % | % | % | **ASSETS** | % | % |
| | | 9.4 | 4.1 | 7.7 | | | Cash & Equivalents | 6.9 | 9.3 |
| | | 22.4 | 22.6 | 24.2 | | | Trade Receivables (net) | 22.4 | 24.6 |
| | | 34.6 | 48.4 | 44.9 | | | Inventory | 40.2 | 38.7 |
| | | 5.4 | 3.9 | 3.0 | | | All Other Current | 4.3 | 5.4 |
| | | 71.8 | 78.9 | 79.8 | | | Total Current | 73.9 | 78.0 |
| | | 12.6 | 10.4 | 11.5 | | | Fixed Assets (net) | 13.7 | 13.6 |
| | | 3.7 | .7 | 2.2 | | | Intangibles (net) | 7.0 | 2.4 |
| | | 11.9 | 9.9 | 6.5 | | | All Other Non-Current | 5.4 | 6.1 |
| | | 100.0 | 100.0 | 100.0 | | | Total | 100.0 | 100.0 |
| | | | | | | | **LIABILITIES** | | |
| | | 9.8 | 18.7 | 9.5 | | | Notes Payable-Short Term | 16.9 | 13.6 |
| | | 2.0 | 3.8 | 1.9 | | | Cur. Mat.-L.T.D. | 1.5 | 3.0 |
| | | 14.6 | 16.3 | 22.2 | | | Trade Payables | 15.9 | 17.6 |
| | | .0 | .1 | .1 | | | Income Taxes Payable | .2 | .3 |
| | | 16.1 | 8.1 | 8.4 | | | All Other Current | 6.7 | 9.2 |
| | | 42.5 | 47.1 | 42.2 | | | Total Current | 41.2 | 43.6 |
| | | 13.6 | 10.5 | 9.0 | | | Long-Term Debt | 11.6 | 11.2 |
| | | .0 | .4 | .0 | | | Deferred Taxes | .3 | .1 |
| | | 6.2 | 3.3 | 3.9 | | | All Other Non-Current | 4.2 | 5.8 |
| | | 37.7 | 38.7 | 44.9 | | | Net Worth | 42.7 | 39.2 |
| | | 100.0 | 100.0 | 100.0 | | | Total Liabilities & Net Worth | 100.0 | 100.0 |
| | | | | | | | **INCOME DATA** | | |
| | | 100.0 | 100.0 | 100.0 | | | Net Sales | 100.0 | 100.0 |
| | | 42.3 | 34.1 | 38.3 | | | Gross Profit | 31.4 | 34.6 |
| | | 37.5 | 27.9 | 29.4 | | | Operating Expenses | 26.9 | 28.9 |
| | | 4.8 | 6.2 | 9.0 | | | Operating Profit | 4.5 | 5.7 |
| | | .2 | .7 | .8 | | | All Other Expenses (net) | 1.4 | .8 |
| | | 4.7 | 5.5 | 8.1 | | | Profit Before Taxes | 3.1 | 4.9 |
| | | | | | | | **RATIOS** | | |
| | | 5.4 | 2.6 | 3.1 | | | | 4.3 | 4.6 |
| | | 2.3 | 1.7 | 1.9 | | | Current | 1.8 | 1.7 |
| | | 1.1 | 1.4 | 1.4 | | | | 1.3 | 1.2 |
| | | 4.5 | .9 | 1.6 | | | | 1.4 | 2.1 |
| | | .9 | .5 | .9 | | | Quick | .6 | .6 |
| | | .5 | .3 | .4 | | | | .4 | .4 |
| | | 26   14.2 | 30   12.0 | 9   39.2 | | | | 23   15.6 | 13   27.4 |
| | | 30   12.2 | 36   10.1 | 39   9.3 | | | Sales/Receivables | 40   9.2 | 35   10.5 |
| | | 40   9.1 | 52   7.0 | 61   6.0 | | | | 56   6.5 | 51   7.1 |
| | | 49   7.5 | 74   4.9 | 59   6.2 | | | | 58   6.3 | 51   7.2 |
| | | 85   4.3 | 104   3.5 | 96   3.8 | | | Cost of Sales/Inventory | 109   3.4 | 83   4.4 |
| | | 126   2.9 | 228   1.6 | 228   1.6 | | | | 176   2.1 | 155   2.3 |
| | | 10   35.5 | 24   15.1 | 27   13.6 | | | | 18   20.8 | 12   31.0 |
| | | 25   14.4 | 32   11.4 | 60   6.1 | | | Cost of Sales/Payables | 25   14.4 | 23   16.0 |
| | | 49   7.5 | 49   7.5 | 69   5.3 | | | | 48   7.7 | 36   10.1 |
| | | 4.4 | 3.5 | 3.4 | | | | 3.4 | 3.6 |
| | | 5.5 | 7.0 | 5.6 | | | Sales/Working Capital | 6.3 | 7.1 |
| | | 36.5 | 11.6 | 13.3 | | | | 17.0 | 15.0 |
| | | 16.9 | 12.8 | 21.3 | | | | 7.1 | 15.6 |
| | | (15) 3.5 | (27) 4.0 | (20) 8.3 | | | EBIT/Interest | (43) 2.5 | (53) 3.8 |
| | | -1.6 | 1.8 | 3.2 | | | | 1.1 | .1 |
| | | | | | | | Net Profit + Depr., Dep., | 11.5 | 22.0 |
| | | | | | | | Amort./Cur. Mat. L/T/D | (10) 5.2 | (10) 4.5 |
| | | | | | | | | 1.3 | 1.1 |
| | | .1 | .0 | .1 | | | | .1 | .1 |
| | | .3 | .2 | .3 | | | Fixed/Worth | .2 | .2 |
| | | -7.0 | .4 | .6 | | | | .7 | 1.0 |
| | | .4 | .9 | .6 | | | | .4 | .3 |
| | | 1.4 | 1.4 | 1.4 | | | Debt/Worth | 1.5 | 1.4 |
| | | -35.7 | 3.1 | 3.0 | | | | 4.6 | 5.4 |
| | | 63.7 | 35.7 | 56.3 | | | % Profit Before Taxes/Tangible | 35.4 | 66.2 |
| | | (13) 35.4 | (27) 25.1 | (20) 33.7 | | | Net Worth | (38) 7.6 | (55) 18.4 |
| | | 5.8 | 11.2 | 13.5 | | | | .2 | 2.9 |
| | | 37.6 | 16.5 | 27.3 | | | % Profit Before Taxes/Total | 11.6 | 22.9 |
| | | 5.2 | 7.9 | 10.7 | | | Assets | 4.7 | 7.2 |
| | | -5.4 | 2.2 | 5.9 | | | | .1 | -2.3 |
| | | 61.7 | 96.8 | 61.8 | | | | 63.9 | 99.3 |
| | | 27.8 | 41.9 | 29.9 | | | Sales/Net Fixed Assets | 18.8 | 23.0 |
| | | 12.1 | 11.6 | 14.4 | | | | 9.0 | 9.5 |
| | | 3.1 | 3.0 | 2.8 | | | | 3.0 | 3.1 |
| | | 2.7 | 2.0 | 2.0 | | | Sales/Total Assets | 2.1 | 2.3 |
| | | 1.9 | 1.4 | 1.7 | | | | 1.5 | 1.7 |
| | | .3 | .4 | .3 | | | | .4 | .3 |
| | | (12) .5 | (23) .8 | (19) .5 | | | % Depr., Dep., Amort./Sales | (36) 1.2 | (47) .7 |
| | | 1.9 | 1.6 | 1.9 | | | | 1.8 | 1.9 |
| | | | 1.7 | | | | % Officers', Directors' | 1.2 | 1.5 |
| | | | (12) 2.7 | | | | Owners' Comp/Sales | (14) 2.6 | (27) 4.0 |
| | | | 3.5 | | | | | 4.7 | 6.0 |
| | 14827M | 62736M | 339523M | 1147151M | 117049M | 535876M | Net Sales ($) | 2824384M | 3564311M |
| | 1881M | 23527M | 146587M | 482244M | 104433M | 386864M | Total Assets ($) | 1669346M | 1840882M |

M = $ thousand    MM = $ million
See Pages 9 through 22 for Explanation of Ratios and Data

## Comparative Historical Data | Current Data Sorted by Sales

| | 4/1/09-3/31/10 ALL | 4/1/10-3/31/11 ALL | 4/1/11-3/31/12 ALL | Type of Statement | 0-1MM | 1-3MM | 3-5MM | 5-10MM | 10-25MM | 25MM & OVER |
|---|---|---|---|---|---|---|---|---|---|---|
| | | | | | | **7 (4/1-9/30/11)** | | | **71 (10/1/11-3/31/12)** | |
| | 18 | 13 | 12 | Unqualified | | 1 | | | 1 | 10 |
| | 12 | 13 | 18 | Reviewed | 1 | | 3 | 3 | 5 | 6 |
| | 7 | 3 | 5 | Compiled | | 2 | | 1 | 2 | |
| | 8 | 16 | 12 | Tax Returns | 1 | 4 | 1 | 5 | | 1 |
| | 13 | 18 | 31 | Other | | 6 | 5 | 5 | 8 | 7 |
| | 58 | 63 | 78 | **NUMBER OF STATEMENTS** | 2 | 13 | 9 | 14 | 16 | 24 |
| | % | % | % | **ASSETS** | % | % | % | % | % | % |
| | 10.4 | 8.4 | 8.0 | Cash & Equivalents | | 12.3 | | 5.2 | 5.4 | 7.7 |
| | 25.2 | 22.0 | 23.1 | Trade Receivables (net) | | 21.7 | | 28.5 | 22.2 | 23.1 |
| | 38.0 | 41.2 | 41.2 | Inventory | | 29.1 | | 44.4 | 49.2 | 42.0 |
| | 2.6 | 4.1 | 3.7 | All Other Current | | 3.7 | | 5.5 | 2.3 | 3.5 |
| | 76.2 | 75.7 | 76.0 | Total Current | | 66.8 | | 83.6 | 79.1 | 76.4 |
| | 11.9 | 13.2 | 11.1 | Fixed Assets (net) | | 11.3 | | 11.9 | 12.3 | 8.3 |
| | 4.7 | 5.0 | 4.1 | Intangibles (net) | | 9.4 | | .3 | 3.1 | 5.7 |
| | 7.2 | 6.1 | 8.8 | All Other Non-Current | | 12.5 | | 4.2 | 5.5 | 9.6 |
| | 100.0 | 100.0 | 100.0 | Total | | 100.0 | | 100.0 | 100.0 | 100.0 |
| | | | | **LIABILITIES** | | | | | | |
| | 14.7 | 16.2 | 13.5 | Notes Payable-Short Term | | 7.6 | | 24.0 | 12.8 | 10.1 |
| | 2.1 | 4.4 | 2.9 | Cur. Mat.-L.T.D. | | 1.8 | | 3.4 | 4.2 | 2.8 |
| | 16.3 | 15.2 | 17.5 | Trade Payables | | 14.1 | | 16.9 | 14.2 | 22.9 |
| | .1 | .1 | .1 | Income Taxes Payable | | .0 | | .1 | .0 | .2 |
| | 10.4 | 9.1 | 10.4 | All Other Current | | 3.8 | | 12.0 | 8.4 | 10.1 |
| | 43.6 | 44.9 | 44.4 | Total Current | | 27.3 | | 56.3 | 39.6 | 46.1 |
| | 8.0 | 12.2 | 10.1 | Long-Term Debt | | 21.5 | | 2.4 | 14.4 | 5.3 |
| | .5 | .1 | .3 | Deferred Taxes | | .0 | | .2 | .5 | .6 |
| | 5.8 | 9.5 | 5.4 | All Other Non-Current | | 16.2 | | 1.7 | 5.2 | 3.3 |
| | 42.1 | 33.2 | 39.7 | Net Worth | | 35.1 | | 39.5 | 40.4 | 44.7 |
| | 100.0 | 100.0 | 100.0 | Total Liabilities & Net Worth | | 100.0 | | 100.0 | 100.0 | 100.0 |
| | | | | **INCOME DATA** | | | | | | |
| | 100.0 | 100.0 | 100.0 | Net Sales | | 100.0 | | 100.0 | 100.0 | 100.0 |
| | 34.1 | 36.3 | 37.7 | Gross Profit | | 36.9 | | 29.2 | 42.1 | 33.9 |
| | 28.4 | 32.0 | 31.4 | Operating Expenses | | 33.2 | | 26.2 | 32.9 | 26.6 |
| | 5.6 | 4.3 | 6.3 | Operating Profit | | 3.7 | | 3.0 | 9.3 | 7.3 |
| | .8 | .5 | .6 | All Other Expenses (net) | | .3 | | .1 | 1.5 | .8 |
| | 4.8 | 3.8 | 5.7 | Profit Before Taxes | | 3.3 | | 3.0 | 7.8 | 6.5 |
| | | | | **RATIOS** | | | | | | |
| | 3.9 | 3.5 | 3.5 | Current | | 6.3 | | 2.0 | 4.0 | 2.7 |
| | 1.8 | 1.8 | 1.8 | | | 2.3 | | 1.7 | 1.9 | 1.8 |
| | 1.3 | 1.3 | 1.3 | | | 1.4 | | 1.2 | 1.5 | 1.3 |
| | 1.7 | 1.2 | 1.3 | Quick | | 3.9 | | 1.0 | 1.3 | 1.6 |
| | 1.0 | .6 | .7 | | | .9 | | .6 | .7 | .8 |
| | .4 | .4 | .4 | | | .6 | | .3 | .5 | .3 |
| | 20  17.8 | 22  16.2 | 20  18.5 | Sales/Receivables | | 16  22.8 | | 28  12.9 | 31  11.8 | 6  65.2 |
| | 37  9.8 | 37  9.8 | 35  10.5 | | | 26  14.1 | | 35  10.5 | 38  9.6 | 39  9.4 |
| | 49  7.4 | 52  7.0 | 47  7.7 | | | 32  11.3 | | 51  7.1 | 54  6.7 | 54  6.7 |
| | 49  7.4 | 56  6.5 | 54  6.7 | Cost of Sales/Inventory | | 24  15.3 | | 49  7.5 | 89  4.1 | 51  7.1 |
| | 88  4.1 | 106  3.4 | 94  3.9 | | | 72  5.1 | | 76  4.8 | 174  2.1 | 89  4.1 |
| | 133  2.8 | 165  2.2 | 203  1.8 | | | 104  3.5 | | 114  3.2 | 281  1.3 | 159  2.3 |
| | 16  22.2 | 11  32.9 | 19  19.3 | Cost of Sales/Payables | | 15  24.0 | | 5  67.0 | 27  13.7 | 23  15.6 |
| | 28  12.9 | 31  11.8 | 33  11.1 | | | 19  19.3 | | 29  12.8 | 44  8.3 | 47  7.8 |
| | 40  9.2 | 50  7.3 | 58  6.3 | | | 35  10.3 | | 35  10.5 | 64  5.7 | 69  5.3 |
| | 3.4 | 3.7 | 3.9 | Sales/Working Capital | | 4.6 | | 5.2 | 2.2 | 4.2 |
| | 6.4 | 6.5 | 6.4 | | | 6.4 | | 7.4 | 5.0 | 6.6 |
| | 16.0 | 17.7 | 15.8 | | | 32.2 | | 25.2 | 9.7 | 15.3 |
| | 21.9 | 16.5 | 17.2 | EBIT/Interest | | 4.9 | | 14.6 | 18.2 | 19.2 |
| | (51) 5.5 | (59) 5.8 | (70) 4.4 | | | (10) 3.7 | | (13) 4.0 | (15) 4.5 | (23) 7.7 |
| | 1.7 | 2.3 | 2.1 | | | 2.1 | | .5 | 2.2 | 2.4 |
| | | 30.5 | 21.2 | Net Profit + Depr., Dep., Amort./Cur. Mat. L/T/D | | | | | | |
| | | (14) 5.0 | (17) 4.1 | | | | | | | |
| | | 1.4 | 1.6 | | | | | | | |
| | .1 | .1 | .1 | Fixed/Worth | | .1 | | .1 | .1 | .1 |
| | .2 | .2 | .2 | | | .3 | | .2 | .3 | .2 |
| | .5 | .9 | .7 | | | -5.4 | | .4 | .9 | .5 |
| | .4 | .7 | .7 | Debt/Worth | | .5 | | .7 | .7 | .6 |
| | 1.3 | 1.8 | 1.6 | | | 1.8 | | 1.5 | 1.4 | 1.8 |
| | 2.9 | 5.6 | 4.4 | | | -26.0 | | 6.3 | 4.8 | 3.1 |
| | 38.1 | 42.0 | 53.4 | % Profit Before Taxes/Tangible Net Worth | | | | 44.6 | 52.3 | 55.5 |
| | (49) 24.1 | (51) 18.9 | (68) 29.2 | | | | | (13) 25.1 | (15) 29.9 | (21) 31.5 |
| | 5.3 | 7.7 | 13.5 | | | | | -.4 | 20.5 | 11.8 |
| | 20.6 | 15.4 | 20.6 | % Profit Before Taxes/Total Assets | | 17.5 | | 31.3 | 18.1 | 28.7 |
| | 9.9 | 8.8 | 9.8 | | | 7.9 | | 4.8 | 11.3 | 9.1 |
| | .7 | 2.2 | 2.5 | | | 3.3 | | -4.5 | 4.3 | 3.0 |
| | 101.9 | 65.8 | 90.0 | Sales/Net Fixed Assets | | 304.1 | | 102.7 | 66.0 | 102.4 |
| | 34.9 | 26.4 | 35.7 | | | 30.5 | | 38.5 | 27.5 | 37.6 |
| | 11.7 | 11.6 | 12.8 | | | 11.6 | | 11.4 | 10.5 | 16.9 |
| | 3.4 | 2.8 | 3.1 | Sales/Total Assets | | 4.0 | | 3.4 | 2.6 | 3.6 |
| | 2.2 | 2.3 | 2.1 | | | 2.8 | | 2.6 | 1.6 | 2.1 |
| | 1.6 | 1.8 | 1.6 | | | 1.9 | | 1.9 | 1.4 | 1.8 |
| | .3 | .4 | .3 | % Depr., Dep., Amort./Sales | | | | .3 | .6 | .3 |
| | (42) .9 | (47) .7 | (59) .6 | | | | | (13) .5 | (14) 1.1 | (20) .5 |
| | 1.6 | 1.5 | 1.6 | | | | | 1.4 | 2.1 | 1.3 |
| | 1.7 | 1.7 | 1.5 | % Officers', Directors' Owners' Comp/Sales | | | | | | |
| | (27) 3.8 | (34) 2.9 | (28) 2.5 | | | | | | | |
| | 5.3 | 5.9 | 3.7 | | | | | | | |
| | 2277633M | 2165216M | 2217162M | Net Sales ($) | 1585M | 28595M | 36384M | 97545M | 254827M | 1798226M |
| | 1388805M | 1086457M | 1145536M | Total Assets ($) | 2534M | 11854M | 18894M | 40954M | 168704M | 902596M |

M = $ thousand     MM = $ million
See Pages 9 through 22 for Explanation of Ratios and Data

## Current Data Sorted by Assets      Comparative Historical Data

| 0-500M | 500M-2MM | 2-10MM | 10-50MM | 50-100MM | 100-250MM | Type of Statement | 4/1/07-3/31/08 ALL | 4/1/08-3/31/09 ALL |
|---|---|---|---|---|---|---|---|---|
| | | 8 | 16 | 3 | 2 | Unqualified | 27 | 45 |
| | 3 | 25 | 10 | | | Reviewed | 37 | 31 |
| | 3 | 9 | 1 | | | Compiled | 12 | 19 |
| 13 | 17 | 12 | | | | Tax Returns | 23 | 22 |
| 9 | 14 | 20 | 13 | 6 | 4 | Other | 50 | 56 |
| | 34 (4/1-9/30/11) | | 154 (10/1/11-3/31/12) | | | | | |
| 22 | 37 | 74 | 40 | 9 | 6 | NUMBER OF STATEMENTS | 149 | 173 |
| % | % | % | % | % | % | ASSETS | % | % |
| 25.6 | 9.2 | 8.7 | 5.9 | | | Cash & Equivalents | 8.2 | 7.7 |
| 20.0 | 23.5 | 23.2 | 29.2 | | | Trade Receivables (net) | 27.8 | 26.6 |
| 24.9 | 36.6 | 43.3 | 39.9 | | | Inventory | 35.4 | 36.5 |
| 5.1 | 1.8 | 1.9 | 6.3 | | | All Other Current | 3.6 | 3.6 |
| 75.6 | 71.1 | 77.2 | 81.2 | | | Total Current | 74.9 | 74.4 |
| 10.4 | 17.0 | 13.2 | 8.8 | | | Fixed Assets (net) | 12.9 | 14.5 |
| 6.0 | 4.6 | 3.5 | 4.9 | | | Intangibles (net) | 5.1 | 4.5 |
| 8.0 | 7.3 | 6.2 | 5.1 | | | All Other Non-Current | 7.0 | 6.6 |
| 100.0 | 100.0 | 100.0 | 100.0 | | | Total | 100.0 | 100.0 |
| | | | | | | LIABILITIES | | |
| 23.4 | 19.3 | 13.1 | 18.4 | | | Notes Payable-Short Term | 17.2 | 19.7 |
| 3.6 | 2.3 | 2.9 | 2.1 | | | Cur. Mat.-L.T.D. | 3.1 | 1.9 |
| 22.3 | 23.0 | 17.8 | 17.4 | | | Trade Payables | 17.8 | 16.1 |
| .0 | .0 | .2 | .2 | | | Income Taxes Payable | .4 | .2 |
| 15.2 | 6.8 | 10.5 | 7.3 | | | All Other Current | 8.0 | 8.3 |
| 64.4 | 51.4 | 44.6 | 45.4 | | | Total Current | 46.4 | 46.2 |
| 6.5 | 12.7 | 11.3 | 7.2 | | | Long-Term Debt | 11.0 | 11.6 |
| .0 | .0 | .1 | .0 | | | Deferred Taxes | .2 | .2 |
| 25.4 | 12.4 | 6.7 | 4.9 | | | All Other Non-Current | 7.4 | 11.4 |
| 3.7 | 23.5 | 37.4 | 42.5 | | | Net Worth | 35.0 | 30.6 |
| 100.0 | 100.0 | 100.0 | 100.0 | | | Total Liabilties & Net Worth | 100.0 | 100.0 |
| | | | | | | INCOME DATA | | |
| 100.0 | 100.0 | 100.0 | 100.0 | | | Net Sales | 100.0 | 100.0 |
| 47.4 | 42.0 | 36.5 | 35.4 | | | Gross Profit | 37.5 | 36.5 |
| 46.4 | 37.5 | 31.5 | 29.4 | | | Operating Expenses | 32.0 | 32.1 |
| 1.0 | 4.5 | 5.0 | 6.0 | | | Operating Profit | 5.5 | 4.4 |
| .7 | .4 | 1.3 | .7 | | | All Other Expenses (net) | 1.5 | 1.1 |
| .4 | 4.1 | 3.7 | 5.3 | | | Profit Before Taxes | 4.0 | 3.3 |
| | | | | | | RATIOS | | |
| 3.0 | 2.9 | 3.5 | 2.4 | | | Current | 2.7 | 2.7 |
| 1.5 | 1.2 | 1.8 | 1.9 | | | | 1.6 | 1.6 |
| 1.2 | 1.1 | 1.4 | 1.3 | | | | 1.2 | 1.2 |
| 1.9 | 1.2 | 1.7 | 1.1 | | | Quick | 1.4 | 1.3 |
| 1.1 | .7 | .8 | .7 | | | | .8 | .7 |
| .3 | .3 | .3 | .5 | | | | .4 | .4 |
| 0 UND | 10 35.8 | 17 21.6 | 27 13.3 | | | Sales/Receivables | 28 13.0 | 23 15.8 |
| 10 35.6 | 26 13.8 | 38 9.6 | 49 7.4 | | | | 41 8.9 | 38 9.6 |
| 40 9.2 | 40 9.1 | 55 6.6 | 63 5.8 | | | | 60 6.1 | 54 6.7 |
| 0 UND | 27 13.4 | 65 5.6 | 54 6.7 | | | Cost of Sales/Inventory | 43 8.5 | 42 8.6 |
| 55 6.6 | 62 5.9 | 111 3.3 | 99 3.7 | | | | 92 4.0 | 92 4.0 |
| 111 3.3 | 152 2.4 | 152 2.4 | 159 2.3 | | | | 157 2.3 | 141 2.6 |
| 0 UND | 22 16.9 | 15 25.0 | 17 21.0 | | | Cost of Sales/Payables | 15 23.6 | 16 22.6 |
| 20 18.3 | 41 8.8 | 29 12.8 | 33 10.9 | | | | 30 12.2 | 29 12.5 |
| 111 3.3 | 65 5.6 | 69 5.3 | 58 6.3 | | | | 57 6.4 | 48 7.6 |
| 8.9 | 4.6 | 3.7 | 3.6 | | | Sales/Working Capital | 4.3 | 4.8 |
| 18.9 | 20.6 | 6.3 | 6.2 | | | | 7.8 | 8.7 |
| NM | 74.9 | 13.1 | 12.8 | | | | 21.8 | 23.5 |
| 8.2 | 15.2 | 15.9 | 13.8 | | | EBIT/Interest | 15.4 | 10.8 |
| (10) 3.5 | (31) 3.2 | (66) 4.8 | (39) 5.5 | | | | (137) 3.8 | (161) 2.5 |
| -1.1 | 1.0 | 1.7 | 2.0 | | | | 1.4 | 1.0 |
| | | | | | | Net Profit + Depr., Dep., Amort./Cur. Mat. L/T/D | 54.7 | 10.1 |
| | | | | | | | (25) 6.7 | (39) 3.2 |
| | | | | | | | 1.8 | .1 |
| .0 | .1 | .0 | .1 | | | Fixed/Worth | .1 | .1 |
| .4 | .6 | .2 | .2 | | | | .3 | .4 |
| -.3 | -1.4 | .7 | .3 | | | | 1.5 | 1.4 |
| 1.4 | 1.1 | .6 | .6 | | | Debt/Worth | .6 | .9 |
| 7.2 | 3.1 | 1.5 | 1.4 | | | | 1.7 | 2.0 |
| -5.4 | -10.9 | 4.1 | 3.2 | | | | 6.6 | 5.7 |
| 115.7 | 51.9 | 39.7 | 68.4 | | | % Profit Before Taxes/Tangible Net Worth | 63.5 | 44.6 |
| (14) 57.6 | (24) 21.8 | (65) 21.5 | (36) 22.2 | | | | (128) 21.1 | (146) 16.2 |
| -3.7 | 6.3 | 9.4 | 8.8 | | | | 6.4 | 2.5 |
| 26.8 | 15.8 | 18.4 | 21.6 | | | % Profit Before Taxes/Total Assets | 20.5 | 16.5 |
| 11.2 | 8.7 | 7.2 | 10.0 | | | | 6.7 | 4.5 |
| -2.6 | .1 | 1.1 | 3.9 | | | | 1.8 | .3 |
| 449.8 | 99.7 | 139.2 | 91.9 | | | Sales/Net Fixed Assets | 66.1 | 60.9 |
| 70.1 | 36.5 | 32.4 | 44.0 | | | | 25.9 | 24.1 |
| 40.1 | 13.6 | 9.1 | 20.7 | | | | 11.4 | 10.3 |
| 10.1 | 3.6 | 2.7 | 2.7 | | | Sales/Total Assets | 3.0 | 3.5 |
| 3.9 | 2.8 | 2.2 | 2.0 | | | | 2.2 | 2.2 |
| 2.6 | 2.0 | 1.6 | 1.5 | | | | 1.5 | 1.7 |
| | .6 | .4 | .5 | | | % Depr., Dep., Amort./Sales | .5 | .5 |
| | (24) .8 | (60) .9 | (34) .9 | | | | (114) 1.1 | (141) 1.0 |
| | 2.0 | 1.7 | 1.4 | | | | 2.1 | 2.1 |
| 3.6 | 1.5 | 2.2 | | | | % Officers', Directors' Owners' Comp/Sales | 1.6 | 1.8 |
| (10) 6.0 | (21) 2.9 | (33) 3.4 | | | | | (54) 3.2 | (63) 3.0 |
| 12.2 | 5.6 | 5.0 | | | | | 5.9 | 5.4 |
| 29062M | 123028M | 951509M | 1938930M | 1208885M | 1104480M | Net Sales ($) | 6692843M | 8733115M |
| 5610M | 43575M | 408526M | 843194M | 705766M | 872049M | Total Assets ($) | 3389562M | 4283343M |

M = $ thousand    MM = $ million
See Pages 9 through 22 for Explanation of Ratios and Data

## Comparative Historical Data

## Current Data Sorted by Sales

| | | | Type of Statement | | | | | | |
|---|---|---|---|---|---|---|---|---|---|
| 41 | 39 | 29 | Unqualified | | | | 1 | 10 | 18 |
| 23 | 41 | 38 | Reviewed | | 2 | 1 | 7 | 19 | 9 |
| 18 | 15 | 13 | Compiled | | 3 | 2 | 2 | 5 | 1 |
| 28 | 35 | 42 | Tax Returns | | 14 | 10 | 10 | 2 | 1 |
| 59 | 70 | 66 | Other | 5 | 12 | 6 | 11 | 9 | 22 |
| 4/1/09- | 4/1/10- | 4/1/11- | | 6 | 34 (4/1-9/30/11) | | 154 (10/1/11-3/31/12) | | |
| 3/31/10 | 3/31/11 | 3/31/12 | | | | | | | |
| ALL | ALL | ALL | | 0-1MM | 1-3MM | 3-5MM | 5-10MM | 10-25MM | 25MM & OVER |
| 169 | 200 | 188 | NUMBER OF STATEMENTS | 11 | 31 | 19 | 31 | 45 | 51 |
| % | % | % | ASSETS | % | % | % | % | % | % |
| 10.5 | 9.8 | 10.2 | Cash & Equivalents | 26.7 | 16.0 | 6.0 | 10.6 | 5.7 | 8.5 |
| 25.6 | 24.9 | 23.8 | Trade Receivables (net) | 11.3 | 23.0 | 25.1 | 25.4 | 22.6 | 26.6 |
| 36.0 | 40.0 | 38.4 | Inventory | 24.3 | 32.0 | 33.3 | 39.2 | 46.8 | 39.3 |
| 2.6 | 3.2 | 4.1 | All Other Current | 6.3 | 2.2 | 2.8 | 1.9 | 3.0 | 7.6 |
| 74.7 | 78.0 | 76.5 | Total Current | 68.5 | 73.2 | 67.2 | 77.0 | 78.1 | 82.0 |
| 12.6 | 11.3 | 12.2 | Fixed Assets (net) | 12.8 | 14.6 | 21.8 | 13.3 | 10.5 | 7.8 |
| 6.0 | 3.5 | 5.1 | Intangibles (net) | 9.3 | 4.2 | 6.2 | 4.0 | 4.5 | 5.5 |
| 6.7 | 7.2 | 6.2 | All Other Non-Current | 9.3 | 8.0 | 4.8 | 5.8 | 6.9 | 4.7 |
| 100.0 | 100.0 | 100.0 | Total | 100.0 | 100.0 | 100.0 | 100.0 | 100.0 | 100.0 |
| | | | LIABILITIES | | | | | | |
| 19.5 | 17.3 | 16.8 | Notes Payable-Short Term | 25.5 | 17.5 | 11.5 | 21.4 | 12.7 | 17.4 |
| 2.6 | 3.8 | 2.7 | Cur. Mat.-L.T.D. | 1.0 | 3.5 | 4.2 | 1.2 | 3.5 | 2.1 |
| 16.3 | 20.6 | 18.6 | Trade Payables | 26.9 | 15.0 | 20.4 | 16.6 | 20.6 | 17.6 |
| .3 | .3 | .2 | Income Taxes Payable | .0 | .0 | .1 | .1 | .1 | .3 |
| 9.0 | 9.4 | 9.6 | All Other Current | 10.4 | 9.5 | 15.3 | 5.2 | 11.0 | 8.9 |
| 47.7 | 51.4 | 47.8 | Total Current | 63.8 | 45.5 | 51.5 | 44.6 | 48.0 | 46.3 |
| 13.2 | 7.1 | 9.8 | Long-Term Debt | 5.7 | 16.0 | 8.6 | 14.3 | 8.4 | 6.1 |
| .3 | .2 | .2 | Deferred Taxes | .0 | .0 | .0 | .0 | .1 | .6 |
| 7.7 | 8.0 | 9.4 | All Other Non-Current | 28.6 | 19.5 | 12.5 | 4.8 | 4.1 | 5.5 |
| 31.1 | 33.3 | 32.7 | Net Worth | 2.0 | 19.0 | 27.4 | 36.3 | 39.4 | 41.6 |
| 100.0 | 100.0 | 100.0 | Total Liabilities & Net Worth | 100.0 | 100.0 | 100.0 | 100.0 | 100.0 | 100.0 |
| | | | INCOME DATA | | | | | | |
| 100.0 | 100.0 | 100.0 | Net Sales | 100.0 | 100.0 | 100.0 | 100.0 | 100.0 | 100.0 |
| 38.1 | 36.1 | 38.4 | Gross Profit | 43.6 | 48.2 | 43.1 | 35.3 | 35.7 | 33.7 |
| 33.7 | 31.0 | 33.4 | Operating Expenses | 43.6 | 44.2 | 40.5 | 30.2 | 30.4 | 26.7 |
| 4.5 | 5.1 | 4.9 | Operating Profit | .0 | 4.0 | 2.6 | 5.1 | 5.3 | 7.0 |
| 1.2 | .7 | .9 | All Other Expenses (net) | 1.2 | .9 | 1.3 | 1.1 | .9 | .6 |
| 3.2 | 4.4 | 4.0 | Profit Before Taxes | -1.2 | 3.1 | 1.3 | 4.0 | 4.5 | 6.4 |
| | | | RATIOS | | | | | | |
| 3.4 | 3.4 | 3.0 | | 7.5 | 4.1 | 5.0 | 5.1 | 2.6 | 2.6 |
| 1.7 | 1.7 | 1.7 | Current | 1.4 | 1.6 | 1.3 | 2.1 | 1.7 | 1.7 |
| 1.2 | 1.2 | 1.2 | | .8 | 1.1 | .8 | 1.2 | 1.3 | 1.3 |
| 1.8 | 1.5 | 1.4 | | 1.8 | 1.3 | 1.4 | 1.7 | 1.1 | 1.3 |
| .8 | .8 | .8 | Quick | 1.2 | 1.0 | .8 | 1.2 | .7 | .7 |
| .4 | .4 | .4 | | .1 | .4 | .3 | .5 | .3 | .4 |

| | | | | | | | | | | | | Sales/Receivables / Cost of Sales / Payables | | | | | | | | | | | | |
|---|---|---|---|---|---|---|---|---|---|---|---|---|---|---|---|---|---|---|---|---|---|---|---|

| | | | | | | | | | | | | | | | | | |
|---|---|---|---|---|---|---|---|---|---|---|---|---|---|---|---|---|---|
| 25 | 14.9 | 19 | 19.1 | 12 | 29.4 | Sales/Receivables | 4 | 83.0 | 4 | 82.5 | 17 | 21.0 | 18 | 19.8 | 12 | 29.6 | 26 | 14.1 |
| 39 | 9.4 | 34 | 10.6 | 36 | 10.1 | | 12 | 29.5 | 20 | 18.3 | 29 | 12.7 | 40 | 9.2 | 32 | 11.5 | 43 | 8.4 |
| 56 | 6.5 | 55 | 6.7 | 54 | 6.8 | | 39 | 9.3 | 42 | 8.6 | 51 | 7.1 | 55 | 6.6 | 54 | 6.7 | 57 | 6.4 |
| 46 | 7.9 | 49 | 7.4 | 48 | 7.6 | Cost of Sales/Inventory | 5 | 80.8 | 9 | 42.1 | 21 | 17.1 | 58 | 6.3 | 72 | 5.1 | 53 | 6.9 |
| 96 | 3.8 | 95 | 3.8 | 101 | 3.6 | | 52 | 7.0 | 101 | 3.6 | 55 | 6.6 | 81 | 4.5 | 111 | 3.3 | 104 | 3.5 |
| 150 | 2.4 | 137 | 2.7 | 146 | 2.5 | | 166 | 2.2 | 182 | 2.0 | 146 | 2.5 | 130 | 2.8 | 159 | 2.3 | 146 | 2.5 |
| 18 | 20.1 | 17 | 21.2 | 15 | 24.7 | Cost of Sales/Payables | 0 | UND | 9 | 39.5 | 13 | 27.5 | 19 | 19.1 | 14 | 26.2 | 17 | 21.0 |
| 31 | 11.8 | 34 | 10.9 | 31 | 11.7 | | 20 | 18.6 | 38 | 9.5 | 40 | 9.1 | 27 | 13.4 | 27 | 13.5 | 33 | 11.0 |
| 49 | 7.4 | 59 | 6.2 | 66 | 5.5 | | 135 | 2.7 | 65 | 5.6 | 89 | 4.1 | 54 | 6.8 | 81 | 4.5 | 58 | 6.3 |

| | | | | | | | | | | | | |
|---|---|---|---|---|---|---|---|---|---|---|---|---|
| 4.2 | 3.7 | 3.9 | Sales/Working Capital | 3.6 | 4.7 | 4.3 | 3.3 | 3.9 | 4.0 |
| 7.2 | 8.5 | 8.2 | | 12.1 | 14.5 | 30.3 | 5.4 | 8.2 | 6.6 |
| 24.0 | 26.3 | 22.4 | | -48.0 | 49.0 | -7.0 | 21.8 | 16.3 | 12.9 |
| 16.2 | 17.8 | 15.2 | EBIT/Interest | | | | 9.1 | 13.1 | 19.6 | 14.6 | 19.5 |
| (152) 3.4 | (171) 4.4 | (159) 4.8 | | (27) 3.2 | (13) 2.4 | (28) 2.9 | (41) 5.6 | (46) 5.7 |
| .8 | 1.3 | 1.8 | | .1 | .1 | 1.7 | 2.0 | 2.5 |

| | | | | | | | | | | | | |
|---|---|---|---|---|---|---|---|---|---|---|---|---|
| 12.0 | 30.1 | 40.1 | Net Profit + Depr., Dep., Amort./Cur. Mat. L/T/D | | | | | | 60.4 |
| (32) 4.9 | (24) 7.1 | (22) 6.7 | | | | | | (12) 9.7 |
| .8 | 3.5 | 1.1 | | | | | | 1.5 |
| .1 | .1 | .1 | Fixed/Worth | .0 | .1 | .2 | .0 | .0 | .1 |
| .3 | .2 | .2 | | .3 | .7 | 1.0 | .2 | .2 | .4 |
| 2.5 | 1.0 | 1.1 | | 2.0 | -.8 | -1.2 | .8 | .5 | .4 |
| .6 | .5 | .7 | Debt/Worth | 1.3 | 1.4 | 1.1 | .3 | .7 | .6 |
| 2.0 | 1.4 | 1.8 | | 6.6 | 3.3 | 5.3 | 1.3 | 1.4 | 1.7 |
| 13.9 | 5.6 | 6.4 | | 10.3 | -9.2 | -9.9 | 4.4 | 3.2 | 4.5 |
| 46.6 | 49.3 | 47.0 | % Profit Before Taxes/Tangible Net Worth | 65.2 | 48.4 | 37.8 | 45.7 | 45.0 |
| (136) 20.9 | (164) 21.8 | (153) 22.8 | | (19) 17.7 | (12) 27.9 | (27) 18.1 | (40) 23.4 | (46) 24.1 |
| 3.9 | 4.4 | 8.8 | | -4.6 | 4.9 | 3.0 | 8.6 | 13.7 |
| 18.5 | 20.1 | 19.0 | % Profit Before Taxes/Total Assets | 30.2 | 13.9 | 16.0 | 18.1 | 20.2 | 20.5 |
| 4.9 | 7.8 | 8.4 | | 6.2 | 6.4 | 9.9 | 7.1 | 8.6 | 9.5 |
| .0 | 1.1 | 1.8 | | -2.5 | -4.2 | .0 | .7 | 3.6 | 3.8 |
| 80.7 | 109.9 | 111.7 | Sales/Net Fixed Assets | 224.0 | 266.4 | 65.3 | 92.0 | 145.5 | 89.5 |
| 29.8 | 39.6 | 41.2 | | 65.1 | 36.5 | 19.5 | 36.1 | 36.1 | 45.6 |
| 13.1 | 16.5 | 13.4 | | 22.5 | 12.4 | 8.4 | 9.2 | 13.8 | 23.0 |
| 3.1 | 3.5 | 3.2 | Sales/Total Assets | 3.8 | 4.0 | 3.7 | 2.8 | 3.0 | 3.0 |
| 2.2 | 2.4 | 2.2 | | 1.8 | 2.9 | 2.3 | 2.1 | 2.2 | 2.3 |
| 1.5 | 1.8 | 1.6 | | .6 | 1.3 | 1.9 | 1.5 | 1.7 | 1.5 |
| .4 | .4 | .5 | % Depr., Dep., Amort./Sales | .6 | .6 | .4 | .4 | .3 |
| (125) 1.0 | (139) .7 | (140) .9 | | (18) 1.0 | (17) .9 | (25) .9 | (38) .8 | (40) .7 |
| 2.1 | 1.6 | 1.4 | | 2.1 | 2.0 | 2.1 | 1.3 | 1.4 |
| 2.2 | 2.0 | 1.5 | % Officers', Directors' Owners' Comp/Sales | 3.0 | 1.5 | 1.7 | 1.4 | .7 |
| (64) 3.3 | (68) 3.2 | (73) 3.3 | | (19) 4.3 | (10) 2.8 | (20) 2.8 | (10) 3.2 | (11) 1.1 |
| 6.1 | 5.5 | 5.4 | | 6.9 | 5.4 | 5.0 | 4.6 | 3.9 |
| 6522008M | 7224418M | 5355894M | Net Sales ($) | 4864M | 60545M | 68966M | 239318M | 739499M | 4242702M |
| 3547952M | 3541062M | 2878720M | Total Assets ($) | 2760M | 27922M | 35246M | 120241M | 349194M | 2343357M |

M = $ thousand    MM = $ million
See Pages 9 through 22 for Explanation of Ratios and Data

## Current Data Sorted by Assets

## Comparative Historical Data

| Type of Statement | 0-500M | 500M-2MM | 2-10MM | 10-50MM | 50-100MM | 100-250MM | | 12 4/1/07-3/31/08 ALL | 13 4/1/08-3/31/09 ALL |
|---|---|---|---|---|---|---|---|---|---|
| Unqualified | | 1 | 1 | 3 | | 2 | | 6 | 8 |
| Reviewed | | 1 | 5 | 3 | | | | 7 | 7 |
| Compiled | | 1 | 2 | | | | | 4 | 3 |
| Tax Returns | | 3 | | | | | | 4 | 6 |
| Other | 2 | 2 | 4 | 4 | 1 | 1 | | 12 | 13 |
| | 7 (4/1-9/30/11) | | | 29 (10/1/11-3/31/12) | | | | | |
| NUMBER OF STATEMENTS | 2 | 8 | 12 | 10 | 1 | 3 | | 33 | 37 |
| | % | % | % | % | % | % | | % | % |
| **ASSETS** | | | | | | | | | |
| Cash & Equivalents | | | 10.4 | 3.3 | | | | 9.5 | 8.5 |
| Trade Receivables (net) | | | 22.6 | 25.1 | | | | 30.6 | 21.4 |
| Inventory | | | 44.1 | 46.7 | | | | 31.0 | 37.1 |
| All Other Current | | | 3.1 | 2.5 | | | | 2.7 | 2.5 |
| Total Current | | | 80.1 | 77.6 | | | | 73.8 | 69.4 |
| Fixed Assets (net) | | | 6.8 | 14.9 | | | | 13.7 | 15.8 |
| Intangibles (net) | | | 6.2 | 2.8 | | | | 9.9 | 9.4 |
| All Other Non-Current | | | 6.8 | 4.7 | | | | 2.6 | 5.4 |
| Total | | | 100.0 | 100.0 | | | | 100.0 | 100.0 |
| **LIABILITIES** | | | | | | | | | |
| Notes Payable-Short Term | | | 20.9 | 19.4 | | | | 11.7 | 20.7 |
| Cur. Mat.-L.T.D. | | | .4 | 1.9 | | | | 2.2 | 4.2 |
| Trade Payables | | | 14.3 | 22.6 | | | | 16.8 | 16.5 |
| Income Taxes Payable | | | .0 | .6 | | | | .2 | .0 |
| All Other Current | | | 6.9 | 4.9 | | | | 5.4 | 8.6 |
| Total Current | | | 42.6 | 49.3 | | | | 36.4 | 50.1 |
| Long-Term Debt | | | 1.5 | 4.4 | | | | 12.3 | 14.4 |
| Deferred Taxes | | | .4 | .0 | | | | .6 | .9 |
| All Other Non-Current | | | 4.3 | 1.2 | | | | 8.1 | 6.6 |
| Net Worth | | | 51.3 | 45.0 | | | | 42.6 | 28.0 |
| Total Liabilities & Net Worth | | | 100.0 | 100.0 | | | | 100.0 | 100.0 |
| **INCOME DATA** | | | | | | | | | |
| Net Sales | | | 100.0 | 100.0 | | | | 100.0 | 100.0 |
| Gross Profit | | | 24.9 | 22.1 | | | | 25.3 | 29.4 |
| Operating Expenses | | | 20.3 | 19.2 | | | | 19.5 | 28.2 |
| Operating Profit | | | 4.7 | 2.8 | | | | 5.8 | 1.2 |
| All Other Expenses (net) | | | 1.1 | .9 | | | | 1.4 | 1.0 |
| Profit Before Taxes | | | 3.6 | 1.9 | | | | 4.4 | .3 |
| **RATIOS** | | | | | | | | | |
| Current | | | 2.5 | 2.1 | | | | 3.0 | 2.3 |
| | | | 1.8 | 1.5 | | | | 2.0 | 1.5 |
| | | | 1.2 | 1.3 | | | | 1.4 | 1.2 |
| Quick | | | .9 | .8 | | | | 1.5 | 1.5 |
| | | | .7 | .6 | | | | 1.1 | .7 |
| | | | .4 | .4 | | | | .7 | .3 |
| Sales/Receivables | | | 37 / 9.9 | 15 / 23.7 | | | | 26 / 14.1 | 24 / 15.4 |
| | | | 45 / 8.1 | 33 / 11.0 | | | | 40 / 9.2 | 33 / 11.0 |
| | | | 50 / 7.3 | 42 / 8.6 | | | | 53 / 6.9 | 50 / 7.3 |
| Cost of Sales/Inventory | | | 62 / 5.9 | 24 / 15.1 | | | | 27 / 13.4 | 69 / 5.3 |
| | | | 99 / 3.7 | 78 / 4.7 | | | | 63 / 5.8 | 103 / 3.5 |
| | | | 140 / 2.6 | 174 / 2.1 | | | | 89 / 4.1 | 124 / 3.0 |
| Cost of Sales/Payables | | | 6 / 65.9 | 13 / 27.5 | | | | 11 / 34.0 | 17 / 21.7 |
| | | | 19 / 18.9 | 35 / 10.5 | | | | 23 / 16.0 | 31 / 12.0 |
| | | | 50 / 7.3 | 76 / 4.8 | | | | 40 / 9.2 | 56 / 6.5 |
| Sales/Working Capital | | | 3.3 | 6.3 | | | | 4.9 | 4.5 |
| | | | 6.0 | 12.2 | | | | 8.0 | 10.4 |
| | | | 27.8 | 27.7 | | | | 13.3 | 17.2 |
| EBIT/Interest | | | | 25.6 | | | | 12.0 | 6.3 |
| | | | 8.7 | | | | (29) | 3.1 | (34) 1.5 |
| | | | 2.1 | | | | | 1.0 | .0 |
| Net Profit + Depr., Dep., Amort./Cur. Mat. L/T/D | | | | | | | | | |
| Fixed/Worth | | | .1 | .1 | | | | .1 | .1 |
| | | | .1 | .2 | | | | .4 | .6 |
| | | | .5 | .6 | | | | 1.2 | NM |
| Debt/Worth | | | .4 | .7 | | | | .6 | .7 |
| | | | 1.5 | 1.0 | | | | 1.8 | 3.9 |
| | | | 4.3 | 3.4 | | | | 5.7 | NM |
| % Profit Before Taxes/Tangible Net Worth | | | 30.5 | 33.0 | | | | 53.6 | 28.5 |
| | | | 19.5 | 18.2 | | | (27) | 21.8 | (28) 6.6 |
| | | | -2.7 | 7.4 | | | | -.4 | -.5 |
| % Profit Before Taxes/Total Assets | | | 14.6 | 18.4 | | | | 23.1 | 7.7 |
| | | | 5.9 | 6.7 | | | | 6.4 | 2.7 |
| | | | -1.5 | 1.7 | | | | .9 | -1.6 |
| Sales/Net Fixed Assets | | | 101.7 | 168.6 | | | | 68.4 | 61.1 |
| | | | 32.4 | 21.4 | | | | 18.4 | 20.2 |
| | | | 16.3 | 16.7 | | | | 10.8 | 8.7 |
| Sales/Total Assets | | | 2.6 | 5.9 | | | | 3.5 | 2.9 |
| | | | 2.1 | 3.0 | | | | 2.6 | 2.1 |
| | | | 1.6 | 1.6 | | | | 1.6 | 1.4 |
| % Depr., Dep., Amort./Sales | | | .4 | | | | | .4 | .5 |
| | | | (10) 1.3 | | | | (29) | 1.4 | (33) 1.0 |
| | | | 2.4 | | | | | 2.3 | 2.0 |
| % Officers', Directors' Owners' Comp/Sales | | | | | | | | 2.0 | 1.6 |
| | | | | | | | (11) | 3.2 | (12) 4.7 |
| | | | | | | | | 12.4 | 6.6 |
| Net Sales ($) | 717M | 37271M | 132889M | 698623M | 58150M | 1146435M | | 1564717M | 1250868M |
| Total Assets ($) | 350M | 9402M | 60108M | 203927M | 50179M | 572645M | | 711329M | 792987M |

M = $ thousand   MM = $ million
See Pages 9 through 22 for Explanation of Ratios and Data

## Comparative Historical Data | Current Data Sorted by Sales

### Type of Statement

| 11 | 10 | 7 | Unqualified | | 1 | | | 2 | 4 |
|---|---|---|---|---|---|---|---|---|---|
| 5 | 7 | 9 | Reviewed | | 1 | 1 | 2 | 2 | 3 |
| 5 | 4 | 3 | Compiled | | | | | 3 | |
| 5 | 4 | 5 | Tax Returns | 2 | 1 | 1 | 1 | | |
| 11 | 12 | 12 | Other | | 2 | | 3 | 2 | 5 |
| 4/1/09-3/31/10 ALL | 4/1/10-3/31/11 ALL | 4/1/11-3/31/12 ALL | | 0-1MM | 1-3MM | 3-5MM | 5-10MM | 10-25MM | 25MM & OVER |
| | | | | | 7 (4/1-9/30/11) | | 29 (10/1/11-3/31/12) | | |
| 37 | 37 | 36 | NUMBER OF STATEMENTS | 2 | 5 | 2 | 6 | 9 | 12 |

| 09-10 % | 10-11 % | 11-12 % | | 0-1MM % | 1-3MM % | 3-5MM % | 5-10MM % | 10-25MM % | 25MM & OVER % |
|---|---|---|---|---|---|---|---|---|---|
| | | | **ASSETS** | | | | | | |
| 10.3 | 10.7 | 7.5 | Cash & Equivalents | | | | | | 4.7 |
| 29.4 | 23.6 | 25.0 | Trade Receivables (net) | | | | | | 22.8 |
| 33.2 | 37.3 | 41.1 | Inventory | | | | | | 41.0 |
| 2.3 | 3.7 | 2.0 | All Other Current | | | | | | 2.5 |
| 75.2 | 75.3 | 75.6 | Total Current | | | | | | 70.9 |
| 12.7 | 11.1 | 13.4 | Fixed Assets (net) | | | | | | 16.1 |
| 6.3 | 9.2 | 5.7 | Intangibles (net) | | | | | | 7.6 |
| 5.8 | 4.3 | 5.3 | All Other Non-Current | | | | | | 5.4 |
| 100.0 | 100.0 | 100.0 | Total | | | | | | 100.0 |
| | | | **LIABILITIES** | | | | | | |
| 23.4 | 16.1 | 13.6 | Notes Payable-Short Term | | | | | | 11.7 |
| 5.5 | 6.3 | 1.2 | Cur. Mat.-L.T.D. | | | | | | .9 |
| 14.9 | 18.5 | 19.3 | Trade Payables | | | | | | 19.8 |
| .3 | .3 | .5 | Income Taxes Payable | | | | | | .5 |
| 7.8 | 5.0 | 6.6 | All Other Current | | | | | | 6.4 |
| 51.9 | 46.2 | 41.2 | Total Current | | | | | | 39.4 |
| 12.2 | 5.8 | 8.7 | Long-Term Debt | | | | | | 5.9 |
| .3 | .5 | .2 | Deferred Taxes | | | | | | .2 |
| 4.5 | 4.0 | 2.6 | All Other Non-Current | | | | | | 2.3 |
| 31.0 | 43.5 | 47.4 | Net Worth | | | | | | 52.3 |
| 100.0 | 100.0 | 100.0 | Total Liabilities & Net Worth | | | | | | 100.0 |
| | | | **INCOME DATA** | | | | | | |
| 100.0 | 100.0 | 100.0 | Net Sales | | | | | | 100.0 |
| 31.3 | 28.9 | 29.8 | Gross Profit | | | | | | 25.2 |
| 29.4 | 24.1 | 25.0 | Operating Expenses | | | | | | 20.0 |
| 1.8 | 4.8 | 4.8 | Operating Profit | | | | | | 5.3 |
| .9 | 1.8 | .5 | All Other Expenses (net) | | | | | | .4 |
| .9 | 3.0 | 4.3 | Profit Before Taxes | | | | | | 4.9 |
| | | | **RATIOS** | | | | | | |
| 2.3 | 2.6 | 3.1 | | | | | | | 3.3 |
| 1.5 | 1.5 | 1.8 | Current | | | | | | 1.5 |
| 1.1 | 1.2 | 1.3 | | | | | | | 1.3 |
| 1.3 | 1.5 | 1.4 | | | | | | | 1.2 |
| .9 | .7 | .8 | Quick | | | | | | .7 |
| .5 | .4 | .4 | | | | | | | .4 |
| 31  11.7 | 22  16.7 | 22  16.6 | | | | | | | 16  22.6 |
| 40  9.1 | 37  9.8 | 38  9.7 | Sales/Receivables | | | | | | 32  11.3 |
| 62  5.9 | 51  7.1 | 51  7.2 | | | | | | | 38  9.6 |
| 41  8.9 | 44  8.3 | 34  10.7 | | | | | | | 27  13.5 |
| 68  5.3 | 68  5.3 | 96  3.8 | Cost of Sales/Inventory | | | | | | 78  4.7 |
| 114  3.2 | 123  3.0 | 152  2.4 | | | | | | | 159  2.3 |
| 13  27.4 | 16  22.5 | 15  23.7 | | | | | | | 16  22.9 |
| 30  12.2 | 31  11.6 | 33  10.9 | Cost of Sales/Payables | | | | | | 31  11.8 |
| 52  7.0 | 59  6.2 | 61  6.0 | | | | | | | 62  5.9 |
| 4.8 | 4.5 | 3.9 | | | | | | | 4.6 |
| 11.3 | 10.1 | 7.2 | Sales/Working Capital | | | | | | 11.9 |
| 33.5 | 26.6 | 25.4 | | | | | | | 25.4 |
| 5.6 | 6.5 | 25.8 | | | | | | | 29.5 |
| (34)  2.5 | (34)  2.8 | (29)  4.5 | EBIT/Interest | | | | | | (11)  12.5 |
| .7 | .8 | 2.0 | | | | | | | 3.9 |
| | | | Net Profit + Depr., Dep., Amort./Cur. Mat. L/T/D | | | | | | |
| .1 | .1 | .1 | | | | | | | .1 |
| .3 | .3 | .2 | Fixed/Worth | | | | | | .4 |
| 2.5 | .8 | .6 | | | | | | | .6 |
| .8 | .8 | .5 | | | | | | | .7 |
| 2.5 | 2.5 | 1.1 | Debt/Worth | | | | | | .8 |
| 13.8 | 5.5 | 4.0 | | | | | | | 3.3 |
| 48.6 | 45.0 | 40.3 | | | | | | | 67.2 |
| (33)  17.8 | (34)  19.8 | (35)  24.9 | % Profit Before Taxes/Tangible Net Worth | | | | | | 25.2 |
| 3.9 | 2.3 | 8.6 | | | | | | | 9.3 |
| 7.8 | 13.5 | 18.1 | | | | | | | 20.2 |
| 3.4 | 6.4 | 8.3 | % Profit Before Taxes/Total Assets | | | | | | 11.6 |
| -1.9 | -.3 | 1.8 | | | | | | | 2.9 |
| 106.3 | 73.7 | 84.6 | | | | | | | 44.2 |
| 26.4 | 27.0 | 21.4 | Sales/Net Fixed Assets | | | | | | 21.4 |
| 10.9 | 11.3 | 14.4 | | | | | | | 12.7 |
| 3.4 | 3.2 | 3.4 | | | | | | | 5.4 |
| 2.3 | 2.4 | 2.4 | Sales/Total Assets | | | | | | 2.8 |
| 1.8 | 1.7 | 1.6 | | | | | | | 1.9 |
| .5 | .4 | .2 | | | | | | | .3 |
| (27)  1.2 | (26)  1.3 | (32)  1.1 | % Depr., Dep., Amort./Sales | | | | | | .8 |
| 2.0 | 1.8 | 1.7 | | | | | | | 1.7 |
| 3.0 | 1.2 | 1.0 | | | | | | | |
| (14)  4.7 | (11)  3.7 | (14)  4.4 | % Officers', Directors' Owners' Comp/Sales | | | | | | |
| 12.3 | 7.2 | 8.1 | | | | | | | |
| 1736961M | 1830039M | 2074085M | Net Sales ($) | 717M | 10791M | 8411M | 41131M | 155106M | 1857929M |
| 965221M | 923960M | 896611M | Total Assets ($) | 350M | 6863M | 3774M | 15610M | 71138M | 798876M |

© RMA 2012

M = $ thousand    MM = $ million
See Pages 9 through 22 for Explanation of Ratios and Data

## Current Data Sorted by Assets     Comparative Historical Data

| | | | | | | Type of Statement | | |
|---|---|---|---|---|---|---|---|---|
| 1 | | 2 | 21 | 9 | 2 | Unqualified | 46 | 33 |
| 1 | 6 | 27 | 17 | 1 | 3 | Reviewed | 46 | 39 |
| 4 | 8 | 14 | 1 | | | Compiled | 35 | 27 |
| 7 | 9 | 4 | 3 | | | Tax Returns | 23 | 25 |
| 1 | 3 | 17 | 25 | 8 | 4 | Other | 88 | 77 |
| | 35 (4/1-9/30/11) | | 163 (10/1/11-3/31/12) | | | | 4/1/07-3/31/08 | 4/1/08-3/31/09 |
| 0-500M | 500M-2MM | 2-10MM | 10-50MM | 50-100MM | 100-250MM | | ALL | ALL |
| 14 | 26 | 64 | 67 | 18 | 9 | NUMBER OF STATEMENTS | 238 | 201 |
| % | % | % | % | % | % | ASSETS | % | % |
| 10.5 | 3.3 | 5.9 | 3.7 | 3.3 | | Cash & Equivalents | 6.2 | 5.5 |
| 16.9 | 13.6 | 13.9 | 9.9 | 11.0 | | Trade Receivables (net) | 11.1 | 9.2 |
| 26.7 | 26.9 | 29.9 | 28.0 | 29.6 | | Inventory | 27.0 | 25.9 |
| 7.0 | 1.3 | 2.0 | 2.2 | 2.1 | | All Other Current | 3.6 | 2.5 |
| 61.1 | 45.1 | 51.7 | 43.9 | 46.0 | | Total Current | 47.9 | 43.1 |
| 31.4 | 44.5 | 38.4 | 44.6 | 38.5 | | Fixed Assets (net) | 41.9 | 45.4 |
| 4.9 | 3.2 | 1.7 | 1.5 | 3.5 | | Intangibles (net) | 1.5 | 1.3 |
| 2.6 | 7.2 | 8.1 | 10.0 | 12.0 | | All Other Non-Current | 8.8 | 10.2 |
| 100.0 | 100.0 | 100.0 | 100.0 | 100.0 | | Total | 100.0 | 100.0 |
| | | | | | | LIABILITIES | | |
| 23.8 | 25.0 | 13.7 | 15.1 | 13.1 | | Notes Payable-Short Term | 14.0 | 13.5 |
| 2.1 | 4.7 | 4.5 | 4.5 | 3.2 | | Cur. Mat.-L.T.D. | 4.6 | 6.1 |
| 13.5 | 8.1 | 6.8 | 5.1 | 4.6 | | Trade Payables | 6.5 | 5.7 |
| .0 | .0 | .0 | .1 | .2 | | Income Taxes Payable | .1 | .1 |
| 13.5 | 12.6 | 5.3 | 10.5 | 9.2 | | All Other Current | 5.2 | 7.9 |
| 53.0 | 50.5 | 30.3 | 35.2 | 30.3 | | Total Current | 30.3 | 33.2 |
| 41.8 | 29.5 | 19.2 | 20.0 | 20.3 | | Long-Term Debt | 22.5 | 26.1 |
| .0 | .0 | .2 | .7 | .4 | | Deferred Taxes | .7 | .6 |
| 15.4 | 15.9 | 4.7 | 5.0 | 6.4 | | All Other Non-Current | 6.1 | 4.8 |
| -10.7 | 4.0 | 45.5 | 39.0 | 42.5 | | Net Worth | 40.4 | 35.4 |
| 100.0 | 100.0 | 100.0 | 100.0 | 100.0 | | Total Liabilties & Net Worth | 100.0 | 100.0 |
| | | | | | | INCOME DATA | | |
| 100.0 | 100.0 | 100.0 | 100.0 | 100.0 | | Net Sales | 100.0 | 100.0 |
| 37.7 | 27.6 | 21.4 | 15.0 | 12.3 | | Gross Profit | 17.6 | 19.7 |
| 34.0 | 26.9 | 18.6 | 14.6 | 10.2 | | Operating Expenses | 16.2 | 19.2 |
| 3.8 | .8 | 2.8 | .4 | 2.1 | | Operating Profit | 1.4 | .5 |
| 3.4 | 1.3 | .5 | .5 | .1 | | All Other Expenses (net) | 1.3 | 1.4 |
| .4 | -.5 | 2.4 | -.1 | 1.9 | | Profit Before Taxes | .1 | -.9 |
| | | | | | | RATIOS | | |
| 4.0 | 2.7 | 3.0 | 2.0 | 4.2 | | | 3.2 | 3.3 |
| 2.2 | 1.2 | 1.9 | 1.4 | 1.7 | Current | 1.7 | 1.4 |
| .6 | .6 | 1.1 | 1.1 | 1.2 | | 1.1 | .8 |
| 1.8 | 1.1 | 1.3 | .7 | .6 | | | 1.1 | 1.1 |
| .5 | .3 | .6 | .4 | .4 | Quick | .5 | .4 |
| .1 | .2 | .3 | .2 | .3 | | .2 | .2 |

| | | | | | | | | |
|---|---|---|---|---|---|---|---|---|
| 3   109.8 | 8   48.5 | 14   25.5 | 13   27.3 | 12   29.9 | | | 10   34.8 | 10   35.5 |
| 10   36.6 | 13   28.5 | 19   19.1 | 19   19.2 | 21   17.1 | | Sales/Receivables | 17   21.5 | 16   23.3 |
| 21   17.0 | 27   13.4 | 28   13.0 | 29   12.8 | 26   14.0 | | | 27   13.3 | 25   14.7 |
| 0   UND | 19   18.9 | 31   11.7 | 40   9.2 | 48   7.6 | | | 34   10.7 | 31   11.7 |
| 16   23.3 | 48   7.6 | 68   5.4 | 87   4.2 | 76   4.8 | | Cost of Sales/Inventory | 58   6.3 | 60   6.1 |
| 76   4.8 | 89   4.1 | 118   3.1 | 130   2.8 | 135   2.7 | | | 93   3.9 | 100   3.6 |
| 0   UND | 2   193.2 | 5   75.3 | 6   63.6 | 6   61.5 | | | 5   72.1 | 4   97.0 |
| 17   21.6 | 8   46.1 | 10   35.2 | 13   29.0 | 9   39.6 | | Cost of Sales/Payables | 11   33.0 | 9   41.1 |
| 49   7.4 | 19   18.9 | 20   17.9 | 22   16.4 | 18   20.2 | | | 19   19.0 | 19   19.6 |
| 3.7 | 8.6 | 5.6 | 5.5 | 6.1 | | | 5.0 | 6.2 |
| 13.1 | NM | 8.9 | 10.9 | 11.2 | | Sales/Working Capital | 9.5 | 16.4 |
| -11.1 | -17.4 | 61.9 | 44.1 | 28.6 | | | 66.0 | -31.1 |
| 1.6 | 5.9 | 10.9 | 3.9 | 7.9 | | | 2.9 | 2.8 |
| (10)   .8 | (25)   1.3 | (59)   2.7 | (66)   1.4 | (16)   1.3 | | EBIT/Interest | (224)   1.0 | (187)   .8 |
| -.6 | -.3 | .5 | -.7 | -.8 | | | -.8 | -1.7 |
| | | 12.0 | 3.3 | | | | 4.0 | 2.3 |
| | (15)   2.3 | (19)   1.9 | | | Net Profit + Depr., Dep., Amort./Cur. Mat. L/T/D | (61)   1.6 | (56)   1.0 |
| | | .9 | 1.3 | | | | .6 | .1 |
| .1 | .6 | .5 | .6 | .4 | | | .5 | .6 |
| 2.2 | 3.0 | .9 | .9 | 1.2 | | Fixed/Worth | 1.0 | 1.3 |
| -1.1 | -3.6 | 1.5 | 1.6 | 2.8 | | | 2.0 | 3.7 |
| .7 | .8 | .7 | .6 | .7 | | | .6 | .7 |
| 18.2 | 3.9 | 1.4 | 1.3 | 1.8 | | Debt/Worth | 1.5 | 1.7 |
| -2.7 | -9.6 | 2.4 | 3.4 | 5.1 | | | 3.3 | 5.8 |
| | | 25.9 | 20.8 | 11.2 | 18.1 | | 14.5 | 14.7 |
| | (15)   9.2 | (62)   5.8 | (60)   2.1 | 2.8 | % Profit Before Taxes/Tangible Net Worth | (219)   1.3 | (174)   .3 |
| | | .0 | -1.6 | -8.8 | -11.7 | | -14.5 | -11.8 |
| 8.2 | 13.3 | 10.0 | 4.1 | 7.8 | | | 5.9 | 4.3 |
| .4 | 1.3 | 2.9 | 1.0 | 1.2 | % Profit Before Taxes/Total Assets | .1 | -.9 |
| -7.4 | -4.7 | -.7 | -4.5 | -3.7 | | | -5.2 | -5.9 |
| UND | 9.9 | 9.3 | 6.5 | 8.7 | | | 8.2 | 8.6 |
| 16.4 | 6.0 | 5.9 | 3.3 | 5.4 | Sales/Net Fixed Assets | 4.6 | 4.0 |
| 6.3 | 2.7 | 3.3 | 1.9 | 2.6 | | | 2.5 | 2.3 |
| 4.4 | 3.8 | 2.8 | 1.8 | 2.2 | | | 2.5 | 2.6 |
| 3.5 | 2.1 | 2.0 | 1.4 | 1.5 | Sales/Total Assets | 1.6 | 1.7 |
| 2.1 | 1.4 | 1.5 | 1.1 | .9 | | | 1.1 | 1.1 |
| | | 1.2 | 1.7 | 2.3 | 1.6 | | 1.7 | 2.3 |
| | (24)   3.1 | (61)   2.9 | (62)   4.1 | (15)   3.5 | % Depr., Dep., Amort./Sales | (218)   3.7 | (182)   4.0 |
| | | 5.6 | 4.4 | 7.2 | 6.6 | | 5.9 | 6.2 |
| | | 1.8 | .7 | | | | 1.3 | 1.4 |
| | (12)   3.3 | (18)   1.5 | | | % Officers', Directors' Owners' Comp/Sales | (67)   2.3 | (57)   2.6 |
| | | 6.1 | 2.3 | | | | 4.1 | 4.3 |
| 11169M | 79338M | 699402M | 1985238M | 2119046M | 1407113M | Net Sales ($) | 9010451M | 6149687M |
| 3303M | 29074M | 320165M | 1354801M | 1275697M | 1382176M | Total Assets ($) | 6407328M | 4779369M |

© RMA 2012

M = $ thousand    MM = $ million
See Pages 9 through 22 for Explanation of Ratios and Data

## Comparative Historical Data      Current Data Sorted by Sales

| | | | Type of Statement | | | | | | |
|---|---|---|---|---|---|---|---|---|---|
| 36 | 33 | 35 | Unqualified | 1 | 1 | | 1 | 7 | 25 |
| 34 | 40 | 55 | Reviewed | 1 | 5 | 4 | 12 | 24 | 9 |
| 23 | 26 | 27 | Compiled | 4 | 8 | 5 | 5 | 4 | 1 |
| 28 | 22 | 23 | Tax Returns | 4 | 7 | 4 | 4 | 4 | |
| 65 | 79 | 58 | Other | 2 | 2 | 3 | 5 | 18 | 28 |
| 4/1/09-3/31/10 ALL | 4/1/10-3/31/11 ALL | 4/1/11-3/31/12 ALL | | 35 (4/1-9/30/11) | | | 163 (10/1/11-3/31/12) | | |
| | | | | 0-1MM | 1-3MM | 3-5MM | 5-10MM | 10-25MM | 25MM & OVER |
| 186 | 200 | 198 | **NUMBER OF STATEMENTS** | 12 | 23 | 16 | 27 | 57 | 63 |
| % | % | % | **ASSETS** | % | % | % | % | % | % |
| 6.2 | 5.4 | 4.9 | Cash & Equivalents | 8.8 | 4.2 | 9.1 | 3.6 | 4.6 | 4.3 |
| 11.6 | 10.2 | 12.2 | Trade Receivables (net) | 7.0 | 12.5 | 13.8 | 12.6 | 13.5 | 11.4 |
| 24.5 | 27.9 | 28.0 | Inventory | 28.1 | 20.6 | 25.2 | 34.4 | 29.3 | 27.6 |
| 3.0 | 2.4 | 2.5 | All Other Current | 8.1 | 1.2 | 1.8 | 2.2 | 1.8 | 2.7 |
| 45.4 | 46.1 | 47.7 | Total Current | 52.1 | 38.6 | 50.0 | 52.7 | 49.1 | 46.0 |
| 42.1 | 42.7 | 41.0 | Fixed Assets (net) | 37.6 | 49.1 | 38.1 | 41.1 | 40.0 | 40.3 |
| 1.4 | 1.6 | 2.2 | Intangibles (net) | 5.7 | 1.5 | 4.9 | 1.0 | 2.1 | 1.7 |
| 11.2 | 9.6 | 9.1 | All Other Non-Current | 4.6 | 10.8 | 7.0 | 5.2 | 8.7 | 12.0 |
| 100.0 | 100.0 | 100.0 | Total | 100.0 | 100.0 | 100.0 | 100.0 | 100.0 | 100.0 |
| | | | **LIABILITIES** | | | | | | |
| 14.3 | 14.6 | 15.9 | Notes Payable-Short Term | 21.1 | 15.2 | 8.4 | 29.8 | 13.7 | 13.0 |
| 6.6 | 5.7 | 4.3 | Cur. Mat.-L.T.D. | 1.0 | 5.2 | 1.7 | 5.7 | 5.5 | 3.5 |
| 5.8 | 5.6 | 6.5 | Trade Payables | 11.4 | 5.0 | 4.3 | 8.0 | 7.1 | 5.6 |
| .1 | .1 | .1 | Income Taxes Payable | .0 | .0 | .2 | .0 | .0 | .2 |
| 5.4 | 4.7 | 8.9 | All Other Current | 8.2 | 17.7 | 4.1 | 2.1 | 8.0 | 10.7 |
| 32.2 | 30.7 | 35.6 | Total Current | 41.8 | 43.0 | 18.6 | 45.7 | 34.3 | 32.9 |
| 27.4 | 23.7 | 23.0 | Long-Term Debt | 53.5 | 33.2 | 16.0 | 18.9 | 21.1 | 18.7 |
| .5 | .5 | .4 | Deferred Taxes | .0 | .0 | .2 | .0 | .7 | .7 |
| 6.0 | 8.7 | 7.1 | All Other Non-Current | 16.3 | 17.1 | 2.0 | 4.4 | 5.2 | 6.0 |
| 33.8 | 36.3 | 33.8 | Net Worth | -12.3 | 6.7 | 63.1 | 31.0 | 38.7 | 41.7 |
| 100.0 | 100.0 | 100.0 | Total Liabilities & Net Worth | 100.0 | 100.0 | 100.0 | 100.0 | 100.0 | 100.0 |
| | | | **INCOME DATA** | | | | | | |
| 100.0 | 100.0 | 100.0 | Net Sales | 100.0 | 100.0 | 100.0 | 100.0 | 100.0 | 100.0 |
| 17.6 | 24.8 | 19.9 | Gross Profit | 38.5 | 28.0 | 19.6 | 25.1 | 18.3 | 12.8 |
| 20.3 | 21.2 | 18.2 | Operating Expenses | 36.7 | 27.3 | 17.3 | 22.1 | 16.3 | 11.6 |
| -2.8 | 3.6 | 1.7 | Operating Profit | 1.7 | .7 | 2.3 | 3.0 | 2.0 | 1.1 |
| 1.3 | 1.7 | .8 | All Other Expenses (net) | 3.1 | 1.5 | -.5 | 1.0 | .7 | .5 |
| -4.1 | 1.9 | .9 | Profit Before Taxes | -1.4 | -.7 | 2.8 | 2.0 | 1.3 | .6 |
| | | | **RATIOS** | | | | | | |
| 3.0 | 2.7 | 2.7 | | 4.1 | 1.5 | 7.0 | 2.4 | 2.4 | 3.0 |
| 1.6 | 1.6 | 1.6 | Current | 2.8 | 1.0 | 3.0 | 1.6 | 1.5 | 1.6 |
| .9 | 1.0 | 1.0 | | .9 | .5 | 1.8 | .9 | 1.1 | 1.2 |
| 1.3 | 1.0 | 1.0 | | 1.6 | .8 | 3.9 | .6 | .9 | .9 |
| .6 | (199) .5 | .4 | Quick | .3 | .3 | 1.5 | .4 | .4 | .5 |
| .2 | .2 | .2 | | .0 | .2 | .7 | .2 | .2 | .3 |
| 12   31.5 | 12   31.7 | 12   29.2 | | 2   212.1 | 7   53.2 | 9   40.7 | 12   31.1 | 16   23.4 | 13   27.4 |
| 20   17.9 | 18   20.1 | 19   19.4 | Sales/Receivables | 7   56.1 | 13   28.1 | 19   19.3 | 19   19.7 | 23   16.0 | 20   18.4 |
| 31   11.9 | 30   12.2 | 28   13.0 | | 15   23.9 | 28   13.0 | 27   13.5 | 32   13.1 | 32   11.5 | 27   13.6 |
| 33   11.2 | 32   11.3 | 33   11.2 | | 0   UND | 3   108.5 | 12   31.5 | 42   8.6 | 37   9.8 | 36   10.2 |
| 60   6.1 | 66   5.5 | 65   5.6 | Cost of Sales/Inventory | 38   9.6 | 62   5.9 | 46   8.0 | 104   3.5 | 69   5.3 | 65   5.6 |
| 107   3.4 | 126   2.9 | 118   3.1 | | 114   3.2 | 182   2.0 | 83   4.4 | 122   3.0 | 122   3.0 | 114   3.2 |
| 5   75.2 | 5   72.8 | 5   72.8 | | 7   52.3 | 0   UND | 2   224.6 | 4   85.1 | 6   61.6 | 6   57.9 |
| 10   36.9 | 11   32.5 | 11   32.9 | Cost of Sales/Payables | 23   16.1 | 8   44.2 | 5   79.9 | 11   32.8 | 13   27.4 | 11   31.9 |
| 19   19.3 | 21   17.6 | 21   17.2 | | 42   8.7 | 19   19.0 | 13   27.7 | 21   17.1 | 23   15.6 | 18   20.3 |
| 4.7 | 4.5 | 5.5 | | 3.6 | 7.9 | 4.1 | 4.9 | 6.1 | 5.3 |
| 10.8 | 11.2 | 11.5 | Sales/Working Capital | 9.2 | -141.2 | 8.3 | 12.1 | 11.2 | 11.3 |
| -39.5 | -247.8 | 301.5 | | NM | -12.2 | 22.1 | -34.3 | 71.3 | 29.7 |
| 2.5 | 7.7 | 5.8 | | | 1.7 | 15.0 | 4.7 | 7.9 | 4.2 |
| (174) .0 | (187) 2.3 | (182) 1.5 | EBIT/Interest | (22) 1.2 | (11) 7.0 | 2.4 | (55) 2.2 | (58) 1.6 | |
| -3.0 | .6 | -.2 | | -1.0 | .1 | .2 | -.4 | -.1 | |
| 2.5 | 4.7 | 4.4 | Net Profit + Depr., Dep., | | | | | 2.5 | 4.7 |
| (42) 1.4 | (46) 1.7 | (44) 1.7 | Amort./Cur. Mat. L/T/D | | | | (14) 1.6 | (17) 1.9 | |
| .5 | 1.0 | 1.0 | | | | | .8 | .7 | |
| .5 | .5 | .5 | | .1 | .8 | .4 | .5 | .5 | .5 |
| 1.3 | 1.1 | 1.0 | Fixed/Worth | 4.8 | 2.1 | .6 | 1.1 | .9 | .9 |
| 3.3 | 3.0 | 2.4 | | -1.7 | -4.5 | 1.9 | 1.9 | 1.5 | 1.6 |
| .6 | .6 | .7 | | .6 | 1.0 | .1 | .7 | .8 | .6 |
| 1.7 | 1.4 | 1.6 | Debt/Worth | NM | 2.3 | .4 | 1.8 | 1.5 | 1.3 |
| 5.5 | 4.6 | 5.2 | | -4.8 | -11.3 | 2.3 | 2.6 | 3.3 | 3.2 |
| 12.6 | 26.0 | 15.5 | % Profit Before Taxes/Tangible | 10.7 | 25.9 | 15.9 | 20.3 | 11.5 | |
| (160) -4.5 | (170) 9.9 | (172) 4.6 | Net Worth | (14) 3.4 | (15) 7.9 | (25) 5.9 | (50) 5.5 | (62) 2.5 | |
| -18.5 | .6 | -7.1 | | -5.0 | -3.7 | -3.6 | -3.2 | -10.4 | |
| 3.8 | 9.3 | 7.0 | % Profit Before Taxes/Total | 20.7 | 3.2 | 18.5 | 7.8 | 6.9 | 5.7 |
| -3.1 | 2.9 | 1.6 | Assets | -2.5 | .0 | 6.2 | 3.0 | 1.8 | .8 |
| -11.4 | -1.2 | -3.7 | | -14.3 | -5.9 | -2.6 | -2.2 | -2.6 | -3.5 |
| 6.9 | 8.3 | 9.0 | | 38.1 | 7.7 | 14.9 | 7.1 | 9.2 | 8.3 |
| 4.0 | 4.7 | 4.8 | Sales/Net Fixed Assets | 12.4 | 3.6 | 6.0 | 6.0 | 4.6 | 3.7 |
| 1.9 | 2.3 | 2.6 | | 2.1 | 2.1 | 3.1 | 3.0 | 2.6 | 2.5 |
| 2.2 | 2.5 | 2.4 | | 3.6 | 2.2 | 3.7 | 2.5 | 2.2 | 2.0 |
| 1.4 | 1.6 | 1.7 | Sales/Total Assets | 2.1 | 1.4 | 2.3 | 1.9 | 1.6 | 1.6 |
| .9 | 1.0 | 1.1 | | 1.3 | .9 | 1.3 | 1.1 | 1.0 | 1.0 |
| 2.6 | 2.2 | 1.8 | | | 1.7 | 1.3 | 2.6 | 1.7 | 2.1 |
| (172) 4.6 | (176) 3.8 | (177) 3.5 | % Depr., Dep., Amort./Sales | (21) 4.7 | (14) 2.5 | 3.9 | (54) 3.0 | (54) 3.5 | |
| 7.7 | 6.8 | 6.0 | | 6.7 | 5.2 | 4.7 | 5.9 | 6.5 | |
| 1.7 | 1.1 | .9 | | | 2.1 | | | .5 | |
| (57) 2.4 | (50) 1.6 | (45) 2.0 | % Officers', Directors' Owners' Comp/Sales | (10) 3.3 | | | (16) .9 | | |
| 3.9 | 3.1 | 5.1 | | 8.9 | | | 1.6 | | |
| 5024584M | 5532922M | 6301306M | Net Sales ($) | 6763M | 39689M | 67866M | 198219M | 976337M | 5012432M |
| 4710500M | 4221276M | 4365216M | Total Assets ($) | 3997M | 51202M | 36406M | 125108M | 673825M | 3474678M |

M = $ thousand    MM = $ million
See Pages 9 through 22 for Explanation of Ratios and Data

## Current Data Sorted by Assets            Comparative Historical Data

| 0-500M | 500M-2MM | 2-10MM | 10-50MM | 50-100MM | 100-250MM | Type of Statement | 4/1/07-3/31/08 ALL | 4/1/08-3/31/09 ALL |
|---|---|---|---|---|---|---|---|---|
| | 1 | 2 | 6 | | 1 | Unqualified | 22 | 14 |
| | | 7 | | | | Reviewed | 11 | 10 |
| | 1 | 1 | | | | Compiled | 1 | 4 |
| | 2 | 1 | | | | Tax Returns | 2 | 2 |
| 1 | 2 | 6 | 4 | 1 | 1 | Other | 15 | 15 |
| | 7 (4/1-9/30/11) | | 29 (10/1/11-3/31/12) | | | | | |
| 1 | 5 | 17 | 10 | 1 | 2 | **NUMBER OF STATEMENTS** | 51 | 45 |
| % | % | % | % | % | % | **ASSETS** | % | % |
| | | 6.4 | 8.6 | | | Cash & Equivalents | 5.2 | 7.1 |
| | | 21.6 | 18.4 | | | Trade Receivables (net) | 19.4 | 17.2 |
| | | 39.4 | 23.7 | | | Inventory | 38.2 | 37.0 |
| | | 1.4 | 2.4 | | | All Other Current | 2.0 | 2.6 |
| | | 68.8 | 53.1 | | | Total Current | 64.8 | 63.9 |
| | | 22.1 | 34.5 | | | Fixed Assets (net) | 28.1 | 26.3 |
| | | .9 | 4.1 | | | Intangibles (net) | .9 | 3.5 |
| | | 8.3 | 8.3 | | | All Other Non-Current | 6.2 | 6.3 |
| | | 100.0 | 100.0 | | | Total | 100.0 | 100.0 |
| | | | | | | **LIABILITIES** | | |
| | | 12.5 | 4.7 | | | Notes Payable-Short Term | 17.3 | 15.8 |
| | | 1.5 | 1.7 | | | Cur. Mat.-L.T.D. | 4.1 | 2.8 |
| | | 10.3 | 9.1 | | | Trade Payables | 8.2 | 8.0 |
| | | .7 | .0 | | | Income Taxes Payable | .3 | .1 |
| | | 4.3 | 8.7 | | | All Other Current | 6.3 | 6.0 |
| | | 29.4 | 24.2 | | | Total Current | 36.2 | 32.7 |
| | | 14.4 | 30.7 | | | Long-Term Debt | 17.4 | 15.5 |
| | | .0 | .2 | | | Deferred Taxes | .5 | .4 |
| | | .7 | 1.2 | | | All Other Non-Current | 1.3 | .7 |
| | | 55.4 | 43.7 | | | Net Worth | 44.6 | 50.6 |
| | | 100.0 | 100.0 | | | Total Liabilities & Net Worth | 100.0 | 100.0 |
| | | | | | | **INCOME DATA** | | |
| | | 100.0 | 100.0 | | | Net Sales | 100.0 | 100.0 |
| | | 21.0 | 16.1 | | | Gross Profit | 17.4 | 17.8 |
| | | 17.9 | 15.7 | | | Operating Expenses | 12.2 | 13.5 |
| | | 3.1 | .4 | | | Operating Profit | 5.1 | 4.3 |
| | | .3 | 1.5 | | | All Other Expenses (net) | .9 | 1.0 |
| | | 2.8 | -1.1 | | | Profit Before Taxes | 4.2 | 3.3 |
| | | | | | | **RATIOS** | | |
| | | 3.4 | 3.3 | | | | 3.4 | 3.6 |
| | | 2.6 | 1.9 | | | Current | 1.7 | 1.8 |
| | | 1.7 | 1.4 | | | | 1.4 | 1.4 |
| | | 1.5 | 1.7 | | | | 1.4 | 1.3 |
| | | .7 | .7 | | | Quick | .6 | .7 |
| | | .4 | .5 | | | | .4 | .4 |
| | 17 | 22.0 | 24  15.5 | | | | 17  21.4 | 12  31.0 |
| | 25 | 14.7 | 33  10.9 | | | Sales/Receivables | 25  14.4 | 24  14.9 |
| | 34 | 10.8 | 43  8.5 | | | | 33  11.0 | 32  11.3 |
| | 32 | 11.3 | 27  13.4 | | | | 40  9.2 | 37  9.8 |
| | 76 | 4.8 | 52  7.0 | | | Cost of Sales/Inventory | 64  5.7 | 66  5.5 |
| | 122 | 3.0 | 62  5.9 | | | | 83  4.4 | 88  4.1 |
| | 10 | 38.4 | 8  44.9 | | | | 6  62.5 | 6  66.1 |
| | 13 | 28.4 | 14  25.7 | | | Cost of Sales/Payables | 11  33.2 | 10  36.1 |
| | 20 | 18.1 | 32  11.4 | | | | 18  20.0 | 19  18.9 |
| | | 4.5 | 5.7 | | | | 5.1 | 6.2 |
| | | 5.6 | 8.2 | | | Sales/Working Capital | 10.4 | 8.0 |
| | | 8.5 | NM | | | | 15.9 | 19.1 |
| | | 17.8 | | | | | 9.5 | 12.2 |
| | (16) | 7.3 | | | | EBIT/Interest | (49)  5.1 | (42)  3.2 |
| | | .9 | | | | | 1.4 | 1.0 |
| | | | | | | | 6.9 | 13.5 |
| | | | | | | Net Profit + Depr., Dep., Amort./Cur. Mat. L/T/D | (14)  3.9 | (15)  2.1 |
| | | | | | | | 1.4 | .2 |
| | | .2 | .2 | | | | .4 | .3 |
| | | .3 | 1.6 | | | Fixed/Worth | .6 | .5 |
| | | .6 | 4.2 | | | | .8 | 1.0 |
| | | .4 | .6 | | | | .8 | .6 |
| | | .6 | 1.4 | | | Debt/Worth | 1.2 | 1.0 |
| | | 1.4 | 6.8 | | | | 2.1 | 2.5 |
| | | 17.1 | 8.2 | | | | 40.9 | 31.0 |
| | (16) | 6.0 | 4.0 | | | % Profit Before Taxes/Tangible Net Worth | (48)  24.4 | 16.9 |
| | | -.1 | -60.3 | | | | 4.3 | -.2 |
| | | 8.0 | 4.6 | | | | 17.9 | 16.1 |
| | | 3.8 | 2.6 | | | % Profit Before Taxes/Total Assets | 9.3 | 5.7 |
| | | .3 | -5.8 | | | | 1.6 | -.1 |
| | | 25.2 | 22.4 | | | | 19.8 | 26.4 |
| | | 17.2 | 6.7 | | | Sales/Net Fixed Assets | 11.8 | 10.0 |
| | | 8.6 | 2.7 | | | | 7.3 | 5.9 |
| | | 3.0 | 2.6 | | | | 3.4 | 3.4 |
| | | 2.2 | 2.2 | | | Sales/Total Assets | 2.7 | 2.2 |
| | | 1.8 | 1.5 | | | | 1.8 | 1.9 |
| | | 1.0 | | | | | .8 | 1.1 |
| | (15) | 1.4 | | | | % Depr., Dep., Amort./Sales | (47)  1.4 | (39)  1.7 |
| | | 1.8 | | | | | 2.2 | 2.7 |
| | | | | | | % Officers', Directors' Owners' Comp/Sales | | |
| 1629M | 22332M | 279060M | 625864M | 165326M | 647745M | Net Sales ($) | 3564301M | 3269146M |
| 159M | 8531M | 90600M | 301439M | 93647M | 388087M | Total Assets ($) | 1750364M | 1710228M |

M = $ thousand     MM = $ million
See Pages 9 through 22 for Explanation of Ratios and Data

## Comparative Historical Data  &  Current Data Sorted by Sales

| | | | | Type of Statement | 0-1MM | 1-3MM | 3-5MM | 5-10MM | 10-25MM | 25MM & OVER |
|---|---|---|---|---|---|---|---|---|---|---|
| | 14 | 11 | 10 | Unqualified | | 1 | 1 | 1 | 5 | 7 |
| | 7 | 10 | 7 | Reviewed | | | | 2 | | |
| | 6 | 4 | 2 | Compiled | | | 1 | 1 | 1 | 1 |
| | 3 | 3 | 3 | Tax Returns | | | 1 | 1 | | |
| | 22 | 18 | 14 | Other | | 1 | 2 | 2 | 2 | 6 |
| | 4/1/09-3/31/10 ALL | 4/1/10-3/31/11 ALL | 4/1/11-3/31/12 ALL | | | 7 (4/1-9/30/11) | | | 29 (10/1/11-3/31/12) | | |
| | 52 | 46 | 36 | NUMBER OF STATEMENTS | | 2 | 5 | 7 | 8 | 14 |

All current columns except **25MM & OVER** are marked **DATA NOT AVAILABLE**.

| Ratio | 4/1/09-3/31/10 | 4/1/10-3/31/11 | 4/1/11-3/31/12 | 25MM & OVER |
|---|---|---|---|---|
| **ASSETS** %| % | % | % | % |
| Cash & Equivalents | 9.2 | 7.4 | 7.9 | 8.0 |
| Trade Receivables (net) | 15.7 | 21.8 | 20.3 | 20.7 |
| Inventory | 32.2 | 31.4 | 31.5 | 25.5 |
| All Other Current | 3.1 | 2.0 | 1.9 | 2.2 |
| Total Current | 60.2 | 62.6 | 61.6 | 56.3 |
| Fixed Assets (net) | 29.5 | 27.6 | 29.2 | 32.1 |
| Intangibles (net) | 3.3 | .7 | 1.6 | 3.0 |
| All Other Non-Current | 7.0 | 9.1 | 7.6 | 8.6 |
| Total | 100.0 | 100.0 | 100.0 | 100.0 |
| **LIABILITIES** | | | | |
| Notes Payable-Short Term | 10.5 | 16.3 | 13.5 | 8.1 |
| Cur. Mat.-L.T.D. | 2.5 | 2.3 | 2.3 | 1.8 |
| Trade Payables | 7.6 | 9.5 | 10.4 | 10.9 |
| Income Taxes Payable | .2 | .0 | .4 | .0 |
| All Other Current | 7.5 | 12.8 | 6.4 | 6.9 |
| Total Current | 28.2 | 41.0 | 32.8 | 27.7 |
| Long-Term Debt | 17.1 | 15.5 | 21.5 | 25.9 |
| Deferred Taxes | .1 | .4 | .1 | .2 |
| All Other Non-Current | 1.8 | 1.9 | .9 | 1.4 |
| Net Worth | 52.7 | 41.2 | 44.7 | 44.9 |
| Total Liabilities & Net Worth | 100.0 | 100.0 | 100.0 | 100.0 |
| **INCOME DATA** | | | | |
| Net Sales | 100.0 | 100.0 | 100.0 | 100.0 |
| Gross Profit | 16.1 | 22.4 | 20.1 | 16.4 |
| Operating Expenses | 12.7 | 18.1 | 17.0 | 15.1 |
| Operating Profit | 3.3 | 4.4 | 3.1 | 1.3 |
| All Other Expenses (net) | .2 | .1 | .6 | .9 |
| Profit Before Taxes | 3.1 | 4.3 | 2.5 | .4 |
| **RATIOS** | | | | |
| Current | 4.5 / 2.2 / 1.5 | 3.8 / 2.0 / 1.6 | 3.2 / 1.9 / 1.4 | 2.8 / 1.8 / 1.5 |
| Quick | 1.6 / .9 / .5 | 1.6 / .8 / .4 | 1.5 / .7 / .4 | 1.7 / .7 / .4 |
| Sales/Receivables | (16) 22.2 / (24) 15.4 / (35) 10.5 | (14) 25.4 / (27) 13.7 / (34) 10.9 | (17) 21.7 / (27) 13.6 / (41) 9.0 | (24) 15.5 / (33) 11.0 / (42) 8.6 |
| Cost of Sales/Inventory | (39) 9.3 / (57) 6.4 / (89) 4.1 | (32) 11.3 / (60) 6.1 / (88) 4.2 | (28) 13.0 / (59) 6.2 / (107) 3.4 | (27) 13.4 / (52) 7.0 / (72) 5.1 |
| Cost of Sales/Payables | (8) 47.9 / (11) 32.0 / (20) 18.7 | (8) 45.3 / (13) 28.2 / (19) 19.2 | (9) 41.9 / (13) 27.9 / (26) 13.8 | (8) 43.4 / (13) 28.9 / (29) 12.7 |
| Sales/Working Capital | 4.1 / 6.1 / 15.1 | 4.8 / 6.9 / 14.4 | 4.9 / 6.6 / .14.1 | 5.9 / 7.8 / 22.0 |
| EBIT/Interest | 15.7 / (46) 5.0 / 1.2 | 32.9 / (44) 8.9 / 2.4 | 15.2 / (34) 6.6 / .1 | 12.1 / (13) 5.5 / .0 |
| Net Profit + Depr., Dep., Amort./Cur. Mat. L/T/D | 13.3 / (15) 6.1 / 4.2 | 9.1 / (15) 5.5 / 2.0 | | |
| Fixed/Worth | .3 / .5 / 1.0 | .3 / .5 / 1.0 | .2 / .5 / 2.4 | .4 / .6 / 3.6 |
| Debt/Worth | .4 / .9 / 1.7 | .3 / .9 / 1.8 | .4 / .8 / 4.2 | .6 / 1.4 / 5.1 |
| % Profit Before Taxes/Tangible Net Worth | 23.9 / (50) 10.7 / 4.1 | 28.9 / (43) 14.0 / 5.7 | 16.4 / (33) 7.3 / -8.7 | 15.5 / 7.0 / -33.4 |
| % Profit Before Taxes/Total Assets | 11.8 / 7.0 / .5 | 14.8 / 6.9 / 3.3 | 8.5 / 4.2 / -2.9 | 7.0 / 3.9 / -4.0 |
| Sales/Net Fixed Assets | 17.6 / 7.3 / 5.0 | 19.4 / 10.7 / 5.3 | 22.7 / 10.1 / 5.0 | 22.4 / 7.1 / 4.5 |
| Sales/Total Assets | 2.7 / 2.1 / 1.5 | 3.1 / 2.4 / 1.8 | 2.8 / 2.1 / 1.7 | 2.6 / 2.0 / 1.5 |
| % Depr., Dep., Amort./Sales | .9 / (44) 1.7 / 2.4 | .9 / (44) 1.5 / 2.7 | 1.1 / (29) 1.8 / 2.3 | .6 / (12) 2.1 / 3.5 |
| % Officers', Directors' Owners' Comp/Sales | .4 / (13) .8 / 2.7 | .7 / (14) 1.1 / 2.9 | | |

| | 4/1/09-3/31/10 | 4/1/10-3/31/11 | 4/1/11-3/31/12 | 1-3MM | 3-5MM | 5-10MM | 10-25MM | 25MM & OVER |
|---|---|---|---|---|---|---|---|---|
| Net Sales ($) | 3645415M | 2484703M | 1741956M | 3741M | 18035M | 51686M | 147401M | 1521093M |
| Total Assets ($) | 2049125M | 1258119M | 882463M | 1663M | 13988M | 19510M | 59086M | 788216M |

M = $ thousand   MM = $ million
See Pages 9 through 22 for Explanation of Ratios and Data

## Current Data Sorted by Assets        Comparative Historical Data

| 0-500M | 500M-2MM | 2-10MM | 10-50MM | 50-100MM | 100-250MM | | 4/1/07-3/31/08 ALL | 4/1/08-3/31/09 ALL |
|---|---|---|---|---|---|---|---|---|
| | | | | | | **Type of Statement** | | |
| | | 1 | 11 | 4 | 2 | Unqualified | 10 | 12 |
| | 1 | 6 | 4 | 1 | | Reviewed | 12 | 9 |
| 1 | 2 | 4 | 1 | | | Compiled | 3 | 13 |
| 2 | 6 | 5 | | | | Tax Returns | 9 | 10 |
| 2 | 6 | 10 | 8 | 2 | 2 | Other | 37 | 31 |
| | 13 (4/1-9/30/11) | | 68 (10/1/11-3/31/12) | | | | | |
| **5** | **15** | **26** | **23** | **8** | **4** | **NUMBER OF STATEMENTS** | **71** | **75** |
| % | % | % | % | % | % | **ASSETS** | % | % |
| | 6.0 | 7.7 | 5.1 | | | Cash & Equivalents | 5.7 | 5.7 |
| | 32.5 | 26.8 | 15.7 | | | Trade Receivables (net) | 24.2 | 20.9 |
| | 33.8 | 30.8 | 39.1 | | | Inventory | 32.0 | 35.2 |
| | 2.1 | 3.1 | 1.9 | | | All Other Current | 2.6 | 2.8 |
| | 74.4 | 68.3 | 61.7 | | | Total Current | 64.5 | 64.5 |
| | 21.7 | 27.4 | 29.9 | | | Fixed Assets (net) | 27.7 | 27.0 |
| | .3 | 1.2 | 4.8 | | | Intangibles (net) | 2.0 | 1.5 |
| | 3.6 | 3.1 | 3.6 | | | All Other Non-Current | 5.8 | 7.1 |
| | 100.0 | 100.0 | 100.0 | | | Total | 100.0 | 100.0 |
| | | | | | | **LIABILITIES** | | |
| | 15.7 | 15.4 | 11.9 | | | Notes Payable-Short Term | 14.2 | 19.6 |
| | 1.3 | 1.8 | 2.7 | | | Cur. Mat.-L.T.D. | 2.8 | 4.4 |
| | 18.8 | 13.3 | 8.6 | | | Trade Payables | 11.0 | 11.5 |
| | .0 | .0 | .2 | | | Income Taxes Payable | .2 | .0 |
| | 13.6 | 9.7 | 4.2 | | | All Other Current | 5.6 | 4.8 |
| | 49.4 | 40.1 | 27.6 | | | Total Current | 33.8 | 40.4 |
| | 31.8 | 12.7 | 10.7 | | | Long-Term Debt | 16.9 | 16.1 |
| | .0 | .0 | 1.0 | | | Deferred Taxes | .6 | .3 |
| | 16.2 | 3.1 | 3.8 | | | All Other Non-Current | 6.0 | 4.4 |
| | 2.5 | 44.1 | 57.0 | | | Net Worth | 42.7 | 38.7 |
| | 100.0 | 100.0 | 100.0 | | | Total Liabilities & Net Worth | 100.0 | 100.0 |
| | | | | | | **INCOME DATA** | | |
| | 100.0 | 100.0 | 100.0 | | | Net Sales | 100.0 | 100.0 |
| | 23.3 | 21.4 | 19.2 | | | Gross Profit | 20.6 | 22.5 |
| | 22.0 | 18.9 | 16.1 | | | Operating Expenses | 17.5 | 21.1 |
| | 1.3 | 2.5 | 3.1 | | | Operating Profit | 3.0 | 1.5 |
| | 1.5 | .4 | .7 | | | All Other Expenses (net) | .9 | 1.3 |
| | -.3 | 2.1 | 2.4 | | | Profit Before Taxes | 2.2 | .2 |
| | | | | | | **RATIOS** | | |
| | 2.8 | 4.4 | 5.5 | | | | 3.8 | 3.4 |
| | 1.6 | 1.8 | 2.8 | | | Current | 1.8 | 1.7 |
| | 1.1 | 1.0 | 1.5 | | | | 1.4 | 1.1 |
| | 2.8 | 1.9 | 1.6 | | | | 1.8 | 1.3 |
| | .9 | .9 | .8 | | | Quick | .9 | .6 |
| | .4 | .5 | .5 | | | | .5 | .3 |
| | 18   20.7 | 27   13.6 | 24   15.4 | | | | 24   15.2 | 21   17.7 |
| | 30   12.0 | 44   8.3 | 30   12.0 | | | Sales/Receivables | 35   10.3 | 32   11.5 |
| | 62   5.9 | 65   5.6 | 48   7.6 | | | | 46   8.0 | 46   8.0 |
| | 14   26.8 | 31   11.6 | 46   8.0 | | | | 34   10.7 | 38   9.6 |
| | 56   6.5 | 54   6.8 | 104   3.5 | | | Cost of Sales/Inventory | 67   5.4 | 69   5.3 |
| | 89   4.1 | 96   3.8 | 182   2.0 | | | | 105   3.5 | 135   2.7 |
| | 11   34.7 | 13   29.1 | 8   44.9 | | | | 10   36.9 | 6   57.6 |
| | 30   12.0 | 19   19.3 | 13   27.9 | | | Cost of Sales/Payables | 17   21.4 | 17   22.1 |
| | 38   9.7 | 30   12.2 | 19   18.9 | | | | 29   12.7 | 32   11.5 |
| | 5.7 | 3.7 | 2.6 | | | | 4.2 | 3.9 |
| | 10.6 | 7.0 | 6.0 | | | Sales/Working Capital | 8.2 | 9.1 |
| | 34.9 | NM | 9.5 | | | | 15.8 | 22.2 |
| | 5.6 | 16.9 | 10.2 | | | | 8.5 | 6.0 |
| | (13) 2.5 | (22) 3.2 | 2.7 | | | EBIT/Interest | (68) 3.0 | (68) 1.7 |
| | -2.5 | -.6 | 1.2 | | | | .0 | -1.3 |
| | | | | | | Net Profit + Depr., Dep., | 4.8 | 2.6 |
| | | | | | | Amort./Cur. Mat. L/T/D | (21) 1.7 | (17) 2.0 |
| | | | | | | | .1 | -2.2 |
| | .1 | .3 | .3 | | | | .3 | .3 |
| | .8 | .6 | .6 | | | Fixed/Worth | .6 | .7 |
| | -1.2 | 1.2 | .9 | | | | 1.1 | 1.6 |
| | .5 | .4 | .4 | | | | .6 | .5 |
| | 1.5 | 1.1 | .8 | | | Debt/Worth | 1.3 | 1.7 |
| | -6.9 | 10.4 | 1.8 | | | | 3.9 | 5.0 |
| | 65.2 | 24.8 | 19.6 | | | % Profit Before Taxes/Tangible | 29.7 | 20.0 |
| | (10) 16.1 | (24) 7.8 | 8.7 | | | Net Worth | (68) 11.1 | (69) 5.3 |
| | -6.9 | -1.6 | 1.1 | | | | -10.6 | -13.8 |
| | 25.0 | 9.5 | 10.1 | | | % Profit Before Taxes/Total | 12.1 | 11.1 |
| | 7.4 | 1.5 | 3.1 | | | Assets | 3.6 | 1.8 |
| | -6.1 | -.9 | .5 | | | | -3.8 | -9.7 |
| | 72.5 | 21.8 | 11.0 | | | | 17.0 | 19.6 |
| | 40.5 | 7.8 | 5.2 | | | Sales/Net Fixed Assets | 8.6 | 8.7 |
| | 5.0 | 4.4 | 3.0 | | | | 4.0 | 4.2 |
| | 5.1 | 3.0 | 2.1 | | | | 2.9 | 3.0 |
| | 2.9 | 2.3 | 1.4 | | | Sales/Total Assets | 2.2 | 2.1 |
| | 2.0 | 1.3 | 1.0 | | | | 1.4 | 1.2 |
| | | 1.1 | .9 | | | | 1.1 | .9 |
| | | (24) 2.5 | (22) 2.4 | | | % Depr., Dep., Amort./Sales | (64) 2.2 | (68) 2.3 |
| | | 3.2 | 3.6 | | | | 3.8 | 4.1 |
| | | 1.2 | | | | % Officers', Directors' | .8 | 1.8 |
| | | (13) 3.2 | | | | Owners' Comp/Sales | (21) 2.5 | (18) 3.3 |
| | | 4.3 | | | | | 4.8 | 4.7 |
| 3709M | 54186M | 253830M | 845726M | 976963M | 733609M | Net Sales ($) | 3591248M | 2228767M |
| 525M | 15726M | 125268M | 506644M | 579668M | 612851M | Total Assets ($) | 1844858M | 1392535M |

M = $ thousand    MM = $ million
See Pages 9 through 22 for Explanation of Ratios and Data

## Comparative Historical Data | Current Data Sorted by Sales

| 4/1/09-3/31/10 ALL | 4/1/10-3/31/11 ALL | 4/1/11-3/31/12 ALL | Type of Statement | 0-1MM | 1-3MM | 3-5MM | 5-10MM | 10-25MM | 25MM & OVER |
|---|---|---|---|---|---|---|---|---|---|
| 12 | 17 | 18 | Unqualified | | | | 3 | 4 | 14 |
| 6 | 12 | 12 | Reviewed | | 3 | 2 | | 5 | 2 |
| 8 | 6 | 8 | Compiled | | | 4 | 2 | | 1 |
| 13 | 3 | 13 | Tax Returns | | 3 | 4 | 4 | 2 | |
| 36 | 28 | 30 | Other | 1 | 3 | 3 | 4 | 13 | 7 |
| | | | | | 13 (4/1-9/30/11) | | | 68 (10/1/11-3/31/12) | |
| 75 | 66 | 81 | NUMBER OF STATEMENTS | 4 | 8 | 10 | 11 | 24 | 24 |
| % | % | % | **ASSETS** | % | % | % | % | % | % |
| 7.4 | 5.9 | 6.9 | Cash & Equivalents | | | 8.8 | 8.5 | 5.1 | 6.6 |
| 19.0 | 21.3 | 21.6 | Trade Receivables (net) | | | 24.3 | 23.3 | 27.0 | 15.2 |
| 32.3 | 31.5 | 31.9 | Inventory | | | 25.4 | 38.2 | 35.5 | 30.1 |
| 4.0 | 3.1 | 3.2 | All Other Current | | | 6.6 | .8 | 1.7 | 3.4 |
| 62.7 | 61.8 | 63.6 | Total Current | | | 65.1 | 70.8 | 69.4 | 55.3 |
| 27.2 | 31.0 | 29.6 | Fixed Assets (net) | | | 30.3 | 26.4 | 24.0 | 34.8 |
| 2.3 | 1.9 | 2.3 | Intangibles (net) | | | .1 | .3 | 3.8 | 2.9 |
| 7.8 | 5.3 | 4.5 | All Other Non-Current | | | 4.5 | 2.5 | 2.8 | 7.0 |
| 100.0 | 100.0 | 100.0 | Total | | | 100.0 | 100.0 | 100.0 | 100.0 |
| | | | **LIABILITIES** | | | | | | |
| 17.3 | 11.3 | 12.8 | Notes Payable-Short Term | | | 12.7 | 8.5 | 19.3 | 8.8 |
| 4.5 | 4.7 | 2.5 | Cur. Mat.-L.T.D. | | | 1.0 | 1.0 | 2.8 | 2.5 |
| 10.0 | 10.4 | 12.3 | Trade Payables | | | 14.8 | 9.1 | 12.0 | 7.4 |
| .1 | .1 | .0 | Income Taxes Payable | | | .0 | .0 | .2 | .0 |
| 5.9 | 6.5 | 8.9 | All Other Current | | | 7.6 | 9.8 | 7.5 | 4.3 |
| 37.8 | 32.9 | 36.6 | Total Current | | | 36.1 | 28.3 | 41.7 | 23.0 |
| 16.1 | 15.0 | 17.1 | Long-Term Debt | | | 8.6 | 17.9 | 8.9 | 12.4 |
| .4 | .5 | .3 | Deferred Taxes | | | .0 | .1 | .0 | 1.0 |
| 6.7 | 5.1 | 7.3 | All Other Non-Current | | | 14.6 | 1.7 | 5.7 | 8.8 |
| 39.0 | 46.6 | 38.8 | Net Worth | | | 40.7 | 51.9 | 43.8 | 54.8 |
| 100.0 | 100.0 | 100.0 | Total Liabilities & Net Worth | | | 100.0 | 100.0 | 100.0 | 100.0 |
| | | | **INCOME DATA** | | | | | | |
| 100.0 | 100.0 | 100.0 | Net Sales | | | 100.0 | 100.0 | 100.0 | 100.0 |
| 20.4 | 22.0 | 20.6 | Gross Profit | | | 21.7 | 22.7 | 20.0 | 17.1 |
| 23.0 | 18.7 | 18.6 | Operating Expenses | | | 22.2 | 18.6 | 17.6 | 14.6 |
| -2.6 | 3.3 | 2.0 | Operating Profit | | | -.5 | 4.1 | 2.5 | 2.5 |
| 1.1 | .6 | .8 | All Other Expenses (net) | | | .3 | .0 | .8 | .9 |
| -3.7 | 2.7 | 1.2 | Profit Before Taxes | | | -.8 | 4.2 | 1.7 | 1.6 |
| | | | **RATIOS** | | | | | | |
| 3.4 | 4.3 | 3.6 | Current | | | 4.1 | 6.7 | 2.8 | 3.7 |
| 1.8 | 2.2 | 2.1 | | | | 2.4 | 2.3 | 1.6 | 2.6 |
| 1.2 | 1.3 | 1.2 | | | | 1.2 | 1.6 | 1.1 | 1.7 |
| 1.4 | 1.5 | 1.7 | Quick | | | 2.8 | 3.8 | 1.4 | 1.8 |
| .6 | .8 | .8 | | | | .9 | 1.1 | .6 | .8 |
| .4 | .5 | .5 | | | | .7 | .6 | .4 | .6 |
| 25 14.6 | 22 16.9 | 19 19.5 | Sales/Receivables | | | 17 21.9 | 18 20.6 | 27 13.4 | 19 18.8 |
| 37 9.9 | 32 11.3 | 31 11.7 | | | | 25 14.7 | 31 11.6 | 46 8.0 | 29 12.6 |
| 52 7.1 | 45 8.1 | 51 7.1 | | | | 61 6.0 | 56 6.5 | 63 5.8 | 46 8.0 |
| 48 7.7 | 41 8.8 | 33 11.2 | Cost of Sales/Inventory | | | 2 204.0 | 43 8.5 | 28 13.0 | 39 9.3 |
| 80 4.6 | 65 5.6 | 58 6.3 | | | | 25 14.8 | 56 6.5 | 74 4.9 | 55 6.6 |
| 155 2.4 | 125 2.9 | 122 3.0 | | | | 99 3.7 | 79 4.6 | 182 2.0 | 126 2.9 |
| 9 40.9 | 8 44.8 | 10 35.4 | Cost of Sales/Payables | | | 10 36.9 | 11 34.7 | 9 39.9 | 8 44.5 |
| 14 25.5 | 15 24.3 | 16 22.4 | | | | 21 17.2 | 15 25.0 | 19 19.5 | 14 26.6 |
| 33 11.1 | 31 11.7 | 31 11.7 | | | | 37 9.8 | 27 13.3 | 41 8.9 | 21 17.2 |
| 3.1 | 3.6 | 3.5 | Sales/Working Capital | | | 3.7 | 3.3 | 3.4 | 3.0 |
| 6.7 | 7.3 | 8.1 | | | | 7.7 | 5.8 | 8.4 | 5.7 |
| 13.9 | 15.3 | 21.3 | | | | NM | 12.7 | 36.6 | 9.8 |
| 2.9 | 10.6 | 7.5 | EBIT/Interest | | | | | 6.2 | 10.2 |
| (69) .6 | (57) 2.2 | (73) 2.4 | | | | | | (21) 1.8 | (23) 2.2 |
| -3.8 | .2 | -.7 | | | | | | .7 | -.6 |
| 3.1 | 7.6 | 5.3 | Net Profit + Depr., Dep., Amort./Cur. Mat. L/T/D | | | | | | 5.5 |
| (10) 1.7 | (14) 2.6 | (11) 1.6 | | | | | | | (10) 1.6 |
| 1.0 | .5 | .5 | | | | | | | .4 |
| .3 | .3 | .3 | Fixed/Worth | | | .3 | .1 | .2 | .4 |
| .7 | .7 | .6 | | | | .6 | .4 | .5 | .6 |
| 1.5 | 1.1 | 1.1 | | | | NM | .7 | 1.0 | 1.1 |
| .5 | .5 | .5 | Debt/Worth | | | .4 | .3 | .5 | .4 |
| 1.5 | 1.0 | 1.0 | | | | .6 | .5 | 1.6 | .7 |
| 6.0 | 2.6 | 4.7 | | | | NM | 1.5 | 6.3 | 1.8 |
| 6.3 | 23.2 | 19.6 | % Profit Before Taxes/Tangible Net Worth | | | 56.5 | | 16.8 | 16.1 |
| (63) -2.4 | (59) 9.8 | (71) 7.6 | | | | (10) 15.4 | | (23) 1.9 | (23) 8.0 |
| -14.0 | -2.2 | -3.3 | | | | 3.3 | | .2 | -3.7 |
| 3.5 | 10.7 | 9.6 | % Profit Before Taxes/Total Assets | | | 13.0 | 35.7 | 8.7 | 9.7 |
| -2.1 | 3.7 | 2.2 | | | | 3.1 | 9.3 | 1.1 | 3.3 |
| -9.8 | -1.5 | -2.6 | | | | -4.9 | .3 | .2 | -2.2 |
| 13.7 | 14.4 | 16.9 | Sales/Net Fixed Assets | | | 20.7 | 72.5 | 32.9 | 9.1 |
| 6.1 | 7.0 | 7.2 | | | | 7.5 | 14.1 | 6.1 | 6.2 |
| 3.8 | 4.0 | 4.5 | | | | 4.1 | 6.9 | 3.8 | 3.4 |
| 2.4 | 2.7 | 3.1 | Sales/Total Assets | | | 4.2 | 3.5 | 3.0 | 2.4 |
| 1.8 | 1.9 | 2.1 | | | | 2.1 | 2.4 | 1.6 | 1.7 |
| 1.1 | 1.3 | 1.2 | | | | 1.4 | 1.8 | 1.1 | 1.1 |
| 1.2 | 1.0 | 1.0 | % Depr., Dep., Amort./Sales | | | | | .6 | 1.2 |
| (64) 2.2 | (56) 2.2 | (68) 2.5 | | | | | | (22) 2.0 | (22) 2.6 |
| 3.8 | 3.6 | 3.7 | | | | | | 3.4 | 4.5 |
| 1.9 | 1.0 | 1.3 | % Officers', Directors' Owners' Comp/Sales | | | | | .8 | |
| (15) 4.9 | (14) 3.3 | (23) 3.0 | | | | | | (11) 1.5 | |
| 3.8 | 5.5 | 4.6 | | | | | | 3.4 | |
| 2370256M | 3775436M | 2868023M | Net Sales ($) | 2016M | 14101M | 39455M | 79061M | 357307M | 2376083M |
| 1578691M | 1919410M | 1840682M | Total Assets ($) | 1202M | 6994M | 23103M | 38296M | 243606M | 1527481M |

## Current Data Sorted by Assets     Comparative Historical Data

| 0-500M | 500M-2MM | 2-10MM | 10-50MM | 50-100MM | 100-250MM | Type of Statement | 4/1/07-3/31/08 ALL | 4/1/08-3/31/09 ALL |
|---|---|---|---|---|---|---|---|---|
| 1 | | 2 | 1 | 1 | | Unqualified | 9 | 5 |
| 1 | 2 | 8 | 2 | | | Reviewed | 22 | 15 |
| 3 | 3 | 8 | 1 | | | Compiled | 23 | 20 |
| 2 | 6 | 7 | | | | Tax Returns | 13 | 12 |
| 2 | 7 | | 6 | | | Other | 24 | 19 |
| | 5 (4/1-9/30/11) | | 58 (10/1/11-3/31/12) | | | | | |
| 9 | 18 | 25 | 10 | 1 | | NUMBER OF STATEMENTS | 91 | 71 |

| 0-500M % | 500M-2MM % | 2-10MM % | 10-50MM % | 50-100MM % | 100-250MM % | | ALL % | ALL % |
|---|---|---|---|---|---|---|---|---|
| | | | | | | **ASSETS** | | |
| | 5.4 | 11.5 | 10.6 | | | Cash & Equivalents | 8.7 | 10.4 |
| | 24.8 | 23.1 | 20.0 | | D | Trade Receivables (net) | 22.0 | 20.3 |
| | 19.7 | 22.7 | 19.9 | | A | Inventory | 23.2 | 21.0 |
| | 4.9 | 3.1 | 5.1 | | T | All Other Current | 4.5 | 5.0 |
| | 54.7 | 60.4 | 55.6 | | A | Total Current | 58.4 | 56.7 |
| | 32.5 | 32.5 | 28.2 | | | Fixed Assets (net) | 31.2 | 31.9 |
| | 4.1 | .5 | 8.2 | | N | Intangibles (net) | 4.8 | 4.0 |
| | 8.7 | 6.6 | 8.0 | | O | All Other Non-Current | 5.6 | 7.4 |
| | 100.0 | 100.0 | 100.0 | | T | Total | 100.0 | 100.0 |
| | | | | | | **LIABILITIES** | | |
| | 4.9 | 8.5 | 13.2 | | A | Notes Payable-Short Term | 11.0 | 11.1 |
| | 5.4 | 2.6 | 1.8 | | V | Cur. Mat.-L.T.D. | 4.8 | 6.3 |
| | 16.7 | 8.9 | 6.3 | | A | Trade Payables | 7.8 | 7.9 |
| | .0 | .0 | .2 | | I | Income Taxes Payable | .1 | .0 |
| | 13.2 | 6.8 | 8.6 | | L | All Other Current | 9.5 | 9.3 |
| | 40.1 | 26.9 | 30.2 | | A | Total Current | 33.2 | 34.6 |
| | 18.0 | 11.0 | 15.5 | | B | Long-Term Debt | 20.1 | 17.3 |
| | .0 | .3 | .1 | | L | Deferred Taxes | .2 | .3 |
| | 26.1 | 14.7 | 18.1 | | E | All Other Non-Current | 7.4 | 11.5 |
| | 15.9 | 47.1 | 36.0 | | | Net Worth | 39.1 | 36.4 |
| | 100.0 | 100.0 | 100.0 | | | Total Liabilities & Net Worth | 100.0 | 100.0 |
| | | | | | | **INCOME DATA** | | |
| | 100.0 | 100.0 | 100.0 | | | Net Sales | 100.0 | 100.0 |
| | 32.1 | 29.9 | 20.6 | | | Gross Profit | 27.9 | 26.1 |
| | 35.6 | 28.3 | 20.5 | | | Operating Expenses | 28.9 | 31.6 |
| | -3.5 | 1.7 | .2 | | | Operating Profit | -1.0 | -5.5 |
| | .7 | .5 | .9 | | | All Other Expenses (net) | 1.1 | .9 |
| | -4.2 | 1.2 | -.8 | | | Profit Before Taxes | -2.1 | -6.4 |
| | | | | | | **RATIOS** | | |
| | 6.4 | 5.5 | 3.9 | | | | 5.0 | 5.0 |
| | 1.2 | 2.6 | 1.7 | | | Current | 2.1 | 2.2 |
| | 1.0 | 1.2 | 1.1 | | | | 1.2 | 1.1 |
| | 1.5 | 3.0 | 1.8 | | | | 2.5 | 2.5 |
| | .7 | 1.6 | 1.0 | | | Quick | 1.0 | 1.1 |
| | .6 | .6 | .6 | | | | .6 | .6 |
| 18 19.8 | 20 17.9 | 28 13.0 | | | | | 18 20.5 | 17 21.5 |
| 30 12.3 | 33 11.2 | 41 8.9 | | | | Sales/Receivables | 28 12.9 | 28 13.1 |
| 45 8.2 | 46 8.0 | 50 7.3 | | | | | 40 9.1 | 40 9.0 |
| 30 12.2 | 36 10.2 | 31 11.9 | | | | | 31 11.9 | 28 12.9 |
| 54 6.8 | 55 6.6 | 42 8.7 | | | | Cost of Sales/Inventory | 39 9.3 | 41 8.8 |
| 65 5.6 | 66 5.5 | 55 6.6 | | | | | 62 5.9 | 60 6.1 |
| 7 54.3 | 6 56.7 | 7 49.4 | | | | | 5 73.3 | 5 80.5 |
| 19 19.5 | 14 26.0 | 15 24.7 | | | | Cost of Sales/Payables | 9 39.1 | 10 37.9 |
| 54 6.8 | 23 15.6 | 17 21.8 | | | | | 16 22.2 | 18 20.3 |
| | 4.6 | 4.4 | 4.7 | | | | 5.1 | 4.5 |
| | 23.9 | 6.7 | 7.3 | | | Sales/Working Capital | 9.6 | 8.0 |
| | NM | 50.1 | 94.6 | | | | 35.6 | 123.1 |
| | .9 | 5.2 | | | | | 5.2 | 2.7 |
| | (16) -1.8 | (22) 1.4 | | | | EBIT/Interest | (85) 1.1 | (66) -1.4 |
| | -11.6 | .3 | | | | | -3.6 | -6.7 |
| | | | | | | | 3.9 | |
| | | | | | | Net Profit + Depr., Dep., Amort./Cur. Mat. L/T/D | (14) 1.4 | |
| | | | | | | | -.9 | |
| | .6 | .4 | .3 | | | | .4 | .4 |
| | 2.0 | .7 | .5 | | | Fixed/Worth | .8 | .8 |
| | -1.7 | 1.2 | 1.4 | | | | 1.5 | 1.5 |
| | .3 | .4 | .2 | | | | .4 | .4 |
| | 4.8 | .8 | .9 | | | Debt/Worth | 1.5 | 1.2 |
| | -10.5 | 2.5 | 2.6 | | | | 3.2 | 3.7 |
| | 20.8 | -11.5 | | | | | 25.4 | 5.4 |
| | (11) -3.3 | (23) 5.9 | | | | % Profit Before Taxes/Tangible Net Worth | (76) 4.7 | (62) -13.5 |
| | -30.1 | -5.4 | | | | | -21.4 | -39.7 |
| | 1.5 | 6.7 | 7.5 | | | | 9.7 | 1.4 |
| | -6.1 | 2.1 | 2.3 | | | % Profit Before Taxes/Total Assets | -.2 | -7.8 |
| | -13.5 | -1.6 | -18.3 | | | | -15.7 | -25.5 |
| | 18.6 | 17.7 | 11.6 | | | | 15.2 | 14.7 |
| | 9.5 | 8.0 | 7.6 | | | Sales/Net Fixed Assets | 9.1 | 8.2 |
| | 4.2 | 4.0 | 3.9 | | | | 5.6 | 5.0 |
| | 3.4 | 3.2 | 2.8 | | | | 3.4 | 3.1 |
| | 2.2 | 2.4 | 1.6 | | | Sales/Total Assets | 2.6 | 2.2 |
| | 1.7 | 1.5 | 1.2 | | | | 2.0 | 1.8 |
| | 1.0 | 1.7 | | | | | 1.5 | 2.0 |
| | (15) 4.6 | (23) 2.6 | | | | % Depr., Dep., Amort./Sales | (84) 2.6 | (65) 2.8 |
| | 5.3 | 4.0 | | | | | 4.1 | 4.4 |
| | | 1.0 | | | | | 1.6 | 1.1 |
| | | (15) 1.8 | | | | % Officers', Directors' Owners' Comp/Sales | (33) 2.7 | (27) 3.4 |
| | | 6.1 | | | | | 4.9 | 6.7 |
| 9082M | 51452M | 283006M | 445600M | 112496M | | Net Sales ($) | 1277536M | 1034004M |
| 2975M | 21116M | 109731M | 195673M | 91240M | | Total Assets ($) | 574349M | 519959M |

M = $ thousand    MM = $ million
See Pages 9 through 22 for Explanation of Ratios and Data

## Comparative Historical Data      Current Data Sorted by Sales

| Type of Statement | 4/1/09-3/31/10 ALL | 4/1/10-3/31/11 ALL | 4/1/11-3/31/12 ALL | | 0-1MM | 1-3MM | 3-5MM | 5-10MM | 10-25MM | 25MM & OVER |
|---|---|---|---|---|---|---|---|---|---|---|
| Unqualified | 4 | 3 | 5 | | | 1 | | | 2 | 2 |
| Reviewed | 16 | 15 | 13 | | | 2 | 2 | 4 | 4 | 1 |
| Compiled | 6 | 10 | 15 | | 3 | 3 | 1 | 5 | 2 | 1 |
| Tax Returns | 7 | 13 | 8 | | 2 | 3 | 2 | 1 | | |
| Other | 27 | 20 | 22 | | 1 | 7 | 3 | 1 | 5 | 5 |
| | 27 | 20 | 22 | | 5 (4/1-9/30/11) | | | 58 (10/1/11-3/31/12) | | |
| NUMBER OF STATEMENTS | 60 | 61 | 63 | | 6 | 16 | 8 | 11 | 13 | 9 |

Data columns below shown for statement groups with sufficient statements: 1-3MM, 5-10MM, 10-25MM.

| | 4/1/09-3/31/10 % | 4/1/10-3/31/11 % | 4/1/11-3/31/12 % | | 1-3MM % | 5-10MM % | 10-25MM % |
|---|---|---|---|---|---|---|---|
| **ASSETS** | | | | | | | |
| Cash & Equivalents | 9.7 | 9.8 | 9.1 | | 6.3 | 18.3 | 9.9 |
| Trade Receivables (net) | 19.8 | 21.2 | 22.9 | | 28.7 | 24.3 | 19.5 |
| Inventory | 22.4 | 23.7 | 22.7 | | 24.5 | 22.6 | 20.0 |
| All Other Current | 3.5 | 3.9 | 3.9 | | .7 | 2.7 | 4.0 |
| Total Current | 55.4 | 58.6 | 58.5 | | 60.3 | 68.0 | 53.5 |
| Fixed Assets (net) | 35.2 | 33.0 | 30.2 | | 28.7 | 30.2 | 29.6 |
| Intangibles (net) | 3.2 | 1.9 | 4.7 | | 4.9 | .1 | 5.8 |
| All Other Non-Current | 6.2 | 6.4 | 6.6 | | 6.2 | 1.7 | 11.1 |
| Total | 100.0 | 100.0 | 100.0 | | 100.0 | 100.0 | 100.0 |
| **LIABILITIES** | | | | | | | |
| Notes Payable-Short Term | 12.7 | 15.0 | 17.4 | | 14.0 | 1.0 | 11.6 |
| Cur. Mat.-L.T.D. | 5.1 | 3.6 | 3.5 | | 2.1 | 3.5 | 3.3 |
| Trade Payables | 8.3 | 8.6 | 11.5 | | 20.6 | 4.5 | 9.2 |
| Income Taxes Payable | .1 | .0 | .1 | | .0 | .0 | .0 |
| All Other Current | 8.4 | 11.3 | 12.0 | | 16.5 | 23.3 | 5.6 |
| Total Current | 34.6 | 38.5 | 44.5 | | 53.1 | 32.2 | 29.6 |
| Long-Term Debt | 20.0 | 17.7 | 13.8 | | 5.8 | 14.5 | 11.9 |
| Deferred Taxes | .4 | .1 | .1 | | .1 | .2 | .3 |
| All Other Non-Current | 14.3 | 16.5 | 22.5 | | 25.0 | 11.5 | 12.2 |
| Net Worth | 30.7 | 27.3 | 19.0 | | 16.0 | 41.6 | 46.0 |
| Total Liabilities & Net Worth | 100.0 | 100.0 | 100.0 | | 100.0 | 100.0 | 100.0 |
| **INCOME DATA** | | | | | | | |
| Net Sales | 100.0 | 100.0 | 100.0 | | 100.0 | 100.0 | 100.0 |
| Gross Profit | 30.5 | 28.6 | 29.4 | | 30.8 | 31.3 | 24.9 |
| Operating Expenses | 35.0 | 30.8 | 30.2 | | 30.4 | 29.9 | 23.8 |
| Operating Profit | -4.5 | -2.2 | -.8 | | .4 | 1.3 | 1.1 |
| All Other Expenses (net) | 1.4 | .7 | 1.0 | | .7 | .2 | -.1 |
| Profit Before Taxes | -5.9 | -2.8 | -1.8 | | -.4 | 1.2 | 1.2 |
| **RATIOS** | | | | | | | |
| Current | 5.1 | 5.4 | 4.5 | | 7.1 | 9.6 | 3.3 |
| | 1.7 | 2.0 | 1.6 | | 1.4 | 4.8 | 1.6 |
| | 1.1 | 1.1 | 1.1 | | 1.0 | 2.1 | 1.1 |
| Quick | 2.9 | 2.4 | 2.1 | | 3.2 | 7.2 | 1.5 |
| | .9 | 1.1 | .8 | | .8 | 2.1 | 1.0 |
| | .5 | .5 | .5 | | .5 | 1.9 | .6 |
| Sales/Receivables | 23   15.6 | 21   17.0 | 20   18.0 | | 25   14.6 | 19   19.3 | 23   16.1 |
| | 32   11.6 | 34   10.8 | 32   11.4 | | 33   11.1 | 32   11.3 | 33   11.2 |
| | 44   8.2 | 49   7.4 | 43   8.4 | | 51   7.2 | 33   11.0 | 45   8.1 |
| Cost of Sales/Inventory | 34   10.7 | 35   10.3 | 30   12.0 | | 24   15.2 | 30   12.0 | 33   11.0 |
| | 53   6.9 | 55   6.7 | 51   7.2 | | 51   7.2 | 48   7.6 | 42   8.6 |
| | 77   4.8 | 91   4.0 | 66   5.5 | | 64   5.7 | 66   5.5 | 58   6.3 |
| Cost of Sales/Payables | 8   47.6 | 6   64.8 | 7   55.8 | | 12   30.9 | 6   60.1 | 6   59.4 |
| | 14   26.3 | 13   29.0 | 14   25.4 | | 24   15.4 | 7   54.3 | 16   23.2 |
| | 24   15.4 | 24   15.0 | 25   14.4 | | 65   5.6 | 10   36.7 | 24   15.3 |
| Sales/Working Capital | 4.7 | 4.0 | 4.9 | | 5.3 | 3.8 | 4.1 |
| | 9.0 | 8.3 | 9.7 | | 18.8 | 4.9 | 8.8 |
| | 93.8 | 56.9 | 108.7 | | NM | 7.6 | 175.1 |
| EBIT/Interest | 3.3 | 3.1 | 3.9 | | 4.5 | 14.4 | 11.0 |
| | (55) -1.2 | (51) -.3 | (53) 1.1 | | (12) .6 | (10) 3.0 | (10) 1.3 |
| | -9.6 | -3.1 | -2.5 | | -2.6 | -2.1 | -.1 |
| Net Profit + Depr., Dep., Amort./Cur. Mat. L/T/D | | | | | | | |
| Fixed/Worth | .5 | .4 | .5 | | .5 | .4 | .4 |
| | 1.1 | .9 | .8 | | 1.2 | .6 | .6 |
| | 4.5 | 3.2 | 10.5 | | -8.9 | .8 | 1.4 |
| Debt/Worth | .6 | .4 | .4 | | 1.0 | .4 | .5 |
| | 1.5 | 1.1 | 1.6 | | 4.1 | .5 | 1.2 |
| | 12.2 | 6.9 | 13.3 | | -30.4 | 1.7 | 3.3 |
| % Profit Before Taxes/Tangible Net Worth | 4.7 | 14.2 | 21.4 | | 27.7 | 11.1 | 17.7 |
| | (48) -6.5 | (49) -.2 | (48) 5.2 | | (11) 8.0 | (10) 7.5 | (12) 1.5 |
| | -41.2 | -18.3 | -9.9 | | -30.1 | 2.1 | -12.1 |
| % Profit Before Taxes/Total Assets | 2.2 | 4.9 | 5.6 | | 9.4 | 7.4 | 5.0 |
| | -7.9 | -2.0 | .6 | | 1.4 | 4.6 | 1.6 |
| | -28.4 | -11.6 | -9.9 | | -6.6 | -4.7 | -4.0 |
| Sales/Net Fixed Assets | 12.3 | 13.4 | 19.6 | | 24.5 | 37.9 | 15.5 |
| | 6.2 | 6.9 | 8.2 | | 11.3 | 8.0 | 7.4 |
| | 3.9 | 4.3 | 4.7 | | 7.2 | 3.2 | 4.7 |
| Sales/Total Assets | 2.9 | 3.0 | 3.3 | | 3.7 | 4.0 | 3.0 |
| | 2.1 | 2.2 | 2.3 | | 2.8 | 2.7 | 1.9 |
| | 1.4 | 1.5 | 1.5 | | 2.0 | 1.8 | 1.3 |
| % Depr., Dep., Amort./Sales | 1.6 | 2.2 | 2.1 | | 1.3 | 1.2 | 2.0 |
| | (54) 3.7 | (53) 3.1 | (54) 2.7 | | (12) 3.3 | (10) 2.6 | (10) 2.7 |
| | 5.7 | 4.5 | 4.5 | | 4.6 | 4.0 | 3.6 |
| % Officers', Directors' Owners' Comp/Sales | 2.0 | 1.9 | 1.1 | | | | |
| | (22) 3.3 | (27) 3.6 | (27) 3.1 | | | | |
| | 6.4 | 7.1 | 6.3 | | | | |

| | 4/1/09-3/31/10 | 4/1/10-3/31/11 | 4/1/11-3/31/12 | | 0-1MM | 1-3MM | 3-5MM | 5-10MM | 10-25MM | 25MM & OVER |
|---|---|---|---|---|---|---|---|---|---|---|
| Net Sales ($) | 585655M | 800703M | 901636M | | 3432M | 29041M | 31618M | 83777M | 189659M | 564109M |
| Total Assets ($) | 308461M | 462069M | 420735M | | 4604M | 12169M | 18123M | 33347M | 108650M | 243842M |

M = $ thousand     MM = $ million
See Pages 9 through 22 for Explanation of Ratios and Data

## Current Data Sorted by Assets  |  Comparative Historical Data

| | 0-500M | 500M-2MM | 2-10MM | 10-50MM | 50-100MM | 100-250MM | Type of Statement | 4/1/07-3/31/08 ALL | 4/1/08-3/31/09 ALL |
|---|---|---|---|---|---|---|---|---|---|
| | 1 | 5 | 17 | 5 | | 1 | Unqualified | 19 | 17 |
| | 2 | 10 | 13 | 5 | 1 | | Reviewed | 54 | 46 |
| | 14 | 21 | 7 | 1 | | | Compiled | 29 | 34 |
| | 4 | 15 | 18 | 15 | 5 | | Tax Returns | 23 | 27 |
| | | | | | | | Other | 70 | 59 |
| | | 24 (4/1-9/30/11) | | 136 (10/1/11-3/31/12) | | | | | |
| **NUMBER OF STATEMENTS** | 21 | 51 | 55 | 26 | 6 | 1 | | 195 | 183 |
| | % | % | % | % | % | % | **ASSETS** | % | % |
| Cash & Equivalents | 19.3 | 9.6 | 7.0 | 9.5 | | | | 8.3 | 8.5 |
| Trade Receivables (net) | 22.4 | 27.8 | 28.4 | 18.5 | | | | 25.9 | 24.6 |
| Inventory | 24.0 | 22.7 | 25.7 | 22.5 | | | | 26.1 | 24.7 |
| All Other Current | 1.1 | .6 | 1.9 | 3.7 | | | | 2.8 | 3.0 |
| Total Current | 66.6 | 60.6 | 63.0 | 54.2 | | | | 63.0 | 60.8 |
| Fixed Assets (net) | 26.7 | 25.2 | 28.9 | 33.9 | | | | 28.2 | 29.7 |
| Intangibles (net) | .8 | 4.4 | .7 | 5.7 | | | | 2.8 | 3.8 |
| All Other Non-Current | 5.8 | 9.8 | 7.4 | 6.1 | | | | 5.9 | 5.7 |
| Total | 100.0 | 100.0 | 100.0 | 100.0 | | | | 100.0 | 100.0 |
| | | | | | | | **LIABILITIES** | | |
| Notes Payable-Short Term | 17.0 | 16.4 | 13.7 | 9.4 | | | | 12.1 | 15.3 |
| Cur. Mat.-L.T.D. | 3.6 | 3.7 | 4.5 | 3.3 | | | | 3.5 | 3.7 |
| Trade Payables | 17.4 | 15.2 | 12.4 | 8.5 | | | | 12.7 | 12.6 |
| Income Taxes Payable | .3 | .1 | .4 | .1 | | | | .2 | .1 |
| All Other Current | 17.3 | 13.5 | 10.6 | 7.6 | | | | 11.8 | 9.7 |
| Total Current | 55.5 | 48.9 | 41.7 | 28.9 | | | | 40.2 | 41.3 |
| Long-Term Debt | 17.3 | 22.9 | 21.6 | 11.3 | | | | 16.1 | 19.5 |
| Deferred Taxes | .0 | .2 | .4 | .5 | | | | .3 | .3 |
| All Other Non-Current | 21.9 | 10.3 | 7.9 | 18.0 | | | | 8.8 | 9.5 |
| Net Worth | 5.3 | 17.7 | 28.5 | 41.2 | | | | 34.6 | 29.4 |
| Total Liabilities & Net Worth | 100.0 | 100.0 | 100.0 | 100.0 | | | | 100.0 | 100.0 |
| | | | | | | | **INCOME DATA** | | |
| Net Sales | 100.0 | 100.0 | 100.0 | 100.0 | | | | 100.0 | 100.0 |
| Gross Profit | 43.2 | 35.1 | 25.1 | 26.4 | | | | 27.9 | 27.1 |
| Operating Expenses | 42.8 | 33.6 | 24.1 | 22.9 | | | | 24.4 | 26.5 |
| Operating Profit | .4 | 1.5 | 1.0 | 3.5 | | | | 3.5 | .6 |
| All Other Expenses (net) | .9 | .3 | 1.5 | .6 | | | | 1.2 | 1.2 |
| Profit Before Taxes | -.5 | 1.3 | -.4 | 2.9 | | | | 2.3 | -.6 |
| | | | | | | | **RATIOS** | | |
| Current | 6.6 | 3.6 | 2.3 | 3.8 | | | | 3.1 | 3.0 |
| | 1.8 | 1.7 | 1.6 | 1.9 | | | | 1.6 | 1.6 |
| | .9 | .8 | 1.1 | 1.1 | | | | 1.1 | 1.0 |
| Quick | 4.9 | 2.5 | 1.3 | 2.0 | | | | 1.6 | 1.7 |
| | 1.0 | .9 | .9 | .8 | | | | .8 | .9 |
| | .3 | .4 | .5 | .5 | | | | .5 | .4 |
| Sales/Receivables | 0 UND | 19 19.5 | 29 12.5 | 22 16.3 | | | | 21 17.2 | 19 18.9 |
| | 19 19.4 | 30 12.0 | 46 7.9 | 34 10.7 | | | | 32 11.5 | 33 11.1 |
| | 35 10.4 | 52 7.0 | 66 5.5 | 41 8.8 | | | | 45 8.1 | 49 7.5 |
| Cost of Sales/Inventory | 14 26.0 | 21 17.3 | 23 15.7 | 24 15.0 | | | | 27 13.6 | 19 18.7 |
| | 30 12.3 | 36 10.0 | 41 9.0 | 52 7.0 | | | | 50 7.3 | 47 7.7 |
| | 55 6.6 | 61 6.0 | 87 4.2 | 111 3.3 | | | | 73 5.0 | 81 4.5 |
| Cost of Sales/Payables | 0 UND | 7 53.7 | 13 28.8 | 12 29.3 | | | | 10 37.4 | 8 47.2 |
| | 12 29.2 | 20 18.3 | 24 15.4 | 19 19.3 | | | | 18 20.8 | 17 21.8 |
| | 61 6.0 | 43 8.5 | 42 8.7 | 35 10.3 | | | | 33 11.2 | 34 10.8 |
| Sales/Working Capital | 7.2 | 5.8 | 5.6 | 3.9 | | | | 5.9 | 5.7 |
| | 19.4 | 10.9 | 9.4 | 9.2 | | | | 10.9 | 12.8 |
| | -342.3 | -21.4 | 44.1 | 97.4 | | | | 97.9 | 108.3 |
| EBIT/Interest | 7.0 | 7.6 | 5.5 | 13.4 | | | | 7.7 | 6.8 |
| | (15) 1.7 | (45) 2.4 | 1.7 | (22) 3.3 | | | | (180) 2.6 | (173) 1.7 |
| | -8.8 | -.5 | -.9 | .2 | | | | .6 | -1.4 |
| Net Profit + Depr., Dep., Amort./Cur. Mat. L/T/D | | | 1.7 | | | | | 3.6 | 3.6 |
| | | (12) .6 | | | | | | (40) 2.2 | (33) 2.2 |
| | | | -1.1 | | | | | .6 | -1.6 |
| Fixed/Worth | .3 | .3 | .3 | .4 | | | | .3 | .4 |
| | 2.0 | 1.0 | .8 | .7 | | | | .8 | 1.0 |
| | -.5 | -.9 | 3.1 | 1.2 | | | | 2.6 | 4.5 |
| Debt/Worth | .5 | .8 | .9 | .5 | | | | .6 | .8 |
| | 3.2 | 3.9 | 1.9 | .9 | | | | 2.0 | 2.1 |
| | -4.4 | -7.4 | 15.7 | 1.8 | | | | 6.2 | 9.8 |
| % Profit Before Taxes/Tangible Net Worth | 31.3 | 52.8 | 24.4 | 20.5 | | | | 44.7 | 39.7 |
| | (12) 3.1 | (34) 12.4 | (44) 7.8 | (23) 5.0 | | | | (164) 15.7 | (149) 8.6 |
| | -38.7 | -5.7 | -9.0 | -2.3 | | | | 3.5 | -10.3 |
| % Profit Before Taxes/Total Assets | 20.0 | 12.3 | 6.9 | 9.4 | | | | 13.1 | 11.4 |
| | 1.8 | 6.0 | 2.5 | 2.5 | | | | 5.3 | 2.2 |
| | -23.2 | -3.3 | -5.0 | -1.1 | | | | -1.3 | -9.0 |
| Sales/Net Fixed Assets | 47.7 | 38.9 | 19.7 | 13.1 | | | | 24.0 | 19.6 |
| | 20.7 | 11.6 | 12.8 | 6.2 | | | | 10.6 | 10.2 |
| | 8.3 | 6.7 | 4.5 | 3.4 | | | | 5.5 | 5.1 |
| Sales/Total Assets | 7.3 | 3.7 | 3.2 | 2.5 | | | | 3.6 | 3.5 |
| | 3.8 | 2.8 | 2.3 | 2.1 | | | | 2.6 | 2.5 |
| | 2.5 | 1.8 | 1.4 | 1.2 | | | | 1.8 | 1.6 |
| % Depr., Dep., Amort./Sales | .5 | .8 | .9 | 1.6 | | | | 1.0 | 1.1 |
| | (18) 1.6 | (40) 2.0 | (50) 1.7 | (23) 2.5 | | | | (170) 1.8 | (158) 1.9 |
| | 2.6 | 4.4 | 3.0 | 4.5 | | | | 2.9 | 3.0 |
| % Officers', Directors' Owners' Comp/Sales | 3.8 | 2.5 | 1.3 | | | | | 2.2 | 1.9 |
| | (10) 5.4 | (28) 4.0 | (23) 4.4 | | | | | (75) 4.8 | (70) 4.9 |
| | 8.0 | 6.8 | 8.2 | | | | | 7.0 | 7.0 |
| Net Sales ($) | 24675M | 164562M | 562535M | 1102952M | 901021M | 321600M | | 6246532M | 4702492M |
| Total Assets ($) | 5620M | 59428M | 240597M | 562581M | 420047M | 206410M | | 2922596M | 2414806M |

© RMA 2012

M = $ thousand    MM = $ million
See Pages 9 through 22 for Explanation of Ratios and Data

## Comparative Historical Data      Current Data Sorted by Sales

| 12 | 10 | 6 | Type of Statement | | | | | 1 | 5 |
|---|---|---|---|---|---|---|---|---|---|
| | | | Unqualified | | | | | 8 | 6 |
| 35 | 34 | 29 | Reviewed | | 4 | 3 | 8 | 8 | 6 |
| 25 | 21 | 25 | Compiled | 2 | 8 | 4 | 8 | 3 | |
| 46 | 43 | 43 | Tax Returns | 9 | 20 | 7 | 5 | 1 | 1 |
| 57 | 67 | 57 | Other | 3 | 10 | 5 | 15 | 5 | 19 |
| 4/1/09- 3/31/10 ALL | 4/1/10- 3/31/11 ALL | 4/1/11- 3/31/12 ALL | | 0-1MM | 24 (4/1-9/30/11) 1-3MM | 3-5MM | 5-10MM | 136 (10/1/11-3/31/12) 10-25MM | 25MM & OVER |
| 175 | 175 | 160 | **NUMBER OF STATEMENTS** | 14 | 42 | 19 | 36 | 18 | 31 |
| % | % | % | **ASSETS** | % | % | % | % | % | % |
| 8.2 | 11.0 | 9.8 | Cash & Equivalents | 12.6 | 14.8 | 3.7 | 9.4 | 9.6 | 6.3 |
| 24.9 | 24.0 | 25.4 | Trade Receivables (net) | 19.9 | 20.8 | 28.2 | 33.8 | 24.6 | 23.0 |
| 24.5 | 25.5 | 24.2 | Inventory | 26.5 | 19.6 | 23.7 | 26.5 | 25.9 | 26.2 |
| 2.9 | 2.5 | 1.7 | All Other Current | 1.5 | .6 | .4 | .7 | 4.8 | 3.3 |
| 60.4 | 63.1 | 61.1 | Total Current | 60.5 | 55.7 | 56.0 | 70.5 | 64.9 | 58.8 |
| 30.1 | 28.8 | 28.2 | Fixed Assets (net) | 35.3 | 31.0 | 27.3 | 23.1 | 27.1 | 28.2 |
| 3.0 | 2.6 | 3.0 | Intangibles (net) | 1.0 | 4.4 | 2.4 | .5 | .9 | 6.6 |
| 6.5 | 5.5 | 7.7 | All Other Non-Current | 3.3 | 8.9 | 14.3 | 5.9 | 7.0 | 6.3 |
| 100.0 | 100.0 | 100.0 | Total | 100.0 | 100.0 | 100.0 | 100.0 | 100.0 | 100.0 |
| | | | **LIABILITIES** | | | | | | |
| 14.9 | 16.2 | 13.9 | Notes Payable-Short Term | 37.1 | 8.2 | 19.6 | 13.0 | 11.4 | 10.1 |
| 5.0 | 3.8 | 3.8 | Cur. Mat.-L.T.D. | 1.7 | 6.2 | 3.3 | 2.1 | 4.2 | 3.8 |
| 14.0 | 13.9 | 13.1 | Trade Payables | 19.9 | 11.8 | 18.7 | 12.3 | 10.5 | 10.6 |
| .2 | .2 | .2 | Income Taxes Payable | .0 | .2 | .0 | .7 | .0 | .1 |
| 11.3 | 11.8 | 12.2 | All Other Current | 18.2 | 10.6 | 20.4 | 10.0 | 10.0 | 10.2 |
| 45.3 | 45.8 | 43.2 | Total Current | 76.9 | 37.0 | 62.0 | 38.2 | 36.1 | 34.8 |
| 21.8 | 18.2 | 19.4 | Long-Term Debt | 19.3 | 24.9 | 25.5 | 19.1 | 13.8 | 11.7 |
| .4 | .3 | .3 | Deferred Taxes | .0 | .1 | .3 | .6 | .1 | .4 |
| 9.0 | 8.6 | 12.1 | All Other Non-Current | 28.5 | 5.4 | 23.4 | 6.0 | 3.5 | 19.1 |
| 23.5 | 27.1 | 25.0 | Net Worth | -24.7 | 32.6 | -11.2 | 36.1 | 46.5 | 33.9 |
| 100.0 | 100.0 | 100.0 | Total Liabilities & Net Worth | 100.0 | 100.0 | 100.0 | 100.0 | 100.0 | 100.0 |
| | | | **INCOME DATA** | | | | | | |
| 100.0 | 100.0 | 100.0 | Net Sales | 100.0 | 100.0 | 100.0 | 100.0 | 100.0 | 100.0 |
| 26.0 | 29.5 | 30.8 | Gross Profit | 46.5 | 38.4 | 29.4 | 26.0 | 20.0 | 26.0 |
| 27.7 | 29.0 | 29.4 | Operating Expenses | 46.9 | 38.2 | 29.3 | 22.9 | 19.1 | 23.2 |
| -1.6 | .5 | 1.4 | Operating Profit | -.4 | .2 | .0 | 3.1 | .8 | 2.8 |
| 1.0 | .8 | .8 | All Other Expenses (net) | .9 | 1.1 | .7 | .8 | .7 | .3 |
| -2.7 | -.3 | .6 | Profit Before Taxes | -1.3 | -.8 | -.7 | 2.3 | .1 | 2.5 |
| | | | **RATIOS** | | | | | | |
| 2.6 | 3.0 | 3.2 | | 2.3 | 5.3 | 1.7 | 3.7 | 2.3 | 2.5 |
| 1.5 | 1.6 | 1.7 | Current | 1.0 | 2.0 | 1.0 | 2.0 | 1.8 | 1.9 |
| 1.0 | 1.0 | .9 | | .4 | .8 | .5 | 1.4 | 1.2 | 1.1 |
| 1.5 | 1.6 | 1.8 | | 1.2 | 2.9 | .9 | 2.2 | 1.4 | 1.3 |
| (174) .8 | .9 | .9 | Quick | .6 | 1.2 | .5 | 1.1 | .9 | .7 |
| .4 | .4 | .5 | | .1 | .5 | .2 | .6 | .5 | .5 |
| 21 17.4 | 21 17.1 | 19 18.8 | | 8 46.6 | 9 40.9 | 19 19.0 | 27 13.3 | 20 18.5 | 23 15.7 |
| 33 10.9 | 35 10.4 | 34 10.6 | Sales/Receivables | 24 15.1 | 34 10.8 | 34 10.6 | 47 7.7 | 35 10.3 | 36 10.0 |
| 51 7.1 | 50 7.3 | 52 7.0 | | 34 10.6 | 55 6.6 | 52 7.0 | 66 5.5 | 51 7.2 | 41 8.9 |
| 20 18.2 | 24 15.2 | 22 16.4 | | 29 12.5 | 22 16.9 | 17 22.1 | 11 34.2 | 26 13.9 | 26 14.1 |
| 51 7.2 | 48 7.6 | 41 8.9 | Cost of Sales/Inventory | 41 8.8 | 35 10.4 | 45 8.1 | 45 8.1 | 38 9.6 | 49 7.5 |
| 84 4.3 | 93 3.9 | 79 4.6 | | 81 4.5 | 83 4.4 | 78 4.7 | 94 3.9 | 81 4.5 | 79 4.6 |
| 10 36.0 | 12 30.3 | 9 42.2 | | 4 95.5 | 5 78.8 | 11 34.6 | 8 44.5 | 13 28.2 | 13 28.8 |
| 18 19.9 | 19 19.2 | 19 19.3 | Cost of Sales/Payables | 16 22.5 | 20 18.6 | 35 10.5 | 18 20.8 | 18 20.4 | 17 21.6 |
| 37 9.9 | 33 10.9 | 41 8.9 | | 79 4.6 | 47 7.8 | 50 7.3 | 37 9.9 | 22 16.5 | 34 10.7 |
| 5.6 | 5.5 | 5.5 | | 10.0 | 5.5 | 10.9 | 4.4 | 4.6 | 5.4 |
| 11.7 | 10.4 | 10.3 | Sales/Working Capital | NM | 10.1 | -225.1 | 8.1 | 10.0 | 8.9 |
| -136.6 | 181.7 | -42.3 | | -3.9 | -21.3 | -17.4 | 11.7 | 25.0 | 32.4 |
| 3.9 | 6.2 | 7.0 | | | 6.3 | 3.2 | 11.5 | 12.4 | 11.3 |
| (163) .6 | (155) 1.9 | (143) 1.9 | EBIT/Interest | (36) | 1.2 | 1.6 | (34) 2.9 | (17) 2.5 | (28) 3.2 |
| -4.4 | -1.8 | -.5 | | | -2.6 | .0 | 1.2 | -2.8 | -.1 |
| 3.7 | 5.2 | 2.0 | Net Profit + Depr., Dep., | | | | | | |
| (23) 2.1 | (22) 2.2 | (20) 1.2 | Amort./Cur. Mat. L/T/D | | | | | | |
| .3 | .0 | -.5 | | | | | | | |
| .3 | .4 | .3 | | .7 | .3 | .5 | .2 | .4 | .4 |
| 1.0 | .9 | .8 | Fixed/Worth | -4.0 | 1.5 | 7.0 | .5 | .6 | .8 |
| -27.7 | 4.7 | NM | | -.4 | -15.2 | -.6 | 1.3 | .9 | 2.0 |
| .8 | .8 | .8 | | 2.3 | .4 | 2.9 | .7 | .7 | .6 |
| 2.1 | 2.0 | 1.6 | Debt/Worth | -22.3 | 2.9 | 27.4 | 1.5 | 1.1 | 1.2 |
| -59.8 | 12.1 | NM | | -2.7 | -19.6 | -2.6 | 3.4 | 1.8 | 3.0 |
| 18.7 | 26.3 | 27.2 | % Profit Before Taxes/Tangible | | 35.5 | 27.4 | 36.9 | 17.8 | 29.5 |
| (131) .8 | (140) 6.7 | (120) 6.4 | Net Worth | (29) | 2.0 | (10) 5.1 | (32) 12.2 | (17) 2.0 | (26) 6.6 |
| -21.0 | -6.4 | -5.8 | | | -16.9 | -14.4 | 3.5 | -13.7 | -5.6 |
| 5.0 | 8.2 | 10.9 | % Profit Before Taxes/Total | 18.1 | 10.3 | 9.8 | 14.2 | 9.0 | 12.8 |
| -1.0 | 2.2 | 2.8 | Assets | 1.4 | 2.0 | 4.2 | 3.4 | 1.2 | 4.1 |
| -11.1 | -5.7 | -4.1 | | -27.0 | -8.7 | -5.1 | 1.5 | -6.7 | -1.6 |
| 18.1 | 23.0 | 29.5 | | 24.5 | 44.8 | 38.9 | 36.0 | 20.3 | 17.2 |
| 9.4 | 10.2 | 10.4 | Sales/Net Fixed Assets | 12.6 | 9.5 | 12.8 | 15.2 | 10.5 | 9.0 |
| 4.4 | 4.8 | 5.2 | | 6.0 | 3.6 | 8.2 | 6.1 | 5.3 | 5.7 |
| 3.2 | 3.4 | 3.3 | | 5.9 | 2.9 | 4.7 | 3.2 | 3.5 | 2.9 |
| 2.2 | 2.4 | 2.4 | Sales/Total Assets | 2.6 | 2.0 | 3.1 | 2.5 | 2.3 | 2.3 |
| 1.6 | 1.6 | 1.7 | | 1.9 | 1.4 | 1.9 | 1.8 | 1.7 | 1.9 |
| 1.2 | 1.4 | 1.0 | | .9 | 1.3 | .5 | .8 | .8 | 1.1 |
| (143) 2.3 | (144) 2.3 | (138) 2.0 | % Depr., Dep., Amort./Sales | (13) 2.5 | (32) 2.4 | (18) 1.4 | (28) 1.4 | 2.0 | (29) 2.1 |
| 3.7 | 3.7 | 3.5 | | 4.1 | 5.0 | 3.3 | 2.4 | 3.9 | 3.1 |
| 2.1 | 2.2 | 2.0 | % Officers', Directors' | | | 2.6 | 1.3 | | |
| (63) 4.2 | (74) 4.2 | (68) 4.3 | Owners' Comp/Sales | | (22) 4.3 | | (20) 4.4 | | |
| 8.3 | 7.6 | 6.8 | | | | 6.3 | 8.2 | | |
| 3612346M | 3460399M | 3077345M | Net Sales ($) | 9900M | 85965M | 74254M | 244546M | 286676M | 2376004M |
| 2082688M | 1899530M | 1494683M | Total Assets ($) | 4229M | 57331M | 31753M | 130326M | 136294M | 1134750M |

M = $ thousand     MM = $ million
See Pages 9 through 22 for Explanation of Ratios and Data

## Current Data Sorted by Assets

## Comparative Historical Data

| 0-500M | 500M-2MM | 2-10MM | 10-50MM | 50-100MM | 100-250MM | Type of Statement | 4/1/07-3/31/08 ALL | 4/1/08-3/31/09 ALL |
|---|---|---|---|---|---|---|---|---|
| | | 2 | 5 | 1 | | Unqualified | 16 | 6 |
| | | 5 | 4 | | | Reviewed | 14 | 7 |
| | 3 | 5 | | | | Compiled | 18 | 18 |
| 1 | 5 | 1 | 1 | | | Tax Returns | 7 | 5 |
| 2 | | 4 | 5 | | 1 | Other | 24 | 17 |
| 9 (4/1-9/30/11) | | | 36 (10/1/11-3/31/12) | | | | | |
| 3 | 8 | 17 | 15 | 1 | 1 | **NUMBER OF STATEMENTS** | 79 | 53 |
| % | % | % | % | % | % | **ASSETS** | % | % |
| | | 6.0 | 2.7 | | | Cash & Equivalents | 5.9 | 9.1 |
| | | 13.5 | 13.5 | | | Trade Receivables (net) | 13.6 | 14.5 |
| | | 40.7 | 37.4 | | | Inventory | 35.0 | 35.2 |
| | | 2.0 | 1.4 | | | All Other Current | 2.1 | 1.7 |
| | | 62.3 | 55.1 | | | Total Current | 56.6 | 60.5 |
| | | 28.8 | 34.3 | | | Fixed Assets (net) | 34.8 | 30.6 |
| | | 1.3 | .7 | | | Intangibles (net) | 2.1 | 1.1 |
| | | 7.6 | 9.9 | | | All Other Non-Current | 6.5 | 7.8 |
| | | 100.0 | 100.0 | | | Total | 100.0 | 100.0 |
| | | | | | | **LIABILITIES** | | |
| | | 17.2 | 18.6 | | | Notes Payable-Short Term | 17.3 | 18.8 |
| | | 2.9 | 7.0 | | | Cur. Mat.-L.T.D. | 4.0 | 4.7 |
| | | 8.4 | 7.5 | | | Trade Payables | 8.6 | 8.8 |
| | | .1 | .2 | | | Income Taxes Payable | .1 | .1 |
| | | 6.9 | 5.5 | | | All Other Current | 6.8 | 6.7 |
| | | 35.6 | 38.8 | | | Total Current | 36.7 | 39.1 |
| | | 15.9 | 14.6 | | | Long-Term Debt | 21.0 | 24.4 |
| | | .3 | .0 | | | Deferred Taxes | .2 | .1 |
| | | 5.0 | 8.8 | | | All Other Non-Current | 3.2 | 7.7 |
| | | 43.3 | 37.8 | | | Net Worth | 38.8 | 28.7 |
| | | 100.0 | 100.0 | | | Total Liabilties & Net Worth | 100.0 | 100.0 |
| | | | | | | **INCOME DATA** | | |
| | | 100.0 | 100.0 | | | Net Sales | 100.0 | 100.0 |
| | | 17.1 | 22.6 | | | Gross Profit | 20.7 | 21.2 |
| | | 13.5 | 19.6 | | | Operating Expenses | 17.9 | 19.0 |
| | | 3.6 | 3.0 | | | Operating Profit | 2.8 | 2.2 |
| | | 1.0 | 1.7 | | | All Other Expenses (net) | 1.9 | 2.5 |
| | | 2.6 | 1.3 | | | Profit Before Taxes | .9 | -.3 |
| | | | | | | **RATIOS** | | |
| | | 5.0 | 2.3 | | | | 2.3 | 2.7 |
| | | 1.9 | 1.4 | | | Current | 1.4 | 1.5 |
| | | 1.2 | 1.0 | | | | 1.0 | 1.1 |
| | | 1.6 | .9 | | | | .8 | 1.1 |
| | | .6 | .5 | | | Quick | (78) .4 | .5 |
| | | .3 | .3 | | | | .2 | .2 |
| | 14 | 26.1 | 14 · 25.9 | | | | 10 · 35.7 | 10 · 37.6 |
| | 23 | 15.9 | 28 · 13.0 | | | Sales/Receivables | 17 · 21.8 | 20 · 18.5 |
| | 31 | 11.6 | 33 · 10.9 | | | | 28 · 13.0 | 34 · 10.6 |
| | 49 | 7.4 | 54 · 6.7 | | | | 33 · 11.1 | 32 · 11.5 |
| | 89 | 4.1 | 87 · 4.2 | | | Cost of Sales/Inventory | 60 · 6.1 | 63 · 5.8 |
| | 107 | 3.4 | 146 · 2.5 | | | | 122 · 3.0 | 123 · 3.0 |
| | 6 | 59.7 | 8 · 44.3 | | | | 7 · 54.0 | 4 · 82.9 |
| | 11 | 33.1 | 19 · 19.2 | | | Cost of Sales/Payables | 12 · 29.3 | 12 · 31.6 |
| | 32 | 11.4 | 45 · 8.1 | | | | 26 · 14.1 | 26 · 14.0 |
| | | 3.5 | 6.4 | | | | 6.1 | 4.8 |
| | | 9.0 | 15.8 | | | Sales/Working Capital | 11.6 | 8.9 |
| | | 39.1 | 389.9 | | | | 95.7 | 36.9 |
| | | 9.6 | 5.3 | | | | 7.1 | 4.3 |
| | | 2.4 | 1.5 | | | EBIT/Interest | (76) 2.7 | (50) 1.5 |
| | | .7 | .7 | | | | .3 | -1.4 |
| | | | | | | Net Profit + Depr., Dep., Amort./Cur. Mat. L/T/D | 2.4 | |
| | | | | | | | (16) 1.9 | |
| | | | | | | | 1.1 | |
| | | .3 | .5 | | | | .3 | .3 |
| | | .8 | .9 | | | Fixed/Worth | .8 | .9 |
| | | 1.3 | 2.4 | | | | 2.0 | 4.7 |
| | | .5 | 1.3 | | | | .6 | .9 |
| | | 1.8 | 1.5 | | | Debt/Worth | 1.7 | 2.2 |
| | | 3.7 | 5.3 | | | | 5.2 | 24.7 |
| | | 24.7 | 20.9 | | | | 28.8 | 13.6 |
| | (16) | 12.2 | 1.1 | | | % Profit Before Taxes/Tangible Net Worth | (71) 9.6 | (41) 5.5 |
| | | -.5 | -1.6 | | | | -1.7 | -6.3 |
| | | 9.3 | 8.6 | | | | 9.0 | 6.3 |
| | | 4.5 | .4 | | | % Profit Before Taxes/Total Assets | 3.4 | 1.3 |
| | | -.8 | -.7 | | | | -3.7 | -5.5 |
| | | 16.2 | 10.3 | | | | 22.1 | 32.5 |
| | | 8.2 | 7.5 | | | Sales/Net Fixed Assets | 6.9 | 7.2 |
| | | 4.3 | 2.7 | | | | 3.0 | 3.1 |
| | | 2.6 | 2.8 | | | | 3.0 | 2.9 |
| | | 2.0 | 1.7 | | | Sales/Total Assets | 2.2 | 1.9 |
| | | 1.6 | 1.0 | | | | 1.4 | 1.3 |
| | | 1.1 | 1.1 | | | | .9 | 1.0 |
| | (16) | 2.6 | (14) · 2.4 | | | % Depr., Dep., Amort./Sales | (72) 2.2 | (43) 2.1 |
| | | 4.3 | 4.4 | | | | 3.8 | 4.4 |
| | | | | | | | .7 | 1.3 |
| | | | | | | % Officers', Directors' Owners' Comp/Sales | (25) 2.3 | (28) 4.5 |
| | | | | | | | 5.8 | 7.0 |
| 2217M | 29187M | 185900M | 509518M | 81536M | 112857M | Net Sales ($) | 4158455M | 1084026M |
| 264M | 8877M | 87884M | 272527M | 86465M | 114416M | Total Assets ($) | 1528780M | 554769M |

M = $ thousand    MM = $ million
See Pages 9 through 22 for Explanation of Ratios and Data

**Comparative Historical Data**                                   **Current Data Sorted by Sales**

| | | | Type of Statement | | | | | | |
|---|---|---|---|---|---|---|---|---|---|
| 9 | 10 | 8 | Unqualified | | | | 1 | | 7 |
| 12 | 11 | 9 | Reviewed | | 1 | | 3 | 3 | 2 |
| 13 | 9 | 8 | Compiled | | 2 | 1 | 3 | 2 | |
| 4 | 8 | 8 | Tax Returns | 1 | 2 | 4 | 1 | | |
| 23 | 13 | 12 | Other | 1 | | 1 | 3 | 4 | 3 |
| 4/1/09-3/31/10 ALL | 4/1/10-3/31/11 ALL | 4/1/11-3/31/12 ALL | | | | 9 (4/1-9/30/11) | | 36 (10/1/11-3/31/12) | |
| | | | | 0-1MM | 1-3MM | 3-5MM | 5-10MM | 10-25MM | 25MM & OVER |
| 61 | 51 | 45 | NUMBER OF STATEMENTS | 2 | 5 | 6 | 11 | 9 | 12 |
| % | % | % | ASSETS | % | % | % | % | % | % |
| 6.6 | 5.8 | 4.1 | Cash & Equivalents | | | | 5.9 | | 2.1 |
| 12.1 | 15.2 | 14.3 | Trade Receivables (net) | | | | 12.7 | | 14.6 |
| 34.6 | 33.9 | 36.3 | Inventory | | | | 41.0 | | 42.4 |
| 2.2 | 1.1 | 1.9 | All Other Current | | | | 2.6 | | 2.3 |
| 55.6 | 55.9 | 56.6 | Total Current | | | | 62.3 | | 61.4 |
| 34.7 | 36.7 | 31.2 | Fixed Assets (net) | | | | 29.2 | | 24.9 |
| 1.7 | .7 | .9 | Intangibles (net) | | | | 2.0 | | 1.2 |
| 8.1 | 6.6 | 11.2 | All Other Non-Current | | | | 6.5 | | 12.5 |
| 100.0 | 100.0 | 100.0 | Total | | | | 100.0 | | 100.0 |
| | | | LIABILITIES | | | | | | |
| 16.9 | 19.6 | 18.4 | Notes Payable-Short Term | | | | 19.2 | | 17.2 |
| 6.3 | 4.1 | 4.0 | Cur. Mat.-L.T.D. | | | | 8.3 | | 3.7 |
| 8.3 | 12.4 | 9.4 | Trade Payables | | | | 7.4 | | 8.1 |
| .1 | .0 | .1 | Income Taxes Payable | | | | .0 | | .3 |
| 6.8 | 6.0 | 6.9 | All Other Current | | | | 3.5 | | 5.9 |
| 38.4 | 42.1 | 38.8 | Total Current | | | | 38.4 | | 35.3 |
| 19.2 | 17.7 | 20.4 | Long-Term Debt | | | | 11.9 | | 12.9 |
| .6 | .4 | .2 | Deferred Taxes | | | | .5 | | .3 |
| 5.0 | 4.3 | 7.5 | All Other Non-Current | | | | 7.7 | | 10.2 |
| 36.8 | 35.4 | 33.0 | Net Worth | | | | 41.5 | | 41.4 |
| 100.0 | 100.0 | 100.0 | Total Liabilties & Net Worth | | | | 100.0 | | 100.0 |
| | | | INCOME DATA | | | | | | |
| 100.0 | 100.0 | 100.0 | Net Sales | | | | 100.0 | | 100.0 |
| 17.2 | 20.5 | 22.2 | Gross Profit | | | | 19.3 | | 14.9 |
| 18.8 | 18.3 | 19.6 | Operating Expenses | | | | 16.2 | | 13.0 |
| -1.6 | 2.2 | 2.7 | Operating Profit | | | | 3.1 | | 1.9 |
| 1.0 | 2.0 | 1.2 | All Other Expenses (net) | | | | .6 | | 1.2 |
| -2.6 | .2 | 1.4 | Profit Before Taxes | | | | 2.5 | | .8 |
| | | | RATIOS | | | | | | |
| 2.1 | 2.2 | 3.3 | | | | | 3.8 | | 3.9 |
| 1.7 | 1.5 | 1.4 | Current | | | | 1.3 | | 1.5 |
| 1.1 | 1.1 | 1.0 | | | | | 1.1 | | 1.1 |
| .8 | 1.0 | 1.2 | | | | | 1.5 | | .7 |
| .4 | .5 | .5 | Quick | | | | .4 | | .5 |
| .3 | .3 | .3 | | | | | .3 | | .3 |
| 12 30.4 | 13 27.6 | 14 25.6 | | | | | 12 30.8 | | 9 42.4 |
| 23 15.9 | 21 17.4 | 25 14.8 | Sales/Receivables | | | | 20 18.6 | | 27 13.5 |
| 30 12.2 | 36 10.0 | 32 11.5 | | | | | 33 11.2 | | 33 11.1 |
| 43 8.6 | 50 7.3 | 44 8.3 | | | | | 61 6.0 | | 58 6.3 |
| 79 4.6 | 70 5.2 | 85 4.3 | Cost of Sales/Inventory | | | | 89 4.1 | | 89 4.1 |
| 130 2.8 | 104 3.5 | 107 3.4 | | | | | 130 2.8 | | 96 3.8 |
| 7 49.4 | 6 58.1 | 7 53.8 | | | | | 6 58.3 | | 8 44.0 |
| 13 28.6 | 17 21.7 | 17 21.9 | Cost of Sales/Payables | | | | 11 33.1 | | 14 26.7 |
| 30 12.0 | 29 12.7 | 36 10.0 | | | | | 31 11.6 | | 26 13.8 |
| 4.7 | 6.2 | 5.0 | | | | | 3.4 | | 5.3 |
| 8.9 | 11.3 | 11.3 | Sales/Working Capital | | | | 10.3 | | 9.8 |
| 37.9 | 161.1 | NM | | | | | 84.8 | | 37.2 |
| 2.6 | 4.1 | 5.4 | | | | | 7.1 | | 5.4 |
| (59) .0 | (46) 1.6 | (41) 1.5 | EBIT/Interest | | | | 1.8 | | 1.2 |
| -2.9 | -.2 | .4 | | | | | .5 | | .3 |
| 4.5 | | | Net Profit + Depr., Dep., | | | | | | |
| (18) 1.3 | | | Amort./Cur. Mat. L/T/D | | | | | | |
| .5 | | | | | | | | | |
| .4 | .4 | .3 | | | | | .4 | | .2 |
| .8 | .8 | .8 | Fixed/Worth | | | | .8 | | .5 |
| 2.6 | 2.1 | 1.9 | | | | | 1.2 | | 2.4 |
| .6 | .6 | .8 | | | | | .7 | | .8 |
| 1.5 | 1.6 | 1.7 | Debt/Worth | | | | 1.5 | | 1.3 |
| 5.8 | 5.0 | 4.8 | | | | | 2.7 | | 5.1 |
| 12.3 | 21.3 | 21.0 | % Profit Before Taxes/Tangible | | | | 13.3 | | 21.5 |
| (52) -1.8 | (46) 7.6 | (41) 4.7 | Net Worth | | | (10) | 9.5 | | .9 |
| -17.4 | -2.0 | -2.1 | | | | | -1.3 | | -11.7 |
| 4.0 | 7.8 | 8.3 | % Profit Before Taxes/Total | | | | 7.8 | | 10.5 |
| -1.1 | 1.8 | .9 | Assets | | | | 1.8 | | .3 |
| -7.8 | -1.5 | -1.8 | | | | | -1.3 | | -1.6 |
| 16.5 | 19.2 | 20.4 | | | | | 10.9 | | 34.1 |
| 5.0 | 7.1 | 8.2 | Sales/Net Fixed Assets | | | | 6.4 | | 9.0 |
| 3.1 | 3.0 | 3.5 | | | | | 3.1 | | 4.1 |
| 2.7 | 2.9 | 3.1 | | | | | 2.6 | | 3.4 |
| 1.7 | 1.9 | 2.1 | Sales/Total Assets | | | | 1.8 | | 2.4 |
| 1.0 | 1.4 | 1.4 | | | | | 1.3 | | 1.1 |
| 1.9 | 1.1 | 1.1 | | | | | .6 | | |
| (55) 3.8 | (48) 2.8 | (38) 2.5 | % Depr., Dep., Amort./Sales | | | | 2.7 | | |
| 5.0 | 4.5 | 4.5 | | | | | 4.2 | | |
| 1.5 | 1.8 | 1.5 | % Officers', Directors' | | | | | | |
| (19) 4.2 | (17) 3.4 | (19) 2.0 | Owners' Comp/Sales | | | | | | |
| 8.5 | 5.8 | 3.0 | | | | | | | |
| 1310147M | 1501516M | 921215M | Net Sales ($) | 68M | 11685M | 23663M | 88586M | 161338M | 635875M |
| 920769M | 759962M | 570433M | Total Assets ($) | 42M | 4492M | 20720M | 53621M | 101640M | 389918M |

© RMA 2012

M = $ thousand    MM = $ million
See Pages 9 through 22 for Explanation of Ratios and Data

## Current Data Sorted by Assets      Comparative Historical Data

**Type of Statement**

| | 0-500M | 500M-2MM | 2-10MM | 10-50MM | 50-100MM | 100-250MM | | 4/1/07-3/31/08 ALL | 4/1/08-3/31/09 ALL |
|---|---|---|---|---|---|---|---|---|---|
| Unqualified | | | 1 | 3 | | | | 10 | 7 |
| Reviewed | | 3 | 15 | 3 | | | | 22 | 25 |
| Compiled | 1 | 10 | 8 | | | | | 20 | 18 |
| Tax Returns | 10 | 7 | 3 | | | | | 19 | 29 |
| Other | 4 | 13 | 7 | 5 | 1 | 2 | | 41 | 48 |
| | | 15 (4/1-9/30/11) | | 81 (10/1/11-3/31/12) | | | | | |

| 0-500M | 500M-2MM | 2-10MM | 10-50MM | 50-100MM | 100-250MM | | 4/1/07-3/31/08 ALL | 4/1/08-3/31/09 ALL |
|---|---|---|---|---|---|---|---|---|
| 15 | 33 | 34 | 11 | 1 | 2 | **NUMBER OF STATEMENTS** | 112 | 127 |
| % | % | % | % | % | % | **ASSETS** | % | % |
| 14.6 | 5.8 | 4.6 | 3.4 | | | Cash & Equivalents | 5.7 | 6.7 |
| 24.5 | 40.2 | 30.6 | 11.4 | | | Trade Receivables (net) | 27.9 | 26.0 |
| 17.7 | 15.5 | 26.3 | 37.8 | | | Inventory | 22.7 | 25.9 |
| 4.9 | 3.7 | 3.0 | 2.2 | | | All Other Current | 2.9 | 2.5 |
| 61.7 | 65.2 | 64.5 | 54.8 | | | Total Current | 59.2 | 61.2 |
| 19.4 | 28.2 | 24.9 | 32.8 | | | Fixed Assets (net) | 31.3 | 28.7 |
| 3.8 | 2.5 | 3.0 | 7.8 | | | Intangibles (net) | 3.2 | 3.6 |
| 15.1 | 4.2 | 7.6 | 4.7 | | | All Other Non-Current | 6.3 | 6.5 |
| 100.0 | 100.0 | 100.0 | 100.0 | | | Total | 100.0 | 100.0 |
| | | | | | | **LIABILITIES** | | |
| 26.3 | 23.3 | 15.0 | 11.7 | | | Notes Payable-Short Term | 13.2 | 17.5 |
| 12.3 | 3.2 | 3.4 | 11.9 | | | Cur. Mat.-L.T.D. | 6.1 | 5.6 |
| 10.1 | 23.1 | 16.6 | 6.8 | | | Trade Payables | 11.7 | 14.0 |
| 1.3 | .0 | .1 | .2 | | | Income Taxes Payable | .2 | .2 |
| 8.2 | 11.9 | 5.6 | 8.7 | | | All Other Current | 11.9 | 8.7 |
| 58.2 | 61.5 | 40.7 | 39.2 | | | Total Current | 43.2 | 46.1 |
| 24.4 | 18.9 | 12.1 | 12.9 | | | Long-Term Debt | 23.6 | 18.4 |
| .0 | .1 | .3 | 1.3 | | | Deferred Taxes | .3 | .4 |
| 54.0 | 15.2 | 3.1 | 8.6 | | | All Other Non-Current | 6.5 | 6.6 |
| -36.5 | 4.3 | 43.8 | 37.9 | | | Net Worth | 26.4 | 28.5 |
| 100.0 | 100.0 | 100.0 | 100.0 | | | Total Liabilities & Net Worth | 100.0 | 100.0 |
| | | | | | | **INCOME DATA** | | |
| 100.0 | 100.0 | 100.0 | 100.0 | | | Net Sales | 100.0 | 100.0 |
| 45.9 | 29.8 | 23.1 | 19.6 | | | Gross Profit | 27.3 | 26.1 |
| 46.2 | 30.3 | 19.6 | 20.4 | | | Operating Expenses | 23.8 | 25.5 |
| -.2 | -.6 | 3.5 | -.8 | | | Operating Profit | 3.5 | .7 |
| .7 | .6 | .9 | 1.8 | | | All Other Expenses (net) | 2.0 | 1.1 |
| -.9 | -1.2 | 2.6 | -2.6 | | | Profit Before Taxes | 1.6 | -.5 |
| | | | | | | **RATIOS** | | |
| 5.1 | 1.6 | 2.2 | 2.6 | | | | 2.2 | 2.3 |
| 1.1 | 1.1 | 1.5 | 1.8 | | | Current | 1.4 | 1.5 |
| .4 | .9 | 1.1 | 1.1 | | | | 1.1 | 1.0 |
| 2.9 | 1.2 | 1.3 | .8 | | | | 1.3 | 1.4 |
| .7 | .8 | .8 | .5 | | | Quick | (111) .8 | .7 |
| .3 | .6 | .6 | .2 | | | | .5 | .4 |
| 0 UND | 23 15.7 | 30 12.2 | 13 27.7 | | | | 23 16.0 | 18 20.3 |
| 25 14.5 | 47 7.8 | 41 8.8 | 24 15.5 | | | Sales/Receivables | 37 9.8 | 29 12.8 |
| 41 9.0 | 76 4.8 | 70 5.2 | 36 10.0 | | | | 56 6.5 | 49 7.5 |
| 0 UND | 7 53.2 | 16 22.3 | 76 4.8 | | | | 17 21.2 | 14 26.1 |
| 15 24.0 | 19 19.3 | 42 8.6 | 114 3.2 | | | Cost of Sales/Inventory | 46 7.9 | 45 8.1 |
| 34 10.6 | 38 9.5 | 89 4.1 | 122 3.0 | | | | 92 4.0 | 87 4.2 |
| 0 UND | 16 23.5 | 17 21.9 | 8 43.3 | | | | 10 37.7 | 9 40.6 |
| 1 264.0 | 31 11.7 | 23 15.8 | 12 30.7 | | | Cost of Sales/Payables | 19 18.9 | 20 18.2 |
| 38 9.7 | 61 6.0 | 40 9.2 | 24 15.1 | | | | 35 10.5 | 31 11.9 |
| 12.2 | 7.7 | 5.8 | 5.5 | | | | 7.3 | 7.0 |
| 132.7 | 43.3 | 10.9 | 7.4 | | | Sales/Working Capital | 13.9 | 13.3 |
| -29.4 | -43.4 | 33.9 | 67.5 | | | | 224.8 | -196.0 |
| 7.3 | 5.5 | 11.4 | 6.0 | | | | 5.5 | 5.5 |
| (10) 2.2 | (31) .5 | (32) 2.9 | (10) 1.9 | | | EBIT/Interest | (105) 2.3 | (116) 1.4 |
| -2.1 | -4.6 | 1.1 | -.5 | | | | .2 | -1.2 |
| | | | | | | Net Profit + Depr., Dep., | 2.4 | 1.9 |
| | | | | | | Amort./Cur. Mat. L/T/D | (16) 1.8 | (20) .6 |
| | | | | | | | .9 | -.1 |
| .0 | .5 | .2 | .4 | | | | .5 | .4 |
| 1.5 | 3.8 | .7 | .8 | | | Fixed/Worth | 1.1 | .9 |
| -.8 | -32.8 | 1.1 | 2.1 | | | | 3.6 | 2.6 |
| 1.9 | 1.7 | .8 | .6 | | | | 1.1 | 1.0 |
| 14.4 | 19.2 | 1.4 | 1.5 | | | Debt/Worth | 2.8 | 2.3 |
| -2.0 | -103.8 | 3.4 | 3.7 | | | | 10.8 | 8.8 |
| | 31.5 | 30.3 | | | | % Profit Before Taxes/Tangible | 55.1 | 35.0 |
| | (24) 2.6 | (31) 5.4 | | | | Net Worth | (93) 13.9 | (108) 7.0 |
| | -123.9 | .8 | | | | | .0 | -20.2 |
| 26.2 | 13.3 | 15.7 | 5.8 | | | % Profit Before Taxes/Total | 11.8 | 10.0 |
| 7.0 | 2.5 | 3.3 | 2.4 | | | Assets | 4.0 | 1.4 |
| -14.1 | -15.2 | .2 | -3.9 | | | | -3.9 | -7.4 |
| 398.1 | 31.6 | 24.7 | 8.5 | | | | 16.1 | 21.4 |
| 64.4 | 13.0 | 9.9 | 5.6 | | | Sales/Net Fixed Assets | 8.6 | 10.3 |
| 19.4 | 7.2 | 5.7 | 4.0 | | | | 4.0 | 6.0 |
| 11.2 | 4.1 | 3.0 | 1.9 | | | | 3.2 | 3.5 |
| 5.9 | 2.8 | 2.2 | 1.8 | | | Sales/Total Assets | 2.2 | 2.6 |
| 2.7 | 2.1 | 1.5 | 1.4 | | | | 1.7 | 1.9 |
| | .9 | 1.0 | 2.5 | | | | 1.4 | 1.0 |
| | (27) 1.7 | (33) 2.2 | 4.2 | | | % Depr., Dep., Amort./Sales | (86) 2.1 | (111) 1.9 |
| | 3.2 | 2.9 | 5.7 | | | | 3.3 | 3.5 |
| 3.7 | 1.5 | .9 | | | | | 1.5 | 1.6 |
| (12) 6.4 | (17) 3.7 | (15) 2.1 | | | | % Officers', Directors' | (41) 3.2 | (54) 3.3 |
| 10.2 | 5.5 | 3.4 | | | | Owners' Comp/Sales | 5.2 | 5.5 |
| 20124M | 105964M | 331643M | 327552M | 110811M | 533578M | Net Sales ($) | 2561267M | 2302769M |
| 3555M | 36541M | 151446M | 201843M | 74674M | 456180M | Total Assets ($) | 1512582M | 1072040M |

M = $ thousand    MM = $ million
See Pages 9 through 22 for Explanation of Ratios and Data

### Comparative Historical Data     Current Data Sorted by Sales

| 4/1/09-3/31/10 ALL | 4/1/10-3/31/11 ALL | 4/1/11-3/31/12 ALL | | 0-1MM | 1-3MM | 3-5MM | 5-10MM | 10-25MM | 25MM & OVER |
|---|---|---|---|---|---|---|---|---|---|
| | | | **Type of Statement** | | 15 (4/1-9/30/11) | | | 81 (10/1/11-3/31/12) | |
| 7 | 6 | 4 | Unqualified | | | | | 1 | 3 |
| 21 | 17 | 21 | Reviewed | | 2 | 4 | 5 | 6 | 4 |
| 19 | 19 | 19 | Compiled | 2 | 3 | 7 | 5 | 2 | |
| 24 | 15 | 20 | Tax Returns | 5 | 7 | 5 | 2 | 1 | |
| 32 | 36 | 32 | Other | 2 | 10 | 4 | 6 | 5 | 5 |
| 103 | 93 | 96 | **NUMBER OF STATEMENTS** | 9 | 22 | 20 | 18 | 15 | 12 |
| % | % | % | **ASSETS** | % | % | % | % | % | % |
| 7.5 | 7.8 | 6.5 | Cash & Equivalents | | 6.5 | 7.1 | 5.6 | 4.9 | 4.2 |
| 23.2 | 25.7 | 30.1 | Trade Receivables (net) | | 40.9 | 29.0 | 33.0 | 25.1 | 12.4 |
| 26.2 | 25.1 | 22.4 | Inventory | | 14.3 | 20.2 | 29.2 | 27.5 | 32.2 |
| 3.3 | 2.7 | 3.4 | All Other Current | | 4.3 | 1.7 | 3.2 | 4.7 | 1.9 |
| 60.3 | 61.2 | 62.4 | Total Current | | 65.9 | 58.1 | 71.0 | 62.2 | 50.7 |
| 27.9 | 26.9 | 26.8 | Fixed Assets (net) | | 24.5 | 31.0 | 23.6 | 21.2 | 41.3 |
| 4.2 | 3.1 | 3.5 | Intangibles (net) | | .8 | 3.5 | 2.1 | 8.4 | 2.6 |
| 7.7 | 8.8 | 7.2 | All Other Non-Current | | 8.7 | 7.4 | 3.3 | 8.2 | 5.4 |
| 100.0 | 100.0 | 100.0 | Total | | 100.0 | 100.0 | 100.0 | 100.0 | 100.0 |
| | | | **LIABILITIES** | | | | | | |
| 15.5 | 22.2 | 18.8 | Notes Payable-Short Term | | 18.4 | 25.7 | 18.5 | 12.4 | 9.7 |
| 5.9 | 7.5 | 6.4 | Cur. Mat.-L.T.D. | | 1.6 | 11.4 | 3.6 | 2.3 | 17.7 |
| 14.1 | 15.2 | 16.3 | Trade Payables | | 18.6 | 17.0 | 20.6 | 15.6 | 6.4 |
| .1 | .2 | .3 | Income Taxes Payable | | .0 | .0 | .2 | .0 | .1 |
| 8.2 | 8.0 | 8.6 | All Other Current | | 8.4 | 12.5 | 5.8 | 7.7 | 6.7 |
| 43.8 | 53.0 | 50.3 | Total Current | | 46.9 | 66.6 | 48.7 | 38.0 | 40.7 |
| 24.1 | 22.6 | 16.9 | Long-Term Debt | | 19.3 | 17.9 | 14.0 | 8.6 | 16.3 |
| .2 | .1 | .3 | Deferred Taxes | | .0 | .2 | .4 | .9 | .3 |
| 10.7 | 15.7 | 15.9 | All Other Non-Current | | 8.1 | 20.8 | 1.8 | 5.0 | 7.8 |
| 21.2 | 8.6 | 16.6 | Net Worth | | 25.7 | -5.5 | 35.1 | 47.5 | 34.9 |
| 100.0 | 100.0 | 100.0 | Total Liabilties & Net Worth | | 100.0 | 100.0 | 100.0 | 100.0 | 100.0 |
| | | | **INCOME DATA** | | | | | | |
| 100.0 | 100.0 | 100.0 | Net Sales | | 100.0 | 100.0 | 100.0 | 100.0 | 100.0 |
| 27.8 | 28.0 | 28.4 | Gross Profit | | 37.0 | 25.7 | 24.1 | 21.7 | 18.8 |
| 28.5 | 28.5 | 27.5 | Operating Expenses | | 35.5 | 25.5 | 22.8 | 18.2 | 18.9 |
| -.7 | -.4 | 1.0 | Operating Profit | | 1.5 | .3 | 1.3 | 3.5 | -.1 |
| 1.6 | 1.3 | 1.0 | All Other Expenses (net) | | .7 | .6 | 1.1 | .4 | 3.2 |
| -2.3 | -1.7 | .0 | Profit Before Taxes | | .8 | -.3 | .3 | 3.1 | -3.3 |
| | | | **RATIOS** | | | | | | |
| 3.0 | 2.3 | 2.1 | | | 1.9 | 1.5 | 2.5 | 2.3 | 3.0 |
| 1.6 | 1.3 | 1.3 | Current | | 1.2 | 1.0 | 1.4 | 1.8 | 2.0 |
| 1.0 | .8 | .9 | | | 1.0 | .6 | 1.1 | 1.1 | .7 |
| 1.6 | 1.3 | 1.2 | | | 1.5 | 1.1 | 1.4 | 1.0 | .8 |
| .8 | .7 | .7 | Quick | | .9 | .7 | .8 | .7 | .6 |
| .4 | .4 | .5 | | | .5 | .4 | .6 | .5 | .2 |
| 21   17.2 | 21   17.5 | 21   17.1 | | | 26   14.1 | 17   22.0 | 33   11.2 | 18   20.8 | 18   20.6 |
| 36   10.2 | 36   10.2 | 39   9.4 | Sales/Receivables | | 51   7.2 | 34   10.6 | 45   8.2 | 36   10.0 | 27   13.7 |
| 53   6.9 | 49   7.4 | 54   6.7 | | | 91   4.0 | 62   5.9 | 53   6.9 | 41   8.8 | 39   9.3 |
| 15   24.3 | 12   29.2 | 10   38.4 | | 0   UND | 15   24.3 | 13   28.2 | 10   34.8 | 51   7.1 | |
| 50   7.2 | 49   7.5 | 33   10.9 | Cost of Sales/Inventory | 11   34.4 | 27   13.5 | 45   8.2 | 42   8.7 | 94   3.9 | |
| 115   3.2 | 93   3.9 | 83   4.4 | | 47   7.8 | 40   9.2 | 99   3.7 | 107   3.4 | 114   3.2 | |
| 10   36.5 | 10   37.1 | 12   30.8 | | 7   55.2 | 11   33.0 | 18   20.0 | 15   24.7 | 9   42.8 | |
| 20   18.0 | 20   18.3 | 22   16.8 | Cost of Sales/Payables | 31   11.6 | 20   18.1 | 23   16.0 | 24   15.3 | 12   29.8 | |
| 42   8.8 | 47   7.7 | 43   8.4 | | 69   5.3 | 38   9.5 | 40   9.1 | 48   7.6 | 22   16.9 | |
| 4.5 | 6.3 | 6.5 | | | 6.8 | 19.8 | 6.9 | 5.7 | 4.5 |
| 11.2 | 17.7 | 17.0 | Sales/Working Capital | | 31.5 | 229.4 | 12.5 | 8.7 | 7.4 |
| 119.2 | -30.3 | -91.1 | | | NM | -11.2 | -31.8 | 29.3 | -18.5 |
| 3.9 | 3.9 | 6.2 | | | 8.3 | 5.0 | 11.1 | 14.7 | 4.7 |
| (92) 1.1 | (80) 1.0 | (86) 1.7 | EBIT/Interest | | (18) 1.3 | (19) 2.1 | 2.2 | (14) 4.0 | (11) 1.8 |
| -3.9 | -2.8 | -1.6 | | | -4.4 | -1.7 | -1.2 | .4 | .1 |
| 3.3 | 6.0 | 14.8 | Net Profit + Depr., Dep., | | | | | | |
| (19) 1.0 | (15) 3.0 | (11) 3.5 | Amort./Cur. Mat. L/T/D | | | | | | |
| -.3 | .1 | 1.4 | | | | | | | |
| .4 | .4 | .4 | | | .1 | .6 | .2 | .2 | .4 |
| .9 | 1.0 | 1.0 | Fixed/Worth | | 1.5 | 3.3 | .7 | .5 | 3.1 |
| -15.0 | -3.0 | 11.4 | | | 13.7 | -.6 | 9.0 | .9 | 3.5 |
| .7 | 1.0 | 1.1 | | | 1.0 | 1.6 | 1.0 | .7 | .7 |
| 2.5 | 3.2 | 2.8 | Debt/Worth | | 4.8 | 9.2 | 1.8 | 1.2 | 1.7 |
| -30.0 | -7.9 | 56.3 | | | 34.2 | -2.5 | 30.3 | 2.9 | 4.4 |
| 24.4 | 32.9 | 27.3 | % Profit Before Taxes/Tangible | | 46.5 | 25.5 | 21.6 | 54.8 | 12.0 |
| (74) 1.3 | (65) 4.2 | (75) 6.0 | Net Worth | | (19) 8.3 | (12) 14.6 | (15) 3.2 | (14) 19.1 | (11) 6.0 |
| -30.6 | -19.3 | -17.1 | | | -100.0 | -8.7 | -9.3 | -.9 | -17.3 |
| 7.6 | 9.0 | 10.7 | % Profit Before Taxes/Total | | 18.2 | 10.3 | 9.5 | 19.1 | 5.4 |
| .3 | .7 | 2.5 | Assets | | -4.0 | 3.9 | 1.1 | 9.5 | 1.8 |
| -10.8 | -11.4 | -5.9 | | | -11.7 | -4.7 | -5.6 | -1.0 | -6.2 |
| 19.0 | 22.3 | 29.6 | | | 100.0 | 29.1 | 18.5 | 41.5 | 7.9 |
| 8.4 | 10.7 | 10.8 | Sales/Net Fixed Assets | | 18.2 | 10.6 | 11.7 | 9.7 | 4.6 |
| 5.3 | 5.6 | 5.8 | | | 6.3 | 5.8 | 7.0 | 5.3 | 2.5 |
| 3.4 | 3.4 | 3.7 | | | 5.3 | 5.0 | 3.4 | 2.4 | 2.4 |
| 2.2 | 2.2 | 2.4 | Sales/Total Assets | | 2.8 | 2.8 | 2.7 | 2.2 | 1.7 |
| 1.4 | 1.6 | 1.7 | | | 1.9 | 2.2 | 1.6 | 2.0 | 1.2 |
| 1.6 | 1.4 | 1.0 | | | .4 | 1.0 | .9 | .8 | 2.3 |
| (90) 2.5 | (76) 2.3 | (81) 2.1 | % Depr., Dep., Amort./Sales | | (15) 1.6 | (19) 2.1 | (16) 2.2 | 1.8 | (10) 3.3 |
| 4.0 | 3.7 | 3.1 | | | 2.0 | 2.9 | 3.2 | 3.4 | 6.7 |
| 2.0 | 1.1 | 1.4 | % Officers', Directors' | | 3.3 | 1.3 | | | |
| (51) 3.7 | (39) 3.8 | (47) 3.3 | Owners' Comp/Sales | | (11) 5.0 | (12) 2.4 | | | |
| 7.6 | 7.6 | 5.8 | | | 8.1 | 5.9 | | | |
| 1358415M | 1095088M | 1429672M | Net Sales ($) | 5363M | 45147M | 79786M | 132843M | 220088M | 946445M |
| 836125M | 595136M | 924239M | Total Assets ($) | 2309M | 20239M | 31557M | 61429M | 112830M | 695875M |

## Current Data Sorted by Assets

## Comparative Historical Data

| Type of Statement | 0-500M | 500M-2MM | 2-10MM | 10-50MM | 50-100MM | 100-250MM | 4/1/07-3/31/08 ALL | 4/1/08-3/31/09 ALL |
|---|---|---|---|---|---|---|---|---|
| Unqualified | 1 | | 1 | 4 | 4 | | 10 | 7 |
| Reviewed | | 2 | 17 | 7 | | | 42 | 28 |
| Compiled | 1 | 17 | 11 | 1 | | 1 | 28 | 28 |
| Tax Returns | 9 | 15 | 9 | | | | 33 | 38 |
| Other | | 20 | 23 | 7 | 2 | | 63 | 54 |
| | | 32 (4/1-9/30/11) | | 120 (10/1/11-3/31/12) | | | | |
| **NUMBER OF STATEMENTS** | 11 | 54 | 61 | 19 | 6 | 1 | 176 | 155 |
| **ASSETS** | % | % | % | % | % | % | % | % |
| Cash & Equivalents | 11.0 | 5.1 | 7.4 | 6.6 | | | 6.8 | 8.6 |
| Trade Receivables (net) | 43.5 | 35.5 | 30.9 | 21.9 | | | 27.2 | 24.9 |
| Inventory | 14.8 | 25.6 | 25.0 | 16.7 | | | 23.5 | 25.3 |
| All Other Current | 1.0 | .8 | 1.7 | 3.6 | | | 2.7 | 1.3 |
| Total Current | 70.3 | 67.0 | 65.1 | 48.8 | | | 60.2 | 60.1 |
| Fixed Assets (net) | 24.0 | 24.5 | 26.4 | 28.4 | | | 31.3 | 30.0 |
| Intangibles (net) | 2.5 | 3.4 | 2.7 | 10.6 | | | 3.0 | 3.0 |
| All Other Non-Current | 3.2 | 5.1 | 5.9 | 12.1 | | | 5.5 | 6.9 |
| Total | 100.0 | 100.0 | 100.0 | 100.0 | | | 100.0 | 100.0 |
| **LIABILITIES** | | | | | | | | |
| Notes Payable-Short Term | 7.4 | 12.6 | 12.4 | 10.5 | | | 14.2 | 15.9 |
| Cur. Mat.-L.T.D. | 4.3 | 3.4 | 3.2 | 3.4 | | | 4.3 | 4.6 |
| Trade Payables | 29.8 | 17.0 | 13.5 | 8.0 | | | 13.1 | 12.7 |
| Income Taxes Payable | .0 | .1 | .0 | .0 | | | .3 | .1 |
| All Other Current | 33.4 | 7.2 | 8.2 | 5.7 | | | 8.0 | 5.3 |
| Total Current | 74.9 | 40.3 | 37.4 | 27.6 | | | 39.8 | 38.6 |
| Long-Term Debt | 20.7 | 16.2 | 11.1 | 14.8 | | | 19.9 | 19.0 |
| Deferred Taxes | .0 | .1 | .3 | .4 | | | .3 | .2 |
| All Other Non-Current | .4 | 7.7 | 2.8 | 5.0 | | | 4.1 | 7.9 |
| Net Worth | 3.9 | 35.8 | 48.3 | 52.2 | | | 35.9 | 34.4 |
| Total Liabilties & Net Worth | 100.0 | 100.0 | 100.0 | 100.0 | | | 100.0 | 100.0 |
| **INCOME DATA** | | | | | | | | |
| Net Sales | 100.0 | 100.0 | 100.0 | 100.0 | | | 100.0 | 100.0 |
| Gross Profit | 25.0 | 28.0 | 22.8 | 22.6 | | | 25.7 | 24.1 |
| Operating Expenses | 22.0 | 25.0 | 20.1 | 17.6 | | | 22.2 | 21.1 |
| Operating Profit | 3.0 | 3.0 | 2.7 | 5.0 | | | 3.5 | 3.1 |
| All Other Expenses (net) | .8 | .3 | .1 | -.3 | | | .9 | .6 |
| Profit Before Taxes | 2.3 | 2.7 | 2.6 | 5.4 | | | 2.6 | 2.5 |
| **RATIOS** | | | | | | | | |
| Current | 2.8 | 2.4 | 3.2 | 2.4 | | | 2.8 | 2.9 |
| | 1.3 | 1.8 | 1.9 | 1.8 | | | 1.7 | 1.7 |
| | .9 | 1.3 | 1.1 | 1.1 | | | 1.1 | 1.1 |
| Quick | 2.4 | 1.4 | 2.2 | 1.7 | | | 1.8 | 1.7 |
| | 1.0 | 1.2 | 1.0 | .9 | | | .9 | .9 |
| | .4 | .7 | .6 | .6 | | | .5 | .5 |
| Sales/Receivables | 14  25.7 | 23  16.1 | 29  12.8 | 35  10.3 | | | 23  15.9 | 19  18.8 |
| | 24  15.1 | 34  10.6 | 35  10.3 | 39  9.3 | | | 32  11.5 | 29  12.4 |
| | 34  10.8 | 46  8.0 | 45  8.2 | 45  8.2 | | | 40  9.2 | 39  9.3 |
| Cost of Sales/Inventory | 2  154.5 | 15  24.6 | 23  15.8 | 26  14.3 | | | 18  20.4 | 19  18.9 |
| | 9  40.6 | 31  11.7 | 36  10.2 | 40  9.2 | | | 37  9.9 | 34  10.6 |
| | 26  13.8 | 49  7.4 | 63  5.8 | 49  7.5 | | | 55  6.6 | 57  6.4 |
| Cost of Sales/Payables | 7  54.8 | 11  32.8 | 9  42.1 | 9  40.5 | | | 9  41.7 | 6  58.0 |
| | 14  25.5 | 21  17.4 | 18  20.2 | 18  20.6 | | | 17  21.9 | 15  25.0 |
| | 47  7.7 | 32  11.3 | 27  13.5 | 27  13.3 | | | 31  11.9 | 28  12.9 |
| Sales/Working Capital | 11.3 | 9.0 | 6.9 | 6.0 | | | 7.1 | 8.0 |
| | 22.5 | 12.2 | 12.3 | 9.7 | | | 13.2 | 13.8 |
| | -109.5 | 25.9 | 48.8 | 35.0 | | | 59.4 | 52.8 |
| EBIT/Interest | | 8.3 | 12.9 | 11.8 | | | 8.4 | 8.8 |
| | (48) 3.1 | | (56) 3.7 | 7.0 | | | (164) 2.7 | (143) 3.0 |
| | | 1.4 | 1.2 | 4.9 | | | 1.1 | 1.1 |
| Net Profit + Depr., Dep., Amort./Cur. Mat. L/T/D | | | 5.1 | | | | 9.1 | 3.1 |
| | | (13) 1.9 | | | | | (38) 2.5 | (26) 2.0 |
| | | | 1.4 | | | | 1.6 | .7 |
| Fixed/Worth | .1 | .3 | .2 | .3 | | | .4 | .3 |
| | .5 | .6 | .6 | .6 | | | .9 | .8 |
| | -7.1 | 2.0 | 1.3 | 1.5 | | | 1.9 | 2.0 |
| Debt/Worth | .5 | .8 | .5 | .6 | | | .7 | .7 |
| | 9.5 | 1.9 | 1.1 | 1.0 | | | 2.0 | 1.7 |
| | -18.2 | 7.1 | 2.8 | 1.8 | | | 3.9 | 4.1 |
| % Profit Before Taxes/Tangible Net Worth | | 48.4 | 32.8 | 29.9 | | | 42.5 | 35.4 |
| | (47) 13.5 | | (59) 13.3 | (16) 23.5 | | | (156) 18.8 | (135) 14.1 |
| | | 6.6 | 1.8 | 17.8 | | | 3.4 | 2.6 |
| % Profit Before Taxes/Total Assets | 40.4 | 13.9 | 13.4 | 12.8 | | | 18.1 | 13.4 |
| | 10.1 | 5.7 | 3.9 | 10.8 | | | 5.4 | 5.4 |
| | -3.3 | 1.0 | .5 | 6.7 | | | .5 | .3 |
| Sales/Net Fixed Assets | 158.5 | 55.0 | 26.3 | 26.9 | | | 25.2 | 26.9 |
| | 38.5 | 16.7 | 12.6 | 8.0 | | | 11.5 | 13.3 |
| | 12.9 | 9.1 | 6.5 | 3.5 | | | 5.9 | 5.1 |
| Sales/Total Assets | 8.1 | 5.4 | 4.3 | 2.3 | | | 4.0 | 4.4 |
| | 6.0 | 3.8 | 2.9 | 1.9 | | | 3.0 | 3.0 |
| | 3.8 | 2.6 | 2.0 | 1.6 | | | 2.0 | 2.1 |
| % Depr., Dep., Amort./Sales | | .8 | 1.0 | 1.3 | | | 1.1 | .9 |
| | (40) 1.7 | | (57) 2.0 | (17) 3.0 | | | (154) 2.0 | (139) 1.9 |
| | | 3.0 | 3.1 | 4.4 | | | 3.2 | 3.2 |
| % Officers', Directors' Owners' Comp/Sales | | 1.7 | 1.3 | | | | 1.5 | 1.5 |
| | (32) 3.4 | | (23) 2.2 | | | | (73) 2.5 | (77) 2.8 |
| | | 5.1 | 4.0 | | | | 4.5 | 4.9 |
| Net Sales ($) | 18323M | 251389M | 818451M | 968302M | 800696M | 1187703M | 3673773M | 2721399M |
| Total Assets ($) | 2766M | 65144M | 270988M | 486100M | 478775M | 213458M | 1866817M | 1248999M |

M = $ thousand    MM = $ million
See Pages 9 through 22 for Explanation of Ratios and Data

## Comparative Historical Data | Current Data Sorted by Sales

| | | | Type of Statement | | | | | | |
|---|---|---|---|---|---|---|---|---|---|
| 7 | 5 | 10 | Unqualified | 1 | | | | 2 | 7 |
| 30 | 25 | 26 | Reviewed | | 1 | 1 | 6 | 8 | 10 |
| 28 | 25 | 31 | Compiled | 1 | 6 | 7 | 11 | 5 | 1 |
| 35 | 39 | 33 | Tax Returns | 2 | 9 | 5 | 14 | 3 | |
| 44 | 52 | 52 | Other | 1 | 4 | 10 | 9 | 17 | 11 |
| 4/1/09-3/31/10 ALL | 4/1/10-3/31/11 ALL | 4/1/11-3/31/12 ALL | | 0-1MM | 32 (4/1-9/30/11) 1-3MM | 3-5MM | 120 (10/1/11-3/31/12) 5-10MM | 10-25MM | 25MM & OVER |
| 144 | 146 | 152 | **NUMBER OF STATEMENTS** | 5 | 20 | 23 | 40 | 35 | 29 |
| % | % | % | **ASSETS** | % | % | % | % | % | % |
| 8.5 | 8.1 | 6.5 | Cash & Equivalents | | 6.3 | 3.8 | 8.8 | 5.2 | 6.0 |
| 26.1 | 27.1 | 31.6 | Trade Receivables (net) | | 26.9 | 29.6 | 35.1 | 34.6 | 25.4 |
| 22.7 | 22.9 | 23.1 | Inventory | | 30.3 | 20.8 | 22.5 | 27.4 | 17.8 |
| 2.1 | 1.9 | 1.8 | All Other Current | | .5 | 1.0 | 1.2 | 1.4 | 4.9 |
| 59.4 | 60.1 | 63.0 | Total Current | | 63.9 | 55.2 | 67.6 | 68.7 | 54.2 |
| 29.3 | 28.5 | 26.6 | Fixed Assets (net) | | 27.5 | 30.5 | 22.4 | 24.9 | 30.5 |
| 4.6 | 4.7 | 4.4 | Intangibles (net) | | 2.9 | 8.1 | 2.5 | 1.7 | 8.5 |
| 6.7 | 6.7 | 6.1 | All Other Non-Current | | 5.7 | 6.2 | 7.5 | 4.7 | 6.8 |
| 100.0 | 100.0 | 100.0 | Total | | 100.0 | 100.0 | 100.0 | 100.0 | 100.0 |
| | | | **LIABILITIES** | | | | | | |
| 15.7 | 14.2 | 11.7 | Notes Payable-Short Term | | 16.5 | 14.2 | 8.8 | 11.6 | 12.0 |
| 4.5 | 4.2 | 3.4 | Cur. Mat.-L.T.D. | | 4.3 | 4.2 | 3.6 | 2.5 | 3.0 |
| 12.4 | 13.1 | 15.1 | Trade Payables | | 17.8 | 11.5 | 16.7 | 16.2 | 11.0 |
| .2 | .1 | .0 | Income Taxes Payable | | .0 | .1 | .0 | .1 | .0 |
| 6.2 | 7.4 | 9.2 | All Other Current | | 5.8 | 4.9 | 7.8 | 9.7 | 6.4 |
| 39.0 | 38.9 | 39.4 | Total Current | | 44.4 | 35.0 | 37.0 | 40.0 | 32.4 |
| 19.2 | 16.2 | 14.5 | Long-Term Debt | | 22.3 | 16.7 | 13.1 | 9.4 | 15.2 |
| .1 | .2 | .3 | Deferred Taxes | | .0 | .7 | .1 | .1 | .8 |
| 5.6 | 5.3 | 5.0 | All Other Non-Current | | 4.3 | 10.1 | 4.9 | 2.2 | 5.7 |
| 36.0 | 39.5 | 40.8 | Net Worth | | 29.1 | 37.5 | 44.9 | 48.2 | 45.9 |
| 100.0 | 100.0 | 100.0 | Total Liabilties & Net Worth | | 100.0 | 100.0 | 100.0 | 100.0 | 100.0 |
| | | | **INCOME DATA** | | | | | | |
| 100.0 | 100.0 | 100.0 | Net Sales | | 100.0 | 100.0 | 100.0 | 100.0 | 100.0 |
| 28.3 | 26.0 | 24.7 | Gross Profit | | 23.6 | 35.6 | 22.2 | 21.9 | 21.9 |
| 25.1 | 23.3 | 21.5 | Operating Expenses | | 21.7 | 31.9 | 20.1 | 19.9 | 17.3 |
| 3.2 | 2.7 | 3.1 | Operating Profit | | 2.0 | 3.7 | 2.2 | 2.0 | 4.6 |
| .8 | .7 | .2 | All Other Expenses (net) | | .8 | .5 | -.3 | -.2 | .5 |
| 2.4 | 2.1 | 2.9 | Profit Before Taxes | | 1.1 | 3.2 | 2.5 | 2.3 | 4.0 |
| | | | **RATIOS** | | | | | | |
| 3.0 | 2.9 | 2.7 | Current | | 2.1 | 2.7 | 3.2 | 3.0 | 2.0 |
| 1.6 | 1.8 | 1.8 | | | 1.6 | 1.8 | 2.2 | 1.9 | 1.8 |
| 1.1 | 1.2 | 1.2 | | | .9 | 1.2 | 1.3 | 1.1 | 1.2 |
| 2.0 | 2.0 | 1.7 | Quick | | 1.2 | 1.5 | 2.6 | 1.7 | 1.4 |
| .8 | 1.0 | 1.0 | | | .8 | 1.2 | 1.2 | .9 | .9 |
| .5 | .6 | .6 | | | .4 | .4 | .8 | .7 | .5 |
| 25 14.5 | 24 15.2 | 27 13.7 | Sales/Receivables | | 20 18.6 | 21 17.1 | 29 12.5 | 26 13.9 | 33 11.2 |
| 34 10.8 | 33 10.9 | 35 10.3 | | | 33 11.2 | 34 10.7 | 36 10.1 | 34 10.7 | 38 9.5 |
| 44 8.3 | 43 8.5 | 44 8.3 | | | 43 8.4 | 46 7.9 | 45 8.1 | 41 8.8 | 43 8.4 |
| 24 15.4 | 20 18.3 | 17 21.4 | Cost of Sales/Inventory | | 10 37.1 | 21 17.7 | 15 23.7 | 23 15.8 | 15 23.7 |
| 43 8.5 | 37 10.0 | 34 10.8 | | | 40 9.2 | 31 11.8 | 35 10.5 | 34 10.6 | 40 9.2 |
| 74 4.9 | 58 6.3 | 51 7.2 | | | 83 4.4 | 54 6.7 | 48 7.6 | 48 7.6 | 50 7.3 |
| 9 39.3 | 10 38.3 | 10 36.0 | Cost of Sales/Payables | | 7 52.3 | 11 32.1 | 10 36.0 | 9 42.0 | 9 40.1 |
| 19 19.5 | 17 21.7 | 19 19.4 | | | 24 15.1 | 20 18.2 | 21 17.6 | 18 20.5 | 17 21.2 |
| 37 9.9 | 31 11.7 | 29 12.6 | | | 49 7.5 | 27 13.3 | 32 11.4 | 26 13.8 | 28 13.2 |
| 6.3 | 6.9 | 7.9 | Sales/Working Capital | | 9.0 | 8.1 | 6.0 | 7.4 | 8.4 |
| 12.3 | 12.0 | 12.2 | | | 11.3 | 13.1 | 10.2 | 13.2 | 12.1 |
| 130.8 | 39.4 | 31.6 | | | NM | 83.8 | 27.8 | 64.8 | 27.0 |
| 6.4 | 14.5 | 11.0 | EBIT/Interest | | 5.0 | 7.9 | 8.3 | 30.1 | 12.5 |
| (137) 2.3 | (140) 4.2 | (135) 4.0 | | | (18) 2.1 | (21) 2.8 | (34) 4.2 | (31) 6.6 | 6.3 |
| .9 | .5 | 1.2 | | | .9 | -.7 | 1.8 | 1.2 | 2.2 |
| 5.6 | 6.1 | 4.7 | Net Profit + Depr., Dep., Amort./Cur. Mat. L/T/D | | | | | | 5.6 |
| (19) 2.6 | (21) 2.5 | (30) 2.8 | | | | | | (13) | 4.0 |
| 1.5 | 1.0 | 1.6 | | | | | | | 2.1 |
| .3 | .3 | .2 | Fixed/Worth | | .2 | .4 | .2 | .2 | .4 |
| .8 | .7 | .6 | | | .8 | 1.3 | .5 | .6 | 1.0 |
| 3.0 | 1.8 | 1.8 | | | 2.7 | 43.9 | 1.3 | 1.0 | 1.7 |
| .7 | .6 | .6 | Debt/Worth | | .7 | .7 | .5 | .5 | .7 |
| 1.9 | 1.5 | 1.3 | | | 2.0 | 1.8 | 1.4 | 1.0 | 1.0 |
| 7.4 | 3.8 | 4.1 | | | 8.9 | 120.6 | 3.6 | 2.8 | 5.1 |
| 35.8 | 37.8 | 37.0 | % Profit Before Taxes/Tangible Net Worth | | 25.6 | 73.9 | 39.8 | 23.5 | 34.5 |
| (120) 13.2 | (128) 16.4 | (136) 17.9 | | | (17) 8.3 | (19) 19.7 | (36) 13.3 | 13.3 | (25) 23.9 |
| .4 | 2.4 | 3.9 | | | 2.3 | 1.7 | 5.5 | 1.2 | 10.6 |
| 10.6 | 16.0 | 13.6 | % Profit Before Taxes/Total Assets | | 6.2 | 21.3 | 11.8 | 14.5 | 13.1 |
| 3.8 | 6.2 | 6.0 | | | 2.9 | 5.0 | 6.1 | 4.7 | 10.0 |
| -.1 | -1.0 | .9 | | | -.8 | -2.1 | 2.1 | .5 | 4.3 |
| 26.5 | 27.1 | 34.7 | Sales/Net Fixed Assets | | 35.4 | 25.3 | 42.6 | 32.3 | 31.4 |
| 11.5 | 11.6 | 13.7 | | | 16.0 | 10.1 | 13.2 | 19.0 | 8.0 |
| 4.9 | 5.6 | 6.6 | | | 9.9 | 5.5 | 8.3 | 7.8 | 3.5 |
| 3.6 | 4.0 | 4.5 | Sales/Total Assets | | 4.1 | 4.1 | 5.1 | 4.9 | 3.3 |
| 2.6 | 2.8 | 3.1 | | | 3.0 | 3.2 | 3.3 | 3.8 | 2.0 |
| 1.7 | 1.8 | 2.1 | | | 2.1 | 2.1 | 2.2 | 2.5 | 1.7 |
| 1.4 | 1.2 | 1.0 | % Depr., Dep., Amort./Sales | | .8 | .9 | 1.2 | 1.0 | .9 |
| (129) 2.4 | (127) 2.1 | (127) 2.0 | | | (15) 1.6 | (21) 2.2 | (31) 2.2 | (32) 1.6 | (25) 2.1 |
| 4.3 | 3.7 | 3.3 | | | 4.9 | 3.0 | 3.6 | 2.5 | 4.3 |
| 1.7 | 1.6 | 1.5 | % Officers', Directors' Owners' Comp/Sales | | 3.7 | 1.5 | 1.3 | 1.5 | |
| (62) 3.0 | (65) 3.5 | (66) 3.0 | | | (13) 3.9 | (11) 3.3 | (22) 2.4 | (13) 2.4 | |
| 5.9 | 5.2 | 4.8 | | | 5.3 | 4.7 | 4.9 | 4.0 | |
| 2288525M | 2505454M | 4044864M | Net Sales ($) | 2909M | 38977M | 89237M | 288534M | 536093M | 3089114M |
| 1274339M | 1432085M | 1517231M | Total Assets ($) | 1612M | 13776M | 35292M | 114761M | 167502M | 1184288M |

## Current Data Sorted by Assets | Comparative Historical Data

| 0-500M | 500M-2MM | 2-10MM | 10-50MM | 50-100MM | 100-250MM | Type of Statement | 4/1/07-3/31/08 ALL | 4/1/08-3/31/09 ALL |
|---|---|---|---|---|---|---|---|---|
| 1 | 2 | 3 | 5 / 1 | 3 | 1 | Unqualified | | |
| | | 4 | | | | Reviewed | 13 | 13 |
| | | 3 | 5 | 2 | 1 | Compiled | 3 | 11 |
| | | | | | | Tax Returns | 9 | 7 |
| | | | | | | | 2 | 2 |
| | | | | | | Other | 9 | 11 |
| | 9 (4/1-9/30/11) | | 22 (10/1/11-3/31/12) | | | | | |
| 1 | 2 | 10 | 11 | 5 | 2 | **NUMBER OF STATEMENTS** | 36 | 44 |
| % | % | % | % | % | % | **ASSETS** | % | % |
| | | 15.1 | 25.8 | | | Cash & Equivalents | 19.0 | 13.8 |
| | | 24.3 | 15.4 | | | Trade Receivables (net) | 15.7 | 14.8 |
| | | 28.3 | 22.7 | | | Inventory | 26.5 | 25.6 |
| | | 2.2 | 4.3 | | | All Other Current | 1.7 | 4.0 |
| | | 70.0 | 68.1 | | | Total Current | 62.9 | 58.2 |
| | | 26.9 | 23.7 | | | Fixed Assets (net) | 25.1 | 29.5 |
| | | 1.2 | 1.7 | | | Intangibles (net) | 6.2 | 3.6 |
| | | 1.9 | 6.5 | | | All Other Non-Current | 5.7 | 8.7 |
| | | 100.0 | 100.0 | | | Total | 100.0 | 100.0 |
| | | | | | | **LIABILITIES** | | |
| | | 5.5 | 8.5 | | | Notes Payable-Short Term | 12.6 | 12.9 |
| | | 4.5 | .8 | | | Cur. Mat.-L.T.D. | 1.4 | 2.2 |
| | | 14.1 | 9.3 | | | Trade Payables | 7.6 | 7.4 |
| | | .2 | .2 | | | Income Taxes Payable | .3 | .3 |
| | | 15.7 | 20.0 | | | All Other Current | 17.5 | 14.2 |
| | | 40.0 | 38.8 | | | Total Current | 39.4 | 37.0 |
| | | 11.9 | 4.1 | | | Long-Term Debt | 12.3 | 19.4 |
| | | .0 | .3 | | | Deferred Taxes | .6 | .2 |
| | | 5.8 | 4.3 | | | All Other Non-Current | 1.9 | 2.5 |
| | | 42.3 | 52.5 | | | Net Worth | 45.8 | 40.8 |
| | | 100.0 | 100.0 | | | Total Liabilities & Net Worth | 100.0 | 100.0 |
| | | | | | | **INCOME DATA** | | |
| | | 100.0 | 100.0 | | | Net Sales | 100.0 | 100.0 |
| | | 22.3 | 12.2 | | | Gross Profit | 23.6 | 24.9 |
| | | 21.9 | 10.8 | | | Operating Expenses | 19.1 | 22.5 |
| | | .5 | 1.4 | | | Operating Profit | 4.5 | 2.5 |
| | | -.7 | -.1 | | | All Other Expenses (net) | .5 | 1.3 |
| | | 1.2 | 1.4 | | | Profit Before Taxes | 4.0 | 1.1 |
| | | | | | | **RATIOS** | | |
| | | 7.9 | 3.4 | | | | 2.4 | 2.8 |
| | | 2.3 | 1.6 | | | Current | 1.6 | 1.6 |
| | | 1.1 | 1.2 | | | | 1.3 | 1.1 |
| | | 5.7 | 2.9 | | | | 1.5 | 1.9 |
| | | .9 | 1.0 | | | Quick | .8 | .7 |
| | | .4 | .4 | | | | .3 | .3 |
| | | 17   21.2 | 21   17.5 | | | | 9   39.3 | 9   39.5 |
| | | 31   11.6 | 25   14.6 | | | Sales/Receivables | 21   17.7 | 22   16.8 |
| | | 68   5.4 | 33   11.1 | | | | 32   11.5 | 34   10.7 |
| | | 21   17.2 | 16   22.3 | | | | 21   17.3 | 30   12.0 |
| | | 33   11.2 | 20   17.9 | | | Cost of Sales/Inventory | 36   10.2 | 44   8.4 |
| | | 114   3.2 | 101   3.6 | | | | 64   5.7 | 74   4.9 |
| | | 5   70.1 | 5   67.8 | | | | 6   65.2 | 5   69.6 |
| | | 13   27.3 | 11   32.4 | | | Cost of Sales/Payables | 11   33.7 | 11   34.4 |
| | | 49   7.5 | 15   24.4 | | | | 17   21.7 | 27   13.6 |
| | | 2.8 | 5.3 | | | | 6.3 | 4.4 |
| | | 8.5 | 7.8 | | | Sales/Working Capital | 10.9 | 10.9 |
| | | 78.9 | 19.7 | | | | 30.8 | 49.1 |
| | | 11.3 | 71.2 | | | | 17.1 | 7.5 |
| | | 3.6 | 10.3 | | | EBIT/Interest | (30) 4.1 | (36) 2.1 |
| | | -2.6 | -.2 | | | | -.3 | -1.0 |
| | | | | | | Net Profit + Depr., Dep., Amort./Cur. Mat. L/T/D | | |
| | | .2 | .2 | | | | .1 | .2 |
| | | .7 | .3 | | | Fixed/Worth | .5 | .5 |
| | | NM | .5 | | | | 2.1 | 3.0 |
| | | .3 | .4 | | | | .5 | .5 |
| | | 1.0 | 1.1 | | | Debt/Worth | 1.2 | 1.6 |
| | | NM | 1.8 | | | | 4.9 | 4.8 |
| | | | 45.1 | | | | 57.9 | 27.2 |
| | | | 12.1 | | | % Profit Before Taxes/Tangible Net Worth | (31) 14.1 | (37) 6.3 |
| | | | -1.7 | | | | -1.8 | -3.9 |
| | | 7.5 | 14.1 | | | | 25.2 | 8.9 |
| | | 3.2 | 4.7 | | | % Profit Before Taxes/Total Assets | 9.9 | 3.0 |
| | | -1.0 | -.9 | | | | -1.6 | -4.6 |
| | | 18.4 | 50.6 | | | | 38.2 | 37.3 |
| | | 9.7 | 12.5 | | | Sales/Net Fixed Assets | 10.7 | 8.2 |
| | | 4.6 | 5.7 | | | | 5.6 | 4.5 |
| | | 3.4 | 2.6 | | | | 3.1 | 2.9 |
| | | 1.9 | 2.0 | | | Sales/Total Assets | 2.6 | 2.0 |
| | | 1.6 | 1.5 | | | | 1.3 | 1.2 |
| | | | .2 | | | | .4 | .4 |
| | | (10) | .8 | | | % Depr., Dep., Amort./Sales | (29) .9 | (40) 1.1 |
| | | | 2.0 | | | | 1.6 | 1.9 |
| | | | | | | % Officers', Directors' Owners' Comp/Sales | | |
| 1166M | 2929M | 128798M | 425076M | 772834M | 868554M | Net Sales ($) | 1890802M | 2324096M |
| 400M | 2355M | 62157M | 200452M | 386825M | 377093M | Total Assets ($) | 1029272M | 1699091M |

M = $ thousand     MM = $ million
See Pages 9 through 22 for Explanation of Ratios and Data

## Comparative Historical Data | Current Data Sorted by Sales

| | 4/1/09-3/31/10 ALL | 4/1/10-3/31/11 ALL | 4/1/11-3/31/12 ALL | 0-1MM | 1-3MM | 3-5MM | 5-10MM | 10-25MM | 25MM & OVER |
|---|---|---|---|---|---|---|---|---|---|
| **Type of Statement** | | | | 9 (4/1-9/30/11) | | | 22 (10/1/11-3/31/12) | | |
| Unqualified | 10 | 8 | 9 | | | | | | 9 |
| Reviewed | 11 | 6 | 4 | | | | | 3 | 1 |
| Compiled | 8 | 3 | 7 | 1 | 2 | 1 | 1 | 2 | |
| Tax Returns | | 2 | | | | | 2 | 2 | |
| Other | 11 | 8 | 11 | | | | | | 7 |
| **NUMBER OF STATEMENTS** | 40 | 27 | 31 | 1 | 2 | 1 | 3 | 7 | 17 |
| **ASSETS** | % | % | % | % | % | % | % | % | % |
| Cash & Equivalents | 16.8 | 14.5 | 18.4 | | | | | | 21.7 |
| Trade Receivables (net) | 13.3 | 18.5 | 17.8 | | | | | | 14.8 |
| Inventory | 25.1 | 24.4 | 25.6 | | | | | | 25.1 |
| All Other Current | 3.7 | 2.4 | 3.8 | | | | | | 5.2 |
| Total Current | 58.9 | 59.7 | 65.5 | | | | | | 66.8 |
| Fixed Assets (net) | 29.2 | 29.6 | 25.9 | | | | | | 20.1 |
| Intangibles (net) | 3.3 | 3.0 | 2.0 | | | | | | 3.0 |
| All Other Non-Current | 8.6 | 7.7 | 6.6 | | | | | | 10.0 |
| Total | 100.0 | 100.0 | 100.0 | | | | | | 100.0 |
| **LIABILITIES** | | | | | | | | | |
| Notes Payable-Short Term | 9.4 | 7.1 | 4.8 | | | | | | 5.5 |
| Cur. Mat.-L.T.D. | 3.0 | 4.6 | 4.1 | | | | | | 1.7 |
| Trade Payables | 9.2 | 15.6 | 10.3 | | | | | | 8.2 |
| Income Taxes Payable | .1 | .0 | .1 | | | | | | .2 |
| All Other Current | 13.3 | 15.2 | 17.9 | | | | | | 18.1 |
| Total Current | 35.0 | 42.5 | 37.3 | | | | | | 33.7 |
| Long-Term Debt | 26.6 | 29.1 | 14.1 | | | | | | 13.9 |
| Deferred Taxes | .4 | .2 | .3 | | | | | | .5 |
| All Other Non-Current | 6.3 | 7.6 | 5.2 | | | | | | 4.5 |
| Net Worth | 31.7 | 20.5 | 43.1 | | | | | | 47.4 |
| Total Liabilties & Net Worth | 100.0 | 100.0 | 100.0 | | | | | | 100.0 |
| **INCOME DATA** | | | | | | | | | |
| Net Sales | 100.0 | 100.0 | 100.0 | | | | | | 100.0 |
| Gross Profit | 17.5 | 21.8 | 18.3 | | | | | | 15.7 |
| Operating Expenses | 22.1 | 20.5 | 17.4 | | | | | | 11.9 |
| Operating Profit | -4.6 | 1.4 | .9 | | | | | | 3.8 |
| All Other Expenses (net) | 1.0 | 2.6 | .1 | | | | | | .3 |
| Profit Before Taxes | -5.6 | -1.2 | .8 | | | | | | 3.4 |
| **RATIOS** | | | | | | | | | |
| Current | 3.5 / 1.8 / 1.1 | 2.4 / 1.6 / 1.2 | 3.4 / 1.7 / 1.2 | | | | | | 3.9 / 1.8 / 1.4 |
| Quick | 2.4 / .8 / .4 | 1.5 / .8 / .5 | 2.6 / .9 / .4 | | | | | | 2.2 / 1.0 / .5 |
| Sales/Receivables | 11 → 32.1 / 25 → 14.3 / 33 → 11.0 | 14 → 26.1 / 38 → 9.5 / 50 → 7.3 | 17 → 21.2 / 26 → 14.3 / 50 → 7.3 | | | | | | 12 → 29.5 / 23 → 15.9 / 30 → 12.0 |
| Cost of Sales/Inventory | 24 → 15.3 / 53 → 6.8 / 104 → 3.5 | 19 → 19.1 / 56 → 6.5 / 85 → 4.3 | 20 → 18.4 / 38 → 9.6 / 101 → 3.6 | | | | | | 19 → 19.7 / 38 → 9.6 / 104 → 3.5 |
| Cost of Sales/Payables | 5 → 74.7 / 10 → 35.9 / 24 → 15.2 | 9 → 41.9 / 15 → 25.0 / 41 → 8.9 | 7 → 54.6 / 12 → 29.9 / 23 → 15.6 | | | | | | 7 → 51.0 / 12 → 31.1 / 14 → 25.5 |
| Sales/Working Capital | 3.4 / 6.7 / 33.4 | 5.0 / 8.1 / 37.6 | 4.7 / 8.6 / 20.4 | | | | | | 4.1 / 7.8 / 15.9 |
| EBIT/Interest | 4.8 / (36) 1.1 / -9.9 | 15.9 / (22) 1.7 / -.4 | 29.4 / (29) 3.9 / -.2 | | | | | | 50.0 / (16) 10.5 / 1.5 |
| Net Profit + Depr., Dep., Amort./Cur. Mat. L/T/D | | | | | | | | | |
| Fixed/Worth | .3 / .6 / 4.6 | .2 / .8 / 1.9 | .2 / .4 / 1.6 | | | | | | .2 / .3 / .6 |
| Debt/Worth | .7 / 1.0 / 7.2 | .9 / 1.5 / 5.1 | .4 / 1.1 / 4.7 | | | | | | .3 / 1.1 / 2.1 |
| % Profit Before Taxes/Tangible Net Worth | 11.7 / (32) 1.3 / -16.6 | 29.7 / (23) 3.3 / -17.6 | 34.7 / (27) 9.6 / -1.7 | | | | | | 42.8 / (16) 10.9 / -1.3 |
| % Profit Before Taxes/Total Assets | 5.9 / -.3 / -15.4 | 13.9 / 1.8 / -5.3 | 10.3 / 4.2 / -2.7 | | | | | | 15.0 / 4.7 / -.4 |
| Sales/Net Fixed Assets | 15.2 / 6.6 / 3.2 | 28.0 / 8.4 / 4.4 | 20.1 / 9.0 / 5.7 | | | | | | 31.3 / 9.0 / 7.6 |
| Sales/Total Assets | 2.5 / 1.6 / 1.1 | 2.3 / 1.7 / 1.3 | 2.7 / 2.0 / 1.5 | | | | | | 2.6 / 2.0 / 1.6 |
| % Depr., Dep., Amort./Sales | .9 / (32) 1.8 / 2.7 | .6 / (18) 1.7 / 4.2 | .7 / (27) 1.4 / 2.2 | | | | | | .8 / (16) 1.3 / 2.0 |
| % Officers', Directors', Owners' Comp/Sales | | | | | | | | | |
| Net Sales ($) | 1144337M | 1659367M | 2199357M | 491M | 3604M | 4406M | 27139M | 106624M | 2057093M |
| Total Assets ($) | 1043870M | 1229046M | 1029282M | 745M | 2010M | 2183M | 25974M | 45036M | 953334M |

© RMA 2012

M = $ thousand    MM = $ million
See Pages 9 through 22 for Explanation of Ratios and Data

## Current Data Sorted by Assets / Comparative Historical Data

| Type of Statement | 0-500M | 500M-2MM | 2-10MM | 10-50MM | 50-100MM | 100-250MM | | 4/1/07-3/31/08 ALL | 4/1/08-3/31/09 ALL |
|---|---|---|---|---|---|---|---|---|---|
| Unqualified | | | 2 | 5 | | | | 23 | 5 |
| Reviewed | | 2 | 6 | 4 | | | | 16 | 15 |
| Compiled | | 4 | 3 | | | | | 13 | 11 |
| Tax Returns | 1 | | 2 | 1 | | | | 6 | 5 |
| Other | 1 | 3 | 6 | 9 | 1 | | | 29 | 34 |
| | 8 (4/1-9/30/11) | | | 42 (10/1/11-3/31/12) | | | | | |
| NUMBER OF STATEMENTS | 2 | 9 | 19 | 19 | 1 | | | 87 | 70 |

*Current data columns 0-500M, 500M-2MM, 50-100MM and 100-250MM: DATA NOT AVAILABLE*

| | 2-10MM % | 10-50MM % | | 4/1/07-3/31/08 ALL % | 4/1/08-3/31/09 ALL % |
|---|---|---|---|---|---|
| **ASSETS** | | | | | |
| Cash & Equivalents | 5.5 | 10.1 | | 11.2 | 12.5 |
| Trade Receivables (net) | 24.4 | 18.1 | | 16.1 | 19.3 |
| Inventory | 24.4 | 24.1 | | 26.3 | 27.1 |
| All Other Current | .9 | 5.3 | | 3.7 | 4.1 |
| Total Current | 55.2 | 57.7 | | 57.3 | 63.1 |
| Fixed Assets (net) | 29.1 | 32.2 | | 29.5 | 27.8 |
| Intangibles (net) | 5.0 | 6.2 | | 5.3 | 3.2 |
| All Other Non-Current | 10.7 | 4.0 | | 7.9 | 5.9 |
| Total | 100.0 | 100.0 | | 100.0 | 100.0 |
| **LIABILITIES** | | | | | |
| Notes Payable-Short Term | 19.0 | 5.9 | | 11.0 | 13.2 |
| Cur. Mat.-L.T.D. | 2.2 | 1.9 | | 4.4 | 4.3 |
| Trade Payables | 11.7 | 12.1 | | 9.5 | 9.5 |
| Income Taxes Payable | .5 | .1 | | .0 | .0 |
| All Other Current | 13.1 | 15.2 | | 18.7 | 17.8 |
| Total Current | 46.4 | 35.2 | | 43.6 | 44.9 |
| Long-Term Debt | 13.3 | 13.8 | | 17.8 | 15.1 |
| Deferred Taxes | .8 | .1 | | .4 | .2 |
| All Other Non-Current | 12.0 | 6.4 | | 4.4 | 3.0 |
| Net Worth | 27.4 | 44.5 | | 33.8 | 36.8 |
| Total Liabilities & Net Worth | 100.0 | 100.0 | | 100.0 | 100.0 |
| **INCOME DATA** | | | | | |
| Net Sales | 100.0 | 100.0 | | 100.0 | 100.0 |
| Gross Profit | 25.9 | 20.1 | | 27.5 | 26.4 |
| Operating Expenses | 24.9 | 17.9 | | 24.4 | 25.8 |
| Operating Profit | 1.0 | 2.2 | | 3.1 | .6 |
| All Other Expenses (net) | 1.7 | .6 | | 1.0 | 1.0 |
| Profit Before Taxes | -.7 | 1.6 | | 2.1 | -.4 |

### RATIOS

| | 2-10MM | 10-50MM | Ratio | 4/1/07-3/31/08 ALL | 4/1/08-3/31/09 ALL |
|---|---|---|---|---|---|
| | 1.8 | 2.3 | | 2.0 | 2.2 |
| | 1.2 | 1.7 | Current | 1.4 | 1.3 |
| | .9 | 1.0 | | 1.0 | 1.0 |
| | 1.0 | 1.7 | | 1.0 | 1.3 |
| | .5 | 1.0 | Quick | .6 | .7 |
| | .2 | .4 | | .3 | .3 |
| | 14 / 26.6 | 17 / 20.9 | | 9 / 38.4 | 6 / 64.3 |
| | 30 / 12.2 | 35 / 10.5 | Sales/Receivables | 21 / 17.2 | 22 / 16.7 |
| | 54 / 6.7 | 66 / 5.5 | | 36 / 10.1 | 46 / 8.0 |
| | 31 / 11.6 | 18 / 20.1 | | 27 / 13.4 | 31 / 11.9 |
| | 74 / 4.9 | 42 / 8.6 | Cost of Sales/Inventory | 52 / 7.0 | 46 / 7.9 |
| | 111 / 3.3 | 69 / 5.3 | | 91 / 4.0 | 85 / 4.3 |
| | 9 / 39.5 | 16 / 22.8 | | 9 / 41.6 | 5 / 67.3 |
| | 21 / 17.2 | 21 / 17.2 | Cost of Sales/Payables | 15 / 24.7 | 13 / 27.8 |
| | 44 / 8.3 | 36 / 10.0 | | 27 / 13.4 | 28 / 13.2 |
| | 11.4 | 6.9 | | 7.4 | 6.9 |
| | 19.3 | 9.4 | Sales/Working Capital | 14.7 | 14.7 |
| | -111.3 | 52.7 | | 695.5 | 254.0 |
| | 7.8 | 19.6 | | 6.5 | 17.8 |
| | (18) 2.7 | (18) 4.6 | EBIT/Interest | (78) 2.7 | (63) 1.4 |
| | -.5 | .2 | | -1.1 | -2.8 |
| | | | | 3.8 | |
| | | | Net Profit + Depr., Dep., Amort./Cur. Mat. L/T/D | (22) .9 | |
| | | | | -.2 | |
| | .5 | .4 | | .4 | .3 |
| | .8 | .9 | Fixed/Worth | 1.1 | .9 |
| | 3.3 | 1.8 | | 3.6 | 2.5 |
| | 1.3 | .5 | | .8 | .8 |
| | 2.3 | 1.9 | Debt/Worth | 2.3 | 2.2 |
| | 17.0 | 3.9 | | 8.7 | 7.9 |
| | 35.1 | 41.2 | | 41.2 | 34.6 |
| | (17) 6.2 | (17) 15.4 | % Profit Before Taxes/Tangible Net Worth | (73) 12.5 | (64) 5.9 |
| | -15.1 | -14.0 | | -7.0 | -38.8 |
| | 9.5 | 18.0 | | 10.0 | 10.4 |
| | 2.4 | 4.8 | % Profit Before Taxes/Total Assets | 3.4 | 1.5 |
| | -7.0 | -3.8 | | -5.8 | -8.4 |
| | 26.0 | 32.3 | | 16.0 | 28.9 |
| | 7.7 | 8.5 * | Sales/Net Fixed Assets | 8.5 | 9.7 |
| | 3.0 | 2.5 | | 5.2 | 4.4 |
| | 2.2 | 2.6 | | 3.2 | 3.0 |
| | 1.9 | 1.8 | Sales/Total Assets | 2.4 | 2.3 |
| | 1.0 | 1.3 | | 1.6 | 1.6 |
| | .7 | .7 | | 1.1 | 1.0 |
| | (18) 1.7 | (17) 1.5 | % Depr., Dep., Amort./Sales | (77) 1.7 | (53) 1.5 |
| | 2.4 | 3.3 | | 2.7 | 3.1 |
| | | | | 1.6 | 1.8 |
| | | | % Officers', Directors' Owners' Comp/Sales | (13) 2.2 | (17) 2.6 |
| | | | | 3.1 | 4.7 |

| 0-500M | 500M-2MM | 2-10MM | 10-50MM | 50-100MM | 100-250MM | | 4/1/07-3/31/08 ALL | 4/1/08-3/31/09 ALL |
|---|---|---|---|---|---|---|---|---|
| 2115M | 35979M | 162801M | 726359M | 162327M | | Net Sales ($) | 2635592M | 1769760M |
| 541M | 10904M | 88182M | 334631M | 99099M | | Total Assets ($) | 1348181M | 817904M |

M = $ thousand    MM = $ million
See Pages 9 through 22 for Explanation of Ratios and Data

## Comparative Historical Data | Current Data Sorted by Sales

| | | | Type of Statement | | | | | | |
|---|---|---|---|---|---|---|---|---|---|
| 7 | 8 | 7 | Unqualified | | | | 1 | 1 | 3 |
| 15 | 14 | 12 | Reviewed | | 3 | 1 | 3 | 4 | 1 |
| 3 | 3 | 7 | Compiled | | 1 | | 2 | 3 | 1 |
| 6 | 5 | 4 | Tax Returns | 1 | | 2 | 1 | | |
| 14 | 20 | 20 | Other | | 3 | 1 | 3 | 7 | 6 |
| 4/1/09-<br>3/31/10<br>ALL | 4/1/10-<br>3/31/11<br>ALL | 4/1/11-<br>3/31/12<br>ALL | | 0-1MM | 8 (4/1-9/30/11)<br>1-3MM | 3-5MM | 5-10MM | 42 (10/1/11-3/31/12)<br>10-25MM | 25MM & OVER |
| 45 | 50 | 50 | **NUMBER OF STATEMENTS** | 1 | 7 | 5 | 12 | 14 | 11 |
| % | % | % | **ASSETS** | % | % | % | % | % | % |
| 8.4 | 9.1 | 8.9 | Cash & Equivalents | | | | 3.8 | 7.7 | 16.6 |
| 17.2 | 21.2 | 20.6 | Trade Receivables (net) | | | | 25.1 | 26.4 | 15.5 |
| 24.5 | 26.0 | 27.1 | Inventory | | | | 27.7 | 18.7 | 32.5 |
| 2.5 | 4.0 | 2.6 | All Other Current | | | | 1.2 | 1.9 | 8.0 |
| 52.6 | 60.3 | 59.3 | Total Current | | | | 57.8 | 54.8 | 72.7 |
| 32.9 | 28.1 | 28.6 | Fixed Assets (net) | | | | 34.6 | 32.1 | 21.7 |
| 6.1 | 5.1 | 4.4 | Intangibles (net) | | | | 1.6 | 6.9 | 2.0 |
| 8.4 | 6.5 | 7.7 | All Other Non-Current | | | | 6.0 | 6.2 | 3.6 |
| 100.0 | 100.0 | 100.0 | Total | | | | 100.0 | 100.0 | 100.0 |
| | | | **LIABILITIES** | | | | | | |
| 16.2 | 17.3 | 14.6 | Notes Payable-Short Term | | | | 23.6 | 11.2 | 7.6 |
| 3.1 | 3.7 | 1.8 | Cur. Mat.-L.T.D. | | | | 1.3 | 2.2 | 1.4 |
| 10.0 | 10.8 | 11.9 | Trade Payables | | | | 9.4 | 13.3 | 15.0 |
| .1 | .0 | .2 | Income Taxes Payable | | | | .0 | .7 | .0 |
| 19.5 | 14.3 | 17.1 | All Other Current | | | | 10.1 | 14.0 | 13.3 |
| 48.9 | 46.0 | 45.7 | Total Current | | | | 44.4 | 41.4 | 37.3 |
| 18.1 | 13.1 | 12.7 | Long-Term Debt | | | | 15.0 | 11.8 | 8.0 |
| .6 | .3 | .3 | Deferred Taxes | | | | .1 | 1.0 | .1 |
| 5.0 | 7.3 | 7.7 | All Other Non-Current | | | | 8.1 | 5.3 | 4.8 |
| 27.4 | 33.3 | 33.6 | Net Worth | | | | 32.5 | 40.5 | 49.8 |
| 100.0 | 100.0 | 100.0 | Total Liabilities & Net Worth | | | | 100.0 | 100.0 | 100.0 |
| | | | **INCOME DATA** | | | | | | |
| 100.0 | 100.0 | 100.0 | Net Sales | | | | 100.0 | 100.0 | 100.0 |
| 28.1 | 26.5 | 25.0 | Gross Profit | | | | 23.0 | 21.7 | 19.2 |
| 31.9 | 26.6 | 23.6 | Operating Expenses | | | | 23.3 | 19.6 | 16.1 |
| -3.9 | -.1 | 1.4 | Operating Profit | | | | -.4 | 2.0 | 3.1 |
| 1.8 | 1.3 | 1.0 | All Other Expenses (net) | | | | .6 | .7 | .3 |
| -5.6 | -1.4 | .4 | Profit Before Taxes | | | | -.9 | 1.3 | 2.7 |
| | | | **RATIOS** | | | | | | |
| 1.9 | 2.2 | 2.1 | | | | | 1.8 | 2.0 | 4.6 |
| 1.2 | 1.3 | 1.3 | Current | | | | 1.2 | 1.4 | 2.1 |
| .8 | .9 | .9 | | | | | 1.0 | 1.0 | 1.3 |
| 1.0 | 1.0 | 1.2 | | | | | 1.2 | 1.3 | 3.8 |
| .5 | .6 | .7 | Quick | | | | .5 | .8 | 1.0 |
| .2 | .3 | .3 | | | | | .2 | .6 | .3 |
| 9   38.5 | 10   38.2 | 11   34.4 | | | | | 12   31.4 | 30   12.3 | 9   38.6 |
| 29   12.6 | 28   12.8 | 29   12.7 | Sales/Receivables | | | | 21   17.0 | 49   7.4 | 20   18.0 |
| 55   6.6 | 53   6.9 | 51   7.2 | | | | | 70   5.2 | 66   5.5 | 34   10.8 |
| 27   13.5 | 22   16.8 | 21   17.7 | | | | | 16   23.2 | 22   16.9 | 20   18.4 |
| 74   4.9 | 52   7.0 | 56   6.5 | Cost of Sales/Inventory | | | | 54   6.8 | 43   8.4 | 33   11.0 |
| 114   3.2 | 97   3.8 | 101   3.6 | | | | | 107   3.4 | 65   5.6 | 83   4.4 |
| 9   40.1 | 6   57.8 | 9   39.0 | | | | | 8   43.8 | 18   19.8 | 8   47.3 |
| 25   14.5 | 18   19.9 | 21   17.4 | Cost of Sales/Payables | | | | 13   29.1 | 24   15.3 | 20   17.9 |
| 38   9.6 | 40   9.2 | 37   9.9 | | | | | 33   11.1 | 43   8.5 | 22   16.4 |
| 6.8 | 6.8 | 7.1 | | | | | 10.5 | 6.8 | 3.3 |
| 18.9 | 16.8 | 17.9 | Sales/Working Capital | | | | 17.9 | 15.4 | 8.8 |
| -15.6 | -24.4 | -94.0 | | | | | NM | -136.8 | 20.9 |
| 6.7 | 6.5 | 9.4 | | | | | 20.4 | 9.0 | 70.9 |
| (41)   .7 | (48)   1.2 | (47)   4.4 | EBIT/Interest | | (11)   6.0 | | | 3.6 | (10)   7.2 |
| -3.8 | -1.8 | -.9 | | | | | -1.0 | 1.3 | .2 |
| 4.5 | | | | | | | | | |
| (12)   2.2 | | | Net Profit + Depr., Dep.,<br>Amort./Cur. Mat. L/T/D | | | | | | |
| -3.2 | | | | | | | | | |
| .4 | .4 | .4 | | | | | .3 | .5 | .3 |
| .9 | .8 | .9 | Fixed/Worth | | | | 1.0 | 1.1 | .4 |
| 3.7 | 2.1 | 2.4 | | | | | 3.4 | 2.0 | .8 |
| 1.0 | 1.1 | .6 | | | | | 1.0 | .5 | .3 |
| 2.1 | 2.4 | 2.2 | Debt/Worth | | | | 2.5 | 1.9 | .6 |
| 14.4 | 6.0 | 6.3 | | | | | 13.7 | 4.5 | 3.0 |
| 22.4 | 40.2 | 43.1 | | | | | 43.1 | 22.4 | 46.9 |
| (37)   1.4 | (43)   5.4 | (43)   10.6 | % Profit Before Taxes/Tangible<br>Net Worth | | (11)   22.5 | | | (13)   10.1 | (10)   35.9 |
| -28.2 | -11.8 | -10.6 | | | | | -32.3 | -4.5 | -13.2 |
| 5.2 | 8.5 | 13.8 | | | | | 15.9 | 6.3 | 23.1 |
| -.6 | .7 | 2.8 | % Profit Before Taxes/Total<br>Assets | | | | 3.5 | 4.3 | 10.9 |
| -13.7 | -6.0 | -5.0 | | | | | -8.2 | -.3 | -3.8 |
| 13.2 | 27.2 | 26.4 | | | | | 21.9 | 18.1 | 45.3 |
| 5.8 | 10.1 | 9.7 | Sales/Net Fixed Assets | | | | 14.2 | 7.1 | 12.8 |
| 2.7 | 3.1 | 4.1 | | | | | 1.4 | 3.2 | 5.7 |
| 2.6 | 3.0 | 3.4 | | | | | 3.7 | 2.2 | 3.8 |
| 1.6 | 2.0 | 2.1 | Sales/Total Assets | | | | 2.2 | 1.8 | 2.4 |
| .9 | 1.2 | 1.5 | | | | | .9 | 1.5 | 1.8 |
| 1.7 | 1.5 | .7 | | | | | | .8 | |
| (37)   2.8 | (41)   1.9 | (44)   1.5 | % Depr., Dep., Amort./Sales | | | | | 1.8 | |
| 4.3 | 3.9 | 2.3 | | | | | | 2.4 | |
| | 1.5 | | | | | | | | |
| | (10)   2.6 | | % Officers', Directors'<br>Owners' Comp/Sales | | | | | | |
| | 8.4 | | | | | | | | |
| 793099M | 1156259M | 1089581M | Net Sales ($) | 282M | 15205M | 20960M | 86987M | 231479M | 734668M |
| 424912M | 653899M | 533357M | Total Assets ($) | 61M | 8112M | 15666M | 56951M | 135874M | 316693M |

M = $ thousand    MM = $ million
See Pages 9 through 22 for Explanation of Ratios and Data

**Current Data Sorted by Assets**

**Comparative Historical Data**

| | | | | | | Type of Statement | | |
|---|---|---|---|---|---|---|---|---|
| 1 | 4 | 3<br>29 | 12<br>12 | 4 | 1 | Unqualified<br>Reviewed | 26<br>47 | 24<br>42 |
| 2 | 13 | 13 | 2 | | | Compiled | 23 | 34 |
| 18 | 13 | 13 | | | | Tax Returns | 40 | 37 |
| 19 | 19 | 19 | 13 | 2 | | Other | 65 | 59 |
| 4 | 45 (4/1-9/30/11) | | 152 (10/1/11-3/31/12) | | | | 4/1/07-<br>3/31/08 | 4/1/08-<br>3/31/09 |
| 0-500M | 500M-2MM | 2-10MM | 10-50MM | 50-100MM | 100-250MM | | ALL | ALL |
| 25 | 49 | 77 | 39 | 6 | 1 | NUMBER OF STATEMENTS | 201 | 196 |
| % | % | % | % | % | % | ASSETS | % | % |
| 25.3 | 6.7 | 5.4 | 5.3 | | | Cash & Equivalents | 7.7 | 7.2 |
| 21.0 | 23.3 | 21.5 | 15.7 | | | Trade Receivables (net) | 22.2 | 21.0 |
| 19.0 | 28.3 | 31.0 | 32.0 | | | Inventory | 29.8 | 30.3 |
| 1.7 | 3.8 | 3.4 | 2.8 | | | All Other Current | 2.2 | 2.5 |
| 67.0 | 62.1 | 61.3 | 55.7 | | | Total Current | 61.9 | 61.0 |
| 23.3 | 22.3 | 32.0 | 30.2 | | | Fixed Assets (net) | 28.7 | 31.4 |
| 4.4 | 6.4 | 2.2 | 7.5 | | | Intangibles (net) | 3.1 | 2.6 |
| 5.3 | 9.2 | 4.6 | 6.6 | | | All Other Non-Current | 6.2 | 5.0 |
| 100.0 | 100.0 | 100.0 | 100.0 | | | Total | 100.0 | 100.0 |
| | | | | | | LIABILITIES | | |
| 9.4 | 15.2 | 12.1 | 13.2 | | | Notes Payable-Short Term | 16.6 | 15.3 |
| 13.5 | 3.6 | 4.5 | 4.9 | | | Cur. Mat.-L.T.D. | 3.5 | 4.2 |
| 10.3 | 15.8 | 11.6 | 7.5 | | | Trade Payables | 11.1 | 10.8 |
| .1 | .1 | .2 | .1 | | | Income Taxes Payable | .2 | .3 |
| 26.9 | 7.3 | 7.1 | 7.2 | | | All Other Current | 9.6 | 7.8 |
| 60.2 | 42.0 | 35.4 | 32.8 | | | Total Current | 41.0 | 38.5 |
| 10.5 | 16.5 | 16.5 | 12.9 | | | Long-Term Debt | 19.7 | 18.5 |
| .0 | .2 | .3 | .6 | | | Deferred Taxes | .3 | .4 |
| 18.2 | 12.5 | 5.9 | 3.5 | | | All Other Non-Current | 5.9 | 7.1 |
| 11.1 | 28.8 | 42.0 | 50.3 | | | Net Worth | 33.1 | 35.5 |
| 100.0 | 100.0 | 100.0 | 100.0 | | | Total Liabilties & Net Worth | 100.0 | 100.0 |
| | | | | | | INCOME DATA | | |
| 100.0 | 100.0 | 100.0 | 100.0 | | | Net Sales | 100.0 | 100.0 |
| 41.0 | 38.3 | 23.3 | 22.6 | | | Gross Profit | 29.3 | 27.9 |
| 38.8 | 35.7 | 21.1 | 17.7 | | | Operating Expenses | 25.1 | 24.8 |
| 2.2 | 2.6 | 2.1 | 4.9 | | | Operating Profit | 4.2 | 3.0 |
| .2 | 1.1 | .4 | .8 | | | All Other Expenses (net) | 1.5 | 1.4 |
| 2.1 | 1.6 | 1.7 | 4.1 | | | Profit Before Taxes | 2.7 | 1.6 |
| | | | | | | RATIOS | | |
| 7.3 | 2.6 | 3.4 | 3.4 | | | | 2.8 | 2.8 |
| 1.9 | 1.6 | 1.7 | 1.8 | | | Current | 1.6 | 1.6 |
| .7 | .9 | 1.3 | 1.1 | | | | 1.2 | 1.1 |
| 6.0 | 1.3 | 1.4 | 1.4 | | | | 1.6 | 1.3 |
| 1.0 | .8 | .8 | .8 | | | Quick | .7 | .7 |
| .4 | .3 | .3 | .3 | | | | .4 | .3 |
| 0 UND | 14 25.7 | 17 21.8 | 24 15.5 | | | | 16 22.4 | 16 23.1 |
| 14 26.9 | 26 13.8 | 26 14.0 | 38 9.7 | | | Sales/Receivables | 29 12.6 | 27 13.4 |
| 31 11.8 | 41 9.0 | 46 8.0 | 51 7.2 | | | | 48 7.6 | 41 8.8 |
| 0 UND | 14 26.9 | 34 10.6 | 53 6.9 | | | | 24 15.0 | 28 13.0 |
| 16 22.2 | 58 6.3 | 62 5.9 | 96 3.8 | | | Cost of Sales/Inventory | 55 6.6 | 62 5.9 |
| 52 7.0 | 114 3.2 | 111 3.3 | 159 2.3 | | | | 113 3.2 | 110 3.3 |
| 0 UND | 12 29.2 | 11 32.4 | 13 29.0 | | | | 9 42.8 | 8 45.9 |
| 5 69.8 | 31 11.8 | 20 18.7 | 19 19.6 | | | Cost of Sales/Payables | 20 18.3 | 19 19.1 |
| 19 19.3 | 60 6.1 | 31 11.7 | 26 13.9 | | | | 35 10.5 | 34 10.6 |
| 6.8 | 6.4 | 4.5 | 4.5 | | | | 6.0 | 5.6 |
| 13.5 | 14.1 | 8.2 | 6.2 | | | Sales/Working Capital | 9.7 | 10.6 |
| -26.0 | -126.1 | 22.5 | 21.0 | | | | 26.0 | 41.4 |
| 7.7 | 7.8 | 6.0 | 15.0 | | | | 7.8 | 6.1 |
| (17) 1.6 | (42) 2.2 | (73) 2.1 | (34) 3.8 | | | EBIT/Interest | (186) 2.3 | (181) 2.4 |
| -3.0 | .5 | 1.0 | 1.4 | | | | .7 | -.1 |
| | | 3.1 | 11.6 | | | | 5.4 | 4.1 |
| | (15) 1.8 | (13) 3.2 | | | | Net Profit + Depr., Dep.,<br>Amort./Cur. Mat. L/T/D | (44) 2.8 | (45) 1.9 |
| | 1.1 | 1.0 | | | | | .8 | .5 |
| .0 | .2 | .4 | .3 | | | | .4 | .3 |
| .8 | .8 | .7 | .7 | | | Fixed/Worth | .7 | .7 |
| -2.8 | 18.3 | 1.3 | 1.9 | | | | 2.3 | 1.5 |
| .3 | .8 | .7 | .4 | | | | .8 | .8 |
| 3.9 | 2.3 | 1.3 | 1.4 | | | Debt/Worth | 1.9 | 1.6 |
| -3.5 | 265.8 | 3.3 | 2.8 | | | | 5.7 | 3.9 |
| 55.3 | 45.5 | 19.8 | 27.1 | | | | 39.2 | 29.9 |
| (15) 16.5 | (38) 13.0 | (72) 7.8 | (38) 9.8 | | | % Profit Before Taxes/Tangible<br>Net Worth | (170) 16.4 | (175) 11.2 |
| 8.4 | -1.6 | .3 | 2.6 | | | | 2.2 | -2.3 |
| 18.9 | 19.7 | 7.8 | 13.8 | | | | 16.7 | 10.8 |
| 8.1 | 3.6 | 2.1 | 3.6 | | | % Profit Before Taxes/Total<br>Assets | 4.8 | 3.1 |
| -1.0 | -1.6 | -.2 | 1.0 | | | | -.3 | -2.7 |
| 455.6 | 39.4 | 16.7 | 12.5 | | | | 24.2 | 20.2 |
| 37.3 | 15.9 | 7.1 | 7.0 | | | Sales/Net Fixed Assets | 9.2 | 8.9 |
| 13.7 | 6.7 | 4.1 | 2.4 | | | | 4.9 | 4.0 |
| 8.3 | 3.6 | 2.6 | 2.2 | | | | 3.2 | 3.0 |
| 5.0 | 2.8 | 2.1 | 1.6 | | | Sales/Total Assets | 2.2 | 2.2 |
| 3.1 | 1.7 | 1.6 | 1.0 | | | | 1.6 | 1.5 |
| .5 | .8 | 1.2 | 1.0 | | | | 1.1 | 1.1 |
| (14) 1.4 | (38) 1.7 | (68) 2.7 | (38) 2.2 | | | % Depr., Dep., Amort./Sales | (160) 2.2 | (170) 2.5 |
| 3.8 | 3.6 | 4.0 | 6.1 | | | | 3.5 | 4.3 |
| 1.9 | 3.0 | 1.5 | | | | | 2.0 | 1.8 |
| (16) 5.6 | (24) 4.1 | (26) 4.2 | | | | % Officers', Directors'<br>Owners' Comp/Sales | (77) 4.2 | (73) 3.1 |
| 11.3 | 7.9 | 6.2 | | | | | 6.6 | 5.9 |
| 27321M | 161419M | 797787M | 1248903M | 684458M | 89270M | Net Sales ($) | 4635025M | 3670976M |
| 5818M | 53286M | 376978M | 737995M | 411761M | 129421M | Total Assets ($) | 2689599M | 2289005M |

© RMA 2012

M = $ thousand    MM = $ million
See Pages 9 through 22 for Explanation of Ratios and Data

## Comparative Historical Data    Current Data Sorted by Sales

| Type of Statement | 4/1/09-3/31/10 ALL | 4/1/10-3/31/11 ALL | 4/1/11-3/31/12 ALL | 0-1MM | 1-3MM | 3-5MM | 5-10MM | 10-25MM | 25MM & OVER |
|---|---|---|---|---|---|---|---|---|---|
| Unqualified | 20 | 25 | 20 | | | | 2 | 5 | 13 |
| Reviewed | 44 | 35 | 46 | 2 | 1 | 4 | 14 | 18 | 7 |
| Compiled | 24 | 24 | 30 | 3 | 5 | 6 | 9 | 6 | 1 |
| Tax Returns | 47 | 37 | 44 | 9 | 19 | 6 | 6 | 4 | |
| Other | 72 | 58 | 57 | 3 | | 2 | 16 | 10 | 9 |
| | | | | | 45 (4/1-9/30/11) | | 152 (10/1/11-3/31/12) | | |
| NUMBER OF STATEMENTS | 207 | 179 | 197 | 17 | 42 | 18 | 47 | 43 | 30 |
| **ASSETS** | % | % | % | % | % | % | % | % | % |
| Cash & Equivalents | 9.1 | 6.8 | 8.1 | 18.5 | 12.7 | 5.9 | 5.6 | 6.6 | 3.1 |
| Trade Receivables (net) | 18.6 | 18.2 | 20.3 | 11.2 | 20.8 | 21.7 | 25.5 | 18.7 | 18.0 |
| Inventory | 29.8 | 31.6 | 28.8 | 19.6 | 28.0 | 22.6 | 29.7 | 31.8 | 33.0 |
| All Other Current | 2.3 | 2.8 | 3.1 | 10.3 | 1.1 | 3.4 | 3.6 | 1.5 | 3.1 |
| Total Current | 59.8 | 59.5 | 60.3 | 59.6 | 62.7 | 53.5 | 64.4 | 58.6 | 57.3 |
| Fixed Assets (net) | 30.0 | 30.9 | 28.6 | 21.7 | 26.0 | 37.8 | 24.7 | 29.5 | 35.7 |
| Intangibles (net) | 3.5 | 4.4 | 4.9 | 11.7 | 3.7 | 2.9 | 5.3 | 4.1 | 4.2 |
| All Other Non-Current | 6.6 | 5.2 | 6.2 | 6.9 | 7.6 | 5.8 | 5.6 | 7.9 | 2.9 |
| Total | 100.0 | 100.0 | 100.0 | 100.0 | 100.0 | 100.0 | 100.0 | 100.0 | 100.0 |
| **LIABILITIES** | | | | | | | | | |
| Notes Payable-Short Term | 16.5 | 15.0 | 12.5 | 5.5 | 14.4 | 14.6 | 12.5 | 15.1 | 8.4 |
| Cur. Mat.-L.T.D. | 5.2 | 4.4 | 5.5 | 2.5 | 9.3 | 5.4 | 4.7 | 4.9 | 4.1 |
| Trade Payables | 11.5 | 11.5 | 11.5 | 6.7 | 12.3 | 17.7 | 10.8 | 12.3 | 9.2 |
| Income Taxes Payable | .2 | .2 | .1 | .2 | .0 | .4 | .2 | .1 | .1 |
| All Other Current | 7.7 | 8.4 | 9.6 | 21.7 | 14.7 | 6.4 | 5.7 | 6.8 | 7.6 |
| Total Current | 41.0 | 39.5 | 39.2 | 36.6 | 50.8 | 44.4 | 34.0 | 39.1 | 29.4 |
| Long-Term Debt | 19.2 | 19.0 | 15.2 | 15.4 | 15.2 | 18.9 | 13.0 | 15.9 | 15.5 |
| Deferred Taxes | .2 | .5 | .5 | .2 | .0 | .3 | .3 | .8 | 1.1 |
| All Other Non-Current | 8.1 | 8.3 | 8.6 | 16.6 | 14.4 | 10.4 | 7.6 | 3.0 | 4.5 |
| Net Worth | 31.4 | 32.8 | 36.5 | 31.1 | 19.5 | 26.0 | 45.1 | 41.2 | 49.4 |
| Total Liabilities & Net Worth | 100.0 | 100.0 | 100.0 | 100.0 | 100.0 | 100.0 | 100.0 | 100.0 | 100.0 |
| **INCOME DATA** | | | | | | | | | |
| Net Sales | 100.0 | 100.0 | 100.0 | 100.0 | 100.0 | 100.0 | 100.0 | 100.0 | 100.0 |
| Gross Profit | 28.4 | 29.4 | 29.1 | 49.1 | 38.5 | 28.9 | 25.7 | 22.8 | 19.4 |
| Operating Expenses | 25.9 | 26.4 | 26.3 | 46.1 | 35.7 | 28.0 | 22.7 | 19.8 | 15.6 |
| Operating Profit | 2.5 | 3.0 | 2.9 | 3.0 | 2.8 | .9 | 3.0 | 3.0 | 3.8 |
| All Other Expenses (net) | 1.2 | .9 | .7 | .3 | 1.1 | .3 | .5 | .8 | .9 |
| Profit Before Taxes | 1.3 | 2.1 | 2.1 | 2.6 | 1.7 | .6 | 2.5 | 2.2 | 2.9 |
| **RATIOS** | | | | | | | | | |
| Current | 3.1 | 3.2 | 3.4 | 13.4 | 2.8 | 2.6 | 4.7 | 2.6 | 2.8 |
| | 1.6 | 1.7 | 1.7 | 2.9 | 1.8 | 1.4 | 1.7 | 1.6 | 1.8 |
| | 1.0 | 1.1 | 1.1 | 1.3 | .8 | 1.0 | 1.3 | 1.1 | 1.4 |
| Quick | 1.4 | 1.4 | 1.4 | 11.0 | 1.5 | 1.3 | 1.8 | 1.2 | 1.3 |
| | .6 | .7 | .8 | .7 | .8 | .9 | .9 | .7 | .8 |
| | .3 | .3 | .3 | .4 | .3 | .3 | .4 | .3 | .5 |
| Sales/Receivables | 15 24.0 | 17 22.1 | 16 22.9 | 0 UND | 14 26.4 | 15 24.6 | 17 21.0 | 18 19.8 | 17 21.9 |
| | 27 13.5 | 30 12.2 | 27 13.5 | 15 25.1 | 26 14.1 | 20 17.9 | 33 11.2 | 35 10.4 | 27 13.3 |
| | 44 8.3 | 45 8.1 | 43 8.4 | 41 9.0 | 35 10.4 | 34 10.8 | 61 6.0 | 56 6.5 | 44 8.3 |
| Cost of Sales/Inventory | 29 12.6 | 35 10.5 | 23 15.6 | 0 UND | 6 63.3 | 14 25.4 | 19 19.2 | 51 7.2 | 38 9.7 |
| | 63 5.8 | 77 4.8 | 61 6.0 | 49 7.4 | 57 6.4 | 46 7.9 | 58 6.3 | 81 4.5 | 72 5.1 |
| | 133 2.7 | 131 2.8 | 111 3.3 | 87 4.2 | 130 2.8 | 72 5.1 | 130 2.8 | 107 3.4 | 104 3.5 |
| Cost of Sales/Payables | 10 34.9 | 9 41.3 | 10 35.1 | 0 UND | 5 72.6 | 10 37.8 | 11 32.8 | 14 26.4 | 12 30.9 |
| | 21 17.3 | 21 17.6 | 19 19.6 | 10 36.9 | 18 20.0 | 16 23.1 | 18 19.8 | 24 15.5 | 17 22.0 |
| | 37 9.9 | 35 10.6 | 35 10.5 | 76 4.8 | 46 8.0 | 39 9.3 | 30 12.2 | 38 9.7 | 24 15.4 |
| Sales/Working Capital | 4.9 | 4.5 | 4.7 | 2.6 | 5.9 | 9.5 | 4.0 | 4.7 | 4.6 |
| | 10.0 | 8.5 | 9.4 | 6.4 | 12.5 | 15.6 | 6.4 | 9.4 | 10.6 |
| | 186.8 | 40.5 | 43.5 | 33.6 | -28.7 | NM | 20.9 | 47.5 | 20.9 |
| EBIT/Interest | 6.4 | 8.1 | 7.2 | 22.0 | 6.8 | 8.0 | 7.5 | 3.9 | 15.5 |
| | (187) 2.3 | (165) 2.9 | (173) 2.1 | (10) 2.0 | (36) 2.1 | (16) 2.0 | (43) 1.8 | (41) 2.1 | (27) 3.8 |
| | -.3 | .3 | .9 | 1.2 | -1.0 | .1 | .7 | 1.1 | 1.1 |
| Net Profit + Depr., Dep., Amort./Cur. Mat. L/T/D | 3.3 | 4.8 | 4.0 | | | | 4.0 | 4.7 | 9.3 |
| | (45) 1.3 | (34) 2.6 | (43) 2.1 | | | | (11) 1.6 | (11) 3.1 | (11) 2.7 |
| | .5 | 1.1 | 1.1 | | | | 1.1 | 1.1 | 1.6 |
| Fixed/Worth | .3 | .4 | .3 | .1 | .2 | .5 | .2 | .4 | .4 |
| | .7 | .8 | .8 | .8 | .9 | 1.1 | .6 | .8 | .7 |
| | 2.5 | 2.3 | 1.9 | NM | -4.2 | 8.7 | 1.2 | 1.4 | 1.8 |
| Debt/Worth | .8 | .7 | .6 | .1 | .8 | .9 | .6 | .7 | .5 |
| | 1.9 | 1.7 | 1.6 | 1.9 | 4.2 | 1.6 | 1.3 | 1.5 | 1.3 |
| | 8.3 | 5.8 | 5.4 | NM | -8.5 | 260.9 | 3.2 | 5.3 | 2.6 |
| % Profit Before Taxes/Tangible Net Worth | 33.1 | 32.4 | 26.0 | 21.6 | 60.9 | 48.3 | 21.5 | 18.9 | 26.7 |
| | (176) 9.2 | (152) 11.8 | (169) 10.0 | (13) 11.8 | (28) 20.7 | (15) 12.3 | (44) 7.4 | (40) 6.9 | (29) 11.8 |
| | -5.4 | -2.5 | 1.1 | -1.0 | 6.2 | -1.8 | -.3 | .9 | 2.6 |
| % Profit Before Taxes/Total Assets | 10.3 | 12.9 | 12.8 | 17.4 | 19.1 | 10.2 | 11.7 | 5.6 | 14.2 |
| | 2.9 | 4.3 | 3.1 | 7.4 | 3.0 | 4.2 | 1.9 | 2.6 | 4.6 |
| | -4.5 | -2.3 | -.2 | -.4 | -2.4 | -3.1 | -.3 | .2 | .5 |
| Sales/Net Fixed Assets | 23.8 | 20.4 | 26.6 | 199.1 | 37.3 | 28.3 | 39.2 | 15.3 | 18.3 |
| | 7.7 | 8.2 | 8.7 | 16.5 | 18.3 | 5.1 | 8.4 | 7.8 | 8.0 |
| | 3.9 | 3.7 | 4.5 | 4.9 | 6.4 | 3.6 | 4.8 | 4.0 | 3.6 |
| Sales/Total Assets | 3.0 | 2.8 | 3.2 | 4.1 | 4.9 | 3.6 | 3.0 | 2.5 | 3.1 |
| | 1.9 | 1.9 | 2.2 | 1.7 | 2.8 | 2.4 | 2.2 | 1.9 | 2.2 |
| | 1.3 | 1.3 | 1.5 | .9 | 1.6 | 1.7 | 1.5 | 1.4 | 1.4 |
| % Depr., Dep., Amort./Sales | 1.1 | 1.2 | 1.0 | | .8 | 1.5 | 1.0 | 1.3 | .8 |
| | (175) 2.5 | (153) 2.1 | (165) 2.5 | | (34) 1.6 | (15) 1.8 | (37) 2.7 | (40) 2.7 | 1.8 |
| | 4.9 | 5.3 | 4.2 | | 3.6 | 7.1 | 4.8 | 3.9 | 4.5 |
| % Officers', Directors' Owners' Comp/Sales | 2.6 | 2.2 | 2.0 | | 3.2 | | 2.6 | 1.0 | |
| | (77) 4.5 | (76) 3.7 | (75) 4.2 | | (23) 4.7 | | (18) 4.9 | (14) 1.7 | |
| | 6.9 | 7.1 | 7.8 | | 8.3 | | 7.9 | 4.0 | |
| Net Sales ($) | 3301153M | 2825732M | 3009158M | 10730M | 78212M | 72878M | 331498M | 670093M | 1845747M |
| Total Assets ($) | 2233438M | 1895535M | 1715259M | 8140M | 43703M | 38052M | 205775M | 427913M | 991676M |

© RMA 2012    M = $ thousand    MM = $ million
See Pages 9 through 22 for Explanation of Ratios and Data

**Current Data Sorted by Assets**      **Comparative Historical Data**

| Type of Statement | 0-500M | 500M-2MM | 2-10MM | 10-50MM | 50-100MM | 100-250MM | 4/1/07-3/31/08 ALL | 4/1/08-3/31/09 ALL |
|---|---|---|---|---|---|---|---|---|
| Unqualified | | | | 13 | 3 | 5 | 18 | 22 |
| Reviewed | | | 3 | 4 | 1 | | 8 | 10 |
| Compiled | | | 2 | | | | 2 | 6 |
| Tax Returns | | | 2 | | | | 3 | 6 |
| Other | 1 | 1 | 3 | 12 | 7 | 7 | 32 | 29 |
| | 1 (4/1-9/30/11) | | 10 (4/1-9/30/11) | 54 (10/1/11-3/31/12) | | 7 | | |
| NUMBER OF STATEMENTS | 1 | 1 | 10 | 29 | 11 | 12 | 63 | 73 |
| | % | % | % | % | % | % | % | % |
| **ASSETS** | | | | | | | | |
| Cash & Equivalents | | | 6.4 | 3.7 | 3.0 | 3.8 | 5.0 | 5.0 |
| Trade Receivables (net) | | | 37.1 | 21.4 | 18.6 | 11.9 | 22.3 | 23.4 |
| Inventory | | | 26.8 | 24.1 | 25.9 | 19.9 | 24.1 | 24.4 |
| All Other Current | | | .9 | 2.7 | 3.9 | 2.4 | 3.0 | 2.3 |
| Total Current | | | 71.3 | 51.9 | 51.4 | 38.0 | 54.4 | 55.0 |
| Fixed Assets (net) | | | 19.7 | 39.8 | 36.9 | 44.2 | 36.6 | 36.3 |
| Intangibles (net) | | | 1.7 | 3.0 | 7.3 | 8.8 | 2.6 | 3.0 |
| All Other Non-Current | | | 7.3 | 5.3 | 4.4 | 8.9 | 6.3 | 5.6 |
| Total | | | 100.0 | 100.0 | 100.0 | 100.0 | 100.0 | 100.0 |
| **LIABILITIES** | | | | | | | | |
| Notes Payable-Short Term | | | 14.6 | 13.5 | 6.3 | 4.3 | 10.2 | 11.3 |
| Cur. Mat.-L.T.D. | | | 3.1 | 7.1 | 5.7 | 1.9 | 3.8 | 4.3 |
| Trade Payables | | | 25.7 | 18.4 | 17.6 | 8.0 | 18.1 | 17.4 |
| Income Taxes Payable | | | .1 | .6 | .1 | .3 | .1 | .2 |
| All Other Current | | | 5.0 | 7.2 | 8.0 | 7.6 | 6.5 | 5.1 |
| Total Current | | | 48.5 | 46.9 | 37.6 | 22.0 | 38.7 | 38.2 |
| Long-Term Debt | | | 7.4 | 18.0 | 11.8 | 17.3 | 23.9 | 26.0 |
| Deferred Taxes | | | 1.1 | .7 | 4.8 | 2.9 | .8 | .9 |
| All Other Non-Current | | | 6.1 | 8.2 | 4.2 | 9.5 | 6.5 | 7.1 |
| Net Worth | | | 37.0 | 26.2 | 41.5 | 48.4 | 30.1 | 27.6 |
| Total Liabilties & Net Worth | | | 100.0 | 100.0 | 100.0 | 100.0 | 100.0 | 100.0 |
| **INCOME DATA** | | | | | | | | |
| Net Sales | | | 100.0 | 100.0 | 100.0 | 100.0 | 100.0 | 100.0 |
| Gross Profit | | | 19.4 | 14.0 | 18.4 | 16.0 | 21.3 | 20.5 |
| Operating Expenses | | | 17.2 | 11.2 | 9.0 | 11.2 | 18.4 | 16.7 |
| Operating Profit | | | 2.2 | 2.7 | 9.4 | 4.8 | 2.9 | 3.8 |
| All Other Expenses (net) | | | .3 | 1.3 | 2.2 | 2.0 | 1.4 | 1.6 |
| Profit Before Taxes | | | 2.0 | 1.5 | 7.2 | 2.8 | 1.5 | 2.2 |
| **RATIOS** | | | | | | | | |
| Current | | | 2.2 | 1.8 | 2.2 | 3.6 | 2.4 | 2.3 |
| | | | 1.5 | 1.1 | 1.3 | 1.9 | 1.4 | 1.4 |
| | | | 1.0 | .8 | 1.1 | 1.0 | 1.1 | 1.0 |
| Quick | | | 1.7 | 1.0 | 1.0 | 1.8 | 1.2 | 1.2 |
| | | | .9 | .6 | .5 | .8 | .6 | .7 |
| | | | .4 | .4 | .3 | .5 | .4 | .4 |
| Sales/Receivables | | | 28 13.2 | 26 14.0 | 28 13.2 | 26 14.3 | 28 13.0 | 23 16.0 |
| | | | 31 11.9 | 34 10.7 | 34 10.8 | 29 12.6 | 34 10.7 | 30 12.3 |
| | | | 41 9.0 | 49 7.5 | 51 7.1 | 43 8.4 | 43 8.5 | 39 9.4 |
| Cost of Sales/Inventory | | | 18 20.0 | 28 13.1 | 36 10.2 | 42 8.7 | 30 12.2 | 26 14.3 |
| | | | 32 11.4 | 42 8.7 | 56 6.5 | 49 7.5 | 45 8.2 | 39 9.3 |
| | | | 72 5.1 | 63 5.8 | 70 5.2 | 94 3.9 | 68 5.4 | 58 6.3 |
| Cost of Sales/Payables | | | 15 24.9 | 17 21.4 | 13 27.2 | 15 24.2 | 20 18.4 | 20 18.6 |
| | | | 23 16.2 | 28 13.2 | 21 17.2 | 23 15.7 | 30 12.1 | 26 14.0 |
| | | | 42 8.6 | 45 8.2 | 35 10.3 | 36 10.1 | 47 7.8 | 38 9.6 |
| Sales/Working Capital | | | 13.5 | 9.0 | 8.5 | 3.7 | 6.3 | 8.0 |
| | | | 18.4 | 34.4 | 18.6 | 8.4 | 13.5 | 25.5 |
| | | | NM | -22.4 | 42.9 | NM | 76.4 | 265.3 |
| EBIT/Interest | | | 24.3 | 7.0 | | 8.8 | 4.8 | 6.9 |
| | | | 2.6 | 3.6 | | (10) 2.8 | (59) 2.0 | (66) 2.6 |
| | | | 2.0 | -.1 | | .0 | .8 | 1.0 |
| Net Profit + Depr., Dep., Amort./Cur. Mat. L/T/D | | | | 3.6 | | | 2.8 | 3.5 |
| | | | | (11) 2.3 | | | (19) 1.5 | (21) 1.6 |
| | | | | 1.5 | | | .4 | .7 |
| Fixed/Worth | | | .1 | .6 | .6 | .9 | .8 | .4 |
| | | | .7 | 1.8 | 1.0 | 1.3 | 1.2 | 1.4 |
| | | | 1.3 | 3.2 | 2.1 | 2.2 | 3.6 | 10.9 |
| Debt/Worth | | | 1.3 | 1.0 | .9 | .3 | 1.4 | .8 |
| | | | 2.2 | 3.2 | 1.4 | 1.7 | 2.8 | 3.1 |
| | | | 5.1 | 6.6 | 3.6 | 4.2 | 4.4 | 19.3 |
| % Profit Before Taxes/Tangible Net Worth | | | 96.6 | 34.5 | 47.1 | 25.2 | 32.8 | 33.2 |
| | | | 17.8 | (23) 20.1 | (10) 25.8 | (10) 9.3 | (54) 13.0 | (59) 18.0 |
| | | | 2.0 | .4 | 14.1 | -8.3 | -.2 | 2.7 |
| % Profit Before Taxes/Total Assets | | | 17.4 | 12.2 | 19.8 | 8.3 | 10.0 | 9.9 |
| | | | 4.8 | 6.3 | 8.6 | 4.7 | 4.5 | 4.9 |
| | | | .7 | -1.7 | 2.7 | -3.6 | -.9 | -.2 |
| Sales/Net Fixed Assets | | | 97.8 | 8.6 | 19.5 | 8.7 | 12.8 | 16.5 |
| | | | 22.0 | 6.6 | 5.1 | 4.5 | 7.6 | 7.0 |
| | | | 10.3 | 3.4 | 2.7 | 1.4 | 3.3 | 3.8 |
| Sales/Total Assets | | | 5.5 | 3.0 | 3.2 | 1.9 | 3.3 | 3.6 |
| | | | 3.3 | 2.1 | 2.1 | 1.2 | 2.2 | 2.2 |
| | | | 2.3 | 1.6 | 1.3 | .8 | 1.4 | 1.5 |
| % Depr., Dep., Amort./Sales | | | | 1.2 | .8 | 2.7 | 1.3 | 1.1 |
| | | | | 1.9 | (10) 2.7 | 3.3 | (53) 2.1 | (64) 2.1 |
| | | | | 3.4 | 3.6 | 5.6 | 3.6 | 3.5 |
| % Officers', Directors' Owners' Comp/Sales | | | | | | | 1.5 | .7 |
| | | | | | | | (13) 2.5 | (15) 1.5 |
| | | | | | | | 4.4 | 3.2 |
| Net Sales ($) | 1851M | 3542M | 163674M | 1638140M | 1989743M | 1949766M | 4586589M | 5866224M |
| Total Assets ($) | 482M | 1770M | 44005M | 737874M | 802728M | 1525961M | 2588737M | 2808766M |

## Comparative Historical Data | Current Data Sorted by Sales

| | | | Type of Statement | 0-1MM | 1-3MM | 3-5MM | 5-10MM | 10-25MM | 25MM & OVER |
|---|---|---|---|---|---|---|---|---|---|
| 23 | 27 | 21 | Unqualified | | | | | 1 | 20 |
| 13 | 11 | 8 | Reviewed | | | | 1 | 5 | 2 |
| 3 | 5 | 2 | Compiled | | | | | 1 | 1 |
| 3 | 1 | 3 | Tax Returns | | | | | 2 | 1 |
| 43 | 39 | 30 | Other | | | 1 | 1 | 3 | 24 |
| 4/1/09-3/31/10 ALL | 4/1/10-3/31/11 ALL | 4/1/11-3/31/12 ALL | | | 10 (4/1-9/30/11) | | | 54 (10/1/11-3/31/12) | |
| 85 | 83 | 64 | **NUMBER OF STATEMENTS** | | 1 | 1 | 3 | 12 | 47 |
| % | % | % | **ASSETS** | % | % | % | % | % | % |
| 4.7 | 5.8 | 4.3 | Cash & Equivalents | | | | | 2.5 | 3.5 |
| 24.8 | 24.7 | 21.7 | Trade Receivables (net) | | | | | 31.3 | 18.8 |
| 23.5 | 20.9 | 23.4 | Inventory | | | | | 26.2 | 23.6 |
| 2.5 | 3.2 | 2.5 | All Other Current | | | | | 1.1 | 3.0 |
| 55.5 | 54.5 | 52.0 | Total Current | | | | | 61.1 | 48.9 |
| 35.2 | 34.7 | 37.4 | Fixed Assets (net) | | | | | 32.1 | 39.4 |
| 2.4 | 3.9 | 4.5 | Intangibles (net) | | | | | .8 | 5.7 |
| 6.9 | 7.0 | 6.1 | All Other Non-Current | | | | | 6.0 | 6.0 |
| 100.0 | 100.0 | 100.0 | Total | | | | | 100.0 | 100.0 |
| | | | **LIABILITIES** | | | | | | |
| 10.3 | 7.2 | 10.3 | Notes Payable-Short Term | | | | | 22.7 | 8.0 |
| 4.0 | 5.3 | 5.3 | Cur. Mat.-L.T.D. | | | | | 2.8 | 4.9 |
| 17.6 | 16.9 | 17.1 | Trade Payables | | | | | 20.9 | 15.5 |
| .4 | .4 | .4 | Income Taxes Payable | | | | | .6 | .3 |
| 12.5 | 6.1 | 8.8 | All Other Current | | | | | 6.3 | 7.3 |
| 44.9 | 35.9 | 41.8 | Total Current | | | | | 53.3 | 36.0 |
| 20.8 | 17.4 | 21.1 | Long-Term Debt | | | | | 15.5 | 15.6 |
| 1.1 | 1.4 | 1.9 | Deferred Taxes | | | | | 1.2 | 2.2 |
| 5.3 | 7.7 | 7.1 | All Other Non-Current | | | | | 2.6 | 9.0 |
| 27.8 | 37.6 | 28.1 | Net Worth | | | | | 27.4 | 37.1 |
| 100.0 | 100.0 | 100.0 | Total Liabilties & Net Worth | | | | | 100.0 | 100.0 |
| | | | **INCOME DATA** | | | | | | |
| 100.0 | 100.0 | 100.0 | Net Sales | | | | | 100.0 | 100.0 |
| 21.7 | 21.3 | 17.3 | Gross Profit | | | | | 15.3 | 15.3 |
| 15.8 | 15.5 | 13.1 | Operating Expenses | | | | | 14.0 | 10.1 |
| 6.0 | 5.8 | 4.3 | Operating Profit | | | | | 1.3 | 5.2 |
| .9 | 1.5 | 1.4 | All Other Expenses (net) | | | | | 1.5 | 1.4 |
| 5.1 | 4.3 | 2.9 | Profit Before Taxes | | | | | -.2 | 3.8 |
| | | | **RATIOS** | | | | | | |
| 2.2 | 2.3 | 2.1 | | | | | | 1.8 | 2.2 |
| 1.4 | 1.5 | 1.3 | Current | | | | | 1.1 | 1.4 |
| 1.0 | 1.1 | .9 | | | | | | .8 | 1.0 |
| 1.2 | 1.4 | 1.2 | | | | | | 1.4 | 1.2 |
| .7 | .8 | .6 | Quick | | | | | .7 | .6 |
| .5 | .5 | .4 | | | | | | .3 | .4 |
| 27 13.8 | 26 13.9 | 26 13.9 | | | | | | 34 10.8 | 26 14.3 |
| 35 10.3 | 38 9.7 | 32 11.3 | Sales/Receivables | | | | | 42 8.7 | 30 12.3 |
| 45 8.2 | 46 7.9 | 45 8.2 | | | | | | 49 7.4 | 41 9.0 |
| 27 13.6 | 22 16.8 | 28 12.9 | | | | | | 25 14.5 | 33 11.1 |
| 43 8.5 | 36 10.2 | 44 8.3 | Cost of Sales/Inventory | | | | | 36 10.2 | 45 8.1 |
| 65 5.6 | 65 5.7 | 72 5.1 | | | | | | 73 5.0 | 68 5.4 |
| 21 17.2 | 20 18.2 | 17 21.9 | | | | | | 14 25.4 | 17 21.8 |
| 29 12.4 | 28 13.2 | 24 15.3 | Cost of Sales/Payables | | | | | 26 14.2 | 22 16.7 |
| 40 9.1 | 37 9.9 | 41 9.0 | | | | | | 47 7.8 | 40 9.1 |
| 6.9 | 6.5 | 8.5 | | | | | | 15.3 | 7.3 |
| 17.7 | 13.9 | 23.5 | Sales/Working Capital | | | | | 37.7 | 19.5 |
| NM | 75.0 | -40.1 | | | | | | -39.9 | -98.8 |
| 8.0 | 10.7 | 8.4 | | | | | | 15.4 | 10.1 |
| (80) 3.9 | (78) 4.5 | (60) 3.6 | EBIT/Interest | | | | | 2.6 | (43) 4.5 |
| .7 | 1.7 | 1.7 | | | | | | 2.0 | 1.1 |
| 4.8 | 12.1 | 3.8 | Net Profit + Depr., Dep., | | | | | | 4.2 |
| (23) 2.5 | (32) 3.2 | (23) 2.3 | Amort./Cur. Mat. L/T/D | | | | | | (18) 2.3 |
| 1.3 | 1.9 | 1.3 | | | | | | | 1.4 |
| .5 | .5 | .6 | | | | | | .4 | .6 |
| 1.2 | 1.0 | 1.3 | Fixed/Worth | | | | | 1.0 | 1.3 |
| 3.3 | 2.2 | 2.3 | | | | | | 2.6 | 2.2 |
| .8 | 1.1 | 1.0 | | | | | | 1.6 | .9 |
| 2.4 | 2.0 | 2.2 | Debt/Worth | | | | | 2.7 | 1.9 |
| 9.3 | 3.7 | 4.8 | | | | | | 5.9 | 3.6 |
| 48.4 | 48.1 | 41.2 | % Profit Before Taxes/Tangible | | | | | 46.0 | 35.1 |
| (70) 24.2 | (73) 21.0 | (54) 19.0 | Net Worth | | | | | (11) 17.9 | (40) 21.0 |
| 4.6 | 7.0 | 5.1 | | | | | | 6.0 | 1.9 |
| 14.1 | 14.8 | 12.4 | % Profit Before Taxes/Total | | | | | 12.6 | 13.7 |
| 7.2 | 8.9 | 6.2 | Assets | | | | | 4.8 | 6.3 |
| .5 | 1.2 | .1 | | | | | | 1.1 | -1.3 |
| 19.4 | 13.3 | 11.1 | | | | | | 24.7 | 10.0 |
| 6.4 | 7.4 | 6.6 | Sales/Net Fixed Assets | | | | | 8.6 | 6.6 |
| 3.0 | 3.8 | 3.3 | | | | | | 2.9 | 3.3 |
| 3.2 | 3.5 | 3.0 | | | | | | 4.5 | 3.0 |
| 2.2 | 2.2 | 2.0 | Sales/Total Assets | | | | | 2.7 | 2.1 |
| 1.5 | 1.6 | 1.5 | | | | | | 1.5 | 1.3 |
| 1.1 | 1.2 | 1.2 | | | | | | 1.2 | 1.3 |
| (75) 2.2 | (76) 2.1 | (62) 2.3 | % Depr., Dep., Amort./Sales | | | | | (11) 1.6 | (46) 2.5 |
| 4.4 | 4.1 | 3.5 | | | | | | 3.5 | 3.5 |
| | 1.4 | 1.2 | % Officers', Directors' | | | | | | |
| | (13) 2.3 | (11) 2.4 | Owners' Comp/Sales | | | | | | |
| | 2.9 | 2.7 | | | | | | | |
| 7062022M | 8309090M | 5746716M | Net Sales ($) | | 1851M | 3542M | 22801M | 227014M | 5491508M |
| 3517311M | 3719323M | 3112820M | Total Assets ($) | | 482M | 1770M | 20867M | 118770M | 2970931M |

*(For the right-hand columns 0-1MM, 1-3MM, 3-5MM and 5-10MM the Assets, Liabilities, Income Data and most Ratios are marked "DATA NOT AVAILABLE".)*

M = $ thousand    MM = $ million
See Pages 9 through 22 for Explanation of Ratios and Data

## Current Data Sorted by Assets      Comparative Historical Data

| 0-500M | 500M-2MM | 2-10MM | 10-50MM | 50-100MM | 100-250MM | Type of Statement | 4/1/07-3/31/08 ALL | 4/1/08-3/31/09 ALL |
|---|---|---|---|---|---|---|---|---|
|  | 1 | 10 | 15 | 4 | 4 | Unqualified | 39 | 26 |
| 1 | 4 | 45 | 25 | 3 |  | Reviewed | 64 | 77 |
| 9 | 8 | 14 | 4 |  |  | Compiled | 22 | 22 |
| 2 | 14 | 7 |  |  |  | Tax Returns | 13 | 15 |
|  | 4 | 28 | 30 | 3 | 6 | Other | 80 | 87 |
|  | 41 (4/1-9/30/11) |  | 200 (10/1/11-3/31/12) |  |  |  |  |  |
| 12 | 31 | 104 | 74 | 10 | 10 | NUMBER OF STATEMENTS | 218 | 227 |

### ASSETS

| 0-500M % | 500M-2MM % | 2-10MM % | 10-50MM % | 50-100MM % | 100-250MM % |  | % | % |
|---|---|---|---|---|---|---|---|---|
| 13.1 | 12.4 | 7.3 | 5.3 | 3.6 | .7 | Cash & Equivalents | 6.0 | 6.5 |
| 28.1 | 40.2 | 29.0 | 23.6 | 16.2 | 22.5 | Trade Receivables (net) | 28.7 | 26.1 |
| 22.4 | 17.6 | 16.3 | 18.5 | 11.6 | 19.2 | Inventory | 16.6 | 16.4 |
| .0 | .6 | 1.6 | 2.4 | 1.0 | 1.8 | All Other Current | 1.9 | 1.7 |
| 63.5 | 70.8 | 54.2 | 49.8 | 32.3 | 44.1 | Total Current | 53.3 | 50.7 |
| 22.7 | 14.3 | 34.9 | 39.4 | 42.3 | 35.5 | Fixed Assets (net) | 33.8 | 36.3 |
| 6.0 | 1.4 | 3.4 | 1.9 | 20.9 | 17.7 | Intangibles (net) | 5.7 | 4.8 |
| 7.8 | 13.4 | 7.4 | 8.9 | 4.5 | 2.7 | All Other Non-Current | 7.2 | 8.2 |
| 100.0 | 100.0 | 100.0 | 100.0 | 100.0 | 100.0 | Total | 100.0 | 100.0 |

### LIABILITIES

| 0-500M | 500M-2MM | 2-10MM | 10-50MM | 50-100MM | 100-250MM |  |  |  |
|---|---|---|---|---|---|---|---|---|
| 16.9 | 6.4 | 7.7 | 9.7 | 1.2 | 8.7 | Notes Payable-Short Term | 9.9 | 11.6 |
| .9 | 2.4 | 4.4 | 4.6 | 9.1 | 4.0 | Cur. Mat.-L.T.D. | 4.5 | 5.0 |
| 15.9 | 28.2 | 16.4 | 14.6 | 10.0 | 13.5 | Trade Payables | 17.7 | 17.4 |
| .0 | .0 | .1 | .1 | .2 | .1 | Income Taxes Payable | .2 | .1 |
| 8.1 | 13.5 | 6.1 | 6.9 | 7.6 | 4.9 | All Other Current | 7.2 | 5.9 |
| 41.7 | 50.5 | 34.6 | 35.8 | 28.0 | 31.2 | Total Current | 39.5 | 40.0 |
| 11.0 | 12.8 | 19.4 | 21.4 | 18.2 | 22.6 | Long-Term Debt | 20.9 | 21.6 |
| .0 | .1 | .7 | 1.4 | 4.1 | 2.9 | Deferred Taxes | 1.1 | .9 |
| 33.5 | 4.1 | 5.6 | 5.1 | 2.5 | 5.0 | All Other Non-Current | 6.0 | 4.8 |
| 13.9 | 32.4 | 39.7 | 36.3 | 47.3 | 38.3 | Net Worth | 32.5 | 32.7 |
| 100.0 | 100.0 | 100.0 | 100.0 | 100.0 | 100.0 | Total Liabilities & Net Worth | 100.0 | 100.0 |

### INCOME DATA

| 0-500M | 500M-2MM | 2-10MM | 10-50MM | 50-100MM | 100-250MM |  |  |  |
|---|---|---|---|---|---|---|---|---|
| 100.0 | 100.0 | 100.0 | 100.0 | 100.0 | 100.0 | Net Sales | 100.0 | 100.0 |
| 38.4 | 32.5 | 26.2 | 23.0 | 23.0 | 26.6 | Gross Profit | 25.4 | 22.8 |
| 33.3 | 28.8 | 22.3 | 17.6 | 13.8 | 22.3 | Operating Expenses | 21.1 | 20.1 |
| 5.2 | 3.7 | 3.8 | 5.4 | 9.2 | 4.3 | Operating Profit | 4.3 | 2.7 |
| -.1 | .3 | .1 | .5 | .5 | 3.1 | All Other Expenses (net) | 1.2 | .7 |
| 5.3 | 3.4 | 3.8 | 4.9 | 8.7 | 1.2 | Profit Before Taxes | 3.0 | 2.0 |

### RATIOS

| 0-500M | 500M-2MM | 2-10MM | 10-50MM | 50-100MM | 100-250MM |  |  |  |
|---|---|---|---|---|---|---|---|---|
| 2.8 | 3.4 | 2.6 | 2.3 | 2.1 | 2.9 | Current | 2.2 | 2.1 |
| 2.1 | 1.6 | 1.6 | 1.4 | 1.4 | 1.4 |  | 1.4 | 1.3 |
| 1.0 | 1.1 | 1.1 | .9 | 1.1 | .9 |  | 1.0 | 1.0 |
| 1.8 | 2.5 | 2.0 | 1.5 | 1.3 | 1.2 | Quick | 1.4 | 1.3 |
| 1.1 | 1.1 | 1.1 | .8 | .9 | .7 |  | .9 | .8 |
| .7 | .7 | .7 | .6 | .7 | .5 |  | .6 | .6 |
| 16   22.7 | 32   11.5 | 31   11.7 | 31   11.9 | 31   11.9 | 37   9.8 | Sales/Receivables | 33   11.1 | 27   13.6 |
| 29   12.6 | 36   10.1 | 38   9.7 | 40   9.2 | 35   10.3 | 47   7.7 |  | 39   9.5 | 35   10.4 |
| 41   9.0 | 42   8.7 | 45   8.2 | 47   7.7 | 42   8.7 | 55   6.6 |  | 45   8.1 | 42   8.7 |
| 0   UND | 9   39.8 | 15   25.1 | 25   14.8 | 16   22.8 | 39   9.4 | Cost of Sales/Inventory | 17   21.3 | 17   21.2 |
| 24   15.1 | 19   18.8 | 27   13.6 | 37   9.8 | 21   17.3 | 44   8.3 |  | 27   13.7 | 26   14.0 |
| 65   5.6 | 43   8.4 | 40   9.1 | 53   6.9 | 41   9.0 | 83   4.4 |  | 40   9.0 | 39   9.4 |
| 0   UND | 13   27.2 | 14   27.0 | 17   21.6 | 18   20.1 | 24   14.9 | Cost of Sales/Payables | 18   20.8 | 15   24.4 |
| 24   15.1 | 38   9.7 | 26   13.8 | 30   12.0 | 24   15.5 | 50   7.3 |  | 28   13.2 | 25   14.8 |
| 49   7.5 | 58   6.3 | 43   8.5 | 43   8.4 | 34   10.6 | 59   6.2 |  | 44   8.3 | 39   9.4 |
| 6.8 | 9.3 | 7.2 | 7.2 | 9.1 | 5.4 | Sales/Working Capital | 9.1 | 9.8 |
| 17.4 | 15.6 | 13.6 | 16.3 | 37.6 | 48.0 |  | 18.9 | 25.6 |
| NM | 123.4 | 46.0 | -71.9 | 91.5 | -47.8 |  | NM | -428.0 |
|  | 19.5 | 11.8 | 16.2 |  |  | EBIT/Interest | 7.1 | 6.4 |
| (27)   7.1 | (98)   4.8 | (70)   7.5 |  |  |  |  | (209)   3.5 | (218)   2.7 |
| 2.1 | 2.1 | 2.7 |  |  |  |  | 1.6 | 1.0 |
|  |  | 10.2 | 4.6 |  |  | Net Profit + Depr., Dep., Amort./Cur. Mat. L/T/D | 5.5 | 3.4 |
|  | (28)   3.1 | (40)   2.9 |  |  |  |  | (80)   2.5 | (85)   1.8 |
|  | 1.5 | 1.7 |  |  |  |  | 1.3 | .9 |
| .0 | .1 | .4 | .6 | 1.1 | 1.0 | Fixed/Worth | .6 | .6 |
| .9 | .3 | 1.1 | 1.1 | 1.6 | 2.5 |  | 1.2 | 1.4 |
| -1.4 | 1.1 | 2.3 | 1.8 | NM | -1.2 |  | 2.8 | 3.9 |
| .8 | .4 | .6 | .7 | .9 | .9 | Debt/Worth | .9 | 1.0 |
| NM | 1.3 | 1.9 | 1.9 | 1.6 | 5.3 |  | 2.1 | 2.1 |
| -4.3 | 15.5 | 4.3 | 3.9 | NM | -5.7 |  | 7.0 | 7.0 |
|  | 46.8 | 39.1 | 41.4 |  |  | % Profit Before Taxes/Tangible Net Worth | 34.2 | 30.0 |
|  | (24)   20.5 | (92)   20.0 | (71)   25.4 |  |  |  | (183)   19.0 | (185)   11.5 |
|  | 1.6 | 8.7 | 13.5 |  |  |  | 6.9 | 2.0 |
| 34.2 | 22.0 | 14.3 | 16.5 | 17.0 | 8.3 | % Profit Before Taxes/Total Assets | 12.9 | 8.4 |
| 20.9 | 10.2 | 7.2 | 7.9 | 9.8 | 5.1 |  | 6.5 | 3.8 |
| 6.9 | .4 | 2.1 | 4.1 | 6.4 | .9 |  | 2.1 | .0 |
| UND | 146.3 | 14.8 | 11.4 | 7.5 | 8.5 | Sales/Net Fixed Assets | 17.1 | 15.5 |
| 212.6 | 46.3 | 8.2 | 5.4 | 5.1 | 5.5 |  | 8.0 | 7.7 |
| 8.1 | 18.6 | 4.5 | 3.6 | 3.9 | 2.0 |  | 4.3 | 4.4 |
| 6.4 | 4.7 | 3.3 | 2.8 | 2.4 | 2.1 | Sales/Total Assets | 3.4 | 3.4 |
| 3.3 | 4.0 | 2.6 | 2.2 | 2.0 | 1.9 |  | 2.5 | 2.5 |
| 2.5 | 3.5 | 2.0 | 1.7 | 1.1 | 1.0 |  | 2.0 | 2.0 |
|  | .2 | 1.3 | 1.6 | 1.8 |  | % Depr., Dep., Amort./Sales | 1.3 | 1.4 |
|  | (26)   .5 | (96)   2.1 | (71)   2.3 | 2.6 |  |  | (200)   2.3 | (209)   2.3 |
|  | 1.8 | 3.2 | 4.0 | 5.0 |  |  | 3.2 | 3.4 |
|  | 3.2 | 1.8 | 1.6 |  |  | % Officers', Directors' Owners' Comp/Sales | 1.4 | 1.1 |
|  | (20)   4.9 | (35)   3.2 | (12)   3.6 |  |  |  | (77)   2.7 | (70)   2.9 |
|  | 1.8 | 4.9 | 5.5 |  |  |  | 6.5 | 5.8 |
| 15889M | 149930M | 1524242M | 3574109M | 1269254M | 2507350M | Net Sales ($) | 7785557M | 8162256M |
| 2941M | 36680M | 576994M | 1605305M | 663822M | 1451910M | Total Assets ($) | 4055056M | 3789712M |

© RMA 2012

M = $ thousand    MM = $ million
See Pages 9 through 22 for Explanation of Ratios and Data

**Comparative Historical Data** | | | | **Current Data Sorted by Sales** | | | | | |

| 4/1/09-3/31/10 ALL | 4/1/10-3/31/11 ALL | 4/1/11-3/31/12 ALL | Type of Statement | 41 (4/1-9/30/11) 0-1MM | 1-3MM | 200 (10/1/11-3/31/12) 3-5MM | 5-10MM | 10-25MM | 25MM & OVER |
|---|---|---|---|---|---|---|---|---|---|
| 32 | 34 | 34 | Unqualified | 1 | | 1 | 2 | 7 | 23 |
| 73 | 69 | 77 | Reviewed | | | 4 | 14 | 32 | 27 |
| 25 | 31 | 27 | Compiled | | 2 | 5 | 11 | 5 | 4 |
| 14 | 21 | 30 | Tax Returns | 5 | 5 | 5 | 12 | 3 | |
| 72 | 91 | 73 | Other | 2 | 1 | 3 | 5 | 22 | 40 |
| 216 | 246 | 241 | **NUMBER OF STATEMENTS** | 8 | 8 | 18 | 44 | 69 | 94 |
| % | % | % | **ASSETS** | % | % | % | % | % | % |
| 6.9 | 7.0 | 7.2 | Cash & Equivalents | | | 13.5 | 8.1 | 7.6 | 4.9 |
| 28.0 | 29.6 | 28.0 | Trade Receivables (net) | | | 31.9 | 33.0 | 26.0 | 26.0 |
| 15.9 | 17.7 | 17.4 | Inventory | | | 12.8 | 16.7 | 16.4 | 18.9 |
| 1.8 | 1.9 | 1.6 | All Other Current | | | .9 | .8 | 1.9 | 2.2 |
| 52.5 | 56.2 | 54.1 | Total Current | | | 59.0 | 58.5 | 51.9 | 52.0 |
| 36.0 | 32.5 | 33.4 | Fixed Assets (net) | | | 24.0 | 27.2 | 39.1 | 36.1 |
| 4.3 | 4.5 | 4.2 | Intangibles (net) | | | 4.4 | 4.0 | 3.0 | 4.8 |
| 7.3 | 6.7 | 8.3 | All Other Non-Current | | | 12.6 | 10.3 | 5.9 | 7.1 |
| 100.0 | 100.0 | 100.0 | Total | | | 100.0 | 100.0 | 100.0 | 100.0 |
| | | | **LIABILITIES** | | | | | | |
| 9.0 | 9.4 | 8.4 | Notes Payable-Short Term | | | 6.6 | 6.5 | 6.7 | 9.9 |
| 5.2 | 4.2 | 4.2 | Cur. Mat.-L.T.D. | | | 4.1 | 4.1 | 4.0 | 5.1 |
| 18.0 | 20.2 | 16.9 | Trade Payables | | | 21.8 | 20.4 | 14.5 | 16.2 |
| .2 | .1 | .1 | Income Taxes Payable | | | .0 | .0 | .1 | .1 |
| 5.8 | 8.1 | 7.4 | All Other Current | | | 11.2 | 4.8 | 6.2 | 7.4 |
| 38.3 | 42.1 | 37.0 | Total Current | | | 43.7 | 35.9 | 31.5 | 38.7 |
| 19.9 | 18.7 | 18.8 | Long-Term Debt | | | 20.7 | 15.0 | 20.4 | 19.5 |
| .9 | .8 | 1.0 | Deferred Taxes | | | .7 | .2 | 1.0 | 1.6 |
| 7.3 | 5.7 | 6.5 | All Other Non-Current | | | 7.4 | 5.7 | 4.7 | 4.8 |
| 33.6 | 32.8 | 36.7 | Net Worth | | | 27.5 | 43.2 | 42.4 | 35.4 |
| 100.0 | 100.0 | 100.0 | Total Liabilities & Net Worth | | | 100.0 | 100.0 | 100.0 | 100.0 |
| | | | **INCOME DATA** | | | | | | |
| 100.0 | 100.0 | 100.0 | Net Sales | | | 100.0 | 100.0 | 100.0 | 100.0 |
| 24.0 | 26.9 | 26.5 | Gross Profit | | | 31.9 | 27.4 | 26.9 | 22.5 |
| 21.8 | 22.3 | 21.9 | Operating Expenses | | | 28.8 | 24.8 | 21.9 | 17.2 |
| 2.2 | 4.5 | 4.6 | Operating Profit | | | 3.0 | 2.7 | 4.9 | 5.4 |
| .6 | .4 | .4 | All Other Expenses (net) | | | .9 | .0 | .1 | .7 |
| 1.6 | 4.1 | 4.2 | Profit Before Taxes | | | 2.2 | 2.6 | 4.8 | 4.7 |
| | | | **RATIOS** | | | | | | |
| 2.3 | 2.2 | 2.4 | Current | | | 4.4 | 3.3 | 2.7 | 2.1 |
| 1.3 | 1.4 | 1.5 | | | | 1.3 | 1.5 | 1.8 | 1.3 |
| 1.0 | 1.0 | 1.1 | | | | 1.0 | 1.2 | 1.2 | 1.0 |
| 1.5 | 1.5 | 1.7 | Quick | | | 3.4 | 2.0 | 2.0 | 1.3 |
| .9 | .9 | 1.0 | | | | 1.0 | 1.1 | 1.2 | .8 |
| .6 | .6 | .6 | | | | .7 | .7 | .6 | .6 |
| 32  11.3 | 32  11.5 | 31  11.7 | Sales/Receivables | | | 29  12.5 | 32  11.4 | 31  11.7 | 31  11.8 |
| 39  9.3 | 41  9.0 | 38  9.7 | | | | 35  10.3 | 38  9.6 | 36  10.1 | 40  9.1 |
| 47  7.8 | 48  7.6 | 45  8.1 | | | | 41  9.0 | 45  8.2 | 43  8.4 | 48  7.6 |
| 18  20.1 | 18  20.0 | 17  21.2 | Cost of Sales/Inventory | | | 6  58.1 | 14  26.3 | 19  18.9 | 22  16.5 |
| 28  12.9 | 30  12.1 | 30  12.1 | | | | 15  23.7 | 22  16.4 | 30  12.3 | 36  10.1 |
| 42  8.6 | 47  7.8 | 46  8.0 | | | | 49  7.4 | 41  9.0 | 45  8.2 | 47  7.7 |
| 16  22.6 | 19  19.1 | 16  23.2 | Cost of Sales/Payables | | | 7  55.1 | 14  26.6 | 14  26.5 | 18  20.1 |
| 30  12.3 | 31  11.7 | 29  12.5 | | | | 30  12.3 | 31  11.7 | 23  16.0 | 33  11.1 |
| 46  8.0 | 49  7.5 | 46  7.9 | | | | 54  6.7 | 49  7.5 | 41  8.8 | 43  8.4 |
| 7.4 | 8.2 | 7.4 | Sales/Working Capital | | | 8.8 | 7.7 | 6.8 | 7.5 |
| 20.7 | 19.5 | 14.9 | | | | 25.0 | 13.9 | 11.7 | 21.7 |
| -302.6 | -986.1 | 125.1 | | | | NM | 54.0 | 34.2 | -129.0 |
| 7.6 | 16.4 | 16.0 | EBIT/Interest | | | 13.3 | 11.3 | 17.1 | 17.2 |
| (206)  2.8 | (228)  5.0 | (221)  6.1 | | | | (17)  2.1 | (39)  5.3 | (65)  5.3 | (87)  6.9 |
| 1.0 | 2.8 | 2.4 | | | | .0 | 1.3 | 3.0 | 2.8 |
| 4.5 | 6.1 | 5.6 | Net Profit + Depr., Dep., Amort./Cur. Mat. L/T/D | | | | 17.2 | 9.8 | 4.8 |
| (71)  2.3 | (83)  2.9 | (84)  3.0 | | | | | (13)  3.0 | (17)  3.6 | (47)  3.0 |
| 1.3 | 1.4 | 1.5 | | | | | 1.1 | 1.3 | 1.8 |
| .6 | .5 | .5 | Fixed/Worth | | | .2 | .2 | .4 | .6 |
| 1.1 | 1.1 | 1.0 | | | | .8 | .6 | 1.2 | 1.2 |
| 2.8 | 2.7 | 2.1 | | | | -2.8 | 2.6 | 1.8 | 2.1 |
| .9 | .9 | .6 | Debt/Worth | | | .4 | .5 | .5 | .8 |
| 1.9 | 2.0 | 1.9 | | | | 3.3 | 1.7 | 1.6 | 2.0 |
| 5.9 | 5.7 | 5.1 | | | | -13.4 | 4.0 | 2.9 | 4.6 |
| 31.1 | 47.7 | 41.6 | % Profit Before Taxes/Tangible Net Worth | | | 54.5 | 30.1 | 37.6 | 48.8 |
| (185)  12.2 | (212)  23.9 | (208)  23.1 | | | | (12)  1.7 | (38)  13.9 | (64)  21.3 | (85)  28.1 |
| 2.6 | 11.3 | 11.3 | | | | -1.8 | 2.9 | 13.3 | 14.4 |
| 9.3 | 16.8 | 16.6 | % Profit Before Taxes/Total Assets | | | 34.5 | 14.7 | 15.4 | 16.4 |
| 3.8 | 8.2 | 7.6 | | | | 1.5 | 5.8 | 9.6 | 7.6 |
| -.5 | 3.4 | 3.1 | | | | -1.4 | 1.1 | 3.1 | 4.4 |
| 15.0 | 20.9 | 18.6 | Sales/Net Fixed Assets | | | 77.1 | 41.6 | 10.8 | 13.4 |
| 7.3 | 8.4 | 8.2 | | | | 34.0 | 10.8 | 7.0 | 6.7 |
| 4.0 | 4.6 | 4.6 | | | | 7.4 | 5.5 | 3.7 | 4.6 |
| 3.1 | 3.5 | 3.5 | Sales/Total Assets | | | 4.9 | 3.8 | 2.9 | 3.2 |
| 2.4 | 2.5 | 2.5 | | | | 3.7 | 3.0 | 2.4 | 2.4 |
| 1.8 | 1.9 | 1.9 | | | | 1.8 | 2.0 | 1.9 | 1.9 |
| 1.6 | 1.3 | 1.2 | % Depr., Dep., Amort./Sales | | | .2 | .6 | 1.5 | 1.6 |
| (199)  2.5 | (223)  2.2 | (214)  2.1 | | | | (15)  1.3 | (40)  1.8 | (64)  2.3 | (88)  2.1 |
| 3.7 | 3.2 | 3.3 | | | | 3.3 | 3.2 | 3.3 | 3.7 |
| 1.6 | 1.3 | 2.0 | % Officers', Directors' Owners' Comp/Sales | | | 3.5 | 3.7 | 1.6 | .7 |
| (69)  3.2 | (78)  3.3 | (73)  3.7 | | | | (10)  4.9 | (21)  4.8 | (20)  2.7 | (15)  2.3 |
| 6.3 | 5.6 | 5.5 | | | | 6.3 | 5.8 | 3.6 | 5.4 |
| 7401077M | 9779006M | 9040774M | Net Sales ($) | 3848M | 15736M | 73503M | 333048M | 1113337M | 7501302M |
| 3754560M | 4541492M | 4337652M | Total Assets ($) | 2057M | 3428M | 29458M | 265436M | 514106M | 3523167M |

© RMA 2012

M = $ thousand    MM = $ million
See Pages 9 through 22 for Explanation of Ratios and Data

## Current Data Sorted by Assets     Comparative Historical Data

Type of Statement periods (Current Data): 13 (4/1-9/30/11)    54 (10/1/11-3/31/12)

| Type of Statement | 0-500M | 500M-2MM | 2-10MM | 10-50MM | 50-100MM | 100-250MM | 4/1/07-3/31/08 ALL | 4/1/08-3/31/09 ALL |
|---|---|---|---|---|---|---|---|---|
| Unqualified | | | 2 | 7 | 3 | | 14 | 14 |
| Reviewed | | 1 | 9 | 7 | | | 11 | 14 |
| Compiled | 1 | 2 | 4 | | | | 7 | 4 |
| Tax Returns | | 1 | 2 | | | | 3 | 4 |
| Other | | 2 | 5 | 13 | 6 | 2 | 26 | 27 |
| **NUMBER OF STATEMENTS** | 1 | 6 | 22 | 27 | 9 | 2 | 61 | 63 |

| | 0-500M % | 500M-2MM % | 2-10MM % | 10-50MM % | 50-100MM % | 100-250MM % | 4/1/07-3/31/08 ALL % | 4/1/08-3/31/09 ALL % |
|---|---|---|---|---|---|---|---|---|
| **ASSETS** | | | | | | | | |
| Cash & Equivalents | | | 9.4 | 4.0 | | | 6.3 | 5.1 |
| Trade Receivables (net) | | | 27.6 | 19.5 | | | 23.8 | 21.0 |
| Inventory | | | 24.0 | 21.7 | | | 21.7 | 21.4 |
| All Other Current | | | 1.1 | 3.0 | | | 1.1 | 1.1 |
| Total Current | | | 62.0 | 48.2 | | | 53.0 | 48.5 |
| Fixed Assets (net) | | | 31.4 | 45.3 | | | 40.2 | 42.1 |
| Intangibles (net) | | | 2.8 | 1.6 | | | 3.4 | 4.3 |
| All Other Non-Current | | | 3.7 | 4.9 | | | 3.4 | 5.1 |
| Total | | | 100.0 | 100.0 | | | 100.0 | 100.0 |
| **LIABILITIES** | | | | | | | | |
| Notes Payable-Short Term | | | 11.2 | 8.8 | | | 8.0 | 9.3 |
| Cur. Mat.-L.T.D. | | | 5.7 | 5.4 | | | 5.8 | 5.6 |
| Trade Payables | | | 19.1 | 10.5 | | | 12.9 | 11.9 |
| Income Taxes Payable | | | .2 | .2 | | | .0 | .0 |
| All Other Current | | | 7.1 | 7.6 | | | 6.2 | 5.4 |
| Total Current | | | 43.2 | 32.4 | | | 32.8 | 32.1 |
| Long-Term Debt | | | 19.8 | 23.9 | | | 22.5 | 24.6 |
| Deferred Taxes | | | .6 | 2.1 | | | .8 | .7 |
| All Other Non-Current | | | 2.8 | 4.0 | | | 5.6 | 3.6 |
| Net Worth | | | 33.6 | 37.6 | | | 38.1 | 38.9 |
| Total Liabilities & Net Worth | | | 100.0 | 100.0 | | | 100.0 | 100.0 |
| **INCOME DATA** | | | | | | | | |
| Net Sales | | | 100.0 | 100.0 | | | 100.0 | 100.0 |
| Gross Profit | | | 28.8 | 23.7 | | | 22.2 | 23.2 |
| Operating Expenses | | | 23.0 | 17.0 | | | 18.0 | 18.3 |
| Operating Profit | | | 5.7 | 6.6 | | | 4.2 | 4.9 |
| All Other Expenses (net) | | | .7 | 1.2 | | | 1.8 | 1.5 |
| Profit Before Taxes | | | 5.1 | 5.5 | | | 2.4 | 3.4 |
| **RATIOS** | | | | | | | | |
| Current | | | 3.3 | 2.6 | | | 2.4 | 3.0 |
| | | | 1.4 | 1.4 | | | 1.6 | 1.5 |
| | | | 1.1 | 1.0 | | | 1.1 | 1.1 |
| Quick | | | 2.2 | 1.7 | | | 1.3 | 1.4 |
| | | | .9 | .7 | | | .8 | .8 |
| | | | .6 | .4 | | | .5 | .5 |
| Sales/Receivables | | | 37  9.9 | 35  10.5 | | | 29  12.6 | 28  12.8 |
| | | | 42  8.7 | 42  8.7 | | | 36  10.1 | 35  10.3 |
| | | | 54  6.8 | 51  7.1 | | | 46  8.0 | 43  8.5 |
| Cost of Sales/Inventory | | | 29  12.7 | 46  7.9 | | | 31  11.7 | 28  13.0 |
| | | | 47  7.7 | 62  5.9 | | | 49  7.5 | 54  6.7 |
| | | | 99  3.7 | 79  4.6 | | | 71  5.2 | 70  5.2 |
| Cost of Sales/Payables | | | 12  29.9 | 11  33.6 | | | 14  25.7 | 15  24.6 |
| | | | 28  13.1 | 27  13.5 | | | 23  15.8 | 24  14.9 |
| | | | 52  7.0 | 46  8.0 | | | 35  10.3 | 33  11.0 |
| Sales/Working Capital | | | 4.6 | 4.6 | | | 5.8 | 5.1 |
| | | | 12.8 | 11.3 | | | 17.3 | 12.9 |
| | | | 49.9 | 232.4 | | | 65.8 | 65.4 |
| EBIT/Interest | | | 9.3 | 15.1 | | | 6.9 | 8.5 |
| | | | (20) 5.1 | (26) 4.3 | | | (57) 2.8 | (60) 2.7 |
| | | | 2.8 | 1.8 | | | 1.4 | .9 |
| Net Profit + Depr., Dep., Amort./Cur. Mat. L/T/D | | | | 4.3 | | | 4.4 | 5.9 |
| | | | | (14) 1.5 | | | (27) 2.2 | (26) 2.1 |
| | | | | 1.1 | | | 1.1 | .9 |
| Fixed/Worth | | | .4 | .8 | | | .7 | .7 |
| | | | 1.0 | 1.2 | | | 1.2 | 1.3 |
| | | | 4.1 | 2.4 | | | 2.6 | 3.9 |
| Debt/Worth | | | .6 | .9 | | | .9 | .7 |
| | | | 2.0 | 1.9 | | | 1.9 | 2.0 |
| | | | 5.5 | 3.5 | | | 4.8 | 6.3 |
| % Profit Before Taxes/Tangible Net Worth | | | 43.1 | 33.4 | | | 37.4 | 28.5 |
| | | | (18) 17.4 | (24) 19.5 | | | (55) 17.1 | (56) 15.7 |
| | | | 10.5 | 10.1 | | | 6.0 | -1.4 |
| % Profit Before Taxes/Total Assets | | | 17.1 | 17.0 | | | 11.4 | 12.6 |
| | | | 9.3 | 7.5 | | | 4.8 | 5.6 |
| | | | 5.0 | 2.4 | | | 1.6 | -.3 |
| Sales/Net Fixed Assets | | | 11.8 | 4.4 | | | 8.1 | 7.5 |
| | | | 9.4 | 3.7 | | | 5.0 | 4.9 |
| | | | 4.0 | 2.8 | | | 3.2 | 3.2 |
| Sales/Total Assets | | | 3.1 | 1.9 | | | 2.6 | 2.5 |
| | | | 2.2 | 1.7 | | | 2.0 | 1.9 |
| | | | 1.6 | 1.4 | | | 1.6 | 1.5 |
| % Depr., Dep., Amort./Sales | | | 1.6 | 2.4 | | | 2.3 | 1.9 |
| | | | (21) 3.2 | 3.7 | | | (55) 3.5 | (58) 3.3 |
| | | | 5.2 | 5.5 | | | 5.4 | 4.7 |
| % Officers', Directors' Owners' Comp/Sales | | | | | | | .9 | .8 |
| | | | | | | | (13) 2.3 | (13) 1.3 |
| | | | | | | | 3.2 | 2.4 |
| Net Sales ($) | 733M | 22034M | 289898M | 1171428M | 1046040M | 471942M | 1913250M | 2022448M |
| Total Assets ($) | 429M | 6837M | 136399M | 724738M | 607280M | 285768M | 1014068M | 1113274M |

M = $ thousand    MM = $ million
See Pages 9 through 22 for Explanation of Ratios and Data

## Comparative Historical Data | Current Data Sorted by Sales

| 4/1/09-3/31/10 ALL | 4/1/10-3/31/11 ALL | 4/1/11-3/31/12 ALL | Type of Statement | 0-1MM | 1-3MM | 3-5MM | 5-10MM | 10-25MM | 25MM & OVER |
|---|---|---|---|---|---|---|---|---|---|
| 12 | 15 | 12 | Unqualified | | | | | 5 | 7 |
| 18 | 20 | 17 | Reviewed | | | | 4 | 9 | 4 |
| 4 | 6 | 7 | Compiled | 1 | 1 | | 3 | 2 | |
| 4 | 4 | 3 | Tax Returns | | 1 | | 2 | | |
| 28 | 23 | 28 | Other | 1 | | 1 | | 5 | 21 |
| | | | | 13 (4/1-9/30/11) | | | 54 (10/1/11-3/31/12) | | |
| **66** | **68** | **67** | **NUMBER OF STATEMENTS** | **1** | **3** | **1** | **9** | **21** | **32** |
| % | % | % | **ASSETS** | % | % | % | % | % | % |
| 4.9 | 6.8 | 6.3 | Cash & Equivalents | | | | | 8.9 | 4.0 |
| 21.4 | 22.7 | 23.7 | Trade Receivables (net) | | | | | 25.7 | 19.8 |
| 21.9 | 20.4 | 22.6 | Inventory | | | | | 20.9 | 21.5 |
| 2.9 | 2.6 | 1.8 | All Other Current | | | | | 1.3 | 2.9 |
| 51.1 | 52.5 | 54.5 | Total Current | | | | | 56.8 | 48.2 |
| 41.1 | 38.7 | 36.1 | Fixed Assets (net) | | | | | 35.9 | 42.3 |
| 2.9 | 2.9 | 4.9 | Intangibles (net) | | | | | 2.6 | 5.0 |
| 4.9 | 5.9 | 4.5 | All Other Non-Current | | | | | 4.7 | 4.6 |
| 100.0 | 100.0 | 100.0 | Total | | | | | 100.0 | 100.0 |
| | | | **LIABILITIES** | | | | | | |
| 10.5 | 8.5 | 9.9 | Notes Payable-Short Term | | | | | 10.3 | 9.9 |
| 5.5 | 4.9 | 4.8 | Cur. Mat.-L.T.D. | | | | | 5.2 | 4.5 |
| 13.1 | 11.1 | 14.4 | Trade Payables | | | | | 13.9 | 10.9 |
| .1 | .1 | .1 | Income Taxes Payable | | | | | .2 | .1 |
| 5.8 | 8.8 | 7.1 | All Other Current | | | | | 6.0 | 7.0 |
| 35.1 | 33.5 | 36.3 | Total Current | | | | | 35.5 | 32.4 |
| 25.6 | 20.2 | 21.9 | Long-Term Debt | | | | | 20.3 | 23.9 |
| .8 | 1.3 | 1.2 | Deferred Taxes | | | | | 1.3 | 1.6 |
| 5.4 | 3.2 | 4.4 | All Other Non-Current | | | | | 4.2 | 5.1 |
| 33.0 | 41.9 | 36.2 | Net Worth | | | | | 38.7 | 37.0 |
| 100.0 | 100.0 | 100.0 | Total Liabilities & Net Worth | | | | | 100.0 | 100.0 |
| | | | **INCOME DATA** | | | | | | |
| 100.0 | 100.0 | 100.0 | Net Sales | | | | | 100.0 | 100.0 |
| 24.1 | 25.8 | 25.8 | Gross Profit | | | | | 25.3 | 21.5 |
| 20.0 | 19.1 | 19.9 | Operating Expenses | | | | | 19.3 | 15.8 |
| 4.1 | 6.7 | 5.8 | Operating Profit | | | | | 6.0 | 5.7 |
| 1.2 | .9 | .7 | All Other Expenses (net) | | | | | .7 | .8 |
| 2.9 | 5.8 | 5.1 | Profit Before Taxes | | | | | 5.4 | 5.0 |
| | | | **RATIOS** | | | | | | |
| 2.4 | 3.2 | 2.8 | | | | | | 3.4 | 2.3 |
| 1.4 | 1.5 | 1.4 | Current | | | | | 1.4 | 1.4 |
| 1.1 | 1.1 | 1.1 | | | | | | 1.0 | 1.0 |
| 1.2 | 1.6 | 1.7 | | | | | | 1.9 | 1.2 |
| .7 | .8 | .8 | Quick | | | | | .9 | .7 |
| .5 | .6 | .5 | | | | | | .6 | .4 |
| 29  12.5 | 32  11.5 | 33  11.0 | | | | | | 34  10.7 | 32  11.5 |
| 38  9.7 | 39  9.3 | 41  8.8 | Sales/Receivables | | | | | 41  8.9 | 42  8.7 |
| 47  7.8 | 48  7.6 | 51  7.1 | | | | | | 51  7.1 | 51  7.2 |
| 38  9.7 | 36  10.1 | 38  9.5 | | | | | | 30  12.1 | 41  8.8 |
| 52  7.0 | 50  7.3 | 59  6.2 | Cost of Sales/Inventory | | | | | 47  7.7 | 60  6.1 |
| 68  5.3 | 68  5.3 | 81  4.5 | | | | | | 87  4.2 | 69  5.3 |
| 16  23.3 | 14  25.5 | 14  26.3 | | | | | | 11  32.4 | 13  27.8 |
| 29  12.6 | 25  14.7 | 29  12.6 | Cost of Sales/Payables | | | | | 23  16.0 | 30  12.1 |
| 44  8.3 | 38  9.6 | 44  8.3 | | | | | | 42  8.7 | 42  8.6 |
| 6.2 | 5.7 | 4.6 | | | | | | 4.1 | 6.7 |
| 16.4 | 12.1 | 12.9 | Sales/Working Capital | | | | | 12.9 | 15.1 |
| 39.7 | 66.4 | 99.9 | | | | | | NM | 120.1 |
| 6.7 | 21.7 | 13.6 | | | | | | 36.1 | 14.1 |
| (64)  3.2 | (63)  7.1 | (63)  4.9 | EBIT/Interest | | | | | 6.4 | (30)  4.1 |
| 1.3 | 2.8 | 2.3 | | | | | | 1.8 | 2.2 |
| 3.8 | 5.8 | 3.9 | Net Profit + Depr., Dep., | | | | | 4.5 | 4.0 |
| (27)  2.4 | (29)  2.7 | (32)  2.0 | Amort./Cur. Mat. L/T/D | | | | | (10)  2.1 | (19)  2.0 |
| 1.2 | 1.6 | 1.5 | | | | | | 1.4 | 1.4 |
| .7 | .5 | .5 | | | | | | .5 | .8 |
| 1.3 | 1.0 | 1.2 | Fixed/Worth | | | | | .9 | 1.4 |
| 2.8 | 2.3 | 3.2 | | | | | | 3.8 | 2.4 |
| .8 | .6 | .9 | | | | | | .6 | 1.2 |
| 2.0 | 1.8 | 2.1 | Debt/Worth | | | | | 1.9 | 2.2 |
| 5.0 | 3.9 | 5.1 | | | | | | 5.1 | 3.8 |
| 34.4 | 46.3 | 32.6 | % Profit Before Taxes/Tangible | | | | | 37.1 | 31.7 |
| (57)  18.3 | (61)  28.8 | (56)  19.5 | Net Worth | | | | | (18)  19.0 | (27)  19.1 |
| 1.1 | 13.1 | 11.0 | | | | | | 11.4 | 10.8 |
| 11.4 | 17.0 | 16.1 | % Profit Before Taxes/Total | | | | | 15.6 | 16.4 |
| 6.1 | 11.4 | 8.6 | Assets | | | | | 10.1 | 6.5 |
| 2.0 | 4.5 | 3.2 | | | | | | 3.1 | 2.5 |
| 7.3 | 8.7 | 10.6 | | | | | | 10.6 | 5.5 |
| 4.5 | 4.9 | 4.5 | Sales/Net Fixed Assets | | | | | 5.5 | 3.9 |
| 3.2 | 3.3 | 3.4 | | | | | | 3.6 | 2.9 |
| 2.5 | 2.4 | 2.3 | | | | | | 2.5 | 1.9 |
| 1.9 | 1.9 | 1.8 | Sales/Total Assets | | | | | 2.1 | 1.7 |
| 1.6 | 1.6 | 1.5 | | | | | | 1.6 | 1.5 |
| 2.2 | 2.1 | 1.8 | | | | | | 1.8 | 2.2 |
| (60)  3.3 | (62)  2.9 | (65)  3.0 | % Depr., Dep., Amort./Sales | | | | | (20)  4.0 | 3.1 |
| 4.5 | 4.2 | 4.7 | | | | | | 5.9 | 4.4 |
| .8 | 1.3 | 1.1 | % Officers', Directors' | | | | | | |
| (11)  3.5 | (14)  2.2 | (15)  1.3 | Owners' Comp/Sales | | | | | | |
| 6.3 | 4.6 | 6.9 | | | | | | | |
| 2476104M | 2593453M | 3002075M | Net Sales ($) | 733M | 7361M | 3808M | 66411M | 356015M | 2567747M |
| 1485675M | 1537303M | 1761451M | Total Assets ($) | 429M | 2546M | 1252M | 35845M | 195864M | 1525515M |

M = $ thousand    MM = $ million
See Pages 9 through 22 for Explanation of Ratios and Data

## Current Data Sorted by Assets | Comparative Historical Data

| 0-500M | 500M-2MM | 2-10MM | 10-50MM | 50-100MM | 100-250MM | Type of Statement | 14 / 4/1/07-3/31/08 ALL | 10 / 4/1/08-3/31/09 ALL |
|---|---|---|---|---|---|---|---|---|
| | | 1 | 2 | | | Unqualified | 14 | 10 |
| | | 2 | 8 | | | Reviewed | 23 | 16 |
| | | 4 | 1 | | | Compiled | 1 | 3 |
| 2 | | 2 | 2 | | | Tax Returns | 1 | 2 |
| 1 | | 4 | 4 | | | Other | 15 | 16 |
| | 7 (4/1-9/30/11) | | 26 (10/1/11-3/31/12) | 1 | 1 | | 15 | 16 |
| 3 | | 13 | 15 | 1 | 1 | **NUMBER OF STATEMENTS** | 54 | 47 |
| % | % | % | % | % | % | **ASSETS** | % | % |
| | | 6.9 | 5.2 | | | Cash & Equivalents | 5.7 | 5.6 |
| | | 28.1 | 27.4 | | | Trade Receivables (net) | 24.0 | 26.5 |
| | | 22.1 | 15.7 | | | Inventory | 19.2 | 20.3 |
| | | .5 | 1.7 | | | All Other Current | 1.4 | 1.9 |
| | | 57.6 | 50.0 | | | Total Current | 50.3 | 54.4 |
| | | 35.7 | 43.8 | | | Fixed Assets (net) | 39.5 | 36.2 |
| | | 4.7 | .4 | | | Intangibles (net) | 4.0 | 4.1 |
| | | 2.1 | 5.8 | | | All Other Non-Current | 6.3 | 5.3 |
| | | 100.0 | 100.0 | | | Total | 100.0 | 100.0 |
| | | | | | | **LIABILITIES** | | |
| | | 8.1 | 5.3 | | | Notes Payable-Short Term | 7.9 | 8.8 |
| | | 5.4 | 5.6 | | | Cur. Mat.-L.T.D. | 5.6 | 6.6 |
| | | 17.6 | 15.3 | | | Trade Payables | 12.9 | 17.1 |
| | | .2 | .0 | | | Income Taxes Payable | .7 | .0 |
| | | 6.8 | 4.6 | | | All Other Current | 5.4 | 8.7 |
| | | 38.1 | 30.9 | | | Total Current | 32.5 | 41.2 |
| | | 19.1 | 22.3 | | | Long-Term Debt | 22.5 | 20.6 |
| | | .8 | .8 | | | Deferred Taxes | 1.2 | 1.1 |
| | | 5.0 | 7.2 | | | All Other Non-Current | 2.5 | 5.2 |
| | | 37.0 | 38.8 | | | Net Worth | 41.3 | 31.8 |
| | | 100.0 | 100.0 | | | Total Liabilties & Net Worth | 100.0 | 100.0 |
| | | | | | | **INCOME DATA** | | |
| | | 100.0 | 100.0 | | | Net Sales | 100.0 | 100.0 |
| | | 28.5 | 20.6 | | | Gross Profit | 24.1 | 20.6 |
| | | 24.6 | 16.8 | | | Operating Expenses | 17.2 | 17.6 |
| | | 4.0 | 3.8 | | | Operating Profit | 6.9 | 3.0 |
| | | .6 | .4 | | | All Other Expenses (net) | 1.5 | 1.7 |
| | | 3.4 | 3.5 | | | Profit Before Taxes | 5.4 | 1.3 |
| | | | | | | **RATIOS** | | |
| | | 2.4 | 2.7 | | | | 2.4 | 2.4 |
| | | 1.6 | 1.8 | | | Current | 1.6 | 1.6 |
| | | 1.2 | .9 | | | | 1.1 | .9 |
| | | 1.8 | 1.8 | | | | 1.5 | 1.5 |
| | | .9 | 1.3 | | | Quick | .9 | .9 |
| | | .5 | .7 | | | | .5 | .5 |
| | | 29   12.5 | 31   11.7 | | | | 28   12.9 | 28   13.1 |
| | | 44   8.3 | 38   9.5 | | | Sales/Receivables | 37   9.9 | 36   10.1 |
| | | 55   6.6 | 51   7.1 | | | | 47   7.8 | 47   7.8 |
| | | 25   14.4 | 20   17.9 | | | | 22   16.7 | 22   16.3 |
| | | 40   9.1 | 29   12.4 | | | Cost of Sales/Inventory | 31   11.7 | 31   11.8 |
| | | 66   5.5 | 37   9.8 | | | | 57   6.4 | 48   7.7 |
| | | 22   16.9 | 13   28.1 | | | | 14   25.5 | 14   26.6 |
| | | 29   12.7 | 28   12.9 | | | Cost of Sales/Payables | 23   15.9 | 25   14.3 |
| | | 50   7.3 | 42   8.6 | | | | 40   9.2 | 39   9.3 |
| | | 6.4 | 6.8 | | | | 6.7 | 6.9 |
| | | 14.3 | 11.5 | | | Sales/Working Capital | 14.0 | 15.3 |
| | | 40.6 | -45.0 | | | | 43.6 | -85.4 |
| | | 16.5 | 12.7 | | | | 11.3 | 8.3 |
| | | 3.4 | (14) 5.0 | | | EBIT/Interest | (52) 4.2 | (46) 3.9 |
| | | 2.2 | 1.0 | | | | 1.8 | 1.0 |
| | | | | | | Net Profit + Depr., Dep., | 6.1 | 2.8 |
| | | | | | | Amort./Cur. Mat. L/T/D | (27) 1.9 | (17) 1.5 |
| | | | | | | | .9 | .3 |
| | | .5 | .7 | | | | .6 | .7 |
| | | .8 | 1.1 | | | Fixed/Worth | 1.1 | 1.3 |
| | | 2.0 | 2.2 | | | | 2.0 | 1.7 |
| | | .9 | .8 | | | | .7 | .8 |
| | | 1.6 | 1.6 | | | Debt/Worth | 1.7 | 2.2 |
| | | 3.5 | 3.0 | | | | 3.3 | 4.0 |
| | | 38.7 | 42.3 | | | % Profit Before Taxes/Tangible | 39.4 | 39.7 |
| | | (12) 11.0 | 17.4 | | | Net Worth | (49) 23.8 | (43) 14.8 |
| | | 6.4 | .7 | | | | 7.6 | 6.6 |
| | | 13.6 | 15.2 | | | % Profit Before Taxes/Total | 15.5 | 12.4 |
| | | 5.0 | 6.8 | | | Assets | 7.4 | 6.0 |
| | | 2.2 | .2 | | | | 2.2 | -1.5 |
| | | 12.0 | 8.5 | | | | 8.8 | 13.6 |
| | | 5.3 | 5.0 | | | Sales/Net Fixed Assets | 5.4 | 6.1 |
| | | 4.0 | 3.8 | | | | 3.6 | 3.8 |
| | | 2.8 | 2.7 | | | | 2.8 | 3.0 |
| | | 2.5 | 2.2 | | | Sales/Total Assets | 2.1 | 2.5 |
| | | 1.8 | 1.9 | | | | 1.7 | 1.8 |
| | | 1.9 | 2.1 | | | | 1.8 | 1.5 |
| | | (11) 3.6 | 3.2 | | | % Depr., Dep., Amort./Sales | (52) 2.7 | (42) 2.8 |
| | | 6.8 | 4.4 | | | | 3.8 | 3.7 |
| | | | | | | | 1.0 | 1.6 |
| | | | | | | % Officers', Directors' | (19) 2.1 | (17) 2.4 |
| | | | | | | Owners' Comp/Sales | 2.7 | 6.5 |
| | 18614M | 158489M | 656301M | 93325M | 245422M | Net Sales ($) | 1992769M | 1678317M |
| | 4945M | 64950M | 290751M | 71381M | 112769M | Total Assets ($) | 983798M | 812598M |

Note: The 0-500M column is marked **DATA NOT AVAILABLE**.

M = $ thousand   MM = $ million
See Pages 9 through 22 for Explanation of Ratios and Data

## Comparative Historical Data | Current Data Sorted by Sales

| | 4/1/09-3/31/10 ALL | 4/1/10-3/31/11 ALL | 4/1/11-3/31/12 ALL | Type of Statement | 0-1MM | 1-3MM | 3-5MM | 5-10MM | 10-25MM | 25MM & OVER |
|---|---|---|---|---|---|---|---|---|---|---|
| | 3 | 5 | 3 | Unqualified | | | | | | 2 |
| | 10 | 12 | 10 | Reviewed | | | | 1 | 1 | 8 |
| | 3 | 4 | 5 | Compiled | | 1 | | 1 | 2 | 1 |
| | 2 | 2 | 4 | Tax Returns | | | 1 | 2 | | |
| | 18 | 13 | 11 | Other | | 1 | | 1 | 4 | 6 |
| | | | | | | 7 (4/1-9/30/11) | | | 26 (10/1/11-3/31/12) | |
| **NUMBER OF STATEMENTS** | 36 | 36 | 33 | | | 2 | 1 | 5 | 8 | 17 |
| | % | % | % | **ASSETS** | % | % | % | % | % | % |
| Cash & Equivalents | 6.8 | 6.9 | 5.6 | | | | | | | 5.4 |
| Trade Receivables (net) | 26.8 | 24.6 | 27.9 | | | | | | | 26.8 |
| Inventory | 20.0 | 20.4 | 18.2 | | | | | | | 15.4 |
| All Other Current | 3.5 | 1.9 | 1.7 | | | | | | | 1.9 |
| Total Current | 57.1 | 53.9 | 53.3 | | | | | | | 49.6 |
| Fixed Assets (net) | 37.4 | 39.3 | 39.8 | | | DATA NOT AVAILABLE | | | | 43.8 |
| Intangibles (net) | 1.7 | 1.4 | 2.2 | | | | | | | .6 |
| All Other Non-Current | 3.8 | 5.5 | 4.7 | | | | | | | 6.0 |
| Total | 100.0 | 100.0 | 100.0 | | | | | | | 100.0 |
| | | | | **LIABILITIES** | | | | | | |
| Notes Payable-Short Term | 8.5 | 7.8 | 8.9 | | | | | | | 5.3 |
| Cur. Mat.-L.T.D. | 5.0 | 3.5 | 5.0 | | | | | | | 5.2 |
| Trade Payables | 13.5 | 13.3 | 15.5 | | | | | | | 14.1 |
| Income Taxes Payable | .1 | .0 | .1 | | | | | | | .1 |
| All Other Current | 5.9 | 6.8 | 5.7 | | | | | | | 4.7 |
| Total Current | 33.1 | 31.3 | 35.3 | | | | | | | 29.4 |
| Long-Term Debt | 23.1 | 18.9 | 21.2 | | | | | | | 20.7 |
| Deferred Taxes | .7 | 1.2 | 1.0 | | | | | | | 1.3 |
| All Other Non-Current | 2.0 | 6.9 | 5.4 | | | | | | | 6.6 |
| Net Worth | 41.0 | 41.7 | 37.1 | | | | | | | 41.9 |
| Total Liabilities & Net Worth | 100.0 | 100.0 | 100.0 | | | | | | | 100.0 |
| | | | | **INCOME DATA** | | | | | | |
| Net Sales | 100.0 | 100.0 | 100.0 | | | | | | | 100.0 |
| Gross Profit | 23.7 | 24.1 | 23.7 | | | | | | | 20.6 |
| Operating Expenses | 19.9 | 19.2 | 19.8 | | | | | | | 16.2 |
| Operating Profit | 3.8 | 4.9 | 3.9 | | | | | | | 4.3 |
| All Other Expenses (net) | 1.1 | .2 | .5 | | | | | | | .3 |
| Profit Before Taxes | 2.7 | 4.6 | 3.4 | | | | | | | 4.0 |
| | | | | **RATIOS** | | | | | | |
| Current | 2.7 | 3.4 | 2.4 | | | | | | | 2.8 |
| | 1.7 | 1.8 | 1.7 | | | | | | | 1.9 |
| | 1.3 | 1.2 | 1.0 | | | | | | | .9 |
| Quick | 1.8 | 2.1 | 1.8 | | | | | | | 1.9 |
| | 1.1 | 1.3 | 1.2 | | | | | | | 1.3 |
| | .6 | .7 | .6 | | | | | | | .7 |
| Sales/Receivables | 31   11.6 | 31   11.9 | 31   11.7 | | | | | | | 32   11.3 |
| | 39   9.4 | 38   9.7 | 40   9.1 | | | | | | | 40   9.1 |
| | 47   7.8 | 51   7.1 | 51   7.2 | | | | | | | 51   7.1 |
| Cost of Sales/Inventory | 22   16.4 | 22   16.7 | 23   15.9 | | | | | | | 23   16.0 |
| | 34   10.8 | 30   12.0 | 31   11.8 | | | | | | | 29   12.4 |
| | 52   7.1 | 57   6.4 | 49   7.4 | | | | | | | 38   9.5 |
| Cost of Sales/Payables | 14   26.1 | 16   22.8 | 14   26.8 | | | | | | | 13   28.9 |
| | 22   16.4 | 22   16.5 | 26   13.8 | | | | | | | 28   13.1 |
| | 30   12.1 | 33   11.1 | 43   8.5 | | | | | | | 40   9.2 |
| Sales/Working Capital | 5.6 | 5.3 | 7.1 | | | | | | | 6.3 |
| | 11.9 | 9.8 | 12.4 | | | | | | | 10.6 |
| | 28.9 | 36.1 | NM | | | | | | | -115.8 |
| EBIT/Interest | 7.5 | 21.3 | 12.9 | | | | | | | 16.0 |
| | (33) 4.2 | (34) 6.5 | (32) 3.5 | | | | | | | (16) 6.2 |
| | 1.0 | 3.0 | 1.8 | | | | | | | 1.3 |
| Net Profit + Depr., Dep., Amort./Cur. Mat. L/T/D | 4.0 | 8.4 | 4.8 | | | | | | | |
| | (12) 2.9 | (11) 5.8 | (12) 3.0 | | | | | | | |
| | 1.4 | 2.9 | 1.4 | | | | | | | |
| Fixed/Worth | .5 | .5 | .6 | | | | | | | .7 |
| | 1.0 | 1.0 | 1.1 | | | | | | | 1.1 |
| | 1.6 | 1.6 | 2.3 | | | | | | | 1.9 |
| Debt/Worth | .8 | .7 | .8 | | | | | | | .8 |
| | 1.6 | 1.3 | 1.6 | | | | | | | 1.2 |
| | 2.3 | 3.0 | 3.5 | | | | | | | 2.5 |
| % Profit Before Taxes/Tangible Net Worth | 34.2 | 34.3 | 35.0 | | | | | | | 37.5 |
| | (33) 15.9 | (33) 22.6 | (30) 17.2 | | | | | | | 17.4 |
| | 4.5 | 11.8 | 6.1 | | | | | | | 3.7 |
| % Profit Before Taxes/Total Assets | 12.9 | 16.1 | 14.6 | | | | | | | 15.1 |
| | 5.8 | 10.3 | 5.7 | | | | | | | 8.2 |
| | 1.0 | 4.6 | 2.2 | | | | | | | 1.9 |
| Sales/Net Fixed Assets | 11.6 | 11.6 | 9.7 | | | | | | | 7.3 |
| | 5.9 | 5.0 | 5.0 | | | | | | | 4.7 |
| | 4.0 | 4.1 | 3.8 | | | | | | | 3.7 |
| Sales/Total Assets | 2.8 | 2.6 | 2.7 | | | | | | | 2.7 |
| | 2.2 | 2.3 | 2.3 | | | | | | | 2.2 |
| | 2.0 | 2.1 | 1.9 | | | | | | | 1.9 |
| % Depr., Dep., Amort./Sales | 1.4 | 2.0 | 1.9 | | | | | | | 2.1 |
| | (33) 2.5 | (34) 2.5 | (31) 3.2 | | | | | | | 3.2 |
| | 4.0 | 3.7 | 5.3 | | | | | | | 4.9 |
| % Officers', Directors' Owners' Comp/Sales | .8 | .8 | 1.0 | | | | | | | |
| | (17) 1.9 | (17) 1.9 | (17) 2.1 | | | | | | | |
| | 3.0 | 3.0 | 4.1 | | | | | | | |
| Net Sales ($) | 1104727M | 1414188M | 1172151M | | | 5263M | 3871M | 39845M | 128124M | 995048M |
| Total Assets ($) | 528042M | 647101M | 544796M | | | 3348M | 1990M | 19645M | 44912M | 474901M |

M = $ thousand     MM = $ million
See Pages 9 through 22 for Explanation of Ratios and Data

**Current Data Sorted by Assets**                                      **Comparative Historical Data**

| Type of Statement | 0-500M | 500M-2MM | 2-10MM | 10-50MM | 50-100MM | 100-250MM | | 4/1/07-3/31/08 ALL | 4/1/08-3/31/09 ALL |
|---|---|---|---|---|---|---|---|---|---|
| Unqualified | | | 1 | 9 | 8 | 5 | | 19 | 24 |
| Reviewed | | 2 | 9 | 6 | | 1 | | 13 | 14 |
| Compiled | 1 | 1 | 5 | 1 | | | | 5 | 6 |
| Tax Returns | 1 | 3 | 4 | 17 | 3 | | | 10 | 6 |
| Other | | 5 | 13 | | | 8 | | 38 | 54 |
| | | 22 (4/1-9/30/11) | | 81 (10/1/11-3/31/12) | | | | | |

| | 0-500M | 500M-2MM | 2-10MM | 10-50MM | 50-100MM | 100-250MM | | 4/1/07-3/31/08 ALL | 4/1/08-3/31/09 ALL |
|---|---|---|---|---|---|---|---|---|---|
| **NUMBER OF STATEMENTS** | 2 | 11 | 32 | 33 | 11 | 14 | | 85 | 104 |
| | % | % | % | % | % | % | **ASSETS** | % | % |
| | | 11.2 | 5.2 | 5.5 | 6.0 | 4.8 | Cash & Equivalents | 5.9 | 6.2 |
| | | 25.2 | 31.7 | 17.1 | 19.6 | 17.8 | Trade Receivables (net) | 27.2 | 24.0 |
| | | 34.8 | 29.1 | 24.4 | 23.0 | 20.0 | Inventory | 23.5 | 23.8 |
| | | 2.2 | 2.2 | 1.3 | 6.6 | 1.2 | All Other Current | 1.3 | 2.0 |
| | | 73.4 | 68.2 | 48.3 | 55.1 | 43.8 | Total Current | 57.9 | 56.0 |
| | | 18.3 | 26.3 | 37.3 | 33.2 | 31.8 | Fixed Assets (net) | 34.5 | 32.8 |
| | | 1.0 | 1.7 | 9.9 | 9.0 | 19.3 | Intangibles (net) | 4.1 | 6.8 |
| | | 7.3 | 3.8 | 4.5 | 2.7 | 5.1 | All Other Non-Current | 3.6 | 4.4 |
| | | 100.0 | 100.0 | 100.0 | 100.0 | 100.0 | Total | 100.0 | 100.0 |
| | | | | | | | **LIABILITIES** | | |
| | | 4.6 | 13.6 | 13.9 | 8.9 | 5.4 | Notes Payable-Short Term | 13.2 | 11.6 |
| | | 4.3 | 3.7 | 4.4 | 1.7 | 2.4 | Cur. Mat.-L.T.D. | 5.0 | 4.3 |
| | | 28.4 | 19.5 | 14.6 | 9.8 | 8.5 | Trade Payables | 18.9 | 15.7 |
| | | .4 | .2 | .1 | .1 | .9 | Income Taxes Payable | .2 | .2 |
| | | 4.3 | 5.6 | 5.8 | 7.7 | 7.1 | All Other Current | 6.1 | 5.2 |
| | | 42.1 | 42.6 | 38.8 | 28.3 | 24.3 | Total Current | 43.4 | 37.0 |
| | | 18.2 | 15.6 | 22.5 | 15.3 | 20.6 | Long-Term Debt | 22.9 | 19.7 |
| | | .4 | .4 | .5 | 1.5 | 3.0 | Deferred Taxes | .5 | .5 |
| | | 5.7 | 9.4 | 9.0 | 6.1 | 12.5 | All Other Non-Current | 6.3 | 5.7 |
| | | 33.6 | 32.1 | 29.2 | 48.8 | 39.6 | Net Worth | 27.0 | 37.0 |
| | | 100.0 | 100.0 | 100.0 | 100.0 | 100.0 | Total Liabilities & Net Worth | 100.0 | 100.0 |
| | | | | | | | **INCOME DATA** | | |
| | | 100.0 | 100.0 | 100.0 | 100.0 | 100.0 | Net Sales | 100.0 | 100.0 |
| | | 29.0 | 25.5 | 21.9 | 21.9 | 21.5 | Gross Profit | 25.3 | 24.9 |
| | | 25.7 | 21.7 | 17.8 | 15.5 | 14.2 | Operating Expenses | 20.7 | 20.2 |
| | | 3.3 | 3.8 | 4.0 | 6.4 | 7.3 | Operating Profit | 4.6 | 4.8 |
| | | .4 | .5 | 1.8 | .7 | 2.7 | All Other Expenses (net) | 1.5 | 1.3 |
| | | 2.9 | 3.3 | 2.2 | 5.7 | 4.6 | Profit Before Taxes | 3.0 | 3.5 |
| | | | | | | | **RATIOS** | | |
| Current | | 3.3 | 2.5 | 1.8 | 3.1 | 2.3 | | 2.2 | 2.5 |
| | | 1.7 | 1.8 | 1.3 | 2.0 | 1.6 | | 1.4 | 1.6 |
| | | 1.3 | 1.2 | .9 | 1.6 | 1.3 | | 1.0 | 1.1 |
| Quick | | 1.9 | 1.4 | 1.0 | 1.2 | 1.2 | | 1.2 | 1.5 |
| | | .7 | 1.0 | .6 | .9 | .8 | | .7 | .8 |
| | | .3 | .7 | .3 | .5 | .6 | | .5 | .5 |
| Sales/Receivables | | 13  27.3 | 28  13.1 | 27  13.5 | 27  13.7 | 35  10.3 | | 31  11.7 | 27  13.4 |
| | | 28  13.2 | 38  9.5 | 33  11.1 | 36  10.0 | 47  7.8 | | 40  9.0 | 36  10.0 |
| | | 51  7.1 | 52  7.0 | 41  8.8 | 41  9.0 | 51  7.1 | | 47  7.7 | 46  8.0 |
| Cost of Sales/Inventory | | 17  21.7 | 36  10.1 | 40  9.2 | 28  13.0 | 43  8.5 | | 33  10.9 | 31  11.9 |
| | | 56  6.5 | 50  7.3 | 61  6.0 | 47  7.7 | 57  6.4 | | 48  7.6 | 50  7.3 |
| | | 68  5.4 | 73  5.0 | 78  4.7 | 76  4.8 | 76  4.8 | | 67  5.4 | 67  5.4 |
| Cost of Sales/Payables | | 29  12.5 | 17  21.6 | 24  15.5 | 14  26.1 | 21  17.2 | | 21  17.6 | 14  25.9 |
| | | 38  9.7 | 32  11.5 | 34  10.6 | 21  17.2 | 25  14.6 | | 29  12.4 | 24  14.9 |
| | | 64  5.7 | 51  7.2 | 47  7.7 | 27  13.7 | 37  9.9 | | 45  8.2 | 43  8.5 |
| Sales/Working Capital | | 5.3 | 6.2 | 8.6 | 3.8 | 4.5 | | 7.0 | 6.4 |
| | | 9.3 | 9.0 | 18.8 | 7.2 | 10.0 | | 15.0 | 12.0 |
| | | 25.4 | 31.8 | -47.3 | 32.3 | 19.3 | | 999.8 | 88.7 |
| EBIT/Interest | | | 13.6 | 8.3 | | 10.8 | | 6.3 | 8.2 |
| | | | (31) 5.4 | (32) 2.4 | | (13) 2.5 | | (82) 3.6 | (95) 3.7 |
| | | | 3.3 | .8 | | .6 | | 1.6 | 1.4 |
| Net Profit + Depr., Dep., Amort./Cur. Mat. L/T/D | | | | 2.9 | | | | 5.6 | 5.8 |
| | | | | (15) 2.0 | | | | (26) 3.7 | (25) 2.4 |
| | | | | .6 | | | | 1.8 | 1.9 |
| Fixed/Worth | | .0 | .4 | 1.0 | .3 | .6 | | .6 | .5 |
| | | .6 | .6 | 1.8 | 1.0 | 1.8 | | 1.1 | 1.0 |
| | | 2.4 | 2.0 | -7.2 | 1.7 | -5.4 | | 2.9 | 2.5 |
| Debt/Worth | | .7 | .8 | 1.3 | .5 | 1.1 | | 1.3 | .9 |
| | | 2.5 | 2.1 | 2.6 | 1.3 | 2.5 | | 2.4 | 2.0 |
| | | 3.5 | 4.5 | -15.6 | 4.2 | -10.9 | | 6.9 | 6.0 |
| % Profit Before Taxes/Tangible Net Worth | | | 61.5 | 31.5 | 49.7 | | | 51.3 | 40.1 |
| | | | (28) 28.1 | (22) 18.8 | (10) 16.9 | | | (72) 25.7 | (87) 16.6 |
| | | | 10.2 | 2.3 | 8.0 | | | 11.7 | 6.1 |
| % Profit Before Taxes/Total Assets | | 20.6 | 15.2 | 8.7 | 14.8 | 13.1 | | 13.5 | 14.7 |
| | | 7.3 | 10.0 | 5.1 | 5.4 | 8.8 | | 7.7 | 7.2 |
| | | -5.2 | 4.2 | -.5 | 3.3 | -2.3 | | 3.0 | 1.5 |
| Sales/Net Fixed Assets | | 81.0 | 20.6 | 10.1 | 9.9 | 7.9 | | 14.4 | 13.3 |
| | | 26.8 | 10.4 | 4.5 | 7.7 | 4.1 | | 7.0 | 7.6 |
| | | 12.5 | 7.4 | 3.5 | 4.9 | 3.3 | | 4.0 | 3.8 |
| Sales/Total Assets | | 4.6 | 3.3 | 2.3 | 2.6 | 1.8 | | 3.2 | 3.1 |
| | | 3.0 | 2.9 | 1.8 | 1.9 | 1.3 | | 2.4 | 2.2 |
| | | 2.2 | 2.3 | 1.5 | 1.5 | 1.1 | | 1.7 | 1.6 |
| % Depr., Dep., Amort./Sales | | | .8 | 1.5 | 1.0 | 2.7 | | 1.5 | 1.6 |
| | | | (28) 1.4 | (32) 2.9 | (10) 2.1 | (10) 3.3 | | (75) 2.6 | (93) 2.7 |
| | | | 2.4 | 4.0 | 4.0 | 3.5 | | 3.8 | 3.4 |
| % Officers', Directors' Owners' Comp/Sales | | | 1.4 | | | | | 2.7 | 1.0 |
| | | | (17) 5.7 | | | | | (25) 4.0 | (27) 2.3 |
| | | | 9.4 | | | | | 9.7 | 4.1 |
| | 4031M | 48505M | 494915M | 1360945M | 1673967M | 3085410M | Net Sales ($) | 4068703M | 6506244M |
| | 449M | 13853M | 173217M | 722221M | 803824M | 2130423M | Total Assets ($) | 2116773M | 3378912M |

M = $ thousand    MM = $ million
See Pages 9 through 22 for Explanation of Ratios and Data

**Comparative Historical Data**          **Current Data Sorted by Sales**

| | | | Type of Statement | 0-1MM | 1-3MM | 3-5MM | 5-10MM | 10-25MM | 25MM & OVER |
|---|---|---|---|---|---|---|---|---|---|
| 25 | 20 | 23 | Unqualified | | | | | 5 | 18 |
| 17 | 27 | 18 | Reviewed | | 1 | | | 8 | 7 |
| 10 | 8 | 8 | Compiled | 1 | 1 | 2 | 3 | 2 | 1 |
| 9 | 5 | 9 | Tax Returns | 3 | 2 | 1 | 1 | 3 | |
| 35 | 26 | 45 | Other | 2 | 1 | 1 | 3 | 14 | 25 |
| 4/1/09-3/31/10 | 4/1/10-3/31/11 | 4/1/11-3/31/12 | | | 22 (4/1-9/30/11) | | | 81 (10/1/11-3/31/12) | |
| ALL | ALL | ALL | | | | | | | |
| 96 | 86 | 103 | **NUMBER OF STATEMENTS** | | 6 | 5 | 9 | 32 | 51 |
| % | % | % | **ASSETS** | % | % | % | % | % | % |
| 7.1 | 7.1 | 6.6 | Cash & Equivalents | | | | | 7.1 | 4.8 |
| 21.8 | 23.0 | 22.9 | Trade Receivables (net) | | | | | 25.2 | 19.8 |
| 22.4 | 26.0 | 26.1 | Inventory | | | | | 28.0 | 23.9 |
| 2.5 | 2.1 | 2.3 | All Other Current | | | | | .6 | 2.5 |
| 53.9 | 58.2 | 57.9 | Total Current | | | | | 60.9 | 50.9 |
| 32.6 | 32.0 | 30.4 | Fixed Assets (net) | | | | | 26.7 | 35.4 |
| 8.6 | 6.9 | 7.4 | Intangibles (net) | | | | | 8.7 | 9.0 |
| 5.0 | 2.8 | 4.4 | All Other Non-Current | | | | | 3.7 | 4.7 |
| 100.0 | 100.0 | 100.0 | Total | | | | | 100.0 | 100.0 |
| | | | **LIABILITIES** | | | | | | |
| 10.6 | 12.6 | 10.9 | Notes Payable-Short Term | | | | | 12.7 | 11.9 |
| 4.6 | 4.3 | 3.5 | Cur. Mat.-L.T.D. | | | | | 3.6 | 3.2 |
| 13.1 | 15.2 | 16.3 | Trade Payables | | | | | 16.7 | 12.4 |
| .2 | .2 | .3 | Income Taxes Payable | | | | | .1 | .3 |
| 5.5 | 5.4 | 8.9 | All Other Current | | | | | 5.8 | 7.1 |
| 34.0 | 37.6 | 39.8 | Total Current | | | | | 38.9 | 34.9 |
| 21.1 | 19.7 | 18.4 | Long-Term Debt | | | | | 17.8 | 18.5 |
| .8 | .9 | .9 | Deferred Taxes | | | | | .3 | 1.3 |
| 7.0 | 7.3 | 8.8 | All Other Non-Current | | | | | 11.4 | 8.3 |
| 37.0 | 34.5 | 32.1 | Net Worth | | | | | 31.6 | 36.9 |
| 100.0 | 100.0 | 100.0 | Total Liabilities & Net Worth | | | | | 100.0 | 100.0 |
| | | | **INCOME DATA** | | | | | | |
| 100.0 | 100.0 | 100.0 | Net Sales | | | | | 100.0 | 100.0 |
| 25.4 | 23.5 | 23.5 | Gross Profit | | | | | 26.1 | 20.7 |
| 20.1 | 18.5 | 19.0 | Operating Expenses | | | | | 21.7 | 15.3 |
| 5.3 | 5.0 | 4.5 | Operating Profit | | | | | 4.4 | 5.4 |
| 1.9 | 1.0 | 1.2 | All Other Expenses (net) | | | | | 1.4 | 1.3 |
| 3.4 | 4.0 | 3.3 | Profit Before Taxes | | | | | 3.1 | 4.1 |
| | | | **RATIOS** | | | | | | |
| 3.1 | 2.8 | 2.3 | | | | | | 2.5 | 2.1 |
| 1.6 | 1.7 | 1.6 | Current | | | | | 1.8 | 1.4 |
| 1.1 | 1.2 | 1.1 | | | | | | 1.2 | 1.1 |
| 1.7 | 1.6 | 1.2 | | | | | | 1.4 | 1.1 |
| .8 | .8 | .8 | Quick | | | | | .9 | .7 |
| .5 | .5 | .5 | | | | | | .5 | .5 |
| 28 13.2 | 28 13.2 | 27 13.5 | | | | | | 29 12.4 | 29 12.8 |
| 39 9.3 | 36 10.1 | 35 10.5 | Sales/Receivables | | | | | 36 10.1 | 34 10.6 |
| 46 8.0 | 44 8.2 | 48 7.6 | | | | | | 51 7.2 | 43 8.4 |
| 33 11.0 | 37 9.9 | 39 9.4 | | | | | | 42 8.7 | 39 9.4 |
| 49 7.4 | 55 6.6 | 56 6.5 | Cost of Sales/Inventory | | | | | 60 6.1 | 52 7.0 |
| 72 5.0 | 75 4.9 | 73 5.0 | | | | | | 85 4.3 | 73 5.0 |
| 16 23.4 | 18 19.9 | 20 18.4 | | | | | | 17 21.4 | 16 22.4 |
| 26 14.0 | 27 13.5 | 31 11.8 | Cost of Sales/Payables | | | | | 33 10.9 | 25 14.6 |
| 39 9.4 | 39 9.3 | 46 8.0 | | | | | | 53 6.9 | 37 9.8 |
| 6.7 | 6.0 | 6.2 | | | | | | 6.7 | 5.7 |
| 10.9 | 11.8 | 12.3 | Sales/Working Capital | | | | | 9.0 | 16.4 |
| 33.7 | 34.9 | 32.9 | | | | | | 31.7 | 60.6 |
| 10.5 | 10.0 | 9.0 | | | | | | 9.6 | 7.5 |
| (86) 3.8 | (81) 4.7 | (95) 3.8 | EBIT/Interest | | | | | (31) 4.8 | (47) 3.7 |
| 1.5 | 1.7 | 1.2 | | | | | | 1.6 | 1.2 |
| 4.3 | 4.7 | 4.0 | | | | | | 8.4 | 3.0 |
| (19) 2.4 | (26) 2.7 | (33) 2.6 | Net Profit + Depr., Dep., Amort./Cur. Mat. L/T/D | | | | | (10) 4.6 | (20) 2.3 |
| .8 | 1.4 | .8 | | | | | | 1.9 | .6 |
| .4 | .5 | .4 | | | | | | .4 | .8 |
| 1.1 | 1.1 | 1.1 | Fixed/Worth | | | | | 1.1 | 1.4 |
| 3.2 | 2.7 | 3.0 | | | | | | -3.2 | 3.0 |
| .8 | .9 | 1.0 | | | | | | .8 | 1.1 |
| 2.2 | 2.3 | 2.3 | Debt/Worth | | | | | 2.4 | 2.2 |
| 9.0 | 5.5 | 8.3 | | | | | | -15.4 | 7.7 |
| 43.4 | 47.1 | 42.1 | | | | | | 42.9 | 37.9 |
| (77) 20.7 | (69) 26.2 | (79) 23.0 | % Profit Before Taxes/Tangible Net Worth | | | | | (22) 23.6 | (41) 21.5 |
| 3.4 | 8.5 | 7.5 | | | | | | 6.7 | 9.0 |
| 14.9 | 18.0 | 13.2 | | | | | | 15.2 | 12.4 |
| 6.7 | 7.5 | 7.3 | % Profit Before Taxes/Total Assets | | | | | 7.9 | 6.2 |
| 1.4 | 1.3 | .6 | | | | | | 2.1 | .5 |
| 12.7 | 16.2 | 15.8 | | | | | | 18.2 | 10.0 |
| 6.6 | 7.5 | 7.7 | Sales/Net Fixed Assets | | | | | 8.8 | 4.9 |
| 3.4 | 4.1 | 4.0 | | | | | | 6.2 | 3.7 |
| 3.0 | 3.0 | 3.0 | | | | | | 3.2 | 2.6 |
| 1.9 | 2.4 | 2.1 | Sales/Total Assets | | | | | 2.5 | 1.8 |
| 1.4 | 1.6 | 1.6 | | | | | | 1.6 | 1.5 |
| 1.6 | 1.2 | 1.0 | | | | | | 1.1 | 1.2 |
| (79) 2.9 | (75) 2.7 | (89) 2.3 | % Depr., Dep., Amort./Sales | | | | | (29) 1.9 | (46) 2.8 |
| 4.2 | 3.7 | 3.6 | | | | | | 3.8 | 3.7 |
| 1.2 | 2.1 | 2.1 | | | | | | 1.2 | |
| (23) 3.5 | (27) 3.6 | (30) 4.4 | % Officers', Directors' Owners' Comp/Sales | | | | | (12) 4.1 | |
| 7.0 | 6.1 | 8.5 | | | | | | 8.5 | |
| 4887744M | 4847898M | 6667773M | Net Sales ($) | | 11329M | 21492M | 62997M | 548676M | 6023279M |
| 3040989M | 2811652M | 3843987M | Total Assets ($) | | 4089M | 7473M | 32040M | 276260M | 3524125M |

*(DATA NOT AVAILABLE for the 0-1MM, 1-3MM, 3-5MM, and 5-10MM columns in the Assets, Liabilities, Income Data, and upper Ratios sections.)*

## Current Data Sorted by Assets     Comparative Historical Data

| 0-500M | 500M-2MM | 2-10MM | 10-50MM | 50-100MM | 100-250MM | Type of Statement | 4/1/07-3/31/08 ALL | 4/1/08-3/31/09 ALL |
|---|---|---|---|---|---|---|---|---|
| | 1 | 2 | 10 | 1 | 1 | Unqualified | 11 | 16 |
| | 2 | 13 | 7 | | | Reviewed | 19 | 15 |
| 1 | 5 | 5 | | | | Compiled | 11 | 8 |
| 2 | 2 | 7 | | | | Tax Returns | 9 | 3 |
| | 3 | 14 | 11 | 1 | 1 | Other | 26 | 28 |
| | 17 (4/1-9/30/11) | | 72 (10/1/11-3/31/12) | | | | | |
| 3 | 13 | 41 | 28 | 2 | 2 | NUMBER OF STATEMENTS | 76 | 70 |
| % | % | % | % | % | % | **ASSETS** | % | % |
| | 3.3 | 6.4 | 6.9 | | | Cash & Equivalents | 5.0 | 4.7 |
| | 32.7 | 33.2 | 29.9 | | | Trade Receivables (net) | 28.3 | 26.2 |
| | 26.5 | 29.7 | 27.5 | | | Inventory | 25.4 | 26.0 |
| | 2.0 | 2.0 | 2.0 | | | All Other Current | 2.4 | 2.0 |
| | 64.5 | 71.2 | 66.2 | | | Total Current | 61.1 | 58.9 |
| | 22.7 | 22.1 | 23.0 | | | Fixed Assets (net) | 27.7 | 29.7 |
| | 9.9 | 3.7 | 3.6 | | | Intangibles (net) | 5.0 | 4.8 |
| | 3.0 | 2.9 | 7.2 | | | All Other Non-Current | 6.2 | 6.5 |
| | 100.0 | 100.0 | 100.0 | | | Total | 100.0 | 100.0 |
| | | | | | | **LIABILITIES** | | |
| | 13.7 | 14.0 | 12.7 | | | Notes Payable-Short Term | 10.5 | 12.5 |
| | 4.8 | 2.7 | 5.5 | | | Cur. Mat.-L.T.D. | 6.3 | 3.0 |
| | 22.5 | 25.8 | 14.6 | | | Trade Payables | 19.5 | 15.1 |
| | .0 | .2 | .1 | | | Income Taxes Payable | .3 | .2 |
| | 5.8 | 7.7 | 9.0 | | | All Other Current | 9.8 | 7.1 |
| | 46.8 | 50.3 | 42.0 | | | Total Current | 46.3 | 37.8 |
| | 19.1 | 13.8 | 9.1 | | | Long-Term Debt | 21.3 | 16.4 |
| | .0 | .5 | 1.1 | | | Deferred Taxes | .5 | .4 |
| | 4.9 | 6.5 | 4.8 | | | All Other Non-Current | 6.9 | 5.3 |
| | 29.2 | 28.9 | 43.0 | | | Net Worth | 25.0 | 40.0 |
| | 100.0 | 100.0 | 100.0 | | | Total Liabilities & Net Worth | 100.0 | 100.0 |
| | | | | | | **INCOME DATA** | | |
| | 100.0 | 100.0 | 100.0 | | | Net Sales | 100.0 | 100.0 |
| | 38.1 | 29.3 | 20.8 | | | Gross Profit | 28.9 | 25.0 |
| | 32.8 | 25.4 | 16.3 | | | Operating Expenses | 24.5 | 21.5 |
| | 5.3 | 3.9 | 4.5 | | | Operating Profit | 4.4 | 3.5 |
| | 1.1 | .6 | .8 | | | All Other Expenses (net) | 1.7 | 1.2 |
| | 4.2 | 3.4 | 3.8 | | | Profit Before Taxes | 2.7 | 2.3 |
| | | | | | | **RATIOS** | | |
| | 2.9 | 2.4 | 3.1 | | | Current | 2.3 | 2.5 |
| | 1.2 | 1.4 | 1.5 | | | | 1.4 | 1.7 |
| | 1.0 | 1.1 | 1.2 | | | | 1.0 | 1.0 |
| | 1.0 | 1.6 | 1.6 | | | Quick | 1.4 | 1.5 |
| | .7 | .8 | .8 | | | | .7 | .8 |
| | .6 | .6 | .6 | | | | .5 | .5 |
| | 27   13.6 | 33   11.0 | 35   10.4 | | | Sales/Receivables | 32   11.2 | 30   12.0 |
| | 32   11.3 | 45   8.2 | 45   8.2 | | | | 41   9.0 | 38   9.7 |
| | 52   7.0 | 56   6.5 | 63   5.8 | | | | 51   7.1 | 44   8.3 |
| | 31   11.7 | 36   10.1 | 38   9.5 | | | Cost of Sales/Inventory | 28   13.1 | 32   11.3 |
| | 46   7.9 | 54   6.8 | 62   5.9 | | | | 48   7.6 | 44   8.3 |
| | 69   5.3 | 72   5.1 | 81   4.5 | | | | 76   4.8 | 72   5.1 |
| | 24   15.2 | 20   18.2 | 18   20.3 | | | Cost of Sales/Payables | 23   15.5 | 16   23.1 |
| | 35   10.4 | 41   8.9 | 24   15.0 | | | | 36   10.2 | 28   13.0 |
| | 64   5.7 | 56   6.5 | 47   7.8 | | | | 55   6.6 | 41   8.8 |
| | 7.1 | 5.2 | 5.3 | | | Sales/Working Capital | 6.6 | 6.6 |
| | 30.9 | 13.6 | 10.0 | | | | 14.8 | 10.5 |
| | -141.7 | 45.1 | 25.6 | | | | -291.0 | 365.7 |
| | 38.3 | 15.6 | 21.1 | | | EBIT/Interest | 7.3 | 7.9 |
| | 4.2 | (40) 6.0 | (25) 4.6 | | | | (68) 2.8 | (65) 2.1 |
| | 1.1 | 2.0 | 2.0 | | | | .8 | .6 |
| | | 8.4 | | | | Net Profit + Depr., Dep., | 5.3 | 4.3 |
| | | (13) 2.7 | | | | Amort./Cur. Mat. L/T/D | (30) 2.7 | (20) 1.6 |
| | | .6 | | | | | .9 | 1.1 |
| | .2 | .4 | .4 | | | Fixed/Worth | .4 | .4 |
| | 2.0 | .9 | .5 | | | | .9 | .8 |
| | -5.0 | 2.7 | 1.3 | | | | 30.8 | 2.2 |
| | 1.4 | .9 | .6 | | | Debt/Worth | .9 | .6 |
| | 5.8 | 2.0 | 1.5 | | | | 2.3 | 1.6 |
| | -20.6 | 12.3 | 6.0 | | | | 81.7 | 6.4 |
| | | 60.0 | 32.6 | | | % Profit Before Taxes/Tangible | 30.5 | 30.5 |
| | | (34) 23.2 | (26) 14.8 | | | Net Worth | (59) 15.4 | (63) 9.2 |
| | | 5.7 | 6.4 | | | | 4.4 | -3.9 |
| | 32.7 | 19.6 | 15.2 | | | % Profit Before Taxes/Total | 11.8 | 12.1 |
| | 5.2 | 10.5 | 6.4 | | | Assets | 5.3 | 3.1 |
| | .2 | 1.0 | 2.4 | | | | .0 | -.8 |
| | 83.9 | 48.6 | 22.6 | | | Sales/Net Fixed Assets | 18.6 | 14.2 |
| | 23.9 | 12.7 | 9.1 | | | | 10.5 | 8.4 |
| | 5.3 | 7.2 | 6.3 | | | | 5.3 | 5.1 |
| | 4.6 | 3.7 | 2.4 | | | Sales/Total Assets | 3.2 | 3.2 |
| | 3.1 | 2.4 | 2.1 | | | | 2.5 | 2.5 |
| | 2.3 | 2.0 | 1.4 | | | | 1.7 | 1.6 |
| | | .7 | 1.1 | | | % Depr., Dep., Amort./Sales | 1.1 | 1.1 |
| | | (34) 1.8 | (23) 1.9 | | | | (71) 1.8 | (65) 1.7 |
| | | 3.1 | 3.2 | | | | 3.3 | 3.5 |
| | | 2.3 | | | | % Officers', Directors' | 1.8 | 2.2 |
| | | (17) 3.6 | | | | Owners' Comp/Sales | (23) 4.2 | (17) 4.4 |
| | | 5.4 | | | | | 7.3 | 7.6 |
| 3618M | 50980M | 520237M | 1477191M | 113051M | 486424M | Net Sales ($) | 2461810M | 2569110M |
| 904M | 16564M | 201932M | 695365M | 154468M | 308445M | Total Assets ($) | 1403135M | 1298922M |

M = $ thousand     MM = $ million
See Pages 9 through 22 for Explanation of Ratios and Data

## Comparative Historical Data | Current Data Sorted by Sales

| Type of Statement | 4/1/09-3/31/10 ALL | 4/1/10-3/31/11 ALL | 4/1/11-3/31/12 ALL | 0-1MM | 1-3MM | 3-5MM | 5-10MM | 10-25MM | 25MM & OVER |
|---|---|---|---|---|---|---|---|---|---|
| Unqualified | 21 | 18 | 15 | | | | 1 | 2 | 12 |
| Reviewed | 21 | 21 | 22 | | 1 | 2 | 2 | 11 | 6 |
| Compiled | 9 | 8 | 11 | | 2 | 1 | 3 | 5 | |
| Tax Returns | 6 | 13 | 11 | 1 | 2 | 3 | 2 | 3 | |
| Other | 31 | 31 | 30 | | 2 | 2 | 7 | 8 | 11 |
| | | | | 17 (4/1-9/30/11) | | | 72 (10/1/11-3/31/12) | | |
| **NUMBER OF STATEMENTS** | 88 | 91 | 89 | 1 | 7 | 8 | 15 | 29 | 29 |
| **ASSETS** | % | % | % | % | % | % | % | % | % |
| Cash & Equivalents | 5.3 | 7.8 | 5.7 | | | | 7.1 | 6.0 | 5.6 |
| Trade Receivables (net) | 25.1 | 27.8 | 31.2 | | | | 34.4 | 33.5 | 27.6 |
| Inventory | 24.2 | 24.5 | 28.7 | | | | 27.1 | 26.5 | 29.1 |
| All Other Current | 2.8 | 1.6 | 1.9 | | | | 1.0 | 2.7 | 2.0 |
| Total Current | 57.5 | 61.8 | 67.5 | | | | 69.5 | 68.8 | 64.4 |
| Fixed Assets (net) | 29.5 | 25.9 | 22.6 | | | | 25.3 | 22.1 | 22.9 |
| Intangibles (net) | 7.9 | 7.2 | 5.8 | | | | 4.2 | 2.9 | 8.0 |
| All Other Non-Current | 5.1 | 5.1 | 4.1 | | | | 1.0 | 6.2 | 4.8 |
| Total | 100.0 | 100.0 | 100.0 | | | | 100.0 | 100.0 | 100.0 |
| **LIABILITIES** | | | | | | | | | |
| Notes Payable-Short Term | 11.2 | 12.5 | 12.9 | | | | 15.3 | 12.1 | 11.8 |
| Cur. Mat.-L.T.D. | 4.3 | 3.3 | 3.9 | | | | 2.1 | 3.5 | 4.3 |
| Trade Payables | 15.3 | 17.6 | 20.7 | | | | 20.1 | 20.7 | 21.2 |
| Income Taxes Payable | .1 | .1 | .1 | | | | .5 | .0 | .1 |
| All Other Current | 9.8 | 6.8 | 7.6 | | | | 7.2 | 7.4 | 9.5 |
| Total Current | 40.7 | 40.3 | 45.2 | | | | 45.2 | 43.8 | 46.9 |
| Long-Term Debt | 15.1 | 11.6 | 14.3 | | | | 21.1 | 10.5 | 13.5 |
| Deferred Taxes | .7 | .8 | .7 | | | | 1.0 | .1 | 1.4 |
| All Other Non-Current | 7.1 | 6.0 | 5.8 | | | | 5.4 | 7.7 | 5.1 |
| Net Worth | 36.4 | 41.2 | 34.0 | | | | 27.2 | 37.9 | 33.1 |
| Total Liabilities & Net Worth | 100.0 | 100.0 | 100.0 | | | | 100.0 | 100.0 | 100.0 |
| **INCOME DATA** | | | | | | | | | |
| Net Sales | 100.0 | 100.0 | 100.0 | | | | 100.0 | 100.0 | 100.0 |
| Gross Profit | 25.3 | 28.0 | 28.5 | | | | 34.1 | 26.7 | 21.3 |
| Operating Expenses | 23.7 | 22.6 | 24.4 | | | | 27.1 | 22.4 | 16.5 |
| Operating Profit | 1.5 | 5.4 | 4.1 | | | | 7.0 | 4.3 | 4.8 |
| All Other Expenses (net) | 1.0 | .7 | 1.0 | | | | -.2 | .7 | 1.7 |
| Profit Before Taxes | .5 | 4.7 | 3.1 | | | | 7.2 | 3.5 | 3.0 |
| **RATIOS** | | | | | | | | | |
| Current | 2.2 | 2.6 | 2.5 | | | | 3.1 | 2.2 | 2.4 |
| | 1.5 | 1.6 | 1.4 | | | | 1.4 | 1.4 | 1.4 |
| | 1.0 | 1.1 | 1.1 | | | | 1.1 | 1.1 | 1.2 |
| Quick | 1.3 | 1.6 | 1.6 | | | | 1.8 | 1.6 | 1.1 |
| | .7 | .9 | .8 | | | | .8 | .8 | .8 |
| | .4 | .6 | .6 | | | | .5 | .6 | .5 |
| Sales/Receivables | 32 11.4 | 35 10.5 | 33 11.2 | | | | 39 9.3 | 31 11.6 | 34 10.7 |
| | 41 9.0 | 41 8.9 | 45 8.2 | | | | 48 7.6 | 42 8.7 | 44 8.3 |
| | 50 7.4 | 53 6.9 | 56 6.5 | | | | 58 6.3 | 52 7.0 | 63 5.8 |
| Cost of Sales/Inventory | 34 10.8 | 29 12.4 | 37 9.9 | | | | 39 9.3 | 30 12.3 | 43 8.5 |
| | 48 7.6 | 50 7.4 | 57 6.4 | | | | 50 7.3 | 45 8.1 | 64 5.7 |
| | 72 5.1 | 77 4.7 | 79 4.6 | | | | 68 5.4 | 70 5.2 | 85 4.3 |
| Cost of Sales/Payables | 18 19.8 | 19 18.8 | 20 18.5 | | | | 24 15.3 | 15 23.8 | 19 19.7 |
| | 31 11.6 | 32 11.4 | 32 11.4 | | | | 31 11.8 | 41 9.0 | 25 14.7 |
| | 53 6.8 | 44 8.3 | 49 7.4 | | | | 58 6.3 | 47 7.8 | 45 8.2 |
| Sales/Working Capital | 6.0 | 5.3 | 5.7 | | | | 4.8 | 5.4 | 5.6 |
| | 13.0 | 10.9 | 11.3 | | | | 15.7 | 13.6 | 10.3 |
| | NM | 102.5 | 41.7 | | | | 46.4 | 47.5 | 22.0 |
| EBIT/Interest | 5.3 | 25.1 | 16.3 | | | | 35.2 | 8.5 | 13.6 |
| | (82) 1.8 | (82) 5.2 | (83) 4.6 | (14) 9.2 | | (28) 3.9 | | | (27) 4.6 |
| | -1.1 | 1.8 | 1.7 | | | | 3.0 | 1.7 | 1.9 |
| Net Profit + Depr., Dep., Amort./Cur. Mat. L/T/D | 3.8 | 6.1 | 8.3 | | | | | 8.6 | |
| | (27) 1.8 | (19) 2.3 | (23) 2.8 | | | | | (11) 1.7 | |
| | -.1 | 1.4 | .7 | | | | | .5 | |
| Fixed/Worth | .5 | .3 | .3 | | | | .2 | .4 | .4 |
| | 1.2 | .7 | .6 | | | | 1.3 | .6 | .6 |
| | 5.3 | 2.3 | 2.8 | | | | -3.5 | 1.4 | 2.3 |
| Debt/Worth | .8 | .6 | .7 | | | | .8 | .8 | .7 |
| | 2.5 | 1.6 | 2.0 | | | | 4.3 | 1.9 | 1.8 |
| | 12.3 | 7.2 | 10.2 | | | | -16.4 | 6.0 | 7.8 |
| % Profit Before Taxes/Tangible Net Worth | 34.1 | 49.9 | 37.0 | | | | 188.0 | 33.6 | 34.2 |
| | (70) 6.8 | (78) 24.0 | (73) 18.6 | (11) 70.5 | | (27) 14.4 | | | (23) 22.5 |
| | -7.5 | 5.2 | 5.2 | | | | 24.7 | 5.3 | 8.2 |
| % Profit Before Taxes/Total Assets | 7.3 | 18.6 | 16.7 | | | | 28.1 | 19.6 | 10.8 |
| | 1.9 | 6.6 | 5.2 | | | | 14.8 | 4.1 | 5.7 |
| | -4.8 | 1.8 | 1.0 | | | | 5.0 | 1.0 | 2.0 |
| Sales/Net Fixed Assets | 13.2 | 19.8 | 32.4 | | | | 48.6 | 28.3 | 23.3 |
| | 7.3 | 9.9 | 11.7 | | | | 14.9 | 11.6 | 8.4 |
| | 4.7 | 5.1 | 6.2 | | | | 7.1 | 7.0 | 5.1 |
| Sales/Total Assets | 2.6 | 2.9 | 3.2 | | | | 3.7 | 3.8 | 2.5 |
| | 2.0 | 2.2 | 2.3 | | | | 2.4 | 2.5 | 2.1 |
| | 1.6 | 1.6 | 1.8 | | | | 2.2 | 1.8 | 1.5 |
| % Depr., Dep., Amort./Sales | 1.2 | 1.1 | 1.0 | | | | 1.1 | .7 | 1.1 |
| | (79) 2.7 | (80) 2.1 | (71) 1.9 | (14) 1.9 | | (23) 1.9 | | | (23) 1.7 |
| | 3.9 | 3.7 | 3.3 | | | | 3.3 | 4.0 | 2.8 |
| % Officers', Directors' Owners' Comp/Sales | 1.5 | 1.9 | 2.2 | | | | | 1.7 | |
| | (22) 2.4 | (35) 2.7 | (31) 3.6 | | | | | (10) 3.1 | |
| | 5.8 | 4.8 | 5.7 | | | | | 4.5 | |
| Net Sales ($) | 4071201M | 3626437M | 2651501M | 159M | 12965M | 33725M | 115424M | 463771M | 2025457M |
| Total Assets ($) | 2473815M | 2164587M | 1377678M | 188M | 7144M | 12332M | 50596M | 206196M | 1101222M |

© RMA 2012

M = $ thousand    MM = $ million
See Pages 9 through 22 for Explanation of Ratios and Data

## Current Data Sorted by Assets

## Comparative Historical Data

| 0-500M | 500M-2MM | 2-10MM | 10-50MM | 50-100MM | 100-250MM | Type of Statement | 4/1/07-3/31/08 ALL | 4/1/08-3/31/09 ALL |
|---|---|---|---|---|---|---|---|---|
| | | 1 | 7 | 2 | 1 | Unqualified | 15 | 20 |
| | 1 | 6 | 1 | | | Reviewed | 14 | 15 |
| | 1 | 2 | | | | Compiled | 5 | 7 |
| | 2 | 1 | | | | Tax Returns | 2 | 2 |
| | 2 | 8 | | 1 | 3 | Other | 16 | 19 |
| | | 13 (4/1-9/30/11) | 34 (10/1/11-3/31/12) | | | | | |
| 6 | 18 | 16 | 3 | 4 | | NUMBER OF STATEMENTS | 52 | 63 |

**Note:** Columns 0-500M and 500M-2MM (first two left columns) show "DATA NOT AVAILABLE" across the Assets / Liabilities / Income Data section.

| 2-10MM (%) | 10-50MM (%) | ASSETS | Hist ALL (%) | Hist ALL (%) |
|---|---|---|---|---|
| 6.6 | 4.5 | Cash & Equivalents | 6.0 | 4.7 |
| 30.9 | 30.7 | Trade Receivables (net) | 28.2 | 24.9 |
| 32.6 | 27.3 | Inventory | 26.8 | 25.2 |
| .7 | 4.6 | All Other Current | 1.3 | 4.5 |
| 70.8 | 67.1 | Total Current | 62.3 | 59.3 |
| 22.9 | 25.9 | Fixed Assets (net) | 28.9 | 31.9 |
| 2.5 | 2.2 | Intangibles (net) | 2.6 | 3.9 |
| 3.7 | 4.9 | All Other Non-Current | 6.2 | 4.8 |
| 100.0 | 100.0 | Total | 100.0 | 100.0 |
| | | **LIABILITIES** | | |
| 14.4 | 12.8 | Notes Payable-Short Term | 15.6 | 15.1 |
| 4.1 | 3.0 | Cur. Mat.-L.T.D. | 4.0 | 7.1 |
| 22.2 | 24.6 | Trade Payables | 20.8 | 16.8 |
| .1 | .0 | Income Taxes Payable | .4 | .4 |
| 7.5 | 7.6 | All Other Current | 7.0 | 9.0 |
| 48.4 | 47.9 | Total Current | 47.9 | 48.3 |
| 11.1 | 13.3 | Long-Term Debt | 26.0 | 15.4 |
| 1.3 | 1.7 | Deferred Taxes | 1.0 | 1.0 |
| 3.0 | 1.9 | All Other Non-Current | 4.3 | 5.2 |
| 36.3 | 35.2 | Net Worth | 20.9 | 30.1 |
| 100.0 | 100.0 | Total Liabilities & Net Worth | 100.0 | 100.0 |
| | | **INCOME DATA** | | |
| 100.0 | 100.0 | Net Sales | 100.0 | 100.0 |
| 24.8 | 18.9 | Gross Profit | 23.8 | 20.4 |
| 20.3 | 13.2 | Operating Expenses | 20.0 | 17.2 |
| 4.5 | 5.7 | Operating Profit | 3.8 | 3.2 |
| .8 | .7 | All Other Expenses (net) | 1.5 | 1.3 |
| 3.7 | 5.0 | Profit Before Taxes | 2.3 | 2.0 |

### RATIOS

| 2-10MM | 10-50MM | Ratio | Hist (4/1/07-3/31/08) | Hist (4/1/08-3/31/09) |
|---|---|---|---|---|
| 3.3 | 2.4 | | 1.9 | 1.7 |
| 1.4 | 1.3 | Current | 1.3 | 1.3 |
| 1.1 | 1.0 | | 1.0 | .9 |
| 2.1 | 1.0 | | 1.0 | .9 |
| .7 | .7 | Quick | .6 | .6 |
| .5 | .5 | | .5 | .4 |
| 33  10.9 | 35  10.5 | | 34  10.7 | 30  12.0 |
| 36  10.0 | 44  8.3 | Sales/Receivables | 41  8.9 | 37  9.9 |
| 51  7.1 | 53  6.9 | | 51  7.1 | 46  8.0 |
| 39  9.4 | 44  8.3 | | 41  8.9 | 31  11.8 |
| 57  6.4 | 54  6.8 | Cost of Sales/Inventory | 55  6.6 | 53  6.9 |
| 78  4.7 | 65  5.6 | | 73  5.0 | 69  5.3 |
| 17  21.9 | 28  13.1 | | 16  22.8 | 20  18.5 |
| 39  9.3 | 36  10.0 | Cost of Sales/Payables | 34  10.7 | 31  11.6 |
| 59  6.2 | 52  7.0 | | 56  6.5 | 37  9.8 |
| 5.9 | 6.5 | | 6.4 | 8.3 |
| 11.6 | 17.5 | Sales/Working Capital | 13.7 | 25.1 |
| 46.4 | 776.4 | | -187.1 | -47.1 |
| 11.0 | 19.0 | | 6.3 | 5.3 |
| (16) 5.4 | 6.6 | EBIT/Interest | (48) 2.5 | (62) 3.0 |
| 1.3 | 3.3 | | 1.5 | .9 |
| | | | 4.7 | 3.9 |
| | | Net Profit + Depr., Dep., Amort./Cur. Mat. L/T/D | (21) 2.5 | (32) 2.1 |
| | | | 1.8 | 1.2 |
| .2 | .3 | | .4 | .4 |
| .6 | .5 | Fixed/Worth | 1.2 | 1.3 |
| 1.4 | 1.9 | | 3.2 | 3.9 |
| .4 | .9 | | 1.4 | 1.1 |
| 2.1 | 3.0 | Debt/Worth | 3.2 | 3.0 |
| 6.4 | 7.0 | | 8.3 | 10.7 |
| 45.2 | 75.7 | | 32.5 | 29.4 |
| (16) 15.2 | 34.3 | % Profit Before Taxes/Tangible Net Worth | (44) 21.1 | (52) 16.8 |
| 3.5 | 13.4 | | 5.9 | 2.8 |
| 10.9 | 19.1 | | 9.5 | 9.1 |
| 4.0 | 9.1 | % Profit Before Taxes/Total Assets | 4.7 | 4.6 |
| 2.2 | 3.1 | | 1.4 | -.3 |
| 108.9 | 39.3 | | 20.8 | 13.5 |
| 10.4 | 12.0 | Sales/Net Fixed Assets | 8.6 | 8.7 |
| 5.7 | 5.2 | | 4.9 | 5.3 |
| 3.4 | 2.8 | | 3.0 | 2.9 |
| 2.2 | 2.5 | Sales/Total Assets | 2.3 | 2.3 |
| 2.0 | 2.0 | | 1.8 | 1.9 |
| .4 | 1.0 | | 1.0 | 1.3 |
| (15) 2.6 | 1.7 | % Depr., Dep., Amort./Sales | (47) 1.7 | (59) 2.1 |
| 4.6 | 3.6 | | 2.9 | 3.7 |
| | | | 1.4 | 1.9 |
| | | % Officers', Directors' Owners' Comp/Sales | (13) 2.3 | (20) 2.3 |
| | | | | 3.4 |

| 500M-2MM | 2-10MM | 10-50MM | 50-100MM | 100-250MM | | Hist | Hist |
|---|---|---|---|---|---|---|---|
| 35404M | 281590M | 982575M | 358657M | 1030031M | Net Sales ($) | 2704115M | 3594568M |
| 8734M | 111177M | 412558M | 164030M | 510086M | Total Assets ($) | 1319824M | 1693785M |

M = $ thousand   MM = $ million
See Pages 9 through 22 for Explanation of Ratios and Data

## Comparative Historical Data | Current Data Sorted by Sales

| Type of Statement | | | | | | | | | |
|---|---|---|---|---|---|---|---|---|---|
| | | | | **0-1MM** | **1-3MM** | **3-5MM** | **5-10MM** | **10-25MM** | **25MM & OVER** |
| Unqualified | 14 | 12 | 11 | | | | 1 | 1 | 9 |
| Reviewed | 12 | 15 | 8 | | | | 2 | 5 | 1 |
| Compiled | 8 | 4 | 3 | | | | 1 | 1 | 1 |
| Tax Returns | 7 | 2 | 3 | | | 1 | 2 | | |
| Other | 16 | 19 | 22 | | | 1 | 1 | 9 | 11 |
| | 4/1/09-3/31/10 ALL | 4/1/10-3/31/11 ALL | 4/1/11-3/31/12 ALL | 13 (4/1-9/30/11) | | | 34 (10/1/11-3/31/12) | | |
| **NUMBER OF STATEMENTS** | 57 | 52 | 47 | | | 2 | 7 | 16 | 22 |

*Columns 0-1MM and 1-3MM: DATA NOT AVAILABLE.*

| | 4/1/09-3/31/10 ALL % | 4/1/10-3/31/11 ALL % | 4/1/11-3/31/12 ALL % | 3-5MM % | 5-10MM % | 10-25MM % | 25MM & OVER % |
|---|---|---|---|---|---|---|---|
| **ASSETS** | | | | | | | |
| Cash & Equivalents | 5.2 | 5.2 | 5.5 | | | 4.0 | 4.5 |
| Trade Receivables (net) | 27.8 | 26.1 | 31.2 | | | 31.6 | 29.5 |
| Inventory | 23.3 | 23.5 | 29.9 | | | 34.3 | 28.3 |
| All Other Current | 1.6 | 2.6 | 2.0 | | | .7 | 3.7 |
| Total Current | 57.7 | 57.3 | 68.6 | | | 70.6 | 66.0 |
| Fixed Assets (net) | 30.3 | 31.3 | 23.5 | | | 26.0 | 24.9 |
| Intangibles (net) | 5.4 | 6.1 | 3.1 | | | .3 | 4.3 |
| All Other Non-Current | 6.6 | 5.2 | 4.9 | | | 3.0 | 4.8 |
| Total | 100.0 | 100.0 | 100.0 | | | 100.0 | 100.0 |
| **LIABILITIES** | | | | | | | |
| Notes Payable-Short Term | 13.2 | 10.2 | 12.1 | | | 15.3 | 11.3 |
| Cur. Mat.-L.T.D. | 5.7 | 4.5 | 3.4 | | | 3.8 | 3.0 |
| Trade Payables | 19.4 | 19.2 | 21.6 | | | 23.0 | 23.3 |
| Income Taxes Payable | .7 | .1 | .1 | | | .1 | .1 |
| All Other Current | 8.2 | 7.3 | 7.8 | | | 7.9 | 8.2 |
| Total Current | 47.2 | 41.4 | 45.0 | | | 50.1 | 45.9 |
| Long-Term Debt | 18.7 | 20.1 | 12.4 | | | 13.1 | 14.2 |
| Deferred Taxes | 1.0 | 1.7 | 1.3 | | | .8 | 1.7 |
| All Other Non-Current | 7.4 | 4.1 | 3.4 | | | 2.8 | 1.5 |
| Net Worth | 25.8 | 32.8 | 37.8 | | | 33.2 | 36.7 |
| Total Liabilities & Net Worth | 100.0 | 100.0 | 100.0 | | | 100.0 | 100.0 |
| **INCOME DATA** | | | | | | | |
| Net Sales | 100.0 | 100.0 | 100.0 | | | 100.0 | 100.0 |
| Gross Profit | 26.1 | 25.1 | 22.0 | | | 23.5 | 17.5 |
| Operating Expenses | 22.1 | 18.2 | 17.3 | | | 19.3 | 12.5 |
| Operating Profit | 3.9 | 6.9 | 4.7 | | | 4.1 | 4.9 |
| All Other Expenses (net) | 1.0 | 1.2 | .8 | | | 1.0 | .5 |
| Profit Before Taxes | 3.0 | 5.7 | 3.9 | | | 3.1 | 4.4 |
| **RATIOS** | | | | | | | |
| Current | 1.9 | 2.1 | 3.1 | | | 1.7 | 2.4 |
| | 1.3 | 1.4 | 1.4 | | | 1.4 | 1.3 |
| | .9 | 1.1 | 1.0 | | | 1.1 | 1.0 |
| Quick | 1.1 | 1.2 | 1.4 | | | 1.4 | 1.1 |
| | .7 | .8 | .8 | | | .6 | .7 |
| | .5 | .5 | .5 | | | .5 | .5 |
| Sales/Receivables | 32  11.3 | 31  11.9 | 33  11.0 | | | 34  10.8 | 33  11.2 |
| | 41  8.8 | 40  9.1 | 38  9.5 | | | 38  9.6 | 41  8.8 |
| | 52  7.0 | 52  7.0 | 52  7.0 | | | 54  6.8 | 52  7.0 |
| Cost of Sales/Inventory | 28  12.9 | 31  11.8 | 43  8.5 | | | 51  7.2 | 46  8.0 |
| | 48  7.6 | 45  8.1 | 53  6.9 | | | 58  6.3 | 53  6.9 |
| | 73  5.0 | 67  5.4 | 68  5.4 | | | 89  4.1 | 63  5.8 |
| Cost of Sales/Payables | 19  19.2 | 24  15.1 | 22  16.7 | | | 18  20.8 | 27  13.5 |
| | 32  11.5 | 30  12.1 | 33  11.2 | | | 41  8.9 | 32  11.4 |
| | 58  6.3 | 48  7.6 | 46  8.0 | | | 61  6.0 | 45  8.1 |
| Sales/Working Capital | 7.9 | 8.0 | 6.2 | | | 8.4 | 6.6 |
| | 19.1 | 16.9 | 13.6 | | | 13.6 | 16.5 |
| | -91.8 | 52.0 | 106.2 | | | 55.9 | 119.0 |
| EBIT/Interest | 12.4 | 12.9 | 16.9 | | | 9.4 | 16.0 |
| | (53) 5.0 | (51) 5.2 | (45) 5.8 | | | (14) 3.2 | 7.5 |
| | 1.8 | 1.8 | 2.1 | | | 1.2 | 2.9 |
| Net Profit + Depr., Dep., Amort./Cur. Mat. L/T/D | 5.2 | 6.6 | 5.5 | | | | 26.8 |
| | (24) 2.6 | (26) 3.2 | (18) 2.3 | | | | (10) 2.6 |
| | 1.2 | 1.9 | 1.4 | | | | 1.5 |
| Fixed/Worth | .3 | .5 | .2 | | | .1 | .3 |
| | 1.1 | 1.3 | .6 | | | .8 | .5 |
| | 5.1 | 3.7 | 1.7 | | | 1.8 | 1.9 |
| Debt/Worth | 1.0 | 1.0 | .7 | | | .9 | 1.0 |
| | 2.5 | 2.9 | 2.5 | | | 2.1 | 2.8 |
| | 14.9 | 7.9 | 6.5 | | | 6.6 | 6.0 |
| % Profit Before Taxes/Tangible Net Worth | 37.5 | 43.8 | 50.8 | | | 46.6 | 62.4 |
| | (44) 16.0 | (44) 23.2 | (45) 28.0 | | | (15) 15.1 | 31.5 |
| | 6.5 | 9.3 | 6.8 | | | 3.0 | 16.2 |
| % Profit Before Taxes/Total Assets | 12.9 | 18.0 | 16.3 | | | 7.9 | 16.6 |
| | 7.5 | 7.2 | 5.4 | | | 4.4 | 8.6 |
| | 2.5 | 2.1 | 2.5 | | | 2.7 | 2.5 |
| Sales/Net Fixed Assets | 19.4 | 17.2 | 50.5 | | | 93.0 | 27.5 |
| | 8.6 | 7.6 | 10.8 | | | 9.4 | 10.4 |
| | 4.0 | 4.4 | 5.7 | | | 5.7 | 5.2 |
| Sales/Total Assets | 3.0 | 2.8 | 3.4 | | | 3.4 | 2.8 |
| | 2.1 | 2.1 | 2.5 | | | 2.2 | 2.5 |
| | 1.5 | 1.7 | 2.0 | | | 2.0 | 2.0 |
| % Depr., Dep., Amort./Sales | 1.3 | 1.3 | 1.0 | | | 1.0 | 1.1 |
| | (50) 2.9 | (49) 2.5 | (42) 2.1 | | | (13) 2.7 | 1.7 |
| | 4.8 | 3.6 | 3.7 | | | 4.2 | 3.7 |
| % Officers', Directors' Owners' Comp/Sales | 1.6 | .9 | 1.0 | | | | |
| | (17) 2.3 | (16) 2.0 | (14) 3.3 | | | | |
| | 5.7 | 4.5 | 6.4 | | | | |
| Net Sales ($) | 2683410M | 2388147M | 2688257M | 8071M | 48896M | 270524M | 2360766M |
| Total Assets ($) | 1400840M | 1272844M | 1206585M | 2924M | 18424M | 112376M | 1072861M |

© RMA 2012

M = $ thousand     MM = $ million
See Pages 9 through 22 for Explanation of Ratios and Data

## Current Data Sorted by Assets      Comparative Historical Data

| | | | | | | Type of Statement | | |
|---|---|---|---|---|---|---|---|---|
| | | 1 | 7 | 1 | | Unqualified | 11 | 9 |
| | | 6 | 3 | | | Reviewed | 8 | 7 |
| | | 2 | | | | Compiled | 3 | 5 |
| | 3 | | | | | Tax Returns | 1 | 8 |
| | 1 | 3 | 4 | | 2 | Other | 11 | 10 |
| | 9 (4/1-9/30/11) | | 26 (10/1/11-3/31/12) | | | | 4/1/07-3/31/08 | 4/1/08-3/31/09 |
| 0-500M | 500M-2MM | 2-10MM | 10-50MM | 50-100MM | 100-250MM | | ALL | ALL |
| | 6 | 12 | 14 | 1 | 2 | NUMBER OF STATEMENTS | 34 | 39 |
| % | % | % | % | % | % | **ASSETS** | % | % |
| | | 11.0 | 1.6 | | | Cash & Equivalents | 7.4 | 5.0 |
| D | | 29.1 | 30.0 | | | Trade Receivables (net) | 28.4 | 35.6 |
| A | | 14.6 | 21.2 | | | Inventory | 16.9 | 17.0 |
| T | | 6.2 | .7 | | | All Other Current | 1.0 | 2.4 |
| A | | 60.9 | 53.5 | | | Total Current | 53.7 | 60.0 |
| | | 31.7 | 41.4 | | | Fixed Assets (net) | 39.4 | 33.0 |
| N | | 1.8 | 2.0 | | | Intangibles (net) | 2.2 | 2.2 |
| O | | 5.6 | 3.1 | | | All Other Non-Current | 4.6 | 4.8 |
| T | | 100.0 | 100.0 | | | Total | 100.0 | 100.0 |
| A | | | | | | **LIABILITIES** | | |
| V | | 9.4 | 13.2 | | | Notes Payable-Short Term | 7.8 | 15.2 |
| A | | 2.9 | 8.7 | | | Cur. Mat.-L.T.D. | 5.9 | 6.4 |
| I | | 10.3 | 11.3 | | | Trade Payables | 15.0 | 21.9 |
| L | | .5 | .2 | | | Income Taxes Payable | .0 | .0 |
| A | | 3.9 | 6.8 | | | All Other Current | 8.1 | 9.4 |
| B | | 27.0 | 40.2 | | | Total Current | 36.9 | 53.0 |
| L | | 9.3 | 20.4 | | | Long-Term Debt | 32.1 | 26.2 |
| E | | 1.8 | .6 | | | Deferred Taxes | .5 | .5 |
| | | 8.6 | 9.8 | | | All Other Non-Current | 6.0 | 9.9 |
| | | 53.4 | 29.1 | | | Net Worth | 24.5 | 10.3 |
| | | 100.0 | 100.0 | | | Total Liabilities & Net Worth | 100.0 | 100.0 |
| | | | | | | **INCOME DATA** | | |
| | | 100.0 | 100.0 | | | Net Sales | 100.0 | 100.0 |
| | | 28.5 | 20.4 | | | Gross Profit | 24.6 | 23.1 |
| | | 24.2 | 16.4 | | | Operating Expenses | 19.6 | 21.6 |
| | | 4.3 | 3.9 | | | Operating Profit | 4.9 | 1.5 |
| | | .8 | 1.5 | | | All Other Expenses (net) | 1.2 | 1.5 |
| | | 3.5 | 2.4 | | | Profit Before Taxes | 3.7 | .0 |
| | | | | | | **RATIOS** | | |
| | | 4.6 | 1.7 | | | | 1.9 | 2.1 |
| | | 2.1 | 1.3 | | | Current | 1.3 | 1.3 |
| | | 1.5 | 1.0 | | | | 1.0 | .9 |
| | | 2.8 | 1.0 | | | | 1.2 | 1.4 |
| | | 1.5 | .8 | | | Quick | .9 | .8 |
| | | .8 | .7 | | | | .7 | .6 |
| | | 34   10.7 | 36   10.2 | | | | 36   10.2 | 36   10.2 |
| | | 43   8.5 | 45   8.2 | | | Sales/Receivables | 42   8.6 | 45   8.2 |
| | | 48   7.6 | 54   6.8 | | | | 51   7.1 | 50   7.3 |
| | | 20   17.9 | 25   14.5 | | | | 21   17.6 | 17   22.0 |
| | | 29   12.6 | 32   11.4 | | | Cost of Sales/Inventory | 32   11.5 | 23   15.7 |
| | | 43   8.5 | 46   8.0 | | | | 51   7.2 | 44   8.3 |
| | | 12   31.1 | 15   23.8 | | | | 19   19.2 | 18   20.6 |
| | | 18   20.8 | 16   22.3 | | | Cost of Sales/Payables | 26   14.1 | 26   14.3 |
| | | 21   17.0 | 18   20.1 | | | | 39   9.3 | 36   10.0 |
| | | 5.7 | 12.6 | | | | 7.6 | 8.7 |
| | | 7.9 | 22.3 | | | Sales/Working Capital | 19.5 | 18.1 |
| | | 12.1 | NM | | | | 975.7 | -92.6 |
| | | 32.2 | 6.4 | | | | 5.9 | 1.8 |
| | | (11)   4.8 | 3.4 | | | EBIT/Interest | (33)   3.1 | (33)   1.3 |
| | | .2 | 1.5 | | | | 1.1 | .2 |
| | | | | | | Net Profit + Depr., Dep., | 4.6 | 3.1 |
| | | | | | | Amort./Cur. Mat. L/T/D | (10)   2.6 | (10)   1.3 |
| | | | | | | | 1.7 | 1.0 |
| | | .3 | .7 | | | | .7 | .7 |
| | | .6 | 1.4 | | | Fixed/Worth | 1.2 | 1.8 |
| | | 1.1 | 2.9 | | | | -236.7 | 6.0 |
| | | .4 | 1.3 | | | | 1.2 | 1.3 |
| | | .8 | 2.1 | | | Debt/Worth | 2.7 | 3.8 |
| | | 2.7 | 5.5 | | | | -475.7 | 19.2 |
| | | 48.1 | 37.3 | | | | 41.8 | 16.2 |
| | | 8.5   (13) | 18.3 | | | % Profit Before Taxes/Tangible Net Worth | (25)   24.6 | (31)   3.4 |
| | | -1.1 | 2.6 | | | | 14.7 | -13.7 |
| | | 13.3 | 13.7 | | | | 13.0 | 3.5 |
| | | 4.3 | 6.7 | | | % Profit Before Taxes/Total Assets | 5.5 | 1.1 |
| | | -.7 | 1.1 | | | | .6 | -2.8 |
| | | 17.7 | 10.6 | | | | 10.8 | 16.1 |
| | | 8.9 | 6.8 | | | Sales/Net Fixed Assets | 6.0 | 9.6 |
| | | 4.6 | 4.0 | | | | 3.7 | 4.1 |
| | | 3.0 | 3.1 | | | | 2.8 | 3.5 |
| | | 2.4 | 2.4 | | | Sales/Total Assets | 2.2 | 2.9 |
| | | 1.9 | 2.0 | | | | 1.8 | 2.2 |
| | | 1.1 | 2.1 | | | | 2.1 | 1.5 |
| | | 1.9 | 2.6 | | | % Depr., Dep., Amort./Sales | (32)   2.8 | (34)   2.3 |
| | | 2.3 | 5.3 | | | | 4.3 | 3.8 |
| | | | | | | | | 2.6 |
| | | | | | | % Officers', Directors' Owners' Comp/Sales | (13) | 5.1 |
| | | | | | | | | 7.1 |
| | 19745M | 187439M | 808647M | 192002M | 1008664M | Net Sales ($) | 1206123M | 1250840M |
| | 6274M | 76618M | 329660M | 76018M | 365755M | Total Assets ($) | 554736M | 517883M |

M = $ thousand     MM = $ million
See Pages 9 through 22 for Explanation of Ratios and Data

## Comparative Historical Data | Current Data Sorted by Sales

| | 4/1/09-3/31/10 ALL | 4/1/10-3/31/11 ALL | 4/1/11-3/31/12 ALL | 0-1MM | 1-3MM | 3-5MM | 5-10MM | 10-25MM | 25MM & OVER |
|---|---|---|---|---|---|---|---|---|---|
| **Type of Statement** | | | | | | | | 9 (4/1-9/30/11) | 26 (10/1/11-3/31/12) |
| Unqualified | 8 | 9 | 9 | | | | | 1 | 8 |
| Reviewed | 13 | 11 | 10 | | | | 2 | 6 | 2 |
| Compiled | 2 | 2 | 3 | | | 1 | | 2 | |
| Tax Returns | 5 | 2 | 3 | | 1 | 1 | | | |
| Other | 12 | 9 | 10 | | 1 | 1 | 1 | 3 | 5 |
| **NUMBER OF STATEMENTS** | 40 | 33 | 35 | | 2 | 3 | 3 | 12 | 15 |
| | % | % | % | % | % | % | % | % | % |
| **ASSETS** | | | | | | | | | |
| Cash & Equivalents | 6.5 | 7.1 | 7.4 | | | | | 8.7 | 2.9 |
| Trade Receivables (net) | 33.8 | 33.3 | 30.5 | | | | | 26.8 | 32.5 |
| Inventory | 18.3 | 19.7 | 19.7 | | | | | 12.7 | 23.9 |
| All Other Current | 1.8 | 1.7 | 2.6 | | | | | 1.8 | .9 |
| Total Current | 60.4 | 61.7 | 60.2 | | | | | 50.0 | 60.2 |
| Fixed Assets (net) | 34.2 | 31.1 | 33.3 | | | | | 42.5 | 33.0 |
| Intangibles (net) | 2.3 | 3.5 | 2.2 | | | | | 2.5 | 3.0 |
| All Other Non-Current | 3.1 | 3.8 | 4.3 | | | | | 4.9 | 3.8 |
| Total | 100.0 | 100.0 | 100.0 | | | | | 100.0 | 100.0 |
| **LIABILITIES** | | | | | | | | | |
| Notes Payable-Short Term | 16.7 | 11.2 | 11.1 | | | | | 9.2 | 13.9 |
| Cur. Mat.-L.T.D. | 4.7 | 6.9 | 5.3 | | | | | 4.9 | 7.4 |
| Trade Payables | 24.0 | 14.5 | 13.7 | | | | | 9.3 | 14.3 |
| Income Taxes Payable | .0 | .5 | .3 | | | | | .7 | .0 |
| All Other Current | 10.4 | 7.4 | 6.1 | | | | | 3.4 | 7.4 |
| Total Current | 55.8 | 40.5 | 36.4 | | | | | 27.5 | 42.9 |
| Long-Term Debt | 28.1 | 24.7 | 19.3 | | | | | 18.6 | 16.2 |
| Deferred Taxes | .9 | 1.2 | .9 | | | | | 1.9 | .5 |
| All Other Non-Current | 7.0 | 8.1 | 8.7 | | | | | 8.5 | 10.7 |
| Net Worth | 8.2 | 25.5 | 34.7 | | | | | 43.5 | 29.7 |
| Total Liabilities & Net Worth | 100.0 | 100.0 | 100.0 | | | | | 100.0 | 100.0 |
| **INCOME DATA** | | | | | | | | | |
| Net Sales | 100.0 | 100.0 | 100.0 | | | | | 100.0 | 100.0 |
| Gross Profit | 22.4 | 25.6 | 25.7 | | | | | 28.7 | 19.2 |
| Operating Expenses | 21.1 | 22.9 | 22.5 | | | | | 22.9 | 17.3 |
| Operating Profit | 1.3 | 2.6 | 3.2 | | | | | 5.8 | 1.9 |
| All Other Expenses (net) | .8 | .7 | 1.2 | | | | | 1.3 | 1.3 |
| Profit Before Taxes | .5 | 1.9 | 2.0 | | | | | 4.4 | .7 |
| **RATIOS** | | | | | | | | | |
| Current | 2.1 | 2.5 | 2.3 | | | | | 2.7 | 1.7 |
|  | 1.3 | 1.4 | 1.6 | | | | | 1.8 | 1.4 |
|  | .9 | 1.1 | 1.2 | | | | | 1.2 | 1.0 |
| Quick | 1.5 | 1.7 | 2.1 | | | | | 2.2 | .9 |
|  | .8 | .9 | .9 | | | | | 1.2 | .7 |
|  | .6 | .7 | .7 | | | | | .8 | .6 |
| Sales/Receivables | 40  9.0 | 38  9.5 | 35  10.3 | | | | | 36  10.2 | 36  10.2 |
|  | 49  7.4 | 48  7.6 | 43  8.5 | | | | | 45  8.1 | 43  8.5 |
|  | 58  6.3 | 58  6.3 | 47  7.8 | | | | | 51  7.2 | 47  7.8 |
| Cost of Sales/Inventory | 16  22.5 | 29  12.6 | 24  14.9 | | | | | 19  19.0 | 29  12.8 |
|  | 33  10.9 | 38  9.7 | 32  11.4 | | | | | 27  13.7 | 32  11.4 |
|  | 53  6.9 | 49  7.4 | 48  7.6 | | | | | 43  8.5 | 46  8.0 |
| Cost of Sales/Payables | 19  19.2 | 18  20.5 | 16  23.5 | | | | | 14  25.2 | 16  23.5 |
|  | 28  12.9 | 23  15.8 | 18  20.2 | | | | | 17  21.1 | 18  20.6 |
|  | 51  7.2 | 35  10.4 | 37  9.8 | | | | | 21  17.1 | 37  9.8 |
| Sales/Working Capital | 8.2 | 5.1 | 6.3 | | | | | 7.1 | 14.3 |
|  | 23.0 | 13.0 | 14.3 | | | | | 11.0 | 18.7 |
|  | -54.4 | 50.7 | 30.3 | | | | | 28.5 | 803.1 |
| EBIT/Interest | 3.1 | 9.2 | 6.9 | | | | | 26.4 | 8.7 |
|  | (37)  1.6 | (31)  4.0 | (32)  3.0 | | | | | 4.6 | (14)  4.0 |
|  | -1.3 | 2.0 | 1.1 | | | | | 1.7 | -.6 |
| Net Profit + Depr., Dep., Amort./Cur. Mat. L/T/D | | 3.4 | 2.6 | | | | | | |
|  | | (16)  2.2 | (13)  1.7 | | | | | | |
|  | | 1.3 | .8 | | | | | | |
| Fixed/Worth | .6 | .6 | .5 | | | | | .5 | .6 |
|  | 1.6 | 1.4 | 1.1 | | | | | .9 | 1.3 |
|  | NM | 4.9 | 3.7 | | | | | 2.5 | 21.1 |
| Debt/Worth | 1.3 | 1.2 | .9 | | | | | .5 | 1.2 |
|  | 2.7 | 3.3 | 2.2 | | | | | 1.7 | 2.2 |
|  | NM | 12.5 | 6.0 | | | | | 3.1 | 59.8 |
| % Profit Before Taxes/Tangible Net Worth | 22.2 | 40.6 | 44.0 | | | | | 57.9 | 35.8 |
|  | (30)  5.8 | (27)  20.2 | (33)  11.5 | | | | | 11.7 | (14)  18.0 |
|  | -12.5 | .8 | -.7 | | | | | 3.6 | -7.8 |
| % Profit Before Taxes/Total Assets | 6.4 | 9.4 | 8.8 | | | | | 14.5 | 7.3 |
|  | 1.7 | 5.1 | 5.6 | | | | | 4.3 | 6.4 |
|  | -4.4 | -1.2 | .1 | | | | | 1.6 | -1.4 |
| Sales/Net Fixed Assets | 14.1 | 12.6 | 13.0 | | | | | 10.2 | 12.4 |
|  | 8.6 | 8.8 | 8.7 | | | | | 4.9 | 9.6 |
|  | 4.6 | 4.5 | 5.4 | | | | | 2.9 | 5.5 |
| Sales/Total Assets | 2.9 | 2.9 | 3.1 | | | | | 2.9 | 2.9 |
|  | 2.5 | 2.5 | 2.5 | | | | | 2.1 | 2.5 |
|  | 1.9 | 1.9 | 2.0 | | | | | 1.7 | 2.4 |
| % Depr., Dep., Amort./Sales | 1.7 | 1.7 | 1.5 | | | | | 1.4 | 1.5 |
|  | (33)  2.3 | (26)  2.4 | (30)  2.1 | | | | | 2.0 | (13)  2.2 |
|  | 3.4 | 3.8 | 3.1 | | | | | 5.2 | 2.9 |
| % Officers', Directors' Owners' Comp/Sales | 1.9 | | 2.6 | | | | | | |
|  | (12)  4.2 | (10)  3.9 | | | | | | | |
|  | 7.9 | | 13.5 | | | | | | |
| Net Sales ($) | 1796028M | 3340775M | 2216497M | | 3223M | 10960M | 24571M | 193791M | 1983952M |
| Total Assets ($) | 704963M | 1432089M | 854325M | | 1665M | 3411M | 9057M | 97340M | 742852M |

(Note: For the Current Data columns 0-1MM through 5-10MM, the composite percentage and asset/liability figures are marked "DATA NOT AVAILABLE.")

## Current Data Sorted by Assets | Comparative Historical Data

| | 0-500M | 500M-2MM | 2-10MM | 10-50MM | 50-100MM | 100-250MM | Type of Statement | | 4/1/07-3/31/08 ALL | 4/1/08-3/31/09 ALL |
|---|---|---|---|---|---|---|---|---|---|---|
| | | | | 2 | 3 | 1 | Unqualified | | 15 | 12 |
| | | | | 2 | | | Reviewed | | 4 | 6 |
| | | | | 1 | | | Compiled | | 4 | 5 |
| | | 1 | 1 | 2 | | | Tax Returns | | | 2 |
| | 2 | | | 2 | | | Other | | 9 | 7 |
| | 1 | 5 (4/1-9/30/11) | 3 | 26 (10/1/11-3/31/12) | 5 | 2 | | | | |
| | 3 | 1 | 6 | 10 | 8 | 3 | NUMBER OF STATEMENTS | | 32 | 32 |
| | % | % | % | % | % | % | ASSETS | | % | % |
| | | | | 7.5 | | | Cash & Equivalents | | 7.9 | 7.7 |
| | | | | 15.3 | | | Trade Receivables (net) | | 23.4 | 24.8 |
| | | | | 21.4 | | | Inventory | | 21.7 | 23.4 |
| | | | | 2.1 | | | All Other Current | | 5.7 | 5.7 |
| | | | | 46.2 | | | Total Current | | 58.7 | 61.6 |
| | | | | 49.5 | | | Fixed Assets (net) | | 31.6 | 34.4 |
| | | | | .3 | | | Intangibles (net) | | 2.5 | .9 |
| | | | | 4.0 | | | All Other Non-Current | | 7.3 | 3.1 |
| | | | | 100.0 | | | Total | | 100.0 | 100.0 |
| | | | | | | | LIABILITIES | | | |
| | | | | 6.8 | | | Notes Payable-Short Term | | 8.6 | 9.1 |
| | | | | 8.9 | | | Cur. Mat.-L.T.D. | | 3.2 | 3.2 |
| | | | | 15.5 | | | Trade Payables | | 14.7 | 16.4 |
| | | | | .1 | | | Income Taxes Payable | | .1 | .1 |
| | | | | 3.6 | | | All Other Current | | 7.9 | 7.4 |
| | | | | 34.9 | | | Total Current | | 34.5 | 36.2 |
| | | | | 29.6 | | | Long-Term Debt | | 23.2 | 20.2 |
| | | | | .2 | | | Deferred Taxes | | 1.2 | 1.1 |
| | | | | 4.6 | | | All Other Non-Current | | 2.0 | 1.9 |
| | | | | 30.8 | | | Net Worth | | 39.2 | 40.7 |
| | | | | 100.0 | | | Total Liabilties & Net Worth | | 100.0 | 100.0 |
| | | | | | | | INCOME DATA | | | |
| | | | | 100.0 | | | Net Sales | | 100.0 | 100.0 |
| | | | | 25.9 | | | Gross Profit | | 25.1 | 23.5 |
| | | | | 17.9 | | | Operating Expenses | | 18.5 | 17.6 |
| | | | | 8.0 | | | Operating Profit | | 6.5 | 6.0 |
| | | | | 2.0 | | | All Other Expenses (net) | | .9 | 1.1 |
| | | | | 5.9 | | | Profit Before Taxes | | 5.7 | 4.9 |
| | | | | | | | RATIOS | | | |
| | | | | 2.3 | | | | | 3.2 | 2.4 |
| | | | | 1.2 | | | Current | | 1.9 | 1.5 |
| | | | | 1.0 | | | | | 1.2 | 1.2 |
| | | | | 1.4 | | | | | 1.7 | 1.4 |
| | | | | .8 | | | Quick | | .8 | .8 |
| | | | | .3 | | | | | .4 | .5 |
| | | | 16 | 22.9 | | | | 30 | 12.3 | 27 | 13.5 |
| | | | 28 | 12.9 | | | Sales/Receivables | 33 | 10.9 | 33 | 11.0 |
| | | | 53 | 6.9 | | | | 45 | 8.2 | 42 | 8.8 |
| | | | 26 | 13.8 | | | | 26 | 14.1 | 28 | 13.3 |
| | | | 52 | 7.0 | | | Cost of Sales/Inventory | 49 | 7.5 | 53 | 6.9 |
| | | | 72 | 5.1 | | | | 62 | 5.9 | 84 | 4.3 |
| | | | 17 | 21.3 | | | | 26 | 13.9 | 20 | 18.2 |
| | | | 34 | 10.7 | | | Cost of Sales/Payables | 33 | 11.1 | 31 | 11.7 |
| | | | 57 | 6.4 | | | | 48 | 7.5 | 54 | 6.7 |
| | | | | 6.7 | | | | | 4.4 | 6.1 |
| | | | | 20.0 | | | Sales/Working Capital | | 9.0 | 11.5 |
| | | | | NM | | | | | 20.6 | 22.0 |
| | | | | | | | | | 9.3 | 10.3 |
| | | | | | | | EBIT/Interest | (30) | 4.6 | (27) | 6.6 |
| | | | | | | | | | 2.5 | 2.0 |
| | | | | | | | Net Profit + Depr., Dep., Amort./Cur. Mat. L/T/D | | | |
| | | | | 1.0 | | | | | .2 | .2 |
| | | | | 2.3 | | | Fixed/Worth | | .8 | .9 |
| | | | | 3.0 | | | | | 2.0 | 1.7 |
| | | | | 1.8 | | | | | .8 | .7 |
| | | | | 2.8 | | | Debt/Worth | | 2.0 | 1.8 |
| | | | | 5.3 | | | | | 3.4 | 3.9 |
| | | | | 48.3 | | | | | 44.5 | 68.8 |
| | | | | 22.2 | | | % Profit Before Taxes/Tangible Net Worth | (30) | 34.6 | 28.5 |
| | | | | 13.6 | | | | | 10.0 | 9.5 |
| | | | | 19.3 | | | | | 14.1 | 20.5 |
| | | | | 6.1 | | | % Profit Before Taxes/Total Assets | | 8.6 | 10.7 |
| | | | | 2.7 | | | | | 4.9 | 3.7 |
| | | | | 6.2 | | | | | 21.0 | 43.1 |
| | | | | 3.6 | | | Sales/Net Fixed Assets | | 7.1 | 7.1 |
| | | | | 1.7 | | | | | 4.3 | 3.4 |
| | | | | 2.1 | | | | | 2.3 | 2.8 |
| | | | | 1.6 | | | Sales/Total Assets | | 2.1 | 2.2 |
| | | | | 1.1 | | | | | 1.4 | 1.4 |
| | | | | | | | | | 1.0 | .9 |
| | | | | | | | % Depr., Dep., Amort./Sales | (24) | 1.7 | (22) | 2.0 |
| | | | | | | | | | 3.5 | 3.8 |
| | | | | | | | % Officers', Directors' Owners' Comp/Sales | | | |
| | 2324M | 979M | 59474M | 385354M | 919643M | 312143M | Net Sales ($) | | 3392173M | 2601282M |
| | 603M | 1306M | 24187M | 237358M | 545297M | 398286M | Total Assets ($) | | 1792171M | 1475813M |

M = $ thousand  MM = $ million
See Pages 9 through 22 for Explanation of Ratios and Data

## Comparative Historical Data / Current Data Sorted by Sales

| 4/1/09-3/31/10 ALL | 4/1/10-3/31/11 ALL | 4/1/11-3/31/12 ALL | Type of Statement | 0-1MM | 1-3MM | 3-5MM | 5-10MM | 10-25MM | 25MM & OVER |
|---|---|---|---|---|---|---|---|---|---|
| 14 | 8 | 6 | Unqualified | | | | | 1 | 5 |
| 4 | 6 | 2 | Reviewed | | | | | | 2 |
| 6 | 8 | 3 | Compiled | | | | | 2 | |
| | 1 | 4 | Tax Returns | 1 | | | 1 | 1 | |
| 10 | 22 | 16 | Other | 2 | 2 | | 1 | 3 | 10 |
| | | | | 5 (4/1-9/30/11) | | | 26 (10/1/11-3/31/12) | | |
| 34 | 45 | 31 | NUMBER OF STATEMENTS | 3 | 2 | | 2 | 7 | 17 |
| % | % | % | ASSETS | % | % | % | % | % | % |
| 5.2 | 6.1 | 7.5 | Cash & Equivalents | | | | | | 6.7 |
| 20.9 | 20.9 | 18.6 | Trade Receivables (net) | | | | | | 15.9 |
| 19.9 | 22.0 | 20.5 | Inventory | | | | | | 20.9 |
| 4.3 | 2.1 | 2.1 | All Other Current | | | | | | 2.0 |
| 50.4 | 51.1 | 48.8 | Total Current | | | | | | 45.5 |
| 39.5 | 40.9 | 41.4 | Fixed Assets (net) | | | | | | 43.5 |
| 6.1 | 3.9 | 5.8 | Intangibles (net) | | | | | | 8.3 |
| 4.1 | 4.1 | 4.1 | All Other Non-Current | | | | | | 2.7 |
| 100.0 | 100.0 | 100.0 | Total | | | | | | 100.0 |
| | | | LIABILITIES | | | | | | |
| 6.4 | 7.3 | 9.2 | Notes Payable-Short Term | | | | | | 4.9 |
| 4.0 | 4.4 | 4.5 | Cur. Mat.-L.T.D. | | | | | | 5.1 |
| 14.4 | 16.3 | 15.1 | Trade Payables | | | | | | 12.4 |
| .1 | .0 | .0 | Income Taxes Payable | | | | | | .1 |
| 7.1 | 7.4 | 6.9 | All Other Current | | | | | | 5.9 |
| 32.0 | 35.4 | 35.6 | Total Current | | | | | | 28.4 |
| 22.5 | 23.0 | 28.8 | Long-Term Debt | | | | | | 30.3 |
| 1.2 | 1.9 | 1.4 | Deferred Taxes | | | | | | 2.5 |
| 2.3 | 3.6 | 6.0 | All Other Non-Current | | | | | | 7.0 |
| 42.0 | 36.0 | 28.2 | Net Worth | | | | | | 31.8 |
| 100.0 | 100.0 | 100.0 | Total Liabilities & Net Worth | | | | | | 100.0 |
| | | | INCOME DATA | | | | | | |
| 100.0 | 100.0 | 100.0 | Net Sales | | | | | | 100.0 |
| 25.0 | 21.8 | 25.7 | Gross Profit | | | | | | 22.0 |
| 14.0 | 15.3 | 16.2 | Operating Expenses | | | | | | 13.6 |
| 11.0 | 6.5 | 9.5 | Operating Profit | | | | | | 8.4 |
| 1.4 | 1.6 | 2.5 | All Other Expenses (net) | | | | | | 1.8 |
| 9.6 | 4.8 | 6.9 | Profit Before Taxes | | | | | | 6.6 |
| | | | RATIOS | | | | | | |
| 2.2 | 2.1 | 2.7 | Current | | | | | | 2.8 |
| 1.7 | 1.4 | 1.7 | | | | | | | 2.0 |
| 1.1 | .9 | 1.1 | | | | | | | 1.1 |
| 1.3 | 1.1 | 1.4 | Quick | | | | | | 1.8 |
| .8 | .8 | .9 | | | | | | | .8 |
| .5 | .5 | .4 | | | | | | | .4 |
| 26  14.0 | 23  16.2 | 16  22.8 | Sales/Receivables | | | | | | 25  14.5 |
| 32  11.3 | 30  12.0 | 30  12.3 | | | | | | | 33  11.0 |
| 45  8.2 | 41  8.9 | 43  8.5 | | | | | | | 43  8.5 |
| 29  12.5 | 37  9.7 | 33  11.2 | Cost of Sales/Inventory | | | | | | 38  9.6 |
| 48  7.6 | 50  7.4 | 53  6.9 | | | | | | | 65  5.6 |
| 75  4.8 | 72  5.1 | 74  4.9 | | | | | | | 74  4.9 |
| 19  19.1 | 20  18.7 | 16  23.3 | Cost of Sales/Payables | | | | | | 17  21.6 |
| 35  10.4 | 34  10.9 | 31  11.7 | | | | | | | 34  10.8 |
| 46  8.0 | 47  7.8 | 49  7.5 | | | | | | | 44  8.3 |
| 6.7 | 7.5 | 5.5 | Sales/Working Capital | | | | | | 5.9 |
| 12.5 | 15.0 | 10.0 | | | | | | | 8.8 |
| 36.1 | -43.6 | 51.3 | | | | | | | 51.2 |
| 18.0 | 11.5 | 13.2 | EBIT/Interest | | | | | | 14.9 |
| (31)  10.5 | (43)  4.7 | (28)  4.3 | | | | | | | 4.4 |
| 4.0 | 1.8 | 1.7 | | | | | | | 2.3 |
| | 11.1 | | Net Profit + Depr., Dep., Amort./Cur. Mat. L/T/D | | | | | | |
| | (13)  3.1 | | | | | | | | |
| | 1.3 | | | | | | | | |
| .6 | .5 | .7 | Fixed/Worth | | | | | | 1.0 |
| 1.0 | 1.5 | 2.0 | | | | | | | 2.0 |
| 2.4 | 3.0 | 3.6 | | | | | | | 5.5 |
| .8 | 1.0 | 1.3 | Debt/Worth | | | | | | 1.4 |
| 1.7 | 2.3 | 2.7 | | | | | | | 2.2 |
| 3.2 | 4.4 | 10.2 | | | | | | | 9.5 |
| 60.8 | 35.4 | 27.1 | % Profit Before Taxes/Tangible Net Worth | | | | | | 48.3 |
| (32)  46.6 | (42)  16.2 | (25)  16.0 | | | | | | (14)  21.2 | 21.2 |
| 26.2 | 6.1 | 10.1 | | | | | | | 12.4 |
| 21.1 | 13.2 | 18.4 | % Profit Before Taxes/Total Assets | | | | | | 11.9 |
| 12.5 | 5.6 | 6.2 | | | | | | | 7.2 |
| 7.7 | 2.3 | 2.7 | | | | | | | 3.4 |
| 15.4 | 14.7 | 15.6 | Sales/Net Fixed Assets | | | | | | 12.0 |
| 5.7 | 5.0 | 4.7 | | | | | | | 4.3 |
| 2.7 | 3.0 | 1.8 | | | | | | | 1.6 |
| 3.0 | 2.6 | 2.4 | Sales/Total Assets | | | | | | 2.1 |
| 2.1 | 2.1 | 1.8 | | | | | | | 1.8 |
| 1.0 | 1.3 | 1.0 | | | | | | | 1.0 |
| 1.3 | 1.9 | 1.2 | % Depr., Dep., Amort./Sales | | | | | | 1.6 |
| (29)  2.5 | (39)  2.7 | (28)  2.8 | | | | | | (16)  2.8 | 2.8 |
| 4.2 | 5.6 | 5.5 | | | | | | | 5.3 |
| | | | % Officers', Directors' Owners' Comp/Sales | | | | | | |
| 3400060M | 3747873M | 1679917M | Net Sales ($) | 2226M | 2128M | | 13955M | 108371M | 1553237M |
| 2108431M | 2308542M | 1207037M | Total Assets ($) | 1734M | 4044M | | 5917M | 75370M | 1119972M |

*Note: For the Current Data columns 0-1MM through 10-25MM, the ratio/percentage data is marked "DATA NOT AVAILABLE."*

## Current Data Sorted by Assets

## Comparative Historical Data

| | | | | | | | Type of Statement | | |
|---|---|---|---|---|---|---|---|---|---|
| | | 1 | 1 | 16 | 4 | 4 | Unqualified | 30 | 31 |
| | | 18 | 18 | 4 | | | Reviewed | 24 | 17 |
| 2 | 7 | 7 | 8 | 1 | | | Compiled | 10 | 11 |
| 1 | 11 | 11 | 4 | | | | Tax Returns | 4 | 6 |
| 4 | | | 12 | 9 | 6 | 2 | Other | 36 | 52 |
| | | 21 (4/1-9/30/11) | | 94 (10/1/11-3/31/12) | | | | 4/1/07-3/31/08 | 4/1/08-3/31/09 |
| 0-500M | 500M-2MM | 2-10MM | 2-10MM | 10-50MM | 50-100MM | 100-250MM | | ALL | ALL |
| 3 | 23 | 43 | | 30 | 10 | 6 | NUMBER OF STATEMENTS | 104 | 117 |
| % | % | % | % | % | % | % | ASSETS | % | % |
| | 10.0 | 8.1 | | 6.0 | 3.6 | | Cash & Equivalents | 5.3 | 4.4 |
| | 26.1 | 25.6 | | 24.6 | 21.6 | | Trade Receivables (net) | 23.7 | 23.7 |
| | 21.8 | 25.4 | | 27.8 | 21.7 | | Inventory | 23.5 | 28.4 |
| | 3.0 | 1.7 | | 1.4 | 1.2 | | All Other Current | 1.6 | 2.1 |
| | 60.8 | 60.9 | | 59.9 | 48.2 | | Total Current | 54.0 | 58.6 |
| | 30.5 | 31.1 | | 31.9 | 39.2 | | Fixed Assets (net) | 35.4 | 30.9 |
| | 5.1 | 3.7 | | 4.6 | 7.7 | | Intangibles (net) | 4.5 | 5.1 |
| | 3.6 | 4.4 | | 3.7 | 4.9 | | All Other Non-Current | 6.1 | 5.4 |
| | 100.0 | 100.0 | | 100.0 | 100.0 | | Total | 100.0 | 100.0 |
| | | | | | | | LIABILITIES | | |
| | 9.1 | 11.0 | | 13.2 | 5.2 | | Notes Payable-Short Term | 11.0 | 14.5 |
| | 5.2 | 4.1 | | 5.1 | 1.6 | | Cur. Mat.-L.T.D. | 4.4 | 4.6 |
| | 18.3 | 13.6 | | 16.0 | 8.9 | | Trade Payables | 13.5 | 15.6 |
| | .6 | .0 | | .0 | .4 | | Income Taxes Payable | .1 | .0 |
| | 5.4 | 6.0 | | 7.2 | 7.6 | | All Other Current | 7.7 | 8.8 |
| | 38.5 | 34.7 | | 41.6 | 23.7 | | Total Current | 36.7 | 43.5 |
| | 27.9 | 14.1 | | 14.2 | 12.0 | | Long-Term Debt | 20.3 | 17.2 |
| | .4 | .6 | | 1.0 | .4 | | Deferred Taxes | .4 | .5 |
| | 7.9 | 6.6 | | 4.6 | 3.0 | | All Other Non-Current | 3.1 | 5.0 |
| | 25.3 | 44.0 | | 38.6 | 60.9 | | Net Worth | 39.5 | 33.7 |
| | 100.0 | 100.0 | | 100.0 | 100.0 | | Total Liabilities & Net Worth | 100.0 | 100.0 |
| | | | | | | | INCOME DATA | | |
| | 100.0 | 100.0 | | 100.0 | 100.0 | | Net Sales | 100.0 | 100.0 |
| | 35.0 | 25.8 | | 22.2 | 20.0 | | Gross Profit | 24.9 | 23.3 |
| | 31.3 | 20.8 | | 16.2 | 15.9 | | Operating Expenses | 19.7 | 20.4 |
| | 3.7 | 5.0 | | 6.0 | 4.1 | | Operating Profit | 5.2 | 2.9 |
| | .4 | .4 | | 1.1 | .7 | | All Other Expenses (net) | 1.4 | 1.0 |
| | 3.4 | 4.6 | | 4.9 | 3.5 | | Profit Before Taxes | 3.8 | 1.9 |
| | | | | | | | RATIOS | | |
| | 2.9 | 3.7 | | 2.2 | 3.2 | | | 2.3 | 2.2 |
| | 1.7 | 1.8 | | 1.4 | 1.8 | | Current | 1.4 | 1.4 |
| | 1.1 | 1.0 | | 1.1 | 1.1 | | | 1.0 | 1.1 |
| | 1.9 | 1.8 | | 1.2 | 1.9 | | | 1.2 | 1.0 |
| | 1.0 | .8 | | .7 | .9 | | Quick | .8 | .7 |
| | .7 | .5 | | .5 | .8 | | | .5 | .4 |

| | | | | | | | | | | | | | | | |
|---|---|---|---|---|---|---|---|---|---|---|---|---|---|---|---|
| | 21 | 17.7 | 32 | 11.4 | 24 | 15.3 | 35 | 10.5 | | Sales/Receivables | 30 | 12.0 | 30 | 12.3 |
| | 32 | 11.3 | 40 | 9.2 | 38 | 9.5 | 43 | 8.5 | | | 38 | 9.7 | 37 | 9.8 |
| | 42 | 8.7 | 45 | 8.1 | 46 | 7.9 | 53 | 6.9 | | | 48 | 7.6 | 51 | 7.1 |
| | 19 | 18.8 | 31 | 11.9 | 29 | 12.4 | 33 | 11.0 | | Cost of Sales/Inventory | 31 | 11.7 | 33 | 11.0 |
| | 30 | 12.1 | 51 | 7.1 | 42 | 8.6 | 45 | 8.1 | | | 49 | 7.4 | 55 | 6.7 |
| | 70 | 5.2 | 73 | 5.0 | 78 | 4.7 | 78 | 4.7 | | | 69 | 5.3 | 82 | 4.4 |
| | 9 | 42.2 | 15 | 24.0 | 14 | 25.7 | 15 | 24.0 | | Cost of Sales/Payables | 16 | 22.7 | 16 | 22.9 |
| | 23 | 15.6 | 25 | 14.6 | 24 | 15.0 | 24 | 15.3 | | | 25 | 14.4 | 29 | 12.8 |
| | 49 | 7.5 | 38 | 9.6 | 34 | 10.8 | 28 | 13.0 | | | 41 | 9.0 | 46 | 7.9 |
| | | 5.6 | | 4.5 | | 8.4 | | 4.7 | | Sales/Working Capital | | 6.9 | | 7.0 |
| | | 12.7 | | 8.9 | | 19.7 | | 9.7 | | | | 13.7 | | 15.3 |
| | | 58.1 | | 213.1 | | 136.9 | | 37.1 | | | | NM | | 134.1 |
| | | 12.2 | | 12.9 | | 30.4 | | 47.0 | | EBIT/Interest | | 8.6 | | 5.1 |
| | (21) | 3.6 | (39) | 6.7 | (28) | 6.5 | | 10.6 | | | (96) | 3.6 | (108) | 1.9 |
| | | 1.1 | | 2.0 | | 2.7 | | 1.2 | | | | 1.6 | | .3 |
| | | | | | | | | | | Net Profit + Depr., Dep., Amort./Cur. Mat. L/T/D | | 6.0 | | 5.3 |
| | | | | | | | | | | | (27) | 2.4 | (28) | 1.7 |
| | | | | | | | | | | | | 1.2 | | .3 |
| | | .1 | | .3 | | .6 | | .3 | | Fixed/Worth | | .6 | | .4 |
| | | 1.2 | | .8 | | 1.0 | | .8 | | | | .9 | | 1.0 |
| | | -2.4 | | 2.4 | | 2.2 | | 1.4 | | | | 2.9 | | 3.0 |
| | | .5 | | .6 | | .6 | | .4 | | Debt/Worth | | .7 | | .8 |
| | | 2.0 | | 1.5 | | 2.3 | | .6 | | | | 1.6 | | 2.3 |
| | | -4.7 | | 4.9 | | 3.1 | | 1.6 | | | | 5.3 | | 6.5 |
| | | 60.2 | | 42.5 | | 45.0 | | 42.2 | | % Profit Before Taxes/Tangible Net Worth | | 49.1 | | 39.3 |
| | (17) | 13.1 | (40) | 24.3 | (29) | 28.1 | | 12.1 | | | (92) | 20.1 | (98) | 14.3 |
| | | 2.4 | | 8.6 | | 10.9 | | 4.7 | | | | 9.5 | | 1.1 |
| | | 25.8 | | 18.9 | | 17.2 | | 16.2 | | % Profit Before Taxes/Total Assets | | 16.0 | | 10.1 |
| | | 4.6 | | 9.3 | | 9.1 | | 8.5 | | | | 6.6 | | 3.2 |
| | | .1 | | 3.4 | | 5.1 | | 1.7 | | | | 2.7 | | -2.0 |
| | | 64.1 | | 17.2 | | 14.1 | | 9.1 | | Sales/Net Fixed Assets | | 13.2 | | 16.3 |
| | | 9.4 | | 8.6 | | 9.0 | | 5.4 | | | | 7.0 | | 8.6 |
| | | 4.3 | | 2.9 | | 6.2 | | 2.4 | | | | 3.7 | | 4.0 |
| | | 3.8 | | 2.8 | | 3.2 | | 2.0 | | Sales/Total Assets | | 3.0 | | 3.1 |
| | | 2.8 | | 2.2 | | 2.6 | | 1.9 | | | | 2.1 | | 2.1 |
| | | 1.9 | | 1.6 | | 2.0 | | 1.5 | | | | 1.6 | | 1.5 |
| | | .8 | | 1.3 | | 1.0 | | | | % Depr., Dep., Amort./Sales | | 1.2 | | 1.0 |
| | (20) | 1.4 | (38) | 2.6 | (29) | 1.9 | | | | | (92) | 2.4 | (104) | 1.7 |
| | | 3.1 | | 5.6 | | 2.9 | | | | | | 3.4 | | 3.4 |
| | | 2.6 | | | | | | | | % Officers', Directors' Owners' Comp/Sales | | 1.2 | | 1.2 |
| | (11) | 4.6 | | | | | | | | | (22) | 1.7 | (21) | 2.3 |
| | | 11.9 | | | | | | | | | | 4.2 | | 4.4 |

| 2993M | 85005M | 493739M | | 1582472M | 1238323M | 1170014M | Net Sales ($) | 4915119M | 6509702M |
| 702M | 26857M | 221692M | | 595659M | 693324M | 914297M | Total Assets ($) | 2567214M | 3468812M |

M = $ thousand　　MM = $ million
See Pages 9 through 22 for Explanation of Ratios and Data

## Comparative Historical Data

## Current Data Sorted by Sales

| | | | Type of Statement | | | | | | |
|---|---|---|---|---|---|---|---|---|---|
| 30 | 30 | 26 | Unqualified | | 1 | | | 2 | 23 |
| 17 | 25 | 22 | Reviewed | | 2 | 1 | 8 | 7 | 4 |
| 9 | 13 | 18 | Compiled | 1 | 2 | 7 | 4 | 3 | 1 |
| 9 | 10 | 16 | Tax Returns | | 5 | 3 | 6 | 2 | |
| 48 | 31 | 33 | Other | 1 | 2 | 1 | 6 | 7 | 16 |
| 4/1/09-3/31/10 ALL | 4/1/10-3/31/11 ALL | 4/1/11-3/31/12 ALL | | 0-1MM | 21 (4/1-9/30/11) 1-3MM | 3-5MM | 94 (10/1/11-3/31/12) 5-10MM | 10-25MM | 25MM & OVER |
| 113 | 109 | 115 | NUMBER OF STATEMENTS | 2 | 12 | 12 | 24 | 21 | 44 |
| % | % | % | ASSETS | % | % | % | % | % | % |
| 7.5 | 8.9 | 7.4 | Cash & Equivalents | | 19.4 | 9.3 | 5.5 | 9.3 | 4.0 |
| 27.0 | 23.3 | 25.1 | Trade Receivables (net) | | 20.3 | 27.6 | 24.4 | 29.7 | 24.0 |
| 24.6 | 24.7 | 24.7 | Inventory | | 12.9 | 25.1 | 24.8 | 27.1 | 26.5 |
| 1.8 | 2.0 | 1.8 | All Other Current | | .3 | 2.2 | 2.6 | 2.2 | 1.6 |
| 60.8 | 58.8 | 59.1 | Total Current | | 52.8 | 64.3 | 57.3 | 68.3 | 56.2 |
| 29.0 | 29.6 | 31.1 | Fixed Assets (net) | | 40.5 | 28.7 | 32.7 | 24.3 | 32.3 |
| 5.8 | 6.2 | 6.0 | Intangibles (net) | | 1.8 | 5.0 | 4.7 | 4.1 | 7.8 |
| 4.4 | 5.4 | 3.9 | All Other Non-Current | | 4.9 | 2.0 | 5.3 | 3.4 | 3.7 |
| 100.0 | 100.0 | 100.0 | Total | | 100.0 | 100.0 | 100.0 | 100.0 | 100.0 |
| | | | LIABILITIES | | | | | | |
| 10.5 | 10.6 | 10.0 | Notes Payable-Short Term | | 10.5 | 2.6 | 12.7 | 10.5 | 10.4 |
| 4.3 | 3.6 | 4.2 | Cur. Mat.-L.T.D. | | 2.5 | 7.3 | 4.8 | 4.0 | 3.7 |
| 17.1 | 16.2 | 15.3 | Trade Payables | | 15.8 | 15.5 | 16.2 | 16.8 | 14.0 |
| .1 | .1 | .2 | Income Taxes Payable | | .5 | .6 | .0 | .0 | .2 |
| 7.8 | 6.9 | 6.6 | All Other Current | | 7.6 | 3.0 | 9.7 | 4.3 | 6.9 |
| 39.8 | 37.5 | 36.3 | Total Current | | 36.8 | 29.0 | 43.5 | 35.7 | 35.1 |
| 17.3 | 17.9 | 17.2 | Long-Term Debt | | 25.1 | 20.4 | 21.3 | 8.9 | 15.3 |
| .5 | .7 | .6 | Deferred Taxes | | .9 | .4 | .3 | .8 | .7 |
| 5.9 | 5.9 | 6.1 | All Other Non-Current | | 3.2 | 6.6 | 10.0 | 3.4 | 6.3 |
| 36.5 | 37.9 | 39.9 | Net Worth | | 33.9 | 43.5 | 24.9 | 51.3 | 42.7 |
| 100.0 | 100.0 | 100.0 | Total Liabilties & Net Worth | | 100.0 | 100.0 | 100.0 | 100.0 | 100.0 |
| | | | INCOME DATA | | | | | | |
| 100.0 | 100.0 | 100.0 | Net Sales | | 100.0 | 100.0 | 100.0 | 100.0 | 100.0 |
| 23.7 | 24.4 | 25.8 | Gross Profit | | 39.9 | 33.2 | 25.4 | 24.9 | 20.8 |
| 19.2 | 18.7 | 20.8 | Operating Expenses | | 36.4 | 27.2 | 21.8 | 18.6 | 15.4 |
| 4.5 | 5.7 | 5.1 | Operating Profit | | 3.5 | 6.0 | 3.6 | 6.3 | 5.3 |
| 1.4 | .8 | .7 | All Other Expenses (net) | | .7 | .0 | .6 | .0 | 1.3 |
| 3.1 | 4.9 | 4.4 | Profit Before Taxes | | 2.7 | 6.0 | 3.0 | 6.3 | 4.0 |
| | | | RATIOS | | | | | | |
| 2.5 | 2.4 | 2.9 | | 5.4 | 4.4 | 2.5 | 5.4 | 2.9 | |
| 1.7 | 1.6 | 1.5 | Current | 1.3 | 2.8 | 1.4 | 1.7 | 1.5 | |
| 1.1 | 1.1 | 1.1 | | .9 | 1.2 | .8 | 1.2 | 1.1 | |
| 1.4 | 1.4 | 1.6 | | 3.2 | 2.4 | 1.5 | 2.6 | 1.3 | |
| .8 | .9 | .9 | Quick | 1.0 | 1.3 | .7 | 1.1 | .5 | |
| .5 | .5 | .5 | | .6 | .7 | .4 | .5 | .5 | |

| | | | | | | | | | | | | |
|---|---|---|---|---|---|---|---|---|---|---|---|---|
| 30 | 12.0 | 27 | 13.5 | 29 | 12.5 | Sales/Receivables | 17 | 21.0 | 29 12.7 | 26 14.3 | 31 11.7 | 33 11.1 |
| 40 | 9.1 | 37 | 9.9 | 38 | 9.6 | | 32 | 11.5 | 33 11.2 | 34 10.7 | 39 9.3 | 38 9.5 |
| 48 | 7.5 | 48 | 7.7 | 46 | 7.9 | | 46 | 8.0 | 43 8.5 | 46 7.9 | 45 8.1 | 49 7.5 |
| 27 | 13.7 | 28 | 13.0 | 28 | 13.0 | Cost of Sales/Inventory | 0 | UND | 20 18.2 | 28 13.0 | 27 13.4 | 33 11.1 |
| 44 | 8.2 | 46 | 7.9 | 45 | 8.1 | | 39 | 9.4 | 33 10.9 | 42 8.6 | 52 7.0 | 47 7.8 |
| 76 | 4.8 | 78 | 4.7 | 74 | 4.9 | | 69 | 5.3 | 74 4.9 | 78 4.7 | 69 5.3 | 79 4.6 |
| 19 | 18.9 | 17 | 21.0 | 14 | 26.1 | Cost of Sales/Payables | 9 | 39.5 | 13 29.1 | 16 22.4 | 12 29.6 | 14 25.5 |
| 29 | 12.7 | 29 | 12.8 | 25 | 14.7 | | 22 | 16.9 | 22 16.6 | 25 14.8 | 25 14.4 | 25 14.5 |
| 44 | 8.3 | 44 | 8.2 | 35 | 10.3 | | 44 | 8.3 | 38 9.5 | 42 8.6 | 38 9.5 | 33 10.9 |
| | 6.2 | | 6.1 | | 5.8 | Sales/Working Capital | | 5.6 | 4.6 | 6.0 | 4.1 | 6.8 |
| | 10.1 | | 10.8 | | 12.7 | | | 19.7 | 7.1 | 12.3 | 11.5 | 16.1 |
| | 54.4 | | 73.1 | | 55.5 | | | -46.4 | 30.3 | -18.6 | 22.4 | 45.4 |
| | 9.3 | | 21.0 | | 14.2 | EBIT/Interest | | 13.2 | | 9.4 | 68.2 | 15.1 |
| (102) | 3.9 | (100) | 6.1 | (106) | 6.6 | | (11) | 1.3 | | (23) 3.6 | (19) 7.4 | (42) 6.9 |
| | 1.8 | | 2.7 | | 2.0 | | | .4 | | 1.3 | 5.7 | 2.7 |
| | 6.3 | | 7.9 | | 6.3 | Net Profit + Depr., Dep., Amort./Cur. Mat. L/T/D | | | | | | 9.1 |
| (24) | 3.3 | (16) | 3.4 | (26) | 2.8 | | | | | | (15) | 5.1 |
| | 1.7 | | 1.3 | | .9 | | | | | | | 2.6 |
| | .3 | | .3 | | .3 | Fixed/Worth | | .4 | .1 | .4 | .2 | .6 |
| | .8 | | .8 | | .9 | | | 1.1 | .6 | 1.1 | .5 | 1.0 |
| | 2.5 | | 2.7 | | 2.2 | | | 1.7 | 2.2 | 17.0 | 1.2 | 2.2 |
| | .7 | | .7 | | .6 | Debt/Worth | | .7 | .3 | .7 | .4 | .6 |
| | 2.1 | | 1.7 | | 1.7 | | | 3.1 | .8 | 2.4 | 1.0 | 1.9 |
| | 5.5 | | 6.1 | | 4.8 | | | 14.8 | 2.7 | 19.9 | 2.9 | 3.3 |
| | 47.6 | | 51.6 | | 43.8 | % Profit Before Taxes/Tangible Net Worth | | 85.2 | 54.1 | 42.5 | 54.1 | 41.9 |
| (100) | 24.9 | (94) | 26.1 | (102) | 24.3 | | (11) | 10.4 | (10) 33.4 | (19) 15.1 | 32.2 | (40) 24.0 |
| | 8.7 | | 10.8 | | 9.7 | | | .0 | 8.4 | -.4 | 13.8 | 10.7 |
| | 15.5 | | 16.8 | | 17.5 | % Profit Before Taxes/Total Assets | | 12.7 | 32.7 | 15.3 | 25.6 | 15.4 |
| | 7.2 | | 8.6 | | 8.5 | | | 1.8 | 10.4 | 7.1 | 10.2 | 8.4 |
| | 2.7 | | 3.7 | | 3.1 | | | -1.6 | 2.0 | 1.3 | 4.3 | 3.7 |
| | 30.6 | | 18.2 | | 17.2 | Sales/Net Fixed Assets | | 13.5 | 58.1 | 20.0 | 39.3 | 13.6 |
| | 10.5 | | 10.0 | | 8.6 | | | 4.0 | 9.7 | 8.2 | 15.1 | 8.5 |
| | 4.1 | | 4.0 | | 4.3 | | | 2.3 | 5.9 | 4.0 | 7.1 | 4.7 |
| | 3.0 | | 3.0 | | 3.1 | Sales/Total Assets | | 3.2 | 3.4 | 2.7 | 3.9 | 2.9 |
| | 2.2 | | 2.2 | | 2.2 | | | 1.9 | 2.9 | 2.1 | 2.7 | 2.2 |
| | 1.5 | | 1.5 | | 1.7 | | | 1.4 | 2.1 | 1.5 | 1.8 | 1.7 |
| | 1.1 | | 1.0 | | 1.2 | % Depr., Dep., Amort./Sales | | .9 | 1.2 | .9 | 1.4 | |
| (94) | 2.2 | (97) | 2.0 | (102) | 2.2 | | (11) 1.2 | (20) 3.9 | (20) 1.9 | (40) 2.2 | |
| | 4.8 | | 3.9 | | 3.7 | | | 3.2 | 6.9 | 3.5 | 2.9 | |
| | 1.9 | | 2.3 | | 2.1 | % Officers', Directors' Owners' Comp/Sales | | | | | | |
| (26) | 2.9 | (22) | 3.3 | (25) | 2.9 | | | | | | | |
| | 6.0 | | 6.2 | | 7.2 | | | | | | | |
| 5583491M | 6160664M | 4572546M | Net Sales ($) | 1561M | 24505M | 46214M | 171597M | 356483M | 3972186M |
| 2820257M | 3047839M | 2452531M | Total Assets ($) | 997M | 16884M | 17579M | 89725M | 145821M | 2181525M |

M = $ thousand    MM = $ million
See Pages 9 through 22 for Explanation of Ratios and Data

## Current Data Sorted by Assets      Comparative Historical Data

| | | | | | | Type of Statement | | |
|---|---|---|---|---|---|---|---|---|
| | | 11 | 40 | 8 | 4 | Unqualified | 85 | 73 |
| 3 | 17 | 55 | 36 | | | Reviewed | 158 | 142 |
| 6 | 31 | 39 | 4 | | | Compiled | 94 | 102 |
| 47 | 59 | 36 | | | | Tax Returns | 75 | 107 |
| 15 | 44 | 69 | 60 | 7 | 3 | Other | 253 | 232 |
| | 106 (4/1-9/30/11) | | 488 (10/1/11-3/31/12) | | | | 4/1/07-3/31/08 | 4/1/08-3/31/09 |
| 0-500M | 500M-2MM | 2-10MM | 10-50MM | 50-100MM | 100-250MM | | ALL | ALL |
| 71 | 151 | 210 | 140 | 15 | 7 | NUMBER OF STATEMENTS | 665 | 656 |
| % | % | % | % | % | % | ASSETS | % | % |
| 17.5 | 10.9 | 8.5 | 8.8 | 2.2 | | Cash & Equivalents | 8.6 | 8.3 |
| 30.2 | 30.0 | 28.8 | 25.9 | 24.4 | | Trade Receivables (net) | 28.5 | 27.6 |
| 6.8 | 11.7 | 10.4 | 11.5 | 11.5 | | Inventory | 9.9 | 10.3 |
| 4.1 | 1.7 | 2.1 | 2.2 | 4.6 | | All Other Current | 2.3 | 1.8 |
| 58.7 | 54.3 | 49.8 | 48.4 | 42.8 | | Total Current | 49.2 | 47.9 |
| 27.3 | 31.2 | 41.0 | 43.0 | 40.9 | | Fixed Assets (net) | 41.1 | 41.7 |
| 4.5 | 5.2 | 4.0 | 3.4 | 7.9 | | Intangibles (net) | 4.4 | 4.1 |
| 9.4 | 9.4 | 5.2 | 5.2 | 8.4 | | All Other Non-Current | 5.3 | 6.2 |
| 100.0 | 100.0 | 100.0 | 100.0 | 100.0 | | Total | 100.0 | 100.0 |
| | | | | | | LIABILITIES | | |
| 14.1 | 9.6 | 7.2 | 6.5 | 3.5 | | Notes Payable-Short Term | 8.8 | 8.8 |
| 8.0 | 6.9 | 8.1 | 7.3 | 8.8 | | Cur. Mat.-L.T.D. | 7.4 | 7.1 |
| 18.7 | 17.7 | 15.0 | 12.2 | 11.5 | | Trade Payables | 14.7 | 14.5 |
| .0 | .2 | .2 | .2 | .2 | | Income Taxes Payable | .2 | .2 |
| 25.7 | 9.0 | 8.0 | 8.1 | 9.6 | | All Other Current | 8.2 | 7.8 |
| 66.5 | 43.5 | 38.5 | 34.3 | 33.6 | | Total Current | 39.2 | 38.4 |
| 40.7 | 32.4 | 28.0 | 22.6 | 27.0 | | Long-Term Debt | 28.6 | 31.0 |
| .0 | .2 | 1.3 | 1.2 | .5 | | Deferred Taxes | .6 | .9 |
| 15.4 | 7.4 | 5.4 | 8.1 | 10.0 | | All Other Non-Current | 4.0 | 4.7 |
| -22.8 | 16.5 | 26.8 | 33.8 | 28.9 | | Net Worth | 27.6 | 25.1 |
| 100.0 | 100.0 | 100.0 | 100.0 | 100.0 | | Total Liabilties & Net Worth | 100.0 | 100.0 |
| | | | | | | INCOME DATA | | |
| 100.0 | 100.0 | 100.0 | 100.0 | 100.0 | | Net Sales | 100.0 | 100.0 |
| 51.1 | 44.8 | 33.3 | 26.3 | 26.6 | | Gross Profit | 35.5 | 34.5 |
| 48.0 | 41.7 | 30.2 | 22.4 | 21.6 | | Operating Expenses | 31.1 | 31.8 |
| 3.1 | 3.1 | 3.1 | 3.9 | 5.0 | | Operating Profit | 4.3 | 2.7 |
| .8 | 1.1 | 1.1 | 1.4 | 1.7 | | All Other Expenses (net) | 1.4 | 1.4 |
| 2.2 | 2.0 | 2.0 | 2.5 | 3.3 | | Profit Before Taxes | 2.9 | 1.3 |
| | | | | | | RATIOS | | |
| 2.8 | 2.3 | 2.1 | 2.2 | 1.7 | | | 2.0 | 2.1 |
| 1.3 | 1.3 | 1.4 | 1.5 | 1.3 | | Current | 1.4 | 1.3 |
| .5 | .8 | 1.0 | .9 | 1.1 | | | .9 | .9 |
| 2.2 | 1.9 | 1.5 | 1.6 | 1.1 | | | 1.6 | 1.6 |
| 1.1 | .9 | 1.0 | 1.0 | .9 | | Quick | 1.0 | .9 |
| .3 | .6 | .7 | .6 | .6 | | | .7 | .6 |
| 0 UND | 29 12.6 | 33 10.9 | 40 9.2 | 36 10.0 | | | 36 10.2 | 33 11.2 |
| 23 15.9 | 38 9.7 | 42 8.6 | 49 7.4 | 51 7.2 | | Sales/Receivables | 45 8.1 | 42 8.7 |
| 41 9.0 | 47 7.7 | 54 6.7 | 62 5.9 | 63 5.8 | | | 58 6.3 | 54 6.7 |
| 0 UND | 6 65.4 | 11 32.4 | 16 23.3 | 21 17.8 | | | 10 35.1 | 10 37.3 |
| 2 160.0 | 15 24.0 | 20 18.4 | 26 14.3 | 25 14.4 | | Cost of Sales/Inventory | 20 18.5 | 18 19.9 |
| 11 34.1 | 42 8.6 | 32 11.5 | 40 9.1 | 38 9.7 | | | 34 10.8 | 35 10.6 |
| 0 UND | 17 21.8 | 20 18.3 | 18 20.6 | 20 18.7 | | | 19 18.9 | 18 19.9 |
| 16 22.8 | 34 10.6 | 30 12.1 | 27 13.5 | 24 15.3 | | Cost of Sales/Payables | 31 11.9 | 29 12.4 |
| 51 7.1 | 65 5.6 | 44 8.3 | 45 8.2 | 38 9.5 | | | 49 7.4 | 46 8.0 |
| 8.3 | 8.2 | 8.7 | 6.5 | 9.9 | | | 7.9 | 8.6 |
| 39.9 | 22.2 | 19.7 | 13.8 | 18.7 | | Sales/Working Capital | 19.1 | 24.5 |
| -12.4 | -33.1 | 398.6 | -91.5 | 42.8 | | | -74.7 | -60.1 |
| 11.3 | 6.5 | 6.6 | 5.8 | 5.8 | | | 5.8 | 4.4 |
| (56) 2.5 | (142) 2.4 | (205) 2.7 | (135) 2.4 | 4.1 | | EBIT/Interest | (627) 2.4 | (629) 1.8 |
| .4 | 1.0 | .9 | .9 | 1.7 | | | 1.0 | -.1 |
| | 2.6 | 2.9 | 3.4 | | | | 2.9 | 2.7 |
| | (17) 1.4 | (64) 1.6 | (50) 2.0 | | | Net Profit + Depr., Dep., Amort./Cur. Mat. L/T/D | (198) 1.8 | (193) 1.4 |
| | .9 | 1.1 | 1.3 | | | | 1.0 | .7 |
| .3 | .6 | .7 | .7 | 1.1 | | | .8 | .8 |
| 4.8 | 1.6 | 1.6 | 1.5 | 2.4 | | Fixed/Worth | 1.6 | 1.8 |
| -.6 | -2.3 | 4.2 | 3.2 | -15.2 | | | 5.6 | 8.2 |
| 1.0 | 1.4 | 1.0 | .9 | 1.0 | | | 1.2 | 1.2 |
| 23.4 | 4.3 | 2.4 | 2.1 | 5.8 | | Debt/Worth | 2.5 | 2.7 |
| -3.0 | -7.1 | 7.8 | 5.2 | -47.1 | | | 10.5 | 17.2 |
| 108.6 | 76.4 | 33.1 | 26.7 | 111.1 | | | 41.4 | 32.6 |
| (41) 20.7 | (106) 19.6 | (178) 14.5 | (123) 12.0 | (11) 15.8 | | % Profit Before Taxes/Tangible Net Worth | (544) 18.0 | (517) 11.3 |
| .9 | 2.6 | .4 | 1.1 | 9.0 | | | 2.8 | -3.8 |
| 30.2 | 16.0 | 10.8 | 9.3 | 7.4 | | | 12.6 | 9.9 |
| 6.4 | 4.4 | 4.3 | 4.1 | 5.6 | | % Profit Before Taxes/Total Assets | 5.0 | 3.0 |
| -2.0 | -.1 | -.4 | -.1 | 2.7 | | | .2 | -2.9 |
| 55.5 | 24.8 | 10.9 | 6.9 | 6.5 | | | 9.9 | 10.8 |
| 20.2 | 10.0 | 5.3 | 3.9 | 4.6 | | Sales/Net Fixed Assets | 5.3 | 5.2 |
| 9.2 | 5.4 | 3.4 | 2.5 | 3.3 | | | 3.2 | 3.1 |
| 6.1 | 3.8 | 2.8 | 2.3 | 2.2 | | | 2.8 | 2.9 |
| 4.1 | 2.6 | 2.2 | 1.7 | 1.8 | | Sales/Total Assets | 2.1 | 2.2 |
| 3.0 | 2.0 | 1.7 | 1.3 | 1.5 | | | 1.6 | 1.5 |
| .6 | 1.3 | 2.5 | 3.4 | 3.3 | | | 2.7 | 2.6 |
| (48) 1.6 | (119) 2.9 | (196) 4.0 | (134) 4.8 | (12) 4.8 | | % Depr., Dep., Amort./Sales | (609) 4.2 | (587) 4.2 |
| 4.6 | 5.4 | 6.0 | 6.6 | 5.9 | | | 5.9 | 6.5 |
| 4.2 | 3.0 | 2.1 | 1.0 | | | | 2.3 | 2.4 |
| (47) 8.2 | (97) 4.8 | (93) 3.5 | (36) 2.1 | | | % Officers', Directors' Owners' Comp/Sales | (290) 4.2 | (261) 4.3 |
| 14.3 | 6.8 | 5.4 | 4.5 | | | | 7.8 | 7.9 |
| 86095M | 483261M | 2152371M | 5352854M | 2027253M | 1164114M | Net Sales ($) | 12928855M | 11811712M |
| 18141M | 174465M | 956231M | 2879900M | 1114067M | 1025084M | Total Assets ($) | 7176700M | 6414191M |

© RMA 2012

M = $ thousand     MM = $ million
See Pages 9 through 22 for Explanation of Ratios and Data

## Comparative Historical Data

## Current Data Sorted by Sales

| | | | Type of Statement | | | | | | |
|---|---|---|---|---|---|---|---|---|---|
| 72 | 77 | 63 | Unqualified | | | 1 | 1 | 20 | 41 |
| 136 | 135 | 111 | Reviewed | 1 | 8 | 13 | 24 | 47 | 18 |
| 80 | 105 | 80 | Compiled | 5 | 20 | 12 | 24 | 18 | 1 |
| 123 | 112 | 142 | Tax Returns | 31 | 48 | 31 | 21 | 11 | |
| 247 | 228 | 198 | Other | 8 | 30 | 27 | 33 | 43 | 57 |
| 4/1/09-3/31/10 ALL | 4/1/10-3/31/11 ALL | 4/1/11-3/31/12 ALL | | 106 (4/1-9/30/11) | | | 488 (10/1/11-3/31/12) | | |
| | | | | 0-1MM | 1-3MM | 3-5MM | 5-10MM | 10-25MM | 25MM & OVER |
| 658 | 657 | 594 | **NUMBER OF STATEMENTS** | 45 | 106 | 84 | 103 | 139 | 117 |
| % | % | % | **ASSETS** | % | % | % | % | % | % |
| 9.0 | 10.1 | 10.1 | Cash & Equivalents | 15.0 | 12.8 | 11.5 | 8.3 | 9.1 | 7.8 |
| 26.9 | 27.4 | 28.3 | Trade Receivables (net) | 25.2 | 27.4 | 29.9 | 28.2 | 29.8 | 27.6 |
| 9.8 | 10.6 | 10.6 | Inventory | 8.7 | 9.2 | 10.7 | 9.9 | 10.8 | 12.8 |
| 2.2 | 2.1 | 2.3 | All Other Current | 3.4 | 2.5 | 2.0 | 1.9 | 1.9 | 2.8 |
| 48.0 | 50.3 | 51.4 | Total Current | 52.3 | 52.0 | 54.1 | 48.3 | 51.6 | 51.0 |
| 40.6 | 39.1 | 37.4 | Fixed Assets (net) | 28.0 | 33.1 | 34.3 | 40.6 | 41.8 | 39.1 |
| 5.5 | 5.0 | 4.4 | Intangibles (net) | 7.9 | 5.5 | 3.5 | 4.7 | 2.9 | 4.3 |
| 6.0 | 5.6 | 6.8 | All Other Non-Current | 11.7 | 9.5 | 8.1 | 6.4 | 3.8 | 5.6 |
| 100.0 | 100.0 | 100.0 | Total | 100.0 | 100.0 | 100.0 | 100.0 | 100.0 | 100.0 |
| | | | **LIABILITIES** | | | | | | |
| 9.7 | 9.4 | 8.3 | Notes Payable-Short Term | 12.7 | 9.6 | 11.4 | 7.2 | 6.7 | 6.1 |
| 7.8 | 7.5 | 7.6 | Cur. Mat.-L.T.D. | 10.7 | 5.7 | 6.6 | 10.3 | 7.4 | 6.7 |
| 15.1 | 15.0 | 15.3 | Trade Payables | 10.8 | 18.3 | 18.7 | 15.0 | 14.4 | 13.3 |
| .2 | .2 | .2 | Income Taxes Payable | .1 | .1 | .2 | .1 | .3 | .1 |
| 9.2 | 9.7 | 10.4 | All Other Current | 22.4 | 12.3 | 9.3 | 7.9 | 8.5 | 9.5 |
| 42.0 | 41.9 | 41.8 | Total Current | 56.7 | 46.1 | 46.2 | 40.5 | 37.4 | 35.6 |
| 31.0 | 29.9 | 29.3 | Long-Term Debt | 37.7 | 38.3 | 30.6 | 32.3 | 23.9 | 20.9 |
| .8 | .9 | .8 | Deferred Taxes | .0 | .3 | .4 | 1.4 | 1.1 | 1.1 |
| 5.1 | 8.0 | 7.9 | All Other Non-Current | 12.5 | 12.2 | 3.9 | 4.6 | 6.4 | 9.7 |
| 21.2 | 19.2 | 20.1 | Net Worth | -7.2 | 3.1 | 18.9 | 21.3 | 31.2 | 32.6 |
| 100.0 | 100.0 | 100.0 | Total Liabilities & Net Worth | 100.0 | 100.0 | 100.0 | 100.0 | 100.0 | 100.0 |
| | | | **INCOME DATA** | | | | | | |
| 100.0 | 100.0 | 100.0 | Net Sales | 100.0 | 100.0 | 100.0 | 100.0 | 100.0 | 100.0 |
| 35.2 | 36.1 | 36.4 | Gross Profit | 56.9 | 46.4 | 42.9 | 34.3 | 28.6 | 25.8 |
| 34.0 | 33.1 | 33.0 | Operating Expenses | 54.3 | 43.8 | 39.2 | 31.1 | 25.0 | 21.7 |
| 1.2 | 3.1 | 3.4 | Operating Profit | 2.5 | 2.7 | 3.7 | 3.2 | 3.6 | 4.1 |
| 1.6 | 1.3 | 1.2 | All Other Expenses (net) | 1.1 | 1.2 | .9 | 1.3 | 1.2 | 1.2 |
| -.5 | 1.8 | 2.2 | Profit Before Taxes | 1.4 | 1.4 | 2.8 | 1.9 | 2.4 | 2.9 |
| | | | **RATIOS** | | | | | | |
| 2.2 | 2.3 | 2.2 | | 2.7 | 2.5 | 2.3 | 2.1 | 2.1 | 2.1 |
| 1.2 | 1.3 | 1.4 | Current | 1.2 | 1.4 | 1.3 | 1.4 | 1.3 | 1.5 |
| .8 | .9 | .9 | | .3 | .7 | .8 | 1.1 | 1.0 | 1.0 |
| 1.7 | 1.7 | 1.7 | | 2.3 | 1.8 | 2.0 | 1.6 | 1.5 | 1.5 |
| .9 | 1.0 | 1.0 | Quick | .9 | 1.0 | .9 | 1.1 | 1.0 | 1.0 |
| .6 | .6 | .6 | | .3 | .5 | .5 | .8 | .7 | .6 |
| 32  11.5 | 32  11.6 | 31  11.7 | | 0  UND | 24  15.5 | 26  14.1 | 34  10.7 | 37  9.8 | 38  9.5 |
| 43  8.5 | 43  8.4 | 41  8.8 | Sales/Receivables | 25  14.7 | 35  10.5 | 38  9.7 | 42  8.7 | 46  7.9 | 48  7.6 |
| 56  6.6 | 59  6.2 | 54  6.7 | | 45  8.1 | 47  7.8 | 49  7.5 | 57  6.4 | 58  6.3 | 62  5.9 |
| 9  40.3 | 10  35.6 | 8  44.5 | | 0  UND | 2  202.3 | 5  71.7 | 12  30.9 | 12  29.6 | 16  23.1 |
| 19  18.8 | 22  16.5 | 20  18.6 | Cost of Sales/Inventory | 4  91.0 | 10  36.8 | 15  24.0 | 22  16.4 | 21  17.2 | 26  14.1 |
| 36  10.0 | 38  9.5 | 36  10.2 | | 23  15.7 | 41  8.9 | 33  10.9 | 34  10.6 | 31  11.7 | 39  9.3 |
| 19  19.4 | 18  20.4 | 17  21.5 | | 0  UND | 13  28.9 | 17  21.5 | 21  17.8 | 20  18.6 | 18  20.4 |
| 32  11.3 | 31  11.8 | 29  12.6 | Cost of Sales/Payables | 16  22.8 | 34  10.7 | 33  11.2 | 33  11.2 | 29  12.4 | 26  14.3 |
| 52  7.0 | 51  7.1 | 49  7.4 | | 59  6.2 | 63  5.8 | 54  6.7 | 51  7.1 | 41  8.9 | 42  8.6 |
| 7.9 | 8.1 | 7.5 | | 7.2 | 7.8 | 8.2 | 8.9 | 8.4 | 7.5 |
| 28.9 | 21.4 | 19.2 | Sales/Working Capital | 39.9 | 24.5 | 24.9 | 17.9 | 21.9 | 14.2 |
| -24.7 | -42.1 | -66.4 | | -7.8 | -19.3 | -43.4 | 93.6 | -336.7 | 552.5 |
| 3.7 | 5.4 | 6.4 | | 7.2 | 5.0 | 9.1 | 5.9 | 6.7 | 6.7 |
| (619)  1.2 | (624)  1.9 | (559)  2.6 | EBIT/Interest | (33)  2.4 | (97)  2.0 | (82)  3.0 | (101)  2.4 | (135)  2.8 | (111)  3.0 |
| -1.4 | .4 | .9 | | .0 | .5 | 1.0 | .9 | .9 | 1.4 |
| 2.1 | 3.4 | 3.0 | | | | 5.0 | 2.5 | 3.3 | 3.8 |
| (164)  1.3 | (157)  1.8 | (143)  1.7 | Net Profit + Depr., Dep., Amort./Cur. Mat. L/T/D | | (10)  1.7 | (34)  1.5 | (47)  1.9 | (41)  2.3 |
| .3 | 1.0 | 1.1 | | | | 1.4 | .9 | 1.1 | 1.4 |
| .8 | .8 | .7 | | .1 | .6 | .6 | .9 | .7 | .7 |
| 1.9 | 1.6 | 1.6 | Fixed/Worth | 2.7 | 2.4 | 1.4 | 2.0 | 1.5 | 1.5 |
| 27.4 | -111.6 | 7.2 | | -.5 | -1.5 | 9.4 | 9.4 | 3.0 | 3.2 |
| 1.1 | 1.1 | 1.0 | | .7 | 1.4 | 1.2 | 1.1 | 1.1 | .9 |
| 2.9 | 2.8 | 2.7 | Debt/Worth | 6.9 | 4.4 | 3.6 | 3.0 | 2.2 | 2.1 |
| UND | -111.9 | 20.4 | | -2.8 | -4.6 | NM | 25.8 | 5.1 | 6.9 |
| 24.9 | 36.6 | 40.7 | | 81.5 | 55.0 | 87.0 | 27.7 | 34.7 | 31.6 |
| (496)  4.6 | (490)  14.1 | (464)  15.1 | % Profit Before Taxes/Tangible Net Worth | (28)  13.8 | (68)  9.5 | (63)  22.0 | (83)  15.5 | (124)  15.0 | (98)  15.3 |
| -14.3 | -.8 | 1.4 | | -10.4 | .1 | 1.7 | 1.4 | 1.7 | 2.5 |
| 7.4 | 11.1 | 11.9 | | 27.8 | 14.0 | 16.6 | 9.8 | 10.9 | 9.3 |
| .6 | 3.1 | 4.6 | % Profit Before Taxes/Total Assets | 5.4 | 3.0 | 5.7 | 4.4 | 4.4 | 4.9 |
| -7.2 | -2.3 | -.3 | | -4.7 | -2.0 | .1 | -.5 | -.1 | .4 |
| 11.1 | 12.1 | 15.5 | | 69.9 | 24.5 | 18.1 | 11.8 | 9.8 | 8.4 |
| 4.9 | 5.9 | 6.3 | Sales/Net Fixed Assets | 16.7 | 9.5 | 9.7 | 5.4 | 4.2 | 5.1 |
| 2.9 | 3.3 | 3.5 | | 6.1 | 4.1 | 4.9 | 3.1 | 3.1 | 3.4 |
| 2.8 | 2.9 | 3.1 | | 4.8 | 3.9 | 4.1 | 2.7 | 3.0 | 2.4 |
| 2.0 | 2.2 | 2.2 | Sales/Total Assets | 3.2 | 2.6 | 2.6 | 2.1 | 2.1 | 1.9 |
| 1.4 | 1.5 | 1.6 | | 1.6 | 1.8 | 2.0 | 1.5 | 1.6 | 1.5 |
| 2.7 | 2.6 | 2.3 | | .8 | 1.3 | 1.3 | 2.4 | 2.7 | 3.1 |
| (579)  4.7 | (581)  4.2 | (511)  3.9 | % Depr., Dep., Amort./Sales | (32)  3.4 | (80)  3.0 | (67)  3.3 | (97)  4.1 | (129)  4.1 | (106)  4.4 |
| 7.3 | 6.4 | 6.0 | | 5.5 | 6.4 | 6.1 | 6.0 | 6.1 | 5.5 |
| 2.7 | 2.5 | 2.4 | | 5.4 | 3.6 | 3.0 | 2.4 | 1.5 | .5 |
| (296)  4.7 | (274)  4.2 | (275)  4.3 | % Officers', Directors' Owners' Comp/Sales | (27)  10.6 | (66)  5.5 | (56)  4.7 | (51)  3.8 | (50)  2.9 | (25)  1.7 |
| 8.3 | 7.5 | 6.7 | | 16.9 | 9.6 | 6.7 | 5.8 | 4.9 | 2.8 |
| 10498479M | 10793029M | 11265948M | Net Sales ($) | 26454M | 213569M | 337734M | 751244M | 2185050M | 7751897M |
| 6333220M | 6540901M | 6167888M | Total Assets ($) | 15167M | 91868M | 139285M | 396183M | 1164396M | 4360989M |

© RMA 2012

M = $ thousand    MM = $ million
See Pages 9 through 22 for Explanation of Ratios and Data

## Current Data Sorted by Assets

## Comparative Historical Data

| 0-500M | 500M-2MM | 2-10MM | 10-50MM | 50-100MM | 100-250MM | Type of Statement | 4/1/07-3/31/08 ALL | 4/1/08-3/31/09 ALL |
|---|---|---|---|---|---|---|---|---|
| | 1 | | | | | Unqualified | 6 | 3 |
| | 3 | 2 | 3 | 1 | | Reviewed | 3 | 5 |
| 1 | 2 | 3 | 7 | | | Compiled | 2 | 1 |
| 1 | 3 | 3 | 1 | | | Tax Returns | 1 | |
| | 3 | 4 | 6 | 1 | 2 | Other | 4 | 4 |
| | 7 (4/1-9/30/11) | | 40 (10/1/11-3/31/12) | | | | | |
| 2 | 12 | 12 | 17 | 2 | 2 | NUMBER OF STATEMENTS | 16 | 13 |
| % | % | % | % | % | % | ASSETS | % | % |
| | 10.4 | 6.4 | 8.6 | | | Cash & Equivalents | 10.3 | 8.2 |
| | 35.9 | 32.0 | 23.9 | | | Trade Receivables (net) | 27.6 | 22.5 |
| | 13.5 | 13.9 | 13.5 | | | Inventory | 15.1 | 14.9 |
| | .2 | .8 | 4.0 | | | All Other Current | 6.6 | 5.1 |
| | 60.0 | 53.2 | 50.1 | | | Total Current | 59.6 | 50.7 |
| | 34.3 | 33.9 | 36.6 | | | Fixed Assets (net) | 31.8 | 32.8 |
| | .9 | 6.5 | 9.9 | | | Intangibles (net) | 1.8 | 8.9 |
| | 4.8 | 6.4 | 3.5 | | | All Other Non-Current | 6.8 | 7.6 |
| | 100.0 | 100.0 | 100.0 | | | Total | 100.0 | 100.0 |
| | | | | | | LIABILITIES | | |
| | 7.3 | 11.3 | 11.0 | | | Notes Payable-Short Term | 1.6 | 5.9 |
| | 7.0 | 5.4 | 6.9 | | | Cur. Mat.-L.T.D. | 6.7 | 5.1 |
| | 14.1 | 17.9 | 11.4 | | | Trade Payables | 13.9 | 8.0 |
| | .0 | .0 | .0 | | | Income Taxes Payable | .1 | .0 |
| | 8.3 | 9.0 | 7.5 | | | All Other Current | 10.0 | 10.4 |
| | 36.7 | 43.6 | 36.9 | | | Total Current | 32.3 | 29.4 |
| | 7.6 | 14.3 | 14.4 | | | Long-Term Debt | 33.6 | 29.4 |
| | .0 | 1.1 | 2.2 | | | Deferred Taxes | .4 | .3 |
| | 14.8 | 4.8 | 8.8 | | | All Other Non-Current | 1.1 | 12.4 |
| | 40.8 | 36.2 | 37.7 | | | Net Worth | 32.7 | 28.4 |
| | 100.0 | 100.0 | 100.0 | | | Total Liabilities & Net Worth | 100.0 | 100.0 |
| | | | | | | INCOME DATA | | |
| | 100.0 | 100.0 | 100.0 | | | Net Sales | 100.0 | 100.0 |
| | 35.1 | 31.8 | 26.3 | | | Gross Profit | 42.7 | 29.4 |
| | 29.3 | 29.6 | 22.9 | | | Operating Expenses | 37.0 | 24.8 |
| | 5.8 | 2.2 | 3.4 | | | Operating Profit | 5.7 | 4.6 |
| | .1 | .0 | 1.2 | | | All Other Expenses (net) | 1.0 | 2.3 |
| | 5.7 | 2.2 | 2.2 | | | Profit Before Taxes | 4.7 | 2.3 |
| | | | | | | RATIOS | | |
| | 3.3 | 2.2 | 2.7 | | | | 5.4 | 3.4 |
| | 2.0 | 1.3 | 1.1 | | | Current | 1.8 | 1.6 |
| | 1.0 | .9 | 1.0 | | | | .9 | .9 |
| | 2.1 | 1.7 | 2.3 | | | | 1.5 | 1.8 |
| | 1.7 | .9 | .7 | | | Quick | 1.3 | 1.0 |
| | .8 | .6 | .5 | | | | .8 | .6 |
| | 33  11.1 | 35  10.3 | 42  8.6 | | | | 18  19.9 | 20  18.5 |
| | 39  9.3 | 50  7.3 | 49  7.5 | | | Sales/Receivables | 35  10.5 | 28  12.8 |
| | 50  7.3 | 61  6.0 | 55  6.6 | | | | 56  6.5 | 50  7.2 |
| | 13  27.7 | 15  24.6 | 23  15.9 | | | | 2  150.8 | 9  41.6 |
| | 21  17.8 | 30  12.2 | 34  10.7 | | | Cost of Sales/Inventory | 21  17.4 | 22  16.4 |
| | 39  9.3 | 45  8.1 | 49  7.4 | | | | 83  4.4 | 58  6.3 |
| | 10  37.6 | 29  12.4 | 17  21.6 | | | | 2  185.8 | 12  30.6 |
| | 23  15.7 | 36  10.1 | 30  12.3 | | | Cost of Sales/Payables | 27  13.3 | 24  15.4 |
| | 38  9.6 | 45  8.1 | 46  7.9 | | | | 43  8.4 | 31  11.6 |
| | 6.1 | 10.3 | 7.7 | | | | 4.1 | 4.7 |
| | 11.8 | 20.5 | 58.2 | | | Sales/Working Capital | 8.6 | 24.4 |
| | NM | -33.5 | NM | | | | -115.9 | NM |
| | 17.8 | 18.7 | 15.8 | | | | 17.4 | 16.8 |
| | (11)  8.4 | (11)  5.1 | 2.1 | | | EBIT/Interest | (15)  3.5 | 2.7 |
| | 3.8 | .7 | .4 | | | | 1.7 | .6 |
| | | | | | | Net Profit + Depr., Dep., Amort./Cur. Mat. L/T/D | | |
| | .4 | .5 | .8 | | | | .1 | .3 |
| | .8 | 1.8 | 1.4 | | | Fixed/Worth | 1.1 | 4.0 |
| | 2.9 | 2.7 | 7.4 | | | | -82.4 | -2.7 |
| | .4 | .7 | .8 | | | | .4 | .5 |
| | .7 | 3.3 | 1.9 | | | Debt/Worth | 3.0 | 5.8 |
| | 5.7 | 4.6 | 15.4 | | | | -121.7 | -7.0 |
| | 44.7 | 48.2 | 27.9 | | | | 83.9 | |
| | (10)  31.6 | (11)  26.3 | (16)  8.9 | | | % Profit Before Taxes/Tangible Net Worth | (11)  24.3 | |
| | 14.9 | -4.6 | -10.0 | | | | 9.3 | |
| | 25.5 | 13.8 | 9.2 | | | | 19.0 | 13.1 |
| | 15.3 | 5.4 | 2.8 | | | % Profit Before Taxes/Total Assets | 10.0 | 2.5 |
| | 5.7 | -3.3 | -1.6 | | | | 2.1 | -2.3 |
| | 17.6 | 14.3 | 7.0 | | | | 39.6 | 51.5 |
| | 7.6 | 7.5 | 4.3 | | | Sales/Net Fixed Assets | 12.9 | 6.3 |
| | 5.3 | 4.6 | 3.3 | | | | 2.5 | 2.6 |
| | 3.7 | 3.1 | 2.1 | | | | 4.0 | 2.6 |
| | 2.9 | 2.7 | 1.6 | | | Sales/Total Assets | 2.3 | 1.7 |
| | 2.7 | 2.0 | 1.5 | | | | 1.6 | 1.4 |
| | 1.7 | 2.9 | 3.9 | | | | 1.0 | 1.6 |
| | (11)  3.2 | 3.5 | 5.1 | | | % Depr., Dep., Amort./Sales | (14)  2.6 | (11)  5.1 |
| | 5.8 | 5.2 | 6.6 | | | | 6.6 | 10.0 |
| | | | | | | % Officers', Directors' Owners' Comp/Sales | | |
| 2892M | 39969M | 137759M | 714485M | 289029M | 352236M | Net Sales ($) | 606056M | 355247M |
| 643M | 13595M | 58752M | 408253M | 133773M | 270376M | Total Assets ($) | 437565M | 209880M |

M = $ thousand    MM = $ million
See Pages 9 through 22 for Explanation of Ratios and Data

## Comparative Historical Data

| | | | | | | | Type of Statement | | | | | | |
|---|---|---|---|---|---|---|---|---|---|---|---|---|---|
| | 4 | | 2 | | 5 | | Unqualified | | | | | | |
| | 4 | | 2 | | 12 | | Reviewed | | | | | | |
| | | | | | 7 | | Compiled | | | | | | |
| | | | | | 7 | | Tax Returns | | | | | | |
| | 4 | | 6 | | 16 | | Other | | | | | | |
| | 4/1/09-3/31/10 | | 4/1/10-3/31/11 | | 4/1/11-3/31/12 | | | | | | | | |
| | ALL | | ALL | | ALL | | | | | | | | |
| | 12 | | 10 | | 47 | | NUMBER OF STATEMENTS | | | | | | |

## Current Data Sorted by Sales

| | | | | | | | | | | | | | |
|---|---|---|---|---|---|---|---|---|---|---|---|---|---|
| | | | | | | | | | 1 | | | 6 | 4 |
| | | | | | | | | | 2 | 1 | | 3 | 3 |
| | | | | | | | | 2 | | 2 | | 1 | |
| | | | | | | | | 2 | 3 | 1 | | 1 | |
| | | | | | | | | 3 | | 2 | | 2 | 9 |
| | | | | | | | | 7 (4/1-9/30/11) | | 40 (10/1/11-3/31/12) | | | |
| | | | | | | | 0-1MM | 1-3MM | 3-5MM | 5-10MM | 10-25MM | 25MM & OVER | |
| | | | | | | | | 7 | 6 | 6 | 12 | 16 | |

| 4/1/09-3/31/10 % | 4/1/10-3/31/11 % | 4/1/11-3/31/12 % | | 0-1MM % | 1-3MM % | 3-5MM % | 5-10MM % | 10-25MM % | 25MM & OVER % |
|---|---|---|---|---|---|---|---|---|---|
| | | | **ASSETS** | | | | | | |
| 5.8 | 9.3 | 9.0 | Cash & Equivalents | | | | | 9.9 | 8.0 |
| 19.4 | 27.6 | 29.2 | Trade Receivables (net) | | | | | 25.2 | 24.8 |
| 9.0 | 11.6 | 12.9 | Inventory | | | | | 17.0 | 12.2 |
| 4.6 | 2.8 | 1.7 | All Other Current | | | | | 1.7 | 3.6 |
| 38.9 | 51.3 | 52.9 | Total Current | | | | | 53.8 | 48.5 |
| 44.4 | 34.3 | 36.2 | Fixed Assets (net) | | | | | 32.9 | 38.7 |
| 6.4 | 4.0 | 6.5 | Intangibles (net) | | | | | 8.0 | 9.0 |
| 10.2 | 10.4 | 4.4 | All Other Non-Current | | | | | 5.3 | 3.8 |
| 100.0 | 100.0 | 100.0 | Total | | | | | 100.0 | 100.0 |
| | | | **LIABILITIES** | | | | | | |
| 3.4 | 9.0 | 11.5 | Notes Payable-Short Term | | | | | 15.3 | 10.3 |
| 11.6 | 6.8 | 6.1 | Cur. Mat.-L.T.D. | | | | | 7.8 | 5.2 |
| 8.2 | 9.1 | 14.1 | Trade Payables | | | | | 16.1 | 13.1 |
| .0 | .1 | .0 | Income Taxes Payable | | | | | .1 | .0 |
| 6.8 | 5.8 | 8.9 | All Other Current | | | | | 9.6 | 8.9 |
| 30.1 | 30.8 | 40.5 | Total Current | | | | | 48.9 | 37.6 |
| 23.4 | 18.1 | 15.0 | Long-Term Debt | | | | | 13.7 | 19.6 |
| .0 | 1.0 | 1.1 | Deferred Taxes | | | | | 1.7 | 1.1 |
| 2.9 | 3.6 | 8.9 | All Other Non-Current | | | | | 3.9 | 9.4 |
| 43.6 | 46.5 | 34.4 | Net Worth | | | | | 31.8 | 32.2 |
| 100.0 | 100.0 | 100.0 | Total Liabilities & Net Worth | | | | | 100.0 | 100.0 |
| | | | **INCOME DATA** | | | | | | |
| 100.0 | 100.0 | 100.0 | Net Sales | | | | | 100.0 | 100.0 |
| 36.4 | 31.9 | 32.1 | Gross Profit | | | | | 25.2 | 28.6 |
| 30.1 | 26.3 | 28.1 | Operating Expenses | | | | | 21.4 | 25.3 |
| 6.4 | 5.6 | 4.0 | Operating Profit | | | | | 3.8 | 3.3 |
| 1.6 | 1.6 | .7 | All Other Expenses (net) | | | | | 1.0 | 1.5 |
| 4.8 | 4.0 | 3.3 | Profit Before Taxes | | | | | 2.7 | 1.8 |
| | | | **RATIOS** | | | | | | |
| 3.8 | 7.0 | 2.4 | | | | | | 1.5 | 1.6 |
| 1.1 | 1.5 | 1.3 | Current | | | | | 1.2 | 1.1 |
| .6 | .9 | .9 | | | | | | .8 | .9 |
| 2.2 | 6.6 | 2.0 | | | | | | 1.3 | 1.4 |
| .6 | 1.1 | .9 | Quick | | | | | .7 | .8 |
| .4 | .5 | .6 | | | | | | .4 | .6 |
| 18  20.3 | 36  10.2 | 36  10.0 | | | | | 35 | 10.3  39 | 9.3 |
| 43  8.5 | 46  8.0 | 46  7.9 | Sales/Receivables | | | | 47 | 7.7  50 | 7.3 |
| 56  6.6 | 53  6.9 | 55  6.6 | | | | | 60 | 6.1  58 | 6.3 |
| 0  UND | 21  17.7 | 15  24.6 | | | | | 22 | 16.8  22 | 16.8 |
| 14  26.5 | 32  11.5 | 29  12.5 | Cost of Sales/Inventory | | | | 33 | 10.9  30 | 12.0 |
| 42  8.7 | 39  9.3 | 45  8.1 | | | | | 51 | 7.1  51 | 7.2 |
| 9  42.1 | 10  37.1 | 20  18.6 | | | | | 25 | 14.8  23 | 15.7 |
| 23  15.7 | 23  16.0 | 30  12.0 | Cost of Sales/Payables | | | | 35 | 10.4  36 | 10.0 |
| 36  10.0 | 38  9.7 | 45  8.2 | | | | | 64 | 5.7  45 | 8.2 |
| 7.0 | 5.6 | 8.4 | | | | | | 13.2 | 11.4 |
| 178.5 | 14.8 | 20.2 | Sales/Working Capital | | | | | 52.8 | 53.8 |
| -13.6 | -38.9 | -62.8 | | | | | | -25.7 | NM |
| 29.2 | 5.6 | 11.0 | | | | | | 8.6 | 8.8 |
| 3.3 | (43)  3.8 | 3.8 | EBIT/Interest | | | | | 2.0  (14) | 1.9 |
| .0 | | 1.2 | | | | | | .8 | .1 |
| | | 3.2 | Net Profit + Depr., Dep., | | | | | | |
| | (13)  2.0 | 2.0 | Amort./Cur. Mat. L/T/D | | | | | | |
| | | 1.4 | | | | | | | |
| .5 | .3 | .5 | | | | | | .5 | 1.2 |
| 1.7 | 1.4 | 1.4 | Fixed/Worth | | | | | 2.5 | 1.9 |
| NM | 3.7 | 3.3 | | | | | | 6.6 | 6.2 |
| .2 | .2 | .5 | | | | | | .8 | 1.4 |
| 1.5 | 2.3 | 2.0 | Debt/Worth | | | | | 4.0 | 2.5 |
| NM | 6.7 | 7.4 | | | | | | 14.9 | 12.6 |
| | | 36.7 | | | | | | 48.2 | 31.4 |
| | (41)  19.7 | 19.7 | % Profit Before Taxes/Tangible Net Worth | | | | | 11.4  (11) | 11.8  (14) |
| | | 2.5 | | | | | | 1.1 | -15.5 |
| 19.6 | 15.7 | 14.3 | | | | | | 10.2 | 9.7 |
| 7.8 | 8.0 | 6.3 | % Profit Before Taxes/Total Assets | | | | | 2.8 | 2.9 |
| -5.1 | -1.1 | .3 | | | | | | -.5 | -1.9 |
| 11.4 | 19.4 | 11.2 | | | | | | 11.1 | 6.9 |
| 3.4 | 5.9 | 5.7 | Sales/Net Fixed Assets | | | | | 6.7 | 4.4 |
| 2.4 | 3.2 | 3.9 | | | | | | 3.3 | 3.4 |
| 2.4 | 2.7 | 2.9 | | | | | | 2.8 | 2.1 |
| 1.8 | 2.0 | 2.2 | Sales/Total Assets | | | | | 2.1 | 1.8 |
| 1.4 | 1.6 | 1.6 | | | | | | 1.3 | 1.6 |
| 2.4 | 1.8 | 2.9 | | | | | | 3.2 | 3.8 |
| 4.9 | 2.8  (44) | 4.3 | % Depr., Dep., Amort./Sales | | | | | 4.6  (15) | 4.8 |
| 8.4 | 4.8 | 6.0 | | | | | | 5.9 | 6.8 |
| | | 2.5 | % Officers', Directors' | | | | | | |
| | (15)  4.7 | 4.7 | Owners' Comp/Sales | | | | | | |
| | | 6.6 | | | | | | | |
| 388247M | 464245M | 1536370M | Net Sales ($) | | 13369M | 21860M | 45543M | 192483M | 1263115M |
| 233084M | 275897M | 885392M | Total Assets ($) | | 4928M | 10780M | 17115M | 125606M | 726963M |

(Column between Comparative Historical Data and Current Data Sorted by Sales, under 0-1MM/1-3MM/3-5MM/5-10MM: "DATA NOT AVAILABLE")

M = $ thousand    MM = $ million
See Pages 9 through 22 for Explanation of Ratios and Data

## Current Data Sorted by Assets     Comparative Historical Data

| Type of Statement | 0-500M | 500M-2MM | 2-10MM | 10-50MM | 50-100MM | 100-250MM | | 4/1/07-3/31/08 ALL | 4/1/08-3/31/09 ALL |
|---|---|---|---|---|---|---|---|---|---|
| Unqualified | | | 1 | 3 | 3 | 1 | | 8 | 11 |
| Reviewed | | | 14 | 9 | | | | 19 | 18 |
| Compiled | | 6 | 5 | | | | | 14 | 6 |
| Tax Returns | | 4 | 1 | | | | | 10 | 7 |
| Other | 3 | 4 | 6 | 5 | 1 | 2 | | 24 | 38 |
| | 8 (4/1-9/30/11) | | | 64 (10/1/11-3/31/12) | | | | | |
| **NUMBER OF STATEMENTS** | 7 | 14 | 27 | 17 | 4 | 3 | | 75 | 80 |

| | 0-500M % | 500M-2MM % | 2-10MM % | 10-50MM % | 50-100MM % | 100-250MM % | | 07-08 ALL % | 08-09 ALL % |
|---|---|---|---|---|---|---|---|---|---|
| **ASSETS** | | | | | | | | | |
| Cash & Equivalents | | 10.7 | 8.7 | 6.5 | | | | 6.8 | 7.9 |
| Trade Receivables (net) | | 23.5 | 25.7 | 25.5 | | | | 27.0 | 25.3 |
| Inventory | | 10.5 | 15.6 | 21.5 | | | | 12.8 | 15.4 |
| All Other Current | | 1.4 | .8 | 2.7 | | | | 1.3 | 2.8 |
| Total Current | | 46.1 | 50.8 | 56.3 | | | | 47.9 | 51.4 |
| Fixed Assets (net) | | 35.3 | 40.6 | 31.8 | | | | 40.5 | 39.6 |
| Intangibles (net) | | 9.3 | 5.7 | 8.9 | | | | 8.0 | 4.9 |
| All Other Non-Current | | 9.3 | 2.9 | 3.0 | | | | 3.5 | 4.1 |
| Total | | 100.0 | 100.0 | 100.0 | | | | 100.0 | 100.0 |
| **LIABILITIES** | | | | | | | | | |
| Notes Payable-Short Term | | 6.7 | 4.8 | 9.9 | | | | 10.8 | 13.6 |
| Cur. Mat.-L.T.D. | | 4.4 | 4.7 | 3.0 | | | | 6.0 | 5.5 |
| Trade Payables | | 15.5 | 12.1 | 9.6 | | | | 12.1 | 14.1 |
| Income Taxes Payable | | .1 | .0 | .0 | | | | .1 | .0 |
| All Other Current | | 7.1 | 5.0 | 10.5 | | | | 11.1 | 6.4 |
| Total Current | | 33.8 | 26.6 | 33.0 | | | | 40.0 | 39.6 |
| Long-Term Debt | | 31.5 | 21.4 | 12.5 | | | | 24.6 | 21.1 |
| Deferred Taxes | | .0 | .4 | 1.6 | | | | .4 | .5 |
| All Other Non-Current | | 21.8 | 4.4 | 7.5 | | | | 7.0 | 13.8 |
| Net Worth | | 12.9 | 47.4 | 45.4 | | | | 28.0 | 25.0 |
| Total Liabilities & Net Worth | | 100.0 | 100.0 | 100.0 | | | | 100.0 | 100.0 |
| **INCOME DATA** | | | | | | | | | |
| Net Sales | | 100.0 | 100.0 | 100.0 | | | | 100.0 | 100.0 |
| Gross Profit | | 42.6 | 33.9 | 26.3 | | | | 37.7 | 32.8 |
| Operating Expenses | | 38.9 | 26.6 | 20.5 | | | | 33.1 | 30.2 |
| Operating Profit | | 3.7 | 7.3 | 5.8 | | | | 4.7 | 2.6 |
| All Other Expenses (net) | | 1.0 | .5 | 1.2 | | | | 2.1 | 1.8 |
| Profit Before Taxes | | 2.7 | 6.8 | 4.6 | | | | 2.6 | .8 |
| **RATIOS** | | | | | | | | | |
| Current | | 2.3 | 3.1 | 2.4 | | | | 2.3 | 2.5 |
| | | 1.5 | 1.9 | 1.7 | | | | 1.4 | 1.4 |
| | | .6 | 1.4 | 1.1 | | | | .9 | 1.0 |
| Quick | | 2.0 | 1.8 | 1.5 | | | | 1.5 | 1.5 |
| | | .9 | 1.2 | .9 | | | | .9 | .8 |
| | | .6 | .8 | .6 | | | | .6 | .6 |
| Sales/Receivables | | 26   14.3 | 34   10.6 | 33   11.0 | | | | 32   11.5 | 29   12.6 |
| | | 35   10.3 | 42   8.7 | 38   9.6 | | | | 40   9.1 | 39   9.3 |
| | | 39   9.4 | 47   7.8 | 49   7.4 | | | | 53   6.9 | 51   7.2 |
| Cost of Sales/Inventory | | 3   114.0 | 30   12.3 | 28   13.1 | | | | 12   31.6 | 20   18.3 |
| | | 23   16.2 | 38   9.6 | 56   6.5 | | | | 30   12.0 | 37   9.9 |
| | | 38   9.6 | 49   7.5 | 78   4.7 | | | | 50   7.3 | 54   6.7 |
| Cost of Sales/Payables | | 13   28.7 | 19   19.7 | 14   25.7 | | | | 17   21.1 | 18   20.1 |
| | | 34   10.7 | 25   14.6 | 20   18.1 | | | | 25   14.4 | 26   13.9 |
| | | 69   5.3 | 42   8.6 | 29   12.6 | | | | 40   9.1 | 40   9.1 |
| Sales/Working Capital | | 9.1 | 6.1 | 6.4 | | | | 8.0 | 7.9 |
| | | 23.5 | 8.7 | 9.7 | | | | 18.3 | 20.1 |
| | | -26.2 | 16.3 | 39.4 | | | | -47.3 | 424.1 |
| EBIT/Interest | | 6.5 | 20.2 | 39.9 | | | | (74) 4.2 | 4.5 |
| | | 2.7 | 5.6 | 5.7 | | | | 2.3 | (74) 2.3 |
| | | .9 | 2.4 | 2.4 | | | | .7 | -.2 |
| Net Profit + Depr., Dep., Amort./Cur. Mat. L/T/D | | | | | | | | (17) 4.5 | 7.5 |
| | | | | | | | | 2.3 | (23) 1.7 |
| | | | | | | | | 1.0 | 1.1 |
| Fixed/Worth | | .5 | .6 | .6 | | | | .8 | .8 |
| | | NM | .9 | 1.1 | | | | 1.7 | 1.6 |
| | | -1.3 | 1.5 | 2.1 | | | | 8.5 | 4.6 |
| Debt/Worth | | 1.3 | .6 | .5 | | | | 1.0 | .9 |
| | | NM | 1.4 | 1.6 | | | | 2.3 | 2.3 |
| | | -3.1 | 2.8 | 5.8 | | | | 19.2 | 9.6 |
| % Profit Before Taxes/Tangible Net Worth | | | 54.4 | 33.2 | | | | 30.8 | 26.8 |
| | | | (26) 29.1 | (15) 16.4 | | | | (60) 17.3 | (66) 11.3 |
| | | | 9.0 | 11.0 | | | | 1.3 | -5.4 |
| % Profit Before Taxes/Total Assets | | 9.1 | 17.4 | 14.8 | | | | 9.6 | 9.9 |
| | | 4.2 | 10.5 | 8.6 | | | | 3.9 | 4.1 |
| | | .0 | 3.1 | 3.1 | | | | -1.3 | -5.8 |
| Sales/Net Fixed Assets | | 16.4 | 11.0 | 13.1 | | | | 11.6 | 11.9 |
| | | 10.2 | 4.7 | 7.3 | | | | 5.0 | 5.6 |
| | | 4.2 | 3.2 | 3.7 | | | | 3.2 | 3.7 |
| Sales/Total Assets | | 3.3 | 2.6 | 2.5 | | | | 2.8 | 2.9 |
| | | 2.9 | 2.1 | 2.1 | | | | 2.0 | 2.1 |
| | | 2.3 | 1.8 | 1.7 | | | | 1.5 | 1.7 |
| % Depr., Dep., Amort./Sales | | 3.1 | 3.2 | 2.4 | | | | (67) 2.6 | 2.1 |
| | | (11) 4.3 | (25) 3.7 | 3.5 | | | | 3.8 | (72) 3.8 |
| | | 6.5 | 5.0 | 5.1 | | | | 5.3 | 5.0 |
| % Officers', Directors' Owners' Comp/Sales | | | | | | | | (34) 2.0 | 2.8 |
| | | | | | | | | 5.1 | (29) 5.1 |
| | | | | | | | | 8.3 | 6.3 |
| Net Sales ($) | 17414M | 52022M | 296923M | 699357M | 425860M | 699576M | | 1272915M | 1631019M |
| Total Assets ($) | 1936M | 19498M | 135958M | 317428M | 268518M | 531722M | | 856460M | 869119M |

© RMA 2012

M = $ thousand    MM = $ million
See Pages 9 through 22 for Explanation of Ratios and Data

## Comparative Historical Data / Current Data Sorted by Sales

| Type of Statement | | | | | | | | | |
|---|---|---|---|---|---|---|---|---|---|
| Unqualified | 11 | 8 | 8 | | | | | 2 | 6 |
| Reviewed | 19 | 25 | 23 | | | 1 | 3 | 13 | 6 |
| Compiled | 5 | 13 | 11 | | 2 | 3 | 4 | 2 | |
| Tax Returns | 10 | 19 | 9 | 1 | 2 | 5 | 1 | | |
| Other | 22 | 31 | 21 | 1 | 3 | 1 | 6 | 3 | 7 |
| | 4/1/09-3/31/10 ALL | 4/1/10-3/31/11 ALL | 4/1/11-3/31/12 ALL | \_\_8 (4/1-9/30/11)\_\_ | | _____64 (10/1/11-3/31/12)_____ | | | |
| | | | | 0-1MM | 1-3MM | 3-5MM | 5-10MM | 10-25MM | 25MM & OVER |
| NUMBER OF STATEMENTS | 67 | 96 | 72 | 2 | 7 | 10 | 14 | 20 | 19 |

| | % | % | % | % | % | % | % | % | % |
|---|---|---|---|---|---|---|---|---|---|
| **ASSETS** | | | | | | | | | |
| Cash & Equivalents | 11.6 | 11.2 | 9.5 | | | 11.4 | 8.9 | 6.4 | 9.2 |
| Trade Receivables (net) | 24.4 | 26.7 | 23.8 | | | 25.3 | 22.4 | 25.1 | 24.6 |
| Inventory | 11.7 | 12.8 | 14.1 | | | 10.3 | 12.9 | 17.1 | 17.8 |
| All Other Current | 1.0 | 1.4 | 1.4 | | | .2 | .6 | 2.1 | 1.6 |
| Total Current | 48.6 | 52.1 | 48.9 | | | 47.2 | 44.8 | 50.7 | 53.1 |
| Fixed Assets (net) | 33.3 | 34.7 | 36.0 | | | 31.7 | 41.3 | 38.4 | 30.7 |
| Intangibles (net) | 10.1 | 7.8 | 9.2 | | | 9.7 | 5.2 | 8.1 | 11.8 |
| All Other Non-Current | 8.0 | 5.5 | 6.0 | | | 11.4 | 8.7 | 2.9 | 4.4 |
| Total | 100.0 | 100.0 | 100.0 | | | 100.0 | 100.0 | 100.0 | 100.0 |
| **LIABILITIES** | | | | | | | | | |
| Notes Payable-Short Term | 9.6 | 8.3 | 7.8 | | | 10.4 | 10.3 | 6.6 | 6.8 |
| Cur. Mat.-L.T.D. | 5.0 | 3.8 | 4.6 | | | 2.9 | 5.8 | 4.9 | 4.6 |
| Trade Payables | 10.6 | 12.8 | 16.6 | | | 12.9 | 38.9 | 10.8 | 10.5 |
| Income Taxes Payable | .0 | .0 | .1 | | | .0 | .0 | .0 | .1 |
| All Other Current | 7.3 | 8.5 | 8.4 | | | 13.2 | 9.9 | 5.8 | 9.7 |
| Total Current | 32.5 | 33.4 | 37.5 | | | 39.4 | 64.9 | 28.1 | 31.7 |
| Long-Term Debt | 21.8 | 22.8 | 19.5 | | | 24.4 | 32.4 | 13.5 | 17.3 |
| Deferred Taxes | .4 | .8 | .8 | | | .0 | .0 | 1.3 | 1.7 |
| All Other Non-Current | 13.3 | 11.7 | 9.6 | | | 12.5 | 7.6 | 8.8 | 4.2 |
| Net Worth | 31.9 | 31.3 | 32.6 | | | 23.8 | -4.9 | 48.3 | 45.1 |
| Total Liabilities & Net Worth | 100.0 | 100.0 | 100.0 | | | 100.0 | 100.0 | 100.0 | 100.0 |
| **INCOME DATA** | | | | | | | | | |
| Net Sales | 100.0 | 100.0 | 100.0 | | | 100.0 | 100.0 | 100.0 | 100.0 |
| Gross Profit | 38.8 | 38.0 | 35.5 | | | 39.0 | 35.3 | 34.0 | 27.2 |
| Operating Expenses | 35.2 | 33.2 | 29.3 | | | 35.7 | 28.9 | 26.0 | 22.2 |
| Operating Profit | 3.6 | 4.8 | 6.2 | | | 3.3 | 6.4 | 8.0 | 5.0 |
| All Other Expenses (net) | 2.3 | .8 | 1.2 | | | .8 | .9 | .9 | 1.9 |
| Profit Before Taxes | 1.3 | 4.0 | 5.0 | | | 2.5 | 5.5 | 7.1 | 3.1 |

### RATIOS

| Ratio | 4/1/09-3/31/10 ALL | 4/1/10-3/31/11 ALL | 4/1/11-3/31/12 ALL | 0-1MM | 1-3MM | 3-5MM | 5-10MM | 10-25MM | 25MM & OVER |
|---|---|---|---|---|---|---|---|---|---|
| Current | 2.7 | 2.6 | 2.5 | | | 3.4 | 2.6 | 3.0 | 2.4 |
| | 1.4 | 1.6 | 1.7 | | | 1.8 | 1.8 | 1.8 | 1.6 |
| | .9 | 1.1 | 1.1 | | | .6 | .8 | 1.2 | 1.2 |
| Quick | 2.0 | 1.9 | 1.8 | | | 2.8 | 1.8 | 1.7 | 1.5 |
| | 1.0 | 1.2 | 1.0 | | | 1.2 | .9 | 1.0 | .9 |
| | .6 | .8 | .7 | | | .5 | .6 | .7 | .7 |
| Sales/Receivables | 34  10.6 | 30  12.3 | 29  12.8 | | | 24  15.1 | 29  12.7 | 34  10.7 | 34  10.8 |
| | 41  9.0 | 40  9.2 | 38  9.5 | | | 36  10.1 | 38  9.5 | 38  9.5 | 48  7.6 |
| | 51  7.2 | 49  7.4 | 47  7.7 | | | 45  8.1 | 43  8.4 | 45  8.2 | 54  6.8 |
| Cost of Sales/Inventory | 12  29.4 | 11  33.8 | 18  20.5 | | | 0  UND | 7  54.9 | 32  11.3 | 24  15.4 |
| | 26  14.1 | 28  13.2 | 34  10.7 | | | 23  16.2 | 33  11.0 | 38  9.7 | 52  7.0 |
| | 46  7.9 | 46  7.9 | 55  6.6 | | | 38  9.6 | 51  7.2 | 46  7.9 | 73  5.0 |
| Cost of Sales/Payables | 14  25.9 | 16  22.2 | 17  20.9 | | | 6  63.9 | 19  19.0 | 15  23.8 | 18  19.8 |
| | 26  14.0 | 26  13.8 | 26  14.0 | | | 22  16.8 | 34  10.7 | 24  15.5 | 24  15.2 |
| | 39  9.3 | 42  8.7 | 39  9.4 | | | 43  8.4 | 47  7.8 | 33  11.2 | 32  11.3 |
| Sales/Working Capital | 6.7 | 7.5 | 7.1 | | | 6.7 | 6.1 | 6.8 | 6.5 |
| | 17.1 | 12.3 | 11.8 | | | 10.2 | 12.1 | 11.8 | 9.7 |
| | -86.6 | 48.6 | 49.0 | | | -30.3 | -44.9 | 37.4 | 33.9 |
| EBIT/Interest | 6.8 | 12.9 | 20.2 | | | 10.8 | 11.3 | 35.2 | 25.5 |
| | (60) 2.4 | (89) 3.8 | (71) 5.2 | | | 2.4 | 4.9 | 5.4 | 4.1 |
| | -1.1 | 1.3 | 1.9 | | | -.3 | 2.1 | 2.3 | 1.7 |
| Net Profit + Depr., Dep., Amort./Cur. Mat. L/T/D | 2.1 | 7.2 | 5.4 | | | | | | |
| | (16) 1.3 | (26) 2.6 | (22) 2.9 | | | | | | |
| | -.2 | 1.0 | 1.7 | | | | | | |
| Fixed/Worth | .5 | .6 | .6 | | | 1.1 | .7 | .5 | .6 |
| | 1.4 | 1.4 | 1.2 | | | 2.1 | 1.5 | 1.1 | 1.3 |
| | -10.8 | 10.1 | 2.9 | | | -7.3 | -6.1 | 1.7 | 2.4 |
| Debt/Worth | .5 | .9 | .8 | | | 1.5 | 1.1 | .5 | .6 |
| | 2.3 | 2.2 | 1.9 | | | 5.6 | 2.5 | 1.1 | 3.1 |
| | -46.2 | 19.9 | 7.2 | | | -30.5 | -22.4 | 2.9 | 5.9 |
| % Profit Before Taxes/Tangible Net Worth | 40.9 | 50.5 | 47.2 | | | | 47.0 | 53.0 | 30.6 |
| | (48) 22.8 | (76) 21.7 | (57) 16.7 | | | | (10) 18.9 | (17) 23.5 | (17) 15.3 |
| | 3.6 | 3.6 | 8.6 | | | | 7.9 | 3.8 | 9.7 |
| % Profit Before Taxes/Total Assets | 12.5 | 19.8 | 16.1 | | | 20.1 | 29.7 | 18.2 | 12.7 |
| | 5.2 | 7.2 | 8.1 | | | 5.6 | 8.8 | 12.2 | 4.8 |
| | -1.1 | 1.0 | 1.9 | | | -4.1 | 3.6 | 1.8 | 1.8 |
| Sales/Net Fixed Assets | 18.2 | 17.0 | 12.4 | | | 25.8 | 13.7 | 10.6 | 13.7 |
| | 5.6 | 7.0 | 7.0 | | | 10.4 | 6.0 | 6.8 | 6.9 |
| | 4.1 | 4.2 | 3.9 | | | 5.5 | 3.4 | 3.9 | 3.4 |
| Sales/Total Assets | 3.0 | 3.1 | 3.0 | | | 4.7 | 3.1 | 2.7 | 2.4 |
| | 2.1 | 2.4 | 2.2 | | | 2.9 | 2.3 | 2.1 | 2.1 |
| | 1.4 | 1.8 | 1.8 | | | 2.0 | 1.7 | 1.8 | 1.5 |
| % Depr., Dep., Amort./Sales | 2.6 | 2.4 | 2.8 | | | | 2.4 | 2.8 | 2.5 |
| | (58) 4.0 | (82) 4.4 | (64) 3.7 | | | | (13) 3.4 | (19) 4.0 | (18) 3.7 |
| | 6.1 | 5.5 | 5.0 | | | | 4.6 | 5.4 | 5.2 |
| % Officers', Directors', Owners' Comp/Sales | 2.8 | 3.2 | 2.1 | | | | | | |
| | (30) 5.7 | (40) 4.7 | (20) 5.0 | | | | | | |
| | 8.4 | 6.4 | 7.9 | | | | | | |
| Net Sales ($) | 928541M | 1692795M | 2191152M | 1525M | 14662M | 39067M | 97262M | 322250M | 1716386M |
| Total Assets ($) | 566227M | 958167M | 1275060M | 569M | 6353M | 14319M | 44641M | 157654M | 1051524M |

M = $ thousand    MM = $ million
See Pages 9 through 22 for Explanation of Ratios and Data

# MANUFACTURING—Commercial Screen Printing  NAICS 323113

## Current Data Sorted by Assets

## Comparative Historical Data

| Type of Statement | 0-500M | 500M-2MM | 2-10MM | 10-50MM | 50-100MM | 100-250MM | 4/1/07-3/31/08 ALL | 4/1/08-3/31/09 ALL |
|---|---|---|---|---|---|---|---|---|
| Unqualified | 1 | 7 | 10 | 4 | 2 | 3 | 6 | 12 |
| Reviewed | 2 | 10 | 7 | 5 | 2 | 2 | 24 | 25 |
| Compiled | 12 | 9 | 5 | 1 | | | 15 | 19 |
| Tax Returns | 7 | 10 | 16 | | | | 15 | 23 |
| Other | | | | 4 | 2 | 4 | 36 | 36 |
| | 14 (4/1-9/30/11) | | 110 (10/1/11-3/31/12) | | | | | |
| **NUMBER OF STATEMENTS** | 22 | 36 | 39 | 14 | 6 | 7 | 96 | 115 |
| | % | % | % | % | % | % | % | % |
| **ASSETS** | | | | | | | | |
| Cash & Equivalents | 9.6 | 9.5 | 7.0 | 13.5 | | | 8.2 | 7.5 |
| Trade Receivables (net) | 25.7 | 28.7 | 28.3 | 26.0 | | | 29.8 | 29.2 |
| Inventory | 9.2 | 23.9 | 22.8 | 23.6 | | | 18.8 | 18.4 |
| All Other Current | 9.8 | 2.0 | 1.2 | 2.3 | | | 3.5 | 1.9 |
| Total Current | 54.3 | 64.1 | 59.2 | 65.3 | | | 60.3 | 57.0 |
| Fixed Assets (net) | 31.0 | 27.4 | 31.8 | 21.3 | | | 31.3 | 32.3 |
| Intangibles (net) | 4.2 | 3.2 | 5.4 | 9.3 | | | 3.2 | 5.3 |
| All Other Non-Current | 10.5 | 5.3 | 3.5 | 4.1 | | | 5.3 | 5.3 |
| Total | 100.0 | 100.0 | 100.0 | 100.0 | | | 100.0 | 100.0 |
| **LIABILITIES** | | | | | | | | |
| Notes Payable-Short Term | 20.1 | 15.6 | 12.8 | 11.0 | | | 13.9 | 16.8 |
| Cur. Mat.-L.T.D. | 8.4 | 4.6 | 7.0 | 4.9 | | | 4.5 | 5.1 |
| Trade Payables | 20.9 | 14.9 | 20.8 | 15.7 | | | 14.9 | 16.6 |
| Income Taxes Payable | .3 | .1 | .1 | .1 | | | .5 | .1 |
| All Other Current | 9.6 | 8.2 | 9.1 | 8.2 | | | 9.1 | 9.6 |
| Total Current | 59.3 | 43.3 | 49.8 | 39.9 | | | 42.9 | 48.2 |
| Long-Term Debt | 60.0 | 13.7 | 19.8 | 7.5 | | | 20.9 | 20.1 |
| Deferred Taxes | .2 | .0 | .1 | .3 | | | .2 | .3 |
| All Other Non-Current | 6.5 | 7.8 | 5.4 | 17.0 | | | 3.2 | 6.3 |
| Net Worth | -25.9 | 35.2 | 24.8 | 35.4 | | | 32.9 | 25.2 |
| Total Liabilities & Net Worth | 100.0 | 100.0 | 100.0 | 100.0 | | | 100.0 | 100.0 |
| **INCOME DATA** | | | | | | | | |
| Net Sales | 100.0 | 100.0 | 100.0 | 100.0 | | | 100.0 | 100.0 |
| Gross Profit | 50.7 | 40.4 | 31.3 | 29.6 | | | 37.7 | 38.4 |
| Operating Expenses | 46.6 | 37.5 | 27.2 | 24.9 | | | 33.1 | 36.5 |
| Operating Profit | 4.1 | 2.8 | 4.0 | 4.7 | | | 4.6 | 1.9 |
| All Other Expenses (net) | 1.3 | .1 | 1.2 | .8 | | | 1.2 | 1.4 |
| Profit Before Taxes | 2.9 | 2.7 | 2.8 | 3.9 | | | 3.4 | .5 |
| **RATIOS** | | | | | | | | |
| Current | 2.9 | 2.9 | 2.1 | 2.3 | | | 2.8 | 1.9 |
| | 1.2 | 1.6 | 1.5 | 1.6 | | | 1.5 | 1.3 |
| | .4 | 1.1 | 1.0 | 1.3 | | | 1.0 | .8 |
| Quick | 1.4 | 1.8 | 1.6 | 1.6 | | | 1.8 | 1.4 |
| | .9 | .9 | .8 | .8 | | | .9 | .8 |
| | .2 | .6 | .5 | .5 | | | .6 | .5 |
| Sales/Receivables | 5 75.5 | 27 13.3 | 35 10.3 | 30 12.2 | | | 28 13.1 | 27 13.7 |
| | 20 18.0 | 35 10.4 | 45 8.2 | 42 8.6 | | | 40 9.1 | 39 9.3 |
| | 38 9.7 | 47 7.8 | 57 6.4 | 66 5.5 | | | 53 6.9 | 56 6.5 |
| Cost of Sales/Inventory | 0 UND | 18 20.7 | 21 17.6 | 18 20.4 | | | 13 27.9 | 11 34.0 |
| | 12 30.3 | 51 7.2 | 42 8.6 | 46 7.9 | | | 29 12.4 | 33 11.2 |
| | 26 13.8 | 89 4.1 | 78 4.7 | 76 4.8 | | | 68 5.4 | 66 5.5 |
| Cost of Sales/Payables | 3 112.3 | 12 31.6 | 23 16.1 | 19 19.2 | | | 16 23.1 | 16 22.5 |
| | 33 11.2 | 25 14.4 | 33 11.2 | 33 11.1 | | | 26 14.0 | 31 11.7 |
| | 45 8.1 | 51 7.1 | 62 5.9 | 45 8.2 | | | 43 8.5 | 55 6.7 |
| Sales/Working Capital | 11.6 | 7.3 | 7.3 | 6.0 | | | 6.1 | 8.5 |
| | 47.6 | 13.2 | 14.5 | 9.9 | | | 12.1 | 19.9 |
| | -8.1 | 80.1 | 999.8 | 20.1 | | | 999.8 | -30.3 |
| EBIT/Interest | 11.5 | 11.0 | 8.5 | 13.5 | | | 7.2 | 5.0 |
| | (18) 1.6 | (30) 2.9 | (36) 2.1 | (11) 4.1 | | | (85) 3.0 | (105) 1.6 |
| | -.1 | .8 | .8 | 1.6 | | | 1.2 | .1 |
| Net Profit + Depr., Dep., Amort./Cur. Mat. L/T/D | | | | | | | 8.6 | 3.2 |
| | | | | | | | (21) 3.8 | (22) 1.5 |
| | | | | | | | 1.0 | .8 |
| Fixed/Worth | .5 | .4 | .5 | .3 | | | .4 | .5 |
| | 2.4 | .7 | 1.1 | .7 | | | .9 | 1.5 |
| | -.4 | 1.9 | 7.2 | 1.1 | | | 2.2 | 11.3 |
| Debt/Worth | 2.1 | .5 | 1.1 | 1.1 | | | .6 | 1.3 |
| | 39.9 | 1.4 | 3.5 | 1.8 | | | 1.9 | 3.4 |
| | -2.2 | 7.2 | 8.6 | 4.1 | | | 9.0 | 27.5 |
| % Profit Before Taxes/Tangible Net Worth | 101.5 | 37.8 | 43.5 | 27.7 | | | 40.7 | 33.4 |
| | (12) 54.4 | (30) 15.3 | (33) 15.2 | (13) 14.6 | | | (83) 19.1 | (89) 11.5 |
| | -27.1 | 2.9 | .6 | 4.5 | | | 7.3 | -4.2 |
| % Profit Before Taxes/Total Assets | 37.0 | 16.5 | 13.9 | 12.6 | | | 15.5 | 11.0 |
| | 5.8 | 6.4 | 3.7 | 3.8 | | | 6.5 | 2.9 |
| | -2.7 | .4 | -.3 | -.3 | | | 1.2 | -2.8 |
| Sales/Net Fixed Assets | 50.9 | 41.8 | 19.0 | 30.4 | | | 19.6 | 18.1 |
| | 22.3 | 10.5 | 9.5 | 22.2 | | | 9.2 | 8.7 |
| | 9.4 | 6.9 | 3.4 | 5.4 | | | 5.3 | 4.4 |
| Sales/Total Assets | 5.5 | 3.4 | 2.9 | 3.6 | | | 3.4 | 3.3 |
| | 4.3 | 2.8 | 2.2 | 2.3 | | | 2.4 | 2.5 |
| | 2.9 | 2.5 | 1.8 | 1.4 | | | 1.8 | 1.8 |
| % Depr., Dep., Amort./Sales | 1.1 | .7 | 1.3 | .8 | | | 1.5 | 1.6 |
| | (13) 2.0 | (29) 1.9 | (32) 3.2 | (11) 1.4 | | | (85) 2.5 | (105) 2.9 |
| | 6.3 | 3.2 | 5.2 | 3.3 | | | 4.4 | 4.4 |
| % Officers', Directors' Owners' Comp/Sales | 3.2 | 2.8 | 1.6 | | | | 2.6 | 3.2 |
| | (10) 7.2 | (22) 8.3 | (17) 3.1 | | | | (49) 5.7 | (65) 5.1 |
| | 17.6 | 11.0 | 4.4 | | | | 11.1 | 9.8 |
| Net Sales ($) | 21884M | 128836M | 369573M | 749361M | 758482M | 1553604M | 1987536M | 2245588M |
| Total Assets ($) | 5148M | 44998M | 159792M | 328740M | 394432M | 1093803M | 946612M | 999021M |

M = $ thousand    MM = $ million
See Pages 9 through 22 for Explanation of Ratios and Data

## Comparative Historical Data | Current Data Sorted by Sales

| | | | Type of Statement | | | | | | |
|---|---|---|---|---|---|---|---|---|---|
| 10 | 6 | 10 | Unqualified | | | | | 2 | 8 |
| 29 | 25 | 25 | Reviewed | | 3 | 3 | 5 | 7 | 7 |
| 17 | 19 | 20 | Compiled | 1 | 4 | 7 | 6 | 1 | 1 |
| 13 | 24 | 26 | Tax Returns | 10 | 7 | 4 | 4 | 1 | |
| 40 | 34 | 43 | Other | 6 | 7 | 8 | 8 | 5 | 9 |
| 4/1/09-3/31/10 ALL | 4/1/10-3/31/11 ALL | 4/1/11-3/31/12 ALL | | | 14 (4/1-9/30/11) | | 110 (10/1/11-3/31/12) | | |
| | | | | 0-1MM | 1-3MM | 3-5MM | 5-10MM | 10-25MM | 25MM & OVER |
| 109 | 108 | 124 | NUMBER OF STATEMENTS | 17 | 21 | 22 | 23 | 16 | 25 |
| % | % | % | ASSETS | % | % | % | % | % | % |
| 9.8 | 9.4 | 9.1 | Cash & Equivalents | 8.8 | 12.1 | 5.9 | 11.5 | 4.6 | 10.1 |
| 28.3 | 29.1 | 26.7 | Trade Receivables (net) | 19.8 | 33.4 | 28.5 | 24.9 | 32.3 | 22.4 |
| 18.4 | 19.8 | 21.0 | Inventory | 8.1 | 14.8 | 26.1 | 25.3 | 22.5 | 25.4 |
| 3.0 | 1.7 | 3.5 | All Other Current | 12.8 | 1.4 | 2.4 | .5 | 2.5 | 3.5 |
| 59.5 | 59.9 | 60.3 | Total Current | 49.6 | 61.7 | 62.9 | 62.3 | 61.8 | 61.3 |
| 28.9 | 28.4 | 28.0 | Fixed Assets (net) | 30.6 | 31.0 | 31.2 | 28.6 | 26.3 | 21.4 |
| 6.2 | 7.2 | 6.1 | Intangibles (net) | 5.6 | 3.3 | 1.1 | 6.8 | 7.0 | 11.8 |
| 5.5 | 4.4 | 5.7 | All Other Non-Current | 14.3 | 4.0 | 4.8 | 2.3 | 4.9 | 5.5 |
| 100.0 | 100.0 | 100.0 | Total | 100.0 | 100.0 | 100.0 | 100.0 | 100.0 | 100.0 |
| | | | LIABILITIES | | | | | | |
| 9.4 | 10.0 | 14.4 | Notes Payable-Short Term | 25.5 | 12.0 | 12.7 | 15.3 | 13.2 | 10.1 |
| 5.3 | 5.1 | 5.8 | Cur. Mat.-L.T.D. | 9.0 | 5.6 | 4.0 | 4.0 | 10.8 | 4.0 |
| 14.7 | 16.4 | 17.4 | Trade Payables | 9.2 | 21.8 | 16.9 | 21.6 | 21.0 | 13.6 |
| .1 | .1 | .2 | Income Taxes Payable | .5 | .0 | .1 | .1 | .1 | .2 |
| 10.0 | 8.1 | 8.6 | All Other Current | 11.0 | 8.9 | 8.7 | 7.7 | 8.2 | 7.8 |
| 39.6 | 39.6 | 46.4 | Total Current | 55.2 | 48.4 | 42.4 | 48.8 | 53.4 | 35.6 |
| 21.7 | 24.6 | 24.1 | Long-Term Debt | 74.1 | 16.8 | 18.2 | 18.8 | 9.0 | 16.1 |
| .3 | .1 | .1 | Deferred Taxes | .0 | .3 | .0 | .2 | .1 | .3 |
| 6.5 | 5.0 | 8.0 | All Other Non-Current | 7.1 | 12.2 | 5.4 | 1.3 | 6.9 | 14.2 |
| 31.9 | 30.6 | 21.4 | Net Worth | -36.1 | 22.3 | 34.0 | 31.0 | 30.7 | 33.8 |
| 100.0 | 100.0 | 100.0 | Total Liabilties & Net Worth | 100.0 | 100.0 | 100.0 | 100.0 | 100.0 | 100.0 |
| | | | INCOME DATA | | | | | | |
| 100.0 | 100.0 | 100.0 | Net Sales | 100.0 | 100.0 | 100.0 | 100.0 | 100.0 | 100.0 |
| 38.7 | 38.7 | 37.0 | Gross Profit | 50.5 | 45.5 | 37.8 | 35.7 | 23.5 | 29.6 |
| 37.0 | 34.6 | 33.0 | Operating Expenses | 44.7 | 44.4 | 33.7 | 31.2 | 20.3 | 24.5 |
| 1.7 | 4.1 | 4.0 | Operating Profit | 5.7 | 1.1 | 4.1 | 4.6 | 3.2 | 5.1 |
| 1.2 | 1.1 | 1.0 | All Other Expenses (net) | 1.9 | -.1 | 1.0 | .8 | .7 | 1.9 |
| .5 | 3.0 | 3.0 | Profit Before Taxes | 3.9 | 1.2 | 3.1 | 3.8 | 2.5 | 3.2 |
| | | | RATIOS | | | | | | |
| 2.6 | 2.4 | 2.3 | | 3.1 | 5.9 | 2.3 | 2.8 | 2.3 | 2.1 |
| 1.5 | 1.7 | 1.5 | Current | 1.0 | 1.5 | 1.5 | 1.6 | 1.4 | 1.6 |
| 1.1 | 1.1 | 1.1 | | .4 | 1.0 | 1.1 | 1.0 | .9 | 1.3 |
| 1.9 | 1.7 | 1.5 | | 1.4 | 3.0 | 1.2 | 1.3 | 1.6 | 1.5 |
| 1.0 | 1.0 | .9 | Quick | .6 | 1.2 | .9 | 1.0 | .8 | .8 |
| .5 | .6 | .5 | | .1 | .6 | .6 | .4 | .5 | .5 |
| 28 13.0 | 25 14.6 | 25 14.7 | | 0 UND | 26 13.8 | 29 12.7 | 18 20.4 | 38 9.5 | 28 13.1 |
| 41 8.9 | 36 10.0 | 37 9.9 | Sales/Receivables | 20 18.0 | 35 10.3 | 38 9.7 | 36 10.0 | 50 7.3 | 41 8.8 |
| 57 6.4 | 53 6.8 | 51 7.2 | | 42 8.7 | 42 8.6 | 51 7.2 | 49 7.4 | 64 5.7 | 59 6.2 |
| 10 38.2 | 14 26.0 | 14 25.8 | | 0 UND | 5 75.0 | 22 16.5 | 24 15.2 | 20 18.3 | 8 8.9 |
| 41 8.9 | 42 8.7 | 43 8.5 | Cost of Sales/Inventory | 14 25.9 | 14 25.8 | 48 7.6 | 54 6.7 | 34 10.7 | 60 6.1 |
| 77 4.7 | 69 5.3 | 78 4.7 | | 34 10.8 | 78 4.7 | 83 4.4 | 76 4.8 | 46 7.9 | 107 3.4 |
| 17 21.1 | 14 25.3 | 16 22.7 | | 0 UND | 8 46.9 | 18 20.6 | 18 20.7 | 18 20.7 | 19 19.2 |
| 32 11.5 | 27 13.6 | 32 11.5 | Cost of Sales/Payables | 30 12.0 | 19 19.0 | 35 10.3 | 28 13.1 | 38 9.7 | 32 11.4 |
| 43 8.5 | 51 7.2 | 51 7.2 | | 40 9.2 | 55 6.6 | 60 6.1 | 55 6.6 | 54 6.7 | 46 8.0 |
| 5.9 | 7.1 | 7.3 | | 11.0 | 6.9 | 8.6 | 6.6 | 7.5 | 5.5 |
| 12.1 | 11.8 | 13.4 | Sales/Working Capital | UND | 19.2 | 13.9 | 11.7 | 15.2 | 10.1 |
| 99.3 | 77.2 | 94.5 | | -3.9 | NM | 67.2 | 376.2 | NM | 15.1 |
| 5.5 | 9.4 | 9.9 | | 6.0 | 19.1 | 7.3 | 9.6 | 22.2 | 10.2 |
| (97) 1.5 | (98) 2.9 | (107) 2.7 | EBIT/Interest | (15) 1.8 | (14) 3.1 | (21) 2.4 | (20) 4.1 | 2.2 | (21) 3.6 |
| -2.2 | .9 | .8 | | .8 | -1.3 | .3 | 1.5 | .1 | 1.4 |
| 5.4 | 5.2 | 4.8 | Net Profit + Depr., Dep., | | | | | | 5.0 |
| (21) 1.6 | (20) 1.9 | (19) 2.6 | Amort./Cur. Mat. L/T/D | | | | | (11) | 2.6 |
| .5 | .8 | 1.6 | | | | | | | 1.8 |
| .3 | .3 | .4 | | .3 | .5 | .4 | .3 | .3 | .5 |
| 1.0 | 1.0 | 1.0 | Fixed/Worth | 3.1 | .8 | .8 | 1.0 | .8 | .9 |
| 4.0 | 2.3 | 4.3 | | -.4 | -1.8 | 2.5 | 4.5 | 2.4 | 1.4 |
| .8 | .7 | .9 | | 2.8 | .3 | .8 | .5 | 1.0 | 1.2 |
| 2.0 | 1.9 | 2.7 | Debt/Worth | -34.7 | 1.9 | 2.0 | 1.9 | 2.0 | 2.7 |
| 18.6 | 10.5 | 15.5 | | -1.9 | -4.2 | 7.3 | 8.6 | 5.5 | 4.5 |
| 36.8 | 41.9 | 45.7 | | | 57.9 | 39.0 | 36.8 | 49.5 | 43.5 |
| (86) 6.5 | (86) 14.8 | (98) 16.6 | % Profit Before Taxes/Tangible Net Worth | (15) 26.8 | (20) 10.0 | (19) 16.7 | (15) 12.0 | (21) 17.8 |
| -8.5 | 2.1 | 1.2 | | | .2 | -2.1 | 6.5 | -4.9 | 1.1 |
| 11.0 | 14.2 | 15.4 | | 38.4 | 22.4 | 11.5 | 16.9 | 16.7 | 11.6 |
| 1.7 | 5.2 | 4.3 | % Profit Before Taxes/Total Assets | 4.5 | 8.7 | 2.7 | 8.6 | 1.8 | 3.9 |
| -6.5 | -.2 | -.2 | | -.6 | -2.6 | -1.4 | 2.1 | -1.6 | -1.2 |
| 27.1 | 28.9 | 28.8 | | 59.5 | 29.1 | 32.3 | 33.1 | 21.6 | 27.7 |
| 11.5 | 12.3 | 11.1 | Sales/Net Fixed Assets | 15.7 | 10.7 | 10.8 | 12.9 | 11.0 | 10.6 |
| 4.4 | 5.3 | 5.7 | | 4.1 | 7.8 | 5.5 | 5.1 | 5.4 | 5.6 |
| 3.4 | 3.7 | 3.4 | | 5.0 | 4.5 | 3.1 | 3.3 | 3.3 | 2.6 |
| 2.1 | 2.6 | 2.6 | Sales/Total Assets | 3.2 | 3.4 | 2.7 | 2.7 | 2.4 | 1.8 |
| 1.6 | 1.9 | 1.8 | | 1.9 | 2.4 | 2.1 | 1.9 | 1.7 | 1.3 |
| 1.3 | .9 | 1.0 | | 1.1 | .8 | .7 | 1.8 | .9 |
| (92) 2.6 | (96) 2.1 | (96) 2.2 | % Depr., Dep., Amort./Sales | (16) 2.8 | (20) 2.1 | (18) 1.8 | (13) 2.8 | (21) 1.8 |
| 4.5 | 4.1 | 3.9 | | | 6.4 | 3.7 | 3.8 | 3.7 | 3.5 |
| 3.3 | 2.7 | 2.2 | | 5.4 | 2.4 | | | | |
| (46) 5.7 | (55) 4.5 | (54) 4.2 | % Officers', Directors' Owners' Comp/Sales | (13) 8.8 | (14) 3.8 | | | | |
| 9.5 | 10.0 | 10.1 | | 12.0 | 7.6 | | | | |
| 1683417M | 2248477M | 3581740M | Net Sales ($) | 9465M | 42988M | 94287M | 169467M | 242504M | 3023029M |
| 872355M | 1300395M | 2026913M | Total Assets ($) | 4815M | 14525M | 43561M | 68905M | 112659M | 1782448M |

M = $ thousand     MM = $ million
See Pages 9 through 22 for Explanation of Ratios and Data

## Current Data Sorted by Assets

## Comparative Historical Data

| | | | | | | | Type of Statement | | |
|---|---|---|---|---|---|---|---|---|---|
| | | | | | | | Unqualified | | |
| | 4 | 3<br>4 | 3 | 1<br>2 | 1 | | Reviewed | 8<br>20 | 3<br>18 |
| | 7 | 7 | 2 | | | | Compiled | 16 | 15 |
| | 5 | 9 | 9 | 5 | | | Tax Returns | 26 | 23 |
| | | 9 (4/1-9/30/11) | | 53 (10/1/11-3/31/12) | | | Other | 29 | 30 |
| | 0-500M | 500M-2MM | 2-10MM | 10-50MM | 50-100MM | 100-250MM | | 4/1/07-<br>3/31/08<br>ALL | 4/1/08-<br>3/31/09<br>ALL |
| | 16 | 23 | 14 | 8 | 1 | | NUMBER OF STATEMENTS | 99 | 89 |
| | % | % | % | % | % | % | ASSETS | % | % |
| | 8.9 | 7.8 | 8.1 | | | | Cash & Equivalents | 7.6 | 6.6 |
| | 36.9 | 32.7 | 33.8 | | | D | Trade Receivables (net) | 28.2 | 27.6 |
| | 8.0 | 10.8 | 7.4 | | | A | Inventory | 9.6 | 8.4 |
| | 1.3 | .8 | 1.4 | | | T | All Other Current | .8 | 2.0 |
| | 55.1 | 52.1 | 50.7 | | | A | Total Current | 46.3 | 44.7 |
| | 29.9 | 37.8 | 40.1 | | | | Fixed Assets (net) | 40.4 | 43.0 |
| | 12.7 | 4.1 | 3.5 | | | N | Intangibles (net) | 6.3 | 5.7 |
| | 2.3 | 5.9 | 5.7 | | | O | All Other Non-Current | 7.0 | 6.7 |
| | 100.0 | 100.0 | 100.0 | | | T | Total | 100.0 | 100.0 |
| | | | | | | A | LIABILITIES | | |
| | 17.7 | 13.2 | 8.7 | | | V | Notes Payable-Short Term | 11.6 | 10.8 |
| | 12.1 | 4.9 | 9.5 | | | A | Cur. Mat.-L.T.D. | 7.7 | 7.8 |
| | 20.0 | 11.7 | 13.5 | | | I | Trade Payables | 14.3 | 14.2 |
| | .1 | .0 | .1 | | | L | Income Taxes Payable | .1 | .0 |
| | 24.2 | 5.4 | 9.8 | | | A | All Other Current | 7.6 | 8.7 |
| | 74.2 | 35.1 | 41.4 | | | B | Total Current | 41.2 | 41.4 |
| | 82.4 | 41.8 | 22.0 | | | L | Long-Term Debt | 33.9 | 36.2 |
| | .0 | .7 | .3 | | | E | Deferred Taxes | .3 | .5 |
| | 22.9 | 5.0 | 8.0 | | | | All Other Non-Current | 6.0 | 5.9 |
| | -79.4 | 17.4 | 28.3 | | | | Net Worth | 18.6 | 16.0 |
| | 100.0 | 100.0 | 100.0 | | | | Total Liabilties & Net Worth | 100.0 | 100.0 |
| | | | | | | | INCOME DATA | | |
| | 100.0 | 100.0 | 100.0 | | | | Net Sales | 100.0 | 100.0 |
| | | | | | | | Gross Profit | | |
| | 96.1 | 95.9 | 92.6 | | | | Operating Expenses | 96.2 | 95.5 |
| | 3.9 | 4.1 | 7.4 | | | | Operating Profit | 3.8 | 4.5 |
| | 1.3 | 2.3 | .7 | | | | All Other Expenses (net) | 1.6 | 2.6 |
| | 2.5 | 1.8 | 6.7 | | | | Profit Before Taxes | 2.2 | 1.9 |
| | | | | | | | RATIOS | | |
| | 1.6 | 2.7 | 1.8 | | | | | 2.2 | 1.7 |
| | .8 | 1.5 | 1.4 | | | | Current | 1.2 | 1.1 |
| | .4 | .8 | .9 | | | | | .8 | .8 |
| | 1.6 | 2.3 | 1.5 | | | | | 1.8 | 1.4 |
| | .6 | 1.2 | 1.1 | | | | Quick | 1.0 | .9 |
| | .3 | .6 | .7 | | | | | .6 | .6 |
| 19 | 19.2 | 25 | 14.6 | 35 | 10.3 | | | 27 | 13.3 | 24 | 15.5 |
| 28 | 13.1 | 41 | 9.0 | 53 | 6.9 | | Sales/Receivables | 40 | 9.1 | 36 | 10.1 |
| 33 | 11.0 | 56 | 6.5 | 66 | 5.5 | | | 52 | 7.1 | 51 | 7.2 |
| | | | | | | | Cost of Sales/Inventory | | |
| | | | | | | | Cost of Sales/Payables | | |
| | 20.3 | 8.2 | 10.8 | | | | | 9.6 | 13.0 |
| | -48.4 | 12.1 | 17.7 | | | | Sales/Working Capital | 42.1 | 43.6 |
| | -17.3 | -27.0 | -39.6 | | | | | -25.4 | -24.1 |
| | 8.0 | 5.4 | 8.1 | | | | | 4.2 | 4.5 |
| (15) | 3.9 | (20) | 2.3 | | 2.9 | | EBIT/Interest | (93) | 1.9 | (84) | 1.8 |
| | -.6 | -.5 | 1.3 | | | | | .4 | -1.0 |
| | | | | | | | Net Profit + Depr., Dep., | 2.4 | 2.5 |
| | | | | | | | Amort./Cur. Mat. L/T/D | (14) | 1.6 | (20) | 1.6 |
| | | | | | | | | .8 | 1.0 |
| | NM | .4 | 1.0 | | | | | .8 | 1.0 |
| | -.3 | 1.0 | 1.3 | | | | Fixed/Worth | 1.9 | 2.5 |
| | -.1 | -1.7 | 2.6 | | | | | -4.3 | -9.7 |
| | NM | .8 | 1.1 | | | | | 1.7 | 1.3 |
| | -2.2 | 2.6 | 2.7 | | | | Debt/Worth | 3.8 | 4.2 |
| | -1.6 | -4.3 | 5.1 | | | | | -9.4 | -38.6 |
| | | | 17.0 | 50.6 | | | | 42.5 | 41.4 |
| | (14) | 8.8 | (13) | 20.5 | | | % Profit Before Taxes/Tangible | (68) | 17.8 | (64) | 14.0 |
| | | -1.1 | -3.0 | | | | Net Worth | 1.4 | -5.5 |
| | 33.5 | 6.3 | 11.9 | | | | | 13.7 | 10.7 |
| | 10.0 | 2.3 | 6.4 | | | | % Profit Before Taxes/Total | 3.4 | 3.0 |
| | -9.5 | -4.2 | .0 | | | | Assets | -1.0 | -6.8 |
| | 63.2 | 13.6 | 9.1 | | | | | 15.5 | 12.8 |
| | 23.5 | 7.0 | 5.3 | | | | Sales/Net Fixed Assets | 6.6 | 6.4 |
| | 10.3 | 4.5 | 4.8 | | | | | 3.7 | 3.4 |
| | 6.7 | 3.6 | 2.6 | | | | | 3.4 | 3.6 |
| | 5.4 | 2.5 | 2.2 | | | | Sales/Total Assets | 2.4 | 2.4 |
| | 4.0 | 1.9 | 2.0 | | | | | 1.7 | 1.6 |
| | .8 | 1.8 | 3.0 | | | | | 2.4 | 2.9 |
| (10) | 2.1 | (22) | 3.8 | (13) | 4.5 | | % Depr., Dep., Amort./Sales | (84) | 3.8 | (77) | 4.3 |
| | 4.9 | 6.9 | 5.1 | | | | | 6.4 | 6.5 |
| | | | 1.7 | | | | | 3.0 | 2.6 |
| | (11) | 4.9 | | | | | % Officers', Directors' | (50) | 5.3 | (50) | 4.2 |
| | | 7.7 | | | | | Owners' Comp/Sales | 8.2 | 8.3 |
| | 18636M | 62997M | 134492M | 286031M | 83659M | | Net Sales ($) | 1228207M | 951117M |
| | 3307M | 26798M | 65724M | 122072M | 51993M | | Total Assets ($) | 629616M | 510663M |

M = $ thousand    MM = $ million
See Pages 9 through 22 for Explanation of Ratios and Data

## Comparative Historical Data | | | Current Data Sorted by Sales

| | | | Type of Statement | | | | | | |
|---|---|---|---|---|---|---|---|---|---|
| 4 | 2 | 2 | Unqualified | | | | | | 2 |
| 16 | 19 | 8 | Reviewed | | 1 | | 3 | 3 | 1 |
| 15 | 13 | 10 | Compiled | 2 | 5 | 2 | 1 | 1 | |
| 15 | 15 | 14 | Tax Returns | 9 | 4 | 1 | | | |
| 31 | 28 | 28 | Other | 3 | 6 | 6 | 4 | 5 | 4 |
| 4/1/09-3/31/10 | 4/1/10-3/31/11 | 4/1/11-3/31/12 | | | 9 (4/1-9/30/11) | | 53 (10/1/11-3/31/12) | | |
| ALL | ALL | ALL | | 0-1MM | 1-3MM | 3-5MM | 5-10MM | 10-25MM | 25MM & OVER |
| 81 | 77 | 62 | NUMBER OF STATEMENTS | 14 | 16 | 9 | 7 | 9 | 7 |
| % | % | % | ASSETS | % | % | % | % | % | % |
| 7.1 | 6.3 | 7.8 | Cash & Equivalents | 6.0 | 11.2 | | | | |
| 28.1 | 29.8 | 33.1 | Trade Receivables (net) | 31.6 | 35.6 | | | | |
| 9.3 | 9.4 | 9.5 | Inventory | 8.3 | 8.7 | | | | |
| .6 | 2.4 | 1.3 | All Other Current | 1.2 | 1.4 | | | | |
| 45.2 | 47.9 | 51.8 | Total Current | 47.1 | 56.8 | | | | |
| 38.6 | 39.1 | 37.6 | Fixed Assets (net) | 37.1 | 32.4 | | | | |
| 8.2 | 6.6 | 6.0 | Intangibles (net) | 14.8 | 5.1 | | | | |
| 7.9 | 6.4 | 4.7 | All Other Non-Current | 1.0 | 5.7 | | | | |
| 100.0 | 100.0 | 100.0 | Total | 100.0 | 100.0 | | | | |
| | | | LIABILITIES | | | | | | |
| 10.4 | 10.7 | 12.2 | Notes Payable-Short Term | 15.3 | 16.4 | | | | |
| 8.6 | 7.4 | 7.9 | Cur. Mat.-L.T.D. | 6.8 | 9.5 | | | | |
| 15.1 | 14.3 | 14.1 | Trade Payables | 21.9 | 10.8 | | | | |
| .0 | .0 | .0 | Income Taxes Payable | .1 | .0 | | | | |
| 8.8 | 12.0 | 11.7 | All Other Current | 6.0 | 23.7 | | | | |
| 42.9 | 44.5 | 45.9 | Total Current | 50.1 | 60.4 | | | | |
| 32.7 | 32.2 | 44.6 | Long-Term Debt | 107.1 | 31.2 | | | | |
| .6 | .6 | .3 | Deferred Taxes | .0 | .0 | | | | |
| 5.1 | 13.0 | 9.9 | All Other Non-Current | 21.8 | 9.4 | | | | |
| 18.8 | 9.8 | -.8 | Net Worth | -78.9 | -1.0 | | | | |
| 100.0 | 100.0 | 100.0 | Total Liabilities & Net Worth | 100.0 | 100.0 | | | | |
| | | | INCOME DATA | | | | | | |
| 100.0 | 100.0 | 100.0 | Net Sales | 100.0 | 100.0 | | | | |
| | | | Gross Profit | | | | | | |
| 97.8 | 93.3 | 95.1 | Operating Expenses | 89.9 | 96.6 | | | | |
| 2.2 | 6.7 | 4.9 | Operating Profit | 10.1 | 3.4 | | | | |
| 2.1 | 2.1 | 1.5 | All Other Expenses (net) | 6.5 | -1.0 | | | | |
| .1 | 4.6 | 3.4 | Profit Before Taxes | 3.6 | 4.4 | | | | |
| | | | RATIOS | | | | | | |
| 1.6 | 1.7 | 2.0 | | 1.4 | 2.6 | | | | |
| 1.1 | 1.1 | 1.3 | Current | .9 | 1.4 | | | | |
| .7 | .8 | .8 | | .6 | .4 | | | | |
| 1.3 | 1.3 | 1.7 | | 1.4 | 2.4 | | | | |
| .9 | .9 | 1.1 | Quick | .8 | 1.1 | | | | |
| .6 | .5 | .6 | | .3 | .4 | | | | |
| 29 12.4 | 23 15.8 | 26 14.3 | | 0 UND | 25 14.6 | | | | |
| 40 9.2 | 37 9.8 | 38 9.7 | Sales/Receivables | 24 15.5 | 32 11.5 | | | | |
| 54 6.8 | 59 6.2 | 59 6.2 | | 33 10.9 | 58 6.3 | | | | |
| | | | Cost of Sales/Inventory | | | | | | |
| | | | Cost of Sales/Payables | | | | | | |
| 13.0 | 12.2 | 9.7 | | 19.9 | 6.2 | | | | |
| 67.2 | 56.9 | 22.3 | Sales/Working Capital | -62.8 | 19.5 | | | | |
| -18.6 | -23.4 | -25.3 | | -6.7 | -16.7 | | | | |
| 3.0 | 6.2 | 7.8 | | 4.1 | 24.8 | | | | |
| (75) .6 | (70) 2.1 | (57) 3.2 | EBIT/Interest | (11) 1.1 | (15) 5.7 | | | | |
| -2.1 | .1 | .3 | | -.6 | -1.0 | | | | |
| 1.5 | 2.6 | 3.2 | Net Profit + Depr., Dep., | | | | | | |
| (15) .9 | (14) 1.8 | (12) 1.6 | Amort./Cur. Mat. L/T/D | | | | | | |
| .1 | .3 | .9 | | | | | | | |
| .8 | .8 | .7 | | NM | .3 | | | | |
| 3.4 | 1.9 | 1.6 | Fixed/Worth | -.4 | NM | | | | |
| -4.0 | -2.1 | -1.3 | | -.1 | -1.2 | | | | |
| 1.3 | 1.2 | 1.1 | | NM | .8 | | | | |
| 5.0 | 3.6 | 3.6 | Debt/Worth | -2.3 | NM | | | | |
| -10.8 | -5.0 | -4.0 | | -1.6 | -4.4 | | | | |
| 18.5 | 35.5 | 31.8 | % Profit Before Taxes/Tangible | | | | | | |
| (55) .4 | (49) 14.4 | (40) 10.6 | Net Worth | | | | | | |
| -25.9 | -1.1 | -5.0 | | | | | | | |
| 6.1 | 12.9 | 12.5 | % Profit Before Taxes/Total | 20.2 | 12.3 | | | | |
| -1.5 | 4.7 | 4.5 | Assets | 3.3 | 5.6 | | | | |
| -8.5 | -4.0 | -2.6 | | -10.0 | -9.1 | | | | |
| 13.8 | 16.7 | 18.5 | | 69.1 | 31.9 | | | | |
| 5.4 | 6.6 | 7.8 | Sales/Net Fixed Assets | 13.9 | 14.5 | | | | |
| 3.2 | 3.7 | 5.0 | | 2.2 | 8.3 | | | | |
| 3.1 | 3.6 | 4.0 | | 6.2 | 5.4 | | | | |
| 2.2 | 2.3 | 2.6 | Sales/Total Assets | 4.0 | 3.8 | | | | |
| 1.5 | 1.6 | 2.1 | | 1.0 | 2.2 | | | | |
| 2.9 | 2.1 | 1.9 | | .8 | 1.3 | | | | |
| (71) 4.8 | (61) 4.9 | (54) 3.8 | % Depr., Dep., Amort./Sales | (10) 4.1 | (13) 2.8 | | | | |
| 7.0 | 6.9 | 5.5 | | 12.7 | 5.6 | | | | |
| 2.2 | 1.7 | 2.4 | % Officers', Directors' | | | | | | |
| (39) 4.0 | (38) 3.2 | (27) 6.1 | Owners' Comp/Sales | | | | | | |
| 9.4 | 8.3 | 10.4 | | | | | | | |
| 838932M | 691192M | 585815M | Net Sales ($) | 8930M | 32928M | 33991M | 44990M | 122245M | 342731M |
| 480228M | 358456M | 269894M | Total Assets ($) | 5990M | 18813M | 13955M | 19072M | 62454M | 149610M |

M = $ thousand    MM = $ million
See Pages 9 through 22 for Explanation of Ratios and Data

## Current Data Sorted by Assets | Comparative Historical Data

| | 0-500M | 500M-2MM | 2-10MM | 10-50MM | 50-100MM | 100-250MM | | 4/1/07-3/31/08 ALL | 4/1/08-3/31/09 ALL |
|---|---|---|---|---|---|---|---|---|---|
| **Type of Statement** | | | | | | | | | |
| Unqualified | | 4 | 3 | 1 | | 1 | | 4 | 4 |
| Reviewed | 2 | 4 | 3 | 2 | | | | 5 | 5 |
| Compiled | 4 | 5 | 6 | | | | | 4 | 6 |
| Tax Returns | 1 | 4 | 1 | 5 | | | | 4 | 4 |
| Other | | | 6 | | | | | 12 | 9 |
| | | 9 (4/1-9/30/11) | | 43 (10/1/11-3/31/12) | | | | | |
| **NUMBER OF STATEMENTS** | 7 | 17 | 19 | 8 | | 1 | | 29 | 28 |
| | % | % | % | % | % | % | | % | % |
| **ASSETS** | | | | | | | | | |
| Cash & Equivalents | | 9.0 | 10.2 | | | | | 7.3 | 7.0 |
| Trade Receivables (net) | | 31.7 | 27.2 | | | | | 27.6 | 25.6 |
| Inventory | | 5.0 | 11.8 | | | | | 10.2 | 7.4 |
| All Other Current | | 4.1 | 2.9 | | | | | 1.0 | 1.4 |
| Total Current | | 49.8 | 52.2 | | | | | 46.1 | 41.5 |
| Fixed Assets (net) | | 32.0 | 37.5 | | | | | 42.5 | 45.6 |
| Intangibles (net) | | 13.6 | 5.9 | | | | | 6.6 | 9.2 |
| All Other Non-Current | | 4.6 | 4.5 | | | | | 4.8 | 3.6 |
| Total | | 100.0 | 100.0 | | | | | 100.0 | 100.0 |
| **LIABILITIES** | | | | | | | | | |
| Notes Payable-Short Term | | 19.0 | 15.7 | | | | | 8.5 | 13.6 |
| Cur. Mat.-L.T.D. | | 10.6 | 5.9 | | | | | 7.1 | 11.2 |
| Trade Payables | | 15.4 | 17.2 | | | | | 15.8 | 13.2 |
| Income Taxes Payable | | .0 | .2 | | | | | .5 | .1 |
| All Other Current | | 4.9 | 7.7 | | | | | 8.9 | 8.1 |
| Total Current | | 49.9 | 46.8 | | | | | 40.9 | 46.1 |
| Long-Term Debt | | 23.5 | 17.8 | | | | | 28.9 | 28.6 |
| Deferred Taxes | | .0 | 1.4 | | | | | 1.4 | 1.0 |
| All Other Non-Current | | 5.9 | 7.1 | | | | | 4.0 | 6.3 |
| Net Worth | | 20.7 | 27.0 | | | | | 24.9 | 17.9 |
| Total Liabilities & Net Worth | | 100.0 | 100.0 | | | | | 100.0 | 100.0 |
| **INCOME DATA** | | | | | | | | | |
| Net Sales | | 100.0 | 100.0 | | | | | 100.0 | 100.0 |
| Gross Profit | | 45.8 | 38.3 | | | | | 41.4 | 45.1 |
| Operating Expenses | | 45.4 | 35.5 | | | | | 38.8 | 41.2 |
| Operating Profit | | .4 | 2.8 | | | | | 2.6 | 3.9 |
| All Other Expenses (net) | | 1.1 | .7 | | | | | 2.0 | 2.2 |
| Profit Before Taxes | | -.7 | 2.1 | | | | | .6 | 1.7 |
| **RATIOS** | | | | | | | | | |
| Current | | 1.9 | 1.8 | | | | | 1.9 | 1.5 |
| | | 1.1 | 1.1 | | | | | 1.3 | 1.0 |
| | | .7 | .7 | | | | | .8 | .6 |
| Quick | | 1.4 | 1.3 | | | | | 1.6 | 1.1 |
| | | .9 | .6 | | | | | .9 | .7 |
| | | .5 | .5 | | | | | .8 | .5 |
| Sales/Receivables | | 29  12.4 | 30  12.1 | | | | | 34  10.6 | 29  12.6 |
| | | 44  8.3 | 45  8.2 | | | | | 44  8.4 | 43  8.5 |
| | | 54  6.7 | 57  6.4 | | | | | 58  6.3 | 55  6.7 |
| Cost of Sales/Inventory | | 3  139.2 | 9  38.8 | | | | | 12  31.1 | 5  73.7 |
| | | 11  34.5 | 25  14.7 | | | | | 24  15.4 | 14  26.1 |
| | | 23  16.2 | 35  10.3 | | | | | 44  8.4 | 40  9.1 |
| Cost of Sales/Payables | | 20  18.7 | 26  14.3 | | | | | 25  14.4 | 17  21.0 |
| | | 33  11.0 | 40  9.1 | | | | | 38  9.6 | 28  13.1 |
| | | 54  6.7 | 59  6.2 | | | | | 72  5.1 | 57  6.4 |
| Sales/Working Capital | | 10.8 | 11.5 | | | | | 9.3 | 13.5 |
| | | 37.2 | 54.0 | | | | | 22.6 | UND |
| | | -22.1 | -13.0 | | | | | -33.6 | -13.2 |
| EBIT/Interest | | 6.9 | 10.3 | | | | | 6.0 | 4.4 |
| | | (15)  2.9 | 3.3 | | | | | (28)  2.0 | (26)  1.9 |
| | | -2.4 | .6 | | | | | .3 | 1.0 |
| Net Profit + Depr., Dep., Amort./Cur. Mat. L/T/D | | | | | | | | 3.7 | |
| | | | | | | | | (10)  2.2 | |
| | | | | | | | | 1.1 | |
| Fixed/Worth | | .6 | .7 | | | | | 1.0 | 1.1 |
| | | 1.6 | 1.4 | | | | | 2.6 | 2.6 |
| | | -1.4 | 3.6 | | | | | 6.5 | -1.9 |
| Debt/Worth | | .6 | 1.4 | | | | | 1.3 | 1.6 |
| | | 4.5 | 2.4 | | | | | 3.4 | 3.3 |
| | | -3.7 | 12.7 | | | | | 8.7 | -5.3 |
| % Profit Before Taxes/Tangible Net Worth | | 48.3 | 49.8 | | | | | 37.0 | 37.2 |
| | | (10)  13.2 | (15)  11.4 | | | | | (23)  13.2 | (18)  22.3 |
| | | .2 | 2.4 | | | | | 1.5 | 1.7 |
| % Profit Before Taxes/Total Assets | | 11.6 | 13.8 | | | | | 11.2 | 13.2 |
| | | 3.1 | 3.5 | | | | | 4.2 | 4.8 |
| | | -10.0 | -2.0 | | | | | -1.8 | .4 |
| Sales/Net Fixed Assets | | 26.6 | 11.5 | | | | | 10.4 | 10.2 |
| | | 7.4 | 5.9 | | | | | 5.3 | 5.3 |
| | | 4.5 | 3.8 | | | | | 3.2 | 2.8 |
| Sales/Total Assets | | 3.5 | 3.0 | | | | | 3.0 | 3.3 |
| | | 2.2 | 2.4 | | | | | 2.1 | 2.0 |
| | | 1.8 | 1.6 | | | | | 1.4 | 1.4 |
| % Depr., Dep., Amort./Sales | | 2.0 | 2.4 | | | | | 2.5 | 2.6 |
| | | (14)  5.1 | (18)  4.8 | | | | | (26)  3.8 | (25)  4.5 |
| | | 9.9 | 7.2 | | | | | 5.1 | 7.2 |
| % Officers', Directors' Owners' Comp/Sales | | | | | | | | 3.1 | 1.8 |
| | | | | | | | | (12)  5.4 | (10)  5.0 |
| | | | | | | | | 9.0 | 14.7 |
| Net Sales ($) | 8020M | 45685M | 170690M | 215443M | | 96411M | | 736054M | 784331M |
| Total Assets ($) | 1916M | 18359M | 80456M | 162754M | | 110533M | | 517471M | 522103M |

*DATA NOT AVAILABLE* (columns 50-100MM and 100-250MM)

M = $ thousand MM = $ million
See Pages 9 through 22 for Explanation of Ratios and Data

## Comparative Historical Data      Current Data Sorted by Sales

| H1 | H2 | H3 | Type of Statement | 0-1MM | 1-3MM | 3-5MM | 5-10MM | 10-25MM | 25MM & OVER |
|---|---|---|---|---|---|---|---|---|---|
| 5 | 3 | 5 | Unqualified | | | | | 4 | 1 |
| 1 | 11 | 9 | Reviewed | | 3 | 1 | 1 | 3 | 1 |
| 4 | 7 | 12 | Compiled | 1 | 4 | 3 | 3 | 1 | |
| 5 | 5 | 10 | Tax Returns | 2 | 4 | 3 | 1 | | |
| 12 | 10 | 16 | Other | | 5 | | 3 | 5 | 2 |
| 4/1/09- 3/31/10 ALL | 4/1/10- 3/31/11 ALL | 4/1/11- 3/31/12 ALL | | | 9 (4/1-9/30/11) | | | 43 (10/1/11-3/31/12) | |
| 27 | 36 | 52 | NUMBER OF STATEMENTS | 3 | 16 | 8 | 8 | 13 | 4 |
| % | % | % | ASSETS | % | % | % | % | % | % |
| 12.4 | 11.7 | 11.1 | Cash & Equivalents | | 10.8 | | | 8.8 | |
| 21.9 | 22.8 | 28.0 | Trade Receivables (net) | | 27.3 | | | 23.9 | |
| 6.3 | 6.5 | 9.0 | Inventory | | 6.5 | | | 12.2 | |
| 2.1 | 2.7 | 3.0 | All Other Current | | 4.4 | | | 1.9 | |
| 42.8 | 43.7 | 51.1 | Total Current | | 48.9 | | | 46.7 | |
| 43.4 | 39.3 | 32.5 | Fixed Assets (net) | | 34.4 | | | 36.4 | |
| 8.8 | 7.0 | 11.8 | Intangibles (net) | | 11.2 | | | 12.9 | |
| 5.0 | 10.0 | 4.6 | All Other Non-Current | | 5.4 | | | 4.0 | |
| 100.0 | 100.0 | 100.0 | Total | | 100.0 | | | 100.0 | |
| | | | LIABILITIES | | | | | | |
| 7.7 | 15.0 | 14.3 | Notes Payable-Short Term | | 15.4 | | | 13.3 | |
| 6.0 | 8.0 | 7.2 | Cur. Mat.-L.T.D. | | 11.1 | | | 4.8 | |
| 10.8 | 11.7 | 16.0 | Trade Payables | | 17.5 | | | 14.4 | |
| .0 | .0 | .1 | Income Taxes Payable | | .0 | | | .1 | |
| 7.5 | 9.1 | 8.6 | All Other Current | | 7.2 | | | 6.4 | |
| 32.0 | 43.9 | 46.2 | Total Current | | 51.3 | | | 39.1 | |
| 26.0 | 24.8 | 26.8 | Long-Term Debt | | 30.0 | | | 12.4 | |
| .4 | .7 | .7 | Deferred Taxes | | .0 | | | 2.3 | |
| 6.7 | 10.8 | 6.4 | All Other Non-Current | | 3.7 | | | 11.4 | |
| 34.9 | 19.8 | 19.9 | Net Worth | | 15.0 | | | 34.8 | |
| 100.0 | 100.0 | 100.0 | Total Liabilties & Net Worth | | 100.0 | | | 100.0 | |
| | | | INCOME DATA | | | | | | |
| 100.0 | 100.0 | 100.0 | Net Sales | | 100.0 | | | 100.0 | |
| 42.8 | 38.8 | 42.1 | Gross Profit | | 45.3 | | | 31.0 | |
| 39.7 | 36.5 | 40.2 | Operating Expenses | | 45.7 | | | 30.1 | |
| 3.1 | 2.3 | 2.0 | Operating Profit | | -.3 | | | .9 | |
| 2.0 | 1.7 | 1.3 | All Other Expenses (net) | | 1.5 | | | 1.5 | |
| 1.1 | .6 | .7 | Profit Before Taxes | | -1.8 | | | -.6 | |
| | | | RATIOS | | | | | | |
| 2.9 | 1.8 | 1.8 | | | 3.1 | | | 1.7 | |
| 1.6 | 1.3 | 1.2 | Current | | 1.2 | | | 1.2 | |
| .8 | .7 | .8 | | | .6 | | | .8 | |
| 2.2 | 1.4 | 1.4 | | | 2.6 | | | 1.4 | |
| 1.1 | .9 | .8 | Quick | | 1.0 | | | .8 | |
| .6 | .5 | .5 | | | .4 | | | .5 | |
| 16   22.5 | 29   12.6 | 31   11.8 | | 24   15.1 | | | | 36   10.2 | |
| 41   9.0 | 42   8.7 | 46   8.0 | Sales/Receivables | 41   9.0 | | | | 52   7.0 | |
| 61   6.0 | 54   6.8 | 57   6.4 | | 51   7.1 | | | | 59   6.2 | |
| 3   106.3 | 8   47.7 | 7   50.8 | | 0   UND | | | | 17   22.1 | |
| 10   35.5 | 20   18.4 | 19   19.5 | Cost of Sales/Inventory | 9   39.3 | | | | 25   14.4 | |
| 24   15.4 | 27   13.4 | 30   12.3 | | 27   13.6 | | | | 33   11.1 | |
| 16   22.3 | 17   22.0 | 22   16.6 | | 13   28.0 | | | | 19   19.1 | |
| 30   12.3 | 30   12.2 | 36   10.1 | Cost of Sales/Payables | 35   10.4 | | | | 35   10.4 | |
| 45   8.1 | 53   6.9 | 54   6.7 | | 57   6.4 | | | | 47   7.8 | |
| 7.1 | 9.3 | 11.6 | | | 12.4 | | | 8.9 | |
| 21.9 | 19.7 | 35.5 | Sales/Working Capital | | 35.5 | | | 24.1 | |
| -42.5 | -15.9 | -18.2 | | | -7.6 | | | -13.3 | |
| 6.9 | 5.1 | 8.8 | | | 7.1 | | | 21.1 | |
| (25) 2.2 | (34) 1.7 | (49) 2.5 | EBIT/Interest | | (15) 2.9 | | | 1.3 | |
| -2.0 | -.9 | -.4 | | | -2.4 | | | -1.3 | |
| | 1.5 | | Net Profit + Depr., Dep., | | | | | | |
| | (10) .4 | | Amort./Cur. Mat. L/T/D | | | | | | |
| | -.2 | | | | | | | | |
| .6 | .9 | .7 | | | .5 | | | .7 | |
| 1.5 | 1.8 | 1.4 | Fixed/Worth | | 1.2 | | | 1.6 | |
| -9.2 | -4.3 | -1.4 | | | -.7 | | | NM | |
| .6 | 1.5 | 1.2 | | | .6 | | | 1.0 | |
| 2.2 | 2.6 | 2.8 | Debt/Worth | | 2.3 | | | 2.3 | |
| -16.1 | -8.3 | -4.3 | | | -3.2 | | | NM | |
| 33.3 | 51.7 | 49.8 | % Profit Before Taxes/Tangible | | 59.5 | | | 32.1 | |
| (20) 9.1 | (24) 13.4 | (34) 11.3 | Net Worth | | (10) 13.2 | | | (10) 5.0 | |
| -30.4 | .9 | 2.2 | | | 5.1 | | | -4.6 | |
| 10.6 | 19.2 | 12.4 | % Profit Before Taxes/Total | | 9.9 | | | 8.5 | |
| 2.4 | 3.0 | 2.9 | Assets | | 2.9 | | | .6 | |
| -18.1 | -4.7 | -4.1 | | | -16.3 | | | -3.5 | |
| 20.5 | 12.1 | 14.5 | | | 15.7 | | | 10.0 | |
| 4.6 | 5.1 | 6.7 | Sales/Net Fixed Assets | | 8.6 | | | 4.6 | |
| 2.9 | 3.0 | 4.5 | | | 5.2 | | | 2.5 | |
| 2.7 | 2.6 | 3.2 | | | 3.6 | | | 2.9 | |
| 2.3 | 2.1 | 2.3 | Sales/Total Assets | | 2.2 | | | 1.6 | |
| 1.3 | 1.4 | 1.6 | | | 1.8 | | | 1.0 | |
| 4.2 | 3.9 | 2.3 | | | 2.0 | | | 3.0 | |
| (19) 6.5 | (29) 6.3 | (45) 4.4 | % Depr., Dep., Amort./Sales | | (14) 4.6 | | | (12) 6.9 | |
| 8.5 | 9.5 | 8.5 | | | 9.9 | | | 10.2 | |
| | 2.5 | 4.1 | % Officers', Directors' | | | | | | |
| | (14) 4.3 | (15) 6.0 | Owners' Comp/Sales | | | | | | |
| | 9.7 | 9.6 | | | | | | | |
| 612104M | 416063M | 536249M | Net Sales ($) | 1631M | 33086M | 32191M | 54358M | 194620M | 220363M |
| 358072M | 265475M | 374018M | Total Assets ($) | 540M | 14254M | 14576M | 20685M | 160365M | 163598M |

M = $ thousand    MM = $ million
See Pages 9 through 22 for Explanation of Ratios and Data

# MANUFACTURING—Manifold Business Forms Printing  NAICS 323116

**Current Data Sorted by Assets**  |  **Comparative Historical Data**

### Type of Statement

| | 0-500M | 500M-2MM | 2-10MM | 10-50MM | 50-100MM | 100-250MM | | 4/1/07-3/31/08 ALL | 4/1/08-3/31/09 ALL |
|---|---|---|---|---|---|---|---|---|---|
| Unqualified | 1 | 4 | 7 | 5 | | | | | |
| Reviewed | 1 | 2 | 1 | 1 | | | | 8 | 6 |
| Compiled | 1 | 2 | | 2 | | | | 13 | 13 |
| Tax Returns | 1 | 2 | | 3 | | | | 4 | 3 |
| Other | | | | | | | | 2 | 3 |
| | | | | | | | | 11 | 11 |

Current-data dates: 7 (4/1-9/30/11); 25 (10/1/11-3/31/12)

| 0-500M | 500M-2MM | 2-10MM | 10-50MM | 50-100MM | 100-250MM | | 4/1/07-3/31/08 ALL | 4/1/08-3/31/09 ALL |
|---|---|---|---|---|---|---|---|---|
| 3 | 10 | 10 | 9 | | | **NUMBER OF STATEMENTS** | 38 | 36 |
| % | % | % | % | % | % | **ASSETS** | % | % |
| | 12.9 | 9.6 | | DATA | DATA | Cash & Equivalents | 12.4 | 13.0 |
| | 16.6 | 29.7 | | NOT | NOT | Trade Receivables (net) | 33.3 | 30.6 |
| | 18.1 | 16.7 | | AVAILABLE | AVAILABLE | Inventory | 12.2 | 16.3 |
| | 1.9 | 8.1 | | | | All Other Current | 2.9 | 2.1 |
| | 49.5 | 64.0 | | | | Total Current | 60.8 | 61.9 |
| | 25.7 | 23.9 | | | | Fixed Assets (net) | 25.7 | 25.4 |
| | 19.6 | 7.0 | | | | Intangibles (net) | 7.0 | 7.2 |
| | 5.3 | 5.2 | | | | All Other Non-Current | 6.4 | 5.5 |
| | 100.0 | 100.0 | | | | Total | 100.0 | 100.0 |
| | | | | | | **LIABILITIES** | | |
| | 12.5 | 7.2 | | | | Notes Payable-Short Term | 9.6 | 6.6 |
| | 4.1 | 4.2 | | | | Cur. Mat.-L.T.D. | 4.9 | 3.6 |
| | 10.6 | 15.0 | | | | Trade Payables | 13.8 | 14.0 |
| | .3 | 1.7 | | | | Income Taxes Payable | .0 | .0 |
| | 16.4 | 11.8 | | | | All Other Current | 10.8 | 11.6 |
| | 43.9 | 39.9 | | | | Total Current | 39.2 | 35.8 |
| | 22.3 | 13.3 | | | | Long-Term Debt | 13.0 | 17.1 |
| | .3 | .2 | | | | Deferred Taxes | .6 | .6 |
| | 6.1 | 8.9 | | | | All Other Non-Current | 5.7 | 5.7 |
| | 27.4 | 37.7 | | | | Net Worth | 41.6 | 40.7 |
| | 100.0 | 100.0 | | | | Total Liabilities & Net Worth | 100.0 | 100.0 |
| | | | | | | **INCOME DATA** | | |
| | 100.0 | 100.0 | | | | Net Sales | 100.0 | 100.0 |
| | 47.3 | 28.7 | | | | Gross Profit | 36.8 | 32.0 |
| | 45.5 | 26.7 | | | | Operating Expenses | 31.5 | 30.0 |
| | 1.8 | 1.9 | | | | Operating Profit | 5.3 | 2.0 |
| | .8 | .2 | | | | All Other Expenses (net) | .7 | 1.2 |
| | 1.1 | 1.7 | | | | Profit Before Taxes | 4.6 | .8 |
| | | | | | | **RATIOS** | | |
| | 4.6 | 3.0 | | | | | 2.5 | 2.4 |
| | 1.2 | 1.7 | | | | Current | 1.8 | 1.8 |
| | .6 | 1.0 | | | | | 1.1 | 1.1 |
| | 2.1 | 2.2 | | | | | 1.8 | 1.9 |
| | .6 | .8 | | | | Quick | 1.1 | 1.1 |
| | .3 | .5 | | | | | .7 | .7 |
| | 11  32.4 | 41  8.8 | | | | | 33  11.2 | 29  12.7 |
| | 24  14.9 | 45  8.2 | | | | Sales/Receivables | 39  9.4 | 36  10.1 |
| | 31  11.9 | 51  7.2 | | | | | 53  6.8 | 51  7.2 |
| | 22  16.3 | 22  16.9 | | | | | 13  28.8 | 12  30.1 |
| | 40  9.2 | 33  10.9 | | | | Cost of Sales/Inventory | 21  17.4 | 25  14.4 |
| | 60  6.1 | 46  7.9 | | | | | 35  10.5 | 51  7.1 |
| | 8  48.1 | 19  18.9 | | | | | 14  25.8 | 11  34.3 |
| | 20  18.4 | 26  14.0 | | | | Cost of Sales/Payables | 22  16.7 | 20  17.8 |
| | 66  5.5 | 38  9.6 | | | | | 41  8.9 | 53  6.9 |
| | 8.7 | 5.8 | | | | | 6.6 | 7.1 |
| | 36.2 | 13.5 | | | | Sales/Working Capital | 11.4 | 12.6 |
| | -10.2 | NM | | | | | NM | 65.7 |
| | | 95.5 | | | | | 11.9 | 7.4 |
| | | 4.0 | | | | EBIT/Interest | (34) 6.0 | (29) 2.1 |
| | | -1.0 | | | | | 1.6 | .1 |
| | | | | | | Net Profit + Depr., Dep., Amort./Cur. Mat. L/T/D | | |
| | .5 | .2 | | | | | .3 | .2 |
| | NM | .8 | | | | Fixed/Worth | .7 | .6 |
| | -.5 | 6.1 | | | | | 1.9 | 2.1 |
| | .7 | .7 | | | | | .6 | .5 |
| | NM | 2.8 | | | | Debt/Worth | 1.8 | 1.6 |
| | -2.6 | 18.0 | | | | | 3.7 | 10.6 |
| | | | | | | | 46.0 | 35.6 |
| | | | | | | % Profit Before Taxes/Tangible Net Worth | (33) 23.4 | (30) 14.9 |
| | | | | | | | 11.8 | 1.9 |
| | 12.1 | 14.1 | | | | | 18.6 | 15.0 |
| | 3.7 | 5.5 | | | | % Profit Before Taxes/Total Assets | 10.6 | 4.2 |
| | -11.8 | -6.1 | | | | | 4.1 | -.5 |
| | 40.4 | 60.5 | | | | | 21.8 | 36.0 |
| | 12.5 | 8.4 | | | | Sales/Net Fixed Assets | 11.3 | 13.5 |
| | 7.5 | 5.4 | | | | | 6.6 | 6.5 |
| | 3.8 | 3.2 | | | | | 3.4 | 3.8 |
| | 3.0 | 2.5 | | | | Sales/Total Assets | 2.5 | 2.9 |
| | 1.9 | 2.1 | | | | | 2.2 | 2.1 |
| | | .9 | | | | | 1.0 | .9 |
| | | 3.1 | | | | % Depr., Dep., Amort./Sales | (33) 2.5 | (30) 1.6 |
| | | 5.5 | | | | | 3.7 | 3.3 |
| | | | | | | | 2.0 | 1.7 |
| | | | | | | % Officers', Directors' Owners' Comp/Sales | (12) 5.5 | (10) 3.7 |
| | | | | | | | 10.6 | 10.6 |
| 4008M | 39813M | 144768M | 414643M | | | Net Sales ($) | 1018476M | 1039612M |
| 1105M | 13540M | 55895M | 169537M | | | Total Assets ($) | 601975M | 556896M |

© RMA 2012

M = $ thousand    MM = $ million
See Pages 9 through 22 for Explanation of Ratios and Data

## Comparative Historical Data  |  Current Data Sorted by Sales

| 4/1/09-3/31/10 ALL | 4/1/10-3/31/11 ALL | 4/1/11-3/31/12 ALL | Type of Statement | 0-1MM | 1-3MM | 3-5MM | 5-10MM | 10-25MM | 25MM & OVER |
|---|---|---|---|---|---|---|---|---|---|
| 4 | 8 | 5 | Unqualified | | | | | 5 | 5 |
| 11 | 6 | 12 | Reviewed | | 3 | | 2 | | 1 |
| 3 | 4 | 4 | Compiled | | 2 | 1 | 1 | 1 | |
| 2 | 4 | 3 | Tax Returns | 1 | | 1 | 1 | 2 | |
| 11 | 13 | 8 | Other | 1 | | 1 | 2 | | 2 |
| | | | | | 7 (4/1-9/30/11) | | | 25 (10/1/11-3/31/12) | |
| 31 | 35 | 32 | NUMBER OF STATEMENTS | 2 | 5 | 3 | 6 | 8 | 8 |
| % | % | % | ASSETS | % | % | % | % | % | % |
| 8.7 | 11.9 | 12.8 | Cash & Equivalents | | | | | | |
| 30.4 | 29.9 | 28.5 | Trade Receivables (net) | | | | | | |
| 13.1 | 13.2 | 14.8 | Inventory | | | | | | |
| 1.8 | 3.9 | 5.4 | All Other Current | | | | | | |
| 54.0 | 58.9 | 61.5 | Total Current | | | | | | |
| 29.3 | 24.4 | 20.5 | Fixed Assets (net) | | | | | | |
| 10.8 | 10.1 | 13.1 | Intangibles (net) | | | | | | |
| 5.9 | 6.6 | 4.8 | All Other Non-Current | | | | | | |
| 100.0 | 100.0 | 100.0 | Total | | | | | | |
| | | | LIABILITIES | | | | | | |
| 8.6 | 4.8 | 7.7 | Notes Payable-Short Term | | | | | | |
| 5.1 | 4.2 | 3.6 | Cur. Mat.-L.T.D. | | | | | | |
| 15.3 | 14.2 | 11.9 | Trade Payables | | | | | | |
| .1 | .4 | .7 | Income Taxes Payable | | | | | | |
| 10.2 | 13.5 | 14.2 | All Other Current | | | | | | |
| 39.4 | 37.1 | 38.1 | Total Current | | | | | | |
| 21.1 | 13.8 | 16.4 | Long-Term Debt | | | | | | |
| .5 | .8 | .4 | Deferred Taxes | | | | | | |
| 5.6 | 10.5 | 10.6 | All Other Non-Current | | | | | | |
| 33.4 | 37.7 | 34.6 | Net Worth | | | | | | |
| 100.0 | 100.0 | 100.0 | Total Liabilties & Net Worth | | | | | | |
| | | | INCOME DATA | | | | | | |
| 100.0 | 100.0 | 100.0 | Net Sales | | | | | | |
| 32.4 | 32.2 | 36.3 | Gross Profit | | | | | | |
| 30.7 | 29.7 | 33.5 | Operating Expenses | | | | | | |
| 1.7 | 2.5 | 2.8 | Operating Profit | | | | | | |
| .6 | .7 | .3 | All Other Expenses (net) | | | | | | |
| 1.2 | 1.8 | 2.5 | Profit Before Taxes | | | | | | |
| | | | RATIOS | | | | | | |
| 1.8 / 1.4 / 1.0 | 2.4 / 1.4 / 1.1 | 3.7 / 1.6 / 1.1 | Current | | | | | | |
| 1.4 / 1.1 / .6 | 1.7 / 1.0 / .7 | 2.3 / .9 / .6 | Quick | | | | | | |
| (31) 11.8 / (40) 9.2 / (53) 6.9 | (30) 12.1 / (41) 8.9 / (53) 6.8 | (28) 12.9 / (38) 9.5 / (50) 7.3 | Sales/Receivables | | | | | | |
| (13) 28.3 / (21) 17.5 / (41) 8.9 | (12) 29.5 / (30) 12.2 / (41) 8.9 | (14) 25.4 / (32) 11.5 / (44) 8.3 | Cost of Sales/Inventory | | | | | | |
| (16) 23.3 / (24) 15.4 / (42) 8.7 | (15) 25.0 / (22) 16.6 / (37) 9.8 | (17) 21.2 / (21) 17.7 / (36) 10.2 | Cost of Sales/Payables | | | | | | |
| 7.1 / 24.1 / -763.9 | 5.3 / 16.3 / 57.2 | 5.3 / 11.9 / 102.1 | Sales/Working Capital | | | | | | |
| 7.1 / (29) 1.6 / -1.3 | 8.8 / (33) 2.5 / .4 | 13.0 / (27) 3.4 / .5 | EBIT/Interest | | | | | | |
| | 3.2 / (11) 1.5 / .6 | | Net Profit + Depr., Dep., Amort./Cur. Mat. L/T/D | | | | | | |
| .3 / 1.3 / UND | .2 / .8 / 2.3 | .2 / .8 / NM | Fixed/Worth | | | | | | |
| .9 / 1.9 / UND | .7 / 1.9 / 15.8 | .7 / 3.5 / NM | Debt/Worth | | | | | | |
| 30.4 / (24) 8.0 / -6.8 | 31.9 / (27) 6.1 / -3.2 | 53.9 / (24) 9.6 / -14.8 | % Profit Before Taxes/Tangible Net Worth | | | | | | |
| 11.3 / 2.9 / -4.0 | 11.3 / 3.2 / -1.8 | 13.4 / 5.4 / -2.4 | % Profit Before Taxes/Total Assets | | | | | | |
| 30.2 / 8.8 / 4.8 | 42.4 / 13.0 / 5.3 | 58.1 / 14.7 / 7.0 | Sales/Net Fixed Assets | | | | | | |
| 4.2 / 2.4 / 1.7 | 3.7 / 2.5 / 2.0 | 3.6 / 2.5 / 1.8 | Sales/Total Assets | | | | | | |
| 1.4 / (28) 3.2 / 4.4 | 1.1 / (29) 2.6 / 3.9 | 1.0 / (28) 2.4 / 3.7 | % Depr., Dep., Amort./Sales | | | | | | |
| | 2.6 / (13) 6.5 / 12.0 | 1.6 / (10) 3.6 / 7.1 | % Officers', Directors' Owners' Comp/Sales | | | | | | |
| 743851M | 713910M | 603232M | Net Sales ($) | 1197M | 11255M | 11295M | 43552M | 141813M | 394120M |
| 365959M | 290535M | 240077M | Total Assets ($) | 629M | 4919M | 4396M | 17431M | 71439M | 141263M |

© RMA 2012

M = $ thousand    MM = $ million
See Pages 9 through 22 for Explanation of Ratios and Data

## Current Data Sorted by Assets

## Comparative Historical Data

| | | | | | | | Type of Statement | | |
|---|---|---|---|---|---|---|---|---|---|
| | | 1 | 5 | 1 | 1 | | Unqualified | 5 | 6 |
| | | 5 | 1 | | | | Reviewed | 10 | 7 |
| | | 1 | 1 | | | | Compiled | 1 | |
| 2 | 3 | | | | | | Tax Returns | 4 | 5 |
| 1 | 2 | 4 | 6 | | 2 | | Other | 12 | 15 |
| | 9 (4/1-9/30/11) | | 27 (10/1/11-3/31/12) | | | | | 4/1/07- 3/31/08 | 4/1/08- 3/31/09 |
| 0-500M | 500M-2MM | 2-10MM | 10-50MM | 50-100MM | 100-250MM | | | ALL | ALL |
| 3 | 5 | 11 | 13 | 1 | 3 | | NUMBER OF STATEMENTS | 32 | 33 |
| % | % | % | % | % | % | | | % | % |
| | | | | | | | ASSETS | | |
| | | 9.8 | 10.5 | | | | Cash & Equivalents | 8.5 | 5.8 |
| | | 31.4 | 24.9 | | | | Trade Receivables (net) | 31.6 | 31.8 |
| | | 9.2 | 15.4 | | | | Inventory | 10.4 | 10.7 |
| | | .5 | 3.2 | | | | All Other Current | 1.0 | 1.7 |
| | | 50.8 | 54.0 | | | | Total Current | 51.5 | 50.0 |
| | | 41.8 | 33.5 | | | | Fixed Assets (net) | 36.6 | 35.3 |
| | | 1.6 | .3 | | | | Intangibles (net) | 4.4 | 6.5 |
| | | 5.8 | 12.2 | | | | All Other Non-Current | 7.5 | 8.2 |
| | | 100.0 | 100.0 | | | | Total | 100.0 | 100.0 |
| | | | | | | | LIABILITIES | | |
| | | 13.4 | 2.1 | | | | Notes Payable-Short Term | 7.8 | 5.7 |
| | | 9.4 | 6.7 | | | | Cur. Mat.-L.T.D. | 5.6 | 5.2 |
| | | 14.4 | 13.5 | | | | Trade Payables | 14.4 | 12.3 |
| | | .0 | .1 | | | | Income Taxes Payable | .1 | .0 |
| | | 3.6 | 9.5 | | | | All Other Current | 6.8 | 8.2 |
| | | 40.7 | 31.9 | | | | Total Current | 34.7 | 31.4 |
| | | 12.4 | 5.5 | | | | Long-Term Debt | 21.4 | 20.0 |
| | | .1 | 2.4 | | | | Deferred Taxes | .9 | 1.2 |
| | | 5.3 | 10.2 | | | | All Other Non-Current | 9.4 | 5.2 |
| | | 41.5 | 50.0 | | | | Net Worth | 33.6 | 42.2 |
| | | 100.0 | 100.0 | | | | Total Liabilities & Net Worth | 100.0 | 100.0 |
| | | | | | | | INCOME DATA | | |
| | | 100.0 | 100.0 | | | | Net Sales | 100.0 | 100.0 |
| | | 28.9 | 18.4 | | | | Gross Profit | 29.2 | 29.1 |
| | | 26.0 | 19.2 | | | | Operating Expenses | 25.2 | 26.2 |
| | | 2.9 | -.9 | | | | Operating Profit | 4.0 | 2.9 |
| | | .2 | -.1 | | | | All Other Expenses (net) | .8 | .5 |
| | | 2.6 | -.7 | | | | Profit Before Taxes | 3.2 | 2.4 |
| | | | | | | | RATIOS | | |
| | | 1.6 | 3.9 | | | | | 2.9 | 2.9 |
| | | 1.2 | 2.6 | | | | Current | 1.8 | 1.8 |
| | | 1.0 | .9 | | | | | 1.0 | 1.1 |
| | | 1.6 | 3.2 | | | | | 2.1 | 1.9 |
| | | 1.1 | 1.3 | | | | Quick | 1.1 | 1.1 |
| | | .8 | .6 | | | | | .8 | .9 |
| | | 36    10.2 | 49    7.5 | | | | | 41    8.9 | 44    8.4 |
| | | 45    8.1 | 56    6.5 | | | | Sales/Receivables | 52    7.0 | 55    6.7 |
| | | 62    5.9 | 69    5.3 | | | | | 66    5.5 | 67    5.5 |
| | | 0    UND | 20    18.6 | | | | | 7    49.2 | 6    63.6 |
| | | 9    42.8 | 40    9.1 | | | | Cost of Sales/Inventory | 16    23.2 | 21    17.3 |
| | | 31    11.8 | 47    7.8 | | | | | 36    10.1 | 39    9.5 |
| | | 17    22.0 | 19    19.2 | | | | | 19    19.0 | 14    25.4 |
| | | 21    17.2 | 24    15.1 | | | | Cost of Sales/Payables | 23    15.6 | 21    17.6 |
| | | 42    8.6 | 36    10.1 | | | | | 35    10.5 | 36    10.0 |
| | | 9.3 | 3.9 | | | | | 5.6 | 5.6 |
| | | 32.7 | 5.4 | | | | Sales/Working Capital | 15.2 | 8.8 |
| | | -600.0 | NM | | | | | NM | 64.2 |
| | | 10.4 | 1.8 | | | | | 9.8 | 6.0 |
| | | (10)    2.6 | (11)    -1.3 | | | | EBIT/Interest | (29)    1.9 | (29)    1.5 |
| | | 1.0 | -7.9 | | | | | .5 | .1 |
| | | | | | | | Net Profit + Depr., Dep., Amort./Cur. Mat. L/T/D | | |
| | | .6 | .4 | | | | | .5 | .5 |
| | | 1.2 | .6 | | | | Fixed/Worth | .9 | .8 |
| | | 2.8 | 2.3 | | | | | 2.8 | 1.5 |
| | | .8 | .4 | | | | | .5 | .9 |
| | | 1.2 | .6 | | | | Debt/Worth | 1.4 | 1.2 |
| | | 7.5 | 6.4 | | | | | 5.3 | 4.1 |
| | | 18.5 | 5.6 | | | | | 29.2 | 22.9 |
| | | (10)    6.5 | (11)    -1.1 | | | | % Profit Before Taxes/Tangible Net Worth | (26)    7.6 | (31)    7.4 |
| | | 1.6 | -5.0 | | | | | .0 | -3.3 |
| | | 7.9 | 1.7 | | | | | 8.7 | 9.5 |
| | | 1.9 | -.8 | | | | % Profit Before Taxes/Total Assets | 3.0 | 1.4 |
| | | .1 | -4.2 | | | | | -2.8 | -2.0 |
| | | 8.3 | 11.8 | | | | | 14.0 | 11.6 |
| | | 6.3 | 5.0 | | | | Sales/Net Fixed Assets | 5.1 | 5.3 |
| | | 5.4 | 3.2 | | | | | 3.0 | 2.9 |
| | | 2.6 | 1.9 | | | | | 2.5 | 2.5 |
| | | 2.4 | 1.7 | | | | Sales/Total Assets | 1.9 | 1.8 |
| | | 2.2 | 1.3 | | | | | 1.5 | 1.3 |
| | | 2.8 | 2.2 | | | | | 2.6 | 2.6 |
| | | (10)    4.7 | (12)    3.4 | | | | % Depr., Dep., Amort./Sales | (29)    3.9 | (28)    4.5 |
| | | 7.1 | 6.2 | | | | | 5.3 | 5.5 |
| | | | | | | | % Officers', Directors' Owners' Comp/Sales | | |
| 2438M | 19290M | 155832M | 530841M | 59169M | 779635M | | Net Sales ($) | 1088548M | 1175119M |
| 910M | 4916M | 68798M | 315120M | 54020M | 628661M | | Total Assets ($) | 620387M | 781849M |

M = $ thousand    MM = $ million
See Pages 9 through 22 for Explanation of Ratios and Data

## Comparative Historical Data | Current Data Sorted by Sales

| | | | Type of Statement | 0-1MM | 1-3MM | 3-5MM | 5-10MM | 10-25MM | 25MM & OVER |
|---|---|---|---|---|---|---|---|---|---|
| 6 | 11 | 8 | Unqualified | | | | | 2 | 6 |
| 7 | 7 | 6 | Reviewed | | | | 1 | 4 | 1 |
| 1 | 2 | 2 | Compiled | | | 1 | | 1 | 1 |
| 1 | 5 | 5 | Tax Returns | | 1 | | | | |
| 12 | 8 | 15 | Other | 2 | 2 | 1 | 3 | 4 | 6 |
| 4/1/09-3/31/10 | 4/1/10-3/31/11 | 4/1/11-3/31/12 | | | | | 9 (4/1-9/30/11) | 27 (10/1/11-3/31/12) | |
| ALL | ALL | ALL | | | | | | | |
| 27 | 33 | 36 | **NUMBER OF STATEMENTS** | 2 | 3 | 2 | 4 | 11 | 14 |
| % | % | % | **ASSETS** | % | % | % | % | % | % |
| 8.7 | 10.3 | 9.7 | Cash & Equivalents | | | | | 11.9 | 9.0 |
| 24.3 | 29.1 | 28.2 | Trade Receivables (net) | | | | | 31.8 | 22.1 |
| 11.7 | 15.2 | 12.7 | Inventory | | | | | 5.7 | 16.5 |
| 2.3 | 3.3 | 1.9 | All Other Current | | | | | 2.2 | 2.0 |
| 47.0 | 57.9 | 52.6 | Total Current | | | | | 51.6 | 49.6 |
| 41.0 | 30.1 | 33.8 | Fixed Assets (net) | | | | | 35.8 | 40.8 |
| 4.5 | 4.2 | 2.7 | Intangibles (net) | | | | | 1.6 | 2.6 |
| 7.5 | 7.8 | 10.9 | All Other Non-Current | | | | | 11.0 | 7.0 |
| 100.0 | 100.0 | 100.0 | Total | | | | | 100.0 | 100.0 |
| | | | **LIABILITIES** | | | | | | |
| 4.3 | 5.1 | 8.2 | Notes Payable-Short Term | | | | | 10.6 | 2.0 |
| 6.6 | 5.9 | 7.1 | Cur. Mat.-L.T.D. | | | | | 8.2 | 6.2 |
| 9.1 | 13.0 | 14.6 | Trade Payables | | | | | 17.5 | 9.3 |
| .1 | .1 | .1 | Income Taxes Payable | | | | | .1 | .1 |
| 7.7 | 11.3 | 6.4 | All Other Current | | | | | 4.3 | 9.2 |
| 27.8 | 35.4 | 36.4 | Total Current | | | | | 40.7 | 26.8 |
| 20.9 | 11.9 | 13.4 | Long-Term Debt | | | | | 9.8 | 6.6 |
| 1.4 | .9 | .9 | Deferred Taxes | | | | | 1.6 | 1.0 |
| 11.5 | 9.0 | 7.9 | All Other Non-Current | | | | | 8.8 | 7.4 |
| 38.5 | 42.8 | 41.3 | Net Worth | | | | | 39.1 | 58.3 |
| 100.0 | 100.0 | 100.0 | Total Liabilities & Net Worth | | | | | 100.0 | 100.0 |
| | | | **INCOME DATA** | | | | | | |
| 100.0 | 100.0 | 100.0 | Net Sales | | | | | 100.0 | 100.0 |
| 30.8 | 28.0 | 28.2 | Gross Profit | | | | | 30.2 | 18.0 |
| 26.6 | 25.4 | 25.4 | Operating Expenses | | | | | 27.0 | 18.1 |
| 4.2 | 2.6 | 2.8 | Operating Profit | | | | | 3.2 | -.2 |
| 1.1 | -.1 | .2 | All Other Expenses (net) | | | | | .5 | .2 |
| 3.2 | 2.7 | 2.7 | Profit Before Taxes | | | | | 2.7 | -.3 |
| | | | **RATIOS** | | | | | | |
| 2.8 | 3.7 | 3.4 | | | | | | 3.4 | 3.6 |
| 2.2 | 1.7 | 1.6 | Current | | | | | 1.2 | 2.6 |
| 1.0 | 1.0 | 1.0 | | | | | | .9 | 1.5 |
| 2.3 | 2.5 | 2.3 | | | | | | 2.3 | 3.1 |
| 1.3 | 1.1 | 1.1 | Quick | | | | | 1.2 | 1.1 |
| .7 | .6 | .7 | | | | | | .9 | .8 |
| 36  10.2 | 36  10.0 | 36  10.0 | | | | | | 45  8.1 | 47  7.8 |
| 44  8.3 | 53  6.9 | 49  7.4 | Sales/Receivables | | | | | 59  6.2 | 51  7.1 |
| 58  6.2 | 59  6.2 | 58  6.3 | | | | | | 73  5.0 | 57  6.4 |
| 10  37.5 | 9  41.2 | 8  43.3 | | | | | | 0  UND | 20  18.6 |
| 19  19.4 | 28  13.1 | 28  13.1 | Cost of Sales/Inventory | | | | | 9  42.8 | 41  8.8 |
| 44  8.3 | 55  6.6 | 46  8.0 | | | | | | 34  10.7 | 70  5.2 |
| 19  19.5 | 17  21.5 | 19  19.2 | | | | | | 17  22.0 | 19  19.3 |
| 22  16.6 | 25  14.7 | 25  14.4 | Cost of Sales/Payables | | | | | 29  12.6 | 22  16.9 |
| 31  11.6 | 43  8.5 | 39  9.3 | | | | | | 68  5.4 | 36  10.2 |
| 5.0 | 4.0 | 5.2 | | | | | | 5.6 | 4.0 |
| 6.5 | 6.8 | 12.0 | Sales/Working Capital | | | | | 28.0 | 5.3 |
| 232.0 | NM | NM | | | | | | -46.4 | 35.8 |
| 6.1 | 11.0 | 6.5 | | | | | | 11.0 | 1.7 |
| (22)  1.5 | (29)  2.9 | (32)  1.7 | EBIT/Interest | | | | | (10)  3.1 | (12)  -.7 |
| -3.0 | .8 | .0 | | | | | | 1.1 | -6.6 |
| | | | Net Profit + Depr., Dep., Amort./Cur. Mat. L/T/D | | | | | | |
| .6 | .3 | .5 | | | | | | .5 | .6 |
| .7 | .7 | .7 | Fixed/Worth | | | | | 1.2 | .7 |
| 2.5 | 1.9 | 1.5 | | | | | | 2.8 | 1.3 |
| .3 | .4 | .4 | | | | | | .9 | .4 |
| 1.0 | 1.1 | 1.0 | Debt/Worth | | | | | 1.2 | .4 |
| 5.1 | 10.4 | 7.6 | | | | | | 7.5 | 1.9 |
| 37.7 | 35.5 | 20.5 | | | | | | | 5.9 |
| (24)  10.9 | (31)  9.1 | (31)  5.3 | % Profit Before Taxes/Tangible Net Worth | | | | | (13)  -.7 | -.7 |
| -3.7 | -.2 | -.7 | | | | | | | -4.6 |
| 7.9 | 12.5 | 6.7 | | | | | | 7.9 | 3.4 |
| 4.7 | 2.7 | 1.8 | % Profit Before Taxes/Total Assets | | | | | 2.4 | -.4 |
| -1.6 | .0 | -.6 | | | | | | -.6 | -3.9 |
| 7.6 | 15.7 | 12.3 | | | | | | 8.3 | 6.7 |
| 4.0 | 7.5 | 6.6 | Sales/Net Fixed Assets | | | | | 6.3 | 3.2 |
| 3.1 | 3.8 | 3.0 | | | | | | 5.0 | 2.7 |
| 2.3 | 2.4 | 2.6 | | | | | | 2.4 | 1.8 |
| 1.8 | 1.9 | 2.0 | Sales/Total Assets | | | | | 2.2 | 1.4 |
| 1.4 | 1.5 | 1.4 | | | | | | 1.4 | 1.3 |
| 3.6 | 2.5 | 2.6 | | | | | | 2.6 | 2.7 |
| (22)  4.8 | (27)  4.1 | (29)  3.6 | % Depr., Dep., Amort./Sales | | | | | (10)  5.2 | (10)  3.8 |
| 6.1 | 5.7 | 6.2 | | | | | | 7.5 | 6.2 |
| | | 2.2 | | | | | | | |
| | (10)  3.7 | | % Officers', Directors' Owners' Comp/Sales | | | | | | |
| | | 7.3 | | | | | | | |
| 1248912M | 1377868M | 1547205M | Net Sales ($) | 1348M | 4777M | 9233M | 29969M | 191264M | 1310614M |
| 856195M | 897359M | 1072425M | Total Assets ($) | 619M | 1891M | 2088M | 10133M | 109053M | 948641M |

© RMA 2012

M = $ thousand    MM = $ million

See Pages 9 through 22 for Explanation of Ratios and Data

## Current Data Sorted by Assets

## Comparative Historical Data

| | 0-500M | 500M-2MM | 2-10MM | 10-50MM | 50-100MM | 100-250MM | Type of Statement | 4/1/07-3/31/08 ALL | 4/1/08-3/31/09 ALL |
|---|---|---|---|---|---|---|---|---|---|
| | | 1 | 14 | 19 | 3 | 1 | Unqualified | 48 | 43 |
| | | 4 | 31 | 22 | | | Reviewed | 74 | 75 |
| | 7 | 32 | 19 | 3 | | | Compiled | 52 | 45 |
| | 25 | 31 | 13 | | 7 | | Tax Returns | 45 | 52 |
| | 17 | 36 | 52 | 32 | | 2 | Other | 140 | 133 |
| | | 69 (4/1-9/30/11) | | 302 (10/1/11-3/31/12) | | | | | |
| | 49 | 104 | 129 | 76 | 10 | 3 | NUMBER OF STATEMENTS | 359 | 348 |

| 0-500M | 500M-2MM | 2-10MM | 10-50MM | 50-100MM | 100-250MM | | 4/1/07-3/31/08 ALL | 4/1/08-3/31/09 ALL |
|---|---|---|---|---|---|---|---|---|
| % | % | % | % | % | % | **ASSETS** | % | % |
| 9.9 | 12.2 | 10.0 | 9.1 | 10.5 | | Cash & Equivalents | 8.0 | 7.9 |
| 34.1 | 30.3 | 28.0 | 23.8 | 14.5 | | Trade Receivables (net) | 28.3 | 26.6 |
| 7.4 | 10.1 | 13.0 | 12.1 | 10.4 | | Inventory | 11.8 | 12.5 |
| 2.5 | 2.7 | 2.4 | 3.2 | 1.5 | | All Other Current | 1.9 | 1.9 |
| 53.8 | 55.2 | 53.4 | 48.3 | 36.9 | | Total Current | 49.9 | 48.8 |
| 35.8 | 30.9 | 37.1 | 38.8 | 32.6 | | Fixed Assets (net) | 38.0 | 37.8 |
| 5.6 | 8.9 | 4.9 | 6.4 | 25.9 | | Intangibles (net) | 5.3 | 6.2 |
| 4.7 | 5.0 | 4.5 | 6.5 | 4.5 | | All Other Non-Current | 6.8 | 7.2 |
| 100.0 | 100.0 | 100.0 | 100.0 | 100.0 | | Total | 100.0 | 100.0 |
| | | | | | | **LIABILITIES** | | |
| 25.0 | 8.9 | 8.5 | 5.8 | 2.5 | | Notes Payable-Short Term | 9.6 | 11.4 |
| 6.8 | 5.7 | 6.9 | 4.9 | 11.5 | | Cur. Mat.-L.T.D. | 6.6 | 6.8 |
| 29.9 | 20.3 | 14.8 | 11.9 | 12.1 | | Trade Payables | 16.0 | 14.6 |
| .0 | .1 | .3 | .1 | .6 | | Income Taxes Payable | .1 | .1 |
| 14.5 | 9.9 | 7.8 | 9.2 | 4.2 | | All Other Current | 8.5 | 9.5 |
| 76.2 | 44.8 | 38.1 | 32.0 | 30.8 | | Total Current | 40.8 | 42.5 |
| 29.4 | 29.6 | 21.5 | 22.9 | 25.6 | | Long-Term Debt | 26.7 | 27.4 |
| .0 | .2 | .6 | 1.3 | 3.5 | | Deferred Taxes | .7 | .6 |
| 38.5 | 8.6 | 6.9 | 6.9 | 6.5 | | All Other Non-Current | 5.5 | 6.4 |
| -44.1 | 16.8 | 32.9 | 37.0 | 33.6 | | Net Worth | 26.2 | 23.1 |
| 100.0 | 100.0 | 100.0 | 100.0 | 100.0 | | Total Liabilities & Net Worth | 100.0 | 100.0 |
| | | | | | | **INCOME DATA** | | |
| 100.0 | 100.0 | 100.0 | 100.0 | 100.0 | | Net Sales | 100.0 | 100.0 |
| 50.6 | 44.1 | 39.2 | 29.7 | 31.7 | | Gross Profit | 35.2 | 36.9 |
| 48.2 | 39.8 | 34.8 | 23.8 | 27.3 | | Operating Expenses | 31.0 | 34.2 |
| 2.4 | 4.3 | 4.4 | 6.0 | 4.5 | | Operating Profit | 4.2 | 2.8 |
| .6 | 1.1 | 1.0 | 1.8 | 3.1 | | All Other Expenses (net) | 1.3 | 1.4 |
| 1.7 | 3.2 | 3.4 | 4.2 | 1.4 | | Profit Before Taxes | 2.9 | 1.3 |
| | | | | | | **RATIOS** | | |
| 2.1 | 2.2 | 2.5 | 2.5 | 1.7 | | | 2.0 | 1.9 |
| 1.0 | 1.1 | 1.4 | 1.4 | 1.4 | | Current | 1.3 | 1.2 |
| .4 | .8 | 1.0 | 1.1 | .9 | | | .9 | .9 |
| 1.5 | 1.8 | 1.6 | 1.8 | 1.4 | | | 1.4 | 1.3 |
| .9 | .9 | 1.0 | 1.0 | .8 | | Quick | .9 | .9 |
| .3 | .5 | .7 | .7 | .5 | | | .6 | .6 |
| 22  16.4 | 27  13.5 | 33  11.0 | 37  9.8 | 38  9.7 | | | 34  10.8 | 30  12.1 |
| 32  11.4 | 42  8.7 | 45  8.1 | 49  7.5 | 49  7.5 | | Sales/Receivables | 45  8.2 | 42  8.8 |
| 48  7.6 | 51  7.2 | 60  6.1 | 61  6.0 | 57  6.4 | | | 58  6.3 | 53  6.9 |
| 0  UND | 3  108.4 | 12  31.5 | 14  25.5 | 7  49.3 | | | 11  34.7 | 11  33.3 |
| 8  43.4 | 17  21.2 | 27  13.3 | 27  13.4 | 33  11.1 | | Cost of Sales/Inventory | 24  15.1 | 23  16.2 |
| 26  14.1 | 34  10.6 | 45  8.2 | 50  7.3 | 64  5.7 | | | 43  8.6 | 45  8.1 |
| 12  30.8 | 21  17.2 | 24  15.5 | 17  21.3 | 33  10.9 | | | 20  18.2 | 19  18.9 |
| 33  11.1 | 41  8.8 | 34  10.7 | 26  13.9 | 50  7.3 | | Cost of Sales/Payables | 32  11.4 | 31  11.6 |
| 85  4.3 | 73  5.0 | 59  6.2 | 42  8.6 | 63  5.8 | | | 54  6.7 | 52  7.0 |
| 11.0 | 9.4 | 7.0 | 5.8 | 7.7 | | | 8.4 | 9.4 |
| -624.2 | 38.6 | 13.7 | 14.7 | 13.6 | | Sales/Working Capital | 20.3 | 26.2 |
| -10.6 | -22.4 | -175.9 | 39.7 | -50.4 | | | -37.6 | -33.5 |
| 4.3 | 8.4 | 8.5 | 11.1 | | | | 5.6 | 5.4 |
| (43) 2.3 | (90) 2.6 | (121) 2.5 | (73) 4.3 | | | EBIT/Interest | (332) 2.4 | (319) 1.6 |
| -1.2 | -.1 | 1.0 | 1.7 | | | | .8 | -.2 |
| | 4.1 | 4.7 | 3.5 | | | | 3.5 | 2.8 |
| | (11) 2.1 | (29) 1.8 | (33) 2.1 | | | Net Profit + Depr., Dep., Amort./Cur. Mat. L/T/D | (103) 1.9 | (99) 1.5 |
| | 1.0 | .8 | 1.2 | | | | 1.1 | .8 |
| 1.2 | .6 | .6 | .7 | 1.0 | | | .7 | .6 |
| -8.3 | 2.1 | 1.2 | 1.5 | 7.7 | | Fixed/Worth | 1.5 | 1.6 |
| -.5 | -1.9 | 3.3 | 3.1 | -1.1 | | | 7.4 | UND |
| 2.0 | 1.5 | 1.0 | .9 | 1.4 | | | 1.2 | 1.1 |
| -8.2 | 4.9 | 1.9 | 1.8 | 21.7 | | Debt/Worth | 2.5 | 2.9 |
| -2.1 | -5.5 | 8.5 | 6.2 | -3.9 | | | 13.2 | UND |
| 40.9 | 84.3 | 40.4 | 44.4 | | | | 43.1 | 33.2 |
| (22) 5.5 | (70) 29.7 | (109) 11.9 | (64) 21.9 | | | % Profit Before Taxes/Tangible Net Worth | (279) 18.5 | (261) 10.3 |
| -60.3 | .1 | 1.9 | 6.3 | | | | 2.9 | -3.5 |
| 16.3 | 15.1 | 11.7 | 14.2 | 6.7 | | | 12.1 | 9.9 |
| 2.6 | 6.4 | 3.8 | 6.5 | 1.0 | | % Profit Before Taxes/Total Assets | 4.9 | 2.3 |
| -14.3 | -1.0 | .2 | 1.4 | -5.2 | | | -.8 | -4.1 |
| 28.6 | 26.4 | 11.7 | 7.4 | 5.8 | | | 12.3 | 13.9 |
| 11.3 | 10.4 | 6.3 | 4.6 | 4.6 | | Sales/Net Fixed Assets | 5.6 | 5.9 |
| 6.5 | 5.6 | 3.4 | 3.0 | 3.5 | | | 3.2 | 3.5 |
| 5.5 | 3.7 | 2.8 | 2.2 | 1.7 | | | 2.8 | 2.9 |
| 3.8 | 2.7 | 2.1 | 1.6 | 1.3 | | Sales/Total Assets | 2.1 | 2.1 |
| 2.7 | 1.9 | 1.6 | 1.3 | .8 | | | 1.5 | 1.5 |
| 1.2 | 1.2 | 2.0 | 2.9 | 4.9 | | | 2.4 | 2.1 |
| (38) 2.8 | (79) 3.1 | (118) 3.7 | (74) 4.1 | 6.7 | | % Depr., Dep., Amort./Sales | (314) 3.9 | (299) 4.0 |
| 4.5 | 5.5 | 5.7 | 5.5 | 9.2 | | | 5.9 | 5.9 |
| 4.2 | 4.3 | 2.4 | 1.1 | | | | 2.6 | 2.7 |
| (32) 10.1 | (50) 5.4 | (64) 3.9 | (12) 2.6 | | | % Officers', Directors' Owners' Comp/Sales | (132) 4.7 | (128) 4.8 |
| 15.4 | 6.9 | 6.3 | 5.6 | | | | 7.1 | 7.3 |
| 50549M | 324827M | 1262747M | 2736204M | 876933M | 581098M | Net Sales ($) | 9631928M | 7610589M |
| 11757M | 115059M | 594944M | 1574242M | 694085M | 405732M | Total Assets ($) | 5410876M | 4485526M |

© RMA 2012

M = $ thousand    MM = $ million
See Pages 9 through 22 for Explanation of Ratios and Data

## Comparative Historical Data | Current Data Sorted by Sales

| Type of Statement | | | | | | | | | |
|---|---|---|---|---|---|---|---|---|---|
| Unqualified | 47 | 44 | 38 | | 1 | 1 | 4 | 14 | 18 |
| Reviewed | 68 | 65 | 57 | | 3 | 4 | 10 | 24 | 16 |
| Compiled | 51 | 47 | 61 | 4 | 22 | 11 | 13 | 9 | 2 |
| Tax Returns | 45 | 61 | 69 | 16 | 29 | 14 | 8 | 2 | |
| Other | 130 | 130 | 146 | 13 | 35 | 12 | 26 | 31 | 29 |
| | 4/1/09-3/31/10 ALL | 4/1/10-3/31/11 ALL | 4/1/11-3/31/12 ALL | \
| | | | | 69 (4/1-9/30/11) | | | 302 (10/1/11-3/31/12) | | |
| | | | | 0-1MM | 1-3MM | 3-5MM | 5-10MM | 10-25MM | 25MM & OVER |
| **NUMBER OF STATEMENTS** | 341 | 347 | 371 | 33 | 90 | 42 | 61 | 80 | 65 |
| **ASSETS** | % | % | % | % | % | % | % | % | % |
| Cash & Equivalents | 10.3 | 9.5 | 10.4 | 6.7 | 12.0 | 11.4 | 10.5 | 10.8 | 8.7 |
| Trade Receivables (net) | 26.4 | 27.4 | 28.2 | 26.7 | 28.7 | 32.1 | 30.1 | 28.5 | 23.4 |
| Inventory | 12.1 | 11.6 | 11.1 | 6.9 | 9.6 | 8.4 | 12.8 | 13.9 | 12.0 |
| All Other Current | 3.3 | 2.3 | 2.7 | 6.0 | 2.1 | 1.9 | 2.1 | 3.0 | 2.4 |
| Total Current | 52.2 | 50.9 | 52.3 | 46.3 | 52.4 | 53.9 | 55.5 | 56.3 | 46.5 |
| Fixed Assets (net) | 37.1 | 35.9 | 35.4 | 40.8 | 33.9 | 35.3 | 35.5 | 34.2 | 36.4 |
| Intangibles (net) | 5.5 | 6.2 | 7.2 | 8.0 | 8.5 | 6.4 | 4.0 | 5.0 | 11.1 |
| All Other Non-Current | 5.2 | 7.0 | 5.1 | 4.9 | 5.2 | 4.5 | 5.1 | 4.6 | 6.1 |
| Total | 100.0 | 100.0 | 100.0 | 100.0 | 100.0 | 100.0 | 100.0 | 100.0 | 100.0 |
| **LIABILITIES** | | | | | | | | | |
| Notes Payable-Short Term | 11.3 | 9.0 | 10.0 | 15.1 | 15.3 | 6.8 | 9.6 | 8.0 | 4.9 |
| Cur. Mat.-L.T.D. | 7.0 | 6.9 | 6.2 | 7.3 | 5.1 | 6.9 | 8.3 | 5.7 | 5.5 |
| Trade Payables | 16.0 | 16.6 | 17.6 | 21.8 | 20.3 | 20.8 | 19.0 | 14.3 | 12.6 |
| Income Taxes Payable | .2 | .2 | .2 | .2 | .1 | .2 | .3 | .1 | .2 |
| All Other Current | 11.5 | 11.0 | 9.5 | 9.6 | 13.5 | 6.6 | 7.4 | 8.5 | 9.0 |
| Total Current | 46.0 | 43.7 | 43.5 | 54.0 | 54.2 | 41.3 | 44.7 | 36.7 | 32.3 |
| Long-Term Debt | 25.2 | 25.9 | 25.4 | 28.3 | 30.3 | 27.9 | 26.5 | 16.7 | 25.2 |
| Deferred Taxes | .7 | .7 | .6 | .0 | .2 | .6 | .5 | 1.1 | 1.3 |
| All Other Non-Current | 7.6 | 8.6 | 11.5 | 25.9 | 19.2 | 7.5 | 6.6 | 6.5 | 6.7 |
| Net Worth | 20.5 | 21.1 | 18.9 | -8.3 | -3.9 | 22.7 | 21.8 | 39.1 | 34.6 |
| Total Liabilities & Net Worth | 100.0 | 100.0 | 100.0 | 100.0 | 100.0 | 100.0 | 100.0 | 100.0 | 100.0 |
| **INCOME DATA** | | | | | | | | | |
| Net Sales | 100.0 | 100.0 | 100.0 | 100.0 | 100.0 | 100.0 | 100.0 | 100.0 | 100.0 |
| Gross Profit | 35.6 | 38.1 | 39.8 | 55.8 | 47.3 | 40.1 | 39.1 | 33.6 | 29.7 |
| Operating Expenses | 34.1 | 34.1 | 35.4 | 50.1 | 43.4 | 37.0 | 35.2 | 30.0 | 22.9 |
| Operating Profit | 1.5 | 4.0 | 4.4 | 5.7 | 3.9 | 3.0 | 3.9 | 3.6 | 6.8 |
| All Other Expenses (net) | 1.4 | 1.6 | 1.2 | 1.1 | 1.6 | .7 | .8 | .8 | 2.2 |
| Profit Before Taxes | .2 | 2.4 | 3.2 | 4.6 | 2.3 | 2.4 | 3.1 | 2.8 | 4.7 |
| **RATIOS** | | | | | | | | | |
| Current | 1.9 | 2.0 | 2.3 | 2.3 | 2.2 | 2.3 | 2.0 | 2.7 | 2.2 |
| | 1.2 | 1.3 | 1.3 | 1.1 | 1.1 | 1.3 | 1.2 | 1.5 | 1.4 |
| | .8 | .9 | .9 | .5 | .6 | .7 | .9 | 1.1 | 1.0 |
| Quick | 1.3 | 1.5 | 1.6 | 1.5 | 1.6 | 2.0 | 1.5 | 2.0 | 1.5 |
| | .8 | .9 | .9 | .9 | .8 | 1.0 | .9 | 1.1 | .9 |
| | .5 | .6 | .6 | .3 | .5 | .6 | .7 | .7 | .7 |
| Sales/Receivables | 29  12.7 | 31  11.6 | 30  12.1 | 27  13.6 | 27  13.6 | 26  14.0 | 33  10.9 | 36  10.2 | 37  9.9 |
| | 42  8.8 | 42  8.7 | 43  8.4 | 36  10.1 | 36  10.0 | 42  8.6 | 45  8.1 | 47  7.8 | 47  7.8 |
| | 56  6.5 | 57  6.4 | 56  6.5 | 63  5.8 | 52  7.0 | 51  7.2 | 55  6.6 | 59  6.2 | 61  6.0 |
| Cost of Sales/Inventory | 8  44.0 | 9  39.0 | 8  43.4 | 0  UND | 3  143.1 | 4  90.7 | 12  31.0 | 17  21.1 | 14  26.5 |
| | 21  17.5 | 23  15.9 | 21  17.0 | 13  28.2 | 14  26.5 | 11  33.5 | 27  13.6 | 31  11.9 | 26  14.3 |
| | 44  8.3 | 41  8.8 | 40  9.1 | 41  9.0 | 34  10.6 | 26  14.3 | 43  8.4 | 46  7.9 | 49  7.4 |
| Cost of Sales/Payables | 17  21.4 | 21  17.6 | 20  18.2 | 17  21.3 | 21  17.3 | 23  16.2 | 23  15.8 | 16  23.0 | 20  18.4 |
| | 31  11.9 | 33  11.1 | 34  10.7 | 63  5.8 | 41  8.8 | 41  9.0 | 35  10.3 | 29  12.5 | 32  11.5 |
| | 53  6.9 | 54  6.8 | 63  5.8 | 99  3.7 | 73  5.0 | 66  5.5 | 65  5.6 | 42  8.6 | 49  7.5 |
| Sales/Working Capital | 9.1 | 8.3 | 8.0 | 8.4 | 9.2 | 9.1 | 8.1 | 5.9 | 6.7 |
| | 28.3 | 21.9 | 20.9 | 41.3 | 91.3 | 18.5 | 22.1 | 12.3 | 16.1 |
| | -21.2 | -35.2 | -38.6 | -5.8 | -13.2 | -21.4 | -76.0 | 49.2 | 130.3 |
| EBIT/Interest | 4.3 | 5.8 | 8.3 | 4.5 | 4.0 | 9.0 | 6.1 | 10.4 | 11.0 |
| | (312) 1.4 | (319) 2.4 | (338) 2.6 | (27) 2.4 | (77) 1.4 | (40) 3.0 | (57) 2.1 | (76) 3.2 | (61) 3.5 |
| | -.9 | .5 | .8 | -1.4 | -.4 | 1.2 | .9 | 1.1 | 1.7 |
| Net Profit + Depr., Dep., Amort./Cur. Mat. L/T/D | 2.5 | 3.2 | 3.5 | | | | 5.1 | 4.4 | 3.1 |
| | (84) 1.4 | (75) 1.9 | (84) 1.9 | | | | (10) 2.3 | (30) 1.9 | (28) 2.2 |
| | .3 | .9 | .9 | | | | .8 | 1.1 | 1.0 |
| Fixed/Worth | .7 | .7 | .7 | 1.0 | .7 | .6 | .7 | .5 | .7 |
| | 1.6 | 1.8 | 1.7 | 7.0 | 2.2 | 1.9 | 1.9 | 1.0 | 1.8 |
| | -24.7 | 46.9 | -43.4 | -.6 | -1.0 | -12.6 | NM | 2.1 | NM |
| Debt/Worth | 1.1 | 1.1 | 1.1 | 1.1 | 1.5 | 1.2 | 1.4 | .8 | 1.0 |
| | 3.0 | 3.0 | 2.9 | 32.6 | 6.4 | 3.9 | 2.9 | 1.6 | 2.2 |
| | -36.2 | -135.9 | -54.0 | -2.4 | -4.1 | -22.2 | NM | 4.9 | NM |
| % Profit Before Taxes/Tangible Net Worth | 34.6 | 41.7 | 50.3 | 44.7 | 66.9 | 45.7 | 71.3 | 34.6 | 50.6 |
| | (247) 7.2 | (258) 18.3 | (273) 16.5 | (18) 13.3 | (57) 12.5 | (29) 7.2 | (46) 18.6 | (74) 11.8 | (49) 26.2 |
| | -11.5 | .7 | .9 | -9.4 | -7.7 | -3.8 | .2 | 3.1 | 12.2 |
| % Profit Before Taxes/Total Assets | 8.2 | 11.8 | 13.8 | 16.2 | 14.4 | 12.9 | 14.5 | 11.9 | 14.5 |
| | 1.2 | 4.4 | 4.3 | 4.8 | 3.2 | 3.9 | 4.2 | 3.7 | 7.6 |
| | -6.6 | -1.0 | -.3 | -17.7 | -3.4 | .7 | -.3 | .2 | 2.2 |
| Sales/Net Fixed Assets | 15.5 | 14.5 | 15.0 | 15.0 | 20.8 | 27.2 | 15.1 | 11.5 | 8.4 |
| | 5.9 | 6.5 | 6.8 | 6.5 | 10.1 | 6.9 | 6.9 | 7.1 | 5.1 |
| | 3.2 | 3.6 | 3.8 | 2.8 | 4.2 | 3.2 | 4.5 | 3.8 | 3.4 |
| Sales/Total Assets | 3.0 | 3.0 | 3.2 | 3.7 | 3.5 | 4.0 | 3.2 | 2.9 | 2.2 |
| | 2.1 | 2.2 | 2.3 | 2.8 | 2.5 | 2.6 | 2.6 | 2.2 | 1.7 |
| | 1.5 | 1.6 | 1.6 | 1.1 | 1.7 | 1.6 | 1.8 | 1.5 | 1.3 |
| % Depr., Dep., Amort./Sales | 2.4 | 2.4 | 2.0 | 2.3 | 1.4 | 1.0 | 1.7 | 2.1 | 2.8 |
| | (288) 4.2 | (299) 4.0 | (320) 3.7 | (24) 3.1 | (68) 3.3 | (37) 3.3 | (54) 3.8 | (76) 3.7 | (61) 3.7 |
| | 6.6 | 6.3 | 5.5 | 5.5 | 5.6 | 6.4 | 5.1 | 5.8 | 5.7 |
| % Officers', Directors' Owners' Comp/Sales | 2.6 | 2.2 | 3.0 | 9.1 | 3.6 | 3.7 | 2.7 | 2.2 | .9 |
| | (132) 4.8 | (148) 4.6 | (161) 4.9 | (15) 14.0 | (47) 6.1 | (28) 5.1 | (35) 4.3 | (26) 3.3 | (10) 3.2 |
| | 8.7 | 8.0 | 8.0 | 18.7 | 8.1 | 6.8 | 7.6 | 5.0 | 4.7 |
| Net Sales ($) | 5744794M | 7156831M | 5832358M | 17254M | 178427M | 171392M | 448104M | 1271914M | 3745267M |
| Total Assets ($) | 3235691M | 4373395M | 3395819M | 11244M | 94847M | 77936M | 198407M | 660974M | 2352411M |

© RMA 2012

M = $ thousand    MM = $ million
See Pages 9 through 22 for Explanation of Ratios and Data

## Current Data Sorted by Assets      Comparative Historical Data

| 0-500M | 500M-2MM | 2-10MM | 10-50MM | 50-100MM | 100-250MM | Type of Statement | 4/1/07-3/31/08 ALL | 4/1/08-3/31/09 ALL |
|---|---|---|---|---|---|---|---|---|
| | | 2 | 3 | | | Unqualified | 1 | 1 |
| 2 | 3 | 6 | 1 | | | Reviewed | 15 | 17 |
| | 4 | 3 | | | | Compiled | 12 | 7 |
| 1 | 4 | 2 | | | | Tax Returns | 4 | 3 |
| | 5 | 5 | 3 | | | Other | 14 | 13 |
| | 10 (4/1-9/30/11) | | 34 (10/1/11-3/31/12) | | | | | |
| 3 | 16 | 18 | 7 | | | NUMBER OF STATEMENTS | 46 | 41 |
| % | % | % | % | % | % | **ASSETS** | % | % |
| | 9.9 | 8.7 | D | D | | Cash & Equivalents | 10.9 | 6.6 |
| | 36.3 | 23.7 | A | A | | Trade Receivables (net) | 24.9 | 24.9 |
| | 4.7 | 11.1 | T | T | | Inventory | 7.8 | 6.7 |
| | 2.6 | 2.1 | A | A | | All Other Current | 1.3 | 1.2 |
| | 53.4 | 45.7 | | | | Total Current | 45.0 | 39.3 |
| | 24.4 | 46.8 | N | N | | Fixed Assets (net) | 43.5 | 44.7 |
| | 10.9 | 3.3 | O | O | | Intangibles (net) | 5.0 | 9.1 |
| | 11.2 | 4.2 | T | T | | All Other Non-Current | 6.5 | 6.9 |
| | 100.0 | 100.0 | | | | Total | 100.0 | 100.0 |
| | | | A | A | | **LIABILITIES** | | |
| | 5.7 | 10.3 | V | V | | Notes Payable-Short Term | 7.7 | 11.6 |
| | 6.7 | 5.7 | A | A | | Cur. Mat.-L.T.D. | 8.1 | 6.5 |
| | 16.0 | 8.8 | I | I | | Trade Payables | 7.5 | 9.6 |
| | .4 | .1 | L | L | | Income Taxes Payable | .2 | .3 |
| | 6.6 | 6.9 | A | A | | All Other Current | 7.6 | 9.7 |
| | 35.5 | 31.8 | B | B | | Total Current | 31.1 | 37.7 |
| | 18.6 | 29.0 | L | L | | Long-Term Debt | 27.5 | 29.1 |
| | .0 | .4 | E | E | | Deferred Taxes | 1.0 | .6 |
| | 14.4 | 24.8 | | | | All Other Non-Current | 14.2 | 19.7 |
| | 31.6 | 14.1 | | | | Net Worth | 26.3 | 12.9 |
| | 100.0 | 100.0 | | | | Total Liabilities & Net Worth | 100.0 | 100.0 |
| | | | | | | **INCOME DATA** | | |
| | 100.0 | 100.0 | | | | Net Sales | 100.0 | 100.0 |
| | 39.2 | 33.0 | | | | Gross Profit | 36.3 | 32.0 |
| | 36.8 | 27.7 | | | | Operating Expenses | 30.3 | 29.2 |
| | 2.4 | 5.4 | | | | Operating Profit | 6.0 | 2.8 |
| | .2 | 1.3 | | | | All Other Expenses (net) | 1.3 | .8 |
| | 2.2 | 4.1 | | | | Profit Before Taxes | 4.7 | 2.0 |
| | | | | | | **RATIOS** | | |
| | 2.8 | 3.1 | | | | | 2.2 | 2.1 |
| | 1.7 | 1.2 | | | | Current | 1.4 | 1.3 |
| | .9 | .9 | | | | | 1.0 | .8 |
| | 2.6 | 2.1 | | | | | 2.1 | 1.8 |
| | 1.3 | 1.0 | | | | Quick | 1.2 | 1.0 |
| | .7 | .6 | | | | | .7 | .6 |
| | 28   12.9 | 35   10.5 | | | | | 36   10.1 | 35   10.5 |
| | 43   8.5 | 45   8.2 | | | | Sales/Receivables | 46   8.0 | 40   9.1 |
| | 61   6.0 | 61   6.0 | | | | | 64   5.7 | 54   6.7 |
| | 0   UND | 3   110.9 | | | | | 0   UND | 0   UND |
| | 2   168.7 | 9   39.2 | | | | Cost of Sales/Inventory | 6   59.1 | 9   41.3 |
| | 22   16.5 | 43   8.4 | | | | | 31   11.6 | 25   14.7 |
| | 10   35.2 | 9   42.6 | | | | | 8   47.6 | 10   37.1 |
| | 15   23.9 | 20   18.0 | | | | Cost of Sales/Payables | 16   23.2 | 16   23.5 |
| | 32   11.4 | 30   12.1 | | | | | 25   14.7 | 24   15.2 |
| | 5.1 | 5.2 | | | | | 6.9 | 8.0 |
| | 20.0 | 44.9 | | | | Sales/Working Capital | 14.6 | 26.3 |
| | NM | -55.5 | | | | | -195.5 | -22.2 |
| | 2.2 | 5.7 | | | | | 4.9 | 5.0 |
| (13) | .5 | (17)   3.6 | | | | EBIT/Interest | (45)   3.0 | 1.8 |
| | -2.7 | 1.6 | | | | | 1.3 | 1.0 |
| | | | | | | | 3.0 | 2.0 |
| | | | | | | Net Profit + Depr., Dep., Amort./Cur. Mat. L/T/D | (15)   2.1 | (11)   1.5 |
| | | | | | | | 1.1 | .6 |
| | .2 | .6 | | | | | .8 | 1.0 |
| | .7 | 1.8 | | | | Fixed/Worth | 1.3 | 2.1 |
| | NM | 7.4 | | | | | 4.9 | NM |
| | .5 | 1.2 | | | | | .9 | 1.1 |
| | 1.1 | 2.4 | | | | Debt/Worth | 2.3 | 3.4 |
| | NM | 8.6 | | | | | 7.5 | NM |
| | 60.7 | 38.7 | | | | | 37.2 | 27.2 |
| (12) | -.1 | (16)   18.0 | | | | % Profit Before Taxes/Tangible Net Worth | (40)   22.3 | (31)   14.4 |
| | -12.5 | 10.0 | | | | | 6.0 | 3.2 |
| | 20.8 | 11.6 | | | | | 11.9 | 10.0 |
| | -.1 | 7.6 | | | | % Profit Before Taxes/Total Assets | 6.7 | 2.9 |
| | -7.1 | 3.1 | | | | | 1.7 | .0 |
| | 23.3 | 7.1 | | | | | 8.0 | 8.4 |
| | 9.5 | 3.7 | | | | Sales/Net Fixed Assets | 4.3 | 6.0 |
| | 6.8 | 2.3 | | | | | 2.8 | 2.5 |
| | 4.2 | 2.6 | | | | | 2.5 | 2.8 |
| | 2.5 | 1.8 | | | | Sales/Total Assets | 1.9 | 1.8 |
| | 1.9 | 1.3 | | | | | 1.2 | 1.5 |
| | 2.7 | 2.8 | | | | | 2.7 | 2.5 |
| (13) | 4.1 | 4.8 | | | | % Depr., Dep., Amort./Sales | (45)   4.6 | (38)   4.5 |
| | 6.1 | 7.9 | | | | | 6.7 | 6.4 |
| | | | | | | | 3.3 | 2.6 |
| | | | | | | % Officers', Directors' Owners' Comp/Sales | (28)   5.8 | (20)   4.7 |
| | | | | | | | 10.9 | 8.9 |
| 2394M | 50430M | 155656M | 168564M | | | Net Sales ($) | 339577M | 427670M |
| 1022M | 18595M | 82522M | 123032M | | | Total Assets ($) | 204720M | 257344M |

© RMA 2012

M = $ thousand    MM = $ million
See Pages 9 through 22 for Explanation of Ratios and Data

## Comparative Historical Data  |  Current Data Sorted by Sales

### Type of Statement

| 4/1/09-3/31/10 ALL | 4/1/10-3/31/11 ALL | 4/1/11-3/31/12 ALL | Type of Statement | 0-1MM | 1-3MM | 3-5MM | 5-10MM | 10-25MM | 25MM & OVER |
|---|---|---|---|---|---|---|---|---|---|
| 3 | 4 | 5 | Unqualified | | | | 1 | 1 | 3 |
| 10 | 11 | 10 | Reviewed | | 2 | 2 | 4 | 2 | |
| 5 | 9 | 9 | Compiled | 2 | 4 | 2 | 1 | | |
| 5 | 2 | 7 | Tax Returns | 2 | | 1 | | 2 | |
| 11 | 13 | 13 | Other | 2 | 2 | 6 | 3 | 3 | 1 |

Current data periods: 10 (4/1-9/30/11) covers 0-1MM, 1-3MM, 3-5MM; 34 (10/1/11-3/31/12) covers 5-10MM, 10-25MM, 25MM & OVER.

### Main Data

| 4/1/09-3/31/10 ALL | 4/1/10-3/31/11 ALL | 4/1/11-3/31/12 ALL | | 0-1MM | 1-3MM | 3-5MM | 5-10MM | 10-25MM | 25MM & OVER |
|---|---|---|---|---|---|---|---|---|---|
| 34 | 39 | 44 | NUMBER OF STATEMENTS | 4 | 8 | 11 | 9 | 8 | 4 |
| % | % | % | | % | % | % | % | % | % |
| | | | **ASSETS** | | | | | | |
| 8.4 | 9.3 | 9.5 | Cash & Equivalents | | | 11.1 | | | |
| 28.2 | 27.5 | 28.9 | Trade Receivables (net) | | | 37.2 | | | |
| 9.2 | 7.7 | 7.9 | Inventory | | | 3.5 | | | |
| 1.0 | .7 | 2.1 | All Other Current | | | 1.6 | | | |
| 46.8 | 45.2 | 48.4 | Total Current | | | 53.5 | | | |
| 39.9 | 40.6 | 38.0 | Fixed Assets (net) | | | 32.7 | | | |
| 7.0 | 6.1 | 5.7 | Intangibles (net) | | | 11.3 | | | |
| 6.3 | 8.0 | 7.9 | All Other Non-Current | | | 2.6 | | | |
| 100.0 | 100.0 | 100.0 | Total | | | 100.0 | | | |
| | | | **LIABILITIES** | | | | | | |
| 12.0 | 9.5 | 7.9 | Notes Payable-Short Term | | | 2.3 | | | |
| 7.0 | 7.3 | 6.1 | Cur. Mat.-L.T.D. | | | 6.9 | | | |
| 9.3 | 10.5 | 12.5 | Trade Payables | | | 17.7 | | | |
| .2 | .1 | .2 | Income Taxes Payable | | | .6 | | | |
| 10.0 | 8.2 | 7.2 | All Other Current | | | 4.7 | | | |
| 38.5 | 35.5 | 33.9 | Total Current | | | 32.2 | | | |
| 30.3 | 32.6 | 24.6 | Long-Term Debt | | | 30.2 | | | |
| .2 | .3 | .2 | Deferred Taxes | | | .0 | | | |
| 20.6 | 21.1 | 18.0 | All Other Non-Current | | | 23.6 | | | |
| 10.4 | 10.5 | 23.3 | Net Worth | | | 14.0 | | | |
| 100.0 | 100.0 | 100.0 | Total Liabilties & Net Worth | | | 100.0 | | | |
| | | | **INCOME DATA** | | | | | | |
| 100.0 | 100.0 | 100.0 | Net Sales | | | 100.0 | | | |
| 36.2 | 34.1 | 36.2 | Gross Profit | | | 40.2 | | | |
| 34.0 | 30.9 | 32.7 | Operating Expenses | | | 36.4 | | | |
| 2.2 | 3.2 | 3.5 | Operating Profit | | | 3.7 | | | |
| 2.0 | .9 | 1.0 | All Other Expenses (net) | | | 1.0 | | | |
| .2 | 2.3 | 2.6 | Profit Before Taxes | | | 2.7 | | | |
| | | | **RATIOS** | | | | | | |
| 2.5 | 2.6 | 2.8 | Current | | | 2.8 | | | |
| 1.3 | 1.3 | 1.3 | | | | 2.2 | | | |
| .8 | .8 | .9 | | | | 1.3 | | | |
| 2.0 | 2.0 | 2.4 | Quick | | | 2.8 | | | |
| 1.0 | 1.1 | 1.2 | | | | 1.9 | | | |
| .7 | .6 | .7 | | | | 1.2 | | | |
| 34  10.8 | 38  9.5 | 35  10.3 | Sales/Receivables | | | 39  9.3 | | | |
| 52  7.0 | 48  7.6 | 46  8.0 | | | | 50  7.3 | | | |
| 68  5.4 | 66  5.5 | 62  5.9 | | | | 69  5.3 | | | |
| 0  UND | 0  UND | 0  UND | Cost of Sales/Inventory | | | 0  UND | | | |
| 10  37.2 | 5  68.5 | 8  47.3 | | | | 2  151.5 | | | |
| 30  12.4 | 31  11.8 | 36  10.2 | | | | 8  45.5 | | | |
| 8  46.6 | 10  35.5 | 10  36.1 | Cost of Sales/Payables | | | 7  55.5 | | | |
| 17  21.0 | 20  18.6 | 20  18.7 | | | | 15  23.9 | | | |
| 31  12.0 | 32  11.4 | 38  9.5 | | | | 37  9.9 | | | |
| 6.3 | 5.5 | 4.8 | Sales/Working Capital | | | 4.6 | | | |
| 22.2 | 17.0 | 32.5 | | | | 10.6 | | | |
| -24.6 | -38.5 | -52.5 | | | | 37.2 | | | |
| 4.3 | 5.3 | 4.9 | EBIT/Interest | | | 3.8 | | | |
| 1.7 | (38)  2.2 | (39)  1.9 | | | | (10)  1.6 | | | |
| -.6 | .7 | .5 | | | | -.9 | | | |
| | | | Net Profit + Depr., Dep., Amort./Cur. Mat. L/T/D | | | | | | |
| .9 | 1.0 | .4 | Fixed/Worth | | | .2 | | | |
| 1.7 | 1.6 | 1.3 | | | | 1.1 | | | |
| -2.8 | 9.6 | 6.9 | | | | -1.0 | | | |
| 1.3 | 1.2 | .7 | Debt/Worth | | | .7 | | | |
| 2.8 | 2.2 | 1.8 | | | | 2.5 | | | |
| -6.8 | 14.3 | 8.4 | | | | -2.6 | | | |
| 22.1 | 54.3 | 38.1 | % Profit Before Taxes/Tangible Net Worth | | | | | | |
| (24)  1.6 | (31)  9.5 | (36)  14.6 | | | | | | | |
| -18.3 | .7 | .0 | | | | | | | |
| 9.1 | 13.4 | 10.7 | % Profit Before Taxes/Total Assets | | | 10.0 | | | |
| 2.1 | 4.0 | 4.1 | | | | 3.2 | | | |
| -5.4 | -.7 | -.3 | | | | -5.7 | | | |
| 18.4 | 9.5 | 10.9 | Sales/Net Fixed Assets | | | 24.2 | | | |
| 6.1 | 4.5 | 6.4 | | | | 8.5 | | | |
| 2.6 | 3.1 | 2.9 | | | | 3.6 | | | |
| 2.8 | 2.7 | 2.8 | Sales/Total Assets | | | 4.5 | | | |
| 1.8 | 1.9 | 2.0 | | | | 2.4 | | | |
| 1.3 | 1.3 | 1.4 | | | | 1.8 | | | |
| 1.6 | 3.0 | 3.0 | % Depr., Dep., Amort./Sales | | | 3.1 | | | |
| (29)  4.1 | (31)  5.2 | (40)  4.6 | | | | (10)  5.4 | | | |
| 9.1 | 8.8 | 7.7 | | | | 9.4 | | | |
| 2.6 | 2.8 | 3.8 | % Officers', Directors' Owners' Comp/Sales | | | | | | |
| (18)  3.9 | (14)  4.7 | (18)  6.7 | | | | | | | |
| 9.9 | 6.1 | 11.2 | | | | | | | |
| 328119M | 359548M | 377044M | Net Sales ($) | 2953M | 18741M | 39726M | 70454M | 123168M | 122002M |
| 208265M | 228062M | 225171M | Total Assets ($) | 1603M | 11501M | 18829M | 35999M | 71920M | 85319M |

**Current Data Sorted by Assets**      **Comparative Historical Data**

| 0-500M | 500M-2MM | 2-10MM | 10-50MM | 50-100MM | 100-250MM | Type of Statement | 5 / 10 / 1 / 1 / 15 | 3 / 11 / 6 / 2 / 13 |
|---|---|---|---|---|---|---|---|---|
| | | 1 | | | | Unqualified | | |
| | 2 | 4 | 3 | | | Reviewed | | |
| 1 | 2 | 2 | 1 | | | Compiled | | |
| | 1 | 1 | | | | Tax Returns | | |
| | | 5 | | | | Other | | |
| | | 6 (4/1-9/30/11) | 16 (10/1/11-3/31/12) | | | | 4/1/07-3/31/08 | 4/1/08-3/31/09 |
| 1 | 5 | 12 | 4 | | | **NUMBER OF STATEMENTS** | 32 ALL | 35 ALL |
| % | % | % | % | % | % | **ASSETS** | % | % |
| | | 13.4 | | | | Cash & Equivalents | 12.6 | 9.3 |
| | | 30.6 | | D | D | Trade Receivables (net) | 31.2 | 31.2 |
| | | 13.0 | | A | A | Inventory | 8.6 | 8.6 |
| | | 1.9 | | T | T | All Other Current | 1.1 | 1.5 |
| | | 58.8 | | A | A | Total Current | 53.4 | 50.5 |
| | | 24.5 | | | | Fixed Assets (net) | 32.7 | 34.5 |
| | | 3.6 | | N | N | Intangibles (net) | 4.8 | 6.1 |
| | | 13.1 | | O | O | All Other Non-Current | 9.1 | 8.9 |
| | | 100.0 | | T | T | Total | 100.0 | 100.0 |
| | | | | | | **LIABILITIES** | | |
| | | 9.9 | | A | A | Notes Payable-Short Term | 3.7 | 6.6 |
| | | 4.8 | | V | V | Cur. Mat.-L.T.D. | 6.0 | 11.8 |
| | | 16.0 | | A | A | Trade Payables | 12.3 | 13.9 |
| | | .0 | | I | I | Income Taxes Payable | .0 | .0 |
| | | 11.0 | | L | L | All Other Current | 11.0 | 8.1 |
| | | 41.6 | | A | A | Total Current | 33.0 | 40.5 |
| | | 15.1 | | B | B | Long-Term Debt | 14.0 | 24.3 |
| | | .9 | | L | L | Deferred Taxes | .4 | .4 |
| | | 4.5 | | E | E | All Other Non-Current | 5.3 | 4.8 |
| | | 37.9 | | | | Net Worth | 47.4 | 30.1 |
| | | 100.0 | | | | Total Liabilities & Net Worth | 100.0 | 100.0 |
| | | | | | | **INCOME DATA** | | |
| | | 100.0 | | | | Net Sales | 100.0 | 100.0 |
| | | 28.7 | | | | Gross Profit | 38.8 | 33.3 |
| | | 26.9 | | | | Operating Expenses | 35.4 | 31.3 |
| | | 1.7 | | | | Operating Profit | 3.4 | 2.0 |
| | | .0 | | | | All Other Expenses (net) | 1.4 | 1.3 |
| | | 1.7 | | | | Profit Before Taxes | 2.1 | .7 |
| | | | | | | **RATIOS** | | |
| | | 2.3 | | | | Current | 3.8 | 2.9 |
| | | 1.6 | | | | | 1.6 | 1.4 |
| | | .9 | | | | | 1.0 | .8 |
| | | 1.9 | | | | Quick | 3.3 | 2.2 |
| | | 1.1 | | | | | 1.2 | .9 |
| | | .7 | | | | | .9 | .6 |
| | | 39   9.4 | | | | Sales/Receivables | 37   9.8    38   9.5 | |
| | | 43   8.4 | | | | | 45   8.1    47   7.8 | |
| | | 57   6.4 | | | | | 75   4.8    60   6.1 | |
| | | 10   36.1 | | | | Cost of Sales/Inventory | 14   26.9    9   39.1 | |
| | | 25   14.8 | | | | | 20   18.0    20   18.5 | |
| | | 41   9.0 | | | | | 33   11.0    28   13.0 | |
| | | 22   16.7 | | | | Cost of Sales/Payables | 15   23.6    13   28.7 | |
| | | 31   11.6 | | | | | 26   14.0    26   13.8 | |
| | | 44   8.3 | | | | | 49   7.5    45   8.1 | |
| | | 6.8 | | | | Sales/Working Capital | 2.8 | 5.5 |
| | | 19.8 | | | | | 14.6 | 15.8 |
| | | -27.7 | | | | | NM | -35.9 |
| | | 30.1 | | | | EBIT/Interest | 9.2 | 5.4 |
| | | (11)   2.0 | | | | | (28)   2.5   (33)   1.6 | |
| | | -.2 | | | | | .6 | -.1 |
| | | | | | | Net Profit + Depr., Dep., Amort./Cur. Mat. L/T/D | | |
| | | .2 | | | | Fixed/Worth | .3 | .4 |
| | | .6 | | | | | .8 | 1.5 |
| | | 21.8 | | | | | 1.7 | 3.2 |
| | | .6 | | | | Debt/Worth | .3 | .8 |
| | | 1.6 | | | | | 1.2 | 2.7 |
| | | 83.8 | | | | | 7.1 | 20.3 |
| | | 30.4 | | | | % Profit Before Taxes/Tangible Net Worth | 34.9 | 52.2 |
| | | (10)   16.2 | | | | | (27)   5.9   (29)   6.1 | |
| | | -17.0 | | | | | -.6 | -10.6 |
| | | 11.1 | | | | % Profit Before Taxes/Total Assets | 15.2 | 8.5 |
| | | 3.5 | | | | | 5.7 | 1.2 |
| | | -5.1 | | | | | -.7 | -4.1 |
| | | 24.2 | | | | Sales/Net Fixed Assets | 11.1 | 13.4 |
| | | 10.4 | | | | | 6.9 | 7.2 |
| | | 7.8 | | | | | 4.3 | 3.8 |
| | | 3.1 | | | | Sales/Total Assets | 2.6 | 2.8 |
| | | 2.5 | | | | | 2.2 | 2.1 |
| | | 1.7 | | | | | 1.2 | 1.8 |
| | | 2.1 | | | | % Depr., Dep., Amort./Sales | 2.7 | 2.5 |
| | | (10)   3.4 | | | | | (29)   4.0   (29)   4.3 | |
| | | 4.1 | | | | | 5.9 | 6.0 |
| | | | | | | % Officers', Directors' Owners' Comp/Sales | 2.0 | 2.1 |
| | | | | | | | (13)   4.6   (14)   4.3 | |
| | | | | | | | 11.7 | 8.1 |
| 441M | 7415M | 173167M | 85791M | | | Net Sales ($) | 436726M | 497009M |
| 20M | 3743M | 70112M | 61052M | | | Total Assets ($) | 223032M | 236523M |

M = $ thousand     MM = $ million
See Pages 9 through 22 for Explanation of Ratios and Data

## Comparative Historical Data      Current Data Sorted by Sales

| | | | Type of Statement | | | | | | |
|---|---|---|---|---|---|---|---|---|---|
| 2 | 6 | 1 | Unqualified | | | | 1 | 4 | 1 |
| 12 | 11 | 7 | Reviewed | | | 2 | 2 | 1 | 1 |
| 3 | 2 | 5 | Compiled | | 2 | 2 | | | |
| 3 | 3 | 3 | Tax Returns | 2 | 1 | | | | |
| 9 | 9 | 6 | Other | | 1 | | | 5 | |
| 4/1/09- | 4/1/10- | 4/1/11- | | | 6 (4/1-9/30/11) | | 16 (10/1/11-3/31/12) | | |
| 3/31/10 | 3/31/11 | 3/31/12 | | 0-1MM | 1-3MM | 3-5MM | 5-10MM | 10-25MM | 25MM & OVER |
| ALL | ALL | ALL | | | | | | | |
| 29 | 31 | 22 | NUMBER OF STATEMENTS | 2 | 4 | | 4 | 10 | 2 |
| % | % | % | ASSETS | % | % | % | % | % | % |
| 11.3 | 8.3 | 12.5 | Cash & Equivalents | | | D | | 9.7 | |
| 32.8 | 30.6 | 28.6 | Trade Receivables (net) | | | A | | 30.8 | |
| 12.1 | 13.7 | 11.8 | Inventory | | | T | | 10.9 | |
| 4.6 | 3.3 | 1.1 | All Other Current | | | A | | 1.9 | |
| 60.8 | 56.0 | 53.9 | Total Current | | | | | 53.4 | |
| 30.9 | 31.2 | 30.6 | Fixed Assets (net) | | | N | | 31.3 | |
| 1.3 | 3.0 | 2.5 | Intangibles (net) | | | O | | 4.8 | |
| 7.0 | 9.8 | 13.0 | All Other Non-Current | | | T | | 10.6 | |
| 100.0 | 100.0 | 100.0 | Total | | | | | 100.0 | |
| | | | LIABILITIES | | | A | | | |
| 13.1 | 11.0 | 21.8 | Notes Payable-Short Term | | | V | | 10.6 | |
| 8.7 | 4.1 | 4.8 | Cur. Mat.-L.T.D. | | | A | | 4.3 | |
| 15.2 | 12.3 | 15.9 | Trade Payables | | | I | | 11.7 | |
| .2 | .1 | .0 | Income Taxes Payable | | | L | | .0 | |
| 7.3 | 8.6 | 8.9 | All Other Current | | | A | | 11.2 | |
| 44.5 | 36.0 | 51.5 | Total Current | | | B | | 37.8 | |
| 21.6 | 21.9 | 23.6 | Long-Term Debt | | | L | | 20.3 | |
| .4 | .8 | .5 | Deferred Taxes | | | E | | .2 | |
| 2.9 | 4.3 | 4.1 | All Other Non-Current | | | | | 5.8 | |
| 30.5 | 37.0 | 20.3 | Net Worth | | | | | 35.8 | |
| 100.0 | 100.0 | 100.0 | Total Liabilties & Net Worth | | | | | 100.0 | |
| | | | INCOME DATA | | | | | | |
| 100.0 | 100.0 | 100.0 | Net Sales | | | | | 100.0 | |
| 35.6 | 32.5 | 30.9 | Gross Profit | | | | | 29.7 | |
| 31.5 | 28.8 | 30.7 | Operating Expenses | | | | | 24.2 | |
| 4.2 | 3.6 | .2 | Operating Profit | | | | | 5.5 | |
| .9 | .6 | .2 | All Other Expenses (net) | | | | | .6 | |
| 3.3 | 3.1 | .0 | Profit Before Taxes | | | | | 5.0 | |
| | | | RATIOS | | | | | | |
| 3.3 | 3.4 | 2.6 | | | | | | 3.7 | |
| 1.5 | 2.1 | 1.5 | Current | | | | | 1.1 | |
| .9 | 1.0 | .9 | | | | | | .8 | |
| 2.6 | 2.4 | 1.9 | | | | | | 2.4 | |
| 1.0 | 1.2 | 1.1 | Quick | | | | | .9 | |
| .6 | .7 | .7 | | | | | | .6 | |
| 36   10.1 | 42   8.6 | 37   9.8 | | | | | | 42   8.6 | |
| 48   7.6 | 52   7.1 | 46   7.9 | Sales/Receivables | | | | | 53   6.9 | |
| 62   5.9 | 60   6.1 | 59   6.2 | | | | | | 65   5.6 | |
| 15   24.9 | 18   20.3 | 11   32.0 | | | | | | 9   38.8 | |
| 28   13.1 | 27   13.7 | 20   17.9 | Cost of Sales/Inventory | | | | | 15   24.2 | |
| 39   9.4 | 44   8.4 | 41   8.8 | | | | | | 43   8.5 | |
| 12   30.0 | 20   18.3 | 20   18.6 | | | | | | 10   35.4 | |
| 27   13.6 | 25   14.5 | 32   11.5 | Cost of Sales/Payables | | | | | 27   13.7 | |
| 52   7.1 | 50   7.3 | 51   7.2 | | | | | | 40   9.2 | |
| 5.3 | 4.6 | 5.9 | | | | | | 4.8 | |
| 12.7 | 9.0 | 20.0 | Sales/Working Capital | | | | | NM | |
| NM | 765.7 | -38.6 | | | | | | -20.9 | |
| 8.6 | 14.3 | 17.0 | | | | | | | |
| (26)   2.3 | (30)   4.8 | (21)   1.8 | EBIT/Interest | | | | | | |
| -.9 | .9 | -5.8 | | | | | | | |
| | 8.6 | | Net Profit + Depr., Dep., | | | | | | |
| | (10)   2.4 | | Amort./Cur. Mat. L/T/D | | | | | | |
| | 1.4 | | | | | | | | |
| .3 | .3 | .3 | | | | | | .5 | |
| 1.3 | .7 | .9 | Fixed/Worth | | | | | 1.7 | |
| 13.2 | 1.7 | 9.0 | | | | | | NM | |
| .5 | .5 | .6 | | | | | | .5 | |
| 2.2 | 1.8 | 2.1 | Debt/Worth | | | | | 2.3 | |
| 26.7 | 2.9 | 30.7 | | | | | | NM | |
| 29.7 | 60.1 | 29.9 | % Profit Before Taxes/Tangible | | | | | | |
| (23)   18.3 | (28)   15.0 | (18)   9.9 | Net Worth | | | | | | |
| -10.8 | .6 | -32.3 | | | | | | | |
| 13.6 | 15.0 | 15.5 | % Profit Before Taxes/Total | | | | | 16.4 | |
| 4.8 | 5.1 | 1.1 | Assets | | | | | 4.8 | |
| -6.0 | .1 | -13.6 | | | | | | -3.5 | |
| 20.7 | 13.2 | 23.5 | | | | | | 12.3 | |
| 9.2 | 9.5 | 8.6 | Sales/Net Fixed Assets | | | | | 8.1 | |
| 3.9 | 3.8 | 3.7 | | | | | | 3.5 | |
| 2.9 | 2.6 | 3.0 | | | | | | 3.0 | |
| 2.4 | 2.2 | 2.4 | Sales/Total Assets | | | | | 2.0 | |
| 1.8 | 1.4 | 1.5 | | | | | | 1.5 | |
| 2.6 | 1.5 | 2.1 | | | | | | | |
| (24)   4.5 | (28)   2.6 | (18)   3.1 | % Depr., Dep., Amort./Sales | | | | | | |
| 6.1 | 5.1 | 4.4 | | | | | | | |
| | 1.6 | | % Officers', Directors' | | | | | | |
| | (16)   4.4 | | Owners' Comp/Sales | | | | | | |
| | 12.7 | | | | | | | | |
| 381447M | 469865M | 266814M | Net Sales ($) | 1398M | 6458M | | 32415M | 164426M | 62117M |
| 178924M | 271192M | 134927M | Total Assets ($) | 1466M | 2297M | | 15190M | 91367M | 24607M |

© RMA 2012    M = $ thousand    MM = $ million
See Pages 9 through 22 for Explanation of Ratios and Data

## Current Data Sorted by Assets      Comparative Historical Data

**Type of Statement**

| 0-500M | 500M-2MM | 2-10MM | 10-50MM | 50-100MM | 100-250MM | Type of Statement | 4/1/07-3/31/08 ALL | 4/1/08-3/31/09 ALL |
|---|---|---|---|---|---|---|---|---|
| | | 1 | 7 | 3 | 4 | Unqualified | 8 | 15 |
| | 1 | 4 | 4 | | | Reviewed | 8 | 8 |
| | 3 | 1 | | | | Compiled | 3 | 5 |
| | | | | | | Tax Returns | 3 | 3 |
| 3 | 1 | 6 | 6 | 1 | 6 | Other | 22 | 15 |
| | | 11 (4/1-9/30/11) | 40 (10/1/11-3/31/12) | | | | | |
| 3 | 5 | 12 | 17 | 4 | 10 | NUMBER OF STATEMENTS | 44 | 46 |
| % | % | % | % | % | % | **ASSETS** | % | % |
| | | 4.9 | 11.4 | | 18.7 | Cash & Equivalents | 15.9 | 13.2 |
| | | 18.3 | 26.4 | | 19.7 | Trade Receivables (net) | 24.3 | 24.5 |
| | | 16.6 | 19.7 | | 16.0 | Inventory | 21.7 | 17.4 |
| | | 2.0 | 2.1 | | 3.2 | All Other Current | 2.2 | 6.0 |
| | | 41.8 | 59.6 | | 57.6 | Total Current | 64.1 | 61.0 |
| | | 41.9 | 27.4 | | 31.8 | Fixed Assets (net) | 29.7 | 30.3 |
| | | .8 | 4.9 | | 1.1 | Intangibles (net) | 1.0 | 2.8 |
| | | 15.5 | 8.1 | | 9.5 | All Other Non-Current | 5.3 | 5.9 |
| | | 100.0 | 100.0 | | 100.0 | Total | 100.0 | 100.0 |
| | | | | | | **LIABILITIES** | | |
| | | 4.1 | 7.7 | | 2.7 | Notes Payable-Short Term | 3.5 | 5.7 |
| | | 2.5 | 5.1 | | 2.5 | Cur. Mat.-L.T.D. | 2.5 | 2.5 |
| | | 20.0 | 17.0 | | 21.7 | Trade Payables | 24.6 | 19.3 |
| | | .3 | .6 | | 1.3 | Income Taxes Payable | .7 | .8 |
| | | 5.1 | 9.5 | | 4.5 | All Other Current | 9.2 | 14.2 |
| | | 32.1 | 40.0 | | 32.7 | Total Current | 40.5 | 42.5 |
| | | 20.8 | 10.0 | | 8.9 | Long-Term Debt | 9.5 | 14.5 |
| | | .7 | 1.7 | | 1.3 | Deferred Taxes | .5 | 1.4 |
| | | 5.3 | 3.6 | | 5.0 | All Other Non-Current | 4.4 | 6.0 |
| | | 41.2 | 44.8 | | 52.1 | Net Worth | 45.1 | 35.7 |
| | | 100.0 | 100.0 | | 100.0 | Total Liabilties & Net Worth | 100.0 | 100.0 |
| | | | | | | **INCOME DATA** | | |
| | | 100.0 | 100.0 | | 100.0 | Net Sales | 100.0 | 100.0 |
| | | 24.3 | 20.9 | | 17.6 | Gross Profit | 19.8 | 14.8 |
| | | 25.4 | 16.1 | | 7.4 | Operating Expenses | 14.1 | 10.1 |
| | | -1.1 | 4.8 | | 10.2 | Operating Profit | 5.7 | 4.7 |
| | | -1.7 | .3 | | -.3 | All Other Expenses (net) | .9 | -.1 |
| | | .6 | 4.5 | | 10.5 | Profit Before Taxes | 4.8 | 4.8 |
| | | | | | | **RATIOS** | | |
| | | 3.4 | 2.7 | | 2.6 | | 2.4 | 2.7 |
| | | 1.0 | 1.8 | | 2.1 | Current | 1.8 | 1.6 |
| | | .7 | .9 | | 1.3 | | 1.3 | 1.1 |
| | | 1.8 | 1.5 | | 1.9 | | 1.6 | 2.1 |
| | | .7 | .7 | | 1.2 | Quick | 1.1 | .9 |
| | | .4 | .6 | | .8 | | .7 | .5 |
| | | 9   41.1 | 9   39.4 | | 10   35.2 | | 16   23.4 | 9   40.7 |
| | | 19   19.3 | 32   11.5 | | 25   14.7 | Sales/Receivables | 22   16.3 | 17   21.1 |
| | | 42   8.6 | 41   8.9 | | 28   13.1 | | 35   10.3 | 31   11.7 |
| | | 3   126.0 | 9   42.5 | | 7   49.3 | | 10   37.1 | 3   126.2 |
| | | 14   25.2 | 16   23.2 | | 15   24.6 | Cost of Sales/Inventory | 24   15.3 | 10   36.5 |
| | | 61   6.0 | 51   7.1 | | 32   11.4 | | 47   7.8 | 32   11.5 |
| | | 9   38.8 | 15   23.8 | | 8   45.8 | | 14   26.5 | 8   44.0 |
| | | 24   15.0 | 26   13.9 | | 23   15.9 | Cost of Sales/Payables | 25   14.8 | 13   27.5 |
| | | 56   6.5 | 30   12.1 | | 40   9.1 | | 38   9.7 | 25   14.6 |
| | | 17.2 | 7.0 | | 6.0 | | 7.4 | 7.5 |
| | | NM | 14.2 | | 15.7 | Sales/Working Capital | 14.9 | 19.6 |
| | | -36.0 | -72.7 | | 28.9 | | 38.3 | 121.3 |
| | | 15.2 | 36.4 | | | | 49.1 | 22.1 |
| | | (11) 1.1 | (15) 13.2 | | 15.7 | EBIT/Interest | (38) 12.4 | (38) 7.0 |
| | | -6.3 | 4.7 | | | | 1.9 | 2.9 |
| | | | | | | Net Profit + Depr., Dep., Amort./Cur. Mat. L/T/D | 14.5 | 21.6 |
| | | | | | | | (11) 8.1 | (14) 4.2 |
| | | | | | | | 2.0 | 1.2 |
| | | .3 | .2 | | .4 | | .2 | .3 |
| | | 1.5 | .7 | | .7 | Fixed/Worth | .6 | .9 |
| | | 3.8 | 2.0 | | 1.1 | | 1.1 | 1.6 |
| | | .6 | .5 | | .5 | | .6 | .7 |
| | | 1.4 | 1.2 | | 1.0 | Debt/Worth | 1.0 | 1.4 |
| | | 5.7 | 2.8 | | 2.0 | | 2.1 | 5.2 |
| | | 30.5 | 45.7 | | 70.1 | | 64.4 | 51.6 |
| | | 4.9 | (15) 30.8 | | 36.6 | % Profit Before Taxes/Tangible Net Worth | (42) 27.2 | (41) 34.8 |
| | | -41.3 | 11.8 | | 18.5 | | 10.5 | 15.7 |
| | | 16.5 | 17.9 | | 33.0 | | 30.4 | 25.1 |
| | | 2.4 | 12.2 | | 22.6 | % Profit Before Taxes/Total Assets | 14.4 | 11.6 |
| | | -4.2 | 7.2 | | 7.5 | | 3.3 | 3.6 |
| | | 16.5 | 33.9 | | 34.8 | | 40.0 | 34.1 |
| | | 8.5 | 10.3 | | 14.6 | Sales/Net Fixed Assets | 20.9 | 13.9 |
| | | 4.6 | 7.6 | | 3.2 | | 7.3 | 7.4 |
| | | 4.9 | 4.4 | | 6.7 | | 4.8 | 6.2 |
| | | 2.9 | 3.3 | | 3.5 | Sales/Total Assets | 3.7 | 3.8 |
| | | 1.8 | 2.7 | | 1.2 | | 2.0 | 2.3 |
| | | | .5 | | | | .5 | .5 |
| | | | (16) .9 | | | % Depr., Dep., Amort./Sales | (40) .8 | .9 |
| | | | 1.5 | | | | 1.7 | 2.0 |
| | | | | | | % Officers', Directors' Owners' Comp/Sales | | |
| 4524M | 22231M | 222867M | 2118261M | 678992M | 7577472M | Net Sales ($) | 9702187M | 15063251M |
| 861M | 5840M | 56878M | 481497M | 290840M | 1633179M | Total Assets ($) | 2355480M | 2542304M |

M = $ thousand     MM = $ million
See Pages 9 through 22 for Explanation of Ratios and Data

## Comparative Historical Data | Current Data Sorted by Sales

### Type of Statement

| | 4/1/09-3/31/10 ALL | 4/1/10-3/31/11 ALL | 4/1/11-3/31/12 ALL | | 11 (4/1-9/30/11) 0-1MM | 1-3MM | 40 (10/1/11-3/31/12) 3-5MM | 5-10MM | 10-25MM | 25MM & OVER |
|---|---|---|---|---|---|---|---|---|---|---|
| Unqualified | 12 | 8 | 15 | | 1 | | | | 1 | 14 |
| Reviewed | 7 | 4 | 1 | | | | | 1 | 3 | 3 |
| Compiled | 3 | 4 | 9 | | | | 1 | 2 | 2 | |
| Tax Returns | | 2 | 3 | | | | | 2 | | |
| Other | 21 | 15 | 23 | | 4 | | 1 | 2 | | 14 |
| **NUMBER OF STATEMENTS** | 43 | 33 | 51 | | 5 | | 2 | 7 | 6 | 31 |

*Note: For columns 0-1MM through 10-25MM the detail data is marked "DATA NOT AVAILABLE." Only the 25MM & OVER column reports ratio/percent data.*

### ASSETS (%)

| | ALL 3/31/10 | ALL 3/31/11 | ALL 3/31/12 | 25MM & OVER |
|---|---|---|---|---|
| Cash & Equivalents | 13.0 | 13.9 | 10.0 | 13.7 |
| Trade Receivables (net) | 23.4 | 22.6 | 21.6 | 23.6 |
| Inventory | 17.8 | 18.1 | 18.1 | 18.3 |
| All Other Current | 3.0 | 4.5 | 2.9 | 2.5 |
| Total Current | 57.1 | 59.1 | 52.6 | 58.1 |
| Fixed Assets (net) | 32.2 | 31.1 | 30.6 | 30.1 |
| Intangibles (net) | 2.0 | 2.0 | 3.5 | 3.3 |
| All Other Non-Current | 8.7 | 7.8 | 13.3 | 8.5 |
| Total | 100.0 | 100.0 | 100.0 | 100.0 |

### LIABILITIES

| | ALL 3/31/10 | ALL 3/31/11 | ALL 3/31/12 | 25MM & OVER |
|---|---|---|---|---|
| Notes Payable-Short Term | 5.4 | 4.6 | 5.2 | 6.5 |
| Cur. Mat.-L.T.D. | 2.7 | 2.0 | 3.3 | 3.7 |
| Trade Payables | 20.9 | 20.6 | 19.1 | 19.0 |
| Income Taxes Payable | .5 | .2 | .5 | .8 |
| All Other Current | 14.7 | 8.1 | 11.5 | 7.7 |
| Total Current | 44.1 | 35.5 | 39.7 | 37.7 |
| Long-Term Debt | 8.5 | 13.3 | 13.2 | 10.0 |
| Deferred Taxes | 1.2 | .5 | 1.0 | 1.4 |
| All Other Non-Current | 4.5 | 3.7 | 4.0 | 5.2 |
| Net Worth | 41.6 | 46.9 | 42.1 | 45.7 |
| Total Liabilities & Net Worth | 100.0 | 100.0 | 100.0 | 100.0 |

### INCOME DATA

| | ALL 3/31/10 | ALL 3/31/11 | ALL 3/31/12 | 25MM & OVER |
|---|---|---|---|---|
| Net Sales | 100.0 | 100.0 | 100.0 | 100.0 |
| Gross Profit | 17.2 | 18.1 | 22.6 | 17.7 |
| Operating Expenses | 13.5 | 13.2 | 16.9 | 11.4 |
| Operating Profit | 3.7 | 4.9 | 5.7 | 6.2 |
| All Other Expenses (net) | -.3 | .0 | .4 | .1 |
| Profit Before Taxes | 4.1 | 4.9 | 5.3 | 6.1 |

### RATIOS

| | ALL 3/31/10 | ALL 3/31/11 | ALL 3/31/12 | 25MM & OVER |
|---|---|---|---|---|
| Current | 2.4 | 2.6 | 2.4 | 2.5 |
| | 1.3 | 1.7 | 1.3 | 1.8 |
| | 1.0 | 1.2 | .9 | 1.0 |
| Quick | 1.8 | 1.8 | 1.5 | 1.6 |
| | 1.0 | 1.0 | .7 | .9 |
| | .5 | .6 | .4 | .6 |
| Sales/Receivables | 14  26.2 | 16  23.5 | 11  34.4 | 9  41.9 |
| | 23  16.2 | 26  14.1 | 27  13.5 | 26  14.2 |
| | 40  9.1 | 50  7.4 | 37  9.9 | 37  9.9 |
| Cost of Sales/Inventory | 5  71.4 | 7  56.1 | 7  51.8 | 7  49.9 |
| | 15  24.8 | 17  21.1 | 16  23.4 | 16  23.2 |
| | 36  10.2 | 51  7.1 | 39  9.3 | 39  9.3 |
| Cost of Sales/Payables | 13  28.4 | 14  25.4 | 11  32.0 | 11  32.7 |
| | 21  17.3 | 28  13.1 | 26  13.9 | 21  17.3 |
| | 32  11.3 | 39  9.3 | 37  9.9 | 31  11.9 |
| Sales/Working Capital | 6.2 | 5.8 | 9.0 | 7.2 |
| | 31.5 | 15.7 | 30.0 | 20.7 |
| | 999.8 | 60.5 | -98.4 | 115.3 |
| EBIT/Interest | 39.2 | 45.2 | 26.0 | 34.2 |
| | (35) 7.5 | (29) 12.9 | (43) 8.0 | (27) 12.9 |
| | 1.5 | 3.4 | 2.1 | 4.7 |
| Net Profit + Depr., Dep., Amort./Cur. Mat. L/T/D | | | 5.6 | |
| | | | (11) 3.1 | |
| | | | .7 | |
| Fixed/Worth | .3 | .2 | .3 | .2 |
| | .8 | .5 | .8 | .7 |
| | 1.8 | 1.2 | 1.7 | 1.4 |
| Debt/Worth | .4 | .5 | .5 | .5 |
| | 1.0 | .9 | 1.5 | 1.4 |
| | 6.4 | 2.5 | 3.2 | 2.2 |
| % Profit Before Taxes/Tangible Net Worth | 38.1 | 36.1 | 46.0 | 43.2 |
| | (39) 17.9 | (31) 22.3 | (48) 28.7 | (29) 30.7 |
| | 2.5 | 3.9 | 7.5 | 11.4 |
| % Profit Before Taxes/Total Assets | 14.7 | 17.2 | 21.8 | 22.2 |
| | 8.1 | 8.3 | 9.7 | 15.3 |
| | .8 | 2.5 | 3.1 | 6.5 |
| Sales/Net Fixed Assets | 24.7 | 38.1 | 31.9 | 33.9 |
| | 10.9 | 14.8 | 11.4 | 14.1 |
| | 5.5 | 3.1 | 6.9 | 7.4 |
| Sales/Total Assets | 5.4 | 4.9 | 4.5 | 4.8 |
| | 3.3 | 2.5 | 3.2 | 3.3 |
| | 1.5 | 1.2 | 1.8 | 2.7 |
| % Depr., Dep., Amort./Sales | .6 | .4 | .7 | .7 |
| | (36) 1.1 | (27) 1.1 | (42) 1.0 | (26) 1.1 |
| | 2.4 | 2.3 | 2.2 | 2.2 |
| % Officers', Directors' Owners' Comp/Sales | | | | |

### Net Sales / Total Assets ($)

| | ALL 3/31/10 | ALL 3/31/11 | ALL 3/31/12 | 0-1MM | 1-3MM | 3-5MM | 5-10MM | 10-25MM | 25MM & OVER |
|---|---|---|---|---|---|---|---|---|---|
| Net Sales ($) | 8695400M | 8090066M | 10624347M | 2184M | | 8450M | 51688M | 118595M | 10443430M |
| Total Assets ($) | 2205486M | 2322361M | 2469095M | 4252M | | 1304M | 19125M | 136042M | 2308372M |

M = $ thousand    MM = $ million
See Pages 9 through 22 for Explanation of Ratios and Data

## Current Data Sorted by Assets | Comparative Historical Data

| Type of Statement | 0-500M | 500M-2MM | 2-10MM | 10-50MM | 50-100MM | 100-250MM | 4/1/07-3/31/08 ALL | 4/1/08-3/31/09 ALL |
|---|---|---|---|---|---|---|---|---|
| Unqualified | | | 6 | 19 | | 10 | 34 | 27 |
| Reviewed | | 1 | 14 | 11 | | 1 | 23 | 28 |
| Compiled | | 5 | 5 | 3 | | | 7 | 10 |
| Tax Returns | 2 | 2 | 3 | | | | 6 | 11 |
| Other | 2 | 4 | 14 | 12 | 4 | 3 | 31 | 37 |
| | | 15 (4/1-9/30/11) | | 107 (10/1/11-3/31/12) | | | | |
| NUMBER OF STATEMENTS | 4 | 12 | 42 | 42 | 9 | 13 | 101 | 113 |
| | % | % | % | % | % | % | % | % |
| **ASSETS** | | | | | | | | |
| Cash & Equivalents | | 12.1 | 11.1 | 13.8 | | 14.9 | 12.2 | 11.3 |
| Trade Receivables (net) | | 28.0 | 24.0 | 26.5 | | 14.0 | 26.4 | 25.6 |
| Inventory | | 11.6 | 11.4 | 11.7 | | 19.2 | 9.2 | 11.3 |
| All Other Current | | 6.5 | 2.9 | 3.4 | | 2.3 | 3.9 | 4.4 |
| Total Current | | 58.2 | 49.3 | 55.4 | | 50.3 | 51.7 | 52.6 |
| Fixed Assets (net) | | 26.7 | 36.3 | 37.5 | | 31.8 | 36.8 | 38.8 |
| Intangibles (net) | | 3.6 | 3.3 | 1.9 | | 3.6 | 2.7 | 3.3 |
| All Other Non-Current | | 11.5 | 11.0 | 5.2 | | 14.3 | 8.9 | 5.3 |
| Total | | 100.0 | 100.0 | 100.0 | | 100.0 | 100.0 | 100.0 |
| **LIABILITIES** | | | | | | | | |
| Notes Payable-Short Term | | 7.2 | 5.4 | 6.4 | | 10.1 | 7.6 | 6.3 |
| Cur. Mat.-L.T.D. | | 1.5 | 4.6 | 4.0 | | 3.8 | 5.7 | 6.1 |
| Trade Payables | | 13.8 | 14.1 | 14.4 | | 7.9 | 13.9 | 14.0 |
| Income Taxes Payable | | .3 | .2 | .1 | | .3 | .3 | .1 |
| All Other Current | | 10.3 | 6.0 | 5.8 | | 5.4 | 6.9 | 6.1 |
| Total Current | | 33.1 | 30.3 | 30.6 | | 27.5 | 34.5 | 32.6 |
| Long-Term Debt | | 23.5 | 14.4 | 15.2 | | 11.5 | 18.4 | 20.1 |
| Deferred Taxes | | .6 | .8 | .6 | | 1.2 | .7 | .6 |
| All Other Non-Current | | 2.2 | 4.2 | 2.8 | | 2.2 | 4.9 | 4.3 |
| Net Worth | | 40.6 | 50.3 | 50.7 | | 57.6 | 41.6 | 42.5 |
| Total Liabilities & Net Worth | | 100.0 | 100.0 | 100.0 | | 100.0 | 100.0 | 100.0 |
| **INCOME DATA** | | | | | | | | |
| Net Sales | | 100.0 | 100.0 | 100.0 | | 100.0 | 100.0 | 100.0 |
| Gross Profit | | 30.9 | 22.4 | 15.5 | | 11.2 | 21.1 | 19.0 |
| Operating Expenses | | 26.1 | 16.1 | 10.3 | | 7.6 | 14.7 | 15.7 |
| Operating Profit | | 4.9 | 6.2 | 5.2 | | 3.5 | 6.4 | 3.4 |
| All Other Expenses (net) | | 2.6 | .3 | .6 | | -1.3 | .4 | 1.0 |
| Profit Before Taxes | | 2.2 | 5.9 | 4.6 | | 4.8 | 5.9 | 2.3 |
| **RATIOS** | | | | | | | | |
| Current | | 3.5 | 3.4 | 3.2 | | 3.4 | 2.9 | 2.5 |
| | | 1.8 | 1.5 | 2.0 | | 1.8 | 1.8 | 1.6 |
| | | 1.0 | 1.0 | 1.1 | | 1.2 | 1.2 | 1.2 |
| Quick | | 2.0 | 2.2 | 2.6 | | 2.1 | 2.1 | 2.1 |
| | | 1.5 | 1.1 | 1.3 | | 1.3 | (100) 1.4 | 1.2 |
| | | .7 | .7 | .7 | | .6 | .8 | .6 |
| Sales/Receivables | 10 | 35.3 | 19 19.5 | 26 13.8 | | 22 16.3 | 26 14.3 | 22 16.5 |
| | 18 | 20.5 | 34 10.8 | 45 8.1 | | 29 12.7 | 39 9.3 | 35 10.3 |
| | 29 | 12.7 | 61 6.0 | 87 4.2 | | 58 6.3 | 57 6.4 | 52 7.0 |
| Cost of Sales/Inventory | 0 | UND | 6 60.0 | 7 51.5 | | 20 18.7 | 2 191.2 | 3 124.2 |
| | 12 | 29.8 | 17 21.4 | 20 18.0 | | 55 6.6 | 13 27.7 | 16 22.5 |
| | 25 | 14.4 | 33 11.0 | 33 11.1 | | 76 4.8 | 28 13.0 | 33 10.9 |
| Cost of Sales/Payables | 7 | 51.3 | 11 32.3 | 12 30.3 | | 15 24.6 | 14 25.6 | 11 32.8 |
| | 11 | 33.1 | 29 12.4 | 26 14.1 | | 20 17.9 | 22 16.7 | 21 17.0 |
| | 24 | 15.2 | 42 8.6 | 41 8.9 | | 24 15.0 | 40 9.2 | 43 8.5 |
| Sales/Working Capital | | 11.6 | 6.4 | 4.4 | | 3.0 | 6.5 | 7.0 |
| | | 24.0 | 19.1 | 9.0 | | 6.2 | 10.7 | 16.0 |
| | | NM | -766.3 | 43.3 | | 17.8 | 34.9 | 45.2 |
| EBIT/Interest | | 21.3 | 26.3 | 10.0 | | 57.0 | 21.6 | 13.0 |
| | (10) | 7.9 | (40) 7.8 | (37) 4.0 | | 11.8 | (95) 6.6 | (104) 4.1 |
| | | 1.5 | 3.7 | 1.4 | | 3.6 | 2.3 | .7 |
| Net Profit + Depr., Dep., Amort./Cur. Mat. L/T/D | | | 6.7 | 4.5 | | | 8.6 | 6.2 |
| | | | (11) 2.4 | (14) 1.6 | | | (40) 4.0 | (35) 2.8 |
| | | | 1.4 | .7 | | | 1.9 | 1.2 |
| Fixed/Worth | | .1 | .4 | .5 | | .2 | .4 | .5 |
| | | .9 | .8 | .8 | | .8 | .8 | .9 |
| | | 4.5 | 1.6 | 1.5 | | 1.0 | 1.6 | 2.0 |
| Debt/Worth | | .3 | .4 | .4 | | .4 | .4 | .6 |
| | | .9 | 1.1 | 1.0 | | 1.0 | 1.2 | 1.4 |
| | | 22.1 | 2.9 | 2.1 | | 1.7 | 2.8 | 3.3 |
| % Profit Before Taxes/Tangible Net Worth | | 75.7 | 45.0 | 22.3 | | 14.0 | 66.7 | 40.6 |
| | (11) | 42.7 | (40) 18.3 | (40) 12.7 | | 9.3 | (90) 26.9 | (99) 17.7 |
| | | 15.1 | 9.5 | 4.1 | | 5.8 | 13.1 | 2.7 |
| % Profit Before Taxes/Total Assets | | 30.5 | 20.0 | 11.6 | | 7.5 | 24.7 | 15.7 |
| | | 17.0 | 10.4 | 5.0 | | 4.6 | 11.7 | 8.0 |
| | | 4.4 | 3.2 | 1.6 | | 2.9 | 4.5 | -.2 |
| Sales/Net Fixed Assets | | 764.7 | 16.4 | 9.4 | | 7.1 | 12.5 | 13.0 |
| | | 17.9 | 7.1 | 5.2 | | 4.6 | 6.7 | 6.6 |
| | | 6.1 | 3.8 | 3.4 | | 3.5 | 3.6 | 3.4 |
| Sales/Total Assets | | 5.5 | 3.2 | 2.6 | | 2.0 | 3.0 | 3.2 |
| | | 3.8 | 2.4 | 1.8 | | 1.3 | 2.2 | 2.3 |
| | | 2.8 | 1.6 | 1.2 | | .8 | 1.6 | 1.5 |
| % Depr., Dep., Amort./Sales | | | 1.5 | 1.9 | | 2.3 | 1.8 | 1.6 |
| | | | (36) 2.6 | (38) 2.7 | | (11) 2.3 | (93) 2.9 | (108) 2.9 |
| | | | 4.1 | 4.6 | | 3.1 | 4.8 | 4.3 |
| % Officers', Directors' Owners' Comp/Sales | | | 1.0 | .9 | | | 1.2 | 1.3 |
| | | | (11) 2.0 | (10) 1.9 | | | (27) 2.8 | (29) 2.7 |
| | | | 7.3 | 3.7 | | | 5.6 | 4.5 |
| Net Sales ($) | 5374M | 67629M | 591788M | 1912609M | 1125168M | 2767376M | 3989466M | 4876816M |
| Total Assets ($) | 737M | 15288M | 237626M | 835188M | 669061M | 2028852M | 1913896M | 2209285M |

M = $ thousand    MM = $ million
See Pages 9 through 22 for Explanation of Ratios and Data

## Comparative Historical Data | Current Data Sorted by Sales

| Hist 4/1/09-3/31/10 ALL | Hist 4/1/10-3/31/11 ALL | Hist 4/1/11-3/31/12 ALL | Type of Statement | 0-1MM | 1-3MM | 3-5MM | 5-10MM | 10-25MM | 25MM & OVER |
|---|---|---|---|---|---|---|---|---|---|
| 32 | 34 | 39 | Unqualified | | 1 | | 2 | 8 | 28 |
| 27 | 24 | 27 | Reviewed | | 1 | 1 | 5 | 8 | 12 |
| 9 | 8 | 10 | Compiled | | 2 | 3 | 2 | 2 | 1 |
| 13 | 10 | 7 | Tax Returns | 1 | 2 | 1 | 2 | 1 | |
| 42 | 38 | 39 | Other | | 3 | 2 | 6 | 14 | 14 |
| | | | | | 15 (4/1-9/30/11) | | 107 (10/1/11-3/31/12) | | |
| 123 | 114 | 122 | **NUMBER OF STATEMENTS** | 1 | 9 | 7 | 17 | 33 | 55 |
| % | % | % | **ASSETS** | % | % | % | % | % | % |
| 14.9 | 13.7 | 14.3 | Cash & Equivalents | | | | 12.2 | 9.0 | 16.3 |
| 25.5 | 24.1 | 23.1 | Trade Receivables (net) | | | | 21.3 | 28.9 | 22.0 |
| 11.5 | 12.3 | 12.2 | Inventory | | | | 7.7 | 12.7 | 14.2 |
| 4.4 | 3.1 | 3.2 | All Other Current | | | | 2.9 | 3.4 | 3.3 |
| 56.3 | 53.3 | 52.9 | Total Current | | | | 44.2 | 54.1 | 55.8 |
| 33.7 | 35.2 | 34.9 | Fixed Assets (net) | | | | 38.2 | 35.8 | 34.1 |
| 2.0 | 4.8 | 3.2 | Intangibles (net) | | | | 3.4 | 2.6 | 2.9 |
| 8.0 | 6.8 | 8.9 | All Other Non-Current | | | | 14.1 | 7.5 | 7.3 |
| 100.0 | 100.0 | 100.0 | Total | | | | 100.0 | 100.0 | 100.0 |
| | | | **LIABILITIES** | | | | | | |
| 5.9 | 6.2 | 6.9 | Notes Payable-Short Term | | | | 4.1 | 6.4 | 8.4 |
| 3.5 | 3.4 | 4.1 | Cur. Mat.-L.T.D. | | | | 4.2 | 4.2 | 3.9 |
| 14.0 | 13.3 | 13.1 | Trade Payables | | | | 11.3 | 18.8 | 11.3 |
| .3 | .4 | .2 | Income Taxes Payable | | | | .0 | .1 | .3 |
| 8.2 | 4.9 | 6.7 | All Other Current | | | | 7.4 | 5.8 | 6.3 |
| 32.0 | 28.1 | 31.0 | Total Current | | | | 27.0 | 35.2 | 30.1 |
| 14.0 | 17.2 | 15.2 | Long-Term Debt | | | | 17.8 | 14.1 | 12.7 |
| .7 | .7 | .7 | Deferred Taxes | | | | .9 | .4 | .9 |
| 4.3 | 4.6 | 3.7 | All Other Non-Current | | | | 2.7 | 7.8 | 2.2 |
| 48.9 | 49.3 | 49.4 | Net Worth | | | | 51.5 | 42.5 | 54.1 |
| 100.0 | 100.0 | 100.0 | Total Liabilities & Net Worth | | | | 100.0 | 100.0 | 100.0 |
| | | | **INCOME DATA** | | | | | | |
| 100.0 | 100.0 | 100.0 | Net Sales | | | | 100.0 | 100.0 | 100.0 |
| 23.9 | 24.3 | 19.9 | Gross Profit | | | | 21.9 | 18.9 | 13.6 |
| 17.9 | 17.6 | 14.8 | Operating Expenses | | | | 13.3 | 14.6 | 10.4 |
| 6.0 | 6.7 | 5.1 | Operating Profit | | | | 8.6 | 4.4 | 3.2 |
| .5 | .0 | .5 | All Other Expenses (net) | | | | 1.0 | .4 | -.1 |
| 5.5 | 6.7 | 4.6 | Profit Before Taxes | | | | 7.5 | 3.9 | 3.3 |
| | | | **RATIOS** | | | | | | |
| 4.0 | 3.4 | 3.5 | Current | | | | 3.0 | 2.5 | 3.5 |
| 2.0 | 1.7 | 1.7 | | | | | 1.6 | 1.4 | 1.9 |
| 1.2 | 1.3 | 1.1 | | | | | 1.0 | 1.0 | 1.2 |
| 2.9 | 2.5 | 2.2 | Quick | | | | 2.1 | 1.8 | 2.3 |
| 1.4 | 1.3 | 1.3 | | | | | 1.5 | 1.1 | 1.3 |
| .8 | .7 | .7 | | | | | .7 | .6 | .7 |
| 26  14.0 | 20  18.4 | 20  18.7 | Sales/Receivables | | | | 14  26.9 | 24  15.3 | 21  17.3 |
| 38  9.5 | 38  9.5 | 35  10.5 | | | | | 27  13.3 | 36  10.2 | 36  10.0 |
| 60  6.0 | 59  6.2 | 59  6.2 | | | | | 70  5.2 | 60  6.1 | 54  6.7 |
| 4  81.3 | 5  70.2 | 6  59.6 | Cost of Sales/Inventory | | | | 0  UND | 6  58.2 | 8  43.9 |
| 22  16.9 | 19  19.3 | 20  18.3 | | | | | 13  27.1 | 21  17.2 | 21  17.1 |
| 44  8.3 | 46  7.9 | 41  9.0 | | | | | 38  9.5 | 35  10.3 | 55  6.6 |
| 12  30.3 | 14  26.2 | 11  32.0 | Cost of Sales/Payables | | | | 8  44.1 | 17  21.6 | 12  31.4 |
| 24  15.4 | 25  14.7 | 23  15.6 | | | | | 15  24.8 | 31  11.8 | 21  17.0 |
| 44  8.3 | 42  8.6 | 36  10.2 | | | | | 50  7.3 | 41  8.9 | 29  12.5 |
| 4.1 | 4.0 | 5.0 | Sales/Working Capital | | | | 7.8 | 7.1 | 4.4 |
| 8.8 | 9.6 | 11.9 | | | | | 12.6 | 21.3 | 10.9 |
| 31.7 | 30.5 | 55.1 | | | | | NM | NM | 39.2 |
| 26.2 | 21.4 | 21.6 | EBIT/Interest | | | | 34.1 | 19.3 | 16.4 |
| (107)  7.4 | (99)  6.0 | (113)  5.9 | | | | | (16)  8.8 | (32)  5.8 | (50)  4.4 |
| 2.8 | 2.6 | 2.8 | | | | | 3.7 | 2.3 | 2.6 |
| 8.8 | 8.4 | 7.9 | Net Profit + Depr., Dep., Amort./Cur. Mat. L/T/D | | | | | | 9.4 |
| (32)  4.2 | (32)  3.0 | (35)  2.7 | | | | | | | (20)  2.7 |
| 2.6 | 1.9 | 1.3 | | | | | | | 1.1 |
| .3 | .4 | .4 | Fixed/Worth | | | | .4 | .5 | .4 |
| .7 | .9 | .8 | | | | | 1.0 | .8 | .7 |
| 1.4 | 1.8 | 1.5 | | | | | 1.8 | 1.8 | 1.4 |
| .3 | .4 | .4 | Debt/Worth | | | | .4 | .8 | .4 |
| .9 | 1.1 | 1.1 | | | | | .7 | 1.5 | 1.0 |
| 2.6 | 2.5 | 2.4 | | | | | 2.7 | 3.2 | 2.1 |
| 44.0 | 40.7 | 32.4 | % Profit Before Taxes/Tangible Net Worth | | | | 45.3 | 46.3 | 26.3 |
| (115)  20.2 | (106)  19.6 | (116)  15.1 | | | | | 20.2 | (30)  18.1 | 12.2 |
| 6.1 | 8.5 | 7.8 | | | | | 8.6 | 9.6 | 4.1 |
| 20.0 | 20.5 | 16.1 | % Profit Before Taxes/Total Assets | | | | 15.5 | 18.9 | 11.3 |
| 9.8 | 9.7 | 7.2 | | | | | 9.0 | 7.2 | 6.5 |
| 2.0 | 3.5 | 2.6 | | | | | 4.1 | 2.3 | 2.0 |
| 13.4 | 13.7 | 12.0 | Sales/Net Fixed Assets | | | | 21.2 | 17.7 | 9.2 |
| 7.1 | 6.3 | 5.8 | | | | | 5.3 | 7.2 | 5.5 |
| 3.6 | 3.4 | 3.8 | | | | | 3.3 | 3.1 | 4.4 |
| 2.9 | 3.2 | 3.1 | Sales/Total Assets | | | | 3.0 | 3.4 | 2.9 |
| 2.2 | 2.1 | 2.1 | | | | | 1.9 | 2.4 | 2.0 |
| 1.4 | 1.3 | 1.4 | | | | | 1.1 | 1.3 | 1.5 |
| 1.7 | 1.6 | 1.6 | % Depr., Dep., Amort./Sales | | | | 2.1 | 1.4 | 1.7 |
| (109)  2.8 | (98)  2.5 | (100)  2.5 | | | | | (15)  4.0 | (27)  2.0 | (48)  2.5 |
| 4.5 | 4.8 | 4.1 | | | | | 5.5 | 3.9 | 3.7 |
| 2.2 | 1.1 | 1.0 | % Officers', Directors' Owners' Comp/Sales | | | | | | .9 |
| (33)  3.4 | (30)  2.7 | (31)  2.3 | | | | | | | (14)  1.7 |
| 5.3 | 4.8 | 4.3 | | | | | | | 2.9 |
| 5781325M | 5713780M | 6469944M | Net Sales ($) | 995M | 15387M | 30012M | 124169M | 533627M | 5765754M |
| 2813036M | 3239420M | 3786752M | Total Assets ($) | 21M | 27730M | 23033M | 83659M | 320644M | 3331665M |

M = $ thousand    MM = $ million
See Pages 9 through 22 for Explanation of Ratios and Data

**Current Data Sorted by Assets**       **Comparative Historical Data**

| 0-500M | 500M-2MM | 2-10MM | 10-50MM | 50-100MM | 100-250MM | Type of Statement | 4/1/07-3/31/08 ALL | 4/1/08-3/31/09 ALL |
|---|---|---|---|---|---|---|---|---|
| | | 2 | 7 | 4 | 3 | Unqualified | 11 | 10 |
| | 1 | 6 | 4 | | | Reviewed | 8 | 13 |
| | 4 | 1 | 1 | | | Compiled | 4 | 3 |
| 1 | 2 | | | | | Tax Returns | 3 | 3 |
| | 1 | 14 | 11 | | 5 | Other | 22 | 23 |
| | 11 (4/1-9/30/11) | | 56 (10/1/11-3/31/12) | | | | | |
| 1 | 8 | 23 | 23 | 4 | 8 | **NUMBER OF STATEMENTS** | 48 | 52 |
| % | % | % | % | % | % | **ASSETS** | % | % |
| | | 6.5 | 8.3 | | | Cash & Equivalents | 8.1 | 6.7 |
| | | 35.6 | 25.3 | | | Trade Receivables (net) | 29.0 | 25.6 |
| | | 27.7 | 29.0 | | | Inventory | 27.9 | 34.0 |
| | | 1.5 | 3.3 | | | All Other Current | 3.6 | 2.7 |
| | | 71.2 | 65.9 | | | Total Current | 68.6 | 69.0 |
| | | 17.8 | 20.2 | | | Fixed Assets (net) | 23.2 | 22.1 |
| | | 3.7 | 6.5 | | | Intangibles (net) | 4.1 | 3.5 |
| | | 7.3 | 7.4 | | | All Other Non-Current | 4.1 | 5.3 |
| | | 100.0 | 100.0 | | | Total | 100.0 | 100.0 |
| | | | | | | **LIABILITIES** | | |
| | | 8.7 | 10.5 | | | Notes Payable-Short Term | 10.4 | 12.9 |
| | | 3.1 | 1.7 | | | Cur. Mat.-L.T.D. | 3.6 | 3.5 |
| | | 22.1 | 14.8 | | | Trade Payables | 20.8 | 15.9 |
| | | .2 | .2 | | | Income Taxes Payable | .9 | .4 |
| | | 5.7 | 7.8 | | | All Other Current | 6.5 | 7.6 |
| | | 39.8 | 35.0 | | | Total Current | 42.2 | 40.3 |
| | | 11.1 | 9.9 | | | Long-Term Debt | 12.8 | 14.0 |
| | | .6 | .4 | | | Deferred Taxes | .9 | .7 |
| | | 9.9 | 6.3 | | | All Other Non-Current | 3.5 | 7.6 |
| | | 38.6 | 48.4 | | | Net Worth | 40.6 | 37.3 |
| | | 100.0 | 100.0 | | | Total Liabilties & Net Worth | 100.0 | 100.0 |
| | | | | | | **INCOME DATA** | | |
| | | 100.0 | 100.0 | | | Net Sales | 100.0 | 100.0 |
| | | 27.2 | 32.1 | | | Gross Profit | 29.6 | 30.1 |
| | | 22.8 | 24.7 | | | Operating Expenses | 23.9 | 24.8 |
| | | 4.4 | 7.4 | | | Operating Profit | 5.7 | 5.3 |
| | | .0 | .6 | | | All Other Expenses (net) | .6 | .9 |
| | | 4.4 | 6.8 | | | Profit Before Taxes | 5.1 | 4.5 |
| | | | | | | **RATIOS** | | |
| | | 3.0 | 3.3 | | | Current | 2.5 | 3.1 |
| | | 1.8 | 1.9 | | | | 1.7 | 1.7 |
| | | 1.2 | 1.5 | | | | 1.2 | 1.2 |
| | | 1.8 | 1.7 | | | Quick | 1.4 | 1.4 |
| | | 1.1 | .9 | | | | 1.0 | .9 |
| | | .7 | .6 | | | | .6 | .5 |
| | | 38   9.7 | 30   12.3 | | | Sales/Receivables | 27   13.3 | 22   16.4 |
| | | 50   7.3 | 41   9.0 | | | | 41   9.0 | 34   10.6 |
| | | 56   6.5 | 46   7.9 | | | | 51   7.2 | 49   7.5 |
| | | 33   10.9 | 41   9.0 | | | Cost of Sales/Inventory | 35   10.4 | 38   9.5 |
| | | 45   8.1 | 66   5.5 | | | | 61   6.0 | 61   6.0 |
| | | 73   5.0 | 91   4.0 | | | | 84   4.3 | 103   3.5 |
| | | 17   21.6 | 15   23.9 | | | Cost of Sales/Payables | 20   18.3 | 13   27.6 |
| | | 28   13.0 | 29   12.7 | | | | 32   11.4 | 26   14.1 |
| | | 55   6.6 | 44   8.3 | | | | 50   7.4 | 37   9.9 |
| | | 5.2 | 4.7 | | | Sales/Working Capital | 5.6 | 5.3 |
| | | 8.7 | 8.0 | | | | 10.7 | 10.6 |
| | | 27.2 | 18.4 | | | | 25.9 | 31.8 |
| | | 29.8 | 44.2 | | | EBIT/Interest | 11.8 | 11.5 |
| | | (20) 6.6 | (22) 17.6 | | | | (44) 4.0 | (49) 2.7 |
| | | 2.5 | 4.8 | | | | 1.6 | 1.2 |
| | | | | | | Net Profit + Depr., Dep., Amort./Cur. Mat. L/T/D | 11.1 | 9.2 |
| | | | | | | | (19) 3.4 | (20) 4.0 |
| | | | | | | | .9 | 1.1 |
| | | .1 | .2 | | | Fixed/Worth | .3 | .3 |
| | | .3 | .5 | | | | .5 | .6 |
| | | 1.3 | .9 | | | | 1.2 | 1.3 |
| | | 1.0 | .5 | | | Debt/Worth | .7 | .7 |
| | | 1.3 | 1.0 | | | | 2.0 | 1.8 |
| | | 5.1 | 2.0 | | | | 3.3 | 3.3 |
| | | 82.2 | 53.7 | | | % Profit Before Taxes/Tangible Net Worth | 61.4 | 38.4 |
| | | (21) 43.6 | (22) 32.5 | | | | (45) 27.4 | (45) 11.5 |
| | | 12.4 | 16.5 | | | | 9.1 | 3.0 |
| | | 24.2 | 21.0 | | | % Profit Before Taxes/Total Assets | 19.1 | 14.6 |
| | | 9.4 | 12.4 | | | | 9.2 | 4.5 |
| | | 5.8 | 7.6 | | | | 2.1 | 1.1 |
| | | 125.3 | 23.8 | | | Sales/Net Fixed Assets | 20.7 | 27.3 |
| | | 12.9 | 15.1 | | | | 11.5 | 13.2 |
| | | 9.2 | 6.3 | | | | 6.6 | 7.6 |
| | | 3.8 | 3.6 | | | Sales/Total Assets | 3.4 | 3.4 |
| | | 2.8 | 2.3 | | | | 2.5 | 2.8 |
| | | 1.8 | 1.7 | | | | 1.9 | 1.9 |
| | | .2 | .7 | | | % Depr., Dep., Amort./Sales | .7 | .6 |
| | | (21) 1.0 | (19) 1.5 | | | | (38) 1.3 | (46) 1.3 |
| | | 1.8 | 2.2 | | | | 2.1 | 2.7 |
| | | | | | | % Officers', Directors' Owners' Comp/Sales | 1.6 | 2.7 |
| | | | | | | | (14) 3.1 | (13) 3.2 |
| | | | | | | | 5.0 | 6.4 |
| 1169M | 38626M | 402054M | 1563704M | 394169M | 2495468M | Net Sales ($) | 2758432M | 3622616M |
| 266M | 10933M | 137546M | 592947M | 284713M | 1164296M | Total Assets ($) | 1147234M | 1434220M |

## Comparative Historical Data | Current Data Sorted by Sales

| Type of Statement | | | | | | | | | |
|---|---|---|---|---|---|---|---|---|---|
| | | | | 0-1MM | 1-3MM | 3-5MM | 5-10MM | 10-25MM | 25MM & OVER |
| Unqualified | 11 | 13 | 16 | | | | 4 | 3 | 13 |
| Reviewed | 7 | 11 | 11 | | | | 3 | 3 | 4 |
| Compiled | 7 | 5 | 6 | 2 | | | 3 | | 1 |
| Tax Returns | | 3 | 3 | 2 | 1 | | | | |
| Other | 28 | 15 | 31 | | | | 4 | 7 | 20 |
| | 4/1/09-3/31/10 ALL | 4/1/10-3/31/11 ALL | 4/1/11-3/31/12 ALL | 11 (4/1-9/30/11) | | | 56 (10/1/11-3/31/12) | | |
| **NUMBER OF STATEMENTS** | 53 | 47 | 67 | 4 | 1 | | 11 | 13 | 38 |

### ASSETS (%)

| | H1 | H2 | H3 | 0-1MM | 1-3MM | 3-5MM | 5-10MM | 10-25MM | 25MM & OVER |
|---|---|---|---|---|---|---|---|---|---|
| Cash & Equivalents | 11.0 | 10.2 | 8.7 | | | | 6.7 | 7.0 | 8.5 |
| Trade Receivables (net) | 27.6 | 29.0 | 30.5 | | | | 36.3 | 29.5 | 28.3 |
| Inventory | 28.8 | 28.3 | 26.3 | | | | 31.3 | 23.3 | 26.3 |
| All Other Current | 4.2 | 1.8 | 2.1 | | | | .9 | 1.5 | 3.0 |
| Total Current | 71.7 | 69.2 | 67.7 | | | | 75.2 | 61.3 | 66.1 |
| Fixed Assets (net) | 22.3 | 23.1 | 20.2 | | | | 17.6 | 20.8 | 21.2 |
| Intangibles (net) | 2.5 | 3.9 | 6.6 | | | | 3.7 | 6.7 | 7.9 |
| All Other Non-Current | 3.5 | 3.8 | 5.5 | | | | 3.5 | 11.2 | 4.8 |
| Total | 100.0 | 100.0 | 100.0 | | | | 100.0 | 100.0 | 100.0 |

(Current data 0-1MM, 1-3MM, 3-5MM columns: DATA NOT AVAILABLE)

### LIABILITIES (%)

| | H1 | H2 | H3 | 5-10MM | 10-25MM | 25MM & OVER |
|---|---|---|---|---|---|---|
| Notes Payable-Short Term | 14.9 | 10.7 | 8.0 | 10.8 | 6.0 | 8.8 |
| Cur. Mat.-L.T.D. | 2.5 | 3.5 | 2.2 | 4.5 | 1.4 | 2.0 |
| Trade Payables | 15.6 | 16.9 | 18.1 | 22.1 | 18.6 | 16.4 |
| Income Taxes Payable | .2 | .5 | .2 | .2 | .1 | .2 |
| All Other Current | 7.5 | 6.1 | 7.4 | 4.0 | 7.5 | 7.2 |
| Total Current | 40.6 | 37.6 | 35.9 | 41.6 | 33.6 | 34.6 |
| Long-Term Debt | 8.3 | 8.7 | 11.7 | 9.3 | 14.0 | 9.3 |
| Deferred Taxes | .6 | .7 | .8 | .0 | .0 | 1.4 |
| All Other Non-Current | 5.8 | 4.1 | 7.0 | 6.2 | 9.9 | 6.3 |
| Net Worth | 44.6 | 48.8 | 44.6 | 42.8 | 42.5 | 48.5 |
| Total Liabilities & Net Worth | 100.0 | 100.0 | 100.0 | 100.0 | 100.0 | 100.0 |

### INCOME DATA (%)

| | H1 | H2 | H3 | 5-10MM | 10-25MM | 25MM & OVER |
|---|---|---|---|---|---|---|
| Net Sales | 100.0 | 100.0 | 100.0 | 100.0 | 100.0 | 100.0 |
| Gross Profit | 31.8 | 30.8 | 30.2 | 28.3 | 35.3 | 27.3 |
| Operating Expenses | 27.0 | 24.7 | 23.9 | 22.1 | 30.0 | 20.1 |
| Operating Profit | 4.8 | 6.1 | 6.2 | 6.1 | 5.2 | 7.2 |
| All Other Expenses (net) | .6 | .4 | .5 | .2 | .7 | .4 |
| Profit Before Taxes | 4.2 | 5.7 | 5.8 | 5.9 | 4.5 | 6.8 |

### RATIOS

| | H1 | H2 | H3 | 5-10MM | 10-25MM | 25MM & OVER |
|---|---|---|---|---|---|---|
| Current | 3.5 | 4.5 | 3.2 | 3.5 | 3.6 | 3.2 |
| | 2.0 | 1.9 | 1.8 | 1.7 | 2.3 | 1.7 |
| | 1.3 | 1.4 | 1.4 | 1.3 | 1.2 | 1.5 |
| Quick | 2.5 | 2.7 | 2.0 | 2.4 | 2.2 | 1.7 |
| | 1.0 | 1.1 | 1.1 | 1.0 | 1.3 | 1.1 |
| | .6 | .6 | .7 | .7 | .7 | .6 |

| Sales/Receivables | H1 | | H2 | | H3 | | 5-10MM | | 10-25MM | | 25MM & OVER | |
|---|---|---|---|---|---|---|---|---|---|---|---|---|
| | 29 | 12.7 | 31 | 11.9 | 33 | 10.9 | 42 | 8.7 | 29 | 12.6 | 35 | 10.4 |
| | 42 | 8.7 | 43 | 8.4 | 43 | 8.5 | 47 | 7.8 | 43 | 8.5 | 42 | 8.6 |
| | 52 | 7.0 | 50 | 7.3 | 50 | 7.3 | 50 | 7.3 | 56 | 6.5 | 48 | 7.6 |
| Cost of Sales/Inventory | 34 | 10.7 | 41 | 8.9 | 32 | 11.3 | 40 | 9.2 | 15 | 24.7 | 32 | 11.3 |
| | 57 | 6.4 | 65 | 5.6 | 53 | 6.9 | 54 | 6.7 | 45 | 8.1 | 62 | 5.9 |
| | 89 | 4.1 | 88 | 4.1 | 79 | 4.6 | 76 | 4.8 | 61 | 6.0 | 81 | 4.5 |
| Cost of Sales/Payables | 17 | 21.4 | 21 | 17.3 | 16 | 22.7 | 20 | 17.9 | 16 | 22.2 | 16 | 23.0 |
| | 27 | 13.5 | 32 | 11.5 | 27 | 13.4 | 28 | 13.0 | 36 | 10.2 | 26 | 13.8 |
| | 39 | 9.3 | 44 | 8.2 | 50 | 7.3 | 66 | 5.5 | 57 | 6.4 | 41 | 8.8 |

| | H1 | H2 | H3 | 5-10MM | 10-25MM | 25MM & OVER |
|---|---|---|---|---|---|---|
| Sales/Working Capital | 3.6 | 3.9 | 5.0 | 6.4 | 5.1 | 4.6 |
| | 7.0 | 7.6 | 8.4 | 8.4 | 8.0 | 9.0 |
| | 19.8 | 17.3 | 18.0 | 19.3 | 30.2 | 15.6 |

| EBIT/Interest | H1 | | H2 | | H3 | | 5-10MM | | 10-25MM | | 25MM & OVER | |
|---|---|---|---|---|---|---|---|---|---|---|---|---|
| | | 21.4 | | 38.8 | | 42.7 | | 56.9 | | 6.6 | | 65.2 |
| | (50) | 8.6 | (44) | 7.3 | (62) | 10.4 | (10) | 8.0 | (11) | 2.6 | (37) | 19.5 |
| | | 3.1 | | 2.1 | | 3.1 | | 4.9 | | 1.7 | | 5.3 |
| Net Profit + Depr., Dep., Amort./Cur. Mat. L/T/D | | 13.0 | | 24.8 | | 19.1 | | | | | | 24.2 |
| | (17) | 5.5 | (16) | 8.2 | (22) | 3.5 | | | | | (16) | 3.9 |
| | | 2.4 | | 2.9 | | 1.7 | | | | | | 2.5 |

| | H1 | H2 | H3 | 5-10MM | 10-25MM | 25MM & OVER |
|---|---|---|---|---|---|---|
| Fixed/Worth | .2 | .2 | .1 | .1 | .1 | .2 |
| | .4 | .4 | .4 | .4 | .3 | .5 |
| | 1.2 | 1.0 | 1.5 | 1.3 | 1.6 | 1.1 |
| Debt/Worth | .4 | .4 | .8 | .3 | .6 | .6 |
| | 1.1 | 1.0 | 1.3 | 1.9 | 1.1 | 1.3 |
| | 2.4 | 2.0 | 3.8 | 5.8 | 5.1 | 2.5 |

| % Profit Before Taxes/Tangible Net Worth | H1 | | H2 | | H3 | | 5-10MM | | 10-25MM | | 25MM & OVER | |
|---|---|---|---|---|---|---|---|---|---|---|---|---|
| | | 47.4 | | 51.3 | | 61.6 | | 74.4 | | 82.1 | | 55.5 |
| | (50) | 25.1 | (43) | 23.7 | (61) | 33.4 | | 50.3 | (11) | 12.7 | (36) | 40.2 |
| | | 6.0 | | 7.5 | | 11.7 | | 21.0 | | 7.5 | | 18.1 |

| | H1 | H2 | H3 | 5-10MM | 10-25MM | 25MM & OVER |
|---|---|---|---|---|---|---|
| % Profit Before Taxes/Total Assets | 22.1 | 18.6 | 21.0 | 14.1 | 13.6 | 23.8 |
| | 9.5 | 9.3 | 10.3 | 8.5 | 5.8 | 14.3 |
| | 2.6 | 1.6 | 4.9 | 7.2 | 2.7 | 8.1 |
| Sales/Net Fixed Assets | 25.5 | 26.6 | 70.3 | 125.3 | 124.3 | 25.0 |
| | 14.3 | 11.9 | 12.9 | 35.3 | 12.0 | 12.0 |
| | 7.8 | 8.2 | 6.3 | 7.5 | 5.2 | 6.1 |
| Sales/Total Assets | 3.1 | 3.1 | 3.6 | 3.7 | 3.8 | 3.6 |
| | 2.5 | 2.5 | 2.5 | 3.0 | 2.5 | 2.4 |
| | 1.8 | 1.7 | 1.7 | 1.8 | 1.7 | 1.5 |

| % Depr., Dep., Amort./Sales | H1 | | H2 | | H3 | | 5-10MM | | 10-25MM | | 25MM & OVER | |
|---|---|---|---|---|---|---|---|---|---|---|---|---|
| | | .6 | | .8 | | .6 | | .2 | | .3 | | .7 |
| | (49) | 1.3 | (42) | 1.1 | (56) | 1.3 | (10) | .7 | (12) | 1.1 | (31) | 1.5 |
| | | 1.9 | | 1.8 | | 2.1 | | 2.1 | | 1.9 | | 2.2 |
| % Officers', Directors' Owners' Comp/Sales | | 1.4 | | .8 | | 1.5 | | | | | | |
| | (12) | 2.6 | | | (16) | 3.7 | | | | | | |
| | | 14.2 | | | | 6.7 | | | | | | |

| | H1 | H2 | H3 | 0-1MM | 1-3MM | 5-10MM | 10-25MM | 25MM & OVER |
|---|---|---|---|---|---|---|---|---|
| Net Sales ($) | 3144010M | 3820227M | 4895190M | 7805M | 3885M | 82280M | 203670M | 4597550M |
| Total Assets ($) | 1427310M | 1408409M | 2190701M | 3683M | 626M | 32714M | 92198M | 2061480M |

M = $ thousand    MM = $ million
See Pages 9 through 22 for Explanation of Ratios and Data

**Current Data Sorted by Assets**      **Comparative Historical Data**

Sub-period labels: 3 (4/1-9/30/11) — under 500M-2MM columns; 23 (10/1/11-3/31/12) — under 10-50MM columns.

| | 0-500M | 500M-2MM | 2-10MM | 10-50MM | 50-100MM | 100-250MM | 4/1/07-3/31/08 ALL | 4/1/08-3/31/09 ALL |
|---|---|---|---|---|---|---|---|---|
| **Type of Statement** | | | | | | | | |
| Unqualified | | | | 3 | 1 | | 8 | 8 |
| Reviewed | | | 2 | 2 | | | 1 | 5 |
| Compiled | | 3 | 1 | 2 | | | 8 | 4 |
| Tax Returns | | 1 | 3 | 5 | 2 | | 5 | 2 |
| Other | 1 | | | | | | 11 | 12 |
| **NUMBER OF STATEMENTS** | 1 | 4 | 6 | 12 | 3 | | 33 | 31 |
| | % | % | % | % | % | % | % | % |
| **ASSETS** | | | | | | | | |
| Cash & Equivalents | | | | 6.6 | | | 12.1 | 14.0 |
| Trade Receivables (net) | | | | 31.0 | | | 24.3 | 24.8 |
| Inventory | | | | 24.1 | | | 16.3 | 12.4 |
| All Other Current | | | | 6.7 | | | 6.6 | 3.2 |
| Total Current | | | | 68.4 | | | 59.2 | 54.4 |
| Fixed Assets (net) | | | | 25.9 | | | 27.6 | 36.1 |
| Intangibles (net) | | | | 1.3 | | | 4.5 | 3.0 |
| All Other Non-Current | | | | 4.5 | | | 8.6 | 6.5 |
| Total | | | | 100.0 | | | 100.0 | 100.0 |
| **LIABILITIES** | | | | | | | | |
| Notes Payable-Short Term | | | | 12.5 | | | 16.6 | 10.0 |
| Cur. Mat.-L.T.D. | | | | 3.4 | | | 2.8 | 5.4 |
| Trade Payables | | | | 17.8 | | | 20.5 | 16.3 |
| Income Taxes Payable | | | | .0 | | | .2 | .1 |
| All Other Current | | | | 7.7 | | | 7.0 | 7.6 |
| Total Current | | | | 41.4 | | | 47.0 | 39.4 |
| Long-Term Debt | | | | 8.5 | | | 16.2 | 16.5 |
| Deferred Taxes | | | | .1 | | | .2 | .3 |
| All Other Non-Current | | | | 5.9 | | | 3.0 | 4.3 |
| Net Worth | | | | 44.0 | | | 33.6 | 39.5 |
| Total Liabilities & Net Worth | | | | 100.0 | | | 100.0 | 100.0 |
| **INCOME DATA** | | | | | | | | |
| Net Sales | | | | 100.0 | | | 100.0 | 100.0 |
| Gross Profit | | | | 20.6 | | | 28.1 | 25.6 |
| Operating Expenses | | | | 13.1 | | | 20.9 | 20.1 |
| Operating Profit | | | | 7.5 | | | 7.2 | 5.6 |
| All Other Expenses (net) | | | | .8 | | | .7 | .3 |
| Profit Before Taxes | | | | 6.7 | | | 6.6 | 5.2 |
| **RATIOS** | | | | | | | | |
| Current | | | | 3.1 | | | 2.8 | 3.5 |
| | | | | 1.2 | | | 1.3 | 1.5 |
| | | | | 1.1 | | | 1.0 | .8 |
| Quick | | | | 1.8 | | | 1.4 | 2.3 |
| | | | | .9 | | | .8 | 1.1 |
| | | | | .7 | | | .4 | .5 |
| Sales/Receivables | | | | 23   15.8 | | | 11   34.2 | 10   35.1 |
| | | | | 32   11.5 | | | 29   12.7 | 28   12.9 |
| | | | | 64   5.7 | | | 42   8.7 | 44   8.3 |
| Cost of Sales/Inventory | | | | 3   110.7 | | | 1   639.7 | 1   253.1 |
| | | | | 38   9.7 | | | 15   24.5 | 9   39.1 |
| | | | | 101   3.6 | | | 50   7.4 | 44   8.2 |
| Cost of Sales/Payables | | | | 11   32.9 | | | 12   29.3 | 6   61.1 |
| | | | | 31   11.7 | | | 26   13.9 | 15   24.2 |
| | | | | 51   7.2 | | | 40   9.1 | 40   9.1 |
| Sales/Working Capital | | | | 4.9 | | | 6.9 | 5.9 |
| | | | | 13.3 | | | 53.8 | 56.0 |
| | | | | 111.5 | | | -931.8 | -119.0 |
| EBIT/Interest | | | | 19.2 | | | 13.6 | 10.7 |
| | | | | 6.7 | | | (30) 2.2 | (29) 3.9 |
| | | | | 4.8 | | | 1.0 | 1.1 |
| Net Profit + Depr., Dep., Amort./Cur. Mat. L/T/D | | | | | | | | |
| Fixed/Worth | | | | .2 | | | .2 | .4 |
| | | | | .5 | | | .8 | .9 |
| | | | | 1.2 | | | 12.1 | 3.2 |
| Debt/Worth | | | | .5 | | | .5 | .7 |
| | | | | 1.9 | | | 2.2 | 1.7 |
| | | | | 3.0 | | | 26.9 | 5.8 |
| % Profit Before Taxes/Tangible Net Worth | | | | 53.0 | | | 70.4 | 59.1 |
| | | | | 31.0 | | | (27) 25.8 | (28) 24.2 |
| | | | | 13.7 | | | 7.5 | 2.1 |
| % Profit Before Taxes/Total Assets | | | | 14.7 | | | 25.8 | 18.0 |
| | | | | 9.5 | | | 6.5 | 10.9 |
| | | | | 5.0 | | | .3 | .4 |
| Sales/Net Fixed Assets | | | | 40.3 | | | 54.4 | 47.9 |
| | | | | 12.0 | | | 16.4 | 10.8 |
| | | | | 4.5 | | | 5.8 | 4.3 |
| Sales/Total Assets | | | | 6.2 | | | 5.2 | 8.2 |
| | | | | 2.3 | | | 3.2 | 2.9 |
| | | | | 1.3 | | | 1.8 | 1.9 |
| % Depr., Dep., Amort./Sales | | | | | | | .4 | .5 |
| | | | | | | | (25) 1.3 | (26) 1.1 |
| | | | | | | | 2.0 | 2.3 |
| % Officers', Directors' Owners' Comp/Sales | | | | | | | .9 | |
| | | | | | | | (10) 5.6 | |
| | | | | | | | 12.1 | |
| Net Sales ($) | 879M | 33008M | 190816M | 1008667M | 365097M | | 3135675M | 3905331M |
| Total Assets ($) | 158M | 5905M | 36858M | 278125M | 203665M | | 934268M | 1363269M |

Note: In the balance sheet / income / ratio rows the columns 0-500M, 500M-2MM, 2-10MM, 50-100MM and 100-250MM are marked "DATA NOT AVAILABLE."

M = $ thousand     MM = $ million
See Pages 9 through 22 for Explanation of Ratios and Data

## Comparative Historical Data | Current Data Sorted by Sales

| 14 | 10 | 4 | Type of Statement |  |  |  |  |  | 4 |
|---|---|---|---|---|---|---|---|---|---|
| 1 | 1 | 4 | Unqualified |  |  |  |  | 1 | 3 |
| 5 | 4 | 6 | Reviewed |  |  | 3 |  |  | 2 |
| 3 | 4 | 2 | Compiled |  | 1 |  |  | 1 |  |
| 12 | 12 | 10 | Tax Returns | 1 |  |  |  | 2 | 7 |
| 4/1/09-3/31/10 ALL | 4/1/10-3/31/11 ALL | 4/1/11-3/31/12 ALL | Other |  | 3 (4/1-9/30/11) |  |  | 23 (10/1/11-3/31/12) |  |
|  |  |  |  | 0-1MM | 1-3MM | 3-5MM | 5-10MM | 10-25MM | 25MM & OVER |
| 35 | 31 | 26 | NUMBER OF STATEMENTS | 1 |  | 2 | 3 | 4 | 16 |
| % | % | % | | % | % | % | % | % | % |
| | | | **ASSETS** | | | | | | |
| 12.6 | 10.1 | 11.8 | Cash & Equivalents | | | | | | 7.2 |
| 20.8 | 24.1 | 28.2 | Trade Receivables (net) | | | | | | 30.5 |
| 17.2 | 20.6 | 23.2 | Inventory | | | | | | 21.0 |
| 1.6 | 1.7 | 4.3 | All Other Current | | | | | | 6.4 |
| 52.1 | 56.4 | 67.5 | Total Current | | | | | | 65.2 |
| 35.5 | 34.2 | 28.4 | Fixed Assets (net) | | | | | | 29.9 |
| 6.4 | 3.3 | .9 | Intangibles (net) | | | | | | 1.0 |
| 5.9 | 6.1 | 3.3 | All Other Non-Current | | | | | | 3.9 |
| 100.0 | 100.0 | 100.0 | Total | | | | | | 100.0 |
| | | | **LIABILITIES** | | | | | | |
| 11.4 | 5.1 | 9.9 | Notes Payable-Short Term | | | | | | 9.3 |
| 2.8 | 4.1 | 4.2 | Cur. Mat.-L.T.D. | | | | | | 5.0 |
| 11.6 | 15.1 | 16.8 | Trade Payables | | | | | | 19.3 |
| .2 | .1 | .1 | Income Taxes Payable | | | | | | .1 |
| 7.4 | 9.3 | 10.2 | All Other Current | | | | | | 8.3 |
| 33.4 | 33.6 | 41.2 | Total Current | | | | | | 42.1 |
| 22.9 | 18.5 | 21.3 | Long-Term Debt | | | | | | 7.0 |
| .4 | .1 | .3 | Deferred Taxes | | | | | | .3 |
| 2.7 | 3.3 | 6.5 | All Other Non-Current | | | | | | 3.8 |
| 40.6 | 44.5 | 30.7 | Net Worth | | | | | | 46.8 |
| 100.0 | 100.0 | 100.0 | Total Liabilities & Net Worth | | | | | | 100.0 |
| | | | **INCOME DATA** | | | | | | |
| 100.0 | 100.0 | 100.0 | Net Sales | | | | | | 100.0 |
| 29.3 | 24.6 | 20.0 | Gross Profit | | | | | | 14.2 |
| 24.3 | 18.2 | 14.9 | Operating Expenses | | | | | | 9.0 |
| 5.0 | 6.4 | 5.1 | Operating Profit | | | | | | 5.2 |
| 1.5 | 1.7 | .4 | All Other Expenses (net) | | | | | | .2 |
| 3.5 | 4.7 | 4.6 | Profit Before Taxes | | | | | | 5.1 |
| | | | **RATIOS** | | | | | | |
| 3.5 | 4.1 | 3.1 | | | | | | | 2.9 |
| 1.6 | 1.7 | 1.4 | Current | | | | | | 1.2 |
| 1.0 | 1.1 | 1.1 | | | | | | | 1.1 |
| 2.4 | 2.5 | 2.0 | | | | | | | 1.8 |
| 1.1 | (30) .9 | .9 | Quick | | | | | | .9 |
| .6 | .7 | .5 | | | | | | | .4 |
| 16  22.2 | 15  23.7 | 16  23.2 | | | | | | | 16  22.6 |
| 38  9.5 | 36  10.1 | 30  12.3 | Sales/Receivables | | | | | | 30  12.3 |
| 60  6.1 | 53  6.8 | 57  6.4 | | | | | | | 54  6.8 |
| 19  18.9 | 8  44.4 | 3  105.9 | | | | | | | 3  110.7 |
| 37  10.0 | 30  12.2 | 30  12.0 | Cost of Sales/Inventory | | | | | | 30  12.0 |
| 65  5.6 | 79  4.6 | 85  4.3 | | | | | | | 61  6.0 |
| 10  36.8 | 12  30.3 | 10  37.9 | | | | | | | 11  33.1 |
| 27  13.7 | 20  18.0 | 27  13.6 | Cost of Sales/Payables | | | | | | 26  13.9 |
| 34  10.8 | 38  9.6 | 48  7.6 | | | | | | | 34  10.8 |
| 4.8 | 5.1 | 6.5 | | | | | | | 8.1 |
| 7.4 | 9.6 | 17.4 | Sales/Working Capital | | | | | | 30.5 |
| 168.5 | 59.7 | 163.6 | | | | | | | 221.5 |
| 9.2 | 14.5 | 19.2 | | | | | | | 29.0 |
| (32) 3.0 | (27) 3.8 | (24) 5.2 | EBIT/Interest | | | | | | (15) 5.8 |
| .1 | 1.4 | 2.3 | | | | | | | 4.4 |
| | | | Net Profit + Depr., Dep., Amort./Cur. Mat. L/T/D | | | | | | |
| .5 | .2 | .2 | | | | | | | .1 |
| 1.0 | .7 | .6 | Fixed/Worth | | | | | | .5 |
| 4.2 | 1.6 | 1.6 | | | | | | | 1.3 |
| .5 | .6 | .5 | | | | | | | .5 |
| 2.1 | 1.4 | 1.9 | Debt/Worth | | | | | | 1.4 |
| 8.5 | 4.1 | 3.2 | | | | | | | 2.7 |
| 57.3 | 57.6 | 52.9 | | | | | | | 48.8 |
| (28) 19.4 | (30) 21.6 | (25) 25.5 | % Profit Before Taxes/Tangible Net Worth | | | | | | 26.7 |
| -1.9 | 2.2 | 4.7 | | | | | | | 7.8 |
| 14.8 | 11.8 | 23.3 | | | | | | | 14.6 |
| 4.6 | 5.6 | 9.5 | % Profit Before Taxes/Total Assets | | | | | | 9.5 |
| -1.3 | 1.2 | 2.0 | | | | | | | 4.7 |
| 18.2 | 35.2 | 38.1 | | | | | | | 62.8 |
| 7.2 | 10.3 | 15.1 | Sales/Net Fixed Assets | | | | | | 15.3 |
| 2.2 | 3.2 | 4.8 | | | | | | | 4.5 |
| 2.5 | 4.0 | 5.8 | | | | | | | 6.6 |
| 1.9 | 1.8 | 2.6 | Sales/Total Assets | | | | | | 2.6 |
| 1.1 | 1.4 | 1.4 | | | | | | | 1.6 |
| 1.3 | .7 | .6 | | | | | | | .7 |
| (29) 2.5 | (25) 1.9 | (20) 1.7 | % Depr., Dep., Amort./Sales | | | | | | (14) 1.7 |
| 4.9 | 4.5 | 2.8 | | | | | | | 3.1 |
| .5 | | | | | | | | | |
| (10) 2.6 | | | % Officers', Directors' Owners' Comp/Sales | | | | | | |
| 10.0 | | | | | | | | | |
| 1352138M | 2060186M | 1598467M | Net Sales ($) | 879M | | 7613M | 22517M | 67296M | 1500162M |
| 1020180M | 965550M | 524711M | Total Assets ($) | 158M | | 4256M | 30345M | 28962M | 460990M |

M = $ thousand    MM = $ million
See Pages 9 through 22 for Explanation of Ratios and Data

**Current Data Sorted by Assets**      **Comparative Historical Data**

| 0-500M | 500M-2MM | 2-10MM | 10-50MM | 50-100MM | 100-250MM | Type of Statement | 4/1/07-3/31/08 ALL | 4/1/08-3/31/09 ALL |
|---|---|---|---|---|---|---|---|---|
| 1 | | 1 | 10 | 6 | 1 | Unqualified | 22 | 21 |
| | | 9 | 9 | 1 | | Reviewed | 23 | 26 |
| | | 3 | 1 | | | Compiled | 3 | 8 |
| 2 | 1 | 2 | | | | Tax Returns | 4 | 2 |
| 5 | | 14 | 21 | 5 | 6 | Other | 38 | 55 |
| | | 17 (4/1-9/30/11) | 81 (10/1/11-3/31/12) | | | | | |
| 3 | 6 | 29 | 41 | 12 | 7 | **NUMBER OF STATEMENTS** | 90 | 112 |
| % | % | % | % | % | % | **ASSETS** | % | % |
| | | 8.5 | 9.2 | 6.8 | | Cash & Equivalents | 6.7 | 6.4 |
| | | 29.8 | 23.8 | 16.3 | | Trade Receivables (net) | 25.2 | 24.3 |
| | | 28.0 | 24.3 | 14.4 | | Inventory | 24.1 | 24.4 |
| | | .9 | 2.6 | 1.5 | | All Other Current | 2.7 | 1.7 |
| | | 67.2 | 59.8 | 39.0 | | Total Current | 58.7 | 56.8 |
| | | 25.1 | 29.9 | 37.9 | | Fixed Assets (net) | 31.6 | 31.2 |
| | | 5.1 | 2.9 | 15.5 | | Intangibles (net) | 5.0 | 6.1 |
| | | 2.5 | 7.4 | 7.6 | | All Other Non-Current | 4.7 | 5.9 |
| | | 100.0 | 100.0 | 100.0 | | Total | 100.0 | 100.0 |
| | | | | | | **LIABILITIES** | | |
| | | 17.2 | 8.2 | 2.9 | | Notes Payable-Short Term | 8.3 | 9.2 |
| | | 2.6 | 3.6 | 3.7 | | Cur. Mat.-L.T.D. | 3.4 | 4.2 |
| | | 16.3 | 15.0 | 8.5 | | Trade Payables | 15.0 | 15.0 |
| | | .2 | .3 | .2 | | Income Taxes Payable | .4 | .3 |
| | | 4.6 | 10.9 | 5.2 | | All Other Current | 10.3 | 7.5 |
| | | 41.0 | 38.0 | 20.5 | | Total Current | 37.3 | 36.2 |
| | | 14.1 | 13.1 | 16.8 | | Long-Term Debt | 19.3 | 19.7 |
| | | .1 | 1.4 | 3.3 | | Deferred Taxes | .9 | 1.4 |
| | | 7.7 | 14.2 | 10.8 | | All Other Non-Current | 3.9 | 3.1 |
| | | 37.0 | 33.3 | 48.6 | | Net Worth | 38.5 | 39.5 |
| | | 100.0 | 100.0 | 100.0 | | Total Liabilities & Net Worth | 100.0 | 100.0 |
| | | | | | | **INCOME DATA** | | |
| | | 100.0 | 100.0 | 100.0 | | Net Sales | 100.0 | 100.0 |
| | | 38.3 | 30.0 | 27.7 | | Gross Profit | 30.0 | 28.5 |
| | | 31.3 | 22.4 | 15.7 | | Operating Expenses | 21.0 | 22.5 |
| | | 7.0 | 7.7 | 12.0 | | Operating Profit | 9.0 | 6.1 |
| | | .4 | .6 | .6 | | All Other Expenses (net) | 1.5 | 1.1 |
| | | 6.6 | 7.1 | 11.4 | | Profit Before Taxes | 7.6 | 4.9 |
| | | | | | | **RATIOS** | | |
| | | 2.0 | 2.4 | 4.1 | | | 2.5 | 2.3 |
| | | 1.6 | 1.7 | 2.0 | | Current | 1.6 | 1.7 |
| | | 1.3 | 1.1 | 1.0 | | | 1.2 | 1.1 |
| | | 1.2 | 1.4 | 2.2 | | | 1.5 | 1.4 |
| | | .9 | .9 | 1.2 | | Quick | 1.0 | .9 |
| | | .6 | .5 | .6 | | | .6 | .6 |
| | | 33 11.1 | 33 11.2 | 42 8.6 | | | 35 10.5 | 30 12.2 |
| | | 39 9.4 | 43 8.5 | 51 7.2 | | Sales/Receivables | 46 7.9 | 40 9.0 |
| | | 45 8.1 | 57 6.4 | 64 5.7 | | | 59 6.2 | 49 7.4 |
| | | 37 9.9 | 38 9.6 | 29 12.6 | | | 30 12.3 | 28 12.8 |
| | | 65 5.6 | 54 6.7 | 49 7.4 | | Cost of Sales/Inventory | 50 7.3 | 59 6.2 |
| | | 104 3.5 | 87 4.2 | 83 4.4 | | | 89 4.1 | 100 3.7 |
| | | 17 21.3 | 27 13.4 | 22 16.8 | | | 22 16.7 | 23 16.2 |
| | | 33 11.0 | 36 10.0 | 35 10.4 | | Cost of Sales/Payables | 33 11.0 | 31 11.6 |
| | | 53 6.9 | 52 7.0 | 49 7.5 | | | 51 7.1 | 46 7.9 |
| | | 7.2 | 3.8 | 3.7 | | | 5.4 | 5.7 |
| | | 10.7 | 9.7 | 6.6 | | Sales/Working Capital | 9.8 | 11.0 |
| | | 22.9 | 59.3 | NM | | | 26.4 | 27.2 |
| | | 17.3 | 13.1 | 31.1 | | | 14.7 | 14.9 |
| | (27) | 6.8 | (36) 5.3 | (11) 11.0 | | EBIT/Interest | (81) 4.8 | (107) 5.1 |
| | | 2.8 | 2.4 | 5.0 | | | 1.4 | 1.6 |
| | | | 20.1 | | | | 5.8 | 7.7 |
| | | (14) | 3.8 | | | Net Profit + Depr., Dep., Amort./Cur. Mat. L/T/D | (30) 3.0 | (37) 3.5 |
| | | | 2.3 | | | | 1.4 | 1.9 |
| | | .4 | .2 | .7 | | | .4 | .3 |
| | | .7 | .9 | 1.3 | | Fixed/Worth | .9 | 1.0 |
| | | 1.5 | 2.3 | 9.7 | | | 3.0 | 2.0 |
| | | .9 | .7 | .6 | | | .7 | .8 |
| | | 1.9 | 1.7 | 2.2 | | Debt/Worth | 1.6 | 1.7 |
| | | 4.5 | 5.1 | 26.9 | | | 7.0 | 4.9 |
| | | 63.3 | 55.3 | 69.2 | | | 62.5 | 54.2 |
| | (26) | 38.9 | (35) 27.9 | (10) 22.9 | | % Profit Before Taxes/Tangible Net Worth | (82) 26.7 | (100) 26.0 |
| | | 14.4 | 12.5 | 18.7 | | | 10.7 | 7.4 |
| | | 21.8 | 19.8 | 14.5 | | | 19.0 | 16.2 |
| | | 8.3 | 10.0 | 12.8 | | % Profit Before Taxes/Total Assets | 10.4 | 8.1 |
| | | 3.8 | 3.5 | 8.4 | | | 2.0 | 1.4 |
| | | 23.0 | 20.0 | 6.1 | | | 19.2 | 18.1 |
| | | 12.7 | 7.5 | 3.4 | | Sales/Net Fixed Assets | 5.2 | 6.5 |
| | | 5.1 | 3.3 | 1.8 | | | 3.7 | 3.1 |
| | | 3.1 | 2.6 | 1.6 | | | 2.7 | 3.2 |
| | | 2.5 | 1.8 | 1.1 | | Sales/Total Assets | 1.7 | 1.9 |
| | | 1.8 | 1.3 | .9 | | | 1.4 | 1.2 |
| | | 1.0 | .9 | 2.7 | | | 1.2 | 1.1 |
| | (23) | 1.4 | (38) 1.5 | 5.2 | | % Depr., Dep., Amort./Sales | (77) 2.4 | (102) 2.2 |
| | | 2.4 | 3.9 | 8.3 | | | 4.6 | 4.3 |
| | | | | | | | 1.8 | 1.2 |
| | | | | | | % Officers', Directors', Owners' Comp/Sales | (22) 3.3 | (25) 3.8 |
| | | | | | | | 6.4 | 6.3 |
| 648M | 37044M | 394987M | 2032930M | 1095482M | 1240314M | Net Sales ($) | 4773369M | 6643890M |
| 456M | 8600M | 149425M | 934872M | 921969M | 1140799M | Total Assets ($) | 3290871M | 4166481M |

## Comparative Historical Data

## Current Data Sorted by Sales

| | | | Type of Statement | 0-1MM | 1-3MM | 3-5MM | 5-10MM | 10-25MM | 25MM & OVER |
|---|---|---|---|---|---|---|---|---|---|
| 31 | 20 | 19 | Unqualified | | 1 | | 2 | 1 | 15 |
| 20 | 26 | 19 | Reviewed | | | 1 | 2 | 6 | 10 |
| 8 | 4 | 4 | Compiled | | | 1 | | 2 | 1 |
| 8 | 5 | 5 | Tax Returns | | | | | | |
| 47 | 55 | 51 | Other | 2 | 1 | | 7 | 16 | 27 |
| 4/1/09-3/31/10 ALL | 4/1/10-3/31/11 ALL | 4/1/11-3/31/12 ALL | | | 17 (4/1-9/30/11) | | 81 (10/1/11-3/31/12) | | |
| 114 | 110 | 98 | NUMBER OF STATEMENTS | 3 | 2 | 2 | 13 | 25 | 53 |
| % | % | % | ASSETS | % | % | % | % | % | % |
| 9.9 | 9.2 | 7.9 | Cash & Equivalents | | | | 7.2 | 4.9 | 10.3 |
| 24.0 | 23.4 | 25.3 | Trade Receivables (net) | | | | 33.1 | 26.5 | 22.8 |
| 22.4 | 20.9 | 23.1 | Inventory | | | | 22.3 | 27.9 | 22.1 |
| 2.0 | 2.4 | 2.3 | All Other Current | | | | .6 | 2.9 | 2.7 |
| 58.3 | 55.9 | 58.6 | Total Current | | | | 63.2 | 62.2 | 57.9 |
| 28.7 | 33.2 | 29.6 | Fixed Assets (net) | | | | 25.4 | 29.1 | 28.8 |
| 5.0 | 5.2 | 6.1 | Intangibles (net) | | | | 1.0 | 4.3 | 7.4 |
| 7.9 | 5.7 | 5.8 | All Other Non-Current | | | | 10.5 | 4.3 | 5.9 |
| 100.0 | 100.0 | 100.0 | Total | | | | 100.0 | 100.0 | 100.0 |
| | | | LIABILITIES | | | | | | |
| 9.1 | 7.9 | 10.1 | Notes Payable-Short Term | | | | 13.6 | 15.9 | 6.3 |
| 3.7 | 3.2 | 4.1 | Cur. Mat.-L.T.D. | | | | 1.4 | 3.4 | 3.5 |
| 15.9 | 14.0 | 13.8 | Trade Payables | | | | 14.5 | 14.6 | 14.2 |
| .4 | .4 | .5 | Income Taxes Payable | | | | 1.3 | .2 | .5 |
| 9.8 | 6.8 | 8.4 | All Other Current | | | | 7.8 | 7.0 | 10.1 |
| 38.8 | 32.2 | 37.0 | Total Current | | | | 38.5 | 41.2 | 34.6 |
| 14.8 | 16.7 | 14.7 | Long-Term Debt | | | | 11.7 | 16.1 | 11.8 |
| .9 | 1.3 | 1.2 | Deferred Taxes | | | | .4 | 1.1 | 1.5 |
| 7.7 | 4.5 | 10.2 | All Other Non-Current | | | | .5 | 12.0 | 12.9 |
| 37.7 | 45.2 | 36.9 | Net Worth | | | | 48.9 | 29.7 | 39.3 |
| 100.0 | 100.0 | 100.0 | Total Liabilities & Net Worth | | | | 100.0 | 100.0 | 100.0 |
| | | | INCOME DATA | | | | | | |
| 100.0 | 100.0 | 100.0 | Net Sales | | | | 100.0 | 100.0 | 100.0 |
| 32.8 | 33.5 | 33.1 | Gross Profit | | | | 37.3 | 40.1 | 26.5 |
| 24.4 | 24.0 | 25.2 | Operating Expenses | | | | 22.9 | 34.9 | 18.1 |
| 8.4 | 9.5 | 7.9 | Operating Profit | | | | 14.4 | 5.2 | 8.4 |
| 1.0 | .9 | .5 | All Other Expenses (net) | | | | -.3 | .9 | .5 |
| 7.4 | 8.5 | 7.4 | Profit Before Taxes | | | | 14.7 | 4.3 | 7.8 |
| | | | RATIOS | | | | | | |
| 2.5 | 2.9 | 2.3 | Current | | | | 2.9 | 1.8 | 2.9 |
| 1.7 | 1.8 | 1.6 | | | | | 1.6 | 1.4 | 1.8 |
| 1.2 | 1.3 | 1.2 | | | | | 1.3 | 1.1 | 1.2 |
| 1.6 | 1.7 | 1.4 | Quick | | | | 1.9 | 1.0 | 1.8 |
| 1.0 | 1.0 | .9 | | | | | 1.2 | .8 | .9 |
| .6 | .7 | .6 | | | | | .4 | .6 | .6 |
| 35  10.4 | 33  11.1 | 34  10.7 | Sales/Receivables | | | | 27  13.7 | 36  10.0 | 34  10.8 |
| 44  8.3 | 43  8.4 | 43  8.4 | | | | | 39  9.3 | 45  8.2 | 43  8.5 |
| 53  6.9 | 54  6.8 | 56  6.5 | | | | | 56  6.5 | 54  6.7 | 58  6.3 |
| 39  9.4 | 31  11.8 | 36  10.1 | Cost of Sales/Inventory | | | | 14  25.2 | 37  9.8 | 37  9.8 |
| 62  5.8 | 54  6.8 | 60  6.1 | | | | | 55  6.6 | 73  5.0 | 56  6.5 |
| 113  3.2 | 86  4.2 | 91  4.0 | | | | | 94  3.9 | 118  3.1 | 85  4.3 |
| 22  16.3 | 24  15.3 | 22  16.8 | Cost of Sales/Payables | | | | 14  26.8 | 19  19.0 | 25  14.8 |
| 34  10.7 | 30  12.3 | 35  10.5 | | | | | 33  11.0 | 46  7.9 | 35  10.4 |
| 52  7.1 | 47  7.7 | 50  7.3 | | | | | 44  8.3 | 65  5.6 | 48  7.6 |
| 4.6 | 4.3 | 4.4 | Sales/Working Capital | | | | 7.3 | 6.2 | 3.7 |
| 10.4 | 8.6 | 10.8 | | | | | 10.7 | 16.6 | 8.6 |
| 27.1 | 21.7 | 38.2 | | | | | 22.9 | 138.4 | 32.2 |
| 14.2 | 28.2 | 20.7 | EBIT/Interest | | | | 30.4 | 11.1 | 30.1 |
| (104)  6.7 | (98)  8.4 | (86)  6.7 | | | | | (11)  10.0 | 5.4 | (44)  10.0 |
| 2.4 | 3.2 | 2.7 | | | | | 3.4 | 2.7 | 3.5 |
| 9.3 | 11.6 | 13.4 | Net Profit + Depr., Dep., Amort./Cur. Mat. L/T/D | | | | | 4.9 | 16.1 |
| (36)  3.0 | (35)  4.4 | (32)  4.5 | | | | | (10)  2.9 | (18)  6.6 | |
| 1.8 | 2.5 | 2.2 | | | | | | .8 | 2.9 |
| .3 | .4 | .4 | Fixed/Worth | | | | .3 | .6 | .3 |
| .8 | .8 | .9 | | | | | .5 | 1.1 | .8 |
| 1.6 | 1.7 | 2.1 | | | | | .8 | 2.3 | 1.9 |
| .6 | .5 | .8 | Debt/Worth | | | | .4 | 1.2 | .6 |
| 1.6 | 1.4 | 1.7 | | | | | .9 | 2.8 | 1.5 |
| 4.1 | 3.7 | 5.2 | | | | | 2.1 | 5.3 | 4.5 |
| 52.3 | 54.0 | 60.3 | % Profit Before Taxes/Tangible Net Worth | | | | 135.1 | 59.0 | 51.0 |
| (102)  28.3 | (104)  29.9 | (85)  35.2 | | | | | (12)  66.8 | (22)  38.9 | (45)  29.0 |
| 8.1 | 11.2 | 14.0 | | | | | 18.7 | 11.8 | 17.1 |
| 18.9 | 20.8 | 20.0 | % Profit Before Taxes/Total Assets | | | | 52.4 | 14.1 | 19.8 |
| 9.9 | 12.0 | 11.2 | | | | | 28.0 | 6.8 | 12.4 |
| 2.4 | 4.6 | 3.9 | | | | | 5.9 | 2.7 | 5.5 |
| 18.9 | 12.9 | 19.0 | Sales/Net Fixed Assets | | | | 50.5 | 17.6 | 17.4 |
| 6.6 | 5.7 | 6.5 | | | | | 14.2 | 8.0 | 5.5 |
| 3.3 | 3.4 | 3.3 | | | | | 4.1 | 3.7 | 3.3 |
| 2.6 | 2.8 | 2.9 | Sales/Total Assets | | | | 4.2 | 2.7 | 2.6 |
| 1.8 | 1.8 | 1.9 | | | | | 2.9 | 2.0 | 1.7 |
| 1.1 | 1.3 | 1.2 | | | | | 1.4 | 1.5 | 1.1 |
| .8 | 1.1 | 1.0 | % Depr., Dep., Amort./Sales | | | | | 1.0 | 1.0 |
| (99)  2.5 | (101)  2.3 | (83)  2.1 | | | | | (23)  1.5 | (48)  2.7 | |
| 5.0 | 4.5 | 3.9 | | | | | | 2.7 | 3.9 |
| .9 | 1.0 | 1.3 | % Officers', Directors' Owners' Comp/Sales | | | | | | |
| (24)  2.1 | (25)  1.7 | (20)  2.0 | | | | | | | |
| 8.4 | 6.4 | 5.1 | | | | | | | |
| 4391231M | 5029702M | 4801405M | Net Sales ($) | 648M | 4530M | 8037M | 104169M | 406369M | 4277652M |
| 2995224M | 3342265M | 3156121M | Total Assets ($) | 456M | 2190M | 8114M | 51468M | 238941M | 2854952M |

M = $ thousand    MM = $ million

See Pages 9 through 22 for Explanation of Ratios and Data

© RMA 2012

## Current Data Sorted by Assets            Comparative Historical Data

| 0-500M | 16 (4/1-9/30/11) 500M-2MM | 2-10MM | 46 (10/1/11-3/31/12) 10-50MM | 18 50-100MM | 23 100-250MM | Type of Statement | 16 | 25 |
|---|---|---|---|---|---|---|---|---|
| | | | | | | Unqualified | | |
| | | | | | | Reviewed | | |
| | | | | | | Compiled | 1 | |
| | | | | | | Tax Returns | | |
| | | 1 | 1 | 7 | 12 | Other | 6 4/1/07-3/31/08 | 11 4/1/08-3/31/09 |
| | | 1 | 1 | 25 | 35 | NUMBER OF STATEMENTS | ALL 23 | ALL 36 |
| % | % | % | % | % | % | ASSETS | % | % |
| D | D | | | 11.1 | 7.9 | Cash & Equivalents | 7.4 | 7.8 |
| A | A | | | 7.9 | 9.3 | Trade Receivables (net) | 6.4 | 5.5 |
| T | T | | | 10.6 | 11.9 | Inventory | 7.3 | 6.8 |
| A | A | | | 2.2 | 2.6 | All Other Current | 3.6 | 2.0 |
| | | | | 31.8 | 31.6 | Total Current | 24.6 | 22.1 |
| N | N | | | 66.3 | 63.7 | Fixed Assets (net) | 71.0 | 72.6 |
| O | O | | | .7 | .8 | Intangibles (net) | .5 | .6 |
| T | T | | | 1.3 | 3.9 | All Other Non-Current | 3.9 | 4.6 |
| | | | | 100.0 | 100.0 | Total | 100.0 | 100.0 |
| A | A | | | | | LIABILITIES | | |
| V | V | | | .2 | 2.8 | Notes Payable-Short Term | 1.6 | 2.5 |
| A | A | | | 7.6 | 5.2 | Cur. Mat.-L.T.D. | 4.3 | 7.9 |
| I | I | | | 5.9 | 5.2 | Trade Payables | 5.3 | 6.2 |
| L | L | | | .0 | .0 | Income Taxes Payable | .0 | .0 |
| A | A | | | 3.8 | 6.9 | All Other Current | 3.7 | 3.4 |
| B | B | | | 17.5 | 20.1 | Total Current | 14.8 | 20.0 |
| L | L | | | 20.3 | 28.6 | Long-Term Debt | 32.8 | 34.1 |
| E | E | | | .0 | .0 | Deferred Taxes | .1 | .0 |
| | | | | 1.8 | 3.2 | All Other Non-Current | .7 | 1.0 |
| | | | | 60.3 | 48.0 | Net Worth | 51.7 | 44.9 |
| | | | | 100.0 | 100.0 | Total Liabilties & Net Worth | 100.0 | 100.0 |
| | | | | | | INCOME DATA | | |
| | | | | 100.0 | 100.0 | Net Sales | 100.0 | 100.0 |
| | | | | 15.4 | 13.5 | Gross Profit | 21.5 | 9.7 |
| | | | | 7.2 | 8.0 | Operating Expenses | 13.5 | 10.3 |
| | | | | 8.1 | 5.5 | Operating Profit | 7.9 | -.6 |
| | | | | .7 | 1.5 | All Other Expenses (net) | .4 | 2.6 |
| | | | | 7.4 | 4.0 | Profit Before Taxes | 7.5 | -3.1 |
| | | | | | | RATIOS | | |
| | | | | 2.8 | 2.3 | | 2.6 | 2.4 |
| | | | | 2.1 | 1.8 | Current | 1.5 | 1.2 |
| | | | | 1.8 | 1.2 | | 1.0 | 1.0 |
| | | | | 1.6 | 1.1 | | 1.6 | 1.1 |
| | | | | 1.3 | .9 | Quick | .8 | .8 |
| | | | | .9 | .6 | | .5 | .3 |
| | | | 9   39.3 | 6   57.9 | | Sales/Receivables | 17   21.5 | 8   45.5 |
| | | | 12   30.9 | 11   33.5 | | | 25   14.8 | 12   29.4 |
| | | | 17   22.0 | 18   20.2 | | | 51   7.1 | 21   17.6 |
| | | | 13   27.6 | 15   25.1 | | Cost of Sales/Inventory | 17   22.1 | 13   28.7 |
| | | | 17   21.3 | 19   18.9 | | | 31   11.7 | 20   18.7 |
| | | | 30   12.2 | 29   12.6 | | | 52   7.0 | 30   12.2 |
| | | | 5   79.1 | 5   79.7 | | Cost of Sales/Payables | 13   27.3 | 8   48.0 |
| | | | 9   42.2 | 7   51.5 | | | 26   14.0 | 12   30.9 |
| | | | 12   29.7 | 9   39.2 | | | 36   10.1 | 21   17.5 |
| | | | | 8.1 | 12.9 | Sales/Working Capital | 6.0 | 11.7 |
| | | | | 11.4 | 17.3 | | 9.7 | 29.9 |
| | | | | 18.6 | 33.1 | | 82.2 | 757.8 |
| | | | | 21.0 | 8.4 | EBIT/Interest | 13.2 | 2.2 |
| | | | (24) | 7.5 | 5.4 | | 6.9 | (35)   .6 |
| | | | | 3.7 | 1.7 | | 2.0 | -2.3 |
| | | | | | | Net Profit + Depr., Dep., Amort./Cur. Mat. L/T/D | | |
| | | | | .8 | 1.0 | Fixed/Worth | 1.1 | 1.1 |
| | | | | 1.1 | 1.3 | | 1.5 | 1.9 |
| | | | | 1.5 | 2.0 | | 2.0 | 2.8 |
| | | | | .3 | .8 | Debt/Worth | .6 | .8 |
| | | | | .6 | 1.0 | | .9 | 1.5 |
| | | | | 1.1 | 2.1 | | 1.5 | 2.3 |
| | | | | 34.4 | 23.5 | % Profit Before Taxes/Tangible Net Worth | 36.0 | 9.4 |
| | | | | 24.7 | 18.7 | | 17.5 | -2.4 |
| | | | | 17.1 | 8.1 | | 6.6 | -20.4 |
| | | | | 19.5 | 13.8 | % Profit Before Taxes/Total Assets | 20.9 | 3.7 |
| | | | | 12.3 | 9.2 | | 6.2 | -.9 |
| | | | | 8.5 | 1.3 | | 2.4 | -6.5 |
| | | | | 4.2 | 4.0 | Sales/Net Fixed Assets | 2.1 | 2.4 |
| | | | | 2.8 | 2.9 | | 1.2 | 1.8 |
| | | | | 2.4 | 2.3 | | .6 | 1.1 |
| | | | | 2.4 | 2.5 | Sales/Total Assets | 1.3 | 1.7 |
| | | | | 2.2 | 2.0 | | .9 | 1.4 |
| | | | | 1.8 | 1.6 | | .5 | .9 |
| | | | | 2.4 | 2.1 | % Depr., Dep., Amort./Sales | (19)   2.4 | (33)   2.6 |
| | | | (24) | 2.9 | (26)   2.4 | | 3.8 | 3.7 |
| | | | | 3.8 | 2.9 | | 5.7 | 4.5 |
| | | | | | | % Officers', Directors' Owners' Comp/Sales | | |
| 37058M | 218695M | | 3970027M | 3970027M | 15469203M | Net Sales ($) | 1726104M | 7730578M |
| 9817M | 34777M | | 1859374M | 1859374M | 5180800M | Total Assets ($) | 2093096M | 3984549M |

M = $ thousand     MM = $ million
See Pages 9 through 22 for Explanation of Ratios and Data

## Comparative Historical Data / Current Data Sorted by Sales

| Type of Statement | 4/1/09-3/31/10 ALL | 4/1/10-3/31/11 ALL | 4/1/11-3/31/12 ALL | | 16 (4/1-9/30/11) | | 46 (10/1/11-3/31/12) | | 25MM & OVER |
|---|---|---|---|---|---|---|---|---|---|
| | | | | 0-1MM | 1-3MM | 3-5MM | 5-10MM | 10-25MM | |
| Unqualified | 32 | 40 | 41 | | | | | | 41 |
| Reviewed | | 1 | | | | | | | |
| Compiled | 1 | 1 | 1 | | | | | | |
| Tax Returns | | | | | | | | | |
| Other | 10 | 13 | 21 | | | | | | 21 |
| **NUMBER OF STATEMENTS** | 43 | 55 | 62 | | | | | | 62 |
| | % | % | % | % | % | % | % | % | % |
| **ASSETS** | | | | | | | | | |
| Cash & Equivalents | 7.7 | 7.8 | 9.3 | D | D | D | D | D | 9.3 |
| Trade Receivables (net) | 6.2 | 8.7 | 8.7 | A | A | A | A | A | 8.7 |
| Inventory | 8.1 | 10.6 | 12.4 | T | T | T | T | T | 12.4 |
| All Other Current | 1.2 | 3.2 | 2.4 | A | A | A | A | A | 2.4 |
| Total Current | 23.1 | 30.3 | 32.8 | | | | | | 32.8 |
| Fixed Assets (net) | 71.1 | 64.9 | 63.6 | N | N | N | N | N | 63.6 |
| Intangibles (net) | .6 | .7 | .7 | O | O | O | O | O | .7 |
| All Other Non-Current | 5.3 | 4.2 | 2.9 | T | T | T | T | T | 2.9 |
| Total | 100.0 | 100.0 | 100.0 | | | | | | 100.0 |
| **LIABILITIES** | | | | A | A | A | A | A | |
| Notes Payable-Short Term | 2.6 | 4.3 | 2.5 | V | V | V | V | V | 2.5 |
| Cur. Mat.-L.T.D. | 5.9 | 5.4 | 6.0 | A | A | A | A | A | 6.0 |
| Trade Payables | 5.0 | 5.7 | 5.6 | I | I | I | I | I | 5.6 |
| Income Taxes Payable | .0 | .0 | .0 | L | L | L | L | L | .0 |
| All Other Current | 4.1 | 5.3 | 5.4 | A | A | A | A | A | 5.4 |
| Total Current | 17.5 | 20.7 | 19.5 | B | B | B | B | B | 19.5 |
| Long-Term Debt | 33.5 | 27.6 | 24.3 | L | L | L | L | L | 24.3 |
| Deferred Taxes | .0 | .0 | .1 | E | E | E | E | E | .1 |
| All Other Non-Current | 1.6 | 2.3 | 2.9 | | | | | | 2.9 |
| Net Worth | 47.4 | 49.4 | 53.1 | | | | | | 53.1 |
| Total Liabilities & Net Worth | 100.0 | 100.0 | 100.0 | | | | | | 100.0 |
| **INCOME DATA** | | | | | | | | | |
| Net Sales | 100.0 | 100.0 | 100.0 | | | | | | 100.0 |
| Gross Profit | 14.4 | 18.8 | 14.3 | | | | | | 14.3 |
| Operating Expenses | 13.2 | 11.2 | 7.8 | | | | | | 7.8 |
| Operating Profit | 1.2 | 7.6 | 6.5 | | | | | | 6.5 |
| All Other Expenses (net) | 1.8 | 1.2 | 1.1 | | | | | | 1.1 |
| Profit Before Taxes | -.6 | 6.4 | 5.4 | | | | | | 5.4 |
| **RATIOS** | | | | | | | | | |
| Current | 2.0 | 2.7 | 2.4 | | | | | | 2.4 |
| | 1.5 | 1.7 | 1.9 | | | | | | 1.9 |
| | 1.1 | 1.1 | 1.5 | | | | | | 1.5 |
| Quick | 1.3 | 1.6 | 1.3 | | | | | | 1.3 |
| | .9 | .8 | 1.1 | | | | | | 1.1 |
| | .5 | .5 | .7 | | | | | | .7 |
| Sales/Receivables | 11  33.7 | 10  35.3 | 8  46.3 | | | | | | 8  46.3 |
| | 15  24.8 | 15  24.6 | 11  33.2 | | | | | | 11  33.2 |
| | 19  19.0 | 22  16.4 | 17  21.4 | | | | | | 17  21.4 |
| Cost of Sales/Inventory | 13  27.2 | 15  23.7 | 14  26.8 | | | | | | 14  26.8 |
| | 22  16.6 | 23  15.7 | 19  19.2 | | | | | | 19  19.2 |
| | 41  9.0 | 39  9.4 | 29  12.5 | | | | | | 29  12.5 |
| Cost of Sales/Payables | 5  73.2 | 6  57.3 | 5  79.1 | | | | | | 5  79.1 |
| | 11  33.6 | 10  37.5 | 8  47.7 | | | | | | 8  47.7 |
| | 26  14.0 | 21  17.7 | 11  32.9 | | | | | | 11  32.9 |
| Sales/Working Capital | 10.4 | 9.2 | 10.3 | | | | | | 10.3 |
| | 20.9 | 13.1 | 15.7 | | | | | | 15.7 |
| | 149.2 | 92.2 | 25.3 | | | | | | 25.3 |
| EBIT/Interest | 4.5 | 7.9 | 9.6 | | | | | | 9.6 |
| | (42)  1.8 | (53)  4.4 | (60)  6.7 | | | | | (60) | 6.7 |
| | -.5 | 2.9 | 3.0 | | | | | | 3.0 |
| Net Profit + Depr., Dep., Amort./Cur. Mat. L/T/D | | | 3.5 | | | | | | 3.5 |
| | | (10)  2.8 | 2.8 | | | | | (10) | 2.8 |
| | | | .9 | | | | | | .9 |
| Fixed/Worth | 1.1 | 1.0 | .9 | | | | | | .9 |
| | 1.8 | 1.4 | 1.3 | | | | | | 1.3 |
| | 2.1 | 1.8 | 1.7 | | | | | | 1.7 |
| Debt/Worth | .7 | .5 | .4 | | | | | | .4 |
| | 1.4 | 1.0 | .9 | | | | | | .9 |
| | 2.0 | 1.6 | 1.7 | | | | | | 1.7 |
| % Profit Before Taxes/Tangible Net Worth | 17.6 | 26.8 | 27.6 | | | | | | 27.6 |
| | 2.1 | (54)  17.6 | 19.9 | | | | | | 19.9 |
| | -13.5 | 9.4 | 13.9 | | | | | | 13.9 |
| % Profit Before Taxes/Total Assets | 7.4 | 13.8 | 15.6 | | | | | | 15.6 |
| | 1.1 | 9.4 | 11.5 | | | | | | 11.5 |
| | -4.2 | 3.4 | 6.5 | | | | | | 6.5 |
| Sales/Net Fixed Assets | 2.0 | 2.7 | 4.1 | | | | | | 4.1 |
| | 1.6 | 2.0 | 2.9 | | | | | | 2.9 |
| | 1.3 | 1.5 | 2.3 | | | | | | 2.3 |
| Sales/Total Assets | 1.5 | 1.6 | 2.5 | | | | | | 2.5 |
| | 1.2 | 1.3 | 2.1 | | | | | | 2.1 |
| | 1.0 | 1.2 | 1.7 | | | | | | 1.7 |
| % Depr., Dep., Amort./Sales | 3.6 | 3.2 | 2.2 | | | | | | 2.2 |
| | (36)  4.8 | (49)  4.5 | (52)  2.5 | | | | | (52) | 2.5 |
| | 6.1 | 5.1 | 3.3 | | | | | | 3.3 |
| % Officers', Directors' Owners' Comp/Sales | | | | | | | | | |
| Net Sales ($) | 5965772M | 10783174M | 19494983M | | | | | | 19494983M |
| Total Assets ($) | 4515816M | 5659212M | 7084768M | | | | | | 7084768M |

M = $ thousand    MM = $ million
See Pages 9 through 22 for Explanation of Ratios and Data

## Current Data Sorted by Assets        Comparative Historical Data

| | 0-500M | 500M-2MM | 2-10MM | 10-50MM | 50-100MM | 100-250MM | | 4/1/07-3/31/08 ALL | 4/1/08-3/31/09 ALL |
|---|---|---|---|---|---|---|---|---|---|
| **Type of Statement** | | | | | | | | | |
| Unqualified | | 1 | 3 | 13 | 30 | 23 | | 67 | 64 |
| Reviewed | | | 11 | 6 | 1 | 1 | | 15 | 18 |
| Compiled | 1 | 2 | 2 | 3 | 1 | 1 | | 4 | 8 |
| Tax Returns | | 4 | 2 | | | | | 3 | 2 |
| Other | 3 | | 15 | 24 | 5 | 11 | | 37 | 47 |
| | | 35 (4/1-9/30/11) | | 125 (10/1/11-3/31/12) | | | | | |
| **NUMBER OF STATEMENTS** | 4 | 5 | 33 | 46 | 36 | 36 | | 126 | 139 |
| | % | % | % | % | % | % | | % | % |
| **ASSETS** | | | | | | | | | |
| Cash & Equivalents | | | 10.0 | 6.5 | 9.4 | 8.3 | | 6.9 | 6.7 |
| Trade Receivables (net) | | | 25.1 | 23.5 | 10.4 | 10.0 | | 17.8 | 18.8 |
| Inventory | | | 29.4 | 22.7 | 12.0 | 14.1 | | 16.9 | 17.4 |
| All Other Current | | | 1.2 | 2.4 | 2.5 | 2.4 | | 3.7 | 2.6 |
| Total Current | | | 65.7 | 55.0 | 34.3 | 34.9 | | 45.4 | 45.5 |
| Fixed Assets (net) | | | 26.1 | 29.8 | 53.9 | 53.9 | | 42.0 | 41.4 |
| Intangibles (net) | | | 4.7 | 7.2 | 6.2 | 6.5 | | 6.7 | 7.6 |
| All Other Non-Current | | | 3.6 | 7.9 | 5.6 | 4.8 | | 5.9 | 5.5 |
| Total | | | 100.0 | 100.0 | 100.0 | 100.0 | | 100.0 | 100.0 |
| **LIABILITIES** | | | | | | | | | |
| Notes Payable-Short Term | | | 8.7 | 6.1 | 1.7 | 3.3 | | 7.2 | 7.6 |
| Cur. Mat.-L.T.D. | | | 3.2 | 2.3 | 3.9 | 4.2 | | 3.6 | 3.8 |
| Trade Payables | | | 17.0 | 12.6 | 8.2 | 6.9 | | 11.7 | 12.0 |
| Income Taxes Payable | | | .0 | .3 | .1 | .3 | | .2 | .2 |
| All Other Current | | | 6.9 | 5.9 | 4.8 | 5.9 | | 7.2 | 7.9 |
| Total Current | | | 35.7 | 27.2 | 18.7 | 20.6 | | 30.0 | 31.5 |
| Long-Term Debt | | | 12.6 | 16.0 | 18.4 | 22.0 | | 20.3 | 18.1 |
| Deferred Taxes | | | .5 | 1.5 | .9 | .8 | | .7 | .5 |
| All Other Non-Current | | | 5.7 | 10.2 | 2.5 | 3.5 | | 4.7 | 5.3 |
| Net Worth | | | 45.6 | 45.2 | 59.5 | 53.1 | | 44.3 | 44.6 |
| Total Liabilities & Net Worth | | | 100.0 | 100.0 | 100.0 | 100.0 | | 100.0 | 100.0 |
| **INCOME DATA** | | | | | | | | | |
| Net Sales | | | 100.0 | 100.0 | 100.0 | 100.0 | | 100.0 | 100.0 |
| Gross Profit | | | 36.2 | 23.7 | 14.9 | 14.4 | | 27.9 | 19.9 |
| Operating Expenses | | | 28.3 | 18.8 | 7.7 | 6.4 | | 18.4 | 16.1 |
| Operating Profit | | | 7.9 | 4.9 | 7.1 | 8.0 | | 9.5 | 3.9 |
| All Other Expenses (net) | | | .7 | .4 | .8 | 1.1 | | 1.6 | 1.5 |
| Profit Before Taxes | | | 7.3 | 4.5 | 6.4 | 6.8 | | 7.9 | 2.4 |
| **RATIOS** | | | | | | | | | |
| Current | | | 3.3 | 3.3 | 2.9 | 2.2 | | 2.5 | 2.3 |
| | | | 1.7 | 2.1 | 2.0 | 1.7 | | 1.6 | 1.7 |
| | | | 1.3 | 1.4 | 1.4 | 1.3 | | 1.1 | 1.1 |
| Quick | | | 1.9 | 1.7 | 1.6 | 1.1 | | 1.3 | 1.4 |
| | | | .9 | 1.1 | 1.2 | .8 | | .8 | .9 |
| | | | .5 | .7 | .8 | .6 | | .5 | .5 |
| Sales/Receivables | | | 30   12.3 | 43   8.5 | 10   37.4 | 9   41.3 | | 22   17.0 | 18   20.7 |
| | | | 37   9.9 | 49   7.4 | 17   21.2 | 16   22.3 | | 37   9.8 | 34   10.6 |
| | | | 55   6.6 | 58   6.3 | 44   8.3 | 46   7.9 | | 51   7.2 | 51   7.1 |
| Cost of Sales/Inventory | | | 41   8.8 | 37   9.9 | 14   26.6 | 14   25.9 | | 28   12.9 | 19   19.2 |
| | | | 65   5.6 | 66   5.5 | 23   16.2 | 26   14.1 | | 45   8.1 | 38   9.6 |
| | | | 122   3.0 | 89   4.1 | 39   9.3 | 72   5.1 | | 66   5.5 | 63   5.8 |
| Cost of Sales/Payables | | | 25   14.8 | 22   16.5 | 5   79.8 | 6   59.8 | | 16   22.3 | 12   30.9 |
| | | | 38   9.7 | 31   11.8 | 13   28.3 | 14   25.8 | | 31   11.9 | 23   15.6 |
| | | | 59   6.2 | 49   7.5 | 34   10.8 | 31   11.8 | | 47   7.7 | 45   8.1 |
| Sales/Working Capital | | | 4.4 | 3.6 | 7.3 | 7.8 | | 5.4 | 5.7 |
| | | | 8.5 | 5.9 | 11.7 | 18.5 | | 10.2 | 13.9 |
| | | | 18.0 | 17.5 | 21.8 | 32.2 | | 39.9 | 77.1 |
| EBIT/Interest | | | 32.2 | 32.9 | 32.2 | 19.0 | | 18.1 | 13.6 |
| | | | (29) 6.0 | (42) 9.0 | 9.7 | (35) 8.9 | | (117) 5.4 | (131) 3.3 |
| | | | 2.5 | 2.6 | 3.2 | 3.9 | | 2.3 | -.4 |
| Net Profit + Depr., Dep., Amort./Cur. Mat. L/T/D | | | | 17.1 | | 21.4 | | 23.8 | 11.5 |
| | | | | (17) 4.9 | | (12) 3.1 | | (37) 3.6 | (39) 3.3 |
| | | | | 2.7 | | 1.4 | | 1.6 | .4 |
| Fixed/Worth | | | .2 | .2 | .7 | .8 | | .5 | .4 |
| | | | .6 | .7 | 1.0 | 1.1 | | 1.1 | 1.2 |
| | | | 1.3 | 1.6 | 1.9 | 1.8 | | 2.0 | 2.1 |
| Debt/Worth | | | .4 | .5 | .2 | .5 | | .6 | .6 |
| | | | 1.6 | 1.2 | .5 | .8 | | 1.1 | 1.3 |
| | | | 4.0 | 3.1 | 1.7 | 1.5 | | 2.8 | 3.3 |
| % Profit Before Taxes/Tangible Net Worth | | | 111.8 | 45.2 | 24.6 | 25.3 | | 44.4 | 31.1 |
| | | | (29) 40.2 | (40) 20.4 | (31) 18.8 | (32) 20.2 | | (106) 27.6 | (121) 11.7 |
| | | | 14.2 | 10.2 | 7.9 | 13.7 | | 14.0 | -5.1 |
| % Profit Before Taxes/Total Assets | | | 33.2 | 17.7 | 18.0 | 15.5 | | 19.5 | 14.4 |
| | | | 9.1 | 10.3 | 12.3 | 11.1 | | 10.6 | 5.0 |
| | | | 4.1 | 2.8 | 3.3 | 6.6 | | 3.7 | -3.0 |
| Sales/Net Fixed Assets | | | 32.9 | 18.1 | 5.5 | 4.5 | | 11.7 | 13.7 |
| | | | 13.2 | 7.2 | 3.6 | 3.5 | | 4.4 | 4.8 |
| | | | 4.5 | 3.1 | 2.6 | 2.5 | | 2.1 | 2.3 |
| Sales/Total Assets | | | 3.0 | 2.1 | 2.4 | 2.1 | | 2.1 | 2.4 |
| | | | 2.1 | 1.7 | 2.0 | 1.7 | | 1.5 | 1.6 |
| | | | 1.5 | 1.2 | 1.4 | 1.5 | | 1.0 | 1.3 |
| % Depr., Dep., Amort./Sales | | | .5 | 1.0 | 2.5 | 2.3 | | 1.2 | 1.0 |
| | | | (26) 1.5 | (43) 1.9 | (34) 3.4 | (28) 2.6 | | (110) 2.8 | (119) 2.5 |
| | | | 3.3 | 5.2 | 4.6 | 2.8 | | 4.4 | 4.0 |
| % Officers', Directors' Owners' Comp/Sales | | | 1.3 | | | | | 1.5 | 1.2 |
| | | | (10) 2.3 | | | | | (22) 2.8 | (19) 2.9 |
| | | | 4.0 | | | | | 5.6 | 4.6 |
| Net Sales ($) | 5809M | 18209M | 385277M | 2055776M | 4808651M | 9026831M | | 8975523M | 12180578M |
| Total Assets ($) | 1052M | 5095M | 169321M | 1168220M | 2571412M | 5227668M | | 7164486M | 7724999M |

© RMA 2012

M = $ thousand    MM = $ million
See Pages 9 through 22 for Explanation of Ratios and Data

## Comparative Historical Data

## Current Data Sorted by Sales

| | | | Type of Statement | | | | | | |
|---|---|---|---|---|---|---|---|---|---|
| 72 | 69 | 70 | Unqualified | | 1 | | | 6 | 63 |
| 23 | 17 | 18 | Reviewed | | | 4 | | 7 | 7 |
| 12 | 8 | 8 | Compiled | 1 | 2 | 3 | | 2 | 3 |
| 6 | 8 | 6 | Tax Returns | 2 | | 3 | | 1 | |
| 50 | 49 | 58 | Other | 2 | 6 | 6 | | 12 | 32 |
| 4/1/09-3/31/10 | 4/1/10-3/31/11 | 4/1/11-3/31/12 | | | 35 (4/1-9/30/11) | | | 125 (10/1/11-3/31/12) | |
| ALL | ALL | ALL | | 0-1MM | 1-3MM | 3-5MM | 5-10MM | 10-25MM | 25MM & OVER |
| 163 | 151 | 160 | **NUMBER OF STATEMENTS** | 2 | 3 | 9 | 13 | 28 | 105 |
| % | % | % | | % | % | % | % | % | % |
| | | | **ASSETS** | | | | | | |
| 8.8 | 9.2 | 8.7 | Cash & Equivalents | | | | 12.2 | 7.4 | 8.2 |
| 18.0 | 19.0 | 17.7 | Trade Receivables (net) | | | | 22.7 | 22.4 | 16.1 |
| 17.2 | 17.1 | 20.0 | Inventory | | | | 28.8 | 26.2 | 17.0 |
| 2.6 | 3.7 | 2.4 | All Other Current | | | | 1.0 | 3.3 | 2.1 |
| 46.6 | 48.9 | 48.9 | Total Current | | | | 64.7 | 59.3 | 43.4 |
| 42.8 | 39.7 | 39.5 | Fixed Assets (net) | | | | 25.5 | 27.6 | 45.0 |
| 4.9 | 5.7 | 6.2 | Intangibles (net) | | | | 7.3 | 4.5 | 6.1 |
| 5.7 | 5.7 | 5.4 | All Other Non-Current | | | | 2.5 | 8.6 | 5.5 |
| 100.0 | 100.0 | 100.0 | Total | | | | 100.0 | 100.0 | 100.0 |
| | | | **LIABILITIES** | | | | | | |
| 5.9 | 6.8 | 5.1 | Notes Payable-Short Term | | | | 6.3 | 6.1 | 3.9 |
| 4.1 | 3.8 | 3.5 | Cur. Mat.-L.T.D. | | | | 5.4 | 2.6 | 3.3 |
| 12.2 | 12.3 | 12.9 | Trade Payables | | | | 19.2 | 14.1 | 10.1 |
| .2 | .2 | .2 | Income Taxes Payable | | | | .0 | .3 | .2 |
| 6.6 | 8.0 | 7.2 | All Other Current | | | | 7.0 | 7.4 | 5.7 |
| 28.8 | 31.0 | 28.9 | Total Current | | | | 37.9 | 30.4 | 23.3 |
| 19.4 | 17.2 | 17.5 | Long-Term Debt | | | | 9.7 | 16.8 | 17.4 |
| .6 | .8 | .9 | Deferred Taxes | | | | .0 | .9 | 1.1 |
| 5.3 | 6.4 | 6.8 | All Other Non-Current | | | | 9.7 | 6.1 | 4.9 |
| 45.9 | 44.4 | 45.9 | Net Worth | | | | 42.8 | 45.7 | 53.3 |
| 100.0 | 100.0 | 100.0 | Total Liabilities & Net Worth | | | | 100.0 | 100.0 | 100.0 |
| | | | **INCOME DATA** | | | | | | |
| 100.0 | 100.0 | 100.0 | Net Sales | | | | 100.0 | 100.0 | 100.0 |
| 22.3 | 25.1 | 22.4 | Gross Profit | | | | 31.2 | 30.9 | 16.9 |
| 18.3 | 18.3 | 16.1 | Operating Expenses | | | | 25.0 | 24.7 | 9.5 |
| 4.0 | 6.8 | 6.3 | Operating Profit | | | | 6.2 | 6.2 | 7.4 |
| 1.3 | .9 | .7 | All Other Expenses (net) | | | | .4 | .3 | .7 |
| 2.8 | 5.8 | 5.6 | Profit Before Taxes | | | | 5.7 | 5.9 | 6.7 |
| | | | **RATIOS** | | | | | | |
| 2.5 | 2.8 | 2.8 | | | | | 3.5 | 3.2 | 2.7 |
| 1.7 | 1.9 | 1.8 | Current | | | | 1.4 | 1.7 | 1.9 |
| 1.2 | 1.2 | 1.3 | | | | | 1.1 | 1.4 | 1.4 |
| 1.4 | 1.6 | 1.6 | | | | | 2.3 | 1.8 | 1.6 |
| .9 | 1.0 | .9 | Quick | | | | .7 | .9 | 1.0 |
| .6 | .6 | .6 | | | | | .5 | .5 | .7 |
| 19  19.3 | 17  21.1 | 15  24.4 | | 26  14.3 | 32  11.3 | 12  31.3 | | | |
| 37  9.8 | 40  9.2 | 36  10.0 | Sales/Receivables | 34  10.6 | 43  8.4 | 32  11.5 | | | |
| 51  7.1 | 53  6.9 | 52  7.0 | | 65  5.6 | 54  6.7 | 51  7.2 | | | |
| 24  15.1 | 24  15.1 | 21  17.3 | | 34  10.6 | 43  8.4 | 17  21.7 | | | |
| 43  8.5 | 40  9.1 | 41  9.0 | Cost of Sales/Inventory | 61  6.0 | 68  5.4 | 33  10.9 | | | |
| 70  5.2 | 69  5.3 | 81  4.5 | | 107  3.4 | 122  3.0 | 68  5.4 | | | |
| 15  25.1 | 12  30.0 | 10  35.4 | | 37  9.8 | 23  15.7 | 7  51.5 | | | |
| 28  13.0 | 27  13.7 | 25  14.6 | Cost of Sales/Payables | 39  9.4 | 28  13.1 | 22  16.3 | | | |
| 47  7.8 | 41  8.8 | 44  8.3 | | 55  6.6 | 57  6.4 | 35  10.4 | | | |
| 4.9 | 5.2 | 5.3 | | | | | 3.5 | 3.9 | 5.7 |
| 9.9 | 9.1 | 10.2 | Sales/Working Capital | | | | 16.6 | 7.6 | 11.8 |
| 30.4 | 22.3 | 22.7 | | | | | 272.6 | 11.8 | 23.3 |
| | 10.8 | 18.8 | 29.9 | | | | 7.6 | 31.4 | 31.5 |
| (153)  4.7 | (139)  7.8 | (150)  8.6 | EBIT/Interest | (12)  3.1 | (24)  6.9 | (103)  10.1 | | | |
| .7 | 2.7 | 2.6 | | | | | 2.4 | 2.6 | 3.9 |
| 9.7 | 14.8 | 13.1 | | | | | | | 20.6 |
| (42)  3.7 | (38)  4.1 | (39)  3.5 | Net Profit + Depr., Dep., Amort./Cur. Mat. L/T/D | | | (30)  4.7 | | | |
| 1.6 | 2.0 | 1.9 | | | | | | | 2.2 |
| .4 | .4 | .4 | | | | | .2 | .2 | .6 |
| 1.0 | .9 | .9 | Fixed/Worth | | | | .3 | .7 | .9 |
| 2.2 | 1.6 | 1.7 | | | | | 2.8 | 1.4 | 1.6 |
| .5 | .5 | .4 | | | | | .4 | .5 | .4 |
| 1.1 | 1.0 | 1.1 | Debt/Worth | | | | 4.0 | 1.3 | .8 |
| 3.4 | 2.7 | 3.2 | | | | | 15.5 | 3.2 | 1.8 |
| 29.1 | 38.0 | 38.3 | | | | | 107.6 | 80.4 | 27.3 |
| (149)  13.1 | (137)  19.3 | (137)  20.6 | % Profit Before Taxes/Tangible Net Worth | (11)  25.3 | (27)  32.6 | (92)  20.1 | | | |
| -1.0 | 8.4 | 12.7 | | | | | 5.7 | 12.8 | 12.8 |
| 11.3 | 18.9 | 17.3 | | | | | 8.7 | 30.2 | 17.6 |
| 6.2 | 8.8 | 10.7 | % Profit Before Taxes/Total Assets | | | | 6.2 | 10.2 | 12.0 |
| -.8 | 3.4 | 4.2 | | | | | 3.0 | 2.4 | 6.8 |
| 13.9 | 14.2 | 14.5 | | | | | 141.1 | 31.5 | 9.8 |
| 3.5 | 4.4 | 4.6 | Sales/Net Fixed Assets | | | | 17.5 | 8.8 | 4.0 |
| 1.8 | 2.1 | 2.8 | | | | | 3.6 | 2.7 | 2.8 |
| 2.1 | 2.1 | 2.4 | | | | | 2.3 | 2.8 | 2.3 |
| 1.4 | 1.5 | 1.9 | Sales/Total Assets | | | | 1.8 | 1.9 | 1.9 |
| 1.1 | 1.2 | 1.4 | | | | | 1.5 | 1.0 | 1.5 |
| 1.4 | 1.3 | 1.5 | | | | | .4 | 1.0 | 1.8 |
| (139)  3.6 | (129)  3.5 | (136)  2.5 | % Depr., Dep., Amort./Sales | (11)  .8 | (22)  1.8 | (93)  2.6 | | | |
| 5.7 | 5.0 | 3.9 | | | | | 3.2 | 5.6 | 3.5 |
| 1.0 | .9 | 1.2 | | | | | | | |
| (34)  2.4 | (24)  3.4 | (25)  2.4 | % Officers', Directors' Owners' Comp/Sales | | | | | | |
| 5.2 | 5.3 | 3.6 | | | | | | | |
| 10966745M | 11509455M | 16300553M | Net Sales ($) | 558M | 5805M | 33619M | 83671M | 454409M | 15722491M |
| 8233160M | 7839544M | 9142768M | Total Assets ($) | 233M | 1973M | 55695M | 48129M | 430474M | 8606264M |

M = $ thousand     MM = $ million
See Pages 9 through 22 for Explanation of Ratios and Data

## Current Data Sorted by Assets          Comparative Historical Data

| | 0-500M | 500M-2MM | 2-10MM | 10-50MM | 50-100MM | 100-250MM | Type of Statement | 4/1/07-3/31/08 ALL | 4/1/08-3/31/09 ALL |
|---|---|---|---|---|---|---|---|---|---|
| | | 1 | 5 | 34 | 6 | 13 | Unqualified | 48 | 50 |
| | 1 | 4 | 23 | 19 | | | Reviewed | 38 | 45 |
| | | 6 | 9 | 1 | | | Compiled | 16 | 18 |
| | 1 | 7 | 5 | 1 | 1 | | Tax Returns | 14 | 12 |
| | 4 | 10 | 25 | 33 | 7 | 11 | Other | 95 | 104 |
| | | 37 (4/1-9/30/11) | | 190 (10/1/11-3/31/12) | | | | | |
| **NUMBER OF STATEMENTS** | 6 | 28 | 67 | 88 | 14 | 24 | | 211 | 229 |
| | % | % | % | % | % | % | **ASSETS** | % | % |
| | | 16.8 | 12.9 | 5.5 | 8.0 | 7.3 | Cash & Equivalents | 6.5 | 7.0 |
| | | 32.8 | 25.6 | 26.0 | 24.3 | 23.8 | Trade Receivables (net) | 28.4 | 26.0 |
| | | 23.5 | 24.1 | 27.5 | 19.0 | 21.5 | Inventory | 23.0 | 23.7 |
| | | 1.2 | 2.4 | 2.1 | 3.2 | 4.2 | All Other Current | 3.1 | 2.8 |
| | | 74.3 | 65.0 | 61.1 | 54.5 | 56.8 | Total Current | 61.0 | 59.4 |
| | | 18.0 | 28.9 | 27.7 | 27.1 | 27.7 | Fixed Assets (net) | 29.7 | 29.8 |
| | | 3.4 | 1.8 | 6.5 | 2.6 | 10.1 | Intangibles (net) | 5.1 | 5.7 |
| | | 4.3 | 4.2 | 4.7 | 15.8 | 5.3 | All Other Non-Current | 4.2 | 5.1 |
| | | 100.0 | 100.0 | 100.0 | 100.0 | 100.0 | Total | 100.0 | 100.0 |
| | | | | | | | **LIABILITIES** | | |
| | | 9.2 | 7.3 | 11.5 | 6.1 | 5.7 | Notes Payable-Short Term | 11.9 | 11.3 |
| | | 2.5 | 5.9 | 3.1 | 5.9 | 1.4 | Cur. Mat.-L.T.D. | 3.4 | 4.2 |
| | | 17.6 | 17.0 | 16.0 | 18.5 | 16.7 | Trade Payables | 18.8 | 16.8 |
| | | .0 | .2 | .2 | .1 | .2 | Income Taxes Payable | .4 | .6 |
| | | 10.0 | 7.8 | 7.3 | 9.4 | 5.7 | All Other Current | 6.4 | 8.5 |
| | | 39.3 | 38.1 | 38.1 | 39.9 | 29.7 | Total Current | 41.0 | 41.3 |
| | | 12.6 | 12.4 | 16.2 | 9.7 | 17.9 | Long-Term Debt | 18.1 | 16.5 |
| | | .4 | .7 | .7 | 1.7 | 3.1 | Deferred Taxes | .4 | .7 |
| | | 3.8 | 6.4 | 6.0 | 9.7 | 5.3 | All Other Non-Current | 4.8 | 8.8 |
| | | 43.8 | 42.5 | 38.9 | 38.9 | 44.0 | Net Worth | 35.8 | 32.8 |
| | | 100.0 | 100.0 | 100.0 | 100.0 | 100.0 | Total Liabilities & Net Worth | 100.0 | 100.0 |
| | | | | | | | **INCOME DATA** | | |
| | | 100.0 | 100.0 | 100.0 | 100.0 | 100.0 | Net Sales | 100.0 | 100.0 |
| | | 43.4 | 28.6 | 22.5 | 18.1 | 18.7 | Gross Profit | 24.2 | 21.8 |
| | | 34.4 | 21.9 | 16.9 | 14.1 | 12.7 | Operating Expenses | 18.9 | 18.3 |
| | | 9.0 | 6.8 | 5.5 | 3.9 | 6.0 | Operating Profit | 5.3 | 3.5 |
| | | .7 | 1.2 | .8 | .2 | 1.8 | All Other Expenses (net) | 1.3 | 1.8 |
| | | 8.3 | 5.5 | 4.7 | 3.7 | 4.3 | Profit Before Taxes | 4.1 | 1.7 |
| | | | | | | | **RATIOS** | | |
| | | 3.9 | 4.1 | 2.0 | 2.6 | 2.5 | | 2.4 | 2.6 |
| | | 2.4 | 1.8 | 1.6 | 1.4 | 2.0 | Current | 1.5 | 1.4 |
| | | 1.4 | 1.1 | 1.3 | 1.0 | 1.6 | | 1.1 | 1.0 |
| | | 2.6 | 2.6 | 1.1 | 1.9 | 1.4 | | 1.3 | 1.4 |
| | | 1.8 | 1.1 | .8 | .6 | 1.0 | Quick | .9 | .8 |
| | | 1.0 | .5 | .6 | .5 | .8 | | .6 | .5 |
| | | 26   14.0 | 33   11.1 | 35   10.3 | 38   9.7 | 34   10.8 | | 36   10.2 | 30   12.1 |
| | | 35   10.3 | 41   9.0 | 45   8.2 | 47   7.7 | 48   7.6 | Sales/Receivables | 45   8.1 | 38   9.7 |
| | | 57   6.4 | 50   7.3 | 56   6.5 | 57   6.4 | 58   6.3 | | 59   6.2 | 51   7.2 |
| | | 15   24.5 | 31   11.9 | 45   8.1 | 24   14.9 | 36   10.1 | | 32   11.6 | 29   12.4 |
| | | 42   8.6 | 52   7.0 | 63   5.8 | 57   6.4 | 46   8.0 | Cost of Sales/Inventory | 51   7.2 | 52   7.1 |
| | | 87   4.2 | 83   4.4 | 78   4.7 | 72   5.1 | 76   4.8 | | 70   5.2 | 73   5.0 |
| | | 17   21.7 | 16   22.7 | 24   15.3 | 33   10.9 | 27   13.5 | | 23   15.8 | 16   22.6 |
| | | 28   12.9 | 35   10.3 | 32   11.3 | 41   8.8 | 42   8.7 | Cost of Sales/Payables | 37   9.9 | 28   12.9 |
| | | 57   6.4 | 52   7.0 | 43   8.5 | 62   5.9 | 51   7.1 | | 51   7.2 | 45   8.1 |
| | | 4.7 | 3.7 | 5.5 | 5.9 | 4.1 | | 5.5 | 5.9 |
| | | 7.8 | 7.5 | 10.6 | 10.1 | 6.6 | Sales/Working Capital | 10.8 | 13.0 |
| | | 22.6 | 46.6 | 17.4 | NM | 11.0 | | 48.3 | 87.6 |
| | | 42.8 | 24.8 | 17.6 | 18.6 | 21.2 | | 10.1 | 8.6 |
| | (22) 11.4 | (59) 6.9 | (85) 5.4 | (12) 8.6 | (22) 5.0 | | EBIT/Interest | (199) 3.4 | (209) 2.7 |
| | | 4.5 | 2.2 | 2.8 | 4.6 | 1.9 | | 1.4 | .5 |
| | | | 17.0 | 6.0 | | | | 9.0 | 7.6 |
| | | (20) 4.8 | (34) 3.6 | | | | Net Profit + Depr., Dep., Amort./Cur. Mat. L/T/D | (57) 4.0 | (62) 2.6 |
| | | | .8 | 1.0 | | | | 1.4 | 1.0 |
| | | .1 | .2 | .4 | .4 | .4 | | .3 | .3 |
| | | .3 | .6 | .8 | .7 | .7 | Fixed/Worth | .8 | .8 |
| | | 1.7 | 2.1 | 1.9 | 1.4 | 4.1 | | 2.3 | 2.7 |
| | | .4 | .5 | 1.0 | 1.0 | .7 | | .9 | .9 |
| | | 1.3 | 1.2 | 1.8 | 1.7 | 1.3 | Debt/Worth | 2.0 | 2.4 |
| | | 4.3 | 3.4 | 3.9 | 5.0 | 11.5 | | 6.7 | 6.6 |
| | | 80.9 | 42.0 | 45.2 | 34.5 | 25.6 | | 44.6 | 36.7 |
| | (24) 38.2 | (61) 21.0 | (81) 25.6 | (19) 20.3 | 16.2 | | % Profit Before Taxes/Tangible Net Worth | (182) 23.7 | (195) 13.3 |
| | | 14.5 | 10.1 | 10.6 | 7.4 | 6.8 | | 7.3 | .0 |
| | | 43.4 | 15.6 | 15.0 | 10.7 | 10.7 | | 15.4 | 10.8 |
| | | 17.3 | 7.1 | 8.6 | 7.2 | 6.2 | % Profit Before Taxes/Total Assets | 6.2 | 4.5 |
| | | 7.5 | 2.2 | 3.1 | 2.6 | 2.0 | | 1.3 | -1.1 |
| | | 111.3 | 17.5 | 15.0 | 15.1 | 8.5 | | 15.9 | 21.4 |
| | | 20.6 | 9.3 | 8.3 | 6.8 | 5.4 | Sales/Net Fixed Assets | 7.1 | 7.4 |
| | | 7.8 | 3.9 | 5.1 | 4.2 | 3.4 | | 4.2 | 4.1 |
| | | 3.9 | 2.8 | 2.7 | 2.1 | 2.8 | | 2.8 | 2.9 |
| | | 2.6 | 2.2 | 2.0 | 1.7 | 1.6 | Sales/Total Assets | 2.2 | 2.1 |
| | | 2.0 | 1.5 | 1.5 | 1.4 | 1.0 | | 1.5 | 1.5 |
| | | .4 | 1.1 | 1.0 | .7 | 1.2 | | 1.1 | 1.2 |
| | (20) 1.4 | (62) 1.9 | (79) 1.5 | (12) 1.8 | (16) 2.0 | | % Depr., Dep., Amort./Sales | (183) 2.2 | (193) 2.2 |
| | | 2.8 | 4.2 | 3.2 | 3.2 | 4.2 | | 3.7 | 4.0 |
| | | 2.3 | 2.2 | 1.0 | | | | 1.4 | 1.8 |
| | (12) 4.1 | (27) 3.2 | (17) 2.4 | | | | % Officers', Directors' Owners' Comp/Sales | (50) 4.1 | (53) 3.4 |
| | | 7.7 | 5.4 | 4.8 | | | | 8.5 | 6.0 |
| | 4998M | 127358M | 811935M | 4116128M | 1910401M | 7389681M | Net Sales ($) | 11212450M | 15610292M |
| | 1411M | 39361M | 372796M | 1914262M | 1039598M | 4016830M | Total Assets ($) | 6311043M | 7691781M |

© RMA 2012

M = $ thousand     MM = $ million
See Pages 9 through 22 for Explanation of Ratios and Data

## Comparative Historical Data | Current Data Sorted by Sales

| | | | Type of Statement | | | | | | |
|---|---|---|---|---|---|---|---|---|---|
| 52 | 52 | 59 | Unqualified | | | 1 | 2 | 8 | 48 |
| 42 | 45 | 47 | Reviewed | 1 | 1 | 2 | 10 | 19 | 14 |
| 17 | 15 | 16 | Compiled | | 4 | 2 | 4 | 4 | 2 |
| 16 | 14 | 15 | Tax Returns | 1 | 3 | 3 | 3 | 3 | 2 |
| 87 | 86 | 90 | Other | 2 | 6 | 7 | 13 | 18 | 44 |
| 4/1/09-3/31/10 | 4/1/10-3/31/11 | 4/1/11-3/31/12 | | | 37 (4/1-9/30/11) | | | 190 (10/1/11-3/31/12) | |
| ALL | ALL | ALL | | 0-1MM | 1-3MM | 3-5MM | 5-10MM | 10-25MM | 25MM & OVER |
| 214 | 212 | 227 | **NUMBER OF STATEMENTS** | 4 | 14 | 15 | 32 | 52 | 110 |
| % | % | % | **ASSETS** | % | % | % | % | % | % |
| 7.4 | 7.2 | 9.4 | Cash & Equivalents | | 19.9 | 10.5 | 14.6 | 10.5 | 6.0 |
| 25.8 | 27.6 | 26.3 | Trade Receivables (net) | | 21.7 | 27.5 | 25.7 | 25.2 | 27.6 |
| 24.6 | 25.9 | 25.0 | Inventory | | 16.1 | 23.5 | 28.4 | 22.8 | 26.1 |
| 2.9 | 2.5 | 2.4 | All Other Current | | 2.3 | 2.0 | 1.7 | 2.7 | 2.6 |
| 60.7 | 63.2 | 63.2 | Total Current | | 60.1 | 63.6 | 70.4 | 61.1 | 62.2 |
| 29.3 | 27.1 | 26.7 | Fixed Assets (net) | | 25.0 | 29.3 | 23.9 | 28.4 | 26.9 |
| 5.0 | 5.7 | 4.7 | Intangibles (net) | | 7.5 | 2.8 | 1.7 | 5.9 | 5.1 |
| 5.0 | 4.1 | 5.3 | All Other Non-Current | | 7.5 | 4.4 | 4.0 | 4.5 | 5.8 |
| 100.0 | 100.0 | 100.0 | Total | | 100.0 | 100.0 | 100.0 | 100.0 | 100.0 |
| | | | **LIABILITIES** | | | | | | |
| 13.4 | 10.3 | 9.3 | Notes Payable-Short Term | | 10.4 | 6.6 | 7.1 | 7.0 | 10.6 |
| 3.8 | 2.8 | 3.8 | Cur. Mat.-L.T.D. | | 3.9 | 4.4 | 2.2 | 6.4 | 3.1 |
| 16.8 | 17.3 | 16.7 | Trade Payables | | 11.5 | 13.1 | 18.8 | 14.0 | 18.8 |
| .3 | .1 | .1 | Income Taxes Payable | | .0 | .0 | .3 | .1 | .2 |
| 6.7 | 9.2 | 10.1 | All Other Current | | 9.3 | 11.0 | 11.3 | 5.0 | 7.7 |
| 41.0 | 39.7 | 40.1 | Total Current | | 35.1 | 35.1 | 39.7 | 32.5 | 40.3 |
| 14.8 | 13.8 | 14.4 | Long-Term Debt | | 17.3 | 21.4 | 9.3 | 13.6 | 14.7 |
| .7 | .7 | .9 | Deferred Taxes | | .0 | 1.0 | .3 | 1.0 | 1.2 |
| 7.5 | 7.0 | 6.1 | All Other Non-Current | | 5.5 | 12.6 | 7.3 | 2.5 | 6.3 |
| 36.0 | 38.8 | 38.4 | Net Worth | | 42.1 | 30.0 | 43.3 | 50.4 | 37.5 |
| 100.0 | 100.0 | 100.0 | Total Liabilities & Net Worth | | 100.0 | 100.0 | 100.0 | 100.0 | 100.0 |
| | | | **INCOME DATA** | | | | | | |
| 100.0 | 100.0 | 100.0 | Net Sales | | 100.0 | 100.0 | 100.0 | 100.0 | 100.0 |
| 25.3 | 25.9 | 26.4 | Gross Profit | | 54.9 | 36.1 | 34.4 | 25.5 | 19.9 |
| 21.1 | 19.9 | 20.3 | Operating Expenses | | 45.9 | 29.1 | 25.9 | 19.0 | 14.9 |
| 4.2 | 6.0 | 6.1 | Operating Profit | | 9.0 | 7.1 | 8.4 | 6.6 | 5.1 |
| 1.0 | 1.0 | 1.0 | All Other Expenses (net) | | 1.9 | .5 | .5 | 1.7 | .8 |
| 3.1 | 4.9 | 5.1 | Profit Before Taxes | | 7.1 | 6.6 | 7.9 | 4.9 | 4.3 |
| | | | **RATIOS** | | | | | | |
| 2.5 | 2.5 | 3.0 | | | 3.9 | 3.5 | 4.4 | 4.2 | 2.1 |
| 1.6 | 1.7 | 1.7 | Current | | 2.8 | 1.6 | 2.4 | 2.0 | 1.5 |
| 1.1 | 1.1 | 1.3 | | | 1.4 | 1.1 | 1.1 | 1.3 | 1.3 |
| 1.5 | 1.6 | 1.8 | | | 2.8 | 2.0 | 2.4 | 2.2 | 1.1 |
| .8 | .9 | .9 | Quick | | 2.1 | .9 | 1.3 | 1.1 | .8 |
| .5 | .5 | .6 | | | .9 | .6 | .4 | .6 | .6 |
| 36  10.1 | 38  9.6 | 33  11.1 | | 24  15.1 | 29  12.6 | 27  13.5 | 34  10.8 | | 34  10.7 |
| 47  7.8 | 47  7.8 | 42  8.6 | Sales/Receivables | 38  9.6 | 38  9.7 | 40  9.1 | 42  8.6 | | 45  8.1 |
| 57  6.5 | 56  6.5 | 56  6.5 | | 58  6.3 | 59  6.2 | 51  7.1 | 52  7.0 | | 56  6.5 |
| 36  10.0 | 38  9.6 | 36  10.1 | | 14  25.8 | 27  13.5 | 39  9.4 | 31  11.6 | | 37  9.8 |
| 55  6.6 | 58  6.2 | 56  6.5 | Cost of Sales/Inventory | 43  8.4 | 54  6.8 | 59  6.2 | 54  6.7 | | 55  6.6 |
| 83  4.4 | 84  4.4 | 78  4.7 | | 118  3.1 | 99  3.7 | 96  3.8 | 76  4.8 | | 72  5.1 |
| 22  16.3 | 24  15.5 | 22  16.7 | | 14  25.8 | 16  23.1 | 18  20.0 | 15  23.6 | | 27  13.5 |
| 36  10.0 | 36  10.2 | 33  10.9 | Cost of Sales/Payables | 48  7.6 | 25  14.8 | 35  10.3 | 30  12.1 | | 35  10.4 |
| 49  7.4 | 51  7.1 | 49  7.4 | | 61  6.0 | 65  5.6 | 55  6.6 | 40  9.1 | | 49  7.4 |
| 5.4 | 5.5 | 4.6 | | | 3.4 | 5.4 | 3.8 | 3.9 | 5.8 |
| 11.8 | 9.4 | 8.5 | Sales/Working Capital | | 6.3 | 6.5 | 7.5 | 6.8 | 10.7 |
| 77.2 | 29.8 | 21.6 | | | 68.6 | 28.8 | 42.9 | 17.4 | 18.0 |
| 11.1 | 17.1 | 22.7 | | | 19.0 | 20.7 | 47.3 | 32.2 | 17.5 |
| (196)  4.0 | (189)  6.0 | (205)  6.7 | EBIT/Interest | (12)  4.7 | (13)  7.4 | (27)  12.9 | (45)  5.2 | (105)  6.7 |
| 1.0 | 2.0 | 2.6 | | | 2.2 | 3.6 | 2.7 | 1.8 | 2.9 |
| 5.3 | 11.6 | 8.5 | Net Profit + Depr., Dep., | | | | | 6.7 | 9.2 |
| (48)  2.4 | (60)  5.3 | (71)  3.8 | Amort./Cur. Mat. L/T/D | | | | (17)  2.9 | (45)  3.9 |
| .8 | 2.1 | 1.1 | | | | | | -.5 | 1.5 |
| .3 | .3 | .3 | | | .2 | .1 | .2 | .3 | .4 |
| .7 | .7 | .7 | Fixed/Worth | | .7 | .9 | .5 | .6 | .7 |
| 2.1 | 2.3 | 1.8 | | | 1.9 | 4.0 | 2.9 | 1.6 | 1.5 |
| .6 | .7 | .7 | | | .6 | .9 | .4 | .5 | 1.1 |
| 1.9 | 1.7 | 1.6 | Debt/Worth | | 1.6 | 1.7 | 1.5 | .9 | 2.0 |
| 5.8 | 7.1 | 4.4 | | | 3.4 | 7.1 | 4.6 | 2.9 | 4.7 |
| 40.0 | 54.8 | 45.0 | % Profit Before Taxes/Tangible | | 60.2 | 59.7 | 52.0 | 35.7 | 44.6 |
| (187)  18.4 | (182)  24.7 | (203)  22.3 | Net Worth | (12)  28.9 | (13)  35.6 | (27)  22.3 | (47)  21.1 | (101)  21.5 |
| 5.3 | 8.7 | 10.1 | | | 11.6 | 15.3 | 9.8 | 8.2 | 10.6 |
| 12.6 | 16.9 | 15.3 | % Profit Before Taxes/Total | | 20.1 | 28.6 | 31.6 | 16.0 | 13.7 |
| 5.5 | 7.9 | 8.3 | Assets | | 10.7 | 12.4 | 9.8 | 8.4 | 7.8 |
| .0 | 2.4 | 2.8 | | | 5.5 | 2.7 | 2.2 | 2.6 | 3.5 |
| 18.7 | 19.4 | 19.2 | | | 35.7 | 77.9 | 46.8 | 14.4 | 17.4 |
| 6.5 | 7.0 | 8.7 | Sales/Net Fixed Assets | | 12.0 | 8.0 | 12.3 | 7.4 | 8.3 |
| 4.2 | 4.5 | 5.1 | | | 4.7 | 3.2 | 5.2 | 5.1 | 5.0 |
| 2.7 | 2.7 | 2.8 | | | 2.5 | 2.7 | 3.4 | 2.6 | 2.9 |
| 1.9 | 2.1 | 2.1 | Sales/Total Assets | | 1.5 | 2.3 | 2.4 | 1.9 | 2.1 |
| 1.4 | 1.5 | 1.5 | | | 1.2 | 1.2 | 1.4 | 1.5 | 1.5 |
| 1.1 | 1.3 | 1.7 | | | .5 | 1.5 | 1.0 | 1.1 | .9 |
| (181)  2.5 | (178)  2.3 | (192)  1.7 | % Depr., Dep., Amort./Sales | (12)  1.4 | (12)  2.9 | (28)  1.9 | (45)  2.1 | (93)  1.5 |
| 4.5 | 3.9 | 3.4 | | | 5.4 | 5.6 | 4.1 | 4.1 | 2.8 |
| 1.7 | 1.3 | 1.7 | % Officers', Directors' | | | | 2.6 | 1.4 | .5 |
| (57)  3.7 | (59)  3.4 | (57)  3.2 | Owners' Comp/Sales | | | (14)  3.7 | (22)  3.1 | (11)  1.8 |
| 8.0 | 7.0 | 5.2 | | | | | 5.0 | 4.9 | 4.5 |
| 11283485M | 11989088M | 14360501M | Net Sales ($) | 1938M | 29826M | 63539M | 230954M | 874676M | 13159568M |
| 6707986M | 6706966M | 7384258M | Total Assets ($) | 964M | 19879M | 38887M | 119549M | 511318M | 6693661M |

## Current Data Sorted by Assets      Comparative Historical Data

| | 0-500M | 500M-2MM | 2-10MM | 10-50MM | 50-100MM | 100-250MM | Type of Statement | 4/1/07-3/31/08 ALL | 4/1/08-3/31/09 ALL |
|---|---|---|---|---|---|---|---|---|---|
| | | | 3 | 2 | 2 | 3 | Unqualified | 13 | 15 |
| | | | 4 | 3 | | | Reviewed | 9 | 8 |
| | | 2 | 3 | | | | Compiled | 4 | 3 |
| | 3 | 3 | 3 | | | | Tax Returns | 6 | 6 |
| | | | 6 | 7 | 1 | 2 | Other | 11 | 19 |
| | | 14 (4/1-9/30/11) | | 33 (10/1/11-3/31/12) | | | | | |
| NUMBER OF STATEMENTS | 3 | 5 | 19 | 12 | 3 | 5 | | 43 | 51 |
| | % | % | % | % | % | % | ASSETS | % | % |
| | | | 10.6 | 3.5 | | | Cash & Equivalents | 6.9 | 6.7 |
| | | | 21.4 | 16.0 | | | Trade Receivables (net) | 24.8 | 23.4 |
| | | | 29.8 | 37.6 | | | Inventory | 31.3 | 32.9 |
| | | | 1.5 | 4.4 | | | All Other Current | 4.8 | 2.8 |
| | | | 63.4 | 61.5 | | | Total Current | 67.8 | 65.8 |
| | | | 26.8 | 32.0 | | | Fixed Assets (net) | 26.7 | 26.6 |
| | | | 2.6 | 3.2 | | | Intangibles (net) | 1.8 | 3.0 |
| | | | 7.1 | 3.3 | | | All Other Non-Current | 3.8 | 4.5 |
| | | | 100.0 | 100.0 | | | Total | 100.0 | 100.0 |
| | | | | | | | LIABILITIES | | |
| | | | 15.0 | 16.9 | | | Notes Payable-Short Term | 15.8 | 20.2 |
| | | | 6.1 | 2.2 | | | Cur. Mat.-L.T.D. | 4.2 | 5.1 |
| | | | 11.4 | 16.5 | | | Trade Payables | 19.2 | 20.7 |
| | | | .1 | .2 | | | Income Taxes Payable | .5 | .6 |
| | | | 9.3 | 6.4 | | | All Other Current | 9.1 | 6.2 |
| | | | 42.0 | 42.1 | | | Total Current | 48.8 | 52.7 |
| | | | 12.3 | 18.6 | | | Long-Term Debt | 22.0 | 18.6 |
| | | | .7 | 1.1 | | | Deferred Taxes | .8 | .4 |
| | | | 1.1 | 3.9 | | | All Other Non-Current | 5.4 | 5.8 |
| | | | 44.0 | 34.3 | | | Net Worth | 23.0 | 22.5 |
| | | | 100.0 | 100.0 | | | Total Liabilties & Net Worth | 100.0 | 100.0 |
| | | | | | | | INCOME DATA | | |
| | | | 100.0 | 100.0 | | | Net Sales | 100.0 | 100.0 |
| | | | 32.3 | 28.0 | | | Gross Profit | 27.5 | 29.2 |
| | | | 23.8 | 24.0 | | | Operating Expenses | 23.1 | 23.2 |
| | | | 8.4 | 4.0 | | | Operating Profit | 4.4 | 6.0 |
| | | | .1 | .8 | | | All Other Expenses (net) | 2.4 | 1.9 |
| | | | 8.3 | 3.2 | | | Profit Before Taxes | 1.9 | 4.1 |
| | | | | | | | RATIOS | | |
| | | | 2.0 | 1.9 | | | | 2.1 | 2.2 |
| | | | 1.4 | 1.5 | | | Current | 1.3 | 1.3 |
| | | | 1.2 | 1.3 | | | | 1.1 | 1.1 |
| | | | 1.2 | .7 | | | | 1.1 | .9 |
| | | | .7 | .5 | | | Quick | .7 | .7 |
| | | | .5 | .2 | | | | .4 | .3 |
| | | | 18   20.0 | 17   20.9 | | | | 27   13.7 | 26   14.0 |
| | | | 27   13.6 | 31   11.6 | | | Sales/Receivables | 36   10.2 | 38   9.5 |
| | | | 49   7.4 | 48   7.6 | | | | 54   6.7 | 48   7.6 |
| | | | 41   9.0 | 59   6.2 | | | | 42   8.6 | 44   8.4 |
| | | | 72   5.1 | 130   2.8 | | | Cost of Sales/Inventory | 66   5.5 | 77   4.8 |
| | | | 114   3.2 | 203   1.8 | | | | 103   3.5 | 105   3.5 |
| | | | 13   28.2 | 25   14.4 | | | | 20   18.6 | 19   19.3 |
| | | | 22   16.9 | 38   9.7 | | | Cost of Sales/Payables | 42   8.7 | 35   10.5 |
| | | | 50   7.3 | 54   6.7 | | | | 67   5.4 | 52   7.1 |
| | | | 7.4 | 4.8 | | | | 7.0 | 7.8 |
| | | | 14.9 | 8.6 | | | Sales/Working Capital | 10.5 | 15.0 |
| | | | 25.3 | 18.1 | | | | 48.4 | 59.0 |
| | | | 42.6 | 9.1 | | | | 6.6 | 8.0 |
| | | | 8.2 | 3.5 | | | EBIT/Interest | (38)   1.9 | (46)   3.9 |
| | | | 4.1 | 1.4 | | | | .8 | 1.5 |
| | | | | | | | Net Profit + Depr., Dep., | 8.1 | 24.6 |
| | | | | | | | Amort./Cur. Mat. L/T/D | (10)   2.1 | (11)   11.0 |
| | | | | | | | | 1.2 | 2.1 |
| | | | .3 | .5 | | | | .6 | .5 |
| | | | .7 | .8 | | | Fixed/Worth | 1.1 | .8 |
| | | | 1.2 | 1.4 | | | | 3.7 | 4.8 |
| | | | .6 | 1.0 | | | | 1.2 | 1.3 |
| | | | 1.3 | 2.0 | | | Debt/Worth | 4.1 | 2.7 |
| | | | 3.3 | 4.8 | | | | 15.8 | 34.3 |
| | | | 58.4 | 25.0 | | | | 52.1 | 48.7 |
| | | (18) | 28.8 | (11)   18.7 | | | % Profit Before Taxes/Tangible Net Worth | (36)   20.6 | (41)   28.0 |
| | | | 17.8 | 1.9 | | | | 4.5 | 9.4 |
| | | | 23.7 | 11.3 | | | | 11.5 | 16.2 |
| | | | 9.5 | 5.1 | | | % Profit Before Taxes/Total Assets | 2.9 | 6.9 |
| | | | 6.5 | .8 | | | | -.6 | 2.9 |
| | | | 17.4 | 12.4 | | | | 23.2 | 17.4 |
| | | | 10.8 | 7.5 | | | Sales/Net Fixed Assets | 12.3 | 10.6 |
| | | | 5.3 | 3.7 | | | | 6.0 | 6.5 |
| | | | 3.1 | 2.0 | | | | 3.1 | 3.1 |
| | | | 2.1 | 1.7 | | | Sales/Total Assets | 2.2 | 2.1 |
| | | | 1.6 | 1.2 | | | | 1.7 | 1.7 |
| | | | 1.0 | .9 | | | | .6 | .9 |
| | | (18) | 1.8 | 2.0 | | | % Depr., Dep., Amort./Sales | (37)   1.7 | (42)   1.8 |
| | | | 3.3 | 5.6 | | | | 3.0 | 2.9 |
| | | | | | | | | 3.4 | 1.4 |
| | | | | | | | % Officers', Directors' Owners' Comp/Sales | (12)   4.6 | (14)   3.8 |
| | | | | | | | | 6.6 | 6.1 |
| | 3640M | 16102M | 250581M | 450865M | 492415M | 1064145M | Net Sales ($) | 2075756M | 2268082M |
| | 629M | 6355M | 103151M | 249216M | 195858M | 671573M | Total Assets ($) | 833880M | 990805M |

M = $ thousand    MM = $ million
See Pages 9 through 22 for Explanation of Ratios and Data

## Comparative Historical Data         Current Data Sorted by Sales

| 4/1/09-3/31/10 ALL | 4/1/10-3/31/11 ALL | 4/1/11-3/31/12 ALL | Type of Statement | 0-1MM | 1-3MM | 3-5MM | 5-10MM | 10-25MM | 25MM & OVER |
|---|---|---|---|---|---|---|---|---|---|
| 17 | 15 | 10 | Unqualified | | | | | 2 | 7 |
| 13 | 15 | 7 | Reviewed | | 1 | | 1 | 4 | 1 |
| 4 | 7 | 5 | Compiled | | 2 | | 2 | 1 | |
| 3 | 4 | 9 | Tax Returns | 2 | 2 | 1 | 1 | 3 | |
| 10 | 16 | 16 | Other | | | 2 | 2 | 3 | 10 |
| | | | | 14 (4/1-9/30/11) | | | 33 (10/1/11-3/31/12) | | |
| 47 | 57 | 47 | **NUMBER OF STATEMENTS** | 2 | 5 | 3 | 6 | 13 | 18 |
| % | % | % | **ASSETS** | % | % | % | % | % | % |
| 8.5 | 8.6 | 8.5 | Cash & Equivalents | | | | | 7.3 | 7.3 |
| 25.4 | 21.5 | 19.4 | Trade Receivables (net) | | | | | 14.7 | 22.1 |
| 31.4 | 27.0 | 30.9 | Inventory | | | | | 29.8 | 36.3 |
| 1.6 | 3.4 | 2.6 | All Other Current | | | | | 2.8 | 3.7 |
| 66.9 | 60.4 | 61.5 | Total Current | | | | | 54.6 | 69.4 |
| 25.4 | 31.6 | 31.0 | Fixed Assets (net) | | | | | 35.4 | 24.4 |
| 2.8 | 2.7 | 2.6 | Intangibles (net) | | | | | 2.8 | 3.3 |
| 5.0 | 5.3 | 4.9 | All Other Non-Current | | | | | 7.1 | 3.0 |
| 100.0 | 100.0 | 100.0 | Total | | | | | 100.0 | 100.0 |
| | | | **LIABILITIES** | | | | | | |
| 16.0 | 11.2 | 30.4 | Notes Payable-Short Term | | | | | 14.5 | 14.7 |
| 3.5 | 4.2 | 4.3 | Cur. Mat.-L.T.D. | | | | | 3.0 | 4.8 |
| 18.5 | 12.7 | 16.1 | Trade Payables | | | | | 8.6 | 20.4 |
| .5 | .6 | .3 | Income Taxes Payable | | | | | .0 | .8 |
| 7.9 | 7.6 | 9.3 | All Other Current | | | | | 7.2 | 8.2 |
| 46.4 | 36.2 | 60.4 | Total Current | | | | | 33.5 | 49.0 |
| 13.5 | 19.9 | 18.4 | Long-Term Debt | | | | | 21.2 | 15.3 |
| .9 | .6 | .9 | Deferred Taxes | | | | | 1.3 | .9 |
| 2.5 | 3.8 | 4.1 | All Other Non-Current | | | | | .3 | 3.1 |
| 36.7 | 39.4 | 16.1 | Net Worth | | | | | 43.8 | 31.7 |
| 100.0 | 100.0 | 100.0 | Total Liabilities & Net Worth | | | | | 100.0 | 100.0 |
| | | | **INCOME DATA** | | | | | | |
| 100.0 | 100.0 | 100.0 | Net Sales | | | | | 100.0 | 100.0 |
| 30.8 | 33.8 | 31.4 | Gross Profit | | | | | 37.5 | 20.4 |
| 23.9 | 25.9 | 24.5 | Operating Expenses | | | | | 31.1 | 13.3 |
| 6.9 | 7.9 | 6.9 | Operating Profit | | | | | 6.4 | 7.1 |
| 1.6 | 1.1 | 1.1 | All Other Expenses (net) | | | | | .3 | 1.3 |
| 5.3 | 6.8 | 5.8 | Profit Before Taxes | | | | | 6.0 | 5.8 |
| | | | **RATIOS** | | | | | | |
| 2.4 | 2.5 | 2.0 | | | | | | 2.3 | 1.9 |
| 1.7 | 1.7 | 1.4 | Current | | | | | 1.4 | 1.5 |
| 1.2 | 1.2 | 1.2 | | | | | | 1.2 | 1.2 |
| 1.3 | 1.5 | 1.0 | | | | | | .9 | 1.1 |
| .7 | .8 | .6 | Quick | | | | | .7 | .6 |
| .5 | .5 | .4 | | | | | | .4 | .4 |
| 18   20.0 | 19   19.0 | 18   20.7 | | | | | | 18   20.4 | 16   22.7 |
| 30   12.3 | 31   11.7 | 29   12.6 | Sales/Receivables | | | | | 22   16.3 | 30   12.1 |
| 62   5.9 | 58   6.3 | 46   8.0 | | | | | | 41   8.9 | 40   9.2 |
| 44   8.3 | 42   8.8 | 42   8.6 | | | | | | 41   9.0 | 36   10.0 |
| 84   4.3 | 61   6.0 | 78   4.7 | Cost of Sales/Inventory | | | | | 78   4.7 | 79   4.6 |
| 123   3.0 | 102   3.6 | 126   2.9 | | | | | | 203   1.8 | 122   3.0 |
| 21   17.3 | 20   18.2 | 19   19.1 | | | | | | 16   23.4 | 19   18.9 |
| 36   10.1 | 29   12.6 | 28   12.9 | Cost of Sales/Payables | | | | | 25   14.6 | 25   14.4 |
| 71   5.2 | 46   7.9 | 53   6.9 | | | | | | 42   8.7 | 59   6.2 |
| 6.0 | 5.4 | 6.4 | | | | | | 5.4 | 6.3 |
| 8.8 | 9.5 | 11.0 | Sales/Working Capital | | | | | 14.2 | 9.9 |
| 22.4 | 17.5 | 25.3 | | | | | | 23.0 | 22.5 |
| 10.7 | 15.4 | 21.4 | | | | | | 47.0 | 23.4 |
| (44)   4.3 | (51)   4.1 | 6.4 | EBIT/Interest | | | | | 7.6 | 6.4 |
| 1.7 | 1.9 | 2.7 | | | | | | 2.7 | 2.1 |
| 5.6 | 49.1 | 4.7 | Net Profit + Depr., Dep., | | | | | | |
| (14)   2.1 | (14)   3.0 | (15)   1.9 | Amort./Cur. Mat. L/T/D | | | | | | |
| 1.2 | 1.6 | .1 | | | | | | | |
| .4 | .4 | .5 | | | | | | .4 | .5 |
| .6 | .8 | .7 | Fixed/Worth | | | | | .9 | .7 |
| 1.2 | 1.6 | 1.3 | | | | | | 1.3 | 1.2 |
| .6 | .6 | .9 | | | | | | .6 | .9 |
| 1.4 | 1.4 | 1.7 | Debt/Worth | | | | | 1.3 | 2.0 |
| 3.8 | 3.2 | 4.6 | | | | | | 2.1 | 4.5 |
| 37.2 | 40.7 | 53.8 | % Profit Before Taxes/Tangible | | | | | 37.0 | 54.0 |
| (40)   20.3 | (51)   22.3 | (41)   23.6 | Net Worth | | | | | (12)   19.2 | (16)   32.2 |
| 8.5 | 13.0 | 12.4 | | | | | | 9.5 | 14.3 |
| 15.6 | 15.6 | 21.2 | % Profit Before Taxes/Total | | | | | 22.0 | 21.5 |
| 6.7 | 8.0 | 8.1 | Assets | | | | | 7.8 | 8.7 |
| 2.5 | 2.7 | 4.6 | | | | | | 3.2 | 4.4 |
| 17.3 | 12.5 | 16.6 | | | | | | 14.2 | 15.1 |
| 9.5 | 8.2 | 9.8 | Sales/Net Fixed Assets | | | | | 5.9 | 10.5 |
| 5.9 | 4.3 | 4.4 | | | | | | 3.0 | 7.8 |
| 2.8 | 2.7 | 2.9 | | | | | | 2.6 | 3.0 |
| 2.1 | 2.0 | 1.9 | Sales/Total Assets | | | | | 1.8 | 2.0 |
| 1.6 | 1.4 | 1.4 | | | | | | 1.3 | 1.7 |
| .9 | 1.2 | .9 | | | | | | 1.6 | .6 |
| (39)   1.4 | (50)   2.2 | (44)   1.8 | % Depr., Dep., Amort./Sales | | | | | (12)   2.0 | (16)   .9 |
| 2.7 | 3.4 | 3.3 | | | | | | 6.7 | 1.2 |
| 3.2 | 1.9 | 1.4 | % Officers', Directors' | | | | | | |
| (15)   4.5 | (17)   4.6 | (14)   4.2 | Owners' Comp/Sales | | | | | | |
| 6.8 | 9.6 | 9.3 | | | | | | | |
| 2604101M | 1892888M | 2277748M | Net Sales ($) | 948M | 10032M | 11043M | 43131M | 191202M | 2021392M |
| 1109116M | 994920M | 1226782M | Total Assets ($) | 478M | 6847M | 6316M | 23934M | 119715M | 1069492M |

© RMA 2012

**M = $ thousand    MM = $ million**
See Pages 9 through 22 for Explanation of Ratios and Data

**Current Data Sorted by Assets**        **Comparative Historical Data**

### Type of Statement

| 0-500M | 500M-2MM | 2-10MM | 10-50MM | 50-100MM | 100-250MM | | 4/1/07-3/31/08 ALL | 4/1/08-3/31/09 ALL |
|---|---|---|---|---|---|---|---|---|
| | | 1 | 5 | 2 | 3 | Unqualified | 5 | 7 |
| | 1 | 4 | 2 | 1 | | Reviewed | 3 | 2 |
| | 1 | 4 | 1 | | | Compiled | 6 | 6 |
| | 3 | 1' | | | | Tax Returns | 4 | 2 |
| | 1 | 5 | 5 | | | Other | 12 | 11 |
| | **6** | **14** | **14** | **3** | **3** | **NUMBER OF STATEMENTS** | **30** | **28** |
| % | % | % | % | % | % | **ASSETS** | % | % |
| | | 4.7 | 5.7 | | | Cash & Equivalents | 7.7 | 6.3 |
| | | 28.5 | 24.5 | | | Trade Receivables (net) | 24.0 | 23.3 |
| | | 26.4 | 34.4 | | | Inventory | 26.8 | 28.8 |
| | | 1.1 | 5.0 | | | All Other Current | 1.8 | 2.4 |
| | | 60.7 | 69.6 | | | Total Current | 60.3 | 60.9 |
| | | 33.4 | 27.5 | | | Fixed Assets (net) | 33.5 | 31.8 |
| | | 2.1 | 1.1 | | | Intangibles (net) | 1.3 | .9 |
| | | 3.8 | 1.8 | | | All Other Non-Current | 4.9 | 6.4 |
| | | 100.0 | 100.0 | | | Total | 100.0 | 100.0 |
| | | | | | | **LIABILITIES** | | |
| | | 13.8 | 16.6 | | | Notes Payable-Short Term | 15.6 | 17.8 |
| | | 7.4 | 2.6 | | | Cur. Mat.-L.T.D. | 3.1 | 3.2 |
| | | 14.9 | 23.9 | | | Trade Payables | 16.9 | 20.1 |
| | | .5 | .0 | | | Income Taxes Payable | .3 | .2 |
| | | 5.1 | 11.8 | | | All Other Current | 10.7 | 10.0 |
| | | 41.7 | 55.0 | | | Total Current | 46.7 | 51.2 |
| | | 16.4 | 12.6 | | | Long-Term Debt | 16.4 | 21.8 |
| | | 1.8 | .5 | | | Deferred Taxes | .6 | .7 |
| | | 7.6 | .9 | | | All Other Non-Current | 4.1 | 4.1 |
| | | 32.5 | 31.0 | | | Net Worth | 32.2 | 22.2 |
| | | 100.0 | 100.0 | | | Total Liabilities & Net Worth | 100.0 | 100.0 |
| | | | | | | **INCOME DATA** | | |
| | | 100.0 | 100.0 | | | Net Sales | 100.0 | 100.0 |
| | | 38.7 | 21.6 | | | Gross Profit | 27.5 | 27.9 |
| | | 34.4 | 18.2 | | | Operating Expenses | 22.4 | 21.9 |
| | | 4.3 | 3.4 | | | Operating Profit | 5.0 | 6.0 |
| | | -.7 | -.3 | | | All Other Expenses (net) | .6 | 1.5 |
| | | 5.0 | 3.7 | | | Profit Before Taxes | 4.5 | 4.5 |
| | | | | | | **RATIOS** | | |
| | | 2.4 | 1.4 | | | | 1.7 | 1.4 |
| | | 1.5 | 1.3 | | | Current | 1.2 | 1.2 |
| | | 1.1 | 1.2 | | | | .9 | 1.0 |
| | | 1.7 | .8 | | | | 1.1 | .8 |
| | | 1.0 | .6 | | | Quick | .6 | .6 |
| | | .5 | .4 | | | | .4 | .3 |
| | | 29   12.6 | 33   11.0 | | | | 19   19.3 | 20   18.6 |
| | | 43   8.5 | 35   10.4 | | | Sales/Receivables | 32   11.3 | 33   11.1 |
| | | 87   4.2 | 53   6.9 | | | | 58   6.3 | 59   6.2 |
| | | 24   15.1 | 35   10.5 | | | | 40   9.2 | 37   9.9 |
| | | 70   5.2 | 81   4.5 | | | Cost of Sales/Inventory | 60   6.1 | 76   4.8 |
| | | 101   3.6 | 146   2.5 | | | | 92   4.0 | 97   3.8 |
| | | 20   18.1 | 26   14.1 | | | | 19   18.9 | 24   15.0 |
| | | 33   10.9 | 36   10.2 | | | Cost of Sales/Payables | 35   10.6 | 40   9.2 |
| | | 72   5.1 | 91   4.0 | | | | 52   7.1 | 60   6.1 |
| | | 4.2 | 11.8 | | | | 8.3 | 14.5 |
| | | 18.7 | 13.2 | | | Sales/Working Capital | 23.4 | 23.7 |
| | | 40.5 | 26.4 | | | | -44.9 | -194.8 |
| | | 26.2 | 8.9 | | | | 8.1 | 9.1 |
| | | (13) 6.1 | (13) 4.6 | | | EBIT/Interest | (27) 3.4 | 5.6 |
| | | 2.0 | 1.6 | | | | 1.8 | 1.4 |
| | | | | | | Net Profit + Depr., Dep., Amort./Cur. Mat. L/T/D | | |
| | | .8 | .6 | | | | .6 | .4 |
| | | 1.1 | .9 | | | Fixed/Worth | .9 | 1.2 |
| | | 1.9 | 1.5 | | | | 2.6 | 2.8 |
| | | 1.1 | 1.1 | | | | 1.2 | 1.6 |
| | | 1.8 | 2.6 | | | Debt/Worth | 3.4 | 4.0 |
| | | 11.4 | 5.6 | | | | 7.2 | 7.1 |
| | | 44.4 | 70.2 | | | | 67.1 | 64.7 |
| | | (13) 30.0 | (13) 21.5 | | | % Profit Before Taxes/Tangible Net Worth | (27) 28.3 | (25) 48.4 |
| | | 9.6 | 14.1 | | | | 20.4 | 16.1 |
| | | 12.9 | 14.9 | | | | 19.7 | 16.0 |
| | | 8.0 | 6.7 | | | % Profit Before Taxes/Total Assets | 9.1 | 7.4 |
| | | 2.8 | 2.1 | | | | 2.5 | 1.0 |
| | | 12.5 | 19.3 | | | | 14.6 | 15.1 |
| | | 5.8 | 8.5 | | | Sales/Net Fixed Assets | 6.9 | 8.3 |
| | | 4.5 | 4.3 | | | | 4.2 | 3.4 |
| | | 3.1 | 3.7 | | | | 2.9 | 2.9 |
| | | 1.9 | 2.1 | | | Sales/Total Assets | 1.8 | 1.7 |
| | | 1.4 | 1.1 | | | | 1.6 | 1.5 |
| | | 1.7 | .8 | | | | 1.1 | .9 |
| | | (13) 3.1 | (12) 1.9 | | | % Depr., Dep., Amort./Sales | (29) 2.0 | (25) 2.0 |
| | | 5.7 | 3.7 | | | | 2.9 | 5.7 |
| | | | | | | % Officers', Directors' Owners' Comp/Sales | | |
| | 24967M | 158646M | 1032391M | 326081M | 479218M | Net Sales ($) | 1207091M | 2959133M |
| | 8517M | 71874M | 347750M | 222964M | 474654M | Total Assets ($) | 501770M | 1109573M |

M = $ thousand    MM = $ million
See Pages 9 through 22 for Explanation of Ratios and Data

## Comparative Historical Data | Current Data Sorted by Sales

| | | | | | | Type of Statement | | | | | | |
|---|---|---|---|---|---|---|---|---|---|---|---|---|
| | 13 | | 12 | | 11 | Unqualified | | | | 2 | 2 | 9 |
| | 2 | | 7 | | 8 | Reviewed | | | | 2 | 2 | 4 |
| | 6 | | 4 | | 6 | Compiled | | 1 | | 1 | 3 | 1 |
| | 8 | | 4 | | 4 | Tax Returns | | | 3 | | | 1 |
| | 7 | | 10 | | 11 | Other | 1 | 2 | | 4 | 1 | 3 |
| | 4/1/09- | | 4/1/10- | | 4/1/11- | | | 11 (4/1-9/30/11) | | 29 (10/1/11-3/31/12) | | |
| | 3/31/10 | | 3/31/11 | | 3/31/12 | | 0-1MM | 1-3MM | 3-5MM | 5-10MM | 10-25MM | 25MM & OVER |
| | ALL | | ALL | | ALL | | | | | | | |
| | 36 | | 37 | | 40 | NUMBER OF STATEMENTS | 1 | 3 | 3 | 7 | 8 | 18 |
| | % | | % | | % | ASSETS | % | % | % | % | % | % |
| | 8.4 | | 9.5 | | 6.8 | Cash & Equivalents | | | | | | 9.8 |
| | 21.7 | | 24.9 | | 25.6 | Trade Receivables (net) | | | | | | 22.5 |
| | 24.1 | | 26.0 | | 28.0 | Inventory | | | | | | 32.2 |
| | 3.2 | | 2.4 | | 2.7 | All Other Current | | | | | | 3.5 |
| | 57.3 | | 62.7 | | 63.1 | Total Current | | | | | | 67.9 |
| | 34.5 | | 31.1 | | 30.5 | Fixed Assets (net) | | | | | | 23.8 |
| | 3.8 | | 1.4 | | 3.1 | Intangibles (net) | | | | | | 4.8 |
| | 4.4 | | 4.8 | | 3.3 | All Other Non-Current | | | | | | 3.5 |
| | 100.0 | | 100.0 | | 100.0 | Total | | | | | | 100.0 |
| | | | | | | LIABILITIES | | | | | | |
| | 13.0 | | 12.0 | | 12.5 | Notes Payable-Short Term | | | | | | 15.2 |
| | 5.2 | | 3.0 | | 5.6 | Cur. Mat.-L.T.D. | | | | | | 6.1 |
| | 12.9 | | 16.0 | | 16.4 | - Trade Payables | | | | | | 16.7 |
| | .2 | | .1 | | .3 | Income Taxes Payable | | | | | | .3 |
| | 11.6 | | 11.1 | | 9.4 | All Other Current | | | | | | 11.3 |
| | 42.9 | | 42.2 | | 44.2 | Total Current | | | | | | 49.5 |
| | 19.4 | | 20.9 | | 15.9 | Long-Term Debt | | | | | | 15.2 |
| | .8 | | .9 | | 1.6 | Deferred Taxes | | | | | | 1.7 |
| | 5.6 | | 5.5 | | 5.7 | All Other Non-Current | | | | | | 3.4 |
| | 31.3 | | 30.5 | | 32.7 | Net Worth | | | | | | 30.1 |
| | 100.0 | | 100.0 | | 100.0 | Total Liabilties & Net Worth | | | | | | 100.0 |
| | | | | | | INCOME DATA | | | | | | |
| | 100.0 | | 100.0 | | 100.0 | Net Sales | | | | | | 100.0 |
| | 30.8 | | 29.0 | | 31.3 | Gross Profit | | | | | | 23.6 |
| | 27.3 | | 22.0 | | 25.0 | Operating Expenses | | | | | | 14.9 |
| | 3.6 | | 7.0 | | 6.4 | Operating Profit | | | | | | 8.7 |
| | .1 | | .0 | | .1 | All Other Expenses (net) | | | | | | .9 |
| | 3.5 | | 7.0 | | 6.2 | Profit Before Taxes | | | | | | 7.8 |
| | | | | | | RATIOS | | | | | | |
| | 2.1 | | 2.0 | | 2.0 | | | | | | | 1.8 |
| | 1.3 | | 1.5 | | 1.4 | Current | | | | | | 1.3 |
| | 1.0 | | 1.1 | | 1.1 | | | | | | | 1.2 |
| | 1.1 | | 1.3 | | 1.5 | | | | | | | 1.1 |
| | .7 | | .8 | | .7 | Quick | | | | | | .6 |
| | .4 | | .5 | | .5 | | | | | | | .4 |
| 17 | 21.4 | 27 | 13.8 | 27 | 13.3 | | | | | | 18 | 20.5 |
| 30 | 12.0 | 37 | 9.8 | 38 | 9.6 | Sales/Receivables | | | | | 34 | 10.7 |
| 49 | 7.5 | 47 | 7.7 | 62 | 5.9 | | | | | | 46 | 7.9 |
| 21 | 17.6 | 31 | 11.7 | 32 | 11.4 | | | | | | 36 | 10.2 |
| 55 | 6.6 | 61 | 6.0 | 69 | 5.3 | Cost of Sales/Inventory | | | | | 79 | 4.6 |
| 92 | 4.0 | 109 | 3.3 | 122 | 3.0 | | | | | | 126 | 2.9 |
| 14 | 25.7 | 18 | 20.1 | 21 | 17.1 | | | | | | 19 | 18.9 |
| 22 | 16.3 | 27 | 13.3 | 33 | 11.1 | Cost of Sales/Payables | | | | | 32 | 11.5 |
| 49 | 7.5 | 42 | 8.7 | 58 | 6.3 | | | | | | 45 | 8.2 |
| | 7.6 | | 6.8 | | 7.1 | | | | | | | 9.4 |
| | 18.2 | | 12.2 | | 13.2 | Sales/Working Capital | | | | | | 13.2 |
| | -241.8 | | 76.6 | | 34.5 | | | | | | | 35.8 |
| | 9.5 | | 16.4 | | 15.0 | | | | | | | 15.2 |
| (35) | 3.7 | (35) | 6.0 | (38) | 5.8 | EBIT/Interest | | | | | (17) | 4.7 |
| | 1.0 | | 2.4 | | 1.8 | | | | | | | 2.3 |
| | | | 15.5 | | 8.9 | Net Profit + Depr., Dep., | | | | | | |
| | | (10) | 4.5 | (11) | 2.7 | Amort./Cur. Mat. L/T/D | | | | | | |
| | | | 1.4 | | 1.7 | | | | | | | |
| | .6 | | .5 | | .5 | | | | | | | .4 |
| | 1.3 | | .9 | | 1.0 | Fixed/Worth | | | | | | .9 |
| | 3.7 | | 2.0 | | 2.1 | | | | | | | 1.5 |
| | 1.2 | | .9 | | .9 | | | | | | | 1.0 |
| | 3.9 | | 2.7 | | 2.3 | Debt/Worth | | | | | | 2.9 |
| | 12.8 | | 5.4 | | 6.7 | | | | | | | 8.9 |
| | 61.1 | | 55.3 | | 53.9 | | | | | | | 73.7 |
| (33) | 29.9 | (34) | 33.5 | (36) | 29.4 | % Profit Before Taxes/Tangible | | | | | (16) | 36.4 |
| | 3.1 | | 8.7 | | 12.7 | Net Worth | | | | | | 16.9 |
| | 14.8 | | 18.0 | | 18.2 | | | | | | | 26.5 |
| | 8.4 | | 7.7 | | 8.6 | % Profit Before Taxes/Total | | | | | | 10.5 |
| | .5 | | 3.5 | | 2.7 | Assets | | | | | | 3.0 |
| | 18.1 | | 15.3 | | 17.9 | | | | | | | 19.3 |
| | 6.7 | | 11.0 | | 7.8 | Sales/Net Fixed Assets | | | | | | 9.6 |
| | 3.3 | | 4.8 | | 4.2 | | | | | | | 4.3 |
| | 3.3 | | 2.9 | | 3.2 | | | | | | | 3.3 |
| | 2.0 | | 2.1 | | 1.9 | Sales/Total Assets | | | | | | 2.1 |
| | 1.5 | | 1.5 | | 1.2 | | | | | | | 1.2 |
| | .8 | | .9 | | 1.3 | | | | | | | .9 |
| (34) | 2.1 | (34) | 1.9 | (34) | 2.1 | % Depr., Dep., Amort./Sales | | | | | (15) | 1.9 |
| | 3.9 | | 3.3 | | 4.2 | | | | | | | 3.9 |
| | | | 1.6 | | | % Officers', Directors' | | | | | | |
| | | (13) | 3.9 | | | Owners' Comp/Sales | | | | | | |
| | | | 5.1 | | | | | | | | | |
| | 2192171M | | 1672121M | | 2021303M | Net Sales ($) | 914M | 6782M | 11887M | 57180M | 114553M | 1829987M |
| | 1052433M | | 715306M | | 1125759M | Total Assets ($) | 920M | 6911M | 4168M | 36728M | 54735M | 1022297M |

© RMA 2012

M = $ thousand   MM = $ million

See Pages 9 through 22 for Explanation of Ratios and Data

## Current Data Sorted by Assets

## Comparative Historical Data

| 0-500M | 500M-2MM | 2-10MM | 10-50MM | 50-100MM | 100-250MM | Type of Statement | 4/1/07-3/31/08 ALL | 4/1/08-3/31/09 ALL |
|---|---|---|---|---|---|---|---|---|
| | | 2 | 7 | 5 | 5 | Unqualified | 13 | 17 |
| | | 2 | 5 | | | Reviewed | 5 | 10 |
| | | 4 | | | | Compiled | 3 | 4 |
| | 1 | 2 | | 1 | | Tax Returns | 3 | 5 |
| | 2 | 8 | 8 | | 1 | Other | 9 | 13 |
| 16 (4/1-9/30/11) | | | 37 (10/1/11-3/31/12) | | | | | |
| 3 | 18 | 20 | 6 | 6 | | **NUMBER OF STATEMENTS** | 33 | 49 |
| % | % | % | % | % | % | **ASSETS** | % | % |
| | | 12.6 | 16.3 | | | Cash & Equivalents | 9.7 | 13.4 |
| | | 31.9 | 20.4 | | | Trade Receivables (net) | 23.9 | 22.1 |
| | | 33.6 | 29.3 | | | Inventory | 35.6 | 36.3 |
| | | 2.5 | 4.8 | | | All Other Current | 2.7 | 3.5 |
| | | 80.6 | 70.7 | | | Total Current | 71.8 | 75.3 |
| | | 11.0 | 17.5 | | | Fixed Assets (net) | 15.9 | 18.2 |
| | | 1.8 | 8.6 | | | Intangibles (net) | 8.3 | 3.2 |
| | | 6.6 | 3.2 | | | All Other Non-Current | 4.0 | 3.3 |
| | | 100.0 | 100.0 | | | Total | 100.0 | 100.0 |
| | | | | | | **LIABILITIES** | | |
| | | 14.9 | 8.8 | | | Notes Payable-Short Term | 12.9 | 17.6 |
| | | 2.3 | 2.1 | | | Cur. Mat.-L.T.D. | 4.6 | 3.9 |
| | | 17.7 | 14.0 | | | Trade Payables | 17.1 | 15.5 |
| | | .2 | 1.2 | | | Income Taxes Payable | .8 | .3 |
| | | 12.1 | 12.9 | | | All Other Current | 9.1 | 10.7 |
| | | 47.2 | 39.1 | | | Total Current | 44.4 | 48.1 |
| | | 15.1 | 9.0 | | | Long-Term Debt | 13.4 | 14.8 |
| | | .0 | .5 | | | Deferred Taxes | .4 | .4 |
| | | 2.5 | 17.3 | | | All Other Non-Current | 4.1 | 3.0 |
| | | 35.1 | 34.1 | | | Net Worth | 37.7 | 33.7 |
| | | 100.0 | 100.0 | | | Total Liabilties & Net Worth | 100.0 | 100.0 |
| | | | | | | **INCOME DATA** | | |
| | | 100.0 | 100.0 | | | Net Sales | 100.0 | 100.0 |
| | | 41.6 | 34.6 | | | Gross Profit | 32.3 | 30.9 |
| | | 33.9 | 28.2 | | | Operating Expenses | 23.7 | 26.2 |
| | | 7.7 | 6.4 | | | Operating Profit | 8.5 | 4.8 |
| | | .2 | 3.9 | | | All Other Expenses (net) | 1.7 | 1.4 |
| | | 7.5 | 2.5 | | | Profit Before Taxes | 6.9 | 3.3 |
| | | | | | | **RATIOS** | | |
| | | 3.3 | 3.2 | | | | 2.3 | 2.6 |
| | | 1.6 | 2.0 | | | Current | 1.8 | 1.4 |
| | | 1.2 | 1.3 | | | | 1.2 | 1.2 |
| | | 1.4 | 1.7 | | | | 1.3 | 1.7 |
| | | 1.1 | 1.0 | | | Quick | .7 (48) | .6 |
| | | .7 | .5 | | | | .4 | .3 |
| | | 23  16.2 | 33  11.0 | | | | 28  12.9 | 21  17.1 |
| | | 56  6.5 | 37  9.9 | | | Sales/Receivables | 44  8.2 | 34  10.8 |
| | | 78  4.7 | 54  6.8 | | | | 71  5.2 | 49  7.5 |
| | | 73  5.0 | 79  4.6 | | | | 74  5.0 | 61  5.9 |
| | | 94  3.9 | 87  4.2 | | | Cost of Sales/Inventory | 115  3.2 | 99  3.7 |
| | | 126  2.9 | 122  3.0 | | | | 162  2.3 | 140  2.6 |
| | | 16  22.5 | 26  14.2 | | | | 23  15.9 | 22  16.3 |
| | | 45  8.2 | 41  9.0 | | | Cost of Sales/Payables | 44  8.4 | 34  10.8 |
| | | 74  4.9 | 51  7.1 | | | | 56  6.5 | 52  7.0 |
| | | 4.1 | 3.6 | | | | 4.7 | 4.1 |
| | | 8.7 | 5.2 | | | Sales/Working Capital | 7.0 | 10.8 |
| | | 12.6 | 11.3 | | | | 14.3 | 27.0 |
| | | 25.7 | 64.7 | | | | 19.4 | 17.1 |
| | (17) | 5.9 | (16) 2.8 | | | EBIT/Interest | (29) 6.3 | (45) 5.8 |
| | | 2.1 | 1.8 | | | | 1.9 | 1.6 |
| | | | | | | Net Profit + Depr., Dep., Amort./Cur. Mat. L/T/D | | 13.4 |
| | | | | | | | (12) | 6.0 |
| | | | | | | | | 1.9 |
| | | .1 | .2 | | | | .1 | .1 |
| | | .3 | .6 | | | Fixed/Worth | .4 | .4 |
| | | 6.9 | 3.9 | | | | 1.6 | 1.5 |
| | | .6 | .6 | | | | .8 | .9 |
| | | 1.6 | 2.8 | | | Debt/Worth | 1.8 | 2.4 |
| | | 98.5 | 9.2 | | | | 10.6 | 6.3 |
| | | 71.8 | 30.3 | | | | 51.2 | 46.2 |
| | (15) | 33.2 | (16) 19.1 | | | % Profit Before Taxes/Tangible Net Worth | (29) 26.9 | (43) 26.1 |
| | | 7.3 | 7.6 | | | | 13.8 | 9.7 |
| | | 23.9 | 14.9 | | | | 14.8 | 14.9 |
| | | 11.4 | 7.8 | | | % Profit Before Taxes/Total Assets | 10.6 | 8.6 |
| | | 2.8 | 1.5 | | | | 3.1 | 2.2 |
| | | 121.6 | 22.3 | | | | 44.9 | 34.6 |
| | | 34.8 | 12.7 | | | Sales/Net Fixed Assets | 12.9 | 13.7 |
| | | 10.6 | 7.8 | | | | 6.2 | 5.8 |
| | | 3.4 | 2.0 | | | | 2.4 | 3.0 |
| | | 1.9 | 1.7 | | | Sales/Total Assets | 1.5 | 1.9 |
| | | 1.6 | 1.6 | | | | 1.3 | 1.5 |
| | | .2 | 1.5 | | | | .8 | .8 |
| | (12) | 1.4 | (18) 2.2 | | | % Depr., Dep., Amort./Sales | (27) 1.8 | (43) 1.5 |
| | | 3.9 | 2.5 | | | | 2.8 | 2.7 |
| | | | | | | % Officers', Directors' Owners' Comp/Sales | | 1.2 |
| | | | | | | | (14) | 3.7 |
| | | | | | | | | 6.4 |
| | 22938M | 219259M | 740784M | 617989M | 2330343M | Net Sales ($) | 1646637M | 2910263M |
| | 4771M | 94654M | 414223M | 453562M | 887441M | Total Assets ($) | 1072428M | 1376819M |

Left-hand columns 0-500M and 500M-2MM marked: **DATA NOT AVAILABLE**

M = $ thousand    MM = $ million
See Pages 9 through 22 for Explanation of Ratios and Data

**Comparative Historical Data**  |  **Current Data Sorted by Sales**

Note: In the current-data columns, the **0-1MM** and **1-3MM** columns are marked **DATA NOT AVAILABLE**. Period groupings: 16 (4/1-9/30/11) and 37 (10/1/11-3/31/12).

| 4/1/09-3/31/10 ALL | 4/1/10-3/31/11 ALL | 4/1/11-3/31/12 ALL | Type of Statement | 0-1MM | 1-3MM | 3-5MM | 5-10MM | 10-25MM | 25MM & OVER |
|---|---|---|---|---|---|---|---|---|---|
| 21 | 15 | 19 | Unqualified | 1 | 1 | | | 1 | 16 |
| 8 | 8 | 7 | Reviewed | 1 | 2 | | | 2 | 4 |
| 5 | 4 | 4 | Compiled | | | 1 | | 3 | |
| 1 | 5 | 4 | Tax Returns | | | 2 | 1 | 1 | 1 |
| 13 | 17 | 19 | Other | | 2 | 3 | | 6 | 8 |
| 48 | 49 | 53 | **NUMBER OF STATEMENTS** | | | 4 | 7 | 13 | 29 |
| % | % | % | **ASSETS** | % | % | % | % | % | % |
| 15.4 | 14.1 | 14.2 | Cash & Equivalents | | | | | 16.5 | 13.3 |
| 21.2 | 24.8 | 25.6 | Trade Receivables (net) | | | | | 30.6 | 22.1 |
| 29.4 | 26.4 | 31.6 | Inventory | | | | | 29.9 | 32.2 |
| 4.5 | 2.8 | 3.7 | All Other Current | | | | | 2.0 | 3.7 |
| 70.5 | 68.1 | 75.2 | Total Current | | | | | 79.0 | 71.3 |
| 19.9 | 17.0 | 15.6 | Fixed Assets (net) | | | | | 11.0 | 18.3 |
| 6.6 | 8.9 | 4.9 | Intangibles (net) | | | | | 4.1 | 7.0 |
| 3.0 | 6.0 | 4.4 | All Other Non-Current | | | | | 6.0 | 3.5 |
| 100.0 | 100.0 | 100.0 | Total | | | | | 100.0 | 100.0 |
| | | | **LIABILITIES** | | | | | | |
| 8.4 | 6.6 | 9.6 | Notes Payable-Short Term | | | | | 11.8 | 9.2 |
| 2.4 | 2.8 | 2.1 | Cur. Mat.-L.T.D. | | | | | 1.3 | 2.3 |
| 15.7 | 15.3 | 15.5 | Trade Payables | | | | | 17.9 | 12.8 |
| .7 | .4 | .8 | Income Taxes Payable | | | | | .0 | 1.4 |
| 12.5 | 11.6 | 12.5 | All Other Current | | | | | 16.0 | 11.6 |
| 39.7 | 36.6 | 40.4 | Total Current | | | | | 47.0 | 37.3 |
| 14.4 | 14.2 | 11.1 | Long-Term Debt | | | | | 4.4 | 9.2 |
| .4 | .8 | .4 | Deferred Taxes | | | | | .0 | .8 |
| 9.1 | 6.4 | 10.2 | All Other Non-Current | | | | | 14.2 | 10.0 |
| 36.4 | 41.9 | 37.8 | Net Worth | | | | | 34.4 | 42.7 |
| 100.0 | 100.0 | 100.0 | Total Liabilities & Net Worth | | | | | 100.0 | 100.0 |
| | | | **INCOME DATA** | | | | | | |
| 100.0 | 100.0 | 100.0 | Net Sales | | | | | 100.0 | 100.0 |
| 35.0 | 34.8 | 35.5 | Gross Profit | | | | | 31.8 | 33.7 |
| 27.6 | 26.2 | 28.0 | Operating Expenses | | | | | 27.4 | 25.0 |
| 7.4 | 8.6 | 7.4 | Operating Profit | | | | | 4.5 | 8.8 |
| .8 | .6 | 1.8 | All Other Expenses (net) | | | | | 4.2 | 1.2 |
| 6.5 | 8.0 | 5.7 | Profit Before Taxes | | | | | .2 | 7.6 |
| | | | **RATIOS** | | | | | | |
| 3.2 | 3.2 | 3.5 | Current | | | | | 3.3 | 3.5 |
| 1.8 | 2.2 | 2.0 | | | | | | 1.7 | 2.4 |
| 1.2 | 1.3 | 1.3 | | | | | | 1.3 | 1.3 |
| 2.1 | 1.9 | 1.7 | Quick | | | | | 1.5 | 2.0 |
| 1.0 | 1.2 | 1.1 | | | | | | 1.2 | 1.1 |
| .4 | .6 | .6 | | | | | | .6 | .6 |
| 21 17.6 | 26 14.2 | 27 13.5 | Sales/Receivables | | | | | 27 13.7 | 27 13.5 |
| 36 10.3 | 44 8.3 | 41 8.8 | | | | | | 50 7.3 | 36 10.1 |
| 46 7.9 | 61 6.0 | 62 5.9 | | | | | | 69 5.3 | 56 6.5 |
| 54 6.8 | 48 7.5 | 70 5.2 | Cost of Sales/Inventory | | | | | 38 9.6 | 74 4.9 |
| 80 4.6 | 91 4.0 | 91 4.0 | | | | | | 83 4.4 | 91 4.0 |
| 129 2.8 | 133 2.7 | 126 2.9 | | | | | | 126 2.9 | 130 2.8 |
| 14 25.6 | 22 16.4 | 19 19.2 | Cost of Sales/Payables | | | | | 22 16.6 | 17 21.0 |
| 42 8.7 | 34 10.7 | 40 9.2 | | | | | | 40 9.2 | 35 10.3 |
| 65 5.7 | 56 6.5 | 55 6.6 | | | | | | 56 6.5 | 46 8.0 |
| 4.1 | 3.3 | 3.2 | Sales/Working Capital | | | | | 3.8 | 3.0 |
| 7.5 | 5.2 | 5.8 | | | | | | 9.5 | 4.6 |
| 21.8 | 10.5 | 11.2 | | | | | | 20.3 | 11.1 |
| 19.8 | 60.8 | 29.8 | EBIT/Interest | | | | | 36.5 | 58.2 |
| (42) 7.5 | (45) 7.3 | (48) 7.2 | | | | | | (10) 19.5 | (28) 9.9 |
| 3.3 | 2.8 | 2.1 | | | | | | 5.8 | 2.1 |
| 14.0 | 31.6 | 13.6 | Net Profit + Depr., Dep., Amort./Cur. Mat. L/T/D | | | | | | 22.0 |
| (13) 8.4 | (14) 5.2 | (12) 4.7 | | | | | | | (10) 4.7 |
| 3.0 | 3.0 | 2.2 | | | | | | | 2.3 |
| .2 | .1 | .1 | Fixed/Worth | | | | | .1 | .2 |
| .5 | .3 | .3 | | | | | | .3 | .4 |
| 2.3 | 2.0 | 1.7 | | | | | | .7 | 1.7 |
| .5 | .5 | .6 | Debt/Worth | | | | | .6 | .6 |
| 2.0 | 1.8 | 1.6 | | | | | | 1.5 | 1.6 |
| 10.9 | 9.9 | 4.9 | | | | | | 4.5 | 4.6 |
| 58.0 | 47.9 | 53.3 | % Profit Before Taxes/Tangible Net Worth | | | | | 43.5 | 41.7 |
| (40) 35.3 | (41) 26.1 | (46) 27.6 | | | | | | (11) 33.2 | (26) 23.2 |
| 19.9 | 15.9 | 8.3 | | | | | | 2.5 | 9.3 |
| 27.5 | 18.0 | 17.6 | % Profit Before Taxes/Total Assets | | | | | 22.1 | 16.0 |
| 12.1 | 10.9 | 9.2 | | | | | | 14.8 | 8.3 |
| 5.2 | 5.4 | 2.1 | | | | | | -13.8 | 2.7 |
| 34.0 | 29.8 | 40.4 | Sales/Net Fixed Assets | | | | | 107.9 | 22.1 |
| 12.5 | 13.2 | 15.4 | | | | | | 18.9 | 11.9 |
| 5.6 | 6.7 | 7.9 | | | | | | 9.7 | 7.9 |
| 2.8 | 2.3 | 2.5 | Sales/Total Assets | | | | | 3.2 | 2.2 |
| 1.8 | 1.7 | 1.8 | | | | | | 1.7 | 1.8 |
| 1.5 | 1.3 | 1.5 | | | | | | 1.6 | 1.3 |
| .9 | 1.2 | .6 | % Depr., Dep., Amort./Sales | | | | | | 1.3 |
| (41) 1.7 | (41) 2.2 | (43) 2.0 | | | | | | | (28) 2.1 |
| 3.1 | 3.0 | 2.7 | | | | | | | 2.7 |
| 1.0 | 1.0 | 1.3 | % Officers', Directors' Owners' Comp/Sales | | | | | | |
| (11) 1.9 | (11) 1.9 | (11) 4.0 | | | | | | | |
| 7.2 | 5.9 | 5.2 | | | | | | | |
| 2677307M | 3205041M | 3931313M | Net Sales ($) | | | 16449M | 53384M | 210540M | 3650940M |
| 1476161M | 1689373M | 1854651M | Total Assets ($) | | | 9450M | 24390M | 120036M | 1700775M |

**Current Data Sorted by Assets** | **Comparative Historical Data**

| | 0-500M | 500M-2MM | 2-10MM | 10-50MM | 50-100MM | 100-250MM | Type of Statement | 4/1/07-3/31/08 ALL | 4/1/08-3/31/09 ALL |
|---|---|---|---|---|---|---|---|---|---|
| Unqualified | | 3 | 1 | 8 | 5 | 7 | | 17 | 26 |
| Reviewed | | | 5 | 6 | | 1 | | 4 | 11 |
| Compiled | | | 4 | 3 | | | | 6 | 4 |
| Tax Returns | | | 7 | | | | | 6 | 3 |
| Other | | 8 | 11 | 11 | 5 | 9 | | 33 | 35 |
| | | 20 (4/1-9/30/11) | 74 (10/1/11-3/31/12) | | | | | 4/1/07-3/31/08 ALL | 4/1/08-3/31/09 ALL |
| NUMBER OF STATEMENTS | | 11 | 28 | 28 | 10 | 17 | | 66 | 79 |

| 0-500M | 500M-2MM % | 2-10MM % | 10-50MM % | 50-100MM % | 100-250MM % | | 4/1/07-3/31/08 ALL % | 4/1/08-3/31/09 ALL % |
|---|---|---|---|---|---|---|---|---|
| | | | | | | **ASSETS** | | |
| | 13.0 | 13.0 | 10.5 | 10.9 | 23.4 | Cash & Equivalents | 10.3 | 10.8 |
| | 32.3 | 22.4 | 17.7 | 16.0 | 10.6 | Trade Receivables (net) | 18.8 | 18.4 |
| | 25.1 | 34.3 | 28.2 | 25.9 | 16.1 | Inventory | 25.6 | 27.7 |
| D | 3.0 | 1.2 | 3.4 | 2.8 | 2.0 | All Other Current | 3.7 | 4.3 |
| A | 73.4 | 70.8 | 59.8 | 55.6 | 52.1 | Total Current | 58.4 | 61.3 |
| T | 15.1 | 19.9 | 21.0 | 23.0 | 18.0 | Fixed Assets (net) | 27.2 | 23.4 |
| A | 2.1 | 4.7 | 12.4 | 17.5 | 24.9 | Intangibles (net) | 8.4 | 9.8 |
| | 9.3 | 4.6 | 6.8 | 3.9 | 5.0 | All Other Non-Current | 6.0 | 5.6 |
| N | 100.0 | 100.0 | 100.0 | 100.0 | 100.0 | Total | 100.0 | 100.0 |
| O | | | | | | **LIABILITIES** | | |
| T | 2.4 | 11.1 | 7.4 | 7.9 | .8 | Notes Payable-Short Term | 7.9 | 8.6 |
| | 2.1 | 1.6 | 2.9 | 3.1 | 10.9 | Cur. Mat.-L.T.D. | 2.4 | 5.0 |
| A | 23.3 | 19.0 | 14.1 | 8.4 | 8.1 | Trade Payables | 13.6 | 13.6 |
| V | .0 | .3 | .2 | 1.2 | .3 | Income Taxes Payable | .5 | .4 |
| A | 15.4 | 7.9 | 9.1 | 19.2 | 13.6 | All Other Current | 12.1 | 11.9 |
| I | 43.2 | 39.9 | 33.7 | 39.7 | 33.5 | Total Current | 36.4 | 39.4 |
| L | 15.2 | 9.1 | 17.5 | 17.3 | 14.0 | Long-Term Debt | 14.5 | 11.4 |
| A | .1 | .1 | .3 | .2 | 2.7 | Deferred Taxes | .4 | .7 |
| B | 1.8 | 13.0 | 3.6 | 9.0 | 3.6 | All Other Non-Current | 11.9 | 4.0 |
| L | 39.8 | 37.8 | 44.8 | 33.7 | 46.2 | Net Worth | 36.8 | 44.5 |
| E | 100.0 | 100.0 | 100.0 | 100.0 | 100.0 | Total Liabilities & Net Worth | 100.0 | 100.0 |
| | | | | | | **INCOME DATA** | | |
| | 100.0 | 100.0 | 100.0 | 100.0 | 100.0 | Net Sales | 100.0 | 100.0 |
| | 55.9 | 39.7 | 43.5 | 47.0 | 50.0 | Gross Profit | 45.6 | 49.0 |
| | 43.1 | 35.6 | 35.4 | 35.3 | 37.8 | Operating Expenses | 37.7 | 43.6 |
| | 12.8 | 4.1 | 8.1 | 11.7 | 12.3 | Operating Profit | 7.9 | 5.4 |
| | 1.2 | .4 | 4.1 | 2.2 | 2.2 | All Other Expenses (net) | 1.5 | 1.5 |
| | 11.7 | 3.7 | 4.0 | 9.5 | 10.1 | Profit Before Taxes | 6.4 | 3.9 |
| | | | | | | **RATIOS** | | |
| | 2.9 | 3.8 | 3.8 | 2.1 | 2.9 | Current | 2.8 | 3.2 |
| | 2.0 | 2.0 | 2.0 | 1.6 | 2.0 | | 1.8 | 1.7 |
| | 1.5 | 1.1 | 1.3 | 1.3 | 1.4 | | 1.1 | 1.2 |
| | 1.6 | 2.0 | 1.5 | 1.2 | 1.7 | Quick | 1.5 | 1.4 |
| | 1.2 | .9 | .9 | .7 | 1.2 | | .8 | .8 |
| | .7 | .5 | .5 | .5 | .7 | | .5 | .5 |
| 10 37.6 | 21 17.7 | 27 13.3 | 40 9.1 | 16 23.0 | | Sales/Receivables | 20 18.4 | 23 15.7 |
| 36 10.1 | 33 10.9 | 38 9.5 | 48 7.6 | 28 13.0 | | | 35 10.3 | 37 9.8 |
| 51 7.1 | 47 7.8 | 51 7.1 | 51 7.2 | 54 6.8 | | | 49 7.5 | 48 7.6 |
| 0 UND | 54 6.7 | 65 5.6 | 89 4.1 | 47 7.8 | | Cost of Sales/Inventory | 68 5.4 | 72 5.1 |
| 29 12.7 | 89 4.1 | 85 4.3 | 122 3.0 | 99 3.7 | | | 89 4.1 | 98 3.7 |
| 203 1.8 | 140 2.6 | 159 2.3 | 243 1.5 | 159 2.3 | | | 142 2.6 | 147 2.5 |
| 20 18.6 | 26 14.1 | 26 14.1 | 24 15.0 | 27 13.3 | | Cost of Sales/Payables | 23 15.7 | 21 17.6 |
| 43 8.4 | 47 7.7 | 45 8.2 | 41 8.8 | 40 9.2 | | | 40 9.0 | 44 8.4 |
| 70 5.2 | 64 5.7 | 72 5.1 | 62 5.9 | 60 6.1 | | | 57 6.4 | 66 5.5 |
| | 4.7 | 4.6 | 3.5 | 4.6 | 3.5 | Sales/Working Capital | 4.6 | 4.6 |
| | 11.2 | 7.9 | 7.8 | 7.5 | 5.7 | | 8.7 | 7.6 |
| | 31.6 | 52.1 | 15.5 | 28.5 | 12.1 | | 44.9 | 21.6 |
| | | 42.2 | 40.3 | | 45.5 | EBIT/Interest | 17.7 | 25.8 |
| | (24) 14.9 | (25) 8.2 | | (16) 11.8 | | | (57) 5.0 | (70) 7.7 |
| | 3.7 | 2.5 | | 1.9 | | | 1.8 | 2.1 |
| | | | | | | Net Profit + Depr., Dep., Amort./Cur. Mat. L/T/D | 17.1 | 17.9 |
| | | | | | | | (17) 5.7 | (28) 6.1 |
| | | | | | | | 2.1 | 2.3 |
| | .1 | .1 | .3 | .6 | .2 | Fixed/Worth | .4 | .3 |
| | .5 | .6 | .8 | 1.1 | .5 | | .8 | .6 |
| | .9 | NM | NM | 2.8 | NM | | 2.2 | 1.5 |
| | .5 | .5 | .6 | 1.8 | .6 | Debt/Worth | .8 | .5 |
| | 2.0 | 1.4 | 1.2 | 4.5 | 1.1 | | 1.8 | 1.3 |
| | 4.6 | NM | NM | 7.4 | NM | | 12.1 | 4.4 |
| | 254.4 | 45.4 | 40.9 | | 148.3 | % Profit Before Taxes/Tangible Net Worth | 68.0 | 46.0 |
| (10) 32.3 | (21) 21.5 | (21) 29.4 | | (13) 29.7 | | | (53) 26.2 | (69) 22.2 |
| | 9.6 | 10.9 | 4.9 | | 17.9 | | 15.0 | 5.1 |
| | 36.3 | 21.1 | 19.2 | 17.0 | 16.4 | % Profit Before Taxes/Total Assets | 20.5 | 17.5 |
| | 12.0 | 8.0 | 9.3 | 4.2 | 7.1 | | 8.5 | 6.4 |
| | .6 | 2.7 | 1.7 | 1.4 | 5.2 | | 3.6 | 1.3 |
| | 40.1 | 51.4 | 33.2 | 21.9 | 22.5 | Sales/Net Fixed Assets | 21.2 | 24.5 |
| | 18.8 | 20.0 | 9.5 | 5.3 | 11.4 | | 9.1 | 11.0 |
| | 12.4 | 7.2 | 4.9 | 2.7 | 4.6 | | 3.7 | 4.7 |
| | 4.0 | 3.3 | 2.2 | 2.7 | 1.6 | Sales/Total Assets | 2.7 | 2.7 |
| | 2.8 | 2.3 | 1.7 | 1.3 | 1.1 | | 1.9 | 1.9 |
| | 2.4 | 1.6 | 1.3 | .7 | .8 | | 1.3 | 1.3 |
| | | .7 | 1.0 | | 1.3 | % Depr., Dep., Amort./Sales | 1.0 | 1.2 |
| | (24) 1.3 | (24) 1.9 | | (11) 2.4 | | | (55) 2.0 | (67) 2.2 |
| | 3.2 | 2.8 | | 4.8 | | | 3.2 | 3.0 |
| | 1.8 | | | | | % Officers', Directors', Owners' Comp/Sales | 1.3 | 1.3 |
| | (14) 2.4 | | | | | | (17) 4.0 | (15) 2.3 |
| | 6.0 | | | | | | 7.6 | 3.9 |
| | 58774M | 328374M | 967277M | 1018081M | 3577862M | Net Sales ($) | 4156857M | 5790794M |
| | 15171M | 133364M | 568050M | 690298M | 2930010M | Total Assets ($) | 2284541M | 3128958M |

M = $ thousand    MM = $ million
See Pages 9 through 22 for Explanation of Ratios and Data

## Comparative Historical Data / Current Data Sorted by Sales

| 4/1/09-3/31/10 ALL | 4/1/10-3/31/11 ALL | 4/1/11-3/31/12 ALL | Type of Statement | 0-1MM | 1-3MM | 3-5MM | 5-10MM | 10-25MM | 25MM & OVER |
|---|---|---|---|---|---|---|---|---|---|
| 27 | 24 | 21 | Unqualified |  |  |  | 1 | 1 | 19 |
| 11 | 15 | 11 | Reviewed |  |  |  | 3 | 4 | 4 |
| 5 | 7 | 8 | Compiled |  |  |  | 3 | 3 | 2 |
| 10 |  | 10 | Tax Returns |  | 1 | 3 | 4 | 2 |  |
| 33 | 53 | 44 | Other | 1 | 4 | 2 | 7 | 9 | 21 |
|  |  |  |  |  | 20 (4/1-9/30/11) |  | 74 (10/1/11-3/31/12) |  |  |
| 86 | 99 | 94 | **NUMBER OF STATEMENTS** | 1 | 5 | 5 | 18 | 19 | 46 |
| % | % | % | **ASSETS** | % | % | % | % | % | % |
| 12.5 | 12.5 | 13.9 | Cash & Equivalents |  |  |  | 10.8 | 7.8 | 17.4 |
| 17.8 | 18.1 | 19.3 | Trade Receivables (net) |  |  |  | 24.8 | 24.3 | 15.2 |
| 25.7 | 24.8 | 27.2 | Inventory |  |  |  | 24.7 | 33.2 | 24.5 |
| 2.8 | 2.9 | 2.4 | All Other Current |  |  |  | 1.1 | 3.0 | 2.6 |
| 58.8 | 58.3 | 62.8 | Total Current |  |  |  | 61.5 | 68.2 | 59.8 |
| 23.7 | 23.1 | 19.6 | Fixed Assets (net) |  |  |  | 18.2 | 22.2 | 19.0 |
| 11.3 | 12.9 | 11.7 | Intangibles (net) |  |  |  | 13.8 | 4.1 | 16.3 |
| 6.2 | 5.6 | 5.8 | All Other Non-Current |  |  |  | 6.5 | 5.4 | 4.8 |
| 100.0 | 100.0 | 100.0 | Total |  |  |  | 100.0 | 100.0 | 100.0 |
|  |  |  | **LIABILITIES** |  |  |  |  |  |  |
| 6.4 | 8.8 | 6.8 | Notes Payable-Short Term |  |  |  | 4.9 | 3.8 | 6.3 |
| 2.6 | 3.2 | 3.9 | Cur. Mat.-L.T.D. |  |  |  | 3.9 | 2.2 | 5.3 |
| 14.6 | 14.6 | 15.0 | Trade Payables |  |  |  | 19.7 | 18.4 | 12.0 |
| .5 | .5 | .3 | Income Taxes Payable |  |  |  | .2 | .3 | .5 |
| 10.9 | 9.6 | 11.3 | All Other Current |  |  |  | 7.7 | 7.2 | 13.6 |
| 35.0 | 36.8 | 37.3 | Total Current |  |  |  | 36.3 | 31.9 | 37.7 |
| 16.1 | 13.9 | 14.1 | Long-Term Debt |  |  |  | 8.5 | 21.7 | 12.8 |
| .8 | 1.1 | .7 | Deferred Taxes |  |  |  | .2 | .2 | 1.2 |
| 10.3 | 7.4 | 6.8 | All Other Non-Current |  |  |  | 8.4 | 4.6 | 5.6 |
| 37.9 | 40.9 | 41.2 | Net Worth |  |  |  | 46.6 | 41.5 | 42.7 |
| 100.0 | 100.0 | 100.0 | Total Liabilities & Net Worth |  |  |  | 100.0 | 100.0 | 100.0 |
|  |  |  | **INCOME DATA** |  |  |  |  |  |  |
| 100.0 | 100.0 | 100.0 | Net Sales |  |  |  | 100.0 | 100.0 | 100.0 |
| 48.5 | 45.3 | 45.4 | Gross Profit |  |  |  | 45.9 | 35.6 | 45.6 |
| 39.4 | 37.0 | 36.8 | Operating Expenses |  |  |  | 41.1 | 27.6 | 35.4 |
| 9.0 | 8.3 | 8.6 | Operating Profit |  |  |  | 4.8 | 8.0 | 10.2 |
| 1.5 | 1.7 | 2.1 | All Other Expenses (net) |  |  |  | 3.4 | 1.0 | 1.8 |
| 7.5 | 6.6 | 6.5 | Profit Before Taxes |  |  |  | 1.4 | 7.0 | 8.3 |
|  |  |  | **RATIOS** |  |  |  |  |  |  |
| 2.6 | 2.9 | 2.9 | Current |  |  |  | 2.5 | 4.0 | 2.7 |
| 1.7 | 1.8 | 1.9 |  |  |  |  | 1.6 | 2.3 | 1.8 |
| 1.3 | 1.2 | 1.2 |  |  |  |  | .9 | 1.7 | 1.3 |
| 1.4 | 1.4 | 1.6 | Quick |  |  |  | 1.3 | 1.6 | 1.5 |
| .7 | .9 | .9 |  |  |  |  | .7 | 1.2 | .9 |
| .4 | .5 | .6 |  |  |  |  | .4 | .7 | .6 |
| 19  18.7 | 26  13.9 | 23  16.2 | Sales/Receivables |  |  |  | 29  12.5 | 33  11.0 | 21  17.1 |
| 34  10.7 | 38  9.5 | 38  9.5 |  |  |  |  | 41  8.9 | 39  9.3 | 39  9.4 |
| 48  7.5 | 50  7.3 | 49  7.4 |  |  |  |  | 52  7.0 | 49  7.5 | 50  7.3 |
| 59  6.2 | 63  5.8 | 56  6.5 | Cost of Sales/Inventory |  |  |  | 39  9.3 | 57  6.4 | 60  6.1 |
| 102  3.6 | 104  3.5 | 99  3.7 |  |  |  |  | 78  4.7 | 79  4.6 | 99  3.7 |
| 149  2.4 | 143  2.6 | 159  2.3 |  |  |  |  | 146  2.5 | 159  2.3 | 159  2.3 |
| 28  13.1 | 26  14.2 | 26  14.0 | Cost of Sales/Payables |  |  |  | 30  12.1 | 26  14.1 | 26  13.9 |
| 43  8.4 | 40  9.0 | 43  8.5 |  |  |  |  | 50  7.3 | 36  10.2 | 41  9.0 |
| 65  5.6 | 63  5.8 | 66  5.5 |  |  |  |  | 78  4.7 | 52  7.0 | 66  5.5 |
| 4.5 | 4.3 | 4.4 | Sales/Working Capital |  |  |  | 5.2 | 3.7 | 4.1 |
| 8.2 | 7.3 | 6.9 |  |  |  |  | 16.7 | 5.3 | 6.9 |
| 22.0 | 27.0 | 20.8 |  |  |  |  | -52.0 | -8.8 | 16.0 |
| 38.7 | 28.8 | 37.4 | EBIT/Interest |  |  |  | 262.9 | 42.2 | 38.2 |
| (76)  8.9 | (83)  6.9 | (79)  8.6 |  |  |  |  | (13)  15.5 | (16)  10.3 | (43)  7.4 |
| 2.6 | 2.0 | 2.2 |  |  |  |  | 5.4 | 3.5 | 2.0 |
| 18.2 | 7.4 | 6.8 | Net Profit + Depr., Dep., Amort./Cur. Mat. L/T/D |  |  |  |  |  | 8.4 |
| (26)  4.8 | (32)  2.4 | (23)  3.8 |  |  |  |  |  | (16)  4.9 |  |
| 1.5 | 1.2 | 2.2 |  |  |  |  |  |  | 2.2 |
| .3 | .4 | .3 | Fixed/Worth |  |  |  | .0 | .3 | .2 |
| .8 | .8 | .7 |  |  |  |  | .6 | .6 | .7 |
| 2.5 | 6.3 | 4.8 |  |  |  |  | NM | 1.4 | 4.8 |
| .7 | .7 | .6 | Debt/Worth |  |  |  | .8 | .5 | .7 |
| 1.9 | 1.6 | 1.7 |  |  |  |  | 1.9 | 1.3 | 1.8 |
| 5.7 | 36.5 | 17.8 |  |  |  |  | NM | 2.3 | 25.3 |
| 90.8 | 56.2 | 50.6 | % Profit Before Taxes/Tangible Net Worth |  |  |  | 112.8 | 31.6 | 55.1 |
| (72)  42.9 | (78)  29.8 | (74)  27.4 |  |  |  |  | (14)  39.6 | (15)  21.5 | (37)  29.7 |
| 16.0 | 13.4 | 11.3 |  |  |  |  | 8.3 | 11.7 | 12.3 |
| 24.1 | 22.0 | 19.7 | % Profit Before Taxes/Total Assets |  |  |  | 25.7 | 16.4 | 17.9 |
| 10.0 | 9.6 | 8.6 |  |  |  |  | 8.2 | 10.5 | 8.1 |
| 2.9 | 2.9 | 2.8 |  |  |  |  | -2.1 | 4.2 | 3.5 |
| 26.4 | 22.1 | 33.1 | Sales/Net Fixed Assets |  |  |  | 192.7 | 35.1 | 25.9 |
| 9.6 | 9.8 | 12.6 |  |  |  |  | 33.8 | 10.6 | 11.7 |
| 4.0 | 4.2 | 5.3 |  |  |  |  | 6.4 | 4.7 | 5.3 |
| 2.7 | 2.5 | 2.5 | Sales/Total Assets |  |  |  | 3.4 | 2.8 | 2.3 |
| 1.8 | 1.7 | 1.8 |  |  |  |  | 2.0 | 2.2 | 1.6 |
| 1.2 | 1.1 | 1.2 |  |  |  |  | 1.4 | 1.3 | 1.1 |
| 1.3 | 1.3 | 1.0 | % Depr., Dep., Amort./Sales |  |  |  | .8 | 1.0 | 1.0 |
| (71)  2.2 | (81)  2.3 | (74)  1.7 |  |  |  |  | (12)  1.5 | (18)  1.8 | (37)  1.8 |
| 3.7 | 3.7 | 3.1 |  |  |  |  | 5.6 | 2.9 | 3.2 |
| 1.4 | 1.1 | 1.4 | % Officers', Directors' Owners' Comp/Sales |  |  |  |  |  |  |
| (19)  2.9 | (15)  2.1 | (29)  2.5 |  |  |  |  |  |  |  |
| 4.6 | 3.5 | 5.3 |  |  |  |  |  |  |  |
| 5303972M | 7674174M | 5950368M | Net Sales ($) | 375M | 11355M | 21194M | 139044M | 328011M | 5450389M |
| 3205736M | 5014963M | 4336893M | Total Assets ($) | 1275M | 7874M | 9878M | 99940M | 170614M | 4047312M |

M = $ thousand     MM = $ million
See Pages 9 through 22 for Explanation of Ratios and Data

## Current Data Sorted by Assets                                   Comparative Historical Data

| Type of Statement | 0-500M | 500M-2MM | 2-10MM | 10-50MM | 50-100MM | 100-250MM | 4/1/07-3/31/08 ALL | 4/1/08-3/31/09 ALL |
|---|---|---|---|---|---|---|---|---|
| Unqualified | | 1 | 3 | 21 | 5 | 16 | 43 | 49 |
| Reviewed | 1 | 1 | 12 | 11 | 3 | 1 | 22 | 27 |
| Compiled | | 5 | 9 | 4 | 1 | 1 | 10 | 11 |
| Tax Returns | 3 | 7 | 5 | | | | 7 | 18 |
| Other | 1 | 2 | 16 | 36 | 8 | 15 | 76 | 78 |
| | | 33 (4/1-9/30/11) | | 154 (10/1/11-3/31/12) | | | | |
| **NUMBER OF STATEMENTS** | 5 | 16 | 45 | 72 | 17 | 32 | 158 | 183 |
| **ASSETS** | % | % | % | % | % | % | % | % |
| Cash & Equivalents | | 11.4 | 10.3 | 12.5 | 21.7 | 16.2 | 13.1 | 13.2 |
| Trade Receivables (net) | | 29.4 | 27.5 | 18.1 | 18.2 | 15.1 | 22.4 | 21.6 |
| Inventory | | 30.7 | 22.7 | 23.0 | 18.7 | 16.1 | 21.7 | 19.8 |
| All Other Current | | 1.6 | 4.1 | 2.5 | 1.9 | 3.0 | 2.8 | 3.2 |
| Total Current | | 73.0 | 64.6 | 56.1 | 60.6 | 50.5 | 60.0 | 57.8 |
| Fixed Assets (net) | | 14.3 | 24.5 | 29.6 | 25.7 | 22.3 | 24.1 | 23.6 |
| Intangibles (net) | | 5.5 | 4.1 | 10.0 | 12.0 | 21.0 | 8.7 | 11.4 |
| All Other Non-Current | | 7.3 | 6.8 | 4.3 | 1.7 | 6.2 | 7.2 | 7.2 |
| Total | | 100.0 | 100.0 | 100.0 | 100.0 | 100.0 | 100.0 | 100.0 |
| **LIABILITIES** | | | | | | | | |
| Notes Payable-Short Term | | 6.7 | 10.3 | 12.2 | 1.5 | 4.2 | 8.0 | 6.4 |
| Cur. Mat.-L.T.D. | | 4.1 | 1.6 | 4.3 | 1.1 | 1.7 | 3.0 | 3.3 |
| Trade Payables | | 20.5 | 16.3 | 14.4 | 11.6 | 8.2 | 12.5 | 12.9 |
| Income Taxes Payable | | .1 | .7 | .2 | .2 | .3 | .4 | .3 |
| All Other Current | | 8.2 | 15.0 | 13.5 | 11.6 | 8.7 | 11.4 | 12.3 |
| Total Current | | 39.7 | 43.8 | 44.7 | 25.9 | 23.1 | 35.2 | 35.2 |
| Long-Term Debt | | 14.1 | 9.5 | 16.4 | 11.6 | 16.9 | 18.4 | 16.4 |
| Deferred Taxes | | .0 | .3 | .7 | .7 | 1.4 | .8 | .9 |
| All Other Non-Current | | 4.9 | 8.5 | 5.3 | 5.8 | 4.7 | 6.2 | 6.6 |
| Net Worth | | 41.2 | 37.8 | 32.9 | 56.0 | 53.8 | 39.3 | 40.9 |
| Total Liabilities & Net Worth | | 100.0 | 100.0 | 100.0 | 100.0 | 100.0 | 100.0 | 100.0 |
| **INCOME DATA** | | | | | | | | |
| Net Sales | | 100.0 | 100.0 | 100.0 | 100.0 | 100.0 | 100.0 | 100.0 |
| Gross Profit | | 47.7 | 46.9 | 38.3 | 43.5 | 45.2 | 43.5 | 45.6 |
| Operating Expenses | | 43.0 | 42.0 | 29.7 | 30.8 | 34.8 | 36.1 | 38.2 |
| Operating Profit | | 4.7 | 4.9 | 8.7 | 12.6 | 10.4 | 7.4 | 7.4 |
| All Other Expenses (net) | | -.4 | .4 | 1.4 | 1.7 | 2.8 | 1.0 | 1.4 |
| Profit Before Taxes | | 5.1 | 4.5 | 7.3 | 11.0 | 7.6 | 6.5 | 6.0 |
| **RATIOS** | | | | | | | | |
| Current | | 3.0 | 2.8 | 3.5 | 6.3 | 2.9 | 3.0 | 3.1 |
| | | 2.1 | 1.6 | 1.9 | 2.6 | 2.2 | 1.8 | 1.8 |
| | | 1.6 | 1.0 | 1.1 | 1.5 | 1.8 | 1.2 | 1.3 |
| Quick | | 1.8 | 1.4 | 2.5 | 4.2 | 1.8 | 1.7 | 1.8 |
| | | .9 | .9 | .8 | 1.5 | 1.3 | 1.0 | 1.0 |
| | | .7 | .6 | .5 | .8 | .8 | .6 | .6 |
| Sales/Receivables | | 13  28.8 | 31  11.9 | 33  11.0 | 27  13.6 | 43  8.5 | 32  11.3 | 31  11.8 |
| | | 29  12.5 | 41  9.0 | 45  8.1 | 51  7.2 | 55  6.6 | 45  8.2 | 42  8.6 |
| | | 51  7.2 | 63  5.8 | 58  6.3 | 63  5.8 | 68  5.4 | 58  6.3 | 57  6.4 |
| Cost of Sales/Inventory | | 39  9.4 | 33  10.9 | 51  7.2 | 65  5.6 | 81  4.5 | 44  8.2 | 43  8.6 |
| | | 72  5.1 | 83  4.4 | 89  4.1 | 89  4.1 | 114  3.2 | 87  4.2 | 86  4.2 |
| | | 118  3.1 | 135  2.7 | 135  2.7 | 146  2.5 | 159  2.3 | 124  3.0 | 135  2.7 |
| Cost of Sales/Payables | | 13  29.0 | 26  14.1 | 27  13.4 | 21  17.4 | 35  10.5 | 23  15.9 | 21  17.6 |
| | | 31  11.9 | 47  7.7 | 36  10.1 | 38  9.6 | 51  7.2 | 38  9.7 | 34  10.7 |
| | | 87  4.2 | 81  4.5 | 72  5.1 | 65  5.6 | 85  4.3 | 62  5.9 | 68  5.4 |
| Sales/Working Capital | | 6.5 | 5.5 | 3.2 | 1.9 | 2.0 | 3.6 | 3.6 |
| | | 9.7 | 10.0 | 8.3 | 2.9 | 4.0 | 6.9 | 7.4 |
| | | 15.3 | 134.6 | 71.0 | 20.7 | 7.8 | 22.1 | 24.9 |
| EBIT/Interest | | 45.4 | 33.5 | 22.6 | 224.3 | 27.5 | 14.9 | 14.1 |
| | (14) | 7.6 | (38)  7.3 | (64)  7.0 | (16)  28.3 | (31)  5.3 | (135)  4.2 | (155)  4.7 |
| | | 3.6 | -1.1 | 2.0 | 2.4 | 1.6 | 1.2 | .8 |
| Net Profit + Depr., Dep., Amort./Cur. Mat. L/T/D | | | | 6.6 | | | 13.3 | 10.1 |
| | | | (26)  3.3 | | | | (46)  2.5 | (59)  3.3 |
| | | | | 1.8 | | | 1.0 | .9 |
| Fixed/Worth | | .1 | .3 | .3 | .2 | .2 | .3 | .3 |
| | | .2 | .5 | .8 | .5 | .7 | .7 | .7 |
| | | 2.1 | 2.7 | 2.0 | 3.7 | 2.3 | 2.4 | 1.8 |
| Debt/Worth | | .6 | .7 | .6 | .2 | .5 | .6 | .5 |
| | | 1.6 | 1.5 | 1.3 | .9 | 1.0 | 1.5 | 1.7 |
| | | 6.2 | 7.1 | 6.3 | 7.5 | 3.2 | 5.2 | 7.1 |
| % Profit Before Taxes/Tangible Net Worth | | 104.5 | 50.4 | 42.1 | 50.0 | 31.2 | 59.4 | 57.5 |
| | (13) | 59.0 | (38)  30.6 | (57)  20.6 | (14)  28.4 | (27)  18.9 | (131)  17.0 | (151)  18.3 |
| | | 5.9 | 8.8 | 8.5 | 11.6 | 1.4 | 1.8 | .9 |
| % Profit Before Taxes/Total Assets | | 45.3 | 18.8 | 19.2 | 21.4 | 14.9 | 20.7 | 21.2 |
| | | 9.9 | 8.8 | 7.9 | 10.2 | 4.9 | 7.7 | 6.8 |
| | | -4.2 | -1.6 | 1.6 | 1.3 | 1.2 | -.4 | -.5 |
| Sales/Net Fixed Assets | | 136.8 | 24.8 | 17.2 | 11.8 | 17.5 | 26.7 | 27.9 |
| | | 39.3 | 13.8 | 5.5 | 5.5 | 5.9 | 9.2 | 8.0 |
| | | 7.6 | 3.9 | 2.7 | 3.1 | 2.1 | 3.5 | 3.5 |
| Sales/Total Assets | | 4.8 | 2.7 | 1.8 | 1.5 | 1.3 | 2.6 | 2.5 |
| | | 3.8 | 1.9 | 1.5 | 1.2 | .8 | 1.7 | 1.5 |
| | | 2.2 | 1.3 | 1.0 | .7 | .6 | 1.1 | 1.1 |
| % Depr., Dep., Amort./Sales | | .5 | .8 | 1.4 | 1.7 | 2.0 | 1.0 | 1.4 |
| | (11) | .7 | (36)  2.3 | (63)  2.8 | (22)  2.7 | 3.5 | (131)  2.2 | (157)  2.6 |
| | | 4.8 | 5.3 | 4.7 | 4.9 | 7.2 | 4.3 | 4.3 |
| % Officers', Directors', Owners' Comp/Sales | | | 1.7 | .9 | | | 1.6 | 1.9 |
| | | (12)  2.6 | (12)  1.3 | | | | (40)  4.0 | (45)  4.0 |
| | | 5.1 | 1.8 | | | | 9.6 | 8.8 |
| Net Sales ($) | 2224M | 64082M | 520874M | 2554143M | 1849336M | 4887630M | 8356015M | 10435939M |
| Total Assets ($) | 1229M | 18508M | 238064M | 1707832M | 1133570M | 5081975M | 5951400M | 7667393M |

© RMA 2012

M = $ thousand    MM = $ million
See Pages 9 through 22 for Explanation of Ratios and Data

## Comparative Historical Data / Current Data Sorted by Sales

### Type of Statement

| Type of Statement | 4/1/09-3/31/10 ALL | 4/1/10-3/31/11 ALL | 4/1/11-3/31/12 ALL | 0-1MM | 1-3MM | 3-5MM | 5-10MM | 10-25MM | 25MM & OVER |
|---|---|---|---|---|---|---|---|---|---|
| Unqualified | 46 | 50 | 46 |  | 2 |  | 3 | 7 | 34 |
| Reviewed | 27 | 24 | 28 | 1 |  | 1 | 4 | 15 | 7 |
| Compiled | 13 | 20 | 20 |  | 1 | 3 | 5 | 6 | 5 |
| Tax Returns | 17 | 12 | 15 | 4 | 3 | 4 | 1 | 1 | 2 |
| Other | 100 | 90 | 78 | 1 | 1 | 5 | 5 | 13 | 53 |
|  |  |  |  | 33 (4/1-9/30/11) |  | 154 (10/1/11-3/31/12) |  |  |  |
| NUMBER OF STATEMENTS | 203 | 196 | 187 | 6 | 7 | 13 | 18 | 42 | 101 |

### ASSETS (%)

| Item | ALL | ALL | ALL | 0-1MM | 1-3MM | 3-5MM | 5-10MM | 10-25MM | 25MM & OVER |
|---|---|---|---|---|---|---|---|---|---|
| Cash & Equivalents | 14.0 | 15.4 | 13.5 |  |  | 8.5 | 18.7 | 9.8 | 15.0 |
| Trade Receivables (net) | 22.0 | 21.6 | 20.7 |  |  | 21.0 | 24.0 | 25.5 | 18.0 |
| Inventory | 19.8 | 20.1 | 22.0 |  |  | 28.0 | 21.0 | 24.0 | 20.9 |
| All Other Current | 3.2 | 3.6 | 2.8 |  |  | .5 | 5.0 | 3.3 | 2.6 |
| Total Current | 59.0 | 60.8 | 59.1 |  |  | 58.1 | 68.6 | 62.6 | 56.5 |
| Fixed Assets (net) | 24.9 | 24.5 | 24.9 |  |  | 32.0 | 16.3 | 27.2 | 25.8 |
| Intangibles (net) | 11.0 | 8.9 | 10.4 |  |  | 8.8 | 9.7 | 3.3 | 13.4 |
| All Other Non-Current | 5.1 | 5.8 | 5.6 |  |  | 1.1 | 5.3 | 6.9 | 4.3 |
| Total | 100.0 | 100.0 | 100.0 |  |  | 100.0 | 100.0 | 100.0 | 100.0 |

### LIABILITIES

| Item | ALL | ALL | ALL | 0-1MM | 1-3MM | 3-5MM | 5-10MM | 10-25MM | 25MM & OVER |
|---|---|---|---|---|---|---|---|---|---|
| Notes Payable-Short Term | 6.2 | 5.5 | 8.6 |  |  | 14.8 | 5.6 | 8.2 | 9.5 |
| Cur. Mat.-L.T.D. | 3.6 | 2.9 | 2.8 |  |  | 2.0 | 3.8 | 2.0 | 3.2 |
| Trade Payables | 12.1 | 12.6 | 14.0 |  |  | 22.8 | 10.9 | 13.3 | 13.8 |
| Income Taxes Payable | .3 | .3 | .3 |  |  | .2 | .4 | .4 | .3 |
| All Other Current | 12.4 | 10.4 | 12.1 |  |  | 6.1 | 9.4 | 14.2 | 11.8 |
| Total Current | 34.7 | 31.7 | 37.9 |  |  | 45.9 | 30.2 | 38.0 | 38.6 |
| Long-Term Debt | 15.5 | 11.8 | 14.4 |  |  | 18.6 | 8.9 | 14.1 | 15.3 |
| Deferred Taxes | .7 | .6 | .6 |  |  | .6 | .2 | .5 | .9 |
| All Other Non-Current | 5.7 | 6.5 | 5.9 |  |  | 22.7 | 3.9 | 5.2 | 4.9 |
| Net Worth | 43.4 | 49.5 | 41.2 |  |  | 12.1 | 56.8 | 42.2 | 40.3 |
| Total Liabilities & Net Worth | 100.0 | 100.0 | 100.0 |  |  | 100.0 | 100.0 | 100.0 | 100.0 |

### INCOME DATA

| Item | ALL | ALL | ALL | 0-1MM | 1-3MM | 3-5MM | 5-10MM | 10-25MM | 25MM & OVER |
|---|---|---|---|---|---|---|---|---|---|
| Net Sales | 100.0 | 100.0 | 100.0 |  |  | 100.0 | 100.0 | 100.0 | 100.0 |
| Gross Profit | 42.1 | 44.7 | 43.7 |  |  | 42.0 | 48.4 | 44.4 | 40.5 |
| Operating Expenses | 35.2 | 35.8 | 35.7 |  |  | 41.0 | 43.0 | 31.8 | 31.8 |
| Operating Profit | 6.9 | 8.9 | 8.0 |  |  | 1.0 | 5.3 | 12.6 | 8.7 |
| All Other Expenses (net) | 1.7 | .9 | 1.2 |  |  | .3 | -.1 | 1.3 | 1.7 |
| Profit Before Taxes | 5.2 | 8.0 | 6.8 |  |  | .7 | 5.4 | 11.3 | 7.0 |

### RATIOS

| Item | ALL | ALL | ALL | 0-1MM | 1-3MM | 3-5MM | 5-10MM | 10-25MM | 25MM & OVER |
|---|---|---|---|---|---|---|---|---|---|
| Current | 3.1 | 3.5 | 3.3 |  |  | 1.9 | 4.0 | 3.5 | 2.9 |
|  | 1.8 | 2.0 | 2.0 |  |  | 1.1 | 2.4 | 1.8 | 2.1 |
|  | 1.2 | 1.3 | 1.1 |  |  | .8 | 1.6 | 1.2 | 1.1 |
| Quick | 1.9 | 2.1 | 2.1 |  |  | .8 | 2.3 | 2.2 | 2.0 |
|  | 1.0 | 1.2 | 1.0 |  |  | .7 | 1.2 | .8 | 1.0 |
|  | .6 | .7 | .6 |  |  | .3 | .7 | .7 | .5 |
| Sales/Receivables | 30  12.2 | 30  12.1 | 31  11.8 |  |  | 16  23.2 | 25  14.5 | 37  9.8 | 33  11.0 |
|  | 43  8.5 | 41  8.9 | 45  8.1 |  |  | 40  9.1 | 42  8.7 | 47  7.7 | 46  7.9 |
|  | 59  6.2 | 58  6.3 | 60  6.1 |  |  | 51  7.1 | 54  6.8 | 61  6.0 | 59  6.2 |
| Cost of Sales/Inventory | 40  9.0 | 39  9.3 | 51  7.2 |  |  | 35  10.3 | 17  21.6 | 54  6.8 | 54  6.7 |
|  | 74  4.9 | 87  4.2 | 91  4.0 |  |  | 73  5.0 | 54  6.8 | 91  4.0 | 54  4.0 |
|  | 119  3.1 | 131  2.8 | 135  2.7 |  |  | 146  2.5 | 126  2.9 | 126  2.9 | 135  2.7 |
| Cost of Sales/Payables | 20  18.6 | 20  17.9 | 27  13.7 |  |  | 31  11.9 | 14  25.5 | 21  17.6 | 29  12.5 |
|  | 36  10.1 | 36  10.3 | 40  9.1 |  |  | 58  6.3 | 29  12.8 | 37  9.9 | 41  8.9 |
|  | 57  6.4 | 56  6.6 | 73  5.0 |  |  | 118  3.1 | 56  6.5 | 63  5.8 | 73  5.0 |
| Sales/Working Capital | 3.5 | 3.4 | 3.3 |  |  | 9.2 | 3.0 | 3.4 | 3.0 |
|  | 7.2 | 6.0 | 6.7 |  |  | 31.0 | 6.1 | 8.0 | 5.3 |
|  | 22.7 | 18.8 | 30.1 |  |  | -15.1 | 13.8 | 40.5 | 35.0 |
| EBIT/Interest | 17.1 | 32.1 | 28.4 |  |  | 9.7 | 24.5 | 37.8 | 28.4 |
|  | (168) 4.2 | (166) 10.2 | (165) 7.3 |  |  | (12) 5.3 | (15) 7.5 | (34) 7.6 | (96) 7.9 |
|  | 1.6 | 2.6 | 1.8 |  |  | -1.8 | 1.8 | 2.0 | 1.8 |
| Net Profit + Depr., Dep., Amort./Cur. Mat. L/T/D | 6.1 | 13.4 | 15.0 |  |  |  |  | 15.6 | 14.5 |
|  | (57) 1.9 | (66) 3.3 | (50) 6.0 |  |  |  |  | (11) 6.5 | (34) 3.7 |
|  | .7 | 1.6 | 1.9 |  |  |  |  | 1.8 | 1.8 |
| Fixed/Worth | .2 | .2 | .2 |  |  | .1 | .1 | .3 | .2 |
|  | .7 | .6 | .6 |  |  | 2.7 | .3 | .6 | .7 |
|  | 2.4 | 1.5 | 2.3 |  |  | -3.1 | .6 | 1.3 | 2.2 |
| Debt/Worth | .6 | .4 | .5 |  |  | 1.6 | .3 | .6 | .6 |
|  | 1.6 | 1.1 | 1.3 |  |  | 6.9 | 1.0 | 1.2 | 1.3 |
|  | 6.8 | 3.2 | 5.9 |  |  | -5.7 | 3.7 | 4.7 | 5.9 |
| % Profit Before Taxes/Tangible Net Worth | 52.7 | 52.5 | 43.4 |  |  |  | 62.8 | 50.2 | 35.7 |
|  | (173) 23.1 | (176) 28.2 | (152) 21.6 |  |  |  | 28.8 | (35) 31.8 | (82) 21.5 |
|  | 6.2 | 9.1 | 7.3 |  |  |  | 4.8 | 12.6 | 7.5 |
| % Profit Before Taxes/Total Assets | 16.3 | 22.9 | 18.7 |  |  | 44.7 | 23.3 | 27.7 | 17.3 |
|  | 7.6 | 10.1 | 8.2 |  |  | 5.3 | 9.3 | 12.5 | 6.4 |
|  | 2.1 | 3.8 | 1.3 |  |  | -10.7 | 2.2 | 6.7 | 1.2 |
| Sales/Net Fixed Assets | 30.0 | 28.4 | 25.5 |  |  | 99.6 | 60.4 | 21.9 | 18.1 |
|  | 8.3 | 9.5 | 7.5 |  |  | 7.3 | 16.9 | 7.7 | 6.3 |
|  | 3.2 | 3.0 | 3.4 |  |  | 2.0 | 6.1 | 3.3 | 3.0 |
| Sales/Total Assets | 2.6 | 2.5 | 2.1 |  |  | 4.0 | 3.2 | 2.2 | 1.8 |
|  | 1.5 | 1.5 | 1.5 |  |  | 2.2 | 1.9 | 1.7 | 1.3 |
|  | .9 | 1.0 | .9 |  |  | 1.0 | 1.5 | 1.2 | .8 |
| % Depr., Dep., Amort./Sales | 1.1 | 1.2 | 1.3 |  |  |  | 1.5 | .7 | 1.6 |
|  | (161) 2.6 | (170) 2.3 | (151) 2.7 |  |  |  | (12) 2.4 | (35) 2.4 | (85) 2.8 |
|  | 4.7 | 4.3 | 4.8 |  |  |  | 6.4 | 3.2 | 4.6 |
| % Officers', Directors' Owners' Comp/Sales | 1.6 | 1.9 | 1.2 |  |  |  |  |  | .9 |
|  | (36) 3.0 | (43) 2.9 | (35) 2.0 |  |  |  |  |  | (15) 1.3 |
|  | 5.6 | 4.3 | 5.8 |  |  |  |  |  | 2.2 |
| Net Sales ($) | 11077764M | 10372922M | 9878289M | 2756M | 13255M | 51436M | 126869M | 706736M | 8977237M |
| Total Assets ($) | 9093741M | 8045271M | 8181178M | 2112M | 21345M | 31974M | 75031M | 508215M | 7542501M |

M = $ thousand    MM = $ million
See Pages 9 through 22 for Explanation of Ratios and Data

## Current Data Sorted by Assets

## Comparative Historical Data

| Type of Statement | 0-500M | 500M-2MM | 2-10MM | 10-50MM | 50-100MM | 100-250MM | | 4/1/07-3/31/08 ALL | 4/1/08-3/31/09 ALL |
|---|---|---|---|---|---|---|---|---|---|
| Unqualified | | | 6 | 7 | | 5 | | 22 | 17 |
| Reviewed | | 2 | 13 | 12 | | 1 | | 27 | 26 |
| Compiled | 2 | 6 | 10 | | | | | 21 | 18 |
| Tax Returns | 2 | 8 | 7 | | | | | 12 | 12 |
| Other | 3 | 21 | 16 | 16 | 1 | 3 | | 45 | 74 |
| | | 24 (4/1-9/30/11) | | 120 (10/1/11-3/31/12) | | | | | |

| | 0-500M | 500M-2MM | 2-10MM | 10-50MM | 50-100MM | 100-250MM | | 4/1/07-3/31/08 ALL | 4/1/08-3/31/09 ALL |
|---|---|---|---|---|---|---|---|---|---|
| **NUMBER OF STATEMENTS** | 7 | 37 | 52 | 35 | 5 | 8 | | 127 | 147 |
| | % | % | % | % | % | % | **ASSETS** | % | % |
| | | 11.0 | 11.1 | 9.2 | | | Cash & Equivalents | 8.6 | 7.0 |
| | | 25.3 | 26.4 | 24.9 | | | Trade Receivables (net) | 27.5 | 24.8 |
| | | 29.6 | 26.7 | 27.6 | | | Inventory | 25.7 | 26.7 |
| | | 1.0 | 1.8 | 2.4 | | | All Other Current | 2.1 | 2.6 |
| | | 66.9 | 65.9 | 64.1 | | | Total Current | 63.9 | 61.1 |
| | | 23.2 | 20.7 | 19.8 | | | Fixed Assets (net) | 19.5 | 22.2 |
| | | 2.6 | 5.7 | 10.0 | | | Intangibles (net) | 7.5 | 8.2 |
| | | 7.2 | 7.7 | 6.1 | | | All Other Non-Current | 9.1 | 8.6 |
| | | 100.0 | 100.0 | 100.0 | | | Total | 100.0 | 100.0 |
| | | | | | | | **LIABILITIES** | | |
| | | 10.5 | 9.2 | 10.2 | | | Notes Payable-Short Term | 11.3 | 12.1 |
| | | 2.3 | 2.9 | 2.4 | | | Cur. Mat.-L.T.D. | 3.3 | 3.3 |
| | | 17.4 | 14.6 | 12.8 | | | Trade Payables | 17.3 | 15.4 |
| | | .2 | .4 | .3 | | | Income Taxes Payable | .3 | .1 |
| | | 9.0 | 8.1 | 6.8 | | | All Other Current | 7.6 | 8.0 |
| | | 39.4 | 35.1 | 32.4 | | | Total Current | 39.7 | 38.9 |
| | | 16.3 | 15.0 | 13.5 | | | Long-Term Debt | 15.2 | 14.3 |
| | | .1 | .5 | 1.2 | | | Deferred Taxes | .4 | .4 |
| | | 16.2 | 4.1 | 5.3 | | | All Other Non-Current | 6.4 | 10.9 |
| | | 28.1 | 45.3 | 47.6 | | | Net Worth | 38.2 | 35.5 |
| | | 100.0 | 100.0 | 100.0 | | | Total Liabilities & Net Worth | 100.0 | 100.0 |
| | | | | | | | **INCOME DATA** | | |
| | | 100.0 | 100.0 | 100.0 | | | Net Sales | 100.0 | 100.0 |
| | | 40.4 | 32.6 | 31.5 | | | Gross Profit | 35.4 | 32.7 |
| | | 35.0 | 27.7 | 24.6 | | | Operating Expenses | 29.7 | 27.3 |
| | | 5.5 | 4.9 | 6.9 | | | Operating Profit | 5.7 | 5.3 |
| | | .9 | .4 | .9 | | | All Other Expenses (net) | 1.1 | 1.4 |
| | | 4.6 | 4.5 | 6.1 | | | Profit Before Taxes | 4.6 | 3.9 |
| | | | | | | | **RATIOS** | | |
| | | 4.0 | 3.8 | 3.2 | | | | 3.4 | 2.9 |
| | | 1.8 | 1.9 | 2.2 | | | Current | 2.0 | 1.8 |
| | | 1.1 | 1.4 | 1.3 | | | | 1.2 | 1.1 |
| | | 2.5 | 2.4 | 1.7 | | | | 1.7 | 1.6 |
| | | .7 | 1.1 | 1.0 | | | Quick | 1.0 | .9 |
| | | .4 | .7 | .7 | | | | .6 | .5 |
| | 20 | 18.0 | 33  11.2 | 31  11.7 | | | | 30  12.1 | 28  13.1 |
| | 34 | 10.6 | 40  9.1 | 45  8.2 | | | Sales/Receivables | 43  8.5 | 40  9.1 |
| | 50 | 7.3 | 49  7.4 | 54  6.7 | | | | 55  6.7 | 52  7.1 |
| | 33 | 11.0 | 44  8.3 | 54  6.8 | | | | 39  9.3 | 37  9.8 |
| | 65 | 5.6 | 62  5.9 | 73  5.0 | | | Cost of Sales/Inventory | 65  5.6 | 63  5.8 |
| | 107 | 3.4 | 83  4.4 | 99  3.7 | | | | 90  4.1 | 90  4.0 |
| | 22 | 16.3 | 19  18.8 | 19  19.3 | | | | 20  18.3 | 17  21.2 |
| | 38 | 9.6 | 28  13.0 | 34  10.6 | | | Cost of Sales/Payables | 36  10.2 | 29  12.6 |
| | 57 | 6.4 | 53  6.9 | 46  8.0 | | | | 53  6.8 | 47  7.8 |
| | | 3.9 | 4.5 | 4.2 | | | | 4.8 | 5.0 |
| | | 7.2 | 6.6 | 6.5 | | | Sales/Working Capital | 8.3 | 8.6 |
| | | 80.1 | 12.8 | 12.7 | | | | 30.7 | 43.5 |
| | | 22.1 | 15.8 | 22.9 | | | | 13.4 | 9.8 |
| | (30) | 4.8 | (49)  5.8 | (33)  7.1 | | | EBIT/Interest | (117)  4.4 | (129)  2.7 |
| | | 1.5 | 2.8 | 1.6 | | | | 1.7 | .9 |
| | | | 4.7 | 6.1 | | | Net Profit + Depr., Dep., | 6.0 | 6.7 |
| | | (17) | 1.6 | (19)  3.6 | | | Amort./Cur. Mat. L/T/D | (35)  2.9 | (36)  2.1 |
| | | | 1.1 | 1.1 | | | | 1.6 | 1.1 |
| | | .1 | .2 | .2 | | | | .2 | .2 |
| | | .4 | .4 | .5 | | | Fixed/Worth | .5 | .7 |
| | | 4.5 | 1.2 | 1.2 | | | | 1.6 | 2.7 |
| | | .4 | .5 | .7 | | | | .5 | .7 |
| | | 2.3 | 1.3 | 1.8 | | | Debt/Worth | 1.8 | 2.0 |
| | | 15.6 | 3.8 | 2.6 | | | | 6.7 | 8.9 |
| | | 70.2 | 38.1 | 38.0 | | | | 48.5 | 43.6 |
| | (30) | 33.6 | (47)  24.5 | (32)  18.8 | | | % Profit Before Taxes/Tangible Net Worth | (104)  20.6 | (120)  17.4 |
| | | 11.8 | 8.8 | 8.1 | | | | 8.4 | 1.3 |
| | | 20.4 | 16.1 | 12.6 | | | | 16.7 | 12.8 |
| | | 9.1 | 8.0 | 7.1 | | | % Profit Before Taxes/Total Assets | 7.9 | 5.5 |
| | | 2.3 | 2.9 | 2.7 | | | | 1.8 | -.1 |
| | | 57.0 | 29.2 | 18.1 | | | | 31.8 | 28.3 |
| | | 15.5 | 15.1 | 10.1 | | | Sales/Net Fixed Assets | 12.2 | 11.7 |
| | | 5.5 | 7.0 | 7.3 | | | | 7.3 | 5.7 |
| | | 3.4 | 2.8 | 2.3 | | | | 3.0 | 3.1 |
| | | 2.7 | 2.3 | 2.0 | | | Sales/Total Assets | 2.3 | 2.3 |
| | | 1.9 | 1.6 | 1.6 | | | | 1.5 | 1.6 |
| | | .5 | .6 | 1.0 | | | | .8 | 1.0 |
| | (30) | 1.0 | (48)  1.3 | (34)  1.5 | | | % Depr., Dep., Amort./Sales | (116)  1.5 | (125)  1.7 |
| | | 4.2 | 2.0 | 2.2 | | | | 2.3 | 2.5 |
| | | 4.1 | 2.8 | | | | | 1.7 | 2.5 |
| | (22) | 5.5 | (14)  5.3 | | | | % Officers', Directors' Owners' Comp/Sales | (39)  4.1 | (41)  4.2 |
| | | 8.0 | 10.0 | | | | | 7.2 | 7.0 |
| | 9120M | 134510M | 544008M | 1567834M | 467639M | 1467155M | Net Sales ($) | 3603763M | 4529226M |
| | 2302M | 47048M | 250353M | 782080M | 377373M | 1244176M | Total Assets ($) | 2159134M | 2686336M |

© RMA 2012

M = $ thousand    MM = $ million
See Pages 9 through 22 for Explanation of Ratios and Data

## Comparative Historical Data — Current Data Sorted by Sales

| 4/1/09-3/31/10 ALL | 4/1/10-3/31/11 ALL | 4/1/11-3/31/12 ALL | Type of Statement | 0-1MM | 1-3MM | 3-5MM | 5-10MM | 10-25MM | 25MM & OVER |
|---|---|---|---|---|---|---|---|---|---|
| 15 | 14 | 21 | Unqualified | | 1 | 2 | 3 | 13 | 14 |
| 33 | 28 | 28 | Reviewed | | 5 | 2 | 9 | 2 | 9 |
| 16 | 19 | 18 | Compiled | | 5 | 2 | 9 | 2 | |
| 18 | 9 | 17 | Tax Returns | | 5 | 5 | 5 | 2 | |
| 58 | 55 | 60 | Other | 4 | 9 | 8 | | 13 | 17 |
| | | | | | 24 (4/1-9/30/11) | | 120 (10/1/11-3/31/12) | | |
| 140 | 125 | 144 | NUMBER OF STATEMENTS | 4 | 20 | 17 | 30 | 33 | 40 |
| % | % | % | **ASSETS** | % | % | % | % | % | % |
| 9.4 | 7.8 | 10.5 | Cash & Equivalents | | 13.7 | 16.3 | 8.3 | 9.3 | 9.9 |
| 24.4 | 23.4 | 25.1 | Trade Receivables (net) | | 23.6 | 23.9 | 29.2 | 27.7 | 21.5 |
| 25.0 | 28.2 | 26.7 | Inventory | | 30.3 | 22.9 | 28.7 | 26.2 | 25.3 |
| 3.0 | 2.6 | 1.7 | All Other Current | | .6 | 1.1 | 1.4 | 2.4 | 2.3 |
| 61.8 | 62.1 | 64.0 | Total Current | | 68.2 | 64.3 | 67.5 | 65.6 | 59.0 |
| 24.2 | 21.8 | 22.0 | Fixed Assets (net) | | 23.0 | 28.8 | 17.5 | 20.5 | 21.5 |
| 7.1 | 8.3 | 7.2 | Intangibles (net) | | 1.9 | 4.4 | 5.9 | 5.4 | 14.3 |
| 6.9 | 7.9 | 6.8 | All Other Non-Current | | 6.9 | 2.4 | 9.1 | 8.6 | 5.2 |
| 100.0 | 100.0 | 100.0 | Total | | 100.0 | 100.0 | 100.0 | 100.0 | 100.0 |
| | | | **LIABILITIES** | | | | | | |
| 9.5 | 10.2 | 9.6 | Notes Payable-Short Term | | 12.8 | 7.8 | 8.4 | 13.7 | 6.5 |
| 4.5 | 3.5 | 2.5 | Cur. Mat.-L.T.D. | | 1.1 | 2.1 | 3.1 | 3.3 | 2.4 |
| 13.9 | 14.1 | 14.4 | Trade Payables | | 16.4 | 14.1 | 13.7 | 17.7 | 10.9 |
| .2 | .1 | .3 | Income Taxes Payable | | .1 | .0 | .6 | .2 | .5 |
| 7.9 | 8.3 | 8.0 | All Other Current | | 7.6 | 7.5 | 8.0 | 7.9 | 8.0 |
| 35.9 | 36.3 | 35.0 | Total Current | | 38.1 | 31.5 | 33.8 | 42.8 | 28.3 |
| 13.0 | 15.3 | 16.3 | Long-Term Debt | | 19.2 | 21.6 | 12.6 | 14.8 | 15.8 |
| .5 | .6 | .8 | Deferred Taxes | | .0 | .2 | .5 | .6 | 1.8 |
| 9.5 | 7.3 | 9.7 | All Other Non-Current | | 32.0 | 15.6 | 2.9 | 5.1 | 5.2 |
| 41.0 | 40.5 | 38.3 | Net Worth | | 10.7 | 31.1 | 50.2 | 36.7 | 48.8 |
| 100.0 | 100.0 | 100.0 | Total Liabilities & Net Worth | | 100.0 | 100.0 | 100.0 | 100.0 | 100.0 |
| | | | **INCOME DATA** | | | | | | |
| 100.0 | 100.0 | 100.0 | Net Sales | | 100.0 | 100.0 | 100.0 | 100.0 | 100.0 |
| 35.6 | 35.1 | 35.3 | Gross Profit | | 43.2 | 38.9 | 35.0 | 30.2 | 32.8 |
| 31.7 | 28.8 | 29.4 | Operating Expenses | | 36.2 | 33.6 | 30.0 | 25.6 | 25.1 |
| 3.9 | 6.3 | 5.8 | Operating Profit | | 7.0 | 5.2 | 5.0 | 4.6 | 7.7 |
| 1.0 | 1.2 | .8 | All Other Expenses (net) | | 1.8 | .8 | -.2 | .8 | 1.0 |
| 3.0 | 5.1 | 5.0 | Profit Before Taxes | | 5.2 | 4.4 | 5.2 | 3.8 | 6.7 |
| | | | **RATIOS** | | | | | | |
| 3.3 | 3.5 | 3.5 | Current | | 3.9 | 6.6 | 4.4 | 2.7 | 3.4 |
| 1.8 | 2.1 | 1.9 | | | 1.8 | 2.6 | 2.4 | 1.4 | 2.3 |
| 1.2 | 1.2 | 1.3 | | | 1.0 | 1.5 | 1.5 | 1.2 | 1.4 |
| 1.9 | 2.0 | 2.1 | Quick | | 3.5 | 4.6 | 2.5 | 1.4 | 1.8 |
| .9 | .9 | 1.0 | | | .6 | 1.7 | 1.2 | .8 | 1.2 |
| .6 | .6 | .6 | | | .4 | .7 | .6 | .6 | .7 |
| 31  12.0 | 31  11.8 | 31  11.8 | Sales/Receivables | 13  28.1 | 27  13.5 | 31  11.8 | 33  11.2 | 31  11.8 | |
| 41  8.9 | 42  8.7 | 40  9.2 | | 36  10.1 | 39  9.4 | 40  9.1 | 43  8.5 | 41  8.8 | |
| 51  7.1 | 51  7.2 | 52  7.0 | | 59  6.2 | 50  7.3 | 51  7.1 | 54  6.8 | 52  7.0 | |
| 43  8.4 | 50  7.3 | 41  9.0 | Cost of Sales/Inventory | 34  10.7 | 4  82.2 | 43  8.4 | 27  13.5 | 63  5.8 | |
| 68  5.4 | 72  5.1 | 69  5.3 | | 69  5.3 | 81  4.5 | 55  6.6 | 62  5.9 | 74  4.9 | |
| 99  3.7 | 104  3.5 | 94  3.9 | | 122  3.0 | 107  3.4 | 91  4.0 | 85  3.6 | 101  3.6 | |
| 18  20.2 | 21  17.7 | 20  18.6 | Cost of Sales/Payables | 26  14.2 | 13  28.3 | 18  20.8 | 23  15.9 | 19  19.5 | |
| 30  12.2 | 32  11.5 | 30  12.3 | | 46  8.0 | 29  12.5 | 23  16.2 | 33  11.1 | 29  12.4 | |
| 47  7.8 | 48  7.7 | 51  7.2 | | 60  6.1 | 56  6.5 | 36  10.1 | 54  6.7 | 41  8.9 | |
| 4.3 | 4.5 | 4.3 | Sales/Working Capital | | 4.4 | 3.8 | 4.3 | 5.5 | 4.1 |
| 7.3 | 6.9 | 6.8 | | | 9.3 | 4.6 | 6.1 | 10.5 | 5.8 |
| 19.2 | 18.5 | 18.3 | | | 140.7 | 17.6 | 14.1 | 30.0 | 10.2 |
| 11.3 | 15.7 | 17.0 | EBIT/Interest | | 12.4 | 30.2 | 20.9 | 10.4 | 26.8 |
| (127)  3.6 | (111)  5.6 | (130)  5.8 | | (15)  2.0 | (16)  2.8 | (28)  12.5 | (29)  4.1 | (39)  7.0 | |
| -.1 | 1.9 | 1.9 | | | 1.7 | -.5 | 4.8 | 2.5 | 1.6 |
| 8.7 | 6.6 | 6.1 | Net Profit + Depr., Dep., Amort./Cur. Mat. L/T/D | | | | 10.0 | 1.9 | 6.5 |
| (42)  3.2 | (36)  2.9 | (46)  2.3 | | | | (10)  2.8 | (12)  1.3 | (21)  4.1 | |
| 1.2 | 1.1 | 1.1 | | | | | 1.6 | .7 | 1.9 |
| .2 | .2 | .2 | Fixed/Worth | | .2 | .2 | .1 | .3 | .3 |
| .5 | .5 | .5 | | | 1.2 | .5 | .3 | .8 | .5 |
| 2.3 | 2.0 | 2.0 | | | UND | NM | .5 | 1.8 | 1.3 |
| .5 | .5 | .6 | Debt/Worth | | .9 | .3 | .4 | .8 | .7 |
| 1.2 | 1.3 | 1.7 | | | 2.4 | 1.4 | .8 | 2.6 | 1.1 |
| 5.1 | 4.2 | 4.2 | | | UND | NM | 2.2 | 5.3 | 2.9 |
| 28.8 | 45.8 | 44.8 | % Profit Before Taxes/Tangible Net Worth | | 92.7 | 54.7 | 40.5 | 40.4 | 36.6 |
| (118)  11.3 | (105)  21.1 | (123)  25.0 | | (15)  44.8 | (13)  26.0 | (28)  24.1 | (29)  25.8 | (34)  16.6 | |
| 1.6 | 8.7 | 8.8 | | | 12.7 | 3.0 | 9.3 | 10.3 | 6.5 |
| 12.4 | 13.7 | 16.0 | % Profit Before Taxes/Total Assets | | 28.4 | 23.2 | 16.1 | 15.2 | 12.8 |
| 4.4 | 7.3 | 9.0 | | | 9.8 | 4.9 | 9.6 | 6.4 | 7.1 |
| -.2 | 3.2 | 2.8 | | | 4.2 | -2.8 | 3.3 | 2.7 | 2.7 |
| 24.8 | 27.7 | 29.9 | Sales/Net Fixed Assets | | 71.3 | 38.9 | 40.0 | 19.7 | 16.1 |
| 10.9 | 12.9 | 11.8 | | | 22.7 | 6.9 | 22.3 | 13.3 | 9.2 |
| 4.9 | 5.6 | 5.9 | | | 4.6 | 4.6 | 10.2 | 7.6 | 5.4 |
| 2.9 | 2.7 | 2.9 | Sales/Total Assets | | 3.4 | 2.9 | 3.5 | 2.9 | 2.3 |
| 2.0 | 2.1 | 2.2 | | | 2.5 | 2.3 | 2.6 | 2.3 | 1.8 |
| 1.4 | 1.5 | 1.6 | | | 1.9 | 1.7 | 1.5 | 1.7 | 1.4 |
| .9 | .8 | .7 | % Depr., Dep., Amort./Sales | | .5 | .9 | .4 | .7 | 1.1 |
| (126)  1.6 | (110)  1.4 | (126)  1.4 | | (17)  1.5 | 1.8 | (25)  1.0 | (31)  1.3 | (36)  1.7 | |
| 2.7 | 2.3 | 2.2 | | | 4.3 | 3.6 | 1.7 | 1.9 | 2.3 |
| 2.0 | 2.0 | 3.0 | % Officers', Directors' Owners' Comp/Sales | | 4.2 | 4.9 | 2.4 | | |
| (52)  4.9 | (39)  3.4 | (46)  4.9 | | (11)  5.1 | (12)  7.9 | (12)  4.0 | | | |
| 7.9 | 7.2 | 7.6 | | | 7.0 | 10.2 | 6.3 | | |
| 4122661M | 3768406M | 4190266M | Net Sales ($) | 2498M | 37962M | 69391M | 219956M | 502136M | 3358323M |
| 2569791M | 2529773M | 2703332M | Total Assets ($) | 1828M | 16434M | 36287M | 103583M | 237602M | 2307598M |

M = $ thousand    MM = $ million
See Pages 9 through 22 for Explanation of Ratios and Data

## Current Data Sorted by Assets | Comparative Historical Data

Period labels (current): **6 (4/1-9/30/11)** covers 0-500M / 500M-2MM / 2-10MM; **79 (10/1/11-3/31/12)** covers 10-50MM / 50-100MM / 100-250MM. Historical columns: **4/1/07-3/31/08 ALL** and **4/1/08-3/31/09 ALL**.

| | 0-500M | 500M-2MM | 2-10MM | 10-50MM | 50-100MM | 100-250MM | | 4/1/07-3/31/08 ALL | 4/1/08-3/31/09 ALL |
|---|---|---|---|---|---|---|---|---|---|
| **Type of Statement** | | | | | | | | | |
| Unqualified | | | 3 | 10 | 1 | 1 | | 17 | 15 |
| Reviewed | | 1 | 15 | 5 | 1 | | | 15 | 21 |
| Compiled | | 2 | 4 | 1 | | | | 9 | 9 |
| Tax Returns | 1 | 4 | 3 | | | | | 7 | 7 |
| Other | 3 | 5 | 6 | 11 | 4 | 4 | | 35 | 29 |
| NUMBER OF STATEMENTS | 4 | 12 | 31 | 27 | 6 | 5 | | 83 | 81 |
| | % | % | % | % | % | % | | % | % |
| **ASSETS** | | | | | | | | | |
| Cash & Equivalents | | 17.1 | 8.3 | 6.6 | | | | 9.2 | 9.9 |
| Trade Receivables (net) | | 34.3 | 28.1 | 26.0 | | | | 27.7 | 25.1 |
| Inventory | | 30.0 | 32.6 | 26.8 | | | | 26.8 | 27.9 |
| All Other Current | | 2.2 | 1.4 | 2.8 | | | | 2.0 | 1.8 |
| Total Current | | 83.5 | 70.4 | 62.2 | | | | 65.8 | 64.7 |
| Fixed Assets (net) | | 10.1 | 20.7 | 20.7 | | | | 20.6 | 22.1 |
| Intangibles (net) | | 2.9 | 2.9 | 11.2 | | | | 6.2 | 5.8 |
| All Other Non-Current | | 3.5 | 5.9 | 5.9 | | | | 7.4 | 7.4 |
| Total | | 100.0 | 100.0 | 100.0 | | | | 100.0 | 100.0 |
| **LIABILITIES** | | | | | | | | | |
| Notes Payable-Short Term | | 13.9 | 11.1 | 6.5 | | | | 10.2 | 10.8 |
| Cur. Mat.-L.T.D. | | 1.4 | 4.0 | 2.5 | | | | 3.4 | 3.8 |
| Trade Payables | | 27.9 | 17.3 | 12.0 | | | | 15.4 | 15.2 |
| Income Taxes Payable | | .0 | .1 | .4 | | | | .2 | .0 |
| All Other Current | | 16.3 | 6.5 | 7.7 | | | | 8.5 | 7.4 |
| Total Current | | 59.4 | 39.0 | 29.1 | | | | 37.7 | 37.1 |
| Long-Term Debt | | 14.2 | 13.8 | 12.8 | | | | 10.7 | 13.6 |
| Deferred Taxes | | .0 | .4 | 1.7 | | | | .5 | .7 |
| All Other Non-Current | | 1.9 | 5.7 | 8.5 | | | | 11.6 | 6.4 |
| Net Worth | | 24.4 | 41.1 | 47.8 | | | | 39.5 | 42.2 |
| Total Liabilities & Net Worth | | 100.0 | 100.0 | 100.0 | | | | 100.0 | 100.0 |
| **INCOME DATA** | | | | | | | | | |
| Net Sales | | 100.0 | 100.0 | 100.0 | | | | 100.0 | 100.0 |
| Gross Profit | | 32.9 | 29.1 | 29.0 | | | | 33.8 | 29.2 |
| Operating Expenses | | 30.6 | 23.6 | 21.2 | | | | 28.3 | 25.0 |
| Operating Profit | | 2.3 | 5.4 | 7.8 | | | | 5.5 | 4.3 |
| All Other Expenses (net) | | .0 | 1.1 | .9 | | | | 1.3 | .8 |
| Profit Before Taxes | | 2.3 | 4.3 | 6.8 | | | | 4.2 | 3.4 |
| **RATIOS** | | | | | | | | | |
| Current | | 3.7 | 2.5 | 3.8 | | | | 3.1 | 3.1 |
| | | 1.3 | 1.8 | 2.3 | | | | 1.8 | 1.8 |
| | | .9 | 1.4 | 1.7 | | | | 1.1 | 1.2 |
| Quick | | 2.5 | 1.2 | 1.8 | | | | 1.8 | 2.1 |
| | | .8 | .8 | 1.2 | | | | 1.0 | .9 |
| | | .4 | .7 | .7 | | | | .5 | .5 |
| Sales/Receivables | | 26  13.8 | 31  11.6 | 37  9.9 | | | | 33  11.2 | 30  12.4 |
| | | 31  11.9 | 37  9.8 | 45  8.2 | | | | 43  8.5 | 39  9.4 |
| | | 46  7.9 | 49  7.4 | 58  6.3 | | | | 53  6.9 | 49  7.5 |
| Cost of Sales/Inventory | | 27  13.7 | 48  7.6 | 47  7.7 | | | | 44  8.3 | 39  9.3 |
| | | 51  7.1 | 61  6.0 | 72  5.1 | | | | 60  6.1 | 57  6.5 |
| | | 94  3.9 | 81  4.5 | 85  4.3 | | | | 83  4.4 | 84  4.4 |
| Cost of Sales/Payables | | 12  29.4 | 15  23.6 | 21  17.6 | | | | 22  16.7 | 17  21.6 |
| | | 31  11.9 | 29  12.6 | 29  12.5 | | | | 33  10.9 | 27  13.3 |
| | | 54  6.8 | 48  7.6 | 40  9.2 | | | | 48  7.6 | 46  7.9 |
| Sales/Working Capital | | 5.8 | 5.6 | 4.2 | | | | 5.1 | 4.7 |
| | | 15.2 | 9.4 | 5.8 | | | | 8.5 | 8.0 |
| | | -56.0 | 13.9 | 9.9 | | | | 30.0 | 20.9 |
| EBIT/Interest | | | 23.1 | 33.1 | | | | 9.4 | 10.7 |
| | | | (26) 6.4 | (25) 11.0 | | | | (71) 4.2 | (69) 3.5 |
| | | | 3.0 | 1.6 | | | | 1.7 | .8 |
| Net Profit + Depr., Dep., Amort./Cur. Mat. L/T/D | | | | 12.6 | | | | 5.0 | 6.9 |
| | | | | (15) 5.4 | | | | (29) 2.8 | (28) 1.5 |
| | | | | 2.3 | | | | 1.0 | .1 |
| Fixed/Worth | | .0 | .1 | .3 | | | | .2 | .1 |
| | | .3 | .5 | .6 | | | | .4 | .5 |
| | | 5.6 | 1.4 | 1.1 | | | | 1.7 | 1.7 |
| Debt/Worth | | .8 | .5 | .7 | | | | .8 | .7 |
| | | 6.3 | 1.8 | 1.2 | | | | 1.9 | 1.4 |
| | | -19.8 | 2.8 | 3.5 | | | | 4.7 | 3.8 |
| % Profit Before Taxes/Tangible Net Worth | | | 49.2 | 42.9 | | | | 60.0 | 45.5 |
| | | | (27) 22.6 | (24) 24.1 | | | | (75) 21.5 | (73) 17.0 |
| | | | 9.9 | 8.4 | | | | 8.2 | 2.5 |
| % Profit Before Taxes/Total Assets | | 14.0 | 15.6 | 23.8 | | | | 15.0 | 16.2 |
| | | 6.7 | 11.4 | 9.8 | | | | 7.7 | 6.1 |
| | | -6.8 | 2.7 | 1.8 | | | | 2.0 | .1 |
| Sales/Net Fixed Assets | | 999.8 | 33.7 | 16.6 | | | | 42.6 | 30.2 |
| | | 82.7 | 16.4 | 12.3 | | | | 14.3 | 11.4 |
| | | 40.6 | 7.2 | 6.4 | | | | 6.7 | 6.6 |
| Sales/Total Assets | | 4.5 | 3.4 | 2.5 | | | | 3.1 | 2.9 |
| | | 3.7 | 2.6 | 2.0 | | | | 2.3 | 2.3 |
| | | 2.6 | 2.1 | 1.7 | | | | 1.7 | 1.8 |
| % Depr., Dep., Amort./Sales | | | .7 | 1.2 | | | | .4 | .7 |
| | | | (28) 1.5 | (25) 1.4 | | | | (72) 1.1 | (70) 1.5 |
| | | | 2.7 | 2.0 | | | | 2.0 | 2.5 |
| % Officers', Directors' Owners' Comp/Sales | | | 2.2 | | | | | 2.8 | 2.1 |
| | | | (13) 3.0 | | | | | (21) 9.0 | (20) 5.4 |
| | | | 4.3 | | | | | 14.4 | 8.7 |
| Net Sales ($) | 5959M | 58873M | 378346M | 1253693M | 653847M | 1006570M | | 2969444M | 2984928M |
| Total Assets ($) | 1383M | 16098M | 151946M | 650979M | 416081M | 834528M | | 1560080M | 1484127M |

M = $ thousand   MM = $ million
See Pages 9 through 22 for Explanation of Ratios and Data

## Comparative Historical Data      Current Data Sorted by Sales

| | | | Type of Statement | | | | | | |
|---|---|---|---|---|---|---|---|---|---|
| 16 | 13 | 15 | Unqualified | | | | | 4 | 11 |
| 18 | 19 | 22 | Reviewed | | | 2 | 2 | 13 | 5 |
| 4 | 5 | 7 | Compiled | | | 2 | 2 | 2 | 1 |
| 5 | 9 | 8 | Tax Returns | 1 | 1 | 2 | 3 | 1 | |
| 32 | 21 | 33 | Other | | 5 | | 8 | 4 | 16 |
| 4/1/09-3/31/10 ALL | 4/1/10-3/31/11 ALL | 4/1/11-3/31/12 ALL | | 0-1MM | 1-3MM | 3-5MM | 5-10MM | 10-25MM | 25MM & OVER |
| | | | | | 6 (4/1-9/30/11) | | 79 (10/1/11-3/31/12) | | |
| 75 | 67 | 85 | **NUMBER OF STATEMENTS** | 1 | 6 | 6 | 15 | 24 | 33 |
| % | % | % | **ASSETS** | % | % | % | % | % | % |
| 6.2 | 9.0 | 9.3 | Cash & Equivalents | | | | 10.2 | 9.4 | 5.7 |
| 25.9 | 26.8 | 28.2 | Trade Receivables (net) | | | | 30.9 | 27.7 | 25.5 |
| 26.3 | 29.1 | 28.0 | Inventory | | | | 36.1 | 30.4 | 23.1 |
| 3.0 | 1.9 | 2.2 | All Other Current | | | | .9 | 1.8 | 3.0 |
| 61.3 | 66.8 | 67.6 | Total Current | | | | 78.2 | 69.4 | 57.4 |
| 21.4 | 18.4 | 19.6 | Fixed Assets (net) | | | | 19.0 | 19.2 | 23.6 |
| 8.9 | 6.7 | 7.6 | Intangibles (net) | | | | 1.9 | 4.7 | 13.0 |
| 8.3 | 8.1 | 5.3 | All Other Non-Current | | | | 1.0 | 6.7 | 6.0 |
| 100.0 | 100.0 | 100.0 | Total | | | | 100.0 | 100.0 | 100.0 |
| | | | **LIABILITIES** | | | | | | |
| 9.3 | 9.5 | 9.1 | Notes Payable-Short Term | | | | 13.3 | 9.0 | 6.5 |
| 4.1 | 4.9 | 3.0 | Cur. Mat.-L.T.D. | | | | 5.9 | 2.3 | 3.2 |
| 14.3 | 15.5 | 16.6 | Trade Payables | | | | 24.9 | 16.9 | 11.9 |
| .4 | .2 | .2 | Income Taxes Payable | | | | .1 | .1 | .4 |
| 7.6 | 8.5 | 13.9 | All Other Current | | | | 12.5 | 6.2 | 8.9 |
| 35.7 | 38.5 | 42.8 | Total Current | | | | 56.7 | 34.6 | 30.8 |
| 14.5 | 11.4 | 13.9 | Long-Term Debt | | | | 17.7 | 11.6 | 13.8 |
| 1.1 | .7 | .9 | Deferred Taxes | | | | .3 | .3 | 2.0 |
| 8.8 | 8.1 | 8.6 | All Other Non-Current | | | | 5.0 | 6.4 | 14.4 |
| 39.8 | 41.3 | 33.8 | Net Worth | | | | 20.3 | 47.2 | 38.9 |
| 100.0 | 100.0 | 100.0 | Total Liabilities & Net Worth | | | | 100.0 | 100.0 | 100.0 |
| | | | **INCOME DATA** | | | | | | |
| 100.0 | 100.0 | 100.0 | Net Sales | | | | 100.0 | 100.0 | 100.0 |
| 32.8 | 33.6 | 30.6 | Gross Profit | | | | 28.2 | 29.2 | 28.6 |
| 27.3 | 27.4 | 24.7 | Operating Expenses | | | | 23.6 | 22.7 | 21.2 |
| 5.5 | 6.2 | 5.9 | Operating Profit | | | | 4.6 | 6.5 | 7.3 |
| 1.1 | .6 | .9 | All Other Expenses (net) | | | | 1.8 | .6 | 1.4 |
| 4.4 | 5.6 | 5.0 | Profit Before Taxes | | | | 2.8 | 5.9 | 6.0 |
| | | | **RATIOS** | | | | | | |
| 2.7 | 2.7 | 3.0 | Current | | | | 2.0 | 4.1 | 3.0 |
| 1.9 | 1.8 | 1.9 | | | | | 1.4 | 2.0 | 2.0 |
| 1.3 | 1.3 | 1.3 | | | | | 1.2 | 1.5 | 1.3 |
| 1.5 | 1.4 | 1.6 | Quick | | | | .9 | 2.6 | 1.5 |
| .9 | .9 | .9 | | | | | .8 | 1.0 | 1.1 |
| .6 | .6 | .7 | | | | | .6 | .7 | .8 |
| 39  9.4 | 33  10.9 | 32  11.3 | Sales/Receivables | | | | 26  14.2 | 32  11.5 | 41  8.9 |
| 47  7.8 | 44  8.3 | 42  8.7 | | | | | 36  10.0 | 37  9.8 | 46  7.9 |
| 52  7.0 | 55  6.7 | 51  7.1 | | | | | 43  8.5 | 49  7.4 | 62  5.9 |
| 50  7.3 | 55  6.7 | 46  7.9 | Cost of Sales/Inventory | | | | 54  6.8 | 46  8.0 | 48  7.6 |
| 67  5.4 | 70  5.2 | 64  5.7 | | | | | 62  5.9 | 61  6.0 | 66  5.5 |
| 97  3.8 | 103  3.5 | 85  4.3 | | | | | 101  3.6 | 81  4.5 | 85  4.3 |
| 25  14.5 | 22  16.9 | 21  17.2 | Cost of Sales/Payables | | | | 15  24.5 | 17  22.1 | 24  14.9 |
| 32  11.4 | 32  11.3 | 32  11.4 | | | | | 27  13.6 | 29  12.7 | 34  10.7 |
| 45  8.1 | 56  6.5 | 46  8.0 | | | | | 49  7.4 | 43  8.4 | 42  8.6 |
| 5.4 | 4.9 | 4.8 | Sales/Working Capital | | | | 6.1 | 3.5 | 4.8 |
| 7.2 | 7.4 | 7.5 | | | | | 12.3 | 8.4 | 6.6 |
| 22.4 | 20.2 | 15.2 | | | | | 32.7 | 13.7 | 14.7 |
| 12.3 | 18.4 | 24.0 | EBIT/Interest | | | | 14.1 | 20.0 | 29.7 |
| (70)  3.8 | (59)  5.9 | (72)  6.4 | | | | (12)  4.9 | | (19)  9.6 | (32)  6.2 |
| 1.5 | 2.9 | 2.5 | | | | | .3 | 3.7 | 1.6 |
| 7.6 | 5.2 | 7.2 | Net Profit + Depr., Dep., Amort./Cur. Mat. L/T/D | | | | | | 7.2 |
| (24)  2.8 | (19)  2.8 | (26)  3.3 | | | | | | (18) | 3.2 |
| 1.3 | 2.1 | 2.0 | | | | | | | 2.0 |
| .2 | .2 | .2 | Fixed/Worth | | | | .2 | .1 | .4 |
| .7 | .5 | .6 | | | | | 1.4 | .3 | .8 |
| 1.6 | 1.3 | 1.8 | | | | | -5.3 | .8 | 2.3 |
| .8 | .6 | .7 | Debt/Worth | | | | 1.0 | .5 | .9 |
| 1.9 | 1.7 | 1.7 | | | | | 2.7 | 1.1 | 1.7 |
| 4.9 | 3.3 | 4.5 | | | | | -7.5 | 2.8 | 4.4 |
| 41.6 | 54.8 | 49.8 | % Profit Before Taxes/Tangible Net Worth | | | | | 49.8 | 49.2 |
| (68)  20.6 | (62)  31.4 | (70)  23.3 | | | | | (22) | 14.8 (28) | 26.3 |
| 5.5 | 11.1 | 10.7 | | | | | | 9.8 | 13.8 |
| 14.9 | 18.6 | 16.6 | % Profit Before Taxes/Total Assets | | | | 15.6 | 16.0 | 18.0 |
| 6.1 | 8.3 | 9.8 | | | | | 11.4 | 11.2 | 9.3 |
| 1.9 | 3.9 | 3.4 | | | | | -2.7 | 5.0 | 1.7 |
| 23.6 | 41.0 | 31.9 | Sales/Net Fixed Assets | | | | 34.1 | 29.1 | 13.9 |
| 10.9 | 14.6 | 13.4 | | | | | 19.6 | 14.9 | 8.2 |
| 6.0 | 7.1 | 6.0 | | | | | 8.2 | 6.6 | 4.8 |
| 2.5 | 2.6 | 3.2 | Sales/Total Assets | | | | 3.9 | 3.3 | 2.5 |
| 2.0 | 2.1 | 2.4 | | | | | 3.1 | 2.2 | 2.0 |
| 1.6 | 1.6 | 1.7 | | | | | 2.5 | 1.7 | 1.2 |
| .8 | .9 | .9 | % Depr., Dep., Amort./Sales | | | | .7 | .9 | 1.2 |
| (61)  1.7 | (54)  1.4 | (69)  1.5 | | | | (10)  2.5 | | (22)  1.5 (30) | 1.7 |
| 2.5 | 2.1 | 2.6 | | | | | 4.2 | 2.2 | 3.3 |
| 3.0 | 2.8 | 1.9 | % Officers', Directors' Owners' Comp/Sales | | | | | | |
| (20)  6.1 | (26)  4.3 | (21)  3.0 | | | | | | | |
| 8.6 | 7.8 | 4.2 | | | | | | | |
| 2598491M | 2289217M | 3357288M | Net Sales ($) | 979M | 11944M | 24727M | 117676M | 398995M | 2802967M |
| 1634189M | 1275718M | 2071015M | Total Assets ($) | 231M | 4557M | 9846M | 42567M | 197408M | 1816406M |

© RMA 2012

M = $ thousand    MM = $ million
See Pages 9 through 22 for Explanation of Ratios and Data

## Current Data Sorted by Assets | Comparative Historical Data

| 0-500M | 500M-2MM | 2-10MM | 10-50MM | 50-100MM | 100-250MM | Type of Statement | 4/1/07-3/31/08 ALL | 4/1/08-3/31/09 ALL |
|---|---|---|---|---|---|---|---|---|
| | | 3 | 3 | | 2 | Unqualified | 7 | 10 |
| | 1 | 10 | 3 | | | Reviewed | 10 | 7 |
| | | 3 | | | | Compiled | 3 | 5 |
| 5 | 6 | 3 | | | | Tax Returns | 5 | 10 |
| 2 | 4 | 9 | 8 | | 1 | Other | 18 | 22 |
| | 6 (4/1-9/30/11) | | 57 (10/1/11-3/31/12) | | | | | |
| 7 | 11 | 28 | 14 | 1 | 2 | NUMBER OF STATEMENTS | 43 | 54 |
| % | % | % | % | % | % | **ASSETS** | % | % |
| | 8.9 | 9.6 | 8.4 | | | Cash & Equivalents | 7.2 | 5.6 |
| | 35.7 | 27.2 | 23.0 | | | Trade Receivables (net) | 28.8 | 24.5 |
| | 33.9 | 29.0 | 20.3 | | | Inventory | 28.7 | 29.6 |
| | 2.0 | 1.5 | 1.7 | | | All Other Current | 2.3 | 3.0 |
| | 80.4 | 67.2 | 53.4 | | | Total Current | 67.1 | 62.7 |
| | 9.5 | 22.5 | 29.0 | | | Fixed Assets (net) | 20.6 | 21.4 |
| | .9 | 6.6 | 11.6 | | | Intangibles (net) | 6.5 | 11.9 |
| | 9.1 | 3.7 | 6.0 | | | All Other Non-Current | 5.9 | 4.0 |
| | 100.0 | 100.0 | 100.0 | | | Total | 100.0 | 100.0 |
| | | | | | | **LIABILITIES** | | |
| | 18.7 | 8.7 | 8.0 | | | Notes Payable-Short Term | 13.6 | 14.3 |
| | 2.4 | 3.2 | 4.3 | | | Cur. Mat.-L.T.D. | 3.0 | 3.8 |
| | 25.8 | 20.7 | 10.8 | | | Trade Payables | 18.7 | 17.4 |
| | .0 | .7 | .0 | | | Income Taxes Payable | .1 | .2 |
| | 2.3 | 5.2 | 8.7 | | | All Other Current | 8.1 | 8.2 |
| | 49.2 | 38.4 | 31.8 | | | Total Current | 43.6 | 43.9 |
| | 10.9 | 12.3 | 23.9 | | | Long-Term Debt | 12.5 | 17.0 |
| | .3 | .1 | .0 | | | Deferred Taxes | .3 | .2 |
| | 5.6 | 4.3 | 8.8 | | | All Other Non-Current | 6.2 | 3.2 |
| | 34.0 | 45.0 | 35.6 | | | Net Worth | 37.4 | 35.6 |
| | 100.0 | 100.0 | 100.0 | | | Total Liabilties & Net Worth | 100.0 | 100.0 |
| | | | | | | **INCOME DATA** | | |
| | 100.0 | 100.0 | 100.0 | | | Net Sales | 100.0 | 100.0 |
| | 36.5 | 38.1 | 34.0 | | | Gross Profit | 33.3 | 35.7 |
| | 30.8 | 31.6 | 29.5 | | | Operating Expenses | 28.4 | 31.1 |
| | 5.6 | 6.5 | 4.5 | | | Operating Profit | 5.0 | 4.7 |
| | .4 | .3 | -.1 | | | All Other Expenses (net) | 1.4 | 2.0 |
| | 5.3 | 6.1 | 4.6 | | | Profit Before Taxes | 3.5 | 2.7 |
| | | | | | | **RATIOS** | | |
| | 3.9 | 2.9 | 2.7 | | | | 2.7 | 2.6 |
| | 2.2 | 1.6 | 1.5 | | | Current | 1.6 | 1.4 |
| | 1.3 | 1.3 | 1.3 | | | | 1.1 | 1.1 |
| | 2.5 | 1.6 | 2.0 | | | | 1.4 | 1.5 |
| | 1.1 | 1.0 | .8 | | | Quick | .8 | .7 |
| | .7 | .7 | .6 | | | | .5 | .4 |
| | 22　16.9 | 31　11.6 | 32　11.5 | | | | 35　10.3 | 25　14.8 |
| | 35　10.4 | 38　9.6 | 38　9.5 | | | Sales/Receivables | 43　8.5 | 33　11.1 |
| | 48　7.6 | 49　7.4 | 46　7.9 | | | | 54　6.8 | 41　8.9 |
| | 35　10.4 | 34　10.6 | 31　11.8 | | | | 40　9.2 | 37　9.8 |
| | 58　6.3 | 58　6.3 | 57　6.4 | | | Cost of Sales/Inventory | 60　6.0 | 61　6.0 |
| | 74　4.9 | 104　3.5 | 64　5.7 | | | | 89　4.1 | 89　4.1 |
| | 27　13.4 | 23　16.2 | 17　21.0 | | | | 26　14.2 | 19　19.1 |
| | 34　10.7 | 35　10.4 | 25　14.8 | | | Cost of Sales/Payables | 40　9.1 | 37　9.8 |
| | 62　5.9 | 62　5.9 | 36　10.2 | | | | 65　5.6 | 48　7.7 |
| | 6.8 | 4.7 | 5.9 | | | | 5.0 | 6.1 |
| | 8.2 | 10.7 | 11.1 | | | Sales/Working Capital | 9.5 | 15.3 |
| | 20.7 | 25.7 | 25.6 | | | | 45.0 | 40.6 |
| | | 19.8 | 13.6 | | | | 10.4 | 12.0 |
| | | (26)　8.2 | (13)　3.4 | | | EBIT/Interest | (38)　3.7 | (49)　3.5 |
| | | 1.7 | 1.0 | | | | 1.1 | .3 |
| | | | | | | Net Profit + Depr., Dep., Amort./Cur. Mat. L/T/D | | |
| | .0 | .1 | .4 | | | | .2 | .2 |
| | .1 | .5 | .9 | | | Fixed/Worth | .5 | .7 |
| | .5 | 1.1 | NM | | | | 2.0 | 2.9 |
| | .4 | .6 | .6 | | | | .6 | .9 |
| | .9 | 1.4 | 1.5 | | | Debt/Worth | 2.0 | 2.4 |
| | 1.7 | 2.4 | NM | | | | 7.7 | 6.6 |
| | 85.8 | 59.1 | 90.8 | | | | 45.8 | 48.4 |
| | (10)　31.3 | (26)　27.6 | (11)　5.1 | | | % Profit Before Taxes/Tangible Net Worth | (35)　16.6 | (43)　17.9 |
| | 16.4 | 4.1 | -1.7 | | | | 4.6 | 1.4 |
| | 42.4 | 22.8 | 24.7 | | | | 19.0 | 17.4 |
| | 10.6 | 8.9 | 4.8 | | | % Profit Before Taxes/Total Assets | 5.4 | 5.3 |
| | 2.6 | 1.2 | -.3 | | | | .6 | -2.1 |
| | 177.2 | 55.4 | 12.1 | | | | 53.7 | 36.6 |
| | 78.2 | 16.1 | 7.5 | | | Sales/Net Fixed Assets | 14.6 | 13.8 |
| | 33.5 | 6.5 | 4.8 | | | | 5.2 | 6.9 |
| | 4.1 | 3.6 | 2.4 | | | | 3.3 | 3.6 |
| | 3.4 | 2.4 | 2.1 | | | Sales/Total Assets | 2.2 | 2.5 |
| | 3.0 | 2.0 | 1.8 | | | | 1.6 | 1.7 |
| | | .8 | 1.8 | | | | .8 | 1.0 |
| | | (23)　1.3 | (13)　3.4 | | | % Depr., Dep., Amort./Sales | (36)　1.3 | (44)　1.8 |
| | | 2.1 | 4.1 | | | | 2.0 | 2.9 |
| | | 1.9 | | | | | 2.7 | 3.3 |
| | | (13)　3.6 | | | | % Officers', Directors' Owners' Comp/Sales | (13)　5.0 | (15)　5.3 |
| | | 6.8 | | | | | 6.0 | 7.6 |
| 4265M | 58216M | 338319M | 753878M | 156754M | 401413M | Net Sales ($) | 1441986M | 1867735M |
| 1738M | 15240M | 136264M | 357222M | 69274M | 375150M | Total Assets ($) | 906557M | 919395M |

M = $ thousand　MM = $ million
See Pages 9 through 22 for Explanation of Ratios and Data

## Comparative Historical Data                                                 ## Current Data Sorted by Sales

| 6 9 5 13 26 | 3 13 6 17 29 | 8 14 3 14 24 | Type of Statement | | | | 2 1 1 2 2 | 2 8 1 4 5 | 6 2 8 |
|---|---|---|---|---|---|---|---|---|---|
| | | | Unqualified | | | | | 2 | 6 |
| | | | Reviewed | | | 2 | 2 | 8 | 2 |
| | | | Compiled | | | 1 | 1 | 1 | |
| | | | Tax Returns | 5 | 1 | 2 | 2 | 4 | |
| | | | Other | 2 | | 2 | 2 | 5 | 8 |
| 4/1/09-3/31/10 ALL | 4/1/10-3/31/11 ALL | 4/1/11-3/31/12 ALL | | 0-1MM | 6 (4/1-9/30/11) 1-3MM | 3-5MM | 57 (10/1/11-3/31/12) 5-10MM | 10-25MM | 25MM & OVER |
| 59 | 68 | 63 | NUMBER OF STATEMENTS | 7 | 1 | 7 | 10 | 22 | 16 |
| % | % | % | ASSETS | % | % | % | % | % | % |
| 8.0 | 7.4 | 8.9 | Cash & Equivalents | | | | 17.1 | 5.3 | 8.7 |
| 25.7 | 23.5 | 25.8 | Trade Receivables (net) | | | | 32.4 | 27.2 | 24.8 |
| 26.4 | 28.5 | 28.3 | Inventory | | | | 31.2 | 32.9 | 19.3 |
| 2.4 | 1.8 | 1.9 | All Other Current | | | | 2.1 | 1.5 | 1.7 |
| 62.5 | 61.2 | 65.0 | Total Current | | | | 82.7 | 67.0 | 54.5 |
| 22.8 | 25.4 | 22.6 | Fixed Assets (net) | | | | 12.6 | 24.2 | 26.3 |
| 7.3 | 7.7 | 6.7 | Intangibles (net) | | | | 1.6 | 4.6 | 13.9 |
| 7.4 | 5.8 | 5.7 | All Other Non-Current | | | | 3.1 | 4.1 | 5.4 |
| 100.0 | 100.0 | 100.0 | Total | | | | 100.0 | 100.0 | 100.0 |
| | | | LIABILITIES | | | | | | |
| 11.8 | 11.0 | 10.5 | Notes Payable-Short Term | | | | 8.8 | 8.7 | 8.3 |
| 7.1 | 5.2 | 4.3 | Cur. Mat.-L.T.D. | | | | 1.6 | 4.1 | 3.1 |
| 15.0 | 15.8 | 19.5 | Trade Payables | | | | 17.5 | 24.1 | 12.8 |
| .1 | .1 | .3 | Income Taxes Payable | | | | .0 | .9 | .0 |
| 10.1 | 7.4 | 5.8 | All Other Current | | | | 3.8 | 5.3 | 8.3 |
| 44.2 | 39.4 | 40.4 | Total Current | | | | 31.7 | 43.2 | 32.5 |
| 15.6 | 17.7 | 15.9 | Long-Term Debt | | | | 6.5 | 11.5 | 23.2 |
| .6 | .3 | .4 | Deferred Taxes | | | | .0 | .1 | 1.2 |
| 3.9 | 6.4 | 5.7 | All Other Non-Current | | | | 7.9 | 4.9 | 6.2 |
| 35.7 | 36.2 | 37.6 | Net Worth | | | | 53.9 | 40.4 | 37.0 |
| 100.0 | 100.0 | 100.0 | Total Liabilities & Net Worth | | | | 100.0 | 100.0 | 100.0 |
| | | | INCOME DATA | | | | | | |
| 100.0 | 100.0 | 100.0 | Net Sales | | | | 100.0 | 100.0 | 100.0 |
| 42.2 | 38.7 | 36.9 | Gross Profit | | | | 37.3 | 33.1 | 32.8 |
| 34.4 | 32.8 | 31.9 | Operating Expenses | | | | 26.4 | 30.4 | 28.9 |
| 7.7 | 5.9 | 5.1 | Operating Profit | | | | 10.9 | 2.8 | 4.0 |
| 1.0 | 1.0 | .4 | All Other Expenses (net) | | | | .2 | .0 | .1 |
| 6.8 | 4.9 | 4.7 | Profit Before Taxes | | | | 10.7 | 2.7 | 3.9 |
| | | | RATIOS | | | | | | |
| 2.8 | 2.7 | 2.9 | | | | | 3.9 | 2.4 | 2.6 |
| 1.8 | 1.6 | 1.7 | Current | | | | 2.8 | 1.5 | 1.7 |
| 1.0 | 1.2 | 1.3 | | | | | 1.7 | 1.2 | 1.3 |
| 1.9 | 1.4 | 1.7 | | | | | 2.6 | 1.6 | 1.9 |
| .9 | .9 | .9 | Quick | | | | 1.8 | .8 | 1.0 |
| .5 | .5 | .6 | | | | | .8 | .5 | .7 |
| 31 11.9 | 27 13.7 | 28 13.2 | | | | | 33 10.9 | 26 13.8 | 33 10.9 |
| 40 9.2 | 37 9.9 | 38 9.7 | Sales/Receivables | | | | 46 7.9 | 36 10.2 | 41 8.8 |
| 50 7.3 | 49 7.5 | 47 7.8 | | | | | 57 6.4 | 49 7.4 | 46 7.9 |
| 39 9.4 | 38 9.5 | 35 10.4 | | | | | 44 8.3 | 39 9.4 | 33 11.2 |
| 68 5.3 | 66 5.5 | 62 6.3 | Cost of Sales/Inventory | | | | 56 6.5 | 62 5.9 | 49 7.4 |
| 113 3.2 | 109 3.3 | 94 3.9 | | | | | 99 3.7 | 111 3.3 | 58 6.3 |
| 21 17.5 | 20 18.7 | 22 16.3 | | | | | 25 14.7 | 21 17.5 | 19 19.1 |
| 36 10.0 | 36 10.0 | 34 10.7 | Cost of Sales/Payables | | | | 33 11.1 | 33 11.0 | 28 12.9 |
| 59 6.2 | 52 7.0 | 62 5.9 | | | | | 46 8.0 | 63 5.8 | 39 9.3 |
| 4.4 | 5.4 | 5.4 | | | | | 4.4 | 6.3 | 5.4 |
| 10.0 | 9.9 | 9.2 | Sales/Working Capital | | | | 5.0 | 14.0 | 10.7 |
| -999.8 | 24.6 | 25.4 | | | | | 9.2 | 35.8 | 24.0 |
| 17.4 | 19.8 | 17.2 | | | | | | 18.8 | 9.0 |
| (52) 4.9 | (66) 5.0 | (54) 4.3 | EBIT/Interest | | | | | (21) 8.6 | (15) 3.0 |
| 2.5 | 2.5 | 1.3 | | | | | | 2.8 | .5 |
| 4.4 | 3.7 | | Net Profit + Depr., Dep., | | | | | | |
| (15) 1.8 | (16) 1.8 | | Amort./Cur. Mat. L/T/D | | | | | | |
| 1.1 | 1.0 | | | | | | | | |
| .2 | .3 | .1 | | | | | .0 | .3 | .4 |
| .6 | .8 | .5 | Fixed/Worth | | | | .1 | .8 | .9 |
| 2.4 | 2.4 | 1.4 | | | | | .6 | 2.7 | 3.0 |
| .9 | 1.0 | .6 | | | | | .3 | .7 | 1.3 |
| 2.0 | 1.6 | 1.5 | Debt/Worth | | | | .8 | 1.4 | 1.7 |
| 4.3 | 6.5 | 3.0 | | | | | 2.6 | 7.7 | 8.7 |
| 79.0 | 67.9 | 64.1 | % Profit Before Taxes/Tangible | | | | 84.7 | 33.9 | 93.6 |
| (50) 30.0 | (58) 29.6 | (54) 22.5 | Net Worth | | | | 49.2 | (19) 19.4 | (14) 5.3 |
| 8.8 | 10.3 | 2.3 | | | | | 22.1 | 4.9 | -2.0 |
| 22.1 | 19.0 | 24.7 | % Profit Before Taxes/Total | | | | 42.1 | 16.3 | 21.0 |
| 8.6 | 7.4 | 7.7 | Assets | | | | 20.9 | 5.1 | 3.5 |
| 3.3 | 2.6 | .2 | | | | | 6.6 | 2.0 | -.9 |
| 33.7 | 31.4 | 52.9 | | | | | UND | 37.0 | 13.1 |
| 14.6 | 12.4 | 13.4 | Sales/Net Fixed Assets | | | | 65.6 | 14.4 | 9.2 |
| 6.3 | 6.1 | 6.3 | | | | | 9.9 | 6.2 | 6.0 |
| 2.9 | 2.9 | 3.3 | | | | | 3.3 | 3.7 | 2.4 |
| 2.2 | 2.3 | 2.4 | Sales/Total Assets | | | | 2.8 | 2.4 | 2.1 |
| 1.7 | 1.8 | 2.0 | | | | | 2.0 | 2.1 | 1.9 |
| 1.1 | 1.0 | .8 | | | | | | .8 | 1.6 |
| (46) 1.9 | (61) 1.8 | (51) 1.6 | % Depr., Dep., Amort./Sales | | | | | (19) 1.3 | (14) 3.0 |
| 3.1 | 3.1 | 2.7 | | | | | | 2.1 | 4.0 |
| 1.7 | 1.4 | 2.2 | % Officers', Directors' | | | | | 1.2 | |
| (24) 3.5 | (30) 4.4 | (26) 3.5 | Owners' Comp/Sales | | | | | (10) 3.3 | |
| 6.0 | 6.9 | 6.0 | | | | | | 9.0 | |
| 1479425M | 2049846M | 1712845M | Net Sales ($) | 4265M | 2745M | 25975M | 71500M | 294434M | 1313926M |
| 737978M | 1115874M | 954888M | Total Assets ($) | 1738M | 740M | 12138M | 30758M | 122041M | 787473M |

© RMA 2012                     **M = $ thousand     MM = $ million**
See Pages 9 through 22 for Explanation of Ratios and Data

## Current Data Sorted by Assets

## Comparative Historical Data

| | 0-500M | 500M-2MM | 2-10MM | 10-50MM | 50-100MM | 100-250MM | | 4/1/07-3/31/08 ALL | 4/1/08-3/31/09 ALL |
|---|---|---|---|---|---|---|---|---|---|
| **Type of Statement** | | | | | | | | | |
| Unqualified | | | 1 | 3 | 2 | | | 18 | 17 |
| Reviewed | | 1 | 10 | 7 | 1 | | | 13 | 17 |
| Compiled | | 4 | 1 | 2 | | | | 7 | 8 |
| Tax Returns | 2 | 5 | 1 | 1 | | | | 8 | 2 |
| Other | 1 | 1 | 6 | 9 | 2 | 3 | | 16 | 21 |
| | 0-500M | 5 (4/1-9/30/11) 500M-2MM | 2-10MM | 57 (10/1/11-3/31/12) 10-50MM | 50-100MM | 100-250MM | | | |
| **NUMBER OF STATEMENTS** | 3 | 11 | 18 | 22 | 5 | 3 | | 62 | 65 |
| **ASSETS** | % | % | % | % | % | % | | % | % |
| Cash & Equivalents | | 8.6 | 5.8 | 14.2 | | | | 9.2 | 9.3 |
| Trade Receivables (net) | | 34.3 | 30.9 | 24.9 | | | | 31.0 | 27.3 |
| Inventory | | 25.4 | 34.4 | 27.0 | | | | 26.0 | 28.6 |
| All Other Current | | 2.3 | 1.5 | 1.4 | | | | 2.5 | 2.1 |
| Total Current | | 70.5 | 72.5 | 67.5 | | | | 68.7 | 67.2 |
| Fixed Assets (net) | | 15.3 | 15.9 | 22.7 | | | | 21.4 | 21.2 |
| Intangibles (net) | | 2.5 | 4.0 | 7.0 | | | | 4.7 | 5.3 |
| All Other Non-Current | | 11.7 | 7.5 | 2.8 | | | | 5.3 | 6.3 |
| Total | | 100.0 | 100.0 | 100.0 | | | | 100.0 | 100.0 |
| **LIABILITIES** | | | | | | | | | |
| Notes Payable-Short Term | | 8.1 | 15.9 | 8.2 | | | | 9.9 | 11.9 |
| Cur. Mat.-L.T.D. | | 2.5 | 1.9 | 2.4 | | | | 3.1 | 3.4 |
| Trade Payables | | 17.5 | 17.7 | 13.8 | | | | 19.4 | 18.0 |
| Income Taxes Payable | | 1.1 | .6 | .2 | | | | .5 | .2 |
| All Other Current | | 13.7 | 7.0 | 8.4 | | | | 8.7 | 8.3 |
| Total Current | | 43.0 | 43.2 | 33.0 | | | | 41.6 | 41.7 |
| Long-Term Debt | | 8.2 | 7.3 | 9.7 | | | | 13.4 | 15.7 |
| Deferred Taxes | | .1 | .1 | .1 | | | | .6 | .3 |
| All Other Non-Current | | 2.0 | 2.0 | 7.0 | | | | 2.9 | 10.0 |
| Net Worth | | 46.7 | 47.4 | 50.2 | | | | 41.5 | 32.2 |
| Total Liabilities & Net Worth | | 100.0 | 100.0 | 100.0 | | | | 100.0 | 100.0 |
| **INCOME DATA** | | | | | | | | | |
| Net Sales | | 100.0 | 100.0 | 100.0 | | | | 100.0 | 100.0 |
| Gross Profit | | 42.3 | 35.5 | 33.8 | | | | 40.5 | 35.7 |
| Operating Expenses | | 43.0 | 31.7 | 26.2 | | | | 34.8 | 32.2 |
| Operating Profit | | -.7 | 3.8 | 7.7 | | | | 5.7 | 3.5 |
| All Other Expenses (net) | | -1.2 | .3 | .6 | | | | .7 | 1.1 |
| Profit Before Taxes | | .5 | 3.5 | 7.1 | | | | 5.0 | 2.5 |
| **RATIOS** | | | | | | | | | |
| Current | | 4.3 | 2.5 | 3.5 | | | | 2.9 | 2.5 |
| | | 2.2 | 1.8 | 1.9 | | | | 1.8 | 1.8 |
| | | .9 | 1.1 | 1.4 | | | | 1.3 | 1.2 |
| Quick | | 2.4 | 1.5 | 2.7 | | | | 1.5 | 1.5 |
| | | 1.1 | 1.0 | 1.3 | | | | 1.0 | .8 |
| | | .4 | .5 | .7 | | | | .7 | .6 |
| Sales/Receivables | | 26 14.3 | 29 12.7 | 36 10.2 | | | | 33 11.0 | 29 12.4 |
| | | 39 9.3 | 35 10.3 | 40 9.2 | | | | 40 9.0 | 39 9.3 |
| | | 51 7.2 | 49 7.5 | 49 7.5 | | | | 47 7.8 | 48 7.7 |
| Cost of Sales/Inventory | | 20 18.7 | 45 8.1 | 45 8.1 | | | | 42 8.7 | 43 8.6 |
| | | 57 6.4 | 65 5.6 | 55 6.6 | | | | 60 6.1 | 67 5.5 |
| | | 89 4.1 | 87 4.2 | 87 4.2 | | | | 79 4.6 | 91 4.0 |
| Cost of Sales/Payables | | 8 44.8 | 21 17.0 | 16 23.3 | | | | 22 16.4 | 21 17.7 |
| | | 18 20.4 | 39 9.4 | 31 11.9 | | | | 35 10.5 | 35 10.6 |
| | | 49 7.5 | 44 8.3 | 46 7.9 | | | | 51 7.2 | 53 6.9 |
| Sales/Working Capital | | 7.0 | 5.9 | 3.0 | | | | 5.7 | 5.6 |
| | | 8.2 | 8.1 | 7.7 | | | | 9.0 | 9.1 |
| | | -28.2 | 26.9 | 12.9 | | | | 23.0 | 28.1 |
| EBIT/Interest | | | 45.7 | 16.5 | | | | 7.6 | 13.0 |
| | | | (16) 4.7 | (17) 10.1 | | | | (54) 4.5 | (57) 4.8 |
| | | | 1.5 | 2.7 | | | | 2.1 | -.2 |
| Net Profit + Depr., Dep., Amort./Cur. Mat. L/T/D | | | | | | | | 6.8 | 7.1 |
| | | | (23) 3.3 | (19) 2.4 | | | | | |
| | | | | | | | | 1.8 | 1.0 |
| Fixed/Worth | | .0 | .2 | .2 | | | | .2 | .2 |
| | | .2 | .3 | .7 | | | | .5 | .5 |
| | | .5 | .6 | 1.0 | | | | 1.0 | 1.2 |
| Debt/Worth | | .4 | .7 | .3 | | | | .6 | .6 |
| | | .9 | 1.3 | 1.1 | | | | 1.3 | 1.3 |
| | | 4.0 | 3.4 | 2.6 | | | | 3.7 | 3.2 |
| % Profit Before Taxes/Tangible Net Worth | | 52.5 | 40.7 | 50.5 | | | | 45.2 | 41.6 |
| | | (10) 8.3 | (17) 12.6 | 28.8 | | | | (57) 26.5 | (56) 14.8 |
| | | 2.7 | 4.7 | 17.8 | | | | 9.4 | -1.3 |
| % Profit Before Taxes/Total Assets | | 25.7 | 19.3 | 22.8 | | | | 18.7 | 16.4 |
| | | 3.5 | 6.2 | 12.1 | | | | 7.7 | 6.3 |
| | | .2 | 1.4 | 5.6 | | | | 3.3 | -2.3 |
| Sales/Net Fixed Assets | | 502.6 | 49.4 | 18.8 | | | | 36.5 | 35.1 |
| | | 30.2 | 21.5 | 12.1 | | | | 12.5 | 14.7 |
| | | 11.8 | 10.8 | 7.1 | | | | 8.1 | 8.9 |
| Sales/Total Assets | | 4.5 | 3.6 | 2.7 | | | | 3.4 | 3.1 |
| | | 3.5 | 2.8 | 2.1 | | | | 2.5 | 2.6 |
| | | 2.4 | 2.3 | 1.6 | | | | 2.0 | 1.8 |
| % Depr., Dep., Amort./Sales | | | .6 | .9 | | | | .8 | .9 |
| | | | (17) 1.0 | (19) 1.8 | | | | (52) 1.4 | (58) 1.4 |
| | | | 1.6 | 2.5 | | | | 2.3 | 2.1 |
| % Officers', Directors' Owners' Comp/Sales | | | | | | | | 1.7 | 1.0 |
| | | | (19) 3.1 | (15) 2.8 | | | | | |
| | | | | | | | | 3.9 | 4.1 |
| Net Sales ($) | 1952M | 38825M | 254648M | 961644M | 834562M | 463410M | | 3090790M | 2804520M |
| Total Assets ($) | 465M | 11526M | 87410M | 466525M | 341665M | 444047M | | 1384852M | 1266703M |

M = $ thousand    MM = $ million
See Pages 9 through 22 for Explanation of Ratios and Data

## Comparative Historical Data | Current Data Sorted by Sales

| Type of Statement | 4/1/09-3/31/10 ALL | 4/1/10-3/31/11 ALL | 4/1/11-3/31/12 ALL | 0-1MM | 1-3MM | 3-5MM | 5-10MM | 10-25MM | 25MM & OVER |
|---|---|---|---|---|---|---|---|---|---|
| Unqualified | 14 | 16 | 6 | | | | 6 | 1 | 5 |
| Reviewed | 21 | 16 | 19 | | | | 1 | 5 | 8 |
| Compiled | 7 | 11 | 7 | 1 | 2 | | 1 | 2 | 1 |
| Tax Returns | 7 | 10 | 8 | 1 | 3 | 2 | 1 | | 1 |
| Other | 18 | 14 | 22 | 1 | 1 | 1 | 2 | 3 | 14 |
| | | | | 5 (4/1-9/30/11) | | | 57 (10/1/11-3/31/12) | | |
| NUMBER OF STATEMENTS | 67 | 67 | 62 | 3 | 6 | 3 | 10 | 11 | 29 |
| **ASSETS** | % | % | % | % | % | % | % | % | % |
| Cash & Equivalents | 9.8 | 11.4 | 10.3 | | | | 10.7 | 7.9 | 11.6 |
| Trade Receivables (net) | 28.5 | 27.4 | 28.7 | | | | 30.8 | 29.7 | 25.4 |
| Inventory | 25.2 | 26.9 | 28.1 | | | | 29.8 | 30.5 | 26.8 |
| All Other Current | 2.0 | 2.0 | 1.7 | | | | 1.5 | .6 | 2.0 |
| Total Current | 65.5 | 67.7 | 68.9 | | | | 72.8 | 68.7 | 65.7 |
| Fixed Assets (net) | 18.6 | 20.2 | 17.3 | | | | 18.7 | 20.0 | 17.8 |
| Intangibles (net) | 7.4 | 6.8 | 6.7 | | | | 5.9 | 1.1 | 10.9 |
| All Other Non-Current | 8.5 | 5.3 | 7.1 | | | | 2.6 | 10.1 | 5.5 |
| Total | 100.0 | 100.0 | 100.0 | | | | 100.0 | 100.0 | 100.0 |
| **LIABILITIES** | | | | | | | | | |
| Notes Payable-Short Term | 10.9 | 9.2 | 10.9 | | | | 4.7 | 15.5 | 9.4 |
| Cur. Mat.-L.T.D. | 2.3 | 2.4 | 2.4 | | | | 3.3 | 2.0 | 1.8 |
| Trade Payables | 16.3 | 15.4 | 15.5 | | | | 18.2 | 15.6 | 14.9 |
| Income Taxes Payable | .1 | .2 | .5 | | | | .8 | .3 | .2 |
| All Other Current | 8.0 | 8.6 | 9.0 | | | | 8.8 | 11.0 | 6.8 |
| Total Current | 37.7 | 35.9 | 38.3 | | | | 35.8 | 44.3 | 33.1 |
| Long-Term Debt | 12.5 | 10.6 | 8.6 | | | | 7.3 | 8.8 | 9.3 |
| Deferred Taxes | .3 | .3 | .1 | | | | .4 | .0 | .0 |
| All Other Non-Current | 13.8 | 4.3 | 3.7 | | | | 1.5 | 2.0 | 6.0 |
| Net Worth | 35.6 | 49.0 | 49.3 | | | | 54.9 | 45.0 | 51.6 |
| Total Liabilities & Net Worth | 100.0 | 100.0 | 100.0 | | | | 100.0 | 100.0 | 100.0 |
| **INCOME DATA** | | | | | | | | | |
| Net Sales | 100.0 | 100.0 | 100.0 | | | | 100.0 | 100.0 | 100.0 |
| Gross Profit | 37.9 | 40.7 | 36.6 | | | | 35.4 | 33.4 | 32.9 |
| Operating Expenses | 32.1 | 34.9 | 31.2 | | | | 30.9 | 29.3 | 26.1 |
| Operating Profit | 5.8 | 5.7 | 5.4 | | | | 4.5 | 4.1 | 6.9 |
| All Other Expenses (net) | .9 | .6 | .4 | | | | .3 | .4 | 1.0 |
| Profit Before Taxes | 4.9 | 5.1 | 5.0 | | | | 4.2 | 3.7 | 5.8 |

### RATIOS

| Ratio | 4/1/09-3/31/10 ALL | 4/1/10-3/31/11 ALL | 4/1/11-3/31/12 ALL | 5-10MM | 10-25MM | 25MM & OVER |
|---|---|---|---|---|---|---|
| Current | 2.7 | 3.7 | 3.0 | 5.1 | 2.5 | 3.6 |
| | 1.8 | 1.8 | 1.8 | 1.9 | 1.7 | 1.9 |
| | 1.3 | 1.2 | 1.3 | 1.4 | 1.1 | 1.3 |
| Quick | 1.8 | 2.5 | 2.1 | 2.6 | 1.3 | 2.7 |
| | 1.0 | 1.0 | 1.1 | 1.3 | 1.0 | 1.1 |
| | .6 | .6 | .6 | .8 | .5 | .7 |
| Sales/Receivables | 34  10.8 | 31  11.9 | 32  11.3 | 23  15.7 | 30  12.0 | 36  10.2 |
| | 41  8.9 | 39  9.4 | 40  9.2 | 31  11.6 | 38  9.6 | 41  8.9 |
| | 47  7.7 | 50  7.3 | 48  7.6 | 42  8.6 | 45  8.1 | 48  7.6 |
| Cost of Sales/Inventory | 41  8.8 | 48  7.5 | 42  8.6 | 27  13.3 | 38  9.6 | 44  8.3 |
| | 63  5.8 | 62  5.9 | 58  6.3 | 56  6.5 | 54  6.7 | 53  6.9 |
| | 84  4.3 | 102  3.6 | 79  4.6 | 85  4.3 | 76  4.8 | 78  4.7 |
| Cost of Sales/Payables | 19  19.1 | 16  22.4 | 17  21.0 | 9  38.7 | 16  23.0 | 20  18.1 |
| | 35  10.3 | 32  11.3 | 32  11.4 | 37  9.9 | 28  12.9 | 31  11.8 |
| | 50  7.2 | 49  7.5 | 46  8.0 | 48  7.6 | 40  9.2 | 46  7.9 |
| Sales/Working Capital | 5.6 | 4.2 | 5.9 | 5.2 | 6.6 | 3.6 |
| | 8.0 | 8.5 | 8.2 | 8.7 | 10.0 | 8.1 |
| | 22.2 | 18.7 | 15.6 | NM | 33.6 | 15.7 |
| EBIT/Interest | 12.3 | 24.0 | 23.1 | | 30.0 | 16.2 |
| | (59)  7.7 | (57)  6.9 | (51)  6.1 | | (23)  3.2 | 9.8 |
| | 2.6 | 3.0 | 2.0 | | 1.9 | 2.5 |
| Net Profit + Depr., Dep., Amort./Cur. Mat. L/T/D | 8.5 | 4.8 | 16.9 | | | 29.9 |
| | (20)  3.7 | (15)  2.5 | (15)  6.8 | | | (10)  8.7 |
| | 1.1 | 1.0 | 1.6 | | | 5.2 |
| Fixed/Worth | .2 | .2 | .2 | .1 | .2 | .2 |
| | .5 | .4 | .4 | .3 | .4 | .5 |
| | 1.0 | 1.0 | .8 | 4.4 | .8 | 1.0 |
| Debt/Worth | .7 | .5 | .5 | .2 | .9 | .3 |
| | 1.6 | 1.1 | 1.3 | 1.0 | .9 | 1.6 |
| | 4.4 | 2.3 | 3.0 | 8.6 | 2.1 | 2.8 |
| % Profit Before Taxes/Tangible Net Worth | 46.3 | 49.3 | 45.6 | | 46.9 | 37.3 |
| | (58)  24.3 | (60)  24.7 | (59)  20.3 | | (28)  14.8 | 24.7 |
| | 9.5 | 7.4 | 6.7 | | 8.6 | 10.8 |
| % Profit Before Taxes/Total Assets | 24.5 | 19.3 | 21.7 | 23.2 | 11.1 | 21.9 |
| | 9.8 | 10.5 | 7.6 | 13.8 | 6.3 | 7.9 |
| | 2.8 | 4.2 | 2.0 | 3.3 | 1.5 | 3.6 |
| Sales/Net Fixed Assets | 30.4 | 36.8 | 33.8 | 163.3 | 33.2 | 25.7 |
| | 16.6 | 14.6 | 16.0 | 21.5 | 15.3 | 14.9 |
| | 9.1 | 7.2 | 10.2 | 11.8 | 10.2 | 7.7 |
| Sales/Total Assets | 3.1 | 3.2 | 3.3 | 4.5 | 3.1 | 2.7 |
| | 2.4 | 2.4 | 2.5 | 3.2 | 2.7 | 2.2 |
| | 1.7 | 1.5 | 2.0 | 2.2 | 2.4 | 1.6 |
| % Depr., Dep., Amort./Sales | 1.1 | 1.1 | .8 | | 1.0 | .9 |
| | (57)  1.4 | (59)  1.5 | (53)  1.4 | | (10)  1.4 | (26)  1.6 |
| | 2.2 | 2.4 | 2.2 | | 2.2 | 2.4 |
| % Officers', Directors' Owners' Comp/Sales | 1.7 | 2.9 | 2.4 | | | |
| | (22)  3.2 | (23)  5.0 | (19)  3.8 | | | |
| | 8.2 | 8.8 | 10.6 | | | |

| | 4/1/09-3/31/10 ALL | 4/1/10-3/31/11 ALL | 4/1/11-3/31/12 ALL | 0-1MM | 1-3MM | 3-5MM | 5-10MM | 10-25MM | 25MM & OVER |
|---|---|---|---|---|---|---|---|---|---|
| Net Sales ($) | 2881152M | 2461353M | 2555041M | 1502M | 12360M | 11580M | 81546M | 176559M | 2271494M |
| Total Assets ($) | 1388903M | 1217113M | 1351638M | 848M | 7504M | 3898M | 28064M | 73989M | 1237335M |

M = $ thousand     MM = $ million
See Pages 9 through 22 for Explanation of Ratios and Data

## Current Data Sorted by Assets      Comparative Historical Data

| 0-500M | 500M-2MM | 2-10MM | 10-50MM | 50-100MM | 100-250MM | Type of Statement | 4/1/07-3/31/08 ALL | 4/1/08-3/31/09 ALL |
|---|---|---|---|---|---|---|---|---|
|  |  | 4 | 7 | 4 | 4 | Unqualified | 20 | 25 |
|  | 3 | 10 | 8 | 1 |  | Reviewed | 23 | 15 |
| 2 | 1 | 3 | 3 |  |  | Compiled | 9 | 9 |
|  | 3 |  |  |  |  | Tax Returns | 2 | 4 |
| 2 | 4 | 9 | 18 | 4 | 2 | Other | 36 | 36 |
|  | 15 (4/1-9/30/11) |  | 77 (10/1/11-3/31/12) |  |  |  |  |  |
| 4 | 11 | 26 | 36 | 9 | 6 | NUMBER OF STATEMENTS | 90 | 89 |
| % | % | % | % | % | % | **ASSETS** | % | % |
|  | 11.0 | 5.3 | 8.4 |  |  | Cash & Equivalents | 8.6 | 7.9 |
|  | 23.5 | 29.2 | 24.2 |  |  | Trade Receivables (net) | 26.5 | 24.6 |
|  | 30.9 | 36.6 | 30.9 |  |  | Inventory | 29.8 | 30.1 |
|  | 1.0 | 2.2 | 3.1 |  |  | All Other Current | 3.3 | 3.1 |
|  | 66.4 | 73.3 | 66.7 |  |  | Total Current | 68.1 | 65.7 |
|  | 23.3 | 16.9 | 19.8 |  |  | Fixed Assets (net) | 16.2 | 17.4 |
|  | 2.4 | 4.8 | 10.0 |  |  | Intangibles (net) | 8.6 | 11.5 |
|  | 7.8 | 5.0 | 3.6 |  |  | All Other Non-Current | 7.1 | 5.4 |
|  | 100.0 | 100.0 | 100.0 |  |  | Total | 100.0 | 100.0 |
|  |  |  |  |  |  | **LIABILITIES** |  |  |
|  | 6.9 | 16.0 | 11.5 |  |  | Notes Payable-Short Term | 12.1 | 11.2 |
|  | 1.0 | 4.8 | 1.8 |  |  | Cur. Mat.-L.T.D. | 2.5 | 3.1 |
|  | 24.4 | 17.2 | 18.5 |  |  | Trade Payables | 18.6 | 16.8 |
|  | .0 | .0 | .2 |  |  | Income Taxes Payable | .4 | .4 |
|  | 29.8 | 7.4 | 9.1 |  |  | All Other Current | 9.8 | 10.7 |
|  | 62.2 | 45.5 | 41.0 |  |  | Total Current | 43.4 | 42.2 |
|  | 6.5 | 9.3 | 10.0 |  |  | Long-Term Debt | 12.3 | 13.7 |
|  | .0 | .2 | .9 |  |  | Deferred Taxes | .2 | .3 |
|  | 1.5 | 2.2 | 14.9 |  |  | All Other Non-Current | 5.1 | 6.9 |
|  | 29.8 | 42.8 | 33.2 |  |  | Net Worth | 39.0 | 36.9 |
|  | 100.0 | 100.0 | 100.0 |  |  | Total Liabilities & Net Worth | 100.0 | 100.0 |
|  |  |  |  |  |  | **INCOME DATA** |  |  |
|  | 100.0 | 100.0 | 100.0 |  |  | Net Sales | 100.0 | 100.0 |
|  | 40.7 | 35.1 | 38.8 |  |  | Gross Profit | 41.3 | 39.2 |
|  | 37.0 | 28.3 | 30.7 |  |  | Operating Expenses | 34.3 | 32.5 |
|  | 3.6 | 6.8 | 8.1 |  |  | Operating Profit | 7.0 | 6.6 |
|  | .5 | .1 | 1.4 |  |  | All Other Expenses (net) | 1.8 | 1.9 |
|  | 3.1 | 6.7 | 6.7 |  |  | Profit Before Taxes | 5.2 | 4.8 |
|  |  |  |  |  |  | **RATIOS** |  |  |
|  | 2.0 | 2.2 | 2.7 |  |  |  | 2.6 | 2.9 |
|  | 1.3 | 1.6 | 1.6 |  |  | Current | 1.6 | 1.6 |
|  | .9 | 1.3 | 1.2 |  |  |  | 1.1 | 1.1 |
|  | 1.4 | 1.2 | 1.7 |  |  |  | 1.5 | 1.7 |
|  | .6 | .7 | .8 |  |  | Quick | .8 | .7 |
|  | .3 | .5 | .5 |  |  |  | .5 | .5 |
|  | 13  28.9 | 31  11.7 | 36  10.2 |  |  |  | 33  11.0 | 33  11.0 |
|  | 35  10.5 | 46  8.0 | 43  8.5 |  |  | Sales/Receivables | 48  7.6 | 45  8.1 |
|  | 54  6.7 | 54  6.7 | 57  6.4 |  |  |  | 65  5.6 | 57  6.4 |
|  | 22  16.3 | 62  5.9 | 68  5.4 |  |  |  | 64  5.7 | 60  6.1 |
|  | 64  5.7 | 87  4.2 | 94  3.9 |  |  | Cost of Sales/Inventory | 89  4.1 | 91  4.0 |
|  | 192  1.9 | 107  3.4 | 126  2.9 |  |  |  | 141  2.6 | 134  2.7 |
|  | 24  14.9 | 22  16.8 | 31  11.7 |  |  |  | 31  11.7 | 25  14.7 |
|  | 47  7.8 | 36  10.0 | 43  8.4 |  |  | Cost of Sales/Payables | 52  7.0 | 48  7.5 |
|  | 79  4.6 | 68  5.4 | 85  4.3 |  |  |  | 79  4.6 | 73  5.0 |
|  | 8.0 | 5.3 | 4.1 |  |  |  | 4.6 | 4.4 |
|  | 42.4 | 8.6 | 9.1 |  |  | Sales/Working Capital | 7.9 | 8.3 |
|  | -26.8 | 14.4 | 25.4 |  |  |  | 29.9 | 31.6 |
|  |  | 13.0 | 35.1 |  |  |  | 15.4 | 15.6 |
|  |  | (23) 8.3 | (34) 10.0 |  |  | EBIT/Interest | (83) 5.3 | (84) 3.9 |
|  |  | 2.7 | 3.3 |  |  |  | 1.6 | 1.4 |
|  |  |  | 10.9 |  |  | Net Profit + Depr., Dep., | 8.1 | 21.4 |
|  |  |  | (13) 3.5 |  |  | Amort./Cur. Mat. L/T/D | (28) 3.2 | (26) 5.7 |
|  |  |  | 1.7 |  |  |  | .4 | -.1 |
|  | .0 | .1 | .2 |  |  |  | .2 | .3 |
|  | .7 | .4 | .5 |  |  | Fixed/Worth | .4 | .6 |
|  | 1.0 | .7 | 4.1 |  |  |  | 1.4 | 2.4 |
|  | .5 | .9 | .5 |  |  |  | .7 | .7 |
|  | 1.0 | 1.7 | 1.6 |  |  | Debt/Worth | 2.1 | 2.2 |
|  | 6.5 | 2.5 | 11.4 |  |  |  | 7.4 | 14.0 |
|  |  | 67.7 | 52.3 |  |  | % Profit Before Taxes/Tangible | 54.5 | 55.4 |
|  |  | (24) 36.7 | (30) 23.0 |  |  | Net Worth | (76) 24.2 | (71) 17.8 |
|  |  | 10.3 | 8.7 |  |  |  | 7.3 | 6.9 |
|  | 22.2 | 25.9 | 15.0 |  |  | % Profit Before Taxes/Total | 19.9 | 15.4 |
|  | 7.2 | 10.2 | 7.7 |  |  | Assets | 6.3 | 6.8 |
|  | 5.1 | 1.9 | 3.0 |  |  |  | 1.2 | 1.2 |
|  | 401.4 | 40.1 | 58.7 |  |  |  | 45.8 | 23.5 |
|  | 13.0 | 17.4 | 17.1 |  |  | Sales/Net Fixed Assets | 16.1 | 14.0 |
|  | 7.5 | 9.4 | 5.9 |  |  |  | 7.8 | 7.8 |
|  | 3.7 | 3.0 | 2.7 |  |  |  | 2.8 | 2.6 |
|  | 2.7 | 2.4 | 1.8 |  |  | Sales/Total Assets | 2.0 | 2.1 |
|  | 1.4 | 1.6 | 1.4 |  |  |  | 1.3 | 1.3 |
|  |  | .7 | .6 |  |  |  | .5 | 1.1 |
|  |  | (21) 1.6 | (32) 1.6 |  |  | % Depr., Dep., Amort./Sales | (79) 1.4 | (78) 1.7 |
|  |  | 2.4 | 2.1 |  |  |  | 2.2 | 2.6 |
|  |  | 1.7 |  |  |  | % Officers', Directors' | 1.6 | 1.6 |
|  |  | (11) 2.4 |  |  |  | Owners' Comp/Sales | (24) 3.5 | (20) 2.5 |
|  |  | 5.5 |  |  |  |  | 7.3 | 5.1 |
| 6191M | 36416M | 367620M | 1723868M | 706455M | 687507M | Net Sales ($) | 4615734M | 4733329M |
| 1476M | 13713M | 158324M | 927089M | 659467M | 894683M | Total Assets ($) | 2856815M | 3116788M |

M = $ thousand   MM = $ million
See Pages 9 through 22 for Explanation of Ratios and Data

## Comparative Historical Data  |  Current Data Sorted by Sales

| 4/1/09-3/31/10 ALL | 4/1/10-3/31/11 ALL | 4/1/11-3/31/12 ALL | Type of Statement | 0-1MM | 1-3MM | 3-5MM | 5-10MM | 10-25MM | 25MM & OVER |
|---|---|---|---|---|---|---|---|---|---|
| 26 | 16 | 19 | Unqualified |  |  |  | 1 | 5 | 13 |
| 22 | 15 | 22 | Reviewed |  | 1 | 1 | 3 | 8 | 9 |
| 5 | 9 | 9 | Compiled | 1 | 1 | 1 |  | 3 | 3 |
| 3 | 6 | 3 | Tax Returns | 1 | 2 |  |  |  |  |
| 38 | 49 | 39 | Other |  | 3 | 6 | 2 | 5 | 23 |
|  |  |  |  |  | 15 (4/1-9/30/11) | | | 77 (10/1/11-3/31/12) | |
| **94** | **95** | **92** | **NUMBER OF STATEMENTS** | 2 | 7 | 8 | 6 | 21 | 48 |

| % | % | % | ASSETS | % | % | % | % | % | % |
|---|---|---|---|---|---|---|---|---|---|
| 7.0 | 10.1 | 6.9 | Cash & Equivalents |  |  |  |  | 5.1 | 6.5 |
| 25.9 | 25.2 | 24.0 | Trade Receivables (net) |  |  |  |  | 30.6 | 22.5 |
| 30.2 | 29.2 | 31.5 | Inventory |  |  |  |  | 37.0 | 29.2 |
| 4.3 | 2.4 | 2.4 | All Other Current |  |  |  |  | 1.5 | 3.3 |
| 67.4 | 66.9 | 64.8 | Total Current |  |  |  |  | 74.2 | 61.6 |
| 16.3 | 16.7 | 17.3 | Fixed Assets (net) |  |  |  |  | 14.5 | 15.9 |
| 10.4 | 12.5 | 13.4 | Intangibles (net) |  |  |  |  | 9.8 | 18.8 |
| 5.9 | 3.9 | 4.4 | All Other Non-Current |  |  |  |  | 1.5 | 3.7 |
| 100.0 | 100.0 | 100.0 | Total |  |  |  |  | 100.0 | 100.0 |

| | | | LIABILITIES | | | | | | |
|---|---|---|---|---|---|---|---|---|---|
| 13.2 | 9.3 | 11.7 | Notes Payable-Short Term |  |  |  |  | 13.7 | 9.7 |
| 2.8 | 2.3 | 2.5 | Cur. Mat.-L.T.D. |  |  |  |  | 2.7 | 2.6 |
| 21.1 | 16.5 | 17.1 | Trade Payables |  |  |  |  | 15.4 | 16.9 |
| .4 | .2 | .1 | Income Taxes Payable |  |  |  |  | .0 | .2 |
| 9.4 | 10.0 | 13.5 | All Other Current |  |  |  |  | 7.0 | 9.4 |
| 46.9 | 38.2 | 44.9 | Total Current |  |  |  |  | 38.9 | 38.7 |
| 10.4 | 11.8 | 11.0 | Long-Term Debt |  |  |  |  | 5.0 | 14.2 |
| .4 | .5 | .8 | Deferred Taxes |  |  |  |  | .8 | 1.2 |
| 3.6 | 9.7 | 9.1 | All Other Non-Current |  |  |  |  | 4.2 | 11.2 |
| 38.8 | 39.7 | 34.2 | Net Worth |  |  |  |  | 51.2 | 34.7 |
| 100.0 | 100.0 | 100.0 | Total Liabilities & Net Worth |  |  |  |  | 100.0 | 100.0 |

| | | | INCOME DATA | | | | | | |
|---|---|---|---|---|---|---|---|---|---|
| 100.0 | 100.0 | 100.0 | Net Sales |  |  |  |  | 100.0 | 100.0 |
| 37.4 | 40.0 | 38.0 | Gross Profit |  |  |  |  | 36.1 | 38.1 |
| 31.5 | 33.8 | 31.0 | Operating Expenses |  |  |  |  | 27.5 | 29.6 |
| 5.9 | 6.2 | 6.9 | Operating Profit |  |  |  |  | 8.6 | 8.5 |
| 1.3 | 1.5 | 1.1 | All Other Expenses (net) |  |  |  |  | 1.2 | 1.5 |
| 4.6 | 4.7 | 5.9 | Profit Before Taxes |  |  |  |  | 7.4 | 7.0 |

| | | | RATIOS | | | | | | |
|---|---|---|---|---|---|---|---|---|---|
| 2.1 | 2.9 | 2.6 | Current |  |  |  |  | 2.6 | 2.6 |
| 1.5 | 1.9 | 1.6 |  |  |  |  |  | 1.9 | 1.6 |
| 1.1 | 1.3 | 1.2 |  |  |  |  |  | 1.3 | 1.2 |
| 1.2 | 1.6 | 1.3 | Quick |  |  |  |  | 1.2 | 1.4 |
| .8 | .8 | .7 |  |  |  |  |  | .7 | .7 |
| .5 | .6 | .5 |  |  |  |  |  | .6 | .5 |
| 31　11.9 | 31　11.8 | 31　11.7 | Sales/Receivables |  |  |  |  | 38　9.7 | 35　10.3 |
| 43　8.4 | 44　8.2 | 44　8.3 |  |  |  |  |  | 47　7.8 | 42　8.6 |
| 60　6.0 | 61　6.0 | 57　6.4 |  |  |  |  |  | 58　6.3 | 60　6.1 |
| 55　6.6 | 60　6.1 | 64　5.7 | Cost of Sales/Inventory |  |  |  |  | 85　4.3 | 68　5.4 |
| 92　4.0 | 93　3.9 | 89　4.1 |  |  |  |  |  | 99　3.7 | 87　4.2 |
| 141　2.6 | 144　2.5 | 126　2.9 |  |  |  |  |  | 130　2.8 | 126　2.9 |
| 32　11.4 | 24　15.0 | 24　15.0 | Cost of Sales/Payables |  |  |  |  | 13　27.6 | 31　11.6 |
| 50　7.3 | 43　8.5 | 38　9.6 |  |  |  |  |  | 37　9.8 | 41　9.0 |
| 77　4.7 | 73　5.0 | 73　5.0 |  |  |  |  |  | 65　5.6 | 83　4.4 |
| 5.2 | 3.9 | 4.6 | Sales/Working Capital |  |  |  |  | 4.4 | 4.0 |
| 10.1 | 6.3 | 9.5 |  |  |  |  |  | 7.5 | 9.5 |
| 29.9 | 12.9 | 25.8 |  |  |  |  |  | 10.9 | 22.9 |
| 17.5 | 22.7 | 15.8 | EBIT/Interest |  |  |  |  | 16.1 | 21.4 |
| (87) 5.2 | (85) 6.6 | (82) 7.2 |  |  |  |  |  | (19) 7.8 | (46) 9.1 |
| 1.5 | 1.8 | 2.1 |  |  |  |  |  | 2.7 | 2.5 |
| 13.3 | 18.0 | 6.7 | Net Profit + Depr., Dep., Amort./Cur. Mat. L/T/D |  |  |  |  |  | 10.9 |
| (21) 5.9 | (18) 8.1 | (20) 2.3 |  |  |  |  |  |  | (17) 2.4 |
| 2.2 | 1.7 | 1.3 |  |  |  |  |  |  | 1.4 |
| .2 | .2 | .2 | Fixed/Worth |  |  |  |  | .1 | .2 |
| .7 | .5 | .5 |  |  |  |  |  | .4 | .5 |
| 1.5 | 2.0 | 3.7 |  |  |  |  |  | .7 | NM |
| 1.1 | .6 | .8 | Debt/Worth |  |  |  |  | .7 | .9 |
| 2.3 | 1.8 | 1.9 |  |  |  |  |  | 1.5 | 2.5 |
| 4.8 | 5.1 | 14.7 |  |  |  |  |  | 2.3 | NM |
| 53.8 | 54.6 | 57.9 | % Profit Before Taxes/Tangible Net Worth |  |  |  |  | 57.5 | 61.2 |
| (79) 28.2 | (77) 29.4 | (71) 25.6 |  |  |  |  |  | (19) 33.1 | (36) 23.0 |
| 8.0 | 11.3 | 10.6 |  |  |  |  |  | 5.9 | 11.9 |
| 14.6 | 18.9 | 17.6 | % Profit Before Taxes/Total Assets |  |  |  |  | 25.0 | 15.6 |
| 8.1 | 7.4 | 7.0 |  |  |  |  |  | 10.2 | 6.8 |
| 1.1 | 1.3 | 2.7 |  |  |  |  |  | 2.5 | 3.5 |
| 36.3 | 35.1 | 45.3 | Sales/Net Fixed Assets |  |  |  |  | 140.2 | 31.4 |
| 15.4 | 14.2 | 18.5 |  |  |  |  |  | 16.9 | 19.4 |
| 7.6 | 7.7 | 8.2 |  |  |  |  |  | 10.0 | 8.9 |
| 2.6 | 2.8 | 3.0 | Sales/Total Assets |  |  |  |  | 2.9 | 2.7 |
| 2.0 | 2.0 | 1.9 |  |  |  |  |  | 2.1 | 1.7 |
| 1.4 | 1.2 | 1.3 |  |  |  |  |  | 1.5 | 1.2 |
| .8 | .7 | .8 | % Depr., Dep., Amort./Sales |  |  |  |  | .5 | .9 |
| (77) 1.8 | (79) 1.5 | (70) 1.6 |  |  |  |  |  | (17) 1.7 | (40) 1.5 |
| 3.0 | 2.4 | 2.6 |  |  |  |  |  | 2.6 | 2.4 |
| 1.3 | 2.1 | 1.4 | % Officers', Directors' Owners' Comp/Sales |  |  |  |  |  |  |
| (25) 3.2 | (26) 4.2 | (24) 2.5 |  |  |  |  |  |  |  |
| 5.3 | 7.6 | 4.9 |  |  |  |  |  |  |  |
| 4223748M | 4036205M | 3528057M | Net Sales ($) | 1158M | 13417M | 33077M | 45476M | 374644M | 3060285M |
| 2642988M | 2628769M | 2654752M | Total Assets ($) | 946M | 7663M | 13892M | 28559M | 231021M | 2372671M |

M = $ thousand    MM = $ million
See Pages 9 through 22 for Explanation of Ratios and Data

## Current Data Sorted by Assets  —  Comparative Historical Data

| 0-500M | 500M-2MM | 2-10MM | 10-50MM | 50-100MM | 100-250MM | Type of Statement | 4/1/07-3/31/08 ALL | 4/1/08-3/31/09 ALL |
|---|---|---|---|---|---|---|---|---|
| | | 1 | 4 | 1 | 1 | Unqualified | 8 | 12 |
| | 2 | 4 | 3 | | | Reviewed | 10 | 14 |
| | 2 | 1 | | | | Compiled | 5 | |
| 1 | 2 | 2 | | | | Tax Returns | 3 | 9 |
| | 2 | 3 | 4 | 1 | | Other | 14 | 16 |
| | 8 (4/1-9/30/11) | | 26 (10/1/11-3/31/12) | | | | | |
| 1 | 8 | 11 | 11 | 2 | 1 | NUMBER OF STATEMENTS | 40 | 51 |

| 0-500M % | 500M-2MM % | 2-10MM % | 10-50MM % | 50-100MM % | 100-250MM % | | % | % |
|---|---|---|---|---|---|---|---|---|
| | | | | | | **ASSETS** | | |
| | | 3.8 | 1.7 | | | Cash & Equivalents | 5.9 | 10.7 |
| | | 31.0 | 24.1 | | | Trade Receivables (net) | 27.2 | 25.5 |
| | | 36.9 | 33.8 | | | Inventory | 33.2 | 30.2 |
| | | 1.8 | .9 | | | All Other Current | 2.5 | 3.2 |
| | | 73.5 | 60.5 | | | Total Current | 68.8 | 69.6 |
| | | 18.8 | 24.6 | | | Fixed Assets (net) | 20.3 | 19.3 |
| | | 3.2 | 9.4 | | | Intangibles (net) | 7.0 | 7.0 |
| | | 4.6 | 5.5 | | | All Other Non-Current | 3.9 | 4.2 |
| | | 100.0 | 100.0 | | | Total | 100.0 | 100.0 |
| | | | | | | **LIABILITIES** | | |
| | | 12.9 | 10.4 | | | Notes Payable-Short Term | 10.8 | 11.1 |
| | | 2.3 | 2.3 | | | Cur. Mat.-L.T.D. | 2.8 | 3.1 |
| | | 24.7 | 16.8 | | | Trade Payables | 16.4 | 16.8 |
| | | .1 | .2 | | | Income Taxes Payable | .4 | .1 |
| | | 7.0 | 12.4 | | | All Other Current | 13.8 | 11.3 |
| | | 47.0 | 42.1 | | | Total Current | 44.2 | 42.4 |
| | | 16.4 | 8.3 | | | Long-Term Debt | 8.9 | 13.7 |
| | | .9 | .1 | | | Deferred Taxes | .3 | .3 |
| | | 6.1 | 1.2 | | | All Other Non-Current | 5.7 | 5.5 |
| | | 29.5 | 48.3 | | | Net Worth | 40.9 | 38.1 |
| | | 100.0 | 100.0 | | | Total Liabilities & Net Worth | 100.0 | 100.0 |
| | | | | | | **INCOME DATA** | | |
| | | 100.0 | 100.0 | | | Net Sales | 100.0 | 100.0 |
| | | 27.6 | 24.6 | | | Gross Profit | 31.6 | 31.9 |
| | | 25.1 | 18.5 | | | Operating Expenses | 26.5 | 27.2 |
| | | 2.4 | 6.2 | | | Operating Profit | 5.1 | 4.6 |
| | | .9 | .5 | | | All Other Expenses (net) | .9 | 1.0 |
| | | 1.5 | 5.7 | | | Profit Before Taxes | 4.2 | 3.7 |
| | | | | | | **RATIOS** | | |
| | | 2.4 | 2.3 | | | | 2.5 | 2.7 |
| | | 1.4 | 1.8 | | | Current | 1.7 | 1.7 |
| | | 1.3 | 1.1 | | | | 1.1 | 1.2 |
| | | 1.2 | 1.0 | | | | 1.2 | 1.7 |
| | | .6 | .7 | | | Quick | .7 | .9 |
| | | .5 | .4 | | | | .6 | .5 |
| | | 36  10.2 | 34  10.6 | | | | 37  9.9 | 34  10.9 |
| | | 46  7.9 | 40  9.2 | | | Sales/Receivables | 43  8.6 | 41  8.9 |
| | | 59  6.2 | 44  8.3 | | | | 49  7.4 | 49  7.4 |
| | | 38  9.7 | 43  8.5 | | | | 56  6.5 | 47  7.8 |
| | | 76  4.8 | 78  4.7 | | | Cost of Sales/Inventory | 76  4.8 | 65  5.6 |
| | | 126  2.9 | 101  3.6 | | | | 113  3.2 | 88  4.1 |
| | | 26  14.3 | 21  17.2 | | | | 23  16.0 | 17  21.5 |
| | | 51  7.1 | 31  11.7 | | | Cost of Sales/Payables | 35  10.4 | 32  11.3 |
| | | 58  6.3 | 55  6.6 | | | | 50  7.3 | 53  6.9 |
| | | 7.2 | 6.2 | | | | 5.4 | 5.4 |
| | | 8.9 | 11.4 | | | Sales/Working Capital | 8.5 | 8.3 |
| | | 16.8 | 42.5 | | | | 39.8 | 22.4 |
| | | 3.8 | 53.0 | | | | 21.9 | 13.4 |
| | | 2.0 | 12.4 | | | EBIT/Interest | (35) 7.2 | (46) 3.8 |
| | | -8.7 | 6.1 | | | | 2.6 | .9 |
| | | | | | | | 9.8 | 21.6 |
| | | | | | | Net Profit + Depr., Dep., Amort./Cur. Mat. L/T/D | (13) 3.6 | (16) 4.1 |
| | | | | | | | 1.6 | 1.8 |
| | | .4 | .3 | | | | .3 | .3 |
| | | .8 | .8 | | | Fixed/Worth | .5 | .5 |
| | | 1.3 | 1.1 | | | | 1.2 | 1.3 |
| | | 1.5 | .6 | | | | .7 | .8 |
| | | 4.4 | 1.3 | | | Debt/Worth | 1.7 | 2.4 |
| | | 6.3 | 4.3 | | | | 6.2 | 4.9 |
| | | 27.1 | 99.2 | | | | 48.2 | 36.6 |
| | | (10) 10.6 | 42.5 | | | % Profit Before Taxes/Tangible Net Worth | (36) 20.1 | (46) 22.2 |
| | | -8.9 | 20.0 | | | | 7.4 | .1 |
| | | 8.7 | 19.4 | | | | 15.3 | 16.4 |
| | | 1.5 | 16.1 | | | % Profit Before Taxes/Total Assets | 8.1 | 4.4 |
| | | -3.2 | 8.5 | | | | 3.4 | -.2 |
| | | 29.2 | 20.1 | | | | 23.4 | 35.1 |
| | | 15.8 | 12.0 | | | Sales/Net Fixed Assets | 14.5 | 14.6 |
| | | 10.5 | 4.6 | | | | 7.5 | 7.0 |
| | | 3.6 | 2.8 | | | | 2.8 | 2.9 |
| | | 2.3 | 2.1 | | | Sales/Total Assets | 2.3 | 2.4 |
| | | 1.8 | 1.8 | | | | 1.7 | 1.7 |
| | | | | | | | 1.0 | 1.1 |
| | | | | | | % Depr., Dep., Amort./Sales | (37) 1.6 | (42) 1.5 |
| | | | | | | | 2.2 | 2.7 |
| | | | | | | | | 1.0 |
| | | | | | | % Officers', Directors' Owners' Comp/Sales | (10) 2.3 | |
| | | | | | | | | 3.0 |
| 340M | 28064M | 165250M | 488599M | 210281M | 241736M | Net Sales ($) | 1707998M | 1984967M |
| 326M | 8625M | 62299M | 232389M | 109772M | 179620M | Total Assets ($) | 905877M | 1184116M |

M = $ thousand    MM = $ million
See Pages 9 through 22 for Explanation of Ratios and Data

## Comparative Historical Data / Current Data Sorted by Sales

| Comparative Historical Data | | | Type of Statement | Current Data Sorted by Sales | | | | | |
|---|---|---|---|---|---|---|---|---|---|
| | | | Unqualified | | | | | 2 | 5 |
| | | | Reviewed | | 1 | 1 | 1 | 4 | 3 |
| | | | Compiled | | | 1 | 1 | | |
| | | | Tax Returns | 1 | 2 | 1 | 1 | 1 | 1 |
| | | | Other | | 1 | 1 | 2 | | 5 |
| 8 | 8 | 7 | | | | | | | |
| 10 | 9 | 9 | | | | | | | |
| 3 | 5 | 3 | | | | | | | |
| 12 | 2 | 5 | | | | | | | |
| 17 | 12 | 10 | | 1 | 2 | 1 | 1 | 1 | 1 |
| 4/1/09-3/31/10 ALL | 4/1/10-3/31/11 ALL | 4/1/11-3/31/12 ALL | | 8 (4/1-9/30/11) | | | 26 (10/1/11-3/31/12) | | |
| | | | | 0-1MM | 1-3MM | 3-5MM | 5-10MM | 10-25MM | 25MM & OVER |
| 50 | 36 | 34 | NUMBER OF STATEMENTS | 1 | 4 | 3 | 5 | 7 | 14 |
| % | % | % | ASSETS | % | % | % | % | % | % |
| 10.8 | 6.3 | 5.8 | Cash & Equivalents | | | | | | 3.4 |
| 27.5 | 31.2 | 30.3 | Trade Receivables (net) | | | | | | 26.4 |
| 27.5 | 27.2 | 31.1 | Inventory | | | | | | 30.3 |
| 1.9 | 2.3 | 3.0 | All Other Current | | | | | | 3.5 |
| 67.7 | 67.1 | 70.2 | Total Current | | | | | | 63.6 |
| 19.8 | 17.6 | 18.0 | Fixed Assets (net) | | | | | | 23.9 |
| 4.6 | 9.7 | 5.1 | Intangibles (net) | | | | | | 7.4 |
| 7.9 | 5.5 | 6.7 | All Other Non-Current | | | | | | 5.1 |
| 100.0 | 100.0 | 100.0 | Total | | | | | | 100.0 |
| | | | LIABILITIES | | | | | | |
| 9.1 | 11.1 | 11.2 | Notes Payable-Short Term | | | | | | 11.8 |
| 1.9 | 2.0 | 1.9 | Cur. Mat.-L.T.D. | | | | | | 1.9 |
| 18.2 | 18.6 | 20.5 | Trade Payables | | | | | | 18.9 |
| .2 | .2 | .1 | Income Taxes Payable | | | | | | .2 |
| 8.8 | 8.0 | 11.1 | All Other Current | | | | | | 10.0 |
| 38.1 | 39.9 | 44.8 | Total Current | | | | | | 42.7 |
| 12.2 | 18.7 | 15.8 | Long-Term Debt | | | | | | 8.2 |
| 1.4 | .8 | .6 | Deferred Taxes | | | | | | .6 |
| 3.7 | 3.6 | 5.6 | All Other Non-Current | | | | | | 2.0 |
| 44.7 | 36.9 | 33.2 | Net Worth | | | | | | 46.4 |
| 100.0 | 100.0 | 100.0 | Total Liabilities & Net Worth | | | | | | 100.0 |
| | | | INCOME DATA | | | | | | |
| 100.0 | 100.0 | 100.0 | Net Sales | | | | | | 100.0 |
| 36.7 | 32.9 | 29.3 | Gross Profit | | | | | | 25.2 |
| 29.7 | 26.8 | 24.4 | Operating Expenses | | | | | | 18.6 |
| 7.0 | 6.0 | 4.9 | Operating Profit | | | | | | 6.5 |
| .4 | 1.1 | .7 | All Other Expenses (net) | | | | | | .7 |
| 6.6 | 4.9 | 4.2 | Profit Before Taxes | | | | | | 5.8 |
| | | | RATIOS | | | | | | |
| 2.9 | 2.5 | 2.3 | Current | | | | | | 2.3 |
| 1.7 | 1.8 | 1.7 | | | | | | | 2.0 |
| 1.2 | 1.2 | 1.2 | | | | | | | 1.1 |
| 1.5 | 1.6 | 1.2 | Quick | | | | | | 1.1 |
| .9 | .8 | .8 | | | | | | | .8 |
| .7 | .5 | .5 | | | | | | | .5 |
| 32  11.4 | 39  9.3 | 35  10.3 | Sales/Receivables | | | | | | 35  10.3 |
| 42  8.8 | 46  8.0 | 40  9.2 | | | | | | | 40  9.1 |
| 52  7.0 | 58  6.3 | 50  7.3 | | | | | | | 49  7.5 |
| 34  10.8 | 29  12.7 | 38  9.5 | Cost of Sales/Inventory | | | | | | 42  8.7 |
| 59  6.1 | 74  4.9 | 65  5.6 | | | | | | | 70  5.2 |
| 107  3.4 | 109  3.3 | 101  3.6 | | | | | | | 101  3.6 |
| 20  18.5 | 23  15.9 | 25  14.4 | Cost of Sales/Payables | | | | | | 27  13.5 |
| 33  11.0 | 32  11.5 | 45  8.2 | | | | | | | 37  9.9 |
| 55  6.6 | 57  6.4 | 54  6.7 | | | | | | | 55  6.6 |
| 4.9 | 4.7 | 6.2 | Sales/Working Capital | | | | | | 4.7 |
| 7.4 | 9.2 | 10.7 | | | | | | | 10.4 |
| 22.3 | 18.8 | 22.0 | | | | | | | 36.2 |
| 21.5 | 27.4 | 20.4 | EBIT/Interest | | | | | | 53.4 |
| (47)  7.7 | (35)  6.1 | 6.5 | | | | | | | 13.0 |
| 3.0 | 2.3 | 1.7 | | | | | | | 6.7 |
| 15.4 | 26.4 | 16.6 | Net Profit + Depr., Dep., Amort./Cur. Mat. L/T/D | | | | | | |
| (15)  3.7 | (12)  4.7 | (14)  3.2 | | | | | | | |
| 1.6 | 2.8 | 1.8 | | | | | | | |
| .2 | .3 | .2 | Fixed/Worth | | | | | | .3 |
| .5 | .6 | .6 | | | | | | | .7 |
| 1.0 | 1.5 | 1.1 | | | | | | | .9 |
| .5 | .8 | .9 | Debt/Worth | | | | | | .6 |
| 1.2 | 3.2 | 2.3 | | | | | | | 1.2 |
| 3.5 | 5.8 | 5.1 | | | | | | | 4.3 |
| 69.4 | 45.1 | 87.3 | % Profit Before Taxes/Tangible Net Worth | | | | | | 93.6 |
| (46)  25.0 | (31)  30.2 | (31)  24.7 | | | | | | (13) | 26.3 |
| 5.9 | 7.5 | 6.5 | | | | | | | 16.1 |
| 19.8 | 17.1 | 17.4 | % Profit Before Taxes/Total Assets | | | | | | 19.0 |
| 10.5 | 9.1 | 9.2 | | | | | | | 13.9 |
| 3.7 | 1.4 | 1.1 | | | | | | | 7.7 |
| 33.1 | 39.3 | 47.3 | Sales/Net Fixed Assets | | | | | | 22.0 |
| 16.9 | 12.5 | 17.2 | | | | | | | 10.6 |
| 7.2 | 7.0 | 7.1 | | | | | | | 4.6 |
| 3.4 | 2.6 | 3.6 | Sales/Total Assets | | | | | | 2.9 |
| 2.2 | 2.2 | 2.3 | | | | | | | 2.0 |
| 1.8 | 1.6 | 1.8 | | | | | | | 1.7 |
| .9 | .9 | .6 | % Depr., Dep., Amort./Sales | | | | | | .8 |
| (38)  1.4 | (30)  1.6 | (23)  1.1 | | | | | | (11) | 1.1 |
| 3.5 | 2.6 | 1.8 | | | | | | | 2.7 |
| 1.6 | 1.5 | | % Officers', Directors' Owners' Comp/Sales | | | | | | |
| (16)  4.9 | (10)  4.2 | | | | | | | | |
| 12.2 | 8.0 | | | | | | | | |
| 1677961M | 1391165M | 1134270M | Net Sales ($) | 340M | 8444M | 12112M | 39943M | 118401M | 955030M |
| 866795M | 709838M | 593031M | Total Assets ($) | 326M | 3505M | 4897M | 14111M | 50276M | 519916M |

© RMA 2012

M = $ thousand    MM = $ million
See Pages 9 through 22 for Explanation of Ratios and Data

## Current Data Sorted by Assets      Comparative Historical Data

| 0-500M | 500M-2MM | 2-10MM | 10-50MM | 50-100MM | 100-250MM | Type of Statement | 4/1/07-3/31/08 ALL | 4/1/08-3/31/09 ALL |
|---|---|---|---|---|---|---|---|---|
| | | 1 | 4 | | 3 | Unqualified | 7 | 6 |
| | | 1 | 3 | | | Reviewed | 2 | 3 |
| | | 2 | 1 | | | Compiled | 3 | 4 |
| | | 2 | 1 | | | Tax Returns | | 5 |
| 1 | 6 | 4 | 12 | 1 | 1 | Other | 10 | 11 |
| | | 5 (4/1-9/30/11) | 38 (10/1/11-3/31/12) | | | | 10 | 11 |
| 1 | 6 | 10 | 21 | 1 | 4 | **NUMBER OF STATEMENTS** | 22 | 29 |
| % | % | % | % | % | % | **ASSETS** | % | % |
| | | 5.5 | 8.4 | | | Cash & Equivalents | 5.3 | 7.5 |
| | | 29.1 | 25.4 | | | Trade Receivables (net) | 29.7 | 24.4 |
| | | 22.5 | 24.4 | | | Inventory | 17.1 | 22.2 |
| | | 4.8 | 1.6 | | | All Other Current | 4.0 | 6.2 |
| | | 61.8 | 59.9 | | | Total Current | 56.1 | 60.3 |
| | | 22.3 | 29.6 | | | Fixed Assets (net) | 34.0 | 30.6 |
| | | 10.3 | 4.7 | | | Intangibles (net) | 2.4 | 5.4 |
| | | 5.6 | 5.8 | | | All Other Non-Current | 7.5 | 3.8 |
| | | 100.0 | 100.0 | | | Total | 100.0 | 100.0 |
| | | | | | | **LIABILITIES** | | |
| | | 10.1 | 7.7 | | | Notes Payable-Short Term | 13.0 | 10.1 |
| | | 4.2 | 2.9 | | | Cur. Mat.-L.T.D. | 1.6 | 4.6 |
| | | 13.9 | 15.5 | | | Trade Payables | 14.9 | 23.8 |
| | | .0 | .1 | | | Income Taxes Payable | .1 | .1 |
| | | 5.8 | 8.7 | | | All Other Current | 8.8 | 7.5 |
| | | 34.0 | 34.9 | | | Total Current | 38.4 | 46.1 |
| | | 15.1 | 16.7 | | | Long-Term Debt | 10.9 | 20.4 |
| | | .8 | .4 | | | Deferred Taxes | .1 | .1 |
| | | 8.2 | 2.8 | | | All Other Non-Current | 6.7 | 8.2 |
| | | 41.8 | 45.2 | | | Net Worth | 43.9 | 25.2 |
| | | 100.0 | 100.0 | | | Total Liabilities & Net Worth | 100.0 | 100.0 |
| | | | | | | **INCOME DATA** | | |
| | | 100.0 | 100.0 | | | Net Sales | 100.0 | 100.0 |
| | | 33.7 | 18.2 | | | Gross Profit | 24.8 | 30.3 |
| | | 25.8 | 11.3 | | | Operating Expenses | 18.7 | 25.9 |
| | | 7.9 | 6.9 | | | Operating Profit | 6.2 | 4.3 |
| | | -.6 | .7 | | | All Other Expenses (net) | 1.5 | 1.4 |
| | | 8.5 | 6.2 | | | Profit Before Taxes | 4.7 | 3.0 |
| | | | | | | **RATIOS** | | |
| | | 5.4 | 3.0 | | | | 2.3 | 2.2 |
| | | 2.0 | 1.8 | | | Current | 1.7 | 1.9 |
| | | 1.3 | 1.0 | | | | 1.4 | 1.2 |
| | | 3.0 | 1.7 | | | | 1.6 | 1.6 |
| | | 1.2 | .8 | | | Quick | 1.1 | .7 |
| | | .5 | .6 | | | | .9 | .4 |
| | | 13  28.5 | 31  11.9 | | | | 31  11.8 | 26  14.3 |
| | | 38  9.5 | 41  8.8 | | | Sales/Receivables | 45  8.2 | 34  10.9 |
| | | 66  5.5 | 50  7.3 | | | | 69  5.3 | 45  8.1 |
| | | 26  14.1 | 36  10.1 | | | | 10  36.2 | 33  11.1 |
| | | 49  7.5 | 46  7.9 | | | Cost of Sales/Inventory | 40  9.2 | 43  8.5 |
| | | 63  5.8 | 65  5.6 | | | | 54  6.8 | 65  5.6 |
| | | 1  265.5 | 20  18.0 | | | | 17  22.0 | 19  18.9 |
| | | 26  13.9 | 27  13.3 | | | Cost of Sales/Payables | 26  14.2 | 31  11.7 |
| | | 39  9.3 | 41  8.9 | | | | 41  8.9 | 43  8.5 |
| | | 5.0 | 5.4 | | | | 6.7 | 6.3 |
| | | 9.2 | 9.5 | | | Sales/Working Capital | 9.0 | 10.5 |
| | | 57.0 | NM | | | | 26.1 | 32.2 |
| | | | 67.3 | | | | 15.1 | 5.4 |
| | | | (20) 5.8 | | | EBIT/Interest | (18) 4.5 | (23) 3.8 |
| | | | 1.7 | | | | 1.2 | 1.4 |
| | | | | | | Net Profit + Depr., Dep., Amort./Cur. Mat. L/T/D | | |
| | | .1 | .4 | | | | .6 | .3 |
| | | .6 | .5 | | | Fixed/Worth | .7 | 1.1 |
| | | 3.5 | 1.4 | | | | 2.1 | 2.4 |
| | | .8 | .8 | | | | .3 | 1.0 |
| | | 1.2 | 1.4 | | | Debt/Worth | 1.3 | 1.6 |
| | | 7.4 | 3.3 | | | | 4.3 | 8.2 |
| | | | 51.9 | | | | 32.8 | 31.5 |
| | | | 28.5 | | | % Profit Before Taxes/Tangible Net Worth | (20) 24.2 | (26) 17.4 |
| | | | 7.9 | | | | 4.4 | 3.1 |
| | | 45.6 | 29.7 | | | | 12.0 | 11.1 |
| | | 24.0 | 12.4 | | | % Profit Before Taxes/Total Assets | 9.4 | 7.4 |
| | | 3.5 | 2.1 | | | | 1.1 | 1.4 |
| | | 77.1 | 14.8 | | | | 18.8 | 18.0 |
| | | 11.1 | 10.2 | | | Sales/Net Fixed Assets | 7.5 | 11.4 |
| | | 7.6 | 3.0 | | | | 3.9 | 4.4 |
| | | 3.7 | 3.2 | | | | 3.2 | 3.3 |
| | | 2.8 | 2.2 | | | Sales/Total Assets | 2.1 | 2.5 |
| | | 1.8 | 1.4 | | | | 1.5 | 1.8 |
| | | | 1.2 | | | | 1.3 | 1.5 |
| | | | (19) 2.4 | | | % Depr., Dep., Amort./Sales | (19) 1.7 | (26) 2.2 |
| | | | 4.9 | | | | 3.5 | 3.4 |
| | | | | | | | | 2.6 |
| | | | | | | % Officers', Directors' Owners' Comp/Sales | | (13) 5.9 |
| | | | | | | | | 13.6 |
| 2768M | 19998M | 119045M | 1492866M | 115058M | 1645870M | Net Sales ($) | 2091969M | 1832262M |
| 94M | 7157M | 44454M | 606173M | 51031M | 668688M | Total Assets ($) | 998813M | 831723M |

M = $ thousand    MM = $ million
See Pages 9 through 22 for Explanation of Ratios and Data

**Comparative Historical Data**                     **Current Data Sorted by Sales**

| | | | Type of Statement | 0-1MM | 1-3MM | 3-5MM | 5-10MM | 10-25MM | 25MM & OVER |
|---|---|---|---|---|---|---|---|---|---|
| 7 | 7 | 8 | Unqualified | | | | | 1 | 7 |
| 4 | 1 | 4 | Reviewed | | | | | 3 | 1 |
| 2 | 3 | 3 | Compiled | | 1 | | 1 | | 1 |
| 4 | 2 | 3 | Tax Returns | | | 2 | 2 | | 1 |
| 13 | 15 | 25 | Other | | 4 | 3 | 2 | 4 | 12 |
| 4/1/09-3/31/10 | 4/1/10-3/31/11 | 4/1/11-3/31/12 | | | 5 (4/1-9/30/11) | | | 38 (10/1/11-3/31/12) | |
| ALL | ALL | ALL | | | | | | | |
| 30 | 28 | 43 | **NUMBER OF STATEMENTS** | | 4 | 4 | 5 | 8 | 22 |
| % | % | % | **ASSETS** | % | % | % | % | % | % |
| 6.6 | 9.2 | 8.4 | Cash & Equivalents | D | | | | | 9.3 |
| 24.2 | 28.2 | 28.7 | Trade Receivables (net) | A | | | | | 27.5 |
| 18.1 | 23.3 | 21.4 | Inventory | T | | | | | 26.6 |
| 2.0 | 2.3 | 2.1 | All Other Current | A | | | | | 1.3 |
| 50.9 | 63.0 | 60.6 | Total Current | | | | | | 64.7 |
| 39.7 | 26.1 | 27.8 | Fixed Assets (net) | N | | | | | 27.5 |
| 5.5 | 5.5 | 5.0 | Intangibles (net) | O | | | | | 3.9 |
| 3.9 | 5.3 | 6.5 | All Other Non-Current | T | | | | | 3.9 |
| 100.0 | 100.0 | 100.0 | Total | | | | | | 100.0 |
| | | | **LIABILITIES** | A | | | | | |
| 9.1 | 9.4 | 9.3 | Notes Payable-Short Term | V | | | | | 6.7 |
| 6.3 | 2.6 | 3.2 | Cur. Mat.-L.T.D. | A | | | | | 2.4 |
| 15.3 | 19.5 | 18.4 | Trade Payables | I | | | | | 17.7 |
| .6 | .2 | .1 | Income Taxes Payable | L | | | | | .1 |
| 4.8 | 6.1 | 6.5 | All Other Current | A | | | | | 7.9 |
| 36.1 | 37.8 | 37.4 | Total Current | B | | | | | 34.8 |
| 19.7 | 14.6 | 16.0 | Long-Term Debt | L | | | | | 13.1 |
| .3 | .5 | .5 | Deferred Taxes | E | | | | | .5 |
| 3.5 | 8.2 | 4.2 | All Other Non-Current | | | | | | 2.4 |
| 40.4 | 38.9 | 41.9 | Net Worth | | | | | | 49.2 |
| 100.0 | 100.0 | 100.0 | Total Liabilties & Net Worth | | | | | | 100.0 |
| | | | **INCOME DATA** | | | | | | |
| 100.0 | 100.0 | 100.0 | Net Sales | | | | | | 100.0 |
| 25.5 | 28.3 | 27.2 | Gross Profit | | | | | | 16.6 |
| 21.4 | 20.8 | 19.8 | Operating Expenses | | | | | | 9.4 |
| 4.2 | 7.5 | 7.4 | Operating Profit | | | | | | 7.2 |
| 1.3 | .8 | .3 | All Other Expenses (net) | | | | | | .5 |
| 2.9 | 6.7 | 7.1 | Profit Before Taxes | | | | | | 6.7 |
| | | | **RATIOS** | | | | | | |
| 2.3 | 2.4 | 2.8 | | | | | | | 3.2 |
| 1.4 | 1.9 | 1.8 | Current | | | | | | 2.0 |
| .8 | 1.1 | 1.2 | | | | | | | 1.4 |
| 1.4 | 1.5 | 1.7 | | | | | | | 1.7 |
| .7 | 1.1 | 1.1 | Quick | | | | | | 1.1 |
| .4 | .5 | .6 | | | | | | | .7 |
| 37 9.9 | 33 11.1 | 25 14.5 | | | | | | | 31 11.8 |
| 54 6.8 | 42 8.6 | 41 9.0 | Sales/Receivables | | | | | | 41 8.9 |
| 64 5.7 | 60 6.1 | 49 7.4 | | | | | | | 49 7.5 |
| 33 11.2 | 37 9.9 | 20 18.6 | | | | | | | 36 10.0 |
| 46 8.0 | 58 6.3 | 45 8.1 | Cost of Sales/Inventory | | | | | | 46 8.0 |
| 76 4.8 | 77 4.8 | 57 6.4 | | | | | | | 63 5.8 |
| 26 14.2 | 23 15.9 | 19 19.0 | | | | | | | 21 17.7 |
| 42 8.7 | 40 9.2 | 27 13.3 | Cost of Sales/Payables | | | | | | 28 13.1 |
| 61 5.9 | 68 5.4 | 42 8.6 | | | | | | | 40 9.1 |
| 5.7 | 6.3 | 5.5 | | | | | | | 5.3 |
| 15.6 | 7.7 | 10.5 | Sales/Working Capital | | | | | | 7.6 |
| -13.4 | 59.5 | 48.0 | | | | | | | 15.2 |
| 8.0 | 38.8 | 42.7 | | | | | | | 111.3 |
| (28) 1.7 | (24) 7.3 | (37) 11.4 | EBIT/Interest | | | | | | (21) 15.4 |
| -.2 | 1.5 | 1.8 | | | | | | | 3.6 |
| | | | Net Profit + Depr., Dep., Amort./Cur. Mat. L/T/D | | | | | | |
| .6 | .4 | .3 | | | | | | | .4 |
| 1.0 | .6 | .5 | Fixed/Worth | | | | | | .4 |
| 2.8 | 3.0 | 1.4 | | | | | | | 1.2 |
| .7 | .8 | .8 | | | | | | | .5 |
| 1.7 | 1.3 | 1.4 | Debt/Worth | | | | | | 1.2 |
| 3.8 | 8.9 | 3.8 | | | | | | | 2.0 |
| 20.9 | 76.9 | 60.9 | | | | | | | 51.9 |
| (27) 5.2 | (24) 35.3 | (40) 36.2 | % Profit Before Taxes/Tangible Net Worth | | | | | | (21) 36.1 |
| -10.7 | 12.4 | 8.9 | | | | | | | 17.3 |
| 9.1 | 29.7 | 38.3 | | | | | | | 29.3 |
| 3.1 | 16.6 | 13.0 | % Profit Before Taxes/Total Assets | | | | | | 13.5 |
| -3.1 | 3.1 | 2.4 | | | | | | | 3.9 |
| 9.1 | 17.8 | 18.6 | | | | | | | 16.1 |
| 4.7 | 9.7 | 10.5 | Sales/Net Fixed Assets | | | | | | 11.0 |
| 1.9 | 5.1 | 5.8 | | | | | | | 7.3 |
| 2.3 | 3.0 | 3.2 | | | | | | | 3.2 |
| 1.5 | 2.4 | 2.8 | Sales/Total Assets | | | | | | 2.8 |
| 1.1 | 1.6 | 1.7 | | | | | | | 1.7 |
| 1.9 | 1.9 | 1.3 | | | | | | | 1.2 |
| (25) 4.5 | (20) 2.7 | (32) 2.0 | % Depr., Dep., Amort./Sales | | | | | | (20) 1.7 |
| 8.1 | 3.6 | 3.6 | | | | | | | 2.9 |
| 1.4 | 2.3 | 1.0 | | | | | | | |
| (12) 3.8 | (11) 5.2 | (12) 2.1 | % Officers', Directors' Owners' Comp/Sales | | | | | | |
| 6.6 | 6.7 | 4.1 | | | | | | | |
| 1335316M | 1555397M | 3395605M | Net Sales ($) | 10079M | 16390M | 37513M | 155797M | | 3175826M |
| 809849M | 884354M | 1377597M | Total Assets ($) | 2956M | 6774M | 13844M | 86270M | | 1267753M |

© RMA 2012

M = $ thousand     MM = $ million
See Pages 9 through 22 for Explanation of Ratios and Data

### Current Data Sorted by Assets — Comparative Historical Data

| | 0-500M | 500M-2MM | 2-10MM | 10-50MM | 50-100MM | 100-250MM | Type of Statement | 4/1/07-3/31/08 ALL | 4/1/08-3/31/09 ALL |
|---|---|---|---|---|---|---|---|---|---|
| | | | 9 | 19 | 8 | 9 | Unqualified | 41 | 41 |
| | | 4 | 22 | 7 | 1 | | Reviewed | 40 | 43 |
| | 2 | 8 | 9 | 5 | | | Compiled | 21 | 18 |
| | 5 | 11 | 11 | 1 | | | Tax Returns | 17 | 23 |
| | 5 | 20 | 30 | 36 | 11 | 5 | Other | 84 | 94 |
| | | 51 (4/1-9/30/11) | | 187 (10/1/11-3/31/12) | | | | | |
| NUMBER OF STATEMENTS | 12 | 43 | 81 | 68 | 20 | 14 | | 203 | 219 |

| | 0-500M | 500M-2MM | 2-10MM | 10-50MM | 50-100MM | 100-250MM | | 4/1/07-3/31/08 ALL | 4/1/08-3/31/09 ALL |
|---|---|---|---|---|---|---|---|---|---|
| | % | % | % | % | % | % | **ASSETS** | % | % |
| | 15.3 | 11.9 | 10.5 | 8.2 | 10.9 | 4.8 | Cash & Equivalents | 7.7 | 7.6 |
| | 34.4 | 30.8 | 26.7 | 28.2 | 21.1 | 11.7 | Trade Receivables (net) | 28.4 | 25.9 |
| | 30.9 | 24.3 | 25.9 | 23.3 | 19.4 | 19.9 | Inventory | 25.8 | 26.1 |
| | 1.4 | 1.7 | 2.4 | 2.9 | 2.9 | 3.6 | All Other Current | 3.4 | 2.7 |
| | 82.0 | 68.8 | 65.5 | 62.6 | 54.3 | 39.9 | Total Current | 65.2 | 62.2 |
| | 9.1 | 20.8 | 22.8 | 27.1 | 26.6 | 34.8 | Fixed Assets (net) | 23.2 | 23.1 |
| | 1.8 | 4.1 | 6.9 | 5.8 | 13.7 | 16.1 | Intangibles (net) | 6.7 | 7.5 |
| | 7.1 | 6.3 | 4.9 | 4.6 | 5.4 | 9.2 | All Other Non-Current | 4.9 | 7.2 |
| | 100.0 | 100.0 | 100.0 | 100.0 | 100.0 | 100.0 | Total | 100.0 | 100.0 |
| | | | | | | | **LIABILITIES** | | |
| | 11.5 | 9.1 | 8.6 | 7.9 | 3.6 | 1.8 | Notes Payable-Short Term | 11.7 | 10.7 |
| | 2.7 | 6.4 | 3.3 | 2.7 | 2.2 | 3.2 | Cur. Mat.-L.T.D. | 3.5 | 3.8 |
| | 18.4 | 16.7 | 16.7 | 14.8 | 10.7 | 7.4 | Trade Payables | 18.3 | 16.2 |
| | .0 | .3 | .5 | .2 | .0 | .0 | Income Taxes Payable | .4 | .2 |
| | 12.4 | 7.1 | 10.1 | 7.4 | 6.3 | 15.5 | All Other Current | 11.4 | 10.3 |
| | 45.2 | 39.6 | 39.2 | 32.9 | 22.9 | 28.0 | Total Current | 45.3 | 41.3 |
| | 18.3 | 22.0 | 16.4 | 13.0 | 11.7 | 28.5 | Long-Term Debt | 16.3 | 14.6 |
| | .0 | .2 | .5 | 1.0 | 2.3 | 1.5 | Deferred Taxes | .7 | .5 |
| | 11.4 | 7.9 | 5.4 | 5.0 | 6.6 | 5.7 | All Other Non-Current | 5.9 | 5.4 |
| | 25.2 | 30.3 | 38.6 | 48.1 | 56.5 | 36.2 | Net Worth | 31.8 | 38.1 |
| | 100.0 | 100.0 | 100.0 | 100.0 | 100.0 | 100.0 | Total Liabilities & Net Worth | 100.0 | 100.0 |
| | | | | | | | **INCOME DATA** | | |
| | 100.0 | 100.0 | 100.0 | 100.0 | 100.0 | 100.0 | Net Sales | 100.0 | 100.0 |
| | 44.6 | 41.7 | 34.6 | 25.2 | 27.2 | 20.9 | Gross Profit | 33.0 | 32.7 |
| | 35.9 | 37.8 | 29.0 | 17.7 | 17.0 | 13.4 | Operating Expenses | 27.0 | 26.2 |
| | 8.8 | 3.9 | 5.6 | 7.5 | 10.2 | 7.4 | Operating Profit | 5.9 | 6.4 |
| | .8 | .7 | .0 | .6 | 1.2 | 2.1 | All Other Expenses (net) | 1.8 | 1.1 |
| | 8.0 | 3.2 | 5.6 | 6.9 | 9.0 | 5.4 | Profit Before Taxes | 4.1 | 5.3 |
| | | | | | | | **RATIOS** | | |
| | 6.7 | 3.3 | 2.8 | 2.7 | 4.9 | 2.0 | | 2.4 | 2.3 |
| | 2.4 | 1.8 | 1.6 | 1.9 | 2.3 | 1.6 | Current | 1.5 | 1.5 |
| | 1.2 | 1.2 | 1.3 | 1.3 | 1.4 | 1.1 | | 1.0 | 1.1 |
| | 5.6 | 2.5 | 1.8 | 1.6 | 3.6 | 1.1 | | 1.3 | 1.3 |
| | 1.0 | 1.0 | .9 | 1.0 | 1.2 | .8 | Quick | .8 | .8 |
| | .5 | .6 | .6 | .6 | .6 | .3 | | .5 | .5 |
| | 12 30.6 | 28 13.2 | 26 13.8 | 34 10.8 | 34 10.6 | 17 21.7 | | 32 11.3 | 26 13.8 |
| | 31 11.8 | 38 9.6 | 41 8.9 | 47 7.7 | 47 7.8 | 46 7.9 | Sales/Receivables | 42 8.7 | 39 9.4 |
| | 54 6.7 | 51 7.2 | 55 6.6 | 57 6.4 | 64 5.7 | 60 6.1 | | 52 7.1 | 49 7.5 |
| | 28 13.2 | 15 23.7 | 34 10.6 | 32 11.3 | 43 8.5 | 39 9.3 | | 33 10.9 | 28 13.2 |
| | 48 7.6 | 42 8.7 | 53 6.9 | 60 6.1 | 55 6.6 | 64 5.7 | Cost of Sales/Inventory | 55 6.6 | 61 5.9 |
| | 104 3.5 | 85 4.3 | 99 3.7 | 83 4.4 | 91 4.0 | 91 4.0 | | 101 3.7 | 100 3.7 |
| | 17 21.9 | 18 20.5 | 18 20.5 | 18 20.4 | 23 16.0 | 19 18.8 | | 21 17.2 | 18 20.1 |
| | 29 12.4 | 28 13.0 | 33 11.0 | 29 12.7 | 28 12.9 | 27 13.6 | Cost of Sales/Payables | 37 10.0 | 31 11.7 |
| | 63 5.8 | 50 7.3 | 55 6.6 | 46 7.9 | 47 7.8 | 39 9.3 | | 56 6.5 | 52 7.1 |
| | 3.8 | 4.5 | 5.7 | 4.3 | 3.4 | 5.6 | | 6.1 | 6.3 |
| | 9.5 | 8.6 | 10.1 | 9.6 | 6.7 | 6.5 | Sales/Working Capital | 12.3 | 12.5 |
| | 75.8 | 49.5 | 31.5 | 15.4 | 18.9 | 33.8 | | 92.1 | 63.4 |
| | | 9.1 | 24.8 | 38.3 | 24.2 | 10.4 | | 9.6 | 11.8 |
| | | (37) 3.9 | (72) 6.0 | (60) 10.1 | (17) 12.7 | (13) 4.6 | EBIT/Interest | (179) 3.4 | (200) 4.2 |
| | | 1.0 | 2.2 | 2.8 | 3.6 | 2.2 | | 1.5 | 1.4 |
| | | | 3.5 | 6.6 | | | | 8.8 | 7.2 |
| | | | (19) 1.8 | (18) 3.3 | | | Net Profit + Depr., Dep., Amort./Cur. Mat. L/T/D | (65) 3.1 | (68) 2.4 |
| | | | 1.4 | 2.0 | | | | 1.7 | .9 |
| | .0 | .1 | .2 | .2 | .4 | .7 | | .2 | .2 |
| | .4 | .5 | .6 | .6 | .8 | 2.2 | Fixed/Worth | .8 | .7 |
| | -1.8 | 1.6 | 3.1 | 1.3 | 7.9 | 13.1 | | 2.5 | 2.1 |
| | .7 | .5 | .8 | .5 | .3 | 1.0 | | 1.0 | 1.0 |
| | 5.3 | 1.5 | 1.8 | 1.3 | .9 | 3.6 | Debt/Worth | 2.2 | 2.0 |
| | -22.5 | 5.1 | 9.2 | 2.6 | 24.3 | 21.8 | | 12.3 | 5.4 |
| | | 32.7 | 67.6 | 50.2 | 58.1 | 63.5 | | 58.8 | 53.1 |
| | | (36) 11.1 | (66) 34.5 | (62) 26.1 | (17) 22.8 | (12) 35.2 | % Profit Before Taxes/Tangible Net Worth | (171) 29.0 | (191) 20.4 |
| | | 2.4 | 11.7 | 8.8 | 13.3 | 14.0 | | 9.5 | 2.7 |
| | 63.2 | 16.5 | 22.8 | 21.6 | 20.1 | 9.2 | | 16.8 | 20.6 |
| | 7.4 | 6.9 | 9.2 | 8.6 | 10.4 | 7.0 | % Profit Before Taxes/Total Assets | 7.2 | 7.2 |
| | 3.1 | .2 | 2.7 | 2.5 | 5.3 | 3.4 | | 1.8 | 1.6 |
| | UND | 89.8 | 38.4 | 20.4 | 10.9 | 8.0 | | 43.6 | 43.8 |
| | 45.8 | 19.9 | 15.3 | 8.9 | 7.9 | 3.3 | Sales/Net Fixed Assets | 12.7 | 14.2 |
| | 24.0 | 5.9 | 6.7 | 4.8 | 3.9 | 1.9 | | 5.9 | 5.4 |
| | 5.5 | 4.4 | 3.2 | 2.9 | 2.3 | 1.3 | | 3.3 | 3.4 |
| | 3.1 | 3.0 | 2.4 | 2.0 | 1.5 | 1.1 | Sales/Total Assets | 2.3 | 2.3 |
| | 2.5 | 1.6 | 1.5 | 1.4 | 1.3 | .6 | | 1.7 | 1.5 |
| | | .5 | .6 | .7 | 1.6 | | | .6 | .6 |
| | | (27) 1.4 | (64) 1.7 | (58) 1.7 | (18) 2.9 | | % Depr., Dep., Amort./Sales | (178) 1.6 | (181) 1.7 |
| | | 2.6 | 3.2 | 3.2 | 4.2 | | | 3.0 | 3.3 |
| | | 4.7 | 1.2 | .5 | | | | 1.6 | 1.5 |
| | | (23) 6.4 | (35) 2.8 | (11) 1.0 | | | % Officers', Directors' Owners' Comp/Sales | (53) 3.3 | (59) 3.2 |
| | | 9.2 | 4.9 | 1.7 | | | | 6.3 | 6.3 |
| | 19237M | 153235M | 2345759M | 3369180M | 2400007M | 2557878M | Net Sales ($) | 9621034M | 15154316M |
| | 4305M | 51003M | 398792M | 1611166M | 1425942M | 2265427M | Total Assets ($) | 4880927M | 6007778M |

## Comparative Historical Data | Current Data Sorted by Sales

| 4/1/09-3/31/10 ALL | 4/1/10-3/31/11 ALL | 4/1/11-3/31/12 ALL | Type of Statement | 0-1MM | 1-3MM | 3-5MM | 5-10MM | 10-25MM | 25MM & OVER |
|---|---|---|---|---|---|---|---|---|---|
| 48 | 35 | 45 | Unqualified | | 1 | | 1 | 7 | 36 |
| 43 | 48 | 34 | Reviewed | | 1 | 2 | 9 | 13 | 9 |
| 19 | 16 | 24 | Compiled | | 4 | 6 | 4 | 8 | 2 |
| 21 | 22 | 28 | Tax Returns | 2 | 10 | 6 | 7 | 2 | 1 |
| 95 | 108 | 107 | Other | 5 | 10 | 14 | 11 | 18 | 49 |
| 4/1/09-3/31/10 ALL | 4/1/10-3/31/11 ALL | 4/1/11-3/31/12 ALL | | | 51 (4/1-9/30/11) | | 187 (10/1/11-3/31/12) | | |
| 226 | 229 | 238 | NUMBER OF STATEMENTS | 7 | 26 | 28 | 32 | 48 | 97 |
| % | % | % | ASSETS | % | % | % | % | % | % |
| 9.4 | 8.9 | 10.0 | Cash & Equivalents | | 16.3 | 11.9 | 8.4 | 8.1 | 9.5 |
| 26.5 | 28.3 | 26.9 | Trade Receivables (net) | | 25.9 | 29.9 | 26.4 | 29.3 | 26.1 |
| 23.3 | 25.5 | 24.2 | Inventory | | 27.0 | 18.6 | 24.4 | 31.3 | 21.4 |
| 3.5 | 2.8 | 2.5 | All Other Current | | 1.1 | 4.8 | 1.5 | 1.4 | 3.1 |
| 62.8 | 65.5 | 63.6 | Total Current | | 70.3 | 65.2 | 60.8 | 70.1 | 60.1 |
| 25.8 | 22.3 | 24.0 | Fixed Assets (net) | | 19.8 | 21.0 | 29.6 | 20.3 | 26.0 |
| 5.6 | 6.1 | 6.9 | Intangibles (net) | | 6.2 | 10.0 | 3.9 | 4.5 | 8.7 |
| 5.8 | 6.2 | 5.5 | All Other Non-Current | | 3.6 | 3.9 | 5.8 | 5.1 | 5.2 |
| 100.0 | 100.0 | 100.0 | Total | | 100.0 | 100.0 | 100.0 | 100.0 | 100.0 |
| | | | LIABILITIES | | | | | | |
| 10.9 | 9.2 | 7.8 | Notes Payable-Short Term | | 8.0 | 12.2 | 7.1 | 9.1 | 6.2 |
| 3.8 | 3.5 | 3.5 | Cur. Mat.-L.T.D. | | 5.8 | 5.9 | 4.1 | 2.4 | 2.6 |
| 15.8 | 15.4 | 15.2 | Trade Payables | | 14.3 | 15.3 | 14.1 | 19.9 | 13.8 |
| .2 | .3 | .3 | Income Taxes Payable | | .0 | .5 | .3 | .3 | .1 |
| 10.5 | 8.7 | 8.9 | All Other Current | | 5.5 | 6.4 | 11.1 | 9.9 | 8.8 |
| 41.1 | 37.2 | 35.8 | Total Current | | 33.6 | 40.2 | 37.2 | 41.6 | 31.6 |
| 15.1 | 14.3 | 16.8 | Long-Term Debt | | 19.7 | 26.1 | 17.7 | 9.8 | 15.1 |
| .7 | .7 | .8 | Deferred Taxes | | .8 | .0 | .4 | .6 | 1.2 |
| 6.2 | 7.0 | 6.1 | All Other Non-Current | | 12.9 | 4.7 | 4.5 | 5.9 | 5.1 |
| 36.9 | 40.8 | 40.5 | Net Worth | | 33.0 | 29.0 | 40.2 | 42.1 | 47.0 |
| 100.0 | 100.0 | 100.0 | Total Liabilities & Net Worth | | 100.0 | 100.0 | 100.0 | 100.0 | 100.0 |
| | | | INCOME DATA | | | | | | |
| 100.0 | 100.0 | 100.0 | Net Sales | | 100.0 | 100.0 | 100.0 | 100.0 | 100.0 |
| 33.3 | 34.7 | 32.3 | Gross Profit | | 42.5 | 45.6 | 36.9 | 28.7 | 25.1 |
| 27.7 | 27.3 | 25.8 | Operating Expenses | | 35.8 | 41.2 | 32.1 | 23.7 | 16.9 |
| 5.5 | 7.3 | 6.5 | Operating Profit | | 6.7 | 4.5 | 4.8 | 5.0 | 8.2 |
| 1.1 | .8 | .5 | All Other Expenses (net) | | .9 | .0 | -.1 | .1 | 1.0 |
| 4.4 | 6.5 | 5.9 | Profit Before Taxes | | 5.8 | 4.4 | 4.9 | 4.8 | 7.2 |
| | | | RATIOS | | | | | | |
| 2.7 | 3.0 | 2.8 | | | 4.8 | 3.3 | 2.7 | 2.7 | 2.7 |
| 1.7 | 1.8 | 1.8 | Current | | 2.6 | 1.6 | 1.5 | 1.7 | 1.8 |
| 1.2 | 1.3 | 1.3 | | | 1.3 | 1.0 | 1.2 | 1.3 | 1.3 |
| 1.6 | 1.8 | 1.8 | | | 3.0 | 2.7 | 1.5 | 1.6 | 1.8 |
| .9 | 1.0 | 1.0 | Quick | | 1.0 | .9 | .9 | .9 | 1.0 |
| .6 | .6 | .6 | | | .5 | .6 | .6 | .5 | .6 |
| 29 | 31 | 29 | | | 25 | 33 | 22 | 29 | 31 |
| 12.7 | 11.6 | 12.7 | | | 14.8 | 10.9 | 16.4 | 12.8 | 11.9 |
| 42  8.7 | 44  8.3 | 42  8.6 | Sales/Receivables | | 38  9.7 | 42  8.7 | 37  9.8 | 43  8.5 | 46  8.0 |
| 54  6.7 | 55  6.6 | 55  6.6 | | | 63  5.8 | 58  6.3 | 49  7.5 | 55  6.6 | 56  6.5 |
| 28  13.1 | 35  10.5 | 31  11.8 | | | 29  12.5 | 12  29.3 | 35  10.5 | 39  9.3 | 30  12.2 |
| 57  6.4 | 56  6.5 | 54  6.7 | Cost of Sales/Inventory | | 62  5.9 | 47  7.7 | 51  7.2 | 63  5.8 | 54  6.8 |
| 93  3.9 | 96  3.8 | 87  4.2 | | | 99  3.7 | 104  3.5 | 96  3.8 | 83  4.4 | 78  4.7 |
| 20  18.6 | 21  17.7 | 18  20.1 | | | 13  28.1 | 16  22.6 | 21  17.4 | 22  16.7 | 17  21.0 |
| 31  11.6 | 32  11.5 | 29  12.6 | Cost of Sales/Payables | | 28  12.9 | 36  10.1 | 33  11.0 | 30  12.1 | 26  13.8 |
| 50  7.3 | 52  7.1 | 50  7.3 | | | 51  7.2 | 72  5.1 | 51  7.1 | 48  7.6 | 46  8.0 |
| 4.9 | 4.6 | 4.7 | | | 2.9 | 4.5 | 6.6 | 5.5 | 4.6 |
| 10.0 | 8.7 | 8.7 | Sales/Working Capital | | 5.0 | 10.6 | 15.5 | 9.2 | 7.7 |
| 26.8 | 18.9 | 22.3 | | | 26.8 | NM | 28.8 | 23.5 | 17.7 |
| 18.0 | 22.0 | 22.2 | | | 9.3 | 6.9 | 17.6 | 21.2 | 37.2 |
| (197) 5.3 | (197) 6.3 | (206) 6.4 | EBIT/Interest | (20) | 3.8 (24) | 2.9 (31) | 5.5 (39) | 7.8 (87) | 10.5 |
| 1.5 | 2.9 | 2.0 | | | 1.4 | 1.0 | 1.6 | 2.6 | 3.2 |
| 13.9 | 9.6 | 4.8 | | | | | | 8.6 | 5.5 |
| (55) 3.0 | (63) 3.4 | (61) 2.3 | Net Profit + Depr., Dep., Amort./Cur. Mat. L/T/D | | | | (12) | 3.3 (31) | 2.9 |
| 1.1 | 1.8 | 1.4 | | | | | | 1.7 | 1.5 |
| .3 | .2 | .2 | | | .0 | .1 | .2 | .2 | .3 |
| .7 | .5 | .6 | Fixed/Worth | | .5 | .6 | .8 | .5 | .7 |
| 1.6 | 1.5 | 2.1 | | | 5.6 | -11.3 | 3.5 | 1.1 | 2.2 |
| .7 | .7 | .6 | | | .3 | 1.2 | .7 | .8 | .6 |
| 1.6 | 1.5 | 1.6 | Debt/Worth | | 1.3 | 3.0 | 1.6 | 1.5 | 1.4 |
| 4.6 | 5.4 | 6.1 | | | 11.2 | -13.1 | 5.7 | 3.0 | 4.2 |
| 50.0 | 61.4 | 55.3 | | | 31.6 | 67.5 | 72.2 | 51.7 | 57.8 |
| (190) 25.6 | (206) 32.6 | (201) 25.4 | % Profit Before Taxes/Tangible Net Worth | (21) | 12.7 (20) | 14.2 (27) | 19.7 (43) | 33.0 (86) | 26.9 |
| 5.8 | 13.6 | 8.7 | | | 1.8 | 5.0 | 2.9 | 11.8 | 13.5 |
| 20.8 | 22.1 | 20.3 | | | 12.9 | 17.7 | 22.2 | 24.6 | 20.4 |
| 8.5 | 10.8 | 8.4 | % Profit Before Taxes/Total Assets | | 6.9 | 5.4 | 8.0 | 9.3 | 8.7 |
| 1.2 | 4.2 | 2.3 | | | .5 | .4 | 1.2 | 3.6 | 3.7 |
| 30.8 | 42.9 | 40.2 | | | 163.3 | 52.8 | 36.6 | 48.3 | 20.2 |
| 10.4 | 12.1 | 11.7 | Sales/Net Fixed Assets | | 16.6 | 20.8 | 12.1 | 15.4 | 9.2 |
| 4.3 | 5.2 | 5.2 | | | 5.3 | 6.4 | 4.6 | 7.3 | 4.6 |
| 3.0 | 3.0 | 3.1 | | | 3.1 | 3.8 | 3.2 | 3.7 | 2.9 |
| 2.1 | 2.2 | 2.2 | Sales/Total Assets | | 2.3 | 2.0 | 2.3 | 2.6 | 1.9 |
| 1.4 | 1.5 | 1.4 | | | 1.2 | 1.1 | 1.6 | 2.0 | 1.3 |
| .8 | .7 | .8 | | | 1.1 | .5 | .9 | .7 | .8 |
| (185) 1.8 | (193) 1.8 | (181) 1.7 | % Depr., Dep., Amort./Sales | (15) | 1.8 (20) | 1.8 (28) | 2.3 (33) | 1.1 (82) | 1.8 |
| 3.9 | 3.3 | 3.3 | | | 3.9 | 5.6 | 3.2 | 2.0 | 3.4 |
| 2.0 | 1.9 | 1.3 | | | 7.2 | 2.7 | 1.4 | 1.3 | .4 |
| (56) 4.7 | (60) 3.7 | (74) 3.9 | % Officers', Directors', Owners' Comp/Sales | (11) | 9.2 (14) | 6.6 (18) | 2.3 (20) | 2.3 (10) | .7 |
| 8.2 | 6.8 | 7.4 | | | 19.1 | 10.1 | 4.9 | 5.1 | 1.1 |
| 10746757M | 9914218M | 10845296M | Net Sales ($) | 4284M | 46267M | 105795M | 213186M | 831601M | 9644163M |
| 6177397M | 5483814M | 5756635M | Total Assets ($) | 4149M | 29970M | 63284M | 118012M | 381665M | 5159555M |

M = $ thousand   MM = $ million
See Pages 9 through 22 for Explanation of Ratios and Data

## Current Data Sorted by Assets        Comparative Historical Data

Period note: 9 (4/1-9/30/11) covers 500M-2MM; 74 (10/1/11-3/31/12) covers remaining current columns.

| 0-500M | 500M-2MM | 2-10MM | 10-50MM | 50-100MM | 100-250MM | Type of Statement | 4/1/07-3/31/08 ALL | 4/1/08-3/31/09 ALL |
|---|---|---|---|---|---|---|---|---|
| | | 1 | | | | Unqualified | 6 | 10 |
| | 1 | 6 | 8 | | | Reviewed | 5 | 3 |
| | 2 | 2 | 1 | | | Compiled | 4 | 5 |
| 5 | 6 | 6 | 1 | | 2 | Tax Returns | 4 | 3 |
| 1 | 8 | 17 | 8 | 6 | 2 | Other | 10 | 15 |
| 6 | 17 | 32 | 18 | 6 | 4 | **NUMBER OF STATEMENTS** | 29 | 36 |
| % | % | % | % | % | % | **ASSETS** | % | % |
| | 4.4 | 6.8 | 1.9 | | | Cash & Equivalents | 6.6 | 3.3 |
| | 32.5 | 27.1 | 20.1 | | | Trade Receivables (net) | 27.7 | 28.2 |
| | 23.8 | 28.3 | 20.3 | | | Inventory | 23.1 | 26.7 |
| | .3 | 1.9 | 1.7 | | | All Other Current | .9 | 2.7 |
| | 61.1 | 64.1 | 43.9 | | | Total Current | 58.4 | 60.9 |
| | 24.8 | 29.8 | 42.4 | | | Fixed Assets (net) | 31.4 | 30.5 |
| | 1.7 | 2.7 | 5.8 | | | Intangibles (net) | 3.5 | 3.6 |
| | 12.4 | 3.5 | 7.9 | | | All Other Non-Current | 6.8 | 5.0 |
| | 100.0 | 100.0 | 100.0 | | | Total | 100.0 | 100.0 |
| | | | | | | **LIABILITIES** | | |
| | 10.7 | 8.9 | 6.4 | | | Notes Payable-Short Term | 15.6 | 18.9 |
| | 4.1 | 2.9 | 6.9 | | | Cur. Mat.-L.T.D. | 3.4 | 4.0 |
| | 23.9 | 19.6 | 16.7 | | | Trade Payables | 20.4 | 18.3 |
| | .0 | .1 | .0 | | | Income Taxes Payable | .3 | .4 |
| | 9.1 | 14.5 | 4.2 | | | All Other Current | 5.8 | 4.5 |
| | 47.8 | 45.9 | 34.2 | | | Total Current | 45.6 | 46.0 |
| | 24.0 | 16.0 | 20.0 | | | Long-Term Debt | 18.8 | 16.7 |
| | .1 | .4 | .8 | | | Deferred Taxes | 1.2 | 1.1 |
| | 1.5 | 6.4 | 4.8 | | | All Other Non-Current | 4.7 | 5.3 |
| | 26.6 | 31.2 | 40.1 | | | Net Worth | 29.7 | 30.9 |
| | 100.0 | 100.0 | 100.0 | | | Total Liabilities & Net Worth | 100.0 | 100.0 |
| | | | | | | **INCOME DATA** | | |
| | 100.0 | 100.0 | 100.0 | | | Net Sales | 100.0 | 100.0 |
| | 33.9 | 22.4 | 22.1 | | | Gross Profit | 19.5 | 20.7 |
| | 26.2 | 17.0 | 16.5 | | | Operating Expenses | 16.5 | 17.9 |
| | 7.7 | 5.3 | 5.6 | | | Operating Profit | 3.0 | 2.8 |
| | 2.3 | .6 | 1.4 | | | All Other Expenses (net) | 1.4 | 1.5 |
| | 5.4 | 4.8 | 4.2 | | | Profit Before Taxes | 1.5 | 1.2 |
| | | | | | | **RATIOS** | | |
| | 3.9 | 3.0 | 2.0 | | | | 1.6 | 1.6 |
| | 1.4 | 1.6 | 1.4 | | | Current | 1.2 | 1.2 |
| | .6 | 1.1 | 1.0 | | | | 1.0 | 1.1 |
| | 2.3 | 1.3 | 1.0 | | | | 1.3 | .9 |
| | .8 | .8 | .7 | | | Quick | .6 | .6 |
| | .3 | .5 | .5 | | | | .5 | .5 |
| | 20 18.7 | 29 12.4 | 33 11.0 | | | | 34 10.7 | 32 11.2 |
| | 39 9.4 | 36 10.0 | 42 8.7 | | | Sales/Receivables | 40 9.2 | 38 9.5 |
| | 59 6.2 | 43 8.4 | 50 7.3 | | | | 51 7.1 | 45 8.2 |
| | 6 56.6 | 31 11.8 | 40 9.1 | | | | 26 13.9 | 37 9.8 |
| | 33 11.1 | 41 8.8 | 53 6.9 | | | Cost of Sales/Inventory | 44 8.3 | 46 7.9 |
| | 101 3.6 | 69 5.3 | 66 5.5 | | | | 58 6.3 | 63 5.8 |
| | 13 27.8 | 23 15.9 | 29 12.6 | | | | 16 22.3 | 20 18.2 |
| | 31 11.7 | 32 11.5 | 43 8.4 | | | Cost of Sales/Payables | 45 8.1 | 26 13.9 |
| | 72 5.1 | 44 8.3 | 54 6.7 | | | | 59 6.2 | 46 7.9 |
| | 4.4 | 5.6 | 7.6 | | | | 8.0 | 10.5 |
| | 9.7 | 12.5 | 14.8 | | | Sales/Working Capital | 30.5 | 31.6 |
| | -17.8 | 54.8 | NM | | | | NM | 49.5 |
| | 19.6 | 29.3 | 11.3 | | | | 5.4 | 4.3 |
| | (12) 4.4 | (30) 9.6 | 5.6 | | | EBIT/Interest | 1.8 | 2.1 |
| | 2.9 | 3.0 | 1.8 | | | | 1.2 | .8 |
| | | | 3.4 | | | | 2.1 | 6.6 |
| | | | (11) 1.9 | | | Net Profit + Depr., Dep., Amort./Cur. Mat. L/T/D | (13) 1.8 | (15) 2.9 |
| | | | 1.2 | | | | 1.3 | 1.3 |
| | .1 | .4 | .9 | | | | .7 | .8 |
| | .4 | .7 | 1.3 | | | Fixed/Worth | 1.2 | 1.0 |
| | 30.8 | 2.6 | 2.2 | | | | 7.4 | 2.9 |
| | .9 | .8 | 1.0 | | | | 1.2 | 1.2 |
| | 2.8 | 2.1 | 1.6 | | | Debt/Worth | 3.2 | 2.2 |
| | 51.1 | 6.5 | 3.6 | | | | 19.4 | 13.5 |
| | 87.8 | 50.1 | 35.1 | | | | 28.2 | 31.9 |
| | (14) 21.7 | (27) 30.9 | (15) 21.6 | | | % Profit Before Taxes/Tangible Net Worth | (25) 16.1 | (31) 18.7 |
| | 6.4 | 13.6 | 12.5 | | | | 5.8 | 1.7 |
| | 18.7 | 18.5 | 10.8 | | | | 9.2 | 9.4 |
| | 13.0 | 10.4 | 6.1 | | | % Profit Before Taxes/Total Assets | 3.9 | 3.5 |
| | 2.0 | 3.1 | 3.2 | | | | .8 | -.9 |
| | 81.0 | 14.6 | 8.8 | | | | 22.9 | 17.8 |
| | 16.4 | 8.3 | 4.6 | | | Sales/Net Fixed Assets | 7.8 | 7.5 |
| | 7.2 | 4.7 | 2.3 | | | | 4.5 | 5.7 |
| | 3.8 | 3.2 | 2.5 | | | | 3.3 | 3.1 |
| | 2.3 | 2.5 | 1.9 | | | Sales/Total Assets | 2.3 | 2.4 |
| | 1.9 | 1.9 | 1.1 | | | | 1.8 | 2.0 |
| | .9 | 1.2 | 2.3 | | | | 1.1 | 1.2 |
| | (11) 3.2 | (30) 2.3 | 3.3 | | | % Depr., Dep., Amort./Sales | (28) 1.6 | (34) 2.2 |
| | 7.3 | 4.8 | 6.3 | | | | 3.5 | 3.4 |
| | | 1.2 | | | | | 1.7 | |
| | | (13) 2.5 | | | | % Officers', Directors' Owners' Comp/Sales | (12) 3.1 | |
| | | 3.0 | | | | | 4.8 | |
| 8504M | 57145M | 444233M | 765210M | 537827M | 981875M | Net Sales ($) | 1182272M | 2330457M |
| 1513M | 21344M | 169676M | 459692M | 399337M | 569895M | Total Assets ($) | 558422M | 1023726M |

M = $ thousand     MM = $ million
See Pages 9 through 22 for Explanation of Ratios and Data

## Comparative Historical Data | Current Data Sorted by Sales

| Type of Statement | | | | | | | | | |
|---|---|---|---|---|---|---|---|---|---|
| | | | Unqualified | | | | 1 | | 10 |
| 9 | 9 | 11 | Reviewed | | 1 | 1 | 1 | 2 | 2 |
| 3 | 9 | 7 | Compiled | | | 2 | | 2 | 1 |
| 5 | 4 | 5 | Tax Returns | | | 2 | 2 | 3 | 2 |
| 6 | 13 | 18 | Other | 4 | 4 | 2 | 3 | 3 | 2 |
| 21 | 23 | 42 | | | 4 | 3 | 8 | 11 | 16 |

| | | | | 0-1MM | 1-3MM | 3-5MM | 5-10MM | 10-25MM | 25MM & OVER |
|---|---|---|---|---|---|---|---|---|---|
| | | | | 9 (4/1-9/30/11) | | | 74 (10/1/11-3/31/12) | | |
| 4/1/09-3/31/10 ALL | 4/1/10-3/31/11 ALL | 4/1/11-3/31/12 ALL | NUMBER OF STATEMENTS | | | | | | |
| 44 | 58 | 83 | | 4 | 9 | 8 | 13 | 18 | 31 |
| % | % | % | ASSETS | % | % | % | % | % | % |
| 3.5 | 6.9 | 4.8 | Cash & Equivalents | | | | 10.0 | 4.5 | 1.7 |
| 29.5 | 28.0 | 26.7 | Trade Receivables (net) | | | | 21.6 | 29.7 | 21.8 |
| 24.0 | 23.8 | 23.5 | Inventory | | | | 15.6 | 32.2 | 23.9 |
| 2.7 | 3.5 | 1.4 | All Other Current | | | | .5 | 2.7 | 1.9 |
| 59.7 | 62.1 | 56.4 | Total Current | | | | 47.7 | 69.1 | 49.3 |
| 30.9 | 27.0 | 31.9 | Fixed Assets (net) | | | | 36.7 | 27.0 | 37.0 |
| 4.3 | 4.7 | 4.7 | Intangibles (net) | | | | 5.7 | .7 | 7.7 |
| 5.1 | 6.3 | 7.0 | All Other Non-Current | | | | 9.9 | 3.2 | 6.0 |
| 100.0 | 100.0 | 100.0 | Total | | | | 100.0 | 100.0 | 100.0 |
| | | | LIABILITIES | | | | | | |
| 18.4 | 10.1 | 8.2 | Notes Payable-Short Term | | | | 10.8 | 10.5 | 7.6 |
| 3.7 | 6.9 | 4.0 | Cur. Mat.-L.T.D. | | | | 2.0 | 2.7 | 5.4 |
| 19.6 | 19.0 | 19.5 | Trade Payables | | | | 13.7 | 22.1 | 16.8 |
| .1 | .3 | .1 | Income Taxes Payable | | | | .0 | .0 | .1 |
| 7.7 | 4.1 | 9.1 | All Other Current | | | | 5.6 | 19.5 | 6.3 |
| 49.6 | 40.5 | 40.8 | Total Current | | | | 32.1 | 54.8 | 36.2 |
| 16.2 | 17.2 | 20.9 | Long-Term Debt | | | | 24.0 | 16.7 | 18.6 |
| .6 | .8 | .8 | Deferred Taxes | | | | .7 | .3 | 1.7 |
| 3.3 | 6.0 | 7.5 | All Other Non-Current | | | | 10.2 | 3.0 | 4.1 |
| 30.2 | 35.5 | 29.9 | Net Worth | | | | 32.9 | 25.2 | 39.4 |
| 100.0 | 100.0 | 100.0 | Total Liabilities & Net Worth | | | | 100.0 | 100.0 | 100.0 |
| | | | INCOME DATA | | | | | | |
| 100.0 | 100.0 | 100.0 | Net Sales | | | | 100.0 | 100.0 | 100.0 |
| 26.5 | 27.7 | 23.7 | Gross Profit | | | | 28.8 | 21.3 | 16.9 |
| 22.0 | 22.4 | 18.2 | Operating Expenses | | | | 20.9 | 16.3 | 13.6 |
| 4.5 | 5.3 | 5.5 | Operating Profit | | | | 8.0 | 5.0 | 3.4 |
| 1.5 | 1.4 | 1.7 | All Other Expenses (net) | | | | .6 | .5 | 3.0 |
| 3.0 | 3.9 | 3.8 | Profit Before Taxes | | | | 7.3 | 4.5 | .4 |
| | | | RATIOS | | | | | | |
| 1.9 | 2.5 | 2.7 | | | | | 3.3 | 2.8 | 2.2 |
| 1.3 | 1.7 | 1.6 | Current | | | | 1.8 | 1.5 | 1.6 |
| 1.0 | 1.1 | 1.1 | | | | | 1.0 | .7 | 1.1 |
| 1.1 | 1.6 | 1.3 | | | | | 2.4 | 1.2 | 1.0 |
| .6 | .8 | .9 | Quick | | | | 1.3 | .7 | .8 |
| .4 | .5 | .5 | | | | | .6 | .4 | .5 |

| | | | | | | | | | | Sales/Receivables | | | | | |
|---|---|---|---|---|---|---|---|---|---|---|---|---|---|---|---|
| 34 | 10.8 | 28 | 13.3 | 29 | 12.8 | | 28 | 12.9 | 34 | 10.8 | 35 | 10.4 |
| 42 | 8.7 | 41 | 9.0 | 39 | 9.4 | Sales/Receivables | 36 | 10.0 | 38 | 9.6 | 41 | 8.8 |
| 52 | 7.0 | 48 | 7.6 | 49 | 7.5 | | 44 | 8.3 | 45 | 8.2 | 49 | 7.5 |
| 32 | 11.5 | 30 | 12.1 | 27 | 13.5 | | 22 | 16.8 | 34 | 10.7 | 40 | 9.2 |
| 52 | 7.0 | 49 | 7.4 | 43 | 8.5 | Cost of Sales/Inventory | 33 | 11.2 | 45 | 8.1 | 49 | 7.5 |
| 69 | 5.3 | 73 | 5.0 | 69 | 5.3 | | 63 | 5.8 | 73 | 5.0 | 68 | 5.4 |
| 25 | 14.4 | 19 | 19.7 | 22 | 16.5 | | 7 | 48.9 | 22 | 16.7 | 24 | 15.3 |
| 35 | 10.4 | 33 | 11.2 | 33 | 11.2 | Cost of Sales/Payables | 24 | 15.5 | 38 | 9.6 | 34 | 10.6 |
| 50 | 7.2 | 51 | 7.1 | 49 | 7.5 | | 38 | 9.6 | 58 | 6.3 | 46 | 7.9 |

| | | | | 5-10MM | 10-25MM | 25MM & OVER |
|---|---|---|---|---|---|---|
| 10.7 | 5.9 | 6.7 | | 4.0 | 6.6 | 7.4 |
| 21.8 | 12.0 | 13.1 | Sales/Working Capital | 7.9 | 10.1 | 16.6 |
| 269.2 | 50.0 | 59.5 | | NM | -17.3 | 98.6 |

| | | | | | | | | | | EBIT/Interest | | | | | |
|---|---|---|---|---|---|---|---|---|---|---|---|---|---|---|---|
| | 10.0 | | 11.1 | | 14.2 | | | | | | | 42.9 | | 19.2 | | 8.9 |
| (43) | 2.4 | (54) | 4.3 | (75) | 6.8 | EBIT/Interest | (11) | 3.8 | (17) | 11.0 | (30) | 5.7 |
| | 1.4 | | 2.0 | | 2.9 | | | 2.4 | | 4.4 | | 1.8 |

| | | | | | | Net Profit + Depr., Dep., Amort./Cur. Mat. L/T/D | | | | | | |
|---|---|---|---|---|---|---|---|---|---|---|---|---|
| | 4.0 | | 3.5 | | 4.8 | | | | | | | 3.4 |
| (15) | 2.5 | (16) | 2.5 | (20) | 2.7 | Net Profit + Depr., Dep., Amort./Cur. Mat. L/T/D | | | | | (16) | 2.6 |
| | 1.2 | | 1.2 | | 1.6 | | | | | | | 1.6 |

| | | | | 5-10MM | 10-25MM | 25MM & OVER |
|---|---|---|---|---|---|---|
| .5 | .3 | .4 | | .5 | .2 | .8 |
| 1.1 | .9 | 1.0 | Fixed/Worth | 1.1 | .5 | 1.2 |
| 3.3 | 2.6 | 2.7 | | NM | 2.7 | 1.8 |
| .9 | .9 | 1.1 | | .5 | .8 | 1.1 |
| 2.9 | 1.7 | 1.9 | Debt/Worth | 1.8 | 1.8 | 1.7 |
| 9.0 | 5.3 | 7.3 | | NM | 7.5 | 3.1 |

| | | | | | | % Profit Before Taxes/Tangible Net Worth | | | | | | |
|---|---|---|---|---|---|---|---|---|---|---|---|---|
| | 35.6 | | 42.1 | | 42.9 | | | | | | | 50.0 | 50.1 | 35.5 |
| (38) | 18.2 | (49) | 23.9 | (68) | 23.4 | % Profit Before Taxes/Tangible Net Worth | (10) | 28.8 | (15) | 24.7 | (26) | 20.4 |
| | 6.4 | | 7.7 | | 13.8 | | | 13.2 | | 13.6 | | 12.4 |

| | | | | 5-10MM | 10-25MM | 25MM & OVER |
|---|---|---|---|---|---|---|
| 13.5 | 17.6 | 17.3 | | 21.7 | 16.4 | 11.3 |
| 4.6 | 8.6 | 8.1 | % Profit Before Taxes/Total Assets | 10.0 | 8.2 | 6.1 |
| 1.1 | 2.1 | 3.4 | | 3.7 | 4.6 | 1.3 |
| 17.4 | 33.8 | 16.4 | | 14.3 | 36.5 | 9.7 |
| 7.4 | 11.9 | 8.0 | Sales/Net Fixed Assets | 4.8 | 11.5 | 5.5 |
| 4.7 | 5.7 | 4.1 | | 3.7 | 7.0 | 3.6 |
| 2.9 | 3.7 | 3.1 | | 3.1 | 3.2 | 2.6 |
| 2.3 | 2.3 | 2.3 | Sales/Total Assets | 2.3 | 2.7 | 2.0 |
| 1.8 | 1.7 | 1.7 | | 1.3 | 1.8 | 1.3 |

| | | | | | | % Depr., Dep., Amort./Sales | | | | | | |
|---|---|---|---|---|---|---|---|---|---|---|---|---|
| | 1.4 | | .8 | | 1.3 | | | | | | | 3.0 | 1.0 | 1.3 |
| (40) | 2.8 | (51) | 2.0 | (70) | 2.8 | % Depr., Dep., Amort./Sales | (12) | 3.6 | | 1.7 | (28) | 2.9 |
| | 3.6 | | 3.2 | | 5.2 | | | 8.9 | | 3.3 | | 4.8 |

| | | | | | | % Officers', Directors' Owners' Comp/Sales |
|---|---|---|---|---|---|---|
| | 1.7 | | 1.4 | | 1.3 | |
| (16) | 4.5 | (23) | 3.0 | (27) | 2.7 | % Officers', Directors' Owners' Comp/Sales |
| | 7.8 | | 4.6 | | 4.7 | |

| | | | | 0-1MM | 1-3MM | 3-5MM | 5-10MM | 10-25MM | 25MM & OVER |
|---|---|---|---|---|---|---|---|---|---|
| 1491034M | 1702900M | 2794794M | Net Sales ($) | 1812M | 19954M | 29824M | 89799M | 239623M | 2413782M |
| 735641M | 923715M | 1621457M | Total Assets ($) | 1691M | 8774M | 10815M | 52866M | 102315M | 1444996M |

© RMA 2012

**M = $ thousand    MM = $ million**
See Pages 9 through 22 for Explanation of Ratios and Data

## Current Data Sorted by Assets     Comparative Historical Data

| | | | | | | Type of Statement | | |
|---|---|---|---|---|---|---|---|---|
| | | 1 | 5 | 1 | 5 | Unqualified | 8 | 5 |
| | | 3 | 4 | | | Reviewed | 2 | 4 |
| | | 2 | | | | Compiled | 1 | 1 |
| | | 2 | | | | Tax Returns | 4 | 3 |
| 3 | 4 | 4 | 5 | 8 | 3 | Other | 7 | 12 |
| 1 | 2 | | 48 (10/1/11-3/31/12) | | | | 4/1/07- | 4/1/08- |
| 2 | 5 (4/1-9/30/11) | | | | | | 3/31/08 | 3/31/09 |
| 0-500M | 500M-2MM | 2-10MM | 10-50MM | 50-100MM | 100-250MM | | ALL | ALL |
| 4 | 6 | 12 | 14 | 9 | 8 | NUMBER OF STATEMENTS | 22 | 25 |
| % | % | % | % | % | % | ASSETS | % | % |
| | | 7.3 | 4.0 | | | Cash & Equivalents | 4.4 | 3.5 |
| | | 33.4 | 25.4 | | | Trade Receivables (net) | 23.9 | 27.3 |
| | | 26.9 | 22.3 | | | Inventory | 23.7 | 28.6 |
| | | 1.6 | 6.9 | | | All Other Current | 2.2 | 3.4 |
| | | 69.2 | 58.5 | | | Total Current | 54.2 | 62.7 |
| | | 28.4 | 34.3 | | | Fixed Assets (net) | 38.8 | 31.7 |
| | | .1 | 1.4 | | | Intangibles (net) | 2.1 | 2.3 |
| | | 2.3 | 5.7 | | | All Other Non-Current | 5.0 | 3.4 |
| | | 100.0 | 100.0 | | | Total | 100.0 | 100.0 |
| | | | | | | LIABILITIES | | |
| | | 13.6 | 10.7 | | | Notes Payable-Short Term | 6.7 | 12.4 |
| | | 2.9 | 5.0 | | | Cur. Mat.-L.T.D. | 6.1 | 3.8 |
| | | 23.2 | 21.9 | | | Trade Payables | 17.6 | 17.4 |
| | | .0 | 1.9 | | | Income Taxes Payable | .1 | .0 |
| | | 7.2 | 7.4 | | | All Other Current | 6.5 | 5.3 |
| | | 46.8 | 46.9 | | | Total Current | 37.1 | 38.8 |
| | | 12.1 | 13.1 | | | Long-Term Debt | 28.3 | 20.1 |
| | | .4 | 3.2 | | | Deferred Taxes | .7 | .9 |
| | | 7.3 | 5.9 | | | All Other Non-Current | 3.0 | 2.8 |
| | | 33.3 | 30.9 | | | Net Worth | 30.9 | 37.4 |
| | | 100.0 | 100.0 | | | Total Liabilties & Net Worth | 100.0 | 100.0 |
| | | | | | | INCOME DATA | | |
| | | 100.0 | 100.0 | | | Net Sales | 100.0 | 100.0 |
| | | 22.6 | 22.5 | | | Gross Profit | 25.6 | 20.4 |
| | | 18.1 | 19.0 | | | Operating Expenses | 22.7 | 16.8 |
| | | 4.5 | 3.5 | | | Operating Profit | 2.9 | 3.6 |
| | | .3 | 1.9 | | | All Other Expenses (net) | .8 | 1.2 |
| | | 4.2 | 1.6 | | | Profit Before Taxes | 2.1 | 2.4 |
| | | | | | | RATIOS | | |
| | | 2.3 | 2.3 | | | | 2.5 | 3.2 |
| | | 1.3 | 1.6 | | | Current | 1.8 | 1.6 |
| | | 1.1 | .7 | | | | 1.2 | 1.2 |
| | | 1.5 | 1.1 | | | | 1.3 | 1.5 |
| | | .8 | .7 | | | Quick | .9 | .7 |
| | | .6 | .4 | | | | .6 | .5 |
| | 31 | 11.6 | 29   12.4 | | | | 30   12.0 | 30   12.3 |
| | 41 | 8.8 | 46   8.0 | | | Sales/Receivables | 35   10.3 | 40   9.0 |
| | 50 | 7.3 | 55   6.6 | | | | 45   8.2 | 45   8.1 |
| | 35 | 10.3 | 41   8.9 | | | | 39   9.4 | 33   11.1 |
| | 43 | 8.4 | 57   6.4 | | | Cost of Sales/Inventory | 52   7.0 | 43   8.5 |
| | 54 | 6.7 | 89   4.1 | | | | 68   5.4 | 62   5.9 |
| | 23 | 16.1 | 21   17.8 | | | | 17   21.5 | 18   20.2 |
| | 36 | 10.0 | 41   8.8 | | | Cost of Sales/Payables | 37   9.8 | 30   12.1 |
| | 46 | 7.9 | 70   5.2 | | | | 59   6.2 | 44   8.3 |
| | | 6.8 | 6.9 | | | | 5.6 | 5.8 |
| | | 15.1 | 14.5 | | | Sales/Working Capital | 9.3 | 10.2 |
| | | 73.8 | -10.1 | | | | 42.9 | 44.1 |
| | | 50.4 | 41.7 | | | | 10.7 | 6.7 |
| | (11) | 6.9 | (13)   2.2 | | | EBIT/Interest | (24)   3.4 | (24)   3.3 |
| | | 2.6 | 1.0 | | | | 1.1 | 1.1 |
| | | | | | | Net Profit + Depr., Dep., | | 3.8 |
| | | | | | | Amort./Cur. Mat. L/T/D | (11)   2.2 | 2.2 |
| | | | | | | | | 1.2 |
| | | .4 | .4 | | | | .5 | .5 |
| | | .9 | 1.0 | | | Fixed/Worth | .9 | .8 |
| | | 6.6 | 3.9 | | | | 3.3 | 1.8 |
| | | .8 | .7 | | | | .8 | .9 |
| | | 1.8 | 2.6 | | | Debt/Worth | 1.6 | 1.8 |
| | | 14.6 | 17.0 | | | | 6.2 | 3.3 |
| | | 48.2 | 29.7 | | | | 40.9 | 37.6 |
| | (10) | 27.7 | (12)   26.4 | | | % Profit Before Taxes/Tangible Net Worth | (19)   24.1 | (23)   19.4 |
| | | 13.3 | 9.8 | | | | 6.7 | 4.2 |
| | | 18.7 | 13.8 | | | | 11.4 | 10.1 |
| | | 10.5 | 4.0 | | | % Profit Before Taxes/Total Assets | 5.0 | 5.9 |
| | | 4.1 | .4 | | | | .8 | .5 |
| | | 16.8 | 18.8 | | | | 8.3 | 14.3 |
| | | 10.9 | 7.0 | | | Sales/Net Fixed Assets | 4.3 | 7.2 |
| | | 7.2 | 2.3 | | | | 2.6 | 4.6 |
| | | 4.2 | 3.4 | | | | 2.6 | 3.2 |
| | | 2.9 | 1.8 | | | Sales/Total Assets | 1.9 | 2.2 |
| | | 2.4 | 1.2 | | | | 1.5 | 1.8 |
| | | .7 | 1.2 | | | | 2.0 | 1.8 |
| | (10) | 2.1 | 2.6 | | | % Depr., Dep., Amort./Sales | (16)   3.2 | (18)   2.7 |
| | | 2.9 | 6.0 | | | | 4.5 | 3.9 |
| | | | | | | % Officers', Directors' Owners' Comp/Sales | | |
| 5822M | 27789M | 207224M | 599568M | 1046431M | 1948682M | Net Sales ($) | 1531812M | 1965843M |
| 1274M | 7404M | 64780M | 330418M | 617381M | 1498389M | Total Assets ($) | 855200M | 931092M |

© RMA 2012

M = $ thousand     MM = $ million
See Pages 9 through 22 for Explanation of Ratios and Data

### Comparative Historical Data        Current Data Sorted by Sales

| | 4/1/09-3/31/10 ALL | 4/1/10-3/31/11 ALL | 4/1/11-3/31/12 ALL | 0-1MM | 1-3MM | 3-5MM | 5-10MM | 10-25MM | 25MM & OVER |
|---|---|---|---|---|---|---|---|---|---|
| **Type of Statement** | | | | | | | | | |
| Unqualified | 8 | 12 | 12 | | | | | 2 | 10 |
| Reviewed | 8 | 8 | 7 | | | | | 3 | 4 |
| Compiled | 1 | 3 | 2 | | | | 1 | 1 | |
| Tax Returns | 2 | 4 | 9 | | | | 1 | 2 | |
| Other | 11 | 17 | 23 | 2 | 3 | 3 | 3 | 2 | 16 |
| | | | | *5 (4/1-9/30/11)* | | | *48 (10/1/11-3/31/12)* | | |
| **NUMBER OF STATEMENTS** | 30 | 44 | 53 | 2 | 3 | 3 | 5 | 10 | 30 |
| | % | % | % | % | % | % | % | % | % |
| **ASSETS** | | | | | | | | | |
| Cash & Equivalents | 7.5 | 6.8 | 5.7 | | | | | 3.9 | 4.3 |
| Trade Receivables (net) | 28.9 | 27.7 | 26.7 | | | | | 27.9 | 23.3 |
| Inventory | 21.7 | 25.9 | 22.2 | | | | | 26.4 | 21.3 |
| All Other Current | 2.6 | 2.7 | 3.4 | | | | | 2.1 | 5.1 |
| Total Current | 60.7 | 63.0 | 58.0 | | | | | 60.4 | 54.1 |
| Fixed Assets (net) | 27.2 | 26.4 | 29.8 | | | | | 34.0 | 32.8 |
| Intangibles (net) | 4.4 | 5.9 | 6.1 | | | | | 1.3 | 8.8 |
| All Other Non-Current | 7.7 | 4.6 | 6.0 | | | | | 4.3 | 4.4 |
| Total | 100.0 | 100.0 | 100.0 | | | | | 100.0 | 100.0 |
| **LIABILITIES** | | | | | | | | | |
| Notes Payable-Short Term | 11.5 | 9.5 | 10.8 | | | | | 14.9 | 11.4 |
| Cur. Mat.-L.T.D. | 4.7 | 2.1 | 4.2 | | | | | 2.6 | 5.1 |
| Trade Payables | 16.0 | 19.1 | 17.8 | | | | | 18.3 | 17.8 |
| Income Taxes Payable | .4 | .3 | .7 | | | | | .0 | 1.3 |
| All Other Current | 6.8 | 10.9 | 5.9 | | | | | 11.2 | 5.4 |
| Total Current | 39.4 | 41.9 | 39.5 | | | | | 47.0 | 41.0 |
| Long-Term Debt | 16.4 | 20.4 | 18.4 | | | | | 18.3 | 17.6 |
| Deferred Taxes | .7 | 1.0 | 1.1 | | | | | .5 | 1.8 |
| All Other Non-Current | 8.8 | 8.7 | 8.1 | | | | | 4.2 | 4.3 |
| Net Worth | 34.9 | 28.0 | 32.9 | | | | | 30.0 | 35.4 |
| Total Liabilities & Net Worth | 100.0 | 100.0 | 100.0 | | | | | 100.0 | 100.0 |
| **INCOME DATA** | | | | | | | | | |
| Net Sales | 100.0 | 100.0 | 100.0 | | | | | 100.0 | 100.0 |
| Gross Profit | 25.9 | 24.8 | 22.5 | | | | | 23.9 | 18.1 |
| Operating Expenses | 21.5 | 19.4 | 17.8 | | | | | 21.2 | 13.6 |
| Operating Profit | 4.4 | 5.4 | 4.7 | | | | | 2.8 | 4.4 |
| All Other Expenses (net) | 1.7 | 1.1 | 1.3 | | | | | 1.9 | 1.5 |
| Profit Before Taxes | 2.8 | 4.3 | 3.4 | | | | | .9 | 3.0 |
| **RATIOS** | | | | | | | | | |
| Current | 2.6 | 2.5 | 2.2 | | | | | 2.1 | 2.1 |
| | 1.8 | 1.6 | 1.5 | | | | | 1.3 | 1.3 |
| | 1.1 | 1.1 | 1.1 | | | | | .9 | 1.1 |
| Quick | 1.5 | 1.5 | 1.3 | | | | | 1.1 | 1.1 |
| | .8 | .8 | .8 | | | | | .7 | .6 |
| | .6 | .6 | .5 | | | | | .4 | .5 |
| Sales/Receivables | 33  11.2 | 37  10.0 | 33  11.2 | | | | | 37  9.9 | 35  10.5 |
| | 45  8.1 | 43  8.5 | 40  9.2 | | | | | 49  7.5 | 40  9.2 |
| | 53  6.9 | 49  7.4 | 49  7.4 | | | | | 54  6.7 | 47  7.7 |
| Cost of Sales/Inventory | 33  10.9 | 43  8.4 | 35  10.4 | | | | | 40  9.1 | 41  9.0 |
| | 49  7.5 | 56  6.5 | 49  7.4 | | | | | 54  6.7 | 51  7.1 |
| | 68  5.4 | 77  4.8 | 65  5.6 | | | | | 85  4.3 | 66  5.5 |
| Cost of Sales/Payables | 22  16.8 | 24  15.1 | 19  19.2 | | | | | 29  12.7 | 19  19.3 |
| | 36  10.2 | 33  11.2 | 35  10.3 | | | | | 41  8.9 | 31  11.8 |
| | 52  7.0 | 50  7.3 | 47  7.8 | | | | | 51  7.1 | 47  7.7 |
| Sales/Working Capital | 7.2 | 4.8 | 6.6 | | | | | 9.2 | 7.3 |
| | 9.3 | 9.1 | 12.3 | | | | | 17.1 | 18.5 |
| | 55.5 | 33.6 | 65.4 | | | | | -89.1 | 87.5 |
| EBIT/Interest | 24.5 | 18.4 | 26.1 | | | | | | 14.2 |
| | (28) 4.4 | (39) 5.5 | (49) 6.9 | | | | | | (29) 6.5 |
| | 1.8 | 2.0 | 1.8 | | | | | | 1.8 |
| Net Profit + Depr., Dep., Amort./Cur. Mat. L/T/D | 16.9 | 15.7 | | | | | | | |
| | (12) 5.5 | (16) 4.6 | | | | | | | |
| | 1.0 | 1.4 | | | | | | | |
| Fixed/Worth | .3 | .4 | .4 | | | | | .4 | .5 |
| | .8 | .7 | 1.1 | | | | | .8 | 1.2 |
| | 3.3 | 7.0 | 4.3 | | | | | NM | 3.8 |
| Debt/Worth | .7 | .8 | .9 | | | | | .6 | 1.1 |
| | 1.9 | 2.3 | 2.9 | | | | | 2.3 | 2.8 |
| | 8.6 | 13.2 | 17.1 | | | | | NM | 9.6 |
| % Profit Before Taxes/Tangible Net Worth | 68.3 | 63.6 | 49.2 | | | | | | 44.7 |
| | (26) 25.3 | (35) 33.5 | (43) 28.5 | | | | | | (25) 26.6 |
| | 8.0 | 15.9 | 12.9 | | | | | | 12.5 |
| % Profit Before Taxes/Total Assets | 17.6 | 18.2 | 18.6 | | | | | 18.6 | 12.2 |
| | 6.7 | 8.1 | 9.9 | | | | | 9.3 | 8.6 |
| | .7 | 3.7 | 2.5 | | | | | -4.2 | 2.3 |
| Sales/Net Fixed Assets | 18.4 | 11.6 | 40.1 | | | | | 22.2 | 12.5 |
| | 7.3 | 7.4 | 8.1 | | | | | 6.6 | 7.3 |
| | 4.3 | 5.7 | 4.1 | | | | | 2.2 | 4.0 |
| Sales/Total Assets | 2.7 | 2.6 | 3.8 | | | | | 3.0 | 2.7 |
| | 2.0 | 2.0 | 2.2 | | | | | 2.5 | 1.8 |
| | 1.4 | 1.5 | 1.4 | | | | | 1.2 | 1.3 |
| % Depr., Dep., Amort./Sales | 1.1 | 1.8 | 1.2 | | | | | | 1.3 |
| | (24) 1.8 | (40) 2.5 | (43) 2.6 | | | | | | (27) 2.7 |
| | 4.4 | 3.5 | 3.6 | | | | | | 3.2 |
| % Officers', Directors' Owners' Comp/Sales | | 1.6 | 1.2 | | | | | | |
| | | (12) 3.9 | (13) 2.4 | | | | | | |
| Net Sales ($) | 2409572M | 5191951M | 3835516M | 1137M | 5030M | 10461M | 36802M | 178932M | 3603154M |
| Total Assets ($) | 1359816M | 2176469M | 2519646M | 731M | 1094M | 4676M | 10765M | 119806M | 2382574M |

## Current Data Sorted by Assets | Comparative Historical Data

| 0-500M | 500M-2MM | 2-10MM | 10-50MM | 50-100MM | 100-250MM | Type of Statement | 4/1/07-3/31/08 | 4/1/08-3/31/09 |
|---|---|---|---|---|---|---|---|---|
| 1 |  | 2 | 7 | 5 | 3 | Unqualified | 21 | 21 |
|  | 1 | 11 | 4 |  | 1 | Reviewed | 19 | 22 |
| 1 | 1 | 6 |  |  |  | Compiled | 9 | 10 |
| 1 | 3 | 5 |  |  |  | Tax Returns | 5 | 14 |
| 3 | 3 | 11 | 15 | 6 | 2 | Other | 35 | 32 |
|  | 12 (4/1-9/30/11) |  | 77 (10/1/11-3/31/12) |  |  |  | ALL | ALL |
| 3 | 8 | 35 | 26 | 11 | 6 | NUMBER OF STATEMENTS | 89 | 99 |
| % | % | % | % | % | % | **ASSETS** | % | % |
|  |  | 9.0 | 3.5 | 3.0 |  | Cash & Equivalents | 5.7 | 7.7 |
|  |  | 27.6 | 23.9 | 15.5 |  | Trade Receivables (net) | 26.1 | 25.7 |
|  |  | 27.3 | 25.8 | 14.6 |  | Inventory | 28.1 | 26.4 |
|  |  | 1.1 | 1.5 | 5.4 |  | All Other Current | 1.7 | 1.6 |
|  |  | 65.0 | 54.7 | 38.5 |  | Total Current | 61.6 | 61.4 |
|  |  | 28.5 | 38.7 | 40.3 |  | Fixed Assets (net) | 29.2 | 29.3 |
|  |  | 1.1 | 2.7 | 16.1 |  | Intangibles (net) | 4.3 | 2.8 |
|  |  | 5.4 | 3.9 | 5.2 |  | All Other Non-Current | 4.9 | 6.4 |
|  |  | 100.0 | 100.0 | 100.0 |  | Total | 100.0 | 100.0 |
|  |  |  |  |  |  | **LIABILITIES** |  |  |
|  |  | 10.8 | 14.5 | 4.7 |  | Notes Payable-Short Term | 11.2 | 10.5 |
|  |  | 2.9 | 3.9 | 3.6 |  | Cur. Mat.-L.T.D. | 4.1 | 4.3 |
|  |  | 20.0 | 17.7 | 9.8 |  | Trade Payables | 18.0 | 16.4 |
|  |  | .4 | .2 | .1 |  | Income Taxes Payable | .3 | .2 |
|  |  | 8.5 | 6.2 | 6.5 |  | All Other Current | 7.5 | 7.5 |
|  |  | 42.7 | 42.6 | 24.6 |  | Total Current | 41.0 | 38.8 |
|  |  | 16.3 | 17.8 | 26.9 |  | Long-Term Debt | 16.2 | 16.7 |
|  |  | .6 | .5 | 1.1 |  | Deferred Taxes | .6 | .8 |
|  |  | 2.7 | 2.9 | 8.9 |  | All Other Non-Current | 5.7 | 4.2 |
|  |  | 37.7 | 36.2 | 38.6 |  | Net Worth | 36.4 | 39.5 |
|  |  | 100.0 | 100.0 | 100.0 |  | Total Liabilities & Net Worth | 100.0 | 100.0 |
|  |  |  |  |  |  | **INCOME DATA** |  |  |
|  |  | 100.0 | 100.0 | 100.0 |  | Net Sales | 100.0 | 100.0 |
|  |  | 25.1 | 18.9 | 26.7 |  | Gross Profit | 23.8 | 22.9 |
|  |  | 19.7 | 13.9 | 20.3 |  | Operating Expenses | 19.4 | 18.0 |
|  |  | 5.3 | 5.0 | 6.4 |  | Operating Profit | 4.4 | 4.8 |
|  |  | .3 | .0 | 1.4 |  | All Other Expenses (net) | 1.5 | 1.1 |
|  |  | 5.0 | 5.0 | 5.0 |  | Profit Before Taxes | 2.9 | 3.7 |
|  |  |  |  |  |  | **RATIOS** |  |  |
|  |  | 2.2 | 2.3 | 2.4 |  | Current | 2.5 | 2.4 |
|  |  | 1.6 | 1.2 | 1.6 |  |  | 1.6 | 1.6 |
|  |  | 1.1 | 1.0 | 1.4 |  |  | 1.1 | 1.2 |
|  |  | 1.2 | .9 | 1.1 |  | Quick | 1.2 | 1.4 |
|  |  | .8 | .6 | .9 |  |  | .8 | .9 |
|  |  | .6 | .5 | .5 |  |  | .5 | .5 |
|  |  | 31  11.8 | 32  11.3 | 27  13.6 |  | Sales/Receivables | 35  10.5 | 30  12.1 |
|  |  | 41  8.9 | 42  8.7 | 32  11.5 |  |  | 44  8.3 | 38  9.7 |
|  |  | 46  7.9 | 49  7.4 | 55  6.6 |  |  | 53  6.9 | 49  7.5 |
|  |  | 35  10.5 | 43  8.5 | 38  9.5 |  | Cost of Sales/Inventory | 42  8.7 | 31  11.8 |
|  |  | 53  6.9 | 54  6.8 | 52  7.0 |  |  | 56  6.5 | 51  7.2 |
|  |  | 65  5.6 | 72  5.1 | 60  6.1 |  |  | 81  4.5 | 76  4.8 |
|  |  | 18  20.4 | 22  16.9 | 18  19.8 |  | Cost of Sales/Payables | 23  15.6 | 19  19.7 |
|  |  | 34  10.6 | 39  9.4 | 33  11.0 |  |  | 35  10.4 | 26  14.2 |
|  |  | 49  7.5 | 53  6.9 | 45  8.2 |  |  | 51  7.1 | 45  8.0 |
|  |  | 7.4 | 9.6 | 7.7 |  | Sales/Working Capital | 5.8 | 5.7 |
|  |  | 10.5 | 20.6 | 9.1 |  |  | 10.6 | 10.8 |
|  |  | 56.5 | -91.2 | 16.5 |  |  | 42.0 | 28.0 |
|  |  | 26.7 | 13.7 |  |  | EBIT/Interest | 9.5 | 11.0 |
|  |  | (31) 6.5 | 5.9 |  |  |  | (83) 3.3 | (92) 3.0 |
|  |  | 2.2 | 2.4 |  |  |  | 1.8 | 1.1 |
|  |  |  | 4.8 |  |  | Net Profit + Depr., Dep., Amort./Cur. Mat. L/T/D | 3.5 | 4.0 |
|  |  |  | (17) 3.6 |  |  |  | (26) 2.3 | (32) 2.1 |
|  |  |  | 2.2 |  |  |  | 1.2 | .5 |
|  |  | .3 | .8 | .8 |  | Fixed/Worth | .4 | .5 |
|  |  | .6 | 1.2 | 1.5 |  |  | .9 | .8 |
|  |  | 1.8 | 2.3 | -13.3 |  |  | 2.0 | 2.3 |
|  |  | .7 | .8 | .7 |  | Debt/Worth | .9 | .6 |
|  |  | 1.9 | 2.3 | 2.5 |  |  | 2.1 | 1.8 |
|  |  | 4.0 | 5.9 | -26.2 |  |  | 4.6 | 5.7 |
|  |  | 58.9 | 38.1 |  |  | % Profit Before Taxes/Tangible Net Worth | 39.2 | 43.3 |
|  |  | (33) 34.4 | (25) 29.4 |  |  |  | (79) 22.8 | (90) 22.5 |
|  |  | 13.5 | 16.4 |  |  |  | 7.9 | 1.0 |
|  |  | 19.1 | 13.5 | 14.0 |  | % Profit Before Taxes/Total Assets | 14.9 | 15.3 |
|  |  | 11.2 | 10.5 | 7.0 |  |  | 6.6 | 6.4 |
|  |  | 3.0 | 2.7 | -2.1 |  |  | 2.0 | .3 |
|  |  | 34.5 | 9.0 | 4.4 |  | Sales/Net Fixed Assets | 16.7 | 16.7 |
|  |  | 11.6 | 5.2 | 3.4 |  |  | 8.7 | 8.9 |
|  |  | 4.8 | 3.7 | 2.6 |  |  | 4.7 | 4.7 |
|  |  | 3.3 | 2.8 | 1.9 |  | Sales/Total Assets | 2.8 | 2.8 |
|  |  | 2.3 | 2.1 | 1.4 |  |  | 2.2 | 2.3 |
|  |  | 1.7 | 1.5 | .9 |  |  | 1.7 | 1.9 |
|  |  | .8 | 1.8 | 2.2 |  | % Depr., Dep., Amort./Sales | 1.2 | 1.2 |
|  |  | (30) 2.6 | (25) 3.2 | 4.5 |  |  | (78) 2.3 | (87) 2.6 |
|  |  | 3.8 | 4.5 | 7.1 |  |  | 3.8 | 4.4 |
|  |  | 1.0 |  |  |  | % Officers', Directors' Owners' Comp/Sales | 1.9 | 1.5 |
|  |  | (13) 2.1 |  |  |  |  | (21) 4.0 | (30) 3.0 |
|  |  | 3.3 |  |  |  |  | 6.1 | 4.9 |
| 2866M | 31874M | 467133M | 1263560M | 1130769M | 1507927M | Net Sales ($) | 3946948M | 5829730M |
| 984M | 10601M | 179900M | 609629M | 772660M | 1055114M | Total Assets ($) | 2237107M | 3047510M |

M = $ thousand    MM = $ million
See Pages 9 through 22 for Explanation of Ratios and Data

## Comparative Historical Data | | | Current Data Sorted by Sales

| | | | | Type of Statement | | | | | | |
|---|---|---|---|---|---|---|---|---|---|---|
| 21 | | 19 | 18 | Unqualified | 1 | | | 1 | 1 | 15 |
| 23 | | 24 | 17 | Reviewed | | | | 2 | 10 | 5 |
| 10 | | 7 | 8 | Compiled | 1 | | 2 | 3 | 2 | |
| 21 | | 16 | 9 | Tax Returns | | 3 | 2 | 3 | | 1 |
| 41 | | 36 | 37 | Other | 1 | | 2 | 5 | 5 | 23 |
| 4/1/09-3/31/10 ALL | | 4/1/10-3/31/11 ALL | 4/1/11-3/31/12 ALL | | | 12 (4/1-9/30/11) | | 77 (10/1/11-3/31/12) | | |
| | | | | | 0-1MM | 1-3MM | 3-5MM | 5-10MM | 10-25MM | 25MM & OVER |
| 116 | | 102 | 89 | NUMBER OF STATEMENTS | 3 | 3 | 6 | 15 | 18 | 44 |
| % | | % | % | | % | % | % | % | % | % |
| | | | | ASSETS | | | | | | |
| 8.3 | | 7.4 | 5.9 | Cash & Equivalents | | | | 8.7 | 7.9 | 3.6 |
| 27.3 | | 27.1 | 25.2 | Trade Receivables (net) | | | | 26.1 | 28.6 | 23.1 |
| 23.9 | | 27.5 | 25.5 | Inventory | | | | 25.1 | 27.5 | 24.2 |
| 2.4 | | 2.5 | 2.1 | All Other Current | | | | 2.1 | .7 | 2.9 |
| 61.8 | | 64.6 | 58.7 | Total Current | | | | 62.0 | 64.8 | 53.8 |
| 30.0 | | 28.6 | 32.5 | Fixed Assets (net) | | | | 28.3 | 28.7 | 35.2 |
| 3.1 | | 2.6 | 4.1 | Intangibles (net) | | | | 4.7 | .2 | 6.1 |
| 5.1 | | 4.3 | 4.8 | All Other Non-Current | | | | 5.0 | 6.3 | 4.9 |
| 100.0 | | 100.0 | 100.0 | Total | | | | 100.0 | 100.0 | 100.0 |
| | | | | LIABILITIES | | | | | | |
| 9.0 | | 8.4 | 11.2 | Notes Payable-Short Term | | | | 10.9 | 11.1 | 11.4 |
| 4.4 | | 3.4 | 3.6 | Cur. Mat.-L.T.D. | | | | 5.2 | 3.0 | 3.2 |
| 17.4 | | 15.9 | 18.4 | Trade Payables | | | | 21.1 | 19.3 | 16.7 |
| .3 | | .3 | .3 | Income Taxes Payable | | | | 1.0 | .0 | .2 |
| 9.3 | | 16.0 | 7.1 | All Other Current | | | | 9.6 | 5.2 | 6.9 |
| 40.4 | | 43.9 | 40.6 | Total Current | | | | 47.9 | 38.7 | 38.4 |
| 14.1 | | 17.1 | 17.9 | Long-Term Debt | | | | 20.5 | 13.5 | 18.4 |
| .5 | | .5 | .8 | Deferred Taxes | | | | .8 | .5 | .9 |
| 3.8 | | 3.8 | 3.6 | All Other Non-Current | | | | 4.4 | 3.6 | 4.2 |
| 41.1 | | 34.6 | 37.1 | Net Worth | | | | 26.4 | 43.6 | 38.1 |
| 100.0 | | 100.0 | 100.0 | Total Liabilties & Net Worth | | | | 100.0 | 100.0 | 100.0 |
| | | | | INCOME DATA | | | | | | |
| 100.0 | | 100.0 | 100.0 | Net Sales | | | | 100.0 | 100.0 | 100.0 |
| 27.0 | | 25.3 | 24.5 | Gross Profit | | | | 30.3 | 21.8 | 20.2 |
| 21.6 | | 19.4 | 19.5 | Operating Expenses | | | | 26.3 | 16.6 | 14.9 |
| 5.4 | | 5.8 | 5.0 | Operating Profit | | | | 3.9 | 5.2 | 5.3 |
| .7 | | 1.0 | .4 | All Other Expenses (net) | | | | 1.1 | .0 | .6 |
| 4.7 | | 4.9 | 4.7 | Profit Before Taxes | | | | 2.8 | 5.2 | 4.7 |
| | | | | RATIOS | | | | | | |
| 2.3 | | 2.7 | 2.3 | | | | | 2.1 | 2.4 | 2.4 |
| 1.6 | | 1.9 | 1.5 | Current | | | | 1.4 | 1.9 | 1.5 |
| 1.1 | | 1.2 | 1.0 | | | | | 1.0 | 1.3 | 1.1 |
| 1.6 | | 1.7 | 1.2 | | | | | 1.2 | 1.3 | 1.1 |
| .9 | | .9 | .7 | Quick | | | | .6 | 1.1 | .7 |
| .6 | | .5 | .5 | | | | | .4 | .7 | .5 |
| 34 10.8 | 32 | 11.3 | 30 12.1 | | 33 10.9 | 31 11.9 | 30 12.2 | | | |
| 45 8.2 | 41 | 8.8 | 42 8.6 | Sales/Receivables | 43 8.5 | 42 8.6 | 42 8.7 | | | |
| 54 6.8 | 52 | 7.0 | 50 7.3 | | 58 6.3 | 47 7.8 | 54 6.8 | | | |
| 36 10.2 | 37 | 9.9 | 39 9.3 | | 31 11.9 | 35 10.5 | 41 9.0 | | | |
| 54 6.8 | 54 | 6.8 | 53 6.9 | Cost of Sales/Inventory | 56 6.5 | 46 7.9 | 52 7.0 | | | |
| 73 5.0 | 72 | 5.1 | 72 5.1 | | 96 3.8 | 72 5.1 | 65 5.6 | | | |
| 23 16.2 | 18 | 20.8 | 23 15.9 | | 16 23.0 | 20 18.1 | 23 15.9 | | | |
| 37 9.8 | 29 | 12.6 | 34 10.6 | Cost of Sales/Payables | 45 8.2 | 33 11.1 | 33 11.0 | | | |
| 51 7.2 | 44 | 8.4 | 51 7.1 | | 62 5.9 | 41 8.9 | 49 7.5 | | | |
| 5.6 | | 5.7 | 7.5 | | | | | 8.8 | 6.7 | 7.6 |
| 11.0 | | 8.6 | 11.4 | Sales/Working Capital | | | | 12.0 | 9.1 | 11.0 |
| 41.7 | | 23.5 | 160.2 | | | | | 253.2 | 21.8 | 83.1 |
| 21.7 | | 14.8 | 23.1 | | | | | 15.7 | 68.5 | 16.5 |
| (105) 4.9 | (89) | 5.5 | (81) 5.7 | EBIT/Interest | (13) 3.3 | (17) 9.2 | (40) 5.5 | | | |
| 2.1 | | 2.0 | 1.7 | | | | | -.3 | 2.6 | 1.6 |
| 5.4 | | 5.4 | 6.4 | | | | | | | 5.1 |
| (34) 2.4 | (28) | 3.9 | (30) 3.9 | Net Profit + Depr., Dep., Amort./Cur. Mat. L/T/D | | | (22) 3.5 | | | |
| .4 | | 2.0 | 2.1 | | | | | | | 2.1 |
| .3 | | .3 | .4 | | | | | .3 | .3 | .7 |
| .7 | | .8 | 1.0 | Fixed/Worth | | | | 1.7 | .6 | 1.2 |
| 1.3 | | 1.7 | 2.2 | | | | | 3.4 | 1.1 | 2.3 |
| .7 | | .7 | .7 | | | | | 1.0 | .6 | .8 |
| 1.6 | | 1.6 | 2.1 | Debt/Worth | | | | 2.9 | 1.1 | 2.2 |
| 3.7 | | 3.6 | 5.6 | | | | | 15.2 | 3.0 | 7.1 |
| 38.7 | | 40.8 | 42.6 | | | | | 51.4 | 56.3 | 37.1 |
| (110) 20.8 | (90) | 25.0 | (81) 30.0 | % Profit Before Taxes/Tangible Net Worth | (12) 38.0 | | (40) 31.2 | 25.9 | | |
| 5.4 | | 9.0 | 10.7 | | | | | 11.6 | 11.2 | 11.2 |
| 16.0 | | 17.6 | 16.4 | | | | | 11.6 | 20.5 | 13.8 |
| 7.0 | | 8.2 | 9.2 | % Profit Before Taxes/Total Assets | | | | 4.6 | 10.4 | 9.6 |
| 2.2 | | 3.0 | 2.2 | | | | | -.3 | 3.0 | 2.4 |
| 25.1 | | 20.7 | 15.0 | | | | | 42.6 | 21.7 | 10.5 |
| 8.3 | | 9.4 | 6.5 | Sales/Net Fixed Assets | | | | 8.8 | 11.4 | 4.9 |
| 4.0 | | 5.1 | 3.7 | | | | | 3.3 | 5.5 | 3.5 |
| 2.8 | | 3.0 | 3.0 | | | | | 2.5 | 3.6 | 2.7 |
| 2.2 | | 2.3 | 2.1 | Sales/Total Assets | | | | 2.1 | 2.8 | 1.9 |
| 1.6 | | 1.7 | 1.5 | | | | | 1.5 | 1.9 | 1.5 |
| 1.3 | | 1.1 | 1.5 | | | | | 1.5 | 1.2 | 1.7 |
| (98) 2.4 | (86) | 2.2 | (79) 2.8 | % Depr., Dep., Amort./Sales | (13) 2.8 | (17) 2.8 | (40) 3.2 | | | |
| 4.1 | | 3.8 | 4.2 | | | | | 5.9 | 3.5 | 4.7 |
| 1.2 | | 1.1 | .9 | % Officers', Directors' Owners' Comp/Sales | | | | | | |
| (46) 2.6 | (28) | 2.3 | (22) 1.8 | | | | | | | |
| 4.6 | | 5.3 | 4.0 | | | | | | | |
| 5303131M | | 3912484M | 4404129M | Net Sales ($) | 1961M | 6164M | 25164M | 102794M | 301312M | 3966734M |
| 3044119M | | 2121116M | 2628888M | Total Assets ($) | 2149M | 2017M | 12950M | 69876M | 129135M | 2412761M |

M = $ thousand    MM = $ million
See Pages 9 through 22 for Explanation of Ratios and Data

**Current Data Sorted by Assets**      **Comparative Historical Data**

Date ranges (Current Data): 10 (4/1-9/30/11) over 500M-2MM; 62 (10/1/11-3/31/12) over 10-50MM.
Date ranges (Historical): 4/1/07-3/31/08 ALL; 4/1/08-3/31/09 ALL.

| 0-500M | 500M-2MM | 2-10MM | 10-50MM | 50-100MM | 100-250MM | | 4/1/07-3/31/08 ALL | 4/1/08-3/31/09 ALL |
|---|---|---|---|---|---|---|---|---|
| | | | | | | **Type of Statement** | 15 | 16 |
| | | | | | | Unqualified | 15 | 16 |
| | 2 | 9 | 3 | 2 | | Reviewed | 20 | 17 |
| | 2 | 6 | 2 | | | Compiled | 20 | 14 |
| | 5 | 4 | | | | Tax Returns | 3 | 10 |
| 2 | 3 | 10 | 7 | | 3 | Other | 22 | 21 |
| | | 2 | 3 | 3 | 4 | (Unqualified) | | |
| 2 | 12 | 31 | 15 | 5 | 7 | **NUMBER OF STATEMENTS** | 80 | 78 |
| % | % | % | % | % | % | **ASSETS** | % | % |
| | 7.3 | 8.5 | 7.2 | | | Cash & Equivalents | 7.3 | 6.6 |
| | 29.8 | 24.1 | 24.7 | | | Trade Receivables (net) | 26.1 | 25.5 |
| | 29.3 | 23.8 | 29.0 | | | Inventory | 24.8 | 24.2 |
| | 2.3 | 2.4 | 2.4 | | | All Other Current | 1.3 | 1.8 |
| | 68.7 | 58.7 | 63.2 | | | Total Current | 59.5 | 58.2 |
| | 19.3 | 32.4 | 30.0 | | | Fixed Assets (net) | 32.9 | 32.0 |
| | 6.7 | 5.4 | 2.1 | | | Intangibles (net) | 1.8 | 3.0 |
| | 5.4 | 3.6 | 4.6 | | | All Other Non-Current | 5.8 | 6.8 |
| | 100.0 | 100.0 | 100.0 | | | Total | 100.0 | 100.0 |
| | | | | | | **LIABILITIES** | | |
| | 11.5 | 8.3 | 9.3 | | | Notes Payable-Short Term | 11.9 | 10.7 |
| | 4.6 | 4.0 | 5.0 | | | Cur. Mat.-L.T.D. | 4.6 | 4.8 |
| | 21.1 | 15.3 | 14.4 | | | Trade Payables | 16.0 | 14.7 |
| | .0 | .2 | .1 | | | Income Taxes Payable | .3 | .3 |
| | 4.3 | 7.1 | 6.2 | | | All Other Current | 8.1 | 10.5 |
| | 41.5 | 34.9 | 35.0 | | | Total Current | 40.9 | 40.9 |
| | 5.9 | 14.4 | 11.4 | | | Long-Term Debt | 18.2 | 17.1 |
| | 1.2 | .5 | 1.0 | | | Deferred Taxes | .4 | .6 |
| | 18.4 | 5.6 | 12.7 | | | All Other Non-Current | 6.0 | 5.5 |
| | 33.1 | 44.6 | 39.8 | | | Net Worth | 34.6 | 35.9 |
| | 100.0 | 100.0 | 100.0 | | | Total Liabilities & Net Worth | 100.0 | 100.0 |
| | | | | | | **INCOME DATA** | | |
| | 100.0 | 100.0 | 100.0 | | | Net Sales | 100.0 | 100.0 |
| | 33.6 | 27.1 | 22.9 | | | Gross Profit | 25.6 | 27.0 |
| | 36.7 | 21.5 | 17.1 | | | Operating Expenses | 22.1 | 23.4 |
| | -3.1 | 5.6 | 5.8 | | | Operating Profit | 3.5 | 3.6 |
| | .8 | .9 | -.2 | | | All Other Expenses (net) | 1.0 | .7 |
| | -3.9 | 4.7 | 6.0 | | | Profit Before Taxes | 2.5 | 2.9 |
| | | | | | | **RATIOS** | | |
| | 3.1 | 2.7 | 3.7 | | | | 2.3 | 2.6 |
| | 2.1 | 1.5 | 2.0 | | | Current | 1.6 | 1.5 |
| | 1.0 | 1.1 | 1.1 | | | | 1.0 | 1.0 |
| | 2.2 | 1.4 | 2.2 | | | | 1.3 | 1.4 |
| | .8 | 1.1 | 1.0 | | | Quick | .8 | .7 |
| | .4 | .6 | .6 | | | | .5 | .5 |
| 27 | 13.7 | 26 14.1 | 34 10.6 | | | | 33 11.1 | 25 14.8 |
| 35 | 10.3 | 40 9.2 | 47 7.7 | | | Sales/Receivables | 41 8.9 | 38 9.7 |
| 65 | 5.6 | 48 7.6 | 55 6.6 | | | | 52 7.0 | 49 7.4 |
| 41 | 8.9 | 42 8.7 | 49 7.4 | | | | 39 9.5 | 35 10.4 |
| 51 | 7.1 | 54 6.7 | 69 5.3 | | | Cost of Sales/Inventory | 52 7.1 | 50 7.3 |
| 68 | 5.4 | 81 4.5 | 89 4.1 | | | | 75 4.9 | 75 4.8 |
| 25 | 14.5 | 21 17.5 | 16 22.9 | | | | 18 20.5 | 17 21.7 |
| 40 | 9.2 | 29 12.8 | 46 7.9 | | | Cost of Sales/Payables | 33 11.0 | 27 13.8 |
| 52 | 7.0 | 39 9.4 | 48 7.6 | | | | 48 7.5 | 48 7.6 |
| | 5.8 | 4.8 | 4.2 | | | | 6.1 | 7.0 |
| | 10.5 | 7.8 | 5.7 | | | Sales/Working Capital | 10.7 | 13.4 |
| | NM | 27.8 | 30.6 | | | | -131.9 | NM |
| | 30.2 | 15.0 | 24.9 | | | | 8.0 | 6.5 |
| (11) | 5.8 | (26) 4.9 | 14.5 | | | EBIT/Interest | (72) 2.1 | (68) 2.3 |
| | -4.4 | 2.1 | 4.0 | | | | .4 | .8 |
| | | | | | | | 4.2 | 4.1 |
| | | | | | | Net Profit + Depr., Dep., Amort./Cur. Mat. L/T/D | (22) 1.8 | (20) 2.9 |
| | | | | | | | .1 | 1.6 |
| | .2 | .4 | .1 | | | | .3 | .5 |
| | .7 | 1.0 | 1.0 | | | Fixed/Worth | .9 | 1.0 |
| | .9 | 1.7 | 1.5 | | | | 2.4 | 2.3 |
| | .6 | .6 | .6 | | | | .7 | .7 |
| | 1.1 | 2.1 | 1.9 | | | Debt/Worth | 1.6 | 1.6 |
| | 4.5 | 3.7 | 3.5 | | | | 5.1 | 5.6 |
| | 70.3 | 57.7 | 52.9 | | | | 37.2 | 26.4 |
| (10) | 20.8 | 26.6 | (14) 33.9 | | | % Profit Before Taxes/Tangible Net Worth | (69) 10.4 | (68) 10.5 |
| | -24.9 | 6.2 | 16.8 | | | | .8 | 1.9 |
| | 25.0 | 14.7 | 21.5 | | | | 13.4 | 10.9 |
| | 4.0 | 7.0 | 10.0 | | | % Profit Before Taxes/Total Assets | 3.9 | 3.5 |
| | -22.0 | 2.3 | 6.5 | | | | -.5 | .1 |
| | 32.7 | 17.2 | 14.6 | | | | 18.2 | 15.2 |
| | 18.7 | 7.6 | 8.6 | | | Sales/Net Fixed Assets | 6.9 | 7.6 |
| | 8.7 | 4.0 | 3.3 | | | | 3.3 | 4.6 |
| | 4.1 | 2.7 | 2.6 | | | | 2.8 | 3.4 |
| | 2.9 | 2.1 | 2.0 | | | Sales/Total Assets | 2.2 | 2.2 |
| | 1.9 | 1.5 | 1.5 | | | | 1.5 | 1.5 |
| | .2 | 1.7 | 1.3 | | | | 1.8 | 1.6 |
| (10) | 2.8 | (28) 3.1 | 2.7 | | | % Depr., Dep., Amort./Sales | (73) 2.9 | (67) 2.5 |
| | 4.2 | 4.4 | 5.3 | | | | 4.6 | 4.1 |
| | | 2.3 | | | | | 2.1 | 2.4 |
| | | (15) 3.2 | | | | % Officers', Directors' Owners' Comp/Sales | (30) 3.5 | (31) 5.4 |
| | | 7.2 | | | | | 7.0 | 6.7 |
| 2019M | 45990M | 369244M | 635115M | 451105M | 1331991M | Net Sales ($) | 2412150M | 2274218M |
| 478M | 15781M | 169292M | 311048M | 337738M | 915822M | Total Assets ($) | 1479683M | 1369138M |

M = $ thousand    MM = $ million
See Pages 9 through 22 for Explanation of Ratios and Data

## Comparative Historical Data

## Current Data Sorted by Sales

| | | | Type of Statement | | | | | | |
|---|---|---|---|---|---|---|---|---|---|
| | | | Unqualified | | | | 1 | 3 | 8 |
| 16 | 16 | 12 | Reviewed | | 2 | | 4 | 6 | 2 |
| 16 | 19 | 14 | Compiled | | | 2 | 2 | 2 | 2 |
| 10 | 7 | 10 | Tax Returns | 2 | 3 | 2 | 6 | 2 | |
| 5 | 9 | 11 | Other | 2 | | 2 | 2 | 7 | 12 |
| 28 | 19 | 25 | | 2 | 3 | 2 | | | |
| 4/1/09- | 4/1/10- | 4/1/11- | | | | | | | |
| 3/31/10 | 3/31/11 | 3/31/12 | | | 10 (4/1-9/30/11) | | | 62 (10/1/11-3/31/12) | |
| ALL | ALL | ALL | | 0-1MM | 1-3MM | 3-5MM | 5-10MM | 10-25MM | 25MM & OVER |
| 75 | 70 | 72 | **NUMBER OF STATEMENTS** | 2 | 5 | 8 | 15 | 18 | 24 |
| % | % | % | **ASSETS** | % | % | % | % | % | % |
| 7.4 | 7.5 | 7.7 | Cash & Equivalents | | | | 8.6 | 7.6 | 5.1 |
| 22.0 | 22.4 | 24.1 | Trade Receivables (net) | | | | 21.4 | 26.3 | 23.2 |
| 22.8 | 23.7 | 25.0 | Inventory | | | | 27.1 | 26.4 | 26.5 |
| 1.4 | 1.8 | 2.2 | All Other Current | | | | 2.0 | 3.1 | 2.3 |
| 53.6 | 55.4 | 59.0 | Total Current | | | | 59.1 | 63.4 | 57.1 |
| 32.0 | 30.3 | 29.2 | Fixed Assets (net) | | | | 29.2 | 28.6 | 30.6 |
| 6.2 | 5.9 | 7.8 | Intangibles (net) | | | | 6.0 | 4.5 | 9.2 |
| 8.2 | 8.3 | 4.0 | All Other Non-Current | | | | 5.7 | 3.6 | 3.1 |
| 100.0 | 100.0 | 100.0 | Total | | | | 100.0 | 100.0 | 100.0 |
| | | | **LIABILITIES** | | | | | | |
| 11.4 | 11.0 | 9.1 | Notes Payable-Short Term | | | | 6.3 | 8.6 | 9.5 |
| 5.0 | 4.2 | 4.2 | Cur. Mat.-L.T.D. | | | | 4.3 | 5.9 | 2.8 |
| 13.0 | 13.9 | 15.0 | Trade Payables | | | | 17.9 | 17.1 | 12.8 |
| .3 | .1 | .1 | Income Taxes Payable | | | | .2 | .2 | .1 |
| 6.9 | 5.4 | 6.5 | All Other Current | | | | 5.4 | 8.7 | 7.1 |
| 36.6 | 34.6 | 34.9 | Total Current | | | | 34.1 | 40.6 | 32.3 |
| 17.1 | 16.9 | 15.0 | Long-Term Debt | | | | 18.6 | 7.9 | 18.0 |
| .8 | .7 | .6 | Deferred Taxes | | | | .4 | .2 | .7 |
| 5.2 | 8.2 | 8.7 | All Other Non-Current | | | | 7.2 | 12.2 | 4.5 |
| 40.3 | 39.5 | 40.8 | Net Worth | | | | 39.7 | 39.0 | 44.4 |
| 100.0 | 100.0 | 100.0 | Total Liabilties & Net Worth | | | | 100.0 | 100.0 | 100.0 |
| | | | **INCOME DATA** | | | | | | |
| 100.0 | 100.0 | 100.0 | Net Sales | | | | 100.0 | 100.0 | 100.0 |
| 30.3 | 32.3 | 28.4 | Gross Profit | | | | 27.2 | 25.6 | 23.9 |
| 26.8 | 26.5 | 24.8 | Operating Expenses | | | | 21.8 | 22.0 | 17.0 |
| 3.5 | 5.8 | 3.6 | Operating Profit | | | | 5.3 | 3.5 | 6.9 |
| 1.3 | 1.4 | .8 | All Other Expenses (net) | | | | .5 | .0 | 1.3 |
| 2.2 | 4.3 | 2.8 | Profit Before Taxes | | | | 4.8 | 3.6 | 5.7 |
| | | | **RATIOS** | | | | | | |
| 2.7 | 2.4 | 3.0 | | | | | 3.5 | 2.8 | 3.5 |
| 1.6 | 1.5 | 1.7 | Current | | | | 2.2 | 1.4 | 1.6 |
| 1.1 | 1.1 | 1.1 | | | | | .9 | 1.2 | 1.1 |
| 1.6 | 1.3 | 1.6 | | | | | 2.1 | 1.2 | 1.8 |
| .9 | .8 | .9 | Quick | | | | .9 | .9 | .9 |
| .5 | .5 | .6 | | | | | .4 | .6 | .6 |
| 35 10.6 | 34 10.6 | 28 12.9 | | | | 24 15.3 | 29 12.6 | 38 9.7 | |
| 42 8.7 | 45 8.1 | 40 9.2 | Sales/Receivables | | | 35 10.4 | 39 9.3 | 46 7.9 | |
| 52 7.0 | 53 6.9 | 51 7.1 | | | | 42 8.6 | 49 7.4 | 53 6.9 | |
| 48 7.6 | 43 8.4 | 43 8.4 | | | | 41 8.9 | 41 8.9 | 47 7.7 | |
| 68 5.4 | 68 5.4 | 64 5.7 | Cost of Sales/Inventory | | | 55 6.6 | 70 5.2 | 69 5.3 | |
| 110 3.3 | 97 3.8 | 83 4.4 | | | | 87 4.2 | 85 4.3 | 91 4.0 | |
| 20 18.1 | 20 18.5 | 21 17.5 | | | | 19 19.0 | 22 16.4 | 17 21.6 | |
| 37 9.9 | 34 10.7 | 30 12.2 | Cost of Sales/Payables | | | 29 12.8 | 30 12.3 | 31 11.7 | |
| 51 7.1 | 55 6.7 | 47 7.8 | | | | 44 8.3 | 42 8.7 | 47 7.8 | |
| 4.8 | 4.5 | 4.8 | | | | | 3.7 | 4.6 | 4.3 |
| 9.5 | 9.7 | 9.8 | Sales/Working Capital | | | | 8.8 | 13.6 | 10.7 |
| 54.9 | 79.0 | 29.9 | | | | | -30.5 | 24.8 | 25.7 |
| 7.0 | 10.6 | 19.0 | | | | | 21.1 | 23.6 | 23.1 |
| (69) 2.5 | (62) 3.7 | (65) 5.3 | EBIT/Interest | | (14) 4.2 | (15) 7.6 | (23) 5.3 | | |
| .6 | 1.3 | 1.8 | | | | | 1.7 | 3.8 | 1.8 |
| 4.1 | 4.1 | 8.5 | Net Profit + Depr., Dep., | | | | | | 17.4 |
| (22) 2.1 | (22) 3.0 | (23) 4.5 | Amort./Cur. Mat. L/T/D | | | | | (12) | 4.7 |
| .9 | 1.8 | 2.0 | | | | | | | 1.8 |
| .4 | .3 | .4 | | | | | .3 | .4 | .5 |
| .9 | .9 | .9 | Fixed/Worth | | | | .8 | .8 | 1.1 |
| 2.1 | 2.2 | 1.9 | | | | | 5.8 | 1.7 | 2.6 |
| .6 | .7 | .7 | | | | | .7 | .6 | .5 |
| 1.4 | 1.5 | 1.9 | Debt/Worth | | | | 1.4 | 2.0 | 2.0 |
| 4.8 | 4.5 | 4.7 | | | | | 10.5 | 4.2 | 4.7 |
| 34.9 | 49.7 | 46.3 | % Profit Before Taxes/Tangible | | | | 74.4 | 67.7 | 40.4 |
| (66) 14.5 | (63) 19.7 | (65) 26.6 | Net Worth | | (14) 30.2 | (17) 31.8 | (21) 29.2 | | |
| -3.2 | 3.2 | 8.0 | | | | | 4.4 | 11.8 | 12.2 |
| 10.8 | 13.7 | 16.1 | % Profit Before Taxes/Total | | | | 26.3 | 20.2 | 17.7 |
| 4.2 | 6.4 | 6.8 | Assets | | | | 6.9 | 7.8 | 6.9 |
| -1.5 | 1.5 | 1.7 | | | | | 2.3 | 3.1 | 2.5 |
| 13.2 | 16.8 | 17.1 | | | | | 27.2 | 22.6 | 8.7 |
| 5.6 | 7.0 | 7.6 | Sales/Net Fixed Assets | | | | 10.5 | 7.7 | 5.8 |
| 3.7 | 3.4 | 4.0 | | | | | 3.9 | 5.4 | 3.6 |
| 2.2 | 2.4 | 2.7 | | | | | 3.8 | 3.0 | 2.6 |
| 1.8 | 1.7 | 1.9 | Sales/Total Assets | | | | 2.5 | 2.1 | 1.7 |
| 1.1 | 1.2 | 1.4 | | | | | 1.4 | 1.7 | 1.4 |
| 1.8 | 1.4 | 1.5 | | | | | 1.3 | 1.7 | 1.4 |
| (63) 3.3 | (63) 3.2 | (62) 3.0 | % Depr., Dep., Amort./Sales | | (14) 2.8 | (16) 3.0 | (20) 2.6 | | |
| 5.1 | 4.6 | 4.8 | | | | | 4.6 | 4.2 | 5.0 |
| 1.9 | 3.2 | 3.0 | % Officers', Directors' | | | | | | |
| (29) 3.7 | (28) 5.8 | (26) 4.8 | Owners' Comp/Sales | | | | | | |
| 7.4 | 7.5 | 8.2 | | | | | | | |
| 2066496M | 1429814M | 2835464M | Net Sales ($) | 1139M | 10173M | 33313M | 102209M | 304721M | 2383909M |
| 1574492M | 1008948M | 1750159M | Total Assets ($) | 842M | 4747M | 21154M | 53078M | 147954M | 1522384M |

M = $ thousand    MM = $ million
See Pages 9 through 22 for Explanation of Ratios and Data

## Current Data Sorted by Assets | Comparative Historical Data

| | 0-500M | 500M-2MM | 2-10MM | 10-50MM | 50-100MM | 100-250MM | Type of Statement | ALL 4/1/07-3/31/08 | ALL 4/1/08-3/31/09 |
|---|---|---|---|---|---|---|---|---|---|
| | | | 4 | 6 | 4 | 8 | Unqualified | 31 | 28 |
| | | 3 | 19 | 6 | 1 | | Reviewed | 32 | 27 |
| | 2 | 8 | 9 | 2 | | 1 | Compiled | 18 | 14 |
| | 1 | 1 | | 2 | | | Tax Returns | 5 | 4 |
| | 1 | 8 | 10 | 12 | 3 | 3 | Other | 45 | 40 |
| | | 14 (4/1-9/30/11) | | 99 (10/1/11-3/31/12) | | | | | |
| NUMBER OF STATEMENTS | 3 | 20 | 42 | 28 | 8 | 12 | | 131 | 113 |
| **ASSETS** | % | % | % | % | % | % | | % | % |
| Cash & Equivalents | | 9.6 | 7.5 | 4.3 | | 3.5 | | 5.7 | 5.9 |
| Trade Receivables (net) | | 26.4 | 24.5 | 25.9 | | 28.0 | | 26.6 | 21.4 |
| Inventory | | 32.9 | 26.0 | 30.4 | | 23.2 | | 24.9 | 25.6 |
| All Other Current | | .4 | 1.9 | 3.2 | | 4.7 | | 1.8 | 1.8 |
| Total Current | | 69.3 | 60.0 | 63.8 | | 59.4 | | 59.1 | 54.8 |
| Fixed Assets (net) | | 23.1 | 29.8 | 30.4 | | 26.3 | | 30.5 | 31.9 |
| Intangibles (net) | | 1.9 | 1.7 | .9 | | 9.5 | | 4.9 | 6.4 |
| All Other Non-Current | | 5.7 | 8.6 | 4.9 | | 4.9 | | 5.6 | 7.0 |
| Total | | 100.0 | 100.0 | 100.0 | | 100.0 | | 100.0 | 100.0 |
| **LIABILITIES** | | | | | | | | | |
| Notes Payable-Short Term | | 15.7 | 11.7 | 11.5 | | 12.0 | | 10.4 | 13.2 |
| Cur. Mat.-L.T.D. | | 2.2 | 3.9 | 2.3 | | 2.3 | | 5.1 | 5.0 |
| Trade Payables | | 12.5 | 14.3 | 15.7 | | 16.0 | | 14.2 | 10.8 |
| Income Taxes Payable | | .0 | .2 | .2 | | .1 | | .2 | .0 |
| All Other Current | | 7.8 | 5.4 | 5.5 | | 10.8 | | 8.1 | 9.2 |
| Total Current | | 38.2 | 35.4 | 35.2 | | 41.2 | | 38.0 | 38.3 |
| Long-Term Debt | | 26.4 | 12.3 | 10.5 | | 10.9 | | 16.9 | 18.1 |
| Deferred Taxes | | .0 | .7 | .8 | | .6 | | .8 | .7 |
| All Other Non-Current | | 15.1 | 9.8 | 10.1 | | 10.5 | | 6.5 | 7.5 |
| Net Worth | | 20.3 | 41.9 | 43.4 | | 36.9 | | 37.8 | 35.3 |
| Total Liabilities & Net Worth | | 100.0 | 100.0 | 100.0 | | 100.0 | | 100.0 | 100.0 |
| **INCOME DATA** | | | | | | | | | |
| Net Sales | | 100.0 | 100.0 | 100.0 | | 100.0 | | 100.0 | 100.0 |
| Gross Profit | | 28.4 | 26.9 | 23.7 | | 23.7 | | 24.7 | 24.9 |
| Operating Expenses | | 28.7 | 22.2 | 18.0 | | 16.8 | | 20.2 | 21.0 |
| Operating Profit | | -.3 | 4.7 | 5.8 | | 6.9 | | 4.5 | 3.9 |
| All Other Expenses (net) | | -.1 | .8 | .4 | | 1.3 | | 1.4 | 1.3 |
| Profit Before Taxes | | -.2 | 3.8 | 5.3 | | 5.6 | | 3.1 | 2.5 |
| **RATIOS** | | | | | | | | | |
| Current | | 3.9 | 2.7 | 3.1 | | 1.9 | | 2.7 | 2.8 |
| | | 1.8 | 1.6 | 1.5 | | 1.4 | | 1.6 | 1.5 |
| | | 1.1 | 1.3 | 1.2 | | 1.2 | | 1.1 | 1.0 |
| Quick | | 1.9 | 1.7 | 1.4 | | .9 | | 1.5 | 1.4 |
| | | 1.1 | .8 | .8 | | .6 | | .9 | .7 |
| | | .5 | .5 | .6 | | .6 | | .5 | .5 |
| Sales/Receivables | | 22   16.9 | 31   11.6 | 39   9.4 | | 47   7.8 | | 31   11.6 | 27   13.5 |
| | | 38   9.6 | 43   8.4 | 43   8.5 | | 54   6.7 | | 45   8.1 | 35   10.3 |
| | | 61   6.0 | 57   6.4 | 55   6.6 | | 83   4.4 | | 57   6.4 | 47   7.7 |
| Cost of Sales/Inventory | | 33   11.2 | 37   9.9 | 41   8.9 | | 25   14.6 | | 32   11.4 | 37   9.9 |
| | | 64   5.7 | 53   6.9 | 70   5.2 | | 76   4.8 | | 53   6.9 | 56   6.5 |
| | | 159   2.3 | 94   3.9 | 107   3.4 | | 140   2.6 | | 76   4.8 | 95   3.8 |
| Cost of Sales/Payables | | 11   31.9 | 17   20.9 | 15   23.7 | | 20   18.7 | | 17   22.0 | 12   29.4 |
| | | 23   15.9 | 30   12.2 | 29   12.5 | | 38   9.5 | | 32   11.6 | 22   16.8 |
| | | 35   10.5 | 49   7.5 | 53   6.9 | | 91   4.0 | | 45   8.2 | 35   10.3 |
| Sales/Working Capital | | 3.4 | 3.8 | 5.0 | | 4.4 | | 5.3 | 5.1 |
| | | 7.6 | 9.5 | 10.9 | | 10.3 | | 9.0 | 11.7 |
| | | 37.7 | 25.7 | 22.5 | | 18.3 | | 60.9 | 230.8 |
| EBIT/Interest | | 13.5 | 9.2 | 15.6 | | 9.5 | | 11.8 | 7.1 |
| | | (17) 5.1 | (39) 4.7 | (26) 9.0 | | 4.4 | | (122) 3.1 | (106) 2.6 |
| | | -.9 | 1.8 | 3.4 | | 2.5 | | .9 | .3 |
| Net Profit + Depr., Dep., Amort./Cur. Mat. L/T/D | | | (11) 7.0 | | | | | 8.0 | 4.0 |
| | | | 3.7 | | | | | (41) 2.5 | (31) 1.9 |
| | | | 1.6 | | | | | 1.5 | .8 |
| Fixed/Worth | | .2 | .4 | .3 | | .4 | | .4 | .4 |
| | | .5 | .8 | .7 | | .9 | | .7 | 1.0 |
| | | 5.7 | 1.2 | 1.3 | | 2.4 | | 2.6 | 3.9 |
| Debt/Worth | | .5 | .6 | .4 | | 1.8 | | .7 | .5 |
| | | 1.2 | 1.5 | 1.2 | | 2.1 | | 1.3 | 1.6 |
| | | 10.3 | 2.8 | 2.7 | | 3.9 | | 6.0 | 9.4 |
| % Profit Before Taxes/Tangible Net Worth | | 41.7 | 31.4 | 36.1 | | 44.1 | | 35.6 | 29.2 |
| | | (16) 15.8 | (40) 15.0 | (25) 20.7 | | (11) 38.8 | | (112) 17.9 | (91) 12.1 |
| | | 5.4 | 2.5 | 14.8 | | 3.6 | | 1.4 | -1.7 |
| % Profit Before Taxes/Total Assets | | 11.6 | 12.9 | 16.8 | | 9.6 | | 15.1 | 13.0 |
| | | 5.7 | 5.3 | 8.8 | | 7.4 | | 6.9 | 4.2 |
| | | -2.5 | 1.6 | 4.6 | | .9 | | .2 | -1.6 |
| Sales/Net Fixed Assets | | 21.9 | 15.0 | 12.1 | | 11.0 | | 14.9 | 13.7 |
| | | 12.4 | 5.6 | 6.9 | | 7.9 | | 7.8 | 6.2 |
| | | 6.7 | 3.5 | 4.7 | | 3.0 | | 4.0 | 3.9 |
| Sales/Total Assets | | 3.3 | 2.6 | 2.6 | | 2.2 | | 2.7 | 2.6 |
| | | 2.5 | 1.8 | 2.2 | | 1.3 | | 2.0 | 2.0 |
| | | 1.7 | 1.2 | 1.6 | | 1.1 | | 1.6 | 1.4 |
| % Depr., Dep., Amort./Sales | | .9 | 1.1 | 1.3 | | 1.2 | | 1.6 | 1.8 |
| | | (17) 2.9 | (38) 3.3 | (27) 2.8 | | (10) 2.1 | | (116) 2.8 | (101) 2.9 |
| | | 3.9 | 5.0 | 3.2 | | 3.8 | | 4.2 | 4.4 |
| % Officers', Directors' Owners' Comp/Sales | | 2.6 | 1.2 | | | | | 1.4 | 1.7 |
| | | (10) 4.5 | (22) 2.1 | | | | | (45) 3.8 | (39) 3.8 |
| | | 6.6 | 6.6 | | | | | 7.3 | |
| Net Sales ($) | 1334M | 60957M | 438726M | 1318687M | 993228M | 2757140M | | 5760168M | 5166648M |
| Total Assets ($) | 504M | 24421M | 225641M | 679646M | 510023M | 1925580M | | 3190810M | 3023015M |

M = $ thousand    MM = $ million
See Pages 9 through 22 for Explanation of Ratios and Data

## Comparative Historical Data / Current Data Sorted by Sales

Periods (current): **14 (4/1-9/30/11)** covers 0-1MM & 1-3MM; **99 (10/1/11-3/31/12)** covers 3-5MM, 5-10MM, 10-25MM, 25MM & Over.

| Type of Statement | 4/1/09-3/31/10 ALL | 4/1/10-3/31/11 ALL | 4/1/11-3/31/12 ALL | 0-1MM | 1-3MM | 3-5MM | 5-10MM | 10-25MM | 25MM & OVER |
|---|---|---|---|---|---|---|---|---|---|
| Unqualified | 30 | 27 | 22 | | | | | 3 | 19 |
| Reviewed | 19 | 23 | 29 | 2 | 2 | 6 | 3 | 11 | 7 |
| Compiled | 22 | 24 | 22 | | 6 | 6 | 4 | 3 | 1 |
| Tax Returns | 6 | 2 | 3 | | | 1 | | | 2 |
| Other | 38 | 31 | 37 | 2 | 2 | 7 | | 7 | 17 |
| **NUMBER OF STATEMENTS** | 115 | 107 | 113 | 4 | 10 | 20 | 9 | 24 | 46 |

### ASSETS (%)

| | 4/1/09-3/31/10 | 4/1/10-3/31/11 | 4/1/11-3/31/12 | 1-3MM | 3-5MM | 10-25MM | 25MM & OVER |
|---|---|---|---|---|---|---|---|
| Cash & Equivalents | 7.6 | 7.9 | 6.9 | 9.4 | 8.8 | 9.2 | 4.0 |
| Trade Receivables (net) | 23.0 | 24.4 | 25.4 | 23.3 | 23.6 | 27.6 | 27.4 |
| Inventory | 26.5 | 27.3 | 27.9 | 37.4 | 20.5 | 31.3 | 27.1 |
| All Other Current | 2.8 | 1.1 | 2.2 | .2 | 1.7 | .9 | 3.1 |
| Total Current | 59.9 | 60.7 | 62.4 | 70.4 | 54.4 | 69.0 | 61.6 |
| Fixed Assets (net) | 29.2 | 29.0 | 28.6 | 22.3 | 31.0 | 25.9 | 29.4 |
| Intangibles (net) | 4.5 | 5.0 | 2.7 | 1.8 | 1.8 | 1.7 | 3.9 |
| All Other Non-Current | 6.4 | 5.3 | 6.3 | 5.5 | 12.9 | 3.4 | 5.1 |
| Total | 100.0 | 100.0 | 100.0 | 100.0 | 100.0 | 100.0 | 100.0 |

### LIABILITIES

| | 4/1/09-3/31/10 | 4/1/10-3/31/11 | 4/1/11-3/31/12 | 1-3MM | 3-5MM | 10-25MM | 25MM & OVER |
|---|---|---|---|---|---|---|---|
| Notes Payable-Short Term | 12.3 | 11.2 | 11.9 | 7.8 | 12.2 | 9.8 | 11.9 |
| Cur. Mat.-L.T.D. | 3.7 | 4.6 | 2.9 | .5 | 3.9 | 3.4 | 2.3 |
| Trade Payables | 12.6 | 12.4 | 14.5 | 8.9 | 10.3 | 14.8 | 16.6 |
| Income Taxes Payable | .1 | .1 | .2 | .1 | .3 | .3 | .1 |
| All Other Current | 8.5 | 8.6 | 7.0 | 7.4 | 6.6 | 4.8 | 7.6 |
| Total Current | 37.2 | 36.9 | 36.4 | 24.7 | 33.3 | 33.1 | 38.4 |
| Long-Term Debt | 14.5 | 15.9 | 14.7 | 15.2 | 15.4 | 11.5 | 10.7 |
| Deferred Taxes | .7 | .8 | .7 | .0 | .2 | .6 | 1.0 |
| All Other Non-Current | 8.5 | 8.4 | 10.2 | 29.1 | 4.2 | 13.7 | 8.7 |
| Net Worth | 39.2 | 37.9 | 38.0 | 30.9 | 46.8 | 41.1 | 41.1 |
| Total Liabilities & Net Worth | 100.0 | 100.0 | 100.0 | 100.0 | 100.0 | 100.0 | 100.0 |

### INCOME DATA

| | 4/1/09-3/31/10 | 4/1/10-3/31/11 | 4/1/11-3/31/12 | 1-3MM | 3-5MM | 10-25MM | 25MM & OVER |
|---|---|---|---|---|---|---|---|
| Net Sales | 100.0 | 100.0 | 100.0 | 100.0 | 100.0 | 100.0 | 100.0 |
| Gross Profit | 24.2 | 26.9 | 25.8 | 34.2 | 28.9 | 27.7 | 23.1 |
| Operating Expenses | 22.9 | 22.0 | 21.2 | 35.2 | 26.2 | 20.0 | 16.9 |
| Operating Profit | 1.3 | 4.9 | 4.6 | -1.0 | 2.7 | 7.7 | 6.3 |
| All Other Expenses (net) | 1.5 | 1.0 | .6 | .7 | .7 | .7 | .6 |
| Profit Before Taxes | -.3 | 3.9 | 3.9 | -1.7 | 2.0 | 7.0 | 5.6 |

### RATIOS

| Ratio | 4/1/09-3/31/10 | 4/1/10-3/31/11 | 4/1/11-3/31/12 | 1-3MM | 3-5MM | 10-25MM | 25MM & OVER |
|---|---|---|---|---|---|---|---|
| Current | 3.3 | 3.4 | 3.0 | 11.9 | 2.5 | 5.1 | 2.9 |
| | 1.7 | 1.6 | 1.6 | 3.1 | 1.6 | 2.3 | 1.5 |
| | 1.1 | 1.2 | 1.2 | 1.7 | 1.1 | 1.3 | 1.2 |
| Quick | 1.8 | 1.8 | 1.6 | 3.4 | 1.9 | 2.2 | 1.2 |
| | .8 | .9 | .8 | 1.3 | 1.1 | 1.3 | .8 |
| | .5 | .5 | .6 | .7 | .5 | .7 | .7 |
| Sales/Receivables | 36 / 10.2 | 36 / 10.2 | 35 / 10.4 | 28 / 13.1 | 24 / 15.2 | 31 / 11.7 | 42 / 8.6 |
| | 48 / 7.7 | 43 / 8.4 | 46 / 7.9 | 41 / 8.8 | 50 / 7.3 | 40 / 9.2 | 49 / 7.5 |
| | 63 / 5.8 | 59 / 6.2 | 57 / 6.4 | 63 / 5.8 | 58 / 6.3 | 55 / 6.6 | 59 / 6.2 |
| Cost of Sales/Inventory | 41 / 8.8 | 43 / 8.6 | 35 / 10.4 | 62 / 5.9 | 29 / 12.7 | 42 / 8.6 | 39 / 9.4 |
| | 64 / 5.7 | 59 / 6.2 | 62 / 5.9 | 146 / 2.5 | 51 / 7.1 | 53 / 6.9 | 68 / 5.4 |
| | 98 / 3.7 | 106 / 3.4 | 107 / 3.4 | 192 / 1.9 | 83 / 4.4 | 101 / 3.6 | 99 / 3.7 |
| Cost of Sales/Payables | 17 / 21.4 | 15 / 24.4 | 17 / 21.3 | 10 / 37.9 | 13 / 28.7 | 16 / 22.6 | 20 / 18.5 |
| | 30 / 12.1 | 27 / 13.7 | 30 / 12.0 | 19 / 19.1 | 25 / 14.4 | 27 / 13.5 | 33 / 11.2 |
| | 43 / 8.4 | 41 / 8.8 | 48 / 7.6 | 50 / 7.3 | 43 / 8.5 | 41 / 8.8 | 54 / 6.8 |
| Sales/Working Capital | 4.2 | 4.1 | 4.4 | 2.4 | 3.2 | 3.3 | 5.1 |
| | 7.6 | 9.5 | 9.7 | 3.8 | 7.4 | 8.5 | 10.9 |
| | 25.5 | 22.3 | 23.1 | 7.1 | 49.0 | 22.8 | 20.9 |
| EBIT/Interest | 6.4 | 9.4 | 12.7 | | 7.4 | 14.0 | 18.0 |
| | (107) 1.2 | (97) 3.9 | (105) 5.1 | | (18) 3.8 | (21) 6.5 | (45) 8.2 |
| | -5.3 | 1.3 | 1.9 | | 1.0 | 2.8 | 3.3 |
| Net Profit + Depr., Dep., Amort./Cur. Mat. L/T/D | 3.1 | 7.4 | 7.6 | | | | 10.7 |
| | (34) 1.3 | (31) 3.5 | (33) 4.2 | | | | (21) 4.9 |
| | .0 | 1.6 | 1.9 | | | | 2.3 |
| Fixed/Worth | .3 | .4 | .4 | .1 | .2 | .3 | .4 |
| | .7 | .8 | .7 | .4 | .6 | .7 | .7 |
| | 1.8 | 1.7 | 1.5 | NM | 2.3 | 1.1 | 1.4 |
| Debt/Worth | .4 | .6 | .6 | .2 | .4 | .4 | .6 |
| | 1.5 | 1.5 | 1.4 | .8 | 1.3 | 1.2 | 1.7 |
| | 4.6 | 3.4 | 3.3 | NM | 3.2 | 2.2 | 3.4 |
| % Profit Before Taxes/Tangible Net Worth | 24.4 | 33.7 | 39.5 | | 29.5 | 39.8 | 44.4 |
| | (100) 1.8 | (95) 16.4 | (102) 20.5 | | (19) 8.7 | (22) 25.0 | (42) 21.4 |
| | -19.6 | 3.8 | 6.1 | | -.1 | 16.9 | 11.5 |
| % Profit Before Taxes/Total Assets | 9.6 | 13.8 | 14.5 | 16.5 | 10.5 | 22.7 | 14.9 |
| | .9 | 6.6 | 6.9 | 3.9 | 2.9 | 13.0 | 7.9 |
| | -9.4 | 1.2 | 2.1 | -7.6 | .0 | 4.9 | 4.5 |
| Sales/Net Fixed Assets | 13.1 | 13.1 | 13.0 | 17.4 | 15.4 | 20.6 | 11.5 |
| | 6.4 | 6.6 | 6.9 | 10.8 | 4.6 | 8.6 | 7.1 |
| | 3.6 | 4.2 | 4.2 | 5.6 | 3.3 | 5.5 | 4.6 |
| Sales/Total Assets | 2.2 | 2.4 | 2.6 | 2.8 | 2.7 | 3.0 | 2.3 |
| | 1.7 | 1.9 | 2.1 | 1.8 | 1.7 | 2.3 | 2.0 |
| | 1.3 | 1.4 | 1.4 | 1.3 | 1.0 | 1.8 | 1.4 |
| % Depr., Dep., Amort./Sales | 1.8 | 1.6 | 1.4 | | .9 | 1.2 | 1.3 |
| | (103) 3.4 | (94) 2.9 | (102) 2.8 | | (18) 2.6 | (20) 2.8 | (43) 2.6 |
| | 5.4 | 4.5 | 3.8 | | 5.1 | 3.6 | 3.3 |
| % Officers', Directors' Owners' Comp/Sales | 1.9 | 1.7 | 1.6 | | 4.3 | 1.1 | |
| | (34) 4.2 | (40) 4.3 | (43) 3.0 | | (12) 6.9 | (11) 1.8 | |
| | 5.8 | 6.3 | 6.2 | | 11.9 | 3.5 | |

| | 4/1/09-3/31/10 | 4/1/10-3/31/11 | 4/1/11-3/31/12 | 0-1MM | 1-3MM | 3-5MM | 5-10MM | 10-25MM | 25MM & OVER |
|---|---|---|---|---|---|---|---|---|---|
| Net Sales ($) | 4101749M | 4428017M | 5570072M | 1918M | 21333M | 79920M | 62391M | 373774M | 5030736M |
| Total Assets ($) | 2980570M | 2898334M | 3365815M | 1153M | 12586M | 60361M | 36126M | 168121M | 3087468M |

M = $ thousand     MM = $ million
See Pages 9 through 22 for Explanation of Ratios and Data

## Current Data Sorted by Assets

## Comparative Historical Data

| | | | | | | Type of Statement | | |
|---|---|---|---|---|---|---|---|---|
| | | 1 | 5 | 2 | 2 | Unqualified | 11 | 11 |
| | 1 | 7 | 4 | | | Reviewed | 12 | 9 |
| | | 1 | | | | Compiled | 4 | 3 |
| | | 1 | 1 | | | Tax Returns | 8 | 4 |
| 1 | 1 | 5 | 6 | 1 | 1 | Other | 16 | 21 |
| | 13 (4/1-9/30/11) | | 28 (10/1/11-3/31/12) | | | | 4/1/07-3/31/08 | 4/1/08-3/31/09 |
| 0-500M | 500M-2MM | 2-10MM | 10-50MM | 50-100MM | 100-250MM | | ALL | ALL |
| 1 | 4 | 15 | 15 | 3 | 3 | NUMBER OF STATEMENTS | 51 | 48 |
| % | % | % | % | % | % | ASSETS | % | % |
| | | 6.1 | 11.3 | | | Cash & Equivalents | 7.6 | 4.5 |
| | | 28.3 | 18.4 | | | Trade Receivables (net) | 23.7 | 21.5 |
| | | 37.5 | 31.5 | | | Inventory | 25.9 | 31.7 |
| | | 1.4 | 1.5 | | | All Other Current | 2.2 | 2.3 |
| | | 73.3 | 62.6 | | | Total Current | 59.3 | 60.0 |
| | | 20.5 | 29.1 | | | Fixed Assets (net) | 27.7 | 28.2 |
| | | .3 | 2.2 | | | Intangibles (net) | 6.0 | 6.7 |
| | | 5.9 | 6.1 | | | All Other Non-Current | 6.9 | 5.1 |
| | | 100.0 | 100.0 | | | Total | 100.0 | 100.0 |
| | | | | | | LIABILITIES | | |
| | | 14.5 | 8.8 | | | Notes Payable-Short Term | 12.3 | 10.8 |
| | | 1.9 | 3.7 | | | Cur. Mat.-L.T.D. | 4.9 | 5.6 |
| | | 16.3 | 14.8 | | | Trade Payables | 15.7 | 15.9 |
| | | .1 | .1 | | | Income Taxes Payable | .2 | .1 |
| | | 5.4 | 4.5 | | | All Other Current | 8.2 | 7.0 |
| | | 38.2 | 31.8 | | | Total Current | 41.3 | 39.4 |
| | | 7.7 | 15.6 | | | Long-Term Debt | 18.7 | 24.7 |
| | | 1.3 | 1.3 | | | Deferred Taxes | 1.0 | .9 |
| | | 8.0 | 3.0 | | | All Other Non-Current | 8.0 | 7.0 |
| | | 44.9 | 48.3 | | | Net Worth | 31.0 | 28.0 |
| | | 100.0 | 100.0 | | | Total Liabilities & Net Worth | 100.0 | 100.0 |
| | | | | | | INCOME DATA | | |
| | | 100.0 | 100.0 | | | Net Sales | 100.0 | 100.0 |
| | | 26.1 | 26.4 | | | Gross Profit | 23.7 | 28.2 |
| | | 20.6 | 19.5 | | | Operating Expenses | 19.5 | 23.2 |
| | | 5.5 | 7.0 | | | Operating Profit | 4.3 | 5.0 |
| | | .8 | 1.0 | | | All Other Expenses (net) | 1.8 | 2.3 |
| | | 4.6 | 6.0 | | | Profit Before Taxes | 2.5 | 2.7 |
| | | | | | | RATIOS | | |
| | | 4.1 | 4.0 | | | | 2.4 | 2.9 |
| | | 2.0 | 1.9 | | | Current | 1.5 | 1.6 |
| | | 1.2 | 1.2 | | | | 1.2 | 1.1 |
| | | 1.4 | 1.8 | | | | 1.5 | 1.3 |
| | | .9 | .7 | | | Quick | .9 | .8 |
| | | .5 | .4 | | | | .5 | .4 |
| | | 31  11.9 | 33  10.9 | | | | 29  12.6 | 23  16.2 |
| | | 35  10.3 | 38  9.6 | | | Sales/Receivables | 41  8.9 | 37  9.9 |
| | | 48  7.6 | 47  7.8 | | | | 50  7.3 | 51  7.2 |
| | | 47  7.8 | 63  5.8 | | | | 31  11.7 | 39  9.3 |
| | | 87  4.2 | 96  3.8 | | | Cost of Sales/Inventory | 52  7.0 | 71  5.2 |
| | | 130  2.8 | 114  3.2 | | | | 91  4.0 | 108  3.4 |
| | | 27  13.3 | 23  15.8 | | | | 22  16.8 | 21  17.1 |
| | | 34  10.7 | 39  9.4 | | | Cost of Sales/Payables | 32  11.4 | 31  11.8 |
| | | 45  8.1 | 45  8.1 | | | | 47  7.8 | 43  8.5 |
| | | 3.7 | 2.9 | | | | 6.3 | 5.4 |
| | | 6.5 | 6.6 | | | Sales/Working Capital | 11.5 | 11.7 |
| | | 17.9 | 14.8 | | | | 30.7 | 58.1 |
| | | 11.7 | 18.6 | | | | 14.2 | 8.3 |
| | | (13)  4.3 | (14)  8.5 | | | EBIT/Interest | (47)  3.7 | (46)  1.8 |
| | | 1.6 | 1.9 | | | | 1.0 | -.5 |
| | | | | | | Net Profit + Depr., Dep., | 3.7 | 3.5 |
| | | | | | | Amort./Cur. Mat. L/T/D | (18)  2.4 | (14)  1.1 |
| | | | | | | | .7 | .0 |
| | | .2 | .2 | | | | .4 | .6 |
| | | .6 | .9 | | | Fixed/Worth | 1.0 | 1.4 |
| | | .8 | 1.4 | | | | 3.3 | -8.0 |
| | | .7 | .3 | | | | .9 | 1.0 |
| | | 1.4 | 1.4 | | | Debt/Worth | 2.4 | 3.4 |
| | | 3.3 | 3.6 | | | | 9.2 | -20.6 |
| | | 42.6 | 62.3 | | | % Profit Before Taxes/Tangible | 48.5 | 41.7 |
| | | 20.8 | 17.5 | | | Net Worth | (40)  17.6 | (34)  17.7 |
| | | 1.7 | 8.6 | | | | 5.1 | -14.1 |
| | | 17.0 | 19.6 | | | % Profit Before Taxes/Total | 14.6 | 16.4 |
| | | 5.9 | 6.6 | | | Assets | 6.2 | 4.0 |
| | | 1.0 | 2.3 | | | | .1 | -4.1 |
| | | 24.9 | 13.5 | | | | 17.9 | 16.1 |
| | | 15.3 | 8.0 | | | Sales/Net Fixed Assets | 8.2 | 7.5 |
| | | 7.5 | 3.3 | | | | 4.9 | 4.6 |
| | | 2.5 | 1.9 | | | | 2.5 | 2.7 |
| | | 2.4 | 1.7 | | | Sales/Total Assets | 2.1 | 2.2 |
| | | 1.8 | 1.4 | | | | 1.5 | 1.6 |
| | | .7 | 1.0 | | | | 1.5 | 1.2 |
| | | (13)  1.4 | (14)  1.5 | | | % Depr., Dep., Amort./Sales | (46)  2.6 | (44)  2.3 |
| | | 3.2 | 3.2 | | | | 4.5 | 3.6 |
| | | | | | | % Officers', Directors' | 1.2 | 1.7 |
| | | | | | | Owners' Comp/Sales | (17)  1.9 | (15)  2.7 |
| | | | | | | | 6.3 | 7.5 |
| 1304M | 13182M | 212344M | 525839M | 353247M | 693186M | Net Sales ($) | 1751145M | 2624494M |
| 284M | 5269M | 90308M | 310037M | 185532M | 459436M | Total Assets ($) | 1053354M | 1674757M |

M = $ thousand    MM = $ million
See Pages 9 through 22 for Explanation of Ratios and Data

## Comparative Historical Data / Current Data Sorted by Sales

| 10 / 13 / 8 / 2 / 23 | 13 / 14 / 2 / 4 / 16 | 10 / 12 / 1 / 3 / 15 | Type of Statement<br>Unqualified<br>Reviewed<br>Compiled<br>Tax Returns<br>Other | 0-1MM | 1-3MM | 3-5MM | 5-10MM | 10-25MM | 25MM & OVER |
|---|---|---|---|---|---|---|---|---|---|
| | | | Unqualified | | | | | 1 | 9 |
| | | | Reviewed | | | | 1 | 7 | 2 |
| | | | Compiled | | | | | 1 | |
| | | | Tax Returns | 2 | | 1 | 1 | | |
| | | | Other | | 2 | 1 | | 5 | 7 |
| **4/1/09-3/31/10 ALL** | **4/1/10-3/31/11 ALL** | **4/1/11-3/31/12 ALL** | | | **13 (4/1-9/30/11)** | | | **28 (10/1/11-3/31/12)** | |
| 56 | 49 | 41 | **NUMBER OF STATEMENTS** | 2 | 2 | 4 | 4 | 13 | 18 |
| % | % | % | **ASSETS** | % | % | % | % | % | % |
| 4.4 | 7.5 | 7.9 | Cash & Equivalents | | | | | 9.3 | 7.2 |
| 23.5 | 23.3 | 23.5 | Trade Receivables (net) | | | | | 28.6 | 19.2 |
| 26.6 | 29.3 | 33.8 | Inventory | | | | | 31.5 | 31.3 |
| 1.4 | 2.5 | 1.3 | All Other Current | | | | | .6 | 1.5 |
| 55.9 | 62.6 | 66.5 | Total Current | | | | | 69.9 | 59.3 |
| 26.5 | 26.4 | 24.5 | Fixed Assets (net) | | | | | 22.1 | 28.2 |
| 12.3 | 5.1 | 4.1 | Intangibles (net) | | | | | .8 | 8.9 |
| 5.3 | 5.9 | 4.8 | All Other Non-Current | | | | | 7.2 | 3.6 |
| 100.0 | 100.0 | 100.0 | Total | | | | | 100.0 | 100.0 |
| | | | **LIABILITIES** | | | | | | |
| 9.4 | 9.1 | 10.2 | Notes Payable-Short Term | | | | | 11.8 | 8.8 |
| 8.3 | 3.7 | 2.5 | Cur. Mat.-L.T.D. | | | | | 1.5 | 3.6 |
| 15.3 | 14.2 | 17.0 | Trade Payables | | | | | 15.7 | 16.5 |
| .2 | .4 | .1 | Income Taxes Payable | | | | | .1 | .0 |
| 7.1 | 6.5 | 5.7 | All Other Current | | | | | 5.7 | 4.8 |
| 40.4 | 33.9 | 35.5 | Total Current | | | | | 34.8 | 33.8 |
| 22.2 | 18.7 | 17.9 | Long-Term Debt | | | | | 7.4 | 24.1 |
| .9 | 1.1 | 1.2 | Deferred Taxes | | | | | 1.0 | 1.5 |
| 7.3 | 6.8 | 6.5 | All Other Non-Current | | | | | 6.5 | 8.3 |
| 29.3 | 39.5 | 38.9 | Net Worth | | | | | 50.2 | 32.3 |
| 100.0 | 100.0 | 100.0 | Total Liabilities & Net Worth | | | | | 100.0 | 100.0 |
| | | | **INCOME DATA** | | | | | | |
| 100.0 | 100.0 | 100.0 | Net Sales | | | | | 100.0 | 100.0 |
| 27.8 | 27.4 | 26.2 | Gross Profit | | | | | 23.8 | 26.9 |
| 23.2 | 22.0 | 20.3 | Operating Expenses | | | | | 19.0 | 19.7 |
| 4.6 | 5.4 | 5.8 | Operating Profit | | | | | 4.7 | 7.2 |
| 1.7 | 1.7 | .8 | All Other Expenses (net) | | | | | .8 | .8 |
| 2.9 | 3.7 | 5.0 | Profit Before Taxes | | | | | 3.9 | 6.4 |
| | | | **RATIOS** | | | | | | |
| 2.4 | 2.5 | 3.0 | Current | | | | | 4.2 | 2.7 |
| 1.3 | 1.9 | 2.0 | | | | | | 1.9 | 1.8 |
| 1.0 | 1.3 | 1.3 | | | | | | 1.4 | 1.2 |
| 1.4 | 1.6 | 1.6 | Quick | | | | | 3.2 | 1.5 |
| .7 | 1.0 | .8 | | | | | | .9 | .7 |
| .5 | .5 | .5 | | | | | | .5 | .4 |
| 32  11.5 | 29  12.4 | 31  11.9 | Sales/Receivables | | | | | 24  15.0 | 34  10.7 |
| 40  9.2 | 42  8.8 | 38  9.6 | | | | | | 46  8.0 | 38  9.5 |
| 51  7.1 | 54  6.7 | 47  7.7 | | | | | | 60  6.1 | 46  7.9 |
| 39  9.3 | 43  8.5 | 57  6.4 | Cost of Sales/Inventory | | | | | 29  12.8 | 63  5.8 |
| 57  6.5 | 65  5.6 | 89  4.1 | | | | | | 87  4.2 | 94  3.9 |
| 100  3.6 | 116  3.2 | 118  3.1 | | | | | | 104  3.5 | 111  3.3 |
| 20  18.1 | 20  18.0 | 27  13.4 | Cost of Sales/Payables | | | | | 23  15.6 | 30  12.2 |
| 35  10.4 | 30  12.3 | 35  10.4 | | | | | | 35  10.4 | 41  8.9 |
| 48  7.6 | 51  7.2 | 47  7.7 | | | | | | 45  8.2 | 50  7.3 |
| 5.2 | 5.3 | 4.1 | Sales/Working Capital | | | | | 3.6 | 4.9 |
| 14.6 | 7.7 | 6.5 | | | | | | 6.1 | 7.3 |
| 536.7 | 12.7 | 15.1 | | | | | | 14.4 | 22.6 |
| 4.2 | 15.8 | 13.1 | EBIT/Interest | | | | | 14.2 | 19.6 |
| (50) 1.7 | (46) 3.0 | (38) 4.1 | | | | | | (11) 6.1 | (17) 3.6 |
| .9 | .7 | 1.8 | | | | | | 2.0 | 1.9 |
| 2.8 | 6.4 | 11.7 | Net Profit + Depr., Dep., Amort./Cur. Mat. L/T/D | | | | | | |
| (18) 1.6 | (19) 2.0 | (12) 2.5 | | | | | | | |
| .2 | 1.4 | 1.0 | | | | | | | |
| .6 | .4 | .3 | Fixed/Worth | | | | | .2 | .5 |
| 1.3 | .6 | .8 | | | | | | .4 | 1.1 |
| -5.2 | 2.1 | 1.5 | | | | | | .8 | NM |
| 1.2 | .7 | .8 | Debt/Worth | | | | | .3 | .9 |
| 3.3 | 1.6 | 1.6 | | | | | | 1.4 | 2.9 |
| -15.4 | 10.4 | 4.6 | | | | | | 3.1 | NM |
| 41.4 | 48.8 | 43.7 | % Profit Before Taxes/Tangible Net Worth | | | | | 45.4 | 63.9 |
| (40) 15.0 | (42) 14.6 | (36) 19.1 | | | | | | 13.0 | (14) 21.4 |
| 2.7 | 2.9 | 7.3 | | | | | | 1.8 | 14.4 |
| 8.7 | 16.5 | 15.7 | % Profit Before Taxes/Total Assets | | | | | 14.6 | 16.2 |
| 3.1 | 6.3 | 4.8 | | | | | | 5.9 | 6.3 |
| .1 | .4 | 1.3 | | | | | | .9 | 3.1 |
| 17.1 | 18.4 | 16.8 | Sales/Net Fixed Assets | | | | | 24.1 | 13.3 |
| 7.8 | 8.9 | 8.6 | | | | | | 13.7 | 7.6 |
| 4.8 | 3.6 | 5.5 | | | | | | 5.6 | 3.9 |
| 2.5 | 2.4 | 2.5 | Sales/Total Assets | | | | | 2.4 | 2.4 |
| 2.0 | 1.9 | 1.9 | | | | | | 1.9 | 1.7 |
| 1.5 | 1.5 | 1.5 | | | | | | 1.6 | 1.4 |
| 1.4 | 1.2 | 1.0 | % Depr., Dep., Amort./Sales | | | | | .7 | 1.1 |
| (48) 2.3 | (43) 2.3 | (36) 1.7 | | | | | | (12) 1.4 | (17) 1.8 |
| 4.2 | 4.3 | 3.9 | | | | | | 2.8 | 4.5 |
| 1.8 | .4 | 1.8 | % Officers', Directors' Owners' Comp/Sales | | | | | | |
| (18) 4.3 | (18) 2.7 | (13) 3.0 | | | | | | | |
| 6.0 | 4.9 | 5.1 | | | | | | | |
| 2017690M | 1909197M | 1799102M | Net Sales ($) | | 2576M | 16780M | 29231M | 231910M | 1518605M |
| 1342283M | 1177700M | 1050866M | Total Assets ($) | | 1528M | 6780M | 15616M | 112234M | 914708M |

M = $ thousand    MM = $ million
See Pages 9 through 22 for Explanation of Ratios and Data

**Current Data Sorted by Assets**       **Comparative Historical Data**

Date groupings: 9 (4/1-9/30/11) over 500M-2MM; 51 (10/1/11-3/31/12) over 2-10MM through 100-250MM.

| | 0-500M | 500M-2MM | 2-10MM | 10-50MM | 50-100MM | 100-250MM | | 4/1/07-3/31/08 ALL | 4/1/08-3/31/09 ALL |
|---|---|---|---|---|---|---|---|---|---|
| **Type of Statement** | | | | | | | | | |
| Unqualified | | | 4 | 8 | 3 | 2 | | 20 | 20 |
| Reviewed | | 2 | 5 | 1 | | | | 18 | 13 |
| Compiled | | 2 | 3 | | 1 | | | 8 | 13 |
| Tax Returns | | 2 | | | | | | 3 | 3 |
| Other | | 3 | 12 | 7 | 3 | 2 | | 31 | 40 |
| **NUMBER OF STATEMENTS** | 9 | 9 | 24 | 16 | 7 | 4 | | 80 | 89 |
| | % | % | % | % | % | % | | % | % |
| **ASSETS** | | | | | | | | | |
| Cash & Equivalents | | | 9.8 | 4.5 | | | | 8.5 | 4.8 |
| Trade Receivables (net) | | | 26.8 | 28.7 | | | | 25.7 | 25.9 |
| Inventory | | | 22.9 | 24.4 | | | | 20.7 | 24.0 |
| All Other Current | | | 2.5 | 1.8 | | | | 3.1 | 4.1 |
| Total Current | | | 62.0 | 59.4 | | | | 58.1 | 58.8 |
| Fixed Assets (net) | | | 31.3 | 33.8 | | | | 33.6 | 33.2 |
| Intangibles (net) | | | 2.3 | 3.4 | | | | 2.3 | 3.2 |
| All Other Non-Current | | | 4.4 | 3.4 | | | | 6.0 | 4.8 |
| Total | | | 100.0 | 100.0 | | | | 100.0 | 100.0 |
| **LIABILITIES** | | | | | | | | | |
| Notes Payable-Short Term | | | 7.3 | 8.4 | | | | 5.9 | 12.0 |
| Cur. Mat.-L.T.D. | | | 3.2 | 2.7 | | | | 3.3 | 4.7 |
| Trade Payables | | | 10.4 | 13.1 | | | | 14.7 | 14.4 |
| Income Taxes Payable | | | .0 | .2 | | | | .1 | .1 |
| All Other Current | | | 9.2 | 7.6 | | | | 7.7 | 7.5 |
| Total Current | | | 30.2 | 32.0 | | | | 31.6 | 38.7 |
| Long-Term Debt | | | 14.1 | 18.7 | | | | 22.1 | 19.5 |
| Deferred Taxes | | | .1 | 1.0 | | | | .4 | .6 |
| All Other Non-Current | | | 5.7 | 3.8 | | | | 5.2 | 6.5 |
| Net Worth | | | 49.9 | 44.5 | | | | 40.6 | 34.8 |
| Total Liabilities & Net Worth | | | 100.0 | 100.0 | | | | 100.0 | 100.0 |
| **INCOME DATA** | | | | | | | | | |
| Net Sales | | | 100.0 | 100.0 | | | | 100.0 | 100.0 |
| Gross Profit | | | 28.0 | 17.5 | | | | 23.2 | 23.6 |
| Operating Expenses | | | 22.3 | 12.6 | | | | 18.3 | 21.3 |
| Operating Profit | | | 5.7 | 4.8 | | | | 4.9 | 2.2 |
| All Other Expenses (net) | | | 1.3 | .5 | | | | 1.1 | 1.1 |
| Profit Before Taxes | | | 4.4 | 4.3 | | | | 3.8 | 1.1 |
| **RATIOS** | | | | | | | | | |
| Current | | | 3.9 | 2.4 | | | | 2.7 | 2.6 |
| | | | 2.2 | 1.7 | | | | 1.8 | 1.5 |
| | | | 1.4 | 1.2 | | | | 1.2 | 1.2 |
| Quick | | | 2.4 | 1.4 | | | | 1.6 | 1.4 |
| | | | 1.2 | 1.1 | | | | 1.1 | .8 |
| | | | .8 | .7 | | | | .6 | .5 |
| Sales/Receivables | | | 30   12.2 | 34   10.7 | | | | 30   12.1 | 25   14.4 |
| | | | 38   9.5 | 47   7.7 | | | | 42   8.8 | 37   9.9 |
| | | | 55   6.6 | 60   6.1 | | | | 52   7.1 | 50   7.3 |
| Cost of Sales/Inventory | | | 30   12.2 | 29   12.5 | | | | 24   15.3 | 30   12.2 |
| | | | 45   8.1 | 46   8.0 | | | | 40   9.1 | 38   9.7 |
| | | | 59   6.2 | 63   5.8 | | | | 57   6.5 | 67   5.5 |
| Cost of Sales/Payables | | | 11   33.2 | 15   24.5 | | | | 16   22.5 | 14   26.5 |
| | | | 18   19.8 | 27   13.3 | | | | 28   13.3 | 25   14.9 |
| | | | 32   11.4 | 40   9.2 | | | | 39   9.4 | 34   10.6 |
| Sales/Working Capital | | | 5.3 | 4.6 | | | | 6.0 | 6.2 |
| | | | 6.9 | 10.9 | | | | 10.3 | 13.1 |
| | | | 15.1 | 22.1 | | | | 24.3 | 55.6 |
| EBIT/Interest | | | 16.3 | 38.5 | | | | 7.7 | 9.0 |
| | | | (21) 2.5 | 7.8 | | | | (74) 3.9 | (84) 3.3 |
| | | | .8 | 1.5 | | | | .7 | -.1 |
| Net Profit + Depr., Dep., Amort./Cur. Mat. L/T/D | | | | | | | | 5.5 | 4.5 |
| | | | | | | | | (27) 2.5 | (28) 2.8 |
| | | | | | | | | 1.3 | 1.7 |
| Fixed/Worth | | | .4 | .5 | | | | .4 | .5 |
| | | | .6 | .7 | | | | .9 | .9 |
| | | | 1.7 | 1.8 | | | | 1.8 | 5.3 |
| Debt/Worth | | | .5 | .5 | | | | .5 | .7 |
| | | | .8 | 1.1 | | | | 1.4 | 1.9 |
| | | | 3.3 | 3.2 | | | | 4.8 | 10.8 |
| % Profit Before Taxes/Tangible Net Worth | | | 41.2 | 35.4 | | | | 36.1 | 32.3 |
| | | | (23) 15.8 | (15) 11.3 | | | | (73) 20.0 | (76) 14.6 |
| | | | 2.0 | -1.2 | | | | .3 | 3.3 |
| % Profit Before Taxes/Total Assets | | | 19.2 | 16.4 | | | | 16.0 | 12.8 |
| | | | 6.9 | 6.1 | | | | 7.9 | 4.4 |
| | | | .6 | .4 | | | | -.7 | -1.8 |
| Sales/Net Fixed Assets | | | 13.2 | 12.1 | | | | 13.7 | 15.5 |
| | | | 7.8 | 5.5 | | | | 7.4 | 8.3 |
| | | | 4.4 | 4.2 | | | | 3.5 | 4.1 |
| Sales/Total Assets | | | 3.0 | 2.5 | | | | 3.0 | 3.3 |
| | | | 2.0 | 2.1 | | | | 2.3 | 2.4 |
| | | | 1.8 | 1.8 | | | | 1.5 | 1.7 |
| % Depr., Dep., Amort./Sales | | | 1.1 | 1.9 | | | | 1.5 | 1.4 |
| | | | (23) 2.5 | (15) 2.6 | | | | (74) 2.7 | (77) 2.1 |
| | | | 5.0 | 3.7 | | | | 4.4 | 3.9 |
| % Officers', Directors' Owners' Comp/Sales | | | | | | | | 1.0 | 1.7 |
| | | | | | | | | (22) 2.7 | (22) 3.4 |
| | | | | | | | | 4.7 | 4.8 |
| Net Sales ($) | | 37245M | 309999M | 815377M | 804049M | 1001796M | | 4432832M | 4188094M |
| Total Assets ($) | | 10450M | 129773M | 384622M | 477081M | 672030M | | 2227113M | 2095623M |

Note: "DATA NOT AVAILABLE" printed vertically across the 0-500M and 500M-2MM columns.

## Comparative Historical Data / Current Data Sorted by Sales

| | | | Type of Statement | 0-1MM | 1-3MM | 3-5MM | 5-10MM | 10-25MM | 25MM & OVER |
|---|---|---|---|---|---|---|---|---|---|
| 18 | 15 | 17 | Unqualified | | | | | 5 | 12 |
| 14 | 13 | 8 | Reviewed | | 2 | | 3 | 3 | 1 |
| 8 | 5 | 6 | Compiled | 1 | 2 | 1 | 1 | 1 | |
| 3 | 4 | 2 | Tax Returns | 1 | | 1 | | | |
| 23 | 33 | 27 | Other | | 2 | 2 | 7 | 5 | 13 |
| 4/1/09- 3/31/10 ALL | 4/1/10- 3/31/11 ALL | 4/1/11- 3/31/12 ALL | | | 9 (4/1-9/30/11) | | 51 (10/1/11-3/31/12) | | |
| 66 | 70 | 60 | **NUMBER OF STATEMENTS** | | 4 | 4 | 12 | 14 | 26 |
| % | % | % | **ASSETS** | % | % | % | % | % | % |
| 7.5 | 6.0 | 8.4 | Cash & Equivalents | | | | 10.8 | 7.7 | 6.0 |
| 25.1 | 26.4 | 27.0 | Trade Receivables (net) | | | | 25.4 | 31.4 | 25.9 |
| 19.8 | 22.0 | 23.6 | Inventory | | | | 26.1 | 19.3 | 22.3 |
| 2.6 | 1.9 | 2.2 | All Other Current | | DATA | | .6 | 4.2 | 1.5 |
| 55.0 | 56.3 | 61.1 | Total Current | | NOT | | 62.9 | 62.7 | 55.7 |
| 34.0 | 30.8 | 30.5 | Fixed Assets (net) | | AVAILABLE | | 28.7 | 33.4 | 32.8 |
| 5.5 | 5.9 | 2.8 | Intangibles (net) | | | | 3.8 | .7 | 4.1 |
| 5.5 | 7.1 | 5.6 | All Other Non-Current | | | | 4.6 | 3.3 | 7.5 |
| 100.0 | 100.0 | 100.0 | Total | | | | 100.0 | 100.0 | 100.0 |
| | | | **LIABILITIES** | | | | | | |
| 9.0 | 12.1 | 6.8 | Notes Payable-Short Term | | | | 10.7 | 5.4 | 6.6 |
| 6.0 | 4.5 | 3.3 | Cur. Mat.-L.T.D. | | | | 4.4 | 3.9 | 2.6 |
| 14.5 | 16.9 | 12.0 | Trade Payables | | | | 9.6 | 14.0 | 11.6 |
| .0 | .0 | .0 | Income Taxes Payable | | | | .0 | .0 | .1 |
| 7.0 | 8.5 | 7.2 | All Other Current | | | | 5.8 | 11.5 | 6.7 |
| 36.6 | 42.1 | 29.4 | Total Current | | | | 30.5 | 34.8 | 27.6 |
| 17.0 | 19.3 | 17.8 | Long-Term Debt | | | | 23.3 | 13.5 | 17.7 |
| .5 | .7 | .6 | Deferred Taxes | | | | .0 | .2 | 1.4 |
| 8.6 | 8.8 | 7.6 | All Other Non-Current | | | | 8.0 | 1.3 | 6.7 |
| 37.2 | 29.1 | 44.6 | Net Worth | | | | 38.2 | 50.2 | 46.6 |
| 100.0 | 100.0 | 100.0 | Total Liabilities & Net Worth | | | | 100.0 | 100.0 | 100.0 |
| | | | **INCOME DATA** | | | | | | |
| 100.0 | 100.0 | 100.0 | Net Sales | | | | 100.0 | 100.0 | 100.0 |
| 25.8 | 26.0 | 24.4 | Gross Profit | | | | 29.9 | 26.7 | 18.0 |
| 23.4 | 21.0 | 19.3 | Operating Expenses | | | | 25.7 | 20.2 | 12.8 |
| 2.4 | 5.0 | 5.1 | Operating Profit | | | | 4.2 | 6.5 | 5.1 |
| 1.6 | 1.2 | 1.1 | All Other Expenses (net) | | | | 1.2 | 1.4 | 1.0 |
| .8 | 3.8 | 4.0 | Profit Before Taxes | | | | 3.0 | 5.1 | 4.2 |
| | | | **RATIOS** | | | | | | |
| 2.8 | 2.4 | 3.9 | | | | | 4.4 | 2.6 | 3.7 |
| 1.6 | 1.5 | 1.9 | Current | | | | 2.1 | 1.9 | 1.8 |
| 1.0 | 1.1 | 1.5 | | | | | 1.5 | 1.4 | 1.3 |
| 1.7 | 1.3 | 2.0 | | | | | 2.1 | 1.8 | 2.0 |
| .9 | .8 | 1.2 | Quick | | | | 1.3 | 1.2 | 1.1 |
| .5 | .5 | .7 | | | | | .4 | .8 | .7 |
| 32  11.3 | 32  11.3 | 29  12.4 | | | | | 27  13.5 | 33  11.1 | 31  11.6 |
| 47  7.8 | 45  8.2 | 41  8.8 | Sales/Receivables | | | | 30  12.2 | 45  8.2 | 45  8.1 |
| 57  6.4 | 53  6.9 | 56  6.5 | | | | | 36  10.1 | 57  6.4 | 59  6.2 |
| 30  12.0 | 32  11.6 | 33  10.9 | | | | | 29  12.6 | 29  12.8 | 36  10.1 |
| 43  8.5 | 44  8.3 | 47  7.8 | Cost of Sales/Inventory | | | | 44  8.3 | 40  9.2 | 47  7.7 |
| 67  5.5 | 72  5.1 | 59  6.2 | | | | | 94  3.9 | 53  6.9 | 58  6.3 |
| 15  24.7 | 20  18.1 | 13  28.2 | | | | | 7  55.0 | 13  28.5 | 14  26.9 |
| 28  13.0 | 31  11.7 | 23  16.2 | Cost of Sales/Payables | | | | 12  29.3 | 28  13.2 | 27  13.3 |
| 44  8.3 | 45  8.1 | 38  9.5 | | | | | 21  17.3 | 46  7.9 | 40  9.2 |
| 5.3 | 6.1 | 4.4 | | | | | 5.7 | 5.5 | 4.1 |
| 12.0 | 12.5 | 7.5 | Sales/Working Capital | | | | 7.4 | 7.1 | 8.7 |
| NM | 45.2 | 16.9 | | | | | 16.2 | 17.2 | 20.7 |
| 8.6 | 14.3 | 21.9 | | | | | 5.5 | 20.5 | 63.5 |
| (57) 2.7 | (68) 4.9 | (55) 4.6 | EBIT/Interest | | | | (11) 1.9 | (13) 9.9 | (24) 7.0 |
| -1.2 | 1.2 | 1.5 | | | | | .4 | 2.1 | 1.5 |
| 7.8 | 6.4 | 12.4 | | | | | | | 22.6 |
| (22) 3.7 | (23) 3.5 | (22) 3.0 | Net Profit + Depr., Dep., Amort./Cur. Mat. L/T/D | | | | | (11) | 3.0 |
| 1.1 | 1.4 | 1.9 | | | | | | | 1.5 |
| .5 | .5 | .4 | | | | | .2 | .5 | .4 |
| 1.1 | 1.1 | .6 | Fixed/Worth | | | | 1.3 | .6 | .6 |
| 3.8 | 3.5 | 1.9 | | | | | 4.3 | .8 | 1.6 |
| .8 | .7 | .5 | | | | | .5 | .5 | .5 |
| 1.8 | 1.8 | 1.2 | Debt/Worth | | | | 3.4 | .8 | 1.2 |
| 8.4 | 7.2 | 3.4 | | | | | 15.6 | 1.6 | 2.6 |
| 42.8 | 47.9 | 33.7 | | | | | 45.2 | 41.2 | 26.8 |
| (57) 15.7 | (57) 17.7 | (54) 17.5 | % Profit Before Taxes/Tangible Net Worth | | | | (11) 17.5 | (13) 28.1 | (24) 17.3 |
| -8.8 | 2.5 | 4.8 | | | | | -10.1 | 3.4 | 8.4 |
| 15.0 | 12.4 | 15.7 | | | | | 8.8 | 22.6 | 16.2 |
| 3.9 | 6.5 | 6.8 | % Profit Before Taxes/Total Assets | | | | 6.8 | 11.1 | 6.4 |
| -10.1 | .4 | 1.9 | | | | | -1.6 | 1.8 | 2.3 |
| 13.2 | 14.5 | 13.6 | | | | | 23.0 | 14.8 | 10.3 |
| 7.1 | 6.4 | 6.6 | Sales/Net Fixed Assets | | | | 7.6 | 7.3 | 6.1 |
| 3.4 | 4.0 | 4.2 | | | | | 3.8 | 3.9 | 4.1 |
| 2.6 | 2.6 | 2.6 | | | | | 3.9 | 3.3 | 2.5 |
| 2.0 | 1.9 | 2.0 | Sales/Total Assets | | | | 1.9 | 2.3 | 1.9 |
| 1.5 | 1.5 | 1.8 | | | | | 1.8 | 1.8 | 1.6 |
| 2.2 | 1.6 | 1.5 | | | | | 1.7 | .7 | 1.9 |
| (62) 3.1 | (63) 2.8 | (54) 2.5 | % Depr., Dep., Amort./Sales | | | | (11) 4.8 | 2.4 | (22) 2.6 |
| 5.3 | 4.7 | 4.8 | | | | | 6.6 | 4.7 | 4.1 |
| .7 | .9 | .9 | | | | | | | |
| (16) 4.4 | (17) 2.3 | (14) 3.7 | % Officers', Directors' Owners' Comp/Sales | | | | | | |
| 9.0 | 4.2 | 5.6 | | | | | | | |
| 2526183M | 2696067M | 2968466M | Net Sales ($) | | 8924M | 17248M | 85577M | 239968M | 2616749M |
| 1500331M | 1478391M | 1673956M | Total Assets ($) | | 3910M | 8222M | 38749M | 103051M | 1520024M |

**Current Data Sorted by Assets**      **Comparative Historical Data**

| 0-500M | 500M-2MM | 2-10MM | 10-50MM | 50-100MM | 100-250MM | Type of Statement | 4/1/07-3/31/08 | 4/1/08-3/31/09 |
|---|---|---|---|---|---|---|---|---|
| | | 3 | 6 | 2 | 3 | Unqualified | 10 | 11 |
| | | 5 | 1 | 1 | | Reviewed | 7 | 6 |
| | | 1 | 1 | | | Compiled | 1 | 1 |
| | | 1 | | | | Tax Returns | | 3 |
| | 2 | 4 | 4 | 1 | 1 | Other | 10 | 13 |
| | 7 (4/1-9/30/11) | | 29 (10/1/11-3/31/12) | | | | ALL | ALL |
| 0-500M | 500M-2MM | 2-10MM | 10-50MM | 50-100MM | 100-250MM | **NUMBER OF STATEMENTS** | 28 | 34 |
| | 2 | 14 | 12 | 4 | 4 | | | |
| % | % | % | % | % | % | **ASSETS** | % | % |
| | | 5.7 | 6.8 | | | Cash & Equivalents | 7.3 | 7.0 |
| | | 23.1 | 25.9 | | | Trade Receivables (net) | 22.8 | 21.6 |
| | | 17.1 | 20.2 | | | Inventory | 15.1 | 16.3 |
| | | 4.0 | 1.9 | | | All Other Current | 1.9 | 2.0 |
| | | 50.0 | 54.8 | | | Total Current | 47.1 | 46.9 |
| | | 45.9 | 34.0 | | | Fixed Assets (net) | 40.8 | 41.3 |
| | | .1 | 3.9 | | | Intangibles (net) | 5.1 | 5.3 |
| | | 4.0 | 7.4 | | | All Other Non-Current | 7.0 | 6.5 |
| | | 100.0 | 100.0 | | | Total | 100.0 | 100.0 |
| | | | | | | **LIABILITIES** | | |
| | | 4.4 | 9.8 | | | Notes Payable-Short Term | 7.7 | 7.7 |
| | | 4.3 | 5.7 | | | Cur. Mat.-L.T.D. | 4.0 | 3.7 |
| | | 15.1 | 17.3 | | | Trade Payables | 13.8 | 13.6 |
| | | .6 | .0 | | | Income Taxes Payable | .1 | .1 |
| | | 9.3 | 6.8 | | | All Other Current | 6.1 | 7.6 |
| | | 33.6 | 39.6 | | | Total Current | 31.7 | 32.8 |
| | | 27.1 | 13.8 | | | Long-Term Debt | 27.8 | 21.2 |
| | | 1.5 | 1.0 | | | Deferred Taxes | 1.0 | .9 |
| | | 1.4 | 10.6 | | | All Other Non-Current | 3.9 | 3.6 |
| | | 36.5 | 35.0 | | | Net Worth | 35.6 | 41.5 |
| | | 100.0 | 100.0 | | | Total Liabilities & Net Worth | 100.0 | 100.0 |
| | | | | | | **INCOME DATA** | | |
| | | 100.0 | 100.0 | | | Net Sales | 100.0 | 100.0 |
| | | 25.3 | 22.2 | | | Gross Profit | 23.4 | 22.6 |
| | | 19.8 | 16.6 | | | Operating Expenses | 16.9 | 17.7 |
| | | 5.5 | 5.6 | | | Operating Profit | 6.6 | 4.9 |
| | | 1.4 | .6 | | | All Other Expenses (net) | 1.8 | 1.4 |
| | | 4.1 | 5.1 | | | Profit Before Taxes | 4.7 | 3.5 |
| | | | | | | **RATIOS** | | |
| | | 2.3 | 2.5 | | | Current | 1.7 | 2.4 |
| | | 1.6 | 1.2 | | | | 1.3 | 1.4 |
| | | 1.0 | 1.0 | | | | 1.0 | .9 |
| | | 1.2 | 1.5 | | | Quick | 1.1 | 1.4 |
| | | .9 | .8 | | | | .7 | .7 |
| | | .7 | .5 | | | | .6 | .5 |
| | | 28   13.2 | 27   13.6 | | | Sales/Receivables | 30   12.1 | 24   15.4 |
| | | 38   9.7 | 41   8.8 | | | | 42   8.6 | 32   11.4 |
| | | 42   8.6 | 52   7.0 | | | | 54   6.7 | 45   8.1 |
| | | 19   19.0 | 23   15.7 | | | Cost of Sales/Inventory | 28   13.2 | 23   16.1 |
| | | 46   8.0 | 31   11.8 | | | | 35   10.4 | 30   12.1 |
| | | 60   6.1 | 56   6.5 | | | | 51   7.1 | 43   8.4 |
| | | 24   15.4 | 19   19.7 | | | Cost of Sales/Payables | 22   16.3 | 17   22.1 |
| | | 27   13.5 | 37   9.8 | | | | 33   11.2 | 30   12.1 |
| | | 36   10.1 | 46   7.9 | | | | 54   6.8 | 39   9.4 |
| | | 7.7 | 5.7 | | | Sales/Working Capital | 8.8 | 7.3 |
| | | 13.0 | 22.7 | | | | 20.0 | 12.0 |
| | | NM | NM | | | | 91.0 | -36.8 |
| | | 9.7 | 40.6 | | | EBIT/Interest | 8.0 | 10.4 |
| | | 3.8 | 9.0 | | | | (27) 2.8 | (32) 1.9 |
| | | 1.0 | .6 | | | | 1.3 | 1.2 |
| | | | | | | Net Profit + Depr., Dep., | 13.7 | 3.3 |
| | | | | | | Amort./Cur. Mat. L/T/D | (12) 3.4 | (12) 2.1 |
| | | | | | | | 1.6 | 1.0 |
| | | .5 | .3 | | | Fixed/Worth | .6 | .4 |
| | | 1.5 | 1.1 | | | | 1.6 | 1.2 |
| | | 3.0 | 2.4 | | | | 2.5 | 2.4 |
| | | 1.0 | 1.2 | | | Debt/Worth | 1.3 | .8 |
| | | 1.5 | 2.4 | | | | 2.1 | 2.1 |
| | | 4.6 | 2.5 | | | | 4.4 | 3.8 |
| | | 64.3 | 73.6 | | | % Profit Before Taxes/Tangible | 30.2 | 36.1 |
| | | (13) 13.0 | (11) 33.4 | | | Net Worth | (25) 12.8 | (31) 6.9 |
| | | 2.8 | 5.7 | | | | 1.8 | .2 |
| | | 16.5 | 14.1 | | | % Profit Before Taxes/Total | 10.9 | 18.0 |
| | | 5.3 | 7.9 | | | Assets | 4.3 | 2.8 |
| | | .1 | -1.9 | | | | 1.0 | .8 |
| | | 12.2 | 18.2 | | | Sales/Net Fixed Assets | 8.8 | 17.6 |
| | | 4.8 | 9.0 | | | | 4.3 | 4.5 |
| | | 1.9 | 4.2 | | | | 2.4 | 2.7 |
| | | 3.2 | 2.6 | | | Sales/Total Assets | 2.2 | 2.8 |
| | | 2.1 | 2.4 | | | | 1.6 | 2.0 |
| | | 1.2 | 1.4 | | | | 1.1 | 1.5 |
| | | 2.3 | 1.5 | | | % Depr., Dep., Amort./Sales | 1.6 | 1.7 |
| | | (13) 3.3 | (11) 2.8 | | | | (24) 3.9 | (29) 2.9 |
| | | 4.8 | 5.4 | | | | 5.4 | 5.2 |
| | | | | | | % Officers', Directors' Owners' Comp/Sales | | |
| 5888M | | 160378M | 595568M | 740811M | 999233M | Net Sales ($) | 2143560M | 2587317M |
| 2377M | | 69275M | 260497M | 262427M | 705190M | Total Assets ($) | 1372486M | 1466133M |

*(The 0-500M and 500M-2MM columns are marked "DATA NOT AVAILABLE" for most rows.)*

M = $ thousand    MM = $ million
See Pages 9 through 22 for Explanation of Ratios and Data

## Comparative Historical Data

## Current Data Sorted by Sales

| 4/1/09-3/31/10 ALL | 4/1/10-3/31/11 ALL | 4/1/11-3/31/12 ALL | Type of Statement | 0-1MM | 1-3MM | 3-5MM | 5-10MM | 10-25MM | 25MM & OVER |
|---|---|---|---|---|---|---|---|---|---|
| 12 | 12 | 14 | Unqualified | | 1 | | 1 | 2 | 10 |
| 7 | 5 | 7 | Reviewed | 1 | | | 2 | 1 | 3 |
| | 1 | 2 | Compiled | | | | 1 | | 1 |
| 2 | 1 | 1 | Tax Returns | | | | 1 | | |
| 13 | 15 | 12 | Other | 2 | 1 | | 1 | 3 | 5 |
| | | | | 7 (4/1-9/30/11) | | | 29 (10/1/11-3/31/12) | | |
| 34 | 34 | 36 | **NUMBER OF STATEMENTS** | 3 | 2 | | 6 | 6 | 19 |
| % | % | % | **ASSETS** | % | % | % | % | % | % |
| 7.0 | 7.3 | 7.0 | Cash & Equivalents | | | | | | 7.4 |
| 18.3 | 21.9 | 21.6 | Trade Receivables (net) | | | | | | 21.5 |
| 17.2 | 20.3 | 17.5 | Inventory | | | | | | 18.3 |
| 4.4 | 4.1 | 4.8 | All Other Current | | | | | | 6.0 |
| 46.9 | 53.6 | 51.0 | Total Current | | | | | | 53.3 |
| 43.6 | 37.3 | 36.4 | Fixed Assets (net) | | | | | | 28.4 |
| 5.5 | 3.2 | 7.1 | Intangibles (net) | | | | | | 11.4 |
| 4.0 | 5.9 | 5.5 | All Other Non-Current | | | | | | 7.0 |
| 100.0 | 100.0 | 100.0 | Total | | | | | | 100.0 |
| | | | **LIABILITIES** | | | | | | |
| 5.0 | 8.3 | 6.6 | Notes Payable-Short Term | | | | | | 7.4 |
| 4.3 | 5.6 | 4.2 | Cur. Mat.-L.T.D. | | | | | | 4.7 |
| 11.2 | 13.6 | 15.4 | Trade Payables | | | | | | 15.4 |
| .2 | | .3 | Income Taxes Payable | | | | | | .0 |
| 14.2 | 10.7 | 10.0 | All Other Current | | | | | | 12.1 |
| 34.9 | 38.1 | 36.5 | Total Current | | | | | | 39.8 |
| 22.1 | 16.5 | 20.9 | Long-Term Debt | | | | | | 15.8 |
| .7 | .5 | 1.3 | Deferred Taxes | | | | | | 1.2 |
| 1.8 | 8.9 | 6.1 | All Other Non-Current | | | | | | 10.3 |
| 40.6 | 36.0 | 35.3 | Net Worth | | | | | | 32.9 |
| 100.0 | 100.0 | 100.0 | Total Liabilities & Net Worth | | | | | | 100.0 |
| | | | **INCOME DATA** | | | | | | |
| 100.0 | 100.0 | 100.0 | Net Sales | | | | | | 100.0 |
| 23.0 | 24.8 | 24.6 | Gross Profit | | | | | | 23.0 |
| 17.2 | 18.8 | 18.7 | Operating Expenses | | | | | | 16.6 |
| 5.8 | 6.0 | 5.9 | Operating Profit | | | | | | 6.4 |
| 1.7 | 1.2 | 1.4 | All Other Expenses (net) | | | | | | 1.5 |
| 4.1 | 4.9 | 4.5 | Profit Before Taxes | | | | | | 5.0 |
| | | | **RATIOS** | | | | | | |
| 2.6 | 2.4 | 2.3 | | | | | | | 2.4 |
| 1.3 | 1.4 | 1.5 | Current | | | | | | 1.3 |
| .9 | .9 | 1.0 | | | | | | | 1.0 |
| 1.3 | 1.4 | 1.6 | | | | | | | 1.6 |
| .8 | .7 | .8 | Quick | | | | | | .7 |
| .4 | .4 | .5 | | | | | | | .4 |
| (28) 12.9 | (27) 13.5 | (24) 15.1 | | | | | | | (24) 15.2 |
| 37 10.0 | 36 10.2 | 38 9.5 | Sales/Receivables | | | | | | 41 8.9 |
| 47 7.8 | 46 7.9 | 52 7.0 | | | | | | | 52 7.0 |
| 27 13.6 | 24 15.1 | 21 17.7 | | | | | | | 21 17.0 |
| 39 9.3 | 39 9.3 | 34 10.8 | Cost of Sales/Inventory | | | | | | 35 10.4 |
| 77 4.7 | 85 4.3 | 56 6.5 | | | | | | | 54 6.8 |
| 16 23.3 | 15 23.6 | 24 14.9 | | | | | | | 24 15.0 |
| 31 11.9 | 24 15.2 | 32 11.5 | Cost of Sales/Payables | | | | | | 37 9.9 |
| 44 8.3 | 55 6.6 | 49 7.4 | | | | | | | 49 7.5 |
| 5.9 | 6.9 | 6.4 | | | | | | | 4.7 |
| 14.0 | 17.2 | 14.7 | Sales/Working Capital | | | | | | 22.1 |
| -74.1 | -19.2 | 289.8 | | | | | | | 342.8 |
| 15.9 | 16.2 | 16.0 | | | | | | | 49.2 |
| (30) 4.4 | (30) 3.7 | 4.2 | EBIT/Interest | | | | | | 6.3 |
| 1.8 | 1.9 | 1.2 | | | | | | | .4 |
| | 8.1 | 4.0 | | | | | | | 6.3 |
| | (11) 2.3 | (15) 2.5 | Net Profit + Depr., Dep., Amort./Cur. Mat. L/T/D | | | | | | (11) 2.6 |
| | 1.2 | 1.7 | | | | | | | 1.9 |
| .7 | .2 | .3 | | | | | | | .4 |
| 1.4 | 1.5 | 1.5 | Fixed/Worth | | | | | | 1.1 |
| 3.2 | 3.8 | 4.5 | | | | | | | -4.6 |
| .6 | .7 | 1.1 | | | | | | | 1.4 |
| 2.1 | 2.1 | 2.4 | Debt/Worth | | | | | | 2.5 |
| 6.2 | 9.1 | 10.5 | | | | | | | -18.8 |
| 33.8 | 58.1 | 57.4 | | | | | | | 61.2 |
| (30) 18.0 | (29) 23.5 | (30) 24.9 | % Profit Before Taxes/Tangible Net Worth | | | | | | (14) 33.6 |
| 11.5 | 11.3 | 6.9 | | | | | | | 10.0 |
| 16.9 | 22.4 | 13.1 | | | | | | | 13.3 |
| 7.0 | 6.9 | 5.4 | % Profit Before Taxes/Total Assets | | | | | | 5.8 |
| 2.7 | 3.4 | .4 | | | | | | | -3.0 |
| 8.2 | 32.7 | 12.3 | | | | | | | 14.3 |
| 3.4 | 5.7 | 5.3 | Sales/Net Fixed Assets | | | | | | 6.2 |
| 2.1 | 2.5 | 2.3 | | | | | | | 3.7 |
| 2.8 | 3.4 | 2.9 | | | | | | | 2.7 |
| 1.6 | 2.0 | 1.9 | Sales/Total Assets | | | | | | 2.3 |
| 1.2 | 1.2 | 1.2 | | | | | | | 1.2 |
| .8 | 1.1 | 2.3 | | | | | | | 1.8 |
| (22) 2.9 | (27) 2.8 | (29) 3.7 | % Depr., Dep., Amort./Sales | | | | | | (14) 3.2 |
| 5.7 | 5.9 | 5.3 | | | | | | | 7.5 |
| | | | % Officers', Directors' Owners' Comp/Sales | | | | | | |
| 2406121M | 1924576M | 2501878M | Net Sales ($) | 7134M | 7849M | | 46670M | 107422M | 2332803M |
| 1748470M | 1084282M | 1299766M | Total Assets ($) | 7767M | 4432M | | 27418M | 48115M | 1212034M |

Note: Columns 0-1MM through 10-25MM for asset, liability, income, and ratio data are marked "DATA NOT AVAILABLE."

M = $ thousand    MM = $ million
See Pages 9 through 22 for Explanation of Ratios and Data

## Current Data Sorted by Assets      Comparative Historical Data

| 0-500M | 500M-2MM | 2-10MM | 10-50MM | 50-100MM | 100-250MM | Type of Statement | 4/1/07-3/31/08 ALL | 4/1/08-3/31/09 ALL |
|---|---|---|---|---|---|---|---|---|
| | | 2 | 2 | 3 | 2 | Unqualified | 4 | 6 |
| | | 1 | 1 | | | Reviewed | 4 | 3 |
| | 1 | | | | | Compiled | 1 | |
| | 2 | | | | | Tax Returns | 2 | 2 |
| 1 | | 5 | 2 | 2 | | Other | 9 | 10 |
| | 4 (4/1-9/30/11) | | 20 (10/1/11-3/31/12) | | | | | |
| **1** | **3** | **8** | **5** | **5** | **2** | **NUMBER OF STATEMENTS** | **20** | **21** |
| % | % | % | % | % | % | | % | % |
| | | | | | | **ASSETS** | | |
| | | | | | | Cash & Equivalents | 5.7 | 4.0 |
| | | | | | | Trade Receivables (net) | 17.7 | 23.5 |
| | | | | | | Inventory | 31.6 | 30.8 |
| | | | | | | All Other Current | 3.1 | 4.0 |
| | | | | | | Total Current | 58.1 | 62.4 |
| | | | | | | Fixed Assets (net) | 29.4 | 24.6 |
| | | | | | | Intangibles (net) | 8.3 | 6.4 |
| | | | | | | All Other Non-Current | 4.3 | 6.6 |
| | | | | | | Total | 100.0 | 100.0 |
| | | | | | | **LIABILITIES** | | |
| | | | | | | Notes Payable-Short Term | 11.4 | 11.4 |
| | | | | | | Cur. Mat.-L.T.D. | 4.5 | 2.4 |
| | | | | | | Trade Payables | 15.0 | 12.6 |
| | | | | | | Income Taxes Payable | .0 | .8 |
| | | | | | | All Other Current | 11.6 | 8.6 |
| | | | | | | Total Current | 42.5 | 35.8 |
| | | | | | | Long-Term Debt | 13.4 | 16.9 |
| | | | | | | Deferred Taxes | .9 | .1 |
| | | | | | | All Other Non-Current | 5.5 | 7.2 |
| | | | | | | Net Worth | 37.6 | 39.9 |
| | | | | | | Total Liabilities & Net Worth | 100.0 | 100.0 |
| | | | | | | **INCOME DATA** | | |
| | | | | | | Net Sales | 100.0 | 100.0 |
| | | | | | | Gross Profit | 24.8 | 24.5 |
| | | | | | | Operating Expenses | 24.4 | 22.6 |
| | | | | | | Operating Profit | .5 | 1.9 |
| | | | | | | All Other Expenses (net) | 1.9 | 1.6 |
| | | | | | | Profit Before Taxes | -1.4 | .3 |
| | | | | | | **RATIOS** | | |
| | | | | | | Current | 2.7 | 3.0 |
| | | | | | | | 1.6 | 1.8 |
| | | | | | | | 1.0 | 1.2 |
| | | | | | | Quick | 1.3 | 1.4 |
| | | | | | | | .6 | .7 |
| | | | | | | | .3 | .4 |
| | | | | | | Sales/Receivables | (14) 25.8   (23) 15.9 | |
| | | | | | | | (25) 14.5   (35) 10.6 | |
| | | | | | | | (39) 9.4   (49) 7.5 | |
| | | | | | | Cost of Sales/Inventory | (47) 7.7   (42) 8.7 | |
| | | | | | | | (64) 5.7   (56) 6.5 | |
| | | | | | | | (78) 4.7   (78) 4.7 | |
| | | | | | | Cost of Sales/Payables | (12) 30.3   (10) 36.6 | |
| | | | | | | | (23) 16.0   (25) 14.6 | |
| | | | | | | | (43) 8.4   (35) 10.5 | |
| | | | | | | Sales/Working Capital | 6.9 | 6.1 |
| | | | | | | | 13.3 | 8.3 |
| | | | | | | | -95.3 | 27.4 |
| | | | | | | EBIT/Interest | 11.1 | 2.7 |
| | | | | | | | (17) .3   (20) -.4 | |
| | | | | | | | -2.0 | -3.7 |
| | | | | | | Net Profit + Depr., Dep., Amort./Cur. Mat. L/T/D | | |
| | | | | | | Fixed/Worth | .4 | .3 |
| | | | | | | | 1.4 | .6 |
| | | | | | | | 3.7 | 233.6 |
| | | | | | | Debt/Worth | .9 | .7 |
| | | | | | | | 1.4 | 1.7 |
| | | | | | | | 6.7 | 501.7 |
| | | | | | | % Profit Before Taxes/Tangible Net Worth | 42.9 | 25.9 |
| | | | | | | | (17) 5.7   (17) -1.7 | |
| | | | | | | | -44.6 | -18.0 |
| | | | | | | % Profit Before Taxes/Total Assets | 15.5 | 5.9 |
| | | | | | | | -.2 | -3.4 |
| | | | | | | | -11.8 | -12.9 |
| | | | | | | Sales/Net Fixed Assets | 28.0 | 23.5 |
| | | | | | | | 8.3 | 13.3 |
| | | | | | | | 5.6 | 5.4 |
| | | | | | | Sales/Total Assets | 3.5 | 3.1 |
| | | | | | | | 2.8 | 2.3 |
| | | | | | | | 1.7 | 1.9 |
| | | | | | | % Depr., Dep., Amort./Sales | 1.2 | 1.1 |
| | | | | | | | (17) 2.5   (19) 1.4 | |
| | | | | | | | 4.3 | 2.1 |
| | | | | | | % Officers', Directors' Owners' Comp/Sales | | |
| 3988M | 6830M | 96848M | 199809M | 645137M | 475832M | Net Sales ($) | 495672M | 1031152M |
| 217M | 2441M | 34714M | 105254M | 351498M | 283978M | Total Assets ($) | 326018M | 518675M |

## Comparative Historical Data | Current Data Sorted by Sales

| 4/1/09-3/31/10 ALL | 4/1/10-3/31/11 ALL | 4/1/11-3/31/12 ALL | Type of Statement | 0-1MM | 1-3MM | 3-5MM | 5-10MM | 10-25MM | 25MM & OVER |
|---|---|---|---|---|---|---|---|---|---|
| 8 | 7 | 7 | Unqualified | | | | | | 7 |
| 6 | 3 | 3 | Reviewed | | | 1 | 1 | 1 | |
| 1 | 4 | 1 | Compiled | | | | | 1 | |
| 2 | 1 | 3 | Tax Returns | 1 | 1 | 1 | | | |
| 14 | 12 | 10 | Other | | | | 3 | 4 | 3 |
| | | | | | 4 (4/1-9/30/11) | | 20 (10/1/11-3/31/12) | | |
| 31 | 27 | 24 | **NUMBER OF STATEMENTS** | 1 | 1 | 2 | 4 | 6 | 10 |
| % | % | % | **ASSETS** | % | % | % | % | % | % |
| 6.5 | 6.5 | 9.9 | Cash & Equivalents | | | | | | 8.9 |
| 23.7 | 18.4 | 20.4 | Trade Receivables (net) | | | | | | 26.8 |
| 25.9 | 25.7 | 25.4 | Inventory | | | | | | 19.4 |
| 5.5 | 3.0 | 2.9 | All Other Current | | | | | | 2.9 |
| 61.6 | 53.6 | 58.6 | Total Current | | | | | | 58.1 |
| 24.8 | 28.0 | 22.2 | Fixed Assets (net) | | | | | | 26.8 |
| 8.8 | 12.4 | 14.8 | Intangibles (net) | | | | | | 13.5 |
| 4.8 | 6.0 | 4.4 | All Other Non-Current | | | | | | 1.7 |
| 100.0 | 100.0 | 100.0 | Total | | | | | | 100.0 |
| | | | **LIABILITIES** | | | | | | |
| 9.8 | 9.1 | 8.6 | Notes Payable-Short Term | | | | | | 5.0 |
| 3.3 | 3.8 | 2.9 | Cur. Mat.-L.T.D. | | | | | | 4.7 |
| 15.4 | 11.2 | 13.6 | Trade Payables | | | | | | 14.6 |
| .2 | .6 | .1 | Income Taxes Payable | | | | | | .2 |
| 9.7 | 10.3 | 11.4 | All Other Current | | | | | | 11.1 |
| 38.4 | 34.9 | 36.5 | Total Current | | | | | | 35.6 |
| 15.8 | 18.1 | 29.3 | Long-Term Debt | | | | | | 28.1 |
| .3 | 1.2 | .6 | Deferred Taxes | | | | | | .8 |
| 7.8 | 11.3 | 12.8 | All Other Non-Current | | | | | | 15.9 |
| 37.8 | 34.5 | 20.8 | Net Worth | | | | | | 19.6 |
| 100.0 | 100.0 | 100.0 | Total Liabilities & Net Worth | | | | | | 100.0 |
| | | | **INCOME DATA** | | | | | | |
| 100.0 | 100.0 | 100.0 | Net Sales | | | | | | 100.0 |
| 29.9 | 30.6 | 28.3 | Gross Profit | | | | | | 27.6 |
| 25.2 | 25.9 | 24.9 | Operating Expenses | | | | | | 21.8 |
| 4.6 | 4.7 | 3.5 | Operating Profit | | | | | | 5.8 |
| 1.0 | 2.8 | 1.1 | All Other Expenses (net) | | | | | | 1.5 |
| 3.6 | 1.9 | 2.4 | Profit Before Taxes | | | | | | 4.3 |
| | | | **RATIOS** | | | | | | |
| 2.9 | 2.4 | 2.8 | Current | | | | | | 2.5 |
| 1.7 | 1.7 | 1.9 | | | | | | | 1.9 |
| 1.1 | 1.2 | 1.1 | | | | | | | 1.3 |
| 1.7 | 1.2 | 1.5 | Quick | | | | | | 1.4 |
| 1.1 | .8 | 1.0 | | | | | | | 1.2 |
| .5 | .4 | .6 | | | | | | | .8 |
| 30  12.2 | 25  14.7 | 18  20.2 | Sales/Receivables | | | | | | 37  9.9 |
| 40  9.1 | 41  9.0 | 37  9.9 | | | | | | | 46  8.0 |
| 59  6.2 | 52  7.0 | 52  7.0 | | | | | | | 65  5.6 |
| 44  8.4 | 43  8.6 | 31  11.9 | Cost of Sales/Inventory | | | | | | 31  11.6 |
| 63  5.8 | 61  6.0 | 58  6.3 | | | | | | | 38  9.6 |
| 79  4.6 | 92  4.0 | 76  4.8 | | | | | | | 62  5.9 |
| 27  13.3 | 23  15.8 | 16  22.8 | Cost of Sales/Payables | | | | | | 32  11.4 |
| 32  11.3 | 33  11.0 | 30  12.2 | | | | | | | 38  9.7 |
| 42  8.7 | 48  7.6 | 42  8.7 | | | | | | | 45  8.1 |
| 4.2 | 4.1 | 5.0 | Sales/Working Capital | | | | | | 5.3 |
| 12.1 | 7.6 | 8.6 | | | | | | | 7.6 |
| 48.0 | 27.3 | 64.3 | | | | | | | NM |
| 22.3 | 9.1 | 5.6 | EBIT/Interest | | | | | | |
| (27) 4.9 | (23) 2.2 | (22) 3.3 | | | | | | | |
| .3 | 1.2 | 1.9 | | | | | | | |
| 6.7 | | | Net Profit + Depr., Dep., Amort./Cur. Mat. L/T/D | | | | | | |
| (10) 2.6 | | | | | | | | | |
| .5 | | | | | | | | | |
| .3 | .4 | .5 | Fixed/Worth | | | | | | .7 |
| .9 | 1.1 | 1.2 | | | | | | | 1.1 |
| 7.3 | -1.9 | -.7 | | | | | | | -1.5 |
| .7 | .8 | 1.5 | Debt/Worth | | | | | | 1.7 |
| 1.6 | 2.0 | 8.2 | | | | | | | 6.0 |
| 33.7 | -5.7 | -4.0 | | | | | | | -4.1 |
| 50.1 | 35.6 | 57.7 | % Profit Before Taxes/Tangible Net Worth | | | | | | |
| (24) 22.4 | (19) 16.8 | (15) 16.8 | | | | | | | |
| 3.5 | 6.1 | 11.0 | | | | | | | |
| 19.8 | 12.5 | 11.5 | % Profit Before Taxes/Total Assets | | | | | | 6.9 |
| 5.3 | 3.4 | 6.2 | | | | | | | 5.7 |
| -3.4 | .5 | 2.1 | | | | | | | 2.1 |
| 16.5 | 12.5 | 25.5 | Sales/Net Fixed Assets | | | | | | 15.6 |
| 8.3 | 6.4 | 12.1 | | | | | | | 8.9 |
| 6.1 | 3.7 | 7.7 | | | | | | | 4.2 |
| 2.9 | 2.5 | 3.0 | Sales/Total Assets | | | | | | 2.4 |
| 2.1 | 1.7 | 2.1 | | | | | | | 1.8 |
| 1.5 | 1.2 | 1.5 | | | | | | | 1.4 |
| 1.6 | 1.4 | 1.1 | % Depr., Dep., Amort./Sales | | | | | | |
| (26) 2.3 | (19) 2.6 | (21) 1.9 | | | | | | | |
| 4.6 | 4.5 | 3.6 | | | | | | | |
| | | | % Officers', Directors' Owners' Comp/Sales | | | | | | |
| 1402315M | 1238139M | 1428444M | Net Sales ($) | 318M | 1121M | 7399M | 28051M | 99055M | 1292500M |
| 909841M | 1126126M | 778102M | Total Assets ($) | 636M | 728M | 15934M | 11653M | 39085M | 710066M |

© RMA 2012

M = $ thousand    MM = $ million

See Pages 9 through 22 for Explanation of Ratios and Data

## Current Data Sorted by Assets      Comparative Historical Data

### Type of Statement

| | 1 | 2 | 30 | 65 | 26 | 26 | | 155 | 152 |
|---|---|---|---|---|---|---|---|---|---|
| Unqualified | 1 | 2 | 30 | 65 | 26 | 26 | | 155 | 152 |
| Reviewed | 3 | 15 | 107 | 54 | 4 | 2 | | 178 | 171 |
| Compiled | 20 | 30 | 57 | 13 | 3 | | | 89 | 98 |
| Tax Returns | | 44 | 33 | 1 | | | | 50 | 72 |
| Other | 9 | 59 | 92 | 90 | 27 | 21 | | 300 | 335 |

| 0-500M | 500M-2MM 119 (4/1-9/30/11) | 2-10MM | 10-50MM 715 (10/1/11-3/31/12) | 50-100MM | 100-250MM | | 4/1/07-3/31/08 ALL | 4/1/08-3/31/09 ALL |
|---|---|---|---|---|---|---|---|---|
| | | | | | | | 300 | 335 |

| 0-500M | 500M-2MM | 2-10MM | 10-50MM | 50-100MM | 100-250MM | | 4/1/07-3/31/08 ALL | 4/1/08-3/31/09 ALL |
|---|---|---|---|---|---|---|---|---|
| 33 | 150 | 319 | 223 | 60 | 49 | NUMBER OF STATEMENTS | 772 | 828 |
| % | % | % | % | % | % | **ASSETS** | % | % |
| 19.5 | 10.5 | 8.6 | 6.9 | 4.6 | 3.3 | Cash & Equivalents | 7.2 | 6.6 |
| 24.7 | 27.7 | 26.5 | 25.7 | 20.3 | 20.5 | Trade Receivables (net) | 26.2 | 24.2 |
| 19.1 | 24.6 | 24.3 | 24.1 | 20.9 | 19.4 | Inventory | 22.9 | 24.5 |
| 2.1 | 2.2 | 1.9 | 2.4 | 2.3 | 3.9 | All Other Current | 2.3 | 2.7 |
| 65.4 | 65.1 | 61.4 | 59.2 | 48.2 | 47.1 | Total Current | 58.6 | 58.0 |
| 23.1 | 28.0 | 30.0 | 31.9 | 30.4 | 30.4 | Fixed Assets (net) | 31.8 | 31.6 |
| 1.7 | 2.6 | 3.7 | 4.9 | 14.1 | 17.6 | Intangibles (net) | 4.4 | 5.2 |
| 9.7 | 4.3 | 4.9 | 4.0 | 7.3 | 4.8 | All Other Non-Current | 5.1 | 5.3 |
| 100.0 | 100.0 | 100.0 | 100.0 | 100.0 | 100.0 | Total | 100.0 | 100.0 |
| | | | | | | **LIABILITIES** | | |
| 22.0 | 11.4 | 10.3 | 9.1 | 5.7 | 4.9 | Notes Payable-Short Term | 10.9 | 12.2 |
| 2.7 | 3.8 | 3.8 | 4.1 | 2.7 | 3.0 | Cur. Mat.-L.T.D. | 5.0 | 4.8 |
| 18.6 | 20.3 | 14.5 | 14.2 | 12.0 | 13.6 | Trade Payables | 16.2 | 15.1 |
| .0 | .2 | .1 | .3 | .1 | .4 | Income Taxes Payable | .2 | .2 |
| 16.4 | 8.7 | 7.9 | 9.1 | 8.7 | 8.0 | All Other Current | 8.0 | 9.3 |
| 59.8 | 44.3 | 36.6 | 36.8 | 29.2 | 29.9 | Total Current | 40.4 | 41.6 |
| 24.7 | 18.9 | 15.6 | 14.3 | 14.5 | 21.2 | Long-Term Debt | 19.1 | 17.9 |
| .0 | .1 | .5 | 1.0 | 1.4 | 2.2 | Deferred Taxes | .6 | .6 |
| 6.6 | 8.6 | 6.8 | 8.6 | 6.8 | 10.5 | All Other Non-Current | 6.8 | 7.0 |
| 9.1 | 28.1 | 40.5 | 39.2 | 48.1 | 36.2 | Net Worth | 33.1 | 32.9 |
| 100.0 | 100.0 | 100.0 | 100.0 | 100.0 | 100.0 | Total Liabilities & Net Worth | 100.0 | 100.0 |
| | | | | | | **INCOME DATA** | | |
| 100.0 | 100.0 | 100.0 | 100.0 | 100.0 | 100.0 | Net Sales | 100.0 | 100.0 |
| 45.4 | 34.4 | 28.1 | 22.6 | 25.0 | 22.8 | Gross Profit | 26.7 | 25.3 |
| 39.0 | 30.1 | 22.0 | 16.3 | 19.3 | 17.0 | Operating Expenses | 21.5 | 21.5 |
| 6.4 | 4.3 | 6.1 | 6.2 | 5.7 | 5.8 | Operating Profit | 5.2 | 3.8 |
| .9 | .6 | 1.0 | 1.2 | 1.5 | 2.3 | All Other Expenses (net) | 1.5 | 1.4 |
| 5.5 | 3.7 | 5.2 | 5.1 | 4.2 | 3.5 | Profit Before Taxes | 3.7 | 2.4 |
| | | | | | | **RATIOS** | | |
| 3.3 | 2.8 | 3.2 | 2.7 | 2.4 | 2.4 | Current | 2.4 | 2.4 |
| 1.4 | 1.6 | 1.8 | 1.7 | 1.6 | 1.7 | | 1.5 | 1.5 |
| .8 | 1.1 | 1.1 | 1.2 | 1.2 | 1.3 | | 1.1 | 1.0 |
| 2.5 | 1.7 | 2.0 | 1.4 | 1.3 | 1.1 | Quick | 1.4 | 1.3 |
| .8 | 1.0 | 1.0 | .9 | 1.0 | .8 | | .8 | .8 |
| .4 | .6 | .6 | .6 | .5 | .6 | | .5 | .5 |
| 5   71.2 | 21   17.7 | 33   11.2 | 37   9.8 | 38   9.5 | 39   9.4 | Sales/Receivables | 32   11.4 | 30   12.1 |
| 21   17.2 | 35   10.5 | 43   8.5 | 46   7.9 | 44   8.3 | 47   7.7 | | 43   8.5 | 40   9.1 |
| 41   8.8 | 46   7.9 | 55   6.6 | 59   6.2 | 56   6.5 | 60   6.1 | | 53   6.9 | 51   7.2 |
| 0   UND | 20   18.1 | 35   10.4 | 37   9.9 | 42   8.6 | 43   8.5 | Cost of Sales/Inventory | 32   11.2 | 34   10.7 |
| 34   10.8 | 43   8.4 | 53   6.9 | 54   6.7 | 62   5.9 | 65   5.6 | | 51   7.2 | 52   7.0 |
| 53   6.9 | 78   4.7 | 81   4.5 | 79   4.6 | 85   4.3 | 94   3.9 | | 76   4.8 | 79   4.6 |
| 5   68.8 | 17   21.6 | 18   20.7 | 21   17.5 | 23   16.0 | 28   13.1 | Cost of Sales/Payables | 20   18.0 | 18   20.1 |
| 25   14.8 | 34   10.8 | 30   12.2 | 30   12.3 | 32   11.4 | 38   9.6 | | 32   11.3 | 29   12.5 |
| 65   5.6 | 51   7.1 | 46   8.0 | 45   8.2 | 50   7.3 | 52   7.0 | | 47   7.7 | 44   8.3 |
| 5.8 | 6.7 | 4.6 | 5.4 | 5.2 | 4.9 | Sales/Working Capital | 5.9 | 5.8 |
| 27.0 | 11.5 | 8.1 | 8.4 | 7.7 | 7.7 | | 12.1 | 12.4 |
| -31.0 | 119.9 | 29.2 | 27.1 | 22.3 | 20.5 | | 82.2 | 999.8 |
| 9.7 | 11.8 | 16.1 | 19.9 | 22.0 | 11.6 | EBIT/Interest | 8.5 | 7.7 |
| (24) 4.9 | (132) 4.2 | (288) 6.3 | (207) 7.0 | (55) 4.9 | (48) 3.0 | | (709) 2.9 | (769) 2.6 |
| 1.8 | 1.4 | 2.1 | 2.3 | 1.0 | 1.1 | | 1.1 | .7 |
| | 7.7 | 6.1 | 7.9 | 9.7 | 7.3 | Net Profit + Depr., Dep., Amort./Cur. Mat. L/T/D | 5.4 | 4.3 |
| | (12) 3.3 | (69) 3.1 | (94) 3.8 | (36) 3.7 | (20) 3.1 | | (228) 2.5 | (267) 2.4 |
| | 2.5 | 1.6 | 1.8 | 1.5 | 1.8 | | 1.3 | 1.0 |
| .0 | .3 | .4 | .4 | .5 | .7 | Fixed/Worth | .5 | .4 |
| 1.4 | .8 | .8 | .8 | 1.0 | 1.7 | | 1.1 | 1.1 |
| -.8 | 8.3 | 1.9 | 2.1 | 1.9 | -3.7 | | 3.7 | 3.5 |
| 1.0 | .7 | .6 | .6 | .7 | 1.4 | Debt/Worth | .8 | .9 |
| 2.8 | 2.1 | 1.6 | 1.4 | 1.6 | 2.6 | | 2.1 | 2.0 |
| -3.1 | 38.0 | 4.0 | 4.2 | 4.8 | -11.6 | | 8.7 | 7.7 |
| 98.2 | 52.1 | 44.1 | 44.3 | 33.8 | 38.9 | % Profit Before Taxes/Tangible Net Worth | 42.4 | 34.9 |
| (20) 24.0 | (117) 23.9 | (281) 23.3 | (198) 23.8 | (50) 16.5 | (35) 17.8 | | (638) 22.4 | (682) 15.6 |
| 2.2 | 4.2 | 8.5 | 11.5 | 4.4 | 9.4 | | 5.2 | .7 |
| 30.5 | 21.2 | 16.8 | 15.7 | 14.7 | 7.7 | % Profit Before Taxes/Total Assets | 15.5 | 12.0 |
| 14.7 | 6.8 | 8.5 | 8.3 | 6.1 | 4.5 | | 6.2 | 4.6 |
| 1.6 | .7 | 2.6 | 3.4 | 1.2 | .3 | | .5 | -1.0 |
| 157.3 | 36.5 | 14.9 | 11.4 | 8.1 | 7.6 | Sales/Net Fixed Assets | 13.9 | 14.5 |
| 27.9 | 11.3 | 7.6 | 6.0 | 5.3 | 4.9 | | 6.9 | 6.9 |
| 9.2 | 6.1 | 4.4 | 3.9 | 3.5 | 3.4 | | 4.2 | 4.0 |
| 5.7 | 3.8 | 2.6 | 2.4 | 2.0 | 1.8 | Sales/Total Assets | 2.8 | 2.8 |
| 3.5 | 2.9 | 2.0 | 1.9 | 1.6 | 1.5 | | 2.1 | 2.1 |
| 2.2 | 2.1 | 1.6 | 1.5 | 1.2 | 1.1 | | 1.6 | 1.5 |
| .6 | .9 | 1.4 | 1.8 | 2.3 | 2.1 | % Depr., Dep., Amort./Sales | 1.7 | 1.7 |
| (17) 2.3 | (115) 2.2 | (290) 2.6 | (208) 2.9 | (56) 3.5 | (32) 2.9 | | (684) 2.9 | (724) 3.0 |
| 5.6 | 4.2 | 4.0 | 4.6 | 5.0 | 3.9 | | 4.5 | 4.6 |
| 3.3 | 3.0 | 1.5 | 1.6 | | | % Officers', Directors' Owners' Comp/Sales | 1.4 | 1.7 |
| (18) 6.9 | (73) 5.2 | (113) 3.3 | (38) 3.1 | | | | (241) 3.2 | (242) 3.8 |
| 10.2 | 7.6 | 5.4 | 4.8 | | | | 6.1 | 6.2 |
| 43395M | 539739M | 3591832M | 9292490M | 6943651M | 10733829M | Net Sales ($) | 28074274M | 31305117M |
| 9584M | 182944M | 1684490M | 4776705M | 4458176M | 7531494M | Total Assets ($) | 15758336M | 18684007M |

M = $ thousand    MM = $ million
See Pages 9 through 22 for Explanation of Ratios and Data

## Comparative Historical Data | Current Data Sorted by Sales

| Hist 1 | Hist 2 | Hist 3 | Type of Statement | 0-1MM | 1-3MM | 3-5MM | 5-10MM | 10-25MM | 25MM & OVER |
|---|---|---|---|---|---|---|---|---|---|
| 150 | 137 | 149 | Unqualified | | | 3 | 12 | 29 | 105 |
| 187 | 179 | 183 | Reviewed | 3 | 7 | 12 | 37 | 77 | 47 |
| 76 | 91 | 106 | Compiled | 1 | 12 | 22 | 32 | 23 | 16 |
| 61 | 95 | 98 | Tax Returns | 8 | 33 | 23 | 21 | 11 | 2 |
| 311 | 320 | 298 | Other | 12 | 29 | 29 | 43 | 59 | 126 |
| 4/1/09-3/31/10 ALL | 4/1/10-3/31/11 ALL | 4/1/11-3/31/12 ALL | | 119 (4/1-9/30/11) | | | 715 (10/1/11-3/31/12) | | |
| 785 | 822 | 834 | **NUMBER OF STATEMENTS** | 24 | 81 | 89 | 145 | 199 | 296 |
| % | % | % | **ASSETS** | % | % | % | % | % | % |
| 8.3 | 8.1 | 8.3 | Cash & Equivalents | 16.6 | 12.8 | 8.7 | 9.8 | 8.5 | 5.5 |
| 24.4 | 26.1 | 25.7 | Trade Receivables (net) | 17.7 | 24.2 | 25.1 | 25.0 | 28.8 | 25.1 |
| 22.7 | 22.7 | 23.6 | Inventory | 14.2 | 21.8 | 24.8 | 25.6 | 23.2 | 23.7 |
| 2.3 | 2.3 | 2.3 | All Other Current | 1.5 | 3.6 | 2.1 | 1.4 | 2.1 | 2.6 |
| 57.8 | 59.1 | 59.9 | Total Current | 50.0 | 62.3 | 60.7 | 61.8 | 62.6 | 56.9 |
| 32.1 | 30.4 | 29.9 | Fixed Assets (net) | 38.6 | 28.1 | 30.0 | 30.4 | 29.3 | 29.9 |
| 5.3 | 5.7 | 5.3 | Intangibles (net) | 1.9 | 3.5 | 3.1 | 3.6 | 4.0 | 8.4 |
| 4.9 | 4.8 | 4.9 | All Other Non-Current | 9.5 | 6.0 | 6.1 | 4.2 | 4.1 | 4.8 |
| 100.0 | 100.0 | 100.0 | Total | 100.0 | 100.0 | 100.0 | 100.0 | 100.0 | 100.0 |
| | | | **LIABILITIES** | | | | | | |
| 11.3 | 9.6 | 10.0 | Notes Payable-Short Term | 12.4 | 11.3 | 13.1 | 10.3 | 10.7 | 7.9 |
| 4.7 | 4.2 | 3.7 | Cur. Mat.-L.T.D. | 1.8 | 4.4 | 3.0 | 4.0 | 4.0 | 3.6 |
| 14.5 | 15.1 | 15.4 | Trade Payables | 11.7 | 16.1 | 18.2 | 16.0 | 15.1 | 14.6 |
| .2 | .2 | .2 | Income Taxes Payable | .1 | .2 | .2 | .1 | .1 | .3 |
| 8.1 | 7.8 | 8.8 | All Other Current | 16.2 | 7.8 | 8.1 | 8.0 | 8.4 | 9.3 |
| 38.7 | 37.0 | 38.1 | Total Current | 42.2 | 39.7 | 42.6 | 38.4 | 38.2 | 35.7 |
| 18.2 | 17.7 | 16.5 | Long-Term Debt | 36.8 | 21.1 | 20.4 | 16.6 | 13.4 | 14.4 |
| .7 | .7 | .7 | Deferred Taxes | .1 | .1 | .2 | .5 | .8 | 1.2 |
| 6.6 | 7.5 | 7.8 | All Other Non-Current | 5.8 | 10.5 | 4.6 | 8.4 | 6.8 | 8.6 |
| 35.8 | 37.1 | 37.0 | Net Worth | 15.6 | 28.6 | 32.3 | 36.2 | 40.8 | 40.2 |
| 100.0 | 100.0 | 100.0 | Total Liabilties & Net Worth | 100.0 | 100.0 | 100.0 | 100.0 | 100.0 | 100.0 |
| | | | **INCOME DATA** | | | | | | |
| 100.0 | 100.0 | 100.0 | Net Sales | 100.0 | 100.0 | 100.0 | 100.0 | 100.0 | 100.0 |
| 27.6 | 28.7 | 27.9 | Gross Profit | 51.2 | 38.9 | 34.5 | 29.4 | 24.9 | 22.4 |
| 23.5 | 22.7 | 22.1 | Operating Expenses | 38.0 | 34.3 | 29.7 | 24.2 | 18.9 | 16.3 |
| 4.1 | 6.0 | 5.8 | Operating Profit | 13.2 | 4.5 | 4.8 | 5.1 | 6.0 | 6.0 |
| 1.5 | 1.2 | 1.1 | All Other Expenses (net) | 4.4 | .9 | .8 | .5 | .8 | 1.4 |
| 2.6 | 4.8 | 4.7 | Profit Before Taxes | 8.8 | 3.6 | 4.0 | 4.6 | 5.2 | 4.6 |
| | | | **RATIOS** | | | | | | |
| 2.5 | 2.8 | 2.8 | Current | 3.2 | 3.5 | 2.9 | 3.0 | 2.7 | 2.5 |
| 1.6 | 1.7 | 1.7 | | 1.4 | 1.8 | 1.7 | 1.9 | 1.7 | 1.6 |
| 1.1 | 1.2 | 1.1 | | .8 | 1.0 | 1.1 | 1.1 | 1.2 | 1.2 |
| 1.5 | 1.7 | 1.6 | Quick | 2.3 | 2.3 | 1.9 | 1.8 | 1.8 | 1.3 |
| .8 | .9 | .9 | | 1.2 | 1.0 | .9 | 1.1 | .9 | .9 |
| .5 | .6 | .6 | | .3 | .6 | .6 | .6 | .6 | .6 |
| 34  10.8 | 34  10.8 | 33  11.2 | Sales/Receivables | 8  44.2 | 21  17.4 | 25  14.5 | 30  12.2 | 36  10.2 | 37  9.9 |
| 46  8.0 | 44  8.2 | 42  8.6 | | 37  9.8 | 36  10.2 | 36  10.2 | 42  8.7 | 45  8.1 | 45  8.1 |
| 59  6.2 | 58  6.3 | 55  6.6 | | 72  5.1 | 47  7.8 | 46  8.0 | 54  6.8 | 60  6.1 | 56  6.5 |
| 36  10.0 | 33  10.9 | 34  10.8 | Cost of Sales/Inventory | 0  UND | 20  18.0 | 23  16.2 | 36  10.0 | 33  11.2 | 38  9.7 |
| 57  6.5 | 52  7.0 | 53  6.9 | | 35  10.4 | 49  7.4 | 49  7.4 | 59  6.2 | 49  7.4 | 54  6.7 |
| 84  4.3 | 80  4.6 | 79  4.6 | | 126  2.9 | 94  3.9 | 85  4.3 | 91  4.0 | 72  5.1 | 79  4.6 |
| 20  18.1 | 19  19.3 | 19  19.1 | Cost of Sales/Payables | 5  77.9 | 13  27.4 | 19  19.5 | 18  20.6 | 20  18.6 | 22  16.9 |
| 33  11.2 | 31  11.9 | 31  11.8 | | 29  12.8 | 34  10.7 | 32  11.3 | 30  12.2 | 30  12.2 | 31  11.7 |
| 49  7.4 | 47  7.7 | 47  7.7 | | 96  3.8 | 56  6.5 | 49  7.5 | 51  7.2 | 45  8.1 | 47  7.8 |
| 5.0 | 5.1 | 5.2 | Sales/Working Capital | 3.7 | 4.5 | 6.2 | 4.7 | 4.9 | 5.5 |
| 9.8 | 8.8 | 9.0 | | 14.6 | 9.3 | 11.8 | 8.3 | 9.3 | 8.5 |
| 43.6 | 27.2 | 32.7 | | -15.9 | 378.0 | 52.0 | 31.9 | 28.4 | 26.5 |
| 8.9 | 14.6 | 16.3 | EBIT/Interest | 6.2 | 9.5 | 9.7 | 12.6 | 19.6 | 20.5 |
| (716)  3.2 | (734)  4.8 | (754)  5.6 | | (15)  4.1 | (66)  3.0 | (82)  3.8 | (128)  6.3 | (183)  6.4 | (280)  6.7 |
| .7 | 1.7 | 1.8 | | 1.3 | 1.1 | 1.4 | 2.0 | 2.7 | 1.9 |
| 5.6 | 6.8 | 6.9 | Net Profit + Depr., Dep., Amort./Cur. Mat. L/T/D | | | 4.0 | 7.0 | 5.5 | 9.2 |
| (244)  2.3 | (260)  3.1 | (232)  3.3 | | | (12)  2.7 | (23)  3.4 | (58)  3.1 | | (134)  3.8 |
| .9 | 1.7 | 1.7 | | | 1.3 | 2.0 | 1.6 | | 1.8 |
| .4 | .4 | .4 | Fixed/Worth | .4 | .2 | .4 | .4 | .4 | .4 |
| 1.0 | .9 | .9 | | 1.8 | .9 | .7 | .8 | .9 | .9 |
| 2.8 | 2.3 | 2.3 | | -8.4 | -9.2 | 4.2 | 2.1 | 1.8 | 2.3 |
| .7 | .7 | .7 | Debt/Worth | 1.2 | .5 | .8 | .6 | .7 | .6 |
| 1.9 | 1.7 | 1.6 | | 3.2 | 1.5 | 2.2 | 1.5 | 1.6 | 1.6 |
| 6.0 | 5.1 | 5.4 | | -31.5 | -24.3 | 53.1 | 5.2 | 3.8 | 4.8 |
| 35.5 | 45.8 | 44.6 | % Profit Before Taxes/Tangible Net Worth | 47.9 | 38.3 | 47.3 | 47.1 | 46.5 | 41.8 |
| (664)  14.2 | (712)  22.5 | (701)  22.3 | | (16)  24.0 | (58)  12.4 | (71)  17.9 | (125)  25.7 | (180)  25.0 | (251)  22.1 |
| .7 | 8.2 | 7.5 | | 6.3 | -.5 | 5.0 | 6.1 | 9.8 | 10.7 |
| 12.8 | 15.7 | 16.3 | % Profit Before Taxes/Total Assets | 19.9 | 16.7 | 18.6 | 18.5 | 16.9 | 15.2 |
| 4.3 | 7.8 | 7.5 | | 5.3 | 6.5 | 6.2 | 8.9 | 8.8 | 7.3 |
| -1.0 | 2.0 | 2.0 | | 1.9 | -.5 | 1.1 | 2.2 | 3.2 | 2.1 |
| 13.0 | 15.1 | 14.6 | Sales/Net Fixed Assets | 25.3 | 45.2 | 20.8 | 16.1 | 14.0 | 11.4 |
| 5.9 | 7.2 | 7.1 | | 5.1 | 10.4 | 9.1 | 7.6 | 7.3 | 6.3 |
| 3.4 | 4.0 | 4.3 | | 1.4 | 4.9 | 5.4 | 3.9 | 4.3 | 4.1 |
| 2.5 | 2.6 | 2.8 | Sales/Total Assets | 2.2 | 3.8 | 3.5 | 2.9 | 2.6 | 2.4 |
| 1.8 | 2.0 | 2.0 | | 1.3 | 2.3 | 2.7 | 2.1 | 2.0 | 1.9 |
| 1.3 | 1.5 | 1.5 | | .8 | 1.6 | 1.8 | 1.5 | 1.6 | 1.4 |
| 1.8 | 1.6 | 1.5 | % Depr., Dep., Amort./Sales | 1.2 | 1.1 | 1.2 | 1.4 | 1.5 | 1.7 |
| (670)  3.3 | (725)  3.0 | (718)  2.7 | | (13)  11.4 | (62)  2.7 | (70)  2.4 | (131)  2.8 | (182)  2.7 | (260)  2.7 |
| 5.2 | 4.7 | 4.4 | | 19.1 | 5.6 | 4.7 | 4.7 | 4.0 | 4.3 |
| 2.0 | 2.0 | 2.0 | % Officers', Directors' Owners' Comp/Sales | | 3.5 | 3.4 | 2.2 | 1.2 | 1.0 |
| (223)  3.9 | (257)  3.8 | (248)  3.9 | | | (48)  6.0 | (47)  5.4 | (52)  3.8 | (57)  2.3 | (38)  2.5 |
| 7.0 | 6.4 | 6.2 | | | 10.7 | 7.3 | 5.4 | 4.7 | |
| 25551409M | 27678018M | 31144936M | Net Sales ($) | 13640M | 166886M | 346244M | 1036172M | 3105541M | 26476453M |
| 16177132M | 17154736M | 18643393M | Total Assets ($) | 20510M | 85954M | 158570M | 555783M | 1615703M | 16206873M |

M = $ thousand   MM = $ million
See Pages 9 through 22 for Explanation of Ratios and Data

## Current Data Sorted by Assets

## Comparative Historical Data

| | | | | | | Type of Statement | | |
|---|---|---|---|---|---|---|---|---|
| | | | 1 | 1 | 1 | Unqualified | 3 | 5 |
| | 1 | 1 | 5 | 3 | 1 | Reviewed | 5 | 4 |
| 1 | 1 | 2 | 2 | 1 | | Compiled | 9 | 6 |
| 3 | 1 | | 1 | | | Tax Returns | 6 | 11 |
| | 1 | 1 | | 3 | 1 | Other | 16 | 12 |
| | 5 (4/1-9/30/11) | | | 24 (10/1/11-3/31/12) | | | 4/1/07-3/31/08 | 4/1/08-3/31/09 |
| 0-500M | .500M-2MM | 2-10MM | 10-50MM | 50-100MM | 100-250MM | | ALL | ALL |
| 4 | 5 | 9 | 8 | 2 | 1 | NUMBER OF STATEMENTS | 39 | 38 |
| % | % | % | % | % | % | | % | % |
| | | | | | | **ASSETS** | | |
| | | | | | | Cash & Equivalents | 8.3 | 5.3 |
| | | | | | | Trade Receivables (net) | 26.3 | 25.4 |
| | | | | | | Inventory | 31.6 | 40.3 |
| | | | | | | All Other Current | 2.4 | 1.7 |
| | | | | | | Total Current | 68.7 | 72.7 |
| | | | | | | Fixed Assets (net) | 27.2 | 19.6 |
| | | | | | | Intangibles (net) | 1.4 | 4.2 |
| | | | | | | All Other Non-Current | 2.8 | 3.6 |
| | | | | | | Total | 100.0 | 100.0 |
| | | | | | | **LIABILITIES** | | |
| | | | | | | Notes Payable-Short Term | 10.7 | 11.1 |
| | | | | | | Cur. Mat.-L.T.D. | 3.5 | 2.2 |
| | | | | | | Trade Payables | 28.3 | 27.1 |
| | | | | | | Income Taxes Payable | .2 | .0 |
| | | | | | | All Other Current | 9.1 | 9.3 |
| | | | | | | Total Current | 51.8 | 49.7 |
| | | | | | | Long-Term Debt | 15.5 | 13.0 |
| | | | | | | Deferred Taxes | .5 | .2 |
| | | | | | | All Other Non-Current | 3.7 | 5.6 |
| | | | | | | Net Worth | 28.4 | 31.5 |
| | | | | | | Total Liabilties & Net Worth | 100.0 | 100.0 |
| | | | | | | **INCOME DATA** | | |
| | | | | | | Net Sales | 100.0 | 100.0 |
| | | | | | | Gross Profit | 34.5 | 31.0 |
| | | | | | | Operating Expenses | 30.3 | 28.8 |
| | | | | | | Operating Profit | 4.2 | 2.2 |
| | | | | | | All Other Expenses (net) | .9 | -.3 |
| | | | | | | Profit Before Taxes | 3.3 | 2.5 |
| | | | | | | **RATIOS** | | |
| | | | | | | Current | 1.6 | 2.0 |
| | | | | | | | 1.3 | 1.3 |
| | | | | | | | 1.0 | 1.2 |
| | | | | | | Quick | 1.0 | .8 |
| | | | | | | | .7 | .5 |
| | | | | | | | .4 | .4 |
| | | | | | | Sales/Receivables | 21　17.5 | 21　17.5 |
| | | | | | | | 35　10.6 | 34　10.7 |
| | | | | | | | 50　7.3 | 46　7.9 |
| | | | | | | Cost of Sales/Inventory | 54　6.7 | 59　6.2 |
| | | | | | | | 67　5.5 | 79　4.6 |
| | | | | | | | 95　3.8 | 116　3.1 |
| | | | | | | Cost of Sales/Payables | 27　13.5 | 29　12.5 |
| | | | | | | | 66　5.6 | 52　7.0 |
| | | | | | | | 83　4.4 | 73　5.0 |
| | | | | | | Sales/Working Capital | 10.7 | 7.6 |
| | | | | | | | 19.6 | 15.4 |
| | | | | | | | -122.8 | 25.8 |
| | | | | | | EBIT/Interest | 8.6 | 6.7 |
| | | | | | | | (35)　3.1 | (36)　2.7 |
| | | | | | | | 1.3 | 1.0 |
| | | | | | | Net Profit + Depr., Dep., Amort./Cur. Mat. L/T/D | 3.7 | 6.5 |
| | | | | | | | (13)　1.7 | (11)　1.7 |
| | | | | | | | 1.0 | 1.2 |
| | | | | | | Fixed/Worth | .4 | .3 |
| | | | | | | | .9 | .6 |
| | | | | | | | 3.4 | 1.6 |
| | | | | | | Debt/Worth | 1.2 | 1.3 |
| | | | | | | | 3.3 | 2.8 |
| | | | | | | | 9.7 | 6.6 |
| | | | | | | % Profit Before Taxes/Tangible Net Worth | 69.3 | 40.0 |
| | | | | | | | (34)　22.4 | (34)　18.3 |
| | | | | | | | 10.8 | 2.4 |
| | | | | | | % Profit Before Taxes/Total Assets | 9.7 | 9.7 |
| | | | | | | | 4.9 | 3.2 |
| | | | | | | | 1.4 | .0 |
| | | | | | | Sales/Net Fixed Assets | 26.3 | 37.1 |
| | | | | | | | 10.3 | 15.9 |
| | | | | | | | 5.5 | 8.2 |
| | | | | | | Sales/Total Assets | 3.2 | 3.3 |
| | | | | | | | 2.5 | 2.7 |
| | | | | | | | 1.9 | 2.0 |
| | | | | | | % Depr., Dep., Amort./Sales | 1.2 | .8 |
| | | | | | | | (36)　2.0 | (33)　1.5 |
| | | | | | | | 3.1 | 2.4 |
| | | | | | | % Officers', Directors' Owners' Comp/Sales | .6 | .5 |
| | | | | | | | (17)　.9 | (17)　1.0 |
| | | | | | | | 4.3 | 2.0 |
| 5220M | 14033M | 160481M | 364575M | 409364M | 252133M | Net Sales ($) | 989823M | 1510190M |
| 1481M | 5501M | 51434M | 145922M | 105851M | 118711M | Total Assets ($) | 418367M | 615928M |

M = $ thousand　　MM = $ million
See Pages 9 through 22 for Explanation of Ratios and Data

## Comparative Historical Data  |  Current Data Sorted by Sales

### Type of Statement

| 4/1/09-3/31/10 ALL | 4/1/10-3/31/11 ALL | 4/1/11-3/31/12 ALL | Type of Statement | 0-1MM | 1-3MM | 3-5MM | 5-10MM | 10-25MM | 25MM & OVER |
|---|---|---|---|---|---|---|---|---|---|
| 4 | 4 | 3 | Unqualified | | | | | 1 | 2 |
| 4 | 10 | 10 | Reviewed | | 1 | | 1 | 4 | 4 |
| 8 | 4 | 5 | Compiled | | 4 | 1 | 1 | 1 | 1 |
| 14 | 12 | 5 | Tax Returns | 1 | 1 | | | | |
| 13 | 10 | 6 | Other | 1 | | | 1 | | 4 |

Period columns (current data): 5 (4/1-9/30/11) · 24 (10/1/11-3/31/12)

| 4/1/09-3/31/10 ALL | 4/1/10-3/31/11 ALL | 4/1/11-3/31/12 ALL | | 0-1MM | 1-3MM | 3-5MM | 5-10MM | 10-25MM | 25MM & OVER |
|---|---|---|---|---|---|---|---|---|---|
| **43** | **40** | **29** | **NUMBER OF STATEMENTS** | **2** | **6** | **1** | **3** | **6** | **11** |
| % | % | % | **ASSETS** | % | % | % | % | % | % |
| 9.5 | 11.5 | 10.7 | Cash & Equivalents | | | | | | 6.6 |
| 22.4 | 20.4 | 20.9 | Trade Receivables (net) | | | | | | 26.6 |
| 34.5 | 32.0 | 33.6 | Inventory | | | | | | 29.8 |
| 1.4 | 2.7 | 2.9 | All Other Current | | | | | | 1.1 |
| 67.9 | 66.7 | 68.0 | Total Current | | | | | | 64.1 |
| 20.5 | 24.0 | 23.9 | Fixed Assets (net) | | | | | | 24.7 |
| 4.1 | 4.0 | 3.7 | Intangibles (net) | | | | | | 8.9 |
| 7.5 | 5.3 | 4.3 | All Other Non-Current | | | | | | 2.3 |
| 100.0 | 100.0 | 100.0 | Total | | | | | | 100.0 |
| | | | **LIABILITIES** | | | | | | |
| 8.2 | 7.8 | 8.7 | Notes Payable-Short Term | | | | | | 10.2 |
| 4.4 | 3.1 | 2.4 | Cur. Mat.-L.T.D. | | | | | | 2.4 |
| 26.6 | 29.4 | 26.3 | Trade Payables | | | | | | 32.8 |
| .1 | .1 | .1 | Income Taxes Payable | | | | | | .0 |
| 9.1 | 5.9 | 8.2 | All Other Current | | | | | | 9.2 |
| 48.4 | 46.3 | 45.6 | Total Current | | | | | | 54.5 |
| 20.2 | 18.5 | 14.5 | Long-Term Debt | | | | | | 13.0 |
| .1 | .2 | .3 | Deferred Taxes | | | | | | .2 |
| 4.6 | 4.7 | 1.4 | All Other Non-Current | | | | | | 1.4 |
| 26.7 | 30.3 | 38.1 | Net Worth | | | | | | 30.8 |
| 100.0 | 100.0 | 100.0 | Total Liabilities & Net Worth | | | | | | 100.0 |
| | | | **INCOME DATA** | | | | | | |
| 100.0 | 100.0 | 100.0 | Net Sales | | | | | | 100.0 |
| 31.2 | 31.7 | 32.4 | Gross Profit | | | | | | 28.4 |
| 29.0 | 28.9 | 27.3 | Operating Expenses | | | | | | 23.8 |
| 2.2 | 2.8 | 5.0 | Operating Profit | | | | | | 4.6 |
| .5 | .1 | 1.4 | All Other Expenses (net) | | | | | | .1 |
| 1.7 | 2.7 | 3.6 | Profit Before Taxes | | | | | | 4.5 |
| | | | **RATIOS** | | | | | | |
| 2.2 | 1.8 | 1.9 | Current | | | | | | 1.6 |
| 1.4 | 1.4 | 1.5 | | | | | | | 1.1 |
| 1.0 | 1.1 | 1.1 | | | | | | | 1.0 |
| 1.3 | 1.0 | 1.0 | Quick | | | | | | .8 |
| .6 | .6 | .6 | | | | | | | .6 |
| .3 | .4 | .4 | | | | | | | .3 |
| 12  29.6 | 19  18.8 | 10  36.1 | Sales/Receivables | | | | | | 17  21.5 |
| 32  11.6 | 30  12.1 | 26  14.2 | | | | | | | 27  13.5 |
| 46  7.9 | 39  9.4 | 40  9.2 | | | | | | | 56  6.5 |
| 33  11.2 | 41  9.0 | 31  11.7 | Cost of Sales/Inventory | | | | | | 31  11.7 |
| 64  5.7 | 60  6.1 | 53  6.9 | | | | | | | 51  7.2 |
| 97  3.7 | 91  4.0 | 94  3.9 | | | | | | | 94  3.9 |
| 31  11.8 | 33  11.1 | 23  15.7 | Cost of Sales/Payables | | | | | | 33  11.0 |
| 54  6.7 | 63  5.8 | 49  7.4 | | | | | | | 52  7.0 |
| 76  4.8 | 78  4.7 | 87  4.2 | | | | | | | 69  5.3 |
| 6.8 | 8.4 | 6.5 | Sales/Working Capital | | | | | | 11.3 |
| 16.4 | 15.6 | 15.5 | | | | | | | 16.2 |
| 106.0 | 42.4 | 47.7 | | | | | | | -194.1 |
| 8.6 | 11.8 | 35.6 | EBIT/Interest | | | | | | 65.8 |
| (38) 2.7 | (34) 5.2 | (27) 8.6 | | | | | | | 6.9 |
| .8 | 3.0 | 2.9 | | | | | | | 4.0 |
| 4.1 | 16.2 | | Net Profit + Depr., Dep., Amort./Cur. Mat. L/T/D | | | | | | |
| (10) 1.0 | (10) 7.3 | | | | | | | | |
| .4 | 3.2 | | | | | | | | |
| .2 | .3 | .2 | Fixed/Worth | | | | | | .7 |
| .5 | .8 | .7 | | | | | | | 1.4 |
| 6.8 | 4.0 | 1.4 | | | | | | | 1.7 |
| .8 | 1.0 | .9 | Debt/Worth | | | | | | 1.6 |
| 2.7 | 2.3 | 1.7 | | | | | | | 5.3 |
| 12.3 | 9.3 | 4.7 | | | | | | | 10.4 |
| 42.7 | 41.9 | 66.1 | % Profit Before Taxes/Tangible Net Worth | | | | | | 141.3 |
| (37) 10.2 | (34) 17.1 | (28) 25.1 | | | | | | | 34.0 |
| 1.2 | 8.5 | 7.9 | | | | | | | 19.7 |
| 9.0 | 9.2 | 12.5 | % Profit Before Taxes/Total Assets | | | | | | 14.1 |
| 3.1 | 5.3 | 8.0 | | | | | | | 8.0 |
| .3 | 2.4 | 3.6 | | | | | | | 3.4 |
| 37.1 | 27.7 | 30.5 | Sales/Net Fixed Assets | | | | | | 28.3 |
| 14.4 | 14.9 | 16.2 | | | | | | | 16.2 |
| 7.2 | 7.0 | 7.1 | | | | | | | 6.1 |
| 3.9 | 3.2 | 3.4 | Sales/Total Assets | | | | | | 4.2 |
| 2.8 | 2.7 | 2.8 | | | | | | | 2.8 |
| 1.9 | 1.9 | 2.1 | | | | | | | 2.1 |
| .8 | .7 | .9 | % Depr., Dep., Amort./Sales | | | | | | .9 |
| (37) 1.6 | (35) 1.5 | (27) 1.6 | | | | | | | 1.6 |
| 2.8 | 2.6 | 2.5 | | | | | | | 2.9 |
| .7 | .8 | | % Officers', Directors' Owners' Comp/Sales | | | | | | |
| (16) 1.3 | (16) 1.5 | | | | | | | | |
| 3.0 | 2.3 | | | | | | | | |
| 1411025M | 1425960M | 1205806M | Net Sales ($) | 1376M | 13491M | 4386M | 28294M | 108136M | 1050123M |
| 552404M | 705932M | 428900M | Total Assets ($) | 862M | 4845M | 1275M | 10271M | 43283M | 368364M |

M = $ thousand     MM = $ million
See Pages 9 through 22 for Explanation of Ratios and Data

© RMA 2012

## Current Data Sorted by Assets     Comparative Historical Data

| 0-500M | 500M-2MM 5 (4/1-9/30/11) | 2-10MM | 10-50MM 35 (10/1/11-3/31/12) | 50-100MM | 100-250MM | Type of Statement | 4/1/07-3/31/08 ALL | 4/1/08-3/31/09 ALL |
|---|---|---|---|---|---|---|---|---|
| | | 1 | 1 | | 2 | Unqualified | 15 | 13 |
| | 1 | 3 | 3 | 1 | | Reviewed | 10 | 8 |
| | 1 | 2 | 1 | | 2 | Compiled | 2 | 7 |
| | | 2 | | | | Tax Returns | 2 | 4 |
| 1 | 1 | 4 | 9 | 2 | 2 | Other | 13 | 16 |
| 1 | 3 | 12 | 14 | 4 | 6 | **NUMBER OF STATEMENTS** | 42 | 48 |
| % | % | % | % | % | % | | % | % |
| | | | | | | **ASSETS** | | |
| | | 9.5 | 9.8 | | | Cash & Equivalents | 9.6 | 8.4 |
| | | 30.5 | 21.3 | | | Trade Receivables (net) | 24.3 | 22.3 |
| | | 32.7 | 31.2 | | | Inventory | 32.8 | 29.1 |
| | | .8 | 2.2 | | | All Other Current | 2.6 | 3.0 |
| | | 73.5 | 64.6 | | | Total Current | 69.3 | 62.8 |
| | | 19.4 | 23.7 | | | Fixed Assets (net) | 18.4 | 21.0 |
| | | 3.2 | 5.9 | | | Intangibles (net) | 5.8 | 7.7 |
| | | 3.9 | 5.8 | | | All Other Non-Current | 6.4 | 8.5 |
| | | 100.0 | 100.0 | | | Total | 100.0 | 100.0 |
| | | | | | | **LIABILITIES** | | |
| | | 7.4 | 5.2 | | | Notes Payable-Short Term | 7.2 | 10.2 |
| | | 1.6 | 2.1 | | | Cur. Mat.-L.T.D. | 3.0 | 2.7 |
| | | 18.9 | 11.2 | | | Trade Payables | 12.7 | 12.0 |
| | | .1 | .1 | | | Income Taxes Payable | .2 | .2 |
| | | 6.2 | 6.3 | | | All Other Current | 10.5 | 8.5 |
| | | 34.3 | 24.9 | | | Total Current | 33.7 | 33.6 |
| | | 7.9 | 11.0 | | | Long-Term Debt | 15.5 | 12.8 |
| | | .8 | 1.0 | | | Deferred Taxes | .6 | .5 |
| | | .5 | 3.2 | | | All Other Non-Current | 7.0 | 8.7 |
| | | 56.4 | 59.9 | | | Net Worth | 43.2 | 44.4 |
| | | 100.0 | 100.0 | | | Total Liabilities & Net Worth | 100.0 | 100.0 |
| | | | | | | **INCOME DATA** | | |
| | | 100.0 | 100.0 | | | Net Sales | 100.0 | 100.0 |
| | | 26.8 | 25.9 | | | Gross Profit | 30.6 | 29.6 |
| | | 20.6 | 19.1 | | | Operating Expenses | 24.1 | 22.1 |
| | | 6.2 | 6.8 | | | Operating Profit | 6.6 | 7.5 |
| | | .1 | .1 | | | All Other Expenses (net) | .9 | .9 |
| | | 6.1 | 6.7 | | | Profit Before Taxes | 5.7 | 6.6 |
| | | | | | | **RATIOS** | | |
| | | 4.5 | 5.5 | | | Current | 3.2 | 3.8 |
| | | 2.3 | 2.5 | | | | 2.4 | 2.2 |
| | | 1.4 | 1.4 | | | | 1.7 | 1.3 |
| | | 2.9 | 3.3 | | | Quick | 1.9 | 1.9 |
| | | 1.3 | .9 | | | | 1.2 | .9 |
| | | .7 | .5 | | | | .7 | .5 |
| | | 30   12.0 | 33   11.2 | | | Sales/Receivables | 35   10.3 | 30   12.0 |
| | | 51   7.1 | 42   8.6 | | | | 43   8.5 | 38   9.5 |
| | | 56   6.5 | 54   6.8 | | | | 52   7.0 | 51   7.2 |
| | | 35   10.5 | 61   6.0 | | | Cost of Sales/Inventory | 55   6.6 | 51   7.1 |
| | | 68   5.4 | 94   3.9 | | | | 67   5.4 | 68   5.4 |
| | | 79   4.6 | 140   2.6 | | | | 113   3.2 | 105   3.5 |
| | | 20   18.1 | 18   20.8 | | | Cost of Sales/Payables | 15   23.9 | 18   19.9 |
| | | 33   11.1 | 31   11.9 | | | | 29   12.7 | 29   12.5 |
| | | 43   8.4 | 51   7.2 | | | | 38   9.5 | 41   9.0 |
| | | 4.1 | 2.8 | | | Sales/Working Capital | 3.0 | 4.2 |
| | | 5.6 | 4.5 | | | | 5.7 | 7.6 |
| | | 11.9 | 10.2 | | | | 10.1 | 21.9 |
| | | | 37.4 | | | EBIT/Interest | 16.8 | 24.9 |
| | | | (12)   9.1 | | | | (38)   3.6 | (44)   9.4 |
| | | | 4.0 | | | | 2.2 | 3.0 |
| | | | | | | Net Profit + Depr., Dep., Amort./Cur. Mat. L/T/D | 10.0 | 8.7 |
| | | | | | | | (18)   4.7 | (17)   4.4 |
| | | | | | | | 2.1 | 2.6 |
| | | .1 | .2 | | | Fixed/Worth | .2 | .2 |
| | | .4 | .5 | | | | .5 | .4 |
| | | .5 | .7 | | | | 1.0 | 1.8 |
| | | .5 | .4 | | | Debt/Worth | .5 | .5 |
| | | .8 | .9 | | | | 1.4 | 1.4 |
| | | 2.0 | 1.6 | | | | 3.7 | 3.7 |
| | | 37.3 | 37.3 | | | % Profit Before Taxes/Tangible Net Worth | 36.9 | 41.8 |
| | | 20.6 | 20.2 | | | | (36)   24.0 | (43)   24.1 |
| | | 12.4 | 15.3 | | | | 10.7 | 10.3 |
| | | 21.6 | 16.9 | | | % Profit Before Taxes/Total Assets | 18.7 | 16.8 |
| | | 11.6 | 10.8 | | | | 8.1 | 10.2 |
| | | 4.9 | 6.8 | | | | 3.4 | 4.4 |
| | | 123.9 | 18.3 | | | Sales/Net Fixed Assets | 27.8 | 24.9 |
| | | 16.3 | 8.9 | | | | 10.7 | 10.1 |
| | | 7.4 | 4.0 | | | | 6.9 | 6.5 |
| | | 3.3 | 2.1 | | | Sales/Total Assets | 2.8 | 2.6 |
| | | 2.3 | 1.6 | | | | 1.9 | 1.9 |
| | | 1.9 | 1.2 | | | | 1.4 | 1.4 |
| | | .2 | .5 | | | % Depr., Dep., Amort./Sales | .5 | .5 |
| | | (11)   1.5 | 1.4 | | | | (37)   1.6 | (45)   1.1 |
| | | 1.9 | 2.0 | | | | 2.8 | 2.5 |
| | | | | | | % Officers', Directors' Owners' Comp/Sales | 2.3 | 1.5 |
| | | | | | | | (10)   3.9 | (13)   3.5 |
| | | | | | | | 9.8 | 4.8 |
| 769M | 7606M | 129644M | 379426M | 526757M | 989077M | Net Sales ($) | 1959491M | 1867386M |
| 450M | 3050M | 53800M | 220177M | 304356M | 692715M | Total Assets ($) | 1152968M | 1168204M |

© RMA 2012

M = $ thousand    MM = $ million
See Pages 9 through 22 for Explanation of Ratios and Data

## Comparative Historical Data | Current Data Sorted by Sales

| Type of Statement | | | | | | | | | | |
|---|---|---|---|---|---|---|---|---|---|---|
| Unqualified | 11 | 12 | 5 | | | | | 1 | | 4 |
| Reviewed | 6 | 12 | 8 | | 1 | | | 3 | | 4 |
| Compiled | 5 | 6 | 6 | 1 | | | 1 | 2 | | 2 |
| Tax Returns | 2 | 4 | 2 | | | | 1 | 1 | | |
| Other | 16 | 18 | 19 | 1 | 1 | | | 10 | | 7 |
| | 4/1/09-3/31/10 ALL | 4/1/10-3/31/11 ALL | 4/1/11-3/31/12 ALL | 0-1MM | 5 (4/1-9/30/11) 1-3MM | 3-5MM | 35 (10/1/11-3/31/12) 5-10MM | 10-25MM | | 25MM & OVER |
| NUMBER OF STATEMENTS | 40 | 52 | 40 | 1 | 2 | 1 | 3 | 16 | | 17 |
| | % | % | % | % | % | % | % | % | | % |

### ASSETS

| | 4/1/09-3/31/10 | 4/1/10-3/31/11 | 4/1/11-3/31/12 | 0-1MM | 1-3MM | 3-5MM | 5-10MM | 10-25MM | 25MM & OVER |
|---|---|---|---|---|---|---|---|---|---|
| Cash & Equivalents | 8.1 | 9.3 | 9.1 | | | | | 8.7 | 9.2 |
| Trade Receivables (net) | 22.8 | 22.5 | 24.4 | | | | | 22.6 | 23.7 |
| Inventory | 29.7 | 28.7 | 31.3 | | | | | 32.3 | 28.0 |
| All Other Current | 4.1 | 1.7 | 1.7 | | | | | 1.4 | 2.3 |
| Total Current | 64.6 | 62.2 | 66.5 | | | | | 65.0 | 63.2 |
| Fixed Assets (net) | 20.7 | 22.3 | 21.4 | | | | | 23.6 | 21.2 |
| Intangibles (net) | 6.4 | 9.6 | 8.2 | | | | | 6.8 | 12.9 |
| All Other Non-Current | 8.3 | 5.9 | 3.9 | | | | | 4.7 | 2.7 |
| Total | 100.0 | 100.0 | 100.0 | | | | | 100.0 | 100.0 |

### LIABILITIES

| | 4/1/09-3/31/10 | 4/1/10-3/31/11 | 4/1/11-3/31/12 | 0-1MM | 1-3MM | 3-5MM | 5-10MM | 10-25MM | 25MM & OVER |
|---|---|---|---|---|---|---|---|---|---|
| Notes Payable-Short Term | 9.0 | 7.9 | 7.7 | | | | | 5.2 | 4.0 |
| Cur. Mat.-L.T.D. | 3.4 | 4.5 | 2.6 | | | | | 2.1 | 3.4 |
| Trade Payables | 11.2 | 13.9 | 15.2 | | | | | 15.0 | 11.5 |
| Income Taxes Payable | .1 | .4 | .3 | | | | | .1 | .5 |
| All Other Current | 8.7 | 8.2 | 8.0 | | | | | 7.0 | 10.0 |
| Total Current | 32.4 | 35.0 | 33.8 | | | | | 29.5 | 29.4 |
| Long-Term Debt | 11.4 | 11.3 | 8.8 | | | | | 8.6 | 10.4 |
| Deferred Taxes | .5 | .7 | 1.4 | | | | | 1.2 | 2.0 |
| All Other Non-Current | 8.7 | 5.6 | 4.0 | | | | | 2.6 | 6.5 |
| Net Worth | 47.0 | 47.4 | 52.0 | | | | | 58.1 | 51.6 |
| Total Liabilties & Net Worth | 100.0 | 100.0 | 100.0 | | | | | 100.0 | 100.0 |

### INCOME DATA

| | 4/1/09-3/31/10 | 4/1/10-3/31/11 | 4/1/11-3/31/12 | 0-1MM | 1-3MM | 3-5MM | 5-10MM | 10-25MM | 25MM & OVER |
|---|---|---|---|---|---|---|---|---|---|
| Net Sales | 100.0 | 100.0 | 100.0 | | | | | 100.0 | 100.0 |
| Gross Profit | 31.7 | 30.8 | 27.6 | | | | | 28.3 | 24.3 |
| Operating Expenses | 24.7 | 22.0 | 20.8 | | | | | 22.1 | 15.9 |
| Operating Profit | 7.1 | 8.8 | 6.8 | | | | | 6.2 | 8.4 |
| All Other Expenses (net) | .8 | .5 | .1 | | | | | .1 | -.2 |
| Profit Before Taxes | 6.3 | 8.3 | 6.7 | | | | | 6.2 | 8.6 |

### RATIOS

| | 4/1/09-3/31/10 | 4/1/10-3/31/11 | 4/1/11-3/31/12 | 0-1MM | 1-3MM | 3-5MM | 5-10MM | 10-25MM | 25MM & OVER |
|---|---|---|---|---|---|---|---|---|---|
| Current | 3.9 | 3.1 | 3.8 | | | | | 3.9 | 3.7 |
| | 2.1 | 2.1 | 2.1 | | | | | 2.3 | 2.2 |
| | 1.4 | 1.2 | 1.3 | | | | | 1.3 | 1.4 |
| Quick | 1.9 | 1.8 | 2.0 | | | | | 2.5 | 2.3 |
| | (39) 1.1 | .9 | .9 | | | | | .8 | 1.0 |
| | .7 | .5 | .5 | | | | | .5 | .5 |
| Sales/Receivables | 40 9.1 | 36 10.2 | 33 11.0 | | | | | 26 14.0 | 41 8.9 |
| | 48 7.6 | 46 8.0 | 44 8.3 | | | | | 35 10.4 | 47 7.8 |
| | 56 6.5 | 53 6.9 | 54 6.8 | | | | | 51 7.1 | 54 6.7 |
| Cost of Sales/Inventory | 63 5.8 | 59 6.2 | 51 7.2 | | | | | 54 6.8 | 44 8.3 |
| | 99 3.7 | 81 4.5 | 79 4.6 | | | | | 83 4.4 | 87 4.2 |
| | 140 2.6 | 118 3.1 | 135 2.7 | | | | | 135 2.7 | 146 2.5 |
| Cost of Sales/Payables | 18 19.8 | 18 19.9 | 19 18.9 | | | | | 20 18.1 | 16 23.1 |
| | 30 12.3 | 35 10.5 | 32 11.4 | | | | | 33 11.1 | 26 14.1 |
| | 41 9.0 | 58 6.3 | 53 6.9 | | | | | 43 8.4 | 55 6.6 |
| Sales/Working Capital | 2.8 | 3.4 | 3.3 | | | | | 4.0 | 3.0 |
| | 6.1 | 6.9 | 6.0 | | | | | 5.6 | 5.9 |
| | 10.5 | 19.9 | 13.5 | | | | | 13.5 | 13.0 |
| EBIT/Interest | 16.8 | 34.2 | 41.4 | | | | | 30.7 | 49.9 |
| | (37) 8.6 | (48) 11.6 | (34) 12.2 | | | | | (13) 12.8 | (16) 20.4 |
| | 2.2 | 3.7 | 6.5 | | | | | 5.3 | 9.5 |
| Net Profit + Depr., Dep., Amort./Cur. Mat. L/T/D | 6.6 | 7.5 | 6.6 | | | | | | |
| | (15) 4.0 | (20) 5.2 | (16) 4.2 | | | | | | |
| | 2.0 | 1.2 | 1.5 | | | | | | |
| Fixed/Worth | .2 | .2 | .2 | | | | | .1 | .4 |
| | .5 | .6 | .5 | | | | | .4 | .7 |
| | .9 | 1.5 | 1.0 | | | | | .6 | 2.0 |
| Debt/Worth | .7 | .5 | .5 | | | | | .5 | .5 |
| | 1.2 | 1.4 | 1.0 | | | | | .9 | 1.5 |
| | 2.4 | 3.7 | 2.8 | | | | | 1.8 | 7.8 |
| % Profit Before Taxes/Tangible Net Worth | 39.5 | 50.2 | 40.4 | | | | | 40.1 | 75.1 |
| | (35) 21.4 | (47) 23.1 | (39) 24.0 | | | | | 17.5 | (16) 31.8 |
| | 5.0 | 16.2 | 14.0 | | | | | 12.4 | 18.4 |
| % Profit Before Taxes/Total Assets | 18.4 | 18.6 | 16.4 | | | | | 16.4 | 18.5 |
| | 7.2 | 11.7 | 10.7 | | | | | 10.3 | 11.8 |
| | 2.1 | 5.7 | 5.9 | | | | | 4.6 | 7.0 |
| Sales/Net Fixed Assets | 17.6 | 16.1 | 22.0 | | | | | 29.0 | 12.0 |
| | 7.8 | 8.8 | 9.6 | | | | | 12.2 | 8.7 |
| | 4.7 | 5.3 | 5.5 | | | | | 3.9 | 5.5 |
| Sales/Total Assets | 2.1 | 2.3 | 2.4 | | | | | 2.4 | 2.3 |
| | 1.6 | 1.8 | 1.8 | | | | | 2.0 | 1.7 |
| | 1.1 | 1.2 | 1.3 | | | | | 1.3 | 1.2 |
| % Depr., Dep., Amort./Sales | .7 | .9 | .6 | | | | | .4 | .9 |
| | (33) 1.5 | (48) 1.7 | (38) 1.5 | | | | | (15) 1.6 | 1.5 |
| | 2.6 | 2.6 | 2.3 | | | | | 2.4 | 2.3 |
| % Officers', Directors' Owners' Comp/Sales | 1.9 | 1.8 | 1.4 | | | | | | |
| | (12) 3.1 | (18) 2.5 | (10) 1.9 | | | | | | |
| | 5.6 | 4.1 | 5.0 | | | | | | |
| Net Sales ($) | 1495493M | 2816813M | 2033279M | 769M | 4064M | 3542M | 22865M | 233104M | 1768935M |
| Total Assets ($) | 1050821M | 1792060M | 1274548M | 450M | 2130M | 920M | 11784M | 137120M | 1122144M |

M = $ thousand     MM = $ million
See Pages 9 through 22 for Explanation of Ratios and Data

## Current Data Sorted by Assets      Comparative Historical Data

### Type of Statement

| | 0-500M | 500M-2MM | 2-10MM | 10-50MM | 50-100MM | 100-250MM | | 4/1/07-3/31/08 ALL | 4/1/08-3/31/09 ALL |
|---|---|---|---|---|---|---|---|---|---|
| Unqualified | | | 4 | 1 | 1 | 2 | | 8 | 7 |
| Reviewed | | | 7 | 1 | | | | 8 | 8 |
| Compiled | | 1 | 6 | | | | | 2 | 7 |
| Tax Returns | | 1 | 4 | | | | | 2 | 2 |
| Other | | 2 | 5 | | | | | 22 | 13 |
| | | 5 (4/1-9/30/11) | | 37 (10/1/11-3/31/12) | | | | 22 | 13 |
| NUMBER OF STATEMENTS | | 4 | 26 | 6 | 3 | 3 | | 42 | 37 |

| 0-500M | 500M-2MM | 2-10MM | 10-50MM | 50-100MM | 100-250MM | | 4/1/07-3/31/08 ALL | 4/1/08-3/31/09 ALL |
|---|---|---|---|---|---|---|---|---|
| % | % | % | % | % | % | **ASSETS** | % | % |
| | | 9.7 | | | | Cash & Equivalents | 8.4 | 7.0 |
| | | 32.8 | | | | Trade Receivables (net) | 27.8 | 24.3 |
| | | 22.7 | | | | Inventory | 20.0 | 25.5 |
| | | 1.4 | | | | All Other Current | 2.0 | 1.7 |
| | | 66.6 | | | | Total Current | 58.1 | 58.5 |
| | | 27.1 | | | | Fixed Assets (net) | 34.1 | 34.7 |
| DATA | | 2.4 | | | | Intangibles (net) | 2.0 | 2.3 |
| NOT | | 3.9 | | | | All Other Non-Current | 5.8 | 4.5 |
| | | 100.0 | | | | Total | 100.0 | 100.0 |
| AVAILABLE | | | | | | **LIABILITIES** | | |
| | | 9.2 | | | | Notes Payable-Short Term | 18.4 | 16.1 |
| | | 3.0 | | | | Cur. Mat.-L.T.D. | 2.4 | 3.1 |
| | | 13.5 | | | | Trade Payables | 14.3 | 16.9 |
| | | .4 | | | | Income Taxes Payable | .2 | .3 |
| | | 6.5 | | | | All Other Current | 9.4 | 12.0 |
| | | 32.6 | | | | Total Current | 44.8 | 48.4 |
| | | 9.3 | | | | Long-Term Debt | 16.9 | 15.1 |
| | | 1.5 | | | | Deferred Taxes | .8 | 1.0 |
| | | 7.1 | | | | All Other Non-Current | 6.6 | 8.1 |
| | | 49.5 | | | | Net Worth | 30.9 | 27.4 |
| | | 100.0 | | | | Total Liabilities & Net Worth | 100.0 | 100.0 |
| | | | | | | **INCOME DATA** | | |
| | | 100.0 | | | | Net Sales | 100.0 | 100.0 |
| | | 27.6 | | | | Gross Profit | 29.3 | 26.7 |
| | | 19.1 | | | | Operating Expenses | 23.4 | 22.0 |
| | | 8.5 | | | | Operating Profit | 6.0 | 4.7 |
| | | .6 | | | | All Other Expenses (net) | 1.5 | 1.8 |
| | | 7.9 | | | | Profit Before Taxes | 4.4 | 2.9 |
| | | | | | | **RATIOS** | | |
| | | 3.5 | | | | | 2.4 | 2.0 |
| | | 2.4 | | | | Current | 1.3 | 1.2 |
| | | 1.5 | | | | | 1.0 | .9 |
| | | 2.1 | | | | | 1.3 | 1.1 |
| | | 1.3 | | | | Quick | .7 | .6 |
| | | .9 | | | | | .5 | .4 |
| | 40 | 9.1 | | | | | 35   10.3 | 31   11.9 |
| | 50 | 7.3 | | | | Sales/Receivables | 46   8.0 | 37   9.8 |
| | 61 | 6.0 | | | | | 54   6.7 | 46   7.9 |
| | 34 | 10.8 | | | | | 28   12.8 | 31   11.8 |
| | 54 | 6.7 | | | | Cost of Sales/Inventory | 39   9.3 | 51   7.1 |
| | 79 | 4.6 | | | | | 76   4.8 | 65   5.6 |
| | 14 | 26.6 | | | | | 17   21.1 | 20   18.4 |
| | 22 | 16.5 | | | | Cost of Sales/Payables | 26   13.9 | 26   14.1 |
| | 38 | 9.7 | | | | | 44   8.2 | 43   8.5 |
| | | 3.9 | | | | | 6.6 | 6.5 |
| | | 6.8 | | | | Sales/Working Capital | 20.5 | 24.9 |
| | | 13.3 | | | | | -141.8 | -44.2 |
| | | 24.9 | | | | | 11.6 | 9.6 |
| | (24) | 10.5 | | | | EBIT/Interest | (39) 2.9 | (33) 2.4 |
| | | 4.0 | | | | | .5 | .3 |
| | | | | | | Net Profit + Depr., Dep., | 5.5 | 3.2 |
| | | | | | | Amort./Cur. Mat. L/T/D | (10) 2.3 | (13) 1.9 |
| | | | | | | | 1.1 | .5 |
| | | .2 | | | | | .5 | .6 |
| | | .6 | | | | Fixed/Worth | 1.2 | 1.2 |
| | | 1.3 | | | | | 2.9 | 2.3 |
| | | .5 | | | | | .8 | .8 |
| | | 1.0 | | | | Debt/Worth | 2.5 | 2.4 |
| | | 2.4 | | | | | 5.9 | 4.6 |
| | | 58.0 | | | | % Profit Before Taxes/Tangible | 44.9 | 49.4 |
| | (25) | 37.5 | | | | Net Worth | (35) 23.1 | (32) 24.8 |
| | | 14.1 | | | | | -3.4 | -2.3 |
| | | 23.9 | | | | | 19.5 | 14.2 |
| | | 15.9 | | | | % Profit Before Taxes/Total | 7.2 | 5.2 |
| | | 7.0 | | | | Assets | -1.9 | -3.8 |
| | | 34.9 | | | | | 14.0 | 15.8 |
| | | 7.7 | | | | Sales/Net Fixed Assets | 5.8 | 7.2 |
| | | 4.2 | | | | | 3.5 | 3.5 |
| | | 2.8 | | | | | 2.6 | 2.9 |
| | | 2.1 | | | | Sales/Total Assets | 2.0 | 2.0 |
| | | 1.7 | | | | | 1.6 | 1.6 |
| | | 1.3 | | | | | 2.3 | 1.3 |
| | (23) | 2.3 | | | | % Depr., Dep., Amort./Sales | (35) 3.1 | (34) 2.8 |
| | | 3.0 | | | | | 4.7 | 4.9 |
| | | | | | | % Officers', Directors' | 2.6 | 1.4 |
| | | | | | | Owners' Comp/Sales | (12) 8.4 | (10) 3.5 |
| | | | | | | | 11.8 | 9.7 |
| 16945M | 357908M | 130406M | 229186M | 572274M | | Net Sales ($) | 1053442M | 844131M |
| 5181M | 150648M | 67447M | 184343M | 424319M | | Total Assets ($) | 685534M | 523617M |

## Comparative Historical Data                                   Current Data Sorted by Sales

| 4/1/09-3/31/10 ALL | 4/1/10-3/31/11 ALL | 4/1/11-3/31/12 ALL | Type of Statement | 0-1MM | 1-3MM | 3-5MM | 5-10MM | 10-25MM | 25MM & OVER |
|---|---|---|---|---|---|---|---|---|---|
| 14 | 6 | 8 | Unqualified | | | | | 4 | 4 |
| 4 | 9 | 8 | Reviewed | | | | 5 | 3 | |
| 5 | 5 | 7 | Compiled | | | 2 | 3 | 2 | |
| 5 | 3 | 5 | Tax Returns | | | 1 | 1 | 3 | |
| 18 | 14 | 14 | Other | | 1 | 1 | 1 | 5 | 6 |
| | | | | | 5 (4/1-9/30/11) | | 37 (10/1/11-3/31/12) | | |
| 46 | 37 | 42 | NUMBER OF STATEMENTS | | 1 | 4 | 10 | 17 | 10 |
| % | % | % | ASSETS | % | % | % | % | % | % |
| 8.0 | 10.0 | 10.4 | Cash & Equivalents | | | | 13.8 | 7.8 | 4.1 |
| 25.0 | 29.2 | 30.6 | Trade Receivables (net) | | | | 31.3 | 35.5 | 28.6 |
| 24.6 | 21.5 | 22.0 | Inventory | | | | 22.7 | 25.6 | 19.6 |
| 3.8 | 2.7 | 1.6 | All Other Current | | | | 1.2 | .6 | 3.7 |
| 61.5 | 63.5 | 64.6 | Total Current | | | | 69.0 | 69.6 | 56.0 |
| 27.9 | 25.1 | 25.6 | Fixed Assets (net) | | | | 23.8 | 23.8 | 22.7 |
| 3.4 | 5.7 | 6.7 | Intangibles (net) | | | | 3.0 | 2.7 | 20.3 |
| 7.2 | 5.8 | 3.1 | All Other Non-Current | | | | 4.2 | 4.0 | 1.1 |
| 100.0 | 100.0 | 100.0 | Total | | | | 100.0 | 100.0 | 100.0 |
| | | | LIABILITIES | | | | | | |
| 12.8 | 11.6 | 8.9 | Notes Payable-Short Term | | | | 9.8 | 9.3 | 11.7 |
| 4.0 | 4.3 | 2.8 | Cur. Mat.-L.T.D. | | | | 1.5 | 3.7 | 3.1 |
| 13.2 | 13.2 | 12.0 | Trade Payables | | | | 8.1 | 15.5 | 11.3 |
| .4 | .5 | .3 | Income Taxes Payable | | | | .1 | .4 | .0 |
| 14.1 | 10.9 | 11.3 | All Other Current | | | | 5.7 | 8.0 | 24.5 |
| 44.6 | 40.5 | 35.3 | Total Current | | | | 25.2 | 36.8 | 50.6 |
| 9.3 | 10.6 | 13.8 | Long-Term Debt | | | | 7.1 | 10.6 | 27.3 |
| .8 | 1.3 | 1.3 | Deferred Taxes | | | | .8 | 1.0 | 1.4 |
| 13.9 | 7.5 | 11.5 | All Other Non-Current | | | | 3.2 | 2.6 | 30.4 |
| 31.4 | 40.1 | 38.0 | Net Worth | | | | 63.6 | 49.0 | -9.7 |
| 100.0 | 100.0 | 100.0 | Total Liabilities & Net Worth | | | | 100.0 | 100.0 | 100.0 |
| | | | INCOME DATA | | | | | | |
| 100.0 | 100.0 | 100.0 | Net Sales | | | | 100.0 | 100.0 | 100.0 |
| 33.7 | 30.3 | 28.5 | Gross Profit | | | | 33.7 | 26.5 | 22.3 |
| 28.2 | 20.7 | 19.4 | Operating Expenses | | | | 23.9 | 20.6 | 12.4 |
| 5.5 | 9.7 | 9.1 | Operating Profit | | | | 9.8 | 5.9 | 10.0 |
| .8 | 1.1 | .9 | All Other Expenses (net) | | | | .5 | .0 | 2.3 |
| 4.7 | 8.5 | 8.3 | Profit Before Taxes | | | | 9.2 | 5.9 | 7.7 |
| | | | RATIOS | | | | | | |
| 3.3 | 3.5 | 3.5 | Current | | | | 7.7 | 2.5 | 2.6 |
| 1.4 | 1.8 | 2.2 | | | | | 3.7 | 2.1 | 1.6 |
| 1.0 | 1.2 | 1.5 | | | | | 1.7 | 1.4 | .8 |
| 1.3 | 2.3 | 2.2 | Quick | | | | 4.1 | 1.7 | 1.6 |
| .7 | 1.0 | 1.3 | | | | | 2.6 | 1.1 | 1.1 |
| .5 | .6 | .9 | | | | | 1.3 | .8 | .3 |
| 30  12.3 | 37  9.9 | 42  8.7 | Sales/Receivables | | | | 43  8.5 | 46  7.9 | 43  8.4 |
| 47  7.8 | 48  7.6 | 49  7.4 | | | | | 49  7.4 | 54  6.7 | 50  7.3 |
| 58  6.3 | 59  6.2 | 61  6.0 | | | | | 65  5.6 | 66  5.5 | 55  6.6 |
| 35  10.3 | 41  8.9 | 35  10.4 | Cost of Sales/Inventory | | | | 28  13.2 | 41  9.0 | 31  11.8 |
| 59  6.2 | 47  7.8 | 57  6.4 | | | | | 68  5.4 | 56  6.5 | 57  6.4 |
| 82  4.4 | 65  5.6 | 73  5.0 | | | | | 83  4.4 | 65  5.6 | 65  5.6 |
| 17  21.9 | 17  21.7 | 14  26.4 | Cost of Sales/Payables | | | | 13  29.1 | 20  18.5 | 17  21.6 |
| 29  12.8 | 24  15.1 | 22  16.8 | | | | | 15  24.2 | 32  11.3 | 24  15.1 |
| 46  7.9 | 38  9.6 | 35  10.3 | | | | | 26  13.9 | 46  7.9 | 33  11.2 |
| 5.0 | 4.5 | 3.9 | Sales/Working Capital | | | | 3.2 | 6.1 | 6.7 |
| 13.2 | 7.6 | 6.9 | | | | | 4.0 | 7.0 | 9.5 |
| -296.1 | 23.7 | 17.7 | | | | | 10.2 | 14.6 | -10.2 |
| 10.1 | 18.9 | 17.0 | EBIT/Interest | | | | | 86.0 | 8.6 |
| (41)  3.6 | (34)  7.6 | (39)  7.2 | | | | | | (16)  11.7 | 5.9 |
| 1.6 | 5.3 | 4.1 | | | | | | 3.6 | 3.8 |
| 8.7 | 4.5 | 9.8 | Net Profit + Depr., Dep., Amort./Cur. Mat. L/T/D | | | | | | |
| (15)  3.6 | (13)  3.2 | (11)  4.7 | | | | | | | |
| .9 | 1.3 | 1.4 | | | | | | | |
| .2 | .3 | .2 | Fixed/Worth | | | | .2 | .1 | .8 |
| 1.0 | .7 | .8 | | | | | .5 | .5 | NM |
| 2.5 | 1.7 | 1.8 | | | | | .8 | 1.3 | -.1 |
| .6 | .5 | .6 | Debt/Worth | | | | .2 | .6 | 3.4 |
| 2.0 | 1.5 | 1.3 | | | | | .6 | 1.1 | NM |
| 6.1 | 3.9 | 4.3 | | | | | 1.3 | 2.0 | -1.7 |
| 44.9 | 62.7 | 59.9 | % Profit Before Taxes/Tangible Net Worth | | | | 47.5 | 47.3 | |
| (37)  17.7 | (33)  35.5 | (36)  30.3 | | | | | 25.5 | (16)  33.0 | |
| 4.0 | 19.8 | 13.1 | | | | | 11.5 | 14.1 | |
| 13.7 | 22.1 | 24.0 | % Profit Before Taxes/Total Assets | | | | 20.0 | 23.9 | 27.8 |
| 6.7 | 12.6 | 14.2 | | | | | 9.5 | 14.4 | 12.5 |
| 1.1 | 8.6 | 6.7 | | | | | 6.5 | 6.6 | 4.6 |
| 21.4 | 17.5 | 16.1 | Sales/Net Fixed Assets | | | | 41.0 | 29.4 | 12.6 |
| 8.2 | 8.2 | 8.2 | | | | | 10.1 | 8.2 | 7.9 |
| 3.5 | 4.8 | 4.9 | | | | | 3.3 | 5.0 | 6.7 |
| 2.6 | 2.9 | 2.9 | Sales/Total Assets | | | | 2.9 | 2.8 | 2.9 |
| 1.8 | 2.1 | 2.1 | | | | | 2.5 | 2.1 | 1.9 |
| 1.3 | 1.4 | 1.4 | | | | | 1.3 | 1.8 | 1.2 |
| 1.7 | 1.1 | 1.4 | % Depr., Dep., Amort./Sales | | | | | 1.3 | |
| (37)  3.4 | (35)  2.2 | (36)  2.5 | | | | | | (15)  2.1 | |
| 5.3 | 4.4 | 3.7 | | | | | | 2.8 | |
| 2.6 | | 1.6 | % Officers', Directors' Owners' Comp/Sales | | | | | | |
| | (13)  4.1 | (14)  3.1 | | | | | | | |
| | | 4.9 5.0 | | | | | | | |
| 728776M | 964564M | 1306719M | Net Sales ($) | | 2002M | 14163M | 71822M | 278451M | 940281M |
| 547832M | 569730M | 831938M | Total Assets ($) | | 927M | 10443M | 43415M | 128535M | 648618M |

(For the 0-1MM column, the notation "DATA NOT AVAILABLE" spans the Assets, Liabilities and Income Data sections.)

M = $ thousand    MM = $ million
See Pages 9 through 22 for Explanation of Ratios and Data

## Current Data Sorted by Assets

## Comparative Historical Data

| Type of Statement | 0-500M | 500M-2MM | 2-10MM | 10-50MM | 50-100MM | 100-250MM | | 4/1/07-3/31/08 ALL | 4/1/08-3/31/09 ALL |
|---|---|---|---|---|---|---|---|---|---|
| Unqualified | | | 3 | 8 | 3 | 2 | | 24 | 15 |
| Reviewed | | 1 | 18 | 8 | | | | 34 | 36 |
| Compiled | 1 | 3 | 14 | 7 | | 1 | | 12 | 16 |
| Tax Returns | 2 | 6 | 7 | 20 | | | | 7 | 7 |
| Other | 4 | 2 | 20 | 9 | 4 | 2 | | 46 | 60 |
| | | 15 (4/1-9/30/11) | | 103 (10/1/11-3/31/12) | | | | | |
| **NUMBER OF STATEMENTS** | 7 | 12 | 62 | 25 | 7 | 5 | | 123 | 134 |
| | % | % | % | % | % | % | | % | % |
| **ASSETS** | | | | | | | | | |
| Cash & Equivalents | | 15.1 | 11.1 | 5.2 | | | | 6.9 | 8.1 |
| Trade Receivables (net) | | 31.2 | 27.2 | 27.5 | | | | 27.5 | 26.1 |
| Inventory | | 31.0 | 25.5 | 26.8 | | | | 25.2 | 24.7 |
| All Other Current | | 1.3 | 1.3 | 1.7 | | | | 2.2 | 2.3 |
| Total Current | | 78.6 | 65.1 | 61.3 | | | | 61.9 | 61.2 |
| Fixed Assets (net) | | 17.7 | 23.0 | 28.3 | | | | 26.8 | 25.8 |
| Intangibles (net) | | 1.3 | 2.4 | 5.6 | | | | 4.5 | 5.4 |
| All Other Non-Current | | 2.4 | 9.5 | 4.8 | | | | 6.9 | 7.5 |
| Total | | 100.0 | 100.0 | 100.0 | | | | 100.0 | 100.0 |
| **LIABILITIES** | | | | | | | | | |
| Notes Payable-Short Term | | 3.3 | 9.8 | 12.7 | | | | 11.5 | 12.1 |
| Cur. Mat.-L.T.D. | | 5.2 | 2.2 | 3.3 | | | | 3.0 | 3.5 |
| Trade Payables | | 14.8 | 15.7 | 14.4 | | | | 14.7 | 14.6 |
| Income Taxes Payable | | .1 | .4 | .1 | | | | .2 | .2 |
| All Other Current | | 18.6 | 9.0 | 8.0 | | | | 9.6 | 11.3 |
| Total Current | | 41.9 | 37.2 | 38.4 | | | | 39.1 | 41.7 |
| Long-Term Debt | | 8.1 | 10.2 | 9.1 | | | | 14.5 | 14.0 |
| Deferred Taxes | | .0 | 1.0 | 1.0 | | | | .6 | .6 |
| All Other Non-Current | | 4.2 | 3.3 | 10.8 | | | | 8.0 | 8.2 |
| Net Worth | | 45.7 | 48.3 | 40.7 | | | | 37.8 | 35.6 |
| Total Liabilties & Net Worth | | 100.0 | 100.0 | 100.0 | | | | 100.0 | 100.0 |
| **INCOME DATA** | | | | | | | | | |
| Net Sales | | 100.0 | 100.0 | 100.0 | | | | 100.0 | 100.0 |
| Gross Profit | | 36.9 | 30.3 | 24.9 | | | | 26.6 | 27.2 |
| Operating Expenses | | 31.3 | 26.1 | 18.8 | | | | 22.7 | 22.7 |
| Operating Profit | | 5.6 | 4.2 | 6.2 | | | | 3.9 | 4.4 |
| All Other Expenses (net) | | .0 | .6 | .8 | | | | 1.4 | 1.2 |
| Profit Before Taxes | | 5.5 | 3.6 | 5.4 | | | | 2.6 | 3.3 |
| **RATIOS** | | | | | | | | | |
| Current | | 5.0 | 3.3 | 2.7 | | | | 2.8 | 3.0 |
| | | 2.3 | 2.0 | 1.7 | | | | 1.7 | 1.7 |
| | | 1.4 | 1.3 | 1.2 | | | | 1.1 | 1.1 |
| Quick | | 4.2 | 2.2 | 1.7 | | | | 1.7 | 1.8 |
| | | 1.3 | 1.0 | .9 | | | | (122) .9 | 1.0 |
| | | .7 | .6 | .6 | | | | .5 | .5 |
| Sales/Receivables | 31 11.6 | 32 11.3 | 41 8.9 | | | | | 37 10.0 | 31 11.9 |
| | 38 9.6 | 40 9.1 | 52 7.0 | | | | | 45 8.1 | 40 9.0 |
| | 43 8.5 | 53 6.9 | 58 6.3 | | | | | 56 6.6 | 50 7.3 |
| Cost of Sales/Inventory | 33 11.2 | 37 9.9 | 32 11.4 | | | | | 32 11.2 | 31 11.7 |
| | 52 7.0 | 56 6.5 | 62 5.9 | | | | | 53 6.9 | 51 7.2 |
| | 64 5.7 | 81 4.5 | 94 3.9 | | | | | 97 3.8 | 88 4.1 |
| Cost of Sales/Payables | 14 27.0 | 20 18.5 | 21 17.2 | | | | | 18 20.5 | 18 20.1 |
| | 27 13.3 | 31 11.8 | 31 11.6 | | | | | 29 12.7 | 26 13.8 |
| | 43 8.5 | 45 8.1 | 51 7.1 | | | | | 42 8.6 | 39 9.4 |
| Sales/Working Capital | | 4.7 | 4.2 | 5.5 | | | | 5.0 | 5.2 |
| | | 6.8 | 7.3 | 8.1 | | | | 9.6 | 9.9 |
| | | 17.9 | 26.0 | 16.9 | | | | 32.2 | 59.6 |
| EBIT/Interest | | | 19.3 | 29.1 | | | | 9.5 | 10.5 |
| | | (48) 6.1 | (23) 9.6 | | | | | (108) 2.8 | (120) 3.3 |
| | | 1.9 | 2.7 | | | | | 1.0 | 1.2 |
| Net Profit + Depr., Dep., Amort./Cur. Mat. L/T/D | | | 7.3 | 5.4 | | | | 5.1 | 5.0 |
| | | (13) 3.2 | (10) 3.7 | | | | | (31) 2.0 | (41) 2.8 |
| | | .5 | .5 | | | | | .8 | 1.6 |
| Fixed/Worth | | .1 | .2 | .3 | | | | .2 | .2 |
| | | .4 | .5 | .9 | | | | .6 | .6 |
| | | 1.5 | 1.3 | 1.5 | | | | 2.0 | 3.0 |
| Debt/Worth | | .3 | .3 | .7 | | | | .6 | .5 |
| | | 1.1 | .9 | 1.8 | | | | 1.8 | 1.6 |
| | | 7.8 | 2.8 | 4.9 | | | | 5.9 | 14.9 |
| % Profit Before Taxes/Tangible Net Worth | | 43.7 | 31.0 | 40.8 | | | | 42.3 | 37.9 |
| | (10) 23.3 | (57) 11.1 | (22) 32.3 | | | | | (107) 15.1 | (106) 15.4 |
| | 15.2 | 4.0 | 16.0 | | | | | 2.1 | 3.2 |
| % Profit Before Taxes/Total Assets | | 20.3 | 13.9 | 15.7 | | | | 14.0 | 14.6 |
| | | 12.8 | 5.2 | 11.9 | | | | 5.6 | 5.2 |
| | | 5.0 | 1.2 | 4.8 | | | | -.1 | .4 |
| Sales/Net Fixed Assets | | 124.7 | 27.8 | 19.4 | | | | 20.4 | 21.0 |
| | | 18.8 | 12.7 | 6.1 | | | | 10.1 | 11.2 |
| | | 9.4 | 5.9 | 3.5 | | | | 4.5 | 5.2 |
| Sales/Total Assets | | 3.6 | 3.0 | 2.6 | | | | 2.9 | 3.0 |
| | | 3.3 | 2.2 | 1.8 | | | | 2.0 | 2.1 |
| | | 2.6 | 1.6 | 1.5 | | | | 1.6 | 1.7 |
| % Depr., Dep., Amort./Sales | | | .9 | .6 | | | | 1.1 | 1.1 |
| | | (57) 1.3 | 2.8 | | | | | (105) 2.0 | (115) 1.9 |
| | | 2.6 | 4.6 | | | | | 3.3 | 3.9 |
| % Officers', Directors' Owners' Comp/Sales | | | 2.0 | | | | | 2.8 | 1.9 |
| | | (22) 3.7 | | | | | | (36) 4.2 | (38) 3.9 |
| | | 6.3 | | | | | | 6.4 | 7.6 |
| Net Sales ($) | 7465M | 55849M | 705497M | 1174156M | 659369M | 886095M | | 3634434M | 4548540M |
| Total Assets ($) | 1546M | 17858M | 300566M | 620985M | 408423M | 616282M | | 1967695M | 2324881M |

M = $ thousand     MM = $ million
See Pages 9 through 22 for Explanation of Ratios and Data

## Comparative Historical Data | Current Data Sorted by Sales

| | | | Type of Statement | 0-1MM | 1-3MM | 3-5MM | 5-10MM | 10-25MM | 25MM & OVER |
|---|---|---|---|---|---|---|---|---|---|
| 25 | 24 | 16 | Unqualified | | | 2 | | 1 | 13 |
| 24 | 35 | 27 | Reviewed | | | 4 | 6 | 9 | 8 |
| 14 | 18 | 19 | Compiled | 1 | 1 | 2 | 11 | 4 | 1 |
| 14 | 10 | 15 | Tax Returns | | | 6 | 5 | 3 | |
| 45 | 44 | 41 | Other | 3 | 1 | 4 | 6 | 13 | 14 |
| 4/1/09-3/31/10 | 4/1/10-3/31/11 | 4/1/11-3/31/12 | | | | 15 (4/1-9/30/11) | | 103 (10/1/11-3/31/12) | |
| ALL | ALL | ALL | | | | | | | |
| 122 | 131 | 118 | **NUMBER OF STATEMENTS** | 4 | 2 | 18 | 28 | 30 | 36 |
| % | % | % | **ASSETS** | % | % | % | % | % | % |
| 9.2 | 9.4 | 9.5 | Cash & Equivalents | | | 14.2 | 14.0 | 8.6 | 5.0 |
| 26.7 | 25.0 | 27.5 | Trade Receivables (net) | | | 26.8 | 24.1 | 31.3 | 26.2 |
| 24.2 | 26.9 | 27.2 | Inventory | | | 28.1 | 26.2 | 25.1 | 28.2 |
| 2.7 | 2.6 | 1.6 | All Other Current | | | 1.1 | 2.0 | .6 | 2.2 |
| 62.9 | 63.8 | 65.8 | Total Current | | | 70.3 | 66.3 | 65.6 | 61.6 |
| 27.2 | 25.7 | 23.9 | Fixed Assets (net) | | | 17.7 | 22.6 | 24.9 | 27.3 |
| 4.1 | 4.4 | 3.6 | Intangibles (net) | | | 1.4 | .9 | 4.0 | 6.9 |
| 5.9 | 6.0 | 6.7 | All Other Non-Current | | | 10.6 | 10.2 | 5.5 | 4.2 |
| 100.0 | 100.0 | 100.0 | Total | | | 100.0 | 100.0 | 100.0 | 100.0 |
| | | | **LIABILITIES** | | | | | | |
| 12.5 | 11.6 | 10.2 | Notes Payable-Short Term | | | 5.0 | 4.8 | 13.8 | 11.5 |
| 3.2 | 2.8 | 2.7 | Cur. Mat.-L.T.D. | | | 4.5 | 1.3 | 2.4 | 3.0 |
| 14.8 | 13.6 | 14.9 | Trade Payables | | | 10.3 | 13.6 | 18.6 | 14.1 |
| .1 | .2 | .3 | Income Taxes Payable | | | .1 | .6 | .3 | .2 |
| 7.9 | 8.1 | 9.1 | All Other Current | | | 9.8 | 10.6 | 10.3 | 6.9 |
| 38.6 | 36.3 | 37.2 | Total Current | | | 29.6 | 30.9 | 45.4 | 35.8 |
| 16.2 | 14.0 | 10.1 | Long-Term Debt | | | 12.9 | 10.6 | 7.7 | 8.7 |
| .7 | .9 | 1.1 | Deferred Taxes | | | .2 | 2.0 | .2 | 1.9 |
| 10.2 | 9.5 | 8.4 | All Other Non-Current | | | 3.2 | .9 | 2.2 | 11.6 |
| 34.3 | 39.3 | 43.3 | Net Worth | | | 54.1 | 55.6 | 44.5 | 41.9 |
| 100.0 | 100.0 | 100.0 | Total Liabilities & Net Worth | | | 100.0 | 100.0 | 100.0 | 100.0 |
| | | | **INCOME DATA** | | | | | | |
| 100.0 | 100.0 | 100.0 | Net Sales | | | 100.0 | 100.0 | 100.0 | 100.0 |
| 29.6 | 30.8 | 30.1 | Gross Profit | | | 40.2 | 32.0 | 28.3 | 25.0 |
| 25.1 | 24.6 | 24.8 | Operating Expenses | | | 35.1 | 27.6 | 24.0 | 17.7 |
| 4.5 | 6.1 | 5.3 | Operating Profit | | | 5.1 | 4.5 | 4.3 | 7.3 |
| 1.6 | 1.0 | .6 | All Other Expenses (net) | | | .0 | .4 | .9 | .8 |
| 2.9 | 5.2 | 4.7 | Profit Before Taxes | | | 5.1 | 4.0 | 3.4 | 6.5 |
| | | | **RATIOS** | | | | | | |
| 3.3 | 3.6 | 3.2 | | | | 12.5 | 3.8 | 2.9 | 2.8 |
| 1.9 | 2.1 | 2.0 | Current | | | 2.7 | 2.4 | 1.4 | 2.0 |
| 1.2 | 1.3 | 1.3 | | | | 1.3 | 1.5 | 1.1 | 1.3 |
| 2.0 | 2.1 | 2.1 | | | | 7.2 | 2.8 | 2.0 | 1.6 |
| 1.0 | 1.0 | 1.0 | Quick | | | 1.7 | 1.2 | 1.0 | 1.0 |
| .6 | .6 | .6 | | | | .7 | .6 | .6 | .6 |
| 35  10.3 | 33  10.9 | 33  11.2 | | | | 30  12.1 | 30  12.2 | 34  10.6 | 38  9.6 |
| 45  8.0 | 43  8.5 | 42  8.7 | Sales/Receivables | | | 34  10.8 | 41  9.0 | 46  7.9 | 45  8.1 |
| 56  6.5 | 53  6.8 | 54  6.8 | | | | 45  8.1 | 51  7.2 | 54  6.7 | 57  6.4 |
| 34  10.6 | 35  10.3 | 37  9.9 | | | | 51  7.1 | 37  9.8 | 35  10.4 | 35  10.3 |
| 54  6.8 | 66  5.5 | 60  6.1 | Cost of Sales/Inventory | | | 70  5.2 | 55  6.6 | 49  7.4 | 73  5.0 |
| 92  4.0 | 110  3.3 | 96  3.8 | | | | 111  3.3 | 83  4.4 | 64  5.7 | 111  3.3 |
| 20  18.3 | 19  19.5 | 20  18.2 | | | | 9  39.6 | 20  18.6 | 22  16.8 | 21  17.0 |
| 29  12.7 | 29  12.7 | 30  12.2 | Cost of Sales/Payables | | | 27  13.3 | 32  11.3 | 30  12.3 | 28  13.1 |
| 43  8.6 | 42  8.8 | 44  8.3 | | | | 45  8.1 | 43  8.5 | 51  7.1 | 44  8.3 |
| 4.4 | 4.3 | 4.6 | | | | 4.1 | 3.7 | 5.4 | 4.8 |
| 7.9 | 7.4 | 7.3 | Sales/Working Capital | | | 6.6 | 5.7 | 10.8 | 6.9 |
| 26.9 | 16.7 | 18.3 | | | | 13.4 | 12.4 | 50.3 | 14.4 |
| 11.4 | 13.1 | 23.8 | | | | 8.7 | 27.8 | 19.3 | 38.1 |
| (105)  3.3 | (109)  5.4 | (94)  7.6 | EBIT/Interest | | | (12)  6.1 | (20)  6.4 | (24)  8.2 | (35)  10.5 |
| 1.1 | 2.3 | 2.0 | | | | 2.3 | 1.4 | 2.0 | 2.7 |
| 7.0 | 4.5 | 8.4 | | | | | | | 10.3 |
| (32)  3.1 | (32)  3.2 | (30)  4.4 | Net Profit + Depr., Dep., Amort./Cur. Mat. L/T/D | | | | | (15)  4.7 | 4.7 |
| .6 | 1.7 | .7 | | | | | | | .8 |
| .3 | .2 | .2 | | | | .1 | .1 | .3 | .3 |
| .8 | .5 | .5 | Fixed/Worth | | | .4 | .3 | .7 | .8 |
| 2.6 | 1.5 | 1.3 | | | | 1.2 | .7 | 1.4 | 1.4 |
| .5 | .4 | .4 | | | | .1 | .3 | .4 | .7 |
| 1.7 | 1.3 | 1.1 | Debt/Worth | | | 1.0 | .6 | 1.6 | 1.5 |
| 10.1 | 3.6 | 2.9 | | | | 4.4 | 1.2 | 3.8 | 3.7 |
| 32.8 | 36.4 | 36.3 | | | | 27.1 | 28.8 | 35.2 | 41.6 |
| (98)  15.6 | (117)  18.5 | (105)  18.3 | % Profit Before Taxes/Tangible Net Worth | | | (17)  18.3 | (26)  11.3 | (27)  16.5 | (32)  30.5 |
| .4 | 7.0 | 5.4 | | | | 5.2 | 2.8 | 5.7 | 15.3 |
| 13.9 | 14.7 | 16.6 | | | | 17.5 | 15.8 | 14.0 | 21.8 |
| 5.2 | 8.6 | 8.8 | % Profit Before Taxes/Total Assets | | | 11.2 | 5.5 | 6.1 | 12.5 |
| .0 | 3.2 | 1.9 | | | | 1.0 | .8 | 2.8 | 4.6 |
| 25.3 | 30.2 | 27.1 | | | | 36.2 | 35.4 | 37.0 | 18.4 |
| 9.0 | 9.9 | 9.9 | Sales/Net Fixed Assets | | | 14.6 | 10.6 | 14.5 | 6.5 |
| 4.7 | 5.2 | 5.1 | | | | 8.1 | 5.8 | 5.6 | 4.1 |
| 2.9 | 2.8 | 3.2 | | | | 3.4 | 2.9 | 3.5 | 2.5 |
| 2.0 | 1.9 | 2.2 | Sales/Total Assets | | | 2.1 | 2.1 | 2.6 | 1.7 |
| 1.4 | 1.5 | 1.6 | | | | 1.6 | 1.7 | 1.8 | 1.4 |
| 1.3 | 1.0 | .9 | | | | .6 | 1.0 | .7 | .9 |
| (101)  2.0 | (113)  2.1 | (105)  1.6 | % Depr., Dep., Amort./Sales | | | (15)  1.4 | (26)  1.7 | (26)  1.3 | (35)  2.2 |
| 4.1 | 3.4 | 3.7 | | | | 2.4 | 3.8 | 2.8 | 4.6 |
| 1.9 | 1.8 | 1.2 | | | | 3.3 | 1.8 | | |
| (33)  4.0 | (37)  4.4 | (39)  3.6 | % Officers', Directors' Owners' Comp/Sales | | | (13)  4.1 | (10)  2.7 | | |
| 6.3 | 8.7 | 7.2 | | | | 10.8 | 6.5 | | |
| 4246318M | 4313680M | 3488431M | Net Sales ($) | 863M | 3599M | 70077M | 204386M | 469216M | 2740290M |
| 2517611M | 2392069M | 1965660M | Total Assets ($) | 275M | 830M | 42885M | 100849M | 208332M | 1612489M |

© RMA 2012

M = $ thousand    MM = $ million
See Pages 9 through 22 for Explanation of Ratios and Data

## Current Data Sorted by Assets

## Comparative Historical Data

| 0-500M | 500M-2MM | 2-10MM | 10-50MM | 50-100MM | 100-250MM | Type of Statement | 4/1/07-3/31/08 ALL | 4/1/08-3/31/09 ALL |
|---|---|---|---|---|---|---|---|---|
| | | 1 | 4 | 3 | 1 | Unqualified | 18 | 16 |
| | 1 | 1 | 3 | | | Reviewed | 10 | 9 |
| | 1 | | | | | Compiled | 4 | 6 |
| 1 | | 2 | | | | Tax Returns | 3 | 2 |
| 1 | 3 | 4 | 4 | 4 | 4 | Other | 18 | 20 |
| | | | 9 (4/1-9/30/11) | | 29 (10/1/11-3/31/12) | | | |
| 2 | 5 | 8 | 11 | 7 | 5 | **NUMBER OF STATEMENTS** | 53 | 53 |
| % | % | % | % | % | % | | % | % |

**ASSETS**

| 10-50MM | Account | 4/1/07-3/31/08 ALL | 4/1/08-3/31/09 ALL |
|---|---|---|---|
| 5.7 | Cash & Equivalents | 8.5 | 10.9 |
| 11.6 | Trade Receivables (net) | 20.1 | 17.6 |
| 25.8 | Inventory | 23.5 | 25.4 |
| 1.3 | All Other Current | 1.5 | 1.8 |
| 44.3 | Total Current | 53.7 | 55.8 |
| 46.3 | Fixed Assets (net) | 36.2 | 35.2 |
| 3.6 | Intangibles (net) | 4.7 | 4.0 |
| 5.8 | All Other Non-Current | 5.5 | 5.0 |
| 100.0 | Total | 100.0 | 100.0 |

**LIABILITIES**

| 10-50MM | Account | 4/1/07-3/31/08 ALL | 4/1/08-3/31/09 ALL |
|---|---|---|---|
| 4.9 | Notes Payable-Short Term | 6.5 | 6.7 |
| 10.8 | Cur. Mat.-L.T.D. | 2.4 | 5.2 |
| 3.5 | Trade Payables | 11.9 | 10.0 |
| .1 | Income Taxes Payable | .2 | .4 |
| 7.7 | All Other Current | 7.1 | 8.4 |
| 26.9 | Total Current | 28.0 | 30.7 |
| 25.7 | Long-Term Debt | 24.2 | 19.8 |
| .6 | Deferred Taxes | 1.6 | 1.2 |
| 2.9 | All Other Non-Current | 3.5 | 6.5 |
| 43.9 | Net Worth | 42.6 | 41.8 |
| 100.0 | Total Liabilities & Net Worth | 100.0 | 100.0 |

**INCOME DATA**

| 10-50MM | Account | 4/1/07-3/31/08 ALL | 4/1/08-3/31/09 ALL |
|---|---|---|---|
| 100.0 | Net Sales | 100.0 | 100.0 |
| 22.7 | Gross Profit | 33.1 | 29.3 |
| 29.5 | Operating Expenses | 24.9 | 26.1 |
| -6.7 | Operating Profit | 8.3 | 3.1 |
| .9 | All Other Expenses (net) | 2.0 | 1.6 |
| -7.6 | Profit Before Taxes | 6.2 | 1.5 |

**RATIOS**

| 2-10MM | 10-50MM | Ratio | 4/1/07-3/31/08 ALL | 4/1/08-3/31/09 ALL |
|---|---|---|---|---|
| | 6.5 | Current | 3.7 | 3.9 |
| | 2.3 | | 2.3 | 2.0 |
| | 1.5 | | 1.4 | 1.2 |
| | 3.5 | Quick | 1.8 | 1.8 |
| | .7 | | .9 | 1.0 |
| | .4 | | .4 | .4 |
| 36 | 10.0 | Sales/Receivables | 29   12.7 | 23   15.7 |
| 45 | 8.2 | | 37   10.0 | 28   12.9 |
| 49 | 7.5 | | 48   7.7 | 39   9.3 |
| 118 | 3.1 | Cost of Sales/Inventory | 58   6.3 | 39   9.3 |
| 174 | 2.1 | | 82   4.5 | 90   4.1 |
| 228 | 1.6 | | 152   2.4 | 158   2.3 |
| 15 | 24.5 | Cost of Sales/Payables | 15   23.7 | 15   24.9 |
| 19 | 19.7 | | 28   13.2 | 21   17.0 |
| 21 | 17.1 | | 45   8.0 | 33   11.0 |
| | 1.7 | Sales/Working Capital | 3.4 | 3.2 |
| | 3.1 | | 7.0 | 5.8 |
| | 7.1 | | 14.6 | 31.5 |
| | 3.5 | EBIT/Interest | 5.0 | 7.7 |
| | -1.4 | | (47)   2.3 | (48)   2.2 |
| | -2.9 | | 1.0 | -.8 |
| | | Net Profit + Depr., Dep., Amort./Cur. Mat. L/T/D | 4.2 | |
| | | | (11)   2.1 | |
| | | | 1.4 | |
| | .6 | Fixed/Worth | .3 | .4 |
| | 1.1 | | 1.0 | .9 |
| | 2.3 | | 2.3 | 2.4 |
| | .4 | Debt/Worth | .5 | .6 |
| | 1.4 | | 2.0 | 1.4 |
| | 3.4 | | 3.7 | 4.8 |
| | 14.9 | % Profit Before Taxes/Tangible Net Worth | 39.4 | 30.9 |
| | (10)   -10.8 | | (48)   14.9 | (49)   6.3 |
| | -17.4 | | .2 | -8.4 |
| | 5.0 | % Profit Before Taxes/Total Assets | 16.5 | 12.6 |
| | -5.7 | | 5.2 | 4.0 |
| | -7.1 | | .1 | -2.5 |
| | 3.2 | Sales/Net Fixed Assets | 19.1 | 20.9 |
| | 1.6 | | 3.4 | 5.1 |
| | .8 | | 1.4 | 1.4 |
| | 1.3 | Sales/Total Assets | 2.3 | 2.3 |
| | .7 | | 1.6 | 1.4 |
| | .5 | | .8 | .8 |
| | 5.2 | % Depr., Dep., Amort./Sales | 1.4 | 1.1 |
| | 8.3 | | (44)   3.6 | (41)   3.7 |
| | 16.7 | | 7.2 | 8.8 |
| | | % Officers', Directors' Owners' Comp/Sales | 1.2 | 2.9 |
| | | | (12)   3.4 | (13)   4.4 |
| | | | 5.2 | 9.3 |

| 0-500M | 500M-2MM | 2-10MM | 10-50MM | 50-100MM | 100-250MM | | 4/1/07-3/31/08 ALL | 4/1/08-3/31/09 ALL |
|---|---|---|---|---|---|---|---|---|
| 1593M | 12983M | 82780M | 174535M | 499160M | 429082M | Net Sales ($) | 2268332M | 1565121M |
| 769M | 6683M | 44502M | 232384M | 564444M | 732431M | Total Assets ($) | 2250966M | 1580363M |

M = $ thousand    MM = $ million
See Pages 9 through 22 for Explanation of Ratios and Data

## Comparative Historical Data | Current Data Sorted by Sales

| | | | Type of Statement | 0-1MM | 1-3MM | 3-5MM | 5-10MM | 10-25MM | 25MM & OVER |
|---|---|---|---|---|---|---|---|---|---|
| 12 | 10 | 9 | Unqualified | | | 1 | 1 | 2 | 5 |
| 8 | 7 | 5 | Reviewed | | 1 | | | 3 | 1 |
| 5 | 2 | 1 | Compiled | | | | 1 | | |
| 7 | 3 | 3 | Tax Returns | | | 1 | 1 | | |
| 22 | 19 | 20 | Other | 1 | 3 | 1 | 1 | 7 | 8 |
| 4/1/09-3/31/10 ALL | 4/1/10-3/31/11 ALL | 4/1/11-3/31/12 ALL | | | 9 (4/1-9/30/11) | | | 29 (10/1/11-3/31/12) | |
| 54 | 41 | 38 | NUMBER OF STATEMENTS | 2 | 4 | 4 | 5 | 10 | 13 |
| % | % | % | ASSETS | % | % | % | % | % | % |
| 8.1 | 10.8 | 6.1 | Cash & Equivalents | | | | | 10.0 | 1.7 |
| 15.0 | 12.9 | 15.6 | Trade Receivables (net) | | | | | 19.2 | 8.8 |
| 29.7 | 24.8 | 28.2 | Inventory | | | | | 26.0 | 28.0 |
| 1.5 | 1.8 | 1.4 | All Other Current | | | | | .5 | 2.4 |
| 54.3 | 50.3 | 51.4 | Total Current | | | | | 55.6 | 41.0 |
| 34.2 | 37.8 | 38.9 | Fixed Assets (net) | | | | | 32.1 | 45.6 |
| 5.6 | 4.3 | 4.0 | Intangibles (net) | | | | | 9.5 | 3.9 |
| 5.9 | 7.9 | 5.7 | All Other Non-Current | | | | | 2.8 | 9.5 |
| 100.0 | 100.0 | 100.0 | Total | | | | | 100.0 | 100.0 |
| | | | LIABILITIES | | | | | | |
| 6.9 | 7.1 | 6.9 | Notes Payable-Short Term | | | | | 10.2 | 1.5 |
| 5.4 | 3.6 | 7.5 | Cur. Mat.-L.T.D. | | | | | 2.5 | 6.3 |
| 9.1 | 7.2 | 7.1 | Trade Payables | | | | | 6.1 | 5.2 |
| .1 | .1 | .0 | Income Taxes Payable | | | | | .1 | .0 |
| 12.0 | 8.5 | 9.6 | All Other Current | | | | | 6.1 | 18.3 |
| 33.5 | 26.4 | 31.1 | Total Current | | | | | 25.0 | 31.3 |
| 19.1 | 21.7 | 19.3 | Long-Term Debt | | | | | 13.8 | 22.5 |
| 1.1 | 1.2 | 1.3 | Deferred Taxes | | | | | 1.7 | 1.4 |
| 4.7 | 7.3 | 8.4 | All Other Non-Current | | | | | 7.7 | 7.7 |
| 41.6 | 43.4 | 39.9 | Net Worth | | | | | 51.8 | 37.1 |
| 100.0 | 100.0 | 100.0 | Total Liabilities & Net Worth | | | | | 100.0 | 100.0 |
| | | | INCOME DATA | | | | | | |
| 100.0 | 100.0 | 100.0 | Net Sales | | | | | 100.0 | 100.0 |
| 30.5 | 31.0 | 25.0 | Gross Profit | | | | | 27.2 | 22.2 |
| 30.7 | 31.9 | 27.2 | Operating Expenses | | | | | 24.3 | 25.2 |
| -.3 | -1.0 | -2.1 | Operating Profit | | | | | 2.9 | -3.0 |
| 1.9 | 1.5 | 2.1 | All Other Expenses (net) | | | | | .8 | 2.4 |
| -2.2 | -2.5 | -4.3 | Profit Before Taxes | | | | | 2.1 | -5.4 |
| | | | RATIOS | | | | | | |
| 3.0 | 5.7 | 4.8 | | | | | | 6.6 | 3.0 |
| 1.9 | 2.3 | 2.3 | Current | | | | | 3.6 | 2.3 |
| 1.2 | 1.2 | 1.3 | | | | | | 1.4 | 1.0 |
| 1.1 | 2.2 | 2.1 | | | | | | 4.6 | .8 |
| .7 | .8 | .7 | Quick | | | | | 1.2 | .7 |
| .3 | .4 | .3 | | | | | | .4 | .1 |
| 27 13.3 | 32 11.6 | 34 10.6 | | | | | | 37 9.9 | 28 13.2 |
| 34 10.6 | 38 9.6 | 42 8.6 | Sales/Receivables | | | | | 43 8.5 | 40 9.1 |
| 43 8.4 | 47 7.8 | 49 7.4 | | | | | | 53 6.9 | 47 7.8 |
| 80 4.6 | 71 5.1 | 81 4.5 | | | | | | 69 5.3 | 96 3.8 |
| 115 3.2 | 117 3.1 | 118 3.1 | Cost of Sales/Inventory | | | | | 96 3.8 | 146 2.5 |
| 233 1.6 | 217 1.7 | 203 1.8 | | | | | | 135 2.7 | 228 1.6 |
| 13 28.3 | 12 30.7 | 15 23.8 | | | | | | 17 21.7 | 12 31.3 |
| 24 15.2 | 22 16.5 | 21 17.3 | Cost of Sales/Payables | | | | | 20 18.2 | 19 19.0 |
| 38 9.5 | 32 11.5 | 33 10.9 | | | | | | 29 12.8 | 42 8.6 |
| 2.6 | 2.1 | 2.3 | | | | | | 1.8 | 2.5 |
| 6.5 | 4.2 | 4.5 | Sales/Working Capital | | | | | 4.7 | 5.0 |
| 22.8 | 19.8 | 20.5 | | | | | | 14.3 | NM |
| 4.7 | 4.7 | 3.5 | | | | | | | 1.5 |
| (48) 1.1 | (35) -.8 | (35) -1.2 | EBIT/Interest | | | | | | (12) -1.6 |
| -1.4 | -2.1 | -2.9 | | | | | | | -11.2 |
| | | | Net Profit + Depr., Dep., Amort./Cur. Mat. L/T/D | | | | | | |
| .3 | .5 | .5 | | | | | | .2 | .8 |
| .8 | 1.0 | 1.2 | Fixed/Worth | | | | | .6 | 1.2 |
| 2.6 | 2.1 | 2.6 | | | | | | 2.4 | 2.2 |
| .5 | .5 | .5 | | | | | | .4 | .6 |
| 1.6 | 1.3 | 2.2 | Debt/Worth | | | | | .9 | 2.4 |
| 4.7 | 3.1 | 4.3 | | | | | | 3.0 | 3.2 |
| 21.2 | 13.6 | 17.9 | | | | | | | 5.8 |
| (47) .6 | (35) -.2 | (33) -9.8 | % Profit Before Taxes/Tangible Net Worth | | | | | | (12) -13.8 |
| -31.8 | -11.8 | -17.8 | | | | | | | -26.1 |
| 5.7 | 9.2 | 8.1 | | | | | | 17.3 | 5.2 |
| .2 | -.2 | -3.0 | % Profit Before Taxes/Total Assets | | | | | 5.9 | -3.9 |
| -9.9 | -6.2 | -9.0 | | | | | | -2.8 | -7.0 |
| 17.5 | 16.9 | 11.9 | | | | | | 40.8 | 4.5 |
| 2.9 | 3.0 | 2.8 | Sales/Net Fixed Assets | | | | | 7.0 | 1.3 |
| 1.0 | .8 | .9 | | | | | | .8 | .9 |
| 2.1 | 1.9 | 1.8 | | | | | | 2.1 | 1.2 |
| 1.1 | 1.0 | 1.0 | Sales/Total Assets | | | | | 1.3 | .9 |
| .6 | .5 | .5 | | | | | | .6 | .4 |
| 1.6 | 1.8 | 2.9 | | | | | | | 5.2 |
| (38) 5.3 | (33) 4.9 | (32) 6.4 | % Depr., Dep., Amort./Sales | | | | | | (10) 8.8 |
| 10.6 | 12.6 | 12.3 | | | | | | | 15.5 |
| | 2.7 | 2.6 | | | | | | | |
| | (11) 3.8 | (12) 3.4 | % Officers', Directors' Owners' Comp/Sales | | | | | | |
| | 5.1 | 6.1 | | | | | | | |
| 1565213M | 1115609M | 1200133M | Net Sales ($) | 1593M | 8170M | 15049M | 38635M | 169131M | 967555M |
| 1894832M | 1510261M | 1581213M | Total Assets ($) | 769M | 5036M | 16633M | 77194M | 226349M | 1255232M |

M = $ thousand    MM = $ million
See Pages 9 through 22 for Explanation of Ratios and Data

**Current Data Sorted by Assets**      **Comparative Historical Data**

| 0-500M | 500M-2MM | 2-10MM | 10-50MM | 50-100MM | 100-250MM | Type of Statement | 4/1/07-3/31/08 ALL | 4/1/08-3/31/09 ALL |
|---|---|---|---|---|---|---|---|---|
| 3 | 3 | 1 | 3 | | | Unqualified | 3 | 5 |
| | 2 | 4 | 2 | | | Reviewed | 3 | 3 |
| | 3 | 2 | 7 | | | Compiled | 4 | 3 |
| 1 | | 2 | | | | Tax Returns | 2 | 2 |
| | | 6 | | | 1 | Other | 15 | 9 |
| 10 (4/1-9/30/11) | | | 30 (10/1/11-3/31/12) | | | | | |
| 4 | 8 | 15 | 12 | | 1 | NUMBER OF STATEMENTS | 27 | 22 |
| % | % | % | % | % | % | **ASSETS** | % | % |
| | | 11.8 | 7.4 | | | Cash & Equivalents | 9.2 | 9.6 |
| | | 30.1 | 21.5 | | | Trade Receivables (net) | 29.5 | 30.3 |
| | | 17.6 | 27.5 | | | Inventory | 24.6 | 19.7 |
| | | 3.0 | 4.1 | | | All Other Current | 1.5 | 2.2 |
| | | 62.5 | 60.5 | | | Total Current | 64.8 | 61.7 |
| | | 34.1 | 29.6 | | | Fixed Assets (net) | 24.9 | 30.1 |
| | | 1.3 | 5.9 | | | Intangibles (net) | 7.6 | 6.3 |
| | | 2.1 | 4.0 | | | All Other Non-Current | 2.7 | 2.0 |
| | | 100.0 | 100.0 | | | Total | 100.0 | 100.0 |
| | | | | | | **LIABILITIES** | | |
| | | 6.5 | 8.0 | | | Notes Payable-Short Term | 9.9 | 11.2 |
| | | 5.1 | 3.3 | | | Cur. Mat.-L.T.D. | 2.1 | 3.5 |
| | | 12.7 | 13.2 | | | Trade Payables | 16.2 | 11.9 |
| | | .1 | .0 | | | Income Taxes Payable | .2 | .4 |
| | | 7.0 | 9.2 | | | All Other Current | 5.0 | 6.1 |
| | | 31.4 | 33.8 | | | Total Current | 33.4 | 33.2 |
| | | 12.9 | 14.2 | | | Long-Term Debt | 15.0 | 15.9 |
| | | .2 | 1.1 | | | Deferred Taxes | .3 | .3 |
| | | 14.3 | 2.3 | | | All Other Non-Current | 3.4 | 8.0 |
| | | 41.2 | 48.5 | | | Net Worth | 47.9 | 42.6 |
| | | 100.0 | 100.0 | | | Total Liabilities & Net Worth | 100.0 | 100.0 |
| | | | | | | **INCOME DATA** | | |
| | | 100.0 | 100.0 | | | Net Sales | 100.0 | 100.0 |
| | | 39.9 | 28.4 | | | Gross Profit | 36.2 | 34.9 |
| | | 35.0 | 24.3 | | | Operating Expenses | 33.1 | 29.8 |
| | | 4.9 | 4.1 | | | Operating Profit | 3.1 | 5.0 |
| | | .5 | .7 | | | All Other Expenses (net) | .9 | 1.5 |
| | | 4.4 | 3.4 | | | Profit Before Taxes | 2.1 | 3.5 |
| | | | | | | **RATIOS** | | |
| | | 3.4 | 5.7 | | | Current | 4.4 | 4.9 |
| | | 2.0 | 2.0 | | | | 2.1 | 1.7 |
| | | 1.5 | 1.4 | | | | 1.2 | 1.1 |
| | | 2.6 | 2.3 | | | Quick | 3.1 | 3.3 |
| | | 1.3 | .9 | | | | 1.1 | .8 |
| | | .8 | .6 | | | | .7 | .6 |
| | | 36   10.1 | 21   17.1 | | | Sales/Receivables | 27   13.3 | 34   10.7 |
| | | 50   7.3 | 43   8.5 | | | | 45   8.1 | 46   7.9 |
| | | 60   6.1 | 61   6.0 | | | | 64   5.7 | 64   5.7 |
| | | 9   42.5 | 43   8.5 | | | Cost of Sales/Inventory | 22   16.8 | 19   18.8 |
| | | 29   12.7 | 55   6.6 | | | | 43   8.6 | 44   8.3 |
| | | 60   6.1 | 126   2.9 | | | | 120   3.0 | 58   6.3 |
| | | 22   16.3 | 16   22.5 | | | Cost of Sales/Payables | 24   15.4 | 14   26.4 |
| | | 31   11.9 | 33   11.2 | | | | 43   8.5 | 24   15.0 |
| | | 47   7.7 | 47   7.8 | | | | 49   7.4 | 50   7.4 |
| | | 4.8 | 3.1 | | | Sales/Working Capital | 3.1 | 5.4 |
| | | 8.0 | 5.8 | | | | 10.0 | 9.5 |
| | | 11.3 | 14.4 | | | | 21.7 | 39.1 |
| | | 8.7 | 18.4 | | | EBIT/Interest | 13.6 | 8.6 |
| | | (14) 6.1 | (11) 3.6 | | | | (26) 1.8 | 3.3 |
| | | 1.6 | 1.3 | | | | -1.4 | 1.7 |
| | | | | | | Net Profit + Depr., Dep., Amort./Cur. Mat. L/T/D | | |
| | | .7 | .3 | | | Fixed/Worth | .2 | .4 |
| | | .9 | .7 | | | | .5 | 1.1 |
| | | 2.2 | 1.7 | | | | 1.5 | 2.7 |
| | | .5 | .4 | | | Debt/Worth | .3 | .5 |
| | | 1.5 | 1.4 | | | | 1.9 | 2.0 |
| | | 5.2 | 3.2 | | | | 6.4 | 4.8 |
| | | 30.8 | 27.7 | | | % Profit Before Taxes/Tangible Net Worth | 20.0 | 61.2 |
| | | (14) 18.1 | (11) 14.7 | | | | (23) 6.7 | (20) 21.9 |
| | | 6.0 | 6.0 | | | | -27.7 | 7.0 |
| | | 13.1 | 10.1 | | | % Profit Before Taxes/Total Assets | 14.0 | 14.6 |
| | | 9.3 | 5.1 | | | | 1.8 | 5.3 |
| | | 1.4 | 1.1 | | | | -11.5 | 2.2 |
| | | 13.8 | 16.2 | | | Sales/Net Fixed Assets | 26.8 | 14.7 |
| | | 6.7 | 5.5 | | | | 12.8 | 6.8 |
| | | 3.3 | 3.8 | | | | 5.2 | 4.5 |
| | | 2.8 | 2.3 | | | Sales/Total Assets | 3.5 | 3.1 |
| | | 2.4 | 1.5 | | | | 2.0 | 2.0 |
| | | 1.3 | 1.4 | | | | 1.5 | 1.7 |
| | | 2.1 | 1.6 | | | % Depr., Dep., Amort./Sales | 1.3 | 2.1 |
| | | (13) 3.1 | (10) 2.5 | | | | (22) 1.6 | (17) 2.7 |
| | | 4.9 | 3.3 | | | | 3.3 | 3.5 |
| | | | | | | % Officers', Directors' Owners' Comp/Sales | | |
| 6842M | 32386M | 149706M | 445100M | | 264591M | Net Sales ($) | 1287380M | 1252816M |
| 1363M | 9962M | 72206M | 240957M | | 167668M | Total Assets ($) | 569642M | 530203M |

## Comparative Historical Data | Current Data Sorted by Sales

| 6 3 1 6 6 | 4 7 4 2 16 | 4 6 5 7 18 | Type of Statement<br>Unqualified<br>Reviewed<br>Compiled<br>Tax Returns<br>Other | 0-1MM | 1-3MM | 3-5MM | 5-10MM | 10-25MM | 25MM & OVER |
|---|---|---|---|---|---|---|---|---|---|
| | | | Unqualified | | | | | 2 | 2 |
| | | | Reviewed | | | | 3 | 3 | |
| | | | Compiled | | 1 | 2 | 1 | 1 | |
| | | | Tax Returns | 1 | 3 | 2 | 1 | | |
| | | | Other | 1 | 1 | 2 | 3 | 5 | 6 |
| 4/1/09-<br>3/31/10<br>ALL | 4/1/10-<br>3/31/11<br>ALL | 4/1/11-<br>3/31/12<br>ALL | | 10 (4/1-9/30/11) | | | 30 (10/1/11-3/31/12) | | |
| 22 | 33 | 40 | NUMBER OF STATEMENTS | 2 | 5 | 6 | 8 | 11 | 8 |
| % | % | % | ASSETS | % | % | % | % | % | % |
| 8.9 | 7.6 | 11.5 | Cash & Equivalents | | | | | 16.1 | |
| 25.8 | 26.9 | 27.2 | Trade Receivables (net) | | | | | 23.4 | |
| 18.3 | 24.1 | 22.2 | Inventory | | | | | 22.9 | |
| 2.0 | 2.7 | 3.4 | All Other Current | | | | | 2.4 | |
| 55.1 | 61.4 | 64.3 | Total Current | | | | | 64.8 | |
| 36.9 | 30.5 | 29.6 | Fixed Assets (net) | | | | | 29.5 | |
| 5.2 | 5.3 | 2.3 | Intangibles (net) | | | | | 3.8 | |
| 2.9 | 2.8 | 3.7 | All Other Non-Current | | | | | 2.0 | |
| 100.0 | 100.0 | 100.0 | Total | | | | | 100.0 | |
| | | | LIABILITIES | | | | | | |
| 6.7 | 9.8 | 6.2 | Notes Payable-Short Term | | | | | .7 | |
| 5.6 | 3.5 | 3.7 | Cur. Mat.-L.T.D. | | | | | 3.6 | |
| 15.6 | 17.0 | 17.6 | Trade Payables | | | | | 7.8 | |
| .2 | .7 | .0 | Income Taxes Payable | | | | | .0 | |
| 9.5 | 7.1 | 10.8 | All Other Current | | | | | 8.1 | |
| 37.6 | 38.0 | 38.3 | Total Current | | | | | 20.2 | |
| 22.7 | 15.0 | 14.8 | Long-Term Debt | | | | | 11.2 | |
| .7 | .4 | .4 | Deferred Taxes | | | | | .4 | |
| 5.2 | 7.1 | 7.6 | All Other Non-Current | | | | | 8.1 | |
| 33.9 | 39.5 | 38.8 | Net Worth | | | | | 60.1 | |
| 100.0 | 100.0 | 100.0 | Total Liabilities & Net Worth | | | | | 100.0 | |
| | | | INCOME DATA | | | | | | |
| 100.0 | 100.0 | 100.0 | Net Sales | | | | | 100.0 | |
| 34.4 | 31.4 | 35.2 | Gross Profit | | | | | 33.1 | |
| 33.6 | 28.0 | 32.3 | Operating Expenses | | | | | 25.9 | |
| .8 | 3.3 | 2.9 | Operating Profit | | | | | 7.2 | |
| 1.3 | .9 | .5 | All Other Expenses (net) | | | | | .6 | |
| -.5 | 2.4 | 2.4 | Profit Before Taxes | | | | | 6.5 | |
| | | | RATIOS | | | | | | |
| 2.6 | 3.3 | 3.5 | Current | | | | | 6.2 | |
| 1.6 | 1.7 | 1.9 | | | | | | 2.2 | |
| 1.0 | 1.2 | 1.3 | | | | | | 1.9 | |
| 1.5 | 2.1 | 2.4 | Quick | | | | | 4.4 | |
| .9 | 1.2 | 1.1 | | | | | | 1.6 | |
| .6 | .7 | .6 | | | | | | 1.1 | |
| 26 14.1 | 22 16.2 | 23 15.8 | Sales/Receivables | | | | | 19 19.2 | |
| 34 10.7 | 39 9.3 | 39 9.3 | | | | | | 43 8.5 | |
| 58 6.3 | 56 6.5 | 57 6.4 | | | | | | 57 6.4 | |
| 18 20.3 | 18 20.5 | 12 31.1 | Cost of Sales/Inventory | | | | | 26 14.2 | |
| 32 11.2 | 34 10.7 | 43 8.5 | | | | | | 41 9.0 | |
| 78 4.7 | 62 5.9 | 89 4.1 | | | | | | 130 2.8 | |
| 18 20.3 | 18 20.1 | 16 22.5 | Cost of Sales/Payables | | | | | 5 73.0 | |
| 36 10.0 | 30 12.1 | 33 11.2 | | | | | | 22 16.3 | |
| 53 6.8 | 51 7.1 | 59 6.2 | | | | | | 29 12.6 | |
| 5.9 | 5.2 | 4.7 | Sales/Working Capital | | | | | 2.7 | |
| 13.3 | 9.6 | 8.6 | | | | | | 5.5 | |
| NM | 62.5 | 23.8 | | | | | | 8.0 | |
| 3.9 | 10.6 | 8.4 | EBIT/Interest | | | | | 19.7 | |
| (20) 2.6 | (28) 2.2 | (34) 3.6 | | | | | | 11.0 | |
| -1.7 | -1.0 | -2.5 | | | | | | 7.5 | |
| | | | Net Profit + Depr., Dep.,<br>Amort./Cur. Mat. L/T/D | | | | | | |
| .8 | .5 | .5 | Fixed/Worth | | | | | .1 | |
| 1.3 | .7 | .8 | | | | | | .7 | |
| 2.0 | 1.9 | 1.7 | | | | | | 1.2 | |
| 1.1 | .4 | .5 | Debt/Worth | | | | | .2 | |
| 2.2 | 1.4 | 1.7 | | | | | | .6 | |
| 5.2 | 3.5 | 6.2 | | | | | | 1.5 | |
| 24.0 | 54.6 | 27.5 | % Profit Before Taxes/Tangible<br>Net Worth | | | | | 58.2 | |
| (19) 10.6 | (29) 11.7 | (37) 13.7 | | | | | | 26.2 | |
| -25.1 | -1.2 | -5.0 | | | | | | 14.7 | |
| 8.5 | 15.0 | 10.3 | % Profit Before Taxes/Total<br>Assets | | | | | 13.6 | |
| 3.9 | 6.1 | 4.0 | | | | | | 10.8 | |
| -7.3 | -3.1 | -8.2 | | | | | | 10.0 | |
| 22.4 | 27.7 | 20.3 | Sales/Net Fixed Assets | | | | | 20.8 | |
| 6.5 | 9.7 | 7.5 | | | | | | 8.2 | |
| 3.7 | 4.0 | 4.1 | | | | | | 3.7 | |
| 3.3 | 4.0 | 3.0 | Sales/Total Assets | | | | | 2.8 | |
| 2.4 | 2.2 | 2.0 | | | | | | 1.7 | |
| 1.4 | 1.6 | 1.4 | | | | | | 1.4 | |
| 1.7 | 1.2 | 1.7 | % Depr., Dep., Amort./Sales | | | | | | |
| (20) 3.5 | (29) 2.5 | (34) 2.8 | | | | | | | |
| 5.5 | 5.5 | 4.8 | | | | | | | |
| | 2.0 | 2.1 | % Officers', Directors'<br>Owners' Comp/Sales | | | | | | |
| | (10) 6.2 | (19) 3.1 | | | | | | | |
| | 10.7 | 6.9 | | | | | | | |
| 1065927M | 812452M | 898625M | Net Sales ($) | 1011M | 10554M | 23076M | 60531M | 194167M | 609286M |
| 496376M | 400512M | 492156M | Total Assets ($) | 459M | 5900M | 9775M | 36166M | 106595M | 333261M |

M = $ thousand    MM = $ million
See Pages 9 through 22 for Explanation of Ratios and Data

## Current Data Sorted by Assets | Comparative Historical Data

| | 0-500M | 500M-2MM | 2-10MM | 10-50MM | 50-100MM | 100-250MM | Type of Statement | 4/1/07-3/31/08 ALL | 4/1/08-3/31/09 ALL |
|---|---|---|---|---|---|---|---|---|---|
| | 1 | | 1 | 4 | | 1 | Unqualified | 20 | 21 |
| | | | 20 | 5 | | | Reviewed | 22 | 35 |
| | 2 | 5 | 12 | 5 | | | Compiled | 10 | 11 |
| | 6 | 9 | 5 | 1 | | | Tax Returns | 12 | 15 |
| | 4 | 10 | 16 | 12 | 1 | 7 | Other | 38 | 42 |
| | | 19 (4/1-9/30/11) | | 103 (10/1/11-3/31/12) | | | | | |
| | 13 | 24 | 54 | 22 | 1 | 8 | NUMBER OF STATEMENTS | 102 | 124 |
| | % | % | % | % | % | % | ASSETS | % | % |
| Cash & Equivalents | 13.8 | 9.3 | 9.8 | 9.6 | | | | 7.9 | 8.5 |
| Trade Receivables (net) | 35.7 | 29.5 | 29.9 | 18.8 | | | | 24.9 | 26.6 |
| Inventory | 23.1 | 24.1 | 25.1 | 14.6 | | | | 22.4 | 24.2 |
| All Other Current | .1 | 1.2 | 3.2 | 1.8 | | | | 4.0 | 2.7 |
| Total Current | 72.8 | 64.1 | 67.9 | 44.6 | | | | 59.2 | 61.9 |
| Fixed Assets (net) | 12.1 | 20.4 | 26.3 | 37.0 | | | | 28.9 | 27.6 |
| Intangibles (net) | .1 | 7.9 | 2.0 | 9.6 | | | | 6.2 | 4.0 |
| All Other Non-Current | 15.1 | 7.5 | 3.7 | 8.8 | | | | 5.7 | 6.5 |
| Total | 100.0 | 100.0 | 100.0 | 100.0 | | | | 100.0 | 100.0 |
| | | | | | | | LIABILITIES | | |
| Notes Payable-Short Term | 10.9 | 16.8 | 9.3 | 7.1 | | | | 8.2 | 9.2 |
| Cur. Mat.-L.T.D. | 3.7 | 2.6 | 3.0 | 3.9 | | | | 4.5 | 4.0 |
| Trade Payables | 16.3 | 19.2 | 15.4 | 13.4 | | | | 13.0 | 12.9 |
| Income Taxes Payable | .3 | .0 | .3 | .6 | | | | .2 | .2 |
| All Other Current | 19.9 | 8.4 | 12.7 | 6.4 | | | | 10.2 | 9.8 |
| Total Current | 51.1 | 47.0 | 40.6 | 31.4 | | | | 36.1 | 36.1 |
| Long-Term Debt | 18.8 | 21.1 | 13.6 | 32.3 | | | | 19.9 | 18.2 |
| Deferred Taxes | .0 | .0 | .3 | .8 | | | | .7 | .4 |
| All Other Non-Current | 18.2 | 6.1 | 7.2 | 6.5 | | | | 7.0 | 6.1 |
| Net Worth | 11.9 | 25.8 | 38.2 | 29.1 | | | | 36.2 | 39.2 |
| Total Liabilties & Net Worth | 100.0 | 100.0 | 100.0 | 100.0 | | | | 100.0 | 100.0 |
| | | | | | | | INCOME DATA | | |
| Net Sales | 100.0 | 100.0 | 100.0 | 100.0 | | | | 100.0 | 100.0 |
| Gross Profit | 43.5 | 41.7 | 32.5 | 27.1 | | | | 34.8 | 32.3 |
| Operating Expenses | 39.3 | 37.8 | 29.1 | 23.4 | | | | 29.9 | 27.8 |
| Operating Profit | 4.2 | 3.9 | 3.4 | 3.7 | | | | 4.9 | 4.6 |
| All Other Expenses (net) | .4 | .5 | .4 | 2.4 | | | | 1.4 | .7 |
| Profit Before Taxes | 3.8 | 3.4 | 3.0 | 1.3 | | | | 3.5 | 3.9 |
| | | | | | | | RATIOS | | |
| Current | 3.9 | 3.0 | 2.6 | 2.6 | | | | 3.1 | 3.1 |
| | 1.4 | 1.3 | 1.7 | 1.6 | | | | 1.7 | 1.8 |
| | .8 | 1.0 | 1.3 | 1.0 | | | | 1.2 | 1.2 |
| Quick | 2.3 | 1.3 | 1.5 | 1.5 | | | | 1.5 | 1.7 |
| | 1.0 | .8 | .9 | 1.0 | | | | 1.0 | 1.0 |
| | .6 | .5 | .6 | .5 | | | | .6 | .6 |
| Sales/Receivables | 11 33.2 | 23 15.6 | 38 9.7 | 30 12.2 | | | | 30 12.1 | 30 12.1 |
| | 36 10.1 | 35 10.5 | 48 7.6 | 43 8.4 | | | | 42 8.7 | 42 8.7 |
| | 60 6.1 | 54 6.7 | 60 6.1 | 58 6.3 | | | | 52 7.0 | 60 6.1 |
| Cost of Sales/Inventory | 0 UND | 14 26.4 | 30 12.2 | 24 15.3 | | | | 24 15.5 | 23 16.2 |
| | 10 38.2 | 46 7.9 | 58 6.3 | 41 8.9 | | | | 51 7.2 | 48 7.6 |
| | 35 10.5 | 66 5.5 | 101 3.6 | 76 4.8 | | | | 84 4.3 | 100 3.6 |
| Cost of Sales/Payables | 0 UND | 24 15.0 | 20 17.9 | 19 18.8 | | | | 16 23.1 | 15 24.6 |
| | 23 16.0 | 35 10.3 | 33 10.9 | 29 12.8 | | | | 26 13.9 | 26 14.1 |
| | 45 8.2 | 60 6.1 | 50 7.3 | 56 6.5 | | | | 46 7.9 | 45 8.2 |
| Sales/Working Capital | 6.2 | 6.7 | 4.2 | 4.1 | | | | 5.3 | 4.6 |
| | 32.5 | 21.6 | 8.3 | 8.9 | | | | 9.7 | 9.5 |
| | -28.8 | 224.2 | 18.1 | NM | | | | 22.5 | 33.0 |
| EBIT/Interest | | 6.1 | 12.8 | 4.3 | | | | 9.7 | 11.8 |
| | | (18) .3 | (50) 3.8 | (20) 1.7 | | | | (92) 3.3 | (112) 3.4 |
| | | -3.8 | .3 | .0 | | | | 1.1 | .4 |
| Net Profit + Depr., Dep., Amort./Cur. Mat. L/T/D | | | 7.3 | | | | | 5.6 | 6.5 |
| | | | (13) 3.3 | | | | | (27) 2.3 | (36) 1.5 |
| | | | 1.2 | | | | | .9 | .3 |
| Fixed/Worth | .0 | .2 | .3 | .5 | | | | .4 | .3 |
| | .1 | .9 | .6 | 1.8 | | | | 1.1 | .8 |
| | -.4 | -5.2 | 1.7 | NM | | | | 5.6 | 2.0 |
| Debt/Worth | .6 | .9 | .9 | 1.1 | | | | .6 | .6 |
| | 3.8 | 3.3 | 1.6 | 2.6 | | | | 1.8 | 1.8 |
| | -4.0 | -20.4 | 3.9 | NM | | | | 39.8 | 5.1 |
| % Profit Before Taxes/Tangible Net Worth | | 55.2 | 28.8 | 26.7 | | | | 46.0 | 38.3 |
| | | (17) 24.1 | (50) 12.4 | (17) 11.4 | | | | (81) 20.7 | (108) 19.6 |
| | | -16.1 | -3.4 | 1.6 | | | | 4.1 | -1.9 |
| % Profit Before Taxes/Total Assets | 34.6 | 13.1 | 13.6 | 4.7 | | | | 19.3 | 16.1 |
| | 15.3 | 2.4 | 2.6 | 2.4 | | | | 6.3 | 6.4 |
| | 5.8 | -8.7 | -1.3 | -4.1 | | | | .0 | -1.3 |
| Sales/Net Fixed Assets | UND | 77.2 | 24.0 | 8.6 | | | | 16.4 | 20.3 |
| | 87.5 | 18.0 | 10.6 | 4.6 | | | | 9.6 | 9.4 |
| | 32.6 | 6.9 | 4.9 | 2.1 | | | | 4.2 | 5.1 |
| Sales/Total Assets | 8.4 | 3.5 | 2.5 | 1.8 | | | | 2.9 | 2.8 |
| | 4.4 | 2.6 | 2.1 | 1.5 | | | | 2.2 | 2.2 |
| | 1.7 | 2.0 | 1.6 | 1.1 | | | | 1.5 | 1.6 |
| % Depr., Dep., Amort./Sales | | .4 | 1.3 | 2.4 | | | | 1.4 | 1.3 |
| | | (18) 1.1 | (48) 2.6 | (21) 4.0 | | | | (87) 2.5 | (112) 2.3 |
| | | 2.5 | 4.1 | 5.5 | | | | 4.2 | 3.5 |
| % Officers', Directors' Owners' Comp/Sales | | 2.3 | 1.6 | | | | | 2.4 | 2.0 |
| | | (14) 5.3 | (26) 3.7 | | | | | (33) 4.5 | (43) 3.0 |
| | | 6.5 | 5.4 | | | | | 9.4 | 6.0 |
| Net Sales ($) | 13225M | 66483M | 534592M | 713703M | 113340M | 2132479M | | 3249674M | 4104065M |
| Total Assets ($) | 3325M | 24398M | 258103M | 489471M | 62505M | 1378884M | | 1586902M | 2234772M |

M = $ thousand　　MM = $ million
See Pages 9 through 22 for Explanation of Ratios and Data

**Comparative Historical Data**          **Current Data Sorted by Sales**

| | | | Type of Statement | | | | | | |
|---|---|---|---|---|---|---|---|---|---|
| 21 | 9 | 6 | Unqualified | | 1 | 1 | 1 | 1 | 4 |
| 32 | 26 | 26 | Reviewed | 1 | 1 | 1 | 11 | 8 | 4 |
| 10 | 14 | 19 | Compiled | 1 | 5 | 4 | 7 | 2 | |
| 18 | 21 | 21 | Tax Returns | 2 | 12 | 1 | 5 | 1 | |
| 46 | 53 | 50 | Other | 5 | 4 | 6 | 6 | 13 | 16 |
| 4/1/09-3/31/10 ALL | 4/1/10-3/31/11 ALL | 4/1/11-3/31/12 ALL | | | 19 (4/1-9/30/11) | | 103 (10/1/11-3/31/12) | | |
| | | | | 0-1MM | 1-3MM | 3-5MM | 5-10MM | 10-25MM | 25MM & OVER |
| 127 | 123 | 122 | NUMBER OF STATEMENTS | 9 | 22 | 12 | 30 | 25 | 24 |
| % | % | % | ASSETS | % | % | % | % | % | % |
| 8.2 | 10.2 | 10.1 | Cash & Equivalents | | 11.2 | 9.5 | 9.6 | 9.6 | 10.6 |
| 24.7 | 26.1 | 27.6 | Trade Receivables (net) | | 23.9 | 32.8 | 29.4 | 28.6 | 20.8 |
| 21.8 | 22.9 | 22.3 | Inventory | | 23.0 | 27.4 | 24.9 | 25.9 | 14.5 |
| 2.4 | 2.8 | 2.3 | All Other Current | | 1.1 | 1.6 | 3.7 | 2.4 | 2.7 |
| 57.1 | 62.0 | 62.2 | Total Current | | 59.2 | 71.3 | 67.6 | 66.5 | 48.6 |
| 31.4 | 29.5 | 26.1 | Fixed Assets (net) | | 24.9 | 22.6 | 23.9 | 24.2 | 36.6 |
| 4.1 | 3.7 | 4.6 | Intangibles (net) | | 7.3 | .3 | 2.9 | 5.6 | 5.7 |
| 7.4 | 4.8 | 7.1 | All Other Non-Current | | 8.6 | 5.9 | 5.6 | 3.7 | 9.1 |
| 100.0 | 100.0 | 100.0 | Total | | 100.0 | 100.0 | 100.0 | 100.0 | 100.0 |
| | | | LIABILITIES | | | | | | |
| 11.1 | 8.5 | 10.1 | Notes Payable-Short Term | | 13.4 | 15.8 | 9.9 | 8.3 | 6.4 |
| 5.1 | 4.2 | 3.0 | Cur. Mat.-L.T.D. | | 3.1 | 1.3 | 3.1 | 3.6 | |
| 14.2 | 12.9 | 15.7 | Trade Payables | | 18.2 | 17.6 | 16.1 | 14.2 | 16.5 |
| .1 | .3 | .3 | Income Taxes Payable | | .0 | .0 | .0 | .6 | .6 |
| 13.7 | 10.8 | 11.6 | All Other Current | | 12.0 | 13.5 | 14.8 | 8.7 | 9.8 |
| 44.3 | 36.7 | 40.6 | Total Current | | 46.7 | 48.2 | 44.0 | 35.3 | 35.8 |
| 23.4 | 17.0 | 18.8 | Long-Term Debt | | 23.2 | 18.0 | 14.7 | 20.0 | 17.7 |
| .5 | .4 | .6 | Deferred Taxes | | .0 | .2 | .1 | .5 | 2.3 |
| 5.6 | 7.7 | 7.8 | All Other Non-Current | | 3.8 | 7.1 | 3.1 | 15.6 | 3.4 |
| 26.2 | 38.2 | 32.1 | Net Worth | | 26.2 | 26.6 | 38.0 | 28.7 | 40.7 |
| 100.0 | 100.0 | 100.0 | Total Liabilities & Net Worth | | 100.0 | 100.0 | 100.0 | 100.0 | 100.0 |
| | | | INCOME DATA | | | | | | |
| 100.0 | 100.0 | 100.0 | Net Sales | | 100.0 | 100.0 | 100.0 | 100.0 | 100.0 |
| 31.6 | 33.3 | 33.8 | Gross Profit | | 42.8 | 42.4 | 29.1 | 31.4 | 23.5 |
| 30.2 | 29.7 | 30.0 | Operating Expenses | | 40.9 | 38.2 | 26.9 | 26.4 | 18.8 |
| 1.4 | 3.5 | 3.9 | Operating Profit | | 1.8 | 4.1 | 2.2 | 5.0 | 4.7 |
| 1.0 | .8 | .8 | All Other Expenses (net) | | .5 | -.1 | .2 | 1.8 | 1.1 |
| .5 | 2.8 | 3.0 | Profit Before Taxes | | 1.4 | 4.2 | 2.0 | 3.2 | 3.6 |
| | | | RATIOS | | | | | | |
| 2.6 | 3.7 | 2.8 | Current | | 2.2 | 3.3 | 2.8 | 2.9 | 2.5 |
| 1.5 | 1.8 | 1.6 | | | 1.3 | 2.0 | 1.6 | 1.9 | 1.5 |
| .9 | 1.2 | 1.1 | | | 1.0 | 1.1 | 1.2 | 1.4 | .9 |
| 1.4 | 2.2 | 1.5 | Quick | | 1.2 | 2.3 | 1.5 | 1.7 | 1.6 |
| .8 | 1.0 | .9 | | | .8 | .9 | .8 | 1.0 | 1.0 |
| .4 | .6 | .6 | | | .5 | .5 | .5 | .6 | .4 |
| 31  11.9 | 35  10.5 | 30  12.1 | Sales/Receivables | 9  39.9 | 21  17.7 | 37  9.9 | 33  11.1 | 31  11.7 | |
| 42  8.8 | 44  8.3 | 42  8.6 | | 35  10.5 | 42  8.7 | 50  7.3 | 40  9.2 | 46  7.9 | |
| 55  6.7 | 55  6.6 | 57  6.4 | | 44  8.3 | 68  5.4 | 60  6.1 | 49  7.4 | 53  6.9 | |
| 23  16.1 | 24  15.5 | 22  16.4 | Cost of Sales/Inventory | 6  57.2 | 34  10.8 | 26  14.1 | 34  10.7 | 25  14.5 | |
| 47  7.7 | 47  7.7 | 46  8.0 | | 25  14.7 | 58  6.3 | 54  6.8 | 54  6.7 | 40  9.2 | |
| 91  4.0 | 95  3.8 | 83  4.4 | | 76  4.8 | 130  2.8 | 114  3.2 | 94  3.9 | 66  5.5 | |
| 14  26.1 | 17  22.0 | 20  18.0 | Cost of Sales/Payables | 23  15.7 | 16  22.6 | 19  19.1 | 17  21.7 | 25  14.6 | |
| 29  12.7 | 29  12.6 | 33  11.1 | | 30  12.0 | 38  9.7 | 37  9.9 | 29  12.5 | 34  10.8 | |
| 49  7.4 | 45  8.1 | 51  7.1 | | 69  5.3 | 46  8.0 | 51  7.1 | 51  7.2 | 58  6.3 | |
| 5.0 | 4.1 | 4.9 | Sales/Working Capital | | 8.4 | 3.7 | 4.0 | 3.5 | 5.6 |
| 14.4 | 8.0 | 10.3 | | | 21.6 | 7.5 | 9.7 | 7.3 | 9.9 |
| -36.6 | 32.2 | 43.1 | | | UND | 38.9 | 38.9 | 19.3 | NM |
| 7.3 | 9.5 | 9.2 | EBIT/Interest | | 9.8 | | 11.0 | 12.9 | 7.6 |
| (116) 1.9 | (104) 2.9 | (101) 2.6 | | | (18) 1.1 | | (27) 2.9 | (24) 3.8 | (20) 2.8 |
| -1.8 | -.2 | .3 | | | -2.1 | | .3 | .4 | 1.0 |
| 3.3 | 3.8 | 5.8 | Net Profit + Depr., Dep., Amort./Cur. Mat. L/T/D | | | | | | |
| (32) 1.5 | (29) 1.7 | (24) 3.0 | | | | | | | |
| .4 | .4 | 1.3 | | | | | | | |
| .5 | .3 | .3 | Fixed/Worth | | .1 | .2 | .1 | .3 | .5 |
| 1.1 | .7 | .7 | | | .9 | .8 | .6 | .6 | 1.1 |
| 19.5 | 2.0 | 2.5 | | | NM | NM | 2.2 | 2.8 | 2.0 |
| .8 | .6 | .8 | Debt/Worth | | .9 | .5 | .7 | 1.0 | .8 |
| 2.2 | 1.5 | 2.0 | | | 4.9 | 1.8 | 1.7 | 1.5 | 2.1 |
| 73.6 | 4.7 | 7.0 | | | -14.9 | NM | 7.1 | 6.3 | 4.5 |
| 36.2 | 30.5 | 32.1 | % Profit Before Taxes/Tangible Net Worth | | 92.6 | | 25.0 | 33.1 | 30.3 |
| (97) 11.9 | (104) 13.6 | (100) 13.4 | | | (16) 26.3 | | (26) 8.4 | (21) 23.9 | (22) 12.0 |
| -6.1 | -3.3 | -.1 | | | -16.5 | | -7.5 | 2.4 | 2.4 |
| 10.8 | 15.4 | 13.6 | % Profit Before Taxes/Total Assets | | 21.6 | 12.8 | 12.4 | 14.1 | 8.5 |
| 3.1 | 4.1 | 3.2 | | | 4.7 | 1.3 | 2.2 | 6.3 | 3.9 |
| -8.0 | -2.0 | -1.7 | | | -6.3 | -6.6 | -3.8 | -2.6 | .8 |
| 17.1 | 21.4 | 26.5 | Sales/Net Fixed Assets | | 330.1 | 24.1 | 26.5 | 22.3 | 8.3 |
| 7.2 | 8.3 | 10.0 | | | 24.1 | 14.8 | 10.5 | 13.2 | 5.2 |
| 3.5 | 3.9 | 4.6 | | | 5.6 | 6.4 | 3.9 | 5.0 | 3.0 |
| 2.8 | 2.5 | 2.8 | Sales/Total Assets | | 3.9 | 3.2 | 2.7 | 2.6 | 1.8 |
| 1.9 | 1.9 | 2.0 | | | 2.8 | 2.1 | 2.1 | 2.2 | 1.6 |
| 1.3 | 1.4 | 1.5 | | | 1.9 | 1.8 | 1.4 | 1.6 | 1.3 |
| 1.3 | 1.5 | 1.2 | % Depr., Dep., Amort./Sales | | 1.0 | .4 | 1.2 | 1.3 | 2.0 |
| (112) 2.7 | (101) 2.9 | (98) 2.6 | | | (15) 2.0 | (11) 1.4 | (25) 2.2 | (22) 2.6 | (21) 3.1 |
| 5.6 | 4.9 | 4.0 | | | 4.0 | 3.1 | 4.4 | 4.0 | 5.0 |
| 2.1 | 2.0 | 1.9 | % Officers', Directors', Owners' Comp/Sales | | 2.9 | | 1.5 | | |
| (36) 3.6 | (44) 4.1 | (49) 3.9 | | | (13) 6.0 | | (15) 3.6 | | |
| 7.7 | 6.9 | 6.1 | | | 7.0 | | 6.7 | | |
| 3541699M | 2706676M | 3573822M | Net Sales ($) | 4439M | 42043M | 47506M | 217248M | 402918M | 2859668M |
| 2366352M | 1771591M | 2216686M | Total Assets ($) | 2850M | 20429M | 21395M | 134592M | 213085M | 1824335M |

© RMA 2012

M = $ thousand    MM = $ million

See Pages 9 through 22 for Explanation of Ratios and Data

## Current Data Sorted by Assets

## Comparative Historical Data

| Type of Statement | 0-500M | 500M-2MM | 2-10MM | 10-50MM | 50-100MM | 100-250MM | 4/1/07-3/31/08 ALL | 4/1/08-3/31/09 ALL |
|---|---|---|---|---|---|---|---|---|
| Unqualified | | | 3 | 18 | 9 | 7 | 44 | 49 |
| Reviewed | | 9 | 19 | 16 | 2 | 1 | 55 | 58 |
| Compiled | 3 | 9 | 18 | 1 | 1 | 1 | 50 | 41 |
| Tax Returns | 5 | 16 | 15 | 2 | | | 34 | 26 |
| Other | 1 | 5 | 21 | 18 | 10 | 3 | 78 | 101 |
| | | 23 (4/1-9/30/11) | | 190 (10/1/11-3/31/12) | | | | |
| **NUMBER OF STATEMENTS** | 9 | 39 | 76 | 55 | 22 | 12 | 261 | 275 |
| **ASSETS** | % | % | % | % | % | % | % | % |
| Cash & Equivalents | | 9.2 | 8.9 | 8.4 | 5.9 | 1.9 | 8.6 | 8.3 |
| Trade Receivables (net) | | 30.5 | 28.0 | 20.0 | 15.4 | 17.1 | 22.9 | 23.1 |
| Inventory | | 8.0 | 8.7 | 11.1 | 7.7 | 10.8 | 7.1 | 8.6 |
| All Other Current | | 2.7 | 4.1 | 2.4 | 3.2 | 4.4 | 2.8 | 2.9 |
| Total Current | | 50.4 | 49.7 | 41.9 | 32.2 | 34.2 | 41.4 | 43.0 |
| Fixed Assets (net) | | 42.1 | 41.2 | 42.8 | 53.0 | 50.3 | 48.2 | 46.5 |
| Intangibles (net) | | 2.9 | 2.0 | 5.5 | 6.7 | 6.6 | 2.8 | 3.2 |
| All Other Non-Current | | 4.7 | 7.1 | 9.8 | 8.2 | 8.8 | 7.5 | 7.3 |
| Total | | 100.0 | 100.0 | 100.0 | 100.0 | 100.0 | 100.0 | 100.0 |
| **LIABILITIES** | | | | | | | | |
| Notes Payable-Short Term | | 6.9 | 5.4 | 6.3 | 4.0 | 6.0 | 4.9 | 5.6 |
| Cur. Mat.-L.T.D. | | 7.6 | 4.4 | 4.9 | 3.3 | 3.8 | 5.6 | 6.5 |
| Trade Payables | | 19.2 | 16.1 | 11.1 | 6.1 | 8.2 | 11.8 | 13.2 |
| Income Taxes Payable | | .1 | .1 | .1 | .0 | .5 | .2 | .1 |
| All Other Current | | 10.9 | 9.3 | 6.3 | 4.9 | 7.1 | 6.5 | 7.4 |
| Total Current | | 44.6 | 35.3 | 28.6 | 18.3 | 25.7 | 29.0 | 32.8 |
| Long-Term Debt | | 26.8 | 21.2 | 18.6 | 23.9 | 17.6 | 24.5 | 24.8 |
| Deferred Taxes | | .2 | .2 | .7 | .8 | .5 | 1.0 | 1.1 |
| All Other Non-Current | | 4.2 | 7.9 | 5.8 | 5.3 | 5.8 | 3.5 | 4.8 |
| Net Worth | | 24.1 | 35.5 | 46.2 | 51.7 | 50.4 | 42.0 | 36.5 |
| Total Liabilities & Net Worth | | 100.0 | 100.0 | 100.0 | 100.0 | 100.0 | 100.0 | 100.0 |
| **INCOME DATA** | | | | | | | | |
| Net Sales | | 100.0 | 100.0 | 100.0 | 100.0 | 100.0 | 100.0 | 100.0 |
| Gross Profit | | 31.0 | 27.9 | 18.6 | 17.7 | 15.9 | 29.3 | 25.0 |
| Operating Expenses | | 29.5 | 28.8 | 20.6 | 19.4 | 12.4 | 25.1 | 24.8 |
| Operating Profit | | 1.4 | -.9 | -2.0 | -1.7 | 3.6 | 4.1 | .2 |
| All Other Expenses (net) | | .2 | .1 | -.4 | .4 | 1.3 | .8 | .7 |
| Profit Before Taxes | | 1.2 | -1.0 | -1.6 | -2.1 | 2.3 | 3.3 | -.4 |
| **RATIOS** | | | | | | | | |
| | | 3.1 | 2.7 | 2.0 | 2.1 | 2.1 | 2.4 | 2.3 |
| Current | | 1.2 | 1.5 | 1.4 | 1.5 | 1.8 | 1.5 | 1.4 |
| | | .8 | 1.0 | 1.0 | 1.3 | .8 | 1.0 | .9 |
| | | 2.6 | 2.1 | 1.6 | 1.5 | 1.4 | 1.7 | 1.5 |
| Quick | | 1.0 | 1.1 | .9 | 1.1 | 1.1 | (260) 1.1 | .9 |
| | | .6 | .6 | .5 | .5 | .4 | .6 | .6 |
| | | 28  13.2 | 34  10.6 | 36  10.2 | 36  10.2 | 36  10.2 | 29  12.5 | 29  12.6 |
| Sales/Receivables | | 46  8.0 | 46  8.0 | 46  7.9 | 45  8.1 | 43  8.4 | 38  9.6 | 40  9.1 |
| | | 56  6.5 | 59  6.2 | 63  5.8 | 64  5.7 | 65  5.6 | 51  7.1 | 51  7.1 |
| | | 3  120.3 | 8  46.9 | 15  24.2 | 17  21.0 | 18  20.1 | 6  59.1 | 7  52.6 |
| Cost of Sales/Inventory | | 11  34.4 | 14  25.5 | 27  13.6 | 23  16.2 | 27  13.6 | 12  30.0 | 15  23.7 |
| | | 26  13.8 | 34  10.6 | 57  6.4 | 54  6.8 | 50  7.3 | 30  12.0 | 33  11.0 |
| | | 18  20.2 | 21  17.3 | 18  20.1 | 14  26.2 | 13  28.5 | 16  22.3 | 14  25.5 |
| Cost of Sales/Payables | | 33  11.0 | 32  11.3 | 33  11.0 | 19  19.5 | 25  14.6 | 25  14.4 | 24  15.3 |
| | | 60  6.1 | 60  6.1 | 51  7.2 | 30  12.2 | 32  11.4 | 41  9.0 | 41  8.9 |
| | | 7.6 | 6.3 | 5.7 | 4.5 | 7.8 | 7.6 | 7.0 |
| Sales/Working Capital | | 29.9 | 12.2 | 11.0 | 11.2 | 9.7 | 15.9 | 16.5 |
| | | -14.9 | 781.6 | 999.8 | 22.2 | NM | -616.1 | -41.7 |
| | | 8.7 | 5.9 | 3.1 | 4.6 | 7.7 | 9.3 | 4.9 |
| EBIT/Interest | | (36) 3.9 | (68) 1.8 | (52) 1.4 | (20) .9 | 5.4 | (237) 2.7 | (253) 1.4 |
| | | -.8 | -1.5 | -1.9 | -1.3 | .7 | 1.1 | -1.5 |
| | | | | 1.7 | | | 3.7 | 3.3 |
| Net Profit + Depr., Dep., Amort./Cur. Mat. L/T/D | | | | (17) 1.3 | | | (67) 1.7 | (72) 1.6 |
| | | | | .6 | | | 1.2 | .6 |
| | | .5 | .5 | .6 | .7 | .7 | .6 | .7 |
| Fixed/Worth | | 1.9 | 1.0 | 1.1 | 1.2 | 1.1 | 1.3 | 1.3 |
| | | -4.5 | 4.1 | 2.0 | 1.9 | 2.1 | 2.5 | 2.8 |
| | | .4 | .5 | .6 | .6 | .5 | .6 | .7 |
| Debt/Worth | | 2.5 | 1.6 | 1.1 | 1.1 | 1.2 | 1.4 | 1.5 |
| | | -11.9 | 7.5 | 2.8 | 1.8 | 2.4 | 3.5 | 4.8 |
| | | 68.6 | 16.0 | 8.4 | 7.2 | 23.4 | 36.2 | 18.1 |
| % Profit Before Taxes/Tangible Net Worth | | (26) 39.0 | (63) 4.7 | (52) 2.5 | -.5 | 10.0 | (237) 13.7 | (232) 4.3 |
| | | -.8 | -10.0 | -11.5 | -18.9 | -3.4 | 1.3 | -13.6 |
| | | 19.8 | 5.8 | 3.4 | 4.8 | 8.4 | 14.2 | 6.8 |
| % Profit Before Taxes/Total Assets | | 7.0 | 1.5 | .6 | -.2 | 4.8 | 4.3 | .8 |
| | | -10.3 | -7.5 | -5.6 | -4.2 | -.8 | .1 | -6.4 |
| | | 10.9 | 7.6 | 5.5 | 3.4 | 3.6 | 6.1 | 7.1 |
| Sales/Net Fixed Assets | | 5.4 | 5.1 | 3.2 | 1.9 | 2.4 | 4.0 | 3.9 |
| | | 3.6 | 3.3 | 2.0 | 1.1 | 1.8 | 2.6 | 2.5 |
| | | 3.9 | 2.5 | 1.7 | 1.3 | 1.6 | 2.5 | 2.6 |
| Sales/Total Assets | | 2.5 | 1.9 | 1.3 | .9 | 1.3 | 1.8 | 1.8 |
| | | 1.6 | 1.5 | 1.0 | .7 | 1.0 | 1.5 | 1.3 |
| | | 2.0 | 3.2 | 3.6 | 6.0 | | 3.2 | 3.2 |
| % Depr., Dep., Amort./Sales | | (36) 4.0 | (72) 4.6 | (51) 5.1 | (19) 7.5 | | (232) 4.8 | (240) 5.0 |
| | | 7.8 | 6.8 | 7.4 | 10.2 | | 6.4 | 7.3 |
| | | 1.0 | 2.0 | .3 | | | 1.3 | 1.0 |
| % Officers', Directors', Owners' Comp/Sales | | (20) 2.2 | (32) 2.8 | (10) .7 | | | (91) 2.4 | (84) 2.4 |
| | | 4.9 | 5.0 | 1.7 | | | 4.7 | 4.1 |
| Net Sales ($) | 15875M | 144569M | 786886M | 1777280M | 1554282M | 2189035M | 11205252M | 11302451M |
| Total Assets ($) | 2701M | 52111M | 384450M | 1311764M | 1511473M | 1644242M | 7046906M | 7403917M |

## Comparative Historical Data

## Current Data Sorted by Sales

| 4/1/09-3/31/10 ALL | 4/1/10-3/31/11 ALL | 4/1/11-3/31/12 ALL | Type of Statement | 0-1MM | 1-3MM | 3-5MM | 5-10MM | 10-25MM | 25MM & OVER |
|---|---|---|---|---|---|---|---|---|---|
| 46 | 38 | 37 | Unqualified | | | | 3 | 8 | 26 |
| 53 | 40 | 47 | Reviewed | 2 | 3 | 2 | 17 | 8 | 15 |
| 43 | 27 | 33 | Compiled | 2 | 7 | 5 | 8 | 9 | 2 |
| 24 | 30 | 38 | Tax Returns | 2 | 10 | 11 | 10 | 4 | 1 |
| 69 | 95 | 58 | Other | | 2 | 1 | 14 | 15 | 26 |
| | | | | | 23 (4/1-9/30/11) | | 190 (10/1/11-3/31/12) | | |
| 235 | 230 | 213 | NUMBER OF STATEMENTS | 6 | 22 | 19 | 52 | 44 | 70 |
| % | % | % | ASSETS | % | % | % | % | % | % |
| 10.7 | 9.8 | 8.6 | Cash & Equivalents | | 12.9 | 6.3 | 10.0 | 9.0 | 6.8 |
| 20.2 | 21.6 | 24.1 | Trade Receivables (net) | | 21.3 | 20.8 | 29.5 | 29.8 | 18.3 |
| 8.3 | 8.3 | 9.0 | Inventory | | 6.1 | 9.4 | 7.4 | 8.3 | 11.4 |
| 2.6 | 3.1 | 3.2 | All Other Current | | 2.0 | 5.0 | 2.1 | 4.4 | 3.1 |
| 41.8 | 42.7 | 44.9 | Total Current | | 42.3 | 41.5 | 49.1 | 51.4 | 39.5 |
| 46.6 | 45.6 | 43.5 | Fixed Assets (net) | | 45.1 | 49.3 | 40.6 | 39.0 | 45.8 |
| 4.1 | 3.6 | 4.3 | Intangibles (net) | | 6.1 | 4.5 | 2.0 | 3.2 | 6.1 |
| 7.6 | 8.1 | 7.3 | All Other Non-Current | | 6.6 | 4.7 | 8.3 | 6.4 | 8.5 |
| 100.0 | 100.0 | 100.0 | Total | | 100.0 | 100.0 | 100.0 | 100.0 | 100.0 |
| | | | LIABILITIES | | | | | | |
| 5.7 | 7.3 | 5.8 | Notes Payable-Short Term | | 6.2 | 7.4 | 4.6 | 7.3 | 5.0 |
| 5.8 | 5.9 | 6.1 | Cur. Mat.-L.T.D. | | 17.3 | 3.3 | 6.0 | 4.7 | 3.9 |
| 10.2 | 12.6 | 14.0 | Trade Payables | | 12.2 | 20.4 | 16.6 | 16.9 | 8.7 |
| .2 | .2 | .1 | Income Taxes Payable | | .0 | .2 | .0 | .2 | .1 |
| 7.3 | 8.0 | 8.5 | All Other Current | | 12.1 | 18.1 | 4.9 | 8.5 | 6.7 |
| 29.2 | 33.9 | 34.5 | Total Current | | 47.8 | 49.5 | 32.1 | 37.6 | 24.5 |
| 26.0 | 23.9 | 23.8 | Long-Term Debt | | 38.7 | 27.4 | 28.3 | 12.7 | 20.4 |
| .7 | .8 | .4 | Deferred Taxes | | .1 | .1 | .3 | .6 | .6 |
| 4.3 | 5.4 | 6.5 | All Other Non-Current | | 10.1 | 9.0 | 6.1 | 5.5 | 6.1 |
| 39.7 | 35.9 | 34.8 | Net Worth | | 3.3 | 14.0 | 33.2 | 43.7 | 48.4 |
| 100.0 | 100.0 | 100.0 | Total Liabilties & Net Worth | | 100.0 | 100.0 | 100.0 | 100.0 | 100.0 |
| | | | INCOME DATA | | | | | | |
| 100.0 | 100.0 | 100.0 | Net Sales | | 100.0 | 100.0 | 100.0 | 100.0 | 100.0 |
| 27.5 | 26.2 | 25.2 | Gross Profit | | 37.2 | 35.6 | 26.6 | 22.4 | 17.8 |
| 28.3 | 26.0 | 25.6 | Operating Expenses | | 38.4 | 33.4 | 28.3 | 24.1 | 17.2 |
| -.8 | .2 | -.4 | Operating Profit | | -1.2 | 2.1 | -1.6 | -1.6 | .6 |
| .8 | 1.0 | .2 | All Other Expenses (net) | | 1.5 | .7 | -.3 | -.3 | .3 |
| -1.5 | -.7 | -.5 | Profit Before Taxes | | -2.7 | 1.5 | -1.3 | -1.4 | .3 |
| | | | RATIOS | | | | | | |
| 3.0 | 2.8 | 2.5 | Current | | 3.0 | 1.5 | 3.9 | 2.1 | 2.1 |
| 1.5 | 1.4 | 1.4 | | | 1.2 | 1.0 | 1.5 | 1.3 | 1.6 |
| .9 | .9 | 1.0 | | | .4 | .6 | 1.0 | 1.0 | 1.3 |
| 2.1 | 2.0 | 1.8 | Quick | | 2.6 | 1.1 | 2.7 | 1.8 | 1.5 |
| 1.0 | 1.0 | 1.0 | | | .9 | .5 | 1.3 | 1.0 | 1.0 |
| .6 | .6 | .6 | | | .3 | .4 | .6 | .6 | .6 |
| 30  12.3 | 30  12.2 | 34  10.8 | Sales/Receivables | | 22  16.6 | 25  14.5 | 32  11.4 | 41  8.8 | 35  10.5 |
| 42  8.6 | 42  8.6 | 45  8.1 | | | 46  7.9 | 38  9.5 | 43  8.4 | 49  7.4 | 42  8.6 |
| 57  6.4 | 58  6.3 | 60  6.1 | | | 57  6.4 | 57  6.4 | 58  6.3 | 69  5.3 | 59  6.2 |
| 7  49.4 | 7  49.1 | 9  42.4 | Cost of Sales/Inventory | | 2  147.3 | 0  UND | 5  70.9 | 6  59.5 | 17  21.6 |
| 20  18.7 | 17  21.9 | 18  20.1 | | | 14  26.0 | 14  25.6 | 14  26.4 | 15  24.4 | 24  15.2 |
| 39  9.3 | 35  10.3 | 43  8.5 | | | 28  12.9 | 51  7.1 | 27  13.7 | 38  9.7 | 52  7.0 |
| 14  26.6 | 15  24.4 | 18  20.2 | Cost of Sales/Payables | | 14  27.0 | 25  14.7 | 20  17.9 | 22  16.7 | 16  22.4 |
| 26  14.1 | 29  12.7 | 31  11.9 | | | 26  14.2 | 55  6.6 | 33  10.9 | 33  10.9 | 21  17.2 |
| 43  8.5 | 53  6.9 | 56  6.5 | | | 60  6.1 | 104  3.5 | 60  6.1 | 63  5.8 | 33  10.9 |
| 5.3 | 5.7 | 6.8 | Sales/Working Capital | | 7.2 | 13.0 | 5.5 | 8.4 | 5.8 |
| 13.1 | 16.5 | 12.5 | | | 34.5 | -999.8 | 11.5 | 13.7 | 10.1 |
| -43.9 | -33.7 | -207.6 | | | -8.6 | -12.7 | -202.3 | 788.3 | 21.6 |
| 3.9 | 5.1 | 5.5 | EBIT/Interest | | 2.6 | 7.2 | 7.2 | 5.3 | 5.4 |
| (213) 1.1 | (212) 1.4 | (195) 1.9 | | | (16) .9 | (18) 3.8 | (47) 1.9 | (42) 1.5 | (66) 2.2 |
| -1.9 | -2.1 | -1.3 | | | -1.1 | -2.5 | -.8 | -2.1 | -.4 |
| 3.1 | 2.4 | 1.9 | Net Profit + Depr., Dep., Amort./Cur. Mat. L/T/D | | | | | | 1.9 |
| (60) 1.3 | (51) 1.2 | (38) 1.4 | | | | | | | (21) 1.5 |
| .4 | .4 | .4 | | | | | | | 1.0 |
| .6 | .6 | .6 | Fixed/Worth | | .4 | .9 | .4 | .5 | .7 |
| 1.2 | 1.2 | 1.1 | | | 3.8 | 1.9 | 1.2 | 1.0 | 1.1 |
| 3.3 | 3.6 | 4.1 | | | -4.8 | -4.5 | 15.4 | 1.8 | 1.7 |
| .5 | .6 | .6 | Debt/Worth | | .5 | .9 | .4 | .7 | .6 |
| 1.4 | 1.4 | 1.4 | | | 6.6 | 2.5 | 1.9 | 1.4 | 1.0 |
| 5.5 | 5.4 | 7.3 | | | -5.9 | -11.9 | 56.4 | 2.7 | 2.2 |
| 16.1 | 23.9 | 18.0 | % Profit Before Taxes/Tangible Net Worth | | 19.6 | 73.6 | 29.9 | 14.5 | 12.4 |
| (199) 2.2 | (191) 3.8 | (179) 4.7 | | | (13) -11.8 | (13) 46.7 | (40) 8.1 | (43) 3.4 | (66) 4.9 |
| -14.9 | -8.2 | -8.1 | | | -19.2 | -3.4 | -9.7 | -7.4 | -4.5 |
| 5.3 | 8.0 | 7.2 | % Profit Before Taxes/Total Assets | | 7.6 | 15.9 | 10.5 | 4.4 | 6.3 |
| .4 | 1.3 | 1.5 | | | -1.6 | 5.9 | 1.4 | 1.5 | 1.9 |
| -7.0 | -5.9 | -5.2 | | | -12.2 | -7.6 | -7.1 | -2.9 | -2.7 |
| 6.1 | 7.2 | 7.6 | Sales/Net Fixed Assets | | 10.8 | 7.5 | 9.2 | 8.7 | 4.5 |
| 3.2 | 3.7 | 4.0 | | | 4.8 | 4.4 | 5.3 | 5.8 | 3.0 |
| 1.9 | 2.0 | 2.3 | | | 2.8 | 2.1 | 3.2 | 2.7 | 1.9 |
| 2.0 | 2.2 | 2.4 | Sales/Total Assets | | 3.4 | 2.4 | 3.0 | 2.4 | 1.7 |
| 1.5 | 1.5 | 1.7 | | | 2.1 | 1.8 | 2.0 | 1.9 | 1.3 |
| 1.1 | 1.1 | 1.2 | | | 1.3 | 1.4 | 1.5 | 1.3 | .9 |
| 3.5 | 3.6 | 3.0 | % Depr., Dep., Amort./Sales | | 4.2 | 2.5 | 2.9 | 2.7 | 3.9 |
| (210) 5.8 | (212) 5.9 | (193) 5.1 | | | (20) 6.0 | 4.4 | (47) 4.6 | (40) 3.6 | (61) 5.7 |
| 8.9 | 8.3 | 7.5 | | | 8.9 | 7.5 | 7.9 | 6.9 | 7.5 |
| 1.3 | 1.4 | 1.3 | % Officers', Directors' Owners' Comp/Sales | | 2.9 | .5 | 1.9 | 1.6 | |
| (72) 2.8 | (70) 2.6 | (70) 2.5 | | | (10) 5.8 | (13) 2.6 | (23) 2.2 | (13) 2.5 | |
| 6.6 | 5.6 | 5.0 | | | 7.4 | 7.4 | 3.6 | 5.1 | |
| 7509555M | 6252213M | 6467927M | Net Sales ($) | 4369M | 46495M | 76086M | 373269M | 704562M | 5263146M |
| 6044683M | 4996099M | 4906741M | Total Assets ($) | 3285M | 28089M | 46174M | 243238M | 439340M | 4146615M |

M = $ thousand    MM = $ million
See Pages 9 through 22 for Explanation of Ratios and Data

## Current Data Sorted by Assets      Comparative Historical Data

| 0-500M | 500M-2MM | 2-10MM | 10-50MM | 50-100MM | 100-250MM | Type of Statement | 4/1/07-3/31/08 ALL | 4/1/08-3/31/09 ALL |
|---|---|---|---|---|---|---|---|---|
| | 1 | 2 | 5 | 2 | 4 | Unqualified | 33 | 23 |
| 1 | 1 | 15 | 2 | | | Reviewed | 19 | 23 |
| | 5 | 1 | 1 | | | Compiled | 14 | 15 |
| | 4 | 3 | 3 | | | Tax Returns | 9 | 10 |
| 1 | 6 | 14 | 12 | 4 | 4 | Other | 55 | 52 |
| | 10 (4/1-9/30/11) | | 81 (10/1/11-3/31/12) | | | | | |
| 2 | 17 | 35 | 23 | 6 | 8 | NUMBER OF STATEMENTS | 130 | 123 |
| % | % | % | % | % | % | ASSETS | % | % |
| | 5.2 | 6.4 | 11.9 | | | Cash & Equivalents | 9.2 | 7.6 |
| | 19.5 | 20.0 | 15.0 | | | Trade Receivables (net) | 16.3 | 16.5 |
| | 21.4 | 19.1 | 16.8 | | | Inventory | 18.6 | 23.3 |
| | 5.3 | 2.6 | 1.8 | | | All Other Current | 3.7 | 3.4 |
| | 51.4 | 48.1 | 45.5 | | | Total Current | 47.8 | 50.8 |
| | 33.4 | 43.6 | 42.8 | | | Fixed Assets (net) | 43.3 | 39.5 |
| | 4.3 | 1.9 | 6.4 | | | Intangibles (net) | 2.9 | 2.7 |
| | 10.8 | 6.4 | 5.3 | | | All Other Non-Current | 5.9 | 7.0 |
| | 100.0 | 100.0 | 100.0 | | | Total | 100.0 | 100.0 |
| | | | | | | LIABILITIES | | |
| | 15.1 | 6.9 | 5.5 | | | Notes Payable-Short Term | 6.3 | 8.6 |
| | 6.5 | 5.2 | 5.8 | | | Cur. Mat.-L.T.D. | 5.3 | 5.5 |
| | 12.9 | 13.6 | 8.1 | | | Trade Payables | 8.5 | 10.3 |
| | .4 | .0 | .0 | | | Income Taxes Payable | .2 | .1 |
| | 15.4 | 6.2 | 8.5 | | | All Other Current | 9.8 | 6.5 |
| | 50.2 | 32.0 | 28.0 | | | Total Current | 30.0 | 31.0 |
| | 25.1 | 24.1 | 17.7 | | | Long-Term Debt | 22.6 | 22.2 |
| | .1 | .8 | .5 | | | Deferred Taxes | .7 | .9 |
| | 19.2 | 10.9 | 4.7 | | | All Other Non-Current | 7.9 | 6.2 |
| | 5.4 | 32.2 | 49.2 | | | Net Worth | 38.7 | 39.7 |
| | 100.0 | 100.0 | 100.0 | | | Total Liabilities & Net Worth | 100.0 | 100.0 |
| | | | | | | INCOME DATA | | |
| | 100.0 | 100.0 | 100.0 | | | Net Sales | 100.0 | 100.0 |
| | 30.8 | 34.3 | 26.0 | | | Gross Profit | 31.9 | 31.6 |
| | 27.4 | 34.4 | 24.2 | | | Operating Expenses | 25.0 | 29.0 |
| | 3.4 | -.2 | 1.8 | | | Operating Profit | 6.9 | 2.6 |
| | 1.1 | 3.7 | 2.1 | | | All Other Expenses (net) | 2.2 | 1.8 |
| | 2.4 | -3.9 | -.3 | | | Profit Before Taxes | 4.7 | .9 |
| | | | | | | RATIOS | | |
| | 1.9 | 2.8 | 4.1 | | | | 3.4 | 3.3 |
| | 1.1 | 1.6 | 1.9 | | | Current | 1.7 | 1.9 |
| | .7 | 1.0 | 1.2 | | | | 1.0 | 1.1 |
| | 1.0 | 1.7 | 2.2 | | | | 1.6 | 1.7 |
| | .5 | .8 | 1.0 | | | Quick | .9 | .9 |
| | .3 | .5 | .3 | | | | .4 | .4 |
| | 25  14.6 | 28  13.1 | 31  11.6 | | | | 25  14.9 | 23  15.9 |
| | 35  10.5 | 38  9.7 | 36  10.2 | | | Sales/Receivables | 35  10.3 | 31  11.8 |
| | 50  7.3 | 55  6.6 | 51  7.2 | | | | 47  7.8 | 48  7.7 |
| | 24  15.1 | 46  8.0 | 49  7.5 | | | | 36  10.1 | 44  8.3 |
| | 63  5.8 | 64  5.7 | 99  3.7 | | | Cost of Sales/Inventory | 68  5.4 | 78  4.7 |
| | 101  3.6 | 99  3.7 | 130  2.8 | | | | 93  3.9 | 112  3.2 |
| | 12  29.5 | 25  14.6 | 18  20.0 | | | | 15  24.9 | 13  27.3 |
| | 22  16.5 | 41  9.0 | 27  13.7 | | | Cost of Sales/Payables | 25  14.4 | 21  17.2 |
| | 46  8.0 | 57  6.4 | 40  9.2 | | | | 37  9.9 | 42  8.7 |
| | 6.4 | 4.6 | 2.5 | | | | 4.4 | 4.6 |
| | 197.7 | 10.8 | 7.5 | | | Sales/Working Capital | 9.2 | 7.8 |
| | -10.9 | 109.3 | 27.5 | | | | NM | 44.5 |
| | 6.3 | 3.9 | 17.8 | | | | 7.4 | 5.4 |
| | (15) 3.5 | (33) .8 | (22) 1.8 | | | EBIT/Interest | (112) 2.3 | (114) 1.3 |
| | -.3 | -5.7 | -1.8 | | | | 1.0 | -1.0 |
| | | | | | | Net Profit + Depr., Dep., Amort./Cur. Mat. L/T/D | 3.0 | 4.1 |
| | | | | | | | (37) 1.9 | (32) 1.8 |
| | | | | | | | .7 | .4 |
| | 1.1 | .6 | .4 | | | | .6 | .5 |
| | 15.6 | 1.2 | .9 | | | Fixed/Worth | 1.2 | 1.0 |
| | -.5 | 4.9 | 1.9 | | | | 2.8 | 2.2 |
| | 2.4 | .7 | .4 | | | | .5 | .5 |
| | 18.7 | 1.6 | 1.8 | | | Debt/Worth | 1.5 | 1.4 |
| | -4.1 | 17.5 | 2.5 | | | | 4.8 | 4.3 |
| | | 11.0 | 14.3 | | | | 33.9 | 18.1 |
| | | (28) -.3 | (21) 6.6 | | | % Profit Before Taxes/Tangible Net Worth | (113) 14.0 | (108) 5.5 |
| | | -18.3 | -5.2 | | | | 4.4 | -7.9 |
| | 11.0 | 5.3 | 5.6 | | | | 12.5 | 7.7 |
| | 3.3 | -.5 | .7 | | | % Profit Before Taxes/Total Assets | 5.3 | 1.1 |
| | -4.0 | -10.4 | -3.4 | | | | .0 | -4.9 |
| | 13.8 | 5.1 | 8.1 | | | | 7.5 | 8.8 |
| | 6.9 | 3.5 | 2.2 | | | Sales/Net Fixed Assets | 3.9 | 4.1 |
| | 2.9 | 1.8 | 1.6 | | | | 2.4 | 2.1 |
| | 2.3 | 2.1 | 1.5 | | | | 2.1 | 2.1 |
| | 1.8 | 1.5 | 1.0 | | | Sales/Total Assets | 1.5 | 1.4 |
| | 1.3 | 1.0 | .6 | | | | 1.1 | 1.0 |
| | 1.9 | 3.2 | 2.6 | | | | 2.2 | 2.4 |
| | (14) 2.8 | (30) 4.3 | 5.9 | | | % Depr., Dep., Amort./Sales | (117) 3.8 | (112) 4.0 |
| | 4.7 | 8.2 | 7.5 | | | | 5.9 | 5.9 |
| | | | | | | % Officers', Directors' Owners' Comp/Sales | 1.7 | 1.9 |
| | | | | | | | (33) 3.4 | (38) 3.1 |
| | | | | | | | 5.2 | 5.3 |
| 742M | 35730M | 275646M | 558515M | 352919M | 1083868M | Net Sales ($) | 4093921M | 3246691M |
| 897M | 19633M | 177692M | 530968M | 442833M | 1098592M | Total Assets ($) | 3186357M | 2849871M |

M = $ thousand     MM = $ million
See Pages 9 through 22 for Explanation of Ratios and Data

## Comparative Historical Data | Current Data Sorted by Sales

| 4/1/09-3/31/10 ALL | 4/1/10-3/31/11 ALL | 4/1/11-3/31/12 ALL | Type of Statement | 0-1MM | 1-3MM | 3-5MM | 5-10MM | 10-25MM | 25MM & OVER |
|---|---|---|---|---|---|---|---|---|---|
| 16 | 14 | 14 | Unqualified | | 1 | | | 4 | 9 |
| 23 | 27 | 19 | Reviewed | 2 | 2 | 3 | 6 | 6 | 9 |
| 15 | 12 | 9 | Compiled | 1 | 2 | 1 | 1 | 3 | 1 |
| 11 | 9 | 8 | Tax Returns | 2 | 2 | 1 | 1 | | 1 |
| 55 | 45 | 41 | Other | 4 | 7 | 1 | 7 | 9 | 13 |
| | | | | | 10 (4/1-9/30/11) | | 81 (10/1/11-3/31/12) | | |
| 120 | 107 | 91 | NUMBER OF STATEMENTS | 9 | 14 | 7 | 15 | 22 | 24 |
| % | % | % | **ASSETS** | % | % | % | % | % | % |
| 8.5 | 8.1 | 7.8 | Cash & Equivalents | | 3.1 | | 6.5 | 12.9 | 8.5 |
| 16.3 | 16.4 | 17.3 | Trade Receivables (net) | | 17.8 | | 21.3 | 16.6 | 15.9 |
| 21.6 | 18.1 | 18.9 | Inventory | | 28.0 | | 17.0 | 20.3 | 15.6 |
| 4.1 | 2.9 | 2.7 | All Other Current | | 1.8 | | 3.1 | 2.7 | 1.9 |
| 50.6 | 45.4 | 46.8 | Total Current | | 50.7 | | 47.9 | 52.5 | 41.9 |
| 40.1 | 45.0 | 40.9 | Fixed Assets (net) | | 32.7 | | 44.4 | 39.0 | 41.4 |
| 3.2 | 3.9 | 4.7 | Intangibles (net) | | 4.5 | | 2.2 | 5.1 | 7.4 |
| 6.2 | 5.7 | 7.6 | All Other Non-Current | | 12.1 | | 5.4 | 3.4 | 9.3 |
| 100.0 | 100.0 | 100.0 | Total | | 100.0 | | 100.0 | 100.0 | 100.0 |
| | | | **LIABILITIES** | | | | | | |
| 8.3 | 7.9 | 8.2 | Notes Payable-Short Term | | 17.0 | | 7.1 | 6.5 | 7.5 |
| 7.1 | 4.8 | 5.1 | Cur. Mat.-L.T.D. | | 9.0 | | 4.8 | 5.8 | 2.3 |
| 9.5 | 9.4 | 10.6 | Trade Payables | | 12.0 | | 18.8 | 9.6 | 8.7 |
| .0 | .1 | .1 | Income Taxes Payable | | .0 | | .0 | .1 | .0 |
| 8.1 | 8.3 | 9.1 | All Other Current | | 3.6 | | 8.9 | 7.4 | 9.3 |
| 33.0 | 30.4 | 33.2 | Total Current | | 41.6 | | 39.6 | 29.3 | 27.8 |
| 24.2 | 23.5 | 21.2 | Long-Term Debt | | 29.0 | | 23.8 | 11.2 | 16.7 |
| .6 | .4 | .7 | Deferred Taxes | | .2 | | .7 | .7 | 1.3 |
| 9.2 | 8.1 | 10.2 | All Other Non-Current | | 22.8 | | 19.9 | 4.3 | 5.7 |
| 32.9 | 37.6 | 34.7 | Net Worth | | 6.5 | | 16.1 | 54.6 | 48.4 |
| 100.0 | 100.0 | 100.0 | Total Liabilities & Net Worth | | 100.0 | | 100.0 | 100.0 | 100.0 |
| | | | **INCOME DATA** | | | | | | |
| 100.0 | 100.0 | 100.0 | Net Sales | | 100.0 | | 100.0 | 100.0 | 100.0 |
| 33.4 | 29.9 | 30.1 | Gross Profit | | 32.8 | | 30.0 | 28.0 | 25.7 |
| 32.0 | 28.5 | 29.3 | Operating Expenses | | 33.0 | | 33.9 | 25.3 | 22.5 |
| 1.4 | 1.5 | .9 | Operating Profit | | -.3 | | -4.0 | 2.7 | 3.3 |
| 2.2 | 2.5 | 2.4 | All Other Expenses (net) | | 2.0 | | 2.0 | 1.6 | 1.0 |
| -.8 | -1.0 | -1.5 | Profit Before Taxes | | -2.3 | | -6.0 | 1.1 | 2.3 |
| | | | **RATIOS** | | | | | | |
| 3.9 | 3.2 | 2.8 | Current | | 2.2 | | 2.8 | 4.8 | 3.1 |
| 1.9 | 1.9 | 1.7 | | | 1.5 | | 1.3 | 2.4 | 1.8 |
| 1.1 | 1.1 | 1.0 | | | .8 | | .8 | 1.1 | 1.0 |
| 1.9 | 2.0 | 1.8 | Quick | | 1.1 | | 1.7 | 2.3 | 1.9 |
| .8 | .9 | .8 | | | .5 | | .7 | 1.5 | 1.0 |
| .3 | .4 | .3 | | | .3 | | .3 | .6 | .4 |
| 26  14.0 | 27  13.8 | 31  11.7 | Sales/Receivables | 28  13.2 | | 28  13.1 | 28  12.9 | 34  10.7 | |
| 36  10.1 | 40  9.1 | 38  9.5 | | 39  9.4 | | 37  9.8 | 38  9.7 | 39  9.4 | |
| 53  6.9 | 57  6.4 | 51  7.1 | | 54  6.7 | | 64  5.7 | 50  7.3 | 55  6.6 | |
| 40  9.2 | 44  8.4 | 46  8.0 | Cost of Sales/Inventory | 60  6.1 | | 49  7.4 | 37  9.8 | 48  7.6 | |
| 78  4.7 | 78  4.7 | 73  5.0 | | 87  4.2 | | 63  5.8 | 94  3.9 | 60  6.1 | |
| 127  2.9 | 115  3.2 | 122  3.0 | | 146  2.5 | | 96  3.8 | 130  2.8 | 99  3.7 | |
| 14  26.3 | 17  22.1 | 18  19.8 | Cost of Sales/Payables | 20  18.4 | | 30  12.0 | 18  19.8 | 18  20.0 | |
| 26  14.0 | 26  14.0 | 29  12.8 | | 39  9.3 | | 49  7.4 | 25  14.4 | 25  14.5 | |
| 43  8.4 | 43  8.4 | 51  7.1 | | 59  6.2 | | 76  4.8 | 40  9.2 | 41  9.0 | |
| 3.2 | 4.0 | 3.9 | Sales/Working Capital | | 4.6 | | 5.4 | 2.5 | 3.5 |
| 6.1 | 7.3 | 8.3 | | | 16.6 | | 16.5 | 5.8 | 7.9 |
| 62.8 | 45.4 | -68.3 | | | -15.8 | | -11.1 | 43.7 | 240.8 |
| | | | | | 5.1 | | 3.5 | 8.6 | 5.9 |
| (105)  4.4 | (93)  4.8 | (85)  5.5 | EBIT/Interest | (13)  .9 | | .3 | (21)  3.4 | 1.8 | |
| 1.5 | 1.1 | 1.2 | | | | | | | |
| -1.6 | -1.7 | -1.3 | | -3.9 | | -5.7 | -1.9 | .2 | |
| 2.7 | 8.3 | 3.0 | Net Profit + Depr., Dep., | | | | | | |
| (28)  1.4 | (21)  2.2 | (24)  1.1 | Amort./Cur. Mat. L/T/D | | | | | | |
| .2 | 1.1 | -.2 | | | | | | | |
| .5 | .7 | .6 | Fixed/Worth | | 1.2 | | .7 | .4 | .6 |
| 1.2 | 1.4 | 1.2 | | | NM | | 1.7 | .6 | 1.2 |
| 3.6 | 3.3 | 4.9 | | | -.4 | | -2.7 | 1.2 | 1.9 |
| .5 | .6 | .7 | Debt/Worth | | 2.1 | | 1.6 | .4 | .7 |
| 1.6 | 1.6 | 2.0 | | | NM | | 2.6 | .7 | 1.2 |
| 6.1 | 7.1 | 17.5 | | | -3.3 | | -5.0 | 2.5 | 2.2 |
| 16.2 | 14.2 | 15.6 | % Profit Before Taxes/Tangible | | | | 3.9 | 28.8 | 12.5 |
| (101)  5.5 | (88)  3.3 | (73)  3.5 | Net Worth | | | (10)  -4.4 | (21)  7.9 | (23)  3.1 | |
| -10.0 | -11.1 | -7.4 | | | | -39.8 | -4.0 | -2.3 | |
| 6.1 | 6.4 | 6.1 | % Profit Before Taxes/Total | | 7.9 | | 3.8 | 8.3 | 5.8 |
| 1.6 | .2 | .4 | Assets | | .7 | | -1.7 | 4.4 | .9 |
| -6.5 | -6.1 | -5.1 | | | -13.9 | | -17.1 | -3.5 | -1.6 |
| 8.1 | 5.1 | 7.0 | Sales/Net Fixed Assets | | 13.5 | | 9.0 | 9.8 | 4.6 |
| 3.6 | 2.6 | 2.8 | | | 4.0 | | 3.8 | 3.1 | 2.1 |
| 1.8 | 1.5 | 1.7 | | | 2.2 | | 1.3 | 1.8 | 1.7 |
| 1.9 | 1.8 | 1.8 | Sales/Total Assets | | 2.2 | | 2.2 | 1.8 | 1.5 |
| 1.2 | 1.1 | 1.3 | | | 1.5 | | 1.5 | 1.2 | 1.0 |
| .9 | .8 | .8 | | | 1.0 | | .9 | .7 | .8 |
| 2.7 | 3.1 | 2.8 | % Depr., Dep., Amort./Sales | | 2.5 | | 1.7 | 4.0 | 2.8 |
| (105)  4.9 | (87)  5.7 | (80)  5.2 | | (10)  4.3 | | (14)  3.6 | (20)  5.6 | (22)  6.2 | |
| 7.6 | 7.7 | 7.6 | | | 7.6 | | 7.2 | 7.4 | 7.8 |
| 2.1 | 1.5 | 1.9 | % Officers', Directors' | | | | | | |
| (36)  3.4 | (30)  2.8 | (24)  3.8 | Owners' Comp/Sales | | | | | | |
| 5.5 | 4.9 | 5.2 | | | | | | | |
| 3167171M | 2805353M | 2307420M | Net Sales ($) | 5908M | 32237M | 25552M | 96648M | 348993M | 1798082M |
| 3304976M | 2816022M | 2270615M | Total Assets ($) | 11614M | 28451M | 15589M | 84205M | 357714M | 1773042M |

© RMA 2012

M = $ thousand    MM = $ million
See Pages 9 through 22 for Explanation of Ratios and Data

| Current Data Sorted by Assets | | | | | | | Comparative Historical Data | |
|---|---|---|---|---|---|---|---|---|

| | | | | | | | **Type of Statement** | | |
|---|---|---|---|---|---|---|---|---|---|
| | | | 1 | 2 | | | Unqualified | 5 | 5 |
| | 1 | 3 | | | | | Reviewed | 6 | 4 |
| | | 5 | | | | | Compiled | 4 | 4 |
| | | 1 | | | | | Tax Returns | | |
| | 3 | 2 | 6 | 2 | 1 | | Other | 16 | 13 |
| | 5 (4/1-9/30/11) | | 22 (10/1/11-3/31/12) | | | | | 4/1/07-3/31/08 | 4/1/08-3/31/09 |
| 0-500M | 500M-2MM | 2-10MM | 10-50MM | 50-100MM | 100-250MM | | | ALL | ALL |
| | 4 | 11 | 7 | 4 | 1 | **NUMBER OF STATEMENTS** | 31 | 26 |
| % | % | % | % | % | % | **ASSETS** | % | % |
| | | 18.6 | | | | Cash & Equivalents | 8.5 | 7.2 |
| | | 16.4 | | | | Trade Receivables (net) | 20.9 | 23.4 |
| | | 21.4 | | | | Inventory | 17.2 | 16.7 |
| | | 2.5 | | | | All Other Current | 2.2 | 2.0 |
| | | 59.0 | | | | Total Current | 48.9 | 49.2 |
| | | 34.7 | | | | Fixed Assets (net) | 44.6 | 43.9 |
| | | 3.0 | | | | Intangibles (net) | 3.0 | 2.5 |
| | | 3.3 | | | | All Other Non-Current | 3.5 | 4.3 |
| | | 100.0 | | | | Total | 100.0 | 100.0 |
| | | | | | | **LIABILITIES** | | |
| | | 4.1 | | | | Notes Payable-Short Term | 6.5 | 7.1 |
| | | 2.0 | | | | Cur. Mat.-L.T.D. | 5.6 | 5.8 |
| | | 5.2 | | | | Trade Payables | 7.9 | 9.0 |
| | | .7 | | | | Income Taxes Payable | .0 | .2 |
| | | 3.8 | | | | All Other Current | 6.5 | 5.1 |
| | | 15.8 | | | | Total Current | 26.6 | 27.1 |
| | | 15.3 | | | | Long-Term Debt | 19.7 | 20.3 |
| | | .8 | | | | Deferred Taxes | 1.1 | 2.0 |
| | | 8.8 | | | | All Other Non-Current | 6.4 | 5.1 |
| | | 59.3 | | | | Net Worth | 46.2 | 45.5 |
| | | 100.0 | | | | Total Liabilities & Net Worth | 100.0 | 100.0 |
| | | | | | | **INCOME DATA** | | |
| | | 100.0 | | | | Net Sales | 100.0 | 100.0 |
| | | 28.4 | | | | Gross Profit | 29.1 | 21.6 |
| | | 29.9 | | | | Operating Expenses | 22.2 | 21.8 |
| | | -1.5 | | | | Operating Profit | 6.9 | -.2 |
| | | -1.7 | | | | All Other Expenses (net) | 1.4 | 1.6 |
| | | .3 | | | | Profit Before Taxes | 5.5 | -1.8 |
| | | | | | | **RATIOS** | | |
| | | 8.4 | | | | | 3.4 | 3.7 |
| | | 4.4 | | | | Current | 2.2 | 2.0 |
| | | 2.4 | | | | | 1.2 | 1.3 |
| | | 4.6 | | | | | 2.7 | 2.3 |
| | | 2.7 | | | | Quick | 1.1 | 1.1 |
| | | 1.4 | | | | | .6 | .5 |
| | 27 | 13.4 | | | | | 33 | 11.1 | 24 | 15.0 |
| | 34 | 10.7 | | | | Sales/Receivables | 37 | 9.8 | 49 | 7.5 |
| | 58 | 6.3 | | | | | 57 | 6.4 | 67 | 5.4 |
| | 38 | 9.5 | | | | | 22 | 16.7 | 18 | 20.3 |
| | 83 | 4.4 | | | | Cost of Sales/Inventory | 64 | 5.7 | 65 | 5.6 |
| | 107 | 3.4 | | | | | 93 | 3.9 | 89 | 4.1 |
| | 14 | 26.0 | | | | | 18 | 20.7 | 13 | 27.7 |
| | 21 | 17.8 | | | | Cost of Sales/Payables | 24 | 15.2 | 19 | 19.3 |
| | 31 | 11.6 | | | | | 35 | 10.6 | 30 | 12.1 |
| | | 2.4 | | | | | 4.7 | 4.4 |
| | | 3.6 | | | | Sales/Working Capital | 7.2 | 7.5 |
| | | 4.6 | | | | | 20.0 | 28.9 |
| | | 8.7 | | | | | 11.1 | 4.5 |
| | (10) | 2.1 | | | | EBIT/Interest | (30) | 3.6 | (24) | 2.2 |
| | | -3.0 | | | | | .7 | -3.3 |
| | | | | | | Net Profit + Depr., Dep., | 6.7 | 6.2 |
| | | | | | | Amort./Cur. Mat. L/T/D | (14) | 3.7 | (13) | 3.6 |
| | | | | | | | 2.1 | 1.6 |
| | | .3 | | | | | .6 | .7 |
| | | .5 | | | | Fixed/Worth | 1.0 | 1.0 |
| | | .9 | | | | | 1.9 | 1.7 |
| | | .3 | | | | | .6 | .6 |
| | | .7 | | | | Debt/Worth | 1.3 | 1.3 |
| | | 1.1 | | | | | 3.0 | 2.7 |
| | | 21.5 | | | | % Profit Before Taxes/Tangible | 33.8 | 14.3 |
| | | 1.8 | | | | Net Worth | 22.2 | (23) | 8.2 |
| | | -11.0 | | | | | -1.1 | .1 |
| | | 8.1 | | | | % Profit Before Taxes/Total | 19.9 | 6.4 |
| | | 1.6 | | | | Assets | 10.0 | 4.0 |
| | | -8.4 | | | | | -.5 | -7.2 |
| | | 7.5 | | | | | 4.9 | 4.6 |
| | | 3.7 | | | | Sales/Net Fixed Assets | 3.7 | 3.8 |
| | | 2.3 | | | | | 2.3 | 1.9 |
| | | 2.2 | | | | | 1.9 | 2.3 |
| | | 1.2 | | | | Sales/Total Assets | 1.6 | 1.2 |
| | | .9 | | | | | 1.2 | 1.0 |
| | | 1.7 | | | | | 2.6 | 3.8 |
| | | 5.2 | | | | % Depr., Dep., Amort./Sales | (30) | 3.6 | (24) | 5.0 |
| | | 10.2 | | | | | 5.7 | 7.1 |
| | | | | | | % Officers', Directors' | | .8 | |
| | | | | | | Owners' Comp/Sales | (13) | 1.7 | |
| | | | | | | | 4.3 | |
| | 11590M | 69785M | 265804M | 298785M | 102127M | Net Sales ($) | 1089860M | 747309M |
| | 5557M | 47480M | 209625M | 324937M | 135774M | Total Assets ($) | 897547M | 618164M |

M = $ thousand    MM = $ million
See Pages 9 through 22 for Explanation of Ratios and Data

## Comparative Historical Data / Current Data Sorted by Sales

| | | | Type of Statement | | | | | | |
|---|---|---|---|---|---|---|---|---|---|
| 6 | 6 | 3 | Unqualified | | | | | 1 | 2 |
| 3 | 3 | 4 | Reviewed | | | | | 2 | 2 |
| 5 | 5 | 5 | Compiled | | 2 | | | | 2 |
| 1 | 1 | 1 | Tax Returns | | | 1 | | 1 | |
| 8 | 14 | 14 | Other | | 2 | 3 | | | 8 |
| 4/1/09-3/31/10 | 4/1/10-3/31/11 | 4/1/11-3/31/12 | | 0-1MM | 1-3MM | 3-5MM | 5-10MM | 10-25MM | 25MM & OVER |
| ALL | ALL | ALL | | | 5 (4/1-9/30/11) | | 22 (10/1/11-3/31/12) | | |
| 23 | 29 | 27 | **NUMBER OF STATEMENTS** | 4 | 6 | 3 | | 4 | 10 |
| % | % | % | **ASSETS** | % | % | % | % | % | % |
| 9.7 | 9.7 | 14.0 | Cash & Equivalents | | | | | | 6.8 |
| 21.1 | 20.1 | 17.6 | Trade Receivables (net) | | | | | | 16.9 |
| 17.4 | 20.5 | 19.5 | Inventory | | | | | | 17.6 |
| 1.4 | 2.2 | 4.2 | All Other Current | | | | | | 7.7 |
| 49.6 | 52.5 | 55.3 | Total Current | | | | | | 49.0 |
| 41.3 | 34.8 | 36.8 | Fixed Assets (net) | | | | | | 37.6 |
| 3.7 | 6.1 | 2.9 | Intangibles (net) | | | | | | 4.0 |
| 5.4 | 6.6 | 5.0 | All Other Non-Current | | | | | | 9.4 |
| 100.0 | 100.0 | 100.0 | Total | | | | | | 100.0 |
| | | | **LIABILITIES** | | | | | | |
| 4.8 | 9.4 | 4.9 | Notes Payable-Short Term | | | | | | 5.6 |
| 3.3 | 3.2 | 2.8 | Cur. Mat.-L.T.D. | | | | | | 2.6 |
| 9.1 | 9.3 | 8.2 | Trade Payables | | | | | | 9.7 |
| .2 | .0 | .6 | Income Taxes Payable | | | | | | .6 |
| 3.7 | 5.2 | 6.0 | All Other Current | | | | | | 10.5 |
| 21.1 | 27.1 | 22.4 | Total Current | | | | | | 29.1 |
| 25.3 | 16.0 | 14.5 | Long-Term Debt | | | | | | 15.0 |
| .6 | 1.2 | 1.0 | Deferred Taxes | | | | | | 1.8 |
| 4.6 | 9.5 | 7.0 | All Other Non-Current | | | | | | 3.4 |
| 48.3 | 46.2 | 55.1 | Net Worth | | | | | | 50.7 |
| 100.0 | 100.0 | 100.0 | Total Liabilities & Net Worth | | | | | | 100.0 |
| | | | **INCOME DATA** | | | | | | |
| 100.0 | 100.0 | 100.0 | Net Sales | | | | | | 100.0 |
| 25.4 | 24.5 | 27.2 | Gross Profit | | | | | | 30.5 |
| 23.9 | 23.5 | 24.7 | Operating Expenses | | | | | | 23.9 |
| 1.5 | 1.0 | 2.5 | Operating Profit | | | | | | 6.7 |
| 1.2 | 2.0 | -.2 | All Other Expenses (net) | | | | | | .8 |
| .3 | -1.0 | 2.7 | Profit Before Taxes | | | | | | 5.9 |
| | | | **RATIOS** | | | | | | |
| 4.6 | 4.0 | 4.8 | Current | | | | | | 4.1 |
| 2.6 | 2.3 | 2.9 | | | | | | | 1.6 |
| 1.5 | 1.4 | 1.8 | | | | | | | 1.2 |
| 3.4 | 2.1 | 3.5 | Quick | | | | | | 2.5 |
| 1.1 | 1.0 | 1.4 | | | | | | | .8 |
| .7 | .6 | .8 | | | | | | | .5 |
| 39  9.5 | 37  9.8 | 31  11.9 | Sales/Receivables | | | | | | 43  8.5 |
| 51  7.1 | 50  7.3 | 49  7.4 | | | | | | | 61  6.0 |
| 61  6.0 | 67  5.5 | 68  5.4 | | | | | | | 74  4.9 |
| 41  8.9 | 44  8.3 | 38  9.5 | Cost of Sales/Inventory | | | | | | 51  7.2 |
| 74  4.9 | 73  5.0 | 83  4.4 | | | | | | | 96  3.8 |
| 92  4.0 | 91  4.0 | 104  3.5 | | | | | | | 111  3.3 |
| 13  28.7 | 14  26.7 | 19  18.8 | Cost of Sales/Payables | | | | | | 35  10.5 |
| 23  15.9 | 26  14.2 | 31  11.6 | | | | | | | 42  8.6 |
| 42  8.8 | 37  9.8 | 42  8.6 | | | | | | | 54  6.7 |
| 3.2 | 3.5 | 2.5 | Sales/Working Capital | | | | | | 3.5 |
| 4.5 | 5.7 | 4.1 | | | | | | | 7.7 |
| 10.4 | 14.7 | 8.9 | | | | | | | 17.8 |
| 5.2 | 4.6 | 8.9 | EBIT/Interest | | | | | | |
| 1.0 | (28) .2 | (24) 2.1 | | | | | | | |
| -.1 | -2.0 | -1.5 | | | | | | | |
| | 19.3 | | Net Profit + Depr., Dep., Amort./Cur. Mat. L/T/D | | | | | | |
| | (10) 2.1 | | | | | | | | |
| | .5 | | | | | | | | |
| .5 | .6 | .4 | Fixed/Worth | | | | | | .6 |
| 1.1 | 1.0 | .8 | | | | | | | 1.0 |
| 1.6 | 1.6 | 1.1 | | | | | | | 1.2 |
| .4 | .6 | .4 | Debt/Worth | | | | | | .6 |
| 1.0 | .8 | .8 | | | | | | | 1.0 |
| 3.5 | 3.4 | 1.6 | | | | | | | 2.1 |
| 21.2 | 20.2 | 25.4 | % Profit Before Taxes/Tangible Net Worth | | | | | | 38.2 |
| (22) 1.0 | (25) -.7 | 5.5 | | | | | | | 17.1 |
| -9.7 | -8.5 | -6.7 | | | | | | | -2.2 |
| 5.7 | 9.8 | 10.1 | % Profit Before Taxes/Total Assets | | | | | | 12.7 |
| .1 | -.7 | 3.5 | | | | | | | 8.2 |
| -2.9 | -4.9 | -3.7 | | | | | | | -.9 |
| 4.7 | 8.1 | 6.0 | Sales/Net Fixed Assets | | | | | | 4.7 |
| 3.3 | 4.0 | 3.7 | | | | | | | 3.4 |
| 2.0 | 2.2 | 2.3 | | | | | | | 1.7 |
| 1.8 | 2.1 | 1.9 | Sales/Total Assets | | | | | | 1.5 |
| 1.4 | 1.6 | 1.2 | | | | | | | 1.1 |
| 1.0 | .9 | .9 | | | | | | | .7 |
| 3.4 | 2.9 | 2.8 | % Depr., Dep., Amort./Sales | | | | | | 3.1 |
| (22) 5.0 | (26) 4.8 | 4.4 | | | | | | | 4.6 |
| 7.2 | 5.8 | 6.0 | | | | | | | 5.3 |
| 1.2 | 1.5 | 1.7 | % Officers', Directors' Owners' Comp/Sales | | | | | | |
| (12) 2.2 | (10) 2.6 | (11) 3.1 | | | | | | | |
| 4.8 | 5.7 | 6.3 | | | | | | | |
| 700018M | 1094833M | 748091M | Net Sales ($) | 8147M | 24510M | 18656M | | 71951M | 624827M |
| 568819M | 855052M | 723373M | Total Assets ($) | 6788M | 22193M | 10816M | | 54208M | 629368M |

Note: Percentage data for the 0-1MM through 10-25MM columns marked **DATA NOT AVAILABLE**.

M = $ thousand    MM = $ million
See Pages 9 through 22 for Explanation of Ratios and Data

## Current Data Sorted by Assets          Comparative Historical Data

| | | | | | | Type of Statement | | |
|---|---|---|---|---|---|---|---|---|
| | | 5 | 10 | 2 | 3 | Unqualified | 33 | 29 |
| | 9 | 20 | 10 | | | Reviewed | 41 | 41 |
| 1 | 7 | 13 | 1 | | | Compiled | 23 | 23 |
| 8 | 11 | 6 | | | | Tax Returns | 16 | 14 |
| 1 | 11 | 22 | 15 | 4 | 3 | Other | 52 | 53 |
| | 24 (4/1-9/30/11) | | 138 (10/1/11-3/31/12) | | | | 4/1/07-3/31/08 | 4/1/08-3/31/09 |
| 0-500M | 500M-2MM | 2-10MM | 10-50MM | 50-100MM | 100-250MM | | ALL | ALL |
| 10 | 38 | 66 | 36 | 6 | 6 | **NUMBER OF STATEMENTS** | 165 | 160 |
| % | % | % | % | % | % | **ASSETS** | % | % |
| 12.6 | 8.5 | 7.2 | 11.3 | | | Cash & Equivalents | 7.1 | 7.9 |
| 18.8 | 29.2 | 27.9 | 27.3 | | | Trade Receivables (net) | 28.6 | 27.1 |
| 16.4 | 16.9 | 15.2 | 13.1 | | | Inventory | 15.4 | 17.0 |
| 2.2 | 2.1 | 3.1 | 4.5 | | | All Other Current | 2.5 | 3.2 |
| 50.0 | 56.6 | 53.4 | 56.1 | | | Total Current | 53.6 | 55.1 |
| 34.8 | 31.7 | 35.0 | 35.3 | | | Fixed Assets (net) | 35.3 | 36.0 |
| 9.6 | 4.2 | 6.3 | .7 | | | Intangibles (net) | 3.2 | 2.7 |
| 5.6 | 7.4 | 5.3 | 7.9 | | | All Other Non-Current | 7.9 | 6.2 |
| 100.0 | 100.0 | 100.0 | 100.0 | | | Total | 100.0 | 100.0 |
| | | | | | | **LIABILITIES** | | |
| 29.0 | 12.2 | 11.6 | 6.9 | | | Notes Payable-Short Term | 7.6 | 8.8 |
| 1.9 | 3.8 | 3.8 | 3.0 | | | Cur. Mat.-L.T.D. | 4.7 | 4.1 |
| 22.7 | 14.0 | 13.2 | 12.6 | | | Trade Payables | 11.7 | 12.6 |
| .0 | .1 | .2 | .2 | | | Income Taxes Payable | .3 | .2 |
| 6.3 | 10.2 | 6.1 | 10.1 | | | All Other Current | 9.7 | 8.5 |
| 59.9 | 40.3 | 34.8 | 32.8 | | | Total Current | 34.0 | 34.2 |
| 29.5 | 21.9 | 18.3 | 13.6 | | | Long-Term Debt | 19.9 | 20.8 |
| .0 | .2 | .5 | .8 | | | Deferred Taxes | .7 | .6 |
| 17.0 | 5.1 | 6.0 | 6.2 | | | All Other Non-Current | 4.0 | 6.0 |
| -6.4 | 32.4 | 40.3 | 46.6 | | | Net Worth | 41.3 | 38.5 |
| 100.0 | 100.0 | 100.0 | 100.0 | | | Total Liabilties & Net Worth | 100.0 | 100.0 |
| | | | | | | **INCOME DATA** | | |
| 100.0 | 100.0 | 100.0 | 100.0 | | | Net Sales | 100.0 | 100.0 |
| 41.9 | 38.0 | 31.3 | 23.1 | | | Gross Profit | 32.1 | 30.3 |
| 38.3 | 34.9 | 28.3 | 19.2 | | | Operating Expenses | 26.1 | 25.9 |
| 3.6 | 3.1 | 3.0 | 3.9 | | | Operating Profit | 6.0 | 4.4 |
| .0 | 1.2 | 1.5 | .2 | | | All Other Expenses (net) | 1.3 | 1.3 |
| 3.6 | 1.9 | 1.5 | 3.6 | | | Profit Before Taxes | 4.7 | 3.1 |
| | | | | | | **RATIOS** | | |
| 1.5 | 3.5 | 2.5 | 2.9 | | | | 3.0 | 2.8 |
| 1.1 | 1.6 | 1.4 | 1.6 | | | Current | 1.7 | 1.7 |
| .5 | .9 | 1.0 | 1.4 | | | | 1.1 | 1.2 |
| 1.3 | 2.6 | 1.4 | 1.9 | | | | 1.8 | 1.7 |
| .6 (37) | 1.1 | .9 | 1.2 | | | Quick | 1.1 | 1.1 |
| .3 | .4 | .7 | .9 | | | | .7 | .6 |
| 0 UND | 25 14.7 | 39 9.3 | 46 7.9 | | | | 34 10.6 | 38 9.7 |
| 20 17.9 | 42 8.6 | 62 5.9 | 65 5.6 | | | Sales/Receivables | 50 7.3 | 47 7.7 |
| 42 8.6 | 59 6.2 | 87 4.2 | 87 4.2 | | | | 72 5.1 | 68 5.4 |
| 0 UND | 7 49.0 | 16 22.3 | 14 25.8 | | | | 16 22.5 | 16 23.0 |
| 19 19.2 | 26 14.0 | 45 8.1 | 40 9.1 | | | Cost of Sales/Inventory | 35 10.3 | 45 8.1 |
| 36 10.2 | 79 4.6 | 83 4.4 | 87 4.2 | | | | 76 4.8 | 88 4.1 |
| 0 UND | 8 43.9 | 21 17.4 | 22 16.7 | | | | 16 22.8 | 16 22.5 |
| 27 13.3 | 25 14.6 | 41 8.9 | 38 9.7 | | | Cost of Sales/Payables | 25 14.6 | 27 13.7 |
| 38 9.6 | 54 6.8 | 65 5.6 | 54 6.7 | | | | 39 9.3 | 51 7.1 |
| 44.0 | 5.1 | 5.1 | 3.6 | | | | 5.1 | 5.1 |
| 246.5 | 13.6 | 11.3 | 7.6 | | | Sales/Working Capital | 8.4 | 7.7 |
| -17.3 | -55.2 | 316.8 | 10.7 | | | | 39.3 | 21.3 |
| | 5.3 | 13.0 | 8.7 | | | | 11.6 | 7.5 |
| (35) | 1.7 (62) | 2.2 (32) | 2.6 | | | EBIT/Interest | (156) 3.7 (147) | 2.4 |
| | .9 | -.7 | 1.2 | | | | 1.4 | .1 |
| | | 10.1 | 7.0 | | | | 9.5 | 10.3 |
| | (13) | .7 (13) | 2.1 | | | Net Profit + Depr., Dep., Amort./Cur. Mat. L/T/D | (49) 3.4 (41) | 2.7 |
| | | -.9 | 1.0 | | | | 2.0 | 1.5 |
| 1.8 | .4 | .5 | .6 | | | | .4 | .4 |
| 12.2 | .8 | .9 | .7 | | | Fixed/Worth | .9 | .9 |
| -1.7 | 6.0 | 4.4 | 1.4 | | | | 2.3 | 2.2 |
| 5.3 | .6 | .5 | .6 | | | | .7 | .7 |
| 61.9 | 1.5 | 1.8 | 1.2 | | | Debt/Worth | 1.4 | 1.5 |
| -3.6 | NM | 6.2 | 2.0 | | | | 3.3 | 4.8 |
| | 34.7 | 33.4 | 20.8 | | | | 43.0 | 29.4 |
| (29) | 7.5 (56) | 10.8 (35) | 9.8 | | | % Profit Before Taxes/Tangible Net Worth | (147) 22.0 (142) | 11.3 |
| | 1.1 | -6.7 | 1.0 | | | | 6.7 | -1.2 |
| 22.7 | 7.9 | 11.8 | 8.4 | | | | 16.4 | 10.7 |
| 3.5 | 3.0 | 1.6 | 3.3 | | | % Profit Before Taxes/Total Assets | 7.1 | 4.7 |
| -2.8 | -.2 | -4.1 | .4 | | | | 1.3 | -2.3 |
| 47.6 | 20.8 | 9.7 | 8.0 | | | | 10.2 | 10.0 |
| 24.6 | 7.8 | 5.2 | 4.0 | | | Sales/Net Fixed Assets | 5.6 | 4.8 |
| 5.8 | 4.0 | 3.0 | 2.1 | | | | 3.6 | 3.0 |
| 7.4 | 3.2 | 2.2 | 1.8 | | | | 2.5 | 2.3 |
| 4.0 | 2.2 | 1.7 | 1.5 | | | Sales/Total Assets | 1.9 | 1.8 |
| 2.1 | 1.7 | 1.0 | 1.0 | | | | 1.3 | 1.3 |
| | 1.8 | 1.7 | 1.5 | | | | 1.8 | 1.9 |
| (31) | 4.1 (57) | 3.4 (35) | 2.9 | | | % Depr., Dep., Amort./Sales | (152) 3.0 (136) | 3.2 |
| | 7.1 | 5.3 | 4.7 | | | | 4.8 | 5.0 |
| | 1.5 | 1.1 | | | | | 2.0 | 1.8 |
| (24) | 3.9 (28) | 3.1 | | | | % Officers', Directors' Owners' Comp/Sales | (59) 3.2 (49) | 3.4 |
| | 7.2 | 4.5 | | | | | 5.6 | 5.1 |
| 16292M | 117107M | 588324M | 1103001M | 581598M | 1180015M | Net Sales ($) | 6143799M | 6644540M |
| 3138M | 46888M | 350005M | 775728M | 378914M | 893669M | Total Assets ($) | 3940422M | 4132100M |

M = $ thousand    MM = $ million
See Pages 9 through 22 for Explanation of Ratios and Data

## Comparative Historical Data | Current Data Sorted by Sales

| | | | Type of Statement | | | | | | |
|---|---|---|---|---|---|---|---|---|---|
| 29 | 25 | 20 | Unqualified | | | | 5 | 4 | 11 |
| 35 | 30 | 39 | Reviewed | | 4 | 4 | 11 | 14 | 6 |
| 23 | 25 | 22 | Compiled | 1 | 6 | 6 | 5 | 3 | 1 |
| 16 | 19 | 25 | Tax Returns | 4 | 11 | 3 | 6 | 1 | |
| 65 | 52 | 56 | Other | 3 | 10 | 5 | 12 | 9 | 17 |
| 4/1/09-3/31/10 ALL | 4/1/10-3/31/11 ALL | 4/1/11-3/31/12 ALL | | | 24 (4/1-9/30/11) | | 138 (10/1/11-3/31/12) | | |
| 168 | 151 | 162 | NUMBER OF STATEMENTS | 0-1MM 8 | 1-3MM 31 | 3-5MM 18 | 5-10MM 39 | 10-25MM 31 | 25MM & OVER 35 |
| % | % | % | ASSETS | % | % | % | % | % | % |
| 10.2 | 12.1 | 9.4 | Cash & Equivalents | | 6.4 | 10.3 | 10.3 | 8.3 | 11.0 |
| 24.5 | 24.8 | 26.9 | Trade Receivables (net) | | 18.1 | 28.0 | 28.7 | 34.4 | 27.4 |
| 17.0 | 14.8 | 15.0 | Inventory | | 19.5 | 15.6 | 16.3 | 12.4 | 13.8 |
| 3.0 | 3.6 | 3.3 | All Other Current | | 3.2 | .3 | 2.0 | 4.6 | 5.3 |
| 54.6 | 55.3 | 54.6 | Total Current | | 47.2 | 54.2 | 57.3 | 59.7 | 57.5 |
| 36.4 | 35.4 | 34.5 | Fixed Assets (net) | | 34.9 | 36.6 | 31.6 | 32.4 | 34.8 |
| 2.6 | 3.1 | 4.7 | Intangibles (net) | | 7.5 | 4.1 | 7.0 | 2.3 | 2.1 |
| 6.4 | 6.2 | 6.2 | All Other Non-Current | | 10.4 | 5.1 | 4.1 | 5.6 | 5.5 |
| 100.0 | 100.0 | 100.0 | Total | | 100.0 | 100.0 | 100.0 | 100.0 | 100.0 |
| | | | LIABILITIES | | | | | | |
| 9.1 | 8.9 | 11.3 | Notes Payable-Short Term | | 15.7 | 6.5 | 11.3 | 11.0 | 7.3 |
| 5.4 | 4.4 | 3.4 | Cur. Mat.-L.T.D. | | 4.7 | 2.0 | 3.5 | 4.6 | 2.5 |
| 12.4 | 12.0 | 13.5 | Trade Payables | | 12.6 | 13.4 | 12.8 | 16.0 | 11.6 |
| .4 | .4 | .2 | Income Taxes Payable | | .1 | .0 | .3 | .2 | .5 |
| 11.0 | 7.9 | 8.4 | All Other Current | | 9.4 | 4.8 | 7.9 | 7.7 | 11.6 |
| 38.3 | 33.7 | 36.8 | Total Current | | 42.5 | 26.7 | 35.7 | 39.5 | 33.5 |
| 18.3 | 20.4 | 18.2 | Long-Term Debt | | 29.1 | 23.2 | 13.0 | 14.8 | 10.8 |
| .5 | .4 | .5 | Deferred Taxes | | .3 | .1 | .1 | 1.5 | .8 |
| 5.2 | 4.8 | 6.9 | All Other Non-Current | | 6.0 | 5.5 | 7.6 | 2.6 | 6.6 |
| 37.7 | 40.7 | 37.6 | Net Worth | | 22.1 | 44.5 | 43.5 | 41.6 | 48.3 |
| 100.0 | 100.0 | 100.0 | Total Liabilties & Net Worth | | 100.0 | 100.0 | 100.0 | 100.0 | 100.0 |
| | | | INCOME DATA | | | | | | |
| 100.0 | 100.0 | 100.0 | Net Sales | | 100.0 | 100.0 | 100.0 | 100.0 | 100.0 |
| 31.1 | 31.9 | 30.9 | Gross Profit | | 41.9 | 39.5 | 26.9 | 26.5 | 22.4 |
| 28.1 | 28.0 | 27.6 | Operating Expenses | | 39.4 | 34.8 | 25.5 | 23.8 | 17.6 |
| 3.1 | 3.8 | 3.3 | Operating Profit | | 2.4 | 4.7 | 1.5 | 2.7 | 4.8 |
| 1.2 | .8 | 1.0 | All Other Expenses (net) | | 2.1 | .7 | .8 | 1.0 | .2 |
| 1.9 | 3.0 | 2.3 | Profit Before Taxes | | .4 | 4.0 | .6 | 1.7 | 4.6 |
| | | | RATIOS | | | | | | |
| 2.7 | 3.2 | 2.8 | | | 3.4 | 3.2 | 2.6 | 2.9 | 3.2 |
| 1.7 | 1.7 | 1.5 | Current | | 1.1 | 1.9 | 1.7 | 1.5 | 1.5 |
| 1.1 | 1.1 | 1.0 | | | .6 | 1.4 | 1.0 | 1.0 | 1.4 |
| 2.1 | 2.2 | 1.8 | | | 1.3 | 2.6 | 1.8 | 1.7 | 2.2 |
| 1.0 | 1.1 (161) | 1.0 | Quick | (30) | .5 | 1.1 | .9 | 1.1 | 1.0 |
| .5 | .6 | .6 | | | .3 | .9 | .7 | .7 | .7 |
| 33 11.0 | 36 10.2 | 33 11.0 | | 20 18.6 | 31 11.8 | 33 11.0 | 38 9.5 | 51 7.2 | |
| 46 8.0 | 54 6.8 | 54 6.7 | Sales/Receivables | 38 9.5 | 60 6.1 | 56 6.5 | 61 6.0 | 63 5.8 | |
| 68 5.4 | 71 5.2 | 78 4.7 | | 51 7.1 | 76 4.8 | 78 4.7 | 91 4.0 | 73 5.0 | |
| 19 19.7 | 14 25.2 | 12 31.2 | | 9 41.2 | 20 18.4 | 10 37.7 | 9 41.6 | 17 21.8 | |
| 44 8.3 | 44 8.2 | 39 9.3 | Cost of Sales/Inventory | 45 8.1 | 58 6.3 | 41 9.0 | 25 14.8 | 31 11.7 | |
| 89 4.1 | 85 4.3 | 79 4.6 | | 89 4.1 | 101 3.6 | 87 4.2 | 54 6.8 | 78 4.7 | |
| 16 22.6 | 16 23.2 | 17 21.7 | | 10 35.6 | 17 21.6 | 17 21.3 | 13 27.6 | 17 21.7 | |
| 29 12.6 | 31 11.8 | 33 11.1 | Cost of Sales/Payables | 34 10.8 | 48 7.6 | 31 11.6 | 35 10.5 | 30 12.0 | |
| 46 8.0 | 51 7.2 | 55 6.6 | | 53 6.9 | 61 6.0 | 53 6.9 | 62 5.9 | 47 7.7 | |
| 4.3 | 3.9 | 4.9 | | | 5.2 | 4.5 | 5.1 | 4.6 | 3.6 |
| 8.1 | 7.3 | 9.9 | Sales/Working Capital | | 123.9 | 7.7 | 10.1 | 9.3 | 8.2 |
| 47.9 | 48.1 | 127.8 | | | -6.8 | 12.4 | 67.6 | 89.1 | 11.9 |
| 9.0 | 8.8 | 6.2 | | | 4.1 | 10.6 | 6.6 | 22.8 | 8.7 |
| (150) 2.1 | (134) 2.1 | (147) 2.3 | EBIT/Interest | (30) 1.2 | (16) 3.4 | (35) 1.9 | (29) 3.1 | (31) 3.4 | |
| -.2 | -.6 | .2 | | | -.3 | -.7 | .0 | -.6 | 1.2 |
| 7.7 | 5.1 | 8.7 | Net Profit + Depr., Dep., | | | | | 3.3 | |
| (42) 1.8 | (32) 2.0 | (30) 1.5 | Amort./Cur. Mat. L/T/D | | | | (11) 1.0 | | |
| .8 | .4 | .5 | | | | | | .3 | |
| .5 | .4 | .5 | | | .6 | .3 | .4 | .4 | .6 |
| .8 | .8 | .8 | Fixed/Worth | | 2.3 | 1.0 | .7 | .8 | .7 |
| 3.0 | 2.6 | 2.3 | | | -3.0 | 4.2 | 1.4 | 1.9 | 1.0 |
| .6 | .6 | .6 | | | 1.2 | .6 | .4 | .5 | .7 |
| 1.2 | 1.2 | 1.7 | Debt/Worth | | 7.3 | 1.1 | 1.6 | 1.9 | 1.2 |
| 5.5 | 4.6 | 6.9 | | | -8.9 | 6.8 | 4.1 | 4.6 | 1.8 |
| 28.3 | 33.8 | 28.4 | % Profit Before Taxes/Tangible | | 21.7 | 37.0 | 21.5 | 37.1 | 30.6 |
| (143) 8.9 | (132) 9.6 | (137) 8.0 | Net Worth | (20) 3.2 | (16) 13.8 | (34) 6.2 | (28) 12.3 | (34) 8.8 | |
| -3.6 | -4.8 | -1.6 | | | -2.4 | 3.4 | -4.2 | -17.8 | .5 |
| 12.3 | 12.4 | 10.0 | % Profit Before Taxes/Total | | 3.5 | 11.4 | 7.4 | 15.6 | 15.4 |
| 2.4 | 3.5 | 2.6 | Assets | | .7 | 3.1 | 1.3 | 3.8 | 2.7 |
| -2.5 | -1.8 | -1.1 | | | -1.8 | -4.3 | -3.5 | -4.5 | .4 |
| 9.2 | 10.9 | 11.2 | | | 13.3 | 31.5 | 12.8 | 11.1 | 7.2 |
| 4.5 | 4.8 | 5.4 | Sales/Net Fixed Assets | | 5.0 | 5.1 | 6.5 | 6.3 | 4.1 |
| 2.8 | 2.7 | 3.0 | | | 2.6 | 2.3 | 3.2 | 3.3 | 2.9 |
| 2.1 | 2.1 | 2.4 | | | 2.8 | 2.2 | 2.8 | 2.5 | 1.8 |
| 1.6 | 1.6 | 1.7 | Sales/Total Assets | | 1.7 | 1.8 | 1.9 | 1.8 | 1.5 |
| 1.2 | 1.1 | 1.2 | | | 1.0 | 1.0 | 1.0 | 1.6 | 1.2 |
| 2.1 | 2.3 | 1.7 | | | 2.4 | 1.6 | 1.5 | 1.5 | 2.1 |
| (142) 3.5 | (130) 3.8 | (142) 3.4 | % Depr., Dep., Amort./Sales | (26) 5.2 | (15) 3.4 | (31) 3.7 | (30) 2.6 | (33) 3.2 | |
| 5.5 | 5.8 | 5.1 | | | 7.9 | 7.8 | 5.2 | 4.0 | 3.8 |
| 2.1 | 1.5 | 1.3 | % Officers', Directors' | | .8 | 1.5 | 1.6 | | |
| (45) 4.5 | (54) 3.3 | (64) 3.1 | Owners' Comp/Sales | (17) 3.6 | (12) 3.7 | (17) 3.0 | | | |
| 5.9 | 5.7 | 5.6 | | | 7.4 | 4.9 | 5.3 | | |
| 5775116M | 4874716M | 3586337M | Net Sales ($) | 6069M | 57324M | 70300M | 273239M | 507556M | 2671849M |
| 3950254M | 3661902M | 2448342M | Total Assets ($) | 11968M | 39129M | 56118M | 204827M | 276960M | 1859340M |

M = $ thousand    MM = $ million
See Pages 9 through 22 for Explanation of Ratios and Data

## Current Data Sorted by Assets      Comparative Historical Data

| | 0-500M | 500M-2MM | 2-10MM | 10-50MM | 50-100MM | 100-250MM | Type of Statement | 4/1/07-3/31/08 ALL | 4/1/08-3/31/09 ALL |
|---|---|---|---|---|---|---|---|---|---|
| | | 1 | 4 | 2 | 1 | 5 | Unqualified | 15 | 13 |
| | | 3 | 5 | 1 | | | Reviewed | 11 | 12 |
| | | 4 | 7 | | | | Compiled | 8 | 7 |
| | 1 | 6 | 1 | | | | Tax Returns | 4 | 5 |
| | 1 | 4 | 9 | 13 | 4 | 1 | Other | 19 | 14 |
| | | 11 (4/1-9/30/11) | | 62 (10/1/11-3/31/12) | | | | | |
| **NUMBER OF STATEMENTS** | 2 | 18 | 26 | 16 | 5 | 6 | | 57 | 51 |
| | % | % | % | % | % | % | **ASSETS** | % | % |
| | | 5.9 | 11.3 | 12.1 | | | Cash & Equivalents | 8.6 | 7.7 |
| | | 28.8 | 27.8 | 20.7 | | | Trade Receivables (net) | 24.0 | 19.1 |
| | | 31.2 | 23.0 | 27.8 | | | Inventory | 30.6 | 30.3 |
| | | 3.7 | 3.2 | 5.1 | | | All Other Current | 3.6 | 3.3 |
| | | 69.6 | 65.3 | 65.7 | | | Total Current | 66.9 | 60.4 |
| | | 23.4 | 25.9 | 26.3 | | | Fixed Assets (net) | 23.0 | 27.1 |
| | | 2.8 | 4.2 | 3.8 | | | Intangibles (net) | 4.4 | 3.9 |
| | | 4.2 | 4.6 | 4.1 | | | All Other Non-Current | 5.7 | 8.6 |
| | | 100.0 | 100.0 | 100.0 | | | Total | 100.0 | 100.0 |
| | | | | | | | **LIABILITIES** | | |
| | | 17.5 | 7.7 | 10.7 | | | Notes Payable-Short Term | 10.6 | 11.8 |
| | | 3.4 | 2.9 | 2.0 | | | Cur. Mat.-L.T.D. | 3.1 | 4.2 |
| | | 21.7 | 14.4 | 11.9 | | | Trade Payables | 16.9 | 10.7 |
| | | .0 | .0 | .1 | | | Income Taxes Payable | .2 | .5 |
| | | 9.0 | 9.5 | 10.3 | | | All Other Current | 7.2 | 7.9 |
| | | 51.6 | 34.5 | 35.0 | | | Total Current | 38.0 | 35.1 |
| | | 11.0 | 12.3 | 16.3 | | | Long-Term Debt | 11.1 | 15.0 |
| | | .0 | .1 | .2 | | | Deferred Taxes | .5 | .4 |
| | | 5.7 | 3.6 | 3.6 | | | All Other Non-Current | 4.6 | 5.3 |
| | | 31.8 | 49.5 | 44.9 | | | Net Worth | 45.8 | 44.2 |
| | | 100.0 | 100.0 | 100.0 | | | Total Liabilities & Net Worth | 100.0 | 100.0 |
| | | | | | | | **INCOME DATA** | | |
| | | 100.0 | 100.0 | 100.0 | | | Net Sales | 100.0 | 100.0 |
| | | 27.7 | 34.7 | 34.9 | | | Gross Profit | 28.4 | 28.2 |
| | | 23.1 | 27.9 | 24.5 | | | Operating Expenses | 21.1 | 23.7 |
| | | 4.6 | 6.8 | 10.4 | | | Operating Profit | 7.3 | 4.5 |
| | | .4 | .5 | 1.5 | | | All Other Expenses (net) | 1.3 | .9 |
| | | 4.2 | 6.4 | 8.9 | | | Profit Before Taxes | 6.0 | 3.6 |
| | | | | | | | **RATIOS** | | |
| | | 1.8 | 4.1 | 4.1 | | | | 2.7 | 3.7 |
| | | 1.5 | 1.9 | 1.8 | | | Current | 1.7 | 1.8 |
| | | 1.2 | 1.3 | 1.1 | | | | 1.3 | 1.2 |
| | | 1.2 | 1.6 | 1.8 | | | | 1.4 | 1.6 |
| | | .7 | 1.2 | .8 | | | Quick | .9 | .8 |
| | | .3 | .9 | .5 | | | | .5 | .5 |
| | | 32   11.4 | 34   10.8 | 21   17.5 | | | | 31   11.8 | 29   12.8 |
| | | 43   8.4 | 38   9.7 | 43   8.4 | | | Sales/Receivables | 37   9.9 | 35   10.3 |
| | | 54   6.8 | 53   6.9 | 55   6.6 | | | | 50   7.4 | 45   8.1 |
| | | 11   33.8 | 15   23.9 | 1   439.4 | | | | 42   8.7 | 35   10.3 |
| | | 74   4.9 | 47   7.8 | 54   6.7 | | | Cost of Sales/Inventory | 75   4.9 | 81   4.5 |
| | | 99   3.7 | 89   4.1 | 122   3.0 | | | | 101   3.6 | 115   3.2 |
| | | 10   35.2 | 17   21.3 | 12   30.6 | | | | 19   19.4 | 14   25.2 |
| | | 29   12.4 | 27   13.3 | 27   13.6 | | | Cost of Sales/Payables | 31   11.8 | 22   16.5 |
| | | 47   7.7 | 43   8.5 | 45   8.1 | | | | 47   7.8 | 38   9.7 |
| | | 5.6 | 4.1 | 2.6 | | | | 4.4 | 4.6 |
| | | 11.4 | 7.9 | 6.1 | | | Sales/Working Capital | 7.9 | 9.3 |
| | | 37.2 | 18.4 | 37.4 | | | | 21.3 | 36.2 |
| | | 16.2 | 30.7 | 21.2 | | | | 25.6 | 10.8 |
| | | (17) 4.2 | (24) 9.1 | (15) 4.8 | | | EBIT/Interest | (53) 7.0 | (47) 3.7 |
| | | 1.1 | 3.9 | .5 | | | | 2.2 | .8 |
| | | | | | | | Net Profit + Depr., Dep., | 6.9 | 5.6 |
| | | | | | | | Amort./Cur. Mat. L/T/D | (15) 2.2   (14) 2.3 | |
| | | | | | | | | 1.1 | .2 |
| | | .2 | .2 | .2 | | | | .2 | .2 |
| | | .6 | .4 | .7 | | | Fixed/Worth | .5 | .6 |
| | | 1.0 | 1.2 | 1.2 | | | | 1.1 | 1.6 |
| | | 1.1 | .4 | .9 | | | | .6 | .5 |
| | | 2.4 | 1.0 | 1.5 | | | Debt/Worth | 1.3 | 1.3 |
| | | 4.7 | 2.4 | 2.1 | | | | 2.9 | 4.4 |
| | | 78.1 | 50.3 | 56.0 | | | % Profit Before Taxes/Tangible | 46.0 | 39.0 |
| | | (16) 23.0 | (25) 27.4 | (15) 20.1 | | | Net Worth | (50) 23.6 | (46) 12.4 |
| | | 14.9 | 13.1 | -1.5 | | | | 9.9 | 1.5 |
| | | 18.6 | 21.4 | 16.3 | | | % Profit Before Taxes/Total | 23.2 | 14.5 |
| | | 7.5 | 11.3 | 7.5 | | | Assets | 9.6 | 6.4 |
| | | .1 | 5.0 | .8 | | | | 4.2 | -.8 |
| | | 55.9 | 20.9 | 21.2 | | | | 21.4 | 16.4 |
| | | 20.3 | 12.6 | 11.9 | | | Sales/Net Fixed Assets | 11.4 | 10.8 |
| | | 11.4 | 5.5 | 4.4 | | | | 5.3 | 4.1 |
| | | 3.8 | 2.5 | 2.4 | | | | 2.8 | 2.5 |
| | | 2.7 | 2.0 | 2.1 | | | Sales/Total Assets | 2.0 | 1.9 |
| | | 2.2 | 1.6 | 1.3 | | | | 1.6 | 1.4 |
| | | .6 | 1.4 | 1.2 | | | | .9 | 1.0 |
| | | (14) 1.5 | (20) 2.3 | (15) 1.5 | | | % Depr., Dep., Amort./Sales | (49) 1.7 | (45) 1.7 |
| | | 3.4 | 3.2 | 4.8 | | | | 2.7 | 3.4 |
| | | 1.0 | | | | | | 1.1 | 1.9 |
| | | (12) 4.3 | | | | | % Officers', Directors' Owners' Comp/Sales | (22) 2.6 | (12) 3.7 |
| | | 5.7 | | | | | | 7.2 | 8.1 |
| | 2119M | 72874M | 372254M | 780316M | 401629M | 1425729M | Net Sales ($) | 1608811M | 1605590M |
| | 633M | 22658M | 119024M | 429609M | 318003M | 898885M | Total Assets ($) | 1148738M | 1088780M |

© RMA 2012

M = $ thousand     MM = $ million
See Pages 9 through 22 for Explanation of Ratios and Data

## Comparative Historical Data | Current Data Sorted by Sales

| 4/1/09-3/31/10 ALL | 4/1/10-3/31/11 ALL | 4/1/11-3/31/12 ALL | Type of Statement | 0-1MM | 1-3MM | 3-5MM | 5-10MM | 10-25MM | 25MM & OVER |
|---|---|---|---|---|---|---|---|---|---|
| 8 | 9 | 13 | Unqualified | | 2 | | | 2 | 9 |
| 12 | 21 | 9 | Reviewed | | 1 | 1 | 4 | 2 | 1 |
| 6 | 12 | 11 | Compiled | | 1 | 5 | 3 | 2 | |
| 5 | 5 | 8 | Tax Returns | | 1 | 5 | 2 | | |
| 27 | 28 | 32 | Other | 1 | 3 | 1 | 5 | 6 | 16 |
| 4/1/09-3/31/10 | 4/1/10-3/31/11 | 4/1/11-3/31/12 | | 11 (4/1-9/30/11) | | 62 (10/1/11-3/31/12) | | | |
| ALL | ALL | ALL | | | | | | | |
| 58 | 75 | 73 | **NUMBER OF STATEMENTS** | 1 | 8 | 12 | 14 | 12 | 26 |
| % | % | % | **ASSETS** | % | % | % | % | % | % |
| 7.8 | 11.5 | 12.0 | Cash & Equivalents | | | 12.6 | 9.3 | 8.9 | 15.0 |
| 23.5 | 28.0 | 25.0 | Trade Receivables (net) | | | 24.3 | 28.5 | 23.5 | 24.2 |
| 30.4 | 27.8 | 25.1 | Inventory | | | 29.3 | 21.5 | 24.7 | 24.3 |
| 4.3 | 2.0 | 3.8 | All Other Current | | | 2.3 | 4.5 | 5.3 | 4.0 |
| 65.9 | 69.4 | 65.8 | Total Current | | | 68.5 | 63.8 | 62.4 | 67.5 |
| 22.1 | 22.7 | 24.1 | Fixed Assets (net) | | | 18.3 | 29.0 | 33.2 | 19.5 |
| 3.6 | 2.6 | 4.7 | Intangibles (net) | | | 7.7 | 1.2 | 2.4 | 6.4 |
| 8.3 | 5.4 | 5.4 | All Other Non-Current | | | 5.6 | 6.0 | 2.0 | 6.5 |
| 100.0 | 100.0 | 100.0 | Total | | | 100.0 | 100.0 | 100.0 | 100.0 |
| | | | **LIABILITIES** | | | | | | |
| 13.1 | 10.6 | 10.0 | Notes Payable-Short Term | | | 15.1 | 13.8 | 5.3 | 8.0 |
| 4.5 | 4.4 | 3.6 | Cur. Mat.-L.T.D. | | | 3.4 | 3.0 | 3.5 | 1.6 |
| 13.1 | 14.8 | 15.2 | Trade Payables | | | 12.9 | 20.1 | 13.7 | 15.2 |
| .7 | .2 | .0 | Income Taxes Payable | | | .0 | .0 | .0 | .1 |
| 7.5 | 7.8 | 9.8 | All Other Current | | | 6.6 | 7.5 | 11.3 | 12.1 |
| 38.8 | 37.8 | 38.6 | Total Current | | | 38.0 | 44.4 | 33.8 | 36.9 |
| 12.0 | 12.2 | 13.9 | Long-Term Debt | | | 14.4 | 12.7 | 14.8 | 9.6 |
| .5 | .3 | .4 | Deferred Taxes | | | .0 | .0 | .2 | 1.0 |
| 7.5 | 8.6 | 4.1 | All Other Non-Current | | | 9.4 | 1.7 | .7 | 4.1 |
| 41.2 | 41.2 | 42.9 | Net Worth | | | 38.2 | 41.2 | 50.3 | 48.4 |
| 100.0 | 100.0 | 100.0 | Total Liabilities & Net Worth | | | 100.0 | 100.0 | 100.0 | 100.0 |
| | | | **INCOME DATA** | | | | | | |
| 100.0 | 100.0 | 100.0 | Net Sales | | | 100.0 | 100.0 | 100.0 | 100.0 |
| 28.5 | 31.0 | 32.2 | Gross Profit | | | 37.8 | 37.2 | 29.0 | 27.8 |
| 26.7 | 23.6 | 24.8 | Operating Expenses | | | 32.4 | 28.8 | 20.3 | 18.8 |
| 1.8 | 7.5 | 7.5 | Operating Profit | | | 5.3 | 8.4 | 8.7 | 9.0 |
| 1.3 | .8 | .7 | All Other Expenses (net) | | | .7 | .6 | .8 | .7 |
| .5 | 6.7 | 6.8 | Profit Before Taxes | | | 4.6 | 7.8 | 7.8 | 8.3 |
| | | | **RATIOS** | | | | | | |
| 2.9 | 3.5 | 3.5 | Current | | | 3.3 | 4.1 | 3.3 | 3.6 |
| 1.9 | 1.9 | 1.7 | | | | 1.7 | 1.6 | 1.8 | 1.9 |
| 1.2 | 1.4 | 1.2 | | | | 1.1 | 1.1 | 1.3 | 1.1 |
| 1.6 | 2.2 | 1.7 | Quick | | | 1.2 | 2.1 | 1.6 | 1.8 |
| .9 | 1.0 | 1.0 | | | | 1.0 | .9 | 1.2 | 1.0 |
| .5 | .7 | .5 | | | | .7 | .5 | .9 | .5 |
| 32  11.4 | 35  10.4 | 32  11.5 | Sales/Receivables | | | 30  12.0 | 36  10.1 | 33  11.0 | 28  13.1 |
| 51  7.2 | 46  8.0 | 41  8.9 | | | | 37  9.9 | 47  7.7 | 36  10.2 | 41  8.9 |
| 64  5.7 | 57  6.5 | 51  7.1 | | | | 55  6.6 | 63  5.8 | 46  7.9 | 53  6.9 |
| 47  7.7 | 36  10.1 | 15  24.0 | Cost of Sales/Inventory | | | 6  61.4 | 0  UND | 10  38.3 | 38  9.5 |
| 91  4.0 | 69  5.3 | 56  6.5 | | | | 79  4.6 | 50  4.6 | 36  10.1 | 69  5.3 |
| 143  2.6 | 115  3.2 | 99  3.7 | | | | 114  3.2 | 89  4.1 | 104  3.5 | 118  3.1 |
| 16  22.8 | 17  22.1 | 15  24.2 | Cost of Sales/Payables | | | 17  21.0 | 17  21.3 | 17  22.1 | 14  25.9 |
| 27  13.6 | 30  12.0 | 26  13.8 | | | | 36  10.2 | 31  11.8 | 27  13.4 | 26  14.3 |
| 46  8.0 | 44  8.3 | 46  7.9 | | | | 49  7.5 | 49  7.5 | 44  8.3 | 47  7.8 |
| 3.0 | 3.6 | 3.9 | Sales/Working Capital | | | 5.0 | 3.7 | 3.6 | 3.2 |
| 6.9 | 7.1 | 7.4 | | | | 7.0 | -10.3 | 9.1 | 6.1 |
| 16.2 | 16.5 | 32.4 | | | | 32.9 | NM | 17.9 | 43.0 |
| 15.2 | 22.5 | 27.7 | EBIT/Interest | | | 13.4 | 43.2 | 33.7 | 52.7 |
| (53)  2.9 | (66)  7.6 | (67)  8.1 | | | | 3.9 | (13)  9.3 | 14.6 | (23)  10.6 |
| -2.0 | 1.7 | 2.6 | | | | 2.3 | 2.4 | 5.4 | 2.5 |
| 3.6 | 10.8 | 44.3 | Net Profit + Depr., Dep., Amort./Cur. Mat. L/T/D | | | | | | |
| (13)  .1 | (20)  2.8 | (10)  5.0 | | | | | | | |
| -1.1 | 2.1 | 2.1 | | | | | | | |
| .2 | .2 | .2 | Fixed/Worth | | | .2 | .2 | .2 | .2 |
| .4 | .4 | .5 | | | | .4 | .6 | .6 | .4 |
| 2.1 | 1.2 | 1.1 | | | | 3.7 | 2.3 | 1.2 | .9 |
| .4 | .5 | .6 | Debt/Worth | | | .9 | .4 | .6 | .5 |
| 1.2 | 1.1 | 1.4 | | | | 2.0 | 1.8 | 1.0 | 1.4 |
| 5.0 | 3.3 | 3.0 | | | | 5.1 | 4.3 | 1.8 | 2.0 |
| 22.5 | 47.6 | 52.6 | % Profit Before Taxes/Tangible Net Worth | | | 28.7 | 83.3 | 56.9 | 49.0 |
| (50)  5.5 | (68)  22.3 | (67)  23.8 | | | (10)  23.2 | (13)  37.2 | 23.7 | (24)  17.5 |
| -5.9 | 4.6 | 12.6 | | | | 18.2 | 11.8 | 16.5 | 4.6 |
| 9.2 | 19.9 | 19.7 | % Profit Before Taxes/Total Assets | | | 12.0 | 22.5 | 21.8 | 19.1 |
| 1.8 | 9.8 | 8.6 | | | | 6.3 | 11.4 | 12.3 | 7.0 |
| -4.2 | 1.6 | 3.4 | | | | 2.7 | 4.6 | 10.8 | 2.9 |
| 18.9 | 34.7 | 24.7 | Sales/Net Fixed Assets | | | 51.1 | 18.2 | 21.7 | 20.0 |
| 9.1 | 11.4 | 13.9 | | | | 18.6 | 11.7 | 10.4 | 13.2 |
| 4.5 | 6.0 | 6.1 | | | | 9.4 | 6.6 | 5.4 | 5.2 |
| 2.2 | 2.7 | 2.9 | Sales/Total Assets | | | 2.5 | 3.2 | 3.6 | 2.4 |
| 1.5 | 2.1 | 2.1 | | | | 2.1 | 2.0 | 2.2 | 1.8 |
| 1.1 | 1.5 | 1.4 | | | | 1.7 | 1.7 | 1.7 | 1.3 |
| 1.2 | .7 | 1.2 | % Depr., Dep., Amort./Sales | | | | 1.4 | 1.3 | .9 |
| (49)  2.2 | (67)  1.6 | (57)  1.8 | | | | | (11)  3.1 | (11)  1.8 | (21)  1.5 |
| 4.4 | 3.0 | 3.2 | | | | | 4.3 | 2.7 | 3.3 |
| 2.3 | 2.0 | .8 | % Officers', Directors' Owners' Comp/Sales | | | | | | |
| (21)  5.0 | (27)  5.3 | (25)  3.8 | | | | | | | |
| 9.3 | 7.4 | 5.7 | | | | | | | |
| 1013674M | 2115838M | 3054921M | Net Sales ($) | 668M | 14160M | 47236M | 101222M | 172122M | 2719513M |
| 824788M | 1093877M | 1788812M | Total Assets ($) | 182M | 10244M | 23435M | 84476M | 106972M | 1563503M |

© RMA 2012

M = $ thousand    MM = $ million
See Pages 9 through 22 for Explanation of Ratios and Data

## Current Data Sorted by Assets　　　　　Comparative Historical Data

| | 0-500M | 500M-2MM | 2-10MM | 10-50MM | 50-100MM | 100-250MM | Type of Statement | 4/1/07-3/31/08 ALL | 4/1/08-3/31/09 ALL |
|---|---|---|---|---|---|---|---|---|---|
| | | | 3 | 4 | 1 | 1 | Unqualified | 10 | 10 |
| | 2 | 6 | 3 | | | | Reviewed | 20 | 25 |
| 2 | 6 | 5 | 1 | | | | Compiled | 22 | 15 |
| 10 | 7 | 4 | | | | | Tax Returns | 25 | 26 |
| 8 | 11 | 14 | | | | | Other | 46 | 41 |
| | 14 (4/1-9/30/11) | | 84 (10/1/11-3/31/12) | | | | | | |
| 20 | 26 | 32 | 13 | 3 | 4 | NUMBER OF STATEMENTS | 123 | 117 |
| % | % | % | % | % | % | **ASSETS** | % | % |
| 14.3 | 9.6 | 4.6 | 3.7 | | | Cash & Equivalents | 7.2 | 8.0 |
| 23.2 | 21.0 | 23.1 | 23.6 | | | Trade Receivables (net) | 23.1 | 22.5 |
| 22.9 | 23.9 | 30.9 | 22.0 | | | Inventory | 22.9 | 23.4 |
| 4.6 | 6.6 | 3.4 | 3.3 | | | All Other Current | 2.5 | 1.5 |
| 65.0 | 61.0 | 62.0 | 52.6 | | | Total Current | 55.7 | 55.4 |
| 22.6 | 25.6 | 30.6 | 30.2 | | | Fixed Assets (net) | 35.3 | 34.7 |
| 1.5 | 5.1 | 2.1 | 10.7 | | | Intangibles (net) | 3.0 | 3.7 |
| 10.9 | 8.2 | 5.3 | 6.5 | | | All Other Non-Current | 6.0 | 6.3 |
| 100.0 | 100.0 | 100.0 | 100.0 | | | Total | 100.0 | 100.0 |
| | | | | | | **LIABILITIES** | | |
| 16.6 | 12.9 | 14.1 | 8.2 | | | Notes Payable-Short Term | 10.0 | 16.7 |
| 8.2 | 6.2 | 4.0 | 3.4 | | | Cur. Mat.-L.T.D. | 4.1 | 4.1 |
| 13.1 | 19.3 | 19.7 | 8.9 | | | Trade Payables | 14.3 | 14.7 |
| .2 | .3 | .1 | .0 | | | Income Taxes Payable | .4 | .3 |
| 15.0 | 11.3 | 14.4 | 7.3 | | | All Other Current | 10.2 | 11.5 |
| 53.1 | 49.9 | 52.3 | 27.8 | | | Total Current | 39.0 | 47.3 |
| 32.9 | 23.7 | 13.5 | 14.6 | | | Long-Term Debt | 22.6 | 24.9 |
| .0 | .0 | .0 | .5 | | | Deferred Taxes | .6 | .3 |
| 25.8 | 6.0 | 5.4 | 5.7 | | | All Other Non-Current | 5.6 | 4.4 |
| -11.8 | 20.4 | 28.8 | 51.4 | | | Net Worth | 32.2 | 23.1 |
| 100.0 | 100.0 | 100.0 | 100.0 | | | Total Liabilities & Net Worth | 100.0 | 100.0 |
| | | | | | | **INCOME DATA** | | |
| 100.0 | 100.0 | 100.0 | 100.0 | | | Net Sales | 100.0 | 100.0 |
| 56.6 | 38.0 | 34.1 | 24.2 | | | Gross Profit | 35.5 | 34.5 |
| 51.3 | 34.3 | 32.0 | 17.2 | | | Operating Expenses | 30.0 | 32.9 |
| 5.3 | 3.7 | 2.1 | 7.0 | | | Operating Profit | 5.4 | 1.6 |
| 2.2 | .8 | .8 | 1.5 | | | All Other Expenses (net) | 1.6 | 2.0 |
| 3.0 | 2.9 | 1.2 | 5.5 | | | Profit Before Taxes | 3.8 | -.4 |
| | | | | | | **RATIOS** | | |
| 2.8 | 2.8 | 2.0 | 4.2 | | | | 2.7 | 2.7 |
| 1.7 | 1.4 | 1.2 | 2.2 | | | Current | 1.5 | 1.5 |
| .7 | .9 | .9 | 1.1 | | | | .9 | .8 |
| 1.8 | 1.1 | 1.0 | 1.9 | | | | 1.4 | 1.3 |
| .6 | .7 | .6 | .9 | | | Quick | .7 | .7 |
| .3 | .3 | .2 | .5 | | | | .4 | .4 |
| 9　42.6 | 4　89.1 | 25　14.6 | 36　10.0 | | | | 20　17.8 | 22　16.2 |
| 17　21.6 | 22　16.9 | 33　10.9 | 42　8.6 | | | Sales/Receivables | 35　10.4 | 37　9.9 |
| 35　10.3 | 41　8.8 | 65　5.6 | 64　5.7 | | | | 54　6.8 | 51　7.2 |
| 0　UND | 11　33.8 | 33　11.1 | 32　11.4 | | | | 21　17.6 | 19　19.3 |
| 20　18.1 | 41　9.0 | 69　5.3 | 49　7.5 | | | Cost of Sales/Inventory | 49　7.5 | 52　7.1 |
| 74　4.9 | 91　4.0 | 192　1.9 | 107　3.4 | | | | 118　3.1 | 126　2.9 |
| 10　36.8 | 10　35.3 | 19　19.4 | 11　32.3 | | | | 13　28.1 | 10　35.1 |
| 21　17.4 | 36　10.0 | 38　9.5 | 24　14.9 | | | Cost of Sales/Payables | 30　12.2 | 19　19.0 |
| 46　7.9 | 53　6.9 | 89　4.1 | 35　10.3 | | | | 47　7.8 | 40　9.2 |
| 5.8 | 8.1 | 5.4 | 3.4 | | | | 6.0 | 5.2 |
| 20.2 | 19.4 | 26.8 | 6.9 | | | Sales/Working Capital | 11.7 | 15.1 |
| -17.5 | -27.0 | -16.6 | 33.8 | | | | -141.7 | -27.6 |
| 12.7 | 8.4 | 8.8 | 24.2 | | | | 11.1 | 4.4 |
| (17)　4.6 | (25)　3.2 | (29)　2.4 | 3.1 | | | EBIT/Interest | (116)　3.0 | (109)　1.3 |
| -2.3 | 1.0 | 1.1 | .9 | | | | 1.1 | -.9 |
| | | | | | | | 9.0 | 5.1 |
| | | | | | | Net Profit + Depr., Dep., Amort./Cur. Mat. L/T/D | (29)　3.2 | (23)　2.0 |
| | | | | | | | 1.3 | 1.0 |
| .3 | .5 | .4 | .3 | | | | .4 | .4 |
| 1.3 | 1.6 | 1.5 | .7 | | | Fixed/Worth | 1.1 | 1.5 |
| -.3 | -4.2 | 3.1 | 4.9 | | | | 3.4 | 10.7 |
| .7 | 1.4 | 1.2 | .5 | | | | .9 | .9 |
| 11.4 | 3.0 | 2.1 | 1.3 | | | Debt/Worth | 2.0 | 2.3 |
| -5.2 | -29.9 | 8.3 | 9.3 | | | | 5.9 | 19.1 |
| 87.0 | 70.6 | 31.9 | 30.0 | | | | 47.0 | 18.7 |
| (13)　4.5 | (19)　26.6 | (28)　14.7 | (11)　19.8 | | | % Profit Before Taxes/Tangible Net Worth | (104)　21.5 | (92)　6.3 |
| -7.0 | .0 | 2.7 | 2.3 | | | | 6.9 | -10.3 |
| 32.7 | 15.5 | 7.4 | 13.7 | | | | 16.0 | 7.2 |
| 3.8 | 8.1 | 3.3 | 4.8 | | | % Profit Before Taxes/Total Assets | 5.0 | 1.2 |
| -6.0 | .0 | 1.3 | -.5 | | | | .3 | -5.9 |
| 111.0 | 33.3 | 15.8 | 10.6 | | | | 17.1 | 17.7 |
| 33.8 | 16.5 | 8.1 | 4.7 | | | Sales/Net Fixed Assets | 7.0 | 7.1 |
| 13.1 | 8.0 | 4.4 | 2.8 | | | | 3.2 | 3.2 |
| 5.2 | 4.2 | 2.8 | 2.4 | | | | 3.3 | 3.2 |
| 3.5 | 3.2 | 2.0 | 1.7 | | | Sales/Total Assets | 2.1 | 2.0 |
| 2.9 | 1.7 | 1.2 | 1.1 | | | | 1.4 | 1.3 |
| | .8 | 1.6 | 1.8 | | | | 1.4 | 1.5 |
| | (19)　2.6 | (28)　3.6 | (12)　3.6 | | | % Depr., Dep., Amort./Sales | (107)　2.5 | (101)　3.4 |
| | 4.5 | 6.4 | 5.2 | | | | 4.9 | 5.0 |
| 1.6 | 1.9 | 2.0 | | | | | 1.5 | 1.8 |
| (12)　4.4 | (12)　6.7 | (16)　3.9 | | | | % Officers', Directors' Owners' Comp/Sales | (66)　2.9 | (53)　3.0 |
| 10.5 | 8.5 | 5.8 | | | | | 6.2 | 5.6 |
| 23667M | 81133M | 247537M | 368391M | 234706M | 696715M | Net Sales ($) | 1884309M | 2231357M |
| 6135M | 26416M | 133515M | 226826M | 216837M | 505439M | Total Assets ($) | 1136900M | 1306950M |

M = $ thousand　MM = $ million
See Pages 9 through 22 for Explanation of Ratios and Data

## Comparative Historical Data | Current Data Sorted by Sales

| 4/1/09-3/31/10 ALL | 4/1/10-3/31/11 ALL | 4/1/11-3/31/12 ALL | Type of Statement | 0-1MM | 1-3MM | 3-5MM | 5-10MM | 10-25MM | 25MM & OVER |
|---|---|---|---|---|---|---|---|---|---|
| | | | Unqualified | | | 2 | 1 | 1 | 5 |
| | | | Reviewed | | 2 | 2 | 4 | 2 | 1 |
| | | | Compiled | 4 | 3 | 3 | 2 | 1 | 1 |
| | | | Tax Returns | 4 | 9 | 3 | 4 | 1 | 1 |
| 8 | 9 | 9 | Other | 2 | 12 | 6 | 9 | 6 | 8 |
| 17 | 18 | 11 | | | | | | | |
| 17 | 13 | 14 | | 14 (4/1-9/30/11) | | | 84 (10/1/11-3/31/12) | | |
| 20 | 20 | 21 | | | | | | | |
| 52 | 42 | 43 | | | | | | | |
| 114 | 102 | 98 | **NUMBER OF STATEMENTS** | 10 | 26 | 16 | 20 | 11 | 15 |
| % | % | % | **ASSETS** | % | % | % | % | % | % |
| 7.0 | 6.5 | 7.8 | Cash & Equivalents | 16.3 | 9.8 | 7.1 | 6.0 | 3.1 | 5.2 |
| 19.8 | 17.6 | 22.2 | Trade Receivables (net) | 9.3 | 24.0 | 20.5 | 24.4 | 28.4 | 21.8 |
| 24.0 | 27.9 | 25.9 | Inventory | 21.7 | 24.4 | 25.2 | 31.7 | 29.4 | 21.5 |
| 2.8 | 3.3 | 4.3 | All Other Current | 13.8 | 1.1 | 6.9 | 2.5 | 5.5 | 2.5 |
| 53.7 | 55.2 | 60.2 | Total Current | 61.2 | 59.3 | 59.7 | 64.5 | 66.4 | 51.0 |
| 34.1 | 30.7 | 28.3 | Fixed Assets (net) | 23.0 | 28.9 | 23.1 | 29.3 | 23.9 | 38.2 |
| 4.5 | 4.3 | 4.3 | Intangibles (net) | 2.7 | 2.0 | 8.8 | 2.7 | 5.7 | 5.9 |
| 7.7 | 9.8 | 7.2 | All Other Non-Current | 13.1 | 9.8 | 8.4 | 3.5 | 4.0 | 4.9 |
| 100.0 | 100.0 | 100.0 | Total | 100.0 | 100.0 | 100.0 | 100.0 | 100.0 | 100.0 |
| | | | **LIABILITIES** | | | | | | |
| 14.4 | 12.1 | 12.8 | Notes Payable-Short Term | 25.5 | 9.7 | 15.3 | 16.7 | 5.7 | 6.8 |
| 4.6 | 5.2 | 5.3 | Cur. Mat.-L.T.D. | 2.1 | 8.8 | 4.7 | 5.3 | 3.8 | 3.0 |
| 12.5 | 13.1 | 15.9 | Trade Payables | 4.1 | 16.4 | 20.0 | 24.8 | 12.2 | 9.3 |
| .2 | .5 | .2 | Income Taxes Payable | .0 | .4 | .2 | .1 | .0 | .1 |
| 10.9 | 12.0 | 12.4 | All Other Current | 17.6 | 10.3 | 15.4 | 13.4 | 12.9 | 7.9 |
| 42.7 | 42.9 | 46.5 | Total Current | 49.2 | 45.5 | 55.6 | 60.4 | 34.5 | 27.1 |
| 28.3 | 24.4 | 20.6 | Long-Term Debt | 15.1 | 35.4 | 20.5 | 13.8 | 7.4 | 17.6 |
| .2 | .3 | .1 | Deferred Taxes | .0 | .0 | .0 | .0 | .1 | .3 |
| 6.1 | 7.2 | 9.7 | All Other Non-Current | 4.7 | 22.7 | 6.9 | 6.1 | 2.6 | 3.6 |
| 22.7 | 25.2 | 23.1 | Net Worth | 31.0 | -3.6 | 17.0 | 19.6 | 55.4 | 51.3 |
| 100.0 | 100.0 | 100.0 | Total Liabilities & Net Worth | 100.0 | 100.0 | 100.0 | 100.0 | 100.0 | 100.0 |
| | | | **INCOME DATA** | | | | | | |
| 100.0 | 100.0 | 100.0 | Net Sales | 100.0 | 100.0 | 100.0 | 100.0 | 100.0 | 100.0 |
| 37.0 | 34.9 | 37.7 | Gross Profit | 62.2 | 46.8 | 39.1 | 28.5 | 30.3 | 21.9 |
| 35.7 | 32.2 | 33.5 | Operating Expenses | 55.6 | 42.4 | 33.8 | 27.0 | 27.3 | 15.9 |
| 1.3 | 2.7 | 4.2 | Operating Profit | 6.6 | 4.4 | 5.2 | 1.4 | 2.9 | 6.0 |
| 1.7 | 1.2 | 1.2 | All Other Expenses (net) | 3.7 | 1.2 | 1.2 | .8 | .3 | .8 |
| -.4 | 1.5 | 3.0 | Profit Before Taxes | 2.9 | 3.2 | 4.0 | .6 | 2.7 | 5.2 |
| | | | **RATIOS** | | | | | | |
| 2.5 | 2.3 | 2.5 | | 3.7 | 2.1 | 1.9 | 1.8 | 3.1 | 3.1 |
| 1.5 | 1.3 | 1.6 | Current | 2.3 | 1.6 | 1.2 | 1.2 | 2.3 | 1.9 |
| .9 | .9 | .9 | | .5 | .8 | .8 | .9 | 1.0 | 1.5 |
| 1.5 | 1.1 | 1.3 | | 1.2 | 1.8 | 1.0 | .8 | 1.7 | 1.4 |
| .7 | .6 | .7 | Quick | .6 | .6 | .6 | .6 | 1.1 | 1.0 |
| .3 | .3 | .3 | | .3 | .3 | .2 | .3 | | .6 |
| 22  16.3 | 21  17.5 | 16  23.0 | | 0  UND | 9  40.0 | 14  26.5 | 16  22.2 | 27  13.3 | 37  9.8 |
| 34  10.6 | 36  10.3 | 33  11.1 | Sales/Receivables | 8  48.4 | 28  13.0 | 43  8.4 | 28  12.9 | 36  10.0 | 41  8.8 |
| 51  7.2 | 49  7.5 | 51  7.2 | | 20  18.1 | 41  8.8 | 65  5.6 | 65  5.6 | 64  5.7 | 57  6.4 |
| 22  16.7 | 41  8.9 | 20  18.3 | | 0  UND | 5  73.8 | 16  23.4 | 33  11.1 | 32  11.5 | 42  8.6 |
| 60  6.1 | 73  5.0 | 53  6.9 | Cost of Sales/Inventory | 0  UND | 45  8.1 | 49  7.5 | 64  5.7 | 53  6.9 | 49  7.5 |
| 144  2.5 | 142  2.6 | 104  3.5 | | 228  1.6 | 104  3.5 | 152  2.4 | 89  4.1 | 101  3.6 | 101  3.6 |
| 12  30.4 | 16  23.1 | 17  21.4 | | 0  UND | 22  16.5 | 8  43.8 | 21  17.8 | 14  25.5 | 20  18.5 |
| 25  14.5 | 28  13.2 | 29  12.7 | Cost of Sales/Payables | 0  UND | 44  8.3 | 25  14.6 | 32  11.4 | 22  16.5 | 25  14.4 |
| 47  7.8 | 51  7.1 | 51  7.2 | | 61  6.0 | 53  6.9 | 70  5.2 | 83  4.4 | 42  8.7 | 35  10.3 |
| 4.6 | 4.9 | 4.9 | | 3.0 | 7.7 | 7.9 | 9.1 | 5.0 | 3.8 |
| 12.9 | 12.6 | 15.4 | Sales/Working Capital | 13.2 | 16.7 | 27.8 | 34.1 | 6.9 | 6.9 |
| -38.2 | -42.7 | -90.4 | | -11.5 | -20.9 | -15.4 | -16.6 | 297.4 | 12.1 |
| 6.6 | 9.0 | 11.3 | | | 14.2 | 7.5 | 5.8 | 14.0 | 49.1 |
| (107) 1.6 | (93) 1.9 | (91) 3.2 | EBIT/Interest | | (25) 4.6 | (15) 3.2 | (18) 1.8 | (10) 10.5 | 4.0 |
| -1.2 | -.9 | 1.0 | | | .8 | 1.6 | -1.8 | 1.9 | 1.5 |
| 2.0 | 15.9 | 7.7 | Net Profit + Depr., Dep., | | | | | | 15.9 |
| (20) 1.1 | (26) 3.7 | (18) 1.4 | Amort./Cur. Mat. L/T/D | | | | | (10) | 3.3 |
| -.1 | 1.0 | .9 | | | | | | | 1.3 |
| .6 | .4 | .4 | | .1 | .6 | .8 | .6 | .2 | .5 |
| 1.6 | 1.1 | 1.2 | Fixed/Worth | .7 | 1.7 | 3.1 | 1.4 | .3 | .7 |
| -27.2 | 7.2 | 4.1 | | 8.6 | -1.4 | -.5 | 3.7 | 1.1 | 1.7 |
| 1.0 | .8 | .9 | | .5 | 1.4 | 1.9 | 1.8 | .6 | .5 |
| 2.7 | 2.1 | 2.3 | Debt/Worth | 2.2 | 5.3 | 7.3 | 3.0 | .7 | 1.0 |
| -26.6 | 15.5 | 16.5 | | 15.6 | -8.1 | -18.8 | 11.7 | 1.5 | 3.0 |
| 26.6 | 27.8 | 39.8 | % Profit Before Taxes/Tangible | | 71.0 | 50.7 | 42.8 | 37.7 | 27.7 |
| (84) 6.7 | (82) 7.4 | (78) 17.8 | Net Worth | | (17) 37.7 | (10) 19.5 | (17) 17.9 | 13.6 | (14) 18.7 |
| -21.8 | -14.5 | 2.0 | | | 5.2 | -.3 | -5.2 | 2.3 | 2.0 |
| 10.1 | 8.8 | 14.4 | % Profit Before Taxes/Total | 11.6 | 25.8 | 12.5 | 10.8 | 12.8 | 16.2 |
| 2.0 | 2.2 | 4.8 | Assets | 1.2 | 7.5 | 4.7 | 3.2 | 7.5 | 4.8 |
| -9.5 | -6.4 | .0 | | -4.4 | -3.6 | 1.9 | -11.2 | 1.4 | .4 |
| 14.9 | 15.7 | 26.2 | | 117.6 | 31.7 | 31.9 | 12.8 | 35.9 | 8.8 |
| 6.9 | 6.2 | 10.0 | Sales/Net Fixed Assets | 29.5 | 14.5 | 15.1 | 8.8 | 18.6 | 3.8 |
| 2.9 | 3.0 | 4.4 | | 2.5 | 6.7 | 3.0 | 5.6 | 4.7 | 3.1 |
| 3.2 | 2.7 | 3.6 | | 4.3 | 3.9 | 3.7 | 3.4 | 3.8 | 2.3 |
| 1.8 | 1.6 | 2.1 | Sales/Total Assets | 2.1 | 3.2 | 2.2 | 2.1 | 2.2 | 1.5 |
| 1.1 | 1.1 | 1.4 | | 1.1 | 1.7 | 1.1 | 1.6 | 1.5 | 1.2 |
| 1.8 | 1.9 | 1.7 | | | 1.8 | 2.1 | 1.1 | .5 | 3.0 |
| (104) 3.2 | (88) 3.6 | (75) 3.1 | % Depr., Dep., Amort./Sales | | (18) 2.4 | (12) 3.4 | (17) 2.6 | (10) 1.7 | 4.3 |
| 6.1 | 6.5 | 4.7 | | | 4.5 | 4.7 | 6.9 | 3.3 | 4.7 |
| 2.6 | 2.0 | 1.9 | % Officers', Directors' | | 2.5 | | | | |
| (45) 4.7 | (46) 3.4 | (42) 4.3 | Owners' Comp/Sales | | (12) 5.5 | | | | |
| 7.1 | 5.8 | 7.7 | | | 7.1 | | | | |
| 1231173M | 1739160M | 1652149M | Net Sales ($) | 5626M | 46507M | 62097M | 148997M | 162758M | 1226164M |
| 1010825M | 1299224M | 1115168M | Total Assets ($) | 3142M | 23048M | 50537M | 76887M | 81974M | 879580M |

M = $ thousand    MM = $ million
See Pages 9 through 22 for Explanation of Ratios and Data

## Current Data Sorted by Assets      Comparative Historical Data

| | | | | | | | Type of Statement | | | | |
|---|---|---|---|---|---|---|---|---|---|---|---|
| | | 1 | 4 | | | | Unqualified | | 6 | | 3 |
| | | 1 | 8 | | | | Reviewed | | 9 | | 8 |
| | 1 | 1 | 1 | | | | Compiled | | 5 | | 5 |
| 1 | 1 | 1 | 1 | | | | Tax Returns | | 6 | | 3 |
| | | 6 | 5 | 1 | | | Other | | 13 | | 22 |
| | 5 (4/1-9/30/11) | | 26 (10/1/11-3/31/12) | | | | | | 4/1/07-3/31/08 | | 4/1/08-3/31/09 |
| 0-500M | 500M-2MM | 2-10MM | 10-50MM | 50-100MM | 100-250MM | | | | ALL | ALL | ALL |
| 1 | 2 | 10 | 17 | 1 | | | NUMBER OF STATEMENTS | | 39 | | 41 |
| % | % | % | % | % | % | | ASSETS | | % | | % |
| | | 12.1 | 11.8 | | | D | Cash & Equivalents | | 9.1 | | 10.3 |
| | | 31.1 | 19.4 | | | A | Trade Receivables (net) | | 22.9 | | 23.1 |
| | | 21.8 | 22.8 | | | T | Inventory | | 22.6 | | 22.3 |
| | | 1.8 | 4.6 | | | A | All Other Current | | 2.4 | | 1.8 |
| | | 66.8 | 58.7 | | | | Total Current | | 56.9 | | 57.6 |
| | | 10.6 | 29.3 | | | N | Fixed Assets (net) | | 34.6 | | 26.6 |
| | | 12.5 | 6.9 | | | O | Intangibles (net) | | 2.4 | | 5.2 |
| | | 10.1 | 5.1 | | | T | All Other Non-Current | | 6.1 | | 10.6 |
| | | 100.0 | 100.0 | | | | Total | | 100.0 | | 100.0 |
| | | | | | | A | LIABILITIES | | | | |
| | | 10.6 | 7.4 | | | V | Notes Payable-Short Term | | 9.2 | | 11.0 |
| | | .4 | 3.5 | | | A | Cur. Mat.-L.T.D. | | 3.9 | | 4.0 |
| | | 11.9 | 8.8 | | | I | Trade Payables | | 14.9 | | 12.9 |
| | | .0 | .4 | | | L | Income Taxes Payable | | .2 | | .3 |
| | | 13.9 | 8.5 | | | A | All Other Current | | 12.3 | | 17.0 |
| | | 36.8 | 28.5 | | | B | Total Current | | 40.4 | | 45.1 |
| | | 5.8 | 5.2 | | | L | Long-Term Debt | | 19.2 | | 13.5 |
| | | .2 | 2.9 | | | E | Deferred Taxes | | .4 | | .7 |
| | | .8 | 9.0 | | | | All Other Non-Current | | 5.3 | | 5.1 |
| | | 56.4 | 54.4 | | | | Net Worth | | 34.7 | | 35.6 |
| | | 100.0 | 100.0 | | | | Total Liabilities & Net Worth | | 100.0 | | 100.0 |
| | | | | | | | INCOME DATA | | | | |
| | | 100.0 | 100.0 | | | | Net Sales | | 100.0 | | 100.0 |
| | | 33.1 | 29.9 | | | | Gross Profit | | 32.9 | | 28.6 |
| | | 26.2 | 19.6 | | | | Operating Expenses | | 25.5 | | 22.2 |
| | | 6.9 | 10.3 | | | | Operating Profit | | 7.4 | | 6.4 |
| | | .6 | .9 | | | | All Other Expenses (net) | | .8 | | 1.0 |
| | | 6.3 | 9.3 | | | | Profit Before Taxes | | 6.6 | | 5.4 |
| | | | | | | | RATIOS | | | | |
| | | 8.7 | 4.0 | | | | | | 3.1 | | 2.7 |
| | | 2.5 | 2.1 | | | | Current | | 1.9 | | 1.4 |
| | | 1.5 | 1.1 | | | | | | 1.0 | | 1.0 |
| | | 5.7 | 2.6 | | | | | | 2.1 | | 1.4 |
| | | 1.3 | 1.0 | | | | Quick | | 1.0 | | .8 |
| | | .8 | .6 | | | | | | .5 | | .5 |
| | | 35   10.4 | 36   10.1 | | | | | 33   11.0 | | 29   12.4 | |
| | | 46   8.0 | 48   7.6 | | | | Sales/Receivables | 41   9.0 | | 38   9.5 | |
| | | 52   7.0 | 60   6.1 | | | | | 55   6.7 | | 53   6.9 | |
| | | 12   30.8 | 40   9.1 | | | | | 37   9.9 | | 27   13.3 | |
| | | 66   5.5 | 57   6.4 | | | | Cost of Sales/Inventory | 57   6.4 | | 62   5.9 | |
| | | 99   3.7 | 104   3.5 | | | | | 87   4.2 | | 97   3.8 | |
| | | 2   204.2 | 13   28.3 | | | | | 20   18.5 | | 15   23.6 | |
| | | 13   28.8 | 23   16.2 | | | | Cost of Sales/Payables | 35   10.3 | | 26   13.8 | |
| | | 58   6.3 | 35   10.5 | | | | | 53   6.9 | | 59   6.2 | |
| | | 2.8 | 2.8 | | | | | | 4.7 | | 4.2 |
| | | 6.5 | 5.7 | | | | Sales/Working Capital | | 6.8 | | 10.2 |
| | | 258.2 | 42.1 | | | | | | 161.4 | | NM |
| | | | 38.7 | | | | | | 9.4 | | 9.1 |
| | | | (14)   17.9 | | | | EBIT/Interest | (34)   4.8 | | (36)   3.0 | |
| | | | 5.2 | | | | | | 1.4 | | -.8 |
| | | | | | | | Net Profit + Depr., Dep., | | 8.3 | | 7.4 |
| | | | | | | | Amort./Cur. Mat. L/T/D | (16)   3.4 | | (19)   1.9 | |
| | | | | | | | | | 2.4 | | .1 |
| | | .1 | .2 | | | | | | .3 | | .3 |
| | | .2 | .6 | | | | Fixed/Worth | | 1.1 | | .8 |
| | | .4 | 1.4 | | | | | | 2.5 | | 1.6 |
| | | .2 | .3 | | | | | | .6 | | .9 |
| | | .7 | .9 | | | | Debt/Worth | | 1.4 | | 1.7 |
| | | 3.8 | 2.8 | | | | | | 4.2 | | 3.7 |
| | | | 39.2 | | | | % Profit Before Taxes/Tangible | | 43.5 | | 33.1 |
| | | | (16)   24.0 | | | | Net Worth | (32)   22.3 | | (35)   15.5 | |
| | | | 13.3 | | | | | | 11.6 | | -2.7 |
| | | 33.6 | 19.2 | | | | | | 18.5 | | 17.8 |
| | | 17.5 | 12.4 | | | | % Profit Before Taxes/Total Assets | | 8.5 | | 5.2 |
| | | -.4 | 4.3 | | | | | | 2.6 | | -2.0 |
| | | 93.7 | 21.6 | | | | | | 21.7 | | 19.2 |
| | | 15.0 | 6.5 | | | | Sales/Net Fixed Assets | | 7.7 | | 8.6 |
| | | 10.3 | 3.0 | | | | | | 3.2 | | 3.9 |
| | | 3.4 | 2.1 | | | | | | 2.5 | | 2.3 |
| | | 2.0 | 1.4 | | | | Sales/Total Assets | | 2.0 | | 1.8 |
| | | .9 | 1.2 | | | | | | 1.2 | | 1.3 |
| | | | .9 | | | | | | 1.9 | | .9 |
| | | | (16)   2.2 | | | | % Depr., Dep., Amort./Sales | (31)   3.5 | | (37)   2.5 | |
| | | | 5.7 | | | | | | 4.7 | | 3.5 |
| | | | | | | | % Officers', Directors' | | 1.7 | | 3.0 |
| | | | | | | | Owners' Comp/Sales | (13)   8.2 | | (15)   3.8 | |
| | | | | | | | | | 11.7 | | 10.9 |
| 10M | 4035M | 117154M | 505166M | 82299M | | | Net Sales ($) | | 893767M | | 1441500M |
| 10M | 1764M | 46592M | 333049M | 63083M | | | Total Assets ($) | | 627232M | | 800961M |

M = $ thousand   MM = $ million
See Pages 9 through 22 for Explanation of Ratios and Data

## Comparative Historical Data | Current Data Sorted by Sales

| 4/1/09-3/31/10 ALL | 4/1/10-3/31/11 ALL | 4/1/11-3/31/12 ALL | Type of Statement | 0-1MM | 1-3MM | 3-5MM | 5-10MM | 10-25MM | 25MM & OVER |
|---|---|---|---|---|---|---|---|---|---|
| 6 | 4 | 5 | Unqualified | | | | 1 | 1 | 3 |
| 13 | 8 | 9 | Reviewed | | | | 1 | 6 | 2 |
| 3 | 2 | 2 | Compiled | | 1 | | | 1 | |
| 3 | 3 | 3 | Tax Returns | 1 | 1 | 1 | | | |
| 9 | 12 | 12 | Other | | | | 3 | 4 | 5 |
| | | | | 5 (4/1-9/30/11) | | | 26 (10/1/11-3/31/12) | | |
| 34 | 29 | 31 | NUMBER OF STATEMENTS | 1 | 2 | 1 | 5 | 12 | 10 |
| % | % | % | ASSETS | % | % | % | % | % | % |
| 10.9 | 12.9 | 12.1 | Cash & Equivalents | | | | | 9.1 | 14.9 |
| 20.6 | 17.9 | 23.2 | Trade Receivables (net) | | | | | 20.6 | 26.5 |
| 22.5 | 22.4 | 25.3 | Inventory | | | | | 24.6 | 20.9 |
| 3.5 | 3.0 | 3.1 | All Other Current | | | | | 1.4 | 7.0 |
| 57.4 | 56.1 | 63.7 | Total Current | | | | | 55.6 | 69.3 |
| 31.1 | 33.0 | 21.7 | Fixed Assets (net) | | | | | 32.3 | 17.3 |
| 4.2 | 5.9 | 8.4 | Intangibles (net) | | | | | 2.0 | 12.2 |
| 7.3 | 4.9 | 6.1 | All Other Non-Current | | | | | 10.1 | 1.3 |
| 100.0 | 100.0 | 100.0 | Total | | | | | 100.0 | 100.0 |
| | | | LIABILITIES | | | | | | |
| 8.6 | 4.6 | 7.4 | Notes Payable-Short Term | | | | | 8.3 | 9.2 |
| 3.5 | 2.8 | 2.0 | Cur. Mat.-L.T.D. | | | | | 3.6 | 2.0 |
| 12.0 | 11.8 | 10.2 | Trade Payables | | | | | 10.3 | 10.3 |
| .1 | .0 | .2 | Income Taxes Payable | | | | | .5 | .1 |
| 9.9 | 4.3 | 9.8 | All Other Current | | | | | 5.6 | 13.0 |
| 34.1 | 23.6 | 29.7 | Total Current | | | | | 28.2 | 34.6 |
| 15.6 | 15.3 | 4.7 | Long-Term Debt | | | | | 7.2 | 1.5 |
| .3 | 1.5 | 1.7 | Deferred Taxes | | | | | 1.6 | 3.0 |
| 6.6 | 9.9 | 5.9 | All Other Non-Current | | | | | 6.8 | 7.4 |
| 43.4 | 49.8 | 58.0 | Net Worth | | | | | 56.1 | 53.5 |
| 100.0 | 100.0 | 100.0 | Total Liabilities & Net Worth | | | | | 100.0 | 100.0 |
| | | | INCOME DATA | | | | | | |
| 100.0 | 100.0 | 100.0 | Net Sales | | | | | 100.0 | 100.0 |
| 30.0 | 32.8 | 31.1 | Gross Profit | | | | | 30.8 | 28.8 |
| 26.3 | 25.5 | 22.0 | Operating Expenses | | | | | 19.7 | 20.2 |
| 3.7 | 7.3 | 9.1 | Operating Profit | | | | | 11.0 | 8.6 |
| .5 | -.1 | .7 | All Other Expenses (net) | | | | | .6 | 1.0 |
| 3.2 | 7.4 | 8.3 | Profit Before Taxes | | | | | 10.5 | 7.6 |
| | | | RATIOS | | | | | | |
| 3.2 | 4.3 | 5.5 | Current | | | | | 3.8 | 4.3 |
| 2.1 | 2.5 | 3.0 | | | | | | 2.0 | 2.8 |
| 1.2 | 1.5 | 1.7 | | | | | | 1.3 | .9 |
| 2.2 | 2.3 | 4.3 | Quick | | | | | 2.8 | 2.6 |
| 1.0 | 1.2 | 1.2 | | | | | | 1.0 | 1.3 |
| .6 | .7 | .7 | | | | | | .6 | .8 |
| 30  12.3 | 25  14.9 | 34  10.7 | Sales/Receivables | | | | | 35  10.4 | 19  19.3 |
| 44  8.3 | 46  7.9 | 47  7.7 | | | | | | 47  7.8 | 43  8.4 |
| 60  6.0 | 63  5.8 | 56  6.5 | | | | | | 56  6.5 | 59  6.2 |
| 27  13.5 | 35  10.5 | 35  10.5 | Cost of Sales/Inventory | | | | | 37  9.8 | 21  17.6 |
| 65  5.6 | 76  4.8 | 72  5.1 | | | | | | 69  5.3 | 52  7.0 |
| 105  3.3 | 109  3.3 | 104  3.5 | | | | | | 104  3.5 | 78  4.7 |
| 14  25.7 | 16  22.2 | 11  33.2 | Cost of Sales/Payables | | | | | 11  33.9 | 17  22.0 |
| 18  20.3 | 29  12.5 | 22  16.5 | | | | | | 14  26.2 | 22  16.3 |
| 43  8.5 | 53  6.9 | 41  8.9 | | | | | | 53  6.9 | 34  10.7 |
| 3.4 | 2.7 | 2.8 | Sales/Working Capital | | | | | 3.4 | 2.9 |
| 7.4 | 4.7 | 5.7 | | | | | | 7.3 | 5.5 |
| 29.2 | 13.6 | 11.0 | | | | | | 12.3 | NM |
| 20.8 | 25.2 | 46.5 | EBIT/Interest | | | | | 44.4 | |
| (30)  4.7 | (24)  6.7 | (24)  23.7 | | | | | | (11)  22.5 | |
| .8 | .0 | 4.9 | | | | | | 4.6 | |
| 7.3 | | | Net Profit + Depr., Dep., Amort./Cur. Mat. L/T/D | | | | | | |
| (10)  3.8 | | | | | | | | | |
| .5 | | | | | | | | | |
| .4 | .3 | .2 | Fixed/Worth | | | | | .1 | .2 |
| .7 | .8 | .3 | | | | | | .5 | .3 |
| 1.4 | 1.4 | 1.1 | | | | | | 1.2 | 1.9 |
| .6 | .4 | .3 | Debt/Worth | | | | | .3 | .3 |
| 1.3 | 1.3 | .9 | | | | | | .8 | .9 |
| 3.9 | 3.3 | 1.8 | | | | | | 2.1 | 12.0 |
| 32.7 | 39.1 | 46.4 | % Profit Before Taxes/Tangible Net Worth | | | | | 39.2 | |
| (29)  14.5 | (26)  19.4 | (29)  24.7 | | | | | | 29.8 | |
| -2.0 | -1.9 | 10.1 | | | | | | 13.3 | |
| 13.4 | 17.3 | 22.7 | % Profit Before Taxes/Total Assets | | | | | 22.0 | 29.5 |
| 5.9 | 6.4 | 12.4 | | | | | | 17.1 | 14.1 |
| -.3 | -1.2 | 3.7 | | | | | | 4.0 | 7.2 |
| 15.7 | 15.2 | 32.2 | Sales/Net Fixed Assets | | | | | 72.6 | 46.2 |
| 6.6 | 4.6 | 10.5 | | | | | | 5.0 | 16.1 |
| 2.9 | 3.0 | 4.3 | | | | | | 2.9 | 4.9 |
| 2.5 | 2.2 | 2.2 | Sales/Total Assets | | | | | 2.6 | 2.4 |
| 1.6 | 1.4 | 1.6 | | | | | | 1.4 | 2.1 |
| .9 | .8 | 1.1 | | | | | | 1.1 | 1.3 |
| 1.5 | 1.7 | .8 | % Depr., Dep., Amort./Sales | | | | | .7 | |
| (33)  3.3 | (26)  2.7 | (27)  1.6 | | | | | | (10)  4.9 | |
| 4.2 | 5.3 | 5.5 | | | | | | 5.8 | |
| | | | % Officers', Directors', Owners' Comp/Sales | | | | | | |
| 679323M | 526216M | 708664M | Net Sales ($) | 10M | 4035M | 3816M | 34161M | 190653M | 475989M |
| 578745M | 458990M | 444498M | Total Assets ($) | 10M | 1764M | 4100M | 25250M | 149224M | 264150M |

M = $ thousand    MM = $ million
See Pages 9 through 22 for Explanation of Ratios and Data

## Current Data Sorted by Assets      Comparative Historical Data

| 0-500M | 500M-2MM | 2-10MM | 10-50MM | 50-100MM | 100-250MM | Type of Statement | 4/1/07-3/31/08 ALL | 4/1/08-3/31/09 ALL |
|---|---|---|---|---|---|---|---|---|
| 1 | 1 | 7 | 13 | 3 | 5 | Unqualified | 27 | 29 |
|  | 2 | 6 | 9 |  |  | Reviewed | 15 | 27 |
| 1 | 5 | 7 | 1 |  |  | Compiled | 8 | 12 |
| 2 | 3 | 3 |  |  |  | Tax Returns | 13 | 15 |
| 3 | 5 | 13 | 22 | 4 | 6 | Other | 47 | 60 |
|  | 23 (4/1-9/30/11) |  | 99 (10/1/11-3/31/12) |  |  |  |  |  |
| 7 | 16 | 36 | 45 | 7 | 11 | NUMBER OF STATEMENTS | 110 | 143 |
| % | % | % | % | % | % | **ASSETS** | % | % |
|  | 6.1 | 9.6 | 4.3 |  | 8.6 | Cash & Equivalents | 8.0 | 7.1 |
|  | 33.2 | 30.6 | 27.1 |  | 16.2 | Trade Receivables (net) | 29.2 | 27.4 |
|  | 20.5 | 20.9 | 30.5 |  | 42.1 | Inventory | 22.8 | 25.4 |
|  | .5 | 3.5 | 3.3 |  | .9 | All Other Current | 2.5 | 2.9 |
|  | 60.3 | 64.6 | 65.3 |  | 67.8 | Total Current | 62.6 | 62.8 |
|  | 28.0 | 29.6 | 26.5 |  | 21.2 | Fixed Assets (net) | 28.9 | 27.7 |
|  | 2.6 | 1.5 | 1.0 |  | 7.9 | Intangibles (net) | 3.4 | 2.7 |
|  | 9.0 | 4.4 | 7.3 |  | 3.1 | All Other Non-Current | 5.1 | 6.8 |
|  | 100.0 | 100.0 | 100.0 |  | 100.0 | Total | 100.0 | 100.0 |
|  |  |  |  |  |  | **LIABILITIES** |  |  |
|  | 11.3 | 7.4 | 14.5 |  | 7.2 | Notes Payable-Short Term | 12.2 | 12.9 |
|  | 4.7 | 3.2 | 2.3 |  | .0 | Cur. Mat.-L.T.D. | 3.4 | 3.6 |
|  | 22.0 | 18.5 | 17.2 |  | 11.1 | Trade Payables | 19.6 | 15.5 |
|  | .0 | .2 | .5 |  | .4 | Income Taxes Payable | .2 | .5 |
|  | 13.8 | 14.7 | 8.3 |  | 17.9 | All Other Current | 9.5 | 9.0 |
|  | 51.9 | 44.0 | 42.8 |  | 36.6 | Total Current | 44.9 | 41.5 |
|  | 14.2 | 14.2 | 14.1 |  | 16.3 | Long-Term Debt | 15.6 | 14.6 |
|  | .6 | 1.1 | .4 |  | 2.3 | Deferred Taxes | .6 | .6 |
|  | 4.1 | 5.2 | 3.8 |  | 7.2 | All Other Non-Current | 6.3 | 6.4 |
|  | 29.2 | 35.5 | 38.9 |  | 37.6 | Net Worth | 32.8 | 36.9 |
|  | 100.0 | 100.0 | 100.0 |  | 100.0 | Total Liabilities & Net Worth | 100.0 | 100.0 |
|  |  |  |  |  |  | **INCOME DATA** |  |  |
|  | 100.0 | 100.0 | 100.0 |  | 100.0 | Net Sales | 100.0 | 100.0 |
|  | 28.8 | 21.7 | 17.4 |  | 10.3 | Gross Profit | 22.2 | 22.5 |
|  | 24.0 | 17.5 | 12.0 |  | 5.2 | Operating Expenses | 15.8 | 16.7 |
|  | 4.8 | 4.2 | 5.4 |  | 5.1 | Operating Profit | 6.4 | 5.8 |
|  | 1.1 | .4 | .9 |  | .9 | All Other Expenses (net) | 1.1 | 1.0 |
|  | 3.7 | 3.8 | 4.5 |  | 4.2 | Profit Before Taxes | 5.4 | 4.8 |
|  |  |  |  |  |  | **RATIOS** |  |  |
|  | 2.8 | 2.9 | 2.5 |  | 3.7 |  | 2.5 | 2.6 |
|  | 1.5 | 1.7 | 1.5 |  | 2.1 | Current | 1.4 | 1.7 |
|  | 1.0 | 1.0 | 1.1 |  | 1.1 |  | 1.0 | 1.1 |
|  | 1.8 | 1.7 | 1.5 |  | 2.6 |  | 1.6 | 1.4 |
|  | 1.1 | .9 | .6 |  | .5 | Quick | .9 | .9 |
|  | .6 | .6 | .4 |  | .3 |  | .5 | .5 |
| 21 | 17.8 | 32  11.3 | 33  11.2 |  | 23  16.2 |  | 32  11.3 | 23  15.6 |
| 39 | 9.3 | 40  9.2 | 45  8.1 |  | 32  11.4 | Sales/Receivables | 44  8.4 | 39  9.3 |
| 49 | 7.4 | 62  5.9 | 61  6.0 |  | 41  8.9 |  | 56  6.5 | 57  6.4 |
| 0 | UND | 11  34.2 | 43  8.5 |  | 38  9.7 |  | 10  36.5 | 18  20.4 |
| 21 | 17.0 | 30  12.0 | 62  5.9 |  | 87  4.2 | Cost of Sales/Inventory | 39  9.4 | 45  8.1 |
| 81 | 4.5 | 58  6.3 | 78  4.7 |  | 135  2.7 |  | 72  5.1 | 76  4.8 |
| 8 | 44.0 | 18  20.1 | 24  15.1 |  | 7  55.1 |  | 19  18.7 | 12  29.8 |
| 27 | 13.6 | 28  12.9 | 32  11.5 |  | 16  23.1 | Cost of Sales/Payables | 31  11.8 | 25  14.8 |
| 58 | 6.3 | 48  7.6 | 42  8.6 |  | 38  9.5 |  | 46  7.9 | 43  8.6 |
|  | 7.7 | 5.6 | 4.5 |  | 3.7 |  | 5.8 | 5.3 |
|  | 20.6 | 9.3 | 10.0 |  | 7.1 | Sales/Working Capital | 13.4 | 11.2 |
|  | NM | NM | 36.7 |  | 31.9 |  | 246.9 | 67.4 |
|  | 51.7 | 15.5 | 34.9 |  |  |  | 18.5 | 17.3 |
| (14) | 8.2 | (33)  7.8 | (44)  7.0 |  |  | EBIT/Interest | (101)  4.5 | (134)  5.6 |
|  | 2.1 | 2.4 | 1.9 |  |  |  | 1.4 | 2.0 |
|  |  |  | 4.9 |  |  |  | 7.9 | 11.8 |
|  |  |  | (15)  2.8 |  |  | Net Profit + Depr., Dep., Amort./Cur. Mat. L/T/D | (24)  1.9 | (35)  3.7 |
|  |  |  | 1.1 |  |  |  | 1.2 | 2.3 |
|  | .4 | .3 | .4 |  | .3 |  | .3 | .3 |
|  | .7 | .7 | .7 |  | .5 | Fixed/Worth | .8 | .8 |
|  | -3.6 | 2.4 | 1.2 |  | 1.2 |  | 2.6 | 1.8 |
|  | .6 | .7 | .6 |  | .6 |  | 1.0 | .8 |
|  | 1.4 | 1.5 | 1.9 |  | 2.0 | Debt/Worth | 2.2 | 1.7 |
|  | -13.3 | 5.2 | 4.2 |  | -8.7 |  | 6.5 | 4.6 |
|  | 70.5 | 58.2 | 36.9 |  |  |  | 58.8 | 62.0 |
| (11) | 36.6 | (29)  23.2 | (42)  19.7 |  |  | % Profit Before Taxes/Tangible Net Worth | (96)  26.4 | (127)  29.4 |
|  | 17.5 | 9.0 | 6.0 |  |  |  | 7.0 | 11.1 |
|  | 21.6 | 19.3 | 14.5 |  | 14.7 |  | 22.2 | 19.3 |
|  | 13.9 | 6.2 | 7.3 |  | 8.3 | % Profit Before Taxes/Total Assets | 10.1 | 10.8 |
|  | 4.3 | 2.7 | 2.2 |  | .5 |  | 2.1 | 2.6 |
|  | 46.0 | 17.9 | 23.8 |  | 20.5 |  | 23.3 | 23.7 |
|  | 20.7 | 10.3 | 7.9 |  | 9.4 | Sales/Net Fixed Assets | 11.5 | 10.8 |
|  | 4.7 | 5.5 | 4.1 |  | 5.8 |  | 4.3 | 5.5 |
|  | 4.4 | 3.4 | 2.7 |  | 2.5 |  | 2.9 | 3.3 |
|  | 2.7 | 2.3 | 2.0 |  | 2.0 | Sales/Total Assets | 2.3 | 2.4 |
|  | 2.1 | 2.0 | 1.5 |  | 1.5 |  | 1.6 | 1.7 |
|  | 1.1 | .8 | .8 |  |  |  | .7 | .7 |
| (10) | 1.7 | (35)  1.5 | (41)  1.8 |  |  | % Depr., Dep., Amort./Sales | (98)  1.4 | (127)  1.3 |
|  | 5.0 | 3.0 | 2.7 |  |  |  | 2.7 | 2.7 |
|  |  | 1.1 |  |  |  |  | 1.2 | 1.1 |
|  |  | (12)  1.9 |  |  |  | % Officers', Directors' Owners' Comp/Sales | (28)  4.1 | (41)  2.8 |
|  |  | 4.6 |  |  |  |  | 6.3 | 4.7 |
| 5360M | 84806M | 512466M | 2454769M | 1346692M | 3620267M | Net Sales ($) | 6552594M | 10441471M |
| 1682M | 20373M | 207289M | 1223248M | 492676M | 1924275M | Total Assets ($) | 3141943M | 4322972M |

## Comparative Historical Data                    ## Current Data Sorted by Sales

| | | | Type of Statement | | | | | | |
|---|---|---|---|---|---|---|---|---|---|
| 36 | 35 | 30 | Unqualified | 2 | | | | 8 | 20 |
| 24 | 23 | 17 | Reviewed | | 1 | 1 | 2 | 5 | 8 |
| 13 | 9 | 14 | Compiled | 1 | 1 | 1 | 3 | 7 | 1 |
| 5 | 10 | 8 | Tax Returns | 1 | 1 | 1 | 1 | 2 | |
| 64 | 56 | 53 | Other | 3 | 2 | 5 | 1 | 11 | 31 |
| 4/1/09-3/31/10 ALL | 4/1/10-3/31/11 ALL | 4/1/11-3/31/12 ALL | | 23 (4/1-9/30/11) | | | 99 (10/1/11-3/31/12) | | |
| | | | | 0-1MM | 1-3MM | 3-5MM | 5-10MM | 10-25MM | 25MM & OVER |
| 142 | 133 | 122 | **NUMBER OF STATEMENTS** | 7 | 7 | 8 | 7 | 33 | 60 |
| % | % | % | **ASSETS** | % | % | % | % | % | % |
| 8.5 | 8.5 | 7.3 | Cash & Equivalents | | | | | 9.4 | 5.0 |
| 24.5 | 25.1 | 26.9 | Trade Receivables (net) | | | | | 33.3 | 25.8 |
| 22.8 | 23.7 | 27.0 | Inventory | | | | | 19.4 | 34.2 |
| 3.4 | 3.2 | 3.1 | All Other Current | | | | | 1.8 | 3.3 |
| 59.1 | 60.6 | 64.4 | Total Current | | | | | 63.8 | 68.3 |
| 30.9 | 27.2 | 27.0 | Fixed Assets (net) | | | | | 30.1 | 23.8 |
| 3.3 | 3.7 | 2.0 | Intangibles (net) | | | | | .8 | 2.4 |
| 6.7 | 8.6 | 6.6 | All Other Non-Current | | | | | 5.3 | 5.4 |
| 100.0 | 100.0 | 100.0 | Total | | | | | 100.0 | 100.0 |
| | | | **LIABILITIES** | | | | | | |
| 10.7 | 12.6 | 11.1 | Notes Payable-Short Term | | | | | 7.5 | 13.1 |
| 4.6 | 3.4 | 2.5 | Cur. Mat.-L.T.D. | | | | | 2.5 | 1.8 |
| 14.3 | 16.0 | 17.1 | Trade Payables | | | | | 18.2 | 16.8 |
| .2 | .4 | .3 | Income Taxes Payable | | | | | .3 | .5 |
| 11.1 | 10.6 | 16.7 | All Other Current | | | | | 16.5 | 11.9 |
| 40.9 | 43.0 | 47.8 | Total Current | | | | | 45.1 | 44.0 |
| 18.2 | 13.6 | 13.9 | Long-Term Debt | | | | | 11.8 | 13.4 |
| .9 | 1.0 | .8 | Deferred Taxes | | | | | 1.0 | .8 |
| 7.6 | 9.9 | 5.5 | All Other Non-Current | | | | | 5.1 | 4.8 |
| 32.3 | 32.5 | 31.9 | Net Worth | | | | | 36.9 | 37.0 |
| 100.0 | 100.0 | 100.0 | Total Liabilities & Net Worth | | | | | 100.0 | 100.0 |
| | | | **INCOME DATA** | | | | | | |
| 100.0 | 100.0 | 100.0 | Net Sales | | | | | 100.0 | 100.0 |
| 21.5 | 20.2 | 20.7 | Gross Profit | | | | | 19.8 | 16.5 |
| 20.3 | 17.1 | 15.8 | Operating Expenses | | | | | 16.1 | 10.6 |
| 1.2 | 3.0 | 5.0 | Operating Profit | | | | | 3.7 | 5.9 |
| 1.8 | .8 | .7 | All Other Expenses (net) | | | | | .2 | .9 |
| -.7 | 2.3 | 4.3 | Profit Before Taxes | | | | | 3.5 | 5.1 |
| | | | **RATIOS** | | | | | | |
| 3.1 | 3.1 | 2.7 | Current | | | | | 3.0 | 2.5 |
| 1.4 | 1.5 | 1.5 | | | | | | 1.4 | 1.5 |
| 1.0 | 1.1 | 1.1 | | | | | | .9 | 1.1 |
| 1.6 | 1.7 | 1.6 | Quick | | | | | 1.9 | 1.5 |
| .7 | .9 | .7 | | | | | | .7 | .6 |
| .4 | .5 | .4 | | | | | | .6 | .4 |
| 31  12.0 | 31  11.7 | 29  12.8 | Sales/Receivables | | | | | 32  11.3 | 31  11.7 |
| 43  8.6 | 43  8.6 | 40  9.1 | | | | | | 41  8.9 | 41  8.8 |
| 60  6.1 | 61  6.0 | 53  6.9 | | | | | | 61  6.0 | 54  6.8 |
| 20  18.2 | 18  19.9 | 16  23.4 | Cost of Sales/Inventory | | | | | 8  48.3 | 41  8.9 |
| 49  7.4 | 49  7.5 | 49  7.4 | | | | | | 26  13.8 | 65  5.6 |
| 84  4.4 | 89  4.1 | 83  4.4 | | | | | | 51  7.2 | 91  4.0 |
| 16  23.1 | 17  21.7 | 16  23.2 | Cost of Sales/Payables | | | | | 18  20.8 | 19  19.5 |
| 30  12.0 | 34  10.9 | 30  12.3 | | | | | | 30  12.1 | 30  12.2 |
| 46  8.0 | 47  7.8 | 43  8.4 | | | | | | 43  8.4 | 41  8.8 |
| 4.5 | 4.5 | 5.4 | Sales/Working Capital | | | | | 5.6 | 4.5 |
| 10.5 | 10.2 | 11.1 | | | | | | 10.0 | 8.5 |
| -478.2 | 39.2 | 56.6 | | | | | | -102.2 | 39.5 |
| 6.5 | 14.6 | 32.9 | EBIT/Interest | | | | | 17.0 | 40.6 |
| (124)  1.5 | (120)  4.0 | (108)  7.6 | | | | | | (29)  7.8 | (55)  9.8 |
| -1.4 | .2 | 2.3 | | | | | | 1.8 | 2.9 |
| 6.5 | 6.0 | 6.8 | Net Profit + Depr., Dep., Amort./Cur. Mat. L/T/D | | | | | | 8.9 |
| (36)  2.3 | (36)  2.2 | (30)  3.6 | | | | | | | (20)  3.9 |
| .2 | 1.2 | 1.2 | | | | | | | 1.7 |
| .3 | .3 | .3 | Fixed/Worth | | | | | .3 | .3 |
| .8 | .7 | .7 | | | | | | .7 | .7 |
| 2.1 | 2.3 | 1.9 | | | | | | 2.2 | 1.1 |
| .7 | .6 | .6 | Debt/Worth | | | | | .6 | .6 |
| 1.8 | 1.8 | 1.9 | | | | | | 1.3 | 2.0 |
| 5.1 | 10.1 | 8.0 | | | | | | 5.1 | 6.1 |
| 23.8 | 33.8 | 49.4 | % Profit Before Taxes/Tangible Net Worth | | | | | 56.1 | 48.5 |
| (118)  6.0 | (108)  15.1 | (100)  23.5 | | | | | | (27)  22.3 | (54)  24.4 |
| -8.5 | 1.1 | 10.4 | | | | | | 2.7 | 11.6 |
| 8.6 | 12.1 | 18.6 | % Profit Before Taxes/Total Assets | | | | | 19.7 | 16.1 |
| 1.7 | 4.4 | 7.5 | | | | | | 11.1 | 8.1 |
| -7.0 | -2.1 | 2.4 | | | | | | 1.7 | 2.6 |
| 17.6 | 21.5 | 23.2 | Sales/Net Fixed Assets | | | | | 18.4 | 24.7 |
| 7.0 | 8.7 | 9.5 | | | | | | 9.8 | 9.5 |
| 3.1 | 4.3 | 4.9 | | | | | | 5.6 | 5.2 |
| 2.6 | 2.7 | 3.1 | Sales/Total Assets | | | | | 3.6 | 2.8 |
| 1.8 | 1.8 | 2.2 | | | | | | 2.4 | 2.1 |
| 1.2 | 1.3 | 1.7 | | | | | | 2.0 | 1.6 |
| 1.0 | 1.0 | .8 | % Depr., Dep., Amort./Sales | | | | | .8 | .7 |
| (119)  2.2 | (110)  1.8 | (104)  1.4 | | | | | | (29)  1.6 | (54)  1.0 |
| 4.2 | 3.6 | 2.8 | | | | | | 2.8 | 2.2 |
| 1.9 | 1.8 | 1.1 | % Officers', Directors' Owners' Comp/Sales | | | | | 1.1 | |
| (25)  3.3 | (31)  3.2 | (22)  2.1 | | | | | | (13)  1.6 | |
| 6.8 | 6.8 | 5.5 | | | | | | 3.9 | |
| 6024034M | 7785857M | 8024360M | Net Sales ($) | 4064M | 13455M | 30727M | 49236M | 544581M | 7382297M |
| 3702847M | 4801561M | 3869543M | Total Assets ($) | 3225M | 7615M | 11876M | 21833M | 237042M | 3587952M |

M = $ thousand    MM = $ million
See Pages 9 through 22 for Explanation of Ratios and Data

## Current Data Sorted by Assets        Comparative Historical Data

| | | | | | | Type of Statement | | |
|---|---|---|---|---|---|---|---|---|
| | | 2 | 13 | 9 | 7 | Unqualified | 31 | 37 |
| 1 | 2 | 14 | 17 | | 1 | Reviewed | 23 | 26 |
| 1 | 6 | 10 | 4 | | | Compiled | 17 | 23 |
| 4 | 17 | 9 | | | | Tax Returns | 13 | 15 |
| 1 | 6 | 14 | 30 | 5 | 4 | Other | 50 | 70 |
| | 30 (4/1-9/30/11) | | 147 (10/1/11-3/31/12) | | | | 4/1/07-3/31/08 | 4/1/08-3/31/09 |
| 0-500M | 500M-2MM | 2-10MM | 10-50MM | 50-100MM | 100-250MM | | ALL | ALL |
| 7 | 31 | 49 | 64 | 14 | 12 | **NUMBER OF STATEMENTS** | 134 | 171 |
| % | % | % | % | % | % | **ASSETS** | % | % |
| | 12.6 | 8.6 | 4.7 | 7.1 | 6.9 | Cash & Equivalents | 7.3 | 8.2 |
| | 34.9 | 26.8 | 26.9 | 19.7 | 21.2 | Trade Receivables (net) | 27.2 | 26.1 |
| | 24.0 | 24.6 | 29.0 | 35.2 | 27.4 | Inventory | 30.9 | 27.9 |
| | .2 | 1.2 | 1.2 | 2.7 | 3.8 | All Other Current | 4.7 | 4.9 |
| | 71.6 | 61.2 | 61.9 | 64.6 | 59.2 | Total Current | 70.0 | 67.1 |
| | 16.3 | 26.6 | 28.5 | 20.6 | 27.1 | Fixed Assets (net) | 22.9 | 23.9 |
| | 5.1 | 4.8 | 5.1 | 9.8 | 5.9 | Intangibles (net) | 4.0 | 3.9 |
| | 7.0 | 7.4 | 4.6 | 5.0 | 7.8 | All Other Non-Current | 3.1 | 5.2 |
| | 100.0 | 100.0 | 100.0 | 100.0 | 100.0 | Total | 100.0 | 100.0 |
| | | | | | | **LIABILITIES** | | |
| | 14.0 | 9.4 | 10.3 | 8.1 | 8.6 | Notes Payable-Short Term | 12.8 | 12.3 |
| | 4.4 | 2.9 | 3.9 | .4 | .9 | Cur. Mat.-L.T.D. | 2.9 | 2.7 |
| | 15.0 | 14.5 | 13.8 | 15.0 | 11.9 | Trade Payables | 17.6 | 15.9 |
| | .1 | .2 | .3 | .2 | .1 | Income Taxes Payable | .4 | .5 |
| | 9.1 | 13.1 | 10.4 | 14.6 | 9.2 | All Other Current | 8.5 | 10.3 |
| | 42.6 | 40.2 | 38.6 | 38.3 | 30.7 | Total Current | 42.2 | 41.6 |
| | 19.8 | 14.6 | 15.9 | 8.7 | 13.0 | Long-Term Debt | 12.8 | 11.6 |
| | .0 | .5 | .3 | 1.2 | 1.6 | Deferred Taxes | .3 | .4 |
| | 9.7 | 4.3 | 3.5 | 5.7 | 4.1 | All Other Non-Current | 4.0 | 4.6 |
| | 27.9 | 40.5 | 41.6 | 46.1 | 50.6 | Net Worth | 40.7 | 41.8 |
| | 100.0 | 100.0 | 100.0 | 100.0 | 100.0 | Total Liabilities & Net Worth | 100.0 | 100.0 |
| | | | | | | **INCOME DATA** | | |
| | 100.0 | 100.0 | 100.0 | 100.0 | 100.0 | Net Sales | 100.0 | 100.0 |
| | 26.8 | 28.5 | 19.8 | 18.7 | 17.8 | Gross Profit | 23.7 | 24.4 |
| | 22.1 | 22.4 | 14.4 | 11.6 | 10.6 | Operating Expenses | 17.0 | 17.5 |
| | 4.7 | 6.0 | 5.5 | 7.1 | 7.2 | Operating Profit | 6.7 | 6.9 |
| | 1.6 | .5 | .5 | .6 | .7 | All Other Expenses (net) | .9 | 1.2 |
| | 3.2 | 5.5 | 5.0 | 6.5 | 6.5 | Profit Before Taxes | 5.8 | 5.7 |
| | | | | | | **RATIOS** | | |
| | 5.3 | 2.9 | 2.3 | 3.7 | 3.2 | | 3.0 | 3.0 |
| | 1.7 | 1.8 | 1.7 | 2.4 | 2.2 | Current | 1.6 | 1.6 |
| | 1.1 | 1.1 | 1.2 | 1.2 | 1.3 | | 1.2 | 1.1 |
| | 4.0 | 1.7 | 1.6 | 1.5 | 1.3 | | 1.4 | 1.5 |
| | 1.2 | 1.0 | .8 | 1.0 | .9 | Quick | .8 | .8 |
| | .6 | .6 | .6 | .3 | .6 | | .5 | .5 |

| | | | | | | | | | | | | | | Historical | | | |
|---|---|---|---|---|---|---|---|---|---|---|---|---|---|---|---|---|---|
| 26 | 14.1 | 30 | 12.2 | 36 | 10.2 | 35 | 10.4 | 28 | 13.1 | | Sales/Receivables | | 27 | 13.4 | 26 | 14.1 |
| 36 | 10.0 | 42 | 8.6 | 47 | 7.7 | 47 | 7.8 | 41 | 8.8 | | | | 38 | 9.5 | 37 | 10.0 |
| 64 | 5.7 | 59 | 6.2 | 60 | 6.1 | 59 | 6.2 | 52 | 7.0 | | | | 48 | 7.7 | 48 | 7.6 |
| 9 | 42.0 | 27 | 13.3 | 33 | 11.1 | 61 | 6.0 | 38 | 9.5 | | Cost of Sales/Inventory | | 23 | 15.8 | 24 | 15.5 |
| 38 | 9.5 | 49 | 7.4 | 59 | 6.2 | 101 | 3.6 | 62 | 5.9 | | | | 57 | 6.4 | 45 | 8.0 |
| 70 | 5.2 | 78 | 4.7 | 101 | 3.6 | 135 | 2.7 | 99 | 3.7 | | | | 92 | 4.0 | 88 | 4.2 |
| 12 | 31.7 | 14 | 25.3 | 17 | 22.0 | 12 | 29.8 | 21 | 17.5 | | Cost of Sales/Payables | | 15 | 24.2 | 11 | 32.6 |
| 26 | 14.3 | 26 | 14.3 | 29 | 12.8 | 32 | 11.5 | 29 | 12.5 | | | | 28 | 13.1 | 26 | 14.0 |
| 36 | 10.0 | 48 | 7.6 | 40 | 9.1 | 59 | 6.2 | 35 | 10.3 | | | | 41 | 8.8 | 42 | 8.8 |

| | | | | | | | | | | | | | | | |
|---|---|---|---|---|---|---|---|---|---|---|---|---|---|---|---|
| | 5.7 | | 4.5 | | 5.4 | | 3.5 | | 3.7 | Sales/Working Capital | | 5.1 | | 4.9 |
| | 10.4 | | 8.8 | | 8.0 | | 4.3 | | 5.6 | | | 9.6 | | 10.4 |
| | 38.8 | | 50.7 | | 23.3 | | 14.8 | | 32.1 | | | 32.2 | | 50.2 |
| | 11.7 | | 16.9 | | 18.0 | | 64.4 | | 71.2 | EBIT/Interest | | 13.7 | | 24.0 |
| (26) | 4.6 | (42) | 3.0 | (61) | 8.3 | (10) | 15.2 | | 16.5 | | (116) | 5.0 | (142) | 5.2 |
| | 1.6 | | .9 | | 3.3 | | -.5 | | 2.1 | | | 2.0 | | 1.6 |
| | | | 4.4 | | 9.6 | | | | | Net Profit + Depr., Dep., Amort./Cur. Mat. L/T/D | | 12.4 | | 8.0 |
| | | (11) | 1.5 | (19) | 2.4 | | | | | | (32) | 4.7 | (39) | 4.0 |
| | | | -39.6 | | .6 | | | | | | | 1.5 | | 1.6 |
| | .2 | | .2 | | .4 | | .3 | | .3 | Fixed/Worth | | .2 | | .2 |
| | .5 | | .7 | | .7 | | .6 | | .6 | | | .5 | | .6 |
| | UND | | 1.5 | | 1.7 | | 1.0 | | 1.1 | | | 1.5 | | 1.6 |
| | .6 | | .6 | | .7 | | .3 | | .4 | Debt/Worth | | .6 | | .5 |
| | 2.1 | | 1.7 | | 1.5 | | 1.8 | | 1.1 | | | 1.6 | | 1.4 |
| | UND | | 4.7 | | 3.4 | | 38.0 | | 1.7 | | | 4.2 | | 4.5 |

| | | | | | | | | | | | | | | | |
|---|---|---|---|---|---|---|---|---|---|---|---|---|---|---|---|
| | 46.9 | | 49.2 | | 34.8 | | 44.4 | | 47.3 | % Profit Before Taxes/Tangible Net Worth | | 59.2 | | 65.9 |
| (24) | 26.6 | (43) | 25.4 | (57) | 18.6 | (12) | 27.8 | (11) | 27.8 | | (113) | 28.3 | (151) | 28.4 |
| | 8.6 | | 2.2 | | 7.8 | | 13.9 | | 2.6 | | | 11.8 | | 7.7 |
| | 23.2 | | 19.3 | | 15.3 | | 18.0 | | 22.3 | % Profit Before Taxes/Total Assets | | 21.5 | | 24.3 |
| | 7.3 | | 6.9 | | 8.4 | | 9.5 | | 13.0 | | | 10.5 | | 9.7 |
| | -.3 | | .2 | | 3.5 | | -.2 | | 1.4 | | | 2.5 | | 2.0 |
| | 33.0 | | 29.9 | | 18.4 | | 14.3 | | 14.3 | Sales/Net Fixed Assets | | 34.8 | | 32.1 |
| | 18.6 | | 8.3 | | 9.3 | | 8.9 | | 6.6 | | | 15.1 | | 14.0 |
| | 10.8 | | 4.4 | | 4.1 | | 4.4 | | 4.3 | | | 7.4 | | 6.2 |
| | 3.7 | | 3.0 | | 2.5 | | 2.2 | | 2.3 | Sales/Total Assets | | 3.4 | | 3.4 |
| | 3.0 | | 2.0 | | 2.0 | | 1.6 | | 1.7 | | | 2.4 | | 2.4 |
| | 2.3 | | 1.4 | | 1.6 | | 1.1 | | 1.3 | | | 1.8 | | 1.8 |
| | .7 | | 1.4 | | .8 | | 1.1 | | .6 | % Depr., Dep., Amort./Sales | | .5 | | .6 |
| (22) | 1.5 | (42) | 2.0 | (59) | 1.8 | (11) | 1.6 | (11) | 2.0 | | (120) | 1.1 | (147) | 1.4 |
| | 2.7 | | 4.2 | | 2.9 | | 3.0 | | 2.6 | | | 2.3 | | 2.7 |
| | 1.8 | | 1.2 | | 1.2 | | | | | % Officers', Directors' Owners' Comp/Sales | | 1.4 | | 1.9 |
| (21) | 3.2 | (20) | 3.0 | (14) | 1.5 | | | | | | (47) | 2.3 | (50) | 2.7 |
| | 5.9 | | 5.8 | | 3.4 | | | | | | | 5.7 | | 7.8 |

| | | | | | | | |
|---|---|---|---|---|---|---|---|
| 5387M | 110548M | 516603M | 2967176M | 1499628M | 3944384M | Net Sales ($) | 7484970M | 11396480M |
| 1859M | 38253M | 238976M | 1383886M | 892138M | 2101499M | Total Assets ($) | 3537587M | 5027076M |

M = $ thousand    MM = $ million
See Pages 9 through 22 for Explanation of Ratios and Data

## Comparative Historical Data | Current Data Sorted by Sales

| 10 | 11 | 12 | Type of Statement | 0-1MM | 1-3MM | 3-5MM | 5-10MM | 10-25MM | 25MM & OVER |
|---|---|---|---|---|---|---|---|---|---|
| 33 | 36 | 31 | Unqualified | | | | 1 | 3 | 27 |
| 42 | 38 | 35 | Reviewed | 1 | 1 | 1 | 6 | 18 | 8 |
| 14 | 20 | 21 | Compiled | 1 | 2 | 3 | 8 | 4 | 3 |
| 19 | 23 | 30 | Tax Returns | 3 | 12 | 6 | 8 | 1 | |
| 73 | 67 | 60 | Other | 3 | 2 | 2 | 7 | 11 | 35 |
| 4/1/09-3/31/10 ALL | 4/1/10-3/31/11 ALL | 4/1/11-3/31/12 ALL | | \<-- 30 (4/1-9/30/11) --\> | | \<-- 147 (10/1/11-3/31/12) --\> | | | |
| 181 | 184 | 177 | NUMBER OF STATEMENTS | 8 | 17 | 12 | 30 | 37 | 73 |
| % | % | % | ASSETS | % | % | % | % | % | % |
| 8.7 | 8.0 | 7.7 | Cash & Equivalents | | 11.4 | 13.0 | 13.4 | 3.8 | 5.6 |
| 25.7 | 25.8 | 26.9 | Trade Receivables (net) | | 20.9 | 37.1 | 29.6 | 27.5 | 26.1 |
| 26.3 | 25.3 | 27.2 | Inventory | | 29.8 | 20.0 | 17.6 | 29.1 | 30.9 |
| 4.3 | 3.6 | 1.3 | All Other Current | | .1 | .3 | 1.0 | 1.2 | 2.0 |
| 65.0 | 62.8 | 63.0 | Total Current | | 62.2 | 70.3 | 61.6 | 61.5 | 64.5 |
| 25.9 | 25.7 | 25.2 | Fixed Assets (net) | | 19.6 | 22.4 | 29.1 | 26.6 | 25.0 |
| 3.9 | 4.9 | 5.8 | Intangibles (net) | | 4.1 | 3.3 | 3.9 | 8.3 | 4.5 |
| 5.2 | 6.7 | 6.0 | All Other Non-Current | | 14.1 | 3.9 | 5.4 | 3.6 | 6.0 |
| 100.0 | 100.0 | 100.0 | Total | | 100.0 | 100.0 | 100.0 | 100.0 | 100.0 |
| | | | LIABILITIES | | | | | | |
| 10.4 | 10.1 | 10.6 | Notes Payable-Short Term | | 12.7 | 14.8 | 4.4 | 16.0 | 9.2 |
| 3.9 | 3.5 | 3.2 | Cur. Mat.-L.T.D. | | 2.0 | 4.9 | 4.8 | 2.6 | 2.8 |
| 14.1 | 14.4 | 14.0 | Trade Payables | | 7.4 | 16.4 | 13.3 | 17.5 | 14.1 |
| .1 | .1 | .2 | Income Taxes Payable | | .1 | .0 | .2 | .3 | .2 |
| 13.8 | 12.6 | 13.4 | All Other Current | | 5.7 | 8.4 | 13.9 | 14.9 | 10.1 |
| 42.2 | 40.7 | 41.4 | Total Current | | 28.0 | 44.5 | 36.6 | 51.2 | 36.4 |
| 14.8 | 17.2 | 16.2 | Long-Term Debt | | 19.5 | 16.7 | 19.0 | 11.1 | 13.5 |
| .4 | .5 | .5 | Deferred Taxes | | .0 | .0 | .7 | .3 | .7 |
| 4.6 | 5.9 | 5.8 | All Other Non-Current | | 15.8 | 6.2 | 1.7 | 3.6 | 4.8 |
| 37.9 | 35.7 | 36.1 | Net Worth | | 36.8 | 32.6 | 41.9 | 33.7 | 44.5 |
| 100.0 | 100.0 | 100.0 | Total Liabilities & Net Worth | | 100.0 | 100.0 | 100.0 | 100.0 | 100.0 |
| | | | INCOME DATA | | | | | | |
| 100.0 | 100.0 | 100.0 | Net Sales | | 100.0 | 100.0 | 100.0 | 100.0 | 100.0 |
| 25.8 | 25.4 | 23.9 | Gross Profit | | 34.7 | 25.1 | 28.4 | 22.9 | 18.0 |
| 23.3 | 20.9 | 18.4 | Operating Expenses | | 28.5 | 19.7 | 21.8 | 17.7 | 12.5 |
| 2.5 | 4.5 | 5.5 | Operating Profit | | 6.2 | 5.3 | 6.6 | 5.3 | 5.5 |
| 1.3 | .6 | .8 | All Other Expenses (net) | | .5 | .0 | .6 | .6 | .5 |
| 1.2 | 3.9 | 4.8 | Profit Before Taxes | | 5.8 | 5.3 | 5.9 | 4.7 | 4.9 |

### RATIOS

| 10 | 11 | 12 | Ratio | 0-1MM | 1-3MM | 3-5MM | 5-10MM | 10-25MM | 25MM & OVER |
|---|---|---|---|---|---|---|---|---|---|
| 3.1 | 3.2 | 2.9 | Current | | 13.0 | 3.8 | 5.1 | 1.8 | 2.9 |
| 1.7 | 1.7 | 1.7 | | | 2.8 | 1.5 | 2.0 | 1.2 | 2.0 |
| 1.1 | 1.0 | 1.2 | | | 1.5 | 1.1 | 1.3 | .9 | 1.3 |
| 1.6 | 1.9 | 1.7 | Quick | | 5.7 | 3.4 | 3.3 | 1.1 | 1.6 |
| .8 | .8 | .9 | | | 1.2 | 1.3 | 1.2 | .7 | 1.0 |
| .5 | .4 | .6 | | | .4 | .6 | .6 | .4 | .6 |
| 29  12.6 | 32  11.3 | 31  11.8 | Sales/Receivables | | 17  22.1 | 35  10.3 | 32  11.3 | 32  11.4 | 33  11.1 |
| 43  8.5 | 45  8.2 | 43  8.5 | | | 27  13.7 | 50  7.3 | 41  8.8 | 47  7.7 | 43  8.4 |
| 58  6.3 | 57  6.4 | 59  6.2 | | | 45  8.1 | 66  5.5 | 60  6.1 | 64  5.7 | 56  6.5 |
| 25  14.4 | 29  12.4 | 27  13.3 | Cost of Sales/Inventory | | 7  51.5 | 8  47.6 | 18  20.2 | 28  13.2 | 36  10.1 |
| 60  6.1 | 53  6.8 | 55  6.6 | | | 56  6.5 | 27  13.6 | 43  8.5 | 54  6.8 | 63  5.8 |
| 108  3.4 | 97  3.8 | 99  3.7 | | | 174  2.1 | 52  7.0 | 78  4.7 | 89  4.1 | 104  3.5 |
| 15  24.0 | 17  21.7 | 14  26.0 | Cost of Sales/Payables | | 1  537.2 | 16  23.2 | 15  24.9 | 24  15.0 | 16  23.3 |
| 27  13.4 | 29  12.7 | 27  13.5 | | | 12  29.3 | 26  13.9 | 24  15.5 | 31  11.7 | 28  13.2 |
| 47  7.8 | 45  8.0 | 40  9.1 | | | 40  9.2 | 35  10.5 | 35  10.5 | 51  7.2 | 39  9.4 |
| 4.3 | 4.7 | 4.9 | Sales/Working Capital | | 3.2 | 5.1 | 3.7 | 6.8 | 4.3 |
| 8.7 | 8.1 | 8.4 | | | 6.7 | 14.9 | 7.9 | 23.7 | 7.7 |
| 60.0 | 154.0 | 32.9 | | | 11.0 | 37.0 | 26.5 | -52.6 | 14.6 |
| 10.5 | 14.0 | 18.7 | EBIT/Interest | | (11) 7.7 | 17.6 | (26) 19.6 | (34) 13.1 | (68) 42.6 |
| (162) 2.4 | (164) 4.0 | (158) 6.2 | | | 3.5 | 8.4 | 7.3 | 4.7 | 11.1 |
| -1.4 | 1.5 | 1.5 | | | .9 | 4.6 | 1.5 | 1.4 | 2.7 |
| 6.0 | 4.8 | 12.6 | Net Profit + Depr., Dep., Amort./Cur. Mat. L/T/D | | | | | 12.0 | 13.2 |
| (35) 1.5 | (32) 3.1 | (43) 2.9 | | | | | | (14) 1.8 | (22) 5.2 |
| -.1 | 1.6 | .8 | | | | | | .1 | 2.3 |
| .2 | .3 | .3 | Fixed/Worth | | .1 | .4 | .2 | .5 | .3 |
| .7 | .8 | .7 | | | .4 | .9 | .8 | .8 | .6 |
| 2.9 | 2.1 | 1.7 | | | -3.8 | 1.4 | 1.4 | 2.8 | 1.1 |
| .5 | .6 | .7 | Debt/Worth | | .3 | 1.2 | .5 | 1.1 | .5 |
| 1.7 | 1.7 | 1.7 | | | 1.3 | 2.8 | .8 | 2.4 | 1.3 |
| 7.7 | 6.1 | 6.1 | | | -7.4 | 7.2 | 3.5 | 7.8 | 2.9 |
| 34.7 | 39.6 | 41.6 | % Profit Before Taxes/Tangible Net Worth | | 43.3 | 68.4 | 57.7 | 50.3 | 34.0 |
| (152) 8.9 | (152) 17.8 | (149) 21.2 | | | (12) 18.5 | (11) 39.9 | (26) 28.9 | (31) 18.2 | (66) 19.0 |
| -4.6 | 6.0 | 6.4 | | | 8.6 | 24.0 | 6.1 | 2.2 | 7.9 |
| 11.8 | 14.3 | 16.9 | % Profit Before Taxes/Total Assets | | 13.6 | 26.4 | 23.5 | 15.2 | 16.8 |
| 3.5 | 6.6 | 8.3 | | | 6.3 | 12.4 | 8.5 | 5.4 | 8.7 |
| -3.7 | 1.6 | 1.1 | | | 1.2 | 7.9 | 1.6 | .8 | 3.0 |
| 26.1 | 25.2 | 23.7 | Sales/Net Fixed Assets | | 27.0 | 31.9 | 27.8 | 29.3 | 18.3 |
| 8.4 | 9.0 | 10.1 | | | 15.0 | 16.9 | 7.7 | 11.0 | 9.5 |
| 4.1 | 4.6 | 5.2 | | | 6.6 | 7.2 | 3.8 | 4.7 | 5.2 |
| 2.7 | 2.8 | 2.8 | Sales/Total Assets | | 2.8 | 3.7 | 3.1 | 3.0 | 2.6 |
| 1.8 | 2.0 | 2.1 | | | 2.4 | 3.2 | 1.9 | 1.9 | 2.2 |
| 1.3 | 1.4 | 1.6 | | | 1.3 | 2.4 | 1.3 | 1.6 | 1.6 |
| .9 | 1.0 | 1.1 | % Depr., Dep., Amort./Sales | | (13) .9 | | (25) 1.6 | (34) 1.0 | (65) .8 |
| (148) 2.1 | (158) 2.2 | (150) 1.9 | | | 2.1 | | 2.0 | 1.7 | 1.7 |
| 4.4 | 3.4 | 3.5 | | | 3.6 | | 4.3 | 3.8 | 2.7 |
| 1.7 | 1.5 | 1.3 | % Officers', Directors' Owners' Comp/Sales | | | (10) 1.1 | (15) 1.4 | (11) 1.2 | (12) 1.1 |
| (54) 3.4 | (54) 3.7 | (60) 3.0 | | | | 3.1 | 3.2 | 1.3 | 1.5 |
| 7.3 | 8.0 | 5.3 | | | | 3.8 | 7.2 | 2.8 | 3.8 |
| 7609908M | 8068340M | 9043726M | Net Sales ($) | 4934M | 40596M | 48974M | 210020M | 653659M | 8085543M |
| 4298495M | 4643634M | 4656611M | Total Assets ($) | 3413M | 23810M | 19570M | 121467M | 384552M | 4103799M |

M = $ thousand    MM = $ million
See Pages 9 through 22 for Explanation of Ratios and Data

## Current Data Sorted by Assets      Comparative Historical Data

| 0-500M | 500M-2MM | 2-10MM | 10-50MM | 50-100MM | 100-250MM | Type of Statement | 4/1/07-3/31/08 ALL | 4/1/08-3/31/09 ALL |
|---|---|---|---|---|---|---|---|---|
| | | 1 | 13 | 1 | 5 | Unqualified | 18 | 17 |
| | 1 | 7 | 9 | | | Reviewed | 11 | 19 |
| | 3 | 6 | 2 | | | Compiled | 10 | 10 |
| 1 | | 2 | | | | Tax Returns | 2 | 8 |
| 2 | 2 | 4 | 11 | | 2 | Other | 34 | 36 |
| 3 | 6 | 20 | 35 | 1 | 7 | **NUMBER OF STATEMENTS** | 75 | 90 |

Current-period groupings: 15 (4/1-9/30/11), 57 (10/1/11-3/31/12)

| 0-500M % | 500M-2MM % | 2-10MM % | 10-50MM % | 50-100MM % | 100-250MM % | | ALL % | ALL % |
|---|---|---|---|---|---|---|---|---|
| | | | | | | **ASSETS** | | |
| | | 7.5 | 9.4 | | | Cash & Equivalents | 5.3 | 7.3 |
| | | 28.3 | 26.5 | | | Trade Receivables (net) | 25.6 | 25.0 |
| | | 27.2 | 27.8 | | | Inventory | 29.5 | 27.8 |
| | | 1.6 | 1.5 | | | All Other Current | 2.0 | 2.1 |
| | | 64.6 | 65.2 | | | Total Current | 62.3 | 62.2 |
| | | 27.2 | 28.3 | | | Fixed Assets (net) | 29.4 | 29.4 |
| | | .2 | 1.9 | | | Intangibles (net) | 2.7 | 2.4 |
| | | 8.0 | 4.6 | | | All Other Non-Current | 5.7 | 6.0 |
| | | 100.0 | 100.0 | | | Total | 100.0 | 100.0 |
| | | | | | | **LIABILITIES** | | |
| | | 12.6 | 11.6 | | | Notes Payable-Short Term | 13.0 | 13.5 |
| | | 1.2 | 2.0 | | | Cur. Mat.-L.T.D. | 3.3 | 2.7 |
| | | 19.5 | 12.8 | | | Trade Payables | 18.8 | 18.5 |
| | | .0 | .6 | | | Income Taxes Payable | .4 | .2 |
| | | 4.3 | 9.4 | | | All Other Current | 5.8 | 6.7 |
| | | 37.6 | 36.5 | | | Total Current | 41.3 | 41.7 |
| | | 14.8 | 10.8 | | | Long-Term Debt | 14.0 | 17.6 |
| | | .4 | .7 | | | Deferred Taxes | .8 | .4 |
| | | 2.8 | 7.3 | | | All Other Non-Current | 7.5 | 6.2 |
| | | 44.4 | 44.7 | | | Net Worth | 36.4 | 34.1 |
| | | 100.0 | 100.0 | | | Total Liabilities & Net Worth | 100.0 | 100.0 |
| | | | | | | **INCOME DATA** | | |
| | | 100.0 | 100.0 | | | Net Sales | 100.0 | 100.0 |
| | | 22.1 | 18.6 | | | Gross Profit | 20.3 | 21.2 |
| | | 17.8 | 12.2 | | | Operating Expenses | 13.1 | 15.9 |
| | | 4.3 | 6.4 | | | Operating Profit | 7.2 | 5.4 |
| | | .5 | .4 | | | All Other Expenses (net) | 1.4 | 1.3 |
| | | 3.8 | 6.1 | | | Profit Before Taxes | 5.8 | 4.0 |
| | | | | | | **RATIOS** | | |
| | | 3.6 | 3.3 | | | | 2.4 | 2.5 |
| | | 2.0 | 2.1 | | | Current | 1.6 | 1.5 |
| | | 1.1 | 1.2 | | | | 1.1 | 1.1 |
| | | 2.5 | 1.9 | | | | 1.3 | 1.4 |
| | | 1.0 | 1.0 | | | Quick | .7 | .7 |
| | | .6 | .6 | | | | .5 | .5 |
| | | 30   12.2 | 37   9.9 | | | | 33   11.1 | 27   13.7 |
| | | 46   8.0 | 47   7.8 | | | Sales/Receivables | 39   9.3 | 34   10.8 |
| | | 66   5.5 | 62   5.9 | | | | 48   7.6 | 45   8.1 |
| | | 29   12.5 | 36   10.1 | | | | 35   10.4 | 23   16.2 |
| | | 49   7.4 | 62   5.9 | | | Cost of Sales/Inventory | 59   6.2 | 47   7.8 |
| | | 111   3.3 | 83   4.4 | | | | 80   4.6 | 77   4.7 |
| | | 16   22.6 | 15   23.7 | | | | 20   18.5 | 13   27.5 |
| | | 41   8.9 | 26   13.8 | | | Cost of Sales/Payables | 33   10.9 | 26   13.8 |
| | | 56   6.5 | 39   9.4 | | | | 41   9.0 | 43   8.6 |
| | | 3.8 | 3.9 | | | | 5.6 | 6.4 |
| | | 5.7 | 8.9 | | | Sales/Working Capital | 12.3 | 12.6 |
| | | 49.9 | 28.8 | | | | 41.6 | 72.4 |
| | | 11.3 | 25.7 | | | | 17.1 | 11.1 |
| | | (17) 3.7 | (32) 12.2 | | | EBIT/Interest | (67) 4.4 | (83) 3.7 |
| | | -1.1 | 4.8 | | | | 1.9 | 1.6 |
| | | | 6.3 | | | | 8.9 | 14.9 |
| | | | (12) 4.9 | | | Net Profit + Depr., Dep., Amort./Cur. Mat. L/T/D | (31) 3.0 | (22) 2.3 |
| | | | 3.2 | | | | 1.0 | 1.4 |
| | | .2 | .4 | | | | .3 | .3 |
| | | .7 | .6 | | | Fixed/Worth | .6 | .7 |
| | | 1.8 | 1.3 | | | | 1.6 | 1.8 |
| | | .4 | .6 | | | | .6 | .8 |
| | | 1.1 | 1.2 | | | Debt/Worth | 1.5 | 2.0 |
| | | 8.7 | 2.4 | | | | 3.9 | 5.2 |
| | | 46.9 | 40.0 | | | | 47.1 | 45.1 |
| | | (18) 11.8 | (30) 21.5 | | | % Profit Before Taxes/Tangible Net Worth | (66) 25.4 | (81) 24.1 |
| | | 2.6 | 9.7 | | | | 9.3 | 4.7 |
| | | 11.5 | 16.2 | | | | 18.8 | 14.7 |
| | | 4.6 | 10.7 | | | % Profit Before Taxes/Total Assets | 8.6 | 6.8 |
| | | .8 | 4.2 | | | | 2.4 | .8 |
| | | 21.2 | 16.5 | | | | 19.4 | 28.4 |
| | | 9.5 | 10.7 | | | Sales/Net Fixed Assets | 8.1 | 10.8 |
| | | 5.5 | 3.8 | | | | 4.7 | 5.0 |
| | | 2.6 | 2.8 | | | | 2.9 | 3.1 |
| | | 2.3 | 2.1 | | | Sales/Total Assets | 2.2 | 2.5 |
| | | 1.4 | 1.4 | | | | 1.8 | 1.6 |
| | | .3 | .8 | | | | .9 | .7 |
| | | (19) .8 | (34) 1.6 | | | % Depr., Dep., Amort./Sales | (67) 1.7 | (81) 1.4 |
| | | 1.8 | 2.9 | | | | 2.8 | 2.7 |
| | | | | | | | .7 | 1.0 |
| | | | | | | % Officers', Directors' Owners' Comp/Sales | (18) 1.5 | (20) 1.6 |
| | | | | | | | 2.7 | 3.2 |
| 3316M | 15195M | 245029M | 1890007M | 144926M | 2194360M | Net Sales ($) | 4110201M | 5016861M |
| 774M | 6078M | 114430M | 874392M | 57707M | 1028434M | Total Assets ($) | 1954521M | 2363393M |

M = $ thousand    MM = $ million
See Pages 9 through 22 for Explanation of Ratios and Data

## Comparative Historical Data                                   Current Data Sorted by Sales

Current Data period headers: **15 (4/1-9/30/11)** and **57 (10/1/11-3/31/12)**

| 4/1/09-3/31/10 ALL | 4/1/10-3/31/11 ALL | 4/1/11-3/31/12 ALL | Type of Statement | 0-1MM | 1-3MM | 3-5MM | 5-10MM | 10-25MM | 25MM & OVER |
|---|---|---|---|---|---|---|---|---|---|
| 13 | 7 | 20 | Unqualified | | | | | 2 | 18 |
| 21 | 15 | 17 | Reviewed | | | 2 | 1 | 7 | 7 |
| 11 | 10 | 11 | Compiled | | 3 | 2 | 1 | 5 | |
| 12 | 7 | 3 | Tax Returns | | 1 | | 2 | | |
| 35 | 40 | 21 | Other | 1 | 2 | 2 | 2 | 4 | 10 |
| 92 | 79 | 72 | NUMBER OF STATEMENTS | 1 | 6 | 6 | 6 | 18 | 35 |
| % | % | % | **ASSETS** | % | % | % | % | % | % |
| 9.4 | 6.6 | 8.1 | Cash & Equivalents | | | | | 13.9 | 4.7 |
| 23.4 | 26.9 | 28.4 | Trade Receivables (net) | | | | | 28.8 | 27.3 |
| 28.8 | 29.9 | 26.7 | Inventory | | | | | 24.9 | 31.5 |
| 2.9 | .8 | 1.8 | All Other Current | | | | | 2.4 | 1.8 |
| 64.5 | 64.2 | 65.1 | Total Current | | | | | 69.9 | 65.4 |
| 27.1 | 27.5 | 26.8 | Fixed Assets (net) | | | | | 24.1 | 26.0 |
| 3.1 | 2.5 | 1.6 | Intangibles (net) | | | | | .2 | 3.2 |
| 5.3 | 5.8 | 6.4 | All Other Non-Current | | | | | 5.7 | 5.4 |
| 100.0 | 100.0 | 100.0 | Total | | | | | 100.0 | 100.0 |
| | | | **LIABILITIES** | | | | | | |
| 11.5 | 16.0 | 11.3 | Notes Payable-Short Term | | | | | 11.0 | 13.4 |
| 3.0 | 3.0 | 2.0 | Cur. Mat.-L.T.D. | | | | | 1.9 | 1.2 |
| 14.4 | 17.1 | 15.8 | Trade Payables | | | | | 13.9 | 15.3 |
| .2 | .1 | .3 | Income Taxes Payable | | | | | .4 | .5 |
| 7.0 | 7.9 | 8.1 | All Other Current | | | | | 6.9 | 9.0 |
| 36.2 | 44.0 | 37.5 | Total Current | | | | | 34.1 | 39.3 |
| 12.8 | 16.0 | 15.6 | Long-Term Debt | | | | | 11.4 | 14.9 |
| .7 | .4 | .7 | Deferred Taxes | | | | | .7 | .9 |
| 7.0 | 9.0 | 7.1 | All Other Non-Current | | | | | 3.6 | 10.4 |
| 43.3 | 30.6 | 39.0 | Net Worth | | | | | 50.3 | 34.5 |
| 100.0 | 100.0 | 100.0 | Total Liabilties & Net Worth | | | | | 100.0 | 100.0 |
| | | | **INCOME DATA** | | | | | | |
| 100.0 | 100.0 | 100.0 | Net Sales | | | | | 100.0 | 100.0 |
| 20.8 | 22.1 | 21.6 | Gross Profit | | | | | 23.7 | 16.1 |
| 18.3 | 16.9 | 15.9 | Operating Expenses | | | | | 15.9 | 10.4 |
| 2.4 | 5.2 | 5.7 | Operating Profit | | | | | 7.7 | 5.7 |
| 1.0 | 1.2 | .6 | All Other Expenses (net) | | | | | .5 | 1.0 |
| 1.4 | 4.0 | 5.1 | Profit Before Taxes | | | | | 7.2 | 4.7 |
| | | | **RATIOS** | | | | | | |
| 3.9 | 2.3 | 3.2 | Current | | | | | 5.4 | 2.5 |
| 1.8 | 1.3 | 1.8 | | | | | | 2.2 | 1.7 |
| 1.1 | 1.1 | 1.2 | | | | | | 1.1 | 1.2 |
| 1.8 | 1.3 | 1.7 | Quick | | | | | 3.2 | 1.2 |
| .8 | .7 | 1.0 | | | | | | 1.3 | .8 |
| .5 | .4 | .7 | | | | | | .5 | .7 |
| 29 12.7 | 38 9.7 | 38 9.7 | Sales/Receivables | | | | | 39 9.4 | 35 10.5 |
| 43 8.6 | 46 7.9 | 47 7.7 | | | | | | 49 7.5 | 45 8.2 |
| 55 6.7 | 55 6.7 | 61 6.0 | | | | | | 78 4.7 | 57 6.4 |
| 33 11.0 | 36 10.2 | 30 12.0 | Cost of Sales/Inventory | | | | | 38 9.6 | 36 10.2 |
| 61 6.0 | 58 6.3 | 56 6.5 | | | | | | 51 7.2 | 61 6.0 |
| 86 4.2 | 87 4.2 | 81 4.5 | | | | | | 74 4.9 | 81 4.5 |
| 14 25.6 | 21 17.0 | 18 20.8 | Cost of Sales/Payables | | | | | 14 26.4 | 23 15.7 |
| 24 15.1 | 32 11.5 | 30 12.3 | | | | | | 28 13.1 | 29 12.8 |
| 44 8.4 | 47 7.8 | 44 8.3 | | | | | | 45 8.1 | 39 9.4 |
| 3.8 | 4.9 | 4.3 | Sales/Working Capital | | | | | 3.4 | 5.2 |
| 7.9 | 13.7 | 8.6 | | | | | | 5.7 | 9.0 |
| 52.4 | 41.4 | 34.7 | | | | | | 79.2 | 22.4 |
| 7.0 | 9.2 | 16.8 | EBIT/Interest | | | | | 37.7 | 20.6 |
| (82) 2.2 | (73) 3.3 | (63) 7.7 | | | | | (15) | 7.7 | (34) 10.6 |
| -1.1 | 1.5 | 2.9 | | | | | | 2.9 | 4.0 |
| 13.3 | 4.9 | 8.3 | Net Profit + Depr., Dep., Amort./Cur. Mat. L/T/D | | | | | | 30.6 |
| (22) 2.8 | (16) 3.2 | (21) 5.4 | | | | | | | (13) 5.6 |
| .3 | 1.9 | 3.3 | | | | | | | 4.9 |
| .3 | .4 | .4 | Fixed/Worth | | | | | .1 | .4 |
| .6 | .9 | .7 | | | | | | .5 | .6 |
| 1.8 | 1.9 | 1.7 | | | | | | 1.6 | 1.7 |
| .5 | .9 | .6 | Debt/Worth | | | | | .4 | .8 |
| 1.6 | 2.0 | 1.4 | | | | | | 1.1 | 1.7 |
| 3.4 | 7.3 | 8.3 | | | | | | 3.5 | 8.9 |
| 24.0 | 38.6 | 43.2 | % Profit Before Taxes/Tangible Net Worth | | | | | 49.2 | 40.4 |
| (82) 8.6 | (69) 19.0 | (59) 23.2 | | | | | | 29.1 | (27) 23.2 |
| -7.8 | 3.8 | 6.3 | | | | | | 11.2 | 9.7 |
| 8.2 | 13.4 | 15.6 | % Profit Before Taxes/Total Assets | | | | | 21.1 | 14.5 |
| 3.0 | 5.1 | 10.2 | | | | | | 10.9 | 10.0 |
| -5.0 | .8 | 3.5 | | | | | | 3.8 | 4.5 |
| 20.4 | 22.1 | 18.2 | Sales/Net Fixed Assets | | | | | 24.3 | 21.5 |
| 8.2 | 9.8 | 10.2 | | | | | | 10.8 | 10.9 |
| 4.0 | 4.1 | 5.3 | | | | | | 5.6 | 5.8 |
| 2.7 | 2.6 | 2.8 | Sales/Total Assets | | | | | 2.6 | 2.9 |
| 1.9 | 2.1 | 2.2 | | | | | | 2.3 | 2.2 |
| 1.4 | 1.4 | 1.5 | | | | | | 1.4 | 1.7 |
| 1.0 | .8 | .6 | % Depr., Dep., Amort./Sales | | | | | .8 | .7 |
| (76) 1.8 | (72) 1.7 | (65) 1.3 | | | | | | (17) 1.1 | (33) 1.4 |
| 4.0 | 3.6 | 2.8 | | | | | | 2.3 | 2.3 |
| 1.5 | 1.4 | 1.3 | % Officers', Directors' Owners' Comp/Sales | | | | | | |
| (25) 2.3 | (16) 2.7 | (15) 5.0 | | | | | | | |
| 4.2 | 4.7 | 6.7 | | | | | | | |
| 4122993M | 2931624M | 4492833M | Net Sales ($) | 9M | 11630M | 24176M | 42958M | 320459M | 4093601M |
| 2133776M | 1526783M | 2081815M | Total Assets ($) | 24M | 3857M | 23233M | 28817M | 174744M | 1851140M |

M = $ thousand    MM = $ million
See Pages 9 through 22 for Explanation of Ratios and Data

## Current Data Sorted by Assets | Comparative Historical Data

| 0-500M | 500M-2MM | 2-10MM | 10-50MM | 50-100MM | 100-250MM | Type of Statement | | 4/1/07-3/31/08 ALL | 4/1/08-3/31/09 ALL |
|---|---|---|---|---|---|---|---|---|---|
| | | | 2 | 1 | 1 | Unqualified | | 14 | 17 |
| | 2 | 3 | 2 | 1 | | Reviewed | | 8 | 10 |
| | 2 | 1 | 1 | | | Compiled | | 8 | 1 |
| | 2 | | | | | Tax Returns | | 1 | 4 |
| | 2 | | 13 | 3 | 2 | Other | | 17 | 8 |
| | 9 (4/1-9/30/11) | | 29 (10/1/11-3/31/12) | | | | | | |
| 6 | 6 | 6 | 18 | 5 | 3 | NUMBER OF STATEMENTS | | 48 | 40 |
| % | % | % | % | % | % | | | % | % |
| | | | | | | **ASSETS** | | | |
| | | | 7.1 | | | Cash & Equivalents | | 8.0 | 7.8 |
| | | | 25.7 | | | Trade Receivables (net) | | 26.5 | 24.0 |
| | | | 32.8 | | | Inventory | | 31.7 | 35.1 |
| | | | .8 | | | All Other Current | | 2.3 | 3.9 |
| | | | 66.5 | | | Total Current | | 68.4 | 70.8 |
| | | | 25.5 | | | Fixed Assets (net) | | 22.8 | 21.6 |
| | | | 5.1 | | | Intangibles (net) | | 1.4 | 2.2 |
| | | | 3.0 | | | All Other Non-Current | | 7.4 | 5.4 |
| | | | 100.0 | | | Total | | 100.0 | 100.0 |
| | | | | | | **LIABILITIES** | | | |
| | | | 8.2 | | | Notes Payable-Short Term | | 12.3 | 16.7 |
| | | | 1.7 | | | Cur. Mat.-L.T.D. | | 2.5 | 4.1 |
| | | | 15.5 | | | Trade Payables | | 16.1 | 14.0 |
| | | | .1 | | | Income Taxes Payable | | .3 | .2 |
| | | | 6.7 | | | All Other Current | | 5.2 | 5.5 |
| | | | 32.3 | | | Total Current | | 36.3 | 40.5 |
| | | | 11.5 | | | Long-Term Debt | | 9.7 | 10.7 |
| | | | .5 | | | Deferred Taxes | | .5 | .4 |
| | | | 3.6 | | | All Other Non-Current | | 3.2 | 6.7 |
| | | | 52.2 | | | Net Worth | | 50.3 | 41.7 |
| | | | 100.0 | | | Total Liabilities & Net Worth | | 100.0 | 100.0 |
| | | | | | | **INCOME DATA** | | | |
| | | | 100.0 | | | Net Sales | | 100.0 | 100.0 |
| | | | 19.4 | | | Gross Profit | | 20.0 | 19.2 |
| | | | 10.9 | | | Operating Expenses | | 14.5 | 15.7 |
| | | | 8.5 | | | Operating Profit | | 5.5 | 3.5 |
| | | | 1.2 | | | All Other Expenses (net) | | .4 | .6 |
| | | | 7.2 | | | Profit Before Taxes | | 5.1 | 2.9 |
| | | | | | | **RATIOS** | | | |
| | | | 4.9 | | | | | 4.3 | 4.9 |
| | | | 2.3 | | | Current | | 2.0 | 1.7 |
| | | | 1.2 | | | | | 1.3 | 1.1 |
| | | | 1.8 | | | | | 1.8 | 2.1 |
| | | | 1.4 | | | Quick | | 1.0 | .8 |
| | | | .7 | | | | | .5 | .4 |
| | | 38 | 9.6 | | | | 37 | 10.0 | 26 14.2 |
| | | 45 | 8.2 | | | Sales/Receivables | 44 | 8.3 | 36 10.1 |
| | | 51 | 7.1 | | | | 53 | 6.9 | 50 7.3 |
| | | 42 | 8.6 | | | | 43 | 8.5 | 39 9.3 |
| | | 78 | 4.7 | | | Cost of Sales/Inventory | 69 | 5.3 | 69 5.3 |
| | | 111 | 3.3 | | | | 100 | 3.7 | 97 3.8 |
| | | 14 | 25.7 | | | | 17 | 21.3 | 12 31.0 |
| | | 19 | 19.2 | | | Cost of Sales/Payables | 30 | 12.0 | 25 14.4 |
| | | 49 | 7.5 | | | | 45 | 8.1 | 39 9.3 |
| | | | 3.5 | | | | | 3.7 | 4.6 |
| | | | 5.4 | | | Sales/Working Capital | | 6.0 | 8.6 |
| | | | 14.7 | | | | | 14.7 | 28.4 |
| | | | 57.6 | | | | | 15.7 | 8.0 |
| | | (16) | 15.2 | | | EBIT/Interest | (37) | 4.6 | (33) 1.8 |
| | | | 6.0 | | | | | 1.8 | -1.6 |
| | | | | | | Net Profit + Depr., Dep., | | 3.5 | 2.4 |
| | | | | | | Amort./Cur. Mat. L/T/D | (12) | 1.8 | (12) 1.0 |
| | | | | | | | | .9 | .0 |
| | | | .3 | | | | | .2 | .1 |
| | | | .5 | | | Fixed/Worth | | .3 | .4 |
| | | | 1.3 | | | | | 1.0 | 1.0 |
| | | | .4 | | | | | .4 | .4 |
| | | | .7 | | | Debt/Worth | | 1.0 | 1.6 |
| | | | 3.5 | | | | | 2.8 | 4.8 |
| | | | 34.6 | | | % Profit Before Taxes/Tangible | | 32.6 | 37.1 |
| | | (16) | 26.0 | | | Net Worth | (46) | 18.7 | (35) 13.4 |
| | | | 17.0 | | | | | 7.5 | -4.3 |
| | | | 19.4 | | | % Profit Before Taxes/Total | | 20.1 | 17.7 |
| | | | 15.3 | | | Assets | | 7.7 | 4.2 |
| | | | 5.2 | | | | | 2.7 | -2.1 |
| | | | 34.7 | | | | | 23.9 | 57.8 |
| | | | 8.3 | | | Sales/Net Fixed Assets | | 11.7 | 14.2 |
| | | | 4.9 | | | | | 5.6 | 6.7 |
| | | | 2.5 | | | | | 2.8 | 2.9 |
| | | | 1.8 | | | Sales/Total Assets | | 2.0 | 2.2 |
| | | | 1.6 | | | | | 1.4 | 1.8 |
| | | | .4 | | | | | .9 | .4 |
| | | (16) | 1.3 | | | % Depr., Dep., Amort./Sales | (41) | 1.6 | (32) 1.5 |
| | | | 2.3 | | | | | 2.4 | 2.8 |
| | | | | | | | | 1.7 | |
| | | | | | | % Officers', Directors' | (12) | 3.7 | |
| | | | | | | Owners' Comp/Sales | | 5.2 | |
| | 22950M | 84682M | 1177583M | 513895M | 938726M | Net Sales ($) | | 2122318M | 2521552M |
| | 8463M | 33557M | 567255M | 282913M | 469028M | Total Assets ($) | | 1217935M | 1253196M |

M = $ thousand    MM = $ million
See Pages 9 through 22 for Explanation of Ratios and Data

**Comparative Historical Data**                **Current Data Sorted by Sales**

| | | | Type of Statement | 0-1MM | 1-3MM | 3-5MM | 5-10MM | 10-25MM | 25MM & OVER |
|---|---|---|---|---|---|---|---|---|---|
| 5 | 6 | 4 | Unqualified | | | | | | 4 |
| 8 | 12 | 8 | Reviewed | | 1 | 1 | 2 | 2 | 2 |
| 4 | 5 | 4 | Compiled | | 1 | 1 | 1 | | 1 |
| 6 | 1 | 2 | Tax Returns | | | | 2 | | |
| 18 | 13 | 20 | Other | | | | | 2 | 18 |
| 4/1/09-3/31/10 ALL | 4/1/10-3/31/11 ALL | 4/1/11-3/31/12 ALL | | | 9 (4/1-9/30/11) | | 29 (10/1/11-3/31/12) | | |
| 41 | 37 | 38 | **NUMBER OF STATEMENTS** | | 2 | 2 | 5 | 4 | 25 |
| % | % | % | **ASSETS** | % | % | % | % | % | % |
| 9.3 | 7.4 | 6.6 | Cash & Equivalents | | | | | | 6.5 |
| 27.2 | 26.7 | 28.5 | Trade Receivables (net) | | | | | | 24.8 |
| 27.3 | 35.8 | 32.3 | Inventory | | | | | | 33.6 |
| 4.4 | 1.8 | 1.2 | All Other Current | | | | | | .6 |
| 68.2 | 71.7 | 68.7 | Total Current | | | | | | 65.5 |
| 21.7 | 22.5 | 25.1 | Fixed Assets (net) | | | | | | 28.5 |
| 1.8 | 1.5 | 3.6 | Intangibles (net) | | | | | | 3.2 |
| 8.4 | 4.4 | 2.6 | All Other Non-Current | | | | | | 2.8 |
| 100.0 | 100.0 | 100.0 | Total | | | | | | 100.0 |
| | | | **LIABILITIES** | | | | | | |
| 14.8 | 14.7 | 9.2 | Notes Payable-Short Term | | | | | | 9.6 |
| 3.1 | 1.9 | 1.5 | Cur. Mat.-L.T.D. | | | | | | 1.6 |
| 17.8 | 19.4 | 18.5 | Trade Payables | | | | | | 15.6 |
| .1 | .1 | .1 | Income Taxes Payable | | | | | | .2 |
| 5.4 | 7.8 | 6.6 | All Other Current | | | | | | 6.4 |
| 41.1 | 43.9 | 36.0 | Total Current | | | | | | 33.4 |
| 9.2 | 12.2 | 11.7 | Long-Term Debt | | | | | | 12.0 |
| .4 | .5 | .6 | Deferred Taxes | | | | | | .7 |
| 13.7 | 3.5 | 3.6 | All Other Non-Current | | | | | | 2.2 |
| 35.5 | 39.9 | 48.2 | Net Worth | | | | | | 51.7 |
| 100.0 | 100.0 | 100.0 | Total Liabilities & Net Worth | | | | | | 100.0 |
| | | | **INCOME DATA** | | | | | | |
| 100.0 | 100.0 | 100.0 | Net Sales | | | | | | 100.0 |
| 21.8 | 23.4 | 19.9 | Gross Profit | | | | | | 16.6 |
| 21.4 | 18.7 | 14.0 | Operating Expenses | | | | | | 9.3 |
| .3 | 4.8 | 5.8 | Operating Profit | | | | | | 7.3 |
| .2 | .6 | .9 | All Other Expenses (net) | | | | | | .8 |
| .1 | 4.2 | 5.0 | Profit Before Taxes | | | | | | 6.4 |
| | | | **RATIOS** | | | | | | |
| 3.8 | 3.5 | 3.7 | Current | | | | | | 4.5 |
| 1.9 | 1.5 | 2.2 | | | | | | | 2.3 |
| 1.1 | 1.1 | 1.2 | | | | | | | 1.2 |
| 2.3 | 1.5 | 1.6 | Quick | | | | | | 1.7 |
| .9 | .7 | 1.2 | | | | | | | 1.2 |
| .6 | .5 | .6 | | | | | | | .6 |
| 34 10.8 | 37 10.0 | 34 10.6 | Sales/Receivables | | | | | | 33 11.0 |
| 41 8.8 | 46 7.9 | 46 8.0 | | | | | | | 41 8.8 |
| 54 6.8 | 53 6.9 | 56 6.5 | | | | | | | 48 7.6 |
| 34 10.8 | 49 7.4 | 42 8.7 | Cost of Sales/Inventory | | | | | | 41 8.8 |
| 55 6.6 | 68 5.3 | 66 5.5 | | | | | | | 68 5.4 |
| 96 3.8 | 135 2.7 | 107 3.4 | | | | | | | 118 3.1 |
| 13 28.4 | 23 15.7 | 17 21.3 | Cost of Sales/Payables | | | | | | 16 23.0 |
| 26 14.2 | 37 9.7 | 31 11.8 | | | | | | | 24 15.0 |
| 60 6.1 | 58 6.3 | 53 6.9 | | | | | | | 45 8.2 |
| 3.6 | 4.2 | 3.9 | Sales/Working Capital | | | | | | 3.5 |
| 8.2 | 7.9 | 6.0 | | | | | | | 6.3 |
| 62.3 | 78.7 | 24.9 | | | | | | | 27.3 |
| 11.4 | 17.6 | 30.1 | EBIT/Interest | | | | | | 65.1 |
| (33) 2.6 | (34) 4.3 | (34) 9.5 | | | | | | (23) | 10.8 |
| -4.2 | 1.2 | 2.3 | | | | | | | 4.9 |
| | | | Net Profit + Depr., Dep., Amort./Cur. Mat. L/T/D | | | | | | |
| .1 | .2 | .2 | Fixed/Worth | | | | | | .3 |
| .5 | .5 | .6 | | | | | | | .6 |
| 1.1 | 1.6 | 1.1 | | | | | | | 1.2 |
| .5 | .6 | .5 | Debt/Worth | | | | | | .4 |
| 1.4 | 1.7 | 1.0 | | | | | | | 1.0 |
| 4.7 | 5.8 | 3.0 | | | | | | | 2.4 |
| 29.4 | 51.2 | 30.2 | % Profit Before Taxes/Tangible Net Worth | | | | | | 35.0 |
| (36) 9.7 | (36) 17.8 | (34) 21.9 | | | | | | (23) | 24.4 |
| -17.2 | 1.7 | 8.9 | | | | | | | 13.0 |
| 7.5 | 15.5 | 17.5 | % Profit Before Taxes/Total Assets | | | | | | 18.9 |
| 2.8 | 5.0 | 7.0 | | | | | | | 14.9 |
| -10.2 | 1.0 | 2.3 | | | | | | | 4.3 |
| 66.4 | 34.6 | 31.2 | Sales/Net Fixed Assets | | | | | | 15.6 |
| 11.6 | 13.5 | 8.0 | | | | | | | 8.0 |
| 6.4 | 5.3 | 5.1 | | | | | | | 5.1 |
| 3.0 | 3.0 | 2.8 | Sales/Total Assets | | | | | | 2.6 |
| 2.0 | 2.0 | 1.9 | | | | | | | 1.8 |
| 1.5 | 1.5 | 1.6 | | | | | | | 1.6 |
| .8 | 1.0 | .4 | % Depr., Dep., Amort./Sales | | | | | | .7 |
| (31) 1.5 | (32) 1.5 | (35) 1.3 | | | | | | (24) | 1.3 |
| 2.5 | 2.9 | 2.8 | | | | | | | 2.3 |
| | | | % Officers', Directors' Owners' Comp/Sales | | | | | | |
| 2115329M | 1522054M | 2737836M | Net Sales ($) | | 3353M | 8240M | 33500M | 70001M | 2622742M |
| 1295253M | 705620M | 1361216M | Total Assets ($) | | 2297M | 3101M | 17090M | 40588M | 1298140M |

For the Current Data columns 0-1MM through 10-25MM (Assets, Liabilities, Income Data): DATA NOT AVAILABLE.

M = $ thousand     MM = $ million
See Pages 9 through 22 for Explanation of Ratios and Data

## Current Data Sorted by Assets      Comparative Historical Data

| 0-500M | 500M-2MM | 2-10MM | 10-50MM | 50-100MM | 100-250MM | Type of Statement | 4/1/07-3/31/08 ALL | 4/1/08-3/31/09 ALL |
|---|---|---|---|---|---|---|---|---|
|  |  |  | 2 | 3 | 1 | Unqualified | 5 | 7 |
|  |  | 2 | 3 |  |  | Reviewed | 4 | 2 |
|  | 1 |  | 2 |  |  | Compiled | 2 | 1 |
|  |  |  | 1 |  |  | Tax Returns | 1 |  |
|  | 1 | 1 | 4 | 3 |  | Other | 10 | 10 |
| 0 (4/1-9/30/11) |  |  | 24 (10/1/11-3/31/12) |  |  |  |  |  |
|  | 2 | 3 | 12 | 6 | 1 | **NUMBER OF STATEMENTS** | 22 | 20 |
| % | % | % | % | % | % | **ASSETS** | % | % |
|  |  |  | 10.5 |  |  | Cash & Equivalents | 8.0 | 6.8 |
|  |  |  | 28.0 |  |  | Trade Receivables (net) | 39.6 | 37.2 |
|  |  |  | 18.2 |  |  | Inventory | 23.9 | 17.5 |
|  |  |  | 2.4 |  |  | All Other Current | 1.4 | 2.6 |
|  |  |  | 59.0 |  |  | Total Current | 72.9 | 64.1 |
|  |  |  | 36.4 |  |  | Fixed Assets (net) | 21.5 | 30.1 |
|  |  |  | 1.0 |  |  | Intangibles (net) | 1.9 | 2.2 |
|  |  |  | 3.6 |  |  | All Other Non-Current | 3.7 | 3.6 |
|  |  |  | 100.0 |  |  | Total | 100.0 | 100.0 |
|  |  |  |  |  |  | **LIABILITIES** |  |  |
|  |  |  | 19.1 |  |  | Notes Payable-Short Term | 16.7 | 18.8 |
|  |  |  | 2.9 |  |  | Cur. Mat.-L.T.D. | 1.9 | 7.4 |
|  |  |  | 9.6 |  |  | Trade Payables | 20.6 | 17.1 |
|  |  |  | .5 |  |  | Income Taxes Payable | .1 | .0 |
|  |  |  | 6.4 |  |  | All Other Current | 7.1 | 12.6 |
|  |  |  | 38.5 |  |  | Total Current | 46.4 | 55.9 |
|  |  |  | 12.5 |  |  | Long-Term Debt | 14.3 | 17.5 |
|  |  |  | .1 |  |  | Deferred Taxes | .2 | .1 |
|  |  |  | 3.1 |  |  | All Other Non-Current | 3.8 | 5.5 |
|  |  |  | 45.9 |  |  | Net Worth | 35.3 | 20.9 |
|  |  |  | 100.0 |  |  | Total Liabilities & Net Worth | 100.0 | 100.0 |
|  |  |  |  |  |  | **INCOME DATA** |  |  |
|  |  |  | 100.0 |  |  | Net Sales | 100.0 | 100.0 |
|  |  |  | 13.2 |  |  | Gross Profit | 21.6 | 14.6 |
|  |  |  | 13.1 |  |  | Operating Expenses | 14.8 | 12.9 |
|  |  |  | .1 |  |  | Operating Profit | 6.8 | 1.7 |
|  |  |  | .9 |  |  | All Other Expenses (net) | 1.7 | 1.4 |
|  |  |  | -.8 |  |  | Profit Before Taxes | 5.2 | .2 |
|  |  |  |  |  |  | **RATIOS** |  |  |
|  |  |  | 3.8 |  |  | Current | 2.3 | 1.9 |
|  |  |  | 1.2 |  |  |  | 1.5 | 1.1 |
|  |  |  | 1.0 |  |  |  | 1.2 | .8 |
|  |  |  | 2.7 |  |  | Quick | 1.7 | 1.6 |
|  |  |  | .8 |  |  |  | 1.2 | .6 |
|  |  |  | .4 |  |  |  | .6 | .4 |
|  |  | 31 | 11.9 |  |  | Sales/Receivables | 31   11.7 | 18   20.4 |
|  |  | 42 | 8.6 |  |  |  | 45   8.1 | 27   13.3 |
|  |  | 61 | 6.0 |  |  |  | 55   6.6 | 41   8.9 |
|  |  | 13 | 28.2 |  |  | Cost of Sales/Inventory | 10   36.1 | 5   75.6 |
|  |  | 28 | 13.1 |  |  |  | 35   10.5 | 13   27.1 |
|  |  | 50 | 7.3 |  |  |  | 70   5.2 | 43   8.5 |
|  |  | 6 | 60.8 |  |  | Cost of Sales/Payables | 17   21.0 | 6   57.0 |
|  |  | 15 | 23.8 |  |  |  | 30   12.2 | 14   26.1 |
|  |  | 29 | 12.4 |  |  |  | 38   9.6 | 29   12.8 |
|  |  |  | 10.5 |  |  | Sales/Working Capital | 8.7 | 13.6 |
|  |  |  | 38.1 |  |  |  | 13.4 | 43.2 |
|  |  |  | NM |  |  |  | 23.0 | -22.8 |
|  |  |  | 7.2 |  |  | EBIT/Interest | (20)   16.2 | (19)   8.0 |
|  |  | (11) | 3.4 |  |  |  | 5.5 | 2.6 |
|  |  |  | .2 |  |  |  | 1.4 | 1.1 |
|  |  |  |  |  |  | Net Profit + Depr., Dep., Amort./Cur. Mat. L/T/D |  |  |
|  |  |  | .4 |  |  | Fixed/Worth | .3 | .5 |
|  |  |  | 1.0 |  |  |  | .4 | 1.9 |
|  |  |  | 1.5 |  |  |  | 1.6 | NM |
|  |  |  | .3 |  |  | Debt/Worth | .6 | 1.0 |
|  |  |  | 1.3 |  |  |  | 2.2 | 4.7 |
|  |  |  | 3.8 |  |  |  | 12.5 | NM |
|  |  |  | 43.5 |  |  | % Profit Before Taxes/Tangible Net Worth | 46.6 | 90.0 |
|  |  |  | 20.5 |  |  |  | (19)   40.1 | (15)   12.3 |
|  |  |  | -11.0 |  |  |  | 13.6 | 4.0 |
|  |  |  | 11.3 |  |  | % Profit Before Taxes/Total Assets | 23.3 | 15.5 |
|  |  |  | 5.4 |  |  |  | 14.5 | 4.3 |
|  |  |  | -2.6 |  |  |  | 3.4 | .2 |
|  |  |  | 33.0 |  |  | Sales/Net Fixed Assets | 57.8 | 42.4 |
|  |  |  | 9.4 |  |  |  | 18.9 | 18.9 |
|  |  |  | 2.3 |  |  |  | 7.9 | 7.7 |
|  |  |  | 4.0 |  |  | Sales/Total Assets | 4.0 | 5.7 |
|  |  |  | 2.9 |  |  |  | 2.8 | 4.0 |
|  |  |  | 1.5 |  |  |  | 2.1 | 3.3 |
|  |  |  | .3 |  |  | % Depr., Dep., Amort./Sales | .5 | .4 |
|  |  |  | 1.5 |  |  |  | (20)   1.0 | (18)   1.1 |
|  |  |  | 5.3 |  |  |  | 1.8 | 1.8 |
|  |  |  |  |  |  | % Officers', Directors' Owners' Comp/Sales |  |  |
|  | 13561M | 54306M | 905570M | 1602840M | 337522M | Net Sales ($) | 1744102M | 2878759M |
|  | 2321M | 17575M | 296327M | 430110M | 107753M | Total Assets ($) | 579780M | 776183M |

*DATA NOT AVAILABLE* (for the 0-500M column)

M = $ thousand    MM = $ million
See Pages 9 through 22 for Explanation of Ratios and Data

## Comparative Historical Data                    Current Data Sorted by Sales

Note: For all sections below, the columns **0-1MM** and **1-3MM** display "DATA NOT AVAILABLE" (shown as vertical lettering in the source) and are left blank here.

Current Data period groupings: **0 (4/1-9/30/11)** spans 0-1MM, 1-3MM; **24 (10/1/11-3/31/12)** spans 3-5MM, 5-10MM, 10-25MM, 25MM & OVER.

| 4/1/09-3/31/10 ALL | 4/1/10-3/31/11 ALL | 4/1/11-3/31/12 ALL | Type of Statement | 0-1MM | 1-3MM | 3-5MM | 5-10MM | 10-25MM | 25MM & OVER |
|---|---|---|---|---|---|---|---|---|---|
| 10 | 8 | 6 | Unqualified |  |  |  |  |  | 6 |
| 5 | 3 | 5 | Reviewed |  |  |  |  | 1 | 4 |
| 2 | 2 | 3 | Compiled |  |  | 1 |  | 1 | 1 |
|  |  | 1 | Tax Returns |  |  |  |  |  | 1 |
| 11 | 8 | 9 | Other |  |  |  | 1 | 3 | 5 |
| 28 | 21 | 24 | **NUMBER OF STATEMENTS** |  |  | 1 | 1 | 5 | 17 |

| % | % | % | ASSETS | % | % | % | % | % | % |
|---|---|---|---|---|---|---|---|---|---|
| 5.2 | 4.9 | 8.1 | Cash & Equivalents |  |  |  |  |  | 6.8 |
| 32.0 | 31.5 | 32.1 | Trade Receivables (net) |  |  |  |  |  | 30.8 |
| 20.2 | 23.8 | 22.7 | Inventory |  |  |  |  |  | 28.9 |
| 3.4 | 1.6 | 2.6 | All Other Current |  |  |  |  |  | 2.2 |
| 60.9 | 61.8 | 65.5 | Total Current |  |  |  |  |  | 68.8 |
| 34.0 | 35.0 | 30.2 | Fixed Assets (net) |  |  |  |  |  | 26.1 |
| .9 | 1.2 | 1.5 | Intangibles (net) |  |  |  |  |  | 1.7 |
| 4.2 | 2.0 | 2.8 | All Other Non-Current |  |  |  |  |  | 3.5 |
| 100.0 | 100.0 | 100.0 | Total |  |  |  |  |  | 100.0 |

| | | | LIABILITIES | | | | | | |
|---|---|---|---|---|---|---|---|---|---|
| 19.0 | 16.8 | 18.9 | Notes Payable-Short Term |  |  |  |  |  | 20.3 |
| 2.9 | 2.8 | 3.3 | Cur. Mat.-L.T.D. |  |  |  |  |  | 3.7 |
| 18.1 | 19.2 | 22.6 | Trade Payables |  |  |  |  |  | 17.6 |
| .1 | .1 | .3 | Income Taxes Payable |  |  |  |  |  | .4 |
| 7.1 | 6.1 | 6.8 | All Other Current |  |  |  |  |  | 6.8 |
| 47.2 | 45.0 | 52.0 | Total Current |  |  |  |  |  | 48.8 |
| 14.1 | 16.0 | 13.2 | Long-Term Debt |  |  |  |  |  | 13.0 |
| .5 | .2 | .3 | Deferred Taxes |  |  |  |  |  | .4 |
| 4.0 | 3.3 | 2.6 | All Other Non-Current |  |  |  |  |  | 3.2 |
| 34.2 | 35.5 | 32.1 | Net Worth |  |  |  |  |  | 34.7 |
| 100.0 | 100.0 | 100.0 | Total Liabilties & Net Worth |  |  |  |  |  | 100.0 |

| | | | INCOME DATA | | | | | | |
|---|---|---|---|---|---|---|---|---|---|
| 100.0 | 100.0 | 100.0 | Net Sales |  |  |  |  |  | 100.0 |
| 17.3 | 13.1 | 14.8 | Gross Profit |  |  |  |  |  | 10.6 |
| 15.2 | 10.0 | 13.7 | Operating Expenses |  |  |  |  |  | 7.8 |
| 2.1 | 3.1 | 1.1 | Operating Profit |  |  |  |  |  | 2.8 |
| .8 | 1.5 | .7 | All Other Expenses (net) |  |  |  |  |  | .5 |
| 1.3 | 1.6 | .4 | Profit Before Taxes |  |  |  |  |  | 2.3 |

| | | | RATIOS | | | | | | |
|---|---|---|---|---|---|---|---|---|---|
| 2.1 | 2.1 | 2.0 | | | | | | | 2.8 |
| 1.4 | 1.3 | 1.2 | Current | | | | | | 1.2 |
| .9 | 1.0 | 1.0 | | | | | | | 1.1 |
| 1.4 | 1.2 | 1.3 | | | | | | | 1.2 |
| .8 | .7 | .7 | Quick | | | | | | .7 |
| .4 | .5 | .5 | | | | | | | .5 |
| 39  9.4 | 33  11.1 | 27  13.5 | | | | | | | 23  16.1 |
| 46  8.0 | 43  8.6 | 33  11.2 | Sales/Receivables | | | | | | 31  11.6 |
| 60  6.1 | 51  7.1 | 49  7.5 | | | | | | | 43  8.5 |
| 16  22.9 | 23  15.7 | 13  28.2 | | | | | | | 22  16.7 |
| 34  10.6 | 30  12.3 | 32  11.4 | Cost of Sales/Inventory | | | | | | 32  11.4 |
| 63  5.8 | 53  6.9 | 54  6.8 | | | | | | | 51  7.1 |
| 14  26.4 | 17  21.3 | 13  28.8 | | | | | | | 7  52.2 |
| 30  12.2 | 28  13.0 | 25  14.7 | Cost of Sales/Payables | | | | | | 16  23.4 |
| 48  7.7 | 38  9.5 | 40  9.1 | | | | | | | 32  11.4 |
| 8.0 | 8.6 | 11.5 | | | | | | | 13.4 |
| 14.3 | 24.8 | 38.1 | Sales/Working Capital | | | | | | 29.7 |
| -43.2 | NM | NM | | | | | | | 72.9 |
| 14.7 | 8.0 | 7.9 | | | | | | | 11.7 |
| (25) 3.4 | (20) 4.6 | (23) 5.1 | EBIT/Interest | | | | | (16) | 5.5 |
| -1.9 | -.3 | .2 | | | | | | | 2.0 |
| 25.6 | | | | | | | | | |
| (10) 2.6 | | | Net Profit + Depr., Dep., Amort./Cur. Mat. L/T/D | | | | | | |
| -1.1 | | | | | | | | | |
| .5 | .5 | .5 | | | | | | | .4 |
| 1.0 | 1.0 | 1.1 | Fixed/Worth | | | | | | 1.0 |
| 8.8 | 2.1 | 1.7 | | | | | | | 1.7 |
| .8 | .9 | .8 | | | | | | | 1.0 |
| 2.0 | 2.2 | 2.2 | Debt/Worth | | | | | | 2.2 |
| 10.6 | 5.2 | 6.1 | | | | | | | 7.8 |
| 37.7 | 51.3 | 57.2 | | | | | | | 60.4 |
| (24) 21.0 | (20) 16.9 | (22) 24.4 | % Profit Before Taxes/Tangible Net Worth | | | | | (16) | 26.5 |
| .5 | .7 | -2.2 | | | | | | | 9.1 |
| 11.5 | 10.5 | 11.3 | | | | | | | 13.0 |
| 6.5 | 4.6 | 6.0 | % Profit Before Taxes/Total Assets | | | | | | 6.2 |
| -3.2 | -1.0 | -3.0 | | | | | | | 2.5 |
| 15.8 | 22.9 | 36.8 | | | | | | | 36.2 |
| 7.2 | 9.1 | 14.2 | Sales/Net Fixed Assets | | | | | | 15.6 |
| 4.1 | 3.1 | 4.2 | | | | | | | 9.5 |
| 2.8 | 3.4 | 4.3 | | | | | | | 4.2 |
| 2.3 | 2.7 | 3.4 | Sales/Total Assets | | | | | | 3.5 |
| 1.9 | 1.7 | 2.0 | | | | | | | 2.9 |
| .8 | .6 | .4 | | | | | | | .3 |
| (26) 1.9 | (18) 1.5 | (23) 1.1 | % Depr., Dep., Amort./Sales | | | | | | .9 |
| 3.2 | 3.3 | 2.9 | | | | | | | 1.7 |
| | | | % Officers', Directors' Owners' Comp/Sales | | | | | | |
| 1350586M | 2009923M | 2913799M | Net Sales ($) | | | 4705M | 8856M | 75049M | 2825189M |
| 593606M | 850828M | 854086M | Total Assets ($) | | | 1247M | 1074M | 63145M | 788620M |

M = $ thousand    MM = $ million
See Pages 9 through 22 for Explanation of Ratios and Data

## Current Data Sorted by Assets / Comparative Historical Data

| 0-500M | 500M-2MM | 2-10MM | 10-50MM | 50-100MM | 100-250MM | Type of Statement | 4/1/07-3/31/08 ALL | 4/1/08-3/31/09 ALL |
|---|---|---|---|---|---|---|---|---|
| | | 1 | 12 | 6 | 5 | Unqualified | 20 | 23 |
| | | 8 | 9 | 1 | | Reviewed | 8 | 8 |
| | 1 | | | | | Compiled | 4 | 6 |
| | | 1 | | | | Tax Returns | 2 | 3 |
| | 2 | 5 | 12 | 3 | 1 | Other | 44 | 46 |
| | 9 (4/1-9/30/11) | | 58 (10/1/11-3/31/12) | | | | | |
| 3 | 15 | 33 | 10 | 6 | | NUMBER OF STATEMENTS | 78 | 86 |
| % | % | % | % | % | % | **ASSETS** | % | % |
| | | 7.2 | 4.6 | 6.0 | | Cash & Equivalents | 4.2 | 4.6 |
| | | 31.7 | 26.1 | 25.4 | | Trade Receivables (net) | 29.9 | 25.8 |
| | | 35.0 | 24.5 | 19.2 | | Inventory | 24.5 | 26.2 |
| | | 1.9 | 1.5 | 3.5 | | All Other Current | 2.2 | 3.3 |
| | | 75.8 | 56.7 | 54.1 | | Total Current | 60.9 | 59.8 |
| | | 21.6 | 34.2 | 32.8 | | Fixed Assets (net) | 31.8 | 30.5 |
| | | .9 | 5.7 | 3.2 | | Intangibles (net) | 3.5 | 2.6 |
| | | 1.7 | 3.4 | 9.9 | | All Other Non-Current | 3.8 | 7.1 |
| | | 100.0 | 100.0 | 100.0 | | Total | 100.0 | 100.0 |
| | | | | | | **LIABILITIES** | | |
| | | 18.5 | 12.9 | 7.1 | | Notes Payable-Short Term | 15.6 | 14.7 |
| | | 1.4 | 3.3 | 2.7 | | Cur. Mat.-L.T.D. | 4.6 | 3.3 |
| | | 16.5 | 14.2 | 14.7 | | Trade Payables | 17.5 | 14.6 |
| | | .0 | .0 | .7 | | Income Taxes Payable | .2 | .2 |
| | | 11.1 | 4.6 | 8.1 | | All Other Current | 5.8 | 7.5 |
| | | 47.6 | 35.1 | 33.4 | | Total Current | 43.7 | 40.5 |
| | | 12.7 | 15.7 | 14.2 | | Long-Term Debt | 21.6 | 21.3 |
| | | .1 | .8 | 3.5 | | Deferred Taxes | .4 | .8 |
| | | 5.5 | 4.5 | 6.3 | | All Other Non-Current | 5.2 | 5.3 |
| | | 34.1 | 43.9 | 42.5 | | Net Worth | 29.1 | 32.2 |
| | | 100.0 | 100.0 | 100.0 | | Total Liabilities & Net Worth | 100.0 | 100.0 |
| | | | | | | **INCOME DATA** | | |
| | | 100.0 | 100.0 | 100.0 | | Net Sales | 100.0 | 100.0 |
| | | 18.1 | 17.6 | 19.1 | | Gross Profit | 20.1 | 18.7 |
| | | 13.2 | 11.7 | 14.3 | | Operating Expenses | 15.3 | 15.7 |
| | | 4.9 | 5.9 | 4.9 | | Operating Profit | 4.8 | 3.0 |
| | | .5 | .9 | .2 | | All Other Expenses (net) | 1.6 | 1.2 |
| | | 4.4 | 5.0 | 4.7 | | Profit Before Taxes | 3.2 | 1.8 |
| | | | | | | **RATIOS** | | |
| | | 3.2 | 2.1 | 2.5 | | | 2.1 | 2.5 |
| | | 1.5 | 1.6 | 1.9 | | Current | 1.5 | 1.7 |
| | | 1.2 | 1.1 | 1.3 | | | 1.1 | 1.1 |
| | | 2.9 | 1.4 | 1.7 | | | 1.2 | 1.3 |
| | | .8 | .9 | .8 | | Quick | .9 | .8 |
| | | .5 | .4 | .7 | | | .6 | .5 |
| | | 28  13.0 | 28  12.9 | 35  10.5 | | | 34  10.6 | 29  12.6 |
| | | 41  9.0 | 42  8.6 | 41  9.0 | | Sales/Receivables | 42  8.7 | 36  10.1 |
| | | 49  7.4 | 51  7.2 | 55  6.6 | | | 50  7.3 | 46  8.0 |
| | | 27  13.3 | 26  14.2 | 26  14.2 | | | 20  18.6 | 22  16.4 |
| | | 41  8.9 | 40  9.2 | 45  8.2 | | Cost of Sales/Inventory | 41  8.9 | 33  11.0 |
| | | 79  4.6 | 65  5.6 | 76  4.8 | | | 62  5.9 | 83  4.4 |
| | | 14  25.5 | 13  27.1 | 27  13.7 | | | 21  17.3 | 14  26.2 |
| | | 20  18.2 | 21  17.1 | 35  10.3 | | Cost of Sales/Payables | 27  13.3 | 23  16.0 |
| | | 26  13.8 | 31  11.7 | 43  8.5 | | | 36  10.2 | 31  11.9 |
| | | 4.4 | 7.8 | 5.2 | | | 8.2 | 6.4 |
| | | 11.2 | 11.0 | 6.0 | | Sales/Working Capital | 15.5 | 9.9 |
| | | 46.7 | 67.7 | 18.3 | | | 59.4 | 57.6 |
| | | 18.8 | 35.1 | 34.9 | | | 6.9 | 8.5 |
| | (14) | 6.5 | (30) 10.3 | 5.4 | | EBIT/Interest | (77) 2.9 | (81) 2.8 |
| | | 1.4 | 3.2 | 1.3 | | | 1.0 | .0 |
| | | | 6.5 | | | | 4.1 | 6.6 |
| | | | (10) 3.9 | | | Net Profit + Depr., Dep., Amort./Cur. Mat. L/T/D | (25) 2.4 | (27) 2.4 |
| | | | 1.0 | | | | .8 | .0 |
| | | .2 | .5 | .6 | | | .6 | .3 |
| | | .6 | 1.1 | .8 | | Fixed/Worth | 1.3 | .8 |
| | | 1.0 | 1.7 | 3.5 | | | 2.3 | 2.2 |
| | | .8 | .9 | .3 | | | 1.4 | .8 |
| | | 1.1 | 1.5 | 1.0 | | Debt/Worth | 3.0 | 1.9 |
| | | 3.8 | 3.2 | 26.3 | | | 7.5 | 4.7 |
| | | 35.4 | 39.6 | | | | 52.4 | 38.8 |
| | (13) | 16.5 | (29) 30.5 | | | % Profit Before Taxes/Tangible Net Worth | (67) 24.6 | (75) 14.9 |
| | | 6.7 | 12.6 | | | | 2.8 | 1.2 |
| | | 22.5 | 16.6 | 13.2 | | | 12.4 | 12.5 |
| | | 7.1 | 11.2 | 7.3 | | % Profit Before Taxes/Total Assets | 6.9 | 4.5 |
| | | 1.5 | 4.7 | 1.0 | | | .2 | -2.1 |
| | | 45.4 | 10.6 | 9.4 | | | 19.0 | 21.7 |
| | | 24.9 | 7.5 | 4.7 | | Sales/Net Fixed Assets | 7.4 | 7.8 |
| | | 4.6 | 4.4 | 4.0 | | | 4.9 | 4.5 |
| | | 4.1 | 3.2 | 2.2 | | | 3.2 | 3.1 |
| | | 2.8 | 2.2 | 1.7 | | Sales/Total Assets | 2.5 | 2.4 |
| | | 2.0 | 1.9 | 1.4 | | | 1.9 | 1.6 |
| | | .3 | 1.5 | | | | .9 | .9 |
| | (13) | .9 | (31) 1.7 | | | % Depr., Dep., Amort./Sales | (73) 1.7 | (76) 1.5 |
| | | 1.6 | 2.9 | | | | 2.8 | 3.2 |
| | | | | | | | .7 | .9 |
| | | | | | | % Officers', Directors' Owners' Comp/Sales | (19) 1.5 | (21) 2.0 |
| | | | | | | | 3.5 | 5.1 |
| | 10537M | 214648M | 1843545M | 1608828M | 1238685M | Net Sales ($) | 4455405M | 5506351M |
| | 4352M | 71790M | 738835M | 748069M | 949682M | Total Assets ($) | 1912080M | 2738973M |

*(0-500M column: DATA NOT AVAILABLE)*

M = $ thousand    MM = $ million
See Pages 9 through 22 for Explanation of Ratios and Data

## Comparative Historical Data  |  Current Data Sorted by Sales

| 4/1/09-3/31/10 ALL | 4/1/10-3/31/11 ALL | 4/1/11-3/31/12 ALL | Type of Statement | 0-1MM | 1-3MM | 3-5MM | 5-10MM | 10-25MM | 25MM & OVER |
|---|---|---|---|---|---|---|---|---|---|
| 24 | 21 | 24 | Unqualified | | 1 | | 1 | 2 | 22 |
| 10 | 15 | 18 | Reviewed | | | | | 6 | 10 |
| 3 | 5 | 1 | Compiled | | | 1 | | | |
| 3 | 4 | 1 | Tax Returns | | | 1 | | | |
| 32 | 38 | 23 | Other | 2 | 1 | | | 6 | 14 |
| | | | | | 9 (4/1-9/30/11) | | | 58 (10/1/11-3/31/12) | |
| 72 | 83 | 67 | NUMBER OF STATEMENTS | 3 | 3 | | 1 | 14 | 46 |

| % | % | % | ASSETS | % | % | % | % | % | % |
|---|---|---|---|---|---|---|---|---|---|
| 6.8 | 6.5 | 5.5 | Cash & Equivalents | | | | | 5.9 | 5.0 |
| 24.2 | 28.2 | 26.5 | Trade Receivables (net) | | | | | 27.3 | 25.9 |
| 23.7 | 25.2 | 25.0 | Inventory | | | | | 32.6 | 22.5 |
| 3.6 | 2.1 | 1.9 | All Other Current | | | | | 2.3 | 1.9 |
| 58.3 | 62.1 | 58.9 | Total Current | | | | | 68.0 | 55.3 |
| 32.7 | 31.2 | 32.3 | Fixed Assets (net) | | | | | 26.4 | 34.5 |
| 3.2 | 2.0 | 4.6 | Intangibles (net) | | | | | 3.5 | 5.5 |
| 5.8 | 4.7 | 4.2 | All Other Non-Current | | | | | 2.1 | 4.7 |
| 100.0 | 100.0 | 100.0 | Total | | | | | 100.0 | 100.0 |

(Columns 0-1MM through 5-10MM: DATA NOT AVAILABLE)

| | | | LIABILITIES | | | | | | |
|---|---|---|---|---|---|---|---|---|---|
| 14.3 | 13.2 | 13.0 | Notes Payable-Short Term | | | | | 20.1 | 10.2 |
| 4.5 | 4.4 | 3.8 | Cur. Mat.-L.T.D. | | | | | 3.7 | 2.5 |
| 14.7 | 15.9 | 15.6 | Trade Payables | | | | | 15.9 | 14.5 |
| .1 | .2 | .2 | Income Taxes Payable | | | | | .0 | .3 |
| 10.6 | 8.2 | 6.8 | All Other Current | | | | | 9.5 | 5.2 |
| 44.2 | 41.9 | 39.4 | Total Current | | | | | 49.2 | 32.7 |
| 20.7 | 17.0 | 16.8 | Long-Term Debt | | | | | 16.0 | 14.5 |
| .7 | .8 | 1.4 | Deferred Taxes | | | | | .4 | 1.9 |
| 5.8 | 7.0 | 5.2 | All Other Non-Current | | | | | 5.6 | 5.1 |
| 28.6 | 33.3 | 37.2 | Net Worth | | | | | 28.8 | 45.9 |
| 100.0 | 100.0 | 100.0 | Total Liabilities & Net Worth | | | | | 100.0 | 100.0 |

| | | | INCOME DATA | | | | | | |
|---|---|---|---|---|---|---|---|---|---|
| 100.0 | 100.0 | 100.0 | Net Sales | | | | | 100.0 | 100.0 |
| 20.9 | 20.2 | 18.9 | Gross Profit | | | | | 18.4 | 18.0 |
| 18.3 | 16.0 | 13.0 | Operating Expenses | | | | | 15.1 | 11.7 |
| 2.6 | 4.1 | 5.9 | Operating Profit | | | | | 3.4 | 6.4 |
| .9 | .6 | .7 | All Other Expenses (net) | | | | | 1.0 | .7 |
| 1.7 | 3.6 | 5.2 | Profit Before Taxes | | | | | 2.4 | 5.6 |

| | | | RATIOS | | | | | | |
|---|---|---|---|---|---|---|---|---|---|
| 2.4 | 2.5 | 2.3 | Current | | | | | 2.9 | 2.3 |
| 1.6 | 1.7 | 1.6 | | | | | | 1.4 | 1.7 |
| .9 | 1.2 | 1.2 | | | | | | .9 | 1.2 |
| 1.4 | 1.6 | 1.5 | Quick | | | | | 1.6 | 1.5 |
| .8 | .9 | .9 | | | | | | .7 | .9 |
| .4 | .5 | .5 | | | | | | .4 | .6 |
| 31  11.9 | 35  10.6 | 31  11.9 | Sales/Receivables | | | | | 26  14.3 | 33  11.2 |
| 41  8.9 | 43  8.4 | 42  8.6 | | | | | | 38  9.5 | 42  8.6 |
| 51  7.1 | 54  6.8 | 53  6.9 | | | | | | 49  7.4 | 53  6.9 |
| 25  14.6 | 25  14.4 | 26  13.8 | Cost of Sales/Inventory | | | | | 26  13.8 | 26  14.0 |
| 42  8.7 | 42  8.7 | 41  9.0 | | | | | | 48  7.6 | 40  9.2 |
| 82  4.4 | 79  4.6 | 74  4.9 | | | | | | 81  4.5 | 61  6.0 |
| 15  23.7 | 19  19.1 | 16  23.4 | Cost of Sales/Payables | | | | | 14  25.4 | 17  21.6 |
| 25  14.8 | 28  12.9 | 25  14.7 | | | | | | 21  17.1 | 27  13.4 |
| 45  8.1 | 43  8.5 | 36  10.0 | | | | | | 30  12.1 | 39  9.4 |
| 5.8 | 5.0 | 5.9 | Sales/Working Capital | | | | | 5.8 | 5.9 |
| 10.3 | 9.8 | 11.0 | | | | | | 12.0 | 10.6 |
| -66.1 | 34.5 | 46.7 | | | | | | -92.3 | 31.1 |
| 7.2 | 21.2 | 24.6 | EBIT/Interest | | | | | 18.8 | 34.6 |
| (68) 2.1 | (79) 5.7 | (63) 6.4 | | | | | | 6.0 | (43) 6.8 |
| -.6 | 1.5 | 3.0 | | | | | | -.6 | 3.8 |
| 4.2 | 6.3 | 6.2 | Net Profit + Depr., Dep., Amort./Cur. Mat. L/T/D | | | | | | 7.4 |
| (19) 1.8 | (24) 2.9 | (21) 4.1 | | | | | | (17) 4.5 | |
| .1 | .9 | 1.8 | | | | | | | 2.1 |
| .4 | .3 | .5 | Fixed/Worth | | | | | .4 | .5 |
| 1.2 | .8 | 1.0 | | | | | | .9 | 1.0 |
| 3.7 | 2.2 | 1.8 | | | | | | -3.3 | 1.9 |
| .7 | .7 | .8 | Debt/Worth | | | | | .8 | .6 |
| 2.0 | 1.6 | 1.4 | | | | | | 1.5 | 1.3 |
| 7.9 | 4.5 | 3.7 | | | | | | -16.5 | 3.4 |
| 33.8 | 36.9 | 39.6 | % Profit Before Taxes/Tangible Net Worth | | | | | 34.2 | 39.7 |
| (59) 9.1 | (68) 19.2 | (58) 24.5 | | | | | | (10) 12.4 | (42) 24.8 |
| -9.7 | 7.6 | 10.4 | | | | | | .2 | 11.7 |
| 10.6 | 15.3 | 15.8 | % Profit Before Taxes/Total Assets | | | | | 17.5 | 15.1 |
| 2.1 | 7.4 | 10.5 | | | | | | 5.4 | 11.4 |
| -4.2 | 1.3 | 2.6 | | | | | | -2.2 | 4.3 |
| 16.7 | 22.8 | 16.1 | Sales/Net Fixed Assets | | | | | 31.9 | 10.9 |
| 6.4 | 7.7 | 7.5 | | | | | | 14.8 | 6.2 |
| 4.1 | 4.0 | 4.3 | | | | | | 4.3 | 4.2 |
| 2.6 | 2.9 | 3.1 | Sales/Total Assets | | | | | 3.7 | 3.1 |
| 2.1 | 2.1 | 2.1 | | | | | | 2.7 | 2.1 |
| 1.4 | 1.6 | 1.6 | | | | | | 1.8 | 1.6 |
| 1.3 | 1.1 | 1.2 | % Depr., Dep., Amort./Sales | | | | | .7 | 1.5 |
| (58) 2.4 | (71) 2.0 | (60) 1.8 | | | | | | 1.2 | (41) 2.0 |
| 4.2 | 3.3 | 2.6 | | | | | | 2.6 | 2.9 |
| 1.0 | .8 | .7 | % Officers', Directors' Owners' Comp/Sales | | | | | | |
| (15) 1.6 | (20) 1.8 | (12) .9 | | | | | | | |
| 2.7 | 11.5 | 1.7 | | | | | | | |
| 3148993M | 4361094M | 4916243M | Net Sales ($) | 7911M | 12032M | | 8664M | 238839M | 4648797M |
| 1785128M | 2335865M | 2512728M | Total Assets ($) | 6650M | 5879M | | 2124M | 103679M | 2394396M |

M = $ thousand     MM = $ million
See Pages 9 through 22 for Explanation of Ratios and Data

**Current Data Sorted by Assets**            **Comparative Historical Data**

| 0-500M | 4 (4/1-9/30/11) 500M-2MM | 2-10MM | 16 (10/1/11-3/31/12) 10-50MM | 50-100MM | 100-250MM | | 4/1/07-3/31/08 ALL | 4/1/08-3/31/09 ALL |
|---|---|---|---|---|---|---|---|---|
| | | | | | | **Type of Statement** | | |
| | | | | | | Unqualified | 7 | 7 |
| | | | | | | Reviewed | 10 | 12 |
| | | | | | | Compiled | 1 | 2 |
| | | | | | | Tax Returns | 2 | 2 |
| | | | | | | Other | 13 | 19 |
| | 1 | 5 | 5 | 5 | 4 | **NUMBER OF STATEMENTS** | 33 | 42 |
| % | % | % | % | % | % | | % | % |
| D | | | | | | **ASSETS** | | |
| A | | | | | | Cash & Equivalents | 5.4 | 8.6 |
| T | | | | | | Trade Receivables (net) | 31.6 | 27.1 |
| A | | | | | | Inventory | 31.8 | 30.8 |
| | | | | | | All Other Current | 1.2 | 2.2 |
| N | | | | | | Total Current | 69.9 | 68.7 |
| O | | | | | | Fixed Assets (net) | 17.8 | 19.6 |
| T | | | | | | Intangibles (net) | 2.7 | 3.2 |
| | | | | | | All Other Non-Current | 9.5 | 8.5 |
| A | | | | | | Total | 100.0 | 100.0 |
| V | | | | | | **LIABILITIES** | | |
| A | | | | | | Notes Payable-Short Term | 16.3 | 11.8 |
| I | | | | | | Cur. Mat.-L.T.D. | 4.0 | 2.6 |
| L | | | | | | Trade Payables | 19.4 | 18.1 |
| A | | | | | | Income Taxes Payable | 1.6 | .4 |
| B | | | | | | All Other Current | 8.4 | 7.1 |
| L | | | | | | Total Current | 49.7 | 39.9 |
| E | | | | | | Long-Term Debt | 11.0 | 12.0 |
| | | | | | | Deferred Taxes | .4 | .4 |
| | | | | | | All Other Non-Current | 7.1 | 7.1 |
| | | | | | | Net Worth | 31.8 | 40.6 |
| | | | | | | Total Liabilties & Net Worth | 100.0 | 100.0 |
| | | | | | | **INCOME DATA** | | |
| | | | | | | Net Sales | 100.0 | 100.0 |
| | | | | | | Gross Profit | 22.8 | 19.2 |
| | | | | | | Operating Expenses | 19.2 | 16.6 |
| | | | | | | Operating Profit | 3.6 | 2.6 |
| | | | | | | All Other Expenses (net) | 1.1 | .2 |
| | | | | | | Profit Before Taxes | 2.5 | 2.4 |
| | | | | | | **RATIOS** | | |
| | | | | | | Current | 2.2 / 1.6 / 1.1 | 2.8 / 1.8 / 1.2 |
| | | | | | | Quick | 1.2 / .8 / .6 | 1.6 / .9 / .6 |
| | | | | | | Sales/Receivables | 35 10.3 / 39 9.3 / 48 7.6 | 24 14.9 / 33 11.0 / 41 8.9 |
| | | | | | | Cost of Sales/Inventory | 43 8.5 / 54 6.8 / 61 5.9 | 21 17.7 / 47 7.7 / 67 5.5 |
| | | | | | | Cost of Sales/Payables | 19 19.4 / 30 12.2 / 42 8.6 | 15 24.2 / 20 17.9 / 35 10.5 |
| | | | | | | Sales/Working Capital | 6.6 / 9.8 / 46.9 | 5.5 / 9.6 / 28.8 |
| | | | | | | EBIT/Interest | 10.8 / (31) 4.4 / 1.7 | 12.7 / 3.8 / 1.6 |
| | | | | | | Net Profit + Depr., Dep., Amort./Cur. Mat. L/T/D | 9.4 / (14) 4.4 / 1.9 | 11.0 / (14) 3.6 / 1.4 |
| | | | | | | Fixed/Worth | .2 / .4 / 1.4 | .1 / .3 / 1.0 |
| | | | | | | Debt/Worth | 1.2 / 1.8 / 7.2 | .6 / 1.4 / 3.7 |
| | | | | | | % Profit Before Taxes/Tangible Net Worth | 67.0 / (30) 32.5 / 7.4 | 43.5 / (39) 22.5 / 5.5 |
| | | | | | | % Profit Before Taxes/Total Assets | 15.2 / 8.0 / 1.9 | 15.4 / 7.3 / 1.6 |
| | | | | | | Sales/Net Fixed Assets | 42.6 / 22.0 / 8.2 | 48.0 / 26.6 / 10.3 |
| | | | | | | Sales/Total Assets | 3.6 / 3.1 / 2.1 | 4.3 / 3.0 / 1.8 |
| | | | | | | % Depr., Dep., Amort./Sales | .8 / (30) 1.3 / 2.1 | .6 / (36) .9 / 2.3 |
| | | | | | | % Officers', Directors' Owners' Comp/Sales | | 2.1 / (11) 4.6 / 8.3 |
| | 6073M | 65736M | 223780M | 1008466M | 1526988M | Net Sales ($) | 2513937M | 5822310M |
| | 802M | 29124M | 100647M | 350065M | 774378M | Total Assets ($) | 1129457M | 1828683M |

*(Current Data Sorted by Assets columns for asset sizes: DATA NOT AVAILABLE)*

M = $ thousand     MM = $ million
See Pages 9 through 22 for Explanation of Ratios and Data

## Comparative Historical Data  —  Current Data Sorted by Sales

| 11 | 9 | 2 | Type of Statement | | | | | | |
|---|---|---|---|---|---|---|---|---|---|
| 11 | 9 | 2 | Unqualified | | | | | | 2 |
| 9 | 10 | 5 | Reviewed | | | | | 1 | 2 |
| 3 | 1 | 1 | Compiled | | | | 1 | | |
| 4 | 3 | 1 | Tax Returns | | | | | | |
| 15 | 16 | 11 | Other | | | 1 | | 2 | 9 |

| 4/1/09-3/31/10 ALL | 4/1/10-3/31/11 ALL | 4/1/11-3/31/12 ALL | | 4 (4/1-9/30/11) | | | 16 (10/1/11-3/31/12) | | |
|---|---|---|---|---|---|---|---|---|---|
| | | | | 0-1MM | 1-3MM | 3-5MM | 5-10MM | 10-25MM | 25MM & OVER |
| 42 | 39 | 20 | NUMBER OF STATEMENTS | | | 1 | 1 | 5 | 13 |
| % | % | % | **ASSETS** | % | % | % | % | % | % |
| 10.2 | 7.4 | 6.9 | Cash & Equivalents | D | D | | | | 6.7 |
| 28.2 | 30.8 | 31.5 | Trade Receivables (net) | A | A | | | | 32.4 |
| 26.6 | 28.6 | 22.4 | Inventory | T | T | | | | 20.1 |
| 3.9 | 1.6 | .7 | All Other Current | A | A | | | | 1.0 |
| 68.9 | 68.4 | 61.6 | Total Current | | | | | | 60.1 |
| 21.5 | 19.7 | 21.3 | Fixed Assets (net) | N | N | | | | 20.1 |
| 2.6 | 4.2 | 4.7 | Intangibles (net) | O | O | | | | 5.4 |
| 7.0 | 7.8 | 12.4 | All Other Non-Current | T | T | | | | 14.3 |
| 100.0 | 100.0 | 100.0 | Total | | | | | | 100.0 |
| | | | **LIABILITIES** | A | A | | | | |
| 10.0 | 12.8 | 10.9 | Notes Payable-Short Term | V | V | | | | 12.6 |
| 1.8 | 2.1 | 1.4 | Cur. Mat.-L.T.D. | A | A | | | | .7 |
| 18.2 | 18.5 | 21.1 | Trade Payables | I | I | | | | 19.1 |
| .1 | .3 | .7 | Income Taxes Payable | L | L | | | | 1.1 |
| 10.6 | 8.2 | 6.9 | All Other Current | A | A | | | | 6.1 |
| 40.8 | 41.8 | 41.0 | Total Current | B | B | | | | 39.6 |
| 14.1 | 13.2 | 7.6 | Long-Term Debt | L | L | | | | 5.2 |
| .4 | .8 | .9 | Deferred Taxes | E | E | | | | 1.2 |
| 6.2 | 7.0 | 3.8 | All Other Non-Current | | | | | | 1.6 |
| 38.4 | 37.3 | 46.8 | Net Worth | | | | | | 52.4 |
| 100.0 | 100.0 | 100.0 | Total Liabilties & Net Worth | | | | | | 100.0 |
| | | | **INCOME DATA** | | | | | | |
| 100.0 | 100.0 | 100.0 | Net Sales | | | | | | 100.0 |
| 21.8 | 20.9 | 23.1 | Gross Profit | | | | | | 17.3 |
| 19.0 | 17.9 | 16.5 | Operating Expenses | | | | | | 12.6 |
| 2.8 | 3.1 | 6.5 | Operating Profit | | | | | | 4.7 |
| 1.4 | 1.1 | -.5 | All Other Expenses (net) | | | | | | -1.1 |
| 1.4 | 1.9 | 7.0 | Profit Before Taxes | | | | | | 5.7 |
| | | | **RATIOS** | | | | | | |
| 3.1 | 2.7 | 2.8 | | | | | | | 3.1 |
| 1.6 | 1.6 | 1.5 | Current | | | | | | 1.4 |
| 1.2 | 1.1 | 1.1 | | | | | | | 1.2 |
| 1.8 | 1.6 | 1.6 | | | | | | | 1.8 |
| 1.0 | .9 | .8 | Quick | | | | | | .8 |
| .7 | .6 | .6 | | | | | | | .7 |
| 33  10.9 | 41  8.9 | 35  10.4 | | | | | | | 32  11.5 |
| 50  7.3 | 52  7.1 | 46  8.0 | Sales/Receivables | | | | | | 50  7.3 |
| 60  6.1 | 62  5.9 | 58  6.3 | | | | | | | 63  5.8 |
| 32  11.2 | 36  10.1 | 19  19.2 | | | | | | | 15  24.7 |
| 70  5.2 | 54  6.8 | 49  7.5 | Cost of Sales/Inventory | | | | | | 39  9.4 |
| 94  3.9 | 84  4.3 | 72  5.1 | | | | | | | 57  6.4 |
| 22  16.9 | 15  24.9 | 14  26.8 | | | | | | | 10  36.0 |
| 37  9.8 | 32  11.4 | 30  12.0 | Cost of Sales/Payables | | | | | | 27  13.7 |
| 49  7.4 | 51  7.2 | 60  6.1 | | | | | | | 68  5.4 |
| 3.6 | 4.2 | 5.4 | | | | | | | 6.4 |
| 7.4 | 10.7 | 13.6 | Sales/Working Capital | | | | | | 14.5 |
| 20.8 | 37.1 | 51.6 | | | | | | | 42.0 |
| 11.6 | 11.5 | 25.1 | | | | | | | 44.6 |
| (38)  2.6 | (33)  5.6 | (16)  7.3 | EBIT/Interest | | | | | (12)  7.3 | |
| -.4 | 1.5 | 2.3 | | | | | | | 2.8 |
| 7.7 | 5.9 | | Net Profit + Depr., Dep., | | | | | | |
| (12)  2.6 | (10)  4.8 | | Amort./Cur. Mat. L/T/D | | | | | | |
| .5 | -4.6 | | | | | | | | |
| .2 | .1 | .2 | | | | | | | .2 |
| .4 | .5 | .5 | Fixed/Worth | | | | | | .4 |
| 1.5 | 1.3 | .8 | | | | | | | .7 |
| .6 | .5 | .6 | | | | | | | .4 |
| 2.0 | 2.2 | 1.5 | Debt/Worth | | | | | | 1.4 |
| 4.4 | 7.8 | 2.7 | | | | | | | 2.0 |
| 29.6 | 48.2 | 42.5 | | | | | | | 29.4 |
| (39)  12.4 | (36)  26.6 | (19)  20.0 | % Profit Before Taxes/Tangible Net Worth | | | | | | 14.9 |
| -2.8 | 8.0 | 10.7 | | | | | | | 5.9 |
| 8.1 | 9.7 | 14.5 | | | | | | | 11.4 |
| 3.6 | 4.8 | 6.4 | % Profit Before Taxes/Total Assets | | | | | | 6.1 |
| -1.8 | 2.3 | 3.3 | | | | | | | 2.7 |
| 36.6 | 62.1 | 29.8 | | | | | | | 28.7 |
| 16.3 | 22.3 | 21.3 | Sales/Net Fixed Assets | | | | | | 19.4 |
| 4.7 | 5.2 | 7.0 | | | | | | | 7.7 |
| 2.8 | 3.2 | 3.2 | | | | | | | 3.4 |
| 2.0 | 2.1 | 2.5 | Sales/Total Assets | | | | | | 2.5 |
| 1.3 | 1.4 | 1.3 | | | | | | | 1.3 |
| 1.0 | .5 | .5 | | | | | | | .4 |
| (33)  1.6 | (31)  1.7 | (18)  .8 | % Depr., Dep., Amort./Sales | | | | | (12)  .7 | |
| 4.1 | 3.1 | 1.4 | | | | | | | 1.4 |
| 2.5 | 3.4 | | % Officers', Directors' | | | | | | |
| (13)  3.6 | (11)  4.2 | | Owners' Comp/Sales | | | | | | |
| 7.0 | 9.5 | | | | | | | | |
| 2779704M | 3188619M | 2831043M | Net Sales ($) | | | 4421M | 6073M | 82667M | 2737882M |
| 1400287M | 1261656M | 1255016M | Total Assets ($) | | | 2720M | 802M | 37982M | 1213512M |

M = $ thousand    MM = $ million
See Pages 9 through 22 for Explanation of Ratios and Data

## Current Data Sorted by Assets  /  Comparative Historical Data

| 0-500M | 500M-2MM | 2-10MM | 10-50MM | 50-100MM | 100-250MM | Type of Statement | 4/1/07-3/31/08 ALL | 4/1/08-3/31/09 ALL |
|---|---|---|---|---|---|---|---|---|
|  |  | 1 | 3 | 2 | 2 | Unqualified | 7 | 8 |
|  | 2 | 4 | 3 |  |  | Reviewed | 7 | 13 |
|  | 1 | 3 |  |  |  | Compiled |  | 4 |
|  | 3 | 2 |  |  |  | Tax Returns | 2 | 2 |
| 1 | 1 | 5 |  |  |  | Other | 12 | 20 |
|  | 7 (4/1-9/30/11) |  | 36 (10/1/11-3/31/12) |  |  |  |  |  |
| 1 | 7 | 15 | 14 | 4 | 2 | **NUMBER OF STATEMENTS** | 28 | 47 |
| % | % | % | % | % | % | | % | % |
| | | | | | | **ASSETS** | | |
| | | 6.8 | 9.2 | | | Cash & Equivalents | 9.8 | 7.1 |
| | | 27.5 | 22.8 | | | Trade Receivables (net) | 25.0 | 22.8 |
| | | 29.1 | 34.0 | | | Inventory | 32.0 | 30.6 |
| | | 1.1 | 2.2 | | | All Other Current | 3.5 | 3.1 |
| | | 64.5 | 68.2 | | | Total Current | 70.3 | 63.5 |
| | | 18.7 | 20.0 | | | Fixed Assets (net) | 21.9 | 28.7 |
| | | 12.8 | 6.4 | | | Intangibles (net) | 5.0 | 3.2 |
| | | 4.0 | 5.4 | | | All Other Non-Current | 2.8 | 4.6 |
| | | 100.0 | 100.0 | | | Total | 100.0 | 100.0 |
| | | | | | | **LIABILITIES** | | |
| | | 14.1 | 19.7 | | | Notes Payable-Short Term | 14.0 | 12.5 |
| | | 1.7 | 2.6 | | | Cur. Mat.-L.T.D. | 3.0 | 2.4 |
| | | 18.6 | 14.8 | | | Trade Payables | 14.0 | 14.1 |
| | | .3 | .6 | | | Income Taxes Payable | .3 | .2 |
| | | 4.9 | 8.2 | | | All Other Current | 8.3 | 10.3 |
| | | 39.7 | 45.9 | | | Total Current | 39.6 | 39.6 |
| | | 12.9 | 17.3 | | | Long-Term Debt | 9.6 | 15.8 |
| | | .6 | .4 | | | Deferred Taxes | .3 | .7 |
| | | 7.4 | 15.3 | | | All Other Non-Current | 7.7 | 5.4 |
| | | 39.3 | 21.1 | | | Net Worth | 42.8 | 38.5 |
| | | 100.0 | 100.0 | | | Total Liabilities & Net Worth | 100.0 | 100.0 |
| | | | | | | **INCOME DATA** | | |
| | | 100.0 | 100.0 | | | Net Sales | 100.0 | 100.0 |
| | | 26.4 | 22.1 | | | Gross Profit | 24.9 | 23.4 |
| | | 19.2 | 14.9 | | | Operating Expenses | 17.0 | 17.0 |
| | | 7.2 | 7.2 | | | Operating Profit | 7.9 | 6.4 |
| | | 1.5 | .9 | | | All Other Expenses (net) | 1.0 | 1.5 |
| | | 5.7 | 6.3 | | | Profit Before Taxes | 6.9 | 4.9 |
| | | | | | | **RATIOS** | | |
| | | 3.3 | 2.4 | | | Current | 3.4 | 2.8 |
| | | 1.7 | 1.3 | | | | 2.0 | 1.7 |
| | | 1.0 | 1.2 | | | | 1.2 | 1.1 |
| | | 1.7 | 1.5 | | | Quick | 1.7 | 1.2 |
| | | .9 | .7 | | | | .8 | .7 |
| | | .6 | .5 | | | | .5 | .5 |
| | | 38 9.6 | 32 11.3 | | | Sales/Receivables | 30 12.1 | 22 16.3 |
| | | 42 8.6 | 41 9.0 | | | | 36 10.2 | 33 10.9 |
| | | 52 7.0 | 54 6.7 | | | | 47 7.7 | 44 8.4 |
| | | 12 31.3 | 43 8.4 | | | Cost of Sales/Inventory | 27 13.5 | 20 18.6 |
| | | 83 4.4 | 61 6.0 | | | | 54 6.8 | 48 7.6 |
| | | 104 3.5 | 114 3.2 | | | | 112 3.2 | 111 3.3 |
| | | 20 18.6 | 22 16.4 | | | Cost of Sales/Payables | 13 28.0 | 11 33.6 |
| | | 31 11.9 | 30 12.2 | | | | 22 16.9 | 22 16.6 |
| | | 59 6.2 | 49 7.5 | | | | 42 8.8 | 42 8.6 |
| | | 3.7 | 5.1 | | | Sales/Working Capital | 3.6 | 4.7 |
| | | 6.5 | 10.0 | | | | 7.2 | 10.4 |
| | | 60.2 | 17.0 | | | | 21.8 | 60.0 |
| | | 20.1 | 15.4 | | | EBIT/Interest | 15.1 | 13.8 |
| | | (14) 7.0 | 3.7 | | | | (25) 7.3 | (42) 7.2 |
| | | 4.0 | 3.0 | | | | 1.0 | .1 |
| | | | | | | Net Profit + Depr., Dep., Amort./Cur. Mat. L/T/D | 4.2 | 7.7 |
| | | | | | | | (11) 2.0 | (13) 4.3 |
| | | | | | | | .7 | -.2 |
| | | .2 | .3 | | | Fixed/Worth | .3 | .4 |
| | | .8 | .8 | | | | .5 | .9 |
| | | -3.9 | NM | | | | 2.9 | 2.7 |
| | | 1.0 | 1.6 | | | Debt/Worth | .6 | .7 |
| | | 3.4 | 4.2 | | | | 1.2 | 1.9 |
| | | -10.1 | NM | | | | 13.1 | 5.3 |
| | | 62.9 | 49.9 | | | % Profit Before Taxes/Tangible Net Worth | 63.0 | 50.3 |
| | | (11) 42.7 | (11) 20.9 | | | | (23) 26.0 | (41) 27.5 |
| | | 19.8 | 11.4 | | | | 16.7 | 7.5 |
| | | 15.5 | 17.2 | | | % Profit Before Taxes/Total Assets | 25.6 | 19.3 |
| | | 9.3 | 5.9 | | | | 10.7 | 8.8 |
| | | 4.7 | 2.4 | | | | .3 | -.2 |
| | | 23.1 | 27.4 | | | Sales/Net Fixed Assets | 34.4 | 21.9 |
| | | 16.8 | 9.9 | | | | 12.7 | 7.5 |
| | | 6.8 | 4.0 | | | | 5.9 | 4.9 |
| | | 3.0 | 3.2 | | | Sales/Total Assets | 3.6 | 3.3 |
| | | 2.2 | 1.8 | | | | 2.1 | 2.3 |
| | | 1.3 | 1.1 | | | | 1.5 | 1.2 |
| | | .5 | .8 | | | % Depr., Dep., Amort./Sales | .9 | .8 |
| | | (14) 1.1 | 1.6 | | | | (27) 1.6 | (40) 2.3 |
| | | 1.8 | 3.2 | | | | 2.4 | 3.4 |
| | | | | | | % Officers', Directors' Owners' Comp/Sales | .8 | 1.1 |
| | | | | | | | (10) 1.4 | (15) 2.5 |
| | | | | | | | 9.0 | 5.4 |
| 927M | 22390M | 175045M | 785837M | 885262M | 562797M | Net Sales ($) | 1494817M | 2615226M |
| 289M | 8354M | 77839M | 349704M | 343670M | 254561M | Total Assets ($) | 912634M | 1510743M |

© RMA 2012

M = $ thousand    MM = $ million
See Pages 9 through 22 for Explanation of Ratios and Data

| Comparative Historical Data | | | | Current Data Sorted by Sales | | | | | |
|---|---|---|---|---|---|---|---|---|---|
| | | | **Type of Statement** | | | | | | |
| 4 | 8 | 8 | Unqualified | | | | | | 8 |
| 14 | 10 | 9 | Reviewed | | 1 | 1 | 1 | 3 | 3 |
| 4 | 4 | 4 | Compiled | | | | 1 | 3 | |
| 6 | 2 | 6 | Tax Returns | 1 | 1 | 2 | 1 | | |
| 21 | 20 | 16 | Other | 1 | 1 | 2 | 1 | 5 | 7 |
| 4/1/09-3/31/10 ALL | 4/1/10-3/31/11 ALL | 4/1/11-3/31/12 ALL | | 0-1MM | 7 (4/1-9/30/11) 1-3MM | 3-5MM | 5-10MM | 36 (10/1/11-3/31/12) 10-25MM | 25MM & OVER |
| 49 | 44 | 43 | **NUMBER OF STATEMENTS** | 1 | 3 | 6 | 6 | 9 | 18 |
| % | % | % | **ASSETS** | % | % | % | % | % | % |
| 10.9 | 8.2 | 6.7 | Cash & Equivalents | | | | | | 6.3 |
| 23.8 | 23.7 | 26.9 | Trade Receivables (net) | | | | | | 25.0 |
| 26.9 | 27.7 | 29.3 | Inventory | | | | | | 33.9 |
| 2.8 | 2.6 | 2.4 | All Other Current | | | | | | 3.4 |
| 64.4 | 62.2 | 65.2 | Total Current | | | | | | 68.6 |
| 26.7 | 24.5 | 21.9 | Fixed Assets (net) | | | | | | 22.5 |
| 3.7 | 7.9 | 7.9 | Intangibles (net) | | | | | | 4.3 |
| 5.1 | 5.4 | 5.0 | All Other Non-Current | | | | | | 4.5 |
| 100.0 | 100.0 | 100.0 | Total | | | | | | 100.0 |
| | | | **LIABILITIES** | | | | | | |
| 14.2 | 13.1 | 18.7 | Notes Payable-Short Term | | | | | | 18.1 |
| 2.9 | 4.6 | 2.3 | Cur. Mat.-L.T.D. | | | | | | 2.3 |
| 15.4 | 15.3 | 14.7 | Trade Payables | | | | | | 14.8 |
| .2 | .6 | .4 | Income Taxes Payable | | | | | | .7 |
| 7.6 | 7.4 | 7.8 | All Other Current | | | | | | 10.5 |
| 40.4 | 40.9 | 43.9 | Total Current | | | | | | 46.4 |
| 14.6 | 15.5 | 15.5 | Long-Term Debt | | | | | | 16.1 |
| 1.0 | 2.0 | .6 | Deferred Taxes | | | | | | .9 |
| 19.8 | 8.8 | 8.0 | All Other Non-Current | | | | | | 9.3 |
| 24.2 | 32.8 | 31.9 | Net Worth | | | | | | 27.3 |
| 100.0 | 100.0 | 100.0 | Total Liabilities & Net Worth | | | | | | 100.0 |
| | | | **INCOME DATA** | | | | | | |
| 100.0 | 100.0 | 100.0 | Net Sales | | | | | | 100.0 |
| 23.4 | 26.3 | 26.4 | Gross Profit | | | | | | 16.3 |
| 20.0 | 20.3 | 19.9 | Operating Expenses | | | | | | 11.7 |
| 3.4 | 6.0 | 6.5 | Operating Profit | | | | | | 4.6 |
| .6 | 1.6 | 1.2 | All Other Expenses (net) | | | | | | .9 |
| 2.8 | 4.4 | 5.3 | Profit Before Taxes | | | | | | 3.7 |
| | | | **RATIOS** | | | | | | |
| 2.7 | 3.0 | 2.7 | | | | | | | 2.4 |
| 1.6 | 1.4 | 1.5 | Current | | | | | | 1.3 |
| 1.2 | 1.0 | 1.2 | | | | | | | 1.2 |
| 1.5 | 1.3 | 1.5 | | | | | | | 1.4 |
| .9 | .7 | .7 | Quick | | | | | | .6 |
| .5 | .4 | .6 | | | | | | | .5 |
| 29 12.5 | 35 10.5 | 33 10.9 | | | | | | | 29 12.7 |
| 45 8.1 | 44 8.2 | 40 9.1 | Sales/Receivables | | | | | | 37 9.8 |
| 53 6.8 | 52 7.0 | 54 6.8 | | | | | | | 54 6.8 |
| 33 11.1 | 39 9.3 | 34 10.6 | | | | | | | 34 10.7 |
| 55 6.6 | 69 5.3 | 59 6.2 | Cost of Sales/Inventory | | | | | | 61 6.0 |
| 109 3.4 | 101 3.6 | 94 3.9 | | | | | | | 107 3.4 |
| 14 26.9 | 22 16.3 | 21 17.7 | | | | | | | 19 18.8 |
| 27 13.7 | 33 10.9 | 29 12.5 | Cost of Sales/Payables | | | | | | 29 12.5 |
| 44 8.3 | 51 7.2 | 44 8.3 | | | | | | | 43 8.4 |
| 3.5 | 4.8 | 4.8 | | | | | | | 5.1 |
| 9.6 | 10.2 | 10.3 | Sales/Working Capital | | | | | | 12.5 |
| 21.8 | 67.5 | 28.5 | | | | | | | 34.9 |
| 14.1 | 9.3 | 12.7 | | | | | | | 13.4 |
| (46) 2.0 | (40) 3.2 | (41) 4.1 | EBIT/Interest | | | | | (17) | 3.3 |
| .1 | 1.8 | 2.4 | | | | | | | 1.9 |
| 3.9 | 5.0 | 5.6 | Net Profit + Depr., Dep., | | | | | | |
| (12) .6 | (13) 2.2 | (13) 3.2 | Amort./Cur. Mat. L/T/D | | | | | | |
| .1 | .6 | .9 | | | | | | | |
| .3 | .3 | .3 | | | | | | | .4 |
| .7 | .7 | .8 | Fixed/Worth | | | | | | .9 |
| 2.7 | 2.0 | 1.2 | | | | | | | 1.2 |
| .7 | .8 | 1.1 | | | | | | | 1.1 |
| 1.8 | 2.2 | 2.6 | Debt/Worth | | | | | | 3.0 |
| 6.0 | 5.9 | 9.9 | | | | | | | 6.5 |
| 34.7 | 44.8 | 50.4 | % Profit Before Taxes/Tangible | | | | | | 33.7 |
| (40) 10.2 | (37) 20.4 | (35) 26.3 | Net Worth | | | | | (16) | 18.4 |
| -4.4 | 9.8 | 11.4 | | | | | | | 6.8 |
| 12.8 | 12.0 | 15.6 | % Profit Before Taxes/Total | | | | | | 14.5 |
| 3.0 | 6.7 | 8.2 | Assets | | | | | | 5.9 |
| -2.7 | 2.1 | 2.5 | | | | | | | 1.9 |
| 32.0 | 20.2 | 23.1 | | | | | | | 28.5 |
| 9.3 | 12.3 | 13.9 | Sales/Net Fixed Assets | | | | | | 14.6 |
| 4.4 | 4.1 | 4.2 | | | | | | | 4.0 |
| 2.9 | 2.8 | 3.1 | | | | | | | 3.5 |
| 1.9 | 1.9 | 2.5 | Sales/Total Assets | | | | | | 2.7 |
| 1.2 | 1.3 | 1.3 | | | | | | | 1.1 |
| .5 | .9 | .6 | | | | | | | .6 |
| (39) 1.7 | (34) 1.3 | (40) 1.2 | % Depr., Dep., Amort./Sales | | | | | (17) | 1.6 |
| 3.6 | 2.1 | 2.5 | | | | | | | 3.3 |
| 2.4 | | .9 | % Officers', Directors' | | | | | | |
| (11) 4.0 | | (12) 3.2 | Owners' Comp/Sales | | | | | | |
| 6.5 | | 5.6 | | | | | | | |
| 2154322M | 2389894M | 2432258M | Net Sales ($) | 927M | 6285M | 23289M | 41283M | 152137M | 2208337M |
| 1331559M | 1527805M | 1034417M | Total Assets ($) | 289M | 2008M | 18182M | 22339M | 83048M | 908551M |

© RMA 2012    M = $ thousand    MM = $ million

See Pages 9 through 22 for Explanation of Ratios and Data

**Current Data Sorted by Assets**     **Comparative Historical Data**

Note: For the 0-500M column under Current Data, the entry reads "DATA NOT AVAILABLE".

| 0-500M | 500M-2MM | 2-10MM | 10-50MM | 50-100MM | 100-250MM | | 4/1/07-3/31/08 ALL | 4/1/08-3/31/09 ALL |
|---|---|---|---|---|---|---|---|---|
| | | | | | | **Type of Statement** | | |
| | | 1 | 6 | 4 | 5 | Unqualified | 17 | 16 |
| | | 3 | 3 | | | Reviewed | 7 | 8 |
| | 3 | 3 | | | | Compiled | 6 | 1 |
| | 1 | | | | | Tax Returns | 7 | 2 |
| | 1 | 5 | 10 | 2 | 4 | Other | 25 | 17 |
| | 11 (4/1-9/30/11) | | 40 (10/1/11-3/31/12) | | | | | |
| | 5 | 12 | 19 | 6 | 9 | **NUMBER OF STATEMENTS** | 62 | 44 |
| % | % | % | % | % | % | **ASSETS** | % | % |
| | | 13.0 | 9.5 | | | Cash & Equivalents | 8.0 | 11.4 |
| | | 15.2 | 29.7 | | | Trade Receivables (net) | 25.6 | 25.7 |
| | | 48.9 | 31.3 | | | Inventory | 32.2 | 35.6 |
| | | 3.0 | 3.9 | | | All Other Current | 4.2 | 1.7 |
| | | 80.1 | 74.4 | | | Total Current | 70.0 | 74.4 |
| | | 11.9 | 18.7 | | | Fixed Assets (net) | 19.8 | 17.6 |
| | | 2.5 | 1.7 | | | Intangibles (net) | 2.3 | 2.2 |
| | | 5.4 | 5.1 | | | All Other Non-Current | 7.9 | 5.8 |
| | | 100.0 | 100.0 | | | Total | 100.0 | 100.0 |
| | | | | | | **LIABILITIES** | | |
| | | 18.8 | 17.8 | | | Notes Payable-Short Term | 16.0 | 20.6 |
| | | 1.6 | 2.5 | | | Cur. Mat.-L.T.D. | 2.3 | 1.5 |
| | | 11.3 | 24.4 | | | Trade Payables | 17.9 | 15.8 |
| | | .0 | .3 | | | Income Taxes Payable | .4 | .4 |
| | | 13.0 | 6.5 | | | All Other Current | 13.1 | 9.0 |
| | | 44.6 | 51.5 | | | Total Current | 49.8 | 47.1 |
| | | 10.2 | 8.9 | | | Long-Term Debt | 12.4 | 8.2 |
| | | .4 | 1.0 | | | Deferred Taxes | .4 | .6 |
| | | 7.5 | 3.5 | | | All Other Non-Current | 2.8 | 3.8 |
| | | 37.3 | 35.1 | | | Net Worth | 34.6 | 40.2 |
| | | 100.0 | 100.0 | | | Total Liabilities & Net Worth | 100.0 | 100.0 |
| | | | | | | **INCOME DATA** | | |
| | | 100.0 | 100.0 | | | Net Sales | 100.0 | 100.0 |
| | | 27.4 | 12.2 | | | Gross Profit | 18.9 | 13.8 |
| | | 20.6 | 8.2 | | | Operating Expenses | 12.6 | 9.3 |
| | | 6.7 | 4.0 | | | Operating Profit | 6.2 | 4.5 |
| | | -.3 | .6 | | | All Other Expenses (net) | .7 | .6 |
| | | 7.0 | 3.4 | | | Profit Before Taxes | 5.6 | 4.0 |
| | | | | | | **RATIOS** | | |
| | | 6.7 | 3.4 | | | | 2.5 | 2.1 |
| | | 1.8 | 1.6 | | | Current | 1.4 | 1.5 |
| | | 1.4 | 1.1 | | | | 1.1 | 1.2 |
| | | 1.8 | 2.2 | | | | 1.2 | 1.1 |
| | | .9 | .8 | | | Quick | .7 | .8 |
| | | .1 | .5 | | | | .4 | .5 |
| | | (5) 79.0 | (24) 15.3 | | | | (14) 26.2 | (15) 24.3 |
| | | (9) 41.6 | (35) 10.5 | | | Sales/Receivables | (35) 10.5 | (24) 15.4 |
| | | (34) 10.8 | (43) 8.5 | | | | (44) 8.4 | (39) 9.5 |
| | | (36) 10.0 | (23) 15.9 | | | | (16) 22.4 | (16) 22.6 |
| | | (66) 5.5 | (39) 9.4 | | | Cost of Sales/Inventory | (36) 10.1 | (38) 9.5 |
| | | (111) 3.3 | (61) 6.0 | | | | (66) 5.5 | (63) 5.8 |
| | | (5) 74.0 | (8) 45.7 | | | | (8) 46.0 | (9) 40.0 |
| | | (15) 24.8 | (30) 12.2 | | | Cost of Sales/Payables | (24) 15.1 | (15) 24.1 |
| | | (28) 12.9 | (45) 8.1 | | | | (43) 8.5 | (33) 11.0 |
| | | 4.3 | 6.4 | | | | 6.9 | 8.7 |
| | | 8.3 | 16.9 | | | Sales/Working Capital | 16.4 | 15.9 |
| | | 21.5 | 30.3 | | | | 50.7 | 51.5 |
| | | | 36.2 | | | | 19.5 | 15.2 |
| | | | (18) 15.4 | | | EBIT/Interest | (57) 6.6 | (43) 6.3 |
| | | | 1.5 | | | | 3.1 | 1.9 |
| | | | | | | | 12.5 | 11.0 |
| | | | | | | Net Profit + Depr., Dep., Amort./Cur. Mat. L/T/D | (14) 6.2 | (20) 5.7 |
| | | | | | | | 2.7 | 2.5 |
| | | .0 | .2 | | | | .2 | .2 |
| | | .2 | .5 | | | Fixed/Worth | .4 | .4 |
| | | 2.0 | 1.1 | | | | 1.2 | 1.1 |
| | | .6 | .7 | | | | 1.0 | .9 |
| | | 2.3 | 1.4 | | | Debt/Worth | 2.2 | 1.7 |
| | | 5.7 | 4.3 | | | | 4.1 | 4.3 |
| | | 114.0 | 46.7 | | | | 69.3 | 66.7 |
| | | (10) 59.9 | (17) 26.6 | | | % Profit Before Taxes/Tangible Net Worth | (58) 35.0 | (43) 33.6 |
| | | 15.9 | 9.1 | | | | 20.5 | 6.2 |
| | | 46.3 | 19.9 | | | | 21.7 | 20.1 |
| | | 17.8 | 9.1 | | | % Profit Before Taxes/Total Assets | 12.1 | 10.9 |
| | | 3.6 | 1.1 | | | | 5.8 | 2.9 |
| | | 150.3 | 57.9 | | | | 85.3 | 77.4 |
| | | 73.2 | 19.7 | | | Sales/Net Fixed Assets | 34.4 | 31.8 |
| | | 13.1 | 11.3 | | | | 7.5 | 11.5 |
| | | 5.6 | 4.2 | | | | 4.6 | 5.9 |
| | | 3.6 | 3.4 | | | Sales/Total Assets | 3.3 | 3.4 |
| | | 1.7 | 2.6 | | | | 1.7 | 2.2 |
| | | | .3 | | | | .2 | .3 |
| | | (16) | .5 | | | % Depr., Dep., Amort./Sales | (55) .6 | (41) .5 |
| | | | 1.0 | | | | 2.4 | 1.4 |
| | | | | | | | 1.1 | .4 |
| | | | | | | % Officers', Directors' Owners' Comp/Sales | (17) 2.0 | (13) 1.6 |
| | | | | | | | 5.4 | 3.0 |
| | 34484M | 199048M | 2203603M | 1394305M | 3209302M | Net Sales ($) | 5777088M | 6628877M |
| | 4356M | 50914M | 555318M | 482959M | 1758172M | Total Assets ($) | 1827655M | 1748066M |

M = $ thousand    MM = $ million
See Pages 9 through 22 for Explanation of Ratios and Data

## Comparative Historical Data                          Current Data Sorted by Sales

| | | | | | | | Type of Statement | | | | | | |
|---|---|---|---|---|---|---|---|---|---|---|---|---|---|
| | 17 | | 14 | | 16 | | Unqualified | | 1 | | | | 15 |
| | 7 | | 5 | | 6 | | Reviewed | | | 1 | 1 | | 4 |
| | 2 | | 4 | | 6 | | Compiled | | 2 | 1 | 3 | | |
| | 2 | | 4 | | 1 | | Tax Returns | | | 1 | | | |
| | 21 | | 22 | | 22 | | Other | | 1 | | 3 | | 18 |
| | 4/1/09-3/31/10 | | 4/1/10-3/31/11 | | 4/1/11-3/31/12 | | | | 11 (4/1-9/30/11) | | 40 (10/1/11-3/31/12) | | |
| | ALL | | ALL | | ALL | | | 0-1MM | 1-3MM | 3-5MM | 5-10MM | 10-25MM | 25MM & OVER |
| | 49 | | 49 | | 51 | | **NUMBER OF STATEMENTS** | | 4 | | 3 | 7 | 37 |
| | % | | % | | % | | **ASSETS** | % | % | % | % | % | % |
| | 9.2 | | 8.5 | | 9.7 | | Cash & Equivalents | | | | | | 6.8 |
| | 24.3 | | 25.4 | | 22.8 | | Trade Receivables (net) | D | D | | | | 26.8 |
| | 31.5 | | 34.5 | | 36.9 | | Inventory | A | A | | | | 33.8 |
| | 4.0 | | 4.8 | | 4.3 | | All Other Current | T | T | | | | 4.9 |
| | 68.9 | | 73.1 | | 73.8 | | Total Current | A | A | | | | 72.2 |
| | 21.3 | | 20.4 | | 17.3 | | Fixed Assets (net) | | | | | | 18.2 |
| | 2.7 | | 2.3 | | 4.4 | | Intangibles (net) | N | N | | | | 5.2 |
| | 7.1 | | 4.2 | | 4.5 | | All Other Non-Current | O | O | | | | 4.4 |
| | 100.0 | | 100.0 | | 100.0 | | Total | T | T | | | | 100.0 |
| | | | | | | | **LIABILITIES** | | | | | | |
| | 17.8 | | 20.0 | | 16.9 | | Notes Payable-Short Term | A | A | | | | 17.6 |
| | 2.9 | | 2.1 | | 1.7 | | Cur. Mat.-L.T.D. | V | V | | | | 1.9 |
| | 17.3 | | 14.9 | | 17.7 | | Trade Payables | A | A | | | | 19.7 |
| | .2 | | .2 | | .3 | | Income Taxes Payable | I | I | | | | .3 |
| | 11.2 | | 10.9 | | 10.6 | | All Other Current | L | L | | | | 8.0 |
| | 49.6 | | 48.2 | | 47.3 | | Total Current | A | A | | | | 47.5 |
| | 9.8 | | 13.5 | | 9.7 | | Long-Term Debt | B | B | | | | 8.4 |
| | .5 | | .3 | | .8 | | Deferred Taxes | L | L | | | | 1.0 |
| | 4.6 | | 6.9 | | 7.6 | | All Other Non-Current | E | E | | | | 4.4 |
| | 35.5 | | 31.2 | | 34.6 | | Net Worth | | | | | | 38.8 |
| | 100.0 | | 100.0 | | 100.0 | | Total Liabilities & Net Worth | | | | | | 100.0 |
| | | | | | | | **INCOME DATA** | | | | | | |
| | 100.0 | | 100.0 | | 100.0 | | Net Sales | | | | | | 100.0 |
| | 16.7 | | 18.2 | | 19.1 | | Gross Profit | | | | | | 14.5 |
| | 13.3 | | 12.9 | | 14.2 | | Operating Expenses | | | | | | 10.0 |
| | 3.4 | | 5.3 | | 4.9 | | Operating Profit | | | | | | 4.5 |
| | .0 | | .6 | | .2 | | All Other Expenses (net) | | | | | | .3 |
| | 3.4 | | 4.6 | | 4.7 | | Profit Before Taxes | | | | | | 4.2 |
| | | | | | | | **RATIOS** | | | | | | |
| | 2.6 | | 2.4 | | 3.5 | | | | | | | | 3.1 |
| | 1.5 | | 1.6 | | 1.7 | | Current | | | | | | 1.6 |
| | 1.1 | | 1.2 | | 1.3 | | | | | | | | 1.3 |
| | 1.3 | | 1.1 | | 1.6 | | | | | | | | 1.4 |
| | .7 | | .7 | | .8 | | Quick | | | | | | .8 |
| | .5 | | .4 | | .4 | | | | | | | | .4 |
| 20 | 18.6 | 14 | 26.8 | 8 | 43.5 | | | | | | | 20 | 18.6 |
| 36 | 10.2 | 43 | 8.5 | 29 | 12.7 | | Sales/Receivables | | | | | 35 | 10.5 |
| 53 | 6.9 | 56 | 6.6 | 44 | 8.3 | | | | | | | 45 | 8.1 |
| 26 | 14.0 | 23 | 15.8 | 28 | 13.0 | | | | | | | 26 | 13.9 |
| 43 | 8.4 | 52 | 7.0 | 49 | 7.5 | | Cost of Sales/Inventory | | | | | 43 | 8.5 |
| 69 | 5.3 | 78 | 4.7 | 101 | 3.6 | | | | | | | 99 | 3.7 |
| 10 | 35.1 | 9 | 42.8 | 8 | 45.7 | | | | | | | 8 | 44.4 |
| 24 | 15.4 | 24 | 15.2 | 21 | 17.8 | | Cost of Sales/Payables | | | | | 21 | 17.8 |
| 43 | 8.5 | 39 | 9.4 | 39 | 9.4 | | | | | | | 43 | 8.5 |
| | 5.0 | | 5.6 | | 5.1 | | | | | | | | 5.6 |
| | 13.1 | | 12.0 | | 10.5 | | Sales/Working Capital | | | | | | 11.4 |
| | 86.1 | | 38.9 | | 24.7 | | | | | | | | 21.7 |
| | 18.4 | | 33.2 | | 36.0 | | | | | | | | 37.7 |
| (47) | 4.0 | (46) | 9.7 | (43) | 11.2 | | EBIT/Interest | | | | | (33) | 17.2 |
| | -.4 | | 3.7 | | 3.0 | | | | | | | | 3.1 |
| | 10.9 | | 27.5 | | 25.6 | | Net Profit + Depr., Dep., | | | | | | 23.9 |
| (16) | 1.6 | (12) | 13.5 | (17) | 5.0 | | Amort./Cur. Mat. L/T/D | | | | | (15) | 5.0 |
| | .2 | | 2.3 | | 2.0 | | | | | | | | 2.4 |
| | .2 | | .1 | | .2 | | | | | | | | .2 |
| | .5 | | .5 | | .4 | | Fixed/Worth | | | | | | .5 |
| | 1.3 | | 1.7 | | 1.1 | | | | | | | | 1.0 |
| | .7 | | 1.0 | | .7 | | | | | | | | .7 |
| | 2.0 | | 2.3 | | 1.9 | | Debt/Worth | | | | | | 1.8 |
| | 5.7 | | 8.2 | | 6.2 | | | | | | | | 5.0 |
| | 46.7 | | 93.9 | | 68.0 | | % Profit Before Taxes/Tangible | | | | | | 46.7 |
| (43) | 20.5 | (46) | 37.4 | (43) | 29.9 | | Net Worth | | | | | (33) | 26.6 |
| | -.2 | | 18.1 | | 13.1 | | | | | | | | 11.3 |
| | 16.8 | | 20.2 | | 21.8 | | % Profit Before Taxes/Total | | | | | | 18.5 |
| | 6.5 | | 13.4 | | 14.5 | | Assets | | | | | | 10.1 |
| | -2.6 | | 6.4 | | 3.7 | | | | | | | | 3.3 |
| | 55.0 | | 53.6 | | 72.4 | | | | | | | | 58.4 |
| | 14.7 | | 15.4 | | 24.8 | | Sales/Net Fixed Assets | | | | | | 19.7 |
| | 6.8 | | 7.7 | | 10.4 | | | | | | | | 9.4 |
| | 3.9 | | 4.1 | | 5.1 | | | | | | | | 4.6 |
| | 2.7 | | 2.6 | | 3.0 | | Sales/Total Assets | | | | | | 3.0 |
| | 1.5 | | 1.7 | | 1.8 | | | | | | | | 1.9 |
| | .4 | | .2 | | .3 | | | | | | | | .3 |
| (44) | 1.2 | (44) | .7 | (41) | .8 | | % Depr., Dep., Amort./Sales | | | | | (31) | .6 |
| | 3.0 | | 2.2 | | 2.0 | | | | | | | | 1.3 |
| | | | 1.5 | | 1.2 | | % Officers', Directors' | | | | | | |
| | | (11) | 3.7 | (14) | 1.7 | | Owners' Comp/Sales | | | | | | |
| | | | 5.5 | | 4.8 | | | | | | | | |
| | 6001347M | | 6482624M | | 7040742M | | Net Sales ($) | | 9569M | | 20077M | 98041M | 6913055M |
| | 1944277M | | 2314652M | | 2851719M | | Total Assets ($) | | 8461M | | 4807M | 26649M | 2811802M |

© RMA 2012                        **M = $ thousand    MM = $ million**
See Pages 9 through 22 for Explanation of Ratios and Data

## Current Data Sorted by Assets      Comparative Historical Data

| 0-500M | 500M-2MM | 2-10MM | 10-50MM | 50-100MM | 100-250MM | Type of Statement | 4/1/07-3/31/08 ALL | 4/1/08-3/31/09 ALL |
|---|---|---|---|---|---|---|---|---|
| | 1 | 1 | 9 | 3 | 3 | Unqualified | 19 | 20 |
| | | 7 | 3 | | | Reviewed | 13 | 15 |
| | 1 | 5 | | | | Compiled | 8 | 4 |
| | 3 | 1 | | | | Tax Returns | 2 | 2 |
| | 1 | 7 | 12 | 3 | 3 | Other | 31 | 20 |
| | 16 (4/1-9/30/11) | | 47 (10/1/11-3/31/12) | | | | | |
| | 6 | 21 | 24 | 6 | 6 | NUMBER OF STATEMENTS | 73 | 61 |
| % | % | % | % | % | % | **ASSETS** | % | % |
| | | 9.1 | 9.7 | | | Cash & Equivalents | 8.2 | 8.7 |
| | | 28.8 | 27.5 | | | Trade Receivables (net) | 26.0 | 24.9 |
| | | 23.1 | 16.7 | | | Inventory | 16.9 | 18.8 |
| | | 2.4 | 2.3 | | | All Other Current | 2.0 | 1.9 |
| | | 63.4 | 56.2 | | | Total Current | 53.1 | 54.3 |
| | | 33.4 | 35.0 | | | Fixed Assets (net) | 36.2 | 36.1 |
| | | .9 | 2.0 | | | Intangibles (net) | 5.0 | 3.9 |
| | | 2.2 | 6.8 | | | All Other Non-Current | 5.6 | 5.8 |
| | | 100.0 | 100.0 | | | Total | 100.0 | 100.0 |
| | | | | | | **LIABILITIES** | | |
| | | 7.5 | 6.3 | | | Notes Payable-Short Term | 7.8 | 10.3 |
| | | 2.7 | 2.5 | | | Cur. Mat.-L.T.D. | 3.6 | 3.5 |
| | | 14.2 | 14.2 | | | Trade Payables | 13.9 | 14.2 |
| | | .1 | .1 | | | Income Taxes Payable | .3 | .2 |
| | | 9.4 | 9.0 | | | All Other Current | 7.4 | 6.1 |
| | | 33.8 | 32.1 | | | Total Current | 32.9 | 34.3 |
| | | 13.5 | 10.7 | | | Long-Term Debt | 16.2 | 14.2 |
| | | .8 | 2.3 | | | Deferred Taxes | 1.2 | 1.2 |
| | | 3.1 | 5.5 | | | All Other Non-Current | 6.8 | 4.7 |
| | | 48.8 | 49.5 | | | Net Worth | 42.9 | 45.6 |
| | | 100.0 | 100.0 | | | Total Liabilities & Net Worth | 100.0 | 100.0 |
| | | | | | | **INCOME DATA** | | |
| | | 100.0 | 100.0 | | | Net Sales | 100.0 | 100.0 |
| | | 22.5 | 18.2 | | | Gross Profit | 21.9 | 17.7 |
| | | 16.6 | 11.1 | | | Operating Expenses | 15.9 | 12.6 |
| | | 5.9 | 7.1 | | | Operating Profit | 6.0 | 5.0 |
| | | .2 | .3 | | | All Other Expenses (net) | 1.3 | 1.1 |
| | | 5.7 | 6.8 | | | Profit Before Taxes | 4.7 | 3.9 |
| | | | | | | **RATIOS** | | |
| | | 3.5 | 3.2 | | | | 2.5 | 2.9 |
| | | 2.1 | 1.7 | | | Current | 1.6 | 1.6 |
| | | 1.3 | 1.1 | | | | 1.1 | 1.1 |
| | | 2.1 | 2.1 | | | | 1.8 | 1.7 |
| | | 1.3 | 1.2 | | | Quick | 1.1 | 1.0 |
| | | .6 | .8 | | | | .7 | .7 |
| | | 42  8.7 | 41  8.8 | | | | 38  9.6 | 32  11.4 |
| | | 47  7.8 | 49  7.4 | | | Sales/Receivables | 46  7.9 | 42  8.7 |
| | | 53  6.9 | 57  6.4 | | | | 55  6.6 | 57  6.5 |
| | | 21  17.8 | 23  16.2 | | | | 19  19.3 | 21  17.7 |
| | | 40  9.2 | 32  11.3 | | | Cost of Sales/Inventory | 32  11.6 | 33  11.2 |
| | | 61  6.0 | 55  6.6 | | | | 59  6.2 | 62  5.9 |
| | | 16  22.8 | 19  19.6 | | | | 18  20.4 | 14  25.9 |
| | | 26  14.3 | 31  11.7 | | | Cost of Sales/Payables | 29  12.7 | 27  13.8 |
| | | 36  10.0 | 36  10.0 | | | | 40  9.1 | 34  10.8 |
| | | 3.3 | 4.3 | | | | 5.9 | 5.4 |
| | | 8.5 | 9.5 | | | Sales/Working Capital | 11.1 | 11.4 |
| | | 25.2 | 64.4 | | | | 67.2 | 50.5 |
| | | 21.5 | 28.3 | | | | 13.9 | 13.1 |
| | | (19) 8.4 | (20) 7.5 | | | EBIT/Interest | (65) 4.2 | (57) 4.3 |
| | | 2.2 | 3.0 | | | | 1.3 | 1.5 |
| | | | | | | Net Profit + Depr., Dep., | 10.2 | 9.7 |
| | | | | | | Amort./Cur. Mat. L/T/D | (31) 3.3 | (24) 3.0 |
| | | | | | | | 1.5 | .8 |
| | | .4 | .4 | | | | .5 | .4 |
| | | .7 | .8 | | | Fixed/Worth | .9 | 1.0 |
| | | 1.1 | 1.6 | | | | 2.7 | 1.8 |
| | | .6 | .5 | | | | .7 | .4 |
| | | 1.0 | .8 | | | Debt/Worth | 1.3 | 1.2 |
| | | 1.9 | 2.0 | | | | 3.9 | 3.7 |
| | | 47.4 | 40.1 | | | % Profit Before Taxes/Tangible | 36.7 | 34.4 |
| | | 21.6 | 25.2 | | | Net Worth | (66) 17.5 | (57) 16.9 |
| | | 8.4 | 13.2 | | | | 5.0 | 3.3 |
| | | 22.8 | 18.7 | | | % Profit Before Taxes/Total | 16.6 | 15.3 |
| | | 12.2 | 10.6 | | | Assets | 7.4 | 5.1 |
| | | 3.6 | 4.6 | | | | 1.9 | 1.4 |
| | | 12.6 | 11.9 | | | | 10.5 | 10.2 |
| | | 5.3 | 5.9 | | | Sales/Net Fixed Assets | 5.3 | 6.2 |
| | | 3.9 | 4.0 | | | | 3.2 | 3.8 |
| | | 2.6 | 2.4 | | | | 2.5 | 2.5 |
| | | 2.0 | 1.8 | | | Sales/Total Assets | 2.0 | 2.0 |
| | | 1.6 | 1.6 | | | | 1.3 | 1.4 |
| | | 1.8 | 2.2 | | | | 1.7 | 1.5 |
| | | (20) 2.6 | (23) 3.0 | | | % Depr., Dep., Amort./Sales | (63) 2.6 | (57) 2.7 |
| | | 4.7 | 3.9 | | | | 4.2 | 4.0 |
| | | | | | | % Officers', Directors' | 1.3 | .8 |
| | | | | | | Owners' Comp/Sales | (18) 2.5 | (14) 1.9 |
| | | | | | | | 5.3 | 5.9 |
| 19939M | 242695M | 910650M | 916393M | 1190849M | | Net Sales ($) | 4116715M | 2743167M |
| 6162M | 114500M | 467629M | 392834M | 911290M | | Total Assets ($) | 2470641M | 1810612M |

(DATA NOT AVAILABLE for columns 0-500M, 500M-2MM, 50-100MM, and 100-250MM in the Assets, Liabilities, Income Data, and Ratios sections.)

M = $ thousand     MM = $ million
See Pages 9 through 22 for Explanation of Ratios and Data

## Comparative Historical Data      Current Data Sorted by Sales

Note: In the Current Data section the 0-1MM column is marked **DATA NOT AVAILABLE**; the 1-3MM and 3-5MM columns carry statement counts only. Multi-value cells are listed as upper / median / lower figures. For the turnover ratios each pair is "days  times".

| | 13 / 11 / 6 / 1 / 27 | 18 / 9 / 9 / 1 / 27 | 17 / 10 / 6 / 4 / 26 | Type of Statement | 0-1MM | 1-3MM | 3-5MM | 5-10MM | 10-25MM | 25MM & OVER |
|---|---|---|---|---|---|---|---|---|---|---|
| | | | | Unqualified | | 1 | | | 1 | 15 |
| | | | | Reviewed | | | | 4 | 6 | |
| | | | | Compiled | | 1 | | 2 | 3 | |
| | | | | Tax Returns | | 1 | 1 | 2 | 2 | |
| | | | | Other | 1 | 2 | 2 | 4 | | 17 |
| | 4/1/09-3/31/10 ALL | 4/1/10-3/31/11 ALL | 4/1/11-3/31/12 ALL | | | 16 (4/1-9/30/11) | | 47 (10/1/11-3/31/12) | | |
| NUMBER OF STATEMENTS | 58 | 64 | 63 | | | 4 | 3 | 10 | 14 | 32 |
| | % | % | % | **ASSETS** | % | % | % | % | % | % |
| | 7.6 | 8.5 | 8.6 | Cash & Equivalents | | | | 10.6 | 9.1 | 8.6 |
| | 21.2 | 27.6 | 28.7 | Trade Receivables (net) | | | | 28.1 | 30.6 | 27.5 |
| | 18.2 | 17.7 | 18.8 | Inventory | | | | 22.0 | 18.4 | 16.2 |
| | 3.5 | 2.8 | 2.5 | All Other Current | | | | 1.9 | 2.3 | 3.0 |
| | 50.5 | 56.6 | 58.6 | Total Current | | | | 62.6 | 60.4 | 55.3 |
| | 36.9 | 32.2 | 32.4 | Fixed Assets (net) | | | | 35.0 | 34.0 | 31.8 |
| | 4.3 | 4.3 | 3.8 | Intangibles (net) | | | | 1.7 | .6 | 6.1 |
| | 8.2 | 6.9 | 5.2 | All Other Non-Current | | | | .7 | 4.9 | 6.8 |
| | 100.0 | 100.0 | 100.0 | Total | | | | 100.0 | 100.0 | 100.0 |
| | | | | **LIABILITIES** | | | | | | |
| | 10.6 | 8.4 | 6.5 | Notes Payable-Short Term | | | | 6.3 | 5.3 | 6.5 |
| | 4.4 | 4.6 | 2.4 | Cur. Mat.-L.T.D. | | | | 3.2 | 3.5 | 2.0 |
| | 11.0 | 14.2 | 16.5 | Trade Payables | | | | 16.6 | 14.6 | 14.8 |
| | .1 | .3 | .4 | Income Taxes Payable | | | | .2 | .0 | .7 |
| | 7.9 | 9.0 | 8.5 | All Other Current | | | | 7.8 | 8.6 | 8.5 |
| | 34.1 | 36.4 | 34.3 | Total Current | | | | 34.1 | 32.0 | 32.4 |
| | 13.9 | 15.1 | 13.8 | Long-Term Debt | | | | 15.2 | 12.4 | 12.0 |
| | 1.0 | .7 | 1.6 | Deferred Taxes | | | | 1.4 | 1.1 | 2.2 |
| | 6.2 | 3.5 | 4.4 | All Other Non-Current | | | | 2.8 | 6.2 | 3.7 |
| | 44.8 | 44.2 | 45.9 | Net Worth | | | | 46.5 | 48.3 | 49.6 |
| | 100.0 | 100.0 | 100.0 | Total Liabilities & Net Worth | | | | 100.0 | 100.0 | 100.0 |
| | | | | **INCOME DATA** | | | | | | |
| | 100.0 | 100.0 | 100.0 | Net Sales | | | | 100.0 | 100.0 | 100.0 |
| | 20.6 | 21.4 | 20.4 | Gross Profit | | | | 22.4 | 20.5 | 17.8 |
| | 19.6 | 15.5 | 14.2 | Operating Expenses | | | | 17.4 | 13.5 | 11.4 |
| | 1.0 | 5.8 | 6.2 | Operating Profit | | | | 5.0 | 7.0 | 6.4 |
| | 1.5 | 1.0 | .6 | All Other Expenses (net) | | | | .4 | -.1 | .8 |
| | -.5 | 4.9 | 5.6 | Profit Before Taxes | | | | 4.6 | 7.1 | 5.6 |
| | | | | **RATIOS** | | | | | | |
| | 3.5 / 1.8 / 1.0 | 2.9 / 1.9 / 1.0 | 2.8 / 1.8 / 1.1 | Current | | | | 5.1 / 2.3 / 1.1 | 2.7 / 2.0 / 1.4 | 3.1 / 1.7 / 1.1 |
| | 1.8 / .8 / .5 | 2.0 / 1.0 / .6 | 2.0 / 1.2 / .7 | Quick | | | | 3.5 / 1.5 / .5 | 2.0 / 1.2 / .9 | 2.0 / 1.2 / .8 |
| | 38 9.5 / 44 8.3 / 53 6.9 | 44 8.3 / 55 6.7 / 67 5.5 | 41 8.8 / 49 7.5 / 58 6.3 | Sales/Receivables | | | | 40 9.1 / 46 7.9 / 56 6.5 | 41 8.8 / 49 7.5 / 52 7.0 | 42 8.6 / 53 6.9 / 60 6.1 |
| | 25 14.4 / 45 8.2 / 70 5.2 | 23 15.7 / 42 8.7 / 63 5.8 | 20 18.6 / 33 11.2 / 58 6.3 | Cost of Sales/Inventory | | | | 18 20.4 / 46 8.0 / 69 5.3 | 18 20.0 / 29 12.8 / 51 7.2 | 23 16.2 / 32 11.3 / 55 6.6 |
| | 15 24.9 / 21 17.2 / 36 10.1 | 24 15.4 / 31 11.6 / 45 8.1 | 18 20.4 / 30 12.0 / 41 8.8 | Cost of Sales/Payables | | | | 16 23.0 / 22 16.8 / 45 8.2 | 18 20.2 / 26 14.2 / 33 11.2 | 20 18.1 / 33 11.2 / 42 8.7 |
| | 3.3 / 10.5 / -193.3 | 3.8 / 9.0 / -851.2 | 4.3 / 8.6 / 33.6 | Sales/Working Capital | | | | 3.1 / 6.3 / 47.3 | 4.2 / 10.0 / NM | 4.3 / 8.3 / 28.2 |
| | 4.9 / (50) 1.4 / -1.3 | 23.4 / (58) 4.6 / 1.5 | 18.8 / (54) 7.2 / 2.3 | EBIT/Interest | | | | 72.9 / 7.4 / .0 | 20.6 / (12) 8.1 / 6.3 | 21.5 / (27) 7.4 / 2.3 |
| | 4.7 / (16) 2.9 / .9 | 7.7 / (20) 3.7 / 2.5 | 9.3 / (22) 5.5 / 1.9 | Net Profit + Depr., Dep., Amort./Cur. Mat. L/T/D | | | | | | 8.4 / (14) 3.9 / 1.9 |
| | .4 / .9 / 3.3 | .3 / .9 / 1.7 | .4 / .8 / 1.3 | Fixed/Worth | | | | .5 / .6 / 1.8 | .3 / .8 / 1.2 | .4 / .8 / 1.3 |
| | .4 / 1.1 / 8.4 | .6 / 1.2 / 4.3 | .5 / 1.2 / 2.7 | Debt/Worth | | | | .5 / .8 / 6.5 | .6 / 1.0 / 2.0 | .5 / 1.0 / 2.6 |
| | 19.5 / (52) 3.0 / -10.5 | 37.4 / (60) 18.9 / 4.7 | 42.5 / (59) 21.6 / 10.4 | % Profit Before Taxes/Tangible Net Worth | | | | 39.4 / 7.9 / -8.5 | 54.3 / 34.8 / 18.6 | 41.1 / (30) 22.5 / 12.6 |
| | 8.9 / .7 / -6.3 | 16.0 / 8.1 / 1.2 | 18.7 / 9.2 / 3.6 | % Profit Before Taxes/Total Assets | | | | 19.7 / 5.1 / -2.6 | 22.7 / 13.2 / 8.3 | 18.6 / 10.6 / 3.7 |
| | 7.7 / 4.8 / 2.6 | 9.4 / 6.2 / 3.3 | 12.6 / 6.3 / 4.0 | Sales/Net Fixed Assets | | | | 11.0 / 4.7 / 3.9 | 16.0 / 9.7 / 3.6 | 10.6 / 6.3 / 4.0 |
| | 2.0 / 1.6 / 1.0 | 2.0 / 1.7 / 1.3 | 2.5 / 1.9 / 1.5 | Sales/Total Assets | | | | 2.3 / 2.0 / 1.5 | 3.0 / 2.1 / 1.7 | 2.3 / 1.7 / 1.5 |
| | 1.7 / (52) 3.7 / 5.2 | 2.1 / (59) 3.0 / 4.8 | 1.8 / (58) 2.7 / 4.2 | % Depr., Dep., Amort./Sales | | | | 2.4 / 3.2 / 4.9 | 1.3 / (13) 1.9 / 4.3 | 2.1 / (29) 2.9 / 3.8 |
| | 1.4 / (15) 3.3 / 5.3 | .8 / (15) 2.6 / 4.6 | .8 / (13) 1.7 / 3.4 | % Officers', Directors' Owners' Comp/Sales | | | | | | |
| | 2036623M | 2083810M | 3280526M | Net Sales ($) | | 8786M | 10666M | 75844M | 235945M | 2949285M |
| | 1820589M | 1486105M | 1892415M | Total Assets ($) | | 3645M | 7859M | 39686M | 117016M | 1724209M |

© RMA 2012

M = $ thousand    MM = $ million
See Pages 9 through 22 for Explanation of Ratios and Data

## Current Data Sorted by Assets                                                    Comparative Historical Data

| 0-500M | 500M-2MM | 2-10MM | 10-50MM | 50-100MM | 100-250MM | Type of Statement | 4/1/07-3/31/08 ALL | 4/1/08-3/31/09 ALL |
|---|---|---|---|---|---|---|---|---|
| | | 2 | 3 | 3 | 3 | Unqualified | 8 | 10 |
| | | 8 | 2 | | | Reviewed | 13 | 14 |
| | 1 | 2 | 1 | | | Compiled | 5 | 7 |
| | 1 | 5 | 8 | 1 | | Tax Returns | 2 | 2 |
| | | | | | | Other | 12 | 18 |
| | 9 (4/1-9/30/11) | | 31 (10/1/11-3/31/12) | | | | | |
| 2 | 17 | 14 | 4 | 3 | | NUMBER OF STATEMENTS | 40 | 51 |

| 0-500M | 500M-2MM | 2-10MM | 10-50MM | 50-100MM | 100-250MM | | 4/1/07-3/31/08 ALL | 4/1/08-3/31/09 ALL |
|---|---|---|---|---|---|---|---|---|
| % | % | % | % | % | % | **ASSETS** | % | % |
| | | 6.8 | 4.0 | | | Cash & Equivalents | 7.3 | 7.2 |
| | | 30.4 | 31.3 | | | Trade Receivables (net) | 27.6 | 30.1 |
| | | 26.7 | 33.5 | | | Inventory | 23.7 | 27.2 |
| | | 2.9 | 1.5 | | | All Other Current | 2.8 | 2.8 |
| | | 66.8 | 70.3 | | | Total Current | 61.3 | 67.2 |
| | | 24.8 | 25.4 | | | Fixed Assets (net) | 32.6 | 25.0 |
| | | 3.8 | 1.5 | | | Intangibles (net) | 1.7 | 3.2 |
| | | 4.7 | 2.7 | | | All Other Non-Current | 4.4 | 4.5 |
| | | 100.0 | 100.0 | | | Total | 100.0 | 100.0 |
| | | | | | | **LIABILITIES** | | |
| | | 12.8 | 12.6 | | | Notes Payable-Short Term | 9.3 | 11.3 |
| | | 2.5 | 2.9 | | | Cur. Mat.-L.T.D. | 2.7 | 2.5 |
| | | 23.6 | 14.3 | | | Trade Payables | 15.4 | 16.9 |
| | | .3 | .3 | | | Income Taxes Payable | .1 | .2 |
| | | 4.9 | 11.3 | | | All Other Current | 13.1 | 10.9 |
| | | 44.1 | 41.3 | | | Total Current | 40.6 | 41.8 |
| | | 11.3 | 9.1 | | | Long-Term Debt | 16.6 | 11.6 |
| | | .3 | .1 | | | Deferred Taxes | .5 | .4 |
| | | 7.0 | 8.5 | | | All Other Non-Current | 5.2 | 9.1 |
| | | 37.3 | 41.0 | | | Net Worth | 37.2 | 37.1 |
| | | 100.0 | 100.0 | | | Total Liabilities & Net Worth | 100.0 | 100.0 |
| | | | | | | **INCOME DATA** | | |
| | | 100.0 | 100.0 | | | Net Sales | 100.0 | 100.0 |
| | | 25.6 | 19.3 | | | Gross Profit | 24.1 | 21.0 |
| | | 20.0 | 14.6 | | | Operating Expenses | 17.6 | 17.0 |
| | | 5.5 | 4.7 | | | Operating Profit | 6.5 | 4.0 |
| | | .5 | .1 | | | All Other Expenses (net) | 1.1 | .7 |
| | | 5.0 | 4.6 | | | Profit Before Taxes | 5.4 | 3.3 |
| | | | | | | **RATIOS** | | |
| | | 2.7 | 2.4 | | | | 2.3 | 2.6 |
| | | 1.4 | 1.9 | | | Current | 1.6 | 1.6 |
| | | 1.1 | 1.4 | | | | 1.1 | 1.2 |
| | | 1.8 | 1.1 | | | | 1.4 | 1.4 |
| | | .7 | .9 | | | Quick | .9 | .9 |
| | | .5 | .7 | | | | .6 | .6 |
| | | 33 11.2 | 45 8.2 | | | | 34 10.6 | 33 11.0 |
| | | 47 7.7 | 54 6.8 | | | Sales/Receivables | 43 8.5 | 44 8.4 |
| | | 56 6.5 | 60 6.1 | | | | 52 7.0 | 58 6.3 |
| | | 25 14.4 | 42 8.7 | | | | 17 21.0 | 22 16.7 |
| | | 41 9.0 | 72 5.1 | | | Cost of Sales/Inventory | 40 9.0 | 46 7.9 |
| | | 72 5.1 | 130 2.8 | | | | 82 4.4 | 72 5.1 |
| | | 26 13.8 | 21 17.8 | | | | 16 22.1 | 13 28.4 |
| | | 40 9.2 | 31 11.6 | | | Cost of Sales/Payables | 30 12.3 | 27 13.4 |
| | | 58 6.3 | 39 9.3 | | | | 38 9.5 | 44 8.3 |
| | | 5.7 | 5.6 | | | | 6.1 | 5.8 |
| | | 9.8 | 7.0 | | | Sales/Working Capital | 9.4 | 8.5 |
| | | 405.3 | 8.6 | | | | 28.1 | 31.5 |
| | | 9.7 | 15.8 | | | | 16.7 | 14.0 |
| | | (13) 8.1 | (13) 6.8 | | | EBIT/Interest | (38) 4.2 | (46) 4.4 |
| | | 2.1 | 3.1 | | | | 2.1 | 1.8 |
| | | | | | | Net Profit + Depr., Dep., | 7.3 | 11.5 |
| | | | | | | Amort./Cur. Mat. L/T/D | (12) 4.4 | (13) 2.4 |
| | | | | | | | 2.6 | 1.6 |
| | | .1 | .5 | | | | .4 | .4 |
| | | .5 | .6 | | | Fixed/Worth | .8 | .7 |
| | | 2.6 | 1.3 | | | | 1.9 | 1.4 |
| | | .7 | .6 | | | | .8 | .8 |
| | | 2.7 | 1.6 | | | Debt/Worth | 1.7 | 1.8 |
| | | 6.5 | 3.8 | | | | 3.7 | 4.2 |
| | | 60.0 | 52.3 | | | % Profit Before Taxes/Tangible | 52.8 | 53.4 |
| | | (15) 23.6 | (13) 16.3 | | | Net Worth | (37) 25.8 | (45) 28.0 |
| | | 7.8 | 8.2 | | | | 9.0 | 2.3 |
| | | 24.5 | 17.5 | | | % Profit Before Taxes/Total | 18.0 | 16.7 |
| | | 12.2 | 6.6 | | | Assets | 8.5 | 8.3 |
| | | 2.9 | 2.5 | | | | 3.0 | 1.7 |
| | | 31.4 | 12.2 | | | | 12.5 | 21.7 |
| | | 12.3 | 9.8 | | | Sales/Net Fixed Assets | 7.7 | 11.2 |
| | | 6.2 | 6.3 | | | | 5.6 | 6.1 |
| | | 3.4 | 2.6 | | | | 3.0 | 3.2 |
| | | 2.4 | 2.0 | | | Sales/Total Assets | 2.6 | 2.4 |
| | | 2.0 | 1.6 | | | | 1.8 | 1.8 |
| | | .4 | 1.4 | | | | 1.0 | .7 |
| | | (15) 1.6 | 1.6 | | | % Depr., Dep., Amort./Sales | (38) 1.9 | (47) 1.3 |
| | | 2.1 | 2.2 | | | | 3.2 | 2.7 |
| | | | | | | % Officers', Directors' | 3.2 | .6 |
| | | | | | | Owners' Comp/Sales | (11) 4.0 | (12) 2.0 |
| | | | | | | | 6.1 | 4.3 |
| | 3414M | 217167M | 698596M | 454806M | 530463M | Net Sales ($) | 2269488M | 2662556M |
| | 1383M | 89603M | 333660M | 281372M | 365979M | Total Assets ($) | 1128733M | 1275243M |

*(The columns 0-500M and 500M-2MM are marked "DATA NOT AVAILABLE".)*

M = $ thousand    MM = $ million
See Pages 9 through 22 for Explanation of Ratios and Data

## Comparative Historical Data | Current Data Sorted by Sales

Date groups for current data: 9 (4/1–9/30/11) and 31 (10/1/11–3/31/12)

| Type of Statement | | | | 0-1MM | 1-3MM | 3-5MM | 5-10MM | 10-25MM | 25MM & OVER |
|---|---|---|---|---|---|---|---|---|---|
| Unqualified | 9 | 9 | 11 | | | | 1 | 1 | 9 |
| Reviewed | 14 | 16 | 10 | | | | 1 | 7 | 2 |
| Compiled | 8 | 7 | 4 | | | 1 | 1 | 1 | 1 |
| Tax Returns | 1 | 2 | | | | | | | 7 |
| Other | 14 | 10 | 15 | | | | | | |
| | 4/1/09-3/31/10 ALL | 4/1/10-3/31/11 ALL | 4/1/11-3/31/12 ALL | 0-1MM | 1-3MM | 3-5MM | 5-10MM | 10-25MM | 25MM & OVER |
| NUMBER OF STATEMENTS | 46 | 44 | 40 | | 2 | 1 | 3 | 15 | 19 |

*(Columns 0-1MM through 5-10MM for the data rows below are marked "DATA NOT AVAILABLE".)*

| | ALL % | ALL % | ALL % | 10-25MM % | 25MM & OVER % |
|---|---|---|---|---|---|
| **ASSETS** | | | | | |
| Cash & Equivalents | 9.2 | 8.4 | 7.1 | 5.1 | 8.0 |
| Trade Receivables (net) | 27.8 | 31.9 | 29.1 | 30.5 | 26.5 |
| Inventory | 25.5 | 25.9 | 27.7 | 28.0 | 29.2 |
| All Other Current | 2.4 | 2.4 | 1.9 | 2.6 | 1.3 |
| Total Current | 64.9 | 68.6 | 65.9 | 66.2 | 65.1 |
| Fixed Assets (net) | 28.7 | 25.0 | 25.7 | 26.4 | 25.0 |
| Intangibles (net) | 2.9 | 2.1 | 2.9 | 4.1 | 2.6 |
| All Other Non-Current | 3.5 | 4.4 | 5.6 | 3.4 | 7.4 |
| Total | 100.0 | 100.0 | 100.0 | 100.0 | 100.0 |
| **LIABILITIES** | | | | | |
| Notes Payable-Short Term | 9.4 | 9.3 | 10.9 | 15.7 | 9.5 |
| Cur. Mat.-L.T.D. | 3.8 | 2.7 | 2.4 | 3.0 | 2.2 |
| Trade Payables | 16.5 | 18.0 | 17.8 | 24.0 | 13.5 |
| Income Taxes Payable | .1 | .1 | .3 | .5 | .2 |
| All Other Current | 8.7 | 11.2 | 8.2 | 5.0 | 11.6 |
| Total Current | 38.4 | 41.2 | 39.5 | 48.2 | 36.9 |
| Long-Term Debt | 12.7 | 13.9 | 9.9 | 15.2 | 7.4 |
| Deferred Taxes | .1 | .4 | .5 | .3 | .8 |
| All Other Non-Current | 13.6 | 7.4 | 8.1 | 7.7 | 10.1 |
| Net Worth | 35.2 | 37.1 | 42.1 | 28.6 | 44.8 |
| Total Liabilities & Net Worth | 100.0 | 100.0 | 100.0 | 100.0 | 100.0 |
| **INCOME DATA** | | | | | |
| Net Sales | 100.0 | 100.0 | 100.0 | 100.0 | 100.0 |
| Gross Profit | 20.8 | 25.1 | 23.2 | 22.5 | 18.7 |
| Operating Expenses | 20.6 | 19.6 | 16.3 | 16.4 | 12.1 |
| Operating Profit | .1 | 5.5 | 7.0 | 6.1 | 6.6 |
| All Other Expenses (net) | 1.2 | .8 | .3 | .7 | .0 |
| Profit Before Taxes | -1.1 | 4.7 | 6.7 | 5.4 | 6.6 |
| **RATIOS** | | | | | |
| Current | 2.9 | 2.8 | 2.7 | 2.2 | 2.5 |
| | 1.8 | 1.7 | 1.9 | 1.3 | 2.0 |
| | 1.1 | 1.1 | 1.2 | 1.0 | 1.3 |
| Quick | 1.9 | 1.5 | 1.7 | 1.2 | 1.4 |
| | 1.0 | 1.1 | 1.0 | .7 | 1.0 |
| | .6 | .7 | .6 | .5 | .6 |
| Sales/Receivables | 35  10.3 | 41  8.8 | 38  9.5 | 31  11.9 | 41  9.0 |
| | 51  7.2 | 57  6.4 | 49  7.5 | 49  7.5 | 51  7.2 |
| | 58  6.3 | 70  5.2 | 61  6.0 | 64  5.7 | 60  6.1 |
| Cost of Sales/Inventory | 27  13.7 | 30  12.2 | 30  12.1 | 26  14.0 | 40  9.2 |
| | 48  7.6 | 48  7.6 | 56  6.5 | 41  9.0 | 69  5.3 |
| | 96  3.8 | 86  4.2 | 91  4.0 | 70  5.2 | 94  3.9 |
| Cost of Sales/Payables | 17  21.8 | 19  19.7 | 20  18.7 | 27  13.6 | 14  26.7 |
| | 27  13.3 | 33  11.0 | 33  11.1 | 40  9.2 | 31  11.7 |
| | 48  7.6 | 56  6.5 | 48  7.6 | 55  6.6 | 41  8.9 |
| Sales/Working Capital | 4.2 | 4.2 | 5.2 | 5.9 | 4.7 |
| | 7.9 | 6.7 | 7.0 | 9.8 | 6.8 |
| | 27.9 | 38.2 | 23.8 | 748.8 | 8.8 |
| EBIT/Interest | 7.0 | 22.3 | 17.1 | 10.7 | 24.3 |
| | (43) 2.6 | (38) 7.1 | (33) 8.9 | (13) 6.8 | (17) 11.1 |
| | -2.8 | 2.2 | 2.9 | 2.1 | 3.1 |
| Net Profit + Depr., Dep., Amort./Cur. Mat. L/T/D | 5.0 | 8.3 | 12.6 | | |
| | (13) 1.0 | (13) 2.6 | (12) 5.3 | | |
| | -.3 | 1.5 | 2.8 | | |
| Fixed/Worth | .3 | .3 | .4 | .4 | .4 |
| | .6 | .6 | .6 | .9 | .7 |
| | 2.1 | 1.4 | 1.4 | 2.7 | 1.4 |
| Debt/Worth | .6 | .7 | .7 | 1.4 | .6 |
| | 1.5 | 1.4 | 1.6 | 3.2 | .9 |
| | 4.9 | 5.0 | 3.9 | 8.1 | 3.9 |
| % Profit Before Taxes/Tangible Net Worth | 19.3 | 39.5 | 58.3 | 79.9 | 37.4 |
| | (40) 5.9 | (40) 18.7 | (36) 28.5 | (13) 26.7 | (17) 30.2 |
| | -11.6 | 6.5 | 8.8 | 7.5 | 8.2 |
| % Profit Before Taxes/Total Assets | 6.6 | 14.0 | 24.1 | 24.0 | 19.4 |
| | 2.0 | 9.3 | 10.0 | 12.2 | 6.6 |
| | -5.5 | 2.4 | 4.1 | 1.5 | 2.7 |
| Sales/Net Fixed Assets | 16.1 | 21.5 | 14.9 | 20.8 | 12.7 |
| | 7.2 | 9.7 | 9.4 | 8.8 | 9.4 |
| | 4.7 | 5.7 | 5.7 | 5.6 | 4.5 |
| Sales/Total Assets | 2.8 | 2.6 | 2.7 | 3.1 | 2.5 |
| | 1.8 | 2.0 | 2.1 | 2.2 | 1.7 |
| | 1.5 | 1.5 | 1.6 | 1.8 | 1.6 |
| % Depr., Dep., Amort./Sales | .9 | .8 | 1.0 | .4 | 1.4 |
| | (43) 2.4 | (41) 1.8 | (38) 1.6 | (13) 1.6 | 1.7 |
| | 3.6 | 2.6 | 2.2 | 2.2 | 2.5 |
| % Officers', Directors' Owners' Comp/Sales | 2.2 | 1.8 | | | |
| | (10) 3.8 | (12) 3.1 | | | |
| | 4.9 | 5.5 | | | |

| | | | | 1-3MM | 3-5MM | 5-10MM | 10-25MM | 25MM & OVER |
|---|---|---|---|---|---|---|---|---|
| Net Sales ($) | 2120873M | 1934673M | 1904446M | 3414M | 4835M | 26946M | 225907M | 1643344M |
| Total Assets ($) | 1130338M | 1037131M | 1071997M | 1383M | 5770M | 8980M | 100477M | 955387M |

M = $ thousand    MM = $ million
See Pages 9 through 22 for Explanation of Ratios and Data

## Current Data Sorted by Assets    Comparative Historical Data

| 0-500M | 500M-2MM | 2-10MM | 10-50MM | 50-100MM | 100-250MM | | 4/1/07-3/31/08 ALL | 4/1/08-3/31/09 ALL |
|---|---|---|---|---|---|---|---|---|
| | | | | | | **Type of Statement** | | |
| | | 1 | 2 | | | Unqualified | 11 | 12 |
| | | 8 | 4 | | | Reviewed | 16 | 11 |
| 1 | 1 | 4 | 1 | | 1 | Compiled | 9 | 10 |
| 1 | 1 | 1 | | | | Tax Returns | 2 | 4 |
| 1 | 1 | 7 | 9 | 1 | 1 | Other | 22 | 16 |
| 3 | 3 | 5 (4/1-9/30/11) 21 | 45 (10/1/11-3/31/12) 16 | 4 | 3 | **NUMBER OF STATEMENTS** | 60 | 53 |
| % | % | % | % | % | % | **ASSETS** | % | % |
| | | 9.0 | 6.4 | | | Cash & Equivalents | 7.1 | 8.0 |
| | | 26.9 | 31.1 | | | Trade Receivables (net) | 29.8 | 25.7 |
| | | 21.4 | 18.2 | | | Inventory | 21.1 | 21.9 |
| | | 3.8 | 2.8 | | | All Other Current | 1.6 | 2.1 |
| | | 61.1 | 58.5 | | | Total Current | 59.7 | 57.8 |
| | | 32.6 | 29.4 | | | Fixed Assets (net) | 33.5 | 31.6 |
| | | 3.1 | 2.9 | | | Intangibles (net) | .8 | 3.7 |
| | | 3.2 | 9.1 | | | All Other Non-Current | 5.9 | 6.9 |
| | | 100.0 | 100.0 | | | Total | 100.0 | 100.0 |
| | | | | | | **LIABILITIES** | | |
| | | 9.2 | 9.2 | | | Notes Payable-Short Term | 9.6 | 11.7 |
| | | 3.2 | 5.5 | | | Cur. Mat.-L.T.D. | 3.1 | 3.7 |
| | | 15.5 | 18.6 | | | Trade Payables | 16.2 | 15.1 |
| | | .2 | .1 | | | Income Taxes Payable | .2 | .0 |
| | | 10.8 | 7.7 | | | All Other Current | 9.5 | 8.4 |
| | | 38.9 | 41.1 | | | Total Current | 38.6 | 38.9 |
| | | 10.0 | 12.2 | | | Long-Term Debt | 16.4 | 17.0 |
| | | 1.0 | 1.1 | | | Deferred Taxes | .6 | .3 |
| | | 5.2 | 6.3 | | | All Other Non-Current | 5.2 | 5.6 |
| | | 44.9 | 39.3 | | | Net Worth | 39.2 | 38.2 |
| | | 100.0 | 100.0 | | | Total Liabilities & Net Worth | 100.0 | 100.0 |
| | | | | | | **INCOME DATA** | | |
| | | 100.0 | 100.0 | | | Net Sales | 100.0 | 100.0 |
| | | 20.9 | 11.3 | | | Gross Profit | 21.1 | 17.6 |
| | | 15.7 | 8.7 | | | Operating Expenses | 15.9 | 15.3 |
| | | 5.3 | 2.7 | | | Operating Profit | 5.2 | 2.2 |
| | | .4 | .8 | | | All Other Expenses (net) | 1.1 | .9 |
| | | 4.9 | 1.9 | | | Profit Before Taxes | 4.0 | 1.3 |
| | | | | | | **RATIOS** | | |
| | | 2.8 | 2.1 | | | | 2.6 | 2.7 |
| | | 1.8 | 1.5 | | | Current | 1.6 | 1.7 |
| | | 1.1 | 1.1 | | | | 1.0 | 1.1 |
| | | 1.9 | 1.4 | | | | 1.8 | 1.7 |
| | | 1.1 | 1.0 | | | Quick | .9 | .8 |
| | | .6 | .7 | | | | .6 | .6 |
| | | 38  9.5 | 42  8.7 | | | | 40  9.2 | 31  11.7 |
| | | 50  7.3 | 55  6.6 | | | Sales/Receivables | 51  7.2 | 49  7.5 |
| | | 63  5.8 | 66  5.5 | | | | 58  6.2 | 59  6.2 |
| | | 27  13.7 | 24  15.3 | | | | 25  14.6 | 27  13.6 |
| | | 41  9.0 | 35  10.3 | | | Cost of Sales/Inventory | 43  8.5 | 36  10.0 |
| | | 70  5.2 | 45  8.1 | | | | 68  5.4 | 57  6.4 |
| | | 21  17.0 | 28  13.1 | | | | 15  24.2 | 15  24.3 |
| | | 29  12.7 | 38  9.5 | | | Cost of Sales/Payables | 31  11.8 | 23  15.8 |
| | | 45  8.1 | 41  8.9 | | | | 46  7.9 | 42  8.6 |
| | | 4.6 | 5.8 | | | | 5.7 | 5.2 |
| | | 7.8 | 11.0 | | | Sales/Working Capital | 9.5 | 11.3 |
| | | 120.3 | 135.5 | | | | 103.1 | 40.6 |
| | | 16.6 | 13.6 | | | | 4.7 | 4.3 |
| | | (19) 8.4 | (15) 4.5 | | | EBIT/Interest | (53) 2.4 | (48) 2.0 |
| | | 2.0 | .4 | | | | 1.2 | -2.8 |
| | | | | | | | 5.2 | 5.3 |
| | | | | | | Net Profit + Depr., Dep., Amort./Cur. Mat. L/T/D | (21) 3.0 | (23) 1.3 |
| | | | | | | | 1.8 | .2 |
| | | .4 | .4 | | | | .4 | .3 |
| | | .6 | .8 | | | Fixed/Worth | .9 | .8 |
| | | 1.2 | 1.3 | | | | 2.1 | 2.4 |
| | | .5 | .6 | | | | .6 | .5 |
| | | .9 | 1.4 | | | Debt/Worth | 1.6 | 1.3 |
| | | 3.9 | 3.8 | | | | 4.6 | 6.6 |
| | | 49.9 | 24.7 | | | | 37.3 | 24.8 |
| | | (20) 17.4 | (14) 9.2 | | | % Profit Before Taxes/Tangible Net Worth | (56) 13.6 | (44) 9.8 |
| | | 10.0 | -5.8 | | | | 5.4 | -.6 |
| | | 15.3 | 10.3 | | | | 13.4 | 7.5 |
| | | 8.8 | 5.2 | | | % Profit Before Taxes/Total Assets | 5.4 | 3.3 |
| | | 2.2 | -1.0 | | | | 1.2 | -3.2 |
| | | 11.2 | 10.5 | | | | 13.5 | 14.3 |
| | | 6.6 | 7.0 | | | Sales/Net Fixed Assets | 7.3 | 6.6 |
| | | 3.6 | 6.4 | | | | 4.1 | 4.1 |
| | | 2.5 | 2.5 | | | | 2.7 | 2.6 |
| | | 2.0 | 2.0 | | | Sales/Total Assets | 2.1 | 1.9 |
| | | 1.5 | 1.7 | | | | 1.5 | 1.4 |
| | | 1.2 | 1.9 | | | | 1.1 | 1.3 |
| | | (19) 2.5 | 2.9 | | | % Depr., Dep., Amort./Sales | (54) 2.4 | (49) 2.4 |
| | | 3.3 | 3.3 | | | | 4.3 | 4.0 |
| | | .9 | | | | | 1.9 | 1.4 |
| | | (10) 2.3 | | | | % Officers', Directors' Owners' Comp/Sales | (21) 2.6 | (26) 3.8 |
| | | 5.7 | | | | | 4.3 | 5.5 |
| 1411M | 14937M | 227321M | 786996M | 377318M | 851317M | Net Sales ($) | 2776002M | 2180097M |
| 580M | 4923M | 120222M | 370700M | 271955M | 502589M | Total Assets ($) | 1480244M | 1297251M |

M = $ thousand    MM = $ million
See Pages 9 through 22 for Explanation of Ratios and Data

## Comparative Historical Data | Current Data Sorted by Sales

| | | | Type of Statement | | | | 5 (4/1-9/30/11) | | | 45 (10/1/11-3/31/12) | |
|---|---|---|---|---|---|---|---|---|---|---|---|
| | | | | | | | | | | 1 | 6 |
| | 1 | | | | 1 | | | | | 3 | 5 |
| | | | | 1 | | 1 | | 1 | | 3 | 1 |
| | | | | 1 | | 1 | | 1 | | | |
| | | | | 1 | 1 | | | 4 | | 6 | 9 |
| 10 | 12 | 7 | Unqualified | | | | | | | | |
| 12 | 11 | 13 | Reviewed | | | | | | | | |
| 12 | 13 | 7 | Compiled | | | | | | | | |
| 4 | 7 | 3 | Tax Returns | | | | | | | | |
| 16 | 20 | 20 | Other | | | | | | | | |
| 4/1/09-3/31/10 ALL | 4/1/10-3/31/11 ALL | 4/1/11-3/31/12 ALL | | | | | 0-1MM | 1-3MM | 3-5MM | 5-10MM | 10-25MM | 25MM & OVER |
| 54 | 63 | 50 | NUMBER OF STATEMENTS | 3 | 1 | 2 | 10 | 13 | 21 |
| % | % | % | | % | % | % | % | % | % |
| | | | **ASSETS** | | | | | | |
| 10.3 | 8.2 | 9.9 | Cash & Equivalents | | | | 6.2 | 9.8 | 8.7 |
| 22.4 | 29.4 | 28.1 | Trade Receivables (net) | | | | 31.7 | 26.2 | 26.5 |
| 18.3 | 20.3 | 17.9 | Inventory | | | | 21.6 | 18.9 | 16.7 |
| 3.4 | 1.8 | 3.1 | All Other Current | | | | 4.6 | 3.0 | 3.2 |
| 54.4 | 59.8 | 59.1 | Total Current | | | | 64.1 | 57.9 | 55.0 |
| 35.9 | 30.1 | 31.0 | Fixed Assets (net) | | | | 30.6 | 33.0 | 32.6 |
| 2.7 | 3.9 | 2.8 | Intangibles (net) | | | | .2 | 5.5 | 2.2 |
| 7.1 | 6.2 | 7.1 | All Other Non-Current | | | | 5.2 | 3.6 | 10.1 |
| 100.0 | 100.0 | 100.0 | Total | | | | 100.0 | 100.0 | 100.0 |
| | | | **LIABILITIES** | | | | | | |
| 8.5 | 12.4 | 8.7 | Notes Payable-Short Term | | | | 10.1 | 9.6 | 7.5 |
| 3.9 | 4.1 | 3.7 | Cur. Mat.-L.T.D. | | | | 2.6 | 2.4 | 4.6 |
| 12.5 | 15.8 | 15.5 | Trade Payables | | | | 14.7 | 15.1 | 16.5 |
| .1 | .1 | .1 | Income Taxes Payable | | | | .4 | .1 | .0 |
| 10.4 | 8.8 | 9.2 | All Other Current | | | | 7.5 | 11.8 | 9.2 |
| 35.4 | 41.2 | 37.2 | Total Current | | | | 35.2 | 39.0 | 38.0 |
| 21.1 | 15.6 | 10.4 | Long-Term Debt | | | | 7.4 | 12.3 | 9.6 |
| .8 | .4 | .8 | Deferred Taxes | | | | .4 | 1.1 | .8 |
| 8.5 | 5.1 | 6.0 | All Other Non-Current | | | | 3.1 | 7.5 | 8.0 |
| 34.1 | 37.7 | 45.5 | Net Worth | | | | 53.8 | 40.0 | 43.7 |
| 100.0 | 100.0 | 100.0 | Total Liabilities & Net Worth | | | | 100.0 | 100.0 | 100.0 |
| | | | **INCOME DATA** | | | | | | |
| 100.0 | 100.0 | 100.0 | Net Sales | | | | 100.0 | 100.0 | 100.0 |
| 19.9 | 23.3 | 19.1 | Gross Profit | | | | 22.3 | 18.5 | 12.7 |
| 18.0 | 18.1 | 14.7 | Operating Expenses | | | | 16.4 | 13.8 | 9.7 |
| 1.9 | 5.2 | 4.5 | Operating Profit | | | | 5.9 | 4.7 | 3.0 |
| 1.6 | .9 | .4 | All Other Expenses (net) | | | | .4 | .4 | .4 |
| .3 | 4.4 | 4.0 | Profit Before Taxes | | | | 5.5 | 4.2 | 2.6 |
| | | | **RATIOS** | | | | | | |
| 3.4 | 2.9 | 2.8 | Current | | | | 3.7 | 2.7 | 2.4 |
| 1.6 | 1.7 | 1.7 | | | | | 1.8 | 1.7 | 1.5 |
| 1.1 | 1.1 | 1.2 | | | | | 1.2 | 1.0 | 1.2 |
| 1.9 | 2.2 | 1.9 | Quick | | | | 2.4 | 1.9 | 1.5 |
| .9 | .9 | 1.1 | | | | | 1.3 | 1.1 | 1.0 |
| .6 | .6 | .6 | | | | | .6 | .6 | .6 |
| 38  9.6 | 35  10.3 | 38  9.6 | Sales/Receivables | | | | 38  9.7 | 39  9.4 | 39  9.4 |
| 50  7.2 | 54  6.8 | 49  7.4 | | | | | 53  6.9 | 52  7.0 | 47  7.8 |
| 67  5.4 | 62  5.9 | 62  5.9 | | | | | 68  5.4 | 54  6.7 | 58  6.3 |
| 29  12.4 | 24  14.9 | 23  15.9 | Cost of Sales/Inventory | | | | 21  17.7 | 28  13.2 | 21  17.2 |
| 48  7.6 | 45  8.1 | 32  11.3 | | | | | 40  9.2 | 35  10.4 | 30  12.3 |
| 81  4.5 | 64  5.7 | 49  7.5 | | | | | 79  4.6 | 52  7.0 | 47  7.7 |
| 15  23.8 | 17  21.7 | 21  17.0 | Cost of Sales/Payables | | | | 21  17.0 | 21  17.2 | 21  17.2 |
| 29  12.8 | 32  11.3 | 31  11.6 | | | | | 30  12.0 | 26  14.3 | 37  9.8 |
| 48  7.7 | 45  8.2 | 41  9.0 | | | | | 45  8.2 | 40  9.2 | 41  9.0 |
| 4.9 | 5.1 | 4.7 | Sales/Working Capital | | | | 4.0 | 4.7 | 5.4 |
| 7.8 | 9.4 | 9.6 | | | | | 9.2 | 8.8 | 10.3 |
| 31.2 | 41.6 | 25.5 | | | | | 25.5 | 186.3 | 95.4 |
| 6.6 | 15.7 | 14.4 | EBIT/Interest | | | | | 15.8 | 20.6 |
| (60)  1.9 | (46)  4.8 | 7.4 | | | | | | (12)  10.6 | (20)  7.4 |
| -.9 | 2.0 | 1.6 | | | | | | 2.1 | .5 |
| 6.6 | 9.5 | 5.0 | Net Profit + Depr., Dep., Amort./Cur. Mat. L/T/D | | | | | | |
| (17)  2.7 | (17)  2.4 | (19)  2.9 | | | | | | | |
| .0 | 2.0 | 1.5 | | | | | | | |
| .5 | .4 | .4 | Fixed/Worth | | | | .2 | .4 | .5 |
| 1.1 | .8 | .6 | | | | | .6 | .7 | .8 |
| 2.6 | 1.8 | 1.1 | | | | | .9 | 1.8 | 1.1 |
| .5 | .6 | .5 | Debt/Worth | | | | .4 | .6 | .5 |
| 1.8 | 1.6 | 1.0 | | | | | .8 | 1.0 | 1.0 |
| 9.0 | 5.5 | 2.5 | | | | | 2.1 | 3.8 | 3.0 |
| 13.7 | 29.0 | 40.7 | % Profit Before Taxes/Tangible Net Worth | | | | 42.2 | 61.5 | 23.6 |
| (45)  3.9 | (54)  17.8 | (47)  16.8 | | | | | 19.6 | (12)  29.8 | (19)  13.0 |
| -5.7 | 8.9 | 3.2 | | | | | 10.0 | 8.9 | -2.2 |
| 4.9 | 14.0 | 15.2 | % Profit Before Taxes/Total Assets | | | | 19.4 | 19.4 | 13.0 |
| 1.5 | 7.9 | 8.7 | | | | | 11.3 | 9.4 | 7.1 |
| -4.9 | 2.9 | 1.7 | | | | | 3.9 | 3.1 | -1.0 |
| 10.7 | 12.7 | 11.1 | Sales/Net Fixed Assets | | | | 17.1 | 11.4 | 10.6 |
| 3.7 | 6.9 | 6.8 | | | | | 7.1 | 6.6 | 6.8 |
| 2.4 | 4.0 | 4.3 | | | | | 3.5 | 3.5 | 4.3 |
| 2.0 | 2.7 | 2.5 | Sales/Total Assets | | | | 3.1 | 2.5 | 2.3 |
| 1.6 | 1.9 | 2.0 | | | | | 1.9 | 2.0 | 2.0 |
| 1.1 | 1.5 | 1.6 | | | | | 1.5 | 1.6 | 1.6 |
| 2.2 | 1.4 | 1.6 | % Depr., Dep., Amort./Sales | | | | .9 | 1.7 | 2.5 |
| (46)  3.7 | (56)  2.4 | (45)  2.7 | | | | | 1.7 | (11)  2.7 | (20)  3.2 |
| 5.9 | 3.7 | 3.4 | | | | | 3.0 | 3.3 | 4.6 |
| 1.9 | 1.4 | 1.2 | % Officers', Directors' Owners' Comp/Sales | | | | | | |
| (22)  3.7 | (26)  2.7 | (19)  2.8 | | | | | | | |
| 5.2 | 4.6 | 5.1 | | | | | | | |
| 1963616M | 3106671M | 2259300M | Net Sales ($) | 1411M | 2399M | 9605M | 75853M | 196211M | 1973821M |
| 1458891M | 1485622M | 1270969M | Total Assets ($) | 580M | 2135M | 4008M | 42027M | 104246M | 1117973M |

M = $ thousand    MM = $ million
See Pages 9 through 22 for Explanation of Ratios and Data

## Current Data Sorted by Assets

## Comparative Historical Data

| | | | | | | Type of Statement | | |
|---|---|---|---|---|---|---|---|---|
| | | 4 | 2 | 1 | | Unqualified | | |
| | | 6 | 1 | 1 | | Reviewed | 4 | 3 |
| 1 | | 2 | | | | Compiled | 5 | 9 |
| | | 1 | | | | Tax Returns | 5 | 4 |
| | | 5 | 5 | 1 | | Other | 2 | 4 |
| | 6 (4/1-9/30/11) | | 24 (10/1/11-3/31/12) | | | | 13 | 12 |
| | | | | | | | 4/1/07- | 4/1/08- |
| | | | | | | | 3/31/08 | 3/31/09 |
| 0-500M | 500M-2MM | 2-10MM | 10-50MM | 50-100MM | 100-250MM | | ALL | ALL |
| 1 | | 18 | 8 | 3 | | NUMBER OF STATEMENTS | 29 | 32 |
| % | % | % | % | % | % | ASSETS | % | % |
| | | 9.5 | | | | Cash & Equivalents | 5.2 | 11.6 |
| | | 30.9 | | | | Trade Receivables (net) | 33.8 | 28.7 |
| | | 17.4 | | | | Inventory | 20.2 | 20.2 |
| | | .6 | | | | All Other Current | 1.9 | 2.3 |
| | | 58.4 | | | | Total Current | 61.1 | 62.8 |
| | | 34.9 | | | | Fixed Assets (net) | 31.1 | 31.1 |
| | | 2.3 | | | | Intangibles (net) | 2.7 | 1.7 |
| | | 4.4 | | | | All Other Non-Current | 5.1 | 4.4 |
| | | 100.0 | | | | Total | 100.0 | 100.0 |
| | | | | | | LIABILITIES | | |
| | | 4.2 | | | | Notes Payable-Short Term | 24.1 | 10.8 |
| | | 3.7 | | | | Cur. Mat.-L.T.D. | 4.9 | 4.8 |
| | | 13.6 | | | | Trade Payables | 20.9 | 15.8 |
| | | .2 | | | | Income Taxes Payable | .1 | .0 |
| | | 6.9 | | | | All Other Current | 8.6 | 12.1 |
| | | 28.7 | | | | Total Current | 58.6 | 43.6 |
| | | 18.7 | | | | Long-Term Debt | 16.5 | 17.0 |
| | | .5 | | | | Deferred Taxes | .4 | .8 |
| | | 4.9 | | | | All Other Non-Current | 5.8 | 2.1 |
| | | 47.2 | | | | Net Worth | 18.6 | 36.6 |
| | | 100.0 | | | | Total Liabilties & Net Worth | 100.0 | 100.0 |
| | | | | | | INCOME DATA | | |
| | | 100.0 | | | | Net Sales | 100.0 | 100.0 |
| | | 26.5 | | | | Gross Profit | 23.8 | 24.3 |
| | | 18.2 | | | | Operating Expenses | 18.6 | 16.3 |
| | | 8.3 | | | | Operating Profit | 5.2 | 8.0 |
| | | 1.3 | | | | All Other Expenses (net) | 1.3 | .6 |
| | | 7.0 | | | | Profit Before Taxes | 4.0 | 7.4 |
| | | | | | | RATIOS | | |
| | | 4.5 | | | | | 2.2 | 2.9 |
| | | 2.6 | | | | Current | 1.2 | 1.5 |
| | | 1.2 | | | | | .9 | 1.0 |
| | | 2.7 | | | | | 1.5 | 1.6 |
| | | 1.6 | | | | Quick | .7 | 1.0 |
| | | .8 | | | | | .5 | .5 |
| | | 37   9.8 | | | | | 40   9.2 | 35   10.3 |
| | | 50   7.3 | | | | Sales/Receivables | 53   6.9 | 45   8.1 |
| | | 65   5.6 | | | | | 59   6.1 | 62   5.9 |
| | | 25   14.8 | | | | | 20   18.5 | 19   19.2 |
| | | 37   9.9 | | | | Cost of Sales/Inventory | 35   10.3 | 40   9.1 |
| | | 60   6.1 | | | | | 62   5.9 | 56   6.5 |
| | | 17   21.8 | | | | | 18   20.1 | 17   21.1 |
| | | 27   13.4 | | | | Cost of Sales/Payables | 39   9.4 | 27   13.5 |
| | | 37   9.9 | | | | | 59   6.2 | 54   6.8 |
| | | 3.6 | | | | | 7.2 | 5.2 |
| | | 6.2 | | | | Sales/Working Capital | 15.4 | 11.6 |
| | | 26.5 | | | | | -28.7 | NM |
| | | 26.4 | | | | | 14.7 | 32.1 |
| | | (16)   7.9 | | | | EBIT/Interest | (28)   2.1 | (31)   5.3 |
| | | 4.3 | | | | | .6 | 2.1 |
| | | | | | | Net Profit + Depr., Dep., Amort./Cur. Mat. L/T/D | | |
| | | .3 | | | | | .5 | .4 |
| | | .7 | | | | Fixed/Worth | 1.6 | .7 |
| | | 2.2 | | | | | NM | 2.6 |
| | | .4 | | | | | .6 | .5 |
| | | 1.2 | | | | Debt/Worth | 3.1 | 2.3 |
| | | 4.1 | | | | | NM | 6.2 |
| | | 69.8 | | | | | 48.6 | 62.2 |
| | | (17)   20.5 | | | | % Profit Before Taxes/Tangible Net Worth | (22)   19.3 | (30)   29.3 |
| | | 9.3 | | | | | 5.5 | 19.5 |
| | | 20.5 | | | | | 12.4 | 23.5 |
| | | 10.0 | | | | % Profit Before Taxes/Total Assets | 2.2 | 11.8 |
| | | 3.2 | | | | | -1.8 | 2.7 |
| | | 11.8 | | | | | 23.3 | 20.1 |
| | | 5.5 | | | | Sales/Net Fixed Assets | 7.8 | 7.9 |
| | | 4.4 | | | | | 3.8 | 4.4 |
| | | 2.7 | | | | | 3.4 | 3.0 |
| | | 2.2 | | | | Sales/Total Assets | 2.0 | 2.2 |
| | | 1.6 | | | | | 1.6 | 1.6 |
| | | 1.5 | | | | | .7 | .9 |
| | | (15)   1.8 | | | | % Depr., Dep., Amort./Sales | (26)   2.0 | (26)   2.5 |
| | | 4.2 | | | | | 4.0 | 4.8 |
| | | | | | | % Officers', Directors' Owners' Comp/Sales | 1.6 | |
| | | | | | | | (11)   7.3 | |
| | | | | | | | 13.2 | |
| 1091M | | 183597M | 282879M | 247420M | | Net Sales ($) | 562757M | 778545M |
| 372M | | 85740M | 150689M | 189440M | | Total Assets ($) | 256681M | 308547M |

In the left table, under columns 500M-2MM and 100-250MM, the cells spanning the ASSETS through LIABILITIES rows read vertically: **DATA NOT AVAILABLE**.

## Comparative Historical Data

## Current Data Sorted by Sales

| Type of Statement | | | | | 0-1MM | 1-3MM | 3-5MM | 5-10MM | 10-25MM | 25MM & OVER |
|---|---|---|---|---|---|---|---|---|---|---|
| Unqualified | 4 | | 3 | 7 | | | | 1 | 3 | 3 |
| Reviewed | 11 | | 8 | 8 | | 2 | | 3 | 1 | 2 |
| Compiled | 6 | | 5 | 3 | 1 | | | 1 | 1 | |
| Tax Returns | 3 | | 2 | 1 | | 1 | | | | |
| Other | 9 | | 10 | 11 | | | | 3 | 4 | 4 |
| | 4/1/09-3/31/10 ALL | | 4/1/10-3/31/11 ALL | 4/1/11-3/31/12 ALL | | 6 (4/1-9/30/11) | | | 24 (10/1/11-3/31/12) | |
| NUMBER OF STATEMENTS | 33 | | 28 | 30 | | 1 | 3 | 8 | 9 | 9 |
| | % | | % | % | % | % | % | % | % | % |
| **ASSETS** | | | | | | | | | | |
| Cash & Equivalents | 12.1 | | 9.8 | 9.5 | D | | | | | |
| Trade Receivables (net) | 25.5 | | 29.4 | 28.0 | A | | | | | |
| Inventory | 17.0 | | 16.3 | 20.5 | T | | | | | |
| All Other Current | 1.3 | | 1.1 | 1.6 | A | | | | | |
| Total Current | 55.9 | | 56.6 | 59.5 | | | | | | |
| Fixed Assets (net) | 38.2 | | 35.2 | 32.6 | N | | | | | |
| Intangibles (net) | 2.8 | | 3.0 | 4.1 | O | | | | | |
| All Other Non-Current | 3.1 | | 5.1 | 3.8 | T | | | | | |
| Total | 100.0 | | 100.0 | 100.0 | | | | | | |
| **LIABILITIES** | | | | | A | | | | | |
| Notes Payable-Short Term | 8.7 | | 15.0 | 4.5 | V | | | | | |
| Cur. Mat.-L.T.D. | 5.1 | | 3.9 | 3.1 | A | | | | | |
| Trade Payables | 13.3 | | 14.5 | 13.2 | I | | | | | |
| Income Taxes Payable | .0 | | .2 | .2 | L | | | | | |
| All Other Current | 6.9 | | 7.0 | 8.1 | A | | | | | |
| Total Current | 34.0 | | 40.6 | 29.2 | B | | | | | |
| Long-Term Debt | 20.9 | | 16.6 | 14.3 | L | | | | | |
| Deferred Taxes | .7 | | .9 | .8 | E | | | | | |
| All Other Non-Current | 1.8 | | 4.0 | 6.3 | | | | | | |
| Net Worth | 42.7 | | 37.9 | 49.4 | | | | | | |
| Total Liabilities & Net Worth | 100.0 | | 100.0 | 100.0 | | | | | | |
| **INCOME DATA** | | | | | | | | | | |
| Net Sales | 100.0 | | 100.0 | 100.0 | | | | | | |
| Gross Profit | 24.6 | | 27.6 | 28.3 | | | | | | |
| Operating Expenses | 21.9 | | 21.5 | 19.4 | | | | | | |
| Operating Profit | 2.7 | | 6.1 | 8.9 | | | | | | |
| All Other Expenses (net) | 1.2 | | 1.4 | 2.1 | | | | | | |
| Profit Before Taxes | 1.5 | | 4.7 | 6.8 | | | | | | |
| **RATIOS** | | | | | | | | | | |
| Current | 3.4 | | 3.0 | 4.0 | | | | | | |
| | 2.1 | | 1.9 | 2.4 | | | | | | |
| | 1.2 | | 1.0 | 1.3 | | | | | | |
| Quick | 2.5 | | 2.4 | 2.5 | | | | | | |
| | 1.4 | | 1.2 | 1.5 | | | | | | |
| | .6 | | .6 | .8 | | | | | | |
| Sales/Receivables | 38  9.6 | 40  9.2 | 37  9.8 | | | | | | | |
| | 45  8.2 | 53  6.8 | 49  7.4 | | | | | | | |
| | 65  5.6 | 70  5.2 | 62  5.9 | | | | | | | |
| Cost of Sales/Inventory | 29  12.5 | 28  13.2 | 27  13.7 | | | | | | | |
| | 40  9.2 | 42  8.7 | 50  7.3 | | | | | | | |
| | 57  6.4 | 66  5.5 | 70  5.2 | | | | | | | |
| Cost of Sales/Payables | 13  28.1 | 19  19.2 | 18  20.4 | | | | | | | |
| | 24  15.1 | 29  12.5 | 29  12.5 | | | | | | | |
| | 39  9.4 | 54  6.8 | 47  7.7 | | | | | | | |
| Sales/Working Capital | 4.3 | | 5.3 | 3.6 | | | | | | |
| | 8.2 | | 9.0 | 6.4 | | | | | | |
| | 386.1 | | NM | 18.2 | | | | | | |
| EBIT/Interest | 13.1 | | 21.1 | 30.5 | | | | | | |
| | (31) 2.6 | (25) | 4.2 | (27) 8.0 | | | | | | |
| | 1.1 | | 1.2 | 4.0 | | | | | | |
| Net Profit + Depr., Dep., Amort./Cur. Mat. L/T/D | | | | | | | | | | |
| Fixed/Worth | .4 | | .4 | .3 | | | | | | |
| | .8 | | .7 | .7 | | | | | | |
| | 2.3 | | 2.1 | 1.6 | | | | | | |
| Debt/Worth | .4 | | .4 | .4 | | | | | | |
| | 1.6 | | 1.5 | 1.2 | | | | | | |
| | 3.8 | | 4.2 | 2.8 | | | | | | |
| % Profit Before Taxes/Tangible Net Worth | 23.7 | | 32.9 | 50.8 | | | | | | |
| | (28) 7.4 | (24) | 20.9 | (28) 23.6 | | | | | | |
| | .2 | | 2.6 | 11.2 | | | | | | |
| % Profit Before Taxes/Total Assets | 10.7 | | 16.1 | 20.5 | | | | | | |
| | 1.9 | | 6.9 | 10.0 | | | | | | |
| | -1.0 | | .6 | 3.9 | | | | | | |
| Sales/Net Fixed Assets | 12.1 | | 12.6 | 11.8 | | | | | | |
| | 5.1 | | 6.8 | 5.6 | | | | | | |
| | 2.7 | | 3.7 | 4.7 | | | | | | |
| Sales/Total Assets | 2.5 | | 2.6 | 2.7 | | | | | | |
| | 1.8 | | 2.1 | 2.0 | | | | | | |
| | 1.2 | | 1.4 | 1.4 | | | | | | |
| % Depr., Dep., Amort./Sales | 2.4 | | 1.8 | 1.5 | | | | | | |
| | (32) 3.5 | (26) | 3.1 | (25) 1.9 | | | | | | |
| | 5.9 | | 5.0 | 3.8 | | | | | | |
| % Officers', Directors' Owners' Comp/Sales | 2.3 | | | | | | | | | |
| | (11) 5.8 | | | | | | | | | |
| | 10.5 | | | | | | | | | |
| Net Sales ($) | 406035M | | 264766M | 714987M | | 1091M | 12285M | 64500M | 141169M | 495942M |
| Total Assets ($) | 236574M | | 159329M | 426241M | | 372M | 8529M | 30008M | 70167M | 317165M |

M = $ thousand     MM = $ million
See Pages 9 through 22 for Explanation of Ratios and Data

## Current Data Sorted by Assets

## Comparative Historical Data

| | 0-500M | 500M-2MM | 2-10MM | 10-50MM | 50-100MM | 100-250MM | Type of Statement | 4/1/07-3/31/08 ALL | 4/1/08-3/31/09 ALL |
|---|---|---|---|---|---|---|---|---|---|
| | | 1 | | 5 1 | | | Unqualified | 9 | 5 |
| | | 4 | | 3 | | | Reviewed | 11 | 14 |
| | | 3 | | 1 | | | Compiled | 6 | 3 |
| | | 1 | | 2 | | | Tax Returns | | 6 |
| | | 2 | | | | | Other | 12 | 12 |
| | 0-500M | 500M-2MM | 2-10MM | 10-50MM | 50-100MM | 100-250MM | NUMBER OF STATEMENTS | 38 | 40 |
| | | 1 | 10 | 9 | 1 | | | | |
| | % | % | % | % | % | % | ASSETS | % | % |
| | D | | 9.2 | | | D | Cash & Equivalents | 6.3 | 8.9 |
| | A | | 26.1 | | | A | Trade Receivables (net) | 29.6 | 31.2 |
| | T | | 23.3 | | | T | Inventory | 22.7 | 25.2 |
| | A | | 1.0 | | | A | All Other Current | 1.8 | 3.6 |
| | | | 59.6 | | | | Total Current | 60.5 | 68.8 |
| | N | | 25.6 | | | N | Fixed Assets (net) | 31.3 | 26.6 |
| | O | | 6.5 | | | O | Intangibles (net) | 2.2 | .9 |
| | T | | 8.3 | | | T | All Other Non-Current | 6.1 | 3.6 |
| | | | 100.0 | | | | Total | 100.0 | 100.0 |
| | A | | | | | A | LIABILITIES | | |
| | V | | 11.9 | | | V | Notes Payable-Short Term | 15.2 | 10.2 |
| | A | | 2.1 | | | A | Cur. Mat.-L.T.D. | 4.6 | 3.2 |
| | I | | 9.5 | | | I | Trade Payables | 17.2 | 13.6 |
| | L | | .0 | | | L | Income Taxes Payable | .2 | 1.1 |
| | A | | 5.0 | | | A | All Other Current | 8.8 | 11.2 |
| | B | | 28.4 | | | B | Total Current | 45.9 | 39.4 |
| | L | | 10.5 | | | L | Long-Term Debt | 14.0 | 11.9 |
| | E | | .0 | | | E | Deferred Taxes | .4 | .6 |
| | | | .9 | | | | All Other Non-Current | 2.6 | 4.1 |
| | | | 60.2 | | | | Net Worth | 37.1 | 44.0 |
| | | | 100.0 | | | | Total Liabilities & Net Worth | 100.0 | 100.0 |
| | | | | | | | INCOME DATA | | |
| | | | 100.0 | | | | Net Sales | 100.0 | 100.0 |
| | | | 25.8 | | | | Gross Profit | 21.8 | 21.5 |
| | | | 18.5 | | | | Operating Expenses | 15.9 | 15.9 |
| | | | 7.3 | | | | Operating Profit | 6.0 | 5.6 |
| | | | .5 | | | | All Other Expenses (net) | 1.1 | .2 |
| | | | 6.8 | | | | Profit Before Taxes | 4.9 | 5.4 |
| | | | | | | | RATIOS | | |
| | | | 5.2 | | | | | 2.0 | 2.7 |
| | | | 2.1 | | | | Current | 1.4 | 1.9 |
| | | | 1.4 | | | | | 1.0 | 1.3 |
| | | | 3.5 | | | | | 1.3 | 1.5 |
| | | | .9 | | | | Quick | .8 | 1.0 |
| | | | .7 | | | | | .5 | .7 |
| | | 20 | 18.1 | | | | | 30  12.0 | 32  11.3 |
| | | 49 | 7.5 | | | | Sales/Receivables | 50  7.4 | 45  8.1 |
| | | 57 | 6.4 | | | | | 63  5.8 | 55  6.7 |
| | | 30 | 12.0 | | | | | 24  15.3 | 22  16.9 |
| | | 61 | 6.0 | | | | Cost of Sales/Inventory | 48  7.6 | 45  8.1 |
| | | 96 | 3.8 | | | | | 69  5.3 | 77  4.8 |
| | | 1 | 286.6 | | | | | 20  17.9 | 13  27.5 |
| | | 25 | 14.8 | | | | Cost of Sales/Payables | 29  12.5 | 20  18.1 |
| | | 33 | 11.1 | | | | | 39  9.4 | 32  11.5 |
| | | | 4.7 | | | | | 8.2 | 4.6 |
| | | | 5.5 | | | | Sales/Working Capital | 18.4 | 8.3 |
| | | | 20.0 | | | | | -135.6 | 25.1 |
| | | | | | | | | 11.0 | 20.9 |
| | | | | | | | EBIT/Interest | (37) 4.0 | (39) 6.2 |
| | | | | | | | | 2.0 | .9 |
| | | | | | | | Net Profit + Depr., Dep., | 10.2 | 13.8 |
| | | | | | | | Amort./Cur. Mat. L/T/D | (11) 3.8 | (10) 3.3 |
| | | | | | | | | 2.7 | .7 |
| | | | .3 | | | | | .4 | .3 |
| | | | .4 | | | | Fixed/Worth | 1.1 | .5 |
| | | | .8 | | | | | 1.8 | 1.3 |
| | | | .3 | | | | | 1.0 | .6 |
| | | | .7 | | | | Debt/Worth | 1.9 | 1.1 |
| | | | 1.8 | | | | | 4.0 | 2.5 |
| | | | | | | | % Profit Before Taxes/Tangible | 49.8 | 51.0 |
| | | | | | | | Net Worth | (35) 26.1 | (38) 20.8 |
| | | | | | | | | 10.4 | -.1 |
| | | | 19.8 | | | | | 16.0 | 25.4 |
| | | | 16.5 | | | | % Profit Before Taxes/Total Assets | 8.9 | 11.6 |
| | | | 6.6 | | | | | 2.8 | -.2 |
| | | | 12.2 | | | | | 21.1 | 20.9 |
| | | | 8.3 | | | | Sales/Net Fixed Assets | 6.9 | 8.7 |
| | | | 6.1 | | | | | 4.6 | 5.3 |
| | | | 2.8 | | | | | 3.0 | 3.2 |
| | | | 2.1 | | | | Sales/Total Assets | 2.3 | 2.5 |
| | | | 1.7 | | | | | 1.5 | 1.8 |
| | | | | | | | | .9 | .5 |
| | | | | | | | % Depr., Dep., Amort./Sales | (34) 2.2 | (34) 1.5 |
| | | | | | | | | 4.3 | 3.8 |
| | | | | | | | | 1.4 | 2.8 |
| | | | | | | | % Officers', Directors', Owners' Comp/Sales | (12) 3.1 | (15) 4.8 |
| | | | | | | | | 5.2 | 8.0 |
| | | 2941M | 126051M | 504208M | 46728M | | Net Sales ($) | 1120342M | 904472M |
| | | 1579M | 57952M | 248618M | 69305M | | Total Assets ($) | 531872M | 415072M |

M = $ thousand   MM = $ million
See Pages 9 through 22 for Explanation of Ratios and Data

## Comparative Historical Data | Current Data Sorted by Sales

| | | | | | | Type of Statement | | | | | | |
|---|---|---|---|---|---|---|---|---|---|---|---|---|
| | 5 | | 5 | | 5 | Unqualified | | 1 | | 2 | 1 | 4 |
| | 11 | | 7 | | 6 | Reviewed | | 1 | | 2 | 2 | 1 |
| | 3 | | 3 | | 3 | Compiled | | 1 | | | 1 | |
| | 1 | | 1 | | 1 | Tax Returns | | | | | | |
| | 10 | | 7 | | 6 | Other | | | | 1 | 1 | 4 |
| | 4/1/09- 3/31/10 ALL | | 4/1/10- 3/31/11 ALL | | 4/1/11- 3/31/12 ALL | | 0-1MM | 4 (4/1-9/30/11) 1-3MM | 3-5MM | 5-10MM | 17 (10/1/11-3/31/12) 10-25MM | 25MM & OVER |
| | 30 | | 23 | | 21 | NUMBER OF STATEMENTS | | 2 | | 3 | 7 | 9 |
| | % | | % | | % | ASSETS | % | % | % | % | % | % |
| | 9.4 | | 7.2 | | 8.3 | Cash & Equivalents | D | D | | | | |
| | 28.2 | | 29.4 | | 23.1 | Trade Receivables (net) | A | A | | | | |
| | 24.0 | | 25.8 | | 26.6 | Inventory | T | T | | | | |
| | 2.2 | | 2.4 | | 2.9 | All Other Current | A | A | | | | |
| | 63.8 | | 64.8 | | 60.9 | Total Current | | | | | | |
| | 29.7 | | 26.3 | | 25.3 | Fixed Assets (net) | N | N | | | | |
| | 1.4 | | 3.8 | | 5.3 | Intangibles (net) | O | O | | | | |
| | 5.1 | | 5.0 | | 8.5 | All Other Non-Current | T | T | | | | |
| | 100.0 | | 100.0 | | 100.0 | Total | | | | | | |
| | | | | | | LIABILITIES | A | A | | | | |
| | 9.5 | | 12.9 | | 12.3 | Notes Payable-Short Term | V | V | | | | |
| | 6.1 | | 2.7 | | 1.7 | Cur. Mat.-L.T.D. | A | A | | | | |
| | 18.0 | | 14.8 | | 11.5 | Trade Payables | I | I | | | | |
| | .1 | | 1.0 | | .0 | Income Taxes Payable | L | L | | | | |
| | 7.4 | | 8.8 | | 5.1 | All Other Current | A | A | | | | |
| | 41.1 | | 40.3 | | 30.6 | Total Current | B | B | | | | |
| | 10.1 | | 6.4 | | 10.8 | Long-Term Debt | L | L | | | | |
| | .3 | | .1 | | 1.1 | Deferred Taxes | E | E | | | | |
| | 3.8 | | 4.3 | | 6.4 | All Other Non-Current | | | | | | |
| | 44.7 | | 48.9 | | 51.2 | Net Worth | | | | | | |
| | 100.0 | | 100.0 | | 100.0 | Total Liabilties & Net Worth | | | | | | |
| | | | | | | INCOME DATA | | | | | | |
| | 100.0 | | 100.0 | | 100.0 | Net Sales | | | | | | |
| | 18.8 | | 26.6 | | 23.8 | Gross Profit | | | | | | |
| | 17.5 | | 21.5 | | 17.1 | Operating Expenses | | | | | | |
| | 1.3 | | 5.1 | | 6.8 | Operating Profit | | | | | | |
| | 1.2 | | 1.0 | | .3 | All Other Expenses (net) | | | | | | |
| | .1 | | 4.2 | | 6.5 | Profit Before Taxes | | | | | | |
| | | | | | | RATIOS | | | | | | |
| | 3.1 | | 3.4 | | 5.7 | | | | | | | |
| | 1.7 | | 1.6 | | 2.1 | Current | | | | | | |
| | 1.0 | | 1.1 | | 1.3 | | | | | | | |
| | 1.8 | | 1.4 | | 2.4 | | | | | | | |
| | 1.1 | | 1.1 | | .9 | Quick | | | | | | |
| | .5 | | .6 | | .6 | | | | | | | |
| 36 | 10.1 | 35 | 10.4 | 32 | 11.4 | | | | | | | |
| 49 | 7.5 | 45 | 8.1 | 45 | 8.2 | Sales/Receivables | | | | | | |
| 62 | 5.9 | 64 | 5.7 | 54 | 6.8 | | | | | | | |
| 32 | 11.4 | 22 | 16.4 | 36 | 10.1 | | | | | | | |
| 55 | 6.6 | 55 | 6.6 | 64 | 5.7 | Cost of Sales/Inventory | | | | | | |
| 80 | 4.6 | 108 | 3.4 | 122 | 3.0 | | | | | | | |
| 18 | 20.1 | 21 | 17.5 | 20 | 18.6 | | | | | | | |
| 27 | 13.6 | 27 | 13.5 | 24 | 14.9 | Cost of Sales/Payables | | | | | | |
| 63 | 5.8 | 41 | 8.8 | 39 | 9.3 | | | | | | | |
| | 4.3 | | 4.9 | | 4.2 | | | | | | | |
| | 9.1 | | 9.1 | | 5.5 | Sales/Working Capital | | | | | | |
| | -199.9 | | 29.7 | | 31.7 | | | | | | | |
| | 36.0 | | 13.9 | | 21.9 | | | | | | | |
| (29) | 2.9 | (21) | 7.3 | (17) | 6.4 | EBIT/Interest | | | | | | |
| | -2.3 | | 3.6 | | 3.6 | | | | | | | |
| | | | | | | Net Profit + Depr., Dep., Amort./Cur. Mat. L/T/D | | | | | | |
| | .3 | | .3 | | .3 | | | | | | | |
| | .6 | | .5 | | .5 | Fixed/Worth | | | | | | |
| | 1.6 | | .9 | | 1.5 | | | | | | | |
| | .5 | | .5 | | .3 | | | | | | | |
| | 1.0 | | .9 | | .9 | Debt/Worth | | | | | | |
| | 4.9 | | 2.8 | | 2.3 | | | | | | | |
| | 20.8 | | 42.2 | | 43.9 | % Profit Before Taxes/Tangible Net Worth | | | | | | |
| (28) | 6.0 | (21) | 18.1 | (19) | 21.8 | | | | | | | |
| | -12.8 | | 6.2 | | 6.3 | | | | | | | |
| | 10.8 | | 16.5 | | 18.2 | % Profit Before Taxes/Total Assets | | | | | | |
| | 1.0 | | 8.6 | | 13.4 | | | | | | | |
| | -6.1 | | 2.8 | | 3.5 | | | | | | | |
| | 14.8 | | 14.3 | | 13.4 | | | | | | | |
| | 7.1 | | 8.5 | | 7.4 | Sales/Net Fixed Assets | | | | | | |
| | 4.1 | | 6.3 | | 4.4 | | | | | | | |
| | 2.3 | | 3.4 | | 2.5 | | | | | | | |
| | 1.7 | | 2.2 | | 1.8 | Sales/Total Assets | | | | | | |
| | 1.4 | | 1.5 | | 1.2 | | | | | | | |
| | .9 | | 1.1 | | 1.5 | | | | | | | |
| (24) | 2.2 | | 2.1 | (19) | 1.8 | % Depr., Dep., Amort./Sales | | | | | | |
| | 5.1 | | 3.0 | | 3.0 | | | | | | | |
| | | | | | | % Officers', Directors' Owners' Comp/Sales | | | | | | |
| | 1917370M | | 1140139M | | 679928M | Net Sales ($) | | 5141M | | 25338M | 116385M | 533064M |
| | 871603M | | 388018M | | 377454M | Total Assets ($) | | 3758M | | 13238M | 59629M | 300829M |

© RMA 2012

M = $ thousand    MM = $ million
See Pages 9 through 22 for Explanation of Ratios and Data

## Current Data Sorted by Assets     Comparative Historical Data

| 0-500M | 500M-2MM | 2-10MM | 10-50MM | 50-100MM | 100-250MM | Type of Statement | 4/1/07-3/31/08 ALL | 4/1/08-3/31/09 ALL |
|---|---|---|---|---|---|---|---|---|
|  |  | 4 | 16 | 4 | 4 | Unqualified | 22 | 23 |
|  | 1 | 13 | 9 |  |  | Reviewed | 18 | 13 |
| 1 | 3 | 4 | 4 |  |  | Compiled | 11 | 15 |
| 2 | 6 | 5 | 1 | 9 | 5 | Tax Returns | 10 | 10 |
| 3 | 12 | 11 | 24 |  |  | Other | 46 | 44 |
|  | 34 (4/1-9/30/11) | | 107 (10/1/11-3/31/12) | | | | | |
| 6 | 22 | 37 | 54 | 13 | 9 | NUMBER OF STATEMENTS | 107 | 105 |
| % | % | % | % | % | % | ASSETS | % | % |
|  | 11.7 | 6.2 | 9.0 | 8.1 |  | Cash & Equivalents | 5.5 | 7.8 |
|  | 28.6 | 27.9 | 24.3 | 21.0 |  | Trade Receivables (net) | 26.1 | 23.1 |
|  | 20.3 | 27.1 | 29.5 | 21.1 |  | Inventory | 27.2 | 29.5 |
|  | 1.1 | 1.0 | 1.2 | 2.0 |  | All Other Current | 3.5 | 2.3 |
|  | 61.8 | 62.2 | 63.9 | 52.1 |  | Total Current | 62.3 | 62.8 |
|  | 32.4 | 26.0 | 28.4 | 30.5 |  | Fixed Assets (net) | 29.9 | 28.3 |
|  | 2.0 | 4.1 | 4.6 | 14.4 |  | Intangibles (net) | 2.9 | 4.3 |
|  | 3.8 | 7.8 | 3.1 | 2.9 |  | All Other Non-Current | 4.9 | 4.6 |
|  | 100.0 | 100.0 | 100.0 | 100.0 |  | Total | 100.0 | 100.0 |
|  |  |  |  |  |  | **LIABILITIES** | | |
|  | 7.9 | 10.3 | 9.6 | 2.6 |  | Notes Payable-Short Term | 9.7 | 10.4 |
|  | 3.8 | 3.6 | 3.5 | 1.0 |  | Cur. Mat.-L.T.D. | 3.2 | 3.6 |
|  | 21.6 | 19.9 | 14.3 | 11.5 |  | Trade Payables | 15.5 | 12.4 |
|  | .0 | .1 | .2 | .2 |  | Income Taxes Payable | .2 | .1 |
|  | 6.1 | 9.1 | 9.2 | 7.5 |  | All Other Current | 10.7 | 7.9 |
|  | 39.4 | 43.0 | 36.8 | 22.8 |  | Total Current | 39.2 | 34.4 |
|  | 31.7 | 12.1 | 12.9 | 19.9 |  | Long-Term Debt | 20.6 | 14.3 |
|  | .1 | .6 | 1.1 | 2.7 |  | Deferred Taxes | .4 | .8 |
|  | 12.2 | 3.0 | 10.7 | 6.4 |  | All Other Non-Current | 8.6 | 9.2 |
|  | 16.6 | 41.4 | 38.6 | 48.1 |  | Net Worth | 31.2 | 41.4 |
|  | 100.0 | 100.0 | 100.0 | 100.0 |  | Total Liabilities & Net Worth | 100.0 | 100.0 |
|  |  |  |  |  |  | **INCOME DATA** | | |
|  | 100.0 | 100.0 | 100.0 | 100.0 |  | Net Sales | 100.0 | 100.0 |
|  | 34.4 | 24.4 | 22.3 | 21.4 |  | Gross Profit | 25.1 | 25.6 |
|  | 27.6 | 20.0 | 14.0 | 13.6 |  | Operating Expenses | 18.1 | 18.8 |
|  | 6.8 | 4.4 | 8.3 | 7.8 |  | Operating Profit | 7.0 | 6.9 |
|  | .1 | .6 | .4 | 1.4 |  | All Other Expenses (net) | 1.3 | 1.1 |
|  | 6.7 | 3.8 | 7.9 | 6.4 |  | Profit Before Taxes | 5.7 | 5.8 |
|  |  |  |  |  |  | **RATIOS** | | |
|  | 3.0 | 2.3 | 2.9 | 3.0 |  | Current | 2.6 | 3.1 |
|  | 1.8 | 1.4 | 1.8 | 2.4 |  |  | 1.9 | 2.0 |
|  | 1.1 | 1.0 | 1.3 | 1.7 |  |  | 1.2 | 1.3 |
|  | 2.2 | 1.3 | 1.7 | 2.0 |  | Quick | 1.4 | 1.7 |
|  | 1.1 | .8 | .9 | 1.2 |  |  | .9 | .8 |
|  | .7 | .5 | .5 | .8 |  |  | .5 | .5 |
|  | 30  12.3 | 36  10.1 | 39  9.4 | 40  9.1 |  | Sales/Receivables | 36  10.1 | 30  12.0 |
|  | 38  9.7 | 45  8.1 | 50  7.3 | 54  6.7 |  |  | 47  7.8 | 41  8.8 |
|  | 44  8.3 | 59  6.2 | 63  5.8 | 61  6.0 |  |  | 54  6.7 | 49  7.4 |
|  | 9  42.5 | 39  9.3 | 45  8.1 | 48  7.6 |  | Cost of Sales/Inventory | 29  12.4 | 37  9.9 |
|  | 35  10.5 | 62  5.9 | 66  5.5 | 54  6.7 |  |  | 58  6.3 | 68  5.3 |
|  | 79  4.6 | 81  4.5 | 118  3.1 | 96  3.8 |  |  | 93  3.9 | 108  3.4 |
|  | 17  21.8 | 27  13.6 | 18  19.9 | 25  14.8 |  | Cost of Sales/Payables | 21  17.3 | 16  22.9 |
|  | 29  12.8 | 47  7.8 | 33  11.0 | 35  10.5 |  |  | 33  11.2 | 24  14.9 |
|  | 70  5.2 | 63  5.8 | 48  7.6 | 49  7.4 |  |  | 47  7.8 | 41  8.8 |
|  | 5.8 | 6.3 | 3.7 | 3.4 |  | Sales/Working Capital | 5.0 | 4.5 |
|  | 9.6 | 12.8 | 6.7 | 6.1 |  |  | 8.6 | 7.3 |
|  | 66.0 | NM | 14.9 | 9.1 |  |  | 21.7 | 16.8 |
|  | 31.7 | 11.8 | 21.4 | 44.2 |  | EBIT/Interest | 19.7 | 24.5 |
|  | (19) 4.2 | (34) 5.9 | (50) 8.9 | (10) 1.7 |  |  | (100) 4.5 | (95) 5.5 |
|  | 1.8 | 1.5 | 3.1 | .8 |  |  | 1.8 | 1.3 |
|  |  |  | 9.1 |  |  | Net Profit + Depr., Dep., Amort./Cur. Mat. L/T/D | 9.5 | 12.3 |
|  |  | (22) | 4.1 |  |  |  | (36) 4.2 | (31) 4.2 |
|  |  |  | 3.3 |  |  |  | 2.4 | 1.7 |
|  | .4 | .3 | .4 | .4 |  | Fixed/Worth | .4 | .3 |
|  | 1.5 | .6 | .9 | .7 |  |  | .8 | .7 |
|  | -16.7 | 2.1 | 2.4 | NM |  |  | 2.9 | 2.3 |
|  | 1.7 | .6 | .7 | .4 |  | Debt/Worth | .9 | .6 |
|  | 3.8 | 1.9 | 1.9 | .8 |  |  | 1.8 | 1.3 |
|  | -57.2 | 8.8 | 4.8 | NM |  |  | 7.5 | 5.7 |
|  | 108.1 | 42.3 | 50.1 | 37.0 |  | % Profit Before Taxes/Tangible Net Worth | 65.8 | 55.4 |
|  | (15) 77.1 | (36) 21.2 | (49) 32.2 | (10) 17.2 |  |  | (92) 35.2 | (90) 30.6 |
|  | 30.4 | 4.8 | 16.1 | -4.6 |  |  | 10.6 | 3.0 |
|  | 31.4 | 17.2 | 17.3 | 20.5 |  | % Profit Before Taxes/Total Assets | 23.9 | 24.7 |
|  | 18.3 | 8.4 | 12.4 | 5.1 |  |  | 9.5 | 11.2 |
|  | 2.4 | 1.6 | 5.9 | 1.7 |  |  | 3.0 | .4 |
|  | 20.9 | 23.6 | 12.5 | 8.9 |  | Sales/Net Fixed Assets | 15.7 | 16.9 |
|  | 9.5 | 9.7 | 7.1 | 4.3 |  |  | 7.7 | 7.4 |
|  | 5.0 | 5.7 | 3.5 | 3.4 |  |  | 4.4 | 4.3 |
|  | 3.5 | 2.8 | 2.2 | 2.0 |  | Sales/Total Assets | 2.6 | 2.7 |
|  | 2.3 | 2.2 | 1.7 | 1.3 |  |  | 2.0 | 2.1 |
|  | 1.7 | 1.6 | 1.3 | 1.0 |  |  | 1.5 | 1.4 |
|  | 2.0 | 1.0 | 1.4 | 3.2 |  | % Depr., Dep., Amort./Sales | 1.3 | 1.2 |
|  | (15) 2.7 | (33) 1.9 | (50) 2.4 | 3.7 |  |  | (91) 2.3 | (94) 2.1 |
|  | 5.5 | 2.8 | 3.9 | 4.2 |  |  | 4.3 | 4.3 |
|  |  | 1.5 | 1.8 |  |  | % Officers', Directors' Owners' Comp/Sales | 1.9 | 1.8 |
|  | (20) | 2.3 | (14) 5.1 |  |  |  | (27) 3.2 | (30) 2.9 |
|  |  | 3.6 | 8.1 |  |  |  | 6.4 | 7.4 |
| 7182M | 94212M | 420112M | 2058280M | 1311676M | 2473418M | Net Sales ($) | 5127544M | 5005417M |
| 1734M | 27314M | 192829M | 1190737M | 850234M | 1402655M | Total Assets ($) | 2909387M | 2671541M |

## Comparative Historical Data      Current Data Sorted by Sales

| Type of Statement | 4/1/09-3/31/10 ALL | 4/1/10-3/31/11 ALL | 4/1/11-3/31/12 ALL | 0-1MM | 1-3MM | 3-5MM | 5-10MM | 10-25MM | 25MM & OVER |
|---|---|---|---|---|---|---|---|---|---|
| Unqualified | 20 | 22 | 28 | | | | 2 | 4 | 22 |
| Reviewed | 19 | 21 | 23 | 1 | | 2 | 6 | 6 | 8 |
| Compiled | 12 | 11 | 12 | | 3 | 2 | 1 | 3 | 3 |
| Tax Returns | 11 | 12 | 14 | 3 | 4 | 1 | 3 | 3 | |
| Other | 60 | 54 | 64 | 2 | 5 | 7 | 7 | 11 | 32 |
| | | | | 34 (4/1-9/30/11) | | | 107 (10/1/11-3/31/12) | | |
| **NUMBER OF STATEMENTS** | 122 | 120 | 141 | 6 | 12 | 12 | 19 | 27 | 65 |
| | % | % | % | % | % | % | % | % | % |
| **ASSETS** | | | | | | | | | |
| Cash & Equivalents | 9.8 | 8.0 | 8.6 | | 10.6 | 8.1 | 8.2 | 11.3 | 7.4 |
| Trade Receivables (net) | 21.7 | 23.8 | 25.9 | | 28.7 | 30.7 | 30.9 | 23.7 | 23.9 |
| Inventory | 24.2 | 28.0 | 25.7 | | 27.4 | 17.4 | 24.9 | 26.7 | 28.5 |
| All Other Current | 3.0 | 1.4 | 1.2 | | 1.6 | .5 | .9 | 1.3 | 1.3 |
| Total Current | 58.7 | 61.2 | 61.3 | | 68.3 | 56.7 | 64.8 | 63.0 | 61.1 |
| Fixed Assets (net) | 32.0 | 29.9 | 29.0 | | 20.6 | 37.5 | 23.1 | 25.3 | 29.6 |
| Intangibles (net) | 4.5 | 4.2 | 5.3 | | 6.5 | 2.2 | 5.9 | 3.0 | 6.8 |
| All Other Non-Current | 4.8 | 4.7 | 4.4 | | 4.6 | 3.6 | 6.2 | 8.7 | 2.4 |
| Total | 100.0 | 100.0 | 100.0 | | 100.0 | 100.0 | 100.0 | 100.0 | 100.0 |
| **LIABILITIES** | | | | | | | | | |
| Notes Payable-Short Term | 10.3 | 9.4 | 9.2 | | 7.9 | 13.5 | 9.3 | 8.1 | 7.3 |
| Cur. Mat.-L.T.D. | 3.5 | 3.8 | 3.1 | | 1.5 | 3.9 | 3.4 | 3.5 | 2.8 |
| Trade Payables | 10.8 | 14.0 | 16.4 | | 12.4 | 22.1 | 20.1 | 17.1 | 15.2 |
| Income Taxes Payable | .1 | .1 | .1 | | .0 | .1 | .1 | .0 | .2 |
| All Other Current | 10.0 | 10.9 | 8.2 | | 5.0 | 7.6 | 7.9 | 8.7 | 9.0 |
| Total Current | 34.8 | 38.2 | 36.9 | | 26.7 | 47.2 | 40.8 | 37.4 | 34.6 |
| Long-Term Debt | 18.8 | 14.0 | 17.9 | | 28.1 | 27.3 | 12.2 | 11.4 | 13.9 |
| Deferred Taxes | .8 | 1.0 | .9 | | .3 | .4 | .9 | .4 | 1.5 |
| All Other Non-Current | 10.7 | 11.7 | 9.7 | | 6.0 | 8.4 | 4.3 | 5.4 | 8.8 |
| Net Worth | 35.0 | 35.2 | 34.5 | | 38.9 | 16.7 | 41.9 | 45.4 | 41.2 |
| Total Liabilties & Net Worth | 100.0 | 100.0 | 100.0 | | 100.0 | 100.0 | 100.0 | 100.0 | 100.0 |
| **INCOME DATA** | | | | | | | | | |
| Net Sales | 100.0 | 100.0 | 100.0 | | 100.0 | 100.0 | 100.0 | 100.0 | 100.0 |
| Gross Profit | 26.1 | 24.3 | 26.4 | | 40.9 | 29.4 | 27.5 | 22.0 | 21.0 |
| Operating Expenses | 21.4 | 18.4 | 19.4 | | 32.5 | 23.4 | 22.6 | 16.5 | 13.0 |
| Operating Profit | 4.7 | 5.9 | 7.0 | | 8.5 | 6.0 | 4.9 | 5.5 | 8.0 |
| All Other Expenses (net) | 1.3 | 1.6 | .5 | | .8 | 1.5 | .3 | -.2 | .8 |
| Profit Before Taxes | 3.3 | 4.2 | 6.5 | | 7.7 | 4.4 | 4.7 | 5.7 | 7.2 |
| **RATIOS** | | | | | | | | | |
| Current | 3.4 | 2.9 | 2.9 | | 4.8 | 3.3 | 2.3 | 4.4 | 2.4 |
| | 1.9 | 1.8 | 1.9 | | 2.7 | 1.2 | 1.8 | 2.0 | 1.9 |
| | 1.2 | 1.2 | 1.2 | | 1.7 | .8 | 1.1 | 1.0 | 1.4 |
| Quick | 2.1 | 1.8 | 1.8 | | 3.5 | 2.1 | 1.8 | 1.9 | 1.5 |
| | .9 | .8 | .9 | | 1.7 | .8 | .9 | .9 | .9 |
| | .6 | .5 | .6 | | .8 | .4 | .6 | .5 | .9 |
| Sales/Receivables | 33 11.1 | 37 9.8 | 36 10.1 | | 35 10.4 | 34 10.6 | 38 9.6 | 37 9.9 | 37 9.8 |
| | 44 8.4 | 48 7.6 | 45 8.1 | | 42 8.7 | 41 9.0 | 45 8.1 | 47 7.7 | 49 7.5 |
| | 60 6.1 | 58 6.3 | 58 6.3 | | 44 8.3 | 56 6.5 | 64 5.7 | 58 6.3 | 58 6.3 |
| Cost of Sales/Inventory | 35 10.4 | 44 8.4 | 38 9.7 | | 16 22.5 | 22 16.4 | 34 10.8 | 47 7.8 | 43 8.4 |
| | 59 6.2 | 75 4.9 | 62 5.9 | | 59 6.2 | 41 8.8 | 60 6.1 | 62 5.9 | 66 5.5 |
| | 111 3.3 | 123 3.0 | 96 3.8 | | 122 3.0 | 96 3.8 | 85 4.3 | 83 4.4 | 114 3.2 |
| Cost of Sales/Payables | 15 24.6 | 22 16.9 | 19 19.3 | | 6 62.2 | 19 19.7 | 23 15.8 | 23 16.2 | 20 18.7 |
| | 26 13.8 | 33 10.9 | 37 9.9 | | 25 14.5 | 33 10.9 | 47 7.8 | 32 11.4 | 37 9.9 |
| | 42 8.6 | 47 7.8 | 56 6.5 | | 58 6.3 | 70 5.2 | 68 5.4 | 57 6.4 | 49 7.5 |
| Sales/Working Capital | 3.7 | 3.8 | 4.1 | | 3.4 | 7.0 | 6.3 | 3.1 | 4.0 |
| | 7.2 | 7.3 | 8.4 | | 7.9 | 31.3 | 9.4 | 7.2 | 6.4 |
| | 27.9 | 18.8 | 26.9 | | 11.0 | -14.4 | 57.6 | -86.4 | 13.5 |
| EBIT/Interest | 14.6 | 17.2 | 20.1 | | 61.8 | 9.1 | 14.9 | 10.8 | 28.2 |
| | (113) 2.6 | (111) 5.0 | (126) 7.1 | | (10) 5.2 | (10) 3.5 | (18) 7.2 | (24) 7.1 | (59) 10.1 |
| | -.5 | 1.1 | 1.9 | | 1.7 | 1.1 | 1.7 | 2.1 | 2.9 |
| Net Profit + Depr., Dep., Amort./Cur. Mat. L/T/D | 4.1 | 5.4 | 10.3 | | | | | | 10.8 |
| | (28) 1.6 | (29) 2.1 | (44) 5.9 | | | | | | (29) 7.0 |
| | .5 | 1.3 | 3.0 | | | | | | 3.7 |
| Fixed/Worth | .4 | .4 | .3 | | .1 | .8 | .3 | .3 | .5 |
| | .7 | .8 | .8 | | .5 | 5.9 | .3 | .7 | .8 |
| | 3.2 | 2.7 | 2.7 | | 1.3 | NM | 2.7 | 1.8 | 2.4 |
| Debt/Worth | .7 | .6 | .7 | | .9 | 1.0 | .6 | .5 | .6 |
| | 1.5 | 1.8 | 2.1 | | 2.1 | 19.5 | 2.3 | 1.5 | 1.6 |
| | 7.1 | 7.1 | 6.9 | | 7.6 | NM | 6.1 | 3.0 | 5.4 |
| % Profit Before Taxes/Tangible Net Worth | 39.9 | 41.3 | 51.2 | | 105.1 | | 40.1 | 35.8 | 50.1 |
| | (102) 14.5 | (101) 19.5 | (122) 28.2 | | (10) 62.3 | | (18) 18.3 | (26) 22.9 | (57) 28.9 |
| | -6.0 | 4.5 | 12.6 | | 25.0 | | 6.9 | 6.2 | 14.7 |
| % Profit Before Taxes/Total Assets | 14.5 | 17.0 | 19.2 | | 33.2 | 24.9 | 16.7 | 14.9 | 18.3 |
| | 3.3 | 5.5 | 10.5 | | 21.7 | 7.2 | 9.4 | 6.1 | 11.4 |
| | -4.6 | .2 | 3.1 | | 3.6 | -1.2 | 1.4 | 2.9 | 5.0 |
| Sales/Net Fixed Assets | 11.1 | 13.1 | 13.8 | | 75.8 | 9.6 | 24.0 | 13.1 | 10.5 |
| | 5.3 | 6.8 | 7.8 | | 12.0 | 5.7 | 13.8 | 9.6 | 6.7 |
| | 3.4 | 3.5 | 4.0 | | 8.3 | 2.5 | 6.6 | 4.7 | 3.8 |
| Sales/Total Assets | 2.2 | 2.2 | 2.5 | | 3.6 | 3.1 | 2.9 | 2.3 | 2.3 |
| | 1.6 | 1.8 | 1.9 | | 2.1 | 2.3 | 2.2 | 1.9 | 1.8 |
| | 1.2 | 1.2 | 1.3 | | 1.7 | 1.2 | 1.6 | 1.4 | 1.3 |
| % Depr., Dep., Amort./Sales | 1.7 | 1.5 | 1.5 | | | | 1.2 | 1.2 | 1.5 |
| | (103) 3.0 | (110) 2.8 | (121) 2.5 | | | | (17) 2.6 | (26) 2.2 | (60) 2.7 |
| | 5.2 | 4.7 | 4.0 | | | | 3.4 | 3.1 | 4.0 |
| % Officers', Directors' Owners' Comp/Sales | 1.8 | 1.4 | 1.9 | | | | 1.9 | 1.6 | .6 |
| | (34) 3.8 | (33) 2.7 | (45) 2.9 | | | | (11) 3.2 | (12) 3.6 | (11) 2.8 |
| | 8.2 | 4.6 | 5.5 | | | | 3.8 | 5.0 | 9.1 |
| Net Sales ($) | 5149694M | 4663866M | 6364880M | 3845M | 26769M | 49010M | 142344M | 465720M | 5677192M |
| Total Assets ($) | 3388856M | 2999544M | 3665503M | 3332M | 11535M | 28922M | 81319M | 284134M | 3256261M |

M = $ thousand   MM = $ million
See Pages 9 through 22 for Explanation of Ratios and Data

## Current Data Sorted by Assets | Comparative Historical Data

| | | | | | | | Type of Statement | | |
|---|---|---|---|---|---|---|---|---|---|
| 2 | | 3 | 15 | 5 | 3 | | Unqualified | 42 | 36 |
| 2 | 7 | 57 | 24 | 1 | | | Reviewed | 83 | 80 |
| 1 | 8 | 23 | 5 | | | | Compiled | 47 | 37 |
| 5 | 10 | 9 | 1 | | | | Tax Returns | 17 | 20 |
| 5 | 8 | 33 | 36 | 6 | 4 | | Other | 96 | 126 |
| | 52 (4/1-9/30/11) | | 221 (10/1/11-3/31/12) | | | | | 4/1/07-3/31/08 | 4/1/08-3/31/09 |
| 0-500M | 500M-2MM | 2-10MM | 10-50MM | 50-100MM | 100-250MM | | | ALL | ALL |
| 15 | 33 | 125 | 81 | 12 | 7 | | NUMBER OF STATEMENTS | 285 | 299 |
| % | % | % | % | % | % | | ASSETS | % | % |
| 11.1 | 11.5 | 7.0 | 5.5 | 4.0 | | | Cash & Equivalents | 7.3 | 7.4 |
| 34.8 | 30.8 | 27.6 | 24.9 | 22.0 | | | Trade Receivables (net) | 25.9 | 23.0 |
| 17.3 | 24.0 | 24.7 | 26.4 | 21.2 | | | Inventory | 22.5 | 25.0 |
| 1.6 | .6 | 1.4 | 1.6 | 5.3 | | | All Other Current | 1.5 | 1.9 |
| 64.8 | 66.9 | 60.7 | 58.4 | 52.6 | | | Total Current | 57.2 | 57.3 |
| 31.1 | 26.6 | 29.7 | 33.4 | 33.5 | | | Fixed Assets (net) | 32.2 | 32.5 |
| .1 | 1.7 | 3.1 | 3.6 | 5.9 | | | Intangibles (net) | 5.0 | 4.0 |
| 4.1 | 4.8 | 6.5 | 4.6 | 8.0 | | | All Other Non-Current | 5.6 | 6.1 |
| 100.0 | 100.0 | 100.0 | 100.0 | 100.0 | | | Total | 100.0 | 100.0 |
| | | | | | | | LIABILITIES | | |
| 20.5 | 8.8 | 9.5 | 10.1 | 9.5 | | | Notes Payable-Short Term | 9.6 | 10.7 |
| 6.2 | 6.8 | 3.5 | 3.5 | 1.7 | | | Cur. Mat.-L.T.D. | 4.9 | 4.2 |
| 25.9 | 14.4 | 15.5 | 13.9 | 13.9 | | | Trade Payables | 14.5 | 12.6 |
| .0 | .0 | .3 | .1 | .1 | | | Income Taxes Payable | .1 | .2 |
| 40.2 | 9.2 | 6.0 | 7.4 | 7.2 | | | All Other Current | 7.7 | 7.0 |
| 92.8 | 39.2 | 34.8 | 35.0 | 32.2 | | | Total Current | 36.8 | 34.7 |
| 27.6 | 21.2 | 12.5 | 16.1 | 10.4 | | | Long-Term Debt | 16.6 | 18.0 |
| .0 | .0 | .5 | .6 | 1.0 | | | Deferred Taxes | .4 | .5 |
| 12.3 | 4.7 | 5.2 | 6.0 | 3.1 | | | All Other Non-Current | 6.4 | 6.6 |
| -33.1 | 34.9 | 47.0 | 42.3 | 53.3 | | | Net Worth | 39.8 | 40.3 |
| 100.0 | 100.0 | 100.0 | 100.0 | 100.0 | | | Total Liabilities & Net Worth | 100.0 | 100.0 |
| | | | | | | | INCOME DATA | | |
| 100.0 | 100.0 | 100.0 | 100.0 | 100.0 | | | Net Sales | 100.0 | 100.0 |
| 33.2 | 32.4 | 25.1 | 19.8 | 20.0 | | | Gross Profit | 23.8 | 24.2 |
| 27.6 | 27.0 | 20.0 | 13.1 | 14.2 | | | Operating Expenses | 18.8 | 19.6 |
| 5.6 | 5.4 | 5.1 | 6.7 | 5.7 | | | Operating Profit | 5.0 | 4.6 |
| 1.6 | .5 | .2 | .7 | .0 | | | All Other Expenses (net) | 1.1 | 1.1 |
| 4.0 | 4.9 | 4.9 | 6.1 | 5.7 | | | Profit Before Taxes | 4.0 | 3.4 |
| | | | | | | | RATIOS | | |
| 2.0 | 3.2 | 2.9 | 2.5 | 3.2 | | | | 2.7 | 2.7 |
| 1.1 | 1.5 | 1.9 | 1.6 | 1.3 | | | Current | 1.6 | 1.7 |
| .3 | 1.2 | 1.2 | 1.2 | 1.1 | | | | 1.1 | 1.1 |
| 1.4 | 2.0 | 1.9 | 1.3 | 1.4 | | | | 1.5 | 1.4 |
| .7 | 1.1 | 1.0 | .8 | .7 | | | Quick | .9 | .8 |
| .2 | .7 | .6 | .6 | .6 | | | | .6 | .5 |

| | | | | | | | | | | | | | | |
|---|---|---|---|---|---|---|---|---|---|---|---|---|---|---|
| 28 | 13.0 | 33 | 11.1 | 37 | 9.9 | 40 | 9.2 | 36 | 10.2 | | | Sales/Receivables | 36 | 10.3 | 30 | 12.2 |
| 45 | 8.2 | 39 | 9.3 | 46 | 7.9 | 48 | 7.6 | 52 | 7.0 | | | | 45 | 8.2 | 40 | 9.2 |
| 52 | 7.0 | 49 | 7.5 | 57 | 6.4 | 60 | 6.1 | 60 | 6.1 | | | | 55 | 6.7 | 51 | 7.1 |
| 9 | 39.7 | 21 | 17.1 | 36 | 10.0 | 40 | 9.1 | 30 | 12.0 | | | Cost of Sales/Inventory | 30 | 12.3 | 35 | 10.5 |
| 26 | 14.0 | 35 | 10.5 | 54 | 6.7 | 63 | 5.8 | 53 | 6.9 | | | | 48 | 7.6 | 55 | 6.7 |
| 73 | 5.0 | 70 | 5.2 | 85 | 4.3 | 96 | 3.8 | 78 | 4.7 | | | | 72 | 5.1 | 80 | 4.6 |
| 3 | 125.8 | 19 | 19.6 | 20 | 18.0 | 22 | 16.6 | 21 | 17.4 | | | Cost of Sales/Payables | 19 | 19.7 | 16 | 23.3 |
| 41 | 9.0 | 24 | 15.4 | 32 | 11.3 | 30 | 12.0 | 33 | 11.1 | | | | 29 | 12.7 | 24 | 14.9 |
| 62 | 5.9 | 35 | 10.4 | 47 | 7.8 | 46 | 7.9 | 43 | 8.4 | | | | 42 | 8.8 | 39 | 9.5 |

| Col1 | Col2 | Col3 | Col4 | Col5 | Col6 | Ratio | Hist1 | Hist2 |
|---|---|---|---|---|---|---|---|---|
| 7.3 | 5.7 | 5.1 | 4.6 | 5.0 | | Sales/Working Capital | 5.5 | 5.5 |
| 61.0 | 12.8 | 8.1 | 8.6 | 14.7 | | | 10.5 | 9.7 |
| -24.7 | 27.4 | 30.9 | 18.5 | 39.0 | | | 71.8 | 46.6 |
| 13.3 | 10.6 | 20.0 | 16.6 | 25.7 | | EBIT/Interest | 8.7 | 10.0 |
| (11) 3.5 | (29) 4.9 | (118) 7.8 | (77) 6.7 | (11) 9.6 | | | (269) 3.1 | (273) 3.5 |
| 1.2 | 2.3 | 1.9 | 2.6 | 2.3 | | | 1.2 | 1.1 |
| | | 11.1 | 8.6 | | | Net Profit + Depr., Dep., Amort./Cur. Mat. L/T/D | 6.0 | 5.3 |
| | (31) 4.3 | (27) 3.3 | | | | | (79) 2.7 | (85) 2.4 |
| | | 1.1 | 2.0 | | | | .8 | 1.2 |
| .2 | .3 | .3 | .6 | .3 | | Fixed/Worth | .4 | .4 |
| 1.7 | .8 | .7 | .8 | 1.0 | | | .9 | .9 |
| 149.5 | 2.4 | 1.4 | 1.5 | 1.7 | | | 2.3 | 2.0 |
| 3.9 | .9 | .5 | .7 | .3 | | Debt/Worth | .7 | .6 |
| 6.2 | 2.0 | 1.2 | 1.7 | .9 | | | 1.7 | 1.6 |
| -2.1 | 5.8 | 3.1 | 2.9 | 3.7 | | | 5.2 | 3.7 |
| 105.6 | 55.5 | 40.9 | 40.3 | 33.0 | | % Profit Before Taxes/Tangible Net Worth | 41.5 | 36.5 |
| (10) 65.8 | (29) 20.3 | (119) 18.5 | (75) 23.4 | 18.8 | | | (252) 19.0 | (266) 15.0 |
| 11.1 | 8.0 | 5.9 | 13.5 | 14.1 | | | 3.4 | 2.2 |
| 21.3 | 21.3 | 18.3 | 14.6 | 12.2 | | % Profit Before Taxes/Total Assets | 14.1 | 13.7 |
| 11.8 | 7.4 | 9.3 | 10.1 | 9.4 | | | 6.0 | 5.9 |
| 5.5 | 3.0 | 1.6 | 4.4 | 3.0 | | | .5 | .2 |
| 107.4 | 32.3 | 13.8 | 8.7 | 6.3 | | Sales/Net Fixed Assets | 12.4 | 13.1 |
| 10.7 | 12.7 | 7.8 | 5.7 | 4.5 | | | 6.5 | 6.5 |
| 4.8 | 6.9 | 4.7 | 3.8 | 2.8 | | | 4.4 | 4.3 |
| 5.0 | 3.8 | 2.6 | 2.3 | 2.3 | | Sales/Total Assets | 2.6 | 2.5 |
| 2.9 | 2.7 | 2.1 | 1.8 | 1.6 | | | 2.0 | 2.0 |
| 2.1 | 2.0 | 1.7 | 1.4 | 1.1 | | | 1.7 | 1.6 |
| | .9 | 1.6 | 1.9 | 3.1 | | % Depr., Dep., Amort./Sales | 1.8 | 1.7 |
| | (28) 2.0 | (117) 2.6 | (76) 2.6 | (11) 3.9 | | | (260) 2.7 | (273) 2.7 |
| | 5.8 | 3.9 | 3.5 | 4.7 | | | 4.2 | 4.5 |
| | 1.6 | 2.4 | 1.2 | | | % Officers', Directors' Owners' Comp/Sales | 1.4 | 1.6 |
| | (16) 4.1 | (59) 3.9 | (22) 2.2 | | | | (99) 3.2 | (99) 3.6 |
| | 9.0 | 5.7 | 3.8 | | | | 5.3 | 7.1 |

| 16490M | 123939M | 1352763M | 2925622M | 1357730M | 2007075M | | Net Sales ($) | 8015387M | 7614453M |
| 4047M | 44414M | 635175M | 1601599M | 831772M | 1182402M | | Total Assets ($) | 4412735M | 4141483M |

M = $ thousand    MM = $ million
See Pages 9 through 22 for Explanation of Ratios and Data

## Comparative Historical Data | Current Data Sorted by Sales

| Type of Statement | | | | | | | | | |
|---|---|---|---|---|---|---|---|---|---|
| Unqualified | 34 | 30 | 28 | 2 | | | 1 | 7 | 18 |
| Reviewed | 72 | 79 | 91 | 1 | 6 | 8 | 21 | 30 | 25 |
| Compiled | 31 | 37 | 37 | 1 | 3 | 7 | 14 | 9 | 3 |
| Tax Returns | 19 | 30 | 25 | 1 | 8 | 6 | 8 | 1 | 1 |
| Other | 116 | 99 | 92 | 3 | 7 | 4 | 14 | 31 | 33 |
| | 4/1/09-3/31/10 | 4/1/10-3/31/11 | 4/1/11-3/31/12 | \<--- 52 (4/1-9/30/11) | | \---> | \<--- 221 (10/1/11-3/31/12) | | \---> |
| | ALL | ALL | ALL | 0-1MM | 1-3MM | 3-5MM | 5-10MM | 10-25MM | 25MM & OVER |
| **NUMBER OF STATEMENTS** | 272 | 275 | 273 | 8 | 24 | 25 | 58 | 78 | 80 |
| | % | % | % | % | % | % | % | % | % |
| **ASSETS** | | | | | | | | | |
| Cash & Equivalents | 7.2 | 7.8 | 7.2 | 11.4 | 10.4 | 9.2 | 5.3 | 5.1 | |
| Trade Receivables (net) | 23.5 | 25.8 | 27.2 | 28.6 | 27.0 | 29.0 | 28.0 | 25.3 | |
| Inventory | 22.5 | 23.5 | 24.5 | 19.2 | 26.1 | 24.9 | 25.0 | 25.5 | |
| All Other Current | 2.9 | 1.6 | 1.6 | .3 | .9 | .5 | 2.1 | 2.3 | |
| Total Current | 56.0 | 58.7 | 60.4 | 59.5 | 64.3 | 63.6 | 60.4 | 58.2 | |
| Fixed Assets (net) | 33.7 | 31.6 | 30.9 | 31.9 | 27.7 | 26.6 | 31.8 | 33.2 | |
| Intangibles (net) | 5.0 | 3.4 | 3.1 | 1.5 | 1.8 | 3.6 | 3.2 | 3.7 | |
| All Other Non-Current | 5.3 | 6.3 | 5.6 | 7.2 | 6.2 | 6.3 | 4.6 | 5.0 | |
| Total | 100.0 | 100.0 | 100.0 | 100.0 | 100.0 | 100.0 | 100.0 | 100.0 | |
| **LIABILITIES** | | | | | | | | | |
| Notes Payable-Short Term | 11.2 | 9.9 | 10.2 | 10.1 | 10.7 | 9.3 | 8.9 | 10.6 | |
| Cur. Mat.-L.T.D. | 4.7 | 4.4 | 4.0 | 8.1 | 4.9 | 3.2 | 3.0 | 3.7 | |
| Trade Payables | 13.7 | 14.7 | 15.3 | 18.3 | 12.9 | 14.2 | 16.1 | 14.8 | |
| Income Taxes Payable | .1 | .1 | .2 | .0 | .1 | .2 | .3 | .1 | |
| All Other Current | 7.8 | 7.6 | 8.8 | 17.8 | 6.7 | 6.4 | 6.3 | 7.8 | |
| Total Current | 37.6 | 36.8 | 38.5 | 54.4 | 35.3 | 33.4 | 34.7 | 37.0 | |
| Long-Term Debt | 18.5 | 16.2 | 15.5 | 18.5 | 18.6 | 14.7 | 13.4 | 13.0 | |
| Deferred Taxes | .4 | .5 | .5 | .0 | .0 | .5 | .5 | .7 | |
| All Other Non-Current | 7.9 | 5.9 | 5.7 | 4.1 | 3.5 | 4.6 | 6.8 | 5.4 | |
| Net Worth | 35.5 | 40.6 | 39.8 | 22.9 | 42.7 | 46.7 | 44.7 | 43.9 | |
| Total Liabilties & Net Worth | 100.0 | 100.0 | 100.0 | 100.0 | 100.0 | 100.0 | 100.0 | 100.0 | |
| **INCOME DATA** | | | | | | | | | |
| Net Sales | 100.0 | 100.0 | 100.0 | 100.0 | 100.0 | 100.0 | 100.0 | 100.0 | |
| Gross Profit | 23.4 | 25.6 | 24.4 | 31.3 | 30.4 | 26.5 | 23.2 | 18.7 | |
| Operating Expenses | 21.5 | 20.0 | 18.7 | 26.6 | 25.9 | 21.2 | 17.0 | 12.8 | |
| Operating Profit | 1.9 | 5.6 | 5.7 | 4.7 | 4.4 | 5.3 | 6.2 | 5.9 | |
| All Other Expenses (net) | 1.0 | .9 | .5 | 1.1 | .3 | .0 | .7 | .2 | |
| Profit Before Taxes | .9 | 4.7 | 5.3 | 3.6 | 4.2 | 5.3 | 5.5 | 5.7 | |
| **RATIOS** | | | | | | | | | |
| Current | 2.7 | 3.0 | 2.8 | 2.2 | 2.7 | 3.3 | 3.0 | 2.3 | |
| | 1.5 | 1.7 | 1.7 | 1.2 | 1.6 | 2.0 | 1.7 | 1.5 | |
| | 1.0 | 1.1 | 1.2 | .9 | 1.2 | 1.4 | 1.2 | 1.2 | |
| Quick | 1.6 | 1.8 | 1.6 | 1.5 | 1.7 | 2.2 | 1.5 | 1.2 | |
| | .8 | 1.0 | .9 | .8 | 1.1 | 1.2 | .9 | .8 | |
| | .5 | .6 | .6 | .4 | .6 | .7 | .6 | .5 | |
| Sales/Receivables | 35 10.3 | 38 9.6 | 37 9.9 | 34 10.7 | 34 10.7 | 36 10.2 | 37 9.8 | 38 9.6 | |
| | 50 7.3 | 48 7.7 | 46 7.9 | 44 8.3 | 48 7.6 | 43 8.5 | 47 7.7 | 47 7.8 | |
| | 64 5.7 | 60 6.1 | 58 6.3 | 59 6.2 | 65 5.6 | 52 7.0 | 63 5.8 | 57 6.4 | |
| Cost of Sales/Inventory | 36 10.1 | 38 9.7 | 34 10.6 | 18 20.6 | 31 11.8 | 38 9.7 | 34 10.6 | 37 9.9 | |
| | 58 6.3 | 54 6.7 | 54 6.8 | 32 11.3 | 54 6.7 | 51 7.1 | 55 6.6 | 54 6.7 | |
| | 86 4.3 | 80 4.5 | 85 4.3 | 89 4.1 | 114 3.2 | 74 4.9 | 87 4.2 | 79 4.6 | |
| Cost of Sales/Payables | 19 19.1 | 20 18.2 | 20 18.0 | 20 17.9 | 18 20.4 | 19 19.1 | 21 17.4 | 21 17.5 | |
| | 30 12.1 | 32 11.4 | 31 11.9 | 36 10.0 | 34 10.6 | 26 14.3 | 34 10.6 | 30 12.0 | |
| | 50 7.3 | 47 7.7 | 46 7.9 | 62 5.9 | 50 7.3 | 38 9.6 | 54 6.8 | 43 8.4 | |
| Sales/Working Capital | 4.6 | 4.7 | 5.2 | 7.9 | 4.1 | 5.1 | 5.1 | 5.9 | |
| | 9.9 | 8.9 | 9.1 | 27.4 | 7.6 | 8.5 | 8.0 | 9.8 | |
| | 306.2 | 36.1 | 27.4 | -43.2 | 24.9 | 15.3 | 28.3 | 26.1 | |
| EBIT/Interest | 6.5 | 13.0 | 16.7 | 12.4 | 13.0 | 13.3 | 20.2 | 18.1 | |
| | (254) 1.6 | (241) 5.2 | (252) 6.7 | (20) 3.6 | (24) 5.1 | (53) 5.9 | (73) 8.1 | (76) 9.7 | |
| | -1.0 | 1.8 | 2.2 | 1.2 | 1.5 | 2.1 | 2.3 | 3.5 | |
| Net Profit + Depr., Dep., Amort./Cur. Mat. L/T/D | 3.5 | 7.9 | 8.8 | | | 10.8 | 13.3 | 8.3 | |
| | (59) 1.6 | (64) 3.8 | (65) 3.5 | | (10) 3.6 | (29) 4.7 | (20) 4.1 | | |
| | .6 | 1.9 | 1.7 | | | 1.6 | 2.3 | 2.0 | |
| Fixed/Worth | .5 | .4 | .4 | .2 | .3 | .3 | .5 | .5 | |
| | 1.0 | .8 | .8 | 1.0 | .7 | .6 | .9 | .8 | |
| | 2.6 | 1.8 | 1.7 | 2.6 | 1.4 | 1.4 | 1.5 | 1.4 | |
| Debt/Worth | .6 | .5 | .6 | 1.2 | .5 | .6 | .6 | .5 | |
| | 1.7 | 1.5 | 1.6 | 3.8 | 1.4 | 1.2 | 1.2 | 1.6 | |
| | 5.8 | 3.6 | 3.5 | 7.3 | 2.8 | 2.6 | 3.5 | 3.0 | |
| % Profit Before Taxes/Tangible Net Worth | 24.8 | 37.5 | 43.0 | 64.9 | 31.1 | 48.3 | 40.9 | 44.4 | |
| | (236) 6.5 | (246) 19.2 | (251) 21.1 | (23) 18.6 | (23) 15.0 | (55) 16.6 | (71) 24.7 | (76) 23.6 | |
| | -10.8 | 4.7 | 8.1 | 1.1 | 4.0 | 6.6 | 7.6 | 16.2 | |
| % Profit Before Taxes/Total Assets | 8.3 | 14.5 | 16.6 | 19.0 | 17.9 | 19.0 | 18.0 | 14.3 | |
| | 1.4 | 8.4 | 9.7 | 6.0 | 7.4 | 9.9 | 9.0 | 10.6 | |
| | -5.1 | 2.0 | 2.7 | .6 | 1.1 | 2.7 | 2.6 | 5.3 | |
| Sales/Net Fixed Assets | 10.7 | 11.8 | 12.9 | 33.7 | 13.9 | 18.1 | 11.5 | 9.3 | |
| | 5.2 | 6.1 | 7.0 | 10.5 | 6.5 | 10.2 | 6.2 | 6.2 | |
| | 3.2 | 4.2 | 4.6 | 5.1 | 4.7 | 5.7 | 4.2 | 4.4 | |
| Sales/Total Assets | 2.2 | 2.4 | 2.6 | 3.2 | 2.7 | 2.9 | 2.5 | 2.4 | |
| | 1.7 | 1.9 | 2.0 | 2.4 | 1.8 | 2.2 | 2.0 | 2.0 | |
| | 1.2 | 1.4 | 1.6 | 1.4 | 1.3 | 1.7 | 1.6 | 1.6 | |
| % Depr., Dep., Amort./Sales | 2.2 | 1.9 | 1.7 | 1.0 | 1.9 | 1.3 | 1.7 | 2.0 | |
| | (237) 3.8 | (247) 3.1 | (245) 2.6 | (19) 2.7 | (23) 3.6 | (54) 2.3 | (71) 2.6 | (73) 2.7 | |
| | 5.9 | 4.6 | 3.9 | 7.8 | 4.0 | 3.6 | 3.9 | 3.6 | |
| % Officers', Directors' Owners' Comp/Sales | 2.1 | 2.0 | 2.0 | 4.0 | 1.6 | 3.0 | 2.0 | .8 | |
| | (87) 3.7 | (99) 3.3 | (105) 3.8 | (12) 5.9 | (15) 3.8 | (29) 5.0 | (29) 2.9 | (17) 2.3 | |
| | 7.1 | 6.3 | 6.3 | 10.0 | 5.0 | 7.7 | 4.8 | 3.6 | |
| Net Sales ($) | 5747250M | 7123651M | 7783619M | 2826M | 49344M | 102051M | 425476M | 1228022M | 5975900M |
| Total Assets ($) | 4010216M | 4408137M | 4299409M | 2300M | 29479M | 57981M | 213933M | 667351M | 3328365M |

© RMA 2012

M = $ thousand    MM = $ million
See Pages 9 through 22 for Explanation of Ratios and Data

**Current Data Sorted by Assets**          **Comparative Historical Data**

| 0-500M | 500M-2MM | 2-10MM | 10-50MM | 50-100MM | 100-250MM | Type of Statement | 4/1/07-3/31/08 ALL | 4/1/08-3/31/09 ALL |
|---|---|---|---|---|---|---|---|---|
| | | 2 | | | | Unqualified | 7 | 6 |
| | 4 | 4 | 3 | | | Reviewed | 6 | 8 |
| 1 | 3 | 8 | | | | Compiled | 5 | 13 |
| | 4 | 5 | 6 | 1 | | Tax Returns | 3 | 6 |
| | | | | 2 | | Other | 10 | 10 |
| | 11 (4/1-9/30/11) | 32 (10/1/11-3/31/12) | | | | | | |
| 1 | 11 | 19 | 9 | 3 | | **NUMBER OF STATEMENTS** | 31 | 43 |
| % | % | % | % | % | % | | % | % |
| | 9.6 | 7.7 | | | | **ASSETS** Cash & Equivalents | 8.8 | 8.4 |
| | 40.2 | 24.2 | | | | Trade Receivables (net) | 27.1 | 24.1 |
| | 17.2 | 21.3 | | | | Inventory | 24.6 | 23.2 |
| | .2 | .2 | | | | All Other Current | 1.6 | 2.2 |
| | 67.1 | 53.4 | | | | Total Current | 62.1 | 57.9 |
| | 28.1 | 32.3 | | | | Fixed Assets (net) | 25.9 | 32.0 |
| | 4.4 | 5.2 | | | | Intangibles (net) | 6.3 | 4.7 |
| | .4 | 9.1 | | | | All Other Non-Current | 5.8 | 5.4 |
| | 100.0 | 100.0 | | | | Total | 100.0 | 100.0 |
| | 6.6 | 5.4 | | | | **LIABILITIES** Notes Payable-Short Term | 7.6 | 7.6 |
| | 2.5 | 5.8 | | | | Cur. Mat.-L.T.D. | 5.1 | 3.8 |
| | 27.3 | 16.2 | | | | Trade Payables | 13.7 | 15.3 |
| | .0 | .0 | | | | Income Taxes Payable | .0 | .0 |
| | 2.4 | 5.7 | | | | All Other Current | 7.9 | 5.0 |
| | 38.8 | 33.1 | | | | Total Current | 34.3 | 31.7 |
| | 58.4 | 17.4 | | | | Long-Term Debt | 20.7 | 25.2 |
| | .0 | .0 | | | | Deferred Taxes | .7 | .2 |
| | 1.5 | 11.2 | | | | All Other Non-Current | 4.8 | 9.3 |
| | 1.2 | 38.3 | | | | Net Worth | 39.6 | 33.5 |
| | 100.0 | 100.0 | | | | Total Liabilities & Net Worth | 100.0 | 100.0 |
| | 100.0 | 100.0 | | | | **INCOME DATA** Net Sales | 100.0 | 100.0 |
| | 37.3 | 30.0 | | | | Gross Profit | 27.5 | 28.9 |
| | 27.4 | 22.8 | | | | Operating Expenses | 18.5 | 22.6 |
| | 9.9 | 7.2 | | | | Operating Profit | 9.0 | 6.3 |
| | 3.7 | 2.0 | | | | All Other Expenses (net) | .9 | .7 |
| | 6.1 | 5.2 | | | | Profit Before Taxes | 8.1 | 5.6 |
| | 2.3 | 4.4 | | | | **RATIOS** Current | 2.7 | 3.2 |
| | 1.7 | 1.9 | | | | Current | 2.0 | 2.2 |
| | 1.1 | 1.0 | | | | | 1.2 | 1.4 |
| | 1.7 | 2.1 | | | | Quick | 1.8 | 2.1 |
| | 1.1 | 1.3 | | | | Quick | 1.1 | 1.1 |
| | .8 | .7 | | | | | .7 | .7 |
| | 28   13.1 | 32   11.4 | | | | Sales/Receivables | 33   11.0 | 29   12.6 |
| | 38   9.5 | 46   8.0 | | | | Sales/Receivables | 47   7.7 | 39   9.4 |
| | 64   5.7 | 58   6.3 | | | | | 67   5.4 | 55   6.7 |
| | 15   24.9 | 26   14.3 | | | | Cost of Sales/Inventory | 35   10.4 | 33   11.2 |
| | 27   13.4 | 43   8.5 | | | | Cost of Sales/Inventory | 67   5.5 | 65   5.7 |
| | 65   5.6 | 65   5.6 | | | | | 91   4.0 | 88   4.1 |
| | 22   16.5 | 20   18.3 | | | | Cost of Sales/Payables | 17   20.9 | 13   28.2 |
| | 46   8.0 | 33   10.9 | | | | Cost of Sales/Payables | 29   12.7 | 31   11.9 |
| | 83   4.4 | 70   5.2 | | | | | 49   7.5 | 49   7.4 |
| | 6.9 | 5.2 | | | | Sales/Working Capital | 3.6 | 4.3 |
| | 11.6 | 8.1 | | | | Sales/Working Capital | 6.6 | 7.8 |
| | 106.9 | 54.9 | | | | | 17.8 | 18.1 |
| | 9.2 | 15.2 | | | | EBIT/Interest | 18.0 | 11.5 |
| | (10) 6.1 | (17) 4.4 | | | | EBIT/Interest | (28) 4.5 | (38) 4.1 |
| | 2.4 | 1.7 | | | | | 2.6 | 1.7 |
| | | | | | | Net Profit + Depr., Dep., Amort./Cur. Mat. L/T/D | 10.2 | |
| | | | | | | | (10) 3.9 | |
| | | | | | | | 1.9 | |
| | .7 | .5 | | | | Fixed/Worth | .3 | .4 |
| | 2.5 | 1.0 | | | | Fixed/Worth | .7 | .7 |
| | -.2 | 5.7 | | | | | 1.5 | 2.3 |
| | 1.6 | .7 | | | | Debt/Worth | .6 | .5 |
| | 4.2 | 1.8 | | | | Debt/Worth | 1.4 | 1.4 |
| | -5.3 | 13.4 | | | | | 5.4 | 6.9 |
| | | 45.1 | | | | % Profit Before Taxes/Tangible Net Worth | 45.8 | 66.6 |
| | | (15) 25.4 | | | | % Profit Before Taxes/Tangible Net Worth | (26) 23.6 | (37) 28.5 |
| | | 10.8 | | | | | 15.0 | 5.8 |
| | 46.6 | 14.5 | | | | % Profit Before Taxes/Total Assets | 16.8 | 16.8 |
| | 13.0 | 9.1 | | | | % Profit Before Taxes/Total Assets | 13.1 | 7.8 |
| | 1.3 | 1.8 | | | | | 4.0 | 2.1 |
| | 93.3 | 17.3 | | | | Sales/Net Fixed Assets | 16.3 | 15.7 |
| | 18.0 | 6.0 | | | | Sales/Net Fixed Assets | 7.6 | 6.0 |
| | 2.3 | 3.0 | | | | | 4.8 | 3.9 |
| | 3.9 | 2.5 | | | | Sales/Total Assets | 2.4 | 2.6 |
| | 2.9 | 1.9 | | | | Sales/Total Assets | 2.0 | 1.9 |
| | 1.4 | 1.3 | | | | | 1.4 | 1.4 |
| | | 1.2 | | | | % Depr., Dep., Amort./Sales | 1.5 | 1.1 |
| | | (17) 2.9 | | | | % Depr., Dep., Amort./Sales | (27) 2.7 | (39) 2.4 |
| | | 5.3 | | | | | 3.9 | 3.3 |
| | | | | | | % Officers', Directors' Owners' Comp/Sales | | 1.7 |
| | | | | | | | (17) 2.5 | |
| | | | | | | | | 4.4 |
| 268M | 37300M | 201423M | 282710M | 171587M | | Net Sales ($) | 913778M | 845918M |
| 9M | 11878M | 98323M | 148199M | 209469M | | Total Assets ($) | 641629M | 512627M |

(Columns 10-50MM, 50-100MM and 100-250MM indicate "DATA NOT AVAILABLE" for the Assets, Liabilities, Income Data and Ratios sections.)

## Comparative Historical Data | Current Data Sorted by Sales

| 4/1/09-3/31/10 ALL | 4/1/10-3/31/11 ALL | 4/1/11-3/31/12 ALL | Type of Statement | 0-1MM | 1-3MM | 3-5MM | 5-10MM | 10-25MM | 25MM & OVER |
|---|---|---|---|---|---|---|---|---|---|
| 4 | 6 | 4 | Unqualified | | | | | 2 | 2 |
| 2 | 9 | 7 | Reviewed | | 2 | 1 | 1 | 1 | 2 |
| 13 | 14 | 12 | Compiled | | | | 5 | 5 | |
| 6 | 3 | 4 | Tax Returns | 1 | 2 | 1 | | 6 | |
| 12 | 14 | 16 | Other | 1 | 3 | 2 | 3 | | 3 |
| | | | | 11 (4/1-9/30/11) | | | 32 (10/1/11-3/31/12) | | |
| 37 | 46 | 43 | NUMBER OF STATEMENTS | 2 | 7 | 4 | 9 | 14 | 7 |
| % | % | % | **ASSETS** | % | % | % | % | % | % |
| 12.8 | 7.8 | 9.2 | Cash & Equivalents | | | | | 9.1 | |
| 23.2 | 24.3 | 25.6 | Trade Receivables (net) | | | | | 28.5 | |
| 17.8 | 23.4 | 20.8 | Inventory | | | | | 18.3 | |
| .5 | .8 | .8 | All Other Current | | | | | .8 | |
| 54.4 | 56.3 | 56.4 | Total Current | | | | | 56.7 | |
| 31.7 | 31.6 | 29.7 | Fixed Assets (net) | | | | | 30.8 | |
| 9.1 | 6.5 | 6.2 | Intangibles (net) | | | | | 2.2 | |
| 4.8 | 5.7 | 7.7 | All Other Non-Current | | | | | 10.2 | |
| 100.0 | 100.0 | 100.0 | Total | | | | | 100.0 | |
| | | | **LIABILITIES** | | | | | | |
| 4.8 | 7.2 | 12.8 | Notes Payable-Short Term | | | | | 3.9 | |
| 4.9 | 4.6 | 3.8 | Cur. Mat.-L.T.D. | | | | | 2.9 | |
| 14.7 | 16.1 | 17.2 | Trade Payables | | | | | 18.3 | |
| .0 | .4 | .1 | Income Taxes Payable | | | | | .3 | |
| 4.9 | 5.9 | 5.3 | All Other Current | | | | | 6.1 | |
| 29.2 | 34.3 | 39.2 | Total Current | | | | | 31.5 | |
| 30.3 | 26.5 | 24.8 | Long-Term Debt | | | | | 7.1 | |
| .8 | .5 | .1 | Deferred Taxes | | | | | .2 | |
| 15.3 | 7.8 | 14.6 | All Other Non-Current | | | | | 13.4 | |
| 24.5 | 31.0 | 21.2 | Net Worth | | | | | 47.8 | |
| 100.0 | 100.0 | 100.0 | Total Liabilities & Net Worth | | | | | 100.0 | |
| | | | **INCOME DATA** | | | | | | |
| 100.0 | 100.0 | 100.0 | Net Sales | | | | | 100.0 | |
| 28.8 | 28.4 | 31.5 | Gross Profit | | | | | 23.8 | |
| 27.2 | 24.4 | 23.5 | Operating Expenses | | | | | 17.6 | |
| 1.6 | 4.0 | 8.0 | Operating Profit | | | | | 6.2 | |
| 2.2 | 1.9 | 2.3 | All Other Expenses (net) | | | | | 2.1 | |
| -.6 | 2.2 | 5.7 | Profit Before Taxes | | | | | 4.1 | |
| | | | **RATIOS** | | | | | | |
| 4.2 | 3.1 | 3.6 | Current | | | | | 4.8 | |
| 2.5 | 1.8 | 1.7 | | | | | | 2.0 | |
| 1.4 | 1.1 | 1.2 | | | | | | 1.0 | |
| 3.4 | 1.8 | 1.7 | Quick | | | | | 3.0 | |
| 1.5 | 1.1 | 1.1 | | | | | | 1.3 | |
| .9 | .5 | .5 | | | | | | .7 | |
| 31  11.9 | 33  11.2 | 30  12.2 | Sales/Receivables | | | | | 31  11.7 | |
| 45  8.0 | 52  7.0 | 43  8.5 | | | | | | 41  8.9 | |
| 56  6.5 | 62  5.9 | 58  6.3 | | | | | | 54  6.8 | |
| 17  21.0 | 35  10.5 | 26  14.3 | Cost of Sales/Inventory | | | | | 23  15.7 | |
| 52  7.0 | 64  5.7 | 52  7.0 | | | | | | 36  10.2 | |
| 89  4.1 | 117  3.1 | 85  4.3 | | | | | | 76  4.8 | |
| 10  35.3 | 20  18.2 | 20  18.3 | Cost of Sales/Payables | | | | | 21  17.6 | |
| 26  14.1 | 41  8.9 | 34  10.7 | | | | | | 24  15.1 | |
| 42  8.7 | 70  5.2 | 57  6.4 | | | | | | 36  10.0 | |
| 3.5 | 4.1 | 5.0 | Sales/Working Capital | | | | | 3.6 | |
| 6.1 | 7.7 | 8.1 | | | | | | 8.5 | |
| 17.2 | 30.5 | 31.8 | | | | | | NM | |
| 5.3 | 12.0 | 15.3 | EBIT/Interest | | | | | 22.7 | |
| (33)  .5 | (44)  2.5 | (38)  6.5 | | | | | | (12)  9.1 | |
| -1.7 | .3 | 2.1 | | | | | | 5.6 | |
| | | | Net Profit + Depr., Dep., Amort./Cur. Mat. L/T/D | | | | | | |
| .3 | .4 | .4 | Fixed/Worth | | | | | .3 | |
| 1.0 | 1.0 | 1.1 | | | | | | .7 | |
| -10.2 | NM | -31.4 | | | | | | 1.1 | |
| .4 | .5 | .7 | Debt/Worth | | | | | .3 | |
| 2.2 | 2.0 | 2.2 | | | | | | 1.1 | |
| -15.7 | NM | -143.3 | | | | | | 5.9 | |
| 33.3 | 32.3 | 54.7 | % Profit Before Taxes/Tangible Net Worth | | | | | 31.3 | |
| (26)  12.7 | (35)  13.0 | (32)  21.7 | | | | | | (12)  23.7 | |
| -7.8 | -6.1 | 4.3 | | | | | | 9.1 | |
| 10.8 | 13.5 | 20.6 | % Profit Before Taxes/Total Assets | | | | | 18.6 | |
| -.6 | 3.9 | 10.0 | | | | | | 10.1 | |
| -7.3 | -3.0 | 1.3 | | | | | | 5.3 | |
| 13.7 | 13.3 | 31.9 | Sales/Net Fixed Assets | | | | | 11.6 | |
| 6.2 | 6.3 | 7.8 | | | | | | 6.7 | |
| 3.2 | 3.3 | 2.7 | | | | | | 4.4 | |
| 2.6 | 2.5 | 3.1 | Sales/Total Assets | | | | | 3.2 | |
| 1.9 | 1.6 | 1.9 | | | | | | 2.1 | |
| 1.0 | 1.2 | 1.3 | | | | | | 1.5 | |
| 2.1 | 2.0 | 1.0 | % Depr., Dep., Amort./Sales | | | | | 2.5 | |
| (29)  4.1 | (42)  3.6 | (37)  2.7 | | | | | | (11)  2.9 | |
| 7.0 | 6.2 | 5.5 | | | | | | 3.9 | |
| 3.0 | 2.3 | 2.4 | % Officers', Directors' Owners' Comp/Sales | | | | | | |
| (12)  3.9 | (14)  3.4 | (14)  3.4 | | | | | | | |
| 9.1 | 11.9 | 6.3 | | | | | | | |
| 579752M | 695012M | 693288M | Net Sales ($) | 459M | 14436M | 14515M | 70190M | 228090M | 365598M |
| 533166M | 489730M | 467878M | Total Assets ($) | 1975M | 6166M | 11492M | 38339M | 112652M | 297254M |

M = $ thousand    MM = $ million
See Pages 9 through 22 for Explanation of Ratios and Data

## Current Data Sorted by Assets | Comparative Historical Data

| | 0-500M | 500M-2MM | 2-10MM | 10-50MM | 50-100MM | 100-250MM | Type of Statement | 4/1/07-3/31/08 ALL | 4/1/08-3/31/09 ALL |
|---|---|---|---|---|---|---|---|---|---|
| | 1 | 4 | 4 | 6 | 8 | | Unqualified | 13 | 13 |
| | 1 | 2 | 13 | 5 | | | Reviewed | 18 | 21 |
| | | 7 | 4 | | | | Compiled | 17 | 16 |
| | 1 | 4 | 2 | 7 | | 1 | Tax Returns | 9 | 6 |
| | | | 10 | | | | Other | 30 | 34 |
| | | 15 (4/1-9/30/11) | | 65 (10/1/11-3/31/12) | | | | | |
| NUMBER OF STATEMENTS | 3 | 17 | 33 | 18 | 8 | 1 | | 87 | 90 |

### ASSETS (%)

| | 0-500M | 500M-2MM | 2-10MM | 10-50MM | 50-100MM | 100-250MM | | 4/1/07-3/31/08 ALL | 4/1/08-3/31/09 ALL |
|---|---|---|---|---|---|---|---|---|---|
| | | 6.9 | 9.1 | 8.0 | | | Cash & Equivalents | 8.5 | 6.2 |
| | | 25.4 | 23.0 | 21.5 | | | Trade Receivables (net) | 23.9 | 23.1 |
| | | 24.4 | 43.0 | 32.8 | | | Inventory | 34.6 | 33.7 |
| | | .2 | 1.0 | 3.0 | | | All Other Current | 1.4 | 2.3 |
| | | 56.9 | 76.1 | 65.3 | | | Total Current | 68.3 | 65.2 |
| | | 33.9 | 16.3 | 19.7 | | | Fixed Assets (net) | 21.7 | 22.9 |
| | | 4.0 | 5.1 | 5.7 | | | Intangibles (net) | 4.8 | 6.1 |
| | | 5.2 | 2.4 | 9.3 | | | All Other Non-Current | 5.2 | 5.8 |
| | | 100.0 | 100.0 | 100.0 | | | Total | 100.0 | 100.0 |

### LIABILITIES

| | 0-500M | 500M-2MM | 2-10MM | 10-50MM | 50-100MM | 100-250MM | | 4/1/07-3/31/08 ALL | 4/1/08-3/31/09 ALL |
|---|---|---|---|---|---|---|---|---|---|
| | | 12.4 | 8.8 | 5.1 | | | Notes Payable-Short Term | 12.1 | 12.1 |
| | | 5.4 | 3.5 | 2.4 | | | Cur. Mat.-L.T.D. | 3.0 | 3.2 |
| | | 13.2 | 12.1 | 7.7 | | | Trade Payables | 10.7 | 12.0 |
| | | .5 | .0 | .2 | | | Income Taxes Payable | .2 | .0 |
| | | 7.2 | 9.9 | 5.7 | | | All Other Current | 9.3 | 8.5 |
| | | 38.6 | 34.3 | 21.0 | | | Total Current | 35.3 | 35.9 |
| | | 23.6 | 13.2 | 8.9 | | | Long-Term Debt | 13.8 | 17.5 |
| | | .5 | .0 | .0 | | | Deferred Taxes | .7 | .7 |
| | | 9.8 | 8.4 | 6.0 | | | All Other Non-Current | 6.6 | 7.6 |
| | | 27.6 | 44.1 | 64.0 | | | Net Worth | 43.7 | 38.4 |
| | | 100.0 | 100.0 | 100.0 | | | Total Liabilities & Net Worth | 100.0 | 100.0 |

### INCOME DATA

| | 0-500M | 500M-2MM | 2-10MM | 10-50MM | 50-100MM | 100-250MM | | 4/1/07-3/31/08 ALL | 4/1/08-3/31/09 ALL |
|---|---|---|---|---|---|---|---|---|---|
| | | 100.0 | 100.0 | 100.0 | | | Net Sales | 100.0 | 100.0 |
| | | 35.8 | 34.2 | 33.1 | | | Gross Profit | 35.8 | 34.7 |
| | | 29.6 | 28.7 | 23.1 | | | Operating Expenses | 30.3 | 30.6 |
| | | 6.2 | 5.5 | 10.0 | | | Operating Profit | 5.5 | 4.0 |
| | | 1.2 | 1.2 | -.2 | | | All Other Expenses (net) | 1.5 | 1.8 |
| | | 5.0 | 4.3 | 10.2 | | | Profit Before Taxes | 4.0 | 2.2 |

### RATIOS

| | 0-500M | 500M-2MM | 2-10MM | 10-50MM | 50-100MM | 100-250MM | | 4/1/07-3/31/08 ALL | 4/1/08-3/31/09 ALL |
|---|---|---|---|---|---|---|---|---|---|
| | | 2.7 | 4.0 | 5.8 | | | Current | 4.4 | 3.8 |
| | | 1.6 | 2.5 | 3.7 | | | | 2.1 | 1.9 |
| | | .9 | 1.5 | 2.7 | | | | 1.3 | 1.3 |
| | | 1.7 | 2.1 | 2.9 | | | Quick | 2.1 | 1.5 |
| | | .8 | .7 | 1.8 | | | | 1.0 | .8 |
| | | .6 | .5 | .8 | | | | .6 | .4 |
| | | 33　11.0 | 31　11.6 | 33　11.1 | | | Sales/Receivables | 29　12.4 | 27　13.5 |
| | | 43　8.4 | 39　9.4 | 44　8.3 | | | | 40　9.2 | 41　8.9 |
| | | 49　7.4 | 56　6.5 | 60　6.1 | | | | 57　6.4 | 51　7.1 |
| | | 36　10.2 | 78　4.7 | 73　5.0 | | | Cost of Sales/Inventory | 60　6.1 | 50　7.3 |
| | | 60　6.1 | 126　2.9 | 135　2.7 | | | | 98　3.7 | 99　3.7 |
| | | 74　4.9 | 215　1.7 | 174　2.1 | | | | 154　2.4 | 164　2.2 |
| | | 20　18.7 | 12　30.0 | 19　19.7 | | | Cost of Sales/Payables | 15　23.6 | 14　26.5 |
| | | 29　12.7 | 25　14.5 | 24　15.4 | | | | 24　15.2 | 26　14.1 |
| | | 42　8.7 | 47　7.8 | 31　11.8 | | | | 45　8.1 | 48　7.5 |
| | | 5.7 | 2.7 | 2.1 | | | Sales/Working Capital | 3.7 | 3.6 |
| | | 9.2 | 5.1 | 3.4 | | | | 5.3 | 6.4 |
| | | NM | 10.6 | 5.6 | | | | 14.8 | 13.2 |
| | | 10.2 | 17.8 | 133.7 | | | EBIT/Interest | 9.8 | 6.0 |
| | | 4.7 | (32)　7.4 | 19.5 | | | | (77)　2.9 | (83)　1.7 |
| | | 2.0 | 2.4 | 5.8 | | | | 1.0 | .0 |
| | | | 13.6 | | | | Net Profit + Depr., Dep., Amort./Cur. Mat. L/T/D | 5.3 | 5.8 |
| | | (10) | 4.1 | | | | | (26)　2.5 | (31)　1.2 |
| | | | -.5 | | | | | 1.4 | .1 |
| | | .5 | .1 | .1 | | | Fixed/Worth | .2 | .3 |
| | | 1.5 | .3 | .2 | | | | .5 | .6 |
| | | 4.9 | .9 | .5 | | | | 1.2 | 1.6 |
| | | 1.3 | .5 | .3 | | | Debt/Worth | .6 | .7 |
| | | 2.4 | 1.3 | .4 | | | | 1.3 | 1.6 |
| | | 11.0 | 3.9 | 1.0 | | | | 4.2 | 5.4 |
| | | 67.9 | 32.0 | 38.2 | | | % Profit Before Taxes/Tangible Net Worth | 34.2 | 37.6 |
| | | (15)　25.5 | (30)　19.7 | (17)　26.2 | | | | (79)　15.0 | (78)　11.2 |
| | | 6.9 | 8.1 | 6.8 | | | | 3.4 | -6.6 |
| | | 16.9 | 16.5 | 20.4 | | | % Profit Before Taxes/Total Assets | 13.7 | 10.8 |
| | | 8.2 | 9.0 | 9.3 | | | | 6.5 | 2.7 |
| | | 3.3 | 2.7 | 4.3 | | | | .5 | -2.9 |
| | | 26.9 | 65.0 | 42.6 | | | Sales/Net Fixed Assets | 24.9 | 21.0 |
| | | 5.9 | 14.0 | 13.0 | | | | 11.2 | 9.8 |
| | | 2.7 | 6.7 | 4.4 | | | | 5.3 | 4.7 |
| | | 2.5 | 2.2 | 1.8 | | | Sales/Total Assets | 2.6 | 2.4 |
| | | 2.0 | 1.8 | 1.7 | | | | 1.9 | 1.7 |
| | | 1.3 | 1.5 | 1.2 | | | | 1.5 | 1.3 |
| | | .7 | .8 | .9 | | | % Depr., Dep., Amort./Sales | 1.5 | 1.2 |
| | | (13)　2.9 | (28)　1.6 | (17)　1.7 | | | | (74)　2.4 | (80)　2.7 |
| | | 8.7 | 3.3 | 3.5 | | | | 4.1 | 3.9 |
| | | 4.7 | 2.5 | | | | % Officers', Directors' Owners' Comp/Sales | 2.2 | 1.9 |
| | | (10)　5.7 | (17)　3.3 | | | | | (31)　4.4 | (35)　5.6 |
| | | 7.4 | 7.5 | | | | | 7.4 | 8.0 |
| Net Sales ($) | 2094M | 45538M | 308612M | 637630M | 832273M | 261392M | | 1814444M | 1975566M |
| Total Assets ($) | 707M | 21620M | 161261M | 395834M | 558220M | 242191M | | 1188162M | 1428892M |

M = $ thousand　MM = $ million
See Pages 9 through 22 for Explanation of Ratios and Data

## Comparative Historical Data / Current Data Sorted by Sales

| | | | Type of Statement | | | | | | |
|---|---|---|---|---|---|---|---|---|---|
| 18 | 14 | 18 | Unqualified | 1 | 2 | 5 | 2 7 | 4 3 | 12 5 |
| 21 | 26 | 23 | Reviewed | 1 | | 3 | 3 | | 5 |
| 8 | 6 | 7 | Compiled | 1 | 4 | 3 | 3 | 1 | |
| 8 | 8 | 9 | Tax Returns | | 4 | 3 | 1 | | |
| 28 | 27 | 23 | Other | 2 | 4 | 1 | 6 | 6 | 4 |
| 4/1/09-<br>3/31/10<br>ALL | 4/1/10-<br>3/31/11<br>ALL | 4/1/11-<br>3/31/12<br>ALL | | | 15 (4/1-9/30/11) | | 65 (10/1/11-3/31/12) | | |
| | | | | 0-1MM | 1-3MM | 3-5MM | 5-10MM | 10-25MM | 25MM & OVER |
| 83 | 81 | 80 | NUMBER OF STATEMENTS | 5 | 10 | 12 | 19 | 13 | 21 |
| % | % | % | ASSETS | % | % | % | % | % | % |
| 7.0 | 9.0 | 9.1 | Cash & Equivalents | | 12.8 | 6.1 | 8.2 | 6.0 | 10.1 |
| 20.5 | 19.8 | 23.3 | Trade Receivables (net) | | 20.9 | 25.9 | 23.4 | 22.1 | 22.7 |
| 36.5 | 32.5 | 33.9 | Inventory | | 27.0 | 38.2 | 43.1 | 34.7 | 32.5 |
| 2.1 | 1.9 | 1.4 | All Other Current | | .1 | .3 | .3 | 2.9 | 2.7 |
| 66.1 | 63.2 | 67.7 | Total Current | | 60.7 | 70.5 | 75.0 | 65.8 | 67.9 |
| 21.4 | 24.8 | 21.5 | Fixed Assets (net) | | 30.1 | 26.5 | 17.0 | 23.5 | 15.0 |
| 7.3 | 4.1 | 4.8 | Intangibles (net) | | 1.0 | 1.3 | 5.9 | 8.3 | 4.5 |
| 5.2 | 7.9 | 6.0 | All Other Non-Current | | 8.2 | 1.8 | 2.1 | 2.4 | 12.6 |
| 100.0 | 100.0 | 100.0 | Total | | 100.0 | 100.0 | 100.0 | 100.0 | 100.0 |
| | | | LIABILITIES | | | | | | |
| 8.6 | 6.9 | 8.0 | Notes Payable-Short Term | | 9.2 | 13.4 | 8.4 | 8.7 | 4.5 |
| 3.0 | 3.0 | 3.4 | Cur. Mat.-L.T.D. | | 4.1 | 4.0 | 3.1 | 2.9 | 1.7 |
| 9.5 | 11.6 | 11.3 | Trade Payables | | 12.0 | 12.9 | 12.5 | 10.0 | 9.2 |
| .3 | .1 | .2 | Income Taxes Payable | | .2 | .5 | .1 | .0 | .5 |
| 9.0 | 9.2 | 8.2 | All Other Current | | 8.1 | 9.1 | 6.4 | 6.6 | 10.0 |
| 30.4 | 30.8 | 31.1 | Total Current | | 33.7 | 39.9 | 31.7 | 28.2 | 25.9 |
| 15.9 | 13.6 | 14.5 | Long-Term Debt | | 19.1 | 17.6 | 11.3 | 14.0 | 10.2 |
| .7 | .6 | .2 | Deferred Taxes | | .0 | .7 | .0 | .1 | .4 |
| 9.1 | 5.5 | 7.9 | All Other Non-Current | | 13.5 | 2.8 | 6.7 | 8.2 | 9.3 |
| 43.9 | 49.4 | 46.2 | Net Worth | | 33.7 | 39.0 | 50.3 | 49.5 | 54.2 |
| 100.0 | 100.0 | 100.0 | Total Liabilties & Net Worth | | 100.0 | 100.0 | 100.0 | 100.0 | 100.0 |
| | | | INCOME DATA | | | | | | |
| 100.0 | 100.0 | 100.0 | Net Sales | | 100.0 | 100.0 | 100.0 | 100.0 | 100.0 |
| 35.0 | 34.4 | 34.1 | Gross Profit | | 35.2 | 30.0 | 34.6 | 29.8 | 34.6 |
| 32.3 | 29.2 | 27.0 | Operating Expenses | | 29.5 | 26.7 | 28.5 | 22.0 | 24.9 |
| 2.7 | 5.2 | 7.1 | Operating Profit | | 5.7 | 3.4 | 6.1 | 7.9 | 9.7 |
| 1.3 | 1.1 | .9 | All Other Expenses (net) | | 1.2 | 1.2 | .9 | 1.1 | .1 |
| 1.5 | 4.2 | 6.3 | Profit Before Taxes | | 4.5 | 2.2 | -5.1 | 6.7 | 9.6 |
| | | | RATIOS | | | | | | |
| 4.0 | 4.0 | 4.3 | | | 5.2 | 2.8 | 4.3 | 5.1 | 5.4 |
| 2.3 | 2.6 | 2.6 | Current | | 2.3 | 1.9 | 2.5 | 3.7 | 3.3 |
| 1.5 | 1.5 | 1.4 | | | .8 | 1.3 | 1.5 | 1.3 | 1.9 |
| 1.6 | 2.1 | 2.3 | | | 2.8 | 1.1 | 2.1 | 3.1 | 2.4 |
| .9 | 1.0 | 1.1 | Quick | | 1.2 | .7 | .9 | 1.3 | 1.4 |
| .5 | .5 | .6 | | | .5 | .6 | .5 | .4 | .8 |
| 33 11.2 | 31 11.8 | 33 11.0 | | 26 14.3 | 33 11.0 | 30 12.3 | 29 12.7 | 40 9.2 | |
| 42 8.6 | 43 8.4 | 43 8.5 | Sales/Receivables | 44 8.3 | 42 8.6 | 40 9.2 | 38 9.6 | 46 8.0 | |
| 55 6.7 | 57 6.4 | 53 6.9 | | 49 7.5 | 54 6.8 | 53 6.9 | 60 6.1 | 53 6.9 | |
| 79 4.6 | 65 5.6 | 61 6.0 | | 52 7.0 | 49 7.4 | 73 5.0 | 87 4.2 | 65 5.6 | |
| 133 2.8 | 102 3.6 | 91 4.0 | Cost of Sales/Inventory | 74 4.9 | 78 4.7 | 140 2.6 | 126 2.9 | 99 3.7 | |
| 193 1.9 | 166 2.2 | 166 2.2 | | 140 2.6 | 182 2.0 | 215 1.7 | 146 2.5 | 166 2.2 | |
| 16 23.2 | 16 23.3 | 16 22.3 | | 10 35.1 | 13 27.8 | 13 28.6 | 16 23.4 | 19 19.0 | |
| 24 15.3 | 30 12.4 | 27 13.5 | Cost of Sales/Payables | 30 12.1 | 26 14.2 | 25 14.4 | 24 14.9 | 29 12.5 | |
| 41 8.8 | 50 7.3 | 42 8.7 | | 64 5.7 | 43 8.4 | 46 8.0 | 37 9.8 | 40 9.2 | |
| 2.8 | 2.8 | 2.8 | | | 3.1 | 3.0 | 2.3 | 2.4 | 2.4 |
| 5.1 | 4.8 | 5.4 | Sales/Working Capital | | 6.4 | 7.3 | 6.7 | 4.4 | 4.0 |
| 9.1 | 10.0 | 12.1 | | | -13.9 | 16.0 | 12.4 | 10.8 | 6.8 |
| 8.6 | 17.6 | 20.7 | | | 11.2 | 11.4 | 21.1 | 19.9 | 81.5 |
| (76) 2.8 | (77) 5.1 | (76) 9.1 | EBIT/Interest | | 4.1 | 7.3 | 7.8 | (12) 9.2 | (20) 21.6 |
| -.3 | 1.8 | 3.0 | | | .7 | 3.0 | 4.1 | 2.4 | 6.5 |
| 5.1 | 11.2 | 13.3 | Net Profit + Depr., Dep., | | | | | | |
| (26) 1.7 | (23) 7.1 | (26) 4.6 | Amort./Cur. Mat. L/T/D | | | | | | |
| .4 | 1.8 | 1.6 | | | | | | | |
| .2 | .1 | .1 | | | .1 | .2 | .1 | .3 | .1 |
| .6 | .5 | .4 | Fixed/Worth | | 1.0 | .9 | .4 | .4 | .2 |
| 1.7 | .9 | 1.1 | | | 4.6 | 2.0 | .9 | .8 | .5 |
| .6 | .5 | .4 | | | .8 | 1.0 | .4 | .4 | .2 |
| 1.3 | 1.0 | 1.2 | Debt/Worth | | 2.1 | 1.4 | 1.1 | 1.6 | .6 |
| 4.8 | 2.2 | 3.4 | | | 6.7 | 4.1 | 3.5 | 4.6 | 1.2 |
| 21.8 | 26.5 | 37.0 | | | | 32.1 | 30.5 | 39.7 | 35.4 |
| (68) 8.2 | (74) 11.3 | (74) 22.7 | % Profit Before Taxes/Tangible<br>Net Worth | | 22.0 | (17) 21.7 | (12) 23.7 | (20) 26.5 | |
| -3.7 | 3.3 | 9.3 | | | | 11.7 | 7.4 | 16.8 | 10.0 |
| 10.1 | 12.0 | 17.8 | % Profit Before Taxes/Total | | 17.3 | 14.6 | 17.2 | 14.6 | 21.4 |
| 3.6 | 6.3 | 8.7 | Assets | | 6.5 | 6.5 | 10.5 | 9.5 | 12.6 |
| -3.4 | 1.7 | 3.7 | | | -.2 | 3.2 | 1.8 | 3.9 | 5.0 |
| 31.2 | 19.7 | 34.5 | | | 26.5 | 47.5 | 56.8 | 25.8 | 46.6 |
| 8.8 | 8.2 | 11.0 | Sales/Net Fixed Assets | | 11.3 | 6.3 | 21.0 | 7.1 | 14.9 |
| 4.7 | 4.1 | 4.8 | | | 2.4 | 4.7 | 6.5 | 4.3 | 5.1 |
| 2.2 | 1.9 | 2.1 | | | 2.1 | 2.2 | 2.3 | 2.0 | 1.8 |
| 1.6 | 1.6 | 1.7 | Sales/Total Assets | | 1.5 | 2.0 | 1.8 | 1.6 | 1.7 |
| 1.1 | 1.1 | 1.3 | | | 1.2 | 1.4 | 1.5 | 1.2 | 1.3 |
| 1.4 | 1.6 | .9 | | | .6 | .6 | 1.0 | .8 | |
| (68) 2.8 | (69) 3.1 | (68) 2.3 | % Depr., Dep., Amort./Sales | | (11) 1.7 | (15) 3.2 | (12) 1.5 | (20) 1.6 | |
| 4.8 | 4.6 | 4.0 | | | 3.8 | 4.4 | 3.9 | 3.7 | |
| 3.1 | 2.6 | 2.6 | | | | | 3.0 | | |
| (22) 5.5 | (31) 3.5 | (30) 4.4 | % Officers', Directors'<br>Owners' Comp/Sales | | | (10) 3.4 | | | |
| 9.0 | 5.8 | 6.8 | | | | | 6.8 | | |
| 2000748M | 1794159M | 2087539M | Net Sales ($) | 3718M | 20108M | 49300M | 142181M | 215129M | 1657103M |
| 1653543M | 1374804M | 1379833M | Total Assets ($) | 2322M | 14246M | 26894M | 86414M | 140856M | 1109101M |

© RMA 2012          M = $ thousand     MM = $ million<br>See Pages 9 through 22 for Explanation of Ratios and Data

## Current Data Sorted by Assets | Comparative Historical Data

| | 0-500M | 500M-2MM | 2-10MM | 10-50MM | 50-100MM | 100-250MM | Type of Statement | 4/1/07-3/31/08 ALL | 4/1/08-3/31/09 ALL |
|---|---|---|---|---|---|---|---|---|---|
| Unqualified | | 2 | 2 | 5 | 3 | 3 | | 21 | 17 |
| Reviewed | | 4 | 12 | 5 | | | | 20 | 14 |
| Compiled | 1 | | 6 | | | | | 11 | 10 |
| Tax Returns | 4 | 7 | 7 | 2 | | | | 11 | 10 |
| Other | 2 | 4 | 15 | 14 | 3 | | | 32 | 40 |
| | 17 (4/1-9/30/11) | | 84 (10/1/11-3/31/12) | | | | | | |
| **NUMBER OF STATEMENTS** | 7 | 17 | 42 | 26 | 6 | 3 | | 95 | 91 |
| | % | % | % | % | % | % | **ASSETS** | % | % |
| | | 14.1 | 13.4 | 8.8 | | | Cash & Equivalents | 11.0 | 12.8 |
| | | 28.3 | 29.0 | 25.2 | | | Trade Receivables (net) | 27.8 | 28.1 |
| | | 22.1 | 29.1 | 24.9 | | | Inventory | 24.1 | 25.9 |
| | | 1.9 | 1.7 | 4.6 | | | All Other Current | 4.1 | 3.8 |
| | | 66.5 | 73.3 | 63.4 | | | Total Current | 67.0 | 70.6 |
| | | 31.3 | 17.4 | 25.9 | | | Fixed Assets (net) | 25.1 | 21.4 |
| | | .1 | 2.2 | 4.8 | | | Intangibles (net) | 2.7 | 1.8 |
| | | 2.0 | 7.1 | 5.9 | | | All Other Non-Current | 5.2 | 6.1 |
| | | 100.0 | 100.0 | 100.0 | | | Total | 100.0 | 100.0 |
| | | | | | | | **LIABILITIES** | | |
| | | 8.4 | 9.2 | 8.6 | | | Notes Payable-Short Term | 12.7 | 15.8 |
| | | 2.2 | 6.5 | 3.8 | | | Cur. Mat.-L.T.D. | 3.8 | 3.0 |
| | | 15.1 | 16.2 | 12.6 | | | Trade Payables | 14.0 | 16.6 |
| | | .1 | .3 | .0 | | | Income Taxes Payable | .3 | .3 |
| | | 9.2 | 16.8 | 9.5 | | | All Other Current | 19.3 | 19.6 |
| | | 34.9 | 49.0 | 34.5 | | | Total Current | 50.2 | 55.4 |
| | | 25.0 | 8.0 | 10.4 | | | Long-Term Debt | 13.9 | 15.3 |
| | | .0 | .5 | .5 | | | Deferred Taxes | .2 | .4 |
| | | 5.9 | 10.2 | 7.3 | | | All Other Non-Current | 3.1 | 3.2 |
| | | 34.3 | 32.4 | 47.2 | | | Net Worth | 32.6 | 25.7 |
| | | 100.0 | 100.0 | 100.0 | | | Total Liabilities & Net Worth | 100.0 | 100.0 |
| | | | | | | | **INCOME DATA** | | |
| | | 100.0 | 100.0 | 100.0 | | | Net Sales | 100.0 | 100.0 |
| | | 32.4 | 28.3 | 23.3 | | | Gross Profit | 29.1 | 27.5 |
| | | 27.6 | 24.2 | 19.9 | | | Operating Expenses | 23.3 | 24.1 |
| | | 4.8 | 4.1 | 3.5 | | | Operating Profit | 5.8 | 3.4 |
| | | .9 | 1.3 | .4 | | | All Other Expenses (net) | 1.3 | .5 |
| | | 3.9 | 2.9 | 3.1 | | | Profit Before Taxes | 4.5 | 2.9 |
| | | | | | | | **RATIOS** | | |
| | | 3.7 | 3.4 | 3.2 | | | | 2.2 | 2.9 |
| | | 2.1 | 1.9 | 1.7 | | | Current | 1.5 | 1.5 |
| | | 1.1 | 1.2 | 1.2 | | | | 1.1 | 1.1 |
| | | 3.0 | 1.9 | 1.5 | | | | 1.4 | 1.5 |
| | | 1.5 | .9 | .9 | | | Quick | .8 | .7 |
| | | .7 | .5 | .6 | | | | .6 | .5 |
| | 22 16.8 | 31 11.6 | 33 11.0 | | | | | 24 15.2 | 21 17.5 |
| | 29 12.4 | 41 9.0 | 42 8.6 | | | | Sales/Receivables | 38 9.7 | 36 10.3 |
| | 43 8.4 | 64 5.7 | 72 5.1 | | | | | 62 5.8 | 51 7.1 |
| | 6 63.7 | 24 15.1 | 22 16.9 | | | | | 17 21.7 | 24 14.9 |
| | 27 13.6 | 53 6.9 | 56 6.5 | | | | Cost of Sales/Inventory | 41 9.0 | 50 7.3 |
| | 78 4.7 | 104 3.5 | 101 3.6 | | | | | 81 4.5 | 86 4.3 |
| | 10 35.4 | 14 26.0 | 19 19.0 | | | | | 16 23.2 | 12 29.3 |
| | 25 14.8 | 27 13.7 | 29 12.6 | | | | Cost of Sales/Payables | 26 14.2 | 26 14.3 |
| | 46 8.0 | 47 7.7 | 47 7.8 | | | | | 39 9.3 | 40 9.2 |
| | | 4.8 | 3.9 | 3.6 | | | | 6.2 | 5.0 |
| | | 9.9 | 7.2 | 6.5 | | | Sales/Working Capital | 12.0 | 12.1 |
| | | NM | 20.2 | 19.8 | | | | 104.6 | 73.2 |
| | | 16.0 | 15.0 | 12.1 | | | | 19.7 | 13.1 |
| | | (15) 3.1 | (34) 4.7 | (23) 3.0 | | | EBIT/Interest | (85) 5.2 | (79) 4.1 |
| | | -1.0 | -.2 | .6 | | | | 1.4 | 1.3 |
| | | | | | | | Net Profit + Depr., Dep., | 14.9 | 10.7 |
| | | | | | | | Amort./Cur. Mat. L/T/D | (30) 4.2 / (23) 4.6 | |
| | | | | | | | | 1.5 | 1.6 |
| | | .2 | .1 | .3 | | | | .2 | .2 |
| | | .7 | .4 | .7 | | | Fixed/Worth | .6 | .7 |
| | | 10.8 | 1.6 | 1.3 | | | | 1.6 | 2.1 |
| | | .3 | .4 | .5 | | | | .9 | .7 |
| | | 1.0 | 1.4 | 1.3 | | | Debt/Worth | 1.7 | 2.3 |
| | | 12.6 | 6.3 | 2.4 | | | | 4.7 | 4.5 |
| | | 30.5 | 32.9 | 23.4 | | | | 54.5 | 47.8 |
| | | (14) 7.8 | (35) 14.6 | (24) 8.9 | | | % Profit Before Taxes/Tangible Net Worth | (85) 30.3 | (79) 27.8 |
| | | -5.8 | 3.6 | -1.9 | | | | 8.2 | 5.9 |
| | | 17.9 | 15.1 | 10.7 | | | | 19.9 | 19.9 |
| | | 4.1 | 5.8 | 4.8 | | | % Profit Before Taxes/Total Assets | 9.9 | 6.4 |
| | | -.6 | .0 | .0 | | | | .8 | .9 |
| | | 25.3 | 58.0 | 15.9 | | | | 33.4 | 38.4 |
| | | 12.7 | 21.5 | 9.0 | | | Sales/Net Fixed Assets | 12.5 | 14.3 |
| | | 6.7 | 8.2 | 4.1 | | | | 6.4 | 7.5 |
| | | 3.8 | 3.2 | 2.6 | | | | 3.3 | 3.3 |
| | | 2.9 | 2.1 | 1.7 | | | Sales/Total Assets | 2.4 | 2.6 |
| | | 1.8 | 1.6 | 1.1 | | | | 1.7 | 1.9 |
| | | .6 | .5 | 1.1 | | | | .8 | .7 |
| | | (14) 1.0 | (37) 1.2 | (25) 1.9 | | | % Depr., Dep., Amort./Sales | (84) 1.4 | (75) 1.3 |
| | | 2.5 | 1.8 | 3.5 | | | | 2.2 | 1.9 |
| | | 2.3 | 1.6 | | | | | 1.4 | 2.1 |
| | | (14) 4.4 | (23) 3.8 | | | | % Officers', Directors', Owners' Comp/Sales | (22) 3.5 | (24) 3.6 |
| | | 8.7 | 6.3 | | | | | 6.2 | 6.0 |
| | 8434M | 69150M | 461149M | 1089569M | 1005776M | 896375M | Net Sales ($) | 4315287M | 5042422M |
| | 1282M | 20866M | 211476M | 600031M | 498965M | 486258M | Total Assets ($) | 1820120M | 2279140M |

M = $ thousand   MM = $ million
See Pages 9 through 22 for Explanation of Ratios and Data

**Comparative Historical Data** | | | | | **Current Data Sorted by Sales**

| 4/1/09-3/31/10 ALL | 4/1/10-3/31/11 ALL | 4/1/11-3/31/12 ALL | Type of Statement | 0-1MM | 1-3MM | 3-5MM | 5-10MM | 10-25MM | 25MM & OVER |
|---|---|---|---|---|---|---|---|---|---|
| 16 | 15 | 13 | Unqualified | | | | 1 | 4 | 8 |
| 11 | 19 | 19 | Reviewed | | | 1 | 7 | 8 | 3 |
| 12 | 9 | 11 | Compiled | | 3 | 2 | 3 | 3 | |
| 11 | 14 | 20 | Tax Returns | 3 | 3 | 2 | 8 | 3 | 1 |
| 39 | 38 | 38 | Other | 4 | 2 | 1 | 9 | 7 | 15 |
| | | | | 17 (4/1-9/30/11) | | | 84 (10/1/11-3/31/12) | | |
| 89 | 95 | 101 | **NUMBER OF STATEMENTS** | 7 | 8 | 6 | 28 | 25 | 27 |
| % | % | % | **ASSETS** | % | % | % | % | % | % |
| 14.9 | 13.4 | 12.0 | Cash & Equivalents | | | | 18.7 | 11.4 | 5.6 |
| 22.8 | 25.6 | 26.4 | Trade Receivables (net) | | | | 27.5 | 24.7 | 26.1 |
| 25.2 | 23.5 | 25.5 | Inventory | | | | 23.3 | 30.9 | 27.1 |
| 3.2 | 2.8 | 3.1 | All Other Current | | | | 1.9 | 3.2 | 5.6 |
| 66.1 | 65.3 | 67.1 | Total Current | | | | 71.4 | 70.2 | 64.4 |
| 25.1 | 26.3 | 24.2 | Fixed Assets (net) | | | | 21.0 | 16.3 | 27.9 |
| 2.3 | 3.6 | 2.6 | Intangibles (net) | | | | .8 | 6.8 | 1.3 |
| 6.5 | 4.8 | 6.1 | All Other Non-Current | | | | 6.9 | 6.6 | 6.4 |
| 100.0 | 100.0 | 100.0 | Total | | | | 100.0 | 100.0 | 100.0 |
| | | | **LIABILITIES** | | | | | | |
| 10.2 | 9.7 | 16.3 | Notes Payable-Short Term | | | | 8.5 | 8.4 | 8.0 |
| 4.0 | 6.5 | 5.4 | Cur. Mat.-L.T.D. | | | | 2.5 | 2.1 | 10.9 |
| 15.0 | 16.6 | 15.3 | Trade Payables | | | | 11.9 | 18.4 | 15.4 |
| .2 | .3 | .2 | Income Taxes Payable | | | | .1 | .5 | .1 |
| 13.2 | 13.6 | 16.4 | All Other Current | | | | 17.8 | 10.5 | 15.1 |
| 42.7 | 46.7 | 53.5 | Total Current | | | | 40.8 | 39.8 | 49.4 |
| 17.3 | 16.1 | 17.0 | Long-Term Debt | | | | 17.7 | 6.3 | 15.1 |
| .7 | .3 | .3 | Deferred Taxes | | | | .6 | .3 | .4 |
| 11.2 | 4.6 | 8.0 | All Other Non-Current | | | | 3.8 | 10.2 | 10.5 |
| 28.0 | 32.2 | 21.1 | Net Worth | | | | 37.0 | 43.3 | 24.6 |
| 100.0 | 100.0 | 100.0 | Total Liabilities & Net Worth | | | | 100.0 | 100.0 | 100.0 |
| | | | **INCOME DATA** | | | | | | |
| 100.0 | 100.0 | 100.0 | Net Sales | | | | 100.0 | 100.0 | 100.0 |
| 32.2 | 27.7 | 28.3 | Gross Profit | | | | 29.0 | 26.8 | 22.5 |
| 30.1 | 25.8 | 23.6 | Operating Expenses | | | | 25.2 | 22.0 | 18.9 |
| 2.1 | 1.8 | 4.6 | Operating Profit | | | | 3.9 | 4.7 | 3.6 |
| 1.7 | .6 | .8 | All Other Expenses (net) | | | | 1.5 | .1 | .8 |
| .5 | 1.2 | 3.8 | Profit Before Taxes | | | | 2.3 | 4.6 | 2.8 |
| | | | **RATIOS** | | | | | | |
| 3.5 | 3.3 | 3.3 | Current | | | | 3.6 | 3.4 | 2.1 |
| 1.7 | 1.8 | 1.8 | | | | | 2.2 | 2.1 | 1.5 |
| 1.2 | 1.1 | 1.2 | | | | | 1.2 | 1.2 | 1.2 |
| 2.3 | 2.0 | 1.7 | Quick | | | | 3.2 | 2.0 | 1.1 |
| 1.0 | .9 | .8 | | | | | 1.2 | .9 | .7 |
| .4 | .5 | .5 | | | | | .6 | .6 | .5 |
| (19) 19.7 | (24) 15.5 | (27) 13.6 | Sales/Receivables | | | | (30) 12.2 | (33) 10.9 | (27) 13.7 |
| (36) 10.3 | (42) 8.7 | (38) 9.7 | | | | | (43) 8.5 | (39) 9.4 | (35) 10.3 |
| (58) 6.3 | (67) 5.4 | (60) 6.1 | | | | | (65) 5.6 | (59) 6.2 | (57) 6.4 |
| (21) 17.4 | (18) 20.1 | (17) 22.1 | Cost of Sales/Inventory | | | | (15) 24.7 | (33) 11.0 | (18) 19.9 |
| (48) 7.6 | (43) 8.6 | (49) 7.4 | | | | | (49) 7.4 | (68) 5.4 | (55) 6.6 |
| (107) 3.4 | (104) 3.5 | (91) 4.0 | | | | | (96) 3.8 | (114) 3.2 | (74) 4.9 |
| (14) 26.1 | (19) 19.7 | (14) 26.2 | Cost of Sales/Payables | | | | (11) 32.2 | (16) 22.2 | (24) 15.3 |
| (29) 12.7 | (31) 11.8 | (28) 13.0 | | | | | (23) 15.6 | (29) 12.4 | (33) 11.0 |
| (50) 7.3 | (49) 7.4 | (46) 8.0 | | | | | (42) 8.6 | (54) 6.7 | (44) 8.3 |
| 3.8 | 3.6 | 4.4 | Sales/Working Capital | | | | 3.1 | 3.5 | 6.0 |
| 7.5 | 7.8 | 7.9 | | | | | 6.2 | 6.7 | 9.0 |
| 31.1 | 136.6 | 49.4 | | | | | 34.0 | 22.9 | 25.8 |
| 9.1 | 23.0 | 19.5 | EBIT/Interest | | | | 7.6 | 72.6 | 24.0 |
| (81) 1.4 | (84) 3.5 | (87) 4.5 | | | | | (22) 4.2 | (22) 11.9 | (26) 5.0 |
| -2.5 | -.4 | 1.4 | | | | | -.6 | 2.0 | 1.2 |
| 16.7 | 4.9 | 6.2 | Net Profit + Depr., Dep., | | | | | | |
| (26) 2.8 | (22) 1.5 | (20) 3.9 | Amort./Cur. Mat. L/T/D | | | | | | |
| .8 | .6 | .7 | | | | | | | |
| .3 | .3 | .2 | Fixed/Worth | | | | .1 | .1 | .4 |
| .7 | .7 | .6 | | | | | .5 | .3 | .7 |
| 1.5 | 1.9 | 1.9 | | | | | 1.9 | 2.4 | 1.1 |
| .7 | .5 | .5 | Debt/Worth | | | | .4 | .4 | 1.0 |
| 1.8 | 2.0 | 1.3 | | | | | 1.3 | 1.2 | 1.4 |
| 5.3 | 5.1 | 5.5 | | | | | 5.6 | 10.6 | 2.7 |
| 27.5 | 38.3 | 27.8 | % Profit Before Taxes/Tangible | | | | 22.2 | 35.6 | 25.4 |
| (75) 6.1 | (82) 9.1 | (83) 11.8 | Net Worth | | | | (24) 10.2 | (20) 16.9 | (25) 14.3 |
| -13.3 | -3.2 | 2.0 | | | | | 2.8 | 2.2 | 1.0 |
| 11.5 | 15.7 | 13.1 | % Profit Before Taxes/Total | | | | 8.3 | 23.1 | 10.9 |
| 1.6 | 4.4 | 5.7 | Assets | | | | 4.4 | 6.9 | 4.2 |
| -7.4 | -3.9 | 1.4 | | | | | -.6 | 1.5 | .4 |
| 25.2 | 21.0 | 30.9 | Sales/Net Fixed Assets | | | | 66.2 | 32.7 | 12.1 |
| 11.3 | 9.9 | 12.2 | | | | | 11.8 | 20.0 | 8.7 |
| 6.0 | 5.4 | 7.4 | | | | | 6.0 | 9.0 | 7.1 |
| 3.0 | 3.0 | 3.1 | Sales/Total Assets | | | | 2.9 | 3.5 | 2.7 |
| 2.1 | 2.1 | 2.2 | | | | | 2.1 | 2.1 | 2.2 |
| 1.6 | 1.4 | 1.6 | | | | | 1.5 | 1.5 | 1.5 |
| .7 | .9 | .7 | % Depr., Dep., Amort./Sales | | | | .9 | .5 | 1.5 |
| (76) 1.8 | (78) 2.1 | (90) 1.4 | | | | | (24) 1.6 | (23) .9 | (26) 2.1 |
| 2.9 | 3.5 | 2.3 | | | | | 2.8 | 1.6 | 2.5 |
| 2.4 | 2.1 | 2.1 | % Officers', Directors' | | | | 1.6 | 2.7 | |
| (32) 6.0 | (37) 3.7 | (47) 4.3 | Owners' Comp/Sales | | | | (16) 3.4 | (14) 4.8 | |
| 9.5 | 7.0 | 7.9 | | | | | 6.5 | 7.0 | |
| 3756233M | 3157082M | 3530453M | Net Sales ($) | 4570M | 16523M | 24093M | 211122M | 397265M | 2876880M |
| 1957229M | 1779015M | 1818878M | Total Assets ($) | 3305M | 8959M | 8313M | 138377M | 228399M | 1431525M |

© RMA 2012

M = $ thousand    MM = $ million

See Pages 9 through 22 for Explanation of Ratios and Data

## Current Data Sorted by Assets          Comparative Historical Data

| 0-500M | 500M-2MM | 2-10MM | 10-50MM | 50-100MM | 100-250MM | Type of Statement | 4/1/07-3/31/08 ALL | 4/1/08-3/31/09 ALL |
|---|---|---|---|---|---|---|---|---|
| 1 | 2 | 17 | 37 | 5 | 6 | Unqualified | 81 | 81 |
|  | 26 | 70 | 30 | 4 |  | Reviewed | 139 | 148 |
| 3 | 28 | 40 | 3 |  |  | Compiled | 64 | 66 |
| 15 | 28 | 26 | 2 |  |  | Tax Returns | 44 | 47 |
| 9 | 24 | 62 | 51 | 10 | 6 | Other | 174 | 180 |
|  | 88 (4/1-9/30/11) |  | 417 (10/1/11-3/31/12) |  |  |  |  |  |
| 28 | 108 | 215 | 123 | 19 | 12 | NUMBER OF STATEMENTS | 502 | 522 |
| % | % | % | % | % | % | ASSETS | % | % |
| 19.6 | 10.3 | 9.9 | 10.8 | 14.2 | 5.1 | Cash & Equivalents | 10.6 | 10.3 |
| 27.2 | 42.7 | 36.2 | 30.8 | 22.9 | 25.7 | Trade Receivables (net) | 34.4 | 34.2 |
| 8.0 | 15.6 | 19.2 | 18.6 | 21.9 | 15.7 | Inventory | 18.5 | 19.2 |
| 2.9 | 3.4 | 5.2 | 6.9 | 9.5 | 12.6 | All Other Current | 5.3 | 5.3 |
| 57.6 | 72.0 | 70.5 | 67.1 | 68.5 | 59.1 | Total Current | 68.8 | 69.0 |
| 30.0 | 21.6 | 22.8 | 24.2 | 19.7 | 21.4 | Fixed Assets (net) | 23.4 | 23.7 |
| 3.9 | 1.0 | 1.7 | 4.0 | 4.6 | 10.9 | Intangibles (net) | 2.4 | 2.4 |
| 8.5 | 5.4 | 5.0 | 4.8 | 7.2 | 8.7 | All Other Non-Current | 5.5 | 5.0 |
| 100.0 | 100.0 | 100.0 | 100.0 | 100.0 | 100.0 | Total | 100.0 | 100.0 |
|  |  |  |  |  |  | LIABILITIES |  |  |
| 34.5 | 12.3 | 11.4 | 11.0 | 7.3 | 5.5 | Notes Payable-Short Term | 9.7 | 10.2 |
| 8.0 | 3.4 | 3.2 | 2.2 | 1.1 | 11.5 | Cur. Mat.-L.T.D. | 4.3 | 3.2 |
| 26.5 | 18.0 | 17.7 | 14.4 | 14.0 | 11.9 | Trade Payables | 17.3 | 15.9 |
| .0 | .3 | .2 | .2 | .3 | .2 | Income Taxes Payable | .4 | .4 |
| 33.8 | 14.1 | 8.9 | 9.8 | 18.5 | 14.6 | All Other Current | 13.9 | 13.1 |
| 102.8 | 48.1 | 41.4 | 37.7 | 41.3 | 43.6 | Total Current | 45.6 | 42.8 |
| 16.3 | 12.8 | 9.7 | 11.5 | 7.3 | 11.1 | Long-Term Debt | 14.2 | 14.0 |
| .0 | .2 | .3 | .6 | .3 | 2.2 | Deferred Taxes | .3 | .4 |
| 35.3 | 7.4 | 5.3 | 3.1 | 3.6 | .6 | All Other Non-Current | 3.0 | 2.7 |
| -54.5 | 31.6 | 43.3 | 47.2 | 47.4 | 42.5 | Net Worth | 36.9 | 40.1 |
| 100.0 | 100.0 | 100.0 | 100.0 | 100.0 | 100.0 | Total Liabilities & Net Worth | 100.0 | 100.0 |
|  |  |  |  |  |  | INCOME DATA |  |  |
| 100.0 | 100.0 | 100.0 | 100.0 | 100.0 | 100.0 | Net Sales | 100.0 | 100.0 |
| 49.3 | 28.8 | 24.8 | 20.2 | 18.2 | 21.4 | Gross Profit | 27.1 | 26.1 |
| 47.5 | 27.3 | 20.8 | 15.9 | 12.3 | 13.9 | Operating Expenses | 20.4 | 20.1 |
| 1.8 | 1.5 | 4.1 | 4.3 | 5.8 | 7.6 | Operating Profit | 6.7 | 6.0 |
| .2 | .3 | .4 | .3 | .2 | 1.1 | All Other Expenses (net) | .7 | .7 |
| 1.5 | 1.3 | 3.7 | 4.0 | 5.6 | 6.5 | Profit Before Taxes | 6.0 | 5.3 |
|  |  |  |  |  |  | RATIOS |  |  |
| 2.1 | 3.6 | 3.0 | 2.8 | 2.1 | 2.1 |  | 2.4 | 2.6 |
| .9 | 1.6 | 1.7 | 1.7 | 1.4 | 1.6 | Current | 1.6 | 1.7 |
| .5 | 1.1 | 1.2 | 1.3 | 1.2 | 1.2 |  | 1.2 | 1.2 |
| 1.7 | 2.5 | 2.0 | 1.9 | 1.5 | 1.2 |  | 1.6 | 1.7 |
| .9 | 1.1 | 1.1 | 1.0 | .8 | .9 | Quick | 1.0 | 1.0 |
| .4 | .7 | .7 | .7 | .5 | .5 | (501) | .7 | .7 |
| 4  86.0 | 36  10.2 | 42  8.7 | 46  8.0 | 38  9.5 | 51  7.2 |  | 35  10.4 | 32  11.3 |
| 24  15.3 | 56  6.5 | 57  6.4 | 61  6.0 | 58  6.3 | 56  6.5 | Sales/Receivables | 49  7.5 | 49  7.4 |
| 45  8.1 | 76  4.8 | 76  4.7 | 78  4.7 | 68  5.4 | 69  5.3 |  | 66  5.5 | 67  5.4 |
| 0  UND | 1  300.5 | 13  28.8 | 18  20.7 | 41  9.0 | 14  26.3 |  | 9  42.7 | 10  36.6 |
| 3  120.7 | 16  22.8 | 36  10.2 | 43  8.5 | 63  5.8 | 34  10.7 | Cost of Sales/Inventory | 31  11.7 | 32  11.5 |
| 18  20.8 | 50  7.3 | 62  5.9 | 81  4.5 | 81  4.5 | 69  5.3 |  | 65  5.6 | 63  5.8 |
| 7  55.3 | 15  23.9 | 17  21.0 | 22  16.4 | 20  18.3 | 31  11.9 |  | 18  20.4 | 16  22.6 |
| 32  11.3 | 29  12.6 | 35  10.5 | 33  10.9 | 32  11.3 | 38  9.5 | Cost of Sales/Payables | 29  12.6 | 27  13.6 |
| 74  4.9 | 44  8.3 | 58  6.3 | 52  7.0 | 56  6.5 | 45  8.2 |  | 45  8.2 | 42  8.7 |
| 11.6 | 5.5 | 4.7 | 3.6 | 2.5 | 3.9 |  | 5.8 | 5.3 |
| UND | 9.9 | 8.5 | 6.7 | 6.9 | 8.1 | Sales/Working Capital | 9.7 | 8.7 |
| -11.7 | 72.2 | 30.0 | 14.0 | 16.1 | 19.0 |  | 23.9 | 21.9 |
| 6.0 | 14.8 | 14.9 | 16.9 | 37.7 | 15.6 |  | 19.0 | 20.2 |
| (17)  3.4 | (97)  2.6 | (183)  4.5 | (106)  5.0 | (15)  11.2 | (11)  4.5 | EBIT/Interest | (458)  5.8 | (476)  6.5 |
| -2.1 | -1.5 | 1.2 | 1.1 | -2.2 | 1.6 |  | 2.4 | 2.4 |
|  | 2.0 | 5.2 | 6.2 |  |  |  | 9.1 | 10.4 |
|  | (13)  1.4 | (36)  1.2 | (37)  3.3 |  |  | Net Profit + Depr., Dep., Amort./Cur. Mat. L/T/D | (132)  3.4 | (134)  3.9 |
|  | -1.2 | .3 | 1.4 |  |  |  | 1.5 | 1.7 |
| .3 | .2 | .2 | .2 | .2 | .5 |  | .2 | .2 |
| 2.5 | .5 | .5 | .5 | .5 | .6 | Fixed/Worth | .5 | .5 |
| -.5 | 1.9 | 1.1 | 1.1 | 1.1 | NM |  | 1.3 | 1.3 |
| 1.1 | .6 | .6 | .5 | .7 | .8 |  | .8 | .6 |
| 8.1 | 1.6 | 1.3 | 1.2 | 1.1 | 1.2 | Debt/Worth | 1.6 | 1.5 |
| -2.2 | 6.2 | 4.1 | 2.7 | 2.4 | NM |  | 4.0 | 3.6 |
| 140.8 | 41.2 | 41.4 | 33.2 | 31.6 |  | % Profit Before Taxes/Tangible Net Worth | 58.3 | 52.2 |
| (16)  43.7 | (92)  13.0 | (201)  16.8 | (114)  15.2 | (17)  15.5 |  |  | (448)  32.6 | (469)  26.2 |
| 16.4 | -6.5 | 2.9 | 2.9 | 4.6 |  |  | 14.2 | 9.8 |
| 22.6 | 16.5 | 15.8 | 11.9 | 16.4 | 11.5 |  | 24.3 | 19.5 |
| 9.3 | 4.0 | 6.6 | 5.6 | 7.4 | 5.7 | % Profit Before Taxes/Total Assets | 11.4 | 9.4 |
| -6.6 | -3.8 | .3 | 1.3 | 1.5 | 2.3 |  | 4.1 | 3.1 |
| 72.8 | 37.3 | 22.8 | 13.8 | 16.5 | 11.1 |  | 26.5 | 26.7 |
| 21.2 | 16.1 | 12.2 | 7.4 | 8.7 | 7.5 | Sales/Net Fixed Assets | 13.4 | 12.4 |
| 7.9 | 9.6 | 6.2 | 4.4 | 4.2 | 4.7 |  | 6.9 | 6.7 |
| 6.9 | 3.5 | 2.8 | 2.2 | 2.2 | 1.8 |  | 3.1 | 3.1 |
| 4.1 | 2.8 | 2.2 | 1.7 | 1.3 | 1.6 | Sales/Total Assets | 2.5 | 2.3 |
| 2.7 | 2.1 | 1.7 | 1.3 | 1.0 | 1.2 |  | 1.9 | 1.8 |
| .8 | .8 | .8 | 1.0 | 1.1 | 1.6 |  | .7 | .8 |
| (20)  1.4 | (82)  1.6 | (191)  1.8 | (114)  2.0 | (17)  1.8 | (11)  2.4 | % Depr., Dep., Amort./Sales | (441)  1.3 | (457)  1.4 |
| 3.9 | 3.5 | 3.0 | 3.1 | 3.2 | 2.7 |  | 2.4 | 2.5 |
| 4.5 | 2.3 | 1.6 | 1.4 |  |  |  | 1.7 | 1.7 |
| (17)  8.5 | (75)  3.7 | (96)  2.4 | (26)  2.3 |  |  | % Officers', Directors' Owners' Comp/Sales | (201)  3.1 | (202)  3.2 |
| 14.6 | 8.0 | 4.3 | 4.0 |  |  |  | 6.7 | 6.1 |
| 31674M | 388465M | 2430478M | 4556911M | 2217998M | 2965733M | Net Sales ($) | 16970525M | 18167322M |
| 7065M | 138797M | 1083070M | 2688481M | 1389849M | 2010273M | Total Assets ($) | 7847073M | 8290672M |

M = $ thousand     MM = $ million
See Pages 9 through 22 for Explanation of Ratios and Data

## Comparative Historical Data | Current Data Sorted by Sales

| 61 | 64 | 68 | Type of Statement Unqualified | 1 | 1 | 2 | 4 | 19 | 41 |
|---|---|---|---|---|---|---|---|---|---|
| 126 | 150 | 130 | Reviewed | | 6 | 27 | 26 | 49 | 22 |
| 50 | 64 | 74 | Compiled | 3 | 19 | 14 | 18 | 17 | 3 |
| 50 | 68 | 71 | Tax Returns | 8 | 22 | 13 | 18 | 9 | 1 |
| 146 | 155 | 162 | Other | 5 | 14 | 18 | 27 | 43 | 55 |
| 4/1/09-3/31/10 ALL | 4/1/10-3/31/11 ALL | 4/1/11-3/31/12 ALL | | 88 (4/1-9/30/11) 0-1MM | 1-3MM | 3-5MM | 417 (10/1/11-3/31/12) 5-10MM | 10-25MM | 25MM & OVER |
| 433 | 501 | 505 | NUMBER OF STATEMENTS | 17 | 62 | 74 | 93 | 137 | 122 |
| % | % | % | **ASSETS** | % | % | % | % | % | % |
| 14.2 | 12.5 | 10.8 | Cash & Equivalents | 16.7 | 12.9 | 10.0 | 10.3 | 11.3 | 9.2 |
| 29.7 | 30.2 | 35.0 | Trade Receivables (net) | 21.5 | 34.3 | 39.7 | 38.0 | 35.2 | 32.0 |
| 18.1 | 18.3 | 17.7 | Inventory | 9.5 | 14.5 | 14.7 | 18.1 | 19.6 | 19.7 |
| 5.0 | 5.2 | 5.4 | All Other Current | 1.4 | 5.5 | 4.1 | 5.4 | 5.0 | 7.3 |
| 66.9 | 66.2 | 68.9 | Total Current | 49.1 | 67.2 | 68.5 | 71.8 | 71.1 | 68.2 |
| 25.6 | 25.7 | 23.1 | Fixed Assets (net) | 42.2 | 24.9 | 22.9 | 20.4 | 23.0 | 21.9 |
| 2.7 | 2.4 | 2.5 | Intangibles (net) | 2.4 | 2.0 | 1.3 | 2.2 | 2.2 | 4.2 |
| 4.7 | 5.7 | 5.4 | All Other Non-Current | 6.3 | 5.9 | 7.2 | 5.5 | 3.7 | 5.7 |
| 100.0 | 100.0 | 100.0 | Total | 100.0 | 100.0 | 100.0 | 100.0 | 100.0 | 100.0 |
| | | | **LIABILITIES** | | | | | | |
| 9.9 | 11.6 | 12.5 | Notes Payable-Short Term | 37.5 | 17.9 | 8.4 | 13.2 | 10.7 | 10.1 |
| 3.4 | 3.6 | 3.4 | Cur. Mat.-L.T.D. | 2.3 | 4.3 | 4.7 | 3.1 | 2.8 | 3.2 |
| 13.5 | 14.4 | 17.2 | Trade Payables | 26.5 | 18.6 | 17.0 | 19.4 | 14.9 | 16.2 |
| .3 | .3 | .2 | Income Taxes Payable | .0 | .1 | .2 | .3 | .3 | .2 |
| 10.9 | 9.0 | 12.1 | All Other Current | 10.7 | 24.6 | 12.5 | 9.9 | 8.2 | 11.8 |
| 38.0 | 38.9 | 45.4 | Total Current | 76.9 | 65.5 | 42.9 | 45.9 | 36.9 | 41.5 |
| 12.9 | 13.9 | 11.1 | Long-Term Debt | 23.4 | 14.2 | 9.9 | 10.4 | 10.4 | 9.8 |
| .5 | .4 | .4 | Deferred Taxes | .0 | .1 | .2 | .2 | .4 | .7 |
| 4.2 | 4.8 | 6.7 | All Other Non-Current | 39.9 | 12.3 | 7.2 | 4.6 | 4.1 | 3.3 |
| 44.4 | 42.1 | 36.5 | Net Worth | -40.3 | 8.0 | 39.8 | 38.9 | 48.2 | 44.7 |
| 100.0 | 100.0 | 100.0 | Total Liabilties & Net Worth | 100.0 | 100.0 | 100.0 | 100.0 | 100.0 | 100.0 |
| | | | **INCOME DATA** | | | | | | |
| 100.0 | 100.0 | 100.0 | Net Sales | 100.0 | 100.0 | 100.0 | 100.0 | 100.0 | 100.0 |
| 25.1 | 25.9 | 25.6 | Gross Profit | 61.1 | 35.0 | 27.0 | 24.3 | 23.2 | 18.7 |
| 22.8 | 23.9 | 22.0 | Operating Expenses | 55.9 | 32.7 | 26.1 | 20.6 | 18.3 | 14.5 |
| 2.4 | 2.0 | 3.6 | Operating Profit | 5.2 | 2.3 | .9 | 3.7 | 4.8 | 4.2 |
| .7 | .8 | .3 | All Other Expenses (net) | .7 | .4 | .2 | .4 | .3 | .3 |
| 1.7 | 1.3 | 3.3 | Profit Before Taxes | 4.5 | 2.0 | .7 | 3.3 | 4.5 | 3.9 |
| | | | **RATIOS** | | | | | | |
| 3.3 | 3.4 | 2.8 | | 2.8 | 3.5 | 3.4 | 2.5 | 3.5 | 2.4 |
| 1.8 | 1.9 | 1.6 | Current | 1.7 | 1.3 | 1.7 | 1.6 | 1.9 | 1.6 |
| 1.3 | 1.2 | 1.1 | | .4 | .8 | 1.1 | 1.2 | 1.4 | 1.2 |
| 2.1 | 2.3 | 2.0 | | 2.1 | 2.5 | 2.2 | 1.7 | 2.6 | 1.4 |
| 1.1 | 1.1 | 1.1 | Quick | 1.6 | .9 | 1.2 | 1.0 | 1.3 | .9 |
| .7 | .7 | .7 | | .4 | .5 | .7 | .7 | .8 | .7 |
| 34  10.8 | 38  9.7 | 40  9.1 | | 3  106.3 | 26  14.1 | 45  8.2 | 40  9.1 | 45  8.2 | 43  8.4 |
| 49  7.4 | 54  6.8 | 57  6.4 | Sales/Receivables | 31  11.8 | 54  6.7 | 61  6.0 | 56  6.5 | 59  6.2 | 58  6.3 |
| 70  5.2 | 75  4.8 | 74  4.9 | | 46  8.0 | 83  4.4 | 81  4.5 | 69  5.3 | 72  5.1 | 74  4.9 |
| 11  32.8 | 13  28.1 | 8  45.5 | | 0  UND | 0  UND | 3  130.2 | 6  56.8 | 17  21.7 | 20  17.9 |
| 35  10.3 | 37  9.8 | 33  11.0 | Cost of Sales/Inventory | 5  68.6 | 15  24.2 | 17  21.2 | 38  9.6 | 38  9.7 | 45  8.1 |
| 70  5.2 | 72  5.1 | 64  5.7 | | 39  9.3 | 57  6.4 | 60  6.1 | 63  5.8 | 66  5.5 | 70  5.2 |
| 15  24.4 | 17  20.9 | 19  19.7 | | 7  51.0 | 21  17.7 | 14  26.5 | 19  19.0 | 16  22.2 | 22  16.3 |
| 26  14.0 | 32  11.6 | 33  11.1 | Cost of Sales/Payables | 60  6.1 | 35  10.4 | 29  12.5 | 34  10.7 | 28  12.9 | 33  10.9 |
| 41  8.8 | 48  7.6 | 53  6.9 | | 101  3.6 | 59  6.2 | 50  7.3 | 55  6.6 | 47  7.7 | 48  7.6 |
| 4.0 | 3.7 | 4.4 | | 7.8 | 4.6 | 4.8 | 5.2 | 3.6 | 4.2 |
| 7.4 | 6.9 | 8.5 | Sales/Working Capital | 24.3 | -12.3 | 8.2 | 10.1 | 6.4 | 8.6 |
| 19.6 | 18.3 | 31.6 | | -6.8 | -42.6 | 54.8 | 33.3 | 12.5 | 15.3 |
| 13.0 | 13.4 | 15.6 | | 7.3 | 14.9 | 9.4 | 14.6 | 18.2 | 19.4 |
| (389)  3.3 | (444)  3.8 | (429)  4.2 | EBIT/Interest | (10)  3.6 | (50)  3.4 | (66)  2.2 | (82)  4.0 | (118)  5.2 | (103)  4.8 |
| -.1 | -1.0 | .8 | | -2.6 | -1.9 | -1.8 | .3 | 1.8 | 1.5 |
| 8.6 | 4.1 | 5.4 | | | | 1.9 | 3.8 | 5.9 | 7.0 |
| (114)  2.0 | (114)  1.7 | (100)  2.3 | Net Profit + Depr., Dep., Amort./Cur. Mat. L/T/D | | (10)  .6 | (10)  .9 | (28)  2.7 | (45)  3.2 | |
| .7 | .2 | .5 | | | -3.1 | -.6 | .5 | .9 | |
| .2 | .2 | .2 | | .3 | .2 | .2 | .2 | .2 | .2 |
| .5 | .5 | .5 | Fixed/Worth | 3.8 | 1.1 | .5 | .6 | .5 | .6 |
| 1.4 | 1.4 | 1.2 | | -6.2 | -13.3 | 1.2 | 1.1 | .9 | 1.1 |
| .5 | .5 | .6 | | .6 | .7 | .6 | .8 | .4 | .7 |
| 1.2 | 1.2 | 1.4 | Debt/Worth | 8.4 | 2.5 | 1.2 | 1.6 | 1.0 | 1.3 |
| 3.1 | 3.2 | 4.1 | | -3.4 | -32.0 | 3.2 | 4.3 | 2.6 | 2.9 |
| 30.1 | 29.6 | 39.0 | | 210.3 | 51.2 | 35.7 | 53.1 | 38.9 | 33.3 |
| (392)  10.7 | (450)  9.7 | (449)  15.8 | % Profit Before Taxes/Tangible Net Worth | (11)  38.9 | (45)  16.5 | (68)  9.0 | (87)  12.1 | (126)  18.6 | (112)  15.7 |
| -.9 | -4.6 | 1.6 | | 20.9 | -5.5 | -8.6 | .1 | 5.5 | 5.3 |
| 12.5 | 12.0 | 15.3 | | 25.7 | 16.1 | 13.7 | 15.2 | 15.2 | 13.8 |
| 4.4 | 3.9 | 6.1 | % Profit Before Taxes/Total Assets | 16.7 | 3.3 | 2.1 | 5.5 | 7.7 | 6.6 |
| -2.6 | -3.8 | .1 | | -5.1 | -5.5 | -4.1 | -.1 | 1.7 | 1.9 |
| 21.3 | 18.1 | 24.6 | | 35.9 | 37.2 | 31.0 | 28.6 | 20.0 | 20.3 |
| 9.7 | 8.8 | 11.5 | Sales/Net Fixed Assets | 7.5 | 14.9 | 13.4 | 13.8 | 10.2 | 9.3 |
| 4.7 | 5.0 | 5.9 | | 3.3 | 6.9 | 6.2 | 7.0 | 5.5 | 5.8 |
| 2.6 | 2.5 | 2.9 | | 4.1 | 3.9 | 3.1 | 3.1 | 2.7 | 2.4 |
| 2.0 | 2.0 | 2.2 | Sales/Total Assets | 2.4 | 2.5 | 2.3 | 2.4 | 2.1 | 1.9 |
| 1.5 | 1.4 | 1.6 | | 1.8 | 1.6 | 1.7 | 1.8 | 1.6 | 1.4 |
| .9 | 1.1 | .9 | | .6 | .8 | .7 | .8 | 1.0 | 1.0 |
| (386)  1.8 | (456)  2.0 | (435)  1.8 | % Depr., Dep., Amort./Sales | (14)  3.3 | (46)  1.6 | (59)  1.5 | (78)  1.9 | (127)  2.0 | (111)  1.8 |
| 3.6 | 3.7 | 3.1 | | 9.1 | 3.8 | 3.6 | 2.8 | 3.1 | 2.8 |
| 1.8 | 2.1 | 1.7 | | | 2.6 | 2.0 | 1.8 | 1.3 | .5 |
| (175)  3.9 | (200)  4.2 | (219)  3.0 | % Officers', Directors' Owners' Comp/Sales | | (37)  4.8 | (46)  3.5 | (50)  2.7 | (58)  2.3 | (19)  1.3 |
| 7.3 | 7.4 | 6.1 | | | 9.1 | 7.0 | 4.3 | 4.2 | 2.3 |
| 12949647M | 10742603M | 12591259M | Net Sales ($) | 11541M | 127094M | 296159M | 679291M | 2227187M | 9249987M |
| 7552121M | 6692463M | 7317535M | Total Assets ($) | 8491M | 71891M | 151295M | 327460M | 1216621M | 5541777M |

© RMA 2012

M = $ thousand   MM = $ million
See Pages 9 through 22 for Explanation of Ratios and Data

## Current Data Sorted by Assets        Comparative Historical Data

### Type of Statement

| 0-500M | 500M-2MM | 2-10MM | 10-50MM | 50-100MM | 100-250MM | Type of Statement | 4/1/07-3/31/08 ALL | 4/1/08-3/31/09 ALL |
|---|---|---|---|---|---|---|---|---|
| | | 3 | 8 | 2 | | Unqualified | 22 | 26 |
| | 1 | 15 | 11 | | | Reviewed | 35 | 35 |
| | 5 | 10 | 1 | | | Compiled | 20 | 23 |
| 3 | 4 | 4 | | | | Tax Returns | 8 | 12 |
| 2 | 5 | 15 | 10 | 8 | 1 | Other | 42 | 45 |
| | 24 (4/1-9/30/11) | | 84 (10/1/11-3/31/12) | | | | | |
| 5 | 15 | 47 | 30 | 10 | 1 | NUMBER OF STATEMENTS | 127 | 141 |
| % | % | % | % | % | % | | % | % |
| | | | | | | **ASSETS** | | |
| | 11.1 | 12.6 | 12.4 | 3.2 | | Cash & Equivalents | 9.2 | 11.8 |
| | 31.8 | 29.9 | 25.8 | 22.6 | | Trade Receivables (net) | 26.7 | 26.0 |
| | 21.4 | 21.3 | 21.3 | 18.3 | | Inventory | 22.0 | 22.1 |
| | .1 | 3.4 | 5.7 | 4.8 | | All Other Current | 5.2 | 4.1 |
| | 64.4 | 67.3 | 65.1 | 48.9 | | Total Current | 63.1 | 63.9 |
| | 28.5 | 24.3 | 25.3 | 24.8 | | Fixed Assets (net) | 27.2 | 26.9 |
| | 3.7 | 1.1 | 4.1 | 16.0 | | Intangibles (net) | 2.4 | 3.8 |
| | 3.3 | 7.3 | 5.4 | 10.2 | | All Other Non-Current | 7.2 | 5.4 |
| | 100.0 | 100.0 | 100.0 | 100.0 | | Total | 100.0 | 100.0 |
| | | | | | | **LIABILITIES** | | |
| | 8.1 | 9.6 | 7.0 | 6.7 | | Notes Payable-Short Term | 7.9 | 8.7 |
| | 4.5 | 2.6 | 2.5 | 3.5 | | Cur. Mat.-L.T.D. | 2.9 | 4.4 |
| | 17.9 | 12.7 | 10.6 | 7.9 | | Trade Payables | 13.6 | 13.3 |
| | .0 | .1 | .8 | .1 | | Income Taxes Payable | .2 | .2 |
| | 12.0 | 8.7 | 15.5 | 14.1 | | All Other Current | 14.3 | 13.1 |
| | 42.4 | 33.8 | 36.4 | 32.3 | | Total Current | 39.0 | 39.7 |
| | 9.8 | 11.3 | 12.8 | 18.1 | | Long-Term Debt | 16.6 | 16.4 |
| | .0 | .4 | .5 | 1.4 | | Deferred Taxes | .3 | .4 |
| | 10.6 | 4.2 | 5.6 | 10.7 | | All Other Non-Current | 6.0 | 6.0 |
| | 37.2 | 50.3 | 44.6 | 37.5 | | Net Worth | 38.1 | 37.5 |
| | 100.0 | 100.0 | 100.0 | 100.0 | | Total Liabilities & Net Worth | 100.0 | 100.0 |
| | | | | | | **INCOME DATA** | | |
| | 100.0 | 100.0 | 100.0 | 100.0 | | Net Sales | 100.0 | 100.0 |
| | 31.4 | 30.1 | 25.2 | 22.3 | | Gross Profit | 26.3 | 28.4 |
| | 24.9 | 24.9 | 19.5 | 18.3 | | Operating Expenses | 19.7 | 21.5 |
| | 6.6 | 5.3 | 5.7 | 4.0 | | Operating Profit | 6.7 | 6.9 |
| | .3 | 1.2 | 1.3 | 1.2 | | All Other Expenses (net) | 1.0 | .8 |
| | 6.3 | 4.0 | 4.3 | 2.8 | | Profit Before Taxes | 5.7 | 6.1 |
| | | | | | | **RATIOS** | | |
| | 2.6 | 3.3 | 3.0 | 2.4 | | | 2.8 | 2.7 |
| | 1.3 | 2.1 | 2.0 | 1.8 | Current | 1.7 | 1.9 |
| | 1.0 | 1.3 | 1.2 | 1.0 | | 1.2 | 1.3 |
| | 2.0 | 2.8 | 1.7 | 1.2 | | 1.5 | 1.7 |
| | .7 | 1.3 | 1.1 | .9 | Quick | .9 | 1.0 |
| | .6 | .6 | .5 | .6 | | .6 | .6 |
| | 20 17.9 | 36 10.2 | 36 10.0 | 45 8.2 | | | 28 13.1 | 29 12.7 |
| | 39 9.4 | 52 7.0 | 52 7.0 | 59 6.2 | Sales/Receivables | 43 8.6 | 40 9.2 |
| | 54 6.7 | 64 5.7 | 63 5.8 | 70 5.2 | | 62 5.9 | 51 7.2 |
| | 12 30.9 | 17 21.4 | 15 24.1 | 40 9.2 | | | 23 15.8 | 18 20.2 |
| | 38 9.5 | 43 8.4 | 50 7.3 | 79 4.6 | Cost of Sales/Inventory | 47 7.8 | 48 7.6 |
| | 54 6.8 | 70 5.2 | 104 3.5 | 111 3.3 | | 85 4.3 | 84 4.3 |
| | 15 24.5 | 13 28.4 | 23 16.0 | 18 20.3 | | | 16 22.2 | 15 24.0 |
| | 30 12.3 | 23 15.8 | 28 13.2 | 32 11.5 | Cost of Sales/Payables | 27 13.3 | 23 16.0 |
| | 37 9.8 | 40 9.2 | 36 10.2 | 45 8.2 | | 46 8.0 | 39 9.4 |
| | 8.0 | 3.6 | 3.0 | 4.6 | | | 4.4 | 4.6 |
| | 19.9 | 6.2 | 6.3 | 6.8 | Sales/Working Capital | 7.6 | 7.8 |
| | -89.2 | 18.0 | 19.6 | NM | | 20.9 | 16.2 |
| | 46.6 | 27.4 | 47.0 | 26.8 | | | 16.0 | 16.6 |
| | (12) 10.8 | (37) 8.1 | (27) 6.2 | 2.1 | EBIT/Interest | (112) 4.8 | (126) 5.2 |
| | 2.3 | 1.8 | 1.9 | .2 | | 1.4 | 1.9 |
| | | | | | | Net Profit + Depr., Dep., | 28.1 | 10.4 |
| | | | | | | Amort./Cur. Mat. L/T/D | (29) 5.7 | (37) 5.2 |
| | | | | | | | 1.8 | 1.8 |
| | .2 | .2 | .2 | .4 | | | .3 | .3 |
| | .7 | .5 | .7 | 2.0 | Fixed/Worth | .7 | .6 |
| | 1.1 | .9 | 1.4 | -5.6 | | 1.3 | 2.1 |
| | .7 | .4 | .5 | 1.0 | | | .7 | .7 |
| | 1.0 | .9 | 1.2 | 5.8 | Debt/Worth | 1.3 | 1.4 |
| | 3.6 | 2.6 | 4.3 | -13.5 | | 3.2 | 4.4 |
| | 102.4 | 51.9 | 37.5 | | | | 52.5 | 57.9 |
| | (13) 66.4 | (46) 18.4 | (27) 17.7 | | % Profit Before Taxes/Tangible Net Worth | (111) 27.2 | (119) 32.0 |
| | 26.7 | 4.1 | 6.2 | | | 10.4 | 8.4 |
| | 37.9 | 19.2 | 15.5 | 8.1 | | | 21.1 | 22.0 |
| | 24.6 | 5.6 | 8.6 | 1.1 | % Profit Before Taxes/Total Assets | 9.3 | 9.3 |
| | 1.5 | 1.8 | 1.6 | -1.4 | | 1.3 | 1.9 |
| | 119.4 | 24.1 | 14.4 | 10.5 | | | 16.7 | 22.4 |
| | 10.3 | 11.6 | 7.9 | 7.0 | Sales/Net Fixed Assets | 8.5 | 9.2 |
| | 6.0 | 4.6 | 3.8 | 3.4 | | 4.9 | 5.3 |
| | 4.0 | 3.0 | 2.3 | 1.8 | | | 2.5 | 3.0 |
| | 3.0 | 2.0 | 1.7 | 1.3 | Sales/Total Assets | 2.0 | 2.1 |
| | 2.2 | 1.3 | 1.3 | .8 | | 1.6 | 1.6 |
| | .7 | 1.3 | 1.4 | | | | .9 | 1.1 |
| | (12) 1.1 | (40) 2.4 | (28) 2.7 | | % Depr., Dep., Amort./Sales | (114) 1.6 | (118) 2.0 |
| | 2.2 | 3.4 | 4.7 | | | 3.0 | 3.8 |
| | | 2.1 | | | | | 2.0 | 2.1 |
| | (18) 3.0 | | | | | % Officers', Directors' Owners' Comp/Sales | (50) 4.2 | (49) 3.2 |
| | 5.8 | | | | | | 6.2 | 7.2 |
| 10334M | 63467M | 450468M | 969534M | 888492M | 186276M | Net Sales ($) | 3472589M | 5158448M |
| 1550M | 20874M | 231831M | 559876M | 691686M | 211459M | Total Assets ($) | 1805743M | 2632063M |

© RMA 2012

M = $ thousand    MM = $ million
See Pages 9 through 22 for Explanation of Ratios and Data

## Comparative Historical Data / Current Data Sorted by Sales

| | | | Type of Statement | 0-1MM | 1-3MM | 3-5MM | 5-10MM | 10-25MM | 25MM & OVER |
|---|---|---|---|---|---|---|---|---|---|
| 19 | 24 | 13 | Unqualified | | | 1 | 1 | 5 | 6 |
| 27 | 30 | 27 | Reviewed | | | 1 | 8 | 10 | 8 |
| 24 | 16 | 16 | Compiled | | 1 | 4 | 8 | 2 | 1 |
| 15 | 12 | 11 | Tax Returns | 2 | 1 | 3 | 3 | 2 | |
| 49 | 49 | 41 | Other | 2 | 4 | 3 | 3 | 5 | 15 | 12 |
| 4/1/09-3/31/10 ALL | 4/1/10-3/31/11 ALL | 4/1/11-3/31/12 ALL | | | 24 (4/1-9/30/11) | | 84 (10/1/11-3/31/12) | | |
| 134 | 131 | 108 | NUMBER OF STATEMENTS | 4 | 6 | 12 | 25 | 34 | 27 |
| % | % | % | ASSETS | % | % | % | % | % | % |
| 14.1 | 13.3 | 12.1 | Cash & Equivalents | | | 5.7 | 17.7 | 9.6 | 8.6 |
| 21.1 | 23.4 | 28.7 | Trade Receivables (net) | | | 28.5 | 31.7 | 27.3 | 26.8 |
| 18.9 | 23.7 | 20.4 | Inventory | | | 14.3 | 20.8 | 25.2 | 19.8 |
| 4.1 | 4.1 | 3.6 | All Other Current | | | 1.6 | 2.6 | 4.1 | 5.7 |
| 58.2 | 64.5 | 64.8 | Total Current | | | 50.1 | 72.7 | 66.2 | 60.8 |
| 30.7 | 25.5 | 25.2 | Fixed Assets (net) | | | 36.5 | 22.4 | 24.7 | 24.4 |
| 3.4 | 3.5 | 3.6 | Intangibles (net) | | | 5.7 | .9 | 1.9 | 8.7 |
| 7.7 | 6.5 | 6.3 | All Other Non-Current | | | 7.8 | 4.0 | 7.1 | 6.0 |
| 100.0 | 100.0 | 100.0 | Total | | | 100.0 | 100.0 | 100.0 | 100.0 |
| | | | LIABILITIES | | | | | | |
| 7.3 | 10.2 | 8.5 | Notes Payable-Short Term | | | 4.8 | 8.0 | 11.1 | 7.2 |
| 4.2 | 4.0 | 3.0 | Cur. Mat.-L.T.D. | | | 8.1 | 2.8 | 1.8 | 3.4 |
| 10.8 | 12.6 | 12.4 | Trade Payables | | | 13.2 | 15.8 | 10.6 | 11.3 |
| .2 | .2 | .3 | Income Taxes Payable | | | .3 | .0 | .6 | .2 |
| 11.2 | 11.5 | 11.2 | All Other Current | | | 7.2 | 11.5 | 8.9 | 16.8 |
| 33.7 | 38.5 | 35.3 | Total Current | | | 33.6 | 38.1 | 33.0 | 39.0 |
| 17.1 | 13.2 | 13.2 | Long-Term Debt | | | 20.9 | 7.6 | 10.6 | 17.7 |
| .3 | .3 | .4 | Deferred Taxes | | | .9 | .1 | .3 | .9 |
| 8.9 | 6.0 | 6.3 | All Other Non-Current | | | 8.4 | 3.3 | 7.3 | 5.6 |
| 39.9 | 41.9 | 44.7 | Net Worth | | | 36.2 | 50.9 | 48.9 | 36.8 |
| 100.0 | 100.0 | 100.0 | Total Liabilities & Net Worth | | | 100.0 | 100.0 | 100.0 | 100.0 |
| | | | INCOME DATA | | | | | | |
| 100.0 | 100.0 | 100.0 | Net Sales | | | 100.0 | 100.0 | 100.0 | 100.0 |
| 29.5 | 29.2 | 28.4 | Gross Profit | | | 33.1 | 32.6 | 25.1 | 22.8 |
| 26.9 | 24.4 | 22.6 | Operating Expenses | | | 26.1 | 28.9 | 19.9 | 17.9 |
| 2.6 | 4.8 | 5.7 | Operating Profit | | | 7.0 | 3.7 | 5.2 | 5.0 |
| 1.2 | 1.0 | 1.1 | All Other Expenses (net) | | | .8 | .0 | 1.4 | .8 |
| 1.4 | 3.8 | 4.7 | Profit Before Taxes | | | 6.3 | 3.7 | 3.8 | 4.2 |
| | | | RATIOS | | | | | | |
| 3.4 | 3.2 | 2.9 | Current | | | 2.4 | 2.7 | 3.1 | 2.4 |
| 2.0 | 1.8 | 2.0 | | | | 1.4 | 2.1 | 2.0 | 1.6 |
| 1.1 | 1.2 | 1.2 | | | | .9 | 1.2 | 1.3 | 1.0 |
| 2.0 | 2.0 | 2.0 | Quick | | | 1.9 | 2.6 | 1.9 | 1.2 |
| 1.1 | .9 | 1.2 | | | | 1.0 | 1.3 | 1.1 | .9 |
| .5 | .5 | .6 | | | | .4 | .6 | .6 | .5 |
| 26  13.8 | 34  10.6 | 36  10.2 | Sales/Receivables | 11  34.6 | 34  10.7 | | | 39  9.4 | 43  8.4 |
| 44  8.4 | 45  8.2 | 51  7.2 | | 43  8.5 | 45  8.1 | | | 52  7.0 | 56  6.5 |
| 58  6.2 | 58  6.3 | 63  5.8 | | 73  5.0 | 57  6.4 | | | 63  5.8 | 65  5.6 |
| 22  16.7 | 26  13.8 | 16  23.2 | Cost of Sales/Inventory | 0  UND | 15  25.1 | | | 36  10.2 | 21  17.2 |
| 49  7.5 | 60  6.1 | 44  8.3 | | 39  9.4 | 39  9.3 | | | 63  5.8 | 53  6.9 |
| 92  3.9 | 115  3.2 | 79  4.6 | | 58  6.3 | 53  6.9 | | | 104  3.5 | 83  4.4 |
| 15  25.0 | 18  20.4 | 15  23.6 | Cost of Sales/Payables | 14  25.6 | 12  29.2 | | | 16  22.5 | 20  18.0 |
| 25  14.5 | 30  12.2 | 27  13.7 | | 21  17.4 | 29  12.6 | | | 25  14.4 | 31  11.8 |
| 43  8.4 | 43  8.6 | 39  9.4 | | 53  6.9 | 37  9.8 | | | 38  9.7 | 41  8.9 |
| 3.4 | 3.4 | 3.8 | Sales/Working Capital | | | 5.2 | 3.7 | 3.7 | 3.9 |
| 6.0 | 6.3 | 7.0 | | | | 13.1 | 7.3 | 6.3 | 9.2 |
| 146.6 | 17.2 | 25.3 | | | | NM | 37.9 | 18.5 | 213.4 |
| 10.9 | 13.6 | 33.7 | EBIT/Interest | | | 21.8 | 53.3 | 16.1 | 28.7 |
| (116)  2.2 | (114)  4.4 | (91)  7.4 | | | | (10)  8.4 | (18)  15.6 | (31)  5.7 | (25)  5.8 |
| -1.5 | 1.3 | 1.8 | | | | 1.7 | 5.5 | 1.9 | .6 |
| 9.1 | 5.0 | 4.8 | Net Profit + Depr., Dep., Amort./Cur. Mat. L/T/D | | | | | | 21.3 |
| (30)  2.0 | (33)  2.2 | (22)  3.3 | | | | | | (10) | 3.7 |
| .6 | .8 | 1.6 | | | | | | | 1.8 |
| .2 | .2 | .2 | Fixed/Worth | | | .2 | .1 | .3 | .4 |
| .7 | .6 | .6 | | | | .9 | .4 | .5 | .9 |
| 1.8 | 1.4 | 1.2 | | | | 9.0 | .7 | 1.1 | 4.2 |
| .5 | .6 | .5 | Debt/Worth | | | .7 | .5 | .4 | .7 |
| 1.3 | 1.4 | 1.1 | | | | 1.1 | 1.0 | 1.0 | 2.4 |
| 3.9 | 3.3 | 3.7 | | | | 10.5 | 2.5 | 2.4 | 11.9 |
| 36.3 | 30.9 | 59.1 | % Profit Before Taxes/Tangible Net Worth | | | 65.2 | 76.7 | 37.4 | 72.4 |
| (113)  11.3 | (115)  16.0 | (97)  19.4 | | | | (10)  40.1 | (24)  21.3 | (32)  16.8 | (22)  15.4 |
| -2.5 | 4.9 | 3.9 | | | | 6.3 | 3.9 | 3.9 | .6 |
| 12.1 | 13.7 | 19.0 | % Profit Before Taxes/Total Assets | | | 26.1 | 40.8 | 15.9 | 12.5 |
| 3.3 | 6.6 | 7.9 | | | | 10.2 | 10.2 | 7.5 | 7.4 |
| -4.3 | 1.3 | 1.5 | | | | 2.2 | 1.4 | 2.1 | -.9 |
| 16.1 | 18.2 | 19.6 | Sales/Net Fixed Assets | | | 25.2 | 39.2 | 19.0 | 12.1 |
| 6.4 | 8.5 | 10.2 | | | | 4.6 | 18.0 | 9.9 | 7.3 |
| 3.1 | 4.3 | 4.6 | | | | 3.1 | 7.7 | 4.6 | 4.3 |
| 2.3 | 2.4 | 3.0 | Sales/Total Assets | | | 3.2 | 3.8 | 2.3 | 2.4 |
| 1.6 | 1.8 | 1.9 | | | | 1.7 | 2.9 | 1.9 | 1.5 |
| 1.1 | 1.2 | 1.4 | | | | 1.3 | 1.3 | 1.5 | 1.1 |
| 1.3 | 1.6 | 1.3 | % Depr., Dep., Amort./Sales | | | | .8 | 1.4 | 1.8 |
| (115)  2.9 | (117)  2.4 | (90)  2.3 | | | | | (19)  1.4 | (32)  2.7 | (23)  2.7 |
| 4.5 | 4.0 | 3.5 | | | | | 2.8 | 4.0 | 3.7 |
| 2.8 | 2.1 | 1.8 | % Officers', Directors' Owners' Comp/Sales | | | | 2.5 | 1.2 | |
| (43)  5.6 | (41)  3.9 | (37)  3.2 | | | | | (10)  4.4 | (10)  2.3 | |
| 8.3 | 7.0 | 5.8 | | | | | 6.2 | 3.3 | |
| 2909449M | 2883687M | 2568571M | Net Sales ($) | 2625M | 13926M | 46179M | 176110M | 533158M | 1796573M |
| 1970590M | 1988726M | 1717276M | Total Assets ($) | 7636M | 8722M | 30440M | 82915M | 307417M | 1280146M |

M = $ thousand    MM = $ million
See Pages 9 through 22 for Explanation of Ratios and Data

## Current Data Sorted by Assets       Comparative Historical Data

| 0-500M | 500M-2MM | 2-10MM | 10-50MM | 50-100MM | 100-250MM | Type of Statement | 4/1/07-3/31/08 ALL | 4/1/08-3/31/09 ALL |
|---|---|---|---|---|---|---|---|---|
| | | 2 | 10 | 2 | | Unqualified | 20 | 27 |
| | 3 | 15 | 9 | | | Reviewed | 38 | 30 |
| 1 | 1 | 6 | | | | Compiled | 11 | 13 |
| 3 | 11 | 1 | | | | Tax Returns | 15 | 16 |
| 3 | 7 | 22 | 16 | 5 | 3 | Other | 58 | 65 |
| | 19 (4/1-9/30/11) | | 101 (10/1/11-3/31/12) | | | | | |
| 7 | 22 | 46 | 35 | 7 | 3 | NUMBER OF STATEMENTS | 142 | 151 |
| % | % | % | % | % | % | **ASSETS** | % | % |
| | 10.6 | 7.6 | 7.5 | | | Cash & Equivalents | 7.4 | 7.6 |
| | 30.5 | 31.8 | 24.4 | | | Trade Receivables (net) | 31.7 | 28.9 |
| | 29.1 | 28.6 | 20.4 | | | Inventory | 22.5 | 24.8 |
| | 4.1 | 2.3 | 3.1 | | | All Other Current | 3.5 | 3.7 |
| | 74.3 | 70.3 | 55.5 | | | Total Current | 65.1 | 65.0 |
| | 17.4 | 22.7 | 31.8 | | | Fixed Assets (net) | 25.5 | 23.9 |
| | 1.9 | 3.2 | 6.5 | | | Intangibles (net) | 4.8 | 5.7 |
| | 6.4 | 3.9 | 6.2 | | | All Other Non-Current | 4.6 | 5.3 |
| | 100.0 | 100.0 | 100.0 | | | Total | 100.0 | 100.0 |
| | | | | | | **LIABILITIES** | | |
| | 13.1 | 10.7 | 7.1 | | | Notes Payable-Short Term | 12.4 | 13.1 |
| | 2.5 | 1.6 | 5.1 | | | Cur. Mat.-L.T.D. | 3.0 | 3.8 |
| | 31.5 | 14.0 | 11.3 | | | Trade Payables | 14.9 | 14.2 |
| | .0 | .2 | .1 | | | Income Taxes Payable | .1 | .1 |
| | 6.1 | 11.5 | 10.8 | | | All Other Current | 10.5 | 12.4 |
| | 53.3 | 38.0 | 34.3 | | | Total Current | 40.9 | 43.6 |
| | 10.6 | 10.6 | 14.9 | | | Long-Term Debt | 18.8 | 15.5 |
| | .1 | .5 | .3 | | | Deferred Taxes | .6 | .4 |
| | 10.8 | 5.9 | 13.5 | | | All Other Non-Current | 4.6 | 5.8 |
| | 25.3 | 45.0 | 36.9 | | | Net Worth | 35.2 | 34.6 |
| | 100.0 | 100.0 | 100.0 | | | Total Liabilities & Net Worth | 100.0 | 100.0 |
| | | | | | | **INCOME DATA** | | |
| | 100.0 | 100.0 | 100.0 | | | Net Sales | 100.0 | 100.0 |
| | 30.9 | 29.5 | 28.6 | | | Gross Profit | 29.2 | 30.9 |
| | 30.9 | 29.9 | 25.2 | | | Operating Expenses | 24.8 | 27.1 |
| | .0 | -.4 | 3.4 | | | Operating Profit | 4.4 | 3.8 |
| | .2 | .1 | 1.2 | | | All Other Expenses (net) | 1.7 | 1.6 |
| | -.2 | -.5 | 2.2 | | | Profit Before Taxes | 2.8 | 2.1 |
| | | | | | | **RATIOS** | | |
| | 2.4 | 2.8 | 2.9 | | | | 2.7 | 2.8 |
| | 1.7 | 1.9 | 1.6 | | | Current | 1.6 | 1.5 |
| | 1.1 | 1.4 | 1.2 | | | | 1.1 | 1.1 |
| | 1.3 | 1.9 | 1.8 | | | | 1.7 | 1.7 |
| | (21) .9 | 1.1 | .7 | | | Quick | .9 | .8 |
| | .5 | .6 | .6 | | | | .6 | .5 |
| 26 | 13.8 | 33 10.9 | 32 11.4 | | | | 30 12.3 | 29 12.8 |
| 31 | 11.6 | 44 8.3 | 40 9.1 | | | Sales/Receivables | 44 8.3 | 42 8.8 |
| 46 | 7.9 | 64 5.7 | 60 6.1 | | | | 65 5.6 | 59 6.2 |
| 23 | 15.7 | 42 8.7 | 34 10.7 | | | | 24 15.5 | 29 12.8 |
| 41 | 9.0 | 65 5.6 | 51 7.1 | | | Cost of Sales/Inventory | 45 8.2 | 48 7.7 |
| 96 | 3.8 | 99 3.7 | 74 4.9 | | | | 69 5.3 | 83 4.4 |
| 25 | 14.6 | 14 26.8 | 16 23.4 | | | | 16 22.7 | 14 27.0 |
| 47 | 7.7 | 28 13.1 | 24 15.3 | | | Cost of Sales/Payables | 28 13.1 | 22 16.2 |
| 64 | 5.7 | 40 9.2 | 45 8.2 | | | | 44 8.2 | 40 9.2 |
| | 5.8 | 4.5 | 5.3 | | | | 5.5 | 5.9 |
| | 10.1 | 7.0 | 10.5 | | | Sales/Working Capital | 9.7 | 9.7 |
| | NM | 11.5 | 37.0 | | | | 34.1 | 76.1 |
| | 8.8 | 8.6 | 7.2 | | | | 7.1 | 9.3 |
| | (19) 1.2 | (42) 2.4 | (33) 4.2 | | | EBIT/Interest | (126) 2.9 | (137) 2.3 |
| | -2.6 | -4.1 | 1.6 | | | | 1.0 | -.1 |
| | | | 5.9 | | | | 6.3 | 3.7 |
| | | (13) 2.3 | | | | Net Profit + Depr., Dep., Amort./Cur. Mat. L/T/D | (45) 2.3 | (44) 2.2 |
| | | | .6 | | | | 1.4 | .5 |
| | .2 | .2 | .4 | | | | .3 | .3 |
| | .4 | .4 | 1.0 | | | Fixed/Worth | .8 | .8 |
| | 1.8 | 1.4 | 2.4 | | | | 2.0 | 3.1 |
| | .8 | .6 | .8 | | | | 1.0 | .9 |
| | 2.3 | 1.3 | 2.1 | | | Debt/Worth | 1.9 | 1.9 |
| | 8.1 | 3.2 | 4.6 | | | | 6.4 | 7.7 |
| | 24.0 | 23.4 | 27.8 | | | | 44.9 | 36.1 |
| | (18) 1.2 | (42) 6.8 | (31) 17.5 | | | % Profit Before Taxes/Tangible Net Worth | (119) 19.5 | (123) 11.5 |
| | -27.9 | -9.9 | 3.3 | | | | 4.5 | -5.8 |
| | 5.9 | 9.7 | 8.7 | | | | 11.8 | 12.8 |
| | .0 | 2.1 | 5.0 | | | % Profit Before Taxes/Total Assets | 6.0 | 3.1 |
| | -9.3 | -6.2 | .8 | | | | .6 | -3.1 |
| | 69.1 | 35.2 | 14.5 | | | | 25.1 | 28.7 |
| | 25.7 | 14.7 | 6.2 | | | Sales/Net Fixed Assets | 12.1 | 12.0 |
| | 11.8 | 5.4 | 3.1 | | | | 6.0 | 6.3 |
| | 3.7 | 3.1 | 2.6 | | | | 2.9 | 3.1 |
| | 3.1 | 2.4 | 1.7 | | | Sales/Total Assets | 2.4 | 2.3 |
| | 2.5 | 1.6 | 1.4 | | | | 1.8 | 1.7 |
| | .3 | .8 | 1.6 | | | | .8 | .9 |
| | (19) .6 | (41) 1.5 | (32) 2.3 | | | % Depr., Dep., Amort./Sales | (128) 1.8 | (133) 1.5 |
| | 1.2 | 2.8 | 3.2 | | | | 2.7 | 2.6 |
| | 2.6 | .9 | | | | | 1.9 | 1.5 |
| | (15) 4.4 | (16) 2.0 | | | | % Officers', Directors' Owners' Comp/Sales | (45) 2.9 | (47) 3.2 |
| | 5.5 | 3.0 | | | | | 5.9 | 6.1 |
| 13647M | 87038M | 551346M | 1267036M | 748659M | 929104M | Net Sales ($) | 4570846M | 5411060M |
| 2292M | 27097M | 237192M | 676362M | 447234M | 480767M | Total Assets ($) | 2417488M | 2571153M |

© RMA 2012

M = $ thousand    MM = $ million
See Pages 9 through 22 for Explanation of Ratios and Data

## Comparative Historical Data | Current Data Sorted by Sales

Right-hand current-data period headings: **19 (4/1-9/30/11)** covers 0-1MM and 1-3MM; **101 (10/1/11-3/31/12)** covers 3-5MM, 5-10MM, 10-25MM, 25MM & OVER.

| 4/1/09–3/31/10 ALL | 4/1/10–3/31/11 ALL | 4/1/11–3/31/12 ALL | Type of Statement | 0-1MM | 1-3MM | 3-5MM | 5-10MM | 10-25MM | 25MM & OVER |
|---|---|---|---|---|---|---|---|---|---|
| 23 | 20 | 14 | Unqualified | | | | 1 | 2 | 11 |
| 34 | 34 | 27 | Reviewed | | | 2 | 8 | 11 | 6 |
| 16 | 10 | 8 | Compiled | | 2 | | 5 | 1 | |
| 11 | 10 | 15 | Tax Returns | 1 | 6 | 3 | 5 | | |
| 53 | 57 | 56 | Other | 2 | 3 | 7 | 6 | 21 | 17 |
| 137 | 131 | 120 | **NUMBER OF STATEMENTS** | 3 | 11 | 12 | 25 | 35 | 34 |
| % | % | % | **ASSETS** | % | % | % | % | % | % |
| 11.7 | 10.1 | 8.7 | Cash & Equivalents | | 7.4 | 10.1 | 10.1 | 6.4 | 9.9 |
| 25.9 | 29.0 | 28.4 | Trade Receivables (net) | | 26.8 | 29.6 | 28.0 | 34.0 | 23.4 |
| 22.0 | 24.7 | 25.1 | Inventory | | 31.4 | 30.1 | 25.5 | 24.4 | 20.6 |
| 3.9 | 2.7 | 3.5 | All Other Current | | .2 | 1.7 | 6.2 | 2.7 | 3.7 |
| 63.5 | 66.5 | 65.6 | Total Current | | 65.9 | 71.5 | 69.8 | 67.5 | 57.6 |
| 26.4 | 22.9 | 24.6 | Fixed Assets (net) | | 16.2 | 25.2 | 22.3 | 25.4 | 29.0 |
| 4.6 | 4.9 | 4.6 | Intangibles (net) | | .5 | 1.0 | 4.8 | 3.2 | 8.0 |
| 5.5 | 5.7 | 5.2 | All Other Non-Current | | 17.4 | 2.4 | 3.1 | 3.9 | 5.5 |
| 100.0 | 100.0 | 100.0 | Total | | 100.0 | 100.0 | 100.0 | 100.0 | 100.0 |
| | | | **LIABILITIES** | | | | | | |
| 11.6 | 9.0 | 9.1 | Notes Payable-Short Term | | 11.3 | 9.9 | 7.9 | 13.5 | 3.8 |
| 3.3 | 3.3 | 2.8 | Cur. Mat.-L.T.D. | | 2.3 | 2.0 | 1.6 | 3.6 | 3.4 |
| 12.5 | 13.4 | 17.1 | Trade Payables | | 26.7 | 22.7 | 18.1 | 15.2 | 9.8 |
| .1 | .2 | .2 | Income Taxes Payable | | 1.5 | .3 | .1 | .1 | .1 |
| 9.5 | 11.8 | 10.4 | All Other Current | | 7.3 | 7.8 | 10.8 | 10.5 | 11.3 |
| 37.1 | 37.8 | 39.6 | Total Current | | 49.1 | 42.6 | 38.4 | 42.9 | 28.3 |
| 20.0 | 13.2 | 12.1 | Long-Term Debt | | 11.7 | 8.6 | 12.5 | 12.5 | 13.5 |
| .6 | .5 | .5 | Deferred Taxes | | .0 | 1.3 | .1 | .5 | .6 |
| 9.6 | 6.7 | 9.8 | All Other Non-Current | | 3.3 | 12.1 | 9.4 | 7.2 | 10.9 |
| 32.7 | 41.7 | 38.0 | Net Worth | | 35.9 | 35.4 | 39.6 | 36.9 | 46.7 |
| 100.0 | 100.0 | 100.0 | Total Liabilities & Net Worth | | 100.0 | 100.0 | 100.0 | 100.0 | 100.0 |
| | | | **INCOME DATA** | | | | | | |
| 100.0 | 100.0 | 100.0 | Net Sales | | 100.0 | 100.0 | 100.0 | 100.0 | 100.0 |
| 31.2 | 30.3 | 29.4 | Gross Profit | | 30.6 | 35.0 | 28.1 | 29.7 | 27.6 |
| 28.3 | 27.3 | 28.1 | Operating Expenses | | 33.6 | 33.3 | 27.7 | 28.7 | 23.7 |
| 3.0 | 3.0 | 1.3 | Operating Profit | | -3.0 | 1.7 | .4 | 1.0 | 3.9 |
| 1.5 | .9 | .5 | All Other Expenses (net) | | -.2 | .1 | .1 | .8 | .8 |
| 1.4 | 2.1 | .8 | Profit Before Taxes | | -2.8 | 1.5 | .4 | .2 | 3.1 |
| | | | **RATIOS** | | | | | | |
| 3.8 | 3.4 | 2.8 | Current | | 2.2 | 2.9 | 3.4 | 2.3 | 3.5 |
| 1.9 | 1.9 | 1.9 | Current | | 1.5 | 2.2 | 1.9 | 1.6 | 2.5 |
| 1.2 | 1.3 | 1.3 | Current | | .6 | 1.6 | 1.5 | 1.1 | 1.3 |
| 2.2 | 2.2 | 1.9 | Quick | | .9 | 1.8 | 2.1 | 1.7 | 2.2 |
| 1.1 | 1.1 | (119) .9 | Quick | | .7 | 1.0 | (24) .9 | .9 | 1.2 |
| .6 | .6 | .6 | Quick | | .3 | .7 | .6 | .5 | .7 |
| 31  11.7 | 31  11.7 | 28  12.9 | Sales/Receivables | | 28  13.1 | 28  13.0 | 26  13.9 | 32  11.4 | 28  12.9 |
| 40  9.2 | 44  8.4 | 40  9.1 | Sales/Receivables | | 33  10.9 | 38  9.6 | 40  9.1 | 49  7.5 | 38  9.6 |
| 57  6.4 | 62  5.8 | 58  6.3 | Sales/Receivables | | 46  8.0 | 61  6.0 | 60  6.1 | 73  5.0 | 52  7.0 |
| 26  14.1 | 33  11.1 | 33  11.2 | Cost of Sales/Inventory | | 31  11.7 | 21  17.3 | 24  15.3 | 37  9.8 | 33  11.1 |
| 50  7.3 | 51  7.1 | 54  6.7 | Cost of Sales/Inventory | | 69  5.3 | 72  5.1 | 65  5.6 | 58  6.3 | 50  7.3 |
| 78  4.7 | 81  4.5 | 83  4.4 | Cost of Sales/Inventory | | 107  3.4 | 130  2.8 | 101  3.6 | 74  4.9 | 57  6.4 |
| 11  33.1 | 14  25.2 | 14  25.9 | Cost of Sales/Payables | | 26  13.9 | 29  12.7 | 19  19.3 | 13  27.2 | 8  46.3 |
| 23  15.8 | 25  14.8 | 27  13.4 | Cost of Sales/Payables | | 36  10.0 | 39  9.4 | 27  13.7 | 29  12.4 | 19  19.5 |
| 37  9.8 | 40  9.0 | 47  7.7 | Cost of Sales/Payables | | 53  6.9 | 60  6.1 | 49  7.5 | 47  7.7 | 29  12.8 |
| 4.1 | 4.7 | 5.1 | Sales/Working Capital | | 6.5 | 3.8 | 4.5 | 5.3 | 4.4 |
| 8.3 | 7.2 | 8.1 | Sales/Working Capital | | 16.5 | 7.8 | 7.2 | 8.7 | 6.8 |
| 24.1 | 18.3 | 24.2 | Sales/Working Capital | | -14.2 | 11.5 | 11.2 | 83.4 | 18.1 |
| 12.3 | 16.4 | 8.8 | EBIT/Interest | | 5.2 | 19.1 | 12.7 | 7.2 | 20.3 |
| (123) 2.6 | (120) 3.6 | (109) 2.7 | EBIT/Interest | | 1.3 | (10) 3.7 | (22) 2.9 | (32) 2.4 | (32) 4.5 |
| .5 | .1 | -.6 | EBIT/Interest | | -1.5 | -2.4 | -20.2 | -3.0 | 1.7 |
| 4.8 | 6.0 | 5.9 | Net Profit + Depr., Dep., Amort./Cur. Mat. L/T/D | | | | | | 7.2 |
| (37) 1.7 | (40) 2.3 | (29) 2.5 | Net Profit + Depr., Dep., Amort./Cur. Mat. L/T/D | | | | | | (11) 3.1 |
| -.1 | .4 | .6 | Net Profit + Depr., Dep., Amort./Cur. Mat. L/T/D | | | | | | 1.8 |
| .3 | .3 | .3 | Fixed/Worth | | .1 | .3 | .2 | .2 | .3 |
| .7 | .6 | .6 | Fixed/Worth | | .3 | .4 | .7 | .7 | .8 |
| 5.7 | 1.7 | 1.7 | Fixed/Worth | | 1.8 | 1.3 | 1.9 | 1.9 | 1.4 |
| .6 | .6 | .6 | Debt/Worth | | .5 | .4 | .6 | .9 | .4 |
| 1.7 | 1.6 | 1.5 | Debt/Worth | | 1.2 | 1.7 | 1.6 | 1.5 | 1.3 |
| 13.4 | 4.1 | 4.4 | Debt/Worth | | 3.0 | 10.2 | 6.4 | 3.8 | 3.9 |
| 36.0 | 35.2 | 28.0 | % Profit Before Taxes/Tangible Net Worth | | 22.2 | 28.7 | 39.7 | 27.6 | 30.2 |
| (109) 13.9 | (118) 13.1 | (106) 9.2 | % Profit Before Taxes/Tangible Net Worth | | (10) 1.2 | (11) 19.5 | (20) 8.4 | (32) 5.5 | (31) 15.2 |
| -2.5 | .8 | -4.1 | % Profit Before Taxes/Tangible Net Worth | | -12.2 | -10.2 | -11.6 | -12.6 | 3.3 |
| 13.0 | 11.9 | 10.1 | % Profit Before Taxes/Total Assets | | 9.1 | 11.3 | 11.2 | 7.5 | 11.6 |
| 5.6 | 4.2 | 2.4 | % Profit Before Taxes/Total Assets | | .7 | 2.9 | 2.6 | 1.9 | 5.4 |
| -1.7 | -1.5 | -3.8 | % Profit Before Taxes/Total Assets | | -7.1 | -9.2 | -8.2 | -5.8 | 1.2 |
| 24.5 | 27.1 | 31.5 | Sales/Net Fixed Assets | | 43.7 | 66.6 | 42.2 | 35.1 | 14.6 |
| 12.3 | 12.1 | 12.3 | Sales/Net Fixed Assets | | 21.2 | 11.0 | 18.3 | 11.8 | 7.8 |
| 4.8 | 5.7 | 5.2 | Sales/Net Fixed Assets | | 11.2 | 4.9 | 8.0 | 4.4 | 4.6 |
| 3.1 | 2.9 | 3.1 | Sales/Total Assets | | 3.6 | 4.5 | 3.3 | 3.1 | 2.6 |
| 2.2 | 2.3 | 2.3 | Sales/Total Assets | | 2.5 | 2.7 | 2.8 | 2.4 | 2.0 |
| 1.5 | 1.7 | 1.6 | Sales/Total Assets | | 1.8 | 1.4 | 1.5 | 1.6 | 1.6 |
| .8 | .9 | .9 | % Depr., Dep., Amort./Sales | | .1 | .2 | .7 | .8 | 1.6 |
| (120) 1.7 | (114) 1.6 | (105) 1.7 | % Depr., Dep., Amort./Sales | | 1.0 | (10) 1.7 | (20) 1.5 | (32) 1.5 | (30) 2.3 |
| 3.0 | 2.8 | 2.8 | % Depr., Dep., Amort./Sales | | 2.3 | 2.8 | 3.4 | 2.4 | 3.1 |
| 1.7 | 2.1 | 1.7 | % Officers', Directors' Owners' Comp/Sales | | | | 1.6 | .7 | |
| (38) 3.7 | (32) 2.7 | (40) 3.0 | % Officers', Directors' Owners' Comp/Sales | | | | (11) 2.4 | (11) 2.2 | |
| 6.0 | 5.7 | 5.2 | % Officers', Directors' Owners' Comp/Sales | | | | 3.2 | 7.7 | |
| 3845685M | 4147856M | 3596830M | Net Sales ($) | 1506M | 22545M | 46659M | 169386M | 614763M | 2741971M |
| 2388586M | 2310785M | 1870944M | Total Assets ($) | 574M | 11783M | 21968M | 84614M | 314944M | 1437061M |

M = $ thousand    MM = $ million

## Current Data Sorted by Assets      Comparative Historical Data

### Type of Statement

| 0-500M | 500M-2MM | 2-10MM | 10-50MM | 50-100MM | 100-250MM | Type of Statement | 4/1/07-3/31/08 ALL | 4/1/08-3/31/09 ALL |
|---|---|---|---|---|---|---|---|---|
| 2 | 13 | 7 | 16 | 5 | | Unqualified | 39 | 34 |
| 3 | 14 | 58 | 14 | 1 | 1 | Reviewed | 93 | 78 |
| 11 | 23 | 18 | 3 | 1 | | Compiled | 59 | 61 |
| 7 | 16 | 18 | 19 | 2 | 3 | Tax Returns | 41 | 52 |
| | | 46 | | | | Other | 87 | 101 |
| 42 (4/1-9/30/11) | | 259 (10/1/11-3/31/12) | | | | | | |

| 0-500M | 500M-2MM | 2-10MM | 10-50MM | 50-100MM | 100-250MM | | 4/1/07-3/31/08 ALL | 4/1/08-3/31/09 ALL |
|---|---|---|---|---|---|---|---|---|
| 23 | 66 | 147 | 52 | 9 | 4 | **NUMBER OF STATEMENTS** | 319 | 326 |
| % | % | % | % | % | % | **ASSETS** | % | % |
| 13.9 | 11.0 | 10.8 | 9.0 | | | Cash & Equivalents | 8.9 | 9.4 |
| 25.3 | 36.4 | 29.9 | 27.7 | | | Trade Receivables (net) | 32.1 | 29.4 |
| 20.1 | 16.3 | 20.5 | 18.0 | | | Inventory | 21.3 | 22.1 |
| 9.7 | 2.0 | 2.9 | 4.0 | | | All Other Current | 2.5 | 2.7 |
| 69.0 | 65.7 | 64.1 | 58.7 | | | Total Current | 64.8 | 63.7 |
| 22.0 | 25.3 | 28.4 | 24.4 | | | Fixed Assets (net) | 26.5 | 27.4 |
| 2.5 | 1.3 | 3.2 | 11.9 | | | Intangibles (net) | 3.0 | 3.4 |
| 6.5 | 7.8 | 4.3 | 5.0 | | | All Other Non-Current | 5.8 | 5.5 |
| 100.0 | 100.0 | 100.0 | 100.0 | | | Total | 100.0 | 100.0 |
| | | | | | | **LIABILITIES** | | |
| 23.2 | 11.6 | 8.1 | 6.9 | | | Notes Payable-Short Term | 10.8 | 11.2 |
| 4.4 | 5.0 | 4.2 | 2.4 | | | Cur. Mat.-L.T.D. | 4.1 | 4.1 |
| 21.5 | 19.7 | 14.1 | 11.9 | | | Trade Payables | 14.7 | 15.3 |
| .0 | .1 | .0 | .3 | | | Income Taxes Payable | .2 | .3 |
| 6.5 | 8.1 | 8.4 | 7.5 | | | All Other Current | 9.3 | 8.5 |
| 55.5 | 44.6 | 34.8 | 29.0 | | | Total Current | 39.1 | 39.3 |
| 25.2 | 14.4 | 14.5 | 13.7 | | | Long-Term Debt | 16.3 | 17.2 |
| .0 | .3 | .3 | 1.0 | | | Deferred Taxes | .4 | .5 |
| 21.9 | 14.1 | 4.7 | 5.3 | | | All Other Non-Current | 5.2 | 7.1 |
| -2.6 | 26.6 | 45.7 | 51.0 | | | Net Worth | 38.9 | 35.9 |
| 100.0 | 100.0 | 100.0 | 100.0 | | | Total Liabilities & Net Worth | 100.0 | 100.0 |
| | | | | | | **INCOME DATA** | | |
| 100.0 | 100.0 | 100.0 | 100.0 | | | Net Sales | 100.0 | 100.0 |
| 42.9 | 32.4 | 26.9 | 21.6 | | | Gross Profit | 27.9 | 27.8 |
| 36.6 | 29.4 | 21.5 | 17.0 | | | Operating Expenses | 22.5 | 23.2 |
| 6.3 | 3.0 | 5.4 | 4.5 | | | Operating Profit | 5.4 | 4.5 |
| .8 | .0 | .6 | 1.3 | | | All Other Expenses (net) | .9 | .8 |
| 5.6 | 3.0 | 4.8 | 3.3 | | | Profit Before Taxes | 4.5 | 3.7 |
| | | | | | | **RATIOS** | | |
| 2.1 | 2.3 | 3.3 | 3.0 | | | | 2.7 | 2.9 |
| 1.5 | 1.4 | 1.7 | 1.9 | | | Current | 1.7 | 1.7 |
| .8 | 1.0 | 1.3 | 1.4 | | | | 1.2 | 1.1 |
| 1.5 | 1.7 | 2.0 | 1.7 | | | | 1.8 | 1.8 |
| .7 | 1.0 | 1.1 | 1.2 | | | Quick | 1.0 | 1.0 |
| .3 | .7 | .8 | .8 | | | | .6 | .6 |
| 16   23.3 | 36   10.0 | 34   10.7 | 39   9.4 | | | | 33   11.2 | 29   12.5 |
| 23   15.6 | 44   8.3 | 45   8.1 | 54   6.7 | | | Sales/Receivables | 44   8.3 | 41   8.9 |
| 37   9.9 | 56   6.5 | 62   5.9 | 74   4.9 | | | | 60   6.1 | 54   6.8 |
| 0   UND | 4   81.4 | 24   15.5 | 21   17.5 | | | | 17   21.4 | 19   19.5 |
| 33   11.0 | 28   12.9 | 44   8.3 | 46   7.9 | | | Cost of Sales/Inventory | 42   8.8 | 40   9.0 |
| 63   5.8 | 47   7.7 | 72   5.1 | 83   4.4 | | | | 71   5.2 | 72   5.1 |
| 17   21.8 | 18   20.4 | 17   21.7 | 20   18.7 | | | | 16   22.7 | 14   25.2 |
| 30   12.0 | 32   11.5 | 27   13.6 | 30   12.3 | | | Cost of Sales/Payables | 28   13.0 | 25   14.3 |
| 54   6.7 | 49   7.5 | 40   9.2 | 41   8.9 | | | | 42   8.7 | 41   8.8 |
| 8.5 | 6.9 | 4.6 | 3.8 | | | | 5.5 | 5.8 |
| 24.5 | 17.6 | 8.4 | 6.8 | | | Sales/Working Capital | 9.6 | 10.0 |
| -22.6 | -141.4 | 18.9 | 10.3 | | | | 26.9 | 33.2 |
| 28.8 | 18.7 | 17.1 | 17.6 | | | | 12.3 | 13.7 |
| (17) 3.7 | (59) 4.7 | (136) 6.3 | (44) 4.2 | | | EBIT/Interest | (292) 4.7 | (306) 4.0 |
| .0 | 1.5 | 2.5 | 1.4 | | | | 1.6 | 1.3 |
| | | 4.7 | 7.3 | | | | 7.1 | 7.7 |
| | (35) 2.3 | (13) 4.7 | | | | Net Profit + Depr., Dep., Amort./Cur. Mat. L/T/D | (79) 2.8 | (103) 3.8 |
| | | 1.2 | 1.1 | | | | 1.7 | 1.7 |
| .1 | .3 | .3 | .3 | | | | .3 | .3 |
| 1.5 | .7 | .7 | .6 | | | Fixed/Worth | .6 | .8 |
| -.3 | 3.5 | 1.4 | 2.0 | | | | 1.7 | 1.9 |
| .9 | .9 | .5 | .5 | | | | .7 | .7 |
| 3.9 | 1.7 | 1.3 | 1.3 | | | Debt/Worth | 1.6 | 1.9 |
| -3.4 | 19.1 | 3.5 | 3.7 | | | | 4.8 | 4.8 |
| 180.5 | 44.4 | 43.2 | 32.0 | | | | 48.5 | 44.9 |
| (16) 56.1 | (53) 24.6 | (139) 20.6 | (46) 16.5 | | | % Profit Before Taxes/Tangible Net Worth | (284) 21.4 | (290) 21.5 |
| 14.1 | 7.0 | 7.6 | 2.5 | | | | 7.4 | 6.8 |
| 53.2 | 17.6 | 14.9 | 13.6 | | | | 19.4 | 15.9 |
| 20.8 | 6.4 | 7.7 | 6.0 | | | % Profit Before Taxes/Total Assets | 7.9 | 7.8 |
| .0 | 1.7 | 2.7 | 1.0 | | | | 2.4 | 1.2 |
| 85.8 | 44.4 | 18.9 | 23.0 | | | | 21.5 | 19.5 |
| 27.1 | 13.9 | 8.2 | 8.0 | | | Sales/Net Fixed Assets | 11.1 | 10.1 |
| 9.1 | 7.0 | 4.6 | 4.3 | | | | 5.8 | 5.5 |
| 6.7 | 3.6 | 2.7 | 2.3 | | | | 3.1 | 3.1 |
| 3.1 | 2.9 | 2.1 | 1.8 | | | Sales/Total Assets | 2.3 | 2.4 |
| 2.4 | 2.2 | 1.7 | .9 | | | | 1.8 | 1.8 |
| .6 | 1.0 | 1.2 | .9 | | | | 1.1 | 1.3 |
| (11) 2.1 | (51) 1.7 | (135) 2.1 | (47) 2.0 | | | % Depr., Dep., Amort./Sales | (290) 2.0 | (290) 2.1 |
| 3.7 | 3.2 | 3.3 | 3.5 | | | | 3.5 | 3.7 |
| 1.4 | 3.1 | 1.7 | | | | | 2.1 | 2.4 |
| (10) 4.1 | (40) 5.3 | (76) 3.5 | | | | % Officers', Directors' Owners' Comp/Sales | (159) 3.8 | (146) 4.0 |
| 6.3 | 6.9 | 5.5 | | | | | 6.6 | 6.4 |
| 23562M | 237119M | 1507392M | 2069068M | 1054310M | 800411M | Net Sales ($) | 6278311M | 11372069M |
| 5493M | 81453M | 694686M | 1265934M | 648891M | 504679M | Total Assets ($) | 2906512M | 3832592M |

M = $ thousand    MM = $ million
See Pages 9 through 22 for Explanation of Ratios and Data

## Comparative Historical Data

## Current Data Sorted by Sales

### Type of Statement

| | | | Type of Statement | | | | | | |
|---|---|---|---|---|---|---|---|---|---|
| 28 | 24 | 28 | Unqualified | | | 2 | 2 | 7 | 17 |
| 79 | 95 | 89 | Reviewed | 3 | 6 | 10 | 26 | 30 | 14 |
| 54 | 56 | 39 | Compiled | 1 | 8 | 7 | 10 | 10 | 3 |
| 52 | 54 | 52 | Tax Returns | 6 | 15 | 14 | 13 | 4 | |
| 87 | 91 | 93 | Other | 6 | 10 | 8 | 25 | 25 | 19 |
| 4/1/09-3/31/10 ALL | 4/1/10-3/31/11 ALL | 4/1/11-3/31/12 ALL | | 42 (4/1-9/30/11) | | | 259 (10/1/11-3/31/12) | | |
| | | | | 0-1MM | 1-3MM | 3-5MM | 5-10MM | 10-25MM | 25MM & OVER |
| 300 | 320 | 301 | NUMBER OF STATEMENTS | 16 | 39 | 41 | 76 | 76 | 53 |
| % | % | % | **ASSETS** | % | % | % | % | % | % |
| 10.8 | 10.6 | 10.8 | Cash & Equivalents | 8.8 | 14.7 | 9.4 | 11.5 | 10.1 | 9.5 |
| 27.7 | 29.9 | 30.3 | Trade Receivables (net) | 25.7 | 28.9 | 33.0 | 33.3 | 27.9 | 29.8 |
| 20.3 | 18.6 | 19.3 | Inventory | 17.1 | 15.2 | 16.1 | 20.6 | 20.4 | 22.2 |
| 3.3 | 2.6 | 3.4 | All Other Current | 11.2 | 2.3 | 1.9 | 3.3 | 3.0 | 4.0 |
| 62.0 | 61.7 | 63.9 | Total Current | 62.8 | 61.2 | 60.4 | 68.6 | 61.4 | 65.5 |
| 28.5 | 28.3 | 26.4 | Fixed Assets (net) | 23.9 | 28.2 | 31.7 | 22.6 | 28.0 | 24.9 |
| 3.4 | 3.5 | 4.4 | Intangibles (net) | 2.8 | 1.6 | 2.7 | 3.6 | 6.5 | 6.2 |
| 6.2 | 6.5 | 5.4 | All Other Non-Current | 10.5 | 8.9 | 5.2 | 5.2 | 4.0 | 3.5 |
| 100.0 | 100.0 | 100.0 | Total | 100.0 | 100.0 | 100.0 | 100.0 | 100.0 | 100.0 |
| | | | **LIABILITIES** | | | | | | |
| 11.3 | 12.2 | 9.8 | Notes Payable-Short Term | 20.7 | 13.8 | 9.4 | 9.6 | 7.1 | 8.1 |
| 4.8 | 3.8 | 3.9 | Cur. Mat.-L.T.D. | 3.1 | 5.4 | 5.1 | 4.2 | 3.5 | 2.3 |
| 12.9 | 14.7 | 15.4 | Trade Payables | 22.4 | 14.5 | 17.1 | 14.9 | 14.9 | 14.1 |
| .1 | .2 | .1 | Income Taxes Payable | .0 | .0 | .2 | .0 | .1 | .2 |
| 8.1 | 8.2 | 8.1 | All Other Current | 6.6 | 9.6 | 7.5 | 6.9 | 7.8 | 10.2 |
| 37.2 | 39.2 | 37.4 | Total Current | 52.8 | 43.4 | 39.4 | 35.6 | 33.4 | 35.0 |
| 18.8 | 17.0 | 15.0 | Long-Term Debt | 22.1 | 20.3 | 17.0 | 13.4 | 14.0 | 11.3 |
| .4 | .4 | .5 | Deferred Taxes | .0 | .4 | .1 | .4 | .6 | .9 |
| 8.5 | 6.1 | 8.1 | All Other Non-Current | 25.0 | 20.7 | 5.4 | 3.3 | 5.6 | 6.4 |
| 35.0 | 37.3 | 39.0 | Net Worth | .0 | 15.2 | 38.3 | 47.3 | 46.5 | 46.3 |
| 100.0 | 100.0 | 100.0 | Total Liabilities & Net Worth | 100.0 | 100.0 | 100.0 | 100.0 | 100.0 | 100.0 |
| | | | **INCOME DATA** | | | | | | |
| 100.0 | 100.0 | 100.0 | Net Sales | 100.0 | 100.0 | 100.0 | 100.0 | 100.0 | 100.0 |
| 29.7 | 29.9 | 28.4 | Gross Profit | 37.4 | 38.0 | 31.5 | 29.2 | 24.1 | 20.9 |
| 27.0 | 25.7 | 23.5 | Operating Expenses | 30.9 | 32.5 | 28.5 | 23.7 | 20.0 | 15.3 |
| 2.7 | 4.2 | 4.9 | Operating Profit | 6.5 | 5.6 | 3.0 | 5.5 | 4.1 | 5.5 |
| 1.0 | .8 | .6 | All Other Expenses (net) | 1.1 | .1 | .4 | .3 | 1.1 | .9 |
| 1.7 | 3.4 | 4.2 | Profit Before Taxes | 5.3 | 5.5 | 2.6 | 5.2 | 3.0 | 4.7 |
| | | | **RATIOS** | | | | | | |
| 3.7 | 3.2 | 3.0 | | 2.0 | 2.3 | 2.9 | 3.4 | 3.3 | 2.5 |
| 1.8 | 1.7 | 1.7 | Current | 1.4 | 1.3 | 1.7 | 1.8 | 1.7 | 1.9 |
| 1.2 | 1.2 | 1.2 | | .7 | .8 | 1.0 | 1.4 | 1.3 | 1.4 |
| 2.2 | 2.1 | 1.7 | | 1.4 | 1.9 | 1.7 | 2.1 | 1.8 | 1.6 |
| 1.1 | 1.1 | 1.1 | Quick | .7 | 1.1 | 1.2 | 1.2 | 1.1 | 1.1 |
| .6 | .7 | .7 | | .2 | .4 | .8 | .7 | .8 | .8 |
| 29 12.6 | 33 11.0 | 33 11.1 | | 21 17.2 | 23 16.0 | 38 9.7 | 37 9.9 | 27 13.3 | 39 9.3 |
| 42 8.6 | 48 7.5 | 45 8.1 | Sales/Receivables | 28 13.0 | 42 8.7 | 44 8.3 | 47 7.7 | 41 8.9 | 51 7.2 |
| 57 6.4 | 64 5.7 | 62 5.9 | | 43 8.5 | 64 5.7 | 62 5.9 | 65 5.6 | 60 6.1 | 70 5.2 |
| 17 21.4 | 14 26.5 | 15 23.6 | | 6 59.4 | 6 62.8 | 5 74.8 | 22 16.6 | 21 17.1 | 23 15.8 |
| 42 8.6 | 43 8.5 | 41 8.8 | Cost of Sales/Inventory | 26 13.8 | 33 11.2 | 31 11.7 | 45 8.1 | 41 8.9 | 51 7.1 |
| 73 5.0 | 75 4.9 | 70 5.2 | | 50 7.3 | 62 5.9 | 54 6.7 | 73 5.0 | 65 5.6 | 99 3.7 |
| 13 27.9 | 17 21.9 | 18 20.6 | | 17 21.2 | 19 18.9 | 16 22.5 | 17 21.5 | 16 22.8 | 19 18.8 |
| 22 16.4 | 27 13.3 | 28 13.0 | Cost of Sales/Payables | 32 11.3 | 28 12.9 | 29 12.6 | 26 13.8 | 29 12.8 | 32 11.4 |
| 40 9.2 | 43 8.5 | 44 8.3 | | 69 5.3 | 44 8.3 | 56 6.5 | 43 8.5 | 37 9.8 | 42 8.6 |
| 5.0 | 4.6 | 5.0 | | 9.9 | 5.2 | 5.6 | 4.6 | 4.7 | 3.9 |
| 9.0 | 8.8 | 8.6 | Sales/Working Capital | 18.9 | 24.5 | 10.4 | 7.7 | 8.8 | 7.2 |
| 26.2 | 26.9 | 24.2 | | -12.0 | -25.5 | NM | 14.7 | 21.3 | 13.5 |
| 9.1 | 12.3 | 18.0 | | 9.8 | 24.5 | 18.7 | 14.9 | 18.6 | 17.6 |
| (274) 2.7 | (285) 4.2 | (267) 5.6 | EBIT/Interest | (11) 1.8 | (34) 6.2 | (39) 4.4 | (70) 5.6 | (69) 6.3 | (44) 7.8 |
| -.4 | .9 | 1.8 | | -.4 | 1.4 | .8 | 2.1 | 2.2 | 1.6 |
| 7.5 | 4.6 | 5.7 | Net Profit + Depr., Dep., | | | 3.5 | 6.3 | 9.5 | |
| (72) 2.4 | (67) 2.8 | (65) 2.8 | Amort./Cur. Mat. L/T/D | | | (21) 1.7 | (18) 3.1 | (15) 4.8 | |
| .9 | 1.2 | 1.3 | | | | 1.1 | .8 | 3.1 | |
| .3 | .3 | .3 | | .2 | .3 | .3 | .3 | .3 | .3 |
| .7 | .7 | .7 | Fixed/Worth | 3.1 | 1.1 | .8 | .5 | .7 | .5 |
| 2.6 | 1.8 | 1.6 | | NM | -6.6 | 1.7 | 1.2 | 1.6 | 1.3 |
| .7 | .6 | .6 | | 1.0 | .9 | .7 | .5 | .5 | .6 |
| 1.7 | 1.6 | 1.5 | Debt/Worth | 4.7 | 1.9 | 1.5 | 1.3 | 1.4 | 1.5 |
| 6.7 | 4.6 | 4.6 | | NM | -10.8 | 5.5 | 3.8 | 3.8 | 3.0 |
| 38.1 | 40.6 | 44.2 | % Profit Before Taxes/Tangible | 162.9 | 50.9 | 37.3 | 48.9 | 42.4 | 34.2 |
| (250) 13.6 | (275) 14.8 | (266) 20.8 | Net Worth | (12) 36.3 | (29) 24.1 | (34) 14.2 | (74) 20.8 | (68) 21.6 | (49) 19.5 |
| -.3 | 3.2 | 7.0 | | 8.4 | 4.6 | 3.0 | 8.3 | 7.9 | 6.2 |
| 13.7 | 15.2 | 16.5 | % Profit Before Taxes/Total | 42.9 | 24.5 | 19.3 | 15.4 | 14.4 | 15.9 |
| 4.0 | 6.1 | 7.6 | Assets | 9.4 | 10.1 | 5.7 | 8.4 | 7.6 | 6.7 |
| -2.0 | .1 | 1.9 | | .3 | 1.3 | .6 | 2.8 | 2.8 | 1.4 |
| 23.8 | 23.8 | 24.4 | | 54.9 | 35.0 | 25.0 | 21.9 | 20.5 | 21.9 |
| 9.6 | 8.7 | 9.7 | Sales/Net Fixed Assets | 14.2 | 13.3 | 9.4 | 10.6 | 8.5 | 8.8 |
| 4.4 | 4.3 | 5.3 | | 5.4 | 6.0 | 3.6 | 5.9 | 4.5 | 5.1 |
| 3.0 | 2.8 | 3.0 | | 4.4 | 3.5 | 3.2 | 2.8 | 3.0 | 2.5 |
| 2.2 | 2.1 | 2.2 | Sales/Total Assets | 2.5 | 2.7 | 2.4 | 2.2 | 2.2 | 2.0 |
| 1.6 | 1.5 | 1.6 | | 1.5 | 1.5 | 1.7 | 1.7 | 1.7 | 1.4 |
| 1.1 | 1.1 | 1.1 | | | 1.3 | 1.4 | 1.1 | 1.0 | .9 |
| (266) 2.5 | (285) 2.6 | (256) 2.1 | % Depr., Dep., Amort./Sales | | (29) 2.1 | (33) 2.2 | (67) 2.0 | (70) 2.0 | (48) 2.0 |
| 4.4 | 4.4 | 3.3 | | | 3.5 | 4.3 | 3.3 | 3.3 | 3.1 |
| 2.6 | 2.0 | 2.1 | | | 3.7 | 2.5 | 2.3 | 1.5 | |
| (147) 4.4 | (147) 3.3 | (132) 3.7 | % Officers', Directors' Owners' Comp/Sales | | (20) 5.7 | (31) 4.3 | (45) 4.2 | (26) 2.3 | |
| 8.5 | 6.0 | 6.0 | | | 7.7 | 6.3 | 5.7 | 3.4 | |
| 5258063M | 5335244M | 5691862M | Net Sales ($) | 9641M | 79426M | 167981M | 544741M | 1134577M | 3755496M |
| 2775498M | 3021722M | 3201136M | Total Assets ($) | 5283M | 42925M | 79536M | 274143M | 688485M | 2110764M |

© RMA 2012

M = $ thousand     MM = $ million
See Pages 9 through 22 for Explanation of Ratios and Data

### Current Data Sorted by Assets      Comparative Historical Data

| 0-500M | 500M-2MM | 2-10MM | 10-50MM | 50-100MM | 100-250MM | Type of Statement | 4/1/07-3/31/08 ALL | 4/1/08-3/31/09 ALL |
|---|---|---|---|---|---|---|---|---|
| | | 1 | 2 | | | Unqualified | 8 | 9 |
| | 2 | 21 | 3 | | | Reviewed | 29 | 22 |
| 2 | 2 | 1 | 1 | | | Compiled | 12 | 10 |
| 5 | 10 | 2 | | 1 | | Tax Returns | 11 | 11 |
| 5 | 8 | 13 | 7 | | 1 | Other | 21 | 36 |
| | 14 (4/1-9/30/11) | | 77 (10/1/11-3/31/12) | | | | | |
| 13 | 22 | 39 | 15 | 1 | 1 | NUMBER OF STATEMENTS | 81 | 88 |
| % | % | % | % | % | % | **ASSETS** | % | % |
| 6.9 | 8.2 | 6.9 | 9.8 | | | Cash & Equivalents | 9.5 | 8.5 |
| 28.9 | 33.4 | 35.0 | 32.0 | | | Trade Receivables (net) | 34.4 | 37.1 |
| 14.7 | 22.4 | 17.1 | 10.8 | | | Inventory | 23.0 | 19.0 |
| 2.9 | 2.9 | 8.9 | 9.2 | | | All Other Current | 4.9 | 4.7 |
| 53.4 | 67.0 | 67.8 | 61.8 | | | Total Current | 71.7 | 69.3 |
| 23.5 | 21.1 | 18.1 | 24.2 | | | Fixed Assets (net) | 20.5 | 20.0 |
| 14.5 | .3 | 2.4 | 6.8 | | | Intangibles (net) | 2.1 | 5.2 |
| 8.6 | 11.6 | 11.6 | 7.2 | | | All Other Non-Current | 5.6 | 5.5 |
| 100.0 | 100.0 | 100.0 | 100.0 | | | Total | 100.0 | 100.0 |
| | | | | | | **LIABILITIES** | | |
| 9.7 | 10.0 | 13.3 | 7.5 | | | Notes Payable-Short Term | 9.7 | 13.1 |
| 6.6 | 5.7 | 2.3 | 2.6 | | | Cur. Mat.-L.T.D. | 3.8 | 4.8 |
| 20.8 | 16.6 | 15.7 | 13.2 | | | Trade Payables | 15.0 | 15.2 |
| .0 | .0 | .9 | .1 | | | Income Taxes Payable | .5 | .5 |
| 23.7 | 9.5 | 11.7 | 13.6 | | | All Other Current | 17.7 | 14.0 |
| 60.9 | 41.8 | 44.0 | 36.9 | | | Total Current | 46.7 | 47.6 |
| 35.2 | 31.7 | 12.7 | 13.6 | | | Long-Term Debt | 12.0 | 15.0 |
| .0 | .1 | .4 | .2 | | | Deferred Taxes | .6 | .5 |
| .3 | 15.9 | 8.3 | 7.0 | | | All Other Non-Current | 5.6 | 6.3 |
| 3.6 | 10.5 | 34.5 | 42.2 | | | Net Worth | 35.1 | 30.7 |
| 100.0 | 100.0 | 100.0 | 100.0 | | | Total Liabilities & Net Worth | 100.0 | 100.0 |
| | | | | | | **INCOME DATA** | | |
| 100.0 | 100.0 | 100.0 | 100.0 | | | Net Sales | 100.0 | 100.0 |
| 46.7 | 39.6 | 29.0 | 34.6 | | | Gross Profit | 33.8 | 32.5 |
| 47.4 | 39.3 | 29.7 | 24.7 | | | Operating Expenses | 26.9 | 27.7 |
| -.7 | .2 | -.8 | 10.0 | | | Operating Profit | 6.9 | 4.8 |
| .2 | 1.2 | .2 | 1.1 | | | All Other Expenses (net) | .7 | .9 |
| -.9 | -1.0 | -1.0 | 8.8 | | | Profit Before Taxes | 6.2 | 3.9 |
| | | | | | | **RATIOS** | | |
| 1.8 | 3.0 | 2.0 | 3.2 | | | Current | 2.6 | 2.3 |
| .8 | 1.9 | 1.5 | 1.8 | | | | 1.6 | 1.7 |
| .3 | 1.1 | 1.2 | 1.2 | | | | 1.2 | 1.2 |
| 1.6 | 2.4 | 1.5 | 1.8 | | | Quick | 1.6 | 1.6 |
| .7 | 1.0 | .9 | .9 | | | | .9 | 1.0 |
| .1 | .5 | .5 | .7 | | | | .6 | .6 |
| 0 UND | 25 14.5 | 33 10.9 | 39 9.3 | | | Sales/Receivables | 35 10.3 | 33 11.2 |
| 22 16.4 | 36 10.0 | 60 6.1 | 58 6.3 | | | | 50 7.4 | 47 7.8 |
| 56 6.5 | 54 6.8 | 89 4.1 | 96 3.8 | | | | 71 5.2 | 68 5.4 |
| 0 UND | 0 UND | 5 76.0 | 14 25.6 | | | Cost of Sales/Inventory | 15 24.3 | 10 38.4 |
| 3 137.0 | 36 10.1 | 38 9.6 | 27 13.6 | | | | 46 7.9 | 36 10.2 |
| 59 6.2 | 101 3.6 | 83 4.4 | 61 6.0 | | | | 80 4.6 | 65 5.6 |
| 0 UND | 10 36.5 | 20 18.2 | 18 20.6 | | | Cost of Sales/Payables | 15 24.3 | 16 22.1 |
| 25 14.8 | 23 16.2 | 38 9.5 | 31 11.9 | | | | 27 13.5 | 27 13.3 |
| 56 6.5 | 41 8.9 | 50 7.3 | 54 6.7 | | | | 44 8.3 | 39 9.3 |
| 10.7 | 4.7 | 4.7 | 4.6 | | | Sales/Working Capital | 5.5 | 6.2 |
| -108.2 | 8.9 | 11.3 | 9.5 | | | | 9.2 | 9.5 |
| -11.6 | NM | 23.5 | 21.7 | | | | 23.1 | 32.0 |
| 26.1 | 9.9 | 12.9 | 71.0 | | | EBIT/Interest | 20.4 | 10.5 |
| (11) 12.2 | (21) 1.1 | (36) 3.6 | (13) 7.1 | | | | (71) 5.6 | (79) 3.6 |
| 1.7 | -3.3 | -3.2 | 1.4 | | | | 2.1 | 1.5 |
| | | 4.5 | | | | Net Profit + Depr., Dep., | 14.2 | 10.9 |
| | (13) 1.7 | | | | | Amort./Cur. Mat. L/T/D | (23) 4.0 | (16) 2.2 |
| | | .5 | | | | | 1.7 | 1.5 |
| .2 | .3 | .2 | .3 | | | Fixed/Worth | .2 | .2 |
| -1.5 | 5.1 | .4 | .7 | | | | .7 | .6 |
| -.2 | -.9 | 1.1 | 1.6 | | | | 1.9 | 6.7 |
| 1.1 | 1.0 | .8 | .5 | | | Debt/Worth | .7 | .9 |
| -7.8 | 32.3 | 1.8 | 1.9 | | | | 2.2 | 2.3 |
| -2.8 | -4.5 | 8.1 | 4.8 | | | | 6.3 | 28.9 |
| | 108.7 | 44.6 | 111.6 | | | % Profit Before Taxes/Tangible | 77.8 | 65.8 |
| (13) | 29.3 | (34) 11.8 | (13) 36.4 | | | Net Worth | (69) 38.5 | (70) 25.3 |
| | -.2 | -6.6 | 16.6 | | | | 22.0 | 9.8 |
| 49.6 | 17.2 | 11.8 | 26.1 | | | % Profit Before Taxes/Total | 23.4 | 18.5 |
| 16.5 | -.1 | 3.8 | 9.4 | | | Assets | 13.0 | 8.1 |
| -10.2 | -20.7 | -4.2 | 3.1 | | | | 4.3 | 1.2 |
| 168.4 | 66.0 | 37.4 | 37.1 | | | Sales/Net Fixed Assets | 37.2 | 41.3 |
| 33.0 | 18.9 | 16.4 | 9.7 | | | | 13.3 | 19.4 |
| 10.9 | 8.2 | 7.8 | 4.2 | | | | 8.2 | 7.1 |
| 7.0 | 3.9 | 2.7 | 2.4 | | | Sales/Total Assets | 3.2 | 3.6 |
| 4.2 | 2.7 | 2.2 | 1.7 | | | | 2.5 | 2.6 |
| 2.5 | 1.9 | 1.4 | 1.1 | | | | 1.8 | 1.9 |
| | .3 | .7 | .4 | | | % Depr., Dep., Amort./Sales | .6 | .7 |
| (17) | 1.2 | (36) 1.4 | (12) 1.5 | | | | (72) 1.2 | (69) 1.4 |
| | 3.5 | 2.5 | 2.3 | | | | 2.2 | 2.9 |
| | 6.0 | 1.3 | | | | % Officers', Directors' | 1.9 | 1.8 |
| (11) | 7.1 | (18) 2.2 | | | | Owners' Comp/Sales | (43) 3.5 | (30) 4.0 |
| | 10.3 | 3.4 | | | | | 6.9 | 7.0 |
| 16286M | 66010M | 429615M | 461783M | 110178M | 327522M | Net Sales ($) | 2186388M | 2430094M |
| 3647M | 22574M | 205610M | 282964M | 71157M | 182007M | Total Assets ($) | 1054245M | 1180874M |

| Comparative Historical Data | | | | Current Data Sorted by Sales | | | | | |
|---|---|---|---|---|---|---|---|---|---|
| | | | **Type of Statement** | | | | | | |
| 5 | 8 | 7 | Unqualified | | 1 | | 1 | 3 | 2 |
| 29 | 23 | 26 | Reviewed | | 2 | 1 | 10 | 11 | 2 |
| 7 | 8 | 6 | Compiled | | 4 | | | 2 | |
| 5 | 12 | 18 | Tax Returns | 4 | 7 | 3 | 3 | | 1 |
| 42 | 33 | 34 | Other | 4 | 6 | 6 | 5 | 8 | 5 |
| 4/1/09-3/31/10 ALL | 4/1/10-3/31/11 ALL | 4/1/11-3/31/12 ALL | | 0-1MM | 14 (4/1-9/30/11) / 1-3MM | 3-5MM | 77 (10/1/11-3/31/12) / 5-10MM | 10-25MM | 25MM & OVER |
| 88 | 84 | 91 | **NUMBER OF STATEMENTS** | 8 | 20 | 10 | 19 | 24 | 10 |
| % | % | % | **ASSETS** | % | % | % | % | % | % |
| 8.0 | 8.9 | 7.7 | Cash & Equivalents | | 8.4 | 3.8 | 6.0 | 8.9 | 10.4 |
| 32.1 | 29.2 | 33.0 | Trade Receivables (net) | | 24.2 | 29.7 | 42.9 | 34.2 | 37.4 |
| 18.7 | 17.6 | 17.4 | Inventory | | 17.1 | 27.5 | 13.2 | 18.8 | 13.6 |
| 5.8 | 6.2 | 6.6 | All Other Current | | 3.2 | 3.6 | 10.6 | 7.1 | 12.5 |
| 64.6 | 61.9 | 64.6 | Total Current | | 53.0 | 64.6 | 72.6 | 69.0 | 73.9 |
| 23.6 | 22.7 | 20.8 | Fixed Assets (net) | | 22.1 | 21.7 | 16.7 | 18.8 | 24.0 |
| 3.9 | 7.0 | 4.4 | Intangibles (net) | | 6.6 | 8.8 | .1 | 4.5 | .9 |
| 8.0 | 8.4 | 10.2 | All Other Non-Current | | 18.2 | 4.9 | 10.6 | 7.7 | 1.2 |
| 100.0 | 100.0 | 100.0 | Total | | 100.0 | 100.0 | 100.0 | 100.0 | 100.0 |
| | | | **LIABILITIES** | | | | | | |
| 10.0 | 13.6 | 11.2 | Notes Payable-Short Term | | 10.6 | 8.6 | 9.0 | 14.9 | 9.3 |
| 3.1 | 2.3 | 3.8 | Cur. Mat.-L.T.D. | | 4.4 | 7.2 | 4.4 | 2.5 | 1.1 |
| 14.1 | 14.0 | 16.2 | Trade Payables | | 19.4 | 12.6 | 14.5 | 17.2 | 15.1 |
| .5 | .3 | .4 | Income Taxes Payable | | .0 | .0 | .8 | .9 | .2 |
| 13.9 | 11.3 | 13.3 | All Other Current | | 16.9 | 7.9 | 13.0 | 11.9 | 17.2 |
| 41.6 | 41.5 | 44.8 | Total Current | | 51.4 | 36.2 | 41.7 | 47.4 | 42.8 |
| 16.2 | 17.6 | 20.5 | Long-Term Debt | | 25.1 | 35.5 | 11.9 | 8.4 | 12.8 |
| .9 | .2 | .3 | Deferred Taxes | | .0 | .3 | .9 | .1 | .9 |
| 7.5 | 7.4 | 8.6 | All Other Non-Current | | 4.1 | 15.6 | 5.9 | 7.0 | 9.7 |
| 33.9 | 33.3 | 25.7 | Net Worth | | 19.4 | 12.4 | 39.7 | 37.2 | 33.7 |
| 100.0 | 100.0 | 100.0 | Total Liabilities & Net Worth | | 100.0 | 100.0 | 100.0 | 100.0 | 100.0 |
| | | | **INCOME DATA** | | | | | | |
| 100.0 | 100.0 | 100.0 | Net Sales | | 100.0 | 100.0 | 100.0 | 100.0 | 100.0 |
| 33.7 | 33.2 | 34.9 | Gross Profit | | 41.6 | 32.0 | 29.9 | 31.0 | 27.3 |
| 31.1 | 30.3 | 33.5 | Operating Expenses | | 43.2 | 30.6 | 29.1 | 26.6 | 19.3 |
| 2.6 | 2.9 | 1.4 | Operating Profit | | -1.6 | 1.4 | .8 | 4.4 | 8.0 |
| 1.2 | 1.2 | .6 | All Other Expenses (net) | | .0 | 2.0 | -.1 | .9 | .0 |
| 1.4 | 1.7 | .8 | Profit Before Taxes | | -1.6 | -.6 | .9 | 3.5 | 8.0 |
| | | | **RATIOS** | | | | | | |
| 2.5 | 2.7 | 2.8 | | | 2.7 | 3.0 | 3.5 | 1.9 | 2.3 |
| 1.6 | 1.6 | 1.5 | Current | | 1.0 | 1.3 | 1.8 | 1.3 | 1.8 |
| 1.2 | 1.2 | 1.1 | | | .7 | 1.2 | 1.3 | 1.1 | 1.3 |
| 1.7 | 1.7 | 1.7 | | | 2.4 | 1.1 | 1.8 | 1.4 | 1.7 |
| .9 | 1.0 | .9 | Quick | | .7 | .8 | 1.3 | .8 | 1.1 |
| .6 | .6 | .5 | | | .2 | .3 | .7 | .5 | .8 |
| 34 10.8 | 31 11.7 | 29 12.4 | | | 0 UND | 30 12.0 | 54 6.8 | 33 10.9 | 40 9.2 |
| 50 7.2 | 47 7.8 | 49 7.4 | Sales/Receivables | | 32 11.4 | 36 10.0 | 72 5.1 | 54 6.7 | 61 6.0 |
| 69 5.3 | 68 5.4 | 72 5.1 | | | 57 6.4 | 43 8.5 | 99 3.7 | 70 5.4 | 76 4.8 |
| 13 28.7 | 9 38.6 | 5 76.4 | | | 0 UND | 18 20.4 | 5 76.0 | 18 20.1 | 8 44.1 |
| 46 7.9 | 45 8.1 | 30 12.3 | Cost of Sales/Inventory | | 9 41.9 | 65 5.6 | 22 16.7 | 54 6.7 | 17 21.0 |
| 86 4.2 | 75 4.9 | 79 4.6 | | | 83 4.4 | 101 3.6 | 81 4.5 | 72 5.1 | 58 6.3 |
| 17 21.7 | 17 21.1 | 15 24.1 | | | 0 UND | 12 29.5 | 15 24.1 | 20 18.5 | 21 17.3 |
| 28 13.1 | 28 13.3 | 34 10.8 | Cost of Sales/Payables | | 22 16.5 | 23 16.2 | 39 9.4 | 32 11.3 | 35 10.5 |
| 48 7.5 | 49 7.5 | 50 7.3 | | | 101 3.6 | 39 9.4 | 50 7.3 | 47 7.7 | 46 7.9 |
| 4.7 | 4.9 | 5.4 | | | 8.9 | 4.7 | 3.1 | 7.8 | 4.4 |
| 8.4 | 10.1 | 11.9 | Sales/Working Capital | | NM | 12.1 | 6.9 | 12.9 | 8.1 |
| 47.8 | 21.2 | 57.3 | | | -19.2 | 36.5 | 14.3 | 32.0 | 12.6 |
| 8.4 | 11.2 | 18.0 | | | | 20.0 | | 13.2 | 18.9 | |
| (80) 3.1 | (76) 3.4 | (83) 4.1 | EBIT/Interest | | (18) 1.8 | | (18) 3.9 | (23) 5.6 | |
| .4 | .0 | -2.0 | | | -5.4 | | -3.7 | 1.5 | |
| 7.2 | 4.7 | 4.2 | | | | | | | |
| (18) 1.5 | (16) 1.1 | (19) 1.4 | Net Profit + Depr., Dep., Amort./Cur. Mat. L/T/D | | | | | | |
| .4 | .1 | .3 | | | | | | | |
| .3 | .2 | .3 | | | .2 | .1 | .1 | .3 | .4 |
| .7 | .7 | .6 | Fixed/Worth | | 23.8 | 1.4 | .4 | .4 | .6 |
| 3.3 | 14.2 | -26.3 | | | -.4 | -2.1 | .8 | 1.6 | 1.3 |
| .7 | .7 | 1.0 | | | .5 | 2.6 | .7 | 1.0 | .9 |
| 1.8 | 2.3 | 3.1 | Debt/Worth | | 120.4 | 5.3 | 1.7 | 1.8 | 1.6 |
| 11.9 | 34.8 | -94.7 | | | -4.9 | -5.3 | 3.2 | 11.1 | 4.4 |
| 34.6 | 59.3 | 72.6 | | | 120.9 | | 30.8 | 72.0 | |
| (73) 11.6 | (67) 18.6 | (68) 22.9 | % Profit Before Taxes/Tangible Net Worth | | (11) 55.7 | | (17) 7.9 | (21) 22.1 | |
| .3 | 1.6 | .3 | | | -6.1 | | -12.9 | 4.8 | |
| 11.1 | 14.8 | 16.3 | | | 26.8 | 26.5 | 9.6 | 13.9 | 25.0 |
| 4.4 | 5.3 | 6.2 | % Profit Before Taxes/Total Assets | | 7.5 | 5.3 | 1.8 | 7.0 | 11.4 |
| -3.0 | -2.1 | -3.9 | | | -21.7 | -8.6 | -4.2 | .8 | 3.9 |
| 25.3 | 31.7 | 47.6 | | | 140.4 | 50.6 | 50.6 | 37.3 | 25.6 |
| 10.1 | 12.3 | 14.7 | Sales/Net Fixed Assets | | 34.9 | 10.9 | 12.5 | 17.5 | 7.4 |
| 5.7 | 5.5 | 7.7 | | | 8.3 | 7.5 | 7.8 | 9.3 | 5.4 |
| 2.7 | 2.8 | 2.9 | | | 4.7 | 3.9 | 2.6 | 2.9 | 2.6 |
| 2.0 | 2.1 | 2.3 | Sales/Total Assets | | 2.8 | 2.7 | 2.0 | 2.3 | 2.0 |
| 1.4 | 1.6 | 1.5 | | | 1.9 | 1.3 | 1.4 | 1.6 | 1.7 |
| 1.1 | .8 | .7 | | | .4 | | .7 | .7 | |
| (71) 1.7 | (74) 2.0 | (76) 1.4 | % Depr., Dep., Amort./Sales | | (14) 1.2 | | (18) 1.2 | (21) 1.6 | |
| 3.4 | 3.1 | 2.4 | | | 2.2 | | 3.4 | 2.1 | |
| 2.5 | 2.1 | 1.8 | | | 5.3 | | 1.3 | 1.5 | |
| (32) 4.0 | (32) 5.5 | (40) 5.0 | % Officers', Directors' Owners' Comp/Sales | | (10) 7.3 | | (10) 3.7 | (11) 2.1 | |
| 7.3 | 8.4 | 8.5 | | | 10.5 | | 6.7 | 2.9 | |
| 2212404M | 1930195M | 1411394M | Net Sales ($) | 4777M | 38815M | 40868M | 126076M | 440510M | 760348M |
| 1262990M | 1092006M | 767959M | Total Assets ($) | 3082M | 20229M | 24620M | 70616M | 235651M | 413761M |

© RMA 2012

M = $ thousand    MM = $ million
See Pages 9 through 22 for Explanation of Ratios and Data

## Current Data Sorted by Assets      Comparative Historical Data

| 0-500M | 500M-2MM | 2-10MM | 10-50MM | 50-100MM | 100-250MM | Type of Statement | 4/1/07-3/31/08 ALL | 4/1/08-3/31/09 ALL |
|---|---|---|---|---|---|---|---|---|
|  | 1 | 2 | 5 | 1 | 1 | Unqualified | 10 | 12 |
|  | 1 | 4 | 4 | 1 |  | Reviewed | 7 | 12 |
|  | 3 | 4 | 3 | 1 |  | Compiled | 6 | 7 |
| 1 | 1 | 5 | 1 |  |  | Tax Returns | 5 | 6 |
| 1 | 5 | 14 | 8 | 2 | 1 | Other | 17 | 29 |
|  | 8 (4/1-9/30/11) |  | 62 (10/1/11-3/31/12) |  |  |  |  |  |
| 3 | 10 | 29 | 21 | 5 | 2 | NUMBER OF STATEMENTS | 45 | 66 |
| % | % | % | % | % | % | ASSETS | % | % |
|  | 7.3 | 8.9 | 6.3 |  |  | Cash & Equivalents | 9.1 | 7.3 |
|  | 36.9 | 28.7 | 25.1 |  |  | Trade Receivables (net) | 26.9 | 25.2 |
|  | 25.3 | 28.3 | 25.9 |  |  | Inventory | 22.6 | 25.2 |
|  | 1.1 | .5 | 3.1 |  |  | All Other Current | 1.9 | 3.1 |
|  | 70.7 | 66.5 | 60.4 |  |  | Total Current | 60.5 | 60.9 |
|  | 24.4 | 23.6 | 27.0 |  |  | Fixed Assets (net) | 29.1 | 26.8 |
|  | .4 | 5.5 | 7.0 |  |  | Intangibles (net) | 6.6 | 6.5 |
|  | 4.6 | 4.4 | 5.7 |  |  | All Other Non-Current | 3.8 | 5.9 |
|  | 100.0 | 100.0 | 100.0 |  |  | Total | 100.0 | 100.0 |
|  |  |  |  |  |  | LIABILITIES |  |  |
|  | 11.4 | 8.0 | 8.1 |  |  | Notes Payable-Short Term | 15.4 | 10.6 |
|  | 2.6 | 2.7 | 2.0 |  |  | Cur. Mat.-L.T.D. | 4.2 | 2.9 |
|  | 24.6 | 18.9 | 12.4 |  |  | Trade Payables | 15.0 | 12.2 |
|  | .0 | .2 | .6 |  |  | Income Taxes Payable | 1.0 | .3 |
|  | 8.6 | 6.9 | 14.6 |  |  | All Other Current | 8.5 | 11.3 |
|  | 47.2 | 36.9 | 37.7 |  |  | Total Current | 44.2 | 37.2 |
|  | 15.4 | 16.0 | 13.4 |  |  | Long-Term Debt | 20.7 | 16.9 |
|  | .0 | .2 | .4 |  |  | Deferred Taxes | .5 | .9 |
|  | 4.4 | 4.7 | 5.3 |  |  | All Other Non-Current | 6.7 | 6.0 |
|  | 33.0 | 42.3 | 43.3 |  |  | Net Worth | 27.9 | 39.0 |
|  | 100.0 | 100.0 | 100.0 |  |  | Total Liabilities & Net Worth | 100.0 | 100.0 |
|  |  |  |  |  |  | INCOME DATA |  |  |
|  | 100.0 | 100.0 | 100.0 |  |  | Net Sales | 100.0 | 100.0 |
|  | 35.4 | 28.8 | 24.0 |  |  | Gross Profit | 32.7 | 28.2 |
|  | 34.8 | 21.5 | 18.1 |  |  | Operating Expenses | 23.8 | 21.7 |
|  | .7 | 7.3 | 6.0 |  |  | Operating Profit | 8.8 | 6.5 |
|  | .3 | .8 | .9 |  |  | All Other Expenses (net) | 1.8 | 1.2 |
|  | .4 | 6.5 | 5.1 |  |  | Profit Before Taxes | 7.0 | 5.3 |
|  |  |  |  |  |  | RATIOS |  |  |
|  | 2.8 | 3.3 | 2.8 |  |  | Current | 2.1 | 2.5 |
|  | 1.7 | 1.6 | 1.5 |  |  |  | 1.6 | 1.6 |
|  | 1.2 | 1.3 | 1.0 |  |  |  | 1.2 | 1.2 |
|  | 1.8 | 1.9 | 1.3 |  |  | Quick | 1.4 | 1.3 |
|  | 1.0 | 1.0 | .8 |  |  |  | .9 | .9 |
|  | .6 | .6 | .5 |  |  |  | .5 | .6 |
| 21 | 17.3 | 32   11.3 | 34   10.8 |  |  | Sales/Receivables | 32   11.5 | 30   12.0 |
| 39 | 9.3 | 46   8.0 | 39   9.3 |  |  |  | 44   8.3 | 40   9.2 |
| 55 | 6.6 | 57   6.4 | 61   6.0 |  |  |  | 55   6.6 | 51   7.2 |
| 4 | 91.7 | 29   12.6 | 25   14.8 |  |  | Cost of Sales/Inventory | 26   14.0 | 31   11.8 |
| 41 | 9.0 | 52   7.0 | 57   6.4 |  |  |  | 54   6.8 | 55   6.6 |
| 79 | 4.6 | 89   4.1 | 122   3.0 |  |  |  | 83   4.4 | 87   4.2 |
| 21 | 17.8 | 24   14.9 | 15   23.7 |  |  | Cost of Sales/Payables | 22   16.4 | 12   31.7 |
| 47 | 7.8 | 36   10.2 | 28   12.9 |  |  |  | 28   12.9 | 21   17.1 |
| 66 | 5.5 | 58   6.3 | 41   9.0 |  |  |  | 41   9.0 | 36   10.1 |
|  | 6.8 | 4.4 | 3.9 |  |  | Sales/Working Capital | 6.6 | 5.2 |
|  | 10.6 | 11.8 | 8.4 |  |  |  | 11.6 | 9.9 |
|  | NM | 20.3 | 123.7 |  |  |  | 22.4 | 21.4 |
|  |  | 23.1 | 30.1 |  |  | EBIT/Interest | 14.5 | 18.9 |
|  |  | (27)   5.3 | (18)   4.3 |  |  |  | (44)   7.1 | (61)   4.5 |
|  |  | 2.2 | 2.4 |  |  |  | 2.6 | 2.2 |
|  |  |  |  |  |  | Net Profit + Depr., Dep., Amort./Cur. Mat. L/T/D | 7.9 | 18.5 |
|  |  |  |  |  |  |  | (15)   3.1 | (19)   6.0 |
|  |  |  |  |  |  |  | 1.6 | 3.1 |
|  | .2 | .3 | .4 |  |  | Fixed/Worth | .4 | .3 |
|  | .8 | .7 | .8 |  |  |  | .8 | .8 |
|  | 1.9 | 2.1 | 1.8 |  |  |  | 3.5 | 2.3 |
|  | .9 | .7 | .7 |  |  | Debt/Worth | .8 | .8 |
|  | 2.3 | 1.9 | 1.2 |  |  |  | 1.6 | 1.7 |
|  | 6.9 | 6.5 | 3.6 |  |  |  | 6.3 | 6.3 |
|  | 58.3 | 62.2 | 42.2 |  |  | % Profit Before Taxes/Tangible Net Worth | 55.2 | 45.7 |
|  | 15.6 | (26)   35.8 | (18)   23.2 |  |  |  | (37)   22.6 | (54)   24.6 |
|  | -29.6 | 10.1 | 4.9 |  |  |  | 12.5 | 11.2 |
|  | 15.4 | 25.5 | 18.5 |  |  | % Profit Before Taxes/Total Assets | 24.1 | 19.1 |
|  | 7.7 | 8.5 | 6.5 |  |  |  | 9.1 | 8.0 |
|  | -6.0 | 3.1 | 1.3 |  |  |  | 4.5 | 3.8 |
|  | 47.7 | 40.1 | 12.8 |  |  | Sales/Net Fixed Assets | 20.6 | 24.4 |
|  | 24.5 | 13.6 | 7.0 |  |  |  | 9.7 | 9.7 |
|  | 6.6 | 7.3 | 4.2 |  |  |  | 4.9 | 5.6 |
|  | 4.3 | 3.5 | 2.7 |  |  | Sales/Total Assets | 3.4 | 3.0 |
|  | 3.2 | 2.3 | 1.9 |  |  |  | 2.3 | 2.2 |
|  | 2.3 | 1.5 | 1.3 |  |  |  | 1.4 | 1.6 |
|  |  | .8 | 1.1 |  |  | % Depr., Dep., Amort./Sales | 1.0 | .9 |
|  |  | (24)   1.5 | (19)   2.0 |  |  |  | (41)   2.4 | (53)   1.5 |
|  |  | 2.5 | 3.2 |  |  |  | 3.8 | 3.4 |
|  |  | 1.4 |  |  |  | % Officers', Directors' Owners' Comp/Sales | 1.5 | 1.9 |
|  |  | (17)   2.4 |  |  |  |  | (17)   3.7 | (20)   4.0 |
|  |  | 5.1 |  |  |  |  | 4.5 | 8.6 |
| 4852M | 39371M | 350367M | 947657M | 702813M | 537573M | Net Sales ($) | 1506243M | 3333095M |
| 962M | 11584M | 138162M | 484257M | 305303M | 391692M | Total Assets ($) | 959894M | 1515239M |

© RMA 2012

M = $ thousand    MM = $ million
See Pages 9 through 22 for Explanation of Ratios and Data

## Comparative Historical Data / Current Data Sorted by Sales

| 11 | 12 | 10 | Type of Statement | | | | | | |
|---|---|---|---|---|---|---|---|---|---|
| 11 | 12 | 10 | Unqualified | 1 | | | 1 | 1 | 8 |
| 7 | 11 | 10 | Reviewed | | 1 | 2 | 3 | 3 | 3 |
| 6 | 10 | 11 | Compiled | | 2 | | 4 | 2 | 3 |
| 7 | 9 | 8 | Tax Returns | | 1 | | 5 | 1 | 1 |
| 27 | 26 | 31 | Other | | 5 | 3 | 5 | 6 | 12 |
| 4/1/09-3/31/10 ALL | 4/1/10-3/31/11 ALL | 4/1/11-3/31/12 ALL | | | 8 (4/1-9/30/11) | | 62 (10/1/11-3/31/12) | | |
| | | | | 0-1MM | 1-3MM | 3-5MM | 5-10MM | 10-25MM | 25MM & OVER |
| 58 | 68 | 70 | NUMBER OF STATEMENTS | 1 | 9 | 5 | 15 | 13 | 27 |
| % | % | % | **ASSETS** | % | % | % | % | % | % |
| 7.5 | 9.7 | 7.7 | Cash & Equivalents | | | | 12.3 | 8.8 | 3.6 |
| 25.6 | 26.0 | 28.3 | Trade Receivables (net) | | | | 27.4 | 32.9 | 26.8 |
| 22.3 | 24.6 | 26.5 | Inventory | | | | 29.6 | 29.9 | 27.5 |
| 4.0 | 2.3 | 1.8 | All Other Current | | | | .9 | .9 | 3.0 |
| 59.4 | 62.6 | 64.3 | Total Current | | | | 70.1 | 72.5 | 61.0 |
| 28.1 | 27.3 | 24.8 | Fixed Assets (net) | | | | 23.3 | 20.0 | 26.2 |
| 8.7 | 6.2 | 6.1 | Intangibles (net) | | | | 2.7 | 5.5 | 7.0 |
| 3.7 | 3.9 | 4.7 | All Other Non-Current | | | | 3.9 | 2.0 | 5.8 |
| 100.0 | 100.0 | 100.0 | Total | | | | 100.0 | 100.0 | 100.0 |
| | | | **LIABILITIES** | | | | | | |
| 8.1 | 9.9 | 8.2 | Notes Payable-Short Term | | | | 10.8 | 10.8 | 7.5 |
| 3.6 | 3.8 | 2.6 | Cur. Mat.-L.T.D. | | | | 2.5 | 2.1 | 1.8 |
| 13.5 | 14.9 | 17.9 | Trade Payables | | | | 17.6 | 22.6 | 15.4 |
| .2 | .2 | .3 | Income Taxes Payable | | | | .5 | .0 | .5 |
| 8.9 | 13.5 | 9.4 | All Other Current | | | | 9.2 | 8.3 | 12.5 |
| 34.2 | 42.4 | 38.3 | Total Current | | | | 40.6 | 43.8 | 37.6 |
| 18.2 | 20.1 | 14.6 | Long-Term Debt | | | | 15.3 | 11.0 | 13.1 |
| 1.0 | .8 | .6 | Deferred Taxes | | | | .4 | .3 | 1.2 |
| 6.3 | 4.1 | 5.3 | All Other Non-Current | | | | 1.9 | 4.7 | 6.8 |
| 40.3 | 32.6 | 41.2 | Net Worth | | | | 41.9 | 40.3 | 41.3 |
| 100.0 | 100.0 | 100.0 | Total Liabilities & Net Worth | | | | 100.0 | 100.0 | 100.0 |
| | | | **INCOME DATA** | | | | | | |
| 100.0 | 100.0 | 100.0 | Net Sales | | | | 100.0 | 100.0 | 100.0 |
| 29.0 | 28.7 | 27.9 | Gross Profit | | | | 30.4 | 27.3 | 22.5 |
| 25.2 | 24.3 | 22.0 | Operating Expenses | | | | 23.7 | 21.8 | 16.5 |
| 3.8 | 4.4 | 5.8 | Operating Profit | | | | 6.7 | 5.5 | 6.0 |
| 1.8 | 1.0 | .8 | All Other Expenses (net) | | | | .5 | .3 | .9 |
| 2.1 | 3.4 | 5.1 | Profit Before Taxes | | | | 6.3 | 5.2 | 5.1 |
| | | | **RATIOS** | | | | | | |
| 3.2 | 2.3 | 2.6 | Current | | | | 4.7 | 3.6 | 2.3 |
| 1.6 | 1.6 | 1.6 | | | | | 1.6 | 1.4 | 1.7 |
| 1.2 | 1.2 | 1.3 | | | | | 1.2 | 1.2 | 1.1 |
| 1.8 | 1.5 | 1.5 | Quick | | | | 2.3 | 1.5 | 1.2 |
| .9 | .9 | .9 | | | | | .8 | .9 | .8 |
| .6 | .5 | .6 | | | | | .6 | .8 | .6 |
| 37  9.7 | 34  10.8 | 33  11.2 | Sales/Receivables | | | | 31  11.6 | 26  14.1 | 33  11.0 |
| 50  7.4 | 44  8.3 | 41  8.9 | | | | | 43  8.5 | 55  6.6 | 38  9.5 |
| 60  6.1 | 57  6.4 | 57  6.4 | | | | | 52  7.0 | 73  5.0 | 52  7.0 |
| 29  12.6 | 32  11.6 | 25  14.7 | Cost of Sales/Inventory | | | | 17  21.1 | 31  11.9 | 30  12.3 |
| 51  7.1 | 52  7.1 | 47  7.7 | | | | | 42  8.6 | 49  7.5 | 53  6.9 |
| 100  3.7 | 102  3.6 | 94  3.9 | | | | | 122  3.0 | 81  4.5 | 74  4.9 |
| 19  18.8 | 17  21.5 | 23  15.9 | Cost of Sales/Payables | | | | 14  26.6 | 24  15.1 | 19  19.4 |
| 32  11.6 | 31  11.9 | 32  11.3 | | | | | 39  9.3 | 36  10.2 | 27  13.5 |
| 49  7.5 | 52  7.0 | 53  6.9 | | | | | 53  6.9 | 54  6.7 | 42  8.7 |
| 4.1 | 5.6 | 4.9 | Sales/Working Capital | | | | 4.1 | 2.8 | 6.5 |
| 9.3 | 10.1 | 9.9 | | | | | 8.2 | 14.3 | 9.2 |
| 20.0 | 21.2 | 29.9 | | | | | 39.9 | 34.6 | 37.8 |
| 5.5 | 16.8 | 21.3 | EBIT/Interest | | | | 18.6 | 62.3 | 37.5 |
| (55) 2.4 | (62) 4.9 | (62) 4.9 | | | | | (13) 4.6 | 7.7 | (24) 7.0 |
| -1.3 | 1.5 | 2.0 | | | | | 1.5 | 2.3 | 2.7 |
| 6.1 | 7.4 | 12.5 | Net Profit + Depr., Dep., Amort./Cur. Mat. L/T/D | | | | | | |
| (14) 2.1 | (13) 4.5 | (10) 5.1 | | | | | | | |
| -.1 | .9 | 2.0 | | | | | | | |
| .4 | .3 | .3 | Fixed/Worth | | | | .3 | .3 | .4 |
| .9 | .7 | .7 | | | | | .7 | .8 | .8 |
| 1.8 | 2.4 | 2.0 | | | | | 1.5 | 2.1 | 1.4 |
| .9 | .7 | .7 | Debt/Worth | | | | .8 | .4 | .8 |
| 1.7 | 1.7 | 1.7 | | | | | 1.9 | 4.4 | 1.2 |
| 6.7 | 6.4 | 6.0 | | | | | 4.0 | 12.1 | 4.1 |
| 36.8 | 39.7 | 54.3 | % Profit Before Taxes/Tangible Net Worth | | | | 56.2 | 64.4 | 53.7 |
| (49) 14.2 | (57) 12.7 | (62) 29.5 | | | | | 34.6 | (12) 32.2 | (23) 25.5 |
| -2.0 | 3.1 | 6.0 | | | | | 2.1 | 13.1 | 8.3 |
| 11.6 | 10.0 | 20.9 | % Profit Before Taxes/Total Assets | | | | 22.8 | 17.0 | 17.8 |
| 2.7 | 6.4 | 8.5 | | | | | 10.9 | 8.5 | 6.6 |
| -2.2 | 1.3 | 2.2 | | | | | .5 | 4.0 | 3.0 |
| 16.8 | 17.5 | 27.8 | Sales/Net Fixed Assets | | | | 27.3 | 41.9 | 22.9 |
| 7.4 | 10.7 | 12.4 | | | | | 12.3 | 13.0 | 11.8 |
| 3.7 | 5.7 | 6.2 | | | | | 6.4 | 6.2 | 6.0 |
| 2.5 | 2.7 | 3.3 | Sales/Total Assets | | | | 3.4 | 3.7 | 2.9 |
| 1.8 | 2.0 | 2.3 | | | | | 2.3 | 2.3 | 2.3 |
| 1.2 | 1.4 | 1.7 | | | | | 1.5 | 1.7 | 1.8 |
| 1.4 | 1.0 | .8 | % Depr., Dep., Amort./Sales | | | | .8 | 1.0 | .6 |
| (48) 2.6 | (60) 2.1 | (60) 1.6 | | | | | (12) 1.3 | (10) 1.5 | (26) 1.8 |
| 4.2 | 3.3 | 2.7 | | | | | 2.2 | 2.3 | 3.1 |
| 1.3 | 1.3 | 1.2 | % Officers', Directors' Owners' Comp/Sales | | | | | | |
| (15) 7.4 | (21) 3.6 | (29) 2.4 | | | | | | | |
| 11.6 | 11.1 | 4.3 | | | | | | | |
| 2050580M | 2057114M | 2582633M | Net Sales ($) | 45M | 17048M | 21071M | 117352M | 196234M | 2230883M |
| 1537366M | 1355753M | 1331960M | Total Assets ($) | 33M | 13357M | 10770M | 68241M | 88177M | 1151382M |

M = $ thousand    MM = $ million
See Pages 9 through 22 for Explanation of Ratios and Data

| Current Data Sorted by Assets | | | | | | | Comparative Historical Data | |

| | 1 | 3 | 10 | 3 | 2 | | Type of Statement | | |
|---|---|---|---|---|---|---|---|---|---|
| | | 18 | 2 | 1 | | | Unqualified | 14 | 18 |
| 1 | 4 | 8 | | | | | Reviewed | 22 | 20 |
| 4 | 8 | 5 | | | | | Compiled | 12 | 14 |
| 3 | 5 | 10 | 14 | 3 | 4 | | Tax Returns | 21 | 16 |
| | 15 (4/1-9/30/11) | | 94 (10/1/11-3/31/12) | | | | Other | 36 | 39 |
| | | | | | | | | 4/1/07- | 4/1/08- |
| | | | | | | | | 3/31/08 | 3/31/09 |
| 0-500M | 500M-2MM | 2-10MM | 10-50MM | 50-100MM | 100-250MM | | | ALL | ALL |
| 8 | 18 | 44 | 26 | 7 | 6 | | NUMBER OF STATEMENTS | 105 | 107 |
| % | % | % | % | % | % | | ASSETS | % | % |
| | 15.7 | 8.7 | 7.5 | | | | Cash & Equivalents | 7.5 | 8.5 |
| | 27.9 | 25.5 | 20.8 | | | | Trade Receivables (net) | 24.7 | 25.3 |
| | 38.2 | 38.6 | 26.7 | | | | Inventory | 31.8 | 33.9 |
| | .5 | 1.5 | 2.8 | | | | All Other Current | 1.1 | 2.0 |
| | 82.3 | 74.4 | 57.7 | | | | Total Current | 65.2 | 69.7 |
| | 11.4 | 15.7 | 25.7 | | | | Fixed Assets (net) | 22.9 | 20.9 |
| | 1.4 | 3.9 | 11.7 | | | | Intangibles (net) | 5.7 | 4.0 |
| | 4.9 | 6.1 | 4.8 | | | | All Other Non-Current | 6.3 | 5.4 |
| | 100.0 | 100.0 | 100.0 | | | | Total | 100.0 | 100.0 |
| | | | | | | | LIABILITIES | | |
| | 19.0 | 9.9 | 5.6 | | | | Notes Payable-Short Term | 10.1 | 13.5 |
| | 1.8 | 2.3 | 2.4 | | | | Cur. Mat.-L.T.D. | 3.3 | 3.4 |
| | 19.3 | 14.4 | 9.5 | | | | Trade Payables | 15.6 | 13.6 |
| | .0 | .0 | .6 | | | | Income Taxes Payable | .2 | .2 |
| | 3.1 | 8.7 | 6.6 | | | | All Other Current | 7.7 | 9.1 |
| | 43.1 | 35.3 | 24.6 | | | | Total Current | 36.9 | 39.8 |
| | 17.3 | 13.2 | 15.2 | | | | Long-Term Debt | 17.4 | 15.6 |
| | .0 | .2 | 1.0 | | | | Deferred Taxes | .5 | .4 |
| | 4.4 | 6.4 | 17.0 | | | | All Other Non-Current | 9.5 | 5.2 |
| | 35.3 | 45.0 | 42.2 | | | | Net Worth | 35.7 | 39.0 |
| | 100.0 | 100.0 | 100.0 | | | | Total Liabilities & Net Worth | 100.0 | 100.0 |
| | | | | | | | INCOME DATA | | |
| | 100.0 | 100.0 | 100.0 | | | | Net Sales | 100.0 | 100.0 |
| | 32.7 | 33.6 | 29.4 | | | | Gross Profit | 31.5 | 30.7 |
| | 27.5 | 29.9 | 21.0 | | | | Operating Expenses | 25.4 | 25.1 |
| | 5.2 | 3.7 | 8.5 | | | | Operating Profit | 6.2 | 5.6 |
| | 1.0 | .8 | 2.0 | | | | All Other Expenses (net) | 1.5 | 1.4 |
| | 4.3 | 3.0 | 6.5 | | | | Profit Before Taxes | 4.7 | 4.2 |
| | | | | | | | RATIOS | | |
| | 3.9 | 3.9 | 4.0 | | | | | 3.4 | 3.8 |
| | 2.4 | 2.2 | 3.1 | | | | Current | 2.1 | 2.1 |
| | 1.4 | 1.4 | 1.5 | | | | | 1.2 | 1.3 |
| | 3.6 | 2.4 | 2.1 | | | | | 1.7 | 1.9 |
| | 1.0 | .9 | 1.6 | | | | Quick | .9 | .8 |
| | .6 | .5 | .7 | | | | | .6 | .5 |
| 25 | 14.8 | 32 | 11.3 | 36 | 10.1 | | Sales/Receivables | 30 | 12.0 | 25 | 14.9 |

| 0-500M | 500M-2MM | 2-10MM | 10-50MM | Ratio | Hist 07-08 | Hist 08-09 |
|---|---|---|---|---|---|---|
| 25 14.8 | 32 11.3 | 36 10.1 | | Sales/Receivables | 30 12.0 | 25 14.9 |
| 36 10.2 | 40 9.1 | 41 8.8 | | | 38 9.6 | 36 10.2 |
| 49 7.5 | 54 6.8 | 53 6.9 | | | 48 7.5 | 57 6.4 |
| 15 25.0 | 68 5.4 | 49 7.5 | | Cost of Sales/Inventory | 51 7.1 | 44 8.3 |
| 51 7.2 | 114 3.2 | 87 4.2 | | | 82 4.5 | 75 4.9 |
| 174 2.1 | 182 2.0 | 118 3.1 | | | 133 2.7 | 154 2.4 |
| 13 27.5 | 16 22.8 | 20 18.4 | | Cost of Sales/Payables | 15 24.0 | 10 34.9 |
| 22 16.8 | 30 12.0 | 30 12.3 | | | 29 12.4 | 24 15.3 |
| 59 6.2 | 48 7.6 | 37 9.8 | | | 51 7.1 | 42 8.7 |
| 3.3 | 3.2 | 3.3 | | Sales/Working Capital | 4.0 | 4.1 |
| 8.2 | 5.2 | 5.0 | | | 7.1 | 6.4 |
| 10.7 | 9.7 | 9.2 | | | 19.5 | 16.4 |
| 33.7 | 21.1 | 15.6 | | EBIT/Interest | 11.1 | 12.5 |
| (14) 7.1 | (38) 4.9 | (23) 5.1 | | | (93) 3.7 | (91) 3.2 |
| 1.0 | .0 | 2.6 | | | 1.5 | .9 |
| | | | | Net Profit + Depr., Dep., | 11.2 | 12.9 |
| | (24) 2.8 | (21) 1.1 | | Amort./Cur. Mat. L/T/D | | |
| | | | | | 1.7 | .1 |
| .0 | .1 | .3 | | Fixed/Worth | .3 | .2 |
| .1 | .3 | .6 | | | .5 | .5 |
| NM | .6 | 2.0 | | | 2.1 | 1.5 |
| .5 | .4 | .5 | | Debt/Worth | .6 | .5 |
| 1.5 | 1.2 | 1.2 | | | 2.2 | 1.8 |
| NM | 2.4 | 4.7 | | | 6.4 | 5.5 |
| 47.7 | 42.7 | 61.4 | | % Profit Before Taxes/Tangible Net Worth | 43.9 | 50.8 |
| (14) 26.2 | (38) 16.5 | (22) 22.3 | | | (86) 19.6 | (91) 17.7 |
| 9.8 | 2.5 | 8.5 | | | 6.5 | 1.0 |
| 26.8 | 13.6 | 16.3 | | % Profit Before Taxes/Total Assets | 15.3 | 16.2 |
| 8.3 | 5.5 | 7.0 | | | 5.7 | 6.7 |
| -.1 | -.5 | 5.0 | | | 1.2 | -.7 |
| 128.8 | 55.2 | 14.1 | | Sales/Net Fixed Assets | 28.4 | 40.1 |
| 65.8 | 12.5 | 8.9 | | | 12.4 | 12.2 |
| 15.3 | 7.9 | 2.9 | | | 5.7 | 5.5 |
| 3.4 | 2.6 | 2.1 | | Sales/Total Assets | 2.6 | 2.8 |
| 2.4 | 2.0 | 1.8 | | | 2.0 | 2.0 |
| 1.9 | 1.4 | 1.2 | | | 1.5 | 1.5 |
| .2 | 1.0 | 1.4 | | % Depr., Dep., Amort./Sales | .8 | .9 |
| (11) .5 | (35) 1.5 | (24) 2.4 | | | (84) 2.2 | (91) 1.7 |
| 1.9 | 2.5 | 4.0 | | | 3.1 | 3.1 |
| 1.8 | 1.3 | | | % Officers', Directors' Owners' Comp/Sales | 1.8 | 2.3 |
| (12) 3.6 | (15) 3.2 | | | | (40) 2.8 | (43) 3.2 |
| 7.6 | 5.9 | | | | 5.5 | 4.9 |

| 8469M | 58745M | 397899M | 937417M | 737314M | 945581M | | Net Sales ($) | 2440692M | 2885470M |
| 2186M | 21258M | 204557M | 543055M | 492459M | 1050209M | | Total Assets ($) | 1534982M | 1712372M |

M = $ thousand   MM = $ million
See Pages 9 through 22 for Explanation of Ratios and Data

## Comparative Historical Data | Current Data Sorted by Sales

| Hist | Hist | Hist | Type of Statement | 0-1MM | 1-3MM | 3-5MM | 5-10MM | 10-25MM | 25MM & OVER |
|---|---|---|---|---|---|---|---|---|---|
| 18 | 24 | 19 | Unqualified | | | 1 | | 1 | 6 | 11 |
| 14 | 15 | 21 | Reviewed | | | | 4 | 7 | 8 | 2 |
| 20 | 16 | 13 | Compiled | | 1 | 2 | 3 | 5 | 2 | |
| 16 | 17 | 17 | Tax Returns | | 1 | 4 | 7 | 4 | 1 | |
| 37 | 38 | 39 | Other | | 4 | 3 | 2 | 6 | 7 | 17 |
| 4/1/09-3/31/10 ALL | 4/1/10-3/31/11 ALL | 4/1/11-3/31/12 ALL | | 15 (4/1-9/30/11) | | 94 (10/1/11-3/31/12) | | | |
| 105 | 110 | 109 | NUMBER OF STATEMENTS | 6 | 10 | 16 | 23 | 24 | 30 |
| % | % | % | **ASSETS** | % | % | % | % | % | % |
| 9.3 | 8.0 | 9.7 | Cash & Equivalents | | 10.0 | 13.2 | 9.3 | 12.0 | 4.4 |
| 22.4 | 21.5 | 23.3 | Trade Receivables (net) | | 31.7 | 23.1 | 25.6 | 23.4 | 19.9 |
| 34.5 | 32.8 | 33.5 | Inventory | | 31.4 | 40.1 | 40.4 | 30.8 | 27.9 |
| 2.3 | 2.8 | 1.8 | All Other Current | | .4 | 1.7 | .8 | 2.1 | 3.1 |
| 68.6 | 65.2 | 68.4 | Total Current | | 73.5 | 78.1 | 76.1 | 68.4 | 55.3 |
| 20.3 | 19.5 | 17.9 | Fixed Assets (net) | | 15.9 | 13.1 | 15.8 | 18.6 | 23.6 |
| 4.0 | 6.4 | 7.4 | Intangibles (net) | | 1.4 | 2.5 | 2.3 | 9.7 | 13.2 |
| 7.2 | 8.9 | 6.4 | All Other Non-Current | | 9.3 | 6.2 | 5.7 | 3.3 | 8.0 |
| 100.0 | 100.0 | 100.0 | Total | | 100.0 | 100.0 | 100.0 | 100.0 | 100.0 |
| | | | **LIABILITIES** | | | | | | |
| 13.0 | 11.6 | 10.2 | Notes Payable-Short Term | | 19.9 | 18.7 | 7.2 | 8.9 | 7.3 |
| 3.2 | 2.7 | 2.5 | Cur. Mat.-L.T.D. | | 5.1 | 1.7 | 2.6 | 2.2 | 2.6 |
| 11.8 | 11.4 | 13.1 | Trade Payables | | 14.7 | 19.0 | 12.3 | 13.7 | 9.7 |
| .3 | .2 | .2 | Income Taxes Payable | | .0 | .0 | .0 | .1 | .6 |
| 10.9 | 7.8 | 7.2 | All Other Current | | 4.4 | 6.4 | 6.9 | 7.9 | 9.3 |
| 39.2 | 33.7 | 33.1 | Total Current | | 44.1 | 45.8 | 29.0 | 32.9 | 29.6 |
| 12.6 | 14.4 | 13.8 | Long-Term Debt | | 9.0 | 22.1 | 11.0 | 17.3 | 13.2 |
| .5 | .5 | .6 | Deferred Taxes | | .0 | .1 | .2 | 1.0 | 1.3 |
| 8.9 | 7.2 | 10.2 | All Other Non-Current | | 9.1 | 3.6 | 3.2 | 12.9 | 16.5 |
| 38.9 | 44.1 | 42.2 | Net Worth | | 37.8 | 28.4 | 56.5 | 36.0 | 39.4 |
| 100.0 | 100.0 | 100.0 | Total Liabilities & Net Worth | | 100.0 | 100.0 | 100.0 | 100.0 | 100.0 |
| | | | **INCOME DATA** | | | | | | |
| 100.0 | 100.0 | 100.0 | Net Sales | | 100.0 | 100.0 | 100.0 | 100.0 | 100.0 |
| 32.4 | 32.5 | 33.1 | Gross Profit | | 43.1 | 33.1 | 34.4 | 32.1 | 29.3 |
| 29.4 | 26.6 | 27.6 | Operating Expenses | | 39.0 | 28.6 | 30.8 | 25.1 | 22.8 |
| 3.0 | 5.8 | 5.5 | Operating Profit | | 4.1 | 4.5 | 3.6 | 7.0 | 6.5 |
| 1.5 | 1.1 | 1.4 | All Other Expenses (net) | | .9 | 1.8 | .5 | 1.8 | 2.2 |
| 1.5 | 4.7 | 4.1 | Profit Before Taxes | | 3.2 | 2.7 | 3.1 | 5.2 | 4.3 |
| | | | **RATIOS** | | | | | | |
| 3.8 | 3.9 | 4.0 | | | 5.6 | 3.0 | 4.7 | 4.0 | 3.4 |
| 2.4 | 2.2 | 2.4 | Current | | 2.4 | 2.0 | 2.9 | 2.3 | 1.9 |
| 1.3 | 1.3 | 1.5 | | | .9 | 1.2 | 1.8 | 1.5 | 1.4 |
| 1.8 | 2.0 | 2.3 | | | 5.6 | 1.7 | 2.7 | 2.7 | 1.7 |
| .9 | .9 | 1.0 | Quick | | .6 | .8 | 1.0 | 1.3 | .8 |
| .5 | .5 | .6 | | | .4 | .5 | .6 | .5 | .5 |
| 27  13.7 | 27  13.4 | 30  12.3 | | | 8  48.6 | 30  12.2 | 27  13.3 | 34  10.8 | 33  11.1 |
| 39  9.5 | 39  9.3 | 39  9.3 | Sales/Receivables | | 27  13.7 | 41  8.8 | 37  9.9 | 36  10.0 | 41  8.8 |
| 50  7.2 | 52  7.0 | 51  7.1 | | | 55  6.6 | 56  6.5 | 50  7.3 | 45  8.1 | 51  7.1 |
| 50  7.3 | 58  6.3 | 54  6.8 | | | 0  UND | 49  7.4 | 51  7.1 | 62  5.9 | 61  6.0 |
| 87  4.2 | 94  3.9 | 87  4.2 | Cost of Sales/Inventory | | 6  56.8 | 111  3.3 | 135  2.7 | 79  4.6 | 83  4.4 |
| 167  2.2 | 148  2.5 | 146  2.5 | | | 203  1.8 | 159  2.3 | 215  1.7 | 135  2.7 | 122  3.0 |
| 12  30.4 | 14  25.5 | 16  22.2 | | | 0  UND | 21  17.4 | 21  17.2 | 12  30.5 | 20  17.9 |
| 24  15.4 | 29  12.6 | 29  12.8 | Cost of Sales/Payables | | 17  22.1 | 40  9.2 | 29  12.6 | 29  12.8 | 30  12.3 |
| 50  7.3 | 43  8.6 | 45  8.1 | | | 23  16.1 | 59  6.2 | 43  8.5 | 47  7.8 | 44  8.3 |
| 3.3 | 3.6 | 3.4 | | | 3.0 | 3.0 | 2.8 | 3.5 | 4.4 |
| 5.3 | 6.0 | 5.6 | Sales/Working Capital | | 6.8 | 7.3 | 4.0 | 5.5 | 6.9 |
| 12.9 | 11.6 | 9.6 | | | NM | 27.5 | 7.5 | 9.1 | 9.7 |
| 9.6 | 12.0 | 20.8 | | | | 11.7 | 30.1 | 18.1 | 21.4 |
| (91)  2.6 | (89)  5.7 | (91)  5.1 | EBIT/Interest | | | (12)  4.5 | (19)  5.5 | 4.9 | (26)  5.9 |
| .1 | 1.8 | 1.2 | | | | -1.0 | -.1 | 1.8 | 2.1 |
| 45.8 | 11.4 | 8.6 | | | | | | | 7.5 |
| (20)  3.6 | (23)  2.6 | (24)  3.3 | Net Profit + Depr., Dep., Amort./Cur. Mat. L/T/D | | | | | | (13)  3.1 |
| .6 | 1.1 | 1.3 | | | | | | | 1.6 |
| .2 | .2 | .1 | | | .1 | .1 | .1 | .2 | .4 |
| .4 | .4 | .4 | Fixed/Worth | | .2 | .3 | .2 | .4 | .7 |
| 1.0 | .9 | 1.5 | | | -5.5 | NM | .6 | 3.0 | 2.0 |
| .5 | .5 | .4 | | | .4 | .6 | .2 | .6 | .6 |
| 1.3 | 1.1 | 1.2 | Debt/Worth | | .8 | 1.8 | 1.0 | 1.5 | 1.3 |
| 4.1 | 3.6 | 4.3 | | | -107.5 | NM | 1.9 | 5.7 | 6.7 |
| 31.0 | 49.3 | 43.2 | | | | 41.6 | 31.5 | 58.2 | 37.6 |
| (96)  9.1 | (99)  18.1 | (90)  18.8 | % Profit Before Taxes/Tangible Net Worth | | | (12)  24.1 | (22)  11.2 | (19)  20.4 | (24)  18.9 |
| .8 | 7.0 | 4.8 | | | | 11.1 | -1.3 | 4.1 | 9.3 |
| 11.1 | 15.8 | 14.3 | | | 30.5 | 23.8 | 12.6 | 19.0 | 11.3 |
| 3.9 | 7.8 | 6.5 | % Profit Before Taxes/Total Assets | | 6.2 | 6.2 | 6.7 | 7.3 | 6.4 |
| -.6 | 1.7 | .5 | | | -3.4 | -3.0 | -.5 | 2.0 | 1.4 |
| 26.8 | 28.8 | 48.8 | | | 84.9 | 87.9 | 56.6 | 36.5 | 14.1 |
| 10.7 | 11.6 | 11.7 | Sales/Net Fixed Assets | | 53.0 | 17.8 | 14.7 | 11.8 | 8.0 |
| 5.5 | 5.3 | 6.5 | | | 28.7 | 8.1 | 6.1 | 7.9 | 4.6 |
| 2.7 | 2.4 | 2.6 | | | 4.1 | 3.2 | 2.6 | 2.7 | 2.1 |
| 1.8 | 1.7 | 1.8 | Sales/Total Assets | | 2.8 | 2.0 | 2.0 | 2.0 | 1.8 |
| 1.3 | 1.3 | 1.3 | | | 1.8 | 1.2 | 1.5 | 1.3 | 1.3 |
| 1.0 | 1.0 | 1.0 | | | | .4 | 1.3 | 1.3 | 1.4 |
| (88)  2.3 | (90)  1.9 | (84)  1.8 | % Depr., Dep., Amort./Sales | | | (12)  .9 | (18)  1.6 | (19)  2.3 | (27)  2.3 |
| 4.0 | 3.3 | 3.4 | | | | 2.2 | 3.0 | 3.5 | 3.7 |
| 1.9 | 2.7 | 1.6 | | | | 1.3 | | | |
| (48)  3.8 | (36)  3.5 | (35)  3.6 | % Officers', Directors', Owners' Comp/Sales | | | (12)  3.4 | | | |
| 7.4 | 5.2 | 9.6 | | | | 7.3 | | | |
| 2621460M | 2707056M | 3085425M | Net Sales ($) | 3678M | 17336M | 63059M | 174765M | 369315M | 2457272M |
| 1767648M | 1918460M | 2313724M | Total Assets ($) | 5046M | 6649M | 37218M | 93699M | 221751M | 1949361M |

M = $ thousand     MM = $ million

See Pages 9 through 22 for Explanation of Ratios and Data

## Current Data Sorted by Assets      Comparative Historical Data

| Type of Statement | | | |
|---|---|---|---|
| | | Unqualified | 8 | 8 |
| | | Reviewed | 10 | 10 |
| | | Compiled | 11 | 9 |
| | | Tax Returns | 2 | 6 |
| | | Other | 14 | 12 |

| 0-500M | 500M-2MM | 2-10MM | 10-50MM | 50-100MM | 100-250MM | | 4/1/07-3/31/08 ALL | 4/1/08-3/31/09 ALL |
|---|---|---|---|---|---|---|---|---|
| | 9 (4/1-9/30/11) | | 27 (10/1/11-3/31/12) | | | | | |
| | 5 | 23 | 7 | 1 | | **NUMBER OF STATEMENTS** | 45 | 45 |
| % | % | % | % | % | % | **ASSETS** | % | % |
| | | 7.5 | | | | Cash & Equivalents | 8.3 | 6.8 |
| | | 21.2 | | | | Trade Receivables (net) | 23.0 | 21.7 |
| | | 22.2 | | | | Inventory | 24.0 | 32.3 |
| | | 1.0 | | | | All Other Current | .9 | 1.1 |
| | | 51.9 | | | | Total Current | 56.1 | 62.0 |
| | | 31.7 | | | | Fixed Assets (net) | 29.1 | 28.2 |
| | | 7.8 | | | | Intangibles (net) | 6.7 | 2.6 |
| | | 8.6 | | | | All Other Non-Current | 8.1 | 7.3 |
| | | 100.0 | | | | Total | 100.0 | 100.0 |
| | | | | | | **LIABILITIES** | | |
| | | 7.6 | | | | Notes Payable-Short Term | 9.1 | 12.5 |
| | | 4.1 | | | | Cur. Mat.-L.T.D. | 3.4 | 4.2 |
| | | 7.5 | | | | Trade Payables | 8.2 | 11.1 |
| | | .1 | | | | Income Taxes Payable | .1 | .0 |
| | | 6.2 | | | | All Other Current | 7.0 | 7.9 |
| | | 25.5 | | | | Total Current | 27.7 | 35.8 |
| | | 15.0 | | | | Long-Term Debt | 17.2 | 20.2 |
| | | .6 | | | | Deferred Taxes | .7 | .4 |
| | | 9.7 | | | | All Other Non-Current | 5.0 | 7.1 |
| | | 49.2 | | | | Net Worth | 49.5 | 36.5 |
| | | 100.0 | | | | Total Liabilities & Net Worth | 100.0 | 100.0 |
| | | | | | | **INCOME DATA** | | |
| | | 100.0 | | | | Net Sales | 100.0 | 100.0 |
| | | 30.1 | | | | Gross Profit | 26.4 | 25.1 |
| | | 23.0 | | | | Operating Expenses | 20.5 | 21.8 |
| | | 7.1 | | | | Operating Profit | 5.8 | 3.2 |
| | | .8 | | | | All Other Expenses (net) | 1.0 | .8 |
| | | 6.3 | | | | Profit Before Taxes | 4.8 | 2.4 |
| | | | | | | **RATIOS** | | |
| | | 3.4 | | | | | 3.0 | 2.9 |
| | | 1.8 | | | | Current | 2.3 | 2.2 |
| | | 1.3 | | | | | 1.4 | 1.3 |
| | | 2.3 | | | | | 2.1 | 1.7 |
| | | 1.3 | | | | Quick | 1.1 | .9 |
| | | .8 | | | | | .7 | .6 |
| | | (33) 10.9 | | | | | (37) 9.9 | (31) 11.8 |
| | | (46) 7.9 | | | | Sales/Receivables | (46) 7.9 | (40) 9.1 |
| | | (58) 6.3 | | | | | (54) 6.7 | (48) 7.6 |
| | | (38) 9.5 | | | | | (35) 10.3 | (44) 8.3 |
| | | (73) 5.0 | | | | Cost of Sales/Inventory | (56) 6.5 | (70) 5.2 |
| | | (94) 3.9 | | | | | (83) 4.4 | (102) 3.6 |
| | | (13) 27.7 | | | | | (11) 34.1 | (12) 29.3 |
| | | (21) 17.6 | | | | Cost of Sales/Payables | (20) 18.5 | (17) 21.1 |
| | | (34) 10.7 | | | | | (29) 12.7 | (31) 11.8 |
| | | 3.5 | | | | | 4.9 | 4.5 |
| | | 7.6 | | | | Sales/Working Capital | 7.1 | 7.1 |
| | | 25.7 | | | | | 15.2 | 15.6 |
| | | 21.1 | | | | | 9.9 | 6.4 |
| | (22) | 4.6 | | | | EBIT/Interest | (42) 3.9 | (42) 2.7 |
| | | 2.0 | | | | | 1.4 | .3 |
| | | 4.8 | | | | Net Profit + Depr., Dep., | 4.0 | 4.5 |
| | (11) | 4.0 | | | | Amort./Cur. Mat. L/T/D | (11) 3.2 | (14) 2.6 |
| | | 1.8 | | | | | 2.7 | 1.2 |
| | | .5 | | | | | .4 | .3 |
| | | .8 | | | | Fixed/Worth | .7 | .8 |
| | | 1.4 | | | | | 1.2 | 1.7 |
| | | .4 | | | | | .5 | .5 |
| | | 1.2 | | | | Debt/Worth | 1.1 | 2.0 |
| | | 3.4 | | | | | 2.6 | 4.3 |
| | | 25.3 | | | | % Profit Before Taxes/Tangible | 31.6 | 29.2 |
| | (22) | 17.2 | | | | Net Worth | (41) 15.2 | (40) 8.6 |
| | | 10.0 | | | | | 4.3 | -2.6 |
| | | 12.5 | | | | % Profit Before Taxes/Total | 12.8 | 12.1 |
| | | 9.9 | | | | Assets | 8.3 | 3.6 |
| | | 2.5 | | | | | 1.3 | -.9 |
| | | 10.1 | | | | | 11.5 | 16.2 |
| | | 6.0 | | | | Sales/Net Fixed Assets | 7.0 | 7.5 |
| | | 4.1 | | | | | 4.4 | 5.1 |
| | | 2.0 | | | | | 2.3 | 2.6 |
| | | 1.7 | | | | Sales/Total Assets | 1.9 | 1.9 |
| | | 1.3 | | | | | 1.6 | 1.7 |
| | | 2.0 | | | | | 2.3 | 1.5 |
| | | 3.0 | | | | % Depr., Dep., Amort./Sales | (43) 3.0 | (43) 2.8 |
| | | 5.5 | | | | | 4.4 | 4.4 |
| | | | | | | % Officers', Directors' | 1.9 | 1.8 |
| | | | | | | Owners' Comp/Sales | (14) 5.3 | (14) 3.7 |
| | | | | | | | 8.5 | 10.6 |
| | 14549M | 258601M | 226714M | 102729M | | Net Sales ($) | 846020M | 923729M |
| | 5919M | 148401M | 138643M | 64767M | | Total Assets ($) | 480793M | 483366M |

*Note: The 0-500M column and the 10-50MM through 100-250MM columns are marked "DATA NOT AVAILABLE" in the original.*

M = $ thousand    MM = $ million
See Pages 9 through 22 for Explanation of Ratios and Data

| Comparative Historical Data | | | | Current Data Sorted by Sales | | | | | |
|---|---|---|---|---|---|---|---|---|---|

| 7 | 5 | 3 | Type of Statement | | | | 1 | 1 | 1 |
|---|---|---|---|---|---|---|---|---|---|
| 12 | 11 | 12 | Unqualified | | | | 4 | 6 | 2 |
| 9 | 8 | 4 | Reviewed | | | 1 | 1 | 1 | 1 |
| 6 | 6 | 4 | Compiled | | | 2 | | | |
| 12 | 9 | 13 | Tax Returns | 1 | 1 | 2 | | | |
| | | | Other | | 2 | | 3 | 3 | 5 |
| 4/1/09-3/31/10 | 4/1/10-3/31/11 | 4/1/11-3/31/12 | | | 9 (4/1-9/30/11) | | | 27 (10/1/11-3/31/12) | |
| ALL | ALL | ALL | | 0-1MM | 1-3MM | 3-5MM | 5-10MM | 10-25MM | 25MM & OVER |
| 46 | 39 | 36 | NUMBER OF STATEMENTS | 1 | 3 | 3 | 9 | 11 | 9 |
| % | % | % | | % | % | % | % | % | % |
| | | | **ASSETS** | | | | | | |
| 10.1 | 11.1 | 9.6 | Cash & Equivalents | | | | | 10.2 | |
| 22.4 | 21.7 | 21.3 | Trade Receivables (net) | | | | | 24.0 | |
| 24.4 | 24.1 | 21.9 | Inventory | | | | | 29.4 | |
| 3.1 | 2.0 | .9 | All Other Current | | | | | 1.0 | |
| 60.0 | 58.9 | 53.6 | Total Current | | | | | 64.6 | |
| 29.5 | 31.3 | 30.9 | Fixed Assets (net) | | | | | 29.4 | |
| 5.9 | 4.3 | 6.8 | Intangibles (net) | | | | | .9 | |
| 4.6 | 5.5 | 8.6 | All Other Non-Current | | | | | 5.1 | |
| 100.0 | 100.0 | 100.0 | Total | | | | | 100.0 | |
| | | | **LIABILITIES** | | | | | | |
| 10.6 | 10.6 | 6.3 | Notes Payable-Short Term | | | | | 9.1 | |
| 4.7 | 3.0 | 3.8 | Cur. Mat.-L.T.D. | | | | | 4.4 | |
| 8.5 | 10.2 | 8.0 | Trade Payables | | | | | 7.8 | |
| .1 | .2 | .1 | Income Taxes Payable | | | | | .2 | |
| 5.1 | 5.5 | 6.8 | All Other Current | | | | | 5.9 | |
| 29.1 | 29.5 | 25.0 | Total Current | | | | | 27.4 | |
| 15.5 | 17.4 | 13.8 | Long-Term Debt | | | | | 10.9 | |
| .3 | .5 | .6 | Deferred Taxes | | | | | .8 | |
| 8.0 | 7.2 | 7.9 | All Other Non-Current | | | | | 6.9 | |
| 47.1 | 45.5 | 52.6 | Net Worth | | | | | 54.0 | |
| 100.0 | 100.0 | 100.0 | Total Liabilties & Net Worth | | | | | 100.0 | |
| | | | **INCOME DATA** | | | | | | |
| 100.0 | 100.0 | 100.0 | Net Sales | | | | | 100.0 | |
| 29.4 | 33.9 | 30.2 | Gross Profit | | | | | 26.7 | |
| 24.6 | 25.9 | 22.7 | Operating Expenses | | | | | 20.4 | |
| 4.8 | 8.0 | 7.5 | Operating Profit | | | | | 6.2 | |
| 1.5 | .7 | .6 | All Other Expenses (net) | | | | | .2 | |
| 3.3 | 7.3 | 6.9 | Profit Before Taxes | | | | | 6.0 | |
| | | | **RATIOS** | | | | | | |
| 4.7 | 3.6 | 3.4 | | | | | | 4.4 | |
| 2.3 | 2.0 | 2.1 | Current | | | | | 2.8 | |
| 1.4 | 1.4 | 1.3 | | | | | | 1.3 | |
| 2.9 | 2.3 | 2.2 | | | | | | 2.6 | |
| 1.2 | 1.1 | 1.3 | Quick | | | | | 1.6 | |
| .7 | .7 | .8 | | | | | | .6 | |
| 38    9.6 | 34    10.9 | 33    10.9 | | | | | | 46    7.9 | |
| 48    7.6 | 46    7.9 | 46    7.9 | Sales/Receivables | | | | | 52    7.0 | |
| 61    5.9 | 52    7.0 | 54    6.7 | | | | | | 60    6.1 | |
| 50    7.3 | 48    7.5 | 39    9.4 | | | | | | 51    7.1 | |
| 71    5.2 | 67    5.4 | 61    6.0 | Cost of Sales/Inventory | | | | | 87    4.2 | |
| 98    3.7 | 99    3.7 | 94    3.9 | | | | | | 111   3.3 | |
| 13    28.0 | 15    24.0 | 12    29.8 | | | | | | 10    35.2 | |
| 23    15.9 | 23    16.2 | 23    15.7 | Cost of Sales/Payables | | | | | 24    14.9 | |
| 35    10.5 | 38    9.7 | 35    10.5 | | | | | | 34    10.7 | |
| 3.5 | 3.5 | 3.6 | | | | | | 3.1 | |
| 6.0 | 6.3 | 6.5 | Sales/Working Capital | | | | | 4.6 | |
| 14.0 | 12.2 | 17.4 | | | | | | 14.6 | |
| 10.0 | 14.9 | 22.5 | | | | | | 25.8 | |
| (39)  2.0 | (35)  5.1 | (34)  10.5 | EBIT/Interest | | | | | 18.3 | |
| -.3 | 2.7 | 3.3 | | | | | | 2.5 | |
| 31.8 | 14.2 | 10.4 | Net Profit + Depr., Dep., | | | | | | |
| (12)  3.3 | (10)  3.8 | (13)  4.3 | Amort./Cur. Mat. L/T/D | | | | | | |
| 1.2 | 2.1 | 2.2 | | | | | | | |
| .4 | .4 | .4 | | | | | | .3 | |
| 1.0 | .7 | .6 | Fixed/Worth | | | | | .5 | |
| 1.7 | 2.3 | 1.4 | | | | | | 1.3 | |
| .3 | .4 | .4 | | | | | | .3 | |
| 1.8 | 1.4 | 1.2 | Debt/Worth | | | | | .7 | |
| 4.5 | 3.8 | 3.2 | | | | | | 2.7 | |
| 26.6 | 41.7 | 34.2 | % Profit Before Taxes/Tangible | | | | | 20.0 | |
| (41)  5.8 | (35)  23.2 | (35)  20.0 | Net Worth | | | | | 15.5 | |
| -7.8 | 13.0 | 13.4 | | | | | | 14.7 | |
| 7.7 | 16.4 | 16.2 | % Profit Before Taxes/Total | | | | | 15.9 | |
| 2.2 | 10.0 | 10.1 | Assets | | | | | 10.5 | |
| -2.7 | 5.6 | 4.5 | | | | | | 4.0 | |
| 11.3 | 10.3 | 10.0 | | | | | | 8.6 | |
| 6.0 | 5.7 | 6.3 | Sales/Net Fixed Assets | | | | | 6.1 | |
| 3.4 | 3.5 | 4.1 | | | | | | 4.5 | |
| 2.2 | 2.2 | 2.2 | | | | | | 2.0 | |
| 1.6 | 1.7 | 1.7 | Sales/Total Assets | | | | | 1.8 | |
| 1.2 | 1.5 | 1.4 | | | | | | 1.4 | |
| 2.2 | 2.0 | 2.1 | | | | | | 2.2 | |
| (43)  3.3 | (37)  3.1 | (33)  2.7 | % Depr., Dep., Amort./Sales | | | | | 3.1 | |
| 5.4 | 4.4 | 4.3 | | | | | | 4.6 | |
| 3.6 | 2.0 | 1.9 | % Officers', Directors' | | | | | | |
| (17)  6.9 | (18)  4.7 | (12)  5.9 | Owners' Comp/Sales | | | | | | |
| 10.0 | 8.3 | 7.9 | | | | | | | |
| 671457M | 644799M | 602593M | Net Sales ($) | 963M | 5854M | 11749M | 65613M | 146927M | 371487M |
| 443438M | 412006M | 357730M | Total Assets ($) | 639M | 11701M | 4431M | 48300M | 83459M | 209200M |

© RMA 2012

M = $ thousand    MM = $ million
See Pages 9 through 22 for Explanation of Ratios and Data

## Current Data Sorted by Assets | Comparative Historical Data

| | 0-500M | 500M-2MM | 2-10MM | 10-50MM | 50-100MM | 100-250MM | | 4/1/07-3/31/08 ALL | 4/1/08-3/31/09 ALL |
|---|---|---|---|---|---|---|---|---|---|
| **Type of Statement** | | | | | | | | 190 | 117 |
| Unqualified | | | 2 | 11 | 10 | 4 | | 36 | 25 |
| Reviewed | | 6 | 15 | 7 | | | | 33 | 21 |
| Compiled | | 6 | 7 | 2 | | | | 26 | 19 |
| Tax Returns | 4 | 8 | 3 | 1 | | | | 18 | 8 |
| Other | | 7 | 24 | 14 | 1 | | | 77 | 44 |
| | | 29 (4/1-9/30/11) | | 103 (10/1/11-3/31/12) | | | | | |
| **NUMBER OF STATEMENTS** | 4 | 27 | 51 | 35 | 11 | 4 | | 190 | 117 |
| | % | % | % | % | % | % | | % | % |
| **ASSETS** | | | | | | | | | |
| Cash & Equivalents | | 12.4 | 7.2 | 10.6 | 5.7 | | | 7.2 | 7.4 |
| Trade Receivables (net) | | 29.6 | 32.1 | 24.3 | 23.4 | | | 27.7 | 25.5 |
| Inventory | | 29.8 | 30.6 | 34.5 | 30.2 | | | 32.8 | 32.9 |
| All Other Current | | 1.4 | 1.7 | 2.9 | 1.9 | | | 2.2 | 2.0 |
| Total Current | | 73.3 | 71.5 | 72.3 | 61.1 | | | 69.8 | 67.7 |
| Fixed Assets (net) | | 19.8 | 19.8 | 22.9 | 25.8 | | | 21.5 | 24.4 |
| Intangibles (net) | | .4 | 3.7 | 1.7 | 5.6 | | | 3.2 | 3.7 |
| All Other Non-Current | | 6.5 | 5.0 | 3.1 | 7.5 | | | 5.5 | 4.2 |
| Total | | 100.0 | 100.0 | 100.0 | 100.0 | | | 100.0 | 100.0 |
| **LIABILITIES** | | | | | | | | | |
| Notes Payable-Short Term | | 16.8 | 18.0 | 12.4 | 8.0 | | | 13.5 | 15.1 |
| Cur. Mat.-L.T.D. | | 2.0 | 3.8 | 1.8 | 1.9 | | | 3.8 | 2.5 |
| Trade Payables | | 20.0 | 17.4 | 12.9 | 12.6 | | | 18.5 | 15.6 |
| Income Taxes Payable | | .0 | .0 | .2 | .0 | | | .2 | .5 |
| All Other Current | | 9.8 | 10.8 | 8.7 | 8.8 | | | 10.5 | 10.1 |
| Total Current | | 48.5 | 50.0 | 36.0 | 31.3 | | | 46.5 | 43.8 |
| Long-Term Debt | | 13.2 | 9.4 | 12.6 | 24.9 | | | 13.0 | 13.1 |
| Deferred Taxes | | .1 | .1 | .6 | 1.3 | | | .4 | .7 |
| All Other Non-Current | | 13.5 | 6.0 | 2.7 | 4.6 | | | 5.0 | 4.1 |
| Net Worth | | 24.7 | 34.5 | 48.1 | 38.0 | | | 35.1 | 38.3 |
| Total Liabilities & Net Worth | | 100.0 | 100.0 | 100.0 | 100.0 | | | 100.0 | 100.0 |
| **INCOME DATA** | | | | | | | | | |
| Net Sales | | 100.0 | 100.0 | 100.0 | 100.0 | | | 100.0 | 100.0 |
| Gross Profit | | 38.8 | 26.7 | 21.7 | 23.4 | | | 25.6 | 24.5 |
| Operating Expenses | | 32.6 | 22.0 | 16.1 | 15.7 | | | 21.0 | 20.0 |
| Operating Profit | | 6.2 | 4.7 | 5.6 | 7.8 | | | 4.6 | 4.6 |
| All Other Expenses (net) | | -.1 | 1.0 | .5 | .8 | | | 1.0 | .9 |
| Profit Before Taxes | | 6.2 | 3.7 | 5.1 | 6.9 | | | 3.6 | 3.6 |
| **RATIOS** | | | | | | | | | |
| Current | | 2.4 | 2.0 | 3.5 | 3.1 | | | 2.5 | 2.8 |
| | | 1.6 | 1.5 | 1.9 | 1.8 | | | 1.6 | 1.7 |
| | | 1.2 | 1.1 | 1.5 | 1.5 | | | 1.1 | 1.1 |
| Quick | | 1.5 | 1.2 | 1.6 | 1.4 | | | 1.3 | 1.4 |
| | | .9 | .7 | .9 | 1.1 | | | .8 | .7 |
| | | .4 | .4 | .6 | .6 | | | .5 | .4 |
| Sales/Receivables | | 24  15.3 | 33  10.9 | 33  10.9 | 36  10.2 | | | 33  11.1 | 28  12.9 |
| | | 28  13.0 | 46  7.9 | 45  8.1 | 46  8.0 | | | 42  8.8 | 39  9.3 |
| | | 49  7.4 | 68  5.4 | 57  6.4 | 60  6.1 | | | 52  7.0 | 48  7.5 |
| Cost of Sales/Inventory | | 20  18.3 | 38  9.5 | 51  7.2 | 43  8.4 | | | 38  9.5 | 43  8.4 |
| | | 72  5.1 | 66  5.5 | 94  3.9 | 73  5.0 | | | 65  5.6 | 64  5.7 |
| | | 91  4.0 | 107  3.4 | 140  2.6 | 122  3.0 | | | 99  3.7 | 108  3.4 |
| Cost of Sales/Payables | | 22  16.5 | 14  26.2 | 11  32.1 | 26  14.3 | | | 18  20.8 | 17  22.0 |
| | | 35  10.3 | 34  10.7 | 24  15.1 | 31  11.8 | | | 31  11.7 | 28  13.2 |
| | | 66  5.5 | 60  6.1 | 37  9.9 | 39  9.4 | | | 49  7.4 | 43  8.5 |
| Sales/Working Capital | | 5.4 | 5.5 | 3.3 | 4.7 | | | 5.0 | 4.5 |
| | | 12.5 | 9.4 | 5.7 | 6.1 | | | 9.1 | 10.0 |
| | | 22.8 | 49.7 | 9.9 | 12.5 | | | 37.7 | 34.3 |
| EBIT/Interest | | 13.2 | 13.9 | 28.1 | 369.3 | | | 9.1 | 10.6 |
| | | (25) 6.2 | (47) 6.1 | (28) 4.8 | 8.0 | | | (172) 2.4 | (110) 3.3 |
| | | 2.2 | 1.3 | 1.9 | 4.1 | | | .9 | 1.0 |
| Net Profit + Depr., Dep., Amort./Cur. Mat. L/T/D | | | 5.8 | 7.8 | | | | 3.2 | 5.4 |
| | | | (12) 3.9 | (10) 2.0 | | | | (47) 2.1 | (41) 2.6 |
| | | | 2.0 | .5 | | | | .8 | .9 |
| Fixed/Worth | | .2 | .2 | .2 | .4 | | | .2 | .3 |
| | | .6 | .6 | .4 | .6 | | | .6 | .8 |
| | | 1.1 | 2.1 | 1.0 | 1.4 | | | 1.9 | 1.7 |
| Debt/Worth | | .6 | .7 | .5 | .4 | | | .7 | .6 |
| | | 1.6 | 1.8 | 1.1 | 1.6 | | | 1.8 | 1.8 |
| | | 6.8 | 6.1 | 3.1 | 2.1 | | | 7.3 | 6.0 |
| % Profit Before Taxes/Tangible Net Worth | | 73.0 | 38.9 | 32.9 | 34.8 | | | 42.2 | 32.6 |
| | | (23) 22.2 | (43) 20.8 | 23.3 | (10) 20.8 | | | (162) 19.6 | (103) 15.4 |
| | | 6.4 | 3.8 | 7.9 | 10.3 | | | 2.8 | 3.0 |
| % Profit Before Taxes/Total Assets | | 27.5 | 15.5 | 16.3 | 18.1 | | | 15.2 | 13.3 |
| | | 7.2 | 7.5 | 6.3 | 11.4 | | | 4.5 | 5.2 |
| | | 3.6 | 1.2 | 2.2 | 4.1 | | | -.1 | .6 |
| Sales/Net Fixed Assets | | 83.6 | 37.0 | 23.2 | 8.7 | | | 37.7 | 20.2 |
| | | 16.2 | 14.6 | 8.3 | 8.2 | | | 13.0 | 11.2 |
| | | 6.7 | 7.2 | 5.8 | 5.4 | | | 6.2 | 5.3 |
| Sales/Total Assets | | 3.8 | 2.7 | 2.4 | 2.2 | | | 3.0 | 3.1 |
| | | 2.7 | 2.2 | 2.0 | 1.9 | | | 2.2 | 2.3 |
| | | 1.9 | 1.6 | 1.4 | 1.3 | | | 1.7 | 1.6 |
| % Depr., Dep., Amort./Sales | | 1.2 | .8 | .6 | 1.9 | | | .8 | 1.0 |
| | | (19) 1.6 | (45) 1.5 | (32) 1.5 | 2.1 | | | (160) 1.5 | (107) 1.8 |
| | | 2.2 | 2.9 | 3.2 | 3.0 | | | 2.8 | 2.6 |
| % Officers', Directors' Owners' Comp/Sales | | 2.3 | 2.1 | | | | | 2.1 | 2.4 |
| | | (18) 6.1 | (17) 3.2 | | | | | (61) 3.9 | (39) 4.6 |
| | | 10.2 | 6.6 | | | | | 8.0 | 7.8 |
| Net Sales ($) | 4685M | 81124M | 601927M | 1658611M | 1202284M | 882622M | | 7328735M | 4628051M |
| Total Assets ($) | 1218M | 28904M | 262787M | 838029M | 673441M | 510310M | | 3467814M | 2157112M |

© RMA 2012

M = $ thousand    MM = $ million
See Pages 9 through 22 for Explanation of Ratios and Data

## Comparative Historical Data    |    Current Data Sorted by Sales

| Comparative Historical Data | | | | Current Data Sorted by Sales | | | | | |
|---|---|---|---|---|---|---|---|---|---|
| 4/1/09-3/31/10 ALL | 4/1/10-3/31/11 ALL | 4/1/11-3/31/12 ALL | **Type of Statement** | 0-1MM | 1-3MM | 3-5MM | 5-10MM | 10-25MM | 25MM & OVER |
| 24 | 17 | 27 | Unqualified | | 3 | 4 | 7 | 3 | 24 |
| 33 | 35 | 28 | Reviewed | | 3 | 4 | 8 | 8 | 6 |
| 14 | 8 | 15 | Compiled | | 6 | 1 | 4 | 3 | 1 |
| 9 | 12 | 16 | Tax Returns | 1 | 5 | 6 | 2 | 1 | 1 |
| 52 | 54 | 46 | Other | | 3 | 5 | 14 | 1 | 13 |
| | | | | | 29 (4/1-9/30/11) | | 103 (10/1/11-3/31/12) | | |
| **132** | **126** | **132** | **NUMBER OF STATEMENTS** | **1** | **17** | **16** | **27** | **26** | **45** |
| % | % | % | **ASSETS** | % | % | % | % | % | % |
| 8.0 | 8.7 | 9.7 | Cash & Equivalents | | 15.7 | 10.2 | 8.7 | 10.8 | 7.4 |
| 24.5 | 26.4 | 28.6 | Trade Receivables (net) | | 30.7 | 23.4 | 32.4 | 28.6 | 26.5 |
| 31.3 | 30.3 | 31.0 | Inventory | | 27.5 | 31.1 | 30.6 | 30.8 | 32.7 |
| 3.3 | 2.6 | 2.0 | All Other Current | | 1.0 | 1.3 | 2.8 | 2.0 | 1.9 |
| 67.0 | 68.1 | 71.2 | Total Current | | 74.9 | 66.0 | 74.6 | 72.2 | 68.6 |
| 25.4 | 22.9 | 21.4 | Fixed Assets (net) | | 19.9 | 21.5 | 16.4 | 22.9 | 24.5 |
| 3.4 | 2.8 | 2.5 | Intangibles (net) | | .2 | 5.6 | 3.2 | .8 | 2.8 |
| 4.2 | 6.1 | 4.9 | All Other Non-Current | | 4.9 | 6.8 | 5.8 | 4.1 | 4.2 |
| 100.0 | 100.0 | 100.0 | Total | | 100.0 | 100.0 | 100.0 | 100.0 | 100.0 |
| | | | **LIABILITIES** | | | | | | |
| 13.8 | 13.0 | 14.8 | Notes Payable-Short Term | | 20.7 | 12.9 | 16.1 | 12.7 | 14.1 |
| 4.1 | 3.0 | 2.5 | Cur. Mat.-L.T.D. | | 2.3 | 2.8 | 2.1 | 4.5 | 1.8 |
| 15.4 | 16.6 | 16.0 | Trade Payables | | 19.5 | 17.6 | 18.3 | 16.0 | 12.4 |
| .3 | .2 | .1 | Income Taxes Payable | | .0 | .0 | .0 | .0 | .3 |
| 6.7 | 8.7 | 9.5 | All Other Current | | 8.3 | 8.7 | 7.8 | 13.3 | 9.4 |
| 40.3 | 41.5 | 43.0 | Total Current | | 50.7 | 42.0 | 44.3 | 46.5 | 37.9 |
| 13.6 | 12.8 | 13.5 | Long-Term Debt | | 30.2 | 6.3 | 11.8 | 9.9 | 13.0 |
| .4 | .4 | .4 | Deferred Taxes | | .1 | .0 | .1 | .1 | .9 |
| 8.0 | 4.1 | 6.4 | All Other Non-Current | | 17.8 | 8.8 | 6.8 | 1.9 | 3.7 |
| 37.7 | 41.3 | 36.7 | Net Worth | | 1.1 | 42.9 | 37.0 | 41.6 | 44.4 |
| 100.0 | 100.0 | 100.0 | Total Liabilities & Net Worth | | 100.0 | 100.0 | 100.0 | 100.0 | 100.0 |
| | | | **INCOME DATA** | | | | | | |
| 100.0 | 100.0 | 100.0 | Net Sales | | 100.0 | 100.0 | 100.0 | 100.0 | 100.0 |
| 23.8 | 26.0 | 27.9 | Gross Profit | | 36.2 | 43.3 | 26.9 | 25.9 | 20.9 |
| 22.5 | 22.1 | 22.4 | Operating Expenses | | 31.6 | 35.2 | 21.7 | 22.7 | 14.4 |
| 1.3 | 3.9 | 5.4 | Operating Profit | | 4.6 | 8.1 | 5.1 | 3.2 | 6.5 |
| 1.1 | .6 | .6 | All Other Expenses (net) | | .7 | .0 | .6 | .9 | .6 |
| .2 | 3.3 | 4.9 | Profit Before Taxes | | 3.9 | 8.1 | 4.5 | 2.3 | 5.9 |
| | | | **RATIOS** | | | | | | |
| 2.6 / 1.8 / 1.2 | 2.9 / 1.6 / 1.3 | 2.8 / 1.7 / 1.3 | Current | | 2.8 / 2.0 / 1.3 | 2.7 / 1.4 / 1.1 | 2.4 / 1.7 / 1.2 | 3.4 / 1.7 / 1.1 | 2.6 / 1.8 / 1.3 |
| 1.3 / .8 / .5 | 1.3 / .8 / .5 | 1.5 / .9 / .5 | Quick | | 2.0 / 1.0 / .4 | 1.2 / .6 / .4 | 1.5 / .9 / .6 | 2.6 / .8 / .6 | 1.3 / .9 / .6 |
| 32 11.3 / 43 8.6 / 57 6.4 | 34 10.8 / 43 8.5 / 54 6.8 | 31 11.6 / 42 8.6 / 58 6.3 | Sales/Receivables | | 24 15.0 / 42 8.6 / 69 5.3 | 24 15.3 / 30 12.2 / 44 8.3 | 33 11.2 / 49 7.5 / 78 4.7 | 31 11.6 / 47 7.8 / 60 6.1 | 34 10.6 / 44 8.3 / 54 6.7 |
| 43 8.4 / 75 4.9 / 113 3.2 | 35 10.3 / 65 5.6 / 111 3.3 | 39 9.4 / 74 4.9 / 107 3.4 | Cost of Sales/Inventory | | 16 23.4 / 53 6.9 / 107 3.4 | 33 11.1 / 79 4.6 / 146 2.5 | 39 9.4 / 72 5.1 / 118 3.1 | 40 9.2 / 78 4.7 / 107 3.4 | 41 8.8 / 74 4.9 / 114 3.2 |
| 17 21.1 / 30 12.3 / 47 7.8 | 18 19.9 / 31 11.7 / 49 7.4 | 16 23.5 / 31 11.6 / 45 8.1 | Cost of Sales/Payables | | 19 18.8 / 35 10.3 / 76 4.8 | 14 26.7 / 35 10.4 / 74 4.9 | 17 21.1 / 41 8.9 / 60 6.1 | 12 29.5 / 32 11.5 / 49 7.5 | 15 24.2 / 26 14.3 / 36 10.1 |
| 4.0 / 6.7 / 27.5 | 4.4 / 8.6 / 19.6 | 4.7 / 8.1 / 20.2 | Sales/Working Capital | | 5.3 / 9.2 / 19.0 | 5.5 / 15.5 / 76.3 | 4.6 / 7.1 / 17.3 | 4.7 / 7.9 / 28.6 | 4.4 / 6.3 / 12.7 |
| 8.6 / (123) 1.6 / -1.3 | 12.3 / (112) 4.0 / 1.7 | 18.5 / (118) 6.3 / 1.8 | EBIT/Interest | | 10.5 / 4.8 / 1.0 | 10.4 / (14) 5.4 / 3.0 | 33.2 / (23) 7.6 / 1.8 | 14.8 / (22) 2.2 / -.6 | 58.9 / (42) 7.3 / 2.8 |
| 3.6 / (38) 1.5 / .2 | 11.4 / (37) 3.2 / 1.6 | 10.6 / (36) 4.2 / 1.7 | Net Profit + Depr., Dep., Amort./Cur. Mat. L/T/D | | | | | | 12.6 / (21) 4.6 / 2.0 |
| .3 / .6 / 1.4 | .2 / .5 / 1.1 | .2 / .5 / 1.1 | Fixed/Worth | | .4 / .7 / UND | .3 / .6 / .8 | .1 / .5 / 1.3 | .2 / .5 / 1.3 | .3 / .5 / 1.0 |
| .6 / 1.7 / 3.9 | .6 / 1.5 / 4.1 | .5 / 1.6 / 3.5 | Debt/Worth | | 1.3 / 1.9 / UND | .5 / 1.6 / 15.1 | .7 / 1.8 / 6.1 | .4 / 1.5 / 2.7 | .5 / 1.3 / 3.0 |
| 21.9 / (115) 6.1 / -10.9 | 35.5 / (112) 19.4 / 5.4 | 36.6 / (118) 21.7 / 7.1 | % Profit Before Taxes/Tangible Net Worth | | 90.5 / (13) 26.5 / 2.5 | 78.6 / (14) 19.4 / 7.9 | 50.5 / (24) 20.2 / 5.7 | 31.3 / (22) 7.9 / -4.1 | 34.1 / (44) 23.4 / 13.0 |
| 8.5 / 1.5 / -7.2 | 12.7 / 6.5 / 1.2 | 16.1 / 7.8 / 1.7 | % Profit Before Taxes/Total Assets | | 21.4 / 7.4 / -.3 | 13.9 / 6.0 / 4.0 | 16.6 / 10.1 / 1.4 | 14.6 / 3.7 / -2.4 | 17.1 / 9.2 / 4.0 |
| 17.9 / 8.4 / 4.4 | 23.7 / 10.4 / 5.2 | 40.1 / 11.2 / 6.3 | Sales/Net Fixed Assets | | 83.5 / 16.2 / 6.7 | 89.7 / 10.7 / 5.3 | 46.9 / 16.1 / 8.7 | 21.3 / 13.7 / 4.5 | 15.6 / 8.5 / 6.1 |
| 2.4 / 1.8 / 1.4 | 2.8 / 2.0 / 1.5 | 2.7 / 2.1 / 1.6 | Sales/Total Assets | | 3.2 / 2.4 / 1.7 | 3.8 / 2.5 / 1.6 | 3.0 / 2.3 / 1.5 | 2.6 / 2.2 / 1.7 | 2.5 / 2.0 / 1.5 |
| 1.5 / (113) 2.4 / 4.0 | 1.1 / (112) 2.0 / 2.9 | .9 / (113) 1.6 / 2.9 | % Depr., Dep., Amort./Sales | | 1.5 / (12) 2.0 / 2.5 | 1.3 / (12) 2.0 / 3.9 | .6 / (23) 1.2 / 3.1 | 1.0 / (24) 1.9 / 3.1 | .8 / (42) 1.7 / 2.6 |
| 2.0 / (42) 3.0 / 7.9 | 2.8 / (43) 5.3 / 8.3 | 2.2 / (48) 3.6 / 7.3 | % Officers', Directors' Owners' Comp/Sales | | 2.0 / (11) 3.0 / 10.6 | 3.2 / (11) 6.5 / 11.1 | 1.4 / (10) 3.0 / 6.6 | | |
| 4196284M | 8333343M | 4431253M | Net Sales ($) | 520M | 32167M | 62612M | 203905M | 411931M | 3720118M |
| 2581220M | 2088308M | 2314689M | Total Assets ($) | 89M | 14618M | 31072M | 131504M | 202935M | 1934471M |

M = $ thousand    MM = $ million
See Pages 9 through 22 for Explanation of Ratios and Data

## Current Data Sorted by Assets      Comparative Historical Data

| | | | | | | Type of Statement | | |
|---|---|---|---|---|---|---|---|---|
| | | 10 | 18 | 4 | 1 | Unqualified | 41 | 30 |
| 1 | 17 | 91 | 36 | | 1 | Reviewed | 131 | 117 |
| 12 | 68 | 75 | 8 | 1 | | Compiled | 180 | 149 |
| 60 | 114 | 63 | 3 | | 2 | Tax Returns | 169 | 160 |
| 44 | 92 | 122 | 54 | 3 | 5 | Other | 259 | 200 |
| | 159 (4/1-9/30/11) | | 746 (10/1/11-3/31/12) | | | | 4/1/07-3/31/08 | 4/1/08-3/31/09 |
| 0-500M | 500M-2MM | 2-10MM | 10-50MM | 50-100MM | 100-250MM | | ALL | ALL |
| 117 | 291 | 361 | 119 | 8 | 9 | NUMBER OF STATEMENTS | 780 | 656 |
| % | % | % | % | % | % | ASSETS | % | % |
| 15.5 | 12.6 | 10.5 | 8.0 | | | Cash & Equivalents | 9.8 | 9.8 |
| 27.2 | 28.4 | 25.4 | 21.5 | | | Trade Receivables (net) | 24.6 | 23.2 |
| 8.2 | 13.8 | 21.1 | 27.0 | | | Inventory | 18.1 | 17.4 |
| 3.3 | 1.3 | 1.6 | 3.2 | | | All Other Current | 1.8 | 1.9 |
| 54.2 | 56.2 | 58.7 | 59.7 | | | Total Current | 54.4 | 52.3 |
| 33.4 | 34.4 | 33.7 | 32.2 | | | Fixed Assets (net) | 37.2 | 39.2 |
| 4.2 | 4.0 | 2.6 | 4.8 | | | Intangibles (net) | 3.0 | 3.2 |
| 8.2 | 5.5 | 5.0 | 3.3 | | | All Other Non-Current | 5.4 | 5.3 |
| 100.0 | 100.0 | 100.0 | 100.0 | | | Total | 100.0 | 100.0 |
| | | | | | | LIABILITIES | | |
| 25.3 | 9.5 | 7.6 | 9.2 | | | Notes Payable-Short Term | 8.1 | 9.8 |
| 6.2 | 5.6 | 4.8 | 5.5 | | | Cur. Mat.-L.T.D. | 6.3 | 6.4 |
| 12.4 | 11.8 | 11.4 | 11.0 | | | Trade Payables | 11.2 | 10.3 |
| .0 | .2 | .2 | .2 | | | Income Taxes Payable | .3 | .2 |
| 12.1 | 6.1 | 6.8 | 8.6 | | | All Other Current | 7.6 | 6.6 |
| 56.0 | 33.2 | 30.9 | 34.5 | | | Total Current | 33.4 | 33.3 |
| 42.1 | 27.8 | 19.0 | 15.9 | | | Long-Term Debt | 26.2 | 26.8 |
| .0 | .3 | .6 | .9 | | | Deferred Taxes | .4 | .5 |
| 12.4 | 7.0 | 4.5 | 6.8 | | | All Other Non-Current | 5.5 | 5.5 |
| -10.5 | 31.7 | 45.0 | 41.9 | | | Net Worth | 34.4 | 33.9 |
| 100.0 | 100.0 | 100.0 | 100.0 | | | Total Liabilities & Net Worth | 100.0 | 100.0 |
| | | | | | | INCOME DATA | | |
| 100.0 | 100.0 | 100.0 | 100.0 | | | Net Sales | 100.0 | 100.0 |
| 52.0 | 40.6 | 33.3 | 24.4 | | | Gross Profit | 35.7 | 35.1 |
| 42.9 | 33.5 | 25.8 | 15.8 | | | Operating Expenses | 28.2 | 28.9 |
| 9.1 | 7.1 | 7.4 | 8.6 | | | Operating Profit | 7.6 | 6.2 |
| 1.6 | .9 | .6 | 1.1 | | | All Other Expenses (net) | 1.5 | 1.2 |
| 7.5 | 6.2 | 6.8 | 7.5 | | | Profit Before Taxes | 6.0 | 5.0 |
| | | | | | | RATIOS | | |
| 2.2 | 3.3 | 3.7 | 3.0 | | | | 2.9 | 3.2 |
| 1.2 | 1.7 | 1.9 | 1.8 | | | Current | 1.7 | 1.7 |
| .6 | 1.1 | 1.3 | 1.3 | | | | 1.1 | 1.1 |
| 2.0 | 2.6 | 2.4 | 1.6 | | | | 2.0 | 2.2 |
| .9 | 1.2 | 1.1 | .8 | | | Quick | 1.0 | 1.0 |
| .4 | .7 | .7 | .5 | | | | .6 | .5 |
| 4   93.6 | 29   12.4 | 34   10.7 | 38   9.7 | | | | 30   12.0 | 27   13.5 |
| 29   12.7 | 42   8.7 | 47   7.8 | 47   7.7 | | | Sales/Receivables | 43   8.4 | 40   9.1 |
| 45   8.1 | 54   6.7 | 61   6.0 | 61   6.0 | | | | 56   6.5 | 53   6.8 |
| 0   UND | 1   689.0 | 24   15.2 | 46   7.9 | | | | 14   26.3 | 10   38.1 |
| 0   UND | 18   19.9 | 51   7.2 | 70   5.2 | | | Cost of Sales/Inventory | 40   9.1 | 36   10.0 |
| 23   16.1 | 50   7.3 | 94   3.9 | 114   3.2 | | | | 77   4.7 | 70   5.2 |
| 0   UND | 12   29.9 | 16   22.5 | 21   17.5 | | | | 14   25.9 | 11   32.1 |
| 14   27.0 | 25   14.7 | 26   14.2 | 31   11.8 | | | Cost of Sales/Payables | 26   14.2 | 23   16.1 |
| 36   10.0 | 43   8.5 | 43   8.5 | 45   8.1 | | | | 41   8.9 | 39   9.3 |
| 13.1 | 6.0 | 4.1 | 3.7 | | | | 5.4 | 5.5 |
| 92.4 | 11.1 | 7.9 | 6.7 | | | Sales/Working Capital | 10.0 | 11.4 |
| -19.9 | 78.8 | 18.3 | 13.7 | | | | 45.6 | 87.1 |
| 18.5 | 14.8 | 18.5 | 19.2 | | | | 9.6 | 9.8 |
| (101)   5.0 | (259)   5.1 | (328)   6.1 | (112)   7.6 | | | EBIT/Interest | (710)   4.2 | (595)   4.1 |
| 1.5 | 1.7 | 1.9 | 2.7 | | | | 1.6 | 1.3 |
| | 3.2 | 5.0 | 3.9 | | | Net Profit + Depr., Dep., | 5.1 | 4.1 |
| | (23)   1.8 | (74)   2.4 | (37)   2.3 | | | Amort./Cur. Mat. L/T/D | (174)   2.5 | (114)   2.1 |
| | 1.2 | 1.3 | 1.6 | | | | 1.4 | 1.1 |
| .4 | .5 | .3 | .5 | | | | .5 | .5 |
| 2.2 | 1.1 | .8 | .8 | | | Fixed/Worth | 1.1 | 1.1 |
| -.6 | 10.6 | 1.7 | 1.4 | | | | 2.8 | 2.8 |
| 1.1 | .7 | .5 | .8 | | | | .8 | .7 |
| 10.8 | 2.1 | 1.2 | 1.4 | | | Debt/Worth | 2.0 | 1.7 |
| -2.8 | 20.3 | 3.1 | 2.9 | | | | 5.0 | 5.8 |
| 119.9 | 71.1 | 46.9 | 38.1 | | | % Profit Before Taxes/Tangible | 57.3 | 55.8 |
| (61)   54.2 | (228)   36.0 | (333)   24.1 | (108)   20.7 | | | Net Worth | (676)   28.6 | (558)   26.7 |
| 20.4 | 12.4 | 7.9 | 13.0 | | | | 8.6 | 6.0 |
| 43.1 | 24.4 | 19.5 | 16.3 | | | % Profit Before Taxes/Total | 21.0 | 19.8 |
| 19.9 | 11.0 | 10.0 | 8.0 | | | Assets | 9.7 | 9.2 |
| 5.1 | 2.6 | 2.4 | 4.0 | | | | 2.1 | 1.1 |
| 38.5 | 21.9 | 12.3 | 7.5 | | | | 11.4 | 12.0 |
| 17.5 | 7.8 | 6.0 | 4.8 | | | Sales/Net Fixed Assets | 5.8 | 5.6 |
| 7.9 | 4.5 | 3.5 | 3.2 | | | | 3.5 | 3.2 |
| 7.5 | 3.1 | 2.4 | 1.9 | | | | 2.7 | 2.8 |
| 3.9 | 2.5 | 1.9 | 1.5 | | | Sales/Total Assets | 2.0 | 2.0 |
| 2.2 | 1.8 | 1.4 | 1.2 | | | | 1.5 | 1.5 |
| 1.2 | 1.6 | 2.0 | 2.3 | | | | 2.1 | 2.0 |
| (58)   2.5 | (212)   3.6 | (309)   3.4 | (111)   3.9 | | | % Depr., Dep., Amort./Sales | (695)   3.8 | (562)   3.7 |
| 4.4 | 6.4 | 5.7 | 5.8 | | | | 6.3 | 6.2 |
| 4.0 | 2.7 | 2.4 | 1.1 | | | % Officers', Directors' | 2.8 | 2.5 |
| (70)   7.4 | (187)   4.9 | (197)   3.8 | (23)   2.2 | | | Owners' Comp/Sales | (434)   4.8 | (359)   4.8 |
| 11.9 | 7.7 | 6.5 | 5.7 | | | | 8.8 | 7.8 |
| 152115M | 874036M | 3051395M | 4038761M | 820116M | 2294727M | Net Sales ($) | 9680374M | 7702159M |
| 32333M | 339011M | 1602013M | 2464061M | 549399M | 1235408M | Total Assets ($) | 4901691M | 4387194M |

M = $ thousand     MM = $ million
See Pages 9 through 22 for Explanation of Ratios and Data

## Comparative Historical Data      Current Data Sorted by Sales

| Hist 1 | Hist 2 | Hist 3 | Type of Statement | 0-1MM | 1-3MM | 3-5MM | 5-10MM | 10-25MM | 25MM & OVER |
|---|---|---|---|---|---|---|---|---|---|
| 38 | 32 | 33 | Unqualified | 1 | 8 | 2 | 3 | 13 | 15 |
| 141 | 156 | 146 | Reviewed | 11 | 38 | 18 | 45 | 58 | 16 |
| 155 | 175 | 164 | Compiled | 28 | 88 | 45 | 43 | 23 | 4 |
| 170 | 220 | 242 | Tax Returns | 33 | 79 | 58 | 48 | 17 | 3 |
| 245 | 301 | 320 | Other | | | 51 | 68 | 46 | 43 |
| 4/1/09-3/31/10 ALL | 4/1/10-3/31/11 ALL | 4/1/11-3/31/12 ALL | | 159 (4/1-9/30/11) | | | 746 (10/1/11-3/31/12) | | |
| 749 | 884 | 905 | **NUMBER OF STATEMENTS** | 73 | 213 | 174 | 207 | 157 | 81 |
| % | % | % | **ASSETS** | % | % | % | % | % | % |
| 10.3 | 10.5 | 11.4 | Cash & Equivalents | 14.7 | 12.4 | 11.9 | 11.2 | 11.0 | 6.2 |
| 21.9 | 25.6 | 26.0 | Trade Receivables (net) | 25.1 | 26.3 | 25.9 | 26.4 | 25.9 | 25.7 |
| 18.3 | 17.8 | 17.9 | Inventory | 7.8 | 12.5 | 16.8 | 20.5 | 22.9 | 27.3 |
| 2.1 | 1.8 | 2.0 | All Other Current | 3.4 | 1.6 | 1.5 | 1.8 | 2.6 | 1.6 |
| 52.6 | 55.7 | 57.3 | Total Current | 51.1 | 52.9 | 56.1 | 59.9 | 62.3 | 60.9 |
| 38.0 | 35.2 | 33.6 | Fixed Assets (net) | 35.1 | 35.5 | 34.1 | 34.2 | 30.9 | 29.8 |
| 3.5 | 3.6 | 3.8 | Intangibles (net) | 6.0 | 5.2 | 3.4 | 1.6 | 2.7 | 6.2 |
| 5.9 | 5.5 | 5.3 | All Other Non-Current | 7.9 | 6.4 | 6.3 | 4.3 | 4.1 | 3.1 |
| 100.0 | 100.0 | 100.0 | Total | 100.0 | 100.0 | 100.0 | 100.0 | 100.0 | 100.0 |
| | | | **LIABILITIES** | | | | | | |
| 10.0 | 9.1 | 10.7 | Notes Payable-Short Term | 27.4 | 12.3 | 8.1 | 8.5 | 7.3 | 8.8 |
| 6.3 | 6.8 | 5.3 | Cur. Mat.-L.T.D. | 5.1 | 5.9 | 5.9 | 4.7 | 5.1 | 4.9 |
| 10.1 | 10.8 | 11.6 | Trade Payables | 12.5 | 10.4 | 11.4 | 11.4 | 12.3 | 13.4 |
| .2 | .1 | .2 | Income Taxes Payable | .1 | .1 | .1 | .3 | .2 | .1 |
| 7.7 | 6.5 | 7.5 | All Other Current | 16.0 | 5.4 | 6.0 | 7.1 | 8.3 | 8.2 |
| 34.2 | 33.3 | 35.3 | Total Current | 61.1 | 34.1 | 31.5 | 32.1 | 33.2 | 35.4 |
| 26.0 | 24.4 | 24.5 | Long-Term Debt | 35.2 | 34.8 | 25.7 | 19.4 | 14.6 | 17.6 |
| .6 | .6 | .5 | Deferred Taxes | .0 | .2 | .6 | .6 | .8 | .7 |
| 7.0 | 5.8 | 6.6 | All Other Non-Current | 12.2 | 8.9 | 5.7 | 4.8 | 4.3 | 6.5 |
| 32.3 | 35.9 | 33.1 | Net Worth | -8.5 | 22.0 | 36.5 | 43.2 | 47.2 | 39.8 |
| 100.0 | 100.0 | 100.0 | Total Liabilities & Net Worth | 100.0 | 100.0 | 100.0 | 100.0 | 100.0 | 100.0 |
| | | | **INCOME DATA** | | | | | | |
| 100.0 | 100.0 | 100.0 | Net Sales | 100.0 | 100.0 | 100.0 | 100.0 | 100.0 | 100.0 |
| 34.7 | 36.7 | 36.8 | Gross Profit | 55.0 | 43.7 | 38.1 | 33.5 | 29.4 | 22.0 |
| 31.6 | 29.9 | 29.0 | Operating Expenses | 44.6 | 36.8 | 31.0 | 25.5 | 21.4 | 14.4 |
| 3.0 | 6.8 | 7.7 | Operating Profit | 10.4 | 6.9 | 7.0 | 8.0 | 8.0 | 7.7 |
| 1.5 | 1.3 | .9 | All Other Expenses (net) | 2.1 | 1.2 | .8 | .6 | .6 | 1.1 |
| 1.5 | 5.6 | 6.8 | Profit Before Taxes | 8.2 | 5.7 | 6.2 | 7.4 | 7.4 | 6.6 |
| | | | **RATIOS** | | | | | | |
| 3.2 | 3.3 | 3.3 | | 2.2 | 3.1 | 3.2 | 3.7 | 3.6 | 2.8 |
| 1.6 | 1.7 | 1.7 | Current | 1.2 | 1.5 | 1.7 | 1.9 | 1.9 | 1.9 |
| 1.0 | 1.1 | 1.1 | | .5 | .9 | 1.2 | 1.3 | 1.3 | 1.3 |
| 2.1 | 2.2 | 2.2 | | 1.9 | 2.3 | 2.3 | 2.5 | 2.4 | 1.4 |
| 1.0 | 1.1 | 1.1 | Quick | .7 | 1.0 | 1.2 | 1.1 | 1.0 | .9 |
| .5 | .6 | .6 | | .4 | .6 | .7 | .7 | .6 | .6 |
| 29   12.6 | 33   11.2 | 31   11.9 | | 22   16.3 | 27   13.5 | 27   13.7 | 35   10.5 | 34   10.8 | 39   9.3 |
| 43   8.5 | 47   7.8 | 43   8.4 | Sales/Receivables | 36   10.1 | 40   9.2 | 41   8.8 | 47   7.8 | 46   8.0 | 49   7.4 |
| 58   6.2 | 61   6.0 | 57   6.4 | | 54   6.7 | 54   6.7 | 53   6.9 | 59   6.2 | 61   6.0 | 61   6.0 |
| 14   25.5 | 13   28.1 | 8   44.7 | | 0   UND | 0   UND | 4   91.6 | 23   15.7 | 27   13.5 | 46   7.9 |
| 45   8.0 | 43   8.4 | 38   9.6 | Cost of Sales/Inventory | 5   73.0 | 14   25.8 | 24   15.4 | 43   8.4 | 60   6.1 | 62   5.9 |
| 91   4.0 | 84   4.3 | 79   4.6 | | 35   10.3 | 55   6.6 | 70   5.2 | 87   4.2 | 99   3.7 | 89   4.1 |
| 13   28.7 | 13   27.5 | 13   27.1 | | 5   76.1 | 8   43.4 | 13   28.2 | 15   24.5 | 18   19.9 | 22   16.7 |
| 23   15.9 | 27   13.6 | 25   14.5 | Cost of Sales/Payables | 26   14.1 | 23   15.8 | 24   15.1 | 25   14.6 | 26   13.8 | 31   11.8 |
| 42   8.8 | 41   9.0 | 43   8.5 | | 64   5.7 | 46   8.0 | 42   8.7 | 43   8.5 | 39   9.4 | 42   8.7 |
| 4.5 | 4.7 | 4.9 | | 6.1 | 5.6 | 6.0 | 4.4 | 4.0 | 4.8 |
| 9.6 | 9.1 | 9.9 | Sales/Working Capital | 201.0 | 14.8 | 10.9 | 8.0 | 8.0 | 8.0 |
| 160.3 | 42.3 | 46.2 | | -8.5 | -136.6 | 31.7 | 17.5 | 15.6 | 13.3 |
| 6.6 | 12.5 | 17.7 | | 13.2 | 10.3 | 20.2 | 17.6 | 24.0 | 21.7 |
| (686) 2.0 | (802) 4.2 | (817) 6.0 | EBIT/Interest | (62) 3.3 | (190) 3.8 | (159) 7.6 | (182) 6.1 | (146) 6.7 | (78) 8.7 |
| -.7 | 1.5 | 1.9 | | .7 | 1.1 | 2.0 | 2.5 | 2.4 | 3.4 |
| 3.3 | 4.5 | 4.3 | | | | 3.8 | 5.1 | 3.4 | 6.7 |
| (151) 1.6 | (151) 2.0 | (146) 2.3 | Net Profit + Depr., Dep., Amort./Cur. Mat. L/T/D | | | (28) 1.8 | (40) 2.7 | (41) 2.0 | (26) 2.6 |
| .4 | 1.2 | 1.3 | | | | 1.1 | 1.8 | .9 | 1.8 |
| .5 | .4 | .4 | | .3 | .5 | .5 | .4 | .3 | .4 |
| 1.1 | 1.0 | .9 | Fixed/Worth | 3.6 | 1.3 | 1.0 | .8 | .7 | .8 |
| 3.5 | 2.6 | 2.9 | | -.8 | -16.8 | 3.9 | 1.8 | 1.4 | 1.4 |
| .7 | .6 | .6 | | 1.0 | .8 | .6 | .5 | .5 | .8 |
| 1.9 | 1.6 | 1.6 | Debt/Worth | -14.8 | 3.1 | 1.6 | 1.2 | 1.2 | 1.4 |
| 7.4 | 5.4 | 6.5 | | -2.9 | -21.0 | 7.6 | 3.7 | 2.7 | 2.9 |
| 35.5 | 47.4 | 54.2 | | 82.5 | 67.8 | 72.7 | 51.0 | 42.2 | 39.0 |
| (618) 8.9 | (750) 20.6 | (744) 27.2 | % Profit Before Taxes/Tangible Net Worth | (35) 35.3 | (153) 32.2 | (147) 30.1 | (190) 30.2 | (148) 22.3 | (71) 25.6 |
| -7.0 | 5.8 | 11.7 | | 17.8 | 8.4 | 11.6 | 11.3 | 9.9 | 13.9 |
| 12.4 | 18.3 | 21.5 | | 32.8 | 24.2 | 23.4 | 22.4 | 17.7 | 17.6 |
| 3.0 | 7.5 | 10.4 | % Profit Before Taxes/Total Assets | 16.7 | 9.5 | 11.1 | 10.5 | 9.5 | 9.5 |
| -4.6 | 1.3 | 3.0 | | .1 | .9 | 3.1 | 3.0 | 3.7 | 5.4 |
| 10.4 | 12.7 | 16.2 | | 30.0 | 19.9 | 16.8 | 14.5 | 13.1 | 8.7 |
| 4.9 | 6.1 | 6.8 | Sales/Net Fixed Assets | 11.0 | 7.7 | 6.9 | 6.7 | 6.3 | 5.9 |
| 2.8 | 3.3 | 3.8 | | 3.2 | 3.5 | 4.5 | 3.6 | 3.6 | 3.9 |
| 2.4 | 2.6 | 2.9 | | 3.6 | 3.3 | 3.2 | 2.7 | 2.6 | 2.2 |
| 1.7 | 1.9 | 2.1 | Sales/Total Assets | 2.0 | 2.3 | 2.3 | 2.1 | 1.9 | 1.8 |
| 1.2 | 1.4 | 1.5 | | 1.3 | 1.6 | 1.7 | 1.5 | 1.4 | 1.4 |
| 2.3 | 2.2 | 1.9 | | 1.5 | 2.2 | 1.6 | 1.9 | 1.9 | 2.0 |
| (682) 4.5 | (756) 4.0 | (705) 3.5 | % Depr., Dep., Amort./Sales | (37) 3.8 | (150) 3.7 | (131) 3.6 | (174) 3.3 | (140) 3.3 | (73) 3.2 |
| 7.6 | 6.4 | 5.8 | | 8.3 | 7.8 | 5.7 | 5.8 | 5.3 | 5.1 |
| 2.7 | 2.8 | 2.5 | | 3.4 | 4.0 | 2.6 | 2.2 | 1.7 | .3 |
| (405) 5.4 | (463) 5.1 | (480) 4.6 | % Officers', Directors' Owners' Comp/Sales | (26) 8.4 | (138) 5.8 | (114) 4.5 | (128) 3.6 | (60) 3.4 | (14) 1.7 |
| 9.2 | 9.4 | 7.9 | | 14.3 | 8.9 | 7.3 | 6.3 | 5.9 | 5.4 |
| 8498431M | 10198177M | 11231150M | Net Sales ($) | 43589M | 406126M | 686186M | 1468197M | 2379533M | 6247519M |
| 5087063M | 6166129M | 6222225M | Total Assets ($) | 23361M | 205511M | 341827M | 814643M | 1410990M | 3425893M |

M = $ thousand    MM = $ million
See Pages 9 through 22 for Explanation of Ratios and Data

## Current Data Sorted by Assets     Comparative Historical Data

| 0-500M | 500M-2MM | 2-10MM | 10-50MM | 50-100MM | 100-250MM | Type of Statement | 4/1/07-3/31/08 ALL | 4/1/08-3/31/09 ALL |
|---|---|---|---|---|---|---|---|---|
| | | 1 | 3 | 6 | | Unqualified | 16 | 13 |
| | 5 | 39 | 14 | | | Reviewed | 60 | 56 |
| 2 | 13 | 21 | 1 | | | Compiled | 36 | 37 |
| 5 | 11 | 9 | | | | Tax Returns | 18 | 16 |
| 2 | 13 | 26 | 22 | 5 | 1 | Other | 55 | 55 |
| | 46 (4/1-9/30/11) | | 153 (10/1/11-3/31/12) | | | | | |
| 9 | 43 | 98 | 43 | 5 | 1 | **NUMBER OF STATEMENTS** | 185 | 177 |
| % | % | % | % | % | % | **ASSETS** | % | % |
| | 10.8 | 7.1 | 5.8 | | | Cash & Equivalents | 7.5 | 6.4 |
| | 27.3 | 25.7 | 21.6 | | | Trade Receivables (net) | 22.8 | 21.5 |
| | 24.5 | 25.1 | 26.0 | | | Inventory | 23.1 | 24.6 |
| | 1.6 | .9 | 4.5 | | | All Other Current | 1.4 | 1.3 |
| | 64.3 | 58.8 | 57.9 | | | Total Current | 54.8 | 53.9 |
| | 26.7 | 32.2 | 34.5 | | | Fixed Assets (net) | 36.9 | 36.6 |
| | 4.7 | 3.6 | 1.5 | | | Intangibles (net) | 2.8 | 4.6 |
| | 4.4 | 5.4 | 6.0 | | | All Other Non-Current | 5.6 | 4.9 |
| | 100.0 | 100.0 | 100.0 | | | Total | 100.0 | 100.0 |
| | | | | | | **LIABILITIES** | | |
| | 6.5 | 7.9 | 12.2 | | | Notes Payable-Short Term | 9.0 | 12.8 |
| | 6.2 | 4.9 | 4.7 | | | Cur. Mat.-L.T.D. | 6.2 | 6.7 |
| | 12.7 | 12.8 | 13.9 | | | Trade Payables | 12.3 | 11.6 |
| | .1 | .3 | .1 | | | Income Taxes Payable | .1 | .2 |
| | 7.0 | 6.3 | 7.2 | | | All Other Current | 6.3 | 5.5 |
| | 32.5 | 32.1 | 38.1 | | | Total Current | 33.9 | 36.7 |
| | 22.2 | 18.5 | 16.4 | | | Long-Term Debt | 23.3 | 25.0 |
| | 1.0 | .6 | 1.1 | | | Deferred Taxes | 1.0 | .7 |
| | 4.8 | 6.0 | 7.3 | | | All Other Non-Current | 4.7 | 5.0 |
| | 39.6 | 42.7 | 37.1 | | | Net Worth | 37.1 | 32.6 |
| | 100.0 | 100.0 | 100.0 | | | Total Liabilities & Net Worth | 100.0 | 100.0 |
| | | | | | | **INCOME DATA** | | |
| | 100.0 | 100.0 | 100.0 | | | Net Sales | 100.0 | 100.0 |
| | 38.8 | 26.9 | 25.0 | | | Gross Profit | 28.3 | 26.4 |
| | 31.6 | 21.1 | 18.6 | | | Operating Expenses | 23.3 | 22.8 |
| | 7.2 | 5.7 | 6.3 | | | Operating Profit | 5.0 | 3.6 |
| | .1 | .4 | 1.4 | | | All Other Expenses (net) | 1.4 | 1.4 |
| | 7.1 | 5.3 | 5.0 | | | Profit Before Taxes | 3.6 | 2.2 |
| | | | | | | **RATIOS** | | |
| | 3.9 | 2.9 | 2.4 | | | | 2.5 | 2.5 |
| | 1.8 | 1.8 | 1.5 | | | Current | 1.6 | 1.6 |
| | 1.4 | 1.3 | 1.1 | | | | 1.1 | 1.1 |
| | 2.9 | 1.5 | 1.1 | | | | 1.6 | 1.5 |
| | 1.0 | .9 | .7 | | | Quick | .9 | .8 |
| | .6 | .7 | .4 | | | | .5 | .5 |
| 30 | 12.3 | 38   9.7 | 36   10.0 | | | | 33   11.0 | 29   12.4 |
| 49 | 7.5 | 51   7.1 | 46   7.9 | | | Sales/Receivables | 44   8.4 | 40   9.1 |
| 61 | 6.0 | 59   6.2 | 54   6.8 | | | | 53   6.9 | 52   7.1 |
| 16 | 22.3 | 37   9.9 | 46   8.0 | | | | 31   11.9 | 33   11.2 |
| 63 | 5.8 | 58   6.3 | 69   5.3 | | | Cost of Sales/Inventory | 54   6.7 | 59   6.2 |
| 114 | 3.2 | 101   3.6 | 104   3.5 | | | | 93   3.9 | 90   4.0 |
| 19 | 19.5 | 19   19.2 | 28   13.1 | | | | 16   23.0 | 14   26.5 |
| 30 | 12.0 | 29   12.8 | 37   9.9 | | | Cost of Sales/Payables | 27   13.6 | 25   14.5 |
| 45 | 8.1 | 47   7.8 | 51   7.2 | | | | 40   9.2 | 39   9.3 |
| | 4.0 | 4.6 | 4.5 | | | | 5.5 | 5.7 |
| | 7.7 | 7.7 | 10.7 | | | Sales/Working Capital | 10.0 | 9.5 |
| | 19.3 | 16.8 | 38.9 | | | | 36.3 | 52.2 |
| | 18.8 | 16.8 | 12.4 | | | | 6.1 | 5.6 |
| | (39) 4.9 | (94) 5.3 | (40) 4.5 | | | EBIT/Interest | (171) 2.6 | (167) 2.2 |
| | 2.7 | 2.1 | 1.4 | | | | 1.0 | .4 |
| | 6.1 | 3.5 | 6.6 | | | Net Profit + Depr., Dep., | 4.0 | 4.2 |
| | (10) 1.9 | (26) 1.9 | (11) 4.8 | | | Amort./Cur. Mat. L/T/D | (63) 2.3 | (51) 1.9 |
| | .8 | 1.1 | 2.1 | | | | 1.4 | 1.3 |
| | .3 | .4 | .5 | | | | .6 | .6 |
| | .8 | .8 | 1.0 | | | Fixed/Worth | 1.0 | 1.2 |
| | 1.9 | 1.6 | 2.0 | | | | 2.2 | 2.9 |
| | .8 | .7 | .8 | | | | .8 | .8 |
| | 1.7 | 1.3 | 1.7 | | | Debt/Worth | 1.7 | 1.8 |
| | 4.8 | 2.9 | 3.5 | | | | 4.5 | 6.0 |
| | 82.7 | 38.2 | 36.9 | | | % Profit Before Taxes/Tangible | 35.5 | 32.7 |
| | (37) 31.2 | (91) 17.5 | (39) 20.7 | | | Net Worth | (161) 14.6 | (147) 11.1 |
| | 8.7 | 5.3 | 10.5 | | | | .9 | -2.6 |
| | 25.1 | 14.7 | 11.8 | | | % Profit Before Taxes/Total | 14.6 | 11.8 |
| | 13.8 | 6.6 | 8.4 | | | Assets | 6.1 | 3.4 |
| | 4.2 | 2.2 | 1.7 | | | | .0 | -2.5 |
| | 24.7 | 13.9 | 7.9 | | | | 10.7 | 10.3 |
| | 10.6 | 6.4 | 5.2 | | | Sales/Net Fixed Assets | 5.6 | 5.3 |
| | 5.9 | 3.6 | 2.8 | | | | 3.2 | 3.2 |
| | 2.9 | 2.5 | 1.9 | | | | 2.6 | 2.7 |
| | 2.3 | 1.9 | 1.6 | | | Sales/Total Assets | 1.9 | 1.9 |
| | 1.6 | 1.4 | 1.4 | | | | 1.3 | 1.4 |
| | 1.5 | 2.1 | 2.4 | | | | 1.7 | 2.1 |
| | (33) 2.6 | (92) 3.6 | (41) 3.8 | | | % Depr., Dep., Amort./Sales | (174) 3.8 | (165) 4.0 |
| | 5.3 | 5.6 | 5.9 | | | | 6.4 | 6.4 |
| | 3.4 | 1.6 | 1.2 | | | | 2.1 | 2.3 |
| | (28) 6.7 | (42) 3.1 | (11) 2.5 | | | % Officers', Directors' Owners' Comp/Sales | (91) 3.9 | (83) 3.7 |
| | 9.9 | 4.9 | 6.2 | | | | 7.0 | 6.3 |
| 14910M | 130583M | 908275M | 1462437M | 265052M | 88041M | Net Sales ($) | 2565289M | 2435181M |
| 2831M | 56739M | 475942M | 869765M | 338052M | 129723M | Total Assets ($) | 1510989M | 1536238M |

M = $ thousand    MM = $ million
See Pages 9 through 22 for Explanation of Ratios and Data

## Comparative Historical Data      Current Data Sorted by Sales

| | | | Type of Statement | 0-1MM | 1-3MM | 3-5MM | 5-10MM | 10-25MM | 25MM & OVER |
|---|---|---|---|---|---|---|---|---|---|
| 14 | 13 | 10 | Unqualified | | | | 1 | 5 | 4 |
| 56 | 59 | 58 | Reviewed | | 4 | 7 | 18 | 20 | 9 |
| 35 | 45 | 37 | Compiled | 3 | 8 | 5 | 14 | 6 | 1 |
| 21 | 20 | 25 | Tax Returns | 1 | 10 | 3 | 10 | 1 | |
| 48 | 64 | 69 | Other | 2 | 10 | 8 | 11 | 18 | 20 |
| 4/1/09-3/31/10 | 4/1/10-3/31/11 | 4/1/11-3/31/12 | | | 46 (4/1-9/30/11) | | | 153 (10/1/11-3/31/12) | |
| ALL | ALL | ALL | | | | | | | |
| 174 | 201 | 199 | **NUMBER OF STATEMENTS** | 6 | 32 | 23 | 54 | 50 | 34 |
| % | % | % | **ASSETS** | % | % | % | % | % | % |
| 7.7 | 7.6 | 8.2 | Cash & Equivalents | | 15.1 | 6.4 | 7.2 | 9.1 | 3.1 |
| 20.5 | 25.2 | 24.4 | Trade Receivables (net) | | 25.9 | 20.7 | 26.1 | 27.3 | 20.3 |
| 24.1 | 25.0 | 24.2 | Inventory | | 20.2 | 23.3 | 24.8 | 26.1 | 25.1 |
| 1.8 | 1.0 | 1.9 | All Other Current | | .5 | 2.7 | .8 | 2.0 | 4.7 |
| 54.2 | 58.7 | 58.7 | Total Current | | 61.7 | 52.9 | 59.0 | 64.5 | 53.4 |
| 37.1 | 32.5 | 31.4 | Fixed Assets (net) | | 27.4 | 37.6 | 33.3 | 27.3 | 32.1 |
| 3.2 | 3.5 | 4.5 | Intangibles (net) | | 7.3 | 2.7 | 3.0 | 2.4 | 9.7 |
| 5.5 | 5.3 | 5.3 | All Other Non-Current | | 3.7 | 6.7 | 4.8 | 5.9 | 4.8 |
| 100.0 | 100.0 | 100.0 | Total | | 100.0 | 100.0 | 100.0 | 100.0 | 100.0 |
| | | | **LIABILITIES** | | | | | | |
| 10.2 | 9.2 | 8.9 | Notes Payable-Short Term | | 9.6 | 6.7 | 8.2 | 8.9 | 11.4 |
| 7.4 | 5.8 | 5.1 | Cur. Mat.-L.T.D. | | 5.4 | 7.5 | 5.1 | 5.1 | 3.1 |
| 10.8 | 13.3 | 12.7 | Trade Payables | | 10.2 | 14.7 | 12.5 | 14.4 | 13.0 |
| .2 | .2 | .2 | Income Taxes Payable | | .1 | .0 | .4 | .1 | .1 |
| 6.1 | 7.3 | 6.5 | All Other Current | | 4.4 | 5.6 | 7.8 | 6.0 | 8.3 |
| 34.8 | 35.9 | 33.4 | Total Current | | 29.6 | 34.6 | 34.0 | 34.6 | 35.9 |
| 22.3 | 19.6 | 22.5 | Long-Term Debt | | 40.1 | 29.1 | 18.9 | 14.7 | 18.6 |
| .8 | .7 | .9 | Deferred Taxes | | .8 | .7 | .9 | .4 | 1.5 |
| 8.4 | 5.7 | 5.8 | All Other Non-Current | | 5.8 | 5.0 | 4.9 | 6.2 | 8.0 |
| 33.7 | 38.1 | 37.4 | Net Worth | | 23.7 | 30.5 | 41.3 | 44.2 | 36.0 |
| 100.0 | 100.0 | 100.0 | Total Liabilities & Net Worth | | 100.0 | 100.0 | 100.0 | 100.0 | 100.0 |
| | | | **INCOME DATA** | | | | | | |
| 100.0 | 100.0 | 100.0 | Net Sales | | 100.0 | 100.0 | 100.0 | 100.0 | 100.0 |
| 28.0 | 28.0 | 30.0 | Gross Profit | | 42.6 | 27.6 | 28.9 | 25.3 | 24.4 |
| 26.3 | 22.8 | 23.5 | Operating Expenses | | 33.2 | 24.3 | 22.8 | 19.3 | 17.0 |
| 1.8 | 5.2 | 6.5 | Operating Profit | | 9.4 | 3.3 | 6.1 | 6.0 | 7.4 |
| 1.6 | 1.2 | .6 | All Other Expenses (net) | | .9 | .7 | -.1 | .5 | 1.7 |
| .2 | 4.0 | 5.9 | Profit Before Taxes | | 8.5 | 2.6 | 6.2 | 5.5 | 5.7 |
| | | | **RATIOS** | | | | | | |
| 2.6 | 2.6 | 2.9 | Current | | 4.8 | 2.4 | 2.9 | 3.0 | 2.2 |
| 1.6 | 1.6 | 1.7 | | | 1.9 | 1.5 | 1.6 | 2.0 | 1.5 |
| 1.1 | 1.2 | 1.3 | | | 1.4 | 1.0 | 1.3 | 1.4 | 1.1 |
| 1.5 | 1.5 | 1.5 | Quick | | 3.0 | 1.0 | 1.8 | 1.7 | .9 |
| .8 (173) | .9 | .9 | | | 1.2 | .7 | .9 | 1.0 | .7 |
| .4 | .5 | .6 | | | .8 | .4 | .6 | .6 | .4 |
| 30 12.1 | 36 10.3 | 34 10.6 | Sales/Receivables | | 31 11.6 | 30 12.3 | 41 8.9 | 35 10.3 | 34 10.7 |
| 44 8.3 | 49 7.5 | 49 7.5 | | | 53 6.9 | 35 10.4 | 51 7.1 | 46 8.0 | 45 8.2 |
| 59 6.2 | 61 6.0 | 58 6.3 | | | 62 5.9 | 54 6.8 | 57 6.4 | 57 6.4 | 53 6.9 |
| 42 8.7 | 35 10.5 | 35 10.4 | Cost of Sales/Inventory | | 4 94.9 | 28 13.2 | 36 10.2 | 41 9.0 | 44 8.3 |
| 66 5.5 | 59 6.2 | 60 6.1 | | | 42 8.7 | 52 7.0 | 62 5.9 | 54 6.7 | 78 4.7 |
| 106 3.4 | 98 3.7 | 104 3.5 | | | 118 3.1 | 83 4.4 | 107 3.4 | 89 4.1 | 104 3.5 |
| 13 27.6 | 20 18.2 | 19 18.9 | Cost of Sales/Payables | | 14 25.4 | 20 18.6 | 17 21.1 | 18 20.1 | 24 15.0 |
| 27 13.6 | 32 11.2 | 30 12.3 | | | 29 12.5 | 29 12.5 | 30 12.1 | 29 12.8 | 35 10.5 |
| 48 7.6 | 45 8.1 | 44 8.3 | | | 42 8.6 | 43 8.4 | 45 8.1 | 48 7.6 | 43 8.5 |
| 4.6 | 4.9 | 4.6 | Sales/Working Capital | | 2.3 | 5.2 | 4.8 | 4.5 | 5.3 |
| 8.4 | 10.0 | 8.1 | | | 7.1 | 9.0 | 10.9 | 6.9 | 9.9 |
| 46.4 | 21.0 | 19.9 | | | 18.1 | 273.8 | 18.7 | 14.1 | 27.9 |
| 3.6 | 11.5 | 15.2 | EBIT/Interest | | 14.8 | 7.4 | 16.4 | 19.3 | 11.4 |
| .7 (162) | 3.8 (192) | 5.5 (187) | | | 5.6 (30) | 3.5 (22) | 4.2 (52) | 6.9 (46) | 7.1 (31) |
| -2.1 | 1.4 | 1.9 | | | 2.2 | 1.2 | 2.0 | 2.3 | 1.4 |
| 3.1 | 3.9 | 5.0 | Net Profit + Depr., Dep., | | | | 3.4 | 4.0 | 12.9 |
| 1.3 (51) | 1.8 (65) | 2.2 (51) | Amort./Cur. Mat. L/T/D | | | | 1.9 (19) | 2.7 (11) | 4.8 (12) |
| .5 | 1.2 | 1.3 | | | | | 1.2 | .7 | 2.2 |
| .6 | .5 | .4 | Fixed/Worth | | .3 | .4 | .4 | .3 | .6 |
| 1.2 | .9 | .9 | | | 1.2 | 1.0 | 1.0 | .5 | 1.1 |
| 2.6 | 1.7 | 2.0 | | | 10.4 | 8.6 | 1.6 | 1.6 | 7.9 |
| .8 | .8 | .7 | Debt/Worth | | 1.0 | .8 | .7 | .6 | 1.1 |
| 1.8 | 1.5 | 1.7 | | | 2.6 | 1.9 | 1.6 | 1.2 | 1.9 |
| 6.2 | 3.7 | 3.9 | | | 31.6 | 11.7 | 3.2 | 3.2 | 17.8 |
| 21.2 | 41.3 | 47.7 | % Profit Before Taxes/Tangible | | 137.5 | 25.8 | 47.4 | 43.5 | 47.8 |
| 1.3 (145) | 17.4 (183) | 21.4 (175) | Net Worth | | 34.9 (26) | 13.2 (19) | 16.9 (49) | 23.9 (48) | 26.6 (27) |
| -17.0 | 3.2 | 7.4 | | | 6.5 | 1.7 | 6.7 | 10.9 | 13.2 |
| 7.7 | 14.5 | 15.9 | % Profit Before Taxes/Total | | 28.7 | 13.3 | 15.1 | 17.8 | 11.9 |
| .3 | 6.1 | 9.0 | Assets | | 14.5 | 6.0 | 6.2 | 10.5 | 9.1 |
| -7.0 | .5 | 2.3 | | | 3.0 | 1.1 | 2.5 | 4.5 | 2.0 |
| 9.3 | 11.8 | 14.2 | Sales/Net Fixed Assets | | 22.9 | 16.9 | 12.4 | 16.4 | 8.7 |
| 4.6 | 6.1 | 6.4 | | | 8.1 | 6.4 | 5.7 | 8.4 | 5.1 |
| 2.8 | 3.6 | 3.6 | | | 5.2 | 1.9 | 3.8 | 5.1 | 2.8 |
| 2.1 | 2.4 | 2.5 | Sales/Total Assets | | 2.9 | 2.7 | 2.5 | 2.6 | 2.0 |
| 1.6 | 1.8 | 1.8 | | | 1.8 | 2.2 | 1.7 | 2.1 | 1.7 |
| 1.2 | 1.4 | 1.4 | | | 1.2 | 1.2 | 1.5 | 1.5 | 1.1 |
| 3.2 | 2.2 | 2.1 | % Depr., Dep., Amort./Sales | | 1.5 | 2.4 | 2.1 | 1.8 | 2.3 |
| 5.1 (155) | 4.0 (181) | 3.5 (176) | | | 4.0 (25) | 4.5 (19) | 3.6 (49) | 2.8 (45) | 3.8 (33) |
| 7.2 | 6.3 | 5.8 | | | 5.8 | 6.8 | 5.5 | 4.4 | 6.0 |
| 1.9 | 1.8 | 1.8 | % Officers', Directors' | | 3.1 | 2.7 | 2.6 | 1.3 | |
| 4.2 (90) | 3.6 (90) | 3.9 (85) | Owners' Comp/Sales | | 4.4 (15) | 4.9 (11) | 4.0 (26) | 1.6 (22) | |
| 8.1 | 6.1 | 6.7 | | | 10.2 | 7.2 | 6.9 | 3.5 | |
| 2094630M | 3163788M | 2869298M | Net Sales ($) | 3788M | 64365M | 88599M | 389469M | 793250M | 1529827M |
| 1572376M | 1856429M | 1873052M | Total Assets ($) | 4784M | 44747M | 51047M | 217699M | 420687M | 1134088M |

M = $ thousand     MM = $ million
See Pages 9 through 22 for Explanation of Ratios and Data

## Current Data Sorted by Assets      Comparative Historical Data

| 0-500M | 500M-2MM | 2-10MM | 10-50MM | 50-100MM | 100-250MM | | 4/1/07-3/31/08 ALL | 4/1/08-3/31/09 ALL |
|---|---|---|---|---|---|---|---|---|
| | | | | | | **Type of Statement** | | |
| | | 4 | 12 | 2 | 1 | Unqualified | 22 | 27 |
| | 1 | 19 | 9 | | | Reviewed | 36 | 37 |
| 1 | 2 | 6 | | | | Compiled | 16 | 15 |
| 1 | 5 | 2 | | | | Tax Returns | 12 | 12 |
| | 8 | 26 | 14 | 5 | 2 | Other | 36 | 41 |
| | 23 (4/1-9/30/11) | | 97 (10/1/11-3/31/12) | | | | | |
| 2 | 16 | 57 | 35 | 7 | 3 | **NUMBER OF STATEMENTS** | 122 | 132 |
| % | % | % | % | % | % | **ASSETS** | % | % |
| | 8.3 | 7.0 | 5.5 | | | Cash & Equivalents | 6.6 | 6.3 |
| | 30.2 | 26.5 | 24.6 | | | Trade Receivables (net) | 24.8 | 23.2 |
| | 31.9 | 32.6 | 34.0 | | | Inventory | 33.5 | 32.5 |
| | .4 | 1.6 | 2.6 | | | All Other Current | 2.1 | 1.7 |
| | 70.8 | 67.7 | 66.7 | | | Total Current | 67.0 | 63.7 |
| | 18.5 | 25.9 | 23.9 | | | Fixed Assets (net) | 24.4 | 26.8 |
| | 2.6 | 1.0 | 4.7 | | | Intangibles (net) | 2.4 | 3.8 |
| | 8.1 | 5.4 | 4.6 | | | All Other Non-Current | 6.2 | 5.7 |
| | 100.0 | 100.0 | 100.0 | | | Total | 100.0 | 100.0 |
| | | | | | | **LIABILITIES** | | |
| | 7.2 | 10.6 | 12.2 | | | Notes Payable-Short Term | 13.5 | 11.7 |
| | 2.2 | 2.8 | 3.2 | | | Cur. Mat.-L.T.D. | 3.5 | 3.3 |
| | 20.4 | 15.5 | 14.3 | | | Trade Payables | 14.5 | 11.7 |
| | .3 | .3 | .3 | | | Income Taxes Payable | .3 | .4 |
| | 7.5 | 7.8 | 6.8 | | | All Other Current | 5.9 | 5.1 |
| | 37.7 | 37.1 | 36.7 | | | Total Current | 37.8 | 32.1 |
| | 33.8 | 15.7 | 7.5 | | | Long-Term Debt | 14.2 | 14.7 |
| | .0 | .7 | 1.5 | | | Deferred Taxes | .7 | .6 |
| | 10.3 | 4.7 | 5.9 | | | All Other Non-Current | 4.8 | 5.8 |
| | 18.2 | 41.7 | 48.4 | | | Net Worth | 42.5 | 46.8 |
| | 100.0 | 100.0 | 100.0 | | | Total Liabilities & Net Worth | 100.0 | 100.0 |
| | | | | | | **INCOME DATA** | | |
| | 100.0 | 100.0 | 100.0 | | | Net Sales | 100.0 | 100.0 |
| | 40.1 | 27.7 | 21.9 | | | Gross Profit | 28.3 | 25.7 |
| | 34.4 | 21.3 | 15.8 | | | Operating Expenses | 22.6 | 20.7 |
| | 5.8 | 6.3 | 6.1 | | | Operating Profit | 5.7 | 5.0 |
| | 1.3 | .9 | .9 | | | All Other Expenses (net) | 1.3 | 1.0 |
| | 4.4 | 5.4 | 5.2 | | | Profit Before Taxes | 4.4 | 4.0 |
| | | | | | | **RATIOS** | | |
| | 3.4 | 3.1 | 3.3 | | | | 2.8 | 3.6 |
| | 1.8 | 1.8 | 2.1 | | | Current | 1.9 | 2.0 |
| | 1.4 | 1.3 | 1.2 | | | | 1.2 | 1.3 |
| | 2.5 | 1.5 | 1.3 | | | | 1.5 | 1.8 |
| | 1.4 | .9 | .9 | | | Quick | .8 | .9 |
| | .7 | .6 | .5 | | | | .5 | .5 |
| | 29   12.7 | 36   10.0 | 41   8.8 | | | | 35   10.5 | 31   11.6 |
| | 37   9.8 | 46   8.0 | 49   7.4 | | | Sales/Receivables | 44   8.3 | 40   9.1 |
| | 52   7.0 | 54   6.8 | 60   6.1 | | | | 54   6.8 | 49   7.5 |
| | 26   14.0 | 55   6.6 | 56   6.5 | | | | 54   6.8 | 48   7.6 |
| | 70   5.2 | 74   4.9 | 87   4.2 | | | Cost of Sales/Inventory | 83   4.4 | 80   4.5 |
| | 122   3.0 | 104   3.5 | 135   2.7 | | | | 124   3.0 | 123   3.0 |
| | 21   17.7 | 20   18.7 | 18   20.8 | | | | 19   19.0 | 12   29.3 |
| | 34   10.6 | 36   10.0 | 31   11.8 | | | Cost of Sales/Payables | 31   11.9 | 23   16.0 |
| | 70   5.2 | 53   6.9 | 47   7.8 | | | | 46   7.9 | 41   8.8 |
| | 5.0 | 4.0 | 2.9 | | | | 4.9 | 4.0 |
| | 6.2 | 6.7 | 6.0 | | | Sales/Working Capital | 7.3 | 6.0 |
| | 14.0 | 12.4 | 27.7 | | | | 16.7 | 14.3 |
| | 29.0 | 28.5 | 72.5 | | | | 9.4 | 13.3 |
| | (15) 4.4 | (54) 5.8 | (32) 10.3 | | | EBIT/Interest | (113) 3.5 | (121) 3.6 |
| | 1.0 | 2.3 | 2.5 | | | | 1.3 | .8 |
| | | 12.6 | 11.0 | | | Net Profit + Depr., Dep., | 4.1 | 8.5 |
| | (22) 4.8 | (13) 2.7 | | | | Amort./Cur. Mat. L/T/D | (37) 2.7 | (51) 3.2 |
| | | 2.1 | 1.8 | | | | 1.6 | 1.6 |
| | .2 | .2 | .2 | | | | .3 | .3 |
| | .3 | .5 | .6 | | | Fixed/Worth | .6 | .6 |
| | NM | 1.6 | 1.2 | | | | 1.2 | 1.2 |
| | .6 | .7 | .4 | | | | .6 | .5 |
| | 2.1 | 1.2 | 1.1 | | | Debt/Worth | 1.3 | 1.2 |
| | NM | 3.1 | 2.9 | | | | 4.3 | 3.6 |
| | 48.9 | 43.1 | 37.1 | | | | 46.5 | 37.2 |
| | (12) 24.5 | (53) 24.8 | (34) 19.2 | | | % Profit Before Taxes/Tangible Net Worth | (113) 19.7 | (125) 11.5 |
| | 14.0 | 9.2 | 8.3 | | | | 4.5 | 1.4 |
| | 16.3 | 16.0 | 14.4 | | | | 16.0 | 14.9 |
| | 6.1 | 10.6 | 8.7 | | | % Profit Before Taxes/Total Assets | 6.3 | 4.7 |
| | .5 | 3.8 | 3.8 | | | | 1.0 | -.4 |
| | 35.8 | 18.3 | 13.7 | | | | 20.1 | 16.5 |
| | 21.0 | 9.3 | 7.9 | | | Sales/Net Fixed Assets | 9.5 | 7.5 |
| | 6.6 | 4.7 | 5.4 | | | | 5.2 | 4.2 |
| | 3.5 | 2.5 | 2.3 | | | | 2.6 | 2.5 |
| | 2.9 | 2.2 | 1.8 | | | Sales/Total Assets | 2.0 | 2.0 |
| | 1.6 | 1.7 | 1.3 | | | | 1.5 | 1.5 |
| | .5 | 1.0 | 1.4 | | | | 1.3 | 1.0 |
| | (14) 1.2 | (54) 1.9 | (34) 2.3 | | | % Depr., Dep., Amort./Sales | (114) 2.1 | (123) 2.2 |
| | 2.9 | 2.8 | 3.3 | | | | 3.2 | 3.7 |
| | 2.7 | 1.1 | | | | | 1.8 | 1.5 |
| | (10) 4.8 | (15) 3.5 | | | | % Officers', Directors' Owners' Comp/Sales | (51) 3.3 | (48) 4.3 |
| | 8.9 | 5.7 | | | | | 7.9 | |
| 2645M | 44917M | 593383M | 1514241M | 642678M | 794320M | Net Sales ($) | 2905891M | 3561606M |
| 857M | 17661M | 292047M | 893408M | 426276M | 452580M | Total Assets ($) | 1602136M | 2102480M |

© RMA 2012

M = $ thousand    MM = $ million
See Pages 9 through 22 for Explanation of Ratios and Data

## Comparative Historical Data | Current Data Sorted by Sales

| 4/1/09-3/31/10 ALL | 4/1/10-3/31/11 ALL | 4/1/11-3/31/12 ALL | Type of Statement | 0-1MM | 1-3MM | 3-5MM | 5-10MM | 10-25MM | 25MM & OVER |
|---|---|---|---|---|---|---|---|---|---|
| 15 | 19 | 19 | Unqualified | | | | 2 | 2 | 15 |
| 25 | 30 | 29 | Reviewed | | 1 | 4 | 7 | 9 | 8 |
| 8 | 11 | 9 | Compiled | 1 | 2 | 1 | 2 | 3 | |
| 11 | 11 | 8 | Tax Returns | | 5 | | 3 | | |
| 49 | 47 | 55 | Other | | 7 | 3 | 9 | 15 | 21 |
| | | | | | 23 (4/1-9/30/11) | | 97 (10/1/11-3/31/12) | | |
| 108 | 118 | 120 | NUMBER OF STATEMENTS | 1 | 15 | 8 | 23 | 29 | 44 |
| % | % | % | **ASSETS** | % | % | % | % | % | % |
| 9.1 | 6.7 | 6.7 | Cash & Equivalents | | 8.4 | | 7.9 | 4.0 | 6.7 |
| 21.6 | 24.0 | 25.9 | Trade Receivables (net) | | 30.1 | | 25.4 | 28.1 | 23.9 |
| 31.9 | 29.7 | 33.2 | Inventory | | 36.3 | | 28.6 | 38.1 | 32.7 |
| 2.4 | 1.8 | 1.8 | All Other Current | | .7 | | 1.9 | 1.8 | 2.1 |
| 64.9 | 62.2 | 67.6 | Total Current | | 75.5 | | 63.8 | 72.0 | 65.3 |
| 24.7 | 27.2 | 23.2 | Fixed Assets (net) | | 18.0 | | 26.9 | 22.3 | 22.7 |
| 4.4 | 3.5 | 2.5 | Intangibles (net) | | 4.3 | | 1.4 | .9 | 3.9 |
| 6.0 | 7.1 | 6.7 | All Other Non-Current | | 2.2 | | 7.9 | 4.9 | 8.1 |
| 100.0 | 100.0 | 100.0 | Total | | 100.0 | | 100.0 | 100.0 | 100.0 |
| | | | **LIABILITIES** | | | | | | |
| 13.3 | 9.2 | 10.6 | Notes Payable-Short Term | | 12.1 | | 10.1 | 11.6 | 11.1 |
| 3.2 | 4.5 | 2.7 | Cur. Mat.-L.T.D. | | 2.4 | | 2.1 | 3.0 | 2.9 |
| 12.5 | 14.1 | 15.4 | Trade Payables | | 20.9 | | 14.5 | 16.0 | 13.8 |
| .3 | .3 | .3 | Income Taxes Payable | | .1 | | .4 | .5 | .2 |
| 7.4 | 6.0 | 7.6 | All Other Current | | 7.8 | | 10.0 | 7.0 | 7.5 |
| 36.6 | 34.0 | 36.7 | Total Current | | 43.4 | | 37.1 | 38.1 | 35.5 |
| 13.3 | 17.9 | 15.1 | Long-Term Debt | | 29.5 | | 18.6 | 12.7 | 8.5 |
| .8 | .7 | .8 | Deferred Taxes | | .0 | | .8 | .6 | 1.3 |
| 4.4 | 9.2 | 7.1 | All Other Non-Current | | 17.3 | | 3.4 | 6.5 | 6.5 |
| 44.9 | 38.2 | 40.4 | Net Worth | | 9.9 | | 40.1 | 42.2 | 48.1 |
| 100.0 | 100.0 | 100.0 | Total Liabilities & Net Worth | | 100.0 | | 100.0 | 100.0 | 100.0 |
| | | | **INCOME DATA** | | | | | | |
| 100.0 | 100.0 | 100.0 | Net Sales | | 100.0 | | 100.0 | 100.0 | 100.0 |
| 29.4 | 29.8 | 27.7 | Gross Profit | | 36.5 | | 33.9 | 24.1 | 23.5 |
| 27.3 | 24.2 | 21.8 | Operating Expenses | | 33.7 | | 27.7 | 17.7 | 17.6 |
| 2.1 | 5.6 | 6.0 | Operating Profit | | 2.8 | | 6.2 | 6.4 | 5.8 |
| 1.3 | 1.4 | .9 | All Other Expenses (net) | | 1.1 | | 1.7 | .7 | .7 |
| .9 | 4.2 | 5.1 | Profit Before Taxes | | 1.7 | | 4.4 | 5.7 | 5.1 |
| | | | **RATIOS** | | | | | | |
| 4.1 | 2.9 | 3.4 | Current | | 3.4 | | 2.7 | 3.6 | 3.8 |
| 1.9 | 1.9 | 1.9 | | | 1.6 | | 1.9 | 1.9 | 2.0 |
| 1.2 | 1.3 | 1.3 | | | 1.3 | | 1.3 | 1.4 | 1.2 |
| 1.9 | 1.6 | 1.6 | Quick | | 1.7 | | 1.5 | 1.4 | 1.8 |
| .8 | 1.0 | .9 | | | 1.1 | | .9 | .8 | 1.0 |
| .4 | .5 | .6 | | | .5 | | .6 | .5 | .5 |
| 36 10.2 | 39 9.3 | 37 9.8 | Sales/Receivables | 29 12.8 | | 38 9.6 | 35 10.5 | 41 8.8 | |
| 48 7.7 | 46 7.9 | 46 8.0 | | 36 10.0 | | 48 7.6 | 46 8.0 | 49 7.5 | |
| 60 6.0 | 58 6.3 | 57 6.4 | | 70 5.2 | | 57 6.4 | 52 7.0 | 58 6.3 | |
| 58 6.2 | 53 6.9 | 54 6.7 | Cost of Sales/Inventory | 31 11.6 | | 49 7.4 | 57 6.4 | 55 6.6 | |
| 102 3.6 | 82 4.4 | 78 4.7 | | 94 3.9 | | 81 4.5 | 69 5.3 | 81 4.5 | |
| 138 2.6 | 125 2.9 | 118 3.1 | | 166 2.2 | | 118 3.1 | 94 3.9 | 140 2.6 | |
| 15 23.9 | 19 19.1 | 18 20.1 | Cost of Sales/Payables | 21 17.5 | | 17 21.7 | 21 17.5 | 17 20.9 | |
| 31 11.7 | 32 11.4 | 34 10.8 | | 37 9.8 | | 37 9.9 | 31 11.9 | 33 10.9 | |
| 46 7.9 | 50 7.2 | 53 6.9 | | 78 4.7 | | 53 6.9 | 46 7.9 | 47 7.8 | |
| 3.5 | 4.0 | 3.9 | Sales/Working Capital | | 4.4 | | 4.0 | 4.1 | 2.8 |
| 6.0 | 6.1 | 6.3 | | | 5.5 | | 8.7 | 6.9 | 6.2 |
| 18.0 | 14.2 | 13.5 | | | 16.0 | | 14.2 | 15.0 | 20.9 |
| 8.1 | 16.2 | 32.5 | EBIT/Interest | | 6.6 | | 15.7 | 60.2 | 54.9 |
| (92) 1.4 | (109) 4.1 | (110) 6.7 | | | 2.5 | | (22) 5.6 | (27) 12.6 | (38) 10.3 |
| -2.1 | 1.1 | 2.2 | | | .9 | | 2.0 | 2.8 | 2.4 |
| 6.0 | 8.2 | 11.6 | Net Profit + Depr., Dep., Amort./Cur. Mat. L/T/D | | | | | 15.0 | 10.6 |
| (32) 2.6 | (40) 2.5 | (38) 3.5 | | | | | | (11) 8.7 | (15) 2.6 |
| 1.0 | .9 | 1.8 | | | | | | 2.2 | 1.0 |
| .2 | .3 | .2 | Fixed/Worth | | .2 | | .2 | .2 | .2 |
| .6 | .8 | .5 | | | .9 | | .6 | .3 | .6 |
| 1.3 | 2.1 | 1.4 | | | -3.4 | | 1.1 | 1.8 | 1.2 |
| .3 | .5 | .5 | Debt/Worth | | 1.6 | | .7 | .4 | .4 |
| 1.3 | 1.4 | 1.4 | | | 2.5 | | 1.2 | 1.2 | 1.1 |
| 4.8 | 5.9 | 3.3 | | | -13.2 | | 2.3 | 3.1 | 3.1 |
| 23.2 | 42.4 | 41.5 | % Profit Before Taxes/Tangible Net Worth | | 47.1 | | 35.5 | 41.2 | 38.9 |
| (96) 1.5 | (106) 14.5 | (110) 21.8 | | (11) 17.7 | | (20) 22.4 | (27) 25.2 | (43) 14.4 | |
| -8.1 | 3.8 | 8.2 | | | 4.8 | | 8.2 | 14.2 | 7.8 |
| 9.3 | 13.0 | 15.1 | % Profit Before Taxes/Total Assets | | 6.7 | | 17.3 | 16.0 | 11.5 |
| .4 | 6.1 | 8.4 | | | 4.2 | | 7.4 | 12.7 | 8.2 |
| -4.9 | .5 | 2.7 | | | -.8 | | 2.6 | 5.2 | 2.1 |
| 14.9 | 13.7 | 19.9 | Sales/Net Fixed Assets | | 37.3 | | 18.8 | 24.3 | 14.2 |
| 7.8 | 7.4 | 9.6 | | | 20.8 | | 7.5 | 12.5 | 8.7 |
| 4.1 | 3.8 | 5.5 | | | 6.6 | | 4.5 | 6.3 | 5.6 |
| 2.2 | 2.3 | 2.5 | Sales/Total Assets | | 3.5 | | 2.3 | 2.6 | 2.2 |
| 1.6 | 1.8 | 2.1 | | | 2.1 | | 2.0 | 2.4 | 1.8 |
| 1.3 | 1.3 | 1.5 | | | 1.5 | | 1.7 | 2.1 | 1.2 |
| 1.2 | 1.4 | 1.0 | % Depr., Dep., Amort./Sales | | 1.0 | | 1.4 | .9 | 1.2 |
| (94) 2.5 | (110) 2.5 | (111) 1.9 | | (13) 1.4 | | (22) 2.1 | (27) 1.2 | (41) 2.3 | |
| 4.9 | 4.7 | 2.9 | | | 2.4 | | 3.4 | 2.7 | 3.3 |
| 2.5 | 2.4 | 1.9 | % Officers', Directors' Owners' Comp/Sales | | | | | | |
| (34) 6.4 | (36) 5.4 | (33) 4.3 | | | | | | | |
| 11.1 | 11.3 | 7.3 | | | | | | | |
| 2876032M | 2741341M | 3592184M | Net Sales ($) | 717M | 31563M | 34589M | 164450M | 422237M | 2938628M |
| 1778024M | 1721027M | 2082829M | Total Assets ($) | 623M | 21374M | 19380M | 94639M | 187726M | 1759087M |

M = $ thousand    MM = $ million
See Pages 9 through 22 for Explanation of Ratios and Data

## Current Data Sorted by Assets       Comparative Historical Data

| 0-500M | 500M-2MM | 2-10MM | 10-50MM | 50-100MM | 100-250MM | Type of Statement | 4/1/07-3/31/08 ALL | 4/1/08-3/31/09 ALL |
|---|---|---|---|---|---|---|---|---|
| | | 1 | 1 | | 1 | Unqualified | 9 | 10 |
| | 2 | 11 | 8 | | | Reviewed | 14 | 20 |
| 1 | 9 | 8 | | | | Compiled | 17 | 13 |
| 3 | 4 | 3 | | | | Tax Returns | 5 | 6 |
| 4 | 10 | 15 | 5 | 3 | | Other | 27 | 26 |
| | 22 (4/1-9/30/11) | | 67 (10/1/11-3/31/12) | | | | | |
| 8 | 25 | 38 | 14 | 3 | 1 | **NUMBER OF STATEMENTS** | 72 | 75 |
| % | % | % | % | % | % | **ASSETS** | % | % |
| | 8.8 | 9.0 | 9.7 | | | Cash & Equivalents | 8.4 | 8.2 |
| | 32.2 | 24.0 | 19.8 | | | Trade Receivables (net) | 26.9 | 25.1 |
| | 6.7 | 7.3 | 10.1 | | | Inventory | 10.8 | 6.4 |
| | .7 | 1.1 | 1.5 | | | All Other Current | 1.6 | 1.2 |
| | 48.5 | 41.3 | 41.2 | | | Total Current | 47.8 | 41.0 |
| | 34.8 | 43.2 | 43.5 | | | Fixed Assets (net) | 41.5 | 45.3 |
| | 6.5 | 2.1 | 9.0 | | | Intangibles (net) | 5.2 | 5.7 |
| | 10.2 | 13.4 | 6.3 | | | All Other Non-Current | 5.5 | 8.1 |
| | 100.0 | 100.0 | 100.0 | | | Total | 100.0 | 100.0 |
| | | | | | | **LIABILITIES** | | |
| | 7.2 | 7.2 | 5.4 | | | Notes Payable-Short Term | 6.3 | 6.6 |
| | 8.3 | 5.3 | 3.9 | | | Cur. Mat.-L.T.D. | 7.7 | 7.0 |
| | 9.3 | 8.5 | 8.9 | | | Trade Payables | 10.7 | 8.8 |
| | .3 | .1 | .0 | | | Income Taxes Payable | .2 | .1 |
| | 5.7 | 6.2 | 5.2 | | | All Other Current | 10.7 | 5.8 |
| | 30.9 | 27.3 | 23.4 | | | Total Current | 35.5 | 28.4 |
| | 28.3 | 22.8 | 24.3 | | | Long-Term Debt | 25.1 | 22.9 |
| | .0 | .8 | 1.6 | | | Deferred Taxes | 1.4 | 1.0 |
| | 14.6 | 7.4 | 6.1 | | | All Other Non-Current | 6.6 | 7.3 |
| | 26.2 | 41.7 | 44.6 | | | Net Worth | 31.4 | 40.5 |
| | 100.0 | 100.0 | 100.0 | | | Total Liabilities & Net Worth | 100.0 | 100.0 |
| | | | | | | **INCOME DATA** | | |
| | 100.0 | 100.0 | 100.0 | | | Net Sales | 100.0 | 100.0 |
| | 48.6 | 39.6 | 35.2 | | | Gross Profit | 36.5 | 36.0 |
| | 39.8 | 28.8 | 22.2 | | | Operating Expenses | 28.3 | 30.2 |
| | 8.8 | 10.8 | 13.1 | | | Operating Profit | 8.3 | 5.8 |
| | .5 | 1.4 | .9 | | | All Other Expenses (net) | 2.3 | 1.3 |
| | 8.3 | 9.4 | 12.2 | | | Profit Before Taxes | 6.0 | 4.5 |
| | | | | | | **RATIOS** | | |
| | 2.5 | 3.2 | 2.0 | | | | 3.2 | 2.5 |
| | 1.5 | 1.8 | 1.8 | | | Current | 1.7 | 1.5 |
| | .8 | 1.1 | 1.3 | | | | .8 | .8 |
| | 2.4 | 3.2 | 1.8 | | | | 2.2 | 2.1 |
| | 1.1 | 1.6 | 1.3 | | | Quick | 1.1 | 1.0 |
| | .6 | .9 | 1.0 | | | | .7 | .7 |
| | 36  10.1 | 38  9.7 | 42  8.7 | | | | 43  8.5 | 38  9.6 |
| | 48  7.6 | 47  7.7 | 48  7.6 | | | Sales/Receivables | 50  7.3 | 48  7.6 |
| | 56  6.5 | 55  6.6 | 58  6.3 | | | | 62  5.9 | 58  6.3 |
| | 0  UND | 0  UND | 0  UND | | | | 0  UND | 0  UND |
| | 14  26.7 | 0  UND | 12  30.7 | | | Cost of Sales/Inventory | 9  41.1 | 7  50.1 |
| | 36  10.0 | 29  12.5 | 43  8.4 | | | | 53  6.8 | 28  12.8 |
| | 10  36.5 | 14  26.9 | 16  22.8 | | | | 16  23.0 | 15  24.6 |
| | 14  26.8 | 26  14.0 | 27  13.7 | | | Cost of Sales/Payables | 27  13.3 | 24  15.2 |
| | 37  9.9 | 37  9.8 | 35  10.5 | | | | 42  8.7 | 40  9.1 |
| | 8.3 | 6.8 | 5.4 | | | | 4.7 | 6.7 |
| | 20.3 | 10.9 | 8.7 | | | Sales/Working Capital | 12.4 | 13.8 |
| | -46.0 | 45.7 | 23.0 | | | | -25.4 | -22.9 |
| | 10.1 | 22.3 | 52.7 | | | | 6.7 | 9.9 |
| | (20) 4.2 | (33) 6.1 | (13) 8.2 | | | EBIT/Interest | (66) 2.3 | (68) 2.6 |
| | 1.6 | 2.2 | 2.9 | | | | .4 | .2 |
| | | | | | | Net Profit + Depr., Dep., | 1.9 | 3.6 |
| | | | | | | Amort./Cur. Mat. L/T/D | (17) 1.3 | (30) 1.9 |
| | | | | | | | .6 | 1.2 |
| | .4 | .6 | .6 | | | | .6 | .6 |
| | 1.4 | 1.1 | 1.0 | | | Fixed/Worth | 1.5 | 1.3 |
| | 5.5 | 2.6 | 2.0 | | | | 12.6 | 3.2 |
| | .6 | .6 | .6 | | | | .7 | .5 |
| | 2.1 | 1.9 | 1.2 | | | Debt/Worth | 1.9 | 1.3 |
| | 17.2 | 4.3 | 2.7 | | | | 28.5 | 7.0 |
| | 70.4 | 73.6 | 60.7 | | | % Profit Before Taxes/Tangible | 55.3 | 39.5 |
| | (21) 42.7 | (34) 33.2 | (12) 31.3 | | | Net Worth | (55) 25.0 | (65) 16.3 |
| | 9.6 | 16.6 | 13.9 | | | | -.1 | -1.5 |
| | 21.4 | 32.0 | 24.1 | | | % Profit Before Taxes/Total | 15.5 | 16.4 |
| | 14.7 | 14.6 | 13.5 | | | Assets | 6.7 | 6.8 |
| | 2.7 | 5.8 | 5.4 | | | | -.9 | -1.2 |
| | 13.4 | 6.7 | 9.3 | | | | 11.3 | 7.3 |
| | 7.9 | 4.2 | 3.0 | | | Sales/Net Fixed Assets | 4.2 | 4.0 |
| | 3.7 | 2.4 | 1.5 | | | | 2.0 | 1.9 |
| | 3.4 | 2.2 | 1.9 | | | | 2.7 | 3.0 |
| | 2.6 | 1.8 | 1.3 | | | Sales/Total Assets | 1.8 | 1.8 |
| | 1.7 | 1.1 | .9 | | | | 1.1 | 1.0 |
| | 1.1 | 1.9 | 1.5 | | | | 2.5 | 2.9 |
| | (20) 3.3 | (37) 3.6 | 4.8 | | | % Depr., Dep., Amort./Sales | (64) 4.6 | (68) 4.8 |
| | 7.0 | 6.2 | 7.2 | | | | 6.9 | 7.8 |
| | | 1.8 | | | | % Officers', Directors' | 2.6 | 2.4 |
| | | (17) 3.1 | | | | Owners' Comp/Sales | (27) 4.6 | (28) 4.5 |
| | | 6.4 | | | | | | 8.3 |
| 6822M | 74841M | 319873M | 456145M | 284989M | 208891M | Net Sales ($) | 1613019M | 1110014M |
| 1797M | 29475M | 180311M | 311901M | 227875M | 213426M | Total Assets ($) | 1239084M | 864420M |

© RMA 2012

M = $ thousand    MM = $ million
See Pages 9 through 22 for Explanation of Ratios and Data

## Comparative Historical Data | Current Data Sorted by Sales

| Type of Statement | 4/1/09-3/31/10 ALL | 4/1/10-3/31/11 ALL | 4/1/11-3/31/12 ALL | 0-1MM | 1-3MM | 3-5MM | 5-10MM | 10-25MM | 25MM & OVER |
|---|---|---|---|---|---|---|---|---|---|
| Unqualified | 4 | 8 | 3 | | | | | | 3 |
| Reviewed | 20 | 15 | 21 | | | 6 | 1 | 12 | 2 |
| Compiled | 17 | 16 | 18 | | 5 | 7 | 6 | | |
| Tax Returns | 7 | 12 | 10 | 3 | 2 | 2 | 2 | 1 | |
| Other | 40 | 32 | 37 | 6 | 9 | 5 | 5 | 5 | 7 |
| | | | | 22 (4/1-9/30/11) | | | 67 (10/1/11-3/31/12) | | |
| **NUMBER OF STATEMENTS** | 88 | 83 | 89 | 9 | 16 | 20 | 14 | 18 | 12 |

### ASSETS (%)

| | | | | | | | | | |
|---|---|---|---|---|---|---|---|---|---|
| Cash & Equivalents | 9.4 | 11.1 | 8.6 | 6.0 | 5.9 | 11.1 | 12.2 | 9.1 | |
| Trade Receivables (net) | 22.4 | 25.6 | 25.7 | 23.3 | 33.1 | 27.2 | 25.5 | 22.4 | |
| Inventory | 9.4 | 7.6 | 8.3 | 3.6 | 6.4 | 10.0 | 6.6 | 17.1 | |
| All Other Current | 3.3 | 2.2 | 1.0 | .1 | 1.3 | 2.0 | .4 | 1.9 | |
| Total Current | 44.6 | 46.5 | 43.6 | 33.1 | 46.6 | 50.3 | 44.8 | 50.4 | |
| Fixed Assets (net) | 43.5 | 40.4 | 39.7 | 45.9 | 38.4 | 36.9 | 44.2 | 33.5 | |
| Intangibles (net) | 6.4 | 6.4 | 5.8 | 7.3 | 3.1 | 2.5 | 4.0 | 11.6 | |
| All Other Non-Current | 5.5 | 6.7 | 10.9 | 13.8 | 11.9 | 10.3 | 7.1 | 4.5 | |
| Total | 100.0 | 100.0 | 100.0 | 100.0 | 100.0 | 100.0 | 100.0 | 100.0 | |

*(Reading order: Historical 4/1/09-3/31/10, 4/1/10-3/31/11, 4/1/11-3/31/12, then 0-1MM, 1-3MM, 3-5MM, 5-10MM, 10-25MM, 25MM & OVER.)*

### LIABILITIES

| | Hist '10 | Hist '11 | Hist '12 | 0-1MM | 1-3MM | 3-5MM | 5-10MM | 10-25MM | 25MM & OVER |
|---|---|---|---|---|---|---|---|---|---|
| Notes Payable-Short Term | 9.4 | 9.3 | 10.1 | 6.5 | 5.4 | 11.0 | 5.6 | 7.1 | |
| Cur. Mat.-L.T.D. | 6.4 | 6.2 | 5.7 | 8.9 | 5.4 | 8.8 | 5.8 | 2.0 | |
| Trade Payables | 9.5 | 9.4 | 8.9 | 4.9 | 10.8 | 8.1 | 10.7 | 10.4 | |
| Income Taxes Payable | .1 | .3 | .1 | .2 | .3 | .2 | .0 | .1 | |
| All Other Current | 8.1 | 6.9 | 9.3 | 12.7 | 7.3 | 8.7 | 4.1 | 9.5 | |
| Total Current | 33.5 | 32.1 | 34.2 | 33.1 | 29.1 | 36.8 | 26.2 | 29.1 | |
| Long-Term Debt | 24.9 | 29.0 | 24.5 | 30.1 | 32.0 | 16.3 | 18.1 | 28.6 | |
| Deferred Taxes | 1.0 | .9 | .7 | .5 | .5 | 1.0 | .7 | 1.5 | |
| All Other Non-Current | 11.6 | 8.1 | 9.7 | 22.0 | 7.1 | 10.0 | 3.4 | 3.3 | |
| Net Worth | 29.0 | 29.9 | 31.0 | 14.2 | 31.4 | 36.0 | 51.6 | 37.4 | |
| Total Liabilities & Net Worth | 100.0 | 100.0 | 100.0 | 100.0 | 100.0 | 100.0 | 100.0 | 100.0 | |

### INCOME DATA

| | Hist '10 | Hist '11 | Hist '12 | 0-1MM | 1-3MM | 3-5MM | 5-10MM | 10-25MM | 25MM & OVER |
|---|---|---|---|---|---|---|---|---|---|
| Net Sales | 100.0 | 100.0 | 100.0 | 100.0 | 100.0 | 100.0 | 100.0 | 100.0 | |
| Gross Profit | 35.2 | 39.7 | 41.1 | 50.9 | 40.6 | 34.9 | 39.4 | 29.1 | |
| Operating Expenses | 35.5 | 31.4 | 31.3 | 43.5 | 31.1 | 26.3 | 27.1 | 17.3 | |
| Operating Profit | -.3 | 8.4 | 9.8 | 7.3 | 9.5 | 8.5 | 12.3 | 11.8 | |
| All Other Expenses (net) | 1.9 | 1.9 | 1.0 | 2.7 | .4 | 1.9 | .1 | 1.3 | |
| Profit Before Taxes | -2.1 | 6.5 | 8.8 | 4.7 | 9.1 | 6.6 | 12.2 | 10.4 | |

### RATIOS

| | Hist '10 | Hist '11 | Hist '12 | 0-1MM | 1-3MM | 3-5MM | 5-10MM | 10-25MM | 25MM & OVER |
|---|---|---|---|---|---|---|---|---|---|
| Current | 2.6 / 1.4 / .8 | 2.6 / 1.7 / 1.1 | 2.5 / 1.5 / 1.0 | 4.3 / 1.1 / .6 | 2.8 / 1.9 / 1.2 | 2.5 / 1.8 / 1.0 | 3.2 / 2.0 / 1.3 | 2.2 / 1.7 / 1.4 | |
| Quick | 2.0 / .9 / .6 | 2.1 / 1.2 / .7 | 2.4 / 1.1 / .6 | 2.9 / 1.0 / .6 | 2.7 / 1.4 / .9 | 2.5 / 1.6 / .4 | 3.2 / 1.6 / 1.0 | 1.5 / 1.1 / .8 | |
| Sales/Receivables | 34 10.6 / 46 7.9 / 57 6.4 | 40 9.2 / 51 7.2 / 62 5.9 | 37 9.8 / 47 7.7 / 56 6.5 | 38 9.7 / 49 7.4 / 60 6.1 | 38 9.6 / 46 8.0 / 55 6.6 | 36 10.2 / 46 8.0 / 55 6.6 | 41 8.9 / 50 7.3 / 58 6.3 | 36 10.1 / 47 7.7 / 55 6.6 | |
| Cost of Sales/Inventory | 0 UND / 6 59.7 / 35 10.5 | 0 UND / 3 121.3 / 41 8.9 | 0 UND / 6 62.8 / 41 9.9 | 0 UND / 0 UND / 25 14.5 | 0 UND / 6 64.0 / 22 16.7 | 0 UND / 0 UND / 43 8.5 | 0 UND / 0 UND / 34 10.7 | 9 41.3 / 45 8.2 / 107 3.4 | |
| Cost of Sales/Payables | 14 26.8 / 24 15.5 / 41 8.9 | 16 23.3 / 24 14.9 / 48 7.6 | 12 30.3 / 23 16.0 / 36 10.1 | 8 45.1 / 19 19.5 / 35 10.5 | 11 32.2 / 24 15.0 / 37 9.8 | 13 27.3 / 19 18.8 / 34 10.7 | 15 24.9 / 26 13.9 / 41 8.8 | 12 29.9 / 27 13.7 / 40 9.2 | |
| Sales/Working Capital | 5.5 / 30.1 / -18.5 | 5.4 / 11.9 / 33.7 | 6.5 / 12.9 / 126.1 | 7.5 / 40.9 / -7.3 | 8.1 / 12.7 / 34.5 | 5.6 / 11.7 / NM | 6.3 / 7.7 / 21.7 | 5.2 / 9.5 / 19.1 | |
| EBIT/Interest | 4.8 / (79) .6 / -4.7 | 24.2 / (74) 4.5 / 2.1 | 19.4 / (76) 5.8 / 1.9 | 10.1 / (13) 4.5 / 1.8 | 17.6 / (16) 6.3 / 1.6 | 13.4 / (13) 5.0 / 1.8 | 41.9 / (16) 11.3 / 4.6 | 59.6 / (11) 9.6 / 4.1 | |
| Net Profit + Depr., Dep., Amort./Cur. Mat. L/T/D | 3.3 / (22) 1.9 / .7 | 4.8 / (18) 2.1 / 1.4 | 5.5 / (19) 2.5 / 1.6 | | | | | | |
| Fixed/Worth | .6 / 1.3 / 21.3 | .5 / 1.1 / 4.5 | .6 / 1.2 / 4.2 | .9 / 1.8 / NM | .6 / 1.2 / 4.3 | .5 / 1.4 / 8.5 | .6 / .9 / 1.8 | .4 / .7 / NM | |
| Debt/Worth | .5 / 1.3 / NM | .5 / 1.7 / 7.1 | .7 / 2.1 / 7.7 | 1.0 / 2.3 / NM | .6 / 1.9 / 8.5 | .7 / 2.4 / 27.4 | .4 / 1.1 / 2.3 | .7 / 1.1 / NM | |
| % Profit Before Taxes/Tangible Net Worth | 17.1 / (66) 3.2 / -13.6 | 64.0 / (69) 24.7 / 10.2 | 64.9 / (73) 37.3 / 14.0 | 60.7 / (12) 41.2 / 27.5 | 84.0 / (18) 34.3 / 8.1 | 103.2 / (12) 32.6 / 9.5 | 61.0 / (17) 30.0 / 19.2 | | |
| % Profit Before Taxes/Total Assets | 7.7 / .7 / -10.6 | 21.5 / 10.0 / 2.8 | 23.1 / 14.4 / 3.5 | 22.1 / 11.2 / 2.8 | 25.2 / 14.6 / 3.0 | 28.5 / 7.4 / 2.4 | 26.4 / 21.1 / 9.2 | 23.6 / 16.3 / 6.6 | |
| Sales/Net Fixed Assets | 7.9 / 4.1 / 1.8 | 8.4 / 4.5 / 2.5 | 10.5 / 5.0 / 2.6 | 10.7 / 3.8 / 1.4 | 12.3 / 5.5 / 3.1 | 13.7 / 5.4 / 4.1 | 8.6 / 4.1 / 2.2 | 11.0 / 5.1 / 2.8 | |
| Sales/Total Assets | 2.7 / 1.5 / 1.0 | 2.7 / 1.7 / 1.0 | 2.8 / 1.8 / 1.1 | 2.3 / 1.7 / .7 | 3.5 / 2.5 / 1.3 | 2.7 / 1.9 / 1.4 | 2.5 / 1.7 / .9 | 2.4 / 1.5 / 1.2 | |
| % Depr., Dep., Amort./Sales | 2.8 / (73) 4.7 / 9.9 | 2.9 / (66) 4.7 / 7.6 | 1.8 / (76) 3.9 / 6.3 | 2.5 / (13) 6.2 / 9.4 | .9 / (16) 2.3 / 3.4 | 1.6 / (13) 4.2 / 6.4 | 2.0 / 4.8 / 6.9 | 1.1 / (10) 2.5 / 4.5 | |
| % Officers', Directors' Owners' Comp/Sales | 4.6 / (27) 6.1 / 11.6 | 2.8 / (32) 5.3 / 9.4 | 2.0 / (31) 4.5 / 7.3 | | | | | | |
| Net Sales ($) | 1297227M | 1415400M | 1351561M | 4291M | 34026M | 80361M | 93462M | 270395M | 869026M |
| Total Assets ($) | 1122232M | 1183089M | 964785M | 2927M | 31862M | 42155M | 55908M | 187727M | 644206M |

## Current Data Sorted by Assets

## Comparative Historical Data

### Type of Statement

| 0-500M | 500M-2MM | 2-10MM | 10-50MM | 50-100MM | 100-250MM | Type of Statement | ALL 4/1/07-3/31/08 | ALL 4/1/08-3/31/09 |
|---|---|---|---|---|---|---|---|---|
| 1 | 3 | 4 | 6 | 1 | 3 | Unqualified | 11 | 11 |
| 3 | 8 | 18 | 6 | | | Reviewed | 33 | 27 |
| 8 | 10 | 12 | | | | Compiled | 23 | 21 |
| 5 | 10 | 9 | 12 | 4 | 2 | Tax Returns | 16 | 20 |
| | | 23 | | | | Other | 52 | 48 |
| | 28 (4/1-9/30/11) | | 120 (10/1/11-3/31/12) | | | | | |
| 17 | 31 | 66 | 24 | 5 | 5 | **NUMBER OF STATEMENTS** | 135 | 127 |

| 0-500M | 500M-2MM | 2-10MM | 10-50MM | 50-100MM | 100-250MM | | ALL 4/1/07-3/31/08 | ALL 4/1/08-3/31/09 |
|---|---|---|---|---|---|---|---|---|
| % | % | % | % | % | % | **ASSETS** | % | % |
| 15.4 | 10.9 | 10.7 | 10.4 | | | Cash & Equivalents | 8.1 | 7.9 |
| 33.9 | 37.1 | 24.8 | 26.2 | | | Trade Receivables (net) | 28.8 | 26.2 |
| 12.1 | 10.4 | 12.6 | 21.9 | | | Inventory | 13.3 | 11.1 |
| .3 | 3.6 | 1.8 | .9 | | | All Other Current | 2.7 | 3.5 |
| 61.7 | 62.1 | 50.0 | 59.4 | | | Total Current | 52.9 | 48.7 |
| 24.1 | 29.5 | 35.2 | 30.9 | | | Fixed Assets (net) | 33.4 | 40.5 |
| 10.8 | 2.5 | 9.3 | 6.2 | | | Intangibles (net) | 4.9 | 3.8 |
| 3.4 | 5.9 | 5.6 | 3.6 | | | All Other Non-Current | 8.7 | 7.0 |
| 100.0 | 100.0 | 100.0 | 100.0 | | | Total | 100.0 | 100.0 |
| | | | | | | **LIABILITIES** | | |
| 27.3 | 8.7 | 6.5 | 10.5 | | | Notes Payable-Short Term | 10.6 | 12.2 |
| 6.5 | 3.2 | 3.6 | 3.1 | | | Cur. Mat.-L.T.D. | 3.9 | 5.4 |
| 22.9 | 18.0 | 10.6 | 10.4 | | | Trade Payables | 12.3 | 10.5 |
| .0 | .1 | .2 | .0 | | | Income Taxes Payable | .5 | .2 |
| 30.0 | 5.2 | 7.7 | 7.6 | | | All Other Current | 10.7 | 11.3 |
| 86.6 | 35.2 | 28.5 | 31.6 | | | Total Current | 38.1 | 39.6 |
| 17.1 | 29.5 | 15.8 | 13.4 | | | Long-Term Debt | 23.6 | 21.8 |
| .1 | .1 | .5 | .3 | | | Deferred Taxes | .4 | .4 |
| 30.5 | 3.8 | 8.3 | 3.7 | | | All Other Non-Current | 5.2 | 4.5 |
| -34.4 | 31.4 | 46.9 | 51.0 | | | Net Worth | 32.8 | 33.7 |
| 100.0 | 100.0 | 100.0 | 100.0 | | | Total Liabilities & Net Worth | 100.0 | 100.0 |
| | | | | | | **INCOME DATA** | | |
| 100.0 | 100.0 | 100.0 | 100.0 | | | Net Sales | 100.0 | 100.0 |
| 47.4 | 41.9 | 33.3 | 24.5 | | | Gross Profit | 31.4 | 34.5 |
| 40.9 | 35.5 | 26.4 | 14.4 | | | Operating Expenses | 25.4 | 30.3 |
| 6.6 | 6.4 | 6.9 | 10.1 | | | Operating Profit | 5.9 | 4.2 |
| 1.9 | -.1 | 1.0 | .8 | | | All Other Expenses (net) | 1.5 | 1.4 |
| 4.7 | 6.5 | 5.9 | 9.3 | | | Profit Before Taxes | 4.4 | 2.8 |
| | | | | | | **RATIOS** | | |
| 1.7 | 4.0 | 3.6 | 4.0 | | | | 2.5 | 2.6 |
| .6 | 1.8 | 1.9 | 1.8 | | | Current | 1.6 | 1.3 |
| .4 | 1.1 | 1.2 | 1.3 | | | | 1.0 | .8 |
| 1.0 | 2.9 | 2.4 | 3.3 | | | | 1.9 | 1.7 |
| .5 | 1.5 | 1.4 | 1.2 | | | Quick | 1.0 | .9 |
| .3 | .8 | .7 | .7 | | | | .6 | .5 |
| 17   22.1 | 37   9.8 | 38   9.5 | 38   9.5 | | | | 37   9.8 | 32   11.4 |
| 28   13.1 | 48   7.6 | 49   7.4 | 49   7.5 | | | Sales/Receivables | 46   8.0 | 43   8.4 |
| 49   7.4 | 54   6.7 | 58   6.3 | 57   6.4 | | | | 56   6.5 | 54   6.8 |
| 0   UND | 2   158.8 | 7   53.3 | 24   15.5 | | | | 7   49.5 | 8   44.6 |
| 11   33.6 | 19   19.4 | 20   18.7 | 46   8.0 | | | Cost of Sales/Inventory | 25   14.7 | 21   17.1 |
| 56   6.5 | 36   10.1 | 59   6.2 | 58   6.3 | | | | 55   6.6 | 49   7.5 |
| 6   58.7 | 14   26.3 | 19   18.9 | 14   26.0 | | | | 16   22.7 | 14   25.2 |
| 28   13.2 | 32   11.3 | 27   13.7 | 24   15.0 | | | Cost of Sales/Payables | 25   14.4 | 25   14.8 |
| 73   5.0 | 47   7.8 | 39   9.3 | 34   10.8 | | | | 40   9.0 | 41   8.8 |
| 14.4 | 5.8 | 4.8 | 4.3 | | | | 6.5 | 6.5 |
| -15.1 | 11.1 | 8.6 | 8.9 | | | Sales/Working Capital | 13.8 | 21.1 |
| -7.7 | 50.1 | 30.7 | 17.7 | | | | -229.0 | -15.7 |
| 5.1 | 25.1 | 16.9 | 32.1 | | | | 13.5 | 9.8 |
| (15) 2.3 | (27) 6.8 | (61) 6.2 | (21) 13.7 | | | EBIT/Interest | (122) 4.5 | (111) 3.7 |
| 1.3 | 2.0 | 1.6 | 5.9 | | | | 1.4 | 1.1 |
| | | 5.7 | | | | | 2.5 | 2.5 |
| | (16) 2.5 | | | | | Net Profit + Depr., Dep., Amort./Cur. Mat. L/T/D | (28) 1.8 | (22) 1.6 |
| | | 1.7 | | | | | .8 | .9 |
| .3 | .3 | .4 | .4 | | | | .4 | .5 |
| -13.5 | .8 | .9 | .8 | | | Fixed/Worth | 1.0 | 1.1 |
| -.1 | 2.9 | 2.1 | 1.1 | | | | 3.5 | 3.2 |
| 1.6 | .6 | .5 | .6 | | | | .7 | .7 |
| -22.0 | 1.3 | 1.3 | 1.3 | | | Debt/Worth | 1.8 | 1.9 |
| -1.9 | 8.3 | 3.3 | 2.9 | | | | 6.8 | 5.9 |
| | 73.6 | 47.9 | 43.0 | | | | 56.7 | 45.3 |
| | (26) 23.0 | (58) 22.9 | (22) 30.4 | | | % Profit Before Taxes/Tangible Net Worth | (115) 25.7 | (106) 18.1 |
| | 5.7 | 8.2 | 23.1 | | | | 4.0 | .7 |
| 26.8 | 25.9 | 22.7 | 23.5 | | | | 20.9 | 15.8 |
| 12.3 | 11.3 | 9.0 | 15.5 | | | % Profit Before Taxes/Total Assets | 8.1 | 5.5 |
| 1.5 | 2.7 | 2.2 | 7.6 | | | | .8 | -.2 |
| 140.3 | 25.5 | 11.1 | 16.2 | | | | 18.0 | 11.6 |
| 38.8 | 14.1 | 5.5 | 7.6 | | | Sales/Net Fixed Assets | 6.8 | 5.4 |
| 16.0 | 5.8 | 3.3 | 3.1 | | | | 3.8 | 3.1 |
| 6.2 | 4.0 | 2.3 | 2.8 | | | | 2.9 | 3.0 |
| 4.1 | 2.9 | 1.9 | 2.0 | | | Sales/Total Assets | 1.9 | 2.0 |
| 2.6 | 2.0 | 1.4 | 1.3 | | | | 1.4 | 1.3 |
| .3 | 1.0 | 2.0 | 1.1 | | | | 1.3 | 1.6 |
| (12) 1.6 | (25) 1.8 | (60) 3.3 | (22) 2.0 | | | % Depr., Dep., Amort./Sales | (114) 2.8 | (102) 3.0 |
| 3.2 | 2.7 | 5.2 | 4.2 | | | | 4.4 | 5.5 |
| | 4.4 | 2.3 | | | | | 3.4 | 2.7 |
| | (23) 6.0 | (33) 5.5 | | | | % Officers', Directors' Owners' Comp/Sales | (39) 5.2 | (46) 5.7 |
| | 7.5 | 10.7 | | | | | 8.3 | 7.4 |
| 21879M | 113845M | 593946M | 1153146M | 687154M | 1362074M | Net Sales ($) | 3540245M | 2990099M |
| 4714M | 39461M | 333607M | 599636M | 358411M | 637615M | Total Assets ($) | 2207264M | 1944148M |

M = $ thousand    MM = $ million
See Pages 9 through 22 for Explanation of Ratios and Data

## Comparative Historical Data | Current Data Sorted by Sales

Current Data date spans: 28 (4/1-9/30/11) · 120 (10/1/11-3/31/12)

| Type of Statement | 4/1/09-3/31/10 ALL | 4/1/10-3/31/11 ALL | 4/1/11-3/31/12 ALL | 0-1MM | 1-3MM | 3-5MM | 5-10MM | 10-25MM | 25MM & OVER |
|---|---|---|---|---|---|---|---|---|---|
| Unqualified | 17 | 12 | 14 | | | | 3 | 1 | 10 |
| Reviewed | 23 | 31 | 28 | 1 | 2 | 5 | 7 | 9 | 4 |
| Compiled | 22 | 23 | 23 | 1 | 4 | 8 | 6 | 4 | |
| Tax Returns | 17 | 17 | 27 | 4 | 8 | 7 | 8 | | |
| Other | 53 | 51 | 56 | 5 | 6 | 5 | 11 | 12 | 17 |
| **NUMBER OF STATEMENTS** | 132 | 134 | 148 | 11 | 20 | 25 | 35 | 26 | 31 |
| **ASSETS** | % | % | % | % | % | % | % | % | % |
| Cash & Equivalents | 10.7 | 12.0 | 11.4 | 8.1 | 15.1 | 10.6 | 13.0 | 9.8 | 10.4 |
| Trade Receivables (net) | 26.6 | 28.4 | 28.6 | 22.4 | 37.2 | 28.4 | 29.3 | 27.1 | 25.7 |
| Inventory | 11.6 | 12.3 | 13.6 | 11.0 | 7.5 | 10.5 | 13.0 | 17.5 | 18.6 |
| All Other Current | 2.9 | 2.4 | 2.0 | 1.0 | 1.5 | 4.2 | 1.9 | 1.0 | 1.9 |
| Total Current | 51.7 | 55.2 | 55.7 | 42.5 | 61.3 | 53.7 | 57.3 | 55.4 | 56.6 |
| Fixed Assets (net) | 35.4 | 34.1 | 31.5 | 30.3 | 28.1 | 33.1 | 30.2 | 36.3 | 30.2 |
| Intangibles (net) | 5.2 | 4.7 | 7.6 | 16.2 | 6.6 | 8.9 | 7.4 | 3.3 | 8.1 |
| All Other Non-Current | 7.7 | 6.0 | 5.2 | 11.0 | 4.0 | 4.2 | 5.1 | 5.0 | 5.1 |
| Total | 100.0 | 100.0 | 100.0 | 100.0 | 100.0 | 100.0 | 100.0 | 100.0 | 100.0 |
| **LIABILITIES** | | | | | | | | | |
| Notes Payable-Short Term | 12.4 | 10.5 | 9.6 | 14.3 | 13.4 | 13.6 | 4.2 | 10.9 | 7.4 |
| Cur. Mat.-L.T.D. | 4.3 | 3.6 | 3.7 | 5.8 | 4.9 | 2.5 | 3.4 | 4.0 | 3.4 |
| Trade Payables | 10.2 | 11.7 | 13.4 | 7.5 | 19.7 | 13.9 | 14.0 | 13.6 | 10.3 |
| Income Taxes Payable | .2 | .2 | .2 | .0 | .0 | .0 | .4 | .1 | .5 |
| All Other Current | 9.0 | 9.0 | 10.1 | 34.2 | 6.8 | 5.9 | 10.3 | 6.2 | 10.3 |
| Total Current | 36.1 | 35.1 | 37.1 | 61.7 | 44.7 | 35.9 | 32.3 | 34.8 | 31.8 |
| Long-Term Debt | 24.1 | 22.2 | 19.5 | 37.2 | 12.9 | 33.6 | 11.7 | 14.0 | 19.5 |
| Deferred Taxes | .5 | .5 | .3 | .0 | .1 | .2 | .6 | .2 | .5 |
| All Other Non-Current | 5.1 | 9.4 | 9.1 | 34.6 | 15.2 | 5.2 | 7.3 | 4.6 | 4.9 |
| Net Worth | 34.2 | 32.9 | 34.0 | -33.6 | 27.1 | 25.1 | 48.1 | 46.4 | 43.3 |
| Total Liabilities & Net Worth | 100.0 | 100.0 | 100.0 | 100.0 | 100.0 | 100.0 | 100.0 | 100.0 | 100.0 |
| **INCOME DATA** | | | | | | | | | |
| Net Sales | 100.0 | 100.0 | 100.0 | 100.0 | 100.0 | 100.0 | 100.0 | 100.0 | 100.0 |
| Gross Profit | 34.6 | 35.3 | 35.0 | 53.2 | 51.4 | 36.4 | 32.3 | 29.0 | 24.8 |
| Operating Expenses | 31.5 | 29.5 | 27.5 | 42.3 | 43.6 | 32.5 | 26.2 | 20.5 | 15.2 |
| Operating Profit | 3.0 | 5.8 | 7.5 | 10.9 | 7.8 | 4.0 | 6.0 | 8.6 | 9.6 |
| All Other Expenses (net) | 1.6 | .9 | .9 | 2.5 | .7 | .4 | 1.1 | .2 | 1.0 |
| Profit Before Taxes | 1.5 | 4.9 | 6.6 | 8.4 | 7.1 | 3.6 | 4.9 | 8.4 | 8.5 |
| **RATIOS** | | | | | | | | | |
| Current | 3.4 | 3.2 | 3.2 | 2.1 | 5.4 | 3.2 | 3.2 | 3.1 | 2.7 |
| Current | 1.7 | 1.8 | 1.8 | .7 | 2.4 | 1.7 | 1.9 | 1.4 | 1.8 |
| Current | .9 | 1.2 | 1.1 | .5 | 1.0 | .9 | 1.3 | 1.0 | 1.5 |
| Quick | 2.4 | 2.7 | 2.3 | .7 | 4.6 | 2.3 | 2.2 | 2.4 | 1.5 |
| Quick | 1.2 | 1.3 | 1.2 | .5 | 2.0 | 1.4 | 1.6 | .9 | 1.2 |
| Quick | .6 | .7 | .7 | .4 | .7 | .7 | .8 | .5 | .8 |
| Sales/Receivables | 35  10.4 | 37  9.9 | 37  9.9 | 25  14.6 | 34  10.8 | 33  11.0 | 40  9.2 | 33  11.2 | 38  9.7 |
| Sales/Receivables | 43  8.4 | 45  8.1 | 47  7.7 | 29  12.5 | 49  7.5 | 47  7.7 | 50  7.3 | 49  7.4 | 47  7.7 |
| Sales/Receivables | 56  6.5 | 57  6.4 | 57  6.4 | 48  7.6 | 65  5.6 | 64  5.7 | 54  6.7 | 58  6.3 | 57  6.4 |
| Cost of Sales/Inventory | 3  109.8 | 9  38.4 | 8  46.1 | 0  UND | 0  UND | 1  579.3 | 5  67.4 | 12  31.4 | 19  19.2 |
| Cost of Sales/Inventory | 22  16.5 | 26  14.2 | 24  15.5 | 26  14.1 | 11  32.1 | 17  21.2 | 24  15.2 | 25  14.4 | 44  8.3 |
| Cost of Sales/Inventory | 46  7.9 | 50  7.3 | 57  6.4 | 69  5.3 | 33  10.9 | 45  8.1 | 58  6.3 | 66  5.5 | 56  6.5 |
| Cost of Sales/Payables | 12  31.0 | 12  31.5 | 17  22.0 | 12  29.3 | 12  29.7 | 8  45.7 | 17  20.9 | 21  17.6 | 14  25.7 |
| Cost of Sales/Payables | 24  15.5 | 26  14.2 | 27  13.6 | 21  17.5 | 29  12.8 | 29  12.8 | 25  14.7 | 29  12.7 | 24  15.0 |
| Cost of Sales/Payables | 42  8.8 | 38  9.6 | 41  8.8 | 91  4.0 | 49  7.5 | 44  8.3 | 36  10.1 | 47  7.7 | 33  11.2 |
| Sales/Working Capital | 5.0 | 4.9 | 5.2 | 5.8 | 4.1 | 4.6 | 4.8 | 6.0 | 5.2 |
| Sales/Working Capital | 10.8 | 9.1 | 9.4 | -15.1 | 9.2 | 9.6 | 8.6 | 14.0 | 9.1 |
| Sales/Working Capital | -53.6 | 27.1 | 47.3 | -6.8 | NM | -53.1 | 15.7 | NM | 11.7 |
| EBIT/Interest | 9.2 | 21.0 | 19.0 | 6.0 | 27.4 | 5.1 | 17.3 | 27.5 | 24.5 |
| EBIT/Interest | (121)  2.4 | (122)  5.7 | (132)  6.2 | (10)  3.6 | (16)  10.0 | (23)  2.5 | (33)  8.8 | (23)  7.7 | (27)  10.2 |
| EBIT/Interest | -.7 | 1.5 | 1.9 | 1.6 | 1.7 | .4 | 1.7 | 3.3 | 3.3 |
| Net Profit + Depr., Dep., Amort./Cur. Mat. L/T/D | 2.9 | 5.9 | 5.5 | | | | 5.2 | | |
| Net Profit + Depr., Dep., Amort./Cur. Mat. L/T/D | (26)  1.6 | (31)  3.4 | (25)  2.5 | | | | (10)  2.5 | | |
| Net Profit + Depr., Dep., Amort./Cur. Mat. L/T/D | .2 | 2.2 | 1.6 | | | | 2.0 | | |
| Fixed/Worth | .4 | .3 | .4 | .8 | .2 | .4 | .3 | .4 | .4 |
| Fixed/Worth | .9 | .8 | .9 | -13.5 | .8 | 1.4 | .7 | 1.0 | .8 |
| Fixed/Worth | 7.1 | 2.9 | 4.6 | .0 | -.4 | 4.8 | 1.2 | 1.9 | 5.4 |
| Debt/Worth | .5 | .5 | .6 | .9 | .2 | .8 | .5 | .6 | .6 |
| Debt/Worth | 1.4 | 1.3 | 1.5 | -22.0 | .8 | 2.0 | 1.2 | 1.4 | 1.4 |
| Debt/Worth | 9.9 | 5.2 | 7.9 | -2.0 | -2.5 | 8.4 | 2.2 | 3.0 | 6.4 |
| % Profit Before Taxes/Tangible Net Worth | 32.6 | 45.5 | 50.0 | | 63.9 | 41.9 | 54.0 | 72.1 | 44.8 |
| % Profit Before Taxes/Tangible Net Worth | (104)  13.6 | (110)  24.8 | (120)  28.1 | | (14)  15.6 | (21)  16.0 | (32)  20.7 | (23)  35.9 | (25)  30.7 |
| % Profit Before Taxes/Tangible Net Worth | -3.7 | 6.7 | 12.0 | | 2.4 | 4.6 | 6.2 | 14.6 | 26.1 |
| % Profit Before Taxes/Total Assets | 15.6 | 19.2 | 24.1 | 34.9 | 23.4 | 14.4 | 23.1 | 29.6 | 20.1 |
| % Profit Before Taxes/Total Assets | 4.4 | 8.1 | 10.7 | 11.3 | 13.0 | 3.8 | 10.2 | 16.1 | 12.4 |
| % Profit Before Taxes/Total Assets | -6.1 | 1.3 | 3.4 | 2.8 | 2.3 | -1.0 | | 7.9 | 6.5 |
| Sales/Net Fixed Assets | 14.3 | 15.2 | 18.0 | 125.8 | 35.9 | 19.1 | 18.2 | 11.1 | 14.6 |
| Sales/Net Fixed Assets | 6.9 | 7.1 | 7.6 | 34.7 | 13.6 | 8.8 | 6.9 | 6.3 | 6.2 |
| Sales/Net Fixed Assets | 2.8 | 3.2 | 4.1 | 1.1 | 4.0 | 4.2 | 4.5 | 3.6 | 3.2 |
| Sales/Total Assets | 2.9 | 2.9 | 3.0 | 4.0 | 4.4 | 3.7 | 2.7 | 2.6 | 3.0 |
| Sales/Total Assets | 2.0 | 2.1 | 2.1 | 2.9 | 2.3 | 2.1 | 2.0 | 2.0 | 2.0 |
| Sales/Total Assets | 1.2 | 1.4 | 1.5 | .9 | 1.6 | 1.4 | 1.5 | 1.6 | 1.5 |
| % Depr., Dep., Amort./Sales | 1.8 | 1.4 | 1.2 | | .5 | 1.6 | 1.5 | 1.8 | 1.1 |
| % Depr., Dep., Amort./Sales | (110)  3.3 | (117)  2.7 | (127)  2.7 | | (15)  1.2 | (21)  2.8 | (31)  2.8 | (25)  3.1 | (27)  2.6 |
| % Depr., Dep., Amort./Sales | 6.1 | 4.6 | 4.5 | | 2.5 | 4.4 | 4.6 | 5.4 | 4.1 |
| % Officers', Directors' Owners' Comp/Sales | 3.6 | 3.3 | 3.8 | | 6.0 | 4.1 | 3.8 | | |
| % Officers', Directors' Owners' Comp/Sales | (48)  5.7 | (47)  6.7 | (67)  6.1 | | (15)  7.5 | (18)  5.5 | (20)  6.5 | | |
| % Officers', Directors' Owners' Comp/Sales | 10.1 | 9.5 | 9.5 | | 13.2 | 7.6 | 12.2 | | |
| Net Sales ($) | 2170995M | 2635396M | 3932044M | 6192M | 45164M | 97898M | 256913M | 385378M | 3140499M |
| Total Assets ($) | 1546595M | 1577231M | 1973444M | 3466M | 22077M | 59217M | 144691M | 198445M | 1545548M |

© RMA 2012

M = $ thousand    MM = $ million
See Pages 9 through 22 for Explanation of Ratios and Data

## Current Data Sorted by Assets　　　　　　　　　　Comparative Historical Data

### Type of Statement

| | 0-500M | 500M-2MM | 2-10MM | 10-50MM | 50-100MM | 100-250MM | Type of Statement | 4/1/07-3/31/08 ALL | 4/1/08-3/31/09 ALL |
|---|---|---|---|---|---|---|---|---|---|
| | | 1 | 4 | 2 | | 1 | Unqualified | 8 | 13 |
| | | 2 | 24 | 2 | 1 | | Reviewed | 30 | 36 |
| | 3 | 19 | 17 | 1 | | | Compiled | 35 | 32 |
| | 9 | 13 | 8 | | | | Tax Returns | 14 | 15 |
| | 8 | 11 | 18 | 9 | | | Other | 59 | 64 |
| | 28 (4/1-9/30/11) | | | 125 (10/1/11-3/31/12) | | | | | |
| NUMBER OF STATEMENTS | 20 | 46 | 71 | 14 | 1 | 1 | | 146 | 160 |

### ASSETS

| | 0-500M % | 500M-2MM % | 2-10MM % | 10-50MM % | 50-100MM % | 100-250MM % | | ALL % | ALL % |
|---|---|---|---|---|---|---|---|---|---|
| | 7.5 | 13.4 | 9.4 | 4.8 | | | Cash & Equivalents | 9.2 | 8.1 |
| | 39.3 | 31.3 | 27.5 | 28.8 | | | Trade Receivables (net) | 29.3 | 26.5 |
| | 8.4 | 9.1 | 11.8 | 17.6 | | | Inventory | 9.4 | 14.2 |
| | 5.0 | 3.2 | 2.6 | 2.2 | | | All Other Current | 2.5 | 3.3 |
| | 60.1 | 57.0 | 51.3 | 53.3 | | | Total Current | 50.3 | 52.0 |
| | 30.2 | 33.5 | 36.9 | 35.2 | | | Fixed Assets (net) | 39.4 | 37.6 |
| | 5.4 | 3.5 | 5.1 | 6.1 | | | Intangibles (net) | 4.0 | 4.4 |
| | 4.3 | 6.0 | 6.7 | 5.4 | | | All Other Non-Current | 6.3 | 5.9 |
| | 100.0 | 100.0 | 100.0 | 100.0 | | | Total | 100.0 | 100.0 |

### LIABILITIES

| | 0-500M | 500M-2MM | 2-10MM | 10-50MM | | | | ALL | ALL |
|---|---|---|---|---|---|---|---|---|---|
| | 13.9 | 6.5 | 11.9 | 11.1 | | | Notes Payable-Short Term | 12.4 | 11.4 |
| | 3.1 | 2.6 | 3.3 | 3.8 | | | Cur. Mat.-L.T.D. | 5.2 | 5.7 |
| | 22.3 | 17.2 | 13.5 | 18.2 | | | Trade Payables | 14.0 | 14.1 |
| | .0 | .0 | .2 | .0 | | | Income Taxes Payable | .1 | .1 |
| | 50.5 | 18.1 | 8.0 | 7.4 | | | All Other Current | 10.0 | 7.5 |
| | 89.7 | 44.5 | 36.8 | 40.5 | | | Total Current | 41.7 | 38.8 |
| | 17.9 | 35.2 | 14.7 | 15.3 | | | Long-Term Debt | 17.9 | 20.3 |
| | .1 | .3 | .6 | 1.1 | | | Deferred Taxes | .6 | .6 |
| | 13.3 | 11.5 | 9.9 | 10.0 | | | All Other Non-Current | 10.7 | 8.0 |
| | -21.0 | 8.6 | 38.0 | 33.0 | | | Net Worth | 29.1 | 32.2 |
| | 100.0 | 100.0 | 100.0 | 100.0 | | | Total Liabilities & Net Worth | 100.0 | 100.0 |

### INCOME DATA

| | 0-500M | 500M-2MM | 2-10MM | 10-50MM | | | | ALL | ALL |
|---|---|---|---|---|---|---|---|---|---|
| | 100.0 | 100.0 | 100.0 | 100.0 | | | Net Sales | 100.0 | 100.0 |
| | 55.0 | 40.4 | 28.8 | 23.1 | | | Gross Profit | 31.0 | 30.1 |
| | 49.9 | 32.5 | 22.1 | 16.6 | | | Operating Expenses | 25.8 | 25.0 |
| | 5.1 | 8.0 | 6.7 | 6.5 | | | Operating Profit | 5.3 | 5.1 |
| | 1.4 | .8 | .7 | 1.0 | | | All Other Expenses (net) | 1.4 | 1.5 |
| | 3.7 | 7.2 | 6.0 | 5.5 | | | Profit Before Taxes | 3.8 | 3.6 |

### RATIOS

| | 0-500M | 500M-2MM | 2-10MM | 10-50MM | | | | ALL | ALL |
|---|---|---|---|---|---|---|---|---|---|
| | 2.5 | 5.1 | 2.9 | 2.7 | | | Current | 2.2 | 2.4 |
| | 1.4 | 2.2 | 1.5 | 1.6 | | | | 1.3 | 1.3 |
| | .4 | 1.0 | 1.0 | .9 | | | | .9 | .9 |
| | 2.3 | 4.3 | 2.2 | 2.2 | | | Quick | 1.6 | 1.7 |
| | .9 | 1.5 | 1.1 | .9 | | | | 1.0 | .9 |
| | .3 | .7 | .7 | .4 | | | | .6 | .6 |
| | 30 12.1 | 35 10.5 | 37 9.8 | 41 8.8 | | | Sales/Receivables | 38 9.7 | 31 11.7 |
| | 38 9.6 | 46 8.0 | 46 8.0 | 51 7.2 | | | | 46 7.9 | 42 8.7 |
| | 42 8.7 | 53 6.9 | 53 6.9 | 68 5.4 | | | | 55 6.6 | 53 6.9 |
| | 0 UND | 0 UND | 5 71.7 | 7 49.3 | | | Cost of Sales/Inventory | 4 100.9 | 8 44.1 |
| | 4 85.1 | 7 53.4 | 13 29.1 | 28 13.1 | | | | 12 30.7 | 21 17.5 |
| | 19 19.1 | 20 18.2 | 41 8.8 | 65 5.6 | | | | 29 12.4 | 46 7.9 |
| | 14 26.5 | 6 64.5 | 17 22.1 | 23 15.8 | | | Cost of Sales/Payables | 15 24.0 | 13 27.3 |
| | 25 14.4 | 19 19.5 | 28 13.1 | 29 12.6 | | | | 25 14.5 | 25 14.5 |
| | 51 7.2 | 56 6.5 | 43 8.4 | 63 5.8 | | | | 38 9.6 | 41 8.9 |
| | 7.9 | 5.4 | 5.5 | 5.5 | | | Sales/Working Capital | 8.4 | 7.1 |
| | 24.4 | 8.5 | 12.8 | 10.7 | | | | 22.4 | 21.3 |
| | -6.7 | NM | -999.8 | -28.9 | | | | -61.0 | -138.9 |
| | 10.4 | 13.6 | 14.2 | 64.1 | | | EBIT/Interest | 10.4 | 7.6 |
| | (14) 2.0 | (39) 2.8 | (65) 5.1 | (12) 7.3 | | | | (134) 3.4 | (144) 2.7 |
| | -3.3 | 1.3 | 2.6 | 3.2 | | | | 1.0 | 1.0 |
| | | | 12.9 | | | | Net Profit + Depr., Dep., Amort./Cur. Mat. L/T/D | 5.5 | 4.9 |
| | | | (20) 4.3 | | | | | (42) 2.4 | (41) 1.9 |
| | | | 3.7 | | | | | .9 | 1.1 |
| | .6 | .2 | .4 | .4 | | | Fixed/Worth | .6 | .5 |
| | NM | .9 | .9 | 1.2 | | | | 1.0 | 1.0 |
| | -.2 | -2.5 | 2.2 | 4.5 | | | | 3.8 | 3.7 |
| | 1.1 | .3 | .5 | .8 | | | Debt/Worth | .7 | .7 |
| | NM | 1.7 | 1.3 | 2.4 | | | | 1.9 | 1.9 |
| | -2.2 | -3.1 | 3.8 | 8.8 | | | | 10.0 | 9.0 |
| | 87.7 | 51.4 | 43.2 | 64.3 | | | % Profit Before Taxes/Tangible Net Worth | 40.6 | 40.1 |
| | (10) 26.8 | (31) 25.3 | (60) 21.4 | (12) 30.0 | | | | (118) 19.5 | (126) 18.0 |
| | -.8 | 6.1 | 11.3 | 15.1 | | | | 4.1 | 2.9 |
| | 25.5 | 23.5 | 18.1 | 16.7 | | | % Profit Before Taxes/Total Assets | 14.9 | 13.3 |
| | 7.6 | 10.4 | 8.4 | 10.9 | | | | 6.2 | 5.0 |
| | -9.8 | 1.7 | 3.4 | 3.4 | | | | .2 | -.8 |
| | 33.4 | 33.7 | 13.5 | 15.9 | | | Sales/Net Fixed Assets | 12.0 | 13.2 |
| | 14.1 | 7.4 | 5.8 | 4.4 | | | | 6.1 | 6.2 |
| | 8.0 | 4.3 | 3.1 | 2.4 | | | | 3.4 | 3.4 |
| | 5.1 | 3.4 | 2.9 | 2.2 | | | Sales/Total Assets | 3.0 | 3.1 |
| | 3.6 | 2.5 | 2.0 | 1.7 | | | | 2.2 | 2.1 |
| | 2.4 | 1.8 | 1.4 | 1.2 | | | | 1.6 | 1.5 |
| | .8 | .8 | 1.6 | 1.3 | | | % Depr., Dep., Amort./Sales | 1.6 | 1.4 |
| | (13) 1.0 | (39) 2.9 | (67) 2.8 | (12) 2.8 | | | | (134) 2.9 | (147) 2.5 |
| | 1.9 | 5.2 | 4.8 | 4.7 | | | | 4.8 | 4.4 |
| | 5.1 | 2.7 | 1.4 | | | | % Officers', Directors' Owners' Comp/Sales | 2.1 | 2.6 |
| | (13) 13.3 | (29) 7.4 | (31) 3.3 | | | | | (71) 4.9 | (62) 4.8 |
| | 20.8 | 10.5 | 6.6 | | | | | 7.7 | 8.1 |
| | 20498M | 137844M | 819034M | 508792M | 105552M | 175595M | Net Sales ($) | 2076297M | 2702961M |
| | 4989M | 53334M | 353424M | 266718M | 61253M | 105553M | Total Assets ($) | 1045949M | 1342564M |

M = $ thousand　　MM = $ million
See Pages 9 through 22 for Explanation of Ratios and Data

**Comparative Historical Data**                                    **Current Data Sorted by Sales**

| | | | Type of Statement | | | | | | |
|---|---|---|---|---|---|---|---|---|---|
| 11 | 8 | 8 | Unqualified | | 1 | | 1 | 2 | 4 |
| 28 | 24 | 29 | Reviewed | | 1 | 2 | 17 | 5 | 4 |
| 23 | 37 | 40 | Compiled | 2 | 12 | 9 | 11 | 6 | |
| 15 | 21 | 30 | Tax Returns | 5 | 12 | 5 | 6 | 2 | |
| 53 | 46 | 46 | Other | 7 | 8 | 3 | 11 | 10 | 7 |
| 4/1/09-3/31/10 ALL | 4/1/10-3/31/11 ALL | 4/1/11-3/31/12 ALL | | 0-1MM | 28 (4/1-9/30/11) 1-3MM | 3-5MM | 125 (10/1/11-3/31/12) 5-10MM | 10-25MM | 25MM & OVER |
| 130 | 136 | 153 | **NUMBER OF STATEMENTS** | 14 | 34 | 19 | 46 | 25 | 15 |
| % | % | % | **ASSETS** | % | % | % | % | % | % |
| 7.0 | 9.2 | 10.0 | Cash & Equivalents | 10.1 | 7.5 | 18.1 | 9.7 | 9.7 | 6.5 |
| 27.3 | 29.7 | 30.3 | Trade Receivables (net) | 29.6 | 32.2 | 27.1 | 29.6 | 29.6 | 33.6 |
| 12.5 | 11.3 | 11.1 | Inventory | 9.3 | 7.7 | 6.6 | 13.2 | 11.4 | 19.2 |
| 3.3 | 2.5 | 3.0 | All Other Current | 3.3 | 3.9 | 3.4 | 2.4 | 3.4 | 1.9 |
| 50.2 | 52.7 | 54.4 | Total Current | 52.2 | 51.2 | 55.2 | 54.9 | 54.1 | 61.2 |
| 38.1 | 34.6 | 34.9 | Fixed Assets (net) | 31.1 | 34.6 | 36.0 | 37.3 | 34.3 | 31.6 |
| 3.9 | 4.8 | 4.7 | Intangibles (net) | 7.7 | 7.2 | 5.5 | 2.2 | 5.9 | .6 |
| 7.8 | 7.9 | 6.0 | All Other Non-Current | 8.9 | 7.0 | 3.3 | 5.5 | 5.7 | 6.6 |
| 100.0 | 100.0 | 100.0 | Total | 100.0 | 100.0 | 100.0 | 100.0 | 100.0 | 100.0 |
| | | | **LIABILITIES** | | | | | | |
| 12.1 | 8.4 | 10.4 | Notes Payable-Short Term | 8.2 | 8.7 | 8.5 | 13.1 | 6.7 | 16.2 |
| 5.0 | 3.8 | 3.2 | Cur. Mat.-L.T.D. | 3.6 | 3.0 | 2.1 | 3.4 | 2.8 | 4.5 |
| 14.4 | 13.0 | 16.1 | Trade Payables | 13.6 | 19.3 | 14.2 | 15.4 | 13.5 | 20.6 |
| .0 | .1 | .1 | Income Taxes Payable | .0 | .0 | .1 | .2 | .0 | .1 |
| 8.6 | 10.2 | 16.6 | All Other Current | 26.2 | 27.5 | 25.2 | 8.4 | 10.1 | 7.6 |
| 40.2 | 35.5 | 46.3 | Total Current | 51.6 | 58.5 | 50.1 | 40.5 | 33.0 | 49.0 |
| 21.0 | 23.5 | 21.7 | Long-Term Debt | 21.1 | 35.9 | 25.2 | 15.4 | 14.0 | 17.5 |
| .7 | .7 | .5 | Deferred Taxes | .1 | .0 | .8 | .8 | .6 | .7 |
| 10.0 | 5.6 | 10.9 | All Other Non-Current | 18.5 | 6.6 | 19.3 | 6.7 | 4.4 | 26.9 |
| 28.1 | 34.7 | 20.6 | Net Worth | 8.7 | -1.0 | 4.7 | 36.6 | 47.9 | 5.9 |
| 100.0 | 100.0 | 100.0 | Total Liabilities & Net Worth | 100.0 | 100.0 | 100.0 | 100.0 | 100.0 | 100.0 |
| | | | **INCOME DATA** | | | | | | |
| 100.0 | 100.0 | 100.0 | Net Sales | 100.0 | 100.0 | 100.0 | 100.0 | 100.0 | 100.0 |
| 33.5 | 35.5 | 35.2 | Gross Profit | 68.6 | 41.4 | 36.0 | 28.0 | 31.4 | 17.3 |
| 30.8 | 28.8 | 28.3 | Operating Expenses | 60.9 | 34.9 | 27.7 | 21.5 | 23.3 | 13.3 |
| 2.7 | 6.7 | 6.9 | Operating Profit | 7.7 | 6.5 | 8.2 | 6.5 | 8.1 | 4.0 |
| 1.4 | 1.6 | .8 | All Other Expenses (net) | 1.8 | 1.2 | .6 | .5 | .2 | 1.2 |
| 1.3 | 5.1 | 6.0 | Profit Before Taxes | 6.0 | 5.3 | 7.6 | 6.0 | 7.8 | 2.7 |
| | | | **RATIOS** | | | | | | |
| 2.7 | 3.4 | 3.4 | | 3.1 | 4.7 | 6.4 | 3.3 | 3.1 | 1.9 |
| 1.2 | 1.5 | 1.6 | Current | 2.0 | 1.9 | 1.6 | 1.4 | 2.5 | 1.4 |
| .9 | 1.1 | .9 | | .6 | .8 | 1.1 | .9 | 1.2 | .8 |
| 1.8 | 2.5 | 2.5 | | 3.1 | 3.6 | 6.2 | 2.2 | 2.5 | 1.2 |
| .9 | 1.1 | 1.2 | Quick | 1.4 | 1.2 | 1.2 | 1.0 | 1.5 | .9 |
| .6 | .7 | .7 | | .5 | .7 | .9 | .6 | .9 | .5 |
| 38  9.7 | 40  9.2 | 36  10.2 | | 30  12.1 | 30  12.1 | 35  10.3 | 36  10.1 | 41  9.0 | 35  10.3 |
| 47  7.8 | 50  7.3 | 45  8.2 | Sales/Receivables | 38  9.5 | 45  8.1 | 45  8.2 | 46  7.9 | 46  8.0 | 43  8.4 |
| 58  6.3 | 60  6.0 | 54  6.8 | | 45  8.1 | 54  6.8 | 52  7.0 | 52  7.0 | 60  6.1 | 57  6.4 |
| 8  45.5 | 7  55.0 | 2  174.3 | | 0  UND | 0  UND | 0  UND | 6  63.8 | 4  87.9 | 11  33.1 |
| 18  20.7 | 16  23.3 | 11  33.1 | Cost of Sales/Inventory | 0  UND | 6  63.9 | 6  58.0 | 19  18.8 | 12  29.5 | 19  19.4 |
| 45  8.1 | 47  7.7 | 38  9.5 | | 79  4.6 | 16  22.5 | 13  28.2 | 49  7.4 | 33  10.9 | 56  6.5 |
| 17  20.9 | 12  29.8 | 14  27.0 | | 0  UND | 12  31.3 | 0  UND | 18  20.4 | 19  19.3 | 24  15.1 |
| 32  11.4 | 25  14.7 | 28  13.2 | Cost of Sales/Payables | 31  11.8 | 22  16.4 | 20  18.7 | 31  11.9 | 27  13.4 | 28  13.2 |
| 46  8.0 | 41  8.9 | 45  8.2 | | 76  4.8 | 46  7.9 | 34  10.6 | 47  7.8 | 40  9.2 | 38  9.5 |
| 6.4 | 5.0 | 5.9 | | 6.7 | 5.7 | 4.9 | 4.6 | 5.6 | 7.8 |
| 22.1 | 11.7 | 12.2 | Sales/Working Capital | 18.4 | 9.8 | 16.3 | 13.2 | 8.6 | 25.7 |
| -33.5 | 95.1 | -85.5 | | -7.5 | -19.7 | 54.8 | -39.2 | 24.4 | -26.0 |
| 6.9 | 19.0 | 13.2 | | 8.3 | 12.5 | 7.9 | 12.7 | 45.4 | 9.2 |
| (120) 2.4 | (125) 4.2 | (132) 4.4 | EBIT/Interest | (10) 5.0 | (28) 3.0 | (15) 2.7 | (44) 5.2 | (21) 13.2 | (14) 3.4 |
| -.4 | 1.4 | 1.7 | | -6.5 | .9 | 1.7 | 2.3 | 3.1 | 2.1 |
| 3.7 | 6.4 | 11.0 | | | | | 5.6 | | |
| (29) 1.6 | (36) 2.4 | (28) 4.1 | Net Profit + Depr., Dep., Amort./Cur. Mat. L/T/D | | | | (12) 4.2 | | |
| .6 | 1.6 | 3.6 | | | | | 2.4 | | |
| .6 | .5 | .4 | | .2 | .5 | .4 | .4 | .3 | .4 |
| 1.2 | 1.0 | 1.0 | Fixed/Worth | 1.4 | 1.4 | 1.0 | 1.0 | .7 | 1.3 |
| 7.4 | 2.9 | NM | | -.6 | -.7 | 7.7 | 2.8 | 1.6 | -1.3 |
| .8 | .5 | .6 | | .5 | .6 | .3 | .6 | .4 | 1.5 |
| 2.0 | 1.6 | 1.7 | Debt/Worth | 2.3 | 2.2 | 1.6 | 1.3 | .9 | 2.9 |
| 15.9 | 5.0 | -35.1 | | -3.1 | -2.3 | 36.3 | 6.2 | 2.8 | -4.4 |
| 31.5 | 47.9 | 48.1 | % Profit Before Taxes/Tangible Net Worth | | 47.3 | 68.2 | 48.4 | 48.0 | 70.2 |
| (103) 8.5 | (109) 20.4 | (114) 25.0 | | (20) 20.9 | (15) 25.3 | (37) 20.9 | (23) 30.2 | (11) 18.4 |
| -.5 | 5.9 | 11.2 | | | 11.3 | 2.9 | 11.3 | 14.0 | 5.2 |
| 8.8 | 21.9 | 19.5 | % Profit Before Taxes/Total Assets | 27.6 | 19.1 | 23.0 | 16.2 | 26.1 | 14.6 |
| 3.2 | 8.1 | 9.2 | | 11.4 | 8.7 | 5.2 | 8.4 | 16.8 | 10.2 |
| -2.9 | 1.8 | 2.5 | | -6.6 | -.1 | 1.1 | 3.0 | 4.8 | 3.4 |
| 10.8 | 17.0 | 18.2 | | 37.1 | 32.6 | 27.9 | 14.0 | 14.9 | 34.6 |
| 5.3 | 6.0 | 7.0 | Sales/Net Fixed Assets | 12.3 | 6.3 | 6.3 | 5.9 | 7.0 | 8.7 |
| 2.9 | 3.2 | 3.5 | | 3.5 | 3.6 | 4.5 | 3.0 | 3.3 | 4.2 |
| 2.8 | 3.0 | 3.3 | | 3.5 | 3.7 | 3.4 | 3.0 | 3.0 | 4.1 |
| 1.9 | 2.0 | 2.2 | Sales/Total Assets | 2.6 | 2.2 | 2.5 | 2.1 | 2.1 | 2.0 |
| 1.4 | 1.4 | 1.5 | | 1.8 | 1.5 | 1.8 | 1.5 | 1.4 | 1.7 |
| 1.3 | 1.3 | 1.2 | | .8 | 2.0 | 1.7 | 1.3 | .9 |
| (113) 3.3 | (120) 2.5 | (132) 2.6 | % Depr., Dep., Amort./Sales | (29) 2.1 | (17) 3.0 | (43) 3.1 | (24) 2.2 | (12) 2.7 |
| 5.2 | 4.6 | 4.7 | | 6.1 | 3.9 | 5.3 | 4.1 | 3.9 |
| 2.6 | 2.6 | 2.1 | % Officers', Directors' Owners' Comp/Sales | 11.1 | 3.2 | 1.7 | 1.8 | | |
| (62) 5.5 | (61) 6.0 | (75) 5.6 | | (10) 14.3 | (19) 7.6 | (12) 5.1 | (24) 3.1 | | |
| 7.8 | 9.9 | 10.3 | | 23.7 | 11.7 | 10.1 | 7.4 | | |
| 1175684M | 2260223M | 1767315M | Net Sales ($) | 8346M | 67547M | 72436M | 343645M | 403230M | 872111M |
| 728761M | 1130875M | 845271M | Total Assets ($) | 3490M | 32484M | 35932M | 177743M | 196731M | 398891M |

© RMA 2012

**M = $ thousand    MM = $ million**
See Pages 9 through 22 for Explanation of Ratios and Data

## Current Data Sorted by Assets      Comparative Historical Data

| | | | | | | Type of Statement | | |
|---|---|---|---|---|---|---|---|---|
| | 1 | 8 | 4 | 3 | 1 | Unqualified | 16 | 8 |
| | 2 | 12 | 4 | 1 | | Reviewed | 10 | 11 |
| 2 | 12 | 18 | | 1 | | Compiled | 10 | 18 |
| 16 | 21 | 16 | | | | Tax Returns | 8 | 25 |
| 10 | 24 | 20 | 12 | 3 | 2 | Other | 25 | 39 |
| | 27 (4/1-9/30/11) | | 166 (10/1/11-3/31/12) | | | | 4/1/07-3/31/08 | 4/1/08-3/31/09 |
| 0-500M | 500M-2MM | 2-10MM | 10-50MM | 50-100MM | 100-250MM | | ALL | ALL |
| 28 | 60 | 74 | 20 | 8 | 3 | NUMBER OF STATEMENTS | 69 | 101 |
| % | % | % | % | % | % | ASSETS | % | % |
| 19.7 | 10.1 | 10.4 | 11.3 | | | Cash & Equivalents | 6.2 | 8.8 |
| 30.6 | 29.6 | 28.7 | 17.5 | | | Trade Receivables (net) | 28.2 | 26.0 |
| 9.7 | 22.1 | 25.5 | 29.6 | | | Inventory | 32.3 | 30.5 |
| 5.3 | 1.7 | 1.4 | 1.3 | | | All Other Current | 2.7 | 1.5 |
| 65.4 | 63.5 | 66.0 | 59.7 | | | Total Current | 69.5 | 66.9 |
| 22.8 | 23.9 | 25.4 | 25.4 | | | Fixed Assets (net) | 21.0 | 24.2 |
| 3.8 | 4.4 | 3.6 | 10.5 | | | Intangibles (net) | 4.1 | 3.1 |
| 7.8 | 8.2 | 5.0 | 4.4 | | | All Other Non-Current | 5.5 | 5.8 |
| 100.0 | 100.0 | 100.0 | 100.0 | | | Total | 100.0 | 100.0 |
| | | | | | | LIABILITIES | | |
| 16.5 | 8.6 | 8.9 | 5.2 | | | Notes Payable-Short Term | 10.0 | 12.1 |
| 4.8 | 2.5 | 4.4 | 3.6 | | | Cur. Mat.-L.T.D. | 3.7 | 3.4 |
| 15.5 | 15.1 | 13.3 | 9.0 | | | Trade Payables | 12.9 | 16.4 |
| .1 | .3 | .2 | .0 | | | Income Taxes Payable | 1.2 | .3 |
| 35.8 | 11.7 | 8.6 | 4.6 | | | All Other Current | 9.8 | 14.2 |
| 72.7 | 38.1 | 35.4 | 22.4 | | | Total Current | 37.6 | 46.4 |
| 21.8 | 19.6 | 16.9 | 15.6 | | | Long-Term Debt | 16.9 | 15.4 |
| .0 | .4 | .2 | .8 | | | Deferred Taxes | .8 | .7 |
| 12.7 | 9.8 | 5.6 | 4.6 | | | All Other Non-Current | 3.5 | 5.1 |
| -7.2 | 32.2 | 41.9 | 56.6 | | | Net Worth | 41.2 | 32.5 |
| 100.0 | 100.0 | 100.0 | 100.0 | | | Total Liabilities & Net Worth | 100.0 | 100.0 |
| | | | | | | INCOME DATA | | |
| 100.0 | 100.0 | 100.0 | 100.0 | | | Net Sales | 100.0 | 100.0 |
| 53.2 | 41.6 | 35.3 | 28.6 | | | Gross Profit | 34.4 | 35.5 |
| 45.6 | 35.2 | 26.0 | 17.6 | | | Operating Expenses | 24.3 | 28.7 |
| 7.5 | 6.4 | 9.3 | 11.0 | | | Operating Profit | 10.1 | 6.9 |
| .7 | .6 | .8 | 1.6 | | | All Other Expenses (net) | .7 | 1.0 |
| 6.8 | 5.7 | 8.5 | 9.4 | | | Profit Before Taxes | 9.4 | 5.8 |
| | | | | | | RATIOS | | |
| 5.0 | 2.7 | 3.9 | 5.4 | | | | 3.1 | 3.1 |
| 1.6 | 1.9 | 2.0 | 2.6 | | | Current | 2.0 | 1.9 |
| .4 | 1.2 | 1.2 | 1.6 | | | | 1.3 | 1.1 |
| 3.4 | 2.1 | 3.0 | 2.7 | | | | 1.7 | 1.8 |
| .8 | 1.0 | 1.1 | 1.2 | | | Quick | 1.0 | .8 |
| .4 | .7 | .7 | .8 | | | | .6 | .5 |
| 0 UND | 26 13.8 | 38 9.5 | 37 9.8 | | | | 40 9.1 | 30 12.2 |
| 36 10.2 | 36 10.0 | 47 7.7 | 43 8.4 | | | Sales/Receivables | 51 7.2 | 40 9.0 |
| 52 7.0 | 54 6.8 | 62 5.9 | 56 6.5 | | | | 63 5.8 | 51 7.2 |
| 0 UND | 6 60.9 | 26 13.8 | 51 7.1 | | | | 47 7.8 | 26 14.0 |
| 4 84.4 | 45 8.1 | 65 5.6 | 89 4.1 | | | Cost of Sales/Inventory | 96 3.8 | 85 4.3 |
| 37 9.9 | 78 4.7 | 107 3.4 | 152 2.4 | | | | 150 2.4 | 147 2.5 |
| 0 UND | 16 22.7 | 18 20.2 | 14 26.1 | | | | 19 19.7 | 16 22.2 |
| 21 17.5 | 31 11.7 | 29 12.7 | 30 12.3 | | | Cost of Sales/Payables | 33 11.2 | 30 12.3 |
| 66 5.5 | 52 7.0 | 47 7.7 | 45 8.1 | | | | 50 7.2 | 45 8.2 |
| 7.4 | 5.9 | 4.0 | 2.3 | | | | 3.2 | 4.3 |
| 13.7 | 10.6 | 6.1 | 3.7 | | | Sales/Working Capital | 5.7 | 7.8 |
| -7.8 | 25.2 | 20.6 | 11.2 | | | | 14.1 | 40.5 |
| 10.7 | 13.7 | 35.7 | 24.2 | | | | 15.8 | 16.5 |
| (18) 2.9 | (49) 4.8 | (65) 8.6 | (16) 8.4 | | | EBIT/Interest | (63) 5.7 | (91) 5.1 |
| -2.9 | 1.9 | 2.6 | 2.1 | | | | 2.6 | 2.2 |
| | | 7.0 | | | | | 3.6 | 4.1 |
| | (11) | 4.5 | | | | Net Profit + Depr., Dep., Amort./Cur. Mat. L/T/D | (22) 2.5 | (23) 2.5 |
| | | 1.5 | | | | | 1.3 | .8 |
| .2 | .2 | .2 | .2 | | | | .2 | .2 |
| .8 | .6 | .6 | .4 | | | Fixed/Worth | .6 | .7 |
| NM | 3.7 | 2.5 | 1.5 | | | | 1.3 | 4.0 |
| .5 | .6 | .5 | .3 | | | | .7 | .6 |
| 3.4 | 2.1 | 1.8 | 1.2 | | | Debt/Worth | 1.5 | 1.8 |
| -6.8 | 10.6 | 4.7 | 2.0 | | | | 4.6 | 24.7 |
| 163.2 | 66.2 | 68.7 | 44.4 | | | | 48.8 | 62.1 |
| (20) 80.5 | (51) 24.8 | (64) 31.4 | (18) 29.6 | | | % Profit Before Taxes/Tangible Net Worth | (59) 36.9 | (80) 30.8 |
| 33.8 | 6.5 | 14.0 | 14.3 | | | | 20.2 | 11.9 |
| 52.7 | 24.2 | 24.5 | 22.5 | | | | 22.8 | 22.0 |
| 24.5 | 10.5 | 14.5 | 14.4 | | | % Profit Before Taxes/Total Assets | 13.6 | 9.1 |
| 8.7 | 2.1 | 4.0 | 6.5 | | | | 4.9 | 2.8 |
| 60.4 | 58.5 | 22.4 | 15.5 | | | | 28.5 | 26.2 |
| 23.7 | 16.0 | 8.3 | 8.8 | | | Sales/Net Fixed Assets | 12.6 | 12.0 |
| 10.7 | 5.6 | 5.2 | 4.2 | | | | 5.5 | 5.6 |
| 6.3 | 3.6 | 2.6 | 1.8 | | | | 2.5 | 3.0 |
| 3.8 | 2.6 | 2.1 | 1.4 | | | Sales/Total Assets | 1.8 | 2.1 |
| 2.8 | 1.6 | 1.5 | 1.3 | | | | 1.5 | 1.5 |
| .7 | .8 | 1.3 | 1.1 | | | | 1.0 | 1.0 |
| (18) 1.3 | (35) 1.9 | (63) 2.2 | (17) 2.0 | | | % Depr., Dep., Amort./Sales | (59) 1.8 | (85) 2.0 |
| 2.2 | 5.2 | 3.7 | 3.7 | | | | 2.9 | 3.0 |
| 5.3 | 2.9 | 1.9 | | | | | 1.6 | 2.4 |
| (14) 6.8 | (32) 4.6 | (45) 3.5 | | | | % Officers', Directors' Owners' Comp/Sales | (23) 4.0 | (43) 5.3 |
| 11.3 | 7.5 | 6.5 | | | | | 7.2 | 7.9 |
| 35368M | 199718M | 650888M | 696038M | 819096M | 559913M | Net Sales ($) | 2051014M | 1984905M |
| 7354M | 72592M | 333594M | 449125M | 623486M | 356712M | Total Assets ($) | 1391976M | 1202179M |

## Comparative Historical Data  |  Current Data Sorted by Sales

| | | | Type of Statement | 0-1MM | 1-3MM | 3-5MM | 5-10MM | 10-25MM | 25MM & OVER |
|---|---|---|---|---|---|---|---|---|---|
| 13 | 11 | 17 | Unqualified | | 1 | | 2 | 7 | 7 |
| 23 | 20 | 19 | Reviewed | | 1 | 1 | 8 | 7 | 2 |
| 32 | 28 | 33 | Compiled | 3 | 6 | 6 | 13 | 4 | 1 |
| 42 | 38 | 53 | Tax Returns | 13 | 12 | 13 | 12 | 3 | 1 |
| 63 | 77 | 71 | Other | 5 | 18 | 10 | 18 | 7 | 13 |
| 4/1/09-3/31/10 ALL | 4/1/10-3/31/11 ALL | 4/1/11-3/31/12 ALL | | 27 (4/1-9/30/11) | | 166 (10/1/11-3/31/12) | | | |
| 173 | 174 | 193 | **NUMBER OF STATEMENTS** | 21 | 38 | 30 | 53 | 28 | 23 |
| % | % | % | **ASSETS** | % | % | % | % | % | % |
| 10.2 | 10.3 | 11.5 | Cash & Equivalents | 17.9 | 11.0 | 11.4 | 9.1 | 14.3 | 8.6 |
| 23.0 | 26.4 | 27.8 | Trade Receivables (net) | 24.8 | 27.2 | 31.3 | 32.3 | 24.9 | 20.2 |
| 25.9 | 26.1 | 23.1 | Inventory | 15.6 | 19.9 | 19.8 | 25.1 | 22.4 | 35.7 |
| 2.2 | 2.0 | 2.1 | All Other Current | 4.4 | 2.6 | 2.4 | 1.2 | 1.2 | 2.0 |
| 61.2 | 64.8 | 64.5 | Total Current | 62.6 | 60.8 | 64.8 | 67.7 | 62.8 | 66.5 |
| 28.7 | 25.7 | 24.4 | Fixed Assets (net) | 21.9 | 24.2 | 25.6 | 25.0 | 23.9 | 24.7 |
| 3.8 | 4.5 | 4.8 | Intangibles (net) | 6.6 | 7.7 | .7 | 2.7 | 8.7 | 3.8 |
| 6.3 | 4.9 | 6.3 | All Other Non-Current | 8.7 | 7.3 | 8.9 | 4.7 | 4.6 | 5.0 |
| 100.0 | 100.0 | 100.0 | Total | 100.0 | 100.0 | 100.0 | 100.0 | 100.0 | 100.0 |
| | | | **LIABILITIES** | | | | | | |
| 11.1 | 11.9 | 9.3 | Notes Payable-Short Term | 10.3 | 10.8 | 7.9 | 10.4 | 8.9 | 5.9 |
| 5.3 | 5.2 | 3.6 | Cur. Mat.-L.T.D. | 5.9 | 3.3 | 2.3 | 4.2 | 3.7 | 2.5 |
| 13.1 | 12.7 | 13.5 | Trade Payables | 17.6 | 12.4 | 14.1 | 14.6 | 12.6 | 9.8 |
| .3 | .2 | .2 | Income Taxes Payable | .1 | .0 | .6 | .2 | .1 | .5 |
| 11.1 | 9.5 | 13.3 | All Other Current | 15.0 | 17.7 | 25.0 | 8.0 | 7.5 | 8.2 |
| 40.9 | 39.6 | 40.0 | Total Current | 48.9 | 44.2 | 49.9 | 37.3 | 32.8 | 26.8 |
| 24.0 | 19.3 | 17.9 | Long-Term Debt | 23.6 | 28.2 | 10.6 | 18.7 | 9.1 | 13.9 |
| .2 | .3 | .4 | Deferred Taxes | .0 | .4 | .2 | .3 | .5 | .9 |
| 9.8 | 10.3 | 8.1 | All Other Non-Current | 26.5 | 4.6 | 3.2 | 6.0 | 9.5 | 6.4 |
| 25.1 | 30.5 | 33.7 | Net Worth | 1.0 | 22.6 | 36.0 | 37.7 | 48.1 | 52.1 |
| 100.0 | 100.0 | 100.0 | Total Liabilities & Net Worth | 100.0 | 100.0 | 100.0 | 100.0 | 100.0 | 100.0 |
| | | | **INCOME DATA** | | | | | | |
| 100.0 | 100.0 | 100.0 | Net Sales | 100.0 | 100.0 | 100.0 | 100.0 | 100.0 | 100.0 |
| 37.7 | 38.6 | 39.2 | Gross Profit | 59.8 | 45.3 | 38.9 | 33.5 | 32.1 | 32.7 |
| 33.0 | 31.3 | 30.9 | Operating Expenses | 51.3 | 37.5 | 32.1 | 25.4 | 23.0 | 22.3 |
| 4.6 | 7.3 | 8.3 | Operating Profit | 8.5 | 7.8 | 6.8 | 8.1 | 9.1 | 10.4 |
| 1.4 | 1.2 | .9 | All Other Expenses (net) | .9 | .9 | .9 | .8 | .3 | 1.6 |
| 3.3 | 6.1 | 7.4 | Profit Before Taxes | 7.6 | 6.9 | 5.9 | 7.3 | 8.7 | 8.9 |
| | | | **RATIOS** | | | | | | |
| 2.9 | 3.6 | 3.9 | Current | 4.6 | 3.5 | 2.7 | 3.3 | 4.5 | 4.2 |
| 1.7 | 1.9 | 2.0 | | 2.2 | 1.9 | 2.0 | 1.6 | 2.4 | 2.5 |
| 1.1 | 1.1 | 1.2 | | .7 | .9 | 1.2 | 1.3 | 1.1 | 1.5 |
| 1.7 | 1.9 | 2.2 | Quick | 2.6 | 2.4 | 2.4 | 1.9 | 3.1 | 1.8 |
| .8 | 1.1 | 1.1 | | .8 | 1.1 | 1.0 | 1.2 | 1.1 | 1.1 |
| .5 | .5 | .6 | | .5 | .5 | .6 | .8 | .8 | .7 |
| 28  13.0 | 33  11.0 | 33  10.9 | Sales/Receivables | 0  UND | 29  12.4 | 27  13.7 | 40  9.2 | 34  10.7 | 39  9.3 |
| 44  8.2 | 48  7.6 | 45  8.1 | | 36  10.1 | 41  8.9 | 37  9.9 | 49  7.5 | 45  8.1 | 47  7.8 |
| 58  6.3 | 61  6.0 | 59  6.2 | | 61  6.0 | 62  5.9 | 54  6.7 | 62  5.9 | 58  6.3 | 60  6.1 |
| 24  15.2 | 23  15.9 | 13  28.5 | Cost of Sales/Inventory | 0  UND | 0  UND | 4  87.2 | 13  28.7 | 32  11.3 | 85  4.3 |
| 72  5.1 | 68  5.4 | 52  7.0 | | 16  22.7 | 48  7.6 | 39  9.3 | 49  7.5 | 53  6.9 | 130  2.8 |
| 129  2.8 | 138  2.6 | 101  3.6 | | 76  4.8 | 118  3.1 | 72  5.1 | 83  4.4 | 91  4.0 | 203  1.8 |
| 15  24.2 | 18  20.1 | 16  23.2 | Cost of Sales/Payables | 0  UND | 15  24.9 | 14  26.5 | 16  22.3 | 17  21.3 | 21  17.8 |
| 29  12.6 | 31  11.8 | 29  12.5 | | 43  8.4 | 36  10.2 | 29  12.7 | 28  13.2 | 30  12.1 | 30  12.1 |
| 50  7.3 | 53  7.0 | 49  7.5 | | 135  2.7 | 54  6.7 | 45  8.1 | 38  9.7 | 40  9.2 | 47  7.8 |
| 4.1 | 3.5 | 4.0 | Sales/Working Capital | 4.4 | 4.2 | 5.8 | 5.1 | 3.8 | 2.3 |
| 8.3 | 7.0 | 7.4 | | 11.7 | 10.0 | 9.0 | 8.0 | 5.0 | 3.6 |
| 80.1 | 68.3 | 21.6 | | -9.6 | -126.3 | 22.8 | 19.1 | 58.9 | 6.6 |
| 8.7 | 15.7 | 19.4 | EBIT/Interest | 9.1 | 12.6 | 22.1 | 27.1 | 44.6 | 21.7 |
| (162)  2.8 | (154)  4.7 | (157)  6.0 | | (14)  3.8 | (29)  2.8 | (24)  4.3 | (49)  8.9 | (22)  10.1 | (19)  7.7 |
| .1 | 1.6 | 2.0 | | -1.1 | 1.6 | 1.9 | 2.3 | 3.0 | 2.1 |
| 5.7 | 7.9 | 6.7 | Net Profit + Depr., Dep., Amort./Cur. Mat. L/T/D | | | | | | 6.8 |
| (35)  1.8 | (25)  3.4 | (29)  3.1 | | | | | | (10) | 3.2 |
| .9 | 2.0 | 1.6 | | | | | | | 1.8 |
| .3 | .2 | .2 | Fixed/Worth | .2 | .2 | .1 | .2 | .3 | .3 |
| .8 | .8 | .6 | | 1.3 | .8 | .3 | .7 | .6 | .4 |
| 5.6 | 4.8 | 2.4 | | -.5 | -20.5 | 1.2 | 2.8 | 1.5 | .8 |
| .8 | .6 | .6 | Debt/Worth | .6 | .6 | .5 | .6 | .4 | .4 |
| 2.3 | 2.0 | 1.7 | | 6.1 | 3.1 | 1.4 | 1.9 | 1.5 | 1.1 |
| 9.5 | 18.5 | 6.5 | | -2.1 | -28.2 | 2.7 | 7.3 | 5.6 | 1.8 |
| 51.7 | 72.9 | 67.7 | % Profit Before Taxes/Tangible Net Worth | 138.6 | 93.8 | 59.0 | 68.4 | 69.7 | 40.9 |
| (136)  21.3 | (143)  31.4 | (163)  30.2 | | (15)  69.2 | (27)  30.9 | (29)  23.9 | (45)  40.5 | (25)  31.2 | (22)  24.7 |
| -.1 | 11.2 | 12.7 | | 2.2 | -.3 | 7.0 | 17.1 | 16.6 | 8.7 |
| 19.4 | 22.4 | 25.2 | % Profit Before Taxes/Total Assets | 43.7 | 25.4 | 31.3 | 24.0 | 24.8 | 20.5 |
| 5.1 | 10.7 | 13.2 | | 10.4 | 11.5 | 10.7 | 16.1 | 13.8 | 13.2 |
| -2.7 | 1.9 | 3.7 | | 2.7 | 2.3 | 2.1 | 3.7 | 5.9 | 3.4 |
| 18.2 | 18.5 | 29.4 | Sales/Net Fixed Assets | 63.4 | 30.9 | 83.8 | 29.3 | 22.4 | 11.2 |
| 9.4 | 9.3 | 10.5 | | 18.9 | 13.1 | 19.4 | 10.1 | 9.8 | 7.8 |
| 4.4 | 4.9 | 5.4 | | 5.5 | 4.6 | 7.1 | 5.5 | 5.4 | 4.7 |
| 2.5 | 2.7 | 3.3 | Sales/Total Assets | 4.0 | 3.4 | 3.8 | 3.1 | 2.6 | 1.9 |
| 1.9 | 2.0 | 2.2 | | 2.6 | 2.1 | 2.8 | 2.4 | 1.8 | 1.4 |
| 1.3 | 1.4 | 1.4 | | 1.3 | 1.2 | 2.0 | 1.8 | 1.5 | 1.3 |
| 1.3 | 1.1 | 1.1 | % Depr., Dep., Amort./Sales | .5 | 1.1 | .7 | 1.6 | 1.1 | 1.6 |
| (142)  2.6 | (151)  2.3 | (143)  2.1 | | (15)  1.3 | (22)  2.3 | (19)  1.9 | (43)  2.2 | (25)  1.9 | (19)  2.2 |
| 4.8 | 4.5 | 4.0 | | 2.4 | 6.4 | 4.4 | 3.5 | 4.6 | 2.9 |
| 2.7 | 2.4 | 2.5 | % Officers', Directors' Owners' Comp/Sales | 5.7 | 3.6 | 1.9 | 2.1 | 1.9 | |
| (89)  4.5 | (75)  4.5 | (92)  4.3 | | (11)  10.9 | (18)  5.0 | (19)  3.7 | (32)  3.3 | (11)  4.9 | |
| 7.9 | 7.8 | 6.5 | | 14.0 | 6.7 | 7.6 | | | 8.6 |
| 4124465M | 2910968M | 2961021M | Net Sales ($) | 11871M | 74089M | 117350M | 386352M | 456815M | 1914544M |
| 2340692M | 2022480M | 1842863M | Total Assets ($) | 6315M | 47535M | 46383M | 181151M | 274272M | 1287207M |

© RMA 2012

M = $ thousand    MM = $ million
See Pages 9 through 22 for Explanation of Ratios and Data

## Current Data Sorted by Assets        Comparative Historical Data

| 0-500M | 500M-2MM | 2-10MM | 10-50MM | 50-100MM | 100-250MM | Type of Statement | 4/1/07-3/31/08 ALL | 4/1/08-3/31/09 ALL |
|---|---|---|---|---|---|---|---|---|
| | | 1 | 7 | | 4 | Unqualified | 6 | 7 |
| | 1 | 6 | 7 | 1 | 1 | Reviewed | 13 | 15 |
| | 1 | 4 | 1 | 1 | | Compiled | 7 | 13 |
| | 3 | 2 | 1 | | | Tax Returns | 3 | 9 |
| | 3 | 5 | 11 | | 1 | Other | 29 | 22 |
| | 8 (4/1-9/30/11) | | 55 (10/1/11-3/31/12) | | | | | |
| | 8 | 18 | 27 | 4 | 6 | **NUMBER OF STATEMENTS** | 58 | 66 |
| % | % | % | % | % | % | **ASSETS** | % | % |
| | | 2.8 | 11.8 | | | Cash & Equivalents | 7.3 | 11.0 |
| | | 29.2 | 21.8 | | | Trade Receivables (net) | 26.6 | 23.1 |
| | | 34.4 | 30.0 | | | Inventory | 32.6 | 30.7 |
| | | 5.3 | 2.1 | | | All Other Current | 4.1 | 3.3 |
| | | 71.8 | 65.6 | | | Total Current | 70.7 | 68.1 |
| | | 18.5 | 22.5 | | | Fixed Assets (net) | 20.9 | 21.9 |
| | | 7.0 | 5.2 | | | Intangibles (net) | 2.5 | 3.5 |
| | | 2.7 | 6.7 | | | All Other Non-Current | 5.9 | 6.5 |
| | | 100.0 | 100.0 | | | Total | 100.0 | 100.0 |
| | | | | | | **LIABILITIES** | | |
| | | 10.6 | 4.4 | | | Notes Payable-Short Term | 10.8 | 8.4 |
| | | 2.8 | 2.1 | | | Cur. Mat.-L.T.D. | 3.3 | 3.2 |
| | | 12.0 | 9.8 | | | Trade Payables | 12.5 | 10.7 |
| | | .0 | .3 | | | Income Taxes Payable | .7 | .6 |
| | | 9.2 | 9.5 | | | All Other Current | 8.2 | 8.5 |
| | | 34.5 | 26.1 | | | Total Current | 35.6 | 31.4 |
| | | 8.6 | 13.3 | | | Long-Term Debt | 12.6 | 10.4 |
| | | .2 | .4 | | | Deferred Taxes | .5 | .4 |
| | | 4.5 | 7.4 | | | All Other Non-Current | 8.2 | 5.2 |
| | | 52.3 | 52.8 | | | Net Worth | 43.0 | 52.6 |
| | | 100.0 | 100.0 | | | Total Liabilities & Net Worth | 100.0 | 100.0 |
| | | | | | | **INCOME DATA** | | |
| | | 100.0 | 100.0 | | | Net Sales | 100.0 | 100.0 |
| | | 34.3 | 34.7 | | | Gross Profit | 30.1 | 33.5 |
| | | 26.4 | 25.0 | | | Operating Expenses | 21.7 | 24.9 |
| | | 7.9 | 9.7 | | | Operating Profit | 8.5 | 8.7 |
| | | .8 | .5 | | | All Other Expenses (net) | 1.4 | 1.0 |
| | | 7.1 | 9.2 | | | Profit Before Taxes | 7.1 | 7.7 |
| | | | | | | **RATIOS** | | |
| | | 3.2 | 4.3 | | | | 3.3 | 4.1 |
| | | 1.9 | 2.6 | | | Current | 2.1 | 2.3 |
| | | 1.4 | 2.0 | | | | 1.4 | 1.6 |
| | | 1.4 | 2.2 | | | | 1.9 | 2.1 |
| | | .9 | 1.2 | | | Quick | .9 | .9 |
| | | .6 | .8 | | | | .6 | .6 |
| | | 33   11.2 | 40   9.1 | | | | 36   10.1 | 33   11.0 |
| | | 45   8.2 | 49   7.5 | | | Sales/Receivables | 47   7.7 | 42   8.7 |
| | | 60   6.1 | 58   6.3 | | | | 61   6.0 | 52   7.1 |
| | | 54   6.8 | 60   6.1 | | | | 51   7.1 | 43   8.5 |
| | | 83   4.4 | 101   3.6 | | | Cost of Sales/Inventory | 94   3.9 | 89   4.1 |
| | | 118   3.1 | 146   2.5 | | | | 135   2.7 | 136   2.7 |
| | | 15   24.5 | 23   15.9 | | | | 20   18.1 | 16   23.2 |
| | | 24   15.3 | 28   13.0 | | | Cost of Sales/Payables | 29   12.6 | 23   15.6 |
| | | 38   9.6 | 44   8.3 | | | | 39   9.3 | 39   9.4 |
| | | 3.7 | 2.3 | | | | 3.1 | 3.3 |
| | | 7.2 | 4.1 | | | Sales/Working Capital | 5.0 | 5.1 |
| | | 13.9 | 6.4 | | | | 11.9 | 10.2 |
| | | 75.1 | 53.3 | | | | 16.8 | 23.9 |
| | | (16) 13.7 | (26) 15.0 | | | EBIT/Interest | (52) 5.7 | (59) 8.8 |
| | | 5.9 | 4.1 | | | | 2.1 | 3.0 |
| | | | | | | | 11.0 | 14.6 |
| | | | | | | Net Profit + Depr., Dep., Amort./Cur. Mat. L/T/D | (23) 3.4 | (26) 4.2 |
| | | | | | | | 1.7 | 2.2 |
| | | .2 | .3 | | | | .2 | .1 |
| | | .4 | .4 | | | Fixed/Worth | .5 | .4 |
| | | .9 | .9 | | | | 1.0 | .7 |
| | | .4 | .3 | | | | .6 | .5 |
| | | 1.2 | .9 | | | Debt/Worth | 1.2 | 1.0 |
| | | 2.0 | 2.6 | | | | 2.6 | 1.6 |
| | | 55.7 | 42.7 | | | | 42.9 | 48.6 |
| | | (17) 38.9 | (25) 27.7 | | | % Profit Before Taxes/Tangible Net Worth | (52) 25.6 | (63) 29.6 |
| | | 18.7 | 14.1 | | | | 10.3 | 9.7 |
| | | 26.7 | 22.3 | | | | 20.2 | 25.2 |
| | | 15.4 | 11.6 | | | % Profit Before Taxes/Total Assets | 12.1 | 14.3 |
| | | 5.3 | 5.7 | | | | 3.9 | 2.9 |
| | | 37.2 | 20.3 | | | | 28.7 | 26.3 |
| | | 11.8 | 9.1 | | | Sales/Net Fixed Assets | 10.2 | 12.7 |
| | | 7.9 | 5.1 | | | | 5.7 | 5.7 |
| | | 2.8 | 1.9 | | | | 2.4 | 2.7 |
| | | 2.4 | 1.5 | | | Sales/Total Assets | 1.9 | 2.0 |
| | | 1.7 | 1.2 | | | | 1.4 | 1.5 |
| | | .8 | 1.5 | | | | .7 | .7 |
| | | (15) 1.9 | (22) 2.2 | | | % Depr., Dep., Amort./Sales | (55) 1.9 | (56) 2.0 |
| | | 2.1 | 3.3 | | | | 3.9 | 3.5 |
| | | | | | | | 1.6 | 1.8 |
| | | | | | | % Officers', Directors' Owners' Comp/Sales | (21) 2.9 | (15) 3.1 |
| | | | | | | | 6.8 | 16.6 |
| | 31128M | 225701M | 938480M | 459209M | 1207943M | Net Sales ($) | 2511986M | 3114674M |
| | 9402M | 99019M | 597859M | 315900M | 909193M | Total Assets ($) | 1563332M | 2067730M |

M = $ thousand    MM = $ million
See Pages 9 through 22 for Explanation of Ratios and Data

## Comparative Historical Data | Current Data Sorted by Sales

| Type of Statement | 4/1/09-3/31/10 ALL | 4/1/10-3/31/11 ALL | 4/1/11-3/31/12 ALL | 0-1MM | 1-3MM | 3-5MM | 5-10MM | 10-25MM | 25MM & OVER |
|---|---|---|---|---|---|---|---|---|---|
| Unqualified | 8 | 12 | 12 | | | | | 3 | 9 |
| Reviewed | 14 | 18 | 16 | | 1 | | 3 | 6 | 6 |
| Compiled | 7 | 9 | 7 | | | | 3 | 1 | 2 |
| Tax Returns | 10 | 4 | 6 | | 1 | 1 | | 1 | 1 |
| Other | 15 | 23 | 22 | | 2 | 1 | 1 | 6 | 12 |
| | | | | | 8 (4/1-9/30/11) | | 55 (10/1/11-3/31/12) | | |
| NUMBER OF STATEMENTS | 54 | 66 | 63 | | 4 | 3 | 9 | 17 | 30 |
| **ASSETS** | % | % | % | % | % | % | % | % | % |
| Cash & Equivalents | 13.1 | 11.1 | 10.2 | D | | | | 7.6 | 11.6 |
| Trade Receivables (net) | 25.5 | 25.7 | 24.0 | A | | | | 28.8 | 20.2 |
| Inventory | 31.3 | 29.5 | 32.2 | T | | | | 27.5 | 31.4 |
| All Other Current | 3.9 | 3.4 | 2.8 | A | | | | 1.3 | 4.7 |
| Total Current | 73.8 | 69.7 | 69.2 | | | | | 65.3 | 67.8 |
| Fixed Assets (net) | 17.0 | 21.7 | 20.4 | N | | | | 25.7 | 19.4 |
| Intangibles (net) | 3.0 | 3.5 | 6.0 | O | | | | 5.4 | 6.3 |
| All Other Non-Current | 6.2 | 5.0 | 4.4 | T | | | | 3.7 | 6.4 |
| Total | 100.0 | 100.0 | 100.0 | | | | | 100.0 | 100.0 |
| **LIABILITIES** | | | | A | | | | | |
| Notes Payable-Short Term | 6.9 | 9.3 | 6.5 | V | | | | 4.8 | 4.5 |
| Cur. Mat.-L.T.D. | 3.2 | 2.9 | 2.0 | A | | | | 3.0 | 1.8 |
| Trade Payables | 10.7 | 10.9 | 11.1 | I | | | | 9.0 | 10.3 |
| Income Taxes Payable | .5 | .5 | .3 | L | | | | .0 | .6 |
| All Other Current | 10.7 | 8.8 | 10.4 | A | | | | 11.0 | 9.2 |
| Total Current | 31.9 | 32.3 | 30.3 | B | | | | 27.7 | 26.4 |
| Long-Term Debt | 7.9 | 8.7 | 10.6 | L | | | | 11.2 | 11.5 |
| Deferred Taxes | .4 | .7 | .6 | E | | | | .5 | .8 |
| All Other Non-Current | 5.8 | 3.9 | 5.4 | | | | | 8.4 | 5.3 |
| Net Worth | 54.0 | 54.4 | 53.0 | | | | | 52.1 | 56.0 |
| Total Liabilities & Net Worth | 100.0 | 100.0 | 100.0 | | | | | 100.0 | 100.0 |
| **INCOME DATA** | | | | | | | | | |
| Net Sales | 100.0 | 100.0 | 100.0 | | | | | 100.0 | 100.0 |
| Gross Profit | 34.8 | 35.0 | 33.3 | | | | | 36.8 | 32.4 |
| Operating Expenses | 27.9 | 25.3 | 23.7 | | | | | 27.2 | 20.8 |
| Operating Profit | 6.9 | 9.7 | 9.6 | | | | | 9.6 | 11.6 |
| All Other Expenses (net) | .9 | .9 | .6 | | | | | .4 | .6 |
| Profit Before Taxes | 6.1 | 8.8 | 9.0 | | | | | 9.2 | 11.0 |
| **RATIOS** | | | | | | | | | |
| Current | 6.3 / 2.8 / 1.6 | 4.5 / 2.5 / 1.4 | 4.3 / 2.4 / 1.6 | | | | | 3.7 / 2.5 / 1.7 | 5.8 / 2.5 / 2.0 |
| Quick | 3.6 / 1.1 / .7 | 2.4 / 1.2 / .6 | 2.1 / 1.1 / .7 | | | | | 2.0 / 1.2 / .8 | 2.3 / 1.0 / .7 |
| Sales/Receivables | 36 10.1 / 46 7.9 / 60 6.1 | 36 10.1 / 50 7.3 / 60 6.1 | 39 9.4 / 44 8.3 / 56 6.5 | | | | | 40 9.1 / 56 6.5 / 66 5.5 | 40 9.2 / 47 7.8 / 54 6.7 |
| Cost of Sales/Inventory | 53 6.9 / 95 3.8 / 150 2.4 | 44 8.2 / 93 3.9 / 140 2.6 | 52 7.0 / 87 4.2 / 130 2.8 | | | | | 58 6.3 / 85 4.3 / 135 2.7 | 66 5.5 / 104 3.5 / 140 2.6 |
| Cost of Sales/Payables | 13 28.0 / 22 16.3 / 37 10.0 | 17 21.0 / 28 13.0 / 42 8.6 | 21 17.3 / 27 13.7 / 43 8.4 | | | | | 23 15.9 / 26 14.0 / 43 8.5 | 23 15.7 / 27 13.5 / 44 8.3 |
| Sales/Working Capital | 2.5 / 4.0 / 9.2 | 2.5 / 4.8 / 11.3 | 3.0 / 4.6 / 9.8 | | | | | 2.9 / 4.3 / 8.2 | 2.6 / 4.0 / 6.5 |
| EBIT/Interest | 17.4 / (46) 3.8 / -.4 | 21.4 / (52) 11.1 / 4.6 | 58.3 / (55) 12.9 / 4.7 | | | | | 65.3 / (16) 17.4 / 7.3 | 58.8 / (26) 15.9 / 7.0 |
| Net Profit + Depr., Dep., Amort./Cur. Mat. L/T/D | 3.5 / (15) 2.1 / .4 | 12.7 / (17) 5.8 / 1.9 | 14.9 / (14) 8.9 / 1.9 | | | | | | |
| Fixed/Worth | .1 / .3 / .6 | .2 / .4 / .9 | .3 / .4 / .9 | | | | | .3 / .6 / 1.2 | .3 / .4 / .8 |
| Debt/Worth | .3 / 1.1 / 2.0 | .3 / .8 / 1.9 | .3 / .9 / 2.4 | | | | | .5 / 1.1 / 2.3 | .4 / .9 / 2.2 |
| % Profit Before Taxes/Tangible Net Worth | 37.1 / (53) 17.6 / -1.7 | 43.3 / (62) 26.5 / 17.2 | 49.3 / (60) 31.4 / 15.3 | | | | | 45.6 / (16) 31.0 / 15.6 | 52.0 / (29) 33.2 / 19.5 |
| % Profit Before Taxes/Total Assets | 21.1 / 8.0 / -1.4 | 23.6 / 12.6 / 8.8 | 22.3 / 12.9 / 6.4 | | | | | 22.6 / 12.6 / 8.3 | 22.5 / 15.5 / 10.7 |
| Sales/Net Fixed Assets | 40.3 / 13.7 / 6.5 | 28.2 / 10.1 / 4.3 | 23.6 / 10.9 / 5.2 | | | | | 12.7 / 8.0 / 3.9 | 20.8 / 9.4 / 5.2 |
| Sales/Total Assets | 2.4 / 1.6 / 1.3 | 2.4 / 1.6 / 1.2 | 2.4 / 1.7 / 1.3 | | | | | 2.2 / 1.5 / 1.2 | 2.2 / 1.5 / 1.2 |
| % Depr., Dep., Amort./Sales | .6 / (44) 1.5 / 3.0 | 1.4 / (53) 2.7 / 4.3 | 1.0 / (52) 2.0 / 3.2 | | | | | 1.3 / (13) 2.6 / 4.2 | 1.6 / (25) 2.3 / 3.1 |
| % Officers', Directors' Owners' Comp/Sales | 1.7 / (12) 3.5 / 9.9 | 1.7 / (17) 2.1 / 3.8 | 1.1 / (14) 1.8 / 3.1 | | | | | | |
| Net Sales ($) | 1570930M | 2478124M | 2862461M | | 8045M | 11210M | 68608M | 266028M | 2508570M |
| Total Assets ($) | 1160848M | 1860694M | 1931373M | | 6305M | 2745M | 29223M | 177864M | 1715236M |

(The four leftmost current-data columns, 0-1MM through 5-10MM, are marked "DATA NOT AVAILABLE" for the Assets, Liabilities and Income Data sections.)

M = $ thousand    MM = $ million
See Pages 9 through 22 for Explanation of Ratios and Data

## Current Data Sorted by Assets | Comparative Historical Data

### Type of Statement

| | 0-500M | 500M-2MM | 2-10MM | 10-50MM | 50-100MM | 100-250MM | | 4/1/07-3/31/08 ALL | 4/1/08-3/31/09 ALL |
|---|---|---|---|---|---|---|---|---|---|
| Unqualified | | | 1 | 4 | 2 | 2 | | 14 | 10 |
| Reviewed | | 1 | 1 | | | | | 3 | 10 |
| Compiled | 1 | | 2 | | | | | 1 | 1 |
| Tax Returns | | 1 | 3 | 1 | | | | 1 | 6 |
| Other | 1 | 1 | 5 | 6 | 1 | 3 | | 10 | 9 |
| | **9 (4/1-9/30/11)** | | | **27 (10/1/11-3/31/12)** | | | | | |
| **NUMBER OF STATEMENTS** | 2 | 3 | 12 | 11 | 3 | 5 | | 29 | 36 |
| | % | % | % | % | % | % | | % | % |
| **ASSETS** | | | | | | | | | |
| Cash & Equivalents | | | 9.4 | 14.8 | | | | 8.4 | 6.2 |
| Trade Receivables (net) | | | 25.4 | 20.8 | | | | 23.6 | 23.0 |
| Inventory | | | 40.6 | 31.3 | | | | 35.7 | 38.3 |
| All Other Current | | | 1.5 | 3.0 | | | | 3.3 | 3.2 |
| Total Current | | | 76.9 | 69.9 | | | | 70.9 | 70.7 |
| Fixed Assets (net) | | | 18.4 | 19.1 | | | | 16.8 | 18.4 |
| Intangibles (net) | | | 1.6 | 6.4 | | | | 7.1 | 6.4 |
| All Other Non-Current | | | 3.0 | 4.6 | | | | 5.2 | 4.5 |
| Total | | | 100.0 | 100.0 | | | | 100.0 | 100.0 |
| **LIABILITIES** | | | | | | | | | |
| Notes Payable-Short Term | | | 15.0 | 9.5 | | | | 12.5 | 9.9 |
| Cur. Mat.-L.T.D. | | | 1.7 | 1.8 | | | | 2.7 | 3.1 |
| Trade Payables | | | 14.4 | 9.8 | | | | 11.7 | 11.9 |
| Income Taxes Payable | | | .2 | .0 | | | | .7 | .4 |
| All Other Current | | | 5.3 | 11.8 | | | | 11.7 | 10.8 |
| Total Current | | | 36.6 | 32.9 | | | | 39.2 | 36.0 |
| Long-Term Debt | | | 14.4 | 14.5 | | | | 23.4 | 15.0 |
| Deferred Taxes | | | .4 | .4 | | | | .1 | .4 |
| All Other Non-Current | | | 3.3 | 4.3 | | | | 6.2 | 7.4 |
| Net Worth | | | 45.2 | 47.9 | | | | 31.1 | 41.2 |
| Total Liabilities & Net Worth | | | 100.0 | 100.0 | | | | 100.0 | 100.0 |
| **INCOME DATA** | | | | | | | | | |
| Net Sales | | | 100.0 | 100.0 | | | | 100.0 | 100.0 |
| Gross Profit | | | 32.7 | 40.2 | | | | 36.3 | 29.9 |
| Operating Expenses | | | 31.8 | 31.1 | | | | 29.0 | 27.5 |
| Operating Profit | | | .9 | 9.1 | | | | 7.2 | 2.4 |
| All Other Expenses (net) | | | 1.1 | .5 | | | | 1.8 | .6 |
| Profit Before Taxes | | | -.2 | 8.5 | | | | 5.4 | 1.8 |
| **RATIOS** | | | | | | | | | |
| Current | | | 6.2 / 2.1 / 1.2 | 5.7 / 1.7 / 1.5 | | | | 3.2 / 2.5 / 1.5 | 3.7 / 2.1 / 1.6 |
| Quick | | | 1.9 / .8 / .6 | 4.2 / .8 / .3 | | | | 1.7 / .9 / .6 | 1.5 / .7 / .5 |
| Sales/Receivables | | | 31  11.9 / 36  10.0 / 42  8.7 | 30  12.0 / 56  6.5 / 70  5.2 | | | | 31  11.7 / 46  7.9 / 56  6.5 | 26  13.8 / 35  10.5 / 53  6.9 |
| Cost of Sales/Inventory | | | 73  5.0 / 111  3.3 / 152  2.4 | 96  3.8 / 122  3.0 / 182  2.0 | | | | 79  4.6 / 98  3.7 / 124  3.0 | 73  5.0 / 97  3.8 / 147  2.5 |
| Cost of Sales/Payables | | | 16  23.4 / 27  13.5 / 43  8.4 | 26  14.1 / 39  9.3 / 51  7.1 | | | | 17  21.6 / 34  10.7 / 49  7.4 | 12  29.6 / 24  14.9 / 39  9.4 |
| Sales/Working Capital | | | 3.2 / 4.8 / 33.5 | 1.9 / 5.1 / 9.4 | | | | 4.2 / 5.2 / 9.0 | 3.4 / 5.5 / 8.6 |
| EBIT/Interest | | | 6.8 / (11) 2.1 / -.9 | | | | | (25) 8.5 / 3.1 / 1.3 | (32) 13.7 / 2.1 / -1.3 |
| Net Profit + Depr., Dep., Amort./Cur. Mat. L/T/D | | | | | | | | | (11) 4.6 / 2.1 / .6 |
| Fixed/Worth | | | .1 / .4 / 1.4 | .1 / .3 / 1.4 | | | | .2 / .7 / 8.5 | .2 / .5 / 1.1 |
| Debt/Worth | | | .5 / 1.3 / 6.0 | .2 / 1.1 / 4.3 | | | | .9 / 2.9 / 33.5 | .6 / 1.5 / 5.1 |
| % Profit Before Taxes/Tangible Net Worth | | | 13.0 / 5.3 / -24.7 | | | | | (23) 61.1 / 37.8 / 15.8 | (31) 23.5 / 17.1 / -.7 |
| % Profit Before Taxes/Total Assets | | | 6.9 / 3.0 / -5.4 | 26.6 / 10.1 / 1.3 | | | | 19.0 / 11.9 / 3.1 | 13.9 / 4.6 / -3.3 |
| Sales/Net Fixed Assets | | | 42.7 / 17.9 / 7.0 | 20.4 / 10.1 / 6.0 | | | | 22.7 / 14.8 / 7.7 | 20.7 / 11.9 / 8.4 |
| Sales/Total Assets | | | 2.5 / 2.3 / 1.9 | 2.2 / 1.4 / 1.1 | | | | 2.3 / 1.9 / 1.6 | 2.7 / 2.0 / 1.5 |
| % Depr., Dep., Amort./Sales | | | | 1.2 / 1.7 / 4.6 | | | | (23) 1.1 / 1.8 / 2.7 | (33) .7 / 1.4 / 2.4 |
| % Officers', Directors' Owners' Comp/Sales | | | | | | | | | |
| Net Sales ($) | 2202M | 8451M | 156139M | 394968M | 359356M | 1016849M | | 1978979M | 2332914M |
| Total Assets ($) | 797M | 3667M | 69676M | 239891M | 230664M | 759173M | | 1127025M | 1333520M |

© RMA 2012

M = $ thousand    MM = $ million
See Pages 9 through 22 for Explanation of Ratios and Data

## Comparative Historical Data | Current Data Sorted by Sales

| | | | | Type of Statement | | | | | | |
|---|---|---|---|---|---|---|---|---|---|---|
| 11 | 8 | 5 | Unqualified | | | | 1 | 1 | 4 |
| 8 | 8 | 6 | Reviewed | 1 | | 1 | 2 | 2 | 2 |
| | 2 | 3 | Compiled | 1 | | | 1 | | |
| 2 | 3 | 5 | Tax Returns | | 1 | 2 | 2 | | |
| 11 | 10 | 17 | Other | | 1 | 3 | 4 | 9 |
| 4/1/09- | 4/1/10- | 4/1/11- | | | 9 (4/1-9/30/11) | | 27 (10/1/11-3/31/12) | | |
| 3/31/10 | 3/31/11 | 3/31/12 | | 0-1MM | 1-3MM | 3-5MM | 5-10MM | 10-25MM | 25MM & OVER |
| ALL | ALL | ALL | | | | | | | |
| 32 | 31 | 36 | NUMBER OF STATEMENTS | 2 | 2 | 1 | 6 | 10 | 15 |
| % | % | % | ASSETS | % | % | % | % | % | % |
| 11.1 | 8.9 | 10.5 | Cash & Equivalents | | | | | 4.7 | 13.0 |
| 21.8 | 22.7 | 25.6 | Trade Receivables (net) | | | | | 27.0 | 23.3 |
| 31.2 | 28.6 | 31.7 | Inventory | | | | | 41.5 | 28.4 |
| 4.3 | 4.3 | 2.2 | All Other Current | | | | | 3.4 | 2.5 |
| 68.3 | 64.6 | 69.9 | Total Current | | | | | 76.6 | 67.2 |
| 19.5 | 17.5 | 18.3 | Fixed Assets (net) | | | | | 17.7 | 16.5 |
| 7.2 | 10.2 | 7.9 | Intangibles (net) | | | | | 3.9 | 12.4 |
| 4.9 | 7.7 | 3.8 | All Other Non-Current | | | | | 1.8 | 3.8 |
| 100.0 | 100.0 | 100.0 | Total | | | | | 100.0 | 100.0 |
| | | | LIABILITIES | | | | | | |
| 9.8 | 12.0 | 12.0 | Notes Payable-Short Term | | | | | 15.5 | 5.9 |
| 2.4 | 3.4 | 1.6 | Cur. Mat.-L.T.D. | | | | | 3.2 | .4 |
| 10.6 | 8.6 | 15.2 | Trade Payables | | | | | 14.9 | 9.8 |
| .5 | .5 | .1 | Income Taxes Payable | | | | | .2 | .0 |
| 9.8 | 8.7 | 8.5 | All Other Current | | | | | 8.1 | 11.2 |
| 33.2 | 33.2 | 37.4 | Total Current | | | | | 41.8 | 27.3 |
| 16.2 | 18.2 | 16.4 | Long-Term Debt | | | | | 13.5 | 11.2 |
| .2 | .7 | .8 | Deferred Taxes | | | | | .6 | .7 |
| 6.7 | 12.4 | 4.9 | All Other Non-Current | | | | | 3.6 | 5.7 |
| 43.7 | 35.5 | 40.4 | Net Worth | | | | | 40.6 | 55.1 |
| 100.0 | 100.0 | 100.0 | Total Liabilties & Net Worth | | | | | 100.0 | 100.0 |
| | | | INCOME DATA | | | | | | |
| 100.0 | 100.0 | 100.0 | Net Sales | | | | | 100.0 | 100.0 |
| 34.7 | 35.2 | 34.9 | Gross Profit | | | | | 30.8 | 34.1 |
| 30.7 | 31.6 | 30.9 | Operating Expenses | | | | | 30.2 | 24.6 |
| 4.0 | 3.6 | 4.0 | Operating Profit | | | | | .6 | 9.5 |
| 1.3 | .7 | 1.0 | All Other Expenses (net) | | | | | 1.1 | .7 |
| 2.7 | 2.9 | 3.0 | Profit Before Taxes | | | | | -.5 | 8.8 |
| | | | RATIOS | | | | | | |
| 4.4 | 4.8 | 3.9 | | | | | | 5.8 | 5.7 |
| 2.2 | 2.3 | 1.8 | Current | | | | | 1.6 | 2.1 |
| 1.4 | 1.3 | 1.2 | | | | | | 1.1 | 1.3 |
| 2.2 | 2.3 | 1.7 | | | | | | 1.7 | 4.2 |
| .7 | 1.1 | .8 | Quick | | | | | .8 | 1.4 |
| .6 | .5 | .5 | | | | | | .3 | .6 |
| 36  10.0 | 35  10.4 | 35  10.4 | | | | | | 33  10.9 | 35  10.3 |
| 44  8.3 | 43  8.5 | 42  8.7 | Sales/Receivables | | | | | 40  9.1 | 51  7.1 |
| 54  6.8 | 57  6.4 | 61  6.0 | | | | | | 55  6.6 | 70  5.2 |
| 68  5.4 | 52  7.0 | 72  5.1 | | | | | | 83  4.4 | 72  5.1 |
| 102  3.6 | 87  4.2 | 101  3.6 | Cost of Sales/Inventory | | | | | 111  3.3 | 96  3.8 |
| 134  2.7 | 159  2.3 | 130  2.8 | | | | | | 140  2.6 | 126  2.9 |
| 21  17.4 | 11  34.4 | 19  18.8 | | | | | | 20  18.3 | 16  23.4 |
| 25  14.3 | 23  15.7 | 33  11.2 | Cost of Sales/Payables | | | | | 32  11.3 | 32  11.4 |
| 37  9.8 | 34  10.8 | 41  8.9 | | | | | | 47  7.8 | 40  9.1 |
| 3.1 | 2.9 | 3.2 | | | | | | 3.2 | 2.2 |
| 4.9 | 4.5 | 5.0 | Sales/Working Capital | | | | | 5.1 | 4.4 |
| 10.8 | 17.7 | 22.7 | | | | | | NM | 10.0 |
| 16.5 | 12.3 | 21.0 | | | | | | 23.4 | 398.6 |
| (29)  2.6 | (27)  3.0 | (30)  4.7 | EBIT/Interest | | | | | 1.6 | (12)  14.5 |
| 1.1 | -.1 | .2 | | | | | | -1.4 | 5.4 |
| 9.0 | | | Net Profit + Depr., Dep., | | | | | | |
| (16)  4.0 | | | Amort./Cur. Mat. L/T/D | | | | | | |
| .8 | | | | | | | | | |
| .2 | .2 | .2 | | | | | | .2 | .2 |
| .6 | .5 | .5 | Fixed/Worth | | | | | .5 | .3 |
| 2.0 | 11.9 | 1.6 | | | | | | 1.4 | .7 |
| .5 | .6 | .5 | | | | | | .7 | .2 |
| 1.7 | 1.8 | 1.3 | Debt/Worth | | | | | 1.5 | 1.1 |
| 7.8 | 26.5 | 8.4 | | | | | | 7.0 | 4.3 |
| 33.3 | 34.0 | 33.2 | % Profit Before Taxes/Tangible | | | | | 32.0 | 37.7 |
| (27)  13.6 | (24)  20.8 | (29)  13.8 | Net Worth | | | | | 2.7 | (12)  27.7 |
| 3.0 | 9.0 | 2.7 | | | | | | -31.2 | 16.1 |
| 14.1 | 13.6 | 10.8 | % Profit Before Taxes/Total | | | | | 7.5 | 18.0 |
| 4.4 | 6.7 | 6.5 | Assets | | | | | 1.6 | 10.5 |
| .7 | -3.3 | -3.4 | | | | | | -7.9 | 9.7 |
| 16.8 | 27.4 | 32.6 | | | | | | 40.6 | 14.6 |
| 9.9 | 12.6 | 11.4 | Sales/Net Fixed Assets | | | | | 15.1 | 10.8 |
| 6.2 | 7.0 | 6.5 | | | | | | 6.1 | 6.8 |
| 2.2 | 2.3 | 2.4 | | | | | | 2.4 | 2.0 |
| 1.9 | 1.8 | 1.8 | Sales/Total Assets | | | | | 2.1 | 1.6 |
| 1.3 | 1.2 | 1.2 | | | | | | 1.7 | 1.2 |
| 1.2 | .9 | 1.2 | | | | | | | 1.2 |
| (28)  2.0 | (22)  1.7 | (25)  2.0 | % Depr., Dep., Amort./Sales | | | | | | (13)  2.0 |
| 3.3 | 2.7 | 3.8 | | | | | | | 2.6 |
| | | | % Officers', Directors' Owners' Comp/Sales | | | | | | |
| 2084224M | 1685821M | 1937965M | Net Sales ($) | 1764M | 3753M | 4466M | 40190M | 170053M | 1717739M |
| 1377117M | 1170908M | 1303868M | Total Assets ($) | 1519M | 1292M | 2095M | 41453M | 85033M | 1172476M |

M = $ thousand    MM = $ million
See Pages 9 through 22 for Explanation of Ratios and Data

## Current Data Sorted by Assets       Comparative Historical Data

| | 0-500M | 500M-2MM | 2-10MM | 10-50MM | 50-100MM | 100-250MM | Type of Statement | 4/1/07-3/31/08 ALL | 4/1/08-3/31/09 ALL |
|---|---|---|---|---|---|---|---|---|---|
| | | | 1 | 5 | 1 | 2 | Unqualified | 25 | 28 |
| | | 6 | 9 | 4 | | | Reviewed | 10 | 15 |
| | | 4 | 6 | | | | Compiled | 9 | 9 |
| | 4 | 6 | 4 | | | | Tax Returns | 3 | 9 |
| | 1 | 2 | 14 | 5 | 3 | 3 | Other | 34 | 35 |
| | | 16 (4/1-9/30/11) | | 64 (10/1/11-3/31/12) | | | | | |
| NUMBER OF STATEMENTS | 5 | 18 | 34 | 14 | 4 | 5 | | 81 | 96 |
| | % | % | % | % | % | % | ASSETS | % | % |
| | | 17.3 | 9.8 | 10.2 | | | Cash & Equivalents | 8.4 | 9.2 |
| | | 37.9 | 23.7 | 23.9 | | | Trade Receivables (net) | 23.0 | 22.2 |
| | | 17.7 | 37.2 | 33.2 | | | Inventory | 32.0 | 31.7 |
| | | .5 | .7 | 1.9 | | | All Other Current | 3.0 | 3.2 |
| | | 73.5 | 71.4 | 69.1 | | | Total Current | 66.5 | 66.4 |
| | | 16.0 | 18.6 | 18.0 | | | Fixed Assets (net) | 20.5 | 20.2 |
| | | 5.1 | 3.4 | 6.0 | | | Intangibles (net) | 6.9 | 7.5 |
| | | 5.4 | 6.6 | 7.0 | | | All Other Non-Current | 6.1 | 5.9 |
| | | 100.0 | 100.0 | 100.0 | | | Total | 100.0 | 100.0 |
| | | | | | | | LIABILITIES | | |
| | | 5.7 | 11.6 | 4.8 | | | Notes Payable-Short Term | 9.3 | 9.1 |
| | | 5.4 | 3.6 | 3.5 | | | Cur. Mat.-L.T.D. | 3.5 | 3.2 |
| | | 20.0 | 13.9 | 13.4 | | | Trade Payables | 11.8 | 13.1 |
| | | .1 | .1 | .0 | | | Income Taxes Payable | .4 | .5 |
| | | 6.0 | 7.0 | 7.1 | | | All Other Current | 7.7 | 8.8 |
| | | 37.1 | 36.3 | 29.0 | | | Total Current | 32.7 | 34.7 |
| | | 13.9 | 15.8 | 10.4 | | | Long-Term Debt | 15.2 | 13.6 |
| | | .0 | .6 | .6 | | | Deferred Taxes | .4 | .5 |
| | | 1.1 | 4.0 | 8.4 | | | All Other Non-Current | 7.7 | 7.3 |
| | | 47.9 | 43.4 | 51.6 | | | Net Worth | 44.0 | 43.9 |
| | | 100.0 | 100.0 | 100.0 | | | Total Liabilties & Net Worth | 100.0 | 100.0 |
| | | | | | | | INCOME DATA | | |
| | | 100.0 | 100.0 | 100.0 | | | Net Sales | 100.0 | 100.0 |
| | | 39.5 | 31.1 | 26.9 | | | Gross Profit | 33.2 | 34.1 |
| | | 33.9 | 24.9 | 21.1 | | | Operating Expenses | 25.3 | 25.1 |
| | | 5.7 | 6.2 | 5.9 | | | Operating Profit | 7.9 | 8.9 |
| | | .5 | .4 | .5 | | | All Other Expenses (net) | 1.3 | 1.0 |
| | | 5.2 | 5.8 | 5.4 | | | Profit Before Taxes | 6.6 | 7.9 |
| | | | | | | | RATIOS | | |
| | | 5.0 | 3.0 | 3.8 | | | Current | 4.3 | 3.2 |
| | | 1.8 | 2.0 | 2.4 | | | | 2.1 | 2.0 |
| | | 1.3 | 1.6 | 1.7 | | | | 1.3 | 1.3 |
| | | 4.0 | 1.7 | 2.2 | | | Quick | 1.8 | 1.9 |
| | | 1.5 | 1.0 | 1.1 | | | | 1.0 | .9 |
| | | .8 | .7 | .8 | | | | .6 | .5 |
| | | 36   10.0 | 36   10.2 | 43   8.5 | | | Sales/Receivables | 35   10.6 | 30   12.1 |
| | | 53   6.9 | 48   7.6 | 47   7.8 | | | | 45   8.2 | 39   9.5 |
| | | 69   5.3 | 63   5.8 | 65   5.6 | | | | 56   6.5 | 51   7.2 |
| | | 0   UND | 62   5.9 | 66   5.5 | | | Cost of Sales/Inventory | 65   5.6 | 62   5.9 |
| | | 32   11.4 | 107   3.4 | 101   3.6 | | | | 91   4.0 | 99   3.7 |
| | | 83   4.4 | 203   1.8 | 174   2.1 | | | | 124   2.9 | 133   2.7 |
| | | 10   35.8 | 17   22.0 | 28   13.2 | | | Cost of Sales/Payables | 16   22.1 | 14   25.3 |
| | | 33   11.1 | 28   13.2 | 34   10.7 | | | | 29   12.6 | 27   13.6 |
| | | 57   6.4 | 58   6.3 | 47   7.8 | | | | 41   8.9 | 42   8.8 |
| | | 4.7 | 3.2 | 3.1 | | | Sales/Working Capital | 3.5 | 4.3 |
| | | 6.2 | 4.6 | 4.7 | | | | 6.0 | 7.1 |
| | | 23.5 | 7.4 | 5.8 | | | | 12.4 | 14.1 |
| | | 39.0 | 13.4 | 22.9 | | | EBIT/Interest | 19.5 | 21.7 |
| | | (12) 9.3 | (30) 4.0 | (13) 6.3 | | | | (74) 6.3 | (81) 7.0 |
| | | 1.7 | 1.2 | 2.8 | | | | 2.0 | 3.0 |
| | | | 4.4 | | | | Net Profit + Depr., Dep., Amort./Cur. Mat. L/T/D | 11.6 | 9.8 |
| | | (13) 2.4 | | | | | | (28) 3.5 | (42) 3.5 |
| | | | 1.1 | | | | | 1.3 | 1.7 |
| | | .1 | .1 | .1 | | | Fixed/Worth | .2 | .2 |
| | | .3 | .4 | .3 | | | | .5 | .5 |
| | | .6 | 1.0 | 1.0 | | | | 1.4 | 1.7 |
| | | .6 | .6 | .4 | | | Debt/Worth | .4 | .6 |
| | | 1.2 | 1.3 | 1.0 | | | | 1.4 | 1.5 |
| | | 2.8 | 3.5 | 2.5 | | | | 5.6 | 3.8 |
| | | 71.6 | 47.6 | 35.6 | | | % Profit Before Taxes/Tangible Net Worth | 55.0 | 58.4 |
| | | (16) 25.2 | (33) 17.1 | (13) 20.3 | | | | (70) 28.8 | (80) 27.4 |
| | | 5.6 | 2.9 | 1.9 | | | | 10.1 | 10.6 |
| | | 24.9 | 20.1 | 13.3 | | | % Profit Before Taxes/Total Assets | 20.5 | 23.3 |
| | | 13.2 | 5.4 | 12.1 | | | | 12.1 | 10.1 |
| | | 1.7 | .9 | 1.1 | | | | 3.2 | 4.0 |
| | | 173.8 | 23.6 | 28.4 | | | Sales/Net Fixed Assets | 24.1 | 31.9 |
| | | 26.3 | 11.9 | 10.8 | | | | 10.2 | 10.8 |
| | | 8.4 | 4.2 | 4.6 | | | | 5.9 | 6.4 |
| | | 3.7 | 2.4 | 2.1 | | | Sales/Total Assets | 2.3 | 2.4 |
| | | 2.7 | 1.7 | 1.8 | | | | 1.9 | 1.9 |
| | | 2.2 | 1.1 | 1.3 | | | | 1.5 | 1.3 |
| | | .4 | .9 | 1.5 | | | % Depr., Dep., Amort./Sales | 1.1 | .6 |
| | | (14) .9 | (30) 2.0 | (12) 2.6 | | | | (73) 2.0 | (84) 1.5 |
| | | 2.6 | 4.1 | 3.2 | | | | 3.4 | 3.2 |
| | | | 1.0 | | | | % Officers', Directors' Owners' Comp/Sales | 1.2 | 1.2 |
| | | (12) 3.0 | | | | | | (18) 2.5 | (18) 3.8 |
| | | | 6.1 | | | | | 7.0 | 6.6 |
| | 6085M | 51149M | 315561M | 483800M | 319472M | 812637M | Net Sales ($) | 2725889M | 4034028M |
| | 1239M | 19346M | 181785M | 296634M | 269246M | 726294M | Total Assets ($) | 1589412M | 2447944M |

## Comparative Historical Data                         Current Data Sorted by Sales

| 4/1/09-3/31/10 ALL | 4/1/10-3/31/11 ALL | 4/1/11-3/31/12 ALL | Type of Statement | 0-1MM | 1-3MM 16 (4/1-9/30/11) | 3-5MM | 5-10MM 64 (10/1/11-3/31/12) | 10-25MM | 25MM & OVER |
|---|---|---|---|---|---|---|---|---|---|
| 20 | 23 | 9 | Unqualified | | | | 1 | 1 | 7 |
| 16 | 12 | 19 | Reviewed | | 3 | 3 | 5 | 5 | 3 |
| 11 | 9 | 10 | Compiled | | 3 | 4 | 2 | 1 | |
| 13 | 15 | 14 | Tax Returns | 2 | 5 | 3 | 3 | 1 | |
| 38 | 40 | 28 | Other | 2 | 2 | 2 | 5 | 6 | 11 |
| 98 | 99 | 80 | **NUMBER OF STATEMENTS** | 4 | 13 | 12 | 16 | 14 | 21 |
| % | % | % | **ASSETS** | % | % | % | % | % | % |
| 9.7 | 11.1 | 12.1 | Cash & Equivalents | | 7.8 | 9.9 | 16.1 | 9.6 | 12.1 |
| 23.1 | 25.8 | 27.1 | Trade Receivables (net) | | 37.7 | 36.2 | 20.8 | 25.6 | 22.2 |
| 28.1 | 30.2 | 30.2 | Inventory | | 12.9 | 25.9 | 37.4 | 39.1 | 32.2 |
| 2.7 | 2.2 | 1.3 | All Other Current | | .5 | .4 | .5 | 1.1 | 3.3 |
| 63.5 | 69.3 | 70.7 | Total Current | | 58.9 | 72.4 | 74.7 | 75.4 | 69.8 |
| 23.8 | 20.7 | 18.8 | Fixed Assets (net) | | 23.2 | 17.7 | 17.4 | 16.8 | 21.9 |
| 6.3 | 4.4 | 4.4 | Intangibles (net) | | 9.8 | 3.0 | 4.7 | 1.6 | 4.3 |
| 6.3 | 5.6 | 6.1 | All Other Non-Current | | 8.1 | 6.9 | 3.2 | 6.2 | 4.0 |
| 100.0 | 100.0 | 100.0 | Total | | 100.0 | 100.0 | 100.0 | 100.0 | 100.0 |
| | | | **LIABILITIES** | | | | | | |
| 7.5 | 8.7 | 10.2 | Notes Payable-Short Term | | 27.4 | 13.5 | 5.5 | 9.1 | 4.0 |
| 5.4 | 3.2 | 3.6 | Cur. Mat.-L.T.D. | | 2.3 | 6.9 | 4.6 | 2.6 | 3.2 |
| 11.3 | 12.5 | 14.2 | Trade Payables | | 14.5 | 13.8 | 16.3 | 12.4 | 10.7 |
| .1 | .3 | .1 | Income Taxes Payable | | .1 | .1 | .0 | .2 | .1 |
| 7.1 | 7.8 | 8.3 | All Other Current | | 15.4 | 3.9 | 8.9 | 7.0 | 7.8 |
| 31.4 | 32.5 | 36.5 | Total Current | | 59.7 | 38.3 | 35.3 | 31.2 | 25.8 |
| 22.8 | 13.8 | 14.1 | Long-Term Debt | | 18.4 | 16.2 | 17.3 | 8.3 | 10.9 |
| .4 | .4 | .7 | Deferred Taxes | | .0 | .2 | .7 | 1.0 | 1.2 |
| 7.5 | 4.8 | 4.1 | All Other Non-Current | | 3.0 | .6 | 5.3 | 2.6 | 6.5 |
| 37.8 | 48.5 | 44.6 | Net Worth | | 18.9 | 44.7 | 41.4 | 56.9 | 55.5 |
| 100.0 | 100.0 | 100.0 | Total Liabilties & Net Worth | | 100.0 | 100.0 | 100.0 | 100.0 | 100.0 |
| | | | **INCOME DATA** | | | | | | |
| 100.0 | 100.0 | 100.0 | Net Sales | | 100.0 | 100.0 | 100.0 | 100.0 | 100.0 |
| 31.4 | 31.3 | 34.6 | Gross Profit | | 52.4 | 31.4 | 27.3 | 36.6 | 28.1 |
| 27.1 | 25.1 | 26.9 | Operating Expenses | | 45.0 | 25.1 | 22.1 | 27.6 | 18.3 |
| 4.4 | 6.3 | 7.7 | Operating Profit | | 7.3 | 6.3 | 5.2 | 9.1 | 9.9 |
| 1.4 | .7 | .5 | All Other Expenses (net) | | -.2 | 1.2 | .8 | .0 | .5 |
| 3.0 | 5.6 | 7.1 | Profit Before Taxes | | 7.5 | 5.1 | 4.4 | 9.0 | 9.4 |
| | | | **RATIOS** | | | | | | |
| 3.6 | 3.8 | 4.2 | Current | | 5.2 | 3.5 | 2.9 | 5.6 | 4.6 |
| 2.1 | 2.1 | 2.3 | | | 1.9 | 1.7 | 2.4 | 2.6 | 2.9 |
| 1.4 | 1.4 | 1.6 | | | .7 | 1.5 | 1.5 | 1.7 | 1.9 |
| 2.0 | 2.1 | 2.3 | Quick | | 3.9 | 2.6 | 2.4 | 2.5 | 2.2 |
| 1.1 | 1.2 | 1.2 | | | 1.5 | 1.1 | 1.0 | 1.1 | 1.2 |
| .6 | .7 | .8 | | | .3 | .8 | .7 | .7 | .8 |
| 35   10.5 | 37   9.8 | 36   10.0 | Sales/Receivables | | 30   12.1 | 43   8.5 | 30   12.0 | 37   9.9 | 42   8.7 |
| 45   8.1 | 51   7.1 | 50   7.3 | | | 36   10.0 | 55   6.6 | 48   7.6 | 44   8.3 | 54   6.8 |
| 60   6.1 | 66   5.5 | 63   5.8 | | | 69   5.3 | 62   5.9 | 65   5.6 | 63   5.8 | 62   5.9 |
| 47   7.7 | 54   6.7 | 38   9.7 | Cost of Sales/Inventory | | 0   UND | 23   16.0 | 62   5.9 | 79   4.6 | 65   5.6 |
| 85   4.3 | 96   3.8 | 91   4.0 | | | 27   13.4 | 48   7.6 | 87   4.2 | 146   2.5 | 107   3.4 |
| 142   2.6 | 131   2.8 | 166   2.2 | | | 87   4.2 | 126   2.9 | 215   1.7 | 192   1.9 | 146   2.5 |
| 17   21.2 | 19   18.8 | 17   21.3 | Cost of Sales/Payables | | 17   21.8 | 12   29.8 | 22   16.3 | 10   35.2 | 22   16.4 |
| 28   13.2 | 34   10.8 | 31   11.9 | | | 27   13.3 | 27   13.4 | 28   13.2 | 29   12.4 | 31   11.7 |
| 43   8.4 | 52   7.0 | 50   7.3 | | | 59   6.2 | 55   6.6 | 46   8.0 | 66   5.5 | 38   9.7 |
| 3.7 | 2.7 | 3.2 | Sales/Working Capital | | 4.6 | 4.9 | 2.8 | 3.1 | 2.1 |
| 5.3 | 4.8 | 4.8 | | | 13.7 | 6.3 | 4.6 | 4.5 | 3.8 |
| 14.2 | 10.5 | 8.4 | | | -10.1 | 9.3 | 8.1 | 5.1 | 5.8 |
| 10.5 | 21.1 | 23.0 | EBIT/Interest | | | | 15.0 | 11.0 | 37.7 | 37.7 |
| (87)   3.7 | (85)   5.4 | (65)   9.0 | | | | (11)   2.6 | (12)   3.2 | (13)   13.3 | (18)   12.6 |
| .7 | 1.2 | 1.6 | | | | 1.6 | 1.2 | 2.5 | 3.5 |
| 6.7 | 9.2 | 4.8 | Net Profit + Depr., Dep., Amort./Cur. Mat. L/T/D | | | | | | 18.3 |
| (42)   2.0 | (32)   2.8 | (26)   2.8 | | | | | | (11)   4.2 |
| .7 | 1.3 | 1.6 | | | | | | | 1.9 |
| .2 | .2 | .1 | Fixed/Worth | | .2 | .1 | .1 | .1 | .2 |
| .6 | .4 | .3 | | | .7 | .5 | .5 | .3 | .4 |
| 2.2 | 1.0 | .8 | | | -2.2 | 1.0 | .8 | .4 | .7 |
| .7 | .5 | .6 | Debt/Worth | | .8 | .6 | .7 | .3 | .3 |
| 1.6 | 1.1 | 1.2 | | | 2.0 | 1.2 | 1.8 | .7 | 1.0 |
| 6.8 | 3.0 | 2.6 | | | -6.2 | 3.7 | 4.6 | 1.6 | 2.0 |
| 40.2 | 27.8 | 43.3 | % Profit Before Taxes/Tangible Net Worth | | | 42.6 | 65.6 | 58.4 | 31.8 |
| (82)   17.8 | (92)   16.4 | (74)   19.9 | | | | (11)   18.0 | 17.2 | 29.0 | (20)   22.6 |
| -1.6 | 3.3 | 4.8 | | | | 1.7 | 5.7 | 3.8 | 13.7 |
| 12.8 | 14.0 | 20.0 | % Profit Before Taxes/Total Assets | | 22.2 | 16.7 | 15.9 | 28.1 | 14.1 |
| 6.0 | 6.7 | 11.6 | | | 16.3 | 8.7 | 5.3 | 15.4 | 12.7 |
| -1.4 | 1.9 | 2.1 | | | 1.2 | 1.3 | 2.0 | .6 | 8.7 |
| 17.4 | 23.7 | 40.7 | Sales/Net Fixed Assets | | 75.4 | 88.0 | 55.0 | 26.7 | 16.3 |
| 8.4 | 9.6 | 11.9 | | | 22.1 | 13.8 | 11.5 | 12.9 | 6.9 |
| 4.7 | 5.1 | 5.1 | | | 6.2 | 4.7 | 3.8 | 7.7 | 4.4 |
| 2.3 | 2.0 | 2.7 | Sales/Total Assets | | 4.1 | 3.5 | 2.7 | 2.6 | 2.1 |
| 1.8 | 1.6 | 1.8 | | | 2.7 | 2.1 | 1.7 | 1.8 | 1.4 |
| 1.2 | 1.3 | 1.2 | | | 1.7 | 1.4 | 1.1 | 1.4 | 1.2 |
| 1.1 | 1.0 | .8 | % Depr., Dep., Amort./Sales | | .2 | .8 | .9 | .6 | 1.8 |
| (88)   2.0 | (79)   2.3 | (67)   2.1 | | (10)   1.8 | (11)   2.2 | (14)   1.7 | (13)   .9 | (18)   2.6 |
| 5.3 | 3.5 | 3.3 | | | 5.2 | 3.7 | 4.1 | 3.3 | 3.0 |
| 2.7 | 1.6 | 1.7 | % Officers', Directors' Owners' Comp/Sales | | | | | | |
| (30)   4.7 | (21)   4.7 | (24)   6.0 | | | | | | | |
| 8.2 | 9.6 | 10.9 | | | | | | | |
| 2674664M | 3614183M | 1988704M | Net Sales ($) | 1977M | 25386M | 48886M | 112926M | 203260M | 1596269M |
| 1749954M | 2351384M | 1494544M | Total Assets ($) | 3725M | 12992M | 26268M | 75129M | 124715M | 1251715M |

M = $ thousand    MM = $ million
See Pages 9 through 22 for Explanation of Ratios and Data

## Current Data Sorted by Assets      Comparative Historical Data

| 0-500M | 500M-2MM | 2-10MM | 10-50MM | 50-100MM | 100-250MM | Type of Statement | 4/1/07-3/31/08 ALL | 4/1/08-3/31/09 ALL |
|---|---|---|---|---|---|---|---|---|
| | | 2 | 7 | 1 | 1 | Unqualified | 8 | 7 |
| | | 4 | 3 | 1 | | Reviewed | 6 | 7 |
| | 1 | 2 | | | | Compiled | 2 | 4 |
| | 2 | 1 | | | | Tax Returns | 5 | 2 |
| | 1 | 2 | 6 | 2 | | Other | 9 | 14 |
| | 4 (4/1-9/30/11) | | 32 (10/1/11-3/31/12) | | | | | |
| 4 | 11 | 16 | 4 | 1 | | NUMBER OF STATEMENTS | 30 | 34 |

(Left columns 0-500M and 500M-2MM for the sections below: **DATA NOT AVAILABLE**)

| 0-500M | 500M-2MM | 2-10MM | 10-50MM | 50-100MM | 100-250MM | | 4/1/07-3/31/08 ALL | 4/1/08-3/31/09 ALL |
|---|---|---|---|---|---|---|---|---|
| % | % | % | % | % | % | **ASSETS** | % | % |
| | | 14.7 | 9.2 | | | Cash & Equivalents | 12.2 | 8.9 |
| | | 28.8 | 20.0 | | | Trade Receivables (net) | 25.1 | 22.4 |
| | | 31.9 | 34.3 | | | Inventory | 32.1 | 31.7 |
| | | .6 | 3.2 | | | All Other Current | 3.4 | 1.8 |
| | | 76.0 | 66.7 | | | Total Current | 72.7 | 64.8 |
| | | 19.1 | 27.0 | | | Fixed Assets (net) | 18.9 | 20.9 |
| | | 2.1 | 2.2 | | | Intangibles (net) | 3.3 | 4.8 |
| | | 2.8 | 4.1 | | | All Other Non-Current | 5.0 | 9.6 |
| | | 100.0 | 100.0 | | | Total | 100.0 | 100.0 |
| | | | | | | **LIABILITIES** | | |
| | | 6.1 | 6.0 | | | Notes Payable-Short Term | 10.7 | 10.1 |
| | | 2.9 | 2.0 | | | Cur. Mat.-L.T.D. | 2.0 | 1.9 |
| | | 16.4 | 11.1 | | | Trade Payables | 13.3 | 9.9 |
| | | .0 | .0 | | | Income Taxes Payable | .4 | .2 |
| | | 6.9 | 6.8 | | | All Other Current | 12.1 | 9.7 |
| | | 32.3 | 25.9 | | | Total Current | 38.5 | 31.7 |
| | | 8.4 | 9.7 | | | Long-Term Debt | 9.7 | 9.9 |
| | | .3 | .3 | | | Deferred Taxes | .4 | .4 |
| | | 3.9 | 8.8 | | | All Other Non-Current | 8.7 | 7.3 |
| | | 55.1 | 55.3 | | | Net Worth | 42.8 | 50.9 |
| | | 100.0 | 100.0 | | | Total Liabilities & Net Worth | 100.0 | 100.0 |
| | | | | | | **INCOME DATA** | | |
| | | 100.0 | 100.0 | | | Net Sales | 100.0 | 100.0 |
| | | 29.0 | 31.8 | | | Gross Profit | 29.6 | 28.7 |
| | | 21.7 | 23.6 | | | Operating Expenses | 20.3 | 19.4 |
| | | 7.3 | 8.1 | | | Operating Profit | 9.3 | 9.3 |
| | | .3 | .3 | | | All Other Expenses (net) | 1.8 | .9 |
| | | 7.0 | 7.8 | | | Profit Before Taxes | 7.5 | 8.4 |
| | | | | | | **RATIOS** | | |
| | | 8.4 | 3.8 | | | | 4.4 | 4.5 |
| | | 2.5 | 3.0 | | | Current | 2.2 | 2.1 |
| | | 1.4 | 1.7 | | | | 1.4 | 1.5 |
| | | 7.0 | 2.0 | | | | 1.8 | 2.3 |
| | | 1.5 | 1.3 | | | Quick | .9 | 1.0 |
| | | .7 | .7 | | | | .6 | .4 |
| | | 35   10.3 | 27   13.4 | | | | 36   10.2 | 40   9.1 |
| | | 47   7.8 | 43   8.5 | | | Sales/Receivables | 45   8.0 | 45   8.0 |
| | | 49   7.4 | 51   7.2 | | | | 53   6.8 | 58   6.3 |
| | | 43   8.5 | 60   6.1 | | | | 43   8.6 | 42   8.7 |
| | | 63   5.8 | 122   3.0 | | | Cost of Sales/Inventory | 93   3.9 | 115   3.2 |
| | | 101   3.6 | 182   2.0 | | | | 131   2.8 | 159   2.3 |
| | | 18   20.6 | 16   22.5 | | | | 17   21.3 | 17   21.2 |
| | | 30   12.0 | 27   13.4 | | | Cost of Sales/Payables | 30   12.1 | 29   12.6 |
| | | 40   9.1 | 48   7.6 | | | | 47   7.8 | 42   8.7 |
| | | 2.2 | 2.6 | | | | 3.1 | 3.0 |
| | | 4.6 | 4.0 | | | Sales/Working Capital | 4.3 | 4.2 |
| | | 11.4 | 8.7 | | | | 10.5 | 13.6 |
| | | | 70.6 | | | | 18.1 | 28.5 |
| | | | (11)   22.1 | | | EBIT/Interest | (27)   7.2 | (29)   6.1 |
| | | | 2.8 | | | | 2.6 | 2.7 |
| | | | | | | | 51.2 | 13.6 |
| | | | | | | Net Profit + Depr., Dep., Amort./Cur. Mat. L/T/D | (12)   8.1 | (11)   2.6 |
| | | | | | | | 2.7 | 1.4 |
| | | .1 | .2 | | | | .1 | .1 |
| | | .2 | .4 | | | Fixed/Worth | .4 | .5 |
| | | 1.7 | 1.3 | | | | 1.4 | 1.2 |
| | | .1 | .2 | | | | .4 | .3 |
| | | .7 | .7 | | | Debt/Worth | 1.5 | 1.6 |
| | | 5.0 | 2.0 | | | | 3.8 | 2.5 |
| | | 31.8 | 37.5 | | | | 42.4 | 49.8 |
| | (10)   10.2 | | 21.1 | | | % Profit Before Taxes/Tangible Net Worth | (26)   24.5 | (32)   20.2 |
| | | 2.0 | 9.2 | | | | 12.2 | 14.4 |
| | | 25.8 | 19.1 | | | | 16.5 | 15.9 |
| | | 4.4 | 9.5 | | | % Profit Before Taxes/Total Assets | 11.5 | 7.8 |
| | | .2 | 5.3 | | | | 3.1 | 4.2 |
| | | 27.7 | 17.1 | | | | 42.3 | 17.4 |
| | | 14.0 | 6.9 | | | Sales/Net Fixed Assets | 9.4 | 8.0 |
| | | 6.9 | 3.4 | | | | 5.4 | 4.6 |
| | | 4.0 | 2.1 | | | | 2.3 | 1.9 |
| | | 2.2 | 1.6 | | | Sales/Total Assets | 1.6 | 1.7 |
| | | 1.3 | 1.1 | | | | 1.3 | 1.1 |
| | | 1.0 | 1.3 | | | | .9 | 1.0 |
| | (10)   1.7 | | (14)   2.0 | | | % Depr., Dep., Amort./Sales | (24)   1.9 | (29)   1.9 |
| | | 3.5 | 4.2 | | | | 3.0 | 3.4 |
| | | | | | | % Officers', Directors' Owners' Comp/Sales | | |
| | 10723M | 137931M | 551128M | 320961M | 156150M | Net Sales ($) | 1087561M | 1257695M |
| | 4129M | 56036M | 329111M | 270147M | 143388M | Total Assets ($) | 772286M | 1046857M |

M = $ thousand     MM = $ million
See Pages 9 through 22 for Explanation of Ratios and Data

## Comparative Historical Data | Current Data Sorted by Sales

| 4/1/09-3/31/10 ALL | 4/1/10-3/31/11 ALL | 4/1/11-3/31/12 ALL | Type of Statement | 0-1MM | 1-3MM | 3-5MM | 5-10MM | 10-25MM | 25MM & OVER |
|---|---|---|---|---|---|---|---|---|---|
| 12 | 6 | 11 | Unqualified | | | | 1 | 1 | 9 |
| 6 | 6 | 8 | Reviewed | | | | 2 | 4 | 2 |
| 1 | 2 | 3 | Compiled | | | 1 | 2 | | |
| 3 | 3 | 3 | Tax Returns | | 2 | | | 1 | |
| 14 | 12 | 11 | Other | | | 1 | | 4 | 6 |
| | | | | | 4 (4/1-9/30/11) | | 32 (10/1/11-3/31/12) | | |
| 36 | 29 | 36 | **NUMBER OF STATEMENTS** | | 2 | 2 | 5 | 10 | 17 |
| % | % | % | **ASSETS** | % | % | % | % | % | % |
| 10.9 | 9.3 | 10.7 | Cash & Equivalents | | | | | 12.7 | 7.8 |
| 21.5 | 24.0 | 23.7 | Trade Receivables (net) | | | | | 23.6 | 21.9 |
| 28.2 | 31.4 | 33.1 | Inventory | | | | | 30.3 | 36.8 |
| 2.8 | 2.1 | 2.2 | All Other Current | | | | | 3.8 | 1.1 |
| 63.3 | 66.8 | 69.6 | Total Current | | | | | 70.3 | 67.6 |
| 24.2 | 22.1 | 22.6 | Fixed Assets (net) | | | | | 24.6 | 21.2 |
| 4.2 | 8.4 | 4.4 | Intangibles (net) | | | | | 1.5 | 7.3 |
| 8.3 | 2.8 | 3.5 | All Other Non-Current | | | | | 3.6 | 3.9 |
| 100.0 | 100.0 | 100.0 | Total | | | | | 100.0 | 100.0 |
| | | | **LIABILITIES** | | | | | | |
| 9.3 | 11.8 | 7.0 | Notes Payable-Short Term | | | | | 8.4 | 7.8 |
| 3.0 | 2.9 | 2.4 | Cur. Mat.-L.T.D. | | | | | 2.1 | 1.8 |
| 9.3 | 14.3 | 13.4 | Trade Payables | | | | | 11.9 | 14.9 |
| .0 | .1 | .0 | Income Taxes Payable | | | | | .0 | .0 |
| 9.4 | 6.1 | 6.0 | All Other Current | | | | | 4.3 | 7.1 |
| 31.0 | 35.2 | 28.7 | Total Current | | | | | 26.7 | 31.6 |
| 14.6 | 9.3 | 11.1 | Long-Term Debt | | | | | 10.8 | 8.6 |
| .6 | .2 | .2 | Deferred Taxes | | | | | .2 | .3 |
| 4.4 | 5.4 | 6.5 | All Other Non-Current | | | | | 5.1 | 8.7 |
| 49.4 | 49.8 | 53.4 | Net Worth | | | | | 57.2 | 50.8 |
| 100.0 | 100.0 | 100.0 | Total Liabilties & Net Worth | | | | | 100.0 | 100.0 |
| | | | **INCOME DATA** | | | | | | |
| 100.0 | 100.0 | 100.0 | Net Sales | | | | | 100.0 | 100.0 |
| 26.4 | 28.0 | 30.3 | Gross Profit | | | | | 29.5 | 29.7 |
| 22.0 | 20.1 | 23.3 | Operating Expenses | | | | | 21.8 | 23.0 |
| 4.4 | 7.9 | 7.0 | Operating Profit | | | | | 7.7 | 6.7 |
| 1.7 | 1.6 | .6 | All Other Expenses (net) | | | | | .1 | .8 |
| 2.7 | 6.4 | 6.4 | Profit Before Taxes | | | | | 7.6 | 5.9 |
| | | | **RATIOS** | | | | | | |
| 4.2 | 3.6 | 5.0 | | | | | | 6.9 | 3.6 |
| 2.1 | 1.8 | 2.8 | Current | | | | | 3.1 | 2.4 |
| 1.2 | 1.1 | 1.6 | | | | | | 1.4 | 1.5 |
| 2.5 | 2.0 | 3.0 | | | | | | 3.6 | 1.5 |
| .9 | .8 | 1.3 | Quick | | | | | 1.9 | 1.0 |
| .4 | .5 | .6 | | | | | | .7 | .4 |
| 30  12.0 | 40  9.1 | 40  9.1 | | | | | | 24  15.1 | 41  8.9 |
| 47  7.8 | 47  7.8 | 45  8.1 | Sales/Receivables | | | | | 44  8.3 | 43  8.4 |
| 66  5.5 | 58  6.2 | 51  7.2 | | | | | | 52  7.0 | 48  7.6 |
| 46  7.9 | 51  7.2 | 51  7.1 | | | | | | 45  8.1 | 63  5.8 |
| 81  4.5 | 85  4.3 | 101  3.6 | Cost of Sales/Inventory | | | | | 89  4.1 | 122  3.0 |
| 147  2.5 | 143  2.6 | 159  2.3 | | | | | | 192  1.9 | 166  2.2 |
| 12  29.6 | 20  18.0 | 15  23.9 | | | | | | 13  28.0 | 21  17.5 |
| 26  14.1 | 33  11.1 | 29  12.6 | Cost of Sales/Payables | | | | | 24  14.9 | 39  9.3 |
| 46  8.0 | 50  7.2 | 55  6.6 | | | | | | 37  9.8 | 64  5.7 |
| 2.8 | 3.5 | 2.5 | | | | | | 2.2 | 2.9 |
| 5.2 | 8.3 | 4.5 | Sales/Working Capital | | | | | 4.0 | 5.2 |
| 13.8 | 27.8 | 11.2 | | | | | | 14.9 | 11.6 |
| 12.5 | 27.3 | 85.7 | | | | | | | 85.7 |
| (33)  2.9 | (29)  4.6 | 6.0 | EBIT/Interest | | | | | (13) | 22.1 |
| .4 | 1.6 | 1.4 | | | | | | | 2.3 |
| 2.9 | | | | | | | | | |
| (10)  1.1 | | | Net Profit + Depr., Dep., Amort./Cur. Mat. L/T/D | | | | | | |
| .4 | | | | | | | | | |
| .2 | .2 | .2 | | | | | | .1 | .2 |
| .6 | .4 | .3 | Fixed/Worth | | | | | .2 | .4 |
| 1.5 | 1.6 | 1.6 | | | | | | 1.3 | 2.2 |
| .3 | .5 | .2 | | | | | | .2 | .4 |
| 1.9 | 1.4 | .8 | Debt/Worth | | | | | .6 | 1.2 |
| 2.6 | 3.0 | 4.5 | | | | | | 5.5 | 8.0 |
| 16.7 | 33.7 | 36.8 | | | | | | 51.7 | 37.5 |
| (34)  4.5 | (27)  16.5 | (34)  17.1 | % Profit Before Taxes/Tangible Net Worth | | | | | 9.3 | (16)  21.7 |
| -5.6 | 7.3 | 3.4 | | | | | | 3.9 | 2.3 |
| 9.0 | 15.2 | 19.1 | | | | | | 20.4 | 20.1 |
| 1.8 | 7.6 | 6.6 | % Profit Before Taxes/Total Assets | | | | | 6.6 | 10.2 |
| -1.2 | 1.6 | .7 | | | | | | 1.8 | 2.0 |
| 14.1 | 22.2 | 25.4 | | | | | | 56.4 | 26.2 |
| 5.5 | 12.3 | 11.4 | Sales/Net Fixed Assets | | | | | 8.0 | 11.4 |
| 4.2 | 5.2 | 4.6 | | | | | | 3.5 | 4.3 |
| 1.9 | 2.4 | 2.4 | | | | | | 2.8 | 2.1 |
| 1.4 | 1.7 | 1.7 | Sales/Total Assets | | | | | 1.7 | 1.6 |
| 1.1 | 1.3 | 1.2 | | | | | | 1.1 | 1.1 |
| 1.8 | 1.1 | 1.2 | | | | | | | 1.1 |
| (31)  2.6 | (27)  1.9 | (30)  1.9 | % Depr., Dep., Amort./Sales | | | | | (14) | 2.0 |
| 3.3 | 3.5 | 4.1 | | | | | | | 3.0 |
| | | | % Officers', Directors' Owners' Comp/Sales | | | | | | |
| 1843572M | 1683530M | 1176893M | Net Sales ($) | | 3676M | 7047M | 32794M | 149296M | 984080M |
| 1483999M | 1026379M | 802811M | Total Assets ($) | | 1483M | 2646M | 20576M | 101061M | 677045M |

Note: Data for the 0-1MM, 1-3MM, 3-5MM and 5-10MM columns (Assets, Liabilities, Income Data, and Ratios) marked DATA NOT AVAILABLE.

M = $ thousand    MM = $ million
See Pages 9 through 22 for Explanation of Ratios and Data

**Current Data Sorted by Assets**  |  **Comparative Historical Data**

The left-hand "Current Data Sorted by Assets" columns are largely marked **DATA NOT AVAILABLE**.

| | 0-500M | 500M-2MM | 2-10MM | 10-50MM | 50-100MM | 100-250MM | Type of Statement | 4/1/07-3/31/08 ALL | 4/1/08-3/31/09 ALL |
|---|---|---|---|---|---|---|---|---|---|
| | | | | 1 | 4 | 3 | Unqualified | 10 | 14 |
| | | | | 2 | | | Reviewed | 3 | 3 |
| | | | | 1 | | | Compiled | 2 | 3 |
| | | 4 | | 1 | | | Tax Returns | 1 | 1 |
| | | 4 | 1 | 1 | 1 | 3 | Other | 6 | 5 |
| | | 5 (4/1-9/30/11) | | 26 (10/1/11-3/31/12) | | | | | |
| | | 8 | 6 | 6 | 5 | 6 | NUMBER OF STATEMENTS | 22 | 26 |
| | % | % | % | % | % | % | | % | % |
| | | | | | | | **ASSETS** | | |
| | | | | | | | Cash & Equivalents | 6.1 | 7.4 |
| D | | | | | | | Trade Receivables (net) | 21.0 | 21.6 |
| A | | | | | | | Inventory | 31.0 | 31.4 |
| T | | | | | | | All Other Current | 2.4 | 2.0 |
| A | | | | | | | Total Current | 60.5 | 62.4 |
| | | | | | | | Fixed Assets (net) | 17.0 | 20.8 |
| N | | | | | | | Intangibles (net) | 16.6 | 12.1 |
| O | | | | | | | All Other Non-Current | 6.0 | 4.8 |
| T | | | | | | | Total | 100.0 | 100.0 |
| | | | | | | | **LIABILITIES** | | |
| A | | | | | | | Notes Payable-Short Term | 10.1 | 10.0 |
| V | | | | | | | Cur. Mat.-L.T.D. | 4.4 | 3.5 |
| A | | | | | | | Trade Payables | 11.4 | 10.8 |
| I | | | | | | | Income Taxes Payable | .4 | .3 |
| L | | | | | | | All Other Current | 8.6 | 9.4 |
| A | | | | | | | Total Current | 34.8 | 33.9 |
| B | | | | | | | Long-Term Debt | 31.8 | 24.5 |
| L | | | | | | | Deferred Taxes | 1.8 | 1.0 |
| E | | | | | | | All Other Non-Current | 8.9 | 6.9 |
| | | | | | | | Net Worth | 22.8 | 33.7 |
| | | | | | | | Total Liabilities & Net Worth | 100.0 | 100.0 |
| | | | | | | | **INCOME DATA** | | |
| | | | | | | | Net Sales | 100.0 | 100.0 |
| | | | | | | | Gross Profit | 32.4 | 36.5 |
| | | | | | | | Operating Expenses | 20.7 | 26.8 |
| | | | | | | | Operating Profit | 11.6 | 9.8 |
| | | | | | | | All Other Expenses (net) | 3.8 | 1.8 |
| | | | | | | | Profit Before Taxes | 7.8 | 7.9 |

**RATIOS**

| | 4/1/07-3/31/08 ALL | | 4/1/08-3/31/09 ALL | |
|---|---|---|---|---|
| Current | | 2.9 | | 3.9 |
| | | 1.8 | | 2.2 |
| | | 1.4 | | 1.3 |
| Quick | | 1.2 | | 1.8 |
| | | .9 | | .9 |
| | | .6 | | .6 |
| Sales/Receivables | 29 | 12.4 | 26 | 13.8 |
| | 47 | 7.8 | 48 | 7.6 |
| | 71 | 5.1 | 66 | 5.6 |
| Cost of Sales/Inventory | 67 | 5.4 | 67 | 5.5 |
| | 93 | 3.9 | 89 | 4.1 |
| | 141 | 2.6 | 117 | 3.1 |
| Cost of Sales/Payables | 25 | 14.9 | 17 | 22.0 |
| | 33 | 11.0 | 29 | 12.7 |
| | 52 | 7.0 | 42 | 8.7 |
| Sales/Working Capital | | 3.9 | | 4.5 |
| | | 6.2 | | 6.0 |
| | | 10.4 | | 12.6 |
| EBIT/Interest | | 8.1 | | 23.1 |
| | (20) | 2.2 | (23) | 3.4 |
| | | 1.2 | | 1.5 |
| Net Profit + Depr., Dep., Amort./Cur. Mat. L/T/D | | | | |
| Fixed/Worth | | .3 | | .3 |
| | | .8 | | .6 |
| | | -.4 | | -.3 |
| Debt/Worth | | .8 | | .6 |
| | | 2.2 | | 1.7 |
| | | -2.9 | | -4.0 |
| % Profit Before Taxes/Tangible Net Worth | | 63.4 | | 64.1 |
| | (14) | 24.0 | (18) | 28.3 |
| | | 18.9 | | 13.2 |
| % Profit Before Taxes/Total Assets | | 21.5 | | 29.2 |
| | | 8.2 | | 11.0 |
| | | 2.3 | | 4.7 |
| Sales/Net Fixed Assets | | 18.1 | | 19.2 |
| | | 9.2 | | 9.2 |
| | | 6.1 | | 6.7 |
| Sales/Total Assets | | 2.2 | | 2.3 |
| | | 1.7 | | 1.9 |
| | | 1.0 | | 1.4 |
| % Depr., Dep., Amort./Sales | | 1.9 | | 1.4 |
| | (20) | 2.2 | (21) | 2.3 |
| | | 3.2 | | 4.5 |
| % Officers', Directors' Owners' Comp/Sales | | | | |

| | 0-500M | 500M-2MM | 2-10MM | 10-50MM | 50-100MM | 100-250MM | | 4/1/07-3/31/08 ALL | 4/1/08-3/31/09 ALL |
|---|---|---|---|---|---|---|---|---|---|
| Net Sales ($) | | 19376M | 65770M | 162712M | 654643M | 1038532M | | 1487730M | 1550906M |
| Total Assets ($) | | 8344M | 30530M | 116918M | 383164M | 900731M | | 1223937M | 1070987M |

M = $ thousand    MM = $ million
See Pages 9 through 22 for Explanation of Ratios and Data

## Comparative Historical Data / Current Data Sorted by Sales

| | 4/1/09-3/31/10 ALL | 4/1/10-3/31/11 ALL | 4/1/11-3/31/12 ALL | | 5 (4/1-9/30/11) | | | 26 (10/1/11-3/31/12) | |
|---|---|---|---|---|---|---|---|---|---|
| Type of Statement | | | | 0-1MM | 1-3MM | 3-5MM | 5-10MM | 10-25MM | 25MM & OVER |
| Unqualified | 12 | 7 | 9 | | | | | 1 | 8 |
| Reviewed | 2 | 1 | 4 | | | | 1 | 2 | 1 |
| Compiled | 2 | | 1 | | | | 1 | 1 | |
| Tax Returns | | | 5 | | | | 1 | 1 | |
| Other | 5 | 7 | 12 | 1 | 2 | 2 | 1 | 3 | 5 |
| NUMBER OF STATEMENTS | 21 | 15 | 31 | 1 | 4 | 2 | 3 | 7 | 14 |
| **ASSETS** | % | % | % | % | % | % | % | % | % |
| Cash & Equivalents | 12.9 | 15.6 | 7.7 | | | | | | 11.1 |
| Trade Receivables (net) | 18.2 | 15.0 | 16.1 | | | | | | 18.2 |
| Inventory | 34.1 | 27.8 | 36.6 | | | | | | 31.8 |
| All Other Current | 2.1 | 1.3 | 3.3 | | | | | | 3.2 |
| Total Current | 67.4 | 59.7 | 63.7 | | | | | | 64.2 |
| Fixed Assets (net) | 15.6 | 18.7 | 23.3 | | | | | | 21.6 |
| Intangibles (net) | 10.5 | 17.2 | 5.9 | | | | | | 10.1 |
| All Other Non-Current | 6.5 | 4.4 | 7.0 | | | | | | 4.1 |
| Total | 100.0 | 100.0 | 100.0 | | | | | | 100.0 |
| **LIABILITIES** | | | | | | | | | |
| Notes Payable-Short Term | 7.6 | 7.1 | 7.4 | | | | | | 7.8 |
| Cur. Mat.-L.T.D. | 2.7 | 1.6 | 2.2 | | | | | | 3.1 |
| Trade Payables | 9.0 | 5.4 | 16.4 | | | | | | 11.1 |
| Income Taxes Payable | .3 | .3 | .1 | | | | | | .2 |
| All Other Current | 10.3 | 11.2 | 8.0 | | | | | | 8.1 |
| Total Current | 29.9 | 25.6 | 34.0 | | | | | | 30.3 |
| Long-Term Debt | 22.7 | 24.0 | 14.5 | | | | | | 9.5 |
| Deferred Taxes | 1.1 | 2.0 | .5 | | | | | | 1.2 |
| All Other Non-Current | 5.1 | 9.1 | 8.4 | | | | | | 5.6 |
| Net Worth | 41.2 | 39.2 | 42.5 | | | | | | 53.4 |
| Total Liabilties & Net Worth | 100.0 | 100.0 | 100.0 | | | | | | 100.0 |
| **INCOME DATA** | | | | | | | | | |
| Net Sales | 100.0 | 100.0 | 100.0 | | | | | | 100.0 |
| Gross Profit | 32.3 | 33.5 | 35.6 | | | | | | 26.7 |
| Operating Expenses | 19.4 | 20.1 | 28.0 | | | | | | 16.5 |
| Operating Profit | 12.9 | 13.4 | 7.7 | | | | | | 10.2 |
| All Other Expenses (net) | 1.8 | 3.2 | 1.0 | | | | | | 1.2 |
| Profit Before Taxes | 11.0 | 10.3 | 6.7 | | | | | | 9.1 |
| **RATIOS** | | | | | | | | | |
| Current | 3.9 / 2.5 / 1.6 | 3.4 / 2.3 / 1.5 | 3.7 / 1.9 / 1.4 | | | | | | 3.7 / 1.8 / 1.4 |
| Quick | 2.1 / .9 / .6 | 2.7 / 1.3 / .6 | 1.6 / .7 / .4 | | | | | | 1.9 / .8 / .6 |
| Sales/Receivables | 21  17.5 / 31  11.9 / 56  6.5 | 22  16.3 / 40  9.1 / 80  4.5 | 25  14.8 / 32  11.5 / 43  8.4 | | | | | | 29  12.6 / 38  9.6 / 76  4.8 |
| Cost of Sales/Inventory | 70  5.2 / 84  4.3 / 112  3.3 | 68  5.3 / 88  4.2 / 127  2.9 | 79  4.6 / 101  3.6 / 146  2.5 | | | | | | 91  4.0 / 107  3.4 / 140  2.6 |
| Cost of Sales/Payables | 15  24.3 / 20  18.6 / 30  12.2 | 11  33.7 / 26  14.3 / 38  9.6 | 22  16.9 / 38  9.6 / 57  6.4 | | | | | | 18  19.9 / 37  9.9 / 52  7.0 |
| Sales/Working Capital | 3.6 / 5.2 / 8.3 | 2.8 / 5.0 / 13.5 | 3.3 / 6.7 / 13.3 | | | | | | 3.1 / 4.9 / 8.9 |
| EBIT/Interest | 35.7 / (20) 17.3 / 2.5 | 97.3 / 11.4 / 1.8 | 53.5 / (29) 9.9 / 3.1 | | | | | | 93.4 / (13) 17.4 / 5.2 |
| Net Profit + Depr., Dep., Amort./Cur. Mat. L/T/D | | | | | | | | | |
| Fixed/Worth | .2 / .3 / -.6 | .2 / .8 / -.4 | .2 / .6 / 4.0 | | | | | | .2 / .5 / NM |
| Debt/Worth | .4 / 1.0 / -4.9 | .4 / .8 / -3.4 | .6 / 1.1 / 5.8 | | | | | | .4 / 1.1 / NM |
| % Profit Before Taxes/Tangible Net Worth | 72.5 / (15) 46.4 / 33.9 | | 42.7 / (24) 15.6 / 7.3 | | | | | | 40.2 / (11) 15.9 / 5.7 |
| % Profit Before Taxes/Total Assets | 31.6 / 17.3 / 7.6 | 18.1 / 6.1 / 3.5 | 18.0 / 8.9 / 2.9 | | | | | | 19.4 / 10.3 / 5.7 |
| Sales/Net Fixed Assets | 25.3 / 11.1 / 8.6 | 23.8 / 9.8 / 7.3 | 35.6 / 11.5 / 4.8 | | | | | | 13.0 / 8.5 / 5.9 |
| Sales/Total Assets | 2.4 / 1.9 / 1.5 | 1.6 / 1.3 / .7 | 2.2 / 1.8 / 1.4 | | | | | | 1.8 / 1.4 / 1.2 |
| % Depr., Dep., Amort./Sales | .9 / (18) 1.7 / 2.6 | 1.4 / (14) 2.7 / 3.8 | .6 / (27) 1.9 / 4.3 | | | | | | .7 / (13) 2.2 / 3.6 |
| % Officers', Directors' Owners' Comp/Sales | | | | | | | | | |
| Net Sales ($) | 2392921M | 1271661M | 1941033M | 204M | 6938M | 7062M | 20296M | 106444M | 1800089M |
| Total Assets ($) | 1523698M | 1160295M | 1439687M | 605M | 3815M | 2458M | 7497M | 65452M | 1359860M |

© RMA 2012

M = $ thousand    MM = $ million
See Pages 9 through 22 for Explanation of Ratios and Data

## Current Data Sorted by Assets     Comparative Historical Data

Type of Statement

| Type of Statement | 0-500M | 500M-2MM | 2-10MM | 10-50MM | 50-100MM | 100-250MM | 4/1/07-3/31/08 ALL | 4/1/08-3/31/09 ALL |
|---|---|---|---|---|---|---|---|---|
| Unqualified | | | 5 | 7 | 6 | 2 | 16 | 28 |
| Reviewed | | 5 | 10 | 10 | | 1 | 18 | 18 |
| Compiled | | 3 | 5 | 2 | | | 18 | 16 |
| Tax Returns | 2 | | 3 | 1 | | | 9 | 10 |
| Other | | 7 | 16 | 8 | 3 | 2 | 31 | 37 |
| | | 15 (4/1-9/30/11) | | 83 (10/1/11-3/31/12) | | | | |
| **NUMBER OF STATEMENTS** | 2 | 15 | 39 | 28 | 10 | 4 | 92 | 109 |
| **ASSETS** | % | % | % | % | % | % | % | % |
| Cash & Equivalents | | 7.0 | 13.5 | 12.4 | 10.9 | | 11.3 | 11.5 |
| Trade Receivables (net) | | 30.8 | 31.2 | 29.4 | 18.2 | | 32.5 | 28.5 |
| Inventory | | 16.9 | 20.9 | 17.4 | 29.0 | | 21.3 | 26.3 |
| All Other Current | | 5.4 | 2.5 | 4.6 | 1.7 | | 5.3 | 4.0 |
| Total Current | | 60.2 | 68.1 | 63.8 | 59.9 | | 70.3 | 70.4 |
| Fixed Assets (net) | | 26.8 | 25.2 | 23.1 | 18.8 | | 22.4 | 23.2 |
| Intangibles (net) | | .4 | 3.6 | 7.0 | 17.7 | | 3.3 | 2.5 |
| All Other Non-Current | | 12.6 | 3.1 | 6.1 | 3.6 | | 4.0 | 3.9 |
| Total | | 100.0 | 100.0 | 100.0 | 100.0 | | 100.0 | 100.0 |
| **LIABILITIES** | | | | | | | | |
| Notes Payable-Short Term | | 15.2 | 9.9 | 6.0 | 11.0 | | 9.2 | 10.3 |
| Cur. Mat.-L.T.D. | | 3.7 | 3.5 | 5.1 | 5.8 | | 4.0 | 4.1 |
| Trade Payables | | 16.9 | 15.0 | 16.4 | 15.8 | | 14.9 | 14.0 |
| Income Taxes Payable | | .2 | .4 | .8 | .7 | | .5 | .5 |
| All Other Current | | 5.7 | 10.5 | 12.7 | 10.0 | | 13.0 | 10.6 |
| Total Current | | 41.7 | 39.3 | 40.9 | 43.3 | | 41.5 | 39.5 |
| Long-Term Debt | | 20.1 | 12.5 | 10.3 | 12.0 | | 15.5 | 13.6 |
| Deferred Taxes | | .5 | .5 | 1.1 | 2.0 | | .6 | .5 |
| All Other Non-Current | | 8.9 | 4.4 | 5.6 | 11.0 | | 4.7 | 4.5 |
| Net Worth | | 28.9 | 43.3 | 42.1 | 31.7 | | 37.6 | 41.8 |
| Total Liabilities & Net Worth | | 100.0 | 100.0 | 100.0 | 100.0 | | 100.0 | 100.0 |
| **INCOME DATA** | | | | | | | | |
| Net Sales | | 100.0 | 100.0 | 100.0 | 100.0 | | 100.0 | 100.0 |
| Gross Profit | | 30.0 | 31.9 | 24.2 | 20.4 | | 29.6 | 28.7 |
| Operating Expenses | | 25.7 | 25.8 | 17.1 | 12.1 | | 21.0 | 20.1 |
| Operating Profit | | 4.2 | 6.1 | 7.1 | 8.3 | | 8.6 | 8.6 |
| All Other Expenses (net) | | -.2 | .1 | 1.0 | 1.9 | | 1.3 | 1.0 |
| Profit Before Taxes | | 4.4 | 6.0 | 6.1 | 6.3 | | 7.3 | 7.7 |
| **RATIOS** | | | | | | | | |
| Current | | 2.4 | 3.1 | 2.6 | 2.3 | | 2.9 | 3.0 |
| | | 1.4 | 2.1 | 1.5 | 1.3 | | 1.7 | 1.9 |
| | | 1.2 | 1.3 | 1.2 | .9 | | 1.2 | 1.2 |
| Quick | | 1.4 | 2.2 | 1.6 | 2.0 | | 1.8 | 2.1 |
| | | .8 | 1.2 | 1.0 | .5 | | 1.0 | .9 |
| | | .6 | .7 | .7 | .4 | | .7 | .6 |
| Sales/Receivables | | 24   15.0 | 39   9.4 | 44   8.3 | 34   10.8 | | 35   10.5 | 31   11.7 |
| | | 42   8.7 | 48   7.6 | 62   5.9 | 45   8.1 | | 47   7.7 | 40   9.1 |
| | | 51   7.1 | 60   6.1 | 73   5.0 | 53   6.9 | | 66   5.6 | 54   6.8 |
| Cost of Sales/Inventory | | 6   58.2 | 24   15.0 | 12   31.1 | 39   9.3 | | 19   19.5 | 28   13.3 |
| | | 29   12.4 | 49   7.5 | 49   7.4 | 59   6.2 | | 41   8.9 | 50   7.4 |
| | | 65   5.6 | 87   4.2 | 62   5.9 | 146   2.5 | | 69   5.3 | 93   3.9 |
| Cost of Sales/Payables | | 11   34.6 | 21   17.2 | 21   17.0 | 24   15.5 | | 16   22.8 | 15   24.9 |
| | | 34   10.7 | 35   10.4 | 38   9.7 | 39   9.3 | | 26   14.1 | 24   15.2 |
| | | 49   7.5 | 49   7.4 | 54   6.8 | 54   6.7 | | 46   7.9 | 43   8.5 |
| Sales/Working Capital | | 8.0 | 4.4 | 4.8 | 4.6 | | 4.7 | 5.0 |
| | | 13.7 | 7.6 | 8.1 | 11.3 | | 8.2 | 8.4 |
| | | 19.7 | 19.5 | 16.5 | -20.6 | | 22.5 | 23.6 |
| EBIT/Interest | | 12.3 | 20.1 | 15.1 | | | 19.3 | 22.2 |
| | | 3.9 | (34) 10.3 | (21) 3.3 | | | (84) 6.2 | (97) 5.8 |
| | | 1.0 | 3.7 | 1.5 | | | 2.2 | 2.1 |
| Net Profit + Depr., Dep., Amort./Cur. Mat. L/T/D | | | 13.9 | 7.3 | | | 10.8 | 17.2 |
| | | (10) | 5.5 | (14) 2.0 | | | (28) 4.2 | (33) 4.2 |
| | | | 3.2 | 1.4 | | | 1.8 | 2.1 |
| Fixed/Worth | | .2 | .2 | .2 | .0 | | .2 | .2 |
| | | .8 | .6 | .8 | .7 | | .5 | .4 |
| | | 2.8 | 1.8 | 3.4 | NM | | 1.6 | 1.3 |
| Debt/Worth | | 1.0 | .5 | .7 | 2.1 | | .7 | .5 |
| | | 2.0 | 1.2 | 1.5 | 2.9 | | 1.6 | 1.4 |
| | | 4.8 | 3.5 | 7.8 | -6.8 | | 5.4 | 3.0 |
| % Profit Before Taxes/Tangible Net Worth | | 68.5 | 65.1 | 35.6 | | | 59.8 | 64.1 |
| | (12) | 26.4 | (35) 45.4 | (25) 25.0 | | | (81) 42.9 | (100) 37.5 |
| | | 19.8 | 18.4 | 7.4 | | | 12.6 | 14.2 |
| % Profit Before Taxes/Total Assets | | 17.2 | 25.7 | 14.7 | 21.4 | | 25.0 | 26.3 |
| | | 7.0 | 14.5 | 7.7 | 6.8 | | 13.2 | 12.8 |
| | | .1 | 7.4 | 2.4 | -.2 | | 4.5 | 4.9 |
| Sales/Net Fixed Assets | | 38.1 | 34.0 | 27.5 | 377.1 | | 33.0 | 26.3 |
| | | 17.9 | 12.2 | 8.4 | 19.0 | | 13.3 | 11.8 |
| | | 6.2 | 4.5 | 4.9 | 4.0 | | 7.1 | 6.3 |
| Sales/Total Assets | | 3.0 | 2.9 | 2.2 | 1.9 | | 3.1 | 3.2 |
| | | 2.5 | 2.2 | 1.7 | 1.4 | | 2.3 | 2.3 |
| | | 1.7 | 1.8 | 1.2 | 1.1 | | 1.6 | 1.7 |
| % Depr., Dep., Amort./Sales | | .6 | .8 | 1.1 | | | .7 | .6 |
| | (10) | 2.1 | (36) 1.7 | (25) 2.4 | | | (83) 1.4 | (94) 1.7 |
| | | 5.0 | 2.8 | 4.0 | | | 2.5 | 2.9 |
| % Officers', Directors', Owners' Comp/Sales | | | 2.7 | | | | 2.0 | 1.5 |
| | | (16) | 4.3 | | | | (35) 3.0 | (39) 3.4 |
| | | | 8.8 | | | | 8.3 | 5.2 |
| Net Sales ($) | 1625M | 47206M | 429488M | 1048220M | 1200411M | 913844M | 4012676M | 5355596M |
| Total Assets ($) | 288M | 19036M | 184296M | 603107M | 713533M | 468308M | 1954561M | 2467769M |

## Comparative Historical Data  |  Current Data Sorted by Sales

Periods: 4/1/09-3/31/10 ALL · 4/1/10-3/31/11 ALL · 4/1/11-3/31/12 ALL
Current current data periods: 15 (4/1-9/30/11); 83 (10/1/11-3/31/12)

| [22] | [21] | [20] | Type of Statement | 0-1MM | 1-3MM | 3-5MM | 5-10MM | 10-25MM | 25MM & OVER |
|---|---|---|---|---|---|---|---|---|---|
| 22 | 21 | 20 | Unqualified | | | 2 | 2 | 2 | 14 |
| 18 | 17 | 20 | Reviewed | | | | 5 | 8 | 7 |
| 7 | 13 | 13 | Compiled | | 3 | 1 | 3 | 3 | 3 |
| 4 | 8 | 9 | Tax Returns | 1 | 3 | 1 | 2 | 1 | 1 |
| 42 | 38 | 36 | Other | | 4 | 7 | 4 | 11 | 10 |
| 93 | 97 | 98 | **NUMBER OF STATEMENTS** | 1 | 10 | 11 | 16 | 25 | 35 |
| % | % | % | **ASSETS** | % | % | % | % | % | % |
| 11.1 | 12.7 | 11.5 | Cash & Equivalents | | 3.8 | 6.9 | 15.0 | 14.7 | 10.8 |
| 26.6 | 26.6 | 28.7 | Trade Receivables (net) | | 25.8 | 25.6 | 31.1 | 32.5 | 27.5 |
| 24.0 | 24.6 | 21.1 | Inventory | | 21.8 | 16.8 | 17.1 | 21.2 | 24.5 |
| 4.6 | 3.4 | 3.7 | All Other Current | | 3.1 | 5.3 | 3.7 | 2.5 | 4.4 |
| 66.4 | 67.4 | 65.1 | Total Current | | 54.4 | 54.7 | 67.0 | 70.9 | 67.2 |
| 24.6 | 22.0 | 23.9 | Fixed Assets (net) | | 29.9 | 35.7 | 27.5 | 20.4 | 18.1 |
| 4.5 | 5.1 | 5.5 | Intangibles (net) | | .6 | 6.7 | 2.1 | 5.1 | 8.5 |
| 4.5 | 5.5 | 5.5 | All Other Non-Current | | 15.0 | 2.9 | 3.4 | 3.6 | 6.2 |
| 100.0 | 100.0 | 100.0 | Total | | 100.0 | 100.0 | 100.0 | 100.0 | 100.0 |
| | | | **LIABILITIES** | | | | | | |
| 11.3 | 9.8 | 9.4 | Notes Payable-Short Term | | 10.0 | 10.1 | 11.7 | 11.4 | 6.6 |
| 3.1 | 2.6 | 4.5 | Cur. Mat.-L.T.D. | | 3.9 | 2.2 | 5.8 | 3.0 | 5.9 |
| 12.6 | 12.6 | 15.4 | Trade Payables | | 19.0 | 7.9 | 13.7 | 17.8 | 16.3 |
| .6 | .4 | .5 | Income Taxes Payable | | .3 | .8 | .1 | .8 | .4 |
| 9.7 | 10.5 | 10.2 | All Other Current | | 7.1 | 6.8 | 11.6 | 10.2 | 11.6 |
| 37.3 | 35.9 | 39.9 | Total Current | | 40.3 | 27.7 | 42.9 | 43.2 | 40.9 |
| 12.0 | 10.9 | 12.9 | Long-Term Debt | | 25.2 | 17.1 | 13.9 | 7.7 | 11.6 |
| .6 | .7 | .8 | Deferred Taxes | | .0 | 1.4 | .4 | .4 | 1.4 |
| 4.3 | 4.5 | 5.9 | All Other Non-Current | | 8.7 | 4.1 | 7.3 | 3.9 | 6.5 |
| 45.7 | 48.0 | 40.5 | Net Worth | | 25.8 | 49.7 | 35.5 | 44.8 | 39.6 |
| 100.0 | 100.0 | 100.0 | Total Liabilities & Net Worth | | 100.0 | 100.0 | 100.0 | 100.0 | 100.0 |
| | | | **INCOME DATA** | | | | | | |
| 100.0 | 100.0 | 100.0 | Net Sales | | 100.0 | 100.0 | 100.0 | 100.0 | 100.0 |
| 27.2 | 30.9 | 28.1 | Gross Profit | | 32.2 | 39.6 | 30.3 | 27.5 | 21.3 |
| 21.0 | 24.6 | 22.0 | Operating Expenses | | 26.2 | 32.3 | 27.1 | 20.4 | 14.3 |
| 6.2 | 6.4 | 6.1 | Operating Profit | | 6.0 | 7.3 | 3.2 | 7.1 | 7.0 |
| .9 | .9 | .6 | All Other Expenses (net) | | -.3 | .0 | .1 | .3 | 1.4 |
| 5.3 | 5.4 | 5.5 | Profit Before Taxes | | 6.4 | 7.3 | 3.1 | 6.7 | 5.7 |
| | | | **RATIOS** | | | | | | |
| 3.0 | 3.3 | 2.8 | Current | | 2.5 | 2.9 | 3.9 | 2.7 | 2.6 |
| 1.9 | 2.3 | 1.6 | | | 1.5 | 1.6 | 1.9 | 1.6 | 1.6 |
| 1.2 | 1.3 | 1.2 | | | 1.1 | 1.4 | .9 | 1.1 | 1.2 |
| 1.9 | 2.0 | 1.8 | Quick | | 1.4 | 2.2 | 3.0 | 1.7 | 1.6 |
| 1.0 | 1.2 | 1.0 | | | .9 | 1.0 | 1.0 | 1.1 | 1.0 |
| .6 | .7 | .6 | | | .4 | .6 | .4 | .7 | .5 |
| 34 · 10.9 | 37 · 9.7 | 36 · 10.0 | Sales/Receivables | | 23 · 15.8 | 41 · 8.8 | 42 · 8.7 | 30 · 12.2 | 41 · 9.0 |
| 49 · 7.5 | 51 · 7.1 | 49 · 7.4 | | | 32 · 11.4 | 49 · 7.5 | 50 · 7.3 | 49 · 7.5 | 51 · 7.2 |
| 62 · 5.9 | 67 · 5.4 | 62 · 5.9 | | | 56 · 6.5 | 54 · 6.7 | 61 · 6.0 | 73 · 5.0 | 61 · 6.0 |
| 31 · 11.8 | 35 · 10.4 | 23 · 15.7 | Cost of Sales/Inventory | | 20 · 18.0 | 31 · 11.8 | 1 · 258.7 | 23 · 15.9 | 37 · 9.8 |
| 56 · 6.5 | 63 · 5.8 | 49 · 7.5 | | | 35 · 10.4 | 60 · 6.1 | 27 · 13.7 | 39 · 9.4 | 39 · 6.8 |
| 96 · 3.2 | 114 · 3.2 | 83 · 4.4 | | | 60 · 6.1 | 78 · 4.7 | 104 · 3.5 | 89 · 4.1 | 89 · 4.1 |
| 14 · 25.2 | 18 · 20.6 | 20 · 17.9 | Cost of Sales/Payables | | 10 · 38.0 | 12 · 31.4 | 20 · 17.9 | 22 · 16.4 | 21 · 17.3 |
| 24 · 15.1 | 31 · 11.8 | 36 · 10.2 | | | 38 · 9.6 | 25 · 14.6 | 34 · 10.6 | 38 · 9.7 | 36 · 10.0 |
| 40 · 9.1 | 45 · 8.1 | 50 · 7.3 | | | 64 · 5.7 | 49 · 7.4 | 42 · 8.6 | 54 · 6.7 | 50 · 7.3 |
| 4.3 | 3.5 | 4.6 | Sales/Working Capital | | 7.6 | 4.4 | 4.5 | 4.2 | 4.8 |
| 7.2 | 5.9 | 8.7 | | | 15.4 | 8.0 | 7.7 | 9.0 | 6.5 |
| 25.7 | 13.2 | 19.6 | | | NM | 13.1 | NM | 25.8 | 15.6 |
| 14.1 | 20.5 | 18.6 | EBIT/Interest | | 18.2 | 18.0 | 15.0 | 19.5 | 20.6 |
| (85) 4.5 | (78) 6.1 | (84) 6.4 | | | 4.9 | 8.2 | (14) 4.8 | (20) 8.6 | (29) 6.2 |
| 1.5 | 1.7 | 2.5 | | | 2.3 | 3.8 | 1.4 | 3.1 | .5 |
| 8.0 | 6.2 | 11.1 | Net Profit + Depr., Dep., Amort./Cur. Mat. L/T/D | | | | | 24.6 | 5.3 |
| (28) 2.5 | (23) 3.1 | (31) 3.4 | | | | | | (12) 6.2 | (15) 1.9 |
| 1.6 | 1.1 | 1.6 | | | | | | 2.1 | .6 |
| .2 | .2 | .2 | Fixed/Worth | | .3 | .6 | .2 | .1 | .1 |
| .5 | .4 | .6 | | | .7 | .8 | .9 | .5 | .5 |
| 1.6 | 1.0 | 1.8 | | | NM | 2.8 | 2.2 | 1.2 | 1.4 |
| .6 | .4 | .7 | Debt/Worth | | .8 | .2 | .6 | .5 | .9 |
| 1.4 | 1.1 | 1.6 | | | 2.5 | 1.5 | 2.4 | 1.0 | 2.4 |
| 3.3 | 4.1 | 3.7 | | | NM | 3.5 | 5.6 | 3.2 | 9.1 |
| 54.3 | 38.9 | 53.6 | % Profit Before Taxes/Tangible Net Worth | | | 56.0 | 94.2 | 50.3 | 40.5 |
| (86) 20.5 | (88) 18.7 | (85) 29.0 | | | | (10) 24.2 | (14) 64.3 | (22) 29.5 | (30) 27.2 |
| 4.1 | 4.6 | 15.2 | | | | 14.6 | 21.3 | 12.6 | 7.4 |
| 21.2 | 17.6 | 20.5 | % Profit Before Taxes/Total Assets | | 16.7 | 17.2 | 26.0 | 25.9 | 15.8 |
| 7.6 | 8.9 | 11.5 | | | 12.1 | 10.1 | 16.5 | 13.0 | 8.5 |
| .9 | 1.8 | 3.8 | | | 4.9 | 7.0 | 4.6 | 4.8 | .0 |
| 23.8 | 29.4 | 34.2 | Sales/Net Fixed Assets | | 32.3 | 12.3 | 22.0 | 44.5 | 38.9 |
| 9.1 | 11.5 | 12.3 | | | 16.0 | 5.6 | 10.6 | 15.7 | 14.0 |
| 4.5 | 4.8 | 4.9 | | | 2.8 | 3.2 | 4.7 | 5.4 | 5.0 |
| 2.9 | 2.6 | 2.6 | Sales/Total Assets | | 3.0 | 2.5 | 2.8 | 2.9 | 2.3 |
| 2.0 | 1.9 | 2.0 | | | 2.2 | 2.0 | 2.2 | 2.2 | 1.9 |
| 1.4 | 1.3 | 1.6 | | | 1.6 | 1.1 | 1.8 | 1.6 | 1.3 |
| 1.0 | 1.2 | .8 | % Depr., Dep., Amort./Sales | | | | .8 | .7 | .8 |
| (84) 2.2 | (85) 2.1 | (86) 1.7 | | | | | (15) 2.3 | (22) 1.5 | (32) 2.0 |
| 3.2 | 3.5 | 3.7 | | | | | 3.9 | 2.5 | 3.3 |
| 2.1 | 1.8 | 1.9 | % Officers', Directors' Owners' Comp/Sales | | | | | | |
| (28) 3.1 | (24) 3.1 | (31) 3.7 | | | | | | | |
| 5.7 | 4.8 | 6.1 | | | | | | | |
| 5533458M | 2661239M | 3640794M | Net Sales ($) | 386M | 22096M | 44182M | 109311M | 411324M | 3053495M |
| 2251811M | 1884726M | 1988568M | Total Assets ($) | 62M | 10991M | 25180M | 55191M | 216226M | 1680918M |

© RMA 2012     M = $ thousand    MM = $ million

See Pages 9 through 22 for Explanation of Ratios and Data

## Current Data Sorted by Assets | Comparative Historical Data

| Type of Statement | 0-500M | 500M-2MM | 2-10MM | 10-50MM | 50-100MM | 100-250MM | | 4/1/07-3/31/08 ALL | 4/1/08-3/31/09 ALL |
|---|---|---|---|---|---|---|---|---|---|
| Unqualified | | 2 | 13 | 26 | 5 | 8 | | 66 | 55 |
| Reviewed | 9 | 11 | 83 | 33 | | | | 114 | 121 |
| Compiled | 30 | 33 | 36 | 6 | 2 | | | 92 | 79 |
| Tax Returns | 17 | 63 | 37 | 6 | | | | 84 | 83 |
| Other | | 47 | 105 | 50 | 10 | 9 | | 186 | 199 |
| | 106 (4/1-9/30/11) | | 535 (10/1/11-3/31/12) | | | | | | |
| NUMBER OF STATEMENTS | 56 | 156 | 274 | 121 | 17 | 17 | | 542 | 537 |
| **ASSETS** | % | % | % | % | % | % | | % | % |
| Cash & Equivalents | 14.2 | 14.6 | 8.7 | 9.7 | 9.4 | 6.4 | | 9.0 | 9.1 |
| Trade Receivables (net) | 27.9 | 29.0 | 26.0 | 25.0 | 21.4 | 21.0 | | 26.6 | 25.5 |
| Inventory | 17.8 | 20.2 | 26.1 | 28.5 | 23.4 | 17.5 | | 24.5 | 25.6 |
| All Other Current | 2.4 | 2.9 | 3.5 | 3.7 | 3.0 | 3.5 | | 2.5 | 2.9 |
| Total Current | 62.4 | 66.6 | 64.3 | 67.0 | 57.1 | 48.4 | | 62.6 | 63.1 |
| Fixed Assets (net) | 26.9 | 23.3 | 26.4 | 22.4 | 26.0 | 25.6 | | 27.6 | 27.3 |
| Intangibles (net) | 4.3 | 4.6 | 3.9 | 5.8 | 9.8 | 18.6 | | 3.9 | 3.9 |
| All Other Non-Current | 6.4 | 5.5 | 5.3 | 4.8 | 7.0 | 7.4 | | 5.9 | 5.8 |
| Total | 100.0 | 100.0 | 100.0 | 100.0 | 100.0 | 100.0 | | 100.0 | 100.0 |
| **LIABILITIES** | | | | | | | | | |
| Notes Payable-Short Term | 15.5 | 8.8 | 10.5 | 7.7 | 6.9 | 5.2 | | 11.4 | 12.3 |
| Cur. Mat.-L.T.D. | 5.7 | 5.1 | 3.9 | 2.8 | 2.5 | 1.5 | | 3.7 | 4.0 |
| Trade Payables | 15.4 | 14.9 | 15.2 | 12.5 | 7.7 | 22.0 | | 13.6 | 13.3 |
| Income Taxes Payable | .0 | .1 | .3 | .3 | .2 | .1 | | .3 | .2 |
| All Other Current | 10.1 | 6.8 | 10.3 | 11.9 | 9.7 | 6.1 | | 10.0 | 10.0 |
| Total Current | 46.7 | 35.7 | 40.2 | 35.1 | 26.9 | 35.0 | | 39.1 | 39.9 |
| Long-Term Debt | 15.2 | 20.7 | 15.8 | 10.3 | 10.6 | 25.0 | | 17.8 | 16.5 |
| Deferred Taxes | .0 | .1 | .6 | .7 | .4 | 3.5 | | .4 | .5 |
| All Other Non-Current | 29.5 | 7.8 | 5.7 | 5.2 | 8.8 | 20.4 | | 6.2 | 5.4 |
| Net Worth | 8.3 | 35.7 | 37.7 | 48.8 | 53.3 | 16.0 | | 36.5 | 37.7 |
| Total Liabilities & Net Worth | 100.0 | 100.0 | 100.0 | 100.0 | 100.0 | 100.0 | | 100.0 | 100.0 |
| **INCOME DATA** | | | | | | | | | |
| Net Sales | 100.0 | 100.0 | 100.0 | 100.0 | 100.0 | 100.0 | | 100.0 | 100.0 |
| Gross Profit | 49.3 | 38.3 | 30.0 | 23.3 | 24.9 | 26.4 | | 32.0 | 29.2 |
| Operating Expenses | 42.9 | 32.1 | 24.6 | 17.4 | 18.6 | 17.5 | | 25.3 | 23.7 |
| Operating Profit | 6.4 | 6.3 | 5.4 | 5.8 | 6.3 | 8.9 | | 6.7 | 5.5 |
| All Other Expenses (net) | .8 | .7 | .9 | .6 | .5 | 3.2 | | 1.2 | 1.0 |
| Profit Before Taxes | 5.6 | 5.5 | 4.5 | 5.2 | 5.8 | 5.7 | | 5.4 | 4.5 |
| **RATIOS** | | | | | | | | | |
| Current | 4.5 | 3.6 | 2.8 | 3.2 | 4.0 | 3.0 | | 2.9 | 3.0 |
| | 1.9 | 2.2 | 1.6 | 2.0 | 2.2 | 1.8 | | 1.7 | 1.7 |
| | .8 | 1.3 | 1.2 | 1.3 | 1.4 | 1.1 | | 1.2 | 1.1 |
| Quick | 2.3 | 2.8 | 1.5 | 2.0 | 2.5 | 1.3 | | 1.7 | 1.8 |
| | 1.1 | 1.5 | .9 | .9 | 1.3 | .8 | | .9 | .8 |
| | .5 | .7 | .5 | .7 | .6 | .6 | | .6 | .5 |
| Sales/Receivables | 9 42.7 | 24 15.2 | 31 11.7 | 37 9.9 | 41 8.9 | 39 9.4 | | 29 12.6 | 26 14.1 |
| | 31 11.6 | 40 9.1 | 44 8.3 | 47 7.8 | 50 7.3 | 42 8.7 | | 42 8.8 | 38 9.6 |
| | 44 8.3 | 58 6.3 | 55 6.6 | 62 5.9 | 60 6.1 | 57 6.4 | | 56 6.5 | 52 7.0 |
| Cost of Sales/Inventory | 0 UND | 8 44.5 | 29 12.5 | 39 9.3 | 49 7.4 | 32 11.4 | | 23 15.7 | 22 16.8 |
| | 16 22.8 | 33 11.0 | 61 6.0 | 70 5.2 | 73 5.0 | 68 5.4 | | 53 6.9 | 50 7.3 |
| | 66 5.5 | 81 4.5 | 101 3.6 | 107 3.4 | 104 3.5 | 83 4.4 | | 91 4.0 | 94 3.9 |
| Cost of Sales/Payables | 4 86.0 | 13 27.9 | 19 18.9 | 17 21.7 | 10 37.6 | 21 17.4 | | 15 23.6 | 13 28.4 |
| | 25 14.4 | 25 14.4 | 33 11.2 | 28 13.1 | 27 13.4 | 32 11.5 | | 27 13.5 | 23 15.6 |
| | 45 8.1 | 48 7.6 | 50 7.3 | 47 7.8 | 36 10.1 | 43 8.4 | | 43 8.5 | 38 9.6 |
| Sales/Working Capital | 6.6 | 4.5 | 4.8 | 3.5 | 2.8 | 4.4 | | 5.3 | 5.3 |
| | 11.9 | 8.2 | 8.9 | 5.9 | 5.3 | 9.7 | | 9.0 | 9.6 |
| | -124.8 | 24.0 | 20.9 | 16.2 | 12.6 | NM | | 29.8 | 31.7 |
| EBIT/Interest | 18.0 | 17.3 | 14.8 | 22.1 | 25.8 | 22.9 | | 12.8 | 12.4 |
| | (45) 4.5 | (135) 4.4 | (251) 5.6 | (107) 7.8 | (13) 9.3 | (16) 9.6 | | (491) 4.0 | (493) 3.9 |
| | .1 | 1.5 | 1.8 | 1.8 | 1.2 | 1.9 | | 1.7 | 1.2 |
| Net Profit + Depr., Dep., Amort./Cur. Mat. L/T/D | | 7.2 | 6.2 | 8.2 | | | | 8.5 | 6.6 |
| | | (15) 2.7 | (67) 3.0 | (34) 2.6 | | | | (139) 3.1 | (145) 2.8 |
| | | .7 | 1.7 | 1.0 | | | | 1.4 | 1.1 |
| Fixed/Worth | .3 | .2 | .3 | .2 | .3 | .7 | | .3 | .3 |
| | 1.1 | .5 | .7 | .5 | .6 | 3.0 | | .7 | .7 |
| | -1.6 | 3.1 | 1.7 | 1.0 | 1.0 | -.5 | | 2.0 | 1.7 |
| Debt/Worth | .7 | .5 | .7 | .5 | .4 | .9 | | .7 | .7 |
| | 2.7 | 1.5 | 1.8 | 1.1 | 1.0 | 6.4 | | 1.7 | 1.6 |
| | -5.7 | 12.4 | 4.6 | 2.5 | 3.1 | -3.3 | | 5.3 | 4.3 |
| % Profit Before Taxes/Tangible Net Worth | 133.7 | 68.4 | 52.0 | 35.4 | 42.2 | 28.5 | | 53.7 | 49.3 |
| | (37) 54.1 | (125) 26.4 | (246) 21.2 | (110) 19.2 | (16) 13.4 | (10) 19.6 | | (470) 25.4 | (471) 21.9 |
| | 10.1 | 6.0 | 5.4 | 5.2 | 3.5 | 3.7 | | 8.5 | 6.0 |
| % Profit Before Taxes/Total Assets | 41.8 | 23.7 | 16.2 | 17.3 | 14.0 | 12.9 | | 19.6 | 17.9 |
| | 17.4 | 9.4 | 7.2 | 8.9 | 8.7 | 8.1 | | 7.9 | 7.7 |
| | -.3 | 2.2 | 1.4 | 1.9 | 1.0 | -.9 | | 2.6 | 1.6 |
| Sales/Net Fixed Assets | 56.3 | 44.4 | 22.5 | 24.1 | 10.3 | 13.4 | | 23.5 | 23.1 |
| | 24.9 | 14.9 | 9.7 | 8.8 | 6.0 | 6.4 | | 10.0 | 9.4 |
| | 9.1 | 7.2 | 4.6 | 4.9 | 4.4 | 4.1 | | 5.0 | 5.1 |
| Sales/Total Assets | 5.0 | 3.7 | 2.7 | 2.3 | 1.9 | 2.7 | | 2.9 | 3.0 |
| | 3.7 | 2.6 | 2.0 | 1.6 | 1.5 | 1.7 | | 2.2 | 2.2 |
| | 2.2 | 1.8 | 1.6 | 1.3 | 1.0 | .8 | | 1.6 | 1.6 |
| % Depr., Dep., Amort./Sales | .8 | .9 | 1.0 | .9 | 1.4 | 1.5 | | 1.1 | 1.2 |
| | (33) 2.3 | (109) 2.4 | (233) 2.2 | (109) 1.7 | (16) 2.4 | (14) 2.9 | | (466) 2.2 | (446) 2.3 |
| | 3.6 | 4.2 | 4.4 | 3.1 | 4.0 | 4.5 | | 4.1 | 4.1 |
| % Officers', Directors' Owners' Comp/Sales | 3.0 | 3.0 | 1.9 | .9 | | | | 2.3 | 1.9 |
| | (35) 5.4 | (84) 5.6 | (121) 3.2 | (28) 1.4 | | | | (225) 4.2 | (209) 3.7 |
| | 9.3 | 9.0 | 5.3 | 4.6 | | | | 7.5 | 7.6 |
| Net Sales ($) | 58792M | 639566M | 2672626M | 4568764M | 1882436M | 4833908M | | 14233757M | 14298619M |
| Total Assets ($) | 15090M | 180939M | 1245354M | 2416586M | 1205287M | 2553810M | | 7243192M | 7686824M |

## Comparative Historical Data | Current Data Sorted by Sales

| | 4/1/09-3/31/10 ALL | 4/1/10-3/31/11 ALL | 4/1/11-3/31/12 ALL | 0-1MM | 1-3MM | 3-5MM | 5-10MM | 10-25MM | 25MM & OVER |
|---|---|---|---|---|---|---|---|---|---|
| **Type of Statement** | | | | | 106 (4/1-9/30/11) | | | 535 (10/1/11-3/31/12) | |
| Unqualified | 57 | 56 | 54 | | | 2 | 2 | 20 | 30 |
| Reviewed | 109 | 118 | 127 | 1 | 6 | 19 | 31 | 50 | 20 |
| Compiled | 90 | 83 | 86 | 10 | 17 | 13 | 25 | 16 | 5 |
| Tax Returns | 107 | 108 | 136 | 14 | 54 | 23 | 26 | 15 | 4 |
| Other | 173 | 192 | 238 | 14 | 41 | 29 | 39 | 59 | 56 |
| **NUMBER OF STATEMENTS** | 536 | 557 | 641 | 39 | 118 | 86 | 123 | 160 | 115 |
| **ASSETS** | % | % | % | % | % | % | % | % | % |
| Cash & Equivalents | 10.4 | 10.0 | 10.8 | 12.9 | 13.3 | 11.7 | 9.5 | 10.9 | 7.8 |
| Trade Receivables (net) | 22.2 | 26.1 | 26.5 | 20.2 | 26.9 | 27.5 | 25.4 | 27.5 | 27.0 |
| Inventory | 23.4 | 23.0 | 24.1 | 18.5 | 18.1 | 22.2 | 26.5 | 27.4 | 26.4 |
| All Other Current | 2.9 | 2.6 | 3.3 | 1.5 | 3.0 | 3.2 | 2.9 | 4.1 | 3.5 |
| Total Current | 58.8 | 61.7 | 64.6 | 53.1 | 61.4 | 64.6 | 64.2 | 70.0 | 64.7 |
| Fixed Assets (net) | 28.9 | 27.7 | 24.9 | 34.4 | 26.8 | 27.0 | 25.1 | 21.3 | 23.0 |
| Intangibles (net) | 6.0 | 5.4 | 5.0 | 5.4 | 5.3 | 3.3 | 4.5 | 4.1 | 7.6 |
| All Other Non-Current | 6.3 | 5.3 | 5.5 | 7.0 | 6.5 | 5.0 | 6.1 | 4.7 | 4.7 |
| Total | 100.0 | 100.0 | 100.0 | 100.0 | 100.0 | 100.0 | 100.0 | 100.0 | 100.0 |
| **LIABILITIES** | | | | | | | | | |
| Notes Payable-Short Term | 11.9 | 11.0 | 9.8 | 13.2 | 9.0 | 9.9 | 10.6 | 9.9 | 8.3 |
| Cur. Mat.-L.T.D. | 4.6 | 4.7 | 4.0 | 3.2 | 6.0 | 4.9 | 4.8 | 2.8 | 2.6 |
| Trade Payables | 12.0 | 14.6 | 14.6 | 11.7 | 12.8 | 15.6 | 14.6 | 15.8 | 15.0 |
| Income Taxes Payable | .2 | .2 | .2 | .0 | .0 | .2 | .3 | .3 | .3 |
| All Other Current | 8.8 | 8.2 | 9.6 | 11.8 | 6.0 | 7.8 | 9.5 | 11.7 | 10.9 |
| Total Current | 37.5 | 38.7 | 38.2 | 39.9 | 33.8 | 38.4 | 39.9 | 40.5 | 37.2 |
| Long-Term Debt | 19.5 | 17.7 | 16.0 | 16.6 | 21.7 | 20.9 | 17.2 | 9.0 | 14.6 |
| Deferred Taxes | .6 | .5 | .5 | .1 | .1 | .3 | .7 | .5 | 1.1 |
| All Other Non-Current | 7.9 | 7.6 | 8.7 | 37.9 | 9.7 | 7.5 | 4.0 | 5.5 | 7.9 |
| Net Worth | 34.6 | 35.6 | 36.6 | 5.1 | 34.8 | 32.9 | 38.2 | 44.4 | 39.2 |
| Total Liabilities & Net Worth | 100.0 | 100.0 | 100.0 | 100.0 | 100.0 | 100.0 | 100.0 | 100.0 | 100.0 |
| **INCOME DATA** | | | | | | | | | |
| Net Sales | 100.0 | 100.0 | 100.0 | 100.0 | 100.0 | 100.0 | 100.0 | 100.0 | 100.0 |
| Gross Profit | 31.0 | 32.0 | 32.2 | 48.6 | 41.7 | 35.6 | 32.5 | 26.3 | 22.4 |
| Operating Expenses | 27.4 | 27.0 | 26.3 | 40.4 | 36.1 | 30.2 | 27.0 | 20.2 | 16.5 |
| Operating Profit | 3.6 | 5.0 | 5.9 | 8.2 | 5.6 | 5.4 | 5.5 | 6.1 | 5.9 |
| All Other Expenses (net) | 1.7 | 1.0 | .8 | 1.3 | 1.0 | .8 | .8 | .6 | 1.0 |
| Profit Before Taxes | 1.9 | 4.1 | 5.1 | 6.9 | 4.6 | 4.7 | 4.6 | 5.6 | 4.9 |
| **RATIOS** | | | | | | | | | |
| Current | 3.3 / 1.8 / 1.1 | 2.9 / 1.8 / 1.2 | 3.1 / 1.9 / 1.2 | 5.2 / 2.1 / .7 | 4.3 / 2.2 / 1.2 | 3.5 / 1.9 / 1.2 | 2.6 / 1.7 / 1.2 | 2.9 / 1.7 / 1.2 | 3.0 / 1.8 / 1.3 |
| Quick | 2.0 / .9 / .5 | 1.8 / 1.0 / .6 | 1.9 / 1.0 / .6 | 3.5 / 1.3 / .5 | 3.1 / 1.5 / .6 | 2.2 / 1.2 / .6 | 1.5 / .9 / .6 | 1.7 / .9 / .6 | 1.7 / .9 / .7 |
| Sales/Receivables | 27 / 13.5 — 39 / 9.3 — 52 / 7.0 | 31 / 11.7 — 43 / 8.4 — 57 / 6.4 | 30 / 12.3 — 43 / 8.5 — 56 / 6.5 | 10 / 38.3 — 32 / 11.3 — 54 / 6.7 | 26 / 14.2 — 42 / 8.6 — 54 / 6.7 | 28 / 13.0 — 46 / 8.0 — 60 / 6.1 | 28 / 13.0 — 40 / 9.2 — 51 / 7.2 | 33 / 10.9 — 44 / 8.3 — 59 / 6.2 | 36 / 10.0 — 46 / 7.9 — 58 / 6.3 |
| Cost of Sales/Inventory | 26 / 14.1 — 57 / 6.4 — 100 / 3.6 | 24 / 15.3 — 54 / 6.8 — 96 / 3.8 | 22 / 16.5 — 55 / 6.6 — 96 / 3.8 | 0 / UND — 31 / 11.9 — 111 / 3.3 | 5 / 67.4 — 35 / 10.4 — 85 / 4.3 | 24 / 15.4 — 54 / 6.8 — 96 / 3.8 | 27 / 13.5 — 63 / 5.8 — 99 / 3.7 | 29 / 12.7 — 56 / 6.5 — 101 / 3.6 | 36 / 10.0 — 61 / 6.0 — 85 / 4.3 |
| Cost of Sales/Payables | 13 / 27.3 — 24 / 15.5 — 40 / 9.1 | 17 / 21.1 — 30 / 12.2 — 45 / 8.1 | 16 / 22.6 — 29 / 12.7 — 48 / 7.6 | 7 / 50.7 — 27 / 13.4 — 70 / 5.2 | 13 / 28.5 — 29 / 12.6 — 57 / 6.4 | 16 / 22.8 — 29 / 12.4 — 54 / 6.8 | 17 / 21.8 — 29 / 12.5 — 47 / 7.8 | 18 / 20.0 — 29 / 12.8 — 44 / 8.3 | 16 / 22.6 — 28 / 13.2 — 43 / 8.4 |
| Sales/Working Capital | 4.1 / 8.1 / 42.1 | 4.5 / 8.4 / 30.9 | 4.5 / 8.4 / 22.0 | 3.3 / 9.5 / -28.4 | 4.3 / 7.6 / 33.4 | 4.1 / 8.3 / 20.0 | 5.3 / 8.8 / 18.7 | 4.1 / 9.0 / 22.9 | 4.6 / 8.6 / 19.4 |
| EBIT/Interest | 8.5 / (477) 2.2 / -1.0 | 11.7 / (504) 4.0 / 1.0 | 17.5 / (567) 6.0 / 1.5 | 11.2 / (31) 3.5 / .1 | 11.9 / (98) 3.5 / .9 | 16.7 / (80) 4.3 / 1.3 | 11.8 / (114) 5.0 / 1.4 | 24.3 / (144) 9.2 / 2.2 | 21.5 / (100) 8.1 / 1.8 |
| Net Profit + Depr., Dep., Amort./Cur. Mat. L/T/D | 5.1 / (135) 2.1 / .5 | 5.1 / (126) 2.0 / .9 | 7.3 / (130) 2.8 / 1.4 | | | 5.4 / (12) 2.6 / .5 | 4.0 / (32) 2.7 / 1.7 | 7.0 / (42) 3.2 / 2.0 | 8.3 / (36) 3.1 / 1.4 |
| Fixed/Worth | .3 / .8 / 3.6 | .3 / .7 / 2.8 | .3 / .6 / 1.8 | .4 / 1.3 / -2.1 | .2 / .7 / 9.2 | .3 / .9 / 3.3 | .3 / .7 / 1.6 | .2 / .5 / 1.3 | .3 / .6 / 1.4 |
| Debt/Worth | .6 / 1.7 / 14.4 | .6 / 1.5 / 8.3 | .6 / 1.7 / 5.7 | .4 / 2.5 / -4.0 | .5 / 1.9 / NM | .7 / 1.4 / 10.6 | .7 / 1.6 / 4.5 | .5 / 1.7 / 3.9 | .7 / 1.6 / 4.6 |
| % Profit Before Taxes/Tangible Net Worth | 35.4 / (422) 11.2 / -5.2 | 46.4 / (458) 20.2 / 2.4 | 54.2 / (544) 21.9 / 5.9 | 77.0 / (27) 18.1 / 4.9 | 68.1 / (89) 29.5 / 4.3 | 62.7 / (71) 19.8 / 3.7 | 61.7 / (111) 20.2 / 5.2 | 46.8 / (148) 23.0 / 8.0 | 40.6 / (98) 21.5 / 7.8 |
| % Profit Before Taxes/Total Assets | 12.7 / 3.0 / -4.7 | 16.0 / 7.1 / .4 | 18.7 / 8.6 / 1.5 | 26.2 / 6.3 / -1.3 | 24.2 / 6.7 / -.2 | 17.4 / 8.7 / 1.2 | 16.4 / 7.1 / .7 | 19.2 / 9.4 / 2.7 | 16.6 / 8.7 / 1.9 |
| Sales/Net Fixed Assets | 18.6 / 8.2 / 3.9 | 19.3 / 8.4 / 4.3 | 28.4 / 10.4 / 5.2 | 29.0 / 9.1 / 3.3 | 29.9 / 10.6 / 5.7 | 33.9 / 9.2 / 4.4 | 23.9 / 10.0 / 5.3 | 30.9 / 13.1 / 6.0 | 24.1 / 8.9 / 4.8 |
| Sales/Total Assets | 2.6 / 1.8 / 1.3 | 2.7 / 2.0 / 1.4 | 3.0 / 2.1 / 1.5 | 2.8 / 2.0 / 1.0 | 3.5 / 2.3 / 1.6 | 3.1 / 2.1 / 1.5 | 2.9 / 2.1 / 1.7 | 2.8 / 2.1 / 1.6 | 2.9 / 1.9 / 1.4 |
| % Depr., Dep., Amort./Sales | 1.3 / (460) 2.8 / 5.5 | 1.3 / (483) 2.5 / 4.6 | 1.0 / (514) 2.2 / 4.1 | 2.0 / (22) 3.2 / 6.9 | 1.1 / (86) 2.6 / 4.6 | 1.1 / (65) 2.8 / 4.8 | 1.1 / (105) 2.5 / 4.2 | .9 / (138) 1.6 / 3.0 | 2.0 / (98) 2.0 / 3.4 |
| % Officers', Directors', Owners' Comp/Sales | 2.5 / (224) 4.9 / 8.2 | 2.6 / (217) 4.2 / 7.4 | 2.1 / (272) 4.1 / 7.1 | 5.7 / (16) 9.0 / 10.5 | 3.0 / (69) 4.8 / 8.3 | 2.4 / (43) 5.6 / 9.1 | 2.3 / (64) 3.7 / 6.0 | 1.6 / (60) 2.6 / 4.4 | .3 / (20) 1.2 / 4.3 |
| Net Sales ($) | 12005939M | 16934725M | 14656092M | 20812M | 230415M | 342673M | 886142M | 2433243M | 10742807M |
| Total Assets ($) | 7997394M | 6760723M | 7617066M | 15308M | 128980M | 188482M | 453882M | 1276700M | 5553714M |

M = $ thousand    MM = $ million
See Pages 9 through 22 for Explanation of Ratios and Data

**Current Data Sorted by Assets**      **Comparative Historical Data**

| 0-500M | 500M-2MM | 2-10MM | 10-50MM | 50-100MM | 100-250MM | Type of Statement | 4/1/07-3/31/08 ALL | 4/1/08-3/31/09 ALL |
|---|---|---|---|---|---|---|---|---|
|  |  | 7 | 17 | 1 | 5 | Unqualified | 33 | 37 |
|  | 2 | 11 | 13 | 2 |  | Reviewed | 32 | 30 |
| 1 | 7 | 13 | 2 |  |  | Compiled | 23 | 25 |
| 1 | 4 | 12 | 1 |  |  | Tax Returns | 12 | 14 |
| 2 | 14 | 11 | 18 | 5 | 3 | Other | 41 | 44 |
|  | 31 (4/1-9/30/11) |  | 121 (10/1/11-3/31/12) |  |  |  |  |  |
| 4 | 27 | 54 | 51 | 8 | 8 | **NUMBER OF STATEMENTS** | 141 | 150 |
| % | % | % | % | % | % | **ASSETS** | % | % |
|  | 10.8 | 7.1 | 11.3 |  |  | Cash & Equivalents | 5.4 | 5.4 |
|  | 21.8 | 20.7 | 17.0 |  |  | Trade Receivables (net) | 20.0 | 20.9 |
|  | 36.5 | 44.6 | 40.5 |  |  | Inventory | 43.6 | 45.8 |
|  | 2.0 | 1.3 | 2.6 |  |  | All Other Current | 3.2 | 2.2 |
|  | 71.1 | 73.8 | 71.4 |  |  | Total Current | 72.2 | 74.3 |
|  | 18.4 | 18.5 | 19.4 |  |  | Fixed Assets (net) | 18.8 | 18.3 |
|  | 2.9 | 1.9 | 2.4 |  |  | Intangibles (net) | 4.6 | 2.5 |
|  | 7.6 | 5.8 | 6.8 |  |  | All Other Non-Current | 4.5 | 4.8 |
|  | 100.0 | 100.0 | 100.0 |  |  | Total | 100.0 | 100.0 |
|  |  |  |  |  |  | **LIABILITIES** |  |  |
|  | 9.5 | 9.3 | 11.5 |  |  | Notes Payable-Short Term | 16.5 | 15.6 |
|  | 3.0 | 2.3 | 1.8 |  |  | Cur. Mat.-L.T.D. | 2.5 | 3.3 |
|  | 13.1 | 18.5 | 9.1 |  |  | Trade Payables | 11.5 | 11.6 |
|  | .0 | .1 | .3 |  |  | Income Taxes Payable | .2 | .3 |
|  | 10.0 | 10.5 | 15.7 |  |  | All Other Current | 10.2 | 11.5 |
|  | 35.7 | 40.7 | 38.3 |  |  | Total Current | 40.9 | 42.3 |
|  | 19.7 | 11.7 | 10.6 |  |  | Long-Term Debt | 13.8 | 11.4 |
|  | .0 | .4 | .3 |  |  | Deferred Taxes | .3 | .5 |
|  | 5.5 | 2.9 | 1.8 |  |  | All Other Non-Current | 3.8 | 3.6 |
|  | 39.1 | 44.3 | 49.0 |  |  | Net Worth | 41.1 | 42.3 |
|  | 100.0 | 100.0 | 100.0 |  |  | Total Liabilities & Net Worth | 100.0 | 100.0 |
|  |  |  |  |  |  | **INCOME DATA** |  |  |
|  | 100.0 | 100.0 | 100.0 |  |  | Net Sales | 100.0 | 100.0 |
|  | 32.3 | 30.7 | 26.0 |  |  | Gross Profit | 26.6 | 27.5 |
|  | 27.1 | 25.4 | 19.9 |  |  | Operating Expenses | 21.0 | 21.6 |
|  | 5.2 | 5.3 | 6.1 |  |  | Operating Profit | 5.6 | 5.9 |
|  | .4 | .6 | .4 |  |  | All Other Expenses (net) | 1.2 | .8 |
|  | 4.8 | 4.7 | 5.7 |  |  | Profit Before Taxes | 4.4 | 5.1 |
|  |  |  |  |  |  | **RATIOS** |  |  |
|  | 4.7 | 2.7 | 3.4 |  |  | Current | 2.8 | 2.6 |
|  | 1.8 | 1.8 | 1.9 |  |  |  | 1.9 | 1.8 |
|  | 1.2 | 1.4 | 1.2 |  |  |  | 1.2 | 1.4 |
|  | 2.2 | 1.2 | 1.7 |  |  | Quick | 1.2 | 1.2 |
|  | .8 | .7 | .7 |  |  |  | (140) .7 | .7 |
|  | .4 | .4 | .3 |  |  |  | .3 | .4 |
| 11 | 32.6 | 14 / 26.7 | 21 / 17.0 |  |  | Sales/Receivables | 20 / 17.9 | 19 / 18.8 |
| 26 | 14.0 | 33 / 10.9 | 36 / 10.2 |  |  |  | 33 / 11.2 | 34 / 10.8 |
| 48 | 7.6 | 47 / 7.7 | 56 / 6.5 |  |  |  | 54 / 6.8 | 55 / 6.6 |
| 29 | 12.6 | 42 / 8.7 | 72 / 5.1 |  |  | Cost of Sales/Inventory | 70 / 5.2 | 68 / 5.4 |
| 83 | 4.4 | 111 / 3.3 | 118 / 3.1 |  |  |  | 106 / 3.4 | 111 / 3.3 |
| 122 | 3.0 | 166 / 2.2 | 192 / 1.9 |  |  |  | 164 / 2.2 | 164 / 2.2 |
| 11 | 32.7 | 20 / 18.7 | 12 / 30.5 |  |  | Cost of Sales/Payables | 14 / 25.7 | 11 / 31.8 |
| 25 | 14.5 | 31 / 11.6 | 18 / 20.7 |  |  |  | 25 / 14.4 | 23 / 15.7 |
| 36 | 10.1 | 59 / 6.2 | 35 / 10.4 |  |  |  | 39 / 9.3 | 37 / 9.9 |
|  | 3.8 | 4.1 | 2.9 |  |  | Sales/Working Capital | 3.7 | 3.9 |
|  | 7.6 | 7.1 | 5.5 |  |  |  | 6.3 | 6.7 |
|  | 24.8 | 17.2 | 18.7 |  |  |  | 14.0 | 13.1 |
|  | 24.1 | 28.8 | 41.7 |  |  | EBIT/Interest | 8.8 | 16.3 |
|  | (25) 6.7 | (51) 8.9 | (46) 4.7 |  |  |  | (135) 3.7 | (144) 5.6 |
|  | 2.7 | 3.9 | 2.2 |  |  |  | 1.6 | 2.1 |
|  |  |  | 10.0 |  |  | Net Profit + Depr., Dep., | 5.7 | 7.7 |
|  |  | (12) | 3.6 |  |  | Amort./Cur. Mat. L/T/D | (42) 2.6 | (38) 3.2 |
|  |  |  | 2.3 |  |  |  | 1.9 | .8 |
|  | .2 | .1 | .2 |  |  | Fixed/Worth | .2 | .2 |
|  | .4 | .2 | .4 |  |  |  | .5 | .4 |
|  | 1.8 | .8 | .8 |  |  |  | 1.1 | .9 |
|  | .7 | .7 | .5 |  |  | Debt/Worth | .7 | .7 |
|  | 1.2 | 1.3 | 1.0 |  |  |  | 1.5 | 1.4 |
|  | 4.4 | 2.2 | 2.8 |  |  |  | 3.9 | 3.2 |
|  | 64.6 | 46.8 | 34.9 |  |  | % Profit Before Taxes/Tangible Net Worth | 42.5 | 43.7 |
|  | (23) 30.4 | (50) 21.0 | (49) 22.8 |  |  |  | (129) 19.4 | (142) 24.0 |
|  | 8.1 | 9.4 | 2.9 |  |  |  | 6.2 | 6.6 |
|  | 28.7 | 16.7 | 15.9 |  |  | % Profit Before Taxes/Total Assets | 13.6 | 16.8 |
|  | 11.4 | 9.1 | 5.8 |  |  |  | 7.4 | 8.7 |
|  | 1.8 | 3.1 | 2.2 |  |  |  | 2.1 | 2.6 |
|  | 48.2 | 72.3 | 15.2 |  |  | Sales/Net Fixed Assets | 30.7 | 36.6 |
|  | 15.7 | 22.6 | 8.5 |  |  |  | 10.7 | 13.4 |
|  | 8.8 | 6.3 | 5.0 |  |  |  | 6.4 | 6.8 |
|  | 3.3 | 2.8 | 2.2 |  |  | Sales/Total Assets | 2.4 | 2.5 |
|  | 2.3 | 2.2 | 1.6 |  |  |  | 1.8 | 1.9 |
|  | 1.7 | 1.6 | 1.2 |  |  |  | 1.4 | 1.5 |
|  | .4 | .6 | .7 |  |  | % Depr., Dep., Amort./Sales | .8 | .9 |
|  | (19) 1.4 | (42) 1.0 | (48) 1.4 |  |  |  | (123) 1.4 | (127) 1.4 |
|  | 2.6 | 2.4 | 2.6 |  |  |  | 2.3 | 2.3 |
|  | 2.1 | 1.3 | .7 |  |  | % Officers', Directors', Owners' Comp/Sales | 1.2 | 1.0 |
|  | (11) 3.9 | (22) 3.0 | (12) 2.2 |  |  |  | (36) 2.4 | (51) 2.1 |
|  | 4.7 | 5.3 | 2.8 |  |  |  | 4.4 | 4.5 |
| 4970M | 92459M | 544605M | 2135945M | 1049718M | 2647282M | Net Sales ($) | 5004293M | 5953923M |
| 1078M | 34851M | 244300M | 1253039M | 574199M | 1596890M | Total Assets ($) | 3307552M | 3266627M |

© RMA 2012

M = $ thousand    MM = $ million
See Pages 9 through 22 for Explanation of Ratios and Data

## Comparative Historical Data                                          Current Data Sorted by Sales

### Type of Statement

| Hist 1 | Hist 2 | Hist 3 | Type of Statement | 0-1MM | 1-3MM | 3-5MM | 5-10MM | 10-25MM | 25MM & OVER |
|---|---|---|---|---|---|---|---|---|---|
| 31 | 29 | 30 | Unqualified | | 1 | 1 | 1 | 11 | 16 |
| 30 | 22 | 28 | Reviewed | | 1 | 2 | 3 | 11 | 11 |
| 29 | 21 | 23 | Compiled | 1 | 4 | 2 | 8 | 7 | 1 |
| 9 | 22 | 18 | Tax Returns | | 7 | 2 | 2 | 6 | 1 |
| 42 | 54 | 53 | Other | 2 | 7 | 8 | 4 | 9 | 23 |
| 4/1/09-3/31/10 ALL | 4/1/10-3/31/11 ALL | 4/1/11-3/31/12 ALL | | \*31 (4/1-9/30/11)\* | | | \*121 (10/1/11-3/31/12)\* | | |
| 141 | 148 | 152 | **NUMBER OF STATEMENTS** | 3 | 20 | 15 | 18 | 44 | 52 |
| % | % | % | **ASSETS** | % | % | % | % | % | % |
| 7.5 | 9.9 | 9.4 | Cash & Equivalents | | 9.9 | 6.0 | 8.8 | 10.2 | 9.1 |
| 19.4 | 20.6 | 19.9 | Trade Receivables (net) | | 20.7 | 19.8 | 14.2 | 23.2 | 19.0 |
| 42.3 | 40.4 | 40.6 | Inventory | | 34.8 | 44.7 | 46.3 | 38.1 | 41.0 |
| 2.1 | 1.6 | 1.9 | All Other Current | | 2.8 | .2 | 1.2 | 1.8 | 2.3 |
| 71.3 | 72.5 | 71.8 | Total Current | | 68.2 | 70.7 | 70.5 | 73.3 | 71.4 |
| 19.6 | 18.6 | 19.0 | Fixed Assets (net) | | 21.9 | 20.4 | 19.9 | 18.2 | 18.8 |
| 3.8 | 3.0 | 2.8 | Intangibles (net) | | 4.3 | 2.0 | .2 | 2.6 | 3.6 |
| 5.3 | 5.9 | 6.4 | All Other Non-Current | | 5.6 | 6.8 | 9.4 | 5.9 | 6.2 |
| 100.0 | 100.0 | 100.0 | Total | | 100.0 | 100.0 | 100.0 | 100.0 | 100.0 |
| | | | **LIABILITIES** | | | | | | |
| 14.7 | 12.6 | 9.4 | Notes Payable-Short Term | | 8.1 | 20.6 | 5.6 | 7.7 | 10.1 |
| 3.1 | 2.3 | 2.1 | Cur. Mat.-L.T.D. | | 1.4 | 3.8 | 3.6 | 2.1 | 1.6 |
| 9.5 | 10.0 | 14.2 | Trade Payables | | 15.3 | 14.0 | 16.6 | 16.3 | 11.1 |
| .3 | .3 | .2 | Income Taxes Payable | | .0 | .0 | .0 | .2 | .3 |
| 11.6 | 11.3 | 12.4 | All Other Current | | 10.6 | 7.7 | 10.9 | 12.0 | 15.6 |
| 39.2 | 36.5 | 38.3 | Total Current | | 35.4 | 46.1 | 36.6 | 38.3 | 38.7 |
| 13.9 | 12.5 | 14.0 | Long-Term Debt | | 35.1 | 21.1 | 9.1 | 10.8 | 9.2 |
| .6 | .2 | .3 | Deferred Taxes | | .0 | .0 | .8 | .1 | .4 |
| 6.0 | 6.2 | 3.0 | All Other Non-Current | | 5.3 | 3.0 | 4.6 | 1.8 | 2.8 |
| 40.4 | 44.6 | 44.3 | Net Worth | | 24.2 | 29.8 | 48.9 | 49.0 | 48.9 |
| 100.0 | 100.0 | 100.0 | Total Liabilities & Net Worth | | 100.0 | 100.0 | 100.0 | 100.0 | 100.0 |
| | | | **INCOME DATA** | | | | | | |
| 100.0 | 100.0 | 100.0 | Net Sales | | 100.0 | 100.0 | 100.0 | 100.0 | 100.0 |
| 29.4 | 29.2 | 28.5 | Gross Profit | | 31.5 | 34.0 | 30.2 | 29.1 | 24.6 |
| 25.8 | 23.8 | 22.7 | Operating Expenses | | 28.1 | 30.3 | 25.4 | 23.3 | 16.9 |
| 3.7 | 5.4 | 5.8 | Operating Profit | | 3.4 | 3.7 | 4.8 | 5.8 | 7.8 |
| 1.0 | .8 | .5 | All Other Expenses (net) | | 1.8 | 1.0 | -.6 | .5 | .3 |
| 2.6 | 4.6 | 5.3 | Profit Before Taxes | | 1.6 | 2.7 | 5.5 | 5.3 | 7.5 |
| | | | **RATIOS** | | | | | | |
| 3.1 | 3.5 | 3.2 | Current | | 7.1 | 2.5 | 2.5 | 3.0 | 3.0 |
| 2.0 | 2.1 | 1.8 | | | 2.5 | 1.4 | 1.9 | 1.9 | 1.8 |
| 1.3 | 1.4 | 1.3 | | | 1.0 | 1.1 | 1.5 | 1.4 | 1.2 |
| 1.3 | 1.6 | 1.4 | Quick | | 2.9 | 1.4 | 1.0 | 1.6 | 1.2 |
| .7 | .8 | .8 | | | .7 | .8 | .7 | 1.0 | .8 |
| .4 | .4 | .4 | | | .3 | .2 | .2 | .4 | .4 |
| 19  19.2 | 25  14.5 | 18  20.8 | Sales/Receivables | | 12  30.8 | 12  30.1 | 7  53.9 | 25  14.5 | 26  14.0 |
| 34  10.6 | 38  9.6 | 33  10.9 | | | 27  13.6 | 35  10.3 | 18  20.5 | 36  10.0 | 33  10.9 |
| 56  6.5 | 56  6.5 | 54  6.8 | | | 51  7.1 | 43  8.4 | 41  8.9 | 55  6.6 | 60  6.1 |
| 70  5.2 | 67  5.5 | 52  7.0 | Cost of Sales/Inventory | | 16  23.1 | 46  8.0 | 54  6.7 | 41  8.9 | 74  4.9 |
| 126  2.9 | 113  3.2 | 104  3.5 | | | 114  3.2 | 104  3.5 | 89  4.1 | 83  4.4 | 111  3.3 |
| 209  1.7 | 177  2.1 | 166  2.2 | | | 203  1.8 | 203  1.8 | 159  2.3 | 159  2.3 | 159  2.3 |
| 11  31.8 | 13  28.7 | 15  24.2 | Cost of Sales/Payables | | 12  30.2 | 16  22.7 | 18  20.6 | 16  22.7 | 15  24.7 |
| 20  18.0 | 23  15.9 | 26  13.8 | | | 15  23.6 | 26  14.3 | 31  11.9 | 27  13.7 | 26  13.8 |
| 35  10.3 | 35  10.5 | 41  9.0 | | | 40  9.1 | 55  6.6 | 43  8.4 | 41  8.8 | 36  10.0 |
| 3.2 | 3.1 | 3.5 | Sales/Working Capital | | 2.4 | 4.3 | 4.3 | 3.5 | 2.8 |
| 5.5 | 4.6 | 6.7 | | | 5.5 | 20.5 | 7.6 | 6.7 | 6.1 |
| 11.1 | 11.2 | 17.5 | | | NM | 80.4 | 15.1 | 15.8 | 12.9 |
| 10.8 | 20.3 | 31.5 | EBIT/Interest | | 12.1 | 18.3 | 44.1 | 29.2 | 62.4 |
| (129) 3.7 | (134) 5.7 | (139) 8.0 | | | (19) 2.5 | (14) 5.2 | (17) 8.9 | (41) 10.0 | (47) 12.3 |
| .9 | 1.8 | 3.1 | | | -1.6 | .5 | 4.4 | 2.3 | 4.0 |
| 16.7 | 19.1 | 9.1 | Net Profit + Depr., Dep., | | | | | | 11.7 |
| (34) 4.2 | (28) 5.5 | (28) 3.2 | Amort./Cur. Mat. L/T/D | | | | | | (16) 6.2 |
| 1.6 | 2.7 | 1.3 | | | | | | | 2.9 |
| .2 | .1 | .2 | Fixed/Worth | | .2 | .3 | .0 | .1 | .2 |
| .4 | .4 | .3 | | | .7 | .8 | .3 | .2 | .4 |
| 1.0 | .8 | .8 | | | -.5 | 1.8 | .9 | .7 | .8 |
| .6 | .4 | .6 | Debt/Worth | | .4 | 1.2 | .7 | .5 | .6 |
| 1.1 | 1.1 | 1.1 | | | 1.0 | 2.0 | .9 | 1.1 | 1.0 |
| 3.5 | 2.6 | 2.9 | | | -7.7 | 12.2 | 1.6 | 2.1 | 2.7 |
| 29.8 | 41.0 | 46.0 | % Profit Before Taxes/Tangible | | 38.3 | 111.3 | 49.6 | 46.8 | 40.9 |
| (127) 12.1 | (140) 19.2 | (141) 23.1 | Net Worth | | (13) 4.5 | (13) 30.4 | 18.3 | (43) 24.3 | (51) 27.0 |
| 1.2 | 5.6 | 8.9 | | | -.8 | 3.2 | 12.1 | 4.9 | 11.1 |
| 11.4 | 16.8 | 17.6 | % Profit Before Taxes/Total | | 13.9 | 25.6 | 14.4 | 18.9 | 18.9 |
| 5.2 | 7.5 | 8.0 | Assets | | 2.2 | 4.8 | 9.4 | 10.9 | 9.9 |
| -.3 | 1.6 | 3.1 | | | -5.0 | -1.0 | 5.0 | 2.4 | 5.0 |
| 33.8 | 29.7 | 37.4 | Sales/Net Fixed Assets | | 48.0 | 36.5 | 103.6 | 42.5 | 18.1 |
| 11.1 | 12.0 | 13.4 | | | 14.4 | 15.7 | 19.1 | 16.6 | 8.5 |
| 5.1 | 5.3 | 5.9 | | | 8.9 | 5.3 | 5.8 | 5.4 | 5.5 |
| 2.2 | 2.4 | 2.7 | Sales/Total Assets | | 2.4 | 3.1 | 3.3 | 2.8 | 2.2 |
| 1.6 | 1.8 | 2.0 | | | 1.6 | 2.2 | 2.4 | 2.2 | 1.8 |
| 1.2 | 1.2 | 1.3 | | | 1.0 | 1.8 | 1.7 | 1.5 | 1.3 |
| 1.1 | 1.0 | .7 | % Depr., Dep., Amort./Sales | | .7 | .4 | 1.0 | .6 | .7 |
| (126) 1.9 | (125) 1.8 | (125) 1.4 | | | (16) 1.9 | (12) 1.3 | (12) 1.7 | (36) 1.1 | (48) 1.4 |
| 3.2 | 3.0 | 2.5 | | | 2.7 | 3.9 | 4.1 | 2.8 | 2.3 |
| 1.5 | 1.2 | 1.2 | % Officers', Directors' | | | | | 1.8 | 1.8 |
| (39) 2.8 | (43) 2.7 | (47) 2.8 | Owners' Comp/Sales | | | | (10) 2.9 | (15) 2.4 | |
| 5.9 | 4.3 | 4.7 | | | | | | 4.5 | 3.7 |
| 4407935M | 4989419M | 6474979M | Net Sales ($) | 2297M | 35795M | 59736M | 134764M | 694274M | 5548113M |
| 2889923M | 3050177M | 3704357M | Total Assets ($) | 3191M | 26498M | 29318M | 63704M | 397305M | 3184341M |

## Current Data Sorted by Assets    Comparative Historical Data

### Type of Statement

| | 0-500M | 500M-2MM | 2-10MM | 10-50MM | 50-100MM | 100-250MM | | 4/1/07-3/31/08 ALL | 4/1/08-3/31/09 ALL |
|---|---|---|---|---|---|---|---|---|---|
| Unqualified | | | | 4 | 1 | | | 8 | 10 |
| Reviewed | | 2 | 1 | 2 | | | | 9 | 3 |
| Compiled | | 1 | 1 | 1 | | | | 5 | 5 |
| Tax Returns | | 1 | 1 | | | | | 4 | 6 |
| Other | | | | 5 | 1 | | | 24 | 20 |
| | | 5 (4/1-9/30/11) | | 17 (10/1/11-3/31/12) | | | | | |
| NUMBER OF STATEMENTS | | 3 | 5 | 12 | 2 | | | 50 | 44 |

| 0-500M | 500M-2MM | 2-10MM | 10-50MM | 50-100MM | 100-250MM | | 4/1/07-3/31/08 ALL | 4/1/08-3/31/09 ALL |
|---|---|---|---|---|---|---|---|---|
| % | % | % | % | % | % | **ASSETS** | % | % |
| | | | 5.3 | | | Cash & Equivalents | 5.7 | 7.6 |
| | | | 19.9 | | | Trade Receivables (net) | 22.5 | 15.3 |
| | | | 37.3 | | | Inventory | 44.3 | 48.8 |
| | | | 2.9 | | | All Other Current | 1.5 | 2.4 |
| | | | 65.4 | | | Total Current | 74.0 | 74.1 |
| | | | 25.6 | | | Fixed Assets (net) | 15.8 | 15.7 |
| | | | 5.4 | | | Intangibles (net) | 5.9 | 6.3 |
| | | | 3.5 | | | All Other Non-Current | 4.4 | 3.9 |
| | | | 100.0 | | | Total | 100.0 | 100.0 |
| | | | | | | **LIABILITIES** | | |
| | | | 18.0 | | | Notes Payable-Short Term | 19.6 | 17.8 |
| | | | 3.1 | | | Cur. Mat.-L.T.D. | 3.2 | 3.0 |
| | | | 16.2 | | | Trade Payables | 17.6 | 16.8 |
| | | | .0 | | | Income Taxes Payable | .4 | .1 |
| | | | 15.6 | | | All Other Current | 9.4 | 8.5 |
| | | | 52.9 | | | Total Current | 50.2 | 46.3 |
| | | | 19.4 | | | Long-Term Debt | 13.6 | 11.9 |
| | | | .2 | | | Deferred Taxes | .3 | .1 |
| | | | 18.0 | | | All Other Non-Current | 9.6 | 5.9 |
| | | | 9.6 | | | Net Worth | 26.4 | 35.8 |
| | | | 100.0 | | | Total Liabilties & Net Worth | 100.0 | 100.0 |
| | | | | | | **INCOME DATA** | | |
| | | | 100.0 | | | Net Sales | 100.0 | 100.0 |
| | | | 28.7 | | | Gross Profit | 28.1 | 29.7 |
| | | | 19.1 | | | Operating Expenses | 24.6 | 27.7 |
| | | | 9.6 | | | Operating Profit | 3.6 | 2.0 |
| | | | 2.2 | | | All Other Expenses (net) | 2.0 | 1.3 |
| | | | 7.3 | | | Profit Before Taxes | 1.6 | .7 |
| | | | | | | **RATIOS** | | |
| | | | 2.5 | | | Current | 3.1 | 2.8 |
| | | | 1.4 | | | | 1.6 | 1.5 |
| | | | .9 | | | | 1.1 | 1.1 |
| | | | 1.0 | | | Quick | 1.5 | .9 |
| | | | .5 | | | | .5 | .5 |
| | | | .3 | | | | .3 | .3 |
| | | 21 | 17.6 | | | Sales/Receivables | 24 15.0 | 17 21.7 |
| | | 34 | 10.8 | | | | 37 9.9 | 34 10.9 |
| | | 76 | 4.8 | | | | 58 6.3 | 45 8.2 |
| | | 73 | 5.0 | | | Cost of Sales/Inventory | 69 5.3 | 100 3.7 |
| | | 99 | 3.7 | | | | 101 3.6 | 134 2.7 |
| | | 192 | 1.9 | | | | 156 2.3 | 195 1.9 |
| | | 26 | 14.0 | | | Cost of Sales/Payables | 16 22.3 | 18 19.8 |
| | | 51 | 7.1 | | | | 34 10.7 | 31 11.7 |
| | | 73 | 5.0 | | | | 54 6.7 | 71 5.1 |
| | | | 3.8 | | | Sales/Working Capital | 4.0 | 3.4 |
| | | | 7.2 | | | | 8.6 | 7.8 |
| | | | NM | | | | 30.4 | 31.5 |
| | | | 7.7 | | | EBIT/Interest | 5.3 | 5.5 |
| | | | 3.1 | | | | (46) 1.7 | (41) 2.3 |
| | | | 1.8 | | | | .2 | .4 |
| | | | | | | Net Profit + Depr., Dep., Amort./Cur. Mat. L/T/D | | 4.0 |
| | | | | | | | (15) 2.9 | |
| | | | | | | | | 2.3 |
| | | | .5 | | | Fixed/Worth | .2 | .2 |
| | | | 1.8 | | | | .5 | .4 |
| | | | NM | | | | NM | 1.3 |
| | | | 2.3 | | | Debt/Worth | .7 | .6 |
| | | | 4.6 | | | | 2.0 | 1.9 |
| | | | -9.6 | | | | -11.3 | 12.9 |
| | | | | | | % Profit Before Taxes/Tangible Net Worth | 32.3 | 27.7 |
| | | | | | | | (37) 17.3 | (35) 14.4 |
| | | | | | | | 4.0 | 2.6 |
| | | | 11.4 | | | % Profit Before Taxes/Total Assets | 10.4 | 9.3 |
| | | | 6.5 | | | | 5.0 | 4.0 |
| | | | 2.4 | | | | -2.5 | -1.2 |
| | | | 20.9 | | | Sales/Net Fixed Assets | 43.7 | 34.3 |
| | | | 5.7 | | | | 18.0 | 13.7 |
| | | | 3.7 | | | | 8.3 | 8.4 |
| | | | 2.4 | | | Sales/Total Assets | 2.7 | 2.3 |
| | | | 1.5 | | | | 2.0 | 1.7 |
| | | | 1.0 | | | | 1.5 | 1.3 |
| | | | | | | % Depr., Dep., Amort./Sales | .6 | .8 |
| | | | | | | | (38) 1.5 | (37) 1.7 |
| | | | | | | | 2.5 | 2.3 |
| | | | | | | % Officers', Directors' Owners' Comp/Sales | 1.7 | 1.6 |
| | | | | | | | (10) 2.6 | (10) 2.9 |
| | | | | | | | 4.4 | 7.4 |
| | 9669M | 46625M | 458775M | 202711M | | Net Sales ($) | 1921653M | 1927255M |
| | 3627M | 27178M | 278828M | 104218M | | Total Assets ($) | 1011123M | 1040757M |

*(Columns 0-500M, 500M-2MM, 2-10MM, 50-100MM and 100-250MM marked "DATA NOT AVAILABLE".)*

M = $ thousand    MM = $ million
See Pages 9 through 22 for Explanation of Ratios and Data

## Comparative Historical Data / Current Data Sorted by Sales

| | Comparative Historical Data | | | Type of Statement | Current Data Sorted by Sales | | | | | |
|---|---|---|---|---|---|---|---|---|---|---|
| | | | | | | 5 (4/1-9/30/11) | | | 17 (10/1/11-3/31/12) | | |
| | | | | | 0-1MM | 1-3MM | 3-5MM | 5-10MM | 10-25MM | 25MM & OVER |
| Unqualified | 8 | 5 | 5 | | | | | | | 5 |
| Reviewed | 6 | 6 | 3 | | | 2 | | | 2 | 1 |
| Compiled | 5 | 6 | 5 | | | | 3 | | | |
| Tax Returns | 4 | 2 | 2 | | | | 1 | | 1 | |
| Other | 16 | 15 | 7 | | | | 1 | 1 | | 5 |
| | 4/1/09-3/31/10 ALL | 4/1/10-3/31/11 ALL | 4/1/11-3/31/12 ALL | | | | 2 | 5 | 4 | 11 |
| | 39 | 34 | 22 | **NUMBER OF STATEMENTS** | | | 2 | 5 | 4 | 11 |
| | % | % | % | **ASSETS** | % | % | % | % | % | % |
| | 10.4 | 11.1 | 8.0 | Cash & Equivalents | | | | | | 6.3 |
| | 14.8 | 17.3 | 18.0 | Trade Receivables (net) | | | | | | 19.8 |
| | 42.7 | 40.8 | 43.2 | Inventory | D | D | | | | 38.6 |
| | 1.9 | 2.7 | 2.2 | All Other Current | A | A | | | | 3.5 |
| | 69.8 | 71.9 | 71.3 | Total Current | T | T | | | | 68.2 |
| | 17.6 | 18.2 | 19.9 | Fixed Assets (net) | A | A | | | | 19.5 |
| | 5.0 | 6.0 | 5.5 | Intangibles (net) | | | | | | 8.9 |
| | 7.7 | 4.0 | 3.4 | All Other Non-Current | N | N | | | | 3.5 |
| | 100.0 | 100.0 | 100.0 | Total | O | O | | | | 100.0 |
| | | | | **LIABILITIES** | T | T | | | | |
| | 17.5 | 15.0 | 15.5 | Notes Payable-Short Term | A | A | | | | 15.0 |
| | 3.3 | 2.6 | 2.5 | Cur. Mat.-L.T.D. | V | V | | | | 2.5 |
| | 17.4 | 17.3 | 20.2 | Trade Payables | A | A | | | | 16.7 |
| | .4 | .5 | .1 | Income Taxes Payable | I | I | | | | .0 |
| | 10.6 | 7.6 | 10.9 | All Other Current | L | L | | | | 18.7 |
| | 49.2 | 42.9 | 49.1 | Total Current | A | A | | | | 52.8 |
| | 8.1 | 12.2 | 11.7 | Long-Term Debt | B | B | | | | 10.6 |
| | .3 | .3 | .7 | Deferred Taxes | L | L | | | | .4 |
| | 10.7 | 4.2 | 9.9 | All Other Non-Current | E | E | | | | 19.6 |
| | 31.7 | 40.4 | 28.6 | Net Worth | | | | | | 16.6 |
| | 100.0 | 100.0 | 100.0 | Total Liabilities & Net Worth | | | | | | 100.0 |
| | | | | **INCOME DATA** | | | | | | |
| | 100.0 | 100.0 | 100.0 | Net Sales | | | | | | 100.0 |
| | 30.9 | 29.1 | 29.8 | Gross Profit | | | | | | 20.3 |
| | 28.9 | 24.1 | 22.9 | Operating Expenses | | | | | | 15.5 |
| | 2.0 | 5.0 | 6.9 | Operating Profit | | | | | | 4.7 |
| | 1.4 | .8 | 1.5 | All Other Expenses (net) | | | | | | 1.8 |
| | .6 | 4.2 | 5.4 | Profit Before Taxes | | | | | | 2.9 |
| | | | | **RATIOS** | | | | | | |
| | 5.5 | 2.9 | 3.0 | | | | | | | 3.0 |
| | 1.5 | 1.5 | 1.6 | Current | | | | | | 1.7 |
| | 1.2 | 1.2 | 1.1 | | | | | | | 1.1 |
| | 1.6 | 1.3 | 1.1 | | | | | | | 1.2 |
| | .6 | .6 | .4 | Quick | | | | | | .4 |
| | .2 | .3 | .3 | | | | | | | .3 |
| | (8) 48.4 | (13) 29.0 | (11) 32.4 | | | | | | (11) | 33.1 |
| | (27) 13.6 | (36) 10.2 | (33) 11.0 | Sales/Receivables | | | | | (37) | 9.8 |
| | (47) 7.8 | (49) 7.5 | (58) 6.3 | | | | | | (79) | 4.6 |
| | (69) 5.3 | (81) 4.5 | (83) 4.4 | | | | | | (73) | 5.0 |
| | (120) 3.0 | (107) 3.4 | (107) 3.4 | Cost of Sales/Inventory | | | | | (85) | 4.3 |
| | (178) 2.0 | (166) 2.2 | (174) 2.1 | | | | | | (107) | 3.4 |
| | (11) 33.5 | (22) 16.8 | (28) 12.9 | | | | | | (25) | 14.5 |
| | (20) 18.6 | (38) 9.7 | (49) 7.4 | Cost of Sales/Payables | | | | | (35) | 10.4 |
| | (48) 7.6 | (55) 6.6 | (79) 4.6 | | | | | | (51) | 7.1 |
| | 3.5 | 4.3 | 3.9 | | | | | | | 3.7 |
| | 7.2 | 8.2 | 7.2 | Sales/Working Capital | | | | | | 7.5 |
| | 20.2 | 17.1 | 30.2 | | | | | | | 41.1 |
| | 10.3 | 18.2 | 11.1 | | | | | | | 13.7 |
| | (37) 1.6 | (33) 6.0 | (21) 3.8 | EBIT/Interest | | | | | | 2.4 |
| | -1.9 | 1.1 | 1.5 | | | | | | | 1.8 |
| | | | | Net Profit + Depr., Dep., Amort./Cur. Mat. L/T/D | | | | | | |
| | .1 | .1 | .1 | | | | | | | .3 |
| | .4 | .4 | .5 | Fixed/Worth | | | | | | .6 |
| | 1.1 | 1.3 | 2.1 | | | | | | | -1.7 |
| | .7 | .7 | .7 | | | | | | | .7 |
| | 1.2 | 1.8 | 3.4 | Debt/Worth | | | | | | 4.3 |
| | 2.7 | 4.4 | 7.0 | | | | | | | -8.3 |
| | 19.2 | 81.5 | 50.6 | % Profit Before Taxes/Tangible Net Worth | | | | | | |
| | (34) 3.9 | (31) 18.7 | (18) 17.4 | | | | | | | |
| | -19.1 | .3 | 7.3 | | | | | | | |
| | 9.6 | 15.7 | 10.6 | % Profit Before Taxes/Total Assets | | | | | | 9.9 |
| | 1.1 | 7.1 | 4.6 | | | | | | | 4.2 |
| | -6.8 | .2 | 1.8 | | | | | | | 2.0 |
| | 51.8 | 52.8 | 75.2 | | | | | | | 20.9 |
| | 15.6 | 21.6 | 15.7 | Sales/Net Fixed Assets | | | | | | 14.3 |
| | 6.1 | 5.5 | 4.7 | | | | | | | 5.7 |
| | 2.6 | 2.3 | 2.6 | | | | | | | 2.9 |
| | 1.7 | 1.7 | 1.7 | Sales/Total Assets | | | | | | 1.8 |
| | 1.3 | 1.2 | 1.1 | | | | | | | 1.2 |
| | .6 | .6 | .9 | | | | | | | |
| | (38) 1.5 | (27) 1.4 | (15) 1.7 | % Depr., Dep., Amort./Sales | | | | | | |
| | 2.4 | 1.9 | 3.0 | | | | | | | |
| | 1.7 | | 1.1 | % Officers', Directors' Owners' Comp/Sales | | | | | | |
| | (16) 3.0 | (14) 2.4 | | | | | | | | |
| | 6.8 | | 3.6 | | | | | | | |
| | 1634538M | 1566709M | 717780M | Net Sales ($) | 4615M | | 31867M | 55088M | | 626210M |
| | 808964M | 729859M | 413851M | Total Assets ($) | 2111M | | 24804M | 41338M | | 345598M |

M = $ thousand     MM = $ million
See Pages 9 through 22 for Explanation of Ratios and Data

## Current Data Sorted by Assets        Comparative Historical Data

| 0-500M | 500M-2MM | 2-10MM | 10-50MM | 50-100MM | 100-250MM | Type of Statement | 4/1/07-3/31/08 ALL | 4/1/08-3/31/09 ALL |
|---|---|---|---|---|---|---|---|---|
| | 1 | 2 | 5 | 5 | | Unqualified | 37 | 44 |
| | 2 | 13 | 14 | 1 | | Reviewed | 24 | 22 |
| | 2 | 7 | 3 | 1 | | Compiled | 16 | 14 |
| 3 | 3 | 6 | 1 | | | Tax Returns | 7 | 7 |
| 1 | 4 | 11 | 17 | 5 | 3 | Other | 44 | 56 |
| | 17 (4/1-9/30/11) | | 93 (10/1/11-3/31/12) | | | | | |
| 4 | 12 | 39 | 40 | 12 | 3 | **NUMBER OF STATEMENTS** | 128 | 143 |
| % | % | % | % | % | % | **ASSETS** | % | % |
| | 8.3 | 10.7 | 5.3 | 13.0 | | Cash & Equivalents | 7.2 | 6.3 |
| | 26.3 | 20.6 | 18.9 | 14.5 | | Trade Receivables (net) | 22.8 | 18.7 |
| | 26.1 | 35.7 | 33.8 | 38.5 | | Inventory | 31.9 | 38.3 |
| | 1.7 | 3.3 | 3.3 | 4.7 | | All Other Current | 4.5 | 4.1 |
| | 62.5 | 70.3 | 61.3 | 70.8 | | Total Current | 66.4 | 67.3 |
| | 22.5 | 21.0 | 28.8 | 21.2 | | Fixed Assets (net) | 24.4 | 23.2 |
| | 3.3 | 4.2 | 4.2 | 4.0 | | Intangibles (net) | 4.3 | 5.4 |
| | 11.7 | 4.4 | 5.7 | 4.0 | | All Other Non-Current | 5.0 | 4.1 |
| | 100.0 | 100.0 | 100.0 | 100.0 | | Total | 100.0 | 100.0 |
| | | | | | | **LIABILITIES** | | |
| | 13.2 | 9.5 | 15.7 | 10.6 | | Notes Payable-Short Term | 14.9 | 14.9 |
| | 4.6 | 4.7 | 3.9 | 2.2 | | Cur. Mat.-L.T.D. | 4.5 | 2.7 |
| | 20.8 | 17.4 | 11.6 | 10.2 | | Trade Payables | 12.2 | 11.3 |
| | .0 | .2 | .0 | .0 | | Income Taxes Payable | .3 | .3 |
| | 9.2 | 15.8 | 7.5 | 15.1 | | All Other Current | 12.3 | 12.6 |
| | 47.9 | 47.5 | 38.8 | 38.1 | | Total Current | 44.2 | 41.7 |
| | 19.0 | 13.2 | 15.1 | 2.9 | | Long-Term Debt | 15.8 | 15.1 |
| | .0 | .4 | .7 | 1.2 | | Deferred Taxes | .3 | .6 |
| | 7.1 | 3.2 | 3.6 | .7 | | All Other Non-Current | 4.1 | 5.1 |
| | 26.0 | 35.7 | 41.8 | 57.1 | | Net Worth | 35.6 | 37.4 |
| | 100.0 | 100.0 | 100.0 | 100.0 | | Total Liabilities & Net Worth | 100.0 | 100.0 |
| | | | | | | **INCOME DATA** | | |
| | 100.0 | 100.0 | 100.0 | 100.0 | | Net Sales | 100.0 | 100.0 |
| | 32.9 | 27.0 | 25.1 | 22.2 | | Gross Profit | 29.7 | 27.2 |
| | 28.6 | 22.8 | 23.8 | 16.8 | | Operating Expenses | 22.9 | 23.1 |
| | 4.4 | 4.2 | 1.2 | 5.4 | | Operating Profit | 6.7 | 4.1 |
| | 1.5 | .5 | 1.5 | -.4 | | All Other Expenses (net) | 1.3 | 1.1 |
| | 2.8 | 3.7 | -.3 | 5.8 | | Profit Before Taxes | 5.4 | 3.0 |
| | | | | | | **RATIOS** | | |
| | 3.4 | 2.5 | 2.8 | 6.8 | | | 2.4 | 2.9 |
| | 1.6 | 1.5 | 1.6 | 1.8 | | Current | 1.6 | 1.6 |
| | .5 | 1.0 | 1.2 | 1.2 | | | 1.1 | 1.1 |
| | 2.5 | 1.3 | 1.2 | 3.4 | | | 1.2 | 1.0 |
| | .5 | .6 | .6 | .8 | | Quick | .6 | .6 |
| | .3 | .4 | .4 | .3 | | | .3 | .3 |
| 21 17.6 | 21 17.8 | 40 9.1 | 22 16.6 | | | | 26 14.1 | 23 16.0 |
| 36 10.1 | 36 10.0 | 51 7.2 | 45 8.1 | | | Sales/Receivables | 41 8.9 | 37 10.0 |
| 51 7.1 | 58 6.3 | 64 5.7 | 60 6.1 | | | | 57 6.3 | 56 6.6 |
| 7 50.9 | 46 8.0 | 58 6.3 | 96 3.8 | | | | 35 10.3 | 65 5.6 |
| 81 4.5 | 89 4.1 | 135 2.7 | 146 2.5 | | | Cost of Sales/Inventory | 91 4.0 | 107 3.4 |
| 135 2.7 | 203 1.8 | 182 2.0 | 203 1.8 | | | | 149 2.4 | 170 2.1 |
| 26 14.2 | 21 17.0 | 22 16.5 | 14 25.6 | | | | 16 22.5 | 15 24.8 |
| 43 8.4 | 36 10.0 | 38 9.7 | 22 16.6 | | | Cost of Sales/Payables | 29 12.8 | 27 13.6 |
| 55 6.6 | 57 6.4 | 49 7.4 | 38 9.6 | | | | 44 8.4 | 41 9.0 |
| | 3.4 | 3.9 | 3.3 | 1.7 | | | 4.7 | 4.1 |
| | 12.5 | 7.3 | 5.5 | 4.2 | | Sales/Working Capital | 9.3 | 6.7 |
| | -8.9 | 148.8 | 15.6 | 11.4 | | | 24.4 | 21.9 |
| | 13.8 | 10.2 | 13.1 | 999.8 | | | 10.0 | 10.2 |
| | (10) 2.6 | (36) 3.9 | (39) 2.7 | (10) 11.3 | | EBIT/Interest | (121) 4.1 | (132) 3.2 |
| | -.6 | 1.0 | -.3 | 4.9 | | | 1.3 | .4 |
| | | | 5.5 | | | Net Profit + Depr., Dep., | 7.4 | 6.5 |
| | | (15) 1.4 | | | | Amort./Cur. Mat. L/T/D | (45) 2.6 | (44) 3.0 |
| | | | 1.1 | | | | 1.0 | .7 |
| | .1 | .2 | .4 | .1 | | | .2 | .2 |
| | .5 | .8 | .7 | .2 | | Fixed/Worth | .5 | .5 |
| | -5.5 | 1.9 | 1.1 | .8 | | | 1.7 | 1.9 |
| | .5 | .9 | .5 | .2 | | | .8 | .6 |
| | 1.6 | 2.5 | 1.4 | 1.0 | | Debt/Worth | 2.2 | 1.8 |
| | -10.7 | 5.3 | 3.1 | 1.5 | | | 5.2 | 7.7 |
| | | 49.2 | 18.6 | 18.4 | | % Profit Before Taxes/Tangible | 44.3 | 36.4 |
| | (36) 18.7 | (37) 7.0 | | 13.2 | | Net Worth | (116) 22.0 | (122) 16.4 |
| | | .1 | -1.3 | 9.2 | | | 5.3 | 1.8 |
| | 12.2 | 12.1 | 7.3 | 8.9 | | | 15.7 | 13.2 |
| | 3.5 | 4.9 | 2.5 | 6.8 | | % Profit Before Taxes/Total Assets | 7.5 | 5.3 |
| | -2.5 | -.3 | -1.4 | 4.4 | | | 1.5 | -.8 |
| | 74.5 | 26.9 | 11.0 | 15.8 | | | 25.3 | 18.7 |
| | 13.3 | 12.3 | 6.1 | 8.4 | | Sales/Net Fixed Assets | 10.1 | 9.9 |
| | 5.6 | 5.3 | 2.8 | 3.3 | | | 5.1 | 5.1 |
| | 3.0 | 2.4 | 1.7 | 1.4 | | | 2.5 | 2.4 |
| | 2.1 | 1.8 | 1.3 | 1.2 | | Sales/Total Assets | 1.7 | 1.6 |
| | 1.6 | 1.5 | .9 | 1.0 | | | 1.2 | 1.2 |
| | | .7 | 1.3 | 1.5 | | | .9 | 1.0 |
| | (36) 1.6 | (38) 2.2 | | (10) 2.8 | | % Depr., Dep., Amort./Sales | (108) 1.9 | (121) 1.8 |
| | | 3.8 | 7.2 | 4.8 | | | 3.4 | 3.4 |
| | | 1.6 | | | | | 2.2 | 1.1 |
| | (19) 2.5 | | | | | % Officers', Directors' Owners' Comp/Sales | (25) 3.8 | (23) 3.1 |
| | | 4.7 | | | | | 5.4 | 5.7 |
| 8770M | 33925M | 359452M | 1129889M | 1061316M | 237007M | Net Sales ($) | 5064454M | 6771288M |
| 1052M | 15750M | 196651M | 884209M | 879821M | 385831M | Total Assets ($) | 3197587M | 4623437M |

© RMA 2012

M = $ thousand    MM = $ million
See Pages 9 through 22 for Explanation of Ratios and Data

## Comparative Historical Data / Current Data Sorted by Sales

| 4/1/09-3/31/10 ALL | 4/1/10-3/31/11 ALL | 4/1/11-3/31/12 ALL | Type of Statement | 0-1MM | 1-3MM | 3-5MM | 5-10MM | 10-25MM | 25MM & OVER |
|---|---|---|---|---|---|---|---|---|---|
| 36 | 26 | 13 | Unqualified | | 1 | | | 6 | 6 |
| 20 | 23 | 30 | Reviewed | | 1 | 2 | 4 | 16 | 7 |
| 9 | 11 | 13 | Compiled | | | 2 | 3 | 4 | 3 | 1 |
| 9 | 6 | 13 | Tax Returns | 1 | 3 | 2 | 4 | 3 | |
| 59 | 53 | 41 | Other | 1 | 2 | 4 | 8 | 8 | 18 |
| 4/1/09-3/31/10 ALL | 4/1/10-3/31/11 ALL | 4/1/11-3/31/12 ALL | | 17 (4/1-9/30/11) | | 93 (10/1/11-3/31/12) | | | |
| 133 | 119 | 110 | NUMBER OF STATEMENTS | 2 | 9 | 11 | 20 | 36 | 32 |
| % | % | % | ASSETS | % | % | % | % | % | % |
| 10.9 | 10.2 | 9.5 | Cash & Equivalents | | | 7.1 | 10.2 | 7.7 | 12.2 |
| 18.5 | 20.2 | 19.7 | Trade Receivables (net) | | | 17.2 | 21.0 | 18.4 | 18.3 |
| 34.1 | 32.2 | 33.1 | Inventory | | | 28.3 | 33.3 | 33.5 | 37.4 |
| 4.8 | 3.7 | 3.2 | All Other Current | | | 1.0 | 3.5 | 2.4 | 5.3 |
| 68.3 | 66.3 | 65.6 | Total Current | | | 53.5 | 68.0 | 62.1 | 73.3 |
| 23.5 | 23.6 | 23.8 | Fixed Assets (net) | | | 29.1 | 17.3 | 29.0 | 18.7 |
| 3.0 | 5.1 | 4.0 | Intangibles (net) | | | 4.7 | 4.6 | 4.5 | 3.7 |
| 5.3 | 5.0 | 6.5 | All Other Non-Current | | | 12.6 | 10.1 | 4.4 | 4.4 |
| 100.0 | 100.0 | 100.0 | Total | | | 100.0 | 100.0 | 100.0 | 100.0 |
| | | | LIABILITIES | | | | | | |
| 12.5 | 12.5 | 13.3 | Notes Payable-Short Term | | | 7.3 | 17.2 | 11.1 | 14.5 |
| 2.8 | 3.6 | 4.1 | Cur. Mat.-L.T.D. | | | 6.6 | 3.7 | 5.0 | 2.4 |
| 10.6 | 11.2 | 14.4 | Trade Payables | | | 13.4 | 17.6 | 12.5 | 12.7 |
| .2 | .3 | .1 | Income Taxes Payable | | | .1 | .2 | .1 | .0 |
| 14.2 | 13.0 | 11.4 | All Other Current | | | 5.8 | 14.8 | 10.5 | 12.1 |
| 40.3 | 40.5 | 43.2 | Total Current | | | 33.3 | 53.5 | 39.2 | 41.8 |
| 13.1 | 11.5 | 14.1 | Long-Term Debt | | | 30.9 | 10.6 | 15.1 | 6.1 |
| .4 | .5 | .5 | Deferred Taxes | | | .5 | .1 | .8 | .8 |
| 6.3 | 5.8 | 3.9 | All Other Non-Current | | | 8.9 | 1.0 | 3.7 | 4.2 |
| 39.8 | 41.7 | 38.2 | Net Worth | | | 26.4 | 34.7 | 41.3 | 47.2 |
| 100.0 | 100.0 | 100.0 | Total Liabilties & Net Worth | | | 100.0 | 100.0 | 100.0 | 100.0 |
| | | | INCOME DATA | | | | | | |
| 100.0 | 100.0 | 100.0 | Net Sales | | | 100.0 | 100.0 | 100.0 | 100.0 |
| 26.5 | 28.7 | 27.2 | Gross Profit | | | 36.0 | 27.4 | 25.5 | 23.7 |
| 26.6 | 24.8 | 23.9 | Operating Expenses | | | 31.0 | 26.7 | 23.9 | 18.3 |
| -.1 | 4.0 | 3.3 | Operating Profit | | | 5.1 | .7 | 1.6 | 5.4 |
| .6 | .7 | .9 | All Other Expenses (net) | | | 1.9 | .0 | 1.2 | .3 |
| -.7 | 3.3 | 2.5 | Profit Before Taxes | | | 3.2 | .7 | .4 | 5.1 |
| | | | RATIOS | | | | | | |
| 3.5 | 3.4 | 2.9 | Current | | | 2.9 | 2.0 | 3.2 | 3.5 |
| 1.8 | 1.8 | 1.6 | | | | 2.1 | 1.4 | 2.0 | 1.6 |
| 1.2 | 1.3 | 1.1 | | | | 1.1 | .9 | 1.1 | 1.2 |
| 1.5 | 1.5 | 1.3 | Quick | | | 1.6 | 1.0 | 1.4 | 1.3 |
| .7 | .7 | .6 | | | | .8 | .5 | .8 | .6 |
| .3 | .5 | .4 | | | | .5 | .5 | .5 | .6 |
| 29  12.6 | 34  10.7 | 24  15.1 | Sales/Receivables | 18  20.0 | 21  17.6 | 27  13.5 | 25  14.6 | | |
| 45  8.2 | 48  7.6 | 45  8.2 | | 48  7.6 | 38  9.6 | 48  7.6 | 45  8.2 | | |
| 62  5.9 | 59  6.2 | 60  6.1 | | 87  4.2 | 51  7.2 | 61  6.0 | 60  6.1 | | |
| 68  5.3 | 58  6.2 | 46  7.9 | Cost of Sales/Inventory | 7  52.3 | 47  7.8 | 51  7.2 | 65  5.6 | | |
| 118  3.1 | 122  3.0 | 111  3.3 | | 118  3.1 | 83  4.4 | 114  3.2 | 135  2.7 | | |
| 199  1.8 | 178  2.0 | 174  2.1 | | 215  1.7 | 140  2.6 | 182  2.0 | 182  2.0 | | |
| 16  23.5 | 18  19.9 | 20  18.0 | Cost of Sales/Payables | 24  15.5 | 21  17.1 | 19  19.2 | 18  19.8 | | |
| 23  15.6 | 33  10.9 | 36  10.1 | | 35  10.4 | 41  8.9 | 35  10.5 | 33  10.9 | | |
| 46  8.0 | 50  7.3 | 52  7.0 | | 76  4.8 | 56  6.5 | 45  8.2 | 49  7.5 | | |
| 2.6 | 3.0 | 3.2 | Sales/Working Capital | | | 3.9 | 5.3 | 2.8 | 2.5 |
| 5.3 | 5.1 | 6.3 | | | | 5.3 | 8.2 | 4.9 | 4.8 |
| 13.2 | 14.8 | 31.9 | | | | 10.5 | -43.3 | 37.3 | 12.7 |
| 6.7 | 12.2 | 13.8 | EBIT/Interest | | | 13.7 | 15.1 | 8.2 | 95.5 |
| (120) 2.3 | (106) 3.6 | (100) 4.2 | | | | 2.6 | (17) 3.3 | (35) 2.6 | (29) 9.0 |
| -2.9 | 1.8 | 1.0 | | | | -.3 | .5 | -.4 | 3.6 |
| 6.2 | 9.5 | 5.5 | Net Profit + Depr., Dep., Amort./Cur. Mat. L/T/D | | | | | 6.1 | |
| (37) 1.4 | (34) 3.5 | (25) 1.6 | | | | | | (14) 1.5 | |
| .0 | .9 | 1.1 | | | | | | 1.0 | |
| .2 | .2 | .2 | Fixed/Worth | | | .5 | .2 | .4 | .2 |
| .6 | .5 | .6 | | | | .8 | .5 | .8 | .3 |
| 1.8 | 1.3 | 1.5 | | | | 5.5 | 4.0 | 1.1 | .9 |
| .6 | .5 | .7 | Debt/Worth | | | .6 | .9 | .6 | .5 |
| 1.4 | 1.3 | 1.6 | | | | 1.5 | 2.6 | 1.4 | 1.3 |
| 4.1 | 2.8 | 5.3 | | | | 11.2 | 11.8 | 3.1 | 2.9 |
| 21.1 | 25.5 | 31.4 | % Profit Before Taxes/Tangible Net Worth | | | | 60.0 | 21.6 | 25.2 |
| (119) 5.2 | (105) 11.1 | (99) 10.7 | | | | (18) 7.7 | (33) 5.5 | (31) 14.7 | |
| -8.4 | 3.1 | 1.2 | | | | | -6.3 | -1.3 | 9.2 |
| 7.3 | 9.6 | 9.8 | % Profit Before Taxes/Total Assets | | | 11.3 | 12.3 | 10.3 | 8.2 |
| 2.1 | 4.9 | 4.5 | | | | 3.5 | 2.5 | 2.8 | 6.1 |
| -5.0 | 1.2 | -.8 | | | | -1.8 | -2.1 | -1.4 | 3.6 |
| 18.2 | 13.9 | 18.1 | Sales/Net Fixed Assets | | | 12.4 | 80.8 | 12.2 | 22.2 |
| 7.5 | 8.8 | 8.5 | | | | 4.9 | 15.3 | 5.9 | 9.8 |
| 3.7 | 4.6 | 4.2 | | | | 3.8 | 5.2 | 3.0 | 6.6 |
| 2.1 | 2.2 | 2.0 | Sales/Total Assets | | | 2.5 | 2.5 | 1.8 | 1.8 |
| 1.3 | 1.4 | 1.6 | | | | 1.6 | 2.0 | 1.3 | 1.4 |
| .9 | 1.0 | 1.1 | | | | .8 | 1.5 | 1.0 | 1.1 |
| 1.3 | 1.5 | 1.0 | % Depr., Dep., Amort./Sales | | | 1.6 | .6 | 1.4 | 1.6 |
| (112) 2.3 | (104) 2.2 | (99) 2.0 | | | (10) 2.8 | (16) 1.5 | (35) 2.1 | (29) 1.6 | |
| 4.0 | 4.1 | 4.6 | | | | 6.4 | 4.3 | 5.5 | 3.2 |
| 1.2 | 1.9 | 1.5 | % Officers', Directors' Owners' Comp/Sales | | | | 1.5 | .9 | |
| (26) 2.9 | (33) 3.5 | (35) 2.4 | | | | (10) 2.5 | (11) 1.7 | | |
| 4.0 | 5.8 | 4.7 | | | | 3.9 | 2.5 | | |
| 4111564M | 4033972M | 2830359M | Net Sales ($) | 792M | 20221M | 41910M | 151386M | 575936M | 2040114M |
| 3820166M | 3668005M | 2363314M | Total Assets ($) | 407M | 12351M | 55557M | 106973M | 498754M | 1689272M |

M = $ thousand    MM = $ million
See Pages 9 through 22 for Explanation of Ratios and Data

## Current Data Sorted by Assets

## Comparative Historical Data

| 0-500M | 500M-2MM | 2-10MM | 10-50MM | 50-100MM | 100-250MM | Type of Statement | 4/1/07-3/31/08 ALL | 4/1/08-3/31/09 ALL |
|---|---|---|---|---|---|---|---|---|
| 1 | | 1 | 3 | 4 | 1 | Unqualified | 12 | 9 |
| | | 4 | 6 | | | Reviewed | 12 | 14 |
| | | 2 | 1 | | | Compiled | 9 | 8 |
| | 4 | 1 | | | | Tax Returns | 3 | 3 |
| 2 | 10 | 10 | 4 | 2 | | Other | 15 | 22 |
| | 11 (4/1-9/30/11) | | 45 (10/1/11-3/31/12) | | | | | |
| 1 | 6 | 18 | 20 | 8 | 3 | NUMBER OF STATEMENTS | 51 | 56 |
| % | % | % | % | % | % | ASSETS | % | % |
| | | 8.7 | 4.2 | | | Cash & Equivalents | 6.3 | 7.1 |
| | | 25.2 | 21.0 | | | Trade Receivables (net) | 24.1 | 23.9 |
| | | 32.6 | 42.7 | | | Inventory | 33.0 | 33.2 |
| | | 2.5 | 1.3 | | | All Other Current | 3.6 | 2.4 |
| | | 69.0 | 69.2 | | | Total Current | 67.0 | 66.7 |
| | | 24.2 | 25.4 | | | Fixed Assets (net) | 23.2 | 22.8 |
| | | 1.9 | 3.3 | | | Intangibles (net) | 3.2 | 5.1 |
| | | 4.9 | 2.0 | | | All Other Non-Current | 6.5 | 5.5 |
| | | 100.0 | 100.0 | | | Total | 100.0 | 100.0 |
| | | | | | | LIABILITIES | | |
| | | 6.9 | 16.4 | | | Notes Payable-Short Term | 10.4 | 12.7 |
| | | 4.2 | 2.8 | | | Cur. Mat.-L.T.D. | 3.3 | 4.3 |
| | | 15.7 | 14.5 | | | Trade Payables | 15.3 | 15.0 |
| | | .0 | .3 | | | Income Taxes Payable | .1 | .5 |
| | | 14.0 | 8.4 | | | All Other Current | 14.8 | 10.2 |
| | | 40.7 | 42.3 | | | Total Current | 43.9 | 42.7 |
| | | 10.0 | 10.9 | | | Long-Term Debt | 18.3 | 16.6 |
| | | .5 | 1.5 | | | Deferred Taxes | .3 | .2 |
| | | 3.7 | 3.8 | | | All Other Non-Current | 4.0 | 4.2 |
| | | 45.1 | 41.5 | | | Net Worth | 33.4 | 36.4 |
| | | 100.0 | 100.0 | | | Total Liabilties & Net Worth | 100.0 | 100.0 |
| | | | | | | INCOME DATA | | |
| | | 100.0 | 100.0 | | | Net Sales | 100.0 | 100.0 |
| | | 36.7 | 27.9 | | | Gross Profit | 29.0 | 29.5 |
| | | 27.4 | 19.3 | | | Operating Expenses | 22.0 | 24.2 |
| | | 9.2 | 8.6 | | | Operating Profit | 7.0 | 5.2 |
| | | -.5 | 2.5 | | | All Other Expenses (net) | .8 | 1.5 |
| | | 9.8 | 6.1 | | | Profit Before Taxes | 6.2 | 3.7 |
| | | | | | | RATIOS | | |
| | | 2.2 | 2.9 | | | | 2.7 | 2.1 |
| | | 1.6 | 1.6 | | | Current | 1.9 | 1.6 |
| | | 1.3 | 1.2 | | | | 1.3 | 1.2 |
| | | 1.0 | 1.4 | | | | 1.2 | 1.1 |
| | | .7 | .5 | | | Quick | .8 | .7 |
| | | .6 | .3 | | | | .5 | .5 |
| | | 30 12.1 | 39 9.3 | | | | 31 11.8 | 28 12.8 |
| | | 44 8.3 | 46 8.0 | | | Sales/Receivables | 49 7.5 | 39 9.4 |
| | | 59 6.2 | 58 6.3 | | | | 61 5.9 | 53 6.9 |
| | | 61 6.0 | 78 4.7 | | | | 45 8.1 | 35 10.5 |
| | | 94 3.9 | 126 2.9 | | | Cost of Sales/Inventory | 69 5.3 | 76 4.8 |
| | | 135 2.7 | 166 2.2 | | | | 155 2.4 | 136 2.7 |
| | | 15 23.6 | 33 10.9 | | | | 18 20.2 | 14 25.7 |
| | | 32 11.4 | 43 8.5 | | | Cost of Sales/Payables | 32 11.5 | 29 12.5 |
| | | 83 4.4 | 54 6.8 | | | | 63 5.8 | 51 7.2 |
| | | 4.6 | 3.4 | | | | 3.4 | 4.7 |
| | | 7.8 | 7.3 | | | Sales/Working Capital | 6.2 | 9.5 |
| | | 12.5 | 24.7 | | | | 14.4 | 21.6 |
| | | 196.6 | 41.1 | | | | 15.0 | 18.7 |
| | | (17) 11.5 | 5.0 | | | EBIT/Interest | (50) 5.9 | (52) 5.3 |
| | | 4.0 | 1.5 | | | | 1.5 | 1.7 |
| | | | | | | Net Profit + Depr., Dep., | 5.0 | 7.5 |
| | | | | | | Amort./Cur. Mat. L/T/D | (15) 2.9 | (20) 2.6 |
| | | | | | | | .3 | .7 |
| | | .2 | .3 | | | | .3 | .3 |
| | | .5 | .8 | | | Fixed/Worth | .6 | .7 |
| | | 1.0 | 2.2 | | | | 1.8 | 1.4 |
| | | .8 | .8 | | | | .9 | 1.0 |
| | | 1.5 | 1.7 | | | Debt/Worth | 2.0 | 1.7 |
| | | 2.6 | 3.2 | | | | 5.2 | 3.8 |
| | | 54.5 | 47.8 | | | | 49.6 | 59.8 |
| | | 35.0 | (19) 24.7 | | | % Profit Before Taxes/Tangible Net Worth | (44) 25.9 | (46) 31.5 |
| | | 14.0 | 2.5 | | | | 13.2 | 5.5 |
| | | 25.6 | 21.2 | | | | 21.3 | 20.5 |
| | | 12.4 | 7.8 | | | % Profit Before Taxes/Total Assets | 10.1 | 7.3 |
| | | 6.2 | 1.1 | | | | 1.0 | -.8 |
| | | 33.9 | 10.8 | | | | 28.4 | 27.9 |
| | | 8.8 | 7.9 | | | Sales/Net Fixed Assets | 12.4 | 10.9 |
| | | 4.5 | 6.0 | | | | 4.5 | 5.4 |
| | | 2.4 | 2.1 | | | | 2.5 | 2.9 |
| | | 2.0 | 1.7 | | | Sales/Total Assets | 2.0 | 2.1 |
| | | 1.5 | 1.4 | | | | 1.4 | 1.5 |
| | | 1.1 | .9 | | | | .9 | 1.1 |
| | | (15) 2.6 | 1.7 | | | % Depr., Dep., Amort./Sales | (47) 1.6 | (50) 1.7 |
| | | 4.0 | 3.4 | | | | 3.2 | 2.7 |
| | | | | | | | 1.5 | 1.4 |
| | | | | | | % Officers', Directors' Owners' Comp/Sales | (13) 2.2 | (14) 1.7 |
| | | | | | | | 4.1 | 6.3 |
| 32M | 20014M | 212607M | 663468M | 810269M | 620415M | Net Sales ($) | 2025816M | 2177751M |
| 14M | 6876M | 105191M | 413312M | 613429M | 473585M | Total Assets ($) | 1112012M | 1224053M |

M = $ thousand   MM = $ million
See Pages 9 through 22 for Explanation of Ratios and Data

## Comparative Historical Data   |   Current Data Sorted by Sales

| | | | Type of Statement | | | | | | |
|---|---|---|---|---|---|---|---|---|---|
| 12 | 11 | 10 | Unqualified | 1 | | | 1 | | 9 |
| 13 | 10 | 10 | Reviewed | | | | 1 | 5 | 4 |
| 2 | 9 | 3 | Compiled | | 1 | | 1 | | 1 |
| 3 | 3 | 5 | Tax Returns | | 2 | 1 | 2 | | |
| 24 | 26 | 28 | Other | 1 | | 1 | 6 | 7 | 13 |
| 4/1/09-3/31/10 | 4/1/10-3/31/11 | 4/1/11-3/31/12 | | | 11 (4/1-9/30/11) | | 45 (10/1/11-3/31/12) | | |
| ALL | ALL | ALL | | 0-1MM | 1-3MM | 3-5MM | 5-10MM | 10-25MM | 25MM & OVER |
| 54 | 59 | 56 | NUMBER OF STATEMENTS | 2 | 3 | 2 | 10 | 12 | 27 |
| % | % | % | ASSETS | % | % | % | % | % | % |
| 7.4 | 9.3 | 6.5 | Cash & Equivalents | | | | 7.9 | 3.3 | 5.6 |
| 20.2 | 22.5 | 24.7 | Trade Receivables (net) | | | | 26.4 | 18.9 | 25.7 |
| 36.2 | 29.7 | 32.7 | Inventory | | | | 36.2 | 42.7 | 30.8 |
| 4.3 | 4.7 | 3.2 | All Other Current | | | | 1.3 | 3.5 | 4.0 |
| 68.2 | 66.2 | 67.0 | Total Current | | | | 71.9 | 68.5 | 66.2 |
| 24.1 | 24.6 | 24.8 | Fixed Assets (net) | | | | 19.9 | 26.7 | 25.8 |
| 4.0 | 3.1 | 3.2 | Intangibles (net) | | | | 2.0 | 3.0 | 3.9 |
| 3.7 | 6.1 | 5.0 | All Other Non-Current | | | | 6.3 | 1.8 | 4.0 |
| 100.0 | 100.0 | 100.0 | Total | | | | 100.0 | 100.0 | 100.0 |
| | | | LIABILITIES | | | | | | |
| 12.0 | 9.7 | 9.8 | Notes Payable-Short Term | | | | 9.8 | 14.4 | 9.8 |
| 4.5 | 4.5 | 2.8 | Cur. Mat.-L.T.D. | | | | 3.6 | 4.3 | 2.4 |
| 11.6 | 13.9 | 14.7 | Trade Payables | | | | 21.2 | 15.0 | 13.4 |
| .9 | .5 | .2 | Income Taxes Payable | | | | .0 | .0 | .4 |
| 10.3 | 10.6 | 12.3 | All Other Current | | | | 9.4 | 14.9 | 12.4 |
| 39.3 | 39.3 | 39.8 | Total Current | | | | 44.0 | 48.6 | 38.4 |
| 14.6 | 17.6 | 11.3 | Long-Term Debt | | | | 5.5 | 14.0 | 11.2 |
| .6 | .6 | .8 | Deferred Taxes | | | | .4 | 1.1 | 1.1 |
| 7.0 | 3.3 | 5.0 | All Other Non-Current | | | | 4.9 | 1.4 | 4.5 |
| 38.6 | 39.2 | 42.9 | Net Worth | | | | 45.2 | 34.9 | 44.8 |
| 100.0 | 100.0 | 100.0 | Total Liabilities & Net Worth | | | | 100.0 | 100.0 | 100.0 |
| | | | INCOME DATA | | | | | | |
| 100.0 | 100.0 | 100.0 | Net Sales | | | | 100.0 | 100.0 | 100.0 |
| 28.9 | 32.5 | 32.8 | Gross Profit | | | | 32.0 | 29.2 | 31.6 |
| 25.1 | 26.2 | 24.7 | Operating Expenses | | | | 23.7 | 23.0 | 22.0 |
| 3.8 | 6.2 | 8.1 | Operating Profit | | | | 8.2 | 6.2 | 9.6 |
| .7 | 1.6 | 1.2 | All Other Expenses (net) | | | | -.3 | 1.0 | 2.3 |
| 3.0 | 4.7 | 6.9 | Profit Before Taxes | | | | 8.5 | 5.2 | 7.3 |
| | | | RATIOS | | | | | | |
| 2.6 | 2.7 | 2.7 | | | | | 3.9 | 1.8 | 2.8 |
| 1.7 | 1.5 | 1.7 | Current | | | | 1.4 | 1.5 | 1.7 |
| 1.3 | 1.2 | 1.2 | | | | | 1.3 | 1.2 | 1.2 |
| 1.5 | 1.6 | 1.4 | | | | | 1.6 | .8 | 1.4 |
| .7 | .8 | .7 | Quick | | | | .7 | .5 | .8 |
| .3 | .4 | .5 | | | | | .5 | .3 | .5 |
| (29) 12.5 | (37) 9.9 | (39) 9.4 | | (27) 13.6 | | (20) 18.5 | | (44) 8.3 | |
| (41) 8.9 | (52) 7.0 | (46) 8.0 | Sales/Receivables | (38) 9.5 | | (45) 8.2 | | (55) 6.6 | |
| (62) 5.9 | (66) 5.5 | (61) 6.0 | | (59) 6.2 | | (54) 6.8 | | (69) 5.3 | |
| (56) 6.5 | (62) 5.9 | (56) 6.5 | | (31) 11.8 | | (79) 4.6 | | (65) 5.6 | |
| (110) 3.3 | (98) 3.7 | (99) 3.7 | Cost of Sales/Inventory | (104) 3.5 | | (111) 3.3 | | (85) 4.3 | |
| (202) 1.8 | (158) 2.3 | (146) 2.5 | | (135) 2.7 | | (166) 2.2 | | (140) 2.6 | |
| (19) 19.2 | (23) 15.8 | (26) 14.2 | | (11) 33.7 | | (26) 14.0 | | (29) 12.5 | |
| (30) 12.0 | (42) 8.7 | (38) 9.5 | Cost of Sales/Payables | (34) 10.7 | | (40) 9.2 | | (41) 9.0 | |
| (51) 7.2 | (63) 5.8 | (55) 6.6 | | (85) 4.3 | | (73) 5.0 | | (55) 6.6 | |
| 3.0 | 3.2 | 4.0 | | | | | 4.4 | 4.2 | 3.7 |
| 5.8 | 7.0 | 7.0 | Sales/Working Capital | | | | 10.7 | 9.6 | 6.5 |
| 15.6 | 16.9 | 15.3 | | | | | 18.8 | 24.8 | 12.5 |
| 16.0 | 16.7 | 38.5 | | | | | | 10.8 | 41.7 |
| (50) 3.6 | (53) 5.8 | (52) 8.1 | EBIT/Interest | | | | | 5.0 | (26) 13.9 |
| -.7 | 2.0 | 2.9 | | | | | | 1.8 | 3.5 |
| 13.9 | 18.4 | 11.6 | Net Profit + Depr., Dep., | | | | | | 47.0 |
| (18) 3.6 | (19) 2.4 | (17) 3.5 | Amort./Cur. Mat. L/T/D | | | | | | (12) 6.6 |
| 1.3 | 1.1 | 1.2 | | | | | | | 1.9 |
| .3 | .3 | .3 | | | | | .2 | .3 | .3 |
| .7 | .6 | .6 | Fixed/Worth | | | | .4 | .9 | .6 |
| 1.5 | 1.2 | 1.0 | | | | | .8 | 1.7 | 1.1 |
| .7 | .6 | .8 | | | | | .7 | 1.3 | .7 |
| 1.9 | 1.6 | 1.7 | Debt/Worth | | | | 1.5 | 1.8 | 1.6 |
| 3.2 | 4.1 | 2.9 | | | | | 3.3 | 3.0 | 2.9 |
| 37.9 | 37.1 | 47.9 | % Profit Before Taxes/Tangible | | | | 54.5 | 50.3 | 47.8 |
| (48) 18.4 | (52) 21.6 | (54) 27.2 | Net Worth | | | | 36.6 | (11) 24.7 | 35.6 |
| 2.8 | 13.3 | 10.9 | | | | | -6.3 | 7.2 | 11.8 |
| 16.1 | 14.3 | 18.1 | % Profit Before Taxes/Total | | | | 30.1 | 17.2 | 18.9 |
| 5.3 | 7.9 | 9.3 | Assets | | | | 11.6 | 7.7 | 9.8 |
| -3.7 | 2.1 | 3.5 | | | | | -1.8 | 2.1 | 4.7 |
| 13.4 | 19.5 | 23.4 | | | | | 40.9 | 20.0 | 10.7 |
| 7.0 | 7.1 | 7.6 | Sales/Net Fixed Assets | | | | 13.0 | 7.9 | 6.4 |
| 4.2 | 4.4 | 4.7 | | | | | 6.0 | 4.1 | 4.9 |
| 2.1 | 2.1 | 2.3 | | | | | 2.6 | 2.1 | 2.0 |
| 1.6 | 1.5 | 1.8 | Sales/Total Assets | | | | 2.2 | 1.7 | 1.6 |
| 1.0 | 1.1 | 1.3 | | | | | 1.7 | 1.3 | 1.4 |
| 1.5 | 1.4 | 1.2 | | | | | | .9 | 2.1 |
| (50) 2.8 | (53) 2.2 | (52) 2.0 | % Depr., Dep., Amort./Sales | | | | | (11) 1.7 | (26) 2.1 |
| 4.4 | 3.8 | 3.6 | | | | | | 4.0 | 3.6 |
| | .9 | 1.4 | % Officers', Directors' | | | | | | |
| (14) 1.5 | (14) 1.5 | (13) 2.1 | Owners' Comp/Sales | | | | | | |
| 2.6 | 2.6 | 9.8 | | | | | | | |
| 2032245M | 2017088M | 2326805M | Net Sales ($) | 476M | 5010M | 7456M | 73027M | 225396M | 2015440M |
| 1260229M | 1690271M | 1612407M | Total Assets ($) | 718M | 7377M | 2356M | 35715M | 139065M | 1427176M |

M = $ thousand     MM = $ million
See Pages 9 through 22 for Explanation of Ratios and Data

## Current Data Sorted by Assets      Comparative Historical Data

| Type of Statement | 0-500M | 500M-2MM | 2-10MM | 10-50MM | 50-100MM | 100-250MM | | 4/1/07-3/31/08 ALL | 4/1/08-3/31/09 ALL |
|---|---|---|---|---|---|---|---|---|---|
| Unqualified | | | 4 | 12 | 4 | 4 | | 11 | 19 |
| Reviewed | | | 5 | 6 | | | | 17 | 11 |
| Compiled | 1 | 1 | 6 | 3 | | | | 17 | 9 |
| Tax Returns | 1 | 2 | 3 | | | | | 5 | 6 |
| Other | 2 | 5 | 24 | 15 | 9 | 9 | | 47 | 60 |
| | 16 (4/1-9/30/11) | | 100 (10/1/11-3/31/12) | | | | | | |
| **NUMBER OF STATEMENTS** | 4 | 8 | 42 | 36 | 13 | 13 | | 97 | 105 |
| | % | % | % | % | % | % | | % | % |
| **ASSETS** | | | | | | | | | |
| Cash & Equivalents | | | 11.5 | 6.0 | 9.6 | 9.2 | | 8.2 | 9.9 |
| Trade Receivables (net) | | | 31.8 | 22.8 | 22.1 | 20.8 | | 28.8 | 23.2 |
| Inventory | | | 21.7 | 25.4 | 20.5 | 15.0 | | 24.4 | 24.7 |
| All Other Current | | | 10.1 | 5.5 | 3.2 | 7.1 | | 8.0 | 6.3 |
| Total Current | | | 75.2 | 59.7 | 55.4 | 52.2 | | 69.3 | 64.1 |
| Fixed Assets (net) | | | 15.6 | 33.0 | 25.9 | 23.0 | | 22.1 | 23.2 |
| Intangibles (net) | | | 2.5 | 5.2 | 15.3 | 18.1 | | 3.7 | 6.7 |
| All Other Non-Current | | | 6.7 | 2.0 | 3.3 | 6.7 | | 4.9 | 5.9 |
| Total | | | 100.0 | 100.0 | 100.0 | 100.0 | | 100.0 | 100.0 |
| **LIABILITIES** | | | | | | | | | |
| Notes Payable-Short Term | | | 8.9 | 10.1 | 5.6 | 3.6 | | 9.3 | 9.0 |
| Cur. Mat.-L.T.D. | | | 2.1 | 3.9 | 2.8 | 4.1 | | 2.9 | 2.9 |
| Trade Payables | | | 16.3 | 12.0 | 10.7 | 13.5 | | 15.5 | 11.9 |
| Income Taxes Payable | | | .7 | .6 | .3 | 1.9 | | .8 | .8 |
| All Other Current | | | 13.1 | 9.6 | 20.6 | 6.8 | | 11.7 | 12.2 |
| Total Current | | | 41.2 | 36.2 | 40.1 | 29.8 | | 40.2 | 36.9 |
| Long-Term Debt | | | 8.6 | 14.4 | 11.0 | 17.0 | | 13.1 | 12.6 |
| Deferred Taxes | | | .5 | .3 | 1.9 | 2.0 | | .7 | 1.4 |
| All Other Non-Current | | | 7.2 | 2.1 | 1.0 | 3.4 | | 1.9 | 3.8 |
| Net Worth | | | 42.5 | 47.0 | 46.1 | 47.8 | | 44.1 | 45.4 |
| Total Liabilties & Net Worth | | | 100.0 | 100.0 | 100.0 | 100.0 | | 100.0 | 100.0 |
| **INCOME DATA** | | | | | | | | | |
| Net Sales | | | 100.0 | 100.0 | 100.0 | 100.0 | | 100.0 | 100.0 |
| Gross Profit | | | 37.5 | 34.4 | 31.8 | 37.7 | | 37.1 | 37.5 |
| Operating Expenses | | | 27.4 | 21.1 | 20.8 | 21.2 | | 25.1 | 25.2 |
| Operating Profit | | | 10.1 | 13.3 | 11.1 | 16.6 | | 12.0 | 12.3 |
| All Other Expenses (net) | | | .9 | 2.0 | 3.4 | 1.3 | | 1.5 | 1.5 |
| Profit Before Taxes | | | 9.3 | 11.3 | 7.7 | 15.2 | | 10.5 | 10.7 |
| **RATIOS** | | | | | | | | | |
| Current | | | 4.4 | 2.6 | 2.6 | 2.4 | | 2.7 | 2.6 |
| | | | 1.9 | 1.6 | 1.5 | 1.7 | | 1.8 | 1.8 |
| | | | 1.3 | 1.2 | 1.0 | 1.4 | | 1.3 | 1.2 |
| Quick | | | 3.7 | 1.3 | 1.2 | 1.5 | | 1.6 | 1.6 |
| | | | .9 | .8 | .9 | 1.0 | | 1.0 | .9 |
| | | | .5 | .4 | .6 | .6 | | .6 | .5 |
| Sales/Receivables | | | 42   8.7 | 38   9.6 | 43   8.4 | 49   7.5 | | 38   9.7 | 39   9.4 |
| | | | 60   6.1 | 59   6.2 | 68   5.4 | 72   5.1 | | 57   6.4 | 54   6.8 |
| | | | 70   5.2 | 76   4.8 | 104   3.5 | 89   4.1 | | 69   5.3 | 72   5.1 |
| Cost of Sales/Inventory | | | 0   UND | 30   12.3 | 0   UND | 42   8.6 | | 18   19.8 | 16   23.5 |
| | | | 34   10.6 | 81   4.5 | 87   4.2 | 94   3.9 | | 66   5.5 | 83   4.4 |
| | | | 114   3.2 | 174   2.1 | 166   2.2 | 182   2.0 | | 145   2.5 | 154   2.4 |
| Cost of Sales/Payables | | | 19   18.8 | 28   12.9 | 28   12.9 | 35   10.4 | | 22   16.7 | 20   18.4 |
| | | | 32   11.3 | 44   8.3 | 37   9.8 | 59   6.2 | | 40   9.2 | 34   10.7 |
| | | | 64   5.7 | 70   5.2 | 66   5.5 | 83   4.4 | | 60   6.1 | 62   5.9 |
| Sales/Working Capital | | | 3.6 | 3.6 | 4.4 | 2.6 | | 4.5 | 3.6 |
| | | | 5.8 | 5.7 | 5.9 | 5.0 | | 7.3 | 6.2 |
| | | | 19.0 | 15.0 | NM | 10.2 | | 18.2 | 14.3 |
| EBIT/Interest | | | 43.1 | 23.3 | 10.4 | 203.2 | | 23.4 | 44.7 |
| | | | (35) 9.6 | (33) 7.2 | (11) 3.8 | (11) 25.9 | | (85) 8.2 | (94) 12.3 |
| | | | 1.4 | 2.5 | 1.4 | 7.8 | | 3.2 | 4.4 |
| Net Profit + Depr., Dep., Amort./Cur. Mat. L/T/D | | | | 13.1 | | | | 29.2 | 20.1 |
| | | | | (11) 4.1 | | | | (26) 5.2 | (33) 3.3 |
| | | | | 2.4 | | | | 2.7 | 1.5 |
| Fixed/Worth | | | .2 | .4 | .5 | .3 | | .2 | .2 |
| | | | .3 | .8 | 1.2 | .5 | | .5 | .4 |
| | | | .8 | 1.7 | -.6 | NM | | 1.2 | 1.4 |
| Debt/Worth | | | .4 | .4 | .7 | .6 | | .7 | .7 |
| | | | 1.3 | 1.3 | 2.2 | 1.9 | | 1.4 | 1.4 |
| | | | 4.4 | 3.0 | -7.1 | NM | | 3.7 | 3.2 |
| % Profit Before Taxes/Tangible Net Worth | | | 65.3 | 68.6 | | 54.8 | | 75.7 | 64.6 |
| | | | (38) 28.9 | (34) 35.1 | (10) 36.9 | | | (94) 42.7 | (93) 35.0 |
| | | | 8.1 | 11.6 | | 24.2 | | 22.5 | 19.3 |
| % Profit Before Taxes/Total Assets | | | 24.6 | 21.7 | 16.9 | 25.1 | | 28.5 | 27.6 |
| | | | 11.5 | 11.6 | 7.0 | 12.0 | | 15.7 | 13.4 |
| | | | 2.3 | 2.9 | 2.8 | 8.2 | | 5.7 | 7.1 |
| Sales/Net Fixed Assets | | | 58.3 | 10.0 | 13.6 | 15.2 | | 32.6 | 28.1 |
| | | | 15.8 | 5.8 | 7.6 | 5.5 | | 9.6 | 9.2 |
| | | | 8.4 | 3.3 | 3.6 | 3.4 | | 5.5 | 4.3 |
| Sales/Total Assets | | | 2.7 | 2.0 | 1.8 | 1.3 | | 2.7 | 2.2 |
| | | | 2.0 | 1.4 | 1.1 | .9 | | 1.8 | 1.7 |
| | | | 1.6 | 1.0 | .6 | .6 | | 1.3 | 1.0 |
| % Depr., Dep., Amort./Sales | | | .3 | 1.7 | 1.3 | | | .5 | .7 |
| | (28) | | .9 | (31) 3.5 | (11) 2.4 | | | (77) 1.8 | (82) 2.6 |
| | | | 2.8 | 6.4 | 4.8 | | | 4.1 | 5.1 |
| % Officers', Directors' Owners' Comp/Sales | | | 1.0 | | | | | 1.4 | 1.6 |
| | (14) | | 2.3 | | | | | (24) 3.4 | (27) 3.4 |
| | | | 4.9 | | | | | 7.7 | 8.0 |
| Net Sales ($) | 6856M | 22284M | 464481M | 1242546M | 1121206M | 1858122M | | 3450700M | 4239960M |
| Total Assets ($) | 1172M | 9870M | 222663M | 891229M | 972415M | 2066341M | | 2435625M | 3618243M |

© RMA 2012

M = $ thousand    MM = $ million

See Pages 9 through 22 for Explanation of Ratios and Data

## Comparative Historical Data | Current Data Sorted by Sales

| Type of Statement | 4/1/09-3/31/10 ALL | 4/1/10-3/31/11 ALL | 4/1/11-3/31/12 ALL | 0-1MM | 1-3MM | 3-5MM | 5-10MM | 10-25MM | 25MM & OVER |
|---|---|---|---|---|---|---|---|---|---|
| Unqualified | 18 | 25 | 24 | | | | 4 | 4 | 16 |
| Reviewed | 8 | 14 | 12 | 1 | | | 2 | 6 | 3 |
| Compiled | 10 | 8 | 10 | | | 3 | 2 | 2 | 3 |
| Tax Returns | 7 | 12 | 6 | | | 4 | 1 | 1 | |
| Other | 51 | 60 | 64 | 3 | 4 | 4 | 5 | 19 | 29 |
| | | | | 16 (4/1-9/30/11) | | | 100 (10/1/11-3/31/12) | | |
| NUMBER OF STATEMENTS | 94 | 119 | 116 | 4 | 4 | 11 | 14 | 32 | 51 |
| **ASSETS** | % | % | % | % | % | % | % | % | % |
| Cash & Equivalents | 12.1 | 12.1 | 9.8 | | | 22.8 | 10.0 | 9.1 | 7.9 |
| Trade Receivables (net) | 18.2 | 23.4 | 28.7 | | | 36.9 | 25.3 | 29.4 | 24.2 |
| Inventory | 21.8 | 22.3 | 21.2 | | | 17.8 | 18.4 | 25.7 | 20.9 |
| All Other Current | 5.8 | 6.2 | 6.6 | | | .8 | 9.4 | 7.7 | 5.8 |
| Total Current | 58.0 | 64.0 | 66.2 | | | 78.4 | 63.0 | 71.9 | 58.7 |
| Fixed Assets (net) | 24.8 | 22.8 | 23.0 | | | 16.1 | 21.0 | 22.4 | 26.7 |
| Intangibles (net) | 9.2 | 6.6 | 6.3 | | | 2.4 | 3.7 | 3.0 | 10.7 |
| All Other Non-Current | 8.0 | 6.6 | 4.5 | | | 3.1 | 12.3 | 2.7 | 3.8 |
| Total | 100.0 | 100.0 | 100.0 | | | 100.0 | 100.0 | 100.0 | 100.0 |
| **LIABILITIES** | | | | | | | | | |
| Notes Payable-Short Term | 6.3 | 6.7 | 8.3 | | | 2.3 | 5.3 | 12.1 | 6.6 |
| Cur. Mat.-L.T.D. | 2.6 | 3.5 | 3.4 | | | 7.6 | 1.9 | 3.5 | 3.2 |
| Trade Payables | 9.0 | 12.5 | 13.7 | | | 13.3 | 13.7 | 16.0 | 12.6 |
| Income Taxes Payable | .4 | .4 | .7 | | | .1 | 1.8 | .1 | 1.0 |
| All Other Current | 9.6 | 9.3 | 11.6 | | | 10.7 | 10.0 | 7.2 | 13.9 |
| Total Current | 28.0 | 32.5 | 37.7 | | | 34.0 | 32.7 | 39.0 | 37.1 |
| Long-Term Debt | 16.8 | 13.4 | 12.8 | | | 20.7 | 8.9 | 12.3 | 13.3 |
| Deferred Taxes | 1.3 | 1.2 | .7 | | | .9 | .3 | .4 | 1.1 |
| All Other Non-Current | 6.2 | 5.4 | 5.4 | | | 10.3 | 16.0 | 4.0 | 1.6 |
| Net Worth | 47.7 | 47.5 | 43.3 | | | 34.0 | 42.1 | 44.3 | 46.9 |
| Total Liabilities & Net Worth | 100.0 | 100.0 | 100.0 | | | 100.0 | 100.0 | 100.0 | 100.0 |
| **INCOME DATA** | | | | | | | | | |
| Net Sales | 100.0 | 100.0 | 100.0 | | | 100.0 | 100.0 | 100.0 | 100.0 |
| Gross Profit | 35.1 | 37.5 | 36.9 | | | 48.8 | 45.9 | 34.9 | 31.8 |
| Operating Expenses | 29.3 | 28.5 | 24.9 | | | 40.9 | 31.7 | 22.7 | 19.7 |
| Operating Profit | 5.8 | 8.9 | 12.0 | | | 7.9 | 14.2 | 12.2 | 12.1 |
| All Other Expenses (net) | 1.9 | 1.7 | 1.5 | | | .9 | 1.0 | 1.6 | 1.8 |
| Profit Before Taxes | 4.0 | 7.2 | 10.5 | | | 7.0 | 13.2 | 10.7 | 10.3 |
| **RATIOS** | | | | | | | | | |
| Current | 3.6 | 3.3 | 3.3 | | | 6.8 | 6.7 | 3.3 | 2.4 |
| | 2.2 | 2.1 | 1.8 | | | 3.4 | 2.3 | 1.8 | 1.6 |
| | 1.3 | 1.4 | 1.3 | | | 1.8 | 1.2 | 1.3 | 1.1 |
| Quick | 2.0 | 2.0 | 2.0 | | | 5.8 | 5.4 | 2.6 | 1.5 |
| | 1.0 | 1.0 | .9 | | | 3.4 | .9 | 1.0 | .9 |
| | .5 | .7 | .5 | | | .8 | .5 | .5 | .6 |
| Sales/Receivables | 28  13.3 | 38  9.7 | 42  8.6 | 45  8.2 | 36  10.0 | 41  9.0 | 42  8.7 | | |
| | 50  7.3 | 57  6.4 | 61  6.0 | 60  6.1 | 46  7.9 | 54  6.8 | 66  5.5 | | |
| | 66  5.5 | 74  4.9 | 74  4.9 | 66  5.5 | 70  5.2 | 69  5.3 | 85  4.3 | | |
| Cost of Sales/Inventory | 16  22.8 | 13  27.8 | 16  23.5 | 0  UND | 0  UND | 23  15.7 | 30  12.2 | | |
| | 88  4.1 | 78  4.7 | 62  5.9 | 23  16.1 | 32  11.4 | 64  5.7 | 79  4.6 | | |
| | 165  2.2 | 166  2.2 | 140  2.6 | 159  2.3 | 111  3.3 | 159  2.3 | 159  2.3 | | |
| Cost of Sales/Payables | 14  26.7 | 20  18.2 | 21  17.1 | 7  51.3 | 14  26.6 | 23  15.9 | 29  12.8 | | |
| | 26  14.0 | 42  8.7 | 38  9.5 | 19  18.8 | 24  15.2 | 38  9.7 | 50  7.3 | | |
| | 50  7.3 | 66  5.5 | 70  5.2 | 61  6.0 | 68  5.4 | 69  5.3 | 70  5.2 | | |
| Sales/Working Capital | 2.8 | 2.9 | 3.6 | | | 3.4 | 2.7 | 3.8 | 3.6 |
| | 4.7 | 4.8 | 5.9 | | | 7.4 | 5.5 | 6.1 | 5.9 |
| | 11.7 | 10.1 | 16.1 | | | 20.8 | NM | 14.8 | 20.8 |
| EBIT/Interest | 23.1 | 23.1 | 31.7 | | | 48.8 | 61.5 | 28.6 | 39.2 |
| | (81) 4.7 | (101) 7.9 | (99) 9.6 | | | (10) 16.7 | (10) 13.9 | (30) 8.5 | (44) 7.9 |
| | 1.2 | 1.3 | 2.2 | | | 2.1 | -.1 | 1.3 | 3.7 |
| Net Profit + Depr., Dep., Amort./Cur. Mat. L/T/D | 6.4 | 11.4 | 8.6 | | | | | | 11.3 |
| | (20) 1.8 | (26) 3.2 | (25) 3.9 | | | | | (16) | 4.7 |
| | .2 | 1.7 | 2.3 | | | | | | 2.5 |
| Fixed/Worth | .2 | .2 | .2 | | | .1 | .1 | .2 | .3 |
| | .5 | .4 | .6 | | | .4 | .4 | .5 | .6 |
| | 1.3 | 1.4 | 1.3 | | | 1.2 | 1.8 | .9 | 2.2 |
| Debt/Worth | .4 | .5 | .5 | | | .3 | .4 | .5 | .6 |
| | 1.1 | 1.2 | 1.4 | | | .7 | 1.0 | 1.3 | 1.6 |
| | 3.7 | 3.9 | 5.9 | | | 29.3 | 5.1 | 2.4 | 6.2 |
| % Profit Before Taxes/Tangible Net Worth | 30.1 | 55.4 | 69.7 | | | | 48.7 | 77.9 | 63.7 |
| | (82) 14.9 | (106) 17.3 | (99) 33.4 | | | (12) 30.5 | (29) 24.6 | | (44) 36.5 |
| | 2.4 | 4.4 | 11.9 | | | | 12.4 | 6.4 | 15.8 |
| % Profit Before Taxes/Total Assets | 14.3 | 18.2 | 25.3 | | | 34.2 | 24.6 | 30.0 | 21.7 |
| | 6.2 | 8.9 | 10.1 | | | 8.4 | 16.5 | 12.7 | 10.0 |
| | .4 | .7 | 4.1 | | | 2.9 | 3.2 | 1.8 | 5.4 |
| Sales/Net Fixed Assets | 15.6 | 23.3 | 23.1 | | | 115.0 | 52.2 | 46.8 | 14.4 |
| | 7.0 | 7.7 | 10.3 | | | 23.2 | 15.8 | 11.1 | 5.9 |
| | 3.0 | 4.2 | 4.3 | | | 8.6 | 6.3 | 4.6 | 3.6 |
| Sales/Total Assets | 1.8 | 2.1 | 2.2 | | | 4.1 | 2.1 | 2.6 | 1.9 |
| | 1.3 | 1.4 | 1.6 | | | 2.2 | 1.6 | 2.0 | 1.3 |
| | .7 | 1.0 | 1.1 | | | 1.9 | 1.3 | 1.4 | .9 |
| % Depr., Dep., Amort./Sales | 1.2 | 1.2 | 1.1 | | | | | .4 | 1.6 |
| | (77) 3.0 | (88) 2.6 | (85) 2.4 | | | | | (25) 1.5 | (41) 2.7 |
| | 6.3 | 4.9 | 4.1 | | | | | 4.8 | 4.2 |
| % Officers', Directors' Owners' Comp/Sales | 2.6 | 1.8 | .8 | | | | | | 1.0 |
| | (25) 4.3 | (21) 4.1 | (23) 2.2 | | | | | (10) | 2.0 |
| | 7.6 | 7.3 | 6.8 | | | | | | 7.1 |
| Net Sales ($) | 2948531M | 3456107M | 4715495M | 3214M | 8855M | 44936M | 99774M | 506408M | 4052308M |
| Total Assets ($) | 3056738M | 3396330M | 4163690M | 2482M | 11570M | 21359M | 72010M | 323846M | 3732423M |

M = $ thousand    MM = $ million
See Pages 9 through 22 for Explanation of Ratios and Data

## Current Data Sorted by Assets      Comparative Historical Data

| | | | | | | Type of Statement | | |
|---|---|---|---|---|---|---|---|---|
| | | 2 | 5 | | | Unqualified | | |
| | | 1 | 1 | | | Reviewed | 4 | 2 |
| | 1 | 2 | 1 | | | Compiled | 5 | 5 |
| | 1 | 5 | 1 | | | Tax Returns | 1 | 3 |
| | 4 | 3 | 2 | | 1 | Other | 6 | 7 |
| | 5 (4/1-9/30/11) | | 25 (10/1/11-3/31/12) | | | | 4/1/07-3/31/08 | 4/1/08-3/31/09 |
| 0-500M | 500M-2MM | 2-10MM | 10-50MM | 50-100MM | 100-250MM | | ALL | ALL |
| | 6 | 13 | 10 | | 1 | NUMBER OF STATEMENTS | 16 | 17 |
| % | % | % | % | % | % | ASSETS | % | % |
| | | 14.3 | 21.0 | | | Cash & Equivalents | 15.7 | 1.6 |
| | | 21.0 | 24.0 | | | Trade Receivables (net) | 24.6 | 30.4 |
| D | D | 35.3 | 25.9 | D | | Inventory | 37.8 | 32.6 |
| A | A | 2.8 | 1.6 | A | | All Other Current | 2.3 | 2.2 |
| T | T | 73.3 | 72.4 | T | | Total Current | 80.4 | 66.8 |
| A | A | 21.4 | 21.2 | A | | Fixed Assets (net) | 14.3 | 19.7 |
| | | .1 | 1.5 | | | Intangibles (net) | 1.7 | 3.8 |
| N | N | 5.2 | 4.9 | N | | All Other Non-Current | 3.6 | 9.6 |
| O | O | 100.0 | 100.0 | O | | Total | 100.0 | 100.0 |
| T | T | | | T | | LIABILITIES | | |
| | | 4.1 | 1.6 | | | Notes Payable-Short Term | 6.5 | 18.5 |
| A | A | 7.8 | 2.3 | A | | Cur. Mat.-L.T.D. | 2.2 | 2.1 |
| V | V | 11.8 | 11.0 | V | | Trade Payables | 22.0 | 20.5 |
| A | A | .0 | .0 | A | | Income Taxes Payable | .0 | .1 |
| I | I | 10.1 | 22.3 | I | | All Other Current | 19.7 | 12.5 |
| L | L | 33.8 | 37.3 | L | | Total Current | 50.4 | 53.6 |
| A | A | 18.1 | 4.3 | A | | Long-Term Debt | 8.8 | 18.8 |
| B | B | .0 | .7 | B | | Deferred Taxes | .2 | .1 |
| L | L | 8.2 | 10.9 | L | | All Other Non-Current | 8.6 | 14.9 |
| E | E | 39.8 | 46.9 | E | | Net Worth | 32.0 | 12.5 |
| | | 100.0 | 100.0 | | | Total Liabilities & Net Worth | 100.0 | 100.0 |
| | | | | | | INCOME DATA | | |
| | | 100.0 | 100.0 | | | Net Sales | 100.0 | 100.0 |
| | | 40.6 | 28.4 | | | Gross Profit | 29.6 | 35.3 |
| | | 32.7 | 18.4 | | | Operating Expenses | 25.4 | 34.2 |
| | | 7.9 | 10.1 | | | Operating Profit | 4.1 | 1.1 |
| | | 1.2 | .8 | | | All Other Expenses (net) | .6 | .3 |
| | | 6.7 | 9.3 | | | Profit Before Taxes | 3.6 | .8 |
| | | | | | | RATIOS | | |
| | | 4.3 | 3.6 | | | | 2.4 | 2.3 |
| | | 3.2 | 2.1 | | | Current | 1.8 | 1.5 |
| | | 2.0 | 1.5 | | | | 1.2 | 1.0 |
| | | 3.6 | 1.5 | | | | 1.4 | 1.0 |
| | | 1.3 | 1.1 | | | Quick | .9 | .5 |
| | | .5 | 1.0 | | | | .4 | .4 |
| | | 28 13.1 | 26 13.8 | | | | 13 27.6 | 13 27.5 |
| | | 43 8.4 | 54 6.7 | | | Sales/Receivables | 30 12.2 | 25 14.6 |
| | | 47 7.7 | 64 5.7 | | | | 55 6.6 | 38 9.6 |
| | | 62 5.9 | 45 8.2 | | | | 19 19.6 | 12 31.1 |
| | | 96 3.8 | 55 6.6 | | | Cost of Sales/Inventory | 86 4.2 | 78 4.7 |
| | | 166 2.2 | 118 3.1 | | | | 118 3.1 | 141 2.6 |
| | | 15 24.7 | 11 33.7 | | | | 15 23.9 | 10 35.0 |
| | | 23 15.6 | 30 12.2 | | | Cost of Sales/Payables | 22 16.5 | 15 25.1 |
| | | 39 9.4 | 47 7.8 | | | | 50 7.3 | 51 7.1 |
| | | 2.6 | 3.1 | | | | 4.3 | 4.7 |
| | | 4.3 | 4.6 | | | Sales/Working Capital | 6.1 | 17.3 |
| | | 6.5 | 13.6 | | | | 86.4 | 375.9 |
| | | 40.8 | | | | | 28.8 | 30.1 |
| | | (10) 5.6 | | | | EBIT/Interest | (12) 3.9 | (16) 2.0 |
| | | 1.8 | | | | | 2.3 | -2.2 |
| | | | | | | Net Profit + Depr., Dep., Amort./Cur. Mat. L/T/D | | |
| | | .2 | .2 | | | | .1 | .3 |
| | | .4 | .3 | | | Fixed/Worth | .3 | .8 |
| | | NM | .9 | | | | 1.1 | -16.9 |
| | | .3 | .5 | | | | .6 | .7 |
| | | .8 | 1.0 | | | Debt/Worth | 2.3 | 1.6 |
| | | NM | 4.1 | | | | 2.8 | -130.2 |
| | | 44.7 | 91.8 | | | | 46.4 | 23.6 |
| | | (10) 16.8 | 39.7 | | | % Profit Before Taxes/Tangible Net Worth | (14) 21.6 | (12) 3.7 |
| | | 3.0 | 15.9 | | | | 7.7 | -12.3 |
| | | 26.4 | 28.8 | | | | 17.7 | 14.5 |
| | | 5.1 | 14.5 | | | % Profit Before Taxes/Total Assets | 5.9 | 2.4 |
| | | 3.1 | 8.5 | | | | 1.9 | -4.8 |
| | | 34.1 | 31.3 | | | | 63.1 | 49.7 |
| | | 11.2 | 14.4 | | | Sales/Net Fixed Assets | 18.2 | 15.0 |
| | | 6.2 | 6.3 | | | | 13.2 | 9.1 |
| | | 2.7 | 2.2 | | | | 4.6 | 5.5 |
| | | 1.8 | 1.9 | | | Sales/Total Assets | 2.4 | 3.5 |
| | | 1.3 | 1.4 | | | | 1.9 | 1.8 |
| | | .9 | | | | | .4 | .7 |
| | | (10) 2.3 | | | | % Depr., Dep., Amort./Sales | 1.0 | (14) 1.5 |
| | | 4.4 | | | | | 1.9 | 3.4 |
| | | | | | | % Officers', Directors' Owners' Comp/Sales | | |
| 16676M | 125001M | 460474M | | | 248595M | Net Sales ($) | 707921M | 530456M |
| 6607M | 57860M | 233918M | | | 139860M | Total Assets ($) | 369282M | 271091M |

M = $ thousand    MM = $ million
See Pages 9 through 22 for Explanation of Ratios and Data

## Comparative Historical Data   |   Current Data Sorted by Sales

### Type of Statement / Number of Statements

| Type of Statement | 4/1/09-3/31/10 ALL | 4/1/10-3/31/11 ALL | 4/1/11-3/31/12 ALL | | 0-1MM | 1-3MM | 3-5MM | 5-10MM | 10-25MM | 25MM & OVER |
|---|---|---|---|---|---|---|---|---|---|---|
| Unqualified | 1 | | 7 | | | | | | 1 | 4 |
| Reviewed | 5 | 2 | 2 | | | | | 1 | 1 | 1 |
| Compiled | 5 | 3 | 4 | | 1 | | | 1 | 1 | 1 |
| Tax Returns | 2 | 2 | 7 | | 1 | 2 | | 3 | 1 | 1 |
| Other | 6 | 6 | 10 | | 3 | 1 | | 2 | 1 | 3 |
| | | | | | 5 (4/1-9/30/11) | | | 25 (10/1/11-3/31/12) | | |
| **NUMBER OF STATEMENTS** | 19 | 13 | 30 | | 5 | 4 | | 7 | 4 | 10 |

*For the six Current Data columns, only the 25MM & OVER column contains data; all others are marked "DATA NOT AVAILABLE."*

### Assets / Liabilities / Income Data (%)

| | 4/1/09-3/31/10 ALL | 4/1/10-3/31/11 ALL | 4/1/11-3/31/12 ALL | 25MM & OVER |
|---|---|---|---|---|
| | % | % | % | % |
| **ASSETS** | | | | |
| Cash & Equivalents | 16.0 | 8.6 | 15.8 | 18.0 |
| Trade Receivables (net) | 20.9 | 19.6 | 21.1 | 28.4 |
| Inventory | 29.8 | 40.5 | 33.6 | 24.0 |
| All Other Current | 7.5 | .7 | 2.3 | 3.4 |
| Total Current | 74.3 | 69.4 | 72.8 | 73.9 |
| Fixed Assets (net) | 21.6 | 20.7 | 19.6 | 20.4 |
| Intangibles (net) | .9 | 1.9 | .6 | 1.4 |
| All Other Non-Current | 3.3 | 8.0 | 7.0 | 4.3 |
| Total | 100.0 | 100.0 | 100.0 | 100.0 |
| **LIABILITIES** | | | | |
| Notes Payable-Short Term | 17.3 | 9.4 | 6.8 | 1.6 |
| Cur. Mat.-L.T.D. | 4.0 | 5.7 | 4.1 | 8.4 |
| Trade Payables | 15.0 | 7.9 | 13.7 | 16.4 |
| Income Taxes Payable | .1 | .1 | .0 | .0 |
| All Other Current | 10.1 | 14.5 | 16.4 | 22.2 |
| Total Current | 46.6 | 37.6 | 41.1 | 48.6 |
| Long-Term Debt | 12.8 | 38.0 | 10.8 | 1.7 |
| Deferred Taxes | .5 | .1 | .2 | .7 |
| All Other Non-Current | 12.4 | 12.1 | 9.7 | 8.4 |
| Net Worth | 27.7 | 12.2 | 38.2 | 40.6 |
| Total Liabilities & Net Worth | 100.0 | 100.0 | 100.0 | 100.0 |
| **INCOME DATA** | | | | |
| Net Sales | 100.0 | 100.0 | 100.0 | 100.0 |
| Gross Profit | 37.1 | 39.8 | 36.2 | 26.3 |
| Operating Expenses | 32.7 | 34.2 | 28.4 | 16.7 |
| Operating Profit | 4.5 | 5.6 | 7.8 | 9.6 |
| All Other Expenses (net) | .7 | .6 | .7 | .4 |
| Profit Before Taxes | 3.7 | 5.0 | 7.1 | 9.3 |

### Ratios

| | 4/1/09-3/31/10 ALL | 4/1/10-3/31/11 ALL | 4/1/11-3/31/12 ALL | 25MM & OVER |
|---|---|---|---|---|
| Current | 2.6 | 2.6 | 4.2 | 3.6 |
| | 1.7 | 1.9 | 2.0 | 1.9 |
| | 1.1 | 1.5 | 1.4 | 1.1 |
| Quick | 1.7 | 1.3 | 1.8 | 1.5 |
| | .6 | 1.0 | 1.1 | 1.1 |
| | .4 | .3 | .4 | .8 |
| Sales/Receivables | 10   36.8 | 12   30.2 | 26   14.3 | 23   15.8 |
| | 28   12.8 | 41   8.9 | 37   9.8 | 51   7.2 |
| | 41   8.9 | 52   7.1 | 51   7.2 | 64   5.7 |
| Cost of Sales/Inventory | 35   10.3 | 54   6.7 | 51   7.2 | 17   21.8 |
| | 67   5.4 | 163   2.2 | 87   4.2 | 49   7.4 |
| | 118   3.1 | 231   1.6 | 135   2.7 | 96   3.8 |
| Cost of Sales/Payables | 12   30.6 | 9   41.0 | 18   20.8 | 11   33.7 |
| | 24   15.0 | 23   15.6 | 31   11.7 | 39   9.3 |
| | 46   7.9 | 56   6.5 | 47   7.7 | 47   7.7 |
| Sales/Working Capital | 3.6 | 4.0 | 3.5 | 3.7 |
| | 10.0 | 4.8 | 4.8 | 6.0 |
| | 48.5 | 7.4 | 11.4 | 70.3 |
| EBIT/Interest | 14.1 | 8.4 | 84.3 | |
| | (17)   3.2 | 4.7 | (24)   5.6 | |
| | -2.0 | 1.6 | 2.4 | |
| Net Profit + Depr., Dep., Amort./Cur. Mat. L/T/D | | | | |
| Fixed/Worth | .4 | .4 | .2 | .2 |
| | .6 | .9 | .4 | .3 |
| | 4.2 | -.3 | 1.8 | .9 |
| Debt/Worth | .9 | .9 | .5 | .5 |
| | 1.4 | 2.2 | 1.1 | 1.1 |
| | 22.1 | -5.5 | 9.5 | 4.6 |
| % Profit Before Taxes/Tangible Net Worth | 29.7 | | 84.4 | |
| | (15)   11.5 | | (27)   36.1 | |
| | -2.9 | | 15.3 | |
| % Profit Before Taxes/Total Assets | 6.5 | 22.1 | 26.9 | 35.9 |
| | 4.6 | 10.4 | 9.0 | 21.6 |
| | -1.1 | 1.1 | 4.3 | 11.7 |
| Sales/Net Fixed Assets | 32.9 | 35.3 | 38.2 | 31.3 |
| | 12.0 | 21.2 | 13.3 | 17.0 |
| | 5.5 | 5.9 | 7.8 | 10.5 |
| Sales/Total Assets | 3.3 | 2.3 | 2.7 | 2.7 |
| | 2.1 | 1.9 | 1.9 | 2.0 |
| | 1.4 | 1.7 | 1.6 | 1.7 |
| % Depr., Dep., Amort./Sales | .9 | 1.2 | .7 | .8 |
| | (17)   1.9 | (12)   2.9 | (25)   1.4 | 1.2 |
| | 3.2 | 5.0 | 2.4 | 2.4 |
| % Officers', Directors' Owners' Comp/Sales | | | 2.1 | |
| | | | (13)   3.7 | |
| | | | 7.1 | |

### Net Sales ($) / Total Assets ($)

| | 4/1/09-3/31/10 ALL | 4/1/10-3/31/11 ALL | 4/1/11-3/31/12 ALL | 0-1MM | 1-3MM | 3-5MM | 5-10MM | 10-25MM | 25MM & OVER |
|---|---|---|---|---|---|---|---|---|---|
| Net Sales ($) | 1964312M | 114882M | 850746M | | 11804M | 15228M | 49360M | 73248M | 701106M |
| Total Assets ($) | 491918M | 58803M | 438245M | | 7018M | 8192M | 28428M | 51886M | 342721M |

M = $ thousand          MM = $ million

**Current Data Sorted by Assets**      **Comparative Historical Data**

| 0-500M | 500M-2MM | 2-10MM | 10-50MM | 50-100MM | 100-250MM | Type of Statement | 4/1/07-3/31/08 ALL | 4/1/08-3/31/09 ALL |
|---|---|---|---|---|---|---|---|---|
|  |  | 3 | 3 | 1 | 1 | Unqualified | 8 | 15 |
| 1 | 1 | 13 | 4 | 1 | 1 | Reviewed | 16 | 17 |
|  | 1 | 4 | 2 |  |  | Compiled | 6 | 3 |
| 1 | 8 | 1 |  |  |  | Tax Returns | 2 | 7 |
| 2 | 3 | 15 | 7 |  | 1 | Other | 16 | 21 |
|  | 5 (4/1-9/30/11) |  | 67 (10/1/11-3/31/12) |  |  |  |  |  |
| 4 | 13 | 36 | 16 | 1 | 2 | **NUMBER OF STATEMENTS** | 48 | 63 |
| % | % | % | % | % | % | **ASSETS** | % | % |
|  | 16.8 | 11.2 | 7.0 |  |  | Cash & Equivalents | 6.6 | 7.4 |
|  | 29.7 | 26.1 | 25.5 |  |  | Trade Receivables (net) | 25.6 | 24.7 |
|  | 14.4 | 25.7 | 24.6 |  |  | Inventory | 24.7 | 23.7 |
|  | 2.5 | 1.6 | .5 |  |  | All Other Current | 2.1 | 2.6 |
|  | 63.3 | 64.7 | 57.6 |  |  | Total Current | 59.1 | 58.4 |
|  | 27.6 | 26.5 | 31.1 |  |  | Fixed Assets (net) | 29.1 | 26.2 |
|  | .5 | 2.9 | 5.8 |  |  | Intangibles (net) | 5.0 | 6.4 |
|  | 8.5 | 5.9 | 5.6 |  |  | All Other Non-Current | 6.9 | 9.0 |
|  | 100.0 | 100.0 | 100.0 |  |  | Total | 100.0 | 100.0 |
|  |  |  |  |  |  | **LIABILITIES** |  |  |
|  | 15.2 | 8.5 | 11.8 |  |  | Notes Payable-Short Term | 9.8 | 10.4 |
|  | 2.6 | 2.7 | 1.9 |  |  | Cur. Mat.-L.T.D. | 3.8 | 3.7 |
|  | 11.0 | 14.0 | 8.4 |  |  | Trade Payables | 15.5 | 14.1 |
|  | .1 | .0 | .6 |  |  | Income Taxes Payable | .1 | .1 |
|  | 10.4 | 15.4 | 17.9 |  |  | All Other Current | 10.7 | 13.2 |
|  | 39.3 | 40.6 | 40.6 |  |  | Total Current | 39.8 | 41.4 |
|  | 22.6 | 18.8 | 12.9 |  |  | Long-Term Debt | 16.4 | 17.5 |
|  | .3 | .3 | 1.1 |  |  | Deferred Taxes | .2 | .8 |
|  | 9.5 | 6.3 | 1.1 |  |  | All Other Non-Current | 4.0 | 4.9 |
|  | 28.4 | 34.0 | 44.4 |  |  | Net Worth | 39.5 | 35.4 |
|  | 100.0 | 100.0 | 100.0 |  |  | Total Liabilities & Net Worth | 100.0 | 100.0 |
|  |  |  |  |  |  | **INCOME DATA** |  |  |
|  | 100.0 | 100.0 | 100.0 |  |  | Net Sales | 100.0 | 100.0 |
|  | 37.4 | 32.7 | 34.0 |  |  | Gross Profit | 28.8 | 29.0 |
|  | 28.8 | 26.9 | 24.8 |  |  | Operating Expenses | 22.2 | 23.7 |
|  | 8.5 | 5.7 | 9.2 |  |  | Operating Profit | 6.7 | 5.3 |
|  | 2.9 | .8 | 1.0 |  |  | All Other Expenses (net) | 1.3 | 1.8 |
|  | 5.6 | 4.9 | 8.2 |  |  | Profit Before Taxes | 5.3 | 3.5 |
|  |  |  |  |  |  | **RATIOS** |  |  |
|  | 6.0 | 2.5 | 1.9 |  |  |  | 2.0 | 2.0 |
|  | 1.2 | 1.5 | 1.5 |  |  | Current | 1.5 | 1.4 |
|  | .7 | 1.2 | 1.2 |  |  |  | 1.1 | 1.1 |
|  | 3.9 | 1.4 | 1.0 |  |  |  | 1.1 | 1.2 |
|  | 1.0 | .9 | .9 |  |  | Quick | .8 | .8 |
|  | .6 | .5 | .7 |  |  |  | .6 | .6 |
| 20 | 18.6 | 36  10.0 | 39  9.4 |  |  |  | 34  10.6 | 31  11.7 |
| 47 | 7.8 | 44  8.3 | 63  5.8 |  |  | Sales/Receivables | 46  7.9 | 44  8.3 |
| 60 | 6.1 | 53  6.9 | 74  4.9 |  |  |  | 58  6.3 | 55  6.6 |
| 0 | UND | 41  9.0 | 54  6.8 |  |  |  | 35  10.3 | 30  12.0 |
| 35 | 10.3 | 65  5.6 | 68  5.4 |  |  | Cost of Sales/Inventory | 59  6.2 | 54  6.8 |
| 65 | 5.6 | 107  3.4 | 140  2.6 |  |  |  | 81  4.5 | 91  4.0 |
| 14 | 26.4 | 21  17.1 | 23  16.0 |  |  |  | 22  16.7 | 17  21.1 |
| 24 | 15.3 | 31  11.7 | 27  13.5 |  |  | Cost of Sales/Payables | 32  11.3 | 35  10.6 |
| 52 | 7.0 | 56  6.5 | 54  6.7 |  |  |  | 53  6.9 | 43  8.4 |
|  | 5.0 | 4.5 | 5.5 |  |  |  | 6.7 | 6.9 |
|  | 27.2 | 10.1 | 7.9 |  |  | Sales/Working Capital | 12.0 | 11.6 |
|  | -22.2 | 17.4 | 12.2 |  |  |  | 33.4 | 44.1 |
|  | 167.5 | 16.5 | 30.6 |  |  |  | 10.8 | 9.5 |
| (12) | 5.5 | (34)  4.9 | (14)  8.5 |  |  | EBIT/Interest | (44)  3.3 | (58)  4.0 |
|  | 1.5 | 1.5 | 5.6 |  |  |  | 1.4 | 1.6 |
|  |  | 15.5 |  |  |  |  | 3.0 | 8.8 |
|  |  | (11)  9.9 |  |  |  | Net Profit + Depr., Dep., Amort./Cur. Mat. L/T/D | (11)  2.1 | (19)  3.3 |
|  |  | 2.7 |  |  |  |  | 1.8 | 2.5 |
|  | .1 | .3 | .3 |  |  |  | .4 | .4 |
|  | 1.1 | .6 | .8 |  |  | Fixed/Worth | .9 | 1.0 |
|  | NM | 5.0 | 1.4 |  |  |  | 1.7 | 2.3 |
|  | .4 | .9 | .9 |  |  |  | .9 | .9 |
|  | 2.5 | 1.7 | 1.7 |  |  | Debt/Worth | 2.0 | 2.8 |
|  | NM | 7.1 | 2.7 |  |  |  | 3.7 | 6.9 |
|  | 46.1 | 58.3 | 60.3 |  |  |  | 35.3 | 59.8 |
| (10) | 26.5 | (31)  23.0 | 33.7 |  |  | % Profit Before Taxes/Tangible Net Worth | (42)  21.1 | (57)  23.3 |
|  | -13.1 | 9.3 | 12.3 |  |  |  | 9.1 | 6.4 |
|  | 22.0 | 14.6 | 16.6 |  |  |  | 14.9 | 14.6 |
|  | 4.8 | 7.3 | 9.2 |  |  | % Profit Before Taxes/Total Assets | 6.7 | 5.5 |
|  | -.7 | 1.5 | 6.9 |  |  |  | 1.7 | 1.5 |
|  | 44.6 | 16.3 | 13.0 |  |  |  | 15.2 | 18.5 |
|  | 20.0 | 9.9 | 4.2 |  |  | Sales/Net Fixed Assets | 6.8 | 8.7 |
|  | 3.1 | 4.3 | 2.9 |  |  |  | 3.4 | 4.5 |
|  | 3.4 | 2.7 | 1.9 |  |  |  | 2.5 | 2.3 |
|  | 2.6 | 2.0 | 1.2 |  |  | Sales/Total Assets | 1.9 | 1.9 |
|  | 1.4 | 1.5 | 1.1 |  |  |  | 1.4 | 1.5 |
|  | .7 | 1.0 | 1.1 |  |  |  | 1.1 | 1.1 |
| (11) | 2.5 | (34)  1.9 | (15)  2.6 |  |  | % Depr., Dep., Amort./Sales | (44)  2.5 | (58)  2.6 |
|  | 4.4 | 3.7 | 3.8 |  |  |  | 4.4 | 4.3 |
|  |  | 2.6 |  |  |  |  | 2.1 | 1.2 |
|  |  | (10)  3.3 |  |  |  | % Officers', Directors', Owners' Comp/Sales | (11)  3.7 | (15)  2.6 |
|  |  | 5.6 |  |  |  |  | 17.1 | 10.3 |
| 4980M | 36315M | 360701M | 365825M | 141528M | 525399M | Net Sales ($) | 1166512M | 1649618M |
| 1411M | 16448M | 182416M | 264677M | 60983M | 317561M | Total Assets ($) | 768371M | 1052100M |

M = $ thousand    MM = $ million
See Pages 9 through 22 for Explanation of Ratios and Data

## Comparative Historical Data | Current Data Sorted by Sales

| 4/1/09-3/31/10 ALL | 4/1/10-3/31/11 ALL | 4/1/11-3/31/12 ALL | Type of Statement | 0-1MM | 1-3MM | 3-5MM | 5-10MM | 10-25MM | 25MM & OVER |
|---|---|---|---|---|---|---|---|---|---|
| 11 | 9 | 8 | Unqualified | | | 1 | | 3 | 4 |
| 17 | 16 | 19 | Reviewed | | 2 | 1 | 9 | 7 | 1 |
| 4 | 7 | 7 | Compiled | | | 1 | 3 | 2 | |
| 9 | 11 | 10 | Tax Returns | 3 | 3 | 3 | | 1 | |
| 28 | 25 | 28 | Other | 3 | 3 | 5 | 6 | 12 | 2 |
| | | | | | | 5 (4/1-9/30/11) | | 67 (10/1/11-3/31/12) | |
| 69 | 68 | 72 | NUMBER OF STATEMENTS | 3 | 8 | 11 | 18 | 25 | 7 |
| % | % | % | **ASSETS** | % | % | % | % | % | % |
| 9.7 | 11.0 | 11.0 | Cash & Equivalents | | | 10.8 | 13.7 | 8.2 | |
| 21.9 | 24.4 | 27.3 | Trade Receivables (net) | | | 32.3 | 22.5 | 28.8 | |
| 25.9 | 23.0 | 23.1 | Inventory | | | 8.9 | 27.1 | 28.5 | |
| 2.9 | .7 | 1.6 | All Other Current | | | 3.9 | .6 | 1.3 | |
| 60.4 | 59.0 | 63.0 | Total Current | | | 55.9 | 63.9 | 66.8 | |
| 25.2 | 29.1 | 27.4 | Fixed Assets (net) | | | 27.4 | 28.2 | 24.7 | |
| 5.3 | 3.9 | 3.6 | Intangibles (net) | | | 4.8 | 1.7 | 4.6 | |
| 9.0 | 8.1 | 6.0 | All Other Non-Current | | | 11.9 | 6.3 | 3.9 | |
| 100.0 | 100.0 | 100.0 | Total | | | 100.0 | 100.0 | 100.0 | |
| | | | **LIABILITIES** | | | | | | |
| 12.9 | 9.1 | 10.5 | Notes Payable-Short Term | | | 7.2 | 7.8 | 9.2 | |
| 3.4 | 4.2 | 2.3 | Cur. Mat.-L.T.D. | | | 6.0 | 3.0 | 1.4 | |
| 12.4 | 12.4 | 12.8 | Trade Payables | | | 15.3 | 13.8 | 10.9 | |
| .1 | .1 | .2 | Income Taxes Payable | | | .0 | .0 | .4 | |
| 16.8 | 14.1 | 14.7 | All Other Current | | | 19.9 | 10.9 | 19.2 | |
| 45.7 | 39.9 | 40.5 | Total Current | | | 48.5 | 35.5 | 41.2 | |
| 15.9 | 20.4 | 18.0 | Long-Term Debt | | | 22.2 | 23.0 | 11.7 | |
| .8 | .6 | .5 | Deferred Taxes | | | .4 | .2 | .9 | |
| 5.8 | 6.4 | 6.5 | All Other Non-Current | | | 10.1 | 1.8 | 4.9 | |
| 31.9 | 32.7 | 34.6 | Net Worth | | | 18.8 | 39.6 | 41.3 | |
| 100.0 | 100.0 | 100.0 | Total Liabilities & Net Worth | | | 100.0 | 100.0 | 100.0 | |
| | | | **INCOME DATA** | | | | | | |
| 100.0 | 100.0 | 100.0 | Net Sales | | | 100.0 | 100.0 | 100.0 | |
| 30.4 | 30.4 | 33.2 | Gross Profit | | | 30.4 | 34.3 | 34.3 | |
| 26.5 | 23.2 | 26.3 | Operating Expenses | | | 24.5 | 28.4 | 26.3 | |
| 3.9 | 7.2 | 6.9 | Operating Profit | | | 5.9 | 5.9 | 8.0 | |
| 1.4 | 1.9 | 1.2 | All Other Expenses (net) | | | 1.7 | .7 | .6 | |
| 2.5 | 5.3 | 5.7 | Profit Before Taxes | | | 4.1 | 5.2 | 7.3 | |
| | | | **RATIOS** | | | | | | |
| 1.9 | 3.0 | 2.5 | Current | | | 2.5 | 5.2 | 2.1 | |
| 1.4 | 1.6 | 1.5 | | | | 1.2 | 1.5 | 1.7 | |
| .9 | 1.0 | 1.1 | | | | .8 | 1.2 | 1.4 | |
| 1.1 | 1.7 | 1.5 | Quick | | | 1.5 | 3.0 | 1.2 | |
| .6 | 1.0 | .9 | | | | 1.0 | .8 | .9 | |
| .4 | .4 | .6 | | | | .5 | .5 | .6 | |
| 37  10.0 | 33  11.2 | 35  10.4 | Sales/Receivables | | | 24  14.9 | 33  11.1 | 38  9.7 | |
| 49  7.5 | 43  8.5 | 47  7.7 | | | | 55  6.6 | 42  8.6 | 49  7.4 | |
| 64  5.7 | 64  5.7 | 60  6.1 | | | | 74  4.9 | 52  7.0 | 72  5.1 | |
| 39  9.4 | 34  10.6 | 35  10.4 | Cost of Sales/Inventory | | | 6  64.6 | 42  8.7 | 57  6.4 | |
| 70  5.2 | 50  7.3 | 60  6.1 | | | | 24  15.0 | 62  5.9 | 74  4.9 | |
| 147  2.5 | 113  3.2 | 99  3.7 | | | | 46  8.0 | 122  3.0 | 114  3.2 | |
| 16  22.2 | 17  21.1 | 19  19.1 | Cost of Sales/Payables | | | 24  15.3 | 18  20.3 | 24  15.0 | |
| 37  9.9 | 30  12.3 | 28  13.2 | | | | 34  10.8 | 30  12.2 | 30  12.0 | |
| 61  6.0 | 49  7.5 | 55  6.6 | | | | 69  5.3 | 55  6.6 | 51  7.1 | |
| 4.9 | 4.2 | 5.4 | Sales/Working Capital | | | 7.7 | 3.6 | 5.2 | |
| 9.9 | 7.7 | 9.8 | | | | 27.2 | 11.3 | 7.8 | |
| -49.9 | NM | 23.4 | | | | -27.5 | 19.3 | 11.7 | |
| 6.6 | 17.0 | 19.8 | EBIT/Interest | | | 5.2 | 16.3 | 30.6 | |
| (61)  1.5 | (61)  3.3 | (67)  5.7 | | | | 2.2 | (17)  4.3 | (22)  12.9 | |
| -.7 | 1.9 | 2.3 | | | | -2.4 | 1.8 | 6.4 | |
| 2.9 | 4.9 | 15.2 | Net Profit + Depr., Dep., Amort./Cur. Mat. L/T/D | | | | | 17.4 | |
| (22)  1.2 | (23)  1.6 | (23)  7.6 | | | | | | (12)  9.5 | |
| -.4 | 1.0 | 3.0 | | | | | | 3.8 | |
| .3 | .4 | .3 | Fixed/Worth | | | .1 | .4 | .3 | |
| .9 | .9 | .8 | | | | 2.6 | .6 | .5 | |
| UND | 3.7 | 2.5 | | | | -1.0 | 1.6 | 1.2 | |
| .7 | .8 | .9 | Debt/Worth | | | 1.2 | .7 | .9 | |
| 2.8 | 2.4 | 1.7 | | | | 5.7 | 1.7 | 1.6 | |
| UND | 7.8 | 5.6 | | | | -5.5 | 5.3 | 2.6 | |
| 32.8 | 54.4 | 50.6 | % Profit Before Taxes/Tangible Net Worth | | | | 41.5 | 64.8 | |
| (53)  7.0 | (58)  21.4 | (62)  28.8 | | | | | (17)  20.2 | (23)  35.0 | |
| -4.5 | 6.3 | 10.2 | | | | | 9.4 | 16.1 | |
| 10.6 | 18.3 | 16.8 | % Profit Before Taxes/Total Assets | | | 12.3 | 14.4 | 17.6 | |
| 1.6 | 6.8 | 8.0 | | | | 3.5 | 6.3 | 10.1 | |
| -4.7 | 1.6 | 3.6 | | | | -9.2 | 2.6 | 6.8 | |
| 14.8 | 17.0 | 19.3 | Sales/Net Fixed Assets | | | 45.5 | 15.8 | 18.6 | |
| 7.1 | 8.1 | 9.3 | | | | 10.0 | 8.5 | 8.9 | |
| 3.7 | 3.4 | 4.0 | | | | 2.8 | 4.0 | 4.2 | |
| 1.9 | 2.5 | 2.7 | Sales/Total Assets | | | 3.1 | 2.5 | 2.7 | |
| 1.4 | 1.9 | 1.9 | | | | 1.6 | 2.0 | 1.7 | |
| 1.0 | 1.2 | 1.4 | | | | 1.3 | 1.7 | 1.1 | |
| 1.4 | 1.1 | 1.1 | % Depr., Dep., Amort./Sales | | | .6 | 1.6 | .7 | |
| (61)  2.3 | (60)  2.6 | (67)  2.2 | | | | (10)  3.5 | (16)  2.0 | (23)  1.5 | |
| 5.2 | 4.8 | 3.5 | | | | 6.2 | 3.3 | 3.3 | |
| 2.1 | 2.9 | 2.6 | % Officers', Directors' Owners' Comp/Sales | | | | | | |
| (18)  4.8 | (24)  4.2 | (22)  3.7 | | | | | | | |
| 10.8 | 6.8 | 7.6 | | | | | | | |
| 1131458M | 1144990M | 1434748M | Net Sales ($) | 1883M | 15660M | 40863M | 137917M | 434471M | 803954M |
| 831614M | 713022M | 843496M | Total Assets ($) | 2795M | 6962M | 31485M | 74285M | 281626M | 446343M |

M = $ thousand    MM = $ million
See Pages 9 through 22 for Explanation of Ratios and Data

## Current Data Sorted by Assets

## Comparative Historical Data

| 0-500M | 500M-2MM | 2-10MM | 10-50MM | 50-100MM | 100-250MM | Type of Statement | 4/1/07-3/31/08 ALL | 4/1/08-3/31/09 ALL |
|---|---|---|---|---|---|---|---|---|
| | | | | 1 | 2 | Unqualified | 5 | |
| | 1 | 5 | 1 | 1 | | Reviewed | 6 | 7 |
| | 1 | 1 | | | | Compiled | 4 | 7 |
| 1 | | 1 | | | | Tax Returns | 2 | 2 |
| | 3 | 12 | 4 | 1 | 1 | Other | 12 | 15 |
| | 4 (4/1-9/30/11) | | 32 (10/1/11-3/31/12) | | | | | |
| 2 | 4 | 19 | 5 | 3 | 3 | NUMBER OF STATEMENTS | 29 | 31 |
| % | % | % | % | % | % | **ASSETS** | % | % |
| | | 6.1 | | | | Cash & Equivalents | 10.1 | 10.4 |
| | | 20.9 | | | | Trade Receivables (net) | 23.7 | 25.2 |
| | | 30.8 | | | | Inventory | 32.5 | 32.6 |
| | | 4.3 | | | | All Other Current | 3.9 | 3.5 |
| | | 62.0 | | | | Total Current | 70.2 | 71.8 |
| | | 29.7 | | | | Fixed Assets (net) | 19.8 | 20.6 |
| | | 5.1 | | | | Intangibles (net) | 6.8 | 4.2 |
| | | 3.2 | | | | All Other Non-Current | 3.2 | 3.5 |
| | | 100.0 | | | | Total | 100.0 | 100.0 |
| | | | | | | **LIABILITIES** | | |
| | | 9.2 | | | | Notes Payable-Short Term | 5.0 | 10.6 |
| | | 2.8 | | | | Cur. Mat.-L.T.D. | 3.9 | 3.3 |
| | | 9.7 | | | | Trade Payables | 17.2 | 17.2 |
| | | .4 | | | | Income Taxes Payable | .5 | .1 |
| | | 15.5 | | | | All Other Current | 22.4 | 18.8 |
| | | 37.6 | | | | Total Current | 49.1 | 50.0 |
| | | 16.7 | | | | Long-Term Debt | 9.7 | 12.3 |
| | | .4 | | | | Deferred Taxes | .5 | .6 |
| | | 4.5 | | | | All Other Non-Current | 4.2 | 6.3 |
| | | 40.7 | | | | Net Worth | 36.6 | 30.9 |
| | | 100.0 | | | | Total Liabilties & Net Worth | 100.0 | 100.0 |
| | | | | | | **INCOME DATA** | | |
| | | 100.0 | | | | Net Sales | 100.0 | 100.0 |
| | | 32.0 | | | | Gross Profit | 28.6 | 30.4 |
| | | 24.5 | | | | Operating Expenses | 23.1 | 26.0 |
| | | 7.5 | | | | Operating Profit | 5.5 | 4.4 |
| | | 2.3 | | | | All Other Expenses (net) | .9 | .7 |
| | | 5.1 | | | | Profit Before Taxes | 4.6 | 3.7 |
| | | | | | | **RATIOS** | | |
| | | 2.4 | | | | | 2.3 | 2.4 |
| | | 1.9 | | | | Current | 1.8 | 1.3 |
| | | 1.1 | | | | | 1.0 | .9 |
| | | 1.2 | | | | | 1.3 | 1.3 |
| | | .7 | | | | Quick | .7 | .6 |
| | | .5 | | | | | .3 | .4 |
| | | 41  8.9 | | | | | 38  9.5 | 30  12.2 |
| | | 47  7.7 | | | | Sales/Receivables | 49  7.4 | 39  9.5 |
| | | 60  6.1 | | | | | 59  6.2 | 49  7.5 |
| | | 69  5.3 | | | | | 52  7.1 | 43  8.6 |
| | | 96  3.8 | | | | Cost of Sales/Inventory | 81  4.5 | 71  5.1 |
| | | 135  2.7 | | | | | 181  2.0 | 111  3.3 |
| | | 20  18.5 | | | | | 20  18.4 | 20  18.6 |
| | | 32  11.5 | | | | Cost of Sales/Payables | 41  8.9 | 31  11.7 |
| | | 38  9.7 | | | | | 63  5.8 | 52  7.0 |
| | | 4.2 | | | | | 3.4 | 5.0 |
| | | 7.3 | | | | Sales/Working Capital | 9.4 | 11.1 |
| | | 27.7 | | | | | NM | -75.7 |
| | | 36.0 | | | | | 34.4 | 20.5 |
| | | (18) 5.9 | | | | EBIT/Interest | (23) 7.4 | (27) 3.5 |
| | | 2.4 | | | | | .4 | .1 |
| | | | | | | Net Profit + Depr., Dep., Amort./Cur. Mat. L/T/D | | |
| | | .3 | | | | | .2 | .2 |
| | | 1.1 | | | | Fixed/Worth | .6 | .6 |
| | | 2.4 | | | | | 4.7 | -4.9 |
| | | .7 | | | | | .6 | .9 |
| | | 1.4 | | | | Debt/Worth | 2.6 | 2.9 |
| | | 2.8 | | | | | 10.7 | -38.8 |
| | | 37.8 | | | | | 60.8 | 55.5 |
| | | (16) 11.7 | | | | % Profit Before Taxes/Tangible Net Worth | (23) 18.8 | (23) 19.3 |
| | | 5.2 | | | | | -5.3 | 8.4 |
| | | 10.7 | | | | | 14.6 | 13.5 |
| | | 4.7 | | | | % Profit Before Taxes/Total Assets | 8.0 | 7.5 |
| | | 2.3 | | | | | -1.4 | .2 |
| | | 15.4 | | | | | 35.4 | 26.9 |
| | | 8.4 | | | | Sales/Net Fixed Assets | 10.9 | 13.0 |
| | | 2.6 | | | | | 3.7 | 7.7 |
| | | 2.0 | | | | | 2.3 | 3.5 |
| | | 1.6 | | | | Sales/Total Assets | 1.7 | 2.1 |
| | | 1.3 | | | | | 1.1 | 1.7 |
| | | .8 | | | | | .5 | .5 |
| | | (17) 2.0 | | | | % Depr., Dep., Amort./Sales | 1.4 | (24) 1.0 |
| | | 3.8 | | | | | 3.5 | 2.1 |
| | | | | | | % Officers', Directors' Owners' Comp/Sales | | |
| 635M | 14861M | 153238M | 245714M | 235034M | 722773M | Net Sales ($) | 923136M | 817392M |
| 466M | 5260M | 96732M | 77772M | 174666M | 522809M | Total Assets ($) | 934191M | 497241M |

© RMA 2012

M = $ thousand    MM = $ million
See Pages 9 through 22 for Explanation of Ratios and Data

## Comparative Historical Data     Current Data Sorted by Sales

| H1 | H2 | H3 | Type of Statement | 0-1MM | 1-3MM | 3-5MM | 5-10MM | 10-25MM | 25MM & OVER |
|---|---|---|---|---|---|---|---|---|---|
| 5 | 3 | 3 | Unqualified | | | | | | 3 |
| 6 | 6 | 8 | Reviewed | 1 | | 1 | 1 | 4 | 1 |
| 4 | 5 | 2 | Compiled | | 1 | | 1 | | |
| 1 | 1 | 2 | Tax Returns | 1 | | | 1 | | |
| 16 | 19 | 21 | Other | 1 | 2 | 3 | 9 | 2 | 5 |
| 4/1/09-3/31/10 ALL | 4/1/10-3/31/11 ALL | 4/1/11-3/31/12 ALL | | | | 4 (4/1-9/30/11) | | 32 (10/1/11-3/31/12) | |
| 32 | 34 | 36 | NUMBER OF STATEMENTS | 2 | 3 | 4 | 12 | 6 | 9 |
| % | % | % | | % | % | % | % | % | % |
| | | | **ASSETS** | | | | | | |
| 15.2 | 11.4 | 7.9 | Cash & Equivalents | | | | 7.1 | | |
| 20.6 | 23.5 | 25.1 | Trade Receivables (net) | | | | 24.5 | | |
| 30.7 | 28.5 | 31.6 | Inventory | | | | 38.9 | | |
| 2.5 | 6.0 | 3.5 | All Other Current | | | | 1.2 | | |
| 68.9 | 69.4 | 68.1 | Total Current | | | | 71.8 | | |
| 22.2 | 17.7 | 22.2 | Fixed Assets (net) | | | | 19.3 | | |
| 3.5 | 7.1 | 5.4 | Intangibles (net) | | | | 5.3 | | |
| 5.4 | 5.8 | 4.3 | All Other Non-Current | | | | 3.6 | | |
| 100.0 | 100.0 | 100.0 | Total | | | | 100.0 | | |
| | | | **LIABILITIES** | | | | | | |
| 9.9 | 11.6 | 8.0 | Notes Payable-Short Term | | | | 9.9 | | |
| 1.9 | 1.7 | 2.2 | Cur. Mat.-L.T.D. | | | | 2.4 | | |
| 12.2 | 12.1 | 11.6 | Trade Payables | | | | 10.7 | | |
| .0 | .1 | .2 | Income Taxes Payable | | | | .2 | | |
| 17.3 | 16.4 | 18.7 | All Other Current | | | | 20.9 | | |
| 41.3 | 41.9 | 40.7 | Total Current | | | | 44.0 | | |
| 11.2 | 9.1 | 10.2 | Long-Term Debt | | | | 16.9 | | |
| .8 | .8 | .3 | Deferred Taxes | | | | .6 | | |
| 6.1 | 9.5 | 3.0 | All Other Non-Current | | | | 3.5 | | |
| 40.6 | 38.8 | 45.8 | Net Worth | | | | 34.9 | | |
| 100.0 | 100.0 | 100.0 | Total Liabilities & Net Worth | | | | 100.0 | | |
| | | | **INCOME DATA** | | | | | | |
| 100.0 | 100.0 | 100.0 | Net Sales | | | | 100.0 | | |
| 29.9 | 30.8 | 31.8 | Gross Profit | | | | 28.5 | | |
| 28.1 | 25.6 | 24.8 | Operating Expenses | | | | 19.4 | | |
| 1.8 | 5.3 | 7.0 | Operating Profit | | | | 9.1 | | |
| .5 | .8 | 1.5 | All Other Expenses (net) | | | | 3.7 | | |
| 1.3 | 4.4 | 5.5 | Profit Before Taxes | | | | 5.4 | | |
| | | | **RATIOS** | | | | | | |
| 3.8 | 3.3 | 2.9 | | | | | 2.7 | | |
| 1.7 | 1.5 | 1.6 | Current | | | | 1.7 | | |
| 1.1 | 1.0 | 1.1 | | | | | 1.1 | | |
| 2.0 | 1.7 | 1.5 | | | | | 1.2 | | |
| .7 | .8 | .7 | Quick | | | | .7 | | |
| .4 | .5 | .5 | | | | | .5 | | |
| 38  9.7 | 35  10.5 | 41  9.0 | | | | | 34  10.7 | | |
| 44  8.4 | 51  7.2 | 46  8.0 | Sales/Receivables | | | | 43  8.5 | | |
| 57  6.4 | 60  6.1 | 58  6.3 | | | | | 61  6.0 | | |
| 42  8.7 | 54  6.7 | 60  6.1 | | | | | 72  5.1 | | |
| 92  4.0 | 79  4.6 | 99  3.7 | Cost of Sales/Inventory | | | | 101  3.6 | | |
| 164  2.2 | 116  3.1 | 135  2.7 | | | | | 135  2.7 | | |
| 17  21.6 | 21  17.4 | 18  20.6 | | | | | 20  18.3 | | |
| 32  11.3 | 32  11.3 | 29  12.4 | Cost of Sales/Payables | | | | 24  15.0 | | |
| 54  6.8 | 53  6.9 | 43  8.4 | | | | | 36  10.1 | | |
| 2.6 | 3.3 | 3.9 | | | | | 4.2 | | |
| 6.0 | 6.3 | 7.8 | Sales/Working Capital | | | | 7.4 | | |
| 28.8 | 181.9 | 24.2 | | | | | 51.4 | | |
| 8.7 | 19.0 | 62.6 | | | | | 86.4 | | |
| (28) 1.6 | (28) 3.4 | (30) 6.9 | EBIT/Interest | | | | (10) 7.3 | | |
| -1.1 | 1.3 | 2.4 | | | | | 4.4 | | |
| | | | Net Profit + Depr., Dep., Amort./Cur. Mat. L/T/D | | | | | | |
| .2 | .2 | .2 | | | | | .2 | | |
| .4 | .4 | .5 | Fixed/Worth | | | | .8 | | |
| 3.3 | 3.2 | 1.5 | | | | | NM | | |
| .5 | .5 | .5 | | | | | .7 | | |
| 1.0 | 2.2 | 1.3 | Debt/Worth | | | | 1.6 | | |
| 32.9 | 10.6 | 4.2 | | | | | NM | | |
| 17.4 | 37.7 | 47.1 | | | | | | | |
| (26) 3.6 | (27) 20.2 | (32) 18.4 | % Profit Before Taxes/Tangible Net Worth | | | | | | |
| -4.9 | 6.8 | 6.2 | | | | | | | |
| 5.2 | 9.5 | 12.6 | | | | | 25.6 | | |
| 1.6 | 6.4 | 7.7 | % Profit Before Taxes/Total Assets | | | | 7.9 | | |
| -3.9 | .9 | 2.5 | | | | | 2.5 | | |
| 18.5 | 23.8 | 19.6 | | | | | 42.1 | | |
| 8.0 | 9.4 | 9.8 | Sales/Net Fixed Assets | | | | 13.7 | | |
| 5.2 | 5.8 | 4.5 | | | | | 6.3 | | |
| 1.9 | 2.2 | 2.2 | | | | | 2.7 | | |
| 1.5 | 1.6 | 1.6 | Sales/Total Assets | | | | 1.9 | | |
| 1.1 | 1.2 | 1.3 | | | | | 1.4 | | |
| .9 | 1.0 | .7 | | | | | .8 | | |
| (29) 1.6 | (28) 1.5 | (31) 1.5 | % Depr., Dep., Amort./Sales | | | | (11) .9 | | |
| 2.3 | 2.4 | 3.3 | | | | | 2.7 | | |
| | | | % Officers', Directors' Owners' Comp/Sales | | | | | | |
| 934233M | 1430518M | 1372255M | Net Sales ($) | 635M | 5721M | 14819M | 96912M | 87171M | 1166997M |
| 857064M | 1247319M | 877705M | Total Assets ($) | 466M | 6927M | 9469M | 53821M | 55605M | 751417M |

M = $ thousand    MM = $ million
See Pages 9 through 22 for Explanation of Ratios and Data

## Current Data Sorted by Assets

## Comparative Historical Data

| 0-500M | 500M-2MM | 2-10MM | 10-50MM | 50-100MM | 100-250MM | Type of Statement | 4/1/07-3/31/08 ALL | 4/1/08-3/31/09 ALL |
|---|---|---|---|---|---|---|---|---|
| | | | | 2 | 1 | Unqualified | 8 | 6 |
| | | 4 | 1 | | | Reviewed | 18 | 11 |
| | 2 | 4 | | | | Compiled | 7 | 3 |
| | | | | | | Tax Returns | 5 | 9 |
| 1 | 1 | 5 | 5 | 2 | 1 | Other | 26 | 27 |
| | 10 (4/1-9/30/11) | | 19 (10/1/11-3/31/12) | | | | | |
| 1 | 3 | 13 | 6 | 4 | 2 | NUMBER OF STATEMENTS | 64 | 56 |
| % | % | % | % | % | % | **ASSETS** | % | % |
| | | 8.3 | | | | Cash & Equivalents | 7.9 | 8.1 |
| | | 28.5 | | | | Trade Receivables (net) | 27.2 | 21.9 |
| | | 30.7 | | | | Inventory | 29.0 | 30.1 |
| | | 2.3 | | | | All Other Current | 2.7 | 2.3 |
| | | 69.8 | | | | Total Current | 66.8 | 62.5 |
| | | 18.9 | | | | Fixed Assets (net) | 23.3 | 23.1 |
| | | 6.4 | | | | Intangibles (net) | 2.5 | 6.9 |
| | | 5.0 | | | | All Other Non-Current | 7.4 | 7.5 |
| | | 100.0 | | | | Total | 100.0 | 100.0 |
| | | | | | | **LIABILITIES** | | |
| | | 7.1 | | | | Notes Payable-Short Term | 8.3 | 11.2 |
| | | 4.7 | | | | Cur. Mat.-L.T.D. | 4.1 | 4.1 |
| | | 18.2 | | | | Trade Payables | 18.3 | 12.7 |
| | | .1 | | | | Income Taxes Payable | .2 | .3 |
| | | 16.9 | | | | All Other Current | 18.5 | 20.9 |
| | | 46.9 | | | | Total Current | 49.5 | 49.2 |
| | | 6.0 | | | | Long-Term Debt | 16.2 | 18.8 |
| | | .6 | | | | Deferred Taxes | .0 | .1 |
| | | .0 | | | | All Other Non-Current | 4.6 | 8.3 |
| | | 46.5 | | | | Net Worth | 29.7 | 23.7 |
| | | 100.0 | | | | Total Liabilities & Net Worth | 100.0 | 100.0 |
| | | | | | | **INCOME DATA** | | |
| | | 100.0 | | | | Net Sales | 100.0 | 100.0 |
| | | 33.7 | | | | Gross Profit | 35.0 | 34.1 |
| | | 27.7 | | | | Operating Expenses | 30.4 | 29.5 |
| | | 6.0 | | | | Operating Profit | 4.6 | 4.6 |
| | | .0 | | | | All Other Expenses (net) | 1.2 | 1.5 |
| | | 5.9 | | | | Profit Before Taxes | 3.4 | 3.1 |
| | | | | | | **RATIOS** | | |
| | | 2.2 | | | | | 2.4 | 2.9 |
| | | 1.7 | | | | Current | 1.6 | 1.6 |
| | | 1.1 | | | | | 1.0 | 1.0 |
| | | 1.2 | | | | | 1.1 | 1.4 |
| | | .9 | | | | Quick | .8 | .7 |
| | | .5 | | | | | .4 | .3 |
| | 37 | 9.9 | | | | | 32 11.4 | 19 19.7 |
| | 43 | 8.4 | | | | Sales/Receivables | 47 7.8 | 44 8.3 |
| | 74 | 4.9 | | | | | 59 6.2 | 55 6.7 |
| | 53 | 6.9 | | | | | 28 13.1 | 31 11.8 |
| | 104 | 3.5 | | | | Cost of Sales/Inventory | 64 5.7 | 75 4.9 |
| | 140 | 2.6 | | | | | 116 3.2 | 97 3.8 |
| | 29 | 12.7 | | | | | 22 16.3 | 13 27.7 |
| | 37 | 9.8 | | | | Cost of Sales/Payables | 37 10.0 | 26 13.9 |
| | 62 | 5.9 | | | | | 55 6.6 | 39 9.4 |
| | | 4.5 | | | | | 5.6 | 5.1 |
| | | 9.3 | | | | Sales/Working Capital | 8.7 | 7.7 |
| | | 18.7 | | | | | 107.0 | 288.3 |
| | | 87.8 | | | | | 9.9 | 6.5 |
| | (11) | 16.5 | | | | EBIT/Interest | (61) 3.1 | (51) 2.9 |
| | | 1.5 | | | | | 1.0 | .6 |
| | | | | | | Net Profit + Depr., Dep., | 12.7 | 13.9 |
| | | | | | | Amort./Cur. Mat. L/T/D | (17) 7.2 | (18) 3.5 |
| | | | | | | | 1.1 | 1.2 |
| | | .1 | | | | | .2 | .3 |
| | | .3 | | | | Fixed/Worth | .6 | .7 |
| | | 1.1 | | | | | 2.4 | NM |
| | | .6 | | | | | .8 | 1.0 |
| | | 1.2 | | | | Debt/Worth | 2.4 | 3.6 |
| | | 2.8 | | | | | 11.8 | NM |
| | | 82.6 | | | | % Profit Before Taxes/Tangible | 47.4 | 38.8 |
| | | 14.9 | | | | Net Worth | (54) 15.5 | (42) 9.7 |
| | | 2.3 | | | | | 2.1 | -3.8 |
| | | 19.5 | | | | % Profit Before Taxes/Total | 12.9 | 11.1 |
| | | 7.6 | | | | Assets | 3.8 | 3.4 |
| | | .9 | | | | | .2 | -1.5 |
| | | 41.6 | | | | | 51.8 | 48.1 |
| | | 21.2 | | | | Sales/Net Fixed Assets | 13.7 | 12.2 |
| | | 6.5 | | | | | 5.9 | 6.9 |
| | | 2.0 | | | | | 2.8 | 2.7 |
| | | 1.6 | | | | Sales/Total Assets | 2.2 | 2.1 |
| | | 1.3 | | | | | 1.5 | 1.5 |
| | | .5 | | | | | .7 | .7 |
| | (12) | 1.4 | | | | % Depr., Dep., Amort./Sales | (59) 1.2 | (50) 1.7 |
| | | 3.2 | | | | | 3.7 | 3.4 |
| | | | | | | | 1.7 | 2.0 |
| | | | | | | % Officers', Directors' Owners' Comp/Sales | (16) 6.0 | (16) 4.6 |
| | | | | | | | 8.4 | 6.7 |
| 2107M | 13213M | 107987M | 285233M | 338108M | 317656M | Net Sales ($) | 2113365M | 2050886M |
| 380M | 4140M | 66715M | 172300M | 263672M | 227759M | Total Assets ($) | 1228451M | 1277343M |

M = $ thousand   MM = $ million
See Pages 9 through 22 for Explanation of Ratios and Data

## Comparative Historical Data  |  Current Data Sorted by Sales

| | | | Type of Statement | 0-1MM | 1-3MM | 3-5MM | 5-10MM | 10-25MM | 25MM & OVER |
|---|---|---|---|---|---|---|---|---|---|
| 8 | 2 | 3 | Unqualified | | | | | | 3 |
| 11 | 8 | 5 | Reviewed | | | | | | 1 |
| 2 | 5 | 6 | Compiled | | | | 4 | | |
| 8 | 5 | 1 | Tax Returns | | 2 | | 2 | 1 | |
| 23 | 17 | 14 | Other | 1 | 1 | | 2 | 5 | 6 |
| 4/1/09-3/31/10 ALL | 4/1/10-3/31/11 ALL | 4/1/11-3/31/12 ALL | | | 10 (4/1-9/30/11) | | | 19 (10/1/11-3/31/12) | |
| 52 | 37 | 29 | **NUMBER OF STATEMENTS** | 2 | 3 | | 8 | 6 | 10 |
| % | % | % | **ASSETS** | % | % | % | % | % | % |
| 9.9 | 9.3 | 9.4 | Cash & Equivalents | | | | | | 11.0 |
| 21.9 | 25.0 | 26.1 | Trade Receivables (net) | | | | | | 20.3 |
| 30.2 | 25.1 | 27.4 | Inventory | | | | | | 26.2 |
| 2.9 | 4.2 | 3.6 | All Other Current | | | | | | 5.6 |
| 64.9 | 63.7 | 66.4 | Total Current | | | | | | 63.1 |
| 20.6 | 18.0 | 15.8 | Fixed Assets (net) | | | | | | 12.8 |
| 7.9 | 11.0 | 11.9 | Intangibles (net) | | DATA NOT AVAILABLE | | | | 17.9 |
| 6.6 | 7.4 | 5.9 | All Other Non-Current | | | | | | 6.2 |
| 100.0 | 100.0 | 100.0 | Total | | | | | | 100.0 |
| | | | **LIABILITIES** | | | | | | |
| 8.4 | 9.2 | 7.7 | Notes Payable-Short Term | | | | | | 8.5 |
| 7.0 | 6.5 | 4.6 | Cur. Mat.-L.T.D. | | | | | | 1.1 |
| 18.6 | 13.1 | 16.0 | Trade Payables | | | | | | 9.9 |
| .2 | .2 | .1 | Income Taxes Payable | | | | | | .2 |
| 13.3 | 17.9 | 17.0 | All Other Current | | | | | | 18.0 |
| 47.5 | 46.9 | 45.4 | Total Current | | | | | | 37.8 |
| 23.3 | 10.0 | 10.3 | Long-Term Debt | | | | | | 11.0 |
| .3 | .5 | .5 | Deferred Taxes | | | | | | .5 |
| 6.4 | 10.5 | 2.9 | All Other Non-Current | | | | | | 3.8 |
| 22.5 | 32.2 | 40.9 | Net Worth | | | | | | 46.9 |
| 100.0 | 100.0 | 100.0 | Total Liabilities & Net Worth | | | | | | 100.0 |
| | | | **INCOME DATA** | | | | | | |
| 100.0 | 100.0 | 100.0 | Net Sales | | | | | | 100.0 |
| 34.2 | 35.1 | 34.6 | Gross Profit | | | | | | 30.2 |
| 34.1 | 29.0 | 29.9 | Operating Expenses | | | | | | 27.3 |
| .1 | 6.1 | 4.7 | Operating Profit | | | | | | 3.0 |
| 1.9 | 1.4 | 1.0 | All Other Expenses (net) | | | | | | 2.0 |
| -1.8 | 4.7 | 3.8 | Profit Before Taxes | | | | | | 1.0 |
| | | | **RATIOS** | | | | | | |
| 2.2 | 2.3 | 2.1 | | | | | | | 2.3 |
| 1.5 | 1.5 | 1.5 | Current | | | | | | 1.4 |
| 1.1 | .9 | 1.1 | | | | | | | 1.2 |
| 1.4 | 1.0 | 1.2 | | | | | | | 1.2 |
| .7 | .7 | .9 | Quick | | | | | | .7 |
| .4 | .5 | .5 | | | | | | | .6 |
| 32  11.5 | 38  9.5 | 38  9.7 | | | | | | | 45  8.2 |
| 49  7.5 | 46  8.0 | 47  7.7 | Sales/Receivables | | | | | | 51  7.2 |
| 61  6.0 | 59  6.2 | 59  6.2 | | | | | | | 59  6.2 |
| 43  8.5 | 35  10.3 | 52  7.0 | | | | | | | 63  5.8 |
| 77  4.7 | 68  5.4 | 94  3.9 | Cost of Sales/Inventory | | | | | | 70  5.2 |
| 159  2.3 | 105  3.5 | 122  3.0 | | | | | | | 107  3.4 |
| 21  17.5 | 24  15.3 | 25  14.7 | | | | | | | 19  18.8 |
| 39  9.3 | 34  10.7 | 33  11.1 | Cost of Sales/Payables | | | | | | 29  12.4 |
| 54  6.8 | 53  6.9 | 58  6.3 | | | | | | | 55  6.6 |
| 4.6 | 5.3 | 5.0 | | | | | | | 5.2 |
| 8.6 | 11.4 | 9.5 | Sales/Working Capital | | | | | | 8.7 |
| 43.2 | -28.0 | 22.3 | | | | | | | 17.8 |
| 11.1 | 13.3 | 28.0 | | | | | | | |
| (50)  2.1 | (36)  3.4 | (24)  6.4 | EBIT/Interest | | | | | | |
| -.7 | 1.4 | .9 | | | | | | | |
| 5.7 | | | | | | | | | |
| (16)  1.2 | | | Net Profit + Depr., Dep., Amort./Cur. Mat. L/T/D | | | | | | |
| -1.9 | | | | | | | | | |
| .3 | .2 | .2 | | | | | | | .2 |
| .6 | .5 | .4 | Fixed/Worth | | | | | | .5 |
| 5.1 | 21.5 | 1.1 | | | | | | | 1.8 |
| 1.0 | .8 | .7 | | | | | | | .7 |
| 2.5 | 3.2 | 2.2 | Debt/Worth | | | | | | 3.9 |
| 54.5 | NM | 8.5 | | | | | | | 11.3 |
| 38.9 | 69.7 | 91.9 | | | | | | | |
| (40)  14.6 | (28)  29.2 | (26)  12.7 | % Profit Before Taxes/Tangible Net Worth | | | | | | |
| -26.0 | 1.8 | -.1 | | | | | | | |
| 11.8 | 15.0 | 10.0 | | | | | | | 8.2 |
| 1.8 | 4.3 | 6.3 | % Profit Before Taxes/Total Assets | | | | | | 3.1 |
| -9.4 | .5 | -.2 | | | | | | | -7.7 |
| 33.8 | 44.1 | 38.8 | | | | | | | 36.5 |
| 10.4 | 13.3 | 19.2 | Sales/Net Fixed Assets | | | | | | 12.4 |
| 5.6 | 6.3 | 6.5 | | | | | | | 6.9 |
| 2.1 | 2.3 | 2.0 | | | | | | | 1.8 |
| 1.7 | 1.8 | 1.5 | Sales/Total Assets | | | | | | 1.4 |
| 1.2 | 1.3 | 1.3 | | | | | | | 1.2 |
| 1.2 | .6 | .7 | | | | | | | 1.0 |
| (43)  3.0 | (32)  2.2 | (26)  1.7 | % Depr., Dep., Amort./Sales | | | | | | 1.8 |
| 4.7 | 3.7 | 2.4 | | | | | | | 2.5 |
| 1.9 | 1.6 | | | | | | | | |
| (16)  5.7 | (11)  2.9 | | % Officers', Directors' Owners' Comp/Sales | | | | | | |
| 7.1 | 10.0 | | | | | | | | |
| 1647637M | 1358419M | 1064304M | Net Sales ($) | | 3931M | 11915M | 54506M | 87108M | 906844M |
| 1241141M | 912354M | 734966M | Total Assets ($) | | 1614M | 6567M | 30593M | 61048M | 635144M |

M = $ thousand     MM = $ million

See Pages 9 through 22 for Explanation of Ratios and Data

## Current Data Sorted by Assets — Comparative Historical Data

| 0-500M | 500M-2MM | 2-10MM | 10-50MM | 50-100MM | 100-250MM | Type of Statement | 4/1/07-3/31/08 ALL | 4/1/08-3/31/09 ALL |
|---|---|---|---|---|---|---|---|---|
| | | 5 | 4 | 1 | 1 | Unqualified | 10 | 14 |
| | | 9 | 10 | 2 | | Reviewed | 18 | 19 |
| 1 | 1 | 3 | 1 | | | Compiled | 13 | 7 |
| 2 | | 3 | 3 | | | Tax Returns | 6 | 6 |
| 1 | 3 | 16 | 18 | 2 | 3 | Other | 35 | 37 |
| | 12 (4/1-9/30/11) | | 77 (10/1/11-3/31/12) | | | | | |
| 4 | 4 | 36 | 36 | 5 | 4 | **NUMBER OF STATEMENTS** | 82 | 83 |
| % | % | % | % | % | % | **ASSETS** | % | % |
| | | 9.9 | 14.1 | | | Cash & Equivalents | 9.5 | 9.9 |
| | | 27.2 | 19.5 | | | Trade Receivables (net) | 24.9 | 23.1 |
| | | 29.4 | 27.1 | | | Inventory | 29.6 | 31.7 |
| | | 7.0 | 3.7 | | | All Other Current | 4.7 | 4.7 |
| | | 73.5 | 64.4 | | | Total Current | 68.6 | 69.4 |
| | | 14.3 | 18.5 | | | Fixed Assets (net) | 19.5 | 19.1 |
| | | 5.8 | 12.1 | | | Intangibles (net) | 5.4 | 4.6 |
| | | 6.4 | 5.1 | | | All Other Non-Current | 6.5 | 6.8 |
| | | 100.0 | 100.0 | | | Total | 100.0 | 100.0 |
| | | | | | | **LIABILITIES** | | |
| | | 5.5 | 1.7 | | | Notes Payable-Short Term | 6.8 | 7.7 |
| | | 1.8 | 1.3 | | | Cur. Mat.-L.T.D. | 3.3 | 2.1 |
| | | 15.9 | 9.9 | | | Trade Payables | 15.7 | 12.9 |
| | | .3 | .6 | | | Income Taxes Payable | .2 | .5 |
| | | 24.1 | 20.5 | | | All Other Current | 17.3 | 20.6 |
| | | 47.7 | 34.0 | | | Total Current | 43.3 | 43.8 |
| | | 12.3 | 8.9 | | | Long-Term Debt | 14.7 | 11.4 |
| | | .3 | .5 | | | Deferred Taxes | .1 | .4 |
| | | 5.1 | 2.9 | | | All Other Non-Current | 3.0 | 4.4 |
| | | 34.6 | 53.8 | | | Net Worth | 38.9 | 40.0 |
| | | 100.0 | 100.0 | | | Total Liabilities & Net Worth | 100.0 | 100.0 |
| | | | | | | **INCOME DATA** | | |
| | | 100.0 | 100.0 | | | Net Sales | 100.0 | 100.0 |
| | | 30.1 | 34.0 | | | Gross Profit | 35.0 | 32.6 |
| | | 25.6 | 25.5 | | | Operating Expenses | 28.7 | 28.0 |
| | | 4.5 | 8.5 | | | Operating Profit | 6.2 | 4.6 |
| | | .4 | .5 | | | All Other Expenses (net) | .2 | .7 |
| | | 4.2 | 8.0 | | | Profit Before Taxes | 6.0 | 3.8 |
| | | | | | | **RATIOS** | | |
| | | 2.7 | 3.5 | | | Current | 2.7 | 2.6 |
| | | 1.7 | 2.1 | | | | 1.5 | 1.5 |
| | | 1.2 | 1.3 | | | | 1.2 | 1.2 |
| | | 1.3 | 2.2 | | | Quick | 1.5 | 1.4 |
| | | .8 | .9 | | | | .7 | .7 |
| | | .5 | .5 | | | | .5 | .4 |
| | | 26  14.0 | 35  10.5 | | | Sales/Receivables | 31  11.9 | 26  14.0 |
| | | 39  9.3 | 46  8.0 | | | | 39  9.3 | 38  9.7 |
| | | 64  5.7 | 50  7.3 | | | | 50  7.4 | 48  7.6 |
| | | 42  8.7 | 73  5.0 | | | Cost of Sales/Inventory | 43  8.5 | 40  9.1 |
| | | 73  5.0 | 104  3.5 | | | | 76  4.8 | 80  4.5 |
| | | 107  3.4 | 135  2.7 | | | | 117  3.1 | 129  2.8 |
| | | 14  25.5 | 22  16.6 | | | Cost of Sales/Payables | 22  16.8 | 18  20.0 |
| | | 27  13.6 | 34  10.8 | | | | 36  10.1 | 28  13.2 |
| | | 53  6.9 | 43  8.4 | | | | 55  6.7 | 43  8.5 |
| | | 4.1 | 3.1 | | | Sales/Working Capital | 4.8 | 5.1 |
| | | 7.7 | 5.7 | | | | 8.8 | 8.0 |
| | | 20.9 | 14.7 | | | | 27.2 | 25.9 |
| | | 27.6 | 78.0 | | | EBIT/Interest | 15.9 | 20.8 |
| | | (32)  11.7 | (32)  21.5 | | | | (74)  7.1 | (73)  6.1 |
| | | 1.0 | 3.9 | | | | 2.9 | 2.0 |
| | | | 26.7 | | | Net Profit + Depr., Dep., Amort./Cur. Mat. L/T/D | 10.5 | 18.7 |
| | | | (15)  7.1 | | | | (25)  5.4 | (24)  4.7 |
| | | | 3.3 | | | | 1.0 | 2.7 |
| | | .2 | .1 | | | Fixed/Worth | .1 | .2 |
| | | .4 | .5 | | | | .5 | .5 |
| | | .9 | 1.0 | | | | 1.3 | 1.3 |
| | | 1.1 | .4 | | | Debt/Worth | .7 | .6 |
| | | 2.0 | 1.5 | | | | 1.7 | 1.6 |
| | | 6.3 | 2.6 | | | | 5.0 | 4.1 |
| | | 58.9 | 53.3 | | | % Profit Before Taxes/Tangible Net Worth | 55.5 | 42.3 |
| | | (32)  27.6 | (32)  27.7 | | | | (75)  32.5 | (76)  23.2 |
| | | -1.9 | 8.2 | | | | 12.7 | 5.3 |
| | | 20.7 | 20.2 | | | % Profit Before Taxes/Total Assets | 16.4 | 18.2 |
| | | 8.4 | 11.9 | | | | 9.8 | 7.8 |
| | | -1.0 | 5.4 | | | | 3.6 | 2.3 |
| | | 65.2 | 25.2 | | | Sales/Net Fixed Assets | 44.5 | 34.9 |
| | | 20.3 | 11.3 | | | | 14.3 | 14.6 |
| | | 7.0 | 5.9 | | | | 6.9 | 6.5 |
| | | 3.0 | 1.9 | | | Sales/Total Assets | 2.9 | 2.7 |
| | | 1.9 | 1.5 | | | | 2.0 | 2.0 |
| | | 1.6 | 1.0 | | | | 1.5 | 1.5 |
| | | .6 | .7 | | | % Depr., Dep., Amort./Sales | .7 | .7 |
| | | (30)  1.7 | (35)  1.5 | | | | (69)  1.5 | (69)  1.3 |
| | | 2.2 | 3.1 | | | | 2.5 | 2.3 |
| | | | | | | % Officers', Directors' Owners' Comp/Sales | 2.6 | 1.8 |
| | | | | | | | (22)  4.6 | (24)  3.7 |
| | | | | | | | 8.6 | 6.3 |
| 3383M | 15521M | 443680M | 1134411M | 545644M | 1150026M | Net Sales ($) | 2818427M | 3724888M |
| 1028M | 4864M | 202244M | 779263M | 382660M | 708798M | Total Assets ($) | 1528821M | 1984808M |

M = $ thousand    MM = $ million
See Pages 9 through 22 for Explanation of Ratios and Data

## Comparative Historical Data                                  Current Data Sorted by Sales

| | | | Type of Statement | | | | | | |
|---|---|---|---|---|---|---|---|---|---|
| 11 | 12 | 11 | Unqualified | | | | 1 | 4 | 6 |
| 20 | 21 | 21 | Reviewed | | | | 4 | 7 | 10 |
| 8 | 4 | 6 | Compiled | 1 | 1 | 1 | 1 | 1 | 1 |
| 9 | 6 | 8 | Tax Returns | 1 | 1 | | 2 | 3 | 1 |
| 28 | 47 | 43 | Other | 2 | 1 | 1 | 3 | 22 | 14 |
| 4/1/09-3/31/10 | 4/1/10-3/31/11 | 4/1/11-3/31/12 | | 12 (4/1-9/30/11) | | | 77 (10/1/11-3/31/12) | | |
| ALL | ALL | ALL | | 0-1MM | 1-3MM | 3-5MM | 5-10MM | 10-25MM | 25MM & OVER |
| 76 | 90 | 89 | NUMBER OF STATEMENTS | 4 | 3 | 2 | 11 | 37 | 32 |
| % | % | % | **ASSETS** | % | % | % | % | % | % |
| 14.0 | 12.5 | 11.6 | Cash & Equivalents | | | | 13.1 | 7.5 | 17.7 |
| 18.1 | 23.4 | 24.1 | Trade Receivables (net) | | | | 23.3 | 25.0 | 21.3 |
| 29.4 | 28.9 | 27.1 | Inventory | | | | 24.2 | 31.0 | 24.7 |
| 3.3 | 4.0 | 4.9 | All Other Current | | | | 1.0 | 8.9 | 2.9 |
| 64.8 | 68.9 | 67.8 | Total Current | | | | 61.5 | 72.5 | 66.7 |
| 20.1 | 17.8 | 17.5 | Fixed Assets (net) | | | | 24.3 | 15.0 | 16.5 |
| 8.9 | 7.4 | 8.8 | Intangibles (net) | | | | 12.1 | 7.1 | 11.0 |
| 6.2 | 6.0 | 5.9 | All Other Non-Current | | | | 2.1 | 5.4 | 5.8 |
| 100.0 | 100.0 | 100.0 | Total | | | | 100.0 | 100.0 | 100.0 |
| | | | **LIABILITIES** | | | | | | |
| 6.3 | 4.6 | 4.9 | Notes Payable-Short Term | | | | 6.2 | 4.3 | 1.0 |
| 2.6 | 2.2 | 1.6 | Cur. Mat.-L.T.D. | | | | 1.1 | 1.8 | 1.4 |
| 11.3 | 12.1 | 13.0 | Trade Payables | | | | 14.2 | 10.9 | 14.4 |
| .3 | .4 | .4 | Income Taxes Payable | | | | .2 | .4 | .6 |
| 16.1 | 24.3 | 22.3 | All Other Current | | | | 11.7 | 25.8 | 22.3 |
| 36.7 | 43.6 | 42.2 | Total Current | | | | 33.4 | 43.2 | 39.6 |
| 13.6 | 10.2 | 12.2 | Long-Term Debt | | | | 12.6 | 8.7 | 9.7 |
| .4 | .4 | .4 | Deferred Taxes | | | | .2 | .6 | .2 |
| 10.6 | 4.9 | 4.0 | All Other Non-Current | | | | 1.0 | 5.5 | 3.1 |
| 38.8 | 41.0 | 41.2 | Net Worth | | | | 52.8 | 42.0 | 47.3 |
| 100.0 | 100.0 | 100.0 | Total Liabilities & Net Worth | | | | 100.0 | 100.0 | 100.0 |
| | | | **INCOME DATA** | | | | | | |
| 100.0 | 100.0 | 100.0 | Net Sales | | | | 100.0 | 100.0 | 100.0 |
| 35.5 | 32.8 | 32.5 | Gross Profit | | | | 33.2 | 30.7 | 33.8 |
| 32.2 | 27.5 | 26.1 | Operating Expenses | | | | 28.9 | 25.2 | 24.7 |
| 3.3 | 5.3 | 6.4 | Operating Profit | | | | 4.3 | 5.4 | 9.1 |
| 1.2 | 1.0 | .6 | All Other Expenses (net) | | | | .7 | .4 | .7 |
| 2.1 | 4.3 | 5.8 | Profit Before Taxes | | | | 3.6 | 5.1 | 8.4 |
| | | | **RATIOS** | | | | | | |
| 2.9 | 2.6 | 3.1 | Current | | | | 3.9 | 2.6 | 3.4 |
| 1.9 | 1.5 | 1.6 | | | | | 1.7 | 1.7 | 1.7 |
| 1.4 | 1.2 | 1.1 | | | | | 1.2 | 1.2 | 1.3 |
| 1.8 | 1.3 | 1.5 | Quick | | | | 2.7 | 1.1 | 1.9 |
| .9 | .8 | .9 | | | | | 1.1 | .7 | .9 |
| .5 | .5 | .5 | | | | | .7 | .5 | .5 |
| 27  13.3 | 34  10.7 | 31  11.6 | Sales/Receivables | | | | 25  14.8 | 31  11.6 | 33  11.0 |
| 38  9.7 | 43  8.5 | 43  8.5 | | | | | 43  8.5 | 40  9.2 | 45  8.2 |
| 48  7.7 | 61  6.0 | 57  6.4 | | | | | 69  5.3 | 55  6.6 | 52  7.0 |
| 50  7.3 | 43  8.4 | 53  6.9 | Cost of Sales/Inventory | | | | 57  6.4 | 63  5.8 | 54  6.7 |
| 92  4.0 | 93  3.9 | 87  4.2 | | | | | 72  5.1 | 89  4.1 | 96  3.8 |
| 146  2.5 | 147  2.5 | 122  3.0 | | | | | 114  3.2 | 130  2.8 | 122  3.0 |
| 16  23.0 | 20  18.0 | 19  19.4 | Cost of Sales/Payables | | | | 11  34.6 | 15  25.0 | 22  16.4 |
| 29  12.8 | 31  11.8 | 33  11.0 | | | | | 27  13.6 | 31  11.6 | 33  10.9 |
| 48  7.6 | 56  6.5 | 46  7.9 | | | | | 55  6.6 | 43  8.5 | 46  7.9 |
| 4.1 | 4.2 | 3.9 | Sales/Working Capital | | | | 3.8 | 5.2 | 3.5 |
| 6.2 | 7.1 | 7.4 | | | | | 4.1 | 6.9 | 6.6 |
| 10.7 | 17.7 | 21.4 | | | | | 21.2 | 16.4 | 16.5 |
| 23.5 | 31.7 | 41.8 | EBIT/Interest | | | | | 34.9 | 103.1 |
| (67)  6.7 | (77)  12.3 | (80)  13.1 | | | | | | (34)  12.0 | (29)  35.6 |
| 1.3 | 1.3 | 2.9 | | | | | | .1 | 12.8 |
| 13.4 | 12.0 | 12.4 | Net Profit + Depr., Dep., | | | | | 15.3 | 13.3 |
| (20)  4.1 | (29)  5.2 | (29)  5.2 | Amort./Cur. Mat. L/T/D | | | | | (10)  4.5 | (16)  7.7 |
| 2.5 | 1.9 | 3.2 | | | | | | .8 | 3.4 |
| .2 | .2 | .2 | Fixed/Worth | | | | .3 | .1 | .1 |
| .5 | .4 | .5 | | | | | .5 | .4 | .4 |
| 1.3 | 1.8 | 1.2 | | | | | .9 | .9 | 1.7 |
| .6 | .7 | .6 | Debt/Worth | | | | .3 | .9 | .6 |
| 1.3 | 1.7 | 1.8 | | | | | 1.5 | 2.0 | 1.6 |
| 4.7 | 5.9 | 6.8 | | | | | 2.9 | 4.9 | 5.8 |
| 29.4 | 39.2 | 55.2 | % Profit Before Taxes/Tangible | | | | 20.7 | 84.7 | 47.8 |
| (65)  15.5 | (78)  23.4 | (75)  29.9 | Net Worth | | | | (10)  4.2 | (34)  31.8 | (26)  34.0 |
| 4.9 | 4.1 | 7.6 | | | | | -5.6 | -5.4 | 23.1 |
| 13.2 | 15.6 | 20.0 | % Profit Before Taxes/Total | | | | 14.8 | 21.1 | 20.3 |
| 6.2 | 7.2 | 9.2 | Assets | | | | 2.9 | 9.0 | 13.0 |
| .1 | .3 | 2.4 | | | | | -1.4 | -1.7 | 7.6 |
| 22.8 | 32.4 | 30.1 | Sales/Net Fixed Assets | | | | 11.1 | 57.6 | 30.5 |
| 9.4 | 13.3 | 11.9 | | | | | 6.3 | 21.8 | 11.2 |
| 4.8 | 5.6 | 6.4 | | | | | 4.7 | 9.9 | 6.3 |
| 2.2 | 2.4 | 2.3 | Sales/Total Assets | | | | 2.0 | 2.7 | 2.0 |
| 1.6 | 1.6 | 1.8 | | | | | 1.7 | 1.8 | 1.5 |
| 1.2 | 1.3 | 1.3 | | | | | 1.2 | 1.5 | 1.2 |
| 1.0 | .6 | .7 | % Depr., Dep., Amort./Sales | | | | 1.9 | .6 | .5 |
| (64)  2.0 | (71)  1.4 | (77)  1.6 | | | | | (10)  2.4 | (32)  1.4 | (30)  1.4 |
| 3.1 | 2.9 | 2.6 | | | | | 4.1 | 2.2 | 2.6 |
| 3.3 | 1.8 | 1.6 | % Officers', Directors' | | | | | 1.6 | |
| (22)  4.5 | (21)  4.2 | (18)  2.8 | Owners' Comp/Sales | | | | | (10)  2.6 | |
| 9.6 | 5.1 | 5.9 | | | | | | 5.0 | |
| 2510089M | 3709413M | 3292665M | Net Sales ($) | 2530M | 6219M | 9081M | 85445M | 593879M | 2595511M |
| 1706534M | 2505778M | 2078857M | Total Assets ($) | 1863M | 2036M | 6338M | 55559M | 351654M | 1661407M |

M = $ thousand    MM = $ million
See Pages 9 through 22 for Explanation of Ratios and Data

## Current Data Sorted by Assets      Comparative Historical Data

| | 0-500M | 500M-2MM | 2-10MM | 10-50MM | 50-100MM | 100-250MM | Type of Statement | 4/1/07-3/31/08 ALL | 4/1/08-3/31/09 ALL |
|---|---|---|---|---|---|---|---|---|---|
| | | 5 | 8 | 26 | 3 | 2 | Unqualified | 36 | 47 |
| | 1 | 6 | 35 | 24 | 2 | | Reviewed | 38 | 45 |
| | 4 | 16 | 13 | 1 | 1 | | Compiled | 29 | 27 |
| | 3 | 14 | 9 | | | | Tax Returns | 14 | 27 |
| | | | 39 | 32 | 8 | 8 | Other | 75 | 90 |
| | | 49 (4/1-9/30/11) | | 211 (10/1/11-3/31/12) | | | | | |
| NUMBER OF STATEMENTS | 8 | 41 | 104 | 83 | 14 | 10 | | 192 | 236 |
| **ASSETS** | % | % | % | % | % | % | | % | % |
| Cash & Equivalents | | 12.9 | 11.9 | 14.5 | 17.9 | 13.1 | | 11.7 | 9.9 |
| Trade Receivables (net) | | 31.0 | 29.4 | 21.9 | 20.2 | 19.4 | | 26.4 | 25.6 |
| Inventory | | 26.2 | 30.7 | 22.2 | 19.5 | 24.3 | | 25.8 | 25.9 |
| All Other Current | | 3.9 | 5.4 | 8.8 | 8.6 | 12.3 | | 4.6 | 5.4 |
| Total Current | | 74.0 | 77.4 | 67.5 | 66.1 | 69.1 | | 68.4 | 66.7 |
| Fixed Assets (net) | | 17.9 | 15.2 | 17.1 | 15.2 | 14.9 | | 19.9 | 20.3 |
| Intangibles (net) | | 1.8 | 2.6 | 8.1 | 8.3 | 7.8 | | 5.9 | 6.0 |
| All Other Non-Current | | 6.4 | 4.8 | 7.3 | 10.3 | 8.2 | | 5.7 | 6.9 |
| Total | | 100.0 | 100.0 | 100.0 | 100.0 | 100.0 | | 100.0 | 100.0 |
| **LIABILITIES** | | | | | | | | | |
| Notes Payable-Short Term | | 6.0 | 7.0 | 6.2 | 5.0 | 4.0 | | 9.4 | 11.0 |
| Cur. Mat.-L.T.D. | | 2.3 | 2.0 | 3.3 | 1.1 | 1.5 | | 3.1 | 3.8 |
| Trade Payables | | 16.7 | 14.1 | 10.1 | 11.0 | 10.7 | | 16.1 | 13.4 |
| Income Taxes Payable | | .0 | .2 | .5 | .0 | .3 | | .2 | .3 |
| All Other Current | | 15.8 | 20.3 | 22.2 | 19.7 | 24.2 | | 17.2 | 16.5 |
| Total Current | | 40.8 | 43.6 | 42.3 | 36.9 | 40.7 | | 46.1 | 44.9 |
| Long-Term Debt | | 13.5 | 10.1 | 8.4 | 7.6 | 5.7 | | 13.6 | 13.4 |
| Deferred Taxes | | .6 | .3 | .7 | .3 | 2.8 | | .3 | .3 |
| All Other Non-Current | | 12.9 | 6.3 | 7.5 | 11.8 | 8.3 | | 6.6 | 6.6 |
| Net Worth | | 32.2 | 39.6 | 41.0 | 43.5 | 42.5 | | 33.5 | 34.7 |
| Total Liabilties & Net Worth | | 100.0 | 100.0 | 100.0 | 100.0 | 100.0 | | 100.0 | 100.0 |
| **INCOME DATA** | | | | | | | | | |
| Net Sales | | 100.0 | 100.0 | 100.0 | 100.0 | 100.0 | | 100.0 | 100.0 |
| Gross Profit | | 39.7 | 33.2 | 27.9 | 24.1 | 20.1 | | 31.7 | 30.8 |
| Operating Expenses | | 34.7 | 25.3 | 20.2 | 19.1 | 17.5 | | 25.9 | 25.7 |
| Operating Profit | | 5.0 | 7.9 | 7.6 | 5.0 | 2.6 | | 5.7 | 5.0 |
| All Other Expenses (net) | | .2 | .8 | .8 | .6 | 1.4 | | 1.3 | 1.1 |
| Profit Before Taxes | | 4.8 | 7.1 | 6.9 | 4.4 | 1.2 | | 4.4 | 4.0 |
| **RATIOS** | | | | | | | | | |
| Current | | 2.7 | 3.4 | 2.3 | 3.1 | 2.4 | | 2.3 | 2.3 |
| | | 2.0 | 1.8 | 1.7 | 1.7 | 2.0 | | 1.4 | 1.6 |
| | | 1.5 | 1.3 | 1.3 | 1.4 | 1.1 | | 1.1 | 1.1 |
| Quick | | 1.8 | 1.8 | 1.3 | 1.4 | 1.3 | | 1.4 | 1.3 |
| | | 1.2 | .9 | 1.0 | 1.1 | .8 | | (191) .8 | .8 |
| | | .7 | .6 | .7 | .6 | .5 | | .5 | .5 |
| Sales/Receivables | 22 16.9 | 33 10.9 | 32 11.5 | 38 9.7 | 35 10.3 | | | 35 10.6 | 31 11.9 |
| | 41 8.8 | 47 7.7 | 51 7.2 | 56 6.5 | 55 6.6 | | | 47 7.7 | 45 8.0 |
| | 55 6.6 | 60 6.1 | 70 5.2 | 66 5.5 | 78 4.7 | | | 63 5.8 | 59 6.2 |
| Cost of Sales/Inventory | 19 19.6 | 38 9.7 | 39 9.4 | 6 59.7 | 39 9.4 | | | 33 10.9 | 30 12.1 |
| | 54 6.7 | 78 4.7 | 69 5.3 | 89 4.1 | 87 4.2 | | | 76 4.8 | 66 5.5 |
| | 118 3.1 | 126 2.9 | 126 2.9 | 146 2.5 | 118 3.1 | | | 116 3.1 | 111 3.3 |
| Cost of Sales/Payables | 21 17.5 | 16 23.4 | 20 18.5 | 21 17.1 | 17 21.3 | | | 21 17.1 | 17 22.0 |
| | 30 12.2 | 31 11.8 | 32 11.5 | 29 12.4 | 47 7.7 | | | 35 10.4 | 29 12.5 |
| | 42 8.6 | 53 6.9 | 45 8.2 | 59 6.2 | 53 6.9 | | | 54 6.7 | 44 8.2 |
| Sales/Working Capital | | 5.3 | 3.3 | 3.6 | 2.8 | 3.2 | | 4.5 | 4.4 |
| | | 7.7 | 6.1 | 6.2 | 5.6 | 5.1 | | 9.8 | 8.8 |
| | | 18.6 | 16.8 | 10.6 | 7.9 | 25.6 | | 47.0 | 40.7 |
| EBIT/Interest | | 21.4 | 69.1 | 36.7 | 58.2 | | | 11.3 | 16.8 |
| | (30) | 6.7 | (80) 15.3 | (69) 14.2 | 9.4 | | | (164) 4.2 | (202) 3.7 |
| | | 2.0 | 4.0 | 5.1 | 2.1 | | | 1.1 | 1.1 |
| Net Profit + Depr., Dep., Amort./Cur. Mat. L/T/D | | | 16.6 | | | | | 11.7 | 10.1 |
| | | | (21) 9.1 | | | | | (55) 3.7 | (59) 3.3 |
| | | | 3.1 | | | | | 1.4 | 1.0 |
| Fixed/Worth | | .2 | .1 | .2 | .1 | .2 | | .2 | .2 |
| | | .4 | .3 | .5 | .4 | .3 | | .6 | .6 |
| | | 1.2 | .7 | 1.1 | 1.0 | 1.9 | | 2.4 | 2.1 |
| Debt/Worth | | .7 | .6 | .6 | .8 | .7 | | 1.0 | .7 |
| | | 1.4 | 1.4 | 1.7 | 2.1 | 1.0 | | 2.4 | 2.1 |
| | | 6.8 | 4.7 | 4.7 | 3.9 | 14.9 | | 6.4 | 8.3 |
| % Profit Before Taxes/Tangible Net Worth | | 43.5 | 58.6 | 50.4 | 42.7 | | | 55.0 | 42.2 |
| | (34) | 22.8 | (94) 37.9 | (73) 31.0 | (13) 24.3 | | | (164) 26.7 | (191) 21.2 |
| | | 6.3 | 14.0 | 16.7 | .7 | | | 6.6 | 5.0 |
| % Profit Before Taxes/Total Assets | | 15.6 | 21.2 | 17.2 | 11.7 | 7.2 | | 19.1 | 16.7 |
| | | 7.0 | 11.1 | 11.5 | 6.6 | 1.2 | | 7.4 | 7.2 |
| | | 1.7 | 5.0 | 5.1 | 1.2 | -3.5 | | .8 | .4 |
| Sales/Net Fixed Assets | | 51.9 | 62.1 | 24.7 | 17.9 | 24.5 | | 34.1 | 31.7 |
| | | 20.5 | 22.2 | 9.9 | 11.4 | 13.2 | | 12.3 | 13.2 |
| | | 9.6 | 8.2 | 6.3 | 5.8 | 5.1 | | 5.3 | 5.8 |
| Sales/Total Assets | | 3.5 | 2.7 | 1.8 | 1.5 | 1.5 | | 2.6 | 2.6 |
| | | 2.8 | 2.1 | 1.5 | 1.3 | 1.4 | | 1.8 | 1.9 |
| | | 1.9 | 1.6 | 1.2 | 1.0 | 1.0 | | 1.3 | 1.4 |
| % Depr., Dep., Amort./Sales | | 1.0 | .6 | 1.1 | .7 | | | .7 | .8 |
| | (31) | 1.8 | (81) 1.1 | (73) 1.9 | (13) 1.3 | | | (161) 1.5 | (192) 1.6 |
| | | 3.6 | 2.5 | 3.3 | 2.7 | | | 3.1 | 3.0 |
| % Officers', Directors' Owners' Comp/Sales | | 2.3 | 2.2 | | | | | 2.6 | 2.5 |
| | (22) | 4.9 | (25) 3.3 | | | | | (51) 4.4 | (75) 3.4 |
| | | 7.5 | 5.4 | | | | | 7.6 | 6.0 |
| Net Sales ($) | 12490M | 143450M | 1089113M | 3021534M | 1310027M | 2482663M | | 5849345M | 7804340M |
| Total Assets ($) | 2371M | 48390M | 518595M | 1992961M | 1025785M | 1645390M | | 4289625M | 4824063M |

M = $ thousand    MM = $ million
See Pages 9 through 22 for Explanation of Ratios and Data

## Comparative Historical Data | Current Data Sorted by Sales

| Type of Statement | Hist 1 | Hist 2 | Hist 3 | 0-1MM | 1-3MM | 3-5MM | 5-10MM | 10-25MM | 25MM & OVER |
|---|---|---|---|---|---|---|---|---|---|
| Unqualified | 48 | 35 | 39 | | 1 | 4 | 2 | 15 | 22 |
| Reviewed | 48 | 43 | 66 | | 5 | 3 | 18 | 28 | 15 |
| Compiled | 27 | 30 | 22 | | 5 | 8 | 8 | 4 | 2 |
| Tax Returns | 23 | 21 | 29 | 1 | 10 | 10 | 5 | 3 | |
| Other | 89 | 86 | 104 | 2 | 10 | 8 | 20 | 29 | 35 |
| | 4/1/09-3/31/10 ALL | 4/1/10-3/31/11 ALL | 4/1/11-3/31/12 ALL | | 49 (4/1-9/30/11) | | 211 (10/1/11-3/31/12) | | |
| **NUMBER OF STATEMENTS** | 235 | 215 | 260 | 3 | 26 | 25 | 53 | 79 | 74 |

| | Hist 1 % | Hist 2 % | Hist 3 % | 0-1MM % | 1-3MM % | 3-5MM % | 5-10MM % | 10-25MM % | 25MM & OVER % |
|---|---|---|---|---|---|---|---|---|---|
| **ASSETS** | | | | | | | | | |
| Cash & Equivalents | 13.3 | 14.2 | 13.2 | | 11.7 | 15.1 | 10.9 | 15.1 | 12.9 |
| Trade Receivables (net) | 23.3 | 24.2 | 26.7 | | 32.1 | 30.0 | 28.5 | 26.2 | 23.4 |
| Inventory | 25.9 | 25.8 | 26.0 | | 22.5 | 25.3 | 34.1 | 25.2 | 22.6 |
| All Other Current | 5.4 | 4.6 | 6.5 | | 3.8 | 2.2 | 6.9 | 6.4 | 9.0 |
| Total Current | 67.9 | 68.7 | 72.4 | | 70.1 | 72.5 | 80.4 | 72.9 | 67.9 |
| Fixed Assets (net) | 19.8 | 19.4 | 16.3 | | 20.0 | 20.4 | 13.3 | 15.2 | 16.9 |
| Intangibles (net) | 5.1 | 5.3 | 4.7 | | 1.9 | 4.3 | .8 | 5.8 | 7.5 |
| All Other Non-Current | 7.2 | 6.6 | 6.6 | | 8.0 | 2.7 | 5.5 | 6.1 | 7.8 |
| Total | 100.0 | 100.0 | 100.0 | | 100.0 | 100.0 | 100.0 | 100.0 | 100.0 |
| **LIABILITIES** | | | | | | | | | |
| Notes Payable-Short Term | 9.6 | 7.4 | 7.3 | | 11.8 | 6.5 | 8.1 | 6.2 | 5.7 |
| Cur. Mat.-L.T.D. | 3.2 | 3.4 | 2.6 | | 2.6 | 3.0 | 2.0 | 3.5 | 1.7 |
| Trade Payables | 13.0 | 13.6 | 13.3 | | 16.0 | 15.5 | 14.8 | 12.4 | 11.4 |
| Income Taxes Payable | .4 | .4 | .3 | | .0 | .0 | .1 | .4 | .4 |
| All Other Current | 16.4 | 17.8 | 20.0 | | 13.1 | 18.9 | 16.5 | 23.9 | 20.9 |
| Total Current | 42.6 | 42.6 | 43.3 | | 43.4 | 43.9 | 41.5 | 46.4 | 40.1 |
| Long-Term Debt | 13.0 | 10.3 | 10.1 | | 16.4 | 19.6 | 9.7 | 7.6 | 7.9 |
| Deferred Taxes | .4 | .4 | .6 | | .4 | .4 | .3 | .7 | .7 |
| All Other Non-Current | 8.0 | 9.0 | 8.8 | | 11.9 | 17.1 | 7.4 | 7.3 | 7.3 |
| Net Worth | 35.9 | 37.7 | 37.2 | | 27.8 | 19.0 | 41.1 | 38.0 | 43.9 |
| Total Liabilities & Net Worth | 100.0 | 100.0 | 100.0 | | 100.0 | 100.0 | 100.0 | 100.0 | 100.0 |
| **INCOME DATA** | | | | | | | | | |
| Net Sales | 100.0 | 100.0 | 100.0 | | 100.0 | 100.0 | 100.0 | 100.0 | 100.0 |
| Gross Profit | 31.1 | 34.2 | 31.8 | | 46.0 | 40.0 | 33.0 | 29.7 | 25.4 |
| Operating Expenses | 28.0 | 29.2 | 24.9 | | 39.5 | 33.8 | 25.9 | 22.7 | 18.3 |
| Operating Profit | 3.1 | 5.0 | 6.9 | | 6.5 | 6.3 | 7.1 | 7.0 | 7.1 |
| All Other Expenses (net) | 1.4 | 1.1 | .7 | | 1.0 | .5 | .4 | .8 | .8 |
| Profit Before Taxes | 1.7 | 4.0 | 6.2 | | 5.5 | 5.8 | 6.7 | 6.2 | 6.3 |

### RATIOS

| Ratio | Hist 1 | Hist 2 | Hist 3 | 0-1MM | 1-3MM | 3-5MM | 5-10MM | 10-25MM | 25MM & OVER |
|---|---|---|---|---|---|---|---|---|---|
| Current | 2.7 | 2.8 | 2.8 | | 3.2 | 2.4 | 4.2 | 2.4 | 2.5 |
| | 1.6 | 1.7 | 1.8 | | 2.0 | 1.6 | 2.1 | 1.6 | 1.9 |
| | 1.1 | 1.2 | 1.3 | | 1.1 | 1.3 | 1.4 | 1.2 | 1.3 |
| Quick | 1.5 | 1.6 | 1.5 | | 1.9 | 1.7 | 1.9 | 1.5 | 1.3 |
| | .8 | 1.0 | 1.0 | | 1.2 | 1.0 | 1.1 | .9 | 1.0 |
| | .5 | .6 | .6 | | .5 | .7 | .6 | .6 | .6 |
| Sales/Receivables | 28 / 13.0 | 34 / 10.6 | 30 / 12.0 | 19 / 19.7 | 26 / 13.8 | 30 / 12.2 | 33 / 11.0 | 36 / 10.1 | |
| | 45 / 8.1 | 49 / 7.5 | 47 / 7.7 | 43 / 8.5 | 41 / 8.9 | 45 / 8.2 | 51 / 7.2 | 52 / 7.0 | |
| | 61 / 6.0 | 69 / 5.3 | 64 / 5.7 | 59 / 6.2 | 53 / 6.9 | 54 / 6.7 | 66 / 5.5 | 68 / 5.4 | |
| Cost of Sales/Inventory | 33 / 11.0 | 36 / 10.2 | 32 / 11.5 | 5 / 70.9 | 8 / 45.2 | 47 / 7.7 | 35 / 10.3 | 35 / 10.4 | |
| | 75 / 4.9 | 87 / 4.2 | 70 / 5.2 | 74 / 4.9 | 47 / 7.7 | 74 / 4.9 | 78 / 4.7 | 69 / 5.3 | |
| | 143 / 2.6 | 140 / 2.6 | 126 / 2.9 | 174 / 2.1 | 126 / 2.9 | 135 / 2.7 | 130 / 2.8 | 101 / 3.6 | |
| Cost of Sales/Payables | 16 / 22.4 | 22 / 16.9 | 18 / 19.8 | 15 / 24.2 | 16 / 23.1 | 16 / 22.2 | 19 / 19.4 | 20 / 18.6 | |
| | 27 / 13.6 | 33 / 11.2 | 31 / 11.8 | 31 / 11.6 | 30 / 12.1 | 28 / 13.2 | 31 / 11.6 | 32 / 11.5 | |
| | 52 / 7.0 | 57 / 6.4 | 49 / 7.4 | 59 / 6.2 | 48 / 7.6 | 53 / 6.9 | 47 / 7.7 | 47 / 7.7 | |
| Sales/Working Capital | 3.6 | 3.5 | 3.7 | | 3.3 | 5.5 | 3.1 | 4.0 | 3.6 |
| | 7.2 | 5.8 | 6.4 | | 7.5 | 9.7 | 6.0 | 6.2 | 6.2 |
| | 23.8 | 21.0 | 16.4 | | 28.1 | 18.6 | 15.1 | 16.7 | 11.1 |
| EBIT/Interest | 12.0 | 25.1 | 38.6 | | 8.7 | 35.2 | 112.0 | 52.2 | 49.3 |
| | (203) 2.6 | (187) 6.7 | (208) 11.8 | (18) 4.6 | (21) 10.0 | (39) 16.2 | (64) 13.2 | (64) 14.5 | |
| | -.2 | 1.3 | 3.2 | | 1.7 | 2.1 | 4.0 | 3.2 | 5.1 |
| Net Profit + Depr., Dep., Amort./Cur. Mat. L/T/D | 7.0 | 12.6 | 12.6 | | | | | 16.5 | 12.8 |
| | (75) 2.1 | (57) 3.0 | (44) 4.3 | | | | | (12) 5.1 | (25) 4.2 |
| | -.1 | 1.3 | 2.1 | | | | | 1.5 | 2.5 |
| Fixed/Worth | .2 | .2 | .1 | | .1 | .1 | .1 | .2 | .2 |
| | .5 | .5 | .4 | | .4 | .6 | .2 | .5 | .4 |
| | 2.3 | 1.4 | 1.0 | | 2.1 | -9.6 | .6 | .9 | 1.0 |
| Debt/Worth | .6 | .6 | .6 | | .5 | 1.2 | .5 | .7 | .6 |
| | 1.4 | 1.5 | 1.5 | | 1.2 | 1.6 | 1.1 | 1.8 | 1.4 |
| | 10.2 | 6.2 | 5.1 | | 10.8 | -38.7 | 3.6 | 5.2 | 3.5 |
| % Profit Before Taxes/Tangible Net Worth | 31.5 | 43.0 | 50.8 | | 42.6 | 33.1 | 62.8 | 55.3 | 48.7 |
| | (193) 10.1 | (185) 18.5 | (226) 27.7 | (22) 10.0 | (17) 25.0 | (47) 33.5 | (70) 34.3 | (69) 24.8 | |
| | -3.7 | 5.0 | 11.8 | | -9.8 | 9.1 | 14.8 | 18.3 | 10.2 |
| % Profit Before Taxes/Total Assets | 11.4 | 15.6 | 17.5 | | 14.6 | 16.1 | 22.5 | 16.9 | 17.3 |
| | 2.8 | 6.6 | 10.3 | | 5.2 | 8.7 | 13.5 | 10.3 | 9.8 |
| | -3.1 | .9 | 3.6 | | .5 | 2.2 | 4.8 | 4.6 | 2.6 |
| Sales/Net Fixed Assets | 28.0 | 28.2 | 45.0 | | 40.1 | 65.1 | 58.7 | 44.3 | 28.1 |
| | 11.7 | 11.4 | 16.5 | | 16.6 | 27.5 | 22.2 | 15.2 | 13.1 |
| | 5.6 | 5.8 | 7.5 | | 8.0 | 7.9 | 9.8 | 7.3 | 6.0 |
| Sales/Total Assets | 2.4 | 2.2 | 2.6 | | 3.2 | 3.4 | 2.9 | 2.5 | 1.9 |
| | 1.6 | 1.6 | 1.8 | | 1.9 | 2.6 | 2.2 | 1.7 | 1.5 |
| | 1.2 | 1.2 | 1.4 | | 1.1 | 1.8 | 1.7 | 1.2 | 1.3 |
| % Depr., Dep., Amort./Sales | .9 | .8 | .7 | | .4 | .8 | .7 | .7 | .9 |
| | (190) 1.8 | (183) 1.8 | (211) 1.5 | (19) 2.0 | (20) 1.8 | (41) 1.2 | (63) 1.4 | (66) 1.7 | |
| | 4.4 | 3.7 | 2.8 | | 4.1 | 3.4 | 2.5 | 2.8 | 3.4 |
| % Officers', Directors' Owners' Comp/Sales | 2.2 | 2.4 | 2.2 | | 2.6 | 2.6 | 2.4 | 1.3 | |
| | (72) 4.7 | (62) 4.5 | (59) 3.9 | (11) 6.5 | (13) 4.9 | (14) 3.5 | (13) 2.4 | | |
| | 9.0 | 8.6 | 6.5 | | 7.6 | 7.9 | 5.6 | 4.4 | |
| Net Sales ($) | 6517825M | 6030331M | 8059277M | 1866M | 47678M | 98741M | 387212M | 1315263M | 6208517M |
| Total Assets ($) | 4647450M | 4941919M | 5233492M | 1294M | 28924M | 45139M | 186001M | 881949M | 4090185M |

M = $ thousand    MM = $ million
See Pages 9 through 22 for Explanation of Ratios and Data

## Current Data Sorted by Assets      Comparative Historical Data

Type of Statement

| | 500M-2MM | 2-10MM | 10-50MM | 50-100MM | 100-250MM | Type of Statement | 4/1/07-3/31/08 ALL | 4/1/08-3/31/09 ALL |
|---|---|---|---|---|---|---|---|---|
| | | 2 | 8 | 2 | 1 | Unqualified | 10 | 11 |
| | 1 | 7 | 1 | | | Reviewed | 7 | 10 |
| | 1 | 2 | | | | Compiled | 7 | 5 |
| | 2 | 4 | | | | Tax Returns | 4 | 4 |
| | 2 | 8 | 9 | 4 | | Other | 30 | 26 |
| 13 (4/1-9/30/11) | | | 41 (10/1/11-3/31/12) | | | | | |

| 0-500M | 500M-2MM | 2-10MM | 10-50MM | 50-100MM | 100-250MM | | 4/1/07-3/31/08 ALL | 4/1/08-3/31/09 ALL |
|---|---|---|---|---|---|---|---|---|
| | 6 | 23 | 18 | 6 | 1 | NUMBER OF STATEMENTS | 58 | 56 |
| % | % | % | % | % | % | **ASSETS** | % | % |
| | | 13.7 | 8.9 | | | Cash & Equivalents | 13.0 | 8.2 |
| | | 24.8 | 18.3 | | | Trade Receivables (net) | 20.9 | 22.2 |
| | | 26.9 | 28.8 | | | Inventory | 25.4 | 29.4 |
| | | 3.4 | 2.4 | | | All Other Current | 3.6 | 2.6 |
| | | 68.8 | 58.4 | | | Total Current | 62.8 | 62.3 |
| | | 25.3 | 22.1 | | | Fixed Assets (net) | 26.6 | 23.1 |
| | | 1.7 | 13.6 | | | Intangibles (net) | 3.8 | 9.1 |
| | | 4.2 | 6.0 | | | All Other Non-Current | 6.7 | 5.4 |
| | | 100.0 | 100.0 | | | Total | 100.0 | 100.0 |
| | | | | | | **LIABILITIES** | | |
| | | 4.9 | 5.8 | | | Notes Payable-Short Term | 5.1 | 7.5 |
| | | 3.9 | 4.6 | | | Cur. Mat.-L.T.D. | 4.5 | 3.1 |
| | | 12.0 | 11.3 | | | Trade Payables | 14.4 | 14.6 |
| | | .3 | .5 | | | Income Taxes Payable | .2 | .2 |
| | | 8.2 | 10.8 | | | All Other Current | 9.3 | 11.7 |
| | | 29.2 | 32.9 | | | Total Current | 33.6 | 37.0 |
| | | 23.2 | 9.4 | | | Long-Term Debt | 14.8 | 13.2 |
| | | .0 | 1.1 | | | Deferred Taxes | .6 | .5 |
| | | 1.3 | 2.5 | | | All Other Non-Current | 4.8 | 6.1 |
| | | 46.3 | 54.0 | | | Net Worth | 46.3 | 43.2 |
| | | 100.0 | 100.0 | | | Total Liabilities & Net Worth | 100.0 | 100.0 |
| | | | | | | **INCOME DATA** | | |
| | | 100.0 | 100.0 | | | Net Sales | 100.0 | 100.0 |
| | | 37.7 | 34.4 | | | Gross Profit | 41.8 | 38.2 |
| | | 29.4 | 30.6 | | | Operating Expenses | 35.2 | 31.1 |
| | | 8.2 | 3.8 | | | Operating Profit | 6.5 | 7.1 |
| | | .0 | .9 | | | All Other Expenses (net) | 1.4 | 1.3 |
| | | 8.2 | 2.8 | | | Profit Before Taxes | 5.1 | 5.7 |
| | | | | | | **RATIOS** | | |
| | | 5.0 | 2.8 | | | Current | 3.4 | 2.5 |
| | | 2.4 | 1.8 | | | | 1.9 | 1.6 |
| | | 1.5 | 1.4 | | | | 1.4 | 1.3 |
| | | 2.1 | 1.6 | | | Quick | 1.6 | 1.2 |
| | | 1.3 | 1.0 | | | | 1.0 | .8 |
| | | .7 | .5 | | | | .6 | .6 |
| | | 30  12.0 | 28  13.1 | | | Sales/Receivables | 28  12.8 | 35  10.5 |
| | | 43  8.4 | 42  8.6 | | | | 42  8.7 | 47  7.8 |
| | | 52  7.0 | 57  6.4 | | | | 56  6.5 | 56  6.5 |
| | | 27  13.7 | 56  6.5 | | | Cost of Sales/Inventory | 45  8.1 | 59  6.2 |
| | | 72  5.1 | 118  3.1 | | | | 91  4.0 | 93  3.9 |
| | | 89  4.1 | 152  2.4 | | | | 130  2.8 | 140  2.6 |
| | | 19  19.5 | 18  20.7 | | | Cost of Sales/Payables | 23  15.9 | 19  18.8 |
| | | 31  11.8 | 31  11.9 | | | | 37  9.8 | 36  10.0 |
| | | 42  8.6 | 61  6.0 | | | | 59  6.1 | 63  5.8 |
| | | 3.7 | 3.2 | | | Sales/Working Capital | 3.6 | 3.9 |
| | | 6.5 | 5.9 | | | | 7.2 | 8.3 |
| | | 15.3 | 15.0 | | | | 15.5 | 19.6 |
| | | 60.0 | 38.9 | | | EBIT/Interest | 8.6 | 11.4 |
| | | (19) 12.8 | (15) 4.3 | | | | (45) 3.6 | (48) 4.2 |
| | | 2.9 | -.1 | | | | 1.1 | 1.5 |
| | | | | | | Net Profit + Depr., Dep., Amort./Cur. Mat. L/T/D | 2.6 | 4.0 |
| | | | | | | | (20) 2.2 | (19) 2.3 |
| | | | | | | | 1.1 | 1.6 |
| | | .1 | .2 | | | Fixed/Worth | .2 | .2 |
| | | .4 | .6 | | | | .6 | .7 |
| | | 1.6 | 1.2 | | | | 1.5 | 1.6 |
| | | .2 | .5 | | | Debt/Worth | .5 | .9 |
| | | .7 | 1.1 | | | | 1.1 | 1.6 |
| | | 2.4 | 2.8 | | | | 3.3 | 3.8 |
| | | 64.3 | 55.3 | | | % Profit Before Taxes/Tangible Net Worth | 45.6 | 46.3 |
| | | (21) 32.1 | (17) 21.1 | | | | (52) 13.3 | (48) 19.9 |
| | | 11.1 | .2 | | | | .9 | 3.3 |
| | | 36.6 | 21.0 | | | % Profit Before Taxes/Total Assets | 18.1 | 16.3 |
| | | 10.5 | 10.1 | | | | 5.3 | 6.7 |
| | | 5.5 | -4.1 | | | | .5 | 1.9 |
| | | 32.4 | 31.3 | | | Sales/Net Fixed Assets | 39.0 | 28.2 |
| | | 9.1 | 9.3 | | | | 8.5 | 9.7 |
| | | 5.5 | 4.8 | | | | 3.9 | 5.2 |
| | | 2.7 | 1.7 | | | Sales/Total Assets | 2.7 | 2.3 |
| | | 2.1 | 1.4 | | | | 1.8 | 1.8 |
| | | 1.6 | 1.2 | | | | 1.2 | 1.3 |
| | | 1.5 | 1.1 | | | % Depr., Dep., Amort./Sales | .8 | .7 |
| | | (18) 2.5 | (15) 2.4 | | | | (53) 3.0 | (45) 2.2 |
| | | 4.5 | 6.9 | | | | 5.0 | 4.1 |
| | | 1.4 | | | | % Officers', Directors' Owners' Comp/Sales | 2.2 | 1.3 |
| | | (13) 4.1 | | | | | (18) 3.1 | (14) 3.5 |
| | | 6.6 | | | | | 5.7 | 11.6 |
| | 21620M | 222871M | 523537M | 803700M | 138964M | Net Sales ($) | 1946228M | 2396070M |
| | 6393M | 108522M | 332308M | 519760M | 175885M | Total Assets ($) | 1332204M | 1516911M |

*(The 0-500M column is marked: DATA NOT AVAILABLE)*

M = $ thousand    MM = $ million
See Pages 9 through 22 for Explanation of Ratios and Data

## Comparative Historical Data  ·  Current Data Sorted by Sales

| Type of Statement | 4/1/09-3/31/10 ALL | 4/1/10-3/31/11 ALL | 4/1/11-3/31/12 ALL | | 0-1MM | 1-3MM | 3-5MM | 5-10MM | 10-25MM | 25MM & OVER |
|---|---|---|---|---|---|---|---|---|---|---|
| Unqualified | 13 | 14 | 13 | | | | | 1 | 6 | 6 |
| Reviewed | 16 | 19 | 9 | | | 2 | | 4 | 2 | 1 |
| Compiled | 5 | 5 | 3 | | 1 | 1 | | | 1 | |
| Tax Returns | 5 | 6 | 6 | | | 3 | 1 | | 2 | |
| Other | 23 | 26 | 23 | | 1 | 1 | | 4 | 10 | 7 |
| | | | | | 13 (4/1-9/30/11) | | 41 (10/1/11-3/31/12) | | | |
| **NUMBER OF STATEMENTS** | 62 | 70 | 54 | | 2 | 8 | | 9 | 21 | 14 |
| | % | % | % | **ASSETS** | % | % | % | % | % | % |
| Cash & Equivalents | 11.2 | 11.8 | 10.7 | | | | | | 11.6 | 7.8 |
| Trade Receivables (net) | 21.6 | 21.7 | 22.0 | | | | | | 23.6 | 18.7 |
| Inventory | 28.6 | 25.6 | 26.8 | | | | | | 27.9 | 27.0 |
| All Other Current | 2.7 | 2.7 | 3.2 | | | | | | 2.7 | 2.7 |
| Total Current | 64.1 | 61.7 | 62.7 | | | | | | 65.8 | 56.2 |
| Fixed Assets (net) | 22.9 | 22.2 | 24.2 | | | | | | 23.5 | 25.3 |
| Intangibles (net) | 8.5 | 8.5 | 7.2 | | | | | | 5.7 | 13.9 |
| All Other Non-Current | 4.4 | 7.6 | 5.9 | | | | | | 5.0 | 4.7 |
| Total | 100.0 | 100.0 | 100.0 | | | | | | 100.0 | 100.0 |
| | | | | **LIABILITIES** | | | | | | |
| Notes Payable-Short Term | 7.8 | 6.9 | 6.1 | | | | | | 4.1 | 4.4 |
| Cur. Mat.-L.T.D. | 2.9 | 2.1 | 3.6 | | | | | | 3.6 | 3.9 |
| Trade Payables | 12.4 | 11.6 | 11.6 | | | | | | 12.7 | 7.3 |
| Income Taxes Payable | .2 | .3 | .3 | | | | | | .5 | .6 |
| All Other Current | 10.9 | 12.2 | 9.4 | | | | | | 8.8 | 14.0 |
| Total Current | 34.2 | 33.1 | 31.0 | | | | | | 29.6 | 30.2 |
| Long-Term Debt | 11.3 | 14.8 | 15.4 | | | | | | 21.2 | 8.5 |
| Deferred Taxes | .9 | .5 | .5 | | | | | | .1 | 1.7 |
| All Other Non-Current | 6.0 | 9.9 | 2.9 | | | | | | 2.2 | 6.9 |
| Net Worth | 47.6 | 41.7 | 50.1 | | | | | | 46.8 | 52.7 |
| Total Liabilities & Net Worth | 100.0 | 100.0 | 100.0 | | | | | | 100.0 | 100.0 |
| | | | | **INCOME DATA** | | | | | | |
| Net Sales | 100.0 | 100.0 | 100.0 | | | | | | 100.0 | 100.0 |
| Gross Profit | 36.8 | 40.3 | 37.5 | | | | | | 32.5 | 39.9 |
| Operating Expenses | 31.8 | 33.0 | 31.1 | | | | | | 28.6 | 29.2 |
| Operating Profit | 5.0 | 7.2 | 6.4 | | | | | | 4.0 | 10.7 |
| All Other Expenses (net) | 1.5 | .9 | .4 | | | | | | .4 | .9 |
| Profit Before Taxes | 3.4 | 6.3 | 6.1 | | | | | | 3.6 | 9.7 |
| | | | | **RATIOS** | | | | | | |
| Current | 3.4 | 3.4 | 3.1 | | | | | | 4.1 | 2.9 |
| | 2.0 | 1.9 | 1.9 | | | | | | 2.4 | 1.8 |
| | 1.4 | 1.4 | 1.5 | | | | | | 1.6 | 1.5 |
| Quick | 1.6 | 1.8 | 1.7 | | | | | | 1.8 | 1.2 |
| | 1.0 | 1.0 | 1.0 | | | | | | 1.5 | .8 |
| | .6 | .6 | .5 | | | | | | .7 | .5 |
| Sales/Receivables | 34  10.7 | 36  10.1 | 30  12.3 | | | | | | 32  11.3 | 29  12.6 |
| | 42  8.6 | 49  7.5 | 42  8.6 | | | | | | 46  8.0 | 43  8.5 |
| | 53  6.9 | 59  6.2 | 53  6.9 | | | | | | 66  5.5 | 54  6.8 |
| Cost of Sales/Inventory | 53  6.9 | 51  7.2 | 48  7.6 | | | | | | 52  7.0 | 68  5.4 |
| | 92  4.0 | 92  4.0 | 87  4.2 | | | | | | 87  4.2 | 111  3.3 |
| | 140  2.6 | 135  2.7 | 126  2.9 | | | | | | 130  2.8 | 126  2.9 |
| Cost of Sales/Payables | 14  26.5 | 20  18.1 | 19  18.9 | | | | | | 20  18.0 | 16  23.0 |
| | 29  12.7 | 39  9.5 | 31  11.9 | | | | | | 31  11.8 | 24  15.1 |
| | 49  7.4 | 56  6.5 | 44  8.3 | | | | | | 56  6.5 | 35  10.4 |
| Sales/Working Capital | 3.6 | 3.4 | 3.7 | | | | | | 3.2 | 4.0 |
| | 6.2 | 5.8 | 6.1 | | | | | | 5.8 | 6.1 |
| | 10.9 | 16.3 | 12.5 | | | | | | 12.0 | 9.3 |
| EBIT/Interest | 8.9 | 14.2 | 45.0 | | | | | | 31.5 | 47.3 |
| | (49)  3.8 | (57)  6.2 | (44)  10.5 | | | | | | (16)  4.7 | (11)  23.9 |
| | 2.5 | 1.7 | 2.4 | | | | | | 1.6 | 10.2 |
| Net Profit + Depr., Dep., Amort./Cur. Mat. L/T/D | 3.4 | 11.1 | 14.7 | | | | | | | |
| | (16)  2.7 | (22)  5.9 | (14)  4.7 | | | | | | | |
| | 1.6 | 2.6 | 2.1 | | | | | | | |
| Fixed/Worth | .2 | .2 | .2 | | | | | | .2 | .5 |
| | .5 | .5 | .5 | | | | | | .4 | .7 |
| | 1.2 | 1.6 | 1.2 | | | | | | 1.5 | 1.1 |
| Debt/Worth | .5 | .7 | .4 | | | | | | .3 | .9 |
| | 1.2 | 1.2 | 1.0 | | | | | | .7 | 1.2 |
| | 3.0 | 3.8 | 2.3 | | | | | | 4.1 | 1.9 |
| % Profit Before Taxes/Tangible Net Worth | 38.3 | 48.9 | 50.5 | | | | | | 43.0 | 104.0 |
| | (59)  15.5 | (61)  21.6 | (50)  26.1 | | | | | | (19)  21.1 | 34.3 |
| | 3.3 | 5.2 | 6.5 | | | | | | 4.4 | 21.1 |
| % Profit Before Taxes/Total Assets | 9.5 | 17.3 | 23.1 | | | | | | 18.4 | 20.4 |
| | 6.0 | 9.7 | 10.5 | | | | | | 9.6 | 12.0 |
| | .9 | 1.8 | 2.7 | | | | | | -.4 | 10.1 |
| Sales/Net Fixed Assets | 29.5 | 28.5 | 24.0 | | | | | | 30.1 | 9.8 |
| | 10.1 | 8.7 | 8.5 | | | | | | 9.5 | 5.9 |
| | 4.2 | 4.9 | 5.5 | | | | | | 5.0 | 4.8 |
| Sales/Total Assets | 2.3 | 2.1 | 2.5 | | | | | | 2.0 | 2.1 |
| | 1.8 | 1.7 | 1.8 | | | | | | 1.6 | 1.5 |
| | 1.2 | 1.3 | 1.4 | | | | | | 1.4 | 1.0 |
| % Depr., Dep., Amort./Sales | 1.5 | 1.4 | 1.3 | | | | | | 1.5 | 1.2 |
| | (50)  3.3 | (57)  2.6 | (44)  2.5 | | | | | | (15)  2.5 | (12)  3.5 |
| | 4.8 | 5.8 | 4.2 | | | | | | 5.1 | 5.8 |
| % Officers', Directors' Owners' Comp/Sales | 1.5 | 2.9 | 1.8 | | | | | | | |
| | (20)  5.0 | (25)  4.3 | (19)  4.1 | | | | | | | |
| | 8.8 | 7.2 | 7.5 | | | | | | | |
| Net Sales ($) | 2381115M | 2371571M | 1710692M | | 3591M | 35658M | | 61188M | 342355M | 1267900M |
| Total Assets ($) | 1425778M | 1615438M | 1142868M | | 1962M | 23556M | | 28063M | 213857M | 875430M |

(Data for the 0-1MM, 1-3MM, 3-5MM, and 5-10MM size ranges in the ASSETS, LIABILITIES, INCOME DATA, and RATIOS sections are marked "DATA NOT AVAILABLE.")

M = $ thousand    MM = $ million
See Pages 9 through 22 for Explanation of Ratios and Data

## Current Data Sorted by Assets     Comparative Historical Data

| 0-500M | 500M-2MM | 2-10MM | 10-50MM | 50-100MM | 100-250MM | Type of Statement | 4/1/07-3/31/08 ALL | 4/1/08-3/31/09 ALL |
|---|---|---|---|---|---|---|---|---|
| | | 7 | 19 | 7 | 3 | Unqualified | 31 | 39 |
| | 10 | 30 | 11 | | | Reviewed | 44 | 50 |
| 2 | 11 | 24 | 3 | | | Compiled | 34 | 43 |
| 3 | 12 | 10 | 2 | | | Tax Returns | 15 | 49 |
| 5 | 17 | 24 | 21 | 4 | 4 | Other | 63 | 88 |
| | 35 (4/1-9/30/11) | | 194 (10/1/11-3/31/12) | | | | | |
| 10 | 50 | 95 | 56 | 11 | 7 | **NUMBER OF STATEMENTS** | 187 | 269 |
| % | % | % | % | % | % | **ASSETS** | % | % |
| 16.2 | 12.3 | 11.7 | 10.2 | 4.3 | | Cash & Equivalents | 9.5 | 9.8 |
| 37.9 | 30.7 | 28.0 | 27.0 | 22.2 | | Trade Receivables (net) | 27.0 | 26.5 |
| 19.9 | 31.2 | 25.1 | 24.8 | 19.5 | | Inventory | 28.2 | 28.2 |
| 2.3 | .9 | 5.3 | 4.5 | 10.5 | | All Other Current | 3.8 | 3.0 |
| 76.4 | 75.1 | 70.0 | 66.6 | 56.5 | | Total Current | 68.5 | 67.6 |
| 17.4 | 16.1 | 17.9 | 17.9 | 26.4 | | Fixed Assets (net) | 18.5 | 20.2 |
| 1.6 | 4.7 | 6.0 | 8.1 | 15.3 | | Intangibles (net) | 6.1 | 5.8 |
| 4.6 | 4.1 | 6.1 | 7.3 | 1.8 | | All Other Non-Current | 6.9 | 6.4 |
| 100.0 | 100.0 | 100.0 | 100.0 | 100.0 | | Total | 100.0 | 100.0 |
| | | | | | | **LIABILITIES** | | |
| 8.9 | 12.5 | 8.0 | 9.4 | 4.9 | | Notes Payable-Short Term | 11.7 | 10.4 |
| 1.2 | 4.4 | 3.1 | 2.4 | 3.9 | | Cur. Mat.-L.T.D. | 5.4 | 5.4 |
| 14.6 | 18.8 | 15.7 | 11.9 | 8.9 | | Trade Payables | 16.4 | 16.1 |
| .0 | .1 | .2 | .2 | .3 | | Income Taxes Payable | .3 | .4 |
| 11.6 | 13.4 | 14.3 | 15.1 | 20.0 | | All Other Current | 16.7 | 13.7 |
| 36.3 | 49.2 | 41.3 | 39.0 | 38.1 | | Total Current | 50.5 | 46.0 |
| 7.1 | 17.5 | 10.5 | 11.2 | 16.4 | | Long-Term Debt | 17.9 | 15.4 |
| .0 | .0 | .5 | .8 | .6 | | Deferred Taxes | .4 | .4 |
| 35.6 | 7.6 | 6.2 | 3.2 | 10.7 | | All Other Non-Current | 5.4 | 5.2 |
| 21.0 | 25.7 | 41.5 | 45.8 | 34.2 | | Net Worth | 25.8 | 33.0 |
| 100.0 | 100.0 | 100.0 | 100.0 | 100.0 | | Total Liabilities & Net Worth | 100.0 | 100.0 |
| | | | | | | **INCOME DATA** | | |
| 100.0 | 100.0 | 100.0 | 100.0 | 100.0 | | Net Sales | 100.0 | 100.0 |
| 33.9 | 36.1 | 34.9 | 29.7 | 30.3 | | Gross Profit | 31.8 | 32.3 |
| 25.1 | 31.2 | 29.7 | 23.1 | 24.8 | | Operating Expenses | 27.9 | 28.7 |
| 8.8 | 4.9 | 5.2 | 6.6 | 5.5 | | Operating Profit | 4.0 | 3.7 |
| 1.0 | .8 | .7 | .6 | 1.4 | | All Other Expenses (net) | 1.2 | 1.2 |
| 7.8 | 4.1 | 4.5 | 5.9 | 4.0 | | Profit Before Taxes | 2.8 | 2.5 |
| | | | | | | **RATIOS** | | |
| 3.7 | 3.3 | 2.7 | 2.7 | 1.9 | | Current | 2.2 | 2.6 |
| 3.0 | 1.6 | 1.7 | 1.6 | 1.6 | | | 1.5 | 1.6 |
| 1.2 | 1.1 | 1.2 | 1.2 | 1.2 | | | 1.1 | 1.1 |
| 3.2 | 1.9 | 1.4 | 1.7 | .8 | | Quick | 1.3 | 1.5 |
| 1.9 | 1.0 | 1.0 | .9 | .7 | | | (186) .8 | .8 |
| .8 | .6 | .6 | .6 | .6 | | | .5 | .5 |
| 5 81.0 | 26 14.2 | 32 11.4 | 33 11.1 | 46 8.0 | | Sales/Receivables | 29 12.6 | 28 12.8 |
| 13 28.0 | 38 9.6 | 45 8.1 | 51 7.2 | 51 7.1 | | | 43 8.5 | 41 9.0 |
| 45 8.1 | 51 7.2 | 65 5.6 | 65 5.6 | 72 5.1 | | | 58 6.3 | 55 6.6 |
| 1 291.3 | 29 12.7 | 27 13.3 | 30 12.2 | 21 17.7 | | Cost of Sales/Inventory | 29 12.5 | 29 12.5 |
| 8 45.1 | 69 5.3 | 61 6.0 | 61 6.0 | 94 3.9 | | | 64 5.7 | 61 6.0 |
| 72 5.1 | 114 3.2 | 101 3.6 | 122 3.0 | 122 3.0 | | | 102 3.6 | 103 3.5 |
| 5 76.6 | 13 27.1 | 23 16.1 | 13 28.5 | 17 21.7 | | Cost of Sales/Payables | 18 20.5 | 16 23.0 |
| 15 24.0 | 31 11.8 | 37 9.8 | 27 13.3 | 33 11.2 | | | 33 11.1 | 30 12.2 |
| 26 13.8 | 54 6.8 | 55 6.6 | 50 7.3 | 43 8.5 | | | 53 6.9 | 48 7.7 |
| 9.7 | 4.6 | 4.3 | 4.0 | 6.0 | | Sales/Working Capital | 5.7 | 5.2 |
| 16.3 | 10.1 | 7.3 | 6.2 | 9.5 | | | 9.7 | 9.6 |
| UND | 38.5 | 18.2 | 18.0 | 19.3 | | | 42.7 | 79.2 |
| | 18.3 | 12.9 | 43.2 | 6.9 | | EBIT/Interest | 11.7 | 13.9 |
| | (43) 5.6 | (80) 5.1 | (50) 10.8 | 4.1 | | | (168) 3.3 | (234) 3.8 |
| | 1.9 | 1.2 | 4.3 | 2.5 | | | .8 | .8 |
| | | 20.8 | 117.9 | | | Net Profit + Depr., Dep., | 6.8 | 7.1 |
| | (20) 2.2 | (19) 11.8 | | | | Amort./Cur. Mat. L/T/D | (58) 2.9 | (71) 1.6 |
| | .7 | 1.8 | | | | | .8 | .4 |
| .0 | .1 | .1 | .2 | .7 | | Fixed/Worth | .2 | .2 |
| .1 | .4 | .4 | .4 | 1.2 | | | .6 | .5 |
| 2.3 | 1.7 | 1.2 | .8 | 10.3 | | | 2.2 | 2.0 |
| .4 | .9 | .7 | .5 | 1.8 | | Debt/Worth | 1.0 | .8 |
| 2.4 | 1.8 | 1.7 | 1.7 | 2.7 | | | 2.5 | 2.1 |
| NM | 28.0 | 4.3 | 3.3 | 20.8 | | | 11.1 | 6.9 |
| | 90.5 | 47.2 | 43.5 | | | % Profit Before Taxes/Tangible | 54.7 | 45.2 |
| | (39) 28.5 | (88) 23.1 | (53) 26.8 | | | Net Worth | (148) 21.2 | (222) 22.3 |
| | 9.9 | 3.2 | 13.3 | | | | 2.6 | 8.3 |
| 57.3 | 21.2 | 15.4 | 17.1 | 10.9 | | % Profit Before Taxes/Total | 16.7 | 14.4 |
| 3.8 | 9.4 | 9.8 | 8.4 | 6.0 | | Assets | 6.4 | 6.4 |
| -17.9 | 1.1 | .9 | 3.6 | 2.2 | | | -.4 | -.4 |
| UND | 101.7 | 71.6 | 40.4 | 11.2 | | Sales/Net Fixed Assets | 36.4 | 36.6 |
| 153.9 | 31.3 | 18.2 | 12.0 | 7.3 | | | 15.9 | 16.0 |
| 23.3 | 10.2 | 5.9 | 6.6 | 5.0 | | | 7.2 | 7.5 |
| 11.4 | 3.6 | 2.5 | 2.2 | 1.9 | | Sales/Total Assets | 2.9 | 3.0 |
| 4.4 | 2.6 | 1.9 | 1.6 | 1.5 | | | 2.2 | 2.3 |
| 2.1 | 2.2 | 1.4 | 1.2 | 1.1 | | | 1.5 | 1.6 |
| | .4 | .5 | .7 | | | % Depr., Dep., Amort./Sales | .8 | .8 |
| | (35) 1.3 | (75) 1.4 | (47) 1.6 | | | | (157) 1.5 | (224) 1.4 |
| | 3.3 | 2.9 | 2.7 | | | | 2.8 | 2.8 |
| | 3.3 | 2.1 | | | | % Officers', Directors' | 1.9 | 2.5 |
| | (22) 4.6 | (34) 3.5 | | | | Owners' Comp/Sales | (56) 4.5 | (100) 4.9 |
| | 6.6 | 6.4 | | | | | 10.2 | 8.5 |
| 15585M | 206287M | 935844M | 2214134M | 1120111M | 1342436M | Net Sales ($) | 4785446M | 7543137M |
| 2648M | 64500M | 433161M | 1250744M | 740742M | 1202341M | Total Assets ($) | 2715591M | 4072850M |

© RMA 2012

**M = $ thousand    MM = $ million**
See Pages 9 through 22 for Explanation of Ratios and Data

## Comparative Historical Data | Current Data Sorted by Sales

| H: 4/1/09-3/31/10 ALL | H: 4/1/10-3/31/11 ALL | H: 4/1/11-3/31/12 ALL | Type of Statement | 0-1MM | 1-3MM | 3-5MM | 5-10MM | 10-25MM | 25MM & OVER |
|---|---|---|---|---|---|---|---|---|---|
| 35 | 33 | 36 | Unqualified | | | 1 | 3 | 7 | 25 |
| 59 | 39 | 51 | Reviewed | 1 | 3 | 9 | 12 | 19 | 7 |
| 51 | 27 | 40 | Compiled | | 10 | 11 | 13 | 3 | 3 |
| 67 | 27 | 27 | Tax Returns | 1 | 7 | 6 | 6 | 6 | 1 |
| 107 | 87 | 75 | Other | 3 | 6 | 12 | 15 | 18 | 21 |
| | | | | | 35 (4/1-9/30/11) | | 194 (10/1/11-3/31/12) | | |
| 319 | 213 | 229 | **NUMBER OF STATEMENTS** | 5 | 26 | 39 | 49 | 53 | 57 |
| % | % | % | **ASSETS** | % | % | % | % | % | % |
| 10.6 | 11.1 | 11.1 | Cash & Equivalents | | 10.6 | 8.8 | 14.6 | 12.0 | 8.0 |
| 27.2 | 27.3 | 28.3 | Trade Receivables (net) | | 28.4 | 29.2 | 28.3 | 28.4 | 28.0 |
| 25.9 | 24.4 | 25.5 | Inventory | | 28.5 | 22.9 | 27.6 | 28.1 | 22.1 |
| 3.3 | 4.8 | 4.3 | All Other Current | | 1.8 | 5.0 | 3.6 | 4.1 | 5.8 |
| 66.9 | 67.6 | 69.1 | Total Current | | 69.5 | 66.0 | 74.0 | 72.6 | 64.0 |
| 20.6 | 19.9 | 17.9 | Fixed Assets (net) | | 15.1 | 20.9 | 16.9 | 15.3 | 19.1 |
| 4.8 | 5.4 | 6.7 | Intangibles (net) | | 7.9 | 8.1 | 3.8 | 7.1 | 8.0 |
| 7.7 | 7.1 | 6.2 | All Other Non-Current | | 7.6 | 5.0 | 5.3 | 5.1 | 8.9 |
| 100.0 | 100.0 | 100.0 | Total | | 100.0 | 100.0 | 100.0 | 100.0 | 100.0 |
| | | | **LIABILITIES** | | | | | | |
| 10.4 | 9.5 | 9.1 | Notes Payable-Short Term | | 9.3 | 13.4 | 9.3 | 7.4 | 7.5 |
| 3.6 | 3.1 | 3.2 | Cur. Mat.-L.T.D. | | 3.7 | 4.9 | 1.9 | 3.2 | 2.8 |
| 15.1 | 14.1 | 14.9 | Trade Payables | | 12.7 | 14.7 | 16.3 | 17.2 | 12.7 |
| .2 | .2 | .2 | Income Taxes Payable | | .1 | .1 | .2 | .1 | .3 |
| 11.4 | 14.8 | 14.4 | All Other Current | | 12.4 | 16.9 | 12.2 | 14.5 | 15.0 |
| 40.8 | 41.7 | 41.7 | Total Current | | 38.2 | 50.0 | 39.9 | 42.4 | 38.3 |
| 15.2 | 13.6 | 12.4 | Long-Term Debt | | 16.2 | 13.5 | 10.0 | 12.0 | 11.7 |
| .3 | .3 | .5 | Deferred Taxes | | .1 | .1 | .2 | .9 | .8 |
| 5.8 | 7.2 | 7.7 | All Other Non-Current | | 11.4 | 11.6 | 5.5 | 4.5 | 7.0 |
| 37.9 | 37.1 | 37.7 | Net Worth | | 34.2 | 24.7 | 44.4 | 40.2 | 42.1 |
| 100.0 | 100.0 | 100.0 | Total Liabilities & Net Worth | | 100.0 | 100.0 | 100.0 | 100.0 | 100.0 |
| | | | **INCOME DATA** | | | | | | |
| 100.0 | 100.0 | 100.0 | Net Sales | | 100.0 | 100.0 | 100.0 | 100.0 | 100.0 |
| 33.9 | 34.8 | 33.4 | Gross Profit | | 37.3 | 38.2 | 35.8 | 30.1 | 29.8 |
| 31.3 | 29.0 | 27.7 | Operating Expenses | | 32.5 | 33.3 | 28.9 | 25.1 | 22.7 |
| 2.6 | 5.8 | 5.7 | Operating Profit | | 4.8 | 4.9 | 6.9 | 5.0 | 7.1 |
| .8 | .7 | .7 | All Other Expenses (net) | | 1.2 | .8 | .2 | .7 | .8 |
| 1.9 | 5.0 | 5.0 | Profit Before Taxes | | 3.6 | 4.1 | 6.6 | 4.4 | 6.3 |
| | | | **RATIOS** | | | | | | |
| 2.8 | 3.1 | 2.8 | Current | | 3.7 | 2.1 | 3.2 | 2.8 | 2.5 |
| 1.7 | 1.7 | 1.6 | | | 2.5 | 1.5 | 1.7 | 1.7 | 1.5 |
| 1.1 | 1.2 | 1.2 | | | 1.1 | 1.0 | 1.3 | 1.2 | 1.3 |
| 1.7 | 1.9 | 1.6 | Quick | | 3.1 | 1.3 | 2.0 | 1.5 | 1.5 |
| .9 | .9 | 1.0 | | | 1.1 | .7 | 1.0 | 1.0 | .9 |
| .6 | .6 | .6 | | | .5 | .5 | .7 | .6 | .6 |
| 30  12.1 | 28  12.8 | 30  12.2 | Sales/Receivables | | 24  15.1 | 32  11.5 | 30  12.1 | 28  13.1 | 37  9.8 |
| 42  8.7 | 44  8.2 | 44  8.3 | | | 42  8.6 | 42  8.7 | 43  8.4 | 43  8.4 | 51  7.1 |
| 56  6.5 | 65  5.7 | 63  5.8 | | | 64  5.7 | 63  5.8 | 58  6.6 | 58  6.3 | 68  7.1 |
| 28  13.2 | 22  16.3 | 27  13.3 | Cost of Sales/Inventory | | 27  13.5 | 33  11.1 | 24  15.2 | 21  17.0 | 29  12.5 |
| 62  5.9 | 53  6.9 | 62  5.9 | | | 81  4.5 | 55  6.6 | 68  5.4 | 61  6.0 | 54  6.8 |
| 114  3.2 | 102  3.6 | 107  3.4 | | | 130  2.8 | 91  4.0 | 118  3.1 | 114  3.2 | 99  3.7 |
| 17  21.7 | 16  23.2 | 18  20.4 | Cost of Sales/Payables | | 15  23.8 | 28  13.1 | 18  20.6 | 18  19.8 | 17  21.8 |
| 30  12.2 | 29  12.5 | 32  11.3 | | | 30  12.1 | 41  9.0 | 37  9.9 | 33  11.0 | 28  13.2 |
| 52  7.0 | 50  7.4 | 53  6.9 | | | 57  6.4 | 55  6.6 | 56  6.5 | 52  7.0 | 43  8.5 |
| 4.7 | 4.5 | 4.6 | Sales/Working Capital | | 4.7 | 5.0 | 4.0 | 4.2 | 5.2 |
| 8.3 | 8.8 | 8.2 | | | 7.9 | 12.5 | 7.0 | 6.9 | 8.3 |
| 27.9 | 21.5 | 22.2 | | | 32.9 | 999.8 | 21.1 | 18.2 | 17.9 |
| 9.6 | 31.0 | 18.2 | EBIT/Interest | | 18.3 | 12.0 | 13.9 | 13.3 | 33.9 |
| (273) 2.9 | (177) 6.9 | (194) 5.7 | | | (20) 1.9 | (37) 4.1 | (40) 5.9 | (42) 8.6 | (53) 8.8 |
| .2 | 1.6 | 1.8 | | | -.6 | 1.6 | 1.2 | 3.7 | 3.7 |
| 7.5 | 16.8 | 17.8 | Net Profit + Depr., Dep., Amort./Cur. Mat. L/T/D | | | | | 3.9 | 68.1 |
| (61) 2.3 | (45) 2.8 | (51) 4.1 | | | | | | (12) 1.9 | (21) 10.6 |
| .5 | 1.3 | 1.5 | | | | | | .5 | 1.8 |
| .2 | .2 | .1 | Fixed/Worth | | .0 | .2 | .1 | .1 | .2 |
| .5 | .5 | .4 | | | .2 | .6 | .4 | .3 | .5 |
| 1.5 | 1.5 | 1.2 | | | 1.3 | 2.4 | .7 | 1.0 | 1.1 |
| .7 | .6 | .8 | Debt/Worth | | .5 | 1.1 | .5 | .7 | .8 |
| 1.8 | 1.6 | 1.8 | | | 1.8 | 1.8 | 1.5 | 1.7 | 2.1 |
| 4.7 | 4.4 | 4.8 | | | NM | 5.8 | 4.5 | 3.5 | 3.7 |
| 36.6 | 55.7 | 51.4 | % Profit Before Taxes/Tangible Net Worth | | 58.6 | 67.3 | 62.8 | 41.4 | 49.8 |
| (276) 15.2 | (187) 24.3 | (202) 25.7 | | | (20) 23.2 | (32) 29.4 | (46) 15.5 | (48) 26.0 | (52) 29.5 |
| .5 | 8.2 | 7.7 | | | 5.5 | 5.0 | 3.0 | 10.6 | 14.6 |
| 12.1 | 20.3 | 17.0 | % Profit Before Taxes/Total Assets | | 21.1 | 13.7 | 17.1 | 19.4 | 17.0 |
| 4.1 | 8.8 | 8.2 | | | 5.9 | 7.8 | 8.8 | 10.2 | 8.2 |
| -1.6 | 1.7 | 1.9 | | | -3.7 | .7 | .8 | 2.2 | 3.6 |
| 35.7 | 37.0 | 64.9 | Sales/Net Fixed Assets | | 449.8 | 53.0 | 96.6 | 107.8 | 33.0 |
| 15.8 | 15.1 | 16.3 | | | 16.6 | 18.2 | 26.9 | 22.4 | 10.0 |
| 6.1 | 6.5 | 6.9 | | | 6.2 | 7.0 | 6.8 | 7.5 | 6.7 |
| 2.9 | 2.8 | 2.7 | Sales/Total Assets | | 2.6 | 2.7 | 2.9 | 3.0 | 2.4 |
| 2.0 | 2.1 | 2.0 | | | 2.2 | 2.2 | 2.1 | 2.0 | 1.8 |
| 1.4 | 1.5 | 1.4 | | | 1.4 | 1.5 | 1.5 | 1.5 | 1.3 |
| .8 | 1.0 | .6 | % Depr., Dep., Amort./Sales | | .8 | .4 | .5 | .6 | .8 |
| (250) 1.9 | (171) 1.6 | (174) 1.5 | | | (17) 1.4 | (32) 1.4 | (38) 1.1 | (40) 1.3 | (45) 1.7 |
| 3.6 | 2.6 | 2.9 | | | 3.1 | 4.7 | 3.1 | 2.4 | 2.7 |
| 2.5 | 2.7 | 2.1 | % Officers', Directors' Owners' Comp/Sales | | 3.7 | 3.3 | 2.6 | 1.6 | |
| (130) 4.6 | (71) 4.6 | (69) 3.6 | | | (13) 4.4 | (16) 5.1 | (19) 3.5 | (13) 2.2 | |
| 7.8 | 7.9 | 6.1 | | | 8.3 | 10.5 | 6.2 | 3.5 | |
| 6335437M | 5627786M | 5834397M | Net Sales ($) | 2370M | 55419M | 154747M | 341810M | 840236M | 4439815M |
| 3752214M | 3095353M | 3694136M | Total Assets ($) | 2491M | 28928M | 88129M | 191469M | 446251M | 2936868M |

M = $ thousand    MM = $ million
See Pages 9 through 22 for Explanation of Ratios and Data

## Current Data Sorted by Assets       Comparative Historical Data

| 0-500M | 500M-2MM | 2-10MM | 10-50MM | 50-100MM | 100-250MM | Type of Statement | 4/1/07-3/31/08 ALL | 4/1/08-3/31/09 ALL |
|---|---|---|---|---|---|---|---|---|
| | | 2 | 1 | | 1 | Unqualified | 6 | 5 |
| | 2 | 5 | 1 | | | Reviewed | 6 | 3 |
| 1 | | 6 | | | | Compiled | 3 | 3 |
| 1 | 1 | | | | | Tax Returns | 2 | 4 |
| 1 | 2 | 4 | 5 | | 2 | Other | 7 | 10 |
| | | 5 (4/1-9/30/11) | | 30 (10/1/11-3/31/12) | | | 4/1/07- 3/31/08 | 4/1/08- 3/31/09 |
| 3 | 5 | 17 | 7 | | 3 | NUMBER OF STATEMENTS | 24 | 25 |
| % | % | % | % | % | % | **ASSETS** | % | % |
| | | 17.1 | | | | Cash & Equivalents | 8.2 | 9.0 |
| | | 30.7 | | | | Trade Receivables (net) | 27.2 | 29.4 |
| | | 18.4 | | | | Inventory | 23.7 | 19.7 |
| | | 5.4 | | | | All Other Current | 6.2 | 4.9 |
| | | 71.5 | | | | Total Current | 65.3 | 63.1 |
| | | 16.7 | | | | Fixed Assets (net) | 18.2 | 17.3 |
| | | 5.6 | | | | Intangibles (net) | 7.8 | 14.1 |
| | | 6.1 | | | | All Other Non-Current | 8.7 | 5.5 |
| | | 100.0 | | | | Total | 100.0 | 100.0 |
| | | | | | | **LIABILITIES** | | |
| | | 4.2 | | | | Notes Payable-Short Term | 9.6 | 11.8 |
| | | 3.0 | | | | Cur. Mat.-L.T.D. | 2.8 | 4.9 |
| | | 15.7 | | | | Trade Payables | 16.4 | 13.6 |
| | | .2 | | | | Income Taxes Payable | .6 | 1.8 |
| | | 16.4 | | | | All Other Current | 13.5 | 8.9 |
| | | 39.4 | | | | Total Current | 42.9 | 41.0 |
| | | 8.9 | | | | Long-Term Debt | 18.6 | 15.5 |
| | | .3 | | | | Deferred Taxes | 1.1 | .9 |
| | | 8.3 | | | | All Other Non-Current | 4.9 | 3.3 |
| | | 43.1 | | | | Net Worth | 32.5 | 39.4 |
| | | 100.0 | | | | Total Liabilities & Net Worth | 100.0 | 100.0 |
| | | | | | | **INCOME DATA** | | |
| | | 100.0 | | | | Net Sales | 100.0 | 100.0 |
| | | 29.3 | | | | Gross Profit | 35.6 | 31.0 |
| | | 22.6 | | | | Operating Expenses | 25.8 | 25.0 |
| | | 6.7 | | | | Operating Profit | 9.8 | 6.0 |
| | | 1.3 | | | | All Other Expenses (net) | 2.1 | 1.4 |
| | | 5.3 | | | | Profit Before Taxes | 7.7 | 4.6 |
| | | | | | | **RATIOS** | | |
| | | 5.2 | | | | Current | 2.8 | 3.6 |
| | | 1.9 | | | | | 1.9 | 1.4 |
| | | 1.0 | | | | | 1.0 | 1.0 |
| | | 3.6 | | | | Quick | 1.6 | 1.5 |
| | | 1.2 | | | | | .8 | .8 |
| | | .6 | | | | | .4 | .5 |
| | | 29   12.6 | | | | Sales/Receivables | 34   10.7 | 26   14.0 |
| | | 50   7.3 | | | | | 50   7.4 | 48   7.7 |
| | | 72   5.1 | | | | | 63   5.8 | 60   6.0 |
| | | 21   17.3 | | | | Cost of Sales/Inventory | 27   13.6 | 17   22.0 |
| | | 31   11.9 | | | | | 51   7.2 | 50   7.3 |
| | | 60   6.1 | | | | | 87   4.2 | 77   4.7 |
| | | 22   16.9 | | | | Cost of Sales/Payables | 15   24.8 | 14   26.4 |
| | | 32   11.4 | | | | | 44   8.3 | 29   12.6 |
| | | 44   8.3 | | | | | 58   6.2 | 45   8.2 |
| | | 3.0 | | | | Sales/Working Capital | 4.7 | 4.2 |
| | | 5.4 | | | | | 7.7 | 12.5 |
| | | 198.1 | | | | | NM | NM |
| | | 129.6 | | | | EBIT/Interest | 16.2 | 13.9 |
| | | (13)   4.8 | | | | | (22)   5.5 | (22)   5.2 |
| | | 2.5 | | | | | 1.7 | 1.2 |
| | | | | | | Net Profit + Depr., Dep., Amort./Cur. Mat. L/T/D | | |
| | | .1 | | | | Fixed/Worth | .2 | .2 |
| | | .6 | | | | | .6 | .7 |
| | | 1.0 | | | | | NM | -4.8 |
| | | .7 | | | | Debt/Worth | .7 | .7 |
| | | 1.7 | | | | | 2.5 | 3.7 |
| | | 3.4 | | | | | NM | -11.9 |
| | | 76.6 | | | | % Profit Before Taxes/Tangible Net Worth | 70.0 | 48.0 |
| | | (16)   18.5 | | | | | (18)   34.4 | (18)   22.4 |
| | | 6.2 | | | | | 19.2 | 10.8 |
| | | 21.2 | | | | % Profit Before Taxes/Total Assets | 20.9 | 15.7 |
| | | 10.3 | | | | | 13.6 | 6.8 |
| | | 3.4 | | | | | 3.6 | 2.3 |
| | | 77.1 | | | | Sales/Net Fixed Assets | 42.4 | 54.0 |
| | | 20.2 | | | | | 10.6 | 10.7 |
| | | 7.4 | | | | | 6.0 | 7.1 |
| | | 3.0 | | | | Sales/Total Assets | 2.5 | 2.9 |
| | | 2.3 | | | | | 2.1 | 2.0 |
| | | 1.5 | | | | | 1.3 | 1.3 |
| | | .2 | | | | % Depr., Dep., Amort./Sales | .5 | .7 |
| | | .9 | | | | | (22)   1.5 | (21)   1.6 |
| | | 1.3 | | | | | 2.3 | 2.3 |
| | | 2.0 | | | | % Officers', Directors' Owners' Comp/Sales | | |
| | | (10)   2.3 | | | | | | |
| | | 3.2 | | | | | | |
| 858M | 15961M | 214413M | 330407M | | 855486M | Net Sales ($) | 1294773M | 1527618M |
| 388M | 6075M | 99113M | 180495M | | 529040M | Total Assets ($) | 767970M | 926749M |

*Note: For the columns 10-50MM, 50-100MM and 100-250MM, the upper sections are marked "DATA NOT AVAILABLE."*

M = $ thousand    MM = $ million
See Pages 9 through 22 for Explanation of Ratios and Data

## Comparative Historical Data | Current Data Sorted by Sales

| | | | Type of Statement | | | | | | |
|---|---|---|---|---|---|---|---|---|---|
| 3 | 8 | 4 | Unqualified | | | | | 1 | 3 |
| 4 | 6 | 8 | Reviewed | | 1 | 1 | 2 | 3 | 1 |
| 2 | 5 | 7 | Compiled | 1 | | 1 | | 5 | |
| 2 | 4 | 2 | Tax Returns | 1 | 1 | 1 | | | |
| 6 | 7 | 14 | Other | 1 | 1 | 1 | 3 | 2 | 6 |
| 4/1/09-3/31/10 ALL | 4/1/10-3/31/11 ALL | 4/1/11-3/31/12 ALL | | 0-1MM | 1-3MM | 3-5MM | 5-10MM | 10-25MM | 25MM & OVER |
| | | | | | 5 (4/1-9/30/11) | | | 30 (10/1/11-3/31/12) | |
| 17 | 30 | 35 | NUMBER OF STATEMENTS | 3 | 2 | 4 | 5 | 11 | 10 |
| % | % | % | **ASSETS** | % | % | % | % | % | % |
| 9.5 | 16.4 | 18.5 | Cash & Equivalents | | | | | 10.2 | 17.0 |
| 23.6 | 26.1 | 26.8 | Trade Receivables (net) | | | | | 35.3 | 20.2 |
| 26.5 | 23.0 | 22.0 | Inventory | | | | | 19.8 | 19.1 |
| 4.0 | 5.6 | 4.3 | All Other Current | | | | | 7.8 | 4.4 |
| 63.7 | 71.0 | 71.5 | Total Current | | | | | 73.1 | 60.7 |
| 19.3 | 15.9 | 15.5 | Fixed Assets (net) | | | | | 13.6 | 22.5 |
| 5.4 | 5.8 | 5.7 | Intangibles (net) | | | | | 7.9 | 10.4 |
| 11.7 | 7.3 | 7.3 | All Other Non-Current | | | | | 5.3 | 6.4 |
| 100.0 | 100.0 | 100.0 | Total | | | | | 100.0 | 100.0 |
| | | | **LIABILITIES** | | | | | | |
| 6.2 | 4.9 | 5.0 | Notes Payable-Short Term | | | | | 6.3 | 4.9 |
| 1.9 | 1.4 | 2.0 | Cur. Mat.-L.T.D. | | | | | 1.9 | 3.8 |
| 11.4 | 11.8 | 13.9 | Trade Payables | | | | | 21.2 | 10.7 |
| .6 | .3 | .3 | Income Taxes Payable | | | | | .2 | .7 |
| 7.1 | 14.6 | 15.7 | All Other Current | | | | | 19.5 | 16.4 |
| 27.1 | 33.1 | 36.9 | Total Current | | | | | 49.2 | 36.4 |
| 19.0 | 15.0 | 10.3 | Long-Term Debt | | | | | 9.4 | 11.8 |
| 1.0 | .7 | .3 | Deferred Taxes | | | | | .5 | .7 |
| 4.7 | 3.4 | 4.6 | All Other Non-Current | | | | | 6.1 | 3.0 |
| 48.1 | 47.9 | 47.9 | Net Worth | | | | | 34.7 | 48.2 |
| 100.0 | 100.0 | 100.0 | Total Liabilities & Net Worth | | | | | 100.0 | 100.0 |
| | | | **INCOME DATA** | | | | | | |
| 100.0 | 100.0 | 100.0 | Net Sales | | | | | 100.0 | 100.0 |
| 33.9 | 33.6 | 31.3 | Gross Profit | | | | | 28.0 | 27.1 |
| 27.8 | 26.7 | 24.1 | Operating Expenses | | | | | 23.2 | 19.1 |
| 6.0 | 6.9 | 7.2 | Operating Profit | | | | | 4.8 | 8.0 |
| .7 | .3 | 1.0 | All Other Expenses (net) | | | | | .2 | 1.4 |
| 5.4 | 6.7 | 6.3 | Profit Before Taxes | | | | | 4.6 | 6.6 |
| | | | **RATIOS** | | | | | | |
| 5.2 | 3.3 | 4.0 | | | | | | 2.3 | 2.2 |
| 2.2 | 2.0 | 1.9 | Current | | | | | 1.2 | 1.8 |
| 1.4 | 1.4 | 1.2 | | | | | | 1.0 | 1.3 |
| 2.7 | 1.7 | 2.6 | | | | | | 1.6 | 1.4 |
| 1.0 | 1.3 | 1.1 | Quick | | | | | .8 | 1.1 |
| .5 | .7 | .6 | | | | | | .6 | .5 |
| 23  16.1 | 29  12.5 | 29  12.4 | | | | | | 29  12.4 | 27  13.3 |
| 48  7.7 | 46  7.9 | 46  8.0 | Sales/Receivables | | | | | 54  6.7 | 41  9.0 |
| 61  5.9 | 60  6.1 | 62  5.9 | | | | | | 60  6.1 | 58  6.3 |
| 38  9.6 | 19  19.5 | 21  17.8 | | | | | | 21  17.8 | 21  17.7 |
| 63  5.8 | 63  5.8 | 34  10.6 | Cost of Sales/Inventory | | | | | 30  12.2 | 39  9.3 |
| 93  3.9 | 96  3.8 | 74  4.9 | | | | | | 48  7.6 | 107  3.4 |
| 13  28.4 | 14  25.9 | 19  19.4 | | | | | | 31  11.6 | 21  17.2 |
| 22  16.5 | 31  11.9 | 32  11.4 | Cost of Sales/Payables | | | | | 42  8.7 | 31  11.7 |
| 51  7.2 | 48  7.6 | 43  8.5 | | | | | | 55  6.6 | 34  10.6 |
| 4.0 | 3.0 | 3.7 | | | | | | 4.4 | 4.8 |
| 5.6 | 6.1 | 7.0 | Sales/Working Capital | | | | | 12.7 | 7.6 |
| 11.0 | 13.1 | 15.1 | | | | | | 203.4 | 13.9 |
| 17.0 | 24.7 | 49.3 | | | | | | | |
| (15)  5.6 | (23)  3.3 | (27)  17.1 | EBIT/Interest | | | | | | |
| 1.5 | .9 | 2.4 | | | | | | | |
| | | 21.7 | | | | | | | |
| | | (12)  3.1 | Net Profit + Depr., Dep., Amort./Cur. Mat. L/T/D | | | | | | |
| | | 1.5 | | | | | | | |
| .2 | .0 | .1 | | | | | | .1 | .1 |
| .3 | .2 | .3 | Fixed/Worth | | | | | .7 | .4 |
| 1.7 | 1.1 | .8 | | | | | | 1.3 | 1.5 |
| .3 | .4 | .6 | | | | | | 1.2 | .7 |
| 1.2 | 1.2 | 1.2 | Debt/Worth | | | | | 2.6 | 1.2 |
| 4.8 | 3.5 | 2.6 | | | | | | 4.5 | 2.4 |
| 28.4 | 37.6 | 88.1 | | | | | | 98.3 | 96.1 |
| (14)  20.2 | (27)  18.1 | (33)  19.2 | % Profit Before Taxes/Tangible Net Worth | | | | (10)  39.4 | | 28.2 |
| 11.7 | 5.2 | 2.7 | | | | | | 7.1 | 2.6 |
| 12.0 | 15.7 | 26.5 | | | | | | 21.8 | 29.7 |
| 7.1 | 8.7 | 11.0 | % Profit Before Taxes/Total Assets | | | | | 12.1 | 11.7 |
| 3.8 | 1.4 | 2.1 | | | | | | 4.1 | 1.2 |
| 39.8 | 73.3 | 61.3 | | | | | | 92.9 | 24.3 |
| 8.6 | 13.5 | 20.2 | Sales/Net Fixed Assets | | | | | 21.4 | 9.4 |
| 4.6 | 7.1 | 7.6 | | | | | | 8.5 | 6.0 |
| 2.8 | 2.8 | 2.7 | | | | | | 3.3 | 2.5 |
| 1.9 | 1.9 | 2.3 | Sales/Total Assets | | | | | 2.3 | 2.1 |
| 1.0 | 1.3 | 1.4 | | | | | | 1.8 | 1.1 |
| .6 | .3 | .3 | | | | | | .3 | |
| (13)  1.4 | (25)  1.5 | (29)  .9 | % Depr., Dep., Amort./Sales | | | | | .9 | |
| 2.9 | 2.3 | 1.7 | | | | | | 1.0 | |
| | 1.6 | 1.9 | | | | | | | |
| | (10)  5.6 | (13)  2.3 | % Officers', Directors' Owners' Comp/Sales | | | | | | |
| | 8.4 | 5.1 | | | | | | | |
| 558891M | 1394070M | 1417125M | Net Sales ($) | 858M | 3670M | 16644M | 41953M | 147116M | 1206884M |
| 477347M | 783247M | 815111M | Total Assets ($) | 388M | 2555M | 8054M | 39180M | 61606M | 703328M |

M = $ thousand    MM = $ million
See Pages 9 through 22 for Explanation of Ratios and Data

## Current Data Sorted by Assets   |   Comparative Historical Data

### Type of Statement

| 0-500M | 500M-2MM | 2-10MM | 10-50MM | 50-100MM | 100-250MM | Type of Statement | 4/1/07-3/31/08 ALL | 4/1/08-3/31/09 ALL |
|---|---|---|---|---|---|---|---|---|
|  |  | 1 | 4 | 1 | 3 | Unqualified | 14 | 8 |
|  | 2 | 3 | 4 |  | 1 | Reviewed | 7 | 10 |
|  |  | 7 |  |  |  | Compiled | 8 | 9 |
|  | 3 | 2 |  |  |  | Tax Returns | 4 | 8 |
| 1 |  | 6 | 8 |  | 2 | Other | 13 | 21 |
|  | 7 (4/1-9/30/11) |  | 41 (10/1/11-3/31/12) |  |  |  |  |  |
| 1 | 5 | 19 | 16 | 1 | 6 | **NUMBER OF STATEMENTS** | 46 | 56 |

### Main Data

| 0-500M % | 500M-2MM % | 2-10MM % | 10-50MM % | 50-100MM % | 100-250MM % | | 4/1/07-3/31/08 ALL % | 4/1/08-3/31/09 ALL % |
|---|---|---|---|---|---|---|---|---|
|  |  |  |  |  |  | **ASSETS** |  |  |
|  |  | 13.7 | 13.6 |  |  | Cash & Equivalents | 9.8 | 12.2 |
|  |  | 33.0 | 26.7 |  |  | Trade Receivables (net) | 27.8 | 27.6 |
|  |  | 26.9 | 14.5 |  |  | Inventory | 21.3 | 23.6 |
|  |  | 7.5 | 4.0 |  |  | All Other Current | 3.2 | 2.1 |
|  |  | 81.1 | 58.8 |  |  | Total Current | 62.1 | 65.5 |
|  |  | 13.7 | 22.4 |  |  | Fixed Assets (net) | 24.4 | 24.1 |
|  |  | .8 | 7.0 |  |  | Intangibles (net) | 7.3 | 6.0 |
|  |  | 4.3 | 11.8 |  |  | All Other Non-Current | 6.3 | 4.3 |
|  |  | 100.0 | 100.0 |  |  | Total | 100.0 | 100.0 |
|  |  |  |  |  |  | **LIABILITIES** |  |  |
|  |  | 6.5 | 10.3 |  |  | Notes Payable-Short Term | 7.5 | 9.0 |
|  |  | 2.0 | 1.1 |  |  | Cur. Mat.-L.T.D. | 2.2 | 1.6 |
|  |  | 14.5 | 9.5 |  |  | Trade Payables | 14.7 | 14.4 |
|  |  | .5 | .4 |  |  | Income Taxes Payable | .5 | .4 |
|  |  | 20.4 | 12.9 |  |  | All Other Current | 15.1 | 13.7 |
|  |  | 43.9 | 34.2 |  |  | Total Current | 40.0 | 39.1 |
|  |  | 3.9 | 11.5 |  |  | Long-Term Debt | 13.7 | 14.9 |
|  |  | .3 | .5 |  |  | Deferred Taxes | .8 | .5 |
|  |  | 12.3 | 5.7 |  |  | All Other Non-Current | 7.1 | 8.9 |
|  |  | 39.6 | 48.1 |  |  | Net Worth | 38.4 | 36.6 |
|  |  | 100.0 | 100.0 |  |  | Total Liabilities & Net Worth | 100.0 | 100.0 |
|  |  |  |  |  |  | **INCOME DATA** |  |  |
|  |  | 100.0 | 100.0 |  |  | Net Sales | 100.0 | 100.0 |
|  |  | 32.6 | 33.7 |  |  | Gross Profit | 29.0 | 30.6 |
|  |  | 26.7 | 27.4 |  |  | Operating Expenses | 22.5 | 25.1 |
|  |  | 5.9 | 6.3 |  |  | Operating Profit | 6.5 | 5.5 |
|  |  | .4 | .9 |  |  | All Other Expenses (net) | 1.2 | .4 |
|  |  | 5.5 | 5.4 |  |  | Profit Before Taxes | 5.3 | 5.1 |
|  |  |  |  |  |  | **RATIOS** |  |  |
|  |  | 3.4 | 4.2 |  |  |  | 2.3 | 2.7 |
|  |  | 1.8 | 1.9 |  |  | Current | 1.6 | 1.6 |
|  |  | 1.2 | 1.3 |  |  |  | 1.2 | 1.2 |
|  |  | 1.4 | 2.5 |  |  |  | 1.4 | 1.7 |
|  |  | 1.2 | 1.3 |  |  | Quick | .9 | 1.0 |
|  |  | .9 | 1.0 |  |  |  | .6 | .7 |
|  |  | 27  13.3 | 38  9.5 |  |  |  | 37  10.0 | 29  12.8 |
|  |  | 51  7.2 | 58  6.3 |  |  | Sales/Receivables | 53  6.9 | 44  8.4 |
|  |  | 57  6.4 | 73  5.0 |  |  |  | 72  5.1 | 59  6.2 |
|  |  | 30  12.0 | 22  16.7 |  |  |  | 31  11.9 | 28  12.9 |
|  |  | 52  7.0 | 38  9.6 |  |  | Cost of Sales/Inventory | 48  7.6 | 55  6.7 |
|  |  | 96  3.8 | 81  4.5 |  |  |  | 86  4.3 | 79  4.6 |
|  |  | 17  21.3 | 17  21.3 |  |  |  | 17  21.8 | 13  28.2 |
|  |  | 24  15.5 | 26  14.3 |  |  | Cost of Sales/Payables | 35  10.5 | 23  16.1 |
|  |  | 38  9.7 | 44  8.3 |  |  |  | 52  7.0 | 39  9.4 |
|  |  | 5.1 | 5.2 |  |  |  | 5.6 | 5.5 |
|  |  | 7.2 | 8.2 |  |  | Sales/Working Capital | 9.2 | 9.6 |
|  |  | 12.6 | 10.5 |  |  |  | 19.8 | 19.4 |
|  |  | 25.0 | 33.2 |  |  |  | 20.8 | 24.1 |
|  |  | (17)  10.3 | (14)  12.0 |  |  | EBIT/Interest | (41)  5.5 | (49)  7.2 |
|  |  | 2.4 | .5 |  |  |  | 1.7 | 2.4 |
|  |  |  |  |  |  |  | 8.6 | 12.7 |
|  |  |  |  |  |  | Net Profit + Depr., Dep., Amort./Cur. Mat. L/T/D | (17)  3.1 | (19)  6.1 |
|  |  |  |  |  |  |  | 1.6 | 2.3 |
|  |  | .1 | .3 |  |  |  | .2 | .3 |
|  |  | .4 | .5 |  |  | Fixed/Worth | .6 | .6 |
|  |  | .7 | 1.1 |  |  |  | 1.4 | 2.6 |
|  |  | .7 | .5 |  |  |  | 1.0 | .7 |
|  |  | 1.7 | .9 |  |  | Debt/Worth | 1.6 | 1.9 |
|  |  | 4.5 | 1.9 |  |  |  | 2.9 | 19.4 |
|  |  | 47.3 | 60.5 |  |  |  | 49.6 | 48.8 |
|  |  | (18)  15.8 | (14)  30.9 |  |  | % Profit Before Taxes/Tangible Net Worth | (40)  29.8 | (44)  24.0 |
|  |  | 9.0 | 5.6 |  |  |  | 9.1 | 12.3 |
|  |  | 18.3 | 20.1 |  |  |  | 19.5 | 17.9 |
|  |  | 6.4 | 8.1 |  |  | % Profit Before Taxes/Total Assets | 10.5 | 10.4 |
|  |  | 2.4 | .2 |  |  |  | 1.6 | 4.0 |
|  |  | 48.7 | 24.5 |  |  |  | 28.5 | 27.3 |
|  |  | 32.3 | 7.0 |  |  | Sales/Net Fixed Assets | 9.6 | 10.9 |
|  |  | 11.1 | 5.5 |  |  |  | 4.5 | 5.5 |
|  |  | 3.6 | 2.2 |  |  |  | 2.3 | 2.8 |
|  |  | 2.5 | 1.9 |  |  | Sales/Total Assets | 1.8 | 2.4 |
|  |  | 1.9 | 1.1 |  |  |  | 1.3 | 1.7 |
|  |  | .6 | 1.4 |  |  |  | .9 | .9 |
|  |  | (14)  1.1 | (14)  1.7 |  |  | % Depr., Dep., Amort./Sales | (41)  1.6 | (49)  1.4 |
|  |  | 1.7 | 3.7 |  |  |  | 2.1 | 2.2 |
|  |  | 2.6 |  |  |  |  |  |  |
|  |  | (11)  3.6 |  |  |  | % Officers', Directors' Owners' Comp/Sales |  |  |
|  |  | 8.5 |  |  |  |  |  |  |
| 218M | 15853M | 244187M | 616879M | 26014M | 1677552M | Net Sales ($) | 1962418M | 2503145M |
| 125M | 4927M | 95871M | 347514M | 71722M | 872093M | Total Assets ($) | 1189963M | 1263358M |

© RMA 2012

M = $ thousand   MM = $ million
See Pages 9 through 22 for Explanation of Ratios and Data

## Comparative Historical Data  /  Current Data Sorted by Sales

| | | | Type of Statement | | | | | | |
|---|---|---|---|---|---|---|---|---|---|
| 10 | 9 | 9 | Unqualified | | | | 1 | | 8 |
| 8 | 6 | 10 | Reviewed | | | 2 | 2 | 2 | 4 |
| 3 | 3 | 7 | Compiled | | | | 1 | 6 | |
| 8 | 8 | 5 | Tax Returns | | 3 | 1 | 1 | | |
| 20 | 22 | 17 | Other | 1 | | | 3 | 7 | 6 |
| 4/1/09- 3/31/10 ALL | 4/1/10- 3/31/11 ALL | 4/1/11- 3/31/12 ALL | | | 7 (4/1-9/30/11) | | 41 (10/1/11-3/31/12) | | |
| 49 | 48 | 48 | **NUMBER OF STATEMENTS** | 0-1MM | 1-3MM | 3-5MM | 5-10MM | 10-25MM | 25MM & OVER |
| % | % | % | | 1 | 3 | 3 | 8 | 15 | 18 |
| | | | **ASSETS** | % | % | % | % | % | % |
| 13.8 | 12.3 | 14.5 | Cash & Equivalents | | | | | 11.3 | 15.1 |
| 24.2 | 33.7 | 29.3 | Trade Receivables (net) | | | | | 32.3 | 27.5 |
| 22.6 | 21.3 | 21.2 | Inventory | | | | | 24.1 | 15.1 |
| 3.8 | 4.5 | 4.7 | All Other Current | | | | | 6.8 | 3.5 |
| 64.5 | 71.9 | 69.8 | Total Current | | | | | 74.5 | 61.2 |
| 22.5 | 18.8 | 17.6 | Fixed Assets (net) | | | | | 19.2 | 23.1 |
| 6.7 | 5.0 | 3.9 | Intangibles (net) | | | | | 3.7 | 4.9 |
| 6.3 | 4.4 | 8.7 | All Other Non-Current | | | | | 2.6 | 10.8 |
| 100.0 | 100.0 | 100.0 | Total | | | | | 100.0 | 100.0 |
| | | | **LIABILITIES** | | | | | | |
| 5.8 | 6.9 | 7.9 | Notes Payable-Short Term | | | | | 6.4 | 3.3 |
| 1.7 | 2.5 | 1.7 | Cur. Mat.-L.T.D. | | | | | 1.2 | .7 |
| 9.8 | 14.0 | 13.0 | Trade Payables | | | | | 15.3 | 9.2 |
| .2 | .5 | .4 | Income Taxes Payable | | | | | .1 | .4 |
| 13.3 | 16.2 | 15.3 | All Other Current | | | | | 19.7 | 13.6 |
| 30.8 | 40.1 | 38.2 | Total Current | | | | | 42.8 | 27.2 |
| 10.0 | 8.9 | 11.2 | Long-Term Debt | | | | | 5.8 | 17.4 |
| .6 | .7 | .5 | Deferred Taxes | | | | | .6 | .8 |
| 5.8 | 5.4 | 7.9 | All Other Non-Current | | | | | 9.5 | 4.7 |
| 52.8 | 44.9 | 42.2 | Net Worth | | | | | 41.3 | 49.8 |
| 100.0 | 100.0 | 100.0 | Total Liabilities & Net Worth | | | | | 100.0 | 100.0 |
| | | | **INCOME DATA** | | | | | | |
| 100.0 | 100.0 | 100.0 | Net Sales | | | | | 100.0 | 100.0 |
| 36.4 | 32.6 | 32.3 | Gross Profit | | | | | 33.4 | 29.4 |
| 29.9 | 25.8 | 26.0 | Operating Expenses | | | | | 27.5 | 21.6 |
| 6.5 | 6.8 | 6.3 | Operating Profit | | | | | 6.0 | 7.8 |
| .4 | .8 | .6 | All Other Expenses (net) | | | | | .6 | .7 |
| 6.1 | 6.0 | 5.7 | Profit Before Taxes | | | | | 5.4 | 7.1 |
| | | | **RATIOS** | | | | | | |
| 4.2 | 2.7 | 3.3 | Current | | | | | 2.0 | 4.3 |
| 2.1 | 1.9 | 1.9 | | | | | | 1.7 | 2.0 |
| 1.4 | 1.3 | 1.3 | | | | | | 1.5 | 1.7 |
| 2.0 | 1.7 | 1.5 | Quick | | | | | 1.4 | 2.9 |
| 1.2 | 1.1 | 1.2 | | | | | | 1.1 | 1.4 |
| .9 | .9 | .9 | | | | | | .9 | 1.0 |
| 34 10.8 | 47 7.8 | 38 9.7 | Sales/Receivables | | | | | 24 15.5 | 39 9.3 |
| 46 7.9 | 56 6.5 | 52 7.0 | | | | | | 52 7.0 | 54 6.7 |
| 61 6.0 | 73 5.0 | 64 5.7 | | | | | | 69 5.3 | 62 5.9 |
| 35 10.5 | 26 13.8 | 27 13.6 | Cost of Sales/Inventory | | | | | 30 12.0 | 24 15.0 |
| 72 5.1 | 64 5.7 | 47 7.7 | | | | | | 69 5.3 | 33 11.0 |
| 94 3.9 | 92 4.0 | 83 4.4 | | | | | | 99 3.7 | 74 4.9 |
| 13 27.4 | 23 15.8 | 20 18.7 | Cost of Sales/Payables | | | | | 21 17.5 | 13 28.3 |
| 29 12.7 | 31 11.9 | 29 12.8 | | | | | | 24 15.2 | 24 15.0 |
| 40 9.1 | 48 7.6 | 42 8.6 | | | | | | 38 9.7 | 36 10.2 |
| 3.6 | 3.9 | 5.1 | Sales/Working Capital | | | | | 5.1 | 4.7 |
| 5.9 | 6.2 | 7.7 | | | | | | 7.6 | 7.7 |
| 11.3 | 12.3 | 11.5 | | | | | | 14.1 | 9.4 |
| 27.6 | 41.2 | 38.9 | EBIT/Interest | | | | | 28.9 | 55.3 |
| (45) 9.4 | (41) 11.3 | (44) 9.6 | | | | | | (13) 10.3 | (16) 19.1 |
| 2.3 | 3.2 | 2.1 | | | | | | 2.4 | 3.6 |
| 13.7 | 9.3 | 5.0 | Net Profit + Depr., Dep., Amort./Cur. Mat. L/T/D | | | | | | |
| (13) 8.4 | (13) 4.2 | (11) 2.4 | | | | | | | |
| 1.9 | 1.5 | 1.6 | | | | | | | |
| .2 | .2 | .2 | Fixed/Worth | | | | | .2 | .3 |
| .5 | .4 | .5 | | | | | | .5 | .5 |
| .8 | 1.0 | 1.1 | | | | | | 1.1 | .9 |
| .4 | .6 | .5 | Debt/Worth | | | | | .8 | .5 |
| 1.1 | 1.2 | 1.4 | | | | | | 1.6 | .9 |
| 2.3 | 4.3 | 5.5 | | | | | | 3.3 | 3.8 |
| 34.7 | 55.3 | 50.1 | % Profit Before Taxes/Tangible Net Worth | | | | | 47.3 | 62.3 |
| (46) 19.4 | (45) 23.4 | (43) 23.7 | | | | | | (14) 23.3 | (17) 31.3 |
| 7.0 | 8.9 | 9.2 | | | | | | 9.0 | 10.0 |
| 16.4 | 18.6 | 18.8 | % Profit Before Taxes/Total Assets | | | | | 18.3 | 22.3 |
| 7.9 | 9.7 | 8.9 | | | | | | 9.3 | 10.9 |
| 2.5 | 3.4 | 2.2 | | | | | | 4.1 | 4.1 |
| 23.0 | 35.8 | 36.5 | Sales/Net Fixed Assets | | | | | 48.7 | 20.7 |
| 9.9 | 10.6 | 13.7 | | | | | | 14.8 | 6.9 |
| 5.0 | 4.9 | 6.4 | | | | | | 5.5 | 5.5 |
| 2.5 | 2.6 | 2.7 | Sales/Total Assets | | | | | 3.7 | 2.4 |
| 1.8 | 2.1 | 2.2 | | | | | | 2.5 | 2.1 |
| 1.4 | 1.4 | 1.6 | | | | | | 1.8 | 1.2 |
| 1.4 | 1.0 | .8 | % Depr., Dep., Amort./Sales | | | | | .7 | 1.4 |
| (41) 1.8 | (40) 1.7 | (39) 1.5 | | | | | | (12) 1.5 | (16) 1.8 |
| 2.7 | 2.8 | 2.4 | | | | | | 2.8 | 3.4 |
| 3.6 | 3.1 | 2.9 | % Officers', Directors', Owners' Comp/Sales | | | | | | |
| (14) 5.1 | (16) 4.8 | (15) 4.0 | | | | | | | |
| 6.5 | 8.0 | 11.5 | | | | | | | |
| 2027850M | 2424465M | 2580703M | Net Sales ($) | 218M | 6234M | 14007M | 59075M | 246447M | 2254722M |
| 1323571M | 1523122M | 1392252M | Total Assets ($) | 125M | 2170M | 5020M | 45033M | 109695M | 1230209M |

M = $ thousand    MM = $ million
See Pages 9 through 22 for Explanation of Ratios and Data

## Current Data Sorted by Assets      Comparative Historical Data

|  |  | 20 (4/1-9/30/11) |  | 61 (10/1/11-3/31/12) |  |  | Type of Statement | 4/1/07-3/31/08 ALL | 4/1/08-3/31/09 ALL |
|---|---|---|---|---|---|---|---|---|---|
| 0-500M | 500M-2MM | 2-10MM | 10-50MM | 50-100MM | 100-250MM | | | |
|  |  | 3 | 11 | 5 | 2 | Unqualified | 22 | 19 |
|  | 2 | 9 | 4 |  |  | Reviewed | 20 | 17 |
|  | 1 | 5 | 1 |  |  | Compiled | 8 | 13 |
| 1 | 5 | 2 |  |  |  | Tax Returns | 6 | 7 |
| 2 | 7 | 6 | 12 | 1 | 2 | Other | 20 | 37 |
| 3 | 15 | 25 | 28 | 6 | 4 | **NUMBER OF STATEMENTS** | 76 | 93 |
| % | % | % | % | % | % | **ASSETS** | % | % |
|  | 14.0 | 15.1 | 11.2 |  |  | Cash & Equivalents | 8.7 | 9.9 |
|  | 33.4 | 35.9 | 25.3 |  |  | Trade Receivables (net) | 26.4 | 27.2 |
|  | 32.2 | 30.8 | 29.3 |  |  | Inventory | 32.6 | 29.5 |
|  | 1.7 | 1.6 | 3.8 |  |  | All Other Current | 4.9 | 4.1 |
|  | 81.3 | 83.4 | 69.6 |  |  | Total Current | 72.6 | 70.8 |
|  | 11.8 | 11.3 | 14.7 |  |  | Fixed Assets (net) | 15.9 | 19.2 |
|  | 4.8 | 1.3 | 9.7 |  |  | Intangibles (net) | 4.9 | 3.3 |
|  | 2.1 | 3.9 | 6.1 |  |  | All Other Non-Current | 6.6 | 6.7 |
|  | 100.0 | 100.0 | 100.0 |  |  | Total | 100.0 | 100.0 |
|  |  |  |  |  |  | **LIABILITIES** |  |  |
|  | 7.3 | 12.0 | 4.7 |  |  | Notes Payable-Short Term | 9.9 | 13.6 |
|  | 1.5 | 1.2 | 1.3 |  |  | Cur. Mat.-L.T.D. | 3.5 | 2.6 |
|  | 20.3 | 15.6 | 12.8 |  |  | Trade Payables | 15.2 | 12.8 |
|  | .0 | .1 | .1 |  |  | Income Taxes Payable | .3 | .4 |
|  | 11.4 | 16.7 | 19.0 |  |  | All Other Current | 16.1 | 14.4 |
|  | 40.5 | 45.6 | 37.9 |  |  | Total Current | 45.1 | 43.9 |
|  | 19.1 | 7.6 | 6.6 |  |  | Long-Term Debt | 12.3 | 11.2 |
|  | .3 | .1 | 1.4 |  |  | Deferred Taxes | .5 | .4 |
|  | 4.1 | 5.4 | 14.1 |  |  | All Other Non-Current | 5.5 | 6.9 |
|  | 36.1 | 41.3 | 39.9 |  |  | Net Worth | 36.6 | 37.6 |
|  | 100.0 | 100.0 | 100.0 |  |  | Total Liabilities & Net Worth | 100.0 | 100.0 |
|  |  |  |  |  |  | **INCOME DATA** |  |  |
|  | 100.0 | 100.0 | 100.0 |  |  | Net Sales | 100.0 | 100.0 |
|  | 34.1 | 35.7 | 32.0 |  |  | Gross Profit | 30.4 | 30.6 |
|  | 30.2 | 29.6 | 25.3 |  |  | Operating Expenses | 25.2 | 25.4 |
|  | 3.9 | 6.1 | 6.8 |  |  | Operating Profit | 5.2 | 5.2 |
|  | .5 | .3 | 1.5 |  |  | All Other Expenses (net) | 1.5 | 1.0 |
|  | 3.4 | 5.8 | 5.3 |  |  | Profit Before Taxes | 3.7 | 4.2 |
|  |  |  |  |  |  | **RATIOS** |  |  |
|  | 4.2 | 3.1 | 2.4 |  |  |  | 2.6 | 2.6 |
|  | 1.9 | 2.1 | 1.7 |  |  | Current | 1.7 | 1.7 |
|  | 1.3 | 1.3 | 1.4 |  |  |  | 1.2 | 1.3 |
|  | 2.0 | 1.8 | 1.6 |  |  |  | 1.2 | 1.3 |
|  | 1.1 | 1.1 | 1.1 |  |  | Quick | .8 | .9 |
|  | .7 | .8 | .6 |  |  |  | .5 | .5 |
|  | 27   13.4 | 36   10.1 | 38   9.7 |  |  |  | 36   10.3 | 31   11.8 |
|  | 47   7.8 | 45   8.1 | 46   7.9 |  |  | Sales/Receivables | 49   7.5 | 44   8.4 |
|  | 60   6.1 | 83   4.4 | 68   5.4 |  |  |  | 63   5.8 | 60   6.1 |
|  | 25   14.8 | 37   9.9 | 38   9.7 |  |  |  | 51   7.2 | 45   8.1 |
|  | 66   5.5 | 85   4.3 | 87   4.2 |  |  | Cost of Sales/Inventory | 88   4.1 | 73   5.0 |
|  | 94   3.9 | 126   2.9 | 101   3.6 |  |  |  | 131   2.8 | 111   3.3 |
|  | 17   21.0 | 18   20.7 | 18   20.6 |  |  |  | 20   18.5 | 12   29.4 |
|  | 38   9.6 | 31   11.6 | 30   12.0 |  |  | Cost of Sales/Payables | 37   9.9 | 27   13.4 |
|  | 56   6.5 | 38   9.5 | 52   7.0 |  |  |  | 53   6.9 | 41   9.0 |
|  | 4.3 | 3.4 | 3.4 |  |  |  | 4.1 | 4.6 |
|  | 8.5 | 5.4 | 5.8 |  |  | Sales/Working Capital | 7.8 | 7.3 |
|  | 20.2 | 11.2 | 11.8 |  |  |  | 19.2 | 17.6 |
|  | 11.3 | 41.6 | 26.5 |  |  |  | 13.1 | 12.3 |
|  | (12) 2.4 | (21) 8.1 | (24) 6.3 |  |  | EBIT/Interest | (69) 5.0 | (83) 3.6 |
|  | 1.1 | 2.1 | 1.8 |  |  |  | 1.0 | 1.5 |
|  |  |  | 7.7 |  |  | Net Profit + Depr., Dep., | 19.8 | 5.5 |
|  |  |  | (10) 2.6 |  |  | Amort./Cur. Mat. L/T/D | (30) 3.8 | (22) 2.7 |
|  |  |  | 1.1 |  |  |  | .9 | 1.3 |
|  | .1 | .1 | .2 |  |  |  | .2 | .2 |
|  | .4 | .2 | .5 |  |  | Fixed/Worth | .4 | .5 |
|  | -52.5 | .9 | 1.0 |  |  |  | 1.4 | 1.2 |
|  | .5 | .4 | .8 |  |  |  | .9 | .8 |
|  | 1.1 | 1.4 | 2.2 |  |  | Debt/Worth | 2.2 | 1.6 |
|  | -640.5 | 6.3 | 10.6 |  |  |  | 4.5 | 4.2 |
|  | 26.4 | 38.1 | 77.6 |  |  |  | 48.3 | 48.8 |
|  | (11) 7.8 | (24) 23.7 | (25) 31.5 |  |  | % Profit Before Taxes/Tangible Net Worth | (67) 18.1 | (85) 16.6 |
|  | 3.3 | 8.6 | 5.5 |  |  |  | .3 | 4.1 |
|  | 9.0 | 17.8 | 13.6 |  |  |  | 15.9 | 14.0 |
|  | 3.9 | 9.3 | 8.7 |  |  | % Profit Before Taxes/Total Assets | 5.6 | 6.2 |
|  | .3 | 1.7 | 1.0 |  |  |  | .0 | 1.1 |
|  | 83.1 | 56.8 | 32.9 |  |  |  | 41.1 | 35.1 |
|  | 41.7 | 22.1 | 15.2 |  |  | Sales/Net Fixed Assets | 16.6 | 18.4 |
|  | 15.7 | 14.9 | 8.5 |  |  |  | 6.3 | 5.8 |
|  | 4.1 | 2.9 | 2.4 |  |  |  | 2.7 | 2.8 |
|  | 2.8 | 2.2 | 1.8 |  |  | Sales/Total Assets | 1.9 | 2.0 |
|  | 2.4 | 1.5 | 1.3 |  |  |  | 1.4 | 1.5 |
|  | .5 | .7 | .9 |  |  |  | .7 | .6 |
|  | (11) 1.2 | (20) .9 | (24) 1.5 |  |  | % Depr., Dep., Amort./Sales | (67) 1.3 | (82) 1.2 |
|  | 1.5 | 1.4 | 3.1 |  |  |  | 2.4 | 2.6 |
|  |  |  | 1.9 |  |  | % Officers', Directors' | 1.7 | 2.7 |
|  |  |  | (11) 2.9 |  |  | Owners' Comp/Sales | (15) 2.8 | (20) 4.1 |
|  |  |  | 9.0 |  |  |  | 6.1 | 7.5 |
| 6676M | 58812M | 298496M | 1268927M | 566969M | 496579M | Net Sales ($) | 3529520M | 3643920M |
| 674M | 18879M | 133473M | 742005M | 401448M | 643494M | Total Assets ($) | 2123172M | 1880668M |

© RMA 2012

M = $ thousand     MM = $ million
See Pages 9 through 22 for Explanation of Ratios and Data

## Comparative Historical Data / Current Data Sorted by Sales

| | | | | | Type of Statement | | | | | | |
|---|---|---|---|---|---|---|---|---|---|---|---|
| | 19 | | 23 | | 21 | Unqualified | | | | 5 | 16 |
| | 23 | | 22 | | 15 | Reviewed | | 1 | 6 | 5 | 3 |
| | 6 | | 8 | | 7 | Compiled | 3 | | 1 | 3 | |
| | 4 | | 6 | | 8 | Tax Returns | 2 | 2 | 2 | 2 | |
| | 30 | | 23 | | 30 | Other | 3 | 6 | 1 | 4 | 15 |
| | 4/1/09-<br>3/31/10<br>ALL | | 4/1/10-<br>3/31/11<br>ALL | | 4/1/11-<br>3/31/12<br>ALL | | 1 | 20 (4/1-9/30/11)<br>0-1MM   1-3MM   3-5MM | | 61 (10/1/11-3/31/12)<br>5-10MM   10-25MM | 25MM & OVER |

| | | | | | | | 0-1MM | 1-3MM | 3-5MM | 5-10MM | 10-25MM | 25MM & OVER |
|---|---|---|---|---|---|---|---|---|---|---|---|---|
| | 82 | | 82 | | 81 | **NUMBER OF STATEMENTS** | 1 | 8 | 9 | 10 | 19 | 34 |
| | % | | % | | % | **ASSETS** | % | % | % | % | % | % |
| | 10.5 | | 10.8 | | 13.2 | Cash & Equivalents | | | | 21.5 | 9.8 | 11.2 |
| | 26.6 | | 30.6 | | 28.9 | Trade Receivables (net) | | | | 33.2 | 33.3 | 25.1 |
| | 31.8 | | 27.9 | | 27.6 | Inventory | | | | 31.5 | 33.1 | 23.1 |
| | 3.7 | | 3.7 | | 3.5 | All Other Current | | | | 2.2 | 2.2 | 6.1 |
| | 72.6 | | 73.1 | | 73.2 | Total Current | | | | 88.4 | 78.3 | 65.4 |
| | 17.4 | | 14.6 | | 15.2 | Fixed Assets (net) | | | | 7.8 | 12.6 | 17.1 |
| | 3.6 | | 5.1 | | 6.9 | Intangibles (net) | | | | 2.6 | 4.3 | 10.9 |
| | 6.4 | | 7.1 | | 4.7 | All Other Non-Current | | | | 1.1 | 4.8 | 6.5 |
| | 100.0 | | 100.0 | | 100.0 | Total | | | | 100.0 | 100.0 | 100.0 |
| | | | | | | **LIABILITIES** | | | | | | |
| | 12.1 | | 10.5 | | 7.2 | Notes Payable-Short Term | | | | 15.4 | 8.3 | 3.3 |
| | 2.5 | | 2.9 | | 2.4 | Cur. Mat.-L.T.D. | | | | .8 | 1.6 | 3.2 |
| | 13.2 | | 15.8 | | 14.3 | Trade Payables | | | | 16.2 | 14.2 | 12.7 |
| | .2 | | .4 | | .1 | Income Taxes Payable | | | | .0 | .2 | .2 |
| | 12.8 | | 13.9 | | 16.8 | All Other Current | | | | 16.7 | 19.3 | 18.2 |
| | 40.8 | | 43.4 | | 40.9 | Total Current | | | | 49.1 | 43.5 | 37.5 |
| | 10.8 | | 7.8 | | 12.9 | Long-Term Debt | | | | 11.0 | 8.5 | 7.5 |
| | .5 | | .4 | | .6 | Deferred Taxes | | | | .1 | .3 | 1.2 |
| | 8.1 | | 9.1 | | 8.8 | All Other Non-Current | | | | 2.0 | 9.0 | 12.3 |
| | 39.7 | | 39.4 | | 36.7 | Net Worth | | | | 37.8 | 38.7 | 41.5 |
| | 100.0 | | 100.0 | | 100.0 | Total Liabilities & Net Worth | | | | 100.0 | 100.0 | 100.0 |
| | | | | | | **INCOME DATA** | | | | | | |
| | 100.0 | | 100.0 | | 100.0 | Net Sales | | | | 100.0 | 100.0 | 100.0 |
| | 32.2 | | 32.8 | | 33.4 | Gross Profit | | | | 31.5 | 33.3 | 30.3 |
| | 26.9 | | 26.8 | | 27.8 | Operating Expenses | | | | 27.5 | 26.3 | 25.1 |
| | 5.3 | | 6.0 | | 5.6 | Operating Profit | | | | 4.0 | 7.0 | 5.3 |
| | 1.1 | | 1.0 | | .9 | All Other Expenses (net) | | | | .3 | 1.2 | 1.3 |
| | 4.2 | | 5.0 | | 4.7 | Profit Before Taxes | | | | 3.7 | 5.8 | 4.0 |
| | | | | | | **RATIOS** | | | | | | |
| | 3.0 | | 2.5 | | 2.9 | Current | | | | 5.4 | 3.1 | 2.4 |
| | 2.0 | | 1.8 | | 1.8 | | | | | 1.7 | 1.9 | 1.7 |
| | 1.3 | | 1.2 | | 1.3 | | | | | 1.3 | 1.3 | 1.4 |
| | 1.7 | | 1.7 | | 1.6 | Quick | | | | 3.1 | 1.6 | 1.5 |
| | .9 | | .9 | | 1.0 | | | | | 1.0 | 1.2 | 1.0 |
| | .5 | | .5 | | .7 | | | | | .8 | .6 | .7 |
| 34 | 10.8 | 37 | 9.8 | 36 | 10.1 | Sales/Receivables | 31 | 11.9 | 37 | 9.8 | 42 | 8.7 |
| 44 | 8.4 | 50 | 7.4 | 47 | 7.8 | | 36 | 10.1 | 46 | 7.9 | 54 | 6.7 |
| 57 | 6.4 | 67 | 5.5 | 70 | 5.2 | | 48 | 7.6 | 73 | 5.0 | 70 | 5.2 |
| 46 | 8.0 | 34 | 10.8 | 32 | 11.5 | Cost of Sales/Inventory | 26 | 13.9 | 47 | 7.7 | 32 | 11.3 |
| 94 | 3.9 | 69 | 5.3 | 78 | 4.7 | | 62 | 5.9 | 107 | 3.4 | 72 | 5.1 |
| 129 | 2.8 | 107 | 3.4 | 104 | 3.5 | | 91 | 4.0 | 146 | 2.5 | 99 | 3.7 |
| 18 | 20.1 | 19 | 19.6 | 18 | 20.8 | Cost of Sales/Payables | 9 | 40.9 | 21 | 17.7 | 19 | 19.3 |
| 28 | 13.1 | 33 | 11.2 | 32 | 11.3 | | 21 | 17.7 | 32 | 11.3 | 32 | 11.5 |
| 44 | 8.3 | 53 | 6.9 | 51 | 7.1 | | 42 | 8.7 | 47 | 7.7 | 56 | 6.5 |
| | 3.7 | | 3.9 | | 3.6 | Sales/Working Capital | | | | 3.5 | 3.6 | 3.5 |
| | 6.3 | | 7.0 | | 7.0 | | | | | 8.7 | 6.5 | 5.9 |
| | 12.4 | | 23.4 | | 13.8 | | | | | 18.9 | 12.2 | 11.3 |
| | 20.8 | | 19.5 | | 20.0 | EBIT/Interest | | | | | 34.2 | 16.2 |
| (75) | 5.4 | (72) | 7.3 | (70) | 6.0 | | | | | (17) 9.5 | (30) 5.9 | |
| | 1.6 | | 2.0 | | 1.2 | | | | | | 3.0 | .8 |
| | 9.6 | | 8.8 | | 5.7 | Net Profit + Depr., Dep., | | | | | | 5.7 |
| (20) | 2.4 | (22) | 4.0 | (20) | 1.7 | Amort./Cur. Mat. L/T/D | | | | | (16) | 1.7 |
| | .5 | | .7 | | .4 | | | | | | | .3 |
| | .2 | | .1 | | .1 | Fixed/Worth | | | | .0 | .1 | .2 |
| | .5 | | .4 | | .4 | | | | | .2 | .2 | .6 |
| | 1.1 | | 1.1 | | 1.2 | | | | | .5 | 1.3 | 1.0 |
| | .6 | | .7 | | .7 | Debt/Worth | | | | .2 | .6 | .9 |
| | 1.6 | | 1.6 | | 1.7 | | | | | 1.6 | 1.7 | 2.0 |
| | 5.6 | | 5.4 | | 9.5 | | | | | NM | 10.1 | 8.4 |
| | 44.0 | | 51.0 | | 44.2 | % Profit Before Taxes/Tangible | | | | | 66.8 | 54.9 |
| (72) | 10.6 | (73) | 19.1 | (69) | 22.1 | Net Worth | | | | (18) | 26.4 (30) | 24.1 |
| | 3.1 | | 7.8 | | 4.5 | | | | | | 12.4 | -.3 |
| | 17.0 | | 15.2 | | 14.9 | % Profit Before Taxes/Total | | | | 18.5 | 15.5 | 13.2 |
| | 4.4 | | 7.6 | | 7.3 | Assets | | | | 4.3 | 8.9 | 6.9 |
| | .9 | | 1.1 | | .9 | | | | | -.2 | 4.6 | -.1 |
| | 31.8 | | 63.9 | | 45.4 | Sales/Net Fixed Assets | | | | 58.4 | 45.2 | 25.2 |
| | 16.3 | | 23.6 | | 20.1 | | | | | 40.1 | 21.7 | 10.3 |
| | 5.0 | | 7.9 | | 8.7 | | | | | 22.1 | 12.6 | 6.0 |
| | 2.7 | | 2.7 | | 2.8 | Sales/Total Assets | | | | 4.5 | 2.9 | 2.3 |
| | 1.8 | | 2.1 | | 2.1 | | | | | 2.6 | 2.1 | 1.7 |
| | 1.3 | | 1.4 | | 1.4 | | | | | 2.2 | 1.5 | 1.2 |
| | .8 | | .7 | | .8 | % Depr., Dep., Amort./Sales | | | | | .8 | .9 |
| (68) | 1.4 | (69) | 1.1 | (64) | 1.2 | | | | | (16) | 1.1 (28) | 1.5 |
| | 2.6 | | 2.5 | | 2.4 | | | | | | 2.0 | 2.9 |
| | 1.1 | | 1.6 | | 1.9 | % Officers', Directors' | | | | | | |
| (17) | 3.2 | (20) | 3.7 | (21) | 3.3 | Owners' Comp/Sales | | | | | | |
| | 5.0 | | 9.2 | | 6.5 | | | | | | | |
| | 3527014M | | 2758642M | | 2696459M | Net Sales ($) | 689M | 17467M | 35831M | 76287M | 311377M | 2254808M |
| | 1998068M | | 1553290M | | 1939973M | Total Assets ($) | 44M | 10248M | 12307M | 30190M | 156758M | 1730426M |

M = $ thousand     MM = $ million
See Pages 9 through 22 for Explanation of Ratios and Data

## Current Data Sorted by Assets        Comparative Historical Data

| | 0-500M | 500M-2MM | 2-10MM | 10-50MM | 50-100MM | 100-250MM | Type of Statement | 4/1/07-3/31/08 ALL | 4/1/08-3/31/09 ALL |
|---|---|---|---|---|---|---|---|---|---|
| | | 2 | 5 | 21 | 2 | 3 | Unqualified | 33 | 26 |
| | | 3 | 22 | 7 | | | Reviewed | 16 | 34 |
| | 1 | 5 | 5 | 1 | | | Compiled | 9 | 12 |
| | | 5 | 1 | | | | Tax Returns | 7 | 12 |
| | 2 | 4 | 19 | 20 | 3 | 1 | Other | 46 | 50 |
| | | 23 (4/1-9/30/11) | | 109 (10/1/11-3/31/12) | | | | | |
| NUMBER OF STATEMENTS | 3 | 19 | 52 | 49 | 5 | 4 | | 111 | 134 |
| **ASSETS** | % | % | % | % | % | % | | % | % |
| Cash & Equivalents | | 13.3 | 8.3 | 6.5 | | | | 7.9 | 8.3 |
| Trade Receivables (net) | | 34.0 | 35.5 | 25.8 | | | | 31.3 | 28.4 |
| Inventory | | 30.5 | 28.2 | 26.8 | | | | 27.8 | 30.1 |
| All Other Current | | 1.6 | 4.0 | 4.5 | | | | 3.4 | 4.0 |
| Total Current | | 79.4 | 76.0 | 63.6 | | | | 70.4 | 70.8 |
| Fixed Assets (net) | | 13.6 | 18.3 | 24.9 | | | | 17.7 | 19.5 |
| Intangibles (net) | | 1.7 | 3.1 | 7.7 | | | | 5.4 | 6.0 |
| All Other Non-Current | | 5.3 | 2.6 | 3.8 | | | | 6.5 | 3.8 |
| Total | | 100.0 | 100.0 | 100.0 | | | | 100.0 | 100.0 |
| **LIABILITIES** | | | | | | | | | |
| Notes Payable-Short Term | | 10.0 | 10.4 | 6.4 | | | | 8.9 | 9.7 |
| Cur. Mat.-L.T.D. | | 2.5 | 2.0 | 3.3 | | | | 2.4 | 4.0 |
| Trade Payables | | 16.3 | 19.3 | 15.1 | | | | 15.9 | 14.0 |
| Income Taxes Payable | | .7 | .4 | .2 | | | | .2 | .4 |
| All Other Current | | 13.7 | 13.8 | 11.9 | | | | 12.2 | 11.9 |
| Total Current | | 43.2 | 46.0 | 36.9 | | | | 39.6 | 40.0 |
| Long-Term Debt | | 7.7 | 8.0 | 13.0 | | | | 14.2 | 12.5 |
| Deferred Taxes | | .2 | 1.1 | .4 | | | | .9 | .7 |
| All Other Non-Current | | 8.5 | 5.0 | 6.8 | | | | 4.7 | 4.8 |
| Net Worth | | 40.4 | 39.8 | 42.9 | | | | 40.7 | 42.1 |
| Total Liabilties & Net Worth | | 100.0 | 100.0 | 100.0 | | | | 100.0 | 100.0 |
| **INCOME DATA** | | | | | | | | | |
| Net Sales | | 100.0 | 100.0 | 100.0 | | | | 100.0 | 100.0 |
| Gross Profit | | 35.0 | 30.5 | 26.1 | | | | 29.0 | 30.7 |
| Operating Expenses | | 30.5 | 24.2 | 20.1 | | | | 22.9 | 24.3 |
| Operating Profit | | 4.6 | 6.2 | 6.0 | | | | 6.1 | 6.5 |
| All Other Expenses (net) | | .2 | .8 | .9 | | | | 1.1 | 1.0 |
| Profit Before Taxes | | 4.4 | 5.5 | 5.1 | | | | 5.0 | 5.5 |
| **RATIOS** | | | | | | | | | |
| Current | | 3.6 | 2.3 | 2.8 | | | | 2.9 | 2.6 |
| | | 1.5 | 1.6 | 1.8 | | | | 1.9 | 1.8 |
| | | 1.2 | 1.2 | 1.3 | | | | 1.3 | 1.4 |
| Quick | | 2.4 | 1.8 | 1.4 | | | | 1.5 | 1.4 |
| | | 1.0 | .8 | .8 | | | | 1.0 | .9 |
| | | .6 | .5 | .6 | | | | .6 | .5 |
| Sales/Receivables | 12 | 30.7 | 29   12.4 | 29   12.6 | | | | 33   11.1 | 28   12.9 |
| | 33 | 11.0 | 41   8.8 | 41   9.0 | | | | 47   7.8 | 39   9.5 |
| | 63 | 5.8 | 63   5.8 | 59   6.2 | | | | 62   5.9 | 57   6.4 |
| Cost of Sales/Inventory | 5 | 80.8 | 13   27.4 | 38   9.6 | | | | 31   11.6 | 30   12.1 |
| | 41 | 8.8 | 54   6.7 | 57   6.4 | | | | 63   5.8 | 64   5.7 |
| | 89 | 4.1 | 96   3.8 | 83   4.4 | | | | 102   3.6 | 109   3.3 |
| Cost of Sales/Payables | 7 | 48.7 | 19   19.1 | 14   25.2 | | | | 19   19.5 | 16   22.9 |
| | 20 | 18.3 | 33   11.2 | 23   16.2 | | | | 27   13.3 | 28   13.1 |
| | 35 | 10.5 | 51   7.2 | 38   9.5 | | | | 44   8.4 | 41   9.0 |
| Sales/Working Capital | | 5.1 | 4.3 | 4.5 | | | | 4.5 | 4.7 |
| | | 13.1 | 10.8 | 8.9 | | | | 7.5 | 7.9 |
| | | 33.7 | 32.1 | 17.4 | | | | 13.4 | 16.9 |
| EBIT/Interest | | 28.0 | 25.1 | 28.2 | | | | 21.0 | 23.4 |
| | (17) | 15.8 | (41)   6.1 | (44)   6.9 | | | | (101)   4.9 | (120)   7.0 |
| | | 4.1 | 2.0 | 2.2 | | | | 1.5 | 2.6 |
| Net Profit + Depr., Dep., Amort./Cur. Mat. L/T/D | | | | 13.6 | | | | 11.4 | 14.3 |
| | | | (17)   2.2 | | | | | (41)   3.2 | (41)   5.6 |
| | | | | 1.5 | | | | 1.1 | 1.8 |
| Fixed/Worth | | .2 | .2 | .4 | | | | .2 | .2 |
| | | .4 | .5 | .7 | | | | .4 | .5 |
| | | 2.2 | 1.0 | 1.1 | | | | 1.2 | 1.2 |
| Debt/Worth | | .6 | .9 | .7 | | | | .6 | .7 |
| | | 1.0 | 1.7 | 1.5 | | | | 1.8 | 1.6 |
| | | 21.8 | 4.0 | 3.5 | | | | 4.1 | 3.2 |
| % Profit Before Taxes/Tangible Net Worth | | 124.2 | 52.8 | 43.9 | | | | 57.9 | 57.6 |
| | (17) | 32.0 | (48)   23.0 | (43)   20.8 | | | | (95)   24.4 | (120)   27.8 |
| | | 14.6 | 7.3 | 11.6 | | | | 8.4 | 11.5 |
| % Profit Before Taxes/Total Assets | | 30.1 | 21.0 | 15.5 | | | | 18.0 | 18.9 |
| | | 13.8 | 5.3 | 8.5 | | | | 9.5 | 10.2 |
| | | 4.7 | 1.5 | 2.2 | | | | 1.9 | 3.4 |
| Sales/Net Fixed Assets | | 86.2 | 49.2 | 26.1 | | | | 43.5 | 36.5 |
| | | 31.8 | 27.4 | 11.4 | | | | 14.7 | 15.1 |
| | | 15.5 | 6.9 | 4.9 | | | | 6.7 | 7.0 |
| Sales/Total Assets | | 5.5 | 3.9 | 2.9 | | | | 3.2 | 3.1 |
| | | 3.8 | 2.6 | 2.1 | | | | 2.2 | 2.2 |
| | | 2.9 | 1.9 | 1.6 | | | | 1.5 | 1.6 |
| % Depr., Dep., Amort./Sales | | .3 | .4 | .8 | | | | .5 | .6 |
| | (13) | .9 | (43)   1.0 | (47)   1.4 | | | | (97)   1.3 | (116)   1.2 |
| | | 1.2 | 2.0 | 2.2 | | | | 2.0 | 2.1 |
| % Officers', Directors' Owners' Comp/Sales | | 2.8 | 1.3 | | | | | .5 | 1.1 |
| | (11) | 5.2 | (15)   2.1 | | | | | (26)   2.3 | (19)   2.3 |
| | | 9.7 | 6.5 | | | | | 5.2 | 7.3 |
| Net Sales ($) | 486M | 80567M | 669075M | 2680438M | 570955M | 1161690M | | 5492622M | 5512865M |
| Total Assets ($) | 252M | 22255M | 252912M | 1144885M | 327024M | 729501M | | 3049924M | 2921438M |

M = $ thousand     MM = $ million
See Pages 9 through 22 for Explanation of Ratios and Data

## Comparative Historical Data | Current Data Sorted by Sales

| | | | Type of Statement | | | | | | |
|---|---|---|---|---|---|---|---|---|---|
| 26 | 29 | 33 | Unqualified | | 1 | 2 | | 9 | 21 |
| 22 | 29 | 32 | Reviewed | | 4 | 6 | 6 | 14 | 8 |
| 19 | 12 | 12 | Compiled | 2 | 1 | 3 | 1 | 4 | 1 |
| 9 | 6 | 6 | Tax Returns | | | 4 | 2 | | |
| 44 | 48 | 49 | Other | 3 | 1 | 1 | 9 | 14 | 21 |
| 4/1/09- | 4/1/10- | 4/1/11- | | | 23 (4/1-9/30/11) | | 109 (10/1/11-3/31/12) | | |
| 3/31/10 | 3/31/11 | 3/31/12 | | 0-1MM | 1-3MM | 3-5MM | 5-10MM | 10-25MM | 25MM & OVER |
| ALL | ALL | ALL | | | | | | | |
| 120 | 124 | 132 | NUMBER OF STATEMENTS | 5 | 3 | 14 | 18 | 41 | 51 |
| % | % | % | ASSETS | % | % | % | % | % | % |
| 13.7 | 9.5 | 8.4 | Cash & Equivalents | | | 15.4 | 10.5 | 7.0 | 7.0 |
| 29.5 | 30.5 | 31.1 | Trade Receivables (net) | | | 33.4 | 32.4 | 33.7 | 29.3 |
| 25.7 | 26.3 | 27.7 | Inventory | | | 24.7 | 31.9 | 23.1 | 28.8 |
| 3.3 | 3.8 | 3.7 | All Other Current | | | 1.5 | 4.2 | 3.4 | 4.7 |
| 72.2 | 70.1 | 70.9 | Total Current | | | 75.1 | 79.0 | 67.2 | 69.8 |
| 17.7 | 18.4 | 20.7 | Fixed Assets (net) | | | 17.7 | 14.4 | 23.2 | 21.6 |
| 5.6 | 6.0 | 4.8 | Intangibles (net) | | | 1.2 | 3.9 | 6.9 | 4.5 |
| 4.4 | 5.5 | 3.6 | All Other Non-Current | | | 6.1 | 2.7 | 2.7 | 4.1 |
| 100.0 | 100.0 | 100.0 | Total | | | 100.0 | 100.0 | 100.0 | 100.0 |
| | | | LIABILITIES | | | | | | |
| 7.1 | 8.5 | 8.6 | Notes Payable-Short Term | | | 10.4 | 7.8 | 10.1 | 7.1 |
| 3.2 | 2.4 | 2.5 | Cur. Mat.-L.T.D. | | | 2.6 | 3.0 | 2.2 | 2.8 |
| 13.3 | 16.1 | 17.6 | Trade Payables | | | 18.1 | 18.7 | 16.5 | 17.8 |
| .7 | .6 | .4 | Income Taxes Payable | | | 1.2 | .5 | .3 | .2 |
| 12.1 | 12.5 | 12.5 | All Other Current | | | 11.0 | 11.6 | 11.3 | 15.0 |
| 36.5 | 40.0 | 41.6 | Total Current | | | 43.2 | 41.6 | 40.4 | 42.9 |
| 11.4 | 11.3 | 9.6 | Long-Term Debt | | | 11.1 | 2.7 | 9.1 | 11.3 |
| .9 | .5 | .7 | Deferred Taxes | | | .3 | 2.0 | .6 | .6 |
| 7.5 | 6.6 | 7.5 | All Other Non-Current | | | 6.9 | 2.1 | 5.9 | 6.1 |
| 43.7 | 41.6 | 40.6 | Net Worth | | | 38.5 | 51.7 | 43.9 | 39.1 |
| 100.0 | 100.0 | 100.0 | Total Liabilities & Net Worth | | | 100.0 | 100.0 | 100.0 | 100.0 |
| | | | INCOME DATA | | | | | | |
| 100.0 | 100.0 | 100.0 | Net Sales | | | 100.0 | 100.0 | 100.0 | 100.0 |
| 30.1 | 28.7 | 28.6 | Gross Profit | | | 33.0 | 36.9 | 27.5 | 24.6 |
| 24.7 | 23.2 | 23.0 | Operating Expenses | | | 27.4 | 30.5 | 22.3 | 18.8 |
| 5.4 | 5.6 | 5.6 | Operating Profit | | | 5.5 | 6.3 | 5.2 | 5.8 |
| .7 | 1.0 | .7 | All Other Expenses (net) | | | .2 | .1 | .6 | .5 |
| 4.7 | 4.6 | 4.9 | Profit Before Taxes | | | 5.3 | 6.3 | 4.6 | 5.2 |
| | | | RATIOS | | | | | | |
| 3.6 | 2.7 | 2.6 | | | | 3.3 | 5.5 | 2.4 | 2.6 |
| 2.0 | 1.8 | 1.7 | Current | | | 1.5 | 1.9 | 1.8 | 1.7 |
| 1.4 | 1.3 | 1.2 | | | | 1.0 | 1.2 | 1.2 | 1.2 |
| 2.3 | 1.5 | 1.7 | | | | 2.5 | 3.0 | 1.7 | 1.4 |
| 1.2 | 1.0 | .9 | Quick | | | 1.2 | 1.0 | .9 | .9 |
| .8 | .5 | .6 | | | | .5 | .5 | .6 | .6 |

| | | | | | | | | | | | | | | | | | |
|---|---|---|---|---|---|---|---|---|---|---|---|---|---|---|---|---|---|
| 31 | 11.7 | 33 | 11.0 | 28 | 12.9 | Sales/Receivables | 11 | 31.9 | 28 | 13.1 | 30 | 12.1 | 27 | 13.4 |
| 42 | 8.6 | 46 | 7.9 | 41 | 8.8 | | 34 | 10.6 | 36 | 10.0 | 45 | 8.2 | 45 | 8.1 |
| 54 | 6.7 | 69 | 5.3 | 61 | 6.0 | | 64 | 5.7 | 58 | 6.3 | 64 | 5.7 | 60 | 6.1 |
| 26 | 14.1 | 32 | 11.3 | 26 | 14.1 | Cost of Sales/Inventory | 0 | UND | 42 | 8.6 | 11 | 32.4 | 37 | 9.9 |
| 57 | 6.3 | 65 | 5.6 | 56 | 6.5 | | 8 | 43.0 | 72 | 5.1 | 53 | 6.9 | 57 | 6.4 |
| 100 | 3.6 | 99 | 3.7 | 91 | 4.0 | | 91 | 4.0 | 96 | 3.8 | 85 | 4.3 | 81 | 4.5 |
| 14 | 26.5 | 19 | 19.3 | 15 | 24.7 | Cost of Sales/Payables | 5 | 80.1 | 16 | 22.3 | 14 | 25.2 | 15 | 23.9 |
| 28 | 13.1 | 30 | 12.2 | 27 | 13.6 | | 29 | 12.6 | 24 | 15.5 | 32 | 11.3 | 24 | 15.4 |
| 37 | 10.0 | 48 | 7.7 | 47 | 7.8 | | 49 | 7.4 | 46 | 8.0 | 46 | 7.9 | 46 | 7.9 |

| | | | | | | | | | |
|---|---|---|---|---|---|---|---|---|---|
| 3.7 | 4.0 | 4.5 | Sales/Working Capital | | | 6.1 | 3.6 | 4.5 | 4.6 |
| 7.2 | 7.7 | 10.1 | | | | 12.4 | 7.6 | 10.2 | 9.2 |
| 15.9 | 17.3 | 22.7 | | | | NM | 26.6 | 21.4 | 23.0 |
| | 22.6 | | 25.1 | | 28.1 | EBIT/Interest | | 23.8 | | 23.9 | | 25.1 | | 44.8 |
| (104) | 7.2 | (110) | 7.0 | (111) | 7.9 | | (12) | 16.0 | (12) | 9.0 | (37) | 5.0 | (46) | 10.1 |
| | 1.3 | | 1.7 | | 2.5 | | | 1.6 | | 3.9 | | 1.6 | | 4.3 |
| | 12.8 | | 10.8 | | 22.4 | Net Profit + Depr., Dep., Amort./Cur. Mat. L/T/D | | | | | | 4.8 | | 46.5 |
| (32) | 3.5 | (38) | 4.2 | (36) | 4.2 | | | | | | (10) | 2.2 | (19) | 6.2 |
| | 1.0 | | 1.8 | | 1.5 | | | | | | | 1.5 | | 2.1 |

| | | | | | | | | | |
|---|---|---|---|---|---|---|---|---|---|
| .2 | .2 | .3 | Fixed/Worth | | | .3 | .1 | .3 | .3 |
| .4 | .5 | .6 | | | | .5 | .4 | .7 | .7 |
| 1.1 | 1.2 | 1.1 | | | | 2.2 | .7 | 1.1 | 1.1 |
| .5 | .7 | .8 | Debt/Worth | | | .8 | .2 | .8 | .7 |
| 1.4 | 1.5 | 1.5 | | | | 1.2 | 1.0 | 1.1 | 1.8 |
| 3.7 | 3.8 | 4.0 | | | | 8.4 | 3.3 | 3.9 | 3.4 |

| | | | | | | | | | | | | | | | |
|---|---|---|---|---|---|---|---|---|---|---|---|---|---|---|---|
| | 46.5 | | 40.6 | | 49.0 | % Profit Before Taxes/Tangible Net Worth | | 80.8 | | 87.4 | | 46.4 | | 49.5 |
| (107) | 19.2 | (110) | 21.8 | (118) | 22.4 | | (13) | 25.8 | | 25.8 | (37) | 21.7 | (45) | 21.1 |
| | 5.1 | | 7.2 | | 9.0 | | | 7.8 | | 13.3 | | 6.5 | | 13.9 |

| | | | | | | | | | |
|---|---|---|---|---|---|---|---|---|---|
| 18.4 | 15.6 | 18.6 | % Profit Before Taxes/Total Assets | | | 33.0 | 21.3 | 19.8 | 15.9 |
| 7.9 | 6.7 | 8.2 | | | | 11.5 | 12.8 | 5.1 | 11.7 |
| .9 | 2.2 | 2.4 | | | | 1.4 | 3.5 | 2.0 | 5.0 |
| 40.2 | 36.0 | 36.9 | Sales/Net Fixed Assets | | | 84.4 | 75.4 | 35.9 | 27.6 |
| 17.1 | 14.7 | 16.2 | | | | 21.9 | 36.5 | 17.0 | 13.3 |
| 8.1 | 7.7 | 7.2 | | | | 13.0 | 11.8 | 6.2 | 7.3 |
| 3.1 | 2.9 | 3.5 | Sales/Total Assets | | | 5.6 | 3.6 | 3.8 | 3.2 |
| 2.2 | 2.1 | 2.4 | | | | 3.5 | 2.8 | 2.3 | 2.2 |
| 1.6 | 1.4 | 1.7 | | | | 2.3 | 1.9 | 1.6 | 1.8 |

| | | | | | | | | | | | | | | | |
|---|---|---|---|---|---|---|---|---|---|---|---|---|---|---|---|
| | .6 | | .7 | | .6 | % Depr., Dep., Amort./Sales | | .3 | | .4 | | .6 | | .7 |
| (99) | 1.3 | (108) | 1.3 | (111) | 1.2 | | (11) | 1.0 | (12) | .5 | (35) | 1.3 | (49) | 1.3 |
| | 2.5 | | 2.2 | | 2.0 | | | 1.9 | | 1.4 | | 2.4 | | 1.8 |
| | 1.7 | | 1.3 | | 1.3 | % Officers', Directors' Owners' Comp/Sales | | | | | | 1.3 | | |
| (30) | 2.9 | (31) | 2.8 | (31) | 2.6 | | | | | | (13) | 2.3 | | |
| | 5.1 | | 6.0 | | 7.2 | | | | | | | 6.8 | | |

| | | | | | | | | | |
|---|---|---|---|---|---|---|---|---|---|
| 4427381M | 5656547M | 5163211M | Net Sales ($) | 768M | 7594M | 57142M | 138208M | 630025M | 4329474M |
| 2383913M | 3146715M | 2476829M | Total Assets ($) | 3859M | 11215M | 19310M | 60334M | 334809M | 2047302M |

© RMA 2012

M = $ thousand    MM = $ million
See Pages 9 through 22 for Explanation of Ratios and Data

## Current Data Sorted by Assets      Comparative Historical Data

| | | | | | | Type of Statement | | |
|---|---|---|---|---|---|---|---|---|
| 1 | | 1 | 3 | 1 | | Unqualified | 10 | 9 |
| | 5 | 22 | 14 | | | Reviewed | 41 | 35 |
| 3 | 12 | 20 | 2 | | | Compiled | 28 | 23 |
| 8 | 8 | 9 | | | | Tax Returns | 17 | 10 |
| 4 | 7 | 11 | 7 | 5 | | Other | 35 | 54 |
| | 29 (4/1-9/30/11) | | 114 (10/1/11-3/31/12) | | | | 4/1/07-3/31/08 ALL | 4/1/08-3/31/09 ALL |
| 0-500M | 500M-2MM | 2-10MM | 10-50MM | 50-100MM | 100-250MM | | | |
| 16 | 32 | 63 | 26 | 6 | | NUMBER OF STATEMENTS | 131 | 131 |
| % | % | % | % | % | % | ASSETS | % | % |
| 13.2 | 12.8 | 11.8 | 8.1 | | | Cash & Equivalents | 7.1 | 9.3 |
| 35.0 | 30.2 | 29.8 | 27.0 | | | Trade Receivables (net) | 26.8 | 26.2 |
| 23.2 | 16.7 | 20.7 | 23.4 | | | Inventory | 16.9 | 18.0 |
| .0 | 4.0 | 2.0 | 4.4 | | | All Other Current | 2.7 | 2.2 |
| 71.4 | 63.8 | 64.3 | 62.9 | | | Total Current | 53.5 | 55.7 |
| 22.8 | 24.2 | 29.5 | 28.0 | | | Fixed Assets (net) | 37.3 | 34.7 |
| .6 | 3.9 | 3.1 | 5.2 | | | Intangibles (net) | 3.4 | 3.7 |
| 5.2 | 8.1 | 3.1 | 3.9 | | | All Other Non-Current | 5.8 | 5.9 |
| 100.0 | 100.0 | 100.0 | 100.0 | | | Total | 100.0 | 100.0 |
| | | | | | | **LIABILITIES** | | |
| 18.5 | 11.9 | 9.5 | 7.7 | | | Notes Payable-Short Term | 9.1 | 9.4 |
| 15.2 | 4.4 | 3.8 | 5.0 | | | Cur. Mat.-L.T.D. | 5.9 | 5.5 |
| 16.0 | 14.0 | 12.7 | 13.4 | | | Trade Payables | 12.5 | 11.4 |
| .4 | .2 | .2 | .3 | | | Income Taxes Payable | .2 | .2 |
| 14.9 | 7.8 | 12.3 | 14.6 | | | All Other Current | 10.5 | 13.1 |
| 64.9 | 38.3 | 38.4 | 41.0 | | | Total Current | 38.2 | 39.6 |
| 24.7 | 14.2 | 14.1 | 10.9 | | | Long-Term Debt | 22.1 | 23.7 |
| .0 | .7 | .7 | .4 | | | Deferred Taxes | 1.0 | .7 |
| 7.0 | 9.4 | 4.7 | 1.5 | | | All Other Non-Current | 6.8 | 7.4 |
| 3.5 | 37.5 | 42.1 | 46.1 | | | Net Worth | 32.0 | 28.6 |
| 100.0 | 100.0 | 100.0 | 100.0 | | | Total Liabilities & Net Worth | 100.0 | 100.0 |
| | | | | | | **INCOME DATA** | | |
| 100.0 | 100.0 | 100.0 | 100.0 | | | Net Sales | 100.0 | 100.0 |
| 43.6 | 39.7 | 26.5 | 22.0 | | | Gross Profit | 28.0 | 28.1 |
| 39.2 | 32.2 | 19.7 | 16.9 | | | Operating Expenses | 24.4 | 25.0 |
| 4.5 | 7.5 | 6.8 | 5.2 | | | Operating Profit | 3.6 | 3.1 |
| .7 | .7 | .3 | .0 | | | All Other Expenses (net) | 1.5 | 1.3 |
| 3.8 | 6.8 | 6.5 | 5.1 | | | Profit Before Taxes | 2.1 | 1.8 |
| | | | | | | **RATIOS** | | |
| 2.1 | 3.7 | 2.8 | 2.7 | | | | 1.9 | 2.6 |
| 1.5 | 1.7 | 1.8 | 1.6 | | | Current | 1.5 | 1.5 |
| .8 | 1.0 | 1.4 | 1.1 | | | | 1.0 | 1.0 |
| 1.5 | 2.7 | 2.0 | 1.5 | | | | 1.2 | 1.6 |
| .8 | 1.1 | 1.2 | .9 | | | Quick | .9 | .9 |
| .5 | .6 | .7 | .6 | | | | .6 | .6 |
| 15 24.8 | 27 13.4 | 41 9.0 | 43 8.4 | | | | 33 10.9 | 31 11.6 |
| 41 9.0 | 38 9.5 | 56 6.5 | 58 6.3 | | | Sales/Receivables | 47 7.7 | 47 7.7 |
| 59 6.2 | 52 7.0 | 70 5.2 | 104 3.5 | | | | 63 5.8 | 61 6.0 |
| 10 36.7 | 11 33.0 | 28 12.9 | 40 9.2 | | | | 16 22.3 | 19 18.8 |
| 22 16.3 | 28 13.2 | 46 8.0 | 57 6.4 | | | Cost of Sales/Inventory | 38 9.5 | 39 9.4 |
| 69 5.3 | 61 6.0 | 81 4.5 | 87 4.2 | | | | 59 6.2 | 69 5.3 |
| 6 57.5 | 17 21.1 | 17 21.4 | 27 13.6 | | | | 15 24.3 | 13 28.9 |
| 24 15.0 | 25 14.4 | 26 13.9 | 40 9.1 | | | Cost of Sales/Payables | 26 13.8 | 22 16.5 |
| 51 7.1 | 49 7.5 | 39 9.3 | 48 7.6 | | | | 43 8.5 | 36 10.1 |
| 8.9 | 5.4 | 4.1 | 3.5 | | | | 6.7 | 5.8 |
| 20.4 | 9.5 | 7.6 | 8.1 | | | Sales/Working Capital | 13.8 | 13.4 |
| -70.7 | 405.8 | 16.2 | 56.4 | | | | 343.4 | 151.7 |
| 14.8 | 16.8 | 27.8 | 23.6 | | | | 5.9 | 5.9 |
| (14) 4.7 | (26) 6.8 | (60) 8.9 | 8.5 | | | EBIT/Interest | (126) 2.3 | (119) 3.2 |
| 2.2 | 1.4 | 2.7 | 2.5 | | | | .1 | -.1 |
| | | 7.9 | 5.5 | | | Net Profit + Depr., Dep., | 3.2 | 6.8 |
| | | (14) 3.4 | (10) 2.9 | | | Amort./Cur. Mat. L/T/D | (37) 2.0 | (33) 2.7 |
| | | 1.6 | 1.1 | | | | 1.3 | 1.7 |
| .0 | .3 | .2 | .3 | | | | .6 | .6 |
| .7 | .6 | .7 | .7 | | | Fixed/Worth | 1.4 | 1.4 |
| -1.3 | 2.3 | 1.9 | 1.2 | | | | 3.6 | 3.7 |
| 1.1 | .9 | .6 | .4 | | | | 1.0 | .9 |
| 6.5 | 1.4 | 1.1 | 1.2 | | | Debt/Worth | 2.1 | 2.5 |
| -4.5 | 7.1 | 3.1 | 3.8 | | | | 7.5 | 11.1 |
| 107.2 | 89.7 | 53.1 | 44.7 | | | % Profit Before Taxes/Tangible | 37.6 | 42.2 |
| (10) 33.7 | (27) 35.5 | (56) 26.8 | (25) 22.1 | | | Net Worth | (108) 11.8 | (106) 17.7 |
| 1.0 | 10.6 | 11.6 | 8.6 | | | | -1.2 | -.5 |
| 46.3 | 27.7 | 19.0 | 10.0 | | | % Profit Before Taxes/Total | 11.9 | 13.5 |
| 11.0 | 8.8 | 10.7 | 6.8 | | | Assets | 3.7 | 5.0 |
| 2.1 | 3.7 | 4.5 | 3.4 | | | | -1.6 | -2.1 |
| UND | 32.5 | 16.8 | 9.9 | | | | 11.4 | 11.1 |
| 20.1 | 13.3 | 7.4 | 6.6 | | | Sales/Net Fixed Assets | 5.7 | 5.6 |
| 6.6 | 5.5 | 3.9 | 3.2 | | | | 3.1 | 3.6 |
| 6.6 | 3.2 | 2.5 | 1.8 | | | | 2.5 | 2.5 |
| 3.1 | 2.7 | 2.0 | 1.3 | | | Sales/Total Assets | 1.8 | 1.9 |
| 2.3 | 1.8 | 1.4 | 1.1 | | | | 1.4 | 1.3 |
| .2 | .6 | 1.8 | 1.8 | | | | 2.1 | 1.8 |
| (10) 3.5 | (25) 2.6 | (55) 3.1 | 2.9 | | | % Depr., Dep., Amort./Sales | (125) 3.8 | (120) 3.6 |
| 4.6 | 6.2 | 4.6 | 4.2 | | | | 6.3 | 5.9 |
| | 1.9 | 2.5 | 1.2 | | | % Officers', Directors' | 2.7 | 2.5 |
| | (27) 4.4 | (29) 3.9 | (12) 2.2 | | | Owners' Comp/Sales | (64) 5.1 | (58) 4.5 |
| | 9.7 | 6.3 | 2.9 | | | | 7.8 | 7.5 |
| 17618M | 101453M | 575476M | 717190M | 593007M | | Net Sales ($) | 1275390M | 1737766M |
| 5150M | 39960M | 292677M | 488502M | 482240M | | Total Assets ($) | 747340M | 1128144M |

M = $ thousand    MM = $ million

See Pages 9 through 22 for Explanation of Ratios and Data

## Comparative Historical Data | Current Data Sorted by Sales

| 4/1/09-3/31/10 ALL | 4/1/10-3/31/11 ALL | 4/1/11-3/31/12 ALL | Type of Statement | 0-1MM | 1-3MM | 3-5MM | 5-10MM | 10-25MM | 25MM & OVER |
|---|---|---|---|---|---|---|---|---|---|
| 7 | 5 | 6 | Unqualified | | 1 | 1 | 14 | 11 | 4 |
| 38 | 42 | 41 | Reviewed | | 4 | 4 | 10 | 8 | 8 |
| 21 | 37 | 37 | Compiled | 2 | 9 | 7 | 10 | 8 | 1 |
| 12 | 16 | 25 | Tax Returns | 5 | 8 | 2 | 8 | 2 | |
| 33 | 48 | 34 | Other | 2 | 5 | 4 | 7 | 8 | 8 |
| | | | | | 29 (4/1-9/30/11) | | 114 (10/1/11-3/31/12) | | |
| 111 | 148 | 143 | **NUMBER OF STATEMENTS** | 9 | 27 | 18 | 39 | 29 | 21 |
| % | % | % | **ASSETS** | % | % | % | % | % | % |
| 8.5 | 9.5 | 11.4 | Cash & Equivalents | | 14.8 | 10.8 | 12.8 | 11.8 | 5.4 |
| 24.9 | 27.2 | 29.6 | Trade Receivables (net) | | 28.9 | 30.3 | 27.6 | 31.7 | 28.5 |
| 19.1 | 19.5 | 20.2 | Inventory | | 18.2 | 10.1 | 23.1 | 22.9 | 20.3 |
| 1.7 | 3.1 | 2.9 | All Other Current | | 4.3 | 2.8 | 1.6 | 3.1 | 4.2 |
| 54.2 | 59.4 | 64.0 | Total Current | | 66.2 | 54.0 | 65.1 | 69.5 | 58.4 |
| 36.5 | 33.1 | 27.7 | Fixed Assets (net) | | 27.5 | 30.1 | 28.4 | 24.7 | 30.4 |
| 3.9 | 2.9 | 3.6 | Intangibles (net) | | .9 | 9.2 | 2.6 | 2.5 | 7.0 |
| 5.4 | 4.6 | 4.7 | All Other Non-Current | | 5.3 | 6.7 | 3.9 | 3.3 | 4.2 |
| 100.0 | 100.0 | 100.0 | Total | | 100.0 | 100.0 | 100.0 | 100.0 | 100.0 |
| | | | **LIABILITIES** | | | | | | |
| 11.9 | 11.4 | 10.4 | Notes Payable-Short Term | | 13.9 | 8.0 | 8.8 | 10.5 | 9.1 |
| 6.9 | 4.7 | 5.4 | Cur. Mat.-L.T.D. | | 11.3 | 3.9 | 3.6 | 4.3 | 3.8 |
| 12.0 | 12.0 | 13.3 | Trade Payables | | 11.6 | 14.5 | 11.1 | 16.2 | 14.2 |
| .1 | .3 | .2 | Income Taxes Payable | | .3 | .0 | .2 | .3 | .1 |
| 9.6 | 9.9 | 11.8 | All Other Current | | 6.5 | 8.6 | 12.3 | 15.1 | 11.8 |
| 40.5 | 38.3 | 41.2 | Total Current | | 43.5 | 35.1 | 36.0 | 46.3 | 39.0 |
| 23.5 | 19.0 | 15.3 | Long-Term Debt | | 19.8 | 19.3 | 11.8 | 12.3 | 16.2 |
| .7 | .4 | .6 | Deferred Taxes | | .6 | 1.0 | .8 | .4 | .2 |
| 6.4 | 8.9 | 5.4 | All Other Non-Current | | 12.1 | 9.8 | 3.2 | 1.5 | 2.6 |
| 28.9 | 33.4 | 37.4 | Net Worth | | 23.8 | 34.9 | 48.2 | 39.5 | 42.0 |
| 100.0 | 100.0 | 100.0 | Total Liabilities & Net Worth | | 100.0 | 100.0 | 100.0 | 100.0 | 100.0 |
| | | | **INCOME DATA** | | | | | | |
| 100.0 | 100.0 | 100.0 | Net Sales | | 100.0 | 100.0 | 100.0 | 100.0 | 100.0 |
| 27.2 | 28.8 | 30.5 | Gross Profit | | 44.7 | 34.2 | 28.8 | 22.8 | 19.7 |
| 26.2 | 24.7 | 24.0 | Operating Expenses | | 35.6 | 27.7 | 22.9 | 16.2 | 13.2 |
| 1.0 | 4.1 | 6.6 | Operating Profit | | 9.1 | 6.5 | 5.9 | 6.5 | 6.5 |
| 1.5 | 1.0 | .4 | All Other Expenses (net) | | .6 | .8 | .0 | .3 | .5 |
| -.5 | 3.1 | 6.1 | Profit Before Taxes | | 8.5 | 5.7 | 5.9 | 6.2 | 6.0 |
| | | | **RATIOS** | | | | | | |
| 2.3 | 2.7 | 2.8 | Current | | 3.1 | 2.8 | 2.8 | 3.2 | 2.5 |
| 1.4 | 1.7 | 1.7 | | | 1.6 | 2.1 | 2.0 | 1.6 | 1.4 |
| 1.0 | 1.1 | 1.1 | | | 1.1 | .9 | 1.4 | 1.1 | 1.1 |
| 1.3 | 1.7 | 2.0 | Quick | | 2.7 | 2.3 | 1.6 | 2.2 | 1.6 |
| .8 (147) | 1.1 | 1.1 | | | 1.1 | 1.6 | 1.4 | 1.0 | .8 |
| .6 | .6 | .6 | | | .6 | .6 | .8 | .6 | .6 |
| 33 11.1 | 37 9.9 | 36 10.1 | Sales/Receivables | 23 16.0 | 31 11.7 | 38 9.7 | 38 9.5 | 47 7.8 | |
| 44 8.3 | 53 6.9 | 51 7.1 | | 46 8.0 | 47 7.8 | 55 6.6 | 52 7.0 | 55 6.6 | |
| 69 5.3 | 69 5.3 | 68 5.4 | | 59 6.2 | 73 5.0 | 73 5.0 | 61 6.0 | 104 3.5 | |
| 22 16.8 | 20 18.0 | 21 17.3 | Cost of Sales/Inventory | 9 39.4 | 11 34.0 | 30 12.0 | 29 12.5 | 33 11.2 | |
| 40 9.2 | 37 9.9 | 43 8.4 | | 33 11.0 | 19 19.6 | 55 6.6 | 41 8.8 | 51 7.1 | |
| 79 4.6 | 76 4.8 | 79 4.6 | | 89 4.1 | 50 7.3 | 87 4.2 | 76 4.8 | 83 4.4 | |
| 13 28.4 | 15 25.1 | 17 21.4 | Cost of Sales/Payables | 8 48.3 | 21 17.7 | 15 23.9 | 20 18.3 | 28 12.9 | |
| 27 13.4 | 27 13.4 | 27 13.3 | | 25 14.7 | 28 13.0 | 23 15.7 | 32 11.4 | 40 9.1 | |
| 46 7.9 | 43 8.4 | 45 8.1 | | 60 6.1 | 54 6.8 | 30 12.2 | 43 8.4 | 54 6.8 | |
| 5.2 | 4.7 | 4.2 | Sales/Working Capital | | 4.2 | 5.0 | 3.8 | 4.0 | 3.7 |
| 13.8 | 9.5 | 8.3 | | | 8.2 | 8.2 | 6.2 | 8.6 | 9.1 |
| -135.8 | 36.2 | 31.4 | | | 50.5 | -44.9 | 13.8 | 41.1 | 86.2 |
| 5.4 | 9.8 | 18.9 | EBIT/Interest | | 16.8 | 16.3 | 22.8 | 53.4 | 10.9 |
| (103) 1.9 | (135) 3.8 | (132) 8.1 | | (22) 6.0 | (17) 6.9 | 8.6 | (26) 10.4 | 7.8 | |
| -2.2 | 1.2 | 2.5 | | | 1.0 | 2.2 | 4.7 | 1.7 | 2.8 |
| 2.1 | 3.8 | 6.1 | Net Profit + Depr., Dep., Amort./Cur. Mat. L/T/D | | | | | | |
| (34) 1.4 | (41) 2.3 | (33) 3.3 | | | | | | | |
| .6 | 1.0 | 1.6 | | | | | | | |
| .6 | .4 | .3 | Fixed/Worth | | .3 | .5 | .2 | .3 | .5 |
| 1.4 | 1.0 | .7 | | | .7 | 1.0 | .6 | .7 | .9 |
| 3.2 | 2.5 | 1.8 | | | 2.4 | NM | 1.1 | 1.9 | 1.7 |
| .9 | .8 | .7 | Debt/Worth | | .7 | .9 | .5 | .5 | .8 |
| 2.1 | 1.9 | 1.3 | | | 1.6 | 1.6 | 1.0 | 1.4 | 1.3 |
| 8.3 | 6.2 | 5.1 | | | 8.3 | NM | 1.5 | 5.3 | 3.9 |
| 31.8 | 41.7 | 58.7 | % Profit Before Taxes/Tangible Net Worth | | 91.0 | 75.1 | 36.9 | 61.1 | 45.2 |
| (92) 5.8 | (129) 17.3 | (124) 26.7 | | (21) 53.5 | (14) 30.9 | (37) 19.8 | (26) 26.0 | (20) 26.4 | |
| -13.2 | 3.8 | 10.6 | | | 10.5 | 10.2 | 8.6 | 12.6 | 10.9 |
| 7.4 | 13.2 | 19.2 | % Profit Before Taxes/Total Assets | | 37.8 | 20.3 | 17.7 | 15.4 | 12.4 |
| 1.7 | 4.7 | 9.2 | | | 18.1 | 7.2 | 9.4 | 9.5 | 6.9 |
| -6.4 | .4 | 4.2 | | | 1.7 | 3.6 | 5.1 | 3.8 | 3.5 |
| 10.3 | 11.4 | 21.6 | Sales/Net Fixed Assets | | 50.2 | 24.2 | 17.2 | 21.1 | 9.5 |
| 4.8 | 5.3 | 7.9 | | | 10.7 | 6.0 | 7.8 | 9.4 | 6.0 |
| 2.8 | 3.3 | 3.9 | | | 3.2 | 3.6 | 4.4 | 4.8 | 3.0 |
| 2.4 | 2.5 | 2.7 | Sales/Total Assets | | 3.2 | 3.1 | 2.5 | 2.7 | 1.8 |
| 1.7 | 1.8 | 2.1 | | | 2.5 | 2.4 | 1.8 | 2.1 | 1.5 |
| 1.3 | 1.2 | 1.4 | | | 1.6 | 1.4 | 1.3 | 1.4 | 1.1 |
| 2.3 | 2.2 | 1.4 | % Depr., Dep., Amort./Sales | | .3 | 2.5 | 1.4 | 1.4 | 1.9 |
| (105) 4.3 | (134) 3.6 | (122) 3.2 | | (22) 2.1 | (14) 4.3 | (35) 2.7 | (25) 2.7 | 3.6 | |
| 7.3 | 6.1 | 4.6 | | | 6.6 | 6.0 | 4.2 | 4.1 | 5.2 |
| 2.0 | 2.3 | 2.0 | % Officers', Directors' Owners' Comp/Sales | | 3.4 | 1.9 | 1.6 | 1.3 | |
| (57) 4.2 | (69) 4.2 | (74) 4.0 | | (20) 6.1 | (10) 4.6 | (21) 3.2 | (14) 3.4 | | |
| 6.3 | 6.5 | 7.0 | | | 9.6 | 10.8 | 6.1 | 4.4 | |
| 1508111M | 1903505M | 2004744M | Net Sales ($) | 7382M | 53966M | 71894M | 285836M | 448727M | 1136939M |
| 1074581M | 1355116M | 1308529M | Total Assets ($) | 2597M | 27452M | 37047M | 174467M | 242906M | 824060M |

M = $ thousand    MM = $ million
See Pages 9 through 22 for Explanation of Ratios and Data

## Current Data Sorted by Assets  —  Comparative Historical Data

| | 0-500M | 500M-2MM | 2-10MM | 10-50MM | 50-100MM | 100-250MM | Type of Statement | 4/1/07-3/31/08 ALL | 4/1/08-3/31/09 ALL |
|---|---|---|---|---|---|---|---|---|---|
| | 1 | | 6 | 14 | 4 | 1 | Unqualified | 27 | 29 |
| | | 8 | 31 | 10 | | 1 | Reviewed | 54 | 50 |
| | 4 | 20 | 14 | | | | Compiled | 32 | 35 |
| | 11 | 10 | 12 | | | | Tax Returns | 19 | 22 |
| | 3 | 14 | 20 | 13 | 2 | 3 | Other | 73 | 65 |
| | | 34 (4/1-9/30/11) | | | 169 (10/1/11-3/31/12) | | | | |
| NUMBER OF STATEMENTS | 19 | 52 | 83 | 38 | 6 | 5 | | 205 | 201 |
| | % | % | % | % | % | % | ASSETS | % | % |
| | 14.6 | 11.6 | 9.5 | 6.2 | | | Cash & Equivalents | 8.3 | 7.9 |
| | 27.7 | 29.8 | 25.5 | 21.6 | | | Trade Receivables (net) | 25.7 | 23.7 |
| | 16.4 | 19.6 | 24.7 | 24.6 | | | Inventory | 22.1 | 24.4 |
| | 2.3 | 1.3 | 1.1 | 5.6 | | | All Other Current | 3.0 | 2.9 |
| | 61.1 | 62.3 | 60.7 | 58.1 | | | Total Current | 59.0 | 58.9 |
| | 36.2 | 30.1 | 32.0 | 29.2 | | | Fixed Assets (net) | 32.4 | 33.0 |
| | .2 | 3.4 | 2.3 | 8.7 | | | Intangibles (net) | 3.6 | 2.8 |
| | 2.6 | 4.2 | 4.9 | 4.0 | | | All Other Non-Current | 5.0 | 5.3 |
| | 100.0 | 100.0 | 100.0 | 100.0 | | | Total | 100.0 | 100.0 |
| | | | | | | | LIABILITIES | | |
| | 6.8 | 12.7 | 7.7 | 6.8 | | | Notes Payable-Short Term | 10.3 | 11.9 |
| | 10.0 | 5.3 | 5.7 | 4.9 | | | Cur. Mat.-L.T.D. | 4.8 | 5.3 |
| | 15.0 | 15.7 | 12.7 | 12.8 | | | Trade Payables | 11.6 | 11.1 |
| | .0 | .3 | .2 | .1 | | | Income Taxes Payable | .1 | .0 |
| | 30.0 | 7.6 | 10.3 | 11.6 | | | All Other Current | 13.3 | 11.4 |
| | 61.8 | 41.6 | 36.5 | 36.2 | | | Total Current | 40.1 | 39.7 |
| | 29.6 | 18.9 | 17.8 | 19.7 | | | Long-Term Debt | 22.2 | 19.4 |
| | .0 | .3 | .6 | 1.6 | | | Deferred Taxes | .6 | .6 |
| | 2.3 | 5.0 | 3.6 | 5.3 | | | All Other Non-Current | 5.7 | 6.1 |
| | 6.3 | 34.2 | 41.6 | 37.3 | | | Net Worth | 31.5 | 34.1 |
| | 100.0 | 100.0 | 100.0 | 100.0 | | | Total Liabilities & Net Worth | 100.0 | 100.0 |
| | | | | | | | INCOME DATA | | |
| | 100.0 | 100.0 | 100.0 | 100.0 | | | Net Sales | 100.0 | 100.0 |
| | 39.3 | 41.1 | 30.7 | 24.1 | | | Gross Profit | 33.8 | 32.7 |
| | 33.2 | 33.9 | 22.6 | 15.7 | | | Operating Expenses | 27.5 | 28.4 |
| | 6.2 | 7.1 | 8.1 | 8.4 | | | Operating Profit | 6.3 | 4.2 |
| | .9 | .3 | 1.2 | 1.3 | | | All Other Expenses (net) | 1.3 | 1.0 |
| | 5.2 | 6.9 | 7.0 | 7.1 | | | Profit Before Taxes | 4.9 | 3.2 |
| | | | | | | | RATIOS | | |
| | 2.7 | 2.6 | 2.6 | 2.3 | | | Current | 2.5 | 2.6 |
| | 1.5 | 1.6 | 1.8 | 1.5 | | | | 1.6 | 1.7 |
| | .7 | 1.1 | 1.3 | 1.2 | | | | 1.1 | 1.1 |
| | 1.7 | 1.6 | 1.6 | 1.2 | | | Quick | 1.7 | 1.4 |
| | .9 | 1.0 | 1.0 | .6 | | | | .9 | .8 |
| | .4 | .8 | .8 | .5 | | | | .6 | .5 |
| | 0 UND | 34 10.8 | 33 11.0 | 37 9.8 | | | Sales/Receivables | 34 10.6 | 31 11.6 |
| | 32 11.5 | 44 8.3 | 46 7.9 | 52 7.0 | | | | 47 7.7 | 41 8.8 |
| | 42 8.7 | 63 5.8 | 57 6.4 | 65 5.6 | | | | 59 6.2 | 56 6.5 |
| | 0 UND | 5 71.9 | 34 10.6 | 44 8.3 | | | Cost of Sales/Inventory | 16 23.3 | 20 18.7 |
| | 8 44.2 | 41 9.0 | 63 5.8 | 79 4.6 | | | | 47 7.7 | 62 5.9 |
| | 40 9.2 | 101 3.6 | 107 3.4 | 126 2.9 | | | | 103 3.5 | 108 3.4 |
| | 0 UND | 15 24.4 | 17 21.6 | 26 14.0 | | | Cost of Sales/Payables | 15 24.7 | 14 26.6 |
| | 16 23.3 | 35 10.3 | 28 13.0 | 37 9.8 | | | | 27 13.4 | 26 14.3 |
| | 31 11.8 | 61 6.0 | 41 9.0 | 53 6.9 | | | | 42 8.7 | 41 8.9 |
| | 5.4 | 5.6 | 5.0 | 3.9 | | | Sales/Working Capital | 5.1 | 4.8 |
| | 18.1 | 11.1 | 7.7 | 7.1 | | | | 9.3 | 8.9 |
| | -24.1 | 45.5 | 13.4 | 19.4 | | | | 28.2 | 47.7 |
| | 21.3 | 15.6 | 16.8 | 10.1 | | | EBIT/Interest | 9.0 | 7.2 |
| | (12) 7.3 | (47) 5.3 | (74) 6.5 | (35) 4.5 | | | | (187) 3.8 | (187) 3.1 |
| | 4.7 | 3.2 | 3.0 | 2.5 | | | | 1.7 | 1.0 |
| | | | 5.9 | 4.7 | | | Net Profit + Depr., Dep., Amort./Cur. Mat. L/T/D | 5.4 | 5.9 |
| | | | (19) 2.7 | (16) 1.9 | | | | (48) 2.1 | (53) 2.1 |
| | | | 1.5 | 1.6 | | | | 1.4 | .9 |
| | .2 | .3 | .4 | .5 | | | Fixed/Worth | .4 | .4 |
| | 1.1 | 1.1 | .8 | .9 | | | | .9 | .9 |
| | -2.8 | 3.9 | 1.5 | 2.5 | | | | 2.3 | 2.0 |
| | .6 | .7 | .7 | 1.1 | | | Debt/Worth | .8 | .8 |
| | 1.4 | 2.3 | 1.4 | 2.2 | | | | 2.0 | 1.9 |
| | -4.6 | 9.6 | 2.9 | 4.6 | | | | 5.4 | 5.0 |
| | 192.0 | 58.9 | 45.8 | 38.2 | | | % Profit Before Taxes/Tangible Net Worth | 47.0 | 40.3 |
| | (14) 54.0 | (45) 32.7 | (77) 25.1 | (33) 23.3 | | | | (175) 24.4 | (172) 17.2 |
| | 11.2 | 11.5 | 12.6 | 9.1 | | | | 6.6 | 1.9 |
| | 58.9 | 17.3 | 19.3 | 14.0 | | | % Profit Before Taxes/Total Assets | 15.9 | 14.9 |
| | 27.9 | 10.7 | 10.7 | 7.4 | | | | 7.6 | 5.2 |
| | .7 | 3.1 | 5.7 | 2.9 | | | | 1.7 | .3 |
| | 58.9 | 19.8 | 12.7 | 9.5 | | | Sales/Net Fixed Assets | 16.1 | 13.8 |
| | 14.2 | 9.3 | 6.6 | 5.7 | | | | 6.7 | 7.1 |
| | 6.0 | 3.8 | 3.7 | 2.8 | | | | 3.7 | 3.4 |
| | 6.6 | 2.8 | 2.3 | 1.9 | | | Sales/Total Assets | 2.4 | 2.5 |
| | 3.1 | 2.3 | 2.0 | 1.4 | | | | 1.8 | 1.9 |
| | 2.4 | 1.5 | 1.5 | .9 | | | | 1.3 | 1.3 |
| | .8 | 1.2 | 1.8 | 1.3 | | | % Depr., Dep., Amort./Sales | 1.4 | 1.3 |
| | (13) 4.1 | (43) 2.9 | (73) 3.4 | (37) 2.6 | | | | (185) 3.0 | (175) 2.7 |
| | 7.2 | 5.0 | 5.3 | 5.0 | | | | 5.1 | 4.8 |
| | | | 3.9 | 1.9 | | | % Officers', Directors' Owners' Comp/Sales | 3.0 | 2.4 |
| | | (28) 5.2 | (34) 3.7 | | | | | (83) 5.6 | (74) 4.2 |
| | | 9.5 | 6.6 | | | | | 10.8 | 6.8 |
| | 26014M | 141470M | 744527M | 1315561M | 568418M | 723175M | Net Sales ($) | 3798528M | 3941084M |
| | 6429M | 63385M | 383634M | 869432M | 446544M | 815125M | Total Assets ($) | 2318095M | 2416030M |

M = $ thousand   MM = $ million
See Pages 9 through 22 for Explanation of Ratios and Data

| | Comparative Historical Data | | | Current Data Sorted by Sales | | | | | |
|---|---|---|---|---|---|---|---|---|---|
| **Type of Statement** | | | | | | | | | |
| Unqualified | 24 | 22 | 26 | | 1 | | 2 | 9 | 14 |
| Reviewed | 63 | 55 | 50 | | 4 | 6 | 15 | 18 | 7 |
| Compiled | 36 | 43 | 38 | | 15 | 11 | 10 | 2 | |
| Tax Returns | 24 | 24 | 34 | 5 | 14 | 5 | 5 | 5 | |
| Other | 60 | 52 | 55 | 2 | 11 | 8 | 10 | 13 | 11 |
| | 4/1/09-3/31/10 ALL | 4/1/10-3/31/11 ALL | 4/1/11-3/31/12 ALL | | 34 (4/1-9/30/11) | | 169 (10/1/11-3/31/12) | | |
| | | | | 0-1MM | 1-3MM | 3-5MM | 5-10MM | 10-25MM | 25MM & OVER |
| **NUMBER OF STATEMENTS** | 207 | 196 | 203 | 7 | 45 | 30 | 42 | 47 | 32 |
| | % | % | % | % | % | % | % | % | % |
| **ASSETS** | | | | | | | | | |
| Cash & Equivalents | 8.7 | 9.0 | 9.6 | | 11.7 | 16.0 | 7.6 | 7.1 | 7.4 |
| Trade Receivables (net) | 23.2 | 25.0 | 26.0 | | 26.8 | 27.4 | 26.5 | 25.3 | 23.8 |
| Inventory | 24.1 | 23.8 | 22.4 | | 18.5 | 17.9 | 23.8 | 27.1 | 24.0 |
| All Other Current | 4.7 | 2.9 | 2.6 | | 1.5 | .8 | 1.5 | 3.2 | 6.5 |
| Total Current | 60.7 | 60.7 | 60.7 | | 58.4 | 62.1 | 59.4 | 62.6 | 61.7 |
| Fixed Assets (net) | 30.3 | 30.7 | 30.6 | | 33.7 | 32.8 | 31.5 | 27.8 | 24.9 |
| Intangibles (net) | 3.9 | 2.9 | 3.6 | | 3.5 | 2.1 | 3.3 | 4.2 | 5.4 |
| All Other Non-Current | 5.1 | 5.8 | 5.1 | | 4.4 | 3.0 | 5.8 | 5.3 | 7.9 |
| Total | 100.0 | 100.0 | 100.0 | | 100.0 | 100.0 | 100.0 | 100.0 | 100.0 |
| **LIABILITIES** | | | | | | | | | |
| Notes Payable-Short Term | 11.2 | 12.5 | 8.9 | | 13.3 | 6.0 | 7.9 | 7.9 | 10.0 |
| Cur. Mat.-L.T.D. | 3.9 | 5.3 | 5.6 | | 8.0 | 5.2 | 5.2 | 5.9 | 3.3 |
| Trade Payables | 11.5 | 13.2 | 13.5 | | 13.1 | 14.1 | 12.8 | 15.5 | 12.7 |
| Income Taxes Payable | .2 | .1 | .2 | | .3 | .1 | .2 | .1 | .0 |
| All Other Current | 10.4 | 12.8 | 12.1 | | 17.2 | 7.3 | 7.9 | 12.9 | 13.3 |
| Total Current | 37.2 | 43.9 | 40.3 | | 51.9 | 32.8 | 34.0 | 42.4 | 39.4 |
| Long-Term Debt | 16.9 | 18.0 | 18.8 | | 26.1 | 18.7 | 18.4 | 17.9 | 11.2 |
| Deferred Taxes | .7 | .7 | .7 | | .2 | 1.0 | .4 | .9 | 1.4 |
| All Other Non-Current | 5.9 | 7.1 | 4.9 | | 6.2 | 2.1 | 5.8 | 2.1 | 9.5 |
| Net Worth | 39.5 | 30.3 | 35.3 | | 15.6 | 45.5 | 41.4 | 36.8 | 38.5 |
| Total Liabilities & Net Worth | 100.0 | 100.0 | 100.0 | | 100.0 | 100.0 | 100.0 | 100.0 | 100.0 |
| **INCOME DATA** | | | | | | | | | |
| Net Sales | 100.0 | 100.0 | 100.0 | | 100.0 | 100.0 | 100.0 | 100.0 | 100.0 |
| Gross Profit | 30.3 | 32.9 | 32.7 | | 39.2 | 40.9 | 30.6 | 27.6 | 21.8 |
| Operating Expenses | 29.4 | 28.5 | 25.1 | | 31.6 | 34.5 | 21.8 | 19.6 | 15.4 |
| Operating Profit | .9 | 4.4 | 7.7 | | 7.7 | 6.4 | 8.7 | 8.0 | 6.5 |
| All Other Expenses (net) | .9 | .9 | .9 | | .7 | .2 | 1.2 | .9 | .9 |
| Profit Before Taxes | .0 | 3.5 | 6.7 | | 7.0 | 6.1 | 7.6 | 7.1 | 5.5 |
| **RATIOS** | | | | | | | | | |
| Current | 2.6 | 2.5 | 2.5 | | 2.2 | 3.3 | 2.5 | 2.3 | 2.2 |
| | 1.7 | 1.6 | 1.7 | | 1.4 | 2.1 | 1.8 | 1.6 | 1.4 |
| | 1.1 | 1.1 | 1.2 | | .9 | 1.6 | 1.3 | 1.2 | 1.1 |
| Quick | 1.5 | 1.4 | 1.4 | | 1.3 | 2.4 | 1.4 | 1.4 | 1.1 |
| | .8 | .9 | .9 | | .9 | 1.4 | .9 | .8 | .7 |
| | .6 | .6 | .6 | | .6 | .9 | .7 | .5 | .5 |
| Sales/Receivables | 35  10.5 | 36  10.3 | 33  11.0 | | 27  13.4 | 33  11.2 | 35  10.4 | 36  10.1 | 42  8.7 |
| | 47  7.8 | 51  7.2 | 47  7.8 | | 41  8.9 | 41  9.0 | 48  7.6 | 48  7.6 | 58  6.3 |
| | 61  6.0 | 64  5.7 | 61  6.0 | | 65  5.6 | 51  7.1 | 55  6.6 | 62  5.9 | 65  5.6 |
| Cost of Sales/Inventory | 29  12.4 | 31  11.9 | 22  16.7 | | 0  UND | 8  44.7 | 31  11.8 | 43  8.5 | 37  9.9 |
| | 63  5.8 | 64  5.7 | 59  6.2 | | 27  13.5 | 43  8.5 | 62  5.9 | 69  5.3 | 76  4.8 |
| | 110  3.3 | 111  3.3 | 107  3.4 | | 107  3.4 | 87  4.2 | 101  3.6 | 118  3.1 | 118  3.1 |
| Cost of Sales/Payables | 16  23.3 | 20  18.7 | 17  22.1 | | 11  32.8 | 13  27.5 | 18  20.4 | 23  16.2 | 27  13.3 |
| | 28  13.3 | 33  11.0 | 30  12.2 | | 25  14.4 | 25  14.5 | 28  12.9 | 34  10.7 | 35  10.3 |
| | 44  8.3 | 53  6.9 | 46  7.9 | | 47  7.8 | 55  6.6 | 39  9.3 | 49  7.5 | 49  7.5 |
| Sales/Working Capital | 4.1 | 4.3 | 5.1 | | 5.6 | 4.5 | 5.4 | 4.8 | 4.4 |
| | 7.4 | 8.1 | 8.2 | | 13.4 | 7.1 | 8.4 | 7.2 | 7.6 |
| | 45.1 | 46.4 | 28.7 | | -27.8 | 14.6 | 12.7 | 25.3 | 70.8 |
| EBIT/Interest | 6.3 | 9.9 | 15.5 | | 11.5 | 19.6 | 17.5 | 16.8 | 9.4 |
| | (194) 1.6 | (187) 2.9 | (179) 5.7 | | (39) 5.4 | (27) 7.9 | (38) 5.8 | (42) 6.6 | (29) 4.3 |
| | -2.9 | 1.2 | 2.9 | | 3.2 | 2.2 | 2.8 | 3.5 | 2.4 |
| Net Profit + Depr., Dep., Amort./Cur. Mat. L/T/D | 3.5 | 4.6 | 4.5 | | | | | 5.3 | 5.1 |
| | (59) 1.0 | (50) 1.8 | (48) 2.0 | | | | | (12) 2.4 | (14) 2.0 |
| | .4 | 1.2 | 1.6 | | | | | 1.6 | 1.6 |
| Fixed/Worth | .3 | .3 | .4 | | .4 | .3 | .4 | .4 | .4 |
| | .8 | .9 | .8 | | 1.9 | .7 | .9 | .8 | .8 |
| | 2.2 | 2.8 | 2.3 | | NM | 2.3 | 1.7 | 1.4 | 2.0 |
| Debt/Worth | .7 | .8 | .7 | | .8 | .6 | .6 | .9 | .8 |
| | 1.7 | 1.9 | 1.6 | | 3.0 | 1.0 | 1.5 | 1.6 | 2.5 |
| | 4.6 | 6.6 | 4.4 | | NM | 3.9 | 3.8 | 2.9 | 14.0 |
| % Profit Before Taxes/Tangible Net Worth | 23.9 | 36.6 | 49.4 | | 97.6 | 51.1 | 50.1 | 43.0 | 37.7 |
| | (190) 3.8 | (170) 14.3 | (180) 25.3 | | (34) 29.5 | (28) 19.1 | (38) 33.4 | (43) 21.1 | (30) 24.1 |
| | -18.3 | 3.1 | 12.6 | | 14.6 | 5.6 | 11.7 | 12.9 | 11.8 |
| % Profit Before Taxes/Total Assets | 8.9 | 10.3 | 18.0 | | 20.8 | 16.7 | 21.8 | 18.0 | 11.6 |
| | 1.1 | 3.9 | 10.0 | | 10.7 | 8.8 | 11.1 | 11.2 | 6.4 |
| | -6.7 | .6 | 3.7 | | 3.0 | 2.8 | 5.5 | 5.0 | 2.6 |
| Sales/Net Fixed Assets | 13.8 | 15.2 | 16.6 | | 22.6 | 16.9 | 16.4 | 14.9 | 23.0 |
| | 6.3 | 6.2 | 7.6 | | 8.4 | 8.8 | 7.9 | 6.6 | 7.0 |
| | 3.7 | 3.6 | 3.8 | | 3.9 | 3.5 | 3.2 | 4.6 | 4.3 |
| Sales/Total Assets | 2.2 | 2.3 | 2.5 | | 3.0 | 2.6 | 2.5 | 2.3 | 2.0 |
| | 1.6 | 1.8 | 1.9 | | 2.3 | 2.1 | 2.0 | 1.7 | 1.4 |
| | 1.1 | 1.2 | 1.4 | | 1.5 | 1.6 | 1.6 | 1.2 | 1.0 |
| % Depr., Dep., Amort./Sales | 1.3 | 1.5 | 1.6 | | 1.1 | 1.7 | 1.6 | 1.6 | 1.2 |
| | (188) 3.2 | (169) 3.3 | (175) 3.0 | | (38) 4.1 | (23) 3.7 | (36) 3.8 | (43) 2.5 | (30) 2.5 |
| | 5.9 | 6.0 | 5.2 | | 6.8 | 5.4 | 6.6 | 3.5 | 5.0 |
| % Officers', Directors' Owners' Comp/Sales | 3.0 | 2.7 | 2.1 | | 3.3 | 4.4 | 1.9 | 1.5 | |
| | (86) 5.0 | (75) 4.5 | (77) 4.6 | | (19) 5.7 | (18) 5.6 | (20) 3.4 | (13) 2.0 | |
| | 8.2 | 7.9 | 7.3 | | 12.5 | 7.9 | 6.2 | 4.8 | |
| Net Sales ($) | 3961256M | 2959059M | 3519165M | 4584M | 80682M | 111875M | 291540M | 709827M | 2320657M |
| Total Assets ($) | 3072880M | 2239048M | 2584549M | 7879M | 40400M | 57644M | 155772M | 460139M | 1862715M |

M = $ thousand    MM = $ million

See Pages 9 through 22 for Explanation of Ratios and Data

## Current Data Sorted by Assets      Comparative Historical Data

| 0-500M | 500M-2MM | 2-10MM | 10-50MM | 50-100MM | 100-250MM | Type of Statement | 4/1/07-3/31/08 ALL | 4/1/08-3/31/09 ALL |
|---|---|---|---|---|---|---|---|---|
| | | 7 | | | | Unqualified | 17 | 16 |
| | 2 | 11 | 5 | 2 | 1 | Reviewed | 22 | 14 |
| 2 | 5 | 8 | 5 | 1 | 1 | Compiled | 20 | 15 |
| 5 | 10 | 4 | 1 | 1 | | Tax Returns | 6 | 9 |
| | 7 | 11 | 18 | 4 | 1 | Other | 37 | 42 |
| | 19 (4/1-9/30/11) | | 93 (10/1/11-3/31/12) | | | | | |
| 7 | 24 | 41 | 29 | 8 | 3 | NUMBER OF STATEMENTS | 102 | 96 |
| % | % | % | % | % | % | | % | % |
| | | | | | | **ASSETS** | | |
| | 15.5 | 8.0 | 12.8 | | | Cash & Equivalents | 10.0 | 9.6 |
| | 29.1 | 29.4 | 23.9 | | | Trade Receivables (net) | 26.5 | 25.3 |
| | 21.1 | 22.8 | 25.8 | | | Inventory | 25.1 | 26.2 |
| | 2.0 | 2.3 | 8.7 | | | All Other Current | 4.0 | 3.3 |
| | 67.7 | 62.4 | 71.3 | | | Total Current | 65.6 | 64.4 |
| | 24.7 | 28.6 | 19.6 | | | Fixed Assets (net) | 25.2 | 26.3 |
| | 1.9 | 1.4 | 4.0 | | | Intangibles (net) | 3.4 | 4.0 |
| | 5.8 | 7.6 | 5.1 | | | All Other Non-Current | 5.8 | 5.4 |
| | 100.0 | 100.0 | 100.0 | | | Total | 100.0 | 100.0 |
| | | | | | | **LIABILITIES** | | |
| | 9.1 | 11.5 | 8.0 | | | Notes Payable-Short Term | 9.6 | 9.9 |
| | 4.2 | 4.6 | 3.7 | | | Cur. Mat.-L.T.D. | 4.0 | 4.3 |
| | 11.9 | 13.5 | 11.6 | | | Trade Payables | 12.3 | 14.2 |
| | .0 | .6 | .5 | | | Income Taxes Payable | .1 | .4 |
| | 7.7 | 5.7 | 14.9 | | | All Other Current | 12.5 | 13.9 |
| | 32.8 | 35.8 | 38.7 | | | Total Current | 38.5 | 42.6 |
| | 14.5 | 12.8 | 8.8 | | | Long-Term Debt | 17.4 | 15.4 |
| | .0 | .8 | .5 | | | Deferred Taxes | .4 | .4 |
| | 9.7 | 3.4 | 6.9 | | | All Other Non-Current | 5.2 | 12.7 |
| | 43.0 | 47.2 | 45.0 | | | Net Worth | 38.6 | 28.9 |
| | 100.0 | 100.0 | 100.0 | | | Total Liabilities & Net Worth | 100.0 | 100.0 |
| | | | | | | **INCOME DATA** | | |
| | 100.0 | 100.0 | 100.0 | | | Net Sales | 100.0 | 100.0 |
| | 43.5 | 27.9 | 25.1 | | | Gross Profit | 30.0 | 31.2 |
| | 32.9 | 19.5 | 14.8 | | | Operating Expenses | 23.0 | 25.7 |
| | 10.6 | 8.4 | 10.3 | | | Operating Profit | 7.0 | 5.6 |
| | .7 | .8 | .6 | | | All Other Expenses (net) | .9 | 1.5 |
| | 9.9 | 7.6 | 9.8 | | | Profit Before Taxes | 6.1 | 4.1 |
| | | | | | | **RATIOS** | | |
| | 3.1 | 3.1 | 3.1 | | | Current | 3.1 | 2.7 |
| | 2.0 | 1.9 | 1.8 | | | | 1.8 | 1.7 |
| | 1.3 | 1.1 | 1.3 | | | | 1.3 | 1.1 |
| | 2.4 | 1.9 | 1.6 | | | Quick | 1.9 | 1.6 |
| | 1.5 | 1.0 | .8 | | | | 1.0 | .8 |
| | .8 | .6 | .6 | | | | .6 | .5 |
| | 22  16.7 | 35  10.5 | 54  6.8 | | | Sales/Receivables | 35  10.4 | 31  11.6 |
| | 42  8.7 | 45  8.2 | 62  5.9 | | | | 43  8.4 | 43  8.4 |
| | 52  7.0 | 65  5.6 | 79  4.6 | | | | 60  6.1 | 55  6.6 |
| | 0  UND | 21  17.4 | 23  16.2 | | | Cost of Sales/Inventory | 23  15.9 | 25  14.8 |
| | 25  14.8 | 57  6.4 | 94  3.9 | | | | 68  5.4 | 65  5.6 |
| | 65  5.6 | 104  3.5 | 174  2.1 | | | | 109  3.4 | 119  3.1 |
| | 10  36.2 | 17  22.0 | 17  21.7 | | | Cost of Sales/Payables | 17  21.8 | 16  22.6 |
| | 16  22.4 | 28  13.2 | 31  11.8 | | | | 28  13.3 | 29  12.7 |
| | 38  9.7 | 42  8.6 | 53  6.9 | | | | 45  8.2 | 48  7.6 |
| | 6.4 | 4.2 | 2.4 | | | Sales/Working Capital | 3.6 | 3.9 |
| | 8.5 | 7.0 | 4.3 | | | | 8.1 | 7.9 |
| | 26.2 | 53.0 | 11.9 | | | | 14.6 | 90.6 |
| | 30.1 | 28.7 | 30.2 | | | EBIT/Interest | 12.3 | 13.8 |
| | (21) 11.7 | (36) 5.6 | (23) 11.4 | | | | (88) 5.0 | (88) 4.8 |
| | 3.6 | 3.0 | 4.5 | | | | 2.1 | 1.0 |
| | | 6.9 | | | | Net Profit + Depr., Dep., | 6.1 | 10.4 |
| | | (12) 3.3 | | | | Amort./Cur. Mat. L/T/D | (27) 3.5 | (22) 2.8 |
| | | 1.8 | | | | | 1.3 | 1.2 |
| | .1 | .3 | .2 | | | Fixed/Worth | .2 | .3 |
| | .4 | .6 | .5 | | | | .7 | .9 |
| | .8 | 1.6 | 1.0 | | | | 1.6 | 3.1 |
| | .6 | .6 | .5 | | | Debt/Worth | .6 | .8 |
| | 1.3 | 1.1 | 1.8 | | | | 1.7 | 1.5 |
| | 2.4 | 2.3 | 4.1 | | | | 4.5 | 8.8 |
| | 130.0 | 60.0 | 43.2 | | | % Profit Before Taxes/Tangible | 52.3 | 51.0 |
| | (22) 42.5 | (38) 30.6 | (26) 24.0 | | | Net Worth | (92) 27.0 | (79) 22.8 |
| | 26.4 | 14.1 | 14.7 | | | | 10.6 | 3.8 |
| | 38.7 | 22.2 | 16.0 | | | % Profit Before Taxes/Total | 17.6 | 17.9 |
| | 20.2 | 12.1 | 9.8 | | | Assets | 9.1 | 7.6 |
| | 5.8 | 5.1 | 5.1 | | | | 3.6 | .0 |
| | 69.7 | 15.7 | 19.7 | | | Sales/Net Fixed Assets | 18.7 | 22.2 |
| | 17.1 | 8.2 | 8.2 | | | | 8.8 | 7.6 |
| | 5.1 | 4.2 | 4.9 | | | | 5.3 | 4.6 |
| | 3.8 | 2.4 | 1.6 | | | Sales/Total Assets | 2.4 | 2.7 |
| | 2.7 | 2.0 | 1.3 | | | | 1.9 | 1.8 |
| | 1.8 | 1.6 | 1.0 | | | | 1.5 | 1.4 |
| | 1.2 | 1.6 | 1.4 | | | % Depr., Dep., Amort./Sales | 1.1 | 1.2 |
| | (12) 2.1 | (37) 1.9 | (26) 2.0 | | | | (92) 2.0 | (82) 2.5 |
| | 6.1 | 3.4 | 2.6 | | | | 4.2 | 3.7 |
| | 2.8 | 1.5 | | | | % Officers', Directors' | 2.6 | 1.9 |
| | (14) 4.0 | (14) 2.5 | | | | Owners' Comp/Sales | (38) 3.4 | (36) 3.4 |
| | 7.2 | 5.5 | | | | | 9.9 | 9.9 |
| 7371M | 75476M | 420657M | 756269M | 598735M | 549881M | Net Sales ($) | 1985266M | 1733339M |
| 2414M | 28265M | 208890M | 609442M | 561174M | 474306M | Total Assets ($) | 1270384M | 1185835M |

M = $ thousand    MM = $ million
See Pages 9 through 22 for Explanation of Ratios and Data

**Comparative Historical Data**  |  **Current Data Sorted by Sales**

| | | | Type of Statement | | | | | | |
|---|---|---|---|---|---|---|---|---|---|
| 10 | 16 | 16 | Unqualified | | 1 | 6 | 2 | 8 | 6 |
| 18 | 22 | 19 | Reviewed | | 3 | 2 | 6 | 6 | 4 |
| 15 | 12 | 17 | Compiled | 1 | 3 | 5 | 3 | 4 | 1 |
| 9 | 14 | 19 | Tax Returns | 3 | 6 | 7 | 2 | 1 | |
| 30 | 45 | 41 | Other | 1 | 4 | 4 | 5 | 13 | 14 |
| 4/1/09-3/31/10 | 4/1/10-3/31/11 | 4/1/11-3/31/12 | | | 19 (4/1-9/30/11) | | 93 (10/1/11-3/31/12) | | |
| ALL | ALL | ALL | | 0-1MM | 1-3MM | 3-5MM | 5-10MM | 10-25MM | 25MM & OVER |
| 82 | 109 | 112 | **NUMBER OF STATEMENTS** | 5 | 14 | 22 | 14 | 32 | 25 |
| % | % | % | **ASSETS** | % | % | % | % | % | % |
| 9.4 | 11.1 | 11.3 | Cash & Equivalents | | 16.1 | 13.6 | 11.2 | 9.6 | 9.3 |
| 23.8 | 26.8 | 26.8 | Trade Receivables (net) | | 22.6 | 29.4 | 26.2 | 29.0 | 23.6 |
| 27.0 | 24.9 | 23.5 | Inventory | | 26.9 | 15.6 | 23.4 | 28.3 | 24.1 |
| 5.6 | 2.8 | 4.1 | All Other Current | | 5.0 | 3.9 | 2.7 | 2.7 | 7.1 |
| 65.8 | 65.6 | 65.7 | Total Current | | 70.6 | 62.5 | 63.5 | 69.7 | 64.1 |
| 26.2 | 23.9 | 24.9 | Fixed Assets (net) | | 22.1 | 25.6 | 27.1 | 24.1 | 22.7 |
| 3.0 | 4.9 | 3.0 | Intangibles (net) | | 2.8 | 1.5 | 1.8 | 1.9 | 6.5 |
| 5.0 | 5.6 | 6.4 | All Other Non-Current | | 4.5 | 10.4 | 7.6 | 4.3 | 6.7 |
| 100.0 | 100.0 | 100.0 | Total | | 100.0 | 100.0 | 100.0 | 100.0 | 100.0 |
| | | | **LIABILITIES** | | | | | | |
| 13.1 | 10.1 | 9.0 | Notes Payable-Short Term | | 9.5 | 11.1 | 9.0 | 9.7 | 6.8 |
| 4.9 | 3.2 | 4.0 | Cur. Mat.-L.T.D. | | 4.0 | 4.1 | 4.3 | 4.1 | 3.7 |
| 11.4 | 11.1 | 11.9 | Trade Payables | | 6.7 | 12.4 | 10.3 | 15.3 | 10.9 |
| .3 | .1 | .3 | Income Taxes Payable | | .0 | .5 | .0 | .3 | .6 |
| 14.0 | 12.9 | 13.9 | All Other Current | | 10.4 | 4.7 | 6.5 | 9.6 | 20.6 |
| 43.7 | 37.3 | 39.2 | Total Current | | 30.7 | 32.9 | 30.1 | 39.1 | 42.5 |
| 12.1 | 15.1 | 14.0 | Long-Term Debt | | 19.7 | 9.5 | 12.0 | 12.7 | 10.5 |
| .2 | .3 | .6 | Deferred Taxes | | .0 | 1.0 | .7 | .1 | 1.2 |
| 6.5 | 7.9 | 5.5 | All Other Non-Current | | 13.5 | 4.7 | 1.7 | 5.5 | 5.1 |
| 37.4 | 39.5 | 40.7 | Net Worth | | 36.2 | 51.9 | 55.5 | 42.7 | 40.6 |
| 100.0 | 100.0 | 100.0 | Total Liabilities & Net Worth | | 100.0 | 100.0 | 100.0 | 100.0 | 100.0 |
| | | | **INCOME DATA** | | | | | | |
| 100.0 | 100.0 | 100.0 | Net Sales | | 100.0 | 100.0 | 100.0 | 100.0 | 100.0 |
| 31.1 | 32.3 | 30.8 | Gross Profit | | 33.7 | 37.1 | 33.1 | 24.6 | 25.9 |
| 28.8 | 25.1 | 22.4 | Operating Expenses | | 28.6 | 29.0 | 22.9 | 15.1 | 17.4 |
| 2.3 | 7.1 | 8.4 | Operating Profit | | 5.2 | 8.2 | 10.2 | 9.5 | 8.5 |
| 2.0 | 1.0 | .7 | All Other Expenses (net) | | .8 | .6 | .4 | .6 | 1.2 |
| .2 | 6.1 | 7.7 | Profit Before Taxes | | 4.4 | 7.6 | 9.8 | 8.9 | 7.3 |
| | | | **RATIOS** | | | | | | |
| 2.9 | 3.0 | 3.0 | | | 11.3 | 3.0 | 6.5 | 2.9 | 2.1 |
| 1.9 | 1.8 | 1.8 | Current | | 2.2 | 2.1 | 1.8 | 1.8 | 1.4 |
| 1.1 | 1.2 | 1.3 | | | 1.1 | 1.5 | 1.3 | 1.2 | 1.2 |
| 1.6 | 1.7 | 1.9 | | | 6.7 | 2.2 | 3.8 | 1.6 | 1.0 |
| .8 | 1.0 | 1.0 | Quick | | 1.6 | 1.6 | 1.2 | 1.0 | .7 |
| .5 | .6 | .6 | | | .5 | .8 | .6 | .6 | .6 |
| 32  11.4 | 35  10.4 | 37  9.8 | | 8  44.7 | 27  13.5 | 36  10.0 | 45  8.1 | 51  7.2 | |
| 46  8.0 | 51  7.2 | 52  7.0 | Sales/Receivables | 33  10.9 | 46  7.9 | 43  8.5 | 58  6.3 | 57  6.4 | |
| 64  5.7 | 68  5.3 | 69  5.3 | | 46  8.0 | 68  5.4 | 51  7.1 | 81  4.5 | 89  4.1 | |
| 42  8.7 | 30  12.0 | 20  17.9 | | 0  UND | 0  UND | 28  13.1 | 23  15.9 | 41  8.8 | |
| 70  5.2 | 68  5.3 | 58  6.3 | Cost of Sales/Inventory | 55  6.6 | 22  16.9 | 60  6.1 | 63  5.8 | 101  3.6 | |
| 126  2.9 | 127  2.9 | 111  3.3 | | 73  5.0 | 64  5.7 | 122  3.0 | 122  3.0 | 174  2.1 | |
| 14  26.9 | 18  20.4 | 14  25.2 | | 3  104.8 | 14  25.7 | 11  33.0 | 23  16.1 | 22  16.6 | |
| 26  14.3 | 29  12.6 | 27  13.5 | Cost of Sales/Payables | 11  33.2 | 18  19.9 | 21  17.6 | 33  11.0 | 28  12.9 | |
| 45  8.1 | 44  8.2 | 45  8.2 | | 18  20.1 | 46  7.9 | 41  8.9 | 50  7.3 | 54  6.7 | |
| 3.5 | 3.5 | 3.8 | | | 3.2 | 5.9 | 4.4 | 2.9 | 2.8 |
| 8.4 | 6.3 | 7.1 | Sales/Working Capital | | 11.4 | 7.9 | 6.1 | 5.5 | 5.2 |
| 54.0 | 24.4 | 16.8 | | | NM | 12.9 | 36.9 | 15.1 | 15.2 |
| 10.2 | 22.3 | 25.5 | | | 13.1 | 29.9 | 88.5 | 32.2 | 22.8 |
| (73)  2.5 | (99)  6.6 | (96)  8.4 | EBIT/Interest | (13)  4.7 | (18)  4.9 | (10)  6.7 | (29)  15.3 | (21)  11.5 | |
| -2.7 | 2.0 | 3.0 | | | -1.2 | 2.7 | 3.3 | 4.9 | 2.7 |
| 3.7 | 5.1 | 9.0 | Net Profit + Depr., Dep., | | | | | 9.1 | |
| (15)  2.1 | (16)  2.2 | (27)  4.8 | Amort./Cur. Mat. L/T/D | | | | | (10)  5.7 | |
| .5 | -.3 | 2.1 | | | | | | 1.4 | |
| .2 | .3 | .2 | | | .0 | .1 | .2 | .2 | .4 |
| .6 | .6 | .5 | Fixed/Worth | | .4 | .4 | .5 | .5 | .7 |
| 1.8 | 1.5 | 1.4 | | | 1.5 | .8 | 1.5 | 1.0 | 1.6 |
| .6 | .7 | .6 | | | .8 | .5 | .2 | .6 | .7 |
| 1.4 | 1.6 | 1.3 | Debt/Worth | | 2.3 | .8 | 1.1 | 1.3 | 1.9 |
| 3.9 | 3.8 | 3.7 | | | 4.3 | 1.6 | 2.0 | 4.1 | 7.7 |
| 29.1 | 54.6 | 47.7 | % Profit Before Taxes/Tangible | | 109.0 | 61.5 | 59.2 | 45.8 | 40.9 |
| (74)  9.5 | (96)  21.2 | (100)  26.0 | Net Worth | (12)  23.0 | (21)  36.7 | 24.9 | (29)  31.9 | (21)  20.2 | |
| -13.7 | 9.3 | 14.1 | | | 8.7 | 4.0 | 19.7 | 19.8 | 9.6 |
| 13.9 | 20.5 | 20.5 | % Profit Before Taxes/Total | | 24.4 | 29.2 | 22.1 | 21.4 | 13.6 |
| 2.8 | 7.8 | 10.2 | Assets | | 6.2 | 9.6 | 13.4 | 13.2 | 7.7 |
| -6.7 | 1.9 | 4.4 | | | .7 | 1.9 | 6.6 | 8.9 | 3.2 |
| 17.9 | 20.0 | 21.6 | | | 139.7 | 31.1 | 25.3 | 22.8 | 9.7 |
| 9.6 | 8.0 | 8.2 | Sales/Net Fixed Assets | | 18.0 | 6.9 | 10.1 | 8.8 | 6.0 |
| 4.5 | 4.8 | 4.6 | | | 5.5 | 3.7 | 3.7 | 5.5 | 4.6 |
| 2.4 | 2.5 | 2.5 | | | 4.0 | 2.8 | 3.1 | 2.2 | 1.4 |
| 1.7 | 1.7 | 1.7 | Sales/Total Assets | | 2.7 | 2.1 | 1.8 | 1.8 | 1.2 |
| 1.3 | 1.2 | 1.2 | | | 1.7 | 1.4 | 1.5 | 1.3 | 1.1 |
| 1.2 | 1.3 | 1.4 | | | | 1.7 | .9 | .8 | 1.4 |
| (69)  2.5 | (92)  2.5 | (86)  2.1 | % Depr., Dep., Amort./Sales | | (15)  3.1 | (12)  1.8 | (28)  2.0 | (22)  2.1 | |
| 4.5 | 4.5 | 3.5 | | | | 4.5 | 3.6 | 3.0 | 4.1 |
| 2.6 | 1.3 | 1.5 | % Officers', Directors' | | | 2.9 | | | |
| (34)  5.1 | (38)  2.5 | (37)  2.9 | Owners' Comp/Sales | | (12)  5.1 | | | | |
| 11.4 | 4.0 | 6.9 | | | | 8.7 | | | |
| 1135870M | 1735028M | 2408389M | Net Sales ($) | 3512M | 27158M | 86682M | 116847M | 510166M | 1664024M |
| 822409M | 1355099M | 1884491M | Total Assets ($) | 1936M | 11223M | 52466M | 63864M | 333161M | 1421841M |

© RMA 2012    M = $ thousand    MM = $ million
See Pages 9 through 22 for Explanation of Ratios and Data

## Current Data Sorted by Assets | Comparative Historical Data

| 0-500M | 500M-2MM | 2-10MM | 10-50MM | 50-100MM | 100-250MM | Type of Statement | 4/1/07-3/31/08 ALL | 4/1/08-3/31/09 ALL |
|---|---|---|---|---|---|---|---|---|
| | | 5 | 10 | 1 | 4 | Unqualified | 36 | 37 |
| | 15 | 49 | 27 | 1 | | Reviewed | 87 | 90 |
| 5 | 25 | 29 | 5 | | | Compiled | 93 | 65 |
| 12 | 19 | 7 | 1 | | | Tax Returns | 24 | 34 |
| 4 | 27 | 30 | 31 | 7 | 1 | Other | 96 | 118 |
| | 66 (4/1-9/30/11) | | 249 (10/1/11-3/31/12) | | | | | |
| 21 | 86 | 120 | 74 | 9 | 5 | NUMBER OF STATEMENTS | 336 | 344 |
| % | % | % | % | % | % | ASSETS | % | % |
| 13.7 | 10.8 | 9.7 | 5.7 | | | Cash & Equivalents | 7.6 | 8.2 |
| 30.4 | 37.0 | 28.9 | 26.8 | | | Trade Receivables (net) | 30.0 | 28.7 |
| 10.0 | 16.2 | 21.8 | 17.0 | | | Inventory | 17.7 | 18.2 |
| 4.7 | 3.4 | 2.2 | 9.0 | | | All Other Current | 3.4 | 2.8 |
| 58.7 | 67.3 | 62.7 | 58.5 | | | Total Current | 58.6 | 58.0 |
| 35.8 | 26.4 | 30.9 | 27.6 | | | Fixed Assets (net) | 33.4 | 32.3 |
| 2.5 | 1.5 | 2.3 | 6.3 | | | Intangibles (net) | 2.6 | 3.7 |
| 3.0 | 4.7 | 4.2 | 7.6 | | | All Other Non-Current | 5.3 | 6.0 |
| 100.0 | 100.0 | 100.0 | 100.0 | | | Total | 100.0 | 100.0 |
| | | | | | | LIABILITIES | | |
| 22.2 | 12.1 | 8.8 | 12.3 | | | Notes Payable-Short Term | 13.1 | 12.2 |
| 6.1 | 4.2 | 4.0 | 3.2 | | | Cur. Mat.-L.T.D. | 5.7 | 5.9 |
| 10.3 | 14.4 | 13.5 | 11.2 | | | Trade Payables | 13.0 | 12.6 |
| .0 | .1 | .1 | .2 | | | Income Taxes Payable | .2 | .2 |
| 16.3 | 9.4 | 10.5 | 8.6 | | | All Other Current | 10.1 | 8.8 |
| 54.8 | 40.2 | 37.0 | 35.6 | | | Total Current | 42.0 | 39.7 |
| 37.6 | 14.7 | 13.8 | 13.9 | | | Long-Term Debt | 18.3 | 19.6 |
| .0 | .3 | .7 | 1.1 | | | Deferred Taxes | .6 | .7 |
| 10.7 | 12.4 | 6.7 | 4.6 | | | All Other Non-Current | 7.0 | 6.5 |
| -3.0 | 32.4 | 41.8 | 44.8 | | | Net Worth | 32.1 | 33.6 |
| 100.0 | 100.0 | 100.0 | 100.0 | | | Total Liabilities & Net Worth | 100.0 | 100.0 |
| | | | | | | INCOME DATA | | |
| 100.0 | 100.0 | 100.0 | 100.0 | | | Net Sales | 100.0 | 100.0 |
| 44.6 | 32.6 | 27.4 | 22.2 | | | Gross Profit | 27.0 | 26.5 |
| 37.3 | 26.5 | 21.2 | 14.8 | | | Operating Expenses | 22.4 | 22.7 |
| 7.3 | 6.1 | 6.2 | 7.4 | | | Operating Profit | 4.7 | 3.7 |
| 1.9 | .6 | .4 | .2 | | | All Other Expenses (net) | 1.1 | .9 |
| 5.5 | 5.5 | 5.8 | 7.2 | | | Profit Before Taxes | 3.6 | 2.8 |
| | | | | | | RATIOS | | |
| 2.3 | 3.6 | 3.1 | 3.1 | | | Current | 2.5 | 2.7 |
| 1.1 | 2.1 | 1.8 | 1.5 | | | | 1.4 | 1.6 |
| .6 | 1.1 | 1.2 | 1.2 | | | | 1.0 | 1.1 |
| 1.2 | 2.4 | 1.8 | 1.7 | | | Quick | 1.5 | 1.7 |
| .8 | 1.5 | 1.1 | .9 | | | | .9 (343) | .9 |
| .3 | .8 | .6 | .6 | | | | .6 | .6 |
| 22 16.7 | 40 9.1 | 40 9.2 | 46 7.9 | | | Sales/Receivables | 39 9.4 | 36 10.2 |
| 41 9.0 | 50 7.3 | 55 6.6 | 59 6.2 | | | | 52 7.0 | 49 7.4 |
| 51 7.2 | 68 5.4 | 73 5.0 | 81 4.5 | | | | 68 5.4 | 67 5.5 |
| 0 UND | 9 39.5 | 27 13.3 | 23 15.9 | | | Cost of Sales/Inventory | 16 22.2 | 17 21.2 |
| 10 37.7 | 27 13.6 | 56 6.5 | 47 7.8 | | | | 40 9.2 | 39 9.4 |
| 28 13.1 | 57 6.4 | 96 3.8 | 83 4.4 | | | | 69 5.3 | 71 5.1 |
| 0 UND | 13 28.3 | 20 18.5 | 19 19.0 | | | Cost of Sales/Payables | 14 25.4 | 15 25.0 |
| 20 18.7 | 30 12.0 | 33 11.0 | 33 11.2 | | | | 27 13.6 | 26 14.2 |
| 42 8.7 | 45 8.1 | 51 7.2 | 43 8.4 | | | | 43 8.4 | 39 9.4 |
| 7.0 | 4.3 | 3.9 | 4.0 | | | Sales/Working Capital | 4.7 | 4.8 |
| 57.9 | 7.0 | 7.6 | 7.2 | | | | 11.3 | 10.2 |
| -27.5 | 54.2 | 23.0 | 14.9 | | | | UND | 62.5 |
| 11.6 | 15.1 | 19.6 | 21.4 | | | EBIT/Interest | 6.7 | 7.2 |
| (19) 2.9 | (72) 4.4 | (112) 6.9 | (70) 6.8 | | (314) | | 2.9 (325) | 2.9 |
| 1.0 | 1.3 | 2.4 | 3.4 | | | | 1.0 | .5 |
| | 13.8 | 6.6 | 9.9 | | | Net Profit + Depr., Dep., Amort./Cur. Mat. L/T/D | 3.1 | 3.4 |
| | (11) 2.2 | (29) 2.3 | (25) 3.4 | | (84) | | 1.9 (95) | 1.7 |
| | .7 | 1.3 | 2.5 | | | | .8 | .9 |
| .3 | .2 | .4 | .4 | | | Fixed/Worth | .4 | .4 |
| 1.8 | .7 | .8 | .6 | | | | 1.0 | .9 |
| -1.2 | 3.2 | 1.6 | 1.7 | | | | 2.8 | 2.9 |
| 1.4 | .5 | .6 | .7 | | | Debt/Worth | .7 | .8 |
| 3.3 | 1.5 | 1.6 | 1.7 | | | | 2.1 | 2.1 |
| -3.0 | 7.6 | 4.1 | 3.3 | | | | 6.5 | 7.2 |
| 100.0 | 66.6 | 39.3 | 37.4 | | | % Profit Before Taxes/Tangible Net Worth | 34.7 | 33.8 |
| (13) 58.5 | (70) 31.5 | (112) 21.7 | (70) 26.8 | | (288) | | 14.7 (291) | 14.2 |
| 8.8 | 7.3 | 8.3 | 10.9 | | | | 2.5 | -.3 |
| 24.5 | 26.8 | 17.4 | 14.2 | | | % Profit Before Taxes/Total Assets | 12.7 | 11.9 |
| 8.7 | 9.4 | 9.6 | 8.2 | | | | 5.1 | 4.3 |
| .6 | 1.0 | 3.2 | 4.1 | | | | .3 | -1.0 |
| 64.3 | 18.6 | 12.2 | 11.4 | | | Sales/Net Fixed Assets | 12.3 | 12.8 |
| 12.7 | 10.0 | 6.6 | 5.7 | | | | 5.9 | 6.1 |
| 6.6 | 5.9 | 3.6 | 3.3 | | | | 3.5 | 3.6 |
| 4.4 | 3.1 | 2.3 | 1.9 | | | Sales/Total Assets | 2.6 | 2.6 |
| 3.3 | 2.3 | 1.7 | 1.4 | | | | 1.9 | 1.8 |
| 2.4 | 1.7 | 1.3 | 1.0 | | | | 1.3 | 1.3 |
| 1.0 | 1.7 | 1.8 | 1.4 | | | % Depr., Dep., Amort./Sales | 2.0 | 1.9 |
| (13) 1.6 | (75) 2.9 | (107) 3.0 | (70) 2.9 | | (308) | | 3.5 (307) | 3.5 |
| 5.0 | 4.8 | 4.7 | 4.5 | | | | 5.5 | 5.1 |
| 4.9 | 3.5 | 2.3 | 1.5 | | | % Officers', Directors' Owners' Comp/Sales | 2.5 | 2.4 |
| (13) 7.3 | (54) 5.9 | (64) 4.5 | (22) 2.6 | | (180) | | 4.8 (177) | 4.6 |
| 13.5 | 9.2 | 7.8 | 3.5 | | | | 7.6 | 8.3 |
| 23582M | 246409M | 997753M | 2121853M | 755518M | 1208023M | Net Sales ($) | 4844617M | 4808539M |
| 6010M | 105065M | 543366M | 1482849M | 679274M | 972389M | Total Assets ($) | 3107992M | 3407732M |

M = $ thousand   MM = $ million
See Pages 9 through 22 for Explanation of Ratios and Data

## Comparative Historical Data | Current Data Sorted by Sales

| Hist 1 | Hist 2 | Hist 3 | Type of Statement | 0-1MM | 1-3MM | 3-5MM | 5-10MM | 10-25MM | 25MM & OVER |
|---|---|---|---|---|---|---|---|---|---|
| 26 | 26 | 20 | Unqualified | | | 1 | 1 | 8 | 11 |
| 85 | 89 | 92 | Reviewed | 1 | 5 | 18 | 25 | 30 | 13 |
| 57 | 66 | 64 | Compiled | 2 | 20 | 21 | 13 | 4 | 4 |
| 30 | 45 | 39 | Tax Returns | 8 | 15 | 6 | 7 | 2 | 1 |
| 89 | 85 | 100 | Other | 5 | 17 | 15 | 20 | 17 | 26 |
| 4/1/09-3/31/10 ALL | 4/1/10-3/31/11 ALL | 4/1/11-3/31/12 ALL | | \[66 (4/1-9/30/11)\] | | | \[249 (10/1/11-3/31/12)\] | | |
| 287 | 311 | 315 | **NUMBER OF STATEMENTS** | 16 | 57 | 61 | 65 | 61 | 55 |
| % | % | % | **ASSETS** | % | % | % | % | % | % |
| 10.1 | 9.7 | 9.2 | Cash & Equivalents | 12.4 | 11.3 | 9.7 | 11.0 | 7.2 | 5.4 |
| 27.3 | 30.1 | 30.4 | Trade Receivables (net) | 27.5 | 35.6 | 30.4 | 30.6 | 27.4 | 28.6 |
| 17.3 | 16.3 | 18.0 | Inventory | 13.9 | 16.5 | 19.0 | 20.2 | 17.8 | 17.5 |
| 4.4 | 3.7 | 4.6 | All Other Current | 3.5 | 3.1 | 2.9 | 3.2 | 8.5 | 5.7 |
| 59.1 | 59.9 | 62.2 | Total Current | 57.3 | 66.6 | 62.0 | 65.0 | 60.9 | 57.2 |
| 33.2 | 31.7 | 29.3 | Fixed Assets (net) | 37.8 | 26.1 | 31.5 | 27.3 | 29.4 | 30.1 |
| 2.7 | 2.6 | 3.2 | Intangibles (net) | 3.1 | 1.4 | 1.8 | 2.7 | 3.0 | 7.3 |
| 5.0 | 5.8 | 5.3 | All Other Non-Current | 1.7 | 5.9 | 4.6 | 5.0 | 6.7 | 5.3 |
| 100.0 | 100.0 | 100.0 | Total | 100.0 | 100.0 | 100.0 | 100.0 | 100.0 | 100.0 |
| | | | **LIABILITIES** | | | | | | |
| 10.7 | 9.6 | 11.3 | Notes Payable-Short Term | 21.8 | 14.1 | 10.7 | 8.4 | 11.6 | 9.2 |
| 6.0 | 5.4 | 4.0 | Cur. Mat.-L.T.D. | 7.4 | 4.2 | 4.9 | 2.4 | 4.5 | 3.2 |
| 10.9 | 12.8 | 12.9 | Trade Payables | 10.9 | 13.1 | 11.5 | 13.6 | 12.3 | 14.5 |
| .1 | .1 | .1 | Income Taxes Payable | .0 | .0 | .0 | .3 | .1 | .2 |
| 9.6 | 10.6 | 10.0 | All Other Current | 9.4 | 11.7 | 10.3 | 10.5 | 9.4 | 8.4 |
| 37.4 | 38.6 | 38.4 | Total Current | 49.5 | 43.1 | 37.5 | 35.1 | 37.9 | 35.4 |
| 19.7 | 16.3 | 15.9 | Long-Term Debt | 42.2 | 17.3 | 15.4 | 10.4 | 15.2 | 14.5 |
| .7 | .7 | .6 | Deferred Taxes | .0 | .2 | .3 | .9 | .8 | 1.1 |
| 6.3 | 6.0 | 8.0 | All Other Non-Current | 10.3 | 13.4 | 8.4 | 7.4 | 5.3 | 5.3 |
| 36.0 | 38.5 | 37.1 | Net Worth | -1.9 | 26.0 | 38.3 | 46.1 | 40.9 | 43.6 |
| 100.0 | 100.0 | 100.0 | Total Liabilities & Net Worth | 100.0 | 100.0 | 100.0 | 100.0 | 100.0 | 100.0 |
| | | | **INCOME DATA** | | | | | | |
| 100.0 | 100.0 | 100.0 | Net Sales | 100.0 | 100.0 | 100.0 | 100.0 | 100.0 | 100.0 |
| 25.6 | 28.3 | 28.5 | Gross Profit | 44.5 | 32.7 | 29.4 | 31.1 | 23.5 | 21.1 |
| 25.7 | 23.2 | 22.0 | Operating Expenses | 39.2 | 27.8 | 23.9 | 23.1 | 16.2 | 13.9 |
| -.1 | 5.2 | 6.5 | Operating Profit | 5.3 | 4.8 | 5.5 | 8.0 | 7.2 | 7.2 |
| 1.1 | .8 | .5 | All Other Expenses (net) | 2.5 | .8 | .3 | .3 | -.1 | .5 |
| -1.2 | 4.4 | 6.1 | Profit Before Taxes | 2.8 | 4.0 | 5.2 | 7.7 | 7.3 | 6.7 |
| | | | **RATIOS** | | | | | | |
| 3.3 | 3.2 | 3.0 | Current | 2.0 | 3.5 | 3.4 | 3.4 | 3.1 | 2.5 |
| 1.7 | 1.7 | 1.8 | | 1.2 | 1.9 | 1.9 | 2.0 | 1.5 | 1.6 |
| 1.1 | 1.1 | 1.2 | | .5 | 1.0 | 1.1 | 1.4 | 1.2 | 1.2 |
| 2.2 | 2.2 | 1.9 | Quick | 1.3 | 2.4 | 2.1 | 2.3 | 1.8 | 1.6 |
| 1.0 | 1.0 | 1.1 | | .7 | 1.3 | 1.1 | 1.3 | 1.0 | .9 |
| .6 | .7 | .6 | | .3 | .7 | .6 | .7 | .6 | .7 |
| 41 9.0 | 41 8.9 | 41 9.0 | Sales/Receivables | 23 16.0 | 41 9.0 | 40 9.1 | 40 9.1 | 42 8.6 | 46 8.0 |
| 54 6.7 | 54 6.8 | 54 6.8 | | 41 8.9 | 51 7.2 | 54 6.7 | 55 6.6 | 54 6.7 | 56 6.5 |
| 75 4.8 | 72 5.1 | 70 5.2 | | 54 6.8 | 78 4.7 | 73 5.0 | 73 5.0 | 68 5.4 | 72 5.1 |
| 21 17.5 | 15 25.1 | 17 21.7 | Cost of Sales/Inventory | 4 95.6 | 5 74.0 | 18 19.9 | 27 13.7 | 20 17.9 | 29 12.5 |
| 45 8.2 | 36 10.2 | 42 8.7 | | 26 14.0 | 14 26.3 | 47 7.7 | 51 7.1 | 47 7.8 | 44 8.3 |
| 72 5.1 | 63 5.8 | 83 4.4 | | 111 3.3 | 69 5.3 | 91 4.0 | 94 3.9 | 74 4.9 | 68 5.4 |
| 15 23.6 | 16 22.2 | 17 21.0 | Cost of Sales/Payables | 0 UND | 10 35.4 | 17 21.8 | 18 20.1 | 18 20.0 | 24 15.0 |
| 26 14.2 | 28 13.0 | 31 11.7 | | 29 12.4 | 31 11.6 | 28 13.1 | 29 12.5 | 31 11.7 | 34 10.8 |
| 42 8.7 | 43 8.5 | 47 7.7 | | 64 5.7 | 50 7.3 | 40 9.2 | 50 7.3 | 45 8.1 | 49 7.5 |
| 3.4 | 4.0 | 4.2 | Sales/Working Capital | 6.3 | 3.3 | 4.3 | 3.8 | 4.3 | 4.5 |
| 7.4 | 8.0 | 7.4 | | 42.6 | 7.2 | 6.8 | 6.5 | 8.3 | 9.4 |
| 75.2 | 77.9 | 28.2 | | -97.6 | NM | 45.5 | 12.7 | 18.3 | 20.0 |
| 5.5 | 12.2 | 16.8 | EBIT/Interest | 2.9 | 14.4 | 11.7 | 28.3 | 21.7 | 17.1 |
| (266) 1.8 | (285) 4.1 | (285) 6.3 | | (15) 2.0 | (49) 4.9 | (56) 4.3 | (56) 7.3 | (59) 6.4 | (50) 8.9 |
| -1.2 | 1.3 | 2.2 | | .5 | 1.0 | 1.4 | 2.5 | 3.7 | 4.6 |
| 2.6 | 4.1 | 7.7 | Net Profit + Depr., Dep., Amort./Cur. Mat. L/T/D | | | 2.4 | 10.1 | 9.2 | 10.1 |
| (81) 1.6 | (72) 2.4 | (70) 2.7 | | | | (15) 1.5 | (16) 5.1 | (15) 2.6 | (20) 3.1 |
| .5 | 1.1 | 1.7 | | | | 1.0 | 1.7 | 1.9 | 2.3 |
| .3 | .3 | .4 | Fixed/Worth | .3 | .3 | .3 | .3 | .3 | .5 |
| .9 | .8 | .8 | | 2.3 | .7 | .8 | .6 | .9 | 1.0 |
| 2.6 | 1.8 | 1.9 | | -1.3 | 3.0 | 1.9 | 1.5 | 1.9 | 1.9 |
| .6 | .5 | .6 | Debt/Worth | 1.4 | .7 | .5 | .5 | .6 | .7 |
| 1.7 | 1.4 | 1.7 | | 3.7 | 1.6 | 1.7 | .9 | 2.1 | 1.7 |
| 5.9 | 4.6 | 4.4 | | -3.3 | 9.3 | 4.4 | 3.2 | 4.1 | 3.7 |
| 17.7 | 40.2 | 49.5 | % Profit Before Taxes/Tangible Net Worth | 93.4 | 54.6 | 40.8 | 38.2 | 59.7 | 39.2 |
| (249) 4.7 | (271) 17.0 | (278) 25.4 | | (10) 32.4 | (46) 27.8 | (53) 20.7 | (60) 21.9 | (58) 27.7 | (51) 25.9 |
| -12.3 | 3.6 | 8.6 | | -8.8 | 3.3 | 5.2 | 10.8 | 11.3 | 15.4 |
| 6.6 | 14.3 | 17.1 | % Profit Before Taxes/Total Assets | 16.3 | 23.2 | 21.2 | 19.0 | 16.2 | 14.0 |
| 1.4 | 6.4 | 8.7 | | 4.6 | 9.8 | 6.4 | 10.1 | 9.2 | 8.7 |
| -6.7 | .9 | 3.1 | | -.9 | .1 | 1.0 | 3.7 | 4.9 | 4.3 |
| 10.8 | 12.4 | 15.2 | Sales/Net Fixed Assets | 23.0 | 20.9 | 14.3 | 16.4 | 13.0 | 9.1 |
| 5.4 | 6.4 | 7.0 | | 9.5 | 9.0 | 6.8 | 8.0 | 5.6 | 5.6 |
| 2.9 | 3.5 | 4.0 | | 3.4 | 5.3 | 3.9 | 4.2 | 3.3 | 3.6 |
| 2.1 | 2.5 | 2.5 | Sales/Total Assets | 3.4 | 2.8 | 2.5 | 2.6 | 2.1 | 2.0 |
| 1.5 | 1.8 | 1.8 | | 2.4 | 2.2 | 1.7 | 1.9 | 1.5 | 1.6 |
| 1.1 | 1.3 | 1.3 | | 1.2 | 1.5 | 1.2 | 1.3 | 1.2 | 1.2 |
| 2.5 | 2.0 | 1.6 | % Depr., Dep., Amort./Sales | 1.1 | 1.1 | 2.0 | 1.5 | 1.6 | 1.5 |
| (259) 4.5 | (279) 3.8 | (276) 3.0 | | (12) 2.5 | (46) 3.1 | (56) 3.4 | (58) 2.4 | (52) 2.8 | (52) 3.4 |
| 6.7 | 5.9 | 4.7 | | 4.8 | 5.0 | 5.5 | 4.0 | 4.4 | 4.1 |
| 2.5 | 2.4 | 2.6 | % Officers', Directors' Owners' Comp/Sales | | 3.8 | 3.0 | 2.7 | 1.9 | 1.2 |
| (138) 4.5 | (173) 4.7 | (154) 4.8 | | | (38) 7.0 | (37) 4.7 | (33) 6.0 | (25) 3.0 | (13) 1.8 |
| 8.1 | 9.0 | 8.3 | | | 10.5 | 8.0 | 7.9 | 4.5 | 2.7 |
| 3883346M | 4212257M | 5353138M | Net Sales ($) | 10524M | 115963M | 232757M | 455435M | 960209M | 3578250M |
| 3093038M | 2977928M | 3788953M | Total Assets ($) | 5390M | 63705M | 142111M | 274322M | 718272M | 2585153M |

## Current Data Sorted by Assets      Comparative Historical Data

| 0-500M | 500M-2MM | 2-10MM | 10-50MM | 50-100MM | 100-250MM | Type of Statement | | |
|---|---|---|---|---|---|---|---|---|
| | | 2 | 2 | 3 | 1 | Unqualified | 11 | 15 |
| | 4 | 17 | 9 | | 2 | Reviewed | 48 | 41 |
| | 10 | 15 | 3 | | | Compiled | 15 | 22 |
| 1 | 16 | 5 | | | | Tax Returns | 15 | 13 |
| 1 | 8 | 17 | 16 | 3 | 2 | Other | 43 | 36 |
| | 25 (4/1-9/30/11) | | 112 (10/1/11-3/31/12) | | | | 4/1/07-3/31/08 | 4/1/08-3/31/09 |
| 0-500M | 500M-2MM | 2-10MM | 10-50MM | 50-100MM | 100-250MM | | ALL | ALL |
| 2 | 38 | 56 | 30 | 8 | 3 | NUMBER OF STATEMENTS | 132 | 127 |
| % | % | % | % | % | % | **ASSETS** | % | % |
| | 9.1 | 12.8 | 5.1 | | | Cash & Equivalents | 6.6 | 7.4 |
| | 29.8 | 24.9 | 23.5 | | | Trade Receivables (net) | 26.4 | 23.5 |
| | 21.5 | 23.9 | 26.3 | | | Inventory | 27.2 | 31.0 |
| | 1.3 | 2.6 | 2.5 | | | All Other Current | 2.4 | 1.7 |
| | 61.7 | 64.3 | 57.5 | | | Total Current | 62.6 | 63.6 |
| | 24.4 | 23.3 | 31.2 | | | Fixed Assets (net) | 27.5 | 28.0 |
| | 8.0 | 6.4 | 8.5 | | | Intangibles (net) | 3.2 | 2.4 |
| | 5.9 | 6.0 | 2.8 | | | All Other Non-Current | 6.7 | 5.9 |
| | 100.0 | 100.0 | 100.0 | | | Total | 100.0 | 100.0 |
| | | | | | | **LIABILITIES** | | |
| | 5.2 | 7.4 | 7.8 | | | Notes Payable-Short Term | 11.7 | 13.0 |
| | 5.7 | 4.3 | 5.7 | | | Cur. Mat.-L.T.D. | 4.9 | 5.1 |
| | 14.8 | 11.9 | 11.5 | | | Trade Payables | 13.5 | 11.1 |
| | .2 | .1 | .1 | | | Income Taxes Payable | .4 | .2 |
| | 8.7 | 7.4 | 7.5 | | | All Other Current | 9.1 | 8.1 |
| | 34.6 | 31.1 | 32.5 | | | Total Current | 39.6 | 37.5 |
| | 23.1 | 12.7 | 16.3 | | | Long-Term Debt | 17.9 | 15.8 |
| | .2 | .8 | .8 | | | Deferred Taxes | .7 | .8 |
| | 14.1 | 6.3 | 5.9 | | | All Other Non-Current | 5.0 | 8.1 |
| | 27.9 | 49.1 | 44.5 | | | Net Worth | 36.9 | 37.8 |
| | 100.0 | 100.0 | 100.0 | | | Total Liabilities & Net Worth | 100.0 | 100.0 |
| | | | | | | **INCOME DATA** | | |
| | 100.0 | 100.0 | 100.0 | | | Net Sales | 100.0 | 100.0 |
| | 42.7 | 33.9 | 34.2 | | | Gross Profit | 34.6 | 33.6 |
| | 34.8 | 24.9 | 23.5 | | | Operating Expenses | 29.4 | 28.9 |
| | 7.8 | 9.0 | 10.7 | | | Operating Profit | 5.2 | 4.7 |
| | 1.5 | .7 | 1.6 | | | All Other Expenses (net) | 1.7 | 1.1 |
| | 6.3 | 8.3 | 9.1 | | | Profit Before Taxes | 3.5 | 3.6 |
| | | | | | | **RATIOS** | | |
| | 3.0 | 3.9 | 3.3 | | | | 2.4 | 2.8 |
| | 2.0 | 2.3 | 1.8 | | | Current | 1.5 | 1.7 |
| | 1.3 | 1.4 | 1.3 | | | | 1.1 | 1.2 |
| | 2.1 | 2.3 | 1.4 | | | | 1.4 | 1.4 |
| | 1.3 | 1.2 | .8 | | | Quick | .8 | .8 |
| | .6 | .8 | .7 | | | | .5 | .5 |
| | 35   10.4 | 38   9.6 | 42   8.7 | | | | 35   10.3 | 32   11.4 |
| | 49   7.4 | 49   7.4 | 50   7.3 | | | Sales/Receivables | 47   7.8 | 41   9.0 |
| | 58   6.3 | 65   5.6 | 69   5.3 | | | | 62   5.9 | 50   7.3 |
| | 26   14.1 | 35   10.3 | 70   5.2 | | | | 36   10.2 | 37   9.9 |
| | 47   7.7 | 68   5.4 | 91   4.0 | | | Cost of Sales/Inventory | 76   4.8 | 84   4.4 |
| | 107   3.4 | 118   3.1 | 135   2.7 | | | | 128   2.9 | 145   2.5 |
| | 17   22.0 | 20   18.4 | 29   12.5 | | | | 20   17.9 | 15   25.1 |
| | 32   11.5 | 30   12.2 | 41   8.9 | | | Cost of Sales/Payables | 32   11.4 | 27   13.4 |
| | 65   5.6 | 43   8.5 | 53   6.9 | | | | 47   7.8 | 44   8.3 |
| | 5.6 | 3.2 | 3.6 | | | | 5.2 | 4.4 |
| | 7.9 | 4.8 | 6.4 | | | Sales/Working Capital | 10.2 | 7.6 |
| | 17.5 | 10.7 | 10.2 | | | | 24.2 | 17.7 |
| | 12.9 | 17.4 | 23.0 | | | | 6.9 | 9.5 |
| | (36) 6.0 | (47) 9.1 | (27) 11.1 | | | EBIT/Interest | (117) 2.2 | (118) 3.4 |
| | 1.9 | 2.9 | 4.2 | | | | .9 | 1.0 |
| | | 5.0 | | | | Net Profit + Depr., Dep., | 2.2 | 4.1 |
| | | (11) 2.4 | | | | Amort./Cur. Mat. L/T/D | (42) 1.3 | (50) 1.3 |
| | | 1.9 | | | | | .7 | .4 |
| | .3 | .2 | .5 | | | | .3 | .4 |
| | .7 | .5 | .8 | | | Fixed/Worth | .7 | .7 |
| | NM | 1.0 | 1.6 | | | | 1.6 | 1.6 |
| | 1.0 | .5 | .8 | | | | .9 | .8 |
| | 2.1 | 1.5 | 1.4 | | | Debt/Worth | 1.8 | 1.6 |
| | NM | 2.7 | 2.2 | | | | 4.6 | 4.2 |
| | 65.8 | 60.8 | 35.8 | | | % Profit Before Taxes/Tangible | 35.4 | 39.2 |
| | (29) 36.8 | (54) 34.2 | (27) 27.8 | | | Net Worth | (115) 14.4 | (116) 15.4 |
| | 9.7 | 11.6 | 19.2 | | | | .1 | 1.8 |
| | 25.3 | 20.9 | 19.1 | | | % Profit Before Taxes/Total | 13.9 | 14.6 |
| | 8.4 | 11.5 | 11.3 | | | Assets | 4.9 | 6.2 |
| | 1.3 | 5.8 | 5.8 | | | | -.2 | .2 |
| | 41.0 | 21.6 | 7.4 | | | | 17.2 | 15.9 |
| | 10.7 | 7.7 | 5.6 | | | Sales/Net Fixed Assets | 8.1 | 7.3 |
| | 5.2 | 4.1 | 2.9 | | | | 4.3 | 4.2 |
| | 2.9 | 2.0 | 1.9 | | | | 2.5 | 2.4 |
| | 2.2 | 1.6 | 1.6 | | | Sales/Total Assets | 2.0 | 1.9 |
| | 1.4 | 1.3 | 1.1 | | | | 1.4 | 1.4 |
| | 1.0 | .9 | 1.7 | | | | 1.2 | 1.3 |
| | (27) 2.3 | (52) 2.0 | (28) 3.1 | | | % Depr., Dep., Amort./Sales | (117) 2.6 | (118) 2.9 |
| | 4.4 | 4.3 | 3.8 | | | | 4.9 | 4.9 |
| | 4.6 | 1.0 | | | | % Officers', Directors' | 2.5 | 2.3 |
| | (25) 6.3 | (25) 3.2 | | | | Owners' Comp/Sales | (52) 5.4 | (57) 4.7 |
| | 10.1 | 5.7 | | | | | 8.1 | 9.2 |
| 2552M | 96872M | 475929M | 993782M | 689478M | 526431M | Net Sales ($) | 2657695M | 1993863M |
| 734M | 43575M | 279167M | 654759M | 502040M | 547488M | Total Assets ($) | 1623446M | 1371120M |

## Comparative Historical Data

## Current Data Sorted by Sales

| | | | Type of Statement | | | | | | |
|---|---|---|---|---|---|---|---|---|---|
| 13 | 7 | 8 | Unqualified | | | | 1 | 2 | 5 |
| 31 | 25 | 32 | Reviewed | | 3 | 4 | 6 | 11 | 8 |
| 29 | 23 | 28 | Compiled | 1 | 5 | 9 | 11 | 1 | 1 |
| 15 | 11 | 22 | Tax Returns | 2 | 13 | 5 | 1 | 1 | |
| 47 | 46 | 47 | Other | | 6 | 7 | 5 | 12 | 17 |
| 4/1/09-3/31/10 ALL | 4/1/10-3/31/11 ALL | 4/1/11-3/31/12 ALL | | 25 (4/1-9/30/11) | | | 112 (10/1/11-3/31/12) | | |
| | | | | 0-1MM | 1-3MM | 3-5MM | 5-10MM | 10-25MM | 25MM & OVER |
| 135 | 112 | 137 | NUMBER OF STATEMENTS | 3 | 27 | 25 | 24 | 27 | 31 |
| % | % | % | ASSETS | % | % | % | % | % | % |
| 8.7 | 8.4 | 9.7 | Cash & Equivalents | | 8.7 | 16.5 | 10.4 | 7.1 | 7.2 |
| 21.2 | 23.9 | 26.0 | Trade Receivables (net) | | 26.2 | 27.2 | 30.2 | 24.7 | 23.9 |
| 27.1 | 24.9 | 23.6 | Inventory | | 19.2 | 19.7 | 23.5 | 31.1 | 25.6 |
| 3.0 | 2.5 | 2.3 | All Other Current | | 1.5 | 2.5 | 2.8 | 1.5 | 3.3 |
| 60.0 | 59.7 | 61.5 | Total Current | | 55.5 | 65.9 | 66.8 | 64.4 | 59.9 |
| 26.3 | 28.3 | 25.5 | Fixed Assets (net) | | 27.9 | 20.8 | 26.5 | 25.9 | 25.6 |
| 6.0 | 5.4 | 7.6 | Intangibles (net) | | 10.3 | 7.5 | 2.0 | 6.7 | 9.8 |
| 7.7 | 6.6 | 5.3 | All Other Non-Current | | 6.3 | 5.8 | 4.8 | 3.0 | 4.7 |
| 100.0 | 100.0 | 100.0 | Total | | 100.0 | 100.0 | 100.0 | 100.0 | 100.0 |
| | | | LIABILITIES | | | | | | |
| 11.0 | 9.7 | 6.9 | Notes Payable-Short Term | | 4.7 | 6.4 | 8.5 | 6.5 | 8.5 |
| 5.4 | 5.9 | 4.9 | Cur. Mat.-L.T.D. | | 5.4 | 4.2 | 6.1 | 3.9 | 4.9 |
| 9.7 | 11.7 | 12.2 | Trade Payables | | 10.9 | 13.9 | 12.3 | 13.8 | 10.8 |
| .1 | .1 | .1 | Income Taxes Payable | | .3 | .0 | .1 | .2 | .0 |
| 8.5 | 8.4 | 7.8 | All Other Current | | 7.2 | 6.4 | 5.6 | 9.2 | 8.4 |
| 34.7 | 35.8 | 31.9 | Total Current | | 28.5 | 31.0 | 32.7 | 33.6 | 32.6 |
| 16.3 | 16.2 | 16.1 | Long-Term Debt | | 27.6 | 12.3 | 14.0 | 12.4 | 12.5 |
| .8 | .7 | .7 | Deferred Taxes | | .3 | .6 | .8 | .9 | .9 |
| 12.6 | 9.5 | 8.4 | All Other Non-Current | | 16.9 | 7.4 | 7.7 | 3.3 | 7.6 |
| 35.5 | 37.8 | 42.9 | Net Worth | | 26.6 | 48.7 | 44.9 | 49.7 | 46.5 |
| 100.0 | 100.0 | 100.0 | Total Liabilities & Net Worth | | 100.0 | 100.0 | 100.0 | 100.0 | 100.0 |
| | | | INCOME DATA | | | | | | |
| 100.0 | 100.0 | 100.0 | Net Sales | | 100.0 | 100.0 | 100.0 | 100.0 | 100.0 |
| 33.5 | 34.3 | 36.9 | Gross Profit | | 42.2 | 39.3 | 34.0 | 34.5 | 33.3 |
| 33.6 | 28.0 | 27.8 | Operating Expenses | | 35.6 | 31.8 | 22.2 | 23.4 | 24.2 |
| -.1 | 6.2 | 9.1 | Operating Profit | | 6.6 | 7.6 | 11.8 | 11.1 | 9.1 |
| 1.7 | 1.3 | 1.2 | All Other Expenses (net) | | 1.3 | 1.2 | .8 | .8 | 1.6 |
| -1.8 | 5.0 | 7.9 | Profit Before Taxes | | 5.2 | 6.4 | 11.0 | 10.2 | 7.6 |
| | | | RATIOS | | | | | | |
| 3.4 | 3.1 | 3.5 | | | 3.2 | 4.4 | 3.6 | 3.2 | 3.7 |
| 1.8 | 1.7 | 2.1 | Current | | 2.2 | 2.6 | 2.2 | 1.8 | 2.1 |
| 1.2 | 1.2 | 1.4 | | | 1.3 | 1.4 | 1.5 | 1.5 | 1.3 |
| 1.8 | 1.5 | 2.0 | | | 2.0 | 2.9 | 2.0 | 1.3 | 2.0 |
| .8 | .9 | 1.2 | Quick | | 1.3 | 1.4 | 1.2 | 1.1 | .8 |
| .5 | .6 | .7 | | | .6 | .8 | .8 | .5 | .7 |
| 36  10.0 | 42  8.7 | 41  9.0 | | | 36  10.2 | 36  10.0 | 42  8.7 | 36  10.1 | 43  8.4 |
| 48  7.6 | 50  7.3 | 50  7.3 | Sales/Receivables | | 51  7.2 | 50  7.3 | 49  7.4 | 46  7.9 | 51  7.2 |
| 62  5.9 | 62  5.9 | 63  5.8 | | | 62  5.9 | 57  6.4 | 69  5.3 | 57  6.4 | 69  5.3 |
| 39  9.3 | 38  9.6 | 33  10.9 | | | 20  18.1 | 29  12.7 | 28  12.9 | 49  7.4 | 61  6.0 |
| 99  3.7 | 76  4.8 | 74  4.9 | Cost of Sales/Inventory | | 54  6.7 | 44  8.3 | 57  6.4 | 107  3.4 | 85  4.3 |
| 162  2.2 | 135  2.7 | 122  3.0 | | | 101  3.6 | 122  3.0 | 96  3.8 | 182  2.0 | 126  2.9 |
| 15  25.1 | 22  16.9 | 21  17.8 | | | 15  24.3 | 14  26.9 | 21  17.0 | 25  14.5 | 28  13.2 |
| 27  13.6 | 35  10.5 | 32  11.3 | Cost of Sales/Payables | | 25  14.7 | 26  14.1 | 31  11.7 | 37  9.9 | 38  9.7 |
| 43  8.5 | 47  7.8 | 52  7.0 | | | 63  5.8 | 55  6.6 | 41  8.8 | 52  7.0 | 47  7.8 |
| 2.9 | 2.9 | 3.5 | | | 4.6 | 3.6 | 3.4 | 4.0 | 3.3 |
| 5.8 | 7.2 | 6.3 | Sales/Working Capital | | 6.6 | 5.8 | 4.5 | 6.3 | 6.3 |
| 30.2 | 18.3 | 11.2 | | | 12.3 | 10.7 | 11.5 | 9.9 | 10.1 |
| 5.7 | 11.1 | 21.5 | | | 10.9 | 20.4 | 26.9 | 24.4 | 40.6 |
| (121)  1.4 | (103)  3.6 | (123)  9.1 | EBIT/Interest | | (26)  6.6 | (20)  5.8 | (23)  11.6 | (23)  10.2 | (28)  11.3 |
| -2.8 | 1.4 | 2.4 | | | 1.2 | 1.7 | 4.6 | 5.7 | 2.4 |
| 1.9 | 3.4 | 5.5 | Net Profit + Depr., Dep., | | | | | | 9.6 |
| (41)  1.1 | (34)  1.6 | (30)  2.4 | Amort./Cur. Mat. L/T/D | | | | | (10) | 5.6 |
| -.4 | .9 | 1.5 | | | | | | | 2.8 |
| .3 | .4 | .3 | | | .4 | .2 | .3 | .1 | .4 |
| .7 | .9 | .6 | Fixed/Worth | | 1.1 | .6 | .6 | .8 | .6 |
| 2.2 | 1.8 | 1.4 | | | -4.8 | 1.0 | 1.4 | .9 | 1.5 |
| .6 | .6 | .7 | | | 1.0 | .5 | .6 | .8 | .4 |
| 1.6 | 1.8 | 1.5 | Debt/Worth | | 2.3 | 1.5 | 1.8 | 1.4 | 1.3 |
| 9.0 | 4.2 | 3.4 | | | -13.3 | 3.3 | 2.8 | 1.8 | 4.4 |
| 16.0 | 39.9 | 54.3 | % Profit Before Taxes/Tangible | | 62.6 | 56.5 | 78.9 | 50.2 | 34.3 |
| (113)  3.6 | (96)  15.9 | (122)  28.9 | Net Worth | | (19)  28.7 | (24)  21.0 | (23)  49.3 | 35.9 | (27)  26.3 |
| -13.0 | 3.3 | 14.3 | | | 8.9 | 2.9 | 14.2 | 19.6 | 16.6 |
| 6.1 | 14.5 | 20.1 | % Profit Before Taxes/Total | | 19.8 | 17.2 | 23.8 | 23.7 | 15.6 |
| .8 | 5.3 | 11.2 | Assets | | 6.4 | 7.5 | 15.5 | 11.5 | 11.8 |
| -5.9 | .7 | 4.1 | | | -1.0 | 1.3 | 10.2 | 7.6 | 4.2 |
| 14.7 | 14.5 | 17.8 | | | 22.1 | 28.9 | 15.6 | 29.5 | 13.1 |
| 6.9 | 5.8 | 6.8 | Sales/Net Fixed Assets | | 8.5 | 10.9 | 6.4 | 5.8 | 6.0 |
| 3.3 | 3.6 | 3.7 | | | 2.4 | 5.7 | 4.1 | 4.4 | 3.5 |
| 1.9 | 2.0 | 2.2 | | | 2.5 | 2.6 | 2.3 | 2.1 | 1.8 |
| 1.4 | 1.6 | 1.6 | Sales/Total Assets | | 1.5 | 1.9 | 1.8 | 1.7 | 1.5 |
| 1.0 | 1.1 | 1.2 | | | 1.2 | 1.3 | 1.4 | 1.4 | 1.1 |
| 1.7 | 1.7 | 1.0 | | | 2.1 | .9 | .9 | .8 | 1.3 |
| (121)  3.6 | (102)  3.1 | (118)  2.6 | % Depr., Dep., Amort./Sales | | (19)  4.4 | (21)  1.6 | (23)  2.4 | (25)  2.1 | (28)  3.0 |
| 5.8 | 5.3 | 4.2 | | | 8.2 | 3.5 | 4.1 | 3.8 | 4.5 |
| 2.8 | 2.5 | 2.7 | % Officers', Directors' | | 3.2 | 3.0 | 1.2 | | | |
| (57)  5.9 | (42)  6.7 | (56)  5.1 | Owners' Comp/Sales | | (17)  6.3 | (17)  4.6 | (11)  3.4 | | | |
| 9.6 | 9.9 | 7.8 | | | 9.2 | 6.7 | 8.7 | | | |
| 2146988M | 2477793M | 2785044M | Net Sales ($) | 1829M | 47891M | 97585M | 172174M | 410255M | 2055310M |
| 1777538M | 2017759M | 2027763M | Total Assets ($) | 1983M | 33115M | 66201M | 101003M | 246371M | 1579090M |

M = $ thousand    MM = $ million
See Pages 9 through 22 for Explanation of Ratios and Data

**Current Data Sorted by Assets**          **Comparative Historical Data**

| 0-500M | 500M-2MM | 2-10MM | 10-50MM | 50-100MM | 100-250MM | Type of Statement | 4/1/07-3/31/08 ALL | 4/1/08-3/31/09 ALL |
|---|---|---|---|---|---|---|---|---|
| | | 2 | 3 | 3 | 3 | Unqualified | 5 | 10 |
| | 1 | 11 | 2 | 1 | | Reviewed | 19 | 21 |
| 2 | 4 | 14 | 3 | | | Compiled | 12 | 16 |
| 2 | 14 | 10 | | | | Tax Returns | 7 | 8 |
| 1 | 5 | 9 | 7 | 2 | 1 | Other | 18 | 27 |
| 21 (4/1-9/30/11) | | | 79 (10/1/11-3/31/12) | | | | | |
| 5 | 24 | 46 | 15 | 6 | 4 | **NUMBER OF STATEMENTS** | 61 | 82 |
| % | % | % | % | % | % | **ASSETS** | % | % |
| | 12.5 | 12.6 | 6.3 | | | Cash & Equivalents | 6.7 | 7.1 |
| | 21.8 | 28.3 | 27.4 | | | Trade Receivables (net) | 27.8 | 24.5 |
| | 21.8 | 25.1 | 23.3 | | | Inventory | 25.4 | 28.2 |
| | 4.9 | 4.6 | 7.0 | | | All Other Current | 4.3 | 4.4 |
| | 61.0 | 70.6 | 63.9 | | | Total Current | 64.2 | 64.3 |
| | 27.9 | 23.4 | 24.3 | | | Fixed Assets (net) | 25.9 | 22.8 |
| | 8.3 | 2.7 | 8.0 | | | Intangibles (net) | 6.7 | 6.4 |
| | 2.9 | 3.3 | 3.7 | | | All Other Non-Current | 3.2 | 6.5 |
| | 100.0 | 100.0 | 100.0 | | | Total | 100.0 | 100.0 |
| | | | | | | **LIABILITIES** | | |
| | 14.4 | 6.6 | 12.6 | | | Notes Payable-Short Term | 9.9 | 7.5 |
| | 4.1 | 2.4 | 1.3 | | | Cur. Mat.-L.T.D. | 6.3 | 5.0 |
| | 15.1 | 14.2 | 9.4 | | | Trade Payables | 10.7 | 11.1 |
| | .2 | .2 | .3 | | | Income Taxes Payable | .1 | .2 |
| | 6.6 | 9.6 | 12.4 | | | All Other Current | 12.6 | 13.8 |
| | 40.5 | 33.1 | 35.9 | | | Total Current | 39.6 | 37.7 |
| | 21.8 | 14.8 | 7.5 | | | Long-Term Debt | 19.2 | 17.6 |
| | .2 | .4 | .5 | | | Deferred Taxes | .2 | .3 |
| | 7.9 | 3.6 | 8.2 | | | All Other Non-Current | 8.2 | 8.6 |
| | 29.7 | 48.1 | 47.9 | | | Net Worth | 32.8 | 35.9 |
| | 100.0 | 100.0 | 100.0 | | | Total Liabilities & Net Worth | 100.0 | 100.0 |
| | | | | | | **INCOME DATA** | | |
| | 100.0 | 100.0 | 100.0 | | | Net Sales | 100.0 | 100.0 |
| | 39.1 | 35.8 | 28.4 | | | Gross Profit | 29.5 | 30.9 |
| | 35.5 | 26.3 | 17.1 | | | Operating Expenses | 25.9 | 24.6 |
| | 3.6 | 9.5 | 11.4 | | | Operating Profit | 3.6 | 6.3 |
| | 1.5 | .2 | 1.3 | | | All Other Expenses (net) | 1.8 | 1.2 |
| | 2.2 | 9.3 | 10.1 | | | Profit Before Taxes | 1.8 | 5.1 |
| | | | | | | **RATIOS** | | |
| | 2.7 | 4.3 | 2.7 | | | | 2.8 | 3.0 |
| | 1.4 | 2.5 | 1.8 | | | Current | 1.9 | 1.8 |
| | 1.0 | 1.5 | 1.2 | | | | 1.1 | 1.2 |
| | 1.5 | 3.9 | 1.7 | | | | 1.5 | 1.4 |
| | .8 | 1.1 | 1.2 | | | Quick | .9 | .9 |
| | .5 | .7 | .6 | | | | .6 | .6 |
| | 22   16.6 | 33   11.1 | 51   7.1 | | | | 40   9.1 | 31   11.6 |
| | 38   9.6 | 46   7.9 | 59   6.2 | | | Sales/Receivables | 52   7.1 | 43   8.5 |
| | 51   7.2 | 63   5.8 | 78   4.7 | | | | 65   5.6 | 57   6.4 |
| | 14   26.7 | 15   23.8 | 34   10.7 | | | | 23   15.8 | 20   18.1 |
| | 45   8.2 | 54   6.7 | 79   4.6 | | | Cost of Sales/Inventory | 71   5.1 | 78   4.7 |
| | 135   2.7 | 104   3.5 | 152   2.4 | | | | 129   2.8 | 128   2.9 |
| | 20   18.4 | 16   22.9 | 11   33.5 | | | | 14   25.8 | 14   26.9 |
| | 39   9.4 | 27   13.3 | 25   14.4 | | | Cost of Sales/Payables | 27   13.6 | 25   14.4 |
| | 59   6.2 | 48   7.6 | 57   6.4 | | | | 46   8.0 | 38   9.6 |
| | 6.8 | 3.5 | 2.9 | | | | 4.5 | 4.5 |
| | 10.9 | 5.8 | 6.1 | | | Sales/Working Capital | 6.6 | 7.4 |
| | 382.7 | 13.4 | 25.9 | | | | 27.4 | 18.7 |
| | 5.5 | 26.7 | 28.0 | | | | 11.2 | 11.9 |
| | (21) 3.3 | (40) 11.9 | (13) 4.9 | | | EBIT/Interest | (55) 2.9 | (71) 4.8 |
| | 1.3 | 3.8 | 3.4 | | | | .8 | 1.5 |
| | | | | | | | 11.3 | 10.4 |
| | | | | | | Net Profit + Depr., Dep., Amort./Cur. Mat. L/T/D | (14) 2.5 | (20) 2.2 |
| | | | | | | | .7 | 1.1 |
| | .3 | .1 | .2 | | | | .3 | .3 |
| | .9 | .4 | .3 | | | Fixed/Worth | .9 | .6 |
| | 17.4 | 1.0 | 1.3 | | | | 17.8 | 2.8 |
| | .9 | .6 | .5 | | | | .8 | .7 |
| | 2.7 | 1.1 | 1.6 | | | Debt/Worth | 2.0 | 1.8 |
| | NM | 2.1 | 4.4 | | | | 99.4 | 6.2 |
| | 63.7 | 47.6 | 60.2 | | | | 35.7 | 37.9 |
| | (18) 26.2 | (44) 24.4 | (14) 18.5 | | | % Profit Before Taxes/Tangible Net Worth | (47) 14.3 | (66) 21.5 |
| | 5.8 | 9.5 | 11.2 | | | | 3.1 | 7.7 |
| | 12.8 | 23.0 | 14.7 | | | | 13.0 | 15.7 |
| | 8.1 | 8.4 | 5.6 | | | % Profit Before Taxes/Total Assets | 4.4 | 8.7 |
| | .4 | 4.5 | 4.0 | | | | -.5 | 1.5 |
| | 58.4 | 44.7 | 23.6 | | | | 31.6 | 26.9 |
| | 15.1 | 12.7 | 13.1 | | | Sales/Net Fixed Assets | 7.3 | 11.8 |
| | 3.8 | 5.3 | 4.9 | | | | 4.2 | 5.9 |
| | 3.2 | 3.0 | 2.0 | | | | 2.5 | 2.7 |
| | 2.0 | 2.1 | 1.5 | | | Sales/Total Assets | 1.7 | 1.8 |
| | 1.7 | 1.3 | .9 | | | | 1.4 | 1.3 |
| | .4 | .9 | .6 | | | | 1.0 | 1.1 |
| | (17) 1.0 | (39) 1.6 | (14) 1.4 | | | % Depr., Dep., Amort./Sales | (56) 2.4 | (71) 2.0 |
| | 3.3 | 4.2 | 5.1 | | | | 4.7 | 3.9 |
| | 3.4 | 1.9 | | | | | 2.0 | 2.7 |
| | (18) 4.9 | (16) 3.5 | | | | % Officers', Directors' Owners' Comp/Sales | (21) 4.6 | (34) 4.9 |
| | 9.4 | 5.0 | | | | | 8.1 | 6.7 |
| 10584M | 63533M | 431990M | 530441M | 474398M | 772334M | Net Sales ($) | 939716M | 2005985M |
| 1309M | 26906M | 205807M | 365667M | 412379M | 576471M | Total Assets ($) | 705096M | 1413567M |

© RMA 2012

M = $ thousand    MM = $ million
See Pages 9 through 22 for Explanation of Ratios and Data

## Comparative Historical Data / Current Data Sorted by Sales

Note on period groupings (Current Data): **21 (4/1-9/30/11)** and **79 (10/1/11-3/31/12)**

| 4/1/09-3/31/10 ALL | 4/1/10-3/31/11 ALL | 4/1/11-3/31/12 ALL | Type of Statement | 0-1MM | 1-3MM | 3-5MM | 5-10MM | 10-25MM | 25MM & OVER |
|---|---|---|---|---|---|---|---|---|---|
| 7 | 8 | 11 | Unqualified | | | | 1 | 2 | 8 |
| 12 | 24 | 15 | Reviewed | | 2 | 1 | 4 | 7 | 1 |
| 13 | 9 | 23 | Compiled | 1 | 2 | 1 | 10 | 5 | 4 |
| 13 | 15 | 26 | Tax Returns | 3 | 7 | 9 | 5 | 2 | |
| 26 | 21 | 25 | Other | 3 | 4 | 3 | 4 | 4 | 7 |
| 71 | 77 | 100 | **NUMBER OF STATEMENTS** | 7 | 15 | 14 | 24 | 20 | 20 |
| % | % | % | **ASSETS** | % | % | % | % | % | % |
| 13.0 | 15.6 | 11.3 | Cash & Equivalents | | 11.2 | 22.7 | 8.6 | 10.4 | 7.5 |
| 21.8 | 23.1 | 27.0 | Trade Receivables (net) | | 21.5 | 21.2 | 34.5 | 26.7 | 26.8 |
| 21.2 | 21.0 | 22.5 | Inventory | | 24.5 | 17.9 | 23.6 | 25.3 | 22.4 |
| 4.7 | 6.3 | 4.7 | All Other Current | | 3.4 | 3.5 | 3.3 | 8.2 | 3.4 |
| 60.7 | 66.1 | 65.4 | Total Current | | 60.6 | 65.3 | 70.0 | 70.6 | 60.1 |
| 28.9 | 22.8 | 23.6 | Fixed Assets (net) | | 24.9 | 26.2 | 24.0 | 21.2 | 19.1 |
| 5.8 | 5.2 | 6.2 | Intangibles (net) | | 11.2 | 2.4 | 4.5 | 4.1 | 10.6 |
| 4.6 | 5.9 | 4.7 | All Other Non-Current | | 3.3 | 6.1 | 1.6 | 4.1 | 10.3 |
| 100.0 | 100.0 | 100.0 | Total | | 100.0 | 100.0 | 100.0 | 100.0 | 100.0 |
| | | | **LIABILITIES** | | | | | | |
| 8.1 | 7.1 | 10.9 | Notes Payable-Short Term | | 22.3 | 10.4 | 4.9 | 10.9 | 7.4 |
| 4.0 | 4.0 | 3.3 | Cur. Mat.-L.T.D. | | 7.2 | .4 | 3.3 | 2.2 | 4.3 |
| 12.4 | 14.0 | 13.4 | Trade Payables | | 12.0 | 10.0 | 19.6 | 10.9 | 13.1 |
| .1 | .1 | .2 | Income Taxes Payable | | .0 | 1.0 | .0 | .1 | .2 |
| 13.9 | 11.9 | 10.1 | All Other Current | | 3.9 | 8.3 | 8.2 | 17.6 | 13.4 |
| 38.4 | 37.2 | 38.0 | Total Current | | 45.4 | 30.0 | 36.1 | 41.7 | 38.2 |
| 24.7 | 22.3 | 13.9 | Long-Term Debt | | 24.4 | 9.6 | 17.3 | 11.2 | 4.7 |
| .2 | .3 | .4 | Deferred Taxes | | .2 | .3 | .1 | .7 | .8 |
| 9.3 | 6.8 | 10.9 | All Other Non-Current | | 10.8 | 4.1 | 7.2 | 4.5 | 5.6 |
| 27.3 | 33.5 | 36.8 | Net Worth | | 19.1 | 56.0 | 39.3 | 41.9 | 50.7 |
| 100.0 | 100.0 | 100.0 | Total Liabilities & Net Worth | | 100.0 | 100.0 | 100.0 | 100.0 | 100.0 |
| | | | **INCOME DATA** | | | | | | |
| 100.0 | 100.0 | 100.0 | Net Sales | | 100.0 | 100.0 | 100.0 | 100.0 | 100.0 |
| 32.4 | 30.7 | 35.1 | Gross Profit | | 37.1 | 37.4 | 37.2 | 28.0 | 28.3 |
| 30.3 | 25.9 | 27.5 | Operating Expenses | | 31.2 | 30.4 | 28.9 | 19.5 | 20.2 |
| 2.1 | 4.8 | 7.6 | Operating Profit | | 5.9 | 6.9 | 8.3 | 8.5 | 8.0 |
| 1.5 | .8 | .7 | All Other Expenses (net) | | 1.4 | .5 | .1 | 1.0 | .8 |
| .5 | 4.1 | 6.9 | Profit Before Taxes | | 4.5 | 6.4 | 8.2 | 7.5 | 7.2 |
| | | | **RATIOS** | | | | | | |
| 4.3 | 3.7 | 3.2 | Current | | 3.1 | 4.6 | 3.6 | 2.4 | 2.3 |
| 1.9 | 1.6 | 1.9 | | | 1.4 | 2.6 | 2.3 | 1.5 | 1.6 |
| 1.1 | 1.2 | 1.2 | | | .8 | 1.3 | 1.6 | 1.2 | 1.1 |
| 1.9 | 1.9 | 1.8 | Quick | | 1.8 | 4.2 | 2.6 | 1.2 | 1.5 |
| 1.0 | 1.0 | .9 | | | .7 | 1.7 | 1.1 | .8 | .9 |
| .6 | .6 | .6 | | | .4 | .8 | .7 | .6 | .6 |
| 24  15.4 | 24  14.9 | 33  11.1 | Sales/Receivables | | 25  14.4 | 16  22.6 | 26  13.8 | 35  10.5 | 40  9.1 |
| 39  9.3 | 42  8.6 | 48  7.6 | | | 46  7.9 | 42  7.8 | 47  7.8 | 45  8.1 | 53  6.9 |
| 57  6.4 | 60  6.1 | 63  5.8 | | | 54  6.8 | 72  5.1 | 59  6.2 | 59  6.2 | 78  4.7 |
| 13  27.4 | 8  47.5 | 16  22.5 | Cost of Sales/Inventory | | 13  28.0 | 0  UND | 13  28.8 | 10  35.1 | 42  8.6 |
| 50  7.3 | 45  8.2 | 54  6.8 | | | 91  4.0 | 37  9.8 | 47  7.7 | 44  8.3 | 66  5.5 |
| 110  3.3 | 111  3.3 | 107  3.4 | | | 192  1.9 | 87  4.2 | 104  3.5 | 96  3.8 | 104  3.5 |
| 10  38.2 | 16  23.3 | 16  22.3 | Cost of Sales/Payables | | 10  37.0 | 5  72.2 | 21  17.4 | 13  27.6 | 20  18.5 |
| 21  17.4 | 29  12.7 | 29  12.6 | | | 43  8.4 | 24  15.5 | 31  11.9 | 19  19.3 | 32  11.3 |
| 40  9.1 | 47  7.7 | 52  7.0 | | | 60  6.1 | 37  9.8 | 57  6.4 | 40  9.2 | 51  7.1 |
| 3.3 | 3.1 | 4.2 | Sales/Working Capital | | 4.9 | 3.1 | 4.5 | 4.3 | 3.2 |
| 7.0 | 8.0 | 7.6 | | | 10.7 | 6.6 | 7.6 | 7.4 | 7.5 |
| 88.4 | 22.5 | 18.5 | | | -16.8 | 13.8 | 10.9 | 18.0 | 37.0 |
| 6.8 | 14.4 | 19.7 | EBIT/Interest | | 5.0 | 30.4 | 29.3 | 14.7 | 24.4 |
| (62) 2.0 | (65) 4.0 | (85) 5.9 | | | (14) 3.1 | (11) 8.8 | 13.2 | (16) 5.4 | (15) 6.2 |
| -.8 | 1.2 | 2.1 | | | -1.0 | 1.7 | 3.2 | 3.5 | 2.2 |
| 6.1 | 3.1 | 12.8 | Net Profit + Depr., Dep., Amort./Cur. Mat. L/T/D | | | | | | |
| (14) 2.2 | (11) 1.5 | (13) 3.6 | | | | | | | |
| .8 | .8 | 1.4 | | | | | | | |
| .3 | .2 | .2 | Fixed/Worth | | .4 | .1 | .2 | .2 | .2 |
| 1.1 | .6 | .5 | | | 1.8 | .3 | .6 | .3 | .3 |
| 26.4 | 1.9 | 1.4 | | | -1.0 | .9 | 1.3 | 1.9 | 1.0 |
| .8 | .6 | .6 | Debt/Worth | | 1.0 | .2 | .8 | .8 | .5 |
| 1.6 | 1.4 | 1.5 | | | 4.1 | 1.0 | 1.2 | 2.0 | 1.1 |
| 236.0 | 6.4 | 3.7 | | | -10.6 | 1.9 | 2.1 | 4.4 | 2.3 |
| 25.8 | 40.0 | 51.9 | % Profit Before Taxes/Tangible Net Worth | | 65.7 | 46.0 | 58.1 | 46.5 | 30.8 |
| (54) 9.2 | (65) 16.9 | (88) 22.2 | | | (10) 28.0 | 13.1 | (21) 40.5 | (19) 23.9 | (19) 17.5 |
| -2.0 | 2.4 | 8.3 | | | 4.9 | 3.5 | 10.1 | 16.7 | 8.8 |
| 9.2 | 15.3 | 18.8 | % Profit Before Taxes/Total Assets | | 9.8 | 22.0 | 29.2 | 9.6 | 11.0 |
| 1.8 | 5.9 | 7.5 | | | 8.2 | 9.4 | 18.4 | 7.4 | 5.8 |
| -2.9 | 1.1 | 2.5 | | | -5.6 | 1.5 | 4.5 | 4.9 | 3.3 |
| 23.7 | 43.0 | 41.0 | Sales/Net Fixed Assets | | 28.2 | 76.2 | 50.5 | 57.1 | 21.5 |
| 7.7 | 9.5 | 13.0 | | | 11.9 | 14.4 | 14.7 | 22.7 | 11.3 |
| 3.4 | 4.1 | 5.5 | | | 3.3 | 3.6 | 5.6 | 8.7 | 7.3 |
| 2.6 | 2.6 | 3.0 | Sales/Total Assets | | 2.2 | 3.4 | 3.3 | 2.9 | 2.5 |
| 1.5 | 1.7 | 1.9 | | | 1.8 | 2.0 | 2.7 | 1.9 | 1.5 |
| .9 | 1.1 | 1.3 | | | 1.4 | 1.2 | 1.8 | 1.5 | 1.0 |
| 1.0 | .8 | .7 | % Depr., Dep., Amort./Sales | | .6 | | .9 | .3 | 1.1 |
| (60) 2.8 | (59) 2.8 | (81) 1.7 | | | (12) 1.2 | | (18) 1.3 | (19) .9 | (17) 2.9 |
| 5.7 | 5.5 | 3.6 | | | 3.1 | | 3.2 | 3.1 | 4.1 |
| 2.2 | 3.3 | 2.3 | % Officers', Directors', Owners' Comp/Sales | | | | 2.9 | | |
| (30) 4.6 | (27) 5.5 | (38) 3.9 | | | | | (10) 4.0 | | |
| 7.7 | 8.9 | 6.8 | | | | | 5.6 | | |
| 950566M | 1394723M | 2283280M | Net Sales ($) | 3992M | 30662M | 50094M | 174069M | 287435M | 1737028M |
| 922060M | 1070445M | 1588539M | Total Assets ($) | 4992M | 23316M | 39782M | 83934M | 188143M | 1248372M |

M = $ thousand   MM = $ million
See Pages 9 through 22 for Explanation of Ratios and Data

## Current Data Sorted by Assets      Comparative Historical Data

| 0-500M | 500M-2MM | 2-10MM | 10-50MM | 50-100MM | 100-250MM | Type of Statement | 4/1/07-3/31/08 ALL | 4/1/08-3/31/09 ALL |
|---|---|---|---|---|---|---|---|---|
|  | 1 | 3 | 2 | 2 | 1 | Unqualified | 4 | 3 |
|  |  | 3 | 3 |  |  | Reviewed | 2 | 3 |
| 1 | 2 | 3 | 1 | 1 | 3 | Compiled | 3 | 5 |
|  | 2 | 7 |  |  |  | Tax Returns | 1 | 1 |
|  |  |  |  |  |  | Other | 4 | 6 |
|  | 9 (4/1-9/30/11) | | 23 (10/1/11-3/31/12) | | | | | |
| 1 | 5 | 13 | 6 | 3 | 4 | **NUMBER OF STATEMENTS** | 14 | 18 |
| % | % | % | % | % | % | **ASSETS** | % | % |
|  |  | 14.9 |  |  |  | Cash & Equivalents | 10.8 | 11.9 |
|  |  | 28.3 |  |  |  | Trade Receivables (net) | 26.3 | 29.9 |
|  |  | 23.5 |  |  |  | Inventory | 28.8 | 15.7 |
|  |  | 4.4 |  |  |  | All Other Current | 5.5 | 5.5 |
|  |  | 71.1 |  |  |  | Total Current | 71.4 | 63.0 |
|  |  | 25.7 |  |  |  | Fixed Assets (net) | 17.3 | 28.3 |
|  |  | .6 |  |  |  | Intangibles (net) | 4.4 | 4.7 |
|  |  | 2.6 |  |  |  | All Other Non-Current | 6.8 | 3.9 |
|  |  | 100.0 |  |  |  | Total | 100.0 | 100.0 |
|  |  |  |  |  |  | **LIABILITIES** |  |  |
|  |  | 6.0 |  |  |  | Notes Payable-Short Term | 6.4 | 6.8 |
|  |  | 1.2 |  |  |  | Cur. Mat.-L.T.D. | 3.9 | 3.2 |
|  |  | 12.1 |  |  |  | Trade Payables | 12.7 | 26.8 |
|  |  | .2 |  |  |  | Income Taxes Payable | .0 | .0 |
|  |  | 21.3 |  |  |  | All Other Current | 12.3 | 27.6 |
|  |  | 40.8 |  |  |  | Total Current | 35.3 | 64.5 |
|  |  | 8.3 |  |  |  | Long-Term Debt | 14.6 | 13.8 |
|  |  | .5 |  |  |  | Deferred Taxes | .1 | .1 |
|  |  | 2.5 |  |  |  | All Other Non-Current | 12.6 | 4.1 |
|  |  | 48.0 |  |  |  | Net Worth | 37.5 | 17.5 |
|  |  | 100.0 |  |  |  | Total Liabilities & Net Worth | 100.0 | 100.0 |
|  |  |  |  |  |  | **INCOME DATA** |  |  |
|  |  | 100.0 |  |  |  | Net Sales | 100.0 | 100.0 |
|  |  | 24.9 |  |  |  | Gross Profit | 30.7 | 29.2 |
|  |  | 18.5 |  |  |  | Operating Expenses | 22.7 | 26.5 |
|  |  | 6.4 |  |  |  | Operating Profit | 8.0 | 2.8 |
|  |  | .8 |  |  |  | All Other Expenses (net) | 1.3 | 1.0 |
|  |  | 5.6 |  |  |  | Profit Before Taxes | 6.7 | 1.8 |
|  |  |  |  |  |  | **RATIOS** |  |  |
|  |  | 3.9 |  |  |  |  | 5.0 | 2.2 |
|  |  | 1.8 |  |  |  | Current | 2.2 | 1.4 |
|  |  | 1.5 |  |  |  |  | 1.3 | .8 |
|  |  | 1.4 |  |  |  |  | 3.3 | 1.6 |
|  |  | 1.1 |  |  |  | Quick | 1.1 | .8 |
|  |  | .9 |  |  |  |  | .5 | .3 |
|  |  | 34  10.6 |  |  |  |  | 33  11.2 | 18  20.6 |
|  |  | 40  9.1 |  |  |  | Sales/Receivables | 49  7.5 | 56  6.5 |
|  |  | 74  4.9 |  |  |  |  | 61  6.0 | 100  3.6 |
|  |  | 26  14.2 |  |  |  |  | 38  9.6 | 11  32.6 |
|  |  | 51  7.2 |  |  |  | Cost of Sales/Inventory | 81  4.5 | 29  12.5 |
|  |  | 107  3.4 |  |  |  |  | 167  2.2 | 67  5.4 |
|  |  | 18  20.7 |  |  |  |  | 12  29.3 | 14  26.5 |
|  |  | 24  15.3 |  |  |  | Cost of Sales/Payables | 30  12.3 | 27  13.6 |
|  |  | 45  8.1 |  |  |  |  | 42  8.7 | 53  6.8 |
|  |  | 3.7 |  |  |  |  | 2.6 | 5.2 |
|  |  | 6.6 |  |  |  | Sales/Working Capital | 5.9 | 21.4 |
|  |  | 9.3 |  |  |  |  | 11.6 | -14.4 |
|  |  |  |  |  |  |  | 11.0 | 27.0 |
|  |  |  |  |  |  | EBIT/Interest | (12) 5.7 | (14) 6.0 |
|  |  |  |  |  |  |  | 2.5 | -2.4 |
|  |  |  |  |  |  | Net Profit + Depr., Dep., Amort./Cur. Mat. L/T/D |  |  |
|  |  | .2 |  |  |  |  | .1 | .2 |
|  |  | .5 |  |  |  | Fixed/Worth | .3 | .8 |
|  |  | 1.0 |  |  |  |  | 2.4 | 3.7 |
|  |  | .3 |  |  |  |  | .3 | .8 |
|  |  | 1.0 |  |  |  | Debt/Worth | 1.9 | 2.1 |
|  |  | 1.8 |  |  |  |  | 5.3 | NM |
|  |  | 50.2 |  |  |  |  | 47.3 | 65.5 |
|  |  | (12) 8.3 |  |  |  | % Profit Before Taxes/Tangible Net Worth | (12) 28.7 | (14) 22.7 |
|  |  | 5.4 |  |  |  |  | 9.2 | 8.2 |
|  |  | 22.0 |  |  |  |  | 14.7 | 26.2 |
|  |  | 5.6 |  |  |  | % Profit Before Taxes/Total Assets | 10.1 | 5.9 |
|  |  | 2.0 |  |  |  |  | 3.7 | -5.8 |
|  |  | 27.8 |  |  |  |  | 95.7 | 38.1 |
|  |  | 5.5 |  |  |  | Sales/Net Fixed Assets | 20.3 | 9.2 |
|  |  | 4.2 |  |  |  |  | 5.9 | 4.2 |
|  |  | 2.8 |  |  |  |  | 2.2 | 2.8 |
|  |  | 1.8 |  |  |  | Sales/Total Assets | 2.0 | 2.0 |
|  |  | 1.4 |  |  |  |  | 1.2 | 1.2 |
|  |  | .6 |  |  |  |  | .8 | 1.0 |
|  |  | (10) 1.7 |  |  |  | % Depr., Dep., Amort./Sales | (12) 2.0 | (12) 3.4 |
|  |  | 3.0 |  |  |  |  | 3.9 | 6.8 |
|  |  |  |  |  |  | % Officers', Directors' Owners' Comp/Sales |  |  |
| 1206M | 19646M | 125165M | 142979M | 344326M | 745005M | Net Sales ($) | 428745M | 948194M |
| 345M | 7904M | 66093M | 116843M | 189771M | 692246M | Total Assets ($) | 362377M | 709033M |

© RMA 2012

M = $ thousand    MM = $ million
See Pages 9 through 22 for Explanation of Ratios and Data

## Comparative Historical Data

## Current Data Sorted by Sales

| | | | | | | Type of Statement | 0-1MM | 1-3MM | 3-5MM | 5-10MM | 10-25MM | 25MM & OVER |
|---|---|---|---|---|---|---|---|---|---|---|---|---|
| | 5 | | 3 | | 6 | Unqualified | | | | | 3 | 3 |
| | 1 | | 1 | | 6 | Reviewed | | | | 2 | 3 | 1 |
| | 4 | | 2 | | | Compiled | | | | | | |
| | 3 | | 4 | | 6 | Tax Returns | | 1 | 3 | 1 | 1 | |
| | 5 | | 11 | | 14 | Other | | 1 | 3 | 2 | 3 | 5 |
| | 4/1/09-3/31/10 ALL | | 4/1/10-3/31/11 ALL | | 4/1/11-3/31/12 ALL | | | 9 (4/1-9/30/11) | | | 23 (10/1/11-3/31/12) | |
| | 18 | | 21 | | 32 | NUMBER OF STATEMENTS | | 2 | 6 | 8 | 7 | 9 |
| | % | | % | | % | ASSETS | % | % | % | % | % | % |
| | 12.0 | | 14.6 | | 11.4 | Cash & Equivalents | D | | | | | |
| | 19.0 | | 24.6 | | 23.0 | Trade Receivables (net) | A | | | | | |
| | 34.5 | | 25.9 | | 24.7 | Inventory | T | | | | | |
| | 3.1 | | 6.4 | | 3.5 | All Other Current | A | | | | | |
| | 68.6 | | 71.5 | | 62.6 | Total Current | | | | | | |
| | 18.7 | | 22.3 | | 26.5 | Fixed Assets (net) | N | | | | | |
| | 4.9 | | 2.1 | | 7.3 | Intangibles (net) | O | | | | | |
| | 7.8 | | 4.1 | | 3.6 | All Other Non-Current | T | | | | | |
| | 100.0 | | 100.0 | | 100.0 | Total | | | | | | |
| | | | | | | LIABILITIES | A | | | | | |
| | 23.3 | | 8.3 | | 4.5 | Notes Payable-Short Term | V | | | | | |
| | 3.1 | | 3.3 | | 1.6 | Cur. Mat.-L.T.D. | A | | | | | |
| | 18.4 | | 14.1 | | 14.0 | Trade Payables | I | | | | | |
| | .2 | | .2 | | .3 | Income Taxes Payable | L | | | | | |
| | 18.7 | | 13.0 | | 17.3 | All Other Current | A | | | | | |
| | 63.8 | | 39.0 | | 37.6 | Total Current | B | | | | | |
| | 21.6 | | 9.1 | | 24.9 | Long-Term Debt | L | | | | | |
| | .6 | | .0 | | .3 | Deferred Taxes | E | | | | | |
| | 8.9 | | 16.4 | | 5.7 | All Other Non-Current | | | | | | |
| | 5.2 | | 35.5 | | 31.5 | Net Worth | | | | | | |
| | 100.0 | | 100.0 | | 100.0 | Total Liabilties & Net Worth | | | | | | |
| | | | | | | INCOME DATA | | | | | | |
| | 100.0 | | 100.0 | | 100.0 | Net Sales | | | | | | |
| | 32.9 | | 32.4 | | 27.4 | Gross Profit | | | | | | |
| | 27.5 | | 27.6 | | 20.8 | Operating Expenses | | | | | | |
| | 5.4 | | 4.8 | | 6.5 | Operating Profit | | | | | | |
| | 1.1 | | 1.3 | | 2.2 | All Other Expenses (net) | | | | | | |
| | 4.3 | | 3.5 | | 4.3 | Profit Before Taxes | | | | | | |
| | | | | | | RATIOS | | | | | | |
| | 5.0 | | 3.4 | | 2.9 | | | | | | | |
| | 1.7 | | 1.8 | | 1.6 | Current | | | | | | |
| | .9 | | 1.3 | | 1.3 | | | | | | | |
| | 1.5 | | 1.7 | | 1.4 | | | | | | | |
| | .9 | | 1.1 | | .9 | Quick | | | | | | |
| | .5 | | .5 | | .6 | | | | | | | |
| 10 | 37.1 | 37 | 9.7 | 34 | 10.7 | | | | | | | |
| 36 | 10.2 | 46 | 8.0 | 42 | 8.7 | Sales/Receivables | | | | | | |
| 68 | 5.3 | 84 | 4.3 | 59 | 6.2 | | | | | | | |
| 41 | 9.0 | 26 | 13.9 | 36 | 10.0 | | | | | | | |
| 94 | 3.9 | 88 | 4.1 | 63 | 5.8 | Cost of Sales/Inventory | | | | | | |
| 250 | 1.5 | 141 | 2.6 | 122 | 3.0 | | | | | | | |
| 10 | 37.2 | 22 | 16.9 | 21 | 17.6 | | | | | | | |
| 25 | 14.7 | 35 | 10.4 | 31 | 11.8 | Cost of Sales/Payables | | | | | | |
| 56 | 6.5 | 58 | 6.3 | 54 | 6.8 | | | | | | | |
| | 3.0 | | 4.2 | | 4.2 | | | | | | | |
| | 6.5 | | 6.7 | | 6.9 | Sales/Working Capital | | | | | | |
| | -96.9 | | 12.4 | | 13.7 | | | | | | | |
| | 12.7 | | 20.0 | | 29.5 | | | | | | | |
| (16) | 4.8 | (20) | 3.4 | (27) | 5.4 | EBIT/Interest | | | | | | |
| | 3.1 | | .7 | | 2.3 | | | | | | | |
| | | | | | | Net Profit + Depr., Dep., Amort./Cur. Mat. L/T/D | | | | | | |
| | .2 | | .1 | | .3 | | | | | | | |
| | .6 | | .6 | | .9 | Fixed/Worth | | | | | | |
| | NM | | 2.2 | | 2.1 | | | | | | | |
| | 1.1 | | .9 | | .5 | | | | | | | |
| | 2.3 | | 1.9 | | 1.6 | Debt/Worth | | | | | | |
| | NM | | 3.9 | | 4.7 | | | | | | | |
| | 68.5 | | 66.0 | | 49.2 | | | | | | | |
| (14) | 28.0 | (18) | 20.4 | (27) | 15.7 | % Profit Before Taxes/Tangible Net Worth | | | | | | |
| | 11.2 | | -.6 | | 4.6 | | | | | | | |
| | 16.4 | | 30.7 | | 18.4 | | | | | | | |
| | 5.2 | | 4.5 | | 6.2 | % Profit Before Taxes/Total Assets | | | | | | |
| | 2.9 | | -.4 | | 1.8 | | | | | | | |
| | 33.5 | | 31.4 | | 23.7 | | | | | | | |
| | 13.4 | | 10.8 | | 5.7 | Sales/Net Fixed Assets | | | | | | |
| | 5.7 | | 4.1 | | 4.0 | | | | | | | |
| | 2.9 | | 2.4 | | 2.4 | | | | | | | |
| | 1.8 | | 1.6 | | 1.7 | Sales/Total Assets | | | | | | |
| | .9 | | 1.0 | | 1.1 | | | | | | | |
| | 1.0 | | .9 | | 1.3 | | | | | | | |
| (16) | 1.7 | (18) | 2.1 | (25) | 2.9 | % Depr., Dep., Amort./Sales | | | | | | |
| | 4.3 | | 4.4 | | 4.4 | | | | | | | |
| | | | | | | % Officers', Directors' Owners' Comp/Sales | | | | | | |
| | 343188M | | 848469M | | 1378327M | Net Sales ($) | | 3635M | 25574M | 62730M | 110709M | 1175679M |
| | 295803M | | 692229M | | 1073202M | Total Assets ($) | | 1654M | 15089M | 51064M | 62683M | 942712M |

© RMA 2012

M = $ thousand   MM = $ million
See Pages 9 through 22 for Explanation of Ratios and Data

## Current Data Sorted by Assets       Comparative Historical Data

| | | | | | | Type of Statement | | |
|---|---|---|---|---|---|---|---|---|
| | | 3 | 2 | 3 | 1 | Unqualified | 7 | 12 |
| | 4 | 5 | 4 | | | Reviewed | 4 | 6 |
| 1 | 1 | 5 | | | | Compiled | 2 | 4 |
| | | 2 | | | | Tax Returns | 1 | 3 |
| | | 8 | 7 | 1 | 1 | Other | 11 | 14 |
| | 13 (4/1-9/30/11) | | 35 (10/1/11-3/31/12) | | | | 4/1/07-3/31/08 | 4/1/08-3/31/09 |
| 0-500M | 500M-2MM | 2-10MM | 10-50MM | 50-100MM | 100-250MM | | ALL | ALL |
| 1 | 5 | 23 | 13 | 4 | 2 | NUMBER OF STATEMENTS | 25 | 39 |
| % | % | % | % | % | % | ASSETS | % | % |
| | | 8.3 | 9.6 | | | Cash & Equivalents | 5.8 | 4.9 |
| | | 21.9 | 22.0 | | | Trade Receivables (net) | 23.9 | 23.9 |
| | | 25.6 | 30.1 | | | Inventory | 32.7 | 32.8 |
| | | 2.0 | 1.4 | | | All Other Current | 1.4 | 1.9 |
| | | 57.8 | 63.2 | | | Total Current | 63.7 | 63.5 |
| | | 34.7 | 33.4 | | | Fixed Assets (net) | 29.0 | 23.7 |
| | | 3.8 | .5 | | | Intangibles (net) | 3.5 | 6.3 |
| | | 3.7 | 2.9 | | | All Other Non-Current | 3.8 | 6.5 |
| | | 100.0 | 100.0 | | | Total | 100.0 | 100.0 |
| | | | | | | LIABILITIES | | |
| | | 7.4 | 4.3 | | | Notes Payable-Short Term | 9.1 | 13.1 |
| | | 4.4 | 4.0 | | | Cur. Mat.-L.T.D. | 3.5 | 3.9 |
| | | 8.2 | 12.9 | | | Trade Payables | 16.1 | 16.7 |
| | | .1 | .0 | | | Income Taxes Payable | 2.2 | .4 |
| | | 7.5 | 11.2 | | | All Other Current | 9.4 | 9.1 |
| | | 27.5 | 32.4 | | | Total Current | 40.3 | 43.3 |
| | | 23.9 | 13.7 | | | Long-Term Debt | 14.5 | 14.8 |
| | | 1.0 | 1.2 | | | Deferred Taxes | .5 | .7 |
| | | 7.6 | .9 | | | All Other Non-Current | 4.0 | 12.7 |
| | | 40.1 | 51.9 | | | Net Worth | 40.8 | 28.6 |
| | | 100.0 | 100.0 | | | Total Liabilties & Net Worth | 100.0 | 100.0 |
| | | | | | | INCOME DATA | | |
| | | 100.0 | 100.0 | | | Net Sales | 100.0 | 100.0 |
| | | 29.4 | 27.3 | | | Gross Profit | 33.7 | 29.5 |
| | | 26.1 | 16.1 | | | Operating Expenses | 24.4 | 23.0 |
| | | 3.3 | 11.2 | | | Operating Profit | 9.3 | 6.5 |
| | | 1.3 | .6 | | | All Other Expenses (net) | 1.0 | 1.3 |
| | | 2.0 | 10.5 | | | Profit Before Taxes | 8.3 | 5.2 |
| | | | | | | RATIOS | | |
| | | 4.1 | 4.7 | | | | 3.2 | 2.7 |
| | | 2.0 | 1.8 | | | Current | 1.8 | 1.5 |
| | | 1.4 | 1.3 | | | | 1.0 | 1.1 |
| | | 2.1 | 2.9 | | | | 1.5 | 1.0 |
| | | 1.0 | .7 | | | Quick | 1.0 | .7 |
| | | .7 | .5 | | | | .5 | .4 |
| | | 37   9.8 | 44   8.3 | | | | 37   9.9 | 35   10.6 |
| | | 45   8.1 | 57   6.4 | | | Sales/Receivables | 52   7.0 | 43   8.5 |
| | | 54   6.8 | 73   5.0 | | | | 62   5.9 | 55   6.7 |
| | | 34   10.8 | 78   4.7 | | | | 73   5.0 | 70   5.2 |
| | | 70   5.2 | 101   3.6 | | | Cost of Sales/Inventory | 99   3.7 | 85   4.3 |
| | | 122   3.0 | 135   2.7 | | | | 116   3.1 | 106   3.4 |
| | | 15   23.8 | 13   27.9 | | | | 17   21.0 | 19   18.9 |
| | | 22   16.4 | 31   11.9 | | | Cost of Sales/Payables | 36   10.3 | 31   11.7 |
| | | 37   9.8 | 68   5.4 | | | | 70   5.2 | 69   5.3 |
| | | 3.3 | 2.8 | | | | 3.8 | 4.9 |
| | | 5.7 | 5.5 | | | Sales/Working Capital | 6.0 | 7.8 |
| | | 9.0 | 10.2 | | | | NM | 53.0 |
| | | 10.8 | 26.0 | | | | 11.3 | 16.6 |
| | | 2.6 | (12)   10.2 | | | EBIT/Interest | (23)   7.1 | (37)   5.0 |
| | | .8 | 8.2 | | | | 4.5 | 1.6 |
| | | | | | | | | 5.6 |
| | | | | | | Net Profit + Depr., Dep., Amort./Cur. Mat. L/T/D | | (10)   2.9 |
| | | | | | | | | 1.8 |
| | | .3 | .4 | | | | .4 | .5 |
| | | 1.1 | .7 | | | Fixed/Worth | .9 | .8 |
| | | 1.8 | 1.1 | | | | 6.2 | 3.9 |
| | | .9 | .2 | | | | .5 | .9 |
| | | 1.7 | 1.2 | | | Debt/Worth | 1.5 | 2.2 |
| | | 2.3 | 2.4 | | | | 33.6 | 7.1 |
| | | 44.2 | 35.8 | | | | 46.7 | 53.3 |
| | | (22)   23.7 | 28.7 | | | % Profit Before Taxes/Tangible Net Worth | (20)   27.7 | (31)   22.9 |
| | | -.7 | 17.6 | | | | 16.2 | 3.8 |
| | | 13.8 | 17.0 | | | | 20.3 | 21.7 |
| | | 3.9 | 11.7 | | | % Profit Before Taxes/Total Assets | 13.6 | 9.3 |
| | | -.3 | 9.5 | | | | 7.4 | 2.8 |
| | | 11.1 | 11.6 | | | | 11.9 | 20.9 |
| | | 4.2 | 3.3 | | | Sales/Net Fixed Assets | 5.5 | 11.5 |
| | | 3.2 | 1.9 | | | | 3.5 | 4.3 |
| | | 1.9 | 1.8 | | | | 2.1 | 2.5 |
| | | 1.5 | 1.3 | | | Sales/Total Assets | 1.7 | 2.0 |
| | | 1.3 | .9 | | | | 1.2 | 1.3 |
| | | 2.3 | 2.8 | | | | 2.1 | 1.0 |
| | | 4.3 | (11)   4.8 | | | % Depr., Dep., Amort./Sales | (23)   3.0 | (31)   2.2 |
| | | 5.3 | 5.7 | | | | 4.7 | 5.3 |
| | | | | | | | | 1.6 |
| | | | | | | % Officers', Directors' Owners' Comp/Sales | | (10)   4.5 |
| | | | | | | | | 7.8 |
| 1048M | 18737M | 175923M | 423042M | 358421M | 629977M | Net Sales ($) | 909489M | 1689273M |
| 380M | 7794M | 108254M | 292684M | 329767M | 444173M | Total Assets ($) | 579729M | 1159657M |

M = $ thousand    MM = $ million
See Pages 9 through 22 for Explanation of Ratios and Data

## Comparative Historical Data | Current Data Sorted by Sales

| 4/1/09-3/31/10 ALL | 4/1/10-3/31/11 ALL | 4/1/11-3/31/12 ALL | Type of Statement | 0-1MM | 1-3MM | 3-5MM | 5-10MM | 10-25MM | 25MM & OVER |
|---|---|---|---|---|---|---|---|---|---|
| 7 | 10 | 9 | Unqualified | | | | | 3 | 6 |
| 6 | 10 | 13 | Reviewed | | 2 | 1 | 4 | 3 | 3 |
| 5 | 3 | 5 | Compiled | | 2 | 1 | 2 | | |
| 2 | 3 | 4 | Tax Returns | | 2 | | 2 | | |
| 13 | 9 | 17 | Other | | 1 | 1 | 5 | 6 | 4 |
| | | | | | 13 (4/1-9/30/11) | | | 35 (10/1/11-3/31/12) | |
| 33 | 35 | 48 | NUMBER OF STATEMENTS | | 7 | 3 | 13 | 12 | 13 |
| % | % | % | **ASSETS** | % | % | % | % | % | % |
| 8.9 | 8.1 | 9.1 | Cash & Equivalents | | | | 6.0 | 10.9 | 8.4 |
| 20.5 | 21.6 | 22.1 | Trade Receivables (net) | | | | 28.2 | 24.1 | 21.0 |
| 29.9 | 29.9 | 27.4 | Inventory | | DATA NOT AVAILABLE | | 23.8 | 30.9 | 28.6 |
| 2.2 | 2.2 | 1.8 | All Other Current | | | | 2.2 | 1.2 | 2.0 |
| 61.4 | 61.7 | 60.5 | Total Current | | | | 60.3 | 67.1 | 60.0 |
| 29.1 | 30.8 | 32.1 | Fixed Assets (net) | | | | 33.6 | 30.5 | 30.8 |
| 3.9 | 1.9 | 3.6 | Intangibles (net) | | | | 3.9 | .7 | 6.3 |
| 5.6 | 5.6 | 3.9 | All Other Non-Current | | | | 2.2 | 1.7 | 2.9 |
| 100.0 | 100.0 | 100.0 | Total | | | | 100.0 | 100.0 | 100.0 |
| | | | **LIABILITIES** | | | | | | |
| 11.6 | 3.6 | 6.1 | Notes Payable-Short Term | | | | 9.4 | 6.4 | 4.0 |
| 3.4 | 5.0 | 4.1 | Cur. Mat.-L.T.D. | | | | 6.1 | 3.0 | 3.8 |
| 12.0 | 12.1 | 9.6 | Trade Payables | | | | 10.2 | 11.4 | 10.8 |
| .1 | .2 | .0 | Income Taxes Payable | | | | .1 | .0 | .0 |
| 10.7 | 7.0 | 9.3 | All Other Current | | | | 7.8 | 7.5 | 15.5 |
| 37.9 | 27.9 | 29.1 | Total Current | | | | 33.6 | 28.3 | 34.1 |
| 18.3 | 22.3 | 19.0 | Long-Term Debt | | | | 20.0 | 13.0 | 18.5 |
| .7 | .7 | 1.0 | Deferred Taxes | | | | 1.1 | .0 | 1.7 |
| 9.6 | 8.3 | 5.0 | All Other Non-Current | | | | 10.5 | 4.3 | 3.4 |
| 33.4 | 40.8 | 45.9 | Net Worth | | | | 34.8 | 54.3 | 42.3 |
| 100.0 | 100.0 | 100.0 | Total Liabilities & Net Worth | | | | 100.0 | 100.0 | 100.0 |
| | | | **INCOME DATA** | | | | | | |
| 100.0 | 100.0 | 100.0 | Net Sales | | | | 100.0 | 100.0 | 100.0 |
| 26.9 | 26.9 | 30.5 | Gross Profit | | | | 37.7 | 27.3 | 27.8 |
| 27.6 | 20.6 | 24.3 | Operating Expenses | | | | 34.3 | 15.4 | 18.2 |
| -.7 | 6.3 | 6.1 | Operating Profit | | | | 3.3 | 11.9 | 9.6 |
| 1.2 | 1.7 | 1.1 | All Other Expenses (net) | | | | 1.1 | .9 | 1.5 |
| -2.0 | 4.6 | 5.1 | Profit Before Taxes | | | | 2.2 | 11.0 | 8.1 |
| | | | **RATIOS** | | | | | | |
| 4.1 | 3.6 | 4.0 | Current | | | | 3.3 | 3.9 | 3.0 |
| 2.0 | 2.5 | 2.0 | | | | | 1.9 | 2.1 | 1.6 |
| 1.2 | 1.6 | 1.4 | | | | | 1.2 | 1.7 | 1.3 |
| 1.8 | 1.7 | 1.9 | Quick | | | | 1.7 | 2.1 | 1.7 |
| 1.0 | 1.3 | .9 | | | | | .9 | 1.3 | .7 |
| .5 | .7 | .6 | | | | | .8 | .6 | .6 |
| 35  10.3 | 40  9.1 | 37  9.8 | Sales/Receivables | | | | 40  9.1 | 39  9.4 | 38  9.5 |
| 47  7.8 | 52  7.0 | 47  7.7 | | | | | 48  7.6 | 61  6.0 | 53  6.9 |
| 53  6.9 | 62  5.9 | 66  5.5 | | | | | 54  6.8 | 79  4.6 | 72  5.1 |
| 57  6.4 | 82  4.4 | 55  6.6 | Cost of Sales/Inventory | | | | 33  11.0 | 76  4.8 | 66  5.5 |
| 98  3.7 | 96  3.8 | 91  4.0 | | | | | 56  6.5 | 118  3.1 | 87  4.2 |
| 124  2.9 | 119  3.1 | 130  2.8 | | | | | 111  3.3 | 135  2.7 | 126  2.9 |
| 11  31.8 | 17  21.0 | 15  24.5 | Cost of Sales/Payables | | | | 17  21.1 | 11  34.7 | 19  19.2 |
| 25  14.7 | 31  11.6 | 30  12.2 | | | | | 32  11.4 | 28  13.2 | 31  11.9 |
| 54  6.8 | 47  7.7 | 43  8.5 | | | | | 38  9.6 | 54  6.8 | 54  6.7 |
| 2.9 | 3.0 | 3.2 | Sales/Working Capital | | | | 4.5 | 2.8 | 3.7 |
| 4.9 | 4.4 | 5.6 | | | | | 7.4 | 4.7 | 6.8 |
| 32.0 | 7.2 | 9.6 | | | | | 23.8 | 6.2 | 10.3 |
| 5.4 | 9.0 | 12.4 | EBIT/Interest | | | | 6.6 | 21.2 | 58.4 |
| (29) 1.2 | (34) 3.3 | (46) 6.2 | | | | | 1.8 | (11) 11.1 | 12.1 |
| -1.7 | 1.1 | 1.4 | | | | | .7 | 7.9 | 2.6 |
| 3.5 | 19.9 | 10.9 | Net Profit + Depr., Dep., | | | | | | |
| (11) 1.0 | (11) 2.9 | (16) 3.2 | Amort./Cur. Mat. L/T/D | | | | | | |
| -1.4 | 1.6 | 1.2 | | | | | | | |
| .4 | .3 | .4 | Fixed/Worth | | | | .5 | .2 | .5 |
| .9 | .8 | .8 | | | | | 1.1 | .6 | .7 |
| 2.6 | 1.8 | 1.3 | | | | | 7.7 | 1.1 | 2.2 |
| .9 | .9 | .9 | Debt/Worth | | | | .9 | .5 | 1.1 |
| 2.3 | 1.7 | 1.6 | | | | | 1.7 | 1.0 | 2.0 |
| 4.1 | 3.3 | 2.5 | | | | | 14.0 | 1.6 | 4.2 |
| 15.9 | 37.3 | 44.2 | % Profit Before Taxes/Tangible | | | | 47.0 | 42.9 | 45.9 |
| (27) .0 | (46) 12.5 | 25.4 | Net Worth | | | | (12) 20.0 | 32.6 | (12) 27.6 |
| -35.7 | 1.3 | 4.2 | | | | | -.8 | 15.4 | 22.2 |
| 9.5 | 12.2 | 17.1 | % Profit Before Taxes/Total | | | | 9.4 | 20.6 | 19.1 |
| .1 | 5.5 | 9.4 | Assets | | | | 3.1 | 13.2 | 9.5 |
| -9.1 | .5 | 2.3 | | | | | -.4 | 10.1 | 3.7 |
| 22.6 | 15.4 | 10.8 | Sales/Net Fixed Assets | | | | 18.2 | 20.5 | 8.5 |
| 6.8 | 5.2 | 4.5 | | | | | 4.3 | 5.8 | 4.7 |
| 2.1 | 2.3 | 2.5 | | | | | 3.3 | 2.2 | 2.2 |
| 2.1 | 2.1 | 1.8 | Sales/Total Assets | | | | 2.6 | 1.8 | 1.8 |
| 1.5 | 1.5 | 1.5 | | | | | 1.7 | 1.5 | 1.4 |
| 1.0 | 1.1 | 1.3 | | | | | 1.5 | 1.1 | .9 |
| 1.6 | 1.9 | 1.7 | % Depr., Dep., Amort./Sales | | | | 2.0 | 1.2 | 1.4 |
| (29) 3.2 | (33) 3.1 | (45) 3.9 | | | | | 4.3 | (11) 4.3 | (11) 3.9 |
| 5.3 | 6.6 | 5.6 | | | | | 5.2 | 5.3 | 5.7 |
| | | 1.8 | % Officers', Directors' | | | | | | |
| | (15) 4.9 | | Owners' Comp/Sales | | | | | | |
| | | 7.8 | | | | | | | |
| 1021026M | 1120241M | 1607148M | Net Sales ($) | | 13926M | 11823M | 90724M | 194452M | 1296223M |
| 752441M | 860232M | 1183052M | Total Assets ($) | | 14460M | 8322M | 50637M | 150128M | 959505M |

| Current Data Sorted by Assets | | | | | | | Comparative Historical Data | |
|---|---|---|---|---|---|---|---|---|

| 0-500M | 500M-2MM | 2-10MM | 10-50MM | 50-100MM | 100-250MM | Type of Statement | 4/1/07-3/31/08 | 4/1/08-3/31/09 |
|---|---|---|---|---|---|---|---|---|
| | 1 | 2 | 8 | 1 | 1 | Unqualified | 11 | 13 |
| | 1 | 15 | 4 | | | Reviewed | 7 | 7 |
| | 1 | 4 | | | | Compiled | 4 | 1 |
| 2 | 1 | 2 | | | | Tax Returns | 1 | 2 |
| 1 | 1 | 9 | 7 | 1 | 1 | Other | 22 | 20 |
| | 12 (4/1-9/30/11) | | 51 (10/1/11-3/31/12) | | | | ALL | ALL |
| 3 | 5 | 32 | 19 | 2 | 2 | NUMBER OF STATEMENTS | 45 | 43 |
| % | % | % | % | % | % | ASSETS | % | % |
| | | 7.7 | 4.8 | | | Cash & Equivalents | 4.0 | 4.6 |
| | | 26.8 | 26.8 | | | Trade Receivables (net) | 27.1 | 25.3 |
| | | 37.9 | 40.1 | | | Inventory | 30.6 | 31.8 |
| | | 2.6 | .6 | | | All Other Current | 4.7 | 3.2 |
| | | 75.0 | 72.3 | | | Total Current | 66.4 | 65.0 |
| | | 19.0 | 21.1 | | | Fixed Assets (net) | 24.4 | 29.8 |
| | | 2.4 | 2.5 | | | Intangibles (net) | 4.0 | 1.7 |
| | | 3.5 | 4.1 | | | All Other Non-Current | 5.2 | 3.6 |
| | | 100.0 | 100.0 | | | Total | 100.0 | 100.0 |
| | | | | | | LIABILITIES | | |
| | | 12.7 | 9.9 | | | Notes Payable-Short Term | 19.1 | 21.0 |
| | | 1.9 | 2.6 | | | Cur. Mat.-L.T.D. | 3.6 | 3.8 |
| | | 20.7 | 12.9 | | | Trade Payables | 13.3 | 10.0 |
| | | .6 | .2 | | | Income Taxes Payable | .5 | .1 |
| | | 12.2 | 11.6 | | | All Other Current | 12.8 | 14.7 |
| | | 48.1 | 37.2 | | | Total Current | 49.3 | 49.5 |
| | | 11.0 | 13.0 | | | Long-Term Debt | 15.6 | 16.9 |
| | | .9 | .8 | | | Deferred Taxes | .7 | 1.0 |
| | | .8 | 6.1 | | | All Other Non-Current | 5.7 | 1.7 |
| | | 39.2 | 43.0 | | | Net Worth | 28.6 | 30.9 |
| | | 100.0 | 100.0 | | | Total Liabilties & Net Worth | 100.0 | 100.0 |
| | | | | | | INCOME DATA | | |
| | | 100.0 | 100.0 | | | Net Sales | 100.0 | 100.0 |
| | | 33.5 | 28.0 | | | Gross Profit | 33.5 | 30.4 |
| | | 26.1 | 20.1 | | | Operating Expenses | 25.7 | 22.8 |
| | | 7.4 | 7.8 | | | Operating Profit | 7.8 | 7.5 |
| | | 1.0 | 1.2 | | | All Other Expenses (net) | .9 | .8 |
| | | 6.4 | 6.7 | | | Profit Before Taxes | 7.0 | 6.7 |
| | | | | | | RATIOS | | |
| | | 2.7 | 3.1 | | | Current | 2.8 | 2.6 |
| | | 1.9 | 2.2 | | | | 1.9 | 1.7 |
| | | 1.3 | 1.5 | | | | 1.2 | 1.2 |
| | | 1.3 | 1.5 | | | Quick | 1.2 | 1.3 |
| | | .9 | .9 | | | | .7 | .8 |
| | | .4 | .5 | | | | .6 | .4 |
| | | 34   10.7 | 38   9.6 | | | Sales/Receivables | 40   9.2 | 33   11.2 |
| | | 43   8.5 | 49   7.4 | | | | 47   7.8 | 44   8.3 |
| | | 54   6.7 | 59   6.2 | | | | 60   6.1 | 61   6.0 |
| | | 50   7.3 | 79   4.6 | | | Cost of Sales/Inventory | 42   8.8 | 46   7.9 |
| | | 89   4.1 | 107   3.4 | | | | 89   4.1 | 70   5.2 |
| | | 182   2.0 | 152   2.4 | | | | 144   2.5 | 148   2.5 |
| | | 28   13.0 | 20   18.3 | | | Cost of Sales/Payables | 17   22.0 | 16   23.1 |
| | | 39   9.4 | 29   12.8 | | | | 29   12.8 | 27   13.5 |
| | | 54   6.8 | 46   7.9 | | | | 44   8.3 | 38   9.6 |
| | | 4.0 | 3.3 | | | Sales/Working Capital | 3.9 | 4.3 |
| | | 5.5 | 5.5 | | | | 6.0 | 7.5 |
| | | 10.9 | 10.5 | | | | 14.9 | 18.7 |
| | | 48.8 | 23.7 | | | EBIT/Interest | 15.2 | 13.3 |
| | | (29) 11.0 | (16) 11.1 | | | | (38) 6.7 | (41) 5.3 |
| | | 6.0 | 3.5 | | | | 3.3 | 1.3 |
| | | | | | | Net Profit + Depr., Dep., Amort./Cur. Mat. L/T/D | 8.1 | 11.0 |
| | | | | | | | (18) 4.2 | (20) 4.4 |
| | | | | | | | 1.8 | 1.7 |
| | | .1 | .2 | | | Fixed/Worth | .3 | .4 |
| | | .4 | .5 | | | | .7 | .8 |
| | | .9 | 1.0 | | | | 1.1 | 1.1 |
| | | .5 | .7 | | | Debt/Worth | .6 | .9 |
| | | 1.0 | 1.4 | | | | 1.6 | 1.5 |
| | | 2.2 | 2.4 | | | | 8.5 | 2.8 |
| | | 56.5 | 32.6 | | | % Profit Before Taxes/Tangible Net Worth | 62.0 | 65.5 |
| | | (30) 34.0 | (18) 27.9 | | | | (39) 23.8 | (41) 20.8 |
| | | 18.3 | 21.1 | | | | 14.2 | 1.6 |
| | | 23.0 | 18.6 | | | % Profit Before Taxes/Total Assets | 16.7 | 19.3 |
| | | 10.4 | 13.3 | | | | 10.4 | 10.8 |
| | | 6.9 | 4.1 | | | | 5.4 | .8 |
| | | 49.7 | 15.1 | | | Sales/Net Fixed Assets | 19.4 | 11.5 |
| | | 11.7 | 9.3 | | | | 9.1 | 8.1 |
| | | 5.4 | 5.6 | | | | 4.0 | 3.4 |
| | | 2.9 | 2.2 | | | Sales/Total Assets | 2.3 | 2.2 |
| | | 2.0 | 1.9 | | | | 1.9 | 2.0 |
| | | 1.5 | 1.4 | | | | 1.5 | 1.4 |
| | | .9 | .6 | | | % Depr., Dep., Amort./Sales | 1.2 | 1.4 |
| | | (29) 2.4 | (18) 1.7 | | | | (39) 1.9 | (41) 2.0 |
| | | 4.2 | 2.4 | | | | 2.9 | 3.9 |
| | | | | | | % Officers', Directors' Owners' Comp/Sales | | |
| 1209M | 12009M | 313919M | 799323M | 130970M | 311597M | Net Sales ($) | 1206163M | 1425466M |
| 654M | 4605M | 154044M | 409126M | 125676M | 396810M | Total Assets ($) | 811377M | 844326M |

M = $ thousand MM = $ million
See Pages 9 through 22 for Explanation of Ratios and Data

## Comparative Historical Data | Current Data Sorted by Sales

| 4/1/09-3/31/10 ALL | 4/1/10-3/31/11 ALL | 4/1/11-3/31/12 ALL | Type of Statement | 0-1MM | 1-3MM | 3-5MM | 5-10MM | 10-25MM | 25MM & OVER |
|---|---|---|---|---|---|---|---|---|---|
| 12 | 10 | 13 | Unqualified | | | | 1 | 5 | 7 |
| 7 | 15 | 20 | Reviewed | | | 3 | 6 | 9 | 2 |
| 2 | 6 | 5 | Compiled | | | 1 | 3 | 1 | |
| 2 | 1 | 5 | Tax Returns | 2 | 1 | 1 | 1 | | |
| 19 | 19 | 20 | Other | 1 | 1 | | 4 | 7 | 7 |
| | | | | 12 (4/1-9/30/11) | | | 51 (10/1/11-3/31/12) | | |
| 42 | 51 | 63 | **NUMBER OF STATEMENTS** | 4 | 2 | 5 | 14 | 22 | 16 |
| % | % | % | **ASSETS** | % | % | % | % | % | % |
| 7.5 | 8.8 | 5.8 | Cash & Equivalents | | | | 8.2 | 7.3 | 2.8 |
| 21.3 | 26.2 | 24.7 | Trade Receivables (net) | | | | 26.1 | 27.3 | 26.3 |
| 33.9 | 33.6 | 37.1 | Inventory | | | | 35.3 | 38.7 | 34.1 |
| 4.2 | 1.3 | 2.0 | All Other Current | | | | 1.5 | 3.0 | 2.2 |
| 66.9 | 69.9 | 69.5 | Total Current | | | | 71.0 | 76.3 | 65.4 |
| 21.1 | 21.2 | 21.1 | Fixed Assets (net) | | | | 22.4 | 18.0 | 24.9 |
| 5.7 | 1.9 | 4.8 | Intangibles (net) | | | | 3.4 | 2.8 | 5.2 |
| 6.3 | 6.9 | 4.6 | All Other Non-Current | | | | 3.2 | 2.9 | 4.6 |
| 100.0 | 100.0 | 100.0 | Total | | | | 100.0 | 100.0 | 100.0 |
| | | | **LIABILITIES** | | | | | | |
| 13.0 | 6.6 | 10.9 | Notes Payable-Short Term | | | | 6.7 | 17.0 | 8.3 |
| 4.1 | 5.0 | 2.9 | Cur. Mat.-L.T.D. | | | | 2.5 | 2.0 | 3.6 |
| 9.6 | 11.7 | 16.5 | Trade Payables | | | | 23.6 | 17.6 | 13.6 |
| .2 | .4 | .4 | Income Taxes Payable | | | | .5 | .7 | .1 |
| 13.0 | 12.4 | 12.8 | All Other Current | | | | 14.1 | 10.2 | 16.8 |
| 39.8 | 36.0 | 43.4 | Total Current | | | | 47.4 | 47.5 | 42.5 |
| 12.1 | 12.5 | 16.2 | Long-Term Debt | | | | 18.5 | 6.2 | 14.1 |
| 1.1 | .9 | .9 | Deferred Taxes | | | | .7 | 1.5 | .7 |
| 10.3 | 4.9 | 3.6 | All Other Non-Current | | | | .6 | 1.3 | 6.7 |
| 36.6 | 45.6 | 35.9 | Net Worth | | | | 32.8 | 43.5 | 36.0 |
| 100.0 | 100.0 | 100.0 | Total Liabilities & Net Worth | | | | 100.0 | 100.0 | 100.0 |
| | | | **INCOME DATA** | | | | | | |
| 100.0 | 100.0 | 100.0 | Net Sales | | | | 100.0 | 100.0 | 100.0 |
| 33.7 | 33.9 | 33.4 | Gross Profit | | | | 31.6 | 33.7 | 22.7 |
| 29.1 | 25.3 | 26.9 | Operating Expenses | | | | 23.7 | 25.4 | 16.8 |
| 4.6 | 8.6 | 6.5 | Operating Profit | | | | 7.9 | 8.3 | 5.9 |
| 1.5 | .7 | .9 | All Other Expenses (net) | | | | -.1 | 1.5 | 1.3 |
| 3.1 | 7.8 | 5.6 | Profit Before Taxes | | | | 8.0 | 6.8 | 4.5 |
| | | | **RATIOS** | | | | | | |
| 3.2 | 3.3 | 2.4 | | | | | 2.9 | 2.6 | 2.2 |
| 1.9 | 2.0 | 1.9 | Current | | | | 1.9 | 1.8 | 1.6 |
| 1.3 | 1.5 | 1.3 | | | | | 1.7 | 1.2 | 1.1 |
| 1.5 | 2.1 | 1.2 | | | | | 1.3 | 1.3 | .9 |
| .8 | 1.0 | .7 | Quick | | | | .9 | .8 | .7 |
| .4 | .6 | .4 | | | | | .4 | .4 | .5 |
| 34  10.8 | 37  9.9 | 34  10.8 | | 30  12.0 | | 35  10.5 | | 40  9.2 | |
| 47  7.8 | 53  6.9 | 44  8.3 | Sales/Receivables | 40  9.1 | | 49  7.5 | | 54  6.8 | |
| 69  5.3 | 66  5.5 | 56  6.5 | | 58  6.3 | | 55  6.6 | | 62  5.9 | |
| 52  7.0 | 62  5.9 | 54  6.8 | | 52  7.0 | | 51  7.1 | | 59  6.2 | |
| 119  3.1 | 92  4.0 | 101  3.6 | Cost of Sales/Inventory | 85  4.3 | | 130  2.8 | | 91  4.0 | |
| 247  1.5 | 163  2.2 | 166  2.2 | | 174  2.1 | | 174  2.1 | | 107  3.4 | |
| 21  17.4 | 23  15.7 | 22  16.3 | | 26  14.2 | | 29  12.5 | | 20  18.3 | |
| 29  12.7 | 29  12.5 | 38  9.6 | Cost of Sales/Payables | 38  9.5 | | 40  9.1 | | 33  11.2 | |
| 41  8.9 | 49  7.5 | 51  7.1 | | 61  6.0 | | 53  6.9 | | 50  7.3 | |
| 2.6 | 3.0 | 4.0 | | | | | 4.4 | 3.8 | 4.7 |
| 5.0 | 4.5 | 5.9 | Sales/Working Capital | | | | 5.4 | 6.5 | 8.0 |
| 13.5 | 12.6 | 14.0 | | | | | 7.3 | 15.4 | 245.1 |
| 14.3 | 23.0 | 27.1 | | | | | 137.3 | 48.3 | 12.9 |
| (35) 3.0 | (44) 8.4 | (56) 9.8 | EBIT/Interest | | | | 17.4 | (18) 9.8 | (14) 5.2 |
| -.6 | 3.3 | 3.7 | | | | | 10.5 | 5.5 | 2.7 |
| 6.3 | 4.6 | 23.1 | | | | | | | |
| (12) 3.1 | (17) 3.2 | (15) 4.6 | Net Profit + Depr., Dep., Amort./Cur. Mat. L/T/D | | | | | | |
| .8 | 2.2 | 2.4 | | | | | | | |
| .2 | .2 | .2 | | | | | .1 | .1 | .5 |
| .5 | .5 | .5 | Fixed/Worth | | | | .4 | .4 | .7 |
| 1.0 | .7 | 1.0 | | | | | .9 | .9 | 1.4 |
| .6 | .6 | .6 | | | | | .4 | .6 | 1.2 |
| 1.3 | 1.1 | 1.4 | Debt/Worth | | | | .6 | 1.6 | 2.0 |
| 3.3 | 2.1 | 3.7 | | | | | 1.3 | 2.9 | 3.8 |
| 38.3 | 37.2 | 55.3 | | | | | 61.9 | 56.9 | 37.2 |
| (37) 14.0 | (49) 23.4 | (56) 28.9 | % Profit Before Taxes/Tangible Net Worth | (13) 38.8 | | (21) 31.0 | | (15) 28.2 | |
| -.4 | 12.0 | 19.0 | | | | | 21.3 | 20.7 | 11.2 |
| 16.9 | 19.1 | 18.7 | | | | | 28.1 | 19.3 | 15.8 |
| 5.6 | 10.0 | 10.9 | % Profit Before Taxes/Total Assets | | | | 16.1 | 11.7 | 9.3 |
| -4.5 | 5.3 | 4.1 | | | | | 7.6 | 5.8 | 2.9 |
| 24.0 | 21.7 | 32.8 | | | | | 45.2 | 53.3 | 14.4 |
| 6.9 | 9.8 | 9.0 | Sales/Net Fixed Assets | | | | 8.8 | 13.1 | 7.8 |
| 3.6 | 3.9 | 5.3 | | | | | 5.1 | 5.4 | 4.1 |
| 2.0 | 2.1 | 2.5 | | | | | 3.0 | 2.5 | 2.3 |
| 1.3 | 1.7 | 1.9 | Sales/Total Assets | | | | 1.8 | 1.9 | 1.9 |
| .9 | 1.3 | 1.4 | | | | | 1.4 | 1.4 | 1.3 |
| 1.6 | 1.0 | .8 | | | | | 1.1 | 1.1 | .6 |
| (34) 2.9 | (47) 2.0 | (53) 2.1 | % Depr., Dep., Amort./Sales | (12) 3.4 | | (21) 1.9 | | (13) 1.5 | |
| 5.7 | 4.5 | 4.2 | | | | | 5.2 | 3.0 | 3.4 |
| | 1.3 | 1.5 | | | | | | | |
| | (11) 3.0 | (12) 3.7 | % Officers', Directors' Owners' Comp/Sales | | | | | | |
| | 6.4 | 6.4 | | | | | | | |
| 1153264M | 1240847M | 1569027M | Net Sales ($) | 1587M | 4309M | 18543M | 96345M | 329950M | 1118293M |
| 1106907M | 924059M | 1090915M | Total Assets ($) | 1509M | 1483M | 11110M | 54038M | 184942M | 837833M |

M = $ thousand    MM = $ million
See Pages 9 through 22 for Explanation of Ratios and Data

## Current Data Sorted by Assets      Comparative Historical Data

| | | | | | | Type of Statement | | |
|---|---|---|---|---|---|---|---|---|
| | 2 | 5 | 14 | 6 | 2 | Unqualified | 25 | 26 |
| | 1 | 11 | 9 | | | Reviewed | 23 | 24 |
| 1 | 2 | 5 | 2 | 1 | | Compiled | 17 | 13 |
| 1 | 10 | 8 | 1 | | | Tax Returns | 13 | 10 |
| 3 | 7 | 13 | 18 | 4 | | Other | 31 | 35 |
| | 21 (4/1-9/30/11) | | 104 (10/1/11-3/31/12) | | | | 4/1/07-3/31/08 | 4/1/08-3/31/09 |
| 0-500M | 500M-2MM | 2-10MM | 10-50MM | 50-100MM | 100-250MM | | ALL | ALL |
| 5 | 22 | 42 | 44 | 10 | 2 | NUMBER OF STATEMENTS | 109 | 108 |
| % | % | % | % | % | % | ASSETS | % | % |
| | 8.9 | 11.1 | 9.1 | 9.2 | | Cash & Equivalents | 9.2 | 8.9 |
| | 32.2 | 29.6 | 26.4 | 23.5 | | Trade Receivables (net) | 28.2 | 25.1 |
| | 31.5 | 33.8 | 31.4 | 29.6 | | Inventory | 33.2 | 33.6 |
| | 3.8 | 1.3 | 4.2 | 2.2 | | All Other Current | 2.7 | 3.5 |
| | 76.3 | 75.7 | 71.1 | 64.4 | | Total Current | 73.3 | 71.1 |
| | 15.9 | 14.5 | 19.3 | 16.8 | | Fixed Assets (net) | 18.8 | 20.0 |
| | 4.3 | 5.3 | 4.0 | 2.5 | | Intangibles (net) | 3.8 | 4.2 |
| | 3.4 | 4.6 | 5.5 | 16.2 | | All Other Non-Current | 4.2 | 4.7 |
| | 100.0 | 100.0 | 100.0 | 100.0 | | Total | 100.0 | 100.0 |
| | | | | | | LIABILITIES | | |
| | 11.2 | 5.0 | 7.9 | 4.7 | | Notes Payable-Short Term | 8.9 | 9.8 |
| | 2.9 | 3.6 | 2.1 | .2 | | Cur. Mat.-L.T.D. | 2.9 | 2.7 |
| | 20.2 | 20.5 | 12.8 | 14.0 | | Trade Payables | 14.1 | 12.9 |
| | .0 | .5 | .5 | .1 | | Income Taxes Payable | .3 | .3 |
| | 19.4 | 14.5 | 10.1 | 9.8 | | All Other Current | 9.6 | 11.0 |
| | 53.8 | 44.1 | 33.4 | 28.9 | | Total Current | 35.7 | 36.8 |
| | 11.7 | 7.8 | 6.6 | 10.4 | | Long-Term Debt | 12.8 | 11.6 |
| | .2 | .7 | .8 | .9 | | Deferred Taxes | .5 | .5 |
| | 8.1 | 3.3 | 5.0 | .6 | | All Other Non-Current | 3.8 | 5.5 |
| | 26.3 | 44.1 | 54.1 | 59.3 | | Net Worth | 47.1 | 45.5 |
| | 100.0 | 100.0 | 100.0 | 100.0 | | Total Liabilties & Net Worth | 100.0 | 100.0 |
| | | | | | | INCOME DATA | | |
| | 100.0 | 100.0 | 100.0 | 100.0 | | Net Sales | 100.0 | 100.0 |
| | 38.1 | 33.9 | 31.4 | 28.6 | | Gross Profit | 34.1 | 32.8 |
| | 35.9 | 26.9 | 23.9 | 20.9 | | Operating Expenses | 25.5 | 26.2 |
| | 2.1 | 7.0 | 7.6 | 7.8 | | Operating Profit | 8.6 | 6.6 |
| | 1.1 | .4 | .7 | -.4 | | All Other Expenses (net) | .6 | .7 |
| | 1.0 | 6.6 | 6.9 | 8.1 | | Profit Before Taxes | 7.9 | 6.0 |
| | | | | | | RATIOS | | |
| | 3.4 | 2.9 | 3.6 | 6.8 | | | 3.1 | 3.2 |
| | 1.7 | 2.0 | 2.0 | 2.3 | | Current | 2.0 | 2.0 |
| | 1.2 | 1.2 | 1.4 | 1.4 | | | 1.4 | 1.4 |
| | 1.7 | 1.5 | 2.5 | 4.1 | | | 1.7 | 1.6 |
| | 1.2 | .9 | 1.0 | 1.0 | | Quick | .9 | 1.0 |
| | .4 | .7 | .6 | .6 | | | .7 | .6 |
| | 26  14.0 | 37  9.9 | 39  9.3 | 42  8.6 | | | 38  9.6 | 32  11.4 |
| | 45  8.1 | 45  8.1 | 51  7.1 | 47  7.8 | | Sales/Receivables | 49  7.4 | 46  7.9 |
| | 63  5.8 | 59  6.2 | 66  5.5 | 62  5.9 | | | 60  6.0 | 57  6.4 |
| | 34  10.7 | 50  7.3 | 61  6.0 | 76  4.8 | | | 52  7.1 | 57  6.4 |
| | 56  6.5 | 87  4.2 | 89  4.1 | 99  3.7 | | Cost of Sales/Inventory | 87  4.2 | 90  4.1 |
| | 79  4.6 | 114  3.2 | 146  2.5 | 130  2.8 | | | 140  2.6 | 139  2.6 |
| | 17  21.6 | 29  12.4 | 17  21.8 | 13  27.6 | | | 20  18.5 | 18  20.0 |
| | 34  10.6 | 43  8.5 | 34  10.8 | 36  10.2 | | Cost of Sales/Payables | 32  11.2 | 29  12.7 |
| | 73  5.0 | 62  5.9 | 43  8.4 | 61  6.0 | | | 48  7.6 | 43  8.4 |
| | 5.0 | 4.4 | 3.2 | 2.6 | | | 3.5 | 3.7 |
| | 9.9 | 6.3 | 5.2 | 4.7 | | Sales/Working Capital | 6.0 | 6.9 |
| | 30.8 | 18.5 | 10.0 | 8.7 | | | 11.2 | 13.5 |
| | 19.3 | 31.6 | 49.8 | | | | 23.2 | 16.4 |
| | (17) 5.6 | (37) 11.3 | (40) 13.6 | | | EBIT/Interest | (101) 6.4 | (94) 5.3 |
| | 1.7 | 2.8 | 3.5 | | | | 2.7 | 1.7 |
| | | 9.0 | 7.8 | | | Net Profit + Depr., Dep., | 10.0 | 10.3 |
| | | (13) 5.3 | (19) 2.4 | | | Amort./Cur. Mat. L/T/D | (38) 3.2 | (36) 3.1 |
| | | 1.7 | 1.7 | | | | 1.5 | 1.2 |
| | .1 | .1 | .2 | .1 | | | .1 | .2 |
| | .4 | .3 | .4 | .2 | | Fixed/Worth | .3 | .4 |
| | 1.5 | .5 | .6 | .5 | | | .9 | 1.1 |
| | .7 | .6 | .4 | .2 | | | .6 | .6 |
| | 2.0 | 1.4 | .8 | .7 | | Debt/Worth | 1.4 | 1.2 |
| | 11.3 | 4.1 | 2.4 | 1.3 | | | 2.9 | 3.3 |
| | 93.8 | 55.6 | 31.0 | | | % Profit Before Taxes/Tangible | 58.7 | 43.4 |
| | (19) 33.3 | (39) 33.8 | (41) 21.3 | | | Net Worth | (105) 34.8 | (97) 21.8 |
| | 13.2 | 9.4 | 8.8 | | | | 14.4 | 7.2 |
| | 27.8 | 16.5 | 17.6 | 19.4 | | % Profit Before Taxes/Total | 24.1 | 17.4 |
| | 8.6 | 10.7 | 10.4 | 9.2 | | Assets | 12.2 | 8.3 |
| | 2.6 | 4.5 | 5.0 | 6.1 | | | 5.2 | 2.5 |
| | 201.9 | 71.5 | 22.5 | 21.5 | | | 48.9 | 34.5 |
| | 25.1 | 24.7 | 10.3 | 11.4 | | Sales/Net Fixed Assets | 12.9 | 13.8 |
| | 7.0 | 8.5 | 5.7 | 5.2 | | | 5.8 | 6.5 |
| | 4.0 | 2.9 | 2.1 | 2.0 | | | 2.7 | 2.6 |
| | 3.1 | 2.2 | 1.8 | 1.6 | | Sales/Total Assets | 2.1 | 2.0 |
| | 1.6 | 1.6 | 1.3 | 1.1 | | | 1.5 | 1.4 |
| | .8 | .6 | .7 | 1.0 | | | .7 | .8 |
| | (12) 2.7 | (33) 1.3 | (39) 1.8 | 1.4 | | % Depr., Dep., Amort./Sales | (90) 1.3 | (90) 1.6 |
| | 5.2 | 3.7 | 2.7 | 2.5 | | | 2.2 | 2.6 |
| | 1.7 | 2.1 | | | | % Officers', Directors' | 1.8 | 2.0 |
| | (13) 4.3 | (18) 3.3 | | | | Owners' Comp/Sales | (39) 3.5 | (30) 3.9 |
| | 7.7 | 7.0 | | | | | 8.2 | 8.7 |
| 4773M | 78117M | 452740M | 1624227M | 1126795M | 196095M | Net Sales ($) | 2843777M | 3850714M |
| 2017M | 25438M | 206499M | 914107M | 714133M | 209369M | Total Assets ($) | 1680249M | 2306591M |

## Comparative Historical Data | Current Data Sorted by Sales

| | | | Type of Statement | 0-1MM | 1-3MM | 3-5MM | 5-10MM | 10-25MM | 25MM & OVER |
|---|---|---|---|---|---|---|---|---|---|
| 26 | 24 | 29 | Unqualified | | 1 | 3 | 1 | 3 | 21 |
| 25 | 34 | 21 | Reviewed | | 1 | 1 | 3 | 13 | 3 |
| 14 | 12 | 10 | Compiled | | | 3 | 5 | | 2 |
| 14 | 20 | 20 | Tax Returns | 1 | 4 | 4 | 5 | 5 | 1 |
| 38 | 40 | 45 | Other | 2 | 5 | 2 | 10 | 6 | 20 |
| 4/1/09-3/31/10 ALL | 4/1/10-3/31/11 ALL | 4/1/11-3/31/12 ALL | | 21 (4/1-9/30/11) | | 104 (10/1/11-3/31/12) | | | |
| 117 | 130 | 125 | NUMBER OF STATEMENTS | 3 | 14 | 10 | 24 | 27 | 47 |
| % | % | % | ASSETS | % | % | % | % | % | % |
| 10.2 | 10.6 | 9.9 | Cash & Equivalents | | 6.9 | 13.1 | 9.9 | 10.7 | 9.2 |
| 25.5 | 25.6 | 28.0 | Trade Receivables (net) | | 27.4 | 36.1 | 27.7 | 29.4 | 26.4 |
| 31.8 | 31.6 | 32.5 | Inventory | | 31.4 | 36.2 | 34.4 | 34.4 | 30.1 |
| 3.4 | 3.8 | 2.8 | All Other Current | | .9 | .7 | .6 | 4.1 | 3.2 |
| 70.9 | 71.5 | 73.3 | Total Current | | 66.6 | 86.0 | 72.6 | 78.5 | 68.9 |
| 20.1 | 20.3 | 16.5 | Fixed Assets (net) | | 23.3 | 7.7 | 17.4 | 15.2 | 17.6 |
| 3.5 | 2.9 | 4.7 | Intangibles (net) | | 4.6 | 5.1 | 5.3 | 3.5 | 4.6 |
| 5.5 | 5.3 | 5.5 | All Other Non-Current | | 5.5 | 1.1 | 4.7 | 2.7 | 8.9 |
| 100.0 | 100.0 | 100.0 | Total | | 100.0 | 100.0 | 100.0 | 100.0 | 100.0 |
| | | | **LIABILITIES** | | | | | | |
| 8.1 | 5.6 | 8.2 | Notes Payable-Short Term | | 20.1 | 9.8 | 3.8 | 5.8 | 7.3 |
| 3.9 | 2.6 | 2.5 | Cur. Mat.-L.T.D. | | 1.5 | 1.9 | 5.8 | 1.9 | 1.7 |
| 13.3 | 13.9 | 17.1 | Trade Payables | | 16.2 | 20.7 | 17.3 | 21.0 | 13.4 |
| .4 | .3 | .4 | Income Taxes Payable | | .1 | .5 | .2 | .6 | .4 |
| 14.7 | 13.3 | 13.1 | All Other Current | | 25.8 | 15.2 | 8.5 | 14.7 | 11.0 |
| 40.4 | 35.7 | 41.3 | Total Current | | 63.8 | 48.1 | 35.6 | 44.0 | 33.9 |
| 11.6 | 11.5 | 8.5 | Long-Term Debt | | 17.5 | 5.8 | 10.3 | 6.8 | 7.0 |
| .6 | .6 | .6 | Deferred Taxes | | .3 | 1.1 | .3 | .6 | .6 |
| 3.0 | 5.3 | 4.4 | All Other Non-Current | | 2.2 | 5.0 | 4.6 | 1.4 | 4.7 |
| 44.2 | 46.8 | 45.2 | Net Worth | | 16.2 | 40.0 | 49.2 | 47.1 | 53.5 |
| 100.0 | 100.0 | 100.0 | Total Liabilities & Net Worth | | 100.0 | 100.0 | 100.0 | 100.0 | 100.0 |
| | | | **INCOME DATA** | | | | | | |
| 100.0 | 100.0 | 100.0 | Net Sales | | 100.0 | 100.0 | 100.0 | 100.0 | 100.0 |
| 34.2 | 34.7 | 33.8 | Gross Profit | | 36.5 | 36.4 | 38.9 | 32.0 | 29.3 |
| 29.2 | 27.3 | 27.0 | Operating Expenses | | 33.6 | 27.0 | 31.7 | 25.7 | 21.7 |
| 5.1 | 7.3 | 6.8 | Operating Profit | | 2.9 | 9.4 | 7.2 | 6.3 | 7.6 |
| 1.0 | .3 | .6 | All Other Expenses (net) | | .9 | .9 | .5 | .3 | .4 |
| 4.1 | 7.1 | 6.2 | Profit Before Taxes | | 2.0 | 8.4 | 6.7 | 6.0 | 7.2 |
| | | | **RATIOS** | | | | | | |
| 4.0 | 3.8 | 3.2 | Current | | 4.5 | 2.5 | 3.2 | 3.6 | 3.3 |
| 2.0 | 2.1 | 1.9 | | | 1.4 | 2.0 | 2.6 | 1.7 | 1.9 |
| 1.3 | 1.4 | 1.3 | | | .7 | 1.5 | 1.2 | 1.3 | 1.4 |
| 2.0 | 2.0 | 1.7 | Quick | | 1.8 | 1.5 | 2.1 | 1.6 | 1.9 |
| 1.0 | 1.0 | .9 | | | 1.1 | 1.0 | 1.2 | .9 | .9 |
| .6 | .6 | .6 | | | .3 | .8 | .5 | .7 | .6 |
| 33  11.2 | 35  10.5 | 37  9.8 | Sales/Receivables | 27  13.7 | 41  8.8 | 36  10.0 | 32  11.5 | 39  9.3 | |
| 47  7.7 | 47  7.7 | 47  7.8 | | 42  8.7 | 53  6.9 | 42  8.6 | 48  7.6 | 48  7.6 | |
| 65  5.6 | 66  5.6 | 62  5.9 | | 56  6.5 | 62  5.9 | 57  6.4 | 76  4.8 | 64  5.7 | |
| 47  7.7 | 55  6.6 | 54  6.8 | Cost of Sales/Inventory | 30  12.0 | 62  5.9 | 49  7.5 | 46  8.0 | 57  6.4 | |
| 87  4.2 | 91  4.0 | 85  4.3 | | 81  4.5 | 73  5.0 | 85  4.3 | 91  4.0 | 85  4.3 | |
| 146  2.5 | 145  2.5 | 130  2.8 | | 135  2.7 | 122  3.0 | 182  2.0 | 135  2.7 | 130  2.8 | |
| 17  21.7 | 17  21.4 | 21  17.5 | Cost of Sales/Payables | 16  22.9 | 29  12.6 | 20  17.9 | 22  16.7 | 21  17.6 | |
| 28  12.9 | 33  11.1 | 36  10.0 | | 30  12.0 | 40  9.1 | 37  9.8 | 43  8.5 | 34  10.8 | |
| 47  7.8 | 51  7.2 | 54  6.8 | | 87  4.2 | 57  6.4 | 89  4.1 | 54  6.8 | 42  8.6 | |
| 3.0 | 3.2 | 3.6 | Sales/Working Capital | | 3.9 | 3.7 | 3.9 | 4.5 | 3.7 |
| 5.9 | 5.4 | 6.0 | | | 13.6 | 6.0 | 5.4 | 8.1 | 5.2 |
| 13.5 | 11.8 | 13.2 | | | -15.8 | 13.0 | 53.1 | 13.4 | 10.8 |
| 26.6 | 31.8 | 29.5 | EBIT/Interest | | | | 38.8 | 25.8 | 50.0 |
| (108)  5.8 | (116)  8.0 | (103)  10.9 | | | | (22)  7.4 | (23)  10.7 | (39)  13.8 | |
| 1.0 | 2.8 | 2.4 | | | | | 2.2 | 3.6 | 3.5 |
| 9.4 | 16.9 | 8.1 | Net Profit + Depr., Dep., Amort./Cur. Mat. L/T/D | | | | | 6.7 | 17.7 |
| (44)  2.8 | (38)  5.1 | (39)  4.4 | | | | | (10)  3.6 | (19)  2.4 | |
| .9 | 1.4 | 1.8 | | | | | | 2.2 | 1.7 |
| .2 | .2 | .1 | Fixed/Worth | | .2 | .0 | .1 | .1 | .2 |
| .4 | .3 | .3 | | | .6 | .1 | .3 | .4 | .3 |
| 1.0 | .9 | .6 | | | 7.0 | .5 | 1.1 | .6 | .6 |
| .4 | .4 | .5 | Debt/Worth | | 1.0 | .7 | .4 | .5 | .5 |
| 1.4 | 1.1 | 1.2 | | | 3.2 | 1.7 | .9 | 1.3 | 1.0 |
| 2.5 | 2.1 | 3.2 | | | NM | 7.8 | 3.1 | 3.5 | 2.0 |
| 34.3 | 34.5 | 47.3 | % Profit Before Taxes/Tangible Net Worth | | 92.4 | 121.5 | 52.2 | 47.2 | 36.6 |
| (106)  15.7 | (120)  18.2 | (113)  25.0 | | (11)  28.4 | 49.0 | (21)  19.7 | (26)  27.2 | (43)  21.6 | |
| 3.6 | 6.2 | 11.5 | | | 11.7 | 25.7 | 8.6 | 9.3 | 11.4 |
| 15.3 | 19.6 | 19.2 | % Profit Before Taxes/Total Assets | | 23.4 | 23.4 | 23.2 | 18.5 | 18.0 |
| 7.0 | 10.0 | 10.4 | | | 7.5 | 13.0 | 9.5 | 10.7 | 10.4 |
| .0 | 2.3 | 5.2 | | | 2.5 | 10.1 | 4.2 | 5.5 | 5.3 |
| 25.2 | 25.9 | 50.6 | Sales/Net Fixed Assets | | 53.3 | UND | 68.3 | 54.4 | 21.7 |
| 13.0 | 11.7 | 15.5 | | | 8.9 | 133.4 | 18.6 | 21.0 | 11.8 |
| 5.6 | 6.2 | 6.5 | | | 5.4 | 39.5 | 6.8 | 7.4 | 6.6 |
| 2.5 | 2.4 | 2.6 | Sales/Total Assets | | 3.0 | 3.5 | 3.5 | 3.0 | 2.3 |
| 1.8 | 1.9 | 2.0 | | | 2.2 | 2.1 | 2.2 | 2.2 | 1.9 |
| 1.3 | 1.4 | 1.5 | | | 1.4 | 1.4 | 1.5 | 1.4 | 1.5 |
| .8 | .9 | .7 | % Depr., Dep., Amort./Sales | | 1.0 | | .8 | .8 | .7 |
| (98)  1.6 | (115)  1.7 | (98)  1.5 | | | (10)  3.2 | (19)  2.7 | (21)  1.5 | (42)  1.5 | |
| 2.9 | 2.7 | 3.1 | | | 5.8 | | 4.9 | 3.7 | 2.3 |
| 1.9 | .8 | 1.8 | % Officers', Directors' Owners' Comp/Sales | | | | 1.1 | 1.7 | |
| (36)  4.1 | (35)  2.6 | (38)  3.3 | | | | (10)  3.0 | (11)  2.4 | | |
| | | | | | | | 5.1 | 6.8 | |
| 3632628M | 3897707M | 3482747M | Net Sales ($) | 1189M | 24475M | 40703M | 171091M | 432435M | 2812854M |
| 2475141M | 2298859M | 2071563M | Total Assets ($) | 1624M | 12744M | 21321M | 96727M | 254016M | 1685131M |

M = $ thousand    MM = $ million
See Pages 9 through 22 for Explanation of Ratios and Data

## Current Data Sorted by Assets      Comparative Historical Data

| 0-500M | 500M-2MM | 2-10MM | 10-50MM | 50-100MM | 100-250MM | Type of Statement | 4/1/07-3/31/08 ALL | 4/1/08-3/31/09 ALL |
|---|---|---|---|---|---|---|---|---|
|  |  |  | 2 | 1 | 2 | Unqualified | 9 | 7 |
|  | 2 | 1 | 6 |  |  | Reviewed | 5 | 4 |
| 1 | 3 | 2 |  |  |  | Compiled | 4 | 3 |
| 1 | 3 | 2 |  |  |  | Tax Returns | 1 | 1 |
|  | 1 | 3 | 4 |  |  | Other | 12 | 15 |
| 4 (4/1-9/30/11) | | | 30 (10/1/11-3/31/12) | | | | | |
| 2 | 9 | 8 | 12 | 1 | 2 | NUMBER OF STATEMENTS | 31 | 30 |
| % | % | % | % | % | % | **ASSETS** | % | % |
|  |  |  | 12.0 |  |  | Cash & Equivalents | 7.3 | 4.8 |
|  |  |  | 25.3 |  |  | Trade Receivables (net) | 22.5 | 23.6 |
|  |  |  | 32.3 |  |  | Inventory | 30.0 | 33.7 |
|  |  |  | 3.9 |  |  | All Other Current | 1.6 | 3.4 |
|  |  |  | 73.5 |  |  | Total Current | 61.4 | 65.5 |
|  |  |  | 14.5 |  |  | Fixed Assets (net) | 25.1 | 24.8 |
|  |  |  | 6.8 |  |  | Intangibles (net) | 10.5 | 4.1 |
|  |  |  | 5.3 |  |  | All Other Non-Current | 3.0 | 5.6 |
|  |  |  | 100.0 |  |  | Total | 100.0 | 100.0 |
|  |  |  |  |  |  | **LIABILITIES** |  |  |
|  |  |  | 8.5 |  |  | Notes Payable-Short Term | 10.4 | 14.6 |
|  |  |  | 1.1 |  |  | Cur. Mat.-L.T.D. | 4.0 | 3.4 |
|  |  |  | 13.1 |  |  | Trade Payables | 14.4 | 14.7 |
|  |  |  | .0 |  |  | Income Taxes Payable | .2 | .2 |
|  |  |  | 19.4 |  |  | All Other Current | 11.9 | 9.1 |
|  |  |  | 42.0 |  |  | Total Current | 40.9 | 42.0 |
|  |  |  | 5.2 |  |  | Long-Term Debt | 15.7 | 14.0 |
|  |  |  | .4 |  |  | Deferred Taxes | 1.4 | 1.8 |
|  |  |  | 1.8 |  |  | All Other Non-Current | 4.2 | 5.4 |
|  |  |  | 50.7 |  |  | Net Worth | 37.8 | 36.8 |
|  |  |  | 100.0 |  |  | Total Liabilities & Net Worth | 100.0 | 100.0 |
|  |  |  |  |  |  | **INCOME DATA** |  |  |
|  |  |  | 100.0 |  |  | Net Sales | 100.0 | 100.0 |
|  |  |  | 26.0 |  |  | Gross Profit | 33.5 | 31.6 |
|  |  |  | 16.6 |  |  | Operating Expenses | 25.2 | 23.9 |
|  |  |  | 9.4 |  |  | Operating Profit | 8.3 | 7.6 |
|  |  |  | .7 |  |  | All Other Expenses (net) | 2.3 | 1.7 |
|  |  |  | 8.7 |  |  | Profit Before Taxes | 6.0 | 5.9 |
|  |  |  |  |  |  | **RATIOS** |  |  |
|  |  |  | 3.3 |  |  | Current | 2.4 | 2.5 |
|  |  |  | 1.6 |  |  |  | 1.4 | 1.7 |
|  |  |  | 1.3 |  |  |  | 1.0 | 1.0 |
|  |  |  | 1.3 |  |  | Quick | 1.3 | 1.2 |
|  |  |  | .8 |  |  |  | .7 | .6 |
|  |  |  | .7 |  |  |  | .4 | .4 |
|  |  |  | 36  10.1 |  |  | Sales/Receivables | 34  10.7 | 37  9.8 |
|  |  |  | 50  7.3 |  |  |  | 50  7.3 | 49  7.5 |
|  |  |  | 56  6.5 |  |  |  | 65  5.6 | 62  5.9 |
|  |  |  | 50  7.3 |  |  | Cost of Sales/Inventory | 63  5.8 | 67  5.4 |
|  |  |  | 96  3.8 |  |  |  | 98  3.7 | 97  3.8 |
|  |  |  | 140  2.6 |  |  |  | 144  2.5 | 128  2.8 |
|  |  |  | 24  15.2 |  |  | Cost of Sales/Payables | 31  11.7 | 21  17.0 |
|  |  |  | 29  12.4 |  |  |  | 47  7.7 | 37  9.8 |
|  |  |  | 47  7.8 |  |  |  | 59  6.1 | 60  6.1 |
|  |  |  | 2.9 |  |  | Sales/Working Capital | 4.5 | 4.5 |
|  |  |  | 6.3 |  |  |  | 8.1 | 8.1 |
|  |  |  | 13.1 |  |  |  | 62.7 | 64.0 |
|  |  |  | 88.0 |  |  | EBIT/Interest | 9.3 | 14.0 |
|  |  |  | (11) 16.3 |  |  |  | (27) 3.7 | (27) 4.6 |
|  |  |  | 8.6 |  |  |  | 1.1 | 1.5 |
|  |  |  |  |  |  | Net Profit + Depr., Dep., Amort./Cur. Mat. L/T/D | 5.3 | 10.0 |
|  |  |  |  |  |  |  | (10) 3.1 | (12) 2.3 |
|  |  |  |  |  |  |  | -.4 | 1.7 |
|  |  |  | .2 |  |  | Fixed/Worth | .4 | .3 |
|  |  |  | .4 |  |  |  | .7 | .7 |
|  |  |  | .5 |  |  |  | 2.9 | 2.2 |
|  |  |  | .6 |  |  | Debt/Worth | .9 | 1.0 |
|  |  |  | 1.2 |  |  |  | 2.6 | 2.2 |
|  |  |  | 2.7 |  |  |  | 6.6 | 3.5 |
|  |  |  | 53.7 |  |  | % Profit Before Taxes/Tangible Net Worth | 77.7 | 44.7 |
|  |  |  | 26.9 |  |  |  | (29) 21.4 | (27) 20.3 |
|  |  |  | 19.7 |  |  |  | 3.9 | 9.2 |
|  |  |  | 17.9 |  |  | % Profit Before Taxes/Total Assets | 16.3 | 15.0 |
|  |  |  | 13.8 |  |  |  | 8.8 | 10.7 |
|  |  |  | 8.0 |  |  |  | 1.1 | 2.1 |
|  |  |  | 27.5 |  |  | Sales/Net Fixed Assets | 17.0 | 18.9 |
|  |  |  | 12.8 |  |  |  | 8.0 | 8.9 |
|  |  |  | 7.5 |  |  |  | 5.1 | 4.0 |
|  |  |  | 2.1 |  |  | Sales/Total Assets | 2.1 | 2.1 |
|  |  |  | 1.7 |  |  |  | 1.5 | 1.7 |
|  |  |  | 1.5 |  |  |  | 1.1 | 1.3 |
|  |  |  | .6 |  |  | % Depr., Dep., Amort./Sales | 1.2 | .9 |
|  |  |  | 1.2 |  |  |  | (28) 1.9 | (26) 1.8 |
|  |  |  | 2.1 |  |  |  | 2.9 | 2.9 |
|  |  |  |  |  |  | % Officers', Directors' Owners' Comp/Sales | 1.5 |  |
|  |  |  |  |  |  |  | (10) 4.5 |  |
|  |  |  |  |  |  |  | 12.4 |  |
| 2569M | 32902M | 73505M | 549491M | 94754M | 173005M | Net Sales ($) | 700916M | 1022799M |
| 656M | 10169M | 36471M | 273273M | 81319M | 261133M | Total Assets ($) | 539778M | 853880M |

© RMA 2012

**M = $ thousand   MM = $ million**
See Pages 9 through 22 for Explanation of Ratios and Data

## Comparative Historical Data                          Current Data Sorted by Sales

| | | | | | Type of Statement | | | | | | | |
|---|---|---|---|---|---|---|---|---|---|---|---|---|
| | 4 | | 6 | | 5 | Unqualified | | | | 5 | | 5 |
| | 5 | | 12 | | 9 | Reviewed | | 1 | | 1 | 4 | 3 |
| | 2 | | | | 6 | Compiled | | 2 | 2 | 2 | | |
| | 2 | | 4 | | 4 | Tax Returns | | 1 | 1 | | 2 | |
| | 18 | | 13 | | 10 | Other | | 2 | 2 | 3 | | 3 |
| | 4/1/09- 3/31/10 | | 4/1/10- 3/31/11 | | 4/1/11- 3/31/12 | | | 4 (4/1-9/30/11) | | 30 (10/1/11-3/31/12) | | |
| | ALL | | ALL | | ALL | | 0-1MM | 1-3MM | 3-5MM | 5-10MM | 10-25MM | 25MM & OVER |
| | 31 | | 35 | | 34 | NUMBER OF STATEMENTS | | 6 | 5 | 6 | 6 | 11 |
| | % | | % | | % | ASSETS | % | % | % | % | % | % |
| | 9.7 | | 10.8 | | 12.3 | Cash & Equivalents | | | | | | 14.8 |
| | 22.9 | | 24.4 | | 25.1 | Trade Receivables (net) | D | | | | | 24.2 |
| | 29.7 | | 27.4 | | 31.9 | Inventory | A | | | | | 29.1 |
| | 4.8 | | 2.4 | | 2.5 | All Other Current | T | | | | | 5.8 |
| | 67.2 | | 65.0 | | 71.8 | Total Current | A | | | | | 73.9 |
| | 22.3 | | 18.4 | | 16.8 | Fixed Assets (net) | | | | | | 12.5 |
| | 4.3 | | 8.9 | | 6.0 | Intangibles (net) | N | | | | | 7.6 |
| | 6.2 | | 7.6 | | 5.3 | All Other Non-Current | O | | | | | 6.0 |
| | 100.0 | | 100.0 | | 100.0 | Total | T | | | | | 100.0 |
| | | | | | | LIABILITIES | A | | | | | |
| | 11.4 | | 10.3 | | 10.9 | Notes Payable-Short Term | V | | | | | 9.0 |
| | 3.8 | | 3.7 | | 2.6 | Cur. Mat.-L.T.D. | A | | | | | .7 |
| | 11.1 | | 14.3 | | 16.8 | Trade Payables | I | | | | | 13.2 |
| | .1 | | .1 | | .1 | Income Taxes Payable | L | | | | | .2 |
| | 12.0 | | 12.7 | | 14.0 | All Other Current | A | | | | | 23.3 |
| | 38.4 | | 41.2 | | 44.3 | Total Current | B | | | | | 46.4 |
| | 12.7 | | 8.1 | | 11.0 | Long-Term Debt | L | | | | | 6.4 |
| | 1.5 | | 1.2 | | .3 | Deferred Taxes | E | | | | | .5 |
| | 7.6 | | 3.6 | | 2.9 | All Other Non-Current | | | | | | .6 |
| | 39.8 | | 46.0 | | 41.5 | Net Worth | | | | | | 46.1 |
| | 100.0 | | 100.0 | | 100.0 | Total Liabilties & Net Worth | | | | | | 100.0 |
| | | | | | | INCOME DATA | | | | | | |
| | 100.0 | | 100.0 | | 100.0 | Net Sales | | | | | | 100.0 |
| | 35.0 | | 36.4 | | 33.0 | Gross Profit | | | | | | 28.5 |
| | 28.6 | | 28.4 | | 25.2 | Operating Expenses | | | | | | 18.8 |
| | 6.4 | | 8.0 | | 7.8 | Operating Profit | | | | | | 9.6 |
| | .6 | | 3.0 | | 1.1 | All Other Expenses (net) | | | | | | 2.3 |
| | 5.8 | | 5.0 | | 6.6 | Profit Before Taxes | | | | | | 7.4 |
| | | | | | | RATIOS | | | | | | |
| | 3.4 | | 2.7 | | 2.3 | | | | | | | 2.2 |
| | 2.2 | | 1.6 | | 1.8 | Current | | | | | | 1.8 |
| | 1.2 | | 1.2 | | 1.3 | | | | | | | 1.3 |
| | 1.7 | | 1.5 | | 1.3 | | | | | | | 1.3 |
| | 1.0 | | 1.0 | | .8 | Quick | | | | | | .9 |
| | .5 | | .6 | | .6 | | | | | | | .6 |
| 35 | 10.6 | 30 | 12.4 | 27 | 13.5 | | | | | | 35 | 10.4 |
| 46 | 8.0 | 46 | 8.0 | 46 | 8.0 | Sales/Receivables | | | | | 51 | 7.2 |
| 59 | 6.2 | 69 | 5.3 | 52 | 7.0 | | | | | | 56 | 6.5 |
| 62 | 5.9 | 50 | 7.3 | 47 | 7.8 | | | | | | 47 | 7.7 |
| 92 | 4.0 | 100 | 3.6 | 74 | 4.9 | Cost of Sales/Inventory | | | | | 83 | 4.4 |
| 141 | 2.6 | 124 | 2.9 | 126 | 2.9 | | | | | | 140 | 2.6 |
| 20 | 18.5 | 18 | 20.2 | 20 | 18.7 | | | | | | 24 | 15.0 |
| 25 | 14.4 | 33 | 11.0 | 36 | 10.2 | Cost of Sales/Payables | | | | | 36 | 10.0 |
| 49 | 7.5 | 60 | 6.1 | 53 | 6.9 | | | | | | 54 | 6.8 |
| | 3.1 | | 3.3 | | 3.4 | | | | | | | 2.8 |
| | 5.3 | | 6.7 | | 7.9 | Sales/Working Capital | | | | | | 5.7 |
| | 26.0 | | 16.6 | | 12.5 | | | | | | | 13.4 |
| | 19.1 | | 87.8 | | 35.3 | | | | | | | 200.0 |
| (27) | 5.4 | (32) | 12.5 | (29) | 11.8 | EBIT/Interest | | | | | (10) | 30.5 |
| | 3.1 | | 2.1 | | 4.8 | | | | | | | 6.4 |
| | | | | | | Net Profit + Depr., Dep., Amort./Cur. Mat. L/T/D | | | | | | |
| | .2 | | .2 | | .1 | | | | | | | .2 |
| | .4 | | .3 | | .3 | Fixed/Worth | | | | | | .3 |
| | 2.5 | | .8 | | .8 | | | | | | | .6 |
| | .5 | | .6 | | .7 | | | | | | | .7 |
| | 1.7 | | 1.4 | | 1.2 | Debt/Worth | | | | | | 1.2 |
| | 3.2 | | 3.2 | | 5.4 | | | | | | | 3.0 |
| | 34.3 | | 40.1 | | 53.4 | % Profit Before Taxes/Tangible Net Worth | | | | | | 42.0 |
| (27) | 14.1 | (31) | 25.6 | (30) | 27.8 | | | | | | (10) | 28.5 |
| | 4.9 | | 12.2 | | 18.8 | | | | | | | 20.7 |
| | 16.0 | | 15.0 | | 19.0 | % Profit Before Taxes/Total Assets | | | | | | 18.2 |
| | 6.3 | | 8.0 | | 11.2 | | | | | | | 12.8 |
| | 2.9 | | 2.2 | | 7.0 | | | | | | | 7.0 |
| | 31.3 | | 43.0 | | 47.8 | | | | | | | 28.8 |
| | 8.9 | | 11.4 | | 21.4 | Sales/Net Fixed Assets | | | | | | 12.8 |
| | 4.0 | | 7.3 | | 9.7 | | | | | | | 9.1 |
| | 2.2 | | 2.0 | | 3.3 | | | | | | | 2.1 |
| | 1.7 | | 1.7 | | 2.0 | Sales/Total Assets | | | | | | 1.6 |
| | 1.1 | | 1.0 | | 1.5 | | | | | | | 1.0 |
| | 1.1 | | .8 | | .6 | | | | | | | .5 |
| (24) | 1.9 | (29) | 1.8 | (27) | 1.0 | % Depr., Dep., Amort./Sales | | | | | (10) | 1.2 |
| | 3.4 | | 3.1 | | 2.0 | | | | | | | 2.2 |
| | .8 | | 1.4 | | 1.0 | % Officers', Directors' Owners' Comp/Sales | | | | | | |
| (14) | 2.1 | (10) | 2.7 | (13) | 3.1 | | | | | | | |
| | 9.7 | | 9.7 | | 5.0 | | | | | | | |
| | 848497M | | 1285990M | | 926226M | Net Sales ($) | | 13321M | 20716M | 40711M | 101906M | 749572M |
| | 707836M | | 1170167M | | 663021M | Total Assets ($) | | 5291M | 9544M | 20718M | 58926M | 568542M |

M = $ thousand    MM = $ million
See Pages 9 through 22 for Explanation of Ratios and Data

## Current Data Sorted by Assets      Comparative Historical Data

| Type of Statement | 0-500M | 500M-2MM | 2-10MM | 10-50MM | 50-100MM | 100-250MM | 4/1/07-3/31/08 ALL | 4/1/08-3/31/09 ALL |
|---|---|---|---|---|---|---|---|---|
| Unqualified | | 2 | 3 | 10 | 4 | 2 | 26 | 23 |
| Reviewed | | 4 | 22 | 9 | | | 27 | 39 |
| Compiled | 3 | 4 | 9 | 1 | | | 15 | 17 |
| Tax Returns | | 3 | 5 | 1 | | | 4 | 6 |
| Other | 2 | 3 | 15 | 13 | 3 | | 35 | 32 |
| | | 28 (4/1-9/30/11) | | 90 (10/1/11-3/31/12) | | | | |
| NUMBER OF STATEMENTS | 5 | 16 | 54 | 34 | 7 | 2 | 107 | 117 |

| ASSETS | 0-500M % | 500M-2MM % | 2-10MM % | 10-50MM % | 50-100MM % | 100-250MM % | ALL % | ALL % |
|---|---|---|---|---|---|---|---|---|
| Cash & Equivalents | | 12.4 | 13.5 | 17.8 | | | 14.7 | 10.3 |
| Trade Receivables (net) | | 36.5 | 29.1 | 32.8 | | | 33.7 | 32.2 |
| Inventory | | 24.6 | 28.6 | 16.6 | | | 22.7 | 26.5 |
| All Other Current | | 4.2 | 2.8 | 5.2 | | | 3.2 | 5.4 |
| Total Current | | 77.7 | 74.0 | 72.4 | | | 74.4 | 74.5 |
| Fixed Assets (net) | | 16.5 | 17.3 | 15.7 | | | 16.7 | 15.9 |
| Intangibles (net) | | 3.9 | 3.1 | 8.8 | | | 3.8 | 3.6 |
| All Other Non-Current | | 1.8 | 5.5 | 3.2 | | | 5.1 | 6.0 |
| Total | | 100.0 | 100.0 | 100.0 | | | 100.0 | 100.0 |
| **LIABILITIES** | | | | | | | | |
| Notes Payable-Short Term | | 7.5 | 8.6 | 4.2 | | | 8.8 | 11.0 |
| Cur. Mat.-L.T.D. | | 1.7 | 2.7 | 1.0 | | | 2.1 | 2.6 |
| Trade Payables | | 24.8 | 14.7 | 13.5 | | | 17.1 | 16.7 |
| Income Taxes Payable | | .2 | .1 | .1 | | | .7 | .4 |
| All Other Current | | 15.1 | 18.9 | 23.0 | | | 17.7 | 18.9 |
| Total Current | | 49.3 | 44.9 | 41.8 | | | 46.5 | 49.6 |
| Long-Term Debt | | 5.6 | 7.8 | 4.5 | | | 9.9 | 10.3 |
| Deferred Taxes | | .5 | .1 | .7 | | | .4 | .4 |
| All Other Non-Current | | 6.5 | 4.7 | 6.2 | | | 5.5 | 5.2 |
| Net Worth | | 38.1 | 42.4 | 46.8 | | | 37.8 | 34.5 |
| Total Liabilties & Net Worth | | 100.0 | 100.0 | 100.0 | | | 100.0 | 100.0 |
| **INCOME DATA** | | | | | | | | |
| Net Sales | | 100.0 | 100.0 | 100.0 | | | 100.0 | 100.0 |
| Gross Profit | | 30.9 | 30.4 | 29.0 | | | 29.9 | 29.5 |
| Operating Expenses | | 28.5 | 23.8 | 22.9 | | | 23.9 | 24.5 |
| Operating Profit | | 2.4 | 6.6 | 6.1 | | | 6.0 | 5.0 |
| All Other Expenses (net) | | .7 | .4 | .6 | | | .8 | .7 |
| Profit Before Taxes | | 1.6 | 6.2 | 5.5 | | | 5.2 | 4.3 |

| RATIOS | 0-500M | 500M-2MM | 2-10MM | 10-50MM | 50-100MM | 100-250MM | ALL | ALL |
|---|---|---|---|---|---|---|---|---|
| Current | | 3.1 | 2.6 | 2.6 | | | 2.5 | 2.5 |
| | | 1.6 | 1.6 | 1.7 | | | 1.6 | 1.6 |
| | | .9 | 1.2 | 1.4 | | | 1.2 | 1.1 |
| Quick | | 1.9 | 1.5 | 1.6 | | | 1.8 | 1.4 |
| | | 1.1 | 1.0 | 1.2 | | | 1.0 | .8 |
| | | .6 | .7 | .9 | | | .7 | .5 |
| Sales/Receivables | | 22   16.7 | 34   10.7 | 43   8.4 | | | 39   9.5 | 37   9.8 |
| | | 39   9.4 | 49   7.5 | 59   6.2 | | | 52   7.0 | 52   7.1 |
| | | 56   6.5 | 59   6.2 | 79   4.6 | | | 68   5.4 | 71   5.1 |
| Cost of Sales/Inventory | | 9   41.8 | 38   9.7 | 19   19.4 | | | 23   15.8 | 31   11.9 |
| | | 41   9.0 | 65   5.6 | 42   8.6 | | | 56   6.5 | 59   6.2 |
| | | 89   4.1 | 111   3.3 | 79   4.6 | | | 83   4.4 | 109   3.4 |
| Cost of Sales/Payables | | 22   16.5 | 19   19.5 | 18   19.8 | | | 22   16.8 | 20   17.9 |
| | | 35   10.4 | 32   11.4 | 35   10.3 | | | 35   10.3 | 35   10.5 |
| | | 101   3.6 | 42   8.7 | 56   6.5 | | | 60   6.1 | 58   6.2 |
| Sales/Working Capital | | 4.6 | 3.9 | 4.3 | | | 4.4 | 4.3 |
| | | 9.2 | 7.2 | 6.1 | | | 7.6 | 7.4 |
| | | -43.1 | 18.6 | 8.2 | | | 20.9 | 29.4 |
| EBIT/Interest | | 9.0 | 41.1 | 60.9 | | | 24.8 | 22.8 |
| | (12) | 1.0 | (49) 10.8 | (29) 16.6 | | | (86) 7.3 | (97) 5.1 |
| | | -6.0 | 3.3 | 5.3 | | | 1.8 | 1.3 |
| Net Profit + Depr., Dep., Amort./Cur. Mat. L/T/D | | | 44.4 | | | | 18.0 | 9.9 |
| | | | (10) 6.5 | | | | (26) 6.7 | (36) 4.2 |
| | | | 3.9 | | | | 2.1 | 1.9 |
| Fixed/Worth | | .1 | .2 | .2 | | | .2 | .1 |
| | | .9 | .3 | .4 | | | .4 | .4 |
| | | 11.5 | .8 | .6 | | | 1.4 | 1.0 |
| Debt/Worth | | .6 | .6 | .6 | | | .6 | .8 |
| | | 1.8 | 1.6 | 1.4 | | | 1.9 | 2.2 |
| | | 83.5 | 3.1 | 4.3 | | | 5.5 | 6.5 |
| % Profit Before Taxes/Tangible Net Worth | | 67.5 | 44.7 | 46.8 | | | 63.3 | 49.5 |
| | (13) | 9.3 | (50) 27.1 | (32) 22.1 | | | (93) 23.0 | (100) 21.2 |
| | | -3.3 | 9.7 | 3.4 | | | 5.3 | 5.0 |
| % Profit Before Taxes/Total Assets | | 12.7 | 15.6 | 18.9 | | | 20.2 | 16.5 |
| | | 1.9 | 8.7 | 9.1 | | | 9.0 | 7.7 |
| | | -7.0 | 2.8 | 2.1 | | | 1.2 | .9 |
| Sales/Net Fixed Assets | | 500.9 | 44.5 | 29.7 | | | 32.3 | 36.6 |
| | | 27.1 | 13.3 | 19.7 | | | 15.7 | 17.8 |
| | | 11.8 | 7.5 | 6.8 | | | 9.1 | 9.0 |
| Sales/Total Assets | | 3.8 | 2.6 | 2.4 | | | 2.7 | 2.7 |
| | | 2.3 | 2.1 | 1.8 | | | 2.1 | 2.1 |
| | | 1.7 | 1.7 | 1.3 | | | 1.6 | 1.5 |
| % Depr., Dep., Amort./Sales | | .3 | .7 | .7 | | | .6 | .8 |
| | (11) | .5 | (45) 1.3 | (30) 1.5 | | | (96) 1.4 | (106) 1.2 |
| | | 2.7 | 2.2 | 2.2 | | | 2.1 | 2.3 |
| % Officers', Directors' Owners' Comp/Sales | | | 1.6 | | | | 2.1 | 2.2 |
| | | | (17) 2.3 | | | | (33) 4.2 | (25) 3.4 |
| | | | 3.5 | | | | 6.9 | 6.3 |
| Net Sales ($) | 5958M | 60890M | 639307M | 1342675M | 798983M | 600697M | 4585537M | 4516392M |
| Total Assets ($) | 1565M | 22254M | 298514M | 755732M | 457905M | 326063M | 2567486M | 2479482M |

M = $ thousand    MM = $ million
See Pages 9 through 22 for Explanation of Ratios and Data

## Comparative Historical Data | | Current Data Sorted by Sales

| | | | Type of Statement | | | | | | |
|---|---|---|---|---|---|---|---|---|---|
| | | | | | | | | | |
| 21 | 15 | 21 | Unqualified | | 1 | 1 | 2 | 4 | 13 |
| 43 | 38 | 35 | Reviewed | | 1 | 3 | 7 | 19 | 5 |
| 13 | 17 | 17 | Compiled | 1 | 3 | 2 | 6 | 4 | 1 |
| 3 | 4 | 9 | Tax Returns | | 2 | 1 | 4 | 2 | |
| 35 | 39 | 36 | Other | 2 | 1 | 2 | 6 | 14 | 11 |
| 4/1/09-3/31/10 ALL | 4/1/10-3/31/11 ALL | 4/1/11-3/31/12 ALL | | | 28 (4/1-9/30/11) | | 90 (10/1/11-3/31/12) | | |
| | | | | 0-1MM | 1-3MM | 3-5MM | 5-10MM | 10-25MM | 25MM & OVER |
| 115 | 113 | 118 | NUMBER OF STATEMENTS | 3 | 8 | 9 | 25 | 43 | 30 |
| % | % | % | ASSETS | % | % | % | % | % | % |
| 11.3 | 13.2 | 14.6 | Cash & Equivalents | | | | 15.5 | 14.1 | 15.2 |
| 26.9 | 31.3 | 32.0 | Trade Receivables (net) | | | | 30.1 | 29.2 | 36.5 |
| 24.9 | 25.1 | 23.4 | Inventory | | | | 28.9 | 23.3 | 17.7 |
| 5.0 | 3.5 | 4.0 | All Other Current | | | | 2.9 | 3.4 | 6.8 |
| 68.1 | 73.1 | 74.1 | Total Current | | | | 77.4 | 70.0 | 76.2 |
| 20.0 | 17.2 | 16.7 | Fixed Assets (net) | | | | 14.9 | 18.3 | 15.5 |
| 5.3 | 4.3 | 4.8 | Intangibles (net) | | | | 2.1 | 6.4 | 5.5 |
| 6.6 | 5.3 | 4.4 | All Other Non-Current | | | | 5.6 | 5.3 | 2.9 |
| 100.0 | 100.0 | 100.0 | Total | | | | 100.0 | 100.0 | 100.0 |
| | | | LIABILITIES | | | | | | |
| 11.1 | 8.1 | 6.9 | Notes Payable-Short Term | | | | 9.4 | 5.5 | 2.5 |
| 2.6 | 2.9 | 1.9 | Cur. Mat.-L.T.D. | | | | 2.4 | 2.3 | 1.1 |
| 13.2 | 15.9 | 16.7 | Trade Payables | | | | 18.1 | 12.6 | 15.9 |
| .3 | .2 | .2 | Income Taxes Payable | | | | .1 | .2 | .3 |
| 15.6 | 18.9 | 21.1 | All Other Current | | | | 16.5 | 21.5 | 24.0 |
| 42.8 | 46.0 | 46.8 | Total Current | | | | 46.5 | 42.0 | 43.8 |
| 10.0 | 9.6 | 7.7 | Long-Term Debt | | | | 8.0 | 7.0 | 9.5 |
| .3 | .3 | .4 | Deferred Taxes | | | | .1 | .5 | .5 |
| 6.0 | 5.2 | 6.0 | All Other Non-Current | | | | 8.1 | 2.7 | 9.9 |
| 41.0 | 38.8 | 39.0 | Net Worth | | | | 37.3 | 47.8 | 36.3 |
| 100.0 | 100.0 | 100.0 | Total Liabilities & Net Worth | | | | 100.0 | 100.0 | 100.0 |
| | | | INCOME DATA | | | | | | |
| 100.0 | 100.0 | 100.0 | Net Sales | | | | 100.0 | 100.0 | 100.0 |
| 30.1 | 31.6 | 30.0 | Gross Profit | | | | 28.0 | 30.9 | 29.1 |
| 27.8 | 27.3 | 23.9 | Operating Expenses | | | | 24.0 | 23.8 | 20.9 |
| 2.3 | 4.2 | 6.1 | Operating Profit | | | | 4.0 | 7.1 | 8.2 |
| 1.3 | .7 | .6 | All Other Expenses (net) | | | | 1.0 | .2 | 1.0 |
| 1.0 | 3.5 | 5.4 | Profit Before Taxes | | | | 3.0 | 6.9 | 7.2 |
| | | | RATIOS | | | | | | |
| 2.7 | 2.5 | 2.6 | Current | | | | 3.1 | 2.4 | 2.8 |
| 1.7 | 1.6 | 1.6 | | | | | 1.9 | 1.5 | 1.6 |
| 1.2 | 1.2 | 1.2 | | | | | 1.2 | 1.3 | 1.4 |
| 1.6 | 1.7 | 1.6 | Quick | | | | 1.5 | 1.5 | 1.9 |
| .9 | 1.0 | 1.1 | | | | | 1.2 | 1.0 | 1.2 |
| .7 | .6 | .7 | | | | | .8 | .8 | 1.0 |
| 35  10.4 | 43  8.4 | 38  9.6 | Sales/Receivables | | | | 35  10.5 | 41  9.0 | 43  8.5 |
| 49  7.4 | 56  6.5 | 49  7.4 | | | | | 46  8.0 | 50  7.3 | 60  6.1 |
| 71  5.1 | 75  4.9 | 70  5.2 | | | | | 52  7.0 | 70  5.2 | 76  4.8 |
| 35  10.4 | 34  10.6 | 26  14.0 | Cost of Sales/Inventory | | | | 35  10.3 | 34  10.7 | 19  19.4 |
| 60  6.1 | 61  6.0 | 50  7.3 | | | | | 69  5.3 | 53  6.9 | 39  9.3 |
| 105  3.5 | 108  3.4 | 101  3.6 | | | | | 122  3.0 | 94  3.9 | 76  4.8 |
| 17  22.0 | 26  14.1 | 20  18.0 | Cost of Sales/Payables | | | | 15  23.8 | 21  17.8 | 20  18.5 |
| 30  12.2 | 36  10.2 | 33  11.1 | | | | | 30  12.1 | 33  11.2 | 35  10.3 |
| 52  7.1 | 53  6.9 | 46  8.0 | | | | | 45  8.1 | 42  8.6 | 53  6.9 |
| 4.1 | 3.9 | 4.1 | Sales/Working Capital | | | | 3.6 | 3.9 | 4.8 |
| 6.9 | 6.8 | 6.5 | | | | | 6.0 | 7.0 | 6.2 |
| 20.9 | 18.8 | 18.6 | | | | | 17.2 | 17.5 | 9.1 |
| 8.0 | 17.3 | 39.6 | EBIT/Interest | | | | 91.5 | 38.3 | 51.5 |
| (103) 2.6 | (98) 3.9 | (100) 10.7 | | | | | (22) 5.4 | (35) 14.8 | (27) 15.4 |
| -.7 | 1.0 | 2.5 | | | | | 1.9 | 5.0 | 5.5 |
| 3.8 | 10.2 | 35.1 | Net Profit + Depr., Dep., Amort./Cur. Mat. L/T/D | | | | | | |
| (34) 1.4 | (29) 2.5 | (22) 5.6 | | | | | | | |
| .2 | 1.0 | 2.3 | | | | | | | |
| .2 | .2 | .2 | Fixed/Worth | | | | .1 | .2 | .2 |
| .5 | .4 | .4 | | | | | .3 | .4 | .4 |
| 1.3 | 1.0 | 1.1 | | | | | 5.9 | .8 | .8 |
| .6 | .7 | .7 | Debt/Worth | | | | .6 | .7 | .5 |
| 1.9 | 1.6 | 1.7 | | | | | 1.7 | 1.3 | 1.7 |
| 4.1 | 4.3 | 4.7 | | | | | 15.8 | 2.7 | 5.1 |
| 29.9 | 40.1 | 47.3 | % Profit Before Taxes/Tangible Net Worth | | | | 37.2 | 45.9 | 55.2 |
| (104) 8.9 | (99) 13.9 | (105) 24.7 | | | | | (21) 14.9 | (42) 25.9 | (26) 34.9 |
| -3.4 | 2.5 | 9.2 | | | | | 5.9 | 10.5 | 14.3 |
| 10.6 | 15.0 | 16.4 | % Profit Before Taxes/Total Assets | | | | 11.6 | 18.5 | 22.8 |
| 2.2 | 5.0 | 8.5 | | | | | 5.8 | 8.8 | 12.8 |
| -1.7 | .1 | 2.2 | | | | | 2.0 | 3.3 | 6.6 |
| 26.3 | 32.9 | 36.9 | Sales/Net Fixed Assets | | | | 70.4 | 29.6 | 30.6 |
| 12.0 | 12.6 | 14.5 | | | | | 16.2 | 9.9 | 19.7 |
| 5.7 | 6.9 | 7.7 | | | | | 10.4 | 6.5 | 8.2 |
| 2.5 | 2.4 | 2.6 | Sales/Total Assets | | | | 3.2 | 2.5 | 2.6 |
| 1.9 | 1.8 | 2.0 | | | | | 2.0 | 2.0 | 2.0 |
| 1.3 | 1.4 | 1.6 | | | | | 1.5 | 1.5 | 1.7 |
| .9 | .8 | .7 | % Depr., Dep., Amort./Sales | | | | .7 | .9 | .7 |
| (98) 1.6 | (98) 1.6 | (96) 1.4 | | | | | (20) 1.1 | (37) 1.7 | (25) 1.2 |
| 2.8 | 2.7 | 2.4 | | | | | 2.3 | 2.6 | 2.1 |
| 2.0 | 1.8 | 1.6 | % Officers', Directors' Owners' Comp/Sales | | | | | 1.6 | |
| (23) 4.1 | (28) 2.9 | (33) 2.5 | | | | | | (15) 2.0 | |
| 6.1 | 8.6 | 4.5 | | | | | | 3.6 | |
| 3651681M | 3268132M | 3448510M | Net Sales ($) | 1928M | 14908M | 35971M | 179200M | 725211M | 2491292M |
| 2283906M | 1833982M | 1862033M | Total Assets ($) | 1121M | 7623M | 19207M | 96099M | 461382M | 1276601M |

M = $ thousand     MM = $ million
See Pages 9 through 22 for Explanation of Ratios and Data

## Current Data Sorted by Assets           Comparative Historical Data

| 0-500M | 500M-2MM | 2-10MM | 10-50MM | 50-100MM | 100-250MM | Type of Statement | 4/1/07-3/31/08 ALL | 4/1/08-3/31/09 ALL |
|---|---|---|---|---|---|---|---|---|
|  | 2 | 6 | 2 | 1 | 2 | Unqualified | 8 | 7 |
|  | 4 | 5 | 2 |  |  | Reviewed | 9 | 11 |
|  | 1 | 1 | 1 |  |  | Compiled | 11 | 8 |
|  |  |  |  |  |  | Tax Returns | 2 | 3 |
| 1 | 1 | 7 | 10 | 1 | 1 | Other | 16 | 15 |
| 1 | 8 | 19 | 15 | 2 | 3 | **NUMBER OF STATEMENTS** | 46 | 44 |
| % | % | % | % | % | % | | % | % |

### ASSETS

| 2-10MM | 10-50MM | | Comp 1 | Comp 2 |
|---|---|---|---|---|
| 9.6 | 10.4 | Cash & Equivalents | 10.9 | 9.4 |
| 28.9 | 24.4 | Trade Receivables (net) | 31.8 | 30.7 |
| 26.3 | 25.2 | Inventory | 27.8 | 28.6 |
| 3.8 | 7.1 | All Other Current | 5.2 | 6.2 |
| 68.6 | 67.2 | Total Current | 75.7 | 74.9 |
| 17.9 | 24.1 | Fixed Assets (net) | 16.2 | 17.4 |
| 8.5 | 2.4 | Intangibles (net) | 2.9 | 3.4 |
| 4.9 | 6.2 | All Other Non-Current | 5.2 | 4.3 |
| 100.0 | 100.0 | Total | 100.0 | 100.0 |

### LIABILITIES

| 2-10MM | 10-50MM | | Comp 1 | Comp 2 |
|---|---|---|---|---|
| 8.2 | 8.9 | Notes Payable-Short Term | 7.3 | 10.3 |
| 2.3 | 1.7 | Cur. Mat.-L.T.D. | 1.7 | 1.9 |
| 12.6 | 13.2 | Trade Payables | 17.5 | 16.4 |
| .3 | .0 | Income Taxes Payable | .3 | .0 |
| 16.2 | 17.9 | All Other Current | 17.1 | 17.1 |
| 39.6 | 41.7 | Total Current | 43.8 | 45.7 |
| 16.4 | 8.7 | Long-Term Debt | 9.2 | 10.2 |
| .4 | .4 | Deferred Taxes | .1 | .2 |
| 1.8 | 4.4 | All Other Non-Current | 4.1 | 2.6 |
| 41.9 | 44.8 | Net Worth | 42.8 | 41.3 |
| 100.0 | 100.0 | Total Liabilities & Net Worth | 100.0 | 100.0 |

### INCOME DATA

| 2-10MM | 10-50MM | | Comp 1 | Comp 2 |
|---|---|---|---|---|
| 100.0 | 100.0 | Net Sales | 100.0 | 100.0 |
| 34.3 | 22.1 | Gross Profit | 30.0 | 29.5 |
| 27.5 | 17.0 | Operating Expenses | 22.5 | 23.0 |
| 6.8 | 5.1 | Operating Profit | 7.5 | 6.5 |
| .7 | .4 | All Other Expenses (net) | .5 | .7 |
| 6.1 | 4.8 | Profit Before Taxes | 7.0 | 5.8 |

### RATIOS

| 2-10MM | 10-50MM | | Comp 1 | Comp 2 |
|---|---|---|---|---|
| 2.6 | 2.0 | Current | 2.6 | 3.0 |
| 1.5 | 1.5 | | 1.6 | 1.6 |
| 1.1 | 1.1 | | 1.3 | 1.2 |
| 1.4 | 1.2 | Quick | 1.7 | 1.4 |
| .9 | .7 | | 1.0 | .8 |
| .5 | .5 | | .7 | .4 |
| 35   10.3 | 45   8.1 | Sales/Receivables | 36   10.2 | 33   11.2 |
| 54   6.7 | 58   6.3 | | 46   7.9 | 52   7.0 |
| 72   5.1 | 69   5.3 | | 62   5.8 | 61   6.0 |
| 21   17.0 | 22   16.6 | Cost of Sales/Inventory | 34   10.7 | 17   21.7 |
| 63   5.8 | 89   4.1 | | 61   6.0 | 68   5.4 |
| 182   2.0 | 118   3.1 | | 106   3.4 | 118   3.1 |
| 31   11.9 | 25   14.4 | Cost of Sales/Payables | 21   17.6 | 19   19.0 |
| 35   10.3 | 35   10.3 | | 30   12.2 | 33   11.2 |
| 43   8.4 | 47   7.8 | | 45   8.2 | 55   6.6 |
| 3.3 | 4.4 | Sales/Working Capital | 4.4 | 4.3 |
| 7.7 | 7.0 | | 7.7 | 9.0 |
| 30.4 | 16.7 | | 16.3 | 22.0 |
| 26.4 | 185.0 | EBIT/Interest | 31.3 | 34.9 |
| 15.8 | (13) 12.3 | | (42) 7.0 | (40) 9.6 |
| 3.7 | 2.6 | | 3.5 | 3.9 |
|  |  | Net Profit + Depr., Dep., Amort./Cur. Mat. L/T/D | 96.3 | |
|  |  | | (13) 9.8 | |
|  |  | | 3.1 | |
| .1 | .1 | Fixed/Worth | .1 | .2 |
| .6 | .4 | | .2 | .3 |
| 1.3 | 1.6 | | .5 | .8 |
| .6 | .6 | Debt/Worth | .7 | .6 |
| 2.2 | 2.0 | | 1.7 | 1.5 |
| 5.7 | 2.3 | | 2.9 | 4.1 |
| 68.6 | 32.7 | % Profit Before Taxes/Tangible Net Worth | 56.0 | 58.8 |
| (17) 29.6 | 26.1 | | (44) 40.9 | (41) 35.6 |
| 8.2 | 4.7 | | 19.6 | 11.8 |
| 17.1 | 18.9 | % Profit Before Taxes/Total Assets | 20.0 | 21.0 |
| 9.8 | 5.9 | | 12.9 | 11.6 |
| 1.4 | 1.4 | | 6.5 | 4.1 |
| 30.8 | 38.1 | Sales/Net Fixed Assets | 40.6 | 34.1 |
| 14.9 | 8.3 | | 22.4 | 21.6 |
| 9.7 | 3.9 | | 12.8 | 8.1 |
| 2.3 | 1.9 | Sales/Total Assets | 2.8 | 3.0 |
| 2.1 | 1.6 | | 2.4 | 2.5 |
| 1.1 | 1.4 | | 1.9 | 1.7 |
| 1.0 | 1.1 | % Depr., Dep., Amort./Sales | .5 | .5 |
| (17) 1.4 | (14) 2.4 | | (38) 1.0 | (40) 1.0 |
| 2.4 | 3.4 | | 1.5 | 1.5 |
|  |  | % Officers', Directors' Owners' Comp/Sales | 1.7 | 1.5 |
|  |  | | (15) 3.8 | (14) 2.6 |
|  |  | | 5.6 | 5.7 |

| 0-500M | 500M-2MM | 2-10MM | 10-50MM | 50-100MM | 100-250MM | | Comp 1 | Comp 2 |
|---|---|---|---|---|---|---|---|---|
| 840M | 38689M | 177930M | 566683M | 187242M | 374083M | Net Sales ($) | 1255829M | 1535551M |
| 475M | 11757M | 95229M | 340758M | 159048M | 359064M | Total Assets ($) | 744796M | 805443M |

M = $ thousand     MM = $ million
See Pages 9 through 22 for Explanation of Ratios and Data

## Comparative Historical Data  —  Current Data Sorted by Sales

| | 4/1/09-3/31/10 ALL | 4/1/10-3/31/11 ALL | 4/1/11-3/31/12 ALL | 1 0-1MM | 2 1-3MM | 8 3-5MM | 6 (4/1-9/30/11) → 5-10MM | 42 (10/1/11-3/31/12) → 10-25MM | 25MM & OVER |
|---|---|---|---|---|---|---|---|---|---|
| **Type of Statement** | | | | | | | | | |
| Unqualified | | | | | | | | | |
| Reviewed | 5 | 6 | 5 | | | 2 | 4 | 3 | 5 |
| Compiled | 8 | 10 | 10 | | 2 | 2 | 4 | 2 | 1 |
| Tax Returns | 8 | 9 | 10 | | | 2 | 2 | | |
| Other | 3 | 1 | 2 | 1 | | 2 | 2 | 5 | 9 |
| | 17 | 16 | 21 | | | | | | |
| **NUMBER OF STATEMENTS** | 41 | 42 | 48 | 1 | 2 | 8 | 12 | 10 | 15 |
| | % | % | % | % | % | % | % | % | % |
| **ASSETS** | | | | | | | | | |
| Cash & Equivalents | 16.0 | 9.2 | 10.5 | | | | 8.5 | 11.2 | 10.6 |
| Trade Receivables (net) | 23.4 | 35.5 | 29.6 | | | | 24.6 | 36.6 | 24.4 |
| Inventory | 27.9 | 27.3 | 25.9 | | | | 29.9 | 26.4 | 26.1 |
| All Other Current | 4.9 | 4.0 | 4.8 | | | | 3.3 | 5.0 | 7.6 |
| Total Current | 72.2 | 76.0 | 70.8 | | | | 66.4 | 79.2 | 68.8 |
| Fixed Assets (net) | 17.5 | 15.4 | 19.1 | | | | 16.0 | 13.8 | 23.0 |
| Intangibles (net) | 3.8 | 4.3 | 5.2 | | | | 12.3 | .6 | 4.3 |
| All Other Non-Current | 6.6 | 4.3 | 4.9 | | | | 5.3 | 6.4 | 3.9 |
| Total | 100.0 | 100.0 | 100.0 | | | | 100.0 | 100.0 | 100.0 |
| **LIABILITIES** | | | | | | | | | |
| Notes Payable-Short Term | 14.3 | 8.9 | 8.2 | | | | 6.2 | 9.2 | 6.9 |
| Cur. Mat.-L.T.D. | 2.1 | 2.1 | 1.6 | | | | 1.8 | .7 | 1.8 |
| Trade Payables | 10.0 | 17.1 | 15.0 | | | | 13.4 | 15.5 | 14.2 |
| Income Taxes Payable | .0 | .0 | .3 | | | | .4 | .0 | .5 |
| All Other Current | 14.5 | 16.8 | 15.8 | | | | 15.8 | 19.3 | 14.2 |
| Total Current | 40.9 | 44.9 | 40.9 | | | | 37.7 | 44.8 | 37.7 |
| Long-Term Debt | 9.1 | 8.7 | 13.6 | | | | 16.9 | 2.1 | 8.7 |
| Deferred Taxes | .7 | .8 | .4 | | | | .7 | .0 | .7 |
| All Other Non-Current | 2.3 | 3.8 | 2.6 | | | | 3.3 | 3.6 | 1.8 |
| Net Worth | 47.0 | 41.8 | 42.4 | | | | 41.4 | 49.5 | 51.2 |
| Total Liabilities & Net Worth | 100.0 | 100.0 | 100.0 | | | | 100.0 | 100.0 | 100.0 |
| **INCOME DATA** | | | | | | | | | |
| Net Sales | 100.0 | 100.0 | 100.0 | | | | 100.0 | 100.0 | 100.0 |
| Gross Profit | 29.1 | 30.1 | 28.9 | | | | 31.6 | 26.7 | 23.1 |
| Operating Expenses | 24.9 | 27.7 | 22.6 | | | | 29.0 | 19.0 | 14.7 |
| Operating Profit | 4.2 | 2.4 | 6.3 | | | | 2.6 | 7.7 | 8.4 |
| All Other Expenses (net) | 2.1 | 1.2 | .6 | | | | .7 | -.4 | .6 |
| Profit Before Taxes | 2.1 | 1.2 | 5.7 | | | | 1.9 | 8.1 | 7.8 |
| **RATIOS** | | | | | | | | | |
| Current | 4.7 | 3.4 | 2.3 | | | | 2.5 | 2.3 | 2.5 |
| | 2.1 | 1.8 | 1.7 | | | | 1.5 | 1.8 | 1.9 |
| | 1.3 | 1.3 | 1.2 | | | | 1.2 | 1.3 | 1.2 |
| Quick | 2.5 | 1.8 | 1.3 | | | | 1.3 | 1.5 | 1.3 |
| | 1.1 | 1.0 | .9 | | | | .9 | 1.0 | .9 |
| | .6 | .7 | .6 | | | | .4 | .7 | .6 |
| Sales/Receivables | 28  12.8 | 49  7.5 | 39  9.3 | | | | 32  11.4 | 45  8.1 | 45  8.1 |
| | 41  8.9 | 59  6.1 | 57  6.4 | | | | 40  9.2 | 58  6.3 | 60  6.1 |
| | 56  6.6 | 74  4.9 | 70  5.2 | | | | 70  5.2 | 81  4.5 | 70  5.2 |
| Cost of Sales/Inventory | 26  14.3 | 32  11.3 | 22  16.6 | | | | 35  10.5 | 21  17.7 | 7  54.9 |
| | 60  6.1 | 60  6.1 | 63  5.8 | | | | 85  4.3 | 54  6.8 | 83  4.4 |
| | 129  2.8 | 113  3.2 | 126  2.9 | | | | 174  2.1 | 107  3.4 | 152  2.4 |
| Cost of Sales/Payables | 11  32.1 | 25  14.4 | 27  13.5 | | | | 29  12.7 | 29  12.5 | 24  15.5 |
| | 22  16.8 | 41  9.0 | 36  10.2 | | | | 39  9.3 | 36  10.1 | 35  10.3 |
| | 38  9.6 | 57  6.4 | 47  7.7 | | | | 47  7.8 | 43  8.4 | 52  7.0 |
| Sales/Working Capital | 3.0 | 3.7 | 3.7 | | | | 3.4 | 4.7 | 3.2 |
| | 6.1 | 7.3 | 7.8 | | | | 7.0 | 7.8 | 4.4 |
| | 18.8 | 15.4 | 16.5 | | | | 14.7 | 10.6 | 16.7 |
| EBIT/Interest | 13.9 | 13.3 | 65.9 | | | | 21.1 | 167.9 | 147.0 |
| | (34) 4.2 | (37) 1.9 | (43) 12.3 | | | | 9.7 | 41.2 | (11) 10.5 |
| | 1.0 | -.1 | 3.4 | | | | .8 | 22.7 | 2.7 |
| Net Profit + Depr., Dep., Amort./Cur. Mat. L/T/D | 44.8 | | 14.8 | | | | | | |
| | (12) 10.4 | | (11) 8.8 | | | | | | |
| | 1.6 | | 2.2 | | | | | | |
| Fixed/Worth | .1 | .2 | .1 | | | | .1 | .1 | .1 |
| | .4 | .4 | .4 | | | | .4 | .2 | .3 |
| | 1.0 | .8 | 1.1 | | | | 6.1 | .5 | 1.1 |
| Debt/Worth | .3 | .4 | .6 | | | | .7 | .6 | .6 |
| | 1.2 | 1.5 | 1.7 | | | | 2.0 | 1.0 | 1.1 |
| | 3.2 | 4.9 | 5.2 | | | | 10.4 | 2.3 | 2.2 |
| % Profit Before Taxes/Tangible Net Worth | 34.1 | 28.1 | 41.1 | | | | 31.1 | 52.2 | 37.0 |
| | (38) 10.8 | (38) 9.7 | (44) 27.2 | | | | (11) 8.6 | 33.9 | 26.1 |
| | .9 | -4.4 | 8.3 | | | | -2.0 | 10.8 | 10.4 |
| % Profit Before Taxes/Total Assets | 12.7 | 8.5 | 16.4 | | | | 9.6 | 29.2 | 23.4 |
| | 5.8 | 3.0 | 7.7 | | | | 2.8 | 13.5 | 9.2 |
| | .0 | -1.7 | 1.7 | | | | -.5 | 7.0 | 3.5 |
| Sales/Net Fixed Assets | 38.2 | 34.3 | 39.6 | | | | 42.0 | 69.5 | 24.5 |
| | 16.7 | 17.8 | 15.0 | | | | 15.4 | 34.4 | 9.8 |
| | 7.2 | 8.6 | 6.9 | | | | 7.2 | 9.3 | 3.9 |
| Sales/Total Assets | 3.2 | 2.9 | 2.5 | | | | 2.2 | 3.0 | 1.7 |
| | 2.1 | 2.0 | 1.7 | | | | 1.6 | 2.1 | 1.5 |
| | 1.4 | 1.5 | 1.2 | | | | 1.0 | 1.5 | 1.3 |
| % Depr., Dep., Amort./Sales | .9 | .6 | .8 | | | | .8 | | .6 |
| | (34) 1.5 | (37) 1.3 | (43) 1.3 | | | | (11) 1.3 | | (12) 1.9 |
| | 2.5 | 2.3 | 2.6 | | | | 2.3 | | 3.8 |
| % Officers', Directors' Owners' Comp/Sales | 1.9 | 2.3 | 1.8 | | | | | | |
| | (14) 3.1 | (14) 4.8 | (16) 3.2 | | | | | | |
| | 8.0 | 7.8 | 5.4 | | | | | | |
| Net Sales ($) | 1402363M | 1366955M | 1345467M | 840M | 4226M | 33496M | 84941M | 178545M | 1043419M |
| Total Assets ($) | 1016205M | 1097221M | 966331M | 475M | 4541M | 13467M | 59528M | 94782M | 793538M |

M = $ thousand    MM = $ million
See Pages 9 through 22 for Explanation of Ratios and Data

## Current Data Sorted by Assets        Comparative Historical Data

| 0-500M | 500M-2MM | 2-10MM | 10-50MM | 50-100MM | 100-250MM | Type of Statement | 4/1/07-3/31/08 | 4/1/08-3/31/09 |
|---|---|---|---|---|---|---|---|---|
| | | 1 | 5 | | 2 | Unqualified | 17 | 9 |
| | 2 | 6 | 6 | | | Reviewed | 11 | 10 |
| | 1 | 2 | | | | Compiled | 10 | 9 |
| | 1 | 1 | | | 3 | Tax Returns | 6 | 6 |
| 1 | 5 | 9 | 4 | 3 | | Other | 29 | 39 |
| 6 (4/1-9/30/11) | | | 45 (10/1/11-3/31/12) | | | | ALL | ALL |
| 1 | 8 | 19 | 15 | 3 | 5 | **NUMBER OF STATEMENTS** | 73 | 73 |
| % | % | % | % | % | % | **ASSETS** | % | % |
| | | 5.5 | 8.4 | | | Cash & Equivalents | 7.1 | 5.9 |
| | | 21.8 | 22.9 | | | Trade Receivables (net) | 24.3 | 20.4 |
| | | 44.3 | 31.5 | | | Inventory | 35.2 | 38.4 |
| | | 1.8 | 2.8 | | | All Other Current | 3.5 | 2.5 |
| | | 73.3 | 65.6 | | | Total Current | 70.1 | 67.1 |
| | | 17.9 | 23.8 | | | Fixed Assets (net) | 23.2 | 20.6 |
| | | 7.1 | 3.4 | | | Intangibles (net) | 3.7 | 7.7 |
| | | 1.7 | 7.2 | | | All Other Non-Current | 3.0 | 4.5 |
| | | 100.0 | 100.0 | | | Total | 100.0 | 100.0 |
| | | | | | | **LIABILITIES** | | |
| | | 12.0 | 14.5 | | | Notes Payable-Short Term | 14.2 | 13.8 |
| | | 1.5 | 4.9 | | | Cur. Mat.-L.T.D. | 3.9 | 4.8 |
| | | 15.7 | 15.2 | | | Trade Payables | 15.5 | 12.2 |
| | | .2 | .0 | | | Income Taxes Payable | .4 | .3 |
| | | 11.7 | 10.6 | | | All Other Current | 9.8 | 15.6 |
| | | 41.1 | 45.1 | | | Total Current | 43.9 | 46.8 |
| | | 14.8 | 18.4 | | | Long-Term Debt | 17.3 | 15.8 |
| | | .1 | 1.7 | | | Deferred Taxes | .3 | .6 |
| | | 3.6 | 6.1 | | | All Other Non-Current | 4.3 | 4.1 |
| | | 40.5 | 28.6 | | | Net Worth | 34.2 | 32.6 |
| | | 100.0 | 100.0 | | | Total Liabilities & Net Worth | 100.0 | 100.0 |
| | | | | | | **INCOME DATA** | | |
| | | 100.0 | 100.0 | | | Net Sales | 100.0 | 100.0 |
| | | 22.7 | 30.0 | | | Gross Profit | 24.9 | 23.6 |
| | | 18.6 | 23.1 | | | Operating Expenses | 18.9 | 21.9 |
| | | 4.0 | 6.9 | | | Operating Profit | 6.0 | 1.6 |
| | | .1 | .0 | | | All Other Expenses (net) | 1.0 | 1.2 |
| | | 4.0 | 6.8 | | | Profit Before Taxes | 5.0 | .4 |
| | | | | | | **RATIOS** | | |
| | | 3.1 | 2.6 | | | | 2.4 | 2.1 |
| | | 1.5 | 1.5 | | | Current | 1.5 | 1.4 |
| | | 1.2 | 1.1 | | | | 1.1 | 1.1 |
| | | 1.1 | 1.4 | | | | 1.1 | .9 |
| | | .6 | .9 | | | Quick | .6 | .5 |
| | | .3 | .4 | | | | .4 | .3 |
| 29 | 12.8 | 24 | 15.0 | | | | 24   15.2 | 18   20.1 |
| 38 | 9.5 | 41 | 8.9 | | | Sales/Receivables | 37   9.8 | 33   11.2 |
| 49 | 7.5 | 46 | 8.0 | | | | 51   7.2 | 51   7.2 |
| 52 | 7.0 | 41 | 8.8 | | | | 42   8.8 | 52   7.0 |
| 85 | 4.3 | 73 | 5.0 | | | Cost of Sales/Inventory | 66   5.5 | 82   4.5 |
| 140 | 2.6 | 101 | 3.6 | | | | 97   3.8 | 141   2.6 |
| 18 | 20.6 | 28 | 13.1 | | | | 13   28.4 | 10   35.9 |
| 28 | 13.2 | 37 | 9.9 | | | Cost of Sales/Payables | 27   13.4 | 26   13.8 |
| 46 | 8.0 | 43 | 8.4 | | | | 42   8.6 | 41   9.0 |
| | | 4.9 | 5.2 | | | | 5.8 | 5.4 |
| | | 7.5 | 8.4 | | | Sales/Working Capital | 10.3 | 10.9 |
| | | 13.2 | 32.1 | | | | 59.0 | 28.1 |
| | | 55.7 | 13.2 | | | | 8.3 | 7.6 |
| | | 6.7 | 6.4 | | | EBIT/Interest | (63) 3.2 | (65) 1.7 |
| | | .6 | 2.8 | | | | 1.2 | -2.7 |
| | | | | | | | 9.7 | 7.9 |
| | | | | | | Net Profit + Depr., Dep., Amort./Cur. Mat. L/T/D | (17) 3.2 | (15) 5.6 |
| | | | | | | | .9 | 2.2 |
| | | .1 | .3 | | | | .2 | .2 |
| | | .4 | .9 | | | Fixed/Worth | .6 | .7 |
| | | 1.5 | 1.8 | | | | 3.7 | 5.8 |
| | | .7 | 1.6 | | | | .7 | 1.1 |
| | | 2.0 | 2.6 | | | Debt/Worth | 2.4 | 2.8 |
| | | 4.0 | 14.0 | | | | 11.2 | 143.8 |
| | | 63.0 | 63.2 | | | | 52.1 | 44.7 |
| | (17) | 31.2 | (14) 45.1 | | | % Profit Before Taxes/Tangible Net Worth | (60) 23.3 | (56) 10.4 |
| | | -.1 | 21.4 | | | | 9.4 | -9.3 |
| | | 15.8 | 15.9 | | | | 16.7 | 11.6 |
| | | 6.8 | 9.8 | | | % Profit Before Taxes/Total Assets | 7.0 | 2.3 |
| | | -.3 | 3.2 | | | | .8 | -7.0 |
| | | 29.7 | 49.1 | | | | 50.2 | 39.0 |
| | | 14.1 | 13.1 | | | Sales/Net Fixed Assets | 13.2 | 12.6 |
| | | 6.6 | 6.4 | | | | 6.8 | 6.6 |
| | | 2.9 | 3.0 | | | | 3.1 | 3.0 |
| | | 2.4 | 2.2 | | | Sales/Total Assets | 2.4 | 2.2 |
| | | 1.6 | 1.3 | | | | 1.6 | 1.4 |
| | | .4 | .5 | | | | .6 | .8 |
| | (17) | 1.1 | (13) 1.4 | | | % Depr., Dep., Amort./Sales | (63) 1.1 | (60) 1.3 |
| | | 1.7 | 2.7 | | | | 2.0 | 2.8 |
| | | | | | | | .9 | 1.1 |
| | | | | | | % Officers', Directors' Owners' Comp/Sales | (20) 2.7 | (14) 2.9 |
| | | | | | | | 4.2 | 5.0 |
| 1268M | 37094M | 218776M | 692692M | 376038M | 1223133M | Net Sales ($) | 2793468M | 3165029M |
| 486M | 10077M | 98887M | 292046M | 237407M | 673446M | Total Assets ($) | 1312721M | 1566961M |

M = $ thousand     MM = $ million
See Pages 9 through 22 for Explanation of Ratios and Data

## Comparative Historical Data — Current Data Sorted by Sales

| | | | Type of Statement | 0-1MM | 1-3MM | 3-5MM | 5-10MM | 10-25MM | 25MM & OVER |
|---|---|---|---|---|---|---|---|---|---|
| 9 | 13 | 11 | Unqualified | | | | | 1 | 10 |
| 10 | 7 | 12 | Reviewed | | | 2 | 1 | 6 | 3 |
| 6 | 6 | 4 | Compiled | | | 1 | 3 | | |
| 6 | 7 | 3 | Tax Returns | | 1 | | | 2 | |
| 28 | 18 | 21 | Other | | 3 | 1 | 4 | 6 | 7 |
| 4/1/09-3/31/10 ALL | 4/1/10-3/31/11 ALL | 4/1/11-3/31/12 ALL | | | 6 (4/1-9/30/11) | | | 45 (10/1/11-3/31/12) | |
| 59 | 51 | 51 | **NUMBER OF STATEMENTS** | | 4 | 4 | 8 | 15 | 20 |
| % | % | % | **ASSETS** | % | % | % | % | % | % |
| 7.8 | 6.5 | 9.1 | Cash & Equivalents | | | | | 13.5 | 5.2 |
| 18.5 | 22.9 | 23.3 | Trade Receivables (net) | | | | | 18.3 | 28.7 |
| 33.9 | 38.0 | 35.4 | Inventory | | | | | 34.1 | 34.8 |
| 3.8 | 2.7 | 2.2 | All Other Current | | | | | 1.9 | 2.7 |
| 64.0 | 70.1 | 70.0 | Total Current | | | | | 67.8 | 71.4 |
| 25.1 | 20.0 | 19.0 | Fixed Assets (net) | | | | | 22.9 | 14.6 |
| 6.2 | 5.0 | 6.3 | Intangibles (net) | | | | | 3.6 | 8.9 |
| 4.7 | 4.8 | 4.6 | All Other Non-Current | | | | | 5.7 | 5.0 |
| 100.0 | 100.0 | 100.0 | Total | | | | | 100.0 | 100.0 |
| | | | **LIABILITIES** | | | | | | |
| 9.7 | 13.7 | 11.7 | Notes Payable-Short Term | | | | | 7.1 | 11.7 |
| 4.4 | 2.9 | 2.2 | Cur. Mat.-L.T.D. | | | | | 3.4 | 2.5 |
| 9.7 | 18.1 | 14.4 | Trade Payables | | | | | 15.2 | 15.8 |
| .3 | .1 | .2 | Income Taxes Payable | | | | | .1 | .4 |
| 12.2 | 10.4 | 13.5 | All Other Current | | | | | 8.5 | 17.2 |
| 36.3 | 45.3 | 42.0 | Total Current | | | | | 34.3 | 47.6 |
| 16.7 | 15.8 | 13.3 | Long-Term Debt | | | | | 16.8 | 9.5 |
| .4 | .6 | .9 | Deferred Taxes | | | | | 1.7 | .9 |
| 5.8 | 10.8 | 5.3 | All Other Non-Current | | | | | 3.1 | 6.7 |
| 40.7 | 27.5 | 38.6 | Net Worth | | | | | 44.1 | 35.2 |
| 100.0 | 100.0 | 100.0 | Total Liabilties & Net Worth | | | | | 100.0 | 100.0 |
| | | | **INCOME DATA** | | | | | | |
| 100.0 | 100.0 | 100.0 | Net Sales | | | | | 100.0 | 100.0 |
| 23.8 | 24.2 | 27.8 | Gross Profit | | | | | 34.0 | 20.8 |
| 23.7 | 21.3 | 22.5 | Operating Expenses | | | | | 26.4 | 14.8 |
| .2 | 2.9 | 5.3 | Operating Profit | | | | | 7.6 | 5.9 |
| 1.5 | .7 | .3 | All Other Expenses (net) | | | | | .1 | .2 |
| -1.3 | 2.2 | 5.0 | Profit Before Taxes | | | | | 7.5 | 5.7 |
| | | | **RATIOS** | | | | | | |
| 3.1 | 2.5 | 2.8 | | | | | | 3.3 | 2.3 |
| 1.8 | 1.8 | 1.5 | Current | | | | | 2.3 | 1.5 |
| 1.2 | 1.2 | 1.2 | | | | | | 1.5 | 1.1 |
| 1.5 | 1.0 | 1.4 | | | | | | 1.5 | 1.1 |
| .7 | .7 | .9 | Quick | | | | | .9 | .9 |
| .4 | .4 | .5 | | | | | | .6 | .5 |
| 21  17.0 | 23  15.8 | 29  12.8 | | | | | | 17  21.0 | 38  9.5 |
| 36  10.2 | 41  9.0 | 41  8.9 | Sales/Receivables | | | | | 33  11.0 | 45  8.1 |
| 57  6.4 | 55  6.6 | 51  7.2 | | | | | | 46  7.9 | 54  6.7 |
| 51  7.1 | 63  5.8 | 47  7.7 | | | | | | 46  7.9 | 49  7.4 |
| 90  4.1 | 88  4.2 | 74  4.9 | Cost of Sales/Inventory | | | | | 55  6.6 | 73  5.0 |
| 144  2.5 | 113  3.2 | 126  2.9 | | | | | | 135  2.7 | 99  3.7 |
| 13  28.5 | 19  19.1 | 18  20.6 | | | | | | 20  18.5 | 21  17.1 |
| 23  16.2 | 35  10.3 | 29  12.6 | Cost of Sales/Payables | | | | | 33  10.9 | 31  11.9 |
| 36  10.1 | 58  6.3 | 43  8.4 | | | | | | 46  8.0 | 43  8.4 |
| 3.1 | 4.4 | 4.9 | | | | | | 4.9 | 5.1 |
| 7.4 | 7.5 | 10.1 | Sales/Working Capital | | | | | 5.8 | 11.1 |
| 23.0 | 19.9 | 30.2 | | | | | | 12.1 | 31.6 |
| 6.2 | 8.7 | 25.7 | | | | | | 114.8 | 54.3 |
| (54)  1.7 | (49)  3.4 | (50)  7.4 | EBIT/Interest | | | | | 9.7 | 10.9 |
| -3.2 | -.9 | 2.6 | | | | | | 4.1 | 2.7 |
| 10.6 | 3.5 | 18.3 | Net Profit + Depr., Dep., | | | | | | |
| (20)  3.4 | (17)  2.4 | (11)  5.5 | Amort./Cur. Mat. L/T/D | | | | | | |
| .3 | 1.1 | 1.9 | | | | | | | |
| .2 | .2 | .2 | | | | | | .2 | .3 |
| .7 | .6 | .6 | Fixed/Worth | | | | | .3 | .7 |
| 1.8 | -69.6 | 1.4 | | | | | | 1.2 | 1.3 |
| .6 | .7 | .7 | | | | | | .6 | 1.1 |
| 1.6 | 2.3 | 2.0 | Debt/Worth | | | | | 1.5 | 4.1 |
| 9.3 | -325.7 | 7.0 | | | | | | 2.6 | 12.4 |
| 17.2 | 42.6 | 63.0 | | | | | | 78.2 | 61.9 |
| (51)  6.2 | (38)  19.3 | (46)  34.8 | % Profit Before Taxes/Tangible Net Worth | | | | | (14)  39.5 | (19)  44.0 |
| -11.0 | 5.4 | 12.7 | | | | | | 17.9 | 24.8 |
| 5.8 | 13.9 | 14.1 | | | | | | 23.8 | 14.0 |
| 1.3 | 4.6 | 7.1 | % Profit Before Taxes/Total Assets | | | | | 11.5 | 8.0 |
| -8.0 | -5.1 | 2.2 | | | | | | 4.0 | 3.3 |
| 19.9 | 29.1 | 49.1 | | | | | | 40.6 | 47.9 |
| 8.4 | 10.5 | 15.1 | Sales/Net Fixed Assets | | | | | 19.9 | 15.4 |
| 4.4 | 5.8 | 6.6 | | | | | | 6.9 | 10.1 |
| 2.6 | 2.8 | 3.0 | | | | | | 3.4 | 2.9 |
| 1.8 | 2.1 | 2.3 | Sales/Total Assets | | | | | 2.6 | 2.2 |
| 1.2 | 1.4 | 1.6 | | | | | | 1.4 | 1.8 |
| 1.2 | .8 | .5 | | | | | | .6 | .4 |
| (52)  2.7 | (46)  1.5 | (42)  1.2 | % Depr., Dep., Amort./Sales | | | | | (13)  1.5 | (19)  1.0 |
| 4.3 | 2.8 | 1.9 | | | | | | 2.8 | 1.7 |
| 1.8 | 1.2 | 1.1 | % Officers', Directors', | | | | | | |
| (14)  2.9 | (15)  2.2 | (12)  2.2 | Owners' Comp/Sales | | | | | | |
| 4.0 | 4.3 | 8.2 | | | | | | | |
| 1940310M | 1201507M | 2549001M | Net Sales ($) | | 7415M | 14804M | 49864M | 213909M | 2263009M |
| 1280121M | 713684M | 1312349M | Total Assets ($) | | 3764M | 7617M | 30442M | 113615M | 1156911M |

© RMA 2012

M = $ thousand   MM = $ million
See Pages 9 through 22 for Explanation of Ratios and Data

## Current Data Sorted by Assets      Comparative Historical Data

| | | | | | | Type of Statement | | |
|---|---|---|---|---|---|---|---|---|
| | | | | | | | **2** | **5** | Unqualified
| 1 | 1 | 2 | 5 | | | Reviewed | 17 | 14 |
| | | 9 | 3 | | | Compiled | 7 | 4 |
| | 1 | 1 | | | | Tax Returns | 2 | 5 |
| | 2 | | | | | Other | 21 | 26 |
| | 4 | 1 | | | | | 4/1/07- | 4/1/08- |
| 1 | 2 | 13 | 5 | 1 | | | 3/31/08 | 3/31/09 |
| | 4 (4/1-9/30/11) | | 47 (10/1/11-3/31/12) | | | | ALL | ALL |
| 0-500M | 500M-2MM | 2-10MM | 10-50MM | 50-100MM | 100-250MM | **NUMBER OF STATEMENTS** | 49 | 54 |
| 2 | 9 | 26 | 13 | 1 | | | | |
| % | % | % | % | % | % | | % | % |

*Type of Statement counts (Unqualified row): reviewed and other columns as shown above.*

| 0-500M | 500M-2MM | 2-10MM | 10-50MM | 50-100MM | 100-250MM | | 4/1/07-3/31/08 ALL | 4/1/08-3/31/09 ALL |
|---|---|---|---|---|---|---|---|---|
| | | | | | | **ASSETS** | | |
| | | 9.8 | 9.8 | | | Cash & Equivalents | 8.1 | 9.2 |
| | | 20.0 | 29.8 | | | Trade Receivables (net) | 27.6 | 26.0 |
| | | 28.5 | 22.0 | | | Inventory | 28.6 | 28.7 |
| | | 4.3 | 8.4 | | | All Other Current | 3.8 | 3.1 |
| | | 62.6 | 70.1 | | | Total Current | 68.1 | 67.1 |
| | | 22.4 | 18.4 | | | Fixed Assets (net) | 23.9 | 18.6 |
| | | 4.4 | 4.4 | | | Intangibles (net) | 1.9 | 4.8 |
| | | 10.6 | 7.0 | | | All Other Non-Current | 6.0 | 9.5 |
| | | 100.0 | 100.0 | | | Total | 100.0 | 100.0 |
| | | | | | | **LIABILITIES** | | |
| | | 8.6 | 4.7 | | | Notes Payable-Short Term | 13.5 | 13.4 |
| | | 2.3 | 1.2 | | | Cur. Mat.-L.T.D. | 2.8 | 2.2 |
| | | 8.7 | 8.3 | | | Trade Payables | 14.5 | 13.5 |
| | | .2 | .1 | | | Income Taxes Payable | .1 | .1 |
| | | 7.7 | 20.6 | | | All Other Current | 13.1 | 8.8 |
| | | 27.4 | 34.8 | | | Total Current | 44.0 | 38.0 |
| | | 14.2 | 5.3 | | | Long-Term Debt | 11.9 | 7.6 |
| | | .3 | 1.0 | | | Deferred Taxes | .5 | .7 |
| | | 5.2 | 7.2 | | | All Other Non-Current | 5.8 | 6.7 |
| | | 52.9 | 51.7 | | | Net Worth | 37.8 | 47.0 |
| | | 100.0 | 100.0 | | | Total Liabilities & Net Worth | 100.0 | 100.0 |
| | | | | | | **INCOME DATA** | | |
| | | 100.0 | 100.0 | | | Net Sales | 100.0 | 100.0 |
| | | 34.8 | 28.7 | | | Gross Profit | 31.3 | 28.7 |
| | | 27.4 | 18.9 | | | Operating Expenses | 26.8 | 23.0 |
| | | 7.4 | 9.8 | | | Operating Profit | 4.5 | 5.7 |
| | | 3.3 | .2 | | | All Other Expenses (net) | 1.1 | .7 |
| | | 4.1 | 9.6 | | | Profit Before Taxes | 3.4 | 5.0 |
| | | | | | | **RATIOS** | | |
| | | 4.1 | 4.3 | | | | 2.4 | 2.9 |
| | | 2.6 | 2.0 | | | Current | 1.7 | 1.9 |
| | | 1.5 | 1.5 | | | | 1.1 | 1.3 |
| | | 2.0 | 1.9 | | | | 1.4 | 1.5 |
| | | 1.2 | 1.0 | | | Quick | 1.0 | 1.0 |
| | | .5 | .8 | | | | .4 | .6 |
| | | 33   11.1 | 41   8.8 | | | | 37   9.8 | 25   14.5 |
| | | 44   8.3 | 65   5.6 | | | Sales/Receivables | 49   7.5 | 41   8.8 |
| | | 54   6.7 | 83   4.4 | | | | 73   5.0 | 56   6.5 |
| | | 45   8.1 | 12   30.6 | | | | 41   8.8 | 31   11.9 |
| | | 101   3.6 | 94   3.9 | | | Cost of Sales/Inventory | 78   4.7 | 69   5.3 |
| | | 140   2.6 | 159   2.3 | | | | 138   2.6 | 117   3.1 |
| | | 14   25.9 | 15   24.1 | | | | 16   22.9 | 17   21.4 |
| | | 28   13.0 | 28   13.2 | | | Cost of Sales/Payables | 29   12.5 | 24   15.3 |
| | | 42   8.6 | 41   9.0 | | | | 51   7.2 | 38   9.7 |
| | | 2.7 | 3.7 | | | | 3.9 | 3.5 |
| | | 4.9 | 4.5 | | | Sales/Working Capital | 9.4 | 6.2 |
| | | 23.4 | 5.3 | | | | 36.9 | 18.4 |
| | | 25.8 | 21.6 | | | | 10.2 | 11.7 |
| | | (22)   6.0 | (11)   9.6 | | | EBIT/Interest | (40)   5.1 | (45)   5.3 |
| | | 1.4 | 3.2 | | | | 1.8 | 1.6 |
| | | | | | | Net Profit + Depr., Dep., | 7.4 | 6.3 |
| | | | (10)   3.5 | | | Amort./Cur. Mat. L/T/D | (11)   4.1 | |
| | | | | | | | 1.9 | 1.4 |
| | | .1 | .1 | | | | .2 | .1 |
| | | .3 | .3 | | | Fixed/Worth | .6 | .4 |
| | | 1.4 | .7 | | | | 1.3 | 1.3 |
| | | .3 | .5 | | | | .8 | .5 |
| | | .8 | .9 | | | Debt/Worth | 1.7 | 1.3 |
| | | 3.4 | 3.3 | | | | 4.6 | 3.4 |
| | | 44.4 | 69.7 | | | % Profit Before Taxes/Tangible | 57.1 | 51.8 |
| | | (25)   23.7 | 25.8 | | | Net Worth | (45)   31.6 | (49)   25.1 |
| | | 9.2 | 12.8 | | | | 6.8 | 6.5 |
| | | 23.3 | 23.1 | | | % Profit Before Taxes/Total | 18.0 | 17.0 |
| | | 9.9 | 12.2 | | | Assets | 7.8 | 8.1 |
| | | 1.8 | 5.6 | | | | 1.9 | 2.1 |
| | | 29.4 | 26.0 | | | | 28.1 | 35.7 |
| | | 9.3 | 10.5 | | | Sales/Net Fixed Assets | 9.8 | 12.8 |
| | | 7.3 | 6.4 | | | | 4.8 | 7.9 |
| | | 2.0 | 2.1 | | | | 2.5 | 2.7 |
| | | 1.7 | 1.7 | | | Sales/Total Assets | 2.0 | 2.1 |
| | | 1.2 | 1.3 | | | | 1.4 | 1.5 |
| | | 1.0 | .9 | | | | .5 | .5 |
| | | (25)   1.5 | (12)   1.4 | | | % Depr., Dep., Amort./Sales | (42)   .9 | (44)   1.1 |
| | | 2.5 | 2.4 | | | | 2.5 | 2.1 |
| | | | | | | | 1.0 | 1.1 |
| | | | | | | % Officers', Directors' | (15)   2.9 | (15)   2.0 |
| | | | | | | Owners' Comp/Sales | 6.2 | 4.8 |
| 1506M | 35910M | 228612M | 556592M | 40678M | | Net Sales ($) | 873289M | 1320905M |
| 662M | 10425M | 135539M | 331673M | 52361M | | Total Assets ($) | 455562M | 724545M |

*Note: In the 50-100MM and 100-250MM columns for the upper portion of the table, the notation reads vertically: "DATA NOT AVAILABLE".*

M = $ thousand     MM = $ million
See Pages 9 through 22 for Explanation of Ratios and Data

## Comparative Historical Data | Current Data Sorted by Sales

| | | | Type of Statement | 0-1MM | 1-3MM | 3-5MM | 5-10MM | 10-25MM | 25MM & OVER |
|---|---|---|---|---|---|---|---|---|---|
| 7 | 14 | 7 | Unqualified | | | | 2 | 2 | 3 |
| 9 | 19 | 14 | Reviewed | 1 | | 3 | 5 | 2 | 3 |
| 5 | 3 | 3 | Compiled | | 1 | | 2 | | |
| 4 | 11 | 5 | Tax Returns | 1 | 1 | 2 | 1 | | |
| 23 | 26 | 22 | Other | 1 | 3 | 3 | 3 | 7 | 5 |
| 4/1/09-3/31/10 | 4/1/10-3/31/11 | 4/1/11-3/31/12 | | | 4 (4/1-9/30/11) | | | 47 (10/1/11-3/31/12) | |
| ALL | ALL | ALL | | | | | | | |
| 48 | 73 | 51 | **NUMBER OF STATEMENTS** | 3 | 5 | 8 | 13 | 11 | 11 |
| % | % | % | **ASSETS** | % | % | % | % | % | % |
| 11.6 | 11.2 | 9.5 | Cash & Equivalents | | | | 9.0 | 9.3 | 9.8 |
| 26.0 | 27.1 | 26.2 | Trade Receivables (net) | | | | 21.9 | 21.3 | 31.7 |
| 24.2 | 26.1 | 26.4 | Inventory | | | | 22.9 | 34.6 | 20.7 |
| 4.9 | 4.8 | 4.8 | All Other Current | | | | .4 | 5.5 | 10.5 |
| 66.7 | 69.3 | 66.9 | Total Current | | | | 54.2 | 70.7 | 72.6 |
| 21.5 | 19.0 | 20.5 | Fixed Assets (net) | | | | 28.5 | 17.0 | 13.9 |
| 4.6 | 4.1 | 4.1 | Intangibles (net) | | | | 5.1 | 4.2 | 7.8 |
| 7.3 | 7.5 | 8.5 | All Other Non-Current | | | | 12.3 | 8.1 | 5.8 |
| 100.0 | 100.0 | 100.0 | Total | | | | 100.0 | 100.0 | 100.0 |
| | | | **LIABILITIES** | | | | | | |
| 13.0 | 8.8 | 7.7 | Notes Payable-Short Term | | | | 6.4 | 11.2 | 4.9 |
| 4.7 | 2.6 | 1.7 | Cur. Mat.-L.T.D. | | | | 3.0 | 1.0 | .8 |
| 14.1 | 12.3 | 11.5 | Trade Payables | | | | 9.4 | 5.6 | 9.5 |
| .4 | .1 | .1 | Income Taxes Payable | | | | .3 | .0 | .1 |
| 9.4 | 13.4 | 10.3 | All Other Current | | | | 6.7 | 10.2 | 22.9 |
| 41.6 | 37.1 | 31.3 | Total Current | | | | 25.9 | 28.0 | 38.1 |
| 11.4 | 9.2 | 11.8 | Long-Term Debt | | | | 15.2 | 7.5 | 1.9 |
| .7 | .8 | .5 | Deferred Taxes | | | | .0 | .0 | 1.4 |
| 9.1 | 7.1 | 6.7 | All Other Non-Current | | | | 1.7 | 8.1 | 7.5 |
| 37.3 | 45.7 | 49.8 | Net Worth | | | | 57.2 | 56.4 | 51.0 |
| 100.0 | 100.0 | 100.0 | Total Liabilities & Net Worth | | | | 100.0 | 100.0 | 100.0 |
| | | | **INCOME DATA** | | | | | | |
| 100.0 | 100.0 | 100.0 | Net Sales | | | | 100.0 | 100.0 | 100.0 |
| 28.8 | 32.6 | 31.4 | Gross Profit | | | | 27.7 | 37.5 | 30.4 |
| 27.2 | 26.0 | 24.6 | Operating Expenses | | | | 21.0 | 27.0 | 21.1 |
| 1.5 | 6.5 | 6.8 | Operating Profit | | | | 6.7 | 10.5 | 9.3 |
| 1.5 | 1.9 | 1.8 | All Other Expenses (net) | | | | 1.3 | 1.2 | .5 |
| .0 | 4.6 | 4.9 | Profit Before Taxes | | | | 5.4 | 9.3 | 8.8 |
| | | | **RATIOS** | | | | | | |
| 2.9 | 3.2 | 4.0 | | | | | 4.8 | 5.2 | 2.8 |
| 1.7 | 1.9 | 2.0 | Current | | | | 2.5 | 3.7 | 1.9 |
| 1.1 | 1.3 | 1.5 | | | | | 1.5 | 1.1 | 1.5 |
| 2.0 | 2.0 | 1.9 | | | | | 3.3 | 2.9 | 2.2 |
| .8 | 1.0 | 1.1 | Quick | | | | 1.3 | 1.4 | 1.0 |
| .4 | .6 | .7 | | | | | .8 | .3 | .5 |
| 41  8.8 | 41  9.0 | 35  10.4 | | | | | 26  13.8 | 33  11.1 | 53  6.9 |
| 62  5.9 | 58  6.3 | 49  7.4 | Sales/Receivables | | | | 46  8.0 | 35  10.4 | 65  5.6 |
| 67  5.4 | 73  5.0 | 65  5.6 | | | | | 59  6.2 | 49  7.4 | 81  4.5 |
| 28  12.9 | 43  8.5 | 28  12.9 | | | | | 24  15.5 | 94  3.9 | 9  38.6 |
| 80  4.6 | 83  4.4 | 85  4.3 | Cost of Sales/Inventory | | | | 74  4.9 | 140  2.6 | 49  7.4 |
| 146  2.5 | 142  2.6 | 140  2.6 | | | | | 114  3.2 | 174  2.1 | 174  2.1 |
| 15  25.0 | 20  18.2 | 15  24.8 | | | | | 12  29.7 | 9  39.3 | 16  23.4 |
| 27  13.6 | 27  13.6 | 28  12.9 | Cost of Sales/Payables | | | | 28  12.9 | 17  20.9 | 30  12.2 |
| 45  8.1 | 54  6.8 | 45  8.1 | | | | | 42  8.7 | 25  14.5 | 45  8.2 |
| 2.8 | 2.9 | 3.6 | | | | | 4.4 | 2.5 | 3.8 |
| 6.3 | 5.7 | 5.0 | Sales/Working Capital | | | | 5.8 | 3.8 | 4.9 |
| 34.7 | 16.0 | 9.4 | | | | | 27.4 | 57.4 | 5.4 |
| 5.5 | 20.9 | 21.9 | | | | | 22.8 | | |
| (44)  .5 | (67)  6.8 | (42)  8.0 | EBIT/Interest | | | | (11)  9.2 | | |
| -6.9 | 2.1 | 1.7 | | | | | 2.3 | | |
| 2.1 | 11.8 | 12.5 | Net Profit + Depr., Dep., | | | | | | |
| (10)  .2 | (19)  2.2 | (10)  7.2 | Amort./Cur. Mat. L/T/D | | | | | | |
| -2.3 | .5 | 2.7 | | | | | | | |
| .2 | .2 | .1 | | | | | .2 | .1 | .1 |
| .6 | .4 | .3 | Fixed/Worth | | | | .4 | .2 | .3 |
| 5.0 | 1.1 | 1.3 | | | | | .9 | 1.4 | .6 |
| .6 | .6 | .4 | | | | | .3 | .3 | .5 |
| 1.5 | 1.2 | .9 | Debt/Worth | | | | .8 | .7 | 1.1 |
| 19.0 | 3.8 | 4.4 | | | | | 1.4 | 4.4 | 6.0 |
| 23.0 | 45.2 | 44.2 | % Profit Before Taxes/Tangible | | | | 36.7 | 41.8 | 119.2 |
| (39)  .5 | (68)  15.3 | (48)  24.4 | Net Worth | | | | 14.8 | 28.5 | (10)  28.1 |
| -23.7 | 3.5 | 10.4 | | | | | 6.6 | 23.7 | 15.0 |
| 9.5 | 15.7 | 19.0 | % Profit Before Taxes/Total | | | | 12.1 | 27.7 | 26.3 |
| -.9 | 6.5 | 8.9 | Assets | | | | 8.6 | 15.1 | 12.2 |
| -11.0 | 1.9 | 2.4 | | | | | 4.6 | 5.9 | 5.5 |
| 20.5 | 21.7 | 29.2 | | | | | 10.8 | 29.2 | 27.5 |
| 8.9 | 10.3 | 10.0 | Sales/Net Fixed Assets | | | | 9.5 | 11.4 | 11.6 |
| 5.6 | 6.2 | 8.1 | | | | | 5.0 | 8.5 | 8.2 |
| 2.2 | 2.1 | 2.2 | | | | | 2.7 | 2.4 | 2.2 |
| 1.5 | 1.6 | 1.9 | Sales/Total Assets | | | | 1.9 | 1.9 | 1.9 |
| 1.2 | 1.2 | 1.4 | | | | | 1.1 | 1.6 | 1.5 |
| 1.2 | 1.1 | .9 | | | | | .5 | 1.0 | .9 |
| (40)  2.4 | (58)  1.8 | (46)  1.5 | % Depr., Dep., Amort./Sales | | | | 1.5 | (10)  1.5 | (10)  1.1 |
| 3.9 | 3.2 | 2.5 | | | | | 4.9 | 2.2 | 1.9 |
| 1.8 | 1.8 | 2.6 | % Officers', Directors' | | | | | | |
| (16)  2.9 | (18)  4.8 | (17)  4.5 | Owners' Comp/Sales | | | | | | |
| 5.4 | 6.1 | 6.2 | | | | | | | |
| 1487270M | 1458017M | 863298M | Net Sales ($) | 2315M | 9624M | 33270M | 94705M | 179153M | 544231M |
| 833306M | 937268M | 530660M | Total Assets ($) | 1302M | 7080M | 20821M | 62900M | 101586M | 336971M |

M = $ thousand    MM = $ million
See Pages 9 through 22 for Explanation of Ratios and Data

## Current Data Sorted by Assets

## Comparative Historical Data

| | | | | | | Type of Statement | | |
|---|---|---|---|---|---|---|---|---|
| | | 2 | 7 | 2 | | Unqualified | 14 | 17 |
| | | 14 | 4 | | | Reviewed | 20 | 17 |
| | 2 | 8 | 2 | | | Compiled | 9 | 13 |
| 1 | 4 | 4 | | | | Tax Returns | 6 | 5 |
| 1 | 2 | 10 | 11 | | 1 | Other | 25 | 18 |
| | 15 (4/1-9/30/11) | | 60 (10/1/11-3/31/12) | | | | 4/1/07-3/31/08 | 4/1/08-3/31/09 |
| 0-500M | 500M-2MM | 2-10MM | 10-50MM | 50-100MM | 100-250MM | | ALL | ALL |
| 2 | 8 | 38 | 24 | 2 | 1 | **NUMBER OF STATEMENTS** | 74 | 70 |
| % | % | % | % | % | % | **ASSETS** | % | % |
| | | 11.3 | 10.8 | | | Cash & Equivalents | 11.9 | 12.0 |
| | | 22.8 | 22.4 | | | Trade Receivables (net) | 26.9 | 24.9 |
| | | 34.4 | 30.7 | | | Inventory | 32.7 | 31.9 |
| | | 2.0 | 4.4 | | | All Other Current | 4.6 | 4.3 |
| | | 70.5 | 68.3 | | | Total Current | 76.0 | 73.2 |
| | | 20.8 | 13.0 | | | Fixed Assets (net) | 13.3 | 14.5 |
| | | 4.5 | 11.8 | | | Intangibles (net) | 6.5 | 6.5 |
| | | 4.1 | 6.9 | | | All Other Non-Current | 4.2 | 5.8 |
| | | 100.0 | 100.0 | | | Total | 100.0 | 100.0 |
| | | | | | | **LIABILITIES** | | |
| | | 10.2 | 3.8 | | | Notes Payable-Short Term | 9.9 | 10.7 |
| | | 2.9 | 2.1 | | | Cur. Mat.-L.T.D. | 3.3 | 2.8 |
| | | 13.5 | 13.0 | | | Trade Payables | 19.5 | 16.5 |
| | | .0 | .6 | | | Income Taxes Payable | .3 | .4 |
| | | 18.0 | 23.8 | | | All Other Current | 24.2 | 24.2 |
| | | 44.6 | 43.3 | | | Total Current | 57.3 | 54.6 |
| | | 8.9 | 5.4 | | | Long-Term Debt | 8.7 | 6.9 |
| | | .2 | .8 | | | Deferred Taxes | .4 | .5 |
| | | 4.7 | 5.6 | | | All Other Non-Current | 6.3 | 4.6 |
| | | 41.6 | 44.8 | | | Net Worth | 27.3 | 33.5 |
| | | 100.0 | 100.0 | | | Total Liabilities & Net Worth | 100.0 | 100.0 |
| | | | | | | **INCOME DATA** | | |
| | | 100.0 | 100.0 | | | Net Sales | 100.0 | 100.0 |
| | | 34.0 | 25.7 | | | Gross Profit | 30.6 | 29.6 |
| | | 27.9 | 20.4 | | | Operating Expenses | 26.7 | 26.1 |
| | | 6.1 | 5.4 | | | Operating Profit | 3.8 | 3.5 |
| | | .7 | .2 | | | All Other Expenses (net) | .7 | .5 |
| | | 5.4 | 5.2 | | | Profit Before Taxes | 3.2 | 3.0 |
| | | | | | | **RATIOS** | | |
| | | 2.1 | 2.5 | | | | 2.1 | 2.1 |
| | | 1.5 | 1.7 | | | Current | 1.4 | 1.5 |
| | | 1.3 | 1.0 | | | | 1.1 | 1.1 |
| | | 1.2 | 1.2 | | | | 1.0 | 1.0 |
| | | .8 | .8 | | | Quick | .7 | .7 |
| | | .4 | .4 | | | | .5 | .4 |
| | 31 | 11.7 | 37   9.9 | | | | 29   12.8 | 26   13.8 |
| | 43 | 8.5 | 43   8.5 | | | Sales/Receivables | 41   9.0 | 38   9.7 |
| | 51 | 7.2 | 62   5.9 | | | | 56   6.5 | 54   6.8 |
| | 49 | 7.4 | 50   7.3 | | | | 42   8.6 | 39   9.5 |
| | 111 | 3.3 | 74   4.9 | | | Cost of Sales/Inventory | 86   4.3 | 78   4.7 |
| | 152 | 2.4 | 118   3.1 | | | | 137   2.7 | 128   2.8 |
| | 19 | 19.0 | 14   27.0 | | | | 15   23.9 | 15   24.3 |
| | 30 | 12.3 | 27   13.4 | | | Cost of Sales/Payables | 32   11.3 | 26   13.9 |
| | 57 | 6.4 | 38   9.7 | | | | 49   7.4 | 46   8.0 |
| | | 5.4 | 3.9 | | | | 4.6 | 4.5 |
| | | 9.4 | 7.0 | | | Sales/Working Capital | 9.5 | 10.3 |
| | | 17.5 | 30.2 | | | | 50.3 | 25.9 |
| | | 14.3 | 51.8 | | | | 16.0 | 20.2 |
| | (28) | 6.0 | (17)   16.7 | | | EBIT/Interest | (66)   2.6 | (60)   5.2 |
| | | 2.6 | .9 | | | | 1.5 | 1.3 |
| | | 10.1 | | | | | 8.3 | 17.2 |
| | (10) | 2.5 | | | | Net Profit + Depr., Dep., Amort./Cur. Mat. L/T/D | (31)   3.2 | (15)   5.0 |
| | | 1.0 | | | | | .6 | .0 |
| | | .2 | .2 | | | | .2 | .2 |
| | | .7 | .4 | | | Fixed/Worth | .5 | .4 |
| | | 1.3 | 1.4 | | | | 2.1 | 1.6 |
| | | .8 | .7 | | | | .8 | .8 |
| | | 2.2 | 1.1 | | | Debt/Worth | 2.2 | 2.2 |
| | | 3.3 | 6.7 | | | | 8.7 | 11.5 |
| | | 48.8 | 48.7 | | | | 37.2 | 49.3 |
| | (37) | 23.0 | (21)   21.8 | | | % Profit Before Taxes/Tangible Net Worth | (59)   20.6 | (57)   19.1 |
| | | 10.3 | 13.1 | | | | 5.1 | 3.4 |
| | | 16.3 | 15.5 | | | | 15.1 | 14.6 |
| | | 9.7 | 10.5 | | | % Profit Before Taxes/Total Assets | 5.7 | 7.0 |
| | | 2.4 | 3.7 | | | | .7 | .6 |
| | | 33.8 | 29.7 | | | | 45.6 | 41.9 |
| | | 10.8 | 16.0 | | | Sales/Net Fixed Assets | 21.1 | 19.9 |
| | | 7.8 | 9.0 | | | | 11.3 | 9.0 |
| | | 3.0 | 2.2 | | | | 2.8 | 3.0 |
| | | 1.8 | 1.6 | | | Sales/Total Assets | 2.1 | 2.0 |
| | | 1.2 | 1.1 | | | | 1.6 | 1.5 |
| | | .8 | .8 | | | | .5 | .6 |
| | (33) | 1.5 | (22)   1.3 | | | % Depr., Dep., Amort./Sales | (66)   1.1 | (61)   1.0 |
| | | 2.4 | 1.8 | | | | 1.7 | 1.7 |
| | | 2.0 | | | | | 2.5 | 1.9 |
| | (17) | 3.3 | | | | % Officers', Directors' Owners' Comp/Sales | (20)   3.5 | (16)   4.1 |
| | | 5.4 | | | | | 6.0 | 6.7 |
| 977M | 27877M | 414665M | 798919M | 210905M | 353642M | Net Sales ($) | 1816315M | 2081778M |
| 221M | 11078M | 200063M | 496140M | 168830M | 211964M | Total Assets ($) | 951276M | 1176255M |

M = $ thousand    MM = $ million
See Pages 9 through 22 for Explanation of Ratios and Data

## Comparative Historical Data          Current Data Sorted by Sales

| Type of Statement | | | | | 0-1MM | 1-3MM | 3-5MM | 5-10MM | 10-25MM | 25MM & OVER |
|---|---|---|---|---|---|---|---|---|---|---|
| Unqualified | 15 | 16 | 11 | | | | | 4 | 6 | 5 |
| Reviewed | 20 | 26 | 18 | | | 2 | 2 | 4 | 6 | 4 |
| Compiled | 6 | 7 | 12 | | | 1 | 2 | 4 | 3 | 2 |
| Tax Returns | 5 | 14 | 9 | | 1 | 1 | 3 | 2 | 2 | |
| Other | 22 | 33 | 25 | | 1 | 2 | | 4 | 10 | 8 |
| | 4/1/09-3/31/10 ALL | 4/1/10-3/31/11 ALL | 4/1/11-3/31/12 ALL | | 15 (4/1-9/30/11) | | | 60 (10/1/11-3/31/12) | | |
| NUMBER OF STATEMENTS | 68 | 96 | 75 | | 2 | 6 | 7 | 14 | 27 | 19 |
| | % | % | % | ASSETS | % | % | % | % | % | % |
| | 11.6 | 13.4 | 9.9 | Cash & Equivalents | | | | 12.2 | 9.6 | 10.4 |
| | 19.7 | 23.2 | 23.3 | Trade Receivables (net) | | | | 22.1 | 20.7 | 27.1 |
| | 35.6 | 31.4 | 32.3 | Inventory | | | | 30.1 | 33.9 | 28.4 |
| | 4.4 | 5.0 | 3.5 | All Other Current | | | | .7 | 4.5 | 5.7 |
| | 71.3 | 72.9 | 68.9 | Total Current | | | | 65.2 | 68.7 | 71.7 |
| | 15.4 | 15.8 | 16.8 | Fixed Assets (net) | | | | 26.6 | 16.2 | 13.8 |
| | 5.0 | 4.6 | 7.4 | Intangibles (net) | | | | 4.8 | 9.6 | 10.8 |
| | 8.3 | 6.6 | 7.0 | All Other Non-Current | | | | 3.5 | 5.5 | 3.8 |
| | 100.0 | 100.0 | 100.0 | Total | | | | 100.0 | 100.0 | 100.0 |
| | | | | LIABILITIES | | | | | | |
| | 8.1 | 5.9 | 9.4 | Notes Payable-Short Term | | | | 9.8 | 9.2 | 2.3 |
| | 2.2 | 3.9 | 2.3 | Cur. Mat.-L.T.D. | | | | 3.4 | 3.7 | 1.0 |
| | 11.0 | 14.3 | 15.5 | Trade Payables | | | | 16.8 | 12.9 | 12.8 |
| | .3 | .5 | .3 | Income Taxes Payable | | | | .0 | .2 | .6 |
| | 24.2 | 30.3 | 20.1 | All Other Current | | | | 14.1 | 21.1 | 27.2 |
| | 45.8 | 54.9 | 47.6 | Total Current | | | | 44.1 | 47.1 | 43.9 |
| | 6.2 | 6.6 | 8.4 | Long-Term Debt | | | | 9.7 | 8.4 | 6.2 |
| | .4 | .4 | .5 | Deferred Taxes | | | | .4 | .6 | .7 |
| | 8.6 | 12.9 | 5.7 | All Other Non-Current | | | | 2.1 | 4.7 | 5.5 |
| | 39.0 | 25.2 | 37.9 | Net Worth | | | | 43.7 | 39.2 | 43.7 |
| | 100.0 | 100.0 | 100.0 | Total Liabilities & Net Worth | | | | 100.0 | 100.0 | 100.0 |
| | | | | INCOME DATA | | | | | | |
| | 100.0 | 100.0 | 100.0 | Net Sales | | | | 100.0 | 100.0 | 100.0 |
| | 34.7 | 34.3 | 32.3 | Gross Profit | | | | 36.2 | 29.2 | 25.3 |
| | 32.7 | 29.3 | 25.8 | Operating Expenses | | | | 30.0 | 24.5 | 19.0 |
| | 2.0 | 4.9 | 6.5 | Operating Profit | | | | 6.2 | 4.8 | 6.3 |
| | .9 | .7 | .6 | All Other Expenses (net) | | | | .6 | .9 | .3 |
| | 1.1 | 4.2 | 5.9 | Profit Before Taxes | | | | 5.6 | 3.9 | 6.0 |
| | | | | RATIOS | | | | | | |
| | 2.7 | 2.5 | 2.1 | | | | | 2.2 | 1.9 | 2.3 |
| | 1.6 | 1.6 | 1.5 | Current | | | | 1.6 | 1.4 | 1.6 |
| | 1.1 | 1.1 | 1.1 | | | | | .9 | 1.0 | 1.4 |
| | 1.3 | 1.3 | 1.2 | | | | | 1.7 | 1.1 | 1.2 |
| | .7 | .7 | .7 | Quick | | | | .9 | .6 | 1.0 |
| | .4 | .5 | .4 | | | | | .5 | .4 | .5 |
| | 28  12.8 | 28  13.1 | 32  11.5 | | | | | 35  10.4 | 29  12.6 | 38  9.7 |
| | 39  9.5 | 42  8.8 | 42  8.7 | Sales/Receivables | | | | 45  8.1 | 39  9.4 | 45  8.1 |
| | 58  6.3 | 54  6.8 | 52  7.0 | | | | | 51  7.2 | 49  7.4 | 60  6.1 |
| | 55  6.6 | 46  7.9 | 46  8.0 | | | | | 48  7.6 | 51  7.2 | 37  9.8 |
| | 126  2.9 | 78  4.7 | 89  4.1 | Cost of Sales/Inventory | | | | 94  3.9 | 107  3.4 | 70  5.2 |
| | 189  1.9 | 141  2.6 | 130  2.8 | | | | | 159  2.3 | 126  2.9 | 89  4.1 |
| | 11  32.6 | 15  23.9 | 18  20.0 | | | | | 20  18.4 | 16  23.3 | 12  30.3 |
| | 24  15.1 | 30  12.0 | 31  11.7 | Cost of Sales/Payables | | | | 35  10.3 | 28  12.9 | 24  15.2 |
| | 50  7.4 | 52  7.0 | 61  6.0 | | | | | 85  4.3 | 52  7.0 | 33  10.9 |
| | 3.7 | 4.1 | 4.6 | | | | | 5.1 | 6.4 | 4.2 |
| | 6.5 | 8.2 | 10.2 | Sales/Working Capital | | | | 9.9 | 11.2 | 6.9 |
| | 44.2 | 45.1 | 33.5 | | | | | -25.2 | 33.5 | 17.7 |
| | 22.8 | 51.6 | 25.4 | | | | | 44.7 | 11.0 | 251.8 |
| | (58) 5.1 | (82) 8.2 | (54) 5.6 | EBIT/Interest | | | | (10) 7.6 | (22) 4.7 | (13) 33.1 |
| | .1 | 2.6 | 1.6 | | | | | 2.5 | 2.0 | 8.8 |
| | 14.3 | 8.4 | 9.5 | Net Profit + Depr., Dep., | | | | | | |
| | (13) 1.3 | (24) 2.6 | (18) 2.5 | Amort./Cur. Mat. L/T/D | | | | | | |
| | -.8 | .6 | 1.1 | | | | | | | |
| | .1 | .1 | .2 | | | | | .4 | .2 | .2 |
| | .4 | .4 | .5 | Fixed/Worth | | | | .9 | .6 | .4 |
| | 1.4 | .9 | 1.6 | | | | | 1.9 | 1.6 | 1.0 |
| | .6 | .7 | .7 | | | | | .7 | .9 | .7 |
| | 1.8 | 1.8 | 2.2 | Debt/Worth | | | | 2.1 | 2.2 | 1.3 |
| | 5.2 | 4.2 | 4.7 | | | | | 3.3 | 7.7 | 3.4 |
| | 27.9 | 49.4 | 50.2 | % Profit Before Taxes/Tangible | | | | 60.1 | 51.0 | 48.7 |
| | (59) 15.6 | (86) 23.4 | (66) 23.4 | Net Worth | | | | (13) 22.6 | (24) 22.1 | (17) 25.1 |
| | .9 | 8.8 | 10.9 | | | | | 11.5 | 7.8 | 18.0 |
| | 11.2 | 17.6 | 16.2 | % Profit Before Taxes/Total | | | | 17.2 | 14.7 | 22.2 |
| | 4.6 | 8.7 | 9.5 | Assets | | | | 9.0 | 7.2 | 11.8 |
| | -.4 | 2.1 | 2.2 | | | | | 2.8 | 2.2 | 7.5 |
| | 39.1 | 53.8 | 31.1 | | | | | 15.0 | 31.6 | 30.5 |
| | 15.3 | 19.9 | 15.1 | Sales/Net Fixed Assets | | | | 8.6 | 13.1 | 16.4 |
| | 7.7 | 9.1 | 8.5 | | | | | 3.9 | 8.0 | 9.4 |
| | 2.1 | 2.6 | 2.9 | | | | | 2.4 | 2.9 | 2.9 |
| | 1.7 | 1.9 | 1.7 | Sales/Total Assets | | | | 1.6 | 1.7 | 1.8 |
| | 1.2 | 1.3 | 1.3 | | | | | 1.2 | 1.3 | 1.6 |
| | .8 | .8 | .7 | | | | | 1.5 | .8 | .6 |
| | (60) 1.3 | (78) 1.4 | (64) 1.4 | % Depr., Dep., Amort./Sales | | | | (12) 2.3 | (24) 1.4 | (18) 1.0 |
| | 1.8 | 2.4 | 2.0 | | | | | 5.4 | 1.9 | 1.8 |
| | 2.2 | 2.5 | 2.0 | % Officers', Directors' | | | | | | |
| | (20) 4.2 | (30) 4.0 | (26) 3.4 | Owners' Comp/Sales | | | | | | |
| | 6.8 | 6.9 | 4.8 | | | | | | | |
| | 1534465M | 2189584M | 1806985M | Net Sales ($) | 977M | 14687M | 26788M | 102997M | 424471M | 1237065M |
| | 1031965M | 1460732M | 1088296M | Total Assets ($) | 221M | 10929M | 15768M | 62433M | 287664M | 711281M |

© RMA 2012

M = $ thousand     MM = $ million
See Pages 9 through 22 for Explanation of Ratios and Data

**Current Data Sorted by Assets**                                  **Comparative Historical Data**

| 0-500M | 500M-2MM | 2-10MM | 10-50MM | 50-100MM | 100-250MM | Type of Statement | 4/1/07-3/31/08 ALL | 4/1/08-3/31/09 ALL |
|---|---|---|---|---|---|---|---|---|
|  |  | 4 | 6 | 2 | 2 | Unqualified | 9 | 8 |
|  | 2 | 9 | 3 |  |  | Reviewed | 18 | 11 |
| 1 | 2 | 2 |  |  |  | Compiled | 5 | 9 |
|  | 2 | 4 |  |  |  | Tax Returns | 2 | 2 |
|  | 2 | 4 | 6 |  |  | Other | 13 | 13 |
| 10 (4/1-9/30/11) | | | 39 (10/1/11-3/31/12) | | | | | |
| 1 | 6 | 23 | 15 | 2 | 2 | **NUMBER OF STATEMENTS** | 47 | 43 |
| % | % | % | % | % | % | **ASSETS** | % | % |
|  |  | 15.4 | 15.4 |  |  | Cash & Equivalents | 13.9 | 11.9 |
|  |  | 35.8 | 29.9 |  |  | Trade Receivables (net) | 35.3 | 32.9 |
|  |  | 17.7 | 14.2 |  |  | Inventory | 15.3 | 20.5 |
|  |  | 5.7 | 9.7 |  |  | All Other Current | 8.2 | 6.0 |
|  |  | 74.6 | 69.2 |  |  | Total Current | 72.7 | 71.3 |
|  |  | 14.6 | 18.5 |  |  | Fixed Assets (net) | 16.3 | 15.4 |
|  |  | 1.1 | 7.7 |  |  | Intangibles (net) | 5.8 | 4.9 |
|  |  | 9.6 | 4.6 |  |  | All Other Non-Current | 5.2 | 8.5 |
|  |  | 100.0 | 100.0 |  |  | Total | 100.0 | 100.0 |
|  |  |  |  |  |  | **LIABILITIES** |  |  |
|  |  | 6.8 | 3.3 |  |  | Notes Payable-Short Term | 10.6 | 13.0 |
|  |  | 1.8 | 2.3 |  |  | Cur. Mat.-L.T.D. | 2.3 | 2.3 |
|  |  | 15.3 | 15.3 |  |  | Trade Payables | 17.2 | 19.0 |
|  |  | .1 | 1.6 |  |  | Income Taxes Payable | .7 | .2 |
|  |  | 27.7 | 28.0 |  |  | All Other Current | 21.3 | 22.8 |
|  |  | 51.8 | 50.5 |  |  | Total Current | 52.2 | 57.3 |
|  |  | 9.8 | 7.7 |  |  | Long-Term Debt | 8.0 | 8.7 |
|  |  | .1 | .6 |  |  | Deferred Taxes | .3 | .1 |
|  |  | 14.9 | 5.0 |  |  | All Other Non-Current | 5.9 | 6.0 |
|  |  | 23.3 | 36.2 |  |  | Net Worth | 33.7 | 28.0 |
|  |  | 100.0 | 100.0 |  |  | Total Liabilities & Net Worth | 100.0 | 100.0 |
|  |  |  |  |  |  | **INCOME DATA** |  |  |
|  |  | 100.0 | 100.0 |  |  | Net Sales | 100.0 | 100.0 |
|  |  | 28.2 | 32.7 |  |  | Gross Profit | 31.8 | 30.4 |
|  |  | 23.3 | 23.2 |  |  | Operating Expenses | 26.0 | 25.9 |
|  |  | 4.9 | 9.5 |  |  | Operating Profit | 5.8 | 4.5 |
|  |  | -.1 | .3 |  |  | All Other Expenses (net) | .6 | .7 |
|  |  | 5.0 | 9.2 |  |  | Profit Before Taxes | 5.3 | 3.8 |
|  |  |  |  |  |  | **RATIOS** |  |  |
|  |  | 2.2 | 1.9 |  |  |  | 2.1 | 2.2 |
|  |  | 1.3 | 1.3 |  |  | Current | 1.5 | 1.6 |
|  |  | 1.1 | 1.1 |  |  |  | 1.0 | 1.1 |
|  |  | 1.3 | 1.2 |  |  |  | 1.4 | 1.3 |
|  |  | .9 | .9 |  |  | Quick | 1.0 | .9 |
|  |  | .7 | .7 |  |  |  | .7 | .5 |
|  |  | 33  11.0 | 46  8.0 |  |  |  | 35  10.4 | 36  10.1 |
|  |  | 54  6.7 | 60  6.1 |  |  | Sales/Receivables | 53  6.9 | 53  6.9 |
|  |  | 70  5.2 | 79  4.6 |  |  |  | 66  5.5 | 68  5.4 |
|  |  | 18  20.3 | 20  18.1 |  |  |  | 7  49.9 | 7  50.9 |
|  |  | 30  12.3 | 29  12.4 |  |  | Cost of Sales/Inventory | 24  15.3 | 37  9.8 |
|  |  | 74  4.9 | 69  5.3 |  |  |  | 63  5.8 | 84  4.3 |
|  |  | 14  25.8 | 12  31.1 |  |  |  | 21  17.2 | 23  15.8 |
|  |  | 34  10.7 | 41  8.8 |  |  | Cost of Sales/Payables | 33  11.0 | 37  10.0 |
|  |  | 51  7.2 | 59  6.2 |  |  |  | 45  8.2 | 60  6.1 |
|  |  | 4.0 | 5.7 |  |  |  | 6.2 | 5.3 |
|  |  | 9.1 | 14.5 |  |  | Sales/Working Capital | 9.4 | 9.6 |
|  |  | 28.9 | 44.5 |  |  |  | 146.4 | 44.2 |
|  |  | 30.6 | 131.9 |  |  |  | 27.0 | 29.6 |
|  |  | (20)  4.9 | (14)  47.8 |  |  | EBIT/Interest | (43)  10.3 | (37)  3.6 |
|  |  | 1.2 | 4.9 |  |  |  | 1.9 | .7 |
|  |  |  |  |  |  |  | 18.6 | 116.3 |
|  |  |  |  |  |  | Net Profit + Depr., Dep., Amort./Cur. Mat. L/T/D | (10)  6.4 | (10)  3.7 |
|  |  |  |  |  |  |  | 2.5 | -3.1 |
|  |  | .2 | .3 |  |  |  | .2 | .2 |
|  |  | .5 | .7 |  |  | Fixed/Worth | .5 | .5 |
|  |  | 2.3 | 1.5 |  |  |  | 2.2 | 1.4 |
|  |  | .8 | 1.0 |  |  |  | 1.1 | 1.0 |
|  |  | 4.8 | 2.7 |  |  | Debt/Worth | 2.1 | 2.9 |
|  |  | 10.0 | 8.3 |  |  |  | 8.1 | 11.9 |
|  |  | 66.0 | 105.5 |  |  |  | 81.6 | 49.9 |
|  |  | (20)  30.8 | (13)  26.0 |  |  | % Profit Before Taxes/Tangible Net Worth | (40)  27.3 | (35)  28.3 |
|  |  | 1.5 | 20.5 |  |  |  | 5.8 | 5.4 |
|  |  | 21.1 | 27.1 |  |  |  | 16.9 | 15.8 |
|  |  | 3.5 | 13.0 |  |  | % Profit Before Taxes/Total Assets | 9.2 | 5.7 |
|  |  | .0 | 4.1 |  |  |  | 1.9 | .8 |
|  |  | 56.0 | 36.7 |  |  |  | 48.6 | 61.3 |
|  |  | 19.1 | 24.7 |  |  | Sales/Net Fixed Assets | 21.2 | 21.4 |
|  |  | 9.4 | 5.7 |  |  |  | 9.8 | 9.0 |
|  |  | 2.6 | 2.2 |  |  |  | 3.2 | 3.2 |
|  |  | 2.0 | 1.8 |  |  | Sales/Total Assets | 2.4 | 2.0 |
|  |  | 1.6 | 1.3 |  |  |  | 1.6 | 1.4 |
|  |  | .5 | .5 |  |  |  | .4 | .6 |
|  |  | (21)  .9 | (14)  .8 |  |  | % Depr., Dep., Amort./Sales | (40)  1.0 | (35)  1.3 |
|  |  | 1.9 | 3.1 |  |  |  | 2.2 | 2.2 |
|  |  |  |  |  |  |  | 2.3 | 1.9 |
|  |  |  |  |  |  | % Officers', Directors' Owners' Comp/Sales | (12)  3.5 | (12)  4.9 |
|  |  |  |  |  |  |  | 6.8 | 7.8 |
| 1858M | 22708M | 218570M | 540956M | 179582M | 497243M | Net Sales ($) | 1120977M | 1184984M |
| 471M | 8545M | 110358M | 319929M | 123323M | 388985M | Total Assets ($) | 565281M | 641046M |

© RMA 2012

M = $ thousand     MM = $ million
See Pages 9 through 22 for Explanation of Ratios and Data

| Comparative Historical Data | | | Type of Statement | Current Data Sorted by Sales | | | | | |
|---|---|---|---|---|---|---|---|---|---|
| | | | Unqualified | | | 1 | 2 | 3 | 8 |
| 8 | 14 | 14 | | 1 | 1 | 1 | 6 | 4 | 1 |
| 13 | 13 | 14 | Reviewed | | | 2 | 2 | | |
| 5 | 3 | 5 | Compiled | | | 1 | 5 | | |
| 2 | 7 | 6 | Tax Returns | | | 1 | 1 | 4 | 4 |
| 12 | 9 | 10 | Other | | | | | | |
| 4/1/09-3/31/10 | 4/1/10-3/31/11 | 4/1/11-3/31/12 | | | 10 (4/1-9/30/11) | | 39 (10/1/11-3/31/12) | | |
| ALL | ALL | ALL | | 0-1MM | 1-3MM | 3-5MM | 5-10MM | 10-25MM | 25MM & OVER |
| 40 | 46 | 49 | **NUMBER OF STATEMENTS** | 1 | 4 | 4 | 16 | 11 | 13 |
| % | % | % | **ASSETS** | % | % | % | % | % | % |
| 15.1 | 18.3 | 14.8 | Cash & Equivalents | | | | 15.9 | 10.1 | 14.9 |
| 29.3 | 32.5 | 34.2 | Trade Receivables (net) | | | | 37.5 | 39.0 | 30.6 |
| 20.3 | 17.7 | 18.0 | Inventory | | | | 18.1 | 15.2 | 17.3 |
| 4.9 | 5.0 | 5.9 | All Other Current | | | | 4.8 | 7.7 | 9.4 |
| 69.5 | 73.5 | 72.8 | Total Current | | | | 76.4 | 72.0 | 72.2 |
| 17.9 | 15.3 | 15.6 | Fixed Assets (net) | | | | 13.5 | 19.3 | 12.4 |
| 4.9 | 6.5 | 4.6 | Intangibles (net) | | | | 2.3 | 4.9 | 9.2 |
| 7.7 | 4.7 | 6.9 | All Other Non-Current | | | | 7.9 | 3.7 | 6.3 |
| 100.0 | 100.0 | 100.0 | Total | | | | 100.0 | 100.0 | 100.0 |
| | | | **LIABILITIES** | | | | | | |
| 12.2 | 9.9 | 5.6 | Notes Payable-Short Term | | | | 6.1 | 4.1 | 4.8 |
| 4.0 | 3.2 | 1.8 | Cur. Mat.-L.T.D. | | | | 1.5 | 2.1 | 2.3 |
| 12.3 | 14.4 | 14.9 | Trade Payables | | | | 17.7 | 15.8 | 15.7 |
| .9 | .4 | .7 | Income Taxes Payable | | | | .2 | .4 | 2.0 |
| 20.3 | 27.6 | 27.0 | All Other Current | | | | 27.7 | 30.9 | 29.3 |
| 49.7 | 55.5 | 50.1 | Total Current | | | | 53.2 | 53.2 | 54.1 |
| 11.3 | 13.3 | 9.6 | Long-Term Debt | | | | 11.4 | 6.6 | 9.1 |
| .2 | .3 | .4 | Deferred Taxes | | | | .1 | .3 | 1.1 |
| 7.0 | 6.4 | 9.4 | All Other Non-Current | | | | 6.5 | 13.7 | 6.9 |
| 31.8 | 24.5 | 30.5 | Net Worth | | | | 28.8 | 26.2 | 28.8 |
| 100.0 | 100.0 | 100.0 | Total Liabilities & Net Worth | | | | 100.0 | 100.0 | 100.0 |
| | | | **INCOME DATA** | | | | | | |
| 100.0 | 100.0 | 100.0 | Net Sales | | | | 100.0 | 100.0 | 100.0 |
| 30.1 | 34.0 | 30.9 | Gross Profit | | | | 27.5 | 25.9 | 34.5 |
| 26.1 | 27.4 | 24.0 | Operating Expenses | | | | 24.1 | 17.5 | 26.1 |
| 4.0 | 6.7 | 6.9 | Operating Profit | | | | 3.5 | 8.3 | 8.3 |
| 1.4 | .4 | .4 | All Other Expenses (net) | | | | -.3 | .2 | 1.6 |
| 2.7 | 6.3 | 6.4 | Profit Before Taxes | | | | 3.8 | 8.1 | 6.7 |
| | | | **RATIOS** | | | | | | |
| 2.0 | 2.4 | 2.1 | | | | | 2.1 | 2.3 | 1.8 |
| 1.5 | 1.7 | 1.4 | Current | | | | 1.3 | 1.2 | 1.3 |
| 1.1 | 1.1 | 1.1 | | | | | 1.1 | 1.1 | 1.1 |
| 1.4 | 1.9 | 1.3 | | | | | 1.4 | 1.3 | 1.2 |
| .9 | 1.1 | .9 | Quick | | | | .9 | .9 | .8 |
| .6 | .7 | .7 | | | | | .5 | .8 | .6 |
| 38  9.6 | 42  8.7 | 43  8.4 | | | | | 27  13.4 | 46  8.0 | 53  6.9 |
| 50  7.2 | 57  6.5 | 57  6.4 | Sales/Receivables | | | | 56  6.5 | 57  6.4 | 63  5.8 |
| 71  5.1 | 75  4.9 | 73  5.0 | | | | | 70  5.2 | 99  3.7 | 79  4.6 |
| 10  35.9 | 18  20.3 | 20  18.4 | | | | | 17  21.4 | 18  20.3 | 28  13.0 |
| 37  9.8 | 47  7.8 | 38  9.7 | Cost of Sales/Inventory | | | | 33  11.0 | 28  12.9 | 51  7.2 |
| 101  3.6 | 81  4.5 | 73  5.0 | | | | | 69  5.3 | 72  5.1 | 70  5.2 |
| 18  19.9 | 17  21.3 | 19  19.1 | | | | | 15  24.7 | 24  15.3 | 22  16.6 |
| 30  12.0 | 39  9.4 | 34  10.6 | Cost of Sales/Payables | | | | 35  10.4 | 34  10.6 | 41  8.8 |
| 43  8.5 | 59  6.2 | 46  8.0 | | | | | 52  7.0 | 41  8.8 | 64  5.7 |
| 4.4 | 3.9 | 5.5 | | | | | 5.6 | 4.2 | 6.6 |
| 10.9 | 7.5 | 9.3 | Sales/Working Capital | | | | 15.6 | 15.5 | 9.9 |
| 56.1 | 48.5 | 28.6 | | | | | 27.2 | 44.5 | NM |
| 15.7 | 25.1 | 91.5 | | | | | 35.1 | 141.9 | 189.5 |
| (37)  3.2 | (39)  6.8 | (44)  12.4 | EBIT/Interest | | | | (14)  5.2 | 52.0 | (12)  9.7 |
| .8 | 2.1 | 2.5 | | | | | 1.9 | 12.2 | 3.3 |
| 5.3 | | 4.2 | Net Profit + Depr., Dep., | | | | | | |
| (11)  2.3 | | (11)  1.6 | Amort./Cur. Mat. L/T/D | | | | | | |
| -10.5 | | .7 | | | | | | | |
| .2 | .1 | .2 | | | | | .2 | .4 | .1 |
| .7 | .4 | .5 | Fixed/Worth | | | | .4 | .6 | .4 |
| 1.4 | 1.8 | 1.4 | | | | | 1.9 | .7 | NM |
| .9 | 1.0 | .9 | | | | | 1.2 | .8 | 1.2 |
| 2.7 | 2.9 | 2.7 | Debt/Worth | | | | 4.5 | 2.7 | 2.7 |
| 8.7 | 8.7 | 8.3 | | | | | 8.9 | 8.3 | NM |
| 62.5 | 59.7 | 66.9 | | | | | 43.6 | 77.0 | 174.4 |
| (37)  10.0 | (39)  24.4 | (43)  26.0 | % Profit Before Taxes/Tangible Net Worth | | | | (15)  12.9 | (10)  65.1 | (10)  34.5 |
| .2 | 10.4 | 9.4 | | | | | .9 | 25.1 | 18.8 |
| 10.7 | 19.6 | 21.3 | | | | | 9.3 | 25.9 | 20.9 |
| 2.3 | 9.3 | 5.5 | % Profit Before Taxes/Total Assets | | | | 2.3 | 17.3 | 13.0 |
| .0 | 2.1 | 1.5 | | | | | .2 | 3.7 | 3.0 |
| 43.3 | 67.2 | 55.1 | | | | | 153.7 | 36.8 | 52.9 |
| 13.7 | 15.7 | 22.4 | Sales/Net Fixed Assets | | | | 26.4 | 19.0 | 34.0 |
| 5.7 | 9.8 | 8.1 | | | | | 10.1 | 5.5 | 9.1 |
| 2.8 | 3.1 | 2.6 | | | | | 2.8 | 2.7 | 2.3 |
| 1.9 | 1.8 | 1.9 | Sales/Total Assets | | | | 2.2 | 1.9 | 1.8 |
| 1.1 | 1.3 | 1.5 | | | | | 1.6 | 1.7 | 1.4 |
| .7 | .7 | .5 | | | | | .5 | .4 | .5 |
| (36)  1.0 | (36)  1.3 | (45)  .9 | % Depr., Dep., Amort./Sales | | | | (13)  .8 | .7 | (12)  1.3 |
| 2.7 | 2.8 | 2.0 | | | | | 1.7 | 2.3 | 3.2 |
| 1.6 | 2.0 | 2.1 | % Officers', Directors' | | | | | | |
| (13)  4.9 | (12)  2.7 | (12)  3.1 | Owners' Comp/Sales | | | | | | |
| 6.1 | 5.4 | 6.5 | | | | | | | |
| 866085M | 1158252M | 1460917M | Net Sales ($) | 945M | 10295M | 16288M | 115809M | 211716M | 1105864M |
| 545403M | 694442M | 951611M | Total Assets ($) | 749M | 6359M | 18119M | 60990M | 112346M | 753048M |

© RMA 2012          M = $ thousand    MM = $ million
See Pages 9 through 22 for Explanation of Ratios and Data

## Current Data Sorted by Assets      Comparative Historical Data

| Type of Statement | 0-500M | 500M-2MM | 2-10MM | 10-50MM | 50-100MM | 100-250MM | | 4/1/07-3/31/08 ALL | 4/1/08-3/31/09 ALL |
|---|---|---|---|---|---|---|---|---|---|
| Unqualified | 1 | 5 | 38 | 19 | 9 | 2 | | 51 | 62 |
| Reviewed | 3 | 8 | 19 | 11 | 4 | | | 54 | 76 |
| Compiled | 9 | 15 | 11 | | | | | 31 | 63 |
| Tax Returns | | | | | | | | 21 | 46 |
| Other | 8 | 15 | 27 | 25 | 7 | 5 | | 75 | 122 |
| | 42 (4/1-9/30/11) | | | 204 (10/1/11-3/31/12) | | | | | |
| NUMBER OF STATEMENTS | 21 | 43 | 100 | 59 | 16 | 7 | | 232 | 369 |
| | % | % | % | % | % | % | | % | % |
| **ASSETS** | | | | | | | | | |
| Cash & Equivalents | 15.9 | 9.8 | 12.3 | 11.1 | 7.2 | | | 8.6 | 9.9 |
| Trade Receivables (net) | 23.1 | 29.3 | 29.2 | 22.1 | 26.9 | | | 29.6 | 25.7 |
| Inventory | 27.0 | 27.9 | 24.8 | 25.8 | 18.5 | | | 24.4 | 22.7 |
| All Other Current | .9 | 3.7 | 4.3 | 4.2 | 8.8 | | | 4.0 | 3.9 |
| Total Current | 66.9 | 70.8 | 70.7 | 63.2 | 61.3 | | | 66.5 | 62.2 |
| Fixed Assets (net) | 15.5 | 19.2 | 21.1 | 16.0 | 17.8 | | | 24.5 | 27.0 |
| Intangibles (net) | 3.3 | 3.0 | 3.7 | 13.7 | 16.4 | | | 4.0 | 4.9 |
| All Other Non-Current | 14.3 | 7.0 | 4.5 | 7.2 | 4.4 | | | 5.0 | 5.9 |
| Total | 100.0 | 100.0 | 100.0 | 100.0 | 100.0 | | | 100.0 | 100.0 |
| **LIABILITIES** | | | | | | | | | |
| Notes Payable-Short Term | 24.3 | 12.1 | 9.5 | 8.1 | 8.1 | | | 11.6 | 10.6 |
| Cur. Mat.-L.T.D. | .9 | 3.9 | 2.7 | 3.4 | 3.2 | | | 3.5 | 4.4 |
| Trade Payables | 15.0 | 15.6 | 13.7 | 11.4 | 14.3 | | | 15.3 | 12.1 |
| Income Taxes Payable | .1 | .2 | .5 | .1 | .7 | | | .4 | .3 |
| All Other Current | 20.5 | 10.3 | 14.9 | 15.2 | 18.7 | | | 12.9 | 11.9 |
| Total Current | 60.7 | 42.0 | 41.4 | 38.2 | 45.0 | | | 43.7 | 39.4 |
| Long-Term Debt | 7.5 | 10.9 | 10.2 | 11.3 | 8.2 | | | 16.4 | 17.0 |
| Deferred Taxes | .0 | .0 | .7 | .7 | .6 | | | .4 | .6 |
| All Other Non-Current | 25.0 | 12.0 | 4.7 | 7.5 | 4.7 | | | 6.1 | 5.6 |
| Net Worth | 6.8 | 34.9 | 43.0 | 42.3 | 41.5 | | | 33.5 | 37.3 |
| Total Liabilities & Net Worth | 100.0 | 100.0 | 100.0 | 100.0 | 100.0 | | | 100.0 | 100.0 |
| **INCOME DATA** | | | | | | | | | |
| Net Sales | 100.0 | 100.0 | 100.0 | 100.0 | 100.0 | | | 100.0 | 100.0 |
| Gross Profit | 37.2 | 37.7 | 31.6 | 33.5 | 28.1 | | | 32.8 | 32.3 |
| Operating Expenses | 29.6 | 33.7 | 26.0 | 25.5 | 18.9 | | | 26.6 | 25.8 |
| Operating Profit | 7.6 | 3.9 | 5.6 | 8.0 | 9.2 | | | 6.2 | 6.4 |
| All Other Expenses (net) | .8 | .7 | .4 | 1.2 | 1.3 | | | 1.2 | 1.2 |
| Profit Before Taxes | 6.8 | 3.3 | 5.2 | 6.8 | 7.9 | | | 5.0 | 5.2 |
| **RATIOS** | | | | | | | | | |
| Current | 5.9 | 3.3 | 3.2 | 2.8 | 1.8 | | | 2.2 | 2.8 |
| | 1.6 | 1.7 | 1.7 | 1.7 | 1.3 | | | 1.6 | 1.6 |
| | .4 | 1.0 | 1.2 | 1.2 | 1.1 | | | 1.1 | 1.1 |
| Quick | 2.3 | 1.5 | 1.7 | 1.5 | 1.1 | | | 1.4 | 1.6 |
| | .8 | .9 | 1.0 | .9 | .6 | | | .8 | .9 |
| | .3 | .5 | .6 | .5 | .5 | | | .6 | .5 |
| Sales/Receivables | 3 140.0 | 23 15.7 | 33 11.1 | 38 9.5 | 39 9.3 | | | 36 10.1 | 31 11.7 |
| | 34 10.6 | 36 10.1 | 49 7.5 | 51 7.2 | 69 5.3 | | | 48 7.6 | 44 8.3 |
| | 55 6.6 | 54 6.8 | 60 6.1 | 66 5.5 | 96 3.8 | | | 63 5.8 | 58 6.3 |
| Cost of Sales/Inventory | 0 UND | 16 22.6 | 28 13.1 | 49 7.5 | 12 31.6 | | | 22 16.8 | 20 18.3 |
| | 16 22.5 | 62 5.9 | 63 5.8 | 94 3.9 | 62 5.9 | | | 58 6.3 | 55 6.7 |
| | 146 2.5 | 111 3.3 | 104 3.5 | 130 2.8 | 126 2.9 | | | 92 4.0 | 99 3.7 |
| Cost of Sales/Payables | 0 933.9 | 11 34.0 | 19 19.0 | 24 14.9 | 26 14.3 | | | 21 17.7 | 14 26.7 |
| | 13 28.5 | 22 16.9 | 31 11.8 | 34 10.8 | 41 8.9 | | | 30 12.2 | 24 15.2 |
| | 38 9.5 | 54 6.8 | 47 7.7 | 47 7.8 | 54 6.7 | | | 53 6.9 | 44 8.3 |
| Sales/Working Capital | 5.0 | 4.2 | 4.1 | 3.3 | 4.0 | | | 4.9 | 4.6 |
| | 12.6 | 8.1 | 7.6 | 5.9 | 10.4 | | | 10.0 | 8.8 |
| | -11.3 | 137.9 | 19.7 | 17.0 | 69.7 | | | 26.5 | 45.1 |
| EBIT/Interest | 28.4 | 25.2 | 35.4 | 22.4 | 24.6 | | | 10.7 | 15.3 |
| | (13) 6.2 | (39) 5.3 | (89) 10.3 | (49) 6.5 | (13) 4.9 | | | (209) 4.0 | (337) 4.8 |
| | 2.8 | 1.2 | 3.6 | 2.0 | 2.8 | | | 1.6 | 1.6 |
| Net Profit + Depr., Dep., Amort./Cur. Mat. L/T/D | | | 8.5 | 11.8 | | | | 11.9 | 7.5 |
| | | | (32) 5.3 | (20) 7.1 | | | | (60) 3.5 | (103) 2.5 |
| | | | 2.7 | 1.7 | | | | 1.2 | 1.4 |
| Fixed/Worth | .0 | .1 | .2 | .2 | .2 | | | .3 | .3 |
| | .3 | .6 | .5 | .4 | .7 | | | .7 | .7 |
| | -3.7 | 1.7 | .9 | 2.9 | NM | | | 3.0 | 2.4 |
| Debt/Worth | .5 | .6 | .6 | .7 | .9 | | | .9 | .7 |
| | 24.0 | 1.8 | 1.4 | 1.5 | 1.7 | | | 2.1 | 1.7 |
| | -4.9 | 6.4 | 3.6 | 20.8 | NM | | | 8.5 | 6.0 |
| % Profit Before Taxes/Tangible Net Worth | 230.3 | 46.2 | 48.8 | 60.2 | 46.5 | | | 59.1 | 54.3 |
| | (11) 49.2 | (39) 21.8 | (90) 27.8 | (48) 26.0 | (12) 27.1 | | | (201) 26.1 | (311) 25.5 |
| | 8.7 | 11.6 | 10.4 | 10.5 | 14.0 | | | 9.9 | 10.1 |
| % Profit Before Taxes/Total Assets | 43.1 | 14.5 | 17.9 | 16.2 | 19.9 | | | 17.0 | 17.6 |
| | 21.9 | 9.9 | 9.7 | 8.5 | 8.6 | | | 8.7 | 8.3 |
| | 2.6 | 1.9 | 3.8 | 1.2 | 4.6 | | | 2.9 | 2.5 |
| Sales/Net Fixed Assets | UND | 65.6 | 24.9 | 23.5 | 14.5 | | | 25.0 | 21.5 |
| | 39.7 | 16.1 | 10.2 | 10.3 | 10.0 | | | 10.4 | 8.8 |
| | 13.7 | 9.2 | 5.5 | 6.4 | 6.3 | | | 5.2 | 4.6 |
| Sales/Total Assets | 6.2 | 3.6 | 2.6 | 1.9 | 1.9 | | | 2.8 | 2.7 |
| | 3.5 | 2.5 | 2.0 | 1.4 | 1.5 | | | 2.1 | 2.0 |
| | 1.8 | 1.8 | 1.5 | 1.1 | 1.1 | | | 1.6 | 1.5 |
| % Depr., Dep., Amort./Sales | .8 | .5 | .8 | 1.0 | .8 | | | .9 | 1.2 |
| | (11) 1.6 | (31) 1.4 | (85) 1.6 | (55) 1.8 | (15) 1.5 | | | (206) 1.8 | (322) 2.3 |
| | 2.3 | 3.2 | 2.4 | 2.8 | 3.3 | | | 3.5 | 4.2 |
| % Officers', Directors', Owners' Comp/Sales | | 2.9 | 2.7 | | | | | 3.1 | 2.2 |
| | | (26) 4.8 | (39) 4.1 | | | | | (80) 4.5 | (139) 4.4 |
| | | 7.7 | 5.8 | | | | | 6.8 | 7.4 |
| Net Sales ($) | 21375M | 150712M | 1143945M | 2015460M | 1782415M | 1129903M | | 6968061M | 9479556M |
| Total Assets ($) | 5391M | 55375M | 551109M | 1325551M | 1175970M | 1027247M | | 4012450M | 5853905M |

M = $ thousand    MM = $ million
See Pages 9 through 22 for Explanation of Ratios and Data

## Comparative Historical Data | Current Data Sorted by Sales

| Hist 1 | Hist 2 | Hist 3 | Type of Statement | 0-1MM | 1-3MM | 3-5MM | 5-10MM | 10-25MM | 25MM & OVER |
|---|---|---|---|---|---|---|---|---|---|
| 37 | 37 | 35 | Unqualified | 1 | 2 | 5 | 1 | 8 | 26 |
| 58 | 60 | 55 | Reviewed |  | 9 | 3 | 13 | 30 | 4 |
| 39 | 39 | 34 | Compiled | 1 |  |  | 11 | 9 | 1 |
| 34 | 44 | 35 | Tax Returns | 7 | 10 | 10 | 6 | 2 |  |
| 86 | 88 | 87 | Other | 5 | 11 | 6 | 13 | 27 | 25 |
| 4/1/09-3/31/10 ALL | 4/1/10-3/31/11 ALL | 4/1/11-3/31/12 ALL | | 42 (4/1-9/30/11) | | | 204 (10/1/11-3/31/12) | | |
| 254 | 268 | 246 | NUMBER OF STATEMENTS | 14 | 32 | 24 | 44 | 76 | 56 |
| % | % | % | **ASSETS** | % | % | % | % | % | % |
| 10.5 | 11.4 | 11.4 | Cash & Equivalents | 11.6 | 15.0 | 8.3 | 13.4 | 11.7 | 8.9 |
| 23.8 | 26.7 | 26.7 | Trade Receivables (net) | 21.3 | 22.3 | 28.4 | 29.1 | 27.3 | 27.0 |
| 24.2 | 24.0 | 25.3 | Inventory | 38.1 | 20.9 | 33.7 | 20.7 | 25.9 | 23.6 |
| 4.8 | 5.0 | 4.3 | All Other Current | 2.3 | 2.9 | 5.3 | 4.4 | 3.3 | 6.4 |
| 63.4 | 67.1 | 67.7 | Total Current | 73.2 | 61.1 | 75.7 | 67.5 | 68.3 | 65.9 |
| 24.5 | 21.4 | 18.7 | Fixed Assets (net) | 9.3 | 23.5 | 19.8 | 22.8 | 17.6 | 16.0 |
| 5.8 | 5.3 | 7.2 | Intangibles (net) | 3.0 | 5.7 | 1.5 | 2.3 | 9.3 | 12.5 |
| 6.4 | 6.1 | 6.5 | All Other Non-Current | 14.5 | 9.7 | 3.0 | 7.5 | 4.8 | 5.6 |
| 100.0 | 100.0 | 100.0 | Total | 100.0 | 100.0 | 100.0 | 100.0 | 100.0 | 100.0 |
| | | | **LIABILITIES** | | | | | | |
| 11.7 | 9.3 | 10.6 | Notes Payable-Short Term | 17.8 | 16.5 | 13.3 | 9.6 | 9.1 | 6.9 |
| 3.4 | 3.9 | 3.0 | Cur. Mat.-L.T.D. | 1.1 | 3.0 | 5.3 | 1.9 | 2.9 | 3.6 |
| 12.9 | 13.4 | 13.6 | Trade Payables | 15.8 | 10.9 | 13.4 | 14.3 | 13.3 | 14.6 |
| .3 | .3 | .3 | Income Taxes Payable | .1 | .1 | .2 | .7 | .3 | .3 |
| 14.2 | 13.5 | 14.9 | All Other Current | 14.8 | 13.1 | 11.9 | 15.6 | 14.8 | 16.8 |
| 42.4 | 40.4 | 42.4 | Total Current | 49.6 | 43.6 | 44.1 | 42.1 | 40.4 | 42.2 |
| 15.2 | 13.0 | 10.4 | Long-Term Debt | 3.7 | 13.4 | 11.6 | 13.3 | 7.3 | 11.6 |
| .5 | .5 | .5 | Deferred Taxes | .0 | .0 | .3 | .5 | .7 | .9 |
| 8.8 | 10.0 | 8.5 | All Other Non-Current | 38.9 | 10.3 | 10.6 | 3.9 | 6.2 | 5.5 |
| 33.0 | 36.1 | 38.2 | Net Worth | 7.8 | 32.7 | 33.3 | 40.2 | 45.4 | 39.8 |
| 100.0 | 100.0 | 100.0 | Total Liabilities & Net Worth | 100.0 | 100.0 | 100.0 | 100.0 | 100.0 | 100.0 |
| | | | **INCOME DATA** | | | | | | |
| 100.0 | 100.0 | 100.0 | Net Sales | 100.0 | 100.0 | 100.0 | 100.0 | 100.0 | 100.0 |
| 31.4 | 35.0 | 33.3 | Gross Profit | 43.1 | 39.1 | 31.2 | 31.9 | 32.7 | 30.3 |
| 28.6 | 27.9 | 27.0 | Operating Expenses | 33.2 | 36.4 | 28.0 | 25.9 | 25.5 | 22.5 |
| 2.8 | 7.1 | 6.3 | Operating Profit | 10.0 | 2.7 | 3.3 | 6.0 | 7.3 | 7.7 |
| 1.4 | 1.1 | .8 | All Other Expenses (net) | 1.5 | .9 | .1 | .2 | .7 | 1.2 |
| 1.5 | 6.0 | 5.6 | Profit Before Taxes | 8.5 | 1.8 | 3.2 | 5.8 | 6.5 | 6.5 |
| | | | **RATIOS** | | | | | | |
| 3.2 | 3.2 | 3.0 | Current | 6.7 | 5.1 | 2.8 | 3.2 | 3.2 | 2.2 |
| 1.6 | 1.8 | 1.7 | | 2.4 | 2.0 | 1.7 | 1.4 | 1.8 | 1.6 |
| 1.0 | 1.2 | 1.1 | | .7 | .9 | 1.1 | 1.1 | 1.2 | 1.2 |
| 1.9 | 1.8 | 1.6 | Quick | 1.7 | 3.1 | 1.4 | 1.8 | 1.6 | 1.3 |
| .8 | 1.0 | .9 | | .7 | 1.0 | .6 | 1.0 | 1.0 | .8 |
| .5 | .6 | .5 | | .3 | .4 | .5 | .7 | .6 | .5 |
| 29  12.4 | 34  10.8 | 33  11.1 | Sales/Receivables | 22  16.3 | 16  23.5 | 27  13.3 | 33  11.1 | 36  10.1 | 40  9.2 |
| 43  8.4 | 48  7.5 | 49  7.5 | | 42  8.6 | 34  10.8 | 42  8.6 | 40  9.2 | 53  6.9 | 54  6.7 |
| 58  6.3 | 66  5.6 | 63  5.8 | | 57  6.4 | 51  7.1 | 57  6.4 | 58  6.3 | 62  5.9 | 78  4.7 |
| 26  13.9 | 25  14.7 | 28  13.0 | Cost of Sales/Inventory | 12  29.9 | 2  163.2 | 24  15.1 | 9  42.9 | 44  8.3 | 33  10.9 |
| 62  5.9 | 64  5.7 | 72  5.1 | | 146  2.5 | 43  8.5 | 83  4.4 | 46  8.0 | 81  4.5 | 72  5.1 |
| 121  3.0 | 116  3.1 | 118  3.1 | | 406  .9 | 94  3.9 | 135  2.7 | 89  4.1 | 122  3.0 | 114  3.2 |
| 16  23.5 | 18  19.9 | 19  19.6 | Cost of Sales/Payables | 8  43.1 | 2  159.2 | 20  18.3 | 16  22.3 | 21  17.8 | 25  14.5 |
| 27  13.7 | 32  11.2 | 30  12.1 | | 28  13.0 | 11  33.6 | 32  11.5 | 26  14.0 | 31  11.6 | 39  9.3 |
| 44  8.3 | 50  7.3 | 50  7.3 | | 85  4.3 | 39  9.3 | 45  8.1 | 49  7.4 | 47  7.7 | 51  7.1 |
| 4.0 | 3.6 | 3.8 | Sales/Working Capital | 2.1 | 3.8 | 4.1 | 4.7 | 3.5 | 3.6 |
| 9.0 | 6.8 | 7.8 | | 8.7 | 8.1 | 6.8 | 10.2 | 7.5 | 6.1 |
| 264.5 | 21.5 | 32.7 | | -11.0 | -38.4 | 34.2 | 63.8 | 15.8 | 20.0 |
| 8.2 | 15.7 | 24.8 | EBIT/Interest | | 24.6 | 11.0 | 43.1 | 26.3 | 21.7 |
| (227) 2.5 | (230) 5.5 | (210) 7.3 | | | (25) 4.7 | (23) 5.1 | (41) 12.5 | (64) 10.8 | (48) 5.3 |
| -.4 | 1.5 | 2.4 | | | .3 | 1.2 | 3.6 | 4.5 | 2.3 |
| 5.3 | 8.8 | 9.2 | Net Profit + Depr., Dep., Amort./Cur. Mat. L/T/D | | | | 9.0 | 10.4 | 11.5 |
| (53) 1.8 | (56) 3.8 | (70) 4.8 | | | | (12) 5.6 | (25) 5.5 | (27) 4.1 | |
| .9 | 1.8 | 1.9 | | | | 2.9 | 2.4 | 1.5 | |
| .2 | .2 | .2 | Fixed/Worth | .0 | .2 | .1 | .2 | .2 | .2 |
| .7 | .5 | .5 | | .1 | .7 | .6 | .5 | .4 | .6 |
| 4.0 | 2.1 | 1.7 | | NM | 4.2 | 1.6 | 1.7 | .9 | 2.5 |
| .6 | .6 | .7 | Debt/Worth | .5 | .4 | .8 | .5 | .6 | .9 |
| 2.1 | 1.6 | 1.6 | | 14.7 | 1.3 | 1.7 | 2.0 | 1.4 | 2.1 |
| 18.4 | 9.0 | 8.1 | | -5.4 | NM | 4.1 | 4.4 | 4.5 | 17.3 |
| 37.1 | 48.5 | 49.2 | % Profit Before Taxes/Tangible Net Worth | | 47.8 | 26.7 | 45.5 | 51.0 | 62.1 |
| (203) 14.5 | (218) 22.6 | (207) 25.6 | | | (24) 24.3 | (22) 13.6 | (40) 26.6 | (66) 33.6 | (47) 27.5 |
| -.5 | 6.6 | 10.4 | | | .8 | 1.8 | 12.0 | 15.6 | 10.7 |
| 11.7 | 19.0 | 18.2 | % Profit Before Taxes/Total Assets | 28.7 | 26.2 | 13.7 | 15.4 | 19.2 | 16.3 |
| 3.9 | 7.5 | 9.0 | | 10.8 | 11.0 | 5.1 | 8.8 | 10.7 | 8.6 |
| -2.6 | 1.9 | 2.4 | | 1.9 | -.4 | .6 | 4.3 | 4.5 | 2.5 |
| 25.0 | 28.6 | 30.3 | Sales/Net Fixed Assets | UND | 44.5 | 47.4 | 28.8 | 25.9 | 21.0 |
| 9.9 | 11.4 | 12.8 | | 295.1 | 14.3 | 13.3 | 10.1 | 12.6 | 10.9 |
| 4.4 | 5.4 | 6.6 | | 10.3 | 6.3 | 7.5 | 4.6 | 6.7 | 6.7 |
| 2.5 | 2.4 | 2.6 | Sales/Total Assets | 2.6 | 3.7 | 2.7 | 3.3 | 2.4 | 2.0 |
| 1.8 | 1.7 | 1.9 | | 1.8 | 2.4 | 1.9 | 2.2 | 1.8 | 1.6 |
| 1.2 | 1.3 | 1.4 | | 1.0 | 1.4 | 1.7 | 1.5 | 1.4 | 1.2 |
| 1.0 | 1.1 | 1.0 | % Depr., Dep., Amort./Sales | | .8 | .8 | .7 | .9 | 1.0 |
| (216) 2.3 | (221) 2.0 | (204) 1.6 | | | (23) 2.1 | (18) 1.2 | (35) 1.4 | (69) 1.8 | (52) 1.4 |
| 4.3 | 3.6 | 2.8 | | | 4.2 | 2.2 | 2.3 | 2.9 | 2.6 |
| 2.5 | 2.2 | 2.5 | % Officers', Directors', Owners' Comp/Sales | | 3.2 | 2.7 | 3.3 | 2.2 | |
| (86) 4.9 | (100) 4.9 | (81) 4.1 | | | (17) 4.6 | (15) 4.8 | (17) 4.4 | (24) 3.3 | |
| 7.6 | 8.2 | 6.5 | | | 6.9 | 7.2 | 6.8 | 4.9 | |
| 5313990M | 5472542M | 6243810M | Net Sales ($) | 7279M | 63253M | 98042M | 328037M | 1261585M | 4485614M |
| 3509307M | 3759169M | 4140643M | Total Assets ($) | 4524M | 32959M | 49595M | 180652M | 831782M | 3041131M |

## Current Data Sorted by Assets     Comparative Historical Data

| 0-500M | 500M-2MM | 2-10MM | 10-50MM | 50-100MM | 100-250MM | Type of Statement | 4/1/07-3/31/08 ALL | 4/1/08-3/31/09 ALL |
|---|---|---|---|---|---|---|---|---|
| | | 1 | 5 | 1 | 2 | Unqualified | 19 | 15 |
| | 1 | 8 | 1 | | | Reviewed | 4 | 12 |
| | 1 | 7 | 1 | | | Compiled | 5 | 3 |
| 4 | 6 | 6 | | | | Tax Returns | 10 | 12 |
| 5 | 8 | 17 | 9 | 2 | | Other | 27 | 27 |
| | 15 (4/1-9/30/11) | | 70 (10/1/11-3/31/12) | | | | | |
| 9 | 16 | 39 | 16 | 3 | 2 | **NUMBER OF STATEMENTS** | 65 | 69 |
| % | % | % | % | % | % | **ASSETS** | % | % |
| | 19.6 | 15.9 | 7.0 | | | Cash & Equivalents | 14.4 | 14.7 |
| | 31.3 | 30.1 | 31.1 | | | Trade Receivables (net) | 30.9 | 26.5 |
| | 19.8 | 27.4 | 35.8 | | | Inventory | 23.2 | 26.8 |
| | 1.7 | 3.3 | 1.5 | | | All Other Current | 3.2 | 5.3 |
| | 72.3 | 76.7 | 75.4 | | | Total Current | 71.7 | 73.3 |
| | 17.7 | 12.7 | 13.2 | | | Fixed Assets (net) | 12.8 | 14.7 |
| | 3.7 | 2.5 | 3.5 | | | Intangibles (net) | 9.0 | 5.0 |
| | 6.3 | 8.1 | 7.9 | | | All Other Non-Current | 6.5 | 7.1 |
| | 100.0 | 100.0 | 100.0 | | | Total | 100.0 | 100.0 |
| | | | | | | **LIABILITIES** | | |
| | 10.3 | 10.1 | 11.0 | | | Notes Payable-Short Term | 11.2 | 14.7 |
| | 2.4 | 2.1 | 2.7 | | | Cur. Mat.-L.T.D. | 2.2 | 2.9 |
| | 17.0 | 16.8 | 18.8 | | | Trade Payables | 19.1 | 16.5 |
| | 1.0 | .0 | .4 | | | Income Taxes Payable | .2 | .2 |
| | 13.7 | 12.5 | 8.9 | | | All Other Current | 12.1 | 9.1 |
| | 44.3 | 41.5 | 41.8 | | | Total Current | 44.8 | 43.5 |
| | 12.6 | 8.5 | 6.2 | | | Long-Term Debt | 9.2 | 9.2 |
| | .0 | .0 | .9 | | | Deferred Taxes | .1 | .2 |
| | 19.1 | 13.4 | 2.6 | | | All Other Non-Current | 8.7 | 6.1 |
| | 24.0 | 36.6 | 48.5 | | | Net Worth | 37.1 | 41.0 |
| | 100.0 | 100.0 | 100.0 | | | Total Liabilities & Net Worth | 100.0 | 100.0 |
| | | | | | | **INCOME DATA** | | |
| | 100.0 | 100.0 | 100.0 | | | Net Sales | 100.0 | 100.0 |
| | 46.8 | 38.2 | 24.6 | | | Gross Profit | 34.8 | 34.1 |
| | 42.7 | 32.9 | 19.9 | | | Operating Expenses | 29.7 | 31.3 |
| | 4.2 | 5.2 | 4.8 | | | Operating Profit | 5.1 | 2.8 |
| | .3 | 1.2 | .1 | | | All Other Expenses (net) | .1 | 1.2 |
| | 3.8 | 4.0 | 4.6 | | | Profit Before Taxes | 5.0 | 1.6 |
| | | | | | | **RATIOS** | | |
| | 4.0 | 3.8 | 2.5 | | | | 3.0 | 3.3 |
| | 1.7 | 1.9 | 1.8 | | | Current | 1.8 | 1.8 |
| | 1.1 | 1.3 | 1.4 | | | | 1.2 | 1.2 |
| | 2.8 | 1.7 | 1.3 | | | | 1.8 | 1.9 |
| | 1.2 | 1.0 | .9 | | | Quick | 1.1 | .9 |
| | .6 | .7 | .8 | | | | .6 | .5 |
| | 25  14.8 | 30  12.3 | 33  10.9 | | | | 30  12.3 | 25  14.6 |
| | 51  7.2 | 36  10.1 | 41  8.8 | | | Sales/Receivables | 44  8.3 | 38  9.5 |
| | 60  6.1 | 56  6.5 | 54  6.7 | | | | 66  5.5 | 52  7.0 |
| | 11  33.1 | 22  16.8 | 45  8.1 | | | | 27  13.6 | 29  12.4 |
| | 32  11.4 | 48  7.6 | 70  5.2 | | | Cost of Sales/Inventory | 44  8.3 | 52  7.0 |
| | 74  4.9 | 126  2.9 | 99  3.7 | | | | 83  4.4 | 128  2.9 |
| | 9  39.4 | 20  18.4 | 16  22.6 | | | | 21  17.6 | 17  21.6 |
| | 31  11.6 | 28  13.0 | 34  10.8 | | | Cost of Sales/Payables | 42  8.6 | 31  11.9 |
| | 50  7.3 | 46  8.0 | 60  6.1 | | | | 72  5.1 | 54  6.8 |
| | 6.6 | 3.9 | 4.7 | | | | 4.3 | 4.4 |
| | 11.5 | 7.5 | 7.1 | | | Sales/Working Capital | 7.9 | 9.7 |
| | 477.3 | 22.7 | 13.7 | | | | 27.7 | 29.3 |
| | 33.6 | 19.9 | 22.0 | | | | 26.7 | 10.3 |
| | (13) 4.9 | (34) 4.9 | (12) 4.8 | | | EBIT/Interest | (59) 6.3 | (55) 2.2 |
| | -.9 | 2.0 | 2.0 | | | | 1.5 | -1.4 |
| | | | | | | Net Profit + Depr., Dep., | 42.3 | 6.0 |
| | | | | | | Amort./Cur. Mat. L/T/D | (16) 6.5 | (13) 2.0 |
| | | | | | | | 1.8 | .3 |
| | .0 | .1 | .1 | | | | .1 | .0 |
| | .2 | .3 | .2 | | | Fixed/Worth | .4 | .3 |
| | .6 | 1.1 | .8 | | | | 1.5 | 1.3 |
| | .8 | .7 | .7 | | | | .8 | .6 |
| | 1.2 | 1.2 | 1.1 | | | Debt/Worth | 1.8 | 1.5 |
| | 8.5 | 4.5 | 2.3 | | | | 9.0 | 5.5 |
| | 54.3 | 50.8 | 32.7 | | | | 71.6 | 54.3 |
| | (14) 36.7 | (32) 24.6 | 19.8 | | | % Profit Before Taxes/Tangible Net Worth | (53) 26.9 | (59) 14.7 |
| | -11.5 | 5.1 | 4.6 | | | | 8.6 | -5.2 |
| | 30.5 | 21.9 | 14.8 | | | | 21.0 | 18.8 |
| | 13.3 | 8.5 | 8.0 | | | % Profit Before Taxes/Total Assets | 11.8 | 5.1 |
| | 4.3 | 1.7 | 2.0 | | | | 1.3 | -4.0 |
| | 356.2 | 140.9 | 71.7 | | | | 71.6 | 136.7 |
| | 40.2 | 64.2 | 32.7 | | | Sales/Net Fixed Assets | 27.4 | 34.3 |
| | 13.7 | 9.1 | 9.8 | | | | 12.5 | 10.6 |
| | 4.0 | 3.7 | 3.0 | | | | 3.2 | 3.7 |
| | 2.8 | 2.7 | 2.3 | | | Sales/Total Assets | 2.2 | 2.2 |
| | 2.2 | 1.8 | 1.3 | | | | 1.4 | 1.3 |
| | | .2 | .5 | | | | .5 | .3 |
| | | (30) .8 | (14) 1.3 | | | % Depr., Dep., Amort./Sales | (44) 1.3 | (45) 1.5 |
| | | 2.2 | 2.0 | | | | 2.6 | 3.2 |
| | | 1.5 | | | | | 1.5 | 1.9 |
| | | (15) 2.8 | | | | % Officers', Directors' Owners' Comp/Sales | (17) 3.6 | (14) 5.0 |
| | | 6.3 | | | | | 7.1 | 12.6 |
| 14404M | 56245M | 529095M | 861543M | 530050M | 300524M | Net Sales ($) | 3214682M | 2506877M |
| 3370M | 17980M | 169199M | 339172M | 241082M | 331275M | Total Assets ($) | 2078851M | 1434081M |

M = $ thousand    MM = $ million
See Pages 9 through 22 for Explanation of Ratios and Data

## Comparative Historical Data  |  Current Data Sorted by Sales

### Type of Statement

| 4/1/09-3/31/10 ALL | 4/1/10-3/31/11 ALL | 4/1/11-3/31/12 ALL | Type of Statement | 0-1MM | 1-3MM | 3-5MM | 5-10MM | 10-25MM | 25MM & OVER |
|---|---|---|---|---|---|---|---|---|---|
| 14 | 11 | 9 | Unqualified | | 1 | | 1 | 1 | 7 |
| 15 | 10 | 10 | Reviewed | | | 2 | 1 | 5 | 1 |
| 3 | 9 | 9 | Compiled | | | 2 | 5 | 1 | 1 |
| 17 | 14 | 16 | Tax Returns | 2 | 6 | 3 | 3 | 2 | |
| 35 | 28 | 41 | Other | 1 | 8 | 4 | 8 | 8 | 12 |
| | | | | 15 (4/1-9/30/11) | | | 70 (10/1/11-3/31/12) | | |
| 84 | 72 | 85 | NUMBER OF STATEMENTS | 3 | 15 | 11 | 18 | 17 | 21 |

### ASSETS

| % | % | % | | % | % | % | % | % | % |
|---|---|---|---|---|---|---|---|---|---|
| 13.3 | 12.4 | 15.0 | Cash & Equivalents | | 17.3 | 28.0 | 15.0 | 10.5 | 10.9 |
| 29.3 | 30.1 | 32.1 | Trade Receivables (net) | | 37.5 | 23.5 | 35.2 | 28.8 | 32.9 |
| 23.9 | 29.4 | 26.0 | Inventory | | 20.5 | 11.8 | 25.4 | 34.8 | 30.6 |
| 3.3 | 1.7 | 2.4 | All Other Current | | 1.5 | .2 | 1.0 | 3.5 | 4.7 |
| 69.7 | 73.6 | 75.5 | Total Current | | 76.7 | 63.6 | 76.7 | 77.5 | 79.1 |
| 15.3 | 12.5 | 12.7 | Fixed Assets (net) | | 13.6 | 18.9 | 15.0 | 13.7 | 7.9 |
| 7.2 | 5.6 | 3.8 | Intangibles (net) | | 1.4 | 6.6 | .1 | 4.7 | 7.2 |
| 7.8 | 8.3 | 7.9 | All Other Non-Current | | 8.3 | 10.9 | 8.3 | 4.1 | 5.8 |
| 100.0 | 100.0 | 100.0 | Total | | 100.0 | 100.0 | 100.0 | 100.0 | 100.0 |

### LIABILITIES

| 14.2 | 14.5 | 10.4 | Notes Payable-Short Term | | 10.3 | 9.2 | 9.1 | 8.4 | 12.5 |
|---|---|---|---|---|---|---|---|---|---|
| 2.9 | 2.1 | 2.1 | Cur. Mat.-L.T.D. | | 1.2 | 2.8 | 1.4 | 2.4 | 3.1 |
| 14.1 | 15.5 | 18.1 | Trade Payables | | 27.8 | 9.4 | 14.0 | 19.0 | 20.3 |
| .6 | .4 | .3 | Income Taxes Payable | | 1.0 | .1 | .0 | .0 | .4 |
| 12.4 | 12.1 | 13.4 | All Other Current | | 18.1 | 16.1 | 9.7 | 10.1 | 14.8 |
| 44.3 | 44.7 | 44.4 | Total Current | | 58.3 | 37.5 | 34.1 | 40.0 | 51.1 |
| 10.9 | 13.4 | 14.1 | Long-Term Debt | | 29.7 | 9.5 | 6.0 | 9.8 | 17.7 |
| .3 | .1 | .3 | Deferred Taxes | | .0 | .0 | .1 | .6 | .4 |
| 6.7 | 8.1 | 20.0 | All Other Non-Current | | 33.5 | 3.3 | 21.2 | 6.5 | 10.4 |
| 37.8 | 33.7 | 21.3 | Net Worth | | -21.5 | 49.7 | 38.6 | 43.1 | 20.3 |
| 100.0 | 100.0 | 100.0 | Total Liabilities & Net Worth | | 100.0 | 100.0 | 100.0 | 100.0 | 100.0 |

### INCOME DATA

| 100.0 | 100.0 | 100.0 | Net Sales | | 100.0 | 100.0 | 100.0 | 100.0 | 100.0 |
|---|---|---|---|---|---|---|---|---|---|
| 40.2 | 37.3 | 39.2 | Gross Profit | | 54.1 | 49.7 | 44.1 | 30.8 | 25.5 |
| 38.0 | 32.3 | 34.0 | Operating Expenses | | 49.7 | 42.0 | 38.9 | 24.8 | 20.9 |
| 2.1 | 5.0 | 5.2 | Operating Profit | | 4.4 | 7.7 | 5.2 | 6.0 | 4.6 |
| .9 | 1.4 | 1.1 | All Other Expenses (net) | | .0 | .4 | .8 | 2.1 | 1.6 |
| 1.3 | 3.6 | 4.1 | Profit Before Taxes | | 4.4 | 7.3 | 4.5 | 3.9 | 3.0 |

### RATIOS

| 2.4 | 2.6 | 2.9 | Current | | 2.7 | 8.2 | 4.3 | 2.9 | 1.9 |
|---|---|---|---|---|---|---|---|---|---|
| 1.5 | 1.6 | 1.8 | | | 1.7 | 1.7 | 2.1 | 2.1 | 1.7 |
| 1.1 | 1.3 | 1.3 | | | .9 | 1.0 | 1.5 | 1.5 | 1.2 |
| 1.8 | 1.4 | 1.7 | Quick | | 1.7 | 6.9 | 3.8 | 1.6 | 1.1 |
| .9 | .9 | 1.0 | | | 1.0 | 1.4 | 1.3 | 1.2 | .9 |
| .6 | .6 | .7 | | | .6 | .5 | .9 | .6 | .7 |
| 33 / 11.1 | 29 / 12.8 | 29 / 12.4 | Sales/Receivables | | 28 / 13.2 | 24 / 15.2 | 29 / 12.4 | 30 / 12.1 | 30 / 12.1 |
| 47 / 7.8 | 42 / 8.7 | 41 / 8.9 | | | 53 / 6.9 | 49 / 7.4 | 35 / 10.3 | 36 / 10.1 | 44 / 8.3 |
| 62 / 5.9 | 57 / 6.4 | 61 / 6.0 | | | 65 / 5.6 | 54 / 6.8 | 45 / 8.1 | 66 / 5.5 | 66 / 5.5 |
| 26 / 14.2 | 31 / 11.9 | 24 / 15.4 | Cost of Sales/Inventory | | 13 / 28.9 | 2 / 149.6 | 10 / 35.5 | 32 / 11.3 | 23 / 15.7 |
| 59 / 6.2 | 61 / 6.0 | 51 / 7.2 | | | 60 / 6.1 | 47 / 7.8 | 42 / 8.7 | 70 / 5.2 | 48 / 7.6 |
| 106 / 3.5 | 103 / 3.6 | 107 / 3.4 | | | 174 / 2.1 | 174 / 2.1 | 104 / 3.5 | 118 / 3.1 | 73 / 5.0 |
| 17 / 20.9 | 13 / 27.2 | 15 / 24.7 | Cost of Sales/Payables | | 7 / 49.7 | 8 / 48.6 | 19 / 19.6 | 22 / 16.9 | 15 / 24.5 |
| 34 / 10.7 | 32 / 11.5 | 30 / 12.3 | | | 32 / 11.5 | 20 / 18.4 | 29 / 12.8 | 30 / 12.1 | 32 / 11.5 |
| 54 / 6.8 | 58 / 6.2 | 51 / 7.1 | | | 69 / 5.3 | 46 / 8.0 | 36 / 10.0 | 47 / 7.7 | 66 / 5.5 |
| 4.1 | 5.1 | 4.7 | Sales/Working Capital | | 5.3 | 2.2 | 3.8 | 4.7 | 5.6 |
| 9.0 | 9.2 | 8.1 | | | 10.9 | 9.0 | 6.9 | 7.0 | 8.4 |
| 33.7 | 20.4 | 21.3 | | | -70.7 | -575.0 | 15.8 | 11.1 | 24.9 |
| 15.1 | 15.1 | 18.5 | EBIT/Interest | | 10.6 | | 16.0 | 19.4 | 26.9 |
| (66) 3.7 | (60) 4.7 | (68) 4.7 | | | (12) 3.1 | | (15) 3.9 | (15) 8.5 | (16) 8.1 |
| .4 | 1.6 | 1.8 | | | -.9 | | 2.0 | 3.2 | 2.0 |
| 12.3 | 19.8 | | Net Profit + Depr., Dep., Amort./Cur. Mat. L/T/D | | | | | | |
| (16) 1.7 | (10) 2.0 | | | | | | | | |
| -.9 | .4 | | | | | | | | |
| .1 | .1 | .1 | Fixed/Worth | | .0 | .1 | .1 | .1 | .1 |
| .3 | .2 | .2 | | | .8 | .3 | .2 | .2 | .2 |
| 1.6 | 1.0 | 1.2 | | | -.7 | 1.0 | .7 | NM | 1.0 |
| .8 | .6 | .7 | Debt/Worth | | 1.1 | .2 | .3 | .6 | .9 |
| 2.0 | 1.7 | 1.2 | | | 18.5 | 1.1 | 1.1 | 1.2 | 2.5 |
| 4.6 | 3.9 | 8.3 | | | -2.5 | 8.6 | 2.6 | NM | 5.6 |
| 43.2 | 48.2 | 50.2 | % Profit Before Taxes/Tangible Net Worth | | | 82.0 | 35.5 | 63.9 | 48.4 |
| (74) 13.2 | (61) 20.1 | (69) 25.8 | | | | (10) 50.4 | (17) 22.4 | (13) 25.4 | (19) 26.2 |
| -.6 | 4.8 | 4.6 | | | | 13.5 | 8.0 | 10.4 | 3.4 |
| 15.1 | 16.9 | 19.6 | % Profit Before Taxes/Total Assets | | 36.9 | 33.2 | 20.8 | 20.8 | 14.0 |
| 3.6 | 7.3 | 8.0 | | | 4.7 | 10.1 | 8.5 | 12.3 | 5.5 |
| -2.0 | 2.0 | .6 | | | -15.8 | .4 | 3.8 | 4.7 | .1 |
| 68.2 | 130.0 | 178.8 | Sales/Net Fixed Assets | | 411.8 | 105.6 | 85.6 | 314.0 | 134.1 |
| 28.6 | 42.7 | 49.2 | | | 68.6 | 25.5 | 31.2 | 64.0 | 52.0 |
| 10.1 | 15.4 | 13.5 | | | 17.6 | 6.0 | 9.1 | 7.9 | 17.8 |
| 3.5 | 3.5 | 3.7 | Sales/Total Assets | | 4.3 | 2.9 | 3.7 | 3.8 | 4.6 |
| 2.2 | 2.5 | 2.7 | | | 3.2 | 1.9 | 2.8 | 2.3 | 2.8 |
| 1.2 | 1.6 | 1.7 | | | 2.3 | 1.4 | 2.3 | 1.3 | 1.6 |
| .8 | .4 | .4 | % Depr., Dep., Amort./Sales | | | | .8 | .1 | .1 |
| (52) 1.6 | (47) 1.2 | (52) 1.0 | | | | | (12) 1.8 | (14) .4 | (15) .6 |
| 3.2 | 2.1 | 2.5 | | | | | 3.1 | 2.5 | 1.5 |
| 1.9 | 1.2 | 1.5 | % Officers', Directors', Owners' Comp/Sales | | | | | | |
| (27) 3.5 | (22) 2.0 | (31) 3.1 | | | | | | | |
| 8.0 | 4.3 | 6.7 | | | | | | | |
| 2576889M | 2016636M | 2291861M | Net Sales ($) | 2161M | 28513M | 44167M | 139797M | 286933M | 1790290M |
| 1760336M | 1005988M | 1102078M | Total Assets ($) | 1060M | 15890M | 24072M | 54894M | 134167M | 871995M |

M = $ thousand   MM = $ million
See Pages 9 through 22 for Explanation of Ratios and Data

## Current Data Sorted by Assets      Comparative Historical Data

Type of Statement

| | 0-500M | 500M-2MM | 2-10MM | 10-50MM | 50-100MM | 100-250MM | | 4/1/07-3/31/08 ALL | 4/1/08-3/31/09 ALL |
|---|---|---|---|---|---|---|---|---|---|
| Unqualified | | 1 | 3 | 4 | 5 | 4 | | 24 | 35 |
| Reviewed | | 2 | 8 | 2 | | | | 10 | 13 |
| Compiled | 1 | 5 | 4 | | 1 | | | 6 | 4 |
| Tax Returns | 1 | 4 | 5 | | 8 | 7 | | 4 | 6 |
| Other | 1 | | 12 | 12 | | | | 38 | 53 |
| | **15 (4/1-9/30/11)** | | **75 (10/1/11-3/31/12)** | | | | | | |
| NUMBER OF STATEMENTS | 3 | 12 | 32 | 18 | 14 | 11 | | 82 | 111 |
| | % | % | % | % | % | % | | % | % |
| **ASSETS** | | | | | | | | | |
| Cash & Equivalents | | 8.7 | 12.8 | 13.4 | 17.7 | 9.1 | | 10.5 | 11.6 |
| Trade Receivables (net) | | 31.3 | 29.7 | 20.8 | 26.9 | 32.1 | | 28.5 | 29.4 |
| Inventory | | 30.8 | 29.1 | 22.9 | 20.8 | 21.9 | | 26.2 | 25.0 |
| All Other Current | | 5.5 | 1.7 | 5.8 | 5.9 | 5.0 | | 5.2 | 6.3 |
| Total Current | | 76.2 | 73.4 | 62.9 | 71.3 | 68.2 | | 70.4 | 72.2 |
| Fixed Assets (net) | | 19.5 | 14.6 | 13.3 | 7.1 | 7.6 | | 13.8 | 11.7 |
| Intangibles (net) | | .8 | 5.0 | 16.5 | 15.3 | 18.3 | | 9.7 | 9.1 |
| All Other Non-Current | | 3.5 | 7.0 | 7.2 | 6.3 | 5.9 | | 6.2 | 7.0 |
| Total | | 100.0 | 100.0 | 100.0 | 100.0 | 100.0 | | 100.0 | 100.0 |
| **LIABILITIES** | | | | | | | | | |
| Notes Payable-Short Term | | 6.0 | 10.5 | 4.9 | 3.6 | 10.4 | | 9.8 | 9.9 |
| Cur. Mat.-L.T.D. | | 3.3 | 2.0 | 1.4 | 1.2 | 1.0 | | 2.1 | 2.7 |
| Trade Payables | | 18.1 | 17.6 | 10.2 | 18.3 | 17.1 | | 16.0 | 16.2 |
| Income Taxes Payable | | 1.1 | .1 | .1 | .6 | .3 | | .5 | .9 |
| All Other Current | | 5.4 | 10.7 | 11.1 | 20.3 | 12.9 | | 11.9 | 16.2 |
| Total Current | | 34.0 | 40.9 | 27.8 | 43.9 | 41.6 | | 40.3 | 46.0 |
| Long-Term Debt | | 15.8 | 8.3 | 9.9 | 7.7 | 7.8 | | 14.8 | 9.1 |
| Deferred Taxes | | .3 | .5 | .2 | .7 | 1.0 | | .4 | .4 |
| All Other Non-Current | | 6.9 | 5.0 | 18.0 | 6.2 | 3.3 | | 7.0 | 6.7 |
| Net Worth | | 43.0 | 45.4 | 44.1 | 41.5 | 46.4 | | 37.4 | 37.7 |
| Total Liabilities & Net Worth | | 100.0 | 100.0 | 100.0 | 100.0 | 100.0 | | 100.0 | 100.0 |
| **INCOME DATA** | | | | | | | | | |
| Net Sales | | 100.0 | 100.0 | 100.0 | 100.0 | 100.0 | | 100.0 | 100.0 |
| Gross Profit | | 38.1 | 35.3 | 40.6 | 42.1 | 31.0 | | 38.5 | 38.0 |
| Operating Expenses | | 31.6 | 29.4 | 32.5 | 36.0 | 24.0 | | 35.8 | 35.1 |
| Operating Profit | | 6.5 | 5.9 | 8.0 | 6.1 | 7.0 | | 2.7 | 2.9 |
| All Other Expenses (net) | | .7 | .3 | 1.0 | 2.9 | 2.2 | | 1.0 | .7 |
| Profit Before Taxes | | 5.8 | 5.5 | 7.1 | 3.2 | 4.8 | | 1.8 | 2.2 |
| **RATIOS** | | | | | | | | | |
| Current | | 5.4 | 2.7 | 3.9 | 2.8 | 2.6 | | 2.5 | 2.9 |
| | | 3.2 | 1.8 | 2.6 | 1.7 | 2.0 | | 1.8 | 1.8 |
| | | 1.8 | 1.4 | 1.5 | 1.2 | 1.1 | | 1.2 | 1.2 |
| Quick | | 3.1 | 1.7 | 2.6 | 1.9 | 1.9 | | 1.4 | 1.6 |
| | | 1.2 | 1.0 | 1.3 | 1.1 | 1.2 | | .9 | 1.0 |
| | | 1.0 | .8 | .8 | .7 | .7 | | .6 | .6 |
| Sales/Receivables | 25  14.6 | 29  12.7 | 45  8.2 | 45  8.1 | 51  7.2 | | 35  10.5 | 38  9.6 | |
| | 40  9.1 | 46  8.0 | 52  7.0 | 64  5.7 | 62  5.9 | | 50  7.3 | 51  7.2 | |
| | 56  6.5 | 56  6.5 | 65  5.6 | 78  4.7 | 94  3.9 | | 65  5.6 | 64  5.7 | |
| Cost of Sales/Inventory | 17  22.1 | 34  10.7 | 62  5.9 | 58  6.3 | 52  7.0 | | 42  8.6 | 33  11.0 | |
| | 45  8.2 | 73  5.0 | 104  3.5 | 79  4.6 | 62  5.9 | | 75  4.8 | 65  5.6 | |
| | 87  4.2 | 99  3.7 | 174  2.1 | 111  3.3 | 114  3.2 | | 122  3.0 | 102  3.6 | |
| Cost of Sales/Payables | 4  82.9 | 22  16.5 | 22  16.4 | 42  8.6 | 33  10.9 | | 26  13.9 | 23  15.8 | |
| | 15  24.9 | 34  10.6 | 40  9.1 | 56  6.5 | 42  8.6 | | 40  9.2 | 37  9.9 | |
| | 65  5.6 | 54  6.8 | 56  6.5 | 96  3.8 | 54  6.7 | | 61  6.0 | 54  6.8 | |
| Sales/Working Capital | | 3.4 | 4.5 | 2.3 | 4.2 | 3.1 | | 3.7 | 4.2 |
| | | 6.1 | 7.7 | 4.3 | 5.4 | 6.3 | | 7.1 | 6.6 |
| | | 9.7 | 13.2 | 8.2 | 9.7 | 11.1 | | 22.4 | 25.3 |
| EBIT/Interest | | 40.6 | 23.8 | 74.0 | 15.7 | | | 12.6 | 10.6 |
| | | 8.9 | (29) 9.6 | (14) 14.5 | (10) 1.8 | | | (70) 2.5 | (91) 3.8 |
| | | 1.2 | 2.9 | -.5 | -.8 | | | -.3 | .3 |
| Net Profit + Depr., Dep., Amort./Cur. Mat. L/T/D | | | 7.4 | | | | | 18.7 | 9.5 |
| | | | (12) 2.2 | | | | | (27) 3.3 | (36) 2.3 |
| | | | 1.6 | | | | | 1.0 | 1.2 |
| Fixed/Worth | | .0 | .1 | .1 | .1 | .1 | | .1 | .1 |
| | | .1 | .2 | .4 | .3 | .2 | | .3 | .3 |
| | | .7 | .6 | NM | .8 | .5 | | 1.1 | .9 |
| Debt/Worth | | .4 | .7 | .3 | 1.1 | .7 | | .6 | .6 |
| | | .8 | 1.5 | 1.3 | 2.4 | .9 | | 2.0 | 1.9 |
| | | 1.9 | 2.3 | NM | 5.6 | 12.8 | | 5.7 | 5.7 |
| % Profit Before Taxes/Tangible Net Worth | | 44.7 | 41.9 | 40.9 | 62.3 | | | 38.8 | 44.2 |
| | (10) 25.4 | (29) 15.5 | (14) 13.7 | (12) 7.6 | | | | (72) 15.8 | (95) 13.9 | |
| | | 3.3 | 6.2 | -5.6 | -5.5 | | | -8.2 | .1 |
| % Profit Before Taxes/Total Assets | | 27.6 | 14.0 | 14.7 | 10.5 | 14.1 | | 16.0 | 12.9 |
| | | 12.3 | 6.9 | 7.8 | 4.1 | 5.3 | | 3.9 | 4.7 |
| | | .8 | 2.6 | -2.4 | -2.2 | -4.4 | | -3.8 | -.8 |
| Sales/Net Fixed Assets | | 532.0 | 129.7 | 52.2 | 65.8 | 80.9 | | 67.8 | 63.4 |
| | | 56.5 | 33.3 | 19.8 | 20.8 | 41.0 | | 24.5 | 27.7 |
| | | 11.4 | 9.7 | 3.9 | 12.5 | 12.3 | | 8.1 | 18.0 |
| Sales/Total Assets | | 3.7 | 3.4 | 1.7 | 2.2 | 2.3 | | 2.9 | 3.0 |
| | | 2.8 | 2.2 | 1.2 | 1.5 | 1.6 | | 2.0 | 2.2 |
| | | 2.2 | 1.7 | .7 | .9 | 1.2 | | 1.2 | 1.3 |
| % Depr., Dep., Amort./Sales | | | .6 | .9 | | | | .7 | .8 |
| | | | (24) 1.2 | (15) 1.3 | | | | (60) 1.6 | (83) 1.3 |
| | | | 2.2 | 2.2 | | | | 2.9 | 2.5 |
| % Officers', Directors', Owners' Comp/Sales | | | 1.7 | | | | | .9 | 3.2 |
| | | | (13) 3.4 | | | | | (14) 3.5 | (18) 4.6 |
| | | | 5.0 | | | | | 7.7 | 10.4 |
| Net Sales ($) | 2285M | 50121M | 370372M | 507856M | 1559817M | 2852231M | | 4491862M | 7129412M |
| Total Assets ($) | 762M | 13843M | 153629M | 416014M | 1008574M | 1748295M | | 2915406M | 4070890M |

© RMA 2012

M = $ thousand    MM = $ million
See Pages 9 through 22 for Explanation of Ratios and Data

## Comparative Historical Data        Current Data Sorted by Sales

| Hist 1 | Hist 2 | Hist 3 | Type of Statement | 0-1MM | 1-3MM | 3-5MM | 5-10MM | 10-25MM | 25MM & OVER |
|---|---|---|---|---|---|---|---|---|---|
| 26 | 24 | 17 | Unqualified | | 3 | | | 4 | 10 |
| 11 | 13 | 12 | Reviewed | | | | 4 | 7 | 1 |
| 5 | 2 | 5 | Compiled | | | | 1 | 3 | |
| 3 | 13 | 12 | Tax Returns | 1 | 4 | 1 | 2 | 3 | 1 |
| 52 | 41 | 44 | Other | 1 | 3 | 4 | 2 | 14 | 21 |
| 4/1/09-3/31/10 ALL | 4/1/10-3/31/11 ALL | 4/1/11-3/31/12 ALL | | | 15 (4/1-9/30/11) | | 75 (10/1/11-3/31/12) | | |
| 97 | 93 | 90 | **NUMBER OF STATEMENTS** | 2 | 10 | 5 | 9 | 31 | 33 |
| % | % | % | **ASSETS** | % | % | % | % | % | % |
| 14.2 | 15.2 | 12.3 | Cash & Equivalents | | 13.0 | | | 14.5 | 12.6 |
| 26.6 | 24.5 | 29.0 | Trade Receivables (net) | | 26.1 | | | 27.4 | 29.1 |
| 22.9 | 26.3 | 25.3 | Inventory | | 21.2 | | | 24.9 | 23.6 |
| 4.7 | 4.8 | 4.1 | All Other Current | | 6.2 | | | 2.1 | 6.5 |
| 68.3 | 70.7 | 70.7 | Total Current | | 66.4 | | | 68.9 | 71.8 |
| 13.6 | 12.2 | 12.8 | Fixed Assets (net) | | 29.5 | | | 12.6 | 7.9 |
| 10.1 | 9.9 | 9.8 | Intangibles (net) | | 1.5 | | | 11.6 | 14.2 |
| 7.9 | 7.1 | 6.7 | All Other Non-Current | | 2.6 | | | 6.9 | 6.0 |
| 100.0 | 100.0 | 100.0 | Total | | 100.0 | | | 100.0 | 100.0 |
| | | | **LIABILITIES** | | | | | | |
| 9.7 | 7.7 | 7.5 | Notes Payable-Short Term | | 2.1 | | | 8.2 | 6.4 |
| 2.2 | 2.6 | 1.7 | Cur. Mat.-L.T.D. | | 3.2 | | | 2.2 | 1.1 |
| 14.1 | 15.0 | 17.7 | Trade Payables | | 27.6 | | | 14.2 | 17.5 |
| .3 | .3 | .3 | Income Taxes Payable | | 1.3 | | | .1 | .4 |
| 13.8 | 12.8 | 12.1 | All Other Current | | 17.1 | | | 8.6 | 16.8 |
| 40.1 | 38.4 | 39.4 | Total Current | | 51.3 | | | 33.4 | 42.1 |
| 10.4 | 9.6 | 9.6 | Long-Term Debt | | 22.7 | | | 6.4 | 8.5 |
| .5 | .5 | .5 | Deferred Taxes | | .9 | | | .5 | .6 |
| 9.0 | 8.1 | 7.7 | All Other Non-Current | | 7.7 | | | 10.2 | 7.7 |
| 40.0 | 43.4 | 42.9 | Net Worth | | 17.3 | | | 49.5 | 41.1 |
| 100.0 | 100.0 | 100.0 | Total Liabilities & Net Worth | | 100.0 | | | 100.0 | 100.0 |
| | | | **INCOME DATA** | | | | | | |
| 100.0 | 100.0 | 100.0 | Net Sales | | 100.0 | | | 100.0 | 100.0 |
| 36.6 | 37.8 | 37.9 | Gross Profit | | 45.0 | | | 35.4 | 36.3 |
| 35.0 | 35.3 | 31.0 | Operating Expenses | | 31.6 | | | 28.3 | 30.7 |
| 1.6 | 2.5 | 6.9 | Operating Profit | | 13.5 | | | 7.1 | 5.6 |
| .8 | .8 | 1.1 | All Other Expenses (net) | | 1.1 | | | .5 | 2.2 |
| .7 | 1.7 | 5.8 | Profit Before Taxes | | 12.4 | | | 6.6 | 3.4 |
| | | | **RATIOS** | | | | | | |
| 3.5 | 3.3 | 3.4 | Current | | 5.8 | | | 3.5 | 2.8 |
| 1.8 | 1.7 | 1.9 | | | 2.5 | | | 2.1 | 1.8 |
| 1.3 | 1.4 | 1.4 | | | .6 | | | 1.4 | 1.3 |
| 2.1 | 2.0 | 1.9 | Quick | | 2.9 | | | 2.5 | 1.8 |
| 1.0 | 1.0 | 1.1 | | | 1.1 | | | 1.1 | 1.1 |
| .6 | .6 | .8 | | | .5 | | | .8 | .7 |
| 36 10.1 | 35 10.6 | 39 9.4 | Sales/Receivables | | 30 12.0 | | | 35 10.5 | 49 7.4 |
| 49 7.5 | 52 7.1 | 51 7.2 | | | 45 8.1 | | | 50 7.3 | 62 5.9 |
| 60 6.0 | 63 5.8 | 63 5.8 | | | 55 6.6 | | | 58 6.3 | 81 4.5 |
| 31 11.8 | 45 8.0 | 51 7.1 | Cost of Sales/Inventory | | 7 53.0 | | | 31 11.6 | 56 6.5 |
| 65 5.6 | 80 4.5 | 74 4.9 | | | 78 4.7 | | | 61 6.0 | 74 4.9 |
| 114 3.2 | 132 2.8 | 114 3.2 | | | 126 2.9 | | | 146 2.5 | 107 3.4 |
| 21 17.0 | 22 17.0 | 22 16.3 | Cost of Sales/Payables | | 7 51.3 | | | 22 16.6 | 35 10.3 |
| 34 10.7 | 45 8.2 | 41 9.0 | | | 40 9.2 | | | 32 11.5 | 51 7.2 |
| 54 6.7 | 63 5.8 | 59 6.2 | | | 166 2.2 | | | 51 7.2 | 66 5.5 |
| 3.2 | 3.2 | 3.9 | Sales/Working Capital | | 2.7 | | | 3.9 | 3.6 |
| 6.9 | 5.6 | 5.9 | | | 5.9 | | | 6.0 | 5.4 |
| 18.6 | 14.0 | 11.8 | | | -6.1 | | | 13.3 | 9.9 |
| 12.0 | 15.8 | 25.5 | EBIT/Interest | | | | | 36.0 | 17.9 |
| (81) 2.7 | (80) 3.0 | (76) 7.6 | | | | | | (27) 14.7 | (26) 2.7 |
| .3 | .6 | 1.7 | | | | | | 2.8 | -.3 |
| 4.8 | 6.8 | 10.8 | Net Profit + Depr., Dep., Amort./Cur. Mat. L/T/D | | | | | 12.1 | 13.2 |
| (25) 2.1 | (27) 3.2 | (25) 2.0 | | | | | | (11) 3.3 | (10) 1.8 |
| .8 | 1.5 | 1.3 | | | | | | 1.4 | -5.2 |
| .1 | .1 | .1 | Fixed/Worth | | .1 | | | .1 | .1 |
| .4 | .2 | .2 | | | .6 | | | .3 | .2 |
| 1.2 | .9 | .8 | | | -2.8 | | | .8 | .6 |
| .5 | .7 | .6 | Debt/Worth | | .8 | | | .4 | .7 |
| 1.8 | 1.4 | 1.5 | | | 2.5 | | | 1.2 | 2.2 |
| 4.8 | 5.4 | 4.6 | | | -6.1 | | | 2.4 | 6.5 |
| 31.6 | 35.4 | 42.6 | % Profit Before Taxes/Tangible Net Worth | | | | | 44.7 | 45.7 |
| (82) 11.2 | (79) 15.2 | (76) 14.1 | | | | | | (26) 24.3 | (28) 7.6 |
| .7 | 1.4 | 3.5 | | | | | | 4.2 | -7.4 |
| 9.1 | 11.9 | 14.9 | % Profit Before Taxes/Total Assets | | 28.5 | | | 17.5 | 13.2 |
| 2.7 | 5.2 | 6.4 | | | 7.3 | | | 9.7 | 5.0 |
| -2.6 | -.4 | .5 | | | 3.1 | | | 2.3 | -3.0 |
| 45.7 | 61.3 | 79.4 | Sales/Net Fixed Assets | | 51.7 | | | 78.9 | 67.5 |
| 23.2 | 24.1 | 29.3 | | | 10.9 | | | 30.4 | 23.3 |
| 8.9 | 9.6 | 9.9 | | | 2.7 | | | 9.7 | 12.8 |
| 2.5 | 2.5 | 2.7 | Sales/Total Assets | | 2.7 | | | 3.5 | 2.2 |
| 1.9 | 1.7 | 2.0 | | | 2.2 | | | 2.1 | 1.5 |
| 1.2 | 1.1 | 1.2 | | | 1.1 | | | 1.3 | 1.1 |
| .9 | .8 | .7 | % Depr., Dep., Amort./Sales | | | | | .7 | .7 |
| (69) 1.7 | (73) 1.4 | (62) 1.2 | | | | | | (27) 1.3 | (21) 1.2 |
| 3.1 | 3.0 | 2.2 | | | | | | 2.1 | 2.1 |
| 3.7 | 1.0 | 1.3 | % Officers', Directors' Owners' Comp/Sales | | | | | 2.0 | |
| (15) 5.6 | (20) 4.3 | (25) 3.4 | | | | | | (11) 2.8 | |
| 8.4 | 6.6 | 5.5 | | | | | | 5.3 | |
| 4272415M | 4437461M | 5342682M | Net Sales ($) | 651M | 21808M | 18409M | 57960M | 492052M | 4751802M |
| 2570055M | 3200096M | 3341117M | Total Assets ($) | 321M | 14043M | 8620M | 27753M | 331613M | 2958767M |

M = $ thousand     MM = $ million
See Pages 9 through 22 for Explanation of Ratios and Data

## Current Data Sorted by Assets      Comparative Historical Data

| 0-500M | 500M-2MM | 2-10MM | 10-50MM | 50-100MM | 100-250MM | Type of Statement | 4/1/07-3/31/08 ALL | 4/1/08-3/31/09 ALL |
|---|---|---|---|---|---|---|---|---|
| | | 1 | 4 | 1 | 1 | Unqualified | 8 | 12 |
| | | 2 | 2 | | | Reviewed | 3 | 1 |
| | 4 | | | | | Compiled | 5 | 1 |
| | 2 | 2 | | | | Tax Returns | 3 | 7 |
| 1 | | 10 | 6 | 2 | 2 | Other | 18 | 16 |
| | 6 (4/1-9/30/11) | | 34 (10/1/11-3/31/12) | | | | | |
| 1 | 6 | 15 | 12 | 3 | 3 | **NUMBER OF STATEMENTS** | 37 | 37 |
| % | % | % | % | % | % | | % | % |
| | | | | | | **ASSETS** | | |
| | | 17.9 | 13.1 | | | Cash & Equivalents | 16.2 | 17.7 |
| | | 30.4 | 28.5 | | | Trade Receivables (net) | 26.1 | 26.0 |
| | | 29.6 | 27.2 | | | Inventory | 21.9 | 22.6 |
| | | 1.8 | 3.6 | | | All Other Current | 5.3 | 2.7 |
| | | 79.8 | 72.4 | | | Total Current | 69.5 | 69.1 |
| | | 8.4 | 13.5 | | | Fixed Assets (net) | 10.5 | 13.8 |
| | | 5.6 | 7.3 | | | Intangibles (net) | 11.6 | 9.5 |
| | | 6.2 | 6.8 | | | All Other Non-Current | 8.4 | 7.7 |
| | | 100.0 | 100.0 | | | Total | 100.0 | 100.0 |
| | | | | | | **LIABILITIES** | | |
| | | 8.4 | 4.3 | | | Notes Payable-Short Term | 7.2 | 9.7 |
| | | 2.5 | 1.8 | | | Cur. Mat.-L.T.D. | 3.4 | 3.9 |
| | | 20.1 | 28.6 | | | Trade Payables | 17.1 | 24.6 |
| | | .0 | .6 | | | Income Taxes Payable | .3 | .1 |
| | | 16.7 | 16.2 | | | All Other Current | 15.9 | 15.7 |
| | | 47.8 | 51.6 | | | Total Current | 44.0 | 54.0 |
| | | 5.5 | 8.9 | | | Long-Term Debt | 7.4 | 9.4 |
| | | .3 | .4 | | | Deferred Taxes | .2 | .4 |
| | | 3.3 | 4.9 | | | All Other Non-Current | 7.0 | 11.4 |
| | | 43.1 | 34.3 | | | Net Worth | 41.3 | 24.8 |
| | | 100.0 | 100.0 | | | Total Liabilities & Net Worth | 100.0 | 100.0 |
| | | | | | | **INCOME DATA** | | |
| | | 100.0 | 100.0 | | | Net Sales | 100.0 | 100.0 |
| | | 44.7 | 40.0 | | | Gross Profit | 38.8 | 40.7 |
| | | 35.1 | 33.8 | | | Operating Expenses | 36.0 | 41.4 |
| | | 9.6 | 6.2 | | | Operating Profit | 2.8 | -.8 |
| | | .5 | .8 | | | All Other Expenses (net) | 1.4 | .9 |
| | | 9.1 | 5.4 | | | Profit Before Taxes | 1.4 | -1.7 |
| | | | | | | **RATIOS** | | |
| | | 3.3 | 3.5 | | | | 3.0 | 4.0 |
| | | 2.5 | 1.4 | | | Current | 1.5 | 1.6 |
| | | 1.5 | 1.0 | | | | 1.1 | 1.0 |
| | | 2.9 | 1.5 | | | | 1.7 | 2.5 |
| | | 1.1 | .9 | | | Quick | 1.0 | .9 |
| | | .5 | .6 | | | | .6 | .6 |
| | | 29   12.5 | 36   10.0 | | | | 37   9.9 | 33   11.0 |
| | | 43   8.4 | 47   7.7 | | | Sales/Receivables | 58   6.3 | 52   7.1 |
| | | 61   6.0 | 58   6.3 | | | | 79   4.6 | 65   5.6 |
| | | 4   96.9 | 38   9.5 | | | | 30   12.1 | 23   16.0 |
| | | 91   4.0 | 85   4.3 | | | Cost of Sales/Inventory | 80   4.6 | 74   4.9 |
| | | 118   3.1 | 174   2.1 | | | | 128   2.9 | 123   3.0 |
| | | 15   23.8 | 22   16.7 | | | | 27   13.8 | 21   17.1 |
| | | 50   7.3 | 57   6.4 | | | Cost of Sales/Payables | 56   6.5 | 38   9.6 |
| | | 78   4.7 | 104   3.5 | | | | 88   4.2 | 70   5.2 |
| | | 3.9 | 3.8 | | | | 3.0 | 3.4 |
| | | 5.9 | 10.6 | | | Sales/Working Capital | 8.3 | 7.3 |
| | | 16.1 | NM | | | | 96.5 | 255.2 |
| | | 41.4 | 32.3 | | | | 11.1 | 6.2 |
| | | (11) 12.0 | (11) 10.6 | | | EBIT/Interest | (29) 1.0 | (31) 1.2 |
| | | 5.4 | 2.4 | | | | -4.0 | -7.5 |
| | | | | | | Net Profit + Depr., Dep., Amort./Cur. Mat. L/T/D | | |
| | | .0 | .2 | | | | .1 | .1 |
| | | .1 | .4 | | | Fixed/Worth | .2 | .2 |
| | | .5 | .9 | | | | 1.1 | 1.0 |
| | | .4 | .6 | | | | .5 | .4 |
| | | .7 | 2.2 | | | Debt/Worth | 1.3 | 2.3 |
| | | 1.9 | 9.4 | | | | 9.8 | 11.1 |
| | | 64.9 | 167.2 | | | | 24.4 | 50.5 |
| | | (13) 35.4 | (11) 36.7 | | | % Profit Before Taxes/Tangible Net Worth | (31) 5.5 | (30) 5.8 |
| | | 14.3 | 3.1 | | | | -9.3 | -22.1 |
| | | 31.2 | 16.9 | | | | 10.7 | 10.2 |
| | | 16.4 | 8.5 | | | % Profit Before Taxes/Total Assets | .7 | 1.3 |
| | | 5.7 | 2.0 | | | | -3.7 | -13.8 |
| | | 266.6 | 40.6 | | | | 85.8 | 67.5 |
| | | 67.8 | 23.4 | | | Sales/Net Fixed Assets | 33.4 | 20.4 |
| | | 21.1 | 6.2 | | | | 9.8 | 6.6 |
| | | 2.8 | 3.2 | | | | 2.3 | 2.8 |
| | | 2.6 | 1.8 | | | Sales/Total Assets | 1.7 | 1.9 |
| | | 1.8 | 1.5 | | | | .9 | 1.0 |
| | | .6 | | | | | .4 | .9 |
| | | (10) 1.3 | | | | % Depr., Dep., Amort./Sales | (24) 1.4 | (24) 2.0 |
| | | 2.3 | | | | | 4.0 | 4.4 |
| | | | | | | | | 4.4 |
| | | | | | | % Officers', Directors' Owners' Comp/Sales | (12) 7.3 | |
| | | | | | | | | 14.2 |
| 1955M | 25416M | 253275M | 570214M | 313662M | 550005M | Net Sales ($) | 2142730M | 2045527M |
| 387M | 6955M | 77286M | 273651M | 237201M | 515841M | Total Assets ($) | 1785362M | 1497386M |

M = $ thousand     MM = $ million
See Pages 9 through 22 for Explanation of Ratios and Data

## Comparative Historical Data  |  Current Data Sorted by Sales

Type of Statement — counts by period: 6 (4/1-9/30/11) and 34 (10/1/11-3/31/12)

| (#) | 4/1/09-3/31/10 ALL | (#) | 4/1/10-3/31/11 ALL | (#) | 4/1/11-3/31/12 ALL | Type of Statement | 0-1MM | 1-3MM | 3-5MM | 5-10MM | 10-25MM | 25MM & OVER |
|---|---|---|---|---|---|---|---|---|---|---|---|---|
|  | 9 |  | 9 |  | 7 | Unqualified |  |  |  |  |  | 6 |
|  | 4 |  | 3 |  | 4 | Reviewed |  | 1 |  |  | 1 | 2 |
|  | 2 |  |  |  | 1 | Compiled |  |  | 4 | 1 |  |  |
|  | 4 |  | 3 |  | 6 | Tax Returns |  |  |  | 2 | 1 |  |
|  | 22 |  | 21 |  | 22 | Other |  | 2 | 1 | 2 | 7 | 10 |
|  | 41 |  | 36 |  | 40 | **NUMBER OF STATEMENTS** |  | 3 | 5 | 5 | 9 | 18 |

*(ASSETS, LIABILITIES and INCOME DATA for the 0-1MM through 10-25MM columns are marked "DATA NOT AVAILABLE"; values shown only for 25MM & OVER.)*

### ASSETS (%)

| 4/1/09-3/31/10 | 4/1/10-3/31/11 | 4/1/11-3/31/12 | Item | 25MM & OVER |
|---|---|---|---|---|
| % | % | % |  | % |
| 19.3 | 20.0 | 15.6 | Cash & Equivalents | 15.7 |
| 29.0 | 27.7 | 30.1 | Trade Receivables (net) | 28.2 |
| 21.4 | 21.5 | 26.6 | Inventory | 25.7 |
| 6.0 | 2.9 | 2.6 | All Other Current | 3.8 |
| 75.6 | 72.0 | 74.9 | Total Current | 73.3 |
| 12.0 | 11.4 | 12.9 | Fixed Assets (net) | 11.7 |
| 6.1 | 6.6 | 6.4 | Intangibles (net) | 7.5 |
| 6.3 | 10.0 | 5.8 | All Other Non-Current | 7.4 |
| 100.0 | 100.0 | 100.0 | Total | 100.0 |

### LIABILITIES

| 4/1/09-3/31/10 | 4/1/10-3/31/11 | 4/1/11-3/31/12 | Item | 25MM & OVER |
|---|---|---|---|---|
| 7.5 | 4.8 | 7.7 | Notes Payable-Short Term | 3.9 |
| 5.8 | 1.8 | 1.7 | Cur. Mat.-L.T.D. | 1.3 |
| 17.3 | 17.3 | 21.6 | Trade Payables | 23.2 |
| .1 | .2 | .2 | Income Taxes Payable | .4 |
| 16.6 | 16.5 | 15.8 | All Other Current | 13.7 |
| 47.4 | 40.6 | 47.0 | Total Current | 42.5 |
| 6.2 | 6.4 | 7.4 | Long-Term Debt | 9.4 |
| .3 | .3 | .3 | Deferred Taxes | .5 |
| 13.1 | 8.6 | 3.3 | All Other Non-Current | 4.0 |
| 33.1 | 44.1 | 41.9 | Net Worth | 43.6 |
| 100.0 | 100.0 | 100.0 | Total Liabilities & Net Worth | 100.0 |

### INCOME DATA

| 4/1/09-3/31/10 | 4/1/10-3/31/11 | 4/1/11-3/31/12 | Item | 25MM & OVER |
|---|---|---|---|---|
| 100.0 | 100.0 | 100.0 | Net Sales | 100.0 |
| 42.2 | 41.3 | 42.3 | Gross Profit | 40.0 |
| 41.3 | 36.4 | 36.0 | Operating Expenses | 33.9 |
| .9 | 4.9 | 6.3 | Operating Profit | 6.1 |
| 1.7 | 1.5 | .9 | All Other Expenses (net) | 1.6 |
| -.8 | 3.4 | 5.4 | Profit Before Taxes | 4.5 |

### RATIOS

| (#) | 4/1/09-3/31/10 | (#) | 4/1/10-3/31/11 | (#) | 4/1/11-3/31/12 | Ratio | 25MM & OVER |
|---|---|---|---|---|---|---|---|
|  | 3.2 |  | 3.8 |  | 3.3 | Current | 3.9 |
|  | 1.6 |  | 2.1 |  | 2.2 |  | 2.3 |
|  | 1.2 |  | 1.2 |  | 1.1 |  | 1.1 |
|  | 2.0 |  | 2.3 |  | 2.2 | Quick | 2.3 |
|  | 1.0 |  | 1.3 |  | 1.1 |  | 1.3 |
|  | .7 |  | .9 |  | .7 |  | .8 |
| 38 | 9.7 | 39 | 9.4 | 35 | 10.4 | Sales/Receivables | 39 9.3 |
| 54 | 6.7 | 47 | 7.7 | 47 | 7.7 |  | 53 6.9 |
| 63 | 5.8 | 65 | 5.6 | 63 | 5.8 |  | 65 5.6 |
| 34 | 10.7 | 33 | 11.0 | 30 | 12.0 | Cost of Sales/Inventory | 46 8.0 |
| 79 | 4.6 | 84 | 4.4 | 85 | 4.3 |  | 114 3.2 |
| 131 | 2.8 | 138 | 2.6 | 126 | 2.9 |  | 146 2.5 |
| 24 | 15.0 | 24 | 15.1 | 22 | 16.9 | Cost of Sales/Payables | 21 17.6 |
| 43 | 8.4 | 42 | 8.7 | 50 | 7.3 |  | 50 7.3 |
| 71 | 5.2 | 75 | 4.9 | 78 | 4.7 |  | 94 3.9 |
|  | 3.2 |  | 3.1 |  | 3.2 | Sales/Working Capital | 2.8 |
|  | 7.0 |  | 4.3 |  | 6.3 |  | 6.2 |
|  | 31.8 |  | 31.9 |  | 57.6 |  | 22.0 |
|  | 17.4 |  | 36.3 |  | 42.6 | EBIT/Interest | 40.2 |
| (33) | 1.8 | (29) | 5.2 | (34) | 12.0 |  | (17) 10.6 |
|  | -4.6 |  | 1.9 |  | 3.1 |  | -.1 |
|  | 7.5 |  |  |  |  | Net Profit + Depr., Dep., Amort./Cur. Mat. L/T/D |  |
| (13) | 3.4 |  |  |  |  |  |  |
|  | -4.4 |  |  |  |  |  |  |
|  | .1 |  | .1 |  | .1 | Fixed/Worth | .1 |
|  | .2 |  | .2 |  | .2 |  | .3 |
|  | 3.5 |  | 1.3 |  | .9 |  | .8 |
|  | .5 |  | .4 |  | .4 | Debt/Worth | .4 |
|  | 1.5 |  | .9 |  | .9 |  | .9 |
|  | 18.8 |  | 7.8 |  | 8.1 |  | 9.3 |
|  | 25.4 |  | 58.5 |  | 77.5 | % Profit Before Taxes/Tangible Net Worth | 142.8 |
| (33) | 10.3 | (30) | 21.7 | (36) | 32.3 |  | (16) 12.7 |
|  | -22.0 |  | 5.0 |  | 4.8 |  | 3.3 |
|  | 13.4 |  | 19.8 |  | 23.1 | % Profit Before Taxes/Total Assets | 15.8 |
|  | .9 |  | 7.2 |  | 12.7 |  | 6.9 |
|  | -16.2 |  | 1.4 |  | 2.0 |  | -1.1 |
|  | 52.2 |  | 56.3 |  | 169.2 | Sales/Net Fixed Assets | 72.9 |
|  | 26.6 |  | 29.2 |  | 24.4 |  | 22.2 |
|  | 12.0 |  | 9.2 |  | 9.4 |  | 6.3 |
|  | 3.0 |  | 3.1 |  | 3.3 | Sales/Total Assets | 3.1 |
|  | 1.8 |  | 1.9 |  | 2.4 |  | 1.6 |
|  | 1.0 |  | 1.2 |  | 1.6 |  | 1.2 |
|  | .8 |  | .6 |  | 1.3 | % Depr., Dep., Amort./Sales | 1.4 |
| (31) | 1.4 | (27) | 1.4 | (26) | 1.8 |  | (11) 1.8 |
|  | 2.0 |  | 1.8 |  | 2.9 |  | 3.7 |
|  |  |  |  |  | 2.2 | % Officers', Directors' Owners' Comp/Sales |  |
|  |  | (10) | 4.6 |  |  |  |  |
|  |  |  |  |  | 6.9 |  |  |

### Net Sales ($) / Total Assets ($)

| 4/1/09-3/31/10 | 4/1/10-3/31/11 | 4/1/11-3/31/12 | Item | 0-1MM | 1-3MM | 3-5MM | 5-10MM | 10-25MM | 25MM & OVER |
|---|---|---|---|---|---|---|---|---|---|
| 2231526M | 2209204M | 1714527M | Net Sales ($) |  | 6577M | 19278M | 35846M | 161012M | 1491814M |
| 1724293M | 1662396M | 1111321M | Total Assets ($) |  | 2271M | 8306M | 15008M | 62585M | 1023151M |

M = $ thousand    MM = $ million
See Pages 9 through 22 for Explanation of Ratios and Data

**Current Data Sorted by Assets**   |   **Comparative Historical Data**

| Type of Statement | 0-500M | 500M-2MM | 2-10MM | 10-50MM | 50-100MM | 100-250MM | | 4/1/07-3/31/08 | 4/1/08-3/31/09 |
|---|---|---|---|---|---|---|---|---|---|
| Unqualified | | 1 | 3 | 14 | 7 | 5 | | 26 | 38 |
| Reviewed | | 1 | 12 | 6 | 1 | | | 18 | 11 |
| Compiled | | 3 | 3 | | | | | 7 | 7 |
| Tax Returns | 3 | 1 | 5 | 2 | | | | 9 | 7 |
| Other | | 4 | 12 | 20 | 4 | 5 | | 47 | 47 |
| | | 19 (4/1-9/30/11) | | 93 (10/1/11-3/31/12) | | | | ALL | ALL |
| NUMBER OF STATEMENTS | 3 | 10 | 35 | 42 | 12 | 10 | | 107 | 110 |

| 0-500M | 500M-2MM | 2-10MM | 10-50MM | 50-100MM | 100-250MM | | 4/1/07-3/31/08 | 4/1/08-3/31/09 |
|---|---|---|---|---|---|---|---|---|
| % | % | % | % | % | % | **ASSETS** | % | % |
| | 19.8 | 12.7 | 18.1 | 8.3 | 21.7 | Cash & Equivalents | 13.2 | 13.2 |
| | 23.9 | 28.0 | 24.5 | 23.1 | 21.0 | Trade Receivables (net) | 23.8 | 25.0 |
| | 25.5 | 30.8 | 28.6 | 22.9 | 17.5 | Inventory | 26.5 | 27.9 |
| | 2.3 | 2.5 | 4.4 | 6.6 | 3.7 | All Other Current | 3.0 | 3.4 |
| | 71.5 | 74.0 | 75.6 | 61.0 | 63.9 | Total Current | 66.5 | 69.4 |
| | 10.2 | 15.8 | 10.8 | 17.8 | 10.8 | Fixed Assets (net) | 19.1 | 15.8 |
| | 1.1 | 5.5 | 7.7 | 15.3 | 16.7 | Intangibles (net) | 8.9 | 7.8 |
| | 17.3 | 4.7 | 5.9 | 5.9 | 8.6 | All Other Non-Current | 5.4 | 6.9 |
| | 100.0 | 100.0 | 100.0 | 100.0 | 100.0 | Total | 100.0 | 100.0 |
| | | | | | | **LIABILITIES** | | |
| | 11.7 | 7.8 | 7.9 | 2.6 | .2 | Notes Payable-Short Term | 13.6 | 10.5 |
| | 3.1 | 1.1 | 1.9 | 4.4 | 1.0 | Cur. Mat.-L.T.D. | 3.1 | 2.4 |
| | 8.1 | 16.6 | 10.9 | 12.6 | 9.9 | Trade Payables | 12.1 | 13.1 |
| | .0 | .4 | 1.4 | .4 | .6 | Income Taxes Payable | .6 | .3 |
| | 8.2 | 12.3 | 12.5 | 9.7 | 17.7 | All Other Current | 10.5 | 12.7 |
| | 31.1 | 38.3 | 34.7 | 29.8 | 29.3 | Total Current | 39.9 | 39.1 |
| | 3.9 | 9.1 | 7.7 | 21.3 | 13.5 | Long-Term Debt | 10.3 | 13.2 |
| | .0 | .5 | .4 | .5 | 1.1 | Deferred Taxes | .4 | .2 |
| | 5.8 | 6.3 | 15.8 | 4.1 | 5.0 | All Other Non-Current | 5.4 | 10.7 |
| | 59.2 | 45.8 | 41.5 | 44.3 | 51.1 | Net Worth | 44.1 | 36.7 |
| | 100.0 | 100.0 | 100.0 | 100.0 | 100.0 | Total Liabilities & Net Worth | 100.0 | 100.0 |
| | | | | | | **INCOME DATA** | | |
| | 100.0 | 100.0 | 100.0 | 100.0 | 100.0 | Net Sales | 100.0 | 100.0 |
| | 47.6 | 41.1 | 41.7 | 31.7 | 35.1 | Gross Profit | 39.8 | 38.9 |
| | 42.1 | 32.9 | 34.2 | 26.8 | 28.5 | Operating Expenses | 32.1 | 32.7 |
| | 5.5 | 8.2 | 7.5 | 4.9 | 6.7 | Operating Profit | 7.7 | 6.2 |
| | .4 | 1.3 | 1.9 | 2.7 | 1.1 | All Other Expenses (net) | 2.0 | 1.8 |
| | 5.1 | 6.9 | 5.6 | 2.2 | 5.6 | Profit Before Taxes | 5.7 | 4.4 |
| | | | | | | **RATIOS** | | |
| | 3.2 | 4.7 | 4.4 | 3.5 | 5.2 | | 4.0 | 3.4 |
| | 2.4 | 2.0 | 2.4 | 2.3 | 2.4 | Current | 2.0 | 2.2 |
| | 1.7 | 1.3 | 1.4 | 1.5 | 1.2 | | 1.2 | 1.3 |
| | 2.4 | 2.2 | 2.9 | 2.2 | 3.6 | | 2.5 | 1.9 |
| | 1.2 | 1.0 | 1.3 | 1.1 | 1.4 | Quick | 1.0 | 1.2 |
| | .9 | .6 | .7 | .7 | .7 | | .5 | .6 |
| | 0  UND | 29  12.5 | 35  10.3 | 35  10.4 | 47  7.7 | | 31  11.8 | 31  11.8 |
| | 32  11.5 | 43  8.4 | 59  6.2 | 50  7.3 | 68  5.4 | Sales/Receivables | 44  8.3 | 43  8.5 |
| | 51  7.2 | 68  5.4 | 76  4.8 | 79  4.6 | 81  4.5 | | 59  6.1 | 65  5.6 |
| | 16  23.5 | 39  9.3 | 35  10.5 | 38  9.7 | 47  7.8 | | 28  13.0 | 46  7.9 |
| | 63  5.8 | 104  3.5 | 122  3.0 | 89  4.1 | 101  3.6 | Cost of Sales/Inventory | 71  5.1 | 86  4.2 |
| | 166  2.2 | 174  2.1 | 174  2.1 | 111  3.3 | 135  2.7 | | 117  3.1 | 137  2.7 |
| | 0  UND | 22  16.9 | 23  15.7 | 29  12.5 | 21  17.3 | | 16  22.1 | 22  16.4 |
| | 10  35.4 | 41  9.0 | 41  9.0 | 38  9.5 | 48  7.6 | Cost of Sales/Payables | 31  11.6 | 36  10.3 |
| | 60  6.1 | 59  6.2 | 58  6.3 | 44  8.3 | 61  6.0 | | 54  6.7 | 57  6.4 |
| | 4.4 | 3.2 | 2.4 | 2.6 | 1.8 | | 3.5 | 3.0 |
| | 6.0 | 5.9 | 4.2 | 4.5 | 3.1 | Sales/Working Capital | 6.4 | 5.3 |
| | 19.3 | 13.9 | 7.5 | 9.0 | 13.2 | | 23.1 | 13.9 |
| | 63.7 | 37.5 | 40.1 | | | | 16.1 | 17.9 |
| | (33) 8.2 | (33) 15.9 | 9.5 | | | EBIT/Interest | (93) 6.3 | (94) 3.8 |
| | -.1 | 4.0 | .1 | | | | 1.3 | .6 |
| | | | 18.5 | | | Net Profit + Depr., Dep., | 15.9 | 16.3 |
| | | (11) 5.2 | | | | Amort./Cur. Mat. L/T/D | (26) 3.8 | (20) 2.5 |
| | | 2.5 | | | | | -.1 | -.1 |
| | .1 | .1 | .1 | .1 | .1 | | .1 | .1 |
| | .2 | .3 | .2 | .4 | .2 | Fixed/Worth | .4 | .3 |
| | .2 | .8 | .4 | 1.4 | -.5 | | 1.0 | 1.1 |
| | .6 | .5 | .3 | .5 | .2 | | .4 | .4 |
| | .7 | 1.2 | .9 | .9 | .6 | Debt/Worth | 1.4 | 1.3 |
| | 1.0 | 5.1 | 2.4 | 1.7 | -4.3 | | 3.4 | 4.7 |
| | 47.7 | 53.2 | 31.5 | 19.8 | | | 69.7 | 44.7 |
| | (31) 21.3 | (38) 27.3 | (11) 15.8 | 15.6 | | % Profit Before Taxes/Tangible Net Worth | (93) 24.5 | (96) 18.0 |
| | -.8 | 8.3 | -6.8 | -.6 | | | 3.1 | 2.4 |
| | 24.7 | 19.4 | 17.1 | 10.2 | 20.6 | | 23.7 | 21.2 |
| | 11.0 | 10.3 | 6.8 | 5.4 | 6.2 | % Profit Before Taxes/Total Assets | 9.8 | 7.9 |
| | -.5 | 4.9 | -2.6 | -4.9 | -7.9 | | .8 | -.4 |
| | 163.7 | 52.2 | 41.7 | 42.0 | 36.4 | | 44.9 | 47.9 |
| | 29.3 | 25.7 | 18.0 | 16.8 | 13.9 | Sales/Net Fixed Assets | 18.3 | 18.2 |
| | 15.2 | 11.8 | 9.5 | 4.8 | 5.1 | | 6.3 | 8.0 |
| | 4.9 | 3.1 | 1.9 | 2.0 | 1.5 | | 2.8 | 2.6 |
| | 2.6 | 2.4 | 1.5 | 1.6 | 1.1 | Sales/Total Assets | 1.9 | 1.8 |
| | 1.5 | 1.2 | 1.2 | 1.0 | .7 | | 1.2 | 1.3 |
| | | .8 | .6 | | | | .6 | .8 |
| | | (26) 1.4 | (37) 1.6 | | | % Depr., Dep., Amort./Sales | (82) 1.5 | (84) 1.5 |
| | | 2.7 | 3.1 | | | | 2.8 | 2.6 |
| | | 2.6 | | | | | 2.3 | 2.0 |
| | | (10) 3.5 | | | | % Officers', Directors' Owners' Comp/Sales | (24) 5.5 | (18) 4.4 |
| | | 5.1 | | | | | 8.1 | 8.9 |
| 4871M | 43523M | 390477M | 1664147M | 1369375M | 2169580M | Net Sales ($) | 3951466M | 5071150M |
| 966M | 13137M | 174117M | 1015857M | 857742M | 1898461M | Total Assets ($) | 2820366M | 3317319M |

**Comparative Historical Data** | **Current Data Sorted by Sales**

| | 4/1/09-3/31/10 ALL | 4/1/10-3/31/11 ALL | 4/1/11-3/31/12 ALL | 0-1MM | 1-3MM | 3-5MM | 5-10MM | 10-25MM | 25MM & OVER |
|---|---|---|---|---|---|---|---|---|---|
| **Type of Statement** | | | | | 19 (4/1-9/30/11) | | 93 (10/1/11-3/31/12) | | |
| Unqualified | 30 | 28 | 30 | | 2 | 1 | 8 | 5 | 22 |
| Reviewed | 15 | 7 | 20 | | 1 | 1 | | 7 | 4 |
| Compiled | 5 | 6 | 6 | | 1 | | 4 | 1 | |
| Tax Returns | 5 | 6 | 11 | | 4 | | 5 | 1 | 1 |
| Other | 45 | 40 | 45 | 1 | 3 | 2 | 3 | 8 | 27 |
| **NUMBER OF STATEMENTS** | 100 | 87 | 112 | 1 | 11 | 4 | 20 | 22 | 54 |
| | % | % | % | % | % | % | % | % | % |
| **ASSETS** | | | | | | | | | |
| Cash & Equivalents | 13.8 | 17.8 | 16.0 | | 11.4 | | 14.7 | 19.1 | 15.3 |
| Trade Receivables (net) | 22.8 | 21.5 | 24.9 | | 19.3 | | 27.9 | 27.5 | 24.5 |
| Inventory | 26.7 | 26.4 | 27.7 | | 35.6 | | 31.7 | 24.8 | 26.2 |
| All Other Current | 6.0 | 3.5 | 4.0 | | 4.0 | | 2.2 | 5.0 | 4.6 |
| Total Current | 69.3 | 69.2 | 72.6 | | 70.3 | | 76.5 | 76.3 | 70.6 |
| Fixed Assets (net) | 16.9 | 14.5 | 12.9 | | 6.1 | | 17.7 | 11.1 | 12.0 |
| Intangibles (net) | 7.5 | 8.3 | 7.8 | | 7.6 | | 1.1 | 8.5 | 10.6 |
| All Other Non-Current | 6.4 | 8.0 | 6.8 | | 16.0 | | 4.7 | 4.1 | 6.8 |
| Total | 100.0 | 100.0 | 100.0 | | 100.0 | | 100.0 | 100.0 | 100.0 |
| **LIABILITIES** | | | | | | | | | |
| Notes Payable-Short Term | 11.1 | 6.3 | 7.3 | | 10.8 | | 7.7 | 12.2 | 4.6 |
| Cur. Mat.-L.T.D. | 3.0 | 1.7 | 1.9 | | 3.0 | | 1.1 | 1.3 | 2.4 |
| Trade Payables | 13.5 | 11.9 | 13.1 | | 15.1 | | 13.1 | 12.3 | 13.6 |
| Income Taxes Payable | .2 | .3 | .8 | | .3 | | .4 | .2 | 1.3 |
| All Other Current | 10.7 | 12.7 | 12.2 | | 7.6 | | 18.2 | 9.4 | 12.8 |
| Total Current | 38.5 | 32.9 | 35.3 | | 36.8 | | 40.6 | 35.3 | 34.8 |
| Long-Term Debt | 13.0 | 11.6 | 10.5 | | 15.4 | | 8.7 | 9.9 | 10.7 |
| Deferred Taxes | .4 | .3 | .4 | | .8 | | .3 | .1 | .6 |
| All Other Non-Current | 3.8 | 4.7 | 9.3 | | 3.2 | | 1.2 | 7.3 | 13.9 |
| Net Worth | 44.3 | 50.5 | 44.4 | | 43.8 | | 49.3 | 47.3 | 40.0 |
| Total Liabilties & Net Worth | 100.0 | 100.0 | 100.0 | | 100.0 | | 100.0 | 100.0 | 100.0 |
| **INCOME DATA** | | | | | | | | | |
| Net Sales | 100.0 | 100.0 | 100.0 | | 100.0 | | 100.0 | 100.0 | 100.0 |
| Gross Profit | 39.4 | 41.6 | 40.6 | | 48.2 | | 41.6 | 43.7 | 36.4 |
| Operating Expenses | 34.1 | 34.6 | 33.7 | | 40.3 | | 33.7 | 35.6 | 30.1 |
| Operating Profit | 5.4 | 7.0 | 6.9 | | 7.9 | | 7.9 | 8.1 | 6.2 |
| All Other Expenses (net) | 2.0 | 1.4 | 1.5 | | .7 | | .6 | 2.6 | 1.5 |
| Profit Before Taxes | 3.4 | 5.6 | 5.4 | | 7.2 | | 7.2 | 5.5 | 4.7 |
| **RATIOS** | | | | | | | | | |
| Current | 3.5 | 4.3 | 3.9 | | 4.1 | | 4.9 | 5.5 | 3.5 |
| | 2.0 | 2.5 | 2.1 | | 2.0 | | 2.0 | 2.8 | 2.1 |
| | 1.3 | 1.5 | 1.4 | | 1.5 | | 1.4 | 1.4 | 1.4 |
| Quick | 2.0 | 2.4 | 2.3 | | 1.8 | | 2.2 | 3.3 | 2.3 |
| | 1.1 | 1.4 | 1.2 | | 1.2 | | 1.0 | 1.5 | 1.2 |
| | .5 | .6 | .7 | | .5 | | .6 | .6 | .7 |
| Sales/Receivables | 29  12.6 | 30  12.0 | 32  11.5 | | 10  38.3 | | 28  12.9 | 29  12.4 | 39  9.3 |
| | 44  8.4 | 47  7.8 | 48  7.6 | | 35  10.3 | | 35  10.3 | 45  8.1 | 58  6.3 |
| | 62  5.9 | 64  5.7 | 70  5.2 | | 83  4.4 | | 47  7.7 | 78  4.7 | 74  4.9 |
| Cost of Sales/Inventory | 38  9.5 | 61  6.0 | 46  7.9 | | 44  8.3 | | 21  17.1 | 39  9.4 | 47  7.8 |
| | 87  4.2 | 90  4.0 | 104  3.5 | | 159  2.3 | | 114  3.2 | 104  3.5 | 101  3.6 |
| | 148  2.5 | 176  2.1 | 140  2.6 | | 228  1.6 | | 192  1.9 | 152  2.4 | 135  2.7 |
| Cost of Sales/Payables | 20  18.4 | 23  15.8 | 22  16.9 | | 15  24.1 | | 19  19.4 | 18  20.3 | 23  15.6 |
| | 34  10.7 | 37  9.8 | 40  9.2 | | 44  8.3 | | 23  15.6 | 38  9.6 | 43  8.5 |
| | 49  7.5 | 59  6.2 | 57  6.4 | | 59  6.2 | | 47  7.7 | 51  7.2 | 60  6.1 |
| Sales/Working Capital | 2.7 | 2.9 | 2.5 | | 3.4 | | 2.4 | 2.5 | 2.4 |
| | 5.1 | 4.8 | 5.0 | | 5.3 | | 7.1 | 5.3 | 4.6 |
| | 13.8 | 8.0 | 11.0 | | 11.4 | | 14.9 | 11.8 | 10.4 |
| EBIT/Interest | 17.8 | 15.4 | 36.7 | | 35.5 | | 31.9 | 129.6 | 41.2 |
| | (80)  2.6 | (73)  5.3 | (93)  9.5 | | 9.7 | | (17)  17.3 | (21)  3.6 | (40)  10.1 |
| | -1.3 | .0 | 1.8 | | 1.1 | | 5.7 | 1.3 | 1.1 |
| Net Profit + Depr., Dep., Amort./Cur. Mat. L/T/D | 5.2 | 8.9 | 19.0 | | | | | | 19.0 |
| | (26)  2.6 | (20)  2.0 | (22)  4.6 | | | | | (14) | 4.4 |
| | .4 | .4 | 2.3 | | | | | | 2.3 |
| Fixed/Worth | .1 | .1 | .1 | | .0 | | .1 | .1 | .1 |
| | .3 | .3 | .2 | | .2 | | .2 | .3 | .2 |
| | 1.0 | .8 | .6 | | -.9 | | .5 | .9 | .7 |
| Debt/Worth | .4 | .4 | .4 | | .6 | | .5 | .4 | .4 |
| | 1.3 | 1.0 | .9 | | .8 | | .9 | 1.8 | .9 |
| | 4.5 | 3.1 | 2.3 | | -11.8 | | 2.1 | 3.2 | 2.4 |
| % Profit Before Taxes/Tangible Net Worth | 35.6 | 53.1 | 40.3 | | | | 93.2 | 44.9 | 33.6 |
| | (87)  11.6 | (82)  13.2 | (98)  21.1 | | | | 25.9 | (18)  24.2 | (47)  15.8 |
| | -6.3 | -1.2 | 2.8 | | | | 6.2 | -2.3 | -.6 |
| % Profit Before Taxes/Total Assets | 13.1 | 17.8 | 18.0 | | 15.1 | | 21.5 | 18.5 | 14.4 |
| | 4.0 | 6.1 | 7.8 | | 11.4 | | 9.7 | 8.0 | 6.8 |
| | -3.7 | -1.7 | .5 | | .4 | | 4.1 | -.2 | -1.8 |
| Sales/Net Fixed Assets | 38.9 | 33.2 | 46.5 | | 164.1 | | 36.8 | 44.5 | 46.4 |
| | 14.6 | 15.7 | 22.4 | | 52.2 | | 19.3 | 26.2 | 18.8 |
| | 6.4 | 7.3 | 11.4 | | 25.7 | | 9.7 | 12.3 | 8.7 |
| Sales/Total Assets | 2.3 | 2.3 | 2.5 | | 3.4 | | 3.0 | 2.7 | 2.0 |
| | 1.7 | 1.4 | 1.6 | | 1.5 | | 2.4 | 1.7 | 1.5 |
| | 1.2 | 1.0 | 1.2 | | 1.2 | | 1.2 | 1.3 | 1.2 |
| % Depr., Dep., Amort./Sales | .8 | .8 | .6 | | | | .5 | .9 | .5 |
| | (76)  1.8 | (64)  2.0 | (85)  1.6 | | | (16)  1.4 | (17)  1.4 | (42)  2.0 | |
| | 3.1 | 3.3 | 3.0 | | | | 3.1 | 2.3 | 3.1 |
| % Officers', Directors' Owners' Comp/Sales | 2.2 | 1.7 | 2.7 | | | | | | |
| | (21)  6.0 | (16)  7.2 | (22)  4.0 | | | | | | |
| | 13.7 | 9.6 | 6.1 | | | | | | |
| Net Sales ($) | 4589267M | 5211697M | 5641973M | 929M | 23561M | 15320M | 152371M | 343315M | 5106477M |
| Total Assets ($) | 3013765M | 3816153M | 3960280M | 2806M | 17342M | 17726M | 87505M | 209680M | 3625221M |

© RMA 2012

M = $ thousand    MM = $ million
See Pages 9 through 22 for Explanation of Ratios and Data

## Current Data Sorted by Assets | Comparative Historical Data

| 0-500M | 500M-2MM | 2-10MM | 10-50MM | 50-100MM | 100-250MM | Type of Statement | 4/1/07-3/31/08 ALL | 4/1/08-3/31/09 ALL |
|---|---|---|---|---|---|---|---|---|
| | | 1 | 8 | 5 | 4 | Unqualified | 16 | 21 |
| | 1 | 11 | 1 | | | Reviewed | 14 | 15 |
| | 3 | 4 | | | | Compiled | 5 | 8 |
| 1 | 3 | 2 | | | | Tax Returns | 9 | 5 |
| | 4 | 10 | 11 | 4 | 4 | Other | 47 | 40 |
| | 16 (4/1-9/30/11) | | 62 (10/1/11-3/31/12) | | | | | |
| 1 | 11 | 28 | 21 | 9 | 8 | NUMBER OF STATEMENTS | 91 | 89 |
| % | % | % | % | % | % | **ASSETS** | % | % |
| | 6.1 | 9.3 | 12.6 | | | Cash & Equivalents | 14.8 | 11.7 |
| | 30.4 | 28.0 | 33.1 | | | Trade Receivables (net) | 28.6 | 29.4 |
| | 30.3 | 26.0 | 21.3 | | | Inventory | 22.7 | 24.7 |
| | .6 | 1.8 | 10.2 | | | All Other Current | 4.7 | 5.0 |
| | 67.5 | 65.1 | 77.2 | | | Total Current | 70.8 | 70.9 |
| | 23.9 | 20.8 | 9.1 | | | Fixed Assets (net) | 16.8 | 15.3 |
| | .2 | 3.8 | 7.3 | | | Intangibles (net) | 6.2 | 6.5 |
| | 8.3 | 10.3 | 6.4 | | | All Other Non-Current | 6.2 | 7.3 |
| | 100.0 | 100.0 | 100.0 | | | Total | 100.0 | 100.0 |
| | | | | | | **LIABILITIES** | | |
| | 18.8 | 8.5 | 9.3 | | | Notes Payable-Short Term | 10.0 | 8.2 |
| | 1.7 | 2.7 | 2.6 | | | Cur. Mat.-L.T.D. | 2.0 | 3.0 |
| | 21.4 | 15.4 | 15.8 | | | Trade Payables | 17.7 | 14.5 |
| | .0 | .0 | .8 | | | Income Taxes Payable | .6 | .4 |
| | 14.3 | 5.6 | 18.6 | | | All Other Current | 13.6 | 10.7 |
| | 56.1 | 32.2 | 47.2 | | | Total Current | 43.9 | 36.8 |
| | 18.2 | 11.8 | 7.8 | | | Long-Term Debt | 12.6 | 9.0 |
| | .0 | .3 | .1 | | | Deferred Taxes | .5 | .5 |
| | 10.3 | 27.3 | 11.1 | | | All Other Non-Current | 10.0 | 8.7 |
| | 15.4 | 28.4 | 33.8 | | | Net Worth | 33.0 | 45.1 |
| | 100.0 | 100.0 | 100.0 | | | Total Liabilties & Net Worth | 100.0 | 100.0 |
| | | | | | | **INCOME DATA** | | |
| | 100.0 | 100.0 | 100.0 | | | Net Sales | 100.0 | 100.0 |
| | 40.7 | 36.0 | 37.2 | | | Gross Profit | 38.5 | 38.3 |
| | 40.5 | 29.8 | 30.4 | | | Operating Expenses | 34.4 | 33.4 |
| | .1 | 6.2 | 6.8 | | | Operating Profit | 4.1 | 4.9 |
| | .3 | 1.2 | 1.3 | | | All Other Expenses (net) | .9 | 2.1 |
| | -.2 | 5.0 | 5.5 | | | Profit Before Taxes | 3.2 | 2.8 |
| | | | | | | **RATIOS** | | |
| | 2.3 | 3.4 | 2.9 | | | Current | 3.8 | 3.8 |
| | 1.5 | 2.0 | 1.9 | | | | 2.2 | 1.8 |
| | .9 | 1.4 | 1.3 | | | | 1.3 | 1.3 |
| | 1.5 | 1.9 | 1.7 | | | Quick | 2.6 | 2.1 |
| | .8 | 1.2 | .9 | | | | 1.2 | 1.0 |
| | .4 | .8 | .6 | | | | .8 | .6 |
| | 29  12.7 | 38  9.7 | 40  9.1 | | | Sales/Receivables | 30  12.0 | 35  10.4 |
| | 39  9.3 | 48  7.6 | 56  6.5 | | | | 52  7.0 | 51  7.1 |
| | 62  5.9 | 58  6.3 | 66  5.5 | | | | 70  5.2 | 66  5.5 |
| | 18  20.8 | 36  10.2 | 26  14.2 | | | Cost of Sales/Inventory | 26  14.1 | 45  8.0 |
| | 68  5.4 | 65  5.6 | 57  6.4 | | | | 59  6.2 | 79  4.6 |
| | 135  2.7 | 111  3.3 | 91  4.0 | | | | 101  3.6 | 109  3.4 |
| | 18  19.9 | 24  15.0 | 22  16.8 | | | Cost of Sales/Payables | 20  18.2 | 19  18.9 |
| | 58  6.3 | 31  11.8 | 28  13.0 | | | | 31  11.8 | 35  10.5 |
| | 96  3.8 | 53  6.9 | 41  8.8 | | | | 57  6.4 | 49  7.5 |
| | 5.8 | 4.2 | 3.8 | | | Sales/Working Capital | 3.5 | 3.3 |
| | 12.7 | 7.2 | 4.9 | | | | 6.2 | 6.9 |
| | -39.7 | 11.8 | 17.7 | | | | 16.3 | 16.2 |
| | 5.8 | 27.7 | 51.5 | | | EBIT/Interest | 15.4 | 36.8 |
| | (10) 1.5 | (27) 6.7 | (20) 10.6 | | | | (70) 5.0 | (75) 6.6 |
| | -1.5 | 2.1 | .2 | | | | -1.1 | 2.0 |
| | | | | | | Net Profit + Depr., Dep., Amort./Cur. Mat. L/T/D | 6.5 | 8.9 |
| | | | | | | | (19) 2.8 | (21) 3.7 |
| | | | | | | | 1.8 | .7 |
| | .3 | .1 | .2 | | | Fixed/Worth | .1 | .1 |
| | 2.2 | .2 | .3 | | | | .3 | .3 |
| | -35.7 | 1.1 | -7.2 | | | | 1.8 | 1.0 |
| | 1.6 | .4 | .8 | | | Debt/Worth | .5 | .4 |
| | 14.9 | 1.0 | 1.9 | | | | 1.5 | 1.3 |
| | -93.5 | 6.6 | -90.7 | | | | 7.3 | 3.3 |
| | | 33.0 | 79.2 | | | % Profit Before Taxes/Tangible Net Worth | 63.7 | 45.6 |
| | | (24) 19.1 | (15) 45.9 | | | | (77) 25.1 | (75) 20.6 |
| | | 11.8 | .1 | | | | -1.6 | 3.6 |
| | 6.0 | 18.1 | 26.5 | | | % Profit Before Taxes/Total Assets | 22.8 | 22.1 |
| | .6 | 7.1 | 14.4 | | | | 9.1 | 8.4 |
| | -2.5 | 2.8 | -1.5 | | | | -1.9 | -.3 |
| | 26.0 | 48.8 | 52.9 | | | Sales/Net Fixed Assets | 54.8 | 46.1 |
| | 24.3 | 21.5 | 28.3 | | | | 21.6 | 21.3 |
| | 5.8 | 4.3 | 21.1 | | | | 9.2 | 9.0 |
| | 3.0 | 3.0 | 2.6 | | | Sales/Total Assets | 3.1 | 2.8 |
| | 2.4 | 2.0 | 1.8 | | | | 2.2 | 2.1 |
| | 2.2 | 1.3 | 1.5 | | | | 1.4 | 1.4 |
| | | .3 | .6 | | | % Depr., Dep., Amort./Sales | .7 | .5 |
| | | (26) .9 | (19) 1.0 | | | | (67) 1.5 | (70) 1.0 |
| | | 2.1 | 1.7 | | | | 3.2 | 2.4 |
| | | 2.7 | | | | % Officers', Directors' Owners' Comp/Sales | 3.4 | 2.6 |
| | | (10) 4.4 | | | | | (21) 5.7 | (25) 4.9 |
| | | 5.6 | | | | | 9.7 | 7.4 |
| 2662M | 32475M | 271856M | 1073454M | 713292M | 1893103M | Net Sales ($) | 2854767M | 4029757M |
| 478M | 12702M | 127179M | 488210M | 599079M | 1074476M | Total Assets ($) | 2053880M | 2604621M |

M = $ thousand   MM = $ million
See Pages 9 through 22 for Explanation of Ratios and Data

## Comparative Historical Data

## Current Data Sorted by Sales

| | 4/1/09-3/31/10 ALL | 4/1/10-3/31/11 ALL | 4/1/11-3/31/12 ALL | 0-1MM | 1-3MM | 3-5MM | 5-10MM | 10-25MM | 25MM & OVER |
|---|---|---|---|---|---|---|---|---|---|
| **Type of Statement** | | | | | | | | | |
| Unqualified | 21 | 14 | 18 | | | | 1 | 2 | 15 |
| Reviewed | 16 | 11 | 13 | | 1 | 3 | 2 | 6 | 1 |
| Compiled | 5 | 3 | 8 | | 2 | 2 | 2 | 2 | |
| Tax Returns | 6 | 7 | 6 | | 4 | 1 | 1 | | |
| Other | 38 | 48 | 33 | | 2 | 5 | 2 | 7 | 17 |
| | | | | 9 | 11 | 8 (4/1-9/30/11: 16) | | 62 (10/1/11-3/31/12) | |
| **NUMBER OF STATEMENTS** | 86 | 83 | 78 | 9 | 11 | 8 | | 17 | 33 |
| **ASSETS** | % | % | % | % | % | % | | % | % |
| Cash & Equivalents | 13.5 | 12.3 | 11.3 | | | 5.4 | | 7.2 | 14.9 |
| Trade Receivables (net) | 30.4 | 30.5 | 28.2 | | | 23.1 | | 31.6 | 28.2 |
| Inventory | 24.0 | 23.9 | 23.7 | | | 21.2 | | 32.3 | 20.1 |
| All Other Current | 4.5 | 4.9 | 4.7 | | | 1.5 | | 6.4 | 7.0 |
| Total Current | 72.4 | 71.6 | 67.8 | | | 51.3 | | 77.5 | 70.3 |
| Fixed Assets (net) | 14.6 | 14.1 | 16.8 | | | 28.7 | | 14.3 | 11.6 |
| Intangibles (net) | 7.6 | 8.3 | 7.2 | | | 5.3 | | 2.7 | 12.4 |
| All Other Non-Current | 5.4 | 6.0 | 8.2 | | | 14.7 | | 5.5 | 5.8 |
| Total | 100.0 | 100.0 | 100.0 | | | 100.0 | | 100.0 | 100.0 |
| **LIABILITIES** | | | | | | | | | |
| Notes Payable-Short Term | 12.0 | 12.4 | 9.1 | | | 11.3 | | 11.8 | 7.3 |
| Cur. Mat.-L.T.D. | 2.6 | 2.2 | 3.3 | | | 4.9 | | 2.4 | 4.4 |
| Trade Payables | 15.9 | 17.0 | 16.0 | | | 14.0 | | 19.5 | 14.5 |
| Income Taxes Payable | .2 | .1 | .2 | | | .0 | | .2 | .4 |
| All Other Current | 11.0 | 10.9 | 11.1 | | | 2.6 | | 8.2 | 14.7 |
| Total Current | 41.8 | 42.6 | 39.8 | | | 32.9 | | 42.1 | 41.3 |
| Long-Term Debt | 9.5 | 9.0 | 11.0 | | | 19.1 | | 9.2 | 7.5 |
| Deferred Taxes | .4 | .4 | .4 | | | .0 | | .0 | .6 |
| All Other Non-Current | 7.5 | 8.2 | 16.5 | | | 15.6 | | 40.6 | 10.5 |
| Net Worth | 40.8 | 39.8 | 32.4 | | | 32.5 | | 8.0 | 40.1 |
| Total Liabilities & Net Worth | 100.0 | 100.0 | 100.0 | | | 100.0 | | 100.0 | 100.0 |
| **INCOME DATA** | | | | | | | | | |
| Net Sales | 100.0 | 100.0 | 100.0 | | | 100.0 | | 100.0 | 100.0 |
| Gross Profit | 39.5 | 42.0 | 38.6 | | | 44.9 | | 31.1 | 39.7 |
| Operating Expenses | 34.8 | 34.9 | 33.8 | | | 38.4 | | 27.4 | 34.5 |
| Operating Profit | 4.7 | 7.1 | 4.8 | | | 6.5 | | 3.6 | 5.1 |
| All Other Expenses (net) | 1.8 | 1.5 | 1.5 | | | 1.3 | | .8 | 2.2 |
| Profit Before Taxes | 2.9 | 5.6 | 3.3 | | | 5.1 | | 2.8 | 2.9 |
| **RATIOS** | | | | | | | | | |
| Current | 3.1 | 2.9 | 3.0 | | | 2.6 | | 2.8 | 3.3 |
| | 1.9 | 2.0 | 1.9 | | | 1.9 | | 2.0 | 1.9 |
| | 1.2 | 1.2 | 1.3 | | | .9 | | 1.4 | 1.2 |
| Quick | 1.9 | 1.8 | 1.9 | | | 1.6 | | 1.5 | 2.2 |
| | 1.1 | 1.1 | 1.2 | | | 1.0 | | 1.1 | 1.2 |
| | .6 | .6 | .6 | | | .7 | | .6 | .6 |
| Sales/Receivables | (46) 8.0 | (39) 9.4 | (39) 9.4 | | | (34) 10.7 | | (45) 8.1 | (44) 8.3 |
| | (56) 6.6 | (52) 7.0 | (52) 7.0 | | | (45) 8.1 | | (55) 6.6 | (55) 6.6 |
| | (71) 5.1 | (67) 5.4 | (62) 5.9 | | | (62) 5.9 | | (60) 6.1 | (69) 5.3 |
| Cost of Sales/Inventory | (50) 7.3 | (37) 9.8 | (33) 10.9 | | | (35) 10.3 | | (33) 11.2 | (30) 12.0 |
| | (78) 4.7 | (78) 4.7 | (69) 5.3 | | | (99) 3.7 | | (81) 4.5 | (69) 5.3 |
| | (109) 3.3 | (122) 3.0 | (118) 3.1 | | | (152) 2.4 | | (99) 3.7 | (118) 3.1 |
| Cost of Sales/Payables | (24) 15.0 | (23) 16.0 | (25) 14.5 | | | (24) 15.3 | | (27) 13.6 | (25) 14.6 |
| | (39) 9.4 | (43) 8.5 | (37) 9.8 | | | (54) 6.7 | | (39) 9.3 | (38) 9.6 |
| | (62) 5.9 | (73) 5.0 | (62) 5.9 | | | (146) 2.5 | | (55) 6.6 | (65) 5.6 |
| Sales/Working Capital | 3.0 | 3.5 | 3.9 | | | 5.1 | | 3.8 | 3.2 |
| | 6.2 | 5.9 | 6.8 | | | 7.0 | | 7.4 | 5.2 |
| | 17.0 | 16.2 | 16.7 | | | -44.3 | | 11.5 | 18.5 |
| EBIT/Interest | 12.7 | 35.8 | 19.6 | | | 13.7 | | 14.9 | 30.8 |
| | (71) 3.6 | (71) 5.4 | (73) 4.9 | | | 4.9 | | 4.5 | (30) 7.4 |
| | 1.0 | 1.1 | 1.2 | | | 1.4 | | 1.9 | .3 |
| Net Profit + Depr., Dep., Amort./Cur. Mat. L/T/D | 9.0 | 11.6 | 6.4 | | | | | | 9.2 |
| | (22) 4.3 | (20) 2.8 | (19) 2.7 | | | | | | (12) 2.7 |
| | 1.8 | .2 | 1.5 | | | | | | 1.6 |
| Fixed/Worth | .1 | .1 | .1 | | | .3 | | .1 | .2 |
| | .4 | .3 | .3 | | | 1.0 | | .2 | .3 |
| | 1.2 | 2.0 | 3.1 | | | -35.7 | | 1.0 | -7.2 |
| Debt/Worth | .5 | .6 | .5 | | | .6 | | .5 | .5 |
| | 1.5 | 1.5 | 1.6 | | | 14.9 | | 1.6 | 1.8 |
| | 8.1 | 18.5 | 31.3 | | | -70.5 | | 6.3 | -90.7 |
| % Profit Before Taxes/Tangible Net Worth | 51.4 | 60.2 | 47.6 | | | | | 20.6 | 57.4 |
| | (71) 15.0 | (67) 32.7 | (61) 17.5 | | | | | (15) 14.1 | (24) 29.5 |
| | 2.7 | 6.4 | 2.8 | | | | | 3.0 | -2.7 |
| % Profit Before Taxes/Total Assets | 20.3 | 24.8 | 16.1 | | | 9.5 | | 7.9 | 21.6 |
| | 6.3 | 7.3 | 5.2 | | | 6.0 | | 4.4 | 4.0 |
| | -3.0 | .3 | -.2 | | | .6 | | 1.8 | -4.1 |
| Sales/Net Fixed Assets | 53.7 | 51.2 | 35.5 | | | 41.5 | | 65.9 | 32.4 |
| | 17.5 | 20.6 | 22.9 | | | 6.5 | | 26.2 | 23.0 |
| | 7.2 | 10.0 | 8.6 | | | 3.9 | | 12.0 | 10.4 |
| Sales/Total Assets | 2.7 | 2.7 | 2.6 | | | 2.8 | | 3.2 | 2.3 |
| | 1.8 | 1.9 | 1.9 | | | 1.3 | | 2.1 | 1.6 |
| | 1.2 | 1.3 | 1.3 | | | .8 | | 1.6 | 1.1 |
| % Depr., Dep., Amort./Sales | .7 | .8 | .6 | | | | | .2 | .9 |
| | (67) 1.5 | (60) 1.4 | (66) 1.4 | | | | | (16) .9 | (27) 1.9 |
| | 3.6 | 3.1 | 2.6 | | | | | 1.5 | 3.4 |
| % Officers', Directors', Owners' Comp/Sales | 2.9 | 2.0 | 1.4 | | | | | | |
| | (18) 5.1 | (21) 4.6 | (19) 4.2 | | | | | | |
| Net Sales ($) | 3855652M | 4444921M | 3986842M | | 20628M | 42796M | 63637M | 281500M | 3578281M |
| Total Assets ($) | 2760872M | 2877188M | 2302124M | | 10066M | 31120M | 29864M | 135309M | 2095765M |

Note: In the current-data asset/liability/income columns for 0-1MM, 1-3MM and 5-10MM the notation "DATA NOT AVAILABLE" appears.

M = $ thousand   MM = $ million
See Pages 9 through 22 for Explanation of Ratios and Data

## Current Data Sorted by Assets        Comparative Historical Data

| 0-500M | 500M-2MM | 2-10MM | 10-50MM | 50-100MM | 100-250MM | | 4/1/07-3/31/08 ALL | 4/1/08-3/31/09 ALL |
|---|---|---|---|---|---|---|---|---|
| | | | | | | **Type of Statement** | | |
| | 1 | 2 | 12 | 3 | 2 | Unqualified | 13 | 19 |
| | 2 | 11 | 5 | 1 | | Reviewed | 15 | 14 |
| | 1 | 5 | 2 | | | Compiled | 9 | 11 |
| 1 | 12 | 5 | 1 | | | Tax Returns | 7 | 10 |
| 1 | 4 | 15 | 16 | 2 | 6 | Other | 33 | 37 |
| 2 | 20 | 38 | 36 | 6 | 8 | **NUMBER OF STATEMENTS** | 77 | 91 |
| % | % | % | % | % | % | **ASSETS** | % | % |
| | 14.9 | 9.1 | 10.9 | | | Cash & Equivalents | 9.9 | 9.2 |
| | 26.8 | 28.0 | 24.2 | | | Trade Receivables (net) | 29.6 | 29.1 |
| | 31.7 | 35.0 | 33.6 | | | Inventory | 34.2 | 33.2 |
| | 3.4 | 2.1 | 3.7 | | | All Other Current | 3.1 | 4.2 |
| | 76.9 | 74.1 | 72.3 | | | Total Current | 76.8 | 75.7 |
| | 17.7 | 12.2 | 13.1 | | | Fixed Assets (net) | 13.6 | 13.3 |
| | 3.7 | 7.6 | 11.3 | | | Intangibles (net) | 4.7 | 5.5 |
| | 1.7 | 6.0 | 3.3 | | | All Other Non-Current | 4.9 | 5.4 |
| | 100.0 | 100.0 | 100.0 | | | Total | 100.0 | 100.0 |
| | | | | | | **LIABILITIES** | | |
| | 9.3 | 14.8 | 9.9 | | | Notes Payable-Short Term | 15.4 | 15.7 |
| | 2.5 | 1.5 | 3.9 | | | Cur. Mat.-L.T.D. | 1.5 | 3.1 |
| | 15.4 | 19.4 | 10.2 | | | Trade Payables | 16.3 | 14.1 |
| | .0 | .3 | .2 | | | Income Taxes Payable | .4 | .3 |
| | 20.6 | 8.4 | 8.8 | | | All Other Current | 9.4 | 10.3 |
| | 47.7 | 44.3 | 33.0 | | | Total Current | 43.1 | 43.5 |
| | 11.8 | 7.5 | 10.5 | | | Long-Term Debt | 12.2 | 11.5 |
| | .0 | .1 | .4 | | | Deferred Taxes | .1 | .2 |
| | 5.4 | 8.8 | 25.0 | | | All Other Non-Current | 7.0 | 4.2 |
| | 35.1 | 39.3 | 31.0 | | | Net Worth | 37.6 | 40.5 |
| | 100.0 | 100.0 | 100.0 | | | Total Liabilities & Net Worth | 100.0 | 100.0 |
| | | | | | | **INCOME DATA** | | |
| | 100.0 | 100.0 | 100.0 | | | Net Sales | 100.0 | 100.0 |
| | 46.8 | 40.4 | 40.5 | | | Gross Profit | 38.4 | 39.9 |
| | 44.5 | 36.3 | 32.2 | | | Operating Expenses | 33.9 | 35.6 |
| | 2.2 | 4.1 | 8.3 | | | Operating Profit | 4.5 | 4.3 |
| | .6 | .9 | 2.2 | | | All Other Expenses (net) | 1.4 | 1.4 |
| | 1.6 | 3.3 | 6.1 | | | Profit Before Taxes | 3.2 | 2.9 |
| | | | | | | **RATIOS** | | |
| | 3.1 | 3.7 | 3.6 | | | | 3.1 | 3.6 |
| | 1.9 | 1.7 | 2.2 | | | Current | 1.9 | 1.7 |
| | 1.4 | 1.1 | 1.6 | | | | 1.3 | 1.3 |
| | 1.6 | 2.0 | 1.6 | | | | 1.5 | 1.8 |
| | 1.1 | .9 | 1.0 | | | Quick | 1.0 | .8 |
| | .5 | .5 | .6 | | | | .6 | .5 |
| | 25  14.8 | 24  15.0 | 33  11.1 | | | | 32  11.4    32  11.5 | |
| | 39  9.4 | 39  9.3 | 47  7.8 | | | Sales/Receivables | 45  8.2    44  8.3 | |
| | 56  6.5 | 63  5.8 | 65  5.6 | | | | 62  5.9    61  6.0 | |
| | 10  37.2 | 59  6.2 | 87  4.2 | | | | 53  6.9    48  7.7 | |
| | 87  4.2 | 118  3.1 | 111  3.3 | | | Cost of Sales/Inventory | 94  3.9    100  3.7 | |
| | 166  2.2 | 174  2.1 | 146  2.5 | | | | 159  2.3    136  2.7 | |
| | 19  18.8 | 23  15.7 | 15  24.6 | | | | 21  17.0    18  20.5 | |
| | 38  9.6 | 43  8.5 | 32  11.5 | | | Cost of Sales/Payables | 38  9.7    33  11.2 | |
| | 61  6.0 | 69  5.3 | 52  7.0 | | | | 61  6.0    58  6.3 | |
| | 4.9 | 3.8 | 3.2 | | | | 3.9 | 3.8 |
| | 8.3 | 7.2 | 5.3 | | | Sales/Working Capital | 6.8 | 6.5 |
| | 13.8 | 28.4 | 7.0 | | | | 14.9 | 17.2 |
| | 12.9 | 55.1 | 20.4 | | | | 16.9 | 14.4 |
| | (17) 2.3 | (36) 7.7 | (30) 4.8 | | | EBIT/Interest | (70) 2.9    (81) 3.6 | |
| | -.8 | 1.0 | 1.2 | | | | .8 | 1.1 |
| | | | 8.6 | | | | 11.2 | 8.5 |
| | | (12) | 4.5 | | | Net Profit + Depr., Dep., Amort./Cur. Mat. L/T/D | (16) 5.3    (24) 2.9 | |
| | | | .6 | | | | 1.6 | .6 |
| | .1 | .1 | .1 | | | | .1 | .1 |
| | .3 | .4 | .4 | | | Fixed/Worth | .3 | .2 |
| | 1.3 | 1.9 | NM | | | | 1.4 | .7 |
| | .7 | .6 | .7 | | | | .6 | .5 |
| | 1.8 | 1.9 | 1.4 | | | Debt/Worth | 1.6 | 1.5 |
| | 5.7 | 40.3 | -9.6 | | | | 9.3 | 5.0 |
| | 49.8 | 57.1 | 47.7 | | | | 38.8 | 45.1 |
| | (18) 10.2 | (30) 23.0 | (26) 20.6 | | | % Profit Before Taxes/Tangible Net Worth | (66) 18.1    (78) 17.5 | |
| | -.7 | 7.6 | 1.3 | | | | 3.6 | 4.7 |
| | 16.7 | 16.1 | 21.6 | | | | 17.9 | 16.9 |
| | 3.1 | 7.4 | 7.7 | | | % Profit Before Taxes/Total Assets | 5.4 | 6.1 |
| | -3.0 | -1.3 | .4 | | | | -.2 | .3 |
| | 76.3 | 54.8 | 42.7 | | | | 62.9 | 66.4 |
| | 29.7 | 33.8 | 23.7 | | | Sales/Net Fixed Assets | 25.0 | 31.8 |
| | 21.3 | 12.2 | 7.8 | | | | 14.1 | 11.5 |
| | 3.6 | 2.7 | 2.4 | | | | 2.9 | 2.9 |
| | 3.0 | 2.2 | 1.8 | | | Sales/Total Assets | 2.2 | 2.1 |
| | 1.9 | 1.6 | 1.0 | | | | 1.5 | 1.6 |
| | .5 | .5 | .8 | | | | .8 | .6 |
| | (15) 1.2 | (28) 1.1 | (28) 1.5 | | | % Depr., Dep., Amort./Sales | (56) 1.2    (66) 1.3 | |
| | 2.1 | 1.5 | 2.8 | | | | 2.0 | 2.1 |
| | 4.9 | 1.3 | | | | | 2.2 | 3.6 |
| | (15) 6.6 | (12) 3.2 | | | | % Officers', Directors' Owners' Comp/Sales | (20) 3.7    (27) 4.7 | |
| | 19.7 | 6.8 | | | | | 6.3 | 7.2 |
| 4882M | 63163M | 428420M | 1394202M | 585065M | 2104182M | Net Sales ($) | 5550368M | 4593992M |
| 560M | 22216M | 193833M | 779880M | 400512M | 1209370M | Total Assets ($) | 2929230M | 2531105M |

M = $ thousand    MM = $ million
See Pages 9 through 22 for Explanation of Ratios and Data

## Comparative Historical Data / Current Data Sorted by Sales

| Type of Statement | | | | | | | | | |
|---|---|---|---|---|---|---|---|---|---|
| Unqualified | 16 | 21 | 20 | | | 1 | 1 | 2 | 16 |
| Reviewed | 9 | 15 | 19 | | | 3 | 3 | 9 | 4 |
| Compiled | 7 | 5 | 8 | 1 | | | 2 | 4 | 1 |
| Tax Returns | 10 | 9 | 19 | 1 | 5 | 7 | 4 | 1 | 1 |
| Other | 41 | 55 | 44 | 1 | 4 | 4 | 7 | 12 | 16 |
| | 4/1/09-3/31/10 ALL | 4/1/10-3/31/11 ALL | 4/1/11-3/31/12 ALL | 0-1MM | 1-3MM | 3-5MM | 5-10MM | 10-25MM | 25MM & OVER |
| | | | | | | 19 (4/1-9/30/11) | 91 (10/1/11-3/31/12) | | |
| **NUMBER OF STATEMENTS** | 83 | 105 | 110 | 4 | 9 | 15 | 16 | 28 | 38 |

| | % | % | % | % | % | % | % | % | % |
|---|---|---|---|---|---|---|---|---|---|
| **ASSETS** | | | | | | | | | |
| Cash & Equivalents | 13.3 | 11.6 | 11.4 | | | 14.6 | 15.8 | 10.1 | 9.6 |
| Trade Receivables (net) | 29.1 | 29.3 | 26.8 | | | 22.3 | 22.4 | 28.4 | 30.5 |
| Inventory | 31.1 | 32.7 | 33.4 | | | 32.4 | 35.3 | 32.1 | 35.4 |
| All Other Current | 3.4 | 3.1 | 3.1 | | | 2.4 | 1.7 | 2.3 | 4.1 |
| Total Current | 76.9 | 76.7 | 74.6 | | | 71.8 | 75.2 | 72.9 | 79.6 |
| Fixed Assets (net) | 13.0 | 12.3 | 13.1 | | | 17.3 | 10.4 | 13.1 | 11.2 |
| Intangibles (net) | 5.5 | 6.5 | 7.9 | | | 6.5 | 8.7 | 10.3 | 4.9 |
| All Other Non-Current | 4.6 | 4.6 | 4.3 | | | 4.4 | 5.7 | 3.8 | 4.2 |
| Total | 100.0 | 100.0 | 100.0 | | | 100.0 | 100.0 | 100.0 | 100.0 |
| **LIABILITIES** | | | | | | | | | |
| Notes Payable-Short Term | 10.4 | 8.7 | 11.0 | | | 7.3 | 11.1 | 15.7 | 9.6 |
| Cur. Mat.-L.T.D. | 2.6 | 4.6 | 3.1 | | | 2.1 | 1.9 | 2.1 | 4.7 |
| Trade Payables | 15.8 | 17.2 | 15.2 | | | 20.7 | 10.5 | 16.2 | 14.8 |
| Income Taxes Payable | .2 | .5 | .3 | | | .0 | .6 | .1 | .6 |
| All Other Current | 14.2 | 11.6 | 13.2 | | | 10.7 | 8.4 | 10.2 | 10.2 |
| Total Current | 43.2 | 42.6 | 42.7 | | | 40.9 | 32.5 | 44.3 | 39.9 |
| Long-Term Debt | 7.9 | 13.9 | 11.7 | | | 14.8 | 11.3 | 7.4 | 14.2 |
| Deferred Taxes | .1 | .3 | .2 | | | .0 | .0 | .2 | .6 |
| All Other Non-Current | 6.4 | 8.3 | 13.0 | | | 5.0 | 14.5 | 11.1 | 16.8 |
| Net Worth | 42.3 | 34.9 | 32.3 | | | 39.4 | 41.6 | 37.0 | 28.6 |
| Total Liabilities & Net Worth | 100.0 | 100.0 | 100.0 | | | 100.0 | 100.0 | 100.0 | 100.0 |
| **INCOME DATA** | | | | | | | | | |
| Net Sales | 100.0 | 100.0 | 100.0 | | | 100.0 | 100.0 | 100.0 | 100.0 |
| Gross Profit | 41.1 | 40.0 | 40.8 | | | 43.4 | 45.9 | 35.4 | 38.7 |
| Operating Expenses | 37.8 | 33.5 | 35.0 | | | 40.1 | 40.1 | 30.0 | 28.8 |
| Operating Profit | 3.3 | 6.4 | 5.8 | | | 3.3 | 5.7 | 5.4 | 9.9 |
| All Other Expenses (net) | 1.0 | 1.3 | 1.4 | | | 1.0 | .9 | 1.7 | 1.5 |
| Profit Before Taxes | 2.3 | 5.1 | 4.4 | | | 2.3 | 4.8 | 3.7 | 8.4 |
| **RATIOS** | | | | | | | | | |
| Current | 3.9 | 3.3 | 3.5 | | | 3.6 | 6.2 | 3.5 | 3.5 |
| | 1.8 | 2.0 | 1.9 | | | 1.9 | 2.8 | 1.6 | 2.1 |
| | 1.3 | 1.2 | 1.3 | | | 1.1 | 1.4 | 1.1 | 1.5 |
| Quick | 2.0 | 1.7 | 1.7 | | | 2.0 | 3.8 | 1.8 | 1.5 |
| | 1.0 | .9 | .9 | | | 1.1 | .9 | .9 | 1.0 |
| | .6 | .7 | .5 | | | .3 | .5 | .4 | .8 |
| Sales/Receivables | 34  10.7 | 34  10.8 | 27  13.5 | | | 21  17.4 | 18  20.0 | 27  13.6 | 41  8.8 |
| | 45  8.1 | 45  8.1 | 47  7.8 | | | 26  14.0 | 43  8.5 | 47  7.7 | 51  7.2 |
| | 69  5.3 | 64  5.7 | 66  5.5 | | | 47  7.8 | 57  6.4 | 69  5.3 | 69  5.3 |
| Cost of Sales/Inventory | 53  6.9 | 58  6.3 | 62  5.9 | | | 8  46.8 | 68  5.4 | 64  5.7 | 81  4.5 |
| | 85  4.3 | 106  3.4 | 111  3.3 | | | 99  3.7 | 99  3.7 | 94  3.9 | 111  3.3 |
| | 148  2.5 | 141  2.6 | 166  2.2 | | | 243  1.5 | 152  2.4 | 159  2.3 | 140  2.6 |
| Cost of Sales/Payables | 18  20.0 | 23  15.6 | 20  18.5 | | | 18  20.5 | 12  31.7 | 21  17.1 | 21  17.0 |
| | 35  10.5 | 40  9.2 | 38  9.6 | | | 25  14.8 | 35  10.5 | 34  10.6 | 42  8.7 |
| | 57  6.5 | 69  5.3 | 68  5.4 | | | 72  5.1 | 53  6.9 | 59  6.2 | 73  5.0 |
| Sales/Working Capital | 3.2 | 3.6 | 3.7 | | | 4.9 | 3.5 | 4.0 | 3.7 |
| | 7.2 | 5.6 | 6.0 | | | 8.9 | 5.2 | 7.4 | 5.3 |
| | 15.9 | 15.4 | 14.8 | | | 42.3 | 13.8 | 60.1 | 7.4 |
| EBIT/Interest | 16.0 | 24.4 | 17.3 | | | 23.1 | 45.0 | 10.9 | 27.8 |
| | (69) 3.7 | (87) 3.7 | (98) 5.5 | | | (13) 2.8 | 10.9 | (25) 6.0 | (35) 7.8 |
| | .3 | .9 | 1.3 | | | 1.2 | .2 | 1.7 | 3.0 |
| Net Profit + Depr., Dep., Amort./Cur. Mat. L/T/D | 13.8 | 7.2 | 7.7 | | | | | | 8.6 |
| | (19) 3.5 | (24) 2.0 | (27) 3.8 | | | | | | (16) 4.5 |
| | 1.0 | .5 | 1.2 | | | | | | .9 |
| Fixed/Worth | .1 | .1 | .1 | | | .2 | .1 | .2 | .1 |
| | .2 | .2 | .3 | | | .6 | .3 | .4 | .2 |
| | .9 | 1.0 | 2.0 | | | -1.2 | -2.3 | 1.8 | .8 |
| Debt/Worth | .4 | .6 | .7 | | | .6 | .5 | .7 | .7 |
| | 1.2 | 1.6 | 1.8 | | | 1.5 | .8 | 2.4 | 1.4 |
| | 5.2 | 6.9 | 17.9 | | | -10.1 | -18.7 | 28.5 | 4.5 |
| % Profit Before Taxes/Tangible Net Worth | 29.8 | 46.7 | 49.4 | | | 21.9 | 65.7 | 52.9 | 49.2 |
| | (71) 9.7 | (85) 23.2 | (85) 21.0 | | | (11) 8.6 | (11) 19.1 | (23) 23.3 | (31) 34.8 |
| | .7 | 2.0 | 3.5 | | | 2.5 | 4.5 | 4.6 | 9.4 |
| % Profit Before Taxes/Total Assets | 11.1 | 19.2 | 17.1 | | | 11.9 | 19.6 | 15.5 | 25.2 |
| | 4.6 | 8.7 | 7.4 | | | 4.0 | 9.5 | 6.6 | 12.9 |
| | -.2 | .0 | .3 | | | .2 | -2.0 | 1.0 | 4.2 |
| Sales/Net Fixed Assets | 66.4 | 78.0 | 55.5 | | | 39.1 | 76.9 | 40.1 | 57.7 |
| | 27.6 | 35.6 | 28.1 | | | 28.4 | 26.7 | 27.4 | 27.7 |
| | 10.3 | 12.5 | 11.9 | | | 22.3 | 11.0 | 13.2 | 11.8 |
| Sales/Total Assets | 2.8 | 2.7 | 2.7 | | | 3.6 | 2.9 | 2.5 | 2.5 |
| | 2.2 | 2.1 | 2.0 | | | 3.0 | 2.5 | 2.2 | 1.9 |
| | 1.3 | 1.5 | 1.4 | | | 1.4 | 1.5 | 1.2 | 1.6 |
| % Depr., Dep., Amort./Sales | .6 | .6 | .8 | | | .5 | .7 | .5 | .9 |
| | (57) 1.4 | (69) 1.4 | (83) 1.3 | | | (10) 1.2 | (12) 1.1 | (22) 1.3 | (31) 1.5 |
| | 2.5 | 2.3 | 2.1 | | | 1.4 | 1.5 | 2.3 | 2.7 |
| % Officers', Directors' Owners' Comp/Sales | 2.7 | 2.2 | 3.0 | | | | 3.0 | | |
| | (23) 4.7 | (26) 4.4 | (30) 5.3 | | | | (10) 5.2 | | |
| | 6.1 | 7.6 | 8.8 | | | | 8.8 | | |
| Net Sales ($) | 4158422M | 5122526M | 4579914M | 2407M | 18785M | 58849M | 116834M | 460939M | 3922100M |
| Total Assets ($) | 2403481M | 2921870M | 2606371M | 3021M | 28779M | 28991M | 70176M | 288902M | 2186502M |

M = $ thousand    MM = $ million
See Pages 9 through 22 for Explanation of Ratios and Data

© RMA 2012

**Current Data Sorted by Assets**      **Comparative Historical Data**

| Type of Statement | 0-500M | 500M-2MM | 2-10MM | 10-50MM | 50-100MM | 100-250MM | | 4/1/07-3/31/08 ALL | 4/1/08-3/31/09 ALL |
|---|---|---|---|---|---|---|---|---|---|
| Unqualified | | | | 4 | 7 | | 2 | 14 | 12 |
| Reviewed | | 4 | 17 | 3 | 1 | | | 18 | 22 |
| Compiled | | 4 | 6 | 1 | | | | 21 | 18 |
| Tax Returns | | 10 | 9 | | | | | 6 | 19 |
| Other | | 3 | 14 | 16 | 3 | 2 | | 57 | 47 |
| | | 18 (4/1-9/30/11) | | 86 (10/1/11-3/31/12) | | | | | |
| **NUMBER OF STATEMENTS** | | 21 | 49 | 27 | 3 | 4 | | 116 | 118 |
| **ASSETS** | % | % | % | % | % | % | | % | % |
| Cash & Equivalents | | 16.0 | 9.4 | 6.4 | | | | 7.9 | 10.7 |
| Trade Receivables (net) | | 31.8 | 31.0 | 23.2 | | | | 28.9 | 28.3 |
| Inventory | | 26.5 | 28.5 | 30.6 | | | | 26.9 | 23.8 |
| All Other Current | | .3 | 1.4 | 2.0 | | | | 1.8 | 2.4 |
| Total Current | | 74.6 | 70.3 | 62.2 | | | | 65.6 | 65.1 |
| Fixed Assets (net) | | 20.8 | 21.5 | 18.7 | | | | 23.7 | 25.4 |
| Intangibles (net) | | 2.2 | 1.6 | 13.6 | | | | 5.9 | 4.8 |
| All Other Non-Current | | 2.3 | 6.6 | 5.5 | | | | 4.9 | 4.8 |
| Total | | 100.0 | 100.0 | 100.0 | | | | 100.0 | 100.0 |
| **LIABILITIES** | | | | | | | | | |
| Notes Payable-Short Term | | 11.0 | 9.5 | 12.1 | | | | 10.4 | 10.2 |
| Cur. Mat.-L.T.D. | | 1.8 | 3.4 | 2.2 | | | | 4.7 | 4.1 |
| Trade Payables | | 22.7 | 17.4 | 15.1 | | | | 18.0 | 17.1 |
| Income Taxes Payable | | .0 | .5 | .2 | | | | .1 | .1 |
| All Other Current | | 10.2 | 7.2 | 8.9 | | | | 9.2 | 7.9 |
| Total Current | | 45.6 | 37.9 | 38.4 | | | | 42.5 | 39.5 |
| Long-Term Debt | | 11.2 | 10.4 | 9.8 | | | | 15.4 | 14.1 |
| Deferred Taxes | | .0 | .5 | 1.0 | | | | .3 | .4 |
| All Other Non-Current | | 2.6 | 4.6 | 8.3 | | | | 4.5 | 10.6 |
| Net Worth | | 40.5 | 46.6 | 42.5 | | | | 37.4 | 35.3 |
| Total Liabilities & Net Worth | | 100.0 | 100.0 | 100.0 | | | | 100.0 | 100.0 |
| **INCOME DATA** | | | | | | | | | |
| Net Sales | | 100.0 | 100.0 | 100.0 | | | | 100.0 | 100.0 |
| Gross Profit | | 41.4 | 26.8 | 25.4 | | | | 28.5 | 27.3 |
| Operating Expenses | | 35.8 | 21.9 | 18.3 | | | | 22.1 | 22.8 |
| Operating Profit | | 5.5 | 5.0 | 7.1 | | | | 6.4 | 4.5 |
| All Other Expenses (net) | | .4 | 1.2 | 2.0 | | | | 1.2 | .8 |
| Profit Before Taxes | | 5.2 | 3.7 | 5.2 | | | | 5.2 | 3.7 |
| **RATIOS** | | | | | | | | | |
| Current | | 3.3 | 2.8 | 2.8 | | | | 2.9 | 2.9 |
| | | 1.8 | 1.7 | 1.6 | | | | 1.6 | 1.9 |
| | | 1.3 | 1.4 | 1.2 | | | | 1.2 | 1.2 |
| Quick | | 2.4 | 1.8 | 1.4 | | | | 1.7 | 1.9 |
| | | 1.3 | 1.0 | .6 | | | | .8 | 1.0 |
| | | .7 | .7 | .6 | | | | .6 | .6 |
| Sales/Receivables | | 26   14.3 | 37   9.9 | 36   10.1 | | | | 35   10.3 | 34   10.9 |
| | | 37   9.8 | 46   8.0 | 46   7.9 | | | | 48   7.6 | 41   8.9 |
| | | 51   7.2 | 60   6.1 | 62   5.9 | | | | 58   6.3 | 51   7.1 |
| Cost of Sales/Inventory | | 15   24.3 | 32   11.4 | 54   6.8 | | | | 35   10.5 | 20   18.5 |
| | | 32   11.3 | 62   5.9 | 89   4.1 | | | | 53   6.9 | 45   8.1 |
| | | 65   5.6 | 89   4.1 | 122   3.0 | | | | 87   4.2 | 75 |
| Cost of Sales/Payables | | 20   18.7 | 19   18.8 | 25   14.5 | | | | 18   20.1 | 18   20.3 |
| | | 31   11.6 | 28   13.2 | 41   8.9 | | | | 35   10.6 | 31   11.8 |
| | | 49   7.4 | 45   8.2 | 55   6.6 | | | | 56   6.5 | 44   8.3 |
| Sales/Working Capital | | 5.6 | 5.4 | 4.4 | | | | 5.4 | 5.2 |
| | | 13.6 | 8.1 | 8.7 | | | | 8.5 | 9.1 |
| | | 28.3 | 13.7 | 19.2 | | | | 34.4 | 25.7 |
| EBIT/Interest | | 35.9 | 15.1 | 16.9 | | | | 11.9 | 14.2 |
| | (16) | 6.9 | (43) 6.2 | (25) 5.0 | | | | (107) 4.3 | (104) 4.3 |
| | | 2.8 | 2.7 | 2.5 | | | | .8 | 1.0 |
| Net Profit + Depr., Dep., Amort./Cur. Mat. L/T/D | | | 15.8 | 4.8 | | | | 11.9 | 7.2 |
| | | | (10) 3.3 | (11) 2.5 | | | | (28) 2.5 | (28) 3.0 |
| | | | 2.2 | 2.1 | | | | .8 | 1.6 |
| Fixed/Worth | | .1 | .2 | .3 | | | | .3 | .2 |
| | | .5 | .4 | .8 | | | | .5 | .8 |
| | | 4.8 | .8 | 1.3 | | | | 1.5 | 1.8 |
| Debt/Worth | | .5 | .5 | .7 | | | | .8 | .7 |
| | | 1.4 | 1.4 | 1.7 | | | | 1.9 | 1.7 |
| | | 20.1 | 2.2 | 7.5 | | | | 4.2 | 4.5 |
| % Profit Before Taxes/Tangible Net Worth | | 180.8 | 35.6 | 41.3 | | | | 55.9 | 43.8 |
| | (19) | 56.8 | (48) 19.5 | (21) 25.3 | | | | (102) 28.4 | (103) 18.4 |
| | | 13.2 | 4.5 | 10.6 | | | | 2.7 | 5.8 |
| % Profit Before Taxes/Total Assets | | 41.6 | 14.7 | 12.5 | | | | 20.9 | 18.0 |
| | | 12.1 | 6.5 | 6.7 | | | | 8.2 | 7.3 |
| | | 3.7 | 3.2 | 3.1 | | | | .5 | .1 |
| Sales/Net Fixed Assets | | 99.1 | 22.7 | 21.7 | | | | 23.2 | 26.4 |
| | | 39.9 | 14.9 | 11.6 | | | | 12.5 | 13.3 |
| | | 8.8 | 7.1 | 5.5 | | | | 7.3 | 5.5 |
| Sales/Total Assets | | 4.6 | 2.7 | 2.3 | | | | 2.8 | 3.3 |
| | | 3.3 | 2.2 | 1.7 | | | | 2.2 | 2.5 |
| | | 2.1 | 1.8 | 1.3 | | | | 1.8 | 1.9 |
| % Depr., Dep., Amort./Sales | | .8 | 1.1 | 1.2 | | | | 1.2 | 1.3 |
| | (15) | 1.4 | (44) 1.8 | (26) 1.9 | | | | (105) 2.1 | (100) 2.2 |
| | | 2.2 | 2.5 | 2.9 | | | | 3.8 | 3.7 |
| % Officers', Directors' Owners' Comp/Sales | | 2.3 | 1.3 | | | | | 2.2 | 2.0 |
| | (15) | 4.0 | (17) 3.4 | | | | | (38) 5.5 | (43) 4.0 |
| | | 6.3 | 4.2 | | | | | 8.3 | 6.4 |
| Net Sales ($) | | 86819M | 646292M | 1016379M | 531987M | 869812M | | 3483286M | 3519141M |
| Total Assets ($) | | 24973M | 272293M | 594563M | 238278M | 490727M | | 1640985M | 1662355M |

*Note: Data Not Available for the 0-500M asset category.*

© RMA 2012

M = $ thousand    MM = $ million
See Pages 9 through 22 for Explanation of Ratios and Data

## Comparative Historical Data                    Current Data Sorted by Sales

| | | | Type of Statement | | 18 (4/1-9/30/11) | | 86 (10/1/11-3/31/12) | | |
|---|---|---|---|---|---|---|---|---|---|
| 14 | 13 | 12 | Unqualified | | | | | | |
| 22 | 20 | 24 | Reviewed | | | | | | |
| 11 | 18 | 11 | Compiled | | | | | | |
| 6 | 15 | 19 | Tax Returns | | | | | | |
| 49 | 46 | 38 | Other | | | | | | |
| 4/1/09-3/31/10 ALL | 4/1/10-3/31/11 ALL | 4/1/11-3/31/12 ALL | | 0-1MM | 1-3MM | 3-5MM | 5-10MM | 10-25MM | 25MM & OVER |
| 102 | 112 | 104 | NUMBER OF STATEMENTS | | 8 | 12 | 18 | 39 | 27 |
| % | % | % | **ASSETS** | % | % | % | % | % | % |
| 8.0 | 10.7 | 9.5 | Cash & Equivalents | | | 17.2 | 15.7 | 8.1 | 4.1 |
| 28.9 | 27.3 | 29.1 | Trade Receivables (net) | | | 31.3 | 28.9 | 29.3 | 28.6 |
| 26.7 | 27.7 | 28.9 | Inventory | | | 20.8 | 23.6 | 30.0 | 32.2 |
| 1.6 | 1.0 | 1.5 | All Other Current | | | 1.9 | 1.1 | 1.0 | 2.7 |
| 65.1 | 66.8 | 68.9 | Total Current | | | 71.2 | 69.3 | 68.4 | 67.7 |
| 23.8 | 21.4 | 20.4 | Fixed Assets (net) | | | 21.5 | 18.4 | 22.7 | 17.0 |
| 5.9 | 7.0 | 5.4 | Intangibles (net) | | | .4 | 4.2 | 3.9 | 11.8 |
| 5.2 | 4.9 | 5.2 | All Other Non-Current | | | 6.8 | 8.1 | 5.0 | 3.5 |
| 100.0 | 100.0 | 100.0 | Total | | | 100.0 | 100.0 | 100.0 | 100.0 |
| | | | **LIABILITIES** | | | | | | |
| 11.8 | 9.9 | 10.7 | Notes Payable-Short Term | | | 12.0 | 9.5 | 9.4 | 12.8 |
| 4.3 | 3.8 | 2.7 | Cur. Mat.-L.T.D. | | | 1.6 | 3.3 | 3.2 | 2.5 |
| 18.2 | 18.3 | 18.2 | Trade Payables | | | 16.5 | 16.1 | 17.2 | 19.4 |
| .2 | .3 | .3 | Income Taxes Payable | | | .0 | .5 | .4 | .2 |
| 8.3 | 6.3 | 8.4 | All Other Current | | | 13.3 | 5.7 | 8.3 | 8.0 |
| 42.9 | 38.6 | 40.2 | Total Current | | | 43.3 | 35.2 | 38.5 | 42.8 |
| 12.4 | 12.7 | 10.3 | Long-Term Debt | | | 18.5 | 12.0 | 9.1 | 8.7 |
| .5 | .5 | .6 | Deferred Taxes | | | .1 | .0 | .9 | .9 |
| 7.9 | 8.3 | 5.8 | All Other Non-Current | | | .0 | 2.6 | 5.4 | 10.7 |
| 36.3 | 39.9 | 43.2 | Net Worth | | | 38.1 | 50.2 | 46.1 | 36.9 |
| 100.0 | 100.0 | 100.0 | Total Liabilities & Net Worth | | | 100.0 | 100.0 | 100.0 | 100.0 |
| | | | **INCOME DATA** | | | | | | |
| 100.0 | 100.0 | 100.0 | Net Sales | | | 100.0 | 100.0 | 100.0 | 100.0 |
| 26.8 | 29.0 | 28.4 | Gross Profit | | | 44.0 | 30.9 | 23.9 | 21.3 |
| 24.4 | 22.4 | 22.9 | Operating Expenses | | | 38.3 | 25.0 | 18.9 | 15.1 |
| 2.4 | 6.7 | 5.4 | Operating Profit | | | 5.7 | 5.9 | 5.0 | 6.2 |
| 1.5 | .4 | 1.3 | All Other Expenses (net) | | | 3.9 | .6 | .5 | 1.9 |
| .9 | 6.2 | 4.2 | Profit Before Taxes | | | 1.8 | 5.3 | 4.4 | 4.4 |
| | | | **RATIOS** | | | | | | |
| 2.4 | 2.8 | 2.8 | | | | 5.7 | 2.9 | 2.6 | 2.5 |
| 1.6 | 1.8 | 1.7 | Current | | | 1.7 | 2.0 | 1.7 | 1.6 |
| 1.2 | 1.4 | 1.3 | | | | 1.1 | 1.5 | 1.4 | 1.2 |
| 1.4 | 1.8 | 1.6 | | | | 2.4 | 1.8 | 1.6 | 1.1 |
| .9 | .9 | 1.0 | Quick | | | 1.3 | 1.1 | 1.0 | .7 |
| .6 | .6 | .6 | | | | .7 | .7 | .6 | .6 |
| 39  9.4 | 38  9.7 | 36  10.2 | | | | 37  9.9 | 30  12.1 | 35  10.3 | 39  9.4 |
| 48  7.6 | 48  7.6 | 46  7.9 | Sales/Receivables | | | 47  7.8 | 39  9.3 | 48  7.6 | 49  7.5 |
| 62  5.9 | 58  6.3 | 59  6.2 | | | | 64  5.7 | 47  7.7 | 60  6.1 | 63  5.8 |
| 28  12.9 | 31  11.6 | 32  11.4 | | | | 16  22.7 | 18  19.8 | 28  12.9 | 54  6.8 |
| 59  6.2 | 64  5.7 | 62  5.9 | Cost of Sales/Inventory | | | 46  8.0 | 54  6.7 | 68  5.4 | 76  4.8 |
| 93  3.9 | 100  3.6 | 101  3.6 | | | | 89  4.1 | 85  4.3 | 111  3.3 | 94  3.9 |
| 21  17.6 | 22  16.3 | 21  17.0 | | | | 24  15.3 | 17  21.6 | 20  18.3 | 31  11.6 |
| 33  11.2 | 42  8.6 | 33  11.0 | Cost of Sales/Payables | | | 39  9.3 | 25  14.5 | 29  12.5 | 41  8.9 |
| 54  6.7 | 60  6.0 | 51  7.2 | | | | 51  7.1 | 38  9.7 | 51  7.2 | 53  6.9 |
| 5.3 | 4.6 | 5.4 | | | | 3.7 | 5.7 | 5.4 | 5.1 |
| 8.9 | 7.8 | 8.2 | Sales/Working Capital | | | 9.8 | 8.6 | 8.2 | 9.3 |
| 20.1 | 14.7 | 17.8 | | | | 240.7 | 19.4 | 14.2 | 22.0 |
| 6.8 | 27.1 | 19.8 | | | | | 24.2 | 10.8 | 20.4 |
| (95) 1.9 | (103) 8.1 | (91) 5.6 | EBIT/Interest | | | | (16) 6.7 | (34) 6.2 | 5.6 |
| -.4 | 2.8 | 2.7 | | | | | 3.5 | 3.1 | 2.3 |
| 4.8 | 9.5 | 6.5 | Net Profit + Depr., Dep., | | | | | 7.3 | 7.6 |
| (31) 2.3 | (26) 2.2 | (26) 2.9 | Amort./Cur. Mat. L/T/D | | | | | (12) 2.9 | (10) 3.6 |
| 1.3 | 1.5 | 2.1 | | | | | | 1.9 | 2.1 |
| .2 | .2 | .2 | | | | .3 | .2 | .2 | .3 |
| .6 | .6 | .6 | Fixed/Worth | | | .6 | .3 | .5 | .8 |
| 1.9 | 1.8 | 1.1 | | | | 23.9 | .7 | 1.0 | 4.4 |
| .8 | .6 | .5 | | | | .4 | .5 | .6 | 1.1 |
| 1.8 | 1.4 | 1.5 | Debt/Worth | | | 2.2 | 1.5 | 1.4 | 2.0 |
| 4.8 | 5.1 | 3.0 | | | | 38.4 | 2.4 | 2.1 | 63.8 |
| 22.4 | 49.3 | 48.8 | % Profit Before Taxes/Tangible | | | 196.6 | 96.5 | 37.5 | 52.2 |
| (88) 7.6 | (93) 23.6 | (94) 24.7 | Net Worth | | | (11) 18.5 | 24.1 | (37) 20.6 | (21) 34.3 |
| -3.3 | 8.0 | 7.4 | | | | -.1 | 10.5 | 4.8 | 10.6 |
| 8.7 | 23.5 | 19.5 | % Profit Before Taxes/Total | | | 33.3 | 23.3 | 15.1 | 19.8 |
| 2.8 | 9.3 | 7.5 | Assets | | | 7.6 | 10.6 | 6.5 | 7.5 |
| -2.1 | 3.5 | 3.1 | | | | .5 | 4.1 | 3.1 | 3.6 |
| 24.0 | 31.6 | 27.7 | | | | 38.6 | 39.4 | 18.0 | 24.3 |
| 13.1 | 14.8 | 14.3 | Sales/Net Fixed Assets | | | 15.1 | 17.8 | 13.4 | 13.2 |
| 4.2 | 5.7 | 7.1 | | | | 4.7 | 10.3 | 6.0 | 9.0 |
| 2.5 | 2.7 | 2.8 | | | | 4.5 | 3.7 | 2.7 | 2.6 |
| 2.0 | 2.0 | 2.2 | Sales/Total Assets | | | 2.2 | 2.4 | 2.2 | 2.1 |
| 1.5 | 1.6 | 1.7 | | | | 1.5 | 1.8 | 1.9 | 1.5 |
| 1.4 | 1.1 | 1.1 | | | | | 1.1 | 1.2 | 1.0 |
| (89) 2.3 | (92) 1.9 | (91) 1.7 | % Depr., Dep., Amort./Sales | | | | (15) 1.5 | (36) 1.9 | (25) 1.4 |
| 3.8 | 3.2 | 2.5 | | | | | 4.2 | 2.7 | 2.5 |
| 2.9 | 2.2 | 1.9 | % Officers', Directors', | | | | 2.0 | | |
| (30) 4.8 | (40) 3.8 | (35) 3.4 | Owners' Comp/Sales | | | | (12) 3.8 | | |
| 12.6 | 6.0 | 4.4 | | | | | 4.4 | | |
| 3507220M | 4282370M | 3151289M | Net Sales ($) | | 16295M | 45032M | 137336M | 660410M | 2292216M |
| 2235898M | 2599465M | 1620834M | Total Assets ($) | | 10015M | 22992M | 54761M | 342418M | 1190648M |

Note: For the Current Data, the 0-1MM and 1-3MM asset/liability/income columns are marked "DATA NOT AVAILABLE".

## Current Data Sorted by Assets      Comparative Historical Data

| 0-500M | 500M-2MM | 2-10MM | 10-50MM | 50-100MM | 100-250MM | Type of Statement | 24 | 22 |
|---|---|---|---|---|---|---|---|---|
| | 1 | 10 | 10 | | 10 | Unqualified | 24 | 22 |
| | 2 | 4 | 2 | | | Reviewed | 7 | 6 |
| | 4 | 4 | | | | Compiled | 6 | 4 |
| | | 4 | | 1 | | Tax Returns | 5 | 6 |
| 1 | 1 | 11 | 17 | 7 | 6 | Other | 36 | 40 |
| | | 18 (4/1-9/30/11) | 73 (10/1/11-3/31/12) | | | | 4/1/07-3/31/08 ALL | 4/1/08-3/31/09 ALL |
| 1 | 8 | 29 | 29 | 8 | 16 | **NUMBER OF STATEMENTS** | 78 | 78 |
| % | % | % | % | % | % | **ASSETS** | % | % |
| | | 8.2 | 17.9 | | 19.4 | Cash & Equivalents | 16.1 | 19.1 |
| | | 25.8 | 21.0 | | 18.3 | Trade Receivables (net) | 24.6 | 20.0 |
| | | 29.2 | 25.4 | | 22.6 | Inventory | 25.5 | 25.8 |
| | | 3.1 | 2.4 | | 5.3 | All Other Current | 4.1 | 2.8 |
| | | 66.3 | 66.7 | | 65.6 | Total Current | 70.2 | 67.6 |
| | | 21.9 | 23.1 | | 16.8 | Fixed Assets (net) | 21.2 | 21.6 |
| | | 7.5 | 6.1 | | 9.9 | Intangibles (net) | 4.0 | 5.2 |
| | | 4.2 | 4.1 | | 7.7 | All Other Non-Current | 4.6 | 5.6 |
| | | 100.0 | 100.0 | | 100.0 | Total | 100.0 | 100.0 |
| | | | | | | **LIABILITIES** | | |
| | | 6.9 | 4.5 | | 2.2 | Notes Payable-Short Term | 7.1 | 5.7 |
| | | 2.9 | 5.3 | | .3 | Cur. Mat.-L.T.D. | 3.0 | 2.3 |
| | | 14.0 | 11.6 | | 17.2 | Trade Payables | 13.6 | 11.5 |
| | | .3 | .2 | | .5 | Income Taxes Payable | .2 | .2 |
| | | 6.8 | 14.8 | | 8.3 | All Other Current | 12.2 | 12.9 |
| | | 31.0 | 36.5 | | 28.6 | Total Current | 36.2 | 32.6 |
| | | 9.1 | 4.4 | | 8.1 | Long-Term Debt | 9.9 | 9.8 |
| | | .4 | .6 | | .8 | Deferred Taxes | .4 | .4 |
| | | 8.2 | 16.6 | | 8.7 | All Other Non-Current | 8.8 | 5.9 |
| | | 51.3 | 41.9 | | 53.8 | Net Worth | 44.7 | 51.2 |
| | | 100.0 | 100.0 | | 100.0 | Total Liabilities & Net Worth | 100.0 | 100.0 |
| | | | | | | **INCOME DATA** | | |
| | | 100.0 | 100.0 | | 100.0 | Net Sales | 100.0 | 100.0 |
| | | 38.7 | 38.0 | | 33.8 | Gross Profit | 35.3 | 36.2 |
| | | 29.5 | 32.3 | | 28.2 | Operating Expenses | 29.9 | 30.9 |
| | | 9.2 | 5.7 | | 5.6 | Operating Profit | 5.4 | 5.3 |
| | | .3 | 1.4 | | 1.7 | All Other Expenses (net) | .8 | .5 |
| | | 8.9 | 4.3 | | 3.9 | Profit Before Taxes | 4.6 | 4.8 |
| | | | | | | **RATIOS** | | |
| | | 4.0 | 4.4 | | 4.4 | | 3.5 | 4.4 |
| | | 2.5 | 2.0 | | 2.4 | Current | 2.3 | 2.3 |
| | | 1.6 | 1.4 | | 1.6 | | 1.6 | 1.5 |
| | | 2.0 | 2.8 | | 2.5 | | 2.2 | 2.9 |
| | | 1.1 | .9 | | 1.5 | Quick | 1.3 | 1.3 |
| | | .6 | .6 | | .8 | | .9 | .7 |
| | | 35   10.4 | 36   10.0 | | 34   10.7 | | 35   10.3 | 28   12.9 |
| | | 42   8.7 | 48   7.6 | | 48   7.6 | Sales/Receivables | 49   7.5 | 39   9.3 |
| | | 51   7.2 | 58   6.3 | | 64   5.7 | | 63   5.8 | 56   6.6 |
| | | 32   11.5 | 61   6.0 | | 54   6.7 | | 46   8.0 | 52   7.0 |
| | | 74   4.9 | 114   3.2 | | 74   4.9 | Cost of Sales/Inventory | 82   4.5 | 80   4.5 |
| | | 130   2.8 | 152   2.4 | | 182   2.0 | | 122   3.0 | 142   2.6 |
| | | 21   17.6 | 17   21.3 | | 33   10.9 | | 24   15.4 | 20   18.2 |
| | | 33   11.1 | 39   9.4 | | 47   7.8 | Cost of Sales/Payables | 38   9.7 | 32   11.4 |
| | | 45   8.2 | 76   4.8 | | 76   4.8 | | 51   7.1 | 50   7.2 |
| | | 3.6 | 2.9 | | 1.6 | | 2.8 | 2.6 |
| | | 6.3 | 4.2 | | 3.7 | Sales/Working Capital | 4.1 | 4.1 |
| | | 9.5 | 11.9 | | 7.6 | | 9.0 | 9.2 |
| | | 92.8 | 58.0 | | 21.3 | | 27.7 | 31.6 |
| | | (26) 9.8 | (23) 6.2 | | (11) 1.5 | EBIT/Interest | (63) 4.5 | (64) 6.1 |
| | | 3.3 | .5 | | .7 | | 1.2 | .7 |
| | | | | | | | 12.5 | 21.3 |
| | | | | | | Net Profit + Depr., Dep., Amort./Cur. Mat. L/T/D | (25) 7.5 | (18) 9.3 |
| | | | | | | | 2.3 | 2.4 |
| | | .1 | .2 | | .1 | | .2 | .2 |
| | | .3 | .5 | | .3 | Fixed/Worth | .4 | .4 |
| | | 1.0 | -22.1 | | 2.2 | | 1.0 | .9 |
| | | .4 | .3 | | .3 | | .5 | .3 |
| | | 1.1 | 1.5 | | .9 | Debt/Worth | 1.1 | .8 |
| | | 2.8 | -39.7 | | 3.4 | | 3.7 | 2.3 |
| | | 63.8 | 35.8 | | 17.2 | | 43.9 | 42.7 |
| | | (27) 34.9 | (21) 25.7 | | (14) 7.4 | % Profit Before Taxes/Tangible Net Worth | (70) 14.4 | (71) 15.1 |
| | | 7.6 | -3.1 | | -1.8 | | 6.6 | .8 |
| | | 26.5 | 20.1 | | 10.9 | | 14.7 | 21.6 |
| | | 11.9 | 10.8 | | 2.5 | % Profit Before Taxes/Total Assets | 7.6 | 6.6 |
| | | 1.9 | -4.3 | | -.4 | | .7 | -1.3 |
| | | 27.8 | 22.7 | | 30.3 | | 24.4 | 17.6 |
| | | 12.9 | 11.6 | | 9.4 | Sales/Net Fixed Assets | 8.7 | 9.5 |
| | | 6.6 | 2.9 | | 3.4 | | 3.8 | 4.6 |
| | | 2.5 | 1.7 | | 1.9 | | 2.3 | 2.1 |
| | | 2.1 | 1.3 | | 1.1 | Sales/Total Assets | 1.5 | 1.5 |
| | | 1.6 | 1.1 | | .6 | | 1.0 | .9 |
| | | 1.0 | 1.1 | | | | 1.4 | 1.2 |
| | | (23) 2.2 | (27) 2.0 | | | % Depr., Dep., Amort./Sales | (65) 3.2 | (61) 2.6 |
| | | 3.7 | 6.3 | | | | 4.8 | 4.2 |
| | | 2.8 | | | | | 1.7 | 2.2 |
| | | (11) 4.1 | | | | % Officers', Directors' Owners' Comp/Sales | (16) 2.7 | (15) 3.1 |
| | | 5.6 | | | | | 5.6 | 6.3 |
| 1421M | 27528M | 306507M | 988359M | 673259M | 4179940M | Net Sales ($) | 5523053M | 6481287M |
| 383M | 9018M | 148363M | 677480M | 538530M | 2776133M | Total Assets ($) | 3407538M | 4250286M |

M = $ thousand    MM = $ million
See Pages 9 through 22 for Explanation of Ratios and Data

## Comparative Historical Data — Current Data Sorted by Sales

| | 4/1/09-3/31/10 ALL | 4/1/10-3/31/11 ALL | 4/1/11-3/31/12 ALL | Type of Statement | 0-1MM | 1-3MM | 3-5MM | 5-10MM | 10-25MM | 25MM & OVER |
|---|---|---|---|---|---|---|---|---|---|---|
| | 30 | 26 | 21 | Unqualified | | | | 4 | 7 | 14 |
| | 7 | 9 | 13 | Reviewed | | 1 | | 2 | 8 | |
| | 4 | 2 | 6 | Compiled | | | 2 | 1 | 2 | |
| | 9 | 18 | 8 | Tax Returns | | 1 | 4 | 1 | 2 | |
| | 42 | 41 | 43 | Other | 1 | 2 | 2 | 4 | 8 | 26 |
| | | | | | | 18 (4/1-9/30/11) | | 73 (10/1/11-3/31/12) | | |
| NUMBER OF STATEMENTS | 92 | 96 | 91 | | 1 | 4 | 8 | 11 | 27 | 40 |
| ASSETS | % | % | % | | % | % | % | % | % | % |
| Cash & Equivalents | 19.1 | 17.5 | 15.9 | | | | | 6.5 | 14.8 | 19.1 |
| Trade Receivables (net) | 21.4 | 24.7 | 23.5 | | | | | 23.8 | 23.7 | 21.1 |
| Inventory | 20.3 | 24.0 | 26.4 | | | | | 37.3 | 28.0 | 23.3 |
| All Other Current | 3.3 | 3.4 | 3.7 | | | | | 1.2 | 3.9 | 5.3 |
| Total Current | 64.1 | 69.6 | 69.4 | | | | | 68.8 | 70.4 | 68.8 |
| Fixed Assets (net) | 22.1 | 19.8 | 19.7 | | | | | 23.2 | 21.9 | 19.2 |
| Intangibles (net) | 6.4 | 5.4 | 6.4 | | | | | 3.7 | 3.5 | 6.8 |
| All Other Non-Current | 7.5 | 5.1 | 4.6 | | | | | 4.4 | 4.2 | 5.2 |
| Total | 100.0 | 100.0 | 100.0 | | | | | 100.0 | 100.0 | 100.0 |
| **LIABILITIES** | | | | | | | | | | |
| Notes Payable-Short Term | 6.1 | 5.8 | 5.7 | | | | | 9.5 | 4.5 | 4.6 |
| Cur. Mat.-L.T.D. | 2.4 | 3.4 | 3.2 | | | | | 3.7 | 2.3 | 3.7 |
| Trade Payables | 13.5 | 14.2 | 14.6 | | | | | 15.7 | 10.6 | 18.1 |
| Income Taxes Payable | .3 | .2 | .3 | | | | | .9 | .2 | .3 |
| All Other Current | 13.9 | 16.9 | 10.7 | | | | | 4.4 | 13.2 | 11.9 |
| Total Current | 36.2 | 40.6 | 34.4 | | | | | 34.2 | 30.9 | 38.6 |
| Long-Term Debt | 9.6 | 12.8 | 7.5 | | | | | 9.0 | 8.1 | 5.1 |
| Deferred Taxes | .4 | .3 | .6 | | | | | .1 | .8 | .8 |
| All Other Non-Current | 6.7 | 6.9 | 11.8 | | | | | 17.1 | 9.9 | 12.4 |
| Net Worth | 47.2 | 39.4 | 45.7 | | | | | 39.6 | 50.3 | 43.0 |
| Total Liabilties & Net Worth | 100.0 | 100.0 | 100.0 | | | | | 100.0 | 100.0 | 100.0 |
| **INCOME DATA** | | | | | | | | | | |
| Net Sales | 100.0 | 100.0 | 100.0 | | | | | 100.0 | 100.0 | 100.0 |
| Gross Profit | 38.0 | 38.6 | 36.1 | | | | | 35.8 | 40.8 | 31.5 |
| Operating Expenses | 36.6 | 31.6 | 29.9 | | | | | 29.3 | 34.0 | 25.9 |
| Operating Profit | 1.5 | 7.0 | 6.2 | | | | | 6.5 | 6.8 | 5.7 |
| All Other Expenses (net) | .8 | .4 | 1.0 | | | | | .2 | .6 | 2.0 |
| Profit Before Taxes | .7 | 6.6 | 5.2 | | | | | 6.3 | 6.2 | 3.7 |
| **RATIOS** | | | | | | | | | | |
| Current | 3.8 | 3.4 | 4.2 | | | | | 2.8 | 4.3 | 4.0 |
| | 2.1 | 2.2 | 2.2 | | | | | 2.3 | 2.3 | 2.1 |
| | 1.3 | 1.3 | 1.4 | | | | | 1.5 | 1.7 | 1.4 |
| Quick | 2.2 | 2.1 | 2.5 | | | | | 1.9 | 2.4 | 2.5 |
| | 1.3 | 1.2 | 1.2 | | | | | .9 | 1.3 | 1.1 |
| | .8 | .7 | .6 | | | | | .7 | .6 | .6 |
| Sales/Receivables | 30 12.1 | 34 10.9 | 35 10.3 | | | | | 35 10.5 | 35 10.4 | 36 10.0 |
| | 46 7.9 | 48 7.7 | 45 8.2 | | | | | 39 9.3 | 43 8.4 | 48 7.6 |
| | 65 5.6 | 65 5.6 | 60 6.1 | | | | | 49 7.4 | 51 7.1 | 63 5.8 |
| Cost of Sales/Inventory | 42 8.7 | 46 7.9 | 51 7.1 | | | | | 59 6.2 | 64 5.7 | 54 6.7 |
| | 74 4.9 | 78 4.7 | 85 4.3 | | | | | 85 4.3 | 104 3.5 | 81 4.5 |
| | 129 2.8 | 112 3.3 | 135 2.7 | | | | | 152 2.4 | 130 2.8 | 135 2.7 |
| Cost of Sales/Payables | 22 16.8 | 20 18.7 | 21 17.6 | | | | | 21 17.6 | 18 19.9 | 33 11.2 |
| | 43 8.4 | 36 10.0 | 35 10.3 | | | | | 34 10.6 | 29 12.8 | 46 7.9 |
| | 73 5.0 | 63 5.8 | 70 5.2 | | | | | 51 7.2 | 55 6.6 | 83 4.4 |
| Sales/Working Capital | 2.6 | 3.0 | 3.0 | | | | | 3.6 | 3.1 | 2.6 |
| | 5.2 | 4.9 | 4.9 | | | | | 6.3 | 4.5 | 4.2 |
| | 14.9 | 15.3 | 9.5 | | | | | 11.0 | 7.9 | 10.9 |
| EBIT/Interest | 14.0 | 36.9 | 29.7 | | | | | | 315.8 | 21.3 |
| | (76) 3.3 | (73) 9.0 | (71) 6.2 | | | | | | (21) 11.7 | (31) 3.8 |
| | -3.1 | 2.5 | .7 | | | | | | 2.5 | .6 |
| Net Profit + Depr., Dep., Amort./Cur. Mat. L/T/D | 20.9 | 67.9 | 15.7 | | | | | | | 15.7 |
| | (18) 5.5 | (20) 3.5 | (19) 2.3 | | | | | | | (11) 3.3 |
| | .9 | 1.3 | .6 | | | | | | | .8 |
| Fixed/Worth | .2 | .1 | .1 | | | | | .1 | .1 | .2 |
| | .5 | .4 | .3 | | | | | .5 | .3 | .4 |
| | 1.0 | 1.2 | 2.2 | | | | | 1.8 | 1.1 | 2.5 |
| Debt/Worth | .4 | .5 | .3 | | | | | .6 | .3 | .4 |
| | 1.1 | 1.1 | 1.2 | | | | | 1.4 | 1.1 | 1.5 |
| | 3.3 | 3.8 | 5.2 | | | | | 10.1 | 2.9 | 14.9 |
| % Profit Before Taxes/Tangible Net Worth | 28.6 | 64.0 | 37.4 | | | | | | 48.2 | 24.5 |
| | (81) 13.3 | (84) 27.0 | (76) 18.9 | | | | | | (24) 32.8 | (32) 12.2 |
| | -5.4 | 8.5 | .5 | | | | | | 10.7 | -1.0 |
| % Profit Before Taxes/Total Assets | 10.3 | 25.9 | 19.0 | | | | | 28.9 | 23.3 | 12.3 |
| | 3.0 | 9.8 | 7.8 | | | | | 11.4 | 11.9 | 5.6 |
| | -4.9 | 2.0 | -1.1 | | | | | -7.8 | -2.2 | -.9 |
| Sales/Net Fixed Assets | 20.2 | 30.0 | 33.2 | | | | | 21.1 | 24.7 | 32.1 |
| | 10.9 | 13.3 | 13.0 | | | | | 15.8 | 11.5 | 11.9 |
| | 3.8 | 5.2 | 4.5 | | | | | 4.5 | 3.4 | 3.3 |
| Sales/Total Assets | 1.9 | 2.4 | 2.3 | | | | | 2.5 | 2.4 | 1.7 |
| | 1.4 | 1.6 | 1.6 | | | | | 2.0 | 1.7 | 1.3 |
| | .9 | 1.2 | 1.1 | | | | | 1.8 | 1.3 | .9 |
| % Depr., Dep., Amort./Sales | 1.3 | 1.3 | .7 | | | | | | 1.1 | .6 |
| | (64) 3.1 | (70) 2.4 | (68) 1.9 | | | | | | (24) 2.0 | (26) 2.7 |
| | 7.8 | 4.8 | 4.1 | | | | | | 3.1 | 5.3 |
| % Officers', Directors' Owners' Comp/Sales | 1.8 | 3.6 | 3.4 | | | | | | | |
| | (22) 4.4 | (22) 7.2 | (19) 4.7 | | | | | | | |
| | 10.7 | 16.3 | 15.3 | | | | | | | |
| Net Sales ($) | 5369432M | 5313774M | 6177014M | | 983M | 8322M | 31379M | 84955M | 468698M | 5582677M |
| Total Assets ($) | 3782796M | 2993971M | 4149907M | | 2042M | 7979M | 17014M | 42442M | 313428M | 3767002M |

## Current Data Sorted by Assets

## Comparative Historical Data

| | | | | | | Type of Statement | | |
|---|---|---|---|---|---|---|---|---|
| | 1 | 1 | 1 | 3 | 1 | 1 | Unqualified | 8 | 6 |
| | 1 | 2 | 2 | 1 | | | Reviewed | 14 | 5 |
| | 1 | 1 | | | | | Compiled | 3 | 4 |
| | | 1 | | | | | Tax Returns | 2 | 2 |
| 1 | | 3 | 3 | 4 | 1 | | Other | 14 | 10 |
| | 3 (4/1-9/30/11) | | | 18 (10/1/11-3/31/12) | | | | 4/1/07- | 4/1/08- |
| | | | | | | | | 3/31/08 | 3/31/09 |
| 0-500M | 500M-2MM | 2-10MM | 10-50MM | 50-100MM | 100-250MM | | ALL | ALL |
| 1 | 3 | 6 | 8 | 2 | 1 | NUMBER OF STATEMENTS | 41 | 27 |
| % | % | % | % | % | % | | % | % |

| | | | | | | | | |
|---|---|---|---|---|---|---|---|---|
| | | | | | | **ASSETS** | | |
| | | | | | | Cash & Equivalents | 10.3 | 9.8 |
| | | | | | | Trade Receivables (net) | 30.9 | 29.0 |
| | | | | | | Inventory | 28.0 | 28.9 |
| | | | | | | All Other Current | 2.2 | 1.3 |
| | | | | | | Total Current | 71.3 | 68.9 |
| | | | | | | Fixed Assets (net) | 19.3 | 21.4 |
| | | | | | | Intangibles (net) | 4.1 | 5.6 |
| | | | | | | All Other Non-Current | 5.3 | 4.1 |
| | | | | | | Total | 100.0 | 100.0 |
| | | | | | | **LIABILITIES** | | |
| | | | | | | Notes Payable-Short Term | 6.8 | 8.0 |
| | | | | | | Cur. Mat.-L.T.D. | 2.7 | 2.2 |
| | | | | | | Trade Payables | 16.5 | 14.6 |
| | | | | | | Income Taxes Payable | .3 | .2 |
| | | | | | | All Other Current | 9.0 | 8.6 |
| | | | | | | Total Current | 35.3 | 33.7 |
| | | | | | | Long-Term Debt | 14.9 | 11.3 |
| | | | | | | Deferred Taxes | .2 | .1 |
| | | | | | | All Other Non-Current | 7.1 | 9.9 |
| | | | | | | Net Worth | 42.5 | 45.0 |
| | | | | | | Total Liabilities & Net Worth | 100.0 | 100.0 |
| | | | | | | **INCOME DATA** | | |
| | | | | | | Net Sales | 100.0 | 100.0 |
| | | | | | | Gross Profit | 31.9 | 32.2 |
| | | | | | | Operating Expenses | 24.5 | 24.5 |
| | | | | | | Operating Profit | 7.4 | 7.8 |
| | | | | | | All Other Expenses (net) | .7 | .8 |
| | | | | | | Profit Before Taxes | 6.6 | 7.0 |

### RATIOS

| | | | | | | | | | | |
|---|---|---|---|---|---|---|---|---|---|---|
| | | | | | | Current | | 3.2 | | 3.6 |
| | | | | | | | | 2.2 | | 2.2 |
| | | | | | | | | 1.5 | | 1.6 |
| | | | | | | Quick | | 2.0 | | 1.8 |
| | | | | | | | | 1.1 | | 1.1 |
| | | | | | | | | .8 | | .7 |
| | | | | | | Sales/Receivables | 38 | 9.7 | 37 | 10.0 |
| | | | | | | | 47 | 7.7 | 49 | 7.4 |
| | | | | | | | 58 | 6.3 | 61 | 5.9 |
| | | | | | | Cost of Sales/Inventory | 36 | 10.1 | 48 | 7.7 |
| | | | | | | | 66 | 5.5 | 68 | 5.4 |
| | | | | | | | 103 | 3.6 | 87 | 4.2 |
| | | | | | | Cost of Sales/Payables | 20 | 18.6 | 19 | 19.1 |
| | | | | | | | 32 | 11.4 | 26 | 14.3 |
| | | | | | | | 53 | 6.9 | 37 | 10.0 |
| | | | | | | Sales/Working Capital | | 4.1 | | 3.3 |
| | | | | | | | | 8.2 | | 6.0 |
| | | | | | | | | 11.5 | | 10.0 |
| | | | | | | EBIT/Interest | | 23.6 | | 22.0 |
| | | | | | | | (39) | 10.9 | (24) | 7.8 |
| | | | | | | | | 2.1 | | 3.4 |
| | | | | | | Net Profit + Depr., Dep., Amort./Cur. Mat. L/T/D | | 15.6 | | |
| | | | | | | | (11) | 5.4 | | |
| | | | | | | | | 2.5 | | |
| | | | | | | Fixed/Worth | | .3 | | .3 |
| | | | | | | | | .5 | | .5 |
| | | | | | | | | .9 | | 1.4 |
| | | | | | | Debt/Worth | | .5 | | .5 |
| | | | | | | | | 1.3 | | 1.4 |
| | | | | | | | | 2.8 | | 4.6 |
| | | | | | | % Profit Before Taxes/Tangible Net Worth | | 54.4 | | 66.4 |
| | | | | | | | (36) | 27.0 | (23) | 29.3 |
| | | | | | | | | 12.0 | | 8.3 |
| | | | | | | % Profit Before Taxes/Total Assets | | 22.1 | | 24.0 |
| | | | | | | | | 11.4 | | 12.9 |
| | | | | | | | | 3.8 | | 3.3 |
| | | | | | | Sales/Net Fixed Assets | | 27.9 | | 20.2 |
| | | | | | | | | 11.8 | | 13.2 |
| | | | | | | | | 7.3 | | 8.5 |
| | | | | | | Sales/Total Assets | | 3.0 | | 3.0 |
| | | | | | | | | 2.3 | | 2.1 |
| | | | | | | | | 1.7 | | 1.8 |
| | | | | | | % Depr., Dep., Amort./Sales | | .9 | | .6 |
| | | | | | | | (36) | 1.6 | (25) | 1.4 |
| | | | | | | | | 2.5 | | 2.1 |
| | | | | | | % Officers', Directors' Owners' Comp/Sales | | 1.6 | | |
| | | | | | | | (11) | 3.5 | | |
| | | | | | | | | 8.6 | | |

| | | | | | | | | |
|---|---|---|---|---|---|---|---|---|
| 2868M | 11479M | 66575M | 329526M | 180710M | 95023M | Net Sales ($) | 1156786M | 1248846M |
| 496M | 4306M | 28027M | 173585M | 148686M | 108657M | Total Assets ($) | 608528M | 648508M |

© RMA 2012

M = $ thousand    MM = $ million
See Pages 9 through 22 for Explanation of Ratios and Data

## Comparative Historical Data      Current Data Sorted by Sales

| Type of Statement | | | | | | | | | |
|---|---|---|---|---|---|---|---|---|---|
| | 8 | 2 | 6 | | | | | 1 | 5 |
| Unqualified | 6 | 8 | 4 | | | | 1 | 1 | |
| Reviewed | 2 | 2 | 1 | | | 1 | 1 | | |
| Compiled | | 1 | 1 | | | 1 | | | |
| Tax Returns | 16 | 6 | 9 | | | | | | |
| Other | | | | | | | | | |

| | 16 4/1/09- 3/31/10 ALL | 6 4/1/10- 3/31/11 ALL | 9 4/1/11- 3/31/12 ALL | 0-1MM | 3 (4/1-9/30/11) 1-3MM | 3-5MM | 18 (10/1/11-3/31/12) 5-10MM | 10-25MM | 25MM & OVER |
|---|---|---|---|---|---|---|---|---|---|
| NUMBER OF STATEMENTS | 32 | 19 | 21 | | 1 | 3 | 4 | 2 | 11 |
| **ASSETS** | % | % | % | % | % | % | % | % | % |
| Cash & Equivalents | 8.0 | 14.1 | 15.0 | | | | | | 7.5 |
| Trade Receivables (net) | 31.6 | 28.7 | 25.7 | | | | | | 28.3 |
| Inventory | 25.9 | 26.3 | 26.1 | | | | | | 27.9 |
| All Other Current | 3.1 | 1.0 | 3.7 | | | | | | 6.0 |
| Total Current | 68.6 | 70.1 | 70.6 | | | | | | 69.7 |
| Fixed Assets (net) | 22.6 | 22.8 | 20.3 | | | | | | 15.2 |
| Intangibles (net) | 3.0 | 3.4 | 6.3 | | | | | | 11.7 |
| All Other Non-Current | 5.8 | 3.6 | 2.9 | | | | | | 3.4 |
| Total | 100.0 | 100.0 | 100.0 | | | | | | 100.0 |
| **LIABILITIES** | | | | | | | | | |
| Notes Payable-Short Term | 8.7 | 5.8 | 6.0 | | | | | | 6.3 |
| Cur. Mat.-L.T.D. | 2.6 | 2.6 | 4.2 | | | | | | 4.5 |
| Trade Payables | 18.1 | 13.8 | 11.1 | | | | | | 14.0 |
| Income Taxes Payable | .7 | .2 | .2 | | | | | | .5 |
| All Other Current | 15.1 | 9.5 | 9.0 | | | | | | 7.3 |
| Total Current | 45.2 | 31.9 | 30.6 | | | | | | 32.5 |
| Long-Term Debt | 11.5 | 16.9 | 13.6 | | | | | | 1.5 |
| Deferred Taxes | .3 | .3 | .8 | | | | | | 1.6 |
| All Other Non-Current | 6.1 | 3.4 | 7.0 | | | | | | 10.6 |
| Net Worth | 36.9 | 47.5 | 48.0 | | | | | | 53.9 |
| Total Liabilities & Net Worth | 100.0 | 100.0 | 100.0 | | | | | | 100.0 |
| **INCOME DATA** | | | | | | | | | |
| Net Sales | 100.0 | 100.0 | 100.0 | | | | | | 100.0 |
| Gross Profit | 30.6 | 30.0 | 29.5 | | | | | | 20.8 |
| Operating Expenses | 24.9 | 21.6 | 21.6 | | | | | | 14.8 |
| Operating Profit | 5.7 | 8.4 | 7.9 | | | | | | 6.0 |
| All Other Expenses (net) | .8 | .6 | .7 | | | | | | .0 |
| Profit Before Taxes | 4.8 | 7.8 | 7.2 | | | | | | 6.0 |
| **RATIOS** | | | | | | | | | |
| Current | 3.0 | 4.1 | 4.7 | | | | | | 5.1 |
| | 1.7 | 2.9 | 2.4 | | | | | | 2.4 |
| | 1.1 | 1.5 | 1.6 | | | | | | .9 |
| Quick | 1.4 | 2.2 | 2.8 | | | | | | 2.9 |
| | .9 | 1.6 | 1.4 | | | | | | 1.1 |
| | .6 | .7 | .7 | | | | | | .5 |
| Sales/Receivables | 45 8.2 | 34 10.9 | 33 11.1 | | | | | | 41 8.9 |
| | 58 6.3 | 51 7.2 | 41 8.9 | | | | | | 51 7.1 |
| | 70 5.2 | 63 5.8 | 66 5.5 | | | | | | 76 4.8 |
| Cost of Sales/Inventory | 40 9.0 | 33 10.9 | 32 11.4 | | | | | | 50 7.3 |
| | 75 4.9 | 70 5.2 | 65 5.6 | | | | | | 74 4.9 |
| | 110 3.3 | 93 3.9 | 101 3.6 | | | | | | 111 3.3 |
| Cost of Sales/Payables | 23 15.6 | 20 18.5 | 14 26.3 | | | | | | 22 16.6 |
| | 37 9.9 | 28 13.3 | 23 15.6 | | | | | | 29 12.4 |
| | 55 6.6 | 37 9.8 | 37 9.9 | | | | | | 57 6.4 |
| Sales/Working Capital | 4.6 | 4.0 | 3.4 | | | | | | 3.0 |
| | 10.5 | 4.9 | 4.6 | | | | | | 4.0 |
| | 24.1 | 11.8 | 15.4 | | | | | | -40.2 |
| EBIT/Interest | 22.0 | 23.9 | 41.4 | | | | | | |
| | (28) 5.4 | (15) 6.6 | (17) 10.4 | | | | | | |
| | 1.3 | 2.9 | 3.7 | | | | | | |
| Net Profit + Depr., Dep., Amort./Cur. Mat. L/T/D | 23.3 | | | | | | | | |
| | (10) 2.6 | | | | | | | | |
| | 1.3 | | | | | | | | |
| Fixed/Worth | .3 | .3 | .2 | | | | | | .1 |
| | .6 | .4 | .4 | | | | | | .3 |
| | 1.3 | 1.0 | 8.6 | | | | | | 16.6 |
| Debt/Worth | .9 | .3 | .4 | | | | | | .4 |
| | 2.0 | 1.1 | .8 | | | | | | .7 |
| | 3.9 | 2.8 | 22.0 | | | | | | 39.4 |
| % Profit Before Taxes/Tangible Net Worth | 42.1 | 72.5 | 47.7 | | | | | | |
| | (30) 20.6 | (18) 28.7 | (17) 24.4 | | | | | | |
| | .4 | 9.5 | 19.8 | | | | | | |
| % Profit Before Taxes/Total Assets | 19.0 | 22.5 | 27.0 | | | | | | 17.2 |
| | 6.4 | 10.4 | 13.7 | | | | | | 10.3 |
| | -.2 | 5.0 | 9.1 | | | | | | 1.1 |
| Sales/Net Fixed Assets | 21.2 | 19.2 | 32.8 | | | | | | 38.9 |
| | 10.9 | 10.4 | 11.4 | | | | | | 14.0 |
| | 4.5 | 6.1 | 7.2 | | | | | | 6.4 |
| Sales/Total Assets | 2.5 | 2.5 | 2.7 | | | | | | 2.4 |
| | 2.0 | 2.2 | 2.2 | | | | | | 1.9 |
| | 1.3 | 1.6 | 1.5 | | | | | | 1.2 |
| % Depr., Dep., Amort./Sales | .9 | 1.2 | 1.0 | | | | | | 1.0 |
| | (25) 1.8 | 1.6 | (18) 1.4 | | | | | | (10) 1.4 |
| | 3.0 | 2.5 | 2.2 | | | | | | 2.1 |
| % Officers', Directors' Owners' Comp/Sales | | | | | | | | | |
| Net Sales ($) | 1403621M | 323013M | 686181M | | 2868M | 11479M | 27557M | 34196M | 610081M |
| Total Assets ($) | 949570M | 178658M | 463757M | | 496M | 4306M | 13629M | 15239M | 430087M |

(For the current-data columns 0-1MM through 10-25MM the asset, liability, income, and ratio figures are marked "DATA NOT AVAILABLE.")

© RMA 2012

M = $ thousand    MM = $ million
See Pages 9 through 22 for Explanation of Ratios and Data

**Current Data Sorted by Assets**      **Comparative Historical Data**

| 0-500M | 500M-2MM | 2-10MM | 10-50MM | 50-100MM | 100-250MM | Type of Statement | 4/1/07-3/31/08 ALL | 4/1/08-3/31/09 ALL |
|---|---|---|---|---|---|---|---|---|
|  | 1 | 2 | 6 | 3 | 1 | Unqualified | 7 | 12 |
|  | 3 | 4 | 3 | 1 | 1 | Reviewed | 6 | 6 |
| 1 | 4 | 3 | 1 |  |  | Compiled | 5 | 6 |
| 1 | 2 | 11 |  | 2 | 1 | Tax Returns | 8 | 4 |
|  |  |  |  |  |  | Other | 15 | 22 |
|  | 10 (4/1-9/30/11) |  | 38 (10/1/11-3/31/12) |  |  |  | 4/1/07-3/31/08 | 4/1/08-3/31/09 |
| 2 | 10 | 21 | 10 | 4 | 1 | NUMBER OF STATEMENTS | 41 | 50 |
| % | % | % | % | % | % | **ASSETS** | % | % |
|  | 13.0 | 10.1 | 13.2 |  |  | Cash & Equivalents | 15.5 | 10.7 |
|  | 37.5 | 26.9 | 22.9 |  |  | Trade Receivables (net) | 28.6 | 27.3 |
|  | 28.1 | 30.9 | 31.9 |  |  | Inventory | 23.3 | 26.1 |
|  | 11.6 | 4.8 | 2.7 |  |  | All Other Current | 3.4 | 2.6 |
|  | 90.1 | 72.7 | 70.7 |  |  | Total Current | 70.8 | 66.8 |
|  | 5.2 | 19.1 | 16.3 |  |  | Fixed Assets (net) | 18.8 | 20.5 |
|  | 3.0 | 4.8 | 10.7 |  |  | Intangibles (net) | 5.6 | 8.9 |
|  | 1.7 | 3.3 | 2.3 |  |  | All Other Non-Current | 4.9 | 3.8 |
|  | 100.0 | 100.0 | 100.0 |  |  | Total | 100.0 | 100.0 |
|  |  |  |  |  |  | **LIABILITIES** |  |  |
|  | 15.9 | 15.7 | 7.0 |  |  | Notes Payable-Short Term | 10.4 | 20.3 |
|  | 3.3 | 5.0 | 1.6 |  |  | Cur. Mat.-L.T.D. | 2.3 | 4.3 |
|  | 30.7 | 15.4 | 8.3 |  |  | Trade Payables | 14.7 | 13.7 |
|  | .3 | .3 | .6 |  |  | Income Taxes Payable | .2 | .2 |
|  | 6.3 | 6.2 | 6.6 |  |  | All Other Current | 6.7 | 7.4 |
|  | 56.5 | 42.5 | 24.1 |  |  | Total Current | 34.3 | 46.0 |
|  | 19.8 | 12.0 | 11.2 |  |  | Long-Term Debt | 10.5 | 16.8 |
|  | .8 | .0 | 1.4 |  |  | Deferred Taxes | .8 | 1.3 |
|  | 3.9 | 2.8 | 6.7 |  |  | All Other Non-Current | 5.9 | 11.5 |
|  | 19.0 | 42.6 | 56.6 |  |  | Net Worth | 48.4 | 24.4 |
|  | 100.0 | 100.0 | 100.0 |  |  | Total Liabilities & Net Worth | 100.0 | 100.0 |
|  |  |  |  |  |  | **INCOME DATA** |  |  |
|  | 100.0 | 100.0 | 100.0 |  |  | Net Sales | 100.0 | 100.0 |
|  | 39.4 | 37.3 | 33.9 |  |  | Gross Profit | 32.0 | 34.2 |
|  | 37.2 | 29.7 | 25.1 |  |  | Operating Expenses | 24.8 | 26.2 |
|  | 2.2 | 7.6 | 8.8 |  |  | Operating Profit | 7.2 | 8.0 |
|  | 1.8 | 1.2 | .6 |  |  | All Other Expenses (net) | .1 | 1.4 |
|  | .3 | 6.4 | 8.1 |  |  | Profit Before Taxes | 7.1 | 6.6 |
|  |  |  |  |  |  | **RATIOS** |  |  |
|  | 8.3 | 3.7 | 7.8 |  |  |  | 4.2 | 3.9 |
|  | 1.8 | 1.9 | 3.5 |  |  | Current | 2.0 | 2.2 |
|  | 1.0 | 1.2 | 1.9 |  |  |  | 1.4 | 1.3 |
|  | 4.7 | 2.0 | 5.1 |  |  |  | 3.3 | 1.9 |
|  | .8 | 1.0 | 1.5 |  |  | Quick | 1.1 | 1.0 |
|  | .5 | .5 | .9 |  |  |  | .8 | .7 |
|  | 38 9.7 | 30 12.2 | 42 8.7 |  |  |  | 35 10.5 | 30 12.2 |
|  | 49 7.4 | 41 8.9 | 54 6.7 |  |  | Sales/Receivables | 44 8.3 | 42 8.8 |
|  | 56 6.5 | 49 7.5 | 68 5.4 |  |  |  | 58 6.3 | 51 7.2 |
|  | 18 20.4 | 35 10.5 | 96 3.8 |  |  |  | 30 12.0 | 39 9.3 |
|  | 51 7.2 | 73 5.0 | 126 2.9 |  |  | Cost of Sales/Inventory | 59 6.2 | 70 5.2 |
|  | 111 3.3 | 152 2.4 | 159 2.3 |  |  |  | 93 3.9 | 96 3.8 |
|  | 13 28.4 | 20 18.1 | 16 23.2 |  |  |  | 20 18.7 | 16 22.5 |
|  | 46 8.0 | 29 12.6 | 26 14.2 |  |  | Cost of Sales/Payables | 29 12.6 | 28 12.9 |
|  | 130 2.8 | 41 8.8 | 38 9.7 |  |  |  | 47 7.8 | 37 9.9 |
|  | 3.9 | 4.4 | 1.7 |  |  |  | 3.9 | 4.3 |
|  | 6.0 | 6.5 | 3.5 |  |  | Sales/Working Capital | 6.3 | 6.4 |
|  | NM | 25.7 | 6.2 |  |  |  | 15.6 | 21.6 |
|  |  | 24.6 |  |  |  |  | 36.7 | 40.6 |
|  |  | (16) 6.2 |  |  |  | EBIT/Interest | (34) 6.2 | (45) 7.5 |
|  |  | 2.4 |  |  |  |  | 1.4 | 1.7 |
|  |  |  |  |  |  |  |  | 18.6 |
|  |  |  |  |  |  | Net Profit + Depr., Dep., Amort./Cur. Mat. L/T/D |  | (11) 4.3 |
|  |  |  |  |  |  |  |  | 2.1 |
|  | .0 | .1 | .1 |  |  |  | .2 | .2 |
|  | .4 | .2 | .4 |  |  | Fixed/Worth | .3 | .4 |
|  | -.2 | 1.7 | .9 |  |  |  | 1.3 | NM |
|  | .6 | .5 | .3 |  |  |  | .3 | .5 |
|  | 9.4 | 1.1 | .9 |  |  | Debt/Worth | .9 | 1.6 |
|  | -5.0 | 81.1 | 2.5 |  |  |  | 2.7 | -28.3 |
|  |  | 64.5 |  |  |  |  | 57.5 | 57.5 |
|  |  | (17) 26.2 |  |  |  | % Profit Before Taxes/Tangible Net Worth | (34) 24.4 | (37) 34.1 |
|  |  | 15.3 |  |  |  |  | 6.5 | 16.8 |
|  | 11.3 | 21.8 | 18.9 |  |  |  | 29.8 | 24.4 |
|  | 2.8 | 13.7 | 9.4 |  |  | % Profit Before Taxes/Total Assets | 10.8 | 12.7 |
|  | -7.1 | 6.7 | 3.6 |  |  |  | 2.8 | 2.9 |
|  | UND | 46.5 | 27.8 |  |  |  | 37.1 | 43.6 |
|  | 141.8 | 30.0 | 9.7 |  |  | Sales/Net Fixed Assets | 18.1 | 16.3 |
|  | 39.6 | 4.5 | 5.8 |  |  |  | 6.8 | 5.7 |
|  | 4.1 | 3.2 | 1.7 |  |  |  | 3.0 | 3.3 |
|  | 2.9 | 1.9 | 1.4 |  |  | Sales/Total Assets | 2.3 | 2.2 |
|  | 1.9 | 1.6 | 1.0 |  |  |  | 1.5 | 1.6 |
|  |  | .5 | .9 |  |  |  | .5 | 1.0 |
|  |  | (16) 1.4 | 1.5 |  |  | % Depr., Dep., Amort./Sales | (32) 1.4 | (40) 2.5 |
|  |  | 2.1 | 4.0 |  |  |  | 3.0 | 4.0 |
|  |  |  |  |  |  |  | 2.3 | 2.3 |
|  |  |  |  |  |  | % Officers', Directors' Owners' Comp/Sales | (18) 3.8 | (15) 4.0 |
|  |  |  |  |  |  |  | 6.0 | 10.0 |
| 879M | 25840M | 247046M | 392456M | 318009M | 259238M | Net Sales ($) | 1306965M | 1701745M |
| 431M | 9526M | 109270M | 253118M | 303592M | 141738M | Total Assets ($) | 765320M | 1124499M |

M = $ thousand    MM = $ million
See Pages 9 through 22 for Explanation of Ratios and Data

## Comparative Historical Data / Current Data Sorted by Sales

Month span: **10 (4/1-9/30/11)** covers 0-1MM, 1-3MM, 3-5MM. **38 (10/1/11-3/31/12)** covers 5-10MM, 10-25MM, 25MM & OVER.

| Type of Statement | 4/1/09-3/31/10 ALL | 4/1/10-3/31/11 ALL | 4/1/11-3/31/12 ALL | 0-1MM | 1-3MM | 3-5MM | 5-10MM | 10-25MM | 25MM & OVER |
|---|---|---|---|---|---|---|---|---|---|
| Unqualified | 6 | 6 | 13 | | 1 | | 1 | 3 | 8 |
| Reviewed | 4 | 6 | 5 | | | 1 | | 3 | 1 |
| Compiled | 11 | 5 | 7 | | 2 | 2 | 1 | 1 | 1 |
| Tax Returns | 3 | 1 | 6 | 1 | 2 | 2 | 1 | | |
| Other | 23 | 22 | 17 | 1 | 3 | 2 | 1 | 8 | 2 |
| **NUMBER OF STATEMENTS** | 47 | 40 | 48 | 2 | 8 | 6 | 5 | 15 | 12 |
| | % | % | % | % | % | % | % | % | % |
| **ASSETS** | | | | | | | | | |
| Cash & Equivalents | 12.9 | 15.4 | 11.6 | | | | | 15.5 | 10.8 |
| Trade Receivables (net) | 26.8 | 23.2 | 26.8 | | | | | 27.6 | 22.1 |
| Inventory | 29.1 | 25.8 | 30.6 | | | | | 29.0 | 33.1 |
| All Other Current | 2.5 | 3.6 | 6.2 | | | | | 2.7 | 5.5 |
| Total Current | 71.3 | 68.0 | 75.2 | | | | | 74.8 | 71.5 |
| Fixed Assets (net) | 18.3 | 17.2 | 16.9 | | | | | 18.7 | 19.2 |
| Intangibles (net) | 6.4 | 13.1 | 5.5 | | | | | 3.6 | 7.8 |
| All Other Non-Current | 4.0 | 1.7 | 2.4 | | | | | 3.0 | 1.6 |
| Total | 100.0 | 100.0 | 100.0 | | | | | 100.0 | 100.0 |
| **LIABILITIES** | | | | | | | | | |
| Notes Payable-Short Term | 9.9 | 4.6 | 15.0 | | | | | 12.8 | 7.9 |
| Cur. Mat.-L.T.D. | 3.1 | 4.9 | 3.8 | | | | | 5.4 | 3.1 |
| Trade Payables | 14.3 | 12.3 | 18.0 | | | | | 14.4 | 8.5 |
| Income Taxes Payable | .1 | .4 | .3 | | | | | .2 | .3 |
| All Other Current | 7.5 | 6.6 | 6.6 | | | | | 6.2 | 6.5 |
| Total Current | 34.9 | 28.7 | 43.8 | | | | | 39.0 | 26.4 |
| Long-Term Debt | 10.6 | 16.9 | 13.3 | | | | | 8.6 | 10.6 |
| Deferred Taxes | .8 | 1.1 | .5 | | | | | .4 | .9 |
| All Other Non-Current | 5.7 | 5.1 | 4.9 | | | | | 2.5 | 6.3 |
| Net Worth | 48.0 | 48.1 | 37.7 | | | | | 49.4 | 55.8 |
| Total Liabilities & Net Worth | 100.0 | 100.0 | 100.0 | | | | | 100.0 | 100.0 |
| **INCOME DATA** | | | | | | | | | |
| Net Sales | 100.0 | 100.0 | 100.0 | | | | | 100.0 | 100.0 |
| Gross Profit | 35.3 | 35.9 | 36.9 | | | | | 38.2 | 27.5 |
| Operating Expenses | 29.5 | 26.6 | 29.4 | | | | | 30.2 | 20.2 |
| Operating Profit | 5.8 | 9.2 | 7.5 | | | | | 8.0 | 7.3 |
| All Other Expenses (net) | .2 | 1.0 | 1.0 | | | | | .7 | .7 |
| Profit Before Taxes | 5.6 | 8.2 | 6.5 | | | | | 7.3 | 6.6 |
| **RATIOS** | | | | | | | | | |
| Current | 3.6 | 5.7 | 5.2 | | | | | 4.1 | 5.8 |
| | 2.5 | 3.1 | 2.1 | | | | | 2.6 | 3.0 |
| | 1.6 | 1.6 | 1.3 | | | | | 1.0 | 2.0 |
| Quick | 2.1 | 2.9 | 2.2 | | | | | 2.1 | 2.4 |
| | 1.2 | 1.5 | 1.1 | | | | | 1.4 | 1.4 |
| | .6 | .7 | .5 | | | | | .5 | .7 |
| Sales/Receivables | 34  10.8 | 36  10.0 | 38  9.7 | | | | | 39  9.3 | 36  10.1 |
| | 43  8.4 | 45  8.1 | 46  7.9 | | | | | 41  8.9 | 52  7.0 |
| | 55  6.6 | 56  6.5 | 55  6.6 | | | | | 47  7.8 | 58  6.3 |
| Cost of Sales/Inventory | 46  7.9 | 57  6.4 | 47  7.8 | | | | | 36  10.2 | 81  4.5 |
| | 89  4.1 | 87  4.2 | 94  3.9 | | | | | 101  3.6 | 107  3.4 |
| | 112  3.3 | 125  2.9 | 135  2.7 | | | | | 135  2.7 | 126  2.9 |
| Cost of Sales/Payables | 22  16.3 | 21  17.2 | 18  20.4 | | | | | 27  13.4 | 14  25.8 |
| | 33  11.1 | 33  11.1 | 31  11.7 | | | | | 31  11.7 | 20  18.4 |
| | 52  7.0 | 47  7.7 | 46  8.0 | | | | | 43  8.4 | 35  10.3 |
| Sales/Working Capital | 3.5 | 2.8 | 3.3 | | | | | 3.1 | 2.1 |
| | 5.4 | 4.5 | 5.9 | | | | | 6.2 | 3.9 |
| | 11.5 | 8.7 | 17.4 | | | | | -59.4 | 5.6 |
| EBIT/Interest | 18.9 | 59.3 | 20.3 | | | | | 27.4 | 46.7 |
| | (39) 3.8 | (34) 13.8 | (38) 4.7 | | | | | (11) 8.5 | 8.2 |
| | 1.6 | 3.5 | 2.2 | | | | | 3.0 | 2.4 |
| Net Profit + Depr., Dep., Amort./Cur. Mat. L/T/D | 11.3 | 14.3 | 15.9 | | | | | | |
| | (14) 5.2 | (12) 4.4 | (14) 3.5 | | | | | | |
| | 1.9 | 2.5 | 2.1 | | | | | | |
| Fixed/Worth | .1 | .1 | .1 | | | | | .1 | .2 |
| | .2 | .3 | .3 | | | | | .2 | .4 |
| | 1.1 | 1.6 | 2.0 | | | | | 2.0 | .7 |
| Debt/Worth | .4 | .4 | .4 | | | | | .4 | .3 |
| | .8 | .9 | 1.2 | | | | | .6 | 1.0 |
| | 3.7 | 7.1 | 29.5 | | | | | 3.4 | 2.2 |
| % Profit Before Taxes/Tangible Net Worth | 38.7 | 46.1 | 37.3 | | | | | 64.5 | 66.0 |
| | (41) 26.1 | (31) 25.0 | (38) 20.2 | | | | | (13) 29.1 | (11) 22.5 |
| | 7.2 | 14.3 | 4.3 | | | | | 17.7 | 4.1 |
| % Profit Before Taxes/Total Assets | 20.3 | 21.8 | 16.5 | | | | | 24.1 | 25.5 |
| | 11.9 | 13.0 | 8.9 | | | | | 14.3 | 8.3 |
| | 2.1 | 4.5 | 2.4 | | | | | 5.6 | 2.5 |
| Sales/Net Fixed Assets | 61.2 | 31.4 | 76.9 | | | | | 55.0 | 23.1 |
| | 18.3 | 17.8 | 23.3 | | | | | 30.4 | 9.2 |
| | 6.2 | 6.5 | 5.7 | | | | | 4.1 | 4.5 |
| Sales/Total Assets | 2.7 | 2.2 | 3.1 | | | | | 3.4 | 1.8 |
| | 2.0 | 1.6 | 1.8 | | | | | 1.8 | 1.5 |
| | 1.6 | 1.3 | 1.3 | | | | | 1.5 | 1.2 |
| % Depr., Dep., Amort./Sales | .6 | .8 | .7 | | | | | .5 | 1.0 |
| | (36) 2.1 | (30) 2.1 | (33) 1.8 | | | | | (12) 1.5 | (11) 2.3 |
| | 3.7 | 4.0 | 3.3 | | | | | 3.2 | 5.5 |
| % Officers', Directors' Owners' Comp/Sales | 2.7 | | 2.4 | | | | | | |
| | (13) 4.6 | | (16) 5.0 | | | | | | |
| | 7.7 | | 5.8 | | | | | | |
| Net Sales ($) | 1353985M | 1614227M | 1243468M | 879M | 16202M | 23833M | 33143M | 249086M | 920325M |
| Total Assets ($) | 908006M | 1202708M | 817675M | 431M | 9519M | 16632M | 17770M | 137308M | 636015M |

© RMA 2012

M = $ thousand   MM = $ million
See Pages 9 through 22 for Explanation of Ratios and Data

## Current Data Sorted by Assets      Comparative Historical Data

| 0-500M | 500M-2MM | 2-10MM | 10-50MM | 50-100MM | 100-250MM | Type of Statement | 4/1/07-3/31/08 ALL | 4/1/08-3/31/09 ALL |
|---|---|---|---|---|---|---|---|---|
| | | 2 | 2 | | 1 | Unqualified | 8 | 6 |
| | | 4 | 1 | | | Reviewed | 4 | 6 |
| | 2 | 4 | | | | Compiled | | |
| 1 | 4 | 3 | 1 | | | Tax Returns | 3 | 2 |
| 1 | 3 | 8 | 8 | | 2 | Other | 10 | 10 |
| | | 7 (4/1-9/30/11) | 40 (10/1/11-3/31/12) | | | | | |
| 2 | 9 | 21 | 12 | | 3 | NUMBER OF STATEMENTS | 25 | 24 |
| % | % | % | % | % | % | ASSETS | % | % |
| | | 6.1 | 6.2 | | | Cash & Equivalents | 5.1 | 4.6 |
| | | 29.6 | 20.8 | | | Trade Receivables (net) | 28.5 | 26.3 |
| | | 39.0 | 25.7 | | | Inventory | 37.5 | 38.2 |
| | | 1.1 | 20.4 | | | All Other Current | 1.0 | 1.3 |
| | | 75.8 | 73.1 | | | Total Current | 72.1 | 70.4 |
| | | 19.7 | 14.8 | | | Fixed Assets (net) | 16.2 | 15.8 |
| | | 2.0 | 8.1 | | | Intangibles (net) | 7.0 | 11.2 |
| | | 2.4 | 4.0 | | | All Other Non-Current | 4.7 | 2.5 |
| | | 100.0 | 100.0 | | | Total | 100.0 | 100.0 |
| | | | | | | LIABILITIES | | |
| | | 13.0 | 5.6 | | | Notes Payable-Short Term | 11.8 | 18.7 |
| | | 2.0 | .7 | | | Cur. Mat.-L.T.D. | 7.5 | 4.5 |
| | | 18.4 | 10.1 | | | Trade Payables | 24.1 | 16.3 |
| | | .2 | .0 | | | Income Taxes Payable | .1 | .1 |
| | | 7.9 | 10.4 | | | All Other Current | 7.6 | 7.0 |
| | | 41.5 | 26.9 | | | Total Current | 51.2 | 46.6 |
| | | 7.9 | 4.5 | | | Long-Term Debt | 27.4 | 21.7 |
| | | .1 | .2 | | | Deferred Taxes | .1 | .2 |
| | | 3.9 | 13.9 | | | All Other Non-Current | 8.7 | 8.9 |
| | | 46.6 | 54.6 | | | Net Worth | 12.6 | 22.6 |
| | | 100.0 | 100.0 | | | Total Liabilities & Net Worth | 100.0 | 100.0 |
| | | | | | | INCOME DATA | | |
| | | 100.0 | 100.0 | | | Net Sales | 100.0 | 100.0 |
| | | 28.5 | 24.6 | | | Gross Profit | 21.5 | 23.1 |
| | | 22.5 | 13.9 | | | Operating Expenses | 17.1 | 18.9 |
| | | 6.0 | 10.7 | | | Operating Profit | 4.4 | 4.2 |
| | | .0 | .9 | | | All Other Expenses (net) | 1.2 | 1.1 |
| | | 6.0 | 9.8 | | | Profit Before Taxes | 3.2 | 3.0 |
| | | | | | | RATIOS | | |
| | | 2.7 | 6.7 | | | Current | 2.3 | 2.5 |
| | | 2.1 | 2.7 | | | | 1.5 | 1.6 |
| | | 1.4 | 1.7 | | | | 1.2 | 1.2 |
| | | 1.3 | 2.1 | | | Quick | 1.0 | 1.1 |
| | | 1.0 | .8 | | | | .7 | .6 |
| | | .5 | .1 | | | | .4 | .4 |
| | | 34   10.7 | 0   UND | | | Sales/Receivables | 39   9.4   31   11.8 | |
| | | 45   8.1 | 42   8.6 | | | | 48   7.6   45   8.0 | |
| | | 53   6.9 | 58   6.3 | | | | 60   6.0   54   6.8 | |
| | | 56   6.5 | 0   UND | | | Cost of Sales/Inventory | 52   7.1   50   7.3 | |
| | | 83   4.4 | 54   6.7 | | | | 82   4.4   79   4.6 | |
| | | 114   3.2 | 122   3.0 | | | | 119   3.1   105   3.5 | |
| | | 28   12.9 | 0   UND | | | Cost of Sales/Payables | 34   10.8   24   15.3 | |
| | | 39   9.4 | 29   12.4 | | | | 41   8.9   35   10.5 | |
| | | 54   6.7 | 42   8.6 | | | | 54   6.7   42   8.7 | |
| | | 5.3 | 2.7 | | | Sales/Working Capital | 4.2 | 5.4 |
| | | 6.6 | 4.2 | | | | 10.8 | 7.8 |
| | | 11.0 | 9.5 | | | | 16.8 | 19.1 |
| | | 27.9 | | | | EBIT/Interest | 6.8 | 4.6 |
| | | (19) 8.6 | | | | | (23) 2.1   (23) 2.5 | |
| | | 3.8 | | | | | .7 | 1.3 |
| | | | | | | Net Profit + Depr., Dep., Amort./Cur. Mat. L/T/D | 4.0 | 3.6 |
| | | | | | | | (12) 2.0   (13) 2.4 | |
| | | | | | | | -.7 | -.2 |
| | | .2 | .2 | | | Fixed/Worth | .2 | .3 |
| | | .3 | .3 | | | | .4 | .6 |
| | | .7 | .8 | | | | 1.1 | 3.2 |
| | | .7 | .2 | | | Debt/Worth | 1.2 | 1.4 |
| | | 1.4 | 1.2 | | | | 1.8 | 2.4 |
| | | 1.8 | 3.2 | | | | 5.9 | 7.8 |
| | | 45.1 | 47.7 | | | % Profit Before Taxes/Tangible Net Worth | 47.1 | 61.6 |
| | | 28.3 | (11) 32.2 | | | | (21) 27.0   (19) 11.7 | |
| | | 10.0 | 26.8 | | | | 3.1 | 2.7 |
| | | 19.2 | 29.5 | | | % Profit Before Taxes/Total Assets | 13.6 | 11.9 |
| | | 11.7 | 14.5 | | | | 4.4 | 5.6 |
| | | 4.1 | 8.9 | | | | -.3 | 1.0 |
| | | 35.4 | 22.7 | | | Sales/Net Fixed Assets | 26.6 | 30.9 |
| | | 15.5 | 12.5 | | | | 14.5 | 15.1 |
| | | 9.4 | 9.8 | | | | 10.1 | 9.9 |
| | | 2.9 | 2.3 | | | Sales/Total Assets | 3.0 | 2.7 |
| | | 2.4 | 2.1 | | | | 1.9 | 2.2 |
| | | 2.0 | 1.5 | | | | 1.6 | 1.6 |
| | | .8 | 1.1 | | | % Depr., Dep., Amort./Sales | 1.0 | .9 |
| | | (19) 1.3 | (10) 1.7 | | | | (23) 1.8   (21) 1.4 | |
| | | 2.1 | 2.1 | | | | 2.7 | 2.2 |
| | | | | | | % Officers', Directors' Owners' Comp/Sales | | |
| 4821M | 43993M | 242479M | 476157M | | 588001M | Net Sales ($) | 1450873M | 1484042M |
| 690M | 13372M | 103260M | 244886M | | 332230M | Total Assets ($) | 771103M | 794075M |

(Columns for 50-100MM asset size: DATA NOT AVAILABLE)

M = $ thousand    MM = $ million  
See Pages 9 through 22 for Explanation of Ratios and Data

## Comparative Historical Data | Current Data Sorted by Sales

Type of Statement (counts):

| Type of Statement | 4/1/09-3/31/10 ALL | 4/1/10-3/31/11 ALL | 4/1/11-3/31/12 ALL | 0-1MM | 1-3MM | 3-5MM | 5-10MM | 10-25MM | 25MM & OVER |
|---|---|---|---|---|---|---|---|---|---|
| Unqualified | 4 | 3 | 5 | | | | 1 | 1 | 3 |
| Reviewed | 10 | 12 | 5 | | | | 1 | 3 | 1 |
| Compiled | | 2 | 6 | | | 2 | 3 | 1 | |
| Tax Returns | 1 | 3 | 9 | | 3 | 1 | 2 | 2 | 1 |
| Other | 8 | 8 | 22 | | 2 | 2 | 5 | 5 | 6 |
| | | | | 7 (4/1-9/30/11) | | | 40 (10/1/11-3/31/12) | | |
| **NUMBER OF STATEMENTS** | 23 | 28 | 47 | | 3 | 5 | 12 | 16 | 11 |

*(Columns 0-1MM, 1-3MM, 3-5MM marked "DATA NOT AVAILABLE" for the percentage sections below.)*

| | 4/1/09-3/31/10 ALL % | 4/1/10-3/31/11 ALL % | 4/1/11-3/31/12 ALL % | 5-10MM % | 10-25MM % | 25MM & OVER % |
|---|---|---|---|---|---|---|
| **ASSETS** | | | | | | |
| Cash & Equivalents | 5.0 | 7.0 | 7.4 | 6.3 | 5.2 | 5.7 |
| Trade Receivables (net) | 29.7 | 31.2 | 27.5 | 31.2 | 31.8 | 22.3 |
| Inventory | 34.2 | 36.9 | 30.2 | 30.1 | 41.1 | 24.4 |
| All Other Current | 1.6 | 1.5 | 7.9 | 4.4 | 5.7 | 14.9 |
| Total Current | 70.5 | 76.5 | 73.1 | 72.0 | 83.8 | 67.3 |
| Fixed Assets (net) | 18.3 | 15.6 | 19.2 | 22.6 | 12.6 | 15.3 |
| Intangibles (net) | 7.8 | 3.8 | 4.8 | 1.1 | 1.0 | 15.7 |
| All Other Non-Current | 3.4 | 4.0 | 2.9 | 4.2 | 2.6 | 1.7 |
| Total | 100.0 | 100.0 | 100.0 | 100.0 | 100.0 | 100.0 |
| **LIABILITIES** | | | | | | |
| Notes Payable-Short Term | 10.5 | 11.0 | 8.7 | 4.6 | 14.5 | 7.9 |
| Cur. Mat.-L.T.D. | 2.6 | 6.2 | 1.6 | 2.6 | 1.3 | 1.2 |
| Trade Payables | 17.7 | 22.1 | 15.8 | 19.0 | 16.7 | 11.4 |
| Income Taxes Payable | .1 | .8 | .2 | .8 | .0 | .1 |
| All Other Current | 6.5 | 7.2 | 13.1 | 11.2 | 8.0 | 10.6 |
| Total Current | 37.5 | 47.2 | 39.4 | 38.2 | 40.6 | 31.1 |
| Long-Term Debt | 10.4 | 15.3 | 8.9 | 14.3 | 2.3 | 7.9 |
| Deferred Taxes | .8 | .3 | .2 | .0 | .0 | .4 |
| All Other Non-Current | 2.7 | 2.9 | 10.9 | 5.9 | 4.4 | 16.6 |
| Net Worth | 48.6 | 34.3 | 40.6 | 41.5 | 52.7 | 43.9 |
| Total Liabilities & Net Worth | 100.0 | 100.0 | 100.0 | 100.0 | 100.0 | 100.0 |
| **INCOME DATA** | | | | | | |
| Net Sales | 100.0 | 100.0 | 100.0 | 100.0 | 100.0 | 100.0 |
| Gross Profit | 23.9 | 27.6 | 29.7 | 36.8 | 25.5 | 17.5 |
| Operating Expenses | 19.6 | 22.3 | 22.0 | 29.8 | 17.6 | 10.3 |
| Operating Profit | 4.3 | 5.3 | 7.7 | 7.0 | 7.9 | 7.2 |
| All Other Expenses (net) | .8 | .8 | .6 | .5 | .3 | 1.5 |
| Profit Before Taxes | 3.4 | 4.5 | 7.1 | 6.5 | 7.6 | 5.7 |

**RATIOS**

| Ratio | 4/1/09-3/31/10 | 4/1/10-3/31/11 | 4/1/11-3/31/12 | 5-10MM | 10-25MM | 25MM & OVER |
|---|---|---|---|---|---|---|
| Current | 3.3 | 2.7 | 3.0 | 2.6 | 3.1 | 3.1 |
| | 1.9 | 1.9 | 2.3 | 2.2 | 2.4 | 2.4 |
| | 1.4 | 1.3 | 1.4 | 1.5 | 1.4 | 1.3 |
| Quick | 1.7 | 1.4 | 1.4 | 1.4 | 1.7 | 1.1 |
| | .9 | .9 | 1.0 | 1.1 | 1.0 | .7 |
| | .7 | .6 | .6 | .7 | .6 | .6 |
| Sales/Receivables | 43  8.6 | 37  9.9 | 29  12.5 | 23  16.1 | 36  10.2 | 33  10.9 |
| | 54  6.8 | 44  8.2 | 43  8.5 | 38  9.6 | 51  7.2 | 46  8.0 |
| | 62  5.9 | 54  6.7 | 53  6.9 | 49  7.4 | 61  6.0 | 54  6.7 |
| Cost of Sales/Inventory | 47  7.8 | 53  6.9 | 31  11.6 | 35  10.3 | 72  5.1 | 29  12.8 |
| | 90  4.1 | 78  4.7 | 69  5.3 | 58  6.3 | 87  4.2 | 55  6.6 |
| | 112  3.3 | 96  3.8 | 96  3.8 | 94  3.9 | 146  2.5 | 69  5.3 |
| Cost of Sales/Payables | 25  14.6 | 28  13.0 | 21  17.5 | 21  17.1 | 29  12.5 | 3  143.8 |
| | 36  10.2 | 41  8.9 | 32  11.4 | 33  10.9 | 36  10.1 | 28  13.0 |
| | 53  6.8 | 59  6.2 | 46  8.0 | 45  8.2 | 47  7.7 | 35  10.3 |
| Sales/Working Capital | 4.5 | 5.7 | 4.6 | 6.3 | 3.6 | 4.0 |
| | 6.0 | 7.1 | 6.9 | 7.4 | 5.9 | 5.5 |
| | 10.7 | 14.4 | 12.6 | 19.2 | 9.6 | 11.2 |
| EBIT/Interest | 15.1 | 27.9 | 25.4 | 32.0 | 33.0 | |
| | (21) 4.4 | (24) 6.9 | (40) 7.9 | (10) 5.9 | (14) 10.9 | |
| | 1.3 | .7 | 3.1 | 3.7 | 3.7 | |
| Net Profit + Depr., Dep., Amort./Cur. Mat. L/T/D | 4.8 | 15.4 | 13.3 | | | |
| | (12) 3.8 | (11) 5.6 | (11) 8.7 | | | |
| | 1.5 | 1.3 | 4.1 | | | |
| Fixed/Worth | .2 | .1 | .2 | .2 | .2 | .3 |
| | .5 | .4 | .4 | .5 | .2 | .6 |
| | .8 | 1.8 | 1.1 | 1.1 | .3 | 3.3 |
| Debt/Worth | .7 | .7 | .6 | 1.0 | .6 | 1.1 |
| | 1.5 | 1.8 | 1.4 | 1.5 | .9 | 2.9 |
| | 2.1 | 4.0 | 2.9 | 2.1 | 1.8 | 25.5 |
| % Profit Before Taxes/Tangible Net Worth | 31.5 | 77.7 | 50.1 | 93.4 | 42.6 | |
| | (22) 15.9 | (25) 31.9 | (42) 31.7 | 37.1 | 28.7 | |
| | 4.6 | 5.7 | 18.1 | 18.4 | 14.6 | |
| % Profit Before Taxes/Total Assets | 13.0 | 33.6 | 23.4 | 35.5 | 23.2 | 14.7 |
| | 5.1 | 13.3 | 13.0 | 11.3 | 14.7 | 8.5 |
| | 1.0 | .9 | 4.1 | 8.2 | 5.8 | 4.1 |
| Sales/Net Fixed Assets | 28.4 | 62.0 | 33.0 | 36.2 | 39.5 | 23.0 |
| | 12.9 | 18.1 | 13.7 | 14.2 | 16.4 | 17.7 |
| | 8.4 | 11.4 | 9.5 | 9.4 | 12.4 | 8.5 |
| Sales/Total Assets | 2.2 | 2.9 | 3.0 | 3.8 | 2.7 | 2.3 |
| | 2.0 | 2.3 | 2.3 | 3.0 | 2.1 | 2.3 |
| | 1.7 | 1.9 | 1.9 | 2.6 | 1.9 | 1.8 |
| % Depr., Dep., Amort./Sales | 1.3 | 1.2 | 1.0 | | .6 | 1.2 |
| | (22) 2.2 | (22) 2.1 | (38) 1.7 | | (13) 1.1 | 2.0 |
| | 3.1 | 2.7 | 2.2 | | 1.9 | 2.6 |
| % Officers', Directors' Owners' Comp/Sales | | 2.8 | 2.6 | | | |
| | | (12) 3.9 | (19) 4.1 | | | |
| | | 9.9 | 10.4 | | | |

| | 4/1/09-3/31/10 | 4/1/10-3/31/11 | 4/1/11-3/31/12 | 1-3MM | 3-5MM | 5-10MM | 10-25MM | 25MM & OVER |
|---|---|---|---|---|---|---|---|---|
| Net Sales ($) | 1005854M | 995478M | 1355451M | 6077M | 17119M | 81294M | 267891M | 983070M |
| Total Assets ($) | 546574M | 505497M | 694438M | 4887M | 6744M | 27018M | 128225M | 527564M |

**Current Data Sorted by Assets**      **Comparative Historical Data**

Type of Statement periods (left): 38 (4/1-9/30/11) for 500M-2MM; 174 (10/1/11-3/31/12) for 10-50MM. Comparative Historical: 4/1/07-3/31/08 ALL; 4/1/08-3/31/09 ALL.

| | 0-500M | 500M-2MM | 2-10MM | 10-50MM | 50-100MM | 100-250MM | | 4/1/07-3/31/08 ALL | 4/1/08-3/31/09 ALL |
|---|---|---|---|---|---|---|---|---|---|
| **Type of Statement** | | | | | | | | | |
| Unqualified | | | 7 | 20 | 6 | 6 | | 34 | 27 |
| Reviewed | | 3 | 24 | 9 | | | | 34 | 38 |
| Compiled | | 9 | 12 | 2 | | | | 18 | 23 |
| Tax Returns | 3 | 9 | 7 | 7 | | 1 | | 19 | 15 |
| Other | 5 | 13 | 30 | 27 | 6 | 13 | | 71 | 90 |
| **NUMBER OF STATEMENTS** | 8 | 34 | 80 | 58 | 13 | 19 | | 176 | 193 |
| **ASSETS** | % | % | % | % | % | % | | % | % |
| Cash & Equivalents | | 12.2 | 13.2 | 8.8 | 15.3 | 11.1 | | 11.2 | 10.0 |
| Trade Receivables (net) | | 32.9 | 28.7 | 26.6 | 27.6 | 25.7 | | 29.6 | 26.5 |
| Inventory | | 30.7 | 30.7 | 27.7 | 24.5 | 22.0 | | 28.1 | 30.8 |
| All Other Current | | 2.2 | 3.7 | 2.1 | 3.8 | 4.0 | | 2.7 | 2.2 |
| Total Current | | 78.0 | 76.2 | 65.3 | 71.2 | 62.7 | | 71.6 | 69.6 |
| Fixed Assets (net) | | 15.7 | 18.1 | 19.4 | 14.5 | 12.5 | | 18.4 | 19.8 |
| Intangibles (net) | | 2.2 | 2.2 | 10.3 | 5.6 | 18.3 | | 5.2 | 5.5 |
| All Other Non-Current | | 4.2 | 3.4 | 5.0 | 8.7 | 6.5 | | 4.8 | 5.2 |
| Total | | 100.0 | 100.0 | 100.0 | 100.0 | 100.0 | | 100.0 | 100.0 |
| **LIABILITIES** | | | | | | | | | |
| Notes Payable-Short Term | | 9.6 | 7.0 | 9.4 | 6.2 | 1.3 | | 10.0 | 13.3 |
| Cur. Mat.-L.T.D. | | 2.3 | 2.8 | 3.9 | 2.5 | 2.3 | | 2.8 | 2.8 |
| Trade Payables | | 17.6 | 16.5 | 12.6 | 21.6 | 16.5 | | 15.5 | 14.0 |
| Income Taxes Payable | | .1 | .4 | .2 | .4 | .6 | | .3 | .3 |
| All Other Current | | 11.8 | 10.1 | 9.7 | 5.7 | 14.7 | | 9.4 | 9.2 |
| Total Current | | 41.4 | 36.8 | 35.8 | 36.4 | 35.4 | | 38.0 | 39.5 |
| Long-Term Debt | | 12.3 | 10.0 | 11.5 | 30.6 | 12.9 | | 12.0 | 12.8 |
| Deferred Taxes | | .0 | .4 | .8 | .6 | 1.2 | | .2 | .5 |
| All Other Non-Current | | 12.1 | 4.7 | 6.3 | 4.9 | 11.5 | | 5.9 | 6.8 |
| Net Worth | | 34.1 | 48.1 | 45.7 | 27.6 | 39.0 | | 43.9 | 40.4 |
| Total Liabilities & Net Worth | | 100.0 | 100.0 | 100.0 | 100.0 | 100.0 | | 100.0 | 100.0 |
| **INCOME DATA** | | | | | | | | | |
| Net Sales | | 100.0 | 100.0 | 100.0 | 100.0 | 100.0 | | 100.0 | 100.0 |
| Gross Profit | | 37.7 | 34.6 | 32.5 | 28.1 | 31.6 | | 33.7 | 32.6 |
| Operating Expenses | | 33.8 | 26.8 | 22.4 | 18.7 | 29.0 | | 27.0 | 27.5 |
| Operating Profit | | 4.0 | 7.8 | 10.1 | 9.4 | 2.5 | | 6.7 | 5.2 |
| All Other Expenses (net) | | .0 | .6 | 1.2 | .9 | 2.0 | | 1.3 | 1.2 |
| Profit Before Taxes | | 4.0 | 7.1 | 8.9 | 8.5 | .6 | | 5.4 | 3.9 |
| **RATIOS** | | | | | | | | | |
| Current | | 4.3 | 3.7 | 2.8 | 3.4 | 2.5 | | 3.2 | 3.0 |
| | | 2.0 | 2.2 | 2.0 | 2.0 | 2.2 | | 1.8 | 1.9 |
| | | 1.3 | 1.4 | 1.4 | 1.5 | 1.3 | | 1.4 | 1.3 |
| Quick | | 1.9 | 2.4 | 1.7 | 1.9 | 1.3 | | 1.9 | 1.8 |
| | | 1.1 | 1.3 | 1.1 | 1.2 | 1.2 | | 1.0 | .9 |
| | | .7 | .6 | .7 | .8 | .8 | | .7 | .6 |
| Sales/Receivables | 30   12.0 | 33   11.0 | 41   8.9 | 42   8.7 | | 51   7.2 | | 38   9.7 | 34   10.6 |
| | 41   9.0 | 43   8.4 | 54   6.8 | 54   6.7 | 59   6.2 | | | 49   7.4 | 44   8.2 |
| | 55   6.6 | 58   6.3 | 64   5.7 | 65   5.6 | 65   5.6 | | | 61   6.0 | 57   6.4 |
| Cost of Sales/Inventory | 24   15.0 | 38   9.7 | 59   6.2 | 37   9.9 | 42   8.7 | | | 35   10.4 | 46   7.9 |
| | 65   5.6 | 73   5.0 | 81   4.5 | 74   4.9 | 73   5.0 | | | 68   5.3 | 78   4.7 |
| | 130   2.8 | 114   3.2 | 140   2.6 | 114   3.2 | 96   3.8 | | | 114   3.2 | 122   3.0 |
| Cost of Sales/Payables | 13   28.3 | 20   18.0 | 19   18.8 | 33   11.1 | 41   8.8 | | | 21   17.5 | 17   21.9 |
| | 26   13.9 | 29   12.8 | 31   11.7 | 42   8.6 | 45   8.1 | | | 33   11.2 | 29   12.4 |
| | 56   6.5 | 45   8.1 | 45   8.2 | 70   5.2 | 66   5.5 | | | 51   7.2 | 49   7.4 |
| Sales/Working Capital | | 5.0 | 3.5 | 3.7 | 3.1 | 4.0 | | 3.9 | 4.1 |
| | | 8.5 | 6.3 | 5.7 | 5.7 | 4.6 | | 6.9 | 6.5 |
| | | 15.6 | 12.0 | 13.1 | 13.1 | 9.9 | | 14.3 | 16.2 |
| EBIT/Interest | | 11.2 | 27.6 | 25.9 | | 20.8 | | 13.4 | 15.8 |
| | | (28) 4.7 | (64) 7.5 | (53) 9.7 | | (18) 4.6 | | (142) 4.6 | (173) 4.4 |
| | | 1.5 | 2.6 | 2.0 | | -2.7 | | 2.0 | 1.4 |
| Net Profit + Depr., Dep., Amort./Cur. Mat. L/T/D | | | 7.4 | 11.1 | | | | 6.0 | 6.4 |
| | | | (17) 3.5 | (22) 4.1 | | | | (40) 2.8 | (44) 2.1 |
| | | | 1.5 | 2.2 | | | | 1.1 | 1.3 |
| Fixed/Worth | | .1 | .1 | .2 | .2 | .2 | | .2 | .2 |
| | | .3 | .3 | .5 | .4 | .5 | | .4 | .4 |
| | | 1.4 | .8 | 1.5 | .6 | -1.0 | | 1.0 | 1.4 |
| Debt/Worth | | .6 | .5 | .8 | .4 | .8 | | .5 | .7 |
| | | 2.3 | 1.2 | 1.5 | .8 | 1.8 | | 1.3 | 1.4 |
| | | 92.1 | 2.4 | 3.4 | 3.6 | -5.9 | | 3.0 | 5.0 |
| % Profit Before Taxes/Tangible Net Worth | | 74.0 | 55.3 | 66.0 | 32.5 | 27.7 | | 52.6 | 46.8 |
| | | (27) 20.7 | (75) 27.5 | (49) 29.1 | (12) 21.0 | (14) 14.4 | | (156) 25.5 | (164) 21.6 |
| | | -2.5 | 11.5 | 8.3 | 13.6 | 3.1 | | 10.6 | 4.1 |
| % Profit Before Taxes/Total Assets | | 19.0 | 25.9 | 25.2 | 15.1 | 7.9 | | 18.8 | 16.2 |
| | | 9.3 | 12.4 | 13.0 | 11.0 | 3.1 | | 9.8 | 7.0 |
| | | .3 | 3.1 | 1.8 | 6.6 | -3.1 | | 3.8 | .8 |
| Sales/Net Fixed Assets | | 110.2 | 48.3 | 38.0 | 31.1 | 26.4 | | 36.5 | 33.6 |
| | | 23.3 | 23.5 | 11.8 | 9.6 | 16.4 | | 14.8 | 14.9 |
| | | 11.6 | 7.9 | 6.0 | 8.5 | 9.2 | | 7.1 | 6.3 |
| Sales/Total Assets | | 4.0 | 2.9 | 2.2 | 2.5 | 1.9 | | 2.9 | 2.8 |
| | | 3.0 | 2.2 | 1.7 | 1.9 | 1.7 | | 2.1 | 2.0 |
| | | 1.9 | 1.7 | 1.2 | 1.1 | 1.1 | | 1.6 | 1.5 |
| % Depr., Dep., Amort./Sales | | .4 | .6 | 1.2 | 1.2 | 1.2 | | .7 | 1.0 |
| | | (22) .7 | (62) 1.1 | (46) 1.8 | (11) 1.7 | (14) 2.3 | | (142) 1.8 | (155) 2.1 |
| | | 2.5 | 2.9 | 3.3 | 2.9 | 3.6 | | 3.3 | 3.2 |
| % Officers', Directors' Owners' Comp/Sales | | 2.9 | 2.1 | | | | | 2.0 | 2.7 |
| | | (21) 5.6 | (28) 4.4 | | | | | (45) 3.6 | (55) 4.6 |
| | | 9.6 | 7.8 | | | | | 5.8 | 8.6 |
| Net Sales ($) | 10161M | 127003M | 936236M | 2265785M | 1791439M | 3954986M | | 4590926M | 5475372M |
| Total Assets ($) | 1908M | 43729M | 394726M | 1233877M | 854397M | 2636656M | | 2853621M | 3180933M |

## Comparative Historical Data | Current Data Sorted by Sales

| | | | Type of Statement | | | | | | |
|---|---|---|---|---|---|---|---|---|---|
| 31 | 32 | 39 | Unqualified | | | | 1 | 13 | 25 |
| 52 | 42 | 36 | Reviewed | 1 | 3 | 10 | 14 | 9 | 8 |
| 18 | 21 | 23 | Compiled | 5 | 3 | 6 | 9 | | |
| 17 | 23 | 20 | Tax Returns | 7 | 3 | 2 | 3 | 2 | |
| 97 | 95 | 94 | Other | 3 | 8 | 9 | 18 | 22 | 34 |
| 4/1/09-3/31/10 ALL | 4/1/10-3/31/11 ALL | 4/1/11-3/31/12 ALL | | 3 | 38 (4/1-9/30/11) | | 174 (10/1/11-3/31/12) | | |
| | | | | 0-1MM | 1-3MM | 3-5MM | 5-10MM | 10-25MM | 25MM & OVER |
| 215 | 213 | 212 | NUMBER OF STATEMENTS | 6 | 21 | 18 | 37 | 61 | 69 |
| % | % | % | ASSETS | % | % | % | % | % | % |
| 11.2 | 10.1 | 12.8 | Cash & Equivalents | 18.4 | 16.8 | 12.4 | 11.3 | 10.0 | |
| 26.6 | 27.9 | 28.0 | Trade Receivables (net) | 28.6 | 28.7 | 29.8 | 26.6 | 29.5 | |
| 28.4 | 30.2 | 28.5 | Inventory | 28.4 | 24.3 | 34.1 | 29.1 | 26.5 | |
| 3.2 | 2.7 | 3.0 | All Other Current | 2.1 | 1.5 | 2.6 | 3.7 | 3.0 | |
| 69.3 | 70.9 | 72.2 | Total Current | 77.5 | 71.2 | 79.0 | 70.8 | 69.0 | |
| 18.8 | 16.1 | 17.1 | Fixed Assets (net) | 16.7 | 20.7 | 15.3 | 18.9 | 15.0 | |
| 6.2 | 7.2 | 6.1 | Intangibles (net) | 1.5 | 1.7 | 3.4 | 5.8 | 10.5 | |
| 5.7 | 5.9 | 4.7 | All Other Non-Current | 4.2 | 6.4 | 2.4 | 4.5 | 5.4 | |
| 100.0 | 100.0 | 100.0 | Total | 100.0 | 100.0 | 100.0 | 100.0 | 100.0 | |
| | | | LIABILITIES | | | | | | |
| 9.8 | 10.1 | 7.7 | Notes Payable-Short Term | 6.6 | 5.9 | 8.6 | 8.7 | 6.5 | |
| 2.6 | 3.5 | 2.9 | Cur. Mat.-L.T.D. | 2.0 | 4.5 | 2.6 | 2.5 | 3.3 | |
| 15.6 | 14.7 | 15.7 | Trade Payables | 14.5 | 13.0 | 16.4 | 14.5 | 18.2 | |
| .1 | .3 | .3 | Income Taxes Payable | .0 | .2 | .5 | .3 | .3 | |
| 10.9 | 10.2 | 10.6 | All Other Current | 13.9 | 5.0 | 10.3 | 11.7 | 10.4 | |
| 39.1 | 38.7 | 37.1 | Total Current | 37.1 | 28.7 | 38.4 | 37.7 | 38.8 | |
| 13.6 | 13.3 | 12.4 | Long-Term Debt | 19.6 | 13.4 | 8.0 | 10.5 | 14.1 | |
| .4 | .6 | .5 | Deferred Taxes | .0 | .0 | .7 | .4 | .9 | |
| 8.7 | 7.0 | 7.0 | All Other Non-Current | 9.4 | 7.0 | 7.6 | 4.1 | 8.5 | |
| 38.2 | 40.3 | 42.9 | Net Worth | 33.9 | 50.9 | 45.3 | 47.3 | 37.7 | |
| 100.0 | 100.0 | 100.0 | Total Liabilities & Net Worth | 100.0 | 100.0 | 100.0 | 100.0 | 100.0 | |
| | | | INCOME DATA | | | | | | |
| 100.0 | 100.0 | 100.0 | Net Sales | 100.0 | 100.0 | 100.0 | 100.0 | 100.0 | |
| 33.0 | 34.1 | 34.3 | Gross Profit | 42.6 | 44.0 | 35.5 | 32.5 | 29.1 | |
| 27.6 | 26.5 | 27.1 | Operating Expenses | 40.0 | 35.3 | 28.0 | 24.2 | 21.9 | |
| 5.4 | 7.6 | 7.3 | Operating Profit | 2.6 | 8.7 | 7.5 | 8.2 | 7.2 | |
| 1.2 | 1.1 | .8 | All Other Expenses (net) | -.3 | 1.0 | .6 | .8 | 1.2 | |
| 4.3 | 6.5 | 6.5 | Profit Before Taxes | 2.9 | 7.6 | 7.0 | 7.5 | 6.0 | |
| | | | RATIOS | | | | | | |
| 3.2 | 3.1 | 3.1 | | 6.1 | 7.1 | 4.2 | 3.0 | 2.5 | |
| 1.9 | 2.0 | 2.1 | Current | 2.0 | 2.5 | 2.3 | 2.1 | 1.8 | |
| 1.3 | 1.3 | 1.4 | | 1.3 | 1.7 | 1.4 | 1.3 | 1.4 | |
| 1.7 | 1.8 | 1.9 | | 2.3 | 4.9 | 2.5 | 1.8 | 1.4 | |
| 1.0 | 1.0 | 1.2 | Quick | 1.2 | 1.5 | 1.3 | 1.1 | 1.2 | |
| .6 | .6 | .7 | | .8 | .7 | .6 | .6 | .7 | |

| | | | | | | Sales/Receivables | | | | | | | | | | | | |
|---|---|---|---|---|---|---|---|---|---|---|---|---|---|---|---|---|---|---|
| 37 | 9.9 | 36 | 10.2 | 35 | 10.4 | | 30 | 12.3 | 39 | 9.4 | 28 | 13.2 | 35 | 10.5 | 44 | 8.3 | | |
| 49 | 7.5 | 51 | 7.2 | 46 | 7.9 | Sales/Receivables | 39 | 9.4 | 49 | 7.4 | 38 | 9.5 | 46 | 7.9 | 55 | 6.6 | | |
| 61 | 6.0 | 62 | 5.9 | 60 | 6.1 | | 59 | 6.2 | 72 | 5.1 | 49 | 7.4 | 58 | 6.3 | 64 | 5.7 | | |
| 43 | 8.4 | 49 | 7.5 | 40 | 9.1 | | 7 | 55.1 | 17 | 22.1 | 42 | 8.6 | 42 | 8.6 | 43 | 8.4 | | |
| 79 | 4.6 | 79 | 4.6 | 74 | 4.9 | Cost of Sales/Inventory | 99 | 3.7 | 76 | 4.8 | 81 | 4.5 | 73 | 5.0 | 73 | 5.0 | | |
| 122 | 3.0 | 129 | 2.8 | 118 | 3.1 | | 166 | 2.2 | 135 | 2.7 | 118 | 3.1 | 111 | 3.3 | 107 | 3.4 | | |
| 21 | 17.3 | 21 | 17.0 | 20 | 18.1 | | 11 | 31.8 | 15 | 25.1 | 16 | 23.2 | 19 | 19.1 | 30 | 12.2 | | |
| 33 | 11.0 | 33 | 11.0 | 33 | 11.2 | Cost of Sales/Payables | 21 | 17.4 | 22 | 16.6 | 28 | 12.9 | 30 | 12.0 | 42 | 8.6 | | |
| 55 | 6.7 | 52 | 7.0 | 49 | 7.4 | | 55 | 6.6 | 35 | 10.5 | 47 | 7.8 | 43 | 8.5 | 54 | 6.7 | | |

| | | | | | | | | |
|---|---|---|---|---|---|---|---|---|
| 3.9 | 4.0 | 3.7 | | 2.8 | 3.1 | 3.5 | 4.0 | 4.1 |
| 6.1 | 6.3 | 6.4 | Sales/Working Capital | 8.6 | 5.2 | 6.1 | 6.6 | 6.2 |
| 13.1 | 13.9 | 12.7 | | 13.0 | 10.3 | 15.2 | 14.4 | 12.5 |

| | | | | | | | | | | | | | | |
|---|---|---|---|---|---|---|---|---|---|---|---|---|---|---|
| | 14.4 | | 19.8 | | 21.7 | | | 11.2 | | 10.0 | | 28.3 | | 28.9 | | 21.7 |
| (185) | 3.6 | (182) | 7.1 | (174) | 7.6 | EBIT/Interest | (17) | 4.7 | (14) | 4.4 | (27) | 6.0 | (54) | 9.5 | (60) | 9.7 |
| | 1.1 | | 1.9 | | 2.1 | | | -3.2 | | -.6 | | 2.2 | | 2.6 | | 2.0 |

| | | | | | | | | | | | |
|---|---|---|---|---|---|---|---|---|---|---|---|
| | 5.4 | | 8.4 | | 10.6 | Net Profit + Depr., Dep., | | | | 5.8 | | 11.4 |
| (62) | 2.8 | (64) | 2.8 | (56) | 4.5 | Amort./Cur. Mat. L/T/D | | (18) | 3.2 | (28) | 5.1 |
| | .8 | | 1.3 | | 1.8 | | | | 2.0 | | 1.8 |

| | | | | | | | | |
|---|---|---|---|---|---|---|---|---|
| .1 | .2 | .1 | | .1 | .1 | .1 | .2 | .2 |
| .5 | .4 | .4 | Fixed/Worth | .3 | .6 | .2 | .4 | .4 |
| 1.4 | 1.2 | .9 | | 1.2 | 3.2 | .8 | .9 | .9 |
| .6 | .6 | .6 | | .7 | .2 | .4 | .6 | .8 |
| 1.4 | 1.4 | 1.4 | Debt/Worth | 3.0 | 1.0 | 1.3 | 1.3 | 1.5 |
| 4.3 | 5.2 | 3.6 | | 15.0 | 4.2 | 4.8 | 2.9 | 3.6 |

| | | | | | | | | | | | |
|---|---|---|---|---|---|---|---|---|---|---|---|
| | 47.1 | | 52.2 | | 58.0 | % Profit Before Taxes/Tangible | | 95.5 | | 50.6 | | 54.1 | | 61.1 | | 60.6 |
| (186) | 15.7 | (182) | 30.2 | (184) | 26.6 | Net Worth | (18) | 28.1 | (15) | 27.5 | (33) | 29.1 | (55) | 27.0 | (58) | 24.7 |
| | 2.1 | | 8.1 | | 7.8 | | | -6.1 | | 7.6 | | 3.6 | | 8.5 | | 11.9 |

| | | | | | | | | |
|---|---|---|---|---|---|---|---|---|
| 18.9 | 19.9 | 21.9 | | 15.8 | 24.4 | 28.3 | 22.9 | 19.0 |
| 4.5 | 9.4 | 10.1 | % Profit Before Taxes/Total Assets | 9.9 | 9.3 | 11.4 | 13.3 | 8.5 |
| .4 | 2.4 | 1.9 | | .0 | 3.8 | .9 | 3.2 | 1.8 |
| 42.0 | 38.6 | 44.0 | | 240.9 | 99.7 | 104.5 | 47.8 | 35.1 |
| 13.5 | 17.6 | 18.7 | Sales/Net Fixed Assets | 19.3 | 20.1 | 25.6 | 20.4 | 14.2 |
| 6.0 | 8.8 | 7.9 | | 10.4 | 4.5 | 10.0 | 6.8 | 8.7 |
| 2.6 | 2.6 | 2.9 | | 4.1 | 2.8 | 3.2 | 2.6 | 2.6 |
| 1.9 | 1.9 | 2.0 | Sales/Total Assets | 2.1 | 1.8 | 2.8 | 2.1 | 1.9 |
| 1.4 | 1.5 | 1.5 | | 1.5 | 1.4 | 1.7 | 1.7 | 1.3 |

| | | | | | | | | | | | | | | |
|---|---|---|---|---|---|---|---|---|---|---|---|---|---|---|
| | .8 | | .8 | | .7 | | | .5 | | .3 | | .7 | | .6 | | 1.2 |
| (176) | 2.1 | (176) | 1.6 | (158) | 1.5 | % Depr., Dep., Amort./Sales | (14) | 1.4 | (12) | 1.7 | (23) | 1.4 | (51) | 1.1 | (55) | 1.8 |
| | 3.6 | | 2.9 | | 2.9 | | | 3.1 | | 5.3 | | 2.8 | | 2.6 | | 2.7 |

| | | | | | | | | | | | |
|---|---|---|---|---|---|---|---|---|---|---|---|
| | 2.3 | | 3.0 | | 2.2 | % Officers', Directors' | | 3.0 | | | 2.7 | | 1.9 | |
| (69) | 4.5 | (58) | 5.2 | (61) | 4.4 | Owners' Comp/Sales | (12) | 5.5 | (14) | 4.6 | (17) | 3.3 | |
| | 7.4 | | 8.9 | | 8.5 | | | 8.7 | | | 10.2 | | 6.8 | |

| | | | | | | | | |
|---|---|---|---|---|---|---|---|---|
| 5024340M | 8295085M | 9085610M | Net Sales ($) | 3318M | 43525M | 67802M | 254240M | 1017958M | 7698767M |
| 3299563M | 4818885M | 5165293M | Total Assets ($) | 4986M | 21307M | 40406M | 126063M | 563147M | 4409384M |

M = $ thousand    MM = $ million
See Pages 9 through 22 for Explanation of Ratios and Data

## Current Data Sorted by Assets       Comparative Historical Data

| | | | | | | Type of Statement | | |
|---|---|---|---|---|---|---|---|---|
| | | 3 | 6 | 2 | 3 | Unqualified | 17 | 17 |
| | 1 | 1 | 1 | 1 | | Reviewed | 4 | 7 |
| | 1 | 2 | | | | Compiled | 1 | 4 |
| 1 | 3 | 3 | 1 | | | Tax Returns | 2 | 4 |
| | 5 | 13 | 10 | 3 | 4 | Other | 31 | 22 |
| | 15 (4/1-9/30/11) | | 49 (10/1/11-3/31/12) | | | | 4/1/07-3/31/08 | 4/1/08-3/31/09 |
| 0-500M | 500M-2MM | 2-10MM | 10-50MM | 50-100MM | 100-250MM | | ALL | ALL |
| 1 | 10 | 22 | 18 | 6 | 7 | NUMBER OF STATEMENTS | 55 | 54 |
| % | % | % | % | % | % | ASSETS | % | % |
| | 14.8 | 12.2 | 16.9 | | | Cash & Equivalents | 15.4 | 14.7 |
| | 34.0 | 24.2 | 23.4 | | | Trade Receivables (net) | 21.9 | 22.4 |
| | 25.0 | 24.7 | 18.8 | | | Inventory | 18.4 | 21.5 |
| | .9 | 2.1 | 5.8 | | | All Other Current | 4.1 | 2.8 |
| | 74.6 | 63.2 | 64.9 | | | Total Current | 59.8 | 61.4 |
| | 13.2 | 25.3 | 17.1 | | | Fixed Assets (net) | 20.4 | 21.5 |
| | 4.3 | 5.0 | 10.6 | | | Intangibles (net) | 16.4 | 11.3 |
| | 7.9 | 6.4 | 7.4 | | | All Other Non-Current | 3.4 | 5.8 |
| | 100.0 | 100.0 | 100.0 | | | Total | 100.0 | 100.0 |
| | | | | | | LIABILITIES | | |
| | 8.8 | 5.9 | 5.6 | | | Notes Payable-Short Term | 8.3 | 9.6 |
| | 1.4 | 2.3 | 2.6 | | | Cur. Mat.-L.T.D. | 2.3 | 4.5 |
| | 15.4 | 13.8 | 10.8 | | | Trade Payables | 10.0 | 8.4 |
| | .0 | .4 | .6 | | | Income Taxes Payable | .3 | .4 |
| | 20.2 | 8.3 | 10.6 | | | All Other Current | 13.2 | 11.7 |
| | 45.8 | 30.7 | 30.1 | | | Total Current | 34.2 | 34.5 |
| | 9.7 | 16.1 | 10.7 | | | Long-Term Debt | 10.3 | 13.9 |
| | .0 | .0 | .4 | | | Deferred Taxes | .5 | .5 |
| | 2.8 | 7.8 | 4.0 | | | All Other Non-Current | 7.0 | 7.7 |
| | 41.7 | 45.4 | 54.8 | | | Net Worth | 47.9 | 43.3 |
| | 100.0 | 100.0 | 100.0 | | | Total Liabilties & Net Worth | 100.0 | 100.0 |
| | | | | | | INCOME DATA | | |
| | 100.0 | 100.0 | 100.0 | | | Net Sales | 100.0 | 100.0 |
| | 43.3 | 48.4 | 37.4 | | | Gross Profit | 49.0 | 50.0 |
| | 35.6 | 41.1 | 35.0 | | | Operating Expenses | 40.8 | 47.3 |
| | 7.7 | 7.3 | 2.3 | | | Operating Profit | 8.1 | 2.7 |
| | .3 | 1.4 | 1.1 | | | All Other Expenses (net) | 1.3 | 1.1 |
| | 7.4 | 5.8 | 1.2 | | | Profit Before Taxes | 6.9 | 1.6 |
| | | | | | | RATIOS | | |
| | 4.8 | 3.5 | 3.9 | | | | 3.2 | 2.9 |
| | 2.7 | 2.1 | 2.2 | | | Current | 2.2 | 2.0 |
| | 1.0 | 1.5 | 1.5 | | | | 1.1 | 1.3 |
| | 3.8 | 2.9 | 3.0 | | | | 2.2 | 2.0 |
| | 1.3 | 1.1 | 1.3 | | | Quick | 1.1 | 1.4 |
| | .3 | .6 | .8 | | | | .6 | .6 |
| 17 20.9 | | 37 9.9 | 38 9.7 | | | | 34 10.6 | 29 12.4 |
| 46 8.0 | | 42 8.6 | 48 7.6 | | | Sales/Receivables | 48 7.7 | 44 8.2 |
| 59 6.2 | | 58 6.3 | 63 5.8 | | | | 75 4.9 | 59 6.2 |
| 0 UND | | 33 11.0 | 22 16.5 | | | | 37 9.9 | 51 7.2 |
| 49 7.5 | | 91 4.0 | 91 4.0 | | | Cost of Sales/Inventory | 90 4.1 | 87 4.2 |
| 135 2.7 | | 152 2.4 | 130 2.8 | | | | 144 2.5 | 146 2.5 |
| 10 36.5 | | 20 18.0 | 27 13.4 | | | | 25 14.8 | 14 26.8 |
| 26 14.3 | | 28 12.9 | 41 9.0 | | | Cost of Sales/Payables | 37 9.8 | 31 11.8 |
| 41 8.9 | | 45 8.1 | 55 6.6 | | | | 67 5.4 | 53 6.9 |
| | 4.3 | 3.4 | 3.0 | | | | 2.8 | 3.2 |
| | 7.4 | 5.5 | 4.5 | | | Sales/Working Capital | 5.3 | 6.1 |
| | NM | 10.8 | 8.4 | | | | 25.6 | 14.1 |
| | | 9.7 | 11.6 | | | | 24.5 | 9.9 |
| | | (18) 3.8 | (13) 1.1 | | | EBIT/Interest | (46) 5.3 | (42) 2.2 |
| | | 2.7 | -4.7 | | | | 1.4 | -1.1 |
| | | | | | | Net Profit + Depr., Dep., | 45.2 | 4.4 |
| | | | | | | Amort./Cur. Mat. L/T/D | (18) 7.0 | (15) 2.4 |
| | | | | | | | 1.0 | .9 |
| | .1 | .2 | .1 | | | | .2 | .2 |
| | .4 | .6 | .4 | | | Fixed/Worth | .4 | .7 |
| | NM | 1.4 | 1.3 | | | | 1.5 | 2.2 |
| | .4 | .5 | .2 | | | | .5 | .6 |
| | .7 | 1.1 | 1.0 | | | Debt/Worth | 1.4 | 1.4 |
| | NM | 2.5 | 3.5 | | | | 4.8 | 9.7 |
| | | 56.5 | 35.7 | | | % Profit Before Taxes/Tangible | 68.5 | 37.8 |
| | | (19) 20.1 | (16) 9.2 | | | Net Worth | (48) 20.8 | (45) 10.1 |
| | | 8.3 | -9.4 | | | | 8.4 | -16.9 |
| | 49.0 | 19.7 | 17.9 | | | % Profit Before Taxes/Total | 17.4 | 15.2 |
| | 21.7 | 6.6 | 3.7 | | | Assets | 8.2 | 2.9 |
| | 1.5 | 3.0 | -6.0 | | | | 1.0 | -7.6 |
| | 83.0 | 44.0 | 34.3 | | | | 21.9 | 29.2 |
| | 23.6 | 13.5 | 16.2 | | | Sales/Net Fixed Assets | 12.0 | 11.3 |
| | 10.0 | 3.4 | 7.6 | | | | 5.1 | 5.3 |
| | 3.4 | 2.5 | 1.9 | | | | 2.4 | 2.2 |
| | 2.9 | 1.8 | 1.4 | | | Sales/Total Assets | 1.3 | 1.6 |
| | 1.9 | 1.5 | 1.1 | | | | .8 | 1.1 |
| | | 1.0 | 1.1 | | | | 1.4 | 1.1 |
| | | (15) 2.8 | (15) 2.0 | | | % Depr., Dep., Amort./Sales | (49) 2.9 | (41) 2.0 |
| | | 4.4 | 4.0 | | | | 5.5 | 3.8 |
| | | | | | | % Officers', Directors' | | 2.8 |
| | | | | | | Owners' Comp/Sales | | (15) 7.7 |
| | | | | | | | | 11.8 |
| 2803M | 34269M | 190646M | 568346M | 511908M | 989712M | Net Sales ($) | 3006329M | 1897427M |
| 335M | 11730M | 102539M | 353488M | 436800M | 1352161M | Total Assets ($) | 2603989M | 1512811M |

M = $ thousand   MM = $ million
See Pages 9 through 22 for Explanation of Ratios and Data

## Comparative Historical Data

## Current Data Sorted by Sales

| | | | | | | Type of Statement | | | | | | | |
|---|---|---|---|---|---|---|---|---|---|---|---|---|---|
| | 19 | | 13 | | 14 | Unqualified | | | | | 1 | 4 | 9 |
| | 11 | | 7 | | 4 | Reviewed | | | | | 2 | 1 | 1 |
| | 1 | | 1 | | 3 | Compiled | | | | | 1 | 1 | |
| | 5 | | 7 | | 8 | Tax Returns | | 1 | | | 2 | 1 | |
| | 27 | | 35 | | 35 | Other | 1 | 3 | 2 | | 8 | 9 | 13 |
| | 4/1/09-3/31/10 ALL | | 4/1/10-3/31/11 ALL | | 4/1/11-3/31/12 ALL | | | 15 (4/1-9/30/11) | | | | 49 (10/1/11-3/31/12) | |
| | | | | | | | 0-1MM | 1-3MM | 3-5MM | 5-10MM | 10-25MM | | 25MM & OVER |
| | 63 | | 63 | | 64 | NUMBER OF STATEMENTS | 1 | 6 | 4 | | 14 | 16 | 23 |
| | % | | % | | % | ASSETS | % | % | % | | % | % | % |
| | 15.6 | | 16.8 | | 14.7 | Cash & Equivalents | | | | | 11.0 | 12.8 | 17.1 |
| | 23.9 | | 26.3 | | 24.0 | Trade Receivables (net) | | | | | 25.2 | 24.5 | 19.0 |
| | 20.2 | | 21.2 | | 20.7 | Inventory | | | | | 32.3 | 18.9 | 15.5 |
| | 3.4 | | 2.9 | | 3.4 | All Other Current | | | | | .5 | 5.4 | 4.5 |
| | 63.1 | | 67.2 | | 62.9 | Total Current | | | | | 68.9 | 61.6 | 56.1 |
| | 20.0 | | 15.1 | | 19.0 | Fixed Assets (net) | | | | | 14.7 | 26.9 | 14.8 |
| | 10.4 | | 10.8 | | 10.9 | Intangibles (net) | | | | | 5.9 | 2.4 | 23.1 |
| | 6.4 | | 6.9 | | 7.3 | All Other Non-Current | | | | | 10.4 | 9.0 | 6.0 |
| | 100.0 | | 100.0 | | 100.0 | Total | | | | | 100.0 | 100.0 | 100.0 |
| | | | | | | LIABILITIES | | | | | | | |
| | 7.7 | | 5.4 | | 5.1 | Notes Payable-Short Term | | | | | 10.1 | 5.3 | 2.3 |
| | 2.9 | | 1.7 | | 2.2 | Cur. Mat.-L.T.D. | | | | | 2.6 | 2.4 | 2.7 |
| | 10.5 | | 10.8 | | 12.6 | Trade Payables | | | | | 9.0 | 17.0 | 8.7 |
| | .2 | | .3 | | .3 | Income Taxes Payable | | | | | .0 | 1.1 | .1 |
| | 16.1 | | 13.1 | | 11.0 | All Other Current | | | | | 9.5 | 7.9 | 12.3 |
| | 37.4 | | 31.4 | | 31.3 | Total Current | | | | | 31.1 | 33.8 | 26.0 |
| | 8.6 | | 9.0 | | 14.3 | Long-Term Debt | | | | | 9.1 | 14.7 | 14.8 |
| | .8 | | .6 | | .4 | Deferred Taxes | | | | | .0 | .2 | .9 |
| | 8.0 | | 11.5 | | 4.9 | All Other Non-Current | | | | | 10.7 | 1.0 | 4.8 |
| | 45.3 | | 47.5 | | 49.1 | Net Worth | | | | | 49.1 | 50.3 | 53.5 |
| | 100.0 | | 100.0 | | 100.0 | Total Liabilities & Net Worth | | | | | 100.0 | 100.0 | 100.0 |
| | | | | | | INCOME DATA | | | | | | | |
| | 100.0 | | 100.0 | | 100.0 | Net Sales | | | | | 100.0 | 100.0 | 100.0 |
| | 44.0 | | 46.8 | | 44.8 | Gross Profit | | | | | 46.5 | 42.6 | 45.3 |
| | 40.5 | | 41.0 | | 38.1 | Operating Expenses | | | | | 38.8 | 33.9 | 39.8 |
| | 3.5 | | 5.8 | | 6.7 | Operating Profit | | | | | 7.8 | 8.8 | 5.5 |
| | 1.3 | | 1.9 | | 1.1 | All Other Expenses (net) | | | | | 1.4 | 1.0 | 1.3 |
| | 2.2 | | 3.9 | | 5.6 | Profit Before Taxes | | | | | 6.4 | 7.7 | 4.2 |
| | | | | | | RATIOS | | | | | | | |
| | 3.3 | | 4.9 | | 3.8 | | | | | | 3.6 | 3.8 | 3.8 |
| | 1.8 | | 2.6 | | 2.3 | Current | | | | | 2.3 | 2.3 | 1.9 |
| | 1.2 | | 1.5 | | 1.5 | | | | | | 1.5 | 1.2 | 1.5 |
| | 2.5 | | 3.1 | | 2.9 | | | | | | 2.3 | 2.8 | 2.6 |
| | 1.0 | | 1.4 | | 1.2 | Quick | | | | | 1.4 | 1.1 | 1.2 |
| | .5 | | .8 | | .7 | | | | | | .6 | .6 | .8 |
| 35 | 10.4 | 33 | 11.0 | 36 | 10.1 | | | | | 32 | 11.4 | 41 9.0 | 32 11.3 |
| 46 | 7.9 | 47 | 7.7 | 47 | 7.7 | Sales/Receivables | | | | 41 | 8.8 | 48 7.6 | 49 7.4 |
| 57 | 6.5 | 67 | 5.5 | 63 | 5.8 | | | | | 59 | 6.2 | 60 6.1 | 74 4.9 |
| 49 | 7.4 | 49 | 7.5 | 29 | 12.5 | | | | | 46 | 7.9 | 26 13.9 | 61 6.0 |
| 77 | 4.7 | 83 | 4.4 | 89 | 4.1 | Cost of Sales/Inventory | | | | 118 | 3.1 | 78 4.7 | 99 3.7 |
| 123 | 3.0 | 141 | 2.6 | 135 | 2.7 | | | | | 192 | 1.9 | 104 3.5 | 159 2.3 |
| 16 | 23.2 | 21 | 17.7 | 22 | 16.9 | | | | | 15 | 24.9 | 20 18.0 | 27 13.5 |
| 32 | 11.4 | 35 | 10.5 | 33 | 11.1 | Cost of Sales/Payables | | | | 30 | 12.1 | 35 10.4 | 45 8.1 |
| 54 | 6.8 | 63 | 5.8 | 56 | 6.5 | | | | | 40 | 9.2 | 54 6.7 | 68 5.4 |
| | 4.0 | | 2.3 | | 3.5 | | | | | | 2.9 | 3.5 | 3.0 |
| | 6.9 | | 4.8 | | 5.4 | Sales/Working Capital | | | | | 5.5 | 5.1 | 5.4 |
| | 18.1 | | 10.8 | | 12.9 | | | | | | 8.9 | 23.7 | 13.1 |
| | 14.0 | | 44.9 | | 16.9 | | | | | | 29.5 | 26.9 | 16.0 |
| (50) | 3.6 | (52) | 4.9 | (50) | 3.8 | EBIT/Interest | | | (13) | 3.3 | (10) 6.2 | (18) 2.0 |
| | .9 | | -.2 | | 1.2 | | | | | | 2.6 | -.7 | -.3 |
| | 3.2 | | .1 | | 11.1 | | | | | | | | 19.4 |
| (15) | 2.1 | | .1 | (16) | 2.5 | Net Profit + Depr., Dep., Amort./Cur. Mat. L/T/D | | | | | | (10) 2.5 |
| | 1.3 | | .1 | | .7 | | | | | | | | -1.2 |
| | .1 | | .1 | | .1 | | | | | | .1 | .1 | .2 |
| | .5 | | .3 | | .5 | Fixed/Worth | | | | | .4 | .5 | .6 |
| | 1.3 | | 1.3 | | 1.6 | | | | | | .9 | 1.2 | -.8 |
| | .4 | | .3 | | .4 | | | | | | .5 | .2 | .3 |
| | 1.0 | | .9 | | 1.0 | Debt/Worth | | | | | 1.2 | .8 | 1.3 |
| | 4.8 | | 7.9 | | 5.7 | | | | | | 3.0 | 2.5 | -4.2 |
| | 41.3 | | 55.9 | | 56.5 | % Profit Before Taxes/Tangible Net Worth | | | | | 54.6 | 45.0 | 43.9 |
| (52) | 14.9 | (53) | 20.5 | (51) | 20.1 | | | | (12) | 12.5 | (14) 21.3 | (16) 7.1 |
| | 1.5 | | -2.9 | | 1.5 | | | | | | 7.5 | .4 | .6 |
| | 16.0 | | 21.9 | | 22.0 | % Profit Before Taxes/Total Assets | | | | | 31.2 | 22.7 | 8.4 |
| | 3.8 | | 8.8 | | 6.6 | | | | | | 6.5 | 13.5 | 3.7 |
| | -3.7 | | -2.2 | | .9 | | | | | | 3.1 | -2.1 | .1 |
| | 39.6 | | 37.3 | | 36.6 | Sales/Net Fixed Assets | | | | | 121.8 | 44.2 | 21.4 |
| | 13.4 | | 17.1 | | 12.8 | | | | | | 19.6 | 12.8 | 9.8 |
| | 4.2 | | 8.9 | | 4.8 | | | | | | 5.7 | 3.4 | 4.8 |
| | 2.4 | | 2.4 | | 2.4 | Sales/Total Assets | | | | | 2.8 | 2.3 | 1.8 |
| | 1.5 | | 1.6 | | 1.6 | | | | | | 2.1 | 1.7 | .9 |
| | 1.1 | | 1.1 | | 1.1 | | | | | | 1.4 | 1.3 | .7 |
| | 1.3 | | .9 | | 1.3 | % Depr., Dep., Amort./Sales | | | | | | 1.0 | 1.5 |
| (50) | 2.4 | (43) | 2.3 | (47) | 2.5 | | | | | | (13) 2.8 | (18) 2.3 |
| | 5.4 | | 4.9 | | 4.3 | | | | | | | 6.3 | 4.2 |
| | 1.3 | | 4.6 | | 3.7 | % Officers', Directors' Owners' Comp/Sales | | | | | | | |
| (16) | 3.1 | (10) | 7.7 | (13) | 7.9 | | | | | | | |
| | 10.6 | | 10.4 | | 11.8 | | | | | | | | |
| 2249239M | | 2263576M | | 2297684M | | Net Sales ($) | 710M | 14440M | 15042M | | 89832M | 252797M | 1924863M |
| 1882904M | | 1954256M | | 2257053M | | Total Assets ($) | 550M | 5137M | 8316M | | 48865M | 156452M | 2037733M |

M = $ thousand    MM = $ million
See Pages 9 through 22 for Explanation of Ratios and Data

**Current Data Sorted by Assets** | **Comparative Historical Data**

| Type of Statement | 0-500M | 500M-2MM | 2-10MM | 10-50MM | 50-100MM | 100-250MM | | ALL 4/1/07-3/31/08 | ALL 4/1/08-3/31/09 |
|---|---|---|---|---|---|---|---|---|---|
| Unqualified | | | 2 | 7 | 1 | 5 | | 20 | 19 |
| Reviewed | | | 4 | 3 | | | | 5 | 8 |
| Compiled | | 1 | 5 | | | | | 4 | 5 |
| Tax Returns | 1 | 2 | 1 | 1 | | 1 | | 3 | 6 |
| Other | | 3 | 7 | 11 | 1 | 5 | | 24 | 24 |
| | 14 (4/1-9/30/11) | | | 46 (10/1/11-3/31/12) | | | | | |
| **NUMBER OF STATEMENTS** | 1 | 6 | 19 | 22 | 2 | 10 | | 56 | 62 |
| | % | % | % | % | % | % | | % | % |
| **ASSETS** | | | | | | | | | |
| Cash & Equivalents | | | 14.5 | 12.6 | | 10.0 | | 11.6 | 10.9 |
| Trade Receivables (net) | | | 27.1 | 28.0 | | 19.5 | | 25.5 | 24.8 |
| Inventory | | | 28.3 | 28.2 | | 26.0 | | 23.3 | 26.2 |
| All Other Current | | | 3.6 | 5.5 | | 7.4 | | 6.6 | 5.2 |
| Total Current | | | 73.6 | 74.3 | | 62.9 | | 67.0 | 67.1 |
| Fixed Assets (net) | | | 15.1 | 18.5 | | 13.9 | | 16.5 | 15.6 |
| Intangibles (net) | | | 6.6 | 3.7 | | 17.9 | | 10.9 | 10.3 |
| All Other Non-Current | | | 4.7 | 3.5 | | 5.3 | | 5.7 | 7.0 |
| Total | | | 100.0 | 100.0 | | 100.0 | | 100.0 | 100.0 |
| **LIABILITIES** | | | | | | | | | |
| Notes Payable-Short Term | | | 3.2 | 11.9 | | 2.2 | | 6.5 | 7.7 |
| Cur. Mat.-L.T.D. | | | 2.8 | 2.0 | | 1.2 | | 4.1 | 2.6 |
| Trade Payables | | | 16.8 | 12.1 | | 8.9 | | 10.9 | 13.3 |
| Income Taxes Payable | | | .1 | .4 | | .1 | | .3 | .3 |
| All Other Current | | | 10.1 | 11.5 | | 12.4 | | 14.7 | 13.5 |
| Total Current | | | 33.1 | 38.0 | | 24.6 | | 36.6 | 37.3 |
| Long-Term Debt | | | 15.6 | 8.9 | | 14.5 | | 15.2 | 13.6 |
| Deferred Taxes | | | .2 | .3 | | 2.7 | | .9 | 1.1 |
| All Other Non-Current | | | 2.3 | 1.9 | | 6.0 | | 7.4 | 4.5 |
| Net Worth | | | 48.9 | 50.9 | | 52.2 | | 40.0 | 43.6 |
| Total Liabilities & Net Worth | | | 100.0 | 100.0 | | 100.0 | | 100.0 | 100.0 |
| **INCOME DATA** | | | | | | | | | |
| Net Sales | | | 100.0 | 100.0 | | 100.0 | | 100.0 | 100.0 |
| Gross Profit | | | 38.4 | 35.6 | | 25.7 | | 37.6 | 37.8 |
| Operating Expenses | | | 29.3 | 25.2 | | 19.7 | | 28.2 | 31.2 |
| Operating Profit | | | 9.1 | 10.4 | | 6.1 | | 9.4 | 6.6 |
| All Other Expenses (net) | | | 1.0 | .7 | | 2.2 | | 1.5 | 1.0 |
| Profit Before Taxes | | | 8.1 | 9.8 | | 3.8 | | 7.9 | 5.6 |
| **RATIOS** | | | | | | | | | |
| Current | | | 4.4 | 3.3 | | 3.9 | | 3.5 | 3.8 |
| | | | 2.2 | 2.3 | | 2.3 | | 2.0 | 2.2 |
| | | | 1.6 | 1.2 | | 2.1 | | 1.3 | 1.3 |
| Quick | | | 2.9 | 2.1 | | 1.7 | | 1.9 | 2.0 |
| | | | 1.1 | 1.1 | | 1.1 | | 1.0 | .9 |
| | | | .8 | .5 | | .8 | | .6 | .6 |
| Sales/Receivables | | | 42   8.6 | 35   10.3 | | 42   8.7 | | 38   9.6 | 31   11.7 |
| | | | 48   7.6 | 62   5.9 | | 49   7.4 | | 48   7.7 | 50   7.4 |
| | | | 65   5.6 | 76   4.8 | | 89   4.1 | | 67   5.4 | 65   5.6 |
| Cost of Sales/Inventory | | | 28   13.1 | 9   39.4 | | 85   4.3 | | 28   13.2 | 38   9.5 |
| | | | 104   3.5 | 135   2.7 | | 101   3.6 | | 85   4.3 | 103   3.5 |
| | | | 182   2.0 | 174   2.1 | | 135   2.7 | | 146   2.5 | 149   2.4 |
| Cost of Sales/Payables | | | 17   21.2 | 23   16.0 | | 19   19.1 | | 19   18.9 | 19   19.3 |
| | | | 30   12.3 | 42   8.7 | | 31   11.7 | | 30   12.2 | 31   11.6 |
| | | | 41   9.0 | 58   6.3 | | 38   9.7 | | 52   7.1 | 54   6.8 |
| Sales/Working Capital | | | 2.7 | 2.9 | | 1.8 | | 2.6 | 3.2 |
| | | | 5.2 | 3.9 | | 4.1 | | 6.1 | 5.6 |
| | | | 6.3 | 14.5 | | 5.0 | | 17.6 | 13.5 |
| EBIT/Interest | | | 229.8 | 60.2 | | 25.0 | | 41.4 | 23.5 |
| | | | (15) 11.7 | (20) 9.1 | | 7.2 | | (50) 11.3 | (56) 4.4 |
| | | | 3.7 | 3.1 | | -.4 | | 1.9 | 1.2 |
| Net Profit + Depr., Dep., Amort./Cur. Mat. L/T/D | | | | | | | | 28.1 | 18.4 |
| | | | | | | | | (19) 2.2 | (20) 2.8 |
| | | | | | | | | .4 | 1.0 |
| Fixed/Worth | | | .1 | .1 | | .2 | | .1 | .2 |
| | | | .2 | .2 | | .3 | | .3 | .4 |
| | | | 1.2 | 1.0 | | -2.9 | | 1.5 | 1.5 |
| Debt/Worth | | | .3 | .4 | | .4 | | .5 | .5 |
| | | | 1.2 | .9 | | .8 | | 1.6 | 1.4 |
| | | | 4.5 | 2.8 | | -9.0 | | 7.8 | 5.1 |
| % Profit Before Taxes/Tangible Net Worth | | | 59.1 | 64.1 | | | | 80.4 | 57.1 |
| | | | (17) 22.8 | (21) 26.1 | | | | (47) 31.6 | (51) 20.4 |
| | | | 7.7 | 11.0 | | | | 7.6 | 4.7 |
| % Profit Before Taxes/Total Assets | | | 21.2 | 23.3 | | 13.6 | | 25.3 | 19.4 |
| | | | 11.1 | 11.1 | | 2.8 | | 11.0 | 6.4 |
| | | | 2.5 | 4.9 | | -1.4 | | 3.8 | 1.6 |
| Sales/Net Fixed Assets | | | 58.6 | 26.3 | | 18.0 | | 24.1 | 29.5 |
| | | | 18.7 | 14.2 | | 11.1 | | 11.6 | 12.6 |
| | | | 10.7 | 6.4 | | 6.8 | | 7.0 | 7.9 |
| Sales/Total Assets | | | 2.3 | 2.1 | | 1.6 | | 2.3 | 2.7 |
| | | | 2.0 | 1.6 | | 1.3 | | 1.5 | 1.6 |
| | | | 1.4 | 1.4 | | .8 | | 1.0 | 1.2 |
| % Depr., Dep., Amort./Sales | | | .6 | .9 | | | | 1.2 | .8 |
| | | | (17) 1.5 | (18) 1.7 | | | | (45) 1.9 | (52) 1.7 |
| | | | 2.6 | 2.9 | | | | 2.9 | 2.6 |
| % Officers', Directors' Owners' Comp/Sales | | | | | | | | | 2.8 |
| | | | | | | | | (18) 5.7 | |
| | | | | | | | | | 10.5 |
| Net Sales ($) | 2420M | 14188M | 202723M | 771018M | 131274M | 1886416M | | 3072344M | 2549041M |
| Total Assets ($) | 484M | 6014M | 104883M | 451216M | 139749M | 1669840M | | 2246521M | 2096510M |

© RMA 2012

M = $ thousand   MM = $ million
See Pages 9 through 22 for Explanation of Ratios and Data

## Comparative Historical Data | Current Data Sorted by Sales

| 4/1/09-3/31/10 ALL | 4/1/10-3/31/11 ALL | 4/1/11-3/31/12 ALL | Type of Statement | 0-1MM | 1-3MM | 3-5MM | 5-10MM | 10-25MM | 25MM & OVER |
|---|---|---|---|---|---|---|---|---|---|
| 29 | 18 | 15 | Unqualified | | | 1 | 1 | 3 | 10 |
| 16 | 12 | 7 | Reviewed | | 1 | | 2 | 2 | 2 |
| 2 | 2 | 6 | Compiled | 1 | | | 2 | 2 | 1 |
| 1 | 5 | 5 | Tax Returns | | | 3 | | | 1 |
| 21 | 36 | 27 | Other | 1 | 3 | | 3 | 5 | 15 |
| | | | | | 14 (4/1-9/30/11) | | | 46 (10/1/11-3/31/12) | |
| 69 | 73 | 60 | NUMBER OF STATEMENTS | 2 | 4 | 5 | 8 | 12 | 29 |
| % | % | % | ASSETS | % | % | % | % | % | % |
| 14.0 | 13.1 | 12.4 | Cash & Equivalents | | | | | 13.8 | 12.1 |
| 22.1 | 23.9 | 25.0 | Trade Receivables (net) | | | | | 27.5 | 24.6 |
| 27.8 | 26.6 | 29.1 | Inventory | | | | | 28.6 | 28.9 |
| 6.1 | 4.9 | 4.7 | All Other Current | | | | | 8.8 | 4.6 |
| 70.1 | 68.5 | 71.3 | Total Current | | | | | 78.6 | 70.2 |
| 16.2 | 16.2 | 15.7 | Fixed Assets (net) | | | | | 12.0 | 15.7 |
| 9.6 | 9.7 | 8.2 | Intangibles (net) | | | | | 4.0 | 11.0 |
| 4.1 | 5.6 | 4.9 | All Other Non-Current | | | | | 5.5 | 3.1 |
| 100.0 | 100.0 | 100.0 | Total | | | | | 100.0 | 100.0 |
| | | | LIABILITIES | | | | | | |
| 4.9 | 15.2 | 8.2 | Notes Payable-Short Term | | | | | 3.3 | 7.0 |
| 2.7 | 2.6 | 1.9 | Cur. Mat.-L.T.D. | | | | | 1.6 | 1.3 |
| 9.8 | 11.2 | 13.7 | Trade Payables | | | | | 11.7 | 11.2 |
| .9 | .7 | .2 | Income Taxes Payable | | | | | .3 | .3 |
| 12.8 | 15.2 | 10.2 | All Other Current | | | | | 9.9 | 13.2 |
| 31.2 | 44.9 | 34.2 | Total Current | | | | | 26.8 | 33.0 |
| 10.0 | 15.8 | 12.8 | Long-Term Debt | | | | | 9.4 | 9.4 |
| .8 | 1.0 | .6 | Deferred Taxes | | | | | .3 | 1.0 |
| 4.8 | 5.4 | 3.6 | All Other Non-Current | | | | | 1.8 | 3.5 |
| 53.2 | 33.0 | 48.8 | Net Worth | | | | | 61.7 | 53.1 |
| 100.0 | 100.0 | 100.0 | Total Liabilities & Net Worth | | | | | 100.0 | 100.0 |
| | | | INCOME DATA | | | | | | |
| 100.0 | 100.0 | 100.0 | Net Sales | | | | | 100.0 | 100.0 |
| 37.7 | 40.8 | 36.2 | Gross Profit | | | | | 35.5 | 34.0 |
| 30.9 | 33.7 | 27.9 | Operating Expenses | | | | | 24.8 | 24.2 |
| 6.8 | 7.1 | 8.3 | Operating Profit | | | | | 10.6 | 9.8 |
| 2.0 | 1.5 | 1.0 | All Other Expenses (net) | | | | | .6 | 1.0 |
| 4.8 | 5.5 | 7.3 | Profit Before Taxes | | | | | 10.0 | 8.7 |
| | | | RATIOS | | | | | | |
| 4.4 | 3.0 | 3.9 | | | | | | 8.6 | 3.9 |
| 2.6 | 2.0 | 2.2 | Current | | | | | 2.5 | 2.2 |
| 1.5 | 1.4 | 1.6 | | | | | | 2.1 | 1.5 |
| 2.5 | 2.0 | 2.2 | | | | | | 3.2 | 2.1 |
| 1.1 | .9 | 1.1 | Quick | | | | | 1.6 | 1.2 |
| .6 | .7 | .7 | | | | | | .9 | .8 |
| 34  10.6 | 35  10.4 | 38  9.6 | | | | | | 43  8.5 | 38  9.5 |
| 48  7.6 | 48  7.5 | 49  7.4 | Sales/Receivables | | | | | 48  7.6 | 52  7.0 |
| 65  5.6 | 63  5.8 | 68  5.4 | | | | | | 65  5.6 | 78  4.7 |
| 65  5.7 | 45  8.2 | 61  6.0 | | | | | | 29  12.5 | 79  4.6 |
| 123  3.0 | 107  3.4 | 122  3.0 | Cost of Sales/Inventory | | | | | 118  3.1 | 122  3.0 |
| 163  2.2 | 169  2.2 | 166  2.2 | | | | | | 192  1.9 | 166  2.2 |
| 18  20.3 | 18  20.5 | 22  16.7 | | | | | | 17  21.4 | 22  16.3 |
| 28  12.9 | 30  12.3 | 36  10.2 | Cost of Sales/Payables | | | | | 29  12.6 | 36  10.2 |
| 51  7.2 | 55  6.6 | 51  7.2 | | | | | | 36  10.0 | 49  7.5 |
| 2.4 | 3.0 | 2.8 | | | | | | 2.7 | 2.7 |
| 4.0 | 4.8 | 4.7 | Sales/Working Capital | | | | | 3.5 | 4.1 |
| 9.4 | 11.2 | 9.3 | | | | | | 5.4 | 7.2 |
| 66.8 | 28.8 | 32.6 | | | | | | 552.6 | 42.4 |
| (61)  6.5 | (65)  5.4 | (53)  7.5 | EBIT/Interest | | | | (10)  23.1 | (27)  11.7 | |
| .8 | 1.5 | 1.7 | | | | | | 7.3 | 1.4 |
| 10.1 | 67.5 | 56.0 | Net Profit + Depr., Dep., | | | | | . | |
| (19)  2.4 | (23)  4.6 | (13)  3.8 | Amort./Cur. Mat. L/T/D | | | | | | |
| 1.3 | 1.5 | 2.3 | | | | | | | |
| .1 | .1 | .1 | | | | | | .1 | .1 |
| .3 | .4 | .3 | Fixed/Worth | | | | | .2 | .2 |
| .7 | 2.3 | 1.2 | | | | | | .5 | 1.2 |
| .4 | .5 | .4 | | | | | | .1 | .4 |
| 1.0 | 1.4 | 1.0 | Debt/Worth | | | | | .6 | .8 |
| 2.5 | 12.6 | 3.8 | | | | | | 2.5 | 2.1 |
| 36.6 | 50.9 | 56.4 | % Profit Before Taxes/Tangible | | | | | 55.9 | 64.1 |
| (61)  13.6 | (59)  25.5 | (52)  20.7 | Net Worth | | | | (11)  19.0 | (25)  26.1 | |
| 2.1 | 8.5 | 3.9 | | | | | | 12.2 | 5.7 |
| 18.2 | 15.8 | 19.6 | % Profit Before Taxes/Total | | | | | 22.0 | 22.2 |
| 7.0 | 8.3 | 10.5 | Assets | | | | | 16.5 | 10.5 |
| -.6 | 1.2 | .8 | | | | | | 10.0 | 1.0 |
| 23.2 | 30.7 | 34.4 | | | | | | 36.3 | 26.5 |
| 11.9 | 16.2 | 15.6 | Sales/Net Fixed Assets | | | | | 15.6 | 17.3 |
| 6.3 | 7.0 | 7.7 | | | | | | 8.0 | 7.7 |
| 2.0 | 2.2 | 2.3 | | | | | | 2.3 | 1.9 |
| 1.4 | 1.5 | 1.6 | Sales/Total Assets | | | | | 1.7 | 1.6 |
| 1.1 | 1.1 | 1.2 | | | | | | 1.4 | 1.0 |
| 1.2 | 1.1 | .9 | | | | | | 1.1 | .9 |
| (58)  2.1 | (54)  2.3 | (50)  1.7 | % Depr., Dep., Amort./Sales | | | | (11)  1.6 | (24)  2.0 | |
| 3.0 | 3.3 | 2.9 | | | | | | 2.3 | 3.2 |
| 2.4 | 2.5 | 3.3 | % Officers', Directors' | | | | | | |
| (12)  5.1 | (12)  6.9 | (15)  5.7 | Owners' Comp/Sales | | | | | | |
| 7.8 | 10.0 | 10.2 | | | | | | | |
| 3383935M | 3222760M | 3008039M | Net Sales ($) | 1669M | 8193M | 20116M | 60079M | 188901M | 2729081M |
| 2805987M | 2862142M | 2372186M | Total Assets ($) | 1349M | 14098M | 11154M | 43035M | 116428M | 2186122M |

© RMA 2012

M = $ thousand    MM = $ million

See Pages 9 through 22 for Explanation of Ratios and Data

## Current Data Sorted by Assets                                    Comparative Historical Data

| | | | | | | | Type of Statement | | |
|---|---|---|---|---|---|---|---|---|---|
| | | 3 | | 4 | | 2 | Unqualified | 10 | 8 |
| | | 6 | | | | | Reviewed | 12 | 11 |
| 1 | 4 | 4 | | | | | Compiled | 5 | 5 |
| 1 | | 2 | | | | | Tax Returns | 5 | 4 |
| 1 | 6 | 8 | 5 | | | 1 | Other | 20 | 16 |
| | 7 (4/1-9/30/11) | | 41 (10/1/11-3/31/12) | | | | | 4/1/07-3/31/08 | 4/1/08-3/31/09 |
| 0-500M | 500M-2MM | 2-10MM | 10-50MM | 50-100MM | 100-250MM | | | ALL | ALL |
| 3 | 10 | 23 | 9 | | | 3 | **NUMBER OF STATEMENTS** | 52 | 44 |
| % | % | % | % | % | % | % | **ASSETS** | % | % |
| | 14.1 | 15.0 | | | | | Cash & Equivalents | 13.9 | 14.4 |
| | 36.0 | 37.8 | | | | | Trade Receivables (net) | 35.6 | 38.3 |
| | 23.5 | 17.3 | | | | | Inventory | 21.0 | 19.4 |
| | 1.1 | 5.9 | | | | | All Other Current | 4.7 | 3.5 |
| | 74.7 | 75.9 | | | | | Total Current | 75.2 | 75.6 |
| | 16.6 | 15.1 | | | | | Fixed Assets (net) | 13.1 | 14.5 |
| | 3.9 | 1.5 | | | | | Intangibles (net) | 3.4 | 4.1 |
| | 4.7 | 7.5 | | | | | All Other Non-Current | 8.4 | 5.8 |
| | 100.0 | 100.0 | | | | | Total | 100.0 | 100.0 |
| | | | | | | | **LIABILITIES** | | |
| | .7 | 12.0 | | | | | Notes Payable-Short Term | 11.7 | 9.0 |
| | 3.1 | 4.4 | | | | | Cur. Mat.-L.T.D. | 3.1 | 3.9 |
| | 14.8 | 18.8 | | | | | Trade Payables | 16.4 | 14.0 |
| | .0 | .4 | | | | | Income Taxes Payable | .3 | .2 |
| | 22.0 | 10.2 | | | | | All Other Current | 19.6 | 16.0 |
| | 40.6 | 45.9 | | | | | Total Current | 51.0 | 43.1 |
| | 11.9 | 10.8 | | | | | Long-Term Debt | 10.0 | 8.0 |
| | .3 | .4 | | | | | Deferred Taxes | .2 | .3 |
| | 13.9 | 1.8 | | | | | All Other Non-Current | 7.2 | 4.6 |
| | 33.3 | 41.1 | | | | | Net Worth | 31.5 | 44.0 |
| | 100.0 | 100.0 | | | | | Total Liabilities & Net Worth | 100.0 | 100.0 |
| | | | | | | | **INCOME DATA** | | |
| | 100.0 | 100.0 | | | | | Net Sales | 100.0 | 100.0 |
| | 50.1 | 35.2 | | | | | Gross Profit | 36.7 | 36.0 |
| | 38.8 | 28.7 | | | | | Operating Expenses | 30.6 | 28.5 |
| | 11.4 | 6.4 | | | | | Operating Profit | 6.1 | 7.6 |
| | 1.8 | .1 | | | | | All Other Expenses (net) | .6 | .5 |
| | 9.6 | 6.3 | | | | | Profit Before Taxes | 5.5 | 7.1 |
| | | | | | | | **RATIOS** | | |
| | 2.6 | 2.6 | | | | | | 3.6 | 3.4 |
| | 1.8 | 1.5 | | | | | Current | 1.8 | 1.8 |
| | 1.2 | 1.2 | | | | | | 1.3 | 1.2 |
| | 1.9 | 2.4 | | | | | | 2.0 | 2.1 |
| | 1.4 | 1.0 | | | | | Quick | 1.1 | 1.4 |
| | .7 | .6 | | | | | | .8 | .8 |

| | | | | | | | | | | | | |
|---|---|---|---|---|---|---|---|---|---|---|---|---|
| 21 | 17.1 | 46 | 8.0 | | | | Sales/Receivables | 37 | 9.9 | 41 | 8.8 |
| 43 | 8.5 | 55 | 6.6 | | | | | 52 | 7.0 | 51 | 7.1 |
| 63 | 5.8 | 69 | 5.3 | | | | | 71 | 5.1 | 68 | 5.4 |
| 26 | 14.2 | 0 | UND | | | | Cost of Sales/Inventory | 18 | 20.2 | 11 | 31.9 |
| 49 | 7.4 | 26 | 14.2 | | | | | 54 | 6.8 | 48 | 7.6 |
| 81 | 4.5 | 78 | 4.7 | | | | | 94 | 3.9 | 86 | 4.3 |
| 3 | 108.4 | 28 | 12.9 | | | | Cost of Sales/Payables | 18 | 20.4 | 13 | 27.0 |
| 30 | 12.1 | 38 | 9.5 | | | | | 31 | 11.7 | 31 | 11.8 |
| 81 | 4.5 | 58 | 6.3 | | | | | 52 | 7.1 | 49 | 7.5 |

| | | | | | | | | | | | | |
|---|---|---|---|---|---|---|---|---|---|---|---|---|
| | 5.2 | | 4.9 | | | | Sales/Working Capital | | 4.2 | | 4.1 |
| | 9.7 | | 8.4 | | | | | | 6.6 | | 7.3 |
| | 18.7 | | 19.3 | | | | | | 15.7 | | 21.9 |
| | | | 55.7 | | | | EBIT/Interest | | 39.0 | | 44.3 |
| | (21) | | 9.8 | | | | | (44) | 8.1 | (39) | 16.8 |
| | | | 2.1 | | | | | | .8 | | 3.5 |
| | | | | | | | Net Profit + Depr., Dep., Amort./Cur. Mat. L/T/D | | | | |
| | .0 | | .1 | | | | Fixed/Worth | | .1 | | .1 |
| | .4 | | .3 | | | | | | .3 | | .2 |
| | -3.4 | | 2.0 | | | | | | 1.0 | | .9 |
| | .4 | | .6 | | | | Debt/Worth | | .6 | | .5 |
| | 1.6 | | 1.6 | | | | | | 1.6 | | 1.3 |
| | -6.4 | | 4.0 | | | | | | 7.0 | | 4.8 |
| | | | 41.6 | | | | % Profit Before Taxes/Tangible Net Worth | | 67.7 | | 69.8 |
| | (21) | | 24.0 | | | | | (45) | 31.3 | (39) | 37.5 |
| | | | 5.8 | | | | | | 6.0 | | 14.0 |
| | 39.3 | | 19.5 | | | | % Profit Before Taxes/Total Assets | | 24.2 | | 27.2 |
| | 18.5 | | 11.5 | | | | | | 11.3 | | 16.4 |
| | 8.8 | | 2.6 | | | | | | 1.1 | | 5.1 |
| | 446.7 | | 52.0 | | | | Sales/Net Fixed Assets | | 35.8 | | 43.6 |
| | 24.4 | | 19.3 | | | | | | 22.5 | | 25.7 |
| | 12.9 | | 10.2 | | | | | | 11.8 | | 11.4 |
| | 4.3 | | 3.1 | | | | Sales/Total Assets | | 3.0 | | 3.3 |
| | 3.0 | | 2.2 | | | | | | 2.3 | | 2.3 |
| | 1.7 | | 1.7 | | | | | | 1.8 | | 1.7 |
| | | | .5 | | | | % Depr., Dep., Amort./Sales | | .5 | | .4 |
| | (21) | | 1.0 | | | | | (44) | 1.3 | (36) | 1.1 |
| | | | 1.3 | | | | | | 2.2 | | 2.1 |
| | | | | | | | % Officers', Directors' Owners' Comp/Sales | | 2.7 | | 3.0 |
| | | | | | | | | (13) | 4.1 | (12) | 4.1 |
| | | | | | | | | | 7.4 | | 7.3 |

| | | | | | | | | | |
|---|---|---|---|---|---|---|---|---|---|
| 5877M | 36264M | 246599M | 455107M | | 696997M | Net Sales ($) | | 1988884M | 1202524M |
| 1167M | 12473M | 107017M | 206390M | | 440254M | Total Assets ($) | | 1102314M | 664087M |

*Note: In columns 4 (10-50MM), 5 (50-100MM) data shown as "DATA NOT AVAILABLE" vertically.*

M = $ thousand    MM = $ million
See Pages 9 through 22 for Explanation of Ratios and Data

## Comparative Historical Data       Current Data Sorted by Sales

| | 4/1/09-3/31/10 ALL | 4/1/10-3/31/11 ALL | 4/1/11-3/31/12 ALL | 0-1MM | 1-3MM | 3-5MM | 5-10MM | 10-25MM | 25MM & OVER |
|---|---|---|---|---|---|---|---|---|---|
| **Type of Statement** | | | | | | | | | |
| Unqualified | 6 | 7 | 9 | | | | 1 | 4 | 4 |
| Reviewed | 9 | 13 | 6 | | | | 4 | 2 | |
| Compiled | 5 | 7 | 9 | 1 | 2 | 1 | 4 | 1 | |
| Tax Returns | 3 | 6 | 3 | | 1 | | 2 | | |
| Other | 11 | 25 | 21 | 1 | 4 | 2 | 2 | 6 | 6 |
| | 4/1/09-3/31/10 | 4/1/10-3/31/11 | 4/1/11-3/31/12 | 7 (4/1-9/30/11) | | | 41 (10/1/11-3/31/12) | | |
| **NUMBER OF STATEMENTS** | 34 | 58 | 48 | 2 | 7 | 4 | 12 | 13 | 10 |
| **ASSETS** | % | % | % | % | % | % | % | % | % |
| Cash & Equivalents | 13.7 | 10.2 | 12.8 | | | | 17.3 | 7.7 | 8.7 |
| Trade Receivables (net) | 38.3 | 36.0 | 37.1 | | | | 39.1 | 36.8 | 37.7 |
| Inventory | 22.0 | 24.0 | 18.4 | | | | 15.8 | 22.9 | 15.5 |
| All Other Current | 4.6 | 6.9 | 6.1 | | | | 3.1 | 10.3 | 9.3 |
| Total Current | 78.6 | 77.1 | 74.4 | | | | 75.3 | 77.7 | 71.3 |
| Fixed Assets (net) | 12.4 | 13.9 | 16.0 | | | | 17.7 | 15.3 | 13.2 |
| Intangibles (net) | 4.1 | 4.1 | 3.6 | | | | 1.4 | 2.2 | 9.7 |
| All Other Non-Current | 5.0 | 5.0 | 6.1 | | | | 5.6 | 4.8 | 5.8 |
| Total | 100.0 | 100.0 | 100.0 | | | | 100.0 | 100.0 | 100.0 |
| **LIABILITIES** | | | | | | | | | |
| Notes Payable-Short Term | 9.6 | 8.4 | 7.7 | | | | 11.1 | 10.7 | 7.7 |
| Cur. Mat.-L.T.D. | 3.1 | 3.9 | 3.7 | | | | 1.9 | 2.6 | 2.7 |
| Trade Payables | 13.2 | 14.3 | 16.0 | | | | 21.2 | 17.0 | 13.0 |
| Income Taxes Payable | .0 | .3 | .4 | | | | .0 | .6 | 1.2 |
| All Other Current | 16.6 | 13.6 | 14.2 | | | | 9.6 | 13.4 | 19.2 |
| Total Current | 42.6 | 40.5 | 42.0 | | | | 43.9 | 44.2 | 43.8 |
| Long-Term Debt | 6.5 | 8.4 | 9.9 | | | | 10.1 | 6.9 | 3.3 |
| Deferred Taxes | .7 | .3 | .7 | | | | .2 | 1.3 | 1.0 |
| All Other Non-Current | 9.0 | 2.8 | 4.7 | | | | 11.2 | .8 | 3.1 |
| Net Worth | 41.1 | 48.1 | 42.7 | | | | 34.6 | 46.9 | 48.7 |
| Total Liabilities & Net Worth | 100.0 | 100.0 | 100.0 | | | | 100.0 | 100.0 | 100.0 |
| **INCOME DATA** | | | | | | | | | |
| Net Sales | 100.0 | 100.0 | 100.0 | | | | 100.0 | 100.0 | 100.0 |
| Gross Profit | 37.5 | 37.7 | 38.2 | | | | 39.2 | 32.1 | 36.1 |
| Operating Expenses | 29.5 | 31.7 | 30.7 | | | | 31.9 | 26.7 | 31.2 |
| Operating Profit | 7.9 | 6.0 | 7.5 | | | | 7.3 | 5.4 | 5.0 |
| All Other Expenses (net) | .4 | .3 | .4 | | | | -.1 | -.4 | -.2 |
| Profit Before Taxes | 7.5 | 5.7 | 7.2 | | | | 7.4 | 5.8 | 5.2 |
| **RATIOS** | | | | | | | | | |
| Current | 3.6 | 3.3 | 2.7 | | | | 3.8 | 2.7 | 1.9 |
| | 2.0 | 2.1 | 1.8 | | | | 1.7 | 2.2 | 1.6 |
| | 1.2 | 1.3 | 1.2 | | | | 1.2 | 1.3 | 1.3 |
| Quick | 2.2 | 2.0 | 1.9 | | | | 3.4 | 1.7 | 1.3 |
| | 1.3 | 1.1 | 1.2 | | | | 1.3 | 1.1 | 1.2 |
| | .8 | .7 | .7 | | | | .9 | .6 | .8 |
| Sales/Receivables | 36   10.2 | 41   8.9 | 41   8.8 | | | | 37   9.9 | 40   9.1 | 49   7.5 |
| | 48   7.6 | 54   6.8 | 55   6.6 | | | | 52   7.0 | 59   6.2 | 62   5.9 |
| | 62   5.9 | 65   5.6 | 72   5.1 | | | | 74   4.9 | 70   5.2 | 87   4.2 |
| Cost of Sales/Inventory | 7   51.0 | 21   17.7 | 11   33.9 | | | | 14   25.9 | 7   54.6 | 12   29.5 |
| | 50   7.3 | 56   6.5 | 34   10.7 | | | | 31   11.7 | 54   6.8 | 41   8.8 |
| | 96   3.8 | 88   4.2 | 76   4.8 | | | | 87   4.2 | 152   2.4 | 68   5.4 |
| Cost of Sales/Payables | 11   32.7 | 18   20.6 | 22   16.6 | | | | 21   17.4 | 31   11.9 | 16   22.2 |
| | 24   15.0 | 31   11.9 | 38   9.5 | | | | 45   8.1 | 38   9.6 | 43   8.4 |
| | 39   9.3 | 49   7.4 | 57   6.4 | | | | 81   4.5 | 45   8.1 | 66   5.5 |
| Sales/Working Capital | 4.4 | 3.9 | 4.4 | | | | 4.9 | 3.4 | 4.2 |
| | 6.7 | 6.4 | 7.9 | | | | 13.0 | 7.5 | 7.5 |
| | 21.2 | 14.7 | 17.7 | | | | 17.6 | 12.5 | 20.3 |
| EBIT/Interest | 210.9 | 34.1 | 45.3 | | | | 26.7 | 82.1 | |
| | (29) 12.0 | (48) 10.9 | (42) 9.0 | | | | (10) 8.6 | 9.8 | |
| | 1.9 | 1.6 | 3.0 | | | | 1.1 | 5.1 | |
| Net Profit + Depr., Dep., Amort./Cur. Mat. L/T/D | | 6.1 | 10.0 | | | | | | |
| | | (13) 1.9 | (17) 3.6 | | | | | | |
| | | .3 | 2.0 | | | | | | |
| Fixed/Worth | .1 | .1 | .1 | | | | .1 | .1 | .2 |
| | .3 | .2 | .4 | | | | .6 | .5 | .4 |
| | .5 | .8 | 1.3 | | | | 2.6 | .6 | .6 |
| Debt/Worth | .6 | .4 | .6 | | | | .3 | .6 | .9 |
| | 1.0 | 1.0 | 1.4 | | | | 2.1 | .7 | 1.4 |
| | 3.1 | 3.3 | 3.8 | | | | 16.1 | 2.6 | 2.1 |
| % Profit Before Taxes/Tangible Net Worth | 57.3 | 52.1 | 45.7 | | | | 66.2 | 40.4 | |
| | (32) 30.4 | (52) 18.4 | (42) 26.3 | | | | (10) 32.0 | (12) 15.1 | |
| | 9.1 | 6.0 | 14.2 | | | | 18.6 | 4.3 | |
| % Profit Before Taxes/Total Assets | 32.7 | 25.8 | 19.6 | | | | 28.6 | 18.8 | 15.3 |
| | 15.0 | 9.5 | 11.7 | | | | 18.5 | 8.3 | 9.6 |
| | 1.1 | 2.5 | 3.6 | | | | 2.1 | 2.9 | 6.7 |
| Sales/Net Fixed Assets | 63.6 | 50.7 | 41.8 | | | | 87.0 | 57.1 | 26.2 |
| | 25.0 | 19.9 | 19.4 | | | | 24.4 | 15.5 | 20.4 |
| | 12.0 | 13.0 | 9.7 | | | | 7.7 | 5.5 | 11.1 |
| Sales/Total Assets | 3.5 | 3.2 | 3.4 | | | | 3.6 | 2.9 | 2.6 |
| | 2.6 | 2.1 | 2.2 | | | | 2.5 | 2.2 | 1.9 |
| | 1.7 | 1.7 | 1.6 | | | | 1.7 | 1.2 | 1.5 |
| % Depr., Dep., Amort./Sales | .4 | .9 | .7 | | | | .4 | .5 | |
| | (27) 1.1 | (49) 1.4 | (42) 1.2 | | | | (10) 1.1 | 1.0 | |
| | 1.8 | 2.3 | 2.8 | | | | 2.1 | 2.8 | |
| % Officers', Directors' Owners' Comp/Sales | 2.8 | 2.7 | 1.7 | | | | | | |
| | (11) 4.8 | (17) 5.6 | (10) 3.0 | | | | | | |
| | 9.9 | 7.1 | 5.4 | | | | | | |
| Net Sales ($) | 1322198M | 1868725M | 1440844M | 914M | 13537M | 15513M | 86917M | 209187M | 1114776M |
| Total Assets ($) | 592043M | 1060483M | 767301M | 3943M | 5811M | 6243M | 38217M | 117872M | 595215M |

M = $ thousand    MM = $ million
See Pages 9 through 22 for Explanation of Ratios and Data

**Current Data Sorted by Assets**  |  **Comparative Historical Data**

### Type of Statement

| 0-500M | 500M-2MM | 2-10MM | 10-50MM | 50-100MM | 100-250MM | | ALL 4/1/07-3/31/08 | ALL 4/1/08-3/31/09 |
|---|---|---|---|---|---|---|---|---|
| | | 4 | 11 | 4 | 5 | Unqualified | 29 | 30 |
| 2 | 8 | 29 | 10 | | 1 | Reviewed | 36 | 27 |
| | 2 | 7 | | | | Compiled | 12 | 8 |
| 3 | 4 | 2 | 1 | | | Tax Returns | 11 | 5 |
| 2 | 5 | 18 | 16 | 5 | 4 | Other | 39 | 49 |
| | 33 (4/1-9/30/11) | | 110 (10/1/11-3/31/12) | | | | | |
| 7 | 19 | 60 | 38 | 9 | 10 | NUMBER OF STATEMENTS | 127 | 119 |

### ASSETS

| 0-500M | 500M-2MM | 2-10MM | 10-50MM | 50-100MM | 100-250MM | | ALL | ALL |
|---|---|---|---|---|---|---|---|---|
| % | % | % | % | % | % | | % | % |
| | 7.4 | 11.7 | 15.3 | | 15.4 | Cash & Equivalents | 12.4 | 11.9 |
| | 40.3 | 29.6 | 28.8 | | 18.0 | Trade Receivables (net) | 29.6 | 26.9 |
| | 26.9 | 28.3 | 25.8 | | 18.6 | Inventory | 24.1 | 24.9 |
| | .4 | 3.6 | 3.8 | | 4.4 | All Other Current | 5.0 | 5.0 |
| | 75.1 | 73.1 | 73.8 | | 56.5 | Total Current | 71.2 | 68.6 |
| | 17.5 | 13.2 | 12.8 | | 15.8 | Fixed Assets (net) | 15.6 | 14.7 |
| | 1.7 | 7.8 | 6.4 | | 25.0 | Intangibles (net) | 6.7 | 8.6 |
| | 5.7 | 5.9 | 7.0 | | 2.7 | All Other Non-Current | 6.5 | 8.1 |
| | 100.0 | 100.0 | 100.0 | | 100.0 | Total | 100.0 | 100.0 |

### LIABILITIES

| 0-500M | 500M-2MM | 2-10MM | 10-50MM | 50-100MM | 100-250MM | | ALL | ALL |
|---|---|---|---|---|---|---|---|---|
| | 15.4 | 8.3 | 5.6 | | .7 | Notes Payable-Short Term | 12.2 | 9.0 |
| | 1.4 | 2.1 | 1.5 | | 1.8 | Cur. Mat.-L.T.D. | 3.4 | 2.5 |
| | 21.9 | 13.7 | 9.8 | | 8.9 | Trade Payables | 13.4 | 11.0 |
| | .0 | .2 | .7 | | .1 | Income Taxes Payable | .3 | 1.0 |
| | 13.3 | 15.4 | 15.4 | | 12.7 | All Other Current | 15.0 | 13.7 |
| | 52.0 | 39.7 | 33.0 | | 24.1 | Total Current | 44.2 | 37.2 |
| | 6.3 | 8.9 | 3.3 | | 9.0 | Long-Term Debt | 14.0 | 11.4 |
| | .1 | .5 | 1.2 | | 2.3 | Deferred Taxes | .4 | .8 |
| | 11.0 | 6.7 | 4.0 | | 3.5 | All Other Non-Current | 5.6 | 7.7 |
| | 30.6 | 44.1 | 58.5 | | 61.2 | Net Worth | 35.8 | 42.9 |
| | 100.0 | 100.0 | 100.0 | | 100.0 | Total Liabilities & Net Worth | 100.0 | 100.0 |

### INCOME DATA

| 0-500M | 500M-2MM | 2-10MM | 10-50MM | 50-100MM | 100-250MM | | ALL | ALL |
|---|---|---|---|---|---|---|---|---|
| | 100.0 | 100.0 | 100.0 | | 100.0 | Net Sales | 100.0 | 100.0 |
| | 41.2 | 37.0 | 39.0 | | 38.5 | Gross Profit | 42.3 | 42.2 |
| | 35.7 | 29.0 | 28.8 | | 29.5 | Operating Expenses | 34.0 | 34.6 |
| | 5.5 | 7.9 | 10.2 | | 9.0 | Operating Profit | 8.3 | 7.6 |
| | .1 | 1.2 | .7 | | -.1 | All Other Expenses (net) | 1.5 | 1.6 |
| | 5.4 | 6.7 | 9.6 | | 9.2 | Profit Before Taxes | 6.7 | 6.0 |

### RATIOS

| 0-500M | 500M-2MM | 2-10MM | 10-50MM | 50-100MM | 100-250MM | | ALL | ALL |
|---|---|---|---|---|---|---|---|---|
| | 4.6 | 3.4 | 3.8 | | 4.5 | Current | 3.3 | 3.5 |
| | 1.7 | 1.9 | 2.3 | | 2.8 | | 2.0 | 2.0 |
| | 1.2 | 1.2 | 1.6 | | 1.9 | | 1.3 | 1.3 |
| | 2.1 | 2.0 | 2.3 | | 2.2 | Quick | 1.8 | 1.8 |
| | 1.1 | 1.1 | 1.4 | | 1.6 | | 1.1 | 1.1 |
| | .6 | .6 | 1.0 | | 1.1 | | .7 | .7 |
| | 34   10.8 | 34   10.8 | 38   9.6 | | 54   6.8 | Sales/Receivables | 39   9.5 | 38   9.6 |
| | 54   6.8 | 52   7.0 | 55   6.6 | | 59   6.2 | | 48   7.6 | 48   7.6 |
| | 76   4.8 | 65   5.6 | 78   4.7 | | 79   4.6 | | 65   5.6 | 65   5.6 |
| | 30   12.2 | 39   9.4 | 46   8.0 | | 54   6.7 | Cost of Sales/Inventory | 43   8.6 | 52   7.0 |
| | 69   5.3 | 85   4.3 | 101   3.6 | | 111   3.3 | | 79   4.6 | 83   4.4 |
| | 122   3.0 | 122   3.0 | 159   2.3 | | 203   1.8 | | 112   3.3 | 138   2.7 |
| | 17   21.2 | 19   19.5 | 18   20.3 | | 30   12.2 | Cost of Sales/Payables | 23   16.0 | 20   18.6 |
| | 29   12.5 | 33   10.9 | 26   13.9 | | 33   11.2 | | 35   10.3 | 32   11.4 |
| | 66   5.5 | 54   6.8 | 43   8.5 | | 81   4.5 | | 57   6.4 | 48   7.6 |
| | 5.2 | 3.3 | 2.8 | | 1.6 | Sales/Working Capital | 3.6 | 3.2 |
| | 6.8 | 6.1 | 4.0 | | 2.9 | | 6.2 | 5.4 |
| | 19.8 | 18.7 | 7.6 | | 23.3 | | 15.3 | 13.4 |
| | 34.6 | 58.1 | 185.8 | | 240.1 | EBIT/Interest | 14.3 | 27.1 |
| | (17) 7.5 | (53) 10.0 | (32) 35.0 | | 17.2 | | (111) 3.8 | (106) 5.4 |
| | -1.1 | 3.2 | 9.2 | | 5.0 | | 1.8 | 1.6 |
| | | 15.0 | 83.9 | | | Net Profit + Depr., Dep., Amort./Cur. Mat. L/T/D | 13.1 | 15.3 |
| | | (14) 5.2 | (10) 29.4 | | | | (36) 4.7 | (41) 3.3 |
| | | 2.1 | 3.9 | | | | 1.9 | 1.7 |
| | .1 | .1 | .1 | | .2 | Fixed/Worth | .2 | .1 |
| | .3 | .3 | .2 | | .5 | | .5 | .4 |
| | .8 | .9 | .4 | | NM | | 2.4 | 1.9 |
| | .3 | .6 | .3 | | .4 | Debt/Worth | .5 | .5 |
| | 1.5 | 1.6 | .7 | | .6 | | 1.8 | 1.5 |
| | 2.7 | 4.8 | 1.5 | | NM | | 13.0 | 8.9 |
| | 44.9 | 49.3 | 49.4 | | | % Profit Before Taxes/Tangible Net Worth | 51.3 | 50.0 |
| | (18) 19.1 | (54) 25.2 | (36) 29.1 | | | | (105) 29.7 | (98) 22.6 |
| | -3.3 | 11.3 | 13.1 | | | | 9.9 | 7.3 |
| | 17.2 | 20.1 | 23.3 | | 13.8 | % Profit Before Taxes/Total Assets | 19.5 | 19.7 |
| | 7.2 | 8.1 | 12.9 | | 7.5 | | 8.3 | 7.7 |
| | -.8 | 3.7 | 7.1 | | 4.7 | | 2.8 | 1.4 |
| | 31.6 | 51.3 | 36.9 | | 15.6 | Sales/Net Fixed Assets | 49.2 | 28.2 |
| | 21.8 | 21.4 | 14.0 | | 10.3 | | 15.5 | 14.1 |
| | 7.2 | 9.6 | 8.2 | | 4.6 | | 7.5 | 8.1 |
| | 3.3 | 2.6 | 2.4 | | 1.2 | Sales/Total Assets | 2.7 | 2.3 |
| | 2.3 | 2.1 | 1.6 | | 1.0 | | 1.9 | 1.7 |
| | 2.0 | 1.4 | 1.1 | | .8 | | 1.4 | 1.4 |
| | .8 | .6 | .5 | | | % Depr., Dep., Amort./Sales | .8 | 1.2 |
| | (15) 1.4 | (51) 1.0 | (30) 1.0 | | | | (105) 1.5 | (92) 1.7 |
| | 2.6 | 2.1 | 2.3 | | | | 2.3 | 2.5 |
| | | 1.4 | | | | % Officers', Directors' Owners' Comp/Sales | 2.4 | 1.3 |
| | | (19) 2.2 | | | | | (31) 5.9 | (23) 4.1 |
| | | 3.5 | | | | | 8.6 | 6.1 |
| 6535M | 60901M | 660586M | 1403630M | 719293M | 1857773M | Net Sales ($) | 4004238M | 4739494M |
| 1914M | 24530M | 332814M | 783176M | 671970M | 1720036M | Total Assets ($) | 2924124M | 3553653M |

M = $ thousand    MM = $ million
See Pages 9 through 22 for Explanation of Ratios and Data

## Comparative Historical Data      Current Data Sorted by Sales

| 4/1/09-3/31/10 ALL | 4/1/10-3/31/11 ALL | 4/1/11-3/31/12 ALL | Type of Statement | 0-1MM | 1-3MM | 3-5MM | 5-10MM | 10-25MM | 25MM & OVER |
|---|---|---|---|---|---|---|---|---|---|
| 29 | 29 | 24 | Unqualified | | | | 1 | 6 | 17 |
| 32 | 34 | 50 | Reviewed | 1 | 6 | 5 | 12 | 18 | 8 |
| 9 | 11 | 9 | Compiled | | 1 | 2 | 4 | 2 | |
| 3 | 7 | 10 | Tax Returns | 2 | 3 | 3 | 1 | | 1 |
| 50 | 50 | 50 | Other | 1 | 4 | 6 | 5 | 16 | 18 |
| | | | | | 33 (4/1-9/30/11) | | 110 (10/1/11-3/31/12) | | |
| 123 | 131 | 143 | **NUMBER OF STATEMENTS** | 4 | 14 | 16 | 23 | 42 | 44 |
| % | % | % | **ASSETS** | % | % | % | % | % | % |
| 14.0 | 14.0 | 12.8 | Cash & Equivalents | | 14.7 | 6.0 | 11.3 | 15.6 | 11.9 |
| 24.2 | 26.2 | 28.8 | Trade Receivables (net) | | 31.7 | 33.6 | 27.1 | 28.6 | 28.1 |
| 25.2 | 25.7 | 26.1 | Inventory | | 25.0 | 25.0 | 29.1 | 28.6 | 22.4 |
| 5.8 | 5.4 | 3.7 | All Other Current | | 1.2 | 1.7 | 4.5 | 3.4 | 5.4 |
| 69.2 | 71.3 | 71.4 | Total Current | | 72.5 | 66.4 | 72.1 | 76.3 | 67.8 |
| 15.4 | 15.9 | 14.3 | Fixed Assets (net) | | 15.2 | 13.4 | 13.4 | 12.8 | 15.5 |
| 9.0 | 6.8 | 8.5 | Intangibles (net) | | 5.2 | 7.1 | 8.9 | 6.0 | 12.8 |
| 6.4 | 5.9 | 5.7 | All Other Non-Current | | 7.1 | 13.1 | 5.6 | 4.9 | 3.9 |
| 100.0 | 100.0 | 100.0 | Total | | 100.0 | 100.0 | 100.0 | 100.0 | 100.0 |
| | | | **LIABILITIES** | | | | | | |
| 8.9 | 8.8 | 7.8 | Notes Payable-Short Term | | 14.5 | 11.4 | 8.4 | 7.2 | 4.2 |
| 2.6 | 2.6 | 2.2 | Cur. Mat.-L.T.D. | | 1.2 | 1.5 | 2.6 | 2.0 | 2.7 |
| 9.9 | 11.2 | 12.6 | Trade Payables | | 9.4 | 23.7 | 14.4 | 11.6 | 9.9 |
| .9 | .3 | .4 | Income Taxes Payable | | 1.0 | .0 | .2 | .6 | .5 |
| 11.6 | 15.8 | 14.4 | All Other Current | | 4.9 | 21.6 | 17.6 | 13.1 | 14.4 |
| 33.9 | 38.8 | 37.5 | Total Current | | 30.9 | 58.1 | 43.1 | 34.5 | 31.6 |
| 10.8 | 8.0 | 7.3 | Long-Term Debt | | 7.6 | 7.3 | 7.0 | 7.6 | 5.4 |
| .5 | .6 | .8 | Deferred Taxes | | .1 | .0 | .7 | 1.1 | 1.2 |
| 9.6 | 8.3 | 8.3 | All Other Non-Current | | 13.3 | 10.6 | 4.7 | 6.3 | 4.0 |
| 45.2 | 44.3 | 46.1 | Net Worth | | 48.1 | 24.0 | 44.5 | 50.4 | 57.8 |
| 100.0 | 100.0 | 100.0 | Total Liabilities & Net Worth | | 100.0 | 100.0 | 100.0 | 100.0 | 100.0 |
| | | | **INCOME DATA** | | | | | | |
| 100.0 | 100.0 | 100.0 | Net Sales | | 100.0 | 100.0 | 100.0 | 100.0 | 100.0 |
| 41.2 | 39.4 | 39.5 | Gross Profit | | 40.8 | 53.0 | 32.3 | 39.3 | 36.9 |
| 35.1 | 31.8 | 31.2 | Operating Expenses | | 35.1 | 43.8 | 27.5 | 28.8 | 27.5 |
| 6.2 | 7.6 | 8.3 | Operating Profit | | 5.7 | 9.2 | 4.9 | 10.4 | 9.4 |
| 1.4 | 1.2 | .9 | All Other Expenses (net) | | .2 | 1.0 | 1.3 | 1.2 | .6 |
| 4.8 | 6.4 | 7.3 | Profit Before Taxes | | 5.5 | 8.2 | 3.6 | 9.3 | 8.7 |
| | | | **RATIOS** | | | | | | |
| 3.5 | 3.8 | 3.5 | Current | | 4.4 | 3.6 | 3.4 | 3.7 | 3.5 |
| 2.3 | 2.3 | 2.1 | | | 3.3 | 1.4 | 1.6 | 2.4 | 2.2 |
| 1.4 | 1.4 | 1.4 | | | 1.4 | .5 | 1.2 | 1.6 | 1.5 |
| 2.1 | 2.1 | 2.1 | Quick | | 3.3 | 2.0 | 1.3 | 2.5 | 2.0 |
| 1.3 | 1.2 | 1.2 | | | 1.7 | .9 | .9 | 1.5 | 1.3 |
| .7 | .7 | .8 | | | 1.0 | .4 | .5 | .7 | .9 |
| 40  9.1 | 41  8.8 | 36  10.2 | Sales/Receivables | | 30  12.3 | 28  13.0 | 31  11.8 | 35  10.3 | 50  7.3 |
| 51  7.2 | 54  6.8 | 54  6.7 | | | 51  7.2 | 43  8.4 | 47  7.8 | 52  7.0 | 58  6.3 |
| 64  5.7 | 63  5.8 | 72  5.1 | | | 87  4.2 | 68  5.4 | 64  5.7 | 76  4.8 | 76  4.8 |
| 56  6.5 | 50  7.3 | 43  8.5 | Cost of Sales/Inventory | | 25  14.5 | 11  32.7 | 33  11.1 | 49  7.4 | 49  7.5 |
| 88  4.1 | 87  4.2 | 89  4.1 | | | 94  3.9 | 83  4.4 | 72  5.1 | 91  4.0 | 99  3.7 |
| 126  2.9 | 118  3.1 | 135  2.7 | | | 122  3.0 | 152  2.4 | 146  2.5 | 140  2.6 | 130  2.8 |
| 19  19.0 | 19  19.3 | 19  18.8 | Cost of Sales/Payables | | 6  58.5 | 23  16.0 | 22  16.6 | 18  19.9 | 21  17.1 |
| 30  12.0 | 32  11.4 | 32  11.3 | | | 20  18.1 | 49  7.4 | 33  11.0 | 29  12.7 | 33  11.1 |
| 46  8.0 | 50  7.3 | 47  7.7 | | | 58  6.3 | 79  4.6 | 58  6.3 | 42  8.6 | 43  8.5 |
| 2.9 | 2.9 | 3.0 | Sales/Working Capital | | 3.2 | 5.5 | 3.0 | 3.3 | 2.8 |
| 4.4 | 4.5 | 5.3 | | | 6.0 | 11.7 | 7.9 | 4.6 | 3.7 |
| 9.9 | 9.9 | 11.1 | | | 10.1 | -5.6 | 21.8 | 8.3 | 8.6 |
| 26.4 | 25.4 | 79.0 | EBIT/Interest | | 32.3 | 49.5 | 33.1 | 187.8 | 143.3 |
| (108) 3.1 | (115) 8.8 | (124) 13.0 | | | (13) 6.0 | (13) 7.4 | (21) 6.5 | (35) 18.9 | (40) 32.7 |
| .9 | 2.1 | 3.7 | | | .4 | 1.0 | 2.1 | 4.4 | 6.7 |
| 11.1 | 10.6 | 27.0 | Net Profit + Depr., Dep., Amort./Cur. Mat. L/T/D | | | | | | 12.2 | 47.2 |
| (41) 3.9 | (41) 2.6 | (34) 4.7 | | | | | | (11) 4.0 | (18) 4.7 |
| 1.0 | .9 | 2.2 | | | | | | | 1.9 | 2.5 |
| .1 | .1 | .1 | Fixed/Worth | | .1 | .0 | .1 | .1 | .2 |
| .3 | .4 | .3 | | | .3 | .3 | .4 | .3 | .3 |
| 1.6 | 1.3 | .7 | | | .7 | .9 | 1.9 | .7 | .6 |
| .4 | .4 | .4 | Debt/Worth | | .3 | .5 | .9 | .4 | .4 |
| 1.2 | 1.2 | 1.2 | | | 1.7 | 1.5 | 1.5 | 1.0 | .8 |
| 5.9 | 4.2 | 3.2 | | | 2.8 | 6.7 | 6.0 | 4.5 | 1.6 |
| 35.2 | 49.1 | 45.5 | % Profit Before Taxes/Tangible Net Worth | | 50.2 | 87.7 | 28.8 | 55.5 | 43.2 |
| (101) 17.8 | (112) 19.7 | (127) 22.3 | | | (13) 22.0 | (14) 12.2 | (22) 11.1 | (37) 33.8 | (39) 20.7 |
| 5.2 | 10.9 | 10.6 | | | 5.8 | 1.1 | 3.0 | 21.8 | 12.9 |
| 14.5 | 16.9 | 19.6 | % Profit Before Taxes/Total Assets | | 23.5 | 16.2 | 10.6 | 25.8 | 18.0 |
| 5.4 | 8.5 | 8.9 | | | 9.2 | 5.3 | 4.7 | 15.4 | 12.3 |
| .7 | 2.6 | 4.1 | | | -.6 | 2.3 | 1.4 | 5.4 | 6.6 |
| 30.6 | 29.2 | 37.1 | Sales/Net Fixed Assets | | 44.6 | 91.6 | 56.6 | 42.4 | 26.2 |
| 13.0 | 15.6 | 15.9 | | | 14.6 | 23.2 | 15.9 | 20.3 | 11.1 |
| 6.8 | 7.8 | 8.2 | | | 7.3 | 8.2 | 8.9 | 9.6 | 6.0 |
| 2.1 | 2.3 | 2.5 | Sales/Total Assets | | 2.7 | 3.3 | 2.7 | 2.3 | 2.3 |
| 1.6 | 1.8 | 1.8 | | | 2.0 | 2.2 | 2.2 | 1.9 | 1.6 |
| 1.1 | 1.1 | 1.2 | | | 1.6 | 1.7 | 1.3 | 1.3 | 1.1 |
| 1.1 | .9 | .6 | % Depr., Dep., Amort./Sales | | 1.2 | .6 | .6 | .5 | .8 |
| (103) 1.6 | (105) 1.5 | (116) 1.6 | | | (10) 1.9 | (13) 1.4 | (18) 1.0 | (34) 1.4 | (38) 2.0 |
| 2.8 | 2.6 | 2.5 | | | 2.6 | 2.6 | 2.1 | 2.2 | 3.2 |
| 2.5 | 2.5 | 1.8 | % Officers', Directors', Owners' Comp/Sales | | | | | | 1.5 | |
| (22) 6.7 | (29) 3.4 | (36) 3.6 | | | | | | (14) 2.5 | |
| 9.6 | 7.8 | 8.2 | | | | | | | 4.5 | |
| 4138665M | 4677691M | 4708718M | Net Sales ($) | 1643M | 29993M | 62846M | 173938M | 661029M | 3779269M |
| 3684322M | 3490302M | 3534440M | Total Assets ($) | 963M | 17306M | 49487M | 100435M | 393061M | 2973188M |

**M = $ thousand    MM = $ million**
See Pages 9 through 22 for Explanation of Ratios and Data

## Current Data Sorted by Assets      Comparative Historical Data

| | | | | | | Type of Statement | | |
|---|---|---|---|---|---|---|---|---|
| | | 1 | 3 | 2 | 1 | Unqualified | 7 | 6 |
| | 1 | 3 | 4 | | | Reviewed | 9 | 11 |
| | 2 | 4 | | | | Compiled | 3 | 5 |
| | 1 | | | | | Tax Returns | 5 | 3 |
| 1 | 5 | 5 | 5 | 1 | | Other | 17 | 14 |
| | 5 (4/1-9/30/11) | | 29 (10/1/11-3/31/12) | | | | 4/1/07-3/31/08 | 4/1/08-3/31/09 |
| 0-500M | 500M-2MM | 2-10MM | 10-50MM | 50-100MM | 100-250MM | | ALL | ALL |
| 1 | 4 | 13 | 12 | 3 | 1 | NUMBER OF STATEMENTS | 41 | 39 |
| % | % | % | % | % | % | ASSETS | % | % |
| | | 11.3 | 13.6 | | | Cash & Equivalents | 11.8 | 12.8 |
| | | 23.7 | 20.0 | | | Trade Receivables (net) | 26.8 | 24.6 |
| | | 44.5 | 22.1 | | | Inventory | 29.7 | 33.7 |
| | | 2.1 | 4.9 | | | All Other Current | 3.1 | 4.3 |
| | | 81.6 | 60.7 | | | Total Current | 71.5 | 75.4 |
| | | 12.7 | 24.1 | | | Fixed Assets (net) | 15.9 | 16.4 |
| | | 4.8 | 9.9 | | | Intangibles (net) | 6.8 | 4.1 |
| | | 1.0 | 5.3 | | | All Other Non-Current | 5.9 | 4.1 |
| | | 100.0 | 100.0 | | | Total | 100.0 | 100.0 |
| | | | | | | LIABILITIES | | |
| | | 10.9 | 5.0 | | | Notes Payable-Short Term | 7.3 | 9.6 |
| | | 2.6 | 3.5 | | | Cur. Mat.-L.T.D. | 3.0 | 3.3 |
| | | 11.0 | 8.1 | | | Trade Payables | 13.2 | 14.0 |
| | | .2 | .0 | | | Income Taxes Payable | .2 | .2 |
| | | 9.9 | 13.7 | | | All Other Current | 10.6 | 14.6 |
| | | 34.6 | 30.4 | | | Total Current | 34.3 | 41.8 |
| | | 2.7 | 15.4 | | | Long-Term Debt | 12.5 | 16.1 |
| | | .8 | .6 | | | Deferred Taxes | .4 | .5 |
| | | 17.7 | 10.1 | | | All Other Non-Current | 3.7 | 6.8 |
| | | 44.2 | 43.5 | | | Net Worth | 49.1 | 34.8 |
| | | 100.0 | 100.0 | | | Total Liabilities & Net Worth | 100.0 | 100.0 |
| | | | | | | INCOME DATA | | |
| | | 100.0 | 100.0 | | | Net Sales | 100.0 | 100.0 |
| | | 43.1 | 31.7 | | | Gross Profit | 40.6 | 37.3 |
| | | 37.7 | 25.2 | | | Operating Expenses | 34.5 | 33.8 |
| | | 5.4 | 6.5 | | | Operating Profit | 6.0 | 3.5 |
| | | .0 | 2.8 | | | All Other Expenses (net) | .0 | .7 |
| | | 5.5 | 3.7 | | | Profit Before Taxes | 6.1 | 2.8 |
| | | | | | | RATIOS | | |
| | | 4.1 | 3.6 | | | | 4.1 | 3.9 |
| | | 2.3 | 1.8 | | | Current | 2.2 | 2.0 |
| | | 1.7 | 1.5 | | | | 1.4 | 1.4 |
| | | 1.3 | 2.1 | | | | 2.3 | 2.1 |
| | | .9 | 1.0 | | | Quick | 1.1 | 1.0 |
| | | .7 | .8 | | | | .6 | .5 |
| | | 33   10.9 | 33   11.0 | | | | 35   10.5 | 30   12.2 |
| | | 42   8.7 | 46   8.0 | | | Sales/Receivables | 48   7.7 | 41   9.0 |
| | | 52   7.0 | 58   6.3 | | | | 59   6.2 | 49   7.5 |
| | | 114   3.2 | 42   8.6 | | | | 67   5.5 | 86   4.3 |
| | | 130   2.8 | 85   4.3 | | | Cost of Sales/Inventory | 109   3.4 | 111   3.3 |
| | | 166   2.2 | 111   3.3 | | | | 141   2.6 | 164   2.2 |
| | | 19   19.7 | 14   25.3 | | | | 19   18.8 | 20   17.8 |
| | | 24   14.9 | 31   11.8 | | | Cost of Sales/Payables | 34   10.9 | 35   10.5 |
| | | 37   9.8 | 49   7.5 | | | | 51   7.1 | 48   7.6 |
| | | 2.9 | 3.5 | | | | 3.5 | 2.6 |
| | | 4.1 | 6.4 | | | Sales/Working Capital | 5.7 | 5.9 |
| | | 7.4 | 8.2 | | | | 9.9 | 11.3 |
| | | 32.4 | 19.5 | | | | 30.1 | 8.4 |
| | | (12)   8.3 | (10)   10.3 | | | EBIT/Interest | (36)   3.9 | (31)   2.7 |
| | | 3.4 | 1.8 | | | | 1.6 | 1.6 |
| | | | | | | Net Profit + Depr., Dep., | 10.8 | 6.6 |
| | | | | | | Amort./Cur. Mat. L/T/D | (15)   3.9 | (10)   1.4 |
| | | | | | | | 1.3 | -253.1 |
| | | .1 | .2 | | | | .2 | .1 |
| | | .3 | .8 | | | Fixed/Worth | .3 | .2 |
| | | 10.4 | 1.7 | | | | .8 | 1.0 |
| | | .3 | .5 | | | | .3 | .5 |
| | | .7 | 1.3 | | | Debt/Worth | .9 | 1.2 |
| | | 153.0 | 3.7 | | | | 3.2 | 3.7 |
| | | 51.0 | 19.2 | | | % Profit Before Taxes/Tangible | 53.0 | 41.4 |
| | | (11)   13.4 | (10)   14.1 | | | Net Worth | (35)   20.2 | (35)   13.6 |
| | | 3.6 | 9.2 | | | | 6.9 | 4.0 |
| | | 17.8 | 11.4 | | | % Profit Before Taxes/Total | 22.6 | 13.6 |
| | | 8.2 | 6.9 | | | Assets | 7.8 | 5.0 |
| | | 4.7 | 2.9 | | | | 1.7 | 2.0 |
| | | 45.1 | 41.3 | | | | 27.1 | 43.4 |
| | | 16.9 | 11.0 | | | Sales/Net Fixed Assets | 14.9 | 14.8 |
| | | 8.8 | 3.7 | | | | 7.9 | 7.3 |
| | | 2.3 | 1.9 | | | | 2.4 | 2.7 |
| | | 2.0 | 1.5 | | | Sales/Total Assets | 1.9 | 2.1 |
| | | 1.5 | 1.2 | | | | 1.5 | 1.5 |
| | | 1.1 | 1.3 | | | | 1.0 | 1.1 |
| | | (11)   1.6 | (11)   2.0 | | | % Depr., Dep., Amort./Sales | (36)   1.8 | (32)   1.7 |
| | | 2.1 | 7.3 | | | | 2.8 | 2.8 |
| | | | | | | % Officers', Directors' Owners' Comp/Sales | | |
| 581M | 11271M | 130344M | 446438M | 355321M | 262915M | Net Sales ($) | 1149490M | 1602890M |
| 315M | 4878M | 63423M | 297455M | 201808M | 218910M | Total Assets ($) | 748056M | 841765M |

M = $ thousand    MM = $ million

See Pages 9 through 22 for Explanation of Ratios and Data

| Comparative Historical Data | | | | Current Data Sorted by Sales | | | | | |
|---|---|---|---|---|---|---|---|---|---|
| | | | **Type of Statement** | | | | | | |
| 6 | 8 | 7 | Unqualified | | | | | 4 | 6 |
| 10 | 11 | 8 | Reviewed | | 1 | 1 | 1 | 2 | 2 |
| 2 | 3 | 6 | Compiled | 1 | 2 | | 1 | 1 | |
| 4 | 4 | 1 | Tax Returns | | 1 | | | | |
| 13 | 14 | 12 | Other | 1 | | 1 | 2 | 5 | 3 |
| 4/1/09-3/31/10 ALL | 4/1/10-3/31/11 ALL | 4/1/11-3/31/12 ALL | | 1 | 5 (4/1-9/30/11) | | 29 (10/1/11-3/31/12) | | |
| | | | | 0-1MM | 1-3MM | 3-5MM | 5-10MM | 10-25MM | 25MM & OVER |
| 35 | 40 | 34 | NUMBER OF STATEMENTS | 1 | 2 | 4 | 5 | 11 | 11 |
| % | % | % | **ASSETS** | % | % | % | % | % | % |
| 9.0 | 10.1 | 14.0 | Cash & Equivalents | | | | | 18.4 | 10.1 |
| 20.7 | 24.4 | 22.3 | Trade Receivables (net) | | | | | 22.7 | 25.1 |
| 34.6 | 30.2 | 33.7 | Inventory | | | | | 25.1 | 28.1 |
| 6.7 | 6.3 | 3.5 | All Other Current | | | | | 5.2 | 3.2 |
| 70.9 | 71.0 | 73.5 | Total Current | | | | | 71.4 | 66.5 |
| 16.9 | 18.3 | 17.4 | Fixed Assets (net) | | | | | 19.3 | 19.6 |
| 4.1 | 4.9 | 6.2 | Intangibles (net) | | | | | 6.7 | 8.6 |
| 8.1 | 5.8 | 3.0 | All Other Non-Current | | | | | 2.6 | 5.2 |
| 100.0 | 100.0 | 100.0 | Total | | | | | 100.0 | 100.0 |
| | | | **LIABILITIES** | | | | | | |
| 10.3 | 6.3 | 6.3 | Notes Payable-Short Term | | | | | 5.8 | 4.3 |
| 2.4 | 2.8 | 2.7 | Cur. Mat.-L.T.D. | | | | | 3.9 | .8 |
| 11.1 | 13.2 | 10.6 | Trade Payables | | | | | 12.0 | 12.2 |
| .1 | .4 | .1 | Income Taxes Payable | | | | | .2 | .2 |
| 12.6 | 17.2 | 13.5 | All Other Current | | | | | 13.3 | 9.9 |
| 36.5 | 39.9 | 33.2 | Total Current | | | | | 35.2 | 27.5 |
| 6.2 | 11.3 | 7.3 | Long-Term Debt | | | | | 8.4 | 10.6 |
| .4 | .8 | .7 | Deferred Taxes | | | | | .5 | .4 |
| 9.5 | 12.3 | 10.8 | All Other Non-Current | | | | | 1.8 | 11.5 |
| 47.4 | 35.6 | 48.0 | Net Worth | | | | | 54.1 | 50.1 |
| 100.0 | 100.0 | 100.0 | Total Liabilities & Net Worth | | | | | 100.0 | 100.0 |
| | | | **INCOME DATA** | | | | | | |
| 100.0 | 100.0 | 100.0 | Net Sales | | | | | 100.0 | 100.0 |
| 38.8 | 38.5 | 38.4 | Gross Profit | | | | | 37.3 | 33.4 |
| 36.5 | 32.1 | 32.3 | Operating Expenses | | | | | 31.6 | 27.9 |
| 2.3 | 6.5 | 6.1 | Operating Profit | | | | | 5.7 | 5.5 |
| .4 | 1.6 | 1.1 | All Other Expenses (net) | | | | | .3 | 2.4 |
| 1.9 | 4.9 | 5.0 | Profit Before Taxes | | | | | 5.4 | 3.0 |
| | | | **RATIOS** | | | | | | |
| 3.5 | 3.3 | 4.1 | Current | | | | | 2.2 | 4.3 |
| 1.9 | 2.1 | 2.2 | | | | | | 1.8 | 3.4 |
| 1.5 | 1.4 | 1.5 | | | | | | 1.5 | 1.7 |
| 1.4 | 1.7 | 2.0 | Quick | | | | | 1.4 | 2.4 |
| 1.0 | 1.0 | .9 | | | | | | 1.0 | 1.9 |
| .5 | .6 | .8 | | | | | | .8 | .8 |
| 37 10.0 | 36 10.1 | 31 11.8 | Sales/Receivables | | | | | 26 14.0 | 45 8.1 |
| 49 7.5 | 43 8.6 | 45 8.1 | | | | | | 38 9.7 | 57 6.4 |
| 63 5.8 | 65 5.6 | 56 6.5 | | | | | | 54 6.7 | 68 5.4 |
| 75 4.9 | 78 4.7 | 81 4.5 | Cost of Sales/Inventory | | | | | 29 12.5 | 85 4.3 |
| 111 3.3 | 102 3.6 | 111 3.3 | | | | | | 89 4.1 | 101 3.6 |
| 173 2.1 | 143 2.6 | 135 2.7 | | | | | | 122 3.0 | 111 3.3 |
| 21 17.5 | 20 18.4 | 19 19.3 | Cost of Sales/Payables | | | | | 24 15.4 | 21 17.4 |
| 35 10.4 | 38 9.7 | 26 13.8 | | | | | | 25 14.5 | 35 10.5 |
| 51 7.1 | 52 7.1 | 41 9.0 | | | | | | 39 9.4 | 66 5.5 |
| 2.5 | 2.8 | 3.0 | Sales/Working Capital | | | | | 4.0 | 2.5 |
| 4.5 | 5.5 | 4.3 | | | | | | 6.7 | 3.6 |
| 8.2 | 9.8 | 8.2 | | | | | | 10.6 | 8.1 |
| 8.9 | 32.0 | 22.7 | EBIT/Interest | | | | | 78.9 | |
| (26) 3.3 | (32) 5.8 | (27) 9.0 | | | | | (10) | 17.7 | |
| .3 | 2.4 | 3.2 | | | | | | 3.4 | |
| | | | Net Profit + Depr., Dep., Amort./Cur. Mat. L/T/D | | | | | | |
| .1 | .2 | .2 | Fixed/Worth | | | | | .1 | .2 |
| .3 | .4 | .3 | | | | | | .2 | .4 |
| .6 | .9 | .8 | | | | | | 1.0 | .8 |
| .5 | .6 | .4 | Debt/Worth | | | | | .5 | .4 |
| .8 | 1.0 | .9 | | | | | | .9 | 1.0 |
| 1.4 | 4.8 | 2.4 | | | | | | 2.4 | 2.4 |
| 25.0 | 32.6 | 24.1 | % Profit Before Taxes/Tangible Net Worth | | | | | 28.3 | 20.1 |
| (32) 12.4 | (33) 16.7 | (30) 13.2 | | | | | (10) | 13.3 | (10) 14.1 |
| 1.0 | 5.9 | 6.8 | | | | | | 8.4 | 7.5 |
| 11.9 | 17.3 | 12.8 | % Profit Before Taxes/Total Assets | | | | | 12.8 | 8.3 |
| 5.0 | 7.7 | 7.4 | | | | | | 7.5 | 6.6 |
| -1.3 | 2.0 | 2.7 | | | | | | 6.7 | .6 |
| 22.3 | 25.6 | 30.6 | Sales/Net Fixed Assets | | | | | 54.0 | 12.8 |
| 14.0 | 12.4 | 13.4 | | | | | | 36.1 | 10.4 |
| 6.9 | 5.6 | 7.8 | | | | | | 13.5 | 4.0 |
| 2.3 | 2.4 | 2.2 | Sales/Total Assets | | | | | 2.2 | 2.1 |
| 1.5 | 1.8 | 1.8 | | | | | | 1.8 | 1.3 |
| 1.2 | 1.2 | 1.3 | | | | | | 1.3 | 1.2 |
| 1.1 | .9 | 1.1 | % Depr., Dep., Amort./Sales | | | | | | 1.5 |
| (30) 1.8 | (35) 2.1 | (31) 1.6 | | | | | | | 2.0 |
| 2.9 | 3.6 | 3.0 | | | | | | | 4.1 |
| | | | % Officers', Directors' Owners' Comp/Sales | | | | | | |
| 724305M | 1302535M | 1206870M | Net Sales ($) | 581M | 4232M | 13594M | 33164M | 195333M | 959966M |
| 503755M | 910184M | 786789M | Total Assets ($) | 315M | 1377M | 7819M | 17917M | 119174M | 640187M |

M = $ thousand    MM = $ million
See Pages 9 through 22 for Explanation of Ratios and Data

## Current Data Sorted by Assets      Comparative Historical Data

| Type of Statement | 0-500M | 500M-2MM | 2-10MM | 10-50MM | 50-100MM | 100-250MM | 4/1/07-3/31/08 ALL | 4/1/08-3/31/09 ALL |
|---|---|---|---|---|---|---|---|---|
| Unqualified | | | 3 | 6 | 2 | 1 | 16 | 13 |
| Reviewed | | | 11 | 1 | | | 12 | 15 |
| Compiled | | 2 | 1 | | | | 6 | 7 |
| Tax Returns | | 3 | 4 | | | | 3 | 2 |
| Other | | 4 | 6 | 11 | | 1 | 17 | 20 |
| | | 12 (4/1-9/30/11) | | 44 (10/1/11-3/31/12) | | | | |
| NUMBER OF STATEMENTS | | 9 | 25 | 18 | 2 | 2 | 54 | 57 |

| | 0-500M % | 500M-2MM % | 2-10MM % | 10-50MM % | 50-100MM % | 100-250MM % | ALL % | ALL % |
|---|---|---|---|---|---|---|---|---|
| **ASSETS** | | | | | | | | |
| Cash & Equivalents | | | 9.0 | 12.0 | | | 14.9 | 16.0 |
| Trade Receivables (net) | | | 23.6 | 21.6 | | | 23.3 | 28.4 |
| Inventory | | | 41.6 | 19.4 | | | 26.8 | 27.1 |
| All Other Current | | | 4.1 | 9.4 | | | 2.7 | 4.8 |
| Total Current | | | 78.3 | 62.4 | | | 67.7 | 76.3 |
| Fixed Assets (net) | | | 10.8 | 20.2 | | | 15.9 | 12.7 |
| Intangibles (net) | | | 2.8 | 7.9 | | | 9.4 | 4.9 |
| All Other Non-Current | | | 8.1 | 9.5 | | | 7.0 | 6.1 |
| Total | | | 100.0 | 100.0 | | | 100.0 | 100.0 |
| **LIABILITIES** | | | | | | | | |
| Notes Payable-Short Term | | | 8.6 | 1.9 | | | 5.9 | 7.4 |
| Cur. Mat.-L.T.D. | | | 2.2 | 3.4 | | | 2.9 | 1.3 |
| Trade Payables | | | 22.5 | 8.1 | | | 10.0 | 11.7 |
| Income Taxes Payable | | | .4 | .4 | | | .3 | .3 |
| All Other Current | | | 11.9 | 18.3 | | | 11.0 | 13.0 |
| Total Current | | | 45.6 | 32.0 | | | 30.0 | 33.7 |
| Long-Term Debt | | | 11.5 | 7.2 | | | 10.0 | 6.2 |
| Deferred Taxes | | | .4 | .4 | | | .1 | .3 |
| All Other Non-Current | | | 7.0 | 10.5 | | | 4.0 | 4.1 |
| Net Worth | | | 35.5 | 49.9 | | | 55.9 | 55.6 |
| Total Liabilties & Net Worth | | | 100.0 | 100.0 | | | 100.0 | 100.0 |
| **INCOME DATA** | | | | | | | | |
| Net Sales | | | 100.0 | 100.0 | | | 100.0 | 100.0 |
| Gross Profit | | | 38.6 | 43.0 | | | 46.1 | 43.2 |
| Operating Expenses | | | 29.8 | 35.9 | | | 39.2 | 36.4 |
| Operating Profit | | | 8.8 | 7.1 | | | 6.9 | 6.8 |
| All Other Expenses (net) | | | .4 | 1.8 | | | 1.0 | 1.3 |
| Profit Before Taxes | | | 8.4 | 5.4 | | | 5.9 | 5.6 |
| **RATIOS** | | | | | | | | |
| Current | | | 4.0 | 4.4 | | | 4.3 | 4.4 |
| | | | 1.8 | 1.9 | | | 2.2 | 2.3 |
| | | | 1.5 | 1.4 | | | 1.6 | 1.8 |
| Quick | | | 2.1 | 1.9 | | | 2.4 | 2.5 |
| | | | .8 | 1.0 | | | 1.3 | 1.5 |
| | | | .6 | .6 | | | .8 | .9 |
| Sales/Receivables | | | 32   11.5 | 36   10.2 | | | 33   11.2 | 39   9.4 |
| | | | 40   9.1 | 62   5.9 | | | 49   7.4 | 48   7.6 |
| | | | 55   6.6 | 89   4.1 | | | 64   5.7 | 63   5.8 |
| Cost of Sales/Inventory | | | 83   4.4 | 50   7.3 | | | 68   5.4 | 61   6.0 |
| | | | 101   3.6 | 94   3.9 | | | 120   3.0 | 101   3.6 |
| | | | 159   2.3 | 166   2.2 | | | 162   2.3 | 159   2.3 |
| Cost of Sales/Payables | | | 16   22.4 | 15   24.2 | | | 19   19.0 | 18   20.4 |
| | | | 35   10.4 | 44   8.3 | | | 30   12.3 | 24   15.3 |
| | | | 59   6.2 | 63   5.8 | | | 48   7.7 | 39   9.3 |
| Sales/Working Capital | | | 4.0 | 3.1 | | | 2.9 | 2.9 |
| | | | 5.9 | 5.8 | | | 4.4 | 4.3 |
| | | | 8.2 | 7.1 | | | 7.4 | 8.5 |
| EBIT/Interest | | | 75.0 | 160.3 | | | 15.0 | 28.1 |
| | | | (22) 14.0 | (13) 14.9 | | | (44) 5.0 | (45) 8.5 |
| | | | 2.1 | 2.9 | | | 1.1 | 1.5 |
| Net Profit + Depr., Dep., Amort./Cur. Mat. L/T/D | | | | | | | 8.5 | 21.2 |
| | | | | | | | (13) 2.5 | (17) 7.8 |
| | | | | | | | -18.7 | 2.1 |
| Fixed/Worth | | | .1 | .1 | | | .1 | .1 |
| | | | .3 | .4 | | | .3 | .2 |
| | | | .5 | 1.0 | | | .7 | .5 |
| Debt/Worth | | | .5 | .3 | | | .3 | .3 |
| | | | 1.5 | 1.5 | | | 1.0 | .8 |
| | | | 2.3 | 2.9 | | | 1.8 | 1.5 |
| % Profit Before Taxes/Tangible Net Worth | | | 45.4 | 42.5 | | | 35.8 | 44.7 |
| | | | (23) 22.6 | (17) 24.5 | | | (50) 13.9 | (54) 20.1 |
| | | | 7.9 | 7.0 | | | 1.2 | 4.4 |
| % Profit Before Taxes/Total Assets | | | 24.6 | 19.4 | | | 17.8 | 26.5 |
| | | | 12.5 | 10.3 | | | 6.5 | 11.5 |
| | | | 1.9 | 1.7 | | | 1.0 | 1.4 |
| Sales/Net Fixed Assets | | | 63.8 | 22.8 | | | 28.9 | 67.8 |
| | | | 22.8 | 8.0 | | | 13.2 | 16.7 |
| | | | 10.7 | 4.4 | | | 7.9 | 10.6 |
| Sales/Total Assets | | | 2.4 | 1.8 | | | 2.4 | 2.5 |
| | | | 2.0 | 1.4 | | | 1.6 | 1.8 |
| | | | 1.6 | .8 | | | 1.0 | 1.4 |
| % Depr., Dep., Amort./Sales | | | .6 | 1.7 | | | .7 | .9 |
| | | | (23) 1.3 | (14) 1.9 | | | (43) 1.5 | (46) 1.8 |
| | | | 2.0 | 4.6 | | | 2.7 | 2.4 |
| % Officers', Directors' Owners' Comp/Sales | | | | | | | 1.8 | 2.3 |
| | | | | | | | (13) 3.5 | (18) 5.3 |
| | | | | | | | 9.4 | 9.1 |
| Net Sales ($) | | 36758M | 254475M | 606462M | 140556M | 261628M | 1573317M | 1762725M |
| Total Assets ($) | | 12132M | 126797M | 432018M | 144541M | 247496M | 1481991M | 1316941M |

*(Note: Columns 0-500M, 500M-2MM, 50-100MM and 100-250MM are marked "DATA NOT AVAILABLE".)*

## Comparative Historical Data        Current Data Sorted by Sales

| | 09-10 ALL | 10-11 ALL | 11-12 ALL | | 0-1MM | 1-3MM | 3-5MM | 5-10MM | 10-25MM | 25MM & OVER |
|---|---|---|---|---|---|---|---|---|---|---|
| **Type of Statement** | | | | | | 12 (4/1-9/30/11) | | 44 (10/1/11-3/31/12) | | |
| Unqualified | 15 | 7 | 12 | | | | | 1 | 3 | 8 |
| Reviewed | 10 | 9 | 12 | | | | | 7 | 5 | |
| Compiled | 6 | 7 | 3 | | | | | 1 | | |
| Tax Returns | 6 | 3 | 7 | | | 2 | 1 | 4 | 1 | |
| Other | 17 | 23 | 22 | | | 1 | 4 | 6 | 6 | 6 |
| | 4/1/09- 3/31/10 | 4/1/10- 3/31/11 | 4/1/11- 3/31/12 | | | | | | | |
| **NUMBER OF STATEMENTS** | 54 | 49 | 56 | | | 3 | 5 | 19 | 15 | 14 |
| | % | % | % | | | | | % | % | % |
| **ASSETS** | | | | | | | | | | |
| Cash & Equivalents | 14.4 | 10.5 | 11.2 | | | | | 11.1 | 5.1 | 15.3 |
| Trade Receivables (net) | 24.6 | 25.8 | 25.9 | | | | | 24.1 | 23.8 | 24.0 |
| Inventory | 27.6 | 28.2 | 30.9 | | | | | 38.2 | 33.3 | 19.6 |
| All Other Current | 2.5 | 6.3 | 6.1 | | | | | 5.5 | 2.4 | 12.5 |
| Total Current | 69.2 | 70.9 | 74.2 | | | | | 78.9 | 64.7 | 71.4 |
| Fixed Assets (net) | 15.5 | 19.0 | 13.8 | | | | | 11.2 | 16.5 | 19.0 |
| Intangibles (net) | 6.2 | 5.2 | 4.7 | | | | | 3.9 | 7.1 | 5.1 |
| All Other Non-Current | 9.1 | 4.9 | 7.3 | | | | | 6.0 | 11.8 | 4.5 |
| Total | 100.0 | 100.0 | 100.0 | | | | | 100.0 | 100.0 | 100.0 |
| **LIABILITIES** | | | | | | | | | | |
| Notes Payable-Short Term | 7.7 | 9.1 | 6.3 | | | | | 3.5 | 11.8 | .4 |
| Cur. Mat.-L.T.D. | 3.6 | 2.6 | 2.7 | | | | | 2.2 | 2.9 | 4.1 |
| Trade Payables | 10.7 | 13.4 | 18.2 | | | | | 23.9 | 24.0 | 8.6 |
| Income Taxes Payable | .2 | .3 | .3 | | | | | .4 | .4 | .2 |
| All Other Current | 11.9 | 16.2 | 15.1 | | | | | 16.0 | 11.7 | 17.9 |
| Total Current | 34.3 | 41.7 | 42.6 | | | | | 46.0 | 50.9 | 31.2 |
| Long-Term Debt | 11.4 | 11.8 | 9.1 | | | | | 12.2 | 8.9 | 6.2 |
| Deferred Taxes | .4 | .3 | .4 | | | | | .4 | .6 | .6 |
| All Other Non-Current | 6.4 | 8.7 | 7.0 | | | | | 3.6 | 8.7 | 13.2 |
| Net Worth | 47.5 | 37.4 | 40.8 | | | | | 37.9 | 30.9 | 48.9 |
| Total Liabilities & Net Worth | 100.0 | 100.0 | 100.0 | | | | | 100.0 | 100.0 | 100.0 |
| **INCOME DATA** | | | | | | | | | | |
| Net Sales | 100.0 | 100.0 | 100.0 | | | | | 100.0 | 100.0 | 100.0 |
| Gross Profit | 42.6 | 45.7 | 41.5 | | | | | 42.7 | 39.2 | 40.7 |
| Operating Expenses | 37.8 | 35.6 | 33.3 | | | | | 31.2 | 30.6 | 34.8 |
| Operating Profit | 4.8 | 10.1 | 8.2 | | | | | 11.6 | 8.5 | 5.9 |
| All Other Expenses (net) | 1.1 | 1.3 | .9 | | | | | -.1 | 1.9 | 1.4 |
| Profit Before Taxes | 3.7 | 8.8 | 7.3 | | | | | 11.6 | 6.7 | 4.6 |
| **RATIOS** | | | | | | | | | | |
| Current | 3.3 | 2.8 | 4.1 | | | | | 4.4 | 2.1 | 5.1 |
| | 2.1 | 1.9 | 1.9 | | | | | 1.8 | 1.6 | 2.1 |
| | 1.4 | 1.4 | 1.4 | | | | | 1.3 | 1.4 | 1.7 |
| Quick | 2.1 | 1.6 | 2.2 | | | | | 2.2 | 1.0 | 3.8 |
| | 1.2 | .9 | .9 | | | | | .8 | .7 | 1.2 |
| | .7 | .5 | .6 | | | | | .5 | .6 | .7 |
| Sales/Receivables | 34  10.8 | 39  9.3 | 33  11.0 | | | | | 26  13.9 | 43  8.5 | 32  11.5 |
| | 49  7.4 | 49  7.5 | 47  7.8 | | | | | 36  10.2 | 54  6.7 | 61  6.0 |
| | 67  5.4 | 63  5.8 | 70  5.2 | | | | | 43  8.5 | 72  5.1 | 81  4.5 |
| Cost of Sales/Inventory | 72  5.1 | 49  7.4 | 59  6.2 | | | | | 76  4.8 | 91  4.0 | 50  7.3 |
| | 107  3.4 | 104  3.5 | 101  3.6 | | | | | 111  3.3 | 104  3.5 | 62  5.9 |
| | 146  2.5 | 142  2.6 | 159  2.3 | | | | | 174  2.1 | 159  2.3 | 122  3.0 |
| Cost of Sales/Payables | 16  22.3 | 17  21.2 | 15  23.7 | | | | | 19  19.0 | 23  15.6 | 12  29.2 |
| | 32  11.3 | 37  10.0 | 39  9.4 | | | | | 39  9.4 | 54  6.7 | 24  15.3 |
| | 44  8.3 | 64  5.7 | 60  6.1 | | | | | 69  5.3 | 62  5.9 | 50  7.3 |
| Sales/Working Capital | 2.9 | 3.6 | 3.0 | | | | | 2.5 | 4.6 | 2.8 |
| | 4.6 | 6.1 | 5.8 | | | | | 5.9 | 6.0 | 5.5 |
| | 10.4 | 8.7 | 7.7 | | | | | 15.1 | 7.8 | 6.7 |
| EBIT/Interest | 29.3 | 25.6 | 71.8 | | | | | 122.5 | 23.6 | 158.6 |
| | (45) 4.4 | (40) 7.1 | (44) 11.3 | | | | | (15) 18.4 | (14) 5.7 | (10) 11.5 |
| | 1.1 | 3.2 | 2.7 | | | | | 3.7 | 1.5 | 1.8 |
| Net Profit + Depr., Dep., Amort./Cur. Mat. L/T/D | 7.5 | 18.6 | 10.2 | | | | | | | |
| | (17) 3.0 | (13) 5.2 | (13) 4.1 | | | | | | | |
| | .8 | 3.0 | .5 | | | | | | | |
| Fixed/Worth | .1 | .2 | .1 | | | | | .1 | .2 | .1 |
| | .4 | .5 | .3 | | | | | .3 | .3 | .5 |
| | .8 | 1.0 | .7 | | | | | .7 | 1.1 | .8 |
| Debt/Worth | .5 | .7 | .4 | | | | | .4 | 1.0 | .3 |
| | 1.1 | 1.8 | 1.5 | | | | | 1.3 | 1.7 | 1.1 |
| | 2.9 | 4.6 | 2.3 | | | | | 2.5 | 2.5 | 2.2 |
| % Profit Before Taxes/Tangible Net Worth | 44.0 | 70.4 | 46.6 | | | | | 49.8 | 48.0 | 35.1 |
| | (47) 14.1 | (41) 38.3 | (50) 24.3 | | | | | (16) 28.1 | (14) 31.4 | (13) 13.4 |
| | 1.4 | 10.1 | 6.5 | | | | | 16.6 | 4.2 | 6.0 |
| % Profit Before Taxes/Total Assets | 16.1 | 28.5 | 24.2 | | | | | 26.1 | 22.6 | 19.1 |
| | 6.3 | 11.1 | 10.8 | | | | | 16.2 | 5.6 | 7.8 |
| | .0 | 3.0 | 2.3 | | | | | 6.4 | .8 | 2.3 |
| Sales/Net Fixed Assets | 26.5 | 29.1 | 50.6 | | | | | 74.0 | 30.9 | 19.3 |
| | 12.9 | 13.6 | 19.2 | | | | | 22.8 | 20.2 | 9.1 |
| | 6.5 | 7.5 | 7.7 | | | | | 10.7 | 6.6 | 6.3 |
| Sales/Total Assets | 2.3 | 2.5 | 2.3 | | | | | 3.2 | 2.3 | 1.9 |
| | 1.6 | 1.9 | 1.8 | | | | | 2.0 | 1.9 | 1.6 |
| | 1.2 | 1.5 | 1.3 | | | | | 1.3 | .8 | 1.4 |
| % Depr., Dep., Amort./Sales | 1.1 | 1.2 | .7 | | | | | .6 | 1.7 | 1.3 |
| | (44) 2.1 | (42) 1.7 | (42) 1.7 | | | | | (15) 1.0 | (14) 1.9 | (10) 2.0 |
| | 3.4 | 4.0 | 2.2 | | | | | 1.6 | 3.0 | 5.8 |
| % Officers', Directors' Owners' Comp/Sales | 3.1 | | 2.1 | | | | | | | |
| | (14) 5.9 | (11) 2.8 | 2.8 | | | | | | | |
| | 9.6 | | 4.3 | | | | | | | |
| Net Sales ($) | 1390867M | 1128126M | 1299879M | | | 6869M | 19253M | 139545M | 256145M | 878067M |
| Total Assets ($) | 1165929M | 772925M | 962984M | | | 4031M | 31436M | 74472M | 201898M | 651147M |

M = $ thousand    MM = $ million
See Pages 9 through 22 for Explanation of Ratios and Data

## Current Data Sorted by Assets          Comparative Historical Data

| 0-500M | 500M-2MM | 2-10MM | 10-50MM | 50-100MM | 100-250MM | | 4/1/07-3/31/08 ALL | 4/1/08-3/31/09 ALL |
|---|---|---|---|---|---|---|---|---|
| | | 4 | 4 | 1 | 3 | Type of Statement | | |
| | | | | | | Unqualified | 15 | 14 |
| | | 8 | 3 | | | Reviewed | 11 | 3 |
| 1 | 1 | 3 | 2 | | | Compiled | 4 | 4 |
| | | 5 | | | | Tax Returns | 2 | 7 |
| | 2 | 13 | 3 | 4 | 3 | Other | 20 | 25 |
| **1** | **3** | **33** | **12** | **5** | **6** | **NUMBER OF STATEMENTS** | **52** | **53** |
| % | % | % | % | % | % | **ASSETS** | % | % |
| | | 16.8 | 18.9 | | | Cash & Equivalents | 11.3 | 13.8 |
| | | 30.2 | 17.8 | | | Trade Receivables (net) | 23.8 | 25.2 |
| | | 27.4 | 24.2 | | | Inventory | 25.7 | 26.1 |
| | | 2.4 | 3.4 | | | All Other Current | 3.1 | 3.0 |
| | | 76.8 | 64.2 | | | Total Current | 63.9 | 68.2 |
| | | 14.5 | 16.9 | | | Fixed Assets (net) | 15.5 | 17.1 |
| | | 4.2 | 12.8 | | | Intangibles (net) | 14.6 | 9.9 |
| | | 4.5 | 6.0 | | | All Other Non-Current | 6.0 | 4.8 |
| | | 100.0 | 100.0 | | | Total | 100.0 | 100.0 |
| | | | | | | **LIABILITIES** | | |
| | | 6.3 | 5.5 | | | Notes Payable-Short Term | 5.0 | 5.3 |
| | | 1.4 | .6 | | | Cur. Mat.-L.T.D. | 3.0 | 3.1 |
| | | 12.8 | 7.5 | | | Trade Payables | 9.6 | 8.4 |
| | | .2 | .1 | | | Income Taxes Payable | .5 | .6 |
| | | 14.1 | 11.4 | | | All Other Current | 12.6 | 12.7 |
| | | 34.8 | 25.0 | | | Total Current | 30.8 | 30.0 |
| | | 6.7 | 6.7 | | | Long-Term Debt | 10.8 | 7.7 |
| | | .7 | .1 | | | Deferred Taxes | .6 | .3 |
| | | 6.5 | 3.2 | | | All Other Non-Current | 5.1 | 5.2 |
| | | 51.3 | 65.0 | | | Net Worth | 52.7 | 56.8 |
| | | 100.0 | 100.0 | | | Total Liabilties & Net Worth | 100.0 | 100.0 |
| | | | | | | **INCOME DATA** | | |
| | | 100.0 | 100.0 | | | Net Sales | 100.0 | 100.0 |
| | | 49.3 | 45.6 | | | Gross Profit | 47.0 | 47.1 |
| | | 40.7 | 34.5 | | | Operating Expenses | 41.0 | 43.4 |
| | | 8.6 | 11.1 | | | Operating Profit | 6.0 | 3.7 |
| | | .9 | 1.5 | | | All Other Expenses (net) | 1.3 | .9 |
| | | 7.8 | 9.6 | | | Profit Before Taxes | 4.7 | 2.8 |
| | | | | | | **RATIOS** | | |
| | | 5.4 | 4.2 | | | | 3.2 | 4.3 |
| | | 3.0 | 2.7 | | | Current | 2.3 | 2.4 |
| | | 1.4 | 1.8 | | | | 1.6 | 1.6 |
| | | 3.5 | 2.9 | | | | 1.8 | 2.4 |
| | | 2.1 | 1.2 | | | Quick | 1.2 | 1.2 |
| | | .7 | .8 | | | | .9 | .8 |
| | | 46   8.0 | 39   9.3 | | | | 46   8.0 | 40   9.2 |
| | | 61   6.0 | 45   8.1 | | | Sales/Receivables | 53   6.9 | 50   7.3 |
| | | 81   4.5 | 53   6.9 | | | | 65   5.6 | 62   5.9 |
| | | 68   5.4 | 53   6.9 | | | | 72   5.1 | 69   5.3 |
| | | 114   3.2 | 122   3.0 | | | Cost of Sales/Inventory | 110   3.3 | 99   3.7 |
| | | 152   2.4 | 182   2.0 | | | | 151   2.4 | 152   2.4 |
| | | 16   22.5 | 20   18.3 | | | | 22   16.7 | 23   15.5 |
| | | 35   10.5 | 32   11.4 | | | Cost of Sales/Payables | 38   9.5 | 33   11.1 |
| | | 72   5.1 | 46   8.0 | | | | 57   6.4 | 50   7.2 |
| | | 2.4 | 2.2 | | | | 3.1 | 3.0 |
| | | 3.2 | 3.7 | | | Sales/Working Capital | 4.4 | 4.3 |
| | | 10.5 | 5.7 | | | | 9.6 | 8.0 |
| | | 44.8 | 38.0 | | | | 20.5 | 46.9 |
| | | (27) 12.7 | (10) 7.8 | | | EBIT/Interest | (49) 6.6 | (47) 5.9 |
| | | 4.9 | -.4 | | | | 1.8 | .6 |
| | | | | | | Net Profit + Depr., Dep., | 20.2 | 4.9 |
| | | | | | | Amort./Cur. Mat. L/T/D | (23) 7.6 | (17) 2.4 |
| | | | | | | | .9 | -.3 |
| | | .1 | .1 | | | | .1 | .1 |
| | | .3 | .2 | | | Fixed/Worth | .3 | .3 |
| | | .9 | .7 | | | | 1.2 | .6 |
| | | .2 | .3 | | | | .5 | .3 |
| | | 1.0 | .5 | | | Debt/Worth | .8 | .8 |
| | | 3.5 | 1.8 | | | | 4.9 | 1.7 |
| | | 49.2 | 44.0 | | | % Profit Before Taxes/Tangible | 44.4 | 32.8 |
| | | (30) 19.8 | (11) 9.5 | | | Net Worth | (43) 18.9 | (49) 10.0 |
| | | 11.3 | -2.6 | | | | 2.3 | -7.5 |
| | | 18.0 | 28.0 | | | % Profit Before Taxes/Total | 18.1 | 16.2 |
| | | 8.3 | 5.7 | | | Assets | 8.0 | 4.4 |
| | | 3.6 | -.3 | | | | 1.8 | -2.3 |
| | | 46.7 | 23.9 | | | | 33.7 | 35.0 |
| | | 17.2 | 11.6 | | | Sales/Net Fixed Assets | 16.1 | 11.0 |
| | | 7.1 | 4.2 | | | | 7.4 | 5.9 |
| | | 2.3 | 1.6 | | | | 2.3 | 2.4 |
| | | 1.8 | 1.3 | | | Sales/Total Assets | 1.4 | 1.7 |
| | | 1.4 | 1.0 | | | | 1.1 | 1.1 |
| | | .6 | 1.4 | | | | .8 | 1.2 |
| | | (26) 1.1 | (11) 1.8 | | | % Depr., Dep., Amort./Sales | (45) 1.9 | (40) 2.1 |
| | | 3.7 | 3.1 | | | | 3.0 | 3.8 |
| | | 2.0 | | | | % Officers', Directors' | 3.1 | 2.6 |
| | | (11) 2.8 | | | | Owners' Comp/Sales | (12) 6.9 | (10) 5.2 |
| | | 6.5 | | | | | 11.5 | 8.1 |
| 1240M | 14955M | 321919M | 332467M | 399631M | 1124981M | Net Sales ($) | 1977478M | 2085476M |
| 442M | 4234M | 182932M | 258397M | 313998M | 945318M | Total Assets ($) | 1868804M | 1847969M |

M = $ thousand    MM = $ million
See Pages 9 through 22 for Explanation of Ratios and Data

## Comparative Historical Data    Current Data Sorted by Sales

| | | | Type of Statement | | | | | | |
|---|---|---|---|---|---|---|---|---|---|
| 21 | 18 | 12 | Unqualified | | 1 | 2 | 3 | 1 | 8 |
| 6 | 11 | 11 | Reviewed | | | | 3 | 7 | 1 |
| 1 | 4 | 7 | Compiled | | | 2 | 2 | 1 | 1 |
| 3 | 7 | 5 | Tax Returns | | 1 | 1 | 1 | 2 | |
| 25 | 30 | 25 | Other | | | | 8 | 6 | 9 |
| 4/1/09-3/31/10 ALL | 4/1/10-3/31/11 ALL | 4/1/11-3/31/12 ALL | | 0-1MM | 13 (4/1-9/30/11) 1-3MM | 3-5MM | 47 (10/1/11-3/31/12) 5-10MM | 10-25MM | 25MM & OVER |
| 56 | 70 | 60 | NUMBER OF STATEMENTS | | 2 | 5 | 17 | 17 | 19 |
| % | % | % | ASSETS | % | % | % | % | % | % |
| 17.5 | 15.9 | 16.0 | Cash & Equivalents | D | | | 17.6 | 15.0 | 18.6 |
| 23.6 | 24.2 | 25.8 | Trade Receivables (net) | A | | | 29.4 | 29.6 | 18.1 |
| 24.7 | 24.5 | 25.1 | Inventory | T | | | 23.9 | 29.1 | 17.9 |
| 1.6 | 3.5 | 2.4 | All Other Current | A | | | 1.0 | 4.1 | 2.4 |
| 67.5 | 68.1 | 69.3 | Total Current | | | | 71.9 | 77.8 | 57.0 |
| 15.3 | 15.5 | 14.8 | Fixed Assets (net) | N | | | 12.7 | 18.6 | 16.4 |
| 11.6 | 11.2 | 10.0 | Intangibles (net) | O | | | 7.4 | 1.3 | 17.4 |
| 5.6 | 5.2 | 5.9 | All Other Non-Current | T | | | 8.0 | 2.3 | 9.2 |
| 100.0 | 100.0 | 100.0 | Total | | | | 100.0 | 100.0 | 100.0 |
| | | | LIABILITIES | A | | | | | |
| 5.6 | 6.4 | 5.3 | Notes Payable-Short Term | V | | | 7.7 | 6.6 | 3.4 |
| 1.6 | 1.8 | 1.4 | Cur. Mat.-L.T.D. | A | | | 1.8 | 1.4 | 1.5 |
| 10.3 | 11.9 | 10.4 | Trade Payables | I | | | 10.8 | 14.8 | 6.5 |
| .1 | .3 | .2 | Income Taxes Payable | L | | | .2 | .1 | .1 |
| 10.7 | 11.7 | 12.9 | All Other Current | A | | | 9.1 | 17.8 | 12.1 |
| 28.3 | 32.1 | 30.1 | Total Current | B | | | 29.6 | 40.7 | 23.6 |
| 12.7 | 7.5 | 6.9 | Long-Term Debt | L | | | 5.4 | 6.1 | 9.4 |
| .6 | .5 | .6 | Deferred Taxes | E | | | .4 | .9 | .7 |
| 6.5 | 6.0 | 5.6 | All Other Non-Current | | | | 10.8 | 2.6 | 3.9 |
| 52.0 | 54.0 | 56.7 | Net Worth | | | | 53.8 | 49.8 | 62.5 |
| 100.0 | 100.0 | 100.0 | Total Liabilities & Net Worth | | | | 100.0 | 100.0 | 100.0 |
| | | | INCOME DATA | | | | | | |
| 100.0 | 100.0 | 100.0 | Net Sales | | | | 100.0 | 100.0 | 100.0 |
| 47.0 | 46.5 | 49.2 | Gross Profit | | | | 52.9 | 43.2 | 51.2 |
| 41.5 | 38.5 | 39.0 | Operating Expenses | | | | 45.0 | 34.9 | 37.4 |
| 5.5 | 8.0 | 10.2 | Operating Profit | | | | 7.9 | 8.3 | 13.8 |
| 1.2 | .7 | .9 | All Other Expenses (net) | | | | 1.0 | .6 | 1.4 |
| 4.3 | 7.3 | 9.3 | Profit Before Taxes | | | | 6.9 | 7.7 | 12.4 |
| | | | RATIOS | | | | | | |
| 4.5 | 3.7 | 4.8 | | | | | 8.5 | 4.8 | 3.8 |
| 2.7 | 2.6 | 2.8 | Current | | | | 3.0 | 2.7 | 2.4 |
| 1.8 | 1.3 | 1.4 | | | | | 1.2 | 1.4 | 1.6 |
| 2.7 | 2.4 | 3.3 | | | | | 5.1 | 3.1 | 2.8 |
| 1.6 | 1.7 | 1.3 | Quick | | | | 2.1 | 1.0 | 1.2 |
| 1.0 | .7 | .8 | | | | | .9 | .6 | .8 |
| 47 7.8 | 39 9.3 | 44 8.3 | | | | | 39 9.4 | 45 8.2 | 45 8.2 |
| 54 6.8 | 51 7.2 | 52 7.0 | Sales/Receivables | | | | 50 7.3 | 52 7.0 | 51 7.1 |
| 64 5.7 | 71 5.1 | 70 5.2 | | | | | 76 4.8 | 72 5.1 | 59 6.2 |
| 66 5.6 | 63 5.8 | 64 5.7 | | | | | 107 3.4 | 64 5.7 | 64 5.7 |
| 104 3.5 | 100 3.6 | 114 3.2 | Cost of Sales/Inventory | | | | 126 2.9 | 111 3.3 | 104 3.5 |
| 149 2.4 | 147 2.5 | 146 2.5 | | | | | 159 2.3 | 152 2.4 | 130 2.8 |
| 25 14.8 | 24 15.0 | 21 17.3 | | | | | 15 24.9 | 20 18.0 | 31 11.8 |
| 35 10.4 | 38 9.6 | 33 11.1 | Cost of Sales/Payables | | | | 32 11.5 | 36 10.2 | 33 11.1 |
| 60 6.1 | 64 5.7 | 55 6.6 | | | | | 62 5.9 | 64 5.7 | 45 8.1 |
| 2.4 | 2.5 | 2.5 | | | | | 2.5 | 2.7 | 2.5 |
| 3.8 | 3.7 | 3.4 | Sales/Working Capital | | | | 3.2 | 3.7 | 3.5 |
| 6.3 | 14.7 | 11.7 | | | | | 98.2 | 12.8 | 11.7 |
| 12.6 | 21.1 | 49.7 | | | | | 25.4 | 52.4 | 64.5 |
| (49) 3.2 | (53) 8.8 | (50) 11.1 | EBIT/Interest | | | | (13) 8.5 | (15) 12.7 | (16) 7.7 |
| -2.2 | 2.1 | 4.7 | | | | | 5.9 | 3.6 | 1.0 |
| 5.5 | 8.0 | 18.0 | Net Profit + Depr., Dep., | | | | | | |
| (15) 2.4 | (15) 4.6 | (13) 3.8 | Amort./Cur. Mat. L/T/D | | | | | | |
| -1.5 | 2.8 | 2.1 | | | | | | | |
| .2 | .1 | .1 | | | | | .1 | .2 | .1 |
| .3 | .3 | .3 | Fixed/Worth | | | | .2 | .4 | .3 |
| .8 | .7 | .8 | | | | | .8 | 1.0 | 1.6 |
| .3 | .4 | .2 | | | | | .2 | .2 | .4 |
| .9 | .9 | .9 | Debt/Worth | | | | 1.0 | .7 | .6 |
| 2.7 | 3.1 | 3.1 | | | | | 2.1 | 3.5 | 2.0 |
| 36.8 | 42.8 | 48.1 | % Profit Before Taxes/Tangible | | | | 44.5 | 50.9 | 48.5 |
| (48) 8.8 | (63) 20.3 | (54) 20.0 | Net Worth | | | | (15) 24.7 | (16) 17.7 | (17) 20.2 |
| -8.0 | 6.4 | 8.1 | | | | | 8.2 | 10.7 | -.6 |
| 13.6 | 17.3 | 21.5 | % Profit Before Taxes/Total | | | | 18.0 | 19.8 | 21.8 |
| 5.8 | 10.4 | 9.7 | Assets | | | | 7.7 | 8.1 | 13.8 |
| -3.0 | 3.5 | 3.1 | | | | | 4.4 | 3.6 | 1.2 |
| 27.1 | 34.1 | 35.2 | | | | | 65.5 | 34.3 | 16.1 |
| 13.0 | 13.2 | 15.4 | Sales/Net Fixed Assets | | | | 19.0 | 12.6 | 11.8 |
| 5.1 | 5.4 | 6.6 | | | | | 7.5 | 5.7 | 4.2 |
| 1.9 | 2.3 | 2.2 | | | | | 2.2 | 2.6 | 1.6 |
| 1.5 | 1.5 | 1.6 | Sales/Total Assets | | | | 1.9 | 1.8 | 1.3 |
| 1.0 | 1.1 | 1.2 | | | | | 1.2 | 1.4 | .9 |
| 1.4 | .9 | .8 | | | | | .6 | .8 | 1.3 |
| (44) 2.3 | (55) 2.0 | (47) 1.9 | % Depr., Dep., Amort./Sales | | | | (13) 1.9 | (13) 1.7 | (17) 2.5 |
| 3.6 | 3.0 | 3.7 | | | | | 3.8 | 2.7 | 4.6 |
| 3.2 | 2.9 | 2.0 | % Officers', Directors' | | | | | | |
| (12) 6.9 | (15) 5.8 | (15) 3.4 | Owners' Comp/Sales | | | | | | |
| 20.7 | 13.8 | 6.5 | | | | | | | |
| 2128205M | 2563347M | 2195193M | Net Sales ($) | | 2415M | 19485M | 125704M | 244818M | 1802771M |
| 1901666M | 2137070M | 1705321M | Total Assets ($) | | 8734M | 10734M | 87394M | 133179M | 1465280M |

© RMA 2012

**M = $ thousand    MM = $ million**
See Pages 9 through 22 for Explanation of Ratios and Data

## Current Data Sorted by Assets      Comparative Historical Data

| 0-500M | 500M-2MM | 2-10MM | 10-50MM | 50-100MM | 100-250MM | Type of Statement | 4/1/07-3/31/08 ALL | 4/1/08-3/31/09 ALL |
|---|---|---|---|---|---|---|---|---|
| | 1 | 4 | 14 | 3 | 6 | Unqualified | 23 | 18 |
| | 1 | 24 | 13 | | | Reviewed | 24 | 27 |
| | 3 | 4 | 2 | | | Compiled | 5 | 12 |
| 3 | 7 | 3 | | | | Tax Returns | 4 | 4 |
| 2 | 5 | 19 | 9 | 2 | 2 | Other | 42 | 51 |
| | 17 (4/1-9/30/11) | | 110 (10/1/11-3/31/12) | | | | | |
| 5 | 17 | 54 | 38 | 5 | 8 | NUMBER OF STATEMENTS | 98 | 112 |
| % | % | % | % | % | % | **ASSETS** | % | % |
| | 15.5 | 11.9 | 11.8 | | | Cash & Equivalents | 10.1 | 11.0 |
| | 21.5 | 31.2 | 25.4 | | | Trade Receivables (net) | 28.4 | 24.4 |
| | 25.4 | 27.3 | 25.0 | | | Inventory | 27.0 | 27.9 |
| | 1.0 | 4.9 | 5.0 | | | All Other Current | 3.6 | 4.8 |
| | 63.5 | 75.4 | 67.2 | | | Total Current | 69.2 | 68.1 |
| | 20.2 | 13.2 | 18.6 | | | Fixed Assets (net) | 14.1 | 16.9 |
| | 4.1 | 6.5 | 10.5 | | | Intangibles (net) | 8.5 | 7.3 |
| | 12.2 | 4.8 | 3.7 | | | All Other Non-Current | 8.2 | 7.7 |
| | 100.0 | 100.0 | 100.0 | | | Total | 100.0 | 100.0 |
| | | | | | | **LIABILITIES** | | |
| | 11.2 | 7.8 | 5.0 | | | Notes Payable-Short Term | 8.2 | 8.9 |
| | 2.5 | 2.7 | 3.4 | | | Cur. Mat.-L.T.D. | 2.8 | 1.7 |
| | 14.5 | 12.7 | 7.3 | | | Trade Payables | 10.7 | 10.5 |
| | .1 | 1.6 | .5 | | | Income Taxes Payable | .3 | .4 |
| | 9.9 | 14.9 | 17.3 | | | All Other Current | 13.6 | 13.6 |
| | 38.2 | 39.7 | 33.6 | | | Total Current | 35.5 | 35.0 |
| | 15.3 | 7.1 | 11.7 | | | Long-Term Debt | 9.0 | 9.3 |
| | .4 | .3 | .8 | | | Deferred Taxes | .4 | .6 |
| | 6.1 | 2.8 | 3.2 | | | All Other Non-Current | 4.9 | 4.6 |
| | 40.0 | 50.1 | 50.6 | | | Net Worth | 50.2 | 50.5 |
| | 100.0 | 100.0 | 100.0 | | | Total Liabilities & Net Worth | 100.0 | 100.0 |
| | | | | | | **INCOME DATA** | | |
| | 100.0 | 100.0 | 100.0 | | | Net Sales | 100.0 | 100.0 |
| | 45.8 | 41.1 | 37.3 | | | Gross Profit | 41.6 | 44.2 |
| | 41.9 | 32.5 | 28.2 | | | Operating Expenses | 31.8 | 36.7 |
| | 3.9 | 8.5 | 9.1 | | | Operating Profit | 9.9 | 7.5 |
| | .5 | .5 | 1.1 | | | All Other Expenses (net) | 1.2 | 1.0 |
| | 3.4 | 8.0 | 8.0 | | | Profit Before Taxes | 8.7 | 6.5 |
| | | | | | | **RATIOS** | | |
| | 3.5 | 3.3 | 3.6 | | | Current | 3.8 | 3.7 |
| | 2.2 | 1.9 | 2.0 | | | | 2.3 | 2.2 |
| | 1.0 | 1.3 | 1.3 | | | | 1.4 | 1.3 |
| | 2.3 | 2.1 | 1.9 | | | Quick | 2.4 | 2.3 |
| | 1.2 | 1.2 | .9 | | | | 1.2 | 1.1 |
| | .5 | .7 | .6 | | | | .7 | .6 |
| | 20  18.5 | 38  9.7 | 42  8.7 | | | Sales/Receivables | 39  9.5 | 31  11.7 |
| | 38  9.6 | 49  7.4 | 54  6.8 | | | | 53  6.9 | 47  7.8 |
| | 43  8.4 | 65  5.6 | 76  4.8 | | | | 77  4.7 | 61  6.0 |
| | 25  14.5 | 48  7.6 | 51  7.1 | | | Cost of Sales/Inventory | 44  8.2 | 56  6.5 |
| | 68  5.4 | 91  4.0 | 91  4.0 | | | | 102  3.6 | 117  3.1 |
| | 135  2.7 | 159  2.3 | 140  2.6 | | | | 148  2.5 | 160  2.3 |
| | 20  18.5 | 20  18.2 | 17  21.7 | | | Cost of Sales/Payables | 14  25.3 | 16  22.8 |
| | 42  8.6 | 35  10.3 | 23  15.8 | | | | 28  13.2 | 29  12.5 |
| | 66  5.5 | 50  7.3 | 33  10.9 | | | | 46  7.9 | 57  6.4 |
| | 5.3 | 3.3 | 2.9 | | | Sales/Working Capital | 3.0 | 3.1 |
| | 7.2 | 5.9 | 4.7 | | | | 5.3 | 5.3 |
| | NM | 12.9 | 10.4 | | | | 12.9 | 17.3 |
| | 76.8 | 67.4 | 27.9 | | | EBIT/Interest | 20.7 | 27.7 |
| | (16)  5.6 | (42)  17.7 | (27)  4.7 | | | | (76)  6.1 | (86)  6.1 |
| | 1.1 | 3.1 | 2.1 | | | | 2.2 | 2.4 |
| | | 18.6 | 7.1 | | | Net Profit + Depr., Dep., Amort./Cur. Mat. L/T/D | 14.7 | 13.7 |
| | | (14)  2.9 | (13)  5.4 | | | | (26)  5.4 | (26)  4.0 |
| | | .8 | 1.5 | | | | 2.0 | 2.0 |
| | .1 | .1 | .1 | | | Fixed/Worth | .1 | .1 |
| | .5 | .3 | .4 | | | | .3 | .4 |
| | 6.5 | .7 | .8 | | | | .8 | .7 |
| | .6 | .6 | .4 | | | Debt/Worth | .4 | .3 |
| | 1.6 | 1.1 | 1.1 | | | | 1.0 | 1.1 |
| | 10.4 | 2.8 | 2.6 | | | | 3.3 | 3.1 |
| | 66.4 | 61.9 | 46.1 | | | % Profit Before Taxes/Tangible Net Worth | 55.1 | 47.9 |
| | (14)  18.1 | (52)  29.1 | (34)  22.9 | | | | (86)  26.6 | (103)  20.9 |
| | 9.7 | 13.2 | 10.7 | | | | 12.4 | 10.8 |
| | 27.5 | 26.7 | 19.6 | | | % Profit Before Taxes/Total Assets | 26.2 | 18.9 |
| | 7.7 | 13.4 | 11.3 | | | | 10.9 | 10.5 |
| | .7 | 4.2 | 5.4 | | | | 4.1 | 3.9 |
| | 37.7 | 62.2 | 18.2 | | | Sales/Net Fixed Assets | 45.7 | 34.4 |
| | 18.1 | 24.3 | 10.8 | | | | 17.9 | 14.3 |
| | 7.8 | 8.4 | 6.1 | | | | 7.9 | 6.4 |
| | 3.0 | 2.7 | 2.1 | | | Sales/Total Assets | 2.5 | 2.3 |
| | 2.2 | 1.8 | 1.7 | | | | 1.7 | 1.7 |
| | 1.8 | 1.5 | 1.2 | | | | 1.3 | 1.2 |
| | .7 | .7 | 1.1 | | | % Depr., Dep., Amort./Sales | .8 | .7 |
| | (13)  2.0 | (42)  1.3 | (36)  1.5 | | | | (78)  1.6 | (85)  1.6 |
| | 3.1 | 2.5 | 3.0 | | | | 2.3 | 3.0 |
| | 4.2 | 3.0 | | | | % Officers', Directors' Owners' Comp/Sales | 2.7 | 3.4 |
| | (10)  5.8 | (17)  4.6 | | | | | (17)  4.8 | (23)  4.2 |
| | 7.7 | 8.4 | | | | | 6.3 | 8.8 |
| 7636M | 60893M | 562321M | 1236692M | 508136M | 1456485M | Net Sales ($) | 3079775M | 3340485M |
| 1561M | 22951M | 280316M | 780005M | 372644M | 1256505M | Total Assets ($) | 2232572M | 2627305M |

M = $ thousand    MM = $ million
See Pages 9 through 22 for Explanation of Ratios and Data

**Comparative Historical Data**          **Current Data Sorted by Sales**

| 4/1/09-3/31/10 ALL | 4/1/10-3/31/11 ALL | 4/1/11-3/31/12 ALL | Type of Statement | 0-1MM | 1-3MM | 3-5MM | 5-10MM | 10-25MM | 25MM & OVER |
|---|---|---|---|---|---|---|---|---|---|
| 23 | 23 | 28 | Unqualified | | 2 | | 2 | 7 | 17 |
| 27 | 32 | 38 | Reviewed | | 2 | 2 | 7 | 19 | 8 |
| 11 | 15 | 9 | Compiled | | 3 | 1 | 3 | | 2 |
| 8 | 5 | 13 | Tax Returns | | 4 | 5 | 1 | 3 | |
| 34 | 41 | 39 | Other | 1 | 4 | 6 | 8 | 11 | 9 |
| | | | | | 17 (4/1-9/30/11) | | 110 (10/1/11-3/31/12) | | |
| 103 | 116 | 127 | **NUMBER OF STATEMENTS** | 1 | 15 | 14 | 21 | 40 | 36 |
| % | % | % | **ASSETS** | % | % | % | % | % | % |
| 11.4 | 12.6 | 13.3 | Cash & Equivalents | | 19.2 | 9.5 | 12.9 | 12.8 | 13.2 |
| 25.1 | 27.2 | 26.5 | Trade Receivables (net) | | 19.8 | 27.7 | 27.1 | 28.3 | 26.3 |
| 25.4 | 22.3 | 25.1 | Inventory | | 18.6 | 35.3 | 33.0 | 21.5 | 23.6 |
| 4.7 | 6.2 | 4.4 | All Other Current | | 1.8 | 1.3 | 3.3 | 6.6 | 4.9 |
| 66.5 | 68.3 | 69.3 | Total Current | | 59.5 | 73.8 | 76.4 | 69.2 | 68.0 |
| 19.1 | 16.9 | 17.1 | Fixed Assets (net) | | 25.3 | 12.2 | 11.7 | 18.0 | 18.2 |
| 9.2 | 8.9 | 8.1 | Intangibles (net) | | 9.0 | 9.3 | 5.5 | 6.5 | 10.9 |
| 5.1 | 5.8 | 5.5 | All Other Non-Current | | 6.3 | 4.7 | 6.4 | 6.3 | 3.0 |
| 100.0 | 100.0 | 100.0 | Total | | 100.0 | 100.0 | 100.0 | 100.0 | 100.0 |
| | | | **LIABILITIES** | | | | | | |
| 9.1 | 8.3 | 8.5 | Notes Payable-Short Term | | 22.2 | 10.6 | 7.7 | 7.1 | 4.2 |
| 2.7 | 2.1 | 3.0 | Cur. Mat.-L.T.D. | | 4.8 | 1.7 | 1.0 | 3.6 | 3.2 |
| 10.3 | 9.7 | 10.7 | Trade Payables | | 10.1 | 16.0 | 11.4 | 12.0 | 7.3 |
| 1.2 | .5 | .9 | Income Taxes Payable | | .1 | .6 | .5 | 1.9 | .7 |
| 13.4 | 16.5 | 15.3 | All Other Current | | 14.2 | 11.1 | 14.0 | 15.2 | 18.1 |
| 36.7 | 37.2 | 38.4 | Total Current | | 51.5 | 40.0 | 34.6 | 39.9 | 33.4 |
| 11.3 | 7.9 | 10.7 | Long-Term Debt | | 21.6 | 15.0 | 5.8 | 7.2 | 11.5 |
| .5 | .6 | .6 | Deferred Taxes | | .7 | .8 | .0 | .7 | .9 |
| 9.3 | 5.2 | 3.9 | All Other Non-Current | | 9.6 | 5.2 | 2.7 | 2.4 | 3.0 |
| 42.2 | 49.1 | 46.4 | Net Worth | | 16.6 | 39.1 | 56.9 | 49.9 | 51.1 |
| 100.0 | 100.0 | 100.0 | Total Liabilities & Net Worth | | 100.0 | 100.0 | 100.0 | 100.0 | 100.0 |
| | | | **INCOME DATA** | | | | | | |
| 100.0 | 100.0 | 100.0 | Net Sales | | 100.0 | 100.0 | 100.0 | 100.0 | 100.0 |
| 42.9 | 41.3 | 40.9 | Gross Profit | | 49.2 | 45.7 | 45.4 | 35.0 | 39.1 |
| 37.8 | 32.6 | 32.4 | Operating Expenses | | 45.9 | 39.0 | 37.0 | 26.2 | 27.9 |
| 5.1 | 8.7 | 8.4 | Operating Profit | | 3.2 | 6.7 | 8.3 | 8.8 | 11.2 |
| .8 | 1.0 | .8 | All Other Expenses (net) | | 1.8 | 1.2 | .6 | .4 | 1.0 |
| 4.3 | 7.7 | 7.6 | Profit Before Taxes | | 1.5 | 5.4 | 7.7 | 8.5 | 10.2 |
| | | | **RATIOS** | | | | | | |
| 3.5 | 3.1 | 3.3 | Current | | 2.1 | 2.9 | 3.6 | 2.8 | 3.6 |
| 1.9 | 2.1 | 2.0 | | | 1.3 | 2.2 | 2.4 | 1.7 | 2.1 |
| 1.4 | 1.3 | 1.2 | | | .7 | 1.4 | 1.5 | 1.2 | 1.4 |
| 2.1 | 2.2 | 1.9 | Quick | | 1.4 | 1.7 | 2.7 | 1.9 | 2.1 |
| (102) 1.0 | 1.0 | 1.0 | | | .7 | 1.2 | 1.2 | .9 | 1.1 |
| .6 | .6 | .6 | | | .5 | .8 | .7 | .6 | .7 |
| 35  10.3 | 39  9.3 | 37  9.8 | Sales/Receivables | | 21  17.5 | 27  13.6 | 33  11.0 | 39  9.3 | 41  8.8 |
| 50  7.3 | 49  7.5 | 46  7.9 | | | 33  10.9 | 47  7.7 | 46  7.9 | 54  6.8 | 50  7.3 |
| 67  5.5 | 68  5.4 | 64  5.7 | | | 42  8.6 | 96  3.8 | 59  7.6 | 64  5.7 | 73  5.0 |
| 40  9.1 | 34  10.7 | 46  7.9 | Cost of Sales/Inventory | | 6  61.6 | 89  4.1 | 73  5.0 | 26  14.0 | 46  7.9 |
| 94  3.9 | 78  4.7 | 89  4.1 | | | 45  8.1 | 140  2.6 | 135  2.7 | 73  5.0 | 76  4.8 |
| 148  2.5 | 130  2.8 | 146  2.5 | | | 146  2.5 | 228  1.6 | 159  2.3 | 130  2.8 | 118  3.1 |
| 15  25.0 | 16  22.5 | 18  20.0 | Cost of Sales/Payables | | 20  18.1 | 30  12.3 | 21  17.7 | 18  20.6 | 15  24.2 |
| 32  11.3 | 31  11.6 | 30  12.1 | | | 30  12.2 | 43  8.5 | 35  10.3 | 31  11.9 | 20  18.4 |
| 52  7.0 | 45  8.1 | 49  7.4 | | | 66  5.5 | 69  5.3 | 49  7.4 | 50  7.3 | 34  10.6 |
| 3.5 | 3.5 | 3.4 | Sales/Working Capital | | | 2.6 | 3.3 | 4.2 | 3.5 |
| 5.2 | 5.7 | 5.6 | | | 25.4 | 5.6 | 4.9 | 8.6 | 4.4 |
| 11.1 | 21.8 | 17.2 | | | -13.8 | 7.2 | 8.7 | 26.8 | 7.5 |
| 13.7 | 56.3 | 45.5 | EBIT/Interest | | 11.3 | 27.7 | 219.6 | 62.3 | 52.9 |
| (83) 4.0 | (96) 7.4 | (100) 9.6 | | (13) 3.4 | 4.2 | (14) 21.8 | (31) 15.3 | (27) 12.7 | |
| .8 | 1.9 | 2.1 | | | 1.2 | 1.9 | 2.2 | 3.2 | 3.0 |
| 5.9 | 9.7 | 7.2 | Net Profit + Depr., Dep., Amort./Cur. Mat. L/T/D | | | | | 6.2 | 9.7 |
| (22) 2.1 | (36) 4.1 | (32) 3.9 | | | | | (15) 2.4 | (11) 5.4 | |
| 1.6 | 1.6 | 1.6 | | | | | | .9 | 3.7 |
| .1 | .1 | .1 | Fixed/Worth | | .3 | .2 | .0 | .1 | .2 |
| .5 | .4 | .4 | | | 5.6 | .5 | .2 | .4 | .3 |
| 1.5 | 1.2 | .8 | | | -.4 | .6 | .7 | 1.1 | .8 |
| .5 | .5 | .5 | Debt/Worth | | 1.3 | 1.0 | .4 | .4 | .4 |
| 1.2 | 1.1 | 1.1 | | | 7.1 | 2.3 | .8 | 1.1 | 1.0 |
| 3.8 | 3.7 | 3.4 | | | -3.6 | 5.2 | 2.3 | 2.9 | 2.3 |
| 33.8 | 53.5 | 54.2 | % Profit Before Taxes/Tangible Net Worth | | | 67.6 | 57.3 | 57.6 | 47.3 |
| (87) 14.4 | (105) 23.4 | (113) 26.2 | | | (13) 16.8 | (20) 28.6 | (37) 27.1 | (33) 30.9 | |
| 1.9 | 5.6 | 12.5 | | | | 11.6 | 16.2 | 11.8 | 16.6 |
| 15.2 | 22.3 | 21.6 | % Profit Before Taxes/Total Assets | | 15.9 | 14.4 | 29.4 | 27.6 | 20.6 |
| 5.3 | 10.6 | 12.5 | | | 2.8 | 7.0 | 13.3 | 13.3 | 15.9 |
| .3 | 1.6 | 3.7 | | | .2 | 2.1 | 4.8 | 5.0 | 8.0 |
| 26.4 | 38.2 | 37.6 | Sales/Net Fixed Assets | | 74.3 | 46.8 | 82.2 | 32.9 | 26.5 |
| 11.9 | 13.8 | 13.4 | | | 10.8 | 17.9 | 33.2 | 12.8 | 11.4 |
| 6.5 | 6.8 | 6.9 | | | 5.5 | 9.8 | 9.0 | 6.2 | 6.3 |
| 2.4 | 2.4 | 2.4 | Sales/Total Assets | | 3.8 | 2.5 | 2.4 | 2.8 | 2.1 |
| 1.6 | 1.6 | 1.7 | | | 2.2 | 1.6 | 1.9 | 1.8 | 1.7 |
| 1.2 | 1.2 | 1.4 | | | 1.6 | 1.2 | 1.5 | 1.4 | 1.3 |
| 1.0 | .8 | 1.0 | % Depr., Dep., Amort./Sales | | 1.0 | .9 | .3 | .9 | 1.1 |
| (83) 1.8 | (103) 1.3 | (104) 1.5 | | (10) 2.3 | (10) 2.3 | (14) 1.4 | (38) 1.3 | (31) 1.5 | |
| 2.9 | 2.3 | 2.6 | | | 3.8 | 3.6 | 2.6 | 1.9 | 2.3 |
| 2.7 | 2.7 | 3.3 | % Officers', Directors' Owners' Comp/Sales | | | | | 4.1 | |
| (27) 4.7 | (32) 4.5 | (36) 5.2 | | | | | | (12) 4.7 | |
| 7.8 | 6.7 | 7.4 | | | | | | 8.0 | |
| 2876376M | 3478424M | 3832163M | Net Sales ($) | 776M | 30441M | 58473M | 147849M | 630168M | 2964456M |
| 2433800M | 2646904M | 2713982M | Total Assets ($) | 880M | 38628M | 41383M | 83529M | 375024M | 2174538M |

M = $ thousand    MM = $ million
See Pages 9 through 22 for Explanation of Ratios and Data

## Current Data Sorted by Assets | Comparative Historical Data

### Type of Statement

| 0-500M | 500M-2MM | 2-10MM | 10-50MM | 50-100MM | 100-250MM | Type of Statement | 4/1/07-3/31/08 ALL | 4/1/08-3/31/09 ALL |
|---|---|---|---|---|---|---|---|---|
| | | | 5 | 1 | | Unqualified | 11 | 10 |
| | 1 | 6 | 4 | | | Reviewed | 4 | 5 |
| | | 4 | | | | Compiled | 3 | 5 |
| 1 | 3 | 1 | | | | Tax Returns | 7 | 8 |
| 2 | 1 | 2 | 5 | 1 | 1 | Other | 10 | 15 |
| | 4 (4/1-9/30/11) | | 33 (10/1/11-3/31/12) | | | | | |
| 3 | 5 | 12 | 14 | 2 | 1 | NUMBER OF STATEMENTS | 35 | 43 |
| % | % | % | % | % | % | | % | % |

### ASSETS

| 2-10MM | 10-50MM | ASSETS | Hist 1 | Hist 2 |
|---|---|---|---|---|
| 6.6 | 6.0 | Cash & Equivalents | 11.0 | 7.3 |
| 17.5 | 28.0 | Trade Receivables (net) | 24.2 | 23.4 |
| 49.3 | 30.4 | Inventory | 40.3 | 41.0 |
| .8 | 6.2 | All Other Current | 1.4 | 4.0 |
| 74.3 | 70.5 | Total Current | 77.0 | 75.7 |
| 19.6 | 16.7 | Fixed Assets (net) | 13.9 | 16.1 |
| .8 | 8.6 | Intangibles (net) | 5.1 | 4.2 |
| 5.3 | 4.2 | All Other Non-Current | 4.0 | 4.0 |
| 100.0 | 100.0 | Total | 100.0 | 100.0 |

### LIABILITIES

| 2-10MM | 10-50MM | LIABILITIES | Hist 1 | Hist 2 |
|---|---|---|---|---|
| 19.3 | 12.2 | Notes Payable-Short Term | 9.5 | 12.1 |
| 1.3 | 1.6 | Cur. Mat.-L.T.D. | 3.1 | 3.8 |
| 14.8 | 10.5 | Trade Payables | 14.2 | 15.2 |
| 2.7 | .0 | Income Taxes Payable | .8 | .5 |
| 9.0 | 10.5 | All Other Current | 11.4 | 8.5 |
| 47.0 | 34.9 | Total Current | 39.0 | 40.2 |
| 11.4 | 15.7 | Long-Term Debt | 11.3 | 10.8 |
| .5 | .4 | Deferred Taxes | .3 | .4 |
| 4.0 | 4.6 | All Other Non-Current | 7.1 | 6.8 |
| 37.0 | 44.5 | Net Worth | 42.2 | 41.9 |
| 100.0 | 100.0 | Total Liabilties & Net Worth | 100.0 | 100.0 |

### INCOME DATA

| 2-10MM | 10-50MM | INCOME DATA | Hist 1 | Hist 2 |
|---|---|---|---|---|
| 100.0 | 100.0 | Net Sales | 100.0 | 100.0 |
| 46.2 | 35.6 | Gross Profit | 42.1 | 43.6 |
| 42.1 | 29.2 | Operating Expenses | 35.3 | 38.0 |
| 4.1 | 6.4 | Operating Profit | 6.7 | 5.5 |
| .8 | 2.9 | All Other Expenses (net) | 1.4 | 1.5 |
| 3.3 | 3.6 | Profit Before Taxes | 5.3 | 4.0 |

### RATIOS

| 2-10MM | 10-50MM | RATIOS | Hist 1 | Hist 2 |
|---|---|---|---|---|
| 3.0 | 3.9 | Current | 3.3 | 3.0 |
| 1.5 | 2.2 | | 2.0 | 1.9 |
| .9 | 1.5 | | 1.4 | 1.4 |
| 1.0 | 1.6 | Quick | 1.3 | 1.4 |
| .3 | 1.1 | | .9 | .6 |
| .3 | .6 | | .7 | .4 |
| 14  27.0 | 37  9.8 | Sales/Receivables | 21  17.8 | 23  16.1 |
| 27  13.3 | 47  7.8 | | 43  8.4 | 39  9.5 |
| 55  6.6 | 70  5.2 | | 65  5.6 | 60  6.1 |
| 96  3.8 | 57  6.4 | Cost of Sales/Inventory | 96  3.8 | 65  5.6 |
| 174  2.1 | 107  3.4 | | 130  2.8 | 132  2.8 |
| 243  1.5 | 140  2.6 | | 183  2.0 | 182  2.0 |
| 31  11.6 | 19  19.4 | Cost of Sales/Payables | 21  17.2 | 23  15.8 |
| 45  8.1 | 31  11.6 | | 31  11.9 | 38  9.6 |
| 94  3.9 | 49  7.4 | | 54  6.8 | 70  5.2 |
| 4.1 | 3.2 | Sales/Working Capital | 3.5 | 3.4 |
| 10.2 | 5.6 | | 6.0 | 7.0 |
| NM | 9.1 | | 8.8 | 14.0 |
| 10.1 | 16.9 | EBIT/Interest | 20.6 | 9.1 |
| (11)  4.1 | (13)  3.7 | | (31)  4.1 | (39)  2.6 |
| 1.1 | 1.3 | | 1.3 | 1.3 |
| | | Net Profit + Depr., Dep., Amort./Cur. Mat. L/T/D | | 5.8 |
| | | | (13)  1.2 | 1.2 |
| | | | | .3 |
| .0 | .3 | Fixed/Worth | .1 | .1 |
| .1 | .4 | | .4 | .4 |
| .7 | 1.2 | | .8 | 1.0 |
| 1.0 | .8 | Debt/Worth | .8 | .7 |
| 2.0 | 1.3 | | 1.6 | 1.6 |
| 4.2 | 6.8 | | 3.5 | 3.2 |
| 46.2 | 18.2 | % Profit Before Taxes/Tangible Net Worth | 50.8 | 48.1 |
| 8.4 | (12)  8.0 | | (32)  27.6 | (40)  14.5 |
| 1.0 | 4.2 | | 7.3 | 1.6 |
| 9.1 | 7.6 | % Profit Before Taxes/Total Assets | 21.5 | 16.8 |
| 3.0 | 4.1 | | 11.9 | 5.8 |
| .4 | .8 | | 1.1 | .9 |
| 119.3 | 21.7 | Sales/Net Fixed Assets | 49.6 | 35.8 |
| 30.8 | 14.5 | | 22.5 | 22.5 |
| 7.6 | 6.3 | | 7.6 | 7.6 |
| 2.4 | 2.2 | Sales/Total Assets | 2.6 | 2.8 |
| 2.1 | 1.9 | | 2.1 | 1.9 |
| 1.3 | 1.2 | | 1.5 | 1.6 |
| | .6 | % Depr., Dep., Amort./Sales | .8 | .6 |
| (11) | 1.8 | | (27)  1.2 | (34)  1.4 |
| | 3.0 | | 2.4 | 2.7 |
| | | % Officers', Directors' Owners' Comp/Sales | 1.7 | 1.4 |
| | | | (13)  2.6 | (16)  2.6 |
| | | | 5.0 | 6.0 |

| 0-500M | 500M-2MM | 2-10MM | 10-50MM | 50-100MM | 100-250MM | | Hist 1 | Hist 2 |
|---|---|---|---|---|---|---|---|---|
| 6428M | 20398M | 107052M | 473895M | 311544M | 203478M | Net Sales ($) | 1342859M | 1413151M |
| 958M | 8141M | 54608M | 288113M | 174843M | 121044M | Total Assets ($) | 701190M | 733318M |

M = $ thousand    MM = $ million
See Pages 9 through 22 for Explanation of Ratios and Data

## Comparative Historical Data        Current Data Sorted by Sales

| Type of Statement | 4/1/09-3/31/10 ALL | 4/1/10-3/31/11 ALL | 4/1/11-3/31/12 ALL | 0-1MM | 1-3MM | 3-5MM | 5-10MM | 10-25MM | 25MM & OVER |
|---|---|---|---|---|---|---|---|---|---|
| Unqualified | 6 | 10 | 6 | | | | | 1 | 5 |
| Reviewed | 6 | 11 | 11 | | 1 | 1 | 4 | | 5 |
| Compiled | 1 | 4 | 4 | | 1 | | 2 | 1 | |
| Tax Returns | 8 | | 4 | | | 3 | 1 | | |
| Other | 19 | 19 | 12 | 1 | 1 | 2 | | 2 | 6 |
| | 4/1/09-3/31/10 | 4/1/10-3/31/11 | 4/1/11-3/31/12 | | 4 (4/1-9/30/11) | | | 33 (10/1/11-3/31/12) | |
| **NUMBER OF STATEMENTS** | 40 | 44 | 37 | 1 | 3 | 6 | 7 | 4 | 16 |
| **ASSETS** | % | % | % | % | % | % | % | % | % |
| Cash & Equivalents | 9.7 | 8.3 | 6.6 | | | | | | 7.3 |
| Trade Receivables (net) | 21.8 | 22.9 | 24.2 | | | | | | 28.3 |
| Inventory | 36.2 | 33.9 | 39.8 | | | | | | 31.6 |
| All Other Current | 4.4 | 3.1 | 3.2 | | | | | | 3.7 |
| Total Current | 72.1 | 68.1 | 73.8 | | | | | | 71.0 |
| Fixed Assets (net) | 17.6 | 17.1 | 15.4 | | | | | | 15.4 |
| Intangibles (net) | 6.1 | 6.8 | 5.1 | | | | | | 9.9 |
| All Other Non-Current | 4.2 | 7.9 | 5.7 | | | | | | 3.8 |
| Total | 100.0 | 100.0 | 100.0 | | | | | | 100.0 |
| **LIABILITIES** | | | | | | | | | |
| Notes Payable-Short Term | 11.9 | 13.6 | 13.6 | | | | | | 11.5 |
| Cur. Mat.-L.T.D. | 4.8 | 1.6 | 1.2 | | | | | | 1.6 |
| Trade Payables | 10.6 | 12.7 | 12.8 | | | | | | 11.8 |
| Income Taxes Payable | .0 | 1.0 | 1.0 | | | | | | .0 |
| All Other Current | 8.4 | 11.6 | 11.1 | | | | | | 12.0 |
| Total Current | 35.7 | 40.5 | 39.7 | | | | | | 36.9 |
| Long-Term Debt | 15.0 | 17.0 | 10.6 | | | | | | 9.4 |
| Deferred Taxes | .3 | .2 | .3 | | | | | | .2 |
| All Other Non-Current | 5.4 | 3.8 | 5.2 | | | | | | 5.3 |
| Net Worth | 43.6 | 38.4 | 44.1 | | | | | | 48.1 |
| Total Liabilties & Net Worth | 100.0 | 100.0 | 100.0 | | | | | | 100.0 |
| **INCOME DATA** | | | | | | | | | |
| Net Sales | 100.0 | 100.0 | 100.0 | | | | | | 100.0 |
| Gross Profit | 41.6 | 42.4 | 43.4 | | | | | | 36.5 |
| Operating Expenses | 38.4 | 37.3 | 38.0 | | | | | | 31.0 |
| Operating Profit | 3.2 | 5.0 | 5.4 | | | | | | 5.5 |
| All Other Expenses (net) | 1.6 | 1.1 | 1.5 | | | | | | 2.3 |
| Profit Before Taxes | 1.6 | 4.0 | 3.9 | | | | | | 3.1 |
| **RATIOS** | | | | | | | | | |
| Current | 4.4 | 3.3 | 3.8 | | | | | | 3.2 |
| | 1.9 | 1.7 | 2.0 | | | | | | 2.0 |
| | 1.2 | 1.3 | 1.3 | | | | | | 1.5 |
| Quick | 2.3 | 1.5 | 1.4 | | | | | | 1.6 |
| | .8 | .8 | .8 | | | | | | 1.0 |
| | .4 | .4 | .4 | | | | | | .7 |
| Sales/Receivables | 27  13.5 | 28  13.2 | 26  14.2 | | | | | | 39  9.4 |
| | 44  8.4 | 49  7.5 | 43  8.5 | | | | | | 50  7.3 |
| | 59  6.2 | 59  6.2 | 58  6.3 | | | | | | 68  5.4 |
| Cost of Sales/Inventory | 63  5.8 | 66  5.5 | 55  6.6 | | | | | | 54  6.8 |
| | 112  3.3 | 111  3.3 | 135  2.7 | | | | | | 114  3.2 |
| | 187  1.9 | 168  2.2 | 192  1.9 | | | | | | 135  2.7 |
| Cost of Sales/Payables | 21  17.1 | 27  13.7 | 22  16.7 | | | | | | 21  17.1 |
| | 29  12.6 | 35  10.5 | 35  10.5 | | | | | | 31  11.6 |
| | 45  8.2 | 63  5.8 | 54  6.8 | | | | | | 48  7.6 |
| Sales/Working Capital | 2.9 | 3.1 | 3.3 | | | | | | 3.2 |
| | 5.8 | 7.9 | 6.5 | | | | | | 6.5 |
| | 15.9 | 17.5 | 14.2 | | | | | | 10.1 |
| EBIT/Interest | 12.6 | 14.6 | 17.0 | | | | | | 17.9 |
| | (38)  2.4 | (41)  3.8 | (32)  3.9 | | | | | (15)  3.7 | |
| | -1.7 | .4 | 1.3 | | | | | | 1.8 |
| Net Profit + Depr., Dep., Amort./Cur. Mat. L/T/D | | 25.2 | | | | | | | |
| | | (14)  .9 | | | | | | | |
| | | -.4 | | | | | | | |
| Fixed/Worth | .2 | .1 | .1 | | | | | | .2 |
| | .4 | .5 | .3 | | | | | | .4 |
| | .9 | 1.0 | .7 | | | | | | .9 |
| Debt/Worth | .5 | .9 | .5 | | | | | | .6 |
| | 1.7 | 1.9 | 1.4 | | | | | | 1.3 |
| | 4.5 | 3.9 | 3.5 | | | | | | 3.4 |
| % Profit Before Taxes/Tangible Net Worth | 15.4 | 68.4 | 27.3 | | | | | | 11.7 |
| | (35)  4.9 | (39)  8.8 | (33)  9.3 | | | | | (13)  8.6 | |
| | -14.7 | -2.7 | 4.2 | | | | | | 4.7 |
| % Profit Before Taxes/Total Assets | 6.2 | 10.6 | 10.3 | | | | | | 8.5 |
| | 3.2 | 4.6 | 5.1 | | | | | | 5.6 |
| | -4.0 | -1.1 | .8 | | | | | | 1.2 |
| Sales/Net Fixed Assets | 47.1 | 62.1 | 99.3 | | | | | | 52.5 |
| | 12.2 | 14.4 | 19.4 | | | | | | 17.3 |
| | 6.2 | 6.0 | 7.4 | | | | | | 7.0 |
| Sales/Total Assets | 2.4 | 2.2 | 2.3 | | | | | | 2.3 |
| | 1.7 | 1.7 | 2.1 | | | | | | 1.9 |
| | 1.4 | 1.4 | 1.5 | | | | | | 1.6 |
| % Depr., Dep., Amort./Sales | .7 | .7 | .6 | | | | | | .8 |
| | (34)  1.5 | (34)  1.6 | (23)  1.4 | | | | | (13)  1.8 | |
| | 2.7 | 3.5 | 2.5 | | | | | | 2.7 |
| % Officers', Directors' Owners' Comp/Sales | 2.0 | 1.2 | 1.0 | | | | | | |
| | (11)  3.6 | (14)  2.6 | (12)  2.6 | | | | | | |
| | 8.9 | 3.7 | 4.7 | | | | | | |
| Net Sales ($) | 1229861M | 1671436M | 1122795M | 761M | 5999M | 22738M | 50830M | 61795M | 980672M |
| Total Assets ($) | 752605M | 1085201M | 647707M | 300M | 4141M | 15402M | 24912M | 38617M | 564335M |

© RMA 2012

**M = $ thousand    MM = $ million**
See Pages 9 through 22 for Explanation of Ratios and Data

### Current Data Sorted by Assets      Comparative Historical Data

**Type of Statement**

| 0-500M | 500M-2MM | 2-10MM | 10-50MM | 50-100MM | 100-250MM | Type of Statement | 4/1/07-3/31/08 ALL | 4/1/08-3/31/09 ALL |
|---|---|---|---|---|---|---|---|---|
| 1 | 1 | 4 | 6 | 3 | | Unqualified | 15 | 14 |
| 1 | 1 | 7 | 2 | | | Reviewed | 12 | 13 |
| 2 | 4 | 3 | | | | Compiled | 5 | 6 |
| 1 | 6 | 6 | | | | Tax Returns | 7 | 12 |
| 1 | 7 | 13 | 7 | 2 | 2 | Other | 23 | 28 |
| | 16 (4/1-9/30/11) | 63 (10/1/11-3/31/12) | | | | | | |
| **6** | **18** | **33** | **15** | **5** | **2** | **NUMBER OF STATEMENTS** | **62** | **73** |
| % | % | % | % | % | % | **ASSETS** | % | % |
| | 16.1 | 12.3 | 9.0 | | | Cash & Equivalents | 7.2 | 10.5 |
| | 28.2 | 27.1 | 27.4 | | | Trade Receivables (net) | 29.1 | 29.4 |
| | 30.6 | 34.5 | 33.6 | | | Inventory | 29.0 | 28.6 |
| | 5.1 | 2.1 | 3.5 | | | All Other Current | 6.0 | 5.2 |
| | 80.1 | 76.1 | 73.4 | | | Total Current | 71.3 | 73.7 |
| | 16.4 | 16.1 | 16.9 | | | Fixed Assets (net) | 15.8 | 15.4 |
| | 2.3 | 3.6 | 6.1 | | | Intangibles (net) | 7.4 | 4.4 |
| | 1.2 | 4.2 | 3.6 | | | All Other Non-Current | 5.4 | 6.6 |
| | 100.0 | 100.0 | 100.0 | | | Total | 100.0 | 100.0 |
| | | | | | | **LIABILITIES** | | |
| | 14.6 | 10.8 | 12.2 | | | Notes Payable-Short Term | 15.4 | 13.6 |
| | 1.3 | 2.1 | 1.1 | | | Cur. Mat.-L.T.D. | 3.3 | 2.7 |
| | 21.7 | 16.8 | 11.8 | | | Trade Payables | 16.2 | 16.4 |
| | .4 | .1 | .2 | | | Income Taxes Payable | .1 | .3 |
| | 12.6 | 9.8 | 13.6 | | | All Other Current | 11.7 | 11.7 |
| | 50.6 | 39.6 | 38.9 | | | Total Current | 46.8 | 44.6 |
| | 10.2 | 10.9 | 11.3 | | | Long-Term Debt | 14.1 | 12.5 |
| | .0 | .3 | 1.2 | | | Deferred Taxes | .5 | .1 |
| | 12.7 | 4.5 | 2.0 | | | All Other Non-Current | 6.4 | 5.4 |
| | 26.4 | 44.7 | 46.6 | | | Net Worth | 32.3 | 37.3 |
| | 100.0 | 100.0 | 100.0 | | | Total Liabilities & Net Worth | 100.0 | 100.0 |
| | | | | | | **INCOME DATA** | | |
| | 100.0 | 100.0 | 100.0 | | | Net Sales | 100.0 | 100.0 |
| | 41.7 | 39.6 | 31.9 | | | Gross Profit | 40.9 | 38.5 |
| | 37.5 | 34.3 | 25.5 | | | Operating Expenses | 33.7 | 32.3 |
| | 4.1 | 5.3 | 6.4 | | | Operating Profit | 7.2 | 6.2 |
| | -.6 | .5 | 1.7 | | | All Other Expenses (net) | 2.2 | 1.1 |
| | 4.8 | 4.8 | 4.7 | | | Profit Before Taxes | 5.1 | 5.1 |
| | | | | | | **RATIOS** | | |
| | 2.6 | 2.7 | 3.7 | | | Current | 2.8 | 2.6 |
| | 1.5 | 2.1 | 1.6 | | | | 1.4 | 1.7 |
| | 1.2 | 1.4 | 1.4 | | | | 1.1 | 1.2 |
| | 1.3 | 1.3 | 1.6 | | | Quick | 1.2 | 1.5 |
| | .8 | 1.1 | .8 | | | | .7 | .9 |
| | .6 | .7 | .5 | | | | .5 | .5 |
| | 12  31.5 | 29  12.8 | 36  10.1 | | | Sales/Receivables | 37  10.0 | 33  11.1 |
| | 38  9.5 | 40  9.1 | 50  7.3 | | | | 46  8.0 | 44  8.3 |
| | 53  6.9 | 50  7.3 | 56  6.5 | | | | 58  6.3 | 57  6.4 |
| | 17  21.7 | 55  6.6 | 53  6.9 | | | Cost of Sales/Inventory | 43  8.5 | 38  9.6 |
| | 56  6.5 | 83  4.4 | 94  3.9 | | | | 85  4.3 | 71  5.1 |
| | 107  3.4 | 114  3.2 | 140  2.6 | | | | 112  3.3 | 109  3.3 |
| | 19  19.6 | 18  20.5 | 24  15.2 | | | Cost of Sales/Payables | 25  14.8 | 20  17.8 |
| | 38  9.6 | 33  11.1 | 32  11.4 | | | | 35  10.5 | 33  11.1 |
| | 81  4.5 | 57  6.4 | 40  9.2 | | | | 52  7.0 | 54  6.8 |
| | 7.0 | 3.5 | 3.0 | | | Sales/Working Capital | 4.8 | 5.0 |
| | 10.1 | 6.4 | 7.5 | | | | 12.1 | 8.7 |
| | 17.4 | 13.2 | 9.0 | | | | 32.7 | 20.5 |
| | 19.1 | 9.1 | 66.3 | | | EBIT/Interest | 14.6 | 16.5 |
| | (16) 3.4 | (27) 5.3 | (14) 10.9 | | | | (58) 5.9 | (67) 4.2 |
| | 1.6 | 1.4 | 2.3 | | | | 2.1 | 1.9 |
| | | | | | | Net Profit + Depr., Dep., Amort./Cur. Mat. L/T/D | 25.1 | 6.8 |
| | | | | | | | (18) 4.4 | (21) 2.4 |
| | | | | | | | 2.2 | 1.3 |
| | .3 | .1 | .2 | | | Fixed/Worth | .2 | .1 |
| | .6 | .4 | .3 | | | | .7 | .5 |
| | 1.0 | .8 | 1.7 | | | | 2.2 | 1.4 |
| | 1.4 | .6 | .5 | | | Debt/Worth | 1.3 | .7 |
| | 3.1 | 1.1 | 1.1 | | | | 2.9 | 2.1 |
| | 9.1 | 2.7 | 4.5 | | | | 12.5 | 8.3 |
| | 79.7 | 55.0 | 50.2 | | | % Profit Before Taxes/Tangible Net Worth | 75.7 | 76.3 |
| | (16) 8.8 | (32) 11.2 | (13) 17.6 | | | | (53) 41.7 | (64) 26.2 |
| | -4.2 | 2.1 | 13.5 | | | | 21.7 | 9.3 |
| | 27.8 | 14.8 | 18.5 | | | % Profit Before Taxes/Total Assets | 15.8 | 17.0 |
| | 2.7 | 5.1 | 8.3 | | | | 11.0 | 8.1 |
| | .1 | 1.0 | 3.2 | | | | 3.0 | 2.5 |
| | 83.9 | 68.7 | 29.4 | | | Sales/Net Fixed Assets | 43.0 | 54.0 |
| | 28.6 | 18.4 | 15.3 | | | | 22.9 | 23.7 |
| | 10.8 | 8.0 | 6.6 | | | | 8.3 | 9.9 |
| | 4.2 | 3.0 | 2.3 | | | Sales/Total Assets | 2.9 | 3.3 |
| | 3.0 | 2.3 | 1.9 | | | | 2.2 | 2.4 |
| | 1.7 | 1.8 | 1.5 | | | | 1.7 | 1.6 |
| | .9 | .7 | .7 | | | % Depr., Dep., Amort./Sales | .6 | .5 |
| | (13) 1.4 | (23) 1.8 | 1.7 | | | | (49) 1.4 | (53) 1.3 |
| | 2.2 | 2.7 | 2.6 | | | | 2.2 | 2.0 |
| | | 3.2 | | | | % Officers', Directors' Owners' Comp/Sales | 2.8 | 2.3 |
| | | (15) 5.2 | | | | | (18) 3.9 | (20) 2.8 |
| | | 7.6 | | | | | 5.5 | 4.5 |
| 3792M | 60261M | 388086M | 664367M | 650374M | 513590M | Net Sales ($) | 2641097M | 2659525M |
| 1418M | 19645M | 161691M | 345754M | 340398M | 372993M | Total Assets ($) | 1582876M | 1442081M |

## Comparative Historical Data | Current Data Sorted by Sales

| | 4/1/09-3/31/10 ALL | 4/1/10-3/31/11 ALL | 4/1/11-3/31/12 ALL | Type of Statement | 0-1MM | 1-3MM | 3-5MM | 5-10MM | 10-25MM | 25MM & OVER |
|---|---|---|---|---|---|---|---|---|---|---|
| | 14 | 10 | 14 | Unqualified | 1 | | | | 5 | 8 |
| | 21 | 11 | 11 | Reviewed | 1 | 1 | 1 | 1 | 5 | 2 |
| | 5 | 8 | 9 | Compiled | 2 | 2 | 3 | 1 | 1 | |
| | 14 | 14 | 13 | Tax Returns | 1 | 4 | 2 | 4 | 2 | |
| | 31 | 30 | 32 | Other | 1 | 4 | 4 | 6 | 8 | 10 |
| | | | | | 16 (4/1-9/30/11) | | | 63 (10/1/11-3/31/12) | | | |
| | 85 | 73 | 79 | NUMBER OF STATEMENTS | 5 | 11 | 10 | 12 | 21 | 20 |
| | % | % | % | **ASSETS** | % | % | % | % | % | % |
| | 11.0 | 11.2 | 11.7 | Cash & Equivalents | 12.1 | 11.4 | 26.9 | 7.3 | 8.3 | |
| | 24.1 | 26.1 | 29.0 | Trade Receivables (net) | 33.9 | 22.4 | 25.7 | 25.4 | 32.0 | |
| | 29.4 | 33.3 | 33.2 | Inventory | 30.0 | 35.5 | 37.8 | 31.2 | 33.4 | |
| | 2.9 | 3.7 | 3.3 | All Other Current | 3.9 | 5.2 | 1.6 | 2.4 | 3.5 | |
| | 67.5 | 74.3 | 77.1 | Total Current | 79.9 | 74.5 | 91.9 | 66.3 | 77.2 | |
| | 19.6 | 17.8 | 16.1 | Fixed Assets (net) | 19.1 | 15.7 | 5.6 | 21.9 | 15.6 | |
| | 8.0 | 4.3 | 3.6 | Intangibles (net) | .8 | 4.7 | .9 | 7.0 | 3.7 | |
| | 4.9 | 3.6 | 3.1 | All Other Non-Current | .2 | 5.2 | 1.6 | 4.9 | 3.5 | |
| | 100.0 | 100.0 | 100.0 | Total | 100.0 | 100.0 | 100.0 | 100.0 | 100.0 | |
| | | | | **LIABILITIES** | | | | | | |
| | 14.0 | 11.3 | 14.0 | Notes Payable-Short Term | 18.2 | 9.5 | 10.2 | 12.7 | 12.1 | |
| | 2.8 | 4.0 | 2.0 | Cur. Mat.-L.T.D. | 1.0 | 2.9 | .7 | 2.2 | 2.7 | |
| | 16.3 | 15.0 | 16.1 | Trade Payables | 19.3 | 16.4 | 17.8 | 16.1 | 14.0 | |
| | .1 | .1 | .2 | Income Taxes Payable | .7 | .1 | .2 | .1 | .3 | |
| | 11.6 | 15.6 | 13.3 | All Other Current | 8.4 | 13.4 | 8.7 | 12.1 | 14.3 | |
| | 44.9 | 46.1 | 45.7 | Total Current | 47.6 | 42.3 | 37.6 | 43.2 | 43.4 | |
| | 14.3 | 10.6 | 10.1 | Long-Term Debt | 11.4 | 15.9 | 6.9 | 10.9 | 7.6 | |
| | .4 | .4 | .4 | Deferred Taxes | .0 | .0 | .4 | .7 | .5 | |
| | 6.7 | 5.1 | 6.5 | All Other Non-Current | 7.9 | 18.4 | 4.5 | 2.9 | 4.9 | |
| | 33.7 | 37.9 | 37.3 | Net Worth | 33.1 | 23.4 | 50.7 | 42.2 | 43.6 | |
| | 100.0 | 100.0 | 100.0 | Total Liabilities & Net Worth | 100.0 | 100.0 | 100.0 | 100.0 | 100.0 | |
| | | | | **INCOME DATA** | | | | | | |
| | 100.0 | 100.0 | 100.0 | Net Sales | 100.0 | 100.0 | 100.0 | 100.0 | 100.0 | |
| | 37.5 | 37.9 | 37.2 | Gross Profit | 45.6 | 38.0 | 42.1 | 37.7 | 31.9 | |
| | 32.9 | 32.3 | 32.9 | Operating Expenses | 44.4 | 34.1 | 33.6 | 34.1 | 24.6 | |
| | 4.6 | 5.6 | 4.3 | Operating Profit | 1.1 | 3.8 | 8.4 | 3.7 | 7.3 | |
| | 1.4 | 1.3 | .6 | All Other Expenses (net) | -1.1 | .2 | .8 | .7 | 1.5 | |
| | 3.2 | 4.3 | 3.6 | Profit Before Taxes | 2.2 | 3.7 | 7.7 | 3.0 | 5.7 | |
| | | | | **RATIOS** | | | | | | |
| | 2.6 | 2.7 | 2.7 | Current | 2.0 | 2.9 | 4.2 | 2.3 | 3.6 | |
| | 1.6 | 1.9 | 1.7 | | 1.5 | 2.1 | 2.9 | 1.7 | 1.6 | |
| | 1.1 | 1.3 | 1.3 | | 1.3 | 1.3 | 1.7 | 1.3 | 1.4 | |
| | 1.3 | 1.4 | 1.4 | Quick | 1.5 | .9 | 2.4 | 1.2 | 1.9 | |
| | .8 | .8 | .8 | | .8 | .8 | 1.5 | .9 | .8 | |
| | .5 | .6 | .6 | | .7 | .6 | 1.0 | .5 | .5 | |
| | 32 11.3 | 31 11.9 | 34 10.7 | Sales/Receivables | 42 8.6 | 9 39.6 | 8 47.9 | 29 12.8 | 48 7.6 | |
| | 44 8.3 | 46 8.0 | 47 7.8 | | 47 7.7 | 38 9.5 | 38 9.7 | 38 9.5 | 53 6.9 | |
| | 59 6.2 | 59 6.2 | 58 6.3 | | 74 4.9 | 56 6.5 | 52 7.0 | 47 7.7 | 63 5.8 | |
| | 55 6.7 | 54 6.7 | 51 7.2 | Cost of Sales/Inventory | 8 46.3 | 39 9.3 | 42 8.7 | 55 6.6 | 62 5.9 | |
| | 90 4.1 | 89 4.1 | 81 4.5 | | 96 3.8 | 79 4.6 | 99 3.7 | 70 5.2 | 81 4.5 | |
| | 140 2.6 | 140 2.6 | 118 3.1 | | 146 2.5 | 118 3.1 | 130 2.8 | 114 3.2 | 140 2.6 | |
| | 15 23.8 | 18 20.6 | 18 20.2 | Cost of Sales/Payables | 20 18.3 | 12 30.6 | 17 22.0 | 28 13.2 | 18 20.0 | |
| | 36 10.0 | 33 11.1 | 33 11.1 | | 49 7.4 | 21 17.8 | 29 12.4 | 33 11.1 | 33 10.9 | |
| | 61 6.0 | 51 7.2 | 52 7.0 | | 111 3.3 | 61 6.0 | 52 7.0 | 53 6.9 | 47 7.7 | |
| | 3.9 | 3.9 | 3.7 | Sales/Working Capital | 6.3 | 3.5 | 2.9 | 6.0 | 3.5 | |
| | 7.9 | 7.2 | 7.5 | | 7.6 | 12.1 | 4.2 | 10.0 | 6.9 | |
| | 35.5 | 16.6 | 14.8 | | 11.1 | 16.6 | 7.2 | 18.7 | 16.5 | |
| | 6.7 | 16.8 | 15.3 | EBIT/Interest | | | | | 10.0 | 36.6 |
| | (75) 3.0 | (63) 4.7 | (67) 5.3 | | | | | | (19) 5.3 | (19) 9.6 |
| | .7 | 1.7 | 1.8 | | | | | | 2.6 | 3.7 |
| | 4.5 | 3.1 | 10.8 | Net Profit + Depr., Dep., Amort./Cur. Mat. L/T/D | | | | | | |
| | (25) 2.1 | (18) 1.5 | (13) 5.2 | | | | | | | |
| | .9 | .2 | 1.9 | | | | | | | |
| | .2 | .1 | .1 | Fixed/Worth | .1 | .3 | .0 | .3 | .2 | |
| | .8 | .5 | .4 | | .7 | .5 | .1 | .6 | .3 | |
| | 2.3 | 1.3 | .9 | | 1.5 | 1.7 | .4 | .9 | 1.4 | |
| | .9 | .9 | .7 | Debt/Worth | 1.1 | 1.4 | .5 | .8 | .5 | |
| | 1.9 | 1.7 | 1.6 | | 2.7 | 2.7 | 1.0 | 1.1 | 1.4 | |
| | 9.9 | 6.5 | 4.5 | | 3.9 | NM | 3.5 | 3.0 | 5.9 | |
| | 55.6 | 60.0 | 59.1 | % Profit Before Taxes/Tangible Net Worth | 14.0 | | 88.5 | 54.4 | 54.1 | |
| | (67) 11.3 | (62) 17.6 | (71) 13.4 | | 4.6 | 35.9 | | (19) 11.6 | (18) 21.4 | |
| | -.4 | 2.1 | 2.3 | | -13.3 | 4.7 | | 4.1 | 12.5 | |
| | 15.0 | 16.9 | 15.9 | % Profit Before Taxes/Total Assets | 3.1 | 27.3 | 40.6 | 11.5 | 19.8 | |
| | 3.0 | 5.7 | 5.6 | | 1.7 | 5.3 | 14.2 | 4.7 | 10.1 | |
| | -.5 | 1.0 | .9 | | -2.7 | -3.1 | 2.6 | 1.0 | 4.0 | |
| | 36.3 | 53.0 | 49.4 | Sales/Net Fixed Assets | 33.1 | 57.9 | 862.5 | 19.7 | 30.2 | |
| | 13.6 | 15.5 | 17.3 | | 13.1 | 31.8 | 97.9 | 14.8 | 16.3 | |
| | 5.6 | 6.9 | 8.3 | | 10.5 | 7.3 | 29.0 | 6.6 | 6.9 | |
| | 2.4 | 2.7 | 3.2 | Sales/Total Assets | 2.9 | 3.9 | 4.3 | 3.2 | 2.4 | |
| | 2.0 | 2.1 | 2.1 | | 2.0 | 2.8 | 2.7 | 2.3 | 1.9 | |
| | 1.4 | 1.6 | 1.7 | | 1.6 | 1.7 | 1.8 | 1.8 | 1.5 | |
| | .9 | .9 | .8 | % Depr., Dep., Amort./Sales | | | | | .9 | .6 |
| | (67) 1.8 | (54) 1.7 | (58) 1.7 | | | | | (16) | 2.1 | (19) 1.4 |
| | 2.7 | 2.7 | 2.5 | | | | | | 3.2 | 2.4 |
| | 3.0 | 1.9 | 3.3 | % Officers', Directors' Owners' Comp/Sales | | | | | | |
| | (29) 3.8 | (31) 4.2 | (26) 4.9 | | | | | | | |
| | 5.6 | 6.5 | 7.2 | | | | | | | |
| | 2733627M | 2438164M | 2280470M | Net Sales ($) | 2161M | 23315M | 39963M | 86298M | 342987M | 1785746M |
| | 1915509M | 1340634M | 1241899M | Total Assets ($) | 959M | 11513M | 17242M | 35869M | 166408M | 1009908M |

M = $ thousand    MM = $ million
See Pages 9 through 22 for Explanation of Ratios and Data

## Current Data Sorted by Assets      Comparative Historical Data

| 0-500M | 500M-2MM | 2-10MM | 10-50MM | 50-100MM | 100-250MM | Type of Statement | 4/1/07-3/31/08 ALL | 4/1/08-3/31/09 ALL |
|---|---|---|---|---|---|---|---|---|
| | | 2 | 2 | 3 | 2 | Unqualified | 8 | 7 |
| | 3 | 4 | 3 | | | Reviewed | 8 | 13 |
| | 2 | 2 | | | | Compiled | 7 | 5 |
| 2 | 6 | 3 | | | | Tax Returns | 5 | 6 |
| 2 | 1 | 3 | 13 | | 2 | Other | 21 | 32 |
| | 4 (4/1-9/30/11) | | 51 (10/1/11-3/31/12) | | | | | |
| 4 | 12 | 14 | 18 | 5 | 2 | **NUMBER OF STATEMENTS** | 49 | 63 |
| % | % | % | % | % | % | | % | % |
| | | | | | | **ASSETS** | | |
| | 8.1 | 20.2 | 5.9 | | | Cash & Equivalents | 9.9 | 9.4 |
| | 27.6 | 28.1 | 19.5 | | | Trade Receivables (net) | 25.5 | 24.4 |
| | 33.7 | 26.9 | 35.3 | | | Inventory | 32.8 | 32.4 |
| | 2.2 | 2.9 | 6.9 | | | All Other Current | 2.7 | 3.8 |
| | 71.6 | 78.1 | 67.6 | | | Total Current | 70.9 | 70.0 |
| | 25.5 | 14.8 | 21.0 | | | Fixed Assets (net) | 18.0 | 22.0 |
| | 1.0 | .4 | 3.1 | | | Intangibles (net) | 6.2 | 2.3 |
| | 1.9 | 6.7 | 8.3 | | | All Other Non-Current | 4.9 | 5.7 |
| | 100.0 | 100.0 | 100.0 | | | Total | 100.0 | 100.0 |
| | | | | | | **LIABILITIES** | | |
| | 6.4 | 5.5 | 8.9 | | | Notes Payable-Short Term | 14.1 | 12.0 |
| | 1.0 | 1.4 | 2.3 | | | Cur. Mat.-L.T.D. | 2.2 | 2.4 |
| | 18.8 | 18.1 | 11.1 | | | Trade Payables | 16.8 | 15.5 |
| | .0 | .0 | .2 | | | Income Taxes Payable | .1 | .3 |
| | 10.0 | 7.9 | 4.1 | | | All Other Current | 8.2 | 9.2 |
| | 36.2 | 33.0 | 26.6 | | | Total Current | 41.5 | 39.4 |
| | 9.5 | 3.6 | 12.9 | | | Long-Term Debt | 13.3 | 10.4 |
| | .0 | .4 | .2 | | | Deferred Taxes | .2 | .2 |
| | 4.1 | 3.2 | 3.7 | | | All Other Non-Current | 12.9 | 10.0 |
| | 50.2 | 59.8 | 56.5 | | | Net Worth | 32.0 | 40.1 |
| | 100.0 | 100.0 | 100.0 | | | Total Liabilities & Net Worth | 100.0 | 100.0 |
| | | | | | | **INCOME DATA** | | |
| | 100.0 | 100.0 | 100.0 | | | Net Sales | 100.0 | 100.0 |
| | 40.6 | 34.5 | 33.0 | | | Gross Profit | 35.0 | 37.2 |
| | 41.3 | 29.4 | 25.5 | | | Operating Expenses | 30.4 | 31.7 |
| | -.7 | 5.0 | 7.5 | | | Operating Profit | 4.6 | 5.4 |
| | .6 | .1 | 1.3 | | | All Other Expenses (net) | 1.8 | .6 |
| | -1.3 | 4.9 | 6.2 | | | Profit Before Taxes | 2.8 | 4.9 |
| | | | | | | **RATIOS** | | |
| | 6.2 | 6.9 | 5.6 | | | | 2.9 | 2.9 |
| | 2.4 | 2.8 | 2.9 | | | Current | 1.9 | 1.8 |
| | 1.3 | 1.4 | 1.5 | | | | 1.3 | 1.2 |
| | 2.5 | 3.8 | 1.9 | | | | 1.7 | 1.5 |
| | 1.0 | 1.7 | 1.3 | | | Quick | .9 | .8 |
| | .4 | .7 | .5 | | | | .5 | .5 |
| | 2   152.8 | 34   10.8 | 30   12.3 | | | | 28   13.1 | 30   12.2 |
| | 31   11.7 | 45   8.2 | 42   8.7 | | | Sales/Receivables | 41   9.0 | 41   8.9 |
| | 43   8.4 | 58   6.3 | 60   6.1 | | | | 56   6.6 | 51   7.1 |
| | 26   13.8 | 26   14.0 | 83   4.4 | | | | 46   8.0 | 55   6.6 |
| | 38   9.6 | 63   5.8 | 101   3.6 | | | Cost of Sales/Inventory | 91   4.0 | 93   3.9 |
| | 114   3.2 | 126   2.9 | 159   2.3 | | | | 129   2.8 | 126   2.9 |
| | 0   UND | 25   14.5 | 24   15.5 | | | | 24   15.3 | 22   17.0 |
| | 30   12.3 | 33   11.1 | 33   11.2 | | | Cost of Sales/Payables | 36   10.2 | 32   11.5 |
| | 51   7.2 | 56   6.5 | 49   7.5 | | | | 50   7.3 | 55   6.7 |
| | 3.6 | 2.6 | 2.5 | | | | 4.0 | 3.9 |
| | 12.7 | 4.7 | 4.1 | | | Sales/Working Capital | 7.1 | 7.2 |
| | 23.9 | 17.1 | 8.6 | | | | 17.6 | 19.8 |
| | | 82.8 | 9.5 | | | | 13.2 | 28.1 |
| | | (12) 31.5 | (15) 5.1 | | | EBIT/Interest | (43) 5.3 | (51) 9.6 |
| | | 1.8 | 3.4 | | | | 1.4 | 2.4 |
| | | | | | | | 38.3 | 19.6 |
| | | | | | | Net Profit + Depr., Dep., Amort./Cur. Mat. L/T/D | (15) 7.8 | (12) 5.2 |
| | | | | | | | 3.3 | 1.9 |
| | .0 | .1 | .1 | | | | .2 | .2 |
| | .2 | .3 | .4 | | | Fixed/Worth | .4 | .5 |
| | .9 | .5 | .5 | | | | 1.0 | 2.0 |
| | .2 | .1 | .3 | | | | .8 | .5 |
| | .8 | .5 | .8 | | | Debt/Worth | 1.7 | 1.1 |
| | 2.0 | 2.3 | 2.2 | | | | 3.5 | 3.2 |
| | 33.2 | 25.6 | 45.5 | | | | 51.1 | 53.5 |
| | (11) 11.2 | 13.5 | 19.4 | | | % Profit Before Taxes/Tangible Net Worth | (44) 26.2 | (58) 27.1 |
| | .4 | 4.7 | 4.7 | | | | 4.9 | 4.4 |
| | 10.3 | 18.6 | 19.7 | | | | 19.4 | 21.3 |
| | 4.4 | 6.0 | 7.5 | | | % Profit Before Taxes/Total Assets | 8.5 | 9.4 |
| | -6.7 | 1.0 | 2.4 | | | | 1.8 | 2.1 |
| | 278.2 | 34.9 | 43.8 | | | | 46.9 | 41.4 |
| | 30.3 | 16.9 | 8.0 | | | Sales/Net Fixed Assets | 18.2 | 15.6 |
| | 4.3 | 9.2 | 3.8 | | | | 5.6 | 5.5 |
| | 4.8 | 2.9 | 2.1 | | | | 2.8 | 2.7 |
| | 2.7 | 2.6 | 1.7 | | | Sales/Total Assets | 2.2 | 2.0 |
| | .8 | 1.6 | 1.0 | | | | 1.5 | 1.5 |
| | | .5 | .7 | | | | .6 | .7 |
| | (13) | 1.2 | (15) 1.2 | | | % Depr., Dep., Amort./Sales | (37) 1.4 | (49) 1.6 |
| | | 2.8 | 3.0 | | | | 2.4 | 2.8 |
| | | | | | | | 2.9 | 1.6 |
| | | | | | | % Officers', Directors' Owners' Comp/Sales | (15) 4.7 | (22) 3.8 |
| | | | | | | | 9.0 | 8.9 |
| 7733M | 36521M | 148756M | 622526M | 741222M | 510291M | Net Sales ($) | 1350904M | 2220200M |
| 1019M | 12959M | 67333M | 342906M | 410532M | 420010M | Total Assets ($) | 743831M | 1374478M |

M = $ thousand    MM = $ million
See Pages 9 through 22 for Explanation of Ratios and Data

## Comparative Historical Data     Current Data Sorted by Sales

| Type of Statement | | | | | | | | | |
|---|---|---|---|---|---|---|---|---|---|
| 10 | 12 | 9 | Unqualified | 2 | 1 | | 3 | 2 | 7 |
| 12 | 11 | 10 | Reviewed | 2 | | 2 | 4 | 2 | 2 |
| 3 | 7 | 4 | Compiled | | 2 | | | 2 | |
| 8 | 9 | 11 | Tax Returns | 2 | 2 | 2 | | 1 | |
| 18 | 29 | 21 | Other | | 1 | 1 | 2 | 9 | 6 |
| 4/1/09-3/31/10 ALL | 4/1/10-3/31/11 ALL | 4/1/11-3/31/12 ALL | | 0-1MM | 1-3MM | 3-5MM | 4 (4/1-9/30/11) 5-10MM | 51 (10/1/11-3/31/12) 10-25MM | 25MM & OVER |
| 51 | 68 | 55 | **NUMBER OF STATEMENTS** | 6 | 4 | 5 | 9 | 16 | 15 |

| % | % | % | **ASSETS** | % | % | % | % | % | % |
|---|---|---|---|---|---|---|---|---|---|
| 12.9 | 12.4 | 12.3 | Cash & Equivalents | | | | | 15.0 | 8.6 |
| 24.4 | 22.9 | 22.4 | Trade Receivables (net) | | | | | 24.1 | 22.5 |
| 30.3 | 33.8 | 30.9 | Inventory | | | | | 31.1 | 38.9 |
| 2.0 | 3.4 | 3.8 | All Other Current | | | | | 2.5 | 2.5 |
| 69.5 | 72.6 | 69.4 | Total Current | | | | | 72.7 | 72.5 |
| 21.2 | 16.5 | 19.5 | Fixed Assets (net) | | | | | 21.8 | 15.8 |
| 2.6 | 4.7 | 2.9 | Intangibles (net) | | | | | .3 | 8.1 |
| 6.6 | 6.2 | 8.2 | All Other Non-Current | | | | | 5.1 | 3.6 |
| 100.0 | 100.0 | 100.0 | Total | | | | | 100.0 | 100.0 |

| | | | **LIABILITIES** | | | | | | |
|---|---|---|---|---|---|---|---|---|---|
| 14.7 | 12.3 | 8.1 | Notes Payable-Short Term | | | | | 6.8 | 9.1 |
| 2.8 | 2.4 | 1.5 | Cur. Mat.-L.T.D. | | | | | 1.1 | 2.4 |
| 12.7 | 14.5 | 14.1 | Trade Payables | | | | | 12.6 | 11.6 |
| .4 | .2 | .1 | Income Taxes Payable | | | | | .0 | .0 |
| 6.9 | 10.4 | 7.5 | All Other Current | | | | | 6.5 | 6.4 |
| 37.5 | 39.9 | 31.3 | Total Current | | | | | 27.0 | 29.5 |
| 10.0 | 10.7 | 9.7 | Long-Term Debt | | | | | 6.1 | 17.9 |
| .2 | .3 | .3 | Deferred Taxes | | | | | .6 | .4 |
| 4.3 | 5.8 | 3.5 | All Other Non-Current | | | | | 2.3 | 4.9 |
| 48.0 | 43.4 | 55.2 | Net Worth | | | | | 64.0 | 47.3 |
| 100.0 | 100.0 | 100.0 | Total Liabilties & Net Worth | | | | | 100.0 | 100.0 |

| | | | **INCOME DATA** | | | | | | |
|---|---|---|---|---|---|---|---|---|---|
| 100.0 | 100.0 | 100.0 | Net Sales | | | | | 100.0 | 100.0 |
| 36.9 | 39.2 | 38.3 | Gross Profit | | | | | 32.8 | 34.2 |
| 32.9 | 32.9 | 33.4 | Operating Expenses | | | | | 28.8 | 25.6 |
| 4.0 | 6.4 | 4.8 | Operating Profit | | | | | 4.1 | 8.6 |
| .8 | 1.0 | .9 | All Other Expenses (net) | | | | | .1 | 2.0 |
| 3.2 | 5.4 | 3.9 | Profit Before Taxes | | | | | 4.0 | 6.7 |

| | | | **RATIOS** | | | | | | |
|---|---|---|---|---|---|---|---|---|---|
| 3.2 | 3.7 | 4.7 | Current | | | | | 5.3 | 4.6 |
| 2.2 | 1.9 | 2.7 | | | | | | 3.1 | 2.6 |
| 1.3 | 1.2 | 1.4 | | | | | | 1.9 | 1.5 |
| 1.9 | 1.7 | 2.3 | Quick | | | | | 2.4 | 2.3 |
| 1.0 | .9 | 1.3 | | | | | | 1.5 | 1.3 |
| .5 | .5 | .6 | | | | | | 1.0 | .4 |
| 29  12.5 | 28  12.8 | 24  15.2 | Sales/Receivables | | | | | 36  10.2 | 27  13.4 |
| 44  8.3 | 40  9.2 | 40  9.1 | | | | | | 44  8.3 | 50  7.3 |
| 57  6.4 | 57  6.4 | 55  6.6 | | | | | | 55  6.6 | 59  6.2 |
| 54  6.8 | 65  5.6 | 33  11.0 | Cost of Sales/Inventory | | | | | 34  10.7 | 85  4.3 |
| 84  4.4 | 96  3.8 | 85  4.3 | | | | | | 96  3.8 | 107  3.4 |
| 128  2.8 | 159  2.3 | 152  2.4 | | | | | | 152  2.4 | 159  2.3 |
| 15  24.3 | 18  20.6 | 18  20.3 | Cost of Sales/Payables | | | | | 23  15.6 | 16  23.1 |
| 30  12.2 | 37  9.9 | 32  11.3 | | | | | | 28  13.2 | 30  12.0 |
| 43  8.5 | 57  6.4 | 49  7.4 | | | | | | 35  10.3 | 42  8.6 |
| 3.0 | 3.0 | 2.7 | Sales/Working Capital | | | | | 2.6 | 2.7 |
| 6.9 | 5.9 | 5.2 | | | | | | 3.2 | 4.3 |
| 13.7 | 17.9 | 13.2 | | | | | | 7.7 | 10.8 |
| 17.3 | 36.0 | 44.5 | EBIT/Interest | | | | | 85.7 | 33.9 |
| (42) 3.9 | (55) 7.2 | (43) 6.8 | | | | | | (15) 11.2 | (13) 8.8 |
| 1.2 | 2.6 | 1.5 | | | | | | 1.5 | 5.0 |
| | 11.0 | | Net Profit + Depr., Dep., Amort./Cur. Mat. L/T/D | | | | | | |
| | (10) 3.7 | | | | | | | | |
| | 2.5 | | | | | | | | |
| .2 | .1 | .1 | Fixed/Worth | | | | | .1 | .1 |
| .5 | .3 | .3 | | | | | | .4 | .4 |
| 1.0 | .9 | .5 | | | | | | .5 | .6 |
| .4 | .5 | .2 | Debt/Worth | | | | | .3 | .3 |
| 1.1 | 1.1 | .7 | | | | | | .5 | 1.0 |
| 2.3 | 3.8 | 2.0 | | | | | | 1.4 | 3.0 |
| 34.0 | 38.6 | 36.0 | % Profit Before Taxes/Tangible Net Worth | | | | | 20.3 | 65.9 |
| (47) 11.9 | (58) 13.6 | (52) 18.0 | | | | | | 9.2 | (14) 41.8 |
| 1.1 | 3.1 | 5.8 | | | | | | 2.9 | 29.7 |
| 13.7 | 18.8 | 19.8 | % Profit Before Taxes/Total Assets | | | | | 15.7 | 23.7 |
| 5.2 | 5.4 | 6.6 | | | | | | 6.0 | 19.7 |
| .7 | 2.0 | 1.7 | | | | | | 1.2 | 9.2 |
| 38.0 | 51.2 | 43.8 | Sales/Net Fixed Assets | | | | | 31.2 | 43.8 |
| 15.3 | 19.7 | 16.2 | | | | | | 12.0 | 13.4 |
| 4.6 | 6.2 | 6.2 | | | | | | 4.0 | 6.5 |
| 2.6 | 2.8 | 2.8 | Sales/Total Assets | | | | | 2.8 | 2.5 |
| 2.0 | 2.0 | 2.0 | | | | | | 1.8 | 1.9 |
| 1.2 | 1.3 | 1.2 | | | | | | 1.3 | 1.5 |
| .8 | .6 | .7 | % Depr., Dep., Amort./Sales | | | | | .7 | .7 |
| (45) 1.5 | (57) 1.4 | (43) 1.2 | | | | | | (15) 1.2 | (11) 1.5 |
| 3.1 | 2.9 | 2.7 | | | | | | 3.0 | 3.0 |
| 2.1 | 2.0 | 2.9 | % Officers', Directors' Owners' Comp/Sales | | | | | | |
| (13) 5.1 | (25) 5.0 | (19) 7.2 | | | | | | | |
| 9.3 | 8.7 | 11.8 | | | | | | | |
| 1583344M | 2068620M | 2067049M | Net Sales ($) | 4505M | 8083M | 18798M | 66578M | 249258M | 1719827M |
| 988559M | 1274726M | 1254759M | Total Assets ($) | 4459M | 2927M | 24790M | 47233M | 150559M | 1024791M |

M = $ thousand     MM = $ million
See Pages 9 through 22 for Explanation of Ratios and Data

## Current Data Sorted by Assets      Comparative Historical Data

| 0-500M | 500M-2MM | 2-10MM | 10-50MM | 50-100MM | 100-250MM | Type of Statement | 4/1/07-3/31/08 ALL | 4/1/08-3/31/09 ALL |
|---|---|---|---|---|---|---|---|---|
| | | 6 | 8 | 3 | 4 | Unqualified | 19 | 20 |
| | | 9 | 5 | | | Reviewed | 15 | 20 |
| 1 | | 3 | | | | Compiled | 2 | 2 |
| 2 | 1 | 2 | | | | Tax Returns | 5 | 3 |
| 1 | 1 | 10 | 11 | 8 | 1 | Other | 24 | 25 |
| | 10 (4/1-9/30/11) | | 66 (10/1/11-3/31/12) | | | | | |
| 4 | 2 | 30 | 24 | 11 | 5 | **NUMBER OF STATEMENTS** | 65 | 70 |
| % | % | % | % | % | % | | % | % |
| | | | | | | **ASSETS** | | |
| | | 9.4 | 9.2 | 10.3 | | Cash & Equivalents | 8.8 | 8.8 |
| | | 32.0 | 25.2 | 29.4 | | Trade Receivables (net) | 30.3 | 29.9 |
| | | 32.0 | 22.6 | 29.8 | | Inventory | 28.4 | 30.0 |
| | | 4.2 | 4.3 | 2.2 | | All Other Current | 1.6 | 2.8 |
| | | 77.6 | 61.4 | 71.5 | | Total Current | 69.0 | 71.6 |
| | | 12.6 | 24.0 | 21.9 | | Fixed Assets (net) | 15.7 | 16.9 |
| | | 3.1 | 8.9 | .2 | | Intangibles (net) | 9.0 | 6.5 |
| | | 6.7 | 5.7 | 6.4 | | All Other Non-Current | 6.3 | 5.0 |
| | | 100.0 | 100.0 | 100.0 | | Total | 100.0 | 100.0 |
| | | | | | | **LIABILITIES** | | |
| | | 17.1 | 5.0 | 5.6 | | Notes Payable-Short Term | 8.7 | 9.8 |
| | | 1.9 | 2.4 | .6 | | Cur. Mat.-L.T.D. | 2.2 | 2.8 |
| | | 18.0 | 14.7 | 11.1 | | Trade Payables | 16.5 | 17.1 |
| | | .4 | .0 | .2 | | Income Taxes Payable | .2 | .5 |
| | | 7.5 | 9.3 | 16.5 | | All Other Current | 10.6 | 11.4 |
| | | 44.9 | 31.4 | 34.0 | | Total Current | 38.2 | 41.5 |
| | | 5.2 | 8.4 | 4.6 | | Long-Term Debt | 13.5 | 9.9 |
| | | .1 | .6 | .2 | | Deferred Taxes | .4 | .5 |
| | | 4.3 | 12.3 | 1.6 | | All Other Non-Current | 5.9 | 4.4 |
| | | 45.4 | 47.4 | 59.7 | | Net Worth | 42.1 | 43.7 |
| | | 100.0 | 100.0 | 100.0 | | Total Liabilities & Net Worth | 100.0 | 100.0 |
| | | | | | | **INCOME DATA** | | |
| | | 100.0 | 100.0 | 100.0 | | Net Sales | 100.0 | 100.0 |
| | | 27.2 | 26.6 | 15.3 | | Gross Profit | 30.3 | 27.3 |
| | | 21.9 | 18.8 | 13.6 | | Operating Expenses | 21.7 | 19.3 |
| | | 5.3 | 7.8 | 1.6 | | Operating Profit | 8.5 | 7.9 |
| | | .3 | 1.1 | -.1 | | All Other Expenses (net) | 1.1 | 1.0 |
| | | 5.0 | 6.7 | 1.8 | | Profit Before Taxes | 7.4 | 6.9 |
| | | | | | | **RATIOS** | | |
| | | 3.3 | 3.8 | 3.9 | | | 2.5 | 2.7 |
| | | 1.7 | 2.1 | 2.7 | | Current | 1.9 | 1.7 |
| | | 1.2 | 1.4 | 1.3 | | | 1.3 | 1.3 |
| | | 1.8 | 1.7 | 2.4 | | | 1.5 | 1.5 |
| | | .9 | 1.1 | 1.0 | | Quick | 1.0 | 1.0 |
| | | .5 | .6 | .7 | | | .7 | .6 |
| | | 38   9.5 | 42   8.7 | 57   6.4 | | | 36   10.2 | 31   11.7 |
| | | 47   7.7 | 48   7.6 | 64   5.7 | | Sales/Receivables | 49   7.5 | 44   8.2 |
| | | 52   7.0 | 61   6.0 | 76   4.8 | | | 62   5.9 | 59   6.1 |
| | | 35   10.3 | 35   10.4 | 51   7.2 | | | 41   8.9 | 43   8.5 |
| | | 65   5.6 | 63   5.8 | 62   5.9 | | Cost of Sales/Inventory | 64   5.7 | 66   5.5 |
| | | 107   3.4 | 114   3.2 | 146   2.5 | | | 106   3.5 | 85   4.3 |
| | | 18   20.4 | 20   17.9 | 20   18.7 | | | 20   18.1 | 17   21.3 |
| | | 31   11.6 | 29   12.5 | 28   13.1 | | Cost of Sales/Payables | 39   9.4 | 28   12.9 |
| | | 49   7.5 | 47   7.8 | 38   9.6 | | | 52   7.0 | 49   7.4 |
| | | 4.9 | 4.2 | 2.2 | | | 5.1 | 5.0 |
| | | 8.3 | 6.4 | 4.1 | | Sales/Working Capital | 7.8 | 8.0 |
| | | 17.1 | 12.7 | 12.5 | | | 14.7 | 20.2 |
| | | 54.4 | 13.6 | | | | 20.4 | 30.1 |
| | | (29) 13.3 | (22) 4.0 | | | EBIT/Interest | (61) 6.5 | (65) 9.4 |
| | | 2.6 | 1.4 | | | | 2.0 | 3.0 |
| | | | | | | Net Profit + Depr., Dep., | 34.0 | 20.3 |
| | | | | | | Amort./Cur. Mat. L/T/D | (22) 15.6 | (26) 8.8 |
| | | | | | | | 2.9 | 2.8 |
| | | .1 | .2 | .2 | | | .2 | .2 |
| | | .2 | .6 | .3 | | Fixed/Worth | .4 | .4 |
| | | .5 | 1.6 | .9 | | | 1.0 | .9 |
| | | .4 | .5 | .3 | | | .6 | .7 |
| | | .8 | 1.5 | .5 | | Debt/Worth | 1.3 | 1.6 |
| | | 3.3 | 2.8 | 1.7 | | | 4.3 | 3.2 |
| | | 44.5 | 40.2 | 20.4 | | % Profit Before Taxes/Tangible | 60.0 | 62.4 |
| | | (27) 14.2 | (20) 20.6 | 12.5 | | Net Worth | (54) 34.5 | (62) 31.0 |
| | | 7.8 | 3.4 | -9.5 | | | 14.7 | 10.6 |
| | | 27.7 | 22.0 | 14.4 | | % Profit Before Taxes/Total | 26.4 | 23.2 |
| | | 7.4 | 5.0 | 3.8 | | Assets | 12.7 | 11.3 |
| | | 2.6 | 1.4 | -6.5 | | | 4.4 | 4.4 |
| | | 48.3 | 21.5 | 12.1 | | | 31.9 | 41.1 |
| | | 23.1 | 7.4 | 10.9 | | Sales/Net Fixed Assets | 13.9 | 17.9 |
| | | 13.8 | 3.9 | 4.3 | | | 9.2 | 9.1 |
| | | 3.0 | 2.5 | 1.7 | | | 3.0 | 3.2 |
| | | 2.5 | 1.6 | 1.4 | | Sales/Total Assets | 2.2 | 2.4 |
| | | 2.2 | 1.1 | 1.3 | | | 1.7 | 1.8 |
| | | .6 | 1.0 | 1.3 | | | .7 | .7 |
| | | (25) .9 | (22) 1.6 | 1.7 | | % Depr., Dep., Amort./Sales | (56) 1.4 | (58) 1.1 |
| | | 1.3 | 2.4 | 2.3 | | | 2.1 | 2.1 |
| | | 1.5 | | | | | 1.6 | 1.3 |
| | | (11) 2.9 | | | | % Officers', Directors' Owners' Comp/Sales | (15) 3.8 | (14) 2.6 |
| | | 3.2 | | | | | 7.6 | 4.0 |
| 4477M | 7405M | 346647M | 963557M | 1351420M | 1070053M | Net Sales ($) | 3680109M | 3967326M |
| 1007M | 2522M | 144011M | 547628M | 820374M | 709681M | Total Assets ($) | 1970508M | 2166204M |

M = $ thousand     MM = $ million
See Pages 9 through 22 for Explanation of Ratios and Data

## Comparative Historical Data

## Current Data Sorted by Sales

| | | | | | Type of Statement | | | | | | | |
|---|---|---|---|---|---|---|---|---|---|---|---|---|
| | 18 | | 25 | | 21 | Unqualified | | | | 3 | 7 | 11 |
| | 15 | | 15 | | 14 | Reviewed | | | | 2 | 8 | 4 |
| | 2 | | 3 | | 4 | Compiled | | 1 | | 1 | 2 | |
| | 8 | | 7 | | 5 | Tax Returns | 1 | 2 | | 2 | | |
| | 38 | | 32 | | 32 | Other | | 1 | | 10 | 4 | 17 |
| | 4/1/09-3/31/10 ALL | | 4/1/10-3/31/11 ALL | | 4/1/11-3/31/12 ALL | | 0-1MM | 10 (4/1-9/30/11) 1-3MM | 3-5MM | 66 (10/1/11-3/31/12) 5-10MM | 10-25MM | 25MM & OVER |
| | 81 | | 82 | | 76 | NUMBER OF STATEMENTS | 1 | 4 | | 18 | 21 | 32 |
| | % | | % | | % | ASSETS | % | % | % | % | % | % |
| | 12.3 | | 10.4 | | 10.7 | Cash & Equivalents | | | | 4.9 | 13.3 | 10.9 |
| | 24.1 | | 27.0 | | 28.7 | Trade Receivables (net) | | | | 30.0 | 30.9 | 26.1 |
| | 30.5 | | 27.6 | | 28.1 | Inventory | | | | 32.6 | 27.0 | 26.5 |
| | 3.0 | | 3.1 | | 3.6 | All Other Current | | | | 5.2 | 4.1 | 2.5 |
| | 69.8 | | 68.1 | | 71.0 | Total Current | | | | 72.7 | 75.3 | 65.9 |
| | 19.4 | | 19.9 | | 18.7 | Fixed Assets (net) | | | | 15.0 | 15.0 | 22.9 |
| | 5.6 | | 6.4 | | 4.8 | Intangibles (net) | | | | 5.0 | 3.7 | 6.1 |
| | 5.2 | | 5.7 | | 5.6 | All Other Non-Current | | | | 7.2 | 6.1 | 5.1 |
| | 100.0 | | 100.0 | | 100.0 | Total | | | | 100.0 | 100.0 | 100.0 |
| | | | | | | LIABILITIES | | | | | | |
| | 10.9 | | 9.4 | | 10.7 | Notes Payable-Short Term | | | | 19.4 | 11.0 | 4.2 |
| | 2.0 | | 2.6 | | 1.8 | Cur. Mat.-L.T.D. | | | | 2.4 | 1.4 | 1.7 |
| | 15.4 | | 14.1 | | 15.9 | Trade Payables | | | | 19.3 | 16.2 | 12.9 |
| | .3 | | .3 | | .2 | Income Taxes Payable | | | | .4 | .3 | .1 |
| | 12.6 | | 10.9 | | 19.8 | All Other Current | | | | 7.4 | 8.0 | 12.1 |
| | 41.3 | | 37.2 | | 48.5 | Total Current | | | | 49.0 | 36.9 | 31.1 |
| | 9.4 | | 10.3 | | 6.8 | Long-Term Debt | | | | 6.6 | 7.3 | 6.8 |
| | .5 | | .5 | | .3 | Deferred Taxes | | | | .2 | .1 | .6 |
| | 4.7 | | 3.0 | | 5.8 | All Other Non-Current | | | | 6.3 | 5.7 | 6.6 |
| | 44.1 | | 49.1 | | 38.6 | Net Worth | | | | 38.0 | 50.1 | 55.0 |
| | 100.0 | | 100.0 | | 100.0 | Total Liabilties & Net Worth | | | | 100.0 | 100.0 | 100.0 |
| | | | | | | INCOME DATA | | | | | | |
| | 100.0 | | 100.0 | | 100.0 | Net Sales | | | | 100.0 | 100.0 | 100.0 |
| | 28.0 | | 28.6 | | 26.5 | Gross Profit | | | | 27.3 | 26.3 | 23.2 |
| | 24.0 | | 22.8 | | 20.4 | Operating Expenses | | | | 23.7 | 18.5 | 17.6 |
| | 4.0 | | 5.9 | | 6.1 | Operating Profit | | | | 3.6 | 7.8 | 5.7 |
| | 1.0 | | .6 | | .4 | All Other Expenses (net) | | | | -.1 | .9 | .5 |
| | 2.9 | | 5.2 | | 5.6 | Profit Before Taxes | | | | 3.8 | 6.9 | 5.1 |
| | | | | | | RATIOS | | | | | | |
| | 3.3 | | 3.4 | | 3.4 | | | | | 3.2 | 3.8 | 4.0 |
| | 1.8 | | 2.1 | | 1.9 | Current | | | | 1.4 | 1.9 | 2.2 |
| | 1.2 | | 1.4 | | 1.3 | | | | | 1.1 | 1.4 | 1.4 |
| | 1.9 | | 1.8 | | 1.8 | | | | | 1.1 | 2.3 | 1.8 |
| | .9 | | 1.0 | | 1.1 | Quick | | | | .7 | 1.4 | 1.2 |
| | .6 | | .7 | | .6 | | | | | .5 | .6 | .7 |
| 30 | 12.0 | 38 | 9.7 | 41 | 9.0 | | 42 | 8.6 | 41 | 8.9 | 42 | 8.6 |
| 42 | 8.7 | 51 | 7.1 | 48 | 7.6 | Sales/Receivables | 51 | 7.1 | 47 | 7.7 | 53 | 6.9 |
| 53 | 6.9 | 66 | 5.5 | 60 | 6.1 | | 60 | 6.1 | 59 | 6.2 | 65 | 5.6 |
| 44 | 8.2 | 47 | 7.8 | 39 | 9.3 | | 47 | 7.8 | 28 | 13.1 | 49 | 7.5 |
| 66 | 5.6 | 76 | 4.8 | 62 | 5.9 | Cost of Sales/Inventory | 79 | 4.6 | 63 | 5.8 | 60 | 6.1 |
| 105 | 3.5 | 110 | 3.3 | 107 | 3.4 | | 111 | 3.3 | 118 | 3.1 | 85 | 4.3 |
| 15 | 24.3 | 18 | 20.5 | 19 | 19.4 | | 16 | 22.8 | 21 | 17.5 | 20 | 18.7 |
| 28 | 13.0 | 29 | 12.7 | 29 | 12.5 | Cost of Sales/Payables | 34 | 10.6 | 28 | 13.0 | 29 | 12.5 |
| 47 | 7.8 | 47 | 7.7 | 47 | 7.8 | | 49 | 7.5 | 49 | 7.5 | 41 | 9.0 |
| | 4.3 | | 3.9 | | 4.0 | | | | | 4.7 | 4.3 | 2.9 |
| | 7.4 | | 5.5 | | 7.0 | Sales/Working Capital | | | | 12.1 | 5.7 | 6.0 |
| | 17.3 | | 14.4 | | 15.9 | | | | | 36.0 | 12.9 | 11.8 |
| | 20.6 | | 26.9 | | 38.9 | | | | | 27.6 | 86.3 | 38.9 |
| (71) | 6.8 | (70) | 7.3 | (67) | 6.6 | EBIT/Interest | | | (20) | 7.1 | (27) 4.6 | 6.1 |
| | 1.0 | | 2.3 | | 1.7 | | | | | .3 | 2.4 | 1.4 |
| | 10.1 | | 8.8 | | 23.9 | | | | | | | |
| (25) | 5.2 | (26) | 2.5 | (19) | 8.0 | Net Profit + Depr., Dep., Amort./Cur. Mat. L/T/D | | | | | | |
| | 1.3 | | 1.2 | | 1.9 | | | | | | | |
| | .2 | | .2 | | .1 | | | | | .2 | .1 | .2 |
| | .4 | | .4 | | .4 | Fixed/Worth | | | | .4 | .2 | .4 |
| | .8 | | 1.0 | | 1.0 | | | | | .6 | .7 | 1.0 |
| | .5 | | .3 | | .4 | | | | | .4 | .5 | .3 |
| | 1.2 | | 1.1 | | 1.2 | Debt/Worth | | | | 1.6 | .8 | .7 |
| | 3.1 | | 1.9 | | 2.9 | | | | | 4.2 | 2.8 | 2.2 |
| | 50.4 | | 43.1 | | 40.2 | | | | | 48.6 | 39.8 | 34.0 |
| (75) | 16.6 | (73) | 16.1 | (64) | 16.7 | % Profit Before Taxes/Tangible Net Worth | | | (15) | 13.9 | (20) 23.3 | (28) 18.5 |
| | .8 | | 6.3 | | 4.7 | | | | | -2.5 | 7.2 | 1.6 |
| | 16.0 | | 15.0 | | 24.2 | | | | | 16.9 | 28.0 | 18.4 |
| | 5.6 | | 7.7 | | 7.9 | % Profit Before Taxes/Total Assets | | | | 8.5 | 6.4 | 8.7 |
| | -.5 | | 2.4 | | 2.3 | | | | | -1.6 | 2.7 | 1.1 |
| | 38.2 | | 24.5 | | 29.4 | | | | | 34.8 | 46.6 | 14.0 |
| | 13.4 | | 11.4 | | 13.7 | Sales/Net Fixed Assets | | | | 17.5 | 25.7 | 10.9 |
| | 7.5 | | 6.1 | | 7.1 | | | | | 10.8 | 8.4 | 5.7 |
| | 3.2 | | 2.8 | | 3.0 | | | | | 2.9 | 3.1 | 2.5 |
| | 2.1 | | 1.8 | | 2.2 | Sales/Total Assets | | | | 2.4 | 2.3 | 1.6 |
| | 1.4 | | 1.4 | | 1.4 | | | | | 1.8 | 1.4 | 1.3 |
| | .6 | | .8 | | .8 | | | | | .6 | .7 | 1.2 |
| (70) | 1.4 | (76) | 1.7 | (65) | 1.3 | % Depr., Dep., Amort./Sales | | | (15) | .9 | (18) .9 | (30) 1.6 |
| | 2.6 | | 2.5 | | 2.0 | | | | | 1.6 | 1.4 | 2.3 |
| | 2.1 | | 1.9 | | 1.8 | | | | | | | |
| (15) | 3.6 | (18) | 3.5 | (17) | 2.9 | % Officers', Directors' Owners' Comp/Sales | | | | | | |
| | 5.6 | | 7.3 | | 5.6 | | | | | | | |
| | 3121359M | | 3683169M | | 3743559M | Net Sales ($) | 398M | 6440M | | 135561M | 353151M | 3248009M |
| | 1870953M | | 2517753M | | 2225223M | Total Assets ($) | 67M | 1499M | | 71033M | 197242M | 1955382M |

M = $ thousand    MM = $ million
See Pages 9 through 22 for Explanation of Ratios and Data

*(Note: For the 0-1MM column group the entry "DATA NOT AVAILABLE" is printed vertically through the Assets and Liabilities sections.)*

## Current Data Sorted by Assets · Comparative Historical Data

| 0-500M | 500M-2MM | 2-10MM | 10-50MM | 50-100MM | 100-250MM | Type of Statement | 4/1/07-3/31/08 ALL | 4/1/08-3/31/09 ALL |
|---|---|---|---|---|---|---|---|---|
| | | 2 | 9 | | 3 | Unqualified | 15 | 12 |
| | | 3 | 5 | | | Reviewed | 13 | 12 |
| | 3 | 4 | | | | Compiled | 9 | 7 |
| | 3 | 3 | | | | Tax Returns | 6 | 2 |
| 1 | | 10 | 13 | 6 | 1 | Other | 22 | 23 |
| 18 (4/1-9/30/11) | | 48 (10/1/11-3/31/12) | | | | | | |
| | 7 | 22 | 27 | 6 | 4 | NUMBER OF STATEMENTS | 65 | 56 |
| % | % | % | % | % | % | **ASSETS** | % | % |
| | | 7.0 | 10.7 | | | Cash & Equivalents | 8.6 | 8.0 |
| | | 34.7 | 26.2 | | | Trade Receivables (net) | 28.8 | 25.7 |
| | | 31.8 | 28.1 | | | Inventory | 28.9 | 32.7 |
| | | 3.0 | 2.9 | | | All Other Current | 2.4 | 2.4 |
| | | 76.5 | 67.8 | | | Total Current | 68.6 | 68.7 |
| | | 16.5 | 21.7 | | | Fixed Assets (net) | 19.9 | 20.1 |
| | | 2.7 | 5.0 | | | Intangibles (net) | 7.1 | 5.9 |
| | | 4.4 | 5.5 | | | All Other Non-Current | 4.4 | 5.2 |
| | | 100.0 | 100.0 | | | Total | 100.0 | 100.0 |
| | | | | | | **LIABILITIES** | | |
| | | 9.5 | 7.9 | | | Notes Payable-Short Term | 10.1 | 12.0 |
| | | 2.1 | 2.8 | | | Cur. Mat.-L.T.D. | 2.6 | 2.6 |
| | | 18.9 | 9.7 | | | Trade Payables | 14.8 | 13.4 |
| | | .0 | .2 | | | Income Taxes Payable | .1 | .1 |
| | | 7.8 | 14.4 | | | All Other Current | 15.8 | 19.5 |
| | | 38.4 | 34.9 | | | Total Current | 43.4 | 47.7 |
| | | 6.8 | 13.2 | | | Long-Term Debt | 14.6 | 13.1 |
| | | .3 | .6 | | | Deferred Taxes | .3 | .6 |
| | | 4.4 | 1.4 | | | All Other Non-Current | 7.4 | 5.6 |
| | | 50.1 | 49.9 | | | Net Worth | 34.2 | 33.0 |
| | | 100.0 | 100.0 | | | Total Liabilities & Net Worth | 100.0 | 100.0 |
| | | | | | | **INCOME DATA** | | |
| | | 100.0 | 100.0 | | | Net Sales | 100.0 | 100.0 |
| | | 32.2 | 27.6 | | | Gross Profit | 30.2 | 27.8 |
| | | 27.4 | 19.3 | | | Operating Expenses | 25.5 | 23.0 |
| | | 4.9 | 8.3 | | | Operating Profit | 4.8 | 4.7 |
| | | .3 | .7 | | | All Other Expenses (net) | 1.1 | 1.1 |
| | | 4.5 | 7.6 | | | Profit Before Taxes | 3.7 | 3.7 |
| | | | | | | **RATIOS** | | |
| | | 3.6 | 2.9 | | | | 2.8 | 2.5 |
| | | 2.1 | 2.2 | | | Current | 1.9 | 1.8 |
| | | 1.3 | 1.2 | | | | 1.2 | 1.3 |
| | | 1.6 | 2.1 | | | | 1.5 | 1.3 |
| | | .9 | .9 | | | Quick | .9 | .8 |
| | | .8 | .7 | | | | .6 | .6 |
| | | 41  9.0 | 42  8.7 | | | | 40  9.1 | 32  11.4 |
| | | 50  7.3 | 51  7.2 | | | Sales/Receivables | 48  7.5 | 45  8.2 |
| | | 64  5.7 | 61  6.0 | | | | 62  5.9 | 56  6.5 |
| | | 41  9.0 | 41  9.0 | | | | 44  8.3 | 52  7.0 |
| | | 65  5.6 | 87  4.2 | | | Cost of Sales/Inventory | 70  5.2 | 85  4.3 |
| | | 107  3.4 | 111  3.3 | | | | 117  3.1 | 107  3.4 |
| | | 25  14.8 | 15  23.6 | | | | 22  16.8 | 17  21.4 |
| | | 37  9.9 | 22  16.5 | | | Cost of Sales/Payables | 33  11.1 | 26  14.1 |
| | | 48  7.6 | 35  10.4 | | | | 46  7.9 | 42  8.7 |
| | | 4.1 | 3.3 | | | | 3.4 | 4.3 |
| | | 6.2 | 5.5 | | | Sales/Working Capital | 7.5 | 7.2 |
| | | 18.5 | 15.2 | | | | 20.3 | 16.3 |
| | | 23.3 | 41.1 | | | | 13.3 | 16.2 |
| | | (18)  9.0 | (19)  6.3 | | | EBIT/Interest | (57)  3.7 | (53)  3.6 |
| | | 3.6 | 2.9 | | | | 1.4 | 1.3 |
| | | | | | | | 8.3 | 17.7 |
| | | | | | | Net Profit + Depr., Dep., Amort./Cur. Mat. L/T/D | (22)  4.3 | (18)  4.3 |
| | | | | | | | 2.1 | .7 |
| | | .1 | .2 | | | | .3 | .4 |
| | | .3 | .4 | | | Fixed/Worth | .5 | .6 |
| | | .6 | 1.0 | | | | 1.2 | 1.2 |
| | | .5 | .5 | | | | .6 | .7 |
| | | 1.2 | 1.1 | | | Debt/Worth | 1.5 | 1.7 |
| | | 1.9 | 2.6 | | | | 5.6 | 5.0 |
| | | 47.6 | 39.1 | | | | 42.0 | 35.3 |
| | | 28.8 | (25)  16.6 | | | % Profit Before Taxes/Tangible Net Worth | (56)  25.8 | (51)  20.1 |
| | | 9.9 | 8.2 | | | | 7.2 | 3.8 |
| | | 19.3 | 17.3 | | | | 14.0 | 13.4 |
| | | 10.9 | 11.0 | | | % Profit Before Taxes/Total Assets | 8.2 | 5.7 |
| | | 3.6 | 4.5 | | | | 1.6 | 1.1 |
| | | 57.3 | 40.2 | | | | 27.0 | 38.9 |
| | | 17.7 | 8.3 | | | Sales/Net Fixed Assets | 11.8 | 9.7 |
| | | 8.4 | 6.3 | | | | 6.2 | 6.0 |
| | | 3.2 | 2.3 | | | | 2.6 | 2.9 |
| | | 2.4 | 1.7 | | | Sales/Total Assets | 1.9 | 2.0 |
| | | 1.9 | 1.3 | | | | 1.3 | 1.5 |
| | | .5 | .7 | | | | 1.2 | .9 |
| | | (20)  1.0 | (23)  2.3 | | | % Depr., Dep., Amort./Sales | (58)  2.0 | (53)  1.6 |
| | | 2.0 | 2.9 | | | | 3.1 | 2.6 |
| | | 1.0 | | | | | 1.8 | 1.6 |
| | | (10)  4.1 | | | | % Officers', Directors' Owners' Comp/Sales | (22)  4.1 | (15)  5.4 |
| | | 8.2 | | | | | 6.2 | 7.2 |
| | 34739M | 251363M | 1048954M | 582399M | 1112691M | Net Sales ($) | 1974319M | 2657124M |
| | 9133M | 97776M | 615063M | 427697M | 586030M | Total Assets ($) | 1107867M | 1494710M |

M = $ thousand    MM = $ million
See Pages 9 through 22 for Explanation of Ratios and Data

## Comparative Historical Data

## Current Data Sorted by Sales

| 15 | 18 | 14 | Type of Statement | | | | 2 | 3 | 9 |
|----|----|----|-------------------|---|---|---|---|---|---|
| 11 | 7 | 8 | Unqualified | | | | 1 | 4 | 3 |
| 7 | 8 | 7 | Reviewed | 1 | | | 1 | 2 | |
| 2 | 3 | 6 | Compiled | | 3 | | 1 | 2 | |
| 20 | 27 | 31 | Tax Returns | | 1 | | 5 | 9 | 16 |
| | | | Other | | | | | | |

| 4/1/09-3/31/10 ALL | 4/1/10-3/31/11 ALL | 4/1/11-3/31/12 ALL | | 0-1MM | 18 (4/1-9/30/11) 1-3MM | 3-5MM | 48 (10/1/11-3/31/12) 5-10MM | 10-25MM | 25MM & OVER |
|---|---|---|---|---|---|---|---|---|---|
| 55 | 63 | 66 | **NUMBER OF STATEMENTS** | 1 | | 7 | 10 | 20 | 28 |
| % | % | % | **ASSETS** | % | % | % | % | % | % |
| 6.4 | 9.3 | 8.5 | Cash & Equivalents | | | | 6.0 | 11.3 | 9.1 |
| 28.5 | 26.6 | 32.0 | Trade Receivables (net) | | | | 34.6 | 31.3 | 29.2 |
| 26.8 | 28.0 | 29.2 | Inventory | | D A T A | | 33.5 | 23.6 | 30.9 |
| 2.1 | 3.7 | 2.6 | All Other Current | | | | 4.6 | 2.3 | 2.6 |
| 63.8 | 67.7 | 72.3 | Total Current | | N O T | | 78.6 | 68.5 | 71.9 |
| 23.5 | 21.9 | 18.0 | Fixed Assets (net) | | | | 18.9 | 18.5 | 18.3 |
| 7.2 | 5.4 | 4.7 | Intangibles (net) | | A V A I L A B L E | | .5 | 7.4 | 5.6 |
| 5.5 | 5.0 | 4.9 | All Other Non-Current | | | | 2.0 | 5.7 | 4.2 |
| 100.0 | 100.0 | 100.0 | Total | | | | 100.0 | 100.0 | 100.0 |
| | | | **LIABILITIES** | | | | | | |
| 11.4 | 9.1 | 7.4 | Notes Payable-Short Term | | | | 8.8 | 6.3 | 8.5 |
| 2.6 | 2.0 | 2.3 | Cur. Mat.-L.T.D. | | | | 2.3 | 2.8 | 1.1 |
| 14.5 | 16.3 | 15.3 | Trade Payables | | | | 19.3 | 16.0 | 12.1 |
| .5 | .1 | .2 | Income Taxes Payable | | | | .0 | .1 | .2 |
| 9.2 | 11.3 | 12.3 | All Other Current | | | | 7.6 | 11.1 | 17.1 |
| 38.3 | 38.8 | 37.4 | Total Current | | | | 38.0 | 36.4 | 39.1 |
| 14.0 | 11.9 | 10.3 | Long-Term Debt | | | | 16.1 | 9.8 | 8.6 |
| .6 | .6 | .6 | Deferred Taxes | | | | .7 | .6 | .7 |
| 4.5 | 8.2 | 5.6 | All Other Non-Current | | | | 2.4 | 3.8 | 7.3 |
| 42.6 | 40.4 | 46.1 | Net Worth | | | | 42.8 | 49.4 | 44.4 |
| 100.0 | 100.0 | 100.0 | Total Liabilities & Net Worth | | | | 100.0 | 100.0 | 100.0 |
| | | | **INCOME DATA** | | | | | | |
| 100.0 | 100.0 | 100.0 | Net Sales | | | | 100.0 | 100.0 | 100.0 |
| 29.3 | 28.1 | 29.6 | Gross Profit | | | | 28.7 | 28.8 | 27.6 |
| 24.0 | 24.2 | 23.2 | Operating Expenses | | | | 24.8 | 21.3 | 20.2 |
| 5.3 | 3.9 | 6.4 | Operating Profit | | | | 4.0 | 7.5 | 7.4 |
| 2.3 | .7 | .5 | All Other Expenses (net) | | | | .6 | .6 | .4 |
| 3.0 | 3.2 | 5.9 | Profit Before Taxes | | | | 3.4 | 6.9 | 7.0 |
| | | | **RATIOS** | | | | | | |
| 2.4 | 2.7 | 3.0 | | | | | 3.9 | 3.8 | 2.6 |
| 1.8 | 2.1 | 2.2 | Current | | | | 2.3 | 1.9 | 2.1 |
| 1.3 | 1.2 | 1.3 | | | | | 1.3 | 1.2 | 1.2 |
| 1.4 | 1.6 | 1.6 | | | | | 1.6 | 2.1 | 1.6 |
| .9 | 1.0 | 1.0 | Quick | | | | 1.1 | 1.0 | .9 |
| .6 | .6 | .8 | | | | | .9 | .8 | .6 |
| 40 9.1 | 39 9.5 | 42 8.6 | | | | | 33 11.1 | 46 7.9 | 42 8.7 |
| 49 7.4 | 47 7.8 | 51 7.1 | Sales/Receivables | | | | 45 8.2 | 58 6.3 | 49 7.4 |
| 57 6.4 | 58 6.3 | 64 5.7 | | | | | 55 6.6 | 64 5.7 | 60 6.1 |
| 51 7.2 | 50 7.3 | 41 8.9 | | | | | 50 7.3 | 38 9.5 | 52 7.0 |
| 66 5.5 | 66 5.6 | 74 4.9 | Cost of Sales/Inventory | | | | 69 5.3 | 54 6.7 | 91 4.0 |
| 87 4.2 | 111 3.3 | 111 3.3 | | | | | 101 3.6 | 99 3.7 | 118 3.1 |
| 22 17.0 | 20 18.0 | 19 19.1 | | | | | 16 22.3 | 23 16.0 | 17 21.3 |
| 31 11.8 | 35 10.4 | 31 11.9 | Cost of Sales/Payables | | | | 34 10.6 | 31 11.8 | 27 13.5 |
| 44 8.4 | 54 6.8 | 43 8.4 | | | | | 45 8.2 | 44 8.3 | 41 8.8 |
| 4.6 | 3.9 | 3.7 | | | | | 4.1 | 3.2 | 4.1 |
| 7.4 | 6.6 | 5.5 | Sales/Working Capital | | | | 5.5 | 6.1 | 5.6 |
| 15.9 | 18.2 | 16.4 | | | | | 13.0 | 21.7 | 15.7 |
| 11.9 | 17.8 | 30.5 | | | | | 23.3 | 28.9 | 111.7 |
| (49) 3.9 | (56) 6.2 | (50) 9.6 | EBIT/Interest | | | | 9.6 | (13) 4.6 | (20) 23.6 |
| -1.3 | 1.6 | 3.6 | | | | | 3.5 | 2.2 | 7.7 |
| 6.2 | 8.6 | 18.6 | Net Profit + Depr., Dep., | | | | | | |
| (20) 3.0 | (21) 2.6 | (18) 7.3 | Amort./Cur. Mat. L/T/D | | | | | | |
| .5 | 1.1 | 2.6 | | | | | | | |
| .3 | .3 | .2 | | | | | .2 | .1 | .2 |
| .6 | .6 | .4 | Fixed/Worth | | | | .4 | .4 | .4 |
| 1.4 | 1.6 | .9 | | | | | 7.9 | 1.0 | 1.2 |
| .7 | .5 | .6 | | | | | .7 | .4 | .5 |
| 1.3 | 1.4 | 1.3 | Debt/Worth | | | | 1.1 | 1.3 | 1.5 |
| 3.9 | 4.8 | 2.8 | | | | | 26.6 | 2.6 | 4.2 |
| 27.3 | 39.6 | 45.3 | % Profit Before Taxes/Tangible | | | | | 47.6 | 75.3 |
| (48) 10.0 | (55) 18.7 | (60) 24.8 | Net Worth | | | | | (18) 22.4 | (25) 32.1 |
| -8.0 | 5.0 | 9.3 | | | | | | 7.2 | 13.3 |
| 11.8 | 15.8 | 17.6 | % Profit Before Taxes/Total | | | | 19.8 | 17.1 | 19.2 |
| 4.7 | 6.6 | 10.7 | Assets | | | | 8.3 | 9.6 | 14.2 |
| -1.2 | 1.1 | 4.7 | | | | | 5.0 | 3.6 | 6.0 |
| 16.0 | 30.7 | 50.5 | | | | | 53.6 | 69.7 | 32.7 |
| 8.6 | 9.6 | 12.2 | Sales/Net Fixed Assets | | | | 13.9 | 9.7 | 11.3 |
| 6.0 | 5.4 | 6.4 | | | | | 7.7 | 6.3 | 6.4 |
| 2.5 | 2.5 | 3.0 | | | | | 3.2 | 3.3 | 2.5 |
| 1.9 | 1.8 | 2.0 | Sales/Total Assets | | | | 2.6 | 1.9 | 1.9 |
| 1.5 | 1.3 | 1.4 | | | | | 2.0 | 1.3 | 1.3 |
| .9 | .9 | .6 | | | | | | .7 | .6 |
| (50) 1.9 | (59) 1.8 | (57) 1.4 | % Depr., Dep., Amort./Sales | | | | | (18) 1.6 | (25) 1.4 |
| 2.8 | 2.9 | 2.4 | | | | | | 2.5 | 2.3 |
| 1.2 | 1.7 | 1.0 | % Officers', Directors' | | | | | | |
| (13) 2.1 | (18) 5.1 | (17) 4.0 | Owners' Comp/Sales | | | | | | |
| 6.1 | 6.5 | 7.4 | | | | | | | |
| 2074779M | 2716906M | 3030146M | Net Sales ($) | 1530M | | 25210M | 73673M | 361722M | 2568011M |
| 1288442M | 1642577M | 1735699M | Total Assets ($) | 716M | | 13675M | 31746M | 241787M | 1447775M |

M = $ thousand    MM = $ million
See Pages 9 through 22 for Explanation of Ratios and Data

## Current Data Sorted by Assets

## Comparative Historical Data

| | | | | | | Type of Statement | | |
|---|---|---|---|---|---|---|---|---|
| | | | | | | Unqualified | 3 | 5 |
| | | | | | | Reviewed | 9 | 11 |
| | | 2 | 1 | | | Compiled | 7 | 8 |
| 2 | 2 | 6 | 2 | 3 | | Tax Returns | 1 | 4 |
| 2 | 2 | 5 1 8 | 7 | | 2 | Other | 19 | 14 |
| | 12 (4/1-9/30/11) | | 30 (10/1/11-3/31/12) | | | | 4/1/07-3/31/08 | 4/1/08-3/31/09 |
| 0-500M | 500M-2MM | 2-10MM | 10-50MM | 50-100MM | 100-250MM | | ALL | ALL |
| 2 | 4 | 21 | 10 | 3 | 2 | NUMBER OF STATEMENTS | 39 | 42 |
| % | % | % | % | % | % | ASSETS | % | % |
| | | 10.4 | 13.3 | | | Cash & Equivalents | 8.0 | 13.3 |
| | | 39.7 | 32.0 | | | Trade Receivables (net) | 35.5 | 31.5 |
| | | 23.6 | 20.3 | | | Inventory | 28.1 | 28.9 |
| | | 4.7 | 8.5 | | | All Other Current | 3.6 | 3.2 |
| | | 78.3 | 74.1 | | | Total Current | 75.3 | 77.0 |
| | | 14.2 | 15.9 | | | Fixed Assets (net) | 16.1 | 13.9 |
| | | 3.4 | 7.2 | | | Intangibles (net) | 6.2 | 6.0 |
| | | 4.0 | 2.8 | | | All Other Non-Current | 2.5 | 3.1 |
| | | 100.0 | 100.0 | | | Total | 100.0 | 100.0 |
| | | | | | | LIABILITIES | | |
| | | 13.2 | 6.5 | | | Notes Payable-Short Term | 14.2 | 11.5 |
| | | 3.4 | 1.6 | | | Cur. Mat.-L.T.D. | 2.2 | 2.1 |
| | | 18.3 | 14.3 | | | Trade Payables | 18.3 | 14.1 |
| | | .3 | .7 | | | Income Taxes Payable | .2 | .5 |
| | | 7.7 | 7.2 | | | All Other Current | 8.5 | 8.9 |
| | | 42.9 | 30.2 | | | Total Current | 43.5 | 37.0 |
| | | 5.8 | 5.5 | | | Long-Term Debt | 8.6 | 8.0 |
| | | .1 | .8 | | | Deferred Taxes | .1 | .2 |
| | | 3.2 | 8.4 | | | All Other Non-Current | 5.9 | 8.7 |
| | | 47.9 | 55.1 | | | Net Worth | 41.9 | 46.1 |
| | | 100.0 | 100.0 | | | Total Liabilities & Net Worth | 100.0 | 100.0 |
| | | | | | | INCOME DATA | | |
| | | 100.0 | 100.0 | | | Net Sales | 100.0 | 100.0 |
| | | 30.5 | 34.0 | | | Gross Profit | 32.6 | 31.0 |
| | | 24.1 | 24.1 | | | Operating Expenses | 24.0 | 22.3 |
| | | 6.4 | 9.9 | | | Operating Profit | 8.6 | 8.7 |
| | | .2 | .5 | | | All Other Expenses (net) | 1.0 | .9 |
| | | 6.1 | 9.4 | | | Profit Before Taxes | 7.7 | 7.8 |
| | | | | | | RATIOS | | |
| | | 3.7 | 4.6 | | | | 2.8 | 3.9 |
| | | 1.6 | 2.5 | | | Current | 2.0 | 2.2 |
| | | 1.3 | 1.6 | | | | 1.4 | 1.6 |
| | | 2.1 | 2.8 | | | | 1.9 | 2.2 |
| | | 1.0 | 1.5 | | | Quick | 1.2 | 1.5 |
| | | .9 | 1.1 | | | | .6 | .7 |
| | | 45  8.2 | 40  9.1 | | | | 38  9.6 | 37  10.0 |
| | | 54  6.7 | 50  7.3 | | | Sales/Receivables | 55  6.6 | 45  8.2 |
| | | 70  5.2 | 78  4.7 | | | | 64  5.7 | 54  6.8 |
| | | 24  15.4 | 22  16.4 | | | | 31  11.8 | 30  12.0 |
| | | 47  7.8 | 62  5.9 | | | Cost of Sales/Inventory | 58  6.3 | 63  5.8 |
| | | 66  5.5 | 91  4.0 | | | | 81  4.5 | 91  4.0 |
| | | 23  15.7 | 20  18.3 | | | | 20  18.0 | 15  23.6 |
| | | 31  11.8 | 35  10.4 | | | Cost of Sales/Payables | 30  12.2 | 22  16.3 |
| | | 44  8.3 | 51  7.2 | | | | 50  7.2 | 41  9.0 |
| | | 4.6 | 2.9 | | | | 4.7 | 4.4 |
| | | 10.0 | 3.9 | | | Sales/Working Capital | 7.4 | 5.6 |
| | | 13.0 | 8.6 | | | | 12.7 | 9.4 |
| | | 15.0 | | | | | 39.4 | 23.4 |
| | | (19)  7.8 | | | | EBIT/Interest | (38)  6.4 | (35)  9.6 |
| | | 2.3 | | | | | 2.0 | 3.5 |
| | | | | | | | 29.3 | 7.6 |
| | | (13) | | | | Net Profit + Depr., Dep., Amort./Cur. Mat. L/T/D | (13)  4.4 | (11)  5.1 |
| | | | | | | | 2.4 | 1.5 |
| | | .1 | .2 | | | | .1 | .2 |
| | | .2 | .4 | | | Fixed/Worth | .3 | .3 |
| | | .5 | .5 | | | | .9 | .6 |
| | | .6 | .5 | | | | .7 | .3 |
| | | 1.9 | .7 | | | Debt/Worth | 1.3 | 1.1 |
| | | 3.2 | 1.8 | | | | 4.8 | 3.0 |
| | | 38.5 | | | | | 59.4 | 59.3 |
| | | 24.6 | | | | % Profit Before Taxes/Tangible Net Worth | (36)  39.3 | (37)  32.9 |
| | | 8.1 | | | | | 20.5 | 16.0 |
| | | 15.6 | 21.6 | | | | 30.5 | 29.5 |
| | | 8.1 | 13.3 | | | % Profit Before Taxes/Total Assets | 14.7 | 13.1 |
| | | 2.6 | 10.4 | | | | 4.0 | 4.4 |
| | | 117.9 | 29.2 | | | | 64.6 | 61.6 |
| | | 25.2 | 12.6 | | | Sales/Net Fixed Assets | 16.9 | 21.5 |
| | | 9.3 | 7.4 | | | | 11.9 | 10.0 |
| | | 3.2 | 2.1 | | | | 3.2 | 3.0 |
| | | 2.8 | 1.8 | | | Sales/Total Assets | 2.5 | 2.3 |
| | | 1.8 | 1.5 | | | | 1.7 | 1.7 |
| | | .1 | | | | | .4 | .3 |
| | | (19)  .5 | | | | % Depr., Dep., Amort./Sales | (33)  .9 | (32)  1.0 |
| | | 1.4 | | | | | 1.9 | 2.0 |
| | | | | | | | 2.4 | 2.8 |
| | | | | | | % Officers', Directors' Owners' Comp/Sales | (13)  3.6 | (10)  6.3 |
| | | | | | | | 14.5 | 11.9 |
| 2063M | 17696M | 259526M | 359989M | 368417M | 357789M | Net Sales ($) | 1433960M | 1580284M |
| 965M | 5720M | 106053M | 201476M | 199522M | 310268M | Total Assets ($) | 805272M | 1018234M |

M = $ thousand    MM = $ million
See Pages 9 through 22 for Explanation of Ratios and Data

## Comparative Historical Data | Current Data Sorted by Sales

| Type of Statement | 4/1/09-3/31/10 ALL | 4/1/10-3/31/11 ALL | 4/1/11-3/31/12 ALL | 0-1MM | 1-3MM | 3-5MM | 5-10MM | 10-25MM | 25MM & OVER |
|---|---|---|---|---|---|---|---|---|---|
| Unqualified | 10 | 7 | 5 | | | | | 1 | 4 |
| Reviewed | 16 | 14 | 8 | | | | | 5 | 2 |
| Compiled | 9 | 10 | 7 | | | 1 | 1 | 3 | |
| Tax Returns | 6 | 7 | 5 | | 1 | 1 | 2 | 1 | |
| Other | 7 | 9 | 17 | 1 | 1 | 1 | | | |
| | | | | 12 (4/1-9/30/11) | | | 30 (10/1/11-3/31/12) | | |
| **NUMBER OF STATEMENTS** | 48 | 47 | 42 | 1 | 2 | 3 | 8 | 14 | 14 |
| **ASSETS** | % | % | % | % | % | % | % | % | % |
| Cash & Equivalents | 16.2 | 13.6 | 13.1 | | | | | 11.0 | 16.8 |
| Trade Receivables (net) | 30.2 | 33.4 | 34.5 | | | | | 38.1 | 28.9 |
| Inventory | 23.6 | 23.7 | 25.0 | | | | | 20.5 | 25.1 |
| All Other Current | 3.7 | 3.9 | 5.3 | | | | | 5.0 | 8.5 |
| Total Current | 73.7 | 74.6 | 77.9 | | | | | 74.6 | 79.3 |
| Fixed Assets (net) | 17.5 | 17.0 | 14.3 | | | | | 16.6 | 13.7 |
| Intangibles (net) | 4.9 | 2.2 | 4.8 | | | | | 5.3 | 4.4 |
| All Other Non-Current | 4.0 | 6.1 | 3.1 | | | | | 3.4 | 2.6 |
| Total | 100.0 | 100.0 | 100.0 | | | | | 100.0 | 100.0 |
| **LIABILITIES** | | | | | | | | | |
| Notes Payable-Short Term | 14.6 | 14.4 | 11.6 | | | | | 13.1 | 6.1 |
| Cur. Mat.-L.T.D. | 2.7 | 1.8 | 2.3 | | | | | 4.4 | 1.3 |
| Trade Payables | 15.7 | 16.5 | 15.5 | | | | | 16.8 | 12.3 |
| Income Taxes Payable | .3 | .2 | .3 | | | | | .2 | .5 |
| All Other Current | 9.3 | 10.4 | 8.3 | | | | | 8.5 | 9.7 |
| Total Current | 42.6 | 43.3 | 38.0 | | | | | 43.1 | 29.9 |
| Long-Term Debt | 8.2 | 7.8 | 5.9 | | | | | 5.5 | 6.3 |
| Deferred Taxes | .5 | .3 | .4 | | | | | .2 | .7 |
| All Other Non-Current | 8.4 | 5.2 | 8.8 | | | | | 5.7 | 6.1 |
| Net Worth | 40.3 | 43.4 | 46.9 | | | | | 45.6 | 57.0 |
| Total Liabilities & Net Worth | 100.0 | 100.0 | 100.0 | | | | | 100.0 | 100.0 |
| **INCOME DATA** | | | | | | | | | |
| Net Sales | 100.0 | 100.0 | 100.0 | | | | | 100.0 | 100.0 |
| Gross Profit | 30.0 | 31.5 | 33.1 | | | | | 28.7 | 34.1 |
| Operating Expenses | 26.9 | 25.1 | 25.8 | | | | | 24.7 | 23.0 |
| Operating Profit | 3.1 | 6.3 | 7.3 | | | | | 4.0 | 11.1 |
| All Other Expenses (net) | 1.1 | 1.0 | .2 | | | | | .1 | .1 |
| Profit Before Taxes | 2.1 | 5.3 | 7.1 | | | | | 3.9 | 11.0 |
| **RATIOS** | | | | | | | | | |
| Current | 3.6 | 3.4 | 3.7 | | | | | 3.0 | 4.6 |
| | 2.2 | 1.8 | 2.4 | | | | | 1.6 | 3.4 |
| | 1.4 | 1.3 | 1.4 | | | | | 1.3 | 2.2 |
| Quick | 2.5 | 2.3 | 2.2 | | | | | 1.9 | 2.8 |
| | 1.3 | 1.0 | 1.4 | | | | | 1.0 | 1.7 |
| | .8 | .7 | .9 | | | | | .9 | 1.1 |
| Sales/Receivables | 38  9.6 | 41  8.9 | 44  8.3 | | | | | 42  8.6 | 45  8.2 |
| | 46  7.9 | 51  7.2 | 51  7.1 | | | | | 49  7.4 | 51  7.2 |
| | 57  6.5 | 65  5.6 | 69  5.3 | | | | | 57  6.4 | 72  5.1 |
| Cost of Sales/Inventory | 32  11.3 | 29  12.5 | 27  13.5 | | | | | 18  20.1 | 46  8.0 |
| | 53  6.9 | 56  6.5 | 57  6.4 | | | | | 30  12.3 | 70  5.2 |
| | 87  4.2 | 77  4.7 | 79  4.6 | | | | | 61  6.0 | 101  3.6 |
| Cost of Sales/Payables | 20  18.1 | 21  17.6 | 19  19.2 | | | | | 21  17.8 | 20  18.3 |
| | 32  11.2 | 32  11.5 | 30  12.3 | | | | | 30  12.1 | 27  13.4 |
| | 47  7.7 | 49  7.4 | 44  8.3 | | | | | 42  8.7 | 44  8.3 |
| Sales/Working Capital | 4.1 | 4.3 | 3.3 | | | | | 5.0 | 2.6 |
| | 6.4 | 7.8 | 5.5 | | | | | 11.4 | 3.4 |
| | 12.0 | 14.7 | 11.7 | | | | | 15.2 | 5.3 |
| EBIT/Interest | 22.1 | 24.3 | 24.1 | | | | | 11.3 | 96.7 |
| | (41) 2.9 | (42) 6.0 | (36) 10.3 | | | | | (13) 8.2 | (11) 22.3 |
| | -2.5 | 2.1 | 4.9 | | | | | 2.5 | 9.7 |
| Net Profit + Depr., Dep., Amort./Cur. Mat. L/T/D | 10.5 | 8.7 | 7.1 | | | | | | |
| | (15) 3.7 | (14) 2.9 | (16) 3.6 | | | | | | |
| | 1.8 | .8 | 1.5 | | | | | | |
| Fixed/Worth | .1 | .1 | .1 | | | | | .2 | .1 |
| | .3 | .3 | .3 | | | | | .3 | .2 |
| | .8 | .5 | .5 | | | | | .7 | .4 |
| Debt/Worth | .5 | .4 | .5 | | | | | .6 | .5 |
| | 1.1 | 1.4 | 1.0 | | | | | 1.6 | .7 |
| | 2.6 | 3.1 | 3.1 | | | | | 3.1 | 1.8 |
| % Profit Before Taxes/Tangible Net Worth | 32.3 | 35.0 | 44.2 | | | | | 26.9 | 50.3 |
| | (40) 11.5 | (42) 18.9 | (39) 27.7 | | | | | (13) 16.4 | 40.2 |
| | -2.9 | 4.1 | 10.5 | | | | | 5.0 | 22.2 |
| % Profit Before Taxes/Total Assets | 14.2 | 23.4 | 18.8 | | | | | 11.4 | 36.8 |
| | 3.8 | 7.9 | 10.7 | | | | | 7.5 | 15.3 |
| | -5.7 | 1.0 | 4.0 | | | | | 2.5 | 10.2 |
| Sales/Net Fixed Assets | 44.6 | 44.5 | 50.8 | | | | | 56.1 | 22.1 |
| | 16.9 | 18.4 | 18.4 | | | | | 29.0 | 16.2 |
| | 7.1 | 8.9 | 8.5 | | | | | 9.0 | 7.9 |
| Sales/Total Assets | 2.9 | 2.8 | 2.9 | | | | | 3.5 | 2.3 |
| | 2.1 | 2.3 | 2.1 | | | | | 2.8 | 1.9 |
| | 1.4 | 1.8 | 1.7 | | | | | 1.7 | 1.3 |
| % Depr., Dep., Amort./Sales | .6 | .7 | .5 | | | | | .2 | .6 |
| | (41) 1.2 | (42) 1.2 | (38) 1.0 | | | | | .8 | (13) 1.4 |
| | 2.7 | 2.3 | 1.7 | | | | | 1.7 | 2.0 |
| % Officers', Directors' Owners' Comp/Sales | 1.6 | 2.1 | 3.1 | | | | | | |
| | (18) 4.1 | (20) 3.8 | (14) 6.6 | | | | | | |
| | 12.9 | 11.3 | 10.6 | | | | | | |
| Net Sales ($) | 1178867M | 1303929M | 1365480M | 894M | 2513M | 13180M | 56693M | 218357M | 1073843M |
| Total Assets ($) | 884635M | 763031M | 824004M | 495M | 1001M | 5354M | 31057M | 92369M | 693728M |

M = $ thousand    MM = $ million
See Pages 9 through 22 for Explanation of Ratios and Data

## Current Data Sorted by Assets

## Comparative Historical Data

| 0-500M | 500M-2MM | 2-10MM | 10-50MM | 50-100MM | 100-250MM | Type of Statement | 4/1/07-3/31/08 ALL | 4/1/08-3/31/09 ALL |
|---|---|---|---|---|---|---|---|---|
| | | 4 | 8 | 2 | 1 | Unqualified | 19 | 15 |
| 1 | 1 | 10 | 6 | | | Reviewed | 14 | 18 |
| | 2 | 9 | | | | Compiled | 11 | 11 |
| 4 | 2 | 5 | 1 | | 1 | Tax Returns | 2 | 8 |
| | 4 | 7 | 7 | 2 | 1 | Other | 27 | 25 |
| 16 (4/1-9/30/11) | | | 62 (10/1/11-3/31/12) | | | | | |
| 5 | 9 | 35 | 22 | 4 | 3 | **NUMBER OF STATEMENTS** | 73 | 77 |
| % | % | % | % | % | % | **ASSETS** | % | % |
| | | 14.6 | 10.7 | | | Cash & Equivalents | 10.6 | 9.8 |
| | | 34.3 | 28.8 | | | Trade Receivables (net) | 30.9 | 29.1 |
| | | 26.9 | 27.9 | | | Inventory | 27.4 | 29.4 |
| | | 3.2 | 3.3 | | | All Other Current | 3.9 | 4.5 |
| | | 79.0 | 70.7 | | | Total Current | 72.9 | 72.9 |
| | | 12.7 | 18.1 | | | Fixed Assets (net) | 16.6 | 14.5 |
| | | 1.6 | 7.4 | | | Intangibles (net) | 4.7 | 6.4 |
| | | 6.7 | 3.8 | | | All Other Non-Current | 5.8 | 6.3 |
| | | 100.0 | 100.0 | | | Total | 100.0 | 100.0 |
| | | | | | | **LIABILITIES** | | |
| | | 9.0 | 6.8 | | | Notes Payable-Short Term | 7.9 | 10.1 |
| | | 1.3 | 3.2 | | | Cur. Mat.-L.T.D. | 2.2 | 3.6 |
| | | 15.7 | 9.6 | | | Trade Payables | 11.5 | 12.5 |
| | | .3 | .0 | | | Income Taxes Payable | .2 | .3 |
| | | 14.8 | 15.2 | | | All Other Current | 13.9 | 12.5 |
| | | 41.1 | 34.8 | | | Total Current | 35.7 | 39.0 |
| | | 4.9 | 8.6 | | | Long-Term Debt | 11.1 | 8.9 |
| | | .2 | .7 | | | Deferred Taxes | .3 | .2 |
| | | 3.6 | 7.4 | | | All Other Non-Current | 3.4 | 6.5 |
| | | 50.4 | 48.5 | | | Net Worth | 49.5 | 45.3 |
| | | 100.0 | 100.0 | | | Total Liabilities & Net Worth | 100.0 | 100.0 |
| | | | | | | **INCOME DATA** | | |
| | | 100.0 | 100.0 | | | Net Sales | 100.0 | 100.0 |
| | | 33.5 | 32.9 | | | Gross Profit | 32.4 | 32.5 |
| | | 26.4 | 22.5 | | | Operating Expenses | 25.0 | 26.9 |
| | | 7.1 | 10.4 | | | Operating Profit | 7.4 | 5.5 |
| | | .3 | 1.3 | | | All Other Expenses (net) | .8 | 1.0 |
| | | 6.7 | 9.1 | | | Profit Before Taxes | 6.6 | 4.5 |
| | | | | | | **RATIOS** | | |
| | | 4.0 | 3.3 | | | | 3.2 | 3.4 |
| | | 1.9 | 1.8 | | | Current | 1.8 | 2.1 |
| | | 1.3 | 1.3 | | | | 1.5 | 1.4 |
| | | 2.1 | 2.3 | | | | 1.7 | 2.1 |
| | | 1.3 | .9 | | | Quick | 1.1 | .9 |
| | | .8 | .7 | | | | .7 | .6 |
| | | 39  9.4 | 43  8.4 | | | | 42  8.6 | 37  9.8 |
| | | 44  8.3 | 50  7.3 | | | Sales/Receivables | 53  6.9 | 46  7.9 |
| | | 59  6.2 | 61  6.0 | | | | 66  5.5 | 61  6.0 |
| | | 29  12.7 | 42  8.6 | | | | 38  9.6 | 43  8.5 |
| | | 62  5.9 | 87  4.2 | | | Cost of Sales/Inventory | 79  4.6 | 82  4.4 |
| | | 99  3.7 | 130  2.8 | | | | 118  3.1 | 117  3.1 |
| | | 11  32.2 | 13  29.0 | | | | 16  22.8 | 15  23.7 |
| | | 24  15.3 | 26  14.2 | | | Cost of Sales/Payables | 30  12.0 | 28  13.1 |
| | | 40  9.1 | 36  10.1 | | | | 40  9.2 | 40  9.0 |
| | | 3.7 | 3.5 | | | | 3.9 | 4.2 |
| | | 6.7 | 5.5 | | | Sales/Working Capital | 5.7 | 5.9 |
| | | 19.0 | 13.5 | | | | 9.1 | 13.3 |
| | | 51.2 | 61.3 | | | | 14.1 | 24.4 |
| | | (28)  15.6 | (21)  9.1 | | | EBIT/Interest | (62)  5.3 | (67)  5.9 |
| | | 7.8 | 4.1 | | | | 1.3 | 1.7 |
| | | | | | | | 9.4 | 9.4 |
| | | | | | | Net Profit + Depr., Dep., Amort./Cur. Mat. L/T/D | (14)  4.6 | (21)  3.2 |
| | | | | | | | 1.7 | .6 |
| | | .1 | .2 | | | | .1 | .1 |
| | | .2 | .4 | | | Fixed/Worth | .4 | .4 |
| | | .5 | .8 | | | | .7 | 1.1 |
| | | .4 | .4 | | | | .5 | .4 |
| | | .7 | 1.3 | | | Debt/Worth | 1.2 | 1.2 |
| | | 2.4 | 3.4 | | | | 2.1 | 3.3 |
| | | 53.1 | 53.4 | | | | 48.0 | 45.0 |
| | | (32)  28.9 | (20)  30.9 | | | % Profit Before Taxes/Tangible Net Worth | (69)  25.2 | (67)  22.8 |
| | | 13.2 | 21.9 | | | | 9.8 | 5.3 |
| | | 24.8 | 27.1 | | | | 19.7 | 18.4 |
| | | 14.3 | 13.1 | | | % Profit Before Taxes/Total Assets | 11.3 | 6.3 |
| | | 4.6 | 4.0 | | | | 2.4 | 1.0 |
| | | 52.8 | 16.8 | | | | 44.3 | 54.3 |
| | | 28.1 | 10.6 | | | Sales/Net Fixed Assets | 15.9 | 19.2 |
| | | 15.8 | 7.1 | | | | 7.0 | 9.2 |
| | | 3.2 | 2.5 | | | | 2.7 | 2.8 |
| | | 2.6 | 1.9 | | | Sales/Total Assets | 2.1 | 2.2 |
| | | 2.1 | 1.4 | | | | 1.4 | 1.5 |
| | | .6 | .9 | | | | .8 | .6 |
| | | (31)  1.1 | (21)  1.9 | | | % Depr., Dep., Amort./Sales | (62)  1.3 | (62)  1.4 |
| | | 2.3 | 3.0 | | | | 2.4 | 2.2 |
| | | 1.7 | | | | | 2.8 | 3.1 |
| | | (15)  2.8 | | | | % Officers', Directors' Owners' Comp/Sales | (20)  4.8 | (27)  6.7 |
| | | 7.7 | | | | | | 10.3 |
| 2390M | 30247M | 450750M | 956960M | 380407M | 502146M | Net Sales ($) | 2115855M | 2395640M |
| 895M | 11709M | 167972M | 481737M | 322370M | 380729M | Total Assets ($) | 1332757M | 1383535M |

M = $ thousand    MM = $ million
See Pages 9 through 22 for Explanation of Ratios and Data

## Comparative Historical Data                                        ## Current Data Sorted by Sales

| | | | Type of Statement | | | | | | |
|---|---|---|---|---|---|---|---|---|---|
| 13 | 15 | 15 | Unqualified | | | | 1 | 3 | 11 |
| 16 | 20 | 18 | Reviewed | | 1 | 1 | 5 | 8 | 3 |
| 13 | 10 | 11 | Compiled | | | 3 | 3 | 4 | 1 |
| 7 | 13 | 13 | Tax Returns | 4 | 2 | | 3 | 2 | 2 |
| 23 | 32 | 21 | Other | 2 | 2 | 3 | 1 | 5 | 10 |
| 4/1/09- | 4/1/10- | 4/1/11- | | | 16 (4/1-9/30/11) | | 62 (10/1/11-3/31/12) | | |
| 3/31/10 | 3/31/11 | 3/31/12 | | | | | | | |
| ALL | ALL | ALL | | 0-1MM | 1-3MM | 3-5MM | 5-10MM | 10-25MM | 25MM & OVER |
| 72 | 90 | 78 | **NUMBER OF STATEMENTS** | 4 | 5 | 7 | 13 | 22 | 27 |
| % | % | % | **ASSETS** | % | % | % | % | % | % |
| 13.4 | 13.4 | 12.7 | Cash & Equivalents | | | | 13.9 | 14.5 | 11.4 |
| 26.6 | 29.7 | 32.7 | Trade Receivables (net) | | | | 33.6 | 35.2 | 28.1 |
| 28.6 | 27.0 | 25.7 | Inventory | | | | 25.0 | 24.0 | 27.9 |
| 3.5 | 4.9 | 3.0 | All Other Current | | | | 2.0 | 3.9 | 2.4 |
| 72.1 | 75.0 | 74.1 | Total Current | | | | 74.6 | 77.6 | 69.9 |
| 16.1 | 12.9 | 14.3 | Fixed Assets (net) | | | | 16.0 | 11.7 | 17.0 |
| 6.4 | 4.5 | 5.4 | Intangibles (net) | | | | 1.5 | 4.2 | 8.9 |
| 5.4 | 7.7 | 6.2 | All Other Non-Current | | | | 7.9 | 6.5 | 4.3 |
| 100.0 | 100.0 | 100.0 | Total | | | | 100.0 | 100.0 | 100.0 |
| | | | **LIABILITIES** | | | | | | |
| 9.5 | 7.2 | 7.1 | Notes Payable-Short Term | | | | 7.9 | 7.5 | 7.3 |
| 2.6 | 3.1 | 2.0 | Cur. Mat.-L.T.D. | | | | 1.1 | 1.6 | 2.2 |
| 10.5 | 14.2 | 13.8 | Trade Payables | | | | 17.0 | 12.2 | 10.1 |
| .1 | .1 | .4 | Income Taxes Payable | | | | .0 | .5 | .7 |
| 11.8 | 12.4 | 15.2 | All Other Current | | | | 21.1 | 13.3 | 16.7 |
| 34.4 | 37.0 | 38.4 | Total Current | | | | 47.1 | 35.1 | 36.9 |
| 9.9 | 9.7 | 6.0 | Long-Term Debt | | | | 5.7 | 6.0 | 4.1 |
| .3 | .4 | .4 | Deferred Taxes | | | | .2 | .2 | .9 |
| 7.2 | 7.2 | 14.4 | All Other Non-Current | | | | 1.7 | 5.2 | 11.1 |
| 48.2 | 45.7 | 40.8 | Net Worth | | | | 45.3 | 53.5 | 47.0 |
| 100.0 | 100.0 | 100.0 | Total Liabilties & Net Worth | | | | 100.0 | 100.0 | 100.0 |
| | | | **INCOME DATA** | | | | | | |
| 100.0 | 100.0 | 100.0 | Net Sales | | | | 100.0 | 100.0 | 100.0 |
| 35.9 | 37.7 | 35.0 | Gross Profit | | | | 33.4 | 33.7 | 34.1 |
| 30.9 | 30.1 | 26.7 | Operating Expenses | | | | 29.1 | 25.1 | 23.1 |
| 5.0 | 7.6 | 8.3 | Operating Profit | | | | 4.3 | 8.6 | 11.0 |
| 1.0 | .6 | .5 | All Other Expenses (net) | | | | .1 | .5 | 1.1 |
| 4.0 | 7.0 | 7.8 | Profit Before Taxes | | | | 4.3 | 8.1 | 9.8 |
| | | | **RATIOS** | | | | | | |
| 4.2 | 3.5 | 3.5 | | | | | 3.9 | 4.0 | 3.7 |
| 2.1 | 2.1 | 2.0 | Current | | | | 1.3 | 2.6 | 2.0 |
| 1.4 | 1.4 | 1.3 | | | | | 1.1 | 1.4 | 1.3 |
| 2.4 | 2.4 | 2.1 | | | | | 1.9 | 2.5 | 1.8 |
| 1.3 | 1.2 | 1.3 | Quick | | | | 1.0 | 1.7 | 1.3 |
| .7 | .7 | .8 | | | | | .7 | .9 | .7 |

| | | | | | | | | | | | | | | | | | |
|---|---|---|---|---|---|---|---|---|---|---|---|---|---|---|---|---|---|
| 37 | 10.0 | 35 | 10.6 | 38 | 9.5 | Sales/Receivables | | | | | 35 | 10.5 | 42 | 8.7 | 41 | 8.9 |
| 47 | 7.7 | 52 | 7.1 | 46 | 7.9 | | | | | | 43 | 8.5 | 49 | 7.4 | 47 | 7.8 |
| 59 | 6.1 | 64 | 5.7 | 61 | 6.0 | | | | | | 65 | 5.6 | 65 | 5.6 | 59 | 6.2 |
| 50 | 7.3 | 34 | 10.7 | 29 | 12.8 | Cost of Sales/Inventory | | | | | 28 | 13.0 | 27 | 13.5 | 49 | 7.5 |
| 95 | 3.8 | 80 | 4.6 | 66 | 5.5 | | | | | | 69 | 5.3 | 61 | 6.0 | 79 | 4.6 |
| 132 | 2.8 | 140 | 2.6 | 107 | 3.4 | | | | | | 122 | 3.0 | 104 | 3.5 | 104 | 3.5 |
| 13 | 29.1 | 22 | 16.8 | 13 | 27.2 | Cost of Sales/Payables | | | | | 14 | 27.0 | 10 | 36.0 | 13 | 28.8 |
| 23 | 15.9 | 30 | 12.2 | 26 | 13.9 | | | | | | 17 | 21.7 | 25 | 14.7 | 25 | 14.6 |
| 40 | 9.0 | 49 | 7.5 | 40 | 9.2 | | | | | | 49 | 7.4 | 36 | 10.1 | 35 | 10.3 |

| | | | | | | | | | |
|---|---|---|---|---|---|---|---|---|---|
| 3.7 | 3.2 | 3.7 | Sales/Working Capital | | | | 4.4 | 3.6 | 3.6 |
| 5.1 | 5.6 | 6.3 | | | | | 15.8 | 4.9 | 6.0 |
| 10.8 | 11.0 | 17.5 | | | | | 33.2 | 12.1 | 17.4 |

| | | | | | | | | | | | | |
|---|---|---|---|---|---|---|---|---|---|---|---|---|
| | 18.4 | | 40.5 | | 50.6 | EBIT/Interest | | | | 52.3 | 59.5 | 56.8 |
| (61) | 2.7 | (76) | 10.3 | (65) | 14.3 | | (11) | 18.4 | (20) | 14.1 | (24) | 14.2 |
| | .5 | | 1.9 | | 4.8 | | | 4.5 | | 6.6 | | 4.7 |

| | | | | | | |
|---|---|---|---|---|---|---|
| | 11.8 | | 6.7 | | 33.9 | Net Profit + Depr., Dep., |
| (17) | 4.5 | (19) | 4.5 | (19) | 6.5 | Amort./Cur. Mat. L/T/D |
| | .2 | | 1.6 | | 1.1 | |

| | | | | | | | | | |
|---|---|---|---|---|---|---|---|---|---|
| .1 | .1 | .1 | Fixed/Worth | | | | .2 | .1 | .2 |
| .4 | .3 | .3 | | | | | .3 | .2 | .4 |
| .9 | .6 | .8 | | | | | .7 | .6 | .8 |
| .4 | .4 | .4 | Debt/Worth | | | | .4 | .3 | .4 |
| 1.0 | 1.2 | 1.2 | | | | | 1.8 | .6 | 1.1 |
| 3.5 | 2.8 | 2.8 | | | | | 2.5 | 1.9 | 3.7 |

| | | | | | | | | | | | | |
|---|---|---|---|---|---|---|---|---|---|---|---|---|
| | 38.6 | | 49.4 | | 53.8 | % Profit Before Taxes/Tangible | | 48.7 | | 52.3 | | 73.9 |
| (64) | 13.7 | (83) | 22.8 | (68) | 29.4 | Net Worth | (12) | 24.3 | (20) | 28.3 | (24) | 36.2 |
| | -.3 | | 8.9 | | 16.6 | | | 7.3 | | 22.3 | | 22.1 |

| | | | | | | | | | |
|---|---|---|---|---|---|---|---|---|---|
| 16.1 | 22.7 | 25.3 | % Profit Before Taxes/Total | | | | 16.1 | 26.1 | 26.9 |
| 4.6 | 8.5 | 13.1 | Assets | | | | 10.5 | 15.3 | 13.8 |
| -.2 | 2.3 | 4.6 | | | | | 3.3 | 8.6 | 6.4 |
| 40.7 | 60.8 | 45.0 | Sales/Net Fixed Assets | | | | 62.9 | 52.9 | 29.6 |
| 16.2 | 17.5 | 18.6 | | | | | 22.8 | 24.4 | 11.8 |
| 7.2 | 9.1 | 8.2 | | | | | 6.8 | 11.6 | 7.7 |
| 2.8 | 2.7 | 3.0 | Sales/Total Assets | | | | 2.7 | 3.2 | 2.8 |
| 1.9 | 1.9 | 2.3 | | | | | 2.3 | 2.5 | 2.0 |
| 1.4 | 1.3 | 1.7 | | | | | 1.8 | 1.8 | 1.4 |

| | | | | | | | | | | | | |
|---|---|---|---|---|---|---|---|---|---|---|---|---|
| | .6 | | .8 | | .6 | % Depr., Dep., Amort./Sales | | 1.1 | | .5 | | .7 |
| (64) | 1.4 | (77) | 1.3 | (67) | 1.1 | | (12) | 1.2 | (21) | 1.0 | (24) | 2.0 |
| | 2.4 | | 2.6 | | 2.4 | | | 2.8 | | 2.1 | | 3.0 |

| | | | | | | | | | |
|---|---|---|---|---|---|---|---|---|---|
| 2.5 | 2.1 | 1.9 | % Officers', Directors' | | | | | 1.5 | |
| (24) 5.1 | (29) 3.4 | (26) 3.3 | Owners' Comp/Sales | | | | | (13) 2.8 | |
| 11.2 | 10.0 | 8.3 | | | | | | 10.4 | |

| | | | | | | | | | |
|---|---|---|---|---|---|---|---|---|---|
| 1609917M | 1993208M | 2322900M | Net Sales ($) | 1251M | 12118M | 26208M | 91811M | 357214M | 1834298M |
| 1056357M | 1279070M | 1365412M | Total Assets ($) | 477M | 3896M | 14553M | 42078M | 183254M | 1121154M |

M = $ thousand   MM = $ million
See Pages 9 through 22 for Explanation of Ratios and Data

## Current Data Sorted by Assets      Comparative Historical Data

Left columns (0-500M data column is marked vertically: **DATA NOT AVAILABLE**). Sub-period groupings: **8 (4/1-9/30/11)** and **24 (10/1/11-3/31/12)**.

| 0-500M | 500M-2MM | 2-10MM | 10-50MM | 50-100MM | 100-250MM | Type of Statement | 6 4/1/07-3/31/08 ALL | 3 4/1/08-3/31/09 ALL |
|---|---|---|---|---|---|---|---|---|
| | | | 4 | 2 | 1 | Unqualified | 3 | 3 |
| | | 2 | | | | Reviewed | 1 | 1 |
| | | 1 | | | | Compiled | 1 | 2 |
| | 2 | 4 | 4 | 1 | | Tax Returns | | |
| | 5 | 5 | 1 | | | Other | | |
| | 7 | 12 | 9 | 3 | 1 | **NUMBER OF STATEMENTS** | 11 | 9 |
| % | % | % | % | % | % | **ASSETS** | % | % |
| | | 4.1 | | | | Cash & Equivalents | 9.0 | |
| | | 25.1 | | | | Trade Receivables (net) | 27.7 | |
| | | 29.0 | | | | Inventory | 27.5 | |
| | | .2 | | | | All Other Current | 1.0 | |
| | | 58.4 | | | | Total Current | 65.1 | |
| | | 29.8 | | | | Fixed Assets (net) | 17.8 | |
| | | .9 | | | | Intangibles (net) | 13.8 | |
| | | 10.9 | | | | All Other Non-Current | 3.3 | |
| | | 100.0 | | | | Total | 100.0 | |
| | | | | | | **LIABILITIES** | | |
| | | 16.8 | | | | Notes Payable-Short Term | 14.7 | |
| | | 3.5 | | | | Cur. Mat.-L.T.D. | 1.5 | |
| | | 15.9 | | | | Trade Payables | 16.7 | |
| | | .6 | | | | Income Taxes Payable | .0 | |
| | | 4.7 | | | | All Other Current | 8.8 | |
| | | 41.5 | | | | Total Current | 41.7 | |
| | | 29.8 | | | | Long-Term Debt | 13.8 | |
| | | .0 | | | | Deferred Taxes | .3 | |
| | | 7.5 | | | | All Other Non-Current | 14.8 | |
| | | 21.2 | | | | Net Worth | 29.3 | |
| | | 100.0 | | | | Total Liabilities & Net Worth | 100.0 | |
| | | | | | | **INCOME DATA** | | |
| | | 100.0 | | | | Net Sales | 100.0 | |
| | | 38.8 | | | | Gross Profit | 28.7 | |
| | | 35.4 | | | | Operating Expenses | 22.6 | |
| | | 3.5 | | | | Operating Profit | 6.2 | |
| | | 1.6 | | | | All Other Expenses (net) | 1.6 | |
| | | 1.8 | | | | Profit Before Taxes | 4.6 | |
| | | | | | | **RATIOS** | | |
| | | 5.1 | | | | Current | 2.4 | |
| | | 1.6 | | | | | 1.4 | |
| | | 1.1 | | | | | 1.1 | |
| | | 2.3 | | | | Quick | 1.1 | |
| | | .8 | | | | | .7 | |
| | | .5 | | | | | .5 | |
| | | 31  11.7 | | | | Sales/Receivables | 39  9.4 | |
| | | 46  8.0 | | | | | 61  6.0 | |
| | | 55  6.6 | | | | | 64  5.7 | |
| | | 53  6.9 | | | | Cost of Sales/Inventory | 49  7.4 | |
| | | 85  4.3 | | | | | 76  4.8 | |
| | | 159  2.3 | | | | | 98  3.7 | |
| | | 17  21.5 | | | | Cost of Sales/Payables | 25  14.9 | |
| | | 32  11.4 | | | | | 41  8.8 | |
| | | 62  5.9 | | | | | 62  5.9 | |
| | | 3.6 | | | | Sales/Working Capital | 6.1 | |
| | | 11.8 | | | | | 11.1 | |
| | | 48.5 | | | | | 35.5 | |
| | | 3.5 | | | | EBIT/Interest | 11.0 | |
| | | 1.5 | | | | | (10) 1.4 | |
| | | -4.7 | | | | | -1.2 | |
| | | | | | | Net Profit + Depr., Dep., Amort./Cur. Mat. L/T/D | | |
| | | 1.3 | | | | Fixed/Worth | .0 | |
| | | 2.1 | | | | | 1.0 | |
| | | -9.6 | | | | | 1.2 | |
| | | 1.1 | | | | Debt/Worth | 1.3 | |
| | | 13.7 | | | | | 3.1 | |
| | | -39.8 | | | | | -3.7 | |
| | | | | | | % Profit Before Taxes/Tangible Net Worth | | |
| | | 9.7 | | | | % Profit Before Taxes/Total Assets | 10.9 | |
| | | 1.5 | | | | | 2.7 | |
| | | -6.2 | | | | | -5.0 | |
| | | 31.0 | | | | Sales/Net Fixed Assets | 95.5 | |
| | | 8.3 | | | | | 8.7 | |
| | | 2.8 | | | | | 5.4 | |
| | | 2.7 | | | | Sales/Total Assets | 2.1 | |
| | | 2.2 | | | | | 1.8 | |
| | | 1.1 | | | | | 1.5 | |
| | | .7 | | | | % Depr., Dep., Amort./Sales | | |
| | | (11) 1.8 | | | | | | |
| | | 2.7 | | | | | | |
| | | | | | | % Officers', Directors' Owners' Comp/Sales | | |
| | 18703M | 75319M | 467942M | 520385M | 304028M | Net Sales ($) | 607311M | 608683M |
| | 6580M | 38226M | 238401M | 217326M | 166839M | Total Assets ($) | 419035M | 260396M |

## Comparative Historical Data · Current Data Sorted by Sales

| | | | Type of Statement | 0-1MM | 1-3MM | 3-5MM | 5-10MM | 10-25MM | 25MM & OVER |
|---|---|---|---|---|---|---|---|---|---|
| 5 | 6 | 7 | Unqualified | | | | 1 | 1 | 5 |
| 3 | 5 | 3 | Reviewed | | | | 1 | 1 | 1 |
| 1 | 2 | 1 | Compiled | | | | 1 | | |
| 4 | 6 | 6 | Tax Returns | | | 4 | 2 | 1 | |
| 7 | 8 | 15 | Other | 2 | 3 | 2 | 3 | | 4 |
| 4/1/09-<br>3/31/10<br>ALL | 4/1/10-<br>3/31/11<br>ALL | 4/1/11-<br>3/31/12<br>ALL | | | | 8 (4/1-9/30/11) | | 24 (10/1/11-3/31/12) | |
| 20 | 27 | 32 | NUMBER OF STATEMENTS | 2 | 3 | 6 | 8 | 3 | 10 |
| % | % | % | **ASSETS** | % | % | % | % | % | % |
| 12.0 | 7.8 | 6.4 | Cash & Equivalents | | | | | | 8.7 |
| 26.1 | 27.5 | 28.6 | Trade Receivables (net) | | | | | | 29.3 |
| 27.2 | 27.4 | 30.3 | Inventory | | | | | | 30.0 |
| 4.1 | 1.3 | 1.4 | All Other Current | | | | | | 2.6 |
| 69.5 | 64.0 | 66.7 | Total Current | | | | | | 70.6 |
| 17.0 | 21.3 | 23.1 | Fixed Assets (net) | | | | | | 19.7 |
| 4.2 | 6.1 | 4.2 | Intangibles (net) | | | | | | 4.9 |
| 9.3 | 8.6 | 6.0 | All Other Non-Current | | | | | | 4.8 |
| 100.0 | 100.0 | 100.0 | Total | | | | | | 100.0 |
| | | | **LIABILITIES** | | | | | | |
| 10.3 | 6.9 | 11.5 | Notes Payable-Short Term | | | | | | 5.5 |
| 2.8 | 2.2 | 4.0 | Cur. Mat.-L.T.D. | | | | | | 2.7 |
| 17.2 | 15.3 | 18.7 | Trade Payables | | | | | | 16.5 |
| .2 | .1 | .3 | Income Taxes Payable | | | | | | .1 |
| 11.3 | 10.8 | 9.6 | All Other Current | | | | | | 10.0 |
| 41.8 | 35.3 | 44.0 | Total Current | | | | | | 34.8 |
| 16.5 | 16.2 | 20.7 | Long-Term Debt | | | | | | 18.8 |
| .4 | .5 | .5 | Deferred Taxes | | | | | | .7 |
| 15.2 | 7.0 | 3.9 | All Other Non-Current | | | | | | 3.4 |
| 26.1 | 41.1 | 31.0 | Net Worth | | | | | | 42.4 |
| 100.0 | 100.0 | 100.0 | Total Liabilities & Net Worth | | | | | | 100.0 |
| | | | **INCOME DATA** | | | | | | |
| 100.0 | 100.0 | 100.0 | Net Sales | | | | | | 100.0 |
| 35.9 | 35.1 | 34.8 | Gross Profit | | | | | | 22.4 |
| 30.0 | 27.4 | 30.5 | Operating Expenses | | | | | | 15.4 |
| 5.9 | 7.7 | 4.3 | Operating Profit | | | | | | 7.0 |
| 1.3 | 1.3 | .6 | All Other Expenses (net) | | | | | | .8 |
| 4.6 | 6.3 | 3.7 | Profit Before Taxes | | | | | | 6.3 |
| | | | **RATIOS** | | | | | | |
| 2.5 | 3.6 | 3.1 | | | | | | | 3.0 |
| 1.8 | 2.0 | 1.9 | Current | | | | | | 2.3 |
| 1.4 | 1.2 | 1.1 | | | | | | | 1.4 |
| 1.3 | 1.9 | 1.6 | | | | | | | 1.8 |
| .8 | 1.1 | .8 | Quick | | | | | | 1.0 |
| .5 | .6 | .5 | | | | | | | .7 |
| 26  14.1 | 28  13.0 | 34  10.8 | | | | | | | 41  9.0 |
| 50  7.4 | 50  7.3 | 46  7.9 | Sales/Receivables | | | | | | 50  7.3 |
| 56  6.5 | 62  5.9 | 59  6.2 | | | | | | | 61  6.0 |
| 36  10.1 | 44  8.3 | 53  6.9 | | | | | | | 54  6.7 |
| 62  5.9 | 91  4.0 | 78  4.7 | Cost of Sales/Inventory | | | | | | 69  5.3 |
| 117  3.1 | 114  3.2 | 111  3.3 | | | | | | | 91  4.0 |
| 26  13.9 | 24  15.3 | 30  12.2 | | | | | | | 27  13.5 |
| 47  7.8 | 39  9.5 | 38  9.6 | Cost of Sales/Payables | | | | | | 38  9.7 |
| 61  5.9 | 61  6.0 | 55  6.6 | | | | | | | 53  6.9 |
| 4.4 | 3.5 | 4.0 | | | | | | | 4.0 |
| 7.5 | 6.3 | 7.4 | Sales/Working Capital | | | | | | 6.4 |
| 15.8 | 28.1 | 48.5 | | | | | | | 12.6 |
| 14.9 | 15.8 | 11.6 | | | | | | | |
| (18)  3.4 | (24)  5.5 | (28)  4.4 | EBIT/Interest | | | | | | |
| 1.3 | 2.1 | .7 | | | | | | | |
| | | | Net Profit + Depr., Dep.,<br>Amort./Cur. Mat. L/T/D | | | | | | |
| .2 | .2 | .2 | | | | | | | .1 |
| 1.1 | .5 | 1.3 | Fixed/Worth | | | | | | .6 |
| 3.8 | 1.7 | 6.3 | | | | | | | 4.9 |
| .9 | .7 | .8 | | | | | | | .5 |
| 3.2 | 1.3 | 1.8 | Debt/Worth | | | | | | 2.1 |
| 18.1 | 9.0 | 23.1 | | | | | | | 13.4 |
| 61.1 | 52.0 | 60.8 | | | | | | | |
| (16)  24.2 | (23)  29.1 | (25)  36.7 | % Profit Before Taxes/Tangible<br>Net Worth | | | | | | |
| 6.1 | 10.3 | 6.5 | | | | | | | |
| 13.0 | 21.1 | 21.5 | | | | | | | 23.1 |
| 7.0 | 8.5 | 10.5 | % Profit Before Taxes/Total<br>Assets | | | | | | 11.0 |
| 1.8 | 3.4 | 1.4 | | | | | | | 3.7 |
| 76.4 | 45.4 | 36.7 | | | | | | | 33.4 |
| 12.3 | 14.9 | 16.0 | Sales/Net Fixed Assets | | | | | | 11.2 |
| 5.5 | 6.2 | 4.5 | | | | | | | 6.9 |
| 2.7 | 2.6 | 2.7 | | | | | | | 2.6 |
| 2.1 | 2.2 | 2.2 | Sales/Total Assets | | | | | | 1.9 |
| 1.4 | 1.4 | 1.5 | | | | | | | 1.7 |
| .9 | .8 | .7 | | | | | | | |
| (15)  2.2 | (21)  1.8 | (25)  1.8 | % Depr., Dep., Amort./Sales | | | | | | |
| 3.1 | 3.4 | 3.1 | | | | | | | |
| | 2.7 | 2.8 | | | | | | | |
| | (10)  3.8 | (13)  3.3 | % Officers', Directors'<br>Owners' Comp/Sales | | | | | | |
| | 5.9 | 7.0 | | | | | | | |
| 829271M | 1080586M | 1386377M | Net Sales ($) | 1567M | 6623M | 24116M | 52142M | 57672M | 1244257M |
| 446119M | 495412M | 667372M | Total Assets ($) | 3187M | 2576M | 10928M | 35398M | 27138M | 588145M |

© RMA 2012

**M = $ thousand   MM = $ million**
See Pages 9 through 22 for Explanation of Ratios and Data

## Current Data Sorted by Assets          Comparative Historical Data

| | 0-500M | 500M-2MM | 2-10MM | 10-50MM | 50-100MM | 100-250MM | Type of Statement | 4/1/07-3/31/08 ALL | 4/1/08-3/31/09 ALL |
|---|---|---|---|---|---|---|---|---|---|
| | | 1 | 1 | 5 | 5 | 3 | Unqualified | 14 | 15 |
| | | 1 | 7 | 2 | | | Reviewed | 10 | 10 |
| | | 1 | 6 | 1 | | | Compiled | 7 | 8 |
| | | 5 | 3 | | | | Tax Returns | 2 | 1 |
| | | 4 | 7 | 8 | | 3 | Other | 21 | 21 |
| | | 10 (4/1-9/30/11) | | 52 (10/1/11-3/31/12) | | | | | |
| | 11 | 11 | 24 | 16 | 5 | 6 | NUMBER OF STATEMENTS | 54 | 55 |
| | % | % | % | % | % | % | **ASSETS** | % | % |
| | | 5.4 | 7.6 | 11.6 | | | Cash & Equivalents | 7.8 | 10.7 |
| | | 35.9 | 31.6 | 24.8 | | | Trade Receivables (net) | 30.9 | 27.6 |
| | | 30.1 | 39.4 | 26.0 | | | Inventory | 33.0 | 31.3 |
| | | .1 | 1.7 | .9 | | | All Other Current | 2.2 | 2.5 |
| | | 71.5 | 80.3 | 63.2 | | | Total Current | 74.0 | 72.1 |
| | | 16.9 | 15.8 | 27.6 | | | Fixed Assets (net) | 16.8 | 16.1 |
| | | 5.1 | 1.4 | 5.7 | | | Intangibles (net) | 4.7 | 5.3 |
| | | 6.5 | 2.5 | 3.5 | | | All Other Non-Current | 4.4 | 6.5 |
| | | 100.0 | 100.0 | 100.0 | | | Total | 100.0 | 100.0 |
| | | | | | | | **LIABILITIES** | | |
| | | 9.0 | 12.7 | 11.7 | | | Notes Payable-Short Term | 11.8 | 9.1 |
| | | 1.3 | 2.6 | 3.0 | | | Cur. Mat.-L.T.D. | 2.1 | 1.9 |
| | | 14.4 | 14.2 | 11.6 | | | Trade Payables | 17.7 | 15.0 |
| | | .0 | .3 | .1 | | | Income Taxes Payable | .3 | .1 |
| | | 14.3 | 12.2 | 8.8 | | | All Other Current | 7.6 | 9.3 |
| | | 38.9 | 41.9 | 35.2 | | | Total Current | 39.6 | 35.4 |
| | | 13.9 | 8.0 | 6.0 | | | Long-Term Debt | 10.5 | 11.3 |
| | | .1 | .5 | 1.8 | | | Deferred Taxes | .4 | .2 |
| | | 2.4 | 3.4 | 3.3 | | | All Other Non-Current | 4.8 | 3.2 |
| | | 44.7 | 46.2 | 53.7 | | | Net Worth | 44.8 | 49.9 |
| | | 100.0 | 100.0 | 100.0 | | | Total Liabilties & Net Worth | 100.0 | 100.0 |
| | | | | | | | **INCOME DATA** | | |
| | | 100.0 | 100.0 | 100.0 | | | Net Sales | 100.0 | 100.0 |
| | | 34.1 | 29.9 | 31.0 | | | Gross Profit | 27.6 | 29.8 |
| | | 30.9 | 23.1 | 23.1 | | | Operating Expenses | 21.9 | 23.8 |
| | | 3.2 | 6.8 | 7.9 | | | Operating Profit | 5.7 | 6.0 |
| | | -.1 | .5 | 2.5 | | | All Other Expenses (net) | .9 | .4 |
| | | 3.3 | 6.3 | 5.4 | | | Profit Before Taxes | 4.8 | 5.5 |
| | | | | | | | **RATIOS** | | |
| | | 2.9 | 3.2 | 3.8 | | | | 2.7 | 3.3 |
| | | 1.8 | 1.9 | 1.8 | | | Current | 2.0 | 2.2 |
| | | 1.2 | 1.4 | 1.1 | | | | 1.4 | 1.5 |
| | | 2.0 | 1.7 | 2.1 | | | | 1.6 | 1.7 |
| | | 1.1 | .8 | .9 | | | Quick | 1.1 | 1.1 |
| | | .6 | .5 | .6 | | | | .6 | .7 |
| | 38 | 9.5 | 39 9.3 | 41 8.8 | | | | 40 9.1 | 28 13.1 |
| | 43 | 8.4 | 47 7.8 | 47 7.7 | | | Sales/Receivables | 48 7.6 | 40 9.1 |
| | 51 | 7.2 | 52 7.0 | 56 6.5 | | | | 58 6.3 | 49 7.5 |
| | 28 | 13.0 | 65 5.6 | 52 7.0 | | | | 51 7.1 | 43 8.5 |
| | 69 | 5.3 | 81 4.5 | 73 5.0 | | | Cost of Sales/Inventory | 71 5.1 | 66 5.5 |
| | 89 | 4.1 | 111 3.3 | 101 3.6 | | | | 106 3.5 | 105 3.5 |
| | 10 | 36.4 | 18 19.9 | 16 23.4 | | | | 24 15.4 | 17 22.0 |
| | 34 | 10.7 | 28 12.9 | 26 14.2 | | | Cost of Sales/Payables | 32 11.6 | 29 12.7 |
| | 51 | 7.2 | 43 8.4 | 42 8.6 | | | | 44 8.4 | 42 8.6 |
| | | 4.3 | 4.0 | 3.8 | | | | 4.6 | 4.5 |
| | | 7.5 | 7.4 | 7.2 | | | Sales/Working Capital | 7.4 | 7.2 |
| | | 35.7 | 10.8 | 32.8 | | | | 12.5 | 14.8 |
| | | 19.5 | 67.5 | 132.3 | | | | 21.3 | 36.6 |
| | | 5.9 | (22) 10.1 | (12) 19.3 | | | EBIT/Interest | (49) 4.5 | (47) 7.2 |
| | | 1.1 | 2.9 | 8.9 | | | | 1.8 | 1.8 |
| | | | 10.7 | | | | | 8.3 | 8.5 |
| | | | (10) 4.9 | | | | Net Profit + Depr., Dep., Amort./Cur. Mat. L/T/D | (20) 3.6 | (19) 3.4 |
| | | | 1.7 | | | | | 2.2 | 1.3 |
| | | .1 | .1 | .2 | | | | .2 | .1 |
| | | .5 | .3 | .5 | | | Fixed/Worth | .3 | .3 |
| | | 2.3 | .8 | 1.2 | | | | .9 | .8 |
| | | .7 | .6 | .4 | | | | .6 | .5 |
| | | 1.4 | 1.2 | 1.2 | | | Debt/Worth | 1.5 | 1.2 |
| | | 10.8 | 3.3 | 2.4 | | | | 3.9 | 2.4 |
| | | 76.5 | 49.6 | 53.8 | | | | 47.1 | 54.4 |
| | | (10) 6.9 | 27.7 | 36.1 | | | % Profit Before Taxes/Tangible Net Worth | (49) 22.3 | (52) 21.6 |
| | | -4.2 | 11.1 | 7.6 | | | | 7.1 | 6.4 |
| | | 13.5 | 19.5 | 25.4 | | | | 22.6 | 27.6 |
| | | 6.8 | 14.1 | 16.3 | | | % Profit Before Taxes/Total Assets | 9.3 | 11.9 |
| | | .1 | 4.3 | 4.7 | | | | 2.8 | 2.8 |
| | | 45.1 | 60.7 | 20.7 | | | | 40.3 | 57.8 |
| | | 15.6 | 20.0 | 10.2 | | | Sales/Net Fixed Assets | 13.4 | 16.0 |
| | | 9.4 | 10.7 | 4.1 | | | | 9.0 | 8.7 |
| | | 3.5 | 2.9 | 2.3 | | | | 3.0 | 3.5 |
| | | 3.0 | 2.4 | 1.9 | | | Sales/Total Assets | 2.3 | 2.5 |
| | | 2.2 | 2.0 | 1.5 | | | | 1.7 | 1.9 |
| | | .4 | .4 | 1.0 | | | | .7 | .7 |
| | | .8 | (21) 1.9 | (15) 1.3 | | | % Depr., Dep., Amort./Sales | (45) 1.6 | (47) 1.0 |
| | | 2.7 | 2.3 | 2.4 | | | | 2.1 | 2.3 |
| | | | 1.8 | | | | | 1.8 | 2.8 |
| | | | (12) 3.2 | | | | % Officers', Directors' Owners' Comp/Sales | (20) 3.4 | (15) 4.2 |
| | | | 4.1 | | | | | 5.5 | 8.0 |
| | | 35997M | 371318M | 920941M | 671768M | 2022958M | Net Sales ($) | 3826778M | 4308514M |
| | | 13334M | 134935M | 458169M | 358405M | 1035393M | Total Assets ($) | 2011654M | 1940061M |

*(Note: the 0-500M column is marked "DATA NOT AVAILABLE")*

## Comparative Historical Data | Current Data Sorted by Sales

| | | | Type of Statement | 0-1MM | 1-3MM | 3-5MM | 5-10MM | 10-25MM | 25MM & OVER |
|---|---|---|---|---|---|---|---|---|---|
| 15 | 13 | 14 | Unqualified | | | | | 3 | 11 |
| 11 | 16 | 10 | Reviewed | | 1 | | 3 | 4 | 2 |
| 11 | 14 | 8 | Compiled | | 1 | | 3 | 3 | 1 |
| 4 | 8 | 8 | Tax Returns | | 1 | 3 | 3 | 1 | |
| 22 | 21 | 22 | Other | | 2 | 3 | | 6 | 11 |
| 4/1/09-3/31/10 ALL | 4/1/10-3/31/11 ALL | 4/1/11-3/31/12 ALL | | | 10 (4/1-9/30/11) | | | 52 (10/1/11-3/31/12) | |
| 63 | 72 | 62 | **NUMBER OF STATEMENTS** | | 5 | 6 | 9 | 17 | 25 |
| % | % | % | **ASSETS** | % | % | % | % | % | % |
| 10.6 | 12.3 | 8.6 | Cash & Equivalents | | | | | 4.4 | 11.5 |
| 23.9 | 27.2 | 29.2 | Trade Receivables (net) | | | | | 27.8 | 27.8 |
| 29.3 | 30.5 | 32.1 | Inventory | | | | | 37.1 | 27.6 |
| 2.1 | 2.4 | 1.2 | All Other Current | | | | | 1.2 | 1.4 |
| 65.9 | 72.5 | 71.1 | Total Current | | | | | 70.5 | 68.4 |
| 20.2 | 17.2 | 19.8 | Fixed Assets (net) | | | | | 23.8 | 18.5 |
| 6.5 | 5.3 | 4.8 | Intangibles (net) | | | | | 1.9 | 8.4 |
| 7.4 | 5.0 | 4.3 | All Other Non-Current | | | | | 3.8 | 4.7 |
| 100.0 | 100.0 | 100.0 | Total | | | | | 100.0 | 100.0 |
| | | | **LIABILITIES** | | | | | | |
| 7.4 | 10.0 | 10.2 | Notes Payable-Short Term | | | | | 14.0 | 8.2 |
| 3.6 | 2.5 | 2.9 | Cur. Mat.-L.T.D. | | | | | 4.0 | 3.0 |
| 12.1 | 16.5 | 13.5 | Trade Payables | | | | | 13.8 | 13.4 |
| .1 | .2 | .2 | Income Taxes Payable | | | | | .1 | .2 |
| 8.9 | 11.2 | 11.2 | All Other Current | | | | | 9.9 | 12.6 |
| 32.2 | 40.5 | 38.0 | Total Current | | | | | 41.8 | 37.5 |
| 10.3 | 10.8 | 9.7 | Long-Term Debt | | | | | 9.2 | 8.1 |
| 1.0 | .5 | .8 | Deferred Taxes | | | | | .5 | 1.4 |
| 6.2 | 4.6 | 4.0 | All Other Non-Current | | | | | 4.6 | 4.3 |
| 50.2 | 43.6 | 47.6 | Net Worth | | | | | 44.0 | 48.8 |
| 100.0 | 100.0 | 100.0 | Total Liabilities & Net Worth | | | | | 100.0 | 100.0 |
| | | | **INCOME DATA** | | | | | | |
| 100.0 | 100.0 | 100.0 | Net Sales | | | | | 100.0 | 100.0 |
| 30.4 | 32.9 | 30.3 | Gross Profit | | | | | 32.6 | 25.1 |
| 25.1 | 25.9 | 24.4 | Operating Expenses | | | | | 26.1 | 18.6 |
| 5.4 | 7.0 | 5.9 | Operating Profit | | | | | 6.5 | 6.4 |
| 1.0 | 1.0 | 1.2 | All Other Expenses (net) | | | | | .3 | 1.3 |
| 4.4 | 5.9 | 4.7 | Profit Before Taxes | | | | | 6.2 | 5.2 |
| | | | **RATIOS** | | | | | | |
| 3.7 | 3.4 | 3.0 | | | | | | 2.9 | 2.9 |
| 2.2 | 2.0 | 1.9 | Current | | | | | 1.6 | 1.9 |
| 1.3 | 1.3 | 1.3 | | | | | | 1.2 | 1.3 |
| 2.2 | 2.0 | 1.7 | | | | | | 1.2 | 1.9 |
| 1.2 | 1.0 | 1.0 | Quick | | | | | .7 | 1.0 |
| .6 | .5 | .6 | | | | | | .5 | .7 |
| 33   11.1 | 37   9.9 | 40   9.1 | | | | | | 42   8.6 | 38   9.5 |
| 46   7.9 | 45   8.1 | 46   7.9 | Sales/Receivables | | | | | 49   7.5 | 46   7.9 |
| 52   7.0 | 52   7.0 | 53   6.9 | | | | | | 57   6.4 | 52   7.0 |
| 53   6.9 | 49   7.4 | 54   6.8 | | | | | | 68   5.4 | 45   8.2 |
| 84   4.3 | 85   4.3 | 73   5.0 | Cost of Sales/Inventory | | | | | 87   4.2 | 69   5.3 |
| 118   3.1 | 114   3.2 | 101   3.6 | | | | | | 126   2.9 | 94   3.9 |
| 17   21.0 | 23   16.1 | 18   20.1 | | | | | | 20   18.4 | 16   22.3 |
| 28   13.2 | 33   11.0 | 30   12.1 | Cost of Sales/Payables | | | | | 32   11.4 | 25   14.4 |
| 43   8.4 | 47   7.7 | 45   8.1 | | | | | | 45   8.1 | 43   8.5 |
| 3.6 | 3.8 | 4.1 | | | | | | 4.3 | 4.2 |
| 6.2 | 7.1 | 6.9 | Sales/Working Capital | | | | | 8.2 | 6.5 |
| 13.0 | 13.2 | 16.8 | | | | | | 18.9 | 17.9 |
| 16.9 | 17.1 | 36.3 | | | | | | 21.5 | 86.5 |
| (54) 4.4 | (59) 6.8 | (56) 8.2 | EBIT/Interest | | | | | (16) 9.0 | (22) 10.2 |
| .4 | 2.7 | 2.6 | | | | | | 3.2 | 2.2 |
| 8.0 | 4.9 | 9.0 | Net Profit + Depr., Dep., | | | | | | |
| (19) 2.9 | (19) 3.3 | (18) 2.5 | Amort./Cur. Mat. L/T/D | | | | | | |
| .2 | 2.1 | 1.6 | | | | | | | |
| .2 | .1 | .1 | | | | | | .2 | .2 |
| .5 | .4 | .4 | Fixed/Worth | | | | | .4 | .4 |
| .9 | 1.4 | 1.1 | | | | | | .9 | 1.1 |
| .5 | .5 | .6 | | | | | | .7 | .4 |
| 1.1 | 1.4 | 1.2 | Debt/Worth | | | | | 1.4 | 1.1 |
| 3.3 | 6.1 | 3.5 | | | | | | 3.3 | 4.7 |
| 39.9 | 45.0 | 46.0 | % Profit Before Taxes/Tangible | | | | | 39.8 | 51.1 |
| (57) 14.8 | (65) 28.2 | (58) 27.7 | Net Worth | | | | | 27.8 | (22) 30.2 |
| -1.4 | 12.2 | 6.7 | | | | | | 8.6 | 10.3 |
| 18.7 | 20.6 | 18.5 | % Profit Before Taxes/Total | | | | | 18.0 | 21.9 |
| 5.9 | 11.6 | 11.1 | Assets | | | | | 14.0 | 10.4 |
| -.2 | 4.3 | 2.7 | | | | | | 2.3 | 3.3 |
| 34.6 | 46.5 | 34.0 | | | | | | 24.8 | 20.8 |
| 12.0 | 16.1 | 14.0 | Sales/Net Fixed Assets | | | | | 11.2 | 12.9 |
| 5.1 | 7.4 | 6.7 | | | | | | 4.8 | 7.7 |
| 2.4 | 2.7 | 2.8 | | | | | | 2.6 | 2.6 |
| 2.0 | 2.2 | 2.2 | Sales/Total Assets | | | | | 2.0 | 2.1 |
| 1.4 | 1.6 | 1.8 | | | | | | 1.5 | 1.7 |
| .9 | .7 | .6 | | | | | | 1.3 | 1.0 |
| (52) 2.1 | (56) 1.4 | (56) 1.5 | % Depr., Dep., Amort./Sales | | | | | (16) 2.2 | (21) 1.5 |
| 3.4 | 2.6 | 2.7 | | | | | | 2.5 | 2.7 |
| 2.7 | 2.9 | 1.8 | % Officers', Directors' | | | | | | |
| (19) 4.4 | (22) 6.4 | (20) 3.2 | Owners' Comp/Sales | | | | | | |
| 7.0 | 9.8 | 5.7 | | | | | | | |
| 4269545M | 3614802M | 4022982M | Net Sales ($) | | 10526M | 22988M | 64343M | 270613M | 3654512M |
| 2479891M | 1883250M | 2000236M | Total Assets ($) | | 5270M | 51816M | 25254M | 137941M | 1779955M |

M = $ thousand     MM = $ million
See Pages 9 through 22 for Explanation of Ratios and Data

## Current Data Sorted by Assets | Comparative Historical Data

| Type of Statement | 0-500M | 500M-2MM | 2-10MM | 10-50MM | 50-100MM | 100-250MM | 4/1/07-3/31/08 ALL | 4/1/08-3/31/09 ALL |
|---|---|---|---|---|---|---|---|---|
| Unqualified | | 1 | 5 | 20 | 10 | 11 | 35 | 35 |
| Reviewed | | 5 | 33 | 17 | | 1 | 43 | 31 |
| Compiled | | 8 | 26 | 3 | | | 28 | 21 |
| Tax Returns | 11 | 15 | 12 | 2 | | | 26 | 33 |
| Other | 6 | 21 | 41 | 24 | 7 | 4 | 94 | 108 |
| | 51 (4/1-9/30/11) | | | 232 (10/1/11-3/31/12) | | | | |
| NUMBER OF STATEMENTS | 17 | 50 | 117 | 66 | 17 | 16 | 226 | 228 |

| | 0-500M % | 500M-2MM % | 2-10MM % | 10-50MM % | 50-100MM % | 100-250MM % | Item | 4/1/07-3/31/08 ALL % | 4/1/08-3/31/09 ALL % |
|---|---|---|---|---|---|---|---|---|---|
| | | | | | | | **ASSETS** | | |
| | 10.8 | 7.4 | 10.2 | 11.4 | 13.0 | 11.5 | Cash & Equivalents | 9.4 | 8.7 |
| | 31.8 | 35.1 | 28.9 | 27.4 | 20.5 | 23.7 | Trade Receivables (net) | 30.7 | 30.2 |
| | 33.7 | 30.6 | 30.0 | 30.4 | 20.1 | 23.1 | Inventory | 28.5 | 31.5 |
| | 4.2 | 2.7 | 1.8 | 2.9 | 2.8 | 3.0 | All Other Current | 3.3 | 3.0 |
| | 80.6 | 75.8 | 71.0 | 72.1 | 56.3 | 61.3 | Total Current | 71.9 | 73.4 |
| | 6.9 | 16.6 | 17.9 | 17.6 | 10.2 | 18.3 | Fixed Assets (net) | 15.7 | 15.5 |
| | 4.4 | 1.6 | 6.1 | 6.2 | 29.0 | 14.6 | Intangibles (net) | 7.1 | 6.1 |
| | 8.1 | 6.0 | 5.0 | 4.1 | 4.5 | 5.8 | All Other Non-Current | 5.3 | 5.0 |
| | 100.0 | 100.0 | 100.0 | 100.0 | 100.0 | 100.0 | Total | 100.0 | 100.0 |
| | | | | | | | **LIABILITIES** | | |
| | 18.0 | 10.6 | 10.6 | 8.3 | 6.1 | 3.6 | Notes Payable-Short Term | 11.2 | 12.7 |
| | 1.8 | 3.8 | 2.3 | 3.1 | 1.1 | 2.1 | Cur. Mat.-L.T.D. | 2.6 | 2.4 |
| | 26.1 | 17.6 | 15.9 | 12.7 | 9.1 | 19.2 | Trade Payables | 15.1 | 15.8 |
| | .0 | .0 | .1 | .4 | .1 | 1.0 | Income Taxes Payable | .5 | .3 |
| | 3.7 | 11.8 | 13.8 | 12.9 | 10.9 | 11.9 | All Other Current | 11.4 | 11.1 |
| | 49.6 | 43.8 | 42.7 | 37.4 | 27.4 | 37.8 | Total Current | 40.8 | 42.2 |
| | 15.0 | 11.4 | 10.6 | 7.3 | 14.0 | 11.3 | Long-Term Debt | 12.3 | 11.9 |
| | .0 | .0 | .3 | .6 | 2.8 | 2.0 | Deferred Taxes | .4 | .4 |
| | 18.8 | 8.5 | 5.5 | 12.4 | 11.2 | 12.0 | All Other Non-Current | 6.9 | 7.0 |
| | 16.6 | 36.2 | 41.0 | 42.3 | 44.7 | 36.8 | Net Worth | 39.5 | 38.5 |
| | 100.0 | 100.0 | 100.0 | 100.0 | 100.0 | 100.0 | Total Liabilties & Net Worth | 100.0 | 100.0 |
| | | | | | | | **INCOME DATA** | | |
| | 100.0 | 100.0 | 100.0 | 100.0 | 100.0 | 100.0 | Net Sales | 100.0 | 100.0 |
| | 51.0 | 37.0 | 38.5 | 31.8 | 33.6 | 30.4 | Gross Profit | 36.0 | 33.7 |
| | 43.7 | 31.8 | 30.9 | 23.3 | 24.9 | 22.6 | Operating Expenses | 28.7 | 28.1 |
| | 7.3 | 5.2 | 7.6 | 8.6 | 8.7 | 7.8 | Operating Profit | 7.3 | 5.6 |
| | .4 | .7 | .8 | .8 | 1.4 | 2.0 | All Other Expenses (net) | 1.6 | 1.3 |
| | 6.9 | 4.5 | 6.8 | 7.8 | 7.3 | 5.8 | Profit Before Taxes | 5.7 | 4.3 |
| | | | | | | | **RATIOS** | | |
| | 3.9 | 3.3 | 3.0 | 3.5 | 3.0 | 2.8 | Current | 3.2 | 3.0 |
| | 2.1 | 1.8 | 1.6 | 1.8 | 2.5 | 1.8 | | 2.0 | 1.8 |
| | 1.2 | 1.3 | 1.3 | 1.4 | 1.6 | 1.2 | | 1.3 | 1.2 |
| | 2.5 | 1.8 | 1.6 | 1.7 | 1.7 | 1.8 | Quick | 1.9 | 1.7 |
| | 1.0 | 1.0 | 1.0 | 1.0 | 1.5 | 1.0 | | 1.1 | .9 |
| | .5 | .6 | .6 | .7 | .7 | .6 | | .6 | .6 |
| | 14 26.1 | 26 13.9 | 35 10.3 | 40 9.2 | 46 7.9 | 46 7.9 | Sales/Receivables | 34 10.6 | 33 11.1 |
| | 33 11.2 | 43 8.5 | 47 7.7 | 51 7.2 | 51 7.1 | 60 6.1 | | 48 7.6 | 44 8.4 |
| | 54 6.8 | 60 6.1 | 62 5.9 | 62 5.9 | 65 5.6 | 68 5.4 | | 62 5.9 | 56 6.5 |
| | 16 23.3 | 23 16.2 | 41 9.0 | 56 6.5 | 63 5.8 | 60 6.1 | Cost of Sales/Inventory | 43 8.5 | 48 7.6 |
| | 59 6.2 | 60 6.1 | 79 4.6 | 96 3.8 | 81 4.5 | 68 5.4 | | 75 4.9 | 76 4.8 |
| | 122 3.0 | 126 2.9 | 146 2.5 | 130 2.8 | 122 3.0 | 107 3.4 | | 123 3.0 | 113 3.2 |
| | 28 13.1 | 14 26.2 | 24 15.3 | 17 21.9 | 29 12.8 | 29 12.8 | Cost of Sales/Payables | 18 20.1 | 18 19.7 |
| | 39 9.3 | 29 12.7 | 37 9.8 | 29 12.7 | 33 10.9 | 64 5.7 | | 32 11.3 | 32 11.4 |
| | 99 3.7 | 53 6.9 | 55 6.6 | 44 8.3 | 47 7.8 | 79 4.6 | | 51 7.2 | 52 7.1 |
| | 5.4 | 4.2 | 3.9 | 3.4 | 3.1 | 3.2 | Sales/Working Capital | 3.9 | 4.8 |
| | 13.9 | 8.8 | 7.2 | 5.8 | 4.5 | 6.3 | | 6.5 | 7.3 |
| | 19.6 | 20.0 | 20.9 | 11.3 | 6.3 | 18.9 | | 15.0 | 18.3 |
| | 21.0 | 28.9 | 24.2 | 46.2 | 29.7 | 58.4 | EBIT/Interest | 14.7 | 22.5 |
| | (13) 6.5 | (45) 6.1 | (102) 8.7 | (58) 12.6 | (12) 5.6 | 16.0 | | (205) 5.1 | (203) 5.6 |
| | 2.1 | 2.2 | 4.2 | 3.0 | 2.2 | 1.1 | | 1.7 | 1.3 |
| | | | 8.5 | 10.7 | | | Net Profit + Depr., Dep., Amort./Cur. Mat. L/T/D | 9.1 | 17.5 |
| | | (24) 2.5 | (23) 5.5 | | | | | (51) 3.7 | (55) 3.5 |
| | | 1.0 | 1.4 | | | | | 1.3 | 1.2 |
| | .0 | .1 | .1 | .2 | .2 | .4 | Fixed/Worth | .1 | .1 |
| | .1 | .4 | .3 | .4 | .6 | .9 | | .4 | .4 |
| | .8 | 1.1 | 1.4 | .8 | -.4 | -5.3 | | 1.2 | 1.2 |
| | .5 | .6 | .6 | .5 | .9 | .7 | Debt/Worth | .6 | .8 |
| | 3.0 | 1.5 | 1.7 | 1.2 | 3.3 | 2.3 | | 1.7 | 1.6 |
| | -24.0 | 5.8 | 5.0 | 2.7 | -6.3 | -30.2 | | 5.5 | 5.3 |
| | 146.1 | 53.3 | 57.1 | 52.9 | 52.8 | 39.1 | % Profit Before Taxes/Tangible Net Worth | 58.9 | 59.1 |
| | (12) 47.4 | (44) 25.8 | (105) 35.8 | (61) 33.5 | (12) 35.3 | (11) 28.1 | | (196) 29.2 | (200) 25.6 |
| | 14.4 | 5.5 | 17.1 | 9.1 | 14.9 | 3.5 | | 10.4 | 7.5 |
| | 30.4 | 19.4 | 20.2 | 23.0 | 16.3 | 14.8 | % Profit Before Taxes/Total Assets | 19.7 | 19.1 |
| | 14.3 | 10.5 | 11.3 | 11.0 | 7.1 | 9.3 | | 9.8 | 8.9 |
| | 5.0 | 2.2 | 5.3 | 3.5 | 4.5 | .3 | | 2.8 | .9 |
| | UND | 91.8 | 40.6 | 35.7 | 26.3 | 16.4 | Sales/Net Fixed Assets | 54.8 | 59.2 |
| | 54.6 | 35.7 | 16.7 | 10.5 | 13.5 | 9.2 | | 18.3 | 19.9 |
| | 28.0 | 12.9 | 8.1 | 5.8 | 9.4 | 5.5 | | 8.1 | 8.8 |
| | 5.0 | 4.0 | 2.7 | 2.4 | 1.7 | 1.9 | Sales/Total Assets | 3.0 | 3.1 |
| | 3.7 | 2.9 | 2.1 | 1.7 | 1.3 | 1.5 | | 2.2 | 2.3 |
| | 2.5 | 1.9 | 1.5 | 1.3 | .7 | 1.2 | | 1.4 | 1.6 |
| | | .4 | .7 | .8 | .8 | 1.5 | % Depr., Dep., Amort./Sales | .7 | .6 |
| | (36) | 1.0 | (89) 1.3 | (61) 1.9 | (12) 1.7 | (11) 2.1 | | (175) 1.5 | (185) 1.6 |
| | | 2.9 | 2.8 | 3.0 | 3.0 | 3.4 | | 2.3 | 2.6 |
| | 5.7 | 3.9 | 2.0 | .8 | | | % Officers', Directors' Owners' Comp/Sales | 2.0 | 2.0 |
| | (10) 10.0 | (27) 5.6 | (43) 3.6 | (13) 2.5 | | | | (74) 4.6 | (69) 3.9 |
| | 14.1 | 7.4 | 5.6 | 4.9 | | | | 8.3 | 5.6 |
| | 19473M | 190670M | 1263064M | 2490862M | 1684478M | 3938707M | Net Sales ($) | 6995107M | 7779040M |
| | 5298M | 63667M | 571326M | 1368401M | 1309432M | 2562486M | Total Assets ($) | 4344424M | 4224101M |

© RMA 2012

M = $ thousand    MM = $ million
See Pages 9 through 22 for Explanation of Ratios and Data

**Comparative Historical Data** | | | | **Current Data Sorted by Sales** | | | | |

| | | | Type of Statement | | | | | | |
|---|---|---|---|---|---|---|---|---|---|
| 46 | 29 | 47 | Unqualified | | 1 | | 4 | 9 | 33 |
| 38 | 47 | 56 | Reviewed | | 2 | 1 | 18 | 21 | 14 |
| 28 | 32 | 37 | Compiled | | 6 | 10 | 8 | 11 | 2 |
| 33 | 33 | 40 | Tax Returns | 7 | 13 | 6 | 9 | 4 | 1 |
| 101 | 122 | 103 | Other | 5 | 14 | 11 | 17 | 27 | 29 |
| 4/1/09-3/31/10 | 4/1/10-3/31/11 | 4/1/11-3/31/12 | | | 51 (4/1-9/30/11) | | 232 (10/1/11-3/31/12) | | |
| ALL | ALL | ALL | | 0-1MM | 1-3MM | 3-5MM | 5-10MM | 10-25MM | 25MM & OVER |
| 246 | 263 | 283 | **NUMBER OF STATEMENTS** | 12 | 36 | 28 | 56 | 72 | 79 |
| % | % | % | **ASSETS** | % | % | % | % | % | % |
| 10.5 | 11.5 | 10.3 | Cash & Equivalents | 5.5 | 10.9 | 10.0 | 9.9 | 11.6 | 9.9 |
| 26.5 | 29.5 | 29.0 | Trade Receivables (net) | 27.0 | 29.5 | 29.0 | 29.7 | 28.2 | 29.5 |
| 29.4 | 28.3 | 29.4 | Inventory | 26.3 | 34.0 | 30.0 | 29.5 | 27.9 | 29.0 |
| 3.6 | 3.3 | 2.5 | All Other Current | 5.7 | .5 | 4.7 | 1.6 | 2.4 | 2.9 |
| 70.0 | 72.6 | 71.3 | Total Current | 64.6 | 74.9 | 73.7 | 70.7 | 70.0 | 71.3 |
| 17.3 | 14.1 | 16.5 | Fixed Assets (net) | 20.5 | 17.0 | 13.2 | 20.9 | 15.6 | 14.6 |
| 7.6 | 6.9 | 7.1 | Intangibles (net) | 7.7 | 2.0 | 7.5 | 3.1 | 9.6 | 9.7 |
| 5.2 | 6.4 | 5.2 | All Other Non-Current | 7.3 | 6.1 | 5.6 | 5.3 | 4.8 | 4.5 |
| 100.0 | 100.0 | 100.0 | Total | 100.0 | 100.0 | 100.0 | 100.0 | 100.0 | 100.0 |
| | | | **LIABILITIES** | | | | | | |
| 10.9 | 9.6 | 9.9 | Notes Payable-Short Term | 17.1 | 11.6 | 13.6 | 8.4 | 10.3 | 7.3 |
| 3.2 | 2.4 | 2.6 | Cur. Mat.-L.T.D. | 2.7 | 4.3 | 1.5 | 2.8 | 2.0 | 2.7 |
| 14.1 | 15.2 | 15.8 | Trade Payables | 22.2 | 18.6 | 13.4 | 15.6 | 13.8 | 16.5 |
| .3 | .2 | .2 | Income Taxes Payable | .0 | .0 | .0 | .1 | .2 | .3 |
| 12.1 | 10.9 | 12.3 | All Other Current | 3.7 | 12.9 | 10.1 | 9.4 | 15.2 | 13.7 |
| 40.6 | 38.3 | 40.9 | Total Current | 45.7 | 47.5 | 38.6 | 36.3 | 41.5 | 40.6 |
| 12.3 | 10.3 | 10.5 | Long-Term Debt | 18.6 | 20.4 | 5.4 | 11.4 | 8.7 | 7.6 |
| .3 | .4 | .5 | Deferred Taxes | .0 | .0 | .1 | .3 | .6 | 1.2 |
| 5.3 | 4.9 | 9.1 | All Other Non-Current | 16.7 | 12.4 | 9.3 | 5.5 | 6.1 | 11.8 |
| 41.4 | 46.1 | 39.0 | Net Worth | 19.0 | 19.7 | 46.6 | 46.6 | 43.2 | 38.9 |
| 100.0 | 100.0 | 100.0 | Total Liabilities & Net Worth | 100.0 | 100.0 | 100.0 | 100.0 | 100.0 | 100.0 |
| | | | **INCOME DATA** | | | | | | |
| 100.0 | 100.0 | 100.0 | Net Sales | 100.0 | 100.0 | 100.0 | 100.0 | 100.0 | 100.0 |
| 34.6 | 35.8 | 36.7 | Gross Profit | 54.4 | 44.33 | 40.1 | 34.6 | 37.6 | 29.9 |
| 30.1 | 29.1 | 29.2 | Operating Expenses | 46.5 | 38.8 | 34.2 | 27.9 | 28.9 | 21.5 |
| 4.4 | 6.7 | 7.5 | Operating Profit | 7.9 | 5.5 | 5.9 | 6.7 | 8.7 | 8.3 |
| 1.3 | .8 | .9 | All Other Expenses (net) | 1.4 | 1.5 | .5 | .0 | 1.2 | .9 |
| 3.2 | 5.9 | 6.6 | Profit Before Taxes | 6.5 | 4.0 | 5.4 | 6.7 | 7.5 | 7.4 |
| | | | **RATIOS** | | | | | | |
| 3.1 | 3.6 | 3.1 | Current | 3.4 | 2.8 | 5.1 | 3.7 | 3.0 | 2.9 |
| 1.8 | 2.0 | 1.8 | | 2.0 | 1.8 | 2.0 | 1.9 | 1.6 | 1.8 |
| 1.2 | 1.3 | 1.3 | | 1.0 | 1.4 | 1.2 | 1.5 | 1.2 | 1.4 |
| 1.7 | 1.9 | 1.6 | Quick | 1.8 | 2.5 | 2.2 | 1.9 | 1.6 | 1.6 |
| .9 | 1.1 | 1.0 | | .9 | .9 | 1.0 | 1.1 | 1.0 | 1.0 |
| .5 | .6 | .6 | | .4 | .4 | .5 | .7 | .6 | .7 |
| 32  11.6 | 34  10.6 | 35  10.5 | Sales/Receivables | 26  14.2 | 26  14.0 | 26  13.9 | 33  10.9 | 37  9.9 | 43  8.4 |
| 44  8.3 | 48  7.6 | 49  7.5 | | 45  8.2 | 42  8.7 | 44  8.3 | 46  7.9 | 47  7.8 | 54  6.8 |
| 59  6.2 | 60  6.0 | 61  6.0 | | 55  6.6 | 58  6.3 | 66  5.5 | 55  6.6 | 63  5.8 | 62  5.9 |
| 44  8.4 | 39  9.4 | 43  8.4 | Cost of Sales/Inventory | 9  41.7 | 47  7.8 | 30  12.0 | 38  9.7 | 41  8.9 | 54  6.8 |
| 75  4.9 | 72  5.1 | 78  4.7 | | 89  4.1 | 85  4.3 | 81  4.5 | 62  5.9 | 79  4.6 | 74  4.9 |
| 115  3.2 | 120  3.0 | 126  2.9 | | 281  1.3 | 182  2.0 | 166  2.2 | 122  3.0 | 152  2.4 | 111  3.3 |
| 19  19.3 | 18  19.9 | 21  17.2 | Cost of Sales/Payables | 31  11.7 | 23  15.7 | 16  22.3 | 19  19.4 | 18  20.6 | 23  15.7 |
| 31  11.8 | 34  10.7 | 33  11.0 | | 53  6.9 | 34  10.8 | 32  11.5 | 31  11.9 | 33  11.2 | 34  10.7 |
| 50  7.4 | 52  7.0 | 54  6.7 | | 107  3.4 | 89  4.1 | 69  5.3 | 49  7.5 | 53  6.9 | 53  6.9 |
| 3.8 | 3.8 | 3.9 | Sales/Working Capital | 4.5 | 4.0 | 3.3 | 4.0 | 3.6 | 3.7 |
| 7.6 | 6.7 | 6.6 | | 8.0 | 8.0 | 4.8 | 7.1 | 8.1 | 6.3 |
| 18.4 | 18.0 | 15.8 | | NM | 15.4 | 29.4 | 15.8 | 21.1 | 12.6 |
| 15.8 | 28.8 | 30.5 | EBIT/Interest | 7.7 | 15.2 | 30.1 | 36.5 | 25.1 | 53.9 |
| (221)  4.0 | (219)  10.5 | (246)  8.3 | | (10)  4.5 | (30)  5.6 | (24)  5.3 | (50)  9.3 | (63)  9.0 | (69)  14.0 |
| 1.0 | 2.3 | 3.1 | | -1.9 | 2.4 | 1.8 | 3.9 | 3.7 | 3.5 |
| 4.6 | 5.7 | 8.6 | Net Profit + Depr., Dep., Amort./Cur. Mat. L/T/D | | | | 14.3 | 7.7 | 10.7 |
| (56)  2.2 | (54)  2.3 | (62)  2.5 | | | | (10)  2.6 | (20)  2.5 | (24)  6.1 |
| .4 | 1.0 | 1.2 | | | | | 2.0 | 1.3 | 1.0 |
| .2 | .1 | .1 | Fixed/Worth | .0 | .1 | .0 | .1 | .2 | .2 |
| .4 | .3 | .4 | | .6 | .4 | .4 | .4 | .3 | .4 |
| 1.4 | .8 | 1.1 | | 2.0 | 3.2 | 1.1 | .9 | 1.3 | .8 |
| .7 | .5 | .6 | Debt/Worth | .8 | .8 | .4 | .5 | .6 | .7 |
| 1.6 | 1.3 | 1.7 | | 2.6 | 3.1 | 1.5 | 1.1 | 1.9 | 1.7 |
| 5.3 | 3.1 | 5.4 | | NM | -16.1 | 8.5 | 3.5 | 4.8 | 4.6 |
| 45.0 | 55.0 | 55.7 | % Profit Before Taxes/Tangible Net Worth | | 62.4 | 47.9 | 51.1 | 61.6 | 55.5 |
| (212)  18.5 | (230)  28.4 | (245)  32.8 | | (26)  34.9 | (25)  14.5 | (52)  26.3 | (64)  37.7 | (69)  38.6 | |
| 1.9 | 9.0 | 11.9 | | 9.5 | 1.0 | 9.5 | 15.6 | 14.2 | |
| 14.9 | 21.9 | 20.0 | % Profit Before Taxes/Total Assets | 14.2 | 20.6 | 17.4 | 21.2 | 21.5 | 20.0 |
| 6.2 | 10.6 | 11.2 | | 8.2 | 9.6 | 5.3 | 10.8 | 11.9 | 11.9 |
| .1 | 2.5 | 4.4 | | -3.2 | 3.4 | .7 | 4.8 | 4.8 | 5.3 |
| 51.4 | 54.9 | 44.7 | Sales/Net Fixed Assets | 208.1 | 60.4 | 96.0 | 50.2 | 38.1 | 43.0 |
| 16.0 | 20.1 | 16.8 | | 21.5 | 35.8 | 30.0 | 16.2 | 15.7 | 13.5 |
| 6.7 | 10.3 | 7.8 | | 9.7 | 8.1 | 13.8 | 5.4 | 8.4 | 7.7 |
| 3.0 | 3.1 | 2.9 | Sales/Total Assets | 3.6 | 4.1 | 3.1 | 3.3 | 2.7 | 2.6 |
| 2.0 | 2.1 | 2.0 | | 2.3 | 2.3 | 2.0 | 2.2 | 2.0 | 1.9 |
| 1.5 | 1.5 | 1.4 | | .9 | 1.3 | 1.5 | 1.5 | 1.4 | 1.4 |
| .7 | .6 | .6 | % Depr., Dep., Amort./Sales | | .5 | .3 | .6 | 1.0 | .6 |
| (195)  1.6 | (200)  1.4 | (216)  1.4 | | (20)  .9 | (21)  .8 | (48)  1.1 | (56)  1.9 | (63)  1.5 | |
| 3.4 | 2.6 | 2.9 | | 1.7 | 2.8 | 3.0 | 3.1 | 2.5 | |
| 2.5 | 2.3 | 2.4 | % Officers', Directors' Owners' Comp/Sales | | 3.7 | 3.4 | 2.4 | 1.6 | .9 |
| (73)  4.6 | (90)  3.9 | (93)  4.2 | | (18)  6.1 | (12)  5.0 | (23)  4.0 | (23)  3.5 | (10)  1.6 | |
| 9.0 | 6.9 | 7.0 | | 11.4 | 6.9 | 6.6 | 4.8 | 4.7 | |
| 8400981M | 8144131M | 9587254M | Net Sales ($) | 7709M | 79433M | 109603M | 406692M | 1130990M | 7852827M |
| 4978297M | 4959778M | 5880610M | Total Assets ($) | 6521M | 45963M | 76217M | 200501M | 737872M | 4813536M |

## Current Data Sorted by Assets      Comparative Historical Data

|  |  |  |  |  |  | Type of Statement | | |
|---|---|---|---|---|---|---|---|---|
| 1 | 2 | 1 | 2 | 2 | 1 | Unqualified | 12 | 10 |
|  | 1 | 1 | 1 |  |  | Reviewed | 7 | 4 |
| 1 | 1 | 2 |  |  |  | Compiled | 7 | 7 |
| 1 | 1 | 5 | 4 | 3 | 3 | Tax Returns | 1 | 4 |
|  |  |  |  |  |  | Other | 19 | 21 |
| 2 (4/1-9/30/11) | | | 32 (10/1/11-3/31/12) | | | | 4/1/07-3/31/08 | 4/1/08-3/31/09 |
| 0-500M | 500M-2MM | 2-10MM | 10-50MM | 50-100MM | 100-250MM | | ALL | ALL |
| 3 | 5 | 9 | 8 | 5 | 4 | NUMBER OF STATEMENTS | 46 | 46 |
| % | % | % | % | % | % | ASSETS | % | % |
|  |  |  |  |  |  | Cash & Equivalents | 10.4 | 10.7 |
|  |  |  |  |  |  | Trade Receivables (net) | 17.8 | 19.8 |
|  |  |  |  |  |  | Inventory | 33.6 | 30.9 |
|  |  |  |  |  |  | All Other Current | 4.4 | 2.4 |
|  |  |  |  |  |  | Total Current | 66.2 | 63.9 |
|  |  |  |  |  |  | Fixed Assets (net) | 21.7 | 25.2 |
|  |  |  |  |  |  | Intangibles (net) | 4.8 | 3.4 |
|  |  |  |  |  |  | All Other Non-Current | 7.3 | 7.6 |
|  |  |  |  |  |  | Total | 100.0 | 100.0 |
|  |  |  |  |  |  | LIABILITIES | | |
|  |  |  |  |  |  | Notes Payable-Short Term | 12.8 | 13.1 |
|  |  |  |  |  |  | Cur. Mat.-L.T.D. | 5.6 | 8.0 |
|  |  |  |  |  |  | Trade Payables | 13.0 | 13.9 |
|  |  |  |  |  |  | Income Taxes Payable | 1.1 | .3 |
|  |  |  |  |  |  | All Other Current | 14.7 | 13.5 |
|  |  |  |  |  |  | Total Current | 47.2 | 48.8 |
|  |  |  |  |  |  | Long-Term Debt | 15.3 | 10.0 |
|  |  |  |  |  |  | Deferred Taxes | .5 | .3 |
|  |  |  |  |  |  | All Other Non-Current | 11.5 | 16.5 |
|  |  |  |  |  |  | Net Worth | 25.6 | 24.4 |
|  |  |  |  |  |  | Total Liabilties & Net Worth | 100.0 | 100.0 |
|  |  |  |  |  |  | INCOME DATA | | |
|  |  |  |  |  |  | Net Sales | 100.0 | 100.0 |
|  |  |  |  |  |  | Gross Profit | 24.2 | 23.2 |
|  |  |  |  |  |  | Operating Expenses | 19.7 | 21.3 |
|  |  |  |  |  |  | Operating Profit | 4.6 | 1.9 |
|  |  |  |  |  |  | All Other Expenses (net) | 1.0 | 1.6 |
|  |  |  |  |  |  | Profit Before Taxes | 3.5 | .2 |
|  |  |  |  |  |  | RATIOS | | |
|  |  |  |  |  |  | Current | 2.1 | 2.2 |
|  |  |  |  |  |  | | 1.4 | 1.4 |
|  |  |  |  |  |  | | 1.1 | .9 |
|  |  |  |  |  |  | Quick | 1.2 | 1.1 |
|  |  |  |  |  |  | | .5 | .5 |
|  |  |  |  |  |  | | .3 | .3 |
|  |  |  |  |  |  | Sales/Receivables | 13   28.4 | 20   18.7 |
|  |  |  |  |  |  | | 27   13.4 | 33   11.1 |
|  |  |  |  |  |  | | 47   7.7 | 50   7.3 |
|  |  |  |  |  |  | Cost of Sales/Inventory | 31   11.7 | 15   23.9 |
|  |  |  |  |  |  | | 55   6.6 | 48   7.6 |
|  |  |  |  |  |  | | 112   3.3 | 105   3.5 |
|  |  |  |  |  |  | Cost of Sales/Payables | 14   26.0 | 13   28.3 |
|  |  |  |  |  |  | | 26   14.0 | 36   10.2 |
|  |  |  |  |  |  | | 43   8.5 | 59   6.2 |
|  |  |  |  |  |  | Sales/Working Capital | 5.0 | 5.1 |
|  |  |  |  |  |  | | 9.9 | 11.0 |
|  |  |  |  |  |  | | NM | -17.2 |
|  |  |  |  |  |  | EBIT/Interest | 13.0 | 12.3 |
|  |  |  |  |  |  | | (42) 3.7 | (41) 2.7 |
|  |  |  |  |  |  | | .6 | .5 |
|  |  |  |  |  |  | Net Profit + Depr., Dep., Amort./Cur. Mat. L/T/D | 3.2 | 2.5 |
|  |  |  |  |  |  | | (16) 1.3 | (10) .7 |
|  |  |  |  |  |  | | .7 | -1.3 |
|  |  |  |  |  |  | Fixed/Worth | .2 | .2 |
|  |  |  |  |  |  | | 1.2 | .5 |
|  |  |  |  |  |  | | -2.5 | -5.5 |
|  |  |  |  |  |  | Debt/Worth | 1.2 | .8 |
|  |  |  |  |  |  | | 3.6 | 2.3 |
|  |  |  |  |  |  | | -14.9 | -8.2 |
|  |  |  |  |  |  | % Profit Before Taxes/Tangible Net Worth | 36.8 | 36.9 |
|  |  |  |  |  |  | | (34) 23.0 | (34) 19.1 |
|  |  |  |  |  |  | | 10.0 | 6.0 |
|  |  |  |  |  |  | % Profit Before Taxes/Total Assets | 14.4 | 16.8 |
|  |  |  |  |  |  | | 6.3 | 3.1 |
|  |  |  |  |  |  | | -1.8 | -1.2 |
|  |  |  |  |  |  | Sales/Net Fixed Assets | 43.5 | 39.9 |
|  |  |  |  |  |  | | 13.7 | 14.5 |
|  |  |  |  |  |  | | 7.9 | 4.8 |
|  |  |  |  |  |  | Sales/Total Assets | 3.0 | 2.6 |
|  |  |  |  |  |  | | 2.1 | 1.9 |
|  |  |  |  |  |  | | 1.5 | 1.2 |
|  |  |  |  |  |  | % Depr., Dep., Amort./Sales | .6 | .6 |
|  |  |  |  |  |  | | (38) 1.6 | (36) 1.4 |
|  |  |  |  |  |  | | 4.4 | 3.7 |
|  |  |  |  |  |  | % Officers', Directors' Owners' Comp/Sales | .9 | 1.0 |
|  |  |  |  |  |  | | (11) 1.9 | (10) 3.7 |
|  |  |  |  |  |  | | 7.1 | 10.9 |
| 736M | 9880M | 73040M | 309617M | 547948M | 943242M | Net Sales ($) | 3185472M | 2853685M |
| 126M | 3849M | 37934M | 191941M | 355824M | 790488M | Total Assets ($) | 1750852M | 1685617M |

M = $ thousand     MM = $ million
See Pages 9 through 22 for Explanation of Ratios and Data

| Comparative Historical Data | | | | | Current Data Sorted by Sales | | | | | |
|---|---|---|---|---|---|---|---|---|---|---|

### Type of Statement

| | | | | | | | | | | 5 |
|---|---|---|---|---|---|---|---|---|---|---|
| 6 | 4 | 5 | Unqualified | | | | 1 | 1 | | 1 |
| 9 | 3 | 5 | Reviewed | 2 | | | | | 2 | |
| 3 | 3 | 3 | Compiled | | 1 | | | | | |
| 5 | 9 | 4 | Tax Returns | 1 | 1 | 2 | | 3 | 1 | 9 |
| 20 | 16 | 17 | Other | 2 | | | 2 | | | |

| 4/1/09- 3/31/10 ALL | 4/1/10- 3/31/11 ALL | 4/1/11- 3/31/12 ALL | | | 2 (4/1-9/30/11) | | | 32 (10/1/11-3/31/12) | | |
|---|---|---|---|---|---|---|---|---|---|---|
| | | | | 0-1MM | 1-3MM | 3-5MM | 5-10MM | 10-25MM | 25MM & OVER | |
| 43 | 35 | 34 | NUMBER OF STATEMENTS | 5 | 2 | 3 | 6 | 3 | 15 |

| % | % | % | ASSETS | % | % | % | % | % | % |
|---|---|---|---|---|---|---|---|---|---|
| 9.9 | 8.9 | 13.5 | Cash & Equivalents | | | | | | 13.8 |
| 20.1 | 21.4 | 15.8 | Trade Receivables (net) | | | | | | 15.3 |
| 30.7 | 32.8 | 32.2 | Inventory | | | | | | 26.5 |
| 5.2 | 6.1 | 4.5 | All Other Current | | | | | | 6.6 |
| 65.7 | 69.1 | 66.0 | Total Current | | | | | | 62.2 |
| 23.2 | 18.2 | 20.0 | Fixed Assets (net) | | | | | | 22.0 |
| 3.3 | 6.3 | 3.0 | Intangibles (net) | | | | | | 3.8 |
| 7.8 | 6.4 | 11.2 | All Other Non-Current | | | | | | 12.1 |
| 100.0 | 100.0 | 100.0 | Total | | | | | | 100.0 |

| | | | LIABILITIES | | | | | | |
|---|---|---|---|---|---|---|---|---|---|
| 18.0 | 15.6 | 10.9 | Notes Payable-Short Term | | | | | | 6.2 |
| 4.6 | 4.4 | 3.6 | Cur. Mat.-L.T.D. | | | | | | 2.7 |
| 13.7 | 13.4 | 13.2 | Trade Payables | | | | | | 11.9 |
| .2 | .3 | .3 | Income Taxes Payable | | | | | | .7 |
| 14.2 | 14.2 | 16.8 | All Other Current | | | | | | 18.7 |
| 50.7 | 48.0 | 44.9 | Total Current | | | | | | 40.1 |
| 9.3 | 12.1 | 9.5 | Long-Term Debt | | | | | | 6.4 |
| .4 | .3 | .2 | Deferred Taxes | | | | | | .5 |
| 7.9 | 16.4 | 11.4 | All Other Non-Current | | | | | | 16.5 |
| 31.6 | 23.2 | 34.0 | Net Worth | | | | | | 36.5 |
| 100.0 | 100.0 | 100.0 | Total Liabilties & Net Worth | | | | | | 100.0 |

| | | | INCOME DATA | | | | | | |
|---|---|---|---|---|---|---|---|---|---|
| 100.0 | 100.0 | 100.0 | Net Sales | | | | | | 100.0 |
| 21.9 | 28.6 | 26.0 | Gross Profit | | | | | | 20.5 |
| 21.5 | 26.2 | 25.0 | Operating Expenses | | | | | | 16.0 |
| .4 | 2.4 | 1.0 | Operating Profit | | | | | | 4.5 |
| .9 | 1.7 | -.5 | All Other Expenses (net) | | | | | | .0 |
| -.5 | .7 | 1.5 | Profit Before Taxes | | | | | | 4.5 |

| | | | RATIOS | | | | | | |
|---|---|---|---|---|---|---|---|---|---|
| 1.9 | 2.1 | 2.6 | | | | | | | 3.5 |
| 1.4 | 1.8 | 1.5 | Current | | | | | | 1.6 |
| 1.1 | 1.1 | 1.0 | | | | | | | 1.0 |
| 1.0 | 1.2 | 1.3 | | | | | | | 1.5 |
| .5 | .5 | .6 | Quick | | | | | | .6 |
| .2 | .3 | .3 | | | | | | | .3 |
| 15   24.7 | 16   22.8 | 15   24.7 | | | | | | | 16   22.7 |
| 37   9.8 | 38   9.5 | 35   10.4 | Sales/Receivables | | | | | | 41   9.0 |
| 61   6.0 | 63   5.8 | 57   6.4 | | | | | | | 49   7.5 |
| 27   13.6 | 17   21.7 | 31   11.7 | | | | | | | 32   11.5 |
| 57   6.4 | 66   5.5 | 76   4.8 | Cost of Sales/Inventory | | | | | | 58   6.3 |
| 118   3.1 | 169   2.2 | 215   1.7 | | | | | | | 122   3.0 |
| 15   24.9 | 14   25.9 | 12   30.9 | | | | | | | 12   30.5 |
| 31   11.7 | 23   15.9 | 27   13.6 | Cost of Sales/Payables | | | | | | 32   11.5 |
| 53   6.8 | 46   8.0 | 52   7.0 | | | | | | | 63   5.8 |
| 5.6 | 4.5 | 3.8 | | | | | | | 4.2 |
| 11.3 | 7.0 | 7.7 | Sales/Working Capital | | | | | | 8.5 |
| 63.2 | 18.1 | -310.3 | | | | | | | -197.2 |
| 6.6 | 9.4 | 12.9 | | | | | | | 43.8 |
| (40)   2.6 | (32)   3.7 | (27)   5.0 | EBIT/Interest | | | | | | (13)   5.0 |
| -1.6 | -.5 | 1.3 | | | | | | | 1.1 |
| 4.3 | | | Net Profit + Depr., Dep., | | | | | | |
| (13)   1.9 | | | Amort./Cur. Mat. L/T/D | | | | | | |
| -.1 | | | | | | | | | |
| .2 | .2 | .2 | | | | | | | .3 |
| .9 | .7 | .5 | Fixed/Worth | | | | | | .5 |
| 2.2 | -3.7 | 5.0 | | | | | | | .7 |
| 1.0 | 1.0 | .6 | | | | | | | .5 |
| 2.3 | 2.6 | 2.9 | Debt/Worth | | | | | | 2.7 |
| 5.8 | -71.0 | 26.7 | | | | | | | 6.3 |
| 27.2 | 25.7 | 24.8 | % Profit Before Taxes/Tangible | | | | | | 38.7 |
| (35)   7.0 | (26)   13.2 | (28)   9.8 | Net Worth | | | | | | (13)   17.6 |
| -14.2 | -4.1 | .4 | | | | | | | -1.4 |
| 8.3 | 10.6 | 9.0 | % Profit Before Taxes/Total | | | | | | 11.1 |
| 3.1 | 5.9 | 1.7 | Assets | | | | | | 2.7 |
| -4.6 | -3.3 | -.1 | | | | | | | .3 |
| 34.6 | 41.8 | 32.5 | | | | | | | 13.3 |
| 13.1 | 12.4 | 12.6 | Sales/Net Fixed Assets | | | | | | 7.7 |
| 4.0 | 8.5 | 4.8 | | | | | | | 4.1 |
| 2.6 | 2.4 | 2.1 | | | | | | | 2.1 |
| 1.6 | 1.7 | 1.7 | Sales/Total Assets | | | | | | 1.6 |
| 1.1 | 1.2 | 1.1 | | | | | | | 1.1 |
| .9 | .9 | .7 | | | | | | | 1.0 |
| (33)   2.0 | (27)   2.0 | (23)   1.6 | % Depr., Dep., Amort./Sales | | | | | | (11)   1.6 |
| 4.7 | 3.5 | 3.4 | | | | | | | 2.3 |
| 1.9 | 1.6 | 1.7 | % Officers', Directors' | | | | | | |
| (10)   3.4 | (12)   3.2 | (11)   3.7 | Owners' Comp/Sales | | | | | | |
| 7.1 | 6.1 | 5.8 | | | | | | | |
| 1582955M | 1753192M | 1884463M | Net Sales ($) | 1661M | 2628M | 12926M | 43950M | 51166M | 1772132M |
| 1084126M | 874965M | 1380162M | Total Assets ($) | 1433M | 1812M | 13692M | 22738M | 24984M | 1315503M |

M = $ thousand    MM = $ million

© RMA 2012

See Pages 9 through 22 for Explanation of Ratios and Data

## Current Data Sorted by Assets | Comparative Historical Data

### Type of Statement

| | 0-500M | 500M-2MM | 2-10MM | 10-50MM | 50-100MM | 100-250MM | Type of Statement | 4/1/07-3/31/08 ALL | 4/1/08-3/31/09 ALL |
|---|---|---|---|---|---|---|---|---|---|
| Unqualified | 1 | 2 | 5 | 10 | 2 | 9 | | 40 | 32 |
| Reviewed | | 8 | 12 | 8 | | | | 30 | 37 |
| Compiled | | | 9 | | | | | 15 | 13 |
| Tax Returns | 4 | 10 | 1 | 1 | | | | 20 | 10 |
| Other | 8 | 9 | 14 | 10 | 2 | 5 | | 67 | 59 |

Date ranges: **18 (4/1-9/30/11)** · **112 (10/1/11-3/31/12)**

| 0-500M | 500M-2MM | 2-10MM | 10-50MM | 50-100MM | 100-250MM | | 4/1/07-3/31/08 ALL | 4/1/08-3/31/09 ALL |
|---|---|---|---|---|---|---|---|---|
| 13 | 29 | 41 | 29 | 4 | 14 | **NUMBER OF STATEMENTS** | 172 | 151 |

### Main Data (%)

| 0-500M | 500M-2MM | 2-10MM | 10-50MM | 50-100MM | 100-250MM | | 4/1/07-3/31/08 ALL | 4/1/08-3/31/09 ALL |
|---|---|---|---|---|---|---|---|---|
| % | % | % | % | % | % | **ASSETS** | % | % |
| 17.8 | 12.1 | 6.3 | 9.8 | | 4.7 | Cash & Equivalents | 5.9 | 5.7 |
| 29.2 | 20.7 | 22.0 | 22.3 | | 21.4 | Trade Receivables (net) | 22.7 | 20.8 |
| 24.6 | 41.7 | 40.9 | 32.8 | | 28.1 | Inventory | 34.1 | 37.7 |
| 4.7 | 2.0 | 2.5 | 1.3 | | 2.5 | All Other Current | 2.5 | 2.4 |
| 76.4 | 76.5 | 71.7 | 66.1 | | 56.7 | Total Current | 65.2 | 66.6 |
| 13.6 | 10.5 | 21.9 | 21.6 | | 29.3 | Fixed Assets (net) | 24.0 | 22.4 |
| 5.4 | 2.5 | 2.1 | 3.9 | | 8.8 | Intangibles (net) | 5.2 | 5.1 |
| 4.6 | 10.5 | 4.2 | 8.4 | | 5.2 | All Other Non-Current | 5.6 | 5.9 |
| 100.0 | 100.0 | 100.0 | 100.0 | | 100.0 | Total | 100.0 | 100.0 |
| | | | | | | **LIABILITIES** | | |
| 23.1 | 15.6 | 16.5 | 11.0 | | 10.9 | Notes Payable-Short Term | 15.0 | 18.1 |
| 4.4 | 3.3 | 2.9 | 5.3 | | 2.1 | Cur. Mat.-L.T.D. | 3.6 | 4.2 |
| 28.3 | 11.8 | 17.2 | 17.2 | | 15.7 | Trade Payables | 17.6 | 15.2 |
| .0 | .1 | .0 | .1 | | .4 | Income Taxes Payable | .1 | .4 |
| 23.8 | 8.7 | 17.2 | 12.3 | | 12.0 | All Other Current | 14.0 | 13.6 |
| 79.5 | 39.4 | 53.8 | 45.8 | | 41.1 | Total Current | 50.3 | 51.5 |
| 15.8 | 9.1 | 14.4 | 7.2 | | 6.5 | Long-Term Debt | 14.9 | 14.0 |
| .0 | .0 | .1 | .4 | | 1.3 | Deferred Taxes | .5 | .6 |
| 15.0 | 12.2 | 3.2 | 6.1 | | 13.8 | All Other Non-Current | 6.8 | 4.9 |
| -10.4 | 39.3 | 28.4 | 40.5 | | 37.2 | Net Worth | 27.5 | 28.9 |
| 100.0 | 100.0 | 100.0 | 100.0 | | 100.0 | Total Liabilities & Net Worth | 100.0 | 100.0 |
| | | | | | | **INCOME DATA** | | |
| 100.0 | 100.0 | 100.0 | 100.0 | | 100.0 | Net Sales | 100.0 | 100.0 |
| 27.2 | 26.6 | 23.0 | 18.9 | | 16.6 | Gross Profit | 22.8 | 20.2 |
| 21.2 | 21.5 | 21.2 | 13.2 | | 12.4 | Operating Expenses | 19.6 | 18.6 |
| 6.1 | 5.1 | 1.8 | 5.6 | | 4.1 | Operating Profit | 3.2 | 1.6 |
| .5 | .4 | .8 | .7 | | 1.0 | All Other Expenses (net) | 1.4 | 1.7 |
| 5.5 | 4.7 | 1.0 | 4.9 | | 3.1 | Profit Before Taxes | 1.8 | -.1 |

### Ratios

| 0-500M | 500M-2MM | 2-10MM | 10-50MM | 50-100MM | 100-250MM | | 4/1/07-3/31/08 ALL | 4/1/08-3/31/09 ALL |
|---|---|---|---|---|---|---|---|---|
| 4.1 | 4.4 | 2.0 | 3.0 | | 2.2 | | 2.3 | 2.3 |
| 1.0 | 2.0 | 1.3 | 1.8 | | 1.3 | Current | 1.4 | 1.5 |
| .6 | 1.3 | 1.0 | 1.1 | | 1.0 | | 1.1 | 1.1 |
| 3.0 | 2.3 | .9 | 1.7 | | 1.0 | | 1.1 | 1.0 |
| .8 | .8 | .5 | .8 | | .7 | Quick | .6 | .6 |
| .4 | .3 | .3 | .4 | | .4 | | .4 | .3 |
| 11  32.1 | 7  53.6 | 17  21.0 | 19  19.0 | | 32  11.4 | | 23  16.1 | 21  17.7 |
| 27  13.6 | 24  15.1 | 31  11.7 | 31  11.8 | | 41  8.9 | Sales/Receivables | 36  10.0 | 33  11.1 |
| 43  8.5 | 38  9.5 | 53  6.9 | 54  6.8 | | 50  7.3 | | 50  7.3 | 43  8.4 |
| 6  59.9 | 48  7.6 | 54  6.7 | 24  15.1 | | 35  10.4 | | 36  10.1 | 42  8.6 |
| 14  26.9 | 64  5.7 | 83  4.4 | 63  5.8 | | 73  5.0 | Cost of Sales/Inventory | 61  6.0 | 70  5.2 |
| 58  6.3 | 126  2.9 | 146  2.5 | 111  3.3 | | 114  3.2 | | 108  3.4 | 106  3.5 |
| 16  22.8 | 7  51.8 | 18  20.5 | 15  24.9 | | 23  15.8 | | 16  22.8 | 12  29.9 |
| 29  12.4 | 17  21.2 | 32  11.5 | 30  12.3 | | 32  11.3 | Cost of Sales/Payables | 31  11.8 | 25  14.4 |
| 43  8.4 | 35  10.5 | 45  8.1 | 38  9.6 | | 41  8.8 | | 44  8.3 | 41  8.9 |
| 4.8 | 5.3 | 7.8 | 4.2 | | 5.7 | | 5.6 | 5.6 |
| 197.7 | 8.6 | 11.0 | 7.5 | | 27.2 | Sales/Working Capital | 12.7 | 10.8 |
| -10.5 | 20.3 | 128.0 | 36.3 | | 109.7 | | 64.0 | 56.3 |
| | 27.0 | 4.3 | 66.7 | | 26.3 | | 5.5 | 5.8 |
| | (26) 4.3 | (37) 2.2 | (27) 11.1 | | 4.2 | EBIT/Interest | (156) 2.3 | (136) 1.5 |
| | -.3 | 1.2 | 2.8 | | 2.5 | | .8 | -1.1 |
| | | | | | | | 5.1 | 5.4 |
| | | | | | | Net Profit + Depr., Dep., Amort./Cur. Mat. L/T/D | (54) 3.0 | (42) 2.1 |
| | | | | | | | .9 | -.1 |
| .1 | .0 | .3 | .2 | | .4 | | .3 | .3 |
| .6 | .1 | .9 | .5 | | 1.0 | Fixed/Worth | .9 | .7 |
| -1.8 | .5 | 3.2 | 1.5 | | 1.7 | | 3.1 | 7.7 |
| .4 | .4 | 1.4 | .5 | | .7 | | 1.0 | .9 |
| 5.3 | 1.5 | 2.6 | 1.2 | | 1.1 | Debt/Worth | 2.8 | 2.4 |
| -1.9 | 3.5 | 10.6 | 14.7 | | 7.4 | | 13.1 | 16.0 |
| | 58.5 | 31.7 | 37.0 | | 41.5 | | 37.3 | 29.1 |
| | (26) 26.2 | (36) 12.6 | (24) 24.0 | | (12) 14.0 | % Profit Before Taxes/Tangible Net Worth | (137) 17.4 | (118) 8.6 |
| | 3.1 | 2.8 | 6.8 | | 4.5 | | 2.5 | -8.0 |
| 42.1 | 17.2 | 7.9 | 19.1 | | 9.3 | | 11.2 | 9.3 |
| 9.1 | 8.9 | 3.2 | 6.9 | | 4.8 | % Profit Before Taxes/Total Assets | 3.6 | 1.7 |
| -1.0 | -1.3 | .7 | 3.0 | | 1.7 | | -.4 | -4.9 |
| 198.8 | 263.0 | 46.1 | 23.2 | | 14.0 | | 31.5 | 31.0 |
| 56.6 | 53.8 | 16.5 | 9.4 | | 7.9 | Sales/Net Fixed Assets | 12.2 | 13.5 |
| 14.0 | 18.3 | 4.3 | 6.3 | | 4.8 | | 5.8 | 5.4 |
| 6.5 | 4.0 | 3.0 | 3.3 | | 2.3 | | 3.0 | 3.1 |
| 4.0 | 2.9 | 2.1 | 2.3 | | 1.9 | Sales/Total Assets | 2.2 | 2.2 |
| 3.2 | 1.5 | 1.3 | 1.6 | | 1.3 | | 1.7 | 1.6 |
| | .1 | .5 | 1.0 | | 1.3 | | .7 | .7 |
| | (18) .4 | (34) 1.2 | (26) 1.5 | | (12) 1.7 | % Depr., Dep., Amort./Sales | (145) 1.5 | (127) 1.3 |
| | 1.4 | 2.6 | 2.2 | | 3.7 | | 3.0 | 3.0 |
| | | 1.4 | | | | | 1.2 | 1.1 |
| | | (18) 2.4 | | | | % Officers', Directors' Owners' Comp/Sales | (50) 2.6 | (35) 3.3 |
| | | 5.5 | | | | | 5.3 | 4.9 |
| 15681M | 114200M | 454720M | 1654598M | 517512M | 4015168M | Net Sales ($) | 10323874M | 8280571M |
| 3248M | 38129M | 206509M | 688288M | 299443M | 2126419M | Total Assets ($) | 5690788M | 4876854M |

M = $ thousand    MM = $ million
See Pages 9 through 22 for Explanation of Ratios and Data

## Comparative Historical Data | Current Data Sorted by Sales

Current Data groupings: **18 (4/1–9/30/11)** and **112 (10/1/11–3/31/12)**

| 4/1/09–3/31/10 ALL | 4/1/10–3/31/11 ALL | 4/1/11–3/31/12 ALL | Type of Statement | 0-1MM | 1-3MM | 3-5MM | 5-10MM | 10-25MM | 25MM & OVER |
|---|---|---|---|---|---|---|---|---|---|
| 25 | 35 | 26 | Unqualified | | 1 | 4 | 1 | 4 | 21 |
| 32 | 21 | 23 | Reviewed | 1 | | 3 | 5 | 7 | 5 |
| 9 | 17 | 17 | Compiled | | 4 | 3 | 7 | 3 | |
| 13 | 13 | 16 | Tax Returns | 1 | 7 | 3 | 3 | 1 | 1 |
| 54 | 49 | 48 | Other | 5 | 9 | 4 | 3 | 11 | 16 |
| 133 | 135 | 130 | **NUMBER OF STATEMENTS** | 7 | 21 | 14 | 19 | 26 | 43 |
| % | % | % | **ASSETS** | % | % | % | % | % | % |
| 8.4 | 9.7 | 9.5 | Cash & Equivalents | | 11.9 | 8.8 | 10.8 | 8.2 | 8.2 |
| 20.5 | 21.6 | 22.6 | Trade Receivables (net) | | 19.3 | 26.0 | 23.2 | 21.8 | 24.2 |
| 36.0 | 34.6 | 35.7 | Inventory | | 34.8 | 34.9 | 45.8 | 37.5 | 30.4 |
| 3.2 | 3.3 | 2.3 | All Other Current | | 2.6 | .4 | 2.2 | 2.0 | 2.0 |
| 68.1 | 69.2 | 70.2 | Total Current | | 68.6 | 70.2 | 82.0 | 69.6 | 64.7 |
| 20.6 | 19.4 | 19.3 | Fixed Assets (net) | | 16.2 | 14.2 | 11.9 | 23.0 | 24.4 |
| 5.3 | 4.0 | 3.8 | Intangibles (net) | | 5.4 | 1.6 | .7 | 4.0 | 5.5 |
| 6.0 | 7.4 | 6.7 | All Other Non-Current | | 9.9 | 14.0 | 5.3 | 3.5 | 5.4 |
| 100.0 | 100.0 | 100.0 | Total | | 100.0 | 100.0 | 100.0 | 100.0 | 100.0 |
| | | | **LIABILITIES** | | | | | | |
| 15.7 | 14.1 | 14.7 | Notes Payable-Short Term | | 17.0 | 21.4 | 14.7 | 14.0 | 10.1 |
| 4.3 | 3.3 | 3.5 | Cur. Mat.-L.T.D. | | 6.2 | 1.7 | 2.1 | 3.7 | 3.9 |
| 15.7 | 17.2 | 17.2 | Trade Payables | | 14.5 | 14.0 | 17.8 | 16.9 | 18.5 |
| .4 | .3 | .1 | Income Taxes Payable | | .1 | .0 | .0 | .0 | .2 |
| 16.6 | 13.6 | 14.0 | All Other Current | | 17.5 | 16.6 | 12.6 | 15.9 | 12.3 |
| 52.7 | 48.6 | 49.6 | Total Current | | 55.4 | 53.7 | 47.3 | 50.5 | 45.0 |
| 13.8 | 10.9 | 11.1 | Long-Term Debt | | 15.5 | 9.4 | 12.6 | 12.3 | 8.0 |
| .5 | .5 | .3 | Deferred Taxes | | .0 | .1 | .2 | .0 | .8 |
| 7.8 | 7.7 | 8.1 | All Other Non-Current | | 12.7 | 10.5 | 9.4 | 1.3 | 8.5 |
| 25.3 | 32.3 | 30.8 | Net Worth | | 16.4 | 26.3 | 30.5 | 35.9 | 37.6 |
| 100.0 | 100.0 | 100.0 | Total Liabilities & Net Worth | | 100.0 | 100.0 | 100.0 | 100.0 | 100.0 |
| | | | **INCOME DATA** | | | | | | |
| 100.0 | 100.0 | 100.0 | Net Sales | | 100.0 | 100.0 | 100.0 | 100.0 | 100.0 |
| 20.7 | 23.8 | 22.4 | Gross Profit | | 24.3 | 31.8 | 21.3 | 21.6 | 17.3 |
| 20.1 | 20.4 | 18.2 | Operating Expenses | | 23.2 | 27.0 | 18.6 | 17.4 | 12.6 |
| .6 | 3.4 | 4.2 | Operating Profit | | 1.1 | 4.8 | 2.7 | 4.1 | 4.7 |
| 1.6 | .7 | .7 | All Other Expenses (net) | | .8 | .6 | .5 | .7 | .8 |
| -1.0 | 2.7 | 3.5 | Profit Before Taxes | | .3 | 4.2 | 2.2 | 3.4 | 3.9 |
| | | | **RATIOS** | | | | | | |
| 2.1 | 2.7 | 2.9 | | | 3.5 | 5.0 | 3.0 | 2.5 | 2.4 |
| 1.4 | 1.6 | 1.5 | Current | | 1.5 | 1.4 | 1.6 | 1.3 | 1.6 |
| 1.0 | 1.1 | 1.1 | | | .9 | 1.0 | 1.3 | 1.0 | 1.1 |
| 1.1 | 1.4 | 1.4 | | | 2.0 | 3.2 | 1.0 | 1.6 | 1.3 |
| .5 | .7 | .7 | Quick | | .6 | 1.2 | .6 | .6 | .8 |
| .3 | .3 | .3 | | | .2 | .3 | .4 | .3 | .4 |
| 15  24.6 | 18  20.0 | 19  18.9 | | | 12  30.6 | 23  15.8 | 13  28.6 | 13  27.4 | 22  16.5 |
| 37  9.9 | 32  11.3 | 33  11.2 | Sales/Receivables | | 26  13.9 | 35  10.5 | 36  10.2 | 27  13.3 | 38  9.6 |
| 49  7.5 | 51  7.2 | 50  7.3 | | | 51  7.1 | 45  8.2 | 58  6.3 | 40  9.2 | 51  7.2 |
| 43  8.4 | 42  8.7 | 35  10.4 | | | 36  10.1 | 11  32.4 | 60  6.1 | 43  8.4 | 25  14.8 |
| 67  5.4 | 69  5.3 | 66  5.5 | Cost of Sales/Inventory | | 87  4.2 | 64  5.7 | 83  4.4 | 66  5.5 | 55  6.6 |
| 112  3.3 | 113  3.2 | 114  3.2 | | | 140  2.6 | 152  2.4 | 114  3.2 | 118  3.1 | 96  3.8 |
| 12  29.4 | 15  25.0 | 16  22.9 | | | 13  28.0 | 6  58.1 | 14  26.4 | 15  24.1 | 20  18.5 |
| 21  17.1 | 28  13.1 | 31  11.9 | Cost of Sales/Payables | | 29  12.4 | 22  16.6 | 32  11.3 | 23  15.7 | 32  11.3 |
| 47  7.8 | 43  8.6 | 43  8.5 | | | 40  9.2 | 35  10.3 | 61  6.0 | 36  10.1 | 44  8.3 |
| 5.6 | 4.8 | 5.4 | | | 4.3 | 6.3 | 5.2 | 8.9 | 5.5 |
| 10.7 | 9.3 | 10.4 | Sales/Working Capital | | 8.5 | 14.6 | 9.4 | 12.0 | 11.3 |
| -186.1 | 38.5 | 99.3 | | | -510.9 | NM | 20.6 | NM | 60.0 |
| 6.3 | 12.4 | 20.1 | | | 6.3 | 38.6 | 5.8 | 14.7 | 38.6 |
| (117) 1.4 | (122) 4.0 | (117) 3.7 | EBIT/Interest | | (19) 1.4 | (12) 4.0 | (18) 3.3 | (24) 3.0 | (41) 5.5 |
| -1.3 | 1.2 | 1.4 | | | -2.2 | .0 | 1.3 | 1.4 | 2.7 |
| 4.2 | 7.9 | 9.9 | Net Profit + Depr., Dep., | | | | | | 20.8 |
| (33) 1.4 | (33) 2.0 | (24) 3.0 | Amort./Cur. Mat. L/T/D | | | | | | (17) 3.2 |
| -.2 | .7 | 1.8 | | | | | | | 1.9 |
| .2 | .2 | .2 | | | .1 | .0 | .0 | .3 | .3 |
| .6 | .5 | .5 | Fixed/Worth | | .4 | .2 | .3 | .8 | .5 |
| 4.1 | 1.5 | 1.7 | | | 1.4 | 2.6 | 3.2 | 2.5 | 1.7 |
| .8 | .7 | .6 | | | 1.0 | .2 | .6 | .6 | .6 |
| 2.4 | 1.5 | 2.0 | Debt/Worth | | 1.5 | 1.8 | 3.3 | 2.5 | 1.2 |
| 22.0 | 7.9 | 8.9 | | | NM | 7.9 | 8.8 | 9.4 | 7.2 |
| 30.6 | 36.8 | 41.5 | % Profit Before Taxes/Tangible | | 37.8 | 46.0 | 58.8 | 42.6 | 38.8 |
| (102) 5.2 | (111) 13.9 | (109) 14.8 | Net Worth | | (16) 4.0 | (12) 13.6 | (17) 20.5 | (23) 15.5 | (36) 18.7 |
| -9.7 | 4.0 | 4.4 | | | -17.1 | 5.4 | 10.9 | 6.0 | 5.7 |
| 8.3 | 12.7 | 13.6 | % Profit Before Taxes/Total | | 15.9 | 18.8 | 8.9 | 14.3 | 13.9 |
| 1.1 | 5.0 | 5.1 | Assets | | .5 | 7.6 | 5.4 | 4.1 | 5.6 |
| -6.8 | .6 | 1.1 | | | -7.1 | .0 | 1.0 | 1.6 | 2.9 |
| 34.7 | 47.3 | 57.0 | | | 165.1 | 156.9 | 217.6 | 45.7 | 20.1 |
| 15.1 | 14.3 | 16.7 | Sales/Net Fixed Assets | | 32.7 | 42.6 | 47.1 | 14.7 | 10.4 |
| 5.5 | 6.7 | 6.5 | | | 12.0 | 5.9 | 15.7 | 6.0 | 6.1 |
| 3.1 | 3.2 | 3.6 | | | 4.0 | 4.1 | 3.9 | 4.1 | 3.0 |
| 2.1 | 2.3 | 2.3 | Sales/Total Assets | | 2.2 | 2.9 | 2.5 | 2.5 | 2.2 |
| 1.3 | 1.5 | 1.5 | | | 1.3 | 1.0 | 1.7 | 1.5 | 1.7 |
| .7 | .6 | .5 | | | .7 | | .1 | .5 | 1.0 |
| (109) 1.5 | (108) 1.4 | (96) 1.3 | % Depr., Dep., Amort./Sales | | (11) 1.6 | | (16) .5 | (22) 1.3 | (39) 1.6 |
| 3.3 | 2.6 | 2.3 | | | 2.1 | | 1.3 | 2.5 | 2.5 |
| 1.4 | 1.5 | 1.4 | | | 2.4 | | | | |
| (44) 2.6 | (45) 2.4 | (37) 2.4 | % Officers', Directors' Owners' Comp/Sales | | (11) 3.1 | | | | |
| 4.4 | 5.5 | 4.7 | | | 6.2 | | | | |
| 6331370M | 6953406M | 6771879M | Net Sales ($) | 2599M | 40744M | 55249M | 133709M | 398048M | 6141530M |
| 3622413M | 3785140M | 3362036M | Total Assets ($) | 1671M | 22595M | 44732M | 59033M | 181555M | 3052450M |

© RMA 2012

M = $ thousand   MM = $ million
See Pages 9 through 22 for Explanation of Ratios and Data

## Current Data Sorted by Assets      Comparative Historical Data

| 0-500M | 500M-2MM | 2-10MM | 10-50MM | 50-100MM | 100-250MM | Type of Statement | 4/1/07-3/31/08 ALL | 4/1/08-3/31/09 ALL |
|---|---|---|---|---|---|---|---|---|
| | | 1 | 7 | 1 | 3 | Unqualified | 15 | 12 |
| | | 6 | 7 | 1 | | Reviewed | 14 | 11 |
| 1 | 5 | 7 | 2 | | | Compiled | 23 | 19 |
| 2 | 5 | | | | | Tax Returns | 11 | 8 |
| 1 | 6 | 9 | 8 | 3 | 4 | Other | 36 | 28 |
| | 9 (4/1-9/30/11) | | 70 (10/1/11-3/31/12) | | | | | |
| 4 | 16 | 23 | 24 | 5 | 7 | **NUMBER OF STATEMENTS** | 99 | 78 |
| % | % | % | % | % | % | **ASSETS** | % | % |
| | 13.1 | 11.3 | 6.0 | | | Cash & Equivalents | 5.7 | 5.8 |
| | 18.3 | 15.9 | 13.9 | | | Trade Receivables (net) | 15.7 | 12.8 |
| | 46.0 | 44.4 | 44.1 | | | Inventory | 44.7 | 45.6 |
| | 1.0 | 3.2 | 1.8 | | | All Other Current | 2.9 | 2.3 |
| | 78.4 | 74.8 | 65.9 | | | Total Current | 69.0 | 66.5 |
| | 17.1 | 20.8 | 25.6 | | | Fixed Assets (net) | 20.9 | 20.9 |
| | 2.2 | 2.2 | 4.3 | | | Intangibles (net) | 4.9 | 7.5 |
| | 2.2 | 2.3 | 4.2 | | | All Other Non-Current | 5.2 | 5.1 |
| | 100.0 | 100.0 | 100.0 | | | Total | 100.0 | 100.0 |
| | | | | | | **LIABILITIES** | | |
| | 8.2 | 10.9 | 15.2 | | | Notes Payable-Short Term | 14.7 | 21.2 |
| | .5 | 2.1 | 4.1 | | | Cur. Mat.-L.T.D. | 3.2 | 3.5 |
| | 18.6 | 15.3 | 15.0 | | | Trade Payables | 15.0 | 15.6 |
| | .0 | .4 | .2 | | | Income Taxes Payable | .2 | .0 |
| | 28.2 | 6.9 | 10.8 | | | All Other Current | 10.6 | 11.4 |
| | 55.5 | 35.6 | 45.3 | | | Total Current | 43.7 | 51.7 |
| | 12.3 | 10.7 | 14.0 | | | Long-Term Debt | 15.3 | 18.4 |
| | .0 | .2 | 1.0 | | | Deferred Taxes | .3 | .5 |
| | 4.7 | 3.6 | 5.7 | | | All Other Non-Current | 7.9 | 9.1 |
| | 27.6 | 49.8 | 34.0 | | | Net Worth | 32.8 | 20.4 |
| | 100.0 | 100.0 | 100.0 | | | Total Liabilities & Net Worth | 100.0 | 100.0 |
| | | | | | | **INCOME DATA** | | |
| | 100.0 | 100.0 | 100.0 | | | Net Sales | 100.0 | 100.0 |
| | 26.3 | 19.4 | 18.2 | | | Gross Profit | 21.0 | 19.7 |
| | 26.9 | 13.8 | 15.0 | | | Operating Expenses | 17.4 | 17.6 |
| | -.6 | 5.6 | 3.2 | | | Operating Profit | 3.6 | 2.1 |
| | .0 | .5 | .4 | | | All Other Expenses (net) | 1.0 | 1.3 |
| | -.6 | 5.2 | 2.8 | | | Profit Before Taxes | 2.5 | .8 |
| | | | | | | **RATIOS** | | |
| | 9.3 | 5.6 | 2.7 | | | | 3.0 | 3.0 |
| | 3.0 | 2.1 | 1.4 | | | Current | 1.6 | 1.5 |
| | .9 | 1.4 | 1.0 | | | | 1.1 | 1.1 |
| | 2.1 | 1.2 | 1.2 | | | | .9 | .7 |
| | .5 | .7 | .3 | | | Quick | .4 | .4 |
| | .3 | .3 | .2 | | | | .2 | .3 |
| | 4  99.5 | 7  53.3 | 12  31.0 | | | | 8  44.0 | 7  51.2 |
| | 14  25.8 | 19  19.4 | 19  19.2 | | | Sales/Receivables | 18  20.5 | 15  24.0 |
| | 33  11.2 | 27  13.6 | 28  13.0 | | | | 29  12.7 | 27  13.6 |
| | 31  11.8 | 34  10.8 | 60  6.1 | | | | 40  9.1 | 45  8.1 |
| | 58  6.3 | 74  4.9 | 78  4.7 | | | Cost of Sales/Inventory | 64  5.7 | 69  5.3 |
| | 104  3.5 | 126  2.9 | 122  3.0 | | | | 99  3.7 | 115  3.2 |
| | 6  62.2 | 7  49.6 | 14  26.8 | | | | 9  38.9 | 7  51.3 |
| | 18  20.7 | 15  23.6 | 23  15.6 | | | Cost of Sales/Payables | 15  23.8 | 15  24.4 |
| | 38  9.7 | 33  11.1 | 41  9.0 | | | | 32  11.4 | 33  10.9 |
| | 4.4 | 4.5 | 5.8 | | | | 7.2 | 5.5 |
| | 6.7 | 8.9 | 13.8 | | | Sales/Working Capital | 11.0 | 11.0 |
| | -140.9 | 17.7 | NM | | | | 50.5 | 46.8 |
| | 15.1 | 18.3 | 33.4 | | | | 11.2 | 8.3 |
| | (14) 7.2 | (22) 7.1 | (23) 8.4 | | | EBIT/Interest | (92) 3.1 | (72) 1.8 |
| | 1.4 | 1.5 | 1.5 | | | | 1.3 | -.2 |
| | | | | | | Net Profit + Depr., Dep., | 11.6 | 8.5 |
| | | | | | | Amort./Cur. Mat. L/T/D | (19) 5.8 | (18) 2.3 |
| | | | | | | | 1.3 | 1.0 |
| | .2 | .2 | .4 | | | | .2 | .2 |
| | .4 | .6 | .7 | | | Fixed/Worth | .7 | .7 |
| | 1.3 | 1.1 | 2.5 | | | | 2.4 | 3.0 |
| | .5 | .4 | .6 | | | | .8 | .9 |
| | 1.9 | .9 | 2.6 | | | Debt/Worth | 2.4 | 2.0 |
| | NM | 3.7 | 12.4 | | | | 11.6 | 26.1 |
| | 31.7 | 68.1 | 45.2 | | | % Profit Before Taxes/Tangible | 54.4 | 29.9 |
| | (12) 17.2 | (22) 26.9 | (22) 28.7 | | | Net Worth | (83) 19.7 | (60) 8.2 |
| | 4.6 | 2.7 | 10.3 | | | | 3.4 | -6.1 |
| | 15.6 | 28.5 | 11.9 | | | % Profit Before Taxes/Total | 16.2 | 9.5 |
| | 5.8 | 8.8 | 6.8 | | | Assets | 6.9 | 2.1 |
| | .5 | 1.5 | 2.9 | | | | .2 | -3.3 |
| | 79.7 | 49.6 | 31.5 | | | | 46.2 | 39.5 |
| | 23.1 | 16.5 | 10.2 | | | Sales/Net Fixed Assets | 17.4 | 15.1 |
| | 12.3 | 9.7 | 5.0 | | | | 8.8 | 7.2 |
| | 4.4 | 4.0 | 3.4 | | | | 4.1 | 4.1 |
| | 3.6 | 2.6 | 2.6 | | | Sales/Total Assets | 3.0 | 2.7 |
| | 2.0 | 1.9 | 1.5 | | | | 2.1 | 1.8 |
| | .6 | .3 | .9 | | | | .5 | .7 |
| | (13) 1.1 | (20) .8 | (23) 1.4 | | | % Depr., Dep., Amort./Sales | (88) 1.0 | (60) 1.2 |
| | 2.6 | 2.0 | 2.0 | | | | 1.5 | 2.1 |
| | | | | | | % Officers', Directors' | .8 | .9 |
| | | | | | | Owners' Comp/Sales | (30) 1.9 | (21) 2.0 |
| | | | | | | | 3.8 | 4.1 |
| 7999M | 77397M | 407757M | 1326434M | 1087701M | 1990847M | Net Sales ($) | 4410820M | 5057652M |
| 1028M | 18730M | 125256M | 549787M | 384022M | 1339781M | Total Assets ($) | 1826745M | 2389823M |

M = $ thousand    MM = $ million
See Pages 9 through 22 for Explanation of Ratios and Data

## Comparative Historical Data | Current Data Sorted by Sales

### Type of Statement

| | 4/1/09-3/31/10 | 4/1/10-3/31/11 | 4/1/11-3/31/12 | 0-1MM | 1-3MM | 3-5MM | 5-10MM | 10-25MM | 25MM & OVER |
|---|---|---|---|---|---|---|---|---|---|
| Unqualified | 8 | 18 | 12 | | | | | 1 | 11 |
| Reviewed | 8 | 14 | 14 | | | | | 5 | 8 |
| Compiled | 16 | 11 | 15 | | 1 | 6 | 2 | 5 | 1 |
| Tax Returns | 6 | 8 | 7 | | 2 | 3 | 1 | | |
| Other | 33 | 30 | 31 | 1 | 2 | 4 | 2 | 3 | 16 |
| | ALL | ALL | ALL | 9 (4/1-9/30/11) | | | 70 (10/1/11-3/31/12) | | |
| NUMBER OF STATEMENTS | 71 | 81 | 79 | 1 | 7 | 11 | 7 | 17 | 36 |

### ASSETS (%)

| | 09-10 | 10-11 | 11-12 | 0-1MM | 1-3MM | 3-5MM | 5-10MM | 10-25MM | 25MM & OVER |
|---|---|---|---|---|---|---|---|---|---|
| Cash & Equivalents | 7.9 | 8.3 | 9.7 | | | 8.3 | | 13.0 | 5.8 |
| Trade Receivables (net) | 14.4 | 16.4 | 15.9 | | | 21.1 | | 16.0 | 14.7 |
| Inventory | 38.6 | 38.7 | 41.4 | | | 53.0 | | 43.5 | 40.0 |
| All Other Current | 3.6 | 3.6 | 2.0 | | | .9 | | .3 | 3.5 |
| Total Current | 64.5 | 67.1 | 69.0 | | | 83.4 | | 72.8 | 64.0 |
| Fixed Assets (net) | 23.0 | 21.5 | 20.7 | | | 14.2 | | 19.0 | 22.7 |
| Intangibles (net) | 6.0 | 5.5 | 6.5 | | | .0 | | 6.2 | 10.1 |
| All Other Non-Current | 6.6 | 5.9 | 3.8 | | | 2.4 | | 1.9 | 3.2 |
| Total | 100.0 | 100.0 | 100.0 | | | 100.0 | | 100.0 | 100.0 |

### LIABILITIES (%)

| | 09-10 | 10-11 | 11-12 | 3-5MM | 10-25MM | 25MM & OVER |
|---|---|---|---|---|---|---|
| Notes Payable-Short Term | 15.8 | 14.7 | 11.2 | 7.8 | 9.1 | 13.7 |
| Cur. Mat.-L.T.D. | 3.8 | 5.7 | 2.4 | 1.7 | 3.3 | 2.7 |
| Trade Payables | 15.6 | 17.7 | 16.1 | 19.0 | 14.6 | 16.7 |
| Income Taxes Payable | .1 | .2 | .2 | .5 | .1 | .1 |
| All Other Current | 13.7 | 16.5 | 12.7 | 16.9 | 13.9 | 10.4 |
| Total Current | 48.9 | 54.9 | 42.6 | 45.8 | 41.0 | 43.6 |
| Long-Term Debt | 15.5 | 19.6 | 14.1 | 15.7 | 9.3 | 13.0 |
| Deferred Taxes | .8 | .6 | .5 | .3 | 1.3 | .4 |
| All Other Non-Current | 9.5 | 15.5 | 5.5 | 1.9 | 4.3 | 7.3 |
| Net Worth | 25.2 | 9.5 | 37.2 | 36.3 | 44.0 | 35.6 |
| Total Liabilities & Net Worth | 100.0 | 100.0 | 100.0 | 100.0 | 100.0 | 100.0 |

### INCOME DATA (%)

| | 09-10 | 10-11 | 11-12 | 3-5MM | 10-25MM | 25MM & OVER |
|---|---|---|---|---|---|---|
| Net Sales | 100.0 | 100.0 | 100.0 | 100.0 | 100.0 | 100.0 |
| Gross Profit | 18.7 | 19.5 | 20.1 | 27.2 | 17.4 | 16.7 |
| Operating Expenses | 18.2 | 15.2 | 16.5 | 23.2 | 13.1 | 13.0 |
| Operating Profit | .4 | 4.3 | 3.5 | 4.0 | 4.4 | 3.7 |
| All Other Expenses (net) | 1.2 | .7 | .7 | -.1 | .7 | 1.2 |
| Profit Before Taxes | -.8 | 3.6 | 2.8 | 4.1 | 3.7 | 2.6 |

### RATIOS

| | 09-10 | 10-11 | 11-12 | 3-5MM | 10-25MM | 25MM & OVER |
|---|---|---|---|---|---|---|
| Current | 2.8 | 3.8 | 3.5 | 4.1 | 5.7 | 2.5 |
| | 1.8 | 1.7 | 1.8 | 2.9 | 2.0 | 1.3 |
| | 1.1 | 1.0 | 1.1 | 1.7 | 1.1 | 1.1 |
| Quick | 1.0 | 1.2 | 1.2 | 1.2 | 1.5 | 1.0 |
| | .6 | .5 | .6 | .7 | .7 | .5 |
| | .2 | .2 | .3 | .5 | .3 | .2 |
| Sales/Receivables | 7   51.4 | 8   46.1 | 7   51.1 | 3   113.2 | 6   64.5 | 10   35.5 |
| | 20   18.3 | 23   15.8 | 19   18.9 | 27   13.6 | 19   18.9 | 19   18.9 |
| | 31   11.7 | 40   9.1 | 30   12.3 | 43   8.4 | 31   11.7 | 29   12.4 |
| Cost of Sales/Inventory | 46   8.0 | 43   8.4 | 40   9.2 | 53   6.9 | 38   9.5 | 41   8.9 |
| | 68   5.4 | 62   5.9 | 64   5.7 | 101   3.6 | 114   3.2 | 63   5.8 |
| | 108   3.4 | 104   3.5 | 111   3.3 | 111   3.3 | 130   2.8 | 74   4.9 |
| Cost of Sales/Payables | 9   41.2 | 9   42.3 | 8   44.9 | 12   31.3 | 7   53.2 | 14   27.0 |
| | 17   21.3 | 18   20.0 | 21   17.1 | 23   15.8 | 24   14.9 | 29   12.7 |
| | 34   10.8 | 40   9.1 | 37   9.9 | 43   8.5 | 40   9.1 | 37   9.8 |
| Sales/Working Capital | 4.6 | 4.9 | 5.7 | 4.8 | 3.8 | 6.7 |
| | 9.4 | 10.9 | 12.0 | 5.9 | 8.4 | 17.6 |
| | 40.8 | NM | 55.6 | 14.7 | 30.1 | 92.0 |
| EBIT/Interest | 10.6 | 11.3 | 14.0 | 12.1 | 55.1 | 14.3 |
| | (66) 1.9 | (74) 4.8 | (72) 5.5 | 5.2 | (16) 3.6 | (34) 6.8 |
| | -2.8 | 1.4 | 1.6 | 3.0 | 1.5 | 1.4 |
| Net Profit + Depr., Dep., Amort./Cur. Mat. L/T/D | 7.1 | 12.2 | 4.3 | | | 5.8 |
| | (12) 2.8 | (19) 2.0 | (22) 1.2 | | | (13) 1.0 |
| | -.2 | .4 | .4 | | | -1.0 |
| Fixed/Worth | .3 | .3 | .3 | .1 | .1 | .5 |
| | .7 | .9 | .7 | .4 | .5 | .9 |
| | 5.2 | NM | 1.4 | .6 | 1.4 | 3.5 |
| Debt/Worth | .7 | .8 | .6 | .5 | .3 | .7 |
| | 2.6 | 2.3 | 2.4 | 1.0 | 2.7 | 3.9 |
| | 16.8 | NM | 7.5 | 4.1 | 5.8 | 21.5 |
| % Profit Before Taxes/Tangible Net Worth | 27.0 | 43.9 | 50.8 | | 79.0 | 52.7 |
| | (55) 5.1 | (61) 17.8 | (68) 25.5 | | (16) 20.1 | (31) 31.6 |
| | -18.9 | 2.1 | 4.6 | | 4.7 | 2.2 |
| % Profit Before Taxes/Total Assets | 9.9 | 16.2 | 16.0 | 22.5 | 14.2 | 14.2 |
| | 2.2 | 7.2 | 6.9 | 10.5 | 4.1 | 7.0 |
| | -9.0 | 1.4 | 2.3 | 5.3 | 1.6 | 2.5 |
| Sales/Net Fixed Assets | 39.5 | 46.4 | 44.8 | 88.9 | 59.4 | 28.9 |
| | 12.3 | 13.8 | 15.1 | 38.7 | 10.4 | 14.5 |
| | 5.5 | 6.2 | 7.3 | 11.0 | 6.4 | 11.0 |
| Sales/Total Assets | 3.6 | 3.8 | 3.8 | 4.4 | 3.2 | 3.7 |
| | 2.3 | 2.6 | 2.6 | 3.0 | 1.9 | 2.7 |
| | 1.4 | 1.5 | 1.9 | 1.9 | 1.5 | 2.0 |
| % Depr., Dep., Amort./Sales | .8 | .8 | .7 | | .4 | .8 |
| | (57) 1.3 | (65) 1.4 | (68) 1.1 | | (15) 1.1 | (34) 1.0 |
| | 2.5 | 2.7 | 2.0 | | 2.4 | 1.7 |
| % Officers', Directors' Owners' Comp/Sales | 1.2 | 1.1 | 1.0 | | | |
| | (19) 3.0 | (22) 2.3 | (18) 1.8 | | | |
| | 4.5 | 4.0 | 2.8 | | | |

### Net Sales / Total Assets ($)

| | 09-10 | 10-11 | 11-12 | 0-1MM | 1-3MM | 3-5MM | 5-10MM | 10-25MM | 25MM & OVER |
|---|---|---|---|---|---|---|---|---|---|
| Net Sales ($) | 3672471M | 4048113M | 4898135M | 449M | 12075M | 46348M | 47326M | 315197M | 4476740M |
| Total Assets ($) | 1970602M | 2053933M | 2418604M | 44M | 6892M | 16554M | 14464M | 148769M | 2231881M |

M = $ thousand    MM = $ million
See Pages 9 through 22 for Explanation of Ratios and Data

## Current Data Sorted by Assets

## Comparative Historical Data

| | | | | | | Type of Statement | | |
|---|---|---|---|---|---|---|---|---|
| 1 | | 3 | 1 | 4 | | Unqualified | 8 | 8 |
| | 1 | | | | | Reviewed | 8 | 5 |
| | | 1 | | | | Compiled | 15 | 8 |
| | | 1 | | | | Tax Returns | 2 | 3 |
| 4 | 3 | 4 | 4 | 1 | 1 | Other | 23 | 22 |
| | 7 (4/1-9/30/11) | | 22 (10/1/11-3/31/12) | | | | 4/1/07-3/31/08 | 4/1/08-3/31/09 |
| 0-500M | 500M-2MM | 2-10MM | 10-50MM | 50-100MM | 100-250MM | | ALL | ALL |
| 5 | 4 | 6 | 7 | 2 | 5 | NUMBER OF STATEMENTS | 56 | 46 |
| % | % | % | % | % | % | ASSETS | % | % |
| | | | | | | Cash & Equivalents | 9.0 | 12.1 |
| | | | | | | Trade Receivables (net) | 16.9 | 12.4 |
| | | | | | | Inventory | 43.3 | 43.5 |
| | | | | | | All Other Current | 1.0 | 2.7 |
| | | | | | | Total Current | 70.2 | 70.7 |
| | | | | | | Fixed Assets (net) | 16.8 | 16.6 |
| | | | | | | Intangibles (net) | 7.6 | 6.3 |
| | | | | | | All Other Non-Current | 5.4 | 6.4 |
| | | | | | | Total | 100.0 | 100.0 |
| | | | | | | LIABILITIES | | |
| | | | | | | Notes Payable-Short Term | 18.5 | 16.8 |
| | | | | | | Cur. Mat.-L.T.D. | 1.2 | 2.5 |
| | | | | | | Trade Payables | 17.7 | 12.0 |
| | | | | | | Income Taxes Payable | .2 | .1 |
| | | | | | | All Other Current | 13.6 | 15.0 |
| | | | | | | Total Current | 51.3 | 46.3 |
| | | | | | | Long-Term Debt | 12.5 | 15.4 |
| | | | | | | Deferred Taxes | .1 | .1 |
| | | | | | | All Other Non-Current | 10.3 | 6.7 |
| | | | | | | Net Worth | 25.9 | 31.5 |
| | | | | | | Total Liabilties & Net Worth | 100.0 | 100.0 |
| | | | | | | INCOME DATA | | |
| | | | | | | Net Sales | 100.0 | 100.0 |
| | | | | | | Gross Profit | 16.0 | 15.6 |
| | | | | | | Operating Expenses | 14.3 | 16.0 |
| | | | | | | Operating Profit | 1.6 | -.4 |
| | | | | | | All Other Expenses (net) | .9 | 1.4 |
| | | | | | | Profit Before Taxes | .8 | -1.9 |
| | | | | | | RATIOS | | |
| | | | | | | | 2.2 | 2.5 |
| | | | | | | Current | 1.4 | 1.3 |
| | | | | | | | 1.0 | 1.1 |
| | | | | | | | 1.0 | 1.1 |
| | | | | | | Quick | .5 | .4 |
| | | | | | | | .2 | .2 |
| | | | | | | | 8   45.0 | 4   85.1 |
| | | | | | | Sales/Receivables | 15   25.0 | 10   37.0 |
| | | | | | | | 26   14.0 | 17   21.1 |
| | | | | | | | 33   10.9 | 30   12.2 |
| | | | | | | Cost of Sales/Inventory | 49   7.4 | 46   7.9 |
| | | | | | | | 78   4.7 | 90   4.1 |
| | | | | | | | 8   43.6 | 6   65.4 |
| | | | | | | Cost of Sales/Payables | 22   16.5 | 13   29.2 |
| | | | | | | | 40   9.1 | 35   10.4 |
| | | | | | | | 10.3 | 7.5 |
| | | | | | | Sales/Working Capital | 20.0 | 16.3 |
| | | | | | | | NM | 99.5 |
| | | | | | | | 11.9 | 9.6 |
| | | | | | | EBIT/Interest | (51)   2.0 | (43)   1.2 |
| | | | | | | | .3 | -3.2 |
| | | | | | | | 11.5 | |
| | | | | | | Net Profit + Depr., Dep., Amort./Cur. Mat. L/T/D | (10)   7.2 | |
| | | | | | | | 3.0 | |
| | | | | | | | .2 | .2 |
| | | | | | | Fixed/Worth | .5 | .6 |
| | | | | | | | UND | 184.3 |
| | | | | | | | .8 | .8 |
| | | | | | | Debt/Worth | 2.4 | 1.6 |
| | | | | | | | UND | 999.8 |
| | | | | | | | 45.9 | 25.5 |
| | | | | | | % Profit Before Taxes/Tangible Net Worth | (43)   13.2 | (36)   2.5 |
| | | | | | | | -3.7 | -19.3 |
| | | | | | | | 16.7 | 14.0 |
| | | | | | | % Profit Before Taxes/Total Assets | 3.7 | .4 |
| | | | | | | | -2.7 | -9.5 |
| | | | | | | | 58.2 | 68.4 |
| | | | | | | Sales/Net Fixed Assets | 25.8 | 25.5 |
| | | | | | | | 13.5 | 12.0 |
| | | | | | | | 5.4 | 4.7 |
| | | | | | | Sales/Total Assets | 3.4 | 3.2 |
| | | | | | | | 2.2 | 1.8 |
| | | | | | | | .4 | .3 |
| | | | | | | % Depr., Dep., Amort./Sales | (48)   .6 | (36)   .7 |
| | | | | | | | 1.2 | 1.3 |
| | | | | | | | 1.4 | 1.5 |
| | | | | | | % Officers', Directors' Owners' Comp/Sales | (17)   2.2 | (13)   1.9 |
| | | | | | | | 4.5 | 2.7 |
| 3385M | 12886M | 75748M | 618161M | 268453M | 2261102M | Net Sales ($) | 5062746M | 3906028M |
| 237M | 5110M | 24451M | 155634M | 162140M | 833260M | Total Assets ($) | 1633932M | 1212954M |

M = $ thousand    MM = $ million
See Pages 9 through 22 for Explanation of Ratios and Data

## Comparative Historical Data | Current Data Sorted by Sales

| 10 | 8 | 8 | Type of Statement | | | | | | 8 |
|---|---|---|---|---|---|---|---|---|---|
| 10 | 8 | 8 | Unqualified | 1 | | | | | 8 |
| 9 | 8 | 1 | Reviewed | | 1 | | | 1 | |
| 10 | 6 | 2 | Compiled | | | | | 1 | |
| 2 | 2 | 1 | Tax Returns | | | | | | |
| 11 | 18 | 17 | Other | 4 | 2 | 3 | | 1 | 7 |
| 4/1/09-3/31/10 | 4/1/10-3/31/11 | 4/1/11-3/31/12 | | 0-1MM | 1-3MM | 3-5MM | 5-10MM | 10-25MM | 25MM & OVER |
| ALL | ALL | ALL | | | 7 (4/1-9/30/11) | | 22 (10/1/11-3/31/12) | | |
| 42 | 42 | 29 | **NUMBER OF STATEMENTS** | 5 | 3 | 3 | | 3 | 15 |
| % | % | % | **ASSETS** | % | % | % | | % | % |
| 11.2 | 10.4 | 7.9 | Cash & Equivalents | | | | | | 4.2 |
| 13.8 | 19.4 | 21.4 | Trade Receivables (net) | | | | | | 22.0 |
| 48.1 | 40.5 | 40.6 | Inventory | | | | | | 33.8 |
| 3.2 | 3.3 | 3.5 | All Other Current | | | | | | 4.6 |
| 76.3 | 73.7 | 73.4 | Total Current | | | | | | 64.5 |
| 13.0 | 12.6 | 12.9 | Fixed Assets (net) | | | | | | 15.5 |
| 6.0 | 4.8 | 8.5 | Intangibles (net) | | | | | | 15.2 |
| 4.7 | 8.9 | 5.2 | All Other Non-Current | | | | | | 4.8 |
| 100.0 | 100.0 | 100.0 | Total | | | | | | 100.0 |
| | | | **LIABILITIES** | | | | | | |
| 17.7 | 11.0 | 7.7 | Notes Payable-Short Term | | | | | | 6.1 |
| 3.6 | 1.8 | .8 | Cur. Mat.-L.T.D. | | | | | | 1.1 |
| 11.4 | 12.9 | 14.4 | Trade Payables | | | | | | 12.7 |
| .2 | .2 | .2 | Income Taxes Payable | | | | | | .0 |
| 16.5 | 16.6 | 21.1 | All Other Current | | | | | | 17.3 |
| 49.4 | 42.4 | 44.1 | Total Current | | | | | | 37.1 |
| 15.8 | 10.1 | 10.7 | Long-Term Debt | | | | | | 14.1 |
| .0 | .1 | .6 | Deferred Taxes | | | | | | 1.1 |
| 11.1 | 19.0 | 9.1 | All Other Non-Current | | | | | | 12.5 |
| 23.6 | 28.3 | 35.8 | Net Worth | | | | | | 35.2 |
| 100.0 | 100.0 | 100.0 | Total Liabilities & Net Worth | | | | | | 100.0 |
| | | | **INCOME DATA** | | | | | | |
| 100.0 | 100.0 | 100.0 | Net Sales | | | | | | 100.0 |
| 15.4 | 17.5 | 19.2 | Gross Profit | | | | | | 14.5 |
| 18.5 | 15.9 | 17.0 | Operating Expenses | | | | | | 12.1 |
| -3.1 | 1.6 | 2.2 | Operating Profit | | | | | | 2.4 |
| 1.5 | .5 | .7 | All Other Expenses (net) | | | | | | 1.5 |
| -4.6 | 1.0 | 1.5 | Profit Before Taxes | | | | | | .9 |
| | | | **RATIOS** | | | | | | |
| 2.8 | 2.8 | 2.6 | Current | | | | | | 2.5 |
| 1.4 | 1.9 | 1.9 | | | | | | | 1.9 |
| 1.0 | 1.2 | 1.1 | | | | | | | 1.2 |
| 1.1 | 1.2 | 1.0 | Quick | | | | | | 1.0 |
| .5 | .8 | .6 | | | | | | | .6 |
| .3 | .5 | .3 | | | | | | | .4 |
| 6  64.0 | 5  67.2 | 15  24.9 | Sales/Receivables | | | | | | 17  21.9 |
| 14  25.6 | 18  20.0 | 23  16.0 | | | | | | | 22  16.7 |
| 31  11.9 | 33  11.2 | 39  9.3 | | | | | | | 33  10.9 |
| 48  7.7 | 36  10.0 | 39  9.4 | Cost of Sales/Inventory | | | | | | 39  9.4 |
| 70  5.2 | 54  6.7 | 55  6.6 | | | | | | | 46  8.0 |
| 139  2.6 | 79  4.6 | 126  2.9 | | | | | | | 55  6.6 |
| 7  54.8 | 7  49.6 | 8  44.4 | Cost of Sales/Payables | | | | | | 10  35.0 |
| 14  26.1 | 15  24.5 | 17  22.1 | | | | | | | 12  31.2 |
| 28  13.2 | 24  14.9 | 42  8.6 | | | | | | | 26  14.0 |
| 4.7 | 5.7 | 5.7 | Sales/Working Capital | | | | | | 6.8 |
| 21.6 | 10.6 | 8.0 | | | | | | | 9.7 |
| -687.4 | 40.0 | 37.8 | | | | | | | 46.4 |
| 11.6 | 25.8 | 9.4 | EBIT/Interest | | | | | | 4.0 |
| (39) -.5 | (35) 5.3 | (22) 2.0 | | | | | | | (14) .9 |
| -7.7 | .7 | .1 | | | | | | | -.9 |
| | | | Net Profit + Depr., Dep., Amort./Cur. Mat. L/T/D | | | | | | |
| .2 | .1 | .1 | Fixed/Worth | | | | | | .1 |
| .8 | .3 | .3 | | | | | | | .6 |
| 3.9 | 1.8 | 9.1 | | | | | | | -1.3 |
| 1.4 | .9 | .8 | Debt/Worth | | | | | | 1.0 |
| 6.3 | 2.8 | 1.9 | | | | | | | 1.9 |
| 86.9 | NM | 26.5 | | | | | | | -5.5 |
| 80.9 | 80.5 | 31.0 | % Profit Before Taxes/Tangible Net Worth | | | | | | 64.0 |
| (34) .7 | (32) 34.3 | (23) 9.1 | | | | | | | (11) -.2 |
| -66.2 | -.4 | -1.0 | | | | | | | -1.9 |
| 9.9 | 17.4 | 10.7 | % Profit Before Taxes/Total Assets | | | | | | 8.4 |
| -4.3 | 5.3 | 1.8 | | | | | | | -.1 |
| -16.5 | -3.7 | -1.0 | | | | | | | -1.0 |
| 62.1 | 101.4 | 69.0 | Sales/Net Fixed Assets | | | | | | 54.8 |
| 35.5 | 47.6 | 22.0 | | | | | | | 19.8 |
| 12.1 | 17.0 | 9.0 | | | | | | | 7.9 |
| 3.9 | 4.5 | 4.3 | Sales/Total Assets | | | | | | 4.5 |
| 2.8 | 3.4 | 2.8 | | | | | | | 3.7 |
| 1.6 | 2.0 | 1.7 | | | | | | | 1.9 |
| .4 | .4 | .4 | % Depr., Dep., Amort./Sales | | | | | | .4 |
| (33) 1.0 | (35) .6 | (20) 1.1 | | | | | | | (14) 1.2 |
| 1.4 | 1.1 | 1.7 | | | | | | | 2.1 |
| 2.2 | .8 | | % Officers', Directors' Owners' Comp/Sales | | | | | | |
| (11) 2.8 | (10) 2.2 | | | | | | | | |
| 3.7 | 3.6 | | | | | | | | |
| 2309508M | 3099385M | 3239735M | Net Sales ($) | 1146M | 6396M | 12614M | | 40039M | 3179540M |
| 964214M | 1188081M | 1180832M | Total Assets ($) | 2681M | 4307M | 3492M | | 11927M | 1158425M |

*(Columns 0-1MM through 10-25MM for the body rows are marked "DATA NOT AVAILABLE".)*

**Current Data Sorted by Assets**           **Comparative Historical Data**

| | | | | | | Type of Statement | | |
|---|---|---|---|---|---|---|---|---|
| | | 3 | 1 | | | Unqualified | 3 | 4 |
| | 1 | 1 | 1 | | | Reviewed | | 4 |
| | 2 | 1 | | | | Compiled | | 1 |
| 2 | 1 | | 1 | 5 | 2 | Tax Returns | | |
| | 7 (4/1-9/30/11) | | | 15 (10/1/11-3/31/12) | | Other | | |
| 0-500M | 500M-2MM | 2-10MM | 10-50MM | 50-100MM | 100-250MM | | 7<br>4/1/07-<br>3/31/08<br>ALL | 15<br>4/1/08-<br>3/31/09<br>ALL |
| 2 | 4 | 6 | 7 | 2 | 1 | **NUMBER OF STATEMENTS** | 10 | 24 |
| % | % | % | % | % | % | **ASSETS** | % | % |
| | | | | | | Cash & Equivalents | 6.1 | 6.1 |
| | | | | | | Trade Receivables (net) | 26.4 | 25.1 |
| | | | | | | Inventory | 41.1 | 27.2 |
| | | | | | | All Other Current | 4.4 | 3.9 |
| | | | | | | Total Current | 77.9 | 62.4 |
| | | | | | | Fixed Assets (net) | 18.9 | 27.7 |
| | | | | | | Intangibles (net) | 1.1 | 5.1 |
| | | | | | | All Other Non-Current | 2.0 | 4.8 |
| | | | | | | Total | 100.0 | 100.0 |
| | | | | | | **LIABILITIES** | | |
| | | | | | | Notes Payable-Short Term | 15.6 | 12.4 |
| | | | | | | Cur. Mat.-L.T.D. | .3 | 4.3 |
| | | | | | | Trade Payables | 13.7 | 16.6 |
| | | | | | | Income Taxes Payable | .0 | .2 |
| | | | | | | All Other Current | 27.4 | 11.6 |
| | | | | | | Total Current | 57.0 | 45.1 |
| | | | | | | Long-Term Debt | 10.9 | 15.5 |
| | | | | | | Deferred Taxes | .1 | .5 |
| | | | | | | All Other Non-Current | 1.1 | 6.0 |
| | | | | | | Net Worth | 30.9 | 32.9 |
| | | | | | | Total Liabilities & Net Worth | 100.0 | 100.0 |
| | | | | | | **INCOME DATA** | | |
| | | | | | | Net Sales | 100.0 | 100.0 |
| | | | | | | Gross Profit | 28.8 | 22.7 |
| | | | | | | Operating Expenses | 25.3 | 18.9 |
| | | | | | | Operating Profit | 3.5 | 3.8 |
| | | | | | | All Other Expenses (net) | .4 | 1.5 |
| | | | | | | Profit Before Taxes | 3.1 | 2.4 |
| | | | | | | **RATIOS** | | |
| | | | | | | Current | 2.1 | 2.4 |
| | | | | | | | 1.3 | 1.4 |
| | | | | | | | 1.2 | 1.1 |
| | | | | | | Quick | .9 | 1.0 |
| | | | | | | | .6 | .8 |
| | | | | | | | .3 | .4 |
| | | | | | | Sales/Receivables | 38   9.6 | 29   12.8 |
| | | | | | | | 42   8.7 | 37   9.8 |
| | | | | | | | 50   7.3 | 48   7.5 |
| | | | | | | Cost of Sales/Inventory | 41   8.9 | 30   12.3 |
| | | | | | | | 97   3.8 | 51   7.2 |
| | | | | | | | 182   2.0 | 95   3.8 |
| | | | | | | Cost of Sales/Payables | 12   31.5 | 17   21.8 |
| | | | | | | | 31   11.7 | 31   11.8 |
| | | | | | | | 70   5.2 | 45   8.2 |
| | | | | | | Sales/Working Capital | 5.8 | 6.9 |
| | | | | | | | 13.0 | 14.8 |
| | | | | | | | 24.5 | 69.6 |
| | | | | | | EBIT/Interest | 16.6 | 7.1 |
| | | | | | | | 5.4   (23) | 2.5 |
| | | | | | | | 1.2 | -.3 |
| | | | | | | Net Profit + Depr., Dep., Amort./Cur. Mat. L/T/D | | |
| | | | | | | Fixed/Worth | .1 | .3 |
| | | | | | | | .5 | 1.1 |
| | | | | | | | 2.1 | 2.4 |
| | | | | | | Debt/Worth | 1.1 | .7 |
| | | | | | | | 3.3 | 3.4 |
| | | | | | | | 9.4 | 11.3 |
| | | | | | | % Profit Before Taxes/Tangible Net Worth | 36.1 | 43.4 |
| | | | | | | | 22.0   (21) | 13.8 |
| | | | | | | | -10.3 | -7.8 |
| | | | | | | % Profit Before Taxes/Total Assets | 13.9 | 10.1 |
| | | | | | | | 4.2 | 3.6 |
| | | | | | | | .2 | -.8 |
| | | | | | | Sales/Net Fixed Assets | 59.1 | 23.9 |
| | | | | | | | 25.5 | 12.7 |
| | | | | | | | 4.8 | 4.2 |
| | | | | | | Sales/Total Assets | 2.5 | 2.8 |
| | | | | | | | 1.9 | 2.4 |
| | | | | | | | 1.7 | 1.9 |
| | | | | | | % Depr., Dep., Amort./Sales | | 1.0 |
| | | | | | | | (17) | 3.4 |
| | | | | | | | | 4.3 |
| | | | | | | % Officers', Directors' Owners' Comp/Sales | | |
| 6220M | 25655M | 90758M | 385820M | 219692M | 351203M | Net Sales ($) | 631845M | 2428474M |
| 702M | 6338M | 42035M | 165143M | 151067M | 114657M | Total Assets ($) | 294647M | 1030585M |

M = $ thousand    MM = $ million
See Pages 9 through 22 for Explanation of Ratios and Data

## Comparative Historical Data | Current Data Sorted by Sales

| | | | Type of Statement | 0-1MM | 1-3MM | 3-5MM | 5-10MM | 10-25MM | 25MM & OVER |
|---|---|---|---|---|---|---|---|---|---|
| 3 | 4 | 4 | Unqualified | | | | | 3 | 1 |
| 4 | 3 | 3 | Reviewed | | | | 1 | 1 | 1 |
| 2 | 2 | 1 | Compiled | | | | | 1 | |
| | 4 | 2 | Tax Returns | | | 2 | | | |
| 12 | 2 | 12 | Other | | 1 | 2 | | 1 | 8 |
| 4/1/09- | 4/1/10- | 4/1/11- | | | 7 (4/1-9/30/11) | | | 15 (10/1/11-3/31/12) | |
| 3/31/10 | 3/31/11 | 3/31/12 | | | | | | | |
| ALL | ALL | ALL | | | | | | | |
| 21 | 30 | 22 | NUMBER OF STATEMENTS | | 1 | 4 | 1 | 6 | 10 |
| % | % | % | **ASSETS** | % | % | % | % | % | % |
| 10.2 | 10.5 | 8.8 | Cash & Equivalents | D | | | | | 12.3 |
| 25.8 | 28.5 | 33.2 | Trade Receivables (net) | A | | | | | 26.4 |
| 34.1 | 31.1 | 29.8 | Inventory | T | | | | | 28.1 |
| 2.0 | 4.1 | 6.3 | All Other Current | A | | | | | 13.2 |
| 72.1 | 74.2 | 78.2 | Total Current | | | | | | 80.0 |
| 18.7 | 16.5 | 16.9 | Fixed Assets (net) | N | | | | | 15.9 |
| 4.1 | 5.8 | 1.7 | Intangibles (net) | O | | | | | .0 |
| 5.0 | 3.5 | 3.2 | All Other Non-Current | T | | | | | 4.1 |
| 100.0 | 100.0 | 100.0 | Total | | | | | | 100.0 |
| | | | **LIABILITIES** | A | | | | | |
| 9.8 | 8.5 | 8.6 | Notes Payable-Short Term | V | | | | | 6.6 |
| 2.7 | 2.8 | 1.6 | Cur. Mat.-L.T.D. | A | | | | | .7 |
| 15.1 | 19.0 | 21.5 | Trade Payables | I | | | | | 22.7 |
| .0 | .1 | .2 | Income Taxes Payable | L | | | | | .2 |
| 6.2 | 9.2 | 12.5 | All Other Current | A | | | | | 19.6 |
| 33.9 | 39.6 | 44.4 | Total Current | B | | | | | 49.9 |
| 16.0 | 7.6 | 11.1 | Long-Term Debt | L | | | | | 4.0 |
| .3 | .1 | .5 | Deferred Taxes | E | | | | | .2 |
| 10.5 | 8.0 | 4.3 | All Other Non-Current | | | | | | 3.9 |
| 39.3 | 44.6 | 39.7 | Net Worth | | | | | | 41.9 |
| 100.0 | 100.0 | 100.0 | Total Liabilities & Net Worth | | | | | | 100.0 |
| | | | **INCOME DATA** | | | | | | |
| 100.0 | 100.0 | 100.0 | Net Sales | | | | | | 100.0 |
| 30.0 | 26.8 | 25.0 | Gross Profit | | | | | | 21.8 |
| 27.1 | 19.4 | 18.9 | Operating Expenses | | | | | | 14.1 |
| 3.0 | 7.4 | 6.1 | Operating Profit | | | | | | 7.7 |
| 1.4 | 1.4 | 1.0 | All Other Expenses (net) | | | | | | 1.0 |
| 1.5 | 6.0 | 5.0 | Profit Before Taxes | | | | | | 6.6 |
| | | | **RATIOS** | | | | | | |
| 4.5 | 3.2 | 3.4 | | | | | | | 3.6 |
| 2.2 | 2.4 | 2.6 | Current | | | | | | 2.4 |
| 1.3 | 1.5 | 1.6 | | | | | | | 1.2 |
| 1.7 | 2.0 | 2.0 | | | | | | | 2.5 |
| 1.2 | .9 | 1.2 | Quick | | | | | | .8 |
| .6 | .7 | .8 | | | | | | | .5 |
| 35  10.5 | 35  10.3 | 27  13.4 | | | | | | | 25  14.6 |
| 60  6.1 | 43  8.4 | 49  7.4 | Sales/Receivables | | | | | | 41  8.8 |
| 63  5.8 | 57  6.4 | 61  6.0 | | | | | | | 57  6.4 |
| 61  6.0 | 31  11.8 | 27  13.6 | | | | | | | 27  13.6 |
| 99  3.7 | 64  5.7 | 62  5.9 | Cost of Sales/Inventory | | | | | | 49  7.5 |
| 153  2.4 | 128  2.8 | 104  3.5 | | | | | | | 104  3.5 |
| 24  15.1 | 25  14.5 | 20  18.6 | | | | | | | 18  20.8 |
| 40  9.1 | 39  9.3 | 27  13.7 | Cost of Sales/Payables | | | | | | 30  12.2 |
| 54  6.7 | 58  6.3 | 40  9.1 | | | | | | | 48  7.6 |
| 2.1 | 3.6 | 3.8 | | | | | | | 3.4 |
| 5.1 | 6.9 | 5.9 | Sales/Working Capital | | | | | | 7.5 |
| 13.3 | 13.8 | 17.9 | | | | | | | 32.7 |
| 11.4 | 42.6 | 46.3 | | | | | | | |
| (19) 2.9 | (23) 7.9 | (18) 14.2 | EBIT/Interest | | | | | | |
| .3 | 2.2 | 3.4 | | | | | | | |
| | | | Net Profit + Depr., Dep., Amort./Cur. Mat. L/T/D | | | | | | |
| .1 | .1 | .1 | | | | | | | .1 |
| .4 | .4 | .3 | Fixed/Worth | | | | | | .3 |
| 1.4 | 2.1 | .9 | | | | | | | .9 |
| .7 | .5 | .4 | | | | | | | .4 |
| 1.6 | 1.3 | .9 | Debt/Worth | | | | | | .8 |
| 4.5 | 4.4 | 2.2 | | | | | | | 6.7 |
| 21.2 | 66.0 | 52.5 | | | | | | | |
| (19) 6.6 | (27) 36.8 | (19) 27.6 | % Profit Before Taxes/Tangible Net Worth | | | | | | |
| -5.9 | 13.6 | 10.8 | | | | | | | |
| 9.4 | 20.6 | 28.3 | | | | | | | 28.6 |
| 1.7 | 12.6 | 17.7 | % Profit Before Taxes/Total Assets | | | | | | 17.7 |
| -2.4 | 4.2 | 2.7 | | | | | | | 1.6 |
| 35.8 | 49.3 | 85.1 | | | | | | | 75.6 |
| 10.7 | 24.0 | 28.0 | Sales/Net Fixed Assets | | | | | | 16.9 |
| 3.6 | 6.2 | 8.9 | | | | | | | 8.1 |
| 2.1 | 2.9 | 3.2 | | | | | | | 3.2 |
| 1.7 | 2.1 | 2.6 | Sales/Total Assets | | | | | | 2.3 |
| 1.1 | 1.5 | 1.7 | | | | | | | 1.7 |
| 1.3 | .8 | .5 | | | | | | | |
| (14) 2.4 | (25) 1.6 | (16) 1.2 | % Depr., Dep., Amort./Sales | | | | | | |
| 4.3 | 3.7 | 2.0 | | | | | | | |
| | | 1.7 | | | | | | | |
| | (10) 3.4 | 3.4 | % Officers', Directors' Owners' Comp/Sales | | | | | | |
| | | 4.6 | | | | | | | |
| 777131M | 1771965M | 1079348M | Net Sales ($) | | 1859M | 18545M | 5509M | 88854M | 964581M |
| 571404M | 897714M | 479942M | Total Assets ($) | | 339M | 11102M | 1751M | 41060M | 425690M |

© RMA 2012    M = $ thousand    MM = $ million
See Pages 9 through 22 for Explanation of Ratios and Data

## Current Data Sorted by Assets         Comparative Historical Data

### Type of Statement

| | 0-500M | 500M-2MM | 2-10MM | 10-50MM | 50-100MM | 100-250MM | | 4/1/07-3/31/08 ALL | 4/1/08-3/31/09 ALL |
|---|---|---|---|---|---|---|---|---|---|
| Unqualified | | 1 | | 1 | | 1 | | 1 | 2 |
| Reviewed | | | | 4 | | | | 1 | 4 |
| Compiled | | 1 | | 1 | | | | | 2 |
| Tax Returns | | 1 | | 1 | | | | 1 | 1 |
| Other | 1 | 3 | 1 | 7 | 4 | | | 6 | 4 |
| | | | | | | | | 6 | |
| | **0-500M** | **500M-2MM** 6 (4/1-9/30/11) | **2-10MM** | **10-50MM** 24 (10/1/11-3/31/12) | **50-100MM** | **100-250MM** | **NUMBER OF STATEMENTS** | **4/1/07- 3/31/08 ALL** | **4/1/08- 3/31/09 ALL** |
| | 2 | 5 | 7 | 11 | 5 | | | 9 | 13 |
| | % | % | % | % | % | % | | % | % |

| 0-500M | 500M-2MM | 2-10MM | 10-50MM | 50-100MM | 100-250MM | | 4/1/07-3/31/08 | 4/1/08-3/31/09 |
|---|---|---|---|---|---|---|---|---|
| | | | | | | **ASSETS** | | |
| | | | 11.6 | | | Cash & Equivalents | | 5.8 |
| | | | 23.5 | | | Trade Receivables (net) | | 12.9 |
| | | | 26.0 | | | Inventory | | 28.6 |
| | | | 2.0 | | | All Other Current | | 1.0 |
| | | | 63.1 | | | Total Current | | 48.3 |
| | | | 27.4 | | | Fixed Assets (net) | | 35.6 |
| | | | 7.9 | | | Intangibles (net) | | 13.3 |
| | | | 1.6 | | | All Other Non-Current | | 2.9 |
| | | | 100.0 | | | Total | | 100.0 |
| | | | | | | **LIABILITIES** | | |
| | | | 11.3 | | | Notes Payable-Short Term | | 12.5 |
| | | | 4.3 | | | Cur. Mat.-L.T.D. | | 6.5 |
| | | | 14.3 | | | Trade Payables | | 9.1 |
| | | | .1 | | | Income Taxes Payable | | .0 |
| | | | 6.4 | | | All Other Current | | 13.2 |
| | | | 36.6 | | | Total Current | | 41.3 |
| | | | 40.3 | | | Long-Term Debt | | 21.7 |
| | | | 2.0 | | | Deferred Taxes | | .6 |
| | | | 7.9 | | | All Other Non-Current | | 6.4 |
| | | | 13.3 | | | Net Worth | | 30.1 |
| | | | 100.0 | | | Total Liabilities & Net Worth | | 100.0 |
| | | | | | | **INCOME DATA** | | |
| | | | 100.0 | | | Net Sales | | 100.0 |
| | | | 24.3 | | | Gross Profit | | 21.7 |
| | | | 16.0 | | | Operating Expenses | | 20.6 |
| | | | 8.3 | | | Operating Profit | | 1.1 |
| | | | 1.0 | | | All Other Expenses (net) | | 3.1 |
| | | | 7.3 | | | Profit Before Taxes | | -2.0 |
| | | | | | | **RATIOS** | | |
| | | | 4.4 | | | | | 3.3 |
| | | | 1.4 | | | Current | | 1.6 |
| | | | 1.2 | | | | | .9 |
| | | | 1.3 | | | | | 1.2 |
| | | | .8 | | | Quick | | .6 |
| | | | .7 | | | | | .2 |
| | | | 18  20.0 | | | | 17  21.5 | |
| | | | 40  9.2 | | | Sales/Receivables | 24  15.3 | |
| | | | 45  8.1 | | | | 40  9.1 | |
| | | | 31  11.8 | | | | 20  17.9 | |
| | | | 48  7.6 | | | Cost of Sales/Inventory | 93  3.9 | |
| | | | 107  3.4 | | | | 150  2.4 | |
| | | | 21  17.7 | | | | 11  31.9 | |
| | | | 27  13.7 | | | Cost of Sales/Payables | 23  16.0 | |
| | | | 36  10.2 | | | | 32  11.4 | |
| | | | 2.8 | | | | | 3.8 |
| | | | 16.0 | | | Sales/Working Capital | | 7.7 |
| | | | 27.1 | | | | | -35.5 |
| | | | | | | | | 2.6 |
| | | | | | | EBIT/Interest | (11) | .8 |
| | | | | | | | | -3.7 |
| | | | | | | Net Profit + Depr., Dep., Amort./Cur. Mat. L/T/D | | |
| | | | .5 | | | | | .4 |
| | | | 1.6 | | | Fixed/Worth | | 1.7 |
| | | | -1.5 | | | | | -1.8 |
| | | | 1.3 | | | | | .9 |
| | | | 6.0 | | | Debt/Worth | | 3.0 |
| | | | -4.5 | | | | | -4.3 |
| | | | | | | % Profit Before Taxes/Tangible Net Worth | | |
| | | | 18.0 | | | | | 2.1 |
| | | | 15.0 | | | % Profit Before Taxes/Total Assets | | -1.1 |
| | | | 5.0 | | | | | -6.5 |
| | | | 16.7 | | | | | 21.6 |
| | | | 5.8 | | | Sales/Net Fixed Assets | | 5.6 |
| | | | 3.8 | | | | | 1.8 |
| | | | 3.3 | | | | | 2.5 |
| | | | 2.1 | | | Sales/Total Assets | | 1.1 |
| | | | 1.1 | | | | | 1.0 |
| | | | 1.1 | | | | | 1.2 |
| | | | 1.9 | | | % Depr., Dep., Amort./Sales | (11) | 3.2 |
| | | | 5.2 | | | | | 7.9 |
| | | | | | | % Officers', Directors' Owners' Comp/Sales | | |
| 2796M | 15798M | 57606M | 401375M | 687385M | | Net Sales ($) | 191306M | 176626M |
| 721M | 5205M | 30568M | 204414M | 374436M | | Total Assets ($) | 121597M | 141371M |

*(Columns 0-500M, 500M-2MM, 2-10MM, 50-100MM and 100-250MM: DATA NOT AVAILABLE for the Assets, Liabilities and Income Data sections.)*

## Comparative Historical Data | Current Data Sorted by Sales

| Type of Statement | 4/1/09-3/31/10 ALL | 4/1/10-3/31/11 ALL | 4/1/11-3/31/12 ALL | 0-1MM | 1-3MM | 3-5MM | 5-10MM | 10-25MM | 25MM & OVER |
|---|---|---|---|---|---|---|---|---|---|
| Unqualified | 3 | 5 | 3 | 1 | | | 4 | 1 | 2 |
| Reviewed | 1 | 4 | 8 | | | | | | 3 |
| Compiled | 3 | 1 | 1 | | 1 | 1 | 1 | | |
| Tax Returns | | | 2 | | 2 | 2 | 1 | 3 | |
| Other | 9 | 9 | 16 | | | | | | 8 |
| | | | | 6 (4/1-9/30/11) | | | 24 (10/1/11-3/31/12) | | |
| **NUMBER OF STATEMENTS** | 16 | 23 | 30 | 1 | 3 | 3 | 6 | 4 | 13 |
| | % | % | % | % | % | % | % | % | % |
| **ASSETS** | | | | | | | | | |
| Cash & Equivalents | 5.4 | 4.4 | 9.0 | | | | | | 3.8 |
| Trade Receivables (net) | 16.9 | 23.6 | 22.6 | | | | | | 27.6 |
| Inventory | 28.9 | 34.1 | 29.2 | | | | | | 27.9 |
| All Other Current | 3.2 | 4.4 | 2.1 | | | | | | 2.3 |
| Total Current | 54.4 | 66.5 | 62.9 | | | | | | 61.5 |
| Fixed Assets (net) | 29.4 | 21.4 | 27.7 | | | | | | 28.0 |
| Intangibles (net) | 12.6 | 8.7 | 5.7 | | | | | | 6.9 |
| All Other Non-Current | 3.7 | 3.4 | 3.7 | | | | | | 3.6 |
| Total | 100.0 | 100.0 | 100.0 | | | | | | 100.0 |
| **LIABILITIES** | | | | | | | | | |
| Notes Payable-Short Term | 5.9 | 10.2 | 11.9 | | | | | | 11.8 |
| Cur. Mat.-L.T.D. | 4.4 | 3.4 | 3.9 | | | | | | 3.9 |
| Trade Payables | 10.6 | 18.7 | 13.9 | | | | | | 17.3 |
| Income Taxes Payable | .1 | .4 | .1 | | | | | | .1 |
| All Other Current | 7.2 | 8.0 | 11.0 | | | | | | 8.4 |
| Total Current | 28.2 | 40.7 | 40.8 | | | | | | 41.5 |
| Long-Term Debt | 20.5 | 18.4 | 19.9 | | | | | | 24.6 |
| Deferred Taxes | .9 | 1.1 | .8 | | | | | | 1.0 |
| All Other Non-Current | 10.2 | 5.8 | 5.4 | | | | | | 7.2 |
| Net Worth | 40.2 | 34.1 | 33.2 | | | | | | 25.8 |
| Total Liabilities & Net Worth | 100.0 | 100.0 | 100.0 | | | | | | 100.0 |
| **INCOME DATA** | | | | | | | | | |
| Net Sales | 100.0 | 100.0 | 100.0 | | | | | | 100.0 |
| Gross Profit | 25.8 | 27.2 | 25.3 | | | | | | 19.5 |
| Operating Expenses | 20.9 | 20.9 | 20.3 | | | | | | 13.5 |
| Operating Profit | 5.0 | 6.3 | 5.1 | | | | | | 6.0 |
| All Other Expenses (net) | 2.8 | 1.2 | 1.0 | | | | | | 1.0 |
| Profit Before Taxes | 2.2 | 5.1 | 4.1 | | | | | | 5.0 |
| **RATIOS** | | | | | | | | | |
| Current | 2.8 | 3.2 | 2.2 | | | | | | 2.2 |
| | 1.9 | 1.5 | 1.4 | | | | | | 1.3 |
| | 1.3 | 1.2 | 1.2 | | | | | | 1.2 |
| Quick | 1.3 | 1.0 | 1.3 | | | | | | 1.0 |
| | .7 | .8 | .8 | | | | | | .8 |
| | .5 | .5 | .5 | | | | | | .6 |
| Sales/Receivables | 24 15.0 | 27 13.7 | 26 14.1 | | | | | | 37 9.8 |
| | 41 8.9 | 35 10.4 | 38 9.6 | | | | | | 43 8.4 |
| | 59 6.1 | 53 6.9 | 46 7.9 | | | | | | 51 7.2 |
| Cost of Sales/Inventory | 49 7.4 | 42 8.7 | 33 11.1 | | | | | | 39 9.3 |
| | 113 3.2 | 79 4.6 | 53 6.9 | | | | | | 52 7.0 |
| | 149 2.4 | 117 3.1 | 107 3.4 | | | | | | 94 3.9 |
| Cost of Sales/Payables | 20 18.0 | 26 14.0 | 20 18.3 | | | | | | 26 13.9 |
| | 38 9.7 | 31 11.7 | 27 13.4 | | | | | | 31 11.6 |
| | 49 7.5 | 47 7.8 | 34 10.8 | | | | | | 38 9.7 |
| Sales/Working Capital | 3.4 | 4.3 | 5.7 | | | | | | 6.0 |
| | 6.2 | 8.4 | 10.5 | | | | | | 16.0 |
| | 13.0 | 22.8 | 30.1 | | | | | | 29.6 |
| EBIT/Interest | 7.4 | 15.3 | 13.5 | | | | | | 19.5 |
| | (15) 1.3 | (21) 4.9 | (26) 4.2 | | | | | | (10) 7.3 |
| | -1.0 | 2.0 | 1.9 | | | | | | 2.2 |
| Net Profit + Depr., Dep., Amort./Cur. Mat. L/T/D | | | | | | | | | |
| Fixed/Worth | .5 | .2 | .4 | | | | | | .4 |
| | .8 | .8 | .9 | | | | | | 1.0 |
| | NM | 4.9 | 2.7 | | | | | | 2.2 |
| Debt/Worth | .8 | 1.1 | .7 | | | | | | .3 |
| | 1.8 | 2.3 | 2.2 | | | | | | 2.9 |
| | NM | 16.8 | 6.2 | | | | | | 5.8 |
| % Profit Before Taxes/Tangible Net Worth | 39.0 | 121.0 | 63.6 | | | | | | 98.2 |
| | (12) 6.3 | (20) 30.7 | (27) 26.8 | | | | | | (11) 26.8 |
| | -12.4 | 9.7 | 5.1 | | | | | | 5.1 |
| % Profit Before Taxes/Total Assets | 12.8 | 17.3 | 16.1 | | | | | | 21.5 |
| | 1.5 | 8.4 | 10.0 | | | | | | 13.5 |
| | -3.1 | 4.0 | 3.3 | | | | | | 2.7 |
| Sales/Net Fixed Assets | 14.5 | 45.6 | 20.6 | | | | | | 15.8 |
| | 5.0 | 18.4 | 8.7 | | | | | | 5.7 |
| | 2.0 | 4.3 | 4.4 | | | | | | 4.6 |
| Sales/Total Assets | 1.9 | 2.9 | 3.0 | | | | | | 3.0 |
| | 1.3 | 2.2 | 2.1 | | | | | | 2.1 |
| | .9 | 1.3 | 1.5 | | | | | | 1.5 |
| % Depr., Dep., Amort./Sales | 2.0 | .6 | 1.1 | | | | | | 1.3 |
| | (13) 2.7 | (20) 1.5 | (26) 2.3 | | | | | | 4.6 |
| | 5.0 | 5.4 | 5.2 | | | | | | 5.4 |
| % Officers', Directors' Owners' Comp/Sales | | | | | | | | | |
| Net Sales ($) | 606227M | 1545197M | 1164960M | 949M | 5069M | 12576M | 44895M | 63153M | 1038318M |
| Total Assets ($) | 392550M | 746971M | 615344M | 435M | 1759M | 3732M | 23608M | 47750M | 538060M |

M = $ thousand    MM = $ million
See Pages 9 through 22 for Explanation of Ratios and Data

## Current Data Sorted by Assets    Comparative Historical Data

| 0-500M | 500M-2MM | 2-10MM | 10-50MM | 50-100MM | 100-250MM | Type of Statement | 4/1/07-3/31/08 | 4/1/08-3/31/09 |
|---|---|---|---|---|---|---|---|---|
| | | 1 | 4 | 2 | 3 | Unqualified | 7 | 7 |
| | | 4 | 1 | 1 | 1 | Reviewed | 8 | 7 |
| | 1 | 3 | 2 | 1 | 1 | Compiled | 7 | 7 |
| | 1 | 2 | | | | Tax Returns | 2 | 4 |
| 1 | 1 | 3 | 3 | 1 | 1 | Other | 20 | 14 |
| | | 6 (4/1-9/30/11) | 32 (10/1/11-3/31/12) | | | | ALL | ALL |
| 1 | 3 | 13 | 11 | 5 | 5 | **NUMBER OF STATEMENTS** | 44 | 39 |
| % | % | % | % | % | % | **ASSETS** | % | % |
| | | 7.8 | 13.6 | | | Cash & Equivalents | 9.8 | 8.1 |
| | | 29.5 | 29.2 | | | Trade Receivables (net) | 28.4 | 26.8 |
| | | 28.1 | 20.3 | | | Inventory | 29.7 | 29.8 |
| | | .9 | 6.4 | | | All Other Current | 2.5 | 2.8 |
| | | 66.4 | 69.6 | | | Total Current | 70.4 | 67.6 |
| | | 22.3 | 17.4 | | | Fixed Assets (net) | 23.3 | 20.4 |
| | | 7.6 | 6.1 | | | Intangibles (net) | 2.9 | 4.7 |
| | | 3.7 | 6.9 | | | All Other Non-Current | 3.2 | 7.3 |
| | | 100.0 | 100.0 | | | Total | 100.0 | 100.0 |
| | | | | | | **LIABILITIES** | | |
| | | 14.1 | 13.4 | | | Notes Payable-Short Term | 10.1 | 8.1 |
| | | 3.6 | 1.4 | | | Cur. Mat.-L.T.D. | 1.0 | 2.4 |
| | | 20.0 | 16.7 | | | Trade Payables | 17.5 | 16.0 |
| | | .1 | .1 | | | Income Taxes Payable | .0 | .1 |
| | | 6.7 | 16.1 | | | All Other Current | 17.0 | 15.4 |
| | | 44.5 | 47.7 | | | Total Current | 45.6 | 42.1 |
| | | 6.4 | 5.4 | | | Long-Term Debt | 14.9 | 18.3 |
| | | .2 | .9 | | | Deferred Taxes | .1 | .1 |
| | | 1.9 | 10.1 | | | All Other Non-Current | 8.3 | 4.3 |
| | | 47.0 | 36.0 | | | Net Worth | 31.1 | 35.2 |
| | | 100.0 | 100.0 | | | Total Liabilities & Net Worth | 100.0 | 100.0 |
| | | | | | | **INCOME DATA** | | |
| | | 100.0 | 100.0 | | | Net Sales | 100.0 | 100.0 |
| | | 24.7 | 18.1 | | | Gross Profit | 25.5 | 23.7 |
| | | 19.8 | 13.6 | | | Operating Expenses | 21.4 | 23.1 |
| | | 4.9 | 4.5 | | | Operating Profit | 4.2 | .5 |
| | | .7 | .6 | | | All Other Expenses (net) | .7 | 1.7 |
| | | 4.2 | 3.9 | | | Profit Before Taxes | 3.4 | -1.2 |
| | | | | | | **RATIOS** | | |
| | | 3.4 | 3.4 | | | | 3.6 | 2.9 |
| | | 1.6 | 1.4 | | | Current | 1.7 | 1.8 |
| | | .9 | 1.2 | | | | 1.1 | 1.1 |
| | | 1.9 | 2.4 | | | | 1.8 | 1.4 |
| | | .7 | .7 | | | Quick | .9 | .9 |
| | | .4 | .5 | | | | .5 | .5 |
| | | 29 12.6 | 26 14.3 | | | | 22 16.8 | 21 17.5 |
| | | 36 10.1 | 47 7.7 | | | Sales/Receivables | 40 9.2 | 33 11.1 |
| | | 52 7.0 | 58 6.3 | | | | 56 6.5 | 46 7.9 |
| | | 39 9.4 | 20 18.5 | | | | 24 15.2 | 27 13.7 |
| | | 43 8.5 | 28 13.1 | | | Cost of Sales/Inventory | 43 8.4 | 46 7.9 |
| | | 55 6.6 | 60 6.1 | | | | 114 3.2 | 86 4.2 |
| | | 19 19.5 | 13 27.4 | | | | 13 27.2 | 15 24.5 |
| | | 30 12.1 | 28 13.2 | | | Cost of Sales/Payables | 30 12.3 | 23 15.6 |
| | | 53 6.9 | 46 8.0 | | | | 38 9.7 | 38 9.5 |
| | | 5.6 | 7.5 | | | | 4.6 | 5.1 |
| | | 21.4 | 12.9 | | | Sales/Working Capital | 10.2 | 9.8 |
| | | -51.5 | 25.5 | | | | 63.4 | 34.5 |
| | | 63.8 | 21.1 | | | | 20.8 | 15.4 |
| | | (10) 6.5 | 7.1 | | | EBIT/Interest | (39) 7.3 | (37) 1.9 |
| | | 2.2 | 4.4 | | | | 1.3 | -3.4 |
| | | | | | | Net Profit + Depr., Dep., Amort./Cur. Mat. L/T/D | | |
| | | .2 | .3 | | | | .3 | .3 |
| | | .4 | .8 | | | Fixed/Worth | .5 | .5 |
| | | 2.4 | 1.8 | | | | 2.4 | 2.8 |
| | | .3 | .8 | | | | .3 | .6 |
| | | 1.5 | 1.9 | | | Debt/Worth | 1.7 | 2.2 |
| | | 6.4 | 5.7 | | | | 10.5 | 8.4 |
| | | 76.3 | 54.9 | | | | 50.4 | 34.0 |
| | | (12) 14.1 | (10) 39.6 | | | % Profit Before Taxes/Tangible Net Worth | (37) 21.4 | (34) 5.2 |
| | | 5.0 | 15.0 | | | | 9.6 | -16.0 |
| | | 20.1 | 15.1 | | | | 19.0 | 12.7 |
| | | 5.3 | 10.6 | | | % Profit Before Taxes/Total Assets | 8.2 | 1.8 |
| | | 2.8 | 6.0 | | | | 2.0 | -10.9 |
| | | 60.9 | 69.6 | | | | 36.5 | 37.7 |
| | | 11.4 | 13.6 | | | Sales/Net Fixed Assets | 17.3 | 13.6 |
| | | 6.5 | 8.8 | | | | 6.2 | 7.7 |
| | | 3.9 | 3.0 | | | | 3.8 | 3.6 |
| | | 2.5 | 2.6 | | | Sales/Total Assets | 2.6 | 2.9 |
| | | 2.0 | 2.2 | | | | 1.6 | 2.0 |
| | | | .3 | | | | .6 | .9 |
| | | | 1.3 | | | % Depr., Dep., Amort./Sales | (40) 1.5 | (29) 1.4 |
| | | | 1.7 | | | | 2.9 | 3.9 |
| | | | | | | | 1.0 | |
| | | | | | | % Officers', Directors' Owners' Comp/Sales | (13) 3.6 | |
| | | | | | | | 7.3 | |
| 21M | 16031M | 191990M | 640952M | 732904M | 1269295M | Net Sales ($) | 1900503M | 2375292M |
| 10M | 2774M | 68233M | 238257M | 322619M | 795717M | Total Assets ($) | 918341M | 1127128M |

M = $ thousand  MM = $ million
See Pages 9 through 22 for Explanation of Ratios and Data

## Comparative Historical Data / Current Data Sorted by Sales

### Type of Statement

| Comparative Historical Data | | | Type of Statement | 0-1MM | 1-3MM | 3-5MM | 5-10MM | 10-25MM | 25MM & OVER |
|---|---|---|---|---|---|---|---|---|---|
| 14 | 13 | 10 | Unqualified | | | | | 1 | 8 |
| 6 | 7 | 7 | Reviewed | | | | 1 | 3 | 3 |
| 4 | 4 | 5 | Compiled | | | 1 | | 2 | 1 |
| 3 | 4 | 3 | Tax Returns | | | 1 | 1 | 2 | |
| 19 | 27 | 13 | Other | 1 | | | 2 | 2 | 9 |
| 4/1/09-3/31/10 ALL | 4/1/10-3/31/11 ALL | 4/1/11-3/31/12 ALL | | | 6 (4/1-9/30/11) | | | 32 (10/1/11-3/31/12) | 25MM & OVER |
| **46** | **55** | **38** | **NUMBER OF STATEMENTS** | 1 | | 2 | 4 | 10 | 21 |

*Note: For the 0-1MM through 5-10MM columns the percentage/ratio section is marked "DATA NOT AVAILABLE." Values are shown only for the 10-25MM and 25MM & OVER columns (and net sales/total assets figures at the bottom).*

### Assets (%)

| 09-10 | 10-11 | 11-12 | ASSETS | 10-25MM | 25MM & OVER |
|---|---|---|---|---|---|
| 9.0 | 10.2 | 10.5 | Cash & Equivalents | 8.9 | 12.0 |
| 27.2 | 30.3 | 30.6 | Trade Receivables (net) | 26.8 | 28.1 |
| 24.5 | 27.4 | 23.2 | Inventory | 33.0 | 19.8 |
| 2.8 | 3.3 | 3.3 | All Other Current | .9 | 5.4 |
| 63.5 | 71.2 | 67.6 | Total Current | 69.6 | 65.4 |
| 23.8 | 19.3 | 21.8 | Fixed Assets (net) | 22.4 | 23.4 |
| 6.1 | 3.9 | 5.6 | Intangibles (net) | 3.8 | 4.4 |
| 6.7 | 5.6 | 5.0 | All Other Non-Current | 4.2 | 6.8 |
| 100.0 | 100.0 | 100.0 | Total | 100.0 | 100.0 |

### Liabilities

| 09-10 | 10-11 | 11-12 | LIABILITIES | 10-25MM | 25MM & OVER |
|---|---|---|---|---|---|
| 9.3 | 12.5 | 10.7 | Notes Payable-Short Term | 14.1 | 11.1 |
| 3.8 | 1.7 | 2.0 | Cur. Mat.-L.T.D. | 3.7 | 1.2 |
| 14.1 | 21.0 | 18.1 | Trade Payables | 17.9 | 18.0 |
| .1 | .0 | .1 | Income Taxes Payable | .1 | .1 |
| 13.8 | 10.5 | 13.2 | All Other Current | 5.1 | 15.9 |
| 41.1 | 45.8 | 44.0 | Total Current | 40.9 | 46.2 |
| 25.1 | 5.1 | 9.9 | Long-Term Debt | 7.1 | 3.7 |
| .7 | .4 | .7 | Deferred Taxes | .6 | 1.0 |
| 14.3 | 10.5 | 5.8 | All Other Non-Current | 2.5 | 9.2 |
| 18.7 | 38.2 | 39.4 | Net Worth | 49.0 | 39.9 |
| 100.0 | 100.0 | 100.0 | Total Liabilities & Net Worth | 100.0 | 100.0 |

### Income Data

| 09-10 | 10-11 | 11-12 | INCOME DATA | 10-25MM | 25MM & OVER |
|---|---|---|---|---|---|
| 100.0 | 100.0 | 100.0 | Net Sales | 100.0 | 100.0 |
| 22.2 | 24.7 | 19.4 | Gross Profit | 24.9 | 15.8 |
| 21.8 | 19.2 | 14.8 | Operating Expenses | 21.7 | 11.6 |
| .3 | 5.5 | 4.6 | Operating Profit | 3.2 | 4.2 |
| 1.5 | .7 | .4 | All Other Expenses (net) | .7 | .2 |
| -1.2 | 4.8 | 4.2 | Profit Before Taxes | 2.5 | 4.1 |

### Ratios

| 09-10 | 10-11 | 11-12 | RATIOS | 10-25MM | 25MM & OVER |
|---|---|---|---|---|---|
| 2.9 | 2.8 | 3.2 | Current | 3.8 | 2.3 |
| 1.5 | 1.4 | 1.6 | | 1.8 | 1.5 |
| 1.1 | 1.2 | 1.1 | | 1.1 | 1.2 |
| 1.3 | 1.6 | 1.8 | Quick | 2.1 | 1.4 |
| .9 | (54) .9 | .9 | | .7 | .9 |
| .5 | .6 | .5 | | .4 | .5 |
| 32  11.2 | 28  13.3 | 29  12.6 | Sales/Receivables | 25  14.8 | 30  12.0 |
| 55  6.6 | 45  8.1 | 37  9.8 | | 36  10.2 | 47  7.7 |
| 73  5.0 | 58  6.3 | 59  6.2 | | 63  5.8 | 60  6.1 |
| 20  18.3 | 29  12.6 | 23  15.9 | Cost of Sales/Inventory | 41  8.9 | 21  17.8 |
| 41  8.9 | 44  8.4 | 41  9.0 | | 54  6.7 | 36  10.0 |
| 98  3.7 | 64  5.7 | 57  6.4 | | 76  4.8 | 53  6.9 |
| 15  24.9 | 18  20.7 | 15  24.2 | Cost of Sales/Payables | 18  20.6 | 15  24.3 |
| 32  11.5 | 34  10.7 | 30  12.2 | | 26  13.9 | 42  9.2 |
| 58  6.3 | 51  7.2 | 46  8.0 | | 50  7.3 | 46  8.0 |
| 4.9 | 5.9 | 5.2 | Sales/Working Capital | 4.4 | 5.7 |
| 11.9 | 13.9 | 11.6 | | 13.9 | 12.3 |
| 54.1 | 25.6 | 30.6 | | NM | 23.9 |
| 4.0 | 32.6 | 31.2 | EBIT/Interest | 32.8 | |
| (42) 1.4 | (45) 7.6 | (34) 9.5 | | 11.9 | |
| -3.3 | 3.4 | 3.0 | | 3.8 | |
| 2.5 | 32.4 | 9.8 | Net Profit + Depr., Dep., Amort./Cur. Mat. L/T/D | | |
| (11) .9 | (13) 3.1 | (13) 3.4 | | | |
| -1.6 | 1.5 | .8 | | | |
| .2 | .2 | .3 | Fixed/Worth | .3 | .4 |
| .6 | .5 | .5 | | .4 | .8 |
| 2.5 | 1.0 | 1.1 | | .7 | 1.8 |
| .8 | .4 | .6 | Debt/Worth | .4 | .8 |
| 2.0 | 1.7 | 1.4 | | 1.1 | 1.6 |
| 7.7 | 3.6 | 4.7 | | 3.6 | 4.8 |
| 28.1 | 57.5 | 46.7 | % Profit Before Taxes/Tangible Net Worth | 47.1 | |
| (37) 5.8 | (46) 22.4 | (35) 15.9 | | (20) 22.8 | |
| -10.2 | 9.3 | 9.2 | | 10.0 | |
| 5.3 | 18.9 | 16.6 | % Profit Before Taxes/Total Assets | 6.5 | 14.9 |
| 1.7 | 9.7 | 6.9 | | 4.1 | 7.2 |
| -8.9 | 3.9 | 3.0 | | 2.3 | 3.8 |
| 22.5 | 59.7 | 34.5 | Sales/Net Fixed Assets | 57.2 | 19.4 |
| 11.1 | 16.3 | 10.7 | | 11.7 | 9.8 |
| 4.8 | 8.0 | 7.2 | | 7.0 | 6.0 |
| 2.5 | 3.0 | 3.2 | Sales/Total Assets | 3.2 | 2.8 |
| 1.9 | 2.7 | 2.5 | | 2.4 | 2.6 |
| 1.2 | 2.0 | 2.1 | | 2.1 | 1.9 |
| 1.0 | .9 | .9 | % Depr., Dep., Amort./Sales | 1.2 | |
| (36) 2.4 | (46) 1.4 | (31) 1.5 | | (19) 1.5 | |
| 4.6 | 2.6 | 2.6 | | 2.6 | |
| | | | % Officers', Directors' Owners' Comp/Sales | | |

### Net Sales / Total Assets ($)

| 09-10 | 10-11 | 11-12 | | 0-1MM | 1-3MM | 3-5MM | 5-10MM | 10-25MM | 25MM & OVER |
|---|---|---|---|---|---|---|---|---|---|
| 2166401M | 3228228M | 2851193M | Net Sales ($) | 21M | | 7921M | 35138M | 146832M | 2661281M |
| 1304020M | 1470636M | 1427610M | Total Assets ($) | 10M | | 1445M | 13625M | 59357M | 1353173M |

M = $ thousand   MM = $ million
See Pages 9 through 22 for Explanation of Ratios and Data

**Current Data Sorted by Assets**       **Comparative Historical Data**

| 0-500M | 500M-2MM | 2-10MM | 10-50MM | 50-100MM | 100-250MM | Type of Statement | 4/1/07-3/31/08 ALL | 4/1/08-3/31/09 ALL |
|---|---|---|---|---|---|---|---|---|
| | | 1 | 6 | 4 | 4 | Unqualified | 13 | 14 |
| | | 5 | 7 | 1 | | Reviewed | 17 | 12 |
| | 2 | 5 | 1 | | | Compiled | 6 | 11 |
| | | | | | | Tax Returns | 2 | 1 |
| 4 | | 9 | 12 | 7 | 4 | Other | 39 | 38 |
| 8 (4/1-9/30/11) | | 64 (10/1/11-3/31/12) | | | | | 4/1/07-3/31/08 | 4/1/08-3/31/09 |
| | 6 | 20 | 26 | 12 | 8 | NUMBER OF STATEMENTS | 77 ALL | 76 ALL |
| % | % | % | % | % | % | **ASSETS** | % | % |
| | | 7.2 | 7.0 | 1.9 | | Cash & Equivalents | 5.3 | 6.4 |
| | | 28.5 | 27.8 | 31.0 | | Trade Receivables (net) | 26.2 | 23.7 |
| | | 24.0 | 18.2 | 16.1 | | Inventory | 17.8 | 19.0 |
| | | 2.0 | 1.6 | 5.3 | | All Other Current | 2.2 | 2.2 |
| | | 61.6 | 54.6 | 54.3 | | Total Current | 51.5 | 51.3 |
| | | 25.6 | 35.5 | 40.7 | | Fixed Assets (net) | 37.8 | 38.6 |
| | | 6.2 | 1.2 | 2.1 | | Intangibles (net) | 2.9 | 2.8 |
| | | 6.6 | 8.7 | 2.9 | | All Other Non-Current | 7.8 | 7.4 |
| | | 100.0 | 100.0 | 100.0 | | Total | 100.0 | 100.0 |
| | | | | | | **LIABILITIES** | | |
| | | 11.8 | 9.4 | 12.7 | | Notes Payable-Short Term | 12.9 | 12.2 |
| | | 3.2 | 2.7 | 5.0 | | Cur. Mat.-L.T.D. | 4.5 | 5.4 |
| | | 18.4 | 13.8 | 17.3 | | Trade Payables | 16.1 | 15.4 |
| | | .0 | .2 | .0 | | Income Taxes Payable | .1 | .2 |
| | | 11.0 | 11.3 | 11.7 | | All Other Current | 7.3 | 6.7 |
| | | 44.3 | 37.5 | 46.7 | | Total Current | 41.0 | 39.8 |
| | | 10.5 | 11.4 | 13.7 | | Long-Term Debt | 17.1 | 16.5 |
| | | .9 | 1.3 | .9 | | Deferred Taxes | .8 | .6 |
| | | 4.1 | 3.6 | 2.8 | | All Other Non-Current | 6.9 | 5.8 |
| | | 40.2 | 46.2 | 35.8 | | Net Worth | 34.3 | 37.2 |
| | | 100.0 | 100.0 | 100.0 | | Total Liabilities & Net Worth | 100.0 | 100.0 |
| | | | | | | **INCOME DATA** | | |
| | | 100.0 | 100.0 | 100.0 | | Net Sales | 100.0 | 100.0 |
| | | 19.3 | 17.6 | 14.0 | | Gross Profit | 18.8 | 19.6 |
| | | 14.6 | 12.1 | 9.2 | | Operating Expenses | 14.8 | 17.4 |
| | | 4.7 | 5.5 | 4.8 | | Operating Profit | 4.0 | 2.2 |
| | | .5 | -.3 | .8 | | All Other Expenses (net) | 1.2 | 1.0 |
| | | 4.2 | 5.9 | 4.0 | | Profit Before Taxes | 2.8 | 1.3 |
| | | | | | | **RATIOS** | | |
| | | 2.4 | 2.2 | 1.6 | | | 2.2 | 2.0 |
| | | 1.3 | 1.5 | 1.4 | | Current | 1.3 | 1.3 |
| | | 1.1 | 1.1 | 1.0 | | | .9 | 1.0 |
| | | 1.2 | 1.4 | 1.0 | | | 1.5 | 1.3 |
| | | .8 | .9 | .7 | | Quick | .8 | .8 |
| | | .5 | .7 | .6 | | | .5 | .5 |
| | | 44   8.3 | 43   8.4 | 61   6.0 | | | 41   9.0 | 32   11.3 |
| | | 49   7.4 | 59   6.2 | 66   5.5 | | Sales/Receivables | 49   7.4 | 45   8.2 |
| | | 56   6.5 | 73   5.0 | 73   5.0 | | | 58   6.3 | 54   6.7 |
| | | 31   11.7 | 38   9.6 | 18   19.9 | | | 24   15.3 | 24   15.0 |
| | | 43   8.5 | 46   7.9 | 33   11.0 | | Cost of Sales/Inventory | 40   9.2 | 42   8.8 |
| | | 73   5.0 | 55   6.6 | 68   5.4 | | | 58   6.3 | 66   5.6 |
| | | 24   15.2 | 20   18.0 | 34   10.8 | | | 23   16.0 | 18   20.8 |
| | | 34   10.6 | 38   9.6 | 45   8.2 | | Cost of Sales/Payables | 35   10.5 | 28   12.9 |
| | | 57   6.4 | 49   7.4 | 50   7.3 | | | 45   8.1 | 47   7.8 |
| | | 6.0 | 5.1 | 5.6 | | | 6.8 | 7.0 |
| | | 16.3 | 9.3 | 13.4 | | Sales/Working Capital | 15.7 | 19.3 |
| | | 68.1 | NM | NM | | | -36.4 | NM |
| | | 35.6 | 31.4 | 12.1 | | | 6.6 | 4.7 |
| | | (19) 5.4 | (25) 11.4 | 9.0 | | EBIT/Interest | (73) 2.2 | (70) 1.8 |
| | | 1.1 | 2.6 | 2.6 | | | .1 | -1.7 |
| | | | | | | Net Profit + Depr., Dep., | 3.7 | 3.0 |
| | | | | | | Amort./Cur. Mat. L/T/D | (26) 1.7   (26) 1.9 | |
| | | | | | | | 1.2 | .8 |
| | | .3 | .5 | .9 | | | .5 | .6 |
| | | .6 | .8 | 1.1 | | Fixed/Worth | 1.3 | 1.3 |
| | | 1.5 | 1.4 | 1.9 | | | 3.5 | 2.6 |
| | | .6 | .6 | 1.0 | | | .8 | .8 |
| | | 1.6 | 1.1 | 2.0 | | Debt/Worth | 2.0 | 2.2 |
| | | 5.7 | 2.5 | 3.8 | | | 7.3 | 5.5 |
| | | 55.2 | 40.9 | 31.9 | | % Profit Before Taxes/Tangible | 41.6 | 30.2 |
| | | (18) 25.2 | (24) 18.6 | 13.7 | | Net Worth | (65) 15.6 | (68) 7.0 |
| | | 2.7 | 5.0 | 8.4 | | | -.7 | -11.2 |
| | | 18.1 | 20.0 | 13.0 | | % Profit Before Taxes/Total | 12.3 | 9.4 |
| | | 7.5 | 7.7 | 6.3 | | Assets | 5.3 | 1.7 |
| | | .5 | 2.8 | 2.0 | | | -1.3 | -4.8 |
| | | 24.5 | 8.0 | 7.8 | | | 8.9 | 9.8 |
| | | 11.8 | 5.1 | 3.5 | | Sales/Net Fixed Assets | 5.1 | 5.7 |
| | | 5.4 | 3.3 | 2.3 | | | 3.2 | 3.2 |
| | | 2.8 | 2.3 | 2.1 | | | 2.3 | 2.5 |
| | | 2.3 | 1.7 | 1.6 | | Sales/Total Assets | 1.9 | 2.0 |
| | | 1.7 | 1.2 | 1.1 | | | 1.5 | 1.3 |
| | | 1.2 | 2.3 | 2.2 | | | 2.2 | 2.4 |
| | | (19) 2.0 | (25) 3.3 | 4.0 | | % Depr., Dep., Amort./Sales | (64) 3.5 | (65) 3.3 |
| | | 4.0 | 4.7 | 5.1 | | | 5.1 | 4.8 |
| | | | | | | % Officers', Directors' | 1.6 | 2.0 |
| | | | | | | Owners' Comp/Sales | (21) 3.1 | (23) 3.3 |
| | | | | | | | 4.7 | 5.4 |
| | 24648M | 252745M | 1109037M | 1453192M | 2406165M | Net Sales ($) | 4540296M | 4777342M |
| | 8186M | 113841M | 620722M | 859037M | 1180424M | Total Assets ($) | 2412961M | 2510707M |

© RMA 2012

M = $ thousand    MM = $ million
See Pages 9 through 22 for Explanation of Ratios and Data

## Comparative Historical Data                                         Current Data Sorted by Sales

| 4/1/09-3/31/10 ALL | 4/1/10-3/31/11 ALL | 4/1/11-3/31/12 ALL | | 0-1MM | 1-3MM | 3-5MM | 5-10MM | 10-25MM | 25MM & OVER |
|---|---|---|---|---|---|---|---|---|---|
| | | | **Type of Statement** | | | | | | |
| 12 | 15 | 15 | Unqualified | | | | | 3 | 12 |
| 15 | 12 | 13 | Reviewed | | | | 2 | 5 | 6 |
| 3 | 4 | 8 | Compiled | | | 1 | 2 | 5 | |
| 2 | 1 | | Tax Returns | | | | | | |
| 35 | 33 | 36 | Other | | | 3 | 6 | 7 | 20 |
| | | | | **8 (4/1-9/30/11)** | | **64 (10/1/11-3/31/12)** | | | |
| 67 | 65 | 72 | **NUMBER OF STATEMENTS** | | | 4 | 10 | 20 | 38 |
| % | % | % | **ASSETS** | % | % | % | % | % | % |
| 6.2 | 5.7 | 5.5 | Cash & Equivalents | D | D | | 8.8 | 8.9 | 2.9 |
| 25.1 | 26.6 | 28.6 | Trade Receivables (net) | A | A | | 26.3 | 27.3 | 30.7 |
| 16.3 | 17.6 | 19.2 | Inventory | T | T | | 24.8 | 18.8 | 18.0 |
| 2.2 | 3.0 | 2.6 | All Other Current | A | A | | 2.8 | .7 | 3.5 |
| 49.7 | 52.9 | 55.9 | Total Current | | | | 62.7 | 55.7 | 55.1 |
| 40.3 | 38.1 | 33.4 | Fixed Assets (net) | N | N | | 21.3 | 33.2 | 36.7 |
| 3.7 | 3.2 | 4.4 | Intangibles (net) | O | O | | 4.8 | 4.7 | 2.9 |
| 6.3 | 5.8 | 6.3 | All Other Non-Current | T | T | | 11.2 | 6.4 | 5.3 |
| 100.0 | 100.0 | 100.0 | Total | | | | 100.0 | 100.0 | 100.0 |
| | | | **LIABILITIES** | A | A | | | | |
| 10.8 | 12.0 | 10.7 | Notes Payable-Short Term | V | V | | 10.3 | 11.5 | 9.2 |
| 4.6 | 4.5 | 3.1 | Cur. Mat.-L.T.D. | A | A | | 3.4 | 3.2 | 3.3 |
| 15.3 | 18.5 | 16.7 | Trade Payables | I | I | | 19.7 | 15.0 | 17.5 |
| .0 | .2 | .1 | Income Taxes Payable | L | L | | .0 | .0 | .2 |
| 8.7 | 8.5 | 10.8 | All Other Current | A | A | | 13.8 | 7.1 | 11.9 |
| 39.4 | 43.8 | 41.4 | Total Current | B | B | | 47.3 | 36.7 | 42.2 |
| 19.1 | 16.8 | 12.7 | Long-Term Debt | L | L | | 17.4 | 9.6 | 12.6 |
| .7 | .9 | 1.1 | Deferred Taxes | E | E | | .2 | .8 | 1.5 |
| 7.0 | 7.6 | 4.4 | All Other Non-Current | | | | 7.1 | 1.5 | 5.4 |
| 33.8 | 30.9 | 40.3 | Net Worth | | | | 28.0 | 51.3 | 38.3 |
| 100.0 | 100.0 | 100.0 | Total Liabilities & Net Worth | | | | 100.0 | 100.0 | 100.0 |
| | | | **INCOME DATA** | | | | | | |
| 100.0 | 100.0 | 100.0 | Net Sales | | | | 100.0 | 100.0 | 100.0 |
| 16.2 | 19.1 | 18.2 | Gross Profit | | | | 24.0 | 20.3 | 14.8 |
| 16.9 | 14.8 | 13.1 | Operating Expenses | | | | 21.6 | 13.8 | 9.8 |
| -.6 | 4.3 | 5.1 | Operating Profit | | | | 2.4 | 6.5 | 5.0 |
| 1.0 | .4 | .4 | All Other Expenses (net) | | | | .6 | -.5 | .7 |
| -1.6 | 4.0 | 4.8 | Profit Before Taxes | | | | 1.8 | 7.0 | 4.4 |
| | | | **RATIOS** | | | | | | |
| 2.2 | 1.7 | 2.0 | | | | | 2.4 | 3.0 | 1.8 |
| 1.2 | 1.3 | 1.4 | Current | | | | 1.6 | 1.3 | 1.4 |
| .9 | .9 | 1.0 | | | | | .9 | 1.1 | 1.0 |
| 1.2 | 1.0 | 1.2 | | | | | 1.6 | 1.8 | 1.1 |
| .8 | .8 | .8 | Quick | | | | .7 | .8 | .9 |
| .6 | .5 | .6 | | | | | .4 | .6 | .7 |
| 46  7.9 | 40  9.2 | 43  8.4 | | | | | 37  9.8 | 46  7.9 | 50  7.3 |
| 60  6.1 | 52  7.1 | 55  6.6 | Sales/Receivables | | | | 50  7.3 | 53  6.9 | 61  6.0 |
| 69  5.3 | 63  5.8 | 68  5.4 | | | | | 60  6.1 | 61  6.0 | 72  5.1 |
| 29  12.7 | 29  12.8 | 27  13.3 | | | | | 37  9.9 | 31  11.7 | 26  14.0 |
| 38  9.6 | 35  10.3 | 41  9.0 | Cost of Sales/Inventory | | | | 62  5.9 | 41  8.9 | 40  9.2 |
| 64  5.7 | 53  6.9 | 56  6.5 | | | | | 76  4.8 | 53  6.9 | 54  6.7 |
| 24  15.3 | 27  13.5 | 24  15.0 | | | | | 27  13.5 | 15  23.9 | 31  11.9 |
| 41  9.0 | 41  8.9 | 39  9.3 | Cost of Sales/Payables | | | | 38  9.6 | 41  9.0 | 42  8.7 |
| 59  6.2 | 52  7.0 | 51  7.1 | | | | | 62  5.9 | 54  6.8 | 50  7.3 |
| 5.6 | 8.6 | 6.1 | | | | | 5.0 | 4.5 | 6.6 |
| 20.3 | 24.3 | 15.3 | Sales/Working Capital | | | | 9.7 | 17.8 | 13.4 |
| -42.3 | -43.4 | 580.9 | | | | | -431.0 | 68.1 | 246.4 |
| 4.1 | 9.7 | 24.7 | | | | | 9.5 | 41.6 | 23.7 |
| (66)  .5 | (60)  4.8 | (70)  6.7 | EBIT/Interest | | | | 4.6 | (18)  6.1 | 9.0 |
| -2.9 | 1.6 | 2.4 | | | | | -3.8 | 2.4 | 2.6 |
| 1.9 | 4.8 | 8.8 | Net Profit + Depr., Dep., | | | | | | 14.6 |
| (15)  .9 | (23)  3.2 | (23)  4.8 | Amort./Cur. Mat. L/T/D | | | | | (18) | 4.6 |
| .1 | 1.6 | 2.1 | | | | | | | 2.8 |
| .7 | .8 | .6 | | | | | .2 | .3 | .8 |
| 1.3 | 1.3 | .9 | Fixed/Worth | | | | .6 | .7 | 1.0 |
| 2.3 | 5.5 | 1.8 | | | | | NM | 1.7 | 1.8 |
| .8 | .9 | .8 | | | | | .9 | .3 | 1.0 |
| 1.9 | 2.6 | 1.6 | Debt/Worth | | | | 2.9 | 1.2 | 1.6 |
| 4.7 | 9.3 | 4.0 | | | | | NM | 3.9 | 3.2 |
| 14.7 | 37.7 | 42.9 | % Profit Before Taxes/Tangible | | | | | 50.5 | 40.8 |
| (60)  -.3 | (54)  18.3 | (66)  24.0 | Net Worth | | | | | 28.2 | (35)  16.6 |
| -19.2 | 5.1 | 7.9 | | | | | | 3.9 | 9.7 |
| 6.4 | 12.8 | 17.9 | % Profit Before Taxes/Total | | | | 14.8 | 22.8 | 15.6 |
| -.6 | 5.4 | 8.6 | Assets | | | | 5.2 | 7.7 | 9.0 |
| -7.6 | 1.2 | 2.3 | | | | | -3.7 | 3.0 | 2.1 |
| 7.1 | 8.2 | 12.5 | | | | | 27.4 | 20.4 | 8.2 |
| 4.3 | 5.9 | 6.1 | Sales/Net Fixed Assets | | | | 10.5 | 5.5 | 5.3 |
| 2.6 | 3.3 | 3.7 | | | | | 6.4 | 2.6 | 3.6 |
| 2.0 | 2.4 | 2.5 | | | | | 2.9 | 2.7 | 2.3 |
| 1.5 | 1.8 | 2.0 | Sales/Total Assets | | | | 1.9 | 2.0 | 1.9 |
| 1.0 | 1.4 | 1.3 | | | | | 1.2 | 1.2 | 1.5 |
| 2.6 | 2.4 | 1.6 | | | | | | 1.4 | 2.1 |
| (57)  4.3 | (59)  3.3 | (68)  2.8 | % Depr., Dep., Amort./Sales | | | | (19) | 2.9 | (36)  3.1 |
| 5.9 | 5.3 | 4.5 | | | | | | 4.7 | 4.6 |
| 2.2 | .9 | 1.4 | % Officers', Directors' | | | | | | |
| (16)  4.8 | (11)  1.8 | (16)  3.8 | Owners' Comp/Sales | | | | | | |
| 6.4 | 4.9 | 5.1 | | | | | | | |
| 3059438M | 5241893M | 5245787M | Net Sales ($) | | | 14419M | 71421M | 315959M | 4843988M |
| 2036772M | 2805535M | 2782210M | Total Assets ($) | | | 5672M | 40643M | 207119M | 2528776M |

M = $ thousand    MM = $ million
See Pages 9 through 22 for Explanation of Ratios and Data

## Current Data Sorted by Assets      Comparative Historical Data

| | | | | | | Type of Statement | | |
|---|---|---|---|---|---|---|---|---|
| 2 | 3 | 7 | 35 | 16 | 15 | Unqualified | 69 | 77 |
| 2 | 9 | 40 | 22 | 2 | | Reviewed | 66 | 62 |
| 8 | 15 | 21 | 2 | | | Compiled | 34 | 41 |
| 3 | 17 | 11 | | | | Tax Returns | 24 | 32 |
| | | 36 | 45 | 24 | 28 | Other | 165 | 148 |
| | 51 (4/1-9/30/11) | | 310 (10/1/11-3/31/12) | | | | 4/1/07-3/31/08 | 4/1/08-3/31/09 |
| 0-500M | 500M-2MM | 2-10MM | 10-50MM | 50-100MM | 100-250MM | | ALL | ALL |
| 15 | 44 | 115 | 104 | 40 | 43 | NUMBER OF STATEMENTS | 358 | 360 |
| % | % | % | % | % | % | ASSETS | % | % |
| 19.6 | 7.4 | 9.3 | 5.5 | 3.9 | 4.9 | Cash & Equivalents | 6.8 | 7.9 |
| 26.4 | 26.4 | 22.5 | 25.0 | 21.5 | 23.7 | Trade Receivables (net) | 25.3 | 23.4 |
| 9.8 | 33.5 | 33.7 | 24.5 | 22.4 | 18.9 | Inventory | 29.3 | 29.3 |
| 2.7 | 1.5 | 1.3 | 4.8 | 4.4 | 3.7 | All Other Current | 2.6 | 2.5 |
| 58.4 | 68.8 | 66.8 | 59.8 | 52.2 | 51.2 | Total Current | 64.0 | 63.1 |
| 26.3 | 21.9 | 24.1 | 29.5 | 29.1 | 33.4 | Fixed Assets (net) | 26.3 | 26.5 |
| 2.6 | 5.4 | 5.2 | 6.3 | 12.8 | 8.7 | Intangibles (net) | 4.8 | 4.7 |
| 12.7 | 3.9 | 3.9 | 4.5 | 6.0 | 6.7 | All Other Non-Current | 4.9 | 5.7 |
| 100.0 | 100.0 | 100.0 | 100.0 | 100.0 | 100.0 | Total | 100.0 | 100.0 |
| | | | | | | LIABILITIES | | |
| 6.5 | 14.1 | 10.0 | 11.9 | 8.6 | 7.0 | Notes Payable-Short Term | 12.2 | 14.1 |
| .3 | 1.8 | 3.8 | 3.7 | 3.5 | 2.1 | Cur. Mat.-L.T.D. | 4.6 | 4.5 |
| 11.4 | 17.8 | 15.4 | 15.0 | 16.9 | 16.7 | Trade Payables | 17.0 | 16.2 |
| .0 | .2 | .3 | .2 | .5 | .3 | Income Taxes Payable | .2 | .2 |
| 11.0 | 4.0 | 9.3 | 10.1 | 14.3 | 8.4 | All Other Current | 10.0 | 9.3 |
| 29.2 | 37.8 | 38.7 | 40.9 | 43.8 | 34.5 | Total Current | 44.1 | 44.4 |
| 19.9 | 16.8 | 15.6 | 11.9 | 17.7 | 18.4 | Long-Term Debt | 16.3 | 15.3 |
| .2 | .1 | .5 | .6 | 1.3 | 2.2 | Deferred Taxes | .7 | .6 |
| 78.1 | 11.2 | 5.8 | 5.2 | 7.9 | 8.2 | All Other Non-Current | 5.9 | 6.6 |
| -27.4 | 34.1 | 39.3 | 41.5 | 29.2 | 36.8 | Net Worth | 33.0 | 33.1 |
| 100.0 | 100.0 | 100.0 | 100.0 | 100.0 | 100.0 | Total Liabilities & Net Worth | 100.0 | 100.0 |
| | | | | | | INCOME DATA | | |
| 100.0 | 100.0 | 100.0 | 100.0 | 100.0 | 100.0 | Net Sales | 100.0 | 100.0 |
| 47.3 | 37.9 | 32.1 | 19.7 | 17.7 | 16.4 | Gross Profit | 25.3 | 25.8 |
| 40.9 | 34.1 | 25.2 | 14.1 | 11.9 | 11.7 | Operating Expenses | 20.9 | 22.7 |
| 6.5 | 3.8 | 6.8 | 5.6 | 5.8 | 4.7 | Operating Profit | 4.4 | 3.1 |
| 1.0 | .5 | 1.1 | .9 | 2.0 | 1.3 | All Other Expenses (net) | 1.5 | 1.1 |
| 5.5 | 3.3 | 5.7 | 4.7 | 3.8 | 3.4 | Profit Before Taxes | 2.9 | 2.0 |
| | | | | | | RATIOS | | |
| 11.5 | 3.2 | 2.8 | 2.3 | 1.6 | 2.0 | | 2.3 | 2.5 |
| 2.9 | 2.0 | 1.8 | 1.4 | 1.2 | 1.5 | Current | 1.5 | 1.5 |
| 1.2 | 1.4 | 1.2 | 1.1 | .9 | 1.3 | | 1.1 | 1.0 |
| 3.8 | 1.5 | 1.4 | 1.1 | .9 | 1.2 | | 1.2 | 1.2 |
| 1.1 | .8 | .8 | .8 | .5 | .9 | Quick | .7 | .7 |
| 1.0 | .5 | .5 | .5 | .4 | .6 | | .4 | .4 |
| 0 UND | 16 23.5 | 26 13.9 | 40 9.1 | 31 11.8 | 41 9.0 | | 30 12.2 | 25 14.4 |
| 20 18.4 | 33 11.1 | 38 9.5 | 47 7.7 | 43 8.4 | 51 7.2 | Sales/Receivables | 44 8.3 | 38 9.6 |
| 40 9.1 | 46 8.0 | 51 7.1 | 57 6.4 | 55 6.6 | 60 6.1 | | 57 6.4 | 53 6.9 |
| 0 UND | 30 12.3 | 45 8.2 | 34 10.6 | 37 9.9 | 27 13.4 | | 34 10.6 | 31 11.7 |
| 7 53.8 | 62 5.9 | 79 4.6 | 49 7.5 | 57 6.4 | 41 8.8 | Cost of Sales/Inventory | 58 6.3 | 61 6.0 |
| 29 12.6 | 122 3.0 | 140 2.6 | 94 3.9 | 99 3.7 | 66 5.5 | | 115 3.2 | 108 3.4 |
| 0 UND | 18 20.8 | 18 20.1 | 20 18.0 | 18 20.3 | 30 12.0 | | 22 16.8 | 18 20.1 |
| 5 69.9 | 36 10.1 | 31 11.7 | 33 10.9 | 33 11.2 | 38 9.6 | Cost of Sales/Payables | 35 10.4 | 32 11.4 |
| 33 11.0 | 42 8.6 | 52 7.0 | 49 7.4 | 43 8.4 | 53 6.9 | | 52 7.0 | 49 7.5 |
| 9.0 | 5.3 | 4.3 | 6.2 | 8.5 | 5.6 | | 5.2 | 5.4 |
| 13.5 | 8.7 | 7.2 | 10.2 | 29.8 | 9.5 | Sales/Working Capital | 10.9 | 11.1 |
| 69.5 | 16.6 | 22.9 | 114.8 | -86.8 | 25.9 | | 57.6 | 206.9 |
| | 23.2 | 20.4 | 25.4 | 17.6 | 28.3 | | 8.9 | 7.1 |
| | (39) 3.8 | (105) 6.2 | (98) 6.0 | (38) 4.8 | (40) 5.4 | EBIT/Interest | (315) 2.6 | (316) 2.4 |
| | 1.3 | 2.2 | 1.4 | 1.4 | 2.0 | | 1.0 | -.4 |
| | | 12.9 | 6.2 | 4.6 | 25.5 | | 4.6 | 5.1 |
| | | (34) 4.3 | (38) 2.8 | (16) 2.5 | (15) 4.8 | Net Profit + Depr., Dep., Amort./Cur. Mat. L/T/D | (92) 2.1 | (96) 2.2 |
| | | 1.7 | 1.3 | .6 | 1.7 | | 1.2 | .8 |
| .2 | .2 | .2 | .4 | .7 | .7 | | .3 | .3 |
| .4 | .6 | .4 | .8 | 1.4 | 1.1 | Fixed/Worth | .9 | .8 |
| -.3 | 1.4 | 2.1 | 1.7 | 3.7 | 3.6 | | 2.5 | 2.2 |
| .5 | .7 | .6 | .7 | 1.7 | .8 | | .8 | .8 |
| 8.9 | 1.9 | 1.5 | 1.9 | 3.7 | 2.2 | Debt/Worth | 2.3 | 2.2 |
| -2.1 | 6.2 | 4.5 | 3.6 | 13.7 | 10.9 | | 7.4 | 6.9 |
| | 48.9 | 52.5 | 48.6 | 41.9 | 30.7 | | 44.0 | 36.3 |
| | (36) 22.1 | (100) 29.1 | (96) 21.8 | (33) 22.6 | (34) 16.1 | % Profit Before Taxes/Tangible Net Worth | (305) 18.3 | (307) 13.5 |
| | 3.4 | 9.0 | 6.4 | 12.2 | 7.5 | | 2.2 | -4.5 |
| 38.2 | 18.3 | 19.2 | 16.7 | 12.5 | 8.7 | | 14.0 | 11.2 |
| 15.4 | 7.0 | 9.3 | 7.2 | 5.8 | 6.1 | % Profit Before Taxes/Total Assets | 5.7 | 3.5 |
| 2.0 | .4 | 2.2 | 1.7 | 1.7 | 1.9 | | -.1 | -3.2 |
| 106.1 | 43.8 | 32.0 | 12.5 | 11.8 | 10.5 | | 20.9 | 24.2 |
| 28.9 | 13.8 | 11.6 | 6.1 | 6.9 | 6.2 | Sales/Net Fixed Assets | 8.8 | 8.1 |
| 10.3 | 6.4 | 4.2 | 4.1 | 3.8 | 3.4 | | 4.7 | 4.5 |
| 8.2 | 3.6 | 2.6 | 2.3 | 2.2 | 2.1 | | 2.7 | 2.8 |
| 3.5 | 2.7 | 2.0 | 1.8 | 1.8 | 1.7 | Sales/Total Assets | 2.0 | 2.0 |
| 2.5 | 2.1 | 1.3 | 1.3 | 1.2 | 1.3 | | 1.5 | 1.5 |
| | .4 | .9 | 1.8 | 2.0 | 1.6 | | 1.2 | 1.1 |
| | (29) 1.8 | (104) 2.0 | (94) 3.1 | (35) 2.9 | (26) 2.5 | % Depr., Dep., Amort./Sales | (287) 2.4 | (288) 2.5 |
| | 3.5 | 3.4 | 4.8 | 4.4 | 4.2 | | 4.0 | 4.2 |
| | 2.3 | 1.8 | | | | | 1.5 | 2.1 |
| | (26) 4.7 | (52) 3.6 | | | | % Officers', Directors' Owners' Comp/Sales | (92) 3.5 | (94) 3.8 |
| | 7.1 | 5.3 | | | | | 7.5 | 6.8 |
| 12829M | 137703M | 1287252M | 4928619M | 5682662M | 11738496M | Net Sales ($) | 21943075M | 20680657M |
| 3581M | 51636M | 616874M | 2571679M | 2888979M | 6574714M | Total Assets ($) | 10925804M | 10336026M |

M = $ thousand    MM = $ million
See Pages 9 through 22 for Explanation of Ratios and Data

## Comparative Historical Data | Current Data Sorted by Sales

| Type of Statement | Hist 1 | Hist 2 | Hist 3 | | 0-1MM | 1-3MM | 3-5MM | 5-10MM | 10-25MM | 25MM & OVER |
|---|---|---|---|---|---|---|---|---|---|---|
| Unqualified | 73 | 53 | 73 | | 1 | 4 | 3 | 2 | 11 | 60 |
| Reviewed | 61 | 62 | 67 | | 1 | 4 | 8 | 15 | 28 | 16 |
| Compiled | 35 | 37 | 34 | | 7 | 12 | 4 | 12 | 8 | 1 |
| Tax Returns | 20 | 27 | 34 | | 3 | 9 | 14 | 6 | 4 | 1 |
| Other | 161 | 151 | 153 | | | | | 15 | 23 | 89 |
| | 4/1/09-3/31/10 ALL | 4/1/10-3/31/11 ALL | 4/1/11-3/31/12 ALL | | \<— 51 (4/1-9/30/11) —\> | | | \<— 310 (10/1/11-3/31/12) —\> | | |
| NUMBER OF STATEMENTS | 350 | 330 | 361 | | 12 | 29 | 29 | 50 | 74 | 167 |

### ASSETS (%)

| | Hist 1 | Hist 2 | Hist 3 | | 0-1MM | 1-3MM | 3-5MM | 5-10MM | 10-25MM | 25MM & OVER |
|---|---|---|---|---|---|---|---|---|---|---|
| Cash & Equivalents | 8.3 | 9.2 | 7.3 | | 16.0 | 7.6 | 7.1 | 10.7 | 8.7 | 5.0 |
| Trade Receivables (net) | 24.0 | 24.1 | 23.9 | | 14.4 | 26.0 | 25.1 | 21.2 | 22.8 | 25.3 |
| Inventory | 27.9 | 27.9 | 27.0 | | 21.7 | 24.2 | 30.7 | 33.1 | 32.5 | 23.0 |
| All Other Current | 3.0 | 2.9 | 3.0 | | 3.5 | 1.1 | 1.8 | 1.4 | 3.1 | 4.0 |
| Total Current | 63.2 | 64.0 | 61.2 | | 55.6 | 59.0 | 64.6 | 66.3 | 67.2 | 57.2 |
| Fixed Assets (net) | 27.0 | 25.8 | 27.1 | | 24.4 | 30.6 | 25.7 | 21.4 | 23.6 | 30.3 |
| Intangibles (net) | 4.7 | 4.9 | 6.7 | | 4.5 | 8.1 | 5.5 | 6.7 | 5.4 | 7.4 |
| All Other Non-Current | 5.0 | 5.3 | 5.0 | | 15.5 | 2.3 | 4.2 | 5.6 | 3.8 | 5.1 |
| Total | 100.0 | 100.0 | 100.0 | | 100.0 | 100.0 | 100.0 | 100.0 | 100.0 | 100.0 |

### LIABILITIES

| | Hist 1 | Hist 2 | Hist 3 | | 0-1MM | 1-3MM | 3-5MM | 5-10MM | 10-25MM | 25MM & OVER |
|---|---|---|---|---|---|---|---|---|---|---|
| Notes Payable-Short Term | 12.5 | 11.3 | 10.4 | | 7.3 | 11.4 | 12.7 | 8.7 | 11.6 | 9.9 |
| Cur. Mat.-L.T.D. | 4.1 | 3.6 | 3.1 | | .0 | 2.9 | 2.7 | 3.1 | 4.4 | 2.9 |
| Trade Payables | 16.7 | 15.4 | 15.7 | | 5.9 | 12.9 | 19.6 | 14.8 | 14.9 | 16.8 |
| Income Taxes Payable | .1 | .2 | .2 | | .0 | .2 | .0 | .2 | .4 | .3 |
| All Other Current | 10.1 | 9.3 | 9.4 | | 9.2 | 6.3 | 4.9 | 8.7 | 9.5 | 10.9 |
| Total Current | 43.4 | 39.8 | 38.9 | | 22.3 | 33.7 | 39.9 | 35.6 | 40.8 | 40.9 |
| Long-Term Debt | 15.8 | 13.1 | 15.4 | | 22.1 | 22.7 | 17.4 | 18.3 | 11.0 | 14.4 |
| Deferred Taxes | .6 | .8 | .8 | | .3 | .0 | .9 | .4 | .5 | 1.2 |
| All Other Non-Current | 7.4 | 6.0 | 9.8 | | 73.9 | 19.2 | 15.1 | 6.5 | 3.8 | 6.3 |
| Net Worth | 32.8 | 40.3 | 35.1 | | -18.6 | 24.5 | 26.6 | 39.3 | 43.9 | 37.2 |
| Total Liabilities & Net Worth | 100.0 | 100.0 | 100.0 | | 100.0 | 100.0 | 100.0 | 100.0 | 100.0 | 100.0 |

### INCOME DATA

| | Hist 1 | Hist 2 | Hist 3 | | 0-1MM | 1-3MM | 3-5MM | 5-10MM | 10-25MM | 25MM & OVER |
|---|---|---|---|---|---|---|---|---|---|---|
| Net Sales | 100.0 | 100.0 | 100.0 | | 100.0 | 100.0 | 100.0 | 100.0 | 100.0 | 100.0 |
| Gross Profit | 24.9 | 27.8 | 26.4 | | 55.0 | 40.3 | 38.1 | 34.5 | 25.7 | 17.7 |
| Operating Expenses | 22.9 | 22.1 | 20.6 | | 49.6 | 34.4 | 31.4 | 29.3 | 19.1 | 12.4 |
| Operating Profit | 2.0 | 5.7 | 5.7 | | 5.4 | 5.9 | 6.7 | 5.2 | 6.6 | 5.3 |
| All Other Expenses (net) | 1.4 | .9 | 1.1 | | 1.8 | 1.5 | 1.3 | .7 | 1.0 | 1.1 |
| Profit Before Taxes | .6 | 4.9 | 4.6 | | 3.6 | 4.3 | 5.4 | 4.5 | 5.7 | 4.2 |

### RATIOS

| | Hist 1 | Hist 2 | Hist 3 | | 0-1MM | 1-3MM | 3-5MM | 5-10MM | 10-25MM | 25MM & OVER |
|---|---|---|---|---|---|---|---|---|---|---|
| Current | 2.6 | 2.8 | 2.5 | | 8.2 | 3.7 | 2.6 | 3.7 | 2.7 | 2.0 |
| | 1.5 | 1.6 | 1.6 | | 3.3 | 1.6 | 1.8 | 2.1 | 1.6 | 1.4 |
| | 1.1 | 1.1 | 1.1 | | 1.4 | 1.0 | 1.2 | 1.3 | 1.1 | 1.1 |
| Quick | 1.3 | 1.5 | 1.3 | | 2.6 | 1.7 | 1.5 | 1.5 | 1.4 | 1.1 |
| | .8 | .8 | .8 | | 1.0 | .9 | .9 | .8 | .8 | .8 |
| | .5 | .5 | .5 | | .3 | .5 | .4 | .5 | .5 | .5 |
| Sales/Receivables | 30  12.1 | 29  12.8 | 30  12.3 | | 0  UND | 19  19.1 | 18  19.8 | 28  13.1 | 26  13.8 | 38  9.6 |
| | 46  8.0 | 43  8.4 | 43  8.4 | | 1  381.8 | 33  10.9 | 46  8.0 | 36  10.1 | 41  8.9 | 48  7.6 |
| | 63  5.8 | 56  6.6 | 54  6.7 | | 23  16.2 | 43  8.5 | 70  5.2 | 49  7.4 | 52  7.0 | 58  6.3 |
| Cost of Sales/Inventory | 36  10.0 | 34  10.6 | 34  10.7 | | 0  UND | 14  25.4 | 40  9.1 | 55  6.6 | 39  9.3 | 32  11.5 |
| | 66  5.5 | 64  5.7 | 56  6.5 | | 10  36.3 | 44  8.3 | 76  4.8 | 83  4.4 | 69  5.3 | 46  7.9 |
| | 109  3.3 | 112  3.2 | 107  3.4 | | 94  3.9 | 146  2.5 | 135  2.7 | 140  2.6 | 114  3.2 | 79  4.6 |
| Cost of Sales/Payables | 19  19.1 | 18  19.9 | 19  19.5 | | 0  UND | 15  23.6 | 28  13.1 | 16  22.2 | 18  20.1 | 21  17.0 |
| | 35  10.3 | 33  11.1 | 34  10.7 | | 5  74.2 | 25  14.4 | 40  9.1 | 34  10.7 | 28  13.1 | 35  10.5 |
| | 54  6.8 | 51  7.2 | 49  7.5 | | 14  27.0 | 41  8.8 | 85  4.3 | 51  7.2 | 49  7.5 | 47  7.8 |
| Sales/Working Capital | 4.5 | 4.8 | 5.2 | | 8.7 | 4.5 | 4.3 | 4.3 | 4.8 | 6.6 |
| | 9.4 | 9.5 | 9.7 | | 12.1 | 12.5 | 8.3 | 6.2 | 7.5 | 11.2 |
| | 49.7 | 47.2 | 38.7 | | 62.0 | NM | 24.4 | 16.0 | 47.3 | 83.2 |
| EBIT/Interest | 6.4 | 20.1 | 21.1 | | | 17.1 | 22.7 | 18.2 | 22.6 | 27.3 |
| | (322) 2.2 | (304) 5.7 | (327) 5.4 | | | (24) 2.6 | (25) 3.8 | (45) 4.6 | (70) 6.8 | (155) 5.3 |
| | -1.0 | 1.7 | 1.6 | | | 1.0 | 1.3 | 1.4 | 2.2 | 1.8 |
| Net Profit + Depr., Dep., Amort./Cur. Mat. L/T/D | 4.3 | 8.8 | 9.0 | | | | | 31.0 | 11.0 | 9.6 |
| | (100) 2.0 | (97) 3.2 | (108) 3.4 | | | | | (10) 5.4 | (26) 3.8 | (62) 3.4 |
| | .6 | 1.3 | 1.7 | | | | | 1.0 | 1.5 | 1.7 |
| Fixed/Worth | .3 | .3 | .3 | | .1 | .3 | .2 | .1 | .2 | .5 |
| | .8 | .7 | .8 | | NM | .8 | .7 | .4 | .6 | .9 |
| | 2.0 | 1.5 | 2.3 | | -.4 | 3.4 | 18.7 | 4.1 | 1.4 | 2.4 |
| Debt/Worth | .7 | .6 | .7 | | .6 | .7 | .8 | .4 | .7 | .8 |
| | 2.0 | 1.5 | 1.9 | | NM | 2.1 | 3.2 | 1.5 | 1.4 | 2.2 |
| | 5.6 | 4.5 | 5.4 | | -2.4 | 7.7 | 29.3 | 8.6 | 2.8 | 5.0 |
| % Profit Before Taxes/Tangible Net Worth | 33.6 | 46.4 | 47.4 | | | 36.1 | 59.7 | 45.4 | 53.3 | 41.6 |
| | (293) 7.9 | (292) 20.6 | (307) 23.1 | | | (23) 14.0 | (23) 28.3 | (41) 23.2 | (67) 34.8 | (147) 20.0 |
| | -5.7 | 5.8 | 7.6 | | | 2.1 | 5.8 | 7.1 | 7.5 | 9.4 |
| % Profit Before Taxes/Total Assets | 9.8 | 16.3 | 16.4 | | 37.5 | 12.9 | 18.7 | 17.9 | 21.3 | 13.3 |
| | 2.3 | 7.4 | 7.5 | | 12.8 | 2.8 | 9.3 | 8.5 | 9.9 | 6.4 |
| | -4.7 | 1.8 | 1.8 | | -7.0 | .8 | .6 | 2.3 | 2.2 | 1.9 |
| Sales/Net Fixed Assets | 23.3 | 25.8 | 20.2 | | 111.1 | 27.1 | 49.5 | 65.1 | 22.6 | 12.1 |
| | 7.2 | 8.7 | 8.0 | | 30.0 | 6.7 | 11.7 | 10.5 | 10.5 | 6.4 |
| | 3.6 | 4.5 | 4.2 | | 10.4 | 4.2 | 4.1 | 4.3 | 5.4 | 4.0 |
| Sales/Total Assets | 2.5 | 2.6 | 2.6 | | 7.6 | 3.1 | 2.7 | 2.7 | 2.7 | 2.4 |
| | 1.8 | 1.9 | 1.9 | | 3.3 | 2.4 | 2.0 | 1.9 | 2.0 | 1.8 |
| | 1.3 | 1.4 | 1.4 | | 1.3 | 1.3 | 1.3 | 1.2 | 1.6 | 1.4 |
| % Depr., Dep., Amort./Sales | 1.2 | 1.2 | 1.2 | | | .4 | .7 | 1.1 | 1.1 | 1.7 |
| | (278) 2.6 | (275) 2.6 | (296) 2.4 | | | (23) 1.4 | (23) 1.9 | (37) 2.4 | (68) 2.0 | (139) 2.9 |
| | 4.9 | 4.5 | 4.1 | | | 4.0 | 6.1 | 4.0 | 3.8 | 4.1 |
| % Officers', Directors' Owners' Comp/Sales | 2.6 | 1.7 | 2.0 | | | 2.1 | 2.1 | 2.7 | 1.6 | |
| | (88) 4.2 | (83) 3.7 | (92) 4.0 | | | (15) 4.6 | (12) 5.3 | (22) 4.0 | (28) 3.2 | |
| | 7.7 | 6.7 | 6.6 | | | 7.1 | 6.5 | 5.8 | 4.7 | |
| Net Sales ($) | 18713440M | 17890545M | 23787561M | | 7043M | 56942M | 109935M | 364444M | 1214976M | 22034221M |
| Total Assets ($) | 10517118M | 9723292M | 12707463M | | 3744M | 37233M | 67357M | 215592M | 680899M | 11702638M |

© RMA 2012

M = $ thousand    MM = $ million
See Pages 9 through 22 for Explanation of Ratios and Data

## Current Data Sorted by Assets

## Comparative Historical Data

| | | | | | | Type of Statement | | |
|---|---|---|---|---|---|---|---|---|
| | | 1 | 4 | 2 | 1 | Unqualified | 6 | 7 |
| | 1 | 4 | 5 | 1 | | Reviewed | | 3 |
| 1 | 2 | 1 | | | | Compiled | 2 | |
| 1 | 1 | 6 | 1 | | | Tax Returns | | 2 |
| | | 4 | 3 | | 2 | Other | 10 | 6 |
| | 7 (4/1-9/30/11) | | 38 (10/1/11-3/31/12) | | | | 4/1/07-3/31/08 | 4/1/08-3/31/09 |
| 0-500M | 500M-2MM | 2-10MM | 10-50MM | 50-100MM | 100-250MM | | ALL | ALL |
| 2 | 4 | 15 | 14 | 7 | 3 | **NUMBER OF STATEMENTS** | 18 | 18 |
| % | % | % | % | % | % | **ASSETS** | % | % |
| | | 9.2 | 9.7 | | | Cash & Equivalents | 15.3 | 10.9 |
| | | 26.4 | 14.8 | | | Trade Receivables (net) | 19.7 | 14.8 |
| | | 28.3 | 29.1 | | | Inventory | 29.4 | 33.7 |
| | | 2.3 | 4.6 | | | All Other Current | 3.8 | 5.6 |
| | | 66.2 | 58.1 | | | Total Current | 68.1 | 65.0 |
| | | 30.2 | 17.9 | | | Fixed Assets (net) | 22.0 | 16.6 |
| | | .7 | 12.4 | | | Intangibles (net) | 1.5 | 7.6 |
| | | 2.8 | 11.6 | | | All Other Non-Current | 8.4 | 10.8 |
| | | 100.0 | 100.0 | | | Total | 100.0 | 100.0 |
| | | | | | | **LIABILITIES** | | |
| | | 10.4 | 6.7 | | | Notes Payable-Short Term | 9.1 | 10.1 |
| | | 1.2 | 2.8 | | | Cur. Mat.-L.T.D. | 2.2 | 4.4 |
| | | 14.3 | 6.2 | | | Trade Payables | 10.6 | 14.8 |
| | | .0 | .2 | | | Income Taxes Payable | .3 | .0 |
| | | 7.8 | 13.2 | | | All Other Current | 15.1 | 15.6 |
| | | 33.8 | 29.2 | | | Total Current | 37.2 | 44.9 |
| | | 24.5 | 14.8 | | | Long-Term Debt | 12.1 | 17.9 |
| | | .0 | 1.7 | | | Deferred Taxes | .7 | 1.0 |
| | | 9.5 | 4.6 | | | All Other Non-Current | 8.7 | 12.5 |
| | | 32.2 | 49.7 | | | Net Worth | 41.2 | 23.6 |
| | | 100.0 | 100.0 | | | Total Liabilities & Net Worth | 100.0 | 100.0 |
| | | | | | | **INCOME DATA** | | |
| | | 100.0 | 100.0 | | | Net Sales | 100.0 | 100.0 |
| | | 27.0 | 27.5 | | | Gross Profit | 31.8 | 29.9 |
| | | 19.5 | 18.2 | | | Operating Expenses | 22.9 | 26.1 |
| | | 7.5 | 9.3 | | | Operating Profit | 8.9 | 3.8 |
| | | 1.0 | 1.6 | | | All Other Expenses (net) | .7 | 1.8 |
| | | 6.5 | 7.8 | | | Profit Before Taxes | 8.2 | 2.1 |
| | | | | | | **RATIOS** | | |
| | | 3.4 | 3.8 | | | | 5.8 | 2.6 |
| | | 1.7 | 2.5 | | | Current | 1.6 | 1.4 |
| | | 1.3 | 1.3 | | | | 1.1 | 1.1 |
| | | 2.8 | 1.6 | | | | 2.7 | 1.1 |
| | | 1.1 | 1.1 | | | Quick | 1.1 | .6 |
| | | .5 | .4 | | | | .3 | .2 |
| | | 25  14.7 | 20  18.5 | | | | 19  19.4 | 8  47.4 |
| | | 43  8.5 | 41  8.9 | | | Sales/Receivables | 45  8.2 | 32  11.4 |
| | | 63  5.8 | 61  6.0 | | | | 70  5.3 | 49  7.4 |
| | | 26  14.1 | 64  5.7 | | | | 22  16.2 | 45  8.1 |
| | | 47  7.7 | 159  2.3 | | | Cost of Sales/Inventory | 75  4.9 | 104  3.5 |
| | | 159  2.3 | 215  1.7 | | | | 162  2.3 | 183  2.0 |
| | | 13  27.6 | 8  43.4 | | | | 18  20.1 | 25  14.5 |
| | | 25  14.6 | 23  15.7 | | | Cost of Sales/Payables | 30  12.1 | 37  9.8 |
| | | 40  9.1 | 35  10.3 | | | | 47  7.7 | 63  5.8 |
| | | 3.8 | 1.8 | | | | 2.2 | 3.7 |
| | | 6.3 | 4.2 | | | Sales/Working Capital | 8.8 | 15.7 |
| | | 22.1 | 16.0 | | | | 50.0 | 190.4 |
| | | 43.0 | 38.6 | | | | 18.1 | 22.9 |
| | | (13)  3.3 | (12)  8.0 | | | EBIT/Interest | (16)  4.3 | (17)  3.5 |
| | | 1.2 | 2.2 | | | | 2.5 | -.8 |
| | | | | | | Net Profit + Depr., Dep., Amort./Cur. Mat. L/T/D | | |
| | | .2 | .1 | | | | .1 | .1 |
| | | 1.1 | .7 | | | Fixed/Worth | .7 | .9 |
| | | 12.5 | NM | | | | 3.4 | -1.6 |
| | | .6 | .3 | | | | .6 | .9 |
| | | 2.7 | 2.0 | | | Debt/Worth | 1.4 | 4.1 |
| | | 22.0 | NM | | | | 10.4 | -9.8 |
| | | 58.2 | 66.3 | | | % Profit Before Taxes/Tangible Net Worth | 74.8 | 60.4 |
| | | (12)  19.7 | (11)  32.3 | | | | (16)  27.8 | (11)  26.0 |
| | | -.1 | 8.6 | | | | 12.3 | -.3 |
| | | 13.5 | 16.2 | | | % Profit Before Taxes/Total Assets | 17.0 | 10.1 |
| | | 9.7 | 11.2 | | | | 10.5 | 6.1 |
| | | 3.3 | 3.9 | | | | 1.2 | -3.8 |
| | | 19.4 | 33.9 | | | | 59.2 | 79.7 |
| | | 6.3 | 7.9 | | | Sales/Net Fixed Assets | 8.7 | 12.3 |
| | | 3.8 | 3.9 | | | | 3.3 | 4.1 |
| | | 2.7 | 1.8 | | | | 2.3 | 3.0 |
| | | 1.7 | .9 | | | Sales/Total Assets | 1.5 | 1.8 |
| | | 1.4 | .6 | | | | 1.0 | .8 |
| | | .6 | .5 | | | | .5 | .3 |
| | | (13)  2.5 | (13)  2.8 | | | % Depr., Dep., Amort./Sales | (15)  1.6 | (14)  1.9 |
| | | 5.8 | 4.2 | | | | 2.9 | 3.3 |
| | | | | | | % Officers', Directors' Owners' Comp/Sales | | |
| 3887M | 11624M | 141952M | 405222M | 531838M | 500347M | Net Sales ($) | 1762254M | 877796M |
| 493M | 3728M | 70136M | 366920M | 525389M | 474980M | Total Assets ($) | 931415M | 504585M |

M = $ thousand    MM = $ million
See Pages 9 through 22 for Explanation of Ratios and Data

## Comparative Historical Data | Current Data Sorted by Sales

| Type of Statement | 4/1/09-3/31/10 ALL | 4/1/10-3/31/11 ALL | 4/1/11-3/31/12 ALL | | 0-1MM | 1-3MM | 3-5MM | 5-10MM | 10-25MM | 25MM & OVER |
|---|---|---|---|---|---|---|---|---|---|---|
| Unqualified | 4 | 5 | 8 | | | | | 1 | 1 | 6 |
| Reviewed | 5 | 6 | 11 | | | | 3 | 3 | | 5 |
| Compiled | 5 | 2 | 4 | | | 2 | 1 | | 1 | |
| Tax Returns | 3 | 3 | 9 | | | 2 | 2 | 4 | 1 | |
| Other | 11 | 12 | 13 | | | | | 1 | 4 | 8 |
| | | | | | | 7 (4/1-9/30/11) | | 38 (10/1/11-3/31/12) | | |
| NUMBER OF STATEMENTS | 28 | 28 | 45 | | | 4 | 6 | 9 | 7 | 19 |
| **ASSETS** | % | % | % | | | % | % | % | % | % |
| Cash & Equivalents | 9.2 | 11.1 | 10.7 | | | | | | | 12.6 |
| Trade Receivables (net) | 20.9 | 17.7 | 19.2 | | | | | | | 18.8 |
| Inventory | 27.1 | 24.6 | 27.0 | | | | | | | 26.7 |
| All Other Current | 9.1 | 8.0 | 6.1 | | | | | | | 10.0 |
| Total Current | 66.3 | 61.4 | 62.9 | | | | | | | 68.1 |
| Fixed Assets (net) | 21.3 | 27.8 | 22.9 | | | | | | | 16.3 |
| Intangibles (net) | 4.4 | 3.5 | 7.5 | | | | | | | 9.1 |
| All Other Non-Current | 8.1 | 7.3 | 6.6 | | | | | | | 6.5 |
| Total | 100.0 | 100.0 | 100.0 | | | | | | | 100.0 |
| **LIABILITIES** | | | | | | | | | | |
| Notes Payable-Short Term | 10.8 | 14.5 | 9.7 | | | | | | | 10.3 |
| Cur. Mat.-L.T.D. | 4.4 | 3.3 | 1.9 | | | | | | | 3.0 |
| Trade Payables | 12.5 | 12.2 | 11.6 | | | | | | | 10.2 |
| Income Taxes Payable | .0 | .1 | .2 | | | | | | | .2 |
| All Other Current | 16.1 | 16.5 | 15.9 | | | | | | | 14.3 |
| Total Current | 43.7 | 46.6 | 39.3 | | | | | | | 38.1 |
| Long-Term Debt | 16.0 | 18.2 | 18.4 | | | | | | | 15.9 |
| Deferred Taxes | .5 | .2 | .6 | | | | | | | .6 |
| All Other Non-Current | 19.4 | 24.1 | 15.5 | | | | | | | 19.2 |
| Net Worth | 20.3 | 10.9 | 26.2 | | | | | | | 26.2 |
| Total Liabilities & Net Worth | 100.0 | 100.0 | 100.0 | | | | | | | 100.0 |
| **INCOME DATA** | | | | | | | | | | |
| Net Sales | 100.0 | 100.0 | 100.0 | | | | | | | 100.0 |
| Gross Profit | 26.7 | 26.9 | 27.9 | | | | | | | 25.7 |
| Operating Expenses | 24.2 | 21.4 | 20.5 | | | | | | | 16.1 |
| Operating Profit | 2.5 | 5.5 | 7.4 | | | | | | | 9.6 |
| All Other Expenses (net) | 1.9 | 3.3 | 2.0 | | | | | | | 3.5 |
| Profit Before Taxes | .5 | 2.2 | 5.4 | | | | | | | 6.1 |
| **RATIOS** | | | | | | | | | | |
| Current | 2.6 | 2.1 | 3.5 | | | | | | | 3.6 |
| | 1.5 | 1.5 | 1.7 | | | | | | | 2.0 |
| | 1.2 | 1.0 | 1.3 | | | | | | | 1.3 |
| Quick | 1.3 | 1.6 | 1.6 | | | | | | | 1.7 |
| | .7 | .6 | 1.0 | | | | | | | 1.1 |
| | .3 | .2 | .4 | | | | | | | .3 |
| Sales/Receivables | 26 14.0 | 14 25.7 | 23 15.6 | | | | | | | 24 15.2 |
| | 46 8.0 | 45 8.0 | 39 9.3 | | | | | | | 41 8.9 |
| | 73 5.0 | 53 6.9 | 58 6.3 | | | | | | | 58 6.3 |
| Cost of Sales/Inventory | 13 28.7 | 15 24.4 | 19 19.1 | | | | | | | 12 31.0 |
| | 67 5.4 | 84 4.3 | 81 4.5 | | | | | | | 87 4.2 |
| | 152 2.4 | 171 2.1 | 192 1.9 | | | | | | | 203 1.8 |
| Cost of Sales/Payables | 20 17.9 | 18 20.6 | 14 26.1 | | | | | | | 16 23.0 |
| | 32 11.3 | 34 10.7 | 25 14.6 | | | | | | | 28 13.1 |
| | 48 7.6 | 58 6.2 | 41 9.0 | | | | | | | 45 8.2 |
| Sales/Working Capital | 3.8 | 4.9 | 3.2 | | | | | | | 1.6 |
| | 6.7 | 14.4 | 6.3 | | | | | | | 4.0 |
| | 27.8 | -62.9 | 22.1 | | | | | | | 13.5 |
| EBIT/Interest | 7.0 | 12.9 | 19.1 | | | | | | | 27.1 |
| | (26) 3.1 | (27) 5.1 | (39) 3.3 | | | | | | | (17) 9.6 |
| | .7 | .8 | .9 | | | | | | | .9 |
| Net Profit + Depr., Dep., Amort./Cur. Mat. L/T/D | | | | | | | | | | |
| | | | | | | | | | | |
| | | | | | | | | | | |
| Fixed/Worth | .1 | .5 | .2 | | | | | | | .1 |
| | .8 | 1.8 | .9 | | | | | | | .6 |
| | -1.6 | -2.8 | NM | | | | | | | -21.5 |
| Debt/Worth | 1.3 | 1.4 | .7 | | | | | | | .6 |
| | 2.5 | 4.4 | 2.7 | | | | | | | 2.7 |
| | -6.3 | -16.3 | -525.3 | | | | | | | -50.9 |
| % Profit Before Taxes/Tangible Net Worth | 32.4 | 68.9 | 40.6 | | | | | | | 49.3 |
| | (19) 13.0 | (18) 40.4 | (33) 19.8 | | | | | | | (14) 38.7 |
| | 6.3 | 11.3 | 2.8 | | | | | | | 7.1 |
| % Profit Before Taxes/Total Assets | 8.7 | 14.3 | 13.8 | | | | | | | 16.6 |
| | 3.1 | 5.6 | 7.2 | | | | | | | 8.3 |
| | -.7 | -1.2 | -.4 | | | | | | | -.4 |
| Sales/Net Fixed Assets | 56.2 | 9.5 | 19.4 | | | | | | | 19.5 |
| | 7.3 | 6.1 | 8.2 | | | | | | | 8.9 |
| | 2.3 | 2.7 | 4.3 | | | | | | | 4.3 |
| Sales/Total Assets | 1.9 | 2.1 | 2.4 | | | | | | | 1.9 |
| | 1.3 | 1.3 | 1.4 | | | | | | | 1.1 |
| | .9 | 1.1 | .8 | | | | | | | .7 |
| % Depr., Dep., Amort./Sales | .9 | 2.0 | .9 | | | | | | | 1.3 |
| | (25) 2.5 | (25) 3.1 | (40) 2.5 | | | | | | | (18) 2.6 |
| | 4.4 | 6.6 | 4.7 | | | | | | | 4.6 |
| % Officers', Directors' Owners' Comp/Sales | | | 1.2 | | | | | | | |
| | | | (13) 2.3 | | | | | | | |
| | | | 6.3 | | | | | | | |
| Net Sales ($) | 777324M | 1268876M | 1594870M | | | 7599M | 24153M | 69953M | 135618M | 1357547M |
| Total Assets ($) | 614568M | 978452M | 1441646M | | | 2664M | 11641M | 69012M | 131446M | 1226883M |

*In the Current Data section, the columns 0-1MM, 1-3MM, 3-5MM, 5-10MM and 10-25MM are marked "DATA NOT AVAILABLE" for the Assets, Liabilities, Income Data and Ratios rows.*

M = $ thousand    MM = $ million
See Pages 9 through 22 for Explanation of Ratios and Data

## Current Data Sorted by Assets     Comparative Historical Data

| 0-500M | 500M-2MM | 2-10MM | 10-50MM | 50-100MM | 100-250MM | Type of Statement | 4/1/07-3/31/08 ALL | 4/1/08-3/31/09 ALL |
|---|---|---|---|---|---|---|---|---|
| 1 | 1 | 4 | 5 | 7 | 5 | Unqualified | 23 | 30 |
|  | 2 | 16 | 8 | 1 |  | Reviewed | 21 | 21 |
|  |  | 7 |  |  |  | Compiled | 7 | 5 |
| 1 | 4 | 2 |  |  |  | Tax Returns | 7 | 9 |
|  | 5 | 18 | 16 | 5 | 4 | Other | 48 | 52 |
|  | 22 (4/1-9/30/11) |  | 90 (10/1/11-3/31/12) |  |  |  |  |  |
| 2 | 12 | 47 | 29 | 13 | 9 | NUMBER OF STATEMENTS | 106 | 117 |

| 0-500M % | 500M-2MM % | 2-10MM % | 10-50MM % | 50-100MM % | 100-250MM % | | 07-08 ALL % | 08-09 ALL % |
|---|---|---|---|---|---|---|---|---|
|  |  |  |  |  |  | **ASSETS** |  |  |
|  | 3.6 | 10.0 | 3.5 | 5.8 |  | Cash & Equivalents | 6.6 | 7.0 |
|  | 29.9 | 22.7 | 18.7 | 19.6 |  | Trade Receivables (net) | 20.8 | 21.2 |
|  | 18.0 | 38.9 | 40.2 | 36.3 |  | Inventory | 38.5 | 38.7 |
|  | 12.2 | 1.7 | .9 | 3.6 |  | All Other Current | 4.2 | 2.2 |
|  | 63.7 | 73.4 | 63.3 | 65.2 |  | Total Current | 70.1 | 69.1 |
|  | 23.6 | 20.4 | 22.7 | 26.7 |  | Fixed Assets (net) | 21.2 | 22.3 |
|  | 7.6 | 2.5 | 8.6 | 5.6 |  | Intangibles (net) | 4.3 | 4.9 |
|  | 5.1 | 3.7 | 5.4 | 2.5 |  | All Other Non-Current | 4.4 | 3.7 |
|  | 100.0 | 100.0 | 100.0 | 100.0 |  | Total | 100.0 | 100.0 |
|  |  |  |  |  |  | **LIABILITIES** |  |  |
|  | 12.2 | 10.8 | 16.1 | 5.0 |  | Notes Payable-Short Term | 12.1 | 11.6 |
|  | 2.0 | 3.4 | 5.3 | 7.8 |  | Cur. Mat.-L.T.D. | 3.9 | 4.7 |
|  | 15.5 | 12.2 | 9.2 | 10.4 |  | Trade Payables | 13.9 | 12.3 |
|  | .0 | .5 | .1 | .1 |  | Income Taxes Payable | .6 | .6 |
|  | 9.7 | 6.3 | 10.4 | 6.9 |  | All Other Current | 12.7 | 10.2 |
|  | 39.4 | 33.2 | 41.1 | 30.3 |  | Total Current | 43.2 | 39.3 |
|  | 13.7 | 9.4 | 12.3 | 10.4 |  | Long-Term Debt | 15.4 | 18.2 |
|  | .0 | 1.5 | .7 | 1.8 |  | Deferred Taxes | .3 | .6 |
|  | 3.3 | 4.7 | 6.5 | 7.2 |  | All Other Non-Current | 6.9 | 7.2 |
|  | 43.6 | 51.1 | 39.5 | 50.2 |  | Net Worth | 34.2 | 34.7 |
|  | 100.0 | 100.0 | 100.0 | 100.0 |  | Total Liabilities & Net Worth | 100.0 | 100.0 |
|  |  |  |  |  |  | **INCOME DATA** |  |  |
|  | 100.0 | 100.0 | 100.0 | 100.0 |  | Net Sales | 100.0 | 100.0 |
|  | 35.2 | 32.6 | 27.8 | 26.5 |  | Gross Profit | 31.6 | 30.2 |
|  | 31.9 | 24.2 | 17.8 | 14.4 |  | Operating Expenses | 22.4 | 22.0 |
|  | 3.3 | 8.4 | 10.0 | 12.1 |  | Operating Profit | 9.3 | 8.2 |
|  | -.2 | .6 | 2.1 | 1.4 |  | All Other Expenses (net) | 2.2 | 1.4 |
|  | 3.5 | 7.8 | 7.9 | 10.7 |  | Profit Before Taxes | 7.1 | 6.8 |
|  |  |  |  |  |  | **RATIOS** |  |  |
|  | 2.8 | 3.7 | 2.3 | 5.3 |  |  | 2.6 | 2.7 |
|  | 1.6 | 2.4 | 1.6 | 2.0 |  | Current | 1.6 | 1.9 |
|  | .9 | 1.6 | 1.3 | 1.5 |  |  | 1.3 | 1.3 |
|  | 2.6 | 2.1 | .8 | 2.1 |  |  | 1.1 | 1.4 |
|  | .8 | .9 | .5 | .7 |  | Quick | .6 | .7 |
|  | .5 | .6 | .4 | .4 |  |  | .4 | .4 |
|  | 31 11.9 | 32 11.4 | 34 10.7 | 43 8.5 |  |  | 25 14.5 | 29 12.6 |
|  | 35 10.3 | 45 8.1 | 50 7.3 | 62 5.9 |  | Sales/Receivables | 42 8.7 | 42 8.6 |
|  | 51 7.2 | 60 6.1 | 60 6.1 | 73 5.0 |  |  | 55 6.6 | 56 6.5 |
|  | 3 134.2 | 64 5.7 | 107 3.4 | 79 4.6 |  |  | 70 5.2 | 61 6.0 |
|  | 14 26.0 | 114 3.2 | 126 2.9 | 135 2.7 |  | Cost of Sales/Inventory | 109 3.4 | 113 3.2 |
|  | 126 2.9 | 182 2.0 | 192 1.9 | 192 1.9 |  |  | 156 2.3 | 195 1.9 |
|  | 5 70.4 | 13 28.8 | 23 16.1 | 24 15.1 |  |  | 20 18.7 | 19 19.6 |
|  | 25 14.4 | 29 12.7 | 29 12.4 | 41 8.9 |  | Cost of Sales/Payables | 34 10.7 | 30 12.2 |
|  | 79 4.6 | 43 8.4 | 41 8.9 | 46 8.0 |  |  | 54 6.7 | 44 8.2 |
|  | 5.9 | 2.9 | 3.5 | 2.5 |  |  | 3.3 | 3.2 |
|  | 12.2 | 3.8 | 6.0 | 4.4 |  | Sales/Working Capital | 7.0 | 5.2 |
|  | NM | 7.2 | 13.4 | 6.1 |  |  | 15.1 | 15.3 |
|  |  | 29.1 | 22.7 | 178.2 |  |  | 9.7 | 11.1 |
|  |  | (42) 8.7 | (27) 4.7 | (12) 4.4 |  | EBIT/Interest | (95) 3.9 | (100) 4.7 |
|  |  | 2.9 | 2.8 | 1.1 |  |  | 2.0 | 1.8 |
|  |  | 7.5 | 2.5 |  |  | Net Profit + Depr., Dep., | 5.9 | 8.0 |
|  |  | (10) 4.0 | (11) 1.6 |  |  | Amort./Cur. Mat. L/T/D | (31) 2.5 | (34) 2.7 |
|  |  | .8 | 1.2 |  |  |  | .7 | 1.2 |
|  | .2 | .1 | .2 | .2 |  |  | .2 | .2 |
|  | .8 | .3 | .6 | .7 |  | Fixed/Worth | .6 | .6 |
|  | 1.5 | .6 | 1.3 | 1.6 |  |  | 1.7 | 1.8 |
|  | .5 | .5 | 1.3 | .2 |  |  | .8 | .8 |
|  | 1.6 | 1.0 | 2.1 | 1.0 |  | Debt/Worth | 1.7 | 2.0 |
|  | 6.6 | 1.7 | 4.3 | 3.7 |  |  | 4.6 | 5.7 |
|  | 42.9 | 45.1 | 44.4 | 37.5 |  |  | 70.1 | 59.8 |
|  | (11) 9.3 | 24.0 | (27) 25.9 | (12) 26.8 |  | % Profit Before Taxes/Tangible Net Worth | (93) 28.1 | (100) 25.3 |
|  | -6.2 | 11.8 | 9.7 | 6.0 |  |  | 11.4 | 8.7 |
|  | 24.8 | 19.9 | 16.2 | 24.1 |  |  | 17.6 | 20.0 |
|  | 6.0 | 11.3 | 7.4 | 7.0 |  | % Profit Before Taxes/Total Assets | 9.6 | 9.4 |
|  | -2.2 | 4.1 | 3.4 | .5 |  |  | 3.6 | 2.8 |
|  | 32.8 | 49.4 | 22.4 | 8.9 |  |  | 29.3 | 20.6 |
|  | 13.6 | 11.7 | 6.3 | 3.9 |  | Sales/Net Fixed Assets | 9.6 | 9.4 |
|  | 5.5 | 5.0 | 3.7 | 2.7 |  |  | 4.9 | 4.8 |
|  | 3.1 | 2.3 | 1.6 | 1.6 |  |  | 2.6 | 2.3 |
|  | 2.1 | 1.7 | 1.3 | 1.2 |  | Sales/Total Assets | 1.8 | 1.6 |
|  | 1.3 | 1.3 | 1.0 | 1.0 |  |  | 1.2 | 1.2 |
|  |  | .8 | 1.3 | 1.7 |  |  | 1.3 | 1.1 |
|  |  | (39) 1.5 | (26) 2.9 | 3.5 |  | % Depr., Dep., Amort./Sales | (88) 2.2 | (103) 1.9 |
|  |  | 3.2 | 3.8 | 3.9 |  |  | 3.6 | 3.3 |
|  |  | 2.6 |  |  |  |  | 1.6 | 2.1 |
|  |  | (13) 3.2 |  |  |  | % Officers', Directors' Owners' Comp/Sales | (31) 4.4 | (22) 4.9 |
|  |  | 5.1 |  |  |  |  | 9.1 | 8.0 |
| 5650M | 39166M | 479075M | 917391M | 1302720M | 2197402M | Net Sales ($) | 4435095M | 5414105M |
| 788M | 15595M | 271655M | 674561M | 997083M | 1475621M | Total Assets ($) | 2811581M | 3676039M |

M = $ thousand    MM = $ million
See Pages 9 through 22 for Explanation of Ratios and Data

## Comparative Historical Data | Current Data Sorted by Sales

| 4/1/09-3/31/10 ALL | 4/1/10-3/31/11 ALL | 4/1/11-3/31/12 ALL | Type of Statement | 0-1MM | 1-3MM | 3-5MM | 5-10MM | 10-25MM | 25MM & OVER |
|---|---|---|---|---|---|---|---|---|---|
| | | | | | 22 (4/1-9/30/11) | | 90 (10/1/11-3/31/12) | | |
| 24 | 29 | 22 | Unqualified | 1 | | | | 4 | 17 |
| 21 | 22 | 26 | Reviewed | | 2 | 1 | 9 | 10 | 4 |
| 4 | 8 | 9 | Compiled | | 1 | 3 | 2 | 3 | |
| 10 | 9 | 7 | Tax Returns | | 3 | 1 | 2 | 1 | |
| 46 | 61 | 48 | Other | | 4 | 2 | 11 | 13 | 18 |
| 105 | 129 | 112 | **NUMBER OF STATEMENTS** | 1 | 10 | 7 | 24 | 31 | 39 |
| % | % | % | **ASSETS** | % | % | % | % | % | % |
| 7.4 | 9.1 | 7.0 | Cash & Equivalents | | 4.5 | | 11.4 | 6.2 | 6.2 |
| 20.3 | 18.2 | 21.8 | Trade Receivables (net) | | 21.1 | | 21.8 | 22.9 | 20.7 |
| 36.3 | 34.8 | 34.9 | Inventory | | 26.4 | | 36.9 | 35.5 | 37.3 |
| 2.4 | 2.7 | 3.4 | All Other Current | | 10.5 | | .7 | 2.0 | 3.6 |
| 66.4 | 64.8 | 67.0 | Total Current | | 62.5 | | 70.8 | 66.7 | 67.8 |
| 24.7 | 23.8 | 21.8 | Fixed Assets (net) | | 24.2 | | 21.9 | 24.1 | 18.7 |
| 4.2 | 6.4 | 7.0 | Intangibles (net) | | 8.0 | | 4.8 | 5.5 | 8.7 |
| 4.6 | 5.0 | 4.1 | All Other Non-Current | | 5.3 | | 2.5 | 3.7 | 4.8 |
| 100.0 | 100.0 | 100.0 | Total | | 100.0 | | 100.0 | 100.0 | 100.0 |
| | | | **LIABILITIES** | | | | | | |
| 12.5 | 8.9 | 10.9 | Notes Payable-Short Term | | 13.7 | | 10.5 | 13.0 | 9.0 |
| 3.7 | 4.1 | 4.0 | Cur. Mat.-L.T.D. | | 1.8 | | 2.2 | 6.1 | 4.4 |
| 10.4 | 11.1 | 11.7 | Trade Payables | | 13.4 | | 8.3 | 14.7 | 12.0 |
| .6 | .3 | .2 | Income Taxes Payable | | .0 | | .2 | .6 | .1 |
| 8.9 | 9.1 | 8.3 | All Other Current | | 14.2 | | 5.7 | 8.1 | 9.4 |
| 36.0 | 33.5 | 35.1 | Total Current | | 43.2 | | 27.0 | 42.5 | 35.0 |
| 15.8 | 15.8 | 11.8 | Long-Term Debt | | 6.3 | | 10.7 | 10.0 | 13.3 |
| .9 | .6 | 1.1 | Deferred Taxes | | .0 | | .1 | 2.5 | 1.1 |
| 4.2 | 6.8 | 6.7 | All Other Non-Current | | 8.8 | | 2.4 | 3.5 | 9.5 |
| 43.1 | 43.2 | 45.2 | Net Worth | | 41.7 | | 59.9 | 41.5 | 41.2 |
| 100.0 | 100.0 | 100.0 | Total Liabilities & Net Worth | | 100.0 | | 100.0 | 100.0 | 100.0 |
| | | | **INCOME DATA** | | | | | | |
| 100.0 | 100.0 | 100.0 | Net Sales | | 100.0 | | 100.0 | 100.0 | 100.0 |
| 26.1 | 30.5 | 30.0 | Gross Profit | | 40.3 | | 33.7 | 26.5 | 26.3 |
| 18.9 | 22.4 | 21.2 | Operating Expenses | | 33.9 | | 23.9 | 17.9 | 15.8 |
| 7.1 | 8.0 | 8.8 | Operating Profit | | 6.4 | | 9.8 | 8.5 | 10.5 |
| 1.6 | 1.8 | 1.3 | All Other Expenses (net) | | -.2 | | 1.1 | 1.7 | 2.1 |
| 5.5 | 6.2 | 7.4 | Profit Before Taxes | | 6.6 | | 8.6 | 6.9 | 8.4 |
| | | | **RATIOS** | | | | | | |
| 3.1 | 3.1 | 3.1 | Current | | 2.8 | | 3.8 | 2.5 | 3.0 |
| 1.9 | 1.9 | 1.9 | | | 1.6 | | 2.6 | 1.6 | 1.7 |
| 1.3 | 1.3 | 1.4 | | | 1.0 | | 2.0 | 1.2 | 1.5 |
| 1.3 | 1.4 | 1.7 | Quick | | 1.8 | | 2.9 | 1.2 | 1.7 |
| .7 | .7 | .7 | | | .7 | | 1.2 | .7 | .6 |
| .5 | .5 | .5 | | | .6 | | .6 | .4 | .4 |
| 32  11.6 | 25  14.5 | 32  11.3 | Sales/Receivables | 0  UND | 29  12.7 | | 32  11.4 | 34  10.7 | 39  9.3 |
| 42  8.7 | 44  8.2 | 45  8.1 | | | 48  7.6 | | 41  8.9 | 45  8.1 | 52  7.0 |
| 55  6.7 | 58  6.3 | 61  6.0 | | | | | 55  6.6 | 64  5.7 | 64  5.7 |
| 62  5.9 | 68  5.4 | 66  5.5 | Cost of Sales/Inventory | 0  UND | 27  13.5 | | 65  5.6 | 61  6.0 | 96  3.8 |
| 107  3.4 | 117  3.1 | 118  3.1 | | | 192  1.9 | | 122  3.0 | 101  3.6 | 126  2.9 |
| 169  2.2 | 167  2.2 | 182  2.0 | | | | | 215  1.7 | 152  2.4 | 182  2.0 |
| 14  26.1 | 19  18.8 | 16  23.0 | Cost of Sales/Payables | 0  UND | 30  12.3 | | 12  30.1 | 17  21.8 | 26  14.0 |
| 25  14.5 | 32  11.6 | 34  10.8 | | | 111  3.3 | | 18  20.7 | 36  10.2 | 37  9.9 |
| 38  9.6 | 48  7.7 | 45  8.2 | | | | | 41  8.9 | 46  7.9 | 46  7.9 |
| 2.9 | 3.0 | 3.1 | Sales/Working Capital | | 4.5 | | 2.7 | 4.4 | 3.1 |
| 5.4 | 6.0 | 5.0 | | | 44.4 | | 3.5 | 6.4 | 5.7 |
| 12.7 | 12.8 | 9.2 | | | NM | | 5.0 | 27.0 | 7.8 |
| 11.8 | 11.6 | 28.1 | EBIT/Interest | | | | 29.1 | 23.4 | 34.0 |
| (96)  4.1 | (108)  4.0 | (96)  5.2 | | | | | (22)  12.4 | (27)  5.2 | (34)  4.6 |
| 1.8 | 1.9 | 2.0 | | | | | 2.6 | 2.7 | 2.1 |
| 6.1 | 4.4 | 5.9 | Net Profit + Depr., Dep., | | | | | | 2.9 |
| (25)  3.0 | (31)  2.3 | (29)  1.6 | Amort./Cur. Mat. L/T/D | | | | | (16) | 1.3 |
| 1.4 | .7 | .8 | | | | | | | .6 |
| .1 | .1 | .2 | Fixed/Worth | | .1 | | .1 | .1 | .2 |
| .6 | .6 | .4 | | | .8 | | .4 | .5 | .4 |
| 1.5 | 1.5 | 1.2 | | | 52.4 | | .6 | 1.3 | 1.3 |
| .6 | .6 | .6 | Debt/Worth | | .9 | | .4 | .9 | .6 |
| 1.6 | 1.5 | 1.5 | | | 1.5 | | .7 | 1.6 | 1.9 |
| 3.7 | 3.4 | 2.9 | | | 90.7 | | 1.1 | 3.3 | 3.8 |
| 44.8 | 34.1 | 42.7 | % Profit Before Taxes/Tangible | | | | 40.6 | 40.0 | 44.9 |
| (98)  23.3 | (116)  19.0 | (104)  25.4 | Net Worth | | | | 16.3 | (29)  24.0 | (35)  27.1 |
| 8.5 | 7.3 | 10.1 | | | | | 11.4 | 12.4 | 9.7 |
| 16.1 | 14.0 | 18.8 | % Profit Before Taxes/Total | | 24.0 | | 23.4 | 15.6 | 18.0 |
| 7.6 | 6.4 | 8.2 | Assets | | 1.9 | | 9.3 | 9.3 | 7.4 |
| 2.4 | 1.5 | 2.8 | | | -2.0 | | 4.1 | 3.2 | 2.8 |
| 24.7 | 24.3 | 31.0 | Sales/Net Fixed Assets | | 33.8 | | 32.4 | 30.8 | 24.3 |
| 8.2 | 7.6 | 8.1 | | | 17.7 | | 11.4 | 7.9 | 7.7 |
| 3.4 | 3.7 | 4.5 | | | 5.5 | | 3.9 | 3.8 | 4.6 |
| 2.1 | 2.0 | 2.2 | Sales/Total Assets | | 4.1 | | 2.3 | 2.2 | 1.6 |
| 1.5 | 1.5 | 1.5 | | | 1.7 | | 1.7 | 1.6 | 1.3 |
| 1.1 | 1.0 | 1.1 | | | 1.0 | | .9 | 1.3 | 1.1 |
| 1.2 | 1.2 | .9 | % Depr., Dep., Amort./Sales | | | | .9 | 1.1 | 1.0 |
| (94)  2.4 | (114)  2.7 | (95)  2.1 | | | | | (19)  1.6 | (24)  2.1 | (37)  2.2 |
| 4.0 | 4.1 | 3.7 | | | | | 3.2 | 3.8 | 3.7 |
| 2.7 | 1.9 | 1.9 | % Officers', Directors' | | | | | | |
| (22)  4.5 | (37)  4.0 | (25)  3.1 | Owners' Comp/Sales | | | | | | |
| 9.6 | 6.0 | 5.1 | | | | | | | |
| 4582138M | 4413145M | 4941404M | Net Sales ($) | 759M | 22125M | 28099M | 182788M | 487475M | 4220158M |
| 3126932M | 2996453M | 3435303M | Total Assets ($) | 620M | 13415M | 18033M | 127647M | 339067M | 2936521M |

M = $ thousand    MM = $ million
See Pages 9 through 22 for Explanation of Ratios and Data

## Current Data Sorted by Assets      Comparative Historical Data

| Type of Statement | 0-500M | 500M-2MM | 2-10MM | 10-50MM | 50-100MM | 100-250MM | 4/1/07-3/31/08 ALL | 4/1/08-3/31/09 ALL |
|---|---|---|---|---|---|---|---|---|
| Unqualified | | | 7 | 17 | 3 | 6 | 24 | 30 |
| Reviewed | | | 24 | 12 | 1 | 1 | 39 | 35 |
| Compiled | 1 | 6 | 17 | 1 | | | 18 | 20 |
| Tax Returns | 2 | 6 | 6 | 2 | | | 23 | 16 |
| Other | 2 | 6 | 27 | 38 | 4 | 16 | 69 | 85 |
| | | 42 (4/1-9/30/11) | | 163 (10/1/11-3/31/12) | | | 69 | 85 |
| NUMBER OF STATEMENTS | 5 | 18 | 81 | 70 | 9 | 22 | 173 | 186 |

| ASSETS | % | % | % | % | % | % | % | % |
|---|---|---|---|---|---|---|---|---|
| Cash & Equivalents | | 13.0 | 11.9 | 7.8 | | 4.4 | 10.0 | 8.4 |
| Trade Receivables (net) | | 32.0 | 22.9 | 18.6 | | 15.1 | 22.0 | 19.0 |
| Inventory | | 25.5 | 33.7 | 34.8 | | 25.7 | 33.4 | 32.7 |
| All Other Current | | 2.8 | 2.1 | 2.9 | | 6.2 | 3.7 | 4.1 |
| Total Current | | 73.1 | 70.6 | 64.0 | | 51.3 | 69.2 | 64.3 |
| Fixed Assets (net) | | 18.3 | 21.9 | 24.1 | | 15.7 | 21.2 | 24.4 |
| Intangibles (net) | | 3.8 | 4.7 | 6.6 | | 26.7 | 5.6 | 7.3 |
| All Other Non-Current | | 4.7 | 2.8 | 5.3 | | 6.3 | 4.0 | 4.1 |
| Total | | 100.0 | 100.0 | 100.0 | | 100.0 | 100.0 | 100.0 |

| LIABILITIES | | | | | | | | |
|---|---|---|---|---|---|---|---|---|
| Notes Payable-Short Term | | 7.0 | 9.2 | 7.8 | | 3.1 | 8.9 | 9.6 |
| Cur. Mat.-L.T.D. | | 3.7 | 4.9 | 4.7 | | 3.6 | 4.8 | 3.5 |
| Trade Payables | | 10.6 | 10.0 | 9.5 | | 7.9 | 11.4 | 9.5 |
| Income Taxes Payable | | .3 | .1 | .2 | | .3 | .5 | .4 |
| All Other Current | | 10.1 | 6.3 | 8.2 | | 7.2 | 9.2 | 8.9 |
| Total Current | | 31.7 | 30.5 | 30.4 | | 22.0 | 34.7 | 31.9 |
| Long-Term Debt | | 11.9 | 16.6 | 17.7 | | 14.9 | 17.6 | 16.7 |
| Deferred Taxes | | .0 | .6 | 1.2 | | 1.4 | .4 | .7 |
| All Other Non-Current | | 12.1 | 6.6 | 5.1 | | 11.9 | 8.0 | 8.7 |
| Net Worth | | 44.3 | 45.7 | 45.6 | | 49.8 | 39.2 | 42.1 |
| Total Liabilities & Net Worth | | 100.0 | 100.0 | 100.0 | | 100.0 | 100.0 | 100.0 |

| INCOME DATA | | | | | | | | |
|---|---|---|---|---|---|---|---|---|
| Net Sales | | 100.0 | 100.0 | 100.0 | | 100.0 | 100.0 | 100.0 |
| Gross Profit | | 46.3 | 34.7 | 29.1 | | 27.4 | 32.2 | 33.2 |
| Operating Expenses | | 41.0 | 24.7 | 20.7 | | 19.7 | 21.9 | 23.6 |
| Operating Profit | | 5.3 | 10.0 | 8.4 | | 7.7 | 10.2 | 9.6 |
| All Other Expenses (net) | | .3 | 1.1 | 1.1 | | 2.8 | 1.8 | 1.6 |
| Profit Before Taxes | | 4.9 | 8.9 | 7.3 | | 4.9 | 8.5 | 8.0 |

| RATIOS | 0-500M | 500M-2MM | 2-10MM | 10-50MM | 50-100MM | 100-250MM | 4/1/07-3/31/08 ALL | 4/1/08-3/31/09 ALL |
|---|---|---|---|---|---|---|---|---|
| Current | | 5.2 / 2.8 / 1.3 | 4.0 / 2.3 / 1.6 | 3.7 / 2.2 / 1.6 | | 4.4 / 2.9 / 2.0 | 3.6 / 2.1 / 1.4 | 3.3 / 2.1 / 1.5 |
| Quick | | 3.5 / 1.4 / .9 | 2.1 / 1.2 / .6 | 1.5 / .8 / .5 | | 1.9 / 1.3 / .5 | 1.7 / .9 / .5 | 1.4 / .8 / .4 |
| Sales/Receivables | | 26 14.3 / 39 9.3 / 49 7.5 | 33 10.9 / 45 8.1 / 64 5.7 | 36 10.2 / 50 7.3 / 60 6.1 | | 37 9.8 / 57 6.4 / 66 5.5 | 28 12.9 / 44 8.2 / 61 6.0 | 25 14.7 / 40 9.0 / 51 7.1 |
| Cost of Sales/Inventory | | 7 51.2 / 45 8.1 / 166 2.2 | 53 6.9 / 99 3.7 / 174 2.1 | 87 4.2 / 122 3.0 / 192 1.9 | | 87 4.2 / 107 3.4 / 182 2.0 | 54 6.8 / 107 3.4 / 168 2.2 | 67 5.5 / 111 3.3 / 172 2.1 |
| Cost of Sales/Payables | | 1 286.2 / 20 18.4 / 59 6.2 | 14 25.2 / 23 15.7 / 46 8.0 | 22 16.3 / 31 11.8 / 39 9.3 | | 24 15.2 / 31 11.6 / 48 7.6 | 18 19.8 / 28 12.8 / 47 7.8 | 18 20.7 / 27 13.3 / 44 8.2 |
| Sales/Working Capital | | 3.3 / 8.7 / 24.0 | 3.3 / 4.4 / 7.3 | 2.6 / 4.3 / 7.6 | | 2.7 / 3.4 / 6.1 | 3.1 / 5.0 / 10.1 | 3.4 / 5.0 / 10.0 |
| EBIT/Interest | | (15) 54.7 / 13.2 / -.1 | (77) 20.3 / 8.7 / 3.7 | (65) 19.3 / 5.6 / 2.2 | | (21) 24.2 / 2.2 / .9 | (158) 12.6 / 5.3 / 2.4 | (172) 18.1 / 5.2 / 1.9 |
| Net Profit + Depr., Dep., Amort./Cur. Mat. L/T/D | | | (29) 14.2 / 3.6 / 1.6 | (31) 4.8 / 2.7 / 1.3 | | (12) 5.5 / 2.0 / .9 | (48) 14.2 / 3.1 / 1.7 | (66) 9.1 / 3.9 / 1.9 |
| Fixed/Worth | | .1 / .3 / 2.3 | .2 / .6 / 1.4 | .2 / .5 / 1.2 | | .3 / .5 / 4.4 | .2 / .5 / 1.5 | .2 / .6 / 1.5 |
| Debt/Worth | | .4 / .7 / 7.0 | .5 / 1.1 / 4.4 | .5 / 1.1 / 3.2 | | .8 / 1.9 / 15.9 | .8 / 1.7 / 4.6 | .7 / 1.4 / 3.8 |
| % Profit Before Taxes/Tangible Net Worth | | (16) 72.0 / 29.4 / 20.7 | (72) 56.3 / 24.5 / 11.6 | (64) 34.9 / 16.6 / 9.2 | | (18) 36.5 / 22.6 / 1.0 | (151) 58.6 / 33.1 / 13.7 | (165) 51.2 / 27.7 / 8.4 |
| % Profit Before Taxes/Total Assets | | 28.3 / 18.3 / 2.9 | 26.8 / 10.6 / 4.2 | 15.1 / 7.9 / 3.0 | | 12.7 / 4.6 / -.5 | 22.1 / 11.3 / 5.2 | 20.0 / 10.7 / 2.5 |
| Sales/Net Fixed Assets | | 100.3 / 19.9 / 10.4 | 39.2 / 9.5 / 4.6 | 16.1 / 6.3 / 3.4 | | 13.8 / 5.7 / 4.7 | 31.3 / 10.0 / 4.6 | 18.0 / 7.7 / 3.8 |
| Sales/Total Assets | | 4.9 / 2.6 / 2.1 | 2.2 / 1.8 / 1.3 | 1.7 / 1.3 / 1.0 | | 1.3 / 1.0 / .7 | 2.2 / 1.7 / 1.2 | 2.2 / 1.6 / 1.1 |
| % Depr., Dep., Amort./Sales | | (11) .4 / 1.6 / 2.9 | (69) 1.1 / 2.4 / 4.3 | (66) 1.7 / 3.0 / 5.2 | | (19) 2.3 / 3.1 / 7.5 | (151) 1.0 / 2.4 / 4.0 | (160) 1.1 / 2.4 / 4.5 |
| % Officers', Directors' Owners' Comp/Sales | | (13) 1.6 / 3.1 / 5.4 | (35) 3.5 / 5.4 / 6.5 | (12) 2.2 / 5.2 / 7.9 | | | (48) 2.4 / 4.2 / | (55) 1.7 / 3.6 / 6.6 |
| Net Sales ($) | 4681M | 77425M | 825400M | 2165083M | 716405M | 3901951M | 4790994M | 6254351M |
| Total Assets ($) | 1502M | 24407M | 455704M | 1624869M | 643801M | 3730914M | 3757282M | 5017101M |

M = $ thousand    MM = $ million
See Pages 9 through 22 for Explanation of Ratios and Data

## Comparative Historical Data / Current Data Sorted by Sales

### Type of Statement

| 4/1/09-3/31/10 ALL | 4/1/10-3/31/11 ALL | 4/1/11-3/31/12 ALL | Type of Statement | 0-1MM | 1-3MM | 3-5MM | 5-10MM | 10-25MM | 25MM & OVER |
|---|---|---|---|---|---|---|---|---|---|
| 35 | 29 | 33 | Unqualified | | | 1 | 3 | 7 | 22 |
| 34 | 48 | 37 | Reviewed | | 1 | 1 | 11 | 16 | 8 |
| 20 | 19 | 26 | Compiled | 1 | 1 | 6 | 11 | 6 | 1 |
| 18 | 13 | 16 | Tax Returns | 1 | 4 | | 7 | 3 | 1 |
| 92 | 87 | 93 | Other | 1 | 5 | 5 | 11 | 33 | 38 |

Historical periods: 4/1/09-3/31/10 ALL, 4/1/10-3/31/11 ALL, 4/1/11-3/31/12 ALL
Current: 42 (4/1-9/30/11), 163 (10/1/11-3/31/12)

| 4/1/09-3/31/10 ALL | 4/1/10-3/31/11 ALL | 4/1/11-3/31/12 ALL | | 0-1MM | 1-3MM | 3-5MM | 5-10MM | 10-25MM | 25MM & OVER |
|---|---|---|---|---|---|---|---|---|---|
| 199 | 196 | 205 | NUMBER OF STATEMENTS | 3 | 11 | 13 | 43 | 65 | 70 |
| % | % | % | **ASSETS** | % | % | % | % | % | % |
| 9.9 | 10.8 | 10.4 | Cash & Equivalents | | 14.0 | 12.5 | 12.7 | 9.3 | 8.6 |
| 18.9 | 20.1 | 20.7 | Trade Receivables (net) | | 14.5 | 19.4 | 26.5 | 21.0 | 18.6 |
| 33.2 | 30.9 | 31.8 | Inventory | | 36.3 | 31.0 | 32.5 | 32.5 | 30.5 |
| 3.9 | 4.2 | 3.8 | All Other Current | | 2.5 | 3.2 | 1.3 | 3.2 | 6.2 |
| 65.9 | 66.1 | 66.6 | Total Current | | 67.3 | 66.1 | 73.0 | 66.0 | 63.9 |
| 23.9 | 22.9 | 21.5 | Fixed Assets (net) | | 25.2 | 24.4 | 22.1 | 22.1 | 19.7 |
| 6.3 | 7.2 | 7.4 | Intangibles (net) | | 2.7 | 6.6 | 3.2 | 7.0 | 11.2 |
| 3.9 | 3.9 | 4.4 | All Other Non-Current | | 4.7 | 2.9 | 1.6 | 5.0 | 5.2 |
| 100.0 | 100.0 | 100.0 | Total | | 100.0 | 100.0 | 100.0 | 100.0 | 100.0 |
| | | | **LIABILITIES** | | | | | | |
| 9.0 | 8.6 | 7.6 | Notes Payable-Short Term | | 4.4 | 10.7 | 8.5 | 9.2 | 5.7 |
| 4.3 | 3.7 | 4.4 | Cur. Mat.-L.T.D. | | 3.9 | 4.7 | 3.9 | 3.8 | 5.3 |
| 9.4 | 10.2 | 9.4 | Trade Payables | | 9.8 | 9.7 | 10.2 | 9.4 | 9.1 |
| .3 | .3 | .2 | Income Taxes Payable | | .1 | .3 | .1 | .1 | .4 |
| 8.3 | 9.1 | 7.5 | All Other Current | | 4.4 | 9.1 | 5.7 | 7.9 | 8.6 |
| 31.4 | 31.9 | 29.1 | Total Current | | 22.7 | 34.4 | 28.4 | 30.4 | 29.2 |
| 16.3 | 13.6 | 16.2 | Long-Term Debt | | 29.9 | 15.8 | 13.4 | 17.2 | 15.3 |
| .8 | 1.0 | .8 | Deferred Taxes | | .0 | .0 | .8 | 1.2 | .8 |
| 7.3 | 7.0 | 8.0 | All Other Non-Current | | 10.7 | 17.0 | 7.0 | 5.3 | 7.3 |
| 44.3 | 46.5 | 45.9 | Net Worth | | 36.6 | 32.8 | 50.5 | 45.9 | 47.4 |
| 100.0 | 100.0 | 100.0 | Total Liabilties & Net Worth | | 100.0 | 100.0 | 100.0 | 100.0 | 100.0 |
| | | | **INCOME DATA** | | | | | | |
| 100.0 | 100.0 | 100.0 | Net Sales | | 100.0 | 100.0 | 100.0 | 100.0 | 100.0 |
| 31.4 | 31.1 | 33.0 | Gross Profit | | 42.8 | 41.8 | 34.9 | 32.5 | 28.9 |
| 23.9 | 22.7 | 24.0 | Operating Expenses | | 34.4 | 36.6 | 25.4 | 22.5 | 20.1 |
| 7.5 | 8.3 | 9.0 | Operating Profit | | 8.4 | 5.2 | 9.5 | 9.9 | 8.8 |
| 1.7 | 1.9 | 1.1 | All Other Expenses (net) | | .2 | 1.2 | .9 | 1.2 | 1.4 |
| 5.8 | 6.4 | 7.9 | Profit Before Taxes | | 8.2 | 4.0 | 8.7 | 8.8 | 7.4 |
| | | | **RATIOS** | | | | | | |
| 4.1 | 3.9 | 4.1 | Current | | 11.0 | 4.0 | 3.8 | 4.2 | 3.6 |
| 2.3 | 2.2 | 2.3 | | | 2.9 | 2.6 | 2.3 | 2.3 | 2.3 |
| 1.6 | 1.5 | 1.6 | | | 1.4 | 1.2 | 1.7 | 1.5 | 1.5 |
| 1.9 | 1.9 | 2.0 | Quick | | 6.1 | 1.5 | 2.2 | 1.7 | 1.7 |
| .9 | 1.0 | 1.0 | | | 1.2 | .8 | 1.3 | 1.0 | .9 |
| .4 | .5 | .6 | | | .4 | .3 | .7 | .5 | .5 |
| 29  12.8 | 31  11.7 | 33  11.2 | Sales/Receivables | | 18  20.8 | 13  28.0 | 33  11.2 | 33  10.9 | 37  9.8 |
| 41  8.8 | 44  8.4 | 46  8.0 | | | 32  11.3 | 38  9.5 | 47  7.8 | 43  8.5 | 51  7.2 |
| 54  6.7 | 58  6.3 | 62  5.9 | | | 43  8.4 | 61  6.0 | 68  5.4 | 60  6.1 | 63  5.8 |
| 63  5.8 | 58  6.2 | 65  5.6 | Cost of Sales/Inventory | | 41  9.0 | 7  48.9 | 41  8.9 | 61  6.0 | 79  4.6 |
| 105  3.5 | 110  3.3 | 104  3.5 | | | 94  3.9 | 122  3.0 | 99  3.7 | 107  3.4 | 107  3.4 |
| 178  2.1 | 157  2.3 | 174  2.1 | | | 228  1.6 | 304  1.2 | 182  2.0 | 174  2.1 | 182  2.0 |
| 15  24.0 | 16  22.6 | 18  20.8 | Cost of Sales/Payables | | 5  69.5 | 15  24.3 | 14  26.5 | 18  20.4 | 22  16.4 |
| 25  14.6 | 29  12.8 | 29  12.8 | | | 21  17.1 | 19  19.4 | 25  14.8 | 30  12.2 | 30  12.2 |
| 41  8.9 | 46  7.9 | 43  8.5 | | | 74  4.9 | 68  5.4 | 47  7.7 | 38  9.7 | 45  8.2 |
| 2.8 | 2.8 | 2.8 | Sales/Working Capital | | 2.1 | 3.4 | 3.2 | 3.2 | 2.4 |
| 4.3 | 4.5 | 4.3 | | | 5.6 | 4.6 | 4.5 | 4.3 | 3.7 |
| 8.2 | 9.2 | 8.0 | | | 18.0 | 20.7 | 6.5 | 8.8 | 7.2 |
| 12.0 | 13.2 | 24.6 | EBIT/Interest | | 34.0 | 13.8 | 36.7 | 21.8 | 24.7 |
| (185) 4.6 | (175) 4.9 | (190) 8.3 | | | (10) 12.5 | (12) 4.1 | (39) 6.5 | (62) 10.4 | (65) 9.0 |
| 1.9 | 1.9 | 2.3 | | | 3.6 | 1.0 | 3.0 | 2.5 | 2.0 |
| 6.2 | 9.5 | 5.9 | Net Profit + Depr., Dep., Amort./Cur. Mat. L/T/D | | | | 9.2 | 5.8 | 5.5 |
| (63) 2.6 | (70) 2.6 | (78) 3.2 | | | | | (13) 2.1 | (30) 3.3 | (31) 2.7 |
| 1.5 | 1.4 | 1.3 | | | | | 1.6 | 1.2 | 1.2 |
| .2 | .2 | .2 | Fixed/Worth | | | .2 | .3 | .1 | .2 | .2 |
| .6 | .5 | .5 | | | .5 | .6 | .5 | .5 | .5 |
| 1.6 | 1.5 | 1.4 | | | -31.5 | NM | 1.1 | 1.3 | 1.3 |
| .6 | .5 | .5 | Debt/Worth | | .4 | .6 | .5 | .4 | .6 |
| 1.3 | 1.3 | 1.1 | | | 6.3 | 1.2 | .8 | 1.1 | 1.1 |
| 3.7 | 3.6 | 3.8 | | | -51.0 | NM | 2.6 | 3.8 | 4.5 |
| 33.3 | 40.2 | 52.3 | % Profit Before Taxes/Tangible Net Worth | | | | 44.5 | 54.4 | 55.6 | 35.4 |
| (176) 19.7 | (177) 17.8 | (182) 23.3 | | | | (10) 26.0 | (41) 27.0 | (60) 21.3 | (61) 23.0 |
| 7.2 | 7.1 | 10.8 | | | | 5.5 | 12.1 | 11.6 | 10.8 |
| 15.8 | 15.3 | 21.7 | % Profit Before Taxes/Total Assets | | 29.2 | 18.6 | 26.6 | 26.3 | 15.9 |
| 8.9 | 7.7 | 10.4 | | | 19.6 | 13.1 | 13.5 | 10.4 | 8.5 |
| 2.1 | 2.2 | 3.6 | | | 3.8 | .0 | 5.1 | 3.1 | 2.6 |
| 17.0 | 19.2 | 24.0 | Sales/Net Fixed Assets | | 36.4 | 24.4 | 41.8 | 23.6 | 19.9 |
| 6.6 | 7.6 | 8.7 | | | 11.1 | 8.3 | 8.9 | 8.8 | 7.4 |
| 3.7 | 3.8 | 4.4 | | | 5.1 | 4.2 | 4.7 | 4.9 | 3.5 |
| 2.1 | 2.0 | 2.1 | Sales/Total Assets | | 3.1 | 2.4 | 2.7 | 2.1 | 1.6 |
| 1.4 | 1.5 | 1.5 | | | 2.2 | 2.0 | 1.9 | 1.7 | 1.2 |
| 1.0 | 1.0 | 1.1 | | | 1.2 | 1.2 | 1.3 | 1.2 | .9 |
| 1.2 | 1.5 | 1.4 | % Depr., Dep., Amort./Sales | | | | .8 | 1.6 | 1.1 | 1.8 |
| (164) 2.9 | (170) 2.9 | (176) 2.7 | | | | (10) 2.2 | (36) 3.2 | (59) 2.1 | (63) 3.0 |
| 5.2 | 4.7 | 4.5 | | | | 3.1 | 4.7 | 3.4 | 5.5 |
| 1.7 | 1.8 | 2.2 | % Officers', Directors' Owners' Comp/Sales | | | | | 2.8 | 2.4 | |
| (65) 5.0 | (67) 4.0 | (63) 4.5 | | | | | (22) 4.5 | (19) 5.5 | |
| 8.9 | 7.4 | 6.5 | | | | | 6.6 | 9.7 | |
| 6134648M | 5429056M | 7690945M | Net Sales ($) | 1631M | 24015M | 52479M | 310876M | 1098018M | 6203926M |
| 5114060M | 4563828M | 6481197M | Total Assets ($) | 1629M | 14369M | 34206M | 184997M | 772880M | 5473116M |

M = $ thousand    MM = $ million
See Pages 9 through 22 for Explanation of Ratios and Data

## Current Data Sorted by Assets | Comparative Historical Data

| 0-500M | 500M-2MM | 2-10MM | 10-50MM | 50-100MM | 100-250MM | Type of Statement | 4/1/07-3/31/08 ALL | 4/1/08-3/31/09 ALL |
|---|---|---|---|---|---|---|---|---|
| | | | 4 | 2 | 3 | Unqualified | 10 | 14 |
| | 1 | 1 | 2 | | | Reviewed | 3 | 1 |
| | 1 | 1 | | | | Compiled | 2 | 2 |
| | | 1 | | | | Tax Returns | 4 | 4 |
| 1 | 1 | 10 | 7 | 3 | 3 | Other | 23 | 18 |
| | 3 (4/1-9/30/11) | | 38 (10/1/11-3/31/12) | | | | | |
| 1 | 3 | 13 | 13 | 5 | 6 | NUMBER OF STATEMENTS | 42 | 39 |
| % | % | % | % | % | % | ASSETS | % | % |
| | | 7.6 | 8.1 | | | Cash & Equivalents | 12.2 | 9.2 |
| | | 29.6 | 22.1 | | | Trade Receivables (net) | 22.4 | 19.5 |
| | | 29.1 | 32.0 | | | Inventory | 23.7 | 32.3 |
| | | 4.3 | 8.6 | | | All Other Current | 3.0 | 4.4 |
| | | 70.6 | 70.8 | | | Total Current | 61.3 | 65.5 |
| | | 20.3 | 17.9 | | | Fixed Assets (net) | 21.4 | 23.4 |
| | | .8 | 5.1 | | | Intangibles (net) | 10.9 | 7.1 |
| | | 8.2 | 6.2 | | | All Other Non-Current | 6.4 | 4.0 |
| | | 100.0 | 100.0 | | | Total | 100.0 | 100.0 |
| | | | | | | LIABILITIES | | |
| | | 10.1 | 11.6 | | | Notes Payable-Short Term | 8.0 | 9.8 |
| | | 1.6 | 2.2 | | | Cur. Mat.-L.T.D. | 5.1 | 3.4 |
| | | 18.9 | 9.6 | | | Trade Payables | 12.6 | 13.8 |
| | | .0 | 1.1 | | | Income Taxes Payable | .1 | .2 |
| | | 8.7 | 7.3 | | | All Other Current | 11.8 | 14.5 |
| | | 39.3 | 31.9 | | | Total Current | 37.6 | 41.8 |
| | | 7.1 | 9.3 | | | Long-Term Debt | 19.2 | 11.6 |
| | | .2 | .2 | | | Deferred Taxes | .7 | .8 |
| | | 3.6 | 4.8 | | | All Other Non-Current | 2.8 | 12.2 |
| | | 49.8 | 53.9 | | | Net Worth | 39.7 | 33.6 |
| | | 100.0 | 100.0 | | | Total Liabilties & Net Worth | 100.0 | 100.0 |
| | | | | | | INCOME DATA | | |
| | | 100.0 | 100.0 | | | Net Sales | 100.0 | 100.0 |
| | | 31.5 | 32.0 | | | Gross Profit | 34.7 | 27.0 |
| | | 27.4 | 19.7 | | | Operating Expenses | 25.3 | 20.7 |
| | | 4.1 | 12.3 | | | Operating Profit | 9.4 | 6.3 |
| | | .1 | 1.3 | | | All Other Expenses (net) | 2.3 | 1.5 |
| | | 4.0 | 10.9 | | | Profit Before Taxes | 7.1 | 4.8 |
| | | | | | | RATIOS | | |
| | | 3.9 | 3.4 | | | | 3.4 | 2.4 |
| | | 1.8 | 2.0 | | | Current | 2.1 | 1.6 |
| | | 1.3 | 1.6 | | | | 1.2 | 1.1 |
| | | 2.5 | 1.6 | | | | 2.1 | 1.2 |
| | | 1.1 | 1.3 | | | Quick | 1.0 | .8 |
| | | .5 | .4 | | | | .6 | .3 |
| | | 35  10.3 | 54  6.7 | | | | 31  11.9 | 33  11.1 |
| | | 40  9.1 | 63  5.8 | | | Sales/Receivables | 43  8.5 | 38  9.5 |
| | | 60  6.1 | 69  5.3 | | | | 56  6.5 | 53  6.9 |
| | | 42  8.6 | 64  5.7 | | | | 34  10.9 | 49  7.4 |
| | | 83  4.4 | 104  3.5 | | | Cost of Sales/Inventory | 65  5.6 | 88  4.1 |
| | | 96  3.8 | 215  1.7 | | | | 103  3.6 | 171  2.1 |
| | | 25  14.4 | 28  13.2 | | | | 18  20.6 | 23  15.7 |
| | | 46  7.9 | 33  10.9 | | | Cost of Sales/Payables | 29  12.8 | 33  11.0 |
| | | 59  6.2 | 46  7.9 | | | | 47  7.7 | 43  8.5 |
| | | 4.4 | 2.0 | | | | 3.9 | 3.7 |
| | | 5.3 | 4.4 | | | Sales/Working Capital | 7.7 | 6.1 |
| | | 19.2 | 6.1 | | | | 16.1 | 33.7 |
| | | | 37.6 | | | | 19.9 | 21.5 |
| | | | (12) 17.1 | | | EBIT/Interest | (37) 8.2 | (38) 5.6 |
| | | | 4.4 | | | | 1.7 | 2.7 |
| | | | | | | Net Profit + Depr., Dep., | 13.9 | 6.1 |
| | | | | | | Amort./Cur. Mat. L/T/D | (11) 5.0 | (14) 2.6 |
| | | | | | | | 2.8 | 1.4 |
| | | .1 | .2 | | | | .2 | .3 |
| | | .5 | .4 | | | Fixed/Worth | .7 | .7 |
| | | .9 | .7 | | | | 2.1 | 2.3 |
| | | .5 | .4 | | | | .6 | 1.0 |
| | | 1.5 | .9 | | | Debt/Worth | 1.5 | 2.6 |
| | | 1.7 | 1.5 | | | | 5.1 | 7.2 |
| | | 31.2 | 54.0 | | | | 73.4 | 38.2 |
| | | 15.2 | 23.4 | | | % Profit Before Taxes/Tangible Net Worth | (34) 29.0 | (33) 26.8 |
| | | 3.6 | 15.7 | | | | 11.6 | 13.8 |
| | | 16.9 | 20.3 | | | | 30.7 | 16.5 |
| | | 5.5 | 14.9 | | | % Profit Before Taxes/Total Assets | 14.6 | 9.3 |
| | | 1.7 | 6.8 | | | | 2.6 | 1.4 |
| | | 28.3 | 16.6 | | | | 21.0 | 19.1 |
| | | 9.5 | 9.1 | | | Sales/Net Fixed Assets | 10.6 | 8.7 |
| | | 7.3 | 4.2 | | | | 6.6 | 5.2 |
| | | 2.5 | 1.7 | | | | 3.0 | 2.2 |
| | | 2.3 | 1.4 | | | Sales/Total Assets | 1.8 | 1.5 |
| | | 2.0 | .9 | | | | 1.2 | 1.1 |
| | | .8 | 1.3 | | | | .7 | .9 |
| | | (12) 1.6 | 2.0 | | | % Depr., Dep., Amort./Sales | (34) 1.6 | (36) 2.0 |
| | | 3.0 | 3.4 | | | | 2.5 | 3.2 |
| | | | | | | % Officers', Directors' Owners' Comp/Sales | | |
| 222M | 8493M | 134216M | 496295M | 425427M | 870986M | Net Sales ($) | 2388783M | 2530898M |
| 89M | 4469M | 61571M | 362874M | 351759M | 994055M | Total Assets ($) | 1457006M | 2026028M |

© RMA 2012

M = $ thousand   MM = $ million
See Pages 9 through 22 for Explanation of Ratios and Data

## Comparative Historical Data / Current Data Sorted by Sales

| | | | Type of Statement | 3 (4/1-9/30/11) | | | 38 (10/1/11-3/31/12) | | |
|---|---|---|---|---|---|---|---|---|---|
| | | | | 0-1MM | 1-3MM | 3-5MM | 5-10MM | 10-25MM | 25MM & OVER |
| 15 | 10 | 9 | Unqualified | | | | | 1 | 8 |
| 5 | 5 | 4 | Reviewed | | 1 | | | 1 | 1 |
| 5 | 1 | 1 | Compiled | | | | 1 | | |
| 3 | 2 | 2 | Tax Returns | | | 2 | 1 | | |
| 17 | 21 | 25 | Other | 1 | 1 | | 2 | 9 | 11 |
| 4/1/09-3/31/10 ALL | 4/1/10-3/31/11 ALL | 4/1/11-3/31/12 ALL | | | | | | | |
| **45** | **39** | **41** | **NUMBER OF STATEMENTS** | **1** | **2** | **3** | **4** | **11** | **20** |
| % | % | % | **ASSETS** | % | % | % | % | % | % |
| 9.6 | 11.1 | 8.3 | Cash & Equivalents | | | | | 7.6 | 8.3 |
| 19.9 | 20.5 | 21.4 | Trade Receivables (net) | | | | | 26.7 | 16.8 |
| 25.4 | 25.2 | 30.4 | Inventory | | | | | 28.5 | 31.1 |
| 4.1 | 5.1 | 5.6 | All Other Current | | | | | 11.2 | 5.1 |
| 59.0 | 61.9 | 65.7 | Total Current | | | | | 74.0 | 61.2 |
| 25.0 | 25.5 | 24.3 | Fixed Assets (net) | | | | | 16.1 | 29.7 |
| 8.7 | 3.3 | 3.3 | Intangibles (net) | | | | | 4.7 | 3.7 |
| 7.3 | 9.4 | 6.7 | All Other Non-Current | | | | | 5.2 | 5.4 |
| 100.0 | 100.0 | 100.0 | Total | | | | | 100.0 | 100.0 |
| | | | **LIABILITIES** | | | | | | |
| 6.9 | 5.5 | 8.9 | Notes Payable-Short Term | | | | | 12.2 | 9.6 |
| 3.3 | 3.6 | 2.4 | Cur. Mat.-L.T.D. | | | | | 1.3 | 3.4 |
| 9.3 | 10.3 | 12.5 | Trade Payables | | | | | 15.7 | 9.0 |
| .4 | .5 | .4 | Income Taxes Payable | | | | | .2 | .6 |
| 10.9 | 10.3 | 8.5 | All Other Current | | | | | 9.0 | 9.4 |
| 30.8 | 30.2 | 32.8 | Total Current | | | | | 38.4 | 32.0 |
| 12.4 | 9.8 | 11.1 | Long-Term Debt | | | | | 7.5 | 15.3 |
| 1.1 | 1.4 | 1.1 | Deferred Taxes | | | | | .2 | 1.7 |
| 7.2 | 7.3 | 5.1 | All Other Non-Current | | | | | 6.6 | 6.0 |
| 48.5 | 51.3 | 49.9 | Net Worth | | | | | 47.3 | 45.1 |
| 100.0 | 100.0 | 100.0 | Total Liabilities & Net Worth | | | | | 100.0 | 100.0 |
| | | | **INCOME DATA** | | | | | | |
| 100.0 | 100.0 | 100.0 | Net Sales | | | | | 100.0 | 100.0 |
| 32.3 | 30.3 | 28.2 | Gross Profit | | | | | 32.7 | 25.2 |
| 24.0 | 23.0 | 20.4 | Operating Expenses | | | | | 25.3 | 16.0 |
| 8.3 | 7.3 | 7.8 | Operating Profit | | | | | 7.4 | 9.2 |
| 1.3 | .2 | .9 | All Other Expenses (net) | | | | | .4 | 2.1 |
| 7.0 | 7.1 | 6.9 | Profit Before Taxes | | | | | 7.0 | 7.1 |
| | | | **RATIOS** | | | | | | |
| 3.8 | 3.5 | 3.4 | | | | | | 2.9 | 2.9 |
| 2.1 | 2.0 | 2.0 | Current | | | | | 2.0 | 2.1 |
| 1.2 | 1.2 | 1.5 | | | | | | 1.6 | 1.5 |
| 1.6 | 2.0 | 1.7 | | | | | | 1.7 | 1.6 |
| 1.0 | 1.2 | 1.1 | Quick | | | | | 1.0 | 1.0 |
| .5 | .6 | .4 | | | | | | .4 | .3 |
| 29 12.4 | 30 12.2 | 35 10.3 | Sales/Receivables | | | | | 40 9.1 | 30 12.2 |
| 38 9.5 | 46 7.9 | 48 7.6 | | | | | | 50 7.3 | 51 7.2 |
| 63 5.8 | 56 6.5 | 60 6.1 | | | | | | 63 5.8 | 61 6.0 |
| 30 12.1 | 35 10.3 | 54 6.8 | Cost of Sales/Inventory | | | | | 31 11.7 | 64 5.7 |
| 77 4.7 | 65 5.6 | 85 4.3 | | | | | | 83 4.4 | 85 4.3 |
| 138 2.6 | 152 2.4 | 140 2.6 | | | | | | 182 2.0 | 159 2.3 |
| 16 23.4 | 17 21.5 | 27 13.5 | Cost of Sales/Payables | | | | | 27 13.3 | 27 13.6 |
| 27 13.3 | 32 11.3 | 36 10.1 | | | | | | 36 10.1 | 35 10.5 |
| 54 6.8 | 51 7.2 | 49 7.5 | | | | | | 48 7.6 | 48 7.6 |
| 3.2 | 2.3 | 2.8 | Sales/Working Capital | | | | | 2.8 | 2.5 |
| 6.0 | 5.3 | 4.6 | | | | | | 5.3 | 4.1 |
| 12.5 | 12.6 | 10.7 | | | | | | 10.5 | 9.8 |
| 38.7 | 38.4 | 32.2 | EBIT/Interest | | | | | | 34.7 |
| (42) 9.8 | (36) 11.3 | (34) 8.5 | | | | | | | 9.2 |
| 2.0 | 2.4 | 2.8 | | | | | | | 2.8 |
| | 12.5 | | Net Profit + Depr., Dep., Amort./Cur. Mat. L/T/D | | | | | | |
| | (10) 5.4 | | | | | | | | |
| | 1.9 | | | | | | | | |
| .3 | .2 | .2 | Fixed/Worth | | | | | .1 | .2 |
| .6 | .5 | .5 | | | | | | .4 | .5 |
| 1.4 | 1.0 | .9 | | | | | | .8 | 1.7 |
| .3 | .4 | .5 | Debt/Worth | | | | | .6 | .5 |
| 1.7 | .9 | 1.1 | | | | | | 1.5 | 1.3 |
| 3.3 | 2.1 | 1.8 | | | | | | 1.9 | 2.5 |
| 51.0 | 34.4 | 33.2 | % Profit Before Taxes/Tangible Net Worth | | | | | 43.7 | 33.7 |
| (42) 19.4 | 18.7 | (40) 22.6 | | | | | | (19) 19.8 | 22.0 |
| 8.6 | 6.7 | 12.3 | | | | | | 13.5 | 11.9 |
| 17.8 | 20.2 | 17.8 | % Profit Before Taxes/Total Assets | | | | | 17.8 | 19.0 |
| 6.9 | 9.8 | 11.9 | | | | | | 13.7 | 8.8 |
| 2.9 | 1.8 | 3.7 | | | | | | 2.0 | 4.3 |
| 14.6 | 16.0 | 15.5 | Sales/Net Fixed Assets | | | | | 36.3 | 13.5 |
| 6.3 | 7.7 | 8.3 | | | | | | 9.1 | 4.7 |
| 3.9 | 3.1 | 4.3 | | | | | | 6.9 | 2.8 |
| 2.2 | 2.0 | 2.2 | Sales/Total Assets | | | | | 2.5 | 1.6 |
| 1.3 | 1.4 | 1.6 | | | | | | 2.0 | 1.2 |
| .9 | .9 | 1.0 | | | | | | 1.1 | .7 |
| 1.2 | 1.3 | 1.2 | % Depr., Dep., Amort./Sales | | | | | .8 | 1.5 |
| (38) 2.4 | (35) 2.2 | (38) 2.4 | | | | | | (10) 1.7 | (19) 2.9 |
| 3.9 | 3.5 | 3.5 | | | | | | 2.1 | 4.2 |
| | | | % Officers', Directors' Owners' Comp/Sales | | | | | | |
| 2151704M | 1499422M | 1935639M | Net Sales ($) | 222M | 5249M | 10695M | 28251M | 175725M | 1715497M |
| 1857200M | 1290032M | 1774817M | Total Assets ($) | 89M | 3232M | 7744M | 13564M | 119667M | 1630521M |

M = $ thousand    MM = $ million
See Pages 9 through 22 for Explanation of Ratios and Data

## Current Data Sorted by Assets  —  Comparative Historical Data

| 0-500M | 500M-2MM | 2-10MM | 10-50MM | 50-100MM | 100-250MM | Type of Statement | 4/1/07-3/31/08 ALL | 4/1/08-3/31/09 ALL |
|---|---|---|---|---|---|---|---|---|
| | | | 14 | 3 | 5 | Unqualified | 29 | 23 |
| | | 5 | 7 | 1 | 1 | Reviewed | 14 | 10 |
| | 4 | 5 | 1 | | 1 | Compiled | 6 | 9 |
| 2 | 3 | 3 | 1 | | | Tax Returns | 6 | 6 |
| 2 | 3 | 12 | 10 | 8 | 5 | Other | 34 | 28 |
| | 29 (4/1-9/30/11) | | 66 (10/1/11-3/31/12) | | | | | |
| 4 | 10 | 25 | 33 | 12 | 11 | **NUMBER OF STATEMENTS** | 89 | 76 |
| % | % | % | % | % | % | **ASSETS** | % | % |
| | 12.5 | 9.8 | 13.9 | 4.6 | 11.8 | Cash & Equivalents | 13.5 | 11.8 |
| | 18.0 | 19.2 | 19.9 | 18.0 | 9.5 | Trade Receivables (net) | 20.5 | 18.3 |
| | 16.2 | 23.4 | 4.5 | 1.7 | 15.9 | Inventory | 11.9 | 11.4 |
| | 9.7 | 3.8 | 13.4 | 12.6 | 7.7 | All Other Current | 11.9 | 12.6 |
| | 56.4 | 56.2 | 51.7 | 37.0 | 44.9 | Total Current | 57.8 | 54.1 |
| | 19.7 | 32.7 | 37.8 | 47.8 | 46.5 | Fixed Assets (net) | 33.7 | 36.2 |
| | 2.5 | 3.6 | 2.7 | 6.0 | 1.9 | Intangibles (net) | 3.0 | 3.4 |
| | 21.4 | 7.5 | 7.8 | 9.2 | 6.7 | All Other Non-Current | 5.4 | 6.2 |
| | 100.0 | 100.0 | 100.0 | 100.0 | 100.0 | Total | 100.0 | 100.0 |
| | | | | | | **LIABILITIES** | | |
| | 13.7 | 7.7 | 7.9 | 3.2 | 2.4 | Notes Payable-Short Term | 7.7 | 9.4 |
| | 12.3 | 4.0 | 4.7 | 2.4 | 4.7 | Cur. Mat.-L.T.D. | 3.4 | 2.8 |
| | 10.4 | 9.7 | 13.3 | 9.1 | 7.6 | Trade Payables | 11.4 | 10.1 |
| | .0 | .3 | .3 | .1 | .0 | Income Taxes Payable | .8 | .6 |
| | 30.1 | 23.8 | 12.3 | 13.0 | 10.6 | All Other Current | 19.7 | 15.2 |
| | 66.5 | 45.5 | 38.5 | 27.7 | 25.3 | Total Current | 42.9 | 38.2 |
| | 10.7 | 15.4 | 18.5 | 22.4 | 19.2 | Long-Term Debt | 15.5 | 20.8 |
| | .0 | 2.1 | 1.7 | 1.0 | 3.6 | Deferred Taxes | .9 | 1.1 |
| | 2.5 | 8.6 | 1.9 | 9.1 | 1.0 | All Other Non-Current | 7.2 | 2.9 |
| | 20.3 | 28.2 | 39.3 | 39.9 | 50.8 | Net Worth | 33.6 | 37.0 |
| | 100.0 | 100.0 | 100.0 | 100.0 | 100.0 | Total Liabilities & Net Worth | 100.0 | 100.0 |
| | | | | | | **INCOME DATA** | | |
| | 100.0 | 100.0 | 100.0 | 100.0 | 100.0 | Net Sales | 100.0 | 100.0 |
| | 32.0 | 28.9 | 23.9 | 21.5 | 16.7 | Gross Profit | 25.0 | 24.6 |
| | 30.8 | 26.6 | 19.4 | 15.2 | 17.5 | Operating Expenses | 18.5 | 18.5 |
| | 1.2 | 2.3 | 4.5 | 6.3 | -.8 | Operating Profit | 6.5 | 6.1 |
| | .1 | .9 | .6 | 2.5 | .4 | All Other Expenses (net) | .4 | 1.1 |
| | 1.1 | 1.3 | 3.8 | 3.9 | -1.2 | Profit Before Taxes | 6.1 | 5.0 |
| | | | | | | **RATIOS** | | |
| | 2.7 | 2.1 | 2.2 | 1.8 | 2.3 | Current | 2.0 | 2.1 |
| | 1.1 | 1.3 | 1.5 | 1.7 | 1.8 | | 1.5 | 1.4 |
| | .4 | .9 | .9 | 1.2 | 1.4 | | 1.1 | 1.0 |
| | 1.6 | 1.4 | 1.7 | 1.3 | 1.4 | Quick | 1.4 | 1.4 |
| | .3 | .8 | .9 | 1.0 | .9 | | .9 | .7 |
| | .1 | .3 | .4 | .6 | .4 | | .4 | .4 |
| | 3  122.8 | 14  25.5 | 16  23.3 | 11  34.2 | 7  49.6 | Sales/Receivables | 15  25.1 | 14  26.8 |
| | 22  16.3 | 38  9.6 | 31  11.6 | 37  9.9 | 27  13.7 | | 31  11.7 | 31  11.7 |
| | 37  9.8 | 46  7.9 | 49  7.5 | 52  7.0 | 33  10.9 | | 56  6.5 | 46  7.9 |
| | 0  UND | 0  UND | 0  UND | 1  292.9 | 2  175.2 | Cost of Sales/Inventory | 0  999.8 | 0  999.8 |
| | 0  UND | 41  8.8 | 1  343.3 | 3  120.3 | 68  5.4 | | 5  71.1 | 8  43.8 |
| | 19  18.8 | 130  2.8 | 10  36.9 | 5  73.8 | 166  2.2 | | 53  6.9 | 32  11.4 |
| | 0  UND | 14  26.4 | 21  17.3 | 17  20.9 | 18  20.7 | Cost of Sales/Payables | 16  22.4 | 11  34.4 |
| | 15  24.5 | 20  18.6 | 30  12.3 | 28  12.9 | 31  11.8 | | 24  14.9 | 20  18.6 |
| | 38  9.5 | 36  10.2 | 45  8.2 | 31  11.7 | 43  8.5 | | 35  10.5 | 40  9.2 |
| | 9.0 | 5.3 | 6.5 | 6.7 | 2.0 | Sales/Working Capital | 6.5 | 5.5 |
| | 139.9 | 15.2 | 11.6 | 10.8 | 6.1 | | 11.9 | 13.4 |
| | -4.5 | -51.5 | -44.9 | 26.9 | 11.1 | | 59.6 | NM |
| | | 9.7 | 32.1 | 19.4 | 13.3 | EBIT/Interest | 17.3 | 12.4 |
| | | (23) 3.2 | (31) 7.6 | 4.6 | 2.9 | | (78) 5.3 | (69) 6.1 |
| | | -.3 | .8 | .3 | -.6 | | 2.1 | 1.6 |
| | | | 2.8 | | | Net Profit + Depr., Dep., Amort./Cur. Mat. L/T/D | 7.8 | 6.5 |
| | | (10) .6 | | | | | (30) 2.6 | (27) 4.5 |
| | | | -1.5 | | | | 1.4 | 2.1 |
| | .0 | .7 | .4 | .8 | .6 | Fixed/Worth | .5 | .6 |
| | .2 | 1.3 | 1.2 | 1.3 | .8 | | 1.0 | 1.1 |
| | NM | NM | 2.0 | NM | 2.2 | | 2.4 | 2.5 |
| | .5 | .6 | .8 | .7 | .4 | Debt/Worth | .9 | .9 |
| | 6.2 | 2.2 | 1.5 | 1.5 | 1.1 | | 1.8 | 1.9 |
| | NM | NM | 3.6 | NM | 1.9 | | 6.0 | 4.5 |
| | | 21.2 | 44.0 | | 21.7 | % Profit Before Taxes/Tangible Net Worth | 66.0 | 51.8 |
| | | (19) 6.1 | (31) 21.0 | | 11.0 | | (82) 31.1 | (66) 29.6 |
| | | 1.5 | -.5 | | -9.0 | | 11.0 | 8.3 |
| | 25.4 | 17.5 | 14.9 | 13.1 | 6.9 | % Profit Before Taxes/Total Assets | 18.8 | 21.5 |
| | 8.9 | 3.6 | 10.0 | 5.7 | 5.6 | | 8.6 | 10.5 |
| | -20.0 | -1.1 | 1.5 | -2.2 | -3.9 | | 3.7 | .9 |
| | 498.1 | 16.0 | 7.7 | 4.2 | 4.6 | Sales/Net Fixed Assets | 16.2 | 10.1 |
| | 67.1 | 7.2 | 4.2 | 2.9 | 2.9 | | 5.8 | 5.0 |
| | 6.8 | 3.3 | 3.3 | 2.2 | 1.0 | | 3.5 | 3.0 |
| | 3.6 | 2.7 | 2.3 | 2.0 | 1.6 | Sales/Total Assets | 2.8 | 2.4 |
| | 2.4 | 2.1 | 1.7 | 1.6 | 1.0 | | 1.9 | 1.9 |
| | 1.3 | 1.3 | 1.3 | 1.2 | .7 | | 1.3 | 1.3 |
| | | 1.2 | 1.2 | 2.5 | | % Depr., Dep., Amort./Sales | 1.0 | 1.4 |
| | | (23) 2.1 | 2.9 | 3.4 | | | (83) 1.8 | (66) 2.3 |
| | | 3.6 | 4.9 | 4.2 | | | 3.3 | 3.7 |
| | | | | | | % Officers', Directors' Owners' Comp/Sales | 1.0 | 1.6 |
| | | | | | | | (14) 1.9 | (21) 2.3 |
| | | | | | | | 6.9 | 5.6 |
| 2641M | 33066M | 258494M | 1433123M | 1429696M | 1492955M | Net Sales ($) | 6163786M | 5384796M |
| 553M | 13524M | 130385M | 769868M | 864751M | 1462528M | Total Assets ($) | 3875066M | 3313183M |

M = $ thousand    MM = $ million
See Pages 9 through 22 for Explanation of Ratios and Data

## Comparative Historical Data  /  Current Data Sorted by Sales

| | | | Type of Statement | 0-1MM | 1-3MM | 3-5MM | 5-10MM | 10-25MM | 25MM & OVER |
|---|---|---|---|---|---|---|---|---|---|
| 20 | 17 | 22 | Unqualified | | | | 3 | 3 | 19 |
| 12 | 10 | 13 | Reviewed | | 4 | | 3 | 3 | 7 |
| 11 | 7 | 11 | Compiled | | 1 | | 5 | 1 | 2 |
| 6 | 10 | 9 | Tax Returns | 2 | 1 | 2 | 2 | 1 | 1 |
| 41 | 37 | 40 | Other | 1 | 5 | 1 | 5 | 6 | 22 |
| 4/1/09-3/31/10 ALL | 4/1/10-3/31/11 ALL | 4/1/11-3/31/12 ALL | | | 29 (4/1-9/30/11) | | | 66 (10/1/11-3/31/12) | |
| 90 | 81 | 95 | NUMBER OF STATEMENTS | 3 | 10 | 3 | 15 | 13 | 51 |
| % | % | % | ASSETS | % | % | % | % | % | % |
| 11.8 | 11.5 | 11.2 | Cash & Equivalents | | 12.1 | | 13.4 | 8.6 | 11.5 |
| 20.0 | 20.0 | 18.3 | Trade Receivables (net) | | 9.2 | | 22.2 | 19.4 | 18.5 |
| 11.6 | 14.9 | 12.3 | Inventory | | 23.0 | | 21.9 | 9.2 | 6.5 |
| 11.4 | 8.3 | 9.2 | All Other Current | | 9.2 | | 2.2 | 12.6 | 11.4 |
| 54.7 | 54.7 | 51.0 | Total Current | | 53.5 | | 59.8 | 49.8 | 47.9 |
| 36.7 | 34.9 | 36.7 | Fixed Assets (net) | | 32.3 | | 23.9 | 36.5 | 42.0 |
| 2.5 | 3.9 | 3.1 | Intangibles (net) | | 1.2 | | 1.8 | 5.3 | 3.3 |
| 6.0 | 6.5 | 9.2 | All Other Non-Current | | 13.1 | | 14.5 | 8.4 | 6.8 |
| 100.0 | 100.0 | 100.0 | Total | | 100.0 | | 100.0 | 100.0 | 100.0 |
| | | | LIABILITIES | | | | | | |
| 8.5 | 10.2 | 6.9 | Notes Payable-Short Term | | 9.3 | | 7.1 | 6.2 | 6.0 |
| 2.9 | 2.9 | 4.9 | Cur. Mat.-L.T.D. | | 12.3 | | 2.6 | 3.9 | 4.3 |
| 11.1 | 13.6 | 10.8 | Trade Payables | | 7.7 | | 11.3 | 8.5 | 12.2 |
| .4 | .2 | .2 | Income Taxes Payable | | .0 | | .5 | .2 | .2 |
| 13.3 | 11.9 | 18.0 | All Other Current | | 40.0 | | 21.3 | 21.4 | 11.3 |
| 36.1 | 38.9 | 40.9 | Total Current | | 69.3 | | 42.8 | 40.2 | 34.0 |
| 21.1 | 21.0 | 17.2 | Long-Term Debt | | 11.7 | | 11.2 | 18.9 | 19.4 |
| 1.0 | 1.6 | 1.7 | Deferred Taxes | | .6 | | 1.0 | 2.4 | 2.1 |
| 3.0 | 5.8 | 4.5 | All Other Non-Current | | 8.3 | | 3.8 | 11.0 | 2.8 |
| 38.8 | 32.7 | 35.7 | Net Worth | | 10.1 | | 41.2 | 27.4 | 41.7 |
| 100.0 | 100.0 | 100.0 | Total Liabilities & Net Worth | | 100.0 | | 100.0 | 100.0 | 100.0 |
| | | | INCOME DATA | | | | | | |
| 100.0 | 100.0 | 100.0 | Net Sales | | 100.0 | | 100.0 | 100.0 | 100.0 |
| 25.2 | 26.9 | 25.6 | Gross Profit | | 35.0 | | 35.3 | 25.5 | 21.3 |
| 20.7 | 23.4 | 22.3 | Operating Expenses | | 34.4 | | 30.3 | 22.5 | 17.3 |
| 4.5 | 3.5 | 3.3 | Operating Profit | | .6 | | 5.0 | 3.0 | 4.0 |
| .9 | .5 | .9 | All Other Expenses (net) | | 1.7 | | -.2 | 1.0 | .9 |
| 3.6 | 3.0 | 2.5 | Profit Before Taxes | | -1.1 | | 5.1 | 2.0 | 3.0 |
| | | | RATIOS | | | | | | |
| 2.4 | 2.2 | 2.0 | Current | | 2.7 | | 2.7 | 1.7 | 2.0 |
| 1.5 | 1.5 | 1.5 | | | .8 | | 1.7 | 1.3 | 1.6 |
| 1.1 | 1.1 | .9 | | | .4 | | 1.2 | .9 | 1.0 |
| 1.5 | 1.4 | 1.4 | Quick | | .6 | | 2.1 | 1.0 | 1.5 |
| .9 | 1.0 | .8 | | | .2 | | .9 | .8 | .9 |
| .4 | .4 | .4 | | | .1 | | .3 | .4 | .4 |
| 16  23.5 | 18  20.5 | 12  30.1 | Sales/Receivables | | 2  155.8 | | 12  30.1 | 29  12.5 | 12  30.9 |
| 34  10.7 | 33  11.0 | 33  11.0 | | | 22  16.7 | | 36  10.0 | 39  9.4 | 31  11.6 |
| 47  7.7 | 54  6.7 | 45  8.1 | | | 35  10.5 | | 45  8.2 | 45  8.1 | 47  7.7 |
| 1  476.5 | 1  696.4 | 0  UND | Cost of Sales/Inventory | | 0  UND | | 0  UND | 0  UND | 0  999.8 |
| 5  75.7 | 17  20.9 | 4  99.0 | | | 20  18.1 | | 13  29.0 | 26  14.3 | 3  132.0 |
| 45  8.2 | 79  4.6 | 60  6.1 | | | 228  1.6 | | 89  4.1 | 47  7.7 | 13  27.4 |
| 12  30.9 | 14  25.5 | 16  23.5 | Cost of Sales/Payables | | 4  95.8 | | 3  112.7 | 14  26.4 | 21  17.5 |
| 24  15.2 | 27  13.3 | 25  14.4 | | | 16  22.6 | | 20  18.6 | 23  15.7 | 30  12.3 |
| 39  9.5 | 44  8.3 | 40  9.1 | | | 38  9.6 | | 40  9.2 | 43  8.4 | 41  8.8 |
| 5.8 | 5.7 | 5.9 | Sales/Working Capital | | 3.4 | | | 6.9 | 6.0 |
| 10.4 | 10.6 | 11.6 | | | NM | | 13.8 | 15.2 | 10.6 |
| 53.0 | 117.1 | -45.5 | | | -3.3 | | 41.7 | -44.3 | -111.8 |
| 12.9 | 11.5 | 11.3 | EBIT/Interest | | | | 17.3 | 4.7 | 23.2 |
| (83) 5.2 | (72) 3.0 | (87) 5.0 | | | | | (13) 8.4 | (12) 1.6 | (49) 7.3 |
| .8 | 1.1 | .4 | | | | | .0 | .0 | 1.4 |
| 9.2 | 3.9 | 5.1 | Net Profit + Depr., Dep., Amort./Cur. Mat. L/T/D | | | | | | 4.9 |
| (30) 2.7 | (23) 2.0 | (27) 1.5 | | | | | | | (16) 1.3 |
| .9 | .8 | .5 | | | | | | | -.2 |
| .5 | .6 | .5 | Fixed/Worth | | .1 | | .4 | 1.0 | .5 |
| .8 | 1.3 | 1.2 | | | .5 | | .8 | 1.5 | 1.2 |
| 1.9 | 2.5 | 2.0 | | | -8.9 | | 1.5 | 2.2 | 2.0 |
| .7 | .9 | .7 | Debt/Worth | | .5 | | .5 | 1.1 | .7 |
| 1.6 | 1.8 | 1.7 | | | 8.2 | | 1.0 | 2.3 | 1.5 |
| 3.1 | 5.1 | 4.5 | | | -11.5 | | 4.8 | 7.1 | 3.0 |
| 43.8 | 48.0 | 43.0 | % Profit Before Taxes/Tangible Net Worth | | | | 83.5 | 6.1 | 41.5 |
| (82) 16.3 | (69) 11.5 | (81) 17.2 | | | | | (13) 21.2 | (11) 1.5 | (46) 20.1 |
| 1.3 | 1.7 | 1.8 | | | | | 2.3 | -4.4 | 4.7 |
| 15.4 | 13.6 | 13.6 | % Profit Before Taxes/Total Assets | | 8.9 | | 29.5 | 5.8 | 13.5 |
| 5.7 | 3.8 | 6.5 | | | 3.8 | | 13.6 | .8 | 7.3 |
| -.3 | .3 | -.2 | | | -19.1 | | .5 | -1.2 | 1.0 |
| 13.7 | 18.2 | 15.6 | Sales/Net Fixed Assets | | 230.6 | | 93.1 | 7.9 | 5.7 |
| 5.6 | 6.0 | 4.6 | | | 11.2 | | 16.3 | 4.9 | 3.7 |
| 2.6 | 2.7 | 2.9 | | | 1.7 | | 4.6 | 2.1 | 2.9 |
| 2.5 | 2.4 | 2.4 | Sales/Total Assets | | 2.5 | | 3.2 | 2.5 | 2.2 |
| 1.7 | 1.7 | 1.7 | | | 1.2 | | 2.3 | 1.6 | 1.7 |
| 1.2 | 1.1 | 1.1 | | | .9 | | 1.4 | 1.0 | 1.1 |
| 1.2 | 1.2 | 1.2 | % Depr., Dep., Amort./Sales | | | | .2 | 1.5 | 1.5 |
| (81) 2.4 | (72) 2.4 | (84) 2.9 | | | | | (11) 1.6 | 2.3 | (49) 3.2 |
| 3.6 | 4.5 | 4.7 | | | | | 5.1 | 4.4 | 4.8 |
| 1.1 | 2.1 | 2.2 | % Officers', Directors' Owners' Comp/Sales | | | | | | |
| (18) 2.7 | (23) 3.9 | (19) 3.9 | | | | | | | |
| 4.1 | 9.2 | 8.2 | | | | | | | |
| 5654797M | 4624380M | 4649975M | Net Sales ($) | 800M | 19670M | 11433M | 116650M | 212230M | 4289192M |
| 3796277M | 2963922M | 3241609M | Total Assets ($) | 189M | 19366M | 8475M | 60920M | 194498M | 2958161M |

© RMA 2012

M = $ thousand    MM = $ million
See Pages 9 through 22 for Explanation of Ratios and Data

## Current Data Sorted by Assets     Comparative Historical Data

| 0-500M | 500M-2MM | 2-10MM | 10-50MM | 50-100MM | 100-250MM | Type of Statement | 4/1/07-3/31/08 ALL | 4/1/08-3/31/09 ALL |
|---|---|---|---|---|---|---|---|---|
| | | 2 | 11 | 4 | 2 | Unqualified | 23 | 20 |
| | 2 | 5 | 4 | 1 | | Reviewed | 17 | 8 |
| | 2 | 4 | | | | Compiled | 7 | 10 |
| 3 | 4 | 2 | | | | Tax Returns | 5 | 9 |
| 1 | 3 | 3 | 9 | 4 | 2 | Other | 40 | 41 |
| | 19 (4/1-9/30/11) | | 49 (10/1/11-3/31/12) | | | | | |
| 4 | 11 | 16 | 24 | 9 | 4 | **NUMBER OF STATEMENTS** | 92 | 88 |
| % | % | % | % | % | % | **ASSETS** | % | % |
| | 8.3 | 18.4 | 15.5 | | | Cash & Equivalents | 10.5 | 7.1 |
| | 6.1 | 14.9 | 12.5 | | | Trade Receivables (net) | 12.5 | 11.0 |
| | 43.6 | 32.4 | 35.6 | | | Inventory | 32.0 | 37.5 |
| | 2.0 | 2.2 | 5.4 | | | All Other Current | 3.9 | 2.5 |
| | 60.1 | 67.9 | 69.0 | | | Total Current | 59.0 | 58.2 |
| | 29.7 | 27.4 | 20.7 | | | Fixed Assets (net) | 29.8 | 31.4 |
| | 2.6 | 1.0 | 4.7 | | | Intangibles (net) | 5.9 | 5.3 |
| | 7.7 | 3.7 | 5.6 | | | All Other Non-Current | 5.4 | 5.2 |
| | 100.0 | 100.0 | 100.0 | | | Total | 100.0 | 100.0 |
| | | | | | | **LIABILITIES** | | |
| | 17.6 | 5.1 | 6.4 | | | Notes Payable-Short Term | 10.3 | 13.1 |
| | 6.9 | 3.8 | 1.6 | | | Cur. Mat.-L.T.D. | 4.3 | 3.1 |
| | 14.9 | 16.7 | 10.6 | | | Trade Payables | 14.2 | 13.0 |
| | .2 | .4 | .0 | | | Income Taxes Payable | .2 | .1 |
| | 9.5 | 12.6 | 17.4 | | | All Other Current | 16.3 | 11.3 |
| | 49.0 | 38.5 | 36.0 | | | Total Current | 45.2 | 40.6 |
| | 38.3 | 11.3 | 17.3 | | | Long-Term Debt | 17.1 | 21.4 |
| | .0 | .5 | .0 | | | Deferred Taxes | .5 | .3 |
| | 15.3 | 12.5 | 3.6 | | | All Other Non-Current | 3.8 | 5.6 |
| | -2.6 | 37.3 | 43.1 | | | Net Worth | 33.4 | 32.1 |
| | 100.0 | 100.0 | 100.0 | | | Total Liabilties & Net Worth | 100.0 | 100.0 |
| | | | | | | **INCOME DATA** | | |
| | 100.0 | 100.0 | 100.0 | | | Net Sales | 100.0 | 100.0 |
| | 30.9 | 17.0 | 20.0 | | | Gross Profit | 21.6 | 22.2 |
| | 27.7 | 15.2 | 14.9 | | | Operating Expenses | 18.5 | 20.9 |
| | 3.2 | 1.8 | 5.1 | | | Operating Profit | 3.1 | 1.4 |
| | 2.4 | .1 | .5 | | | All Other Expenses (net) | 1.2 | 1.0 |
| | .8 | 1.7 | 4.6 | | | Profit Before Taxes | 1.9 | .3 |
| | | | | | | **RATIOS** | | |
| | 2.4 | 2.4 | 2.8 | | | Current | 2.2 | 2.5 |
| | 1.1 | 1.7 | 1.9 | | | | 1.4 | 1.3 |
| | .8 | 1.3 | 1.4 | | | | 1.1 | 1.0 |
| | .7 | 1.7 | 1.2 | | | Quick | .9 | .8 |
| | .3 | .8 | .9 | | | | .5 | .4 |
| | .2 | .5 | .5 | | | | .2 | .2 |
| | 5   75.4 | 11   33.8 | 9   41.1 | | | Sales/Receivables | 6   63.4 | 6   58.6 |
| | 8   43.3 | 14   26.8 | 15   24.0 | | | | 16   22.9 | 14   25.8 |
| | 12   31.3 | 20   18.0 | 32   11.3 | | | | 26   14.2 | 26   13.8 |
| | 54   6.7 | 22   16.3 | 25   14.7 | | | Cost of Sales/Inventory | 31   11.8 | 40   9.0 |
| | 87   4.2 | 45   8.2 | 74   4.9 | | | | 53   6.8 | 68   5.4 |
| | 118   3.1 | 72   5.1 | 99   3.7 | | | | 84   3.0 | 123   3.0 |
| | 15   24.9 | 11   32.8 | 12   29.7 | | | Cost of Sales/Payables | 13   28.4 | 12   30.8 |
| | 29   12.7 | 20   18.4 | 20   18.4 | | | | 21   17.3 | 22   16.8 |
| | 39   9.3 | 34   10.6 | 28   12.9 | | | | 32   11.4 | 37   9.9 |
| | 6.3 | 7.2 | 4.4 | | | Sales/Working Capital | 6.6 | 6.0 |
| | 40.5 | 12.6 | 7.0 | | | | 13.2 | 13.7 |
| | -24.0 | 23.1 | 11.6 | | | | 265.2 | NM |
| | 4.0 | 40.3 | 24.5 | | | EBIT/Interest | 8.7 | 5.7 |
| | (10) 1.1 | (15) 11.5 | (21) 8.9 | | | | (83) 2.7 | (82) 1.3 |
| | .1 | 1.9 | 3.6 | | | | .7 | -1.1 |
| | | | | | | Net Profit + Depr., Dep., Amort./Cur. Mat. L/T/D | 9.1 | 9.7 |
| | | | | | | | (21) 1.8 | (17) 2.3 |
| | | | | | | | -.1 | .4 |
| | .5 | .4 | .2 | | | Fixed/Worth | .4 | .5 |
| | 3.3 | .8 | .4 | | | | .9 | 1.4 |
| | -.6 | 8.3 | 1.9 | | | | 2.9 | 4.1 |
| | .7 | .7 | .6 | | | Debt/Worth | .6 | 1.0 |
| | 19.5 | 1.6 | 1.0 | | | | 1.9 | 2.6 |
| | -3.0 | 17.5 | 4.8 | | | | 7.4 | 16.0 |
| | | 36.7 | 37.2 | | | % Profit Before Taxes/Tangible Net Worth | 46.4 | 28.7 |
| | | (14) 30.0 | (21) 15.1 | | | | (75) 13.0 | (71) 6.7 |
| | | 10.0 | 6.6 | | | | .0 | -15.5 |
| | 9.6 | 16.1 | 15.2 | | | % Profit Before Taxes/Total Assets | 13.6 | 10.2 |
| | 2.7 | 10.6 | 8.1 | | | | 5.5 | 1.2 |
| | -.8 | 2.9 | 2.7 | | | | -1.0 | -5.7 |
| | 25.5 | 28.2 | 40.4 | | | Sales/Net Fixed Assets | 21.8 | 14.9 |
| | 16.0 | 10.5 | 12.5 | | | | 9.4 | 7.4 |
| | 5.2 | 6.1 | 6.8 | | | | 5.2 | 4.2 |
| | 3.2 | 4.4 | 2.8 | | | Sales/Total Assets | 3.2 | 2.9 |
| | 2.9 | 3.6 | 2.0 | | | | 2.5 | 2.1 |
| | 1.6 | 2.1 | 1.5 | | | | 1.6 | 1.4 |
| | .8 | 1.0 | .6 | | | % Depr., Dep., Amort./Sales | .8 | .9 |
| | (10) 1.3 | (14) 1.6 | (21) 1.4 | | | | (83) 1.3 | (79) 1.6 |
| | 1.9 | 3.1 | 1.9 | | | | 2.4 | 3.1 |
| | | | | | | % Officers', Directors', Owners' Comp/Sales | 1.0 | 1.2 |
| | | | | | | | (21) 2.0 | (21) 1.6 |
| | | | | | | | 5.8 | 2.5 |
| 3279M | 38386M | 215259M | 1110404M | 1010601M | 799220M | Net Sales ($) | 4471746M | 4080234M |
| 785M | 14517M | 73841M | 486111M | 598085M | 665222M | Total Assets ($) | 2424477M | 2369519M |

M = $ thousand    MM = $ million
See Pages 9 through 22 for Explanation of Ratios and Data

## Comparative Historical Data      Current Data Sorted by Sales

| | 16<br>5<br>6<br>7<br>30<br>4/1/09-<br>3/31/10<br>ALL | 15<br>6<br>6<br>12<br>31<br>4/1/10-<br>3/31/11<br>ALL | 19<br>12<br>6<br>9<br>22<br>4/1/11-<br>3/31/12<br>ALL | Type of Statement | 0-1MM | 1-3MM | 3-5MM | 5-10MM | 10-25MM | 25MM & OVER |
|---|---|---|---|---|---|---|---|---|---|---|
| | | | | Unqualified | | | | 1 | 3 | 15 |
| | | | | Reviewed | | 1 | | 2 | 6 | 3 |
| | | | | Compiled | | 2 | | 2 | 3 | |
| | | | | Tax Returns | 2 | | 1 | 2 | 2 | |
| | | | | Other | 1 | 4 | 1 | | 5 | 11 |
| | | | | | 19 (4/1-9/30/11) | | | 49 (10/1/11-3/31/12) | | |
| NUMBER OF STATEMENTS | 64 | 70 | 68 | | 3 | 7 | 3 | 7 | 19 | 29 |
| | % | % | % | **ASSETS** | % | % | % | % | % | % |
| | 9.5 | 11.3 | 12.9 | Cash & Equivalents | | | | | 14.3 | 12.5 |
| | 10.8 | 11.0 | 10.7 | Trade Receivables (net) | | | | | 15.2 | 9.7 |
| | 32.3 | 29.6 | 35.7 | Inventory | | | | | 34.8 | 32.3 |
| | 5.0 | 5.2 | 3.4 | All Other Current | | | | | 2.3 | 5.0 |
| | 57.6 | 57.0 | 62.6 | Total Current | | | | | 66.6 | 59.6 |
| | 33.0 | 29.9 | 26.1 | Fixed Assets (net) | | | | | 26.5 | 24.8 |
| | 4.4 | 7.8 | 5.8 | Intangibles (net) | | | | | 2.8 | 10.5 |
| | 5.0 | 5.3 | 5.5 | All Other Non-Current | | | | | 4.2 | 5.2 |
| | 100.0 | 100.0 | 100.0 | Total | | | | | 100.0 | 100.0 |
| | | | | **LIABILITIES** | | | | | | |
| | 12.3 | 14.9 | 10.8 | Notes Payable-Short Term | | | | | 8.3 | 3.7 |
| | 2.3 | 2.9 | 3.3 | Cur. Mat.-L.T.D. | | | | | 2.8 | 2.2 |
| | 10.9 | 13.6 | 11.8 | Trade Payables | | | | | 14.1 | 9.8 |
| | .4 | .1 | .1 | Income Taxes Payable | | | | | .0 | .0 |
| | 12.4 | 12.4 | 14.6 | All Other Current | | | | | 15.6 | 16.7 |
| | 38.2 | 43.9 | 40.7 | Total Current | | | | | 40.9 | 32.5 |
| | 18.5 | 30.2 | 31.5 | Long-Term Debt | | | | | 16.9 | 19.1 |
| | .1 | .4 | .3 | Deferred Taxes | | | | | .3 | .5 |
| | 7.0 | 11.7 | 8.7 | All Other Non-Current | | | | | 10.5 | 6.4 |
| | 36.2 | 13.9 | 18.8 | Net Worth | | | | | 31.4 | 41.5 |
| | 100.0 | 100.0 | 100.0 | Total Liabilities & Net Worth | | | | | 100.0 | 100.0 |
| | | | | **INCOME DATA** | | | | | | |
| | 100.0 | 100.0 | 100.0 | Net Sales | | | | | 100.0 | 100.0 |
| | 19.9 | 23.8 | 21.3 | Gross Profit | | | | | 21.0 | 17.8 |
| | 23.4 | 21.8 | 18.2 | Operating Expenses | | | | | 15.3 | 14.4 |
| | -3.5 | 2.0 | 3.1 | Operating Profit | | | | | 5.7 | 3.4 |
| | 1.2 | 2.1 | 1.3 | All Other Expenses (net) | | | | | .9 | 1.0 |
| | -4.7 | -.1 | 1.9 | Profit Before Taxes | | | | | 4.8 | 2.4 |
| | | | | **RATIOS** | | | | | | |
| | 3.1 | 2.5 | 2.6 | Current | | | | | 2.1 | 3.0 |
| | 1.5 | 1.4 | 1.6 | | | | | | 1.5 | 1.8 |
| | 1.1 | 1.0 | 1.2 | | | | | | 1.2 | 1.2 |
| | 1.2 | .9 | 1.1 | Quick | | | | | 1.3 | 1.1 |
| | .6 | .6 | .6 | | | | | | .7 | .7 |
| | .2 | .2 | .3 | | | | | | .3 | .3 |
| | 8   46.6 | 9   40.7 | 8   43.1 | Sales/Receivables | | | | | 6   57.8 | 10   36.4 |
| | 16   22.9 | 16   22.6 | 12   30.3 | | | | | | 19   19.3 | 13   28.6 |
| | 38   9.5 | 30   12.0 | 23   16.2 | | | | | | 33   11.1 | 23   15.6 |
| | 34   10.9 | 38   9.6 | 36   10.1 | Cost of Sales/Inventory | | | | | 20   17.9 | 44   8.3 |
| | 86   4.2 | 76   4.8 | 58   6.3 | | | | | | 50   7.3 | 73   5.0 |
| | 185   2.0 | 123   3.0 | 99   3.7 | | | | | | 89   4.1 | 99   3.7 |
| | 15   23.6 | 13   27.9 | 10   36.4 | Cost of Sales/Payables | | | | | 11   34.3 | 10   36.3 |
| | 23   15.6 | 23   15.7 | 20   17.9 | | | | | | 21   17.6 | 18   20.8 |
| | 37   9.9 | 34   10.7 | 31   11.9 | | | | | | 31   11.9 | 27   13.7 |
| | 3.0 | 5.0 | 6.3 | Sales/Working Capital | | | | | 6.2 | 5.0 |
| | 9.5 | 13.2 | 11.8 | | | | | | 12.0 | 8.7 |
| | 57.9 | -108.5 | 36.3 | | | | | | 21.3 | 38.1 |
| | 2.5 | 5.6 | 15.1 | EBIT/Interest | | | | | 27.4 | 17.5 |
| (55) | -.9 | (62) 1.3 | (61) 4.4 | | | | | (18) | 9.8 | (26) 5.0 |
| | -6.0 | -.9 | .9 | | | | | | 2.7 | .8 |
| | 4.8 | 4.2 | 10.1 | Net Profit + Depr., Dep., Amort./Cur. Mat. L/T/D | | | | | | |
| (13) | 1.7 | (12) 1.2 | (18) 5.1 | | | | | | | |
| | -4.9 | -.3 | 1.3 | | | | | | | |
| | .4 | .5 | .3 | Fixed/Worth | | | | | .3 | .3 |
| | 1.0 | 1.4 | .9 | | | | | | .7 | .5 |
| | 6.7 | -2.4 | -5.1 | | | | | | 13.3 | NM |
| | .7 | 1.0 | .6 | Debt/Worth | | | | | .8 | .6 |
| | 1.7 | 3.0 | 1.9 | | | | | | 1.8 | 1.0 |
| | 13.3 | -6.6 | -22.2 | | | | | | 16.6 | NM |
| | 19.1 | 24.3 | 35.0 | % Profit Before Taxes/Tangible Net Worth | | | | | 42.9 | 27.2 |
| (52) | -3.8 | (49) 7.9 | (50) 14.5 | | | | | (16) | 30.2 | (22) 12.6 |
| | -39.2 | -5.9 | 3.5 | | | | | | 13.0 | 2.2 |
| | 5.5 | 6.1 | 11.7 | % Profit Before Taxes/Total Assets | | | | | 17.7 | 9.0 |
| | -2.7 | .8 | 4.6 | | | | | | 9.1 | 3.8 |
| | -19.7 | -7.2 | .1 | | | | | | 4.1 | .0 |
| | 11.4 | 15.3 | 27.3 | Sales/Net Fixed Assets | | | | | 27.6 | 30.0 |
| | 4.2 | 6.0 | 9.9 | | | | | | 10.2 | 9.1 |
| | 2.4 | 3.3 | 5.0 | | | | | | 5.4 | 5.1 |
| | 2.3 | 2.4 | 3.3 | Sales/Total Assets | | | | | 3.8 | 2.7 |
| | 1.3 | 1.6 | 2.1 | | | | | | 2.2 | 2.0 |
| | 1.0 | 1.1 | 1.5 | | | | | | 1.4 | 1.5 |
| | 1.4 | 1.1 | .9 | % Depr., Dep., Amort./Sales | | | | | 1.1 | .9 |
| (58) | 2.5 | (59) 2.6 | (59) 1.7 | | | | | (18) | 1.7 | (25) 1.8 |
| | 4.9 | 3.9 | 2.7 | | | | | | 2.7 | 2.8 |
| | 1.3 | 1.6 | 1.8 | % Officers', Directors' Owners' Comp/Sales | | | | | | |
| (18) | 2.7 | (18) 2.5 | (16) 4.1 | | | | | | | |
| | 4.0 | 3.9 | 7.3 | | | | | | | |
| | 1981851M | 2306371M | 3177149M | Net Sales ($) | 798M | 13248M | 12486M | 54525M | 334134M | 2761958M |
| | 1688944M | 1811469M | 1838561M | Total Assets ($) | 505M | 5275M | 5709M | 24825M | 181153M | 1621094M |

M = $ thousand    MM = $ million
See Pages 9 through 22 for Explanation of Ratios and Data

## Current Data Sorted by Assets      Comparative Historical Data

| 0-500M | 500M-2MM | 2-10MM | 10-50MM | 50-100MM | 100-250MM | | 4/1/07-3/31/08 ALL | 4/1/08-3/31/09 ALL |
|---|---|---|---|---|---|---|---|---|
| | | 2 | 1 | 1 | 2 | Type of Statement | 4 | 3 |
| | 1 | 3 | | | | Unqualified | 4 | 6 |
| | 3 | 1 | | | | Reviewed | 5 | 4 |
| 1 | 9 | 3 | | | | Compiled | 6 | 11 |
| | 2 | 10 | | | | Tax Returns | 13 | 14 |
| | 7 (4/1-9/30/11) | 38 (10/1/11-3/31/12) | 5 (10/1/11-3/31/12) | | | Other | | |
| 1 | 15 | 19 | 6 | 2 | 2 | **NUMBER OF STATEMENTS** | 32 | 38 |
| % | % | % | % | % | % | | % | % |
| | | | | | | **ASSETS** | | |
| | 6.6 | 15.2 | | | | Cash & Equivalents | 6.4 | 6.0 |
| | 19.0 | 15.1 | | | | Trade Receivables (net) | 17.3 | 17.9 |
| | 52.6 | 35.4 | | | | Inventory | 42.1 | 41.3 |
| | .8 | 3.3 | | | | All Other Current | 1.5 | 1.7 |
| | 79.0 | 69.0 | | | | Total Current | 67.3 | 66.8 |
| | 12.9 | 20.8 | | | | Fixed Assets (net) | 14.4 | 17.1 |
| | 2.8 | 5.1 | | | | Intangibles (net) | 11.4 | 9.6 |
| | 5.3 | 5.1 | | | | All Other Non-Current | 6.9 | 6.5 |
| | 100.0 | 100.0 | | | | Total | 100.0 | 100.0 |
| | | | | | | **LIABILITIES** | | |
| | 28.8 | 10.0 | | | | Notes Payable-Short Term | 19.4 | 22.0 |
| | 1.7 | 2.2 | | | | Cur. Mat.-L.T.D. | 1.4 | 3.3 |
| | 14.5 | 11.0 | | | | Trade Payables | 12.6 | 14.1 |
| | .0 | .0 | | | | Income Taxes Payable | .3 | .2 |
| | 9.0 | 10.4 | | | | All Other Current | 13.8 | 9.5 |
| | 54.0 | 33.6 | | | | Total Current | 47.6 | 49.1 |
| | 14.8 | 15.3 | | | | Long-Term Debt | 13.7 | 17.6 |
| | .0 | .1 | | | | Deferred Taxes | .4 | .0 |
| | 15.4 | 22.1 | | | | All Other Non-Current | 11.7 | 14.0 |
| | 15.8 | 28.8 | | | | Net Worth | 26.6 | 19.3 |
| | 100.0 | 100.0 | | | | Total Liabilities & Net Worth | 100.0 | 100.0 |
| | | | | | | **INCOME DATA** | | |
| | 100.0 | 100.0 | | | | Net Sales | 100.0 | 100.0 |
| | 36.8 | 35.4 | | | | Gross Profit | 32.6 | 31.6 |
| | 31.0 | 32.0 | | | | Operating Expenses | 26.8 | 27.6 |
| | 5.8 | 3.4 | | | | Operating Profit | 5.8 | 4.0 |
| | 1.2 | 2.3 | | | | All Other Expenses (net) | 2.0 | 3.3 |
| | 4.6 | 1.1 | | | | Profit Before Taxes | 3.8 | .7 |
| | | | | | | **RATIOS** | | |
| | 4.5 | 4.5 | | | | | 2.7 | 2.3 |
| | 2.0 | 2.1 | | | | Current | 1.4 | 1.5 |
| | 1.2 | 1.5 | | | | | .9 | 1.1 |
| | 1.6 | 2.0 | | | | | 1.0 | 1.0 |
| | .7 | 1.0 | | | | Quick | .6 | .5 |
| | .1 | .6 | | | | | .2 | .2 |
| | 10   37.3 | 3   137.5 | | | | | 9   42.5 | 10   36.2 |
| | 21   17.1 | 18   20.8 | | | | Sales/Receivables | 23   16.0 | 26   14.0 |
| | 38   9.7 | 43   8.5 | | | | | 60   6.1 | 51   7.1 |
| | 49   7.5 | 70   5.2 | | | | | 68   5.4 | 63   5.8 |
| | 118   3.1 | 91   4.0 | | | | Cost of Sales/Inventory | 102   3.6 | 115   3.2 |
| | 166   2.2 | 140   2.6 | | | | | 141   2.6 | 157   2.3 |
| | 8   43.8 | 8   46.8 | | | | | 13   27.1 | 15   24.2 |
| | 22   16.5 | 24   15.5 | | | | Cost of Sales/Payables | 24   15.0 | 27   13.3 |
| | 48   7.6 | 45   8.2 | | | | | 50   7.3 | 47   7.7 |
| | 5.9 | 2.7 | | | | | 6.3 | 7.0 |
| | 9.2 | 6.1 | | | | Sales/Working Capital | 11.1 | 10.6 |
| | 30.3 | 10.0 | | | | | -39.8 | 170.0 |
| | 76.6 | 7.3 | | | | | 12.3 | 7.7 |
| | 6.7 | (17)   1.5 | | | | EBIT/Interest | (29)   3.3 | (37)   1.8 |
| | 1.8 | .4 | | | | | 1.6 | .6 |
| | | | | | | Net Profit + Depr., Dep., Amort./Cur. Mat. L/T/D | | |
| | .0 | .1 | | | | | .2 | .1 |
| | .4 | .5 | | | | Fixed/Worth | .9 | .6 |
| | -415.0 | 2.6 | | | | | -1.1 | -1.7 |
| | .8 | .4 | | | | | 1.8 | 1.0 |
| | 2.3 | 1.9 | | | | Debt/Worth | 4.4 | 3.9 |
| | -999.8 | 3.6 | | | | | -8.4 | -6.2 |
| | 108.9 | 25.7 | | | | | 91.7 | 56.8 |
| | (11)   56.0 | (16)   2.3 | | | | % Profit Before Taxes/Tangible Net Worth | (22)   37.1 | (26)   24.5 |
| | 13.9 | -6.5 | | | | | 8.4 | 7.3 |
| | 28.9 | 11.8 | | | | | 19.9 | 15.2 |
| | 20.4 | 1.0 | | | | % Profit Before Taxes/Total Assets | 7.7 | 2.9 |
| | 1.7 | -2.1 | | | | | .0 | .0 |
| | 197.5 | 66.5 | | | | | 43.1 | 98.7 |
| | 30.9 | 20.8 | | | | Sales/Net Fixed Assets | 28.5 | 26.6 |
| | 13.2 | 6.1 | | | | | 10.4 | 9.7 |
| | 3.9 | 2.9 | | | | | 3.4 | 3.1 |
| | 2.8 | 1.6 | | | | Sales/Total Assets | 1.8 | 2.0 |
| | 2.5 | 1.2 | | | | | 1.2 | 1.3 |
| | | .3 | | | | | .8 | .5 |
| | (17) | .7 | | | | % Depr., Dep., Amort./Sales | (26)   1.3 | (28)   1.0 |
| | | 4.0 | | | | | 2.6 | 2.9 |
| | 2.7 | | | | | | 2.4 | 3.1 |
| | (12)   3.5 | | | | | % Officers', Directors' Owners' Comp/Sales | (12)   5.6 | (14)   4.8 |
| | 5.5 | | | | | | 11.0 | 10.6 |
| 580M | 54753M | 203275M | 218281M | 207959M | 601546M | Net Sales ($) | 1378295M | 1045256M |
| 294M | 18371M | 108956M | 121287M | 122301M | 317934M | Total Assets ($) | 909511M | 730927M |

## Comparative Historical Data | Current Data Sorted by Sales

| | | | | | | Type of Statement | | | | | | |
|---|---|---|---|---|---|---|---|---|---|---|---|---|
| | 2 | | 3 | | 6 | Unqualified | | | | 1 | 1 | 4 |
| | 3 | | 3 | | 4 | Reviewed | | | | | 3 | |
| | 5 | | 6 | | 4 | Compiled | | 1 | | 2 | 1 | |
| | 13 | | 10 | | 13 | Tax Returns | | 3 | 1 | 5 | | |
| | 16 | | 14 | | 18 | Other | 1 | 3 | 4 | 5 | 5 | 5 |
| | 4/1/09-3/31/10 ALL | | 4/1/10-3/31/11 ALL | | 4/1/11-3/31/12 ALL | | 0-1MM | 7 (4/1-9/30/11) 1-3MM | 3-5MM | 38 (10/1/11-3/31/12) 5-10MM | 10-25MM | 25MM & OVER |
| | 39 | | 36 | | 45 | NUMBER OF STATEMENTS | 1 | 6 | 8 | 11 | 10 | 9 |
| | % | | % | | % | ASSETS | % | % | % | % | % | % |
| | 9.6 | | 9.1 | | 9.9 | Cash & Equivalents | | | | 14.9 | 15.7 | |
| | 14.9 | | 16.3 | | 19.3 | Trade Receivables (net) | | | | 17.5 | 20.1 | |
| | 44.7 | | 40.9 | | 40.6 | Inventory | | | | 35.7 | 39.4 | |
| | 1.9 | | 4.8 | | 1.9 | All Other Current | | | | 3.3 | 2.7 | |
| | 71.1 | | 71.1 | | 71.8 | Total Current | | | | 71.4 | 77.9 | |
| | 15.2 | | 16.6 | | 17.2 | Fixed Assets (net) | | | | 20.6 | 13.6 | |
| | 10.1 | | 6.1 | | 5.6 | Intangibles (net) | | | | 1.8 | 6.7 | |
| | 3.6 | | 6.2 | | 5.4 | All Other Non-Current | | | | 6.2 | 1.8 | |
| | 100.0 | | 100.0 | | 100.0 | Total | | | | 100.0 | 100.0 | |
| | | | | | | LIABILITIES | | | | | | |
| | 16.7 | | 10.6 | | 17.4 | Notes Payable-Short Term | | | | 6.3 | 13.2 | |
| | 3.7 | | 2.3 | | 2.0 | Cur. Mat.-L.T.D. | | | | 3.4 | .5 | |
| | 12.6 | | 13.4 | | 14.3 | Trade Payables | | | | 12.8 | 12.7 | |
| | .1 | | .2 | | .1 | Income Taxes Payable | | | | .0 | .0 | |
| | 13.3 | | 10.0 | | 10.8 | All Other Current | | | | 14.4 | 6.3 | |
| | 46.4 | | 36.6 | | 44.6 | Total Current | | | | 36.9 | 32.7 | |
| | 23.1 | | 18.6 | | 13.3 | Long-Term Debt | | | | 24.9 | 5.5 | |
| | .0 | | .1 | | .1 | Deferred Taxes | | | | .2 | .0 | |
| | 6.2 | | 13.0 | | 16.1 | All Other Non-Current | | | | 7.4 | 31.8 | |
| | 24.2 | | 31.8 | | 26.0 | Net Worth | | | | 30.5 | 29.9 | |
| | 100.0 | | 100.0 | | 100.0 | Total Liabilties & Net Worth | | | | 100.0 | 100.0 | |
| | | | | | | INCOME DATA | | | | | | |
| | 100.0 | | 100.0 | | 100.0 | Net Sales | | | | 100.0 | 100.0 | |
| | 32.9 | | 32.1 | | 33.3 | Gross Profit | | | | 34.7 | 30.2 | |
| | 30.2 | | 28.7 | | 29.0 | Operating Expenses | | | | 32.7 | 24.6 | |
| | 2.7 | | 3.4 | | 4.4 | Operating Profit | | | | 2.0 | 5.6 | |
| | 3.1 | | .7 | | 1.8 | All Other Expenses (net) | | | | 2.1 | 2.5 | |
| | -.4 | | 2.6 | | 2.6 | Profit Before Taxes | | | | -.1 | 3.2 | |
| | | | | | | RATIOS | | | | | | |
| | 3.1 | | 4.1 | | 3.9 | | | | | 5.1 | 4.2 | |
| | 1.4 | | 1.8 | | 1.8 | Current | | | | 2.2 | 2.7 | |
| | 1.0 | | 1.3 | | 1.2 | | | | | 1.4 | 1.7 | |
| | 1.1 | | 1.3 | | 1.7 | | | | | 2.0 | 2.1 | |
| | .3 | | .6 | | .7 | Quick | | | | .8 | 1.1 | |
| | .2 | | .3 | | .3 | | | | | .3 | .7 | |
| 11 | 32.2 | 5 | 76.4 | 11 | 33.9 | | 13 | 29.0 | 0 | UND | |
| 22 | 16.9 | 28 | 12.8 | 26 | 14.2 | Sales/Receivables | 27 | 13.4 | 16 | 23.2 | |
| 38 | 9.6 | 38 | 9.6 | 50 | 7.3 | | 43 | 8.5 | 83 | 4.4 | |
| 62 | 5.9 | 61 | 6.0 | 53 | 6.9 | | 65 | 5.6 | 51 | 7.1 | |
| 116 | 3.1 | 90 | 4.1 | 91 | 4.0 | Cost of Sales/Inventory | 91 | 4.0 | 99 | 3.7 | |
| 220 | 1.7 | 135 | 2.7 | 146 | 2.5 | | 152 | 2.4 | 146 | 2.5 | |
| 18 | 20.8 | 11 | 33.0 | 12 | 31.2 | | 14 | 25.9 | 5 | 70.1 | |
| 28 | 12.9 | 23 | 15.9 | 26 | 13.9 | Cost of Sales/Payables | 25 | 14.6 | 28 | 12.9 | |
| 59 | 6.2 | 44 | 8.4 | 47 | 7.8 | | 45 | 8.2 | 47 | 7.8 | |
| | 4.0 | | 3.7 | | 3.8 | | | | | 3.5 | 2.9 | |
| | 8.5 | | 9.7 | | 8.0 | Sales/Working Capital | | | | 6.6 | 4.2 | |
| | 58.0 | | 19.2 | | 18.7 | | | | | 11.9 | 9.2 | |
| | 8.2 | | 7.8 | | 15.9 | | | | | 3.3 | 71.9 | |
| (36) | 2.4 | (33) | 2.3 | (43) | 3.6 | EBIT/Interest | (10) | 1.6 | | 5.4 | |
| | -1.1 | | .6 | | 1.1 | | | | | .2 | .9 | |
| | | | | | | Net Profit + Depr., Dep., Amort./Cur. Mat. L/T/D | | | | | | |
| | .2 | | .1 | | .1 | | | | | .0 | .0 | |
| | .5 | | .5 | | .4 | Fixed/Worth | | | | .4 | .2 | |
| | -1.3 | | NM | | 2.8 | | | | | 1.3 | NM | |
| | .9 | | .9 | | .6 | | | | | .6 | .3 | |
| | 3.4 | | 2.8 | | 2.5 | Debt/Worth | | | | 2.3 | 1.4 | |
| | -9.4 | | NM | | 6.8 | | | | | 4.1 | NM | |
| | 56.2 | | 34.9 | | 56.0 | % Profit Before Taxes/Tangible Net Worth | | | | 16.1 | | |
| (28) | 16.7 | (27) | 5.9 | (35) | 12.7 | | (10) | 1.4 | | | |
| | -1.4 | | -11.3 | | 2.0 | | | | | -10.2 | | |
| | 10.2 | | 11.9 | | 19.2 | % Profit Before Taxes/Total Assets | | | | 11.0 | 19.0 | |
| | 4.0 | | 2.7 | | 5.4 | | | | | .6 | 6.2 | |
| | -8.1 | | -2.6 | | -.2 | | | | | -3.8 | .0 | |
| | 51.9 | | 75.8 | | 89.6 | | | | | 66.5 | 93.1 | |
| | 18.8 | | 31.9 | | 20.9 | Sales/Net Fixed Assets | | | | 20.9 | 47.1 | |
| | 9.5 | | 8.5 | | 9.0 | | | | | 6.1 | 10.5 | |
| | 2.9 | | 3.6 | | 2.9 | | | | | 3.6 | 2.5 | |
| | 1.8 | | 2.2 | | 2.2 | Sales/Total Assets | | | | 2.8 | 2.1 | |
| | 1.3 | | 1.5 | | 1.6 | | | | | 1.1 | 1.5 | |
| | 1.0 | | .6 | | .4 | | | | | | | |
| (25) | 1.6 | (25) | 1.4 | (34) | .9 | % Depr., Dep., Amort./Sales | | | | | | |
| | 4.9 | | 4.6 | | 2.9 | | | | | | | |
| | 1.8 | | 2.2 | | 2.7 | % Officers', Directors' Owners' Comp/Sales | | | | | | |
| (17) | 3.9 | (14) | 3.6 | (18) | 3.5 | | | | | | | |
| | 8.9 | | 9.0 | | 8.2 | | | | | | | |
| | 1332209M | | 977340M | | 1286394M | Net Sales ($) | 580M | 14658M | 30160M | 74440M | 153333M | 1013223M |
| | 726940M | | 488229M | | 689143M | Total Assets ($) | 294M | 8210M | 11688M | 42633M | 75554M | 550764M |

## Current Data Sorted by Assets      Comparative Historical Data

| 0-500M | 500M-2MM | 2-10MM | 10-50MM | 50-100MM | 100-250MM | Type of Statement | 4/1/07-3/31/08 ALL | 4/1/08-3/31/09 ALL |
|---|---|---|---|---|---|---|---|---|
| | 1 | 1 | 5 | 3 | 3 | Unqualified | 10 | 10 |
| | 4 | 5 | 6 | | | Reviewed | 5 | 15 |
| 1 | 11 | 3 | 1 | | | Compiled | 7 | 9 |
| 2 | 5 | 12 | 6 | | | Tax Returns | 11 | 11 |
| 3 | | | | | 1 | Other | 29 | 25 |
| | 9 (4/1-9/30/11) | | 64 (10/1/11-3/31/12) | | | | | |
| 6 | 21 | 21 | 18 | 3 | 4 | **NUMBER OF STATEMENTS** | 62 | 70 |
| % | % | % | % | % | % | **ASSETS** | % | % |
| | 12.2 | 8.0 | 4.8 | | | Cash & Equivalents | 9.8 | 10.6 |
| | 25.8 | 24.3 | 24.2 | | | Trade Receivables (net) | 22.9 | 20.1 |
| | 43.4 | 36.1 | 32.4 | | | Inventory | 34.6 | 36.7 |
| | 1.0 | 3.6 | 2.1 | | | All Other Current | 2.8 | 3.5 |
| | 82.4 | 72.0 | 63.5 | | | Total Current | 70.0 | 71.0 |
| | 12.0 | 19.0 | 23.7 | | | Fixed Assets (net) | 16.7 | 19.5 |
| | 1.9 | 3.6 | 6.9 | | | Intangibles (net) | 9.0 | 4.9 |
| | 3.6 | 5.4 | 6.0 | | | All Other Non-Current | 4.3 | 4.6 |
| | 100.0 | 100.0 | 100.0 | | | Total | 100.0 | 100.0 |
| | | | | | | **LIABILITIES** | | |
| | 22.8 | 15.2 | 18.3 | | | Notes Payable-Short Term | 13.8 | 16.4 |
| | .7 | 1.7 | 3.7 | | | Cur. Mat.-L.T.D. | 3.2 | 3.7 |
| | 22.3 | 16.4 | 13.2 | | | Trade Payables | 16.0 | 11.4 |
| | .1 | .4 | .0 | | | Income Taxes Payable | .2 | .1 |
| | 4.7 | 12.6 | 8.7 | | | All Other Current | 11.1 | 10.7 |
| | 50.7 | 46.3 | 43.9 | | | Total Current | 44.3 | 42.4 |
| | 14.5 | 9.6 | 16.8 | | | Long-Term Debt | 13.3 | 17.8 |
| | .0 | .3 | .5 | | | Deferred Taxes | .1 | .2 |
| | 3.6 | 3.2 | 5.3 | | | All Other Non-Current | 7.4 | 8.7 |
| | 31.3 | 40.5 | 33.4 | | | Net Worth | 34.9 | 31.0 |
| | 100.0 | 100.0 | 100.0 | | | Total Liabilities & Net Worth | 100.0 | 100.0 |
| | | | | | | **INCOME DATA** | | |
| | 100.0 | 100.0 | 100.0 | | | Net Sales | 100.0 | 100.0 |
| | 42.1 | 26.6 | 22.1 | | | Gross Profit | 31.2 | 25.8 |
| | 40.5 | 22.9 | 15.2 | | | Operating Expenses | 24.6 | 21.6 |
| | 1.6 | 3.7 | 6.9 | | | Operating Profit | 6.6 | 4.3 |
| | .5 | .8 | 1.4 | | | All Other Expenses (net) | 1.7 | .7 |
| | 1.0 | 2.9 | 5.5 | | | Profit Before Taxes | 5.0 | 3.5 |
| | | | | | | **RATIOS** | | |
| | 3.9 | 2.0 | 2.0 | | | | 2.7 | 3.1 |
| | 1.8 | 1.6 | 1.3 | | | Current | 1.5 | 1.6 |
| | 1.2 | 1.2 | 1.1 | | | | 1.0 | 1.2 |
| | 1.9 | 1.1 | 1.2 | | | | 1.4 | 1.5 |
| | .7 | (20) .5 | .7 | | | Quick | .7 | .7 |
| | .5 | .3 | .3 | | | | .4 | .3 |
| | 11   32.2 | 11   32.3 | 24   15.0 | | | | 15   24.4 | 7   48.7 |
| | 27   13.5 | 40   9.1 | 41   9.0 | | | Sales/Receivables | 28   13.1 | 31   11.8 |
| | 48   7.6 | 60   6.1 | 59   6.2 | | | | 51   7.2 | 52   7.0 |
| | 49   7.4 | 29   12.6 | 38   9.6 | | | | 25   14.5 | 26   14.2 |
| | 72   5.1 | 66   5.5 | 73   5.0 | | | Cost of Sales/Inventory | 62   5.9 | 69   5.3 |
| | 152   2.4 | 122   3.0 | 122   3.0 | | | | 99   3.7 | 127   2.9 |
| | 19   19.1 | 17   21.5 | 22   16.5 | | | | 11   32.6 | 7   54.4 |
| | 33   11.2 | 23   16.2 | 30   12.0 | | | Cost of Sales/Payables | 29   12.6 | 19   19.2 |
| | 63   5.8 | 58   6.3 | 35   10.3 | | | | 42   8.6 | 34   10.7 |
| | 4.7 | 5.1 | 4.1 | | | | 6.2 | 5.5 |
| | 10.3 | 7.8 | 19.1 | | | Sales/Working Capital | 12.9 | 10.4 |
| | 23.3 | 22.8 | 73.8 | | | | 119.7 | 37.8 |
| | 14.5 | 21.0 | 15.8 | | | | 21.6 | 13.6 |
| | (17) 1.6 | (20) 8.2 | (17) 3.1 | | | EBIT/Interest | (48) 4.3 | (64) 2.0 |
| | -3.3 | 1.7 | 1.4 | | | | 2.1 | .5 |
| | | | | | | Net Profit + Depr., Dep., | 5.9 | 6.5 |
| | | | | | | Amort./Cur. Mat. L/T/D | (12) 3.6 | (20) 1.6 |
| | | | | | | | 1.8 | -.2 |
| | .1 | .2 | .4 | | | | .2 | .2 |
| | .2 | .4 | 1.1 | | | Fixed/Worth | .6 | .6 |
| | 1.7 | 1.2 | -6.1 | | | | 5.0 | 1.9 |
| | .8 | .8 | 1.4 | | | | .7 | .7 |
| | 2.0 | 1.5 | 2.8 | | | Debt/Worth | 2.7 | 2.6 |
| | 18.7 | 3.4 | -20.8 | | | | 19.8 | 7.7 |
| | 62.3 | 38.0 | 77.6 | | | | 64.3 | 48.0 |
| | (17) 15.0 | (13) 25.5 | 20.0 | | | % Profit Before Taxes/Tangible Net Worth | (49) 27.5 | (61) 15.4 |
| | -18.4 | 8.9 | 3.8 | | | | 13.9 | -1.8 |
| | 21.5 | 19.0 | 13.1 | | | | 18.0 | 15.8 |
| | .7 | 7.9 | 7.2 | | | % Profit Before Taxes/Total Assets | 9.0 | 3.8 |
| | -6.9 | 1.6 | 1.1 | | | | 3.1 | -.7 |
| | 142.9 | 35.9 | 12.2 | | | | 39.4 | 38.6 |
| | 42.0 | 16.9 | 8.5 | | | Sales/Net Fixed Assets | 20.1 | 17.5 |
| | 21.8 | 6.9 | 6.5 | | | | 10.3 | 7.4 |
| | 4.9 | 3.3 | 2.6 | | | | 3.9 | 3.5 |
| | 2.8 | 2.4 | 2.1 | | | Sales/Total Assets | 2.4 | 2.6 |
| | 1.9 | 1.8 | 1.4 | | | | 1.5 | 1.4 |
| | .3 | .7 | 1.4 | | | | .7 | .7 |
| | (12) .8 | (18) 1.4 | (15) 1.6 | | | % Depr., Dep., Amort./Sales | (46) 1.0 | (60) 1.2 |
| | 1.2 | 2.9 | 2.2 | | | | 2.4 | 2.4 |
| | 1.7 | | | | | | 2.1 | 1.8 |
| | (11) 4.0 | | | | | % Officers', Directors' Owners' Comp/Sales | (16) 3.9 | (25) 2.8 |
| | 6.6 | | | | | | 6.3 | 4.9 |
| 8321M | 75961M | 268795M | 731913M | 236213M | 1075447M | Net Sales ($) | 2809477M | 3280429M |
| 2103M | 23850M | 110922M | 387148M | 204853M | 576003M | Total Assets ($) | 1237189M | 1620358M |

## Comparative Historical Data | Current Data Sorted by Sales

Comparative Historical Data period columns: **4/1/09-3/31/10 ALL**, **4/1/10-3/31/11 ALL**, **4/1/11-3/31/12 ALL**.
Current Data date groupings: **9 (4/1-9/30/11)** covering 0-1MM / 1-3MM / 3-5MM and **64 (10/1/11-3/31/12)** covering 5-10MM / 10-25MM / 25MM & OVER.

| 4/1/09-3/31/10 ALL | 4/1/10-3/31/11 ALL | 4/1/11-3/31/12 ALL | Type of Statement | 0-1MM | 1-3MM | 3-5MM | 5-10MM | 10-25MM | 25MM & OVER |
|---|---|---|---|---|---|---|---|---|---|
| 9 | 9 | 12 | Unqualified | | | | 2 | | 10 |
| 7 | 12 | 12 | Reviewed | | | 1 | 1 | 3 | 7 |
| 6 | 7 | 6 | Compiled | 2 | 1 | 1 | 1 | 1 | |
| 10 | 11 | 16 | Tax Returns | | 6 | 6 | 2 | 2 | |
| 32 | 21 | 27 | Other | 1 | 5 | 3 | 4 | 7 | 7 |
| 64 | 60 | 73 | **NUMBER OF STATEMENTS** | 3 | 12 | 11 | 10 | 13 | 24 |
| % | % | % | **ASSETS** | % | % | % | % | % | % |
| 8.1 | 12.8 | 8.8 | Cash & Equivalents | | 7.7 | 8.6 | 11.3 | 7.9 | 8.0 |
| 17.7 | 22.6 | 23.6 | Trade Receivables (net) | | 23.5 | 24.0 | 16.8 | 30.8 | 22.0 |
| 35.0 | 38.7 | 36.5 | Inventory | | 33.2 | 48.4 | 40.8 | 31.9 | 34.2 |
| 4.6 | 2.2 | 3.8 | All Other Current | | 9.9 | .6 | 4.0 | 3.0 | 3.0 |
| 65.4 | 76.4 | 72.7 | Total Current | | 74.3 | 81.5 | 72.8 | 73.6 | 67.2 |
| 20.7 | 16.2 | 16.7 | Fixed Assets (net) | | 11.0 | 13.2 | 10.8 | 20.9 | 20.6 |
| 7.6 | 3.1 | 4.9 | Intangibles (net) | | 1.3 | 4.2 | 3.1 | 3.6 | 9.0 |
| 6.3 | 4.3 | 5.7 | All Other Non-Current | | 13.4 | 1.0 | 13.3 | 1.9 | 3.2 |
| 100.0 | 100.0 | 100.0 | Total | | 100.0 | 100.0 | 100.0 | 100.0 | 100.0 |
| | | | **LIABILITIES** | | | | | | |
| 15.5 | 18.2 | 24.5 | Notes Payable-Short Term | | 58.3 | 26.1 | 15.3 | 12.8 | 18.4 |
| 5.4 | 1.6 | 1.8 | Cur. Mat.-L.T.D. | | .7 | .8 | .7 | 3.3 | 2.8 |
| 13.9 | 15.0 | 16.7 | Trade Payables | | 18.3 | 18.3 | 13.1 | 20.2 | 12.3 |
| .5 | .1 | .3 | Income Taxes Payable | | .1 | .1 | .0 | .0 | .9 |
| 10.4 | 14.0 | 12.7 | All Other Current | | 31.2 | 8.6 | 5.7 | 12.6 | 12.3 |
| 45.7 | 48.9 | 56.1 | Total Current | | 108.7 | 53.8 | 34.8 | 48.9 | 43.4 |
| 19.5 | 12.0 | 14.0 | Long-Term Debt | | 12.9 | 11.8 | 11.2 | 9.7 | 18.4 |
| .1 | .5 | .3 | Deferred Taxes | | .0 | .0 | .6 | .1 | .6 |
| 10.8 | 6.2 | 5.7 | All Other Non-Current | | 13.9 | 4.1 | 5.4 | 3.6 | 4.4 |
| 23.7 | 32.5 | 23.9 | Net Worth | | -35.5 | 30.3 | 48.1 | 37.6 | 33.1 |
| 100.0 | 100.0 | 100.0 | Total Liabilities & Net Worth | | 100.0 | 100.0 | 100.0 | 100.0 | 100.0 |
| | | | **INCOME DATA** | | | | | | |
| 100.0 | 100.0 | 100.0 | Net Sales | | 100.0 | 100.0 | 100.0 | 100.0 | 100.0 |
| 31.0 | 29.5 | 31.2 | Gross Profit | | 40.1 | 42.6 | 28.7 | 28.0 | 23.2 |
| 30.2 | 25.0 | 28.1 | Operating Expenses | | 44.4 | 42.2 | 25.8 | 21.3 | 16.6 |
| .8 | 4.5 | 3.1 | Operating Profit | | -4.3 | .3 | 2.9 | 6.7 | 6.6 |
| 1.4 | .3 | 1.0 | All Other Expenses (net) | | 1.1 | .6 | .6 | .9 | 1.5 |
| -.6 | 4.2 | 2.1 | Profit Before Taxes | | -5.4 | -.3 | 2.4 | 5.8 | 5.1 |
| | | | **RATIOS** | | | | | | |
| 2.7 | 2.3 | 2.6 | Current | | 3.8 | 1.9 | 5.6 | 2.0 | 2.2 |
| 1.5 | 1.6 | 1.6 | | | 1.1 | 1.6 | 2.6 | 1.6 | 1.4 |
| 1.0 | 1.2 | 1.1 | | | .4 | 1.2 | 1.4 | 1.2 | 1.1 |
| 1.1 | 1.2 | 1.1 | Quick | | 1.8 | 1.0 | | 1.3 | 1.2 |
| .7 | .7 | (72) .6 | | | .3 | .5 | | .7 | .8 |
| .4 | .3 | .3 | | | .1 | .4 | | .4 | .3 |
| 16  23.4 | 14  25.6 | 15  25.0 | Sales/Receivables | | 10  36.4 | 10  37.3 | 0  UND | 21  17.0 | 24  15.4 |
| 30  12.3 | 37  9.9 | 32  11.5 | | | 22  16.6 | 43  8.4 | 15  24.5 | 42  8.6 | 38  9.5 |
| 50  7.3 | 51  7.2 | 54  6.7 | | | 39  9.4 | 58  6.3 | 40  9.2 | 74  4.9 | 56  6.5 |
| 27  13.6 | 41  8.8 | 40  9.1 | Cost of Sales/Inventory | | 42  8.6 | 60  6.1 | 28  13.0 | 35  10.5 | 39  9.4 |
| 80  4.6 | 61  6.0 | 69  5.3 | | | 74  4.9 | 122  3.0 | 62  5.9 | 59  6.2 | 64  5.7 |
| 128  2.9 | 133  2.7 | 126  2.9 | | | 111  3.3 | 281  1.3 | 126  2.9 | 107  3.4 | 118  3.1 |
| 12  29.5 | 14  26.5 | 20  18.1 | Cost of Sales/Payables | | 4  102.4 | 21  17.3 | 8  44.0 | 22  16.9 | 20  18.4 |
| 26  14.0 | 26  14.1 | 30  12.2 | | | 38  9.7 | 46  7.9 | 21  17.8 | 26  14.3 | 29  12.6 |
| 43  8.4 | 43  8.4 | 46  7.9 | | | 66  5.5 | 68  5.4 | 33  11.1 | 54  6.8 | 36  10.2 |
| 3.8 | 4.8 | 4.9 | Sales/Working Capital | | 5.9 | 4.5 | 4.3 | 6.2 | 4.5 |
| 11.1 | 7.6 | 10.3 | | | NM | 7.1 | 9.3 | 8.8 | 13.9 |
| 85.6 | 29.1 | 34.2 | | | -4.7 | 22.2 | NM | 22.8 | 34.5 |
| 6.1 | 7.7 | 14.9 | EBIT/Interest | | | | | 26.1 | 9.8 |
| (56) 1.8 | (51) 2.7 | (64) 3.5 | | | | | | 11.2 | (22) 3.5 |
| -1.3 | .9 | 1.2 | | | | | | 4.8 | 1.6 |
| 4.3 | 12.3 | 22.5 | Net Profit + Depr., Dep., Amort./Cur. Mat. L/T/D | | | | | | |
| (15) 2.1 | (12) 3.7 | (13) 5.0 | | | | | | | |
| .4 | 1.4 | 2.9 | | | | | | | |
| .2 | .1 | .1 | Fixed/Worth | | .0 | .2 | .1 | .2 | .3 |
| .7 | .4 | .4 | | | .6 | .4 | .1 | .6 | .9 |
| 3.6 | 1.4 | 1.9 | | | -13.8 | 4.2 | 1.1 | 1.3 | NM |
| 1.0 | 1.1 | .9 | Debt/Worth | | 1.3 | .9 | .6 | 1.4 | 1.1 |
| 2.5 | 2.2 | 2.2 | | | -186.9 | 3.1 | 1.2 | 1.6 | 2.8 |
| 12.9 | 7.4 | 18.9 | | | -2.1 | 24.2 | 3.2 | 3.3 | NM |
| 56.6 | 63.5 | 57.9 | % Profit Before Taxes/Tangible Net Worth | | | 17.6 | 99.4 | 38.3 | 74.4 |
| (52) 8.6 | (55) 20.8 | (57) 23.3 | | | (10) 1.7 | 20.8 | (12) 32.4 | | (18) 29.1 |
| -21.4 | 2.1 | 3.1 | | | -36.8 | 6.5 | 19.4 | | 4.0 |
| 9.3 | 12.7 | 15.2 | % Profit Before Taxes/Total Assets | | 20.1 | 1.3 | 34.7 | 18.5 | 13.7 |
| 1.7 | 5.0 | 5.5 | | | -1.7 | .5 | 14.0 | 8.3 | 5.8 |
| -9.5 | .7 | .2 | | | -20.8 | -4.8 | 3.2 | | 1.3 |
| 35.2 | 69.9 | 67.3 | Sales/Net Fixed Assets | | 925.1 | 42.0 | 156.9 | 27.9 | 41.7 |
| 12.8 | 21.8 | 21.5 | | | 78.3 | 33.6 | 34.8 | 10.3 | 11.3 |
| 5.9 | 7.3 | 6.9 | | | 19.5 | 13.0 | 10.3 | 6.8 | 5.9 |
| 3.2 | 3.2 | 3.3 | Sales/Total Assets | | 3.7 | 3.3 | 5.2 | 3.3 | 2.8 |
| 2.0 | 2.3 | 2.5 | | | 3.2 | 2.8 | 2.8 | 2.6 | 2.3 |
| 1.1 | 1.7 | 1.7 | | | 2.1 | 1.7 | 1.4 | 1.9 | 1.5 |
| 1.0 | .7 | .7 | % Depr., Dep., Amort./Sales | | | | | | .4 | .9 |
| (51) 1.5 | (48) 1.1 | (52) 1.3 | | | | | | (11) 1.0 | (19) 1.5 |
| 3.6 | 2.2 | 2.2 | | | | | | 2.4 | 2.2 |
| 2.1 | 1.0 | 1.2 | % Officers', Directors' Owners' Comp/Sales | | | | | | |
| (12) 6.7 | (20) 2.5 | (26) 3.0 | | | | | | | |
| 15.1 | 9.6 | 6.0 | | | | | | | |
| 3654711M | 2803995M | 2396650M | Net Sales ($) | 2394M | 22149M | 45328M | 77410M | 204504M | 2044865M |
| 2044056M | 1270869M | 1304879M | Total Assets ($) | 2900M | 8127M | 24267M | 38752M | 92387M | 1138446M |

M = $ thousand    MM = $ million
See Pages 9 through 22 for Explanation of Ratios and Data

**Current Data Sorted by Assets**            **Comparative Historical Data**

| 0-500M | 500M-2MM | 2-10MM | 10-50MM | 50-100MM | 100-250MM | Type of Statement | 4/1/07-3/31/08 ALL | 4/1/08-3/31/09 ALL |
|---|---|---|---|---|---|---|---|---|
| | | 4 | 10 | | 2 | Unqualified | 25 | 18 |
| 2 | 6 | 25 | 6 | | | Reviewed | 30 | 39 |
| 9 | 15 | 15 | 3 | | | Compiled | 34 | 36 |
| 24 | 22 | 6 | 1 | | | Tax Returns | 53 | 63 |
| 10 | 28 | 13 | 14 | 2 | 1 | Other | 78 | 85 |
| | 41 (4/1-9/30/11) | | 177 (10/1/11-3/31/12) | | | | | |
| 45 | 71 | 63 | 34 | 2 | 3 | NUMBER OF STATEMENTS | 220 | 241 |
| % | % | % | % | % | % | **ASSETS** | % | % |
| 10.3 | 9.1 | 9.3 | 12.2 | | | Cash & Equivalents | 9.2 | 7.8 |
| 25.7 | 27.7 | 23.1 | 19.9 | | | Trade Receivables (net) | 26.9 | 24.0 |
| 17.0 | 20.1 | 28.7 | 20.1 | | | Inventory | 21.1 | 21.1 |
| 1.2 | 2.8 | 1.6 | 3.1 | | | All Other Current | 2.7 | 2.3 |
| 54.2 | 59.7 | 62.7 | 55.4 | | | Total Current | 59.9 | 55.2 |
| 27.8 | 28.7 | 29.6 | 31.9 | | | Fixed Assets (net) | 29.6 | 33.6 |
| 2.7 | 2.8 | 2.8 | 6.5 | | | Intangibles (net) | 4.5 | 3.6 |
| 15.4 | 8.8 | 4.9 | 6.3 | | | All Other Non-Current | 6.0 | 7.5 |
| 100.0 | 100.0 | 100.0 | 100.0 | | | Total | 100.0 | 100.0 |
| | | | | | | **LIABILITIES** | | |
| 19.7 | 16.0 | 11.0 | 10.8 | | | Notes Payable-Short Term | 10.5 | 14.9 |
| 4.2 | 4.5 | 4.5 | 3.1 | | | Cur. Mat.-L.T.D. | 4.4 | 4.4 |
| 22.0 | 16.3 | 12.0 | 8.0 | | | Trade Payables | 13.9 | 14.3 |
| .0 | .2 | .3 | .1 | | | Income Taxes Payable | .2 | .4 |
| 31.7 | 12.2 | 23.5 | 11.3 | | | All Other Current | 13.9 | 16.4 |
| 77.6 | 49.2 | 51.3 | 33.4 | | | Total Current | 43.0 | 50.3 |
| 29.3 | 23.7 | 15.2 | 10.9 | | | Long-Term Debt | 20.4 | 20.6 |
| .0 | .2 | .4 | .5 | | | Deferred Taxes | .4 | .3 |
| 21.2 | 10.1 | 6.5 | 9.9 | | | All Other Non-Current | 6.9 | 6.9 |
| -28.1 | 16.8 | 26.6 | 45.3 | | | Net Worth | 29.3 | 21.9 |
| 100.0 | 100.0 | 100.0 | 100.0 | | | Total Liabilities & Net Worth | 100.0 | 100.0 |
| | | | | | | **INCOME DATA** | | |
| 100.0 | 100.0 | 100.0 | 100.0 | | | Net Sales | 100.0 | 100.0 |
| 44.8 | 33.7 | 27.4 | 28.2 | | | Gross Profit | 32.9 | 32.2 |
| 43.4 | 32.0 | 26.8 | 25.9 | | | Operating Expenses | 29.3 | 31.4 |
| 1.4 | 1.7 | .6 | 2.3 | | | Operating Profit | 3.6 | .9 |
| 1.0 | 1.0 | .7 | .7 | | | All Other Expenses (net) | 1.1 | 1.2 |
| .5 | .7 | -.1 | 1.6 | | | Profit Before Taxes | 2.5 | -.3 |
| | | | | | | **RATIOS** | | |
| 1.7 | 2.2 | 3.2 | 3.6 | | | | 2.7 | 2.4 |
| .9 | 1.6 | 1.5 | 1.8 | | | Current | 1.5 | 1.2 |
| .3 | .7 | .9 | 1.2 | | | | 1.0 | .7 |
| 1.4 | 1.6 | 1.8 | 2.9 | | | | 1.6 | 1.4 |
| .4 | 1.0 | .7 | .9 | | | Quick | .9 (240) | .7 |
| .2 | .3 | .4 | .7 | | | | .4 | .4 |
| 0 UND | 17 21.9 | 20 18.5 | 20 18.1 | | | | 17 20.9 | 14 25.4 |
| 13 27.9 | 35 10.5 | 33 11.1 | 30 12.1 | | | Sales/Receivables | 30 12.2 | 28 13.1 |
| 38 9.5 | 52 7.0 | 41 8.8 | 43 8.4 | | | | 44 8.3 | 44 8.2 |
| 0 UND | 14 25.4 | 25 14.4 | 28 13.1 | | | | 16 22.6 | 16 22.7 |
| 11 32.4 | 30 12.1 | 46 8.0 | 43 8.4 | | | Cost of Sales/Inventory | 31 11.9 | 32 11.4 |
| 35 10.4 | 48 7.6 | 83 4.4 | 66 5.5 | | | | 56 6.5 | 60 6.1 |
| 3 122.8 | 13 27.5 | 10 37.3 | 8 44.7 | | | | 9 40.0 | 9 42.6 |
| 13 27.5 | 29 12.7 | 21 17.2 | 14 26.9 | | | Cost of Sales/Payables | 20 18.0 | 19 19.0 |
| 43 8.4 | 43 8.4 | 32 11.4 | 36 10.2 | | | | 39 9.3 | 34 10.7 |
| 11.4 | 6.8 | 5.7 | 4.4 | | | | 7.8 | 8.4 |
| -183.4 | 16.4 | 12.7 | 7.7 | | | Sales/Working Capital | 16.2 | 30.3 |
| -11.1 | -12.8 | -48.2 | 29.5 | | | | -527.6 | -17.9 |
| 5.5 | 5.1 | 12.8 | 7.4 | | | | 7.3 | 4.9 |
| (36) 2.4 | (60) 1.7 | (56) 2.3 | (30) 3.4 | | | EBIT/Interest | (195) 3.0 | (215) 1.5 |
| -3.9 | -.8 | -.8 | .1 | | | | .6 | -2.1 |
| | | 4.5 | | | | Net Profit + Depr., Dep., | 8.7 | 6.7 |
| | (14) 2.6 | | | | | Amort./Cur. Mat. L/T/D | (38) 1.9 | (37) 2.1 |
| | | .9 | | | | | .9 | .2 |
| .3 | .3 | .4 | .4 | | | | .4 | .5 |
| -27.4 | 1.3 | .9 | .6 | | | Fixed/Worth | 1.0 | 1.5 |
| -.3 | -7.3 | 3.7 | 1.6 | | | | 6.8 | -7.4 |
| 1.2 | .8 | .5 | .3 | | | | .8 | .9 |
| -30.5 | 2.0 | 2.2 | 1.1 | | | Debt/Worth | 2.3 | 3.5 |
| -2.2 | -36.2 | 11.2 | 3.4 | | | | 17.5 | -20.9 |
| 83.7 | 40.9 | 32.5 | 22.9 | | | | 55.9 | 42.6 |
| (21) 43.6 | (52) 11.4 | (51) 13.8 | (31) 7.9 | | | % Profit Before Taxes/Tangible Net Worth | (173) 28.4 | (173) 10.4 |
| -1.5 | -1.9 | -19.8 | -4.2 | | | | 6.9 | -5.1 |
| 28.5 | 13.4 | 10.2 | 9.4 | | | | 18.6 | 10.3 |
| 7.8 | 3.0 | 3.5 | 4.1 | | | % Profit Before Taxes/Total Assets | 7.2 | 2.1 |
| -13.2 | -4.8 | -5.6 | -3.1 | | | | -2.2 | -9.2 |
| 51.7 | 34.9 | 20.7 | 18.0 | | | | 31.5 | 22.3 |
| 31.5 | 13.3 | 9.0 | 5.8 | | | Sales/Net Fixed Assets | 11.5 | 9.5 |
| 13.6 | 4.9 | 4.6 | 3.1 | | | | 6.1 | 4.7 |
| 8.1 | 4.2 | 3.1 | 2.5 | | | | 4.0 | 3.7 |
| 4.3 | 2.8 | 2.4 | 1.9 | | | Sales/Total Assets | 2.7 | 2.7 |
| 3.0 | 1.8 | 1.5 | 1.3 | | | | 2.1 | 2.0 |
| .8 | .9 | 1.3 | 1.0 | | | | 1.0 | 1.2 |
| (34) 1.3 | (59) 1.5 | (60) 2.0 | (31) 2.9 | | | % Depr., Dep., Amort./Sales | (187) 2.0 | (208) 2.1 |
| 3.5 | 2.7 | 2.9 | 5.3 | | | | 3.2 | 3.8 |
| 4.2 | 2.9 | 1.6 | | | | | 1.9 | 2.1 |
| (26) 7.9 | (43) 4.9 | (25) 2.3 | | | | % Officers', Directors' Owners' Comp/Sales | (94) 4.2 | (106) 3.1 |
| 10.5 | 7.1 | 3.9 | | | | | 7.6 | 6.7 |
| 53555M | 246364M | 767760M | 1390243M | 268846M | 942164M | Net Sales ($) | 6531850M | 5689639M |
| 10549M | 82278M | 309690M | 645727M | 123183M | 566721M | Total Assets ($) | 2940134M | 2484522M |

© RMA 2012      M = $ thousand    MM = $ million

See Pages 9 through 22 for Explanation of Ratios and Data

## Comparative Historical Data                    Current Data Sorted by Sales

| | | | Type of Statement | | | | | | |
|---|---|---|---|---|---|---|---|---|---|
| 20 | 20 | 16 | Unqualified | 1 | 1 | | 2 | 4 | 9 |
| 32 | 36 | 39 | Reviewed | 1 | 2 | 6 | 6 | 16 | 8 |
| 38 | 39 | 42 | Compiled | 4 | 16 | 3 | 12 | 5 | 2 |
| 46 | 56 | 53 | Tax Returns | 16 | 22 | 7 | 6 | 1 | 1 |
| 66 | 76 | 68 | Other | 8 | 19 | 4 | 10 | 14 | 13 |
| 4/1/09-3/31/10 ALL | 4/1/10-3/31/11 ALL | 4/1/11-3/31/12 ALL | | 41 (4/1-9/30/11) | | 177 (10/1/11-3/31/12) | | | |
| | | | | 0-1MM | 1-3MM | 3-5MM | 5-10MM | 10-25MM | 25MM & OVER |
| 202 | 227 | 218 | **NUMBER OF STATEMENTS** | 29 | 60 | 20 | 36 | 40 | 33 |
| % | % | % | **ASSETS** | % | % | % | % | % | % |
| 9.4 | 9.1 | 9.8 | Cash & Equivalents | 11.5 | 8.1 | 13.6 | 9.5 | 10.1 | 8.7 |
| 22.0 | 24.6 | 24.7 | Trade Receivables (net) | 17.6 | 27.5 | 22.0 | 27.1 | 24.7 | 24.9 |
| 23.3 | 20.9 | 21.8 | Inventory | 12.4 | 22.2 | 19.2 | 24.8 | 25.0 | 23.9 |
| 1.9 | 2.0 | 2.2 | All Other Current | .8 | 2.4 | 2.2 | 2.0 | 1.9 | 3.3 |
| 56.6 | 56.7 | 58.5 | Total Current | 42.4 | 60.3 | 57.1 | 63.5 | 61.7 | 60.8 |
| 32.1 | 30.8 | 29.2 | Fixed Assets (net) | 36.7 | 26.1 | 33.6 | 27.8 | 31.2 | 24.5 |
| 3.5 | 4.4 | 3.6 | Intangibles (net) | 5.5 | 2.0 | 1.5 | 3.0 | 2.2 | 8.7 |
| 7.8 | 8.1 | 8.7 | All Other Non-Current | 15.5 | 11.6 | 7.8 | 5.7 | 4.8 | 6.0 |
| 100.0 | 100.0 | 100.0 | Total | 100.0 | 100.0 | 100.0 | 100.0 | 100.0 | 100.0 |
| | | | **LIABILITIES** | | | | | | |
| 17.5 | 17.7 | 14.3 | Notes Payable-Short Term | 19.3 | 14.9 | 7.7 | 13.8 | 15.3 | 12.3 |
| 4.6 | 4.4 | 4.2 | Cur. Mat.-L.T.D. | 6.3 | 4.1 | 3.6 | 4.5 | 3.3 | 3.5 |
| 14.0 | 15.2 | 14.7 | Trade Payables | 16.4 | 17.2 | 14.0 | 16.0 | 12.5 | 10.4 |
| .1 | .1 | .2 | Income Taxes Payable | .0 | .1 | .0 | .5 | .2 | .1 |
| 14.8 | 15.4 | 19.3 | All Other Current | 21.9 | 33.2 | 7.1 | 16.5 | 10.6 | 12.4 |
| 51.1 | 52.7 | 52.7 | Total Current | 63.9 | 69.5 | 32.4 | 51.3 | 42.1 | 38.8 |
| 20.2 | 20.5 | 20.9 | Long-Term Debt | 43.6 | 17.4 | 17.7 | 24.7 | 12.4 | 15.5 |
| .6 | .3 | .3 | Deferred Taxes | .0 | .2 | .1 | .3 | .5 | .6 |
| 11.7 | 10.0 | 11.2 | All Other Non-Current | 12.3 | 15.3 | 7.1 | 10.8 | 6.2 | 11.7 |
| 16.4 | 16.5 | 14.9 | Net Worth | -19.8 | -2.4 | 42.7 | 13.0 | 38.8 | 33.4 |
| 100.0 | 100.0 | 100.0 | Total Liabilities & Net Worth | 100.0 | 100.0 | 100.0 | 100.0 | 100.0 | 100.0 |
| | | | **INCOME DATA** | | | | | | |
| 100.0 | 100.0 | 100.0 | Net Sales | 100.0 | 100.0 | 100.0 | 100.0 | 100.0 | 100.0 |
| 31.2 | 33.2 | 33.1 | Gross Profit | 44.9 | 39.2 | 26.9 | 29.9 | 26.5 | 26.7 |
| 32.7 | 32.2 | 31.5 | Operating Expenses | 43.2 | 38.3 | 28.1 | 28.3 | 25.3 | 21.8 |
| -1.5 | 1.0 | 1.6 | Operating Profit | 1.7 | .9 | -1.2 | 1.6 | 1.2 | 4.9 |
| 1.0 | 1.1 | .9 | All Other Expenses (net) | 2.1 | .7 | .4 | 1.0 | .2 | 1.1 |
| -2.5 | -.1 | .7 | Profit Before Taxes | -.3 | .1 | -1.5 | .6 | .9 | 3.8 |
| | | | **RATIOS** | | | | | | |
| 2.5 | 2.3 | 2.8 | | 2.6 | 1.9 | 6.4 | 2.6 | 3.6 | 2.6 |
| 1.2 | 1.3 | 1.5 | Current | .8 | 1.1 | 1.7 | 1.6 | 1.8 | 1.7 |
| .7 | .7 | .7 | | .3 | .6 | .8 | .7 | 1.1 | 1.2 |
| 1.3 | 1.4 | 1.6 | | 1.6 | 1.2 | 3.6 | 1.7 | 2.2 | 1.6 |
| .7 | .8 | .8 | Quick | .4 | .6 | .9 | .8 | .9 | .9 |
| .3 | .4 | .3 | | .2 | .2 | .5 | .4 | .5 | .7 |
| 17  21.0 | 18  20.7 | 15  24.3 | | 4  85.6 | 10  36.3 | 7  51.8 | 22  16.5 | 18  20.7 | 22  16.6 |
| 31  12.0 | 32  11.3 | 29  12.4 | Sales/Receivables | 17  21.9 | 33  11.2 | 27  13.4 | 33  11.0 | 27  13.7 | 36  10.2 |
| 46  8.0 | 52  7.1 | 47  7.8 | | 38  9.5 | 56  6.5 | 42  8.7 | 53  6.9 | 40  9.1 | 44  8.3 |
| 24  15.5 | 20  18.3 | 17  21.6 | | 0  UND | 10  36.5 | 10  38.0 | 22  16.7 | 23  15.6 | 26  14.1 |
| 39  9.4 | 36  10.0 | 35  10.3 | Cost of Sales/Inventory | 15  24.7 | 34  10.7 | 34  10.7 | 35  10.3 | 45  8.2 | 39  9.3 |
| 76  4.8 | 61  5.9 | 60  6.1 | | 34  10.6 | 73  5.0 | 54  6.8 | 78  4.7 | 69  5.3 | 57  6.4 |
| 9  42.2 | 11  33.4 | 9  40.1 | | 3  121.0 | 10  35.8 | 7  54.9 | 15  24.2 | 10  36.5 | 10  37.1 |
| 21  17.4 | 24  15.3 | 21  17.8 | Cost of Sales/Payables | 13  27.5 | 23  15.7 | 16  23.3 | 26  13.8 | 16  23.2 | 14  26.1 |
| 41  9.0 | 45  8.1 | 39  9.4 | | 49  7.4 | 46  7.9 | 36  10.2 | 41  9.0 | 32  11.5 | 29  12.5 |
| 7.3 | 7.4 | 6.4 | | 9.4 | 7.0 | 5.2 | 6.1 | 4.6 | 5.7 |
| 28.3 | 19.8 | 15.7 | Sales/Working Capital | -30.1 | 77.8 | 14.6 | 15.3 | 9.9 | 10.7 |
| -17.5 | -17.7 | -22.4 | | -4.1 | -13.7 | -122.0 | -8.3 | 52.8 | 34.0 |
| 3.5 | 5.5 | 7.7 | | 4.5 | 4.8 | 5.7 | 10.6 | 13.3 | 10.5 |
| (183)  .8 | (202)  1.7 | (187)  2.3 | EBIT/Interest | (26)  1.5 | (46)  1.7 | (16)  -.7 | (32)  2.2 | (35)  3.5 | (32)  3.9 |
| -3.1 | -1.0 | -.8 | | -1.6 | -2.3 | -4.5 | -.7 | -.5 | 1.1 |
| 5.3 | 3.4 | 5.8 | Net Profit + Depr., Dep., Amort./Cur. Mat. L/T/D | | | | | | |
| (36)  .7 | (36)  1.5 | (29)  2.7 | | | | | | | |
| -.1 | -.1 | 1.3 | | | | | | | |
| .4 | .5 | .4 | | .7 | .3 | .2 | .4 | .4 | .3 |
| 1.3 | 1.2 | 1.1 | Fixed/Worth | 5.7 | 1.0 | .5 | 1.2 | .7 | .7 |
| -3.9 | -4.6 | -6.8 | | -.3 | -1.5 | 4.5 | -1.2 | 2.4 | 3.5 |
| .8 | .9 | .7 | | 1.3 | .8 | .3 | .8 | .3 | .5 |
| 2.7 | 2.9 | 2.1 | Debt/Worth | 130.0 | 2.5 | 1.7 | 2.6 | 1.7 | 2.5 |
| -10.3 | -8.7 | -18.7 | | -2.0 | -5.8 | 4.9 | -4.2 | 5.3 | 13.1 |
| 16.0 | 34.0 | 37.5 | | 33.3 | 72.8 | 42.4 | 29.9 | 26.5 | 46.1 |
| (142)  1.8 | (163)  7.0 | (157)  11.6 | % Profit Before Taxes/Tangible Net Worth | (15)  10.2 | (39)  13.0 | (18)  -.2 | (22)  18.4 | (36)  6.1 | (27)  15.7 |
| -26.9 | -9.7 | -4.9 | | -2.6 | -.6 | -30.6 | 2.0 | -13.0 | 1.8 |
| 5.6 | 9.3 | 12.9 | | 9.0 | 19.8 | 12.8 | 9.3 | 10.9 | 14.6 |
| -1.1 | 1.7 | 3.9 | % Profit Before Taxes/Total Assets | 3.2 | 3.5 | -2.8 | 4.2 | 3.7 | 7.2 |
| -10.0 | -8.3 | -5.1 | | -11.7 | -5.6 | -12.4 | -4.4 | -5.1 | .2 |
| 24.1 | 26.9 | 33.5 | | 34.7 | 42.8 | 44.2 | 27.2 | 22.6 | 30.4 |
| 9.8 | 9.0 | 11.9 | Sales/Net Fixed Assets | 19.4 | 14.0 | 13.3 | 12.5 | 7.8 | 12.0 |
| 4.7 | 4.5 | 4.8 | | 3.0 | 5.5 | 4.2 | 4.7 | 4.2 | 5.8 |
| 3.5 | 3.7 | 4.0 | | 4.2 | 4.4 | 4.4 | 3.9 | 3.3 | 3.4 |
| 2.4 | 2.4 | 2.6 | Sales/Total Assets | 2.6 | 2.9 | 2.9 | 2.5 | 2.7 | 2.4 |
| 1.6 | 1.6 | 1.8 | | 1.6 | 1.8 | 1.7 | 1.5 | 1.7 | 1.8 |
| 1.2 | 1.1 | 1.0 | | 1.0 | .8 | 1.3 | 1.0 | .8 | 1.0 |
| (170)  2.3 | (188)  2.1 | (185)  1.7 | % Depr., Dep., Amort./Sales | (24)  1.8 | (44)  1.4 | (16)  2.8 | (35)  2.1 | (39)  1.7 | (27)  2.0 |
| 4.0 | 3.9 | 3.3 | | 4.2 | 2.7 | 3.5 | 2.8 | 2.9 | 4.2 |
| 1.9 | 1.9 | 2.1 | | 4.9 | 3.1 | 2.3 | 2.1 | 1.3 | |
| (100)  3.5 | (108)  3.6 | (103)  4.1 | % Officers', Directors' Owners' Comp/Sales | (17)  8.2 | (34)  5.5 | (16)  2.9 | (16)  3.9 | (14)  1.9 | |
| 7.6 | 7.0 | 7.7 | | 9.8 | 8.3 | 5.0 | 5.7 | 3.7 | |
| 4307628M | 7546906M | 3668932M | Net Sales ($) | 18247M | 120352M | 78100M | 244408M | 663523M | 2544302M |
| 1760586M | 2918765M | 1738148M | Total Assets ($) | 11468M | 49596M | 30899M | 126365M | 318410M | 1201410M |

© RMA 2012

M = $ thousand    MM = $ million
See Pages 9 through 22 for Explanation of Ratios and Data

## Current Data Sorted by Assets      Comparative Historical Data

| 0-500M | 500M-2MM | 2-10MM | 10-50MM | 50-100MM | 100-250MM | Type of Statement | 4/1/07-3/31/08 ALL | 4/1/08-3/31/09 ALL |
|---|---|---|---|---|---|---|---|---|
| 1 | 1 | 1 | 5 | 2 | 2 | Unqualified | 14 | 18 |
| | 1 | 8 | 5 | | | Reviewed | 19 | 15 |
| 1 | 1 | 3 | 1 | | | Compiled | 13 | 10 |
| 3 | 3 | 2 | | | | Tax Returns | 7 | 10 |
| | 4 | 8 | 6 | 3 | 1 | Other | 35 | 35 |
| | 13 (4/1-9/30/11) | | 49 (10/1/11-3/31/12) | | | | | |
| 5 | 10 | 22 | 17 | 5 | 3 | NUMBER OF STATEMENTS | 88 | 88 |
| % | % | % | % | % | % | ASSETS | % | % |
| | 9.3 | 4.1 | 9.3 | | | Cash & Equivalents | 6.9 | 7.7 |
| | 15.3 | 20.5 | 29.9 | | | Trade Receivables (net) | 24.0 | 22.9 |
| | 38.4 | 43.7 | 28.2 | | | Inventory | 35.2 | 37.0 |
| | 1.0 | 2.7 | 3.5 | | | All Other Current | 4.6 | 2.6 |
| | 64.0 | 71.0 | 71.0 | | | Total Current | 70.7 | 70.3 |
| | 23.0 | 15.0 | 16.7 | | | Fixed Assets (net) | 18.4 | 20.6 |
| | .2 | 2.3 | 8.0 | | | Intangibles (net) | 2.7 | 2.1 |
| | 12.8 | 11.7 | 4.4 | | | All Other Non-Current | 8.2 | 7.0 |
| | 100.0 | 100.0 | 100.0 | | | Total | 100.0 | 100.0 |
| | | | | | | LIABILITIES | | |
| | 8.9 | 18.5 | 5.1 | | | Notes Payable-Short Term | 12.9 | 17.6 |
| | .4 | 7.4 | 5.7 | | | Cur. Mat.-L.T.D. | 2.6 | 2.7 |
| | 13.9 | 11.7 | 16.2 | | | Trade Payables | 17.1 | 13.6 |
| | .2 | .4 | .4 | | | Income Taxes Payable | .2 | .1 |
| | 14.6 | 28.0 | 10.8 | | | All Other Current | 14.1 | 13.2 |
| | 38.0 | 65.9 | 38.2 | | | Total Current | 47.0 | 47.2 |
| | 10.7 | 11.3 | 14.8 | | | Long-Term Debt | 16.2 | 19.0 |
| | .1 | .1 | .1 | | | Deferred Taxes | .5 | .3 |
| | 8.9 | 4.9 | 9.0 | | | All Other Non-Current | 5.6 | 7.8 |
| | 42.4 | 17.7 | 38.0 | | | Net Worth | 30.7 | 25.7 |
| | 100.0 | 100.0 | 100.0 | | | Total Liabilties & Net Worth | 100.0 | 100.0 |
| | | | | | | INCOME DATA | | |
| | 100.0 | 100.0 | 100.0 | | | Net Sales | 100.0 | 100.0 |
| | 35.6 | 28.5 | 24.9 | | | Gross Profit | 27.5 | 25.8 |
| | 35.8 | 28.5 | 19.5 | | | Operating Expenses | 25.0 | 25.7 |
| | -.3 | .0 | 5.5 | | | Operating Profit | 2.6 | .1 |
| | 1.0 | .3 | .8 | | | All Other Expenses (net) | .5 | 1.2 |
| | -1.2 | -.3 | 4.6 | | | Profit Before Taxes | 2.1 | -1.1 |
| | | | | | | RATIOS | | |
| | 4.3 | 1.9 | 2.8 | | | | 2.8 | 4.0 |
| | 1.7 | 1.5 | 1.9 | | | Current | 1.7 | 1.8 |
| | 1.0 | 1.1 | 1.6 | | | | 1.1 | 1.0 |
| | | 1.0 | 1.4 | | | | 1.4 | 1.9 |
| | | .4 | 1.0 | | | Quick | .6 | .8 |
| | | .1 | .5 | | | | .4 | .4 |

| | | | | | | | | | Sales/Receivables | | | | |
|---|---|---|---|---|---|---|---|---|---|---|---|---|---|

| 0-500M | 500M-2MM | 2-10MM | 10-50MM | Label | Hist 1 | Hist 2 |
|---|---|---|---|---|---|---|
| 4   89.0 | 9   42.0 | 26   14.0 | | | 12   29.8 | 19   19.3 |
| 18   20.1 | 25   14.5 | 42   8.7 | | Sales/Receivables | 28   12.8 | 31   11.8 |
| 28   12.9 | 41   8.9 | 48   7.6 | | | 40   9.1 | 40   9.1 |
| 15   25.0 | 43   8.5 | 38   9.6 | | | 37   9.9 | 36   10.1 |
| 57   6.4 | 96   3.8 | 53   6.9 | | Cost of Sales/Inventory | 53   6.9 | 60   6.0 |
| 166   2.2 | 152   2.4 | 83   4.4 | | | 81   4.5 | 102   3.6 |
| 9   42.6 | 11   32.2 | 17   21.0 | | | 11   33.6 | 10   38.0 |
| 20   18.7 | 27   13.5 | 25   14.6 | | Cost of Sales/Payables | 20   18.5 | 17   21.5 |
| 45   8.2 | 38   9.5 | 33   11.1 | | | 34   10.6 | 31   11.6 |
| 3.1 | 6.2 | 3.7 | | | 5.7 | 5.0 |
| 19.0 | 11.8 | 7.5 | | Sales/Working Capital | 12.7 | 11.3 |
| -653.2 | NM | 12.6 | | | 79.5 | 202.1 |
| | 9.2 | 36.7 | | | 10.1 | 6.1 |
| | (21)   1.5 | (15)   4.4 | | EBIT/Interest | (79)   2.1 | (79)   1.1 |
| | .0 | 1.4 | | | -.1 | -2.4 |
| | | | | Net Profit + Depr., Dep., | 5.3 | 7.4 |
| | | | | Amort./Cur. Mat. L/T/D | (23)   .8 | (21)   2.3 |
| | | | | | .2 | -5.6 |
| | .0 | .1 | .2 | | .2 | .2 |
| | .4 | .4 | .4 | Fixed/Worth | .6 | .5 |
| | 1.1 | NM | NM | | 1.3 | 2.2 |
| | .5 | 1.1 | .5 | | .5 | .5 |
| | 1.5 | 2.4 | 1.1 | Debt/Worth | 1.9 | 1.5 |
| | 215.9 | NM | NM | | 6.6 | 13.9 |
| | | 28.8 | 38.9 | % Profit Before Taxes/Tangible | 38.5 | 16.0 |
| | (17)   6.7 | (13)   23.2 | | Net Worth | (75)   12.7 | (71)   5.0 |
| | | 3.9 | 4.0 | | -2.0 | -10.2 |
| | 3.4 | 7.3 | 24.1 | % Profit Before Taxes/Total | 17.0 | 7.9 |
| | .1 | 2.5 | 9.1 | Assets | 5.0 | .7 |
| | -13.5 | -2.5 | 1.6 | | -2.2 | -11.8 |
| | 66.4 | 89.2 | 37.7 | | 63.4 | 31.8 |
| | 27.1 | 25.5 | 15.5 | Sales/Net Fixed Assets | 19.7 | 18.3 |
| | 10.2 | 8.7 | 6.2 | | 10.0 | 10.0 |
| | 5.7 | 3.2 | 3.7 | | 4.0 | 4.1 |
| | 3.0 | 2.4 | 2.4 | Sales/Total Assets | 3.0 | 2.9 |
| | 1.8 | 1.8 | 1.6 | | 2.3 | 2.2 |
| | | .4 | .6 | | .4 | .6 |
| | (21)   .9 | (14)   1.0 | | % Depr., Dep., Amort./Sales | (75)   .8 | (80)   .9 |
| | | 1.3 | 1.6 | | 1.4 | 1.5 |
| | | | | % Officers', Directors' | 2.3 | 1.6 |
| | | | | Owners' Comp/Sales | (29)   3.4 | (33)   2.8 |
| | | | | | 5.9 | 5.3 |

| 5298M | 39227M | 270448M | 1081053M | 783878M | 926775M | Net Sales ($) | 5511356M | 4058096M |
|---|---|---|---|---|---|---|---|---|
| 752M | 11202M | 106098M | 445306M | 382634M | 416383M | Total Assets ($) | 2167492M | 1601647M |

M = $ thousand     MM = $ million
See Pages 9 through 22 for Explanation of Ratios and Data

## Comparative Historical Data | Current Data Sorted by Sales

| 4/1/09-3/31/10 ALL | 4/1/10-3/31/11 ALL | 4/1/11-3/31/12 ALL | Type of Statement | 0-1MM | 1-3MM | 3-5MM | 5-10MM | 10-25MM | 25MM & OVER |
|---|---|---|---|---|---|---|---|---|---|
| 19 | 16 | 12 | Unqualified | 1 | | | 1 | 1 | 9 |
| 12 | 13 | 14 | Reviewed | | 1 | | 3 | 5 | 5 |
| 9 | 11 | 6 | Compiled | 1 | | | 2 | 1 | 1 |
| 7 | 8 | 8 | Tax Returns | 2 | 2 | 3 | 1 | | 1 |
| 33 | 34 | 22 | Other | | 2 | 2 | 5 | 3 | 10 |
| | | | | 13 (4/1-9/30/11) | | | 49 (10/1/11-3/31/12) | | |
| 80 | 82 | 62 | NUMBER OF STATEMENTS | 4 | 5 | 6 | 12 | 10 | 25 |
| % | % | % | **ASSETS** | % | % | % | % | % | % |
| 9.5 | 8.3 | 8.1 | Cash & Equivalents | | | | 3.9 | 9.9 | 9.6 |
| 24.2 | 23.6 | 24.2 | Trade Receivables (net) | | | | 10.0 | 28.3 | 28.4 |
| 32.3 | 31.8 | 35.9 | Inventory | | | | 46.4 | 30.1 | 32.8 |
| 2.5 | 4.8 | 2.5 | All Other Current | | | | 2.4 | 4.2 | 2.3 |
| 68.5 | 68.6 | 70.7 | Total Current | | | | 62.8 | 72.4 | 73.1 |
| 19.6 | 19.2 | 17.3 | Fixed Assets (net) | | | | 21.3 | 17.7 | 15.8 |
| 3.4 | 3.5 | 3.0 | Intangibles (net) | | | | .2 | 5.5 | 5.1 |
| 8.5 | 8.7 | 9.0 | All Other Non-Current | | | | 15.8 | 4.3 | 5.9 |
| 100.0 | 100.0 | 100.0 | Total | | | | 100.0 | 100.0 | 100.0 |
| | | | **LIABILITIES** | | | | | | |
| 10.8 | 10.1 | 12.5 | Notes Payable-Short Term | | | | 23.2 | 10.7 | 5.3 |
| 3.3 | 2.7 | 4.9 | Cur. Mat.-L.T.D. | | | | 12.1 | 3.2 | 4.9 |
| 14.0 | 16.8 | 14.4 | Trade Payables | | | | 12.6 | 7.1 | 15.7 |
| .3 | .5 | .5 | Income Taxes Payable | | | | .7 | .1 | .3 |
| 8.0 | 14.2 | 17.8 | All Other Current | | | | 34.2 | 18.5 | 11.1 |
| 36.5 | 44.3 | 50.1 | Total Current | | | | 82.9 | 39.5 | 37.3 |
| 19.7 | 15.4 | 10.3 | Long-Term Debt | | | | 16.3 | 4.0 | 10.1 |
| .3 | .4 | .1 | Deferred Taxes | | | | .2 | .0 | .1 |
| 5.4 | 5.3 | 7.0 | All Other Non-Current | | | | 4.9 | 4.1 | 7.3 |
| 38.1 | 34.6 | 32.5 | Net Worth | | | | -4.2 | 52.4 | 45.2 |
| 100.0 | 100.0 | 100.0 | Total Liabilities & Net Worth | | | | 100.0 | 100.0 | 100.0 |
| | | | **INCOME DATA** | | | | | | |
| 100.0 | 100.0 | 100.0 | Net Sales | | | | 100.0 | 100.0 | 100.0 |
| 26.4 | 25.2 | 28.5 | Gross Profit | | | | 27.4 | 24.9 | 23.1 |
| 23.9 | 24.3 | 26.1 | Operating Expenses | | | | 27.8 | 24.5 | 17.8 |
| 2.5 | .9 | 2.5 | Operating Profit | | | | -.4 | .5 | 5.2 |
| .7 | 1.1 | .6 | All Other Expenses (net) | | | | .7 | -.2 | .6 |
| 1.8 | -.2 | 1.9 | Profit Before Taxes | | | | -1.1 | .6 | 4.7 |
| | | | **RATIOS** | | | | | | |
| 4.1 | 3.4 | 3.0 | Current | | | | 1.7 | 2.5 | 3.4 |
| 2.2 | 1.7 | 1.7 | | | | | 1.1 | 1.9 | 2.1 |
| 1.2 | 1.1 | 1.1 | | | | | .6 | 1.5 | 1.6 |
| 2.1 | 1.5 | 1.5 | Quick | | | | .4 | 1.5 | 1.8 |
| 1.1 | .8 | (61) .7 | | | | | .2 | 1.0 | 1.1 |
| .5 | .4 | .3 | | | | | .0 | .5 | .5 |
| 23  16.1 | 15  24.3 | 14  26.3 | Sales/Receivables | | | 3  111.6 | 19  19.4 | 26  14.0 | |
| 36  10.2 | 34  10.9 | 33  11.2 | | | | 11  32.4 | 35  10.5 | 39  9.3 | |
| 46  7.9 | 46  8.0 | 42  8.6 | | | | 30  12.1 | 42  8.6 | 45  8.1 | |
| 34  10.6 | 35  10.5 | 39  9.4 | Cost of Sales/Inventory | | | 49  7.4 | 26  14.3 | 38  9.5 | |
| 51  7.2 | 56  6.5 | 70  5.2 | | | | 99  3.7 | 57  6.4 | 63  5.8 | |
| 91  4.0 | 96  3.8 | 104  3.5 | | | | 261  1.4 | 104  3.5 | 81  4.5 | |
| 10  35.3 | 15  24.6 | 13  27.1 | Cost of Sales/Payables | | | 8  44.2 | 4  96.0 | 18  19.9 | |
| 22  16.7 | 24  15.0 | 24  15.2 | | | | 31  11.7 | 12  30.4 | 24  15.2 | |
| 35  10.6 | 39  9.4 | 35  10.3 | | | | 47  7.7 | 16  22.9 | 32  11.3 | |
| 4.8 | 4.3 | 4.4 | Sales/Working Capital | | | | 9.3 | 3.8 | 3.9 |
| 8.4 | 9.6 | 10.4 | | | | | 46.9 | 7.5 | 7.5 |
| 31.6 | 45.4 | 45.9 | | | | | -4.5 | 16.1 | 12.6 |
| 11.5 | 13.7 | 8.7 | EBIT/Interest | | | | 6.0 | | 31.7 |
| (71) 2.5 | (75) 2.6 | (54) 2.5 | | | | | 1.4 | (20) 4.6 | |
| -.2 | -.5 | .0 | | | | | -.2 | | 1.3 |
| 4.2 | 10.4 | 35.1 | Net Profit + Depr., Dep., Amort./Cur. Mat. L/T/D | | | | | | |
| (14) 1.1 | (13) 3.9 | (12) 2.4 | | | | | | | |
| -.2 | -.8 | .0 | | | | | | | |
| .2 | .2 | .2 | Fixed/Worth | | | | .3 | .2 | .2 |
| .4 | .4 | .4 | | | | | 2.3 | .3 | .3 |
| 1.4 | 1.2 | 1.1 | | | | | -4.8 | .4 | .6 |
| .4 | .4 | .5 | Debt/Worth | | | | 1.2 | .5 | .4 |
| 1.1 | 1.2 | 1.3 | | | | | 4.6 | 1.0 | 1.1 |
| 4.1 | 9.1 | 4.5 | | | | | -19.4 | 2.1 | 2.3 |
| 40.1 | 37.5 | 31.4 | % Profit Before Taxes/Tangible Net Worth | | | | | 19.8 | 44.5 |
| (68) 8.7 | (69) 9.7 | (51) 6.7 | | | | | | 6.4 | (21) 23.2 |
| -10.0 | -4.3 | .4 | | | | | | -4.2 | 5.5 |
| 14.1 | 12.6 | 11.9 | % Profit Before Taxes/Total Assets | | | | 5.9 | 7.2 | 23.2 |
| 3.7 | 3.6 | 2.8 | | | | | 1.1 | 2.5 | 9.8 |
| -4.0 | -2.7 | -1.6 | | | | | -3.5 | -3.1 | 1.8 |
| 32.3 | 43.6 | 69.1 | Sales/Net Fixed Assets | | | | 61.2 | 145.5 | 36.6 |
| 16.4 | 18.0 | 19.3 | | | | | 17.8 | 13.9 | 15.9 |
| 9.4 | 8.4 | 9.0 | | | | | 7.0 | 6.5 | 9.2 |
| 3.7 | 3.7 | 3.6 | Sales/Total Assets | | | | 2.8 | 3.5 | 3.6 |
| 2.8 | 2.6 | 2.5 | | | | | 2.2 | 2.6 | 2.4 |
| 1.7 | 1.8 | 1.8 | | | | | 1.3 | 1.8 | 1.8 |
| .7 | .6 | .6 | % Depr., Dep., Amort./Sales | | | | .6 | | .6 |
| (65) 1.1 | (73) .9 | (48) 1.0 | | | | | (11) 1.1 | (21) .8 | |
| 2.0 | 1.5 | 1.5 | | | | | 1.4 | | 1.5 |
| 1.4 | 1.6 | 2.9 | % Officers', Directors' Owners' Comp/Sales | | | | | | |
| (18) 3.0 | (20) 3.4 | (22) 4.7 | | | | | | | |
| 3.8 | 5.6 | 9.4 | | | | | | | |
| 4166300M | 4549430M | 3106679M | Net Sales ($) | 2070M | 10288M | 23106M | 87636M | 174553M | 2809026M |
| 1865964M | 1927871M | 1362375M | Total Assets ($) | 984M | 3268M | 9652M | 45174M | 76439M | 1226858M |

© RMA 2012

M = $ thousand    MM = $ million
See Pages 9 through 22 for Explanation of Ratios and Data

## Current Data Sorted by Assets | Comparative Historical Data

| 0-500M | 500M-2MM | 2-10MM | 10-50MM | 50-100MM | 100-250MM | Type of Statement | 4/1/07-3/31/08 ALL | 4/1/08-3/31/09 ALL |
|---|---|---|---|---|---|---|---|---|
| | | 1 | 4 | | 1 | Unqualified | 10 | 9 |
| | | 9 | 1 | | | Reviewed | 19 | 15 |
| | 4 | | 1 | | | Compiled | 15 | 13 |
| 8 | 6 | 3 | | 1 | | Tax Returns | 14 | 21 |
| 2 | 8 | 7 | 4 | 6 | | Other | 39 | 44 |
| | 10 (4/1-9/30/11) | | 56 (10/1/11-3/31/12) | | | | | |
| 10 | 18 | 20 | 10 | 7 | 1 | **NUMBER OF STATEMENTS** | 97 | 102 |
| % | % | % | % | % | % | **ASSETS** | % | % |
| 16.4 | 10.0 | 11.0 | 5.1 | | | Cash & Equivalents | 8.1 | 6.8 |
| 18.5 | 11.4 | 21.9 | 26.6 | | | Trade Receivables (net) | 21.5 | 19.8 |
| 32.8 | 44.2 | 38.7 | 44.2 | | | Inventory | 35.9 | 41.0 |
| .2 | 1.0 | 2.4 | 1.7 | | | All Other Current | 3.9 | 2.6 |
| 67.9 | 66.7 | 74.1 | 77.6 | | | Total Current | 69.4 | 70.2 |
| 20.9 | 24.4 | 16.3 | 12.7 | | | Fixed Assets (net) | 23.0 | 21.8 |
| 1.8 | 1.1 | 6.5 | 1.9 | | | Intangibles (net) | 2.3 | 1.8 |
| 9.4 | 7.8 | 3.1 | 7.9 | | | All Other Non-Current | 5.3 | 6.2 |
| 100.0 | 100.0 | 100.0 | 100.0 | | | Total | 100.0 | 100.0 |
| | | | | | | **LIABILITIES** | | |
| 22.2 | 19.6 | 14.5 | 15.7 | | | Notes Payable-Short Term | 15.9 | 15.4 |
| 6.9 | 1.3 | 1.2 | .6 | | | Cur. Mat.-L.T.D. | 3.4 | 2.5 |
| 16.9 | 15.3 | 8.1 | 14.6 | | | Trade Payables | 14.7 | 13.5 |
| .0 | .0 | .0 | .0 | | | Income Taxes Payable | .2 | .1 |
| 82.8 | 17.4 | 21.4 | 11.5 | | | All Other Current | 13.1 | 14.2 |
| 128.8 | 53.6 | 45.2 | 42.4 | | | Total Current | 47.3 | 45.7 |
| 17.6 | 14.0 | 14.7 | 5.7 | | | Long-Term Debt | 19.5 | 15.0 |
| .0 | .0 | .0 | .0 | | | Deferred Taxes | .1 | .1 |
| 14.1 | 11.6 | 2.4 | 5.6 | | | All Other Non-Current | 6.5 | 6.3 |
| -60.5 | 20.7 | 37.7 | 46.3 | | | Net Worth | 26.7 | 32.9 |
| 100.0 | 100.0 | 100.0 | 100.0 | | | Total Liabilities & Net Worth | 100.0 | 100.0 |
| | | | | | | **INCOME DATA** | | |
| 100.0 | 100.0 | 100.0 | 100.0 | | | Net Sales | 100.0 | 100.0 |
| 52.7 | 43.1 | 33.8 | 26.0 | | | Gross Profit | 31.4 | 29.7 |
| 51.5 | 40.5 | 30.2 | 24.0 | | | Operating Expenses | 28.7 | 29.2 |
| 1.2 | 2.6 | 3.6 | 2.0 | | | Operating Profit | 2.7 | .6 |
| .6 | 1.0 | .3 | .3 | | | All Other Expenses (net) | .4 | .9 |
| .6 | 1.6 | 3.2 | 1.7 | | | Profit Before Taxes | 2.3 | -.3 |
| | | | | | | **RATIOS** | | |
| 1.6 | 2.2 | 5.2 | 4.8 | | | Current | 3.2 | 3.3 |
| 1.0 | 1.5 | 2.4 | 1.9 | | | | 1.7 | 1.6 |
| .4 | .8 | 1.6 | 1.2 | | | | 1.0 | 1.1 |
| .9 | .9 | 2.1 | 1.2 | | | Quick | 1.5 | 1.5 |
| .3 | .3 | 1.3 | .7 | | | | .6 (100) | .6 |
| .0 | .2 | .6 | .4 | | | | .3 | .3 |
| 0 UND | 1 358.8 | 25 14.4 | 15 23.8 | | | Sales/Receivables | 13 27.2 | 10 35.7 |
| 6 63.4 | 16 22.5 | 31 11.8 | 41 8.9 | | | | 27 13.3 | 29 12.8 |
| 33 10.9 | 30 12.1 | 53 6.9 | 53 6.9 | | | | 41 8.8 | 40 9.2 |
| 0 UND | 48 7.6 | 68 5.4 | 41 8.8 | | | Cost of Sales/Inventory | 31 11.8 | 46 8.0 |
| 23 15.7 | 99 3.7 | 104 3.5 | 96 3.8 | | | | 65 5.6 | 81 4.5 |
| 72 5.1 | 215 1.7 | 182 2.0 | 192 1.9 | | | | 99 3.7 | 136 2.7 |
| 0 UND | 20 18.5 | 13 28.3 | 14 26.1 | | | Cost of Sales/Payables | 14 26.8 | 10 34.8 |
| 10 36.9 | 34 10.8 | 16 22.8 | 21 17.1 | | | | 22 16.9 | 21 17.3 |
| 31 11.9 | 56 6.5 | 34 10.6 | 63 5.8 | | | | 39 9.4 | 38 9.6 |
| 25.9 | 5.0 | 3.5 | 2.9 | | | Sales/Working Capital | 4.7 | 4.4 |
| -353.2 | 13.4 | 5.4 | 5.2 | | | | 9.7 | 9.2 |
| -8.3 | -16.5 | 7.8 | 23.3 | | | | 303.0 | 33.9 |
| | 8.1 | 20.2 | 99.8 | | | EBIT/Interest | 7.6 | 7.3 |
| | 1.1 | (19) 4.5 | 3.5 | | | | (86) 2.4 | (91) 1.9 |
| | | 1.1 | -3.0 | | | | .0 | -1.9 |
| | | | | | | Net Profit + Depr., Dep., Amort./Cur. Mat. L/T/D | 7.2 | 6.0 |
| | | | | | | | (21) 1.7 | (19) .7 |
| | | | | | | | -.3 | -8.0 |
| 2.1 | .2 | .1 | .1 | | | Fixed/Worth | .2 | .2 |
| -3.9 | .4 | .3 | .2 | | | | .5 | .5 |
| -.1 | -3.0 | .7 | .6 | | | | 2.2 | 3.0 |
| 13.8 | .7 | .5 | .3 | | | Debt/Worth | .8 | .6 |
| -11.1 | 2.9 | .7 | 1.7 | | | | 2.1 | 1.8 |
| -3.0 | -10.1 | 2.3 | 3.6 | | | | 8.8 | 9.0 |
| | 69.1 | 50.9 | | | | % Profit Before Taxes/Tangible Net Worth | 63.0 | 22.6 |
| (12) 3.3 | | (18) 12.2 | | | | | (81) 18.2 | (83) 7.0 |
| | -23.3 | .9 | | | | | -.1 | -11.7 |
| 24.8 | 19.4 | 16.3 | 11.8 | | | % Profit Before Taxes/Total Assets | 14.4 | 10.8 |
| 5.4 | .3 | 3.5 | 5.0 | | | | 4.5 | 1.9 |
| -8.5 | -10.4 | .0 | -1.1 | | | | -4.4 | -6.9 |
| 238.3 | 35.4 | 59.1 | 52.6 | | | Sales/Net Fixed Assets | 38.1 | 38.7 |
| 54.0 | 13.4 | 20.4 | 31.3 | | | | 12.7 | 15.5 |
| 25.9 | 8.7 | 4.7 | 7.1 | | | | 7.0 | 6.8 |
| 8.3 | 3.3 | 2.3 | 3.1 | | | Sales/Total Assets | 3.8 | 3.5 |
| 7.1 | 2.3 | 1.8 | 2.1 | | | | 2.7 | 2.6 |
| 4.4 | 1.7 | 1.4 | 1.5 | | | | 1.9 | 1.9 |
| | .6 | .5 | .3 | | | % Depr., Dep., Amort./Sales | .6 | .9 |
| (13) | 1.2 | (18) .9 | .7 | | | | (80) 1.4 | (84) 1.6 |
| | 1.6 | 1.8 | 1.3 | | | | 2.5 | 2.7 |
| | 1.6 | | | | | % Officers', Directors' Owners' Comp/Sales | 2.2 | 2.1 |
| (10) | 4.7 | | | | | | (43) 3.7 | (43) 3.6 |
| | 12.7 | | | | | | 6.7 | 5.4 |
| 14166M | 48382M | 183619M | 573185M | 980269M | 254015M | Net Sales ($) | 3846608M | 3604471M |
| 2360M | 18203M | 99249M | 245085M | 492565M | 100849M | Total Assets ($) | 1903848M | 1821421M |

M = $ thousand    MM = $ million
See Pages 9 through 22 for Explanation of Ratios and Data

## Comparative Historical Data / Current Data Sorted by Sales

| | | | Type of Statement | 0-1MM | 1-3MM | 3-5MM | 5-10MM | 10-25MM | 25MM & OVER |
|---|---|---|---|---|---|---|---|---|---|
| 9 | 7 | 6 | Unqualified | | | | 1 | | 5 |
| 11 | 16 | 10 | Reviewed | | | | 4 | 6 | 1 |
| 7 | 7 | 5 | Compiled | 1 | 3 | | | | 1 |
| 17 | 7 | 18 | Tax Returns | 5 | 3 | 9 | | | 1 |
| 31 | 33 | 27 | Other | 3 | 5 | 4 | 3 | 3 | 9 |
| 4/1/09-3/31/10 ALL | 4/1/10-3/31/11 ALL | 4/1/11-3/31/12 ALL | | 10 (4/1-9/30/11) | | | 56 (10/1/11-3/31/12) | | |
| 75 | 70 | 66 | **NUMBER OF STATEMENTS** | 9 | 11 | 13 | 8 | 9 | 16 |
| % | % | % | **ASSETS** | % | % | | | | % |
| 6.5 | 8.5 | 11.2 | Cash & Equivalents | 13.8 | 13.1 | | | | 9.8 |
| 17.9 | 18.9 | 19.8 | Trade Receivables (net) | 19.9 | 12.7 | | | | 28.0 |
| 39.5 | 36.3 | 39.4 | Inventory | 28.4 | 41.8 | | | | 36.9 |
| 3.4 | 3.4 | 1.7 | All Other Current | .6 | 2.0 | | | | 2.6 |
| 67.3 | 67.1 | 72.0 | Total Current | 62.8 | 69.6 | | | | 77.3 |
| 26.6 | 22.9 | 18.9 | Fixed Assets (net) | 28.7 | 22.4 | | | | 15.7 |
| 1.0 | 2.6 | 3.0 | Intangibles (net) | 1.3 | .9 | | | | 1.8 |
| 5.1 | 7.4 | 6.1 | All Other Non-Current | 7.2 | 7.1 | | | | 5.2 |
| 100.0 | 100.0 | 100.0 | Total | 100.0 | 100.0 | | | | 100.0 |
| | | | **LIABILITIES** | | | | | | |
| 14.7 | 13.6 | 17.8 | Notes Payable-Short Term | 18.4 | 13.1 | | | | 17.7 |
| 4.3 | 3.8 | 2.2 | Cur. Mat.-L.T.D. | 5.4 | 1.7 | | | | 2.0 |
| 15.0 | 13.4 | 12.7 | Trade Payables | 17.1 | 17.3 | | | | 13.9 |
| .0 | .1 | .0 | Income Taxes Payable | .0 | .0 | | | | .0 |
| 13.8 | 10.8 | 26.4 | All Other Current | 21.4 | 37.5 | | | | 9.3 |
| 47.8 | 41.6 | 59.1 | Total Current | 62.4 | 69.5 | | | | 42.9 |
| 17.3 | 15.3 | 11.8 | Long-Term Debt | 19.3 | 18.1 | | | | 3.6 |
| .1 | .1 | .0 | Deferred Taxes | .0 | .0 | | | | .1 |
| 8.9 | 9.1 | 7.4 | All Other Non-Current | 3.8 | 9.3 | | | | 5.8 |
| 25.9 | 33.9 | 21.6 | Net Worth | 14.4 | 3.1 | | | | 47.5 |
| 100.0 | 100.0 | 100.0 | Total Liabilities & Net Worth | 100.0 | 100.0 | | | | 100.0 |
| | | | **INCOME DATA** | | | | | | |
| 100.0 | 100.0 | 100.0 | Net Sales | 100.0 | 100.0 | | | | 100.0 |
| 31.7 | 32.3 | 36.8 | Gross Profit | 36.8 | 50.0 | | | | 24.7 |
| 33.1 | 31.2 | 34.6 | Operating Expenses | 38.0 | 45.1 | | | | 24.5 |
| -1.4 | 1.1 | 2.2 | Operating Profit | -1.3 | 4.9 | | | | .2 |
| .3 | .5 | .5 | All Other Expenses (net) | 1.3 | .5 | | | | .2 |
| -1.7 | .6 | 1.7 | Profit Before Taxes | -2.6 | 4.4 | | | | .0 |
| | | | **RATIOS** | | | | | | |
| 3.2 | 3.5 | 3.3 | Current | 2.3 | 2.2 | | | | 3.8 |
| 1.7 | 1.7 | 1.6 | | 1.4 | 1.6 | | | | 1.7 |
| 1.2 | 1.3 | 1.1 | | .6 | .6 | | | | 1.3 |
| 1.4 | 1.5 | 1.4 | Quick | 1.3 | .9 | | | | 1.4 |
| .6 (69) | .7 | .7 | | .8 | .4 | | | | .9 |
| .2 | .4 | .3 | | .3 | .2 | | | | .4 |
| 9  38.6 | 11  32.1 | 6  59.0 | Sales/Receivables | 4  83.9 | 1  415.4 | | | | 28  13.2 |
| 30  12.0 | 29  12.5 | 30  12.1 | | 26  13.9 | 15  24.6 | | | | 41  8.9 |
| 43  8.5 | 47  7.8 | 43  8.5 | | 34  10.8 | 29  12.4 | | | | 61  6.0 |
| 47  7.8 | 43  8.5 | 47  7.8 | Cost of Sales/Inventory | 4  91.9 | 24  15.3 | | | | 29  12.5 |
| 82  4.5 | 87  4.2 | 91  4.0 | | 47  7.8 | 111  3.3 | | | | 85  4.3 |
| 133  2.8 | 127  2.9 | 152  2.4 | | 159  2.3 | 174  2.1 | | | | 122  3.0 |
| 14  27.0 | 14  25.9 | 12  29.2 | Cost of Sales/Payables | 9  39.3 | 18  20.0 | | | | 14  26.2 |
| 26  14.1 | 25  14.6 | 23  16.1 | | 18  20.3 | 35  10.3 | | | | 23  15.8 |
| 39  9.4 | 40  9.2 | 39  9.4 | | 83  4.4 | 62  5.9 | | | | 39  9.4 |
| 4.4 | 4.2 | 3.8 | Sales/Working Capital | 3.8 | 6.2 | | | | 2.7 |
| 8.4 | 8.0 | 8.1 | | 30.2 | 17.0 | | | | 6.5 |
| 18.3 | 26.1 | 35.5 | | -14.2 | -12.5 | | | | 19.4 |
| 3.5 | 12.1 | 13.7 | EBIT/Interest | 3.6 | 14.3 | | | | 14.8 |
| (70) .4 | (66) 2.2 | (62) 2.6 | | (10) .9 | (12) 5.8 | | | | (15) 2.3 |
| -4.1 | -1.7 | .0 | | -6.9 | 1.0 | | | | -.7 |
| 1.9 | 2.9 | | Net Profit + Depr., Dep., Amort./Cur. Mat. L/T/D | | | | | | |
| (12) .8 | (13) 1.4 | | | | | | | | |
| -3.3 | -.2 | | | | | | | | |
| .2 | .2 | .2 | Fixed/Worth | .3 | .3 | | | | .2 |
| .7 | .5 | .4 | | 1.8 | .9 | | | | .3 |
| -43.6 | 1.6 | 2.9 | | -5.8 | -2.4 | | | | .7 |
| .7 | .6 | .6 | Debt/Worth | 2.4 | .7 | | | | .4 |
| 1.8 | 1.4 | 2.0 | | 2.9 | 2.6 | | | | 1.2 |
| -18.3 | 5.1 | 26.3 | | -7.4 | -8.1 | | | | 2.8 |
| 20.7 | 28.7 | 60.5 | % Profit Before Taxes/Tangible Net Worth | | | | | | 45.0 |
| (55) .1 | (58) 7.0 | (51) 6.7 | | | | | | | (15) -.4 |
| -19.8 | -7.0 | -4.6 | | | | | | | -8.8 |
| 5.0 | 12.0 | 16.2 | % Profit Before Taxes/Total Assets | 8.6 | 41.2 | | | | 12.8 |
| -1.7 | 3.0 | 2.3 | | .3 | 4.9 | | | | 2.1 |
| -11.1 | -4.2 | -2.9 | | -9.8 | -1.4 | | | | -3.4 |
| 30.6 | 32.9 | 54.1 | Sales/Net Fixed Assets | 57.2 | 36.9 | | | | 56.2 |
| 11.0 | 10.7 | 20.4 | | 11.9 | 18.0 | | | | 17.6 |
| 4.7 | 6.5 | 6.9 | | 2.1 | 10.6 | | | | 5.7 |
| 3.1 | 3.2 | 3.5 | Sales/Total Assets | 6.1 | 4.2 | | | | 2.7 |
| 2.2 | 2.2 | 2.2 | | 2.2 | 3.0 | | | | 2.0 |
| 1.5 | 1.7 | 1.6 | | 1.3 | 2.3 | | | | 1.6 |
| .8 | .8 | .5 | % Depr., Dep., Amort./Sales | | | | | | .3 |
| (65) 2.1 | (63) 1.6 | (55) 1.1 | | | | | | | .8 |
| 3.2 | 3.0 | 1.7 | | | | | | | 1.6 |
| 2.2 | 2.1 | 1.9 | % Officers', Directors' Owners' Comp/Sales | | | | | | |
| (32) 4.6 | (23) 3.9 | (26) 3.9 | | | | | | | |
| 8.3 | 5.5 | 9.1 | | | | | | | |
| 2819114M | 3168527M | 2053636M | Net Sales ($) | 6543M | 21998M | 51753M | 56533M | 144236M | 1772573M |
| 1511608M | 1680834M | 958311M | Total Assets ($) | 3256M | 14046M | 19615M | 33473M | 75978M | 811943M |

© RMA 2012

M = $ thousand   MM = $ million
See Pages 9 through 22 for Explanation of Ratios and Data

## Current Data Sorted by Assets                                                                 Comparative Historical Data

```
                                  1
                          2       2           4
                  2       2       1
                  2       2       2
          2       2       2       4           2                   2
    3     3       2                           26                  2
          3 (4/1-9/30/11)                     26 (10/1/11-3/31/12)
  0-500M  500M-2MM  2-10MM  10-50MM  50-100MM  100-250MM
    5       6         10      6                  2
```

| Type of Statement | | | | | | | | 4/1/07-3/31/08 ALL | 4/1/08-3/31/09 ALL |
|---|---|---|---|---|---|---|---|---|---|
| Unqualified | | | | | | | | 5 | 4 |
| Reviewed | | | | | | | | 5 | 3 |
| Compiled | | | | | | | | 4 | 2 |
| Tax Returns | | | | | | | | 3 | 5 |
| Other | | | | | | | | 5 | 9 |
| | 0-500M | 500M-2MM | 2-10MM | 10-50MM | 50-100MM | 100-250MM | NUMBER OF STATEMENTS | 22 | 23 |
| | 5 | 6 | 10 | 6 | | 2 | | | |
| | % | % | % | % | % | % | ASSETS | % | % |
| | | | 3.4 | | | | Cash & Equivalents | 8.6 | 5.7 |
| | | | 21.0 | | | | Trade Receivables (net) | 22.0 | 21.7 |
| | | | 29.9 | | | | Inventory | 34.2 | 33.2 |
| | | | 1.5 | | | | All Other Current | 3.7 | 3.2 |
| | | | 55.9 | | | | Total Current | 68.4 | 63.7 |
| | | | 24.6 | DATA | NOT | AVAILABLE | Fixed Assets (net) | 17.5 | 20.0 |
| | | | 7.5 | | | | Intangibles (net) | 6.5 | 5.5 |
| | | | 11.9 | | | | All Other Non-Current | 7.5 | 10.8 |
| | | | 100.0 | | | | Total | 100.0 | 100.0 |
| | | | | | | | LIABILITIES | | |
| | | | 10.2 | | | | Notes Payable-Short Term | 8.7 | 8.5 |
| | | | .9 | | | | Cur. Mat.-L.T.D. | 2.9 | 3.7 |
| | | | 11.7 | | | | Trade Payables | 19.2 | 14.5 |
| | | | .0 | | | | Income Taxes Payable | .0 | .0 |
| | | | 15.6 | | | | All Other Current | 14.8 | 16.5 |
| | | | 38.3 | | | | Total Current | 45.6 | 43.3 |
| | | | 9.5 | | | | Long-Term Debt | 17.4 | 16.2 |
| | | | .0 | | | | Deferred Taxes | .3 | .8 |
| | | | 3.1 | | | | All Other Non-Current | 8.9 | 2.4 |
| | | | 49.1 | | | | Net Worth | 27.8 | 37.4 |
| | | | 100.0 | | | | Total Liabilities & Net Worth | 100.0 | 100.0 |
| | | | | | | | INCOME DATA | | |
| | | | 100.0 | | | | Net Sales | 100.0 | 100.0 |
| | | | 37.1 | | | | Gross Profit | 30.9 | 33.6 |
| | | | 34.0 | | | | Operating Expenses | 27.8 | 32.6 |
| | | | 3.1 | | | | Operating Profit | 3.2 | 1.0 |
| | | | .8 | | | | All Other Expenses (net) | 1.4 | 1.6 |
| | | | 2.3 | | | | Profit Before Taxes | 1.8 | -.6 |
| | | | | | | | RATIOS | | |
| | | | 2.1 | | | | | 2.4 | 2.9 |
| | | | 1.6 | | | | Current | 1.7 | 1.4 |
| | | | 1.0 | | | | | 1.1 | 1.0 |
| | | | 1.1 | | | | | 1.2 | .9 |
| | | | .7 | | | | Quick | .7 | .7 |
| | | | .5 | | | | | .3 | .2 |
| | | 26 | 13.8 | | | | | 19 19.2 | 9 40.4 |
| | | 39 | 9.4 | | | | Sales/Receivables | 37 9.9 | 30 12.1 |
| | | 46 | 7.9 | | | | | 64 5.7 | 46 7.9 |
| | | 45 | 8.1 | | | | | 37 10.0 | 38 9.6 |
| | | 87 | 4.2 | | | | Cost of Sales/Inventory | 83 4.4 | 57 6.4 |
| | | 140 | 2.6 | | | | | 165 2.2 | 130 2.8 |
| | | 19 | 19.7 | | | | | 25 14.7 | 12 30.3 |
| | | 29 | 12.5 | | | | Cost of Sales/Payables | 40 9.1 | 26 13.9 |
| | | 42 | 8.7 | | | | | 69 5.3 | 56 6.5 |
| | | | 5.6 | | | | | 4.0 | 5.1 |
| | | | 11.8 | | | | Sales/Working Capital | 8.7 | 12.4 |
| | | | NM | | | | | 200.4 | -170.1 |
| | | | 51.3 | | | | | 11.1 | 6.3 |
| | | | 16.6 | | | | EBIT/Interest | (21) 2.2 | (21) 1.9 |
| | | | 1.3 | | | | | .4 | -2.3 |
| | | | | | | | Net Profit + Depr., Dep., Amort./Cur. Mat. L/T/D | | |
| | | | .2 | | | | | .2 | .2 |
| | | | .5 | | | | Fixed/Worth | .6 | .4 |
| | | | 1.5 | | | | | -3.0 | .9 |
| | | | .6 | | | | | .9 | .6 |
| | | | 1.1 | | | | Debt/Worth | 1.9 | 2.3 |
| | | | 2.7 | | | | | -13.3 | 4.8 |
| | | | | | | | % Profit Before Taxes/Tangible Net Worth | 41.2 | 30.4 |
| | | | | | | | | (15) 13.2 | (21) 8.0 |
| | | | | | | | | 5.2 | -11.5 |
| | | | 25.1 | | | | | 11.1 | 7.4 |
| | | | 13.4 | | | | % Profit Before Taxes/Total Assets | 2.9 | .4 |
| | | | -1.5 | | | | | -3.7 | -10.2 |
| | | | 29.9 | | | | | 41.5 | 28.8 |
| | | | 13.9 | | | | Sales/Net Fixed Assets | 14.8 | 11.5 |
| | | | 4.8 | | | | | 6.0 | 7.0 |
| | | | 3.4 | | | | | 3.5 | 3.1 |
| | | | 2.2 | | | | Sales/Total Assets | 1.9 | 2.1 |
| | | | .8 | | | | | 1.2 | 1.3 |
| | | | | | | | | .5 | .9 |
| | | | | | | | % Depr., Dep., Amort./Sales | (18) 1.2 | (18) 1.4 |
| | | | | | | | | 1.8 | 3.2 |
| | | | | | | | % Officers', Directors', Owners' Comp/Sales | | |
| 7116M | 17074M | 129351M | 318868M | | 270826M | Net Sales ($) | 776208M | 1106616M |
| 1199M | 5921M | 55193M | 170992M | | 223307M | Total Assets ($) | 555784M | 632102M |

M = $ thousand   MM = $ million
See Pages 9 through 22 for Explanation of Ratios and Data

## Comparative Historical Data

## Current Data Sorted by Sales

| | | | Type of Statement | 0-1MM | 1-3MM | 3-5MM | 5-10MM | 10-25MM | 25MM & OVER |
|---|---|---|---|---|---|---|---|---|---|
| | | | Unqualified | | | | | 1 | |
| 2 | 2 | 1 | Reviewed | | | | 1 | 3 | 2 |
| 4 | 3 | 6 | Compiled | | 1 | | 1 | 1 | |
| 1 | 2 | 3 | Tax Returns | 1 | 2 | 2 | | 1 | |
| | 3 | 6 | Other | 1 | 4 | 2 | | 2 | 4 |
| 11 | 9 | 13 | | 1 | 2 | 2 | 1 | 1 | |
| 4/1/09-3/31/10 ALL | 4/1/10-3/31/11 ALL | 4/1/11-3/31/12 ALL | | 1 | 4 | 2 | | 2 | 4 |
| | | | | | | 3 (4/1-9/30/11) | | 26 (10/1/11-3/31/12) | |
| 18 | 19 | 29 | NUMBER OF STATEMENTS | 2 | 7 | 4 | 2 | 8 | 6 |
| % | % | % | ASSETS | % | % | % | % | % | % |
| 9.6 | 6.6 | 7.2 | Cash & Equivalents | | | | | | |
| 15.6 | 28.7 | 23.1 | Trade Receivables (net) | | | | | | |
| 31.8 | 23.4 | 28.9 | Inventory | | | | | | |
| 3.1 | 3.2 | .8 | All Other Current | | | | | | |
| 60.1 | 62.0 | 60.0 | Total Current | | | | | | |
| 24.0 | 14.9 | 24.1 | Fixed Assets (net) | | | | | | |
| 6.1 | 8.7 | 6.9 | Intangibles (net) | | | | | | |
| 9.7 | 14.5 | 9.0 | All Other Non-Current | | | | | | |
| 100.0 | 100.0 | 100.0 | Total | | | | | | |
| | | | LIABILITIES | | | | | | |
| 10.0 | 11.1 | 8.3 | Notes Payable-Short Term | | | | | | |
| 1.3 | 1.5 | 1.2 | Cur. Mat.-L.T.D. | | | | | | |
| 15.2 | 23.9 | 16.9 | Trade Payables | | | | | | |
| .0 | .0 | .0 | Income Taxes Payable | | | | | | |
| 16.2 | 10.0 | 17.5 | All Other Current | | | | | | |
| 42.7 | 46.6 | 44.0 | Total Current | | | | | | |
| 22.7 | 23.0 | 20.1 | Long-Term Debt | | | | | | |
| .6 | .3 | .0 | Deferred Taxes | | | | | | |
| 12.6 | 7.3 | 15.8 | All Other Non-Current | | | | | | |
| 21.1 | 22.8 | 20.1 | Net Worth | | | | | | |
| 100.0 | 100.0 | 100.0 | Total Liabilties & Net Worth | | | | | | |
| | | | INCOME DATA | | | | | | |
| 100.0 | 100.0 | 100.0 | Net Sales | | | | | | |
| 35.5 | 32.6 | 35.6 | Gross Profit | | | | | | |
| 28.6 | 30.0 | 33.4 | Operating Expenses | | | | | | |
| 6.9 | 2.6 | 2.3 | Operating Profit | | | | | | |
| .4 | 1.3 | .9 | All Other Expenses (net) | | | | | | |
| 6.5 | 1.2 | 1.4 | Profit Before Taxes | | | | | | |
| | | | RATIOS | | | | | | |
| 2.0 | 2.0 | 2.4 | Current | | | | | | |
| 1.6 | 1.5 | 1.4 | | | | | | | |
| .9 | 1.1 | 1.0 | | | | | | | |
| 1.1 | 1.2 | 1.2 | Quick | | | | | | |
| .7 | .8 | .6 | | | | | | | |
| .2 | .6 | .5 | | | | | | | |
| 3  136.1 | 32  11.2 | 24  15.5 | Sales/Receivables | | | | | | |
| 24  15.4 | 46  7.9 | 41  8.8 | | | | | | | |
| 43  8.5 | 69  5.3 | 49  7.4 | | | | | | | |
| 23  16.0 | 39  9.3 | 32  11.5 | Cost of Sales/Inventory | | | | | | |
| 78  4.7 | 51  7.1 | 83  4.4 | | | | | | | |
| 135  2.7 | 103  3.5 | 118  3.1 | | | | | | | |
| 15  24.5 | 30  12.0 | 18  19.9 | Cost of Sales/Payables | | | | | | |
| 25  14.6 | 44  8.3 | 28  13.0 | | | | | | | |
| 53  6.9 | 69  5.3 | 44  8.3 | | | | | | | |
| 7.3 | 5.0 | 5.7 | Sales/Working Capital | | | | | | |
| 11.1 | 10.6 | 11.8 | | | | | | | |
| NM | 62.9 | 69.3 | | | | | | | |
| 22.2 | 12.3 | 21.9 | EBIT/Interest | | | | | | |
| (15) 6.4 | (16) 4.4 | (23) 2.3 | | | | | | | |
| 1.1 | -3.1 | -1.5 | | | | | | | |
| | | | Net Profit + Depr., Dep., Amort./Cur. Mat. L/T/D | | | | | | |
| .4 | .1 | .2 | Fixed/Worth | | | | | | |
| .6 | .4 | .9 | | | | | | | |
| 1.6 | -1.1 | -2.0 | | | | | | | |
| .7 | .9 | 1.0 | Debt/Worth | | | | | | |
| 2.0 | 2.2 | 2.3 | | | | | | | |
| 5.7 | -3.0 | -4.6 | | | | | | | |
| 68.8 | 34.7 | 51.7 | % Profit Before Taxes/Tangible Net Worth | | | | | | |
| (15) 21.9 | (12) 17.9 | (19) 31.1 | | | | | | | |
| 5.1 | 10.9 | 9.1 | | | | | | | |
| 22.0 | 9.8 | 21.9 | % Profit Before Taxes/Total Assets | | | | | | |
| 10.5 | 4.6 | 4.1 | | | | | | | |
| 1.4 | -7.8 | -5.3 | | | | | | | |
| 43.4 | 50.2 | 46.5 | Sales/Net Fixed Assets | | | | | | |
| 12.4 | 12.6 | 13.4 | | | | | | | |
| 5.1 | 8.0 | 6.2 | | | | | | | |
| 3.4 | 3.1 | 3.7 | Sales/Total Assets | | | | | | |
| 2.3 | 1.7 | 2.4 | | | | | | | |
| 1.3 | 1.1 | 1.4 | | | | | | | |
| .6 | .5 | .8 | % Depr., Dep., Amort./Sales | | | | | | |
| (10) 2.5 | (14) 1.5 | (21) 1.8 | | | | | | | |
| 4.5 | 3.3 | 2.8 | | | | | | | |
| | | 2.2 | % Officers', Directors' Owners' Comp/Sales | | | | | | |
| | | (11) 5.1 | | | | | | | |
| | | 14.4 | | | | | | | |
| 891961M | 716645M | 743235M | Net Sales ($) | 1066M | 11674M | 13443M | 14948M | 144931M | 557173M |
| 610275M | 529021M | 456612M | Total Assets ($) | 264M | 9747M | 6314M | 5014M | 75410M | 359863M |

M = $ thousand    MM = $ million
See Pages 9 through 22 for Explanation of Ratios and Data

**Current Data Sorted by Assets**          **Comparative Historical Data**

| 0-500M | 500M-2MM | 2-10MM | 10-50MM | 50-100MM | 100-250MM | | 4/1/07-3/31/08 ALL | 4/1/08-3/31/09 ALL |
|---|---|---|---|---|---|---|---|---|
| | 1 | 4 | 8 | 2 | 4 | Type of Statement | | |
| | | 7 | 5 | 1 | | Unqualified | 23 | 22 |
| 1 | 1 | 6 | 1 | | | Reviewed | 29 | 28 |
| 1 | | 7 | 3 | | | Compiled | 18 | 20 |
| 2 | 4 | 14 | 14 | 7 | | Tax Returns | 14 | 11 |
| | | | | | | Other | 61 | 35 |
| | 19 (4/1-9/30/11) | | 74 (10/1/11-3/31/12) | | | | | |
| 4 | 13 | 34 | 28 | 10 | 4 | **NUMBER OF STATEMENTS** | 145 | 116 |
| % | % | % | % | % | % | **ASSETS** | % | % |
| | 18.0 | 9.1 | 6.7 | 5.1 | | Cash & Equivalents | 6.3 | 7.5 |
| | 26.5 | 26.9 | 23.0 | 18.1 | | Trade Receivables (net) | 30.4 | 28.3 |
| | 22.1 | 31.4 | 29.3 | 13.1 | | Inventory | 25.7 | 25.4 |
| | 3.3 | 2.4 | 3.5 | 2.6 | | All Other Current | 3.3 | 2.8 |
| | 69.9 | 69.8 | 62.5 | 38.8 | | Total Current | 65.7 | 64.1 |
| | 17.3 | 19.7 | 22.7 | 15.5 | | Fixed Assets (net) | 22.6 | 25.7 |
| | 7.1 | 6.0 | 12.2 | 40.4 | | Intangibles (net) | 5.6 | 5.2 |
| | 5.6 | 4.4 | 2.6 | 5.2 | | All Other Non-Current | 6.1 | 5.1 |
| | 100.0 | 100.0 | 100.0 | 100.0 | | Total | 100.0 | 100.0 |
| | | | | | | **LIABILITIES** | | |
| | 7.7 | 8.4 | 12.9 | 14.8 | | Notes Payable-Short Term | 13.6 | 11.1 |
| | 10.0 | 3.6 | 2.3 | 6.0 | | Cur. Mat.-L.T.D. | 2.5 | 3.0 |
| | 16.1 | 16.1 | 11.5 | 6.4 | | Trade Payables | 15.4 | 14.3 |
| | .1 | .1 | .0 | 2.2 | | Income Taxes Payable | .1 | .1 |
| | 15.8 | 14.0 | 11.4 | 13.5 | | All Other Current | 14.9 | 15.4 |
| | 49.6 | 42.1 | 38.1 | 42.8 | | Total Current | 46.5 | 43.9 |
| | 19.3 | 12.0 | 12.4 | 10.4 | | Long-Term Debt | 15.4 | 17.4 |
| | .0 | .4 | .1 | .7 | | Deferred Taxes | .3 | .5 |
| | 3.5 | 9.0 | 3.2 | 9.2 | | All Other Non-Current | 5.4 | 4.9 |
| | 27.7 | 36.4 | 46.3 | 36.9 | | Net Worth | 32.4 | 33.4 |
| | 100.0 | 100.0 | 100.0 | 100.0 | | Total Liabilities & Net Worth | 100.0 | 100.0 |
| | | | | | | **INCOME DATA** | | |
| | 100.0 | 100.0 | 100.0 | 100.0 | | Net Sales | 100.0 | 100.0 |
| | 37.3 | 30.3 | 28.9 | 31.2 | | Gross Profit | 31.2 | 30.2 |
| | 32.8 | 27.2 | 25.7 | 28.4 | | Operating Expenses | 25.9 | 25.1 |
| | 4.4 | 3.1 | 3.2 | 2.8 | | Operating Profit | 5.3 | 5.1 |
| | 1.0 | .8 | .6 | 4.9 | | All Other Expenses (net) | 1.3 | 1.2 |
| | 3.4 | 2.4 | 2.6 | -2.1 | | Profit Before Taxes | 3.9 | 3.9 |
| | | | | | | **RATIOS** | | |
| | 2.1 | 3.2 | 2.2 | 2.8 | | | 2.1 | 2.6 |
| | 1.7 | 1.8 | 1.7 | 1.4 | | Current | 1.5 | 1.6 |
| | .9 | 1.2 | 1.2 | .7 | | | 1.1 | 1.2 |
| | 1.4 | 1.4 | 1.1 | 1.7 | | | 1.3 | 1.6 |
| | 1.1 | .9 | .8 | .6 | | Quick | .8 | .8 |
| | .5 | .5 | .5 | .4 | | | .5 | .5 |
| | 2 150.0 | 24 15.2 | 27 13.4 | 31 11.6 | | | 27 13.3 | 27 13.6 |
| | 40 9.1 | 40 9.2 | 38 9.7 | 48 7.6 | | Sales/Receivables | 41 8.8 | 38 9.6 |
| | 65 5.6 | 56 6.5 | 51 7.2 | 61 6.0 | | | 57 6.4 | 53 6.9 |
| | 12 30.0 | 36 10.1 | 31 11.9 | 26 13.9 | | | 33 11.2 | 29 12.5 |
| | 58 6.3 | 63 5.8 | 63 5.8 | 47 7.8 | | Cost of Sales/Inventory | 49 7.5 | 50 7.3 |
| | 74 4.9 | 96 3.8 | 140 2.6 | 63 5.8 | | | 86 4.3 | 92 4.0 |
| | 18 20.0 | 13 28.7 | 15 24.7 | 15 24.1 | | | 16 23.4 | 14 25.2 |
| | 33 11.1 | 27 13.6 | 26 14.0 | 24 15.4 | | Cost of Sales/Payables | 26 13.9 | 25 14.8 |
| | 58 6.3 | 56 6.5 | 41 8.8 | 38 9.7 | | | 43 8.5 | 39 9.4 |
| | 5.1 | 5.1 | 5.4 | 4.5 | | | 6.4 | 6.2 |
| | 8.0 | 8.7 | 8.5 | 504.3 | | Sales/Working Capital | 12.4 | 11.2 |
| | NM | 27.8 | 20.2 | -7.6 | | | 81.5 | 40.0 |
| | 30.1 | 14.7 | 17.4 | | | | 8.7 | 17.1 |
| | (11) 1.3 | (31) 4.9 | (25) 3.6 | | | EBIT/Interest | (133) 3.8 | (109) 4.7 |
| | -2.2 | -.6 | .1 | | | | 1.6 | 1.4 |
| | | | | | | | 8.4 | 12.9 |
| | | | | | | Net Profit + Depr., Dep., Amort./Cur. Mat. L/T/D | (32) 3.3 | (33) 3.4 |
| | | | | | | | 1.4 | 1.0 |
| | .1 | .2 | .3 | .5 | | | .3 | .3 |
| | .3 | .5 | .4 | 4.1 | | Fixed/Worth | .6 | .8 |
| | NM | 2.4 | 1.9 | -.3 | | | 4.1 | 5.0 |
| | .9 | .6 | .6 | 1.8 | | | .9 | .8 |
| | 2.5 | 1.6 | 1.3 | 10.0 | | Debt/Worth | 2.5 | 2.2 |
| | NM | 11.3 | 4.0 | -3.2 | | | 10.4 | 13.0 |
| | 68.6 | 68.6 | 47.7 | | | | 53.3 | 51.6 |
| | (10) 19.1 | (29) 30.3 | (24) 13.2 | | | % Profit Before Taxes/Tangible Net Worth | (121) 27.9 | (94) 22.5 |
| | -21.2 | 11.2 | 2.7 | | | | 10.2 | 6.5 |
| | 27.5 | 18.4 | 9.8 | 7.7 | | | 16.4 | 17.9 |
| | 1.3 | 7.2 | 5.3 | -1.3 | | % Profit Before Taxes/Total Assets | 9.3 | 7.0 |
| | -15.6 | -.5 | -.2 | -7.3 | | | 2.0 | 1.1 |
| | 37.9 | 80.0 | 24.6 | 20.9 | | | 35.8 | 29.2 |
| | 18.5 | 16.2 | 9.2 | 9.8 | | Sales/Net Fixed Assets | 13.0 | 9.9 |
| | 11.6 | 7.8 | 5.9 | 6.2 | | | 6.5 | 6.4 |
| | 2.7 | 3.4 | 2.8 | 1.8 | | | 3.3 | 3.2 |
| | 2.4 | 2.5 | 1.8 | 1.2 | | Sales/Total Assets | 2.5 | 2.4 |
| | 1.7 | 1.7 | 1.5 | .9 | | | 1.8 | 1.8 |
| | | .5 | 1.2 | | | | .7 | .8 |
| | | (29) 1.1 | (24) 1.6 | | | % Depr., Dep., Amort./Sales | (125) 1.6 | (102) 1.9 |
| | | 2.4 | 2.0 | | | | 2.5 | 2.7 |
| | | .7 | | | | | 1.9 | 1.7 |
| | | (10) 2.3 | | | | % Officers', Directors' Owners' Comp/Sales | (45) 4.0 | (35) 2.9 |
| | | 7.2 | | | | | 6.3 | 5.4 |
| 2388M | 40362M | 544006M | 1116105M | 883913M | 885207M | Net Sales ($) | 4861713M | 3786059M |
| 902M | 16558M | 196002M | 571720M | 694414M | 514632M | Total Assets ($) | 2401610M | 1792355M |

© RMA 2012

M = $ thousand     MM = $ million
See Pages 9 through 22 for Explanation of Ratios and Data

## Comparative Historical Data | Current Data Sorted by Sales

| | 4/1/09-3/31/10 ALL | 4/1/10-3/31/11 ALL | 4/1/11-3/31/12 ALL | Type of Statement | 0-1MM | 1-3MM | 3-5MM | 5-10MM | 10-25MM | 25MM & OVER |
|---|---|---|---|---|---|---|---|---|---|---|
| | 16 | 12 | 19 | Unqualified | | | | 1 | 3 | 15 |
| | 24 | 19 | 13 | Reviewed | | | | 2 | 6 | 5 |
| | 12 | 10 | 9 | Compiled | | 2 | 3 | 1 | 1 | 2 |
| | 6 | 9 | 11 | Tax Returns | 2 | 3 | 1 | 4 | 1 | |
| | 56 | 42 | 41 | Other | 3 | 3 | 3 | | 14 | 18 |
| | | | | | 19 (4/1-9/30/11) | | | 74 (10/1/11-3/31/12) | | |
| **NUMBER OF STATEMENTS** | 114 | 92 | 93 | | 5 | 8 | 7 | 8 | 25 | 40 |
| **ASSETS** | % | % | % | | % | % | % | % | % | % |
| Cash & Equivalents | 9.0 | 7.8 | 9.1 | | | | | | 8.6 | 7.6 |
| Trade Receivables (net) | 24.6 | 27.2 | 24.2 | | | | | | 23.0 | 24.9 |
| Inventory | 27.1 | 28.2 | 26.5 | | | | | | 34.9 | 23.5 |
| All Other Current | 2.5 | 2.4 | 2.9 | | | | | | 1.4 | 3.4 |
| Total Current | 63.2 | 65.6 | 62.7 | | | | | | 67.9 | 59.5 |
| Fixed Assets (net) | 24.1 | 22.8 | 20.1 | | | | | | 21.6 | 20.2 |
| Intangibles (net) | 6.2 | 5.3 | 11.5 | | | | | | 7.5 | 15.8 |
| All Other Non-Current | 6.5 | 6.2 | 5.8 | | | | | | 3.0 | 4.4 |
| Total | 100.0 | 100.0 | 100.0 | | | | | | 100.0 | 100.0 |
| **LIABILITIES** | | | | | | | | | | |
| Notes Payable-Short Term | 12.1 | 10.5 | 11.6 | | | | | | 11.2 | 11.1 |
| Cur. Mat.-L.T.D. | 3.1 | 5.2 | 4.5 | | | | | | 3.1 | 3.3 |
| Trade Payables | 13.4 | 13.2 | 13.6 | | | | | | 14.1 | 11.7 |
| Income Taxes Payable | .2 | .1 | .3 | | | | | | .1 | .6 |
| All Other Current | 11.6 | 12.2 | 15.6 | | | | | | 12.8 | 12.6 |
| Total Current | 40.5 | 41.2 | 45.6 | | | | | | 41.2 | 39.3 |
| Long-Term Debt | 18.1 | 17.5 | 14.8 | | | | | | 10.1 | 12.2 |
| Deferred Taxes | .5 | .2 | .3 | | | | | | .5 | .4 |
| All Other Non-Current | 7.0 | 6.0 | 7.1 | | | | | | 4.6 | 7.2 |
| Net Worth | 33.9 | 35.1 | 32.2 | | | | | | 43.6 | 40.9 |
| Total Liabilities & Net Worth | 100.0 | 100.0 | 100.0 | | | | | | 100.0 | 100.0 |
| **INCOME DATA** | | | | | | | | | | |
| Net Sales | 100.0 | 100.0 | 100.0 | | | | | | 100.0 | 100.0 |
| Gross Profit | 30.4 | 29.8 | 31.5 | | | | | | 34.0 | 26.5 |
| Operating Expenses | 27.8 | 26.7 | 28.2 | | | | | | 29.9 | 23.3 |
| Operating Profit | 2.6 | 3.1 | 3.4 | | | | | | 4.1 | 3.2 |
| All Other Expenses (net) | 1.4 | .7 | 1.2 | | | | | | .4 | 1.7 |
| Profit Before Taxes | 1.1 | 2.4 | 2.1 | | | | | | 3.7 | 1.5 |
| **RATIOS** | | | | | | | | | | |
| Current | 2.7 | 2.4 | 2.2 | | | | | | 2.6 | 2.2 |
| | 1.7 | 1.8 | 1.8 | | | | | | 1.7 | 1.8 |
| | 1.1 | 1.2 | 1.1 | | | | | | 1.2 | 1.2 |
| Quick | 1.6 | 1.3 | 1.3 | | | | | | 1.3 | 1.5 |
| | .8 | .9 | .9 | | | | | | .9 | .9 |
| | .5 | .5 | .4 | | | | | | .4 | .5 |
| Sales/Receivables | 25  14.4 | 26  13.8 | 26  13.8 | | | | | | 21  17.0 | 33  11.1 |
| | 37  9.8 | 41  8.8 | 41  9.0 | | | | | | 32  11.4 | 42  8.7 |
| | 49  7.4 | 56  6.5 | 54  6.8 | | | | | | 46  8.0 | 53  6.9 |
| Cost of Sales/Inventory | 31  11.7 | 32  11.5 | 31  11.6 | | | | | | 42  8.7 | 28  13.1 |
| | 49  7.4 | 57  6.4 | 60  6.1 | | | | | | 69  5.3 | 47  7.8 |
| | 102  3.6 | 92  4.0 | 99  3.7 | | | | | | 130  2.8 | 85  4.3 |
| Cost of Sales/Payables | 14  26.9 | 14  26.0 | 16  22.6 | | | | | | 13  27.1 | 17  21.0 |
| | 24  15.0 | 25  14.5 | 28  13.2 | | | | | | 22  16.8 | 24  15.0 |
| | 40  9.1 | 40  9.2 | 48  7.6 | | | | | | 56  6.5 | 37  9.9 |
| Sales/Working Capital | 4.6 | | 5.2 | | | | | | 5.5 | 5.6 |
| | 10.0 | 10.2 | 8.8 | | | | | | 8.3 | 10.6 |
| | 59.2 | 22.7 | 39.6 | | | | | | 17.7 | 23.7 |
| EBIT/Interest | 12.6 | 11.4 | 15.0 | | | | | | 27.1 | 14.9 |
| | (104) 2.7 | (81) 4.5 | (81) 3.6 | | | | | | 6.9 | (34) 2.7 |
| | -.2 | .2 | -.6 | | | | | | 2.4 | -.5 |
| Net Profit + Depr., Dep., Amort./Cur. Mat. L/T/D | 11.1 | 8.9 | 4.1 | | | | | | | 5.0 |
| | (36) 1.6 | (19) 2.9 | (21) 1.5 | | | | | | | (12) 1.4 |
| | .8 | .7 | .0 | | | | | | | -1.2 |
| Fixed/Worth | .3 | .3 | .2 | | | | | | .3 | .3 |
| | .6 | .5 | .6 | | | | | | .4 | .8 |
| | 4.9 | 1.7 | 4.2 | | | | | | 1.9 | 5.9 |
| Debt/Worth | .8 | .8 | .8 | | | | | | .5 | .7 |
| | 2.1 | 1.6 | 2.0 | | | | | | 1.0 | 2.1 |
| | 12.0 | 5.0 | 16.3 | | | | | | 3.3 | 23.0 |
| % Profit Before Taxes/Tangible Net Worth | 48.4 | 46.2 | 62.2 | | | | | | 48.1 | 67.0 |
| | (93) 15.5 | (82) 18.0 | (74) 20.8 | | | | | (22) | 22.9 | (32) 18.9 |
| | -2.5 | -.2 | 5.3 | | | | | | 10.6 | 4.8 |
| % Profit Before Taxes/Total Assets | 12.7 | 12.8 | 15.2 | | | | | | 17.4 | 9.8 |
| | 4.1 | 7.2 | 5.6 | | | | | | 7.3 | 4.6 |
| | -2.7 | -2.2 | -2.8 | | | | | | 2.3 | -3.0 |
| Sales/Net Fixed Assets | 25.8 | 21.9 | 29.5 | | | | | | 24.4 | 26.9 |
| | 11.3 | 12.4 | 15.1 | | | | | | 10.5 | 10.1 |
| | 6.1 | 6.6 | 7.5 | | | | | | 8.0 | 6.5 |
| Sales/Total Assets | 2.9 | 2.9 | 3.1 | | | | | | 3.1 | 3.1 |
| | 2.2 | 2.1 | 2.1 | | | | | | 2.2 | 1.9 |
| | 1.7 | 1.7 | 1.5 | | | | | | 1.6 | 1.4 |
| % Depr., Dep., Amort./Sales | .8 | 1.2 | .7 | | | | | | .7 | 1.0 |
| | (94) 1.9 | (73) 1.7 | (75) 1.6 | | | | | (22) | 1.2 | (33) 1.7 |
| | 3.0 | 2.7 | 2.8 | | | | | | 1.7 | 3.2 |
| % Officers', Directors', Owners' Comp/Sales | 1.7 | 1.8 | 1.5 | | | | | | | |
| | (34) 3.8 | (35) 3.2 | (24) 3.3 | | | | | | | |
| | 8.2 | 5.7 | 5.9 | | | | | | | |
| Net Sales ($) | 4773864M | 2899595M | 3471981M | | 2605M | 16980M | 25859M | 61501M | 441371M | 2923665M |
| Total Assets ($) | 2521370M | 1521207M | 1994228M | | 5107M | 15668M | 10661M | 32287M | 207906M | 1722599M |

M = $ thousand    MM = $ million
See Pages 9 through 22 for Explanation of Ratios and Data

## Current Data Sorted by Assets | Comparative Historical Data

| 0-500M | 500M-2MM | 2-10MM | 10-50MM | 50-100MM | 100-250MM | Type of Statement | 4/1/07-3/31/08 ALL | 4/1/08-3/31/09 ALL |
|---|---|---|---|---|---|---|---|---|
|  | 1 | 2 | 3 | 1 | 1 | Unqualified | 6 | 5 |
|  | 2 | 8 | 5 |  |  | Reviewed | 14 | 14 |
| 1 | 5 | 5 | 1 |  |  | Compiled | 8 | 8 |
| 3 | 4 | 2 |  |  |  | Tax Returns | 10 | 5 |
| 2 | 5 | 11 | 3 |  | 1 | Other | 15 | 16 |
|  | 18 (4/1-9/30/11) | | 48 (10/1/11-3/31/12) | | | | | |
| 6 | 17 | 28 | 12 | 1 | 2 | NUMBER OF STATEMENTS | 53 | 48 |
| % | % | % | % | % | % | ASSETS | % | % |
|  | 9.1 | 9.0 | 14.2 |  |  | Cash & Equivalents | 7.5 | 6.6 |
|  | 39.2 | 35.7 | 19.7 |  |  | Trade Receivables (net) | 36.9 | 35.0 |
|  | 23.4 | 20.7 | 24.0 |  |  | Inventory | 19.0 | 19.4 |
|  | 3.5 | 3.3 | 1.8 |  |  | All Other Current | 3.9 | 6.6 |
|  | 75.3 | 68.7 | 59.8 |  |  | Total Current | 67.3 | 67.6 |
|  | 21.1 | 26.3 | 32.3 |  |  | Fixed Assets (net) | 25.1 | 27.3 |
|  | .6 | 1.0 | 4.3 |  |  | Intangibles (net) | 1.8 | 1.0 |
|  | 3.0 | 4.0 | 3.5 |  |  | All Other Non-Current | 5.9 | 4.1 |
|  | 100.0 | 100.0 | 100.0 |  |  | Total | 100.0 | 100.0 |
|  |  |  |  |  |  | LIABILITIES |  |  |
|  | 19.8 | 17.5 | 4.9 |  |  | Notes Payable-Short Term | 9.5 | 8.5 |
|  | 4.2 | 4.4 | 3.5 |  |  | Cur. Mat.-L.T.D. | 2.8 | 3.6 |
|  | 23.3 | 16.7 | 8.7 |  |  | Trade Payables | 15.1 | 15.5 |
|  | .0 | .3 | .2 |  |  | Income Taxes Payable | .3 | .1 |
|  | 19.7 | 12.1 | 11.3 |  |  | All Other Current | 15.6 | 13.0 |
|  | 67.1 | 50.9 | 28.5 |  |  | Total Current | 43.3 | 40.8 |
|  | 12.0 | 19.7 | 11.8 |  |  | Long-Term Debt | 16.9 | 19.0 |
|  | .0 | .8 | 1.2 |  |  | Deferred Taxes | .7 | .6 |
|  | 13.9 | 1.5 | 1.1 |  |  | All Other Non-Current | 6.6 | 4.2 |
|  | 7.0 | 27.2 | 57.4 |  |  | Net Worth | 32.5 | 35.5 |
|  | 100.0 | 100.0 | 100.0 |  |  | Total Liabilties & Net Worth | 100.0 | 100.0 |
|  |  |  |  |  |  | INCOME DATA |  |  |
|  | 100.0 | 100.0 | 100.0 |  |  | Net Sales | 100.0 | 100.0 |
|  | 28.2 | 24.3 | 27.9 |  |  | Gross Profit | 31.6 | 28.4 |
|  | 28.6 | 20.9 | 21.7 |  |  | Operating Expenses | 27.5 | 25.0 |
|  | -.4 | 3.4 | 6.2 |  |  | Operating Profit | 4.0 | 3.5 |
|  | .0 | .8 | .5 |  |  | All Other Expenses (net) | .7 | 1.0 |
|  | -.4 | 2.6 | 5.7 |  |  | Profit Before Taxes | 3.3 | 2.5 |
|  |  |  |  |  |  | RATIOS |  |  |
|  | 2.2 | 2.6 | 4.1 |  |  | Current | 2.6 | 2.9 |
|  | 1.2 | 1.4 | 2.5 |  |  |  | 1.5 | 1.7 |
|  | .9 | 1.0 | 1.5 |  |  |  | 1.1 | 1.4 |
|  | 1.8 | 1.4 | 2.8 |  |  | Quick | 1.5 | 1.8 |
|  | 1.1 | 1.1 | 1.1 |  |  |  | 1.0 | 1.1 |
|  | .3 | .6 | .6 |  |  |  | .6 | .7 |
|  | 20 / 18.0 | 28 / 13.2 | 27 / 13.6 |  |  | Sales/Receivables | 29 / 12.4 | 35 / 10.5 |
|  | 51 / 7.1 | 45 / 8.2 | 54 / 6.7 |  |  |  | 44 / 8.3 | 48 / 7.6 |
|  | 68 / 5.4 | 89 / 4.1 | 62 / 5.9 |  |  |  | 63 / 5.8 | 71 / 5.2 |
|  | 7 / 53.4 | 13 / 28.7 | 38 / 9.7 |  |  | Cost of Sales/Inventory | 5 / 67.1 | 9 / 39.0 |
|  | 17 / 21.9 | 31 / 11.7 | 65 / 5.6 |  |  |  | 33 / 10.9 | 23 / 15.6 |
|  | 68 / 5.4 | 51 / 7.2 | 111 / 3.3 |  |  |  | 68 / 5.4 | 66 / 5.6 |
|  | 22 / 16.5 | 22 / 16.9 | 14 / 25.2 |  |  | Cost of Sales/Payables | 14 / 26.6 | 16 / 23.4 |
|  | 31 / 11.6 | 28 / 13.0 | 23 / 15.8 |  |  |  | 23 / 15.9 | 23 / 15.8 |
|  | 51 / 7.1 | 45 / 8.2 | 48 / 7.6 |  |  |  | 37 / 9.9 | 37 / 9.9 |
|  | 7.0 | 4.6 | 2.7 |  |  | Sales/Working Capital | 5.7 | 5.2 |
|  | 19.6 | 9.2 | 4.4 |  |  |  | 12.8 | 9.5 |
|  | -163.3 | -378.5 | 9.2 |  |  |  | 30.4 | 16.2 |
|  | 11.3 | 9.5 | 7.3 |  |  | EBIT/Interest | 12.9 | 10.4 |
|  | 3.1 | (26) 3.0 | (10) 3.1 |  |  |  | (48) 4.4 | (47) 3.5 |
|  | -2.5 | 1.1 | .3 |  |  |  | 2.3 | 1.1 |
|  |  |  |  |  |  | Net Profit + Depr., Dep., Amort./Cur. Mat. L/T/D | 11.2 | 6.6 |
|  |  |  |  |  |  |  | (16) 6.6 | (19) 1.4 |
|  |  |  |  |  |  |  | 2.0 | .3 |
|  | .3 | .5 | .3 |  |  | Fixed/Worth | .3 | .4 |
|  | 1.2 | .7 | .7 |  |  |  | .6 | .7 |
|  | -15.7 | 1.1 | 1.2 |  |  |  | 2.8 | 1.3 |
|  | 1.9 | 1.0 | .4 |  |  | Debt/Worth | .8 | .9 |
|  | 4.1 | 2.1 | .5 |  |  |  | 2.3 | 1.5 |
|  | -54.1 | 4.6 | 2.3 |  |  |  | 6.3 | 3.7 |
|  | 45.0 | 44.2 | 41.0 |  |  | % Profit Before Taxes/Tangible Net Worth | 40.8 | 28.9 |
|  | (12) 13.1 | (25) 11.8 | (11) 11.0 |  |  |  | (43) 22.4 | (43) 15.2 |
|  | -18.7 | 2.5 | -3.5 |  |  |  | 9.8 | 3.2 |
|  | 8.3 | 16.5 | 18.8 |  |  | % Profit Before Taxes/Total Assets | 18.2 | 11.1 |
|  | 4.0 | 3.8 | 6.3 |  |  |  | 8.2 | 6.3 |
|  | -7.2 | .7 | -1.2 |  |  |  | 2.8 | .3 |
|  | 30.9 | 15.8 | 12.4 |  |  | Sales/Net Fixed Assets | 23.7 | 18.3 |
|  | 18.2 | 10.5 | 5.1 |  |  |  | 13.7 | 10.7 |
|  | 9.8 | 5.9 | 2.4 |  |  |  | 6.7 | 4.5 |
|  | 3.4 | 3.2 | 1.7 |  |  | Sales/Total Assets | 3.7 | 3.3 |
|  | 3.0 | 2.2 | 1.6 |  |  |  | 2.7 | 2.4 |
|  | 2.3 | 1.8 | 1.3 |  |  |  | 2.2 | 1.9 |
|  | .4 | 1.4 | 2.0 |  |  | % Depr., Dep., Amort./Sales | .8 | 1.2 |
|  | (14) .7 | (25) 2.1 | (10) 2.4 |  |  |  | (50) 1.5 | (46) 1.8 |
|  | 2.4 | 2.7 | 4.9 |  |  |  | 2.9 | 3.1 |
|  | 2.1 | 1.2 |  |  |  | % Officers', Directors' Owners' Comp/Sales | 2.3 | 2.0 |
|  | (11) 3.3 | (13) 1.7 |  |  |  |  | (29) 4.7 | (23) 5.3 |
|  | 5.0 | 5.6 |  |  |  |  | 8.2 | 7.1 |
| 10530M | 63719M | 311668M | 355345M | 93128M | 613374M | Net Sales ($) | 897453M | 845706M |
| 1618M | 22685M | 129774M | 243693M | 81736M | 315790M | Total Assets ($) | 396110M | 400058M |

© RMA 2012

M = $ thousand   MM = $ million
See Pages 9 through 22 for Explanation of Ratios and Data

## Comparative Historical Data                                    Current Data Sorted by Sales

| 4/1/09-3/31/10 ALL | 4/1/10-3/31/11 ALL | 4/1/11-3/31/12 ALL | Type of Statement | 0-1MM | 1-3MM | 3-5MM | 5-10MM | 10-25MM | 25MM & OVER |
|---|---|---|---|---|---|---|---|---|---|
| 5 | 4 | 8 | Unqualified | | | 1 | | 2 | 5 |
| 15 | 14 | 15 | Reviewed | | 3 | 4 | 4 | 4 | |
| 8 | 11 | 12 | Compiled | | 2 | 4 | 4 | 1 | 1 |
| 5 | 6 | 9 | Tax Returns | 1 | 2 | 2 | 3 | 1 | |
| 14 | 16 | 22 | Other | 1 | 4 | 2 | 2 | 5 | 2 |
| | | | | | 18 (4/1-9/30/11) | | 48 (10/1/11-3/31/12) | | |
| 47 | 51 | 66 | NUMBER OF STATEMENTS | 2 | 9 | 11 | 19 | 13 | 12 |
| % | % | % | ASSETS | % | % | % | % | % | % |
| 5.7 | 8.4 | 10.8 | Cash & Equivalents | | | 7.8 | 9.0 | 14.6 | 9.9 |
| 32.9 | 32.2 | 30.3 | Trade Receivables (net) | | | 33.2 | 32.4 | 37.3 | 22.1 |
| 21.3 | 24.4 | 21.2 | Inventory | | | 24.4 | 25.0 | 20.6 | 18.6 |
| 5.1 | 2.8 | 4.3 | All Other Current | | | 2.5 | 2.9 | 1.9 | 6.6 |
| 65.0 | 67.8 | 66.6 | Total Current | | | 67.8 | 69.3 | 74.4 | 57.1 |
| 28.0 | 25.5 | 25.9 | Fixed Assets (net) | | | 26.9 | 26.3 | 20.9 | 30.3 |
| 1.7 | 1.2 | 2.3 | Intangibles (net) | | | .2 | 1.6 | .7 | 9.0 |
| 5.2 | 5.5 | 5.1 | All Other Non-Current | | | 5.1 | 2.8 | 4.0 | 3.6 |
| 100.0 | 100.0 | 100.0 | Total | | | 100.0 | 100.0 | 100.0 | 100.0 |
| | | | LIABILITIES | | | | | | |
| 11.2 | 16.5 | 16.6 | Notes Payable-Short Term | | | 9.2 | 19.9 | 11.6 | 7.3 |
| 3.6 | 2.7 | 3.6 | Cur. Mat.-L.T.D. | | | 4.1 | 5.8 | 2.5 | 2.7 |
| 16.3 | 14.3 | 17.7 | Trade Payables | | | 19.7 | 19.0 | 16.5 | 9.7 |
| .1 | .1 | .2 | Income Taxes Payable | | | .0 | .1 | .3 | .3 |
| 12.0 | 14.3 | 18.3 | All Other Current | | | 11.1 | 15.1 | 12.3 | 12.4 |
| 43.1 | 47.9 | 56.4 | Total Current | | | 44.1 | 59.9 | 43.3 | 32.4 |
| 20.4 | 13.4 | 15.8 | Long-Term Debt | | | 17.1 | 20.8 | 7.5 | 17.3 |
| .6 | .6 | .6 | Deferred Taxes | | | .2 | .7 | .8 | 1.4 |
| 3.7 | 3.6 | 5.8 | All Other Non-Current | | | 17.0 | 3.4 | 1.7 | 3.5 |
| 32.2 | 34.4 | 21.3 | Net Worth | | | 21.5 | 15.3 | 46.7 | 45.4 |
| 100.0 | 100.0 | 100.0 | Total Liabilties & Net Worth | | | 100.0 | 100.0 | 100.0 | 100.0 |
| | | | INCOME DATA | | | | | | |
| 100.0 | 100.0 | 100.0 | Net Sales | | | 100.0 | 100.0 | 100.0 | 100.0 |
| 25.2 | 29.9 | 28.7 | Gross Profit | | | 25.7 | 26.0 | 25.7 | 31.8 |
| 23.0 | 27.1 | 26.1 | Operating Expenses | | | 24.2 | 24.8 | 20.9 | 23.9 |
| 2.2 | 2.8 | 2.6 | Operating Profit | | | 1.5 | 1.2 | 4.8 | 7.9 |
| .8 | .6 | .7 | All Other Expenses (net) | | | .7 | .8 | -.3 | 1.3 |
| 1.4 | 2.2 | 1.9 | Profit Before Taxes | | | .9 | .4 | 5.1 | 6.6 |
| | | | RATIOS | | | | | | |
| 2.3 | 2.8 | 2.6 | | | | 2.4 | 2.4 | 3.7 | 2.6 |
| 1.6 | 1.8 | 1.5 | Current | | | 2.1 | 1.3 | 1.6 | 2.2 |
| 1.2 | 1.3 | 1.0 | | | | 1.3 | 1.0 | 1.1 | 1.4 |
| 1.3 | 1.7 | 1.7 | | | | 2.0 | 1.3 | 3.1 | 1.3 |
| .9 | 1.0 | .9 | Quick | | | 1.3 | .9 | 1.1 | .9 |
| .6 | .5 | .4 | | | | .4 | .3 | .9 | .5 |
| 33  11.0 | 29  12.7 | 22  16.4 | | | | 23  15.6 | 21  17.1 | 30  12.0 | 26  14.2 |
| 42  8.6 | 48  7.6 | 45  8.2 | Sales/Receivables | | | 51  7.1 | 44  8.3 | 45  8.1 | 47  7.7 |
| 61  6.0 | 65  5.6 | 64  5.7 | | | | 65  5.6 | 61  6.0 | 83  4.4 | 59  6.2 |
| 7  51.8 | 13  29.0 | 13  28.4 | | | | 8  43.2 | 13  28.8 | 12  29.9 | 37  9.8 |
| 35  10.5 | 41  8.8 | 35  10.3 | Cost of Sales/Inventory | | | 29  12.8 | 44  8.3 | 34  10.6 | 62  5.9 |
| 77  4.7 | 104  3.5 | 69  5.3 | | | | 60  6.1 | 83  4.4 | 70  5.2 | 74  4.9 |
| 14  25.9 | 17  22.1 | 20  18.1 | | | | 11  33.4 | 24  15.1 | 16  23.5 | 17  20.9 |
| 22  16.8 | 25  14.5 | 29  12.6 | Cost of Sales/Payables | | | 31  11.9 | 29  12.8 | 30  12.0 | 24  14.9 |
| 38  9.6 | 41  8.8 | 45  8.1 | | | | 60  6.1 | 46  8.0 | 45  8.2 | 46  8.0 |
| 6.1 | 4.0 | 4.8 | | | | 5.6 | 4.8 | 3.9 | 4.0 |
| 11.4 | 7.1 | 9.0 | Sales/Working Capital | | | 7.5 | 20.9 | 10.1 | 6.7 |
| 34.9 | 16.0 | -261.1 | | | | 117.9 | -101.3 | NM | 13.7 |
| 8.5 | 11.0 | 9.7 | | | | 11.8 | 7.3 | 46.7 | 15.6 |
| (43)  1.9 | (45)  3.4 | (60)  3.1 | EBIT/Interest | (10)  2.4 | | 2.8 | (10)  5.2 | (11)  4.5 | |
| .1 | -.3 | .3 | | | | -.4 | .2 | -4.2 | 1.7 |
| 5.3 | 6.4 | 13.8 | Net Profit + Depr., Dep., | | | | | | |
| (13)  3.6 | (12)  2.6 | (14)  2.8 | Amort./Cur. Mat. L/T/D | | | | | | |
| 1.3 | .1 | 1.4 | | | | | | | |
| .5 | .3 | .4 | | | | .6 | .7 | .2 | .3 |
| .8 | .5 | .9 | Fixed/Worth | | | .9 | 1.0 | .5 | .8 |
| 2.0 | 1.3 | 5.7 | | | | -46.3 | 1.6 | .7 | 3.3 |
| .8 | .5 | .9 | | | | 1.5 | 1.1 | .4 | .5 |
| 2.2 | 1.5 | 2.6 | Debt/Worth | | | 2.8 | 3.1 | 1.1 | 1.5 |
| 6.5 | 4.6 | 12.1 | | | | -90.3 | 5.4 | 2.8 | 3.5 |
| 21.1 | 26.2 | 42.8 | % Profit Before Taxes/Tangible | | | | 42.8 | 50.1 | 42.0 |
| (42)  7.1 | (46)  8.1 | (51)  12.7 | Net Worth | | (15)  12.6 | | (12)  6.5 | (10)  30.9 | |
| -6.4 | -2.8 | 1.5 | | | | | 1.5 | -6.4 | 4.9 |
| 10.1 | 11.0 | 11.1 | % Profit Before Taxes/Total | | | 9.2 | 7.9 | 29.4 | 25.5 |
| 2.6 | 4.3 | 4.1 | Assets | | | 4.0 | 3.7 | 5.4 | 6.6 |
| -1.2 | -1.9 | -1.7 | | | | -8.1 | -1.9 | -1.2 | .4 |
| 25.7 | 21.3 | 21.0 | | | | 23.9 | 17.9 | 37.8 | 15.6 |
| 12.2 | 12.7 | 12.0 | Sales/Net Fixed Assets | | | 11.2 | 10.0 | 13.4 | 8.9 |
| 6.2 | 5.4 | 5.7 | | | | 4.8 | 5.7 | 7.8 | 3.6 |
| 3.3 | 3.2 | 3.2 | | | | 3.3 | 3.3 | 3.1 | 2.4 |
| 2.6 | 2.2 | 2.2 | Sales/Total Assets | | | 2.4 | 2.2 | 2.2 | 1.7 |
| 1.9 | 1.6 | 1.7 | | | | 1.9 | 1.9 | 1.8 | 1.5 |
| .7 | 1.0 | .9 | | | | | 1.2 | .4 | |
| (42)  1.5 | (46)  2.2 | (53)  2.1 | % Depr., Dep., Amort./Sales | | (18)  2.2 | | (11)  1.6 | | |
| 3.2 | 3.1 | 2.7 | | | | | 2.6 | 2.0 | |
| 2.1 | 1.8 | 1.5 | % Officers', Directors' | | | | 1.5 | | |
| (18)  2.4 | (23)  2.8 | (30)  2.3 | Owners' Comp/Sales | | (11)  3.3 | | | | |
| 6.4 | 5.2 | 5.3 | | | | | 6.0 | | |
| 936923M | 1064132M | 1447764M | Net Sales ($) | 1024M | 18664M | 44795M | 143409M | 218611M | 1021261M |
| 448715M | 538844M | 795296M | Total Assets ($) | 570M | 8312M | 18496M | 70160M | 102842M | 594916M |

© RMA 2012

M = $ thousand   MM = $ million

See Pages 9 through 22 for Explanation of Ratios and Data

## Current Data Sorted by Assets   |   Comparative Historical Data

| | 2 | 9 | | 1 | | Type of Statement | | 2 |
|---|---|---|---|---|---|---|---|---|
| | 7 | 2 2 | | | | Unqualified | 9 | 8 |
| 1 2 | 5 | 7 | 1 | 1 | | Reviewed | 5 | 3 |
| | 3 (4/1-9/30/11) | | 37 (10/1/11-3/31/12) | | | Compiled | 3 | 4 |
| | | | | | | Tax Returns | 5 | 9 |
| | | | | | | Other | 4/1/07-3/31/08 ALL | 4/1/08-3/31/09 ALL |
| 0-500M | 500M-2MM | 2-10MM | 10-50MM | 50-100MM | 100-250MM | NUMBER OF STATEMENTS | 22 | 26 |
| 3 | 14 | 20 | 1 | 2 | | | | |

| 0-500M | 500M-2MM | 2-10MM | 10-50MM | 50-100MM | 100-250MM | | 4/1/07-3/31/08 ALL | 4/1/08-3/31/09 ALL |
|---|---|---|---|---|---|---|---|---|
| % | % | % | % | % | % | ASSETS | % | % |
| | 3.5 | 8.2 | | | | Cash & Equivalents | 7.9 | 7.6 |
| | 38.9 | 37.7 | | | | Trade Receivables (net) | 42.5 | 37.9 |
| | 15.0 | 16.5 | | | | Inventory | 16.1 | 16.7 |
| | 1.8 | 4.5 | | | | All Other Current | 2.2 | 3.5 |
| | 59.2 | 66.8 | | | | Total Current | 68.7 | 65.8 |
| | 28.4 | 27.7 | | | | Fixed Assets (net) | 26.5 | 24.8 |
| | 5.4 | 1.0 | | | | Intangibles (net) | .4 | 5.9 |
| | 6.9 | 4.4 | | | | All Other Non-Current | 4.3 | 3.5 |
| | 100.0 | 100.0 | | | | Total | 100.0 | 100.0 |
| | | | | | | LIABILITIES | | |
| | 16.3 | 14.0 | | | | Notes Payable-Short Term | 18.2 | 14.5 |
| | 3.0 | 3.9 | | | | Cur. Mat.-L.T.D. | 2.5 | 2.2 |
| | 18.7 | 13.0 | | | | Trade Payables | 14.1 | 14.4 |
| | .0 | .1 | | | | Income Taxes Payable | .2 | .4 |
| | 16.7 | 11.0 | | | | All Other Current | 12.2 | 12.7 |
| | 54.7 | 42.0 | | | | Total Current | 47.2 | 44.2 |
| | 13.8 | 10.3 | | | | Long-Term Debt | 17.0 | 11.4 |
| | .1 | .5 | | | | Deferred Taxes | .2 | 1.2 |
| | 3.8 | 4.3 | | | | All Other Non-Current | 11.3 | 22.4 |
| | 27.6 | 42.8 | | | | Net Worth | 24.3 | 20.9 |
| | 100.0 | 100.0 | | | | Total Liabilties & Net Worth | 100.0 | 100.0 |
| | | | | | | INCOME DATA | | |
| | 100.0 | 100.0 | | | | Net Sales | 100.0 | 100.0 |
| | 34.6 | 24.9 | | | | Gross Profit | 31.0 | 25.9 |
| | 31.1 | 22.8 | | | | Operating Expenses | 27.4 | 24.8 |
| | 3.5 | 2.1 | | | | Operating Profit | 3.6 | 1.1 |
| | 1.1 | .3 | | | | All Other Expenses (net) | .9 | .9 |
| | 2.5 | 1.9 | | | | Profit Before Taxes | 2.7 | .2 |
| | | | | | | RATIOS | | |
| | 2.0 | 2.8 | | | | | 2.3 | 2.3 |
| | 1.0 | 1.9 | | | | Current | 1.5 | 1.5 |
| | .8 | 1.2 | | | | | 1.0 | 1.1 |
| | .9 | 1.8 | | | | | 1.9 | 1.9 |
| | .7 | 1.0 | | | | Quick | 1.2 | 1.1 |
| | .6 | .8 | | | | | .7 | .6 |
| | 24  15.5 | 41  8.8 | | | | | 33  11.1 | 25  14.8 |
| | 40  9.1 | 54  6.8 | | | | Sales/Receivables | 49  7.5 | 47  7.8 |
| | 74  4.9 | 85  4.3 | | | | | 71  5.1 | 70  5.2 |
| | 0  UND | 14  27.0 | | | | | 8  45.5 | 9  41.0 |
| | 13  28.8 | 24  14.9 | | | | Cost of Sales/Inventory | 21  17.4 | 26  13.8 |
| | 29  12.4 | 55  6.6 | | | | | 37  9.8 | 43  8.5 |
| | 20  18.3 | 17  21.6 | | | | | 8  45.2 | 11  33.2 |
| | 38  9.7 | 22  16.7 | | | | Cost of Sales/Payables | 25  14.3 | 20  18.4 |
| | 54  6.7 | 41  8.9 | | | | | 38  9.7 | 33  11.0 |
| | 19.6 | 5.0 | | | | | 6.9 | 6.5 |
| | NM | 7.8 | | | | Sales/Working Capital | 11.8 | 10.2 |
| | -21.5 | 25.2 | | | | | NM | NM |
| | 8.4 | 6.4 | | | | | 20.7 | 3.8 |
| | 1.8 | (17) 5.2 | | | | EBIT/Interest | 4.8 | (25) 1.8 |
| | -.9 | .6 | | | | | -.7 | -1.3 |
| | | | | | | Net Profit + Depr., Dep., Amort./Cur. Mat. L/T/D | | |
| | .3 | .3 | | | | | .4 | .4 |
| | .9 | .7 | | | | Fixed/Worth | .8 | .8 |
| | NM | 1.5 | | | | | 2.9 | NM |
| | .7 | .5 | | | | | 1.1 | .7 |
| | 4.3 | 1.3 | | | | Debt/Worth | 1.8 | 3.3 |
| | NM | 3.4 | | | | | 10.8 | NM |
| | 48.6 | 18.8 | | | | | 68.9 | 36.1 |
| | (11) 1.0 | (19) 13.1 | | | | % Profit Before Taxes/Tangible Net Worth | (18) 30.9 | (20) 1.8 |
| | -7.9 | 2.1 | | | | | -15.8 | -19.6 |
| | 12.4 | 8.4 | | | | | 18.8 | 9.7 |
| | 1.0 | 4.6 | | | | % Profit Before Taxes/Total Assets | 7.2 | 1.9 |
| | -2.9 | -1.2 | | | | | -6.4 | -6.1 |
| | 65.7 | 18.1 | | | | | 21.7 | 22.6 |
| | 15.9 | 9.0 | | | | Sales/Net Fixed Assets | 16.3 | 12.0 |
| | 6.0 | 5.9 | | | | | 7.8 | 7.2 |
| | 3.9 | 2.9 | | | | | 3.8 | 3.5 |
| | 2.9 | 2.3 | | | | Sales/Total Assets | 2.9 | 3.1 |
| | 1.7 | 1.8 | | | | | 2.3 | 2.3 |
| | .7 | .9 | | | | | 1.0 | .7 |
| | (13) 1.7 | (19) 1.4 | | | | % Depr., Dep., Amort./Sales | (17) 1.6 | (22) 1.7 |
| | 2.7 | 2.8 | | | | | 2.8 | 2.7 |
| | | 1.5 | | | | | 2.3 | 1.5 |
| | (11) | 2.8 | | | | % Officers', Directors' Owners' Comp/Sales | (15) 7.7 | (13) 3.7 |
| | | 12.1 | | | | | 11.5 | 8.1 |
| 1370M | 41196M | 206554M | 43937M | 130701M | | Net Sales ($) | 242048M | 441609M |
| 350M | 13541M | 91274M | 15959M | 118303M | | Total Assets ($) | 94507M | 163094M |

Note: In the current-data columns 10-50MM, 50-100MM, and 100-250MM, the cells read vertically "DATA NOT AVAILABLE."

M = $ thousand   MM = $ million
See Pages 9 through 22 for Explanation of Ratios and Data

## Comparative Historical Data | Current Data Sorted by Sales

| 1 | 2 | 3 | Type of Statement | 0-1MM | 1-3MM | 3-5MM | 5-10MM | 10-25MM | 25MM & OVER |
|---|---|---|---|---|---|---|---|---|---|
| | 1 | 2 | Unqualified | | | | | | |
| 6 | 8 | 12 | Reviewed | | | 3 | 3 | 5 | 1 |
| 4 | 5 | 2 | Compiled | | | 2 | | | |
| 5 | 6 | 10 | Tax Returns | 1 | 5 | 2 | 1 | 1 | 2 |
| 12 | 11 | 16 | Other | 3 | 3 | 1 | 5 | 2 | 2 |
| 4/1/09-3/31/10 ALL | 4/1/10-3/31/11 ALL | 4/1/11-3/31/12 ALL | | | 3 (4/1-9/30/11) | | | 37 (10/1/11-3/31/12) | |
| 28 | 32 | 40 | **NUMBER OF STATEMENTS** | 4 | 8 | 8 | 9 | 8 | 3 |
| % | % | % | **ASSETS** | % | % | % | % | % | % |
| 13.4 | 9.5 | 7.0 | Cash & Equivalents | | | | | | |
| 36.7 | 33.8 | 36.1 | Trade Receivables (net) | | | | | | |
| 15.7 | 20.0 | 15.8 | Inventory | | | | | | |
| 6.0 | 3.5 | 3.2 | All Other Current | | | | | | |
| 71.9 | 66.9 | 62.1 | Total Current | | | | | | |
| 22.1 | 24.7 | 28.4 | Fixed Assets (net) | | | | | | |
| 2.1 | 3.3 | 4.0 | Intangibles (net) | | | | | | |
| 4.0 | 5.2 | 5.5 | All Other Non-Current | | | | | | |
| 100.0 | 100.0 | 100.0 | Total | | | | | | |
| | | | **LIABILITIES** | | | | | | |
| 14.2 | 17.4 | 14.6 | Notes Payable-Short Term | | | | | | |
| 4.2 | 1.7 | 3.1 | Cur. Mat.-L.T.D. | | | | | | |
| 14.2 | 17.2 | 16.0 | Trade Payables | | | | | | |
| .9 | .0 | .0 | Income Taxes Payable | | | | | | |
| 20.9 | 19.5 | 11.7 | All Other Current | | | | | | |
| 54.4 | 55.8 | 45.5 | Total Current | | | | | | |
| 11.2 | 12.4 | 12.1 | Long-Term Debt | | | | | | |
| .3 | .3 | .3 | Deferred Taxes | | | | | | |
| 13.9 | 16.0 | 20.1 | All Other Non-Current | | | | | | |
| 20.2 | 15.6 | 22.0 | Net Worth | | | | | | |
| 100.0 | 100.0 | 100.0 | Total Liabilities & Net Worth | | | | | | |
| | | | **INCOME DATA** | | | | | | |
| 100.0 | 100.0 | 100.0 | Net Sales | | | | | | |
| 28.8 | 30.0 | 29.2 | Gross Profit | | | | | | |
| 28.1 | 30.0 | 28.4 | Operating Expenses | | | | | | |
| .7 | .0 | .8 | Operating Profit | | | | | | |
| .0 | 1.0 | .7 | All Other Expenses (net) | | | | | | |
| .7 | -1.0 | .1 | Profit Before Taxes | | | | | | |
| | | | **RATIOS** | | | | | | |
| 2.9 | 3.0 | 2.4 | Current | | | | | | |
| 1.5 | 1.9 | 1.4 | | | | | | | |
| 1.0 | 1.0 | .9 | | | | | | | |
| 2.1 | 2.2 | 1.6 | Quick | | | | | | |
| 1.1 | .9 | .9 | | | | | | | |
| .6 | .7 | .7 | | | | | | | |
| 27  13.5 | 33  10.9 | 32  11.4 | Sales/Receivables | | | | | | |
| 47  7.8 | 46  8.0 | 50  7.3 | | | | | | | |
| 58  6.3 | 73  5.0 | 79  4.6 | | | | | | | |
| 7  50.7 | 13  27.4 | 8  46.3 | Cost of Sales/Inventory | | | | | | |
| 17  21.8 | 35  10.5 | 21  17.6 | | | | | | | |
| 35  10.5 | 70  5.2 | 48  7.6 | | | | | | | |
| 12  29.5 | 20  18.3 | 18  20.6 | Cost of Sales/Payables | | | | | | |
| 18  20.4 | 28  13.2 | 30  12.3 | | | | | | | |
| 35  10.3 | 48  7.6 | 41  8.8 | | | | | | | |
| 4.7 | 4.6 | 6.1 | Sales/Working Capital | | | | | | |
| 20.4 | 8.1 | 13.1 | | | | | | | |
| NM | -387.7 | -61.8 | | | | | | | |
| 15.6 | 14.9 | 6.7 | EBIT/Interest | | | | | | |
| (26)  2.4 | (30)  1.9 | (35)  2.2 | | | | | | | |
| -.5 | -1.7 | -.3 | | | | | | | |
| | | | Net Profit + Depr., Dep., Amort./Cur. Mat. L/T/D | | | | | | |
| .2 | .3 | .3 | Fixed/Worth | | | | | | |
| .8 | 1.0 | .9 | | | | | | | |
| -6.7 | 13.0 | 9.1 | | | | | | | |
| .6 | .6 | .7 | Debt/Worth | | | | | | |
| 2.5 | 1.6 | 2.8 | | | | | | | |
| -20.4 | 61.2 | 23.0 | | | | | | | |
| 33.0 | 32.2 | 18.9 | % Profit Before Taxes/Tangible Net Worth | | | | | | |
| (19)  10.0 | (26)  6.3 | (32)  11.7 | | | | | | | |
| -3.3 | -28.2 | -1.5 | | | | | | | |
| 18.6 | 12.7 | 8.0 | % Profit Before Taxes/Total Assets | | | | | | |
| 1.7 | 1.6 | 1.8 | | | | | | | |
| -4.3 | -9.9 | -3.8 | | | | | | | |
| 33.3 | 26.1 | 28.8 | Sales/Net Fixed Assets | | | | | | |
| 10.1 | 10.5 | 12.4 | | | | | | | |
| 8.7 | 6.9 | 5.9 | | | | | | | |
| 3.2 | 3.2 | 3.1 | Sales/Total Assets | | | | | | |
| 2.7 | 2.5 | 2.6 | | | | | | | |
| 1.9 | 1.6 | 1.7 | | | | | | | |
| .9 | .8 | .9 | % Depr., Dep., Amort./Sales | | | | | | |
| (24)  1.8 | (30)  2.1 | (37)  1.6 | | | | | | | |
| 2.8 | 3.3 | 2.9 | | | | | | | |
| 2.4 | 1.9 | 2.4 | % Officers', Directors' Owners' Comp/Sales | | | | | | |
| (17)  5.7 | (14)  3.9 | (21)  5.7 | | | | | | | |
| 10.4 | 8.0 | 12.3 | | | | | | | |
| 369666M | 393696M | 423758M | Net Sales ($) | 2224M | 15410M | 31860M | 68795M | 130831M | 174638M |
| 169475M | 235237M | 239427M | Total Assets ($) | 881M | 11900M | 16049M | 30026M | 46309M | 134262M |

M = $ thousand    MM = $ million
See Pages 9 through 22 for Explanation of Ratios and Data

## Current Data Sorted by Assets      Comparative Historical Data

| | 0-500M | 500M-2MM | 2-10MM | 10-50MM | 50-100MM | 100-250MM | Type of Statement | 4/1/07-3/31/08 ALL | 4/1/08-3/31/09 ALL |
|---|---|---|---|---|---|---|---|---|---|
| | | | 1 | | | | Unqualified | 12 | 15 |
| | | | 11 | | | 2 | Reviewed | 16 | 12 |
| | | 3 | | 3 | | | Compiled | 6 | 2 |
| | 1 | 2 | 1 | | | | Tax Returns | 3 | 2 |
| | | | 9 | 6 | 1 | 2 | Other | 24 | 29 |
| | | 7 (4/1-9/30/11) | | 37 (10/1/11-3/31/12) | | | | | |
| NUMBER OF STATEMENTS | 1 | 7 | 22 | 9 | 3 | 2 | | 61 | 60 |

| 0-500M | 500M-2MM | 2-10MM | 10-50MM | 50-100MM | 100-250MM | | Hist ALL | Hist ALL |
|---|---|---|---|---|---|---|---|---|
| % | % | % | % | % | % | **ASSETS** | % | % |
| | | 6.6 | | | | Cash & Equivalents | 7.5 | 5.9 |
| | | 30.9 | | | | Trade Receivables (net) | 36.2 | 32.4 |
| | | 32.9 | | | | Inventory | 21.2 | 24.2 |
| | | 4.0 | | | | All Other Current | 3.2 | 3.1 |
| | | 74.4 | | | | Total Current | 68.1 | 65.5 |
| | | 18.3 | | | | Fixed Assets (net) | 19.6 | 21.3 |
| | | 3.4 | | | | Intangibles (net) | 7.6 | 7.3 |
| | | 3.9 | | | | All Other Non-Current | 4.7 | 5.9 |
| | | 100.0 | | | | Total | 100.0 | 100.0 |
| | | | | | | **LIABILITIES** | | |
| | | 5.7 | | | | Notes Payable-Short Term | 14.9 | 11.6 |
| | | 2.3 | | | | Cur. Mat.-L.T.D. | 3.0 | 2.6 |
| | | 16.6 | | | | Trade Payables | 18.3 | 15.3 |
| | | .3 | | | | Income Taxes Payable | .3 | .4 |
| | | 14.8 | | | | All Other Current | 12.8 | 12.4 |
| | | 39.7 | | | | Total Current | 49.3 | 42.3 |
| | | 11.2 | | | | Long-Term Debt | 18.0 | 17.2 |
| | | .2 | | | | Deferred Taxes | .5 | .6 |
| | | 4.5 | | | | All Other Non-Current | 5.2 | 5.3 |
| | | 44.5 | | | | Net Worth | 27.0 | 34.5 |
| | | 100.0 | | | | Total Liabilities & Net Worth | 100.0 | 100.0 |
| | | | | | | **INCOME DATA** | | |
| | | 100.0 | | | | Net Sales | 100.0 | 100.0 |
| | | 33.5 | | | | Gross Profit | 30.4 | 30.3 |
| | | 30.2 | | | | Operating Expenses | 26.6 | 26.0 |
| | | 3.3 | | | | Operating Profit | 3.8 | 4.3 |
| | | .6 | | | | All Other Expenses (net) | 1.4 | 1.2 |
| | | 2.7 | | | | Profit Before Taxes | 2.4 | 3.1 |
| | | | | | | **RATIOS** | | |
| | | 3.2 | | | | | 2.2 | 2.7 |
| | | 1.8 | | | | Current | 1.6 | 1.6 |
| | | 1.5 | | | | | 1.1 | 1.2 |
| | | 1.9 | | | | | 1.4 | 1.4 |
| | | 1.0 | | | | Quick | .9 | .9 |
| | | .5 | | | | | .6 | .6 |
| | | 32   11.4 | | | | | 36   10.0 | 34   10.8 |
| | | 41   8.9 | | | | Sales/Receivables | 48   7.6 | 42   8.6 |
| | | 61   6.0 | | | | | 64   5.7 | 53   7.0 |
| | | 38   9.6 | | | | | 20   18.0 | 22   16.6 |
| | | 62   5.9 | | | | Cost of Sales/Inventory | 36   10.2 | 40   9.2 |
| | | 99   3.7 | | | | | 67   5.4 | 73   5.0 |
| | | 15   24.9 | | | | | 20   18.6 | 14   26.9 |
| | | 29   12.5 | | | | Cost of Sales/Payables | 31   11.6 | 23   15.8 |
| | | 41   8.8 | | | | | 44   8.3 | 42   8.7 |
| | | 4.4 | | | | | 7.4 | 6.6 |
| | | 8.1 | | | | Sales/Working Capital | 12.3 | 11.3 |
| | | 11.8 | | | | | 50.6 | 32.3 |
| | | 52.1 | | | | | 9.1 | 8.0 |
| | | (17)   11.9 | | | | EBIT/Interest | (57)   2.9 | (54)   4.1 |
| | | 2.8 | | | | | 1.2 | 1.5 |
| | | | | | | Net Profit + Depr., Dep., | 11.3 | 8.3 |
| | | | | | | Amort./Cur. Mat. L/T/D | (27)   2.5 | (30)   2.8 |
| | | | | | | | 1.8 | .1 |
| | | .2 | | | | | .5 | .4 |
| | | .3 | | | | Fixed/Worth | 1.0 | .7 |
| | | .8 | | | | | -30.2 | 2.3 |
| | | .4 | | | | | 1.3 | .9 |
| | | 1.3 | | | | Debt/Worth | 3.7 | 2.4 |
| | | 3.9 | | | | | -147.3 | 9.2 |
| | | 39.7 | | | | % Profit Before Taxes/Tangible | 39.1 | 45.7 |
| | | (21)   27.9 | | | | Net Worth | (45)   17.7 | (48)   21.2 |
| | | 9.4 | | | | | 4.9 | 11.0 |
| | | 11.7 | | | | % Profit Before Taxes/Total | 12.5 | 18.8 |
| | | 6.7 | | | | Assets | 5.1 | 7.4 |
| | | 3.7 | | | | | .8 | 3.0 |
| | | 46.5 | | | | | 44.3 | 43.5 |
| | | 14.8 | | | | Sales/Net Fixed Assets | 14.9 | 14.2 |
| | | 11.1 | | | | | 8.6 | 8.5 |
| | | 3.2 | | | | | 3.6 | 3.9 |
| | | 2.5 | | | | Sales/Total Assets | 2.6 | 2.6 |
| | | 2.1 | | | | | 1.9 | 1.9 |
| | | .8 | | | | | .8 | .8 |
| | | (21)   1.2 | | | | % Depr., Dep., Amort./Sales | (51)   1.3 | (54)   1.4 |
| | | 1.7 | | | | | 2.5 | 2.2 |
| | | | | | | % Officers', Directors' | 2.8 | |
| | | | | | | Owners' Comp/Sales | (14)   3.4 | |
| | | | | | | | 6.1 | |
| 945M | 19362M | 301052M | 425175M | 310028M | 194401M | Net Sales ($) | 3209410M | 3030620M |
| 380M | 7728M | 116684M | 191399M | 218622M | 277283M | Total Assets ($) | 1598090M | 1323590M |

M = $ thousand     MM = $ million
See Pages 9 through 22 for Explanation of Ratios and Data

**Comparative Historical Data**                          **Current Data Sorted by Sales**

| Type of Statement | 4/1/09-3/31/10 ALL | 4/1/10-3/31/11 ALL | 4/1/11-3/31/12 ALL | 0-1MM | 1-3MM | 3-5MM | 5-10MM | 10-25MM | 25MM & OVER |
|---|---|---|---|---|---|---|---|---|---|
| Unqualified | 20 | 7 | 3 | | | | | 1 | 2 |
| Reviewed | 17 | 14 | 14 | | | | 1 | 11 | 2 |
| Compiled | 4 | 5 | 3 | | 2 | 1 | 1 | | |
| Tax Returns | 2 | 2 | 4 | 1 | 1 | 1 | 1 | | |
| Other | 24 | 23 | 20 | 1 | 1 | 1 | 4 | 7 | 7 |
| | | | | | 7 (4/1-9/30/11) | | 37 (10/1/11-3/31/12) | | |
| **NUMBER OF STATEMENTS** | 67 | 51 | 44 | 1 | 4 | 3 | 6 | 19 | 11 |
| **ASSETS** | % | % | % | % | % | % | % | % | % |
| Cash & Equivalents | 8.0 | 9.2 | 8.9 | | | | | 6.9 | 11.3 |
| Trade Receivables (net) | 29.9 | 35.1 | 27.0 | | | | | 29.6 | 26.2 |
| Inventory | 25.9 | 21.8 | 32.1 | | | | | 30.7 | 19.3 |
| All Other Current | 3.9 | 3.8 | 2.5 | | | | | 4.4 | 1.0 |
| Total Current | 67.6 | 69.9 | 70.4 | | | | | 71.6 | 57.8 |
| Fixed Assets (net) | 20.4 | 17.4 | 19.7 | | | | | 22.3 | 25.4 |
| Intangibles (net) | 6.5 | 7.9 | 6.5 | | | | | 1.6 | 13.2 |
| All Other Non-Current | 5.5 | 4.9 | 3.4 | | | | | 4.5 | 3.6 |
| Total | 100.0 | 100.0 | 100.0 | | | | | 100.0 | 100.0 |
| **LIABILITIES** | | | | | | | | | |
| Notes Payable-Short Term | 9.0 | 8.2 | 9.7 | | | | | 6.0 | 4.4 |
| Cur. Mat.-L.T.D. | 4.1 | 2.6 | 2.4 | | | | | 2.4 | 3.0 |
| Trade Payables | 15.5 | 18.0 | 15.6 | | | | | 18.0 | 15.1 |
| Income Taxes Payable | .4 | .3 | .2 | | | | | .4 | .2 |
| All Other Current | 13.2 | 11.7 | 12.1 | | | | | 16.7 | 8.6 |
| Total Current | 42.2 | 40.9 | 40.0 | | | | | 43.5 | 31.2 |
| Long-Term Debt | 17.1 | 14.2 | 12.7 | | | | | 14.1 | 14.9 |
| Deferred Taxes | .6 | .5 | .8 | | | | | .3 | 1.5 |
| All Other Non-Current | 8.4 | 4.3 | 3.7 | | | | | 5.3 | 3.0 |
| Net Worth | 31.7 | 40.2 | 42.8 | | | | | 36.9 | 49.4 |
| Total Liabilties & Net Worth | 100.0 | 100.0 | 100.0 | | | | | 100.0 | 100.0 |
| **INCOME DATA** | | | | | | | | | |
| Net Sales | 100.0 | 100.0 | 100.0 | | | | | 100.0 | 100.0 |
| Gross Profit | 31.3 | 30.6 | 34.0 | | | | | 34.0 | 26.7 |
| Operating Expenses | 27.5 | 26.7 | 30.0 | | | | | 30.9 | 20.7 |
| Operating Profit | 3.8 | 4.0 | 4.0 | | | | | 3.2 | 6.0 |
| All Other Expenses (net) | 1.5 | 1.0 | 1.0 | | | | | .7 | 1.9 |
| Profit Before Taxes | 2.3 | 3.0 | 3.0 | | | | | 2.5 | 4.1 |
| **RATIOS** | | | | | | | | | |
| Current | 2.4 | 2.7 | 2.7 | | | | | 2.0 | 2.7 |
| | 1.7 | 1.6 | 1.7 | | | | | 1.7 | 1.8 |
| | 1.3 | 1.3 | 1.3 | | | | | 1.4 | 1.1 |
| Quick | 1.5 | 1.6 | 1.7 | | | | | 1.3 | 1.8 |
| | .9 | 1.0 | .9 | | | | | .9 | 1.2 |
| | .7 | .7 | .6 | | | | | .7 | .7 |
| Sales/Receivables | 33  11.0 | 38  9.6 | 32  11.3 | | | | | 32  11.4 | 42  8.7 |
| | 41  8.8 | 49  7.4 | 42  8.6 | | | | | 36  10.0 | 49  7.5 |
| | 53  6.8 | 64  5.7 | 60  6.1 | | | | | 62  5.9 | 61  6.0 |
| Cost of Sales/Inventory | 25  14.3 | 23  15.8 | 38  9.6 | | | | | 39  9.4 | 38  9.6 |
| | 49  7.5 | 46  7.9 | 64  5.7 | | | | | 60  6.1 | 43  8.4 |
| | 84  4.4 | 73  5.0 | 99  3.7 | | | | | 94  3.9 | 79  4.6 |
| Cost of Sales/Payables | 17  21.8 | 19  19.4 | 18  19.8 | | | | | 15  23.7 | 24  15.2 |
| | 30  12.0 | 33  11.1 | 30  12.2 | | | | | 30  12.3 | 33  11.0 |
| | 45  8.1 | 56  6.5 | 46  8.0 | | | | | 42  8.7 | 55  6.6 |
| Sales/Working Capital | 5.7 | 6.1 | 4.7 | | | | | 4.8 | 5.5 |
| | 10.0 | 9.7 | 7.9 | | | | | 9.6 | 7.3 |
| | 21.9 | 15.7 | 13.0 | | | | | 13.1 | 38.9 |
| EBIT/Interest | 11.8 | 23.1 | 18.0 | | | | | 22.4 | 87.2 |
| | (62)  3.3 | (44)  5.1 | (38)  6.9 | | | | | (17)  9.2 | (10)  11.1 |
| | 1.2 | 2.1 | 1.1 | | | | | 2.8 | -.1 |
| Net Profit + Depr., Dep., Amort./Cur. Mat. L/T/D | 5.5 | 11.2 | 3.2 | | | | | | |
| | (27)  2.3 | (18)  3.6 | (12)  2.1 | | | | | | |
| | .3 | 1.4 | .2 | | | | | | |
| Fixed/Worth | .3 | .2 | .3 | | | | | .3 | .3 |
| | .7 | .5 | .5 | | | | | .5 | .9 |
| | 2.0 | 1.4 | 1.1 | | | | | 1.2 | 2.9 |
| Debt/Worth | .8 | .8 | .7 | | | | | 1.1 | .7 |
| | 1.8 | 1.8 | 1.3 | | | | | 1.5 | 1.0 |
| | 11.6 | 11.3 | 4.2 | | | | | 3.7 | 9.0 |
| % Profit Before Taxes/Tangible Net Worth | 43.3 | 49.3 | 44.9 | | | | | 42.1 | |
| | (54)  18.8 | (43)  20.2 | (40)  25.0 | | | | | (18)  28.5 | |
| | 1.2 | 9.8 | 5.7 | | | | | 9.6 | |
| % Profit Before Taxes/Total Assets | 13.3 | 10.9 | 12.8 | | | | | 11.2 | 26.6 |
| | 4.1 | 5.5 | 5.5 | | | | | 6.5 | 4.9 |
| | -.3 | 2.2 | -.4 | | | | | 4.0 | -3.1 |
| Sales/Net Fixed Assets | 32.6 | 57.0 | 41.7 | | | | | 26.8 | 17.6 |
| | 14.0 | 21.2 | 12.6 | | | | | 12.8 | 6.1 |
| | 6.4 | 8.4 | 7.0 | | | | | 7.6 | 3.9 |
| Sales/Total Assets | 3.3 | 3.2 | 3.0 | | | | | 3.3 | 2.8 |
| | 2.4 | 2.5 | 2.3 | | | | | 2.6 | 2.1 |
| | 1.7 | 1.8 | 1.8 | | | | | 2.1 | 1.1 |
| % Depr., Dep., Amort./Sales | .7 | .6 | .9 | | | | | .9 | |
| | (58)  1.9 | (44)  1.5 | (37)  1.4 | | | | | 1.3 | |
| | 2.6 | 2.3 | 2.5 | | | | | 2.0 | |
| % Officers', Directors' Owners' Comp/Sales | 1.1 | 2.2 | 1.8 | | | | | | |
| | (15)  2.8 | (14)  3.3 | (12)  2.7 | | | | | | |
| | 4.4 | 4.2 | 4.3 | | | | | | |
| Net Sales ($) | 3958712M | 2111698M | 1250963M | 945M | 7295M | 12067M | 48497M | 310942M | 871217M |
| Total Assets ($) | 1910115M | 1099765M | 812096M | 380M | 3320M | 4408M | 27634M | 128088M | 648266M |

M = $ thousand     MM = $ million
See Pages 9 through 22 for Explanation of Ratios and Data

## Current Data Sorted by Assets  |  Comparative Historical Data

| 0-500M | 500M-2MM | 2-10MM | 10-50MM | 50-100MM | 100-250MM | Type of Statement | 4/1/07-3/31/08 ALL | 4/1/08-3/31/09 ALL |
|---|---|---|---|---|---|---|---|---|
| | 2 | 2 | 14 | 2 | 2 | Unqualified | 22 | 21 |
| | 2 | 15 | 3 | | | Reviewed | 42 | 39 |
| | 6 | 5 | | | | Compiled | 27 | 20 |
| 1 | 4 | 1 | | | | Tax Returns | 13 | 12 |
| 3 | 5 | 15 | 20 | 1 | 2 | Other | 47 | 40 |
| | 18 (4/1-9/30/11) | | 85 (10/1/11-3/31/12) | | | | | |
| 4 | 17 | 38 | 37 | 3 | 4 | NUMBER OF STATEMENTS | 151 | 132 |
| % | % | % | % | % | % | **ASSETS** | % | % |
| | 18.6 | 9.8 | 4.5 | | | Cash & Equivalents | 8.3 | 9.6 |
| | 33.1 | 37.2 | 29.1 | | | Trade Receivables (net) | 32.6 | 26.9 |
| | 20.7 | 20.1 | 26.2 | | | Inventory | 23.2 | 23.6 |
| | .5 | 3.0 | 3.5 | | | All Other Current | 3.2 | 2.4 |
| | 72.9 | 70.1 | 63.4 | | | Total Current | 67.3 | 62.5 |
| | 15.8 | 20.9 | 24.6 | | | Fixed Assets (net) | 24.0 | 27.0 |
| | 4.9 | 3.2 | 7.9 | | | Intangibles (net) | 4.5 | 5.0 |
| | 6.4 | 5.8 | 4.1 | | | All Other Non-Current | 4.2 | 5.5 |
| | 100.0 | 100.0 | 100.0 | | | Total | 100.0 | 100.0 |
| | | | | | | **LIABILITIES** | | |
| | 8.6 | 11.3 | 14.7 | | | Notes Payable-Short Term | 16.4 | 11.1 |
| | 2.9 | 2.4 | 3.5 | | | Cur. Mat.-L.T.D. | 3.8 | 3.6 |
| | 23.9 | 16.4 | 14.9 | | | Trade Payables | 17.5 | 14.1 |
| | .1 | .5 | .0 | | | Income Taxes Payable | .5 | .3 |
| | 8.3 | 10.6 | 9.8 | | | All Other Current | 12.7 | 11.5 |
| | 43.8 | 41.2 | 42.9 | | | Total Current | 51.0 | 40.6 |
| | 8.9 | 11.8 | 18.0 | | | Long-Term Debt | 18.7 | 21.7 |
| | .0 | .3 | .4 | | | Deferred Taxes | .2 | .2 |
| | 15.3 | 5.2 | 6.7 | | | All Other Non-Current | 6.3 | 5.8 |
| | 32.0 | 41.6 | 32.0 | | | Net Worth | 23.7 | 31.7 |
| | 100.0 | 100.0 | 100.0 | | | Total Liabilities & Net Worth | 100.0 | 100.0 |
| | | | | | | **INCOME DATA** | | |
| | 100.0 | 100.0 | 100.0 | | | Net Sales | 100.0 | 100.0 |
| | 37.3 | 29.0 | 23.7 | | | Gross Profit | 29.6 | 28.6 |
| | 30.9 | 25.3 | 19.8 | | | Operating Expenses | 24.6 | 25.2 |
| | 6.4 | 3.7 | 3.9 | | | Operating Profit | 4.9 | 3.4 |
| | .5 | .8 | 1.1 | | | All Other Expenses (net) | 1.4 | 1.4 |
| | 5.9 | 2.9 | 2.8 | | | Profit Before Taxes | 3.6 | 2.0 |
| | | | | | | **RATIOS** | | |
| | 2.7 | 2.7 | 1.9 | | | Current | 2.2 | 2.4 |
| | 1.9 | 1.8 | 1.5 | | | | 1.5 | 1.6 |
| | 1.4 | 1.3 | 1.1 | | | | 1.1 | 1.1 |
| | 2.4 | 1.9 | 1.0 | | | Quick | 1.3 | 1.6 |
| | 1.4 | 1.3 | .7 | | | | .8 | .9 |
| | .8 | .9 | .5 | | | | .6 | .5 |
| | 15  24.3 | 33  10.9 | 39  9.3 | | | Sales/Receivables | 28  12.9 | 27  13.6 |
| | 33  11.1 | 55  6.6 | 47  7.7 | | | | 44  8.4 | 38  9.7 |
| | 45  8.1 | 66  5.5 | 73  5.0 | | | | 60  6.1 | 51  7.1 |
| | 3  107.2 | 17  21.6 | 36  10.2 | | | Cost of Sales/Inventory | 20  18.4 | 17  21.4 |
| | 24  15.0 | 34  10.6 | 66  5.5 | | | | 44  8.4 | 49  7.4 |
| | 73  5.0 | 66  5.5 | 87  4.2 | | | | 71  5.1 | 77  4.7 |
| | 19  19.6 | 14  26.3 | 21  17.8 | | | Cost of Sales/Payables | 15  23.9 | 14  25.3 |
| | 43  8.5 | 25  14.5 | 31  11.6 | | | | 26  14.1 | 27  13.4 |
| | 60  6.1 | 47  7.7 | 41  8.9 | | | | 39  9.4 | 37  9.9 |
| | 6.3 | 6.3 | 6.1 | | | Sales/Working Capital | 6.9 | 6.0 |
| | 8.8 | 8.2 | 10.1 | | | | 12.4 | 10.6 |
| | 20.7 | 16.7 | 29.7 | | | | 66.3 | 56.3 |
| | 13.8 | 18.7 | 13.0 | | | EBIT/Interest | 9.1 | 8.8 |
| | (14) 7.1 | (34) 3.4 | 2.6 | | | | (137) 3.5 | (118) 2.2 |
| | 1.6 | .8 | .6 | | | | 1.5 | .0 |
| | | | 5.0 | | | Net Profit + Depr., Dep., Amort./Cur. Mat. L/T/D | 6.8 | 4.4 |
| | | | (10) 3.1 | | | | (42) 3.5 | (39) 2.1 |
| | | | .6 | | | | 1.5 | .7 |
| | .0 | .2 | .5 | | | Fixed/Worth | .3 | .4 |
| | .3 | .3 | 1.1 | | | | .8 | 1.0 |
| | 3.2 | 1.9 | -6.2 | | | | 3.0 | 4.2 |
| | .6 | .6 | 1.2 | | | Debt/Worth | 1.0 | .9 |
| | 1.6 | 1.4 | 2.0 | | | | 2.5 | 2.5 |
| | 7.5 | 3.9 | -27.3 | | | | 10.5 | 10.3 |
| | 96.1 | 57.0 | 37.2 | | | % Profit Before Taxes/Tangible Net Worth | 64.7 | 47.2 |
| | (15) 34.8 | (35) 19.8 | (26) 26.9 | | | | (124) 24.2 | (107) 19.1 |
| | 7.2 | 3.0 | | | | | 9.1 | 2.0 |
| | 25.8 | 15.6 | 12.2 | | | % Profit Before Taxes/Total Assets | 16.7 | 13.8 |
| | 13.3 | 3.7 | 5.1 | | | | 8.7 | 4.5 |
| | 3.3 | .7 | -.9 | | | | 1.5 | -3.0 |
| | 217.3 | 41.8 | 13.8 | | | Sales/Net Fixed Assets | 29.6 | 24.8 |
| | 46.5 | 19.9 | 8.7 | | | | 15.0 | 10.8 |
| | 9.1 | 6.6 | 5.3 | | | | 7.1 | 6.4 |
| | 4.6 | 3.0 | 2.2 | | | Sales/Total Assets | 3.6 | 3.1 |
| | 3.0 | 2.5 | 2.0 | | | | 2.6 | 2.4 |
| | 2.3 | 1.9 | 1.6 | | | | 1.9 | 1.9 |
| | .5 | .8 | 1.2 | | | % Depr., Dep., Amort./Sales | .9 | 1.1 |
| | (13) .8 | (34) 1.4 | (31) 1.6 | | | | (129) 1.5 | (113) 1.6 |
| | 2.0 | 3.1 | 3.1 | | | | 2.9 | 3.1 |
| | 2.2 | 1.7 | | | | % Officers', Directors', Owners' Comp/Sales | 2.2 | 1.9 |
| | (12) 3.7 | (11) 3.0 | | | | | (61) 3.9 | (52) 3.2 |
| | 4.5 | | | | | | 5.9 | 6.0 |
| 4003M | 75801M | 475149M | 1672494M | 369305M | 914822M | Net Sales ($) | 4027661M | 4005616M |
| 1088M | 22318M | 186843M | 886747M | 217811M | 562560M | Total Assets ($) | 1930541M | 1976262M |

© RMA 2012

M = $ thousand    MM = $ million
See Pages 9 through 22 for Explanation of Ratios and Data

## Comparative Historical Data | Current Data Sorted by Sales

| 4/1/09-3/31/10 ALL | 4/1/10-3/31/11 ALL | 4/1/11-3/31/12 ALL | Type of Statement | 0-1MM | 1-3MM | 3-5MM | 5-10MM | 10-25MM | 25MM & OVER |
|---|---|---|---|---|---|---|---|---|---|
| 15 | 17 | 20 | Unqualified |  |  |  |  | 4 | 16 |
| 19 | 26 | 20 | Reviewed |  |  | 2 | 8 | 8 | 2 |
| 12 | 12 | 11 | Compiled |  | 2 | 1 | 6 | 2 |  |
| 9 | 16 | 6 | Tax Returns | 1 | 2 | 1 | 1 | 1 |  |
| 46 | 41 | 46 | Other | 1 | 3 | 6 | 5 | 8 | 23 |
|  |  |  |  |  | 18 (4/1-9/30/11) |  | 85 (10/1/11-3/31/12) |  |  |
| 101 | 112 | 103 | **NUMBER OF STATEMENTS** | 2 | 7 | 10 | 20 | 23 | 41 |
| % | % | % | **ASSETS** | % | % | % | % | % | % |
| 7.7 | 9.9 | 8.9 | Cash & Equivalents |  |  | 8.6 | 13.6 | 10.7 | 3.8 |
| 27.3 | 29.9 | 33.1 | Trade Receivables (net) |  |  | 38.0 | 29.9 | 39.3 | 31.4 |
| 23.7 | 21.9 | 22.0 | Inventory |  |  | 17.6 | 23.0 | 19.9 | 25.8 |
| 2.2 | 2.0 | 2.8 | All Other Current |  |  | 1.1 | 2.3 | 2.3 | 4.1 |
| 61.0 | 63.7 | 66.7 | Total Current |  |  | 65.3 | 68.7 | 72.3 | 65.1 |
| 26.8 | 24.0 | 22.1 | Fixed Assets (net) |  |  | 22.2 | 21.4 | 21.5 | 21.2 |
| 6.8 | 5.8 | 6.0 | Intangibles (net) |  |  | 2.7 | 3.1 | 3.7 | 9.8 |
| 5.4 | 6.5 | 5.2 | All Other Non-Current |  |  | 9.8 | 6.8 | 2.6 | 3.9 |
| 100.0 | 100.0 | 100.0 | Total |  |  | 100.0 | 100.0 | 100.0 | 100.0 |
|  |  |  | **LIABILITIES** |  |  |  |  |  |  |
| 14.8 | 16.7 | 12.0 | Notes Payable-Short Term |  |  | 9.0 | 8.2 | 13.3 | 12.4 |
| 4.1 | 5.5 | 3.2 | Cur. Mat.-L.T.D. |  |  | 4.9 | 3.0 | 1.8 | 3.2 |
| 14.1 | 16.1 | 16.6 | Trade Payables |  |  | 17.4 | 16.0 | 20.3 | 14.9 |
| .1 | .3 | .2 | Income Taxes Payable |  |  | .2 | .4 | .4 | .1 |
| 11.4 | 9.8 | 10.6 | All Other Current |  |  | 8.0 | 8.6 | 10.5 | 11.6 |
| 44.6 | 48.4 | 42.6 | Total Current |  |  | 39.5 | 36.2 | 46.3 | 42.2 |
| 19.4 | 13.9 | 15.4 | Long-Term Debt |  |  | 14.7 | 11.1 | 10.6 | 18.8 |
| .3 | .3 | .3 | Deferred Taxes |  |  | .0 | .6 | .1 | .4 |
| 7.8 | 12.7 | 8.5 | All Other Non-Current |  |  | 15.1 | 5.9 | 9.2 | 7.0 |
| 27.9 | 24.8 | 33.2 | Net Worth |  |  | 30.7 | 46.2 | 33.8 | 31.7 |
| 100.0 | 100.0 | 100.0 | Total Liabilities & Net Worth |  |  | 100.0 | 100.0 | 100.0 | 100.0 |
|  |  |  | **INCOME DATA** |  |  |  |  |  |  |
| 100.0 | 100.0 | 100.0 | Net Sales |  |  | 100.0 | 100.0 | 100.0 | 100.0 |
| 26.9 | 29.4 | 28.7 | Gross Profit |  |  | 36.1 | 30.9 | 26.2 | 24.2 |
| 26.4 | 26.9 | 24.3 | Operating Expenses |  |  | 32.9 | 26.3 | 22.7 | 19.8 |
| .5 | 2.5 | 4.4 | Operating Profit |  |  | 3.2 | 4.6 | 3.5 | 4.4 |
| 1.7 | 1.1 | .9 | All Other Expenses (net) |  |  | 1.2 | .8 | 1.0 | .7 |
| -1.3 | 1.4 | 3.5 | Profit Before Taxes |  |  | 2.0 | 3.8 | 2.5 | 3.7 |
|  |  |  | **RATIOS** |  |  |  |  |  |  |
| 2.6 | 2.3 | 2.5 | Current |  |  | 2.7 | 3.3 | 2.2 | 2.0 |
| 1.6 | 1.5 | 1.7 |  |  |  | 2.0 | 2.0 | 1.6 | 1.6 |
| 1.0 | 1.1 | 1.1 |  |  |  | 1.2 | 1.5 | 1.1 | 1.2 |
| 1.5 | 1.6 | 1.5 | Quick |  |  | 2.3 | 2.2 | 1.5 | 1.3 |
| .8 | .9 | 1.0 |  |  |  | 1.5 | 1.2 | 1.1 | .8 |
| .5 | .5 | .6 |  |  |  | .9 | .9 | .6 | .6 |
| 30  12.2 | 30  12.3 | 34  10.6 | Sales/Receivables |  |  | 17  21.0 | 24  15.1 | 33  10.9 | 40  9.1 |
| 40  9.0 | 45  8.2 | 47  7.8 |  |  |  | 49  7.5 | 40  9.1 | 55  6.6 | 55  6.6 |
| 60  6.1 | 60  6.1 | 70  5.2 |  |  |  | 94  3.9 | 59  6.2 | 70  5.2 | 72  5.1 |
| 22  16.6 | 14  25.3 | 23  16.0 | Cost of Sales/Inventory |  |  | 0  UND | 18  20.0 | 15  23.8 | 34  10.8 |
| 50  7.4 | 45  8.1 | 41  8.8 |  |  |  | 28  13.2 | 45  8.2 | 38  9.7 | 54  6.8 |
| 85  4.3 | 80  4.5 | 79  4.6 |  |  |  | 79  4.6 | 76  4.8 | 78  4.7 | 83  4.4 |
| 14  25.5 | 15  24.7 | 18  20.4 | Cost of Sales/Payables |  |  | 14  27.0 | 14  25.5 | 19  19.2 | 21  17.8 |
| 25  14.7 | 26  14.1 | 31  11.9 |  |  |  | 34  10.7 | 22  16.8 | 33  11.0 | 31  11.6 |
| 39  9.4 | 44  8.2 | 47  7.7 |  |  |  | 78  4.7 | 47  7.7 | 59  6.2 | 38  9.7 |
| 5.4 | 5.8 | 6.2 | Sales/Working Capital |  |  | 4.2 | 4.6 | 7.1 | 6.0 |
| 10.2 | 11.2 | 9.0 |  |  |  | 9.2 | 7.1 | 11.7 | 9.8 |
| 550.2 | 98.2 | 24.8 |  |  |  | NM | 17.3 | 31.8 | 24.9 |
| 7.4 | 8.2 | 15.2 | EBIT/Interest |  |  |  | 9.1 | 16.0 | 20.3 |
| (95)  1.3 | (102)  2.4 | (94)  3.5 |  |  |  |  | (17)  3.4 | (21)  3.3 | (39)  4.9 |
| -2.2 | .7 | 1.2 |  |  |  |  | 1.6 | .8 | 1.5 |
| 5.8 | 6.0 | 5.0 | Net Profit + Depr., Dep., Amort./Cur. Mat. L/T/D |  |  |  |  |  | 6.8 |
| (29)  1.7 | (28)  2.5 | (22)  2.9 |  |  |  |  |  | (12) | 3.1 |
| -.6 | 1.0 | 1.2 |  |  |  |  |  |  | .9 |
| .3 | .3 | .2 | Fixed/Worth |  |  | .1 | .2 | .2 | .4 |
| 1.0 | .9 | .7 |  |  |  | .2 | .4 | .6 | .9 |
| 18.4 | 4.9 | 5.7 |  |  |  | NM | 1.5 | 1.8 | -3.8 |
| .8 | 1.0 | .8 | Debt/Worth |  |  | .4 | .3 | 1.0 | 1.1 |
| 2.9 | 1.8 | 1.9 |  |  |  | .7 | 1.2 | 2.0 | 2.3 |
| 54.9 | 16.6 | 14.5 |  |  |  | NM | 5.8 | 4.0 | -21.4 |
| 28.4 | 36.3 | 51.4 | % Profit Before Taxes/Tangible Net Worth |  |  |  | 43.9 | 69.0 | 35.5 |
| (78)  5.6 | (89)  14.1 | (82)  21.7 |  |  |  |  | (18)  12.5 | (21)  22.4 | (28)  26.2 |
| -31.0 | 2.1 | 3.4 |  |  |  |  | 2.8 | 3.1 | 6.6 |
| 8.2 | 11.3 | 15.4 | % Profit Before Taxes/Total Assets |  |  | 17.1 | 10.2 | 20.7 | 12.2 |
| 1.6 | 3.6 | 5.2 |  |  |  | 9.5 | 3.8 | 4.7 | 6.5 |
| -10.2 | -.6 | .9 |  |  |  | -3.1 | 1.4 | -.3 | 1.0 |
| 25.4 | 30.4 | 33.3 | Sales/Net Fixed Assets |  |  | 87.2 | 44.1 | 63.1 | 22.5 |
| 10.4 | 11.4 | 11.6 |  |  |  | 21.0 | 15.6 | 14.1 | 9.4 |
| 4.6 | 5.8 | 6.3 |  |  |  | 4.6 | 5.6 | 5.0 | 6.3 |
| 2.9 | 3.2 | 2.8 | Sales/Total Assets |  |  | 3.0 | 3.0 | 3.4 | 2.4 |
| 2.1 | 2.3 | 2.2 |  |  |  | 2.3 | 2.4 | 2.5 | 2.1 |
| 1.6 | 1.7 | 1.8 |  |  |  | 1.7 | 1.7 | 1.9 | 1.7 |
| 1.4 | 1.0 | .9 | % Depr., Dep., Amort./Sales |  |  |  | .7 | .4 | 1.0 |
| (90)  2.2 | (97)  2.1 | (86)  1.5 |  |  |  |  | (17)  1.7 | (21)  1.6 | (35)  1.5 |
| 3.8 | 3.2 | 3.0 |  |  |  |  | 3.7 | 2.5 | 2.4 |
| 2.8 | 2.4 | 1.8 | % Officers', Directors' Owners' Comp/Sales |  |  |  |  |  |  |
| (34)  4.6 | (41)  4.7 | (28)  3.5 |  |  |  |  |  |  |  |
| 7.2 | 6.2 | 5.2 |  |  |  |  |  |  |  |
| 2826805M | 2839297M | 3511574M | Net Sales ($) | 1206M | 14215M | 39343M | 138464M | 381427M | 2936919M |
| 1483178M | 1531761M | 1877367M | Total Assets ($) | 480M | 5979M | 21099M | 60927M | 182536M | 1606346M |

M = $ thousand    MM = $ million
See Pages 9 through 22 for Explanation of Ratios and Data

**Current Data Sorted by Assets**     **Comparative Historical Data**

| Type of Statement | 0-500M | 500M-2MM | 2-10MM | 10-50MM | 50-100MM | 100-250MM | | 4/1/07-3/31/08 ALL | 4/1/08-3/31/09 ALL |
|---|---|---|---|---|---|---|---|---|---|
| Unqualified | | | 1 | 2 | | 1 | | 6 | 5 |
| Reviewed | | 6 | 4 | 1 | | | | 11 | 11 |
| Compiled | | 2 | 1 | | | | | 7 | 13 |
| Tax Returns | | 3 | 1 | | | | | 2 | 4 |
| Other | 1 | | 10 | 5 | | 1 | | 11 | 13 |
| | | 5 (4/1-9/30/11) | | 34 (10/1/11-3/31/12) | | | | | |
| NUMBER OF STATEMENTS | 1 | 11 | 17 | 8 | | 2 | | 37 | 46 |

Middle size-columns (10-50MM, 50-100MM, 100-250MM) marked: **DATA NOT AVAILABLE**

| 0-500M % | 500M-2MM % | 2-10MM % | 10-50MM % | 50-100MM % | 100-250MM % | | 4/1/07-3/31/08 ALL % | 4/1/08-3/31/09 ALL % |
|---|---|---|---|---|---|---|---|---|
| | | | | | | **ASSETS** | | |
| | 8.1 | 7.7 | | | | Cash & Equivalents | 12.2 | 8.8 |
| | 28.0 | 26.1 | | | | Trade Receivables (net) | 26.8 | 24.8 |
| | 36.5 | 31.4 | | | | Inventory | 22.1 | 22.3 |
| | .4 | .6 | | | | All Other Current | 3.1 | 3.8 |
| | 73.0 | 65.7 | | | | Total Current | 64.1 | 59.7 |
| | 17.7 | 25.3 | | | | Fixed Assets (net) | 24.4 | 27.8 |
| | 5.5 | 2.4 | | | | Intangibles (net) | 4.8 | 3.8 |
| | 3.8 | 6.5 | | | | All Other Non-Current | 6.6 | 8.7 |
| | 100.0 | 100.0 | | | | Total | 100.0 | 100.0 |
| | | | | | | **LIABILITIES** | | |
| | 11.7 | 8.5 | | | | Notes Payable-Short Term | 8.1 | 12.7 |
| | 2.5 | 1.0 | | | | Cur. Mat.-L.T.D. | 3.5 | 2.0 |
| | 27.1 | 20.3 | | | | Trade Payables | 17.5 | 17.6 |
| | .0 | .0 | | | | Income Taxes Payable | .2 | .7 |
| | 22.7 | 8.3 | | | | All Other Current | 11.2 | 8.5 |
| | 64.0 | 38.2 | | | | Total Current | 40.5 | 41.5 |
| | 3.2 | 12.3 | | | | Long-Term Debt | 14.3 | 17.0 |
| | .2 | .0 | | | | Deferred Taxes | .6 | .4 |
| | 18.2 | 5.0 | | | | All Other Non-Current | 3.8 | 5.7 |
| | 14.5 | 44.5 | | | | Net Worth | 40.8 | 35.4 |
| | 100.0 | 100.0 | | | | Total Liabilities & Net Worth | 100.0 | 100.0 |
| | | | | | | **INCOME DATA** | | |
| | 100.0 | 100.0 | | | | Net Sales | 100.0 | 100.0 |
| | 37.9 | 24.9 | | | | Gross Profit | 33.4 | 30.3 |
| | 37.3 | 24.2 | | | | Operating Expenses | 30.5 | 31.3 |
| | .6 | .7 | | | | Operating Profit | 2.9 | -1.0 |
| | .6 | .2 | | | | All Other Expenses (net) | .5 | .9 |
| | .0 | .4 | | | | Profit Before Taxes | 2.5 | -1.8 |
| | | | | | | **RATIOS** | | |
| | 1.8 | 2.7 | | | | | 3.4 | 3.1 |
| | 1.2 | 1.6 | | | | Current | 1.5 | 1.4 |
| | .8 | 1.1 | | | | | 1.1 | 1.0 |
| | 1.1 | 1.3 | | | | | 2.1 | 1.8 |
| | .6 | .8 | | | | Quick | .9 | .7 |
| | .2 | .6 | | | | | .6 | .5 |
| | 17  22.1 | 20  17.9 | | | | | 17  21.6 | 18  20.1 |
| | 19  18.8 | 29  12.5 | | | | Sales/Receivables | 30  12.0 | 33  11.2 |
| | 35  10.3 | 43  8.4 | | | | | 44  8.4 | 47  7.8 |
| | 31  11.9 | 28  13.0 | | | | | 20  17.9 | 27  13.7 |
| | 61  6.0 | 42  8.7 | | | | Cost of Sales/Inventory | 33  11.1 | 38  9.7 |
| | 79  4.6 | 78  4.7 | | | | | 47  7.8 | 52  7.0 |
| | 16  22.7 | 18  19.9 | | | | | 16  22.2 | 14  26.2 |
| | 36  10.1 | 30  12.0 | | | | Cost of Sales/Payables | 24  15.1 | 24  15.2 |
| | 43  8.5 | 41  8.9 | | | | | 41  8.8 | 46  7.9 |
| | 8.8 | 8.6 | | | | | 5.9 | 5.9 |
| | 32.0 | 14.2 | | | | Sales/Working Capital | 15.8 | 18.7 |
| | -19.0 | 31.1 | | | | | 79.3 | -174.5 |
| | 5.3 | 6.0 | | | | | 14.0 | 4.0 |
| | (10)  2.7 | (14)  2.1 | | | | EBIT/Interest | (32)  2.4 | (40)  .1 |
| | -7.6 | -2.9 | | | | | -.8 | -6.3 |
| | | | | | | | | 2.9 |
| | | | | | | Net Profit + Depr., Dep., Amort./Cur. Mat. L/T/D | | (15)  1.3 |
| | | | | | | | | -10.4 |
| | .3 | .1 | | | | | .3 | .3 |
| | 2.8 | .5 | | | | Fixed/Worth | .5 | .7 |
| | -.2 | 1.3 | | | | | 2.6 | 2.1 |
| | 1.3 | .8 | | | | | .4 | .6 |
| | 9.9 | 1.1 | | | | Debt/Worth | 1.4 | 1.6 |
| | -6.8 | 2.6 | | | | | 4.3 | 7.0 |
| | | 15.5 | | | | | 38.7 | 16.8 |
| | | (15)  8.3 | | | | % Profit Before Taxes/Tangible Net Worth | (32)  18.8 | (39)  1.5 |
| | | -24.0 | | | | | -4.5 | -42.9 |
| | 11.3 | 8.2 | | | | | 18.9 | 6.8 |
| | 2.4 | 2.3 | | | | % Profit Before Taxes/Total Assets | 7.1 | -5.7 |
| | -21.0 | -5.2 | | | | | -1.8 | -18.4 |
| | 72.9 | 56.4 | | | | | 34.4 | 29.9 |
| | 47.0 | 19.1 | | | | Sales/Net Fixed Assets | 16.2 | 12.1 |
| | 14.4 | 6.9 | | | | | 7.9 | 5.3 |
| | 5.5 | 3.9 | | | | | 4.9 | 4.0 |
| | 4.2 | 3.4 | | | | Sales/Total Assets | 3.1 | 3.1 |
| | 2.6 | 1.9 | | | | | 2.1 | 2.1 |
| | .6 | .6 | | | | | 1.1 | 1.1 |
| | (10)  .8 | (14)  1.0 | | | | % Depr., Dep., Amort./Sales | (32)  1.5 | (38)  1.4 |
| | 1.4 | 1.5 | | | | | 2.6 | 2.6 |
| | | | | | | | 1.2 | 1.0 |
| | | | | | | % Officers', Directors' Owners' Comp/Sales | (15)  2.2 | (13)  3.0 |
| | | | | | | | 4.1 | 5.9 |
| 591M | 64188M | 233682M | 565093M | | 612248M | Net Sales ($) | 1808364M | 2355476M |
| 84M | 15163M | 77083M | 227573M | | 277427M | Total Assets ($) | 578486M | 774157M |

M = $ thousand    MM = $ million
See Pages 9 through 22 for Explanation of Ratios and Data

## Comparative Historical Data | Current Data Sorted by Sales

| 3/31/10 ALL | 3/31/11 ALL | 3/31/12 ALL | Type of Statement | 0-1MM | 1-3MM | 3-5MM | 5-10MM | 10-25MM | 25MM & OVER |
|---|---|---|---|---|---|---|---|---|---|
| 3 | 3 | 4 | Unqualified | | | | | 1 | 3 |
| 11 | 9 | 5 | Reviewed | | | | 1 | 3 | 1 |
| 7 | 7 | 8 | Compiled | | 1 | 2 | 3 | 2 | |
| 2 | 4 | 3 | Tax Returns | 1 | | 1 | 1 | | |
| 20 | 21 | 19 | Other | | | 4 | 2 | 7 | 6 |
| 4/1/09-3/31/10 | 4/1/10-3/31/11 | 4/1/11-3/31/12 | | | 5 (4/1-9/30/11) | | | 34 (10/1/11-3/31/12) | |
| 43 | 44 | 39 | **NUMBER OF STATEMENTS** | 1 | 1 | 7 | 7 | 13 | 10 |
| % | % | % | **ASSETS** | % | % | % | % | % | % |
| 12.3 | 10.4 | 9.0 | Cash & Equivalents | | | | | 8.0 | 10.5 |
| 22.2 | 27.2 | 25.4 | Trade Receivables (net) | | | | | 27.2 | 23.8 |
| 25.7 | 27.1 | 30.1 | Inventory | | | | | 30.7 | 22.9 |
| 3.3 | 3.0 | 1.2 | All Other Current | | | | | .6 | 3.4 |
| 63.5 | 67.7 | 65.8 | Total Current | | | | | 66.5 | 60.7 |
| 26.3 | 21.8 | 24.1 | Fixed Assets (net) | | | | | 25.8 | 25.3 |
| 4.9 | 4.6 | 4.6 | Intangibles (net) | | | | | 3.1 | 8.0 |
| 5.4 | 5.8 | 5.5 | All Other Non-Current | | | | | 4.6 | 6.0 |
| 100.0 | 100.0 | 100.0 | Total | | | | | 100.0 | 100.0 |
| | | | **LIABILITIES** | | | | | | |
| 7.1 | 8.8 | 8.2 | Notes Payable-Short Term | | | | | 3.0 | 4.5 |
| 3.4 | 2.1 | 1.7 | Cur. Mat.-L.T.D. | | | | | .7 | 2.0 |
| 18.9 | 16.5 | 19.9 | Trade Payables | | | | | 20.5 | 13.4 |
| .1 | .3 | .2 | Income Taxes Payable | | | | | .0 | .2 |
| 8.3 | 10.9 | 13.2 | All Other Current | | | | | 11.7 | 12.4 |
| 37.9 | 38.6 | 43.1 | Total Current | | | | | 35.8 | 32.4 |
| 15.0 | 10.6 | 10.4 | Long-Term Debt | | | | | 13.3 | 15.6 |
| .3 | .8 | .7 | Deferred Taxes | | | | | .0 | 2.5 |
| 6.3 | 11.4 | 10.9 | All Other Non-Current | | | | | 11.1 | 14.0 |
| 40.4 | 38.5 | 34.9 | Net Worth | | | | | 39.8 | 35.6 |
| 100.0 | 100.0 | 100.0 | Total Liabilties & Net Worth | | | | | 100.0 | 100.0 |
| | | | **INCOME DATA** | | | | | | |
| 100.0 | 100.0 | 100.0 | Net Sales | | | | | 100.0 | 100.0 |
| 33.5 | 30.2 | 30.3 | Gross Profit | | | | | 25.4 | 30.9 |
| 31.4 | 26.2 | 29.5 | Operating Expenses | | | | | 24.9 | 30.3 |
| 2.1 | 4.0 | .9 | Operating Profit | | | | | .5 | .6 |
| .1 | .4 | .4 | All Other Expenses (net) | | | | | .1 | .5 |
| 2.0 | 3.6 | .4 | Profit Before Taxes | | | | | .4 | .1 |
| | | | **RATIOS** | | | | | | |
| 3.2 | 3.2 | 2.7 | Current | | | | | 3.7 | 3.1 |
| 1.7 | 1.9 | 1.6 | | | | | | 1.7 | 1.9 |
| 1.0 | 1.1 | 1.1 | | | | | | 1.3 | 1.1 |
| 2.1 | 2.0 | 1.6 | Quick | | | | | 2.2 | 2.1 |
| .8 | 1.1 | .8 | | | | | | .9 | .8 |
| .4 | .5 | .4 | | | | | | .6 | .4 |
| 16  22.9 | 17  21.0 | 18  20.1 | Sales/Receivables | | | | | 16  22.3 | 19  19.0 |
| 28  13.2 | 33  11.0 | 28  13.1 | | | | | | 25  14.4 | 29  12.6 |
| 43  8.6 | 44  8.2 | 42  8.6 | | | | | | 38  9.6 | 48  7.6 |
| 27  13.3 | 26  13.8 | 26  14.1 | Cost of Sales/Inventory | | | | | 25  14.8 | 24  15.2 |
| 42  8.7 | 44  8.3 | 42  8.7 | | | | | | 34  10.8 | 32  11.5 |
| 79  4.6 | 61  6.0 | 74  4.9 | | | | | | 52  7.0 | 55  6.6 |
| 16  23.0 | 16  22.1 | 17  22.0 | Cost of Sales/Payables | | | | | 17  21.8 | 14  26.5 |
| 27  13.6 | 23  15.6 | 30  12.0 | | | | | | 27  13.5 | 23  15.7 |
| 49  7.5 | 38  9.6 | 42  8.7 | | | | | | 34  10.8 | 42  8.7 |
| 5.2 | 5.1 | 7.7 | Sales/Working Capital | | | | | 8.3 | 4.8 |
| 12.7 | 11.9 | 14.5 | | | | | | 14.2 | 9.0 |
| 247.8 | 42.8 | 76.7 | | | | | | 51.1 | NM |
| 13.7 | 9.0 | 5.7 | EBIT/Interest | | | | | 6.0 | |
| (36)  3.5 | (32)  2.9 | (32)  2.7 | | | | | | (10)  .6 | |
| -.4 | -.2 | -2.4 | | | | | | -20.0 | |
| 5.4 | 6.3 | | Net Profit + Depr., Dep., Amort./Cur. Mat. L/T/D | | | | | | |
| (15)  2.2 | (10)  2.8 | | | | | | | | |
| 1.5 | .3 | | | | | | | | |
| .2 | .2 | .2 | Fixed/Worth | | | | | .1 | .2 |
| .6 | .5 | .9 | | | | | | 1.0 | .9 |
| 3.7 | 4.9 | 4.7 | | | | | | NM | NM |
| .5 | .5 | .7 | Debt/Worth | | | | | .5 | .5 |
| 1.4 | 1.4 | 1.3 | | | | | | 1.3 | .9 |
| 11.6 | 19.8 | 12.5 | | | | | | NM | NM |
| 57.7 | 44.3 | 29.9 | % Profit Before Taxes/Tangible Net Worth | | | | | 18.9 | |
| (37)  17.5 | (34)  14.7 | (30)  8.9 | | | | | | (10)  8.5 | |
| -2.8 | 4.5 | -5.7 | | | | | | -8.4 | |
| 16.0 | 12.6 | 10.4 | % Profit Before Taxes/Total Assets | | | | | 8.2 | 11.6 |
| 6.2 | 4.8 | 2.4 | | | | | | .0 | 4.3 |
| -3.1 | .3 | -6.7 | | | | | | -5.2 | -12.2 |
| 29.5 | 42.3 | 51.1 | Sales/Net Fixed Assets | | | | | 56.4 | 31.8 |
| 14.3 | 17.7 | 19.6 | | | | | | 20.3 | 18.1 |
| 6.6 | 9.7 | 8.2 | | | | | | 9.8 | 4.6 |
| 4.0 | 4.1 | 4.3 | Sales/Total Assets | | | | | 4.3 | 2.9 |
| 2.8 | 2.8 | 3.4 | | | | | | 3.8 | 2.4 |
| 2.0 | 2.2 | 2.1 | | | | | | 2.7 | 2.1 |
| 1.0 | .8 | .6 | % Depr., Dep., Amort./Sales | | | | | .6 | .8 |
| (37)  1.5 | (40)  1.2 | (34)  .9 | | | | | | (12)  .8 | 1.1 |
| 2.7 | 1.9 | 1.4 | | | | | | 1.2 | 2.0 |
| .8 | .8 | .6 | % Officers', Directors' Owners' Comp/Sales | | | | | | |
| (14)  1.7 | (15)  2.9 | (13)  3.1 | | | | | | | |
| 5.8 | 7.5 | 5.3 | | | | | | | |
| 1646937M | 2360188M | 1475802M | Net Sales ($) | 591M | 2606M | 26923M | 56665M | 211676M | 1177341M |
| 574351M | 905274M | 597330M | Total Assets ($) | 84M | 619M | 11974M | 15794M | 63859M | 505000M |

M = $ thousand    MM = $ million
See Pages 9 through 22 for Explanation of Ratios and Data

## Current Data Sorted by Assets      Comparative Historical Data

| 0-500M | 500M-2MM | 2-10MM | 10-50MM | 50-100MM | 100-250MM | Type of Statement | 4/1/07-3/31/08 ALL | 4/1/08-3/31/09 ALL |
|---|---|---|---|---|---|---|---|---|
| | | | 1 | 2 | | Unqualified | 5 | 4 |
| | | 5 | 1 | | | Reviewed | 6 | 4 |
| 1 | 3 | 1 | 4 | | | Compiled | 3 | 4 |
| 1 | 1 | 1 | 3 | | | Tax Returns | 1 | 1 |
| | 1 | 1 | | | | Other | 15 | 13 |
| | 2 (4/1-9/30/11) | | 28 (10/1/11-3/31/12) | | 1 | | | |
| 2 | 5 | 14 | 7 | 1 | 1 | NUMBER OF STATEMENTS | 30 | 26 |
| % | % | % | % | % | % | | % | % |
| | | | | | | **ASSETS** | | |
| | | 7.4 | | | | Cash & Equivalents | 7.4 | 5.0 |
| | | 23.3 | | | | Trade Receivables (net) | 32.1 | 29.3 |
| | | 38.1 | | | | Inventory | 34.3 | 34.9 |
| | | 1.7 | | | | All Other Current | 4.0 | 3.3 |
| | | 70.6 | | | | Total Current | 77.9 | 72.5 |
| | | 18.2 | | | | Fixed Assets (net) | 16.2 | 17.9 |
| | | 9.4 | | | | Intangibles (net) | 3.3 | 4.1 |
| | | 1.8 | | | | All Other Non-Current | 2.7 | 5.5 |
| | | 100.0 | | | | Total | 100.0 | 100.0 |
| | | | | | | **LIABILITIES** | | |
| | | 14.9 | | | | Notes Payable-Short Term | 17.7 | 15.8 |
| | | .6 | | | | Cur. Mat.-L.T.D. | 3.0 | 1.8 |
| | | 19.9 | | | | Trade Payables | 22.1 | 21.0 |
| | | .0 | | | | Income Taxes Payable | .6 | .2 |
| | | 14.3 | | | | All Other Current | 13.8 | 13.2 |
| | | 49.8 | | | | Total Current | 57.2 | 51.9 |
| | | 7.7 | | | | Long-Term Debt | 9.1 | 16.2 |
| | | .1 | | | | Deferred Taxes | .2 | .3 |
| | | 2.9 | | | | All Other Non-Current | 4.8 | 4.1 |
| | | 39.5 | | | | Net Worth | 28.7 | 27.5 |
| | | 100.0 | | | | Total Liabilties & Net Worth | 100.0 | 100.0 |
| | | | | | | **INCOME DATA** | | |
| | | 100.0 | | | | Net Sales | 100.0 | 100.0 |
| | | 31.3 | | | | Gross Profit | 31.8 | 31.5 |
| | | 28.8 | | | | Operating Expenses | 28.2 | 29.5 |
| | | 2.5 | | | | Operating Profit | 3.6 | 2.0 |
| | | .8 | | | | All Other Expenses (net) | 1.6 | 1.5 |
| | | 1.7 | | | | Profit Before Taxes | 1.9 | .5 |
| | | | | | | **RATIOS** | | |
| | | 2.7 | | | | | 2.2 | 2.2 |
| | | 1.3 | | | | Current | 1.4 | 1.5 |
| | | 1.0 | | | | | 1.1 | 1.1 |
| | | 1.2 | | | | | 1.1 | 1.0 |
| | | .7 | | | | Quick | .8 | .8 |
| | | .2 | | | | | .4 | .4 |
| | | 13   28.1 | | | | | 26   13.9 | 26   14.2 |
| | | 28   13.1 | | | | Sales/Receivables | 38   9.5 | 36   10.1 |
| | | 36   10.1 | | | | | 49   7.4 | 49   7.4 |
| | | 45   8.1 | | | | | 36   10.2 | 47   7.7 |
| | | 60   6.1 | | | | Cost of Sales/Inventory | 61   6.0 | 62   5.9 |
| | | 104   3.5 | | | | | 81   4.5 | 89   4.1 |
| | | 18   20.8 | | | | | 20   18.2 | 19   18.9 |
| | | 33   11.0 | | | | Cost of Sales/Payables | 31   11.8 | 32   11.3 |
| | | 52   7.0 | | | | | 56   6.5 | 43   8.4 |
| | | 6.5 | | | | | 7.2 | 6.6 |
| | | 14.5 | | | | Sales/Working Capital | 15.8 | 10.8 |
| | | NM | | | | | 62.4 | 34.4 |
| | | 8.1 | | | | | 7.6 | 4.5 |
| | | (12)   2.8 | | | | EBIT/Interest | (27)   3.6 | (24)   2.2 |
| | | -.8 | | | | | 1.2 | -3.0 |
| | | | | | | Net Profit + Depr., Dep., Amort./Cur. Mat. L/T/D | | |
| | | .2 | | | | | .3 | .3 |
| | | .5 | | | | Fixed/Worth | .4 | .5 |
| | | 2.6 | | | | | 16.0 | NM |
| | | .8 | | | | | .8 | .9 |
| | | 3.3 | | | | Debt/Worth | 2.8 | 2.4 |
| | | 9.5 | | | | | 95.2 | NM |
| | | 15.9 | | | | | 43.9 | 28.4 |
| | | (12)   5.6 | | | | % Profit Before Taxes/Tangible Net Worth | (24)   18.1 | (20)   10.2 |
| | | -3.7 | | | | | 1.9 | -12.2 |
| | | 6.1 | | | | | 13.3 | 8.2 |
| | | 1.8 | | | | % Profit Before Taxes/Total Assets | 5.2 | 4.2 |
| | | -1.9 | | | | | .6 | -6.6 |
| | | 51.9 | | | | | 43.0 | 40.2 |
| | | 20.4 | | | | Sales/Net Fixed Assets | 33.0 | 23.1 |
| | | 8.8 | | | | | 12.1 | 11.8 |
| | | 3.5 | | | | | 4.6 | 4.0 |
| | | 3.0 | | | | Sales/Total Assets | 3.3 | 2.9 |
| | | 2.0 | | | | | 2.3 | 2.2 |
| | | .7 | | | | | .7 | .6 |
| | | (11)   1.2 | | | | % Depr., Dep., Amort./Sales | (23)   1.1 | (19)   1.2 |
| | | 1.7 | | | | | 2.0 | 2.1 |
| | | | | | | | 1.5 | 1.5 |
| | | | | | | % Officers', Directors' Owners' Comp/Sales | (15)   2.8 | (10)   3.4 |
| | | | | | | | 5.7 | 4.8 |
| 2313M | 17175M | 212137M | 348906M | 30759M | 514332M | Net Sales ($) | 736946M | 1782762M |
| 587M | 6078M | 65139M | 167209M | 52385M | 244196M | Total Assets ($) | 296718M | 735327M |

M = $ thousand    MM = $ million
See Pages 9 through 22 for Explanation of Ratios and Data

**Comparative Historical Data**                    **Current Data Sorted by Sales**

| Type of Statement | | | | | | | | | |
|---|---|---|---|---|---|---|---|---|---|
| | 1 | 4 | 3 | | | | | 1 | 2 |
| Unqualified | 1 | 4 | 3 | | | | | | 2 |
| Reviewed | 7 | 8 | 6 | | 1 | | 2 | 2 | 3 |
| Compiled | 2 | 2 | 5 | | 2 | | 2 | 3 | 1 |
| Tax Returns | 1 | 3 | 6 | | 2 | | 3 | 1 | |
| Other | 14 | 13 | 10 | 1 | | 1 | | 4 | 4 |
| | 4/1/09-3/31/10 | 4/1/10-3/31/11 | 4/1/11-3/31/12 | | 2 (4/1-9/30/11) | | | 28 (10/1/11-3/31/12) | |
| | ALL | ALL | ALL | 0-1MM | 1-3MM | 3-5MM | 5-10MM | 10-25MM | 25MM & OVER |
| **NUMBER OF STATEMENTS** | 25 | 30 | 30 | 1 | 4 | 2 | 5 | 8 | 10 |

| | % | % | % | % | % | % | % | % | % |
|---|---|---|---|---|---|---|---|---|---|
| **ASSETS** | | | | | | | | | |
| Cash & Equivalents | 7.1 | 8.5 | 7.6 | | | | | | 9.8 |
| Trade Receivables (net) | 25.5 | 24.1 | 24.7 | | | | | | 20.0 |
| Inventory | 35.4 | 35.9 | 36.0 | | | | | | 31.4 |
| All Other Current | 3.0 | 1.8 | 2.5 | | | | | | 4.6 |
| Total Current | 71.0 | 70.3 | 70.8 | | | | | | 65.8 |
| Fixed Assets (net) | 17.1 | 14.3 | 17.1 | | | | | | 22.6 |
| Intangibles (net) | 7.0 | 11.1 | 10.6 | | | | | | 9.8 |
| All Other Non-Current | 4.9 | 4.4 | 1.5 | | | | | | 1.8 |
| Total | 100.0 | 100.0 | 100.0 | | | | | | 100.0 |
| **LIABILITIES** | | | | | | | | | |
| Notes Payable-Short Term | 20.8 | 21.3 | 12.1 | | | | | | 6.6 |
| Cur. Mat.-L.T.D. | 2.0 | 1.5 | 2.1 | | | | | | 2.2 |
| Trade Payables | 19.2 | 17.7 | 18.6 | | | | | | 14.4 |
| Income Taxes Payable | .1 | .1 | .1 | | | | | | .1 |
| All Other Current | 12.2 | 13.1 | 21.6 | | | | | | 14.5 |
| Total Current | 54.4 | 53.6 | 54.4 | | | | | | 37.9 |
| Long-Term Debt | 12.5 | 14.1 | 18.0 | | | | | | 29.0 |
| Deferred Taxes | .8 | .9 | .5 | | | | | | 1.1 |
| All Other Non-Current | 5.9 | 7.1 | 7.8 | | | | | | 7.6 |
| Net Worth | 26.5 | 24.3 | 19.3 | | | | | | 24.4 |
| Total Liabilities & Net Worth | 100.0 | 100.0 | 100.0 | | | | | | 100.0 |
| **INCOME DATA** | | | | | | | | | |
| Net Sales | 100.0 | 100.0 | 100.0 | | | | | | 100.0 |
| Gross Profit | 34.0 | 36.5 | 33.4 | | | | | | 36.1 |
| Operating Expenses | 32.3 | 34.5 | 30.4 | | | | | | 33.2 |
| Operating Profit | 1.7 | 2.0 | 3.0 | | | | | | 2.9 |
| All Other Expenses (net) | 2.0 | 3.2 | 1.9 | | | | | | 2.9 |
| Profit Before Taxes | -.4 | -1.3 | 1.1 | | | | | | .0 |
| **RATIOS** | | | | | | | | | |
| Current | 2.1 / 1.5 / 1.1 | 2.5 / 1.5 / 1.1 | 2.7 / 1.5 / 1.2 | | | | | | 3.6 / 1.7 / 1.4 |
| Quick | 1.1 / .8 / .3 | 1.2 / .8 / .4 | 1.1 / .7 / .3 | | | | | | 1.3 / 1.0 / .5 |
| Sales/Receivables | 25  14.6 / 34  10.6 / 46  7.9 | 18  20.7 / 29  12.6 / 57  6.4 | 21  17.7 / 30  12.1 / 49  7.4 | | | | | | 12  30.5 / 32  11.4 / 58  6.3 |
| Cost of Sales/Inventory | 55  6.7 / 70  5.2 / 87  4.2 | 53  6.8 / 74  5.0 / 99  3.7 | 46  7.9 / 72  5.1 / 111  3.3 | | | | | | 55  6.6 / 66  5.5 / 96  3.8 |
| Cost of Sales/Payables | 20  18.5 / 35  10.5 / 42  8.6 | 14  26.8 / 31  11.7 / 42  8.7 | 18  20.0 / 34  10.8 / 54  6.8 | | | | | | 18  20.1 / 30  12.0 / 54  6.7 |
| Sales/Working Capital | 6.5 / 12.2 / 45.0 | 4.7 / 15.3 / 34.6 | 6.1 / 11.4 / 30.1 | | | | | | 5.6 / 8.3 / 14.6 |
| EBIT/Interest | (23)  9.5 / 2.3 / -3.5 | (28)  7.9 / 2.0 / .1 | (27)  7.2 / 2.3 / .0 | | | | | | |
| Net Profit + Depr., Dep., Amort./Cur. Mat. L/T/D | | | | | | | | | |
| Fixed/Worth | .3 / .4 / -25.5 | .2 / .7 / -1.0 | .2 / .7 / -4.4 | | | | | | .5 / 1.0 / -4.1 |
| Debt/Worth | .9 / 2.9 / -59.0 | 1.2 / 3.4 / -6.2 | .9 / 4.5 / -28.9 | | | | | | .5 / 3.5 / -25.7 |
| % Profit Before Taxes/Tangible Net Worth | (18)  34.8 / 3.6 / -19.5 | (21)  16.7 / 6.3 / -8.6 | (22)  18.5 / 2.9 / -4.0 | | | | | | |
| % Profit Before Taxes/Total Assets | 11.3 / 1.3 / -10.6 | 6.5 / 1.1 / -3.9 | 7.5 / 1.8 / -1.9 | | | | | | 6.3 / 1.8 / -2.5 |
| Sales/Net Fixed Assets | 48.3 / 20.8 / 12.0 | 55.3 / 26.9 / 11.1 | 50.2 / 20.4 / 8.3 | | | | | | 18.5 / 10.5 / 8.2 |
| Sales/Total Assets | 3.7 / 2.8 / 1.9 | 4.4 / 3.0 / 1.8 | 3.3 / 2.6 / 1.8 | | | | | | 3.4 / 2.6 / 1.9 |
| % Depr., Dep., Amort./Sales | (19)  .8 / 1.3 / 2.5 | (19)  .8 / 1.3 / 1.9 | (22)  .7 / 1.2 / 1.8 | | | | | | |
| % Officers', Directors', Owners' Comp/Sales | (11)  1.9 / 4.2 / 5.6 | (12)  2.1 / 2.8 / 4.7 | (12)  2.2 / 3.0 / 7.3 | | | | | | |
| Net Sales ($) | 983819M | 1137634M | 1125622M | 520M | 7347M | 8430M | 31661M | 110604M | 967060M |
| Total Assets ($) | 437196M | 586914M | 535594M | 527M | 2846M | 6739M | 12159M | 55411M | 457912M |

M = $ thousand     MM = $ million
See Pages 9 through 22 for Explanation of Ratios and Data

## Current Data Sorted by Assets

## Comparative Historical Data

| | 0-500M | 500M-2MM | 2-10MM | 10-50MM | 50-100MM | 100-250MM | Type of Statement | 4/1/07-3/31/08 ALL | 4/1/08-3/31/09 ALL |
|---|---|---|---|---|---|---|---|---|---|
| | | | 10 | 20 | 12 | 7 | Unqualified | 47 | 50 |
| | 1 | | 15 | 15 | | | Reviewed | 18 | 22 |
| | 1 | 5 | 6 | 2 | | | Compiled | 12 | 15 |
| | 3 | 14 | 12 | 1 | | | Tax Returns | 6 | 9 |
| | 3 | 5 | 32 | 25 | 6 | 12 | Other | 68 | 82 |
| | | 27 (4/1-9/30/11) | | 180 (10/1/11-3/31/12) | | | | | |
| NUMBER OF STATEMENTS | 8 | 24 | 75 | 63 | 18 | 19 | | 151 | 178 |
| | % | % | % | % | % | % | **ASSETS** | % | % |
| | | 13.5 | 11.4 | 14.4 | 10.0 | 15.3 | Cash & Equivalents | 12.9 | 11.3 |
| | | 23.5 | 24.2 | 22.9 | 20.6 | 13.1 | Trade Receivables (net) | 22.2 | 23.4 |
| | | 31.4 | 26.5 | 21.7 | 18.9 | 12.2 | Inventory | 23.4 | 23.8 |
| | | 1.7 | 3.3 | 2.4 | 4.7 | 2.2 | All Other Current | 2.6 | 2.3 |
| | | 70.0 | 65.2 | 61.3 | 54.1 | 42.8 | Total Current | 61.0 | 60.7 |
| | | 14.8 | 22.8 | 26.2 | 21.1 | 18.8 | Fixed Assets (net) | 22.2 | 20.1 |
| | | 6.8 | 5.1 | 7.7 | 19.3 | 33.1 | Intangibles (net) | 11.9 | 14.1 |
| | | 8.4 | 6.8 | 4.7 | 5.4 | 5.4 | All Other Non-Current | 4.9 | 5.0 |
| | | 100.0 | 100.0 | 100.0 | 100.0 | 100.0 | Total | 100.0 | 100.0 |
| | | | | | | | **LIABILITIES** | | |
| | | 6.7 | 9.2 | 4.8 | 2.8 | 2.9 | Notes Payable-Short Term | 7.6 | 8.2 |
| | | 1.8 | 2.6 | 3.0 | 4.5 | 2.0 | Cur. Mat.-L.T.D. | 3.2 | 3.6 |
| | | 16.8 | 12.7 | 10.3 | 6.1 | 5.1 | Trade Payables | 11.2 | 12.2 |
| | | .0 | .0 | .1 | .5 | .1 | Income Taxes Payable | .3 | .3 |
| | | 9.4 | 10.8 | 8.3 | 11.7 | 6.1 | All Other Current | 10.2 | 10.8 |
| | | 34.7 | 35.4 | 26.5 | 25.4 | 16.3 | Total Current | 32.5 | 35.1 |
| | | 11.0 | 14.8 | 17.4 | 14.5 | 17.6 | Long-Term Debt | 14.8 | 17.0 |
| | | .0 | .4 | .6 | 1.4 | 1.9 | Deferred Taxes | .7 | .7 |
| | | 10.9 | 8.1 | 6.4 | 13.0 | 17.8 | All Other Non-Current | 6.9 | 7.5 |
| | | 43.4 | 41.3 | 49.1 | 45.8 | 46.4 | Net Worth | 45.1 | 39.6 |
| | | 100.0 | 100.0 | 100.0 | 100.0 | 100.0 | Total Liabilities & Net Worth | 100.0 | 100.0 |
| | | | | | | | **INCOME DATA** | | |
| | | 100.0 | 100.0 | 100.0 | 100.0 | 100.0 | Net Sales | 100.0 | 100.0 |
| | | 50.4 | 45.6 | 44.5 | 49.1 | 49.9 | Gross Profit | 45.2 | 44.8 |
| | | 44.7 | 40.5 | 33.6 | 38.2 | 38.5 | Operating Expenses | 37.5 | 36.6 |
| | | 5.8 | 5.2 | 10.9 | 10.9 | 11.4 | Operating Profit | 7.6 | 8.2 |
| | | .6 | 1.0 | 1.4 | 2.1 | 6.9 | All Other Expenses (net) | 1.6 | 2.1 |
| | | 5.1 | 4.2 | 9.5 | 8.7 | 4.5 | Profit Before Taxes | 6.0 | 6.2 |
| | | | | | | | **RATIOS** | | |
| | | 3.4 | 3.5 | 4.3 | 4.7 | 5.5 | | 3.5 | 3.4 |
| | | 2.2 | 1.7 | 2.3 | 1.9 | 3.1 | Current | 2.2 | 1.9 |
| | | 1.3 | 1.1 | 1.5 | 1.5 | 1.9 | | 1.3 | 1.2 |
| | | 2.4 | 2.0 | 2.6 | 2.9 | 3.2 | | 2.1 | 2.2 |
| | | 1.0 | 1.0 | 1.3 | 1.0 | 2.0 | Quick | 1.2 | 1.1 |
| | | .5 | .6 | .8 | .7 | .9 | | .6 | .6 |
| | | 15  25.0 | 30  12.1 | 36  10.0 | 41  8.8 | 33  10.9 | | 37  9.9 | 38  9.7 |
| | | 35  10.5 | 40  9.2 | 47  7.7 | 49  7.4 | 47  7.8 | Sales/Receivables | 47  7.8 | 46  7.9 |
| | | 44  8.3 | 50  7.3 | 58  6.3 | 56  6.5 | 68  5.4 | | 60  6.1 | 58  6.3 |
| | | 47  7.7 | 49  7.4 | 55  6.6 | 66  5.5 | 55  6.6 | | 60  6.1 | 60  6.1 |
| | | 78  4.7 | 76  4.8 | 87  4.2 | 99  3.7 | 79  4.6 | Cost of Sales/Inventory | 91  4.0 | 84  4.4 |
| | | 122  3.0 | 126  2.9 | 130  2.8 | 174  2.1 | 140  2.6 | | 148  2.5 | 131  2.8 |
| | | 14  25.5 | 24  15.1 | 24  15.0 | 20  18.5 | 19  19.3 | | 20  18.4 | 22  16.8 |
| | | 30  12.2 | 35  10.4 | 34  10.7 | 29  12.6 | 33  10.9 | Cost of Sales/Payables | 33  11.2 | 35  10.5 |
| | | 89  4.1 | 53  6.9 | 52  7.0 | 55  6.6 | 65  5.6 | | 57  6.4 | 56  6.5 |
| | | 4.6 | 4.1 | 3.4 | 2.3 | 2.0 | | 3.4 | 3.5 |
| | | 7.2 | 8.6 | 4.7 | 4.4 | 3.5 | Sales/Working Capital | 5.4 | 5.8 |
| | | 16.9 | 23.3 | 8.8 | 8.9 | 8.9 | | 13.6 | 16.2 |
| | | 18.4 | 20.6 | 42.6 | 13.7 | 8.1 | | 15.8 | 14.2 |
| | (14) | 6.6 | (63) 7.6 | (54) 7.9 | (16) 7.9 | (15) 1.5 | EBIT/Interest | (124) 4.0 | (153) 4.3 |
| | | 1.7 | 1.9 | 1.1 | 2.2 | -.4 | | 1.4 | 1.8 |
| | | | | 5.7 | 8.5 | | | 6.8 | 14.9 |
| | | | (24) 1.7 | (11) 2.1 | | | Net Profit + Depr., Dep., Amort./Cur. Mat. L/T/D | (42) 2.5 | (52) 3.7 |
| | | | | 1.0 | 1.0 | | | 1.4 | 1.9 |
| | | .2 | .2 | .2 | .1 | .4 | | .2 | .2 |
| | | .3 | .6 | .6 | .9 | 10.5 | Fixed/Worth | .5 | .6 |
| | | 1.9 | 1.4 | 1.2 | -9.3 | -.4 | | 1.9 | 6.6 |
| | | .5 | .7 | .3 | .3 | .2 | | .4 | .5 |
| | | 1.4 | 1.7 | 1.0 | 1.5 | 20.6 | Debt/Worth | 1.2 | 1.6 |
| | | 13.4 | 4.4 | 2.4 | -33.0 | -2.0 | | 3.9 | 18.3 |
| | | 73.3 | 55.8 | 61.1 | 35.0 | 32.1 | | 40.9 | 46.2 |
| | (20) | 30.8 | (68) 32.9 | (55) 29.2 | (11) 20.7 | (10) 19.8 | % Profit Before Taxes/Tangible Net Worth | (125) 19.0 | (138) 26.7 |
| | | 11.1 | 6.8 | 4.0 | 10.3 | -9.3 | | 6.9 | 12.5 |
| | | 20.5 | 21.2 | 26.4 | 20.0 | 21.6 | | 20.1 | 19.4 |
| | | 8.2 | 9.2 | 11.5 | 8.1 | 4.3 | % Profit Before Taxes/Total Assets | 9.2 | 8.2 |
| | | 1.7 | 2.2 | 1.7 | 3.7 | -2.6 | | 1.6 | 2.5 |
| | | 40.4 | 31.3 | 19.1 | 19.9 | 14.7 | | 21.7 | 23.1 |
| | | 21.8 | 14.2 | 8.7 | 6.8 | 5.3 | Sales/Net Fixed Assets | 8.8 | 10.1 |
| | | 14.1 | 5.7 | 3.7 | 4.2 | 3.3 | | 4.0 | 4.6 |
| | | 3.5 | 2.7 | 2.1 | 1.6 | 1.2 | | 2.3 | 2.5 |
| | | 2.5 | 2.1 | 1.6 | 1.1 | .8 | Sales/Total Assets | 1.6 | 1.6 |
| | | 1.7 | 1.5 | 1.3 | .8 | .6 | | 1.0 | 1.0 |
| | | .8 | 1.1 | 1.4 | 2.3 | 2.4 | | 1.2 | .9 |
| | (16) | 1.0 | (64) 2.2 | (56) 2.2 | (17) 3.3 | (11) 3.0 | % Depr., Dep., Amort./Sales | (127) 2.9 | (142) 2.3 |
| | | 1.5 | 3.9 | 5.4 | 4.7 | 5.8 | | 4.6 | 4.2 |
| | | 3.3 | 2.6 | 2.6 | | | | 3.2 | 2.9 |
| | (13) | 7.8 | (30) 5.4 | (11) 3.7 | | | % Officers', Directors' Owners' Comp/Sales | (26) 5.4 | (34) 5.6 |
| | | 15.7 | 7.1 | | | | | 11.5 | 9.2 |
| | 17641M | 92252M | 763440M | 2384009M | 1720382M | 2639590M | Net Sales ($) | 5493474M | 8755231M |
| | 2067M | 30611M | 370295M | 1456167M | 1265251M | 2983253M | Total Assets ($) | 5010160M | 6984919M |

M = $ thousand     MM = $ million
See Pages 9 through 22 for Explanation of Ratios and Data

## Comparative Historical Data     Current Data Sorted by Sales

| | Comparative Historical Data | | | | Current Data Sorted by Sales | | | | |
|---|---|---|---|---|---|---|---|---|---|
| Type of Statement | 4/1/09-3/31/10 ALL | 4/1/10-3/31/11 ALL | 4/1/11-3/31/12 ALL | 0-1MM | 1-3MM | 3-5MM | 5-10MM | 10-25MM | 25MM & OVER |
| | | | | | 27 (4/1-9/30/11) | | 180 (10/1/11-3/31/12) | | |
| Unqualified | 54 | 50 | 49 | | | 3 | 2 | 8 | 36 |
| Reviewed | 26 | 30 | 31 | | 1 | 1 | 9 | 12 | 8 |
| Compiled | 23 | 17 | 14 | | 4 | 3 | 1 | 6 | |
| Tax Returns | 14 | 14 | 30 | 3 | 4 | 9 | 9 | 5 | |
| Other | 80 | 79 | 83 | 2 | 6 | 4 | 12 | 24 | 35 |
| **NUMBER OF STATEMENTS** | 197 | 190 | 207 | 5 | 15 | 20 | 33 | 55 | 79 |
| **ASSETS** | % | % | % | % | % | % | % | % | % |
| Cash & Equivalents | 12.2 | 12.8 | 13.3 | | 18.4 | 14.2 | 13.2 | 10.0 | 13.3 |
| Trade Receivables (net) | 23.7 | 23.5 | 22.4 | | 20.2 | 25.0 | 21.7 | 24.9 | 21.2 |
| Inventory | 22.8 | 20.8 | 23.7 | | 14.8 | 28.4 | 27.6 | 28.4 | 19.3 |
| All Other Current | 2.9 | 2.7 | 2.7 | | .9 | 5.0 | 1.5 | 3.0 | 2.9 |
| Total Current | 61.5 | 59.7 | 62.1 | | 54.2 | 72.6 | 64.0 | 66.3 | 56.8 |
| Fixed Assets (net) | 20.4 | 20.9 | 21.8 | | 21.3 | 13.8 | 25.0 | 24.8 | 21.2 |
| Intangibles (net) | 11.7 | 13.1 | 9.8 | | 9.8 | 8.3 | 3.4 | 4.8 | 17.0 |
| All Other Non-Current | 6.4 | 6.3 | 6.2 | | 14.7 | 5.2 | 7.6 | 4.1 | 5.1 |
| Total | 100.0 | 100.0 | 100.0 | | 100.0 | 100.0 | 100.0 | 100.0 | 100.0 |
| **LIABILITIES** | | | | | | | | | |
| Notes Payable-Short Term | 8.3 | 6.3 | 6.5 | | 6.2 | 5.3 | 8.9 | 9.2 | 3.2 |
| Cur. Mat.-L.T.D. | 3.5 | 3.6 | 2.6 | | 1.8 | 1.3 | 3.0 | 2.9 | 3.0 |
| Trade Payables | 10.7 | 11.1 | 11.3 | | 11.7 | 13.0 | 10.8 | 13.9 | 9.2 |
| Income Taxes Payable | .3 | .2 | .1 | | .0 | .0 | .0 | .0 | .2 |
| All Other Current | 10.4 | 10.3 | 9.7 | | 7.4 | 19.8 | 8.6 | 7.8 | 9.4 |
| Total Current | 33.3 | 31.5 | 30.3 | | 27.1 | 39.3 | 31.3 | 33.9 | 25.0 |
| Long-Term Debt | 13.6 | 14.2 | 15.3 | | 16.3 | 8.2 | 14.1 | 15.3 | 17.1 |
| Deferred Taxes | .9 | .7 | .6 | | .0 | .4 | .6 | .0 | 1.2 |
| All Other Non-Current | 8.1 | 8.8 | 9.0 | | 20.5 | 14.7 | 3.0 | 4.4 | 11.4 |
| Net Worth | 44.1 | 44.8 | 44.8 | | 36.1 | 37.4 | 51.0 | 46.3 | 45.3 |
| Total Liabilities & Net Worth | 100.0 | 100.0 | 100.0 | | 100.0 | 100.0 | 100.0 | 100.0 | 100.0 |
| **INCOME DATA** | | | | | | | | | |
| Net Sales | 100.0 | 100.0 | 100.0 | | 100.0 | 100.0 | 100.0 | 100.0 | 100.0 |
| Gross Profit | 46.0 | 45.2 | 46.8 | | 49.5 | 46.9 | 49.6 | 43.3 | 46.3 |
| Operating Expenses | 37.4 | 37.3 | 38.7 | | 41.6 | 45.3 | 43.6 | 33.9 | 36.5 |
| Operating Profit | 8.6 | 7.9 | 8.1 | | 7.9 | 1.6 | 6.0 | 9.5 | 9.8 |
| All Other Expenses (net) | 2.1 | 1.7 | 1.7 | | 2.1 | 1.1 | .5 | 1.0 | 2.9 |
| Profit Before Taxes | 6.5 | 6.2 | 6.4 | | 5.8 | .5 | 5.6 | 8.5 | 6.9 |
| **RATIOS** | | | | | | | | | |
| Current | 3.9 / 2.1 / 1.2 | 3.9 / 2.0 / 1.2 | 4.1 / 2.2 / 1.3 | | 3.5 / 1.7 / 1.2 | 4.5 / 2.2 / 1.2 | 5.5 / 1.9 / 1.2 | 3.5 / 2.3 / 1.3 | 4.3 / 2.2 / 1.6 |
| Quick | 2.2 / 1.1 / .6 | 2.4 / 1.2 / .6 | 2.5 / 1.2 / .7 | | 1.9 / .9 / .6 | 3.0 / 1.2 / .5 | 2.4 / 1.0 / .4 | 2.0 / .9 / .6 | 2.7 / 1.4 / .8 |
| Sales/Receivables | 34 10.7 / 44 8.2 / 58 6.3 | 36 10.2 / 47 7.8 / 58 6.3 | 32 11.5 / 43 8.5 / 54 6.8 | | 14 26.6 / 34 10.8 / 38 9.7 | 29 12.7 / 42 8.7 / 54 6.7 | 29 12.7 / 40 9.2 / 51 7.2 | 32 11.5 / 41 9.0 / 51 7.1 | 40 9.2 / 49 7.4 / 58 6.3 |
| Cost of Sales/Inventory | 50 7.3 / 90 4.1 / 134 2.7 | 44 8.3 / 77 4.7 / 120 3.0 | 51 7.1 / 79 4.6 / 130 2.8 | | 6 60.0 / 46 8.0 / 159 2.3 | 48 7.6 / 78 4.7 / 146 2.5 | 54 6.8 / 78 4.7 / 152 2.4 | 49 7.4 / 79 4.6 / 122 3.0 | 54 6.7 / 81 4.5 / 135 2.7 |
| Cost of Sales/Payables | 19 19.4 / 32 11.5 / 49 7.5 | 18 20.5 / 32 11.4 / 55 6.7 | 22 16.9 / 33 10.9 / 54 6.7 | | 14 26.7 / 46 7.9 / 114 3.2 | 24 14.9 / 29 12.8 / 51 7.1 | 20 18.7 / 37 9.9 / 53 6.9 | 23 15.8 / 33 11.1 / 50 7.3 | 22 16.7 / 33 10.9 / 56 6.5 |
| Sales/Working Capital | 3.2 / 6.4 / 19.7 | 3.2 / 6.3 / 16.1 | 3.5 / 5.9 / 16.2 | | 4.5 / 12.1 / 41.2 | 4.2 / 5.7 / 10.0 | 3.3 / 8.8 / 28.1 | 4.0 / 6.9 / 18.4 | 3.0 / 4.7 / 8.7 |
| EBIT/Interest | 17.6 / (169) 5.7 / 1.7 | 24.5 / (168) 6.0 / 1.2 | 20.7 / (165) 7.0 / 1.5 | | 8.7 / (10) 6.6 / 1.6 | 18.5 / (11) 4.5 / 1.4 | 24.5 / (28) 8.2 / 1.9 | 25.0 / (47) 8.3 / 2.0 | 16.9 / (67) 7.2 / 1.1 |
| Net Profit + Depr., Dep., Amort./Cur. Mat. L/T/D | 6.3 / (67) 3.3 / 1.6 | 13.6 / (52) 2.7 / 1.3 | 6.5 / (50) 2.2 / 1.1 | | | | | | 8.1 / (39) 1.9 / 1.0 |
| Fixed/Worth | .2 / .5 / 2.3 | .2 / .6 / 3.0 | .2 / .6 / 2.0 | | .2 / .3 / -2.7 | .2 / .4 / 1.0 | .1 / .5 / 1.1 | .2 / .6 / 1.2 | .2 / .6 / -12.1 |
| Debt/Worth | .4 / 1.5 / 8.9 | .5 / 1.4 / 12.3 | .4 / 1.5 / 5.3 | | .4 / 3.0 / -5.3 | .9 / 2.6 / 5.7 | .4 / 1.3 / 2.2 | .5 / 1.2 / 4.0 | .3 / 1.5 / -42.8 |
| % Profit Before Taxes/Tangible Net Worth | 45.1 / (158) 22.2 / 6.5 | 49.7 / (150) 27.2 / 8.0 | 58.9 / (171) 29.2 / 6.3 | | 60.5 / (11) 35.9 / 13.1 | 59.2 / (18) 25.2 / -3.4 | 56.0 / (31) 25.2 / 3.6 | 64.6 / (51) 37.1 / 12.5 | 39.8 / (56) 23.1 / 5.4 |
| % Profit Before Taxes/Total Assets | 21.6 / 8.6 / 1.6 | 20.3 / 9.3 / 1.1 | 21.6 / 9.8 / 1.7 | | 21.1 / 7.2 / 3.3 | 11.6 / 6.4 / .8 | 22.4 / 11.6 / 1.7 | 30.1 / 12.6 / 4.6 | 19.9 / 9.0 / .8 |
| Sales/Net Fixed Assets | 26.4 / 10.8 / 4.6 | 27.9 / 10.3 / 4.4 | 25.0 / 12.4 / 4.8 | | 62.2 / 15.6 / 5.4 | 42.0 / 18.5 / 7.6 | 26.4 / 11.6 / 4.0 | 28.5 / 12.9 / 4.4 | 18.7 / 8.9 / 4.3 |
| Sales/Total Assets | 2.3 / 1.7 / 1.1 | 2.3 / 1.6 / 1.1 | 2.5 / 1.7 / 1.2 | | 3.4 / 1.8 / 1.0 | 3.1 / 2.2 / 1.3 | 2.5 / 1.9 / 1.3 | 3.1 / 1.9 / 1.5 | 2.1 / 1.4 / 1.0 |
| % Depr., Dep., Amort./Sales | 1.1 / (155) 2.3 / 4.7 | 1.1 / (153) 2.6 / 4.7 | 1.2 / (164) 2.3 / 4.3 | | | 1.0 / (15) 1.6 / 3.6 | 1.1 / (28) 2.2 / 4.9 | 1.0 / (47) 2.2 / 5.1 | 1.5 / (65) 2.5 / 4.3 |
| % Officers', Directors' Owners' Comp/Sales | 2.6 / (39) 5.9 / 9.4 | 2.4 / (49) 4.4 / 4.7 | 2.6 / (58) 5.4 / 8.9 | | | | 2.3 / (10) 4.6 / 13.6 | 4.2 / (16) 6.2 / 9.8 | 1.9 / (17) 3.0 / 7.0 |
| Net Sales ($) | 7804768M | 7752169M | 7617314M | 3900M | 29140M | 84316M | 247733M | 868981M | 6383244M |
| Total Assets ($) | 5993680M | 6135205M | 6107644M | 1373M | 17651M | 53426M | 158603M | 476968M | 5399623M |

© RMA 2012

M = $ thousand    MM = $ million
See Pages 9 through 22 for Explanation of Ratios and Data

## Current Data Sorted by Assets      Comparative Historical Data

| | | | | | | Type of Statement | | |
|---|---|---|---|---|---|---|---|---|
| | | 1 | 5 | 16 | 5 | 6   Unqualified | 40 | 34 |
| | | 1 | 16 | 8 | 5 |   Reviewed | 22 | 32 |
| | | 4 | 8 | 1 | 1 |   Compiled | 21 | 26 |
| 7 | | 15 | 4 | 1 | 1 |   Tax Returns | 12 | 27 |
| 5 | | 13 | 20 | 13 | 4 | 11   Other | 49 | 72 |
| | 26 (4/1-9/30/11) | | | 136 (10/1/11-3/31/12) | | | 4/1/07-3/31/08 ALL | 4/1/08-3/31/09 ALL |
| 0-500M | 500M-2MM | 2-10MM | 10-50MM | 50-100MM | 100-250MM | | | |
| 12 | 34 | 53 | 36 | 10 | 17 | NUMBER OF STATEMENTS | 144 | 191 |
| % | % | % | % | % | % | ASSETS | % | % |
| 12.4 | 11.7 | 9.3 | 9.8 | 8.8 | 12.9 | Cash & Equivalents | 11.5 | 9.3 |
| 45.5 | 30.9 | 26.8 | 23.8 | 30.7 | 11.1 | Trade Receivables (net) | 26.6 | 26.2 |
| 18.0 | 30.7 | 31.6 | 23.6 | 14.8 | 19.6 | Inventory | 22.7 | 25.5 |
| 5.1 | 5.9 | 1.4 | 2.5 | 2.2 | 2.5 | All Other Current | 3.4 | 3.0 |
| 81.0 | 79.3 | 69.2 | 59.7 | 56.5 | 46.1 | Total Current | 64.3 | 64.0 |
| 16.2 | 13.5 | 17.7 | 20.3 | 14.7 | 19.8 | Fixed Assets (net) | 19.7 | 21.1 |
| 1.1 | 2.0 | 7.6 | 14.5 | 18.6 | 26.9 | Intangibles (net) | 10.4 | 8.9 |
| 1.5 | 5.2 | 5.5 | 5.4 | 10.2 | 7.1 | All Other Non-Current | 5.7 | 5.9 |
| 100.0 | 100.0 | 100.0 | 100.0 | 100.0 | 100.0 | Total | 100.0 | 100.0 |
| | | | | | | LIABILITIES | | |
| 21.7 | 10.5 | 14.8 | 8.6 | 7.1 | 3.0 | Notes Payable-Short Term | 8.2 | 9.6 |
| .9 | 2.9 | 2.7 | 3.0 | 3.4 | 1.4 | Cur. Mat.-L.T.D. | 2.2 | 2.6 |
| 15.4 | 15.5 | 10.4 | 9.1 | 12.2 | 3.9 | Trade Payables | 13.8 | 12.7 |
| .7 | .2 | .4 | .2 | .5 | .3 | Income Taxes Payable | .3 | .2 |
| 20.6 | 11.7 | 11.5 | 13.6 | 6.6 | 10.8 | All Other Current | 8.6 | 11.6 |
| 59.2 | 40.7 | 39.8 | 34.4 | 29.7 | 19.4 | Total Current | 33.1 | 36.6 |
| 10.4 | 11.4 | 8.0 | 10.6 | 26.7 | 11.8 | Long-Term Debt | 14.1 | 14.7 |
| .4 | .1 | .2 | .5 | .0 | 2.7 | Deferred Taxes | .5 | .2 |
| 16.4 | 4.1 | 12.3 | 4.2 | 6.2 | 6.5 | All Other Non-Current | 4.7 | 7.5 |
| 13.5 | 43.7 | 39.8 | 50.2 | 37.3 | 59.6 | Net Worth | 47.6 | 41.0 |
| 100.0 | 100.0 | 100.0 | 100.0 | 100.0 | 100.0 | Total Liabilties & Net Worth | 100.0 | 100.0 |
| | | | | | | INCOME DATA | | |
| 100.0 | 100.0 | 100.0 | 100.0 | 100.0 | 100.0 | Net Sales | 100.0 | 100.0 |
| 50.6 | 50.0 | 44.6 | 42.6 | 39.6 | 46.5 | Gross Profit | 42.1 | 41.3 |
| 50.4 | 45.9 | 36.1 | 34.2 | 33.0 | 38.3 | Operating Expenses | 35.7 | 34.6 |
| .1 | 4.1 | 8.5 | 8.4 | 6.6 | 8.3 | Operating Profit | 6.4 | 6.7 |
| .2 | -.2 | 1.1 | 1.6 | 1.4 | 2.6 | All Other Expenses (net) | 1.4 | 1.3 |
| -.1 | 4.3 | 7.5 | 6.8 | 5.2 | 5.7 | Profit Before Taxes | 5.0 | 5.4 |
| | | | | | | RATIOS | | |
| 4.7 | 4.1 | 3.8 | 3.4 | 3.4 | 4.9 | | 3.5 | 3.3 |
| 2.2 | 2.3 | 2.3 | 2.1 | 2.0 | 2.9 | Current | 2.2 | 1.9 |
| .8 | 1.4 | 1.3 | 1.4 | 1.3 | 1.4 | | 1.4 | 1.1 |
| 3.8 | 2.8 | 1.9 | 2.0 | 2.3 | 2.3 | | 2.0 | 2.0 |
| 1.6 | 1.0 | .9 | 1.0 | 1.3 | 1.6 | Quick | 1.1 | 1.0 |
| .5 | .7 | .6 | .6 | .9 | .7 | | .7 | .5 |
| 33   10.9 | 34   10.6 | 34   10.6 | 39   9.3 | 54   6.7 | 36   10.1 | | 34   10.7 | 30   12.2 |
| 37   9.8 | 44   8.3 | 43   8.5 | 45   8.2 | 74   4.9 | 47   7.8 | Sales/Receivables | 45   8.1 | 41   8.9 |
| 52   7.0 | 59   6.2 | 59   6.2 | 53   6.9 | 99   3.7 | 54   6.8 | | 59   6.1 | 55   6.7 |
| 6   62.0 | 25   14.7 | 56   6.5 | 47   7.7 | 45   8.2 | 78   4.7 | | 31   11.8 | 30   12.1 |
| 27   13.7 | 87   4.2 | 76   4.8 | 87   4.2 | 68   5.4 | 159   2.3 | Cost of Sales/Inventory | 65   5.6 | 64   5.7 |
| 60   6.1 | 182   2.0 | 126   2.9 | 126   2.9 | 91   4.0 | 261   1.4 | | 121   3.0 | 121   3.0 |
| 0   UND | 15   24.6 | 12   30.9 | 22   16.3 | 18   19.8 | 20   18.0 | | 18   20.4 | 17   21.4 |
| 10   37.4 | 32   11.5 | 29   12.8 | 31   11.9 | 36   10.0 | 31   11.9 | Cost of Sales/Payables | 32   11.5 | 29   12.6 |
| 49   7.4 | 78   4.7 | 52   7.0 | 49   7.4 | 70   5.2 | 55   6.6 | | 52   7.0 | 48   7.6 |
| 6.1 | 3.6 | 4.0 | 3.4 | 4.0 | 1.7 | | 4.0 | 4.4 |
| 10.0 | 6.4 | 5.8 | 6.5 | 4.9 | 2.9 | Sales/Working Capital | 6.5 | 7.3 |
| NM | 15.9 | 19.4 | 16.0 | 11.5 | 11.3 | | 19.5 | 43.7 |
| 19.4 | | 23.6 | 21.9 | 23.9 | 27.8 | | 15.8 | 13.3 |
| | (32) 6.9 | (46) 8.4 | (27) 5.0 | 5.7 | (15) 8.9 | EBIT/Interest | (126) 4.9 | (167) 4.0 |
| | 1.7 | 2.8 | 2.0 | 1.1 | 1.5 | | 2.1 | 1.4 |
| | | | 9.3 | | | Net Profit + Depr., Dep., | 9.7 | 10.5 |
| | | | (15) 3.4 | | | Amort./Cur. Mat. L/T/D | (51) 4.0 | (45) 4.1 |
| | | | .9 | | | | 1.7 | 1.6 |
| .0 | .1 | .1 | .2 | .5 | .3 | | .2 | .2 |
| 14.2 | .3 | .4 | .5 | .7 | .6 | Fixed/Worth | .5 | .6 |
| -.8 | .8 | 3.3 | 1.3 | NM | NM | | 1.5 | 2.1 |
| .4 | .5 | .3 | .5 | 1.4 | .4 | | .5 | .6 |
| NM | 1.1 | 1.2 | 1.1 | 2.6 | .8 | Debt/Worth | 1.3 | 1.7 |
| -4.4 | 4.5 | 9.0 | 2.7 | NM | NM | | 4.0 | 11.4 |
| | 41.1 | 66.3 | 45.0 | | 32.6 | % Profit Before Taxes/Tangible | 50.6 | 51.3 |
| (30) 19.0 | (43) 21.5 | (29) 25.0 | | | (13) 24.5 | Net Worth | (123) 23.5 | (157) 22.5 |
| 3.8 | 8.9 | 10.1 | | | 7.2 | | 8.0 | 6.6 |
| 39.5 | 18.3 | 24.2 | 26.7 | 12.0 | 11.6 | % Profit Before Taxes/Total | 19.0 | 17.2 |
| 14.6 | 8.6 | 11.2 | 8.1 | 6.2 | 5.7 | Assets | 9.3 | 8.8 |
| -13.7 | 1.4 | 1.6 | 3.3 | -.5 | -.4 | | 2.4 | 1.1 |
| UND | 131.0 | 58.2 | 20.6 | 18.6 | 13.1 | | 32.4 | 32.6 |
| 42.1 | 31.8 | 27.5 | 9.7 | 9.9 | 4.8 | Sales/Net Fixed Assets | 12.6 | 12.5 |
| 17.0 | 9.2 | 7.5 | 5.7 | 6.0 | 3.2 | | 6.4 | 6.0 |
| 5.1 | 3.6 | 2.7 | 2.1 | 1.8 | 1.2 | | 2.9 | 3.3 |
| 4.3 | 2.3 | 2.0 | 1.7 | 1.5 | .7 | Sales/Total Assets | 2.0 | 2.1 |
| 3.3 | 1.6 | 1.4 | 1.2 | 1.1 | .6 | | 1.3 | 1.5 |
| | .5 | .6 | 1.2 | | 3.6 | | .9 | .9 |
| (21) .8 | (38) 1.6 | (31) 2.0 | | | (10) 4.8 | % Depr., Dep., Amort./Sales | (115) 1.8 | (159) 1.7 |
| 1.0 | 3.2 | 3.3 | | | 6.8 | | 3.5 | 3.4 |
| | 4.8 | 1.3 | | | | % Officers', Directors' | 2.5 | 1.9 |
| (24) 6.9 | (17) 3.5 | | | | | Owners' Comp/Sales | (50) 4.3 | (53) 4.8 |
| 11.8 | 5.1 | | | | | | 8.2 | 9.8 |
| 15759M | 108995M | 546150M | 1411716M | 908728M | 2191439M | Net Sales ($) | 5123530M | 6469088M |
| 3318M | 44118M | 256935M | 831438M | 646897M | 2640681M | Total Assets ($) | 3872816M | 4742981M |

© RMA 2012

M = $ thousand    MM = $ million
See Pages 9 through 22 for Explanation of Ratios and Data

## Comparative Historical Data | Current Data Sorted by Sales

| | | | Type of Statement | 0-1MM | 1-3MM | 3-5MM | 5-10MM | 10-25MM | 25MM & OVER |
|---|---|---|---|---|---|---|---|---|---|
| 24 | 29 | 33 | Unqualified | | 1 | 1 | 4 | 3 | 24 |
| 31 | 28 | 22 | Reviewed | 1 | 1 | 1 | 8 | 8 | 3 |
| 16 | 18 | 13 | Compiled | | 1 | 4 | 4 | 4 | |
| 22 | 16 | 28 | Tax Returns | 4 | 11 | 7 | 2 | 3 | 1 |
| 66 | 63 | 66 | Other | 3 | 11 | 4 | 14 | 9 | 25 |
| 4/1/09-3/31/10 ALL | 4/1/10-3/31/11 ALL | 4/1/11-3/31/12 ALL | | \multicolumn{2}{} 26 (4/1-9/30/11) | | 136 (10/1/11-3/31/12) | | | |
| 159 | 154 | 162 | NUMBER OF STATEMENTS | 8 | 25 | 17 | 32 | 27 | 53 |
| % | % | % | ASSETS | % | % | % | % | % | % |
| 11.0 | 10.9 | 10.5 | Cash & Equivalents | | 12.5 | 9.2 | 10.0 | 6.3 | 11.9 |
| 28.0 | 26.6 | 27.0 | Trade Receivables (net) | | 28.6 | 29.2 | 28.5 | 28.4 | 22.5 |
| 24.1 | 24.6 | 26.3 | Inventory | | 29.5 | 21.7 | 28.4 | 34.5 | 21.0 |
| 3.0 | 3.2 | 3.0 | All Other Current | | 5.6 | 1.1 | 1.5 | 2.6 | 2.3 |
| 66.1 | 65.3 | 66.9 | Total Current | | 76.2 | 61.2 | 68.4 | 71.8 | 57.6 |
| 20.5 | 19.5 | 17.4 | Fixed Assets (net) | | 16.4 | 25.0 | 15.2 | 16.7 | 18.8 |
| 8.0 | 10.1 | 10.2 | Intangibles (net) | | 4.7 | 7.9 | 9.7 | 7.3 | 16.6 |
| 5.3 | 5.1 | 5.6 | All Other Non-Current | | 2.7 | 6.0 | 6.7 | 4.2 | 7.0 |
| 100.0 | 100.0 | 100.0 | Total | | 100.0 | 100.0 | 100.0 | 100.0 | 100.0 |
| | | | LIABILITIES | | | | | | |
| 8.4 | 9.6 | 11.3 | Notes Payable-Short Term | | 17.4 | 9.0 | 8.9 | 21.2 | 6.5 |
| 3.0 | 3.0 | 2.6 | Cur. Mat.-L.T.D. | | 1.1 | 7.2 | 1.9 | 2.9 | 2.3 |
| 14.0 | 11.5 | 11.0 | Trade Payables | | 11.5 | 13.5 | 10.7 | 12.0 | 8.5 |
| .2 | .1 | .4 | Income Taxes Payable | | .6 | .4 | .5 | .1 | .3 |
| 11.5 | 9.7 | 12.3 | All Other Current | | 9.5 | 13.9 | 11.8 | 12.1 | 9.9 |
| 37.1 | 33.9 | 37.5 | Total Current | | 40.1 | 44.1 | 33.8 | 48.4 | 27.6 |
| 12.1 | 13.7 | 11.0 | Long-Term Debt | | 6.2 | 23.1 | 7.9 | 8.2 | 13.3 |
| .5 | .6 | .5 | Deferred Taxes | | .2 | .1 | .1 | .1 | 1.2 |
| 6.5 | 8.3 | 8.1 | All Other Non-Current | | 5.8 | 2.1 | 9.4 | 10.9 | 6.0 |
| 43.7 | 43.6 | 42.9 | Net Worth | | 47.7 | 30.5 | 48.8 | 32.4 | 51.9 |
| 100.0 | 100.0 | 100.0 | Total Liabilities & Net Worth | | 100.0 | 100.0 | 100.0 | 100.0 | 100.0 |
| | | | INCOME DATA | | | | | | |
| 100.0 | 100.0 | 100.0 | Net Sales | | 100.0 | 100.0 | 100.0 | 100.0 | 100.0 |
| 43.3 | 44.6 | 45.6 | Gross Profit | | 47.3 | 48.6 | 47.4 | 44.7 | 42.5 |
| 35.9 | 36.7 | 38.8 | Operating Expenses | | 43.0 | 46.3 | 38.8 | 36.2 | 33.8 |
| 7.4 | 7.9 | 6.8 | Operating Profit | | 4.3 | 2.3 | 8.6 | 8.5 | 8.6 |
| 1.2 | 1.1 | 1.0 | All Other Expenses (net) | | .6 | -.2 | 1.3 | 1.5 | 1.4 |
| 6.2 | 6.7 | 5.8 | Profit Before Taxes | | 3.7 | 2.5 | 7.3 | 6.9 | 7.2 |
| | | | RATIOS | | | | | | |
| 3.4 | 3.9 | 3.6 | | | 5.8 | 2.4 | 4.2 | 3.4 | 3.6 |
| 2.1 | 2.3 | 2.2 | Current | | 2.3 | 1.5 | 2.3 | 2.2 | 2.2 |
| 1.3 | 1.3 | 1.3 | | | 1.2 | 1.0 | 1.2 | 1.4 | 1.5 |
| 2.2 | 2.3 | 2.3 | | | 3.4 | 1.8 | 2.3 | 1.5 | 2.2 |
| 1.1 | 1.1 | 1.0 | Quick | | .9 | .8 | 1.0 | .7 | 1.4 |
| .7 | .7 | .6 | | | .6 | .5 | .8 | .5 | .8 |
| 34   10.6 | 35   10.4 | 36   10.2 | | | 34   10.8 | 35   10.5 | 36   10.1 | 36   10.2 | 38   9.6 |
| 45   8.1 | 47   7.7 | 45   8.2 | Sales/Receivables | | 42   8.7 | 40   9.2 | 43   8.5 | 43   8.5 | 49   7.4 |
| 63   5.8 | 57   6.4 | 57   6.4 | | | 57   6.4 | 55   6.6 | 62   5.9 | 51   7.1 | 66   5.5 |
| 35   10.4 | 44   8.3 | 43   8.5 | | | 20   18.7 | 11   34.4 | 34   10.6 | 62   5.9 | 49   7.4 |
| 70   5.2 | 73   5.0 | 81   4.5 | Cost of Sales/Inventory | | 91   4.0 | 43   8.5 | 85   4.3 | 96   3.8 | 81   4.5 |
| 117   3.1 | 116   3.1 | 140   2.6 | | | 228   1.6 | 111   3.3 | 114   3.2 | 215   1.7 | 135   2.7 |
| 18   20.8 | 17   21.2 | 14   25.8 | | | 3   106.1 | 18   20.2 | 12   29.9 | 23   15.9 | 20   18.0 |
| 31   11.9 | 28   13.1 | 30   12.1 | Cost of Sales/Payables | | 19   18.9 | 31   11.6 | 29   12.6 | 30   12.2 | 33   10.9 |
| 52   7.0 | 46   8.0 | 52   7.0 | | | 57   6.4 | 54   6.8 | 49   7.5 | 51   7.1 | 51   7.1 |
| 4.0 | 3.8 | 3.5 | | | 2.6 | 5.6 | 4.0 | 3.8 | 3.1 |
| 6.7 | 6.1 | 5.9 | Sales/Working Capital | | 5.7 | 14.9 | 6.7 | 5.8 | 4.6 |
| 18.3 | 17.6 | 16.7 | | | 23.3 | NM | 27.5 | 12.8 | 11.9 |
| 24.6 | 21.7 | 20.5 | | | 17.3 | 16.5 | 30.4 | 20.3 | 31.9 |
| (134)   6.3 | (130)   5.9 | (138)   6.6 | EBIT/Interest | | (19)   4.8 | (16)   5.6 | (27)   7.6 | (25)   8.1 | (45)   9.2 |
| 2.0 | 1.8 | 1.9 | | | 1.0 | 1.4 | 2.4 | 3.0 | 1.7 |
| 13.7 | 14.3 | 13.5 | Net Profit + Depr., Dep., | | | | | | 14.8 |
| (41)   4.5 | (30)   3.6 | (40)   4.6 | Amort./Cur. Mat. L/T/D | | | | | | (25)   6.8 |
| 1.5 | 2.7 | 1.0 | | | | | | | .9 |
| .2 | .2 | .2 | | | .1 | .1 | .1 | .1 | .3 |
| .5 | .5 | .4 | Fixed/Worth | | .4 | .5 | .4 | .4 | .5 |
| 1.4 | 1.9 | 1.6 | | | 1.0 | 16.4 | 8.3 | 1.7 | 1.5 |
| .4 | .5 | .5 | | | .3 | .9 | .3 | .5 | .5 |
| 1.2 | 1.4 | 1.2 | Debt/Worth | | .7 | 1.9 | 1.1 | 1.1 | 1.1 |
| 4.7 | 5.4 | 9.1 | | | 6.9 | 49.3 | 15.6 | 3.0 | 4.4 |
| 50.1 | 48.3 | 51.1 | % Profit Before Taxes/Tangible | | 42.6 | 135.2 | 62.7 | 46.2 | 47.2 |
| (136)   25.0 | (126)   26.0 | (129)   23.6 | Net Worth | | (20)   10.5 | (14)   21.8 | (25)   27.5 | (23)   13.8 | (43)   30.0 |
| 7.3 | 8.9 | 6.7 | | | 1.1 | 8.3 | 13.1 | 8.9 | 8.1 |
| 23.9 | 22.7 | 22.5 | % Profit Before Taxes/Total | | 16.3 | 30.1 | 26.9 | 20.1 | 23.5 |
| 9.8 | 8.8 | 8.5 | Assets | | 4.6 | 7.0 | 12.4 | 8.6 | 8.4 |
| 1.5 | 1.9 | 1.2 | | | -.1 | .9 | 3.7 | 3.2 | 1.4 |
| 28.5 | 30.8 | 49.6 | | | 195.3 | 74.1 | 71.1 | 47.8 | 19.4 |
| 12.3 | 12.7 | 15.3 | Sales/Net Fixed Assets | | 20.2 | 20.3 | 30.2 | 15.8 | 8.7 |
| 5.5 | 5.8 | 6.7 | | | 8.7 | 6.1 | 9.0 | 7.3 | 4.9 |
| 2.9 | 2.7 | 2.7 | | | 4.1 | 3.4 | 3.0 | 2.7 | 2.0 |
| 2.1 | 1.9 | 1.8 | Sales/Total Assets | | 1.7 | 2.5 | 2.0 | 2.2 | 1.6 |
| 1.5 | 1.4 | 1.3 | | | 1.3 | 1.6 | 1.5 | 1.5 | .9 |
| 1.0 | 1.1 | 1.1 | | | .8 | .6 | .6 | .5 | 1.3 |
| (132)   1.9 | (120)   1.9 | (114)   1.7 | % Depr., Dep., Amort./Sales | | (16)   .9 | (12)   1.5 | (16)   1.8 | (24)   1.4 | (42)   2.3 |
| 3.6 | 3.5 | 3.3 | | | 2.1 | 3.4 | 3.0 | 3.1 | 4.6 |
| 2.6 | 3.7 | 2.7 | % Officers', Directors' | | 3.2 | 3.6 | 2.0 | 2.3 | |
| (51)   4.4 | (39)   6.4 | (56)   4.9 | Owners' Comp/Sales | | (14)   6.9 | (12)   7.3 | (11)   4.9 | (10)   3.6 | |
| 9.9 | 10.0 | 8.8 | | | 10.7 | 11.8 | 6.1 | 4.8 | |
| 6258573M | 5302568M | 5182787M | Net Sales ($) | 5161M | 47135M | 68558M | 237929M | 468100M | 4355904M |
| 4374966M | 3848382M | 4423387M | Total Assets ($) | 3875M | 31083M | 42840M | 136334M | 253189M | 3956066M |

© RMA 2012

M = $ thousand    MM = $ million
See Pages 9 through 22 for Explanation of Ratios and Data

## Current Data Sorted by Assets      Comparative Historical Data

| 0-500M | 500M-2MM | 2-10MM | 10-50MM | 50-100MM | 100-250MM | Type of Statement | 4/1/07-3/31/08 ALL | 4/1/08-3/31/09 ALL |
|---|---|---|---|---|---|---|---|---|
| | 1 | 2 | 1 | 2 | 3 | Unqualified | 8 | 9 |
| | 2 | 6 | 1 | | | Reviewed | 4 | 4 |
| | 2 | 2 | | | | Compiled | 2 | 2 |
| 2 | 1 | 3 | | | | Tax Returns | 2 | 5 |
| 1 | 4 | 4 | 6 | 2 | 5 | Other | 22 | 22 |
| | 6 (4/1-9/30/11) | | 44 (10/1/11-3/31/12) | | | | | |
| 3 | 10 | 17 | 8 | 4 | 8 | **NUMBER OF STATEMENTS** | 38 | 42 |
| % | % | % | % | % | % | **ASSETS** | % | % |
| | 13.5 | 9.0 | | | | Cash & Equivalents | 12.6 | 10.6 |
| | 30.4 | 25.6 | | | | Trade Receivables (net) | 24.8 | 24.2 |
| | 25.9 | 30.2 | | | | Inventory | 22.5 | 22.9 |
| | 2.1 | 3.0 | | | | All Other Current | 3.2 | 2.4 |
| | 71.9 | 67.8 | | | | Total Current | 63.1 | 60.1 |
| | 13.3 | 24.2 | | | | Fixed Assets (net) | 22.3 | 22.3 |
| | 5.2 | 4.9 | | | | Intangibles (net) | 12.1 | 13.0 |
| | 9.6 | 3.1 | | | | All Other Non-Current | 2.5 | 4.7 |
| | 100.0 | 100.0 | | | | Total | 100.0 | 100.0 |
| | | | | | | **LIABILITIES** | | |
| | 15.3 | 8.5 | | | | Notes Payable-Short Term | 13.2 | 9.2 |
| | .8 | 4.2 | | | | Cur. Mat.-L.T.D. | 3.0 | 9.4 |
| | 9.8 | 10.3 | | | | Trade Payables | 8.4 | 10.8 |
| | .0 | 1.0 | | | | Income Taxes Payable | .2 | .2 |
| | 11.2 | 8.1 | | | | All Other Current | 8.9 | 12.1 |
| | 37.0 | 32.0 | | | | Total Current | 33.8 | 41.8 |
| | 8.4 | 12.0 | | | | Long-Term Debt | 13.7 | 22.0 |
| | .0 | 1.2 | | | | Deferred Taxes | .7 | .8 |
| | 3.4 | .9 | | | | All Other Non-Current | 5.2 | 3.9 |
| | 51.2 | 53.9 | | | | Net Worth | 46.6 | 31.4 |
| | 100.0 | 100.0 | | | | Total Liabilities & Net Worth | 100.0 | 100.0 |
| | | | | | | **INCOME DATA** | | |
| | 100.0 | 100.0 | | | | Net Sales | 100.0 | 100.0 |
| | 52.4 | 44.9 | | | | Gross Profit | 44.3 | 46.0 |
| | 50.1 | 38.3 | | | | Operating Expenses | 36.4 | 39.2 |
| | 2.3 | 6.6 | | | | Operating Profit | 7.9 | 6.8 |
| | -.4 | .5 | | | | All Other Expenses (net) | 1.5 | 2.1 |
| | 2.6 | 6.1 | | | | Profit Before Taxes | 6.5 | 4.7 |
| | | | | | | **RATIOS** | | |
| | 2.6 | 4.6 | | | | | 2.7 | 3.2 |
| | 1.8 | 2.4 | | | | Current | 1.8 | 1.9 |
| | 1.6 | 1.3 | | | | | 1.3 | 1.2 |
| | 2.3 | 1.7 | | | | | 1.5 | 1.4 |
| | 1.2 | 1.2 | | | | Quick | 1.1 | 1.1 |
| | .6 | .6 | | | | | .7 | .7 |
| | 35   10.3 | 29   12.7 | | | | | 34   10.9 | 30   12.2 |
| | 39   9.4 | 46   7.9 | | | | Sales/Receivables | 47   7.8 | 39   9.4 |
| | 43   8.5 | 55   6.6 | | | | | 53   6.9 | 45   8.1 |
| | 17   21.6 | 56   6.5 | | | | | 31   11.9 | 45   8.1 |
| | 91   4.0 | 104   3.5 | | | | Cost of Sales/Inventory | 76   4.8 | 81   4.5 |
| | 243   1.5 | 159   2.3 | | | | | 121   3.0 | 151   2.4 |
| | 14   26.5 | 20   18.0 | | | | | 14   26.4 | 16   23.0 |
| | 29   12.5 | 28   13.1 | | | | Cost of Sales/Payables | 27   13.5 | 31   11.9 |
| | 47   7.8 | 36   10.2 | | | | | 48   7.6 | 48   7.7 |
| | 4.1 | 3.5 | | | | | 3.8 | 4.5 |
| | 6.9 | 6.6 | | | | Sales/Working Capital | 8.3 | 8.4 |
| | 13.1 | 13.4 | | | | | 21.3 | 24.5 |
| | | 44.9 | | | | | 12.2 | 11.1 |
| | (16) | 5.5 | | | | EBIT/Interest | (37)   3.9 | (41)   3.1 |
| | | 2.1 | | | | | 2.0 | .8 |
| | | 8.5 | | | | Net Profit + Depr., Dep., | 10.9 | 10.7 |
| | (12) | 3.9 | | | | Amort./Cur. Mat. L/T/D | (14)   3.8 | (12)   3.8 |
| | | 2.0 | | | | | 1.5 | .9 |
| | .1 | .1 | | | | | .2 | .2 |
| | .1 | .5 | | | | Fixed/Worth | .7 | .7 |
| | .5 | 1.4 | | | | | 1.8 | 2.5 |
| | .5 | .3 | | | | | .9 | .8 |
| | 1.2 | 1.0 | | | | Debt/Worth | 1.4 | 1.5 |
| | 2.9 | 2.6 | | | | | 4.0 | NM |
| | 76.3 | 41.3 | | | | % Profit Before Taxes/Tangible | 55.1 | 66.7 |
| | 25.9 | 23.6 | | | | Net Worth | (34)   24.3 | (32)   12.2 |
| | -2.3 | 8.6 | | | | | 10.3 | .1 |
| | 26.7 | 17.3 | | | | % Profit Before Taxes/Total | 16.6 | 13.3 |
| | 12.2 | 10.8 | | | | Assets | 9.9 | 4.8 |
| | -1.5 | 3.3 | | | | | 3.7 | -.9 |
| | 61.4 | 18.4 | | | | | 21.0 | 19.8 |
| | 27.8 | 12.2 | | | | Sales/Net Fixed Assets | 10.2 | 11.7 |
| | 14.0 | 5.2 | | | | | 5.2 | 5.3 |
| | 3.6 | 2.5 | | | | | 2.8 | 2.9 |
| | 2.4 | 2.1 | | | | Sales/Total Assets | 1.9 | 2.0 |
| | 1.6 | 1.5 | | | | | 1.2 | 1.2 |
| | | 1.3 | | | | | 1.2 | 1.6 |
| | (16) | 2.2 | | | | % Depr., Dep., Amort./Sales | (34)   1.9 | (34)   2.1 |
| | | 3.4 | | | | | 4.3 | 3.3 |
| | | | | | | % Officers', Directors' | 2.4 | 1.5 |
| | | | | | | Owners' Comp/Sales | (12)   5.4 | (10)   5.1 |
| | | | | | | | 9.0 | 7.1 |
| 4691M | 36905M | 210663M | 330703M | 448027M | 1153082M | Net Sales ($) | 2824284M | 3171281M |
| 777M | 13414M | 105389M | 276187M | 260852M | 1239622M | Total Assets ($) | 1789806M | 1609088M |

M = $ thousand    MM = $ million
See Pages 9 through 22 for Explanation of Ratios and Data

## Comparative Historical Data                    Current Data Sorted by Sales

Current Data size brackets: 6 (4/1-9/30/11) covers 0-1MM, 1-3MM, 3-5MM; 44 (10/1/11-3/31/12) covers 5-10MM, 10-25MM, 25MM & OVER.

| Type of Statement | 4/1/09-3/31/10 ALL | 4/1/10-3/31/11 ALL | 4/1/11-3/31/12 ALL | 0-1MM | 1-3MM | 3-5MM | 5-10MM | 10-25MM | 25MM & OVER |
|---|---|---|---|---|---|---|---|---|---|
| Unqualified | 9 | 5 | 9 | | | | 1 | 2 | 6 |
| Reviewed | 6 | 8 | 9 | | 1 | | 1 | 6 | |
| Compiled | 1 | 4 | 4 | 1 | | | 1 | 1 | |
| Tax Returns | 5 | 8 | 6 | | 3 | 1 | 3 | | |
| Other | 20 | 20 | 22 | 1 | 1 | 1 | 3 | 7 | 10 |
| NUMBER OF STATEMENTS | 41 | 45 | 50 | 2 | 5 | 2 | 9 | 16 | 16 |
| **ASSETS** | % | % | % | % | % | % | % | % | % |
| Cash & Equivalents | 6.8 | 8.6 | 10.5 | | | | | 7.3 | 6.4 |
| Trade Receivables (net) | 22.0 | 26.0 | 23.2 | | | | | 24.2 | 17.2 |
| Inventory | 27.0 | 18.7 | 24.4 | | | | | 26.5 | 20.0 |
| All Other Current | 2.7 | 2.2 | 2.4 | | | | | 3.4 | 2.0 |
| Total Current | 58.4 | 55.6 | 60.5 | | | | | 61.4 | 45.7 |
| Fixed Assets (net) | 20.1 | 25.4 | 20.4 | | | | | 21.9 | 22.5 |
| Intangibles (net) | 16.3 | 14.6 | 14.0 | | | | | 10.3 | 29.4 |
| All Other Non-Current | 5.3 | 4.3 | 5.1 | | | | | 6.4 | 2.5 |
| Total | 100.0 | 100.0 | 100.0 | | | | | 100.0 | 100.0 |
| **LIABILITIES** | | | | | | | | | |
| Notes Payable-Short Term | 10.4 | 10.4 | 9.5 | | | | | 8.6 | 6.5 |
| Cur. Mat.-L.T.D. | 2.6 | 3.7 | 2.3 | | | | | 3.3 | 1.8 |
| Trade Payables | 9.1 | 13.3 | 9.8 | | | | | 10.8 | 9.3 |
| Income Taxes Payable | .3 | .2 | .4 | | | | | .4 | .0 |
| All Other Current | 10.7 | 9.8 | 10.0 | | | | | 9.3 | 8.3 |
| Total Current | 33.2 | 37.5 | 31.9 | | | | | 32.4 | 26.0 |
| Long-Term Debt | 13.7 | 18.7 | 11.5 | | | | | 11.5 | 11.1 |
| Deferred Taxes | .5 | 1.2 | 1.3 | | | | | 1.6 | 2.2 |
| All Other Non-Current | 2.8 | 3.2 | 3.8 | | | | | 2.6 | 6.1 |
| Net Worth | 49.7 | 39.4 | 51.5 | | | | | 51.8 | 54.6 |
| Total Liabilities & Net Worth | 100.0 | 100.0 | 100.0 | | | | | 100.0 | 100.0 |
| **INCOME DATA** | | | | | | | | | |
| Net Sales | 100.0 | 100.0 | 100.0 | | | | | 100.0 | 100.0 |
| Gross Profit | 45.5 | 44.2 | 49.1 | | | | | 43.0 | 49.6 |
| Operating Expenses | 40.9 | 39.9 | 42.7 | | | | | 39.1 | 39.3 |
| Operating Profit | 4.6 | 4.3 | 6.4 | | | | | 3.8 | 10.3 |
| All Other Expenses (net) | 1.4 | 1.4 | 1.0 | | | | | 2.3 | 1.6 |
| Profit Before Taxes | 3.2 | 2.9 | 5.4 | | | | | 1.6 | 8.7 |
| **RATIOS** | | | | | | | | | |
| Current | 2.7 | 2.6 | 3.6 | | | | | 3.8 | 3.9 |
| | 1.7 | 1.7 | 1.9 | | | | | 2.1 | 2.0 |
| | 1.4 | 1.2 | 1.4 | | | | | 1.3 | 1.3 |
| Quick | 1.4 | 1.7 | 1.7 | | | | | 1.4 | 1.7 |
| | .8 | 1.0 | 1.2 | | | | | 1.2 | 1.1 |
| | .6 | .7 | .6 | | | | | .6 | .6 |
| Sales/Receivables | 30  12.3 | 37  9.9 | 35  10.5 | | | | | 28  13.0 | 35  10.4 |
| | 41  8.9 | 43  8.4 | 41  8.9 | | | | | 38  9.5 | 42  8.6 |
| | 50  7.2 | 49  7.4 | 50  7.3 | | | | | 65  5.6 | 47  7.7 |
| Cost of Sales/Inventory | 59  6.2 | 20  18.6 | 60  6.1 | | | | | 54  6.7 | 74  4.9 |
| | 98  3.7 | 64  5.7 | 114  3.2 | | | | | 99  3.7 | 126  2.9 |
| | 142  2.6 | 118  3.1 | 159  2.3 | | | | | 159  2.3 | 146  2.5 |
| Cost of Sales/Payables | 16  23.0 | 17  21.1 | 19  18.8 | | | | | 20  18.1 | 27  13.7 |
| | 30  12.2 | 30  12.0 | 30  12.0 | | | | | 27  13.6 | 40  9.2 |
| | 58  6.3 | 52  7.0 | 45  8.1 | | | | | 43  8.4 | 61  6.0 |
| Sales/Working Capital | 6.2 | 5.7 | 4.0 | | | | | 3.8 | 4.1 |
| | 8.1 | 12.0 | 6.6 | | | | | 6.8 | 5.2 |
| | 14.3 | 24.5 | 14.5 | | | | | 14.2 | 16.6 |
| EBIT/Interest | 11.9 | 15.7 | 42.6 | | | | | 41.6 | 64.9 |
| | (38) 4.8 | (42) 7.2 | (46) 8.4 | | | | | 5.5 | 9.6 |
| | 1.2 | 1.3 | 2.1 | | | | | 2.1 | 2.7 |
| Net Profit + Depr., Dep., Amort./Cur. Mat. L/T/D | 4.1 | 7.0 | 11.9 | | | | | 8.0 | |
| | (14) 2.2 | (12) 3.3 | (19) 6.7 | | | | | (11) 3.3 | |
| | 1.5 | .5 | 2.4 | | | | | 1.9 | |
| Fixed/Worth | .2 | .3 | .2 | | | | | .2 | .5 |
| | .6 | .9 | .5 | | | | | .6 | .9 |
| | 1.2 | 2.0 | 1.5 | | | | | 1.9 | NM |
| Debt/Worth | .8 | .9 | .5 | | | | | .3 | .7 |
| | 1.2 | 1.7 | 1.4 | | | | | 1.2 | 1.6 |
| | 3.3 | 5.5 | 3.3 | | | | | 4.0 | NM |
| % Profit Before Taxes/Tangible Net Worth | 55.5 | 74.1 | 61.6 | | | | | 33.5 | 63.5 |
| | (37) 24.5 | (39) 34.6 | (45) 25.5 | | | | | (15) 22.7 | (12) 30.0 |
| | 5.9 | 8.7 | 7.0 | | | | | 8.1 | 18.6 |
| % Profit Before Taxes/Total Assets | 17.6 | 16.8 | 18.0 | | | | | 15.5 | 17.0 |
| | 7.5 | 8.4 | 9.9 | | | | | 6.4 | 13.2 |
| | .8 | -.8 | 2.8 | | | | | 3.2 | 5.0 |
| Sales/Net Fixed Assets | 26.0 | 36.1 | 21.3 | | | | | 21.1 | 12.0 |
| | 11.4 | 9.5 | 11.3 | | | | | 11.6 | 5.5 |
| | 5.2 | 3.9 | 5.0 | | | | | 4.2 | 3.4 |
| Sales/Total Assets | 2.8 | 3.2 | 2.4 | | | | | 2.4 | 1.8 |
| | 1.9 | 1.9 | 1.8 | | | | | 2.0 | 1.3 |
| | 1.1 | 1.4 | 1.3 | | | | | 1.4 | .7 |
| % Depr., Dep., Amort./Sales | .9 | 1.0 | 1.5 | | | | | 1.3 | 1.9 |
| | (33) 2.5 | (34) 2.3 | (37) 2.2 | | | | | (14) 2.0 | (12) 3.6 |
| | 3.9 | 4.1 | 3.6 | | | | | 3.3 | 5.1 |
| % Officers', Directors' Owners' Comp/Sales | | | (15) 4.7 | | | | | | |
| | | | 6.6 | | | | | | |
| | | | 9.0 | | | | | | |
| Net Sales ($) | 2551656M | 2470934M | 2184071M | 1933M | 9169M | 8177M | 60697M | 259483M | 1844612M |
| Total Assets ($) | 1806568M | 1774173M | 1896241M | 1139M | 3220M | 3589M | 32339M | 276401M | 1579553M |

M = $ thousand   MM = $ million
See Pages 9 through 22 for Explanation of Ratios and Data

## Current Data Sorted by Assets        Comparative Historical Data

| | | | | | | Type of Statement | | | |
|---|---|---|---|---|---|---|---|---|---|
| | | | 1 | 1 | 1 | 3 | Unqualified | 9 | 11 |
| | | 1 | 2 | | | | Reviewed | 5 | 4 |
| | 1 | 1 | | | | | Compiled | 6 | 3 |
| 1 | 3 | | | | | | Tax Returns | 2 | 2 |
| | 1 | | 6 | 2 | 1 | | Other | 15 | 11 |
| | 4 (4/1-9/30/11) | | 20 (10/1/11-3/31/12) | | | | | 4/1/07-3/31/08 | 4/1/08-3/31/09 |
| 0-500M | 500M-2MM | 2-10MM | 10-50MM | 50-100MM | 100-250MM | | | ALL | ALL |
| 1 | 5 | 2 | 9 | 3 | 4 | | NUMBER OF STATEMENTS | 37 | 31 |
| % | % | % | % | % | % | | | % | % |
| | | | | | | | **ASSETS** | | |
| | | | | | | | Cash & Equivalents | 7.9 | 7.6 |
| | | | | | | | Trade Receivables (net) | 24.3 | 20.7 |
| | | | | | | | Inventory | 25.5 | 26.6 |
| | | | | | | | All Other Current | 3.1 | 2.9 |
| | | | | | | | Total Current | 60.7 | 57.8 |
| | | | | | | | Fixed Assets (net) | 20.4 | 22.6 |
| | | | | | | | Intangibles (net) | 9.7 | 9.3 |
| | | | | | | | All Other Non-Current | 9.3 | 10.3 |
| | | | | | | | Total | 100.0 | 100.0 |
| | | | | | | | **LIABILITIES** | | |
| | | | | | | | Notes Payable-Short Term | 7.6 | 10.7 |
| | | | | | | | Cur. Mat.-L.T.D. | 3.8 | 4.0 |
| | | | | | | | Trade Payables | 16.6 | 15.8 |
| | | | | | | | Income Taxes Payable | .1 | .3 |
| | | | | | | | All Other Current | 11.3 | 6.3 |
| | | | | | | | Total Current | 39.5 | 37.0 |
| | | | | | | | Long-Term Debt | 20.5 | 15.7 |
| | | | | | | | Deferred Taxes | .8 | .8 |
| | | | | | | | All Other Non-Current | 2.6 | 3.0 |
| | | | | | | | Net Worth | 36.6 | 43.4 |
| | | | | | | | Total Liabilities & Net Worth | 100.0 | 100.0 |
| | | | | | | | **INCOME DATA** | | |
| | | | | | | | Net Sales | 100.0 | 100.0 |
| | | | | | | | Gross Profit | 43.8 | 47.0 |
| | | | | | | | Operating Expenses | 36.5 | 38.6 |
| | | | | | | | Operating Profit | 7.3 | 8.3 |
| | | | | | | | All Other Expenses (net) | 1.3 | 1.1 |
| | | | | | | | Profit Before Taxes | 6.0 | 7.2 |
| | | | | | | | **RATIOS** | | |
| | | | | | | | | 2.4 | 3.0 |
| | | | | | | | Current | 1.6 | 1.4 |
| | | | | | | | | 1.0 | 1.1 |
| | | | | | | | | 1.1 | 1.3 |
| | | | | | | | Quick | .7 | .7 |
| | | | | | | | | .5 | .4 |
| | | | | | | | | 31   11.7 | 26   13.8 |
| | | | | | | | Sales/Receivables | 44   8.4 | 40   9.0 |
| | | | | | | | | 51   7.1 | 49   7.5 |
| | | | | | | | | 32   11.5 | 27   13.6 |
| | | | | | | | Cost of Sales/Inventory | 86   4.2 | 97   3.7 |
| | | | | | | | | 136   2.7 | 156   2.3 |
| | | | | | | | | 26   14.1 | 28   13.2 |
| | | | | | | | Cost of Sales/Payables | 46   8.0 | 46   7.9 |
| | | | | | | | | 85   4.3 | 84   4.4 |
| | | | | | | | | 4.9 | 5.9 |
| | | | | | | | Sales/Working Capital | 9.5 | 9.7 |
| | | | | | | | | NM | 56.9 |
| | | | | | | | | 9.7 | 13.5 |
| | | | | | | | EBIT/Interest | (35)   3.6 | (27)   2.2 |
| | | | | | | | | 1.2 | 1.1 |
| | | | | | | | | 38.0 | 3.8 |
| | | | | | | | Net Profit + Depr., Dep., Amort./Cur. Mat. L/T/D | (13)   3.6 | (13)   2.2 |
| | | | | | | | | 1.5 | .9 |
| | | | | | | | | .2 | .2 |
| | | | | | | | Fixed/Worth | .8 | .7 |
| | | | | | | | | 2.9 | 1.0 |
| | | | | | | | | 1.0 | .8 |
| | | | | | | | Debt/Worth | 2.0 | 1.4 |
| | | | | | | | | 9.7 | 4.9 |
| | | | | | | | | 53.0 | 50.4 |
| | | | | | | | % Profit Before Taxes/Tangible Net Worth | (31)   20.1 | (27)   17.6 |
| | | | | | | | | 3.5 | 3.9 |
| | | | | | | | | 16.2 | 17.4 |
| | | | | | | | % Profit Before Taxes/Total Assets | 6.0 | 7.3 |
| | | | | | | | | 1.0 | 1.5 |
| | | | | | | | | 54.7 | 24.3 |
| | | | | | | | Sales/Net Fixed Assets | 11.3 | 9.0 |
| | | | | | | | | 6.2 | 4.7 |
| | | | | | | | | 3.4 | 2.4 |
| | | | | | | | Sales/Total Assets | 2.0 | 1.9 |
| | | | | | | | | 1.2 | 1.4 |
| | | | | | | | | .8 | 1.3 |
| | | | | | | | % Depr., Dep., Amort./Sales | (30)   2.1 | (25)   2.1 |
| | | | | | | | | 3.6 | 3.9 |
| | | | | | | | % Officers', Directors' Owners' Comp/Sales | | |
| 858M | 16219M | 37134M | 347866M | 247398M | 800205M | | Net Sales ($) | 2063753M | 1795085M |
| 404M | 4571M | 15021M | 239788M | 221539M | 591963M | | Total Assets ($) | 1561789M | 1246214M |

© RMA 2012

M = $ thousand    MM = $ million
See Pages 9 through 22 for Explanation of Ratios and Data

**Comparative Historical Data**  |  **Current Data Sorted by Sales**

| | 4/1/09-3/31/10 ALL | 4/1/10-3/31/11 ALL | 4/1/11-3/31/12 ALL | Type of Statement | 0-1MM | 1-3MM | 3-5MM | 5-10MM | 10-25MM | 25MM & OVER |
|---|---|---|---|---|---|---|---|---|---|---|
| | 14 | 7 | 5 | Unqualified | | | | | 1 | 4 |
| | 3 | 5 | 3 | Reviewed | | | | 1 | 2 | |
| | 4 | 4 | 2 | Compiled | | | | 1 | 1 | |
| | 3 | 2 | 4 | Tax Returns | 2 | 2 | 1 | | 1 | |
| | 12 | 16 | 10 | Other | | | | | | 8 |
| | | | | | | 4 (4/1-9/30/11) | | | 20 (10/1/11-3/31/12) | |
| | 36 | 34 | 24 | NUMBER OF STATEMENTS | 2 | 2 | 1 | 2 | 5 | 12 |
| | % | % | % | **ASSETS** | % | % | % | % | % | % |
| | 7.8 | 7.2 | 8.3 | Cash & Equivalents | | | | | | 10.0 |
| | 23.2 | 24.2 | 24.6 | Trade Receivables (net) | | | | | | 22.6 |
| | 21.5 | 24.0 | 22.4 | Inventory | | | | | | 24.6 |
| | 3.8 | 2.7 | 4.0 | All Other Current | | | | | | 5.0 |
| | 56.3 | 58.1 | 59.3 | Total Current | | | | | | 62.1 |
| | 21.6 | 20.2 | 19.3 | Fixed Assets (net) | | | | | | 22.6 |
| | 14.0 | 13.4 | 15.0 | Intangibles (net) | | | | | | 7.4 |
| | 8.1 | 8.3 | 6.5 | All Other Non-Current | | | | | | 8.0 |
| | 100.0 | 100.0 | 100.0 | Total | | | | | | 100.0 |
| | | | | **LIABILITIES** | | | | | | |
| | 8.0 | 6.6 | 6.5 | Notes Payable-Short Term | | | | | | 4.6 |
| | 3.7 | 3.4 | 5.7 | Cur. Mat.-L.T.D. | | | | | | 5.5 |
| | 16.3 | 18.4 | 13.9 | Trade Payables | | | | | | 14.0 |
| | .4 | .1 | .3 | Income Taxes Payable | | | | | | .6 |
| | 9.6 | 8.2 | 6.6 | All Other Current | | | | | | 8.3 |
| | 38.0 | 36.6 | 33.0 | Total Current | | | | | | 32.9 |
| | 14.7 | 16.7 | 14.9 | Long-Term Debt | | | | | | 4.2 |
| | .5 | .9 | .5 | Deferred Taxes | | | | | | 1.0 |
| | 7.9 | 4.6 | 10.8 | All Other Non-Current | | | | | | 9.0 |
| | 38.8 | 41.2 | 40.9 | Net Worth | | | | | | 53.0 |
| | 100.0 | 100.0 | 100.0 | Total Liabilities & Net Worth | | | | | | 100.0 |
| | | | | **INCOME DATA** | | | | | | |
| | 100.0 | 100.0 | 100.0 | Net Sales | | | | | | 100.0 |
| | 44.9 | 43.0 | 48.6 | Gross Profit | | | | | | 44.5 |
| | 38.4 | 34.9 | 39.6 | Operating Expenses | | | | | | 35.7 |
| | 6.5 | 8.0 | 9.1 | Operating Profit | | | | | | 8.8 |
| | 1.3 | 1.5 | 1.9 | All Other Expenses (net) | | | | | | 2.9 |
| | 5.1 | 6.5 | 7.1 | Profit Before Taxes | | | | | | 5.9 |
| | | | | **RATIOS** | | | | | | |
| | 2.7 | 2.5 | 2.6 | Current | | | | | | 3.2 |
| | 1.4 | 1.6 | 1.9 | | | | | | | 2.1 |
| | 1.1 | 1.2 | 1.3 | | | | | | | 1.4 |
| | 1.3 | 1.4 | 1.9 | Quick | | | | | | 1.8 |
| | .8 | .8 | .9 | | | | | | | .9 |
| | .5 | .6 | .6 | | | | | | | .6 |
| | 30 12.1 | 33 11.2 | 36 10.0 | Sales/Receivables | | | | | | 37 9.8 |
| | 39 9.5 | 43 8.6 | 45 8.1 | | | | | | | 47 7.8 |
| | 45 8.1 | 49 7.5 | 51 7.1 | | | | | | | 78 4.7 |
| | 34 10.8 | 31 11.8 | 32 11.4 | Cost of Sales/Inventory | | | | | | 76 4.8 |
| | 81 4.5 | 76 4.8 | 111 3.3 | | | | | | | 118 3.1 |
| | 126 2.9 | 136 2.7 | 146 2.5 | | | | | | | 159 2.3 |
| | 25 14.9 | 26 14.0 | 27 13.7 | Cost of Sales/Payables | | | | | | 34 10.6 |
| | 41 8.9 | 60 6.1 | 53 6.9 | | | | | | | 59 6.2 |
| | 67 5.5 | 80 4.5 | 85 4.3 | | | | | | | 85 4.3 |
| | 4.6 | 4.3 | 3.7 | Sales/Working Capital | | | | | | 3.3 |
| | 12.1 | 9.6 | 5.9 | | | | | | | 4.7 |
| | 67.5 | 26.0 | 21.3 | | | | | | | 7.7 |
| | 15.9 | 12.9 | 31.3 | EBIT/Interest | | | | | | 47.0 |
| | (35) 2.5 | (32) 4.8 | (21) 7.7 | | | | | | (10) | 10.1 |
| | 1.0 | 1.5 | 1.6 | | | | | | | 2.2 |
| | 8.8 | 6.7 | | Net Profit + Depr., Dep., Amort./Cur. Mat. L/T/D | | | | | | |
| | (13) 3.1 | (12) 2.5 | | | | | | | | |
| | .6 | 1.2 | | | | | | | | |
| | .3 | .3 | .4 | Fixed/Worth | | | | | | .2 |
| | .7 | .6 | .7 | | | | | | | .5 |
| | 4.0 | 2.9 | NM | | | | | | | .8 |
| | .7 | .6 | .8 | Debt/Worth | | | | | | .3 |
| | 1.8 | 1.5 | 2.1 | | | | | | | .8 |
| | 16.3 | 15.9 | NM | | | | | | | 2.2 |
| | 38.1 | 38.8 | 54.5 | % Profit Before Taxes/Tangible Net Worth | | | | | | 30.0 |
| | (29) 10.4 | (27) 18.0 | (18) 22.3 | | | | | | (11) | 13.3 |
| | -1.0 | 6.4 | 1.3 | | | | | | | 4.3 |
| | 12.9 | 11.8 | 14.1 | % Profit Before Taxes/Total Assets | | | | | | 14.1 |
| | 4.0 | 8.0 | 9.0 | | | | | | | 10.5 |
| | .1 | 2.4 | 2.4 | | | | | | | 2.4 |
| | 34.9 | 48.0 | 18.6 | Sales/Net Fixed Assets | | | | | | 11.2 |
| | 12.7 | 15.9 | 10.2 | | | | | | | 6.7 |
| | 5.1 | 6.2 | 6.1 | | | | | | | 5.3 |
| | 3.1 | 2.7 | 2.4 | Sales/Total Assets | | | | | | 1.8 |
| | 1.6 | 1.9 | 1.5 | | | | | | | 1.4 |
| | .9 | 1.2 | 1.1 | | | | | | | 1.1 |
| | 1.2 | .7 | 1.7 | % Depr., Dep., Amort./Sales | | | | | | |
| | (28) 2.0 | (25) 2.2 | (19) 2.3 | | | | | | | |
| | 3.0 | 3.3 | 5.0 | | | | | | | |
| | | 3.1 | | % Officers', Directors' Owners' Comp/Sales | | | | | | |
| | | (11) 4.9 | | | | | | | | |
| | | 6.3 | | | | | | | | |
| | 1769103M | 2131627M | 1449680M | Net Sales ($) | 1478M | 4764M | 3084M | 17632M | 81660M | 1341062M |
| | 1339203M | 1413330M | 1073286M | Total Assets ($) | 1394M | 1282M | 1131M | 22500M | 73413M | 973566M |

© RMA 2012

M = $ thousand    MM = $ million
See Pages 9 through 22 for Explanation of Ratios and Data

## Current Data Sorted by Assets

## Comparative Historical Data

| 0-500M | 500M-2MM | 2-10MM | 10-50MM | 50-100MM | 100-250MM | Type of Statement | | 4/1/07-3/31/08 ALL | 4/1/08-3/31/09 ALL |
|---|---|---|---|---|---|---|---|---|---|
| | | | | 1 | | Unqualified | | 1 | 2 |
| 2 | 1 | 1 | | | | Reviewed | | 3 | 3 |
| 9 | 5 | | 1 | | | Compiled | | 6 | 10 |
| 5 | 9 | 1 | 2 | 1 | 1 | Tax Returns | | 9 | 15 |
| | 8 | 2 | | | | Other | | 14 | 10 |
| | 8 (4/1-9/30/11) | | | 38 (10/1/11-3/31/12) | | | | | |
| 16 | 23 | 4 | 1 | 1 | 1 | **NUMBER OF STATEMENTS** | | 33 | 40 |
| % | % | % | % | % | % | **ASSETS** | | % | % |
| 23.6 | 12.4 | | | | | Cash & Equivalents | | 11.1 | 18.2 |
| 26.7 | 25.7 | | | | | Trade Receivables (net) | | 25.9 | 21.2 |
| 3.3 | 4.6 | | | | | Inventory | | 9.2 | 6.3 |
| .9 | 1.3 | | | | | All Other Current | | 2.0 | 2.5 |
| 54.4 | 43.9 | | | | | Total Current | | 48.2 | 48.2 |
| 32.9 | 32.3 | | | | | Fixed Assets (net) | | 34.1 | 31.3 |
| 7.2 | 17.4 | | | | | Intangibles (net) | | 3.2 | 8.5 |
| 5.5 | 6.4 | | | | | All Other Non-Current | | 14.4 | 12.1 |
| 100.0 | 100.0 | | | | | Total | | 100.0 | 100.0 |
| | | | | | | **LIABILITIES** | | | |
| 26.2 | 9.1 | | | | | Notes Payable-Short Term | | 16.3 | 22.6 |
| 5.9 | 5.4 | | | | | Cur. Mat.-L.T.D. | | 4.6 | 3.0 |
| 13.1 | 12.0 | | | | | Trade Payables | | 9.8 | 8.8 |
| .0 | .1 | | | | | Income Taxes Payable | | .5 | .4 |
| 19.9 | 10.8 | | | | | All Other Current | | 9.1 | 9.0 |
| 65.1 | 37.3 | | | | | Total Current | | 40.3 | 43.9 |
| 23.6 | 31.2 | | | | | Long-Term Debt | | 17.5 | 22.6 |
| .0 | .2 | | | | | Deferred Taxes | | 1.3 | .8 |
| 1.2 | 3.0 | | | | | All Other Non-Current | | 1.6 | 1.9 |
| 10.1 | 28.2 | | | | | Net Worth | | 39.2 | 30.9 |
| 100.0 | 100.0 | | | | | Total Liabilties & Net Worth | | 100.0 | 100.0 |
| | | | | | | **INCOME DATA** | | | |
| 100.0 | 100.0 | | | | | Net Sales | | 100.0 | 100.0 |
| | | | | | | Gross Profit | | | |
| 84.3 | 91.4 | | | | | Operating Expenses | | 92.6 | 94.9 |
| 15.7 | 8.6 | | | | | Operating Profit | | 7.4 | 5.1 |
| 7.7 | 1.9 | | | | | All Other Expenses (net) | | 1.5 | 1.2 |
| 8.0 | 6.7 | | | | | Profit Before Taxes | | 5.9 | 3.9 |
| | | | | | | **RATIOS** | | | |
| 2.1 | 1.4 | | | | | | | 2.5 | 2.3 |
| .7 | 1.3 | | | | | Current | | 1.6 | 1.4 |
| .5 | .5 | | | | | | | .7 | 1.1 |
| 2.0 | 1.3 | | | | | | | 2.0 | 1.9 |
| .6 | 1.1 | | | | | Quick | | 1.3 | 1.1 |
| .4 | .4 | | | | | | | .4 | .8 |
| 0   UND | 0   UND | | | | | | 24   15.1 | 0   UND | |
| 20   17.9 | 33   10.9 | | | | | Sales/Receivables | 35   10.3 | 32   11.3 | |
| 39   9.4 | 41   8.8 | | | | | | 41   9.0 | 42   8.8 | |
| | | | | | | Cost of Sales/Inventory | | | |
| | | | | | | Cost of Sales/Payables | | | |
| 25.2 | 19.8 | | | | | | | 10.7 | 14.1 |
| -60.7 | 35.7 | | | | | Sales/Working Capital | | 19.8 | 27.7 |
| -11.2 | -15.7 | | | | | | | -14.1 | 479.2 |
| 12.4 | 17.2 | | | | | | | 11.8 | 21.9 |
| (11)   4.1 | (22)   7.3 | | | | | EBIT/Interest | (31)   6.1 | (36)   3.6 | |
| 1.5 | 1.6 | | | | | | | 1.1 | .1 |
| | | | | | | Net Profit + Depr., Dep., Amort./Cur. Mat. L/T/D | | 4.8 | 2.0 |
| | | | | | | | (10)   2.3 | (10)   1.1 | |
| | | | | | | | | 1.8 | .5 |
| .5 | 1.0 | | | | | | | .5 | .3 |
| 38.2 | 3.1 | | | | | Fixed/Worth | | .9 | .7 |
| -.6 | -.8 | | | | | | | 1.9 | 4.0 |
| .7 | 1.6 | | | | | | | .7 | .6 |
| 94.2 | 6.4 | | | | | Debt/Worth | | 1.7 | 1.4 |
| -3.5 | -4.1 | | | | | | | 5.0 | 6.5 |
| | 68.4 | | | | | | | 74.6 | 58.8 |
| | (14)   27.3 | | | | | % Profit Before Taxes/Tangible Net Worth | (30)   30.1 | (35)   24.8 | |
| | 15.8 | | | | | | | 7.5 | 2.7 |
| 65.9 | 29.7 | | | | | | | 27.6 | 28.8 |
| 28.3 | 12.4 | | | | | % Profit Before Taxes/Total Assets | | 10.5 | 8.0 |
| 3.5 | 1.4 | | | | | | | 1.0 | -1.1 |
| 44.9 | 31.1 | | | | | | | 23.9 | 42.0 |
| 21.1 | 14.7 | | | | | Sales/Net Fixed Assets | | 12.4 | 16.1 |
| 12.1 | 7.3 | | | | | | | 5.9 | 7.6 |
| 8.1 | 4.9 | | | | | | | 4.0 | 6.1 |
| 5.0 | 3.5 | | | | | Sales/Total Assets | | 3.2 | 3.9 |
| 4.0 | 2.1 | | | | | | | 1.9 | 2.2 |
| 1.1 | 1.1 | | | | | | | 1.2 | 1.3 |
| (11)   1.8 | (20)   2.0 | | | | | % Depr., Dep., Amort./Sales | (29)   1.8 | (30)   2.0 | |
| 3.3 | 3.9 | | | | | | | 3.4 | 3.3 |
| 3.0 | 2.9 | | | | | | | 6.6 | 6.1 |
| (11)   9.2 | (17)   5.6 | | | | | % Officers', Directors' Owners' Comp/Sales | (22)   12.6 | (23)   8.2 | |
| 14.0 | 11.2 | | | | | | | 17.2 | 14.3 |
| 19928M | 77746M | 37026M | 9554M | 251872M | 64461M | Net Sales ($) | | 591272M | 1452494M |
| 4103M | 23820M | 15821M | 11788M | 57087M | 137996M | Total Assets ($) | | 377354M | 509397M |

© RMA 2012

M = $ thousand     MM = $ million
See Pages 9 through 22 for Explanation of Ratios and Data

## Comparative Historical Data | Current Data Sorted by Sales

| | | | Type of Statement | | | | | | |
|---|---|---|---|---|---|---|---|---|---|
| 2 | 3 | 1 | Unqualified | | | 1 | | 1 | 1 |
| 2 | 2 | 2 | Reviewed | | | 1 | 1 | | |
| 5 | 4 | 7 | Compiled | 1 | 4 | 1 | 1 | | |
| 17 | 21 | 19 | Tax Returns | 5 | 11 | 1 | 2 | | |
| 19 | 10 | 17 | Other | 2 | 6 | 4 | 3 | 1 | 1 |
| 4/1/09-3/31/10 ALL | 4/1/10-3/31/11 ALL | 4/1/11-3/31/12 ALL | | 8 (4/1-9/30/11) | | | 38 (10/1/11-3/31/12) | | |
| | | | | 0-1MM | 1-3MM | 3-5MM | 5-10MM | 10-25MM | 25MM & OVER |
| 45 | 40 | 46 | NUMBER OF STATEMENTS | 8 | 21 | 7 | 6 | 2 | 2 |
| % | % | % | ASSETS | % | % | % | % | % | % |
| 13.7 | 15.1 | 16.5 | Cash & Equivalents | | 13.2 | | | | |
| 27.0 | 23.6 | 25.7 | Trade Receivables (net) | | 28.2 | | | | |
| 7.1 | 4.2 | 4.6 | Inventory | | 5.5 | | | | |
| 3.9 | 3.1 | 1.5 | All Other Current | | .1 | | | | |
| 51.6 | 46.0 | 48.2 | Total Current | | 47.0 | | | | |
| 29.2 | 35.2 | 30.5 | Fixed Assets (net) | | 26.3 | | | | |
| 7.5 | 10.4 | 14.4 | Intangibles (net) | | 17.7 | | | | |
| 11.7 | 8.4 | 7.0 | All Other Non-Current | | 8.9 | | | | |
| 100.0 | 100.0 | 100.0 | Total | | 100.0 | | | | |
| | | | LIABILITIES | | | | | | |
| 12.9 | 12.4 | 15.5 | Notes Payable-Short Term | | 20.8 | | | | |
| 4.8 | 8.0 | 5.0 | Cur. Mat.-L.T.D. | | 5.8 | | | | |
| 8.7 | 13.4 | 11.8 | Trade Payables | | 12.3 | | | | |
| .4 | .4 | .0 | Income Taxes Payable | | .0 | | | | |
| 10.4 | 12.1 | 13.8 | All Other Current | | 21.3 | | | | |
| 37.3 | 46.3 | 46.1 | Total Current | | 60.2 | | | | |
| 27.4 | 25.1 | 24.2 | Long-Term Debt | | 32.0 | | | | |
| .4 | .5 | .1 | Deferred Taxes | | .1 | | | | |
| 3.2 | 6.0 | 2.8 | All Other Non-Current | | 3.3 | | | | |
| 31.7 | 22.1 | 26.9 | Net Worth | | 4.3 | | | | |
| 100.0 | 100.0 | 100.0 | Total Liabilties & Net Worth | | 100.0 | | | | |
| | | | INCOME DATA | | | | | | |
| 100.0 | 100.0 | 100.0 | Net Sales | | 100.0 | | | | |
| | | | Gross Profit | | | | | | |
| 93.7 | 95.6 | 88.8 | Operating Expenses | | 94.5 | | | | |
| 6.3 | 4.4 | 11.2 | Operating Profit | | 5.5 | | | | |
| .9 | 1.7 | 3.7 | All Other Expenses (net) | | 1.6 | | | | |
| 5.5 | 2.6 | 7.4 | Profit Before Taxes | | 3.8 | | | | |
| | | | RATIOS | | | | | | |
| 3.4 | 2.2 | 1.6 | | | 1.3 | | | | |
| 1.5 | 1.1 | 1.1 | Current | | .7 | | | | |
| .8 | .5 | .5 | | | .5 | | | | |
| 2.6 | 1.7 | 1.4 | | | 1.2 | | | | |
| 1.1 | .9 | .8 | Quick | | .6 | | | | |
| .6 | .5 | .4 | | | .4 | | | | |
| 1  309.9 | 0  UND | 0  UND | | | 0  UND | | | | |
| 35  10.5 | 33  10.9 | 33  11.0 | Sales/Receivables | | 33  11.1 | | | | |
| 40  9.0 | 41  9.0 | 42  8.7 | | | 39  9.3 | | | | |
| | | | Cost of Sales/Inventory | | | | | | |
| | | | Cost of Sales/Payables | | | | | | |
| 8.2 | 14.1 | 19.1 | | | 35.1 | | | | |
| 31.2 | 74.5 | NM | Sales/Working Capital | | -40.2 | | | | |
| -56.3 | -12.7 | -14.4 | | | -10.7 | | | | |
| 24.2 | 9.8 | 15.5 | | | 10.1 | | | | |
| (37)  5.0 | (30)  3.5 | (39)  7.4 | EBIT/Interest | | (19)  2.8 | | | | |
| 1.7 | .6 | 1.8 | | | 1.5 | | | | |
| | | | Net Profit + Depr., Dep., Amort./Cur. Mat. L/T/D | | | | | | |
| .3 | .6 | .6 | | | 2.0 | | | | |
| 1.0 | 3.0 | 3.1 | Fixed/Worth | | -2.1 | | | | |
| UND | NM | -.8 | | | -.4 | | | | |
| .4 | .8 | .8 | | | 6.2 | | | | |
| 3.7 | 6.7 | 5.3 | Debt/Worth | | -8.7 | | | | |
| UND | -5.9 | -4.0 | | | -2.6 | | | | |
| 109.6 | 172.8 | 109.6 | | | | | | | |
| (35)  52.2 | (29)  43.1 | (28)  39.3 | % Profit Before Taxes/Tangible Net Worth | | | | | | |
| 19.7 | 17.8 | 19.5 | | | | | | | |
| 36.1 | 30.8 | 38.5 | | | 30.2 | | | | |
| 12.9 | 11.5 | 13.5 | % Profit Before Taxes/Total Assets | | 11.4 | | | | |
| 3.0 | .5 | 1.4 | | | .2 | | | | |
| 51.7 | 40.0 | 36.6 | | | 37.0 | | | | |
| 18.2 | 16.7 | 14.9 | Sales/Net Fixed Assets | | 19.2 | | | | |
| 6.5 | 6.1 | 10.1 | | | 12.6 | | | | |
| 5.5 | 5.2 | 5.1 | | | 5.3 | | | | |
| 3.6 | 3.9 | 4.1 | Sales/Total Assets | | 4.4 | | | | |
| 2.2 | 2.5 | 2.1 | | | 2.8 | | | | |
| 1.2 | 1.1 | 1.2 | | | 1.2 | | | | |
| (31)  1.8 | (29)  2.0 | (37)  2.0 | % Depr., Dep., Amort./Sales | | (16)  2.1 | | | | |
| 3.6 | 3.3 | 3.6 | | | 3.6 | | | | |
| 5.0 | 4.1 | 3.1 | | | 3.4 | | | | |
| (30)  8.6 | (24)  6.5 | (30)  5.5 | % Officers', Directors' Owners' Comp/Sales | | (16)  9.4 | | | | |
| 13.5 | 10.3 | 11.1 | | | 13.1 | | | | |
| 421439M | 709382M | 460587M | Net Sales ($) | 3817M | 38240M | 28346M | 43945M | 29906M | 316333M |
| 270208M | 464337M | 250615M | Total Assets ($) | 5003M | 11105M | 7582M | 20270M | 11572M | 195083M |

© RMA 2012     M = $ thousand     MM = $ million
See Pages 9 through 22 for Explanation of Ratios and Data

## Current Data Sorted by Assets                         Comparative Historical Data

| | 0-500M | 500M-2MM | 2-10MM | 10-50MM | 50-100MM | 100-250MM | Type of Statement | 4/1/07-3/31/08 ALL | 4/1/08-3/31/09 ALL |
|---|---|---|---|---|---|---|---|---|---|
| | 1 | | 7 | 16 | 3 | 1 | Unqualified | 25 | 28 |
| | 6 | 10 | 22 | 5 | | | Reviewed | 46 | 36 |
| | 13 | 23 | 11 | 4 | | | Compiled | 14 | 15 |
| | 6 | 19 | 9 | 3 | | | Tax Returns | 17 | 25 |
| | | 34 (4/1-9/30/11) | 32 | 170 (10/1/11-3/31/12) 9 | 2 | 2 | Other | 32 | 68 |
| | 26 | 52 | 81 | 37 | 5 | 3 | NUMBER OF STATEMENTS | 134 | 172 |
| | % | % | % | % | % | % | ASSETS | % | % |
| | 13.2 | 11.2 | 8.5 | 10.9 | | | Cash & Equivalents | 5.8 | 7.2 |
| | 26.0 | 30.2 | 23.6 | 19.6 | | | Trade Receivables (net) | 27.7 | 23.9 |
| | 31.9 | 34.0 | 36.9 | 36.3 | | | Inventory | 47.1 | 43.0 |
| | .8 | .5 | 2.2 | 1.3 | | | All Other Current | 1.8 | 1.5 |
| | 72.0 | 75.9 | 71.2 | 68.0 | | | Total Current | 82.4 | 75.6 |
| | 14.6 | 16.7 | 19.0 | 17.4 | | | Fixed Assets (net) | 10.2 | 14.2 |
| | 3.9 | 1.7 | 2.2 | 1.9 | | | Intangibles (net) | 1.9 | 2.5 |
| | 9.5 | 5.7 | 7.6 | 12.7 | | | All Other Non-Current | 5.6 | 7.7 |
| | 100.0 | 100.0 | 100.0 | 100.0 | | | Total | 100.0 | 100.0 |
| | | | | | | | LIABILITIES | | |
| | 14.1 | 10.2 | 10.7 | 10.1 | | | Notes Payable-Short Term | 25.7 | 23.9 |
| | 1.6 | 3.3 | 2.2 | 1.8 | | | Cur. Mat.-L.T.D. | 2.4 | 3.1 |
| | 14.0 | 25.4 | 16.8 | 15.3 | | | Trade Payables | 18.7 | 14.2 |
| | .1 | .1 | .1 | .0 | | | Income Taxes Payable | .5 | .5 |
| | 33.8 | 9.9 | 16.2 | 10.2 | | | All Other Current | 7.8 | 14.0 |
| | 63.5 | 48.9 | 46.0 | 37.4 | | | Total Current | 55.1 | 55.6 |
| | 43.9 | 13.1 | 12.8 | 6.6 | | | Long-Term Debt | 5.8 | 10.4 |
| | .1 | .0 | .3 | .5 | | | Deferred Taxes | .3 | .3 |
| | 15.7 | 6.7 | 5.6 | 5.2 | | | All Other Non-Current | 5.2 | 3.7 |
| | -23.2 | 31.3 | 35.3 | 50.4 | | | Net Worth | 33.6 | 30.0 |
| | 100.0 | 100.0 | 100.0 | 100.0 | | | Total Liabilities & Net Worth | 100.0 | 100.0 |
| | | | | | | | INCOME DATA | | |
| | 100.0 | 100.0 | 100.0 | 100.0 | | | Net Sales | 100.0 | 100.0 |
| | 42.9 | 36.0 | 33.6 | 26.4 | | | Gross Profit | 27.4 | 33.2 |
| | 40.6 | 30.9 | 29.3 | 21.2 | | | Operating Expenses | 23.6 | 29.2 |
| | 2.3 | 5.1 | 4.2 | 5.2 | | | Operating Profit | 3.8 | 3.9 |
| | .6 | .9 | .8 | .6 | | | All Other Expenses (net) | 1.2 | 1.6 |
| | 1.7 | 4.2 | 3.4 | 4.6 | | | Profit Before Taxes | 2.6 | 2.4 |
| | | | | | | | RATIOS | | |
| | 4.8 | 2.6 | 3.3 | 4.1 | | | Current | 2.0 | 2.3 |
| | 1.6 | 1.9 | 1.8 | 1.8 | | | | 1.4 | 1.5 |
| | .8 | 1.1 | 1.2 | 1.2 | | | | 1.2 | 1.1 |
| | 2.2 | 1.3 | 1.3 | 2.0 | | | Quick | 1.0 | 1.0 |
| | .9 | .8 | .8 | .9 | | | | .6 | .5 |
| | .2 | .5 | .5 | .5 | | | | .3 | .4 |
| | 0 UND | 24 15.4 | 23 15.8 | 33 10.9 | | | Sales/Receivables | 24 15.0 | 18 20.5 |
| | 23 15.7 | 31 11.9 | 39 9.3 | 45 8.2 | | | | 48 7.6 | 40 9.1 |
| | 36 10.1 | 45 8.1 | 54 6.8 | 58 6.3 | | | | 82 4.5 | 62 5.9 |
| | 0 UND | 17 21.0 | 40 9.1 | 42 8.7 | | | Cost of Sales/Inventory | 58 6.3 | 51 7.1 |
| | 42 8.7 | 50 7.3 | 87 4.2 | 89 4.1 | | | | 116 3.1 | 114 3.2 |
| | 140 2.6 | 91 4.0 | 174 2.1 | 228 1.6 | | | | 225 1.6 | 236 1.5 |
| | 1 517.7 | 17 22.0 | 19 19.5 | 17 22.1 | | | Cost of Sales/Payables | 11 34.2 | 9 40.8 |
| | 19 19.7 | 41 8.9 | 38 9.6 | 30 12.0 | | | | 40 9.2 | 25 14.5 |
| | 49 7.5 | 68 5.4 | 66 5.5 | 54 6.7 | | | | 81 4.5 | 58 6.3 |
| | 7.0 | 4.7 | 3.6 | 2.1 | | | Sales/Working Capital | 3.8 | 3.9 |
| | 61.1 | 11.0 | 6.8 | 6.4 | | | | 7.9 | 8.1 |
| | -21.7 | 48.8 | 24.7 | 21.4 | | | | 17.2 | 37.1 |
| | 12.3 | 14.6 | 13.9 | 48.8 | | | EBIT/Interest | 4.9 | 5.4 |
| (14) 3.5 | | (44) 5.6 | (74) 4.2 | (27) 6.6 | | | | (123) 1.9 | (157) 2.2 |
| | .5 | 2.3 | 1.0 | 1.9 | | | | 1.1 | .9 |
| | | | 8.5 | | | | Net Profit + Depr., Dep., Amort./Cur. Mat. L/T/D | 14.1 | 7.7 |
| | | (17) 3.4 | | | | | | (20) 3.6 | (31) 2.3 |
| | | | .4 | | | | | .8 | .6 |
| | .0 | .1 | .1 | .1 | | | Fixed/Worth | .1 | .1 |
| | .2 | .4 | .4 | .2 | | | | .2 | .2 |
| | -.2 | 1.0 | 1.1 | .6 | | | | .5 | .8 |
| | .8 | 1.0 | .7 | .3 | | | Debt/Worth | 1.2 | .8 |
| | 11.9 | 1.9 | 1.7 | 1.3 | | | | 2.3 | 1.9 |
| | -2.1 | 8.5 | 4.2 | 2.9 | | | | 4.6 | 3.8 |
| | 98.1 | 61.4 | 40.1 | 35.8 | | | % Profit Before Taxes/Tangible Net Worth | 28.7 | 31.5 |
| (15) 26.0 | | (45) 27.4 | (74) 15.3 | (36) 15.2 | | | | (128) 8.7 | (158) 8.4 |
| | 5.7 | 5.3 | 4.9 | 3.2 | | | | 1.1 | .4 |
| | 22.7 | 16.8 | 14.6 | 16.6 | | | % Profit Before Taxes/Total Assets | 8.1 | 10.7 |
| | 5.3 | 7.7 | 4.9 | 9.6 | | | | 2.5 | 3.0 |
| | -5.5 | 2.3 | .5 | .9 | | | | .3 | -.1 |
| | UND | 82.4 | 79.7 | 38.3 | | | Sales/Net Fixed Assets | 133.7 | 98.5 |
| | 35.3 | 24.3 | 22.7 | 18.1 | | | | 40.8 | 31.3 |
| | 16.3 | 12.7 | 5.5 | 7.0 | | | | 14.6 | 10.7 |
| | 6.7 | 4.2 | 2.9 | 2.3 | | | Sales/Total Assets | 2.6 | 3.0 |
| | 3.8 | 3.0 | 2.1 | 1.4 | | | | 1.8 | 1.9 |
| | 2.2 | 2.1 | 1.3 | .9 | | | | 1.2 | 1.2 |
| | .4 | .4 | .5 | .5 | | | % Depr., Dep., Amort./Sales | .2 | .3 |
| (16) 1.1 | | (35) 1.0 | (58) 1.0 | (34) 1.0 | | | | (111) .7 | (141) 1.0 |
| | 2.0 | 2.6 | 3.2 | 2.2 | | | | 1.2 | 1.8 |
| | 3.5 | 2.0 | 1.4 | | | | % Officers', Directors' Owners' Comp/Sales | 1.1 | 1.7 |
| (16) 7.9 | | (37) 4.1 | (40) 3.4 | | | | | (69) 2.7 | (82) 3.4 |
| | 10.0 | 7.9 | 6.0 | | | | | 6.4 | 6.3 |
| | 28284M | 225933M | 849596M | 1356691M | 529798M | 826380M | Net Sales ($) | 5586316M | 4749716M |
| | 6808M | 67906M | 383311M | 823526M | 309120M | 524448M | Total Assets ($) | 2894524M | 2658158M |

M = $ thousand    MM = $ million
See Pages 9 through 22 for Explanation of Ratios and Data

## Comparative Historical Data / Current Data Sorted by Sales

| | | | Type of Statement | | | | | | |
|---|---|---|---|---|---|---|---|---|---|
| 33 | 20 | 27 | Unqualified | | 1 | | 6 | 8 | 12 |
| 36 | 34 | 28 | Reviewed | 1 | | 4 | 9 | 11 | 3 |
| 20 | 16 | 31 | Compiled | 5 | 6 | 8 | 4 | 5 | 3 |
| 43 | 29 | 48 | Tax Returns | 10 | 15 | 8 | 9 | 5 | 1 |
| 62 | 51 | 70 | Other | 3 | 6 | 14 | 15 | 20 | 12 |
| 4/1/09-3/31/10 ALL | 4/1/10-3/31/11 ALL | 4/1/11-3/31/12 ALL | | 0-1MM | 1-3MM | 3-5MM | 5-10MM | 10-25MM | 25MM & OVER |
| | | | | | 34 (4/1-9/30/11) | | 170 (10/1/11-3/31/12) | | |
| 194 | 150 | 204 | NUMBER OF STATEMENTS | 19 | 28 | 34 | 43 | 49 | 31 |
| % | % | % | **ASSETS** | % | % | % | % | % | % |
| 8.8 | 10.1 | 10.2 | Cash & Equivalents | 11.4 | 11.3 | 8.1 | 8.6 | 12.0 | 10.3 |
| 25.6 | 25.4 | 24.6 | Trade Receivables (net) | 23.2 | 18.6 | 31.2 | 25.9 | 24.4 | 21.9 |
| 37.9 | 35.9 | 35.1 | Inventory | 34.2 | 41.3 | 32.7 | 35.5 | 34.5 | 33.1 |
| 1.0 | 1.6 | 1.4 | All Other Current | .0 | 2.7 | 1.1 | .9 | 1.3 | 1.9 |
| 73.3 | 73.0 | 71.2 | Total Current | 68.8 | 73.9 | 73.1 | 70.9 | 72.3 | 67.2 |
| 18.0 | 17.1 | 17.8 | Fixed Assets (net) | 14.6 | 17.6 | 17.2 | 21.6 | 14.9 | 19.9 |
| 1.9 | 3.2 | 2.8 | Intangibles (net) | 4.4 | 2.8 | 1.1 | 1.8 | 3.0 | 4.8 |
| 6.8 | 6.6 | 8.2 | All Other Non-Current | 12.2 | 5.8 | 8.7 | 5.7 | 9.8 | 8.2 |
| 100.0 | 100.0 | 100.0 | Total | 100.0 | 100.0 | 100.0 | 100.0 | 100.0 | 100.0 |
| | | | **LIABILITIES** | | | | | | |
| 18.1 | 13.5 | 10.7 | Notes Payable-Short Term | 14.4 | 8.7 | 15.0 | 9.8 | 10.2 | 7.4 |
| 3.4 | 2.2 | 2.3 | Cur. Mat.-L.T.D. | .4 | 4.3 | 4.0 | 1.9 | 1.3 | 2.1 |
| 16.6 | 16.1 | 18.1 | Trade Payables | 11.9 | 18.3 | 22.0 | 18.8 | 16.2 | 19.6 |
| .1 | .2 | .1 | Income Taxes Payable | .1 | .0 | .1 | .3 | .0 | .0 |
| 11.0 | 11.2 | 15.6 | All Other Current | 35.3 | 12.6 | 7.7 | 17.8 | 16.3 | 10.4 |
| 49.2 | 43.1 | 46.8 | Total Current | 62.0 | 43.9 | 48.9 | 48.6 | 44.0 | 39.6 |
| 11.4 | 12.2 | 15.6 | Long-Term Debt | 43.7 | 26.0 | 13.6 | 13.9 | 6.7 | 7.9 |
| .2 | .4 | .2 | Deferred Taxes | .1 | .0 | .0 | .3 | .5 | .3 |
| 5.0 | 4.9 | 7.3 | All Other Non-Current | 15.5 | 11.1 | 4.8 | 9.4 | 3.8 | 4.0 |
| 34.1 | 39.4 | 30.1 | Net Worth | -21.3 | 19.0 | 32.7 | 27.7 | 45.1 | 48.2 |
| 100.0 | 100.0 | 100.0 | Total Liabilities & Net Worth | 100.0 | 100.0 | 100.0 | 100.0 | 100.0 | 100.0 |
| | | | **INCOME DATA** | | | | | | |
| 100.0 | 100.0 | 100.0 | Net Sales | 100.0 | 100.0 | 100.0 | 100.0 | 100.0 | 100.0 |
| 33.2 | 35.8 | 34.2 | Gross Profit | 48.6 | 37.9 | 35.7 | 34.6 | 30.1 | 26.4 |
| 30.5 | 31.2 | 29.8 | Operating Expenses | 43.4 | 35.5 | 32.2 | 28.3 | 27.2 | 20.1 |
| 2.7 | 4.6 | 4.4 | Operating Profit | 5.1 | 2.4 | 3.5 | 6.3 | 2.9 | 6.2 |
| 1.2 | .9 | .9 | All Other Expenses (net) | 1.6 | .1 | 1.1 | 1.1 | .6 | 1.0 |
| 1.5 | 3.7 | 3.5 | Profit Before Taxes | 3.5 | 2.4 | 2.4 | 5.2 | 2.3 | 5.2 |
| | | | **RATIOS** | | | | | | |
| 2.9 | 3.0 | 3.3 | | 6.1 | 3.8 | 2.6 | 3.1 | 4.1 | 3.2 |
| 1.6 | 1.7 | 1.8 | Current | 2.1 | 2.0 | 1.5 | 1.8 | 1.9 | 1.6 |
| 1.1 | 1.2 | 1.1 | | .8 | 1.0 | 1.1 | 1.1 | 1.2 | 1.2 |
| 1.5 | 1.4 | 1.5 | | 3.8 | 1.4 | 1.2 | 1.4 | 2.4 | 1.3 |
| .7 | .8 | .8 | Quick | 1.0 | .6 | .7 | .8 | .8 | .9 |
| .4 | .5 | .5 | | .3 | .2 | .5 | .5 | .5 | .5 |
| 30  12.2 | 25  14.5 | 21  17.2 | | 6  63.2 | 0  UND | 30  12.3 | 24  15.5 | 27  13.7 | 21  17.4 |
| 48  7.5 | 43  8.5 | 37  9.8 | Sales/Receivables | 30  12.3 | 25  14.6 | 38  9.7 | 39  9.4 | 41  9.0 | 38  9.7 |
| 70  5.2 | 72  5.1 | 51  7.1 | | 54  6.8 | 36  10.0 | 56  6.5 | 53  6.9 | 59  6.2 | 47  7.7 |
| 35  10.3 | 33  10.9 | 30  12.2 | | 0  UND | 25  14.8 | 22  16.7 | 26  14.0 | 47  7.7 | 33  11.0 |
| 92  4.0 | 92  4.0 | 74  4.9 | Cost of Sales/Inventory | 91  4.0 | 65  5.6 | 62  5.9 | 73  5.0 | 91  4.0 | 78  4.7 |
| 212  1.7 | 195  1.9 | 159  2.3 | | 261  1.4 | 261  1.4 | 174  2.1 | 159  2.3 | 140  2.6 | 130  2.8 |
| 14  25.6 | 14  25.4 | 17  22.1 | | 3  145.5 | 11  34.0 | 28  13.0 | 15  23.7 | 18  20.7 | 15  23.7 |
| 31  11.8 | 32  11.5 | 34  10.8 | Cost of Sales/Payables | 27  13.4 | 46  7.9 | 49  7.5 | 33  11.1 | 33  10.9 | 32  11.5 |
| 61  6.0 | 75  4.9 | 61  6.0 | | 59  6.2 | 73  5.0 | 79  4.6 | 54  6.7 | 50  7.3 | 61  6.0 |
| 3.5 | 3.4 | 4.0 | | 2.8 | 3.6 | 3.9 | 4.2 | 3.2 | 5.1 |
| 6.8 | 7.7 | 8.5 | Sales/Working Capital | 12.7 | 6.9 | 11.5 | 8.1 | 6.9 | 10.7 |
| 27.9 | 19.1 | 38.4 | | -9.1 | NM | 81.5 | 39.2 | 25.5 | 22.2 |
| 7.7 | 11.8 | 15.4 | | 12.3 | 7.5 | 9.0 | 25.5 | 27.8 | 54.4 |
| (170)  2.0 | (131)  4.0 | (166)  4.6 | EBIT/Interest | (10)  4.2 | (23)  4.3 | (30)  3.4 | (38)  5.6 | (38)  4.1 | (27)  12.2 |
| -.2 | 1.6 | 1.3 | | 1.2 | .1 | 1.4 | 2.2 | .5 | 2.8 |
| 5.9 | 7.9 | 12.9 | Net Profit + Depr., Dep., | | | | | | |
| (30)  1.3 | (30)  2.4 | (31)  4.5 | Amort./Cur. Mat. L/T/D | | | | | | |
| .1 | .7 | 1.1 | | | | | | | |
| .1 | .1 | .1 | | .0 | .0 | .0 | .2 | .1 | .2 |
| .3 | .3 | .3 | Fixed/Worth | .2 | .4 | .4 | .6 | .2 | .4 |
| 1.1 | 1.0 | 1.1 | | -7.8 | NM | 1.2 | 1.2 | .6 | .8 |
| .7 | .7 | .7 | | .3 | .8 | 1.1 | 1.1 | .5 | .4 |
| 1.7 | 1.9 | 1.8 | Debt/Worth | 6.1 | 2.3 | 1.9 | 1.9 | 1.2 | 1.5 |
| 6.8 | 3.7 | 6.1 | | -2.1 | -15.3 | 5.4 | 10.5 | 3.1 | 3.2 |
| 32.7 | 39.7 | 42.2 | % Profit Before Taxes/Tangible | 51.4 | 38.1 | 41.9 | 74.8 | 23.1 | 49.1 |
| (171)  8.8 | (137)  14.3 | (177)  16.0 | Net Worth | (11)  11.4 | (20)  15.1 | (32)  17.6 | (38)  29.4 | (46)  11.2 | (30)  26.6 |
| -.4 | 4.0 | 4.7 | | -16.1 | 2.3 | 2.7 | 5.2 | 3.3 | 12.0 |
| 11.5 | 13.3 | 16.2 | % Profit Before Taxes/Total | 22.2 | 16.5 | 11.2 | 16.9 | 13.1 | 21.4 |
| 2.5 | 5.1 | 6.9 | Assets | 3.3 | 5.2 | 4.1 | 8.8 | 5.9 | 12.6 |
| -3.1 | 1.2 | .5 | | -1.4 | -1.9 | 1.1 | .8 | .4 | 4.7 |
| 74.0 | 61.2 | 67.8 | | UND | 153.4 | 99.9 | 67.6 | 95.3 | 31.5 |
| 21.0 | 23.2 | 22.1 | Sales/Net Fixed Assets | 32.7 | 31.6 | 23.6 | 16.8 | 27.5 | 16.8 |
| 7.4 | 7.7 | 9.7 | | 16.0 | 12.9 | 8.4 | 6.0 | 10.7 | 7.1 |
| 2.8 | 2.8 | 3.4 | | 5.7 | 3.9 | 3.4 | 3.4 | 3.0 | 2.9 |
| 1.8 | 1.9 | 2.2 | Sales/Total Assets | 2.2 | 2.7 | 2.3 | 2.2 | 2.0 | 2.0 |
| 1.2 | 1.2 | 1.4 | | 1.3 | 1.7 | 1.6 | 1.5 | 1.1 | 1.6 |
| .5 | .5 | .5 | | .7 | .4 | .4 | .4 | .3 | .7 |
| (165)  1.2 | (114)  1.1 | (150)  1.1 | % Depr., Dep., Amort./Sales | (12)  1.1 | (18)  1.1 | (22)  1.0 | (32)  1.5 | (38)  1.1 | (28)  1.0 |
| 2.8 | 3.0 | 2.6 | | 3.0 | 2.0 | 2.9 | 3.2 | 2.4 | 2.3 |
| 1.4 | 1.7 | 1.9 | % Officers', Directors' | 6.5 | 2.9 | 3.1 | 1.1 | 1.6 | |
| (97)  3.5 | (71)  3.8 | (101)  4.0 | Owners' Comp/Sales | (10)  8.9 | (19)  4.4 | (24)  4.3 | (19)  1.9 | (21)  3.2 | |
| 5.6 | 3.0 | 7.6 | | 12.0 | 10.2 | 7.0 | 4.3 | 6.5 | |
| 3721836M | 3642435M | 3816682M | Net Sales ($) | 9973M | 59002M | 138706M | 300186M | 734413M | 2574402M |
| 2174498M | 2306027M | 2115119M | Total Assets ($) | 6749M | 28770M | 69760M | 164758M | 491661M | 1353421M |

M = $ thousand   MM = $ million
See Pages 9 through 22 for Explanation of Ratios and Data

## Current Data Sorted by Assets      Comparative Historical Data

| | | 4 (4/1-9/30/11) | | 25 (10/1/11-3/31/12) | | Type of Statement | 4/1/07-3/31/08 | 4/1/08-3/31/09 |
|---|---|---|---|---|---|---|---|---|
| 0-500M | 500M-2MM | 2-10MM | 10-50MM | 50-100MM | 100-250MM | | | |
| 1 | | | 2 | | | Unqualified | | |
| | 1 | 8 | | | | Reviewed | 3 | 3 |
| | 1 | 2 | | | | Compiled | 11 | 11 |
| 1 | 1 | 3 | | | | Tax Returns | 4 | 5 |
| | 2 | 6 | 1 | | | Other | 3 | 5 |
| 2 | 5 | 19 | 3 | | | **NUMBER OF STATEMENTS** | **22 ALL** | **26 ALL** |
| % | % | % | % | % | % | | % | % |

| 0-500M | 500M-2MM | 2-10MM | 10-50MM | 50-100MM | 100-250MM | | 4/1/07-3/31/08 ALL | 4/1/08-3/31/09 ALL |
|---|---|---|---|---|---|---|---|---|
| | | | | D | D | **ASSETS** | | |
| | | 11.4 | | A | A | Cash & Equivalents | 14.8 | 9.3 |
| | | 36.2 | | T | T | Trade Receivables (net) | 33.8 | 30.3 |
| | | 31.2 | | A | A | Inventory | 30.0 | 32.3 |
| | | 3.1 | | | | All Other Current | 1.0 | 2.4 |
| | | 82.0 | | N | N | Total Current | 79.6 | 74.2 |
| | | 9.5 | | O | O | Fixed Assets (net) | 11.7 | 14.2 |
| | | 2.5 | | T | T | Intangibles (net) | 4.0 | 3.4 |
| | | 6.0 | | | | All Other Non-Current | 4.6 | 8.1 |
| | | 100.0 | | A | A | Total | 100.0 | 100.0 |
| | | | | V | V | **LIABILITIES** | | |
| | | 7.4 | | A | A | Notes Payable-Short Term | 19.0 | 17.0 |
| | | 1.8 | | I | I | Cur. Mat.-L.T.D. | 1.4 | 4.8 |
| | | 20.8 | | L | L | Trade Payables | 16.6 | 18.2 |
| | | .1 | | A | A | Income Taxes Payable | .0 | .0 |
| | | 7.9 | | B | B | All Other Current | 9.2 | 9.7 |
| | | 37.9 | | L | L | Total Current | 46.2 | 49.8 |
| | | 3.4 | | E | E | Long-Term Debt | 4.9 | 12.8 |
| | | .1 | | | | Deferred Taxes | .3 | .3 |
| | | 4.1 | | | | All Other Non-Current | 30.3 | 6.5 |
| | | 54.5 | | | | Net Worth | 18.2 | 30.6 |
| | | 100.0 | | | | Total Liabilities & Net Worth | 100.0 | 100.0 |
| | | | | | | **INCOME DATA** | | |
| | | 100.0 | | | | Net Sales | 100.0 | 100.0 |
| | | 40.4 | | | | Gross Profit | 35.6 | 38.0 |
| | | 35.9 | | | | Operating Expenses | 31.9 | 34.8 |
| | | 4.5 | | | | Operating Profit | 3.6 | 3.2 |
| | | -.1 | | | | All Other Expenses (net) | .5 | 1.2 |
| | | 4.6 | | | | Profit Before Taxes | 3.1 | 2.0 |
| | | | | | | **RATIOS** | | |
| | | 4.1 | | | | | 3.1 | 2.7 |
| | | 2.4 | | | | Current | 2.0 | 1.7 |
| | | 1.6 | | | | | 1.1 | 1.1 |
| | | 2.2 | | | | | 1.9 | 1.3 |
| | | 1.5 | | | | Quick | .9 | .7 |
| | | .8 | | | | | .8 | .4 |
| | | 41   8.9 | | | | | 26   14.0 | 28   12.9 |
| | | 49   7.4 | | | | Sales/Receivables | 50   7.2 | 38   9.6 |
| | | 68   5.4 | | | | | 71   5.1 | 57   6.4 |
| | | 17   21.2 | | | | | 28   13.0 | 27   13.5 |
| | | 83   4.4 | | | | Cost of Sales/Inventory | 57   6.4 | 57   6.4 |
| | | 166   2.2 | | | | | 124   2.9 | 123   3.0 |
| | | 24   15.4 | | | | | 16   22.3 | 27   13.7 |
| | | 41   9.0 | | | | Cost of Sales/Payables | 30   12.1 | 37   9.7 |
| | | 72   5.1 | | | | | 44   8.3 | 55   6.7 |
| | | 3.9 | | | | | 5.4 | 5.0 |
| | | 4.8 | | | | Sales/Working Capital | 8.4 | 8.5 |
| | | 9.0 | | | | | 23.7 | 34.0 |
| | | 37.4 | | | | | 9.5 | 12.5 |
| | | (17)   16.3 | | | | EBIT/Interest | (21)   2.7 | 2.2 |
| | | 2.0 | | | | | .3 | .7 |
| | | | | | | Net Profit + Depr., Dep., Amort./Cur. Mat. L/T/D | | |
| | | .1 | | | | | .1 | .1 |
| | | .1 | | | | Fixed/Worth | .2 | .3 |
| | | .4 | | | | | .5 | .8 |
| | | .3 | | | | | .5 | .9 |
| | | .7 | | | | Debt/Worth | 1.6 | 2.6 |
| | | 1.4 | | | | | 3.8 | 6.6 |
| | | 78.9 | | | | | 94.2 | 77.0 |
| | | 18.8 | | | | % Profit Before Taxes/Tangible Net Worth | (20)   17.6 | (22)   16.9 |
| | | 3.8 | | | | | -3.3 | 3.2 |
| | | 25.4 | | | | | 34.0 | 20.9 |
| | | 10.7 | | | | % Profit Before Taxes/Total Assets | 8.6 | 4.3 |
| | | 1.8 | | | | | -2.2 | .1 |
| | | 80.1 | | | | | 76.2 | 102.3 |
| | | 30.4 | | | | Sales/Net Fixed Assets | 34.2 | 23.8 |
| | | 19.8 | | | | | 14.6 | 13.7 |
| | | 3.7 | | | | | 3.8 | 3.7 |
| | | 2.9 | | | | Sales/Total Assets | 2.7 | 2.8 |
| | | 1.9 | | | | | 1.9 | 1.9 |
| | | .1 | | | | | .4 | .4 |
| | | (14)   .6 | | | | % Depr., Dep., Amort./Sales | (19)   .6 | (24)   .8 |
| | | .9 | | | | | 1.2 | 2.2 |
| | | 1.9 | | | | | 2.3 | 2.3 |
| | | (10)   3.3 | | | | % Officers', Directors' Owners' Comp/Sales | (12)   4.7 | (14)   3.3 |
| | | 5.3 | | | | | 8.1 | 5.4 |
| 3324M | 11509M | 233824M | 213109M | | | Net Sales ($) | 450803M | 604524M |
| 453M | 4945M | 83411M | 97959M | | | Total Assets ($) | 208636M | 302129M |

M = $ thousand     MM = $ million
See Pages 9 through 22 for Explanation of Ratios and Data

## Comparative Historical Data | Current Data Sorted by Sales

| | | | Type of Statement | 0-1MM | 1-3MM | 3-5MM | 5-10MM | 10-25MM | 25MM & OVER |
|---|---|---|---|---|---|---|---|---|---|
| 3 | 1 | 3 | Unqualified | 1 | | | | 1 | 1 |
| 6 | 8 | 9 | Reviewed | | 1 | 2 | 1 | 5 | |
| 4 | 1 | 3 | Compiled | | | 1 | 1 | 1 | |
| 1 | 1 | 5 | Tax Returns | | | 2 | 1 | 1 | 1 |
| 7 | 12 | 9 | Other | | 2 | 1 | 3 | 1 | 2 |
| 4/1/09- 3/31/10 | 4/1/10- 3/31/11 | 4/1/11- 3/31/12 | | | 4 (4/1-9/30/11) | | 25 (10/1/11-3/31/12) | | |
| ALL | ALL | ALL | | | | | | | |
| 21 | 23 | 29 | **NUMBER OF STATEMENTS** | 1 | 3 | 6 | 6 | 9 | 4 |
| % | % | % | **ASSETS** | % | % | % | % | % | % |
| 14.5 | 12.3 | 10.4 | Cash & Equivalents | | | | | | |
| 33.1 | 38.0 | 38.0 | Trade Receivables (net) | | | | | | |
| 29.9 | 24.4 | 30.6 | Inventory | | | | | | |
| 4.2 | 2.9 | 2.9 | All Other Current | | | | | | |
| 81.8 | 77.6 | 81.8 | Total Current | | | | | | |
| 9.9 | 11.1 | 8.1 | Fixed Assets (net) | | | | | | |
| 1.7 | 5.9 | 4.4 | Intangibles (net) | | | | | | |
| 6.6 | 5.4 | 5.6 | All Other Non-Current | | | | | | |
| 100.0 | 100.0 | 100.0 | Total | | | | | | |
| | | | **LIABILITIES** | | | | | | |
| 16.8 | 14.4 | 11.2 | Notes Payable-Short Term | | | | | | |
| 3.0 | 2.5 | 1.6 | Cur. Mat.-L.T.D. | | | | | | |
| 16.9 | 16.9 | 20.7 | Trade Payables | | | | | | |
| .1 | .1 | .1 | Income Taxes Payable | | | | | | |
| 9.6 | 11.2 | 7.5 | All Other Current | | | | | | |
| 46.3 | 45.0 | 41.1 | Total Current | | | | | | |
| 6.6 | 5.5 | 3.3 | Long-Term Debt | | | | | | |
| .0 | .1 | .1 | Deferred Taxes | | | | | | |
| 8.8 | 7.7 | 4.5 | All Other Non-Current | | | | | | |
| 38.3 | 41.7 | 51.2 | Net Worth | | | | | | |
| 100.0 | 100.0 | 100.0 | Total Liabilities & Net Worth | | | | | | |
| | | | **INCOME DATA** | | | | | | |
| 100.0 | 100.0 | 100.0 | Net Sales | | | | | | |
| 37.7 | 38.6 | 38.9 | Gross Profit | | | | | | |
| 31.8 | 32.6 | 33.9 | Operating Expenses | | | | | | |
| 5.8 | 6.0 | 5.0 | Operating Profit | | | | | | |
| .2 | .6 | .1 | All Other Expenses (net) | | | | | | |
| 5.7 | 5.4 | 4.9 | Profit Before Taxes | | | | | | |
| | | | **RATIOS** | | | | | | |
| 3.4 | 2.8 | 3.9 | Current | | | | | | |
| 1.9 | 1.5 | 2.3 | | | | | | | |
| 1.2 | 1.2 | 1.5 | | | | | | | |
| 2.1 | 1.6 | 1.9 | Quick | | | | | | |
| 1.0 | 1.0 | 1.2 | | | | | | | |
| .5 | .7 | .7 | | | | | | | |
| 33  11.0 | 41  9.0 | 39  9.4 | Sales/Receivables | | | | | | |
| 57  6.4 | 53  6.8 | 54  6.8 | | | | | | | |
| 70  5.2 | 78  4.7 | 76  4.8 | | | | | | | |
| 25  14.8 | 21  17.3 | 30  12.2 | Cost of Sales/Inventory | | | | | | |
| 66  5.5 | 61  6.0 | 63  5.8 | | | | | | | |
| 133  2.7 | 137  2.7 | 152  2.4 | | | | | | | |
| 21  17.7 | 30  12.0 | 21  17.3 | Cost of Sales/Payables | | | | | | |
| 31  11.7 | 41  9.0 | 37  9.8 | | | | | | | |
| 68  5.4 | 56  6.5 | 62  5.9 | | | | | | | |
| 3.1 | 4.4 | 3.9 | Sales/Working Capital | | | | | | |
| 6.0 | 10.2 | 6.1 | | | | | | | |
| 19.4 | 17.4 | 10.5 | | | | | | | |
| 18.2 | 13.9 | 35.7 | EBIT/Interest | | | | | | |
| (18)  4.5 | (19)  4.9 | (24)  12.4 | | | | | | | |
| 1.3 | 1.4 | 1.8 | | | | | | | |
| | | | Net Profit + Depr., Dep., Amort./Cur. Mat. L/T/D | | | | | | |
| .1 | .1 | .1 | Fixed/Worth | | | | | | |
| .2 | .3 | .1 | | | | | | | |
| .6 | .7 | .4 | | | | | | | |
| .8 | 1.0 | .5 | Debt/Worth | | | | | | |
| 1.7 | 1.4 | .9 | | | | | | | |
| 4.1 | 3.9 | 1.9 | | | | | | | |
| 53.6 | 65.0 | 76.2 | % Profit Before Taxes/Tangible Net Worth | | | | | | |
| (19)  13.2 | (19)  31.9 | (28)  21.5 | | | | | | | |
| 5.8 | 5.3 | 3.9 | | | | | | | |
| 24.4 | 28.8 | 23.0 | % Profit Before Taxes/Total Assets | | | | | | |
| 7.3 | 10.7 | 9.3 | | | | | | | |
| 2.1 | 1.5 | 2.0 | | | | | | | |
| 120.9 | 60.1 | 154.9 | Sales/Net Fixed Assets | | | | | | |
| 35.6 | 35.1 | 46.5 | | | | | | | |
| 15.2 | 11.9 | 19.0 | | | | | | | |
| 3.3 | 2.7 | 3.5 | Sales/Total Assets | | | | | | |
| 2.3 | 2.2 | 2.5 | | | | | | | |
| 1.6 | 1.7 | 1.8 | | | | | | | |
| .2 | .6 | .1 | % Depr., Dep., Amort./Sales | | | | | | |
| (17)  .9 | (17)  1.1 | (20)  .6 | | | | | | | |
| 1.5 | 1.4 | 1.2 | | | | | | | |
| 1.1 | 2.2 | 2.2 | % Officers', Directors' Owners' Comp/Sales | | | | | | |
| (12)  4.2 | (10)  3.4 | (15)  3.7 | | | | | | | |
| 6.9 | 6.6 | 5.4 | | | | | | | |
| 333210M | 578932M | 461766M | Net Sales ($) | 91M | 4269M | 22856M | 42690M | 141691M | 250169M |
| 147855M | 256994M | 186768M | Total Assets ($) | 35M | 2595M | 10548M | 20480M | 49751M | 103359M |

© RMA 2012

M = $ thousand    MM = $ million
See Pages 9 through 22 for Explanation of Ratios and Data

## Current Data Sorted by Assets      Comparative Historical Data

| | | | | | | Type of Statement | | |
|---|---|---|---|---|---|---|---|---|
| | | 8 | 22 | 6 | 4 | Unqualified | 41 | 39 |
| | 3 | 11 | 12 | | | Reviewed | 34 | 29 |
| 2 | 5 | 14 | 8 | 1 | | Compiled | 17 | 16 |
| 4 | 14 | 8 | 12 | | | Tax Returns | 14 | 22 |
| 5 | 18 | 29 | 6 | 5 | 3 | Other | 61 | 90 |
| | 37 (4/1-9/30/11) | | | 163 (10/1/11-3/31/12) | | | 61 4/1/07- 3/31/08 ALL | 90 4/1/08- 3/31/09 ALL |
| 0-500M | 500M-2MM | 2-10MM | 10-50MM | 50-100MM | 100-250MM | | | |
| 11 | 40 | 70 | 60 | 12 | 7 | NUMBER OF STATEMENTS | 167 | 196 |
| % | % | % | % | % | % | ASSETS | % | % |
| 9.2 | 10.1 | 7.0 | 8.2 | 12.3 | | Cash & Equivalents | 6.8 | 7.6 |
| 21.5 | 22.6 | 23.6 | 19.8 | 20.1 | | Trade Receivables (net) | 24.1 | 21.7 |
| 34.8 | 40.1 | 43.1 | 36.3 | 22.9 | | Inventory | 39.2 | 40.0 |
| 3.6 | 4.8 | 2.2 | 4.2 | 4.7 | | All Other Current | 3.0 | 3.1 |
| 69.0 | 77.6 | 75.9 | 68.6 | 60.0 | | Total Current | 73.1 | 72.5 |
| 14.1 | 15.9 | 15.0 | 14.3 | 11.9 | | Fixed Assets (net) | 13.3 | 13.9 |
| 12.6 | 3.8 | 4.0 | 11.5 | 23.4 | | Intangibles (net) | 6.7 | 7.8 |
| 4.3 | 2.7 | 5.1 | 5.6 | 4.7 | | All Other Non-Current | 6.9 | 5.8 |
| 100.0 | 100.0 | 100.0 | 100.0 | 100.0 | | Total | 100.0 | 100.0 |
| | | | | | | LIABILITIES | | |
| 9.4 | 18.0 | 13.9 | 11.3 | 3.6 | | Notes Payable-Short Term | 19.3 | 17.7 |
| 8.2 | 3.1 | 2.8 | 3.7 | 4.4 | | Cur. Mat.-L.T.D. | 2.9 | 2.9 |
| 11.4 | 13.7 | 13.7 | 11.7 | 11.8 | | Trade Payables | 13.5 | 13.8 |
| .0 | .2 | .4 | .3 | .2 | | Income Taxes Payable | .6 | .5 |
| 16.8 | 7.3 | 12.0 | 11.4 | 10.0 | | All Other Current | 10.9 | 10.4 |
| 45.7 | 42.4 | 42.7 | 38.4 | 30.1 | | Total Current | 47.1 | 45.4 |
| 20.3 | 25.6 | 9.1 | 13.1 | 25.9 | | Long-Term Debt | 13.1 | 13.0 |
| .0 | .0 | .2 | .6 | .8 | | Deferred Taxes | .3 | .3 |
| 16.5 | 15.5 | 6.1 | 6.1 | 12.5 | | All Other Non-Current | 7.5 | 9.4 |
| 17.4 | 16.4 | 41.9 | 41.8 | 30.7 | | Net Worth | 32.0 | 32.0 |
| 100.0 | 100.0 | 100.0 | 100.0 | 100.0 | | Total Liabilities & Net Worth | 100.0 | 100.0 |
| | | | | | | INCOME DATA | | |
| 100.0 | 100.0 | 100.0 | 100.0 | 100.0 | | Net Sales | 100.0 | 100.0 |
| 46.9 | 41.6 | 35.3 | 35.8 | 38.2 | | Gross Profit | 36.5 | 35.5 |
| 43.5 | 36.3 | 30.9 | 30.2 | 31.2 | | Operating Expenses | 30.5 | 32.6 |
| 3.4 | 5.2 | 4.4 | 5.5 | 7.0 | | Operating Profit | 6.0 | 2.9 |
| 1.9 | .6 | .6 | 1.8 | 1.8 | | All Other Expenses (net) | 1.8 | 1.9 |
| 1.5 | 4.7 | 3.7 | 3.7 | 5.2 | | Profit Before Taxes | 4.2 | 1.0 |
| | | | | | | RATIOS | | |
| 2.9 | 3.7 | 3.6 | 3.8 | 4.8 | | | 3.0 | 3.3 |
| 1.6 | 1.9 | 1.9 | 1.9 | 2.5 | | Current | 1.7 | 1.7 |
| .8 | 1.3 | 1.3 | 1.4 | 1.5 | | | 1.1 | 1.2 |
| 1.2 | 1.6 | 1.3 | 1.9 | 1.9 | | | 1.4 | 1.4 |
| .6 | .9 | .7 | .7 | 1.4 | | Quick | .6 | .7 |
| .4 | .4 | .4 | .4 | .5 | | | .4 | .4 |
| 4   86.7 | 15   25.0 | 21   17.0 | 27   13.4 | 46   7.9 | | | 24   15.0 | 22   16.4 |
| 15   23.8 | 33   10.9 | 33   11.2 | 45   8.1 | 51   7.2 | | Sales/Receivables | 41   8.9 | 37   9.9 |
| 55   6.6 | 46   7.9 | 53   6.9 | 64   5.7 | 63   5.8 | | | 62   5.9 | 56   6.5 |
| 15   24.9 | 39   9.3 | 76   4.8 | 87   4.2 | 54   6.7 | | | 73   5.0 | 75   4.8 |
| 35   10.3 | 96   3.8 | 114   3.2 | 114   3.2 | 101   3.6 | | Cost of Sales/Inventory | 110   3.3 | 112   3.3 |
| 166   2.2 | 140   2.6 | 152   2.4 | 174   2.1 | 166   2.2 | | | 167   2.2 | 161   2.3 |
| 11   32.5 | 6   57.4 | 11   33.8 | 18   20.3 | 15   24.6 | | | 13   27.3 | 16   23.0 |
| 20   17.9 | 26   14.0 | 24   15.1 | 32   11.5 | 24   15.0 | | Cost of Sales/Payables | 28   13.2 | 30   12.1 |
| 28   13.0 | 56   6.5 | 43   8.5 | 53   6.9 | 89   4.1 | | | 52   7.1 | 50   7.2 |
| 8.0 | 4.5 | 3.7 | 3.1 | 2.4 | | | 4.0 | 3.8 |
| 14.1 | 7.5 | 5.8 | 4.8 | 3.7 | | Sales/Working Capital | 8.1 | 7.0 |
| -54.2 | 17.2 | 14.1 | 8.8 | 10.8 | | | 23.3 | 17.7 |
| | 15.3 | 18.8 | 16.8 | 67.0 | | | 8.9 | 6.5 |
| | (34)   3.4 | (66)   4.8 | (53)   3.4 | 3.2 | | EBIT/Interest | (149)   3.0 | (179)   1.9 |
| | .7 | 1.2 | 1.3 | 1.0 | | | 1.1 | .0 |
| | | 3.9 | 7.0 | | | Net Profit + Depr., Dep., | | 11.8   5.9 |
| | | (11)   2.8 | (22)   1.7 | | | Amort./Cur. Mat. L/T/D | (46)   2.1 | (38)   1.7 |
| | | 1.2 | .5 | | | | .4 | .4 |
| .0 | .1 | .1 | .2 | .3 | | | .1 | .1 |
| .1 | .3 | .2 | .5 | -3.8 | | Fixed/Worth | .3 | .4 |
| -1.9 | NM | 1.4 | 2.2 | -.2 | | | 1.6 | 1.7 |
| 1.1 | .8 | .5 | .6 | 1.3 | | | .7 | .7 |
| 5.6 | 2.2 | 1.6 | 1.3 | -14.0 | | Debt/Worth | 2.3 | 1.9 |
| -3.2 | -14.8 | 4.2 | 10.2 | -3.6 | | | 10.6 | 11.8 |
| | 67.9 | 44.6 | 53.3 | | | % Profit Before Taxes/Tangible | 46.6 | 36.7 |
| | (29)   33.3 | (61)   23.3 | (50)   19.0 | | | Net Worth | (134)   18.9 | (157)   13.0 |
| | 12.9 | 8.2 | 7.7 | | | | 4.3 | -3.7 |
| 42.0 | 21.9 | 17.1 | 12.9 | 10.6 | | | 15.7 | 10.8 |
| 2.6 | 9.8 | 7.8 | 4.7 | 5.4 | | % Profit Before Taxes/Total Assets | 6.6 | 3.2 |
| -7.3 | .4 | .3 | 1.6 | -1.0 | | | .7 | -2.4 |
| UND | 230.8 | 96.0 | 29.9 | 57.8 | | | 55.7 | 48.5 |
| 82.2 | 31.5 | 24.3 | 11.3 | 22.5 | | Sales/Net Fixed Assets | 22.3 | 21.8 |
| 13.1 | 10.8 | 10.9 | 7.4 | 5.9 | | | 10.0 | 8.9 |
| 7.8 | 3.3 | 2.8 | 1.9 | 1.7 | | | 2.8 | 2.6 |
| 3.8 | 2.6 | 2.1 | 1.5 | 1.3 | | Sales/Total Assets | 2.0 | 1.8 |
| 1.5 | 1.9 | 1.6 | 1.2 | .9 | | | 1.4 | 1.4 |
| | .8 | .6 | .9 | .8 | | | .7 | .8 |
| | (23)   1.5 | (56)   1.2 | (54)   2.0 | (10)   3.3 | | % Depr., Dep., Amort./Sales | (132)   1.5 | (150)   1.5 |
| | 2.3 | 2.7 | 3.7 | 5.7 | | | 2.6 | 2.7 |
| | 3.5 | 2.3 | | | | | 3.1 | 1.9 |
| | (20)   6.2 | (27)   4.2 | | | | % Officers', Directors' Owners' Comp/Sales | (41)   5.6 | (48)   4.5 |
| | 8.0 | 8.3 | | | | | 10.8 | 8.0 |
| 12838M | 109563M | 801710M | 2464754M | 1155827M | 1058203M | Net Sales ($) | 5142252M | 6999057M |
| 3153M | 41535M | 362571M | 1555684M | 852541M | 1294288M | Total Assets ($) | 3262106M | 4317975M |

M = $ thousand    MM = $ million
See Pages 9 through 22 for Explanation of Ratios and Data

## Comparative Historical Data / Current Data Sorted by Sales

| Type of Statement | 4/1/09–3/31/10 ALL | 4/1/10–3/31/11 ALL | 4/1/11–3/31/12 ALL | 0-1MM | 1-3MM | 3-5MM | 5-10MM | 10-25MM | 25MM & OVER |
|---|---|---|---|---|---|---|---|---|---|
| Unqualified | 34 | 40 | 40 | | | | 3 | 8 | 29 |
| Reviewed | 31 | 25 | 26 | | 2 | 3 | 5 | 10 | 6 |
| Compiled | 14 | 17 | 16 | | 7 | 3 | 3 | 3 | |
| Tax Returns | 23 | 22 | 30 | 3 | 10 | 8 | 9 | | |
| Other | 94 | 88 | 88 | 3 | 15 | 7 | 7 | 26 | 30 |
| | | | | 37 (4/1-9/30/11) | | | 163 (10/1/11-3/31/12) | | |
| | | | | 0-1MM | 1-3MM | 3-5MM | 5-10MM | 10-25MM | 25MM & OVER |
| **NUMBER OF STATEMENTS** | 196 | 192 | 200 | 6 | 34 | 21 | 27 | 47 | 65 |
| **ASSETS** | % | % | % | % | % | % | % | % | % |
| Cash & Equivalents | 8.0 | 9.1 | 8.4 | | 11.4 | 9.8 | 6.4 | 6.3 | 9.3 |
| Trade Receivables (net) | 21.9 | 21.7 | 21.5 | | 20.5 | 23.7 | 21.0 | 23.5 | 19.8 |
| Inventory | 33.4 | 37.0 | 38.1 | | 40.8 | 31.0 | 50.4 | 38.5 | 34.5 |
| All Other Current | 3.2 | 3.5 | 3.6 | | 5.2 | 2.6 | 1.5 | 3.4 | 4.4 |
| Total Current | 66.5 | 71.3 | 71.7 | | 77.8 | 67.1 | 79.3 | 71.6 | 68.0 |
| Fixed Assets (net) | 16.4 | 14.0 | 14.7 | | 15.7 | 19.0 | 11.1 | 14.9 | 13.6 |
| Intangibles (net) | 10.5 | 8.9 | 8.7 | | 4.7 | 7.5 | 4.7 | 7.5 | 13.5 |
| All Other Non-Current | 6.6 | 5.8 | 4.8 | | 1.9 | 6.4 | 4.9 | 6.0 | 4.8 |
| Total | 100.0 | 100.0 | 100.0 | | 100.0 | 100.0 | 100.0 | 100.0 | 100.0 |
| **LIABILITIES** | | | | | | | | | |
| Notes Payable-Short Term | 15.6 | 12.4 | 12.8 | | 21.6 | 11.7 | 13.1 | 13.2 | 8.9 |
| Cur. Mat.-L.T.D. | 2.7 | 3.5 | 3.5 | | 3.8 | 2.4 | 6.4 | 1.9 | 3.4 |
| Trade Payables | 12.0 | 13.0 | 12.6 | | 11.5 | 13.7 | 9.7 | 15.0 | 13.1 |
| Income Taxes Payable | .2 | .2 | .3 | | .0 | .5 | .5 | .3 | .3 |
| All Other Current | 10.3 | 10.4 | 10.7 | | 9.6 | 9.3 | 8.6 | 12.0 | 11.5 |
| Total Current | 40.8 | 39.5 | 40.0 | | 46.6 | 37.6 | 38.2 | 42.3 | 37.2 |
| Long-Term Debt | 18.2 | 12.3 | 15.4 | | 24.0 | 18.5 | 10.1 | 10.2 | 14.1 |
| Deferred Taxes | .4 | .5 | .4 | | .0 | .1 | .1 | .4 | .9 |
| All Other Non-Current | 8.9 | 11.6 | 8.9 | | 16.9 | 7.0 | 7.9 | 6.6 | 7.6 |
| Net Worth | 31.7 | 36.1 | 35.3 | | 12.6 | 36.8 | 43.7 | 40.5 | 40.3 |
| Total Liabilities & Net Worth | 100.0 | 100.0 | 100.0 | | 100.0 | 100.0 | 100.0 | 100.0 | 100.0 |
| **INCOME DATA** | | | | | | | | | |
| Net Sales | 100.0 | 100.0 | 100.0 | | 100.0 | 100.0 | 100.0 | 100.0 | 100.0 |
| Gross Profit | 38.0 | 37.8 | 37.4 | | 40.9 | 38.4 | 39.8 | 34.0 | 35.7 |
| Operating Expenses | 33.9 | 31.9 | 32.4 | | 37.3 | 32.6 | 33.1 | 29.7 | 29.7 |
| Operating Profit | 4.1 | 5.9 | 5.1 | | 3.5 | 5.7 | 6.7 | 4.3 | 6.0 |
| All Other Expenses (net) | 2.6 | 1.6 | 1.2 | | .5 | .9 | .5 | 2.0 | 1.3 |
| Profit Before Taxes | 1.4 | 4.3 | 3.9 | | 3.0 | 4.8 | 6.2 | 2.3 | 4.8 |
| **RATIOS** | | | | | | | | | |
| Current | 3.3 / 1.7 / 1.2 | 3.7 / 1.9 / 1.3 | 3.7 / 1.9 / 1.3 | | 3.6 / 1.7 / 1.2 | 5.1 / 1.7 / 1.2 | 3.7 / 2.2 / 1.5 | 3.0 / 1.9 / 1.2 | 4.0 / 2.1 / 1.5 |
| Quick | 1.5 / .8 / .4 | 1.6 / .8 / .4 | 1.6 / .8 / .4 | | 1.5 / .7 / .3 | 2.5 / 1.0 / .3 | 1.1 / .7 / .4 | 1.1 / .7 / .4 | 1.8 / .9 / .5 |
| Sales/Receivables | 24  15.4 / 41  9.0 / 58  6.3 | 26  14.1 / 40  9.2 / 57  6.4 | 23  15.8 / 40  9.2 / 58  6.3 | | 13  27.1 / 36  10.0 / 47  7.8 | 17  21.4 / 31  11.8 / 49  7.5 | 23  15.9 / 30  12.3 / 51  7.1 | 21  17.8 / 31  11.6 / 61  6.0 | 34  10.6 / 47  7.8 / 59  6.2 |
| Cost of Sales/Inventory | 65  5.6 / 98  3.7 / 146  2.3 | 69  5.3 / 109  3.4 / 156  2.3 | 73  5.0 / 107  3.4 / 166  2.2 | | 52  7.0 / 104  3.5 / 215  1.7 | 35  10.4 / 69  5.3 / 146  2.5 | 94  3.9 / 122  3.0 / 182  2.0 | 68  5.4 / 104  3.5 / 146  2.5 | 87  4.2 / 107  3.4 / 166  2.2 |
| Cost of Sales/Payables | 14  26.4 / 29  12.5 / 45  8.1 | 16  22.5 / 29  12.4 / 48  7.6 | 14  25.8 / 27  13.3 / 50  7.3 | | 5  73.5 / 23  15.6 / 48  7.6 | 7  55.8 / 18  20.4 / 55  6.6 | 10  36.2 / 16  23.5 / 29  12.6 | 15  24.9 / 32  11.4 / 48  7.6 | 20  18.3 / 31  11.6 / 54  6.8 |
| Sales/Working Capital | 3.7 / 6.4 / 21.6 | 3.4 / 5.7 / 14.3 | 3.2 / 5.9 / 12.8 | | 3.2 / 6.3 / 17.8 | 4.4 / 10.0 / 27.9 | 3.7 / 5.9 / 9.6 | 4.0 / 6.8 / 16.2 | 3.0 / 4.9 / 9.1 |
| EBIT/Interest | 9.6 / (176) 2.3 / -.2 | 16.4 / (166) 4.6 / 1.4 | 16.5 / (179) 3.9 / 1.3 | | 5.7 / (29) 1.5 / -.5 | 30.3 / (19) 7.1 / -3.3 | 20.7 / (25) 6.6 / 2.7 | 18.0 / (44) 4.1 / .9 | 17.1 / (59) 3.6 / 1.8 |
| Net Profit + Depr., Dep., Amort./Cur. Mat. L/T/D | 3.9 / (38) 1.7 / .0 | 11.1 / (38) 2.6 / .8 | 7.4 / (40) 2.5 / 1.0 | | | | | 5.8 / (13) 1.7 / -1.3 | 9.8 / (22) 2.5 / 1.1 |
| Fixed/Worth | .1 / .4 / NM | .1 / .3 / 3.6 | .1 / .3 / 2.3 | | .0 / .4 / -20.3 | .1 / .3 / NM | .1 / .2 / .4 | .1 / .3 / 2.2 | .2 / .4 / 6.0 |
| Debt/Worth | .6 / 1.9 / -63.2 | .4 / 1.5 / 17.8 | .6 / 1.7 / 22.6 | | .6 / 3.3 / -4.7 | .6 / 1.4 / NM | .3 / 1.2 / 3.5 | .6 / 1.7 / 4.1 | .7 / 1.7 / 33.3 |
| % Profit Before Taxes/Tangible Net Worth | 33.3 / (146) 12.7 / -2.9 | 43.5 / (151) 20.0 / 8.6 | 45.5 / (157) 22.1 / 8.0 | | 50.4 / (22) 19.1 / -3.1 | 76.2 / (16) 23.8 / 2.4 | 43.7 / (24) 23.2 / 8.9 | 36.8 / (39) 22.1 / 8.2 | 58.7 / (52) 22.5 / 10.6 |
| % Profit Before Taxes/Total Assets | 11.4 / 3.6 / -3.0 | 15.7 / 7.4 / 1.7 | 15.9 / 5.8 / .4 | | 16.2 / 3.1 / -3.1 | 27.4 / 15.7 / -3.0 | 17.4 / 12.4 / 4.1 | 13.7 / 5.8 / .4 | 12.9 / 5.4 / 2.4 |
| Sales/Net Fixed Assets | 49.3 / 15.8 / 7.4 | 54.3 / 19.3 / 9.0 | 78.8 / 21.0 / 7.9 | | 355.5 / 32.6 / 9.8 | 136.6 / 13.8 / 5.6 | 147.2 / 23.1 / 16.6 | 72.2 / 24.1 / 7.5 | 54.8 / 11.4 / 7.4 |
| Sales/Total Assets | 2.5 / 1.7 / 1.3 | 2.4 / 1.9 / 1.3 | 2.7 / 1.8 / 1.3 | | 3.0 / 2.3 / 1.3 | 3.7 / 2.1 / 1.4 | 3.4 / 2.4 / 1.8 | 2.7 / 1.9 / 1.3 | 2.2 / 1.6 / 1.2 |
| % Depr., Dep., Amort./Sales | 1.0 / (138) 2.1 / 3.4 | .9 / (142) 1.8 / 3.2 | .8 / (155) 1.6 / 3.2 | | .7 / (19) 1.3 / 2.3 | 1.1 / (15) 2.8 / 3.3 | .8 / (20) 1.1 / 2.6 | .7 / (39) 1.3 / 2.4 | .6 / (58) 2.1 / 4.0 |
| % Officers', Directors' Owners' Comp/Sales | 2.3 / (42) 4.5 / 7.7 | 2.0 / (52) 4.3 / 7.4 | 2.3 / (60) 4.9 / 8.3 | | 3.4 / (14) 5.1 / 6.9 | 1.9 / (11) 7.9 / 9.3 | 2.3 / (19) 4.4 / 6.7 | | |
| Net Sales ($) | 7755975M | 6875019M | 5602895M | 2295M | 65380M | 79952M | 205276M | 771232M | 4478760M |
| Total Assets ($) | 5458449M | 4975927M | 4109772M | 1919M | 38573M | 46500M | 102935M | 474220M | 3445625M |

© RMA 2012

M = $ thousand    MM = $ million
See Pages 9 through 22 for Explanation of Ratios and Data

## Current Data Sorted by Assets | Comparative Historical Data

| Type of Statement | 0-500M | 500M-2MM | 2-10MM | 10-50MM | 50-100MM | 100-250MM | | 4/1/07-3/31/08 ALL | | 4/1/08-3/31/09 ALL |
|---|---|---|---|---|---|---|---|---|---|---|
| Unqualified | | | 1 | 6 | | 1 | | 15 | | 15 |
| Reviewed | | 1 | 7 | 3 | | | | 8 | | 10 |
| Compiled | | 1 | 1 | | | | | 2 | | 3 |
| Tax Returns | 2 | 4 | 7 | 8 | 2 | 3 | | 4 | | 1 |
| Other | | | | | | | | 18 | | 27 |
| | 5 (4/1-9/30/11) | | | 42 (10/1/11-3/31/12) | | | | | | |
| NUMBER OF STATEMENTS | 2 | 6 | 16 | 17 | 2 | 4 | | 47 | | 56 |
| **ASSETS** | % | % | % | % | % | % | | % | | % |
| Cash & Equivalents | | | 5.4 | 11.0 | | | | 12.2 | | 10.1 |
| Trade Receivables (net) | | | 29.3 | 29.5 | | | | 27.0 | | 27.0 |
| Inventory | | | 33.5 | 28.6 | | | | 33.5 | | 32.8 |
| All Other Current | | | 2.7 | 2.4 | | | | 2.9 | | 2.9 |
| Total Current | | | 70.9 | 71.5 | | | | 75.6 | | 72.8 |
| Fixed Assets (net) | | | 19.6 | 16.7 | | | | 13.3 | | 12.8 |
| Intangibles (net) | | | 1.7 | 6.7 | | | | 7.6 | | 7.5 |
| All Other Non-Current | | | 7.8 | 5.2 | | | | 3.5 | | 6.9 |
| Total | | | 100.0 | 100.0 | | | | 100.0 | | 100.0 |
| **LIABILITIES** | | | | | | | | | | |
| Notes Payable-Short Term | | | 12.4 | 11.1 | | | | 16.0 | | 15.5 |
| Cur. Mat.-L.T.D. | | | 2.8 | 1.4 | | | | 6.2 | | 1.5 |
| Trade Payables | | | 14.8 | 12.7 | | | | 14.4 | | 16.1 |
| Income Taxes Payable | | | .6 | .5 | | | | .1 | | .1 |
| All Other Current | | | 10.4 | 5.7 | | | | 11.0 | | 19.5 |
| Total Current | | | 41.0 | 31.5 | | | | 47.8 | | 52.7 |
| Long-Term Debt | | | 8.4 | 10.5 | | | | 10.1 | | 9.8 |
| Deferred Taxes | | | .1 | .8 | | | | .8 | | .5 |
| All Other Non-Current | | | 9.0 | 5.1 | | | | 6.7 | | 8.0 |
| Net Worth | | | 41.6 | 52.1 | | | | 34.7 | | 29.0 |
| Total Liabilities & Net Worth | | | 100.0 | 100.0 | | | | 100.0 | | 100.0 |
| **INCOME DATA** | | | | | | | | | | |
| Net Sales | | | 100.0 | 100.0 | | | | 100.0 | | 100.0 |
| Gross Profit | | | 41.0 | 35.6 | | | | 36.4 | | 34.7 |
| Operating Expenses | | | 36.2 | 29.0 | | | | 32.1 | | 35.0 |
| Operating Profit | | | 4.8 | 6.7 | | | | 4.3 | | -.3 |
| All Other Expenses (net) | | | -.2 | 1.2 | | | | 1.5 | | 1.2 |
| Profit Before Taxes | | | 5.0 | 5.5 | | | | 2.8 | | -1.5 |
| **RATIOS** | | | | | | | | | | |
| Current | | | 2.8 | 4.6 | | | | 3.1 | | 2.7 |
| | | | 1.9 | 2.1 | | | | 2.0 | | 1.5 |
| | | | 1.2 | 1.4 | | | | 1.2 | | 1.2 |
| Quick | | | 1.5 | 3.4 | | | | 1.7 | | 1.2 |
| | | | .8 | 1.1 | | | | .9 | | .7 |
| | | | .5 | .5 | | | | .5 | | .5 |
| Sales/Receivables | | | 29  12.7 | 53  6.9 | | | | 28  12.8 | | 31  11.9 |
| | | | 47  7.8 | 70  5.2 | | | | 49  7.4 | | 51  7.2 |
| | | | 65  5.6 | 96  3.8 | | | | 79  4.6 | | 73  5.0 |
| Cost of Sales/Inventory | | | 38  9.6 | 69  5.3 | | | | 58  6.3 | | 61  6.0 |
| | | | 99  3.7 | 107  3.4 | | | | 102  3.6 | | 100  3.7 |
| | | | 159  2.3 | 135  2.7 | | | | 122  3.0 | | 133  2.7 |
| Cost of Sales/Payables | | | 17  21.6 | 21  17.0 | | | | 13  27.7 | | 17  21.1 |
| | | | 34  10.8 | 47  7.7 | | | | 38  9.7 | | 38  9.7 |
| | | | 54  6.7 | 74  4.9 | | | | 66  5.5 | | 63  5.8 |
| Sales/Working Capital | | | 4.7 | 2.5 | | | | 3.8 | | 4.2 |
| | | | 8.2 | 4.5 | | | | 6.0 | | 9.2 |
| | | | 11.0 | 8.4 | | | | 18.1 | | 23.0 |
| EBIT/Interest | | | 46.5 | 30.4 | | | | 9.3 | | 8.7 |
| | | | (13) 4.5 | (16) 5.5 | | | | (40) 3.9 | | (51) 2.4 |
| | | | -1.1 | 1.8 | | | | .3 | | 1.0 |
| Net Profit + Depr., Dep., Amort./Cur. Mat. L/T/D | | | | | | | | 9.3 | | 7.7 |
| | | | | | | | | (11) 2.4 | | (15) 3.3 |
| | | | | | | | | 1.8 | | 1.8 |
| Fixed/Worth | | | .1 | .1 | | | | .1 | | .1 |
| | | | .3 | .4 | | | | .4 | | .4 |
| | | | 1.1 | .9 | | | | UND | | 1.3 |
| Debt/Worth | | | .6 | .3 | | | | .5 | | .8 |
| | | | 1.4 | 1.4 | | | | 2.7 | | 2.4 |
| | | | 2.6 | 3.5 | | | | UND | | 19.3 |
| % Profit Before Taxes/Tangible Net Worth | | | 55.3 | 33.1 | | | | 56.0 | | 46.1 |
| | | | (13) 23.6 | (15) 17.2 | | | | (37) 17.5 | | (44) 11.0 |
| | | | 1.4 | 3.7 | | | | -2.9 | | .1 |
| % Profit Before Taxes/Total Assets | | | 21.8 | 19.2 | | | | 16.9 | | 11.5 |
| | | | 6.1 | 3.6 | | | | 7.3 | | 2.8 |
| | | | -1.3 | .4 | | | | -2.9 | | -4.7 |
| Sales/Net Fixed Assets | | | 45.8 | 67.0 | | | | 57.9 | | 85.3 |
| | | | 14.5 | 21.2 | | | | 18.6 | | 25.2 |
| | | | 6.7 | 5.8 | | | | 9.4 | | 6.8 |
| Sales/Total Assets | | | 2.6 | 2.0 | | | | 2.7 | | 2.6 |
| | | | 2.4 | 1.6 | | | | 2.0 | | 2.0 |
| | | | 1.5 | 1.0 | | | | 1.5 | | 1.4 |
| % Depr., Dep., Amort./Sales | | | .7 | .4 | | | | .9 | | .6 |
| | | | (14) 1.8 | (16) 1.2 | | | | (35) 1.8 | | (46) 1.4 |
| | | | 3.1 | 3.4 | | | | 3.3 | | 2.8 |
| % Officers', Directors', Owners' Comp/Sales | | | | | | | | 2.4 | | 2.1 |
| | | | | | | | | (10) 4.1 | | (11) 2.8 |
| | | | | | | | | 7.8 | | 5.2 |
| Net Sales ($) | 22M | 20823M | 203541M | 576921M | 161683M | 617808M | | 1923559M | | 2248261M |
| Total Assets ($) | 44M | 8006M | 95391M | 382636M | 154875M | 628512M | | 1116828M | | 1358878M |

M = $ thousand    MM = $ million
See Pages 9 through 22 for Explanation of Ratios and Data

## Comparative Historical Data | Current Data Sorted by Sales

| | | | Type of Statement | | | | | | |
|---|---|---|---|---|---|---|---|---|---|
| 14 | 7 | 8 | Unqualified | | | | 1 | 8 | 7 |
| 11 | 21 | 11 | Reviewed | | 1 | 2 | | 1 | |
| 3 | 4 | 1 | Compiled | 1 | | | | | |
| 5 | 4 | 1 | Tax Returns | | | | 1 | | |
| 20 | 24 | 26 | Other | 2 | 2 | 2 | 4 | 6 | 10 |
| 4/1/09-3/31/10 | 4/1/10-3/31/11 | 4/1/11-3/31/12 | | 0-1MM | 1-3MM | 5 (4/1-9/30/11) 3-5MM | 5-10MM | 42 (10/1/11-3/31/12) 10-25MM | 25MM & OVER |
| ALL | ALL | ALL | | | | | | | |
| 53 | 60 | 47 | NUMBER OF STATEMENTS | 2 | 3 | 4 | 6 | 15 | 17 |
| % | % | % | | % | % | % | % | % | % |
| | | | **ASSETS** | | | | | | |
| 10.1 | 9.6 | 7.2 | Cash & Equivalents | | | | | 9.7 | 5.2 |
| 26.1 | 28.1 | 26.6 | Trade Receivables (net) | | | | | 33.8 | 26.1 |
| 28.5 | 31.7 | 30.1 | Inventory | | | | | 26.0 | 28.5 |
| 3.7 | 2.2 | 3.4 | All Other Current | | | | | 4.3 | 1.6 |
| 68.4 | 71.5 | 67.3 | Total Current | | | | | 73.7 | 61.4 |
| 15.1 | 15.4 | 18.6 | Fixed Assets (net) | | | | | 17.7 | 12.4 |
| 8.0 | 6.6 | 9.5 | Intangibles (net) | | | | | 3.5 | 22.1 |
| 8.6 | 6.4 | 4.6 | All Other Non-Current | | | | | 5.1 | 4.1 |
| 100.0 | 100.0 | 100.0 | Total | | | | | 100.0 | 100.0 |
| | | | **LIABILITIES** | | | | | | |
| 12.5 | 23.5 | 10.1 | Notes Payable-Short Term | | | | | 10.1 | 10.8 |
| 1.9 | 2.9 | 1.5 | Cur. Mat.-L.T.D. | | | | | .9 | 1.2 |
| 14.7 | 17.6 | 14.1 | Trade Payables | | | | | 13.8 | 13.2 |
| .3 | .1 | .4 | Income Taxes Payable | | | | | .4 | .5 |
| 10.5 | 9.1 | 9.0 | All Other Current | | | | | 10.6 | 6.4 |
| 39.9 | 53.2 | 35.1 | Total Current | | | | | 35.8 | 32.2 |
| 9.7 | 12.0 | 15.4 | Long-Term Debt | | | | | 10.7 | 19.8 |
| .4 | .5 | .4 | Deferred Taxes | | | | | .3 | .9 |
| 6.3 | 4.8 | 6.5 | All Other Non-Current | | | | | 8.2 | 5.8 |
| 43.9 | 29.4 | 42.7 | Net Worth | | | | | 45.0 | 41.4 |
| 100.0 | 100.0 | 100.0 | Total Liabilities & Net Worth | | | | | 100.0 | 100.0 |
| | | | **INCOME DATA** | | | | | | |
| 100.0 | 100.0 | 100.0 | Net Sales | | | | | 100.0 | 100.0 |
| 38.7 | 34.9 | 37.8 | Gross Profit | | | | | 39.2 | 30.7 |
| 33.3 | 31.2 | 31.9 | Operating Expenses | | | | | 33.5 | 24.6 |
| 5.3 | 3.7 | 5.8 | Operating Profit | | | | | 5.7 | 6.1 |
| 2.0 | 1.0 | 1.0 | All Other Expenses (net) | | | | | .3 | 2.1 |
| 3.4 | 2.7 | 4.8 | Profit Before Taxes | | | | | 5.4 | 4.0 |
| | | | **RATIOS** | | | | | | |
| 3.2 | 2.4 | 3.3 | | | | | | 3.0 | 4.9 |
| 1.9 | 1.5 | 2.1 | Current | | | | | 2.3 | 2.1 |
| 1.2 | 1.1 | 1.3 | | | | | | 1.6 | 1.3 |
| 1.9 | 1.3 | 2.1 | | | | | | 2.1 | 3.4 |
| .9 | .7 | .9 | Quick | | | | | 1.4 | .8 |
| .6 | .4 | .5 | | | | | | .6 | .5 |
| 28  13.2 | 35  10.4 | 37  9.9 | | | | | | 49  7.5 | 47  7.7 |
| 51  7.1 | 52  7.1 | 52  7.0 | Sales/Receivables | | | | | 55  6.6 | 55  6.6 |
| 66  5.5 | 68  5.3 | 79  4.6 | | | | | | 94  3.9 | 81  4.5 |
| 51  7.2 | 46  8.0 | 69  5.3 | | | | | | 37  9.9 | 66  5.5 |
| 92  4.0 | 93  3.9 | 101  3.6 | Cost of Sales/Inventory | | | | | 96  3.8 | 107  3.4 |
| 124  2.9 | 145  2.5 | 135  2.7 | | | | | | 126  2.9 | 135  2.7 |
| 15  24.1 | 19  19.7 | 19  19.2 | | | | | | 24  15.4 | 12  30.3 |
| 33  10.9 | 36  10.0 | 39  9.3 | Cost of Sales/Payables | | | | | 39  9.3 | 34  10.6 |
| 58  6.3 | 71  5.2 | 74  4.9 | | | | | | 68  5.4 | 73  5.0 |
| 4.1 | 4.9 | 3.9 | | | | | | 3.9 | 3.7 |
| 6.8 | 9.0 | 5.8 | Sales/Working Capital | | | | | 4.8 | 5.6 |
| 16.5 | 20.5 | 10.7 | | | | | | 8.5 | 9.5 |
| 18.3 | 10.2 | 27.7 | | | | | | 57.0 | 23.5 |
| (48)  6.8 | (52)  4.2 | (39)  4.0 | EBIT/Interest | | | | | (12)  5.6 | (16)  2.5 |
| 1.3 | .9 | .2 | | | | | | 1.3 | -.8 |
| 13.9 | | | Net Profit + Depr., Dep., | | | | | | |
| (15)  4.5 | | | Amort./Cur. Mat. L/T/D | | | | | | |
| 2.4 | | | | | | | | | |
| .1 | .1 | .1 | | | | | | .1 | .3 |
| .3 | .3 | .3 | Fixed/Worth | | | | | .2 | .6 |
| 1.1 | 1.9 | UND | | | | | | 2.8 | -1.1 |
| .6 | .6 | .5 | | | | | | .4 | .5 |
| 1.5 | 1.8 | 1.5 | Debt/Worth | | | | | 1.4 | 3.6 |
| 8.7 | 122.9 | UND | | | | | | 4.0 | -5.1 |
| 75.0 | 40.8 | 56.4 | % Profit Before Taxes/Tangible | | | | | 45.0 | 47.6 |
| (47)  37.5 | (47)  18.8 | (36)  22.1 | Net Worth | | | | | (12)  21.0 | (10)  18.8 |
| 2.8 | 2.1 | .8 | | | | | | 7.2 | 1.5 |
| 24.2 | 13.6 | 20.0 | % Profit Before Taxes/Total | | | | | 22.9 | 15.4 |
| 11.2 | 6.5 | 6.4 | Assets | | | | | 5.1 | 3.6 |
| .5 | .3 | -1.8 | | | | | | .2 | -4.1 |
| 69.5 | 55.3 | 60.1 | | | | | | 49.2 | 75.0 |
| 25.8 | 23.3 | 18.0 | Sales/Net Fixed Assets | | | | | 18.0 | 21.2 |
| 7.8 | 8.5 | 5.9 | | | | | | 8.9 | 6.4 |
| 2.7 | 2.6 | 2.5 | | | | | | 2.6 | 2.0 |
| 1.9 | 1.9 | 1.8 | Sales/Total Assets | | | | | 2.3 | 1.6 |
| 1.3 | 1.4 | 1.1 | | | | | | 1.3 | 1.1 |
| .7 | .8 | .7 | | | | | | .7 | .3 |
| (38)  1.6 | (49)  1.9 | (34)  1.8 | % Depr., Dep., Amort./Sales | | | | | (14)  1.3 | (13)  1.3 |
| 3.3 | 3.3 | 3.4 | | | | | | 3.2 | 3.2 |
| 1.5 | | | % Officers', Directors' | | | | | | |
| (19)  3.3 | | | Owners' Comp/Sales | | | | | | |
| 4.9 | | | | | | | | | |
| 2537216M | 2223666M | 1580798M | Net Sales ($) | 22M | 6861M | 16793M | 44992M | 267541M | 1244589M |
| 1599258M | 1495217M | 1269464M | Total Assets ($) | 44M | 5238M | 5245M | 37331M | 170310M | 1051296M |

© RMA 2012

**M = $ thousand     MM = $ million**
See Pages 9 through 22 for Explanation of Ratios and Data

## Current Data Sorted by Assets

## Comparative Historical Data

| 0-500M | 500M-2MM | 2-10MM | 10-50MM | 50-100MM | 100-250MM | Type of Statement | ALL 4/1/07-3/31/08 | ALL 4/1/08-3/31/09 |
|---|---|---|---|---|---|---|---|---|
|  |  | 5 | 10 | 2 | 1 | Unqualified | 23 | 23 |
|  | 7 | 29 | 15 |  |  | Reviewed | 42 | 51 |
| 7 | 11 | 10 | 2 |  |  | Compiled | 36 | 36 |
| 24 | 13 | 8 |  |  | 1 | Tax Returns | 28 | 40 |
| 14 | 13 | 37 | 15 |  | 1 | Other | 75 | 92 |
| 0-500M | 40 (4/1-9/30/11) 500M-2MM | 2-10MM | 185 (10/1/11-3/31/12) 10-50MM | 50-100MM | 100-250MM |  | 4/1/07-3/31/08 | 4/1/08-3/31/09 |
| 45 | 44 | 89 | 42 | 2 | 3 | NUMBER OF STATEMENTS | 204 | 242 |
| % | % | % | % | % | % | ASSETS | % | % |
| 11.8 | 6.1 | 13.4 | 7.8 |  |  | Cash & Equivalents | 8.8 | 9.5 |
| 20.6 | 38.8 | 35.7 | 29.0 |  |  | Trade Receivables (net) | 34.8 | 30.7 |
| 9.0 | 19.0 | 18.2 | 21.5 |  |  | Inventory | 17.2 | 18.9 |
| 7.5 | 2.7 | 3.4 | 4.7 |  |  | All Other Current | 3.6 | 4.0 |
| 48.8 | 66.6 | 70.6 | 63.1 |  |  | Total Current | 64.3 | 63.1 |
| 27.4 | 24.3 | 22.1 | 25.1 |  |  | Fixed Assets (net) | 25.1 | 25.7 |
| 11.4 | 3.3 | 1.6 | 5.3 |  |  | Intangibles (net) | 4.8 | 4.7 |
| 12.3 | 5.9 | 5.7 | 6.5 |  |  | All Other Non-Current | 5.7 | 6.5 |
| 100.0 | 100.0 | 100.0 | 100.0 |  |  | Total | 100.0 | 100.0 |
|  |  |  |  |  |  | LIABILITIES |  |  |
| 15.0 | 14.6 | 11.1 | 13.0 |  |  | Notes Payable-Short Term | 13.5 | 13.1 |
| 6.5 | 3.9 | 3.2 | 3.4 |  |  | Cur. Mat.-L.T.D. | 6.6 | 5.7 |
| 16.6 | 16.2 | 15.6 | 13.8 |  |  | Trade Payables | 15.8 | 15.1 |
| .0 | .1 | .2 | .2 |  |  | Income Taxes Payable | .6 | .2 |
| 19.6 | 10.4 | 15.6 | 11.6 |  |  | All Other Current | 14.8 | 13.5 |
| 57.7 | 45.1 | 45.7 | 42.0 |  |  | Total Current | 51.4 | 47.6 |
| 44.4 | 18.6 | 12.2 | 17.4 |  |  | Long-Term Debt | 21.1 | 20.5 |
| .0 | .1 | .5 | .6 |  |  | Deferred Taxes | .3 | .3 |
| 18.6 | 12.7 | 4.1 | 4.8 |  |  | All Other Non-Current | 7.8 | 5.3 |
| -20.7 | 23.5 | 37.5 | 35.2 |  |  | Net Worth | 19.4 | 26.3 |
| 100.0 | 100.0 | 100.0 | 100.0 |  |  | Total Liabilities & Net Worth | 100.0 | 100.0 |
|  |  |  |  |  |  | INCOME DATA |  |  |
| 100.0 | 100.0 | 100.0 | 100.0 |  |  | Net Sales | 100.0 | 100.0 |
| 59.8 | 44.7 | 34.8 | 29.0 |  |  | Gross Profit | 39.6 | 38.2 |
| 57.5 | 42.5 | 30.0 | 25.5 |  |  | Operating Expenses | 35.0 | 34.8 |
| 2.4 | 2.1 | 4.8 | 3.5 |  |  | Operating Profit | 4.6 | 3.4 |
| 1.6 | .4 | .5 | 1.4 |  |  | All Other Expenses (net) | 1.4 | 1.0 |
| .8 | 1.7 | 4.2 | 2.1 |  |  | Profit Before Taxes | 3.2 | 2.4 |
|  |  |  |  |  |  | RATIOS |  |  |
| 2.1 | 2.3 | 2.3 | 2.2 |  |  | Current | 2.1 | 2.2 |
| 1.0 | 1.5 | 1.6 | 1.4 |  |  |  | 1.4 | 1.5 |
| .5 | 1.1 | 1.2 | 1.1 |  |  |  | 1.0 | 1.1 |
| 1.4 | 1.5 | 1.7 | 1.3 |  |  | Quick | 1.4 | 1.5 |
| .6 | .9 | 1.1 | .9 |  |  |  | .9 | .9 |
| .3 | .6 | .7 | .6 |  |  |  | .6 | .6 |
| 6  56.5 | 36  10.1 | 33  11.0 | 45  8.2 |  |  | Sales/Receivables | 31  11.8 | 26  14.3 |
| 20  18.7 | 46  7.9 | 49  7.4 | 60  6.1 |  |  |  | 47  7.8 | 40  9.2 |
| 35  10.4 | 59  6.2 | 70  5.2 | 73  5.0 |  |  |  | 61  6.0 | 56  6.5 |
| 0  UND | 16  23.3 | 13  28.0 | 23  16.0 |  |  | Cost of Sales/Inventory | 16  23.5 | 15  23.8 |
| 9  42.5 | 38  9.6 | 36  10.1 | 54  6.8 |  |  |  | 35  10.5 | 36  10.2 |
| 35  10.5 | 58  6.3 | 58  6.3 | 89  4.1 |  |  |  | 58  6.3 | 63  5.8 |
| 0  UND | 18  20.0 | 19  19.4 | 28  13.0 |  |  | Cost of Sales/Payables | 17  21.6 | 17  21.3 |
| 24  15.3 | 29  12.5 | 30  12.1 | 36  10.0 |  |  |  | 31  11.7 | 28  13.2 |
| 59  6.2 | 51  7.2 | 47  7.7 | 47  7.8 |  |  |  | 49  7.5 | 45  8.2 |
| 10.9 | 8.6 | 6.1 | 5.6 |  |  | Sales/Working Capital | 7.8 | 6.9 |
| -164.2 | 13.4 | 10.6 | 10.5 |  |  |  | 15.1 | 13.9 |
| -14.4 | 96.2 | 25.6 | 46.9 |  |  |  | NM | 106.6 |
| 5.7 | 6.1 | 21.3 | 17.4 |  |  | EBIT/Interest | 11.6 | 9.6 |
| (39) 2.6 | (39) 3.8 | (79) 6.6 | (38) 2.7 |  |  |  | (191) 3.3 | (222) 3.1 |
| .7 | 1.1 | 2.6 | 1.0 |  |  |  | 1.0 | .9 |
|  |  | 8.5 | 24.4 |  |  | Net Profit + Depr., Dep., Amort./Cur. Mat. L/T/D | 9.4 | 6.4 |
|  | (22) 3.5 | (11) 5.4 |  |  |  |  | (45) 2.1 | (52) 2.0 |
|  |  | .7 | .3 |  |  |  | 1.4 | 1.0 |
| .7 | .4 | .2 | .3 |  |  | Fixed/Worth | .3 | .3 |
| -1.2 | .9 | .5 | 1.1 |  |  |  | 1.0 | .8 |
| -.3 | 5.8 | 1.4 | 1.8 |  |  |  | 88.5 | 3.1 |
| 1.8 | .9 | .7 | .9 |  |  | Debt/Worth | 1.2 | .9 |
| -4.8 | 2.4 | 1.7 | 2.4 |  |  |  | 3.2 | 2.4 |
| -1.9 | 24.0 | 4.0 | 5.4 |  |  |  | NM | 9.5 |
| 170.8 | 37.9 | 48.9 | 32.7 |  |  | % Profit Before Taxes/Tangible Net Worth | 57.6 | 50.3 |
| (19) 40.6 | (34) 13.1 | (81) 25.8 | (39) 16.3 |  |  |  | (153) 26.0 | (197) 21.9 |
| 4.7 | 1.7 | 9.4 | 2.8 |  |  |  | 7.1 | 5.7 |
| 24.6 | 11.6 | 18.7 | 13.7 |  |  | % Profit Before Taxes/Total Assets | 17.1 | 15.4 |
| 5.6 | 4.7 | 8.9 | 3.4 |  |  |  | 6.4 | 6.3 |
| -2.9 | .4 | 3.2 | -.3 |  |  |  | .3 | -.5 |
| 40.2 | 41.6 | 29.1 | 25.2 |  |  | Sales/Net Fixed Assets | 31.6 | 30.7 |
| 18.4 | 12.4 | 15.6 | 7.5 |  |  |  | 14.6 | 13.7 |
| 7.6 | 8.1 | 8.1 | 4.6 |  |  |  | 7.2 | 6.7 |
| 4.9 | 3.6 | 3.4 | 2.2 |  |  | Sales/Total Assets | 3.4 | 3.5 |
| 3.6 | 2.9 | 2.5 | 1.6 |  |  |  | 2.6 | 2.6 |
| 2.3 | 2.4 | 2.0 | 1.4 |  |  |  | 1.9 | 2.0 |
| .9 | .9 | .9 | 1.3 |  |  | % Depr., Dep., Amort./Sales | .9 | .9 |
| (32) 2.3 | (35) 1.5 | (81) 1.6 | (37) 2.4 |  |  |  | (173) 1.6 | (209) 2.0 |
| 5.1 | 3.1 | 2.5 | 2.9 |  |  |  | 3.1 | 3.0 |
| 4.1 | 2.8 | 1.8 |  |  |  | % Officers', Directors' Owners' Comp/Sales | 3.2 | 2.7 |
| (33) 6.8 | (25) 3.9 | (33) 3.9 |  |  |  |  | (84) 4.8 | (103) 5.2 |
| 10.1 | 7.3 | 4.8 |  |  |  |  | 8.3 | 9.3 |
| 42276M | 132995M | 1132907M | 1626774M | 250429M | 731049M | Net Sales ($) | 4204965M | 4548104M |
| 11979M | 46194M | 441220M | 865524M | 136996M | 588717M | Total Assets ($) | 2026325M | 2154924M |

M = $ thousand    MM = $ million
See Pages 9 through 22 for Explanation of Ratios and Data

## Comparative Historical Data — Current Data Sorted by Sales

| 4/1/09-3/31/10 ALL | 4/1/10-3/31/11 ALL | 4/1/11-3/31/12 ALL | Type of Statement | 0-1MM | 1-3MM | 3-5MM | 5-10MM | 10-25MM | 25MM & OVER |
|---|---|---|---|---|---|---|---|---|---|
| 20 | 21 | 18 | Unqualified | | | | | 10 | 8 |
| 42 | 54 | 51 | Reviewed | | 2 | 8 | 7 | 23 | 11 |
| 31 | 26 | 30 | Compiled | 5 | 10 | 6 | 2 | 6 | 1 |
| 33 | 38 | 46 | Tax Returns | 18 | 15 | 6 | 3 | 3 | 1 |
| 85 | 80 | 80 | Other | 7 | 14 | 7 | 7 | 30 | 15 |
| | | | | 40 (4/1-9/30/11) | | | 185 (10/1/11-3/31/12) | | |
| 211 | 219 | 225 | NUMBER OF STATEMENTS | 30 | 41 | 27 | 19 | 72 | 36 |
| % | % | % | **ASSETS** | % | % | % | % | % | % |
| 9.7 | 10.2 | 10.4 | Cash & Equivalents | 9.8 | 10.5 | 8.5 | 9.1 | 13.5 | 6.4 |
| 30.4 | 30.5 | 31.7 | Trade Receivables (net) | 18.3 | 32.7 | 34.1 | 36.8 | 35.2 | 30.2 |
| 17.2 | 16.9 | 17.1 | Inventory | 6.7 | 14.5 | 19.1 | 17.5 | 19.9 | 21.7 |
| 3.6 | 3.6 | 4.3 | All Other Current | 10.6 | 1.6 | .7 | 7.1 | 3.3 | 5.1 |
| 60.8 | 61.2 | 63.5 | Total Current | 45.5 | 59.3 | 62.4 | 70.5 | 71.9 | 63.4 |
| 25.8 | 26.8 | 24.5 | Fixed Assets (net) | 27.7 | 27.9 | 26.5 | 24.6 | 19.3 | 27.0 |
| 5.6 | 4.9 | 4.7 | Intangibles (net) | 14.1 | 5.4 | 3.1 | .3 | 3.0 | 3.1 |
| 7.8 | 7.1 | 7.3 | All Other Non-Current | 12.6 | 7.5 | 8.0 | 4.6 | 5.7 | 6.6 |
| 100.0 | 100.0 | 100.0 | Total | 100.0 | 100.0 | 100.0 | 100.0 | 100.0 | 100.0 |
| | | | **LIABILITIES** | | | | | | |
| 12.4 | 11.9 | 12.9 | Notes Payable-Short Term | 9.7 | 16.9 | 13.6 | 8.8 | 13.8 | 10.5 |
| 4.5 | 4.2 | 4.0 | Cur. Mat.-L.T.D. | 6.4 | 5.3 | 3.4 | 4.1 | 3.0 | 2.8 |
| 13.5 | 15.6 | 15.5 | Trade Payables | 10.9 | 21.0 | 10.3 | 16.2 | 16.8 | 13.9 |
| .2 | .1 | .1 | Income Taxes Payable | .0 | .0 | .1 | .9 | .1 | .2 |
| 12.0 | 12.7 | 14.8 | All Other Current | 15.7 | 16.7 | 12.5 | 8.9 | 15.1 | 15.8 |
| 42.6 | 44.5 | 47.2 | Total Current | 42.7 | 60.0 | 39.8 | 38.9 | 48.9 | 43.3 |
| 19.8 | 19.9 | 21.2 | Long-Term Debt | 51.4 | 27.4 | 15.9 | 17.5 | 9.7 | 18.2 |
| .5 | .5 | .4 | Deferred Taxes | .0 | .4 | .9 | .3 | .3 | .5 |
| 7.3 | 9.3 | 8.8 | All Other Non-Current | 18.5 | 15.8 | 7.0 | 1.5 | 5.9 | 3.9 |
| 29.7 | 25.8 | 22.3 | Net Worth | -12.8 | -3.5 | 36.4 | 41.9 | 35.3 | 34.1 |
| 100.0 | 100.0 | 100.0 | Total Liabilities & Net Worth | 100.0 | 100.0 | 100.0 | 100.0 | 100.0 | 100.0 |
| | | | **INCOME DATA** | | | | | | |
| 100.0 | 100.0 | 100.0 | Net Sales | 100.0 | 100.0 | 100.0 | 100.0 | 100.0 | 100.0 |
| 40.2 | 39.0 | 40.6 | Gross Profit | 63.3 | 48.5 | 42.2 | 34.6 | 32.7 | 30.7 |
| 37.7 | 35.2 | 37.1 | Operating Expenses | 61.1 | 46.3 | 39.0 | 29.8 | 28.0 | 27.3 |
| 2.5 | 3.8 | 3.5 | Operating Profit | 2.3 | 2.2 | 3.1 | 4.8 | 4.6 | 3.4 |
| 1.2 | 1.2 | .9 | All Other Expenses (net) | 1.8 | .9 | .7 | .7 | .7 | .9 |
| 1.4 | 2.6 | 2.6 | Profit Before Taxes | .5 | 1.3 | 2.4 | 4.1 | 4.0 | 2.5 |
| | | | **RATIOS** | | | | | | |
| 2.5 | 2.2 | 2.2 | Current | 2.0 | 2.3 | 2.2 | 3.0 | 2.2 | 2.0 |
| 1.6 | 1.5 | 1.5 | | 1.0 | 1.2 | 1.6 | 1.7 | 1.4 | 1.5 |
| 1.1 | 1.1 | 1.0 | | .7 | .8 | 1.2 | 1.1 | 1.1 | 1.2 |
| 1.7 | 1.4 | 1.5 | Quick | 1.4 | 1.5 | 1.4 | 2.1 | 1.6 | 1.2 |
| 1.0 | 1.0 | .9 | | .7 | .8 | 1.0 | 1.1 | 1.0 | .9 |
| .6 | .6 | .6 | | .4 | .4 | .7 | .6 | .6 | .6 |
| 27  13.3 | 31  11.6 | 27  13.5 | Sales/Receivables | 0  UND | 21  17.7 | 32  11.3 | 36  10.2 | 33  10.9 | 44  8.3 |
| 42  8.6 | 48  7.6 | 47  7.6 | | 20  18.3 | 38  9.7 | 51  7.1 | 49  7.4 | 49  7.5 | 61  6.0 |
| 63  5.8 | 68  5.3 | 63  5.8 | | 43  8.5 | 50  7.3 | 76  4.8 | 70  5.2 | 65  5.6 | 76  4.8 |
| 16  22.6 | 13  27.4 | 9  38.5 | Cost of Sales/Inventory | 0  UND | 7  52.5 | 16  22.6 | 15  23.8 | 13  28.5 | 18  20.0 |
| 39  9.5 | 38  9.6 | 35  10.4 | | 8  44.6 | 25  14.7 | 46  8.0 | 30  12.2 | 39  9.3 | 54  6.8 |
| 68  5.4 | 63  5.8 | 60  6.1 | | 49  7.5 | 46  7.9 | 72  5.1 | 54  6.8 | 62  5.9 | 99  3.7 |
| 18  20.1 | 17  21.7 | 19  19.7 | Cost of Sales/Payables | 0  UND | 16  23.1 | 11  33.0 | 17  22.0 | 23  15.9 | 20  18.5 |
| 29  12.6 | 30  12.1 | 30  12.0 | | 27  13.7 | 31  11.8 | 20  18.4 | 30  12.2 | 31  11.8 | 35  10.4 |
| 48  7.5 | 51  7.2 | 50  7.3 | | 57  6.4 | 60  6.1 | 48  7.6 | 51  7.2 | 49  7.5 | 46  8.0 |
| 5.6 | 5.8 | 7.0 | Sales/Working Capital | 8.1 | 10.3 | 6.3 | 5.1 | 7.0 | 5.8 |
| 11.1 | 11.4 | 12.3 | | NM | 40.2 | 12.3 | 8.4 | 11.8 | 8.9 |
| 70.6 | 79.6 | 352.0 | | -22.7 | -23.8 | 28.5 | 32.7 | 48.4 | 26.9 |
| 8.5 | 11.4 | 13.1 | EBIT/Interest | 5.9 | 5.5 | 6.5 | 15.7 | 25.2 | 21.2 |
| (187)  2.9 | (196)  2.9 | (199)  4.2 | | (26)  3.0 | (37)  1.8 | (24)  4.8 | (16)  5.6 | (63)  6.9 | (33)  3.3 |
| -.9 | .5 | 1.4 | | .7 | .6 | 1.9 | 1.6 | 2.5 | 1.8 |
| 4.6 | 7.2 | 7.8 | Net Profit + Depr., Dep., Amort./Cur. Mat. L/T/D | | | | | 59.5 | 19.6 |
| (41)  2.0 | (58)  3.2 | (41)  2.9 | | | | | | (14)  6.2 | (10)  4.9 |
| -.6 | 1.0 | .8 | | | | | | 1.5 | 1.3 |
| .3 | .3 | .3 | Fixed/Worth | .5 | .6 | .4 | .1 | .2 | .3 |
| .8 | .8 | .8 | | -2.0 | 2.8 | .8 | .7 | .5 | .7 |
| 5.4 | 2.4 | 5.4 | | -.2 | -.8 | 2.6 | 1.2 | 1.7 | 1.7 |
| .8 | .9 | .9 | Debt/Worth | 1.8 | 1.4 | .8 | .5 | .7 | .9 |
| 1.9 | 2.0 | 2.4 | | -8.2 | 12.1 | 1.8 | 1.5 | 1.9 | 2.2 |
| 9.8 | 6.7 | 14.4 | | -1.8 | -3.3 | 6.4 | 2.9 | 5.5 | 4.9 |
| 35.9 | 34.6 | 44.7 | % Profit Before Taxes/Tangible Net Worth | 235.5 | 58.0 | 26.7 | 36.1 | 51.7 | 32.5 |
| (167)  12.3 | (179)  14.2 | (176)  20.3 | | (14)  29.1 | (25)  18.1 | (22)  10.9 | (18)  21.5 | (64)  27.2 | (33)  16.3 |
| -1.0 | -.3 | 4.8 | | -2.2 | 1.3 | 5.2 | 4.2 | 14.0 | 2.1 |
| 13.7 | 14.5 | 16.3 | % Profit Before Taxes/Total Assets | 24.2 | 14.5 | 11.7 | 13.7 | 18.9 | 17.0 |
| 4.0 | 4.5 | 6.0 | | 5.8 | 2.4 | 6.0 | 7.7 | 10.4 | 4.6 |
| -4.9 | -.9 | .7 | | -3.2 | -1.2 | 2.1 | 1.4 | 2.1 | .7 |
| 27.8 | 24.8 | 29.0 | Sales/Net Fixed Assets | 47.3 | 27.2 | 19.1 | 44.9 | 32.9 | 23.7 |
| 11.1 | 11.5 | 13.7 | | 13.2 | 16.6 | 11.2 | 15.2 | 17.6 | 8.9 |
| 5.6 | 6.3 | 6.1 | | 6.4 | 7.1 | 7.3 | 4.4 | 9.1 | 3.8 |
| 3.1 | 3.1 | 3.5 | Sales/Total Assets | 4.4 | 4.3 | 3.3 | 3.1 | 3.4 | 2.4 |
| 2.3 | 2.3 | 2.5 | | 2.5 | 3.3 | 2.4 | 2.6 | 2.6 | 1.7 |
| 1.6 | 1.8 | 1.8 | | 1.9 | 2.6 | 1.5 | 1.8 | 2.2 | 1.4 |
| 1.1 | 1.1 | 1.0 | % Depr., Dep., Amort./Sales | 1.3 | 1.1 | .9 | .4 | 1.1 | 1.0 |
| (168)  2.2 | (185)  2.1 | (187)  1.8 | | (22)  3.7 | (30)  2.3 | (23)  1.5 | 1.5 | (62)  1.5 | (31)  2.2 |
| 3.5 | 3.5 | 2.9 | | 6.6 | 3.2 | 3.5 | 2.5 | 2.4 | 2.8 |
| 2.6 | 2.1 | 2.4 | % Officers', Directors' Owners' Comp/Sales | 1.9 | 3.9 | 2.6 | | 1.7 | |
| (78)  4.4 | (95)  4.8 | (97)  4.3 | | (22) | (28)  5.7 | (15)  4.4 | | (22)  2.7 | |
| 7.9 | 8.0 | 6.8 | | 10.5 | 9.1 | 5.2 | | 4.4 | |
| 4402482M | 4393402M | 3916430M | Net Sales ($) | 17828M | 80913M | 107983M | 132576M | 1162949M | 2414181M |
| 2495686M | 2220856M | 2090630M | Total Assets ($) | 7521M | 30671M | 61087M | 56751M | 496775M | 1437825M |

M = $ thousand   MM = $ million
See Pages 9 through 22 for Explanation of Ratios and Data

## Current Data Sorted by Assets

## Comparative Historical Data

| | 0-500M | 500M-2MM | 2-10MM | 10-50MM | 50-100MM | 100-250MM | | Type of Statement | 4/1/07-3/31/08 | 4/1/08-3/31/09 |
|---|---|---|---|---|---|---|---|---|---|---|
| | | 1 | 3 | 3 | 2 | 2 | | Unqualified | 9 | 14 |
| | | 3 | 8 | 4 | | | | Reviewed | 21 | 18 |
| | 3 | 8 | 7 | | | | | Compiled | 14 | 12 |
| | 1 | 6 | 2 | | | | | Tax Returns | 7 | 9 |
| | | | 11 | 9 | 2 | 9 | | Other | 19 | 27 |
| | | 19 (4/1-9/30/11) | | 65 (10/1/11-3/31/12) | | | | | ALL | ALL |
| | 4 | 18 | 31 | 16 | 4 | 11 | | NUMBER OF STATEMENTS | 70 | 80 |
| | % | % | % | % | % | % | | **ASSETS** | % | % |
| | | 10.2 | 7.1 | 5.7 | | 10.0 | | Cash & Equivalents | 10.5 | 9.6 |
| | | 34.8 | 25.2 | 18.8 | | 20.5 | | Trade Receivables (net) | 24.4 | 25.8 |
| | | 28.1 | 27.7 | 24.5 | | 17.3 | | Inventory | 25.1 | 23.6 |
| | | .9 | 1.0 | 3.4 | | 2.8 | | All Other Current | 2.4 | 2.9 |
| | | 74.0 | 60.9 | 52.4 | | 50.6 | | Total Current | 62.5 | 61.9 |
| | | 20.4 | 24.6 | 18.2 | | 18.4 | | Fixed Assets (net) | 24.8 | 21.7 |
| | | 1.9 | 10.5 | 16.7 | | 18.9 | | Intangibles (net) | 6.2 | 10.1 |
| | | 3.7 | 4.0 | 12.7 | | 12.2 | | All Other Non-Current | 6.5 | 6.3 |
| | | 100.0 | 100.0 | 100.0 | | 100.0 | | Total | 100.0 | 100.0 |
| | | | | | | | | **LIABILITIES** | | |
| | | 13.3 | 7.9 | 11.5 | | 2.7 | | Notes Payable-Short Term | 11.8 | 7.2 |
| | | 4.6 | 2.5 | 2.1 | | 2.7 | | Cur. Mat.-L.T.D. | 3.2 | 3.5 |
| | | 15.0 | 14.0 | 9.8 | | 7.9 | | Trade Payables | 16.0 | 12.7 |
| | | .2 | .4 | .3 | | .5 | | Income Taxes Payable | .2 | .2 |
| | | 7.3 | 12.2 | 8.2 | | 8.1 | | All Other Current | 7.5 | 6.8 |
| | | 40.4 | 37.0 | 32.0 | | 22.0 | | Total Current | 38.6 | 30.4 |
| | | 11.9 | 13.1 | 10.3 | | 13.9 | | Long-Term Debt | 14.9 | 15.2 |
| | | .4 | .4 | 1.6 | | 2.7 | | Deferred Taxes | .6 | .7 |
| | | 7.0 | 2.2 | 16.1 | | 13.9 | | All Other Non-Current | 7.2 | 10.4 |
| | | 40.3 | 47.3 | 40.1 | | 47.5 | | Net Worth | 38.7 | 43.3 |
| | | 100.0 | 100.0 | 100.0 | | 100.0 | | Total Liabilties & Net Worth | 100.0 | 100.0 |
| | | | | | | | | **INCOME DATA** | | |
| | | 100.0 | 100.0 | 100.0 | | 100.0 | | Net Sales | 100.0 | 100.0 |
| | | 33.6 | 31.9 | 29.0 | | 34.4 | | Gross Profit | 30.1 | 33.4 |
| | | 28.4 | 26.9 | 19.2 | | 22.6 | | Operating Expenses | 25.8 | 27.8 |
| | | 5.2 | 5.0 | 9.8 | | 11.8 | | Operating Profit | 4.3 | 5.6 |
| | | .1 | .5 | 3.6 | | 1.8 | | All Other Expenses (net) | 1.1 | 1.0 |
| | | 5.0 | 4.5 | 6.2 | | 9.9 | | Profit Before Taxes | 3.3 | 4.6 |
| | | | | | | | | **RATIOS** | | |
| | | 4.0 | 2.6 | 3.2 | | 3.5 | | | 3.4 | 3.8 |
| | | 2.2 | 1.8 | 2.0 | | 2.4 | | Current | 1.8 | 2.0 |
| | | 1.2 | 1.3 | 1.0 | | 1.9 | | | 1.2 | 1.3 |
| | | 2.1 | 1.6 | 2.2 | | 2.1 | | | 2.4 | 2.1 |
| | | 1.4 | .9 | 1.0 | | 1.3 | | Quick | .9 | 1.1 |
| | | .8 | .6 | .5 | | 1.0 | | | .6 | .7 |
| | 38 9.7 | 38 9.7 | 36 10.0 | | 43 8.4 | | | | 33 11.0 | 33 11.1 |
| | 43 8.4 | 43 8.5 | 41 8.8 | | 51 7.2 | | | Sales/Receivables | 42 8.7 | 41 8.9 |
| | 55 6.6 | 54 6.8 | 50 7.3 | | 64 5.7 | | | | 49 7.4 | 48 7.7 |
| | 20 18.7 | 43 8.4 | 32 11.3 | | 60 6.1 | | | | 33 11.1 | 27 13.3 |
| | 51 7.1 | 64 5.7 | 63 5.8 | | 78 4.7 | | | Cost of Sales/Inventory | 54 6.7 | 52 7.0 |
| | 101 3.6 | 104 3.5 | 122 3.0 | | 104 3.5 | | | | 89 4.1 | 87 4.2 |
| | 9 39.7 | 23 16.1 | 16 22.4 | | 22 16.4 | | | | 20 18.4 | 18 19.8 |
| | 21 17.6 | 29 12.7 | 25 14.4 | | 24 14.9 | | | Cost of Sales/Payables | 28 12.9 | 26 13.9 |
| | 42 8.7 | 50 7.3 | 48 7.6 | | 36 10.1 | | | | 41 8.8 | 39 9.4 |
| | | 4.7 | 4.7 | 4.9 | | 2.9 | | | 4.7 | 5.0 |
| | | 7.8 | 7.0 | 7.2 | | 5.5 | | Sales/Working Capital | 8.9 | 8.8 |
| | | 23.7 | 28.9 | NM | | 7.2 | | | 21.5 | 16.7 |
| | | 50.7 | 10.8 | 19.8 | | | | | 8.2 | 10.9 |
| | (15) 14.1 | (28) 7.2 | 7.5 | | | | EBIT/Interest | (63) 4.3 | (70) 2.9 |
| | | 1.2 | 3.1 | 1.4 | | | | | 1.2 | 1.6 |
| | | | | | | | | Net Profit + Depr., Dep., | 5.8 | 2.0 |
| | | | | | | | | Amort./Cur. Mat. L/T/D | (21) 2.2 | (16) 1.2 |
| | | | | | | | | | .7 | .6 |
| | | .2 | .3 | .4 | | .1 | | | .3 | .2 |
| | | .4 | .5 | .5 | | 1.2 | | Fixed/Worth | .6 | .7 |
| | | 4.1 | 1.2 | NM | | -.9 | | | 2.6 | 2.1 |
| | | .4 | .7 | .7 | | .3 | | | .6 | .6 |
| | | 1.1 | 1.1 | 2.8 | | 2.1 | | Debt/Worth | 1.7 | 1.8 |
| | | 7.0 | 3.2 | NM | | -9.9 | | | 5.0 | 6.2 |
| | | 76.1 | 43.3 | 48.7 | | | | % Profit Before Taxes/Tangible | 37.9 | 33.0 |
| | (15) 15.8 | (28) 32.1 | (12) 25.9 | | | | Net Worth | (60) 16.0 | (67) 15.9 |
| | | 1.3 | 5.8 | 4.2 | | | | | 6.5 | 6.0 |
| | | 34.1 | 16.7 | 13.5 | | 15.1 | | % Profit Before Taxes/Total | 14.6 | 11.9 |
| | | 12.7 | 10.1 | 5.1 | | 11.5 | | Assets | 6.2 | 6.4 |
| | | -.8 | 2.5 | 1.4 | | 6.2 | | | .8 | 2.0 |
| | | 51.8 | 20.5 | 14.5 | | 20.0 | | | 28.8 | 51.0 |
| | | 22.9 | 10.9 | 8.0 | | 5.9 | | Sales/Net Fixed Assets | 10.3 | 11.4 |
| | | 7.7 | 6.0 | 5.9 | | 4.2 | | | 4.4 | 5.3 |
| | | 3.4 | 2.5 | 1.9 | | 1.7 | | | 2.8 | 3.0 |
| | | 2.7 | 1.9 | 1.6 | | 1.3 | | Sales/Total Assets | 2.1 | 2.2 |
| | | 2.0 | 1.6 | 1.0 | | .7 | | | 1.5 | 1.6 |
| | | .9 | .9 | 1.0 | | 1.1 | | | .8 | .8 |
| | (13) 1.8 | (29) 1.4 | (15) 1.4 | | 2.5 | | % Depr., Dep., Amort./Sales | (62) 1.7 | (65) 1.7 |
| | | 4.2 | 2.4 | 3.2 | | 3.8 | | | 3.0 | 3.0 |
| | 3.0 | | | | | | | % Officers', Directors', | 3.0 | 2.9 |
| | (13) 5.4 | | | | | | Owners' Comp/Sales | (25) 6.2 | (29) 4.6 |
| | 8.0 | | | | | | | | 9.8 | 7.8 |
| | 6830M | 57966M | 336956M | 534004M | 413169M | 1971563M | | Net Sales ($) | 1641741M | 2279084M |
| | 1764M | 20569M | 162181M | 349887M | 255988M | 1673364M | | Total Assets ($) | 1168963M | 1505367M |

M = $ thousand    MM = $ million
See Pages 9 through 22 for Explanation of Ratios and Data

## Comparative Historical Data | Current Data Sorted by Sales

| 11 | 10 | 10 | Type of Statement | | | | | | |
|---|---|---|---|---|---|---|---|---|---|
| 19 | 19 | 13 | Unqualified | | | | 1 | 3 | 6 |
| 14 | 8 | 10 | Reviewed | | 1 | 1 | 5 | 5 | 2 |
| 6 | 7 | 13 | Compiled | 1 | 7 | 3 | 3 | 3 | |
| 33 | 43 | 38 | Tax Returns | 3 | 3 | 3 | 3 | | |
| | | | Other | 1 | | 5 | 3 | 9 | 17 |
| 4/1/09-3/31/10 | 4/1/10-3/31/11 | 4/1/11-3/31/12 | | | 19 (4/1-9/30/11) | | 65 (10/1/11-3/31/12) | | |
| ALL | ALL | ALL | | 0-1MM | 1-3MM | 3-5MM | 5-10MM | 10-25MM | 25MM & OVER |
| 83 | 87 | 84 | NUMBER OF STATEMENTS | 1 | 11 | 12 | 15 | 20 | 25 |
| % | % | % | **ASSETS** | % | % | % | % | % | % |
| 10.4 | 9.1 | 8.5 | Cash & Equivalents | | 9.9 | 10.1 | 7.7 | 6.1 | 9.6 |
| 24.4 | 26.9 | 26.0 | Trade Receivables (net) | | 28.6 | 34.8 | 22.5 | 25.5 | 22.4 |
| 22.8 | 24.3 | 25.6 | Inventory | | 30.1 | 23.6 | 32.2 | 24.0 | 21.8 |
| 2.9 | 3.0 | 1.6 | All Other Current | | 1.5 | .4 | .4 | 1.3 | 3.3 |
| 60.5 | 63.3 | 61.8 | Total Current | | 70.1 | 68.9 | 62.7 | 56.9 | 57.1 |
| 25.2 | 21.7 | 20.2 | Fixed Assets (net) | | 19.4 | 23.6 | 17.5 | 22.1 | 19.8 |
| 7.8 | 9.1 | 11.6 | Intangibles (net) | | 9.7 | 2.5 | 11.5 | 15.0 | 13.9 |
| 6.4 | 5.9 | 6.4 | All Other Non-Current | | .8 | 5.0 | 8.3 | 6.0 | 9.1 |
| 100.0 | 100.0 | 100.0 | Total | | 100.0 | 100.0 | 100.0 | 100.0 | 100.0 |
| | | | **LIABILITIES** | | | | | | |
| 7.5 | 8.8 | 8.7 | Notes Payable-Short Term | | 13.9 | 10.6 | 6.8 | 7.7 | 7.6 |
| 4.3 | 3.5 | 2.9 | Cur. Mat.-L.T.D. | | 3.2 | 5.8 | 1.6 | 2.8 | 2.4 |
| 12.4 | 13.8 | 12.8 | Trade Payables | | 13.4 | 15.7 | 14.8 | 12.6 | 9.4 |
| .2 | .4 | .3 | Income Taxes Payable | | .4 | .0 | .3 | .5 | .4 |
| 7.3 | 9.7 | 9.8 | All Other Current | | 12.7 | 6.7 | 12.0 | 7.3 | 11.2 |
| 31.7 | 36.1 | 34.5 | Total Current | | 43.6 | 38.8 | 35.5 | 30.8 | 31.1 |
| 13.2 | 12.8 | 11.8 | Long-Term Debt | | 14.5 | 12.4 | 14.4 | 8.8 | 11.8 |
| .9 | .9 | .9 | Deferred Taxes | | .1 | .5 | .4 | .7 | 1.9 |
| 6.9 | 4.7 | 8.9 | All Other Non-Current | | 9.1 | 5.2 | .6 | 8.6 | 12.7 |
| 47.4 | 45.5 | 43.9 | Net Worth | | 32.7 | 43.2 | 49.1 | 51.2 | 42.4 |
| 100.0 | 100.0 | 100.0 | Total Liabilities & Net Worth | | 100.0 | 100.0 | 100.0 | 100.0 | 100.0 |
| | | | **INCOME DATA** | | | | | | |
| 100.0 | 100.0 | 100.0 | Net Sales | | 100.0 | 100.0 | 100.0 | 100.0 | 100.0 |
| 30.7 | 32.2 | 32.0 | Gross Profit | | 38.1 | 35.0 | 29.7 | 31.1 | 30.4 |
| 26.8 | 24.8 | 25.0 | Operating Expenses | | 31.8 | 34.8 | 25.1 | 21.5 | 20.1 |
| 3.9 | 7.4 | 7.0 | Operating Profit | | 6.3 | .2 | 4.6 | 9.6 | 10.2 |
| .7 | 1.2 | 1.1 | All Other Expenses (net) | | -.1 | -.1 | .6 | 1.8 | 2.1 |
| 3.2 | 6.2 | 5.9 | Profit Before Taxes | | 6.3 | .3 | 4.0 | 7.8 | 8.2 |
| | | | **RATIOS** | | | | | | |
| 3.5 | 2.6 | 3.0 | Current | | 4.7 | 5.0 | 2.9 | 2.6 | 2.9 |
| 2.0 | 1.8 | 1.9 | | | 2.0 | 2.3 | 1.8 | 1.6 | 2.1 |
| 1.3 | 1.3 | 1.3 | | | 1.2 | 1.0 | 1.7 | 1.2 | 1.4 |
| 2.1 | 1.6 | 1.7 | Quick | | 1.7 | 3.3 | 1.6 | 1.6 | 1.7 |
| 1.2 | 1.0 | 1.1 | | | 1.2 | 1.5 | .9 | 1.0 | 1.1 |
| .7 | .7 | .7 | | | .8 | .6 | .6 | .6 | .7 |
| 38  9.7 | 39  9.5 | 38  9.7 | Sales/Receivables | | 25  14.4 | 38  9.7 | 38  9.7 | 36  10.1 | 41  8.8 |
| 43  8.5 | 46  7.9 | 45  8.2 | | | 45  8.1 | 42  8.6 | 40  9.2 | 43  8.4 | 51  7.2 |
| 54  6.8 | 56  6.5 | 54  6.8 | | | 58  6.3 | 48  7.6 | 50  7.3 | 54  6.8 | 56  6.5 |
| 39  9.3 | 43  8.4 | 39  9.3 | Cost of Sales/Inventory | | 14  26.3 | 39  9.3 | 45  8.2 | 39  9.4 | 41  8.8 |
| 61  6.0 | 69  5.3 | 64  5.7 | | | 54  6.7 | 49  7.4 | 79  4.6 | 47  7.7 | 72  5.1 |
| 90  4.0 | 95  3.9 | 104  3.5 | | | 146  2.5 | 76  4.8 | 122  3.0 | 87  4.2 | 101  3.6 |
| 19  18.8 | 19  18.9 | 17  21.3 | Cost of Sales/Payables | | 13  27.1 | 8  45.4 | 17  21.3 | 22  16.6 | 20  18.3 |
| 28  13.0 | 31  11.7 | 25  14.4 | | | 20  18.3 | 21  17.3 | 27  13.5 | 27  13.4 | 23  15.6 |
| 44  8.4 | 44  8.4 | 46  7.9 | | | 41  9.0 | 45  8.2 | 65  5.6 | 47  7.8 | 39  9.4 |
| 3.7 | 4.3 | 4.6 | Sales/Working Capital | | 3.4 | 4.7 | 5.5 | 4.7 | 3.9 |
| 6.3 | 7.8 | 7.0 | | | 15.2 | 8.3 | 6.5 | 10.4 | 6.0 |
| 16.9 | 17.5 | 15.8 | | | 45.6 | 757.3 | 8.3 | 34.4 | 11.4 |
| 8.3 | 17.6 | 22.1 | EBIT/Interest | | | 24.0 | 24.8 | 13.8 | 33.9 |
| (70) 3.6 | (74) 8.1 | (73) 8.6 | | | | (11) 1.5 | (14) 9.0 | (18) 7.9 | (20) 9.6 |
| .9 | 3.5 | 1.6 | | | | -2.0 | 4.1 | 3.8 | 1.6 |
| 2.8 | 9.2 | 7.0 | Net Profit + Depr., Dep., Amort./Cur. Mat. L/T/D | | | | | | 9.6 |
| (20) 1.4 | (17) 2.2 | (19) 2.7 | | | | | | | (11) 2.7 |
| .3 | 1.1 | .7 | | | | | | | .4 |
| .3 | .3 | .2 | Fixed/Worth | | | .1 | .2 | .1 | .3 | .4 |
| .6 | .6 | .5 | | | | 1.1 | .4 | .4 | .6 | .5 |
| 1.3 | 1.3 | 2.1 | | | | 4.4 | 2.5 | .7 | 1.2 | NM |
| .5 | .7 | .6 | Debt/Worth | | | .5 | .3 | .9 | .6 | .7 |
| 1.4 | 1.4 | 1.9 | | | | 4.9 | 1.0 | .9 | 1.5 | 2.5 |
| 3.0 | 4.7 | 6.3 | | | | 8.4 | 3.5 | 3.2 | 3.1 | NM |
| 34.6 | 57.3 | 49.5 | % Profit Before Taxes/Tangible Net Worth | | | 15.8 | 40.5 | 54.1 | 50.5 |
| (74) 8.5 | (73) 27.8 | (68) 28.3 | | | (10) 6.2 | (13) 11.1 | (17) 35.9 | (19) 34.7 |
| .1 | 10.8 | 6.6 | | | | -16.1 | 5.5 | 16.5 | 18.4 |
| 11.1 | 18.4 | 17.1 | % Profit Before Taxes/Total Assets | | | 32.5 | 12.0 | 15.3 | 23.2 | 16.1 |
| 3.6 | 9.7 | 11.1 | | | | 14.1 | 2.6 | 5.0 | 13.0 | 11.5 |
| .2 | 4.5 | 2.4 | | | | 2.5 | -8.8 | 1.3 | 4.9 | 4.2 |
| 18.3 | 25.0 | 21.7 | Sales/Net Fixed Assets | | | 57.9 | 49.4 | 20.6 | 17.5 | 19.3 |
| 7.9 | 9.8 | 10.9 | | | | 24.4 | 17.2 | 15.1 | 10.9 | 7.7 |
| 3.9 | 5.3 | 6.0 | | | | 7.6 | 5.0 | 6.9 | 6.0 | 5.2 |
| 2.4 | 2.5 | 2.5 | Sales/Total Assets | | | 2.8 | 4.1 | 2.2 | 2.7 | 1.9 |
| 1.7 | 1.8 | 1.9 | | | | 2.4 | 2.8 | 2.0 | 1.9 | 1.7 |
| 1.3 | 1.5 | 1.5 | | | | 1.4 | 1.9 | 1.6 | 1.5 | 1.1 |
| 1.0 | .9 | 1.0 | % Depr., Dep., Amort./Sales | | | | | .8 | .9 | 1.1 |
| (69) 2.6 | (74) 2.0 | (73) 2.0 | | | | | (12) 1.3 | (19) 1.4 | 2.1 |
| 4.0 | 3.1 | 3.2 | | | | | | 2.3 | 3.9 | 3.1 |
| 2.6 | 2.6 | 2.1 | % Officers', Directors' Owners' Comp/Sales | | | | | | |
| (28) 4.8 | (27) 5.5 | (28) 5.1 | | | | | | | |
| 8.2 | 10.2 | 7.1 | | | | | | | |
| 2769891M | 3504613M | 3320488M | Net Sales ($) | 904M | 21547M | 45809M | 105477M | 312985M | 2833766M |
| 2051638M | 2348505M | 2463753M | Total Assets ($) | 417M | 10069M | 18097M | 67796M | 194249M | 2173125M |

M = $ thousand    MM = $ million
See Pages 9 through 22 for Explanation of Ratios and Data

## Current Data Sorted by Assets      Comparative Historical Data

| 0-500M | 500M-2MM | 2-10MM | 10-50MM | 50-100MM | 100-250MM | Type of Statement | 4/1/07-3/31/08 ALL | 4/1/08-3/31/09 ALL |
|---|---|---|---|---|---|---|---|---|
| | | | 4 | 2 | 1 | Unqualified | 6 | 5 |
| | | | 1 | | | Reviewed | 7 | 9 |
| | | 1 | 1 | | | Compiled | 7 | 4 |
| 1 | 1 | 2 | | | | Tax Returns | 1 | 1 |
| 1 | 1 | 5 | 4 | 1 | | Other | 10 | 19 |
| 5 (4/1-9/30/11) | | | 20 (10/1/11-3/31/12) | | | | | |
| 1 | 2 | 8 | 10 | 3 | 1 | NUMBER OF STATEMENTS | 31 | 38 |
| % | % | % | % | % | % | | % | % |
| | | | | | | **ASSETS** | | |
| | | | 15.0 | | | Cash & Equivalents | 5.5 | 8.1 |
| | | | 16.5 | | | Trade Receivables (net) | 23.6 | 22.1 |
| | | | 39.9 | | | Inventory | 39.2 | 38.0 |
| | | | 3.0 | | | All Other Current | 2.5 | 2.5 |
| | | | 74.5 | | | Total Current | 70.8 | 70.7 |
| | | | 19.0 | | | Fixed Assets (net) | 18.5 | 19.2 |
| | | | 2.9 | | | Intangibles (net) | 2.9 | 1.7 |
| | | | 3.5 | | | All Other Non-Current | 7.8 | 8.3 |
| | | | 100.0 | | | Total | 100.0 | 100.0 |
| | | | | | | **LIABILITIES** | | |
| | | | 2.9 | | | Notes Payable-Short Term | 25.1 | 10.9 |
| | | | 3.7 | | | Cur. Mat.-L.T.D. | 3.4 | 2.7 |
| | | | 7.9 | | | Trade Payables | 9.6 | 9.1 |
| | | | .1 | | | Income Taxes Payable | .2 | .4 |
| | | | 11.7 | | | All Other Current | 10.7 | 11.7 |
| | | | 26.3 | | | Total Current | 48.9 | 34.8 |
| | | | 7.5 | | | Long-Term Debt | 16.3 | 14.2 |
| | | | .1 | | | Deferred Taxes | .3 | .4 |
| | | | 4.2 | | | All Other Non-Current | 7.8 | 7.3 |
| | | | 61.9 | | | Net Worth | 26.7 | 43.3 |
| | | | 100.0 | | | Total Liabilities & Net Worth | 100.0 | 100.0 |
| | | | | | | **INCOME DATA** | | |
| | | | 100.0 | | | Net Sales | 100.0 | 100.0 |
| | | | 31.4 | | | Gross Profit | 38.5 | 36.6 |
| | | | 27.1 | | | Operating Expenses | 32.3 | 30.8 |
| | | | 4.3 | | | Operating Profit | 6.2 | 5.8 |
| | | | 1.1 | | | All Other Expenses (net) | 1.7 | 1.2 |
| | | | 3.1 | | | Profit Before Taxes | 4.5 | 4.6 |
| | | | | | | **RATIOS** | | |
| | | | 8.1 | | | | 3.2 | 3.8 |
| | | | 3.1 | | | Current | 2.2 | 2.1 |
| | | | 2.1 | | | | 1.5 | 1.4 |
| | | | 3.7 | | | | 1.3 | 1.5 |
| | | | 1.4 | | | Quick | .9 | .8 |
| | | | .7 | | | | .6 | .5 |
| | | 15 | 24.6 | | | | 31  11.6 | 31  11.7 |
| | | 47 | 7.7 | | | Sales/Receivables | 45  8.1 | 41  9.0 |
| | | 60 | 6.1 | | | | 61  6.0 | 63  5.8 |
| | | 114 | 3.2 | | | | 96  3.8 | 97  3.8 |
| | | 152 | 2.4 | | | Cost of Sales/Inventory | 136  2.7 | 134  2.7 |
| | | 215 | 1.7 | | | | 186  2.0 | 186  2.0 |
| | | 6 | 56.3 | | | | 10  35.5 | 10  35.1 |
| | | 26 | 13.9 | | | Cost of Sales/Payables | 26  14.0 | 22  16.3 |
| | | 41 | 9.0 | | | | 61  6.0 | 49  7.4 |
| | | | 2.1 | | | | 3.0 | 3.2 |
| | | | 2.7 | | | Sales/Working Capital | 5.2 | 4.8 |
| | | | 4.6 | | | | 9.0 | 9.9 |
| | | | | | | | 11.9 | 8.3 |
| | | | | | | EBIT/Interest | (28)  2.6 | (33)  3.2 |
| | | | | | | | 1.4 | 1.6 |
| | | | | | | | 10.7 | 12.1 |
| | | | | | | Net Profit + Depr., Dep., Amort./Cur. Mat. L/T/D | (11)  4.2 | (16)  9.0 |
| | | | | | | | 1.2 | 2.5 |
| | | | .1 | | | | .2 | .2 |
| | | | .2 | | | Fixed/Worth | .3 | .3 |
| | | | .8 | | | | 5.8 | 1.1 |
| | | | .2 | | | | .4 | .4 |
| | | | .5 | | | Debt/Worth | 1.1 | .8 |
| | | | 1.5 | | | | -43.0 | 5.3 |
| | | | 16.2 | | | | 25.6 | 26.7 |
| | | | 1.3 | | | % Profit Before Taxes/Tangible Net Worth | (23)  9.2 | (32)  12.4 |
| | | | -9.3 | | | | 1.5 | 2.1 |
| | | | 14.4 | | | | 14.3 | 16.3 |
| | | | .8 | | | % Profit Before Taxes/Total Assets | 4.6 | 6.2 |
| | | | -1.7 | | | | 1.0 | .8 |
| | | | 18.1 | | | | 25.8 | 25.9 |
| | | | 11.9 | | | Sales/Net Fixed Assets | 10.9 | 9.6 |
| | | | 3.2 | | | | 6.6 | 5.6 |
| | | | 1.8 | | | | 1.9 | 2.1 |
| | | | 1.4 | | | Sales/Total Assets | 1.6 | 1.6 |
| | | | 1.1 | | | | 1.3 | 1.2 |
| | | | | | | | .9 | .7 |
| | | | | | | % Depr., Dep., Amort./Sales | (28)  1.9 | (35)  1.7 |
| | | | | | | | 3.1 | 2.8 |
| | | | | | | % Officers', Directors' Owners' Comp/Sales | | |
| 1534M | 5801M | 87885M | 415596M | 314935M | 308613M | Net Sales ($) | 1386547M | 2308964M |
| 461M | 2143M | 47932M | 297305M | 246494M | 162813M | Total Assets ($) | 918876M | 1365003M |

M = $ thousand     MM = $ million
See Pages 9 through 22 for Explanation of Ratios and Data

## Comparative Historical Data | Current Data Sorted by Sales

| | | | | | Type of Statement | | | | | | 2 | 5 |
|---|---|---|---|---|---|---|---|---|---|---|---|---|
| | 9 | | 11 | | 7 | Unqualified | | | | | | 1 |
| | 2 | | 2 | | 1 | Reviewed | | | | | | 1 |
| | 5 | | 4 | | 2 | Compiled | | | | | 1 | |
| | 3 | | 2 | | 4 | Tax Returns | | | | 1 | 2 | |
| | 13 | | 10 | | 11 | Other | 1 | 1 | 2 | 2 | 1 | 5 |
| | 4/1/09-3/31/10 ALL | | 4/1/10-3/31/11 ALL | | 4/1/11-3/31/12 ALL | | 2 | | 20 (10/1/11-3/31/12) | | | |
| | | | | | | | 5 (4/1-9/30/11) | | | | | |
| | | | | | | 0-1MM | 1-3MM | 3-5MM | 5-10MM | 10-25MM | | 25MM & OVER |
| | 32 | | 29 | | 25 | NUMBER OF STATEMENTS | 3 | 1 | 4 | 5 | | 12 |
| | % | | % | | % | | % | % | % | % | | % |
| | | | | | | ASSETS | | | | | | |
| | 13.9 | | 10.5 | | 11.7 | Cash & Equivalents | | | | | | 9.8 |
| | 16.3 | | 19.5 | | 17.7 | Trade Receivables (net) | D | | | | | 18.2 |
| | 34.9 | | 35.6 | | 38.4 | Inventory | A | | | | | 33.5 |
| | 3.5 | | 2.5 | | 2.6 | All Other Current | T | | | | | 1.9 |
| | 68.6 | | 68.1 | | 70.5 | Total Current | A | | | | | 63.5 |
| | 20.6 | | 19.2 | | 17.2 | Fixed Assets (net) | | | | | | 21.7 |
| | 4.1 | | 3.9 | | 3.6 | Intangibles (net) | N | | | | | 6.9 |
| | 6.7 | | 8.8 | | 8.7 | All Other Non-Current | O | | | | | 8.0 |
| | 100.0 | | 100.0 | | 100.0 | Total | T | | | | | 100.0 |
| | | | | | | LIABILITIES | A | | | | | |
| | 9.7 | | 11.6 | | 11.6 | Notes Payable-Short Term | V | | | | | 3.7 |
| | 1.4 | | 3.3 | | 2.3 | Cur. Mat.-L.T.D. | A | | | | | 2.9 |
| | 10.4 | | 10.1 | | 8.1 | Trade Payables | I | | | | | 9.1 |
| | .2 | | .4 | | .2 | Income Taxes Payable | L | | | | | .3 |
| | 6.3 | | 8.8 | | 9.4 | All Other Current | A | | | | | 11.1 |
| | 28.1 | | 34.3 | | 31.5 | Total Current | B | | | | | 27.0 |
| | 16.4 | | 24.4 | | 14.3 | Long-Term Debt | L | | | | | 12.9 |
| | .3 | | .1 | | .1 | Deferred Taxes | E | | | | | .1 |
| | 7.3 | | 8.5 | | 4.6 | All Other Non-Current | | | | | | 6.7 |
| | 48.0 | | 32.6 | | 49.5 | Net Worth | | | | | | 53.2 |
| | 100.0 | | 100.0 | | 100.0 | Total Liabilties & Net Worth | | | | | | 100.0 |
| | | | | | | INCOME DATA | | | | | | |
| | 100.0 | | 100.0 | | 100.0 | Net Sales | | | | | | 100.0 |
| | 38.2 | | 41.7 | | 36.8 | Gross Profit | | | | | | 34.7 |
| | 33.2 | | 36.6 | | 32.1 | Operating Expenses | | | | | | 28.2 |
| | 5.0 | | 5.1 | | 4.7 | Operating Profit | | | | | | 6.5 |
| | 1.4 | | 1.6 | | 1.1 | All Other Expenses (net) | | | | | | 1.4 |
| | 3.6 | | 3.6 | | 3.6 | Profit Before Taxes | | | | | | 5.1 |
| | | | | | | RATIOS | | | | | | |
| | 6.3 | | 4.0 | | 3.9 | | | | | | | 3.9 |
| | 2.6 | | 2.1 | | 2.3 | Current | | | | | | 2.4 |
| | 1.5 | | 1.2 | | 1.9 | | | | | | | 2.0 |
| | 1.8 | | 1.7 | | 1.8 | | | | | | | 2.2 |
| | 1.1 | | .8 | | 1.0 | Quick | | | | | | 1.0 |
| | .6 | | .6 | | .6 | | | | | | | .8 |
| 27 | 13.8 | 29 | 12.5 | 27 | 13.3 | | | | | | 31 | 11.6 |
| 38 | 9.7 | 48 | 7.7 | 38 | 9.6 | Sales/Receivables | | | | | 46 | 8.0 |
| 53 | 6.8 | 53 | 6.9 | 57 | 6.4 | | | | | | 56 | 6.5 |
| 92 | 4.0 | 97 | 3.8 | 99 | 3.7 | | | | | | 99 | 3.7 |
| 123 | 3.0 | 140 | 2.6 | 146 | 2.5 | Cost of Sales/Inventory | | | | | 118 | 3.1 |
| 184 | 2.0 | 209 | 1.7 | 174 | 2.1 | | | | | | 182 | 2.0 |
| 12 | 30.2 | 18 | 20.3 | 15 | 24.3 | | | | | | 15 | 23.6 |
| 21 | 17.7 | 37 | 9.8 | 23 | 16.1 | Cost of Sales/Payables | | | | | 26 | 13.9 |
| 58 | 6.3 | 56 | 6.5 | 36 | 10.0 | | | | | | 52 | 7.0 |
| | 2.4 | | 2.5 | | 2.4 | | | | | | | 2.7 |
| | 3.6 | | 4.0 | | 4.2 | Sales/Working Capital | | | | | | 4.5 |
| | 7.3 | | 13.8 | | 7.3 | | | | | | | 6.7 |
| | 15.2 | | 14.0 | | 9.8 | | | | | | | |
| (26) | 3.4 | (26) | 2.6 | (19) | 4.4 | EBIT/Interest | | | | | | |
| | .5 | | 1.2 | | .9 | | | | | | | |
| | | | 18.4 | | | Net Profit + Depr., Dep., | | | | | | |
| | | (11) | 1.8 | | | Amort./Cur. Mat. L/T/D | | | | | | |
| | | | .7 | | | | | | | | | |
| | .1 | | .2 | | .1 | | | | | | | .2 |
| | .4 | | .8 | | .3 | Fixed/Worth | | | | | | .4 |
| | 1.5 | | -1.1 | | 1.3 | | | | | | | 3.7 |
| | .2 | | .4 | | .3 | | | | | | | .3 |
| | .8 | | 1.7 | | .7 | Debt/Worth | | | | | | .7 |
| | 3.6 | | -7.6 | | 6.0 | | | | | | | 9.3 |
| | 19.2 | | 21.5 | | 23.8 | | | | | | | 24.2 |
| (27) | 10.8 | (18) | 8.4 | (22) | 6.6 | % Profit Before Taxes/Tangible Net Worth | | | | | (10) | 3.3 |
| | .9 | | 1.9 | | .6 | | | | | | | -9.3 |
| | 13.4 | | 12.9 | | 13.9 | | | | | | | 17.9 |
| | 7.3 | | 4.7 | | 5.4 | % Profit Before Taxes/Total Assets | | | | | | 4.3 |
| | .1 | | .7 | | .1 | | | | | | | -.8 |
| | 26.1 | | 21.6 | | 30.0 | | | | | | | 15.7 |
| | 8.1 | | 8.0 | | 14.7 | Sales/Net Fixed Assets | | | | | | 7.6 |
| | 5.3 | | 5.5 | | 6.2 | | | | | | | 4.1 |
| | 1.9 | | 2.1 | | 2.2 | | | | | | | 1.9 |
| | 1.6 | | 1.7 | | 1.4 | Sales/Total Assets | | | | | | 1.6 |
| | 1.0 | | 1.1 | | 1.2 | | | | | | | 1.1 |
| | .7 | | .7 | | .5 | | | | | | | |
| (28) | 2.0 | (26) | 1.8 | (20) | .9 | % Depr., Dep., Amort./Sales | | | | | | |
| | 3.0 | | 3.2 | | 2.6 | | | | | | | |
| | | | | | | % Officers', Directors' Owners' Comp/Sales | | | | | | |
| | 1584082M | | 1759549M | | 1134364M | Net Sales ($) | 5427M | 4258M | 32080M | 93187M | | 999412M |
| | 1074835M | | 1116276M | | 757148M | Total Assets ($) | 3466M | 1222M | 21675M | 67571M | | 663214M |

M = $ thousand     MM = $ million
See Pages 9 through 22 for Explanation of Ratios and Data

## Current Data Sorted by Assets      Comparative Historical Data

| Type of Statement | 0-500M | 500M-2MM | 2-10MM | 10-50MM | 50-100MM | 100-250MM | 4/1/07-3/31/08 ALL | 4/1/08-3/31/09 ALL |
|---|---|---|---|---|---|---|---|---|
| Unqualified | | | 17 | 41 | 9 | 11 | 83 | 92 |
| Reviewed | 2 | 10 | 64 | 27 | | | 76 | 79 |
| Compiled | 9 | 18 | 31 | 7 | | | 62 | 50 |
| Tax Returns | 41 | 56 | 31 | 3 | | | 71 | 85 |
| Other | 13 | 42 | 77 | 68 | 15 | 13 | 179 | 213 |
| | 93 (4/1-9/30/11) | | | 512 (10/1/11-3/31/12) | | | | |
| NUMBER OF STATEMENTS | 65 | 126 | 220 | 146 | 24 | 24 | 471 | 519 |
| **ASSETS** | % | % | % | % | % | % | % | % |
| Cash & Equivalents | 14.6 | 12.6 | 8.2 | 8.8 | 6.5 | 7.4 | 9.5 | 9.3 |
| Trade Receivables (net) | 24.3 | 30.5 | 27.4 | 23.3 | 20.1 | 22.2 | 24.8 | 23.9 |
| Inventory | 21.5 | 26.0 | 30.2 | 27.8 | 23.1 | 19.8 | 27.5 | 28.9 |
| All Other Current | 1.8 | 2.9 | 2.5 | 2.9 | 1.9 | 4.0 | 3.1 | 3.0 |
| Total Current | 62.2 | 72.0 | 68.3 | 62.8 | 51.7 | 53.5 | 64.9 | 65.1 |
| Fixed Assets (net) | 24.2 | 17.7 | 20.3 | 22.9 | 28.3 | 19.0 | 23.2 | 21.6 |
| Intangibles (net) | 5.4 | 4.5 | 4.2 | 7.4 | 14.1 | 16.0 | 5.3 | 6.8 |
| All Other Non-Current | 8.2 | 5.8 | 7.2 | 6.9 | 6.0 | 11.5 | 6.6 | 6.5 |
| Total | 100.0 | 100.0 | 100.0 | 100.0 | 100.0 | 100.0 | 100.0 | 100.0 |
| **LIABILITIES** | | | | | | | | |
| Notes Payable-Short Term | 25.6 | 13.2 | 10.2 | 9.3 | 10.2 | 2.3 | 12.9 | 13.2 |
| Cur. Mat.-L.T.D. | 2.3 | 2.7 | 3.1 | 2.6 | 2.3 | 1.9 | 4.3 | 3.4 |
| Trade Payables | 22.1 | 17.7 | 15.2 | 11.4 | 9.6 | 10.5 | 13.2 | 14.3 |
| Income Taxes Payable | .3 | .1 | .3 | .4 | .3 | .6 | .2 | .3 |
| All Other Current | 10.2 | 12.9 | 9.7 | 12.9 | 10.3 | 14.9 | 11.8 | 11.1 |
| Total Current | 60.5 | 46.7 | 38.6 | 36.6 | 32.7 | 30.2 | 42.4 | 42.3 |
| Long-Term Debt | 40.5 | 16.4 | 12.7 | 13.9 | 21.4 | 20.7 | 16.0 | 18.0 |
| Deferred Taxes | .0 | .1 | .4 | .8 | 1.2 | 1.5 | .4 | .3 |
| All Other Non-Current | 20.7 | 11.3 | 6.2 | 7.0 | 4.3 | 9.5 | 4.8 | 7.1 |
| Net Worth | -21.7 | 25.5 | 42.2 | 41.6 | 40.5 | 38.1 | 36.4 | 32.3 |
| Total Liabilities & Net Worth | 100.0 | 100.0 | 100.0 | 100.0 | 100.0 | 100.0 | 100.0 | 100.0 |
| **INCOME DATA** | | | | | | | | |
| Net Sales | 100.0 | 100.0 | 100.0 | 100.0 | 100.0 | 100.0 | 100.0 | 100.0 |
| Gross Profit | 46.1 | 39.0 | 35.6 | 29.2 | 27.0 | 28.7 | 35.1 | 32.9 |
| Operating Expenses | 42.9 | 33.5 | 30.0 | 22.1 | 20.7 | 20.7 | 28.7 | 27.9 |
| Operating Profit | 3.2 | 5.5 | 5.6 | 7.2 | 6.3 | 8.0 | 6.4 | 4.9 |
| All Other Expenses (net) | .6 | .7 | .5 | .8 | 3.1 | 1.0 | 1.3 | 1.4 |
| Profit Before Taxes | 2.7 | 4.8 | 5.1 | 6.4 | 3.2 | 7.0 | 5.1 | 3.5 |
| **RATIOS** | | | | | | | | |
| Current | 2.8 | 4.1 | 2.9 | 3.2 | 2.8 | 2.5 | 2.6 | 2.9 |
| | 1.5 | 1.6 | 1.8 | 2.0 | 1.8 | 2.1 | 1.7 | 1.7 |
| | .8 | 1.1 | 1.3 | 1.3 | 1.1 | 1.3 | 1.1 | 1.1 |
| Quick | 2.0 | 2.3 | 1.6 | 1.6 | 1.2 | 1.4 | 1.5 | 1.7 |
| | .8 | .9 | .9 | .9 | .9 | 1.1 | .8 | .8 |
| | .3 | .6 | .5 | .6 | .5 | .7 | .5 | .5 |
| Sales/Receivables | 1   473.4 | 21   17.3 | 31   11.9 | 31   11.9 | 38   9.7 | 33   11.2 | 26   14.0 | 25   14.5 |
| | 22   16.7 | 36   10.0 | 42   8.6 | 47   7.8 | 49   7.4 | 51   7.1 | 40   9.1 | 37   9.7 |
| | 40   9.1 | 52   7.0 | 58   6.3 | 58   6.3 | 60   6.1 | 62   5.9 | 58   6.2 | 54   6.8 |
| Cost of Sales/Inventory | 1   698.4 | 17   21.7 | 40   9.2 | 43   8.5 | 49   7.4 | 38   9.7 | 36   10.2 | 37   9.9 |
| | 14   25.2 | 51   7.1 | 70   5.2 | 72   5.1 | 87   4.2 | 70   5.2 | 64   5.7 | 73   5.0 |
| | 74   4.9 | 96   3.8 | 122   3.0 | 122   3.0 | 107   3.4 | 94   3.9 | 113   3.2 | 109   3.4 |
| Cost of Sales/Payables | 6   59.2 | 12   29.2 | 20   18.5 | 17   22.0 | 23   15.7 | 14   25.5 | 16   22.4 | 15   24.5 |
| | 21   17.8 | 26   14.3 | 33   11.1 | 29   12.6 | 31   11.9 | 29   12.5 | 29   12.7 | 27   13.4 |
| | 49   7.5 | 51   7.1 | 51   7.2 | 45   8.2 | 41   9.0 | 42   8.6 | 47   7.8 | 48   7.6 |
| Sales/Working Capital | 7.6 | 4.9 | 4.3 | 3.7 | 3.7 | 4.2 | 4.7 | 4.6 |
| | 20.6 | 13.0 | 7.7 | 6.3 | 6.8 | 5.8 | 8.6 | 9.0 |
| | -45.6 | 94.0 | 17.3 | 15.9 | 22.4 | 12.9 | 32.5 | 34.3 |
| EBIT/Interest | 11.8 | 15.3 | 18.4 | 21.7 | 43.1 | 21.2 | 10.8 | 10.7 |
| | (51) 4.4 | (102) 4.6 | (182) 5.3 | (128) 6.6 | (21) 9.1 | (22) 5.2 | (414) 3.7 | (455) 3.2 |
| | .9 | 1.1 | 2.0 | 2.2 | .3 | 1.8 | 1.3 | .8 |
| Net Profit + Depr., Dep., Amort./Cur. Mat. L/T/D | | 8.0 | 4.5 | 10.6 | 8.0 | 20.0 | 6.5 | 6.2 |
| | | (11) 1.2 | (44) 2.5 | (47) 5.2 | (11) 2.7 | (13) 7.1 | (121) 2.7 | (119) 3.0 |
| | | .6 | 1.3 | 2.3 | 1.3 | 2.1 | .9 | 1.1 |
| Fixed/Worth | .2 | .1 | .1 | .2 | .5 | .3 | .2 | .2 |
| | 2.5 | .4 | .4 | .6 | .7 | .7 | .6 | .6 |
| | -.3 | 5.6 | 1.4 | 1.6 | -27.5 | 3.7 | 1.5 | 2.2 |
| Debt/Worth | 1.1 | .8 | .5 | .5 | .6 | 1.0 | .6 | .7 |
| | 7.8 | 2.4 | 1.4 | 1.4 | 1.9 | 2.1 | 1.7 | 1.8 |
| | -2.5 | 26.9 | 4.0 | 4.4 | -37.4 | 20.8 | 5.5 | 8.0 |
| % Profit Before Taxes/Tangible Net Worth | 100.0 | 66.9 | 54.4 | 44.9 | 59.2 | 72.5 | 58.6 | 43.6 |
| | (35) 35.6 | (102) 34.0 | (203) 24.3 | (120) 24.1 | (17) 13.3 | (19) 24.4 | (410) 25.5 | (429) 19.4 |
| | 8.3 | 9.6 | 5.9 | 7.9 | 5.6 | 4.6 | 5.3 | 1.7 |
| % Profit Before Taxes/Total Assets | 36.1 | 24.9 | 19.3 | 17.5 | 14.8 | 15.5 | 19.0 | 16.3 |
| | 12.8 | 10.2 | 7.0 | 9.1 | 4.9 | 9.1 | 7.7 | 5.9 |
| | .7 | .5 | 2.2 | 1.6 | -.2 | 2.2 | 1.3 | -.1 |
| Sales/Net Fixed Assets | 92.8 | 102.6 | 45.6 | 29.8 | 11.3 | 18.3 | 32.5 | 34.5 |
| | 33.6 | 31.0 | 15.7 | 8.4 | 6.2 | 9.3 | 12.2 | 13.0 |
| | 10.3 | 9.5 | 5.6 | 4.9 | 3.7 | 6.3 | 5.5 | 6.0 |
| Sales/Total Assets | 6.1 | 4.1 | 2.9 | 2.4 | 2.0 | 1.9 | 3.0 | 2.9 |
| | 4.1 | 2.8 | 2.1 | 1.8 | 1.4 | 1.5 | 2.1 | 2.1 |
| | 2.4 | 1.9 | 1.5 | 1.3 | 1.1 | 1.1 | 1.4 | 1.4 |
| % Depr., Dep., Amort./Sales | .7 | .5 | .9 | .9 | 1.6 | 1.2 | .9 | .8 |
| | (36) 2.0 | (80) 1.0 | (171) 1.7 | (127) 1.8 | (23) 2.5 | (21) 2.3 | (394) 1.9 | (425) 1.8 |
| | 4.1 | 2.0 | 3.3 | 3.5 | 3.9 | 3.7 | 3.3 | 3.1 |
| % Officers', Directors' Owners' Comp/Sales | 5.0 | 3.4 | 1.9 | .7 | | | 2.2 | 1.9 |
| | (37) 7.2 | (73) 4.8 | (77) 3.7 | (21) 1.0 | | | (157) 3.9 | (156) 3.8 |
| | 11.4 | 9.9 | 6.5 | 2.9 | | | 6.8 | 7.3 |
| Net Sales ($) | 79486M | 457305M | 2471854M | 5837271M | 2499164M | 6447805M | 12453260M | 18464887M |
| Total Assets ($) | 17683M | 150841M | 1084960M | 3065041M | 1754419M | 3639408M | 7296445M | 11019501M |

© RMA 2012

M = $ thousand    MM = $ million
See Pages 9 through 22 for Explanation of Ratios and Data

## Comparative Historical Data · Current Data Sorted by Sales

### Type of Statement

|  | | | | 93 (4/1-9/30/11) | | | 512 (10/1/11-3/31/12) | | |
|---|---|---|---|---|---|---|---|---|---|
| Type of Statement | | | | | | | | | |
| Unqualified | 97 | 87 | 78 | | | 2 | 5 | 16 | 55 |
| Reviewed | 90 | 101 | 103 | 1 | 9 | 6 | 22 | 44 | 21 |
| Compiled | 43 | 62 | 65 | 5 | 11 | 10 | 22 | 11 | 6 |
| Tax Returns | 100 | 96 | 131 | 23 | 47 | 26 | 25 | 10 | |
| Other | 257 | 244 | 228 | 9 | 27 | 30 | 31 | 60 | 71 |
|  | 4/1/09-3/31/10 ALL | 4/1/10-3/31/11 ALL | 4/1/11-3/31/12 ALL | 0-1MM | 1-3MM | 3-5MM | 5-10MM | 10-25MM | 25MM & OVER |
| NUMBER OF STATEMENTS | 587 | 590 | 605 | 38 | 94 | 74 | 105 | 141 | 153 |

### ASSETS

|  | % | % | % | % | % | % | % | % | % |
|---|---|---|---|---|---|---|---|---|---|
| Cash & Equivalents | 9.8 | 10.1 | 9.9 | 8.0 | 14.6 | 10.3 | 10.7 | 9.0 | 7.4 |
| Trade Receivables (net) | 23.4 | 25.5 | 26.2 | 28.8 | 23.3 | 26.6 | 27.6 | 27.0 | 25.5 |
| Inventory | 26.7 | 28.0 | 27.1 | 21.4 | 24.9 | 27.5 | 28.5 | 29.4 | 26.7 |
| All Other Current | 3.4 | 2.2 | 2.6 | .3 | 3.7 | 2.7 | 2.1 | 2.5 | 3.0 |
| Total Current | 63.4 | 65.7 | 65.8 | 58.5 | 66.5 | 67.1 | 68.8 | 68.0 | 62.5 |
| Fixed Assets (net) | 23.8 | 21.6 | 21.1 | 28.1 | 20.8 | 20.2 | 20.2 | 19.6 | 21.9 |
| Intangibles (net) | 6.6 | 6.4 | 6.0 | 8.6 | 5.1 | 4.1 | 3.6 | 5.7 | 9.0 |
| All Other Non-Current | 6.2 | 6.3 | 7.1 | 4.8 | 7.6 | 8.6 | 7.4 | 6.8 | 6.6 |
| Total | 100.0 | 100.0 | 100.0 | 100.0 | 100.0 | 100.0 | 100.0 | 100.0 | 100.0 |

### LIABILITIES

|  | | | | | | | | | |
|---|---|---|---|---|---|---|---|---|---|
| Notes Payable-Short Term | 12.4 | 13.0 | 12.0 | 19.5 | 14.0 | 11.4 | 15.1 | 9.7 | 9.1 |
| Cur. Mat.-L.T.D. | 4.1 | 3.0 | 2.7 | 1.8 | 3.4 | 3.9 | 2.6 | 2.2 | 2.7 |
| Trade Payables | 14.8 | 15.0 | 15.1 | 24.4 | 14.8 | 18.0 | 13.1 | 13.8 | 14.4 |
| Income Taxes Payable | .2 | .3 | .3 | .5 | .0 | .1 | .5 | .5 | .2 |
| All Other Current | 12.5 | 10.5 | 11.4 | 6.6 | 9.4 | 14.4 | 11.8 | 10.2 | 13.4 |
| Total Current | 44.1 | 41.7 | 41.6 | 52.8 | 41.5 | 47.7 | 43.0 | 36.2 | 39.9 |
| Long-Term Debt | 17.6 | 16.1 | 17.4 | 39.1 | 24.5 | 19.2 | 11.9 | 12.6 | 14.9 |
| Deferred Taxes | .4 | .4 | .5 | .0 | .1 | .2 | .4 | .5 | .9 |
| All Other Non-Current | 8.0 | 7.9 | 9.1 | 29.4 | 10.6 | 3.1 | 10.5 | 5.9 | 8.0 |
| Net Worth | 30.0 | 33.9 | 31.5 | -21.3 | 23.4 | 29.8 | 34.2 | 44.8 | 36.3 |
| Total Liabilties & Net Worth | 100.0 | 100.0 | 100.0 | 100.0 | 100.0 | 100.0 | 100.0 | 100.0 | 100.0 |

### INCOME DATA

|  | | | | | | | | | |
|---|---|---|---|---|---|---|---|---|---|
| Net Sales | 100.0 | 100.0 | 100.0 | 100.0 | 100.0 | 100.0 | 100.0 | 100.0 | 100.0 |
| Gross Profit | 34.2 | 35.0 | 35.3 | 52.9 | 43.5 | 37.6 | 37.2 | 32.1 | 26.3 |
| Operating Expenses | 30.4 | 29.7 | 29.5 | 49.4 | 36.8 | 34.1 | 32.3 | 25.7 | 19.3 |
| Operating Profit | 3.8 | 5.3 | 5.8 | 3.5 | 6.7 | 3.5 | 5.0 | 6.4 | 7.0 |
| All Other Expenses (net) | 1.8 | 1.2 | .7 | .6 | 1.1 | .9 | .0 | .4 | 1.4 |
| Profit Before Taxes | 2.0 | 4.1 | 5.1 | 2.9 | 5.6 | 2.6 | 5.0 | 6.0 | 5.7 |

### RATIOS

|  | | | | | | | | | |
|---|---|---|---|---|---|---|---|---|---|
| Current | 3.1 | 2.8 | 2.9 | 2.8 | 4.9 | 2.9 | 3.3 | 3.0 | 2.7 |
|  | 1.7 | 1.8 | 1.8 | 1.5 | 1.9 | 1.5 | 1.8 | 2.0 | 1.8 |
|  | 1.1 | 1.2 | 1.2 | .8 | 1.2 | 1.1 | 1.3 | 1.4 | 1.2 |
| Quick | 1.7 | 1.6 | 1.6 | 2.1 | 2.4 | 1.5 | 2.0 | 1.4 | 1.4 |
|  | .8 | .9 | .9 | .8 | 1.0 | .8 | .9 | 1.0 | .9 |
|  | .5 | | .5 | .3 | .5 | .5 | .5 | .6 | .6 |
| Sales/Receivables | 27  13.3 | 27  13.4 | 26  13.8 | 13  27.3 | 20  18.3 | 19  19.5 | 25  14.8 | 32  11.5 | 30  12.0 |
|  | 43  8.6 | 44  8.3 | 41  8.9 | 29  12.4 | 36  10.0 | 37  9.8 | 41  8.8 | 45  8.1 | 44  8.3 |
|  | 58  6.3 | 58  6.3 | 56  6.5 | 54  6.8 | 53  6.9 | 55  6.6 | 58  6.3 | 57  6.4 | 57  6.4 |
| Cost of Sales/Inventory | 38  9.7 | 35  10.4 | 33  11.1 | 0  UND | 11  34.5 | 29  12.6 | 33  11.1 | 40  9.1 | 38  9.5 |
|  | 76  4.8 | 70  5.2 | 62  5.9 | 22  16.7 | 53  6.9 | 65  5.6 | 65  5.6 | 72  5.1 | 63  5.8 |
|  | 123  3.0 | 113  3.2 | 111  3.3 | 122  3.0 | 118  3.1 | 135  2.7 | 111  3.3 | 118  3.1 | 89  4.1 |
| Cost of Sales/Payables | 17  21.2 | 18  20.8 | 15  23.7 | 7  55.0 | 15  24.9 | 15  24.5 | 14  27.0 | 16  23.5 | 18  19.9 |
|  | 30  12.4 | 30  12.0 | 29  12.4 | 22  16.7 | 29  12.7 | 37  9.9 | 29  12.7 | 29  12.6 | 29  12.4 |
|  | 52  7.0 | 49  7.4 | 47  7.7 | 78  4.7 | 50  7.3 | 56  6.5 | 47  7.8 | 46  7.9 | 43  8.4 |
| Sales/Working Capital | 4.1 | 4.4 | 4.4 | 4.8 | 3.7 | 5.0 | 4.4 | 3.9 | 4.9 |
|  | 8.3 | 8.5 | 8.1 | 12.5 | 9.0 | 13.2 | 7.6 | 6.8 | 7.6 |
|  | 61.9 | 28.6 | 26.6 | -58.4 | 41.7 | 114.4 | 27.1 | 14.4 | 18.7 |
| EBIT/Interest | 9.9 | 12.3 | 18.5 | 9.9 | 16.4 | 8.3 | 23.4 | 22.6 | 23.8 |
|  | (519)  2.7 | (514)  3.9 | (506)  5.3 | (29)  4.4 | (73)  3.8 | (64)  3.2 | (83)  5.3 | (120)  6.6 | (137)  7.6 |
|  | .0 | 1.1 | 1.8 | .8 | 1.2 | 1.1 | 2.1 | 2.2 | 2.0 |
| Net Profit + Depr., Dep., Amort./Cur. Mat. L/T/D | 5.7 | 6.3 | 9.7 | | | | 10.4 | 9.0 | 10.7 |
|  | (129)  2.4 | (138)  2.7 | (127)  3.4 | | | (15)  1.8 | (43)  3.3 | (56)  4.8 | |
|  | .6 | .9 | 1.6 | | | 1.1 | 1.7 | 1.9 | |
| Fixed/Worth | .2 | .2 | .2 | .2 | .1 | .2 | .1 | .1 | .3 |
|  | .7 | .6 | .5 | 15.5 | .6 | .5 | .4 | .4 | .6 |
|  | 3.3 | 2.3 | 2.3 | -.3 | 18.3 | 4.2 | 1.3 | 1.4 | 2.1 |
| Debt/Worth | .7 | .7 | .6 | 1.7 | .5 | .8 | .5 | .5 | .7 |
|  | 2.0 | 1.7 | 1.7 | 41.8 | 2.4 | 2.7 | 1.3 | 1.3 | 2.0 |
|  | 14.8 | 8.0 | 6.7 | -2.8 | -29.2 | 9.9 | 3.8 | 3.7 | 6.3 |
| % Profit Before Taxes/Tangible Net Worth | 38.6 | 52.7 | 58.1 | 102.4 | 69.4 | 41.5 | 57.8 | 46.1 | 60.3 |
|  | (467)  15.9 | (486)  18.9 | (496)  25.7 | (20)  32.3 | (70)  36.2 | (62)  23.0 | (93)  23.3 | (128)  24.2 | (123)  27.2 |
|  | 1.7 | 3.4 | 6.9 | -4.0 | 7.4 | 11.7 | 4.6 | 7.9 | 11.9 |
| % Profit Before Taxes/Total Assets | 12.1 | 17.0 | 20.8 | 30.9 | 25.6 | 13.8 | 20.5 | 22.6 | 17.7 |
|  | 4.4 | 6.4 | 8.2 | 7.1 | 9.3 | 6.0 | 7.9 | 8.2 | 10.0 |
|  | -2.5 | .6 | 1.7 | -.9 | .7 | .4 | 1.4 | 2.4 | 2.7 |
| Sales/Net Fixed Assets | 29.7 | 34.9 | 50.8 | 67.6 | 72.7 | 59.4 | 56.5 | 55.5 | 32.0 |
|  | 10.2 | 14.2 | 14.2 | 22.6 | 18.6 | 16.5 | 21.0 | 13.4 | 10.6 |
|  | 4.5 | 5.4 | 6.1 | 6.0 | 6.6 | 6.6 | 6.9 | 5.6 | 6.0 |
| Sales/Total Assets | 2.6 | 2.9 | 3.1 | 4.2 | 3.8 | 3.1 | 3.5 | 2.7 | 2.7 |
|  | 1.9 | 2.0 | 2.2 | 2.4 | 2.5 | 2.4 | 2.2 | 2.0 | 2.0 |
|  | 1.2 | 1.4 | 1.5 | 1.5 | 1.4 | 1.5 | 1.6 | 1.5 | 1.5 |
| % Depr., Dep., Amort./Sales | 1.0 | .9 | .8 | .7 | .7 | .6 | .7 | .9 | 1.0 |
|  | (465)  2.3 | (478)  1.8 | (458)  1.7 | (21)  2.3 | (61)  1.6 | (53)  1.3 | (76)  1.4 | (112)  1.9 | (135)  1.7 |
|  | 4.4 | 3.6 | 3.4 | 5.8 | 3.1 | 3.4 | 3.4 | 3.2 | 3.4 |
| % Officers', Directors' Owners' Comp/Sales | 1.6 | 2.2 | 2.2 | 6.7 | 3.8 | 2.9 | 2.2 | 1.0 | .3 |
|  | (171)  3.5 | (195)  3.8 | (210)  4.4 | (19)  10.2 | (55)  6.2 | (37)  4.5 | (40)  3.6 | (46)  2.5 | (13)  .7 |
|  | 6.8 | 7.1 | 7.5 | 18.7 | 9.6 | 7.1 | 6.4 | 4.8 | 1.6 |
| Net Sales ($) | 16106926M | 15716564M | 17792885M | 21856M | 184465M | 292623M | 757230M | 2264800M | 14271911M |
| Total Assets ($) | 10297634M | 9576502M | 9712352M | 12244M | 99364M | 161852M | 385571M | 1309725M | 7743596M |

© RMA 2012

M = $ thousand    MM = $ million
See Pages 9 through 22 for Explanation of Ratios and Data

# WHOLESALE TRADE

## Current Data Sorted by Assets        Comparative Historical Data

Type of Statement counts (Unqualified / Reviewed / Compiled / Tax Returns / Other) by column:

| Type of Statement | 0-500M | 500M-2MM | 2-10MM | 10-50MM | 50-100MM | 100-250MM | | 4/1/07-3/31/08 ALL | 4/1/08-3/31/09 ALL |
|---|---|---|---|---|---|---|---|---|---|
| Unqualified | | 1 | 7 | 22 | 9 | 10 | | 39 | 41 |
| Reviewed | | 2 | 34 | 42 | 3 | 2 | | 62 | 62 |
| Compiled | 1 | 9 | 21 | 5 | 2 | 1 | | 50 | 54 |
| Tax Returns | 9 | 39 | 30 | 2 | 1 | | | 57 | 70 |
| Other | 5 | 37 | 48 | 53 | 12 | 10 | | 137 | 168 |
| | 57 (4/1-9/30/11) | | | 360 (10/1/11-3/31/12) | | | | | |
| **NUMBER OF STATEMENTS** | 15 | 88 | 140 | 124 | 27 | 23 | | 345 | 395 |
| **ASSETS** | % | % | % | % | % | % | | % | % |
| Cash & Equivalents | 17.1 | 10.8 | 11.5 | 9.3 | 6.5 | 10.2 | | 8.1 | 8.3 |
| Trade Receivables (net) | 9.8 | 23.2 | 20.2 | 18.0 | 14.9 | 11.1 | | 18.0 | 17.0 |
| Inventory | 51.9 | 45.2 | 45.3 | 43.8 | 45.5 | 44.5 | | 44.9 | 45.4 |
| All Other Current | .0 | .8 | 3.1 | 3.0 | 3.3 | 4.2 | | 3.2 | 3.1 |
| Total Current | 78.7 | 79.9 | 80.1 | 74.2 | 70.2 | 70.0 | | 74.2 | 73.8 |
| Fixed Assets (net) | 15.0 | 13.2 | 12.1 | 17.9 | 15.7 | 16.5 | | 17.7 | 17.1 |
| Intangibles (net) | 2.2 | 2.6 | 2.8 | 3.5 | 6.4 | 5.6 | | 2.9 | 2.6 |
| All Other Non-Current | 4.5 | 4.3 | 5.1 | 4.4 | 7.7 | 7.9 | | 5.3 | 6.4 |
| Total | 100.0 | 100.0 | 100.0 | 100.0 | 100.0 | 100.0 | | 100.0 | 100.0 |
| **LIABILITIES** | | | | | | | | | |
| Notes Payable-Short Term | 38.3 | 18.9 | 24.1 | 29.6 | 37.6 | 35.1 | | 30.6 | 26.4 |
| Cur. Mat.-L.T.D. | 1.2 | 1.3 | 2.6 | 3.9 | 2.6 | 5.1 | | 3.3 | 4.1 |
| Trade Payables | 21.6 | 20.3 | 17.9 | 11.6 | 17.9 | 6.4 | | 10.4 | 11.3 |
| Income Taxes Payable | .0 | .2 | .1 | .4 | .2 | .1 | | .1 | .1 |
| All Other Current | 1.8 | 8.7 | 9.8 | 9.4 | 10.8 | 6.6 | | 9.3 | 12.4 |
| Total Current | 63.0 | 49.5 | 54.5 | 54.9 | 69.2 | 53.3 | | 53.7 | 54.4 |
| Long-Term Debt | 15.2 | 13.5 | 6.4 | 8.5 | 12.8 | 12.9 | | 13.2 | 15.9 |
| Deferred Taxes | .0 | .0 | .2 | .6 | 1.3 | 1.3 | | .5 | .3 |
| All Other Non-Current | 4.7 | 4.8 | 3.3 | 3.4 | 2.4 | 1.9 | | 4.8 | 5.9 |
| Net Worth | 17.1 | 32.2 | 35.6 | 32.7 | 14.3 | 30.6 | | 27.9 | 23.5 |
| Total Liabilities & Net Worth | 100.0 | 100.0 | 100.0 | 100.0 | 100.0 | 100.0 | | 100.0 | 100.0 |
| **INCOME DATA** | | | | | | | | | |
| Net Sales | 100.0 | 100.0 | 100.0 | 100.0 | 100.0 | 100.0 | | 100.0 | 100.0 |
| Gross Profit | 31.0 | 28.9 | 22.0 | 22.3 | 23.5 | 16.3 | | 24.3 | 23.8 |
| Operating Expenses | 27.2 | 25.4 | 18.8 | 18.1 | 20.8 | 13.0 | | 20.2 | 21.4 |
| Operating Profit | 3.7 | 3.4 | 3.1 | 4.2 | 2.7 | 3.3 | | 4.1 | 2.4 |
| All Other Expenses (net) | -.8 | .5 | -.1 | .2 | .4 | .5 | | .9 | 1.1 |
| Profit Before Taxes | 4.6 | 2.9 | 3.3 | 3.9 | 2.3 | 2.8 | | 3.2 | 1.4 |
| **RATIOS** | | | | | | | | | |
| Current | 2.1 | 3.1 | 2.0 | 1.8 | 1.3 | 1.5 | | 2.0 | 1.9 |
| | 1.3 | 1.7 | 1.4 | 1.2 | 1.1 | 1.2 | | 1.3 | 1.4 |
| | .8 | 1.1 | 1.1 | 1.1 | .9 | 1.0 | | 1.1 | 1.1 |
| Quick | .7 | 1.3 | .9 | .7 | .5 | .4 | | 1.0 | .8 |
| | .3 | .6 | .5 | .4 | .3 | .3 | | (344) .4 | .4 |
| | .2 | .3 | .3 | .3 | .2 | .2 | | .2 | .2 |
| Sales/Receivables | 0 UND | 5 67.3 | 7 52.6 | 9 42.5 | 10 37.9 | 12 31.5 | | 5 70.4 | 7 52.7 |
| | 2 179.5 | 20 18.7 | 15 24.1 | 15 24.0 | 20 18.2 | 17 21.5 | | 16 23.3 | 15 23.7 |
| | 13 28.0 | 36 10.2 | 33 11.2 | 30 12.1 | 33 11.1 | 28 13.1 | | 31 11.8 | 29 12.5 |
| Cost of Sales/Inventory | 9 42.5 | 22 16.3 | 34 10.6 | 43 8.4 | 49 7.4 | 61 6.0 | | 35 10.4 | 34 10.6 |
| | 49 7.4 | 57 6.4 | 64 5.7 | 63 5.8 | 81 4.5 | 87 4.2 | | 64 5.7 | 65 5.6 |
| | 94 3.9 | 135 2.7 | 96 3.8 | 96 3.8 | 118 3.1 | 104 3.5 | | 105 3.5 | 102 3.6 |
| Cost of Sales/Payables | 0 826.0 | 1 286.6 | 5 68.1 | 7 54.1 | 9 40.0 | 7 51.9 | | 3 125.5 | 4 86.5 |
| | 4 87.5 | 18 20.5 | 17 21.0 | 12 30.8 | 14 26.0 | 11 34.1 | | 9 40.1 | 11 33.1 |
| | 64 5.7 | 44 8.3 | 40 9.1 | 20 18.0 | 33 11.0 | 21 17.5 | | 23 15.7 | 28 13.2 |
| Sales/Working Capital | 14.5 | 4.9 | 8.5 | 8.6 | 17.6 | 6.5 | | 7.1 | 7.9 |
| | 26.4 | 14.8 | 14.1 | 17.1 | 42.1 | 18.6 | | 18.3 | 18.2 |
| | -101.5 | 68.5 | 47.0 | 58.1 | -36.5 | 93.3 | | 60.8 | 128.5 |
| EBIT/Interest | | 11.4 | 14.8 | 15.6 | 5.8 | 11.4 | | 5.2 | 5.5 |
| | | (72) 4.6 | (125) 5.4 | (109) 5.2 | (25) 3.5 | (22) 4.0 | | (308) 2.4 | (363) 2.2 |
| | | 1.6 | 2.2 | 2.5 | 2.1 | 2.1 | | 1.3 | .9 |
| Net Profit + Depr., Dep., Amort./Cur. Mat. L/T/D | | | 17.8 | 14.2 | 1.5 | | | 4.1 | 4.8 |
| | | | (22) 4.9 | (30) 2.3 | (10) 1.3 | | | (58) 1.5 | (66) 1.5 |
| | | | 2.1 | 1.0 | 1.1 | | | .9 | .8 |
| Fixed/Worth | .0 | .0 | .1 | .2 | .2 | .2 | | .1 | .1 |
| | .8 | .2 | .2 | .4 | 1.4 | 1.2 | | .5 | .5 |
| | -4.3 | 1.1 | .8 | 1.3 | 3.9 | 1.8 | | 1.5 | 2.0 |
| Debt/Worth | .8 | .8 | 1.0 | 1.3 | 2.7 | 1.4 | | 1.4 | 1.5 |
| | 19.9 | 2.3 | 2.0 | 3.2 | 4.7 | 5.5 | | 3.3 | 3.3 |
| | -8.0 | 9.4 | 3.8 | 6.8 | 19.6 | 12.9 | | 8.3 | 9.6 |
| % Profit Before Taxes/Tangible Net Worth | 565.0 | 72.5 | 40.8 | 41.1 | 68.3 | 43.0 | | 45.9 | 40.3 |
| | (10) 47.4 | (70) 26.0 | (129) 20.7 | (118) 23.6 | (22) 36.2 | (21) 19.7 | | (308) 19.7 | (341) 15.4 |
| | 13.4 | 5.7 | 9.3 | 13.2 | 12.6 | 13.2 | | 6.7 | 3.7 |
| % Profit Before Taxes/Total Assets | 48.6 | 18.1 | 11.9 | 11.3 | 7.8 | 8.4 | | 13.0 | 10.2 |
| | 7.7 | 5.6 | 5.8 | 5.9 | 4.1 | 5.4 | | 4.4 | 3.7 |
| | 2.2 | .9 | 2.6 | 2.9 | 2.2 | 2.0 | | 1.3 | -.3 |
| Sales/Net Fixed Assets | UND | 314.2 | 162.6 | 61.3 | 72.0 | 80.6 | | 106.9 | 109.0 |
| | 106.0 | 67.1 | 57.1 | 23.7 | 21.1 | 18.1 | | 32.7 | 31.1 |
| | 25.0 | 21.2 | 19.9 | 10.1 | 6.8 | 6.9 | | 9.9 | 10.0 |
| Sales/Total Assets | 6.2 | 6.3 | 4.5 | 3.9 | 2.8 | 3.0 | | 4.2 | 4.0 |
| | 5.3 | 3.5 | 3.2 | 2.8 | 2.2 | 2.3 | | 2.9 | 2.9 |
| | 4.0 | 2.1 | 2.3 | 1.9 | 1.5 | 1.4 | | 1.9 | 2.0 |
| % Depr., Dep., Amort./Sales | | .1 | .2 | .3 | .3 | .2 | | .3 | .3 |
| | | (50) .4 | (110) .4 | (109) .8 | (26) .7 | (14) .6 | | (264) .6 | (310) .7 |
| | | 1.0 | 1.3 | 2.1 | 2.8 | 1.4 | | 1.7 | 2.1 |
| % Officers', Directors' Owners' Comp/Sales | | 1.6 | .5 | .4 | | | | .6 | .8 |
| | | (50) 2.4 | (62) 1.3 | (27) .8 | | | | (115) 1.4 | (152) 1.7 |
| | | 4.0 | 3.2 | 1.7 | | | | 3.1 | 3.3 |
| Net Sales ($) | 21775M | 578039M | 2755098M | 8733859M | 4555310M | 8875216M | | 19387565M | 15443253M |
| Total Assets ($) | 3510M | 102360M | 721661M | 2987665M | 1860722M | 3847452M | | 6360001M | 6447458M |

M = $ thousand     MM = $ million
See Pages 9 through 22 for Explanation of Ratios and Data

## Comparative Historical Data | Current Data Sorted by Sales

| Type of Statement | | | | | | | | | |
|---|---|---|---|---|---|---|---|---|---|
| | 48 | 41 | 49 | Unqualified | | 1 | 1 | 4 | 43 |
| | 57 | 80 | 83 | Reviewed | 1 | | 10 | 18 | 54 |
| | 51 | 54 | 39 | Compiled | 1 | 5 | 11 | 11 | 11 |
| | 74 | 81 | 81 | Tax Returns | 5 | 20 | 11 | 16 | 19 | 10 |
| | 148 | 153 | 165 | Other | 5 | 19 | 9 | 14 | 36 | 82 |
| | 4/1/09-3/31/10 ALL | 4/1/10-3/31/11 ALL | 4/1/11-3/31/12 ALL | | 57 (4/1-9/30/11) | | 360 (10/1/11-3/31/12) | | | |
| | | | | | 0-1MM | 1-3MM | 3-5MM | 5-10MM | 10-25MM | 25MM & OVER |
| NUMBER OF STATEMENTS | 378 | 409 | 417 | | 10 | 41 | 26 | 52 | 88 | 200 |

| | % | % | % | ASSETS | % | % | % | % | % | % |
|---|---|---|---|---|---|---|---|---|---|---|
| | 12.2 | 11.4 | 10.5 | Cash & Equivalents | 15.5 | 11.6 | 9.2 | 10.3 | 10.6 | 10.2 |
| | 16.8 | 17.0 | 19.0 | Trade Receivables (net) | 6.3 | 22.1 | 20.5 | 26.5 | 18.8 | 16.9 |
| | 41.5 | 41.9 | 45.0 | Inventory | 45.4 | 45.2 | 44.6 | 42.6 | 45.5 | 45.4 |
| | 3.0 | 3.1 | 2.6 | All Other Current | .0 | .7 | .2 | 1.2 | 2.3 | 3.9 |
| | 73.5 | 73.3 | 77.1 | Total Current | 67.2 | 79.5 | 74.5 | 80.6 | 77.1 | 76.5 |
| | 16.2 | 17.5 | 14.6 | Fixed Assets (net) | 27.3 | 12.8 | 11.7 | 14.4 | 13.1 | 15.5 |
| | 3.5 | 3.8 | 3.3 | Intangibles (net) | 2.8 | 3.6 | 2.1 | 2.4 | 5.6 | 2.7 |
| | 6.8 | 5.4 | 5.0 | All Other Non-Current | 3.2 | 4.1 | 11.8 | 2.6 | 4.1 | 5.4 |
| | 100.0 | 100.0 | 100.0 | Total | 100.0 | 100.0 | 100.0 | 100.0 | 100.0 | 100.0 |

| | | | | LIABILITIES | | | | | | |
|---|---|---|---|---|---|---|---|---|---|---|
| | 26.4 | 24.7 | 26.6 | Notes Payable-Short Term | 21.7 | 19.8 | 20.3 | 22.1 | 26.9 | 30.1 |
| | 3.4 | 2.4 | 2.8 | Cur. Mat.-L.T.D. | .0 | 1.6 | 3.4 | 2.6 | 1.8 | 3.6 |
| | 12.4 | 15.3 | 16.1 | Trade Payables | 14.1 | 16.4 | 19.8 | 19.6 | 18.1 | 13.8 |
| | .1 | .2 | .2 | Income Taxes Payable | .0 | .0 | .1 | .0 | .2 | .4 |
| | 10.6 | 11.5 | 9.0 | All Other Current | 4.6 | 10.2 | 7.4 | 9.2 | 7.7 | 9.7 |
| | 52.9 | 54.2 | 54.7 | Total Current | 40.5 | 48.0 | 50.9 | 53.5 | 54.7 | 57.6 |
| | 12.3 | 11.1 | 9.6 | Long-Term Debt | 17.4 | 20.1 | 13.5 | 6.1 | 5.9 | 9.1 |
| | .4 | .5 | .4 | Deferred Taxes | .0 | .0 | .0 | .3 | .3 | .7 |
| | 4.7 | 5.5 | 3.6 | All Other Non-Current | 7.8 | 4.3 | 4.0 | 2.0 | 5.0 | 2.9 |
| | 29.6 | 28.8 | 31.7 | Net Worth | 34.3 | 27.7 | 31.7 | 38.2 | 34.1 | 29.7 |
| | 100.0 | 100.0 | 100.0 | Total Liabilities & Net Worth | 100.0 | 100.0 | 100.0 | 100.0 | 100.0 | 100.0 |

| | | | | INCOME DATA | | | | | | |
|---|---|---|---|---|---|---|---|---|---|---|
| | 100.0 | 100.0 | 100.0 | Net Sales | 100.0 | 100.0 | 100.0 | 100.0 | 100.0 | 100.0 |
| | 25.3 | 25.5 | 23.6 | Gross Profit | 48.5 | 38.2 | 37.4 | 23.3 | 23.8 | 17.6 |
| | 22.8 | 22.3 | 20.1 | Operating Expenses | 42.1 | 34.7 | 30.5 | 20.6 | 19.7 | 14.8 |
| | 2.5 | 3.2 | 3.5 | Operating Profit | 6.4 | 3.4 | 7.0 | 2.7 | 4.1 | 2.9 |
| | .8 | .5 | .2 | All Other Expenses (net) | -.2 | .5 | -.7 | .1 | .3 | .2 |
| | 1.7 | 2.8 | 3.4 | Profit Before Taxes | 6.5 | 2.9 | 7.7 | 2.6 | 3.8 | 2.7 |

| | | | | RATIOS | | | | | | |
|---|---|---|---|---|---|---|---|---|---|---|
| | 2.1 | 1.9 | 2.0 | Current | 6.5 | 3.9 | 3.2 | 2.3 | 2.0 | 1.7 |
| | 1.4 | 1.3 | 1.3 | | 1.6 | 1.8 | 1.6 | 1.5 | 1.4 | 1.2 |
| | 1.1 | 1.1 | 1.1 | | .7 | 1.1 | 1.0 | 1.1 | 1.1 | 1.1 |
| | 1.0 | .8 | .9 | Quick | .8 | 1.5 | 1.0 | 1.2 | .9 | .7 |
| (377) | .5 | .5 | .5 | | .3 | .7 | .5 | .6 | .5 | .4 |
| | .2 | .3 | .2 | | .2 | .3 | .2 | .3 | .2 | .2 |
| | 5  66.6 | 6  59.1 | 7  50.2 | Sales/Receivables | 0  UND | 4  88.1 | 1  266.6 | 14  26.1 | 7  52.6 | 8  48.1 |
| | 16  23.0 | 16  22.2 | 16  23.1 | | 6  61.2 | 30  12.0 | 13  27.8 | 27  13.3 | 15  24.6 | 14  26.3 |
| | 32  11.3 | 30  12.3 | 32  11.4 | | 23  15.8 | 59  6.2 | 39  9.4 | 42  8.7 | 31  11.8 | 26  13.8 |
| | 31  11.9 | 32  11.4 | 37  9.9 | Cost of Sales/Inventory | 0  UND | 49  7.4 | 19  19.2 | 25  14.7 | 29  12.5 | 39  9.3 |
| | 62  5.9 | 64  5.7 | 64  5.7 | | 89  4.1 | 118  3.1 | 76  4.8 | 61  6.0 | 61  6.0 | 63  5.8 |
| | 107  3.4 | 99  3.7 | 104  3.5 | | 406  .9 | 166  2.2 | 140  2.6 | 126  2.9 | 94  3.9 | 94  3.9 |
| | 3  113.5 | 5  80.5 | 5  66.4 | Cost of Sales/Payables | 0  UND | 2  155.6 | 1  305.0 | 4  88.1 | 5  67.3 | 7  55.9 |
| | 13  27.7 | 15  24.5 | 14  26.1 | | 13  28.6 | 21  17.5 | 20  18.2 | 25  14.8 | 16  23.4 | 12  30.4 |
| | 30  12.3 | 37  9.8 | 33  10.9 | | 62  6.5 | 56  4.7 | 78  4.7 | 46  7.9 | 47  7.7 | 20  18.2 |
| | 7.4 | 8.0 | 8.2 | Sales/Working Capital | 3.6 | 3.3 | 3.3 | 6.8 | 8.4 | 10.9 |
| | 15.9 | 17.3 | 17.3 | | 10.5 | 5.8 | 11.5 | 11.2 | 15.5 | 23.1 |
| | 89.1 | 98.3 | 71.9 | | -52.6 | 67.8 | 305.4 | 33.4 | 46.6 | 76.8 |
| | 5.5 | 8.0 | 13.7 | EBIT/Interest | | 8.2 | 22.8 | 14.6 | 14.6 | 13.9 |
| (325) 2.2 | (359) 3.6 | (361) 4.7 | | | (27) 3.0 | (20) 6.1 | (49) 4.6 | (82) 6.1 | (177) 4.7 | |
| | 1.1 | 1.6 | 2.2 | | | .8 | 2.1 | 1.3 | 2.1 | 2.6 |
| | 4.9 | 5.8 | 13.4 | Net Profit + Depr., Dep., Amort./Cur. Mat. L/T/D | | | | | 28.5 | 10.3 |
| (62) 1.6 | (69) 1.7 | (71) 2.7 | | | | | | (12) 7.1 | (51) 1.9 | |
| | .8 | 1.0 | 1.3 | | | | | | 1.8 | 1.3 |
| | .1 | .1 | .1 | Fixed/Worth | .0 | .1 | .0 | .0 | .1 | .1 |
| | .4 | .5 | .4 | | .9 | .4 | .2 | .2 | .3 | .4 |
| | 1.7 | 2.0 | 1.3 | | 2.6 | -3.4 | .9 | .9 | 1.0 | 1.4 |
| | 1.1 | 1.3 | 1.2 | Debt/Worth | .6 | .8 | .8 | .9 | 1.3 | 1.4 |
| | 2.8 | 2.9 | 2.7 | | 2.9 | 3.2 | 2.4 | 1.6 | 2.7 | 3.2 |
| | 11.7 | 9.0 | 7.0 | | 62.0 | -11.0 | 5.7 | 3.4 | 4.8 | 8.2 |
| | 34.9 | 43.4 | 47.0 | % Profit Before Taxes/Tangible Net Worth | | 50.6 | 65.8 | 37.9 | 44.1 | 46.9 |
| (329) 13.8 | (355) 21.7 | (370) 22.7 | | | (28) 13.6 | (22) 25.2 | (46) 13.5 | (78) 24.0 | (187) 25.1 | |
| | 3.5 | 7.2 | 11.1 | | | -2.0 | 8.5 | 3.6 | 11.3 | 13.9 |
| | 8.5 | 10.6 | 12.1 | % Profit Before Taxes/Total Assets | 51.7 | 10.3 | 19.0 | 10.5 | 12.8 | 11.4 |
| | 3.0 | 5.5 | 5.5 | | 12.8 | 3.8 | 10.8 | 5.1 | 6.2 | 5.6 |
| | .4 | 1.4 | 2.4 | | .8 | -1.5 | 2.9 | .8 | 3.0 | 2.8 |
| | 121.6 | 111.5 | 123.9 | Sales/Net Fixed Assets | UND | 106.7 | 253.8 | 287.9 | 139.7 | 101.1 |
| | 32.7 | 35.2 | 40.9 | | 26.9 | 38.8 | 52.8 | 52.9 | 45.0 | 33.1 |
| | 9.4 | 10.8 | 14.5 | | 3.0 | 12.6 | 18.1 | 21.8 | 17.1 | 10.8 |
| | 4.3 | 4.3 | 4.4 | Sales/Total Assets | 5.2 | 3.5 | 4.7 | 5.4 | 4.3 | 4.4 |
| | 2.8 | 2.9 | 3.0 | | 3.2 | 2.1 | 2.8 | 3.0 | 3.3 | 3.0 |
| | 1.7 | 1.8 | 2.0 | | .9 | 1.3 | 1.8 | 2.0 | 2.4 | 2.2 |
| | .3 | .3 | .3 | % Depr., Dep., Amort./Sales | | .3 | .2 | .2 | .2 | .3 |
| (285) .9 | (325) .7 | (318) .6 | | | (23) .7 | (16) .8 | (35) .5 | (76) .4 | (163) .7 | |
| | 2.1 | 1.9 | 1.6 | | | 1.6 | 1.2 | 1.7 | 1.3 | 1.9 |
| | .8 | .7 | .6 | % Officers', Directors' Owners' Comp/Sales | | 1.6 | 2.0 | 1.6 | .5 | .3 |
| (134) 1.6 | (155) 1.7 | (156) 1.6 | | | (19) 2.9 | (15) 2.9 | (28) 2.3 | (42) 1.1 | (49) .6 | |
| | 4.0 | 4.1 | 3.4 | | | 8.3 | 4.3 | 3.5 | 2.1 | 1.6 |
| | 18952473M | 20071196M | 25519297M | Net Sales ($) | 4858M | 85854M | 100596M | 363630M | 1436881M | 23527478M |
| | 7569302M | 7976447M | 9523370M | Total Assets ($) | 3766M | 53264M | 59702M | 149932M | 611460M | 8645246M |

M = $ thousand     MM = $ million
See Pages 9 through 22 for Explanation of Ratios and Data

## Current Data Sorted by Assets        Comparative Historical Data

| | | | | | | | Type of Statement | | |
|---|---|---|---|---|---|---|---|---|---|
| | | | 10 | 27 | 9 | 10 | Unqualified | 65 | 69 |
| | 7 | | 52 | 44 | 3 | | Reviewed | 104 | 108 |
| 6 | 20 | | 38 | 9 | | 1 | Compiled | 101 | 101 |
| 20 | 52 | | 43 | 5 | | 1 | Tax Returns | 58 | 64 |
| 7 | 30 | | 70 | 82 | 9 | 12 | Other | 164 | 197 |
| | 80 (4/1-9/30/11) | | | 487 (10/1/11-3/31/12) | | | | 4/1/07-3/31/08 | 4/1/08-3/31/09 |
| 0-500M | 500M-2MM | 2-10MM | 10-50MM | 50-100MM | 100-250MM | | ALL | ALL |
| 33 | 109 | 213 | 167 | 21 | 24 | NUMBER OF STATEMENTS | 492 | 539 |
| % | % | % | % | % | % | ASSETS | % | % |
| 12.2 | 8.2 | 6.8 | 4.3 | 4.1 | 4.7 | Cash & Equivalents | 6.0 | 5.6 |
| 23.5 | 24.8 | 24.2 | 23.6 | 20.8 | 23.6 | Trade Receivables (net) | 23.9 | 22.7 |
| 43.5 | 46.8 | 52.0 | 49.5 | 39.0 | 38.9 | Inventory | 49.3 | 50.8 |
| 3.6 | 3.3 | 1.8 | 2.5 | 2.8 | 2.3 | All Other Current | 2.1 | 2.6 |
| 82.9 | 83.1 | 84.9 | 80.0 | 66.8 | 69.6 | Total Current | 81.2 | 81.7 |
| 9.2 | 9.5 | 9.4 | 10.8 | 12.9 | 15.3 | Fixed Assets (net) | 11.3 | 10.6 |
| 4.3 | 2.7 | 2.0 | 4.2 | 14.7 | 11.8 | Intangibles (net) | 3.7 | 3.7 |
| 3.7 | 4.7 | 3.8 | 5.0 | 5.7 | 3.4 | All Other Non-Current | 3.8 | 4.0 |
| 100.0 | 100.0 | 100.0 | 100.0 | 100.0 | 100.0 | Total | 100.0 | 100.0 |
| | | | | | | LIABILITIES | | |
| 15.8 | 11.3 | 14.1 | 16.7 | 15.2 | 13.9 | Notes Payable-Short Term | 17.9 | 19.0 |
| 1.3 | 1.9 | 1.9 | 1.8 | 3.9 | 1.6 | Cur. Mat.-L.T.D. | 2.2 | 2.4 |
| 18.6 | 19.4 | 23.1 | 20.6 | 19.2 | 20.9 | Trade Payables | 21.7 | 19.7 |
| .0 | .3 | .3 | .3 | .0 | .0 | Income Taxes Payable | .2 | .2 |
| 14.4 | 9.2 | 6.7 | 7.7 | 6.6 | 7.7 | All Other Current | 6.7 | 7.9 |
| 50.0 | 42.0 | 46.1 | 47.0 | 44.9 | 44.1 | Total Current | 48.7 | 49.2 |
| 15.7 | 13.3 | 9.0 | 7.7 | 12.5 | 16.2 | Long-Term Debt | 11.0 | 10.0 |
| .1 | .1 | .1 | .3 | .2 | 1.4 | Deferred Taxes | .2 | .1 |
| 14.2 | 5.2 | 5.6 | 4.7 | 5.1 | 4.2 | All Other Non-Current | 6.7 | 5.1 |
| 20.2 | 39.4 | 39.2 | 40.3 | 37.3 | 34.1 | Net Worth | 33.5 | 35.5 |
| 100.0 | 100.0 | 100.0 | 100.0 | 100.0 | 100.0 | Total Liabilties & Net Worth | 100.0 | 100.0 |
| | | | | | | INCOME DATA | | |
| 100.0 | 100.0 | 100.0 | 100.0 | 100.0 | 100.0 | Net Sales | 100.0 | 100.0 |
| 35.3 | 34.5 | 30.1 | 28.3 | 29.0 | 28.0 | Gross Profit | 30.4 | 31.0 |
| 32.2 | 31.4 | 26.9 | 23.4 | 24.1 | 22.1 | Operating Expenses | 26.5 | 27.9 |
| 3.1 | 3.2 | 3.2 | 4.9 | 4.9 | 5.9 | Operating Profit | 3.9 | 3.0 |
| 1.2 | .3 | .3 | .5 | 1.3 | .8 | All Other Expenses (net) | 1.0 | .8 |
| 1.9 | 2.9 | 2.9 | 4.4 | 3.6 | 5.1 | Profit Before Taxes | 2.9 | 2.2 |
| | | | | | | RATIOS | | |
| 3.2 | 3.8 | 2.9 | 2.4 | 2.0 | 2.9 | | 2.6 | 2.6 |
| 2.0 | 2.2 | 1.9 | 1.8 | 1.7 | 1.4 | Current | 1.6 | 1.7 |
| 1.1 | 1.5 | 1.4 | 1.3 | 1.3 | 1.0 | | 1.3 | 1.2 |
| 1.2 | 1.4 | 1.0 | 1.0 | .7 | 1.0 | | 1.0 | .9 |
| .8 | (108) .8 | .6 | .6 | .4 | .6 | Quick | .6 | .5 |
| .4 | .4 | .4 | .4 | .4 | .4 | | .4 | .3 |
| 10   36.6 | 20   17.9 | 22   16.7 | 27   13.3 | 24   14.9 | 33   11.0 | | 23   15.6 | 21   17.0 |
| 27   13.3 | 30   12.2 | 31   11.8 | 36   10.2 | 40   9.2 | 41   8.8 | Sales/Receivables | 33   11.2 | 31   11.8 |
| 39   9.3 | 41   8.9 | 43   8.4 | 49   7.4 | 44   8.3 | 49   7.4 | | 45   8.1 | 44   8.4 |
| 38   9.7 | 52   7.0 | 66   5.5 | 81   4.5 | 62   5.9 | 52   7.0 | | 67   5.4 | 70   5.2 |
| 76   4.8 | 91   4.0 | 101   3.6 | 122   3.0 | 96   3.8 | 126   2.9 | Cost of Sales/Inventory | 109   3.4 | 114   3.2 |
| 130   2.8 | 146   2.5 | 159   2.3 | 174   2.1 | 146   2.5 | 182   2.0 | | 157   2.3 | 179   2.0 |
| 5   74.0 | 13   29.1 | 23   15.8 | 24   15.2 | 27   13.7 | 27   13.3 | | 24   15.3 | 20   18.6 |
| 27   13.3 | 31   11.6 | 41   9.0 | 43   8.4 | 40   9.1 | 45   8.1 | Cost of Sales/Payables | 41   8.9 | 34   10.9 |
| 54   6.8 | 58   6.3 | 62   5.9 | 68   5.4 | 66   5.5 | 68   5.4 | | 62   5.8 | 56   6.6 |
| 4.1 | 4.2 | 4.2 | 3.9 | 6.3 | 3.1 | | 4.6 | 4.3 |
| 11.3 | 6.5 | 6.7 | 6.7 | 8.8 | 12.2 | Sales/Working Capital | 7.7 | 7.6 |
| 104.7 | 14.5 | 13.3 | 12.3 | 11.1 | 74.1 | | 15.1 | 18.6 |
| 9.9 | 20.4 | 14.8 | 24.0 | 14.1 | 24.6 | | 6.6 | 7.5 |
| (23) 3.4 | (88) 4.5 | (195) 5.5 | (156) 8.1 | (20) 7.0 | (23) 4.3 | EBIT/Interest | (444) 2.6 | (495) 2.9 |
| 1.0 | 1.2 | 2.2 | 3.1 | 1.5 | 1.2 | | 1.4 | 1.1 |
| | | 5.1 | 8.0 | | 17.1 | | 5.5 | 6.8 |
| | (38) 2.3 | (46) 2.8 | | (13) 3.7 | | Net Profit + Depr., Dep., Amort./Cur. Mat. L/T/D | (136) 2.5 | (144) 3.0 |
| | | 1.0 | 1.2 | | 1.7 | | .8 | .9 |
| .0 | .0 | .1 | .1 | .1 | .3 | | .1 | .1 |
| .2 | .1 | .2 | .2 | .4 | .5 | Fixed/Worth | .3 | .2 |
| 2.0 | .7 | .5 | .6 | NM | 1.7 | | .8 | .7 |
| 1.1 | .6 | .8 | .9 | 1.6 | 1.4 | | 1.0 | .9 |
| 2.3 | 1.4 | 1.6 | 1.8 | 2.8 | 2.8 | Debt/Worth | 2.1 | 2.0 |
| UND | 4.6 | 3.7 | 4.3 | NM | 7.4 | | 5.5 | 5.6 |
| 143.5 | 42.8 | 35.4 | 40.8 | 46.7 | 37.0 | | 39.3 | 33.3 |
| (25) 16.2 | (93) 14.6 | (197) 14.9 | (156) 21.5 | (16) 24.4 | (21) 24.5 | % Profit Before Taxes/Tangible Net Worth | (442) 17.4 | (480) 14.5 |
| 2.0 | 2.8 | 4.4 | 9.9 | 10.5 | 6.9 | | 5.7 | 2.9 |
| 27.9 | 14.1 | 12.8 | 13.8 | 10.5 | 16.2 | | 13.0 | 10.7 |
| 7.6 | 5.5 | 6.2 | 7.2 | 6.4 | 5.9 | % Profit Before Taxes/Total Assets | 5.1 | 4.6 |
| .0 | .8 | 1.3 | 2.8 | 2.4 | .8 | | 1.4 | .2 |
| UND | 243.7 | 133.6 | 87.9 | 88.4 | 36.3 | | 86.5 | 92.1 |
| 81.5 | 50.3 | 47.1 | 43.1 | 33.2 | 19.3 | Sales/Net Fixed Assets | 36.9 | 37.1 |
| 29.8 | 20.2 | 23.4 | 15.1 | 8.1 | 9.1 | | 17.5 | 17.3 |
| 5.7 | 3.5 | 3.2 | 2.8 | 2.4 | 2.7 | | 3.2 | 3.2 |
| 3.3 | 2.8 | 2.5 | 2.1 | 2.1 | 1.8 | Sales/Total Assets | 2.4 | 2.4 |
| 1.7 | 2.1 | 1.9 | 1.6 | 1.4 | 1.4 | | 1.8 | 1.7 |
| .3 | .3 | .3 | .4 | .5 | .6 | | .4 | .4 |
| (19) .7 | (74) .7 | (162) .6 | (140) .6 | (17) 1.1 | (20) 1.2 | % Depr., Dep., Amort./Sales | (422) .8 | (445) .7 |
| 1.6 | 1.2 | 1.1 | 1.1 | 1.3 | 1.4 | | 1.3 | 1.2 |
| 4.4 | 2.2 | 1.3 | .6 | | | | 1.5 | 1.4 |
| (17) 7.4 | (66) 5.1 | (98) 2.3 | (36) 1.4 | | | % Officers', Directors' Owners' Comp/Sales | (191) 2.8 | (206) 2.6 |
| 9.7 | 7.3 | 4.0 | 2.1 | | | | 5.1 | 4.7 |
| 39025M | 381273M | 2876680M | 8758630M | 2745887M | 8227030M | Net Sales ($) | 16845240M | 21023396M |
| 9163M | 128158M | 1077081M | 3867006M | 1377335M | 3610047M | Total Assets ($) | 7905636M | 9561307M |

M = $ thousand     MM = $ million
See Pages 9 through 22 for Explanation of Ratios and Data

## Comparative Historical Data

## Current Data Sorted by Sales

| | | | Type of Statement | | | | | 13 | 43 |
|---|---|---|---|---|---|---|---|---|---|
| 66 | 54 | 56 | Unqualified | 1 | 1 | 7 | 10 | 44 | 43 |
| 110 | 132 | 106 | Reviewed | | | | | 21 | 9 |
| 85 | 79 | 74 | Compiled | 3 | 10 | 10 | 21 | 19 | 9 |
| 63 | 82 | 121 | Tax Returns | 14 | 31 | 22 | 26 | 48 | 94 |
| 197 | 199 | 210 | Other | 7 | 18 | 17 | 26 | | |
| 4/1/09-3/31/10 ALL | 4/1/10-3/31/11 ALL | 4/1/11-3/31/12 ALL | | 80 (4/1-9/30/11) | | | 487 (10/1/11-3/31/12) | | |
| | | | | 0-1MM | 1-3MM | 3-5MM | 5-10MM | 10-25MM | 25MM & OVER |
| 521 | 546 | 567 | NUMBER OF STATEMENTS | 25 | 60 | 56 | 83 | 145 | 198 |
| % | % | % | **ASSETS** | % | % | % | % | % | % |
| 7.0 | 6.7 | 6.5 | Cash & Equivalents | 12.3 | 8.9 | 8.3 | 7.4 | 5.2 | 4.9 |
| 22.9 | 23.5 | 24.0 | Trade Receivables (net) | 20.0 | 23.0 | 23.2 | 23.9 | 24.4 | 24.7 |
| 47.8 | 48.3 | 48.8 | Inventory | 43.2 | 46.5 | 48.0 | 51.5 | 50.8 | 47.7 |
| 2.5 | 2.7 | 2.5 | All Other Current | 2.5 | 3.5 | 3.9 | 2.2 | 1.6 | 2.5 |
| 80.2 | 81.2 | 81.7 | Total Current | 78.1 | 81.9 | 83.5 | 85.1 | 82.0 | 79.8 |
| 11.6 | 10.2 | 10.2 | Fixed Assets (net) | 12.5 | 11.5 | 8.1 | 10.1 | 9.5 | 10.7 |
| 4.1 | 4.2 | 3.8 | Intangibles (net) | 5.2 | 2.7 | 3.3 | 1.4 | 2.7 | 5.9 |
| 4.1 | 4.4 | 4.4 | All Other Non-Current | 4.4 | 3.8 | 5.2 | 3.5 | 5.8 | 3.6 |
| 100.0 | 100.0 | 100.0 | Total | 100.0 | 100.0 | 100.0 | 100.0 | 100.0 | 100.0 |
| | | | **LIABILITIES** | | | | | | |
| 19.4 | 16.2 | 14.5 | Notes Payable-Short Term | 12.2 | 14.1 | 12.7 | 12.4 | 14.6 | 16.2 |
| 2.3 | 2.0 | 1.9 | Cur. Mat.-L.T.D. | 1.7 | 2.0 | 1.9 | 1.1 | 2.5 | 1.7 |
| 19.6 | 20.1 | 21.1 | Trade Payables | 12.1 | 22.6 | 15.5 | 21.3 | 22.3 | 22.6 |
| .2 | .2 | .2 | Income Taxes Payable | .6 | .0 | .2 | .3 | .2 | .3 |
| 6.9 | 7.0 | 8.0 | All Other Current | 13.5 | 7.0 | 13.6 | 6.8 | 5.9 | 8.0 |
| 48.5 | 45.5 | 45.7 | Total Current | 40.0 | 45.7 | 43.8 | 41.9 | 45.5 | 48.7 |
| 9.4 | 9.4 | 10.3 | Long-Term Debt | 26.2 | 16.6 | 7.6 | 6.8 | 10.0 | 8.7 |
| .2 | .2 | .2 | Deferred Taxes | .1 | .1 | .1 | .1 | .2 | .4 |
| 7.1 | 6.2 | 5.7 | All Other Non-Current | 16.7 | 7.3 | 5.5 | 4.1 | 5.7 | 4.5 |
| 34.7 | 38.8 | 38.2 | Net Worth | 17.4 | 30.3 | 43.0 | 47.3 | 38.6 | 37.8 |
| 100.0 | 100.0 | 100.0 | Total Liabilities & Net Worth | 100.0 | 100.0 | 100.0 | 100.0 | 100.0 | 100.0 |
| | | | **INCOME DATA** | | | | | | |
| 100.0 | 100.0 | 100.0 | Net Sales | 100.0 | 100.0 | 100.0 | 100.0 | 100.0 | 100.0 |
| 31.2 | 31.3 | 30.6 | Gross Profit | 35.7 | 39.0 | 32.7 | 31.9 | 29.3 | 27.2 |
| 28.5 | 27.2 | 26.7 | Operating Expenses | 32.9 | 35.8 | 28.4 | 28.2 | 26.3 | 22.4 |
| 2.8 | 4.1 | 3.9 | Operating Profit | 2.7 | 3.1 | 4.3 | 3.7 | 3.1 | 4.8 |
| 1.0 | .5 | .4 | All Other Expenses (net) | 1.5 | 1.2 | -.1 | .1 | .2 | .5 |
| 1.7 | 3.5 | 3.4 | Profit Before Taxes | 1.2 | 1.9 | 4.4 | 3.5 | 2.8 | 4.2 |
| | | | **RATIOS** | | | | | | |
| 2.9 | 2.9 | 2.9 | Current | 4.8 | 3.3 | 3.6 | 3.3 | 2.8 | 2.4 |
| 1.7 | 1.8 | 1.8 | | 2.3 | 2.2 | 2.0 | 2.2 | 1.8 | 1.6 |
| 1.2 | 1.3 | 1.3 | | 1.2 | 1.1 | 1.5 | 1.5 | 1.4 | 1.2 |
| 1.1 | 1.1 | 1.1 | Quick | 1.5 | 1.2 | 1.3 | 1.3 | 1.0 | .9 |
| .6 (545) | .6 (566) | .6 | | .8 | .8 (55) | .7 | .7 | .6 | .6 |
| .4 | .4 | .4 | | .4 | .4 | .4 | .5 | .4 | .4 |
| 23  16.0 | 22  16.3 | 23  15.6 | Sales/Receivables | 13  28.9 | 20  18.6 | 21  17.7 | 21  17.6 | 25  14.7 | 27  13.4 |
| 34  10.8 | 34  10.7 | 33  11.1 | | 28  12.9 | 31  11.9 | 28  13.1 | 30  12.2 | 32  11.4 | 36  10.0 |
| 46  8.0 | 47  7.7 | 45  8.2 | | 46  7.9 | 40  9.1 | 45  8.1 | 41  8.8 | 47  7.7 | 45  8.1 |
| 69  5.3 | 64  5.7 | 64  5.7 | Cost of Sales/Inventory | 59  6.2 | 50  6.9 | 47  7.7 | 72  5.1 | 70  5.2 | 63  5.8 |
| 109  3.4 | 112  3.3 | 104  3.5 | | 122  3.0 | 101  3.6 | 96  3.8 | 104  3.5 | 107  3.4 | 104  3.5 |
| 178  2.0 | 170  2.2 | 159  2.3 | | 243  1.5 | 159  2.3 | 174  2.1 | 152  2.4 | 166  2.2 | 146  2.5 |
| 21  17.6 | 22  16.8 | 21  17.1 | Cost of Sales/Payables | 8  43.4 | 21  17.2 | 9  42.6 | 21  17.1 | 26  13.9 | 24  15.2 |
| 36  10.1 | 38  9.6 | 40  9.1 | | 23  16.1 | 47  7.8 | 33  11.1 | 44  8.3 | 44  8.3 | 42  8.6 |
| 61  6.0 | 61  6.0 | 64  5.7 | | 48  7.6 | 74  4.9 | 50  7.3 | 51  7.1 | 65  5.6 | 64  5.7 |
| 4.0 | 4.1 | 4.1 | Sales/Working Capital | 1.7 | 3.7 | 4.2 | 3.6 | 4.1 | 4.8 |
| 6.8 | 6.6 | 6.8 | | 6.1 | 5.9 | 6.5 | 6.2 | 6.2 | 8.5 |
| 15.8 | 13.6 | 14.8 | | 60.6 | 54.5 | 14.5 | 10.9 | 12.0 | 17.8 |
| 8.7 | 14.1 | 17.7 | EBIT/Interest | 6.7 | 8.4 | 29.8 | 16.5 | 14.9 | 23.0 |
| (471)  3.3 | (485)  4.4 | (505)  5.9 | | (16)  1.3 | (50)  3.0 | (46)  5.4 | (71)  5.4 | (134)  5.4 | (188)  8.2 |
| 1.1 | 1.8 | 2.0 | | -2.3 | 1.1 | 2.2 | 2.2 | 1.5 | 3.2 |
| 7.3 | 7.7 | 6.8 | Net Profit + Depr., Dep., | | | | 20.2 | 4.4 | 8.4 |
| (128)  2.7 | (121)  2.7 | (112)  2.7 | Amort./Cur. Mat. L/T/D | | | | (12)  3.0 | (28)  2.1 | (62)  3.0 |
| 1.0 | 1.2 | 1.2 | | | | | 1.6 | .9 | 1.6 |
| .1 | .1 | .1 | Fixed/Worth | .0 | .1 | .0 | .0 | .1 | .1 |
| .2 | .2 | .2 | | .1 | .2 | .1 | .1 | .1 | .2 |
| .7 | .7 | .7 | | UND | 1.3 | .5 | .3 | .6 | .7 |
| .9 | .8 | .8 | Debt/Worth | .8 | .7 | .5 | .5 | .9 | 1.1 |
| 2.0 | 1.8 | 1.8 | | 2.5 | 2.2 | 1.3 | 1.0 | 1.7 | 2.0 |
| 5.5 | 4.9 | 4.4 | | -13.2 | 16.1 | 4.1 | 2.4 | 4.3 | 4.4 |
| 28.0 | 37.9 | 41.0 | % Profit Before Taxes/Tangible | 102.8 | 26.1 | 65.0 | 31.6 | 31.3 | 48.1 |
| (452)  11.9 | (493)  17.0 | (508)  17.6 | Net Worth | (18)  15.7 | (47)  9.8 | (50)  21.7 | (78)  13.5 | (135)  13.0 | (180)  25.9 |
| 2.1 | 5.2 | 5.0 | | .0 | 1.3 | 4.7 | 3.6 | 3.3 | 11.7 |
| 9.7 | 12.4 | 13.4 | % Profit Before Taxes/Total | 21.0 | 9.3 | 19.3 | 13.0 | 11.8 | 13.9 |
| 3.7 | 5.9 | 6.5 | Assets | 1.8 | 3.2 | 10.1 | 5.0 | 5.1 | 7.7 |
| .3 | 1.6 | 1.6 | | -5.1 | .4 | 1.7 | 1.3 | .6 | 3.5 |
| 89.3 | 95.3 | 119.7 | Sales/Net Fixed Assets | 668.5 | 172.9 | 173.1 | 267.8 | 125.0 | 85.2 |
| 39.3 | 42.1 | 45.8 | | 35.5 | 51.1 | 46.3 | 51.1 | 47.5 | 42.1 |
| 16.3 | 19.6 | 19.3 | | 13.7 | 18.5 | 20.0 | 20.2 | 24.5 | 15.5 |
| 2.9 | 3.1 | 3.2 | Sales/Total Assets | 2.9 | 3.3 | 3.6 | 3.2 | 3.1 | 2.9 |
| 2.3 | 2.3 | 2.4 | | 1.6 | 2.5 | 2.8 | 2.5 | 2.4 | 2.4 |
| 1.6 | 1.7 | 1.8 | | 1.2 | 1.9 | 2.0 | 1.9 | 1.8 | 1.8 |
| .4 | .4 | .3 | % Depr., Dep., Amort./Sales | .5 | .4 | .2 | .4 | .3 | .4 |
| (427)  .8 | (433)  .7 | (432)  .7 | | (17)  1.5 | (42)  .8 | (41)  .5 | (51)  .8 | (114)  .6 | (167)  .7 |
| 1.4 | 1.3 | 1.2 | | 2.6 | 1.4 | .9 | 1.5 | 1.0 | 1.2 |
| 1.6 | 1.3 | 1.4 | % Officers', Directors' | 5.0 | 3.2 | 2.1 | 1.2 | 1.4 | .6 |
| (201)  2.8 | (199)  2.3 | (222)  2.7 | Owners' Comp/Sales | (12)  6.7 | (39)  6.0 | (31)  3.3 | (39)  2.0 | (60)  2.3 | (41)  1.1 |
| 5.4 | 4.0 | 6.0 | | 8.2 | 9.0 | 7.2 | 4.8 | 3.8 | 2.4 |
| 15288872M | 18337050M | 23028525M | Net Sales ($) | 15176M | 123550M | 218709M | 588545M | 2365473M | 19717072M |
| 7696110M | 8998468M | 10068790M | Total Assets ($) | 9073M | 62593M | 91461M | 266852M | 1155547M | 8483264M |

M = $ thousand     MM = $ million
See Pages 9 through 22 for Explanation of Ratios and Data

## Current Data Sorted by Assets     Comparative Historical Data

| | | | | | | Type of Statement | | |
|---|---|---|---|---|---|---|---|---|
| 2 | 1 | 11 | 3 | 4 | | Unqualified | 18 | 21 |
| | 1 | 13 | 3 | | | Reviewed | 34 | 35 |
| | 4 | 13 | 4 | 1 | | Compiled | 41 | 35 |
| 7 | 8 | 16 | 2 | | | Tax Returns | 16 | 11 |
| 1 | 2 | 14 | 23 | 9 | 11 | Other | 55 | 57 |
| | 25 (4/1-9/30/11) | | 142 (10/1/11-3/31/12) | | | | 4/1/07-3/31/08 | 4/1/08-3/31/09 |
| 0-500M | 500M-2MM | 2-10MM | 10-50MM | 50-100MM | 100-250MM | | ALL | ALL |
| 10 | 15 | 57 | 54 | 16 | 15 | NUMBER OF STATEMENTS | 164 | 159 |
| % | % | % | % | % | % | ASSETS | % | % |
| 9.9 | 7.8 | 5.6 | 5.9 | .8 | 4.3 | Cash & Equivalents | 5.3 | 5.1 |
| 21.6 | 25.6 | 31.3 | 27.1 | 24.8 | 21.8 | Trade Receivables (net) | 27.5 | 24.7 |
| 45.7 | 52.5 | 46.2 | 42.7 | 50.2 | 49.3 | Inventory | 41.4 | 44.7 |
| 1.4 | .6 | 1.8 | 2.3 | 1.3 | 1.4 | All Other Current | 3.3 | 3.0 |
| 78.6 | 86.5 | 84.9 | 77.9 | 77.0 | 76.8 | Total Current | 77.5 | 77.6 |
| 16.5 | 7.7 | 9.5 | 14.1 | 13.0 | 17.6 | Fixed Assets (net) | 15.5 | 15.7 |
| .4 | .5 | 1.1 | 1.3 | 7.1 | 1.8 | Intangibles (net) | 2.5 | 1.9 |
| 4.4 | 5.4 | 4.6 | 6.8 | 2.9 | 3.8 | All Other Non-Current | 4.5 | 4.9 |
| 100.0 | 100.0 | 100.0 | 100.0 | 100.0 | 100.0 | Total | 100.0 | 100.0 |
| | | | | | | LIABILITIES | | |
| 8.3 | 8.8 | 12.7 | 14.5 | 18.8 | 9.6 | Notes Payable-Short Term | 13.0 | 14.8 |
| .7 | 1.5 | 2.5 | 1.8 | 1.2 | 2.3 | Cur. Mat.-L.T.D. | 3.1 | 2.6 |
| 26.2 | 37.4 | 36.1 | 27.2 | 30.3 | 29.0 | Trade Payables | 32.5 | 30.9 |
| .0 | .2 | .3 | .3 | .1 | .2 | Income Taxes Payable | .1 | .1 |
| 31.3 | 12.4 | 8.9 | 7.0 | 5.4 | 5.5 | All Other Current | 6.9 | 7.1 |
| 66.5 | 60.4 | 60.6 | 50.8 | 55.8 | 46.6 | Total Current | 55.5 | 55.5 |
| 21.7 | 16.0 | 6.8 | 7.8 | 11.8 | 38.6 | Long-Term Debt | 10.3 | 10.0 |
| .0 | .0 | .2 | .5 | .1 | .4 | Deferred Taxes | .3 | .2 |
| 24.6 | 2.9 | 2.9 | 3.7 | 2.7 | 1.4 | All Other Non-Current | 4.4 | 4.7 |
| -13.2 | 20.7 | 29.6 | 37.3 | 29.5 | 13.0 | Net Worth | 29.5 | 29.6 |
| 100.0 | 100.0 | 100.0 | 100.0 | 100.0 | 100.0 | Total Liabilties & Net Worth | 100.0 | 100.0 |
| | | | | | | INCOME DATA | | |
| 100.0 | 100.0 | 100.0 | 100.0 | 100.0 | 100.0 | Net Sales | 100.0 | 100.0 |
| 39.2 | 26.2 | 20.6 | 23.7 | 18.5 | 18.5 | Gross Profit | 24.7 | 25.2 |
| 40.5 | 25.0 | 18.5 | 19.9 | 15.0 | 13.9 | Operating Expenses | 22.4 | 23.3 |
| -1.3 | 1.2 | 2.1 | 3.8 | 3.5 | 4.6 | Operating Profit | 2.3 | 2.0 |
| .3 | .4 | .0 | .0 | .3 | .3 | All Other Expenses (net) | .3 | .4 |
| -1.6 | .8 | 2.1 | 3.8 | 3.3 | 4.3 | Profit Before Taxes | 2.0 | 1.6 |
| | | | | | | RATIOS | | |
| 2.5 | 3.3 | 1.7 | 1.9 | 2.1 | 2.4 | | 1.7 | 1.9 |
| 1.3 | 1.3 | 1.4 | 1.5 | 1.5 | 1.6 | Current | 1.4 | 1.4 |
| .7 | 1.0 | 1.2 | 1.3 | 1.2 | 1.1 | | 1.1 | 1.1 |
| 1.2 | .8 | .7 | .7 | .8 | | | .7 | .7 |
| .6 | .6 | .6 | .5 | .5 | | Quick | .5 | .5 |
| .3 | .3 | .5 | .3 | .5 | | | .4 | .3 |
| 0   UND | 16   23.4 | 21   17.1 | 26   14.1 | 27   13.3 | 10   34.8 | | 23   15.9 | 18   20.7 |
| 10   38.1 | 19   19.5 | 32   11.3 | 31   11.6 | 37   9.8 | 35   10.4 | Sales/Receivables | 33   11.2 | 30   12.1 |
| 26   14.0 | 29   12.8 | 47   7.7 | 46   8.0 | 54   6.8 | 41   8.9 | | 43   8.4 | 41   8.8 |
| 34   10.6 | 46   7.9 | 41   8.8 | 54   6.7 | 64   5.7 | 69   5.3 | | 49   7.5 | 53   6.8 |
| 44   8.3 | 68   5.4 | 83   4.4 | 76   4.8 | 81   4.5 | 76   4.8 | Cost of Sales/Inventory | 69   5.3 | 73   5.0 |
| 60   6.1 | 94   3.9 | 107   3.4 | 114   3.2 | 107   3.4 | 96   3.8 | | 93   3.9 | 97   3.7 |
| 0   UND | 15   23.7 | 37   9.9 | 30   12.2 | 37   9.8 | 23   16.1 | | 32   11.3 | 29   12.6 |
| 21   17.1 | 38   9.5 | 52   7.0 | 45   8.1 | 52   7.0 | 52   7.0 | Cost of Sales/Payables | 53   6.9 | 51   7.2 |
| 50   7.3 | 76   4.8 | 79   4.6 | 72   5.1 | 61   6.0 | 76   4.8 | | 73   5.0 | 69   5.3 |
| 13.0 | 7.7 | 7.4 | 5.6 | 6.1 | 5.8 | | 8.2 | 7.7 |
| 47.5 | 20.0 | 13.3 | 11.0 | 11.8 | 8.5 | Sales/Working Capital | 15.5 | 14.6 |
| -37.5 | 108.1 | 24.8 | 17.5 | 18.9 | 25.8 | | 42.0 | 34.3 |
| | 4.8 | 11.9 | 19.6 | 8.8 | 13.2 | | 7.9 | 7.6 |
| (13)   2.4 | (53)   5.3 | (46)   7.5 | (14)   5.6 | (14)   8.4 | | EBIT/Interest | (154)   3.3 | (150)   3.4 |
| .3 | 2.1 | 3.8 | 3.9 | 3.0 | | | 1.7 | 1.4 |
| | 9.5 | 13.7 | | | | | 6.3 | 4.4 |
| (14)   3.9 | (17)   6.9 | | | | Net Profit + Depr., Dep., | (43)   3.1 | (48)   2.2 |
| 1.1 | 2.1 | | | | | Amort./Cur. Mat. L/T/D | 1.5 | 1.3 |
| .0 | .0 | .1 | .1 | .2 | .3 | | .2 | .2 |
| .6 | .1 | .3 | .3 | .5 | .9 | Fixed/Worth | .4 | .5 |
| -6.8 | .8 | .7 | .6 | 1.3 | 4.3 | | 1.1 | 1.1 |
| 3.0 | .5 | 1.6 | 1.0 | 2.4 | 1.2 | | 1.3 | 1.3 |
| -65.4 | 4.3 | 2.4 | 1.6 | 3.3 | 5.2 | Debt/Worth | 2.5 | 2.6 |
| -2.6 | 20.0 | 4.5 | 3.2 | 5.8 | 7.5 | | 4.9 | 5.9 |
| | 34.0 | 38.9 | 39.4 | 49.5 | 34.4 | | 34.3 | 31.7 |
| (13)   10.7 | (54)   22.4 | 26.5 | (15)   26.9 | (12)   21.8 | % Profit Before Taxes/Tangible Net Worth | (151)   16.1 | (147)   13.2 |
| 3.1 | 11.5 | 14.2 | 18.0 | 11.7 | | | 6.9 | 3.8 |
| 9.4 | 6.7 | 10.8 | 15.0 | 10.6 | 11.5 | | 9.4 | 8.3 |
| -7.2 | 3.3 | 5.5 | 8.3 | 5.8 | 7.3 | % Profit Before Taxes/Total Assets | 5.2 | 4.3 |
| -20.7 | .2 | 1.0 | 4.2 | 4.4 | 4.9 | | 1.7 | .9 |
| UND | 999.8 | 145.8 | 64.8 | 61.0 | 137.0 | | 55.2 | 61.8 |
| 88.5 | 114.3 | 51.2 | 23.3 | 29.7 | 21.6 | Sales/Net Fixed Assets | 29.4 | 28.1 |
| 18.2 | 25.7 | 22.0 | 11.7 | 9.2 | 7.5 | | 13.1 | 13.2 |
| 9.0 | 4.7 | 3.9 | 3.3 | 3.6 | 3.0 | | 3.8 | 3.6 |
| 4.9 | 4.0 | 3.1 | 2.6 | 2.5 | 2.4 | Sales/Total Assets | 3.0 | 2.9 |
| 3.8 | 3.3 | 2.2 | 2.0 | 1.9 | 2.3 | | 2.3 | 2.2 |
| | .2 | .4 | .4 | .3 | | | .5 | .5 |
| (49)   .7 | (52)   .8 | (15)   .8 | (13)   .7 | | % Depr., Dep., Amort./Sales | (147)   .9 | (142)   .8 |
| 1.4 | 1.3 | 1.6 | 1.1 | | | | 1.4 | 1.3 |
| 1.4 | .7 | .6 | | | | | .6 | 1.0 |
| (11)   2.5 | (28)   1.5 | (13)   .9 | | | % Officers', Directors' Owners' Comp/Sales | (68)   1.2 | (57)   1.6 |
| 4.6 | 2.4 | 1.6 | | | | | 3.0 | 3.5 |
| 13876M | 86584M | 903869M | 3693126M | 2938060M | 7425941M | Net Sales ($) | 9808360M | 13499898M |
| 2119M | 19855M | 285188M | 1382021M | 1136205M | 2556831M | Total Assets ($) | 4004875M | 4678550M |

© RMA 2012

M = $ thousand    MM = $ million
See Pages 9 through 22 for Explanation of Ratios and Data

## Comparative Historical Data | Current Data Sorted by Sales

| | | | Type of Statement | | | | | | |
|---|---|---|---|---|---|---|---|---|---|
| 23 | 21 | 21 | Unqualified | 2 | | | | 2 | 17 |
| 26 | 38 | 31 | Reviewed | | | 1 | 5 | 4 | 21 |
| 30 | 26 | 22 | Compiled | | 2 | 1 | 5 | 6 | 8 |
| 10 | 18 | 33 | Tax Returns | 1 | 8 | | 11 | 10 | 3 |
| 49 | 55 | 60 | Other | | 2 | 1 | 11 | 11 | 43 |
| 4/1/09-3/31/10 ALL | 4/1/10-3/31/11 ALL | 4/1/11-3/31/12 ALL | | 25 (4/1-9/30/11) | | | 142 (10/1/11-3/31/12) | | |
| | | | | 0-1MM | 1-3MM | 3-5MM | 5-10MM | 10-25MM | 25MM & OVER |
| 138 | 158 | 167 | NUMBER OF STATEMENTS | 3 | 12 | 3 | 24 | 33 | 92 |
| % | % | % | ASSETS | % | % | % | % | % | % |
| 5.9 | 6.6 | 5.6 | Cash & Equivalents | | 6.2 | | 4.2 | 8.5 | 4.5 |
| 26.0 | 28.6 | 27.4 | Trade Receivables (net) | | 17.6 | | 24.6 | 29.4 | 28.7 |
| 41.4 | 42.6 | 46.3 | Inventory | | 59.7 | | 52.2 | 41.4 | 45.5 |
| 2.7 | 2.6 | 1.7 | All Other Current | | 1.2 | | 1.5 | 2.7 | 1.6 |
| 76.0 | 80.4 | 80.9 | Total Current | | 84.7 | | 82.6 | 82.0 | 80.3 |
| 16.9 | 13.8 | 12.3 | Fixed Assets (net) | | 9.0 | | 8.5 | 10.8 | 13.4 |
| 2.9 | 2.0 | 1.7 | Intangibles (net) | | .4 | | .9 | 1.1 | 2.3 |
| 4.2 | 3.7 | 5.1 | All Other Non-Current | | 5.9 | | 8.0 | 6.2 | 4.1 |
| 100.0 | 100.0 | 100.0 | Total | | 100.0 | | 100.0 | 100.0 | 100.0 |
| | | | LIABILITIES | | | | | | |
| 12.6 | 12.6 | 13.0 | Notes Payable-Short Term | | 6.3 | | 10.3 | 13.7 | 14.6 |
| 2.5 | 2.0 | 1.9 | Cur. Mat.-L.T.D. | | .9 | | 2.6 | 1.0 | 1.7 |
| 32.1 | 35.1 | 31.5 | Trade Payables | | 34.4 | | 35.8 | 35.6 | 29.8 |
| .3 | .2 | .3 | Income Taxes Payable | | .0 | | .4 | .4 | .2 |
| 8.1 | 9.9 | 9.3 | All Other Current | | 18.6 | | 11.4 | 6.3 | 6.7 |
| 55.5 | 59.8 | 56.0 | Total Current | | 60.3 | | 60.5 | 57.1 | 53.0 |
| 11.3 | 9.0 | 12.2 | Long-Term Debt | | 14.3 | | 13.2 | 7.7 | 12.6 |
| .2 | .2 | .3 | Deferred Taxes | | .0 | | .1 | .2 | .4 |
| 3.8 | 5.0 | 4.3 | All Other Non-Current | | 20.0 | | 4.1 | 1.4 | 3.0 |
| 29.1 | 26.0 | 27.2 | Net Worth | | 5.4 | | 22.2 | 33.6 | 31.1 |
| 100.0 | 100.0 | 100.0 | Total Liabilities & Net Worth | | 100.0 | | 100.0 | 100.0 | 100.0 |
| | | | INCOME DATA | | | | | | |
| 100.0 | 100.0 | 100.0 | Net Sales | | 100.0 | | 100.0 | 100.0 | 100.0 |
| 24.1 | 22.8 | 22.8 | Gross Profit | | 39.2 | | 21.8 | 22.5 | 20.6 |
| 22.6 | 20.2 | 20.1 | Operating Expenses | | 40.0 | | 20.8 | 19.7 | 17.0 |
| 1.5 | 2.7 | 2.7 | Operating Profit | | -.8 | | 1.0 | 2.8 | 3.7 |
| .0 | .0 | .1 | All Other Expenses (net) | | .3 | | .1 | -.1 | .1 |
| 1.5 | 2.7 | 2.6 | Profit Before Taxes | | -1.1 | | .9 | 2.8 | 3.6 |
| | | | RATIOS | | | | | | |
| 1.8 | 1.9 | 1.9 | | | 3.6 | | 2.0 | 1.9 | 1.9 |
| 1.4 | 1.4 | 1.5 | Current | | 1.3 | | 1.3 | 1.4 | 1.5 |
| 1.1 | 1.1 | 1.2 | | | .8 | | 1.1 | 1.2 | 1.2 |
| .8 | .8 | .8 | | | .9 | | .7 | .8 | .8 |
| .6 | .6 (166) | .6 | Quick | | .4 | | .5 | .6 | .6 |
| .4 | .4 | .4 | | | .3 | | .4 | .4 | .5 |
| 20 18.0 | 21 17.5 | 20 18.1 | | 0 UND | | 18 19.9 | 21 17.1 | 26 14.1 | |
| 34 10.7 | 34 10.9 | 31 11.8 | Sales/Receivables | 13 28.9 | | 27 13.5 | 37 9.8 | 34 10.7 | |
| 44 8.3 | 50 7.4 | 45 8.1 | | 29 12.6 | | 38 9.7 | 48 7.6 | 46 8.0 | |
| 53 6.9 | 48 7.6 | 52 7.0 | | 47 7.7 | | 55 6.6 | 37 9.9 | 55 6.6 | |
| 71 5.1 | 68 5.4 | 76 4.8 | Cost of Sales/Inventory | 62 5.9 | | 78 4.7 | 87 4.2 | 76 4.8 | |
| 96 3.8 | 93 3.9 | 104 3.5 | | 159 2.3 | | 118 3.1 | 107 3.4 | 96 3.8 | |
| 32 11.5 | 36 10.2 | 30 12.2 | | 13 27.4 | | 34 10.7 | 36 10.0 | 29 12.8 | |
| 52 7.0 | 52 7.0 | 49 7.4 | Cost of Sales/Payables | 43 8.5 | | 52 7.0 | 53 6.9 | 47 7.7 | |
| 71 5.1 | 74 5.0 | 70 5.2 | | 70 5.2 | | 74 4.9 | 91 4.0 | 66 5.5 | |
| 7.2 | 7.5 | 7.0 | | | 9.8 | | 8.1 | 7.3 | 6.5 |
| 14.1 | 12.7 | 12.9 | Sales/Working Capital | | 30.0 | | 16.3 | 11.0 | 12.3 |
| 77.1 | 41.8 | 25.8 | | | -25.4 | | 37.6 | 32.3 | 19.9 |
| 10.9 | 11.4 | 13.0 | | | 9.8 | | 7.3 | 13.8 | 13.9 |
| (132) 4.1 | (144) 5.7 | (147) 5.5 | EBIT/Interest | (23) 2.1 | | (29) 5.5 | (82) 7.3 | | |
| 1.8 | 2.5 | 2.7 | | | .1 | | 3.2 | 4.2 | |
| 9.8 | 11.1 | 12.3 | | | | | | | 13.2 |
| (40) 2.6 | (40) 5.8 | (42) 4.0 | Net Profit + Depr., Dep., Amort./Cur. Mat. L/T/D | | | | | (26) 4.0 | |
| .8 | 1.8 | 1.9 | | | | | | | 1.9 |
| .2 | .1 | .1 | | | .0 | | .1 | .1 | .1 |
| .5 | .4 | .3 | Fixed/Worth | | .5 | | .2 | .3 | .3 |
| 1.4 | 1.1 | .9 | | | -2.7 | | 1.2 | .5 | .9 |
| 1.4 | 1.3 | 1.3 | | | 1.1 | | 1.6 | 1.2 | 1.3 |
| 2.5 | 2.7 | 2.5 | Debt/Worth | | NM | | 3.8 | 2.3 | 2.4 |
| 5.8 | 6.1 | 5.2 | | | -6.3 | | 14.0 | 3.9 | 4.2 |
| 30.4 | 37.7 | 39.3 | | | 35.5 | | 37.3 | 41.4 | |
| (127) 13.5 | (142) 24.4 | (152) 23.8 | % Profit Before Taxes/Tangible Net Worth | (22) 6.6 | | 23.8 | (88) 25.7 | | |
| 6.4 | 10.7 | 12.3 | | | .8 | | 13.0 | 17.6 | |
| 8.8 | 11.8 | 11.5 | | | 7.0 | | 3.8 | 10.8 | 14.2 |
| 4.1 | 6.9 | 5.8 | % Profit Before Taxes/Total Assets | | -5.0 | | 1.9 | 6.4 | 7.5 |
| 1.7 | 2.1 | 2.8 | | | -11.6 | | -2.2 | 3.7 | 4.4 |
| 62.1 | 100.6 | 108.2 | | | UND | | 246.6 | 107.4 | 86.3 |
| 25.8 | 39.0 | 36.6 | Sales/Net Fixed Assets | | 88.5 | | 52.5 | 36.7 | 29.7 |
| 9.9 | 15.9 | 15.6 | | | 20.2 | | 23.6 | 16.1 | 12.6 |
| 3.5 | 3.9 | 4.1 | | | 8.1 | | 4.1 | 3.8 | 3.7 |
| 2.8 | 2.9 | 3.0 | Sales/Total Assets | | 4.0 | | 3.2 | 2.6 | 2.8 |
| 2.1 | 2.2 | 2.2 | | | 3.2 | | 2.3 | 2.1 | 2.1 |
| .5 | .4 | .3 | | | .3 | | .3 | .2 | .4 |
| (123) .9 | (136) .7 | (142) .7 | % Depr., Dep., Amort./Sales | | (17) .8 | (29) .7 | (85) .7 | | |
| 1.6 | 1.3 | 1.3 | | | 1.1 | | 1.1 | 1.5 | 1.2 |
| .8 | .7 | .7 | | | 1.4 | | .7 | .6 | |
| (52) 1.4 | (57) 1.6 | (63) 1.4 | % Officers', Directors' Owners' Comp/Sales | | (15) 2.3 | (18) 1.2 | (21) .9 | | |
| 3.2 | 3.0 | 2.7 | | | 2.7 | | 1.8 | 1.6 | |
| 10654643M | 14164374M | 15061456M | Net Sales ($) | 829M | 24310M | 13485M | 176592M | 521426M | 14324814M |
| 4191399M | 5193459M | 5382219M | Total Assets ($) | 234M | 6897M | 13352M | 59353M | 216528M | 5085855M |

© RMA 2012

M = $ thousand    MM = $ million
See Pages 9 through 22 for Explanation of Ratios and Data

## Current Data Sorted by Assets

## Comparative Historical Data

| 0-500M | 500M-2MM | 2-10MM | 10-50MM | 50-100MM | 100-250MM | Type of Statement | 4/1/07-3/31/08 ALL | 4/1/08-3/31/09 ALL |
|---|---|---|---|---|---|---|---|---|
| | | 1 | 1 | 1 | 1 | Unqualified | 4 | 5 |
| | 2 | 5 | 4 | | | Reviewed | 14 | 13 |
| | 8 | 8 | 1 | | | Compiled | 14 | 21 |
| 4 | 5 | 2 | 1 | | | Tax Returns | 10 | 11 |
| 1 | | 7 | | | | Other | 11 | 7 |
| | 15 (4/1-9/30/11) | | 37 (10/1/11-3/31/12) | | | | | |
| 5* | 15 | 23 | 7 | 1 | 1 | NUMBER OF STATEMENTS | 53 | 57 |
| % | % | % | % | % | % | ASSETS | % | % |
| | 15.1 | 9.2 | | | | Cash & Equivalents | 4.8 | 6.9 |
| | 17.1 | 19.1 | | | | Trade Receivables (net) | 17.5 | 20.5 |
| | 41.7 | 40.7 | | | | Inventory | 45.4 | 45.2 |
| | .3 | .6 | | | | All Other Current | 3.3 | 2.6 |
| | 74.2 | 69.6 | | | | Total Current | 71.0 | 75.1 |
| | 12.2 | 19.9 | | | | Fixed Assets (net) | 19.0 | 16.5 |
| | 8.2 | 8.1 | | | | Intangibles (net) | 2.8 | 1.8 |
| | 5.4 | 2.4 | | | | All Other Non-Current | 7.1 | 6.5 |
| | 100.0 | 100.0 | | | | Total | 100.0 | 100.0 |
| | | | | | | LIABILITIES | | |
| | 9.7 | 9.8 | | | | Notes Payable-Short Term | 15.7 | 14.6 |
| | 1.5 | 3.3 | | | | Cur. Mat.-L.T.D. | 3.7 | 3.7 |
| | 12.3 | 14.4 | | | | Trade Payables | 10.6 | 14.9 |
| | .6 | .5 | | | | Income Taxes Payable | .0 | .3 |
| | 4.4 | 7.5 | | | | All Other Current | 13.4 | 13.1 |
| | 28.4 | 35.6 | | | | Total Current | 43.5 | 46.5 |
| | 5.1 | 10.9 | | | | Long-Term Debt | 12.1 | 11.2 |
| | .2 | .3 | | | | Deferred Taxes | .2 | .3 |
| | 4.3 | 4.9 | | | | All Other Non-Current | 3.8 | 4.1 |
| | 62.0 | 48.3 | | | | Net Worth | 40.4 | 38.0 |
| | 100.0 | 100.0 | | | | Total Liabilities & Net Worth | 100.0 | 100.0 |
| | | | | | | INCOME DATA | | |
| | 100.0 | 100.0 | | | | Net Sales | 100.0 | 100.0 |
| | 37.7 | 33.1 | | | | Gross Profit | 34.3 | 31.3 |
| | 33.3 | 28.6 | | | | Operating Expenses | 29.3 | 27.7 |
| | 4.5 | 4.5 | | | | Operating Profit | 5.0 | 3.6 |
| | .5 | .5 | | | | All Other Expenses (net) | 1.0 | .7 |
| | 3.9 | 4.0 | | | | Profit Before Taxes | 4.0 | 2.9 |
| | | | | | | RATIOS | | |
| | 22.2 | 4.5 | | | | | 2.7 | 2.7 |
| | 3.0 | 2.2 | | | | Current | 1.7 | 1.7 |
| | 1.7 | 1.4 | | | | | 1.3 | 1.2 |
| | 11.4 | 2.7 | | | | | .8 | 1.4 |
| | 1.2 | .7 | | | | Quick | .5 | .6 |
| | .5 | .4 | | | | | .3 | .3 |
| | 4   96.0 | 5   76.8 | | | | | 9   41.6 | 10   38.0 |
| | 22   16.7 | 19   18.8 | | | | Sales/Receivables | 23   16.0 | 25   14.5 |
| | 29   12.4 | 36   10.2 | | | | | 36   10.1 | 38   9.6 |
| | 38   9.7 | 54   6.7 | | | | | 54   6.8 | 51   7.1 |
| | 72   5.1 | 85   4.3 | | | | Cost of Sales/Inventory | 97   3.8 | 81   4.5 |
| | 107   3.4 | 111   3.3 | | | | | 200   1.8 | 131   2.8 |
| | 2   187.1 | 5   71.9 | | | | | 7   54.1 | 7   51.2 |
| | 11   34.6 | 21   17.6 | | | | Cost of Sales/Payables | 17   21.0 | 18   20.2 |
| | 28   12.9 | 43   8.4 | | | | | 42   8.8 | 47   7.8 |
| | 3.9 | 5.5 | | | | | 3.9 | 5.0 |
| | 7.8 | 7.7 | | | | Sales/Working Capital | 8.1 | 10.1 |
| | 13.2 | 16.1 | | | | | 20.3 | 24.9 |
| | 114.3 | 64.6 | | | | | 8.0 | 9.1 |
| | (12) 7.9 | (19) 20.7 | | | | EBIT/Interest | (45) 3.6 | (50) 3.9 |
| | 2.6 | 8.6 | | | | | 1.5 | 1.7 |
| | | | | | | Net Profit + Depr., Dep., Amort./Cur. Mat. L/T/D | 2.6 | 4.1 |
| | | | | | | | (12) 1.6 | (13) 1.3 |
| | | | | | | | .6 | .1 |
| | .1 | .1 | | | | | .1 | .1 |
| | .2 | .4 | | | | Fixed/Worth | .3 | .3 |
| | .4 | 1.0 | | | | | .8 | .9 |
| | .1 | .5 | | | | | .6 | .6 |
| | .8 | 1.0 | | | | Debt/Worth | 1.7 | 1.8 |
| | 1.6 | 5.6 | | | | | 2.6 | 3.7 |
| | 36.1 | 61.3 | | | | | 38.2 | 35.7 |
| | 21.0 | (21) 33.1 | | | | % Profit Before Taxes/Tangible Net Worth | (52) 14.1 | (52) 16.3 |
| | 5.2 | 17.8 | | | | | 4.4 | 5.8 |
| | 25.3 | 21.3 | | | | | 13.2 | 14.1 |
| | 8.6 | 13.8 | | | | % Profit Before Taxes/Total Assets | 6.2 | 5.1 |
| | 2.9 | 5.2 | | | | | 1.4 | 1.4 |
| | 148.6 | 137.0 | | | | | 55.5 | 86.5 |
| | 46.4 | 19.6 | | | | Sales/Net Fixed Assets | 29.1 | 30.3 |
| | 17.2 | 11.4 | | | | | 6.6 | 10.0 |
| | 4.3 | 3.8 | | | | | 3.5 | 3.9 |
| | 3.6 | 3.0 | | | | Sales/Total Assets | 2.3 | 2.8 |
| | 2.5 | 2.5 | | | | | 1.5 | 1.6 |
| | .4 | .3 | | | | | .7 | .3 |
| | (11) 1.1 | (18) 1.0 | | | | % Depr., Dep., Amort./Sales | (45) 1.1 | (49) 1.0 |
| | 1.4 | 2.3 | | | | | 2.2 | 2.1 |
| | 1.9 | | | | | | 2.7 | 2.4 |
| | (11) 5.8 | | | | | % Officers', Directors' Owners' Comp/Sales | (19) 4.9 | (27) 4.2 |
| | 7.7 | | | | | | 11.0 | 7.9 |
| 7224M | 63314M | 281334M | 381743M | 344927M | 352436M | Net Sales ($) | 1087990M | 1655383M |
| 1933M | 17363M | 98550M | 149046M | 86236M | 172717M | Total Assets ($) | 487047M | 638739M |

© RMA 2012

M = $ thousand    MM = $ million
See Pages 9 through 22 for Explanation of Ratios and Data

## Comparative Historical Data      Current Data Sorted by Sales

### Type of Statement

| Type of Statement | 4/1/09-3/31/10 ALL | 4/1/10-3/31/11 ALL | 4/1/11-3/31/12 ALL | 0-1MM | 1-3MM | 3-5MM | 5-10MM | 10-25MM | 25MM & OVER |
|---|---|---|---|---|---|---|---|---|---|
| Unqualified | 7 | 6 | 4 | | | | | 1 | 3 |
| Reviewed | 15 | 9 | 9 | | | | 1 | 4 | 4 |
| Compiled | 12 | 10 | 11 | | | 1 | | 5 | 1 |
| Tax Returns | 12 | 14 | 14 | 1 | 4 | 5 | 4 | | |
| Other | 14 | 9 | 14 | 1 | 4 | 1 | 5 | 2 | 1 |
| | | | | 15 (4/1-9/30/11) | | | 37 (10/1/11-3/31/12) | | |
| **NUMBER OF STATEMENTS** | 60 | 48 | 52 | 2 | 9 | 7 | 13 | 12 | 9 |

### ASSETS (%)

| | 4/1/09-3/31/10 ALL | 4/1/10-3/31/11 ALL | 4/1/11-3/31/12 ALL | 0-1MM | 1-3MM | 3-5MM | 5-10MM | 10-25MM | 25MM & OVER |
|---|---|---|---|---|---|---|---|---|---|
| Cash & Equivalents | 7.2 | 6.5 | 9.9 | | | | 11.8 | 7.6 | |
| Trade Receivables (net) | 21.9 | 20.0 | 19.3 | | | | 7.9 | 25.7 | |
| Inventory | 46.6 | 44.3 | 43.9 | | | | 34.7 | 49.5 | |
| All Other Current | 3.2 | 2.1 | .6 | | | | .2 | 1.0 | |
| Total Current | 78.9 | 72.9 | 73.7 | | | | 54.6 | 83.8 | |
| Fixed Assets (net) | 13.4 | 15.4 | 14.7 | | | | 28.4 | 10.5 | |
| Intangibles (net) | 2.9 | 4.4 | 7.3 | | | | 11.9 | 1.5 | |
| All Other Non-Current | 4.8 | 7.4 | 4.4 | | | | 5.1 | 4.2 | |
| Total | 100.0 | 100.0 | 100.0 | | | | 100.0 | 100.0 | |

### LIABILITIES

| | 4/1/09-3/31/10 ALL | 4/1/10-3/31/11 ALL | 4/1/11-3/31/12 ALL | 0-1MM | 1-3MM | 3-5MM | 5-10MM | 10-25MM | 25MM & OVER |
|---|---|---|---|---|---|---|---|---|---|
| Notes Payable-Short Term | 15.5 | 13.1 | 13.4 | | | | 4.6 | 14.1 | |
| Cur. Mat.-L.T.D. | 3.6 | 4.8 | 2.2 | | | | 4.7 | 1.7 | |
| Trade Payables | 16.0 | 19.4 | 14.6 | | | | 6.1 | 21.8 | |
| Income Taxes Payable | .1 | .4 | .4 | | | | .1 | .9 | |
| All Other Current | 9.2 | 5.4 | 5.7 | | | | 3.8 | 2.9 | |
| Total Current | 44.5 | 43.1 | 36.3 | | | | 19.2 | 41.3 | |
| Long-Term Debt | 7.9 | 11.6 | 10.2 | | | | 13.1 | 8.4 | |
| Deferred Taxes | .2 | .2 | .2 | | | | .2 | .5 | |
| All Other Non-Current | 8.7 | 3.1 | 4.8 | | | | 3.5 | 3.1 | |
| Net Worth | 38.6 | 42.0 | 48.4 | | | | 64.0 | 46.7 | |
| Total Liabilities & Net Worth | 100.0 | 100.0 | 100.0 | | | | 100.0 | 100.0 | |

### INCOME DATA

| | 4/1/09-3/31/10 ALL | 4/1/10-3/31/11 ALL | 4/1/11-3/31/12 ALL | 0-1MM | 1-3MM | 3-5MM | 5-10MM | 10-25MM | 25MM & OVER |
|---|---|---|---|---|---|---|---|---|---|
| Net Sales | 100.0 | 100.0 | 100.0 | | | | 100.0 | 100.0 | |
| Gross Profit | 35.3 | 33.3 | 34.5 | | | | 36.5 | 32.2 | |
| Operating Expenses | 32.7 | 30.1 | 30.2 | | | | 31.3 | 27.2 | |
| Operating Profit | 2.6 | 3.3 | 4.3 | | | | 5.2 | 5.1 | |
| All Other Expenses (net) | .7 | .0 | .5 | | | | .9 | .0 | |
| Profit Before Taxes | 1.9 | 3.3 | 3.8 | | | | 4.3 | 5.1 | |

### RATIOS

| | 4/1/09-3/31/10 ALL | 4/1/10-3/31/11 ALL | 4/1/11-3/31/12 ALL | 0-1MM | 1-3MM | 3-5MM | 5-10MM | 10-25MM | 25MM & OVER |
|---|---|---|---|---|---|---|---|---|---|
| Current | 2.7 | 3.1 | 4.4 | | | | 4.5 | 4.6 | |
| | 1.6 | 1.7 | 2.2 | | | | 3.1 | 2.4 | |
| | 1.3 | 1.4 | 1.5 | | | | 2.1 | 1.3 | |
| Quick | 1.2 | 1.3 | 2.0 | | | | 2.2 | 3.1 | |
| | .6 | .6 | .8 | | | | .7 | .9 | |
| | .3 | .4 | .4 | | | | .5 | .4 | |
| Sales/Receivables | 14   25.7 | 8   48.4 | 6   64.1 | | | | 0   UND | 9   42.7 | |
| | 30   12.1 | 24   14.9 | 22   16.5 | | | | 2   149.1 | 34   10.8 | |
| | 40   9.0 | 40   9.1 | 33   11.2 | | | | 17   22.0 | 52   7.0 | |
| Cost of Sales/Inventory | 56   6.5 | 34   10.6 | 50   7.3 | | | | 19   19.3 | 57   6.4 | |
| | 102   3.6 | 91   4.0 | 85   4.3 | | | | 65   5.6 | 87   4.2 | |
| | 164   2.2 | 137   2.7 | 122   3.0 | | | | 91   4.0 | 107   3.4 | |
| Cost of Sales/Payables | 7   50.2 | 9   41.4 | 4   102.1 | | | | 1   260.6 | 10   35.2 | |
| | 25   14.5 | 23   15.7 | 20   18.3 | | | | 8   46.4 | 36   10.0 | |
| | 61   6.0 | 50   7.2 | 42   8.7 | | | | 23   15.9 | 65   5.6 | |
| Sales/Working Capital | 3.9 | 4.4 | 4.8 | | | | 7.4 | 5.3 | |
| | 7.2 | 9.0 | 7.8 | | | | 7.8 | 8.9 | |
| | 15.3 | 18.1 | 15.8 | | | | 16.6 | 15.2 | |
| EBIT/Interest | 13.8 | 23.9 | 42.6 | | | | 77.5 | | |
| | (53) 3.7 | (45) 7.2 | (45) 9.1 | | | | (11) 14.1 | | |
| | 2.3 | 2.4 | 4.0 | | | | 8.6 | | |
| Net Profit + Depr., Dep., Amort./Cur. Mat. L/T/D | 7.1 | 11.4 | 11.4 | | | | | | |
| | (18) 2.3 | (13) 3.6 | (10) 4.3 | | | | | | |
| | 1.1 | 1.4 | 1.9 | | | | | | |
| Fixed/Worth | .1 | .1 | .1 | | | | .3 | .0 | |
| | .2 | .2 | .3 | | | | .5 | .2 | |
| | .8 | .5 | .5 | | | | .9 | .5 | |
| Debt/Worth | .8 | .6 | .4 | | | | .2 | .4 | |
| | 2.0 | 1.1 | 1.2 | | | | .6 | 1.0 | |
| | 3.2 | 2.5 | 2.6 | | | | 2.8 | 5.7 | |
| % Profit Before Taxes/Tangible Net Worth | 24.9 | 43.2 | 52.1 | | | | 56.6 | 54.5 | |
| | (53) 13.4 | (45) 21.9 | (48) 26.7 | | | | 27.3 | (11) 33.4 | |
| | 5.3 | 8.3 | 12.7 | | | | 8.7 | 18.6 | |
| % Profit Before Taxes/Total Assets | 11.2 | 14.4 | 20.9 | | | | 21.9 | 25.2 | |
| | 4.7 | 9.0 | 11.5 | | | | 11.1 | 15.6 | |
| | 1.9 | 3.3 | 3.3 | | | | 3.4 | 6.7 | |
| Sales/Net Fixed Assets | 93.2 | 138.6 | 125.8 | | | | 26.4 | 265.5 | |
| | 34.7 | 37.1 | 28.7 | | | | 13.8 | 36.0 | |
| | 11.1 | 11.4 | 14.5 | | | | 10.4 | 16.7 | |
| Sales/Total Assets | 3.4 | 3.8 | 4.1 | | | | 4.0 | 4.0 | |
| | 2.5 | 2.7 | 3.2 | | | | 3.6 | 2.8 | |
| | 1.8 | 1.8 | 2.2 | | | | 3.3 | 2.5 | |
| % Depr., Dep., Amort./Sales | .4 | .5 | .4 | | | | .5 | | |
| | (51) .9 | (38) .9 | (42) .9 | | | | (12) 1.7 | | |
| | 2.1 | 1.9 | 1.4 | | | | 3.6 | | |
| % Officers', Directors' Owners' Comp/Sales | 1.7 | 1.9 | 1.7 | | | | | | |
| | (28) 5.4 | (21) 5.0 | (27) 4.5 | | | | | | |
| | 9.0 | 10.0 | 7.8 | | | | | | |
| Net Sales ($) | 1684532M | 1541179M | 1430978M | 1122M | 16891M | 28660M | 106820M | 198379M | 1079106M |
| Total Assets ($) | 728861M | 586463M | 525845M | 803M | 8050M | 9156M | 33138M | 66699M | 407999M |

M = $ thousand    MM = $ million
See Pages 9 through 22 for Explanation of Ratios and Data

## Current Data Sorted by Assets     Comparative Historical Data

| | | | | | | Type of Statement | | |
|---|---|---|---|---|---|---|---|---|
| | 2 | 7 | 15 | 2 | 2 | Unqualified | 38 | 33 |
| 1 | 10 | 48 | 20 | | | Reviewed | 59 | 71 |
| 5 | 14 | 17 | 1 | | | Compiled | 37 | 43 |
| 11 | 27 | 25 | | | | Tax Returns | 28 | 32 |
| 2 | 24 | 53 | 33 | 3 | 2 | Other | 82 | 106 |
| | 46 (4/1-9/30/11) | | 278 (10/1/11-3/31/12) | | | | 4/1/07-3/31/08 ALL | 4/1/08-3/31/09 ALL |
| 0-500M | 500M-2MM | 2-10MM | 10-50MM | 50-100MM | 100-250MM | | | |
| 19 | 77 | 150 | 69 | 5 | 4 | NUMBER OF STATEMENTS | 244 | 285 |
| % | % | % | % | % | % | **ASSETS** | % | % |
| 17.6 | 13.4 | 8.3 | 5.0 | | | Cash & Equivalents | 8.1 | 7.6 |
| 21.0 | 28.9 | 39.2 | 41.4 | | | Trade Receivables (net) | 40.4 | 36.7 |
| 43.7 | 37.4 | 30.9 | 28.1 | | | Inventory | 29.3 | 31.1 |
| 3.2 | 2.9 | 3.8 | 4.4 | | | All Other Current | 3.7 | 4.6 |
| 85.5 | 82.6 | 82.2 | 78.9 | | | Total Current | 81.5 | 80.0 |
| 11.5 | 9.0 | 10.1 | 6.9 | | | Fixed Assets (net) | 10.2 | 11.1 |
| .0 | 1.3 | 2.0 | 7.4 | | | Intangibles (net) | 2.8 | 3.6 |
| 3.5 | 7.1 | 5.7 | 6.8 | | | All Other Non-Current | 5.4 | 5.3 |
| 100.0 | 100.0 | 100.0 | 100.0 | | | Total | 100.0 | 100.0 |
| | | | | | | **LIABILITIES** | | |
| 22.9 | 12.4 | 14.5 | 16.0 | | | Notes Payable-Short Term | 19.1 | 17.0 |
| .5 | 1.9 | 1.0 | 1.2 | | | Cur. Mat.-L.T.D. | 2.1 | 1.6 |
| 26.5 | 20.2 | 19.7 | 21.6 | | | Trade Payables | 19.2 | 19.8 |
| .0 | .0 | .2 | .2 | | | Income Taxes Payable | .2 | .2 |
| 9.2 | 13.2 | 15.8 | 17.2 | | | All Other Current | 14.8 | 15.4 |
| 59.2 | 47.7 | 51.2 | 56.2 | | | Total Current | 55.4 | 54.1 |
| .6 | 8.6 | 5.0 | 8.7 | | | Long-Term Debt | 5.6 | 6.0 |
| .0 | .0 | .1 | .1 | | | Deferred Taxes | .1 | .1 |
| 21.3 | 7.1 | 4.8 | 4.5 | | | All Other Non-Current | 5.2 | 5.4 |
| 18.8 | 36.5 | 38.8 | 30.5 | | | Net Worth | 33.7 | 34.5 |
| 100.0 | 100.0 | 100.0 | 100.0 | | | Total Liabilities & Net Worth | 100.0 | 100.0 |
| | | | | | | **INCOME DATA** | | |
| 100.0 | 100.0 | 100.0 | 100.0 | | | Net Sales | 100.0 | 100.0 |
| 40.6 | 29.5 | 26.5 | 26.6 | | | Gross Profit | 28.4 | 28.6 |
| 35.2 | 26.2 | 23.5 | 23.9 | | | Operating Expenses | 25.2 | 26.3 |
| 5.4 | 3.4 | 3.0 | 2.7 | | | Operating Profit | 3.2 | 2.3 |
| .7 | .4 | .3 | .4 | | | All Other Expenses (net) | .6 | .3 |
| 4.7 | 2.9 | 2.7 | 2.3 | | | Profit Before Taxes | 2.5 | 2.0 |
| | | | | | | **RATIOS** | | |
| 2.4 | 3.7 | 2.4 | 1.9 | | | Current | 2.2 | 2.2 |
| 1.7 | 1.9 | 1.5 | 1.4 | | | | 1.5 | 1.5 |
| .9 | 1.2 | 1.2 | 1.1 | | | | 1.1 | 1.2 |
| 1.8 | 1.9 | 1.4 | 1.2 | | | Quick | 1.3 | 1.3 |
| .6 | .9 | 1.0 | .9 | | | | .9 | .8 |
| .4 | .5 | .6 | .5 | | | | .6 | .5 |
| 0 UND | 10 36.5 | 29 12.8 | 35 10.3 | | | Sales/Receivables | 23 15.5 | 23 15.8 |
| 4 87.2 | 26 13.8 | 39 9.3 | 49 7.5 | | | | 40 9.1 | 35 10.6 |
| 21 17.5 | 38 9.6 | 54 6.8 | 62 5.9 | | | | 57 6.4 | 51 7.2 |
| 3 124.0 | 19 19.4 | 11 34.0 | 17 21.6 | | | Cost of Sales/Inventory | 11 34.7 | 11 32.6 |
| 22 16.7 | 53 6.9 | 37 9.9 | 33 11.0 | | | | 33 11.1 | 35 10.5 |
| 122 3.0 | 101 3.6 | 118 3.1 | 91 4.0 | | | | 90 4.1 | 92 4.0 |
| 0 UND | 8 46.7 | 14 26.4 | 17 21.0 | | | Cost of Sales/Payables | 12 29.4 | 12 31.3 |
| 10 35.9 | 21 17.5 | 21 17.3 | 26 14.2 | | | | 24 15.2 | 21 17.3 |
| 41 9.0 | 41 8.9 | 40 9.2 | 43 8.5 | | | | 37 10.0 | 37 9.8 |
| 7.2 | 6.8 | 6.3 | 8.1 | | | Sales/Working Capital | 7.4 | 7.9 |
| 20.9 | 10.1 | 11.5 | 14.9 | | | | 14.4 | 14.2 |
| -103.1 | 32.1 | 32.1 | 45.3 | | | | 32.3 | 34.7 |
| 26.3 | 36.0 | 16.4 | 16.0 | | | EBIT/Interest | 8.1 | 11.5 |
| (16) 3.8 | (61) 4.0 | (123) 5.1 | (63) 4.9 | | | | (220) 3.7 | (261) 3.9 |
| 1.4 | .5 | 2.2 | 2.2 | | | | 1.4 | 1.1 |
| | | 18.5 | 11.2 | | | Net Profit + Depr., Dep., Amort./Cur. Mat. L/T/D | 13.4 | 8.4 |
| | | (24) 6.7 | (14) 2.7 | | | | (42) 4.0 | (38) 4.1 |
| | | 1.7 | 1.5 | | | | 1.1 | 2.2 |
| .1 | .0 | .1 | .1 | | | Fixed/Worth | .1 | .1 |
| .1 | .1 | .2 | .3 | | | | .2 | .3 |
| .9 | .6 | .5 | .9 | | | | .7 | .7 |
| .8 | .5 | .7 | 1.3 | | | Debt/Worth | .9 | .9 |
| 1.5 | 1.5 | 1.8 | 3.8 | | | | 2.3 | 2.2 |
| -7.4 | 9.4 | 4.0 | 14.1 | | | | 5.9 | 5.1 |
| 165.8 | 59.5 | 44.4 | 57.4 | | | % Profit Before Taxes/Tangible Net Worth | 49.2 | 42.3 |
| (13) 37.5 | (67) 19.3 | (141) 17.2 | (60) 29.9 | | | | (217) 23.5 | (263) 19.1 |
| 12.1 | 3.5 | 6.6 | 5.5 | | | | 5.4 | 2.9 |
| 30.0 | 17.5 | 14.7 | 11.8 | | | % Profit Before Taxes/Total Assets | 14.3 | 13.8 |
| 5.5 | 8.7 | 6.0 | 6.8 | | | | 6.6 | 5.9 |
| 1.4 | .2 | 1.6 | 1.7 | | | | 1.3 | .5 |
| 900.0 | 408.2 | 172.6 | 130.2 | | | Sales/Net Fixed Assets | 118.9 | 105.9 |
| 132.6 | 101.0 | 62.8 | 64.3 | | | | 56.1 | 52.5 |
| 57.3 | 30.1 | 25.7 | 34.1 | | | | 26.4 | 24.9 |
| 10.8 | 5.5 | 4.6 | 3.9 | | | Sales/Total Assets | 4.5 | 4.8 |
| 7.0 | 4.1 | 3.2 | 3.1 | | | | 3.4 | 3.4 |
| 2.7 | 2.7 | 2.2 | 2.0 | | | | 2.5 | 2.4 |
| | .2 | .3 | .2 | | | % Depr., Dep., Amort./Sales | .3 | .3 |
| | (51) .4 | (109) .4 | (63) .4 | | | | (211) .5 | (231) .5 |
| | .8 | .8 | .8 | | | | .9 | 1.0 |
| 3.0 | 1.6 | 1.0 | .8 | | | % Officers', Directors', Owners' Comp/Sales | 1.4 | 1.1 |
| (10) 4.2 | (45) 2.7 | (56) 2.4 | (14) 2.2 | | | | (92) 3.1 | (98) 2.6 |
| 10.4 | 5.6 | 4.1 | 4.9 | | | | 5.4 | 4.8 |
| 37045M | 405976M | 2561004M | 4505593M | 845871M | 1142840M | Net Sales ($) | 8736602M | 8791888M |
| 4660M | 94765M | 761712M | 1446523M | 293164M | 604030M | Total Assets ($) | 2501692M | 2709360M |

M = $ thousand    MM = $ million
See Pages 9 through 22 for Explanation of Ratios and Data

## Comparative Historical Data  |  Current Data Sorted by Sales

| Type of Statement | 4/1/09-3/31/10 ALL | 4/1/10-3/31/11 ALL | 4/1/11-3/31/12 ALL | 0-1MM | 1-3MM | 3-5MM | 5-10MM | 10-25MM | 25MM & OVER |
|---|---|---|---|---|---|---|---|---|---|
| Unqualified | 33 | 22 | 28 | | 1 | | 1 | 5 | 21 |
| Reviewed | 77 | 88 | 79 | 1 | 1 | 4 | 15 | 28 | 30 |
| Compiled | 29 | 40 | 37 | 3 | 6 | 8 | 5 | 14 | 1 |
| Tax Returns | 41 | 47 | 63 | 7 | 14 | 15 | 15 | 11 | 1 |
| Other | 97 | 121 | 117 | | 8 | 8 | 16 | 38 | 47 |
| | | | | 46 (4/1-9/30/11) | | 278 (10/1/11-3/31/12) | | | |
| **NUMBER OF STATEMENTS** | 277 | 318 | 324 | 11 | 30 | 35 | 52 | 96 | 100 |

| ASSETS | % | % | % | % | % | % | % | % | % |
|---|---|---|---|---|---|---|---|---|---|
| Cash & Equivalents | 10.4 | 9.6 | 9.4 | 15.4 | 11.5 | 13.4 | 12.4 | 8.0 | 6.5 |
| Trade Receivables (net) | 33.5 | 35.2 | 35.9 | 10.9 | 20.9 | 26.4 | 31.5 | 38.2 | 46.6 |
| Inventory | 30.2 | 30.5 | 32.5 | 47.6 | 45.7 | 36.5 | 36.1 | 32.5 | 23.7 |
| All Other Current | 3.6 | 3.7 | 3.8 | .6 | 3.2 | 4.5 | 4.4 | 3.6 | 3.9 |
| Total Current | 77.8 | 79.0 | 81.6 | 74.5 | 81.4 | 80.8 | 84.4 | 82.3 | 80.7 |
| Fixed Assets (net) | 12.2 | 11.6 | 9.4 | 17.8 | 11.3 | 9.0 | 9.6 | 10.0 | 7.4 |
| Intangibles (net) | 3.9 | 3.5 | 2.8 | .3 | .1 | 1.7 | .5 | 3.1 | 5.2 |
| All Other Non-Current | 6.1 | 5.8 | 6.2 | 8.3 | 7.2 | 8.5 | 5.5 | 4.6 | 6.6 |
| Total | 100.0 | 100.0 | 100.0 | 100.0 | 100.0 | 100.0 | 100.0 | 100.0 | 100.0 |

| LIABILITIES | | | | | | | | | |
|---|---|---|---|---|---|---|---|---|---|
| Notes Payable-Short Term | 16.5 | 15.1 | 14.8 | 20.6 | 21.7 | 9.5 | 11.7 | 14.3 | 16.1 |
| Cur. Mat.-L.T.D. | 2.1 | 2.0 | 1.3 | .6 | .6 | .9 | 1.8 | 1.5 | 1.1 |
| Trade Payables | 18.6 | 20.3 | 20.5 | 11.9 | 20.5 | 26.0 | 17.4 | 21.7 | 19.9 |
| Income Taxes Payable | .2 | .3 | .2 | .0 | .1 | .0 | .1 | .1 | .3 |
| All Other Current | 13.0 | 16.1 | 15.0 | 2.8 | 10.6 | 20.1 | 13.5 | 14.7 | 16.9 |
| Total Current | 50.4 | 53.8 | 51.7 | 35.8 | 53.4 | 56.5 | 44.5 | 52.4 | 54.3 |
| Long-Term Debt | 8.3 | 7.1 | 6.6 | 8.1 | 4.0 | 8.8 | 7.7 | 6.7 | 5.9 |
| Deferred Taxes | .2 | .1 | .1 | .0 | .0 | .1 | .0 | .2 | .1 |
| All Other Non-Current | 6.9 | 6.3 | 6.2 | 23.5 | 12.9 | 4.9 | 3.9 | 6.3 | 3.9 |
| Net Worth | 34.2 | 32.7 | 35.4 | 32.7 | 29.6 | 29.6 | 43.9 | 34.5 | 35.9 |
| Total Liabilities & Net Worth | 100.0 | 100.0 | 100.0 | 100.0 | 100.0 | 100.0 | 100.0 | 100.0 | 100.0 |

| INCOME DATA | | | | | | | | | |
|---|---|---|---|---|---|---|---|---|---|
| Net Sales | 100.0 | 100.0 | 100.0 | 100.0 | 100.0 | 100.0 | 100.0 | 100.0 | 100.0 |
| Gross Profit | 29.0 | 29.3 | 28.0 | 48.3 | 38.5 | 30.1 | 27.8 | 25.5 | 24.3 |
| Operating Expenses | 27.9 | 26.7 | 24.9 | 34.8 | 34.4 | 28.3 | 23.9 | 23.1 | 21.8 |
| Operating Profit | 1.1 | 2.6 | 3.1 | 13.4 | 4.1 | 1.7 | 3.9 | 2.4 | 2.5 |
| All Other Expenses (net) | .7 | .4 | .4 | 2.6 | 1.1 | .0 | .2 | .4 | .2 |
| Profit Before Taxes | .4 | 2.2 | 2.7 | 10.8 | 3.0 | 1.7 | 3.7 | 2.0 | 2.3 |

| RATIOS | | | | | | | | | |
|---|---|---|---|---|---|---|---|---|---|
| Current | 2.8 | 2.3 | 2.5 | 42.5 | 2.4 | 3.6 | 3.4 | 2.3 | 2.1 |
| | 1.6 | 1.5 | 1.6 | 5.0 | 1.6 | 1.3 | 2.1 | 1.5 | 1.5 |
| | 1.1 | 1.1 | 1.2 | 2.0 | 1.1 | 1.0 | 1.2 | 1.2 | 1.2 |
| Quick | 1.6 | 1.3 | 1.4 | 6.0 | 1.1 | 1.2 | 1.9 | 1.3 | 1.5 |
| | (276) .9 | .9 | 1.0 | .8 | .5 | .7 | 1.0 | .9 | 1.0 |
| | .5 | .5 | .5 | .2 | .2 | .3 | .6 | .6 | .7 |
| Sales/Receivables | 22  16.6 | 21  17.2 | 21  17.2 | 0  UND | 0  UND | 13  28.4 | 17  21.2 | 26  13.9 | 36  10.0 |
| | 36  10.0 | 39  9.3 | 37  9.9 | 1  246.0 | 27  13.4 | 27  13.4 | 30  12.2 | 37  9.8 | 48  7.6 |
| | 53  6.9 | 58  6.2 | 51  7.1 | 24  15.0 | 43  8.5 | 38  9.6 | 49  7.5 | 49  7.4 | 58  6.3 |
| Cost of Sales/Inventory | 13  28.9 | 13  28.4 | 14  27.0 | 22  16.7 | 38  9.5 | 17  21.4 | 22  16.3 | 12  29.4 | 10  35.8 |
| | 36  10.2 | 36  10.1 | 38  9.7 | 192  1.9 | 94  3.9 | 38  9.7 | 58  6.3 | 38  9.6 | 22  16.7 |
| | 103  3.5 | 108  3.4 | 104  3.5 | 912  .4 | 159  2.3 | 111  3.3 | 114  3.2 | 114  3.2 | 58  6.3 |
| Cost of Sales/Payables | 12  30.7 | 12  29.7 | 12  29.7 | 0  UND | 2  229.2 | 17  21.8 | 11  32.7 | 12  29.5 | 16  23.2 |
| | 22  16.3 | 25  14.3 | 22  16.6 | 5  70.7 | 27  13.6 | 28  13.2 | 18  19.8 | 23  16.0 | 21  17.2 |
| | 41  8.9 | 44  8.2 | 41  9.0 | 41  9.0 | 61  6.0 | 51  7.1 | 39  9.3 | 49  7.4 | 33  11.1 |
| Sales/Working Capital | 5.5 | 6.7 | 6.9 | 1.4 | 4.7 | 7.9 | 5.0 | 6.8 | 8.5 |
| | 11.5 | 12.3 | 12.2 | 3.8 | 10.4 | 17.5 | 8.5 | 14.0 | 13.5 |
| | 43.8 | 41.8 | 34.3 | 7.5 | 198.1 | 117.0 | 28.5 | 34.3 | 31.1 |
| EBIT/Interest | 9.1 | 14.7 | 17.0 | | 12.0 | 23.3 | 32.0 | 15.7 | 20.3 |
| | (245) 2.4 | (265) 3.9 | (272) 4.7 | | (27) 2.1 | (27) 2.7 | (41) 4.9 | (82) 4.5 | (88) 7.2 |
| | -.1 | 1.3 | 1.9 | | -1.3 | .1 | 2.1 | 2.0 | 2.6 |
| Net Profit + Depr., Dep., Amort./Cur. Mat. L/T/D | 6.8 | 9.1 | 10.5 | | | | | 7.9 | 16.1 |
| | (42) 2.5 | (38) 2.6 | (48) 3.7 | | | | | (18) 3.4 | (23) 7.3 |
| | .3 | .2 | 1.4 | | | | | .7 | 1.9 |
| Fixed/Worth | .1 | .1 | .1 | .0 | .1 | .0 | .0 | .1 | .1 |
| | .3 | .3 | .2 | .1 | .2 | .1 | .1 | .2 | .2 |
| | 1.1 | .8 | .6 | .3 | -8.9 | 1.3 | .3 | .8 | .5 |
| Debt/Worth | .8 | .9 | .8 | .1 | .1 | .4 | .5 | .8 | .9 |
| | 2.1 | 1.9 | 2.0 | 1.3 | 1.3 | 3.5 | 1.0 | 2.2 | 2.3 |
| | 7.1 | 7.8 | 6.0 | 16.2 | -52.1 | 22.8 | 4.3 | 4.7 | 6.7 |
| % Profit Before Taxes/Tangible Net Worth | 35.3 | 42.4 | 52.1 | | 29.1 | 63.8 | 52.8 | 45.7 | 56.6 |
| | (238) 10.5 | (283) 16.9 | (289) 19.2 | | (22) 9.1 | (30) 14.2 | (50) 15.8 | (86) 18.9 | (92) 25.6 |
| | -2.7 | 2.7 | 6.0 | | 3.2 | .6 | 3.0 | 8.8 | 9.6 |
| % Profit Before Taxes/Total Assets | 10.0 | 14.4 | 14.9 | 30.0 | 15.8 | 24.6 | 15.5 | 13.9 | 14.0 |
| | 3.2 | 5.2 | 6.0 | 4.7 | 3.1 | 3.2 | 5.8 | 6.2 | 7.2 |
| | -1.8 | .6 | 1.5 | 1.4 | -.3 | -1.6 | 1.5 | 1.3 | 2.4 |
| Sales/Net Fixed Assets | 114.3 | 154.5 | 188.6 | 900.0 | 209.3 | 377.0 | 363.5 | 200.5 | 142.9 |
| | 48.3 | 55.5 | 69.0 | 57.3 | 84.0 | 68.2 | 75.1 | 68.7 | 69.0 |
| | 20.2 | 22.0 | 27.9 | 3.2 | 18.9 | 31.9 | 25.8 | 26.6 | 35.6 |
| Sales/Total Assets | 4.4 | 4.5 | 4.7 | 4.4 | 5.8 | 5.3 | 4.6 | 5.0 | 4.6 |
| | 3.1 | 3.1 | 3.4 | 1.5 | 2.7 | 3.3 | 3.4 | 3.4 | 3.6 |
| | 2.2 | 2.2 | 2.3 | .7 | 2.1 | 2.3 | 2.1 | 2.2 | 2.7 |
| % Depr., Dep., Amort./Sales | .3 | .3 | .2 | .2 | .2 | .2 | .2 | .3 | .3 |
| | (231) .5 | (243) .5 | (240) .4 | | (21) .4 | (20) .4 | (34) .4 | (73) .4 | (87) .4 |
| | 1.1 | .9 | .8 | | .9 | .8 | .8 | .8 | .7 |
| % Officers', Directors' Owners' Comp/Sales | 1.4 | 1.1 | 1.2 | | 3.3 | 1.9 | 1.5 | .9 | .7 |
| | (100) 2.6 | (108) 2.4 | (125) 2.6 | | (18) 5.6 | (18) 2.4 | (32) 2.9 | (35) 1.3 | (18) 1.6 |
| | 5.5 | 4.3 | 4.8 | | 11.2 | 4.8 | 4.8 | 1.8 | 3.0 |
| Net Sales ($) | 6983518M | 7281046M | 9498329M | 5528M | 64810M | 140848M | 396192M | 1508377M | 7382574M |
| Total Assets ($) | 2450873M | 2713631M | 3204854M | 4942M | 28858M | 47740M | 143080M | 526434M | 2453800M |

M = $ thousand    MM = $ million
See Pages 9 through 22 for Explanation of Ratios and Data

## Current Data Sorted by Assets

## Comparative Historical Data

| | | | | | | Type of Statement | | |
|---|---|---|---|---|---|---|---|---|
| 1 | 2 | 5 | 23 | 6 | 5 | Unqualified | 56 | 47 |
| | 4 | 48 | 27 | 2 | | Reviewed | 69 | 84 |
| 4 | 10 | 24 | 3 | | | Compiled | 38 | 39 |
| 7 | 21 | 23 | 3 | | | Tax Returns | 35 | 46 |
| 8 | 23 | 43 | 34 | 11 | 2 | Other | 129 | 121 |
| | 49 (4/1-9/30/11) | | 290 (10/1/11-3/31/12) | | | | 4/1/07-3/31/08 | 4/1/08-3/31/09 |
| 0-500M | 500M-2MM | 2-10MM | 10-50MM | 50-100MM | 100-250MM | | ALL | ALL |
| 20 | 60 | 143 | 90 | 19 | 7 | NUMBER OF STATEMENTS | 327 | 337 |
| % | % | % | % | % | % | ASSETS | % | % |
| 19.3 | 9.0 | 6.5 | 6.3 | 3.5 | | Cash & Equivalents | 8.0 | 8.4 |
| 23.7 | 28.1 | 28.1 | 28.5 | 21.2 | | Trade Receivables (net) | 28.8 | 28.3 |
| 34.6 | 41.6 | 45.9 | 42.4 | 39.0 | | Inventory | 40.3 | 40.9 |
| 2.4 | 3.2 | 1.9 | 3.2 | 3.3 | | All Other Current | 3.0 | 3.9 |
| 80.0 | 82.0 | 82.3 | 80.4 | 67.2 | | Total Current | 80.1 | 81.5 |
| 9.4 | 7.6 | 11.2 | 8.2 | 6.2 | | Fixed Assets (net) | 10.3 | 9.8 |
| 2.6 | 1.1 | 1.8 | 6.2 | 20.1 | | Intangibles (net) | 4.1 | 2.5 |
| 7.9 | 9.3 | 4.6 | 5.3 | 6.5 | | All Other Non-Current | 5.5 | 6.3 |
| 100.0 | 100.0 | 100.0 | 100.0 | 100.0 | | Total | 100.0 | 100.0 |
| | | | | | | LIABILITIES | | |
| 14.3 | 15.2 | 18.2 | 15.0 | 14.2 | | Notes Payable-Short Term | 17.7 | 18.1 |
| .9 | 2.1 | 1.2 | 2.1 | 2.1 | | Cur. Mat.-L.T.D. | 2.5 | 2.8 |
| 13.6 | 22.9 | 18.9 | 16.4 | 15.1 | | Trade Payables | 18.5 | 17.8 |
| .0 | .2 | .2 | .2 | .2 | | Income Taxes Payable | .1 | .2 |
| 9.9 | 10.8 | 7.0 | 9.5 | 7.9 | | All Other Current | 10.0 | 10.2 |
| 38.6 | 51.2 | 45.4 | 43.2 | 39.5 | | Total Current | 48.7 | 49.1 |
| 11.4 | 10.2 | 9.7 | 9.0 | 11.5 | | Long-Term Debt | 9.3 | 6.3 |
| .0 | .0 | .2 | .2 | .5 | | Deferred Taxes | .3 | .1 |
| 15.6 | 6.4 | 5.2 | 4.8 | 9.3 | | All Other Non-Current | 6.3 | 6.3 |
| 34.5 | 32.1 | 39.5 | 42.9 | 39.1 | | Net Worth | 35.6 | 38.2 |
| 100.0 | 100.0 | 100.0 | 100.0 | 100.0 | | Total Liabilties & Net Worth | 100.0 | 100.0 |
| | | | | | | INCOME DATA | | |
| 100.0 | 100.0 | 100.0 | 100.0 | 100.0 | | Net Sales | 100.0 | 100.0 |
| 35.2 | 33.8 | 32.1 | 30.8 | 30.4 | | Gross Profit | 32.8 | 31.4 |
| 29.9 | 30.6 | 29.5 | 25.8 | 23.0 | | Operating Expenses | 28.8 | 28.5 |
| 5.3 | 3.1 | 2.6 | 5.0 | 7.4 | | Operating Profit | 4.1 | 2.8 |
| .5 | .4 | .6 | .8 | 1.2 | | All Other Expenses (net) | 1.3 | .9 |
| 4.8 | 2.7 | 2.0 | 4.2 | 6.2 | | Profit Before Taxes | 2.8 | 2.0 |
| | | | | | | RATIOS | | |
| 7.1 | 3.0 | 3.0 | 3.0 | 3.0 | | | 2.8 | 2.7 |
| 2.4 | 1.7 | 1.8 | 1.8 | 1.6 | | Current | 1.6 | 1.7 |
| 1.2 | 1.2 | 1.3 | 1.3 | 1.2 | | | 1.2 | 1.3 |
| 6.0 | 1.6 | 1.2 | 1.5 | 1.3 | | | 1.2 | 1.3 |
| 1.2 | .6 | .8 | .8 | .6 | | Quick | .7 | .7 |
| .5 | .4 | .4 | .5 | .4 | | | .5 | .5 |

| | | | | | | | | | | | | | | |
|---|---|---|---|---|---|---|---|---|---|---|---|---|---|---|
| 2 | 183.9 | 15 | 24.7 | 25 | 14.8 | 28 | 13.2 | 34 | 10.8 | | | 27 | 13.8 | 26 | 14.1 |

Continuing ratios (Sales/Receivables, etc.):

| 0-500M | 500M-2MM | 2-10MM | 10-50MM | 50-100MM | 100-250MM | Ratio | ALL 4/1/07-3/31/08 | ALL 4/1/08-3/31/09 |
|---|---|---|---|---|---|---|---|---|
| 2 / 183.9 | 15 / 24.7 | 25 / 14.8 | 28 / 13.2 | 34 / 10.8 | | Sales/Receivables | 27 / 13.8 | 26 / 14.1 |
| 22 / 16.5 | 30 / 12.3 | 39 / 9.4 | 43 / 8.4 | 41 / 8.9 | | | 40 / 9.2 | 37 / 9.9 |
| 52 / 7.0 | 58 / 6.3 | 56 / 6.5 | 60 / 6.1 | 51 / 7.2 | | | 60 / 6.1 | 55 / 6.7 |
| 6 / 66.0 | 36 / 10.0 | 53 / 6.9 | 62 / 5.9 | 89 / 4.1 | | Cost of Sales/Inventory | 51 / 7.1 | 44 / 8.3 |
| 43 / 8.4 | 79 / 4.6 | 96 / 3.8 | 99 / 3.7 | 104 / 3.5 | | | 85 / 4.3 | 87 / 4.2 |
| 166 / 2.2 | 152 / 2.4 | 182 / 2.0 | 152 / 2.4 | 174 / 2.1 | | | 142 / 2.6 | 142 / 2.6 |
| 4 / 94.5 | 9 / 42.6 | 13 / 27.3 | 15 / 24.5 | 17 / 22.0 | | Cost of Sales/Payables | 16 / 22.7 | 13 / 28.2 |
| 14 / 25.9 | 28 / 13.2 | 28 / 13.0 | 36 / 10.2 | 35 / 10.5 | | | 28 / 12.9 | 26 / 14.2 |
| 33 / 11.0 | 63 / 5.8 | 55 / 6.6 | 57 / 6.4 | 60 / 6.1 | | | 52 / 7.0 | 47 / 7.8 |
| 4.4 | 4.5 | 3.6 | 4.3 | 3.5 | | Sales/Working Capital | 4.6 | 4.6 |
| 8.8 | 8.5 | 6.7 | 6.8 | 8.4 | | | 8.5 | 8.1 |
| 28.4 | 43.0 | 15.8 | 13.2 | 17.1 | | | 20.3 | 18.3 |
| 43.9 | 8.0 | 9.4 | 13.6 | 15.7 | | EBIT/Interest | 6.0 | 6.2 |
| (13) 3.0 | (48) 3.1 | (130) 3.2 | (82) 3.6 | (18) 5.9 | | | (286) 2.9 | (293) 2.3 |
| -4.3 | 1.5 | 1.5 | 2.0 | 2.0 | | | 1.3 | .3 |
| | | 17.2 | 11.0 | | | Net Profit + Depr., Dep., Amort./Cur. Mat. L/T/D | 8.7 | 6.3 |
| | (22) 6.5 | (22) 5.5 | | | | (64) 3.1 | (58) 1.6 |
| | 2.0 | 1.8 | | | | 1.4 | -.1 |
| .0 | .0 | .1 | .1 | .2 | | Fixed/Worth | .1 | .1 |
| .1 | .2 | .2 | .1 | .4 | | | .2 | .2 |
| .6 | .6 | .6 | .5 | -.4 | | | .7 | .5 |
| .3 | .8 | .6 | .6 | 1.1 | | Debt/Worth | .8 | .8 |
| .9 | 2.1 | 1.7 | 2.0 | 5.7 | | | 2.0 | 1.8 |
| NM | 7.1 | 4.8 | 5.0 | -22.6 | | | 4.2 | 4.6 |
| 95.5 | 55.4 | 33.9 | 38.1 | 93.4 | | % Profit Before Taxes/Tangible Net Worth | 37.0 | 31.6 |
| (15) 64.8 | (53) 16.4 | (133) 15.8 | (80) 17.1 | (13) 16.6 | | | (289) 16.2 | (307) 11.1 |
| 12.5 | 2.7 | 4.3 | 3.8 | 11.7 | | | 4.2 | .0 |
| 43.2 | 12.7 | 9.3 | 14.5 | 11.4 | | % Profit Before Taxes/Total Assets | 12.7 | 11.1 |
| 9.8 | 4.9 | 4.2 | 4.8 | 7.8 | | | 4.9 | 2.8 |
| -1.5 | .9 | .8 | .9 | 4.7 | | | .9 | -1.9 |
| UND | 243.2 | 112.4 | 121.6 | 108.5 | | Sales/Net Fixed Assets | 111.4 | 121.8 |
| 104.6 | 75.2 | 46.9 | 57.1 | 37.6 | | | 44.3 | 47.4 |
| 22.8 | 26.3 | 19.4 | 24.0 | 24.5 | | | 20.0 | 20.0 |
| 4.3 | 3.8 | 3.4 | 2.8 | 2.3 | | Sales/Total Assets | 3.5 | 3.5 |
| 3.1 | 2.8 | 2.3 | 2.2 | 1.7 | | | 2.5 | 2.5 |
| 1.7 | 1.9 | 1.7 | 1.6 | 1.3 | | | 1.8 | 1.8 |
| .3 | .2 | .3 | .3 | .5 | | % Depr., Dep., Amort./Sales | .3 | .3 |
| (10) .9 | (35) .4 | (120) .5 | (75) .5 | (14) .9 | | | (271) .6 | (263) .6 |
| 1.1 | .8 | 1.0 | .9 | 1.6 | | | 1.1 | 1.2 |
| | 1.8 | 1.0 | .6 | | | % Officers', Directors' Owners' Comp/Sales | 1.6 | 1.1 |
| | (32) 3.1 | (72) 1.9 | (28) 1.6 | | | (121) 2.9 | (138) 2.4 |
| | 5.9 | 4.1 | 4.3 | | | | 6.8 | 5.5 |
| 22684M | 213757M | 1771551M | 4403696M | 2542803M | 1248225M | Net Sales ($) | 12231275M | 13416415M |
| 5821M | 68148M | 704218M | 1893872M | 1365680M | 1099918M | Total Assets ($) | 5411266M | 5697910M |

M = $ thousand    MM = $ million
See Pages 9 through 22 for Explanation of Ratios and Data

## Comparative Historical Data | Current Data Sorted by Sales

| | 4/1/09-3/31/10 ALL | 4/1/10-3/31/11 ALL | 4/1/11-3/31/12 ALL | Type of Statement | 0-1MM | 1-3MM | 3-5MM | 5-10MM | 10-25MM | 25MM & OVER |
|---|---|---|---|---|---|---|---|---|---|---|
| | | | | | | 49 (4/1-9/30/11) | | 290 (10/1/11-3/31/12) | | |
| | 36 | 46 | 42 | Unqualified | 1 | 2 | 1 | 1 | 8 | 29 |
| | 79 | 91 | 81 | Reviewed | 2 | 1 | 4 | 14 | 36 | 26 |
| | 41 | 37 | 41 | Compiled | | 6 | 10 | 7 | 13 | 3 |
| | 41 | 36 | 54 | Tax Returns | 5 | 12 | 14 | 13 | 8 | 2 |
| | 106 | 109 | 121 | Other | 4 | 17 | 11 | 14 | 31 | 44 |
| | 303 | 319 | 339 | **NUMBER OF STATEMENTS** | 12 | 38 | 40 | 49 | 96 | 104 |
| | % | % | % | **ASSETS** | % | % | % | % | % | % |
| | 8.5 | 8.5 | 7.4 | Cash & Equivalents | 17.2 | 8.9 | 8.5 | 6.0 | 8.0 | 5.4 |
| | 28.0 | 26.4 | 27.5 | Trade Receivables (net) | 17.7 | 20.0 | 31.5 | 26.9 | 31.2 | 26.7 |
| | 39.7 | 41.4 | 42.6 | Inventory | 36.3 | 46.1 | 39.7 | 48.4 | 41.6 | 41.4 |
| | 3.6 | 3.7 | 2.7 | All Other Current | 4.5 | 1.8 | 3.0 | 2.0 | 2.5 | 3.1 |
| | 79.7 | 80.0 | 80.2 | Total Current | 75.7 | 76.9 | 82.7 | 83.2 | 83.2 | 76.6 |
| | 9.7 | 9.7 | 9.4 | Fixed Assets (net) | 3.5 | 13.7 | 8.6 | 10.9 | 9.8 | 7.8 |
| | 3.8 | 4.4 | 4.4 | Intangibles (net) | 3.8 | .9 | .7 | 1.6 | 3.4 | 9.4 |
| | 6.8 | 5.9 | 6.0 | All Other Non-Current | 16.9 | 8.6 | 8.0 | 4.2 | 3.6 | 6.1 |
| | 100.0 | 100.0 | 100.0 | Total | 100.0 | 100.0 | 100.0 | 100.0 | 100.0 | 100.0 |
| | | | | **LIABILITIES** | | | | | | |
| | 18.7 | 17.3 | 16.3 | Notes Payable-Short Term | 13.3 | 16.7 | 16.2 | 18.4 | 17.2 | 14.5 |
| | 2.6 | 2.6 | 1.8 | Cur. Mat.-L.T.D. | .8 | 1.3 | 2.8 | 1.4 | 1.1 | 2.5 |
| | 18.3 | 19.0 | 18.3 | Trade Payables | 12.6 | 17.2 | 15.6 | 21.1 | 19.8 | 17.6 |
| | .3 | .2 | .2 | Income Taxes Payable | .0 | .2 | .2 | .0 | .2 | .3 |
| | 11.2 | 9.9 | 8.6 | All Other Current | 8.1 | 10.8 | 8.5 | 6.7 | 8.5 | 9.0 |
| | 51.1 | 48.9 | 45.1 | Total Current | 34.8 | 46.1 | 43.3 | 47.6 | 46.7 | 44.0 |
| | 8.6 | 8.2 | 9.7 | Long-Term Debt | 7.1 | 16.3 | 11.5 | 8.9 | 8.6 | 8.4 |
| | .2 | .2 | .2 | Deferred Taxes | .0 | .0 | .0 | .1 | .2 | .3 |
| | 6.2 | 6.0 | 6.2 | All Other Non-Current | 27.8 | 4.2 | 6.4 | 6.8 | 5.1 | 4.9 |
| | 34.0 | 36.6 | 38.9 | Net Worth | 30.4 | 33.4 | 38.8 | 36.6 | 39.4 | 42.4 |
| | 100.0 | 100.0 | 100.0 | Total Liabilities & Net Worth | 100.0 | 100.0 | 100.0 | 100.0 | 100.0 | 100.0 |
| | | | | **INCOME DATA** | | | | | | |
| | 100.0 | 100.0 | 100.0 | Net Sales | 100.0 | 100.0 | 100.0 | 100.0 | 100.0 | 100.0 |
| | 31.6 | 33.1 | 32.2 | Gross Profit | 32.9 | 42.9 | 31.9 | 32.5 | 29.7 | 30.4 |
| | 29.2 | 30.0 | 28.4 | Operating Expenses | 29.2 | 38.7 | 29.7 | 30.5 | 26.3 | 24.9 |
| | 2.4 | 3.1 | 3.8 | Operating Profit | 3.7 | 4.2 | 2.3 | 2.0 | 3.4 | 5.5 |
| | 1.1 | 1.0 | .7 | All Other Expenses (net) | .3 | 1.0 | .1 | .5 | .7 | .9 |
| | 1.3 | 2.1 | 3.1 | Profit Before Taxes | 3.4 | 3.3 | 2.1 | 1.5 | 2.7 | 4.6 |
| | | | | **RATIOS** | | | | | | |
| | 2.5 | 2.9 | 3.0 | Current | 8.5 | 3.0 | 4.4 | 3.1 | 3.0 | 2.9 |
| | 1.7 | 1.8 | 1.8 | | 3.1 | 1.8 | 2.0 | 1.8 | 1.7 | 1.7 |
| | 1.2 | 1.2 | 1.3 | | 1.4 | 1.1 | 1.3 | 1.3 | 1.3 | 1.3 |
| | 1.3 | 1.3 | 1.4 | Quick | 5.5 | 1.1 | 2.0 | 1.2 | 1.3 | 1.4 |
| | .7 | .7 | .8 | | 1.6 | .6 | .8 | .7 | .8 | .7 |
| | .4 | .4 | .4 | | .4 | .3 | .4 | .4 | .5 | .4 |
| | 25 14.4 | 24 15.3 | 25 14.8 | Sales/Receivables | 8 46.3 | 7 50.6 | 25 14.4 | 22 16.6 | 26 14.2 | 30 12.2 |
| | 39 9.4 | 39 9.4 | 39 9.4 | | 36 10.2 | 22 16.6 | 54 6.7 | 40 9.2 | 40 9.1 | 41 9.0 |
| | 58 6.3 | 56 6.5 | 57 6.4 | | 61 6.0 | 51 7.1 | 69 5.3 | 60 6.1 | 59 6.2 | 54 6.7 |
| | 49 7.4 | 55 6.6 | 54 6.7 | Cost of Sales/Inventory | 32 11.5 | 64 5.7 | 35 10.5 | 72 5.1 | 41 8.8 | 62 5.9 |
| | 81 4.5 | 90 4.0 | 96 3.8 | | 146 2.5 | 130 2.8 | 96 3.8 | 130 2.8 | 87 4.2 | 89 4.1 |
| | 147 2.5 | 147 2.5 | 159 2.3 | | 243 1.5 | 228 1.6 | 192 1.9 | 228 1.6 | 140 2.6 | 135 2.7 |
| | 15 24.2 | 16 22.5 | 13 27.3 | Cost of Sales/Payables | 9 40.8 | 6 58.0 | 6 65.2 | 17 20.9 | 19 19.7 | 17 21.9 |
| | 29 12.8 | 30 12.3 | 31 11.8 | | 16 22.7 | 23 15.6 | 19 19.4 | 33 10.9 | 31 11.9 | 33 11.2 |
| | 58 6.3 | 57 6.4 | 56 6.5 | | 57 6.4 | 74 4.9 | 50 7.3 | 83 4.4 | 53 6.9 | 55 6.6 |
| | 4.4 | 4.0 | 3.9 | Sales/Working Capital | 2.6 | 4.3 | 3.2 | 3.5 | 3.9 | 4.7 |
| | 7.4 | 7.6 | 7.0 | | 4.0 | 7.7 | 6.0 | 6.5 | 7.8 | 7.8 |
| | 18.8 | 17.5 | 16.9 | | 13.4 | 35.1 | 13.4 | 17.6 | 16.4 | 14.4 |
| | 7.4 | 12.1 | 10.3 | EBIT/Interest | | 5.2 | 7.0 | 12.5 | 11.4 | 16.5 |
| | (270) 2.8 | (274) 3.7 | (298) 3.5 | | (31) 2.6 | (34) 1.8 | (44) 3.1 | (86) 3.8 | (96) 4.9 | |
| | .8 | 1.3 | 1.6 | | | -.5 | .9 | 1.6 | 2.0 | 2.1 |
| | 6.1 | 11.3 | 13.3 | Net Profit + Depr., Dep., Amort./Cur. Mat. L/T/D | | | | | 11.6 | 26.6 |
| | (44) 1.8 | (56) 3.3 | (52) 4.3 | | | | | (14) 7.4 | (29) 3.1 | |
| | .1 | .8 | 1.8 | | | | | | 1.9 | 1.7 |
| | .1 | .1 | .1 | Fixed/Worth | .0 | .0 | .0 | .1 | .1 | .1 |
| | .2 | .2 | .2 | | .0 | .2 | .2 | .2 | .1 | .2 |
| | .7 | .7 | .6 | | NM | .7 | .6 | .9 | .6 | .8 |
| | .8 | .7 | .6 | Debt/Worth | .4 | .6 | .7 | .6 | .6 | .6 |
| | 1.9 | 1.7 | 1.9 | | 1.5 | 1.1 | 1.9 | 2.0 | 2.0 | 2.1 |
| | 4.6 | 6.5 | 5.9 | | -13.5 | 7.2 | 5.1 | 6.1 | 4.8 | 5.8 |
| | 30.9 | 39.8 | 39.8 | % Profit Before Taxes/Tangible Net Worth | | 54.2 | 35.2 | 37.9 | 38.3 | 40.6 |
| | (258) 8.3 | (279) 14.7 | (299) 16.6 | | (35) 19.4 | (36) 8.3 | (44) 15.1 | (87) 17.5 | (89) 17.9 | |
| | 1.0 | 1.7 | 4.4 | | | 7.3 | -1.8 | 4.2 | 4.5 | 5.8 |
| | 10.5 | 12.5 | 11.4 | % Profit Before Taxes/Total Assets | 21.3 | 10.9 | 9.9 | 10.1 | 10.0 | 13.3 |
| | 2.8 | 4.5 | 4.9 | | 5.4 | 6.2 | 1.8 | 3.7 | 4.7 | 6.8 |
| | -.2 | .4 | 1.2 | | -3.9 | .3 | -.4 | 1.3 | 1.3 | 2.0 |
| | 104.9 | 115.3 | 129.9 | Sales/Net Fixed Assets | UND | 391.0 | 168.8 | 101.6 | 119.5 | 114.6 |
| | 46.4 | 52.1 | 52.8 | | 126.5 | 44.3 | 63.0 | 39.0 | 51.6 | 53.7 |
| | 22.1 | 21.9 | 21.1 | | 47.1 | 13.1 | 19.6 | 17.2 | 20.9 | 26.8 |
| | 3.4 | 3.2 | 3.3 | Sales/Total Assets | 2.1 | 3.7 | 3.3 | 3.3 | 3.5 | 3.2 |
| | 2.3 | 2.3 | 2.3 | | 1.5 | 2.6 | 2.3 | 2.1 | 2.6 | 2.3 |
| | 1.7 | 1.7 | 1.7 | | 1.0 | 1.7 | 1.5 | 1.7 | 1.8 | 1.6 |
| | .3 | .3 | .3 | % Depr., Dep., Amort./Sales | | .3 | .3 | .4 | .2 | .3 |
| | (229) .6 | (249) .6 | (259) .5 | | (23) .7 | (29) .6 | (36) .6 | (82) .4 | (85) .6 | |
| | 1.1 | 1.1 | 1.0 | | | 1.3 | .9 | 1.2 | .8 | 1.0 |
| | 1.3 | 1.1 | 1.0 | % Officers', Directors' Owners' Comp/Sales | | 1.1 | 2.1 | 1.1 | .9 | .5 |
| | (141) 2.3 | (123) 2.1 | (139) 2.1 | | (16) 3.5 | (25) 3.8 | (28) 1.7 | (42) 2.1 | (23) 1.4 | |
| | 4.2 | 5.3 | 4.6 | | | 10.3 | 4.2 | 2.9 | 4.2 | 2.5 |
| | 9285708M | 10694806M | 10202716M | Net Sales ($) | 5882M | 69693M | 155111M | 359133M | 1580764M | 8032133M |
| | 4710449M | 5400466M | 5137657M | Total Assets ($) | 3804M | 39250M | 77828M | 181087M | 710647M | 4125041M |

© RMA 2012

M = $ thousand    MM = $ million
See Pages 9 through 22 for Explanation of Ratios and Data

**Current Data Sorted by Assets**      **Comparative Historical Data**

| 0-500M | 500M-2MM | 2-10MM | 10-50MM | 50-100MM | 100-250MM | Type of Statement | 4/1/07-3/31/08 ALL | 4/1/08-3/31/09 ALL |
|---|---|---|---|---|---|---|---|---|
| | 3 | 18 | 47 | 21 | 8 | Unqualified | 139 | 127 |
| 2 | 15 | 101 | 46 | 2 | | Reviewed | 260 | 233 |
| 8 | 43 | 51 | 14 | | | Compiled | 132 | 127 |
| 16 | 45 | 23 | 3 | 1 | | Tax Returns | 90 | 85 |
| 18 | 48 | 106 | 81 | 24 | 6 | Other | 353 | 365 |
| | 109 (4/1-9/30/11) | | 641 (10/1/11-3/31/12) | | | | | |
| 44 | 154 | 299 | 191 | 48 | 14 | NUMBER OF STATEMENTS | 974 | 937 |
| % | % | % | % | % | % | **ASSETS** | % | % |
| 15.9 | 7.9 | 6.3 | 4.6 | 4.5 | 5.3 | Cash & Equivalents | 6.6 | 6.5 |
| 29.1 | 35.9 | 31.3 | 27.1 | 26.2 | 25.7 | Trade Receivables (net) | 32.1 | 29.4 |
| 29.5 | 33.9 | 35.7 | 38.2 | 33.2 | 22.7 | Inventory | 34.7 | 35.7 |
| .7 | 2.4 | 2.1 | 3.0 | 3.6 | 2.6 | All Other Current | 2.7 | 2.9 |
| 75.3 | 80.2 | 75.5 | 72.9 | 67.4 | 56.3 | Total Current | 76.2 | 74.5 |
| 16.3 | 12.8 | 15.4 | 17.7 | 16.6 | 24.0 | Fixed Assets (net) | 16.1 | 16.8 |
| 1.5 | 2.2 | 2.0 | 2.5 | 4.6 | 8.3 | Intangibles (net) | 2.1 | 2.0 |
| 7.2 | 4.8 | 7.1 | 6.9 | 11.4 | 11.5 | All Other Non-Current | 5.7 | 6.6 |
| 100.0 | 100.0 | 100.0 | 100.0 | 100.0 | 100.0 | Total | 100.0 | 100.0 |
| | | | | | | **LIABILITIES** | | |
| 21.3 | 22.9 | 19.3 | 21.3 | 17.9 | 11.9 | Notes Payable-Short Term | 20.4 | 21.9 |
| 3.0 | 2.3 | 2.4 | 1.9 | 1.4 | 5.6 | Cur. Mat.-L.T.D. | 2.4 | 2.8 |
| 22.2 | 18.4 | 12.7 | 11.6 | 12.1 | 16.6 | Trade Payables | 13.0 | 11.8 |
| .2 | .0 | .1 | .1 | .0 | .4 | Income Taxes Payable | .1 | .2 |
| 12.5 | 8.6 | 7.4 | 7.8 | 6.8 | 8.4 | All Other Current | 9.0 | 8.1 |
| 59.3 | 52.3 | 41.8 | 42.7 | 38.2 | 42.8 | Total Current | 45.0 | 44.8 |
| 14.0 | 8.8 | 8.8 | 8.6 | 10.7 | 13.8 | Long-Term Debt | 9.6 | 9.6 |
| .0 | .0 | .2 | .3 | .6 | 1.4 | Deferred Taxes | .2 | .2 |
| 30.8 | 9.3 | 7.8 | 4.2 | 5.7 | 4.8 | All Other Non-Current | 5.6 | 5.4 |
| -3.9 | 29.6 | 41.4 | 44.2 | 44.7 | 37.2 | Net Worth | 39.6 | 40.0 |
| 100.0 | 100.0 | 100.0 | 100.0 | 100.0 | 100.0 | Total Liabilties & Net Worth | 100.0 | 100.0 |
| | | | | | | **INCOME DATA** | | |
| 100.0 | 100.0 | 100.0 | 100.0 | 100.0 | 100.0 | Net Sales | 100.0 | 100.0 |
| 30.2 | 23.4 | 21.8 | 20.1 | 18.5 | 18.7 | Gross Profit | 21.5 | 21.2 |
| 27.8 | 23.2 | 20.6 | 18.7 | 17.0 | 18.8 | Operating Expenses | 19.7 | 21.0 |
| 2.4 | .1 | 1.3 | 1.3 | 1.5 | -.1 | Operating Profit | 1.7 | .2 |
| .8 | .2 | .3 | .3 | .3 | .9 | All Other Expenses (net) | .6 | .6 |
| 1.6 | -.1 | .9 | 1.0 | 1.2 | -1.0 | Profit Before Taxes | 1.2 | -.4 |
| | | | | | | **RATIOS** | | |
| 3.1 | 3.2 | 3.2 | 2.7 | 3.0 | 2.8 | | 2.9 | 3.1 |
| 1.5 | 1.8 | 1.8 | 1.7 | 1.7 | 1.2 | Current | 1.7 | 1.7 |
| .8 | 1.2 | 1.3 | 1.2 | 1.3 | 1.1 | | 1.2 | 1.2 |
| 1.7 | 1.6 | 1.6 | 1.3 | 1.3 | 1.2 | | 1.5 | 1.6 |
| .9 | .9 | .8 | .7 | .8 | .7 | Quick | .8 | .8 |
| .3 | .4 | .5 | .5 | .4 | .5 | | .5 | .4 |
| 2   148.3 | 19   19.3 | 24   15.2 | 27   13.4 | 25   14.4 | 24   15.5 | | 22   16.4 | 20   17.9 |
| 22   16.3 | 32   11.3 | 35   10.5 | 33   10.4 | 33   11.2 | 33   10.9 | Sales/Receivables | 32   11.5 | 29   12.5 |
| 36   10.0 | 44   8.3 | 47   7.7 | 45   8.1 | 46   7.9 | 45   8.1 | | 44   8.3 | 41   8.8 |
| 0   UND | 16   22.2 | 33   11.0 | 40   9.1 | 43   8.4 | 22   16.4 | | 28   12.8 | 30   12.2 |
| 26   14.1 | 40   9.1 | 54   6.8 | 64   5.7 | 60   6.1 | 43   8.4 | Cost of Sales/Inventory | 48   7.6 | 51   7.2 |
| 68   5.4 | 79   4.6 | 89   4.1 | 96   3.8 | 83   4.4 | 54   6.8 | | 75   4.8 | 78   4.7 |
| 3   120.8 | 8   43.3 | 9   41.3 | 10   35.8 | 10   38.2 | 13   28.7 | | 8   47.1 | 6   60.2 |
| 18   20.1 | 17   21.2 | 16   22.8 | 15   23.6 | 18   20.2 | 23   15.7 | Cost of Sales/Payables | 15   25.0 | 13   27.6 |
| 38   9.5 | 36   10.1 | 29   12.8 | 25   14.6 | 29   12.7 | 41   9.0 | | 25   14.7 | 23   15.9 |
| 8.4 | 5.6 | 5.5 | 5.3 | 4.9 | 6.6 | | 6.3 | 6.0 |
| 20.0 | 11.7 | 9.8 | 9.7 | 9.6 | 25.2 | Sales/Working Capital | 11.3 | 10.6 |
| -27.6 | 34.3 | 21.5 | 20.7 | 20.3 | 269.1 | | 25.6 | 27.7 |
| 19.3 | 6.4 | 6.5 | 6.8 | 8.9 | 1.8 | | 5.8 | 4.4 |
| (30)   3.9 | (135)   1.9 | (274)   2.1 | (177)   2.4 | (46)   2.1 | (13)   .6 | EBIT/Interest | (920)   2.1 | (871)   1.4 |
| -.3 | -1.1 | .4 | 1.0 | .5 | -2.0 | | .8 | -.9 |
| | 4.2 | 6.4 | 5.1 | 6.9 | | | 7.2 | 4.7 |
| | (13)   .1 | (53)   1.7 | (60)   1.9 | (17)   3.6 | | Net Profit + Depr., Dep., Amort./Cur. Mat. L/T/D | (245)   2.7 | (224)   1.4 |
| | -2.7 | .2 | .5 | 1.4 | | | .8 | -.3 |
| .0 | .1 | .1 | .2 | .2 | .5 | | .1 | .1 |
| .2 | .2 | .3 | .3 | .4 | .7 | Fixed/Worth | .4 | .3 |
| -.9 | 1.3 | .7 | .8 | .6 | 5.5 | | .9 | .9 |
| .8 | .6 | .6 | .6 | .6 | .8 | | .7 | .6 |
| 2.0 | 1.9 | 1.5 | 1.4 | 1.5 | 2.7 | Debt/Worth | 1.6 | 1.5 |
| -6.2 | 12.4 | 3.6 | 3.2 | 3.3 | 16.4 | | 3.8 | 3.6 |
| 79.3 | 17.9 | 21.3 | 17.7 | 17.7 | 11.0 | % Profit Before Taxes/Tangible Net Worth | 25.9 | 17.6 |
| (29)   25.2 | (123)   4.1 | (282)   5.2 | (186)   6.1 | (45)   5.7 | (12)   -1.8 | | (894)   10.5 | (858)   3.5 |
| 2.8 | -8.9 | -2.0 | .2 | -2.5 | -35.3 | | .0 | -9.6 |
| 22.9 | 7.6 | 7.0 | 8.1 | 7.1 | 3.0 | % Profit Before Taxes/Total Assets | 10.5 | 7.0 |
| 5.6 | 1.7 | 2.1 | 2.6 | 2.3 | -.4 | | 3.7 | 1.0 |
| -3.7 | -4.1 | -1.2 | .0 | -.9 | -6.3 | | -.7 | -5.0 |
| 894.4 | 154.8 | 113.0 | 50.1 | 46.8 | 23.2 | | 83.2 | 79.9 |
| 116.1 | 52.6 | 31.1 | 20.1 | 26.4 | 10.5 | Sales/Net Fixed Assets | 29.0 | 28.6 |
| 23.0 | 20.6 | 11.8 | 8.2 | 7.7 | 5.2 | | 11.8 | 10.5 |
| 7.4 | 5.3 | 3.9 | 3.1 | 3.5 | 3.6 | | 4.2 | 4.1 |
| 4.6 | 3.5 | 2.9 | 2.5 | 2.2 | 2.1 | Sales/Total Assets | 3.2 | 3.0 |
| 2.8 | 2.7 | 2.1 | 1.9 | 1.7 | 1.6 | | 2.4 | 2.2 |
| .3 | .2 | .4 | .5 | .4 | .6 | | .3 | .4 |
| (24)   .6 | (111)   .6 | (263)   .8 | (177)   .8 | (44)   .8 | (11)   1.3 | % Depr., Dep., Amort./Sales | (857)   .8 | (824)   .9 |
| 1.7 | 1.2 | 1.4 | 1.3 | 1.5 | 1.9 | | 1.4 | 1.7 |
| 2.6 | 1.6 | .9 | .4 | | | % Officers', Directors' Owners' Comp/Sales | 1.2 | 1.1 |
| (19)   6.0 | (83)   3.1 | (114)   1.8 | (49)   1.1 | | | | (354)   2.3 | (352)   2.2 |
| 9.1 | 4.9 | 2.8 | 2.2 | | | | 4.7 | 4.0 |
| 59695M | 752821M | 4741896M | 11034950M | 8035360M | 7455491M | Net Sales ($) | 46893140M | 40857294M |
| 11826M | 191463M | 1484277M | 4078762M | 3159246M | 2273445M | Total Assets ($) | 15218062M | 13386766M |

© RMA 2012      M = $ thousand    MM = $ million

See Pages 9 through 22 for Explanation of Ratios and Data

## Comparative Historical Data

## Current Data Sorted by Sales

| | | | Type of Statement | | | | | | |
|---|---|---|---|---|---|---|---|---|---|
| 110 | 111 | 97 | Unqualified | | 1 | | 5 | 12 | 79 |
| 216 | 223 | 166 | Reviewed | 2 | 5 | 8 | 34 | 58 | 59 |
| 115 | 118 | 116 | Compiled | 6 | 16 | 17 | 38 | 26 | 13 |
| 98 | 93 | 88 | Tax Returns | 9 | 18 | 20 | 25 | 14 | 2 |
| 305 | 273 | 283 | Other | 8 | 26 | 20 | 40 | 77 | 112 |
| 4/1/09-3/31/10 ALL | 4/1/10-3/31/11 ALL | 4/1/11-3/31/12 ALL | | | 109 (4/1-9/30/11) | | 641 (10/1/11-3/31/12) | | |
| | | | | 0-1MM | 1-3MM | 3-5MM | 5-10MM | 10-25MM | 25MM & OVER |
| 844 | 818 | 750 | **NUMBER OF STATEMENTS** | 25 | 66 | 65 | 142 | 187 | 265 |
| % | % | % | **ASSETS** | % | % | % | % | % | % |
| 7.7 | 6.8 | 6.6 | Cash & Equivalents | 18.8 | 9.0 | 8.8 | 6.7 | 6.3 | 4.6 |
| 29.1 | 29.4 | 30.6 | Trade Receivables (net) | 11.8 | 30.2 | 35.0 | 31.4 | 31.4 | 30.5 |
| 33.3 | 35.3 | 35.2 | Inventory | 31.8 | 35.2 | 31.2 | 36.2 | 35.1 | 36.1 |
| 3.5 | 2.5 | 2.4 | All Other Current | .9 | 2.3 | 1.1 | 2.2 | 2.6 | 2.9 |
| 73.6 | 74.0 | 74.9 | Total Current | 63.3 | 76.7 | 76.1 | 76.4 | 75.4 | 74.1 |
| 17.6 | 16.9 | 15.7 | Fixed Assets (net) | 22.4 | 15.0 | 17.6 | 13.9 | 16.1 | 15.6 |
| 2.2 | 2.4 | 2.4 | Intangibles (net) | 2.4 | 2.4 | 1.5 | 2.7 | 1.5 | 3.1 |
| 6.7 | 6.6 | 6.9 | All Other Non-Current | 12.2 | 5.9 | 4.8 | 7.0 | 7.0 | 7.2 |
| 100.0 | 100.0 | 100.0 | Total | 100.0 | 100.0 | 100.0 | 100.0 | 100.0 | 100.0 |
| | | | **LIABILITIES** | | | | | | |
| 19.6 | 19.1 | 20.4 | Notes Payable-Short Term | 17.3 | 22.3 | 24.3 | 18.2 | 19.4 | 21.2 |
| 2.5 | 2.1 | 2.3 | Cur. Mat.-L.T.D. | 2.6 | 3.2 | 2.9 | 1.6 | 2.6 | 2.1 |
| 12.7 | 13.7 | 14.2 | Trade Payables | 15.6 | 20.9 | 15.4 | 14.6 | 12.8 | 12.8 |
| .2 | .2 | .1 | Income Taxes Payable | .4 | .0 | .0 | .1 | .0 | .2 |
| 8.3 | 9.1 | 8.0 | All Other Current | 13.8 | 11.1 | 6.8 | 6.5 | 7.8 | 7.9 |
| 43.3 | 44.3 | 45.0 | Total Current | 49.6 | 57.5 | 49.4 | 41.1 | 42.7 | 44.1 |
| 10.4 | 10.5 | 9.3 | Long-Term Debt | 30.6 | 11.5 | 12.4 | 7.8 | 7.7 | 7.8 |
| .3 | .2 | .2 | Deferred Taxes | .0 | .0 | .1 | .1 | .2 | .4 |
| 6.5 | 6.1 | 8.3 | All Other Non-Current | 34.5 | 14.0 | 9.2 | 6.9 | 8.2 | 5.1 |
| 39.5 | 38.9 | 37.2 | Net Worth | -14.4 | 16.9 | 28.9 | 44.0 | 41.2 | 42.7 |
| 100.0 | 100.0 | 100.0 | Total Liabilities & Net Worth | 100.0 | 100.0 | 100.0 | 100.0 | 100.0 | 100.0 |
| | | | **INCOME DATA** | | | | | | |
| 100.0 | 100.0 | 100.0 | Net Sales | 100.0 | 100.0 | 100.0 | 100.0 | 100.0 | 100.0 |
| 21.9 | 22.0 | 21.9 | Gross Profit | 36.7 | 27.9 | 25.8 | 23.0 | 20.6 | 18.4 |
| 22.4 | 21.2 | 20.8 | Operating Expenses | 34.8 | 28.3 | 23.7 | 21.9 | 19.7 | 17.1 |
| -.5 | .8 | 1.1 | Operating Profit | 1.9 | -.4 | 2.1 | 1.0 | 1.0 | 1.3 |
| .6 | .4 | .3 | All Other Expenses (net) | 1.5 | .4 | .8 | .1 | .3 | .2 |
| -1.1 | .4 | .8 | Profit Before Taxes | .4 | -.8 | 1.3 | .9 | .6 | 1.1 |
| | | | **RATIOS** | | | | | | |
| 3.2 | 3.1 | 2.9 | Current | 3.6 | 3.3 | 3.3 | 3.4 | 2.8 | 2.7 |
| 1.8 | 1.7 | 1.7 | | 1.5 | 1.6 | 1.7 | 1.8 | 1.8 | 1.7 |
| 1.2 | 1.2 | 1.2 | | .7 | 1.0 | 1.2 | 1.4 | 1.2 | 1.2 |
| 1.6 | 1.4 | 1.4 | Quick | 2.3 | 1.2 | 1.7 | 1.7 | 1.6 | 1.3 |
| .8 | .8 | .8 | | .6 | .8 | .9 | .9 | .8 | .8 |
| .5 | .5 | .5 | | .3 | .3 | .5 | .5 | .5 | .5 |
| 23  16.1 | 23  15.9 | 23  15.6 | Sales/Receivables | 0  UND | 20  18.7 | 20  17.9 | 21  17.3 | 24  15.2 | 25  14.5 |
| 34  10.8 | 33  11.1 | 34  10.7 | | 10  37.4 | 33  10.9 | 36  10.2 | 32  11.3 | 35  10.4 | 34  10.7 |
| 47  7.7 | 45  8.1 | 46  8.0 | | 41  8.8 | 46  7.9 | 51  7.2 | 46  7.9 | 48  7.6 | 44  8.3 |
| 30  12.3 | 31  11.9 | 31  11.9 | Cost of Sales/Inventory | 0  UND | 24  15.2 | 23  15.7 | 30  12.0 | 29  12.4 | 33  10.9 |
| 54  6.8 | 55  6.6 | 53  6.9 | | 49  7.5 | 58  6.3 | 51  7.2 | 53  6.9 | 52  7.0 | 55  6.6 |
| 84  4.3 | 88  4.2 | 87  4.2 | | 146  2.5 | 104  3.5 | 96  3.8 | 87  4.2 | 94  3.9 | 78  4.7 |
| 9  41.7 | 9  41.1 | 9  39.2 | Cost of Sales/Payables | 0  UND | 13  29.1 | 8  43.4 | 10  38.2 | 8  43.7 | 9  38.9 |
| 16  22.7 | 16  22.2 | 16  22.3 | | 10  36.5 | 31  11.8 | 19  19.2 | 17  21.2 | 16  23.1 | 15  24.5 |
| 26  14.0 | 28  13.1 | 29  12.4 | | 49  7.5 | 52  7.0 | 37  9.9 | 31  11.6 | 27  13.5 | 25  14.7 |
| 5.1 | 5.6 | 5.6 | Sales/Working Capital | 7.1 | 4.5 | 4.3 | 5.2 | 5.5 | 6.0 |
| 9.9 | 10.1 | 10.3 | | 15.2 | 9.8 | 11.6 | 9.7 | 9.6 | 11.3 |
| 25.6 | 24.7 | 25.1 | | -22.2 | -92.6 | 36.6 | 19.1 | 23.8 | 22.7 |
| 3.8 | 6.0 | 6.8 | EBIT/Interest | 5.2 | 7.6 | 4.2 | 8.8 | 6.1 | 8.2 |
| (769)  1.0 | (741)  1.9 | (675)  2.2 | | (13)  2.2 | (55)  1.0 | (57)  2.0 | (132)  2.0 | (169)  2.0 | (249)  2.4 |
| -2.7 | -.5 | .4 | | -1.8 | -3.1 | .6 | .2 | .2 | 1.0 |
| 3.3 | 5.1 | 5.5 | Net Profit + Depr., Dep., Amort./Cur. Mat. L/T/D | | | | 5.4 | 5.3 | 6.8 |
| (179)  .8 | (169)  1.9 | (148)  1.8 | | | | (26)  .8 | (27)  2.9 | (83)  2.0 | |
| -.9 | -.1 | .3 | | | | | .0 | 1.0 | .4 |
| .1 | .1 | .1 | Fixed/Worth | .0 | .1 | .1 | .1 | .1 | .1 |
| .3 | .3 | .3 | | .3 | .6 | .2 | .2 | .3 | .3 |
| .9 | .9 | .9 | | UND | -.9 | 2.3 | .7 | .8 | .7 |
| .6 | .6 | .6 | Debt/Worth | .5 | .8 | .7 | .6 | .6 | .7 |
| 1.4 | 1.5 | 1.5 | | 4.3 | 2.8 | 1.9 | 1.3 | 1.5 | 1.5 |
| 4.0 | 4.0 | 3.8 | | -40.3 | -6.3 | 7.2 | 3.3 | 3.7 | 3.5 |
| 12.6 | 18.9 | 19.2 | % Profit Before Taxes/Tangible Net Worth | 75.1 | 23.4 | 24.1 | 15.6 | 20.5 | 17.8 |
| (764)  .8 | (734)  4.6 | (677)  5.8 | | (18)  11.2 | (45)  6.2 | (53)  7.1 | (132)  3.2 | (175)  5.8 | (254)  6.6 |
| -15.1 | -5.0 | -1.2 | | .0 | -23.2 | -1.5 | -5.8 | -.5 | .0 |
| 4.7 | 7.0 | 7.8 | % Profit Before Taxes/Total Assets | 7.5 | 10.0 | 7.3 | 7.3 | 7.5 | 7.8 |
| .1 | 1.6 | 2.2 | | 1.7 | 1.4 | 2.1 | 1.6 | 2.0 | 2.7 |
| -7.2 | -3.3 | -1.1 | | -4.5 | -12.1 | -1.5 | -2.6 | -.8 | .0 |
| 76.4 | 89.9 | 102.5 | Sales/Net Fixed Assets | 579.3 | 110.2 | 117.2 | 147.1 | 93.5 | 65.7 |
| 24.8 | 29.7 | 31.3 | | 43.6 | 34.3 | 29.3 | 40.1 | 26.7 | 29.8 |
| 8.2 | 9.2 | 11.4 | | 4.4 | 11.6 | 8.3 | 12.6 | 11.6 | 10.8 |
| 3.7 | 3.9 | 4.0 | Sales/Total Assets | 5.4 | 4.2 | 4.8 | 3.8 | 3.9 | 4.0 |
| 2.7 | 2.8 | 2.9 | | 2.3 | 2.8 | 3.1 | 3.1 | 2.7 | 2.9 |
| 1.9 | 2.0 | 2.1 | | .8 | 1.9 | 1.8 | 2.4 | 2.0 | 2.1 |
| .4 | .4 | .4 | % Depr., Dep., Amort./Sales | .6 | .3 | .3 | .3 | .5 | .3 |
| (723)  .9 | (705)  .9 | (630)  .8 | | (12)  .9 | (47)  1.0 | (51)  .7 | (118)  .6 | (160)  .8 | (242)  .7 |
| 1.9 | 1.6 | 1.3 | | 7.8 | 1.8 | 1.4 | 1.4 | 1.4 | 1.2 |
| 1.4 | 1.0 | .9 | % Officers', Directors' Owners' Comp/Sales | 2.7 | 2.1 | 1.7 | 1.3 | .8 | .4 |
| (308)  2.6 | (313)  1.9 | (269)  2.0 | | (10)  7.1 | (28)  3.2 | (36)  3.0 | (73)  2.2 | (65)  1.7 | (57)  1.0 |
| 4.8 | 4.0 | 4.1 | | 15.2 | 6.1 | 5.7 | 3.9 | 3.1 | 1.6 |
| 30402572M | 30065106M | 32080213M | Net Sales ($) | 13925M | 131314M | 262749M | 1036096M | 3053235M | 27582894M |
| 11183799M | 10695050M | 11199019M | Total Assets ($) | 11050M | 53532M | 112878M | 372583M | 1313479M | 9335497M |

© RMA 2012

M = $ thousand    MM = $ million
See Pages 9 through 22 for Explanation of Ratios and Data

## Current Data Sorted by Assets      Comparative Historical Data

| 0-500M | 500M-2MM | 2-10MM | 10-50MM | 50-100MM | 100-250MM | Type of Statement | 4/1/07-3/31/08 ALL | 4/1/08-3/31/09 ALL |
|---|---|---|---|---|---|---|---|---|
| | 1 | 5 | 8 | 1 | 3 | Unqualified | 37 | 28 |
| 1 | 8 | 37 | 17 | 1 | | Reviewed | 71 | 68 |
| 7 | 7 | 17 | 4 | | | Compiled | 47 | 41 |
| 9 | 30 | 20 | | | | Tax Returns | 48 | 41 |
| 5 | 24 | 38 | 30 | 2 | 1 | Other | 101 | 102 |
| | 38 (4/1-9/30/11) | | 238 (10/1/11-3/31/12) | | | | | |
| 22 | 70 | 117 | 59 | 4 | 4 | **NUMBER OF STATEMENTS** | 304 | 280 |
| % | % | % | % | % | % | **ASSETS** | % | % |
| 12.3 | 8.8 | 6.8 | 5.8 | | | Cash & Equivalents | 6.4 | 7.4 |
| 23.0 | 28.9 | 22.8 | 24.6 | | | Trade Receivables (net) | 26.9 | 25.7 |
| 32.4 | 33.9 | 40.0 | 30.1 | | | Inventory | 33.5 | 33.8 |
| 6.3 | 1.4 | 1.4 | 3.2 | | | All Other Current | 2.9 | 3.2 |
| 74.0 | 72.9 | 71.0 | 63.8 | | | Total Current | 69.8 | 70.2 |
| 21.7 | 15.9 | 20.2 | 27.2 | | | Fixed Assets (net) | 21.8 | 22.1 |
| 1.2 | 2.0 | 3.3 | 3.5 | | | Intangibles (net) | 2.8 | 2.0 |
| 3.0 | 9.1 | 5.5 | 5.6 | | | All Other Non-Current | 5.6 | 5.7 |
| 100.0 | 100.0 | 100.0 | 100.0 | | | Total | 100.0 | 100.0 |
| | | | | | | **LIABILITIES** | | |
| 25.0 | 12.3 | 12.6 | 12.4 | | | Notes Payable-Short Term | 12.5 | 13.5 |
| 5.4 | 3.4 | 2.7 | 3.1 | | | Cur. Mat.-L.T.D. | 3.7 | 3.1 |
| 31.6 | 28.2 | 20.5 | 18.6 | | | Trade Payables | 20.4 | 20.2 |
| .7 | .1 | .0 | .6 | | | Income Taxes Payable | .1 | .3 |
| 20.7 | 9.0 | 9.0 | 5.3 | | | All Other Current | 9.2 | 9.7 |
| 83.4 | 53.0 | 44.9 | 40.1 | | | Total Current | 45.9 | 46.8 |
| 30.3 | 11.2 | 11.6 | 10.4 | | | Long-Term Debt | 15.4 | 12.5 |
| .0 | .0 | .2 | .7 | | | Deferred Taxes | .4 | .4 |
| 42.6 | 8.9 | 6.5 | 3.2 | | | All Other Non-Current | 5.1 | 6.0 |
| -56.3 | 27.0 | 36.8 | 45.5 | | | Net Worth | 33.2 | 34.3 |
| 100.0 | 100.0 | 100.0 | 100.0 | | | Total Liabilties & Net Worth | 100.0 | 100.0 |
| | | | | | | **INCOME DATA** | | |
| 100.0 | 100.0 | 100.0 | 100.0 | | | Net Sales | 100.0 | 100.0 |
| 40.5 | 34.3 | 30.8 | 27.1 | | | Gross Profit | 30.4 | 30.8 |
| 35.8 | 32.8 | 28.9 | 24.2 | | | Operating Expenses | 27.3 | 29.4 |
| 4.7 | 1.5 | 1.8 | 2.9 | | | Operating Profit | 3.2 | 1.4 |
| 1.1 | .2 | .4 | -.2 | | | All Other Expenses (net) | .8 | .5 |
| 3.6 | 1.3 | 1.4 | 3.1 | | | Profit Before Taxes | 2.3 | .9 |
| | | | | | | **RATIOS** | | |
| 7.6 | 2.6 | 2.7 | 2.9 | | | Current | 2.4 | 2.6 |
| 2.0 | 1.4 | 1.6 | 1.6 | | | | 1.6 | 1.7 |
| .8 | .9 | 1.2 | 1.1 | | | | 1.1 | 1.2 |
| 2.6 | 1.4 | 1.0 | 1.4 | | | Quick | 1.2 | 1.2 |
| .5 | .7 | .6 | .7 | | | | .7 | .7 |
| .2 | .4 | .4 | .4 | | | | .4 | .4 |
| 0 UND | 20 18.1 | 24 15.3 | 35 10.4 | | | Sales/Receivables | 25 14.4 | 23 16.0 |
| 21 17.2 | 31 11.6 | 37 9.8 | 49 7.4 | | | | 37 10.0 | 35 10.3 |
| 35 10.3 | 53 6.9 | 53 6.9 | 68 5.4 | | | | 52 7.1 | 53 6.9 |
| 0 UND | 15 23.6 | 46 7.9 | 39 9.3 | | | Cost of Sales/Inventory | 33 11.2 | 33 10.9 |
| 51 7.2 | 56 6.5 | 96 3.8 | 66 5.5 | | | | 65 5.6 | 69 5.3 |
| 99 3.7 | 99 3.7 | 192 1.9 | 146 2.5 | | | | 122 3.0 | 118 3.1 |
| 5 72.2 | 18 20.1 | 24 15.1 | 24 15.5 | | | Cost of Sales/Payables | 18 19.7 | 19 19.4 |
| 38 9.7 | 45 8.2 | 40 9.2 | 51 7.1 | | | | 32 11.3 | 31 11.6 |
| 73 5.0 | 69 5.3 | 73 5.0 | 78 4.7 | | | | 60 6.1 | 56 6.5 |
| 4.5 | 6.0 | 4.1 | 3.8 | | | Sales/Working Capital | 5.9 | 4.9 |
| 6.2 | 15.3 | 7.6 | 7.4 | | | | 10.3 | 8.8 |
| -31.1 | -58.6 | 20.7 | 28.0 | | | | 39.5 | 28.9 |
| 3.8 | 10.4 | 4.8 | 11.7 | | | EBIT/Interest | 7.2 | 5.6 |
| (15) .3 | (54) 4.4 | (107) 1.9 | (56) 3.2 | | | | (284) 2.5 | (252) 2.0 |
| -4.3 | -.3 | .5 | 1.1 | | | | .6 | -.1 |
| | | 2.9 | 7.7 | | | Net Profit + Depr., Dep., | 6.8 | 6.0 |
| | | (19) 1.5 | (17) 2.8 | | | Amort./Cur. Mat. L/T/D | (76) 2.5 | (64) 2.8 |
| | | .3 | 1.2 | | | | .8 | .7 |
| .1 | .1 | .1 | .1 | | | Fixed/Worth | .2 | .2 |
| -7.9 | .4 | .4 | .6 | | | | .6 | .5 |
| -.2 | 9.0 | 1.8 | 1.4 | | | | 1.9 | 1.3 |
| 1.8 | .9 | .7 | .6 | | | Debt/Worth | .8 | .8 |
| -11.6 | 2.4 | 1.7 | 1.2 | | | | 2.3 | 1.8 |
| -2.4 | -17.7 | 4.7 | 3.5 | | | | 6.7 | 4.5 |
| | 65.6 | 19.5 | 20.4 | | | % Profit Before Taxes/Tangible | 38.8 | 23.4 |
| | (52) 18.3 | (101) 4.6 | (56) 11.1 | | | Net Worth | (263) 16.7 | (248) 8.2 |
| | 1.8 | .2 | 2.8 | | | | 1.8 | -2.8 |
| 13.2 | 12.5 | 6.8 | 7.9 | | | % Profit Before Taxes/Total | 13.5 | 8.2 |
| 1.8 | 4.9 | .9 | 3.1 | | | Assets | 4.7 | 2.4 |
| -39.0 | -1.8 | -1.2 | .3 | | | | -.8 | -2.7 |
| UND | 92.2 | 48.5 | 27.5 | | | Sales/Net Fixed Assets | 45.0 | 50.7 |
| 44.8 | 24.4 | 15.1 | 7.1 | | | | 16.1 | 16.6 |
| 15.1 | 13.4 | 5.2 | 3.4 | | | | 6.9 | 6.5 |
| 6.5 | 3.8 | 2.4 | 2.0 | | | Sales/Total Assets | 3.4 | 3.1 |
| 3.2 | 2.7 | 1.8 | 1.7 | | | | 2.4 | 2.4 |
| 1.7 | 1.9 | 1.2 | 1.2 | | | | 1.6 | 1.6 |
| | .6 | .7 | .6 | | | % Depr., Dep., Amort./Sales | .7 | .7 |
| | (46) 1.5 | (103) 1.5 | (54) 1.8 | | | | (250) 1.4 | (231) 1.6 |
| | 2.6 | 3.4 | 3.6 | | | | 2.6 | 3.5 |
| | 3.0 | 1.8 | .9 | | | % Officers', Directors', | 1.5 | 1.5 |
| | (40) 4.1 | (41) 2.8 | (19) 2.4 | | | Owners' Comp/Sales | (121) 2.8 | (117) 2.9 |
| | 7.4 | 5.7 | 4.0 | | | | 6.3 | 4.6 |
| 39320M | 268023M | 1103638M | 2310282M | 377203M | 877450M | Net Sales ($) | 9310961M | 6962194M |
| 6364M | 84644M | 585195M | 1297254M | 319841M | 661602M | Total Assets ($) | 4242952M | 3475496M |

M = $ thousand    MM = $ million
See Pages 9 through 22 for Explanation of Ratios and Data

## Comparative Historical Data | Current Data Sorted by Sales

| Type of Statement | 4/1/09-3/31/10 ALL | 4/1/10-3/31/11 ALL | 4/1/11-3/31/12 ALL | 0-1MM | 1-3MM | 3-5MM | 5-10MM | 10-25MM | 25MM & OVER |
|---|---|---|---|---|---|---|---|---|---|
| Unqualified | 23 | 30 | 18 | | | 1 | 1 | 4 | 12 |
| Reviewed | 66 | 59 | 64 | 1 | 2 | 5 | 21 | 25 | 10 |
| Compiled | 39 | 38 | 35 | 7 | 4 | 8 | 6 | 7 | 3 |
| Tax Returns | 62 | 39 | 59 | 4 | 24 | 9 | 16 | 6 | |
| Other | 104 | 101 | 100 | 5 | 13 | 16 | 22 | 24 | 20 |
| | | | | 38 (4/1-9/30/11) | | | 238 (10/1/11-3/31/12) | | |
| NUMBER OF STATEMENTS | 294 | 267 | 276 | 17 | 43 | 39 | 66 | 66 | 45 |
| **ASSETS** | % | % | % | % | % | % | % | % | % |
| Cash & Equivalents | 6.6 | 8.0 | 7.4 | 7.9 | 6.4 | 12.0 | 7.0 | 6.8 | 6.4 |
| Trade Receivables (net) | 23.4 | 23.9 | 24.5 | 22.3 | 22.1 | 24.4 | 24.0 | 27.2 | 24.6 |
| Inventory | 35.2 | 34.0 | 35.2 | 33.7 | 39.9 | 35.8 | 38.0 | 34.7 | 27.6 |
| All Other Current | 3.0 | 2.3 | 2.2 | 4.1 | 2.2 | 1.3 | 1.5 | 2.2 | 3.6 |
| Total Current | 68.2 | 68.2 | 69.4 | 68.0 | 70.6 | 73.4 | 70.4 | 70.9 | 61.8 |
| Fixed Assets (net) | 23.0 | 22.9 | 21.2 | 26.7 | 18.6 | 18.3 | 19.7 | 20.4 | 27.3 |
| Intangibles (net) | 2.9 | 3.0 | 2.9 | 3.5 | 1.4 | 1.9 | 3.4 | 2.7 | 4.6 |
| All Other Non-Current | 6.0 | 6.0 | 6.5 | 1.9 | 9.4 | 6.4 | 6.4 | 6.0 | 6.3 |
| Total | 100.0 | 100.0 | 100.0 | 100.0 | 100.0 | 100.0 | 100.0 | 100.0 | 100.0 |
| **LIABILITIES** | | | | | | | | | |
| Notes Payable-Short Term | 12.6 | 14.5 | 13.6 | 16.6 | 10.9 | 11.6 | 14.2 | 15.6 | 12.7 |
| Cur. Mat.-L.T.D. | 3.3 | 3.0 | 3.1 | 7.0 | 2.6 | 3.0 | 4.1 | 2.3 | 2.0 |
| Trade Payables | 21.9 | 24.2 | 22.6 | 20.9 | 24.0 | 18.1 | 21.6 | 29.9 | 16.5 |
| Income Taxes Payable | .1 | .1 | .2 | .9 | .0 | .2 | .0 | .2 | .6 |
| All Other Current | 8.5 | 9.1 | 9.0 | 10.4 | 13.5 | 13.3 | 6.1 | 8.8 | 5.1 |
| Total Current | 46.5 | 50.9 | 48.5 | 55.7 | 51.0 | 46.2 | 46.0 | 56.9 | 36.9 |
| Long-Term Debt | 18.1 | 12.0 | 12.9 | 28.3 | 12.7 | 15.1 | 12.4 | 10.1 | 10.3 |
| Deferred Taxes | .4 | .3 | .3 | .0 | .0 | .0 | .2 | .5 | .6 |
| All Other Non-Current | 7.4 | 6.7 | 9.7 | 27.2 | 23.8 | 7.0 | 6.1 | 3.7 | 6.3 |
| Net Worth | 27.7 | 30.1 | 28.5 | -11.3 | 12.4 | 31.8 | 35.3 | 28.8 | 45.9 |
| Total Liabilties & Net Worth | 100.0 | 100.0 | 100.0 | 100.0 | 100.0 | 100.0 | 100.0 | 100.0 | 100.0 |
| **INCOME DATA** | | | | | | | | | |
| Net Sales | 100.0 | 100.0 | 100.0 | 100.0 | 100.0 | 100.0 | 100.0 | 100.0 | 100.0 |
| Gross Profit | 30.9 | 30.9 | 31.7 | 44.6 | 38.4 | 29.1 | 33.1 | 27.7 | 26.4 |
| Operating Expenses | 31.9 | 30.1 | 29.5 | 38.6 | 36.3 | 28.5 | 31.4 | 25.4 | 23.7 |
| Operating Profit | -1.0 | .7 | 2.2 | 5.9 | 2.1 | .6 | 1.6 | 2.3 | 2.7 |
| All Other Expenses (net) | .8 | .5 | .3 | 1.5 | .4 | .3 | .2 | .1 | .4 |
| Profit Before Taxes | -1.7 | .2 | 1.8 | 4.4 | 1.8 | .3 | 1.5 | 2.2 | 2.3 |
| **RATIOS** | | | | | | | | | |
| Current | 2.7 | 2.6 | 2.7 | 5.0 | 4.2 | 3.1 | 2.6 | 2.1 | 3.0 |
| | 1.6 | 1.6 | 1.5 | 1.9 | 1.6 | 1.5 | 1.6 | 1.4 | 1.7 |
| | 1.1 | 1.0 | 1.1 | .8 | .8 | 1.2 | 1.1 | 1.1 | 1.2 |
| Quick | 1.3 | 1.3 | 1.2 | 4.2 | 1.1 | 1.5 | 1.0 | 1.2 | 1.4 |
| | .6 | .6 | .6 | .5 | .5 | .8 | .6 | .5 | .8 |
| | .4 | .4 | .4 | .2 | .4 | .4 | .4 | .4 | .5 |
| Sales/Receivables | 24  15.1 | 23  15.5 | 24  15.3 | 0  UND | 15  24.5 | 24  15.1 | 20  18.3 | 31  11.9 | 32  11.3 |
| | 37  9.8 | 38  9.6 | 37  9.9 | 26  13.9 | 26  13.8 | 34  10.6 | 37  9.9 | 43  8.5 | 48  7.6 |
| | 54  6.8 | 52  7.0 | 55  6.6 | 130  2.8 | 52  7.0 | 53  6.9 | 51  7.1 | 55  6.6 | 62  5.9 |
| Cost of Sales/Inventory | 40  9.1 | 34  10.9 | 35  10.4 | 0  UND | 30  12.1 | 47  7.7 | 34  10.8 | 42  8.6 | 29  12.8 |
| | 83  4.4 | 73  5.0 | 69  5.3 | 57  6.4 | 65  5.6 | 70  5.2 | 91  4.0 | 73  5.0 | 59  6.2 |
| | 148  2.5 | 148  2.5 | 146  2.5 | 304  1.2 | 215  1.7 | 118  3.1 | 174  2.1 | 122  3.0 | 130  2.8 |
| Cost of Sales/Payables | 19  19.0 | 22  16.3 | 22  16.3 | 21  17.3 | 10  37.5 | 14  26.9 | 26  14.1 | 27  13.7 | 21  17.2 |
| | 35  10.4 | 41  8.8 | 41  8.9 | 56  6.5 | 32  11.4 | 33  11.0 | 45  8.2 | 47  7.7 | 37  9.8 |
| | 67  5.4 | 71  5.1 | 74  4.9 | 140  2.6 | 114  3.2 | 76  4.8 | 61  6.0 | 76  4.8 | 64  5.7 |
| Sales/Working Capital | 4.2 | 4.5 | 4.2 | 3.1 | 3.0 | 4.1 | 4.5 | 5.1 | 3.8 |
| | 8.8 | 8.9 | 8.3 | 6.1 | 7.6 | 7.5 | 7.9 | 10.1 | 8.1 |
| | 36.6 | 130.5 | 33.0 | -11.0 | -18.8 | 36.5 | 31.4 | 32.5 | 20.5 |
| EBIT/Interest | 3.4 | 4.9 | 7.5 | 6.5 | 7.8 | 5.2 | 9.0 | 6.5 | 12.1 |
| | (264)  .8 | (224)  1.3 | (239)  2.3 | (12)  .0 | (32)  2.0 | (32)  2.4 | (59)  2.4 | (61)  2.3 | (43)  2.9 |
| | -3.3 | -1.8 | .3 | -3.7 | -3.1 | -1.2 | -.1 | 1.0 | .2 |
| Net Profit + Depr., Dep., Amort./Cur. Mat. L/T/D | 2.6 | 4.2 | 4.5 | | | | 2.9 | 4.6 | 9.6 |
| | (58)  .6 | (43)  1.3 | (42)  2.1 | | | | (11)  1.1 | (13)  2.8 | (15)  2.5 |
| | -.4 | .3 | .5 | | | | -.1 | 1.7 | .6 |
| Fixed/Worth | .2 | .1 | .1 | .0 | .1 | .2 | .1 | .1 | .2 |
| | .6 | .6 | .5 | 3.1 | .6 | .4 | .6 | .4 | .7 |
| | 2.5 | 2.2 | 2.1 | -1.0 | -.8 | 8.2 | 1.6 | 1.9 | 1.5 |
| Debt/Worth | .9 | .7 | .8 | 1.8 | .7 | .7 | .9 | 1.0 | .5 |
| | 2.2 | 1.9 | 2.0 | -15.3 | 3.1 | 2.4 | 1.6 | 2.3 | 1.1 |
| | 8.1 | 6.2 | 9.0 | -3.2 | -6.7 | 32.4 | 4.5 | 4.8 | 3.8 |
| % Profit Before Taxes/Tangible Net Worth | 14.6 | 17.5 | 23.3 | | 24.2 | 31.9 | 20.4 | 23.3 | 19.5 |
| | (240)  1.2 | (223)  3.2 | (224)  8.1 | | (27)  15.1 | (31)  8.1 | (58)  5.0 | (60)  11.5 | (40)  8.4 |
| | -13.8 | -8.3 | .7 | | 1.7 | .5 | -.5 | 1.3 | -1.0 |
| % Profit Before Taxes/Total Assets | 4.3 | 6.1 | 8.1 | 17.0 | 11.3 | 8.5 | 7.3 | 7.4 | 8.8 |
| | -.3 | .7 | 2.5 | -.2 | 3.0 | 1.7 | 2.4 | 2.7 | 2.8 |
| | -8.5 | -4.4 | -1.2 | -26.1 | -1.3 | -3.7 | -1.7 | .1 | -1.3 |
| Sales/Net Fixed Assets | 44.6 | 43.7 | 56.1 | UND | 106.2 | 44.9 | 61.0 | 57.7 | 32.0 |
| | 15.4 | 15.1 | 17.1 | 19.4 | 22.5 | 16.3 | 19.3 | 19.7 | 7.9 |
| | 4.8 | 4.8 | 5.1 | 1.8 | 7.1 | 7.7 | 6.8 | 4.9 | 3.5 |
| Sales/Total Assets | 2.8 | 2.9 | 2.8 | 3.7 | 2.8 | 3.0 | 3.1 | 2.8 | 2.2 |
| | 1.9 | 1.9 | 2.0 | 1.4 | 2.1 | 2.1 | 2.1 | 2.0 | 1.7 |
| | 1.3 | 1.4 | 1.4 | .6 | 1.4 | 1.2 | 1.3 | 1.5 | 1.3 |
| % Depr., Dep., Amort./Sales | .7 | .7 | .6 | | .5 | .7 | .7 | .5 | .6 |
| | (239)  1.7 | (223)  1.8 | (216)  1.5 | | (29)  1.3 | (30)  1.8 | (55)  1.7 | (58)  1.1 | (37)  1.6 |
| | 3.6 | 4.1 | 3.3 | | 5.2 | 2.5 | 3.4 | 2.3 | 3.4 |
| % Officers', Directors' Owners' Comp/Sales | 2.0 | 1.8 | 2.1 | | 2.9 | 2.9 | 2.1 | 1.3 | .7 |
| | (129)  3.3 | (95)  3.2 | (104)  3.6 | | (21)  5.6 | (16)  3.8 | (29)  3.8 | (24)  2.4 | (11)  2.5 |
| | 5.0 | 5.0 | 5.0 | | 9.3 | 8.1 | 5.7 | 3.8 | 6.0 |
| Net Sales ($) | 4938246M | 4587004M | 4975916M | 8291M | 83051M | 158037M | 467932M | 1042211M | 3216394M |
| Total Assets ($) | 2742055M | 2778464M | 2954900M | 6437M | 52744M | 94924M | 272596M | 582370M | 1945829M |

M = $ thousand    MM = $ million
See Pages 9 through 22 for Explanation of Ratios and Data

## Current Data Sorted by Assets | Comparative Historical Data

| 0-500M | 500M-2MM | 2-10MM | 10-50MM | 50-100MM | 100-250MM | Type of Statement | 4/1/07-3/31/08 ALL | 4/1/08-3/31/09 ALL |
|---|---|---|---|---|---|---|---|---|
|  |  | 4 | 6 | 3 | 4 | Unqualified | 19 | 23 |
|  | 3 | 20 | 12 | 1 |  | Reviewed | 32 | 33 |
| 1 | 6 | 10 | 4 |  |  | Compiled | 30 | 23 |
| 1 | 9 | 14 | 2 |  |  | Tax Returns | 13 | 16 |
| 1 | 9 | 11 | 29 | 5 | 2 | Other | 56 | 60 |
|  | 18 (4/1-9/30/11) |  | 139 (10/1/11-3/31/12) |  |  |  |  |  |
| 3 | 27 | 59 | 53 | 9 | 6 | **NUMBER OF STATEMENTS** | 150 | 155 |
| % | % | % | % | % | % | **ASSETS** | % | % |
|  | 9.5 | 8.0 | 5.7 |  |  | Cash & Equivalents | 7.9 | 7.4 |
|  | 31.7 | 35.1 | 36.0 |  |  | Trade Receivables (net) | 33.5 | 31.3 |
|  | 29.6 | 38.4 | 34.4 |  |  | Inventory | 33.1 | 34.9 |
|  | 2.7 | 1.3 | 2.6 |  |  | All Other Current | 3.6 | 2.4 |
|  | 73.5 | 82.8 | 78.7 |  |  | Total Current | 78.1 | 76.0 |
|  | 18.8 | 11.5 | 11.7 |  |  | Fixed Assets (net) | 14.2 | 14.9 |
|  | 1.4 | 1.7 | 3.5 |  |  | Intangibles (net) | 2.6 | 3.8 |
|  | 6.4 | 4.0 | 6.2 |  |  | All Other Non-Current | 5.0 | 5.4 |
|  | 100.0 | 100.0 | 100.0 |  |  | Total | 100.0 | 100.0 |
|  |  |  |  |  |  | **LIABILITIES** |  |  |
|  | 12.5 | 13.1 | 8.3 |  |  | Notes Payable-Short Term | 13.7 | 13.9 |
|  | 2.1 | 1.3 | 1.3 |  |  | Cur. Mat.-L.T.D. | 1.7 | 2.4 |
|  | 20.3 | 20.9 | 23.5 |  |  | Trade Payables | 19.9 | 18.8 |
|  | .1 | .0 | .2 |  |  | Income Taxes Payable | .2 | .2 |
|  | 9.8 | 8.4 | 9.5 |  |  | All Other Current | 10.0 | 8.9 |
|  | 44.8 | 43.7 | 42.7 |  |  | Total Current | 45.4 | 44.2 |
|  | 13.0 | 6.1 | 13.7 |  |  | Long-Term Debt | 9.6 | 12.5 |
|  | .0 | .1 | .4 |  |  | Deferred Taxes | .2 | .8 |
|  | 8.5 | 6.1 | 3.1 |  |  | All Other Non-Current | 4.0 | 3.7 |
|  | 33.7 | 44.0 | 40.0 |  |  | Net Worth | 40.7 | 38.8 |
|  | 100.0 | 100.0 | 100.0 |  |  | Total Liabilities & Net Worth | 100.0 | 100.0 |
|  |  |  |  |  |  | **INCOME DATA** |  |  |
|  | 100.0 | 100.0 | 100.0 |  |  | Net Sales | 100.0 | 100.0 |
|  | 29.1 | 23.8 | 24.2 |  |  | Gross Profit | 24.9 | 25.1 |
|  | 26.5 | 21.0 | 20.2 |  |  | Operating Expenses | 21.7 | 22.1 |
|  | 2.7 | 2.8 | 4.0 |  |  | Operating Profit | 3.2 | 3.0 |
|  | .0 | -.1 | -.2 |  |  | All Other Expenses (net) | .1 | .5 |
|  | 2.7 | 2.9 | 4.2 |  |  | Profit Before Taxes | 3.1 | 2.5 |
|  |  |  |  |  |  | **RATIOS** |  |  |
|  | 2.7 | 2.7 | 2.4 |  |  | Current | 2.6 | 2.9 |
|  | 1.8 | 2.1 | 1.9 |  |  |  | 1.8 | 1.8 |
|  | 1.1 | 1.4 | 1.4 |  |  |  | 1.3 | 1.3 |
|  | 1.8 | 1.6 | 1.4 |  |  | Quick | 1.5 | 1.4 |
|  | (26) .9 | .9 | 1.0 |  |  |  | .9 | .8 |
|  | .5 | .7 | .6 |  |  |  | .6 | .5 |
|  | 16 22.7 | 30 12.0 | 35 10.4 |  |  | Sales/Receivables | 26 14.0 | 24 15.1 |
|  | 30 12.2 | 40 9.2 | 49 7.4 |  |  |  | 39 9.3 | 38 9.5 |
|  | 56 6.5 | 49 7.4 | 60 6.1 |  |  |  | 53 6.8 | 55 6.7 |
|  | 22 16.9 | 40 9.1 | 46 8.0 |  |  | Cost of Sales/Inventory | 33 11.1 | 36 10.1 |
|  | 47 7.8 | 60 6.1 | 61 6.0 |  |  |  | 50 7.4 | 54 6.8 |
|  | 66 5.5 | 94 3.9 | 74 4.9 |  |  |  | 75 4.8 | 79 4.6 |
|  | 10 34.9 | 21 17.2 | 23 15.7 |  |  | Cost of Sales/Payables | 16 23.3 | 14 25.5 |
|  | 27 13.7 | 31 11.6 | 32 11.3 |  |  |  | 29 12.5 | 27 13.4 |
|  | 57 6.4 | 47 7.7 | 59 6.2 |  |  |  | 44 8.3 | 45 8.1 |
|  | 6.7 | 5.8 | 5.3 |  |  | Sales/Working Capital | 6.0 | 5.9 |
|  | 9.9 | 7.2 | 7.2 |  |  |  | 8.9 | 8.8 |
|  | 73.1 | 13.6 | 13.1 |  |  |  | 18.8 | 18.1 |
|  | 15.2 | 13.9 | 21.4 |  |  | EBIT/Interest | 11.0 | 11.3 |
|  | (26) 3.7 | (53) 4.8 | (50) 11.2 |  |  |  | (138) 3.9 | (144) 3.7 |
|  | -.4 | 1.6 | 4.2 |  |  |  | 1.4 | 1.3 |
|  |  |  | 9.6 |  |  | Net Profit + Depr., Dep., Amort./Cur. Mat. L/T/D | 12.9 | 4.1 |
|  |  |  | (12) 4.8 |  |  |  | (38) 3.3 | (31) 2.4 |
|  |  |  | 1.8 |  |  |  | 1.5 | 1.1 |
|  | .1 | .1 | .2 |  |  | Fixed/Worth | .1 | .1 |
|  | .3 | .2 | .3 |  |  |  | .3 | .3 |
|  | 1.2 | .4 | .5 |  |  |  | .8 | .8 |
|  | .5 | .6 | .7 |  |  | Debt/Worth | .6 | .7 |
|  | 2.8 | 1.3 | 1.6 |  |  |  | 1.5 | 1.7 |
|  | 6.6 | 3.1 | 3.0 |  |  |  | 3.8 | 4.1 |
|  | 54.4 | 38.4 | 53.2 |  |  | % Profit Before Taxes/Tangible Net Worth | 48.6 | 40.1 |
|  | (22) 23.3 | (57) 17.6 | (49) 27.4 |  |  |  | (140) 18.3 | (141) 18.0 |
|  | 5.3 | 5.8 | 12.0 |  |  |  | 4.1 | 5.3 |
|  | 18.0 | 11.2 | 14.2 |  |  | % Profit Before Taxes/Total Assets | 15.5 | 14.9 |
|  | 6.6 | 6.4 | 10.5 |  |  |  | 8.3 | 5.9 |
|  | -1.3 | 1.3 | 5.4 |  |  |  | 1.0 | .9 |
|  | 118.3 | 109.8 | 51.0 |  |  | Sales/Net Fixed Assets | 68.5 | 71.4 |
|  | 31.4 | 36.9 | 26.8 |  |  |  | 28.4 | 30.8 |
|  | 9.4 | 16.3 | 19.2 |  |  |  | 15.7 | 12.2 |
|  | 4.0 | 3.7 | 3.2 |  |  | Sales/Total Assets | 3.7 | 3.6 |
|  | 3.0 | 3.0 | 2.6 |  |  |  | 3.0 | 2.9 |
|  | 2.4 | 2.3 | 2.4 |  |  |  | 2.3 | 2.2 |
|  | .3 | .4 | .5 |  |  | % Depr., Dep., Amort./Sales | .4 | .5 |
|  | (19) .7 | (52) .7 | (51) .6 |  |  |  | (134) .9 | (132) .9 |
|  | 1.1 | 1.0 | 1.0 |  |  |  | 1.4 | 1.4 |
|  | 1.7 | 1.2 | 2.0 |  |  | % Officers', Directors' Owners' Comp/Sales | 1.4 | 1.1 |
|  | (17) 2.9 | (25) 2.1 | (11) 3.0 |  |  |  | (60) 2.4 | (53) 2.5 |
|  | 4.9 | 4.0 | 8.4 |  |  |  | 4.1 | 4.3 |
| 3644M | 117859M | 832407M | 3047663M | 1412745M | 1865274M | Net Sales ($) | 6781047M | 6709454M |
| 718M | 35136M | 261482M | 1123442M | 603190M | 872579M | Total Assets ($) | 2437540M | 2604509M |

M = $ thousand    MM = $ million
See Pages 9 through 22 for Explanation of Ratios and Data

## Comparative Historical Data | Current Data Sorted by Sales

| | | | Type of Statement | 0-1MM | 1-3MM | 3-5MM | 5-10MM | 10-25MM | 25MM & OVER |
|---|---|---|---|---|---|---|---|---|---|
| 18 | 20 | 17 | Unqualified | | | | 1 | 3 | 13 |
| 33 | 42 | 36 | Reviewed | | | 2 | 5 | 13 | 16 |
| 23 | 29 | 21 | Compiled | | 2 | 4 | 4 | 6 | 5 |
| 23 | 23 | 26 | Tax Returns | 1 | 2 | 3 | 13 | 5 | 2 |
| 46 | 53 | 57 | Other | 1 | 4 | 4 | 4 | 9 | 35 |
| 4/1/09-3/31/10 | 4/1/10-3/31/11 | 4/1/11-3/31/12 | | | | 18 (4/1-9/30/11) | 139 (10/1/11-3/31/12) | | |
| ALL | ALL | ALL | | | | | | | |
| 143 | 167 | 157 | **NUMBER OF STATEMENTS** | 2 | 8 | 13 | 27 | 36 | 71 |
| % | % | % | **ASSETS** | % | % | % | % | % | % |
| 9.2 | 9.4 | 7.8 | Cash & Equivalents | | | 7.9 | 11.6 | 7.6 | 6.7 |
| 30.0 | 32.9 | 34.1 | Trade Receivables (net) | | | 30.6 | 32.7 | 36.9 | 35.5 |
| 34.1 | 34.7 | 34.5 | Inventory | | | 36.7 | 35.5 | 33.5 | 34.1 |
| 4.3 | 3.2 | 2.1 | All Other Current | | | 2.6 | 1.3 | 2.3 | 2.4 |
| 77.6 | 80.2 | 78.5 | Total Current | | | 77.7 | 81.1 | 80.2 | 78.6 |
| 13.2 | 13.0 | 12.8 | Fixed Assets (net) | | | 14.6 | 14.5 | 11.5 | 10.6 |
| 3.1 | 2.3 | 3.6 | Intangibles (net) | | | .9 | .9 | 2.9 | 5.6 |
| 6.1 | 4.6 | 5.1 | All Other Non-Current | | | 6.8 | 3.6 | 5.4 | 5.2 |
| 100.0 | 100.0 | 100.0 | Total | | | 100.0 | 100.0 | 100.0 | 100.0 |
| | | | **LIABILITIES** | | | | | | |
| 13.9 | 12.0 | 11.0 | Notes Payable-Short Term | | | 12.1 | 9.6 | 13.1 | 9.9 |
| 2.7 | 2.2 | 1.4 | Cur. Mat.-L.T.D. | | | 1.3 | 2.0 | 1.6 | .9 |
| 19.5 | 20.6 | 21.8 | Trade Payables | | | 21.9 | 22.8 | 21.8 | 22.8 |
| .1 | .1 | .1 | Income Taxes Payable | | | .0 | .0 | .1 | .1 |
| 7.7 | 7.5 | 8.8 | All Other Current | | | 5.9 | 8.0 | 8.1 | 9.2 |
| 43.9 | 42.5 | 43.1 | Total Current | | | 41.1 | 42.5 | 44.7 | 42.9 |
| 12.0 | 11.0 | 9.9 | Long-Term Debt | | | 17.8 | 5.9 | 8.1 | 10.5 |
| .4 | .4 | .3 | Deferred Taxes | | | .0 | .1 | .1 | .5 |
| 5.0 | 4.9 | 5.2 | All Other Non-Current | | | 12.6 | 9.9 | 3.3 | 3.1 |
| 38.7 | 41.2 | 41.5 | Net Worth | | | 28.4 | 41.5 | 43.8 | 43.0 |
| 100.0 | 100.0 | 100.0 | Total Liabilties & Net Worth | | | 100.0 | 100.0 | 100.0 | 100.0 |
| | | | **INCOME DATA** | | | | | | |
| 100.0 | 100.0 | 100.0 | Net Sales | | | 100.0 | 100.0 | 100.0 | 100.0 |
| 26.7 | 25.5 | 25.0 | Gross Profit | | | 24.4 | 25.0 | 24.0 | 23.9 |
| 25.0 | 23.6 | 21.6 | Operating Expenses | | | 21.2 | 22.5 | 20.8 | 20.2 |
| 1.6 | 1.9 | 3.4 | Operating Profit | | | 3.2 | 2.5 | 3.2 | 3.7 |
| .2 | .2 | -.1 | All Other Expenses (net) | | | -.5 | .0 | .0 | -.1 |
| 1.5 | 1.7 | 3.5 | Profit Before Taxes | | | 3.7 | 2.5 | 3.2 | 3.8 |
| | | | **RATIOS** | | | | | | |
| 3.2 | 3.0 | 2.8 | | | | 2.8 | 2.8 | 2.7 | 2.5 |
| 1.7 | 1.9 | 1.9 | Current | | | 1.8 | 2.1 | 2.2 | 1.8 |
| 1.3 | 1.4 | 1.3 | | | | 1.4 | 1.3 | 1.3 | 1.4 |
| 1.8 | 1.7 | 1.5 | | | | 1.7 | 2.0 | 1.7 | 1.4 |
| .8 (166) | 1.0 (156) | 1.0 | Quick | | | .8 | 1.0 | 1.0 | 1.0 |
| .5 | .7 | .6 | | | | .5 | .5 | .7 | .7 |
| 27 13.4 | 26 14.3 | 29 12.6 | | | | 21 17.2 | 23 15.6 | 31 11.6 | 30 12.1 |
| 36 10.0 | 41 9.0 | 43 8.5 | Sales/Receivables | | | 33 11.0 | 41 9.0 | 39 9.4 | 49 7.5 |
| 54 6.7 | 59 6.2 | 56 6.5 | | | | 59 6.2 | 53 6.9 | 49 7.4 | 59 6.2 |
| 37 9.9 | 42 8.6 | 40 9.2 | | | | 46 7.9 | 38 9.7 | 31 11.8 | 42 8.6 |
| 58 6.3 | 59 6.2 | 58 6.3 | Cost of Sales/Inventory | | | 54 6.8 | 53 6.9 | 50 7.3 | 60 6.1 |
| 84 4.4 | 79 4.6 | 76 4.8 | | | | 83 4.4 | 104 3.5 | 69 5.3 | 73 5.0 |
| 16 22.4 | 20 18.0 | 22 16.7 | | | | 13 27.5 | 13 28.3 | 23 15.7 | 23 16.0 |
| 32 11.5 | 32 11.4 | 32 11.3 | Cost of Sales/Payables | | | 29 12.5 | 41 8.9 | 28 12.9 | 33 11.2 |
| 50 7.4 | 49 7.5 | 55 6.6 | | | | 52 7.0 | 61 6.0 | 49 7.4 | 55 6.6 |
| 5.1 | 4.7 | 5.4 | | | | 5.8 | 5.1 | 6.2 | 5.1 |
| 9.2 | 7.9 | 7.8 | Sales/Working Capital | | | 8.1 | 6.9 | 8.0 | 7.8 |
| 21.0 | 17.7 | 15.6 | | | | 17.1 | 13.4 | 18.9 | 15.2 |
| 10.7 | 11.6 | 17.8 | | | | 17.9 | 10.0 | 23.9 | 20.9 |
| (133) 3.4 | (149) 4.4 | (144) 6.0 | EBIT/Interest | | | (23) 3.6 | (33) 3.7 | (67) 5.8 | 10.8 |
| .6 | 1.2 | 2.1 | | | | -.3 | 1.4 | 2.5 | 3.4 |
| 6.5 | 6.2 | 15.2 | | | | | | | 19.7 |
| (23) 2.5 | (28) 2.2 | (28) 3.8 | Net Profit + Depr., Dep., Amort./Cur. Mat. L/T/D | | | | | (15) | 5.8 |
| .9 | .7 | 1.7 | | | | | | | 2.0 |
| .1 | .1 | .1 | | | | .0 | .2 | .1 | .2 |
| .3 | .2 | .3 | Fixed/Worth | | | .2 | .3 | .2 | .3 |
| .8 | .7 | .5 | | | | 2.6 | .6 | .3 | .4 |
| .7 | .6 | .7 | | | | 1.6 | .6 | .6 | .7 |
| 1.8 | 1.5 | 1.6 | Debt/Worth | | | 4.1 | 1.4 | 1.3 | 1.5 |
| 4.6 | 3.8 | 3.8 | | | | 6.1 | 4.0 | 4.1 | 2.9 |
| 38.9 | 30.5 | 41.9 | | | | 43.4 | 33.3 | 46.9 | 36.9 |
| (133) 13.0 | (153) 11.9 | (145) 22.2 | % Profit Before Taxes/Tangible Net Worth | | (11) 38.0 | (25) 14.9 | (35) 19.8 | (66) 25.8 |
| 1.4 | 3.7 | 8.8 | | | | -5.5 | 2.5 | 12.0 | 11.6 |
| 11.6 | 10.9 | 13.3 | | | | 13.7 | 12.1 | 11.9 | 14.5 |
| 3.7 | 3.9 | 7.7 | % Profit Before Taxes/Total Assets | | | 6.6 | 4.4 | 9.1 | 9.4 |
| -.3 | .5 | 1.6 | | | | -3.1 | 1.0 | 4.6 | 3.0 |
| 61.8 | 80.9 | 64.9 | | | | 725.7 | 117.1 | 87.6 | 60.9 |
| 33.9 | 37.2 | 32.1 | Sales/Net Fixed Assets | | | 55.4 | 32.1 | 38.7 | 29.8 |
| 16.4 | 16.0 | 16.9 | | | | 8.6 | 11.2 | 17.2 | 23.1 |
| 3.6 | 3.5 | 3.6 | | | | 3.3 | 3.8 | 3.7 | 3.4 |
| 2.7 | 2.9 | 2.7 | Sales/Total Assets | | | 2.9 | 2.7 | 3.1 | 2.6 |
| 2.1 | 2.2 | 2.3 | | | | 2.3 | 2.1 | 2.5 | 2.3 |
| .5 | .5 | .4 | | | | | .4 | .4 | .4 |
| (117) .8 | (141) .7 | (134) .7 | % Depr., Dep., Amort./Sales | | | (22) .8 | (33) .7 | (65) .6 |
| 1.4 | 1.5 | 1.0 | | | | | 1.4 | .9 | 1.0 |
| 1.3 | 1.3 | 1.4 | | | | | 1.8 | 1.0 | 1.4 |
| (57) 2.9 | (61) 3.2 | (55) 2.4 | % Officers', Directors' Owners' Comp/Sales | | | (16) 3.3 | (14) 1.3 | (12) 2.9 |
| 4.8 | 5.2 | 5.3 | | | | | 4.2 | 2.2 | 7.8 |
| 5643477M | 5903390M | 7279592M | Net Sales ($) | 604M | 17868M | 53381M | 183531M | 547419M | 6476789M |
| 2085012M | 2313158M | 2896547M | Total Assets ($) | 905M | 7152M | 20008M | 68996M | 207662M | 2591824M |

M = $ thousand    MM = $ million
See Pages 9 through 22 for Explanation of Ratios and Data

## Current Data Sorted by Assets      Comparative Historical Data

| | | | | | | | Type of Statement | | |
|---|---|---|---|---|---|---|---|---|---|
| 1 | 1 | 8 | 8 | 7 | 4 | | Unqualified | 41 | 42 |
| | 9 | 39 | 8 | 2 | | | Reviewed | 68 | 73 |
| 7 | 17 | 22 | 2 | | | | Compiled | 46 | 55 |
| 19 | 35 | 28 | | | | | Tax Returns | 45 | 62 |
| 7 | 24 | 41 | 20 | 3 | 4 | | Other | 99 | 108 |
| | 41 (4/1-9/30/11) | | 275 (10/1/11-3/31/12) | | | | | 4/1/07-3/31/08 | 4/1/08-3/31/09 |
| 0-500M | 500M-2MM | 2-10MM | 10-50MM | 50-100MM | 100-250MM | | | ALL | ALL |
| 34 | 86 | 138 | 38 | 12 | 8 | | NUMBER OF STATEMENTS | 299 | 340 |
| % | % | % | % | % | % | | ASSETS | % | % |
| 11.7 | 9.3 | 8.6 | 7.4 | 6.0 | | | Cash & Equivalents | 7.2 | 8.4 |
| 29.5 | 35.3 | 34.5 | 27.3 | 24.6 | | | Trade Receivables (net) | 34.7 | 31.0 |
| 25.0 | 32.7 | 34.3 | 32.9 | 32.7 | | | Inventory | 31.1 | 32.5 |
| 4.9 | 1.6 | 2.0 | 1.5 | 2.3 | | | All Other Current | 2.8 | 3.1 |
| 71.1 | 78.8 | 79.4 | 69.1 | 65.6 | | | Total Current | 75.7 | 75.0 |
| 15.9 | 14.2 | 13.4 | 19.4 | 26.4 | | | Fixed Assets (net) | 15.5 | 17.2 |
| 4.5 | 1.2 | 2.4 | 6.0 | 5.3 | | | Intangibles (net) | 3.2 | 3.3 |
| 8.5 | 5.9 | 4.8 | 5.5 | 2.7 | | | All Other Non-Current | 5.6 | 4.5 |
| 100.0 | 100.0 | 100.0 | 100.0 | 100.0 | | | Total | 100.0 | 100.0 |
| | | | | | | | LIABILITIES | | |
| 18.1 | 16.1 | 15.8 | 13.4 | 14.7 | | | Notes Payable-Short Term | 16.8 | 16.6 |
| 3.1 | 1.7 | 2.1 | 2.3 | 1.3 | | | Cur. Mat.-L.T.D. | 3.6 | 3.4 |
| 17.0 | 21.3 | 20.1 | 14.1 | 10.2 | | | Trade Payables | 18.2 | 15.4 |
| .1 | .1 | .1 | .1 | .0 | | | Income Taxes Payable | .2 | .2 |
| 15.9 | 7.0 | 7.2 | 7.0 | 7.8 | | | All Other Current | 9.1 | 7.9 |
| 54.1 | 46.2 | 45.3 | 37.0 | 34.1 | | | Total Current | 47.9 | 43.6 |
| 12.0 | 12.5 | 7.1 | 9.4 | 7.0 | | | Long-Term Debt | 11.2 | 12.2 |
| .0 | .0 | .3 | .1 | .7 | | | Deferred Taxes | .3 | .4 |
| 12.3 | 8.3 | 7.3 | 4.8 | 2.1 | | | All Other Non-Current | 4.1 | 4.1 |
| 21.6 | 33.0 | 40.2 | 48.7 | 56.1 | | | Net Worth | 36.5 | 39.8 |
| 100.0 | 100.0 | 100.0 | 100.0 | 100.0 | | | Total Liabilties & Net Worth | 100.0 | 100.0 |
| | | | | | | | INCOME DATA | | |
| 100.0 | 100.0 | 100.0 | 100.0 | 100.0 | | | Net Sales | 100.0 | 100.0 |
| 34.8 | 28.1 | 27.3 | 27.2 | 25.9 | | | Gross Profit | 27.5 | 27.8 |
| 33.2 | 26.0 | 24.8 | 23.9 | 21.5 | | | Operating Expenses | 24.1 | 25.3 |
| 1.6 | 2.1 | 2.6 | 3.3 | 4.3 | | | Operating Profit | 3.4 | 2.6 |
| .5 | .1 | .2 | .6 | .7 | | | All Other Expenses (net) | .4 | .6 |
| 1.1 | 1.9 | 2.4 | 2.8 | 3.6 | | | Profit Before Taxes | 3.0 | 2.0 |
| | | | | | | | RATIOS | | |
| 4.2 | 2.7 | 3.2 | 4.2 | 3.4 | | | | 2.8 | 3.2 |
| 1.5 | 1.8 | 1.7 | 2.0 | 2.2 | | | Current | 1.7 | 1.8 |
| .9 | 1.2 | 1.2 | 1.3 | 1.4 | | | | 1.2 | 1.3 |
| 3.1 | 1.5 | 1.5 | 2.4 | 2.0 | | | | 1.5 | 1.6 |
| .7 | .9 | .9 | .9 | 1.1 | | | Quick | .9 | .9 |
| .4 | .6 | .6 | .6 | .4 | | | | .6 | .5 |

| | | | | | | | | | | | | | | | |
|---|---|---|---|---|---|---|---|---|---|---|---|---|---|---|---|
| 9 | 42.7 | 26 | 14.0 | 30 | 12.0 | 31 | 11.6 | 31 | 11.9 | | | Sales/Receivables | 30 | 12.3 | 24 | 15.1 |
| 38 | 9.7 | 37 | 9.8 | 45 | 8.1 | 41 | 8.8 | 41 | 8.9 | | | | 39 | 9.4 | 37 | 10.0 |
| 54 | 6.7 | 63 | 5.8 | 65 | 5.6 | 52 | 7.0 | 49 | 7.4 | | | | 53 | 6.9 | 51 | 7.1 |

Sales/Receivables, Cost of Sales/Inventory, Cost of Sales/Payables etc. follow:

| Left count | Value | | | | | | | | | Center label | Hist count | Value | count | Value |
|---|---|---|---|---|---|---|---|---|---|---|---|---|---|---|
| 7 | 54.0 | 17 | 21.7 | 36 | 10.2 | 43 | 8.4 | 48 | 7.6 | Cost of Sales/Inventory | 29 | 12.7 | 28 | 13.3 |
| 27 | 13.4 | 56 | 6.5 | 62 | 5.9 | 64 | 5.7 | 59 | 6.2 | | 51 | 7.2 | 54 | 6.8 |
| 99 | 3.7 | 94 | 3.9 | 91 | 4.0 | 89 | 4.1 | 94 | 3.9 | | 75 | 4.9 | 82 | 4.4 |
| 0 | UND | 15 | 24.7 | 18 | 20.1 | 18 | 20.3 | 12 | 29.4 | Cost of Sales/Payables | 16 | 22.9 | 11 | 32.8 |
| 20 | 17.9 | 25 | 14.4 | 29 | 12.7 | 26 | 13.8 | 24 | 15.1 | | 24 | 15.5 | 20 | 18.3 |
| 54 | 6.7 | 48 | 7.6 | 47 | 7.7 | 39 | 9.4 | 33 | 10.9 | | 40 | 9.1 | 38 | 9.7 |

| | | | | | | | | | |
|---|---|---|---|---|---|---|---|---|---|
| 6.2 | 4.7 | 5.0 | 4.0 | 4.9 | | Sales/Working Capital | 6.0 | 5.3 |
| 20.1 | 8.0 | 8.4 | 9.0 | 7.5 | | | 10.4 | 9.1 |
| -39.2 | 34.0 | 18.8 | 18.9 | 11.7 | | | 22.5 | 20.1 |

| count | Value | count | Value | count | Value | count | Value | | | Center | count | Value | count | Value |
|---|---|---|---|---|---|---|---|---|---|---|---|---|---|---|
| | 11.3 | | 10.1 | | 12.8 | | 15.2 | | | EBIT/Interest | | 10.6 | | 10.7 |
| (27) | 3.0 | (73) | 3.5 | (116) | 3.6 | (35) | 4.6 | | | | (278) | 3.5 | (306) | 3.3 |
| | -1.2 | | 1.1 | | 1.2 | | 1.7 | | | | | 1.5 | | .9 |
| | | | | | 4.2 | | | | | Net Profit + Depr., Dep., Amort./Cur. Mat. L/T/D | | 7.1 | | 5.9 |
| | | (19) | 1.9 | | | | | | | | (69) | 3.0 | (70) | 2.1 |
| | | | .9 | | | | | | | | | 1.1 | | .4 |

| | | | | | | | | | |
|---|---|---|---|---|---|---|---|---|---|
| .0 | .1 | .1 | .1 | .2 | | Fixed/Worth | .1 | .1 |
| .2 | .2 | .2 | .4 | .4 | | | .3 | .3 |
| 1.0 | 1.0 | 1.1 | .9 | .8 | | | .9 | .9 |
| .7 | .7 | .6 | .4 | .3 | | Debt/Worth | .8 | .7 |
| 2.8 | 2.0 | 1.6 | 1.5 | 1.0 | | | 1.7 | 1.7 |
| -28.3 | 11.2 | 4.6 | 3.4 | 1.9 | | | 4.3 | 4.7 |

| count | Value | count | Value | count | Value | count | Value | | | Center | count | Value | count | Value |
|---|---|---|---|---|---|---|---|---|---|---|---|---|---|---|
| | 47.2 | | 30.5 | | 37.0 | | 23.7 | | 25.7 | % Profit Before Taxes/Tangible Net Worth | | 45.5 | | 34.3 |
| (25) | 20.0 | (77) | 9.3 | (125) | 13.1 | (36) | 11.4 | | 8.2 | | (275) | 21.3 | (311) | 15.6 |
| | -1.6 | | .3 | | 1.9 | | 5.0 | | 2.6 | | | 7.0 | | 1.4 |

| | | | | | | | | | |
|---|---|---|---|---|---|---|---|---|---|
| 15.3 | 12.0 | 12.6 | 11.0 | 7.4 | | % Profit Before Taxes/Total Assets | 16.8 | 14.7 |
| 6.6 | 4.6 | 5.2 | 5.2 | 4.1 | | | 6.9 | 5.1 |
| -4.8 | .1 | .3 | .4 | .9 | | | 1.7 | -.1 |
| 380.0 | 156.5 | 88.2 | 41.9 | 32.9 | | Sales/Net Fixed Assets | 74.1 | 72.0 |
| 70.3 | 55.5 | 37.2 | 16.7 | 12.1 | | | 30.5 | 28.8 |
| 24.0 | 18.6 | 14.4 | 8.1 | 5.3 | | | 13.5 | 11.3 |
| 6.1 | 3.7 | 3.3 | 2.9 | 2.6 | | Sales/Total Assets | 3.8 | 3.7 |
| 3.6 | 3.0 | 2.5 | 2.3 | 2.4 | | | 2.9 | 2.9 |
| 2.3 | 1.9 | 2.0 | 1.7 | 2.1 | | | 2.2 | 2.1 |

| count | Value | count | Value | count | Value | count | Value | | | Center | count | Value | count | Value |
|---|---|---|---|---|---|---|---|---|---|---|---|---|---|---|
| | .1 | | .3 | | .4 | | .4 | | 1.4 | % Depr., Dep., Amort./Sales | | .5 | | .5 |
| (20) | .4 | (61) | .6 | (111) | .9 | (36) | .8 | | 1.7 | | (258) | .9 | (282) | .9 |
| | 1.9 | | 1.1 | | 1.7 | | 1.5 | | 2.5 | | | 1.8 | | 2.0 |
| | 3.6 | | 2.2 | | 1.5 | | | | | % Officers', Directors' Owners' Comp/Sales | | 1.2 | | 1.8 |
| (18) | 5.3 | (48) | 3.2 | (64) | 2.3 | | | | | | (105) | 2.6 | (141) | 2.8 |
| | 9.2 | | 6.1 | | 4.1 | | | | | | | 5.4 | | 4.9 |

| | | | | | | | | | |
|---|---|---|---|---|---|---|---|---|---|
| 38113M | 311614M | 1686081M | 2091791M | 1760482M | 2682831M | Net Sales ($) | 10948669M | 13065514M |
| 9891M | 98448M | 621153M | 817306M | 790310M | 1323641M | Total Assets ($) | 4219611M | 4337331M |

## Comparative Historical Data | Current Data Sorted by Sales

| | | | Type of Statement | | | | | | |
|---|---|---|---|---|---|---|---|---|---|
| 34 | 36 | 29 | Unqualified | 1 | 1 | | 2 | 7 | 18 |
| 75 | 68 | 58 | Reviewed | | 4 | 6 | 16 | 21 | 11 |
| 38 | 51 | 48 | Compiled | 3 | 11 | 4 | 14 | 13 | 3 |
| 42 | 56 | 82 | Tax Returns | 10 | 26 | 15 | 14 | 16 | 1 |
| 114 | 114 | 99 | Other | 7 | 15 | 11 | 23 | 19 | 24 |
| 4/1/09-3/31/10 ALL | 4/1/10-3/31/11 ALL | 4/1/11-3/31/12 ALL | | 41 (4/1-9/30/11) | | | 275 (10/1/11-3/31/12) | | |
| | | | | 0-1MM | 1-3MM | 3-5MM | 5-10MM | 10-25MM | 25MM & OVER |
| 303 | 325 | 316 | NUMBER OF STATEMENTS | 21 | 57 | 36 | 69 | 76 | 57 |
| % | % | % | **ASSETS** | % | % | % | % | % | % |
| 8.9 | 10.0 | 8.7 | Cash & Equivalents | 13.5 | 9.1 | 9.1 | 8.2 | 9.4 | 6.1 |
| 29.4 | 30.7 | 32.7 | Trade Receivables (net) | 27.1 | 32.1 | 30.7 | 34.8 | 36.9 | 28.5 |
| 31.6 | 33.5 | 32.3 | Inventory | 30.8 | 27.2 | 29.8 | 35.0 | 34.7 | 33.0 |
| 2.5 | 3.0 | 2.2 | All Other Current | 5.1 | 2.3 | 2.3 | 1.6 | 1.5 | 2.4 |
| 72.4 | 77.2 | 75.9 | Total Current | 76.6 | 70.7 | 71.8 | 79.7 | 82.5 | 69.9 |
| 19.2 | 14.8 | 15.5 | Fixed Assets (net) | 11.3 | 20.6 | 20.4 | 12.3 | 10.6 | 19.5 |
| 3.0 | 3.2 | 2.9 | Intangibles (net) | 4.2 | 1.2 | 4.4 | 2.1 | 2.6 | 4.5 |
| 5.3 | 4.9 | 5.7 | All Other Non-Current | 7.9 | 7.5 | 3.3 | 5.8 | 4.4 | 6.0 |
| 100.0 | 100.0 | 100.0 | Total | 100.0 | 100.0 | 100.0 | 100.0 | 100.0 | 100.0 |
| | | | **LIABILITIES** | | | | | | |
| 14.4 | 16.5 | 15.5 | Notes Payable-Short Term | 16.3 | 17.1 | 10.6 | 16.9 | 16.7 | 13.5 |
| 2.8 | 2.3 | 2.1 | Cur. Mat.-L.T.D. | .8 | 2.6 | 4.6 | 1.6 | 1.5 | 1.9 |
| 15.7 | 18.2 | 19.0 | Trade Payables | 16.3 | 17.9 | 15.5 | 24.5 | 19.5 | 15.9 |
| .1 | .1 | .1 | Income Taxes Payable | .0 | .1 | .1 | .1 | .1 | .2 |
| 7.3 | 8.0 | 8.1 | All Other Current | 17.7 | 11.2 | 4.5 | 5.6 | 6.9 | 8.2 |
| 40.3 | 45.1 | 44.8 | Total Current | 51.1 | 48.8 | 35.3 | 48.7 | 44.7 | 39.7 |
| 12.5 | 9.1 | 9.5 | Long-Term Debt | 15.5 | 14.8 | 11.2 | 7.1 | 5.7 | 9.0 |
| .2 | .2 | .2 | Deferred Taxes | .0 | .0 | .1 | .2 | .2 | .5 |
| 5.9 | 7.3 | 7.5 | All Other Non-Current | 20.9 | 10.6 | 6.0 | 5.8 | 7.1 | 2.8 |
| 41.0 | 38.2 | 38.0 | Net Worth | 12.5 | 25.7 | 47.4 | 38.1 | 42.3 | 48.0 |
| 100.0 | 100.0 | 100.0 | Total Liabilities & Net Worth | 100.0 | 100.0 | 100.0 | 100.0 | 100.0 | 100.0 |
| | | | **INCOME DATA** | | | | | | |
| 100.0 | 100.0 | 100.0 | Net Sales | 100.0 | 100.0 | 100.0 | 100.0 | 100.0 | 100.0 |
| 28.2 | 28.4 | 28.0 | Gross Profit | 37.2 | 32.3 | 28.5 | 26.9 | 27.4 | 22.2 |
| 26.5 | 26.6 | 25.6 | Operating Expenses | 37.1 | 29.3 | 25.6 | 26.1 | 23.6 | 19.6 |
| 1.7 | 1.8 | 2.4 | Operating Profit | .1 | 3.0 | 2.9 | .8 | 3.8 | 2.6 |
| .5 | .3 | .3 | All Other Expenses (net) | .6 | .5 | -.3 | .2 | .3 | .5 |
| 1.2 | 1.5 | 2.1 | Profit Before Taxes | -.6 | 2.5 | 3.2 | .6 | 3.5 | 2.1 |
| | | | **RATIOS** | | | | | | |
| 3.2 | 3.3 | 3.1 | | 4.4 | 3.3 | 4.6 | 2.4 | 3.3 | 2.9 |
| 1.9 | 1.8 | 1.7 | Current | 1.8 | 1.6 | 2.2 | 1.6 | 1.7 | 1.9 |
| 1.3 | 1.3 | 1.2 | | .9 | 1.1 | 1.4 | 1.2 | 1.3 | 1.4 |
| 1.7 | 1.7 | 1.5 | | 3.7 | 1.7 | 2.2 | 1.3 | 1.7 | 1.7 |
| 1.0 | .9 | .9 | Quick | .8 | .9 | 1.1 | .9 | 1.0 | .9 |
| .6 | .6 | .6 | | .5 | .5 | .7 | .6 | .6 | .6 |
| 26  14.2 | 24  15.2 | 29  12.8 | | 22  16.7 | 27  13.3 | 25  14.8 | 28  12.9 | 28  12.9 | 31  11.6 |
| 37  9.9 | 40  9.1 | 41  9.0 | Sales/Receivables | 53  6.9 | 40  9.2 | 37  9.9 | 41  8.9 | 40  9.1 | 41  9.0 |
| 54  6.7 | 57  6.4 | 61  6.0 | | 87  4.2 | 69  5.3 | 60  6.1 | 65  5.6 | 60  6.0 | 50  7.3 |
| 31  11.9 | 31  11.9 | 29  12.5 | | 14  25.4 | 8  46.1 | 27  13.7 | 33  11.2 | 33  10.9 | 42  8.7 |
| 57  6.4 | 60  6.0 | 59  6.2 | Cost of Sales/Inventory | 126  2.9 | 50  7.3 | 53  6.9 | 63  5.8 | 60  6.1 | 57  6.4 |
| 91  4.0 | 99  3.7 | 91  4.0 | | 243  1.5 | 99  3.7 | 78  4.7 | 99  3.7 | 85  4.3 | 79  4.6 |
| 13  29.2 | 15  24.9 | 16  23.1 | | 0  UND | 14  25.6 | 18  20.1 | 18  19.8 | 17  21.3 | 16  23.0 |
| 24  15.5 | 27  13.5 | 27  13.4 | Cost of Sales/Payables | 30  12.0 | 27  13.4 | 24  15.3 | 31  11.6 | 26  14.1 | 26  14.0 |
| 38  9.5 | 46  7.9 | 46  8.0 | | 87  4.2 | 68  5.4 | 38  9.6 | 53  6.9 | 45  8.2 | 36  10.0 |
| 5.0 | 4.6 | 4.8 | | 3.4 | 4.8 | 4.3 | 5.1 | 5.1 | 4.7 |
| 8.3 | 8.6 | 9.2 | Sales/Working Capital | 9.6 | 11.1 | 7.0 | 11.2 | 9.3 | 9.1 |
| 16.5 | 17.1 | 24.1 | | -26.9 | 145.3 | 14.1 | 24.0 | -16.3 | 15.7 |
| 7.1 | 11.3 | 11.2 | | 8.4 | 11.5 | 9.3 | 7.5 | 26.1 | 11.0 |
| (271)  1.8 | (282)  3.4 | (268)  3.6 | EBIT/Interest | (16)  2.0 | (48)  3.6 | (27)  3.7 | (63)  2.5 | (63)  4.8 | (51)  5.0 |
| -.6 | .8 | 1.1 | | -5.1 | .9 | .8 | .5 | 1.6 | 1.3 |
| 4.5 | 5.4 | 5.5 | Net Profit + Depr., Dep., | | | | 2.6 | 54.8 | 5.7 |
| (62)  1.7 | (43)  1.8 | (38)  2.2 | Amort./Cur. Mat. L/T/D | | | (10)  2.0 | (10)  3.3 | (15)  2.7 |
| .0 | .7 | 1.2 | | | | | .9 | 1.2 | .9 |
| .1 | .1 | .1 | | .0 | .1 | .0 | .1 | .1 | .2 |
| .4 | .3 | .3 | Fixed/Worth | .2 | .3 | .3 | .2 | .2 | .4 |
| 1.2 | .9 | 1.0 | | NM | 2.3 | 1.4 | 1.0 | .8 | .7 |
| .6 | .6 | .6 | | .6 | .9 | .5 | .7 | .6 | .5 |
| 1.6 | 1.5 | 1.6 | Debt/Worth | 3.1 | 2.7 | 1.4 | 1.9 | 1.6 | 1.4 |
| 3.6 | 3.7 | 5.1 | | -6.8 | 19.2 | 7.3 | 4.5 | 3.6 | 3.4 |
| 23.4 | 28.8 | 31.6 | % Profit Before Taxes/Tangible | 28.4 | 45.7 | 45.2 | 23.9 | 46.4 | 17.8 |
| (274)  7.4 | (289)  10.7 | (282)  11.6 | Net Worth | (12)  4.9 | (47)  16.6 | (35)  15.0 | (64)  8.0 | (70)  15.2 | (54)  11.3 |
| -5.9 | .6 | 1.0 | | -1.2 | .0 | 2.0 | -1.4 | 5.6 | 1.9 |
| 9.4 | 11.3 | 12.1 | % Profit Before Taxes/Total | 11.0 | 13.5 | 13.9 | 8.7 | 15.6 | 9.7 |
| 2.6 | 3.9 | 5.0 | Assets | 5.8 | 4.9 | 8.6 | 2.6 | 6.1 | 4.9 |
| -3.0 | -1.1 | .1 | | -5.6 | -.6 | .8 | -1.3 | 1.0 | .4 |
| 55.1 | 90.4 | 103.6 | | 596.5 | 133.3 | 165.1 | 79.1 | 178.6 | 37.9 |
| 21.7 | 32.3 | 34.0 | Sales/Net Fixed Assets | 94.0 | 40.4 | 35.2 | 38.3 | 65.4 | 17.4 |
| 7.9 | 12.8 | 11.7 | | 17.8 | 9.3 | 5.3 | 14.9 | 22.6 | 7.8 |
| 3.5 | 3.4 | 3.5 | | 2.8 | 3.8 | 3.6 | 3.4 | 3.7 | 3.2 |
| 2.5 | 2.6 | 2.6 | Sales/Total Assets | 1.8 | 2.6 | 2.6 | 2.6 | 3.1 | 2.5 |
| 1.7 | 1.8 | 1.9 | | 1.2 | 1.7 | 1.9 | 2.0 | 2.3 | 1.9 |
| .5 | .5 | .4 | | .1 | .3 | .4 | .4 | .4 | .5 |
| (252)  1.1 | (258)  .8 | (246)  .8 | % Depr., Dep., Amort./Sales | (12)  .4 | (42)  .6 | (22)  1.0 | (59)  .8 | (57)  .8 | (54)  1.0 |
| 2.3 | 1.7 | 1.7 | | 2.9 | 1.9 | 2.8 | 1.3 | 1.3 | 1.7 |
| 2.1 | 1.9 | 1.6 | | | 3.1 | 2.5 | 1.6 | 1.2 | .9 |
| (126)  3.6 | (127)  3.3 | (137)  2.9 | % Officers', Directors' Owners' Comp/Sales | (31)  4.9 | (18)  3.9 | (31)  2.8 | (38)  2.0 | (10)  1.4 |
| 6.5 | 5.9 | 5.5 | | | 6.5 | 5.8 | 4.0 | 3.8 | 4.1 |
| 8156121M | 7729226M | 8570912M | Net Sales ($) | 11571M | 105672M | 143013M | 493637M | 1223108M | 6593911M |
| 3640964M | 3162869M | 3660749M | Total Assets ($) | 7106M | 49004M | 71594M | 211109M | 447626M | 2874310M |

M = $ thousand   MM = $ million
See Pages 9 through 22 for Explanation of Ratios and Data

**Current Data Sorted by Assets** — **Comparative Historical Data**

| 0-500M | 500M-2MM | 2-10MM | 10-50MM | 50-100MM | 100-250MM | Type of Statement | 4/1/07-3/31/08 ALL | 4/1/08-3/31/09 ALL |
|---|---|---|---|---|---|---|---|---|
| | | 2 | 3 | | 1 | Unqualified | 5 | 7 |
| | 1 | 13 | 2 | | | Reviewed | 11 | 15 |
| 1 | 2 | 2 | | | | Compiled | 5 | 2 |
| | 9 | 9 | | | | Tax Returns | 5 | 4 |
| 1 | 7 | 6 | 6 | | | Other | 13 | 13 |
| | 15 (4/1-9/30/11) | | 50 (10/1/11-3/31/12) | | | | | |
| 2 | 19 | 32 | 11 | | 1 | **NUMBER OF STATEMENTS** | 39 | 41 |
| % | % | % | % | % | % | **ASSETS** | % | % |
| | 7.9 | 8.2 | 7.8 | | | Cash & Equivalents | 7.6 | 8.2 |
| | 39.4 | 34.1 | 26.6 | | | Trade Receivables (net) | 35.5 | 31.9 |
| | 29.1 | 40.5 | 37.2 | | | Inventory | 30.4 | 33.6 |
| | .0 | 1.2 | 2.0 | | | All Other Current | 3.4 | 1.6 |
| | 76.4 | 84.0 | 73.6 | | | Total Current | 76.8 | 75.2 |
| | 10.3 | 10.1 | 14.8 | | | Fixed Assets (net) | 13.6 | 12.2 |
| | 4.5 | 2.5 | 6.9 | | | Intangibles (net) | 3.7 | 7.4 |
| | 8.8 | 3.3 | 4.7 | | | All Other Non-Current | 5.9 | 5.3 |
| | 100.0 | 100.0 | 100.0 | | | Total | 100.0 | 100.0 |
| | | | | | | **LIABILITIES** | | |
| | 9.9 | 11.4 | 14.9 | | | Notes Payable-Short Term | 16.9 | 13.2 |
| | 3.1 | 1.4 | 1.7 | | | Cur. Mat.-L.T.D. | 1.8 | 3.2 |
| | 29.5 | 24.2 | 23.5 | | | Trade Payables | 22.2 | 17.1 |
| | .0 | .3 | .3 | | | Income Taxes Payable | .3 | .1 |
| | 8.6 | 7.8 | 8.0 | | | All Other Current | 15.4 | 13.3 |
| | 51.0 | 45.0 | 48.4 | | | Total Current | 56.5 | 46.8 |
| | 16.0 | 9.0 | 5.9 | | | Long-Term Debt | 7.4 | 9.6 |
| | .0 | .0 | .0 | | | Deferred Taxes | .1 | .0 |
| | 4.4 | 1.3 | 6.5 | | | All Other Non-Current | 6.0 | 4.1 |
| | 28.5 | 44.7 | 39.2 | | | Net Worth | 30.1 | 39.5 |
| | 100.0 | 100.0 | 100.0 | | | Total Liabilities & Net Worth | 100.0 | 100.0 |
| | | | | | | **INCOME DATA** | | |
| | 100.0 | 100.0 | 100.0 | | | Net Sales | 100.0 | 100.0 |
| | 24.3 | 27.1 | 30.2 | | | Gross Profit | 27.8 | 29.3 |
| | 21.6 | 23.2 | 25.3 | | | Operating Expenses | 24.2 | 26.6 |
| | 2.6 | 3.8 | 4.9 | | | Operating Profit | 3.6 | 2.7 |
| | 2.4 | -.2 | .4 | | | All Other Expenses (net) | 1.4 | .6 |
| | .2 | 4.1 | 4.5 | | | Profit Before Taxes | 2.2 | 2.1 |
| | | | | | | **RATIOS** | | |
| | 3.0 | 3.1 | 2.2 | | | | 1.9 | 2.3 |
| | 1.8 | 2.2 | 1.5 | | | Current | 1.4 | 1.6 |
| | 1.0 | 1.4 | 1.3 | | | | 1.1 | 1.2 |
| | 1.7 | 1.8 | 1.0 | | | | 1.0 | 1.1 |
| | .9 | 1.0 | .8 | | | Quick | .8 | .8 |
| | .7 | .6 | .5 | | | | .6 | .5 |
| | 13 28.4 | 25 14.4 | 28 13.2 | | | | 28 12.9 | 27 13.8 |
| | 27 13.3 | 38 9.6 | 43 8.5 | | | Sales/Receivables | 41 8.8 | 36 10.2 |
| | 42 8.6 | 50 7.3 | 52 7.0 | | | | 54 6.8 | 56 6.5 |
| | 0 UND | 32 11.4 | 61 6.0 | | | | 30 12.3 | 30 12.3 |
| | 36 10.0 | 54 6.7 | 73 5.0 | | | Cost of Sales/Inventory | 45 8.1 | 48 7.7 |
| | 69 5.3 | 91 4.0 | 89 4.1 | | | | 88 4.2 | 87 4.2 |
| | 9 40.6 | 17 21.6 | 30 12.0 | | | | 18 20.3 | 13 27.8 |
| | 28 12.9 | 36 10.1 | 43 8.5 | | | Cost of Sales/Payables | 29 12.4 | 24 15.2 |
| | 85 4.3 | 47 7.8 | 63 5.8 | | | | 47 7.8 | 52 7.0 |
| | 6.8 | 5.6 | 6.2 | | | | 8.7 | 5.8 |
| | 15.2 | 9.0 | 11.3 | | | Sales/Working Capital | 11.4 | 12.3 |
| | 163.2 | 12.8 | 13.0 | | | | 51.6 | 25.8 |
| | 33.6 | 61.2 | 16.7 | | | | 11.1 | 11.0 |
| | (16) 8.9 | (30) 6.5 | (10) 6.4 | | | EBIT/Interest | (37) 4.7 | (37) 2.3 |
| | .4 | 2.5 | 1.4 | | | | 1.7 | .0 |
| | | | | | | Net Profit + Depr., Dep., | 5.9 | |
| | | | | | | Amort./Cur. Mat. L/T/D | (13) 3.2 | |
| | | | | | | | 1.3 | |
| | .1 | .0 | .2 | | | | .1 | .1 |
| | .1 | .1 | .3 | | | Fixed/Worth | .4 | .4 |
| | 6.6 | .5 | .9 | | | | 1.5 | .9 |
| | .8 | .5 | .8 | | | | 1.0 | 1.0 |
| | 3.3 | 1.3 | 2.1 | | | Debt/Worth | 2.7 | 2.8 |
| | 18.2 | 3.3 | 4.2 | | | | 9.1 | 6.6 |
| | 87.1 | 36.4 | 52.6 | | | | 51.2 | 41.2 |
| | (16) 38.3 | (30) 22.4 | 26.2 | | | % Profit Before Taxes/Tangible Net Worth | (33) 23.9 | (35) 17.2 |
| | 10.1 | 4.9 | 12.7 | | | | 5.6 | -4.1 |
| | 26.5 | 22.1 | 14.4 | | | | 13.0 | 14.8 |
| | 11.2 | 6.2 | 7.0 | | | % Profit Before Taxes/Total Assets | 5.6 | 4.8 |
| | -1.6 | 2.3 | 1.4 | | | | 1.6 | -2.3 |
| | 296.7 | 170.3 | 57.2 | | | | 183.5 | 157.7 |
| | 129.6 | 71.3 | 16.8 | | | Sales/Net Fixed Assets | 43.0 | 44.9 |
| | 35.7 | 37.3 | 8.4 | | | | 14.2 | 19.3 |
| | 8.0 | 4.5 | 3.0 | | | | 3.9 | 4.2 |
| | 4.3 | 3.3 | 2.3 | | | Sales/Total Assets | 3.0 | 2.8 |
| | 3.2 | 2.6 | 1.8 | | | | 2.3 | 2.1 |
| | .3 | .2 | .3 | | | | .3 | .5 |
| | (10) .5 | (24) .5 | .9 | | | % Depr., Dep., Amort./Sales | (31) .7 | (30) 1.0 |
| | 1.5 | 1.2 | 1.1 | | | | 1.5 | 1.6 |
| | 1.5 | | | | | | .8 | 1.3 |
| | (13) 2.0 | | | | | % Officers', Directors' Owners' Comp/Sales | (14) 2.7 | (15) 2.4 |
| | 4.8 | | | | | | 6.0 | 6.4 |
| 1315M | 154706M | 561281M | 595321M | | 183577M | Net Sales ($) | 1934990M | 1597524M |
| 362M | 22457M | 146685M | 240296M | | 239700M | Total Assets ($) | 782547M | 729891M |

M = $ thousand    MM = $ million
See Pages 9 through 22 for Explanation of Ratios and Data

## Comparative Historical Data | Current Data Sorted by Sales

| H1 | H2 | H3 | Type of Statement | 0-1MM | 1-3MM | 3-5MM | 5-10MM | 10-25MM | 25MM & OVER |
|---|---|---|---|---|---|---|---|---|---|
| 8 | 7 | 6 | Unqualified | | | | | 1 | 5 |
| 18 | 20 | 16 | Reviewed | | 1 | | 4 | 7 | 4 |
| 5 | 6 | 5 | Compiled | | 1 | | 3 | | 1 |
| 14 | 14 | 18 | Tax Returns | 2 | 2 | | 5 | 4 | 2 |
| 11 | 16 | 20 | Other | 2 | | | 6 | 3 | 9 |
| 4/1/09-3/31/10 ALL | 4/1/10-3/31/11 ALL | 4/1/11-3/31/12 ALL | | 15 (4/1-9/30/11) | | | 50 (10/1/11-3/31/12) | | |
| 56 | 63 | 65 | **NUMBER OF STATEMENTS** | 4 | 4 | 3 | 18 | 15 | 21 |
| % | % | % | **ASSETS** | % | % | % | % | % | % |
| 13.5 | 11.8 | 7.7 | Cash & Equivalents | | | | 4.8 | 11.3 | 8.9 |
| 26.6 | 30.1 | 33.5 | Trade Receivables (net) | | | | 37.3 | 36.7 | 33.1 |
| 33.3 | 33.6 | 35.1 | Inventory | | | | 40.6 | 39.7 | 34.5 |
| 1.4 | 1.3 | 1.1 | All Other Current | | | | .6 | .2 | 2.1 |
| 74.9 | 76.8 | 77.4 | Total Current | | | | 83.3 | 87.9 | 78.6 |
| 13.6 | 12.7 | 11.2 | Fixed Assets (net) | | | | 9.8 | 7.6 | 9.8 |
| 6.0 | 5.1 | 4.9 | Intangibles (net) | | | | 2.3 | 2.2 | 7.2 |
| 5.6 | 5.4 | 6.5 | All Other Non-Current | | | | 4.6 | 2.3 | 4.3 |
| 100.0 | 100.0 | 100.0 | Total | | | | 100.0 | 100.0 | 100.0 |
| | | | **LIABILITIES** | | | | | | |
| 9.5 | 12.4 | 12.1 | Notes Payable-Short Term | | | | 17.1 | 4.3 | 13.3 |
| 3.1 | 2.0 | 1.9 | Cur. Mat.-L.T.D. | | | | 2.6 | .7 | 1.5 |
| 25.2 | 23.5 | 24.8 | Trade Payables | | | | 30.7 | 21.6 | 23.5 |
| .4 | .3 | .2 | Income Taxes Payable | | | | .0 | .6 | .2 |
| 11.2 | 7.8 | 8.7 | All Other Current | | | | 6.4 | 7.0 | 10.4 |
| 49.4 | 45.9 | 47.7 | Total Current | | | | 56.8 | 34.3 | 48.9 |
| 7.3 | 10.9 | 10.7 | Long-Term Debt | | | | 11.7 | 7.1 | 7.1 |
| .1 | .1 | .1 | Deferred Taxes | | | | .0 | .0 | .1 |
| 4.8 | 2.3 | 3.3 | All Other Non-Current | | | | 2.0 | 2.1 | 4.8 |
| 38.5 | 40.9 | 38.3 | Net Worth | | | | 29.5 | 56.5 | 39.1 |
| 100.0 | 100.0 | 100.0 | Total Liabilties & Net Worth | | | | 100.0 | 100.0 | 100.0 |
| | | | **INCOME DATA** | | | | | | |
| 100.0 | 100.0 | 100.0 | Net Sales | | | | 100.0 | 100.0 | 100.0 |
| 29.1 | 29.2 | 27.8 | Gross Profit | | | | 27.9 | 27.9 | 23.3 |
| 25.8 | 23.6 | 24.3 | Operating Expenses | | | | 24.1 | 24.0 | 19.5 |
| 3.3 | 5.6 | 3.5 | Operating Profit | | | | 3.8 | 3.9 | 3.8 |
| .2 | .6 | .6 | All Other Expenses (net) | | | | .4 | -1.3 | .5 |
| 3.1 | 5.0 | 2.9 | Profit Before Taxes | | | | 3.4 | 5.2 | 3.3 |
| | | | **RATIOS** | | | | | | |
| 2.4 | 2.7 | 2.7 | | | | | 2.4 | 3.3 | 2.1 |
| 1.6 | 1.7 | 1.8 | Current | | | | 1.4 | 2.7 | 1.6 |
| 1.1 | 1.2 | 1.3 | | | | | 1.0 | 2.1 | 1.4 |
| 1.4 | 1.5 | 1.6 | | | | | 1.1 | 1.8 | 1.1 |
| .8 | .9 | .9 | Quick | | | | .8 | 1.3 | .9 |
| .5 | .6 | .6 | | | | | .5 | .9 | .6 |
| 16 22.5 | 19 19.4 | 20 18.4 | | | | | 27 13.6 | 20 18.1 | 9 42.2 |
| 32 11.6 | 34 10.7 | 36 10.1 | Sales/Receivables | | | | 38 9.6 | 34 10.6 | 35 10.5 |
| 46 7.9 | 50 7.3 | 47 7.7 | | | | | 49 7.4 | 51 7.1 | 47 7.7 |
| 25 14.8 | 29 12.8 | 27 13.7 | | | | | 30 12.2 | 35 10.4 | 28 13.0 |
| 46 7.9 | 51 7.1 | 55 6.6 | Cost of Sales/Inventory | | | | 70 5.2 | 55 6.6 | 54 6.8 |
| 93 3.9 | 93 3.9 | 87 4.2 | | | | | 91 4.0 | 94 3.9 | 76 4.8 |
| 17 21.2 | 13 27.4 | 16 22.7 | | | | | 27 13.3 | 15 25.0 | 14 25.7 |
| 37 9.8 | 31 11.7 | 36 10.1 | Cost of Sales/Payables | | | | 41 8.9 | 25 14.5 | 30 12.0 |
| 66 5.6 | 55 6.6 | 56 6.5 | | | | | 68 5.4 | 40 9.2 | 57 6.4 |
| 6.1 | 5.6 | 6.5 | | | | | 6.9 | 4.6 | 7.4 |
| 14.0 | 9.9 | 10.9 | Sales/Working Capital | | | | 12.3 | 6.2 | 11.4 |
| 106.9 | 35.5 | 24.3 | | | | | NM | 10.9 | 20.8 |
| 22.8 | 34.1 | 37.0 | | | | | 37.0 | 112.4 | 25.8 |
| (51) 7.0 | (54) 6.7 | (58) 7.1 | EBIT/Interest | | | | 5.6 | (13) 14.0 | (19) 6.0 |
| 2.7 | 3.4 | 1.9 | | | | | 1.5 | 5.5 | 1.6 |
| 13.4 | 90.8 | 21.7 | | | | | | | |
| (17) 3.3 | (14) 10.9 | (16) 10.0 | Net Profit + Depr., Dep., Amort./Cur. Mat. L/T/D | | | | | | |
| .7 | 2.8 | 2.1 | | | | | | | |
| .1 | .0 | .1 | | | | | .1 | .0 | .1 |
| .3 | .2 | .2 | Fixed/Worth | | | | .2 | .1 | .3 |
| .9 | 1.0 | .9 | | | | | 2.4 | .2 | .4 |
| .7 | .7 | .6 | | | | | .9 | .3 | 1.2 |
| 2.6 | 1.5 | 2.0 | Debt/Worth | | | | 3.6 | .5 | 2.1 |
| 6.3 | 4.1 | 5.0 | | | | | 12.7 | 1.6 | 3.4 |
| 50.4 | 63.9 | 53.6 | | | | | 76.8 | 58.9 | 59.5 |
| (49) 22.1 | (57) 27.7 | (58) 26.3 | % Profit Before Taxes/Tangible Net Worth | | | | (15) 26.5 | 21.0 | (20) 28.2 |
| 11.4 | 9.3 | 6.2 | | | | | 4.8 | 8.6 | 9.3 |
| 14.2 | 23.1 | 23.3 | | | | | 26.7 | 30.5 | 19.5 |
| 6.1 | 8.6 | 7.9 | % Profit Before Taxes/Total Assets | | | | 8.1 | 10.2 | 5.9 |
| 2.8 | 2.8 | 1.6 | | | | | .8 | 3.2 | 1.9 |
| 184.0 | 312.4 | 192.7 | | | | | 173.5 | 220.2 | 216.0 |
| 57.5 | 63.6 | 70.5 | Sales/Net Fixed Assets | | | | 72.0 | 66.4 | 66.3 |
| 18.0 | 23.9 | 24.5 | | | | | 32.8 | 34.0 | 20.9 |
| 4.0 | 4.2 | 4.6 | | | | | 3.8 | 5.6 | 4.8 |
| 2.9 | 2.9 | 3.3 | Sales/Total Assets | | | | 3.3 | 3.4 | 3.9 |
| 2.1 | 1.8 | 2.3 | | | | | 2.1 | 2.5 | 2.3 |
| .2 | .4 | .3 | | | | | .1 | .3 | .3 |
| (45) .8 | (42) .7 | (46) .6 | % Depr., Dep., Amort./Sales | | | | (13) .4 | (10) .8 | (16) .5 |
| 2.0 | 1.2 | 1.2 | | | | | 1.4 | 1.5 | 1.0 |
| .9 | .9 | 1.6 | | | | | 1.9 | | |
| (25) 2.7 | (25) 1.8 | (24) 2.7 | % Officers', Directors' Owners' Comp/Sales | | | | (10) 2.2 | | |
| 4.5 | 4.1 | 4.6 | | | | | 4.6 | | |
| 1440546M | 1375532M | 1496200M | Net Sales ($) | 1551M | 8052M | 12508M | 129156M | 224356M | 1120577M |
| 655047M | 417589M | 649500M | Total Assets ($) | 2831M | 2371M | 5851M | 38833M | 69072M | 530542M |

M = $ thousand     MM = $ million
See Pages 9 through 22 for Explanation of Ratios and Data

## Current Data Sorted by Assets | Comparative Historical Data

| | 0-500M | 500M-2MM | 2-10MM | 10-50MM | 50-100MM | 100-250MM | 4/1/07-3/31/08 ALL | 4/1/08-3/31/09 ALL |
|---|---|---|---|---|---|---|---|---|
| **Type of Statement** | | | | | | | | |
| Unqualified | | | 4 | 11 | | | 36 | 27 |
| Reviewed | 1 | 5 | 28 | 8 | 2 | | 46 | 40 |
| Compiled | 1 | 12 | 16 | | | | 25 | 32 |
| Tax Returns | 7 | 6 | 10 | | | | 18 | 24 |
| Other | 6 | 18 | 20 | 14 | 5 | 2 | 65 | 81 |
| | | 38 (4/1-9/30/11) | | 138 (10/1/11-3/31/12) | | | | |
| **NUMBER OF STATEMENTS** | 15 | 41 | 78 | 33 | 7 | 2 | 190 | 204 |
| | % | % | % | % | % | % | % | % |
| **ASSETS** | | | | | | | | |
| Cash & Equivalents | 10.4 | 12.6 | 13.1 | 6.6 | | | 8.3 | 7.9 |
| Trade Receivables (net) | 29.8 | 32.0 | 30.0 | 31.1 | | | 31.8 | 30.8 |
| Inventory | 30.6 | 28.4 | 26.3 | 27.4 | | | 29.8 | 28.5 |
| All Other Current | 4.5 | 2.4 | 4.0 | 4.7 | | | 5.4 | 4.2 |
| Total Current | 75.3 | 75.4 | 73.3 | 69.9 | | | 75.3 | 71.3 |
| Fixed Assets (net) | 10.9 | 12.0 | 13.7 | 13.3 | | | 14.5 | 14.8 |
| Intangibles (net) | 2.8 | 6.4 | 4.8 | 10.8 | | | 3.9 | 5.9 |
| All Other Non-Current | 11.0 | 6.3 | 8.2 | 6.0 | | | 6.3 | 7.9 |
| Total | 100.0 | 100.0 | 100.0 | 100.0 | | | 100.0 | 100.0 |
| **LIABILITIES** | | | | | | | | |
| Notes Payable-Short Term | 39.3 | 10.3 | 9.7 | 11.4 | | | 13.6 | 15.7 |
| Cur. Mat.-L.T.D. | 5.4 | 1.8 | 3.9 | 3.5 | | | 3.7 | 3.1 |
| Trade Payables | 26.6 | 20.1 | 17.8 | 16.8 | | | 20.2 | 16.9 |
| Income Taxes Payable | .0 | .3 | .2 | .3 | | | .4 | .2 |
| All Other Current | 25.4 | 12.3 | 12.5 | 11.4 | | | 17.0 | 15.4 |
| Total Current | 96.7 | 44.8 | 44.1 | 43.4 | | | 54.9 | 51.3 |
| Long-Term Debt | 15.3 | 7.6 | 11.7 | 9.4 | | | 11.4 | 11.7 |
| Deferred Taxes | .0 | .3 | .5 | .4 | | | .3 | .2 |
| All Other Non-Current | 13.7 | 5.7 | 4.5 | 4.6 | | | 5.8 | 5.4 |
| Net Worth | -25.6 | 41.6 | 39.2 | 42.3 | | | 27.6 | 31.4 |
| Total Liabilities & Net Worth | 100.0 | 100.0 | 100.0 | 100.0 | | | 100.0 | 100.0 |
| **INCOME DATA** | | | | | | | | |
| Net Sales | 100.0 | 100.0 | 100.0 | 100.0 | | | 100.0 | 100.0 |
| Gross Profit | 46.3 | 40.8 | 37.6 | 34.1 | | | 37.9 | 37.6 |
| Operating Expenses | 44.6 | 38.4 | 33.0 | 28.7 | | | 34.1 | 34.5 |
| Operating Profit | 1.7 | 2.4 | 4.6 | 5.4 | | | 3.7 | 3.1 |
| All Other Expenses (net) | .5 | .1 | .1 | .4 | | | .5 | .5 |
| Profit Before Taxes | 1.2 | 2.3 | 4.5 | 5.0 | | | 3.2 | 2.6 |
| **RATIOS** | | | | | | | | |
| Current | 2.0 | 2.5 | 2.8 | 2.5 | | | 2.0 | 2.1 |
| | 1.5 | 1.8 | 1.6 | 1.6 | | | 1.4 | 1.4 |
| | .6 | 1.2 | 1.3 | 1.2 | | | 1.1 | 1.1 |
| Quick | 1.0 | 1.6 | 1.4 | 1.5 | | | 1.1 | 1.2 |
| | .6 | 1.0 | 1.0 | .8 | | | .7 | .8 |
| | .2 | .6 | .6 | .5 | | | .5 | .5 |
| Sales/Receivables | 16 23.1 | 23 16.2 | 23 15.7 | 35 10.5 | | | 26 13.8 | 26 14.0 |
| | 21 17.6 | 29 12.7 | 32 11.4 | 42 8.7 | | | 35 10.3 | 35 10.5 |
| | 26 14.0 | 40 9.2 | 40 9.1 | 50 7.3 | | | 47 7.8 | 46 7.9 |
| Cost of Sales/Inventory | 10 38.1 | 14 27.0 | 27 13.4 | 45 8.2 | | | 34 10.8 | 28 13.1 |
| | 41 8.8 | 47 7.7 | 54 6.7 | 63 5.8 | | | 59 6.1 | 58 6.2 |
| | 59 6.2 | 81 4.5 | 87 4.2 | 83 4.4 | | | 83 4.4 | 89 4.1 |
| Cost of Sales/Payables | 9 42.2 | 15 23.8 | 14 25.8 | 17 21.9 | | | 17 21.6 | 14 25.5 |
| | 14 25.6 | 30 12.2 | 26 13.8 | 31 11.8 | | | 30 12.0 | 24 15.1 |
| | 68 5.4 | 49 7.5 | 43 8.4 | 47 7.7 | | | 50 7.3 | 48 7.7 |
| Sales/Working Capital | 6.2 | 8.2 | 5.8 | 4.9 | | | 7.5 | 8.2 |
| | 34.2 | 12.5 | 10.5 | 9.4 | | | 13.9 | 16.2 |
| | -11.9 | 28.4 | 25.5 | 24.3 | | | 59.4 | 85.4 |
| EBIT/Interest | 16.7 | 18.3 | 34.3 | 21.2 | | | 9.6 | 8.2 |
| | (10) 8.5 | (34) 7.2 | (71) 9.1 | (32) 10.1 | | | (160) 3.5 | (178) 3.0 |
| | 1.1 | .9 | 2.5 | 4.3 | | | 1.7 | 1.2 |
| Net Profit + Depr., Dep., Amort./Cur. Mat. L/T/D | | | 19.9 | 9.3 | | | 5.9 | 10.2 |
| | | | (17) 2.2 | (10) 2.6 | | | (46) 1.7 | (44) 2.9 |
| | | | .9 | 2.1 | | | .6 | .9 |
| Fixed/Worth | .0 | .1 | .1 | .1 | | | .1 | .1 |
| | .2 | .2 | .3 | .2 | | | .4 | .4 |
| | .9 | 1.9 | .7 | 1.1 | | | 1.6 | 1.5 |
| Debt/Worth | 1.0 | .6 | .8 | 1.3 | | | 1.0 | 1.1 |
| | 2.4 | 1.3 | 1.6 | 1.8 | | | 2.2 | 2.3 |
| | -3.4 | 4.3 | 5.0 | 3.5 | | | 9.0 | 10.2 |
| % Profit Before Taxes/Tangible Net Worth | 226.0 | 40.0 | 58.3 | 50.5 | | | 45.8 | 40.4 |
| | (11) 18.2 | (33) 10.5 | (71) 21.3 | (30) 27.1 | | | (156) 19.3 | (166) 19.5 |
| | 4.7 | 1.6 | 11.9 | 12.0 | | | 6.8 | 5.1 |
| % Profit Before Taxes/Total Assets | 47.2 | 14.2 | 19.9 | 15.9 | | | 14.3 | 12.4 |
| | -11.1 | 7.8 | 9.4 | 7.5 | | | 6.7 | 5.4 |
| | -1.7 | 1.0 | 3.0 | 4.0 | | | 1.6 | .7 |
| Sales/Net Fixed Assets | UND | 112.2 | 104.0 | 107.4 | | | 82.3 | 83.4 |
| | 120.1 | 41.9 | 38.9 | 29.4 | | | 35.2 | 35.5 |
| | 45.1 | 20.4 | 11.9 | 14.3 | | | 12.6 | 11.9 |
| Sales/Total Assets | 7.1 | 4.8 | 4.3 | 3.6 | | | 4.0 | 4.1 |
| | 6.2 | 3.6 | 3.1 | 2.5 | | | 3.1 | 3.0 |
| | 3.3 | 2.8 | 1.9 | 1.7 | | | 2.2 | 2.1 |
| % Depr., Dep., Amort./Sales | | .4 | .3 | .3 | | | .5 | .5 |
| | | (32) .7 | (59) .7 | (30) .8 | | | (163) .9 | (169) 1.0 |
| | | 1.8 | 2.4 | 2.4 | | | 2.0 | 2.4 |
| % Officers', Directors' Owners' Comp/Sales | | 2.7 | 1.6 | | | | 2.4 | 1.9 |
| | | (17) 5.7 | (33) 2.7 | | | | (56) 4.2 | (71) 3.6 |
| | | 10.4 | 6.1 | | | | 6.6 | 6.8 |
| Net Sales ($) | 20215M | 214885M | 1194914M | 1976756M | 863102M | 257843M | 5913624M | 5176938M |
| Total Assets ($) | 3788M | 52285M | 372512M | 766441M | 459140M | 323637M | 2237934M | 2158204M |

M = $ thousand    MM = $ million
See Pages 9 through 22 for Explanation of Ratios and Data

## Comparative Historical Data  —  Current Data Sorted by Sales

**Type of Statement**

| | | | | 0-1MM | 1-3MM | 3-5MM | 5-10MM | 10-25MM | 25MM & OVER |
|---|---|---|---|---|---|---|---|---|---|
| 19 | 21 | 15 | Unqualified | | | | | 3 | 12 |
| 40 | 48 | 44 | Reviewed | 1 | 7 | 3 | 13 | 16 | 11 |
| 28 | 32 | 29 | Compiled | | | 3 | 9 | 9 | 1 |
| 70 | 58 | 65 | Tax Returns | 2 | 6 | 5 | 7 | 2 | 1 |
| 4/1/09-3/31/10 ALL | 4/1/10-3/31/11 ALL | 4/1/11-3/31/12 ALL | Other | 4 | 5 | 9 | 11 | 10 | 26 |
| | | | | | 38 (4/1-9/30/11) | | 138 (10/1/11-3/31/12) | | |
| 180 | 186 | 176 | NUMBER OF STATEMENTS | 7 | 18 | 20 | 40 | 40 | 51 |

| % | % | % | | % | % | % | % | % | % |
|---|---|---|---|---|---|---|---|---|---|
| | | | **ASSETS** | | | | | | |
| 10.0 | 10.4 | 12.1 | Cash & Equivalents | | 14.9 | 11.2 | 16.8 | 10.2 | 10.2 |
| 31.0 | 31.3 | 30.1 | Trade Receivables (net) | | 30.5 | 24.1 | 27.7 | 33.4 | 32.7 |
| 26.9 | 29.3 | 27.2 | Inventory | | 31.5 | 29.9 | 24.4 | 26.5 | 27.0 |
| 5.4 | 4.8 | 3.8 | All Other Current | | .0 | 2.0 | 4.4 | 4.7 | 3.8 |
| 73.3 | 75.8 | 73.2 | Total Current | | 76.9 | 67.2 | 73.3 | 74.8 | 73.7 |
| 12.4 | 13.1 | 12.6 | Fixed Assets (net) | | 11.4 | 18.8 | 15.4 | 10.5 | 10.4 |
| 5.7 | 4.9 | 6.5 | Intangibles (net) | | 3.4 | 3.8 | 6.0 | 4.9 | 9.5 |
| 8.6 | 6.2 | 7.7 | All Other Non-Current | | 8.3 | 10.1 | 5.2 | 9.7 | 6.4 |
| 100.0 | 100.0 | 100.0 | Total | | 100.0 | 100.0 | 100.0 | 100.0 | 100.0 |
| | | | **LIABILITIES** | | | | | | |
| 12.0 | 10.6 | 12.6 | Notes Payable-Short Term | | 28.5 | 12.6 | 8.9 | 8.3 | 11.4 |
| 4.0 | 2.8 | 3.3 | Cur. Mat.-L.T.D. | | 5.3 | 1.9 | 4.3 | 3.9 | 2.4 |
| 19.9 | 18.0 | 18.7 | Trade Payables | | 23.2 | 13.8 | 17.0 | 19.7 | 19.3 |
| .2 | .3 | .2 | Income Taxes Payable | | .5 | .2 | .4 | .0 | .2 |
| 16.0 | 14.2 | 13.2 | All Other Current | | 19.5 | 12.4 | 12.0 | 13.0 | 12.2 |
| 52.1 | 45.8 | 48.0 | Total Current | | 77.1 | 41.0 | 42.6 | 44.8 | 45.4 |
| 10.7 | 12.3 | 10.4 | Long-Term Debt | | 16.5 | 15.0 | 10.4 | 9.6 | 7.4 |
| .3 | .3 | .4 | Deferred Taxes | | .1 | .2 | .8 | .3 | .5 |
| 5.7 | 6.6 | 5.5 | All Other Non-Current | | 11.5 | 7.5 | 4.1 | 3.2 | 5.8 |
| 31.3 | 35.0 | 35.6 | Net Worth | | -5.1 | 36.3 | 42.1 | 42.1 | 41.0 |
| 100.0 | 100.0 | 100.0 | Total Liabilities & Net Worth | | 100.0 | 100.0 | 100.0 | 100.0 | 100.0 |
| | | | **INCOME DATA** | | | | | | |
| 100.0 | 100.0 | 100.0 | Net Sales | | 100.0 | 100.0 | 100.0 | 100.0 | 100.0 |
| 39.5 | 40.0 | 38.2 | Gross Profit | | 44.4 | 41.8 | 38.4 | 36.2 | 34.0 |
| 35.2 | 35.7 | 34.2 | Operating Expenses | | 43.7 | 40.3 | 33.8 | 32.4 | 28.9 |
| 4.3 | 4.2 | 4.0 | Operating Profit | | .6 | 1.5 | 4.6 | 3.8 | 5.1 |
| .6 | .1 | .2 | All Other Expenses (net) | | .3 | -.1 | .0 | .1 | .4 |
| 3.7 | 4.1 | 3.8 | Profit Before Taxes | | .3 | 1.6 | 4.6 | 3.7 | 4.7 |
| | | | **RATIOS** | | | | | | |
| 2.2 | 2.4 | 2.6 | Current | | 4.0 | 2.4 | 2.9 | 2.8 | 2.6 |
| 1.4 | 1.7 | 1.6 | | | 1.7 | 1.9 | 1.7 | 1.8 | 1.5 |
| 1.1 | 1.2 | 1.3 | | | 1.1 | 1.4 | 1.3 | 1.3 | 1.2 |
| 1.3 | 1.5 | 1.5 | Quick | | 1.5 | 1.5 | 1.6 | 1.8 | 1.4 |
| (179) .8 | .9 | .9 | | | .9 | .9 | 1.0 | .9 | .9 |
| .5 | .6 | .6 | | | .4 | .5 | .7 | .5 | .6 |
| 25 14.7 | 24 15.4 | 23 15.6 | Sales/Receivables | | 21 17.0 | 19 19.1 | 24 15.4 | 22 16.8 | 31 11.6 |
| 35 10.5 | 35 10.5 | 33 11.2 | | | 28 13.2 | 27 13.6 | 31 11.7 | 30 12.1 | 38 9.5 |
| 46 8.0 | 47 7.8 | 42 8.7 | | | 34 10.7 | 41 9.0 | 39 9.3 | 50 7.3 | 48 7.6 |
| 29 12.7 | 35 10.4 | 26 14.1 | Cost of Sales/Inventory | | 17 21.4 | 22 16.5 | 17 21.7 | 21 17.0 | 40 9.1 |
| 57 6.4 | 63 5.8 | 55 6.6 | | | 59 6.2 | 70 5.2 | 52 7.0 | 48 7.6 | 63 5.8 |
| 90 4.1 | 89 4.1 | 83 4.4 | | | 104 3.5 | 101 3.6 | 78 4.7 | 81 4.5 | 74 4.9 |
| 18 20.3 | 16 22.5 | 14 25.6 | Cost of Sales/Payables | | 17 22.1 | 14 25.2 | 9 40.1 | 13 28.2 | 16 22.7 |
| 33 11.1 | 30 12.2 | 28 13.2 | | | 30 12.0 | 32 11.5 | 31 11.9 | 25 14.8 | 28 13.2 |
| 58 6.3 | 49 7.5 | 46 8.0 | | | 63 5.8 | 44 8.3 | 43 8.4 | 43 8.5 | 46 8.0 |
| 6.3 | 5.7 | 6.1 | Sales/Working Capital | | 5.9 | 5.7 | 6.3 | 6.2 | 4.9 |
| 12.8 | 10.5 | 11.0 | | | 14.0 | 9.4 | 10.9 | 11.3 | 10.4 |
| 82.7 | 27.4 | 27.9 | | | 76.9 | 30.5 | 18.0 | 32.2 | 31.3 |
| 17.4 | 18.5 | 24.3 | EBIT/Interest | | 17.2 | 9.2 | 22.8 | 85.0 | 28.4 |
| (158) 5.6 | (159) 7.4 | (155) 8.8 | | | (13) 8.3 | (19) 2.8 | (34) 8.0 | (34) 10.1 | (50) 12.5 |
| 1.8 | 2.5 | 2.5 | | | 1.3 | -2.8 | 3.2 | 2.1 | 4.8 |
| 11.9 | 16.7 | 10.7 | Net Profit + Depr., Dep., Amort./Cur. Mat. L/T/D | | | | | | 17.2 |
| (38) 3.8 | (41) 3.2 | (39) 2.5 | | | | | | | (15) 2.8 |
| 1.8 | 1.0 | 1.2 | | | | | | | 2.1 |
| .1 | .1 | .1 | Fixed/Worth | | .1 | .2 | .1 | .1 | .1 |
| .3 | .2 | .2 | | | .3 | .6 | .4 | .2 | .2 |
| 2.4 | 1.3 | .8 | | | -1.6 | 2.2 | .8 | .5 | .8 |
| 1.0 | .8 | .8 | Debt/Worth | | .4 | .8 | .8 | .7 | 1.1 |
| 2.5 | 1.9 | 1.7 | | | 1.5 | 2.2 | 1.3 | 1.3 | 2.0 |
| 8.1 | 5.5 | 4.6 | | | -34.2 | 7.5 | 3.9 | 4.0 | 5.0 |
| 47.2 | 50.2 | 47.8 | % Profit Before Taxes/Tangible Net Worth | | 41.9 | 20.2 | 58.4 | 38.5 | 64.3 |
| (152) 24.0 | (159) 21.6 | (153) 20.3 | | | (13) 18.2 | (17) 8.7 | (36) 29.3 | (35) 17.4 | (47) 30.6 |
| 9.3 | 7.4 | 8.4 | | | 3.4 | -19.3 | 10.0 | 7.9 | 11.9 |
| 15.0 | 16.3 | 18.2 | % Profit Before Taxes/Total Assets | | 14.2 | 8.9 | 21.3 | 17.8 | 16.5 |
| 7.2 | 6.6 | 8.3 | | | 7.9 | 2.0 | 12.3 | 7.5 | 9.9 |
| 1.0 | 2.1 | 2.3 | | | .7 | -3.2 | 4.9 | 1.9 | 4.1 |
| 90.6 | 97.5 | 118.0 | Sales/Net Fixed Assets | | 163.8 | 58.4 | 67.8 | 114.6 | 151.5 |
| 41.7 | 43.6 | 41.3 | | | 53.8 | 25.3 | 21.9 | 51.1 | 56.1 |
| 16.1 | 16.7 | 15.2 | | | 23.7 | 8.5 | 11.6 | 19.5 | 16.9 |
| 4.0 | 4.2 | 4.3 | Sales/Total Assets | | 6.4 | 3.7 | 4.1 | 4.7 | 4.0 |
| 2.9 | 3.0 | 3.2 | | | 3.7 | 2.8 | 3.1 | 3.6 | 2.8 |
| 2.2 | 2.1 | 2.1 | | | 2.6 | 1.6 | 2.1 | 2.2 | 1.8 |
| .5 | .4 | .3 | % Depr., Dep., Amort./Sales | | .5 | .6 | .4 | .2 | .2 |
| (139) 1.0 | (149) .8 | (134) .7 | | | (11) 1.3 | (15) 1.0 | (32) 1.1 | (31) .6 | (43) .6 |
| 2.3 | 2.1 | 2.1 | | | 2.7 | 1.9 | 3.0 | .9 | 2.3 |
| 1.4 | 2.2 | 1.7 | % Officers', Directors' Owners' Comp/Sales | | 4.3 | 1.2 | 1.4 | 1.2 | |
| (77) 2.9 | (68) 4.2 | (65) 4.5 | | | (13) 5.5 | (11) 4.3 | (16) 1.8 | (13) 2.9 | |
| 7.7 | 7.0 | 7.1 | | | 12.4 | 6.5 | 7.2 | 6.3 | |
| 4578564M | 5082971M | 4527715M | Net Sales ($) | 2758M | 38237M | 76158M | 299747M | 676792M | 3434023M |
| 2073318M | 2372363M | 1977803M | Total Assets ($) | 1585M | 12268M | 30934M | 110376M | 249429M | 1573211M |

M = $ thousand   MM = $ million
See Pages 9 through 22 for Explanation of Ratios and Data

## Current Data Sorted by Assets             Comparative Historical Data

| | 0-500M | 500M-2MM | 2-10MM | 10-50MM | 50-100MM | 100-250MM | Type of Statement | 4/1/07-3/31/08 ALL | 4/1/08-3/31/09 ALL |
|---|---|---|---|---|---|---|---|---|---|
| | | 32 (4/1-9/30/11) | | 222 (10/1/11-3/31/12) | | | | | |
| Unqualified | | 1 | 8 | 30 | 5 | 6 | | 49 | 58 |
| Reviewed | 1 | 2 | 22 | 13 | | | | 33 | 38 |
| Compiled | 2 | 8 | 10 | 1 | | | | 16 | 21 |
| Tax Returns | 6 | 14 | 7 | 2 | | | | 20 | 31 |
| Other | 4 | 26 | 44 | 28 | 5 | 9 | | 111 | 110 |
| **NUMBER OF STATEMENTS** | 13 | 51 | 91 | 74 | 10 | 15 | | 229 | 258 |
| | % | % | % | % | % | % | **ASSETS** | % | % |
| Cash & Equivalents | 20.5 | 19.8 | 15.0 | 9.5 | 7.3 | 9.5 | | 12.3 | 13.4 |
| Trade Receivables (net) | 23.0 | 37.7 | 46.7 | 44.9 | 34.7 | 32.6 | | 43.7 | 41.7 |
| Inventory | 17.1 | 22.4 | 20.1 | 24.1 | 23.5 | 26.2 | | 18.4 | 20.3 |
| All Other Current | 2.9 | 2.2 | 2.6 | 3.6 | 7.2 | 5.4 | | 4.3 | 3.6 |
| Total Current | 63.4 | 82.1 | 84.4 | 82.1 | 72.7 | 73.8 | | 78.8 | 79.0 |
| Fixed Assets (net) | 13.2 | 9.0 | 7.6 | 6.7 | 10.1 | 4.3 | | 8.6 | 8.3 |
| Intangibles (net) | 12.2 | 3.6 | 3.7 | 7.0 | 5.0 | 14.0 | | 7.1 | 6.2 |
| All Other Non-Current | 11.1 | 5.4 | 4.3 | 4.2 | 12.1 | 7.9 | | 5.5 | 6.5 |
| Total | 100.0 | 100.0 | 100.0 | 100.0 | 100.0 | 100.0 | | 100.0 | 100.0 |
| | | | | | | | **LIABILITIES** | | |
| Notes Payable-Short Term | 36.2 | 11.2 | 10.6 | 15.3 | 22.4 | 12.9 | | 14.0 | 12.1 |
| Cur. Mat.-L.T.D. | .8 | 3.0 | 2.4 | 1.4 | 1.1 | .3 | | 2.0 | 2.3 |
| Trade Payables | 14.3 | 30.2 | 30.7 | 27.9 | 23.6 | 27.3 | | 25.0 | 26.4 |
| Income Taxes Payable | .0 | .7 | .4 | .1 | 1.2 | .1 | | .4 | .3 |
| All Other Current | 40.1 | 12.5 | 13.1 | 15.1 | 18.7 | 11.8 | | 12.8 | 12.2 |
| Total Current | 91.4 | 57.7 | 57.2 | 59.7 | 67.0 | 52.5 | | 54.2 | 53.3 |
| Long-Term Debt | 20.3 | 8.2 | 7.6 | 6.1 | 7.4 | 7.5 | | 7.6 | 9.4 |
| Deferred Taxes | .2 | .2 | .1 | .1 | .2 | .9 | | .2 | .2 |
| All Other Non-Current | 9.9 | 5.4 | 6.5 | 2.9 | 8.4 | 2.0 | | 6.8 | 6.4 |
| Net Worth | -21.8 | 28.5 | 28.5 | 31.1 | 17.0 | 37.2 | | 31.2 | 30.8 |
| Total Liabilities & Net Worth | 100.0 | 100.0 | 100.0 | 100.0 | 100.0 | 100.0 | | 100.0 | 100.0 |
| | | | | | | | **INCOME DATA** | | |
| Net Sales | 100.0 | 100.0 | 100.0 | 100.0 | 100.0 | 100.0 | | 100.0 | 100.0 |
| Gross Profit | 40.2 | 36.5 | 30.0 | 23.9 | 33.8 | 18.8 | | 32.4 | 29.2 |
| Operating Expenses | 38.9 | 32.5 | 24.9 | 19.3 | 29.7 | 15.0 | | 27.5 | 25.2 |
| Operating Profit | 1.3 | 4.0 | 5.1 | 4.6 | 4.1 | 3.8 | | 4.9 | 4.0 |
| All Other Expenses (net) | .8 | .3 | .5 | .4 | 1.1 | .8 | | .6 | .8 |
| Profit Before Taxes | .5 | 3.7 | 4.6 | 4.2 | 3.0 | 3.0 | | 4.2 | 3.2 |
| | | | | | | | **RATIOS** | | |
| Current | 1.2 | 2.4 | 2.2 | 1.7 | 1.6 | 2.0 | | 2.1 | 2.2 |
| | .9 | 1.5 | 1.5 | 1.3 | 1.0 | 1.4 | | 1.4 | 1.4 |
| | .3 | 1.2 | 1.2 | 1.1 | .7 | 1.1 | | 1.1 | 1.1 |
| Quick | 1.0 | 1.7 | 1.4 | 1.2 | 1.0 | 1.1 | | 1.6 | 1.6 |
| | .5 | 1.2 | 1.1 | .9 | .6 | .8 | | 1.1 | 1.0 |
| | .1 | .5 | .8 | .6 | .4 | .6 | | .7 | .7 |
| Sales/Receivables | 0 UND | 17 21.3 | 29 12.8 | 38 9.6 | 30 12.1 | 34 10.7 | | 32 11.5 | 27 13.6 |
| | 7 53.8 | 32 11.5 | 45 8.1 | 49 7.5 | 53 6.9 | 41 8.8 | | 44 8.3 | 41 8.9 |
| | 41 8.9 | 46 7.9 | 64 5.7 | 73 5.0 | 65 5.6 | 61 6.0 | | 63 5.8 | 58 6.2 |
| Cost of Sales/Inventory | 0 UND | 4 88.1 | 2 214.7 | 6 57.4 | 0 UND | 11 32.8 | | 2 163.8 | 2 173.1 |
| | 4 101.5 | 21 17.6 | 13 28.3 | 30 12.2 | 45 8.1 | 40 9.1 | | 21 17.3 | 21 17.7 |
| | 24 15.3 | 51 7.2 | 51 7.2 | 73 5.0 | 81 4.5 | 72 5.1 | | 50 7.2 | 47 7.8 |
| Cost of Sales/Payables | 0 UND | 21 17.5 | 19 19.3 | 21 17.8 | 11 34.3 | 27 13.6 | | 19 19.2 | 17 21.3 |
| | 6 64.7 | 33 10.9 | 36 10.2 | 34 10.6 | 47 7.7 | 31 11.6 | | 33 11.1 | 30 12.2 |
| | 41 8.9 | 52 7.0 | 62 5.9 | 61 6.0 | 73 5.0 | 45 8.1 | | 54 6.8 | 51 7.1 |
| Sales/Working Capital | 90.3 | 7.4 | 7.0 | 8.7 | 12.2 | 8.9 | | 8.2 | 8.1 |
| | -45.6 | 16.1 | 13.9 | 16.6 | 81.3 | 13.3 | | 13.8 | 16.0 |
| | -8.8 | 50.3 | 35.3 | 49.8 | -9.0 | 45.2 | | 44.7 | 51.3 |
| EBIT/Interest | 9.4 | 20.4 | 39.2 | 23.5 | | 16.4 | | 17.2 | 21.7 |
| | (10) 3.4 | (37) 8.5 | (81) 9.4 | (62) 8.8 | | (13) 3.7 | | (193) 5.4 | (216) 4.7 |
| | -1.0 | 3.0 | 2.9 | 2.6 | | 1.7 | | 1.6 | 1.7 |
| Net Profit + Depr., Dep., Amort./Cur. Mat. L/T/D | | | 6.1 | 69.1 | | | | 27.2 | 28.5 |
| | | (15) 1.9 | | (16) 9.8 | | | | (46) 5.3 | (46) 4.1 |
| | | 1.2 | | 1.5 | | | | 1.4 | 1.3 |
| Fixed/Worth | .5 | .1 | .0 | .1 | .2 | .1 | | .1 | .1 |
| | -1.8 | .2 | .1 | .2 | 1.0 | .2 | | .2 | .2 |
| | -.2 | .7 | .9 | 1.0 | -9.2 | -1.3 | | .8 | .7 |
| Debt/Worth | 27.1 | .8 | 1.2 | 1.7 | 2.8 | .8 | | .9 | .9 |
| | -4.0 | 1.9 | 2.5 | 2.9 | 10.0 | 2.7 | | 2.4 | 2.2 |
| | -2.3 | 5.5 | 6.3 | 6.2 | -85.9 | -29.7 | | 7.2 | 6.1 |
| % Profit Before Taxes/Tangible Net Worth | | 56.2 | 76.2 | 69.6 | | 32.9 | | 74.7 | 65.1 |
| | | (42) 31.8 | (78) 43.8 | (64) 36.2 | | (11) 19.6 | | (193) 34.1 | (219) 23.0 |
| | | 14.3 | 12.3 | 12.3 | | 4.6 | | 8.7 | 6.3 |
| % Profit Before Taxes/Total Assets | 26.2 | 20.4 | 22.3 | 15.6 | 11.1 | 12.2 | | 20.7 | 16.2 |
| | 16.5 | 10.2 | 11.5 | 8.9 | 6.1 | 2.8 | | 8.8 | 6.4 |
| | .0 | 3.1 | 3.3 | 3.6 | -.1 | .8 | | 1.9 | 1.8 |
| Sales/Net Fixed Assets | 493.5 | 224.4 | 510.1 | 284.5 | 141.9 | 217.1 | | 193.6 | 290.7 |
| | 85.9 | 84.2 | 118.7 | 102.4 | 26.1 | 70.0 | | 71.7 | 84.1 |
| | 38.2 | 32.8 | 38.6 | 30.2 | 12.9 | 43.4 | | 30.6 | 33.3 |
| Sales/Total Assets | 11.9 | 5.7 | 5.5 | 4.4 | 3.5 | 4.2 | | 4.8 | 5.2 |
| | 5.5 | 4.3 | 3.7 | 3.2 | 2.1 | 3.2 | | 3.5 | 3.6 |
| | 3.8 | 2.9 | 2.4 | 1.9 | 1.5 | 1.2 | | 2.4 | 2.3 |
| % Depr., Dep., Amort./Sales | | .2 | .1 | .2 | | .1 | | .2 | .1 |
| | | (30) .5 | (61) .3 | (58) .3 | | (12) .6 | | (171) .5 | (191) .4 |
| | | 1.1 | .8 | .9 | | 2.0 | | 1.0 | 1.0 |
| % Officers', Directors' Owners' Comp/Sales | | 3.6 | | .3 | | | | 1.1 | 1.0 |
| | | (22) 4.4 | (27) 1.8 | (14) .7 | | | | (59) 2.5 | (68) 2.3 |
| | | 8.0 | 3.3 | 1.6 | | | | 6.8 | 4.7 |
| Net Sales ($) | 28998M | 294692M | 1924724M | 5425397M | 1880454M | 7121882M | | 17426211M | 19252775M |
| Total Assets ($) | 3662M | 64799M | 465222M | 1666762M | 728201M | 2452276M | | 5657814M | 5930116M |

M = $ thousand     MM = $ million
See Pages 9 through 22 for Explanation of Ratios and Data

## Comparative Historical Data  |  Current Data Sorted by Sales

Type of Statement counts and date ranges — Current Data: 32 (4/1-9/30/11); 222 (10/1/11-3/31/12)

| | 4/1/09-3/31/10 ALL | 4/1/10-3/31/11 ALL | 4/1/11-3/31/12 ALL | 0-1MM | 1-3MM | 3-5MM | 5-10MM | 10-25MM | 25MM & OVER |
|---|---|---|---|---|---|---|---|---|---|
| **Type of Statement** | | | | | | | | | |
| Unqualified | 54 | 48 | 50 | | 1 | | 2 | 4 | 43 |
| Reviewed | 42 | 53 | 38 | 1 | | 1 | 5 | 9 | 22 |
| Compiled | 19 | 25 | 21 | | 2 | 4 | 4 | 5 | 6 |
| Tax Returns | 30 | 40 | 29 | 3 | 6 | 8 | 4 | 4 | 4 |
| Other | 108 | 119 | 116 | 2 | 6 | 12 | 15 | 31 | 50 |
| **NUMBER OF STATEMENTS** | 253 | 285 | 254 | 6 | 15 | 25 | 30 | 53 | 125 |
| | % | % | % | % | % | % | % | % | % |
| **ASSETS** | | | | | | | | | |
| Cash & Equivalents | 15.5 | 14.3 | 14.0 | | 30.1 | 24.2 | 10.7 | 13.1 | 11.5 |
| Trade Receivables (net) | 41.0 | 42.3 | 41.8 | | 21.5 | 32.0 | 46.9 | 44.3 | 44.9 |
| Inventory | 19.6 | 20.2 | 22.1 | | 18.2 | 20.2 | 20.5 | 22.8 | 23.0 |
| All Other Current | 3.8 | 3.6 | 3.1 | | 2.7 | 2.2 | 3.7 | 3.2 | 3.3 |
| Total Current | 79.9 | 80.4 | 81.1 | | 72.5 | 78.5 | 81.7 | 83.4 | 82.7 |
| Fixed Assets (net) | 8.2 | 8.0 | 7.8 | | 21.0 | 7.6 | 8.3 | 9.2 | 5.8 |
| Intangibles (net) | 5.7 | 5.2 | 5.7 | | 1.7 | 5.7 | 4.3 | 3.2 | 6.6 |
| All Other Non-Current | 6.2 | 6.4 | 5.4 | | 4.8 | 8.2 | 5.6 | 4.1 | 4.9 |
| Total | 100.0 | 100.0 | 100.0 | | 100.0 | 100.0 | 100.0 | 100.0 | 100.0 |
| **LIABILITIES** | | | | | | | | | |
| Notes Payable-Short Term | 14.2 | 13.9 | 14.0 | | 23.6 | 12.4 | 9.9 | 11.6 | 14.8 |
| Cur. Mat.-L.T.D. | 2.2 | 1.9 | 2.0 | | 2.3 | 2.1 | 4.2 | 2.6 | 1.2 |
| Trade Payables | 27.2 | 28.9 | 28.5 | | 14.7 | 21.6 | 27.7 | 25.4 | 33.0 |
| Income Taxes Payable | .2 | .3 | .4 | | .2 | .1 | 1.7 | .2 | .2 |
| All Other Current | 12.8 | 13.6 | 15.1 | | 30.3 | 12.9 | 12.1 | 16.3 | 14.3 |
| Total Current | 56.6 | 58.7 | 59.9 | | 71.1 | 49.0 | 55.7 | 56.1 | 63.4 |
| Long-Term Debt | 6.5 | 6.2 | 7.9 | | 20.3 | 5.6 | 11.7 | 6.5 | 6.3 |
| Deferred Taxes | .2 | .2 | .2 | | .1 | .0 | .7 | .0 | .2 |
| All Other Non-Current | 7.6 | 6.4 | 5.2 | | 6.6 | 5.6 | 3.4 | 8.5 | 4.2 |
| Net Worth | 29.1 | 28.5 | 26.8 | | 1.9 | 39.8 | 28.4 | 28.8 | 25.9 |
| Total Liabilties & Net Worth | 100.0 | 100.0 | 100.0 | | 100.0 | 100.0 | 100.0 | 100.0 | 100.0 |
| **INCOME DATA** | | | | | | | | | |
| Net Sales | 100.0 | 100.0 | 100.0 | | 100.0 | 100.0 | 100.0 | 100.0 | 100.0 |
| Gross Profit | 28.8 | 29.1 | 29.5 | | 50.6 | 36.6 | 33.8 | 35.9 | 21.1 |
| Operating Expenses | 25.7 | 24.8 | 25.1 | | 44.3 | 32.6 | 29.1 | 30.5 | 17.2 |
| Operating Profit | 3.2 | 4.3 | 4.4 | | 6.3 | 3.9 | 4.7 | 5.4 | 3.9 |
| All Other Expenses (net) | .4 | .4 | .5 | | .9 | .3 | .7 | .6 | .4 |
| Profit Before Taxes | 2.7 | 3.9 | 3.9 | | 5.4 | 3.6 | 4.0 | 4.8 | 3.5 |
| **RATIOS** | | | | | | | | | |
| Current | 2.1 / 1.4 / 1.1 | 2.0 / 1.3 / 1.1 | 2.0 / 1.4 / 1.1 | | 2.3 / 1.9 / .6 | 3.8 / 1.6 / 1.0 | 1.8 / 1.5 / 1.2 | 2.2 / 1.5 / 1.2 | 1.7 / 1.3 / 1.1 |
| Quick | 1.5 / 1.0 / .7 | 1.4 / 1.0 / .7 | 1.4 / 1.0 / .6 | | 2.0 / 1.0 / .4 | 2.5 / 1.2 / .5 | 1.4 / 1.1 / .9 | 1.4 / 1.1 / .7 | 1.3 / .9 / .6 |
| Sales/Receivables | 25 14.5 / 42 8.7 / 63 5.8 | 26 13.9 / 42 8.7 / 63 5.8 | 29 12.8 / 42 8.6 / 60 6.1 | | 10 35.1 / 20 18.6 / 41 8.9 | 18 19.9 / 31 11.7 / 49 7.5 | 31 11.6 / 42 8.7 / 61 6.0 | 31 11.7 / 47 7.7 / 69 5.3 | 31 11.7 / 43 8.4 / 57 6.4 |
| Cost of Sales/Inventory | 2 215.9 / 18 20.0 / 48 7.5 | 3 113.6 / 21 17.4 / 52 7.1 | 3 111.9 / 22 16.8 / 54 6.8 | | 0 UND / 23 15.8 / 91 4.0 | 2 240.5 / 20 18.3 / 51 7.1 | 4 91.7 / 17 21.0 / 41 9.0 | 3 141.0 / 25 14.5 / 64 5.7 | 4 96.1 / 22 16.7 / 55 6.6 |
| Cost of Sales/Payables | 17 21.2 / 33 11.0 / 54 6.8 | 20 18.5 / 37 9.9 / 58 6.3 | 19 18.8 / 34 10.6 / 54 6.8 | | 9 42.8 / 40 9.2 / 61 6.0 | 6 61.0 / 34 10.7 / 51 7.2 | 25 14.7 / 36 10.2 / 52 7.0 | 18 19.8 / 36 10.2 / 69 5.3 | 21 17.3 / 34 10.8 / 50 7.3 |
| Sales/Working Capital | 7.5 / 16.9 / 50.3 | 8.6 / 18.5 / 53.2 | 7.9 / 17.4 / 56.7 | | 3.9 / 8.7 / -9.4 | 6.0 / 16.1 / 178.4 | 7.8 / 18.1 / 35.1 | 6.3 / 11.2 / 27.9 | 12.0 / 20.8 / 56.2 |
| EBIT/Interest | (213) 22.1 / 5.5 / 1.5 | (234) 22.6 / 7.4 / 2.8 | (212) 25.0 / 8.5 / 2.4 | | (13) 13.0 / 5.3 / 2.7 | (16) 14.6 / 6.1 / .5 | (25) 39.3 / 8.4 / 3.1 | (45) 22.4 / 8.7 / 2.1 | (110) 26.5 / 9.1 / 2.6 |
| Net Profit + Depr., Dep., Amort./Cur. Mat. L/T/D | (44) 20.0 / 3.2 / 1.2 | (43) 20.3 / 5.7 / 3.0 | (38) 18.0 / 3.6 / 1.2 | | | | | (11) 7.7 / 2.4 / 1.2 | (25) 64.4 / 6.1 / 1.2 |
| Fixed/Worth | .1 / .2 / .7 | .0 / .1 / .7 | .1 / .2 / 1.0 | | .1 / .8 / -.3 | .0 / .1 / 1.1 | .1 / .3 / 1.4 | .1 / .3 / 1.2 | .0 / .2 / .6 |
| Debt/Worth | 1.0 / 2.7 / 7.7 | 1.1 / 3.0 / 7.8 | 1.3 / 2.8 / 10.8 | | .7 / 1.3 / -3.2 | .5 / 2.3 / 12.6 | 1.3 / 2.8 / 13.0 | 1.3 / 2.4 / 8.1 | 1.6 / 2.9 / 7.4 |
| % Profit Before Taxes/Tangible Net Worth | (218) 54.4 / 21.4 / 4.2 | (240) 67.1 / 32.9 / 10.3 | (207) 66.7 / 36.4 / 12.4 | | | (21) 56.9 / 31.7 / 18.1 | (25) 62.1 / 33.8 / 11.8 | (44) 64.0 / 39.4 / 14.4 | (105) 76.1 / 37.2 / 10.1 |
| % Profit Before Taxes/Total Assets | 14.8 / 5.8 / .8 | 18.2 / 8.3 / 1.7 | 18.4 / 9.8 / 2.7 | | 24.1 / 16.5 / 2.7 | 25.3 / 9.8 / .7 | 20.8 / 8.0 / 3.3 | 19.3 / 10.2 / 2.6 | 16.9 / 9.0 / 2.6 |
| Sales/Net Fixed Assets | 314.1 / 103.3 / 36.6 | 366.7 / 106.5 / 35.9 | 313.9 / 86.8 / 32.6 | | 63.9 / 32.8 / 9.9 | 339.4 / 85.9 / 34.4 | 201.1 / 89.3 / 35.6 | 200.8 / 52.7 / 23.5 | 401.8 / 119.0 / 38.9 |
| Sales/Total Assets | 4.9 / 3.3 / 2.3 | 4.9 / 3.4 / 2.3 | 5.0 / 3.6 / 2.2 | | 4.6 / 3.5 / 1.7 | 5.7 / 3.2 / 2.3 | 5.0 / 4.1 / 2.2 | 4.5 / 3.3 / 2.3 | 5.4 / 3.9 / 2.2 |
| % Depr., Dep., Amort./Sales | (182) .1 / .5 / 1.1 | (192) .1 / .4 / .8 | (175) .1 / .3 / .9 | | | (14) .2 / .4 / .7 | (21) .2 / .5 / 1.0 | (38) .2 / .6 / 1.2 | (92) .1 / .2 / .8 |
| % Officers', Directors' Owners' Comp/Sales | (68) 1.0 / 2.4 / 5.4 | (95) .9 / 2.4 / 4.2 | (69) .9 / 2.4 | | (11) 2.4 / 4.3 / 8.6 | (12) 1.3 / 3.9 / 4.7 | (14) 1.2 / 2.7 / 4.1 | (23) .3 / .7 / 1.3 | |
| Net Sales ($) | 13948886M | 16386918M | 16676147M | 2522M | 32419M | 104867M | 218844M | 861498M | 15455997M |
| Total Assets ($) | 4985789M | 5281680M | 5380922M | 2538M | 12653M | 34806M | 75771M | 326023M | 4929131M |

M = $ thousand    MM = $ million
See Pages 9 through 22 for Explanation of Ratios and Data

## Current Data Sorted by Assets      Comparative Historical Data

| 0-500M | 500M-2MM | 2-10MM | 10-50MM | 50-100MM | 100-250MM | Type of Statement | 4/1/07-3/31/08 ALL | 4/1/08-3/31/09 ALL |
|---|---|---|---|---|---|---|---|---|
| | | 3 | 17 | 5 | 4 | Unqualified | 19 | 23 |
| | 6 | 37 | 16 | 3 | | Reviewed | 41 | 55 |
| | 16 | 21 | 3 | | | Compiled | 26 | 35 |
| 2 | 29 | 10 | | | 1 | Tax Returns | 29 | 29 |
| 15 | 22 | 35 | 15 | 3 | 4 | Other | 89 | 80 |
| 3 | | | | | | | | |

43 (4/1-9/30/11)      227 (10/1/11-3/31/12)

| 0-500M | 500M-2MM | 2-10MM | 10-50MM | 50-100MM | 100-250MM | | 4/1/07-3/31/08 ALL | 4/1/08-3/31/09 ALL |
|---|---|---|---|---|---|---|---|---|
| 20 | 73 | 106 | 51 | 11 | 9 | NUMBER OF STATEMENTS | 204 | 222 |
| % | % | % | % | % | % | **ASSETS** | % | % |
| 17.9 | 13.2 | 9.0 | 10.1 | 2.7 | | Cash & Equivalents | 7.6 | 8.9 |
| 22.3 | 33.4 | 32.0 | 27.0 | 26.8 | | Trade Receivables (net) | 31.9 | 28.3 |
| 37.2 | 32.0 | 35.8 | 33.6 | 28.9 | | Inventory | 33.6 | 34.0 |
| .9 | 1.6 | 3.1 | 3.7 | 3.2 | | All Other Current | 3.4 | 3.2 |
| 78.3 | 80.2 | 79.8 | 74.5 | 61.5 | | Total Current | 76.4 | 74.5 |
| 11.6 | 9.9 | 13.5 | 14.3 | 7.9 | | Fixed Assets (net) | 15.6 | 15.5 |
| 4.6 | 2.4 | 2.1 | 4.1 | 25.3 | | Intangibles (net) | 3.1 | 4.0 |
| 5.5 | 7.6 | 4.5 | 7.0 | 5.3 | | All Other Non-Current | 4.9 | 6.1 |
| 100.0 | 100.0 | 100.0 | 100.0 | 100.0 | | Total | 100.0 | 100.0 |
| | | | | | | **LIABILITIES** | | |
| 21.2 | 11.7 | 14.0 | 13.7 | 11.3 | | Notes Payable-Short Term | 13.8 | 14.7 |
| 8.9 | 2.5 | 2.8 | 1.6 | 3.6 | | Cur. Mat.-L.T.D. | 2.9 | 2.8 |
| 31.1 | 21.8 | 20.5 | 17.5 | 9.9 | | Trade Payables | 20.9 | 17.3 |
| .1 | .1 | .3 | .2 | .3 | | Income Taxes Payable | .2 | .2 |
| 27.3 | 8.6 | 11.5 | 12.2 | 12.7 | | All Other Current | 13.3 | 12.6 |
| 88.7 | 44.7 | 49.0 | 45.2 | 37.8 | | Total Current | 51.0 | 47.6 |
| 3.7 | 8.4 | 8.8 | 7.8 | 24.2 | | Long-Term Debt | 10.2 | 12.5 |
| .0 | .0 | .2 | .3 | 3.1 | | Deferred Taxes | .3 | .2 |
| 19.1 | 7.0 | 5.1 | 5.0 | 9.7 | | All Other Non-Current | 4.0 | 5.5 |
| -11.5 | 39.9 | 36.8 | 41.7 | 25.2 | | Net Worth | 34.5 | 34.2 |
| 100.0 | 100.0 | 100.0 | 100.0 | 100.0 | | Total Liabilities & Net Worth | 100.0 | 100.0 |
| | | | | | | **INCOME DATA** | | |
| 100.0 | 100.0 | 100.0 | 100.0 | 100.0 | | Net Sales | 100.0 | 100.0 |
| 34.1 | 31.6 | 28.5 | 28.1 | 28.4 | | Gross Profit | 31.3 | 31.3 |
| 34.4 | 26.6 | 25.5 | 21.5 | 21.0 | | Operating Expenses | 26.4 | 26.7 |
| -.3 | 5.0 | 3.0 | 6.7 | 7.4 | | Operating Profit | 5.0 | 4.6 |
| -.6 | -.3 | .1 | .4 | 2.3 | | All Other Expenses (net) | .7 | .6 |
| .3 | 5.3 | 2.9 | 6.3 | 5.1 | | Profit Before Taxes | 4.2 | 4.1 |
| | | | | | | **RATIOS** | | |
| 5.0 | 2.8 | 2.5 | 3.0 | 2.7 | | | 2.2 | 2.4 |
| 1.6 | 1.9 | 1.5 | 1.5 | 1.6 | | Current | 1.6 | 1.6 |
| .9 | 1.2 | 1.2 | 1.2 | 1.5 | | | 1.1 | 1.1 |
| 2.1 | 1.6 | 1.3 | 1.2 | 1.4 | | | 1.2 | 1.3 |
| .6 | .9 | .9 | .7 | .8 | | Quick | .9 | .8 |
| .3 | .7 | .5 | .5 | .5 | | | .5 | .4 |
| 2   226.6 | 15   24.7 | 28   12.9 | 33   11.2 | 30   12.3 | | | 24   15.5 | 24   15.2 |
| 13   27.7 | 31   11.6 | 41   8.8 | 39   9.3 | 47   7.7 | | Sales/Receivables | 37   9.9 | 34   10.6 |
| 23   15.6 | 48   7.6 | 58   6.3 | 51   7.1 | 58   6.3 | | | 52   7.1 | 46   7.9 |
| 0   UND | 16   22.5 | 41   8.8 | 38   9.5 | 37   9.9 | | | 28   13.0 | 30   12.1 |
| 42   8.6 | 42   8.6 | 63   5.8 | 69   5.3 | 50   7.3 | | Cost of Sales/Inventory | 59   6.2 | 63   5.8 |
| 91   4.0 | 96   3.8 | 99   3.7 | 118   3.1 | 83   4.4 | | | 93   3.9 | 96   3.8 |
| 0   821.4 | 15   25.0 | 18   20.0 | 15   24.4 | 8   45.6 | | | 15   23.6 | 12   29.2 |
| 14   26.1 | 32   11.5 | 33   11.1 | 25   14.7 | 26   13.8 | | Cost of Sales/Payables | 28   12.8 | 25   14.6 |
| 59   6.2 | 54   6.7 | 51   7.1 | 44   8.3 | 34   10.6 | | | 48   7.6 | 46   8.0 |
| 9.5 | 5.9 | 5.0 | 5.8 | 5.6 | | | 6.3 | 6.5 |
| 33.2 | 10.6 | 10.0 | 9.4 | 7.0 | | Sales/Working Capital | 10.4 | 10.9 |
| NM | 28.0 | 21.8 | 17.5 | 13.2 | | | 37.4 | 35.2 |
| 5.0 | 27.4 | 12.4 | 49.3 | 9.8 | | | 10.5 | 9.8 |
| (15)   3.0 | (63)   12.0 | (94)   4.8 | (46)   9.8 | 4.5 | | EBIT/Interest | (181)   4.4 | (198)   3.3 |
| .5 | 1.7 | 1.3 | 4.2 | 1.7 | | | 1.8 | 1.6 |
| | | 13.9 | 27.5 | | | | 18.3 | 9.6 |
| | | (23)   4.6 | (14)   9.1 | | | Net Profit + Depr., Dep., Amort./Cur. Mat. L/T/D | (40)   4.3 | (44)   2.6 |
| | | .6 | 1.6 | | | | 1.2 | .7 |
| .1 | .0 | .1 | .1 | .1 | | | .1 | .1 |
| 1.0 | .1 | .2 | .3 | .9 | | Fixed/Worth | .3 | .3 |
| NM | .7 | .9 | .6 | -.1 | | | 1.1 | 1.2 |
| .7 | .7 | .8 | .6 | 2.4 | | | .8 | .8 |
| 3.1 | 1.4 | 2.1 | 2.2 | 4.4 | | Debt/Worth | 2.0 | 2.1 |
| NM | 4.4 | 4.4 | 4.1 | -2.2 | | | 5.6 | 5.3 |
| 83.3 | 74.6 | 38.0 | 68.4 | | | | 51.7 | 55.2 |
| (15)   24.0 | (65)   38.9 | (98)   12.4 | (49)   29.8 | | | % Profit Before Taxes/Tangible Net Worth | (177)   25.8 | (191)   21.2 |
| -1.0 | 10.0 | 1.4 | 18.7 | | | | 9.1 | 5.7 |
| 11.6 | 31.4 | 13.9 | 17.6 | 12.3 | | | 15.7 | 16.4 |
| 2.7 | 10.2 | 4.8 | 11.0 | 6.7 | | % Profit Before Taxes/Total Assets | 7.7 | 5.8 |
| -4.8 | 3.2 | .6 | 4.8 | 3.7 | | | 2.4 | 1.4 |
| 258.1 | 322.5 | 119.1 | 111.4 | 61.8 | | | 123.4 | 102.4 |
| 72.4 | 71.8 | 48.5 | 27.5 | 27.7 | | Sales/Net Fixed Assets | 44.2 | 34.2 |
| 24.8 | 28.8 | 16.9 | 11.3 | 16.4 | | | 14.7 | 13.7 |
| 7.5 | 4.9 | 3.6 | 3.0 | 2.8 | | | 4.1 | 3.8 |
| 5.5 | 3.6 | 2.6 | 2.3 | 2.4 | | Sales/Total Assets | 2.9 | 2.9 |
| 4.1 | 2.4 | 2.0 | 1.8 | 1.1 | | | 2.0 | 2.0 |
| .1 | .3 | .3 | .3 | .4 | | | .3 | .3 |
| (15)   .3 | (40)   .6 | (95)   .6 | (47)   .8 | | | % Depr., Dep., Amort./Sales | (167)   .7 | (187)   .7 |
| 1.0 | .9 | 1.0 | 1.6 | | | | 1.4 | 1.6 |
| 2.6 | 2.3 | 1.3 | 1.5 | | | | 1.8 | 1.8 |
| (12)   5.2 | (44)   4.2 | (38)   2.5 | (11)   2.0 | | | % Officers', Directors' Owners' Comp/Sales | (69)   3.2 | (80)   3.4 |
| 12.5 | 7.1 | 4.8 | 4.6 | | | | 6.1 | 6.4 |
| 46673M | 362529M | 1402321M | 2434502M | 1386106M | 4002963M | Net Sales ($) | 6216107M | 7768600M |
| 5317M | 85126M | 496669M | 998383M | 674898M | 1544629M | Total Assets ($) | 2397226M | 3011899M |

M = $ thousand     MM = $ million
See Pages 9 through 22 for Explanation of Ratios and Data

## Comparative Historical Data | Current Data Sorted by Sales

### Type of Statement

| 4/1/09-3/31/10 ALL | 4/1/10-3/31/11 ALL | 4/1/11-3/31/12 ALL | Type of Statement | 0-1MM | 1-3MM | 3-5MM | 5-10MM | 10-25MM | 25MM & OVER |
|---|---|---|---|---|---|---|---|---|---|
| 27 | 19 | 29 | Unqualified | | | | 1 | 7 | 21 |
| 55 | 59 | 62 | Reviewed | | 2 | 4 | 18 | 19 | 19 |
| 37 | 38 | 42 | Compiled | | 11 | 8 | 11 | 9 | 3 |
| 33 | 42 | 55 | Tax Returns | 6 | 18 | 13 | 10 | 4 | 4 |
| 80 | 87 | 82 | Other | | 10 | 9 | 17 | 26 | 20 |
| 4/1/09-3/31/10 ALL | 4/1/10-3/31/11 ALL | 4/1/11-3/31/12 ALL | | | 43 (4/1-9/30/11) | | 227 (10/1/11-3/31/12) | | |
| 232 | 245 | 270 | NUMBER OF STATEMENTS | 6 | 41 | 34 | 57 | 65 | 67 |

### ASSETS

| % | % | % | | % | % | % | % | % | % |
|---|---|---|---|---|---|---|---|---|---|
| 9.8 | 9.3 | 10.5 | Cash & Equivalents | | 13.2 | 13.8 | 10.9 | 10.1 | 7.5 |
| 30.0 | 32.0 | 30.5 | Trade Receivables (net) | | 24.6 | 26.7 | 30.9 | 37.0 | 30.8 |
| 32.6 | 31.6 | 33.8 | Inventory | | 31.8 | 33.0 | 37.8 | 33.1 | 31.1 |
| 3.6 | 2.5 | 2.7 | All Other Current | | 1.5 | 1.4 | 2.7 | 3.3 | 3.5 |
| 75.9 | 75.4 | 77.5 | Total Current | | 71.1 | 74.8 | 82.4 | 83.6 | 72.9 |
| 14.2 | 14.4 | 12.3 | Fixed Assets (net) | | 13.5 | 18.5 | 10.8 | 9.8 | 11.5 |
| 5.1 | 4.8 | 4.3 | Intangibles (net) | | 5.7 | 1.4 | 1.0 | 2.6 | 9.6 |
| 4.8 | 5.3 | 5.9 | All Other Non-Current | | 9.8 | 5.3 | 5.9 | 4.0 | 5.9 |
| 100.0 | 100.0 | 100.0 | Total | | 100.0 | 100.0 | 100.0 | 100.0 | 100.0 |

### LIABILITIES

| | | | | | | | | | |
|---|---|---|---|---|---|---|---|---|---|
| 13.7 | 13.6 | 13.6 | Notes Payable-Short Term | | 15.7 | 11.8 | 16.4 | 13.0 | 12.2 |
| 2.7 | 3.3 | 2.9 | Cur. Mat.-L.T.D. | | 3.9 | 2.1 | 4.2 | 2.5 | 2.3 |
| 17.3 | 19.3 | 20.6 | Trade Payables | | 23.6 | 19.9 | 19.6 | 22.4 | 18.2 |
| .1 | .1 | .2 | Income Taxes Payable | | .3 | .6 | .0 | .2 | .2 |
| 11.6 | 10.9 | 12.0 | All Other Current | | 18.1 | 7.7 | 13.0 | 10.2 | 12.0 |
| 45.4 | 47.1 | 49.3 | Total Current | | 61.5 | 42.0 | 53.3 | 48.3 | 44.9 |
| 12.1 | 10.2 | 9.4 | Long-Term Debt | | 9.4 | 17.0 | 7.6 | 5.6 | 11.8 |
| .4 | .4 | .3 | Deferred Taxes | | .0 | .0 | .3 | .2 | .9 |
| 5.1 | 6.5 | 6.9 | All Other Non-Current | | 13.7 | 7.0 | 3.5 | 5.9 | 5.0 |
| 37.0 | 35.7 | 34.0 | Net Worth | | 15.4 | 34.0 | 35.4 | 39.9 | 37.4 |
| 100.0 | 100.0 | 100.0 | Total Liabilities & Net Worth | | 100.0 | 100.0 | 100.0 | 100.0 | 100.0 |

### INCOME DATA

| | | | | | | | | | |
|---|---|---|---|---|---|---|---|---|---|
| 100.0 | 100.0 | 100.0 | Net Sales | | 100.0 | 100.0 | 100.0 | 100.0 | 100.0 |
| 30.4 | 30.7 | 29.6 | Gross Profit | | 32.8 | 36.7 | 28.9 | 25.7 | 25.7 |
| 27.2 | 26.3 | 25.4 | Operating Expenses | | 29.0 | 31.1 | 25.5 | 22.6 | 20.1 |
| 3.2 | 4.4 | 4.2 | Operating Profit | | 3.8 | 5.6 | 3.5 | 3.1 | 5.5 |
| .7 | .4 | .2 | All Other Expenses (net) | | -.2 | .4 | .2 | -.1 | .6 |
| 2.4 | 4.0 | 4.0 | Profit Before Taxes | | 3.9 | 5.2 | 3.3 | 3.2 | 4.9 |

### RATIOS

| | | | | | | | | | |
|---|---|---|---|---|---|---|---|---|---|
| 3.1 | 2.5 | 2.6 | Current | | 2.4 | 2.4 | 2.2 | 3.0 | 2.5 |
| 1.8 | 1.6 | 1.7 | | | 1.7 | 2.0 | 1.5 | 1.7 | 1.5 |
| 1.2 | 1.2 | 1.2 | | | 1.1 | 1.2 | 1.2 | 1.3 | 1.2 |
| 1.6 | 1.4 | 1.4 | Quick | | 1.4 | 1.4 | 1.0 | 1.7 | 1.2 |
| .9 | .8 | .9 | | | .8 | .9 | .8 | .9 | .8 |
| .5 | .6 | .6 | | | .4 | .6 | .5 | .7 | .6 |
| 24  14.9 | 26  14.2 | 22  16.9 | Sales/Receivables | | 12  29.7 | 9  39.0 | 20  18.2 | 29  12.4 | 29  12.4 |
| 37  9.8 | 39  9.5 | 39  9.4 | | | 28  13.2 | 33  10.9 | 39  9.4 | 41  8.9 | 40  9.1 |
| 54  6.8 | 55  6.7 | 51  7.2 | | | 47  7.8 | 55  6.6 | 48  7.6 | 64  5.7 | 51  7.1 |
| 30  12.1 | 28  13.0 | 26  13.8 | Cost of Sales/Inventory | | 15  24.0 | 28  13.0 | 29  12.8 | 23  16.0 | 31  11.7 |
| 60  6.1 | 57  6.4 | 58  6.3 | | | 46  8.0 | 63  5.8 | 64  5.7 | 54  6.8 | 53  6.9 |
| 99  3.7 | 99  3.7 | 99  3.7 | | | 83  4.4 | 126  2.9 | 122  3.0 | 78  4.7 | 87  4.2 |
| 14  26.2 | 16  23.1 | 15  24.5 | Cost of Sales/Payables | | 13  28.5 | 17  21.9 | 19  19.6 | 15  24.1 | 15  24.4 |
| 28  13.3 | 27  13.4 | 31  11.7 | | | 38  9.7 | 39  9.4 | 28  13.2 | 32  11.3 | 27  13.7 |
| 46  8.0 | 50  7.2 | 51  7.2 | | | 58  6.3 | 70  5.2 | 40  9.1 | 47  7.8 | 42  8.7 |
| 5.1 | 5.6 | 5.7 | Sales/Working Capital | | 6.0 | 5.3 | 5.5 | 5.1 | 6.2 |
| 8.7 | 9.8 | 10.3 | | | 13.8 | 9.0 | 11.0 | 10.2 | 10.2 |
| 23.8 | 31.8 | 25.2 | | | 103.0 | 18.1 | 21.2 | 21.4 | 25.2 |
| 9.3 | 13.2 | 20.7 | EBIT/Interest | | 21.2 | 19.1 | 11.9 | 29.5 | 35.0 |
| (198) 2.5 | (217) 4.2 | (238) 5.8 | | | (32) 4.1 | (30) 5.8 | (52) 5.0 | (57) 9.0 | (63) 6.9 |
| .6 | 1.7 | 1.7 | | | 1.2 | 1.2 | 1.3 | 2.1 | 2.7 |
| 6.6 | 9.4 | 14.9 | Net Profit + Depr., Dep., Amort./Cur. Mat. L/T/D | | | | 10.9 | 14.9 | 27.2 |
| (40) 1.9 | (43) 2.7 | (47) 4.6 | | | | (12) 4.5 | (11) 8.3 | (19) 4.7 |
| 1.1 | 1.1 | 1.1 | | | | | .9 | .6 | 1.7 |
| .1 | .1 | .1 | Fixed/Worth | | .1 | .0 | .1 | .1 | .1 |
| .2 | .3 | .2 | | | .2 | .2 | .2 | .2 | .3 |
| 1.1 | 1.1 | .9 | | | 10.7 | 2.3 | .7 | .6 | .9 |
| .6 | .7 | .8 | Debt/Worth | | .7 | 1.0 | 1.0 | .7 | 1.1 |
| 1.8 | 2.1 | 2.1 | | | 1.5 | 2.1 | 2.5 | 1.7 | 2.4 |
| 5.4 | 6.6 | 4.8 | | | 56.7 | 7.2 | 4.2 | 4.2 | 5.5 |
| 40.9 | 48.9 | 63.8 | % Profit Before Taxes/Tangible Net Worth | | 83.4 | 59.9 | 38.1 | 64.2 | 69.4 |
| (201) 12.7 | (211) 19.2 | (239) 26.0 | | | (32) 36.6 | (30) 28.1 | (54) 15.5 | (60) 24.4 | (57) 29.6 |
| 1.1 | 4.7 | 4.6 | | | 13.0 | 2.4 | 2.8 | 1.7 | 18.6 |
| 12.6 | 14.7 | 17.3 | % Profit Before Taxes/Total Assets | | 24.0 | 29.5 | 13.0 | 17.9 | 17.6 |
| 3.6 | 5.6 | 7.2 | | | 6.5 | 4.2 | 5.3 | 8.5 | 9.5 |
| -.8 | 1.4 | 1.2 | | | .7 | .4 | .9 | .9 | 4.4 |
| 105.9 | 144.3 | 146.0 | Sales/Net Fixed Assets | | 147.7 | 158.6 | 153.8 | 162.7 | 128.8 |
| 34.5 | 49.3 | 52.7 | | | 61.2 | 41.9 | 53.9 | 70.4 | 33.4 |
| 13.2 | 12.7 | 17.2 | | | 19.9 | 7.9 | 16.6 | 23.9 | 14.9 |
| 3.7 | 3.7 | 3.9 | Sales/Total Assets | | 4.7 | 3.7 | 3.7 | 4.0 | 3.8 |
| 2.8 | 2.8 | 2.8 | | | 3.0 | 2.6 | 2.9 | 2.8 | 2.7 |
| 1.9 | 1.9 | 2.0 | | | 1.9 | 1.9 | 1.9 | 2.3 | 1.8 |
| .4 | .4 | .3 | % Depr., Dep., Amort./Sales | | .4 | .3 | .2 | .3 | .3 |
| (187) .8 | (179) .8 | (210) .6 | | | (26) .8 | (25) .6 | (44) .5 | (53) .6 | (56) .7 |
| 1.5 | 1.5 | 1.1 | | | 1.0 | 2.0 | 1.0 | .9 | 1.3 |
| 1.6 | 1.8 | 1.6 | % Officers', Directors' Owners' Comp/Sales | | 2.4 | 2.8 | 2.3 | .8 | .6 |
| (91) 3.5 | (99) 3.0 | (109) 3.0 | | | (21) 5.0 | (17) 4.0 | (27) 4.1 | (20) 1.6 | (18) 1.5 |
| 6.7 | 6.0 | 6.1 | | | 10.0 | 7.8 | 6.2 | 2.7 | 2.1 |
| 7168031M | 6677472M | 9635094M | Net Sales ($) | 4436M | 85234M | 134033M | 417268M | 1112369M | 7881754M |
| 3330617M | 3138695M | 3805022M | Total Assets ($) | 1274M | 37379M | 87539M | 169466M | 396911M | 3112453M |

M = $ thousand    MM = $ million
See Pages 9 through 22 for Explanation of Ratios and Data

## Current Data Sorted by Assets      Comparative Historical Data

| Type of Statement | 0-500M | 500M-2MM | 2-10MM | 10-50MM | 50-100MM | 100-250MM | ALL 4/1/07-3/31/08 | ALL 4/1/08-3/31/09 |
|---|---|---|---|---|---|---|---|---|
| Unqualified | | 1 | 13 | 25 | 16 | 11 | 53 | 52 |
| Reviewed | | 9 | 41 | 14 | 2 | | 49 | 63 |
| Compiled | 2 | 25 | 25 | 6 | 1 | | 45 | 55 |
| Tax Returns | 13 | 42 | 24 | 1 | | | 53 | 65 |
| Other | 13 | 35 | 72 | 43 | 11 | 8 | 122 | 168 |
| | 51 (4/1-9/30/11) | | | 402 (10/1/11-3/31/12) | | | | |
| NUMBER OF STATEMENTS | 28 | 112 | 175 | 89 | 30 | 19 | 322 | 403 |
| **ASSETS** | % | % | % | % | % | % | % | % |
| Cash & Equivalents | 15.6 | 10.5 | 9.5 | 10.8 | 6.9 | 7.1 | 9.2 | 8.7 |
| Trade Receivables (net) | 34.5 | 33.5 | 33.8 | 32.8 | 26.5 | 29.0 | 33.1 | 33.7 |
| Inventory | 23.6 | 28.6 | 30.0 | 28.2 | 20.8 | 25.2 | 29.2 | 28.7 |
| All Other Current | 1.5 | 2.3 | 2.4 | 2.4 | 4.8 | 2.6 | 2.0 | 3.2 |
| Total Current | 75.2 | 74.8 | 75.8 | 74.2 | 59.0 | 64.0 | 73.6 | 74.3 |
| Fixed Assets (net) | 9.3 | 13.4 | 13.4 | 12.5 | 17.2 | 11.4 | 13.7 | 14.0 |
| Intangibles (net) | 1.1 | 4.8 | 4.5 | 8.9 | 19.3 | 20.8 | 7.1 | 6.1 |
| All Other Non-Current | 14.1 | 7.0 | 6.4 | 4.4 | 4.5 | 3.8 | 5.6 | 5.6 |
| Total | 100.0 | 100.0 | 100.0 | 100.0 | 100.0 | 100.0 | 100.0 | 100.0 |
| **LIABILITIES** | | | | | | | | |
| Notes Payable-Short Term | 18.1 | 14.4 | 12.8 | 11.9 | 8.9 | 9.4 | 13.8 | 15.2 |
| Cur. Mat.-L.T.D. | 2.0 | 2.8 | 3.5 | 1.7 | 3.2 | 1.5 | 3.2 | 4.1 |
| Trade Payables | 23.0 | 25.5 | 23.6 | 22.5 | 15.2 | 14.7 | 21.7 | 21.4 |
| Income Taxes Payable | .0 | .1 | .1 | .3 | .5 | .1 | .2 | .2 |
| All Other Current | 7.3 | 9.0 | 7.5 | 10.6 | 12.2 | 13.7 | 10.3 | 9.6 |
| Total Current | 50.5 | 51.7 | 47.5 | 47.1 | 39.9 | 39.4 | 49.1 | 50.5 |
| Long-Term Debt | 23.9 | 12.8 | 10.6 | 9.9 | 17.7 | 13.0 | 12.0 | 12.0 |
| Deferred Taxes | .0 | .3 | .1 | .6 | 2.5 | 1.2 | .2 | .2 |
| All Other Non-Current | 10.7 | 9.0 | 5.4 | 4.0 | 6.2 | 4.5 | 5.8 | 4.8 |
| Net Worth | 15.2 | 26.2 | 36.3 | 38.3 | 33.7 | 41.9 | 32.9 | 32.5 |
| Total Liabilities & Net Worth | 100.0 | 100.0 | 100.0 | 100.0 | 100.0 | 100.0 | 100.0 | 100.0 |
| **INCOME DATA** | | | | | | | | |
| Net Sales | 100.0 | 100.0 | 100.0 | 100.0 | 100.0 | 100.0 | 100.0 | 100.0 |
| Gross Profit | 48.7 | 41.6 | 40.2 | 34.5 | 43.0 | 30.7 | 40.1 | 40.2 |
| Operating Expenses | 38.3 | 37.0 | 34.4 | 29.1 | 35.3 | 24.7 | 34.2 | 34.5 |
| Operating Profit | 10.4 | 4.6 | 5.8 | 5.4 | 7.6 | 6.0 | 5.9 | 5.7 |
| All Other Expenses (net) | .1 | .9 | .5 | .4 | 1.1 | 2.0 | 1.5 | .9 |
| Profit Before Taxes | 10.3 | 3.7 | 5.3 | 5.0 | 6.6 | 4.0 | 4.4 | 4.7 |
| **RATIOS** | | | | | | | | |
| Current | 5.8 | 2.5 | 2.6 | 2.4 | 2.2 | 2.3 | 2.4 | 2.4 |
| | 1.4 | 1.5 | 1.5 | 1.7 | 1.5 | 1.4 | 1.5 | 1.5 |
| | 1.0 | 1.0 | 1.2 | 1.2 | 1.2 | 1.2 | 1.1 | 1.1 |
| Quick | 4.2 | 1.5 | 1.5 | 1.5 | 1.3 | 1.1 | 1.4 | 1.5 |
| | 1.0 | .9 | .9 | .9 | 1.0 | .9 | .9 | .8 |
| | .5 | .5 | .6 | .6 | .6 | .6 | .6 | .5 |
| Sales/Receivables | 10   36.4 | 24   15.1 | 31   11.7 | 36   10.2 | 38   9.5 | 35   10.4 | 32   11.5 | 30   12.1 |
| | 33   10.9 | 35   10.4 | 43   8.4 | 44   8.3 | 50   7.3 | 52   7.0 | 42   8.7 | 42   8.6 |
| | 45   8.1 | 51   7.1 | 59   6.2 | 59   6.2 | 62   5.9 | 69   5.3 | 58   6.2 | 59   6.2 |
| Cost of Sales/Inventory | 0   UND | 26   14.2 | 32   11.5 | 35   10.5 | 34   10.7 | 40   9.1 | 32   11.3 | 29   12.4 |
| | 23   16.0 | 53   6.9 | 59   6.2 | 62   5.9 | 51   7.2 | 60   6.1 | 60   6.1 | 54   6.7 |
| | 78   4.7 | 101   3.6 | 118   3.1 | 107   3.4 | 126   2.9 | 130   2.8 | 105   3.5 | 101   3.6 |
| Cost of Sales/Payables | 2   218.6 | 21   17.5 | 26   13.8 | 24   15.5 | 23   16.1 | 19   18.8 | 24   15.4 | 21   17.1 |
| | 25   14.7 | 41   8.9 | 44   8.3 | 38   9.5 | 38   9.7 | 35   10.3 | 39   9.3 | 38   9.6 |
| | 58   6.3 | 79   4.6 | 74   4.9 | 74   4.9 | 101   3.6 | 68   5.4 | 66   5.5 | 67   5.5 |
| Sales/Working Capital | 10.3 | 6.5 | 5.2 | 5.5 | 4.7 | 5.4 | 6.0 | 6.0 |
| | 28.2 | 15.5 | 10.6 | 9.1 | 9.1 | 8.5 | 11.9 | 12.3 |
| | UND | 182.2 | 30.1 | 25.4 | 32.7 | 17.1 | 37.2 | 48.1 |
| EBIT/Interest | 36.5 | 16.8 | 27.2 | 40.2 | 29.9 | 10.4 | 12.3 | 14.9 |
| | (15) 1.7 | (92) 4.3 | (148) 7.3 | (77) 9.2 | (27) 4.4 | (18) 3.8 | (286) 4.1 | (346) 4.5 |
| | -.8 | 1.0 | 2.4 | 3.0 | 1.3 | 1.6 | 1.7 | 1.6 |
| Net Profit + Depr., Dep., Amort./Cur. Mat. L/T/D | | 6.4 | 4.8 | 29.5 | | | 8.5 | 10.4 |
| | | (10) 1.1 | (22) 2.5 | (28) 6.3 | | | (55) 3.4 | (70) 3.0 |
| | | .2 | 1.1 | 2.9 | | | 1.5 | 1.0 |
| Fixed/Worth | .0 | .0 | .1 | .1 | .3 | .2 | .1 | .1 |
| | .4 | .3 | .3 | .3 | 1.0 | 1.0 | .4 | .4 |
| | UND | 3.0 | 1.2 | 1.0 | -1.5 | -7.7 | 1.6 | 1.7 |
| Debt/Worth | 1.1 | 1.0 | .9 | .7 | 1.1 | 1.1 | .9 | .9 |
| | 4.5 | 3.1 | 2.2 | 1.9 | 6.5 | 4.3 | 2.3 | 2.6 |
| | UND | 41.1 | 5.9 | 5.1 | -15.5 | -109.7 | 9.3 | 10.3 |
| % Profit Before Taxes/Tangible Net Worth | 274.6 | 71.6 | 74.3 | 54.7 | 45.0 | 33.3 | 61.7 | 61.1 |
| | (21) 87.2 | (87) 20.5 | (153) 28.6 | (75) 34.3 | (20) 23.9 | (14) 21.3 | (265) 27.9 | (333) 27.4 |
| | -4.5 | 4.3 | 9.6 | 14.1 | 16.2 | 11.7 | 8.9 | 9.2 |
| % Profit Before Taxes/Total Assets | 72.3 | 17.1 | 21.4 | 19.2 | 11.5 | 10.0 | 19.2 | 18.2 |
| | 18.5 | 4.3 | 10.8 | 9.0 | 7.9 | 5.0 | 7.8 | 6.9 |
| | -3.4 | .4 | 1.8 | 4.3 | 1.6 | 1.4 | 1.9 | 1.8 |
| Sales/Net Fixed Assets | UND | 259.4 | 138.8 | 138.5 | 61.9 | 27.0 | 133.1 | 130.4 |
| | 87.1 | 51.6 | 52.1 | 29.3 | 20.2 | 16.7 | 34.9 | 36.9 |
| | 27.5 | 18.6 | 14.6 | 9.9 | 5.8 | 14.9 | 12.1 | 14.0 |
| Sales/Total Assets | 6.3 | 4.4 | 3.9 | 3.4 | 2.1 | 2.9 | 3.8 | 3.9 |
| | 4.5 | 3.1 | 2.7 | 2.2 | 1.7 | 1.7 | 2.8 | 2.8 |
| | 2.8 | 2.3 | 1.8 | 1.6 | 1.4 | 1.2 | 1.7 | 1.8 |
| % Depr., Dep., Amort./Sales | .3 | .3 | .3 | .2 | .7 | .9 | .3 | .3 |
| | (12) .7 | (70) .9 | (131) .8 | (79) .6 | (19) 1.7 | (14) 1.5 | (240) .8 | (299) .7 |
| | 2.6 | 2.0 | 1.9 | 2.0 | 3.1 | 2.4 | 2.0 | 1.9 |
| % Officers', Directors', Owners' Comp/Sales | 4.8 | 3.4 | 1.4 | 1.0 | | | 2.5 | 2.0 |
| | (13) 7.3 | (62) 5.2 | (73) 3.0 | (11) 1.7 | | | (109) 4.2 | (146) 3.6 |
| | 9.1 | 9.5 | 4.8 | 2.3 | | | 7.6 | 7.4 |
| Net Sales ($) | 31697M | 456882M | 2431354M | 5058997M | 4066891M | 6362757M | 10781124M | 21124280M |
| Total Assets ($) | 6644M | 130474M | 855604M | 1974523M | 2143799M | 3126008M | 4431483M | 6455148M |

M = $ thousand     MM = $ million
See Pages 9 through 22 for Explanation of Ratios and Data

## Comparative Historical Data | Current Data Sorted by Sales

| Type of Statement | 4/1/09-3/31/10 ALL | 4/1/10-3/31/11 ALL | 4/1/11-3/31/12 ALL | 0-1MM | 1-3MM | 3-5MM | 5-10MM | 10-25MM | 25MM & OVER |
|---|---|---|---|---|---|---|---|---|---|
| Unqualified | 54 | 58 | 66 | | 1 | | 2 | 13 | 50 |
| Reviewed | 63 | 62 | 66 | | 3 | 8 | 11 | 27 | 17 |
| Compiled | 53 | 63 | 59 | 3 | 8 | 9 | 15 | 14 | 10 |
| Tax Returns | 64 | 73 | 80 | 7 | 24 | 16 | 18 | 13 | 2 |
| Other | 165 | 176 | 182 | 10 | 20 | 21 | 32 | 37 | 62 |
| | | | | 51 (4/1-9/30/11) | | | 402 (10/1/11-3/31/12) | | |
| **NUMBER OF STATEMENTS** | 399 | 432 | 453 | 20 | 56 | 54 | 78 | 104 | 141 |
| **ASSETS** | % | % | % | % | % | % | % | % | % |
| Cash & Equivalents | 10.4 | 10.4 | 10.1 | 16.0 | 11.8 | 8.9 | 9.4 | 9.8 | 9.7 |
| Trade Receivables (net) | 32.8 | 32.1 | 32.9 | 29.3 | 27.4 | 34.3 | 34.5 | 33.6 | 33.5 |
| Inventory | 27.6 | 26.1 | 28.1 | 17.1 | 29.9 | 24.9 | 31.4 | 31.1 | 26.1 |
| All Other Current | 2.8 | 2.9 | 2.5 | 1.0 | 2.1 | 3.9 | 1.8 | 2.0 | 3.1 |
| Total Current | 73.6 | 71.5 | 73.6 | 63.4 | 71.3 | 72.0 | 77.1 | 76.5 | 72.4 |
| Fixed Assets (net) | 14.8 | 14.0 | 13.1 | 19.8 | 12.1 | 14.2 | 14.3 | 11.6 | 12.6 |
| Intangibles (net) | 7.0 | 8.2 | 6.9 | 1.5 | 5.0 | 5.4 | 4.3 | 6.0 | 11.1 |
| All Other Non-Current | 4.7 | 6.3 | 6.4 | 14.8 | 11.7 | 8.4 | 4.3 | 5.8 | 3.9 |
| Total | 100.0 | 100.0 | 100.0 | 100.0 | 100.0 | 100.0 | 100.0 | 100.0 | 100.0 |
| **LIABILITIES** | | | | | | | | | |
| Notes Payable-Short Term | 14.4 | 13.6 | 12.9 | 17.9 | 14.0 | 14.7 | 13.9 | 11.9 | 11.4 |
| Cur. Mat.-L.T.D. | 3.2 | 3.1 | 2.8 | 2.4 | 2.1 | 3.9 | 4.8 | 2.4 | 1.9 |
| Trade Payables | 21.2 | 21.0 | 22.9 | 14.7 | 21.5 | 23.7 | 22.3 | 26.8 | 21.7 |
| Income Taxes Payable | .2 | .2 | .2 | .0 | .1 | .1 | .0 | .2 | .2 |
| All Other Current | 9.7 | 10.5 | 9.0 | 7.7 | 5.2 | 6.8 | 8.4 | 10.3 | 11.1 |
| Total Current | 48.6 | 48.4 | 47.8 | 42.7 | 42.8 | 49.3 | 49.4 | 51.6 | 46.3 |
| Long-Term Debt | 12.1 | 12.3 | 12.4 | 14.0 | 23.8 | 11.7 | 10.3 | 10.0 | 10.9 |
| Deferred Taxes | .2 | .4 | .4 | .0 | .0 | .5 | .0 | .1 | 1.1 |
| All Other Non-Current | 5.5 | 5.3 | 6.4 | 10.2 | 13.3 | 11.1 | 4.2 | 4.2 | 4.1 |
| Net Worth | 33.5 | 33.6 | 33.0 | 33.6 | 20.2 | 27.4 | 36.1 | 34.0 | 37.6 |
| Total Liabilities & Net Worth | 100.0 | 100.0 | 100.0 | 100.0 | 100.0 | 100.0 | 100.0 | 100.0 | 100.0 |
| **INCOME DATA** | | | | | | | | | |
| Net Sales | 100.0 | 100.0 | 100.0 | 100.0 | 100.0 | 100.0 | 100.0 | 100.0 | 100.0 |
| Gross Profit | 39.9 | 41.2 | 39.7 | 55.7 | 47.1 | 45.2 | 41.9 | 36.1 | 33.9 |
| Operating Expenses | 34.1 | 34.9 | 33.9 | 41.6 | 40.8 | 41.0 | 37.7 | 30.6 | 27.7 |
| Operating Profit | 5.9 | 6.2 | 5.8 | 14.1 | 6.4 | 4.1 | 4.3 | 5.5 | 6.2 |
| All Other Expenses (net) | .7 | .8 | .7 | .0 | 1.5 | .6 | .5 | .3 | .8 |
| Profit Before Taxes | 5.1 | 5.4 | 5.2 | 14.1 | 4.8 | 3.6 | 3.8 | 5.2 | 5.4 |
| **RATIOS** | | | | | | | | | |
| Current | 2.4 | 2.6 | 2.5 | 7.9 | 4.0 | 3.0 | 2.5 | 2.1 | 2.4 |
| | 1.5 | 1.6 | 1.5 | 1.3 | 1.8 | 1.5 | 1.6 | 1.5 | 1.5 |
| | 1.2 | 1.1 | 1.1 | .9 | 1.2 | 1.0 | 1.2 | 1.1 | 1.2 |
| Quick | 1.5 | 1.5 | 1.5 | 6.1 | 1.8 | 1.6 | 1.5 | 1.3 | 1.4 |
| | .9 | .9 | .9 | 1.0 | .9 | .9 | .9 | .9 | .9 |
| | .6 | .5 | .6 | .5 | .5 | .5 | .6 | .5 | .7 |
| Sales/Receivables | 30  12.4 | 28  13.1 | 30  12.3 | 11  33.8 | 21  17.0 | 29  12.6 | 27  13.5 | 31  11.6 | 34  10.8 |
| | 42  8.7 | 41  8.9 | 42  8.7 | 41  8.8 | 38  9.7 | 48  7.6 | 41  9.0 | 39  9.3 | 44  8.3 |
| | 57  6.4 | 56  6.6 | 58  6.3 | 104  3.5 | 53  6.9 | 66  5.5 | 61  6.0 | 51  7.1 | 58  6.3 |
| Cost of Sales/Inventory | 28  13.1 | 30  12.3 | 29  12.4 | 0  UND | 28  13.0 | 17  22.1 | 29  12.5 | 33  11.0 | 27  13.6 |
| | 52  7.0 | 51  7.1 | 55  6.6 | 56  6.5 | 69  5.3 | 54  6.8 | 64  5.7 | 54  6.7 | 51  7.2 |
| | 96  3.8 | 99  3.7 | 107  3.4 | 96  3.8 | 152  2.4 | 118  3.1 | 122  3.0 | 101  3.6 | 89  4.1 |
| Cost of Sales/Payables | 20  18.5 | 21  17.1 | 23  15.7 | 4  87.9 | 12  30.9 | 29  12.8 | 26  14.2 | 24  15.1 | 22  16.5 |
| | 40  9.2 | 38  9.7 | 41  8.9 | 31  11.6 | 41  8.9 | 52  7.0 | 45  8.2 | 40  9.2 | 35  10.3 |
| | 67  5.5 | 63  5.8 | 74  4.9 | 126  2.9 | 89  4.1 | 81  4.5 | 76  4.8 | 70  5.2 | 72  5.1 |
| Sales/Working Capital | 6.0 | 5.8 | 5.8 | 4.0 | 4.8 | 4.3 | 6.1 | 6.3 | 5.7 |
| | 11.3 | 12.4 | 10.8 | 20.7 | 10.5 | 12.1 | 10.6 | 13.1 | 10.0 |
| | 33.9 | 54.9 | 35.4 | -103.0 | 30.4 | 181.4 | 38.1 | 41.1 | 28.3 |
| EBIT/Interest | 21.6 | 30.7 | 23.4 | | 9.7 | 13.9 | 34.9 | 25.6 | 38.2 |
| | (348) 6.1 | (373) 5.6 | (377) 6.4 | (41) 2.1 | (49) 4.3 | (68) 6.5 | (86) 7.8 | (124) 7.5 | |
| | 2.0 | 2.0 | 1.8 | | .7 | 1.0 | 1.6 | 2.8 | 2.6 |
| Net Profit + Depr., Dep., Amort./Cur. Mat. L/T/D | 12.2 | 12.6 | 13.0 | | | | | 4.5 | 26.2 |
| | (72) 4.2 | (72) 4.8 | (74) 3.7 | | | | (16) 2.8 | (40) 5.4 | |
| | 1.8 | 1.8 | 1.3 | | | | | 1.3 | 3.0 |
| Fixed/Worth | .1 | .1 | .1 | .0 | .1 | .0 | .1 | .1 | .1 |
| | .3 | .4 | .4 | .4 | .6 | .3 | .3 | .3 | .4 |
| | 1.5 | 1.7 | 2.2 | 3.0 | -3.5 | 2.4 | 1.9 | 1.1 | 1.4 |
| Debt/Worth | .9 | .8 | .9 | .4 | 1.2 | 1.0 | .8 | .9 | .9 |
| | 2.1 | 2.2 | 2.5 | 2.1 | 3.5 | 2.2 | 2.6 | 2.1 | 2.5 |
| | 8.2 | 13.7 | 12.9 | 12.0 | -20.5 | 23.4 | 9.9 | 6.4 | 8.3 |
| % Profit Before Taxes/Tangible Net Worth | 65.1 | 68.8 | 71.2 | 192.9 | 98.1 | 36.9 | 87.4 | 80.3 | 56.7 |
| | (332) 30.7 | (363) 29.9 | (370) 28.6 | (17) 57.2 | (39) 17.3 | (44) 14.0 | (68) 37.3 | (90) 29.2 | (112) 32.0 |
| | 11.2 | 11.4 | 9.4 | -4.5 | .3 | 3.1 | 2.5 | 13.2 | 16.1 |
| % Profit Before Taxes/Total Assets | 20.6 | 21.5 | 19.5 | 63.8 | 16.2 | 15.5 | 23.4 | 19.5 | 18.5 |
| | 9.6 | 9.0 | 8.3 | 7.5 | 3.5 | 5.3 | 7.9 | 10.6 | 8.7 |
| | 2.6 | 2.0 | 1.8 | -1.0 | -.1 | .7 | .7 | 2.5 | 4.2 |
| Sales/Net Fixed Assets | 134.2 | 146.0 | 145.5 | UND | 127.5 | 262.0 | 155.8 | 138.8 | 143.9 |
| | 33.0 | 35.0 | 41.4 | 37.6 | 51.5 | 44.0 | 38.6 | 55.0 | 31.8 |
| | 11.0 | 12.0 | 13.4 | 6.3 | 17.5 | 11.7 | 11.9 | 17.0 | 12.6 |
| Sales/Total Assets | 3.8 | 3.9 | 3.9 | 4.3 | 4.0 | 3.7 | 4.0 | 4.0 | 3.7 |
| | 2.7 | 2.8 | 2.7 | 2.5 | 2.3 | 2.5 | 2.9 | 2.9 | 2.4 |
| | 1.8 | 1.8 | 1.8 | 1.3 | 1.5 | 1.7 | 1.9 | 2.0 | 1.6 |
| % Depr., Dep., Amort./Sales | .3 | .3 | .3 | | .3 | .7 | .4 | .3 | .3 |
| | (298) .8 | (312) .8 | (325) .9 | | (32) .9 | (30) 1.4 | (56) 1.3 | (84) .6 | (114) .7 |
| | 1.8 | 1.9 | 2.0 | | 2.4 | 4.1 | 2.2 | 1.7 | 2.0 |
| % Officers', Directors' Owners' Comp/Sales | 1.9 | 1.7 | 1.8 | | 3.5 | 4.0 | 2.3 | 1.2 | .5 |
| | (144) 3.6 | (153) 3.4 | (163) 3.9 | | (34) 6.4 | (30) 6.0 | (32) 3.7 | (45) 2.7 | (17) 1.5 |
| | 6.9 | 6.0 | 7.1 | | 8.8 | 10.8 | 6.4 | 4.2 | 2.4 |
| Net Sales ($) | 15516500M | 15521468M | 18408578M | 11854M | 110144M | 203143M | 557542M | 1686774M | 15839121M |
| Total Assets ($) | 6612639M | 7333154M | 8237052M | 7110M | 52891M | 100272M | 246826M | 684018M | 7145935M |

M = $ thousand    MM = $ million
See Pages 9 through 22 for Explanation of Ratios and Data

# WHOLESALE—Ophthalmic Goods Merchant Wholesalers  NAICS 423460

| | Current Data Sorted by Assets | | | | | | Comparative Historical Data | |
|---|---|---|---|---|---|---|---|---|
| | | | 2 | 3 | | 1 | | |
| | | 1 | 3 | 3 | | | | |
| | | 1 | 3 | | | | | |
| | 1 | 3 | 3 | | | | | |
| | 1 | 2 | 11 | 5 | | | | |
| Type of Statement | 0-500M | 7 (4/1-9/30/11) 500M-2MM | 2-10MM | 36 (10/1/11-3/31/12) 10-50MM | 50-100MM | 100-250MM | 4/1/07-3/31/08 ALL | 4/1/08-3/31/09 ALL |
| Unqualified | | | 2 | 3 | | 1 | 4 | 5 |
| Reviewed | | 1 | 3 | 3 | | | 3 | 6 |
| Compiled | | 1 | 3 | | | | 4 | 4 |
| Tax Returns | 1 | 3 | 3 | | | | 2 | 3 |
| Other | 1 | 2 | 11 | 5 | | | 9 | 10 |
| NUMBER OF STATEMENTS | 2 | 7 | 22 | 11 | | 1 | 22 | 28 |
| | % | % | % | % | % | % | % | % |
| **ASSETS** | | | | | | | | |
| Cash & Equivalents | | | 5.5 | 3.8 | | | 8.2 | 6.6 |
| Trade Receivables (net) | | | 32.6 | 29.5 | | | 31.6 | 28.9 |
| Inventory | | | 38.3 | 42.1 | | | 35.7 | 37.6 |
| All Other Current | | | 4.3 | 1.9 | | | 3.2 | 3.2 |
| Total Current | | | 80.6 | 77.3 | | | 78.7 | 76.3 |
| Fixed Assets (net) | | | 7.9 | 9.9 | | | 10.1 | 7.5 |
| Intangibles (net) | | | 7.4 | 5.8 | | | 7.6 | 5.2 |
| All Other Non-Current | | | 4.0 | 7.0 | | | 3.5 | 11.0 |
| Total | | | 100.0 | 100.0 | | | 100.0 | 100.0 |
| **LIABILITIES** | | | | | | | | |
| Notes Payable-Short Term | | | 14.4 | 13.8 | | | 13.3 | 19.0 |
| Cur. Mat.-L.T.D. | | | 1.2 | 2.4 | | | .7 | .9 |
| Trade Payables | | | 30.5 | 20.4 | | | 25.8 | 31.1 |
| Income Taxes Payable | | | .1 | .4 | | | .2 | .3 |
| All Other Current | | | 6.8 | 11.8 | | | 21.5 | 11.2 |
| Total Current | | | 53.0 | 48.7 | | | 61.5 | 62.5 |
| Long-Term Debt | | | 5.3 | 8.3 | | | 6.1 | 7.3 |
| Deferred Taxes | | | .0 | .0 | | | .2 | .0 |
| All Other Non-Current | | | 1.2 | 1.7 | | | 3.4 | 1.7 |
| Net Worth | | | 40.5 | 41.3 | | | 28.8 | 28.5 |
| Total Liabilties & Net Worth | | | 100.0 | 100.0 | | | 100.0 | 100.0 |
| **INCOME DATA** | | | | | | | | |
| Net Sales | | | 100.0 | 100.0 | | | 100.0 | 100.0 |
| Gross Profit | | | 40.9 | 41.4 | | | 37.3 | 40.4 |
| Operating Expenses | | | 35.3 | 34.0 | | | 33.7 | 35.4 |
| Operating Profit | | | 5.7 | 7.4 | | | 3.6 | 5.0 |
| All Other Expenses (net) | | | .5 | .5 | | | 1.0 | .6 |
| Profit Before Taxes | | | 5.2 | 6.9 | | | 2.6 | 4.4 |
| **RATIOS** | | | | | | | | |
| Current | | | 2.3 | 2.2 | | | 1.8 | 1.9 |
| | | | 1.4 | 1.7 | | | 1.3 | 1.2 |
| | | | 1.2 | 1.2 | | | 1.1 | .9 |
| Quick | | | 1.1 | .9 | | | 1.0 | .9 |
| | | | .8 | .6 | | | .7 | .6 |
| | | | .4 | .5 | | | .4 | .4 |
| Sales/Receivables | | | 35  10.3 | 34  10.7 | | | 28  13.0 | 33  11.0 |
| | | | 44  8.3 | 41  8.9 | | | 40  9.2 | 41  8.8 |
| | | | 57  6.4 | 47  7.8 | | | 60  6.1 | 59  6.2 |
| Cost of Sales/Inventory | | | 54  6.8 | 47  7.8 | | | 48  7.5 | 54  6.8 |
| | | | 122  3.0 | 140  2.6 | | | 68  5.3 | 107  3.4 |
| | | | 182  2.0 | 182  2.0 | | | 136  2.7 | 193  1.9 |
| Cost of Sales/Payables | | | 34  10.8 | 30  12.1 | | | 23  16.0 | 31  11.9 |
| | | | 59  6.2 | 43  8.5 | | | 44  8.3 | 59  6.2 |
| | | | 78  4.7 | 81  4.5 | | | 87  4.2 | 107  3.4 |
| Sales/Working Capital | | | 4.9 | 4.7 | | | 7.4 | 6.4 |
| | | | 8.8 | 7.0 | | | 14.7 | 16.2 |
| | | | 20.6 | 23.4 | | | 55.2 | -82.2 |
| EBIT/Interest | | | 19.7 | 173.0 | | | 12.1 | 10.5 |
| | | | (20) 8.4 | 19.1 | | | (20) 3.9 | (25) 4.9 |
| | | | 1.8 | 5.1 | | | 1.3 | 1.2 |
| Net Profit + Depr., Dep., Amort./Cur. Mat. L/T/D | | | | | | | | |
| Fixed/Worth | | | .1 | .1 | | | .1 | .1 |
| | | | .2 | .2 | | | .2 | .2 |
| | | | .4 | .8 | | | 1.8 | .6 |
| Debt/Worth | | | .8 | 1.1 | | | 1.5 | 1.8 |
| | | | 1.7 | 1.8 | | | 2.8 | 2.7 |
| | | | 3.4 | 3.4 | | | 7.8 | 5.5 |
| % Profit Before Taxes/Tangible Net Worth | | | 56.0 | 46.1 | | | 118.5 | 61.9 |
| | | | (20) 27.3 | 42.8 | | | (19) 21.8 | (26) 29.4 |
| | | | 8.9 | 24.6 | | | 8.1 | 6.2 |
| % Profit Before Taxes/Total Assets | | | 27.7 | 23.6 | | | 15.1 | 15.1 |
| | | | 8.4 | 12.8 | | | 4.5 | 5.8 |
| | | | .6 | 6.9 | | | 1.7 | .9 |
| Sales/Net Fixed Assets | | | 201.9 | 82.2 | | | 211.6 | 162.5 |
| | | | 61.6 | 44.9 | | | 47.9 | 42.6 |
| | | | 18.7 | 11.4 | | | 23.3 | 20.2 |
| Sales/Total Assets | | | 3.0 | 3.8 | | | 3.8 | 3.3 |
| | | | 2.2 | 2.6 | | | 2.8 | 2.3 |
| | | | 1.6 | 1.5 | | | 2.0 | 1.6 |
| % Depr., Dep., Amort./Sales | | | .2 | .2 | | | .1 | .2 |
| | | | (16) .3 | .6 | | | (16) .3 | (24) .5 |
| | | | 1.6 | 1.6 | | | .7 | 1.2 |
| % Officers', Directors' Owners' Comp/Sales | | | | | | | | 2.7 |
| | | | | | | | (13) 3.9 | |
| | | | | | | | | 6.4 |
| Net Sales ($) | 4060M | 28198M | 292093M | 462138M | | 479019M | 541467M | 472084M |
| Total Assets ($) | 410M | 7407M | 108861M | 166577M | | 182961M | 311171M | 202685M |

M = $ thousand   MM = $ million
See Pages 9 through 22 for Explanation of Ratios and Data

## Comparative Historical Data  /  Current Data Sorted by Sales

### Type of Statement

| 4/1/09-3/31/10 ALL | 4/1/10-3/31/11 ALL | 4/1/11-3/31/12 ALL | Type of Statement | 0-1MM | 1-3MM | 3-5MM | 5-10MM | 10-25MM | 25MM & OVER |
|---|---|---|---|---|---|---|---|---|---|
| 2 | 7 | 6 | Unqualified | | | | 1 | 1 | 4 |
| 5 | 8 | 7 | Reviewed | 1 | | | | 5 | 1 |
| 5 | 9 | 4 | Compiled | | | 3 | | | 1 |
| 3 | 5 | 7 | Tax Returns | | 1 | 2 | 4 | | |
| 12 | 12 | 19 | Other | 1 | | | 4 | 9 | 5 |
| | | | | | 7 (4/1-9/30/11) | | 36 (10/1/11-3/31/12) | | |
| 27 | 41 | 43 | NUMBER OF STATEMENTS | 2 | 1 | 5 | 9 | 15 | 11 |

### Main Data

| 4/1/09-3/31/10 ALL % | 4/1/10-3/31/11 ALL % | 4/1/11-3/31/12 ALL % | | 0-1MM % | 1-3MM % | 3-5MM % | 5-10MM % | 10-25MM % | 25MM & OVER % |
|---|---|---|---|---|---|---|---|---|---|
| | | | **ASSETS** | | | | | | |
| 3.4 | 9.6 | 5.1 | Cash & Equivalents | | | | | 4.9 | 4.5 |
| 30.9 | 33.0 | 30.7 | Trade Receivables (net) | | | | | 25.8 | 40.3 |
| 37.5 | 34.5 | 41.9 | Inventory | | | | | 44.8 | 33.0 |
| 3.8 | 2.4 | 2.8 | All Other Current | | | | | 3.0 | 3.0 |
| 75.7 | 79.4 | 80.6 | Total Current | | | | | 78.5 | 80.9 |
| 6.3 | 7.3 | 8.4 | Fixed Assets (net) | | | | | 7.3 | 9.1 |
| 11.8 | 8.8 | 6.2 | Intangibles (net) | | | | | 7.3 | 7.5 |
| 6.2 | 4.5 | 4.8 | All Other Non-Current | | | | | 6.9 | 2.4 |
| 100.0 | 100.0 | 100.0 | Total | | | | | 100.0 | 100.0 |
| | | | **LIABILITIES** | | | | | | |
| 17.6 | 13.8 | 15.9 | Notes Payable-Short Term | | | | | 14.9 | 10.1 |
| 1.5 | 1.7 | 1.4 | Cur. Mat.-L.T.D. | | | | | 2.1 | 1.6 |
| 28.0 | 31.3 | 26.8 | Trade Payables | | | | | 26.7 | 28.2 |
| .1 | .1 | .1 | Income Taxes Payable | | | | | .0 | .4 |
| 7.8 | 6.5 | 8.4 | All Other Current | | | | | 5.3 | 14.6 |
| 55.0 | 53.3 | 52.6 | Total Current | | | | | 49.0 | 54.8 |
| 6.7 | 9.2 | 9.1 | Long-Term Debt | | | | | 7.7 | 7.8 |
| .5 | .0 | .0 | Deferred Taxes | | | | | .0 | .0 |
| 4.1 | 3.4 | 1.4 | All Other Non-Current | | | | | 1.5 | .9 |
| 33.7 | 34.1 | 36.9 | Net Worth | | | | | 41.8 | 36.4 |
| 100.0 | 100.0 | 100.0 | Total Liabilities & Net Worth | | | | | 100.0 | 100.0 |
| | | | **INCOME DATA** | | | | | | |
| 100.0 | 100.0 | 100.0 | Net Sales | | | | | 100.0 | 100.0 |
| 40.2 | 38.0 | 39.4 | Gross Profit | | | | | 41.1 | 33.7 |
| 37.4 | 33.9 | 33.9 | Operating Expenses | | | | | 34.7 | 26.4 |
| 2.8 | 4.2 | 5.5 | Operating Profit | | | | | 6.4 | 7.2 |
| 1.1 | 1.0 | .5 | All Other Expenses (net) | | | | | .7 | .3 |
| 1.7 | 3.2 | 5.0 | Profit Before Taxes | | | | | 5.7 | 6.9 |
| | | | **RATIOS** | | | | | | |
| 1.9 / 1.3 / 1.1 | 2.0 / 1.5 / 1.1 | 2.2 / 1.5 / 1.2 | Current | | | | | 2.2 / 1.7 / 1.3 | 2.2 / 1.5 / 1.2 |
| .9 / .6 / .4 | 1.0 / .8 / .5 | 1.1 / .7 / .4 | Quick | | | | | .9 / .5 / .4 | 1.1 / .9 / .6 |
| 32 11.3 / 41 8.9 / 49 7.4 | 33 11.2 / 39 9.4 / 57 6.5 | 34 10.8 / 41 8.9 / 52 7.0 | Sales/Receivables | | | | | 34 10.8 / 46 8.0 / 49 7.5 | 34 10.7 / 36 10.2 / 47 7.8 |
| 50 7.3 / 90 4.1 / 175 2.1 | 44 8.3 / 83 4.4 / 158 2.3 | 47 7.8 / 107 3.4 / 174 2.1 | Cost of Sales/Inventory | | | | | 81 4.5 / 159 2.3 / 215 1.7 | 29 12.6 / 51 7.1 / 152 2.4 |
| 40 9.1 / 56 6.5 / 80 4.5 | 36 10.3 / 50 7.3 / 72 5.0 | 32 11.4 / 44 8.3 / 78 4.7 | Cost of Sales/Payables | | | | | 34 10.7 / 73 5.0 / 79 4.6 | 32 11.4 / 37 9.9 / 58 6.3 |
| 8.1 / 12.8 / 50.3 | 5.6 / 12.7 / 30.6 | 5.0 / 9.6 / 21.4 | Sales/Working Capital | | | | | 5.0 / 6.5 / 19.7 | 7.0 / 17.3 / 34.6 |
| 15.3 / 7.6 / 1.0 | (35) 18.7 / 8.4 / 2.7 | (39) 22.0 / 8.5 / 2.6 | EBIT/Interest | | | | | 16.5 / 10.6 / 5.1 | (10) 191.8 / 20.6 / 2.5 |
| | (16) 8.3 / 3.9 / 1.9 | (13) 11.3 / 3.3 / 2.1 | Net Profit + Depr., Dep., Amort./Cur. Mat. L/T/D | | | | | | |
| .1 / .2 / .7 | .1 / .2 / .4 | .1 / .2 / .4 | Fixed/Worth | | | | | .1 / .1 / .3 | .1 / .4 / 2.0 |
| 1.8 / 2.7 / 12.6 | 1.2 / 2.2 / 8.3 | 1.1 / 2.0 / 4.1 | Debt/Worth | | | | | 1.1 / 1.7 / 3.2 | 1.6 / 2.2 / 13.0 |
| (22) 73.9 / 25.9 / 2.5 | (36) 53.8 / 36.9 / 10.3 | (40) 56.0 / 32.2 / 7.7 | % Profit Before Taxes/Tangible Net Worth | | | | | 49.1 / 29.7 / 9.3 | 380.0 / 43.9 / 36.2 |
| 14.5 / 5.8 / .1 | 15.9 / 7.0 / 2.4 | 23.6 / 10.1 / 1.1 | % Profit Before Taxes/Total Assets | | | | | 14.8 / 10.5 / 3.8 | 27.7 / 12.8 / 1.2 |
| 148.1 / 63.8 / 22.5 | 197.4 / 54.7 / 21.3 | 198.5 / 56.7 / 19.2 | Sales/Net Fixed Assets | | | | | 177.5 / 57.4 / 20.7 | 198.5 / 71.6 / 11.4 |
| 3.8 / 2.5 / 1.4 | 3.9 / 2.6 / 1.8 | 3.8 / 2.6 / 1.8 | Sales/Total Assets | | | | | 2.9 / 2.3 / 1.6 | 5.9 / 2.7 / 2.6 |
| (19) .3 / .6 / 1.2 | (35) .3 / .7 / 1.0 | (33) .2 / .6 / 1.4 | % Depr., Dep., Amort./Sales | | | | | (12) .2 / .6 / 2.9 | |
| (11) 1.6 / 4.0 / 5.4 | (16) .9 / 2.1 / 1.0 | (15) .8 / 1.5 / 2.9 | % Officers', Directors', Owners' Comp/Sales | | | | | | |
| 1163852M | 1586022M | 1265508M | Net Sales ($) | 829M | 2803M | 20309M | 64593M | 207618M | 969356M |
| 601041M | 715742M | 466216M | Total Assets ($) | 643M | 947M | 5870M | 35237M | 97442M | 326077M |

M = $ thousand    MM = $ million
See Pages 9 through 22 for Explanation of Ratios and Data

**Current Data Sorted by Assets**      **Comparative Historical Data**

| Type of Statement | 0-500M | 500M-2MM | 2-10MM | 10-50MM | 50-100MM | 100-250MM | | 4/1/07-3/31/08 ALL | 4/1/08-3/31/09 ALL |
|---|---|---|---|---|---|---|---|---|---|
| Unqualified | | 1 | 3 | 11 | 2 | 1 | | 13 | 12 |
| Reviewed | | 5 | 14 | 4 | 1 | 1 | | 26 | 23 |
| Compiled | 1 | 5 | 5 | | 1 | | | 17 | 11 |
| Tax Returns | 3 | 9 | 5 | | 1 | | | 12 | 15 |
| Other | 2 | 14 | 19 | 8 | | | | 29 | 34 |
| | | 20 (4/1-9/30/11) | 96 (10/1/11-3/31/12) | | | 1 | | | |
| **NUMBER OF STATEMENTS** | 6 | 34 | 46 | 24 | 4 | 2 | | 97 | 95 |
| | % | % | % | % | % | % | | % | % |
| **ASSETS** | | | | | | | | | |
| Cash & Equivalents | | 9.8 | 10.7 | 7.4 | | | | 9.3 | 7.4 |
| Trade Receivables (net) | | 36.2 | 39.3 | 31.2 | | | | 29.2 | 28.5 |
| Inventory | | 30.1 | 31.6 | 26.7 | | | | 31.8 | 35.9 |
| All Other Current | | 2.6 | 3.0 | 4.5 | | | | 2.4 | 3.8 |
| Total Current | | 78.8 | 84.5 | 69.8 | | | | 72.8 | 75.7 |
| Fixed Assets (net) | | 9.3 | 7.1 | 13.3 | | | | 13.9 | 12.5 |
| Intangibles (net) | | 3.7 | 3.6 | 7.4 | | | | 8.6 | 7.4 |
| All Other Non-Current | | 8.2 | 4.7 | 9.4 | | | | 4.6 | 4.4 |
| Total | | 100.0 | 100.0 | 100.0 | | | | 100.0 | 100.0 |
| **LIABILITIES** | | | | | | | | | |
| Notes Payable-Short Term | | 18.5 | 11.3 | 9.9 | | | | 14.3 | 21.1 |
| Cur. Mat.-L.T.D. | | 2.4 | 1.7 | 4.1 | | | | 2.7 | 2.0 |
| Trade Payables | | 20.3 | 25.9 | 19.5 | | | | 22.8 | 19.5 |
| Income Taxes Payable | | .1 | .0 | .3 | | | | .3 | .2 |
| All Other Current | | 11.9 | 12.7 | 13.8 | | | | 11.3 | 10.1 |
| Total Current | | 53.2 | 51.6 | 47.6 | | | | 51.4 | 52.9 |
| Long-Term Debt | | 11.8 | 2.8 | 6.3 | | | | 10.6 | 11.4 |
| Deferred Taxes | | .1 | .1 | .3 | | | | .1 | .2 |
| All Other Non-Current | | 12.3 | 4.1 | 6.4 | | | | 7.1 | 6.4 |
| Net Worth | | 22.6 | 41.4 | 39.4 | | | | 30.7 | 29.2 |
| Total Liabilities & Net Worth | | 100.0 | 100.0 | 100.0 | | | | 100.0 | 100.0 |
| **INCOME DATA** | | | | | | | | | |
| Net Sales | | 100.0 | 100.0 | 100.0 | | | | 100.0 | 100.0 |
| Gross Profit | | 38.2 | 29.8 | 31.5 | | | | 36.0 | 33.5 |
| Operating Expenses | | 33.9 | 26.3 | 28.7 | | | | 32.3 | 30.5 |
| Operating Profit | | 4.3 | 3.5 | 2.9 | | | | 3.7 | 2.9 |
| All Other Expenses (net) | | .8 | .4 | .7 | | | | 1.3 | 1.5 |
| Profit Before Taxes | | 3.5 | 3.1 | 2.2 | | | | 2.4 | 1.5 |
| **RATIOS** | | | | | | | | | |
| Current | | 2.6 | 2.1 | 2.2 | | | | 2.2 | 2.0 |
| | | 1.6 | 1.7 | 1.5 | | | | 1.6 | 1.5 |
| | | 1.2 | 1.2 | 1.2 | | | | 1.1 | 1.1 |
| Quick | | 2.0 | 1.3 | 1.3 | | | | 1.1 | 1.1 |
| | | .8 | .9 | .7 | | | | .8 | .7 |
| | | .5 | .7 | .5 | | | | .5 | .5 |
| Sales/Receivables | | 27   13.4 | 31   11.7 | 30   12.1 | | | | 28   13.1 | 25   14.4 |
| | | 40   9.2 | 40   9.2 | 41   8.8 | | | | 40   9.2 | 37   9.8 |
| | | 58   6.3 | 56   6.5 | 63   5.8 | | | | 52   7.0 | 50   7.3 |
| Cost of Sales/Inventory | | 5   76.3 | 17   21.2 | 14   26.2 | | | | 35   10.4 | 34   10.7 |
| | | 51   7.1 | 48   7.6 | 70   5.2 | | | | 70   5.2 | 66   5.5 |
| | | 130   2.8 | 85   4.3 | 114   3.2 | | | | 111   3.3 | 122   3.0 |
| Cost of Sales/Payables | | 9   39.0 | 20   18.0 | 21   17.0 | | | | 24   15.2 | 18   20.3 |
| | | 34   10.8 | 36   10.1 | 29   12.5 | | | | 36   10.2 | 32   11.5 |
| | | 64   5.7 | 68   5.4 | 64   5.7 | | | | 70   5.2 | 56   6.6 |
| Sales/Working Capital | | 5.6 | 5.9 | 7.1 | | | | 6.5 | 6.1 |
| | | 9.7 | 9.9 | 10.1 | | | | 11.6 | 12.6 |
| | | 21.0 | 28.0 | 23.9 | | | | 59.2 | 34.5 |
| EBIT/Interest | | 8.5 | 18.1 | 18.6 | | | | 9.9 | 7.9 |
| | | (29) 3.0 | (39) 3.6 | (21) 10.8 | | | | (88) 3.7 | (83) 4.3 |
| | | 1.6 | 2.0 | 3.7 | | | | 1.3 | 1.8 |
| Net Profit + Depr., Dep., Amort./Cur. Mat. L/T/D | | | | | | | | 11.5 | 8.0 |
| | | | | | | | | (18) 3.4 | (20) 3.2 |
| | | | | | | | | 1.8 | 1.2 |
| Fixed/Worth | | .1 | .0 | .1 | | | | .1 | .1 |
| | | .2 | .1 | .3 | | | | .4 | .3 |
| | | 1.1 | .3 | 3.9 | | | | 3.9 | 1.1 |
| Debt/Worth | | .8 | .9 | .8 | | | | 1.1 | 1.4 |
| | | 2.2 | 1.7 | 1.9 | | | | 2.7 | 2.6 |
| | | 24.1 | 4.2 | 23.6 | | | | 95.3 | 11.0 |
| % Profit Before Taxes/Tangible Net Worth | | 51.4 | 40.4 | 86.6 | | | | 43.9 | 42.6 |
| | | (27) 16.6 | (45) 22.3 | (21) 18.7 | | | | (78) 18.3 | (82) 21.9 |
| | | 4.7 | 4.7 | 7.0 | | | | 5.4 | 7.7 |
| % Profit Before Taxes/Total Assets | | 14.2 | 17.2 | 13.1 | | | | 13.9 | 10.9 |
| | | 4.1 | 4.7 | 6.9 | | | | 6.6 | 5.8 |
| | | 1.4 | 1.6 | 2.9 | | | | .7 | 1.7 |
| Sales/Net Fixed Assets | | 464.2 | 208.4 | 52.0 | | | | 82.6 | 93.2 |
| | | 60.3 | 69.5 | 23.9 | | | | 33.9 | 38.6 |
| | | 23.4 | 27.8 | 9.7 | | | | 11.3 | 15.4 |
| Sales/Total Assets | | 4.2 | 3.9 | 3.2 | | | | 3.5 | 3.8 |
| | | 2.7 | 3.0 | 2.5 | | | | 2.6 | 2.7 |
| | | 2.0 | 2.5 | 1.6 | | | | 1.9 | 1.9 |
| % Depr., Dep., Amort./Sales | | .2 | .1 | .5 | | | | .5 | .3 |
| | | (25) .6 | (36) .3 | (21) 1.2 | | | | (74) 1.1 | (78) .6 |
| | | 1.0 | .9 | 1.7 | | | | 2.8 | 1.3 |
| % Officers', Directors' Owners' Comp/Sales | | 3.2 | .9 | | | | | 2.4 | 2.5 |
| | | (16) 6.2 | (23) 2.7 | | | | | (37) 3.9 | (31) 4.0 |
| | | 8.6 | 6.6 | | | | | 6.5 | 6.5 |
| Net Sales ($) | 7098M | 141881M | 688618M | 1185248M | 385710M | 915285M | | 1860265M | 2914159M |
| Total Assets ($) | 1677M | 42651M | 207498M | 510235M | 245268M | 283583M | | 930534M | 1397772M |

© RMA 2012

M = $ thousand     MM = $ million
See Pages 9 through 22 for Explanation of Ratios and Data

## Comparative Historical Data | Current Data Sorted by Sales

Date spans: Historical columns = 4/1/09-3/31/10 ALL, 4/1/10-3/31/11 ALL, 4/1/11-3/31/12 ALL. Current columns: "20 (4/1-9/30/11)" covers 0-1MM and 1-3MM; "96 (10/1/11-3/31/12)" covers 3-5MM, 5-10MM, 10-25MM, 25MM & OVER.

| | 4/1/09-3/31/10 ALL | 4/1/10-3/31/11 ALL | 4/1/11-3/31/12 ALL | 0-1MM | 1-3MM | 3-5MM | 5-10MM | 10-25MM | 25MM & OVER |
|---|---|---|---|---|---|---|---|---|---|
| **Type of Statement** | | | | | | | | | |
| Unqualified | 12 | 12 | 18 | | | 1 | 1 | 2 | 14 |
| Reviewed | 19 | 27 | 24 | | 1 | 3 | 4 | 11 | 5 |
| Compiled | 17 | 10 | 12 | 1 | 5 | 2 | 6 | 2 | 1 |
| Tax Returns | 21 | 18 | 18 | 2 | | 3 | 5 | 2 | 1 |
| Other | 45 | 42 | 44 | 2 | 6 | 7 | 7 | 11 | 11 |
| **NUMBER OF STATEMENTS** | 114 | 109 | 116 | 5 | 12 | 16 | 23 | 28 | 32 |
| **ASSETS** | % | % | % | % | % | % | % | % | % |
| Cash & Equivalents | 7.1 | 10.4 | 10.0 | | 14.7 | 10.7 | 10.6 | 9.8 | 7.7 |
| Trade Receivables (net) | 32.9 | 35.0 | 36.1 | | 31.3 | 37.3 | 38.1 | 41.4 | 32.3 |
| Inventory | 31.1 | 28.4 | 30.8 | | 25.7 | 34.3 | 28.8 | 30.7 | 29.4 |
| All Other Current | 3.5 | 3.1 | 3.0 | | .8 | 2.0 | 2.1 | 3.9 | 4.0 |
| Total Current | 74.7 | 76.8 | 79.8 | | 72.6 | 84.3 | 79.6 | 85.9 | 73.5 |
| Fixed Assets (net) | 13.0 | 10.7 | 8.9 | | 10.0 | 9.1 | 6.9 | 7.8 | 11.4 |
| Intangibles (net) | 6.0 | 6.6 | 4.6 | | 9.0 | .6 | 4.5 | 1.6 | 8.4 |
| All Other Non-Current | 6.3 | 5.9 | 6.6 | | 8.4 | 6.1 | 9.0 | 4.7 | 6.7 |
| Total | 100.0 | 100.0 | 100.0 | | 100.0 | 100.0 | 100.0 | 100.0 | 100.0 |
| **LIABILITIES** | | | | | | | | | |
| Notes Payable-Short Term | 17.2 | 13.8 | 14.2 | | 11.2 | 18.8 | 18.3 | 10.8 | 10.4 |
| Cur. Mat.-L.T.D. | 2.4 | 1.6 | 2.4 | | 3.4 | 2.5 | .9 | 3.8 | 1.9 |
| Trade Payables | 20.2 | 21.2 | 21.7 | | 11.7 | 22.1 | 17.8 | 29.0 | 23.4 |
| Income Taxes Payable | .1 | .2 | .1 | | .0 | .1 | .1 | .0 | .4 |
| All Other Current | 9.3 | 10.4 | 12.5 | | 12.5 | 11.8 | 11.7 | 13.7 | 13.2 |
| Total Current | 49.2 | 47.1 | 50.9 | | 38.7 | 55.2 | 48.7 | 57.3 | 49.3 |
| Long-Term Debt | 10.9 | 8.7 | 7.2 | | 18.0 | 10.2 | 2.2 | 3.3 | 6.8 |
| Deferred Taxes | .1 | .2 | .2 | | .0 | .1 | .2 | .1 | .3 |
| All Other Non-Current | 6.3 | 10.0 | 7.0 | | 6.3 | 21.8 | 5.7 | 2.1 | 5.7 |
| Net Worth | 33.4 | 34.0 | 34.8 | | 37.0 | 12.7 | 43.2 | 37.2 | 37.8 |
| Total Liabilities & Net Worth | 100.0 | 100.0 | 100.0 | | 100.0 | 100.0 | 100.0 | 100.0 | 100.0 |
| **INCOME DATA** | | | | | | | | | |
| Net Sales | 100.0 | 100.0 | 100.0 | | 100.0 | 100.0 | 100.0 | 100.0 | 100.0 |
| Gross Profit | 33.7 | 34.2 | 32.9 | | 50.0 | 34.1 | 34.6 | 26.9 | 29.0 |
| Operating Expenses | 29.9 | 29.9 | 29.3 | | 43.1 | 32.0 | 32.2 | 24.3 | 23.9 |
| Operating Profit | 3.8 | 4.3 | 3.6 | | 6.9 | 2.1 | 2.4 | 2.6 | 5.1 |
| All Other Expenses (net) | .6 | .5 | .6 | | .6 | 1.0 | .5 | .5 | .5 |
| Profit Before Taxes | 3.2 | 3.8 | 3.0 | | 6.3 | 1.1 | 1.8 | 2.1 | 4.6 |
| **RATIOS** | | | | | | | | | |
| Current | 2.6 / 1.5 / 1.2 | 2.6 / 1.6 / 1.2 | 2.3 / 1.6 / 1.2 | | 8.3 / 2.1 / 1.3 | 2.3 / 1.7 / 1.3 | 5.2 / 1.8 / 1.3 | 2.0 / 1.5 / 1.1 | 2.1 / 1.6 / 1.2 |
| Quick | 1.3 / .8 / .5 | 1.5 / .9 / .6 | 1.5 / .9 / .5 | | 3.5 / 1.4 / .7 | 1.7 / 1.0 / .4 | 2.2 / 1.1 / .5 | 1.2 / .8 / .7 | 1.3 / .7 / .4 |
| Sales/Receivables | 30 12.3 / 42 8.8 / 58 6.2 | 26 14.1 / 39 9.3 / 56 6.5 | 30 12.0 / 41 9.0 / 57 6.4 | | 36 10.0 / 49 7.4 / 64 5.7 | 24 15.0 / 35 10.5 / 53 6.9 | 28 13.0 / 40 9.1 / 65 5.6 | 34 10.6 / 40 9.2 / 54 6.7 | 28 13.1 / 39 9.4 / 56 6.5 |
| Cost of Sales/Inventory | 21 17.2 / 61 6.0 / 118 3.1 | 22 16.2 / 58 6.3 / 95 3.8 | 16 22.2 / 60 6.1 / 114 3.2 | | 9 42.5 / 101 3.6 / 228 1.6 | 3 129.5 / 70 5.2 / 152 2.4 | 15 24.8 / 45 8.2 / 135 2.4 | 18 19.9 / 45 8.2 / 72 5.1 | 12 31.5 / 65 5.6 / 96 3.8 |
| Cost of Sales/Payables | 18 20.5 / 32 11.2 / 57 6.4 | 20 18.5 / 36 10.3 / 58 6.3 | 18 20.5 / 34 10.7 / 64 5.7 | | 3 111.4 / 24 15.3 / 69 5.3 | 17 21.4 / 38 9.7 / 73 5.0 | 18 20.7 / 31 11.8 / 66 5.5 | 22 16.7 / 37 9.8 / 69 5.3 | 24 15.5 / 31 11.6 / 61 6.0 |
| Sales/Working Capital | 5.6 / 11.6 / 25.3 | 5.7 / 9.1 / 23.1 | 5.7 / 9.7 / 24.2 | | 4.2 / 5.5 / 20.4 | 5.9 / 9.7 / 19.2 | 4.5 / 8.7 / 15.1 | 7.2 / 13.5 / 41.7 | 7.1 / 10.7 / 23.9 |
| EBIT/Interest | (100) 12.3 / 4.4 / 1.2 | (98) 24.2 / 6.5 / 2.4 | (100) 17.0 / 5.0 / 2.0 | | | 9.4 / 2.6 / 1.6 | (21) 13.6 / 2.9 / -.1 | (24) 32.3 / 3.4 / 2.0 | (27) 18.8 / 10.8 / 3.8 |
| Net Profit + Depr., Dep., Amort./Cur. Mat. L/T/D | (25) 7.2 / 3.5 / .4 | (19) 8.1 / 3.2 / 2.4 | (21) 9.9 / 2.3 / .6 | | | | | | (11) 11.5 / 4.7 / .6 |
| Fixed/Worth | .1 / .3 / 1.3 | .1 / .3 / .8 | .1 / .2 / .6 | | .0 / .2 / NM | .1 / .2 / .6 | .0 / .1 / .4 | .0 / .2 / .3 | .1 / .3 / 3.9 |
| Debt/Worth | 1.2 / 2.3 / 12.5 | .8 / 1.9 / 8.2 | .9 / 2.0 / 6.0 | | .7 / 2.3 / NM | 1.0 / 2.4 / 4.8 | .5 / 1.7 / 4.0 | .9 / 1.8 / 5.9 | 1.0 / 2.0 / 23.7 |
| % Profit Before Taxes/Tangible Net Worth | (95) 49.9 / 23.0 / 5.6 | (91) 58.6 / 23.5 / 8.9 | (103) 49.9 / 21.2 / 5.5 | | | (14) 39.7 / 8.8 / 4.1 | (21) 38.2 / 8.2 / 1.7 | 37.0 / 23.2 / 4.0 | (28) 107.9 / 21.6 / 14.8 |
| % Profit Before Taxes/Total Assets | 14.9 / 6.8 / 1.0 | 16.8 / 6.7 / 2.1 | 14.2 / 5.5 / 1.8 | | 31.9 / 14.3 / 6.0 | 6.9 / 2.5 / 1.0 | 10.0 / 4.3 / .2 | 16.6 / 3.6 / 1.6 | 14.2 / 8.3 / 4.7 |
| Sales/Net Fixed Assets | 120.6 / 38.3 / 15.3 | 131.6 / 51.1 / 21.4 | 190.3 / 54.4 / 22.3 | | 197.6 / 46.9 / 16.2 | 235.5 / 52.2 / 22.7 | 580.5 / 86.5 / 22.2 | 190.3 / 63.7 / 27.2 | 104.2 / 35.5 / 13.1 |
| Sales/Total Assets | 3.6 / 2.6 / 1.9 | 3.7 / 2.9 / 2.0 | 3.7 / 2.8 / 2.0 | | 2.3 / 1.9 / 1.4 | 4.2 / 2.7 / 2.5 | 4.2 / 2.9 / 2.0 | 4.1 / 3.2 / 2.7 | 3.3 / 2.9 / 1.9 |
| % Depr., Dep., Amort./Sales | (91) .3 / .6 / 1.7 | (85) .2 / .5 / 1.3 | (90) .3 / .6 / 1.2 | | | (13) .2 / .5 / .9 | (17) .2 / .5 / .9 | (21) .3 / .5 / 1.0 | (28) .3 / .6 / 1.5 |
| % Officers', Directors', Owners' Comp/Sales | (52) 1.3 / 3.1 / 5.0 | (45) 1.4 / 3.4 / 5.0 | (45) 2.2 / 4.7 / 8.7 | | | | | (14) 2.6 / 4.7 / 11.5 | (12) .9 / 1.8 / 3.4 |
| Net Sales ($) | 3049980M | 3029967M | 3323840M | 3174M | 23665M | 63112M | 159643M | 437753M | 2636493M |
| Total Assets ($) | 1434509M | 1270706M | 1290912M | 2013M | 15374M | 22277M | 68881M | 144208M | 1038159M |

© RMA 2012

M = $ thousand    MM = $ million
See Pages 9 through 22 for Explanation of Ratios and Data

## Current Data Sorted by Assets

## Comparative Historical Data

| | | | | | | Type of Statement | | |
|---|---|---|---|---|---|---|---|---|
| 1 | 1 | 7 | 63 | 22 | 21 | Unqualified | 130 | 116 |
| 1 | 6 | 77 | 72 | 5 | 5 | Reviewed | 168 | 172 |
| 4 | 22 | 46 | 14 | | | Compiled | 108 | 101 |
| 14 | 31 | 40 | 5 | | | Tax Returns | 56 | 55 |
| 4 | 27 | 99 | 109 | 35 | 20 | Other | 211 | 269 |
| | 108 (4/1-9/30/11) | | 643 (10/1/11-3/31/12) | | | | 4/1/07-3/31/08 ALL | 4/1/08-3/31/09 ALL |
| 0-500M | 500M-2MM | 2-10MM | 10-50MM | 50-100MM | 100-250MM | | | |
| 24 | 87 | 269 | 263 | 62 | 46 | NUMBER OF STATEMENTS | 673 | 713 |
| % | % | % | % | % | % | ASSETS | % | % |
| 18.9 | 11.2 | 7.7 | 5.4 | 3.0 | 5.5 | Cash & Equivalents | 6.2 | 8.0 |
| 32.3 | 36.0 | 34.1 | 29.7 | 28.8 | 25.4 | Trade Receivables (net) | 33.4 | 29.8 |
| 20.5 | 33.5 | 39.0 | 44.4 | 45.5 | 47.9 | Inventory | 39.8 | 40.7 |
| .9 | 2.3 | 2.2 | 2.1 | 1.9 | 2.6 | All Other Current | 2.0 | 2.7 |
| 72.6 | 83.0 | 83.0 | 81.6 | 79.3 | 81.4 | Total Current | 81.4 | 81.2 |
| 16.7 | 11.3 | 10.8 | 12.8 | 11.6 | 11.2 | Fixed Assets (net) | 12.0 | 12.7 |
| 3.5 | 1.3 | 2.8 | 2.0 | 5.0 | 4.3 | Intangibles (net) | 2.3 | 2.2 |
| 7.3 | 4.4 | 3.4 | 3.6 | 4.1 | 3.1 | All Other Non-Current | 4.3 | 3.9 |
| 100.0 | 100.0 | 100.0 | 100.0 | 100.0 | 100.0 | Total | 100.0 | 100.0 |
| | | | | | | LIABILITIES | | |
| 13.1 | 18.6 | 17.8 | 22.2 | 18.7 | 17.3 | Notes Payable-Short Term | 20.1 | 20.6 |
| 17.6 | 3.1 | 2.6 | 1.5 | 1.7 | .6 | Cur. Mat.-L.T.D. | 2.0 | 2.1 |
| 22.4 | 24.7 | 22.3 | 17.8 | 20.6 | 14.7 | Trade Payables | 21.5 | 18.9 |
| .1 | .1 | .1 | .1 | .2 | .2 | Income Taxes Payable | .2 | .2 |
| 16.3 | 5.4 | 5.5 | 6.5 | 5.1 | 8.0 | All Other Current | 7.6 | 8.0 |
| 69.5 | 51.9 | 48.4 | 48.1 | 46.4 | 40.9 | Total Current | 51.4 | 49.8 |
| 21.5 | 8.3 | 7.1 | 7.8 | 11.7 | 9.6 | Long-Term Debt | 8.4 | 8.8 |
| .0 | .1 | .1 | .3 | .5 | .7 | Deferred Taxes | .3 | .2 |
| 11.3 | 4.2 | 5.1 | 4.9 | 4.5 | 4.8 | All Other Non-Current | 3.8 | 5.2 |
| -2.3 | 35.5 | 39.3 | 39.0 | 36.9 | 44.0 | Net Worth | 36.0 | 36.1 |
| 100.0 | 100.0 | 100.0 | 100.0 | 100.0 | 100.0 | Total Liabilities & Net Worth | 100.0 | 100.0 |
| | | | | | | INCOME DATA | | |
| 100.0 | 100.0 | 100.0 | 100.0 | 100.0 | 100.0 | Net Sales | 100.0 | 100.0 |
| 32.3 | 20.8 | 20.7 | 16.1 | 14.4 | 15.9 | Gross Profit | 19.3 | 19.5 |
| 25.4 | 17.4 | 16.3 | 11.9 | 9.5 | 9.5 | Operating Expenses | 14.5 | 14.7 |
| 6.9 | 3.5 | 4.4 | 4.2 | 5.0 | 6.4 | Operating Profit | 4.9 | 4.9 |
| 1.7 | .6 | .6 | .6 | .7 | .8 | All Other Expenses (net) | .9 | .9 |
| 5.1 | 2.9 | 3.8 | 3.6 | 4.2 | 5.6 | Profit Before Taxes | 3.9 | 3.9 |
| | | | | | | RATIOS | | |
| 3.2 | 2.4 | 2.9 | 3.0 | 2.7 | 3.6 | | 2.4 | 2.8 |
| 1.9 | 1.7 | 1.6 | 1.6 | 1.8 | 2.2 | Current | 1.5 | 1.7 |
| .6 | 1.2 | 1.2 | 1.2 | 1.3 | 1.4 | | 1.2 | 1.2 |
| 2.2 | 1.4 | 1.5 | 1.2 | 1.1 | 1.1 | | 1.3 | 1.4 |
| 1.0 | .8 | .9 | .7 | .7 | .9 | Quick | .7 (712) | .7 |
| .5 | .6 | .5 | .4 | .5 | .5 | | .5 | .5 |
| 0 UND | 19 19.2 | 30 12.3 | 32 11.5 | 35 10.5 | 32 11.5 | | 30 12.0 | 22 16.5 |
| 13 27.1 | 31 11.7 | 39 9.3 | 40 9.2 | 41 8.8 | 42 8.7 | Sales/Receivables | 39 9.4 | 32 11.6 |
| 40 9.2 | 54 6.7 | 50 7.3 | 49 7.5 | 51 7.1 | 53 6.9 | | 49 7.4 | 43 8.4 |
| 0 UND | 9 41.1 | 31 11.8 | 47 7.7 | 56 6.5 | 60 6.1 | | 35 10.5 | 30 12.3 |
| 6 56.7 | 38 9.6 | 64 5.7 | 79 4.6 | 81 4.5 | 96 3.8 | Cost of Sales/Inventory | 62 5.9 | 58 6.3 |
| 30 12.0 | 85 4.3 | 104 3.5 | 111 3.3 | 135 2.7 | 135 2.7 | | 102 3.6 | 99 3.7 |
| 0 UND | 9 38.5 | 17 21.1 | 15 23.8 | 19 18.8 | 14 26.7 | | 17 21.7 | 10 37.6 |
| 10 35.6 | 26 13.9 | 32 11.5 | 27 13.6 | 30 12.0 | 27 13.4 | Cost of Sales/Payables | 30 12.3 | 21 17.1 |
| 42 8.6 | 43 8.5 | 49 7.4 | 41 9.0 | 45 8.2 | 41 8.8 | | 44 8.4 | 39 9.4 |
| 7.1 | 6.3 | 5.1 | 4.5 | 4.0 | 3.5 | | 5.7 | 5.3 |
| 17.0 | 11.7 | 10.2 | 8.6 | 7.3 | 5.0 | Sales/Working Capital | 10.5 | 10.9 |
| -62.3 | 34.5 | 21.8 | 18.6 | 15.9 | 10.2 | | 25.7 | 29.2 |
| 36.2 | 14.2 | 15.0 | 21.0 | 16.2 | 42.8 | | 10.7 | 13.2 |
| (17) 5.7 | (76) 5.6 | (240) 6.5 | (247) 6.6 | (61) 6.3 | (43) 8.9 | EBIT/Interest | (617) 4.0 | (656) 5.1 |
| 2.0 | 2.2 | 2.5 | 2.4 | 2.5 | 3.2 | | 1.7 | 1.6 |
| | | 9.9 | 11.8 | 25.4 | 46.8 | Net Profit + Depr., Dep., | 10.2 | 13.2 |
| | (48) 3.3 | (60) 4.2 | (18) 7.8 | (15) 36.0 | | Amort./Cur. Mat. L/T/D | (174) 4.0 | (153) 4.3 |
| | 1.6 | 1.9 | 2.5 | 3.9 | | | 1.7 | 1.6 |
| .0 | .0 | .0 | .0 | .1 | .0 | | .1 | .1 |
| 1.2 | .1 | .2 | .2 | .3 | .2 | Fixed/Worth | .2 | .2 |
| UND | .8 | .5 | .7 | .8 | .5 | | .6 | .7 |
| .6 | 1.1 | .7 | .8 | 1.1 | .6 | | .9 | .8 |
| 5.1 | 2.0 | 1.7 | 2.0 | 2.3 | 1.5 | Debt/Worth | 2.2 | 1.9 |
| -28.7 | 5.0 | 4.8 | 3.7 | 3.9 | 5.9 | | 5.1 | 5.0 |
| 196.4 | 75.8 | 50.5 | 38.0 | 42.1 | 55.7 | % Profit Before Taxes/Tangible | 51.0 | 57.5 |
| (17) 62.1 | (82) 20.4 | (246) 24.8 | (250) 20.5 | (58) 22.2 | (43) 25.1 | Net Worth | (634) 27.7 | (649) 27.1 |
| 5.2 | 4.9 | 8.2 | 9.2 | 10.7 | 13.3 | | 11.2 | 8.0 |
| 62.5 | 16.1 | 15.4 | 13.1 | 13.3 | 19.2 | % Profit Before Taxes/Total | 17.4 | 19.9 |
| 15.8 | 6.5 | 7.7 | 6.8 | 7.7 | 10.7 | Assets | 8.8 | 8.5 |
| .6 | 1.4 | 2.5 | 2.7 | 3.3 | 4.2 | | 2.3 | 1.9 |
| UND | 999.8 | 273.0 | 220.2 | 134.1 | 113.6 | | 200.7 | 228.3 |
| 177.0 | 95.4 | 59.8 | 30.8 | 32.8 | 34.2 | Sales/Net Fixed Assets | 38.1 | 42.6 |
| 23.9 | 21.9 | 18.3 | 12.2 | 10.7 | 9.5 | | 14.7 | 16.6 |
| 15.0 | 4.9 | 3.8 | 3.2 | 3.2 | 2.9 | | 3.9 | 4.4 |
| 6.4 | 3.3 | 2.8 | 2.5 | 2.2 | 2.2 | Sales/Total Assets | 2.8 | 3.1 |
| 3.9 | 2.4 | 2.1 | 1.9 | 1.7 | 1.7 | | 2.1 | 2.2 |
| .2 | .2 | .2 | .2 | .2 | .1 | | .2 | .2 |
| (11) 1.6 | (53) .6 | (200) .6 | (230) .7 | (56) .7 | (39) .3 | % Depr., Dep., Amort./Sales | (568) .6 | (577) .6 |
| 2.4 | 1.3 | 1.2 | 1.2 | 1.4 | 1.4 | | 1.1 | 1.1 |
| 4.3 | 1.4 | 1.4 | .7 | .5 | | % Officers', Directors', | 1.1 | 1.0 |
| (10) 6.4 | (45) 2.5 | (132) 1.8 | (69) 1.4 | (13) .9 | | Owners' Comp/Sales | (256) 2.3 | (269) 2.2 |
| 14.4 | 4.3 | 4.1 | 3.1 | 2.6 | | | 3.9 | 4.7 |
| 43974M | 500826M | 4622495M | 16798424M | 11192521M | 16214052M | Net Sales ($) | 41914843M | 53073352M |
| 4645M | 109695M | 1350156M | 6241103M | 4425317M | 7441525M | Total Assets ($) | 15379804M | 17351241M |

M = $ thousand    MM = $ million
See Pages 9 through 22 for Explanation of Ratios and Data

## Comparative Historical Data | Current Data Sorted by Sales

| | | | Type of Statement | | | | | | |
|---|---|---|---|---|---|---|---|---|---|
| 119 | 128 | 115 | Unqualified | 1 | 1 | 1 | 2 | 6 | 105 |
| 148 | 168 | 166 | Reviewed | 1 | 4 | 2 | 15 | 60 | 84 |
| 100 | 95 | 86 | Compiled | 5 | 4 | 10 | 23 | 26 | 18 |
| 59 | 80 | 90 | Tax Returns | 7 | 12 | 9 | 32 | 21 | 9 |
| 266 | 250 | 294 | Other | 4 | 14 | 16 | 29 | 72 | 159 |
| 4/1/09-3/31/10 ALL | 4/1/10-3/31/11 ALL | 4/1/11-3/31/12 ALL | | 108 (4/1-9/30/11) | | | 643 (10/1/11-3/31/12) | | |
| | | | | 0-1MM | 1-3MM | 3-5MM | 5-10MM | 10-25MM | 25MM & OVER |
| 692 | 721 | 751 | NUMBER OF STATEMENTS | 17 | 35 | 38 | 101 | 185 | 375 |
| % | % | % | ASSETS | % | % | % | % | % | % |
| 8.9 | 8.1 | 7.1 | Cash & Equivalents | 20.5 | 11.0 | 10.8 | 8.4 | 8.2 | 4.9 |
| 28.4 | 30.0 | 31.8 | Trade Receivables (net) | 21.3 | 35.7 | 30.0 | 31.5 | 31.5 | 32.2 |
| 38.1 | 39.9 | 40.8 | Inventory | 23.3 | 26.7 | 41.0 | 38.8 | 40.6 | 43.5 |
| 2.5 | 2.3 | 2.1 | All Other Current | 1.0 | 3.7 | 2.7 | 2.4 | 1.9 | 2.0 |
| 77.9 | 80.3 | 81.8 | Total Current | 66.0 | 77.2 | 84.4 | 81.0 | 82.1 | 82.7 |
| 15.1 | 12.5 | 11.8 | Fixed Assets (net) | 17.0 | 14.9 | 10.8 | 13.0 | 11.3 | 11.3 |
| 2.6 | 2.6 | 2.6 | Intangibles (net) | 4.4 | 2.4 | 2.1 | 1.9 | 3.3 | 2.5 |
| 4.5 | 4.5 | 3.8 | All Other Non-Current | 12.6 | 5.5 | 2.7 | 4.1 | 3.3 | 3.4 |
| 100.0 | 100.0 | 100.0 | Total | 100.0 | 100.0 | 100.0 | 100.0 | 100.0 | 100.0 |
| | | | LIABILITIES | | | | | | |
| 18.2 | 18.4 | 19.3 | Notes Payable-Short Term | 8.3 | 23.5 | 15.5 | 17.2 | 18.1 | 21.0 |
| 3.1 | 2.3 | 2.5 | Cur. Mat.-L.T.D. | 6.9 | 3.1 | 3.1 | 6.2 | 2.1 | 1.4 |
| 18.4 | 21.1 | 20.4 | Trade Payables | 12.6 | 23.7 | 23.5 | 20.8 | 21.0 | 19.8 |
| .2 | .2 | .1 | Income Taxes Payable | .0 | .1 | .0 | .1 | .2 | .2 |
| 6.4 | 5.9 | 6.3 | All Other Current | 6.0 | 13.3 | 5.5 | 5.2 | 5.2 | 6.6 |
| 46.3 | 47.9 | 48.7 | Total Current | 33.9 | 63.7 | 47.7 | 49.5 | 46.7 | 48.9 |
| 9.8 | 8.3 | 8.5 | Long-Term Debt | 22.7 | 9.7 | 7.4 | 10.6 | 7.8 | 7.6 |
| .4 | .3 | .3 | Deferred Taxes | .1 | .0 | .1 | .1 | .1 | .4 |
| 5.5 | 5.8 | 5.0 | All Other Non-Current | 20.4 | 2.4 | 2.2 | 6.1 | 4.3 | 4.9 |
| 38.0 | 37.8 | 37.5 | Net Worth | 23.0 | 24.2 | 42.6 | 33.6 | 41.1 | 38.2 |
| 100.0 | 100.0 | 100.0 | Total Liabilities & Net Worth | 100.0 | 100.0 | 100.0 | 100.0 | 100.0 | 100.0 |
| | | | INCOME DATA | | | | | | |
| 100.0 | 100.0 | 100.0 | Net Sales | 100.0 | 100.0 | 100.0 | 100.0 | 100.0 | 100.0 |
| 19.6 | 19.5 | 18.7 | Gross Profit | 34.6 | 28.9 | 21.2 | 24.3 | 20.2 | 14.5 |
| 18.1 | 15.8 | 14.2 | Operating Expenses | 21.6 | 24.5 | 19.1 | 19.3 | 15.7 | 10.3 |
| 1.5 | 3.7 | 4.5 | Operating Profit | 13.0 | 4.5 | 2.0 | 5.0 | 4.4 | 4.2 |
| .8 | .7 | .6 | All Other Expenses (net) | 4.2 | .9 | .5 | .9 | .5 | .5 |
| .7 | 3.0 | 3.8 | Profit Before Taxes | 8.8 | 3.5 | 1.6 | 4.1 | 3.9 | 3.7 |
| | | | RATIOS | | | | | | |
| 3.1 | 2.9 | 2.9 | Current | 5.2 | 2.4 | 2.9 | 3.1 | 2.9 | 2.6 |
| 1.7 | 1.7 | 1.7 | | 2.1 | 1.4 | 1.8 | 1.7 | 1.7 | 1.6 |
| 1.2 | 1.2 | 1.2 | | 1.5 | 1.0 | 1.3 | 1.2 | 1.2 | 1.3 |
| 1.4 | 1.3 | 1.4 | Quick | 2.8 | 2.1 | 1.5 | 1.5 | 1.5 | 1.2 |
| .8 | .8 | .8 | | 1.1 | .8 | .8 | .8 | .9 | .7 |
| .5 | .5 | .5 | | .6 | .4 | .6 | .5 | .5 | .5 |
| 31  11.9 | 31  11.7 | 30  12.3 | Sales/Receivables | 0  UND | 24  14.9 | 21  17.7 | 29  12.4 | 30  12.1 | 30  12.0 |
| 39  9.3 | 42  8.7 | 40  9.2 | | 13  27.5 | 49  7.4 | 40  9.1 | 40  9.1 | 39  9.3 | 39  9.3 |
| 52  7.0 | 52  7.1 | 50  7.3 | | 62  5.9 | 65  5.6 | 55  6.6 | 53  6.9 | 49  7.4 | 49  7.5 |
| 39  9.5 | 40  9.1 | 36  10.0 | Cost of Sales/Inventory | 0  UND | 0  UND | 34  10.8 | 30  12.0 | 36  10.2 | 42  8.6 |
| 70  5.2 | 74  4.9 | 70  5.2 | | 33  11.0 | 36  10.1 | 65  5.6 | 69  5.3 | 69  5.3 | 74  4.9 |
| 113  3.2 | 121  3.0 | 107  3.4 | | 118  3.1 | 111  3.3 | 146  2.5 | 114  3.2 | 107  3.4 | 107  3.4 |
| 15  24.2 | 18  20.3 | 15  24.5 | Cost of Sales/Payables | 0  UND | 8  43.9 | 7  50.9 | 17  21.9 | 18  20.2 | 15  24.4 |
| 27  13.4 | 31  11.8 | 28  13.0 | | 17  21.1 | 43  8.5 | 29  12.7 | 35  10.5 | 30  12.0 | 26  14.0 |
| 44  8.3 | 49  7.5 | 45  8.2 | | 55  6.6 | 79  4.6 | 45  8.2 | 48  7.6 | 45  8.2 | 40  9.1 |
| 4.0 | 4.2 | 4.8 | Sales/Working Capital | 1.6 | 7.2 | 4.4 | 4.4 | 4.5 | 4.9 |
| 8.3 | 8.5 | 9.2 | | 4.4 | 14.3 | 7.8 | 8.5 | 9.8 | 9.0 |
| 21.0 | 21.4 | 21.6 | | 9.5 | 89.9 | 14.2 | 22.5 | 21.4 | 21.1 |
| 8.8 | 12.9 | 17.5 | EBIT/Interest | 32.3 | 7.9 | 8.4 | 13.7 | 16.7 | 22.3 |
| (629)  2.3 | (652)  4.7 | (684)  6.6 | | (10)  6.4 | (29)  3.8 | (32)  3.1 | (89)  5.5 | (169)  6.8 | (355)  7.3 |
| -.7 | 1.8 | 2.4 | | 2.3 | 1.7 | 1.1 | 2.2 | 2.7 | 2.7 |
| 6.3 | 10.3 | 15.0 | Net Profit + Depr., Dep., Amort./Cur. Mat. L/T/D | | | | 17.2 | 8.6 | 21.4 |
| (161)  1.9 | (154)  3.2 | (149)  4.9 | | | | | (12)  8.5 | (37)  3.1 | (95)  5.6 |
| .3 | 1.2 | 1.9 | | | | | 1.8 | 1.7 | 2.0 |
| .1 | .0 | .0 | Fixed/Worth | .0 | .1 | .0 | .1 | .0 | .0 |
| .3 | .2 | .2 | | .1 | .5 | .1 | .2 | .2 | .2 |
| .8 | .7 | .7 | | NM | 4.2 | .5 | 1.1 | .5 | .6 |
| .7 | .7 | .8 | Debt/Worth | .2 | .9 | .7 | .7 | .7 | .9 |
| 1.7 | 1.9 | 1.9 | | 1.0 | 1.6 | 1.6 | 2.0 | 1.7 | 2.0 |
| 4.6 | 4.3 | 4.7 | | -53.8 | 9.1 | 3.2 | 5.9 | 4.6 | 4.2 |
| 28.1 | 39.6 | 48.6 | % Profit Before Taxes/Tangible Net Worth | 33.5 | 126.3 | 41.0 | 47.3 | 52.1 | 47.4 |
| (627)  8.7 | (653)  16.7 | (696)  22.6 | | (12)  13.0 | (29)  29.0 | (37)  8.1 | (89)  24.3 | (172)  20.9 | (357)  23.0 |
| -5.3 | 5.4 | 8.6 | | .3 | 6.1 | .7 | 6.5 | 8.6 | 11.0 |
| 10.0 | 12.0 | 14.8 | % Profit Before Taxes/Total Assets | 15.8 | 14.1 | 9.0 | 17.3 | 14.1 | 14.5 |
| 2.8 | 5.8 | 7.3 | | 3.3 | 6.2 | 2.8 | 7.5 | 7.9 | 7.5 |
| -3.3 | 1.5 | 2.6 | | .0 | 1.3 | .3 | 2.5 | 3.3 | 2.9 |
| 142.7 | 209.9 | 266.0 | Sales/Net Fixed Assets | UND | 120.3 | 366.7 | 164.3 | 217.2 | 288.8 |
| 28.4 | 40.2 | 43.7 | | 62.8 | 45.9 | 69.6 | 49.3 | 48.9 | 39.6 |
| 9.0 | 11.6 | 15.0 | | 14.3 | 14.8 | 21.3 | 13.7 | 17.4 | 13.7 |
| 3.2 | 3.3 | 3.6 | Sales/Total Assets | 4.2 | 4.5 | 3.9 | 3.6 | 3.7 | 3.5 |
| 2.4 | 2.4 | 2.7 | | 1.8 | 2.9 | 2.5 | 2.6 | 2.8 | 2.7 |
| 1.7 | 1.8 | 2.0 | | .3 | 1.7 | 1.8 | 2.0 | 2.0 | 2.0 |
| .3 | .3 | .2 | % Depr., Dep., Amort./Sales | .4 | .2 | .3 | .3 | .1 |  |
| (575)  .9 | (575)  .8 | (589)  .6 | | (22)  .8 | (25)  .8 | (73)  .9 | (137)  .6 | (323)  .6 |  |
| 1.8 | 1.5 | 1.2 | | 1.8 | 1.1 | 1.5 | 1.3 | 1.0 |  |
| 1.3 | 1.1 | .9 | % Officers', Directors' Owners' Comp/Sales | 2.0 | 1.3 | 1.5 | .9 | .5 |  |
| (249)  2.3 | (267)  2.1 | (273)  1.8 | | (12)  4.1 | (19)  3.6 | (54)  2.4 | (88)  1.9 | (96)  1.1 |  |
| 4.4 | 4.3 | 4.1 | | 6.7 | 5.7 | 4.0 | 4.2 | 2.4 |  |
| 38713803M | 39300877M | 49372292M | Net Sales ($) | 9042M | 74889M | 149088M | 764661M | 3072888M | 45301724M |
| 16272173M | 17072856M | 19572441M | Total Assets ($) | 14449M | 31934M | 63312M | 328472M | 1263259M | 17871015M |

M = $ thousand    MM = $ million
See Pages 9 through 22 for Explanation of Ratios and Data

# WHOLESALE—Coal and Other Mineral and Ore Merchant Wholesalers   NAICS 423520

## Current Data Sorted by Assets     Comparative Historical Data

### Type of Statement

| Type of Statement | 0-500M | 500M-2MM | 2-10MM | 10-50MM | 50-100MM | 100-250MM | | 4/1/07-3/31/08 ALL | 4/1/08-3/31/09 ALL |
|---|---|---|---|---|---|---|---|---|---|
| Unqualified | | 1 | 1 | 4 | 1 | 1 | | 12 | 9 |
| Reviewed | | 2 | 6 | 7 | | | | 9 | 13 |
| Compiled | | 2 | 1 | 1 | | | | 10 | 5 |
| Tax Returns | 2 | | 3 | | | | | 4 | 3 |
| Other | 1 | 2 | 3 | 9 | 9 | 2 | | 15 | 20 |

Date ranges: 5 (4/1-9/30/11) · 53 (10/1/11-3/31/12)

| | 0-500M | 500M-2MM | 2-10MM | 10-50MM | 50-100MM | 100-250MM | | 4/1/07-3/31/08 ALL | 4/1/08-3/31/09 ALL |
|---|---|---|---|---|---|---|---|---|---|
| **NUMBER OF STATEMENTS** | 3 | 7 | 14 | 21 | 10 | 3 | | 50 | 50 |
| | % | % | % | % | % | % | | % | % |
| **ASSETS** | | | | | | | | | |
| Cash & Equivalents | | | 27.4 | 6.2 | 5.5 | | | 12.4 | 9.2 |
| Trade Receivables (net) | | | 35.7 | 44.2 | 21.8 | | | 31.6 | 33.1 |
| Inventory | | | 14.4 | 25.6 | 28.5 | | | 23.8 | 23.6 |
| All Other Current | | | 1.4 | 2.3 | 2.4 | | | 2.6 | 7.4 |
| Total Current | | | 78.9 | 78.2 | 58.1 | | | 70.4 | 73.3 |
| Fixed Assets (net) | | | 14.8 | 14.4 | 29.3 | | | 22.6 | 17.4 |
| Intangibles (net) | | | .6 | 1.2 | 3.3 | | | 1.8 | 2.5 |
| All Other Non-Current | | | 5.6 | 6.2 | 9.3 | | | 5.3 | 6.8 |
| Total | | | 100.0 | 100.0 | 100.0 | | | 100.0 | 100.0 |
| **LIABILITIES** | | | | | | | | | |
| Notes Payable-Short Term | | | 5.7 | 12.0 | 5.2 | | | 12.9 | 13.7 |
| Cur. Mat.-L.T.D. | | | .8 | 1.4 | 2.3 | | | 2.2 | 1.5 |
| Trade Payables | | | 23.1 | 28.9 | 23.0 | | | 20.1 | 25.2 |
| Income Taxes Payable | | | .1 | .1 | .0 | | | .1 | .3 |
| All Other Current | | | 6.4 | 8.4 | 10.8 | | | 10.6 | 14.1 |
| Total Current | | | 36.1 | 50.9 | 41.3 | | | 45.9 | 54.9 |
| Long-Term Debt | | | 9.5 | 9.1 | 13.2 | | | 13.2 | 7.3 |
| Deferred Taxes | | | .0 | .1 | .0 | | | .0 | .1 |
| All Other Non-Current | | | 3.9 | .5 | 4.5 | | | 4.9 | 4.3 |
| Net Worth | | | 50.5 | 39.5 | 40.9 | | | 35.9 | 33.3 |
| Total Liabilities & Net Worth | | | 100.0 | 100.0 | 100.0 | | | 100.0 | 100.0 |
| **INCOME DATA** | | | | | | | | | |
| Net Sales | | | 100.0 | 100.0 | 100.0 | | | 100.0 | 100.0 |
| Gross Profit | | | 16.4 | 10.6 | 14.2 | | | 21.8 | 12.4 |
| Operating Expenses | | | 11.2 | 7.1 | 5.5 | | | 16.9 | 8.2 |
| Operating Profit | | | 5.2 | 3.5 | 8.7 | | | 4.9 | 4.2 |
| All Other Expenses (net) | | | 1.8 | .0 | .5 | | | .9 | .6 |
| Profit Before Taxes | | | 3.4 | 3.5 | 8.2 | | | 4.1 | 3.6 |
| **RATIOS** | | | | | | | | | |
| Current | | | 3.8 | 3.0 | 2.5 | | | 2.5 | 2.4 |
| | | | 1.9 | 1.9 | 1.1 | | | 1.5 | 1.3 |
| | | | 1.6 | 1.1 | .8 | | | 1.0 | 1.0 |
| Quick | | | 3.1 | 1.7 | 1.2 | | | 1.7 | 1.3 |
| | | | 1.7 | 1.0 | .7 | | | .9 | 1.0 |
| | | | 1.1 | .8 | .1 | | | .5 | .4 |
| Sales/Receivables | | | 17  21.5 | 25  14.7 | 3  116.7 | | | 21  17.7 | 18  20.4 |
| | | | 33  10.9 | 41  9.0 | 29  12.4 | | | 33  11.1 | 26  14.1 |
| | | | 56  6.5 | 49  7.5 | 37  9.9 | | | 44  8.3 | 43  8.5 |
| Cost of Sales/Inventory | | | 0  UND | 3  110.8 | 7  53.1 | | | 0  UND | 0  UND |
| | | | 1  279.0 | 40  9.2 | 31  11.9 | | | 28  12.8 | 15  24.4 |
| | | | 47  7.8 | 55  6.6 | 61  6.0 | | | 52  7.0 | 56  6.6 |
| Cost of Sales/Payables | | | 15  24.5 | 16  22.9 | 21  17.8 | | | 11  32.6 | 10  36.3 |
| | | | 30  12.0 | 25  14.7 | 27  13.4 | | | 22  16.6 | 23  16.1 |
| | | | 36  10.0 | 33  11.2 | 42  8.6 | | | 39  9.3 | 39  9.2 |
| Sales/Working Capital | | | 4.6 | 5.8 | 6.8 | | | 7.4 | 7.6 |
| | | | 7.6 | 18.1 | NM | | | 18.2 | 23.6 |
| | | | 27.9 | 96.7 | -31.6 | | | NM | 926.7 |
| EBIT/Interest | | | 40.4 | 30.7 | 185.8 | | | 35.9 | 28.5 |
| | | | (10) 13.1 | 6.3 | 26.5 | | | (49) 6.5 | (47) 6.8 |
| | | | 3.8 | 4.6 | 4.3 | | | 1.9 | 1.4 |
| Net Profit + Depr., Dep., Amort./Cur. Mat. L/T/D | | | | | | | | | |
| Fixed/Worth | | | .0 | .0 | .1 | | | .0 | .0 |
| | | | .3 | .2 | .3 | | | .3 | .3 |
| | | | .6 | .7 | 2.9 | | | .8 | 1.5 |
| Debt/Worth | | | .4 | .6 | .7 | | | .7 | .9 |
| | | | 1.0 | 1.3 | 2.1 | | | 2.0 | 2.9 |
| | | | 2.3 | 5.7 | 3.3 | | | 4.5 | 6.4 |
| % Profit Before Taxes/Tangible Net Worth | | | 60.4 | 64.9 | 93.8 | | | 50.3 | 61.2 |
| | | | (13) 33.1 | (20) 31.3 | 45.9 | | | (47) 25.7 | (47) 28.5 |
| | | | 4.6 | 11.5 | 21.4 | | | 15.1 | 4.0 |
| % Profit Before Taxes/Total Assets | | | 21.2 | 18.9 | 28.2 | | | 16.8 | 21.3 |
| | | | 14.5 | 10.7 | 13.4 | | | 9.1 | 6.8 |
| | | | 1.0 | 4.8 | 8.8 | | | 3.3 | .7 |
| Sales/Net Fixed Assets | | | 999.8 | 945.2 | 66.0 | | | 765.3 | 986.7 |
| | | | 329.8 | 115.1 | 41.8 | | | 50.8 | 45.8 |
| | | | 8.2 | 10.8 | 3.0 | | | 5.7 | 9.8 |
| Sales/Total Assets | | | 5.1 | 5.8 | 4.2 | | | 5.0 | 6.4 |
| | | | 3.2 | 3.9 | 2.7 | | | 3.4 | 3.6 |
| | | | 1.8 | 2.5 | 1.7 | | | 1.7 | 2.4 |
| % Depr., Dep., Amort./Sales | | | .0 | .0 | .4 | | | .1 | .1 |
| | | | (10) .5 | (17) .5 | 1.0 | | | (39) .8 | (39) .7 |
| | | | 3.3 | 1.8 | 2.4 | | | 5.1 | 1.7 |
| % Officers', Directors' Owners' Comp/Sales | | | | | | | | 1.0 | .3 |
| | | | | | | | | (11) 1.6 | (12) 1.1 |
| | | | | | | | | 4.1 | 2.4 |
| Net Sales ($) | 10314M | 121603M | 273128M | 2428896M | 2796596M | 1727855M | | 4610038M | 5939018M |
| Total Assets ($) | 1096M | 8400M | 74907M | 512273M | 772908M | 435978M | | 1153000M | 1312159M |

M = $ thousand    MM = $ million
See Pages 9 through 22 for Explanation of Ratios and Data

## Comparative Historical Data / Current Data Sorted by Sales

| 4/1/09-3/31/10 ALL | 4/1/10-3/31/11 ALL | 4/1/11-3/31/12 ALL | Type of Statement | 0-1MM | 1-3MM | 3-5MM | 5-10MM | 10-25MM | 25MM & OVER |
|---|---|---|---|---|---|---|---|---|---|
| 10 | 7 | 8 | Unqualified | | | | | | 8 |
| 14 | 11 | 15 | Reviewed | | 1 | | 1 | 3 | 10 |
| 5 | 7 | 4 | Compiled | | | 1 | 1 | 1 | 1 |
| 7 | 4 | 7 | Tax Returns | | | | 4 | 2 | 1 |
| 20 | 33 | 24 | Other | 1 | | | | | 22 |
| | | | | 5 (4/1-9/30/11) | | | 53 (10/1/11-3/31/12) | | |
| 56 | 62 | 58 | NUMBER OF STATEMENTS | | 3 | 1 | 6 | 7 | 41 |
| % | % | % | ASSETS | % | % | % | % | % | % |
| 14.5 | 12.7 | 18.0 | Cash & Equivalents | | | | | | 12.0 |
| 29.2 | 30.5 | 33.5 | Trade Receivables (net) | | | | | | 37.5 |
| 24.0 | 22.5 | 21.1 | Inventory | | | | | | 24.2 |
| 5.7 | 3.5 | 2.8 | All Other Current | | | | | | 2.5 |
| 73.4 | 69.3 | 75.4 | Total Current | | | | | | 76.1 |
| 16.5 | 19.6 | 16.7 | Fixed Assets (net) | | DATA NOT AVAILABLE | | | | 15.8 |
| 2.5 | 2.1 | 1.2 | Intangibles (net) | | | | | | 1.4 |
| 7.6 | 9.0 | 6.7 | All Other Non-Current | | | | | | 6.7 |
| 100.0 | 100.0 | 100.0 | Total | | | | | | 100.0 |
| | | | LIABILITIES | | | | | | |
| 14.5 | 12.4 | 8.1 | Notes Payable-Short Term | | | | | | 9.0 |
| 3.5 | 4.9 | 2.1 | Cur. Mat.-L.T.D. | | | | | | 1.4 |
| 16.0 | 19.3 | 24.3 | Trade Payables | | | | | | 26.2 |
| .5 | .1 | .1 | Income Taxes Payable | | | | | | .1 |
| 11.3 | 8.6 | 8.2 | All Other Current | | | | | | 9.2 |
| 45.8 | 45.4 | 42.8 | Total Current | | | | | | 45.9 |
| 14.9 | 11.2 | 10.7 | Long-Term Debt | | | | | | 8.6 |
| .0 | .2 | .0 | Deferred Taxes | | | | | | .0 |
| 3.5 | 4.3 | 3.4 | All Other Non-Current | | | | | | 3.8 |
| 35.7 | 39.0 | 43.1 | Net Worth | | | | | | 41.7 |
| 100.0 | 100.0 | 100.0 | Total Liabilities & Net Worth | | | | | | 100.0 |
| | | | INCOME DATA | | | | | | |
| 100.0 | 100.0 | 100.0 | Net Sales | | | | | | 100.0 |
| 18.6 | 21.7 | 14.0 | Gross Profit | | | | | | 10.8 |
| 13.0 | 17.1 | 9.0 | Operating Expenses | | | | | | 5.8 |
| 5.6 | 4.6 | 5.0 | Operating Profit | | | | | | 5.1 |
| 1.7 | .5 | .5 | All Other Expenses (net) | | | | | | .1 |
| 3.9 | 4.2 | 4.4 | Profit Before Taxes | | | | | | 5.0 |
| | | | RATIOS | | | | | | |
| 3.0 | 3.2 | 3.1 | | | | | | | 2.9 |
| 1.7 | 1.7 | 1.9 | Current | | | | | | 1.9 |
| 1.1 | 1.0 | 1.1 | | | | | | | 1.1 |
| 1.7 | 1.6 | 1.8 | | | | | | | 1.7 |
| 1.0 | 1.0 | 1.1 | Quick | | | | | | 1.0 |
| .6 | .6 | .7 | | | | | | | .7 |
| 19  18.8 | 23  15.9 | 16  22.3 | | | | | | | 19  19.7 |
| 33  11.1 | 36  10.1 | 33  11.2 | Sales/Receivables | | | | | | 34  10.7 |
| 46  8.0 | 47  7.7 | 46  7.9 | | | | | | | 45  8.2 |
| 0  UND | 0  UND | 0  UND | | | | | | | 1  353.5 |
| 35  10.5 | 35  10.3 | 19  19.1 | Cost of Sales/Inventory | | | | | | 28  13.0 |
| 72  5.0 | 72  5.1 | 50  7.3 | | | | | | | 54  6.8 |
| 8  44.1 | 15  23.7 | 15  24.5 | | | | | | | 15  24.0 |
| 22  16.8 | 24  15.0 | 24  15.2 | Cost of Sales/Payables | | | | | | 23  16.2 |
| 35  10.3 | 42  8.8 | 35  10.5 | | | | | | | 30  12.0 |
| 4.9 | 5.7 | 6.1 | | | | | | | 7.2 |
| 10.8 | 9.6 | 18.0 | Sales/Working Capital | | | | | | 21.4 |
| 43.0 | 313.8 | 88.7 | | | | | | | 103.6 |
| 20.8 | 25.1 | 38.9 | | | | | | | 68.7 |
| (52)  6.4 | (53)  8.2 | (49)  12.6 | EBIT/Interest | | | | | | (38)  13.5 |
| 1.6 | 1.0 | 4.6 | | | | | | | 4.4 |
| 10.0 | 17.0 | | Net Profit + Depr., Dep., | | | | | | |
| (13)  2.3 | (13)  3.1 | | Amort./Cur. Mat. L/T/D | | | | | | |
| -.7 | .3 | | | | | | | | |
| .0 | .0 | .0 | | | | | | | .0 |
| .3 | .2 | .2 | Fixed/Worth | | | | | | .1 |
| 1.4 | 1.1 | 1.2 | | | | | | | 1.1 |
| .7 | .4 | .6 | | | | | | | .6 |
| 1.9 | 1.4 | 1.3 | Debt/Worth | | | | | | 1.3 |
| 8.3 | 5.6 | 4.1 | | | | | | | 4.5 |
| 37.9 | 43.3 | 63.4 | % Profit Before Taxes/Tangible | | | | | | 70.2 |
| (48)  19.2 | (56)  22.2 | (54)  33.9 | Net Worth | | | | | | (39)  38.5 |
| 4.3 | 5.1 | 16.7 | | | | | | | 21.8 |
| 15.6 | 20.0 | 26.1 | % Profit Before Taxes/Total | | | | | | 28.8 |
| 7.0 | 11.1 | 13.8 | Assets | | | | | | 13.8 |
| 1.4 | .1 | 4.9 | | | | | | | 5.3 |
| 543.9 | 477.5 | 999.8 | | | | | | | 999.8 |
| 45.0 | 39.6 | 58.0 | Sales/Net Fixed Assets | | | | | | 115.1 |
| 9.4 | 6.5 | 9.4 | | | | | | | 10.8 |
| 4.7 | 4.2 | 5.9 | | | | | | | 6.6 |
| 2.9 | 2.8 | 3.9 | Sales/Total Assets | | | | | | 4.0 |
| 1.6 | 1.4 | 2.4 | | | | | | | 2.5 |
| .1 | .1 | .1 | | | | | | | .0 |
| (40)  .9 | (46)  .8 | (45)  .6 | % Depr., Dep., Amort./Sales | | | | | | (33)  .5 |
| 4.3 | 2.7 | 1.9 | | | | | | | 1.8 |
| .8 | 1.1 | .7 | % Officers', Directors' | | | | | | .5 |
| (17)  1.5 | (15)  3.5 | (18)  1.7 | Owners' Comp/Sales | | | | | | (10)  1.7 |
| 3.1 | 5.5 | 3.5 | | | | | | | 1.8 |
| 3936119M | 3953463M | 7358392M | Net Sales ($) | | 4401M | 4573M | 41662M | 94133M | 7213623M |
| 1533598M | 1743237M | 1805562M | Total Assets ($) | | 6752M | 1141M | 17422M | 31258M | 1748989M |

M = $ thousand   MM = $ million
See Pages 9 through 22 for Explanation of Ratios and Data

## Current Data Sorted by Assets      Comparative Historical Data

| 0-500M | 500M-2MM | 2-10MM | 10-50MM | 50-100MM | 100-250MM | Type of Statement | 4/1/07-3/31/08 ALL | 4/1/08-3/31/09 ALL |
|---|---|---|---|---|---|---|---|---|
| | 2 | 9 | 29 | 14 | 11 | Unqualified | 69 | 75 |
| 8 | 14 | 93 | 42 | 2 | 2 | Reviewed | 129 | 135 |
| 4 | 32 | 48 | 11 | | | Compiled | 104 | 100 |
| 28 | 54 | 45 | 7 | | | Tax Returns | 62 | 83 |
| 17 | 37 | 88 | 58 | 15 | 14 | Other | 170 | 203 |
| | 103 (4/1-9/30/11) | | 581 (10/1/11-3/31/12) | | | | | |
| 57 | 139 | 283 | 147 | 31 | 27 | **NUMBER OF STATEMENTS** | 534 | 596 |
| % | % | % | % | % | % | **ASSETS** | % | % |
| 17.9 | 14.0 | 8.7 | 6.7 | 6.9 | 6.6 | Cash & Equivalents | 7.4 | 8.3 |
| 30.4 | 32.2 | 38.2 | 38.2 | 32.2 | 34.8 | Trade Receivables (net) | 37.4 | 35.2 |
| 23.4 | 33.9 | 33.9 | 34.2 | 30.4 | 28.6 | Inventory | 33.5 | 34.7 |
| 6.0 | 2.9 | 2.4 | 2.8 | 3.1 | 2.9 | All Other Current | 2.2 | 2.3 |
| 77.7 | 83.1 | 83.3 | 81.9 | 72.5 | 72.9 | Total Current | 80.6 | 80.5 |
| 11.4 | 9.0 | 9.2 | 9.3 | 11.6 | 11.6 | Fixed Assets (net) | 11.8 | 11.0 |
| 3.6 | 3.3 | 2.3 | 3.9 | 10.1 | 9.4 | Intangibles (net) | 3.2 | 2.9 |
| 7.3 | 4.7 | 5.3 | 5.0 | 5.8 | 6.2 | All Other Non-Current | 4.5 | 5.6 |
| 100.0 | 100.0 | 100.0 | 100.0 | 100.0 | 100.0 | Total | 100.0 | 100.0 |
| | | | | | | **LIABILITIES** | | |
| 28.3 | 13.4 | 12.7 | 14.3 | 7.4 | 7.8 | Notes Payable-Short Term | 14.2 | 14.9 |
| 3.4 | 2.0 | 1.6 | 1.5 | .5 | 1.6 | Cur. Mat.-L.T.D. | 2.4 | 2.1 |
| 17.3 | 24.1 | 24.1 | 23.1 | 19.2 | 20.4 | Trade Payables | 23.6 | 21.6 |
| .0 | .3 | .2 | .2 | .1 | .4 | Income Taxes Payable | .4 | .1 |
| 14.0 | 10.2 | 8.6 | 8.1 | 8.3 | 8.6 | All Other Current | 9.1 | 8.9 |
| 63.0 | 50.0 | 47.2 | 47.2 | 35.5 | 38.8 | Total Current | 49.6 | 47.7 |
| 7.0 | 7.1 | 5.9 | 5.7 | 10.7 | 17.0 | Long-Term Debt | 10.0 | 9.7 |
| .0 | .1 | .1 | .2 | .2 | .9 | Deferred Taxes | .1 | .2 |
| 8.4 | 9.4 | 4.6 | 2.8 | 3.5 | 5.8 | All Other Non-Current | 5.5 | 4.2 |
| 21.6 | 33.4 | 42.1 | 44.1 | 50.1 | 37.5 | Net Worth | 34.9 | 38.2 |
| 100.0 | 100.0 | 100.0 | 100.0 | 100.0 | 100.0 | Total Liabilities & Net Worth | 100.0 | 100.0 |
| | | | | | | **INCOME DATA** | | |
| 100.0 | 100.0 | 100.0 | 100.0 | 100.0 | 100.0 | Net Sales | 100.0 | 100.0 |
| 40.4 | 34.0 | 30.0 | 23.6 | 27.4 | 23.2 | Gross Profit | 28.9 | 28.9 |
| 35.1 | 30.2 | 25.2 | 19.5 | 20.1 | 18.5 | Operating Expenses | 24.2 | 25.1 |
| 5.3 | 3.7 | 4.9 | 4.2 | 7.3 | 4.7 | Operating Profit | 4.7 | 3.8 |
| -.2 | .5 | .2 | .2 | .6 | .9 | All Other Expenses (net) | .5 | .4 |
| 5.5 | 3.2 | 4.7 | 4.0 | 6.7 | 3.9 | Profit Before Taxes | 4.2 | 3.3 |
| | | | | | | **RATIOS** | | |
| 3.1 | 2.8 | 2.8 | 2.7 | 4.2 | 3.0 | Current | 2.5 | 2.6 |
| 1.5 | 1.8 | 1.8 | 1.8 | 2.0 | 2.0 | | 1.7 | 1.7 |
| .7 | 1.2 | 1.3 | 1.3 | 1.4 | 1.4 | | 1.3 | 1.3 |
| 2.2 | 1.7 | 1.5 | 1.6 | 2.0 | 1.8 | Quick | 1.4 | 1.4 |
| .9 | .9 | 1.0 | .9 | .9 | 1.2 | | .9 | .9 |
| .4 | .6 | .7 | .6 | .7 | .6 | | .6 | .6 |
| 0 UND | 17 21.0 | 35 10.4 | 43 8.4 | 41 9.0 | 42 8.6 | Sales/Receivables | 34 10.7 | 32 11.3 |
| 25 14.4 | 35 10.3 | 47 7.7 | 52 7.0 | 55 6.6 | 53 6.9 | | 46 7.9 | 40 9.0 |
| 48 7.6 | 51 7.2 | 60 6.1 | 64 5.7 | 65 5.6 | 63 5.8 | | 59 6.2 | 53 6.8 |
| 0 UND | 8 43.2 | 31 11.8 | 40 9.2 | 44 8.3 | 38 9.5 | Cost of Sales/Inventory | 34 10.9 | 32 11.3 |
| 13 28.6 | 59 6.2 | 62 5.9 | 59 6.2 | 76 4.8 | 60 6.1 | | 55 6.6 | 57 6.5 |
| 91 4.0 | 114 3.2 | 96 3.8 | 94 3.9 | 107 3.4 | 89 4.1 | | 92 4.0 | 90 4.0 |
| 3 107.3 | 18 20.8 | 25 14.6 | 28 13.2 | 29 12.6 | 28 13.2 | Cost of Sales/Payables | 24 14.9 | 20 18.3 |
| 17 21.3 | 37 9.8 | 38 9.7 | 38 9.7 | 35 10.5 | 37 9.8 | | 36 10.0 | 31 11.7 |
| 43 8.4 | 62 5.9 | 55 6.6 | 48 7.6 | 52 7.0 | 49 7.5 | | 53 6.9 | 47 7.7 |
| 6.4 | 5.2 | 4.9 | 4.9 | 3.9 | 4.7 | Sales/Working Capital | 6.0 | 5.5 |
| 31.0 | 8.9 | 7.7 | 7.8 | 6.7 | 7.6 | | 9.7 | 9.1 |
| -37.8 | 23.1 | 17.6 | 13.2 | 10.9 | 10.3 | | 18.7 | 18.4 |
| 13.7 | 23.8 | 26.5 | 32.3 | 113.3 | 24.2 | EBIT/Interest | 13.9 | 16.3 |
| (34) 3.6 | (108) 4.7 | (244) 8.6 | (132) 12.2 | (27) 12.8 | (24) 8.5 | | (481) 5.1 | (531) 5.4 |
| -1.2 | 1.6 | 3.2 | 4.0 | 5.1 | 4.0 | | 1.8 | 1.7 |
| | | 7.6 | 17.7 | | | Net Profit + Depr., Dep., Amort./Cur. Mat. L/T/D | 14.3 | 12.6 |
| | | (49) 3.7 | (41) 5.1 | | | | (156) 4.7 | (154) 4.2 |
| | | 1.4 | 1.7 | | | | 1.8 | 1.9 |
| .0 | .0 | .0 | .1 | .1 | .1 | Fixed/Worth | .1 | .1 |
| .2 | .1 | .1 | .2 | .2 | .3 | | .2 | .2 |
| 2.9 | .5 | .4 | .4 | .6 | .5 | | .6 | .6 |
| .6 | .7 | .7 | .7 | .3 | .7 | Debt/Worth | .9 | .7 |
| 4.0 | 1.7 | 1.4 | 1.4 | 1.4 | 1.5 | | 1.8 | 1.6 |
| UND | 6.1 | 3.5 | 3.0 | 2.6 | 4.1 | | 4.3 | 4.1 |
| 158.5 | 53.6 | 49.6 | 44.8 | 42.2 | 51.2 | % Profit Before Taxes/Tangible Net Worth | 48.2 | 43.8 |
| (43) 62.1 | (118) 22.4 | (268) 23.5 | (140) 19.5 | (28) 20.4 | (23) 23.0 | | (486) 26.1 | (544) 23.0 |
| 30.2 | 4.2 | 7.1 | 9.7 | 12.7 | 18.6 | | 8.9 | 6.9 |
| 36.5 | 22.8 | 17.9 | 13.0 | 15.1 | 13.1 | % Profit Before Taxes/Total Assets | 17.1 | 16.0 |
| 16.5 | 6.2 | 7.6 | 7.9 | 9.1 | 8.9 | | 9.0 | 7.5 |
| -2.7 | 1.5 | 2.5 | 4.3 | 5.3 | 5.7 | | 2.3 | 1.6 |
| UND | 436.9 | 162.4 | 114.2 | 56.7 | 65.8 | Sales/Net Fixed Assets | 95.1 | 115.3 |
| 89.0 | 79.3 | 60.5 | 49.6 | 34.9 | 30.0 | | 41.1 | 47.0 |
| 27.2 | 31.4 | 22.1 | 18.0 | 8.5 | 10.9 | | 19.0 | 20.2 |
| 7.0 | 4.2 | 3.7 | 3.2 | 2.7 | 3.5 | Sales/Total Assets | 3.6 | 3.8 |
| 3.7 | 3.2 | 2.8 | 2.6 | 2.2 | 2.7 | | 2.9 | 3.0 |
| 2.1 | 2.3 | 2.1 | 2.0 | 1.3 | 1.7 | | 2.2 | 2.3 |
| .4 | .2 | .2 | .2 | .4 | .3 | % Depr., Dep., Amort./Sales | .3 | .3 |
| (20) .7 | (88) .5 | (219) .5 | (133) .5 | (29) .5 | (24) .7 | | (437) .6 | (476) .6 |
| 2.2 | 1.0 | 1.0 | .9 | 1.5 | 1.2 | | 1.1 | 1.0 |
| 5.8 | 2.0 | 1.5 | 1.1 | | | % Officers', Directors' Owners' Comp/Sales | 1.7 | 1.7 |
| (21) 10.2 | (78) 4.2 | (117) 2.6 | (37) 1.6 | | | | (216) 3.5 | (224) 3.4 |
| 14.8 | 6.6 | 4.3 | 3.6 | | | | 6.0 | 6.9 |
| 88134M | 601065M | 4268650M | 8773177M | 4615865M | 10233300M | Net Sales ($) | 26241237M | 29206552M |
| 16425M | 167156M | 1447860M | 3332434M | 2152349M | 4197547M | Total Assets ($) | 9225007M | 10307329M |

## Comparative Historical Data / Current Data Sorted by Sales

| Type of Statement | | | | | | | | | |
|---|---|---|---|---|---|---|---|---|---|
| Unqualified | 61 | 70 | 65 | | | 1 | 4 | 5 | 55 |
| Reviewed | 147 | 144 | 161 | 6 | 7 | 6 | 22 | 62 | 58 |
| Compiled | 90 | 90 | 95 | 1 | 12 | 12 | 23 | 33 | 14 |
| Tax Returns | 86 | 110 | 134 | 19 | 19 | 34 | 37 | 19 | 6 |
| Other | 219 | 232 | 229 | 10 | 25 | 21 | 25 | 53 | 95 |
| | 4/1/09-3/31/10 ALL | 4/1/10-3/31/11 ALL | 4/1/11-3/31/12 ALL | 103 (4/1-9/30/11) 0-1MM | 1-3MM | 3-5MM | 581 (10/1/11-3/31/12) 5-10MM | 10-25MM | 25MM & OVER |
| **NUMBER OF STATEMENTS** | 603 | 646 | 684 | 36 | 63 | 74 | 111 | 172 | 228 |
| **ASSETS** | % | % | % | % | % | % | % | % | % |
| Cash & Equivalents | 9.1 | 9.0 | 10.0 | 12.3 | 14.6 | 15.6 | 11.9 | 8.4 | 6.8 |
| Trade Receivables (net) | 34.9 | 36.5 | 36.0 | 25.9 | 31.7 | 30.5 | 34.6 | 38.5 | 39.3 |
| Inventory | 33.7 | 32.8 | 32.7 | 28.1 | 31.2 | 31.3 | 35.9 | 34.1 | 31.7 |
| All Other Current | 2.5 | 2.7 | 3.0 | 6.9 | 4.4 | 2.6 | 1.9 | 2.0 | 3.3 |
| Total Current | 80.2 | 80.9 | 81.6 | 73.2 | 81.9 | 80.0 | 84.3 | 82.9 | 81.0 |
| Fixed Assets (net) | 11.2 | 10.2 | 9.5 | 18.4 | 8.3 | 8.4 | 8.7 | 9.5 | 9.3 |
| Intangibles (net) | 3.3 | 3.2 | 3.6 | 4.8 | 3.2 | 3.7 | 3.2 | 2.0 | 4.8 |
| All Other Non-Current | 5.3 | 5.6 | 5.3 | 3.6 | 6.6 | 7.9 | 3.8 | 5.6 | 4.9 |
| Total | 100.0 | 100.0 | 100.0 | 100.0 | 100.0 | 100.0 | 100.0 | 100.0 | 100.0 |
| **LIABILITIES** | | | | | | | | | |
| Notes Payable-Short Term | 14.3 | 13.4 | 14.1 | 22.3 | 17.0 | 15.8 | 12.2 | 13.9 | 12.4 |
| Cur. Mat.-L.T.D. | 2.4 | 1.7 | 1.7 | 4.0 | 2.8 | 1.6 | 1.8 | 1.4 | 1.4 |
| Trade Payables | 21.1 | 21.9 | 23.0 | 11.1 | 22.6 | 22.5 | 23.1 | 23.8 | 24.5 |
| Income Taxes Payable | .1 | .2 | .2 | .0 | .4 | .2 | .0 | .3 | .2 |
| All Other Current | 8.4 | 8.6 | 9.2 | 11.0 | 9.9 | 6.5 | 13.3 | 7.7 | 8.9 |
| Total Current | 46.2 | 45.8 | 48.2 | 48.4 | 52.7 | 46.7 | 50.4 | 47.0 | 47.4 |
| Long-Term Debt | 7.9 | 7.8 | 6.8 | 11.8 | 7.2 | 7.8 | 6.2 | 5.6 | 6.9 |
| Deferred Taxes | .2 | .2 | .2 | .0 | .1 | .1 | .1 | .2 | .2 |
| All Other Non-Current | 5.1 | 4.6 | 5.5 | 11.8 | 5.4 | 12.4 | 4.6 | 4.8 | 3.3 |
| Net Worth | 40.7 | 41.5 | 39.2 | 28.1 | 34.6 | 32.9 | 38.8 | 42.4 | 42.2 |
| Total Liabilities & Net Worth | 100.0 | 100.0 | 100.0 | 100.0 | 100.0 | 100.0 | 100.0 | 100.0 | 100.0 |
| **INCOME DATA** | | | | | | | | | |
| Net Sales | 100.0 | 100.0 | 100.0 | 100.0 | 100.0 | 100.0 | 100.0 | 100.0 | 100.0 |
| Gross Profit | 29.5 | 29.0 | 29.9 | 45.1 | 40.5 | 34.4 | 32.1 | 27.4 | 24.0 |
| Operating Expenses | 26.6 | 25.2 | 25.3 | 38.1 | 36.1 | 30.4 | 27.3 | 22.9 | 19.4 |
| Operating Profit | 2.9 | 3.8 | 4.6 | 7.0 | 4.5 | 4.0 | 4.8 | 4.5 | 4.5 |
| All Other Expenses (net) | .4 | .4 | .3 | .8 | .2 | .3 | .1 | .3 | .3 |
| Profit Before Taxes | 2.5 | 3.4 | 4.4 | 6.2 | 4.3 | 3.7 | 4.7 | 4.3 | 4.3 |
| **RATIOS** | | | | | | | | | |
| Current | 2.8 | 2.8 | 2.8 | 6.6 | 2.7 | 3.0 | 2.9 | 2.8 | 2.6 |
| | 1.8 | 1.8 | 1.8 | 2.8 | 1.8 | 1.7 | 1.9 | 1.8 | 1.8 |
| | 1.3 | 1.3 | 1.3 | .8 | 1.1 | 1.2 | 1.3 | 1.3 | 1.3 |
| Quick | 1.6 | 1.7 | 1.6 | 4.2 | 1.8 | 1.7 | 1.5 | 1.5 | 1.6 |
| | .9 | 1.0 | 1.0 | 1.3 | .7 | 1.0 | .9 | 1.0 | 1.0 |
| | .6 | .7 | .6 | .2 | .4 | .7 | .5 | .7 | .6 |
| Sales/Receivables | 35  10.3 | 36  10.1 | 33  11.2 | 0  UND | 20  18.2 | 17  22.0 | 32  11.4 | 34  10.7 | 40  9.1 |
| | 47  7.8 | 48  7.5 | 46  7.9 | 27  13.5 | 38  9.5 | 36  10.2 | 46  7.9 | 46  8.0 | 51  7.1 |
| | 59  6.1 | 61  6.0 | 60  6.1 | 83  4.4 | 60  6.1 | 54  6.8 | 61  6.0 | 57  6.4 | 63  5.8 |
| Cost of Sales/Inventory | 36  10.2 | 31  11.7 | 29  12.8 | 0  UND | 3  125.1 | 8  44.7 | 33  11.1 | 29  12.6 | 32  11.3 |
| | 60  6.1 | 59  6.2 | 59  6.2 | 89  4.1 | 69  5.3 | 48  7.6 | 70  5.2 | 61  6.0 | 55  6.6 |
| | 105  3.5 | 97  3.8 | 99  3.7 | 215  1.7 | 146  2.5 | 101  3.6 | 118  3.1 | 96  3.8 | 83  4.4 |
| Cost of Sales/Payables | 23  15.7 | 23  15.6 | 24  15.4 | 5  69.1 | 9  39.6 | 18  20.1 | 23  15.8 | 23  15.8 | 28  13.2 |
| | 36  10.2 | 37  10.0 | 37  9.9 | 29  12.7 | 41  8.8 | 38  9.7 | 36  10.0 | 36  10.2 | 37  9.9 |
| | 50  7.3 | 52  7.0 | 54  6.8 | 56  6.5 | 70  5.2 | 62  5.9 | 61  6.0 | 50  7.3 | 48  7.6 |
| Sales/Working Capital | 4.9 | 4.8 | 5.0 | 3.0 | 4.1 | 5.2 | 4.6 | 5.2 | 5.1 |
| | 7.8 | 7.9 | 8.1 | 6.4 | 8.9 | 8.8 | 7.3 | 8.0 | 8.2 |
| | 16.0 | 14.8 | 17.9 | UND | 35.4 | 30.7 | 15.4 | 17.5 | 15.3 |
| EBIT/Interest | 12.9 | 19.9 | 26.2 | 14.4 | 20.7 | 16.3 | 30.0 | 25.7 | 35.0 |
| | (536)  3.7 | (554)  6.0 | (569)  8.9 | (16)  2.7 | (46)  5.4 | (61)  4.0 | (90)  7.6 | (153)  8.6 | (203)  12.4 |
| | 1.0 | 2.0 | 2.7 | -2.6 | 1.7 | .7 | 2.0 | 3.3 | 4.7 |
| Net Profit + Depr., Dep., Amort./Cur. Mat. L/T/D | 6.4 | 10.2 | 12.7 | | | | 7.7 | 13.0 | 14.0 |
| | (128)  2.5 | (129)  3.8 | (113)  3.8 | | | | (14)  2.8 | (30)  3.9 | (60)  5.2 |
| | .9 | 1.6 | 1.4 | | | | 1.3 | 1.3 | 1.7 |
| Fixed/Worth | .1 | .1 | .0 | .0 | .0 | .0 | .0 | .0 | .1 |
| | .2 | .2 | .2 | .2 | .1 | .2 | .1 | .2 | .2 |
| | .5 | .5 | .5 | 3.4 | .8 | .6 | .4 | .4 | .5 |
| Debt/Worth | .6 | .7 | .7 | .5 | .8 | .6 | .6 | .7 | .7 |
| | 1.6 | 1.5 | 1.5 | 2.2 | 1.7 | 1.8 | 1.5 | 1.4 | 1.5 |
| | 3.6 | 3.5 | 4.2 | UND | 6.1 | 7.7 | 5.1 | 2.6 | 3.9 |
| % Profit Before Taxes/Tangible Net Worth | 30.8 | 39.4 | 50.3 | 94.7 | 77.6 | 43.2 | 49.9 | 49.5 | 48.2 |
| | (556)  10.5 | (594)  16.7 | (620)  23.5 | (27)  39.2 | (54)  44.7 | (62)  17.1 | (100)  23.5 | (164)  23.1 | (213)  22.0 |
| | .7 | 4.0 | 8.7 | 4.6 | 7.5 | 4.1 | 5.5 | 7.3 | 11.8 |
| % Profit Before Taxes/Total Assets | 11.2 | 14.0 | 16.9 | 29.4 | 25.2 | 16.5 | 16.1 | 20.1 | 13.8 |
| | 3.7 | 5.9 | 8.0 | 6.6 | 9.1 | 5.2 | 9.0 | 7.3 | 8.6 |
| | .1 | 1.6 | 2.6 | -5.6 | 1.3 | 1.3 | 1.8 | 2.7 | 4.8 |
| Sales/Net Fixed Assets | 114.0 | 148.5 | 162.1 | UND | 293.4 | 687.7 | 207.7 | 150.7 | 116.0 |
| | 43.4 | 50.4 | 59.9 | 30.2 | 79.3 | 72.2 | 69.6 | 59.4 | 52.6 |
| | 17.7 | 19.1 | 21.4 | 7.7 | 30.9 | 31.2 | 21.0 | 20.8 | 20.0 |
| Sales/Total Assets | 3.5 | 3.4 | 3.7 | 3.1 | 3.9 | 4.2 | 3.7 | 3.8 | 3.5 |
| | 2.7 | 2.7 | 2.8 | 1.9 | 2.9 | 3.0 | 2.6 | 3.0 | 2.8 |
| | 2.0 | 2.1 | 2.1 | 1.2 | 2.1 | 2.1 | 2.0 | 2.3 | 2.1 |
| % Depr., Dep., Amort./Sales | .4 | .3 | .2 | .7 | .3 | .3 | .2 | .3 | .2 |
| | (485)  .6 | (499)  .6 | (513)  .5 | (16)  1.6 | (32)  .6 | (50)  .6 | (87)  .4 | (131)  .6 | (197)  .5 |
| | 1.2 | 1.1 | 1.0 | 4.1 | 1.1 | .9 | 1.0 | 1.0 | .9 |
| % Officers', Directors' Owners' Comp/Sales | 1.8 | 1.6 | 1.6 | 5.9 | 3.2 | 2.1 | 1.9 | 1.3 | 1.0 |
| | (239)  3.5 | (264)  3.3 | (261)  3.1 | (12)  10.8 | (30)  6.2 | (48)  4.4 | (55)  3.8 | (63)  2.3 | (53)  1.6 |
| | 7.4 | 6.3 | 5.8 | 15.7 | 9.6 | 5.8 | 6.4 | 3.1 | 3.7 |
| Net Sales ($) | 27561436M | 28651042M | 28580191M | 19075M | 125168M | 278527M | 812796M | 2740349M | 24604276M |
| Total Assets ($) | 10855210M | 11329911M | 11313771M | 13276M | 51458M | 103637M | 360993M | 994733M | 9789674M |

## Current Data Sorted by Assets  —  Comparative Historical Data

| | | | | | | Type of Statement | | |
|---|---|---|---|---|---|---|---|---|
| | | 2 | 5 | 4 | 2 | Unqualified | 22 | 26 |
| | 3 | 17 | 11 | 1 | | Reviewed | 26 | 31 |
| | 8 | 13 | 1 | | | Compiled | 16 | 20 |
| 1 | 7 | 6 | 1 | | | Tax Returns | 12 | 20 |
| 1 | 13 | 21 | 26 | 8 | 5 | Other | 51 | 44 |
| | 29 (4/1-9/30/11) | | 126 (10/1/11-3/31/12) | | | | 4/1/07-3/31/08 ALL | 4/1/08-3/31/09 ALL |
| 0-500M | 500M-2MM | 2-10MM | 10-50MM | 50-100MM | 100-250MM | | | |
| 2 | 31 | 59 | 44 | 12 | 7 | NUMBER OF STATEMENTS | 127 | 141 |
| % | % | % | % | % | % | ASSETS | % | % |
| | 14.5 | 9.6 | 11.2 | 5.1 | | Cash & Equivalents | 6.5 | 7.4 |
| | 27.2 | 34.9 | 25.3 | 26.0 | | Trade Receivables (net) | 32.0 | 29.4 |
| | 40.0 | 39.6 | 42.0 | 44.5 | | Inventory | 44.1 | 42.4 |
| | 2.7 | 2.0 | 2.1 | 1.8 | | All Other Current | 1.9 | 3.0 |
| | 84.4 | 86.0 | 80.6 | 77.4 | | Total Current | 84.4 | 82.1 |
| | 6.4 | 7.3 | 9.4 | 12.0 | | Fixed Assets (net) | 8.1 | 10.0 |
| | 4.4 | 3.1 | 6.0 | 5.1 | | Intangibles (net) | 4.7 | 3.8 |
| | 4.8 | 3.6 | 3.9 | 5.6 | | All Other Non-Current | 2.8 | 4.1 |
| | 100.0 | 100.0 | 100.0 | 100.0 | | Total | 100.0 | 100.0 |
| | | | | | | LIABILITIES | | |
| | 15.0 | 16.8 | 12.0 | 14.0 | | Notes Payable-Short Term | 17.0 | 18.2 |
| | 4.1 | 1.5 | .7 | .4 | | Cur. Mat.-L.T.D. | 1.4 | 2.4 |
| | 28.0 | 28.1 | 20.3 | 22.3 | | Trade Payables | 24.9 | 23.1 |
| | .1 | .0 | .0 | .0 | | Income Taxes Payable | .3 | .2 |
| | 5.9 | 8.4 | 8.1 | 9.8 | | All Other Current | 10.4 | 10.1 |
| | 53.0 | 54.8 | 41.0 | 46.5 | | Total Current | 53.9 | 54.0 |
| | 9.6 | 3.7 | 4.5 | 3.2 | | Long-Term Debt | 6.3 | 7.8 |
| | .0 | .1 | .2 | .0 | | Deferred Taxes | .1 | .2 |
| | 6.4 | 8.0 | 8.7 | 6.6 | | All Other Non-Current | 3.6 | 3.1 |
| | 31.0 | 33.5 | 45.6 | 43.6 | | Net Worth | 36.0 | 34.9 |
| | 100.0 | 100.0 | 100.0 | 100.0 | | Total Liabilities & Net Worth | 100.0 | 100.0 |
| | | | | | | INCOME DATA | | |
| | 100.0 | 100.0 | 100.0 | 100.0 | | Net Sales | 100.0 | 100.0 |
| | 26.9 | 23.3 | 25.1 | 16.8 | | Gross Profit | 25.4 | 23.8 |
| | 24.0 | 20.5 | 20.5 | 13.2 | | Operating Expenses | 22.0 | 22.1 |
| | 2.9 | 2.8 | 4.6 | 3.6 | | Operating Profit | 3.4 | 1.7 |
| | .1 | .1 | .1 | .6 | | All Other Expenses (net) | 1.0 | .9 |
| | 2.8 | 2.7 | 4.4 | 3.0 | | Profit Before Taxes | 2.4 | .8 |
| | | | | | | RATIOS | | |
| | 2.8 | 2.3 | 3.0 | 2.0 | | Current | 2.2 | 2.6 |
| | 1.7 | 1.6 | 2.0 | 1.7 | | | 1.6 | 1.6 |
| | 1.2 | 1.2 | 1.5 | 1.4 | | | 1.2 | 1.2 |
| | 1.6 | 1.3 | 1.3 | .9 | | Quick | 1.1 | 1.1 |
| | .8 | .8 | .8 | .7 | | | .7 | .7 |
| | .3 | .5 | .6 | .4 | | | .5 | .4 |
| 18 20.7 | 22 16.4 | 22 16.6 | 20 17.9 | | | Sales/Receivables | 26 14.3 | 21 17.2 |
| 33 11.2 | 34 10.8 | 35 10.5 | 32 11.4 | | | | 34 10.6 | 32 11.6 |
| 47 7.8 | 62 5.9 | 52 7.0 | 51 7.1 | | | | 47 7.8 | 47 7.8 |
| 44 8.3 | 28 13.1 | 54 6.8 | 50 7.3 | | | Cost of Sales/Inventory | 46 7.9 | 41 8.9 |
| 63 5.8 | 60 6.1 | 83 4.4 | 78 4.7 | | | | 69 5.3 | 60 6.1 |
| 85 4.3 | 94 3.9 | 114 3.2 | 101 3.6 | | | | 102 3.6 | 106 3.4 |
| 16 22.2 | 21 17.1 | 17 21.4 | 18 20.7 | | | Cost of Sales/Payables | 19 19.7 | 18 20.8 |
| 44 8.3 | 36 10.0 | 28 13.0 | 30 12.0 | | | | 32 11.3 | 30 12.0 |
| 56 6.5 | 53 6.9 | 56 6.5 | 45 8.2 | | | | 50 7.3 | 46 8.0 |
| | 5.0 | 6.5 | 4.9 | 6.0 | | Sales/Working Capital | 6.6 | 5.7 |
| | 11.4 | 10.6 | 7.4 | 8.2 | | | 10.5 | 11.4 |
| | 30.2 | 24.3 | 11.3 | 17.9 | | | 22.4 | 27.8 |
| | 5.3 | 19.3 | 21.7 | 41.5 | | EBIT/Interest | 8.0 | 13.8 |
| (19) 3.0 | (55) 4.8 | (40) 5.6 | (11) 10.6 | | | | (111) 3.7 | (129) 3.6 |
| | .2 | 1.9 | 1.6 | 2.3 | | | 1.3 | 1.0 |
| | | | | | | Net Profit + Depr., Dep., Amort./Cur. Mat. L/T/D | 14.1 | 19.9 |
| | | | | | | | (23) 7.0 | (24) 6.0 |
| | | | | | | | 1.1 | .8 |
| | .0 | .1 | .0 | .0 | | Fixed/Worth | .1 | .1 |
| | .1 | .1 | .2 | .3 | | | .2 | .2 |
| | -3.3 | .7 | .4 | .5 | | | .5 | .5 |
| | .6 | 1.2 | .5 | 1.0 | | Debt/Worth | .9 | .8 |
| | 2.2 | 2.0 | 1.4 | 1.5 | | | 2.3 | 2.1 |
| | -16.6 | 7.9 | 3.5 | 2.4 | | | 5.0 | 5.6 |
| | 42.3 | 46.8 | 34.3 | 50.4 | | % Profit Before Taxes/Tangible Net Worth | 49.7 | 31.6 |
| (22) 18.1 | (53) 20.9 | (40) 19.3 | 15.4 | | | | (115) 23.0 | (124) 13.4 |
| | -6.9 | 6.9 | 5.1 | 7.9 | | | 6.9 | 1.9 |
| | 13.4 | 11.5 | 14.2 | 12.8 | | % Profit Before Taxes/Total Assets | 13.7 | 8.5 |
| | 6.0 | 4.7 | 6.3 | 6.0 | | | 7.2 | 4.3 |
| | -3.1 | 2.6 | 2.2 | 3.5 | | | 1.2 | .0 |
| | 433.1 | 230.0 | 118.9 | 260.1 | | Sales/Net Fixed Assets | 178.3 | 168.0 |
| | 117.2 | 101.9 | 64.6 | 45.6 | | | 63.8 | 62.0 |
| | 45.9 | 40.1 | 23.8 | 15.2 | | | 25.7 | 22.9 |
| | 4.3 | 4.0 | 3.5 | 3.1 | | Sales/Total Assets | 4.0 | 4.3 |
| | 3.2 | 3.1 | 2.8 | 2.7 | | | 3.0 | 3.1 |
| | 2.7 | 2.4 | 2.1 | 2.2 | | | 2.3 | 2.0 |
| | .1 | .1 | .2 | | | % Depr., Dep., Amort./Sales | .2 | .2 |
| (20) | .3 | (47) .3 | (36) .5 | | | | (105) .4 | (116) .4 |
| | 1.1 | .7 | 1.0 | | | | .9 | .8 |
| | 1.6 | .7 | .5 | | | % Officers', Directors' Owners' Comp/Sales | 1.3 | 1.2 |
| (14) | 2.7 | (26) 1.7 | (11) .7 | | | | (41) 2.6 | (49) 1.8 |
| | 4.5 | 5.1 | 2.0 | | | | 4.1 | 4.0 |
| 4810M | 140590M | 1168882M | 2745582M | 2358415M | 3083764M | Net Sales ($) | 6973602M | 7797522M |
| 720M | 40784M | 331259M | 861078M | 832364M | 1029026M | Total Assets ($) | 2711124M | 2817052M |

M = $ thousand    MM = $ million
See Pages 9 through 22 for Explanation of Ratios and Data

## Comparative Historical Data | Current Data Sorted by Sales

**Type of Statement**

| 19 | 21 | 13 | Unqualified | | | | 1 | 4 | 1 | 12 |
| 25 | 34 | 31 | Reviewed | | | | 3 | 6 | 16 | 10 |
| 18 | 19 | 22 | Compiled | | | 1 | 1 | 8 | 9 | 3 |
| 22 | 20 | 15 | Tax Returns | | | 3 | 4 | 5 | 1 | 2 |
| 61 | 59 | 74 | Other | | | 4 | 9 | 5 | 12 | 44 |
| 4/1/09-3/31/10 ALL | 4/1/10-3/31/11 ALL | 4/1/11-3/31/12 ALL | | | 29 (4/1-9/30/11) | | 126 (10/1/11-3/31/12) | | | |
| | | | | 0-1MM | 1-3MM | 3-5MM | 5-10MM | 10-25MM | 25MM & OVER |
| 145 | 153 | 155 | **NUMBER OF STATEMENTS** | | 8 | 14 | 23 | 39 | 71 |

(0-1MM and 1-3MM columns: DATA NOT AVAILABLE for ratio/percentage data)

| H 09-10 | H 10-11 | H 11-12 | | 3-5MM | 5-10MM | 10-25MM | 25MM & OVER |
|---|---|---|---|---|---|---|---|
| % | % | % | **ASSETS** | % | % | % | % |
| 9.9 | 9.4 | 10.4 | Cash & Equivalents | 11.2 | 7.0 | 7.9 | 11.4 |
| 31.4 | 27.7 | 30.2 | Trade Receivables (net) | 30.6 | 26.3 | 39.5 | 27.0 |
| 40.6 | 43.5 | 40.6 | Inventory | 41.3 | 43.4 | 38.2 | 41.4 |
| 2.4 | 2.5 | 2.1 | All Other Current | 2.1 | 1.4 | 2.7 | 1.9 |
| 84.2 | 83.1 | 83.4 | Total Current | 85.3 | 78.0 | 88.4 | 81.7 |
| 8.9 | 9.1 | 8.1 | Fixed Assets (net) | 6.3 | 10.3 | 6.5 | 8.7 |
| 3.0 | 2.9 | 4.5 | Intangibles (net) | 4.6 | 6.7 | 1.3 | 5.3 |
| 3.9 | 4.8 | 4.1 | All Other Non-Current | 3.8 | 5.0 | 3.9 | 4.2 |
| 100.0 | 100.0 | 100.0 | Total | 100.0 | 100.0 | 100.0 | 100.0 |
| | | | **LIABILITIES** | | | | |
| 16.5 | 14.8 | 14.6 | Notes Payable-Short Term | 16.2 | 17.5 | 20.8 | 9.8 |
| 2.0 | 1.8 | 1.6 | Cur. Mat.-L.T.D. | 2.0 | 4.9 | 1.4 | .7 |
| 23.4 | 24.3 | 25.5 | Trade Payables | 27.9 | 27.5 | 24.8 | 25.1 |
| .2 | .1 | .0 | Income Taxes Payable | .1 | .0 | .0 | .0 |
| 9.4 | 11.4 | 7.8 | All Other Current | 4.7 | 6.8 | 7.1 | 9.5 |
| 51.6 | 52.4 | 49.5 | Total Current | 50.9 | 56.7 | 54.2 | 45.2 |
| 6.1 | 7.3 | 5.5 | Long-Term Debt | 4.4 | 9.9 | 2.9 | 5.1 |
| .0 | .1 | .1 | Deferred Taxes | .0 | .1 | .1 | .1 |
| 6.7 | 6.1 | 7.6 | All Other Non-Current | 21.9 | 7.5 | 6.9 | 6.0 |
| 35.6 | 34.1 | 37.4 | Net Worth | 22.8 | 25.7 | 35.9 | 43.8 |
| 100.0 | 100.0 | 100.0 | Total Liabilities & Net Worth | 100.0 | 100.0 | 100.0 | 100.0 |
| | | | **INCOME DATA** | | | | |
| 100.0 | 100.0 | 100.0 | Net Sales | 100.0 | 100.0 | 100.0 | 100.0 |
| 23.5 | 24.5 | 24.0 | Gross Profit | 28.1 | 26.0 | 23.0 | 22.1 |
| 21.6 | 22.1 | 20.6 | Operating Expenses | 25.9 | 26.0 | 19.7 | 17.8 |
| 1.9 | 2.3 | 3.4 | Operating Profit | 2.2 | .0 | 3.2 | 4.3 |
| .4 | .2 | .1 | All Other Expenses (net) | -.2 | .5 | .1 | .1 |
| 1.5 | 2.1 | 3.2 | Profit Before Taxes | 2.4 | -.5 | 3.1 | 4.2 |
| | | | **RATIOS** | | | | |
| 2.6 | 2.5 | 2.6 | | 2.9 | 2.1 | 2.5 | 2.7 |
| 1.6 | 1.7 | 1.7 | Current | 2.0 | 1.4 | 1.6 | 2.0 |
| 1.2 | 1.3 | 1.3 | | 1.0 | 1.0 | 1.2 | 1.5 |
| 1.5 | 1.2 | 1.3 | | 1.5 | 1.0 | 1.3 | 1.3 |
| .8 | .8 | .8 | Quick | .8 | .7 | 1.0 | .8 |
| .6 | .4 | .5 | | .5 | .3 | .5 | .6 |
| 23  15.9 | 20  18.6 | 21  17.6 | | 21  17.8 | 18  20.6 | 27  13.6 | 21  17.7 |
| 31  11.9 | 30  12.4 | 34  10.8 | Sales/Receivables | 36  10.1 | 27  13.5 | 54  6.7 | 33  11.0 |
| 49  7.5 | 45  8.1 | 52  7.0 | | 47  7.7 | 35  10.4 | 85  4.3 | 47  7.7 |
| 39  9.3 | 41  9.0 | 43  8.4 | | 55  6.6 | 40  9.2 | 28  13.1 | 45  8.1 |
| 62  5.9 | 67  5.4 | 69  5.3 | Cost of Sales/Inventory | 81  4.5 | 63  5.8 | 63  5.8 | 69  5.3 |
| 96  3.8 | 102  3.6 | 101  3.6 | | 101  3.6 | 94  3.9 | 118  3.1 | 94  3.9 |
| 17  21.9 | 16  22.4 | 20  18.7 | | 29  12.6 | 17  21.3 | 23  15.7 | 17  21.9 |
| 31  11.7 | 30  12.2 | 34  10.6 | Cost of Sales/Payables | 46  7.9 | 45  8.2 | 37  9.9 | 29  12.4 |
| 46  7.9 | 50  7.4 | 53  6.9 | | 53  6.9 | 70  5.2 | 58  6.3 | 45  8.1 |
| 5.5 | 5.4 | 5.5 | | 4.7 | 11.1 | 5.3 | 5.7 |
| 9.7 | 10.7 | 9.3 | Sales/Working Capital | 6.2 | 15.6 | 9.3 | 8.4 |
| 20.7 | 21.2 | 19.7 | | -229.9 | -501.5 | 20.7 | 18.8 |
| 14.1 | 17.3 | 15.8 | | | 5.1 | 12.6 | 48.5 |
| (133)  4.0 | (136)  4.3 | (134)  5.0 | EBIT/Interest | | (21)  1.7 | (37)  4.8 | (64)  9.4 |
| .5 | 1.2 | 1.8 | | | -1.9 | 2.3 | 2.3 |
| 54.2 | 37.8 | 20.3 | Net Profit + Depr., Dep., | | | | |
| (22)  2.8 | (26)  6.2 | (18)  3.5 | Amort./Cur. Mat. L/T/D | | | | |
| .0 | 1.1 | 1.8 | | | | | |
| .0 | .1 | .0 | | .0 | .1 | .0 | .1 |
| .2 | .2 | .2 | Fixed/Worth | .9 | .5 | .1 | .2 |
| .4 | .4 | .7 | | -.8 | -3.3 | .5 | .4 |
| .8 | .8 | .8 | | .8 | 1.2 | 1.2 | .6 |
| 1.9 | 1.7 | 1.7 | Debt/Worth | 8.5 | 5.0 | 1.8 | 1.4 |
| 5.0 | 4.1 | 7.2 | | -3.6 | -16.6 | 5.0 | 3.5 |
| 31.1 | 31.8 | 45.1 | % Profit Before Taxes/Tangible | 20.7 | 39.3 | 46.6 | |
| (129)  11.6 | (135)  20.0 | (135)  18.3 | Net Worth | (16)  8.8 | (37)  17.8 | (66)  19.3 | |
| 2.2 | 5.0 | 6.7 | | -24.4 | 7.4 | 8.1 | |
| 10.0 | 13.5 | 13.4 | % Profit Before Taxes/Total | 18.3 | 8.9 | 11.0 | 14.6 |
| 3.7 | 5.9 | 6.0 | Assets | 6.7 | 2.8 | 4.1 | 7.0 |
| -.8 | .9 | 2.2 | | -5.0 | -9.8 | 2.7 | 2.4 |
| 223.7 | 164.7 | 228.6 | | 425.6 | 136.7 | 239.4 | 137.9 |
| 68.7 | 61.3 | 88.9 | Sales/Net Fixed Assets | 100.3 | 47.8 | 105.0 | 74.6 |
| 29.9 | 26.9 | 26.9 | | 62.6 | 22.3 | 46.0 | 25.3 |
| 4.3 | 4.1 | 3.8 | | 3.4 | 4.3 | 3.4 | 4.2 |
| 2.9 | 3.1 | 3.0 | Sales/Total Assets | 2.8 | 3.4 | 2.5 | 3.0 |
| 2.2 | 2.5 | 2.3 | | 2.6 | 2.9 | 2.2 | 2.4 |
| .2 | .2 | .2 | | | .4 | .1 | .2 |
| (103)  .4 | (125)  .4 | (117)  .4 | % Depr., Dep., Amort./Sales | | (18)  .7 | (31)  .2 | (57)  .4 |
| .8 | .9 | .8 | | | 1.5 | .6 | .7 |
| 1.0 | .8 | .7 | % Officers', Directors' | | 1.9 | .5 | .6 |
| (47)  2.0 | (54)  1.7 | (55)  1.7 | Owners' Comp/Sales | | (12)  4.1 | (21)  1.3 | (12)  1.0 |
| 3.6 | 3.6 | 4.3 | | | 5.7 | 3.9 | 1.2 |

| 8335990M | 10406296M | 9502043M | Net Sales ($) | | 15490M | 56551M | 155826M | 679227M | 8594949M |
| 2608827M | 2944652M | 3095231M | Total Assets ($) | | 6266M | 20117M | 54083M | 268210M | 2746555M |

M = $ thousand     MM = $ million
See Pages 9 through 22 for Explanation of Ratios and Data

## Current Data Sorted by Assets

## Comparative Historical Data

| Type of Statement | 0-500M | 500M-2MM | 2-10MM | 10-50MM | 50-100MM | 100-250MM | | 4/1/07-3/31/08 ALL | 4/1/08-3/31/09 ALL |
|---|---|---|---|---|---|---|---|---|---|
| Unqualified | | 1 | 16 | 26 | 9 | 8 | | 63 | 80 |
| Reviewed | 2 | 8 | 51 | 24 | | 1 | | 78 | 84 |
| Compiled | 2 | 9 | 19 | 3 | | | | 46 | 42 |
| Tax Returns | 5 | 29 | 25 | 2 | | | | 34 | 44 |
| Other | 12 | 38 | 62 | 62 | 5 | 7 | | 105 | 142 |
| | | 71 (4/1-9/30/11) | | 355 (10/1/11-3/31/12) | | | | | |
| NUMBER OF STATEMENTS | 21 | 85 | 173 | 117 | 14 | 16 | | 326 | 392 |
| **ASSETS** | % | % | % | % | % | % | | % | % |
| Cash & Equivalents | 12.0 | 11.3 | 9.1 | 8.0 | 8.4 | 11.4 | | 8.9 | 9.9 |
| Trade Receivables (net) | 29.2 | 35.5 | 36.9 | 34.5 | 31.5 | 31.0 | | 37.9 | 35.0 |
| Inventory | 40.9 | 34.5 | 34.8 | 35.2 | 30.4 | 26.4 | | 33.7 | 33.6 |
| All Other Current | .6 | 1.4 | 1.9 | 2.9 | 4.8 | 3.9 | | 2.8 | 2.5 |
| Total Current | 82.7 | 82.6 | 82.8 | 80.5 | 75.2 | 72.7 | | 83.2 | 81.1 |
| Fixed Assets (net) | 9.7 | 9.3 | 8.1 | 7.5 | 9.0 | 6.1 | | 8.8 | 8.9 |
| Intangibles (net) | 1.6 | 2.6 | 3.3 | 6.1 | 8.3 | 17.8 | | 3.3 | 3.9 |
| All Other Non-Current | 6.1 | 5.5 | 5.8 | 5.9 | 7.5 | 3.4 | | 4.7 | 6.1 |
| Total | 100.0 | 100.0 | 100.0 | 100.0 | 100.0 | 100.0 | | 100.0 | 100.0 |
| **LIABILITIES** | | | | | | | | | |
| Notes Payable-Short Term | 57.4 | 15.1 | 12.0 | 15.0 | 17.1 | 10.0 | | 15.2 | 14.4 |
| Cur. Mat.-L.T.D. | 1.8 | 1.1 | 1.6 | 1.5 | .2 | .7 | | 1.5 | 1.8 |
| Trade Payables | 27.7 | 27.6 | 25.4 | 22.1 | 22.4 | 21.9 | | 23.9 | 22.8 |
| Income Taxes Payable | .0 | .6 | .5 | .2 | .2 | .2 | | .3 | .2 |
| All Other Current | 9.8 | 7.5 | 7.8 | 8.2 | 10.2 | 10.8 | | 10.3 | 9.3 |
| Total Current | 96.7 | 51.9 | 47.3 | 47.0 | 50.1 | 43.5 | | 51.3 | 48.6 |
| Long-Term Debt | 14.2 | 9.3 | 6.5 | 7.9 | 2.6 | 5.6 | | 7.6 | 7.7 |
| Deferred Taxes | .0 | .0 | .2 | .3 | .3 | .4 | | .2 | .1 |
| All Other Non-Current | 13.7 | 9.7 | 4.4 | 8.7 | 3.3 | 2.3 | | 4.2 | 4.3 |
| Net Worth | -24.6 | 29.1 | 41.6 | 36.1 | 43.7 | 48.1 | | 36.8 | 39.3 |
| Total Liabilities & Net Worth | 100.0 | 100.0 | 100.0 | 100.0 | 100.0 | 100.0 | | 100.0 | 100.0 |
| **INCOME DATA** | | | | | | | | | |
| Net Sales | 100.0 | 100.0 | 100.0 | 100.0 | 100.0 | 100.0 | | 100.0 | 100.0 |
| Gross Profit | 36.7 | 33.9 | 27.1 | 25.2 | 24.6 | 30.0 | | 28.6 | 28.6 |
| Operating Expenses | 30.5 | 29.4 | 23.5 | 20.0 | 15.4 | 21.1 | | 24.9 | 25.3 |
| Operating Profit | 6.2 | 4.4 | 3.6 | 5.2 | 9.3 | 8.9 | | 3.7 | 3.4 |
| All Other Expenses (net) | 1.0 | .3 | .2 | .6 | .6 | .2 | | .5 | .4 |
| Profit Before Taxes | 5.2 | 4.1 | 3.4 | 4.6 | 8.6 | 8.7 | | 3.1 | 3.0 |
| **RATIOS** | | | | | | | | | |
| Current | 2.0 | 2.5 | 2.7 | 2.5 | 2.0 | 2.1 | | 2.4 | 2.6 |
| | 1.2 | 1.7 | 1.8 | 1.7 | 1.4 | 1.6 | | 1.6 | 1.7 |
| | .6 | 1.2 | 1.3 | 1.3 | 1.2 | 1.2 | | 1.2 | 1.2 |
| Quick | 1.3 | 1.6 | 1.6 | 1.4 | 1.1 | 1.3 | | 1.4 | 1.5 |
| | .7 | 1.0 | 1.0 | .9 | .8 | .9 | | .9 | .9 |
| | .6 | .6 | .7 | .6 | .6 | .6 | | .6 | .6 |
| Sales/Receivables | 0 UND | 24 15.2 | 30 12.0 | 31 11.6 | 26 14.3 | 38 9.5 | | 34 10.8 | 31 11.9 |
| | 20 18.2 | 35 10.4 | 41 8.9 | 45 8.2 | 44 8.3 | 47 7.8 | | 44 8.3 | 42 8.7 |
| | 29 12.6 | 45 8.1 | 54 6.8 | 68 5.4 | 57 6.4 | 55 6.6 | | 58 6.3 | 54 6.7 |
| Cost of Sales/Inventory | 14 25.8 | 16 23.4 | 30 12.3 | 40 9.2 | 33 11.0 | 17 21.0 | | 31 11.9 | 30 12.2 |
| | 43 8.4 | 45 8.1 | 57 6.4 | 63 5.8 | 66 5.5 | 45 8.2 | | 56 6.6 | 54 6.7 |
| | 101 3.6 | 94 3.9 | 85 4.3 | 104 3.5 | 96 3.8 | 89 4.1 | | 90 4.1 | 96 3.8 |
| Cost of Sales/Payables | 2 180.8 | 17 21.8 | 17 21.4 | 20 18.0 | 26 14.3 | 28 12.9 | | 20 18.5 | 20 18.7 |
| | 19 19.0 | 36 10.1 | 33 11.1 | 36 10.2 | 34 10.6 | 47 7.7 | | 36 10.1 | 32 11.5 |
| | 42 8.7 | 59 6.2 | 54 6.7 | 60 6.1 | 54 6.8 | 58 6.3 | | 53 6.9 | 52 7.0 |
| Sales/Working Capital | 13.7 | 6.6 | 5.5 | 4.7 | 5.9 | 4.3 | | 5.5 | 5.3 |
| | 45.8 | 14.3 | 9.0 | 8.8 | 19.1 | 10.6 | | 10.1 | 9.5 |
| | -19.3 | 32.5 | 18.8 | 15.6 | 25.8 | 27.9 | | 20.7 | 23.2 |
| EBIT/Interest | 10.0 | 26.5 | 27.9 | 36.1 | 24.4 | 105.4 | | 17.0 | 14.0 |
| | (16) 3.7 | (63) 4.8 | (151) 6.6 | (101) 7.0 | (13) 8.9 | (13) 20.3 | | (289) 4.2 | (322) 4.2 |
| | 1.2 | 1.6 | 2.6 | 2.6 | 4.3 | 6.0 | | 1.4 | 1.5 |
| Net Profit + Depr., Dep., Amort./Cur. Mat. L/T/D | | | 5.9 | 22.1 | | | | 18.6 | 13.7 |
| | | | (20) 2.6 | (23) 5.4 | | | | (64) 4.9 | (83) 4.4 |
| | | | 1.2 | 1.2 | | | | 1.9 | 1.2 |
| Fixed/Worth | .0 | .0 | .0 | .1 | .1 | .1 | | .1 | .1 |
| | .7 | .2 | .1 | .1 | .3 | .2 | | .2 | .2 |
| | -.2 | .7 | .3 | .7 | .5 | .5 | | .5 | .5 |
| Debt/Worth | 1.4 | 1.1 | .8 | .9 | .7 | .9 | | .8 | .7 |
| | 4.7 | 2.4 | 1.6 | 2.2 | 1.7 | 2.1 | | 1.9 | 1.8 |
| | -3.5 | 6.1 | 3.7 | 6.3 | 5.5 | 11.5 | | 4.7 | 4.3 |
| % Profit Before Taxes/Tangible Net Worth | 208.7 | 91.8 | 51.1 | 49.7 | 71.2 | 82.2 | | 45.1 | 38.7 |
| | (12) 46.0 | (74) 20.7 | (162) 18.3 | (100) 24.9 | (13) 31.3 | (13) 33.1 | | (296) 22.1 | (347) 17.6 |
| | 17.2 | 5.8 | 6.2 | 9.6 | 10.4 | 23.6 | | 7.2 | 3.8 |
| % Profit Before Taxes/Total Assets | 34.7 | 20.9 | 17.6 | 18.7 | 19.3 | 18.5 | | 15.7 | 15.4 |
| | 16.0 | 8.3 | 6.8 | 8.9 | 8.5 | 13.9 | | 6.8 | 5.4 |
| | 1.2 | 1.6 | 2.1 | 3.5 | 5.7 | 4.8 | | 1.3 | .9 |
| Sales/Net Fixed Assets | UND | 568.7 | 184.0 | 157.3 | 138.8 | 126.8 | | 156.8 | 149.7 |
| | 104.1 | 91.4 | 68.8 | 68.5 | 37.5 | 34.2 | | 55.5 | 51.9 |
| | 42.3 | 22.8 | 31.4 | 29.5 | 14.0 | 19.9 | | 21.7 | 24.9 |
| Sales/Total Assets | 12.1 | 4.7 | 3.8 | 3.3 | 4.5 | 3.6 | | 3.8 | 4.0 |
| | 5.1 | 3.7 | 3.0 | 2.5 | 2.5 | 2.0 | | 3.0 | 3.0 |
| | 3.1 | 2.5 | 2.4 | 1.8 | 1.3 | .9 | | 2.2 | 2.1 |
| % Depr., Dep., Amort./Sales | | .1 | .2 | .2 | .1 | .3 | | .2 | .2 |
| | | (52) .5 | (129) .4 | (99) .4 | | (13) .7 | | (267) .4 | (319) .5 |
| | | .9 | .8 | .7 | 1.1 | 1.6 | | 1.0 | 1.1 |
| % Officers', Directors', Owners' Comp/Sales | | 2.0 | .9 | .8 | | | | 1.2 | 1.4 |
| | | (55) 4.1 | (66) 2.4 | (22) 1.2 | | | | (111) 2.6 | (130) 3.2 |
| | | 6.3 | 4.1 | 3.3 | | | | 5.7 | 6.0 |
| Net Sales ($) | 52360M | 419675M | 2894609M | 6420711M | 2905748M | 6484013M | | 14538678M | 21097761M |
| Total Assets ($) | 6134M | 104642M | 885632M | 2362469M | 992741M | 2800456M | | 5306933M | 7304452M |

## Comparative Historical Data | Current Data Sorted by Sales

| | | | Type of Statement | 0-1MM | 1-3MM | 3-5MM | 5-10MM | 10-25MM | 25MM & OVER |
|---|---|---|---|---|---|---|---|---|---|
| 59 | 64 | 60 | Unqualified | | 1 | 1 | 15 | 43 | |
| 92 | 97 | 86 | Reviewed | 2 | 3 | 16 | 36 | 29 | |
| 47 | 51 | 33 | Compiled | 1 | 3 | 3 | 10 | 13 | 3 |
| 40 | 52 | 61 | Tax Returns | 2 | 15 | 9 | 13 | 16 | 6 |
| 175 | 154 | 186 | Other | 6 | 13 | 16 | 26 | 54 | 71 |
| 4/1/09-3/31/10 ALL | 4/1/10-3/31/11 ALL | 4/1/11-3/31/12 ALL | | 71 (4/1-9/30/11) | | | 355 (10/1/11-3/31/12) | | |
| 413 | 418 | 426 | NUMBER OF STATEMENTS | 11 | 31 | 32 | 66 | 134 | 152 |
| % | % | % | ASSETS | % | % | % | % | % | % |
| 10.5 | 10.1 | 9.4 | Cash & Equivalents | 6.7 | 9.6 | 14.3 | 11.4 | 8.9 | 8.2 |
| 33.2 | 34.9 | 35.2 | Trade Receivables (net) | 27.8 | 23.5 | 31.8 | 38.1 | 36.4 | 36.4 |
| 34.1 | 34.3 | 34.7 | Inventory | 46.4 | 39.6 | 29.6 | 32.3 | 36.2 | 33.6 |
| 3.3 | 3.0 | 2.2 | All Other Current | .1 | 1.7 | .9 | 1.4 | 2.3 | 2.9 |
| 81.0 | 82.2 | 81.5 | Total Current | 81.0 | 74.4 | 76.6 | 83.1 | 83.8 | 81.2 |
| 8.2 | 8.2 | 8.2 | Fixed Assets (net) | 13.2 | 11.9 | 10.9 | 8.2 | 7.3 | 7.2 |
| 5.1 | 4.5 | 4.6 | Intangibles (net) | .5 | 5.2 | 1.2 | 3.8 | 3.4 | 6.8 |
| 5.6 | 5.0 | 5.8 | All Other Non-Current | 5.3 | 8.5 | 11.2 | 4.8 | 5.4 | 4.8 |
| 100.0 | 100.0 | 100.0 | Total | 100.0 | 100.0 | 100.0 | 100.0 | 100.0 | 100.0 |
| | | | LIABILITIES | | | | | | |
| 14.6 | 13.4 | 15.8 | Notes Payable-Short Term | 61.8 | 18.0 | 15.8 | 9.4 | 16.1 | 14.5 |
| 1.9 | 1.5 | 1.4 | Cur. Mat.-L.T.D. | .0 | 2.8 | .5 | 1.3 | 1.5 | 1.3 |
| 24.1 | 24.3 | 24.8 | Trade Payables | 16.9 | 19.6 | 26.0 | 29.0 | 25.1 | 24.2 |
| .2 | .2 | .4 | Income Taxes Payable | .0 | .4 | 1.0 | .7 | .4 | .2 |
| 9.0 | 10.1 | 8.1 | All Other Current | 8.9 | 7.8 | 9.5 | 7.3 | 7.2 | 9.0 |
| 49.7 | 49.6 | 50.5 | Total Current | 87.5 | 48.7 | 52.8 | 47.6 | 50.2 | 49.3 |
| 7.8 | 7.9 | 7.7 | Long-Term Debt | 5.6 | 24.4 | 8.8 | 6.3 | 5.6 | 6.6 |
| .2 | .2 | .2 | Deferred Taxes | .0 | .2 | .0 | .2 | .2 | .3 |
| 6.2 | 5.5 | 7.0 | All Other Non-Current | 6.6 | 15.6 | 9.1 | 7.5 | 6.6 | 4.9 |
| 36.1 | 36.9 | 34.7 | Net Worth | .2 | 11.1 | 29.3 | 38.5 | 37.5 | 39.0 |
| 100.0 | 100.0 | 100.0 | Total Liabilities & Net Worth | 100.0 | 100.0 | 100.0 | 100.0 | 100.0 | 100.0 |
| | | | INCOME DATA | | | | | | |
| 100.0 | 100.0 | 100.0 | Net Sales | 100.0 | 100.0 | 100.0 | 100.0 | 100.0 | 100.0 |
| 28.3 | 28.2 | 28.4 | Gross Profit | 39.5 | 43.5 | 38.1 | 30.4 | 26.3 | 23.5 |
| 25.9 | 23.8 | 23.7 | Operating Expenses | 29.8 | 39.4 | 31.9 | 26.2 | 22.3 | 18.5 |
| 2.4 | 4.3 | 4.7 | Operating Profit | 9.7 | 4.0 | 6.2 | 4.2 | 4.1 | 5.0 |
| .5 | .4 | .4 | All Other Expenses (net) | 1.5 | 1.0 | .3 | .3 | .2 | .4 |
| 1.9 | 3.9 | 4.3 | Profit Before Taxes | 8.1 | 3.0 | 5.9 | 3.9 | 3.9 | 4.6 |
| | | | RATIOS | | | | | | |
| 2.6 | 2.6 | 2.5 | | 4.7 | 2.7 | 3.0 | 2.5 | 2.5 | 2.4 |
| 1.6 | 1.7 | 1.7 | Current | 1.3 | 1.6 | 1.7 | 1.7 | 1.8 | 1.5 |
| 1.2 | 1.2 | 1.3 | | .7 | 1.2 | 1.1 | 1.4 | 1.3 | 1.2 |
| 1.5 | 1.5 | 1.5 | | 2.0 | 1.1 | 1.6 | 1.6 | 1.5 | 1.3 |
| .8 | (417) .9 | 1.0 | Quick | .7 | .7 | 1.0 | 1.1 | 1.0 | .9 |
| .5 | .6 | .6 | | .7 | .4 | .4 | .7 | .7 | .6 |
| 31 12.0 | 34 10.8 | 28 12.9 | | 13 27.8 | 9 40.0 | 25 14.5 | 27 13.4 | 31 11.9 | 31 11.8 |
| 43 8.6 | 45 8.2 | 40 9.2 | Sales/Receivables | 23 15.8 | 37 9.9 | 36 10.2 | 36 10.2 | 41 8.9 | 44 8.3 |
| 60 6.1 | 56 6.5 | 54 6.7 | | 47 7.8 | 52 7.0 | 51 7.2 | 47 7.7 | 54 6.8 | 61 6.0 |
| 28 12.8 | 34 10.8 | 29 12.4 | | 46 8.0 | 43 8.4 | 4 84.0 | 20 18.5 | 29 12.7 | 31 11.9 |
| 55 6.7 | 57 6.4 | 56 6.5 | Cost of Sales/Inventory | 104 3.5 | 91 4.0 | 53 6.9 | 41 9.0 | 60 6.1 | 52 7.0 |
| 104 3.5 | 94 3.9 | 94 3.9 | | 228 1.6 | 152 2.4 | 104 3.5 | 79 4.6 | 96 3.8 | 83 4.4 |
| 22 16.6 | 22 16.4 | 18 20.0 | | 2 240.0 | 9 42.7 | 16 22.8 | 23 16.0 | 15 24.8 | 21 17.6 |
| 38 9.6 | 36 10.1 | 34 10.8 | Cost of Sales/Payables | 19 19.0 | 39 9.3 | 41 8.8 | 37 9.9 | 33 11.2 | 32 11.5 |
| 59 6.2 | 58 6.3 | 56 6.5 | | 43 8.5 | 83 4.4 | 63 5.8 | 56 6.5 | 62 5.9 | 49 7.4 |
| 5.0 | 5.0 | 5.4 | | 3.8 | 3.9 | 5.4 | 6.2 | 5.4 | 5.5 |
| 10.4 | 9.6 | 10.7 | Sales/Working Capital | 43.4 | 11.0 | 11.6 | 11.1 | 9.1 | 10.7 |
| 24.5 | 21.0 | 21.5 | | -3.1 | 36.9 | 66.6 | 18.2 | 17.0 | 21.8 |
| 16.5 | 22.8 | 28.4 | | | 7.9 | 22.3 | 27.5 | 37.4 | 27.5 |
| (360) 3.7 | (355) 6.3 | (357) 6.6 | EBIT/Interest | (25) 2.6 | (24) 6.7 | (51) 8.5 | (120) 6.4 | (129) 8.1 | |
| 1.2 | 2.1 | 2.3 | | | 1.0 | 1.6 | 2.3 | 2.5 | 3.0 |
| 14.5 | 23.5 | 17.0 | | | | | | 17.0 | 22.6 |
| (79) 2.3 | (76) 5.3 | (59) 4.6 | Net Profit + Depr., Dep., Amort./Cur. Mat. L/T/D | | | | | (15) 4.7 | (35) 4.7 |
| .8 | 1.3 | 1.4 | | | | | | 1.4 | 1.6 |
| .0 | .0 | .0 | | .0 | .1 | .0 | .0 | .0 | .1 |
| .2 | .1 | .1 | Fixed/Worth | .7 | .4 | .2 | .1 | .1 | .2 |
| .6 | .6 | .5 | | -.2 | UND | 1.1 | .5 | .4 | .5 |
| .9 | .8 | .9 | | .2 | 1.5 | .7 | .7 | .9 | .9 |
| 2.2 | 1.8 | 2.0 | Debt/Worth | 3.0 | 3.9 | 2.2 | 1.9 | 1.6 | 2.1 |
| 5.4 | 4.5 | 4.9 | | -3.2 | UND | 9.2 | 4.4 | 3.8 | 5.4 |
| 35.1 | 50.7 | 58.0 | | | 58.0 | 128.3 | 64.1 | 47.7 | 58.2 |
| (359) 15.3 | (372) 21.7 | (374) 23.5 | % Profit Before Taxes/Tangible Net Worth | | (24) 9.9 | (26) 31.7 | (59) 25.1 | (123) 20.6 | (135) 28.4 |
| 1.9 | 6.5 | 7.4 | | | -1.4 | 4.5 | 10.0 | 6.5 | 10.9 |
| 12.8 | 16.3 | 18.7 | | 36.2 | 14.4 | 36.0 | 19.4 | 18.4 | 18.3 |
| 4.2 | 7.2 | 8.3 | % Profit Before Taxes/Total Assets | 19.4 | 3.6 | 7.3 | 8.2 | 7.0 | 8.9 |
| .3 | 1.9 | 2.4 | | .3 | -.6 | 1.1 | 2.4 | 2.1 | 3.7 |
| 176.8 | 242.4 | 226.1 | | UND | 136.1 | 999.8 | 351.6 | 187.6 | 206.3 |
| 62.6 | 65.2 | 71.5 | Sales/Net Fixed Assets | 61.9 | 48.5 | 59.7 | 82.4 | 68.5 | 80.3 |
| 24.2 | 26.8 | 28.9 | | 22.2 | 13.0 | 18.0 | 38.1 | 29.5 | 30.5 |
| 3.7 | 3.8 | 4.0 | | 4.9 | 3.7 | 4.5 | 4.4 | 3.8 | 3.8 |
| 2.8 | 2.8 | 2.9 | Sales/Total Assets | 2.7 | 2.6 | 3.0 | 3.4 | 2.9 | 2.9 |
| 1.9 | 2.1 | 2.2 | | 1.3 | 1.7 | 2.1 | 2.4 | 2.2 | 2.2 |
| .2 | .2 | .2 | | | .3 | .1 | .2 | .2 | .2 |
| (306) .5 | (330) .4 | (314) .4 | % Depr., Dep., Amort./Sales | | (18) .8 | (17) .5 | (45) .5 | (97) .4 | (133) .4 |
| 1.1 | .9 | .8 | | | 1.3 | 1.1 | .9 | .7 | .7 |
| 1.8 | 1.3 | 1.1 | | | 4.2 | 1.8 | 1.3 | .9 | .8 |
| (120) 3.0 | (145) 2.7 | (155) 2.8 | % Officers', Directors' Owners' Comp/Sales | | (24) 5.6 | (17) 3.9 | (34) 2.7 | (46) 2.2 | (31) 1.2 |
| 6.0 | 5.1 | 5.0 | | | 10.8 | 4.8 | 4.9 | 3.5 | 3.5 |
| 19489850M | 21243650M | 19177116M | Net Sales ($) | 5903M | 63364M | 123534M | 482841M | 2200345M | 16301129M |
| 7508373M | 7626780M | 7152074M | Total Assets ($) | 2935M | 34758M | 46644M | 167008M | 849139M | 6051590M |

© RMA 2012

M = $ thousand    MM = $ million
See Pages 9 through 22 for Explanation of Ratios and Data

## Current Data Sorted by Assets        Comparative Historical Data

| | 0-500M | 500M-2MM | 2-10MM | 10-50MM | 50-100MM | 100-250MM | | ALL 4/1/07-3/31/08 | ALL 4/1/08-3/31/09 |
|---|---|---|---|---|---|---|---|---|---|
| | | | | | | | **Type of Statement** | | |
| | | 1 | 7 | 22 | 3 | | Unqualified | 33 | 41 |
| | 1 | 4 | 60 | 21 | 1 | | Reviewed | 61 | 81 |
| | 4 | 12 | 27 | 2 | | | Compiled | 39 | 38 |
| | 11 | 22 | 20 | 3 | | | Tax Returns | 37 | 47 |
| | 6 | 13 | 56 | 33 | 3 | 4 | Other | 86 | 107 |
| | 51 (4/1-9/30/11) | | 285 (10/1/11-3/31/12) | | | | | | |
| | 22 | 52 | 170 | 81 | 7 | 4 | **NUMBER OF STATEMENTS** | 256 | 314 |
| | % | % | % | % | % | % | **ASSETS** | % | % |
| | 14.2 | 10.1 | 7.8 | 6.3 | | | Cash & Equivalents | 7.0 | 6.8 |
| | 22.1 | 35.7 | 29.5 | 26.4 | | | Trade Receivables (net) | 28.9 | 28.5 |
| | 30.5 | 37.9 | 45.4 | 42.7 | | | Inventory | 43.9 | 44.9 |
| | 2.1 | 1.9 | 2.3 | 2.4 | | | All Other Current | 1.9 | 2.2 |
| | 68.8 | 85.6 | 85.1 | 77.8 | | | Total Current | 81.6 | 82.4 |
| | 14.4 | 9.5 | 9.2 | 12.2 | | | Fixed Assets (net) | 11.2 | 10.7 |
| | 6.6 | .5 | 1.4 | 4.5 | | | Intangibles (net) | 2.4 | 3.0 |
| | 10.2 | 4.4 | 4.3 | 5.5 | | | All Other Non-Current | 4.8 | 3.9 |
| | 100.0 | 100.0 | 100.0 | 100.0 | | | Total | 100.0 | 100.0 |
| | | | | | | | **LIABILITIES** | | |
| | 18.5 | 17.1 | 17.6 | 15.5 | | | Notes Payable-Short Term | 17.9 | 19.2 |
| | 7.0 | 2.8 | 1.8 | 1.3 | | | Cur. Mat.-L.T.D. | 5.2 | 2.2 |
| | 25.3 | 21.9 | 18.5 | 16.3 | | | Trade Payables | 19.4 | 16.7 |
| | .0 | .0 | .1 | .0 | | | Income Taxes Payable | .2 | .3 |
| | 19.6 | 5.7 | 7.6 | 6.5 | | | All Other Current | 7.2 | 7.8 |
| | 70.4 | 47.5 | 45.6 | 39.6 | | | Total Current | 49.9 | 46.3 |
| | 25.5 | 9.1 | 8.1 | 10.1 | | | Long-Term Debt | 10.3 | 9.0 |
| | .0 | .0 | .2 | .3 | | | Deferred Taxes | .2 | .2 |
| | 12.1 | 3.3 | 5.7 | 3.9 | | | All Other Non-Current | 5.2 | 4.2 |
| | -8.0 | 40.0 | 40.5 | 46.0 | | | Net Worth | 34.4 | 40.4 |
| | 100.0 | 100.0 | 100.0 | 100.0 | | | Total Liabilities & Net Worth | 100.0 | 100.0 |
| | | | | | | | **INCOME DATA** | | |
| | 100.0 | 100.0 | 100.0 | 100.0 | | | Net Sales | 100.0 | 100.0 |
| | 33.5 | 32.5 | 31.8 | 30.7 | | | Gross Profit | 31.7 | 31.4 |
| | 31.6 | 29.4 | 28.1 | 25.6 | | | Operating Expenses | 27.4 | 28.0 |
| | 1.9 | 3.1 | 3.7 | 5.1 | | | Operating Profit | 4.2 | 3.5 |
| | .2 | .4 | .3 | .5 | | | All Other Expenses (net) | .7 | .6 |
| | 1.7 | 2.7 | 3.4 | 4.5 | | | Profit Before Taxes | 3.6 | 2.9 |
| | | | | | | | **RATIOS** | | |
| | 1.6 | 3.1 | 3.1 | 3.7 | | | | 2.9 | 3.1 |
| | 1.0 | 2.0 | 2.0 | 2.2 | | | Current | 1.8 | 1.8 |
| | .6 | 1.3 | 1.3 | 1.4 | | | | 1.3 | 1.3 |
| | 1.2 | 1.9 | 1.3 | 1.5 | | | | 1.3 | 1.3 |
| | .6 | .9 | .8 | .8 | | | Quick | .7 | .8 |
| | .2 | .5 | .5 | .5 | | | | .5 | .4 |
| | 4  94.1 | 27  13.7 | 30  12.2 | 33  11.1 | | | | 30  12.2 | 28  13.2 |
| | 18  20.7 | 36  10.2 | 41  9.0 | 42  8.7 | | | Sales/Receivables | 38  9.6 | 37  9.9 |
| | 31  11.6 | 51  7.1 | 54  6.8 | 53  6.9 | | | | 51  7.2 | 48  7.6 |
| | 0  UND | 25  14.6 | 55  6.6 | 69  5.3 | | | | 61  6.0 | 55  6.7 |
| | 24  14.9 | 78  4.7 | 101  3.6 | 101  3.6 | | | Cost of Sales/Inventory | 97  3.8 | 95  3.9 |
| | 140  2.6 | 111  3.3 | 159  2.3 | 146  2.5 | | | | 128  2.8 | 144  2.5 |
| | 2  187.4 | 14  26.6 | 18  20.3 | 23  15.9 | | | | 20  18.2 | 16  23.0 |
| | 49  7.5 | 30  12.1 | 34  10.6 | 33  11.1 | | | Cost of Sales/Payables | 34  10.7 | 30  12.2 |
| | 76  4.8 | 47  7.8 | 53  6.9 | 46  7.9 | | | | 50  7.3 | 45  8.1 |
| | 8.8 | 4.8 | 3.9 | 3.9 | | | | 5.0 | 4.8 |
| | NM | 8.1 | 6.5 | 6.4 | | | Sales/Working Capital | 7.8 | 7.6 |
| | -64.5 | 15.1 | 13.1 | 10.9 | | | | 14.7 | 15.0 |
| | 3.3 | 14.3 | 10.4 | 16.3 | | | | 10.7 | 9.4 |
| | (14)  1.8 | (39)  3.4 | (149)  3.6 | (73)  5.0 | | | EBIT/Interest | (227)  3.3 | (271)  3.0 |
| | -14.7 | 1.1 | 1.8 | 2.1 | | | | 1.5 | 1.5 |
| | | | 8.8 | 50.4 | | | | 6.7 | 7.5 |
| | | (39)  3.1 | (21)  4.9 | | | | Net Profit + Depr., Dep., Amort./Cur. Mat. L/T/D | (63)  3.2 | (76)  4.0 |
| | | 1.1 | 1.8 | | | | | .9 | .8 |
| | .0 | .0 | .1 | .1 | | | | .1 | .1 |
| | .1 | .1 | .2 | .3 | | | Fixed/Worth | .2 | .2 |
| | 4.8 | .8 | .5 | .7 | | | | .6 | .5 |
| | 1.4 | .6 | .6 | .4 | | | | .7 | .6 |
| | 9.4 | 1.6 | 1.6 | 1.5 | | | Debt/Worth | 1.7 | 1.8 |
| | -4.5 | 4.6 | 3.1 | 3.9 | | | | 3.8 | 4.1 |
| | 173.3 | 31.6 | 36.6 | 33.9 | | | | 37.5 | 35.2 |
| | (15)  87.5 | (44)  10.3 | (158)  17.3 | (74)  13.9 | | | % Profit Before Taxes/Tangible Net Worth | (235)  16.0 | (289)  14.6 |
| | 14.9 | .3 | 5.0 | 6.2 | | | | 4.4 | 3.2 |
| | 26.2 | 16.0 | 13.6 | 13.6 | | | | 14.5 | 12.9 |
| | 6.8 | 4.4 | 4.8 | 5.1 | | | % Profit Before Taxes/Total Assets | 6.3 | 4.3 |
| | -7.6 | .2 | 1.5 | 1.8 | | | | 1.2 | .9 |
| | UND | 264.4 | 94.0 | 83.1 | | | | 92.8 | 96.0 |
| | 163.8 | 71.9 | 41.4 | 29.8 | | | Sales/Net Fixed Assets | 41.3 | 38.6 |
| | 21.0 | 28.9 | 19.3 | 12.7 | | | | 18.7 | 16.6 |
| | 4.9 | 4.2 | 3.1 | 2.8 | | | | 3.3 | 3.3 |
| | 3.8 | 3.1 | 2.5 | 2.1 | | | Sales/Total Assets | 2.6 | 2.6 |
| | 2.0 | 2.4 | 1.9 | 1.7 | | | | 2.1 | 2.0 |
| | .1 | .3 | .3 | .3 | | | | .3 | .4 |
| | (10)  .4 | (35)  .5 | (148)  .5 | (70)  .5 | | | % Depr., Dep., Amort./Sales | (216)  .6 | (264)  .6 |
| | .9 | 1.1 | 1.2 | 1.0 | | | | 1.1 | 1.1 |
| | 3.2 | 2.6 | 1.5 | 1.1 | | | | 2.1 | 2.1 |
| | (11)  6.4 | (32)  4.1 | (79)  3.0 | (18)  1.4 | | | % Officers', Directors' Owners' Comp/Sales | (116)  3.5 | (122)  3.8 |
| | 10.4 | 7.1 | 6.0 | 4.7 | | | | 7.3 | 7.0 |
| | 24707M | 194963M | 2078883M | 3890011M | 1000245M | 707281M | Net Sales ($) | 7640239M | 10309827M |
| | 6438M | 59891M | 843630M | 1771138M | 473539M | 491508M | Total Assets ($) | 3232255M | 4578978M |

M = $ thousand    MM = $ million
See Pages 9 through 22 for Explanation of Ratios and Data

## Comparative Historical Data | Current Data Sorted by Sales

| H1 | H2 | H3 | Type of Statement | 0-1MM | 1-3MM | 3-5MM | 5-10MM | 10-25MM | 25MM & OVER |
|---|---|---|---|---|---|---|---|---|---|
| 43 | 29 | 33 | Unqualified | | 1 | | 1 | 8 | 23 |
| 80 | 86 | 87 | Reviewed | 1 | 3 | 5 | 14 | 45 | 19 |
| 44 | 48 | 45 | Compiled | | 9 | 7 | 18 | 10 | 1 |
| 61 | 55 | 56 | Tax Returns | 4 | 16 | 8 | 15 | 11 | 2 |
| 117 | 118 | 115 | Other | 6 | 9 | 7 | 16 | 41 | 36 |
| 4/1/09-3/31/10 ALL | 4/1/10-3/31/11 ALL | 4/1/11-3/31/12 ALL | | 51 (4/1-9/30/11) | | | 285 (10/1/11-3/31/12) | | |
| 345 | 336 | 336 | NUMBER OF STATEMENTS | 11 | 38 | 27 | 64 | 115 | 81 |
| % | % | % | ASSETS | % | % | % | % | % | % |
| 7.9 | 7.9 | 8.2 | Cash & Equivalents | 19.7 | 11.7 | 7.9 | 10.1 | 6.6 | 5.8 |
| 27.1 | 29.1 | 28.9 | Trade Receivables (net) | 17.3 | 26.0 | 23.3 | 32.3 | 30.9 | 28.1 |
| 42.9 | 43.5 | 42.7 | Inventory | 33.4 | 36.1 | 50.1 | 41.5 | 44.7 | 42.8 |
| 3.0 | 2.1 | 2.2 | All Other Current | .2 | 4.4 | 3.2 | 2.1 | 1.4 | 2.4 |
| 80.8 | 82.6 | 82.0 | Total Current | 70.6 | 78.3 | 84.6 | 86.0 | 83.7 | 79.1 |
| 11.4 | 10.3 | 10.6 | Fixed Assets (net) | 8.7 | 12.3 | 11.5 | 8.1 | 11.0 | 11.1 |
| 2.9 | 2.4 | 2.3 | Intangibles (net) | 9.3 | 1.4 | 1.2 | 1.2 | 1.6 | 4.0 |
| 4.9 | 4.7 | 5.0 | All Other Non-Current | 11.4 | 8.0 | 2.7 | 4.7 | 3.7 | 5.8 |
| 100.0 | 100.0 | 100.0 | Total | 100.0 | 100.0 | 100.0 | 100.0 | 100.0 | 100.0 |
| | | | LIABILITIES | | | | | | |
| 17.2 | 16.7 | 17.2 | Notes Payable-Short Term | 15.7 | 20.3 | 18.2 | 13.5 | 18.9 | 16.2 |
| 2.8 | 2.1 | 2.2 | Cur. Mat.-L.T.D. | 3.7 | 4.8 | 2.1 | 2.4 | 1.6 | 1.3 |
| 17.4 | 18.6 | 18.8 | Trade Payables | 25.2 | 18.4 | 25.1 | 18.6 | 17.6 | 18.0 |
| .2 | .1 | .1 | Income Taxes Payable | .0 | .0 | .0 | .1 | .1 | .1 |
| 7.6 | 6.9 | 7.8 | All Other Current | 30.6 | 5.7 | 8.1 | 8.3 | 6.5 | 7.0 |
| 45.1 | 44.4 | 46.1 | Total Current | 75.2 | 49.2 | 53.5 | 43.0 | 44.8 | 42.6 |
| 9.2 | 8.8 | 9.8 | Long-Term Debt | 33.9 | 8.9 | 16.3 | 7.5 | 8.6 | 8.4 |
| .2 | .2 | .2 | Deferred Taxes | .0 | .0 | .2 | .0 | .2 | .3 |
| 5.0 | 5.8 | 5.4 | All Other Non-Current | 4.1 | 8.5 | 5.9 | 7.5 | 3.9 | 4.4 |
| 40.6 | 40.8 | 38.5 | Net Worth | -13.3 | 33.5 | 24.1 | 42.0 | 42.5 | 44.4 |
| 100.0 | 100.0 | 100.0 | Total Liabilities & Net Worth | 100.0 | 100.0 | 100.0 | 100.0 | 100.0 | 100.0 |
| | | | INCOME DATA | | | | | | |
| 100.0 | 100.0 | 100.0 | Net Sales | 100.0 | 100.0 | 100.0 | 100.0 | 100.0 | 100.0 |
| 31.2 | 31.9 | 31.4 | Gross Profit | 46.2 | 28.1 | 34.5 | 32.6 | 32.1 | 28.0 |
| 29.2 | 28.9 | 27.6 | Operating Expenses | 44.3 | 25.1 | 32.8 | 28.0 | 28.2 | 23.7 |
| 2.1 | 3.0 | 3.8 | Operating Profit | 1.9 | 3.0 | 1.7 | 4.7 | 3.9 | 4.3 |
| .4 | .5 | .4 | All Other Expenses (net) | 1.2 | -.1 | .5 | .6 | .2 | .7 |
| 1.7 | 2.5 | 3.4 | Profit Before Taxes | .7 | 3.1 | 1.2 | 4.0 | 3.7 | 3.6 |
| | | | RATIOS | | | | | | |
| 3.3 | 3.5 | 3.1 | Current | 1.6 | 4.1 | 2.5 | 3.3 | 3.0 | 3.4 |
| 2.0 | 2.0 | 2.0 | | 1.3 | 1.7 | 1.9 | 2.2 | 2.0 | 2.0 |
| 1.3 | 1.3 | 1.3 | | .9 | 1.0 | 1.1 | 1.4 | 1.3 | 1.3 |
| 1.5 | 1.6 | 1.4 | Quick | 1.5 | 1.5 | .8 | 1.5 | 1.3 | 1.4 |
| (344) .7 | .8 | .8 | | .6 | .7 | .5 | 1.0 | .8 | .8 |
| .5 | .5 | .5 | | .1 | .4 | .4 | .6 | .5 | .5 |
| 29 12.8 | 30 12.0 | 29 12.6 | Sales/Receivables | 0 UND | 20 18.0 | 22 16.4 | 31 11.8 | 30 12.1 | 33 11.1 |
| 38 9.5 | 40 9.1 | 39 9.3 | | 19 19.6 | 29 12.6 | 35 10.5 | 41 8.9 | 41 9.0 | 42 8.7 |
| 50 7.2 | 54 6.8 | 52 7.0 | | 36 10.0 | 48 7.6 | 51 7.2 | 54 6.8 | 54 6.8 | 52 7.0 |
| 55 6.7 | 54 6.8 | 52 7.0 | Cost of Sales/Inventory | 0 UND | 19 19.4 | 70 5.2 | 49 7.4 | 54 6.7 | 63 5.8 |
| 95 3.8 | 96 3.8 | 96 3.8 | | 76 4.8 | 83 4.4 | 140 2.6 | 83 4.4 | 99 3.7 | 101 3.6 |
| 142 2.6 | 148 2.5 | 152 2.4 | | 261 1.4 | 140 2.6 | 228 1.6 | 130 2.8 | 159 2.3 | 135 2.7 |
| 18 20.0 | 20 17.9 | 19 19.7 | Cost of Sales/Payables | 38 9.6 | 3 137.2 | 18 19.8 | 19 19.7 | 18 20.3 | 24 14.9 |
| 32 11.3 | 34 10.8 | 33 11.0 | | 66 5.5 | 23 15.9 | 45 8.2 | 31 11.8 | 33 11.2 | 33 11.0 |
| 48 7.6 | 50 7.3 | 50 7.3 | | 104 3.5 | 52 7.0 | 76 4.8 | 47 7.8 | 49 7.4 | 46 7.9 |
| 4.3 | 4.1 | 4.0 | Sales/Working Capital | 4.6 | 3.8 | 4.7 | 3.7 | 4.2 | 4.0 |
| 6.4 | 6.5 | 7.4 | | 14.1 | 9.4 | 7.7 | 5.9 | 6.9 | 7.7 |
| 14.3 | 12.6 | 14.1 | | -68.6 | -930.8 | 21.2 | 11.4 | 13.5 | 12.7 |
| 9.6 | 11.9 | 10.5 | EBIT/Interest | | 6.7 | 7.6 | 9.8 | 11.8 | 18.1 |
| (303) 2.8 | (290) 3.4 | (284) 3.6 | | (23) 3.3 | (25) 2.7 | (54) 3.2 | (102) 4.4 | (73) 3.9 | |
| .9 | 1.2 | 1.7 | | .2 | 1.1 | 1.9 | 1.9 | 1.5 | |
| 6.7 | 4.3 | 12.6 | Net Profit + Depr., Dep., Amort./Cur. Mat. L/T/D | | | | | 9.6 | 17.8 |
| (82) 2.6 | (72) 1.8 | (66) 3.3 | | | | | (33) 3.1 | (23) 4.9 | |
| .7 | .4 | 1.5 | | | | | 1.4 | 1.7 | |
| .1 | .1 | .1 | Fixed/Worth | .0 | .0 | .1 | .0 | .1 | .1 |
| .2 | .2 | .2 | | .0 | .1 | .3 | .1 | .2 | .3 |
| .6 | .6 | .6 | | .8 | 1.9 | 1.6 | .3 | .5 | .7 |
| .6 | .5 | .6 | Debt/Worth | .9 | .5 | .9 | .7 | .6 | .4 |
| 1.4 | 1.5 | 1.8 | | 2.8 | 2.5 | 2.3 | 1.6 | 1.4 | 1.6 |
| 4.0 | 3.7 | 4.1 | | -9.4 | 21.0 | 9.4 | 3.1 | 3.0 | 4.1 |
| 25.5 | 30.9 | 36.3 | % Profit Before Taxes/Tangible Net Worth | | 88.1 | 21.4 | 38.0 | 38.9 | 29.4 |
| (316) 8.2 | (305) 11.1 | (302) 15.4 | | (32) 19.1 | (21) 12.7 | (58) 16.7 | (109) 17.2 | (74) 13.6 | |
| -.2 | 1.8 | 4.8 | | 3.7 | 4.0 | 3.9 | 5.0 | 4.7 | |
| 11.2 | 11.9 | 13.9 | % Profit Before Taxes/Total Assets | 23.3 | 17.8 | 7.8 | 13.9 | 14.7 | 12.3 |
| 3.3 | 3.8 | 5.0 | | 7.2 | 4.1 | 4.1 | 4.4 | 6.3 | 4.9 |
| -.4 | .2 | 1.4 | | -8.5 | -.5 | .4 | 1.8 | 1.6 | 1.1 |
| 84.2 | 94.8 | 103.0 | Sales/Net Fixed Assets | UND | 999.8 | 62.7 | 114.1 | 80.0 | 83.1 |
| 36.4 | 40.7 | 42.4 | | 270.7 | 151.6 | 27.6 | 49.9 | 37.2 | 39.0 |
| 16.7 | 18.2 | 18.4 | | 13.1 | 25.2 | 15.6 | 27.1 | 17.2 | 14.4 |
| 3.2 | 3.1 | 3.2 | Sales/Total Assets | 3.2 | 4.0 | 3.7 | 3.5 | 3.2 | 2.9 |
| 2.4 | 2.4 | 2.5 | | 1.8 | 2.7 | 2.3 | 2.6 | 2.6 | 2.3 |
| 1.8 | 1.8 | 1.9 | | 1.3 | 1.9 | 1.5 | 1.8 | 1.9 | 1.8 |
| .4 | .3 | .3 | % Depr., Dep., Amort./Sales | | .1 | .4 | .3 | .3 | .3 |
| (292) .7 | (295) .6 | (273) .5 | | (23) .5 | (23) .6 | (52) .4 | (102) .6 | (70) .5 | |
| 1.3 | 1.1 | 1.1 | | 1.1 | 1.3 | .9 | 1.2 | 1.0 | |
| 2.0 | 1.8 | 1.7 | % Officers', Directors' Owners' Comp/Sales | | 3.1 | 2.5 | 1.9 | 1.2 | 1.0 |
| (152) 3.9 | (156) 3.6 | (141) 3.5 | | (20) 4.7 | (13) 6.4 | (37) 3.8 | (52) 2.8 | (15) 1.2 | |
| 6.8 | 6.5 | 6.4 | | 7.0 | 10.5 | 6.3 | 5.0 | 3.9 | |
| 9170963M | 7595038M | 7896090M | Net Sales ($) | 6274M | 77032M | 107552M | 460990M | 1838525M | 5405717M |
| 4230835M | 3298176M | 3646144M | Total Assets ($) | 3721M | 37900M | 53623M | 202497M | 784965M | 2563438M |

© RMA 2012        M = $ thousand    MM = $ million
See Pages 9 through 22 for Explanation of Ratios and Data

## Current Data Sorted by Assets

## Comparative Historical Data

| | | | | | | Type of Statement | | |
|---|---|---|---|---|---|---|---|---|
| | | 4 | 22 | 9 | 3 | Unqualified | 38 | 36 |
| | 7 | 57 | 27 | | 1 | Reviewed | 101 | 123 |
| 2 | 25 | 33 | 3 | 1 | | Compiled | 85 | 74 |
| 9 | 25 | 27 | 1 | | | Tax Returns | 37 | 50 |
| 7 | 22 | 54 | 42 | 5 | 4 | Other | 100 | 104 |
| | 56 (4/1-9/30/11) | | 334 (10/1/11-3/31/12) | | | | 4/1/07-3/31/08 ALL | 4/1/08-3/31/09 ALL |
| 0-500M | 500M-2MM | 2-10MM | 10-50MM | 50-100MM | 100-250MM | | | |
| 18 | 79 | 175 | 95 | 15 | 8 | NUMBER OF STATEMENTS | 361 | 387 |
| % | % | % | % | % | % | ASSETS | % | % |
| 8.8 | 10.5 | 6.9 | 4.8 | 6.5 | | Cash & Equivalents | 7.0 | 7.2 |
| 29.5 | 29.2 | 32.2 | 31.7 | 29.3 | | Trade Receivables (net) | 33.2 | 31.3 |
| 40.6 | 38.7 | 40.8 | 41.9 | 31.0 | | Inventory | 39.7 | 40.4 |
| 3.0 | 1.5 | 2.1 | 2.6 | 4.8 | | All Other Current | 2.7 | 2.5 |
| 81.9 | 79.8 | 82.0 | 80.9 | 71.6 | | Total Current | 82.7 | 81.3 |
| 9.5 | 10.7 | 10.2 | 12.8 | 17.0 | | Fixed Assets (net) | 11.2 | 11.1 |
| 4.3 | 4.8 | 2.7 | 1.9 | 2.2 | | Intangibles (net) | 1.8 | 2.1 |
| 4.3 | 4.8 | 5.1 | 4.4 | 9.2 | | All Other Non-Current | 4.4 | 5.5 |
| 100.0 | 100.0 | 100.0 | 100.0 | 100.0 | | Total | 100.0 | 100.0 |
| | | | | | | LIABILITIES | | |
| 15.8 | 12.9 | 13.1 | 20.8 | 16.6 | | Notes Payable-Short Term | 16.9 | 17.0 |
| 3.1 | 1.6 | 2.2 | 2.4 | 1.7 | | Cur. Mat.-L.T.D. | 2.2 | 2.6 |
| 23.3 | 18.1 | 21.0 | 17.8 | 10.6 | | Trade Payables | 20.3 | 18.9 |
| .1 | .3 | .1 | .2 | .2 | | Income Taxes Payable | .3 | .2 |
| 15.4 | 8.9 | 7.9 | 6.1 | 12.1 | | All Other Current | 7.8 | 8.8 |
| 57.7 | 41.8 | 44.3 | 47.5 | 41.2 | | Total Current | 47.3 | 47.5 |
| 15.6 | 10.1 | 6.1 | 7.7 | 5.6 | | Long-Term Debt | 8.1 | 9.0 |
| .0 | .1 | .2 | .7 | .5 | | Deferred Taxes | .2 | .4 |
| 7.1 | 4.4 | 5.7 | 5.7 | 7.4 | | All Other Non-Current | 4.3 | 4.2 |
| 19.6 | 43.6 | 43.8 | 38.4 | 45.3 | | Net Worth | 40.1 | 38.8 |
| 100.0 | 100.0 | 100.0 | 100.0 | 100.0 | | Total Liabilities & Net Worth | 100.0 | 100.0 |
| | | | | | | INCOME DATA | | |
| 100.0 | 100.0 | 100.0 | 100.0 | 100.0 | | Net Sales | 100.0 | 100.0 |
| 37.2 | 36.3 | 27.4 | 26.4 | 31.0 | | Gross Profit | 29.2 | 28.8 |
| 33.9 | 34.1 | 24.7 | 23.0 | 27.4 | | Operating Expenses | 25.6 | 26.4 |
| 3.3 | 2.1 | 2.7 | 3.4 | 3.6 | | Operating Profit | 3.6 | 2.5 |
| .6 | .1 | .0 | .4 | .5 | | All Other Expenses (net) | .2 | .3 |
| 2.7 | 2.1 | 2.7 | 3.0 | 3.1 | | Profit Before Taxes | 3.4 | 2.1 |
| | | | | | | RATIOS | | |
| 5.1 | 3.6 | 2.8 | 2.4 | 3.5 | | | 2.7 | 2.6 |
| 1.4 | 2.3 | 2.0 | 1.6 | 2.1 | Current | 1.8 | 1.7 |
| 1.1 | 1.5 | 1.4 | 1.3 | 1.4 | | 1.4 | 1.3 |
| 1.6 | 1.8 | 1.5 | 1.2 | 1.8 | | | 1.4 | 1.3 |
| .7 | 1.0 | .9 | .7 | 1.2 | Quick | .8 | .8 |
| .2 | .5 | .6 | .7 | .7 | | .5 | .5 |
| 10 38.2 | 23 16.2 | 32 11.5 | 36 10.0 | 43 8.4 | | | 32 11.4 | 29 12.4 |
| 26 14.0 | 33 11.0 | 40 9.2 | 45 8.2 | 56 6.5 | Sales/Receivables | 40 9.0 | 38 9.7 |
| 44 8.3 | 42 8.6 | 51 7.1 | 63 5.8 | 62 5.9 | | 51 7.2 | 48 7.6 |
| 23 16.1 | 34 10.6 | 47 7.7 | 61 6.0 | 64 5.7 | | 51 7.2 | 46 8.0 |
| 66 5.5 | 70 5.2 | 74 4.9 | 91 4.0 | 87 4.2 | Cost of Sales/Inventory | 73 5.0 | 76 4.8 |
| 122 3.0 | 140 2.6 | 111 3.3 | 118 3.1 | 107 3.4 | | 102 3.6 | 103 3.6 |
| 10 38.0 | 19 19.5 | 24 15.3 | 26 14.2 | 14 25.4 | | 21 17.1 | 19 19.5 |
| 40 9.1 | 31 11.6 | 33 11.2 | 34 10.6 | 31 11.7 | Cost of Sales/Payables | 33 11.1 | 27 13.3 |
| 66 5.5 | 50 7.3 | 52 7.0 | 47 7.8 | 37 9.9 | | 46 7.9 | 44 8.2 |
| 4.8 | 5.2 | 4.2 | 4.8 | 3.5 | | | 5.0 | 5.1 |
| 14.9 | 7.4 | 7.2 | 7.8 | 5.5 | Sales/Working Capital | 8.2 | 9.6 |
| NM | 13.4 | 14.3 | 13.7 | 9.2 | | 15.3 | 15.8 |
| 5.1 | 18.7 | 16.5 | 12.2 | 7.5 | | | 10.9 | 9.8 |
| (12) 1.4 | (65) 4.3 | (162) 4.8 | (89) 4.9 | (12) 5.1 | EBIT/Interest | (328) 4.0 | (350) 3.4 |
| -.1 | 1.3 | 1.9 | 1.9 | 2.3 | | 1.6 | 1.2 |
| | | 18.2 | 8.3 | | | | 7.4 | 6.0 |
| | | (41) 4.0 | (29) 3.7 | | | Net Profit + Depr., Dep., Amort./Cur. Mat. L/T/D | (114) 3.5 | (104) 2.5 |
| | | 1.1 | 1.5 | | | | 1.6 | 1.2 |
| .0 | .1 | .1 | .1 | .2 | | | .1 | .1 |
| .3 | .2 | .2 | .2 | .4 | Fixed/Worth | .2 | .2 |
| NM | .5 | .4 | .6 | .5 | | .5 | .5 |
| .9 | .4 | .6 | .9 | .6 | | | .7 | .8 |
| 3.5 | 1.3 | 1.4 | 1.8 | 1.4 | Debt/Worth | 1.4 | 1.5 |
| -7.6 | 4.8 | 3.0 | 3.8 | 2.1 | | 3.3 | 3.2 |
| 55.8 | 27.4 | 35.4 | 33.9 | 20.2 | | | 34.2 | 27.4 |
| (13) 9.0 | (69) 10.0 | (167) 13.7 | (89) 14.3 | (14) 11.0 | % Profit Before Taxes/Tangible Net Worth | (336) 20.8 | (353) 15.1 |
| -10.2 | 3.0 | 4.2 | 6.4 | 4.1 | | 6.6 | 2.4 |
| 12.2 | 11.9 | 12.8 | 9.5 | 8.1 | | | 14.8 | 11.8 |
| 5.4 | 4.9 | 6.5 | 5.7 | 5.0 | % Profit Before Taxes/Total Assets | 7.4 | 5.2 |
| -3.2 | .7 | 1.6 | 1.6 | 1.4 | | 2.1 | .5 |
| UND | 133.8 | 94.9 | 57.6 | 22.9 | | | 65.6 | 74.4 |
| 60.7 | 59.4 | 45.6 | 28.4 | 14.1 | Sales/Net Fixed Assets | 36.3 | 38.8 |
| 12.0 | 22.3 | 21.7 | 12.9 | 7.4 | | 19.8 | 19.2 |
| 3.9 | 4.2 | 3.4 | 2.8 | 2.3 | | | 3.5 | 3.6 |
| 2.9 | 3.1 | 2.7 | 2.4 | 2.0 | Sales/Total Assets | 2.8 | 2.9 |
| 2.1 | 2.1 | 1.9 | 2.0 | 1.6 | | 2.2 | 2.2 |
| | .3 | .3 | .4 | .5 | | | .4 | .4 |
| | (55) .6 | (145) .6 | (89) .6 | (14) 1.1 | % Depr., Dep., Amort./Sales | (315) .7 | (330) .6 |
| | 1.1 | 1.0 | .9 | 1.8 | | 1.0 | 1.0 |
| | 2.5 | 1.6 | .8 | | | | 1.5 | 1.5 |
| | (46) 4.5 | (87) 2.4 | (24) | | | % Officers', Directors' Owners' Comp/Sales | (152) 2.6 | (164) 2.8 |
| | 7.4 | 3.9 | 2.5 | | | | 5.5 | 5.6 |
| 21567M | 314697M | 2400673M | 5000544M | 1815057M | 2059681M | Net Sales ($) | 11999810M | 14160590M |
| 6427M | 97313M | 900721M | 2117952M | 938854M | 1150914M | Total Assets ($) | 4461018M | 5326975M |

M = $ thousand    MM = $ million
See Pages 9 through 22 for Explanation of Ratios and Data

## Comparative Historical Data | Current Data Sorted by Sales

| | | | Type of Statement | | | | | | |
|---|---|---|---|---|---|---|---|---|---|
| 42 | 29 | 38 | Unqualified | | 1 | 5 | 1 | 5 | 32 |
| 102 | 106 | 92 | Reviewed | | 11 | 10 | 17 | 35 | 34 |
| 59 | 60 | 64 | Compiled | 1 | 13 | 16 | 19 | 19 | 4 |
| 60 | 64 | 62 | Tax Returns | 4 | 15 | 7 | 19 | 9 | 1 |
| 137 | 118 | 134 | Other | 4 | | | 16 | 43 | 49 |
| 4/1/09-3/31/10 ALL | 4/1/10-3/31/11 ALL | 4/1/11-3/31/12 ALL | | | 56 (4/1-9/30/11) | | 334 (10/1/11-3/31/12) | | |
| | | | | 0-1MM | 1-3MM | 3-5MM | 5-10MM | 10-25MM | 25MM & OVER |
| 400 | 377 | 390 | **NUMBER OF STATEMENTS** | 9 | 40 | 38 | 72 | 111 | 120 |
| % | % | % | **ASSETS** | % | % | % | % | % | % |
| 7.6 | 7.6 | 7.1 | Cash & Equivalents | | 7.6 | 11.5 | 10.6 | 4.4 | 5.4 |
| 30.3 | 31.6 | 31.1 | Trade Receivables (net) | | 20.1 | 28.8 | 31.9 | 33.4 | 33.1 |
| 40.5 | 38.7 | 40.1 | Inventory | | 44.0 | 38.2 | 39.3 | 40.9 | 40.1 |
| 2.7 | 2.2 | 2.2 | All Other Current | | 2.4 | 1.9 | 1.1 | 2.8 | 2.6 |
| 81.1 | 80.2 | 80.5 | Total Current | | 74.0 | 80.4 | 82.8 | 81.5 | 81.2 |
| 11.5 | 12.1 | 11.2 | Fixed Assets (net) | | 16.4 | 8.2 | 9.0 | 12.0 | 10.9 |
| 1.8 | 2.1 | 3.3 | Intangibles (net) | | 3.7 | 7.5 | 2.5 | 2.2 | 3.1 |
| 5.6 | 5.7 | 4.9 | All Other Non-Current | | 5.9 | 4.0 | 5.7 | 4.3 | 4.8 |
| 100.0 | 100.0 | 100.0 | Total | | 100.0 | 100.0 | 100.0 | 100.0 | 100.0 |
| | | | **LIABILITIES** | | | | | | |
| 17.4 | 15.2 | 15.2 | Notes Payable-Short Term | | 15.1 | 11.9 | 10.2 | 16.6 | 17.5 |
| 2.1 | 2.1 | 2.1 | Cur. Mat.-L.T.D. | | 1.5 | 4.2 | 2.0 | 1.4 | 2.2 |
| 19.1 | 19.1 | 19.2 | Trade Payables | | 16.8 | 16.7 | 22.5 | 19.8 | 18.4 |
| .2 | .2 | .2 | Income Taxes Payable | | .5 | .1 | .2 | .1 | .2 |
| 8.6 | 7.9 | 8.2 | All Other Current | | 15.0 | 5.6 | 8.1 | 7.8 | 7.6 |
| 47.3 | 44.5 | 44.8 | Total Current | | 48.8 | 38.5 | 43.0 | 45.6 | 45.9 |
| 8.4 | 9.1 | 8.0 | Long-Term Debt | | 15.3 | 12.1 | 4.5 | 7.4 | 6.5 |
| .3 | .3 | .3 | Deferred Taxes | | .1 | .3 | .3 | .1 | .7 |
| 5.0 | 6.2 | 5.5 | All Other Non-Current | | 6.4 | 4.8 | 4.5 | 5.6 | 5.4 |
| 39.0 | 40.0 | 41.4 | Net Worth | | 29.4 | 44.2 | 47.6 | 41.3 | 41.5 |
| 100.0 | 100.0 | 100.0 | Total Liabilties & Net Worth | | 100.0 | 100.0 | 100.0 | 100.0 | 100.0 |
| | | | **INCOME DATA** | | | | | | |
| 100.0 | 100.0 | 100.0 | Net Sales | | 100.0 | 100.0 | 100.0 | 100.0 | 100.0 |
| 30.2 | 30.4 | 29.5 | Gross Profit | | 40.3 | 35.3 | 27.2 | 27.9 | 25.8 |
| 29.1 | 28.2 | 26.7 | Operating Expenses | | 39.0 | 32.1 | 26.4 | 24.2 | 22.5 |
| 1.1 | 2.2 | 2.8 | Operating Profit | | 1.4 | 3.2 | .8 | 3.7 | 3.4 |
| .4 | .2 | .2 | All Other Expenses (net) | | .0 | .3 | .1 | .0 | .3 |
| .7 | 2.0 | 2.7 | Profit Before Taxes | | 1.4 | 2.9 | .8 | 3.6 | 3.0 |
| | | | **RATIOS** | | | | | | |
| 2.6 | 2.8 | 2.9 | | | 3.3 | 4.5 | 3.1 | 2.4 | 2.8 |
| 1.8 | 1.9 | 1.8 | Current | | 1.7 | 2.3 | 2.0 | 1.9 | 1.7 |
| 1.3 | 1.4 | 1.3 | | | 1.2 | 1.6 | 1.4 | 1.3 | 1.4 |
| 1.4 | 1.5 | 1.5 | | | 1.3 | 2.0 | 1.8 | 1.3 | 1.5 |
| .8 | .9 | .8 | Quick | | .7 | 1.0 | 1.0 | .8 | .8 |
| .5 | .6 | .5 | | | .3 | .6 | .6 | .5 | .6 |

| | | | | | | | | | | | | | | | |
|---|---|---|---|---|---|---|---|---|---|---|---|---|---|---|---|
| 31 | 11.6 | 34 | 10.8 | 31 | 11.9 | Sales/Receivables | 21 | 17.5 | 27 | 13.3 | 29 | 12.4 | 32 | 11.5 | 36 | 10.0 |
| 41 | 8.9 | 43 | 8.6 | 41 | 9.0 | | 30 | 12.3 | 35 | 10.5 | 38 | 9.6 | 40 | 9.2 | 45 | 8.2 |
| 52 | 7.0 | 54 | 6.8 | 53 | 6.9 | | 43 | 8.5 | 48 | 7.6 | 49 | 7.5 | 55 | 6.6 | 57 | 6.4 |
| 52 | 7.0 | 50 | 7.2 | 49 | 7.5 | Cost of Sales/Inventory | 59 | 6.2 | 43 | 8.4 | 42 | 8.7 | 47 | 7.7 | 51 | 7.2 |
| 81 | 4.5 | 81 | 4.5 | 79 | 4.6 | | 122 | 3.0 | 74 | 4.9 | 73 | 5.0 | 79 | 4.6 | 81 | 4.5 |
| 121 | 3.0 | 114 | 3.2 | 118 | 3.1 | | 192 | 1.9 | 140 | 2.6 | 107 | 3.4 | 114 | 3.2 | 104 | 3.5 |
| 22 | 16.6 | 24 | 15.3 | 23 | 15.8 | Cost of Sales/Payables | 24 | 15.3 | 17 | 21.4 | 21 | 17.1 | 22 | 16.6 | 25 | 14.8 |
| 32 | 11.4 | 33 | 11.1 | 33 | 11.2 | | 36 | 10.0 | 36 | 10.0 | 33 | 10.9 | 32 | 11.4 | 31 | 11.8 |
| 46 | 7.9 | 51 | 7.2 | 49 | 7.5 | | 64 | 5.7 | 54 | 6.8 | 56 | 6.5 | 47 | 7.7 | 40 | 9.1 |

| | | | | | | | | | |
|---|---|---|---|---|---|---|---|---|---|
| 4.8 | 4.5 | 4.6 | Sales/Working Capital | | 4.5 | 4.1 | 4.5 | 4.8 | 5.0 |
| 7.9 | 7.3 | 7.4 | | | 6.9 | 6.8 | 7.7 | 7.2 | 7.7 |
| 16.7 | 12.7 | 14.3 | | | 30.8 | 11.6 | 14.3 | 15.3 | 11.6 |

| | | | | | | | | | | | |
|---|---|---|---|---|---|---|---|---|---|---|---|
| | 9.8 | | 11.0 | | 14.5 | EBIT/Interest | | 12.5 | | 12.6 | | 15.8 | | 15.4 | | 14.5 |

| Hist count | Hist val | Hist count | Hist val | Hist count | Hist val | Ratio | Cur count | Cur val | Cur count | Cur val | Cur count | Cur val | Cur count | Cur val |
|---|---|---|---|---|---|---|---|---|---|---|---|---|---|---|
| | 9.8 | | 11.0 | | 14.5 | EBIT/Interest | | 12.5 | | 12.6 | | 15.8 | 15.4 | 14.5 |
| (361) | 2.4 | (335) | 3.5 | (348) | 4.7 | | (34) 2.4 | (31) 3.5 | (62) 4.8 | (104) 4.8 | (112) 5.9 |
| | -.3 | | 1.2 | | 1.7 | | 1.2 | 1.6 | .7 | 2.1 | 2.2 |
| | 7.0 | | 8.1 | | 9.0 | Net Profit + Depr., Dep., Amort./Cur. Mat. L/T/D | | 11.5 | 7.8 | 11.8 |
| (98) | 2.2 | (94) | 2.8 | (88) | 3.4 | | (14) 2.6 | (31) 3.3 | (38) 5.0 |
| | .4 | | .9 | | 1.4 | | .6 | .9 | 1.9 |
| | .1 | | .1 | | .1 | Fixed/Worth | | .1 | .1 | .1 | .1 | .1 |
| | .2 | | .2 | | .2 | | .4 | .2 | .1 | .2 | .2 |
| | .6 | | .5 | | .5 | | 11.8 | .6 | .3 | .5 | .5 |
| | .7 | | .6 | | .7 | Debt/Worth | | 1.1 | .4 | .5 | .7 | .8 |
| | 1.5 | | 1.4 | | 1.5 | | 1.9 | 1.7 | 1.2 | 1.6 | 1.5 |
| | 3.4 | | 3.0 | | 3.6 | | NM | 5.6 | 2.3 | 3.1 | 3.0 |
| | 19.3 | | 21.1 | | 31.9 | % Profit Before Taxes/Tangible Net Worth | | 27.8 | 23.4 | 27.4 | 41.2 | 30.4 |
| (360) | 6.4 | (340) | 9.0 | (358) | 13.3 | | (30) 8.9 | (33) 9.9 | (69) 10.7 | (108) 16.4 | (111) 13.5 |
| | -4.1 | | 2.0 | | 4.6 | | 3.0 | 2.8 | -.7 | 4.7 | 6.6 |
| | 8.4 | | 8.9 | | 11.4 | % Profit Before Taxes/Total Assets | | 11.4 | 11.1 | 11.1 | 12.6 | 10.7 |
| | 2.4 | | 3.8 | | 5.4 | | 3.1 | 5.8 | 4.2 | 7.1 | 6.1 |
| | -3.2 | | .7 | | 1.4 | | .2 | 1.2 | -.1 | 2.1 | 1.8 |
| | 70.9 | | 74.8 | | 89.7 | Sales/Net Fixed Assets | | 73.3 | 144.8 | 126.8 | 103.9 | 57.8 |
| | 37.0 | | 34.0 | | 37.8 | | 28.6 | 45.0 | 58.9 | 41.5 | 30.5 |
| | 16.1 | | 15.1 | | 15.3 | | 7.0 | 19.8 | 24.4 | 17.2 | 15.2 |
| | 3.3 | | 3.2 | | 3.3 | Sales/Total Assets | | 2.9 | 3.7 | 3.9 | 3.4 | 3.0 |
| | 2.6 | | 2.5 | | 2.6 | | 2.3 | 2.5 | 2.7 | 2.7 | 2.5 |
| | 2.0 | | 2.0 | | 1.9 | | 1.5 | 1.8 | 2.0 | 1.9 | 2.1 |
| | .4 | | .4 | | .3 | % Depr., Dep., Amort./Sales | | .6 | .3 | .2 | .3 | .4 |
| (339) | .7 | (329) | .7 | (318) | .6 | | (29) 1.1 | (26) .5 | (54) .5 | (92) .6 | (112) .6 |
| | 1.2 | | 1.1 | | 1.1 | | 2.2 | .9 | 1.1 | 1.0 | .9 |
| | 1.5 | | 1.5 | | 1.5 | % Officers', Directors' Owners' Comp/Sales | | 3.5 | 1.6 | 2.0 | 1.3 | .8 |
| (162) | 3.1 | (157) | 3.4 | (167) | 2.6 | | (17) 4.6 | (23) 4.7 | (46) 2.9 | (49) 2.6 | (29) 1.3 |
| | 6.3 | | 6.4 | | 4.7 | | 12.2 | 8.0 | 4.7 | 3.7 | 2.2 |
| 11497174M | 11539742M | 11612219M | Net Sales ($) | 6103M | 73909M | 148964M | 523149M | 1812010M | 9048084M |
| 4840325M | 4803773M | 5212181M | Total Assets ($) | 3272M | 41846M | 66029M | 255777M | 792248M | 4053009M |

© RMA 2012          M = $ thousand    MM = $ million
See Pages 9 through 22 for Explanation of Ratios and Data

## Current Data Sorted by Assets          Comparative Historical Data

| 0-500M | 500M-2MM | 2-10MM | 10-50MM | 50-100MM | 100-250MM | Type of Statement | 4/1/07-3/31/08 ALL | 4/1/08-3/31/09 ALL |
|---|---|---|---|---|---|---|---|---|
| 1 | | 1 | 22 | 7 | 3 | Unqualified | 36 | 37 |
| | 7 | 40 | 27 | 1 | 1 | Reviewed | 64 | 80 |
| | 14 | 19 | 4 | 1 | | Compiled | 39 | 36 |
| 8 | 16 | 12 | 1 | | | Tax Returns | 25 | 41 |
| 2 | 16 | 43 | 26 | 6 | 3 | Other | 70 | 82 |
| | 36 (4/1-9/30/11) | | 244 (10/1/11-3/31/12) | | | | | |
| 11 | 53 | 115 | 80 | 15 | 6 | NUMBER OF STATEMENTS | 234 | 276 |
| % | % | % | % | % | % | **ASSETS** | % | % |
| 11.1 | 11.6 | 7.6 | 4.7 | 6.3 | | Cash & Equivalents | 5.9 | 6.6 |
| 47.4 | 35.6 | 39.6 | 31.2 | 30.2 | | Trade Receivables (net) | 37.7 | 37.1 |
| 5.3 | 36.9 | 31.2 | 44.7 | 39.9 | | Inventory | 38.1 | 37.1 |
| 5.1 | 1.4 | 4.2 | 2.7 | 3.0 | | All Other Current | 2.9 | 2.7 |
| 68.9 | 85.6 | 82.7 | 83.3 | 79.3 | | Total Current | 84.6 | 83.4 |
| 23.1 | 6.9 | 8.6 | 9.0 | 13.6 | | Fixed Assets (net) | 9.7 | 9.3 |
| .8 | 1.7 | 2.7 | 3.3 | 3.3 | | Intangibles (net) | 1.6 | 2.0 |
| 7.1 | 5.9 | 6.0 | 4.5 | 3.8 | | All Other Non-Current | 4.1 | 5.4 |
| 100.0 | 100.0 | 100.0 | 100.0 | 100.0 | | Total | 100.0 | 100.0 |
| | | | | | | **LIABILITIES** | | |
| 37.1 | 16.2 | 12.9 | 19.3 | 16.4 | | Notes Payable-Short Term | 17.9 | 20.1 |
| 2.7 | 2.1 | 1.9 | 1.1 | .3 | | Cur. Mat.-L.T.D. | 1.6 | 2.0 |
| 29.7 | 24.7 | 24.1 | 17.0 | 13.3 | | Trade Payables | 22.2 | 21.4 |
| .0 | .3 | .3 | .2 | .1 | | Income Taxes Payable | .2 | .3 |
| 20.4 | 17.8 | 11.3 | 9.2 | 9.8 | | All Other Current | 9.9 | 11.8 |
| 89.9 | 61.1 | 50.5 | 46.7 | 39.8 | | Total Current | 51.8 | 55.6 |
| 10.4 | 6.4 | 6.8 | 7.6 | 10.7 | | Long-Term Debt | 7.6 | 7.2 |
| .0 | .1 | .4 | .2 | .0 | | Deferred Taxes | .2 | .2 |
| 9.1 | 4.3 | 4.4 | 4.8 | 2.6 | | All Other Non-Current | 4.0 | 3.9 |
| -9.1 | 28.1 | 37.9 | 40.6 | 46.9 | | Net Worth | 36.4 | 33.0 |
| 100.0 | 100.0 | 100.0 | 100.0 | 100.0 | | Total Liabilities & Net Worth | 100.0 | 100.0 |
| | | | | | | **INCOME DATA** | | |
| 100.0 | 100.0 | 100.0 | 100.0 | 100.0 | | Net Sales | 100.0 | 100.0 |
| 31.8 | 30.8 | 28.5 | 25.5 | 24.7 | | Gross Profit | 27.9 | 27.0 |
| 30.8 | 28.1 | 25.2 | 22.9 | 20.5 | | Operating Expenses | 24.2 | 24.3 |
| 1.0 | 2.7 | 3.3 | 2.7 | 4.2 | | Operating Profit | 3.6 | 2.6 |
| .7 | .0 | .1 | -.1 | .3 | | All Other Expenses (net) | .3 | .1 |
| .3 | 2.7 | 3.2 | 2.7 | 3.9 | | Profit Before Taxes | 3.3 | 2.5 |
| | | | | | | **RATIOS** | | |
| 1.1 | 2.2 | 2.4 | 2.7 | 3.1 | | Current | 2.2 | 2.2 |
| .9 | 1.5 | 1.7 | 1.8 | 2.3 | | | 1.6 | 1.5 |
| .4 | 1.1 | 1.2 | 1.3 | 1.3 | | | 1.3 | 1.2 |
| 1.0 | 1.2 | 1.3 | 1.3 | 1.3 | | Quick | 1.2 | 1.2 |
| .7 | .8 | 1.0 | .8 | .9 | | | .8 | .7 |
| .2 | .5 | .6 | .6 | .7 | | | .6 | .5 |
| 24 14.9 | 23 15.9 | 31 11.6 | 34 10.7 | 41 8.9 | | Sales/Receivables | 33 11.1 | 31 11.8 |
| 37 9.8 | 32 11.3 | 45 8.1 | 40 9.1 | 46 8.0 | | | 42 8.7 | 41 8.9 |
| 66 5.5 | 47 7.8 | 60 6.1 | 51 7.1 | 56 6.5 | | | 55 6.6 | 55 6.7 |
| 0 UND | 29 12.5 | 14 25.4 | 73 5.0 | 59 6.2 | | Cost of Sales/Inventory | 33 11.0 | 27 13.4 |
| 0 UND | 61 6.0 | 57 6.4 | 94 3.9 | 78 4.7 | | | 70 5.2 | 67 5.4 |
| 10 38.1 | 89 4.1 | 104 3.5 | 118 3.1 | 118 3.1 | | | 100 3.6 | 100 3.7 |
| 5 70.4 | 16 22.9 | 22 16.5 | 19 19.1 | 13 27.7 | | Cost of Sales/Payables | 19 19.1 | 18 20.7 |
| 46 8.0 | 37 9.9 | 34 10.8 | 30 12.0 | 19 19.3 | | | 31 11.9 | 29 12.4 |
| 87 4.2 | 57 6.4 | 58 6.3 | 43 8.5 | 35 10.3 | | | 48 7.7 | 49 7.4 |
| 113.0 | 6.3 | 5.9 | 4.4 | 4.0 | | Sales/Working Capital | 6.2 | 6.1 |
| -71.1 | 11.7 | 8.7 | 7.5 | 5.3 | | | 8.7 | 10.1 |
| -24.0 | 72.3 | 24.4 | 14.0 | 16.9 | | | 17.6 | 24.3 |
| | 20.0 | 23.4 | 14.2 | 234.6 | | EBIT/Interest | 13.3 | 11.1 |
| | (47) 6.2 | (102) 6.2 | (76) 5.1 | (12) 8.8 | | | (221) 4.6 | (257) 4.2 |
| | 1.4 | 2.2 | 2.4 | 1.6 | | | 2.1 | 1.5 |
| | | 13.8 | 6.3 | | | Net Profit + Depr., Dep., Amort./Cur. Mat. L/T/D | 14.8 | 12.5 |
| | | (26) 4.5 | (20) 3.6 | | | | (66) 4.1 | (62) 4.8 |
| | | 1.7 | 2.3 | | | | 2.0 | 2.1 |
| .8 | .0 | .1 | .1 | .1 | | Fixed/Worth | .1 | .1 |
| 4.4 | .2 | .2 | .2 | .3 | | | .2 | .2 |
| -.5 | .6 | .5 | .4 | .6 | | | .5 | .5 |
| 7.1 | .9 | .7 | .8 | .7 | | Debt/Worth | .9 | 1.0 |
| -37.4 | 2.3 | 1.7 | 1.6 | 1.3 | | | 1.8 | 2.1 |
| -4.0 | 17.7 | 5.1 | 4.0 | 4.0 | | | 3.9 | 5.1 |
| | 71.6 | 37.9 | 29.2 | 27.4 | | % Profit Before Taxes/Tangible Net Worth | 46.3 | 38.5 |
| | (45) 26.0 | (102) 15.1 | (74) 17.0 | 14.6 | | | (217) 22.8 | (249) 16.4 |
| | 7.6 | 5.2 | 8.1 | 8.5 | | | 10.6 | 4.8 |
| 22.5 | 21.5 | 16.0 | 11.0 | 13.2 | | % Profit Before Taxes/Total Assets | 16.1 | 12.6 |
| 7.3 | 7.3 | 5.6 | 5.3 | 6.1 | | | 7.7 | 5.5 |
| 3.9 | 1.7 | 1.6 | 2.3 | 3.2 | | | 3.6 | .9 |
| 504.4 | 764.3 | 148.8 | 97.4 | 80.4 | | Sales/Net Fixed Assets | 128.3 | 118.8 |
| 32.2 | 74.2 | 49.0 | 50.3 | 28.4 | | | 51.7 | 49.3 |
| 23.7 | 35.1 | 24.4 | 21.1 | 8.1 | | | 23.8 | 25.2 |
| 10.3 | 4.4 | 3.5 | 3.0 | 3.1 | | Sales/Total Assets | 3.6 | 3.7 |
| 4.6 | 3.4 | 3.0 | 2.6 | 2.4 | | | 2.9 | 3.0 |
| 3.1 | 2.7 | 2.3 | 1.9 | 1.7 | | | 2.5 | 2.4 |
| | .2 | .2 | .3 | .5 | | % Depr., Dep., Amort./Sales | .3 | .3 |
| | (41) .5 | (92) .5 | (75) .5 | (13) 1.0 | | | (194) .5 | (237) .5 |
| | 1.0 | 1.0 | .8 | 1.1 | | | .9 | .8 |
| | 3.1 | 1.5 | 1.0 | | | % Officers', Directors' Owners' Comp/Sales | 1.3 | 1.4 |
| | (23) 4.5 | (48) 2.7 | (16) 2.5 | | | | (91) 2.8 | (99) 2.9 |
| | 7.7 | 5.2 | 4.3 | | | | 5.1 | 5.1 |
| 34116M | 216003M | 1681598M | 4571578M | 2520623M | 3061452M | Net Sales ($) | 10222574M | 10890428M |
| 3130M | 62550M | 578599M | 1794029M | 1059094M | 1202348M | Total Assets ($) | 3687623M | 3948396M |

M = $ thousand    MM = $ million
See Pages 9 through 22 for Explanation of Ratios and Data

## Comparative Historical Data | Current Data Sorted by Sales

| | | | Type of Statement | 0-1MM | 1-3MM | 3-5MM | 5-10MM | 10-25MM | 25MM & OVER |
|---|---|---|---|---|---|---|---|---|---|
| 38 | 35 | 34 | Unqualified | 1 | | | | 3 | 30 |
| 77 | 79 | 75 | Reviewed | | 2 | 3 | 11 | 31 | 28 |
| 39 | 42 | 38 | Compiled | | 5 | 5 | 9 | 15 | 4 |
| 31 | 31 | 37 | Tax Returns | 2 | 10 | 6 | 11 | 6 | 2 |
| 77 | 79 | 96 | Other | 1 | 7 | 10 | 11 | 33 | 34 |
| 4/1/09-3/31/10 ALL | 4/1/10-3/31/11 ALL | 4/1/11-3/31/12 ALL | | 36 (4/1-9/30/11) | | | 244 (10/1/11-3/31/12) | | |
| 262 | 266 | 280 | NUMBER OF STATEMENTS | 4 | 24 | 24 | 42 | 88 | 98 |
| % | % | % | ASSETS | % | % | % | % | % | % |
| 7.3 | 7.4 | 7.5 | Cash & Equivalents | | 10.4 | 12.9 | 7.4 | 8.1 | 4.9 |
| 36.5 | 37.1 | 36.1 | Trade Receivables (net) | | 30.7 | 34.8 | 36.2 | 38.3 | 34.7 |
| 36.9 | 35.7 | 35.6 | Inventory | | 36.9 | 30.3 | 33.6 | 33.2 | 40.8 |
| 2.6 | 2.4 | 3.3 | All Other Current | | 2.2 | 5.3 | 3.5 | 3.1 | 3.1 |
| 83.4 | 82.5 | 82.5 | Total Current | | 80.3 | 83.4 | 80.7 | 82.7 | 83.5 |
| 9.6 | 8.7 | 9.3 | Fixed Assets (net) | | 13.9 | 6.7 | 9.3 | 8.8 | 9.0 |
| 2.3 | 3.4 | 2.8 | Intangibles (net) | | .3 | 3.2 | 3.0 | 2.9 | 3.3 |
| 4.7 | 5.3 | 5.4 | All Other Non-Current | | 5.6 | 6.7 | 6.9 | 5.7 | 4.3 |
| 100.0 | 100.0 | 100.0 | Total | | 100.0 | 100.0 | 100.0 | 100.0 | 100.0 |
| | | | LIABILITIES | | | | | | |
| 15.5 | 15.0 | 16.4 | Notes Payable-Short Term | | 18.7 | 17.6 | 12.0 | 14.9 | 18.1 |
| 1.9 | 1.7 | 1.6 | Cur. Mat.-L.T.D. | | 3.8 | 1.5 | 2.6 | 1.4 | .9 |
| 22.6 | 22.7 | 22.0 | Trade Payables | | 16.5 | 27.5 | 24.0 | 24.1 | 18.1 |
| .2 | .3 | .2 | Income Taxes Payable | | .7 | .1 | .1 | .3 | .2 |
| 11.4 | 11.2 | 12.1 | All Other Current | | 21.9 | 14.7 | 11.9 | 10.4 | 9.7 |
| 51.6 | 51.0 | 52.3 | Total Current | | 61.6 | 61.4 | 50.5 | 51.2 | 47.0 |
| 5.7 | 6.4 | 7.2 | Long-Term Debt | | 9.7 | 6.5 | 7.5 | 6.9 | 6.8 |
| .2 | .3 | .3 | Deferred Taxes | | .1 | .0 | .9 | .1 | .3 |
| 5.2 | 4.1 | 4.6 | All Other Non-Current | | 7.8 | 1.1 | 1.8 | 6.0 | 3.8 |
| 37.3 | 38.2 | 35.6 | Net Worth | | 20.8 | 31.0 | 39.3 | 35.7 | 42.0 |
| 100.0 | 100.0 | 100.0 | Total Liabilities & Net Worth | | 100.0 | 100.0 | 100.0 | 100.0 | 100.0 |
| | | | INCOME DATA | | | | | | |
| 100.0 | 100.0 | 100.0 | Net Sales | | 100.0 | 100.0 | 100.0 | 100.0 | 100.0 |
| 27.4 | 27.4 | 27.9 | Gross Profit | | 34.4 | 28.2 | 29.0 | 28.4 | 24.9 |
| 25.3 | 24.9 | 24.9 | Operating Expenses | | 32.7 | 25.1 | 26.0 | 24.7 | 22.1 |
| 2.0 | 2.5 | 3.0 | Operating Profit | | 1.7 | 3.1 | 2.9 | 3.7 | 2.8 |
| .0 | .2 | .1 | All Other Expenses (net) | | .8 | -.9 | .2 | .1 | .0 |
| 2.0 | 2.3 | 2.9 | Profit Before Taxes | | .9 | 4.0 | 2.7 | 3.6 | 2.8 |
| | | | RATIOS | | | | | | |
| 2.4 | 2.5 | 2.4 | | 3.0 | 2.1 | 2.4 | 2.3 | 2.8 | |
| 1.6 | 1.6 | 1.6 | Current | 1.3 | 1.4 | 1.7 | 1.7 | 1.8 | |
| 1.2 | 1.3 | 1.2 | | .9 | 1.0 | 1.2 | 1.2 | 1.3 | |
| 1.3 | 1.3 | 1.3 | | 1.1 | 1.2 | 1.3 | 1.3 | 1.3 | |
| .8 | .9 | .9 | Quick | .7 | .9 | .8 | 1.0 | .8 | |
| .5 | .6 | .5 | | .4 | .5 | .6 | .5 | .5 | |
| 33  11.0 | 34  10.7 | 30  12.3 | | 23  16.0 | 22  16.4 | 29  12.6 | 30  12.0 | 35  10.4 | |
| 43  8.5 | 46  7.9 | 41  8.9 | Sales/Receivables | 31  11.9 | 32  11.3 | 38  9.6 | 42  8.6 | 43  8.5 | |
| 57  6.5 | 58  6.3 | 58  6.3 | | 49  7.4 | 56  6.5 | 54  6.7 | 59  6.2 | 56  6.5 | |
| 30  12.2 | 32  11.5 | 27  13.7 | | 21  17.5 | 14  25.8 | 23  16.1 | 15  24.8 | 58  6.3 | |
| 77  4.8 | 70  5.2 | 72  5.1 | Cost of Sales/Inventory | 78  4.7 | 57  6.4 | 52  7.0 | 65  5.6 | 85  4.3 | |
| 109  3.3 | 102  3.6 | 104  3.5 | | 101  3.6 | 83  4.4 | 96  3.8 | 111  3.3 | 107  3.4 | |
| 20  18.2 | 21  17.1 | 20  18.5 | | 6  57.2 | 12  30.0 | 23  15.8 | 22  16.6 | 18  20.8 | |
| 33  11.0 | 37  9.9 | 32  11.5 | Cost of Sales/Payables | 31  11.9 | 42  8.6 | 33  10.9 | 34  10.6 | 29  12.5 | |
| 55  6.6 | 58  6.3 | 51  7.2 | | 49  7.5 | 61  6.0 | 56  6.5 | 51  7.2 | 41  8.8 | |
| 5.4 | 5.0 | 5.3 | | 5.0 | 6.7 | 6.0 | 6.1 | 4.5 | |
| 8.8 | 8.7 | 9.4 | Sales/Working Capital | 13.6 | 12.3 | 9.9 | 8.7 | 7.6 | |
| 18.5 | 17.3 | 24.1 | | -55.6 | 85.7 | 36.3 | 19.2 | 15.1 | |
| 13.3 | 16.5 | 19.6 | | 11.6 | 15.7 | 13.9 | 25.3 | 23.8 | |
| (241)  4.3 | (241)  4.3 | (252)  6.0 | EBIT/Interest | (23)  4.1 | (18)  6.2 | (41)  3.5 | (76)  6.5 | (92)  6.1 | |
| 1.1 | 1.9 | 2.1 | | .2 | 2.0 | 1.4 | 2.6 | 2.6 | |
| 9.0 | 11.6 | 10.6 | | | | | | 13.9 | 21.4 |
| (60)  2.9 | (72)  3.4 | (56)  3.8 | Net Profit + Depr., Dep., Amort./Cur. Mat. L/T/D | | | | (18)  5.1 | (25)  3.9 | |
| .4 | 1.5 | 1.8 | | | | | | 2.6 | 2.6 |
| .1 | .1 | .1 | | .1 | .0 | .1 | .1 | .1 | |
| .2 | .2 | .2 | Fixed/Worth | .4 | .2 | .2 | .2 | .2 | |
| .6 | .6 | .6 | | 2.8 | .6 | .5 | .8 | .4 | |
| .8 | .7 | .8 | | 1.2 | 1.0 | .7 | .7 | .8 | |
| 1.7 | 1.7 | 1.8 | Debt/Worth | 3.0 | 2.4 | 1.4 | 1.8 | 1.6 | |
| 4.3 | 4.9 | 5.3 | | 107.8 | 9.9 | 4.5 | 7.1 | 3.6 | |
| 28.4 | 34.4 | 37.4 | | 56.4 | 55.9 | 38.1 | 50.6 | 30.4 | |
| (242)  12.1 | (238)  15.1 | (247)  17.1 | % Profit Before Taxes/Tangible Net Worth | (19)  16.0 | (20)  34.7 | (38)  8.3 | (75)  21.4 | (94)  17.0 | |
| 2.9 | 3.6 | 7.0 | | 6.3 | 2.5 | 2.0 | 8.0 | 8.6 | |
| 9.8 | 12.2 | 14.9 | | 18.9 | 18.2 | 17.3 | 17.9 | 11.9 | |
| 4.0 | 5.4 | 6.1 | % Profit Before Taxes/Total Assets | 6.4 | 7.5 | 3.1 | 7.0 | 5.4 | |
| .3 | 1.0 | 2.1 | | -1.6 | 1.5 | .8 | 2.2 | 2.6 | |
| 121.8 | 128.7 | 146.2 | | 535.5 | 905.1 | 135.4 | 149.6 | 110.5 | |
| 49.1 | 51.3 | 50.6 | Sales/Net Fixed Assets | 37.5 | 166.1 | 46.0 | 52.7 | 49.5 | |
| 22.6 | 23.9 | 23.3 | | 21.9 | 36.0 | 23.5 | 22.6 | 21.7 | |
| 3.5 | 3.3 | 3.5 | | 3.9 | 4.4 | 3.6 | 4.0 | 3.1 | |
| 2.7 | 2.7 | 2.8 | Sales/Total Assets | 2.9 | 3.1 | 3.0 | 3.0 | 2.7 | |
| 2.2 | 2.2 | 2.3 | | 2.3 | 2.3 | 2.3 | 2.2 | 2.2 | |
| .3 | .3 | .3 | | .2 | .1 | .3 | .2 | .3 | |
| (232)  .6 | (226)  .5 | (232)  .5 | % Depr., Dep., Amort./Sales | (20)  .9 | (15)  .4 | (32)  .7 | (73)  .5 | (90)  .5 | |
| .9 | 1.0 | 1.0 | | 1.3 | .9 | 1.0 | .9 | .9 | |
| 1.5 | 1.3 | 1.5 | | 3.9 | 2.1 | 1.9 | 1.5 | 1.2 | |
| (83)  2.9 | (96)  3.0 | (95)  3.3 | % Officers', Directors', Owners' Comp/Sales | (12)  5.4 | (11)  4.3 | (20)  3.3 | (36)  2.5 | (15)  2.6 | |
| 5.9 | 5.8 | 5.6 | | 10.3 | 7.7 | 5.6 | 5.0 | 4.6 | |
| 9568577M | 11397319M | 12085370M | Net Sales ($) | 2653M | 53103M | 94446M | 293827M | 1489138M | 10152203M |
| 3642777M | 4744338M | 4699750M | Total Assets ($) | 933M | 19816M | 37942M | 101769M | 556463M | 3982827M |

M = $ thousand    MM = $ million
See Pages 9 through 22 for Explanation of Ratios and Data

## Current Data Sorted by Assets          Comparative Historical Data

| Type of Statement | | | | | | | | |
|---|---|---|---|---|---|---|---|---|
| | | 3 | 8 | 2 | | Unqualified | | |
| | 1 | 12 | 8 | | | Reviewed | 15 | 20 |
| 2 | 4 | 3 | 3 | | | Compiled | 14 | 12 |
| 3 | 12 | 2 | 1 | | | Tax Returns | 2 | 17 |
| 1 | 3 | 10 | 4 | | 1 | Other | 18 | 23 |
| | 10 (4/1-9/30/11) | | 73 (10/1/11-3/31/12) | | | | 4/1/07-3/31/08 | 4/1/08-3/31/09 |
| 0-500M | 500M-2MM | 2-10MM | 10-50MM | 50-100MM | 100-250MM | | ALL | ALL |
| 6 | 20 | 30 | 24 | 3 | | NUMBER OF STATEMENTS | 56 | 80 |

| 0-500M | 500M-2MM | 2-10MM | 10-50MM | 50-100MM | 100-250MM | | Hist ALL | Hist ALL |
|---|---|---|---|---|---|---|---|---|
| % | % | % | % | % | % | **ASSETS** | % | % |
| | 11.8 | 10.6 | 6.4 | | | Cash & Equivalents | 10.1 | 10.6 |
| | 30.0 | 28.0 | 22.6 | | | Trade Receivables (net) | 27.2 | 24.6 |
| | 34.9 | 33.5 | 50.3 | | | Inventory | 37.0 | 38.0 |
| | 1.7 | 3.0 | 3.3 | | | All Other Current | 3.5 | 3.0 |
| | 78.3 | 75.1 | 82.7 | | | Total Current | 77.9 | 76.2 |
| | 10.0 | 16.6 | 10.1 | | | Fixed Assets (net) | 13.3 | 12.9 |
| | 6.1 | 2.7 | 2.3 | | | Intangibles (net) | 4.4 | 6.0 |
| | 5.5 | 5.6 | 4.9 | | | All Other Non-Current | 4.5 | 5.0 |
| | 100.0 | 100.0 | 100.0 | | | Total | 100.0 | 100.0 |
| | | | | | | **LIABILITIES** | | |
| | 13.3 | 11.1 | 16.1 | | | Notes Payable-Short Term | 17.3 | 20.0 |
| | 6.0 | 1.6 | 1.5 | | | Cur. Mat.-L.T.D. | 2.0 | 2.4 |
| | 17.3 | 19.1 | 16.5 | | | Trade Payables | 16.7 | 17.2 |
| | .1 | .2 | .3 | | | Income Taxes Payable | .4 | .2 |
| | 7.2 | 8.8 | 5.9 | | | All Other Current | 8.7 | 9.0 |
| | 43.9 | 40.7 | 40.3 | | | Total Current | 45.0 | 48.8 |
| | 17.6 | 4.7 | 3.2 | | | Long-Term Debt | 8.9 | 11.8 |
| | .0 | .3 | .6 | | | Deferred Taxes | .1 | .2 |
| | 3.6 | 5.1 | 2.2 | | | All Other Non-Current | 6.1 | 5.5 |
| | 34.9 | 49.3 | 53.7 | | | Net Worth | 39.8 | 33.7 |
| | 100.0 | 100.0 | 100.0 | | | Total Liabilties & Net Worth | 100.0 | 100.0 |
| | | | | | | **INCOME DATA** | | |
| | 100.0 | 100.0 | 100.0 | | | Net Sales | 100.0 | 100.0 |
| | 33.1 | 27.5 | 24.5 | | | Gross Profit | 32.0 | 28.6 |
| | 29.4 | 24.9 | 19.8 | | | Operating Expenses | 25.1 | 25.1 |
| | 3.7 | 2.5 | 4.8 | | | Operating Profit | 6.9 | 3.5 |
| | -.4 | .5 | .0 | | | All Other Expenses (net) | .9 | .3 |
| | 4.1 | 2.0 | 4.8 | | | Profit Before Taxes | 6.0 | 3.2 |
| | | | | | | **RATIOS** | | |
| | 3.7 | 2.8 | 3.9 | | | | 2.6 | 2.8 |
| | 2.3 | 2.0 | 2.1 | | | Current | 1.8 | 1.7 |
| | 1.2 | 1.3 | 1.5 | | | | 1.4 | 1.2 |
| | 1.8 | 1.3 | 1.1 | | | | 1.3 | 1.1 |
| | 1.2 | .8 | .7 | | | Quick | .8 | .7 |
| | .7 | .6 | .5 | | | | .4 | .4 |
| 21 17.1 | 20 18.0 | 23 15.6 | | | | | 24 15.4 | 21 17.8 |
| 30 12.3 | 30 12.0 | 34 10.8 | | | | Sales/Receivables | 35 10.6 | 27 13.5 |
| 42 8.6 | 47 7.8 | 39 9.3 | | | | | 45 8.2 | 39 9.4 |
| 16 22.5 | 37 9.8 | 68 5.4 | | | | | 31 11.8 | 34 10.8 |
| 62 5.9 | 56 6.5 | 111 3.3 | | | | Cost of Sales/Inventory | 76 4.8 | 59 6.1 |
| 101 3.6 | 91 4.0 | 146 2.5 | | | | | 127 2.9 | 123 3.0 |
| 11 33.7 | 21 17.8 | 16 22.6 | | | | | 14 26.4 | 11 34.5 |
| 19 18.9 | 27 13.3 | 27 13.3 | | | | Cost of Sales/Payables | 28 13.1 | 26 13.8 |
| 37 9.9 | 48 7.6 | 41 8.9 | | | | | 46 7.9 | 36 10.1 |
| | 3.6 | 5.0 | 3.5 | | | | 4.8 | 4.6 |
| | 6.6 | 8.5 | 6.3 | | | Sales/Working Capital | 8.7 | 10.8 |
| | 92.1 | 17.6 | 10.0 | | | | 12.5 | 36.4 |
| | 26.5 | 32.3 | 21.6 | | | | 9.7 | 9.8 |
| | (17) 7.5 | (23) 8.2 | (21) 7.0 | | | EBIT/Interest | (53) 4.0 | (73) 3.5 |
| | 2.6 | 2.2 | 4.6 | | | | 2.4 | 1.6 |
| | | | | | | Net Profit + Depr., Dep., | 31.4 | 42.1 |
| | | | | | | Amort./Cur. Mat. L/T/D | (18) 10.7 | (19) 5.6 |
| | | | | | | | 1.4 | 2.0 |
| | .1 | .1 | .1 | | | | .2 | .1 |
| | .2 | .3 | .2 | | | Fixed/Worth | .3 | .3 |
| | NM | .6 | .4 | | | | .8 | 1.4 |
| | .6 | .5 | .5 | | | | .9 | .7 |
| | 1.1 | 1.3 | 1.0 | | | Debt/Worth | 1.7 | 1.6 |
| | NM | 2.2 | 1.8 | | | | 3.4 | 7.0 |
| | 53.4 | 37.2 | 35.3 | | | | 56.7 | 38.3 |
| | (15) 15.7 | 16.8 | 16.7 | | | % Profit Before Taxes/Tangible Net Worth | (50) 24.8 | (66) 16.5 |
| | 6.3 | 4.3 | 9.2 | | | | 8.8 | 7.1 |
| | 22.2 | 15.9 | 16.6 | | | | 16.4 | 12.9 |
| | 7.5 | 8.2 | 8.8 | | | % Profit Before Taxes/Total Assets | 8.4 | 5.8 |
| | 3.4 | 3.0 | 4.2 | | | | 3.1 | 2.1 |
| | 114.2 | 106.1 | 101.5 | | | | 63.4 | 93.3 |
| | 56.1 | 26.4 | 27.9 | | | Sales/Net Fixed Assets | 32.2 | 43.7 |
| | 31.1 | 12.8 | 15.3 | | | | 12.8 | 18.4 |
| | 4.4 | 3.7 | 2.9 | | | | 3.4 | 3.9 |
| | 3.1 | 3.1 | 2.3 | | | Sales/Total Assets | 2.7 | 2.9 |
| | 2.6 | 2.3 | 2.0 | | | | 2.0 | 2.1 |
| | .4 | .5 | .3 | | | | .4 | .4 |
| | (15) .8 | (23) .8 | (21) .7 | | | % Depr., Dep., Amort./Sales | (49) .8 | (66) .7 |
| | .9 | 1.4 | | | | | 1.2 | 1.0 |
| | 1.9 | | | | | | 1.8 | 2.1 |
| | (13) 3.2 | | | | | % Officers', Directors' Owners' Comp/Sales | (24) 3.8 | (35) 4.5 |
| | 4.9 | | | | | | 5.9 | 6.8 |
| 7933M | 107559M | 420914M | 1343137M | 451405M | | Net Sales ($) | 1537966M | 2273007M |
| 1944M | 27180M | 147360M | 548688M | 245658M | | Total Assets ($) | 622284M | 993486M |

*(Leftmost data column 0-500M shows: DATA NOT AVAILABLE)*

M = $ thousand    MM = $ million
See Pages 9 through 22 for Explanation of Ratios and Data

## Comparative Historical Data      Current Data Sorted by Sales

### Type of Statement

| 4/1/09-3/31/10 ALL | 4/1/10-3/31/11 ALL | 4/1/11-3/31/12 ALL | Type of Statement | 0-1MM | 1-3MM | 3-5MM | 5-10MM | 10-25MM | 25MM & OVER |
|---|---|---|---|---|---|---|---|---|---|
| 11 | 9 | 13 | Unqualified | | | | | 4 | 9 |
| 18 | 16 | 21 | Reviewed | 1 | 2 | | 2 | 10 | 8 |
| 12 | 10 | 12 | Compiled | 1 | 4 | 1 | 4 | 2 | 2 |
| 5 | 7 | 18 | Tax Returns | 1 | 5 | 5 | 3 | 2 | 2 |
| 26 | 22 | 19 | Other | | | 2 | 4 | 5 | 6 |
| | | | | 10 (4/1-9/30/11) | | | 73 (10/1/11-3/31/12) | | |
| 72 | 64 | 83 | NUMBER OF STATEMENTS | 3 | 8 | 9 | 13 | 23 | 27 |

### ASSETS

| % | % | % | | % | % | % | % | % | % |
|---|---|---|---|---|---|---|---|---|---|
| 11.7 | 11.5 | 9.8 | Cash & Equivalents | | | | 7.8 | 11.7 | 8.4 |
| 26.4 | 27.3 | 26.2 | Trade Receivables (net) | | | | 33.5 | 30.5 | 23.5 |
| 38.5 | 36.0 | 38.4 | Inventory | | | | 35.0 | 34.6 | 44.3 |
| 3.4 | 3.8 | 2.7 | All Other Current | | | | 3.0 | 3.3 | 2.7 |
| 80.0 | 78.6 | 77.2 | Total Current | | | | 79.3 | 80.1 | 78.8 |
| 11.2 | 10.2 | 12.9 | Fixed Assets (net) | | | | 10.8 | 11.0 | 12.3 |
| 4.7 | 5.0 | 3.8 | Intangibles (net) | | | | 3.6 | 2.4 | 4.4 |
| 4.1 | 6.2 | 6.1 | All Other Non-Current | | | | 6.2 | 6.5 | 4.5 |
| 100.0 | 100.0 | 100.0 | Total | | | | 100.0 | 100.0 | 100.0 |

### LIABILITIES

| | | | | | | | | | |
|---|---|---|---|---|---|---|---|---|---|
| 13.3 | 10.5 | 13.6 | Notes Payable-Short Term | | | | 10.8 | 10.6 | 14.7 |
| 2.2 | 3.0 | 3.0 | Cur. Mat.-L.T.D. | | | | 1.7 | 2.1 | 1.7 |
| 18.5 | 18.7 | 16.9 | Trade Payables | | | | 19.3 | 21.3 | 17.0 |
| .1 | .4 | .3 | Income Taxes Payable | | | | .2 | .0 | .3 |
| 8.4 | 8.6 | 7.3 | All Other Current | | | | 7.1 | 10.9 | 7.5 |
| 42.5 | 41.3 | 41.1 | Total Current | | | | 39.1 | 45.0 | 41.1 |
| 7.8 | 8.2 | 8.0 | Long-Term Debt | | | | 7.0 | 4.4 | 4.5 |
| .2 | .2 | .4 | Deferred Taxes | | | | .0 | .2 | 1.1 |
| 6.7 | 5.6 | 3.8 | All Other Non-Current | | | | 5.4 | 3.6 | 3.1 |
| 42.7 | 44.8 | 46.7 | Net Worth | | | | 48.5 | 46.9 | 50.2 |
| 100.0 | 100.0 | 100.0 | Total Liabilities & Net Worth | | | | 100.0 | 100.0 | 100.0 |

### INCOME DATA

| | | | | | | | | | |
|---|---|---|---|---|---|---|---|---|---|
| 100.0 | 100.0 | 100.0 | Net Sales | | | | 100.0 | 100.0 | 100.0 |
| 28.7 | 30.0 | 28.3 | Gross Profit | | | | 30.8 | 24.5 | 23.5 |
| 25.0 | 25.9 | 24.8 | Operating Expenses | | | | 28.0 | 20.7 | 19.2 |
| 3.7 | 4.1 | 3.5 | Operating Profit | | | | 2.9 | 3.8 | 4.3 |
| .3 | .2 | .2 | All Other Expenses (net) | | | | .3 | .2 | .2 |
| 3.4 | 3.8 | 3.3 | Profit Before Taxes | | | | 2.6 | 3.7 | 4.1 |

### RATIOS

| 4/1/09-3/31/10 | 4/1/10-3/31/11 | 4/1/11-3/31/12 | Ratio | 0-1MM | 1-3MM | 3-5MM | 5-10MM | 10-25MM | 25MM & OVER |
|---|---|---|---|---|---|---|---|---|---|
| 3.1 | 3.3 | 3.3 | Current | | | | 3.1 | 2.7 | 2.7 |
| 2.0 | 1.8 | 2.1 | | | | | 2.2 | 1.7 | 1.9 |
| 1.4 | 1.4 | 1.3 | | | | | 1.5 | 1.3 | 1.3 |
| 1.4 | 1.4 | 1.5 | Quick | | | | 1.5 | 1.3 | 1.0 |
| .9 | 1.0 | .8 | | | | | 1.2 | .9 | .7 |
| .6 | .6 | .6 | | | | | .6 | .7 | .5 |
| 24   15.1 | 23   16.0 | 21   17.5 | Sales/Receivables | | | | 28   12.9 | 22   16.3 | 20   18.3 |
| 34   10.8 | 31   11.7 | 32   11.5 | | | | | 35   10.3 | 29   12.4 | 33   11.0 |
| 40   9.0 | 40   9.1 | 45   8.2 | | | | | 48   7.6 | 45   8.2 | 39   9.3 |
| 44   8.2 | 26   14.2 | 40   9.1 | Cost of Sales/Inventory | | | | 28   13.1 | 35   10.5 | 47   7.8 |
| 75   4.8 | 75   4.9 | 72   5.1 | | | | | 63   5.8 | 52   7.0 | 78   4.7 |
| 124   2.9 | 123   3.0 | 111   3.3 | | | | | 94   3.9 | 96   3.8 | 135   2.7 |
| 17   21.8 | 17   21.5 | 15   23.9 | Cost of Sales/Payables | | | | 18   20.1 | 18   20.8 | 16   23.1 |
| 31   11.8 | 32   11.6 | 26   14.3 | | | | | 26   13.8 | 28   13.1 | 24   15.2 |
| 48   7.6 | 44   8.3 | 38   9.5 | | | | | 46   7.9 | 41   8.9 | 40   9.1 |
| 4.3 | 4.8 | 4.0 | Sales/Working Capital | | | | 4.0 | 5.7 | 3.6 |
| 6.7 | 7.7 | 7.3 | | | | | 7.3 | 9.2 | 7.0 |
| 11.8 | 17.1 | 19.6 | | | | | 19.5 | 20.7 | 16.1 |
| 12.6 | 31.6 | 26.7 | EBIT/Interest | | | | 13.1 | 36.7 | 69.6 |
| (64) 5.5 | (54) 9.0 | (70) 7.5 | | | | | (11) 3.3 | (17) 7.7 | (25) 8.6 |
| 2.7 | 3.8 | 3.1 | | | | | 2.0 | 3.1 | 4.6 |
| 6.6 | 6.5 | 9.6 | Net Profit + Depr., Dep., Amort./Cur. Mat. L/T/D | | | | | | |
| (16) 5.2 | (17) 2.8 | (15) 3.6 | | | | | | | |
| 2.8 | 1.7 | 2.3 | | | | | | | |
| .1 | .1 | .1 | Fixed/Worth | | | | .1 | .1 | .1 |
| .2 | .2 | .2 | | | | | .2 | .2 | .2 |
| .5 | .6 | .5 | | | | | .6 | .4 | .5 |
| .5 | .5 | .5 | Debt/Worth | | | | .4 | .7 | .6 |
| 1.2 | 1.2 | 1.1 | | | | | .9 | 1.4 | 1.1 |
| 3.2 | 3.3 | 2.7 | | | | | 2.7 | 2.5 | 1.8 |
| 26.9 | 38.7 | 37.5 | % Profit Before Taxes/Tangible Net Worth | | | | 22.4 | 38.4 | 44.4 |
| (64) 13.9 | (57) 16.9 | (76) 16.3 | | | | | (11) 6.3 | 17.6 | (26) 17.4 |
| 4.7 | 9.6 | 6.3 | | | | | 3.4 | 6.6 | 9.5 |
| 11.4 | 14.8 | 16.1 | % Profit Before Taxes/Total Assets | | | | 12.0 | 23.7 | 17.0 |
| 5.8 | 8.6 | 7.3 | | | | | 3.8 | 8.7 | 10.3 |
| 2.1 | 3.8 | 3.3 | | | | | 1.5 | 3.5 | 4.2 |
| 73.0 | 106.1 | 95.4 | Sales/Net Fixed Assets | | | | 97.3 | 143.7 | 44.8 |
| 38.2 | 36.6 | 32.7 | | | | | 33.0 | 38.6 | 26.6 |
| 16.6 | 20.1 | 17.6 | | | | | 26.1 | 22.0 | 12.9 |
| 3.3 | 3.5 | 3.7 | Sales/Total Assets | | | | 4.3 | 4.2 | 3.0 |
| 2.6 | 2.6 | 2.8 | | | | | 3.3 | 3.3 | 2.6 |
| 1.9 | 2.2 | 2.0 | | | | | 2.3 | 2.4 | 1.9 |
| .5 | .4 | .4 | % Depr., Dep., Amort./Sales | | | | | .4 | .3 |
| (58) .8 | (53) .8 | (65) .8 | | | | | | (18) .7 | (23) .7 |
| 1.3 | 1.1 | 1.1 | | | | | | 1.3 | .9 |
| 1.6 | 2.4 | 1.9 | % Officers', Directors' Owners' Comp/Sales | | | | | | |
| (14) 2.5 | (20) 3.4 | (29) 2.8 | | | | | | | |
| 4.4 | 5.1 | 3.9 | | | | | | | |
| 2200014M | 1688555M | 2330948M | Net Sales ($) | 1629M | 16787M | 34704M | 92596M | 365052M | 1820180M |
| 939613M | 667377M | 970830M | Total Assets ($) | 1601M | 6238M | 20860M | 37998M | 122940M | 781193M |

## Current Data Sorted by Assets | | | | | | Comparative Historical Data

| | | | | | | Type of Statement | | |
|---|---|---|---|---|---|---|---|---|
| 3 | | 19 | 38 | 22 | 21 | Unqualified | 120 | 145 |
| | 11 | 71 | 52 | 6 | | Reviewed | 118 | 128 |
| 6 | 11 | 50 | 5 | | | Compiled | 70 | 63 |
| 21 | 37 | 32 | 5 | | | Tax Returns | 45 | 49 |
| 11 | 37 | 81 | 46 | 24 | 30 | Other | 177 | 222 |
| | 92 (4/1-9/30/11) | | 547 (10/1/11-3/31/12) | | | | 4/1/07-3/31/08 | 4/1/08-3/31/09 |
| 0-500M | 500M-2MM | 2-10MM | 10-50MM | 50-100MM | 100-250MM | | ALL | ALL |
| 41 | 96 | 253 | 146 | 52 | 51 | NUMBER OF STATEMENTS | 530 | 607 |
| % | % | % | % | % | % | ASSETS | % | % |
| 22.1 | 13.3 | 9.7 | 7.1 | 3.1 | 3.1 | Cash & Equivalents | 5.6 | 5.4 |
| 21.1 | 26.8 | 20.6 | 16.1 | 14.4 | 17.1 | Trade Receivables (net) | 16.9 | 16.0 |
| 25.2 | 39.0 | 47.4 | 48.0 | 49.2 | 47.8 | Inventory | 49.5 | 49.9 |
| 4.1 | 2.9 | 1.6 | 2.5 | 1.6 | 2.5 | All Other Current | 2.0 | 2.1 |
| 72.5 | 81.9 | 79.3 | 73.8 | 68.3 | 70.4 | Total Current | 74.0 | 73.5 |
| 16.2 | 12.0 | 15.0 | 19.0 | 26.4 | 24.4 | Fixed Assets (net) | 21.3 | 20.9 |
| 2.4 | 2.0 | 2.3 | 1.8 | 2.1 | 1.0 | Intangibles (net) | 1.4 | 1.5 |
| 8.9 | 4.0 | 3.5 | 5.4 | 3.2 | 4.2 | All Other Non-Current | 3.3 | 4.2 |
| 100.0 | 100.0 | 100.0 | 100.0 | 100.0 | 100.0 | Total | 100.0 | 100.0 |
| | | | | | | LIABILITIES | | |
| 17.4 | 16.6 | 20.8 | 27.3 | 27.2 | 24.1 | Notes Payable-Short Term | 27.8 | 29.5 |
| 1.3 | 2.2 | 3.5 | 3.5 | 5.1 | 3.2 | Cur. Mat.-L.T.D. | 5.2 | 4.4 |
| 17.0 | 19.9 | 14.6 | 9.9 | 9.3 | 11.1 | Trade Payables | 12.7 | 11.2 |
| .2 | .2 | .3 | .5 | 1.1 | .2 | Income Taxes Payable | .3 | .3 |
| 26.4 | 9.4 | 9.3 | 6.4 | 6.1 | 7.4 | All Other Current | 7.5 | 7.8 |
| 62.3 | 48.3 | 48.5 | 47.6 | 48.9 | 46.1 | Total Current | 53.6 | 53.1 |
| 17.7 | 11.2 | 10.0 | 9.9 | 12.2 | 11.5 | Long-Term Debt | 14.0 | 13.1 |
| .0 | .2 | .5 | 1.3 | 1.2 | 1.1 | Deferred Taxes | .5 | .6 |
| 5.4 | 5.8 | 4.2 | 3.7 | 2.8 | 2.9 | All Other Non-Current | 3.8 | 3.0 |
| 14.5 | 34.6 | 36.8 | 37.5 | 34.9 | 38.4 | Net Worth | 28.2 | 30.2 |
| 100.0 | 100.0 | 100.0 | 100.0 | 100.0 | 100.0 | Total Liabilities & Net Worth | 100.0 | 100.0 |
| | | | | | | INCOME DATA | | |
| 100.0 | 100.0 | 100.0 | 100.0 | 100.0 | 100.0 | Net Sales | 100.0 | 100.0 |
| 39.6 | 29.4 | 27.9 | 24.2 | 23.1 | 23.3 | Gross Profit | 26.0 | 26.0 |
| 31.0 | 25.4 | 23.6 | 19.5 | 18.1 | 17.6 | Operating Expenses | 20.7 | 21.9 |
| 8.6 | 4.0 | 4.3 | 4.7 | 5.0 | 5.7 | Operating Profit | 5.3 | 4.1 |
| .6 | .9 | .6 | .4 | .3 | .1 | All Other Expenses (net) | 1.3 | 1.1 |
| 8.0 | 3.1 | 3.7 | 4.3 | 4.7 | 5.6 | Profit Before Taxes | 3.9 | 3.0 |
| | | | | | | RATIOS | | |
| 3.2 | 3.4 | 2.3 | 2.1 | 2.0 | 1.9 | | 1.8 | 2.0 |
| 1.7 | 1.7 | 1.6 | 1.5 | 1.4 | 1.5 | Current | 1.3 | 1.3 |
| .8 | 1.2 | 1.2 | 1.2 | 1.1 | 1.2 | | 1.1 | 1.1 |
| 2.0 | 1.8 | 1.0 | .8 | .6 | .7 | | .7 | .7 |
| .9 | 1.0 | .6 | .4 | .3 | .4 | Quick | .4 | .3 |
| .3 | .4 | .3 | .3 | .2 | .3 | | .2 | .2 |

Note: some Quick/Current cells carry counts (95), (606).

| | | | | | | | | | | | | Sales/Receivables, etc. | | | | |
|---|---|---|---|---|---|---|---|---|---|---|---|---|---|---|---|---|
| 0 | UND | 16 | 22.8 | 20 | 18.6 | 23 | 16.0 | 27 | 13.5 | 32 | 11.4 | Sales/Receivables | 17 | 21.1 | 17 | 21.2 |
| 20 | 17.9 | 30 | 12.2 | 34 | 10.7 | 35 | 10.5 | 37 | 9.8 | 40 | 9.1 | | 30 | 12.4 | 28 | 13.0 |
| 40 | 9.2 | 42 | 8.7 | 47 | 7.8 | 51 | 7.2 | 49 | 7.5 | 50 | 7.3 | | 45 | 8.1 | 43 | 8.5 |
| 0 | UND | 22 | 16.9 | 56 | 6.5 | 91 | 4.0 | 78 | 4.7 | 94 | 3.9 | Cost of Sales/Inventory | 59 | 6.2 | 69 | 5.3 |
| 15 | 23.7 | 59 | 6.2 | 118 | 3.1 | 159 | 2.3 | 140 | 2.6 | 159 | 2.3 | | 124 | 2.9 | 136 | 2.7 |
| 99 | 3.7 | 118 | 3.1 | 203 | 1.8 | 215 | 1.7 | 228 | 1.6 | 215 | 1.7 | | 207 | 1.8 | 219 | 1.7 |
| 2 | 175.9 | 8 | 44.6 | 10 | 35.7 | 13 | 28.1 | 13 | 29.0 | 18 | 20.5 | Cost of Sales/Payables | 11 | 34.2 | 9 | 42.1 |
| 35 | 10.5 | 28 | 12.9 | 26 | 13.9 | 22 | 16.6 | 23 | 15.7 | 32 | 11.4 | | 22 | 16.8 | 19 | 19.4 |
| 57 | 6.4 | 56 | 6.5 | 48 | 7.6 | 40 | 9.2 | 41 | 8.9 | 42 | 8.7 | | 47 | 7.8 | 42 | 8.7 |

| | | | | | | Sales/Working Capital, etc. | | |
|---|---|---|---|---|---|---|---|---|
| 6.2 | 5.1 | 4.0 | 3.9 | 4.2 | 4.2 | Sales/Working Capital | 5.2 | 4.9 |
| 17.4 | 9.6 | 7.0 | 6.0 | 7.6 | 7.0 | | 9.8 | 9.3 |
| -96.7 | 26.4 | 15.2 | 12.5 | 22.1 | 15.3 | | 27.8 | 24.9 |
| 29.2 | 13.5 | 10.9 | 10.2 | 10.4 | 12.9 | | 4.9 | 5.2 |
| (29) 5.8 | (74) 4.6 | (233) 4.6 | (140) 4.1 | 6.3 | 7.1 | EBIT/Interest | (509) 2.4 | (578) 2.3 |
| -1.5 | 1.2 | 1.9 | 1.9 | 3.7 | 4.4 | | 1.3 | 1.2 |
| | | 11.2 | 11.2 | 46.2 | | Net Profit + Depr., Dep., | 7.0 | 6.5 |
| | (32) 2.5 | (46) 2.8 | (12) 6.9 | | | Amort./Cur. Mat. L/T/D | (137) 2.0 | (144) 1.9 |
| | 1.0 | 1.5 | 1.1 | | | | .7 | .5 |
| .0 | .0 | .1 | .1 | .2 | .2 | | .1 | .2 |
| .4 | .2 | .2 | .3 | .4 | .6 | Fixed/Worth | .4 | .5 |
| 3.3 | .8 | .9 | .9 | 1.7 | 1.1 | | 1.5 | 1.4 |
| .6 | .6 | 1.0 | 1.1 | 1.4 | 1.1 | | 1.6 | 1.4 |
| 2.6 | 1.8 | 1.9 | 2.1 | 2.3 | 1.7 | Debt/Worth | 3.0 | 2.8 |
| -7.5 | 7.0 | 3.7 | 3.5 | 3.5 | 2.6 | | 5.9 | 5.6 |
| 179.4 | 66.1 | 38.6 | 26.7 | 23.8 | 30.0 | % Profit Before Taxes/Tangible | 39.1 | 28.8 |
| (29) 94.4 | (84) 25.8 | (242) 18.4 | (142) 14.9 | (51) 18.7 | (49) 20.4 | Net Worth | (498) 18.8 | (572) 13.7 |
| 26.2 | 4.5 | 5.7 | 7.9 | 11.2 | 12.7 | | 6.5 | 3.6 |
| 84.4 | 19.9 | 11.9 | 8.3 | 8.2 | 9.9 | % Profit Before Taxes/Total | 9.6 | 8.8 |
| 27.7 | 7.6 | 5.3 | 5.0 | 5.8 | 8.0 | Assets | 4.5 | 3.3 |
| -1.2 | .5 | 2.2 | 2.4 | 3.7 | 4.8 | | 1.1 | .4 |
| UND | 287.9 | 83.8 | 42.1 | 33.5 | 28.8 | Sales/Net Fixed Assets | 51.9 | 41.0 |
| 46.0 | 72.3 | 29.9 | 15.3 | 14.4 | 9.4 | | 19.4 | 16.8 |
| 11.3 | 16.5 | 10.5 | 5.0 | 2.6 | 3.5 | | 5.4 | 5.1 |
| 8.1 | 4.1 | 2.8 | 1.9 | 1.9 | 1.6 | | 2.5 | 2.4 |
| 3.4 | 2.8 | 1.9 | 1.5 | 1.4 | 1.4 | Sales/Total Assets | 1.8 | 1.7 |
| 2.0 | 1.9 | 1.4 | 1.1 | 1.0 | 1.3 | | 1.3 | 1.2 |
| .8 | .3 | .6 | .6 | 1.1 | .6 | | .6 | .7 |
| (15) 2.6 | (50) .7 | (169) 1.2 | (109) 1.2 | (32) 3.5 | (19) .7 | % Depr., Dep., Amort./Sales | (405) 1.1 | (443) 1.3 |
| 3.4 | 2.4 | 3.2 | 5.3 | 10.3 | 3.7 | | 4.8 | 4.4 |
| 2.7 | 2.2 | 1.6 | 1.1 | | | | 1.0 | 1.3 |
| (18) 5.1 | (49) 3.5 | (100) 2.6 | (30) 1.8 | | | % Officers', Directors' Owners' Comp/Sales | (121) 2.2 | (155) 2.1 |
| 8.6 | 6.2 | 3.9 | 4.9 | | | | 4.9 | 4.2 |
| 46683M | 369305M | 2643541M | 5349178M | 5447760M | 12565113M | Net Sales ($) | 26164916M | 32829823M |
| 9753M | 114063M | 1263193M | 3457122M | 3660311M | 8372491M | Total Assets ($) | 15861361M | 20495425M |

M = $ thousand    MM = $ million
See Pages 9 through 22 for Explanation of Ratios and Data

## Comparative Historical Data  —  Current Data Sorted by Sales

| 4/1/09-3/31/10 ALL | 4/1/10-3/31/11 ALL | 4/1/11-3/31/12 ALL | Type of Statement | 0-1MM | 1-3MM | 3-5MM | 5-10MM | 10-25MM | 25MM & OVER |
|---|---|---|---|---|---|---|---|---|---|
| 124 | 113 | 103 | Unqualified | 2 | 1 | | 7 | 17 | 76 |
| 127 | 140 | 140 | Reviewed | | 6 | 8 | 31 | 57 | 38 |
| 75 | 63 | 72 | Compiled | 5 | 11 | 11 | 27 | 15 | 3 |
| 59 | 69 | 95 | Tax Returns | 15 | 23 | 17 | 18 | 17 | 5 |
| 227 | 215 | 229 | Other | 9 | 25 | 25 | 40 | 46 | 84 |
| | | | | 92 (4/1-9/30/11) | | | 547 (10/1/11-3/31/12) | | |
| 612 | 600 | 639 | **NUMBER OF STATEMENTS** | 31 | 66 | 61 | 123 | 152 | 206 |
| % | % | % | **ASSETS** | % | % | % | % | % | % |
| 7.3 | 7.6 | 9.4 | Cash & Equivalents | 12.3 | 15.3 | 13.3 | 10.0 | 11.1 | 4.4 |
| 17.0 | 18.4 | 19.7 | Trade Receivables (net) | 20.5 | 19.3 | 21.7 | 19.3 | 22.3 | 17.6 |
| 46.9 | 47.4 | 45.0 | Inventory | 32.2 | 37.4 | 43.4 | 48.2 | 42.6 | 49.8 |
| 1.9 | 1.8 | 2.2 | All Other Current | 5.1 | 2.8 | 3.0 | 1.3 | 2.0 | 2.0 |
| 73.2 | 75.2 | 76.4 | Total Current | 70.1 | 74.8 | 81.4 | 78.7 | 78.0 | 73.8 |
| 20.0 | 18.0 | 17.2 | Fixed Assets (net) | 20.1 | 18.0 | 14.2 | 13.2 | 16.6 | 20.2 |
| 1.9 | 2.1 | 2.0 | Intangibles (net) | 2.9 | .8 | 2.6 | 3.4 | 1.4 | 1.8 |
| 4.9 | 4.7 | 4.4 | All Other Non-Current | 6.9 | 6.4 | 1.8 | 4.6 | 4.0 | 4.3 |
| 100.0 | 100.0 | 100.0 | Total | 100.0 | 100.0 | 100.0 | 100.0 | 100.0 | 100.0 |
| | | | **LIABILITIES** | | | | | | |
| 23.8 | 24.0 | 22.2 | Notes Payable-Short Term | 12.9 | 21.5 | 20.7 | 20.7 | 19.2 | 27.4 |
| 4.5 | 4.2 | 3.3 | Cur. Mat.-L.T.D. | 1.6 | 2.7 | 2.4 | 3.1 | 4.1 | 3.4 |
| 11.0 | 12.5 | 13.8 | Trade Payables | 22.9 | 13.1 | 15.7 | 13.7 | 15.6 | 10.8 |
| .3 | .4 | .4 | Income Taxes Payable | .3 | .0 | .5 | .3 | .3 | .6 |
| 9.0 | 7.6 | 9.4 | All Other Current | 28.1 | 8.4 | 11.0 | 9.0 | 9.2 | 6.7 |
| 48.6 | 48.8 | 49.0 | Total Current | 65.8 | 45.8 | 50.2 | 46.8 | 48.4 | 48.9 |
| 13.1 | 11.0 | 10.9 | Long-Term Debt | 16.8 | 18.9 | 12.2 | 8.7 | 8.3 | 10.4 |
| .7 | .7 | .7 | Deferred Taxes | .0 | .2 | .2 | .8 | .9 | .9 |
| 3.6 | 4.5 | 4.2 | All Other Non-Current | 1.3 | 8.1 | 6.3 | 4.1 | 3.5 | 3.3 |
| 34.0 | 34.9 | 35.2 | Net Worth | 16.1 | 27.1 | 31.0 | 39.6 | 38.9 | 36.4 |
| 100.0 | 100.0 | 100.0 | Total Liabilities & Net Worth | 100.0 | 100.0 | 100.0 | 100.0 | 100.0 | 100.0 |
| | | | **INCOME DATA** | | | | | | |
| 100.0 | 100.0 | 100.0 | Net Sales | 100.0 | 100.0 | 100.0 | 100.0 | 100.0 | 100.0 |
| 28.3 | 27.5 | 27.3 | Gross Profit | 46.1 | 33.4 | 32.6 | 27.9 | 24.6 | 22.5 |
| 26.5 | 24.1 | 22.5 | Operating Expenses | 39.2 | 29.7 | 26.3 | 24.0 | 19.8 | 17.7 |
| 1.9 | 3.5 | 4.8 | Operating Profit | 6.9 | 3.7 | 6.3 | 3.9 | 4.8 | 4.9 |
| 1.1 | .9 | .5 | All Other Expenses (net) | 1.1 | 1.2 | 1.1 | .7 | .1 | .2 |
| .7 | 2.6 | 4.3 | Profit Before Taxes | 5.8 | 2.5 | 5.2 | 3.3 | 4.7 | 4.6 |
| | | | **RATIOS** | | | | | | |
| 2.3 | 2.1 | 2.3 | | 2.5 | 3.0 | 3.2 | 2.6 | 2.1 | 2.0 |
| 1.5 | 1.5 | 1.5 | Current | 1.4 | 1.8 | 1.6 | 1.7 | 1.6 | 1.4 |
| 1.2 | 1.2 | 1.2 | | .9 | 1.2 | 1.1 | 1.3 | 1.3 | 1.2 |
| .9 | .9 | 1.0 | | 1.1 | 1.5 | 1.6 | 1.1 | 1.2 | .7 |
| .4 | .5 (638) | .5 | Quick | .4 | .8 (60) | .6 | .6 | .7 | .4 |
| .2 | .3 | .3 | | .2 | .3 | .3 | .3 | .4 | .2 |
| 20 18.3 | 22 16.8 | 20 17.9 | | 25 14.8 | 12 31.3 | 16 22.7 | 18 20.4 | 24 14.9 | 25 14.6 |
| 33 11.0 | 36 10.2 | 34 10.7 | Sales/Receivables | 34 10.6 | 29 12.4 | 31 11.6 | 31 11.9 | 35 10.4 | 36 10.0 |
| 48 7.6 | 51 7.2 | 47 7.8 | | 46 8.0 | 47 7.7 | 51 7.1 | 46 8.0 | 45 8.2 | 50 7.3 |
| 67 5.5 | 64 5.7 | 53 6.9 | | 0 UND | 8 46.8 | 41 8.8 | 51 7.1 | 46 7.9 | 81 4.5 |
| 156 2.3 | 134 2.7 | 118 3.1 | Cost of Sales/Inventory | 85 4.3 | 85 4.3 | 104 3.5 | 118 3.1 | 96 3.8 | 146 2.5 |
| 253 1.4 | 224 1.6 | 203 1.8 | | 261 1.4 | 182 2.0 | 203 1.8 | 215 1.7 | 166 2.2 | 215 1.7 |
| 10 35.9 | 12 31.1 | 11 33.3 | | 41 9.0 | 7 55.9 | 6 58.1 | 10 36.5 | 11 32.0 | 13 28.7 |
| 20 18.0 | 24 15.1 | 26 14.0 | Cost of Sales/Payables | 51 7.2 | 28 13.2 | 23 16.2 | 26 13.8 | 26 14.0 | 23 16.2 |
| 41 8.9 | 46 8.0 | 45 8.1 | | 140 2.6 | 47 7.7 | 61 6.0 | 50 7.3 | 40 9.1 | 40 9.1 |
| 3.5 | 3.8 | 4.2 | | 4.9 | 4.6 | 4.4 | 3.8 | 4.6 | 4.2 |
| 6.8 | 6.9 | 7.5 | Sales/Working Capital | 11.7 | 8.6 | 6.4 | 6.2 | 7.8 | 7.7 |
| 17.8 | 17.1 | 17.1 | | -18.6 | 26.6 | 23.9 | 13.6 | 15.7 | 14.8 |
| 4.1 | 7.9 | 12.3 | | 24.9 | 6.1 | 13.4 | 8.2 | 14.8 | 12.3 |
| (567) 1.7 | (565) 2.9 | (579) 4.8 | EBIT/Interest | (22) 4.2 | (52) 2.7 | (54) 4.4 | (111) 3.5 | (138) 5.3 | (202) 6.2 |
| .3 | 1.3 | 2.0 | | -1.7 | .4 | 1.2 | 1.8 | 2.6 | 3.0 |
| 5.1 | 8.0 | 12.8 | Net Profit + Depr., Dep., | | | | 5.7 | 12.0 | 19.7 |
| (119) 1.7 | (123) 3.1 | (102) 2.9 | Amort./Cur. Mat. L/T/D | | | | (16) 1.7 | (29) 2.6 | (51) 4.6 |
| .5 | 1.0 | 1.1 | | | | | 1.0 | .9 | 2.0 |
| .1 | .1 | .1 | | .0 | .0 | .0 | .1 | .1 | .1 |
| .4 | .3 | .3 | Fixed/Worth | .6 | .4 | .2 | .2 | .3 | .4 |
| 1.2 | 1.1 | 1.0 | | 4.4 | 1.7 | 1.2 | .7 | .8 | 1.1 |
| 1.0 | 1.0 | 1.0 | | .9 | .8 | 1.0 | .9 | 1.0 | 1.2 |
| 2.1 | 1.9 | 2.0 | Debt/Worth | 3.1 | 2.2 | 2.3 | 1.7 | 1.7 | 2.2 |
| 4.4 | 3.9 | 3.8 | | -22.5 | 16.3 | 5.9 | 3.2 | 3.2 | 3.5 |
| 17.8 | 24.0 | 37.5 | % Profit Before Taxes/Tangible | 174.3 | 91.3 | 52.8 | 29.4 | 42.4 | 28.3 |
| (568) 5.6 | (549) 9.5 | (597) 18.9 | Net Worth | (23) 24.2 | (54) 26.9 | (54) 25.7 | (117) 14.1 | (149) 23.0 | (200) 18.0 |
| -3.6 | 2.5 | 8.0 | | .4 | 4.2 | 4.1 | 4.5 | 8.0 | 11.4 |
| 5.6 | 8.2 | 11.9 | % Profit Before Taxes/Total | 47.7 | 17.9 | 17.1 | 10.5 | 13.6 | 9.2 |
| 1.6 | 3.5 | 6.0 | Assets | 4.0 | 5.2 | 7.3 | 4.4 | 6.1 | 6.3 |
| -1.7 | .6 | 2.5 | | -8.9 | -.5 | .7 | 1.9 | 2.8 | 3.6 |
| 39.8 | 49.7 | 79.5 | | 154.7 | 301.9 | 247.6 | 104.6 | 73.2 | 42.1 |
| 16.5 | 20.9 | 24.7 | Sales/Net Fixed Assets | 14.3 | 31.1 | 38.6 | 34.3 | 25.0 | 16.1 |
| 5.2 | 6.4 | 7.6 | | 7.6 | 6.4 | 10.4 | 13.8 | 8.1 | 4.9 |
| 2.2 | 2.4 | 2.6 | | 2.7 | 3.7 | 3.1 | 2.8 | 2.9 | 2.0 |
| 1.4 | 1.6 | 1.8 | Sales/Total Assets | 2.0 | 2.2 | 2.2 | 1.8 | 2.1 | 1.6 |
| 1.0 | 1.1 | 1.3 | | 1.1 | 1.4 | 1.4 | 1.4 | 1.5 | 1.3 |
| .7 | .7 | .6 | | 1.8 | .5 | .4 | .6 | .6 | .6 |
| (421) 1.5 | (405) 1.3 | (394) 1.2 | % Depr., Dep., Amort./Sales | (18) 2.9 | (37) 1.4 | (29) 1.0 | (72) 1.2 | (114) 1.1 | (124) 1.1 |
| 4.7 | 4.7 | 3.7 | | 4.2 | 5.9 | 3.2 | 3.1 | 3.2 | 4.0 |
| 1.5 | 1.5 | 1.6 | % Officers', Directors' | | 3.3 | 2.3 | 1.7 | 1.2 | .7 |
| (183) 2.9 | (168) 2.6 | (204) 2.7 | Owners' Comp/Sales | | (32) 4.7 | (31) 3.4 | (52) 2.9 | (51) 1.9 | (29) 1.6 |
| 5.8 | 4.5 | 4.9 | | | 7.9 | 5.1 | 4.5 | 3.1 | 3.7 |
| 23930316M | 24733078M | 26421580M | Net Sales ($) | 18033M | 136298M | 240428M | 898980M | 2399741M | 22728100M |
| 18153636M | 17334370M | 16876933M | Total Assets ($) | 13522M | 94004M | 135938M | 535501M | 1371043M | 14726925M |

M = $ thousand    MM = $ million
See Pages 9 through 22 for Explanation of Ratios and Data

## Current Data Sorted by Assets     Comparative Historical Data

| 0-500M | 500M-2MM | 2-10MM | 10-50MM | 50-100MM | 100-250MM | Type of Statement | 4/1/07-3/31/08 ALL | 4/1/08-3/31/09 ALL |
|---|---|---|---|---|---|---|---|---|
|  | 4 | 8 | 26 | 7 | 6 | Unqualified | 36 | 39 |
| 3 | 6 | 31 | 36 | 3 |  | Reviewed | 69 | 75 |
| 2 | 16 | 38 | 13 | 3 | 1 | Compiled | 94 | 74 |
| 2 | 6 | 21 | 3 |  |  | Tax Returns | 43 | 49 |
|  |  | 42 | 35 | 11 | 3 | Other | 105 | 91 |
|  | 52 (4/1-9/30/11) | | 271 (10/1/11-3/31/12) | | | | | |
| 7 | 32 | 140 | 113 | 21 | 10 | **NUMBER OF STATEMENTS** | 347 | 328 |
| % | % | % | % | % | % | **ASSETS** | % | % |
|  | 7.9 | 8.6 | 6.1 | 4.1 | 3.7 | Cash & Equivalents | 5.7 | 6.7 |
|  | 20.9 | 15.6 | 14.2 | 9.3 | 16.9 | Trade Receivables (net) | 15.0 | 14.0 |
|  | 48.4 | 59.8 | 61.2 | 65.1 | 43.7 | Inventory | 58.3 | 60.2 |
|  | .7 | 1.5 | 2.1 | 2.5 | 2.9 | All Other Current | 2.4 | 2.4 |
|  | 77.8 | 85.6 | 83.6 | 81.1 | 67.1 | Total Current | 81.5 | 83.3 |
|  | 15.2 | 9.2 | 11.9 | 14.6 | 21.9 | Fixed Assets (net) | 12.3 | 11.3 |
|  | .4 | 1.2 | 1.6 | 1.4 | 7.5 | Intangibles (net) | 1.6 | 1.1 |
|  | 6.6 | 4.0 | 2.9 | 3.0 | 3.5 | All Other Non-Current | 4.6 | 4.2 |
|  | 100.0 | 100.0 | 100.0 | 100.0 | 100.0 | Total | 100.0 | 100.0 |
|  |  |  |  |  |  | **LIABILITIES** | | |
|  | 16.0 | 22.0 | 26.4 | 21.1 | 13.7 | Notes Payable-Short Term | 24.2 | 25.2 |
|  | 3.2 | 1.7 | 1.6 | 1.1 | 2.9 | Cur. Mat.-L.T.D. | 2.5 | 2.7 |
|  | 18.1 | 15.4 | 18.8 | 20.2 | 23.4 | Trade Payables | 18.5 | 18.5 |
|  | .1 | .1 | .3 | .1 | .6 | Income Taxes Payable | .1 | .3 |
|  | 7.8 | 9.1 | 10.2 | 12.4 | 20.5 | All Other Current | 9.9 | 9.2 |
|  | 45.1 | 48.4 | 57.3 | 54.9 | 61.2 | Total Current | 55.2 | 55.9 |
|  | 11.3 | 8.0 | 5.6 | 6.3 | 10.5 | Long-Term Debt | 8.7 | 7.2 |
|  | .2 | .3 | .4 | .3 | .5 | Deferred Taxes | .2 | .1 |
|  | 5.3 | 3.3 | 4.1 | 2.3 | 2.5 | All Other Non-Current | 4.0 | 4.0 |
|  | 38.2 | 40.1 | 32.6 | 36.2 | 25.4 | Net Worth | 31.8 | 32.8 |
|  | 100.0 | 100.0 | 100.0 | 100.0 | 100.0 | Total Liabilities & Net Worth | 100.0 | 100.0 |
|  |  |  |  |  |  | **INCOME DATA** | | |
|  | 100.0 | 100.0 | 100.0 | 100.0 | 100.0 | Net Sales | 100.0 | 100.0 |
|  | 27.9 | 24.1 | 18.8 | 15.7 | 20.7 | Gross Profit | 22.9 | 22.3 |
|  | 27.0 | 20.9 | 15.1 | 11.2 | 14.8 | Operating Expenses | 20.0 | 19.0 |
|  | .9 | 3.2 | 3.8 | 4.5 | 5.8 | Operating Profit | 2.9 | 3.3 |
|  | -.4 | .1 | .0 | .0 | .9 | All Other Expenses (net) | .6 | .3 |
|  | 1.3 | 3.1 | 3.7 | 4.5 | 4.9 | Profit Before Taxes | 2.3 | 3.0 |
|  |  |  |  |  |  | **RATIOS** | | |
|  | 2.5 | 2.5 | 1.7 | 1.7 | 1.2 |  | 1.9 | 2.0 |
|  | 1.8 | 1.7 | 1.4 | 1.4 | 1.1 | Current | 1.5 | 1.5 |
|  | 1.3 | 1.3 | 1.3 | 1.3 | 1.0 |  | 1.2 | 1.2 |
|  | 1.2 | 1.0 | .6 | .3 | .5 |  | .7 | .6 |
|  | .6 | .5 | .3 | .2 | .2 | Quick | .3 | .3 |
|  | .3 | .2 | .2 | .1 | .1 |  | .1 | .1 |
| 11 33.7 | 7 50.4 | 7 51.6 | 5 73.8 | 8 48.0 | | Sales/Receivables | 7 52.8 | 6 64.1 |
| 29 12.5 | 18 20.2 | 14 25.4 | 7 51.2 | 25 14.5 | | | 17 20.9 | 15 24.6 |
| 43 8.4 | 36 10.2 | 34 10.7 | 19 19.6 | 57 6.4 | | | 35 10.4 | 31 11.9 |
| 58 6.3 | 85 4.3 | 79 4.6 | 83 4.4 | 87 4.2 | | Cost of Sales/Inventory | 80 4.6 | 76 4.8 |
| 96 3.8 | 130 2.8 | 111 3.3 | 107 3.4 | 101 3.6 | | | 116 3.1 | 117 3.1 |
| 166 2.2 | 174 2.1 | 159 2.3 | 122 3.0 | 130 2.8 | | | 168 2.2 | 168 2.2 |
| 11 34.2 | 8 45.8 | 10 36.3 | 8 44.2 | 2 159.9 | | Cost of Sales/Payables | 9 40.0 | 7 48.9 |
| 25 14.4 | 21 17.6 | 24 15.5 | 32 11.4 | 45 8.2 | | | 26 14.1 | 22 16.3 |
| 58 6.3 | 46 8.0 | 55 6.6 | 59 6.2 | 99 3.7 | | | 54 6.8 | 53 6.8 |
|  | 5.3 | 4.5 | 6.6 | 7.3 | 16.1 | Sales/Working Capital | 5.5 | 5.8 |
|  | 7.9 | 7.2 | 9.8 | 12.4 | 49.8 | | 9.6 | 10.1 |
|  | 15.2 | 12.2 | 15.1 | 17.3 | NM | | 17.3 | 19.3 |
|  | 7.5 | 16.2 | 20.3 | 71.0 | 14.2 | EBIT/Interest | 5.7 | 8.6 |
|  | (31) 2.3 | (129) 4.0 | (111) 5.8 | 13.1 | 5.6 | | (337) 2.6 | (317) 4.0 |
|  | 1.4 | 1.9 | 3.1 | 6.6 | 4.1 | | 1.4 | 1.7 |
|  |  | 12.3 | 8.3 |  |  | Net Profit + Depr., Dep., | 5.1 | 5.1 |
|  |  | (36) 3.4 | (34) 4.7 |  |  | Amort./Cur. Mat. L/T/D | (100) 2.6 | (84) 2.9 |
|  |  | 1.4 | 1.8 |  |  | | 1.2 | 1.5 |
|  | .0 | .1 | .1 | .2 | .3 | Fixed/Worth | .1 | .1 |
|  | .3 | .2 | .3 | .3 | .7 | | .3 | .3 |
|  | .7 | .4 | .6 | .6 | 2.6 | | .7 | .6 |
|  | 1.0 | .8 | 1.4 | 1.3 | 3.0 | Debt/Worth | 1.1 | 1.1 |
|  | 1.6 | 1.8 | 2.3 | 2.1 | 4.0 | | 2.6 | 2.1 |
|  | 2.7 | 3.9 | 3.6 |  | 8.8 | | 4.5 | 4.4 |
|  | 28.9 | 29.7 | 38.0 | 41.6 |  | % Profit Before Taxes/Tangible | 28.7 | 35.4 |
|  | (30) 9.7 | (135) 13.4 | (109) 27.6 | 28.2 |  | Net Worth | (323) 13.9 | (309) 18.2 |
|  | 2.4 | 6.0 | 14.4 | 22.0 |  | | 4.9 | 6.4 |
|  | 8.1 | 10.9 | 13.0 | 13.7 | 11.1 | % Profit Before Taxes/Total | 9.6 | 12.0 |
|  | 3.0 | 5.0 | 7.7 | 9.5 | 8.6 | Assets | 3.8 | 5.1 |
|  | 1.0 | 2.0 | 3.7 | 7.7 | 5.9 | | 1.2 | 1.9 |
|  | 150.9 | 93.9 | 74.2 | 62.5 | 76.2 | Sales/Net Fixed Assets | 72.3 | 74.8 |
|  | 32.7 | 45.4 | 31.5 | 28.5 | 25.0 | | 31.9 | 38.0 |
|  | 9.6 | 21.2 | 16.0 | 15.4 | 2.7 | | 14.4 | 16.5 |
|  | 3.4 | 2.9 | 3.0 | 3.3 | 2.4 | Sales/Total Assets | 2.9 | 3.2 |
|  | 2.5 | 2.2 | 2.4 | 2.4 | 1.8 | | 2.3 | 2.5 |
|  | 1.9 | 1.7 | 1.9 | 2.0 | 1.5 | | 1.8 | 1.8 |
|  | .5 | .4 | .3 | .3 |  | % Depr., Dep., Amort./Sales | .4 | .4 |
|  | (22) 1.0 | (116) .5 | (98) .6 | (18) .5 |  | | (293) .8 | (273) .7 |
|  | 1.6 | .9 | 1.1 | .8 |  | | 1.4 | 1.3 |
|  | 1.4 | .5 | .5 |  |  | % Officers', Directors' | 1.0 | .9 |
|  | (17) 3.9 | (71) 2.1 | (38) .9 |  |  | Owners' Comp/Sales | (148) 1.8 | (129) 1.8 |
|  | 6.5 | 3.9 | 1.6 |  |  | | 3.5 | 3.4 |
| 11156M | 109295M | 1702391M | 6678457M | 3549560M | 3311027M | Net Sales ($) | 11011927M | 12846978M |
| 2215M | 37548M | 710398M | 2686103M | 1342202M | 1701125M | Total Assets ($) | 4713147M | 5195260M |

M = $ thousand     MM = $ million
See Pages 9 through 22 for Explanation of Ratios and Data

## Comparative Historical Data | | | | Current Data Sorted by Sales

| Yr1 | Yr2 | Yr3 | Type of Statement | 0-1MM | 1-3MM | 3-5MM | 5-10MM | 10-25MM | 25MM & OVER |
|---|---|---|---|---|---|---|---|---|---|
| 43 | 39 | 47 | Unqualified | | | 2 | 9 | | 36 |
| 72 | 81 | 74 | Reviewed | | 1 | 5 | 9 | 21 | 38 |
| 51 | 62 | 61 | Compiled | 2 | 4 | 7 | 20 | 16 | 12 |
| 43 | 41 | 42 | Tax Returns | 1 | 15 | 2 | 9 | 13 | 2 |
| 93 | 103 | 99 | Other | | 7 | 7 | 14 | 25 | 46 |
| 4/1/09-3/31/10 ALL | 4/1/10-3/31/11 ALL | 4/1/11-3/31/12 ALL | | 52 (4/1-9/30/11) | | | 271 (10/1/11-3/31/12) | | |
| 302 | 326 | 323 | NUMBER OF STATEMENTS | 3 | 27 | 21 | 54 | 84 | 134 |
| % | % | % | ASSETS | % | % | % | % | % | % |
| 6.5 | 7.0 | 7.2 | Cash & Equivalents | | 6.2 | 5.9 | 11.9 | 7.0 | 5.9 |
| 14.3 | 14.1 | 15.4 | Trade Receivables (net) | | 19.6 | 17.6 | 14.0 | 18.0 | 13.3 |
| 57.9 | 60.4 | 59.1 | Inventory | | 56.2 | 51.8 | 57.3 | 58.0 | 61.8 |
| 2.0 | 2.3 | 1.8 | All Other Current | | 1.8 | .5 | 1.8 | 1.2 | 2.4 |
| 80.7 | 83.8 | 83.4 | Total Current | | 83.9 | 75.8 | 85.0 | 84.2 | 83.3 |
| 12.9 | 11.3 | 11.4 | Fixed Assets (net) | | 13.9 | 16.6 | 10.3 | 9.5 | 11.9 |
| 1.7 | 1.3 | 1.5 | Intangibles (net) | | .3 | .0 | .6 | 2.1 | 1.9 |
| 4.7 | 3.7 | 3.7 | All Other Non-Current | | 1.9 | 7.6 | 4.1 | 4.2 | 3.0 |
| 100.0 | 100.0 | 100.0 | Total | | 100.0 | 100.0 | 100.0 | 100.0 | 100.0 |
| | | | LIABILITIES | | | | | | |
| 26.8 | 25.6 | 22.8 | Notes Payable-Short Term | | 15.5 | 25.9 | 20.3 | 24.1 | 23.6 |
| 2.1 | 1.8 | 1.8 | Cur. Mat.-L.T.D. | | 1.2 | 3.0 | 1.8 | 1.7 | 1.6 |
| 17.0 | 16.4 | 17.3 | Trade Payables | | 21.5 | 12.0 | 13.6 | 16.4 | 19.8 |
| .2 | .1 | .2 | Income Taxes Payable | | .0 | .2 | .2 | .2 | .3 |
| 7.1 | 9.2 | 9.8 | All Other Current | | 5.7 | 3.5 | 9.2 | 8.7 | 12.6 |
| 53.3 | 53.2 | 51.9 | Total Current | | 43.9 | 44.6 | 45.0 | 51.0 | 57.9 |
| 8.2 | 7.6 | 7.4 | Long-Term Debt | | 13.9 | 9.1 | 9.2 | 6.7 | 5.7 |
| .4 | .2 | .3 | Deferred Taxes | | .1 | .2 | .5 | .4 | .3 |
| 4.2 | 3.8 | 4.2 | All Other Non-Current | | 6.7 | 5.7 | 3.8 | 2.4 | 4.1 |
| 34.0 | 35.2 | 36.2 | Net Worth | | 35.5 | 40.4 | 41.4 | 39.6 | 32.1 |
| 100.0 | 100.0 | 100.0 | Total Liabilities & Net Worth | | 100.0 | 100.0 | 100.0 | 100.0 | 100.0 |
| | | | INCOME DATA | | | | | | |
| 100.0 | 100.0 | 100.0 | Net Sales | | 100.0 | 100.0 | 100.0 | 100.0 | 100.0 |
| 22.7 | 23.6 | 22.2 | Gross Profit | | 31.7 | 25.4 | 25.7 | 22.2 | 18.3 |
| 20.2 | 20.6 | 18.7 | Operating Expenses | | 28.3 | 22.9 | 21.9 | 19.3 | 14.4 |
| 2.5 | 3.0 | 3.5 | Operating Profit | | 3.3 | 2.4 | 3.8 | 2.9 | 3.9 |
| .4 | .3 | .2 | All Other Expenses (net) | | 1.4 | -.2 | .2 | -.1 | .1 |
| 2.1 | 2.7 | 3.3 | Profit Before Taxes | | 2.0 | 2.7 | 3.5 | 3.0 | 3.8 |
| | | | RATIOS | | | | | | |
| 2.2 | 2.1 | 2.2 | Current | | 2.5 | 2.4 | 3.6 | 2.2 | 1.7 |
| 1.5 | 1.5 | 1.5 | | | 1.9 | 1.7 | 2.0 | 1.5 | 1.4 |
| 1.2 | 1.3 | 1.3 | | | 1.4 | 1.3 | 1.3 | 1.3 | 1.2 |
| .8 | .7 | .8 | Quick | | .7 | 1.0 | 1.3 | .9 | .5 |
| .3 | .3 | .4 | | | .5 | .6 | .6 | .5 | .3 |
| .1 | .1 | .2 | | | | | | | |
| 7 50.9 | 7 52.3 | 7 52.3 | Sales/Receivables | | 14 25.8 | 8 43.9 | 7 49.1 | 7 51.9 | 6 65.9 |
| 16 22.9 | 16 23.4 | 16 23.2 | | | 32 11.5 | 16 22.7 | 17 20.9 | 18 20.1 | 13 29.0 |
| 35 10.4 | 36 10.2 | 35 10.3 | | | 43 8.4 | 42 8.6 | 35 10.4 | 41 8.9 | 29 12.8 |
| 78 4.7 | 86 4.2 | 81 4.5 | Cost of Sales/Inventory | | 91 4.0 | 57 6.4 | 91 4.0 | 78 4.7 | 78 4.7 |
| 119 3.1 | 125 2.9 | 114 3.2 | | | 140 2.6 | 130 2.8 | 135 2.7 | 122 3.0 | 107 3.4 |
| 184 2.0 | 176 2.1 | 166 2.2 | | | 304 1.2 | 228 1.6 | 174 2.1 | 166 2.2 | 140 2.6 |
| 9 39.1 | 7 52.9 | 8 44.2 | Cost of Sales/Payables | | 22 16.4 | 8 45.0 | 5 69.2 | 9 40.8 | 9 41.9 |
| 24 14.9 | 23 15.7 | 22 16.4 | | | 54 6.7 | 17 21.0 | 18 20.4 | 19 19.3 | 25 14.8 |
| 53 6.9 | 47 7.8 | 53 6.9 | | | 111 3.3 | 47 7.8 | 43 8.4 | 46 8.0 | 56 6.5 |
| 5.0 | 4.9 | 5.4 | Sales/Working Capital | | 3.0 | 4.7 | 3.5 | 5.7 | 7.3 |
| 8.5 | 8.2 | 9.2 | | | 5.9 | 6.3 | 5.6 | 8.9 | 10.9 |
| 15.3 | 14.3 | 14.1 | | | 9.6 | 12.6 | 10.1 | 13.4 | 16.3 |
| 8.1 | 11.0 | 16.3 | EBIT/Interest | | 7.4 | 8.9 | 18.1 | 11.7 | 22.6 |
| (287) 3.0 | (313) 3.8 | (307) 4.9 | | | (26) 2.2 | (20) 3.2 | (48) 3.7 | (79) 4.2 | (132) 6.6 |
| 1.1 | 1.7 | 2.3 | | | 1.5 | 1.8 | 1.6 | 1.9 | 3.5 |
| 6.1 | 7.1 | 9.4 | Net Profit + Depr., Dep., Amort./Cur. Mat. L/T/D | | | | 13.2 | 8.0 | 8.7 |
| (86) 3.4 | (75) 3.4 | (80) 4.1 | | | | | (12) 4.0 | (24) 3.7 | (37) 5.4 |
| 1.1 | 1.6 | 1.7 | | | | | .8 | 2.1 | 1.9 |
| .1 | .1 | .1 | Fixed/Worth | | .0 | .1 | .1 | .1 | .1 |
| .2 | .2 | .2 | | | .2 | .2 | .2 | .2 | .3 |
| .6 | .5 | .5 | | | .7 | .5 | .5 | .4 | .6 |
| 1.0 | 1.0 | 1.1 | Debt/Worth | | 1.1 | 1.1 | .6 | .8 | 1.5 |
| 2.1 | 2.2 | 2.1 | | | 1.7 | 1.8 | 1.2 | 1.9 | 2.3 |
| 4.6 | 3.9 | 3.7 | | | 4.8 | 2.8 | 6.3 | 3.7 | 3.6 |
| 28.5 | 30.5 | 34.9 | % Profit Before Taxes/Tangible Net Worth | | 29.0 | 28.5 | 31.1 | 29.8 | 43.8 |
| (285) 13.5 | (310) 14.6 | (309) 20.4 | | | (24) 9.5 | 15.6 | (51) 12.8 | (82) 15.8 | (129) 28.5 |
| 1.7 | 5.7 | 9.1 | | | 3.5 | 5.6 | 5.5 | 6.7 | 17.4 |
| 9.2 | 10.0 | 11.7 | % Profit Before Taxes/Total Assets | | 7.5 | 8.7 | 10.2 | 11.9 | 13.1 |
| 3.7 | 4.1 | 6.2 | | | 3.0 | 4.6 | 5.3 | 5.3 | 8.0 |
| .3 | 1.5 | 2.6 | | | 1.3 | 2.2 | 1.5 | 1.9 | 4.4 |
| 66.6 | 76.4 | 89.2 | Sales/Net Fixed Assets | | 131.5 | 58.8 | 95.5 | 109.3 | 67.6 |
| 31.2 | 35.0 | 39.9 | | | 35.0 | 28.8 | 43.9 | 47.0 | 31.8 |
| 13.4 | 14.6 | 16.8 | | | 8.6 | 11.2 | 17.7 | 22.0 | 18.0 |
| 2.9 | 3.0 | 3.0 | Sales/Total Assets | | 3.0 | 2.5 | 2.6 | 3.1 | 3.2 |
| 2.2 | 2.3 | 2.3 | | | 2.1 | 2.1 | 2.1 | 2.3 | 2.5 |
| 1.6 | 1.7 | 1.8 | | | 1.1 | 1.4 | 1.7 | 1.9 | 2.1 |
| .4 | .4 | .3 | % Depr., Dep., Amort./Sales | | .5 | .4 | .4 | .4 | .3 |
| (253) .8 | (261) .7 | (264) .6 | | | (17) .9 | (16) .6 | (45) .6 | (70) .6 | (115) .5 |
| 1.6 | 1.3 | 1.0 | | | 1.9 | 1.5 | 1.0 | 1.3 | .8 |
| .9 | 1.0 | .7 | % Officers', Directors', Owners' Comp/Sales | | 2.4 | 1.1 | 1.3 | | .5 |
| (115) 1.9 | (140) 1.8 | (133) 1.6 | | | (14) 4.2 | (10) 1.6 | (28) 2.4 | (42) 1.4 | (37) .9 |
| 4.0 | 3.5 | 3.8 | | | 6.7 | 3.5 | 5.5 | 3.2 | 2.2 |
| 11774119M | 12841619M | 15361886M | Net Sales ($) | 1456M | 56133M | 83224M | 393186M | 1391026M | 13436861M |
| 5588385M | 5805152M | 6479591M | Total Assets ($) | 923M | 33329M | 43412M | 208300M | 628276M | 5565351M |

## Current Data Sorted by Assets        Comparative Historical Data

### Type of Statement

| | 0-500M | 500M-2MM | 2-10MM | 10-50MM | 50-100MM | 100-250MM | 4/1/07-3/31/08 ALL | 4/1/08-3/31/09 ALL |
|---|---|---|---|---|---|---|---|---|
| Unqualified | | | 32 | 64 | 27 | 25 | 205 | 206 |
| Reviewed | | 33 | 188 | 99 | 2 | | 284 | 317 |
| Compiled | 9 | 73 | 101 | 19 | 1 | | 208 | 224 |
| Tax Returns | 37 | 102 | 78 | 4 | 1 | | 118 | 159 |
| Other | 16 | 92 | 194 | 137 | 22 | 21 | 416 | 533 |
| | 248 (4/1-9/30/11) | | | 1,129 (10/1/11-3/31/12) | | | | |
| **NUMBER OF STATEMENTS** | 62 | 300 | 593 | 323 | 53 | 46 | 1231 | 1439 |

### ASSETS

| | 0-500M % | 500M-2MM % | 2-10MM % | 10-50MM % | 50-100MM % | 100-250MM % | ALL % | ALL % |
|---|---|---|---|---|---|---|---|---|
| Cash & Equivalents | 20.8 | 10.7 | 9.3 | 7.0 | 5.8 | 5.7 | 7.6 | 8.0 |
| Trade Receivables (net) | 34.8 | 33.8 | 32.3 | 27.8 | 27.2 | 21.9 | 31.1 | 29.6 |
| Inventory | 20.8 | 34.1 | 37.4 | 34.5 | 39.6 | 31.5 | 35.7 | 35.7 |
| All Other Current | 5.1 | 2.0 | 1.8 | 3.4 | 2.7 | 4.5 | 2.7 | 3.0 |
| Total Current | 81.5 | 80.5 | 80.7 | 72.7 | 75.3 | 63.6 | 77.2 | 76.3 |
| Fixed Assets (net) | 10.7 | 12.0 | 12.1 | 17.1 | 16.5 | 18.6 | 15.2 | 15.4 |
| Intangibles (net) | 1.5 | 2.6 | 2.2 | 4.0 | 5.0 | 12.1 | 2.6 | 3.0 |
| All Other Non-Current | 6.4 | 5.0 | 5.0 | 6.2 | 3.2 | 5.7 | 5.1 | 5.3 |
| Total | 100.0 | 100.0 | 100.0 | 100.0 | 100.0 | 100.0 | 100.0 | 100.0 |

### LIABILITIES

| | 0-500M | 500M-2MM | 2-10MM | 10-50MM | 50-100MM | 100-250MM | ALL | ALL |
|---|---|---|---|---|---|---|---|---|
| Notes Payable-Short Term | 13.7 | 13.8 | 14.7 | 14.1 | 18.4 | 12.0 | 17.1 | 17.5 |
| Cur. Mat.-L.T.D. | 3.0 | 2.9 | 2.4 | 3.4 | 2.0 | 3.1 | 3.3 | 3.2 |
| Trade Payables | 24.5 | 24.5 | 19.8 | 15.4 | 16.4 | 13.3 | 19.0 | 18.7 |
| Income Taxes Payable | .2 | .1 | .3 | .3 | .4 | .2 | .3 | .2 |
| All Other Current | 13.7 | 10.4 | 9.9 | 12.1 | 14.5 | 13.0 | 10.8 | 10.4 |
| Total Current | 55.1 | 51.7 | 47.2 | 45.3 | 51.7 | 41.6 | 50.4 | 50.0 |
| Long-Term Debt | 11.5 | 12.0 | 7.3 | 9.7 | 8.9 | 15.9 | 9.9 | 10.1 |
| Deferred Taxes | .0 | .1 | .4 | .9 | 1.1 | 1.8 | .3 | .3 |
| All Other Non-Current | 4.1 | 6.3 | 4.9 | 4.3 | 2.6 | 2.9 | 4.0 | 4.5 |
| Net Worth | 29.4 | 30.0 | 40.3 | 39.8 | 35.7 | 37.8 | 35.4 | 35.1 |
| Total Liabilties & Net Worth | 100.0 | 100.0 | 100.0 | 100.0 | 100.0 | 100.0 | 100.0 | 100.0 |

### INCOME DATA

| | 0-500M | 500M-2MM | 2-10MM | 10-50MM | 50-100MM | 100-250MM | ALL | ALL |
|---|---|---|---|---|---|---|---|---|
| Net Sales | 100.0 | 100.0 | 100.0 | 100.0 | 100.0 | 100.0 | 100.0 | 100.0 |
| Gross Profit | 35.5 | 33.2 | 30.3 | 28.2 | 25.7 | 26.3 | 29.7 | 29.7 |
| Operating Expenses | 32.2 | 30.1 | 25.7 | 23.0 | 20.3 | 20.0 | 25.1 | 26.0 |
| Operating Profit | 3.2 | 3.2 | 4.7 | 5.3 | 5.4 | 6.3 | 4.6 | 3.6 |
| All Other Expenses (net) | .0 | .3 | .3 | .5 | .7 | 1.1 | .7 | .6 |
| Profit Before Taxes | 3.2 | 2.8 | 4.4 | 4.8 | 4.7 | 5.2 | 3.9 | 3.0 |

### RATIOS

| | 0-500M | 500M-2MM | 2-10MM | 10-50MM | 50-100MM | 100-250MM | ALL | ALL |
|---|---|---|---|---|---|---|---|---|
| Current | 4.8 | 2.7 | 2.6 | 2.3 | 2.0 | 2.4 | 2.2 | 2.3 |
| | 1.7 | 1.7 | 1.7 | 1.6 | 1.4 | 1.6 | 1.6 | 1.5 |
| | 1.1 | 1.2 | 1.3 | 1.2 | 1.2 | 1.3 | 1.2 | 1.2 |
| Quick | 3.5 | 1.3 | 1.5 | 1.2 | 1.0 | 1.2 | 1.2 | 1.2 |
| | 1.2 | .9 | .9 | .8 | .7 | .7 | .8 (1438) | .8 |
| | .7 | .6 | .6 | .5 | .4 | .3 | .5 | .5 |
| Sales/Receivables | 11   32.7 | 24   15.5 | 32   11.5 | 36   10.2 | 39   9.4 | 37   9.8 | 30   12.2 | 27   13.7 |
| | 29   12.8 | 37   9.9 | 42   8.6 | 46   8.0 | 49   7.4 | 45   8.2 | 40   9.2 | 38   9.7 |
| | 51   7.2 | 51   7.2 | 54   6.8 | 56   6.5 | 59   6.2 | 59   6.2 | 51   7.1 | 51   7.2 |
| Cost of Sales/Inventory | 2   226.6 | 26   14.3 | 38   9.7 | 46   7.9 | 59   6.2 | 55   6.6 | 35   10.4 | 33   11.1 |
| | 24   15.0 | 55   6.6 | 69   5.3 | 74   4.9 | 85   4.3 | 74   4.9 | 63   5.8 | 64   5.7 |
| | 57   6.4 | 99   3.7 | 122   3.0 | 126   2.9 | 140   2.6 | 146   2.5 | 107   3.4 | 114   3.2 |
| Cost of Sales/Payables | 4   83.0 | 19   19.4 | 18   19.8 | 19   19.6 | 24   15.0 | 22   16.9 | 18   20.7 | 16   23.0 |
| | 26   14.1 | 35   10.5 | 33   10.9 | 29   12.6 | 35   10.5 | 35   10.4 | 31   11.9 | 28   13.2 |
| | 40   9.2 | 57   6.4 | 51   7.1 | 42   8.6 | 45   8.2 | 48   7.6 | 47   7.8 | 47   7.8 |
| Sales/Working Capital | 5.6 | 5.5 | 4.7 | 4.9 | 4.7 | 4.6 | 5.9 | 5.7 |
| | 15.5 | 10.9 | 8.2 | 9.0 | 9.0 | 7.0 | 10.2 | 10.6 |
| | 161.8 | 32.1 | 16.7 | 18.5 | 20.1 | 13.3 | 25.9 | 25.8 |
| EBIT/Interest | 23.0 | 16.4 | 21.9 | 28.2 | 28.2 | 26.9 | 10.1 | 12.0 |
| | (35) 7.1 | (258) 4.4 | (515) 6.7 | (295) 10.2 | (49) 10.4 | 9.1 | (1109) 3.8 | (1296) 3.5 |
| | .3 | 1.6 | 2.4 | 3.8 | 3.2 | 3.5 | 1.7 | 1.4 |
| Net Profit + Depr., Dep., Amort./Cur. Mat. L/T/D | | 9.7 | 8.2 | 14.3 | 8.6 | 88.2 | 6.8 | 8.7 |
| | (25) 2.7 | (117) 2.7 | (82) 5.3 | (12) 4.1 | (11) 39.3 | | (329) 2.8 | (342) 3.1 |
| | 1.6 | 1.3 | 2.1 | 1.5 | 7.5 | | 1.3 | 1.1 |
| Fixed/Worth | .0 | .1 | .1 | .1 | .2 | .2 | .1 | .1 |
| | .2 | .2 | .2 | .3 | .4 | .6 | .3 | .3 |
| | 1.3 | .9 | .5 | 1.1 | .8 | 1.3 | 1.0 | 1.0 |
| Debt/Worth | .4 | .9 | .7 | .9 | 1.3 | 1.2 | .9 | .9 |
| | 1.8 | 2.1 | 1.6 | 1.8 | 2.4 | 2.1 | 1.9 | 2.1 |
| | 12.4 | 7.1 | 3.4 | 3.6 | 4.8 | 7.4 | 4.8 | 4.8 |
| % Profit Before Taxes/Tangible Net Worth | 90.7 | 58.1 | 45.7 | 44.3 | 55.2 | 40.7 | 44.2 | 40.2 |
| | (50) 31.9 | (253) 18.8 | (562) 23.0 | (294) 24.7 | (51) 25.2 | (40) 31.9 | (1130) 21.1 | (1317) 16.6 |
| | -.8 | 5.9 | 8.2 | 11.8 | 15.8 | 13.3 | 7.4 | 4.1 |
| % Profit Before Taxes/Total Assets | 31.0 | 15.5 | 16.5 | 15.4 | 14.8 | 12.0 | 14.7 | 13.3 |
| | 9.5 | 6.3 | 7.9 | 8.6 | 7.2 | 7.1 | 6.7 | 5.2 |
| | -1.0 | 1.4 | 2.7 | 3.8 | 3.4 | 3.6 | 2.0 | 1.1 |
| Sales/Net Fixed Assets | UND | 196.4 | 109.6 | 56.0 | 39.1 | 53.6 | 75.1 | 81.4 |
| | 122.1 | 55.4 | 41.9 | 21.1 | 17.5 | 18.4 | 32.8 | 32.1 |
| | 27.9 | 17.7 | 15.2 | 7.8 | 8.7 | 6.1 | 11.7 | 11.9 |
| Sales/Total Assets | 6.8 | 4.5 | 3.4 | 2.8 | 2.4 | 2.3 | 3.6 | 3.6 |
| | 4.6 | 3.2 | 2.6 | 2.1 | 1.9 | 1.5 | 2.7 | 2.7 |
| | 2.2 | 2.3 | 1.9 | 1.5 | 1.4 | .9 | 1.9 | 1.9 |
| % Depr., Dep., Amort./Sales | .2 | .3 | .3 | .5 | .5 | .4 | .4 | .4 |
| | (32) .6 | (202) .7 | (467) .7 | (272) 1.1 | (40) 1.0 | (29) 1.1 | (1023) .7 | (1151) .8 |
| | 1.4 | 1.6 | 1.5 | 2.5 | 3.8 | 2.1 | 1.8 | 1.9 |
| % Officers', Directors' Owners' Comp/Sales | 4.0 | 2.5 | 1.8 | .7 | | | 1.8 | 1.8 |
| | (35) 6.3 | (180) 4.6 | (255) 3.4 | (51) 1.3 | | | (438) 3.9 | (475) 3.4 |
| | 11.3 | 7.4 | 5.5 | 3.6 | | | | |
| Net Sales ($) | 112268M | 1212049M | 7880828M | 15456449M | 7224609M | 10829061M | 41247601M | 50340857M |
| Total Assets ($) | 19869M | 358228M | 2920639M | 7151589M | 3646071M | 6708664M | 19071611M | 23402505M |

## Comparative Historical Data | Current Data Sorted by Sales

| 175 | 164 | 148 | Type of Statement — Unqualified | | 1 | 1 | 4 | 32 | 110 |
|---|---|---|---|---|---|---|---|---|---|
| 284 | 307 | 322 | Reviewed | | 12 | 22 | 57 | 131 | 100 |
| 204 | 210 | 203 | Compiled | 8 | 27 | 38 | 62 | 52 | 16 |
| 145 | 187 | 222 | Tax Returns | 21 | 56 | 43 | 63 | 31 | 8 |
| 436 | 481 | 482 | Other | 11 | 47 | 48 | 88 | 118 | 170 |
| 4/1/09-3/31/10 ALL | 4/1/10-3/31/11 ALL | 4/1/11-3/31/12 ALL | | 248 (4/1-9/30/11) | | | 1,129 (10/1/11-3/31/12) | | |
| | | | | 0-1MM | 1-3MM | 3-5MM | 5-10MM | 10-25MM | 25MM & OVER |
| 1244 | 1349 | 1377 | **NUMBER OF STATEMENTS** | 40 | 143 | 152 | 274 | 364 | 404 |
| % | % | % | **ASSETS** | % | % | % | % | % | % |
| 8.4 | 9.4 | 9.3 | Cash & Equivalents | 14.2 | 11.8 | 12.2 | 9.3 | 9.6 | 6.7 |
| 27.8 | 30.7 | 31.1 | Trade Receivables (net) | 29.5 | 27.2 | 32.6 | 30.7 | 33.9 | 30.0 |
| 34.9 | 34.0 | 35.1 | Inventory | 25.1 | 35.2 | 32.6 | 39.2 | 35.0 | 34.3 |
| 3.2 | 2.5 | 2.5 | All Other Current | 7.0 | 2.4 | 2.3 | 1.2 | 1.8 | 3.5 |
| 74.4 | 76.6 | 78.0 | Total Current | 75.9 | 76.6 | 79.6 | 80.4 | 80.4 | 74.5 |
| 16.8 | 14.9 | 13.6 | Fixed Assets (net) | 15.3 | 14.0 | 12.4 | 11.6 | 13.5 | 15.1 |
| 3.2 | 3.0 | 3.1 | Intangibles (net) | 1.8 | 2.9 | 2.1 | 2.3 | 2.0 | 5.2 |
| 5.5 | 5.5 | 5.3 | All Other Non-Current | 7.1 | 6.5 | 5.9 | 5.6 | 4.2 | 5.2 |
| 100.0 | 100.0 | 100.0 | Total | 100.0 | 100.0 | 100.0 | 100.0 | 100.0 | 100.0 |
| | | | **LIABILITIES** | | | | | | |
| 15.9 | 15.3 | 14.4 | Notes Payable-Short Term | 13.8 | 13.6 | 15.0 | 16.0 | 13.2 | 14.4 |
| 3.3 | 2.9 | 2.8 | Cur. Mat.-L.T.D. | 4.2 | 2.2 | 3.2 | 2.2 | 3.2 | 2.6 |
| 16.8 | 19.0 | 19.7 | Trade Payables | 17.8 | 18.9 | 21.9 | 23.8 | 18.9 | 17.1 |
| .2 | .2 | .3 | Income Taxes Payable | .4 | .1 | .1 | .3 | .3 | .4 |
| 9.4 | 10.7 | 11.0 | All Other Current | 15.1 | 10.5 | 10.2 | 8.3 | 11.0 | 12.9 |
| 45.6 | 48.1 | 48.1 | Total Current | 51.3 | 45.3 | 50.4 | 50.7 | 46.6 | 47.4 |
| 10.7 | 9.7 | 9.4 | Long-Term Debt | 18.8 | 15.2 | 10.6 | 7.8 | 6.5 | 9.8 |
| .4 | .4 | .5 | Deferred Taxes | .0 | .1 | .2 | .3 | .5 | .9 |
| 4.6 | 4.7 | 4.8 | All Other Non-Current | 6.2 | 8.0 | 5.3 | 4.2 | 5.2 | 3.5 |
| 38.6 | 37.1 | 37.2 | Net Worth | 23.7 | 31.4 | 33.6 | 37.0 | 41.2 | 38.4 |
| 100.0 | 100.0 | 100.0 | Total Liabilities & Net Worth | 100.0 | 100.0 | 100.0 | 100.0 | 100.0 | 100.0 |
| | | | **INCOME DATA** | | | | | | |
| 100.0 | 100.0 | 100.0 | Net Sales | 100.0 | 100.0 | 100.0 | 100.0 | 100.0 | 100.0 |
| 31.0 | 31.1 | 30.4 | Gross Profit | 45.0 | 36.2 | 34.2 | 31.2 | 28.4 | 26.7 |
| 28.8 | 27.5 | 25.9 | Operating Expenses | 39.7 | 33.0 | 30.1 | 27.2 | 23.6 | 21.6 |
| 2.2 | 3.6 | 4.5 | Operating Profit | 5.3 | 3.2 | 4.1 | 4.0 | 4.9 | 5.1 |
| .7 | .4 | .4 | All Other Expenses (net) | .6 | .6 | .4 | .2 | .3 | .5 |
| 1.5 | 3.2 | 4.1 | Profit Before Taxes | 4.7 | 2.6 | 3.7 | 3.8 | 4.6 | 4.6 |
| | | | **RATIOS** | | | | | | |
| 2.7 | 2.6 | 2.5 | Current | 5.4 | 3.7 | 2.7 | 2.4 | 2.7 | 2.1 |
| 1.7 | 1.6 | 1.6 | | 2.1 | 1.9 | 1.8 | 1.6 | 1.6 | 1.5 |
| 1.2 | 1.2 | 1.2 | | 1.3 | 1.2 | 1.2 | 1.2 | 1.3 | 1.2 |
| 1.4 | 1.4 | 1.4 | Quick | 3.1 | 1.6 | 1.4 | 1.2 | 1.6 | 1.2 |
| .8 | .9 | .8 | | 1.1 | .9 | .9 | .8 | .9 | .8 |
| .5 | .5 | .5 | | .6 | .4 | .6 | .5 | .6 | .5 |
| 29  12.6 | 33  11.1 | 31  11.8 | Sales/Receivables | 18  19.8 | 18  20.1 | 25  14.7 | 27  13.6 | 35  10.5 | 35  10.5 |
| 40  9.1 | 43  8.4 | 42  8.6 | | 46  8.0 | 38  9.5 | 40  9.1 | 38  9.6 | 45  8.1 | 45  8.2 |
| 53  6.9 | 56  6.5 | 54  6.7 | | 73  5.0 | 55  6.6 | 52  7.0 | 52  7.0 | 55  6.6 | 55  6.6 |
| 37  9.8 | 39  9.4 | 36  10.2 | Cost of Sales/Inventory | 9  39.6 | 30  12.1 | 22  16.8 | 37  9.9 | 37  9.9 | 42  8.7 |
| 72  5.1 | 71  5.2 | 66  5.5 | | 87  4.2 | 89  4.1 | 56  6.5 | 73  5.0 | 61  6.0 | 66  5.5 |
| 135  2.7 | 121  3.0 | 118  3.1 | | 182  2.0 | 152  2.4 | 99  3.7 | 126  2.9 | 107  3.4 | 111  3.3 |
| 16  22.5 | 19  18.9 | 18  20.0 | Cost of Sales/Payables | 5  70.5 | 15  24.1 | 17  21.3 | 21  17.7 | 18  20.6 | 20  18.7 |
| 30  12.3 | 33  11.2 | 32  11.4 | | 29  12.5 | 32  11.3 | 34  10.6 | 38  9.7 | 31  11.6 | 30  12.1 |
| 47  7.7 | 51  7.1 | 50  7.3 | | 101  3.6 | 72  5.1 | 50  7.3 | 61  6.0 | 45  8.1 | 42  8.6 |
| 4.5 | 4.7 | 5.0 | Sales/Working Capital | 1.8 | 3.8 | 4.9 | 5.0 | 5.3 | 5.7 |
| 8.2 | 8.6 | 9.0 | | 4.8 | 6.5 | 9.4 | 10.0 | 8.4 | 9.8 |
| 22.7 | 22.4 | 19.9 | | 16.9 | 23.3 | 28.7 | 21.7 | 16.9 | 19.7 |
| 9.2 | 17.3 | 21.9 | EBIT/Interest | 14.8 | 8.7 | 10.5 | 20.8 | 27.1 | 29.1 |
| (1125) 2.3 | (1195) 4.8 | (1198) 7.0 | | (25) 2.8 | (115) 2.8 | (127) 4.7 | (244) 5.9 | (316) 9.1 | (371) 10.2 |
| .3 | 1.8 | 2.4 | | -.2 | 1.1 | 1.5 | 2.2 | 3.2 | 3.7 |
| 8.7 | 8.3 | 11.3 | Net Profit + Depr., Dep., Amort./Cur. Mat. L/T/D | | 3.3 | 4.0 | 10.9 | 7.7 | 24.4 |
| (304) 2.3 | (291) 3.0 | (247) 3.8 | | | (12) 2.0 | (11) 2.6 | (50) 3.2 | (75) 2.6 | (99) 6.7 |
| .7 | 1.2 | 1.6 | | | 1.6 | .4 | 1.5 | 1.1 | 2.8 |
| .1 | .1 | .1 | Fixed/Worth | .0 | .1 | .0 | .1 | .1 | .1 |
| .3 | .3 | .2 | | .1 | .3 | .2 | .2 | .2 | .3 |
| 1.0 | .9 | .8 | | 1.3 | 1.5 | .7 | .6 | .6 | 1.0 |
| .7 | .8 | .8 | Debt/Worth | .6 | .7 | .7 | .8 | .7 | 1.0 |
| 1.7 | 1.8 | 1.9 | | 1.9 | 2.3 | 1.9 | 2.0 | 1.6 | 2.0 |
| 4.3 | 4.1 | 4.1 | | 78.6 | 10.3 | 5.2 | 4.4 | 3.1 | 4.1 |
| 25.0 | 38.2 | 47.0 | % Profit Before Taxes/Tangible Net Worth | 50.8 | 37.4 | 48.2 | 47.5 | 45.6 | 51.2 |
| (1139) 7.9 | (1231) 16.5 | (1250) 23.8 | | (32) 15.5 | (114) 13.3 | (133) 17.1 | (251) 19.6 | (344) 24.2 | (376) 28.2 |
| -1.7 | 4.8 | 9.0 | | -1.8 | 4.0 | 4.8 | 7.8 | 9.4 | 13.4 |
| 9.3 | 13.4 | 15.9 | % Profit Before Taxes/Total Assets | 12.5 | 13.9 | 15.9 | 14.8 | 17.3 | 16.2 |
| 2.6 | 5.7 | 7.5 | | 3.5 | 4.4 | 6.3 | 6.9 | 8.9 | 9.0 |
| -1.2 | 1.4 | 2.7 | | -1.2 | .6 | .9 | 2.3 | 3.4 | 4.4 |
| 67.9 | 86.5 | 100.3 | Sales/Net Fixed Assets | UND | 110.4 | 181.8 | 121.7 | 94.6 | 71.2 |
| 26.0 | 30.2 | 36.4 | | 22.0 | 30.8 | 59.5 | 45.7 | 34.6 | 25.7 |
| 8.6 | 10.9 | 13.0 | | 8.7 | 11.8 | 15.3 | 15.8 | 15.1 | 10.8 |
| 3.3 | 3.2 | 3.4 | Sales/Total Assets | 2.3 | 3.5 | 4.1 | 3.7 | 3.5 | 3.1 |
| 2.3 | 2.4 | 2.5 | | 1.5 | 2.3 | 2.8 | 2.6 | 2.7 | 2.4 |
| 1.5 | 1.6 | 1.8 | | 1.0 | 1.5 | 1.9 | 1.8 | 1.9 | 1.7 |
| .5 | .4 | .4 | % Depr., Dep., Amort./Sales | .6 | .6 | .3 | .4 | .3 | .4 |
| (997) 1.0 | (1060) .9 | (1042) .8 | | (19) 1.5 | (96) 1.1 | (108) .6 | (199) .7 | (297) .8 | (323) .8 |
| 2.6 | 2.4 | 1.9 | | 5.8 | 2.4 | 1.5 | 1.5 | 2.0 | 1.9 |
| 1.8 | 2.0 | 2.0 | % Officers', Directors' Owners' Comp/Sales | 5.5 | 3.2 | 2.8 | 2.0 | 1.5 | .7 |
| (429) 3.7 | (491) 3.9 | (526) 3.8 | | (19) 9.3 | (76) 4.6 | (91) 4.6 | (148) 3.9 | (133) 3.3 | (59) 1.3 |
| 6.5 | 6.8 | 6.3 | | 12.5 | 8.2 | 6.7 | 6.2 | 5.0 | 3.3 |
| 34660009M | 37292081M | 42715264M | Net Sales ($) | 23397M | 292276M | 614071M | 1985458M | 6013448M | 33786614M |
| 19367366M | 19321970M | 20805060M | Total Assets ($) | 21413M | 159757M | 270809M | 870472M | 2669629M | 16812980M |

M = $ thousand     MM = $ million
See Pages 9 through 22 for Explanation of Ratios and Data

# WHOLESALE—Industrial Supplies Merchant Wholesalers  NAICS 423840

**Current Data Sorted by Assets**  |  **Comparative Historical Data**

| 0-500M | 500M-2MM | 2-10MM | 10-50MM | 50-100MM | 100-250MM | | 4/1/07-3/31/08 ALL | 4/1/08-3/31/09 ALL |
|---|---|---|---|---|---|---|---|---|
| | | | | | | **Type of Statement** | | |
| | 1 | 15 | 41 | 10 | 4 | Unqualified | 70 | 73 |
| | 11 | 87 | 47 | 1 | 1 | Reviewed | 141 | 157 |
| 2 | 31 | 52 | 11 | 1 | | Compiled | 91 | 102 |
| 15 | 40 | 30 | 3 | | | Tax Returns | 51 | 70 |
| 12 | 37 | 75 | 53 | 8 | 9 | Other | 151 | 183 |
| 99 (4/1-9/30/11) | | | 497 (10/1/11-3/31/12) | | | | | |
| 29 | 120 | 259 | 155 | 20 | 13 | **NUMBER OF STATEMENTS** | 504 | 585 |
| % | % | % | % | % | % | **ASSETS** | % | % |
| 21.7 | 8.9 | 8.3 | 5.1 | 4.9 | 2.2 | Cash & Equivalents | 6.4 | 6.8 |
| 38.9 | 35.2 | 32.2 | 31.1 | 31.7 | 29.7 | Trade Receivables (net) | 32.9 | 32.2 |
| 24.7 | 38.6 | 38.1 | 37.1 | 31.3 | 28.4 | Inventory | 37.9 | 38.4 |
| 1.5 | 1.2 | 1.6 | 2.7 | 2.4 | 4.0 | All Other Current | 2.2 | 2.1 |
| 86.8 | 83.9 | 80.2 | 76.0 | 70.4 | 64.3 | Total Current | 79.5 | 79.4 |
| 7.1 | 9.6 | 11.2 | 13.3 | 15.8 | 10.3 | Fixed Assets (net) | 12.6 | 11.7 |
| 2.0 | 2.4 | 3.9 | 4.4 | 9.4 | 20.9 | Intangibles (net) | 2.8 | 3.6 |
| 3.8 | 4.1 | 4.7 | 6.3 | 4.4 | 4.5 | All Other Non-Current | 5.2 | 5.3 |
| 100.0 | 100.0 | 100.0 | 100.0 | 100.0 | 100.0 | Total | 100.0 | 100.0 |
| | | | | | | **LIABILITIES** | | |
| 14.9 | 12.7 | 12.3 | 17.5 | 19.7 | 7.4 | Notes Payable-Short Term | 16.1 | 17.5 |
| .5 | 2.4 | 2.4 | 2.0 | 1.0 | .6 | Cur. Mat.-L.T.D. | 2.4 | 2.2 |
| 27.0 | 27.4 | 18.2 | 17.9 | 13.4 | 13.8 | Trade Payables | 21.1 | 19.7 |
| .1 | .3 | .2 | .3 | .1 | .5 | Income Taxes Payable | .2 | .2 |
| 9.3 | 7.2 | 7.4 | 7.3 | 8.8 | 6.6 | All Other Current | 7.2 | 7.7 |
| 51.7 | 50.1 | 40.6 | 45.0 | 43.1 | 28.9 | Total Current | 46.9 | 47.3 |
| 9.5 | 10.8 | 7.0 | 7.1 | 8.2 | 17.9 | Long-Term Debt | 9.7 | 8.2 |
| .0 | .1 | .2 | .4 | .7 | 1.4 | Deferred Taxes | .3 | .2 |
| 8.2 | 4.9 | 5.7 | 3.0 | 7.9 | 2.6 | All Other Non-Current | 4.3 | 5.2 |
| 30.5 | 34.2 | 46.6 | 44.6 | 40.1 | 49.1 | Net Worth | 38.8 | 39.2 |
| 100.0 | 100.0 | 100.0 | 100.0 | 100.0 | 100.0 | Total Liabilities & Net Worth | 100.0 | 100.0 |
| | | | | | | **INCOME DATA** | | |
| 100.0 | 100.0 | 100.0 | 100.0 | 100.0 | 100.0 | Net Sales | 100.0 | 100.0 |
| 33.1 | 30.3 | 29.8 | 30.0 | 26.2 | 27.3 | Gross Profit | 29.8 | 29.6 |
| 26.7 | 27.0 | 25.3 | 23.4 | 21.0 | 21.7 | Operating Expenses | 25.0 | 25.0 |
| 6.5 | 3.3 | 4.6 | 6.6 | 5.1 | 5.5 | Operating Profit | 4.8 | 4.6 |
| .1 | .0 | .3 | .4 | 1.0 | .7 | All Other Expenses (net) | .6 | .6 |
| 6.3 | 3.3 | 4.3 | 6.2 | 4.2 | 4.8 | Profit Before Taxes | 4.2 | 4.0 |
| | | | | | | **RATIOS** | | |
| 3.2 | 2.6 | 3.6 | 2.3 | 2.6 | 4.1 | | 2.8 | 2.7 |
| 2.0 | 1.7 | 2.1 | 1.6 | 1.5 | 2.3 | Current | 1.7 | 1.7 |
| 1.3 | 1.3 | 1.4 | 1.3 | 1.3 | 1.3 | | 1.3 | 1.2 |
| 2.4 | 1.5 | 1.8 | 1.3 | 1.3 | 1.7 | | 1.4 | 1.3 |
| 1.2 | 1.0 | 1.0 | .8 | .9 | 1.2 | Quick | .9 | .9 |
| .9 | .6 | .6 | .5 | .6 | .8 | | .6 | .5 |
| 21  17.5 | 27  13.7 | 32  11.5 | 38  9.6 | 41  8.8 | 47  7.8 | | 33  10.9 | 30  12.2 |
| 35  10.3 | 37  9.8 | 40  9.2 | 47  7.7 | 49  7.4 | 58  6.3 | Sales/Receivables | 41  9.0 | 38  9.5 |
| 49  7.4 | 47  7.8 | 48  7.6 | 54  6.8 | 55  6.6 | 69  5.3 | | 50  7.4 | 48  7.6 |
| 2  188.9 | 29  12.6 | 38  9.5 | 44  8.3 | 53  6.9 | 48  7.6 | | 42  8.8 | 37  9.8 |
| 17  21.0 | 60  6.1 | 66  5.5 | 76  4.8 | 70  5.2 | 62  5.9 | Cost of Sales/Inventory | 68  5.4 | 63  5.8 |
| 61  6.0 | 94  3.9 | 104  3.5 | 146  2.5 | 126  2.9 | 140  2.6 | | 101  3.6 | 110  3.3 |
| 17  21.8 | 21  17.4 | 19  19.3 | 25  14.6 | 21  17.4 | 22  16.3 | | 21  17.2 | 19  19.6 |
| 31  11.8 | 37  9.8 | 28  12.9 | 35  10.4 | 37  9.9 | 35  10.4 | Cost of Sales/Payables | 33  11.0 | 30  12.3 |
| 42  8.7 | 54  6.7 | 45  8.2 | 49  7.5 | 42  8.7 | 40  9.2 | | 47  7.7 | 45  8.1 |
| 5.0 | 5.6 | 4.4 | 5.1 | 5.6 | 3.9 | | 5.3 | 5.5 |
| 14.8 | 10.8 | 7.7 | 8.2 | 8.5 | 6.6 | Sales/Working Capital | 8.8 | 9.6 |
| 41.3 | 20.7 | 14.6 | 15.5 | 13.8 | 36.7 | | 19.7 | 21.8 |
| 26.5 | 18.5 | 21.2 | 25.8 | 23.7 | 25.3 | | 11.5 | 14.5 |
| (18) 14.0 | (103) 6.6 | (228) 5.7 | (143) 9.4 | 9.7 | (12) 7.4 | EBIT/Interest | (458) 4.4 | (535) 4.8 |
| 2.6 | 2.3 | 1.9 | 3.7 | 2.4 | 2.0 | | 1.9 | 1.7 |
| | 4.7 | 8.3 | 9.6 | | | | 10.8 | 11.4 |
| | (14) 1.7 | (62) 3.0 | (57) 4.7 | | | Net Profit + Depr., Dep., Amort./Cur. Mat. L/T/D | (128) 3.4 | (142) 3.3 |
| | .6 | 1.4 | 2.0 | | | | 1.6 | 1.4 |
| .0 | .1 | .1 | .1 | .2 | .1 | | .1 | .1 |
| .1 | .2 | .2 | .3 | .5 | .2 | Fixed/Worth | .2 | .3 |
| 2.7 | .7 | .6 | .6 | 1.1 | NM | | .7 | .7 |
| .5 | .9 | .4 | .7 | .9 | .8 | | .7 | .7 |
| 1.9 | 2.1 | 1.2 | 1.5 | 1.5 | 1.7 | Debt/Worth | 1.7 | 1.7 |
| 159.2 | 6.4 | 3.1 | 2.8 | 4.3 | NM | | 4.0 | 4.5 |
| 134.1 | 63.3 | 42.8 | 48.9 | 53.0 | 41.8 | | 42.0 | 46.0 |
| (23) 43.0 | (103) 29.1 | (234) 16.3 | (148) 26.8 | (18) 20.3 | (10) 22.3 | % Profit Before Taxes/Tangible Net Worth | (458) 22.8 | (517) 24.7 |
| 27.7 | 6.6 | 6.1 | 13.0 | 6.4 | 5.5 | | 9.8 | 6.9 |
| 58.3 | 20.8 | 19.9 | 17.6 | 15.0 | 14.9 | | 15.7 | 17.1 |
| 20.5 | 8.3 | 7.3 | 11.4 | 10.0 | 8.0 | % Profit Before Taxes/Total Assets | 7.9 | 7.6 |
| 8.3 | 1.8 | 2.0 | 5.0 | 1.6 | 1.5 | | 2.8 | 1.6 |
| UND | 185.5 | 120.6 | 62.6 | 41.0 | 111.7 | | 90.8 | 108.7 |
| 266.8 | 67.7 | 44.3 | 27.6 | 18.1 | 61.6 | Sales/Net Fixed Assets | 40.3 | 43.5 |
| 58.3 | 23.6 | 15.8 | 10.2 | 6.1 | 15.6 | | 17.0 | 18.2 |
| 7.2 | 4.5 | 3.6 | 3.2 | 2.5 | 2.6 | | 3.7 | 3.8 |
| 4.6 | 3.4 | 2.8 | 2.2 | 2.2 | 2.2 | Sales/Total Assets | 2.8 | 2.9 |
| 2.6 | 2.5 | 2.1 | 1.6 | 1.5 | 1.4 | | 2.1 | 2.1 |
| .3 | .3 | .3 | .4 | .5 | .3 | | .4 | .3 |
| (11) .8 | (75) .6 | (206) .6 | (146) .7 | (18) 1.3 | (11) .6 | % Depr., Dep., Amort./Sales | (430) .6 | (493) .6 |
| 3.0 | 1.0 | 1.2 | 1.2 | 1.8 | 1.3 | | 1.1 | 1.2 |
| 5.0 | 2.2 | 1.5 | 1.2 | | | | 1.9 | 1.6 |
| (14) 5.7 | (71) 3.6 | (107) 3.0 | (34) 2.3 | | | % Officers', Directors' Owners' Comp/Sales | (194) 3.4 | (233) 3.0 |
| 13.0 | 6.6 | 5.8 | 5.6 | | | | 6.0 | 6.2 |
| 43009M | 537637M | 3447633M | 7846055M | 2879528M | 4575167M | Net Sales ($) | 15481090M | 22410395M |
| 7432M | 149325M | 1227668M | 3267959M | 1418126M | 2216400M | Total Assets ($) | 5892633M | 7872875M |

M = $ thousand    MM = $ million
See Pages 9 through 22 for Explanation of Ratios and Data

## Comparative Historical Data                                   Current Data Sorted by Sales

| | | | Type of Statement | 0-1MM | 1-3MM | 3-5MM | 5-10MM | 10-25MM | 25MM & OVER |
|---|---|---|---|---|---|---|---|---|---|
| 72 | 54 | 71 | Unqualified | | 1 | | 3 | 14 | 53 |
| 132 | 161 | 146 | Reviewed | | 3 | 7 | 36 | 55 | 45 |
| 99 | 94 | 97 | Compiled | 2 | 10 | 11 | 26 | 38 | 10 |
| 56 | 68 | 88 | Tax Returns | 10 | 18 | 14 | 26 | 17 | 3 |
| 194 | 213 | 194 | Other | 5 | 23 | 15 | 34 | 51 | 66 |
| 4/1/09-3/31/10 | 4/1/10-3/31/11 | 4/1/11-3/31/12 | | 99 (4/1-9/30/11) | | | 497 (10/1/11-3/31/12) | | |
| ALL | ALL | ALL | | | | | | | |
| 553 | 590 | 596 | NUMBER OF STATEMENTS | 17 | 55 | 47 | 125 | 175 | 177 |
| % | % | % | | % | % | % | % | % | % |
| | | | **ASSETS** | | | | | | |
| 8.2 | 7.7 | 8.0 | Cash & Equivalents | 21.5 | 10.4 | 11.2 | 8.0 | 8.3 | 4.7 |
| 30.4 | 33.1 | 32.7 | Trade Receivables (net) | 34.9 | 32.7 | 30.6 | 30.6 | 33.1 | 34.3 |
| 37.1 | 36.1 | 36.9 | Inventory | 27.3 | 37.8 | 40.2 | 37.8 | 38.5 | 34.3 |
| 2.5 | 2.1 | 1.9 | All Other Current | .5 | 2.3 | 1.8 | 1.1 | 1.5 | 2.9 |
| 78.2 | 78.9 | 79.5 | Total Current | 84.3 | 83.3 | 83.9 | 77.4 | 81.4 | 76.2 |
| 12.4 | 11.6 | 11.3 | Fixed Assets (net) | 7.7 | 9.7 | 9.1 | 13.3 | 10.1 | 12.7 |
| 4.0 | 4.1 | 4.2 | Intangibles (net) | 3.4 | 3.7 | 3.5 | 2.9 | 3.7 | 6.1 |
| 5.5 | 5.4 | 4.9 | All Other Non-Current | 4.1 | 3.3 | 3.5 | 6.4 | 4.8 | 5.0 |
| 100.0 | 100.0 | 100.0 | Total | 100.0 | 100.0 | 100.0 | 100.0 | 100.0 | 100.0 |
| | | | **LIABILITIES** | | | | | | |
| 16.0 | 14.3 | 14.0 | Notes Payable-Short Term | 9.6 | 11.4 | 14.4 | 11.9 | 14.4 | 16.2 |
| 2.8 | 2.5 | 2.1 | Cur. Mat.-L.T.D. | .6 | .8 | 2.8 | 2.9 | 2.3 | 1.7 |
| 18.3 | 21.5 | 20.2 | Trade Payables | 21.9 | 25.9 | 24.2 | 20.2 | 19.1 | 18.3 |
| .2 | .3 | .3 | Income Taxes Payable | .2 | .3 | .1 | .2 | .3 | .3 |
| 7.1 | 8.2 | 7.5 | All Other Current | 10.5 | 6.6 | 5.7 | 6.9 | 8.0 | 7.7 |
| 44.4 | 46.8 | 44.0 | Total Current | 42.8 | 45.2 | 47.1 | 42.1 | 44.1 | 44.2 |
| 9.2 | 8.6 | 8.2 | Long-Term Debt | 4.7 | 13.5 | 10.7 | 8.9 | 6.2 | 7.7 |
| .2 | .3 | .2 | Deferred Taxes | .0 | .0 | .1 | .2 | .3 | .4 |
| 4.7 | 4.7 | 4.9 | All Other Non-Current | 14.9 | 6.0 | 2.4 | 7.8 | 3.7 | 3.6 |
| 41.5 | 39.7 | 42.6 | Net Worth | 37.6 | 35.4 | 39.7 | 41.1 | 45.8 | 44.2 |
| 100.0 | 100.0 | 100.0 | Total Liabilities & Net Worth | 100.0 | 100.0 | 100.0 | 100.0 | 100.0 | 100.0 |
| | | | **INCOME DATA** | | | | | | |
| 100.0 | 100.0 | 100.0 | Net Sales | 100.0 | 100.0 | 100.0 | 100.0 | 100.0 | 100.0 |
| 31.1 | 31.1 | 30.0 | Gross Profit | 42.5 | 32.8 | 32.7 | 30.8 | 28.9 | 27.6 |
| 27.8 | 26.9 | 25.0 | Operating Expenses | 35.5 | 28.5 | 27.1 | 27.0 | 23.8 | 22.0 |
| 3.3 | 4.2 | 5.0 | Operating Profit | 6.9 | 4.3 | 5.6 | 3.8 | 5.1 | 5.6 |
| .6 | .5 | .3 | All Other Expenses (net) | .4 | .8 | .3 | .2 | .1 | .4 |
| 2.7 | 3.7 | 4.7 | Profit Before Taxes | 6.5 | 3.5 | 5.3 | 3.6 | 5.0 | 5.2 |
| | | | **RATIOS** | | | | | | |
| 3.2 | 2.8 | 3.1 | | 3.6 | 3.3 | 3.0 | 3.7 | 3.5 | 2.5 |
| 1.8 | 1.7 | 1.8 | Current | 2.6 | 2.2 | 1.9 | 1.8 | 1.9 | 1.7 |
| 1.3 | 1.3 | 1.3 | | 1.3 | 1.3 | 1.4 | 1.3 | 1.3 | 1.3 |
| 1.6 | 1.5 | 1.6 | | 2.6 | 1.9 | 1.5 | 1.6 | 1.7 | 1.4 |
| .9 | .9 | 1.0 | Quick | 1.3 | 1.0 | 1.0 | .9 | 1.0 | .9 |
| .6 | .6 | .6 | | .8 | .6 | .6 | .6 | .6 | .6 |
| 31  11.7 | 35  10.6 | 32  11.4 | | 27  13.4 | 28  13.2 | 26  13.8 | 27  13.3 | 33  11.1 | 38  9.5 |
| 40  9.2 | 44  8.4 | 42  8.7 | Sales/Receivables | 42  8.6 | 37  9.8 | 39  9.3 | 38  9.7 | 41  9.0 | 47  7.7 |
| 50  7.3 | 52  7.0 | 51  7.2 | | 56  6.5 | 49  7.4 | 49  7.4 | 48  7.6 | 48  7.6 | 54  6.8 |
| 37  10.0 | 38  9.5 | 36  10.0 | | 7  54.1 | 26  14.1 | 28  13.1 | 45  8.1 | 38  9.7 | 39  9.3 |
| 67  5.4 | 67  5.5 | 65  5.6 | Cost of Sales/Inventory | 32  11.4 | 69  5.3 | 79  4.6 | 66  5.5 | 64  5.7 | 62  5.9 |
| 121  3.0 | 116  3.1 | 107  3.4 | | 174  2.1 | 146  2.5 | 111  3.3 | 104  3.5 | 114  3.2 | 91  4.0 |
| 19  19.2 | 23  16.0 | 21  17.4 | | 24  15.1 | 22  16.9 | 19  19.1 | 18  20.0 | 21  17.7 | 24  15.5 |
| 30  12.1 | 34  10.6 | 31  11.6 | Cost of Sales/Payables | 33  10.9 | 41  9.0 | 36  10.0 | 29  12.4 | 28  12.9 | 33  11.0 |
| 46  7.9 | 54  6.8 | 48  7.6 | | 69  5.3 | 59  6.2 | 52  7.0 | 50  7.3 | 47  7.8 | 42  8.6 |
| 4.4 | 4.9 | 4.7 | | 2.6 | 3.9 | 4.9 | 4.5 | 4.5 | 6.1 |
| 8.1 | 8.6 | 8.3 | Sales/Working Capital | 4.7 | 7.4 | 8.6 | 9.4 | 7.9 | 8.5 |
| 18.2 | 18.4 | 16.6 | | 21.5 | 20.5 | 21.8 | 18.6 | 17.4 | 14.7 |
| 13.0 | 19.0 | 23.4 | | 26.8 | 18.3 | 28.4 | 14.8 | 21.8 | 27.3 |
| (504) 3.7 | (535) 6.3 | (524) 7.0 | EBIT/Interest | (10) 10.4 | (42) 4.5 | (41) 7.8 | (111) 4.7 | (156) 6.7 | (164) 10.9 |
| 1.2 | 2.1 | 2.4 | | -1.7 | -.3 | 2.9 | 1.6 | 2.6 | 3.6 |
| 8.2 | 10.9 | 9.8 | | | | | 4.4 | 9.9 | 21.7 |
| (138) 2.9 | (138) 3.4 | (144) 3.7 | Net Profit + Depr., Dep., Amort./Cur. Mat. L/T/D | | | | (25) 1.6 | (47) 3.4 | (64) 6.1 |
| 1.0 | 1.5 | 1.6 | | | | | 1.1 | 1.9 | 2.4 |
| .1 | .1 | .1 | | .0 | .0 | .0 | .1 | .0 | .1 |
| .3 | .2 | .2 | Fixed/Worth | .1 | .1 | .1 | .2 | .2 | .2 |
| .7 | .7 | .6 | | NM | .7 | .9 | .9 | .5 | .6 |
| .6 | .6 | .6 | | .5 | .6 | .8 | .5 | .4 | .8 |
| 1.6 | 1.6 | 1.5 | Debt/Worth | 1.3 | 1.6 | 1.2 | 1.8 | 1.3 | 1.5 |
| 4.0 | 4.2 | 3.4 | | NM | 8.5 | 5.5 | 3.7 | 3.0 | 3.1 |
| 30.2 | 43.2 | 49.8 | | 83.1 | 43.0 | 72.8 | 47.3 | 45.8 | 51.5 |
| (491) 13.9 | (523) 21.6 | (536) 23.6 | % Profit Before Taxes/Tangible Net Worth | (13) 27.7 | (44) 29.4 | (42) 30.6 | (113) 13.8 | (158) 21.6 | (166) 26.8 |
| 2.8 | 8.0 | 8.4 | | 9.2 | 3.2 | 14.4 | 3.8 | 9.1 | 11.7 |
| 11.8 | 15.2 | 19.5 | | 27.2 | 23.4 | 26.7 | 14.0 | 21.3 | 17.6 |
| 5.2 | 8.1 | 9.0 | % Profit Before Taxes/Total Assets | 9.1 | 8.4 | 12.4 | 5.4 | 8.4 | 11.1 |
| .5 | 2.3 | 2.7 | | -6.2 | -.2 | 3.9 | 1.4 | 3.0 | 4.6 |
| 93.6 | 92.7 | 121.2 | | UND | 266.8 | 409.4 | 97.2 | 125.7 | 72.0 |
| 36.1 | 34.6 | 41.7 | Sales/Net Fixed Assets | 65.3 | 41.7 | 75.8 | 41.6 | 43.4 | 35.4 |
| 15.3 | 15.5 | 15.3 | | 19.0 | 16.9 | 22.7 | 14.1 | 15.7 | 13.2 |
| 3.4 | 3.5 | 3.7 | | 4.2 | 3.8 | 4.3 | 3.8 | 3.9 | 3.4 |
| 2.6 | 2.6 | 2.7 | Sales/Total Assets | 2.4 | 2.7 | 2.9 | 2.9 | 2.8 | 2.5 |
| 1.8 | 1.9 | 2.0 | | 1.5 | 1.9 | 2.1 | 2.0 | 2.0 | 2.0 |
| .4 | .4 | .4 | | | .4 | .3 | .3 | .3 | .4 |
| (445) .8 | (475) .8 | (467) .6 | % Depr., Dep., Amort./Sales | | (29) .6 | (26) .6 | (97) .7 | (146) .6 | (160) .6 |
| 1.5 | 1.4 | 1.2 | | | 2.0 | 1.0 | 1.3 | 1.1 | 1.2 |
| 1.9 | 1.7 | 1.8 | | | 3.1 | 2.8 | 1.8 | 1.2 | .7 |
| (198) 3.4 | (208) 3.3 | (228) 3.3 | % Officers', Directors' Owners' Comp/Sales | | (23) 4.3 | (26) 4.4 | (64) 3.6 | (78) 2.9 | (28) 2.1 |
| 6.6 | 6.7 | 6.1 | | | 9.7 | 5.8 | 8.0 | 4.2 | 5.0 |
| 15164013M | 16106702M | 19329029M | Net Sales ($) | 10546M | 116815M | 191270M | 923891M | 2739360M | 15347147M |
| 6270446M | 6975289M | 8286910M | Total Assets ($) | 5155M | 48920M | 80486M | 380995M | 1155302M | 6616052M |

© RMA 2012

**M = $ thousand     MM = $ million**
See Pages 9 through 22 for Explanation of Ratios and Data

## Current Data Sorted by Assets        Comparative Historical Data

| Type of Statement | 0-500M | 500M-2MM | 2-10MM | 10-50MM | 50-100MM | 100-250MM | | 4/1/07-3/31/08 ALL | 4/1/08-3/31/09 ALL |
|---|---|---|---|---|---|---|---|---|---|
| Unqualified | | 1 | 3 | 7 | 2 | 1 | | 14 | 15 |
| Reviewed | | 5 | 31 | 10 | | | | 44 | 43 |
| Compiled | 2 | 15 | 25 | 4 | | | | 25 | 30 |
| Tax Returns | 9 | 19 | 10 | | | | | 15 | 33 |
| Other | 6 | 16 | 18 | 18 | 2 | 3 | | 54 | 56 |
| | | 43 (4/1-9/30/11) | | 164 (10/1/11-3/31/12) | | | | | |
| **NUMBER OF STATEMENTS** | 17 | 56 | 87 | 39 | 4 | 4 | | 152 | 177 |

| ASSETS | % | % | % | % | % | % | | % | % |
|---|---|---|---|---|---|---|---|---|---|
| Cash & Equivalents | 15.9 | 9.9 | 7.8 | 6.3 | | | | 7.2 | 7.4 |
| Trade Receivables (net) | 22.2 | 31.8 | 33.7 | 31.3 | | | | 33.1 | 31.7 |
| Inventory | 32.9 | 32.9 | 31.2 | 30.8 | | | | 34.2 | 32.5 |
| All Other Current | .3 | 3.2 | 2.9 | 4.1 | | | | 3.9 | 3.7 |
| Total Current | 71.3 | 77.7 | 75.6 | 72.5 | | | | 78.5 | 75.2 |
| Fixed Assets (net) | 18.2 | 12.0 | 13.4 | 13.0 | | | | 11.4 | 12.1 |
| Intangibles (net) | 3.6 | 4.2 | 4.0 | 8.2 | | | | 5.7 | 5.5 |
| All Other Non-Current | 6.9 | 6.1 | 7.0 | 6.3 | | | | 4.4 | 7.1 |
| Total | 100.0 | 100.0 | 100.0 | 100.0 | | | | 100.0 | 100.0 |

| LIABILITIES | | | | | | | | | |
|---|---|---|---|---|---|---|---|---|---|
| Notes Payable-Short Term | 19.9 | 10.2 | 16.4 | 20.1 | | | | 14.8 | 16.0 |
| Cur. Mat.-L.T.D. | 5.9 | 2.5 | 2.2 | 2.1 | | | | 2.6 | 2.6 |
| Trade Payables | 18.5 | 21.9 | 19.3 | 19.1 | | | | 22.7 | 18.2 |
| Income Taxes Payable | .0 | .5 | .1 | .4 | | | | .2 | .2 |
| All Other Current | 6.3 | 16.7 | 9.7 | 6.9 | | | | 12.6 | 12.0 |
| Total Current | 50.6 | 51.8 | 47.8 | 48.6 | | | | 52.8 | 49.0 |
| Long-Term Debt | 21.2 | 11.3 | 7.6 | 5.9 | | | | 9.5 | 9.2 |
| Deferred Taxes | .0 | .0 | .1 | .4 | | | | .2 | .2 |
| All Other Non-Current | 11.2 | 3.3 | 3.8 | 6.6 | | | | 5.4 | 5.1 |
| Net Worth | 16.9 | 33.7 | 40.7 | 38.5 | | | | 32.0 | 36.6 |
| Total Liabilities & Net Worth | 100.0 | 100.0 | 100.0 | 100.0 | | | | 100.0 | 100.0 |

| INCOME DATA | | | | | | | | | |
|---|---|---|---|---|---|---|---|---|---|
| Net Sales | 100.0 | 100.0 | 100.0 | 100.0 | | | | 100.0 | 100.0 |
| Gross Profit | 41.6 | 31.4 | 31.2 | 28.3 | | | | 30.2 | 32.7 |
| Operating Expenses | 39.6 | 29.3 | 29.1 | 25.7 | | | | 27.3 | 29.5 |
| Operating Profit | 2.0 | 2.1 | 2.1 | 2.6 | | | | 2.8 | 3.2 |
| All Other Expenses (net) | .2 | .2 | -.5 | .2 | | | | .4 | .5 |
| Profit Before Taxes | 1.8 | 2.0 | 2.6 | 2.5 | | | | 2.4 | 2.7 |

| RATIOS | | | | | | | | | |
|---|---|---|---|---|---|---|---|---|---|
| Current | 2.9 | 3.1 | 2.4 | 2.4 | | | | 2.0 | 2.3 |
| | 1.7 | 1.6 | 1.5 | 1.3 | | | | 1.5 | 1.5 |
| | 1.2 | 1.0 | 1.1 | 1.1 | | | | 1.1 | 1.1 |
| Quick | 1.1 | 1.6 | 1.3 | 1.3 | | | | 1.1 | 1.3 |
| | .7 | .7 | .8 | .7 | | | | .7 | .8 |
| | .5 | .5 | .6 | .5 | | | | .5 | .5 |
| Sales/Receivables | 9   41.8 | 20   18.1 | 30   12.2 | 33   11.0 | | | | 25   14.4 | 22   16.4 |
| | 21   17.5 | 32   11.3 | 38   9.6 | 43   8.5 | | | | 38   9.7 | 35   10.4 |
| | 35   10.4 | 44   8.3 | 54   6.7 | 54   6.8 | | | | 49   7.5 | 45   8.1 |
| Cost of Sales/Inventory | 24   14.9 | 29   12.8 | 30   12.1 | 36   10.1 | | | | 33   11.0 | 27   13.6 |
| | 38   9.7 | 47   7.7 | 48   7.6 | 60   6.1 | | | | 49   7.4 | 50   7.3 |
| | 114   3.2 | 78   4.7 | 85   4.3 | 91   4.0 | | | | 80   4.6 | 85   4.3 |
| Cost of Sales/Payables | 4   94.4 | 14   25.9 | 19   19.7 | 17   20.9 | | | | 18   19.8 | 14   26.8 |
| | 19   19.5 | 30   12.2 | 32   11.4 | 24   15.0 | | | | 29   12.7 | 23   15.9 |
| | 49   7.5 | 49   7.4 | 45   8.1 | 43   8.5 | | | | 48   7.6 | 39   9.4 |
| Sales/Working Capital | 5.4 | 6.9 | 6.9 | 7.4 | | | | 7.3 | 7.4 |
| | 19.7 | 14.3 | 11.3 | 14.5 | | | | 12.9 | 13.7 |
| | 514.9 | 756.4 | 39.4 | 38.1 | | | | 44.7 | 53.5 |
| EBIT/Interest | (12)   11.6 | (44)   22.6 | (80)   10.2 | (35)   7.6 | | | | (136)   7.4 | (156)   12.8 |
| | 5.3 | 4.6 | 4.4 | 4.5 | | | | 3.0 | 4.1 |
| | -.7 | .0 | 1.2 | 2.6 | | | | 1.3 | 1.4 |
| Net Profit + Depr., Dep., Amort./Cur. Mat. L/T/D | | | (23)   5.8 | (11)   1.7 | | | | (47)   5.0 | (48)   10.1 |
| | | | 3.4 | 1.0 | | | | 2.4 | 3.5 |
| | | | 1.0 | .8 | | | | .9 | 1.0 |
| Fixed/Worth | .2 | .0 | .1 | .1 | | | | .1 | .1 |
| | .5 | .2 | .3 | .4 | | | | .3 | .3 |
| | -.8 | 1.4 | .6 | 1.1 | | | | 1.2 | .9 |
| Debt/Worth | .4 | .8 | .9 | .9 | | | | 1.2 | .8 |
| | 1.8 | 1.9 | 1.7 | 2.6 | | | | 2.6 | 2.1 |
| | -3.7 | 6.2 | 4.7 | 4.2 | | | | 8.1 | 6.7 |
| % Profit Before Taxes/Tangible Net Worth | (11)   95.5 | (43)   38.3 | (83)   30.3 | (37)   32.2 | | | | (129)   44.2 | (151)   36.8 |
| | 14.6 | 16.4 | 9.9 | 19.0 | | | | 18.3 | 17.9 |
| | .0 | 3.2 | 2.4 | 8.4 | | | | 5.8 | 6.3 |
| % Profit Before Taxes/Total Assets | 14.9 | 11.7 | 9.3 | 10.9 | | | | 12.0 | 13.2 |
| | 5.6 | 4.4 | 3.7 | 5.2 | | | | 5.0 | 6.4 |
| | -10.6 | -2.1 | 1.2 | 2.8 | | | | 1.3 | 1.1 |
| Sales/Net Fixed Assets | 93.6 | 192.9 | 82.8 | 83.9 | | | | 86.6 | 107.6 |
| | 19.6 | 74.5 | 41.3 | 30.3 | | | | 43.8 | 47.0 |
| | 14.2 | 23.0 | 14.3 | 10.3 | | | | 20.9 | 20.7 |
| Sales/Total Assets | 5.6 | 4.9 | 3.6 | 3.5 | | | | 4.2 | 4.2 |
| | 4.1 | 3.4 | 3.0 | 2.9 | | | | 3.2 | 3.2 |
| | 2.2 | 2.3 | 2.4 | 1.7 | | | | 2.4 | 2.5 |
| % Depr., Dep., Amort./Sales | | (38)   .2 | (70)   .4 | (34)   .4 | | | | (125)   .4 | (139)   .4 |
| | | .7 | .7 | .6 | | | | .7 | .7 |
| | | 1.0 | 1.2 | 2.0 | | | | 1.1 | 1.2 |
| % Officers', Directors', Owners' Comp/Sales | (10)   2.2 | (36)   3.1 | (40)   1.8 | | | | | (60)   1.6 | (84)   1.8 |
| | 4.3 | 5.0 | 3.3 | | | | | 3.4 | 3.3 |
| | 9.5 | 6.9 | 6.3 | | | | | 6.0 | 6.1 |
| Net Sales ($) | 18131M | 250002M | 1229107M | 2363160M | 736550M | 1871403M | | 5524602M | 6960256M |
| Total Assets ($) | 4668M | 70884M | 401296M | 779581M | 311436M | 751849M | | 1734646M | 2090554M |

M = $ thousand    MM = $ million
See Pages 9 through 22 for Explanation of Ratios and Data

## Comparative Historical Data | Current Data Sorted by Sales

| | | Comparative Historical Data | | Type of Statement | | Current Data Sorted by Sales | | | | |
|---|---|---|---|---|---|---|---|---|---|---|
| 17 | 13 | 14 | | Unqualified | | 1 | | 1 | 1 | 11 |
| 45 | 41 | 46 | | Reviewed | | 1 | | 12 | 16 | 15 |
| 41 | 38 | 46 | | Compiled | 1 | 6 | 6 | 11 | 18 | 4 |
| 26 | 33 | 38 | | Tax Returns | 6 | 10 | 5 | 9 | 7 | 1 |
| 62 | 63 | 63 | | Other | 4 | 12 | 5 | 10 | 10 | 22 |
| 4/1/09-3/31/10 | 4/1/10-3/31/11 | 4/1/11-3/31/12 | | | 43 (4/1-9/30/11) | | | 164 (10/1/11-3/31/12) | | |
| ALL | ALL | ALL | | | 0-1MM | 1-3MM | 3-5MM | 5-10MM | 10-25MM | 25MM & OVER |
| 191 | 188 | 207 | | NUMBER OF STATEMENTS | 11 | 30 | 18 | 43 | 52 | 53 |
| % | % | % | | ASSETS | % | % | % | % | % | % |
| 6.9 | 8.3 | 8.5 | | Cash & Equivalents | 18.3 | 7.8 | 13.1 | 9.8 | 7.2 | 5.4 |
| 30.9 | 30.7 | 31.5 | | Trade Receivables (net) | 12.9 | 25.9 | 32.9 | 34.2 | 33.4 | 34.1 |
| 33.3 | 31.7 | 31.4 | | Inventory | 31.7 | 30.6 | 30.5 | 33.4 | 34.8 | 27.0 |
| 3.7 | 3.5 | 3.1 | | All Other Current | .1 | 4.4 | 1.4 | 2.0 | 3.6 | 4.0 |
| 74.9 | 74.2 | 74.5 | | Total Current | 62.9 | 68.6 | 77.9 | 79.5 | 79.0 | 70.5 |
| 13.3 | 12.1 | 13.2 | | Fixed Assets (net) | 27.3 | 17.1 | 14.3 | 11.3 | 10.4 | 12.0 |
| 5.0 | 6.4 | 5.7 | | Intangibles (net) | 6.0 | 5.9 | 2.4 | 2.2 | 4.5 | 10.9 |
| 6.8 | 7.3 | 6.6 | | All Other Non-Current | 3.7 | 8.4 | 5.4 | 7.0 | 6.1 | 6.6 |
| 100.0 | 100.0 | 100.0 | | Total | 100.0 | 100.0 | 100.0 | 100.0 | 100.0 | 100.0 |
| | | | | LIABILITIES | | | | | | |
| 15.3 | 14.3 | 15.7 | | Notes Payable-Short Term | 25.5 | 12.4 | 9.4 | 11.7 | 16.7 | 20.0 |
| 2.7 | 2.2 | 2.5 | | Cur. Mat.-L.T.D. | 9.5 | 2.0 | 2.0 | 2.8 | 1.7 | 2.1 |
| 20.2 | 20.9 | 19.8 | | Trade Payables | 11.5 | 19.0 | 20.1 | 22.1 | 20.7 | 19.2 |
| .2 | .3 | .3 | | Income Taxes Payable | .0 | .8 | .0 | .1 | .1 | .3 |
| 13.1 | 12.6 | 10.8 | | All Other Current | 4.5 | 11.8 | 25.5 | 11.2 | 9.6 | 7.4 |
| 51.5 | 50.2 | 49.1 | | Total Current | 51.0 | 46.0 | 57.0 | 48.0 | 48.8 | 49.0 |
| 13.5 | 10.0 | 9.5 | | Long-Term Debt | 26.0 | 13.5 | 11.4 | 8.6 | 7.2 | 6.2 |
| .2 | .1 | .1 | | Deferred Taxes | .0 | .0 | .0 | .1 | .1 | .5 |
| 6.1 | 6.9 | 5.0 | | All Other Non-Current | 14.1 | 6.3 | 2.4 | 3.2 | 2.4 | 7.3 |
| 28.7 | 32.8 | 36.2 | | Net Worth | 8.6 | 34.1 | 29.2 | 40.2 | 41.6 | 37.0 |
| 100.0 | 100.0 | 100.0 | | Total Liabilities & Net Worth | 100.0 | 100.0 | 100.0 | 100.0 | 100.0 | 100.0 |
| | | | | INCOME DATA | | | | | | |
| 100.0 | 100.0 | 100.0 | | Net Sales | 100.0 | 100.0 | 100.0 | 100.0 | 100.0 | 100.0 |
| 31.6 | 33.1 | 31.3 | | Gross Profit | 48.1 | 37.5 | 27.5 | 30.6 | 30.2 | 27.4 |
| 29.7 | 30.3 | 29.0 | | Operating Expenses | 48.0 | 34.6 | 25.4 | 27.7 | 28.8 | 24.3 |
| 1.9 | 2.8 | 2.3 | | Operating Profit | .1 | 2.9 | 2.1 | 2.9 | 1.4 | 3.0 |
| .4 | .1 | .0 | | All Other Expenses (net) | .5 | .4 | -.9 | .1 | -.4 | .4 |
| 1.5 | 2.7 | 2.3 | | Profit Before Taxes | -.4 | 2.5 | 3.0 | 2.8 | 1.8 | 2.7 |
| | | | | RATIOS | | | | | | |
| 2.6 | 2.3 | 2.5 | | Current | 3.1 | 3.3 | 3.4 | 2.6 | 2.5 | 2.0 |
| 1.5 | 1.5 | 1.5 | | | 1.7 | 1.4 | 1.4 | 1.7 | 1.5 | 1.3 |
| 1.1 | 1.1 | 1.1 | | | 1.0 | .9 | .9 | 1.2 | 1.1 | 1.1 |
| 1.2 | 1.3 | 1.3 | | Quick | 1.1 | 1.3 | 1.5 | 1.6 | 1.3 | 1.1 |
| .8 | .8 | .7 | | | .7 | .7 | .8 | .8 | .7 | .7 |
| .5 | .5 | .5 | | | .5 | .4 | .5 | .5 | .5 | .6 |
| 23  15.9 | 23  15.6 | 25  14.5 | | Sales/Receivables | 0  UND | 21  17.7 | 16  23.0 | 25  14.6 | 31  11.6 | 31  11.7 |
| 34  10.9 | 35  10.4 | 36  10.0 | | | 13  27.3 | 34  10.7 | 31  11.8 | 37  9.9 | 38  9.7 | 42  8.7 |
| 46  8.0 | 47  7.7 | 49  7.5 | | | 24  14.9 | 47  7.8 | 48  7.6 | 53  6.9 | 48  7.6 | 49  7.4 |
| 31  11.6 | 29  12.8 | 29  12.4 | | Cost of Sales/Inventory | 36  10.1 | 32  11.4 | 23  16.2 | 29  12.7 | 36  10.2 | 26  14.1 |
| 52  7.0 | 51  7.2 | 48  7.6 | | | 104  3.5 | 55  6.6 | 48  7.6 | 49  7.4 | 48  7.6 | 43  8.4 |
| 79  4.6 | 89  4.1 | 85  4.3 | | | 182  2.0 | 96  3.8 | 69  5.3 | 83  4.4 | 85  4.3 | 78  4.7 |
| 16  23.1 | 16  23.1 | 16  22.7 | | Cost of Sales/Payables | 1  504.0 | 16  23.5 | 7  50.2 | 19  19.4 | 19  19.3 | 17  21.2 |
| 28  13.3 | 30  12.3 | 28  13.2 | | | 14  25.7 | 25  14.6 | 29  12.8 | 28  13.0 | 33  10.9 | 26  13.9 |
| 43  8.4 | 50  7.3 | 45  8.2 | | | 57  6.4 | 64  5.7 | 51  7.2 | 50  7.3 | 41  8.9 | 41  9.0 |
| 6.6 | 6.5 | 7.1 | | Sales/Working Capital | 4.6 | 6.6 | 5.7 | 6.9 | 6.8 | 8.5 |
| 14.3 | 12.8 | 12.9 | | | 18.4 | 15.6 | 23.2 | 8.9 | 11.3 | 15.4 |
| 73.3 | 54.0 | 50.0 | | | UND | -161.7 | -40.4 | 17.6 | 38.3 | 44.2 |
| 9.1 | 10.5 | 10.2 | | EBIT/Interest | | 9.9 | 22.6 | 7.4 | 10.4 | 8.9 |
| (170)  2.9 | (169)  3.1 | (179)  4.4 | | | (21)  5.3 | (16)  3.0 | (38)  4.4 | (48)  4.4 | (49)  4.6 | |
| .9 | 1.3 | 1.2 | | | | .5 | -4.5 | 1.8 | 1.1 | 1.7 |
| 7.3 | 8.0 | 5.1 | | Net Profit + Depr., Dep., Amort./Cur. Mat. L/T/D | | | | 3.4 | 6.0 | 4.0 |
| (41)  2.1 | (28)  2.2 | (42)  2.2 | | | | | | (12)  2.5 | (11)  4.8 | (16)  1.6 |
| 1.2 | 1.1 | .9 | | | | | | .5 | 1.3 | .8 |
| .1 | .1 | .1 | | Fixed/Worth | .2 | .1 | .1 | .1 | .1 | .2 |
| .4 | .3 | .3 | | | .9 | .3 | .2 | .2 | .2 | .2 |
| 2.4 | 2.0 | 1.0 | | | -.4 | NM | NM | .4 | .6 | 1.6 |
| .9 | 1.0 | .9 | | Debt/Worth | .2 | .8 | .8 | 1.2 | .7 | 1.2 |
| 2.6 | 2.5 | 2.0 | | | -6.8 | 1.7 | 2.1 | 1.7 | 1.7 | 2.9 |
| 23.6 | 14.9 | 6.0 | | | -2.4 | NM | -8.1 | 3.2 | 5.9 | 9.2 |
| 32.3 | 29.6 | 33.6 | | % Profit Before Taxes/Tangible Net Worth | | 56.7 | 62.9 | 28.0 | 34.3 | 41.7 |
| (151)  17.8 | (151)  12.8 | (179)  13.3 | | | (23)  14.6 | (13)  14.8 | (41)  13.3 | (51)  8.4 | (46)  21.5 | |
| 3.3 | 3.0 | 2.5 | | | | 3.2 | -6.8 | 7.5 | .9 | 7.8 |
| 10.7 | 11.9 | 10.1 | | % Profit Before Taxes/Total Assets | 7.8 | 10.2 | 14.6 | 9.5 | 10.1 | 11.1 |
| 4.8 | 4.9 | 4.3 | | | .0 | 5.4 | 1.9 | 5.5 | 3.4 | 5.6 |
| -.4 | .8 | .3 | | | -24.9 | -.5 | -5.4 | 2.4 | .2 | 1.5 |
| 106.0 | 95.7 | 95.8 | | Sales/Net Fixed Assets | 79.9 | 88.8 | 159.2 | 183.0 | 112.7 | 83.4 |
| 46.1 | 41.3 | 40.6 | | | 14.7 | 28.2 | 54.5 | 50.6 | 41.5 | 37.4 |
| 19.5 | 19.1 | 14.7 | | | 4.7 | 8.4 | 28.4 | 15.3 | 27.0 | 13.2 |
| 4.2 | 4.1 | 4.2 | | Sales/Total Assets | 5.6 | 4.1 | 5.0 | 4.6 | 3.6 | 4.3 |
| 3.2 | 3.1 | 3.0 | | | 2.3 | 2.8 | 3.3 | 3.0 | 3.2 | 3.1 |
| 2.4 | 2.2 | 2.3 | | | 1.5 | 1.6 | 2.4 | 2.4 | 2.4 | 2.4 |
| .3 | .4 | .4 | | % Depr., Dep., Amort./Sales | | .5 | .3 | .3 | .3 | .4 |
| (160)  .7 | (154)  .7 | (159)  .7 | | | (20)  .8 | (14)  .9 | (31)  .7 | (42)  .5 | (46)  .6 | |
| 1.4 | 1.3 | 1.3 | | | | 2.4 | 1.2 | 1.5 | 1.0 | 1.4 |
| 1.8 | 2.3 | 2.2 | | % Officers', Directors' Owners' Comp/Sales | | 2.3 | 2.4 | 2.2 | 2.2 | .7 |
| (86)  4.1 | (98)  4.5 | (93)  4.2 | | | (16)  4.8 | (12)  5.3 | (25)  3.8 | (23)  3.7 | (10)  2.2 | |
| 7.1 | 7.8 | 6.6 | | | | 6.2 | 12.7 | 7.0 | 6.5 | 3.8 |
| 6607243M | 4929956M | 6468353M | | Net Sales ($) | 6075M | 62486M | 72385M | 316156M | 766058M | 5245193M |
| 2039301M | 1660990M | 2319714M | | Total Assets ($) | 2683M | 34734M | 24492M | 112051M | 269628M | 1876126M |

© RMA 2012

M = $ thousand    MM = $ million
See Pages 9 through 22 for Explanation of Ratios and Data

## Current Data Sorted by Assets | Comparative Historical Data

| Type of Statement | 0-500M | 500M-2MM | 2-10MM | 10-50MM | 50-100MM | 100-250MM | | 4/1/07-3/31/08 ALL | 4/1/08-3/31/09 ALL |
|---|---|---|---|---|---|---|---|---|---|
| Unqualified | | | 8 | 11 | 5 | 3 | | 32 | 37 |
| Reviewed | 1 | 1 | 19 | 15 | 2 | | | 48 | 53 |
| Compiled | 3 | 9 | 8 | 2 | | | | 29 | 28 |
| Tax Returns | 10 | 12 | 17 | 2 | | | | 14 | 24 |
| Other | 5 | 12 | 22 | 30 | 7 | 3 | | 89 | 89 |
| | | 33 (4/1-9/30/11) | | 174 (10/1/11-3/31/12) | | | | | |
| NUMBER OF STATEMENTS | 19 | 34 | 74 | 60 | 14 | 6 | | 212 | 231 |
| **ASSETS** | % | % | % | % | % | % | | % | % |
| Cash & Equivalents | 19.3 | 10.6 | 11.0 | 7.8 | 3.9 | | | 6.3 | 8.2 |
| Trade Receivables (net) | 19.0 | 24.1 | 24.4 | 20.7 | 23.8 | | | 22.0 | 22.6 |
| Inventory | 42.1 | 50.4 | 42.6 | 43.7 | 44.7 | | | 44.2 | 43.9 |
| All Other Current | .5 | 2.9 | 1.9 | 3.9 | 4.4 | | | 2.8 | 2.4 |
| Total Current | 80.8 | 88.0 | 79.9 | 76.1 | 76.8 | | | 75.3 | 77.1 |
| Fixed Assets (net) | 11.0 | 6.8 | 10.8 | 13.4 | 12.2 | | | 16.1 | 15.0 |
| Intangibles (net) | 4.0 | 1.4 | 2.5 | 4.0 | 4.4 | | | 2.3 | 1.9 |
| All Other Non-Current | 4.2 | 3.8 | 6.9 | 6.5 | 6.6 | | | 6.3 | 6.0 |
| Total | 100.0 | 100.0 | 100.0 | 100.0 | 100.0 | | | 100.0 | 100.0 |
| **LIABILITIES** | | | | | | | | | |
| Notes Payable-Short Term | 27.5 | 15.8 | 12.3 | 13.1 | 21.1 | | | 22.3 | 19.5 |
| Cur. Mat.-L.T.D. | 2.4 | 2.6 | 1.5 | 2.6 | 1.0 | | | 3.5 | 3.3 |
| Trade Payables | 10.2 | 23.7 | 18.8 | 13.4 | 12.1 | | | 15.3 | 15.6 |
| Income Taxes Payable | .0 | .0 | .1 | .1 | .1 | | | .2 | .2 |
| All Other Current | 32.3 | 7.8 | 11.0 | 9.4 | 7.5 | | | 9.3 | 11.5 |
| Total Current | 72.4 | 49.9 | 43.7 | 38.7 | 41.8 | | | 50.6 | 50.1 |
| Long-Term Debt | 16.7 | 10.7 | 6.9 | 9.4 | 10.7 | | | 11.0 | 10.9 |
| Deferred Taxes | .1 | .0 | .1 | .1 | .3 | | | .2 | .3 |
| All Other Non-Current | 9.7 | 5.2 | 6.5 | 4.3 | 11.5 | | | 5.1 | 4.6 |
| Net Worth | 1.1 | 34.3 | 42.7 | 47.6 | 35.6 | | | 33.1 | 34.2 |
| Total Liabilties & Net Worth | 100.0 | 100.0 | 100.0 | 100.0 | 100.0 | | | 100.0 | 100.0 |
| **INCOME DATA** | | | | | | | | | |
| Net Sales | 100.0 | 100.0 | 100.0 | 100.0 | 100.0 | | | 100.0 | 100.0 |
| Gross Profit | 34.2 | 36.7 | 26.5 | 29.5 | 26.3 | | | 29.0 | 28.4 |
| Operating Expenses | 31.2 | 32.7 | 21.4 | 20.9 | 18.3 | | | 22.6 | 23.4 |
| Operating Profit | 3.0 | 4.0 | 5.1 | 8.6 | 8.0 | | | 6.4 | 5.0 |
| All Other Expenses (net) | .5 | .6 | .3 | 1.0 | .2 | | | 1.3 | 1.1 |
| Profit Before Taxes | 2.5 | 3.4 | 4.8 | 7.6 | 7.8 | | | 5.1 | 3.9 |
| **RATIOS** | | | | | | | | | |
| Current | 3.2 | 3.3 | 2.6 | 3.8 | 3.1 | | | 2.4 | 2.4 |
| | 1.8 | 1.9 | 1.8 | 2.0 | 1.6 | | | 1.5 | 1.5 |
| | .9 | 1.2 | 1.3 | 1.4 | 1.3 | | | 1.1 | 1.2 |
| Quick | 1.5 | 1.3 | 1.2 | 1.3 | 1.3 | | | .9 | 1.1 |
| | .6 | .8 | .8 | .7 | .6 | | (211) | .6 | .6 |
| | .1 | .3 | .5 | .3 | .5 | | | .3 | .3 |
| Sales/Receivables | 0 UND | 17 21.0 | 17 21.6 | 30 12.1 | 31 11.7 | | 14 | 26.1 / 14 | 26.5 |
| | 7 50.7 | 27 13.5 | 36 10.1 | 41 8.9 | 43 8.4 | | 32 | 11.3 / 32 | 11.3 |
| | 37 9.8 | 42 8.7 | 47 7.8 | 60 6.1 | 57 6.4 | | 47 | 7.8 / 48 | 7.6 |
| Cost of Sales/Inventory | 15 24.4 | 38 9.5 | 41 9.0 | 61 6.0 | 104 3.5 | | 41 | 8.9 / 37 | 9.8 |
| | 45 8.2 | 94 3.9 | 76 4.8 | 122 3.0 | 126 2.9 | | 80 | 4.6 / 95 | 3.8 |
| | 104 3.5 | 174 2.1 | 126 2.9 | 228 1.6 | 182 2.0 | | 158 | 2.3 / 175 | 2.1 |
| Cost of Sales/Payables | 0 UND | 20 18.6 | 19 19.0 | 21 17.3 | 13 28.4 | | 10 | 34.8 / 11 | 32.6 |
| | 11 33.4 | 34 10.8 | 31 11.8 | 35 10.4 | 27 13.3 | | 23 | 15.8 / 27 | 13.6 |
| | 41 8.8 | 56 6.5 | 46 8.0 | 59 6.2 | 41 8.8 | | 42 | 8.6 / 49 | 7.4 |
| Sales/Working Capital | 6.2 | 4.2 | 5.1 | 2.3 | 3.1 | | | 5.0 | 4.5 |
| | 13.4 | 6.5 | 7.6 | 5.0 | 6.0 | | | 11.1 | 9.4 |
| | -29.9 | 19.3 | 14.0 | 14.4 | 12.0 | | | 42.8 | 30.7 |
| EBIT/Interest | 34.1 | 19.5 | 32.5 | 28.6 | 25.2 | | | 9.4 | 10.5 |
| | (13) 6.9 | (28) 6.0 | (69) 9.5 | (51) 10.3 | (13) 3.9 | | (194) | 3.3 / (209) | 3.0 |
| | 2.1 | .5 | 3.7 | 3.6 | 2.5 | | | 1.8 | 1.3 |
| Net Profit + Depr., Dep., Amort./Cur. Mat. L/T/D | | | 7.6 | 19.3 | | | | 8.0 | 13.2 |
| | | (14) 4.5 | (14) 7.5 | | | | (41) | 2.3 / (50) | 2.8 |
| | | 3.6 | 2.6 | | | | | 1.2 | .9 |
| Fixed/Worth | .0 | .0 | .0 | .0 | .1 | | | .1 | .1 |
| | .1 | .1 | .2 | .2 | .2 | | | .3 | .3 |
| | 3.8 | .6 | .5 | .5 | 1.7 | | | 1.0 | .8 |
| Debt/Worth | .6 | .7 | .7 | .4 | 1.1 | | | .9 | 1.0 |
| | 1.6 | 1.4 | 1.5 | 1.5 | 2.8 | | | 2.1 | 2.2 |
| | -7.3 | 6.9 | 3.2 | 2.9 | 5.0 | | | 5.1 | 4.9 |
| % Profit Before Taxes/Tangible Net Worth | 99.6 | 66.2 | 47.4 | 51.4 | 66.8 | | | 46.4 | 45.9 |
| | (13) 17.5 | (29) 22.1 | (71) 24.7 | (58) 25.5 | 32.7 | | (196) | 25.4 / (213) | 22.8 |
| | -10.7 | 2.6 | 10.1 | 9.5 | 10.1 | | | 9.2 | 3.4 |
| % Profit Before Taxes/Total Assets | 47.4 | 18.9 | 15.8 | 19.5 | 18.5 | | | 15.7 | 13.9 |
| | 9.8 | 11.9 | 8.9 | 11.7 | 9.9 | | | 6.7 | 5.3 |
| | -5.7 | -.3 | 3.3 | 3.4 | 2.6 | | | 2.2 | .9 |
| Sales/Net Fixed Assets | UND | 667.2 | 191.0 | 113.9 | 62.4 | | | 113.3 | 123.0 |
| | 277.7 | 90.3 | 49.2 | 31.7 | 26.2 | | | 33.4 | 39.9 |
| | 11.5 | 24.8 | 18.5 | 7.0 | 9.9 | | | 10.5 | 11.0 |
| Sales/Total Assets | 5.5 | 4.0 | 3.7 | 2.3 | 2.2 | | | 3.6 | 3.4 |
| | 3.4 | 2.8 | 2.8 | 1.6 | 1.8 | | | 2.3 | 2.3 |
| | 2.2 | 2.3 | 1.9 | 1.0 | 1.3 | | | 1.6 | 1.5 |
| % Depr., Dep., Amort./Sales | | .4 | .2 | .3 | .6 | | | .3 | .3 |
| | (17) | .8 / (59) | .5 / (46) | .6 | 1.1 | | (169) | .7 / (175) | .7 |
| | | 1.7 | 1.3 | 2.3 | 1.9 | | | 1.6 | 1.7 |
| % Officers', Directors' Owners' Comp/Sales | | 3.8 | 1.2 | .9 | | | | 1.0 | 1.3 |
| | (19) | 7.1 / (36) | 2.5 / (13) | 2.3 | | | (68) | 2.3 / (89) | 4.0 |
| | | 11.7 | 5.6 | 5.7 | | | | 4.8 | 7.9 |
| Net Sales ($) | 22271M | 118235M | 1081632M | 2799610M | 1875899M | 1108137M | | 6892841M | 7049465M |
| Total Assets ($) | 5128M | 37039M | 367563M | 1393962M | 1059749M | 899113M | | 3239597M | 3563493M |

M = $ thousand   MM = $ million
See Pages 9 through 22 for Explanation of Ratios and Data

## Comparative Historical Data | Current Data Sorted by Sales

### Type of Statement

| Hist 1 | Hist 2 | Hist 3 | Type of Statement | 0-1MM | 1-3MM | 3-5MM | 5-10MM | 10-25MM | 25MM & OVER |
|---|---|---|---|---|---|---|---|---|---|
| 31 | 34 | 27 | Unqualified | 1 | 1 | 3 | 1 | 6 | 20 |
| 27 | 45 | 38 | Reviewed | | | | 8 | 9 | 16 |
| 21 | 33 | 22 | Compiled | 2 | 5 | 2 | 7 | 5 | 1 |
| 20 | 27 | 41 | Tax Returns | 7 | 8 | 5 | 11 | 8 | 2 |
| 92 | 65 | 79 | Other | 3 | 13 | 6 | 7 | 15 | 35 |
| 4/1/09-3/31/10 ALL | 4/1/10-3/31/11 ALL | 4/1/11-3/31/12 ALL | | 33 (4/1-9/30/11) 0-1MM | 1-3MM | 3-5MM | 174 (10/1/11-3/31/12) 5-10MM | 10-25MM | 25MM & OVER |
| 191 | 204 | 207 | NUMBER OF STATEMENTS | 13 | 27 | 16 | 34 | 43 | 74 |
| % | % | % | ASSETS | % | % | % | % | % | % |
| 7.8 | 9.3 | 10.0 | Cash & Equivalents | 19.2 | 9.9 | 12.4 | 10.6 | 7.1 | 9.4 |
| 22.2 | 22.4 | 22.5 | Trade Receivables (net) | 13.3 | 23.0 | 21.2 | 24.8 | 23.5 | 22.6 |
| 42.6 | 42.9 | 44.4 | Inventory | 36.5 | 49.8 | 46.3 | 43.5 | 44.2 | 43.9 |
| 3.0 | 4.0 | 2.7 | All Other Current | .9 | 2.2 | 1.9 | 3.7 | 1.8 | 3.3 |
| 75.6 | 78.6 | 79.6 | Total Current | 69.8 | 84.9 | 81.9 | 82.5 | 76.7 | 79.2 |
| 15.4 | 13.5 | 11.2 | Fixed Assets (net) | 15.9 | 6.5 | 8.3 | 9.2 | 14.6 | 11.8 |
| 2.6 | 3.1 | 3.2 | Intangibles (net) | 1.1 | 3.6 | 3.2 | 2.7 | 2.2 | 4.3 |
| 6.4 | 4.7 | 6.0 | All Other Non-Current | 13.3 | 5.0 | 6.7 | 5.6 | 6.6 | 4.7 |
| 100.0 | 100.0 | 100.0 | Total | 100.0 | 100.0 | 100.0 | 100.0 | 100.0 | 100.0 |
| | | | **LIABILITIES** | | | | | | |
| 19.7 | 15.1 | 15.4 | Notes Payable-Short Term | 32.0 | 15.1 | 18.1 | 9.7 | 13.1 | 16.0 |
| 3.2 | 3.4 | 2.0 | Cur. Mat.-L.T.D. | 5.0 | 2.0 | 1.0 | 1.8 | 2.6 | 1.5 |
| 15.8 | 14.9 | 16.5 | Trade Payables | 6.4 | 17.3 | 14.7 | 23.1 | 15.3 | 16.1 |
| .1 | .1 | .1 | Income Taxes Payable | .0 | .1 | .0 | .0 | .2 | .1 |
| 11.0 | 11.4 | 11.6 | All Other Current | 38.6 | 12.7 | 6.8 | 9.8 | 8.8 | 9.9 |
| 49.9 | 44.9 | 45.6 | Total Current | 81.9 | 47.2 | 40.6 | 44.5 | 40.1 | 43.6 |
| 9.2 | 8.3 | 9.9 | Long-Term Debt | 20.0 | 12.5 | 5.2 | 8.0 | 10.5 | 8.6 |
| .1 | .2 | .1 | Deferred Taxes | .1 | .0 | .1 | .1 | .1 | .2 |
| 5.9 | 6.8 | 6.2 | All Other Non-Current | 26.7 | 4.8 | 4.1 | 3.9 | 5.1 | 5.2 |
| 34.9 | 39.8 | 38.2 | Net Worth | -28.7 | 35.5 | 49.9 | 43.5 | 44.3 | 42.5 |
| 100.0 | 100.0 | 100.0 | Total Liabilities & Net Worth | 100.0 | 100.0 | 100.0 | 100.0 | 100.0 | 100.0 |
| | | | **INCOME DATA** | | | | | | |
| 100.0 | 100.0 | 100.0 | Net Sales | 100.0 | 100.0 | 100.0 | 100.0 | 100.0 | 100.0 |
| 29.2 | 30.5 | 29.8 | Gross Profit | 41.5 | 35.9 | 34.0 | 30.3 | 29.3 | 24.7 |
| 25.3 | 24.9 | 23.7 | Operating Expenses | 39.4 | 30.8 | 29.0 | 24.0 | 23.2 | 17.5 |
| 3.9 | 5.6 | 6.1 | Operating Profit | 2.0 | 5.1 | 5.0 | 6.3 | 6.1 | 7.2 |
| .9 | 1.1 | .7 | All Other Expenses (net) | 1.0 | .6 | .6 | .6 | .6 | .7 |
| 3.0 | 4.5 | 5.4 | Profit Before Taxes | 1.1 | 4.5 | 4.4 | 5.6 | 5.5 | 6.5 |

### RATIOS

| Hist 1 | Hist 2 | Hist 3 | Ratio | 0-1MM | 1-3MM | 3-5MM | 5-10MM | 10-25MM | 25MM & OVER |
|---|---|---|---|---|---|---|---|---|---|
| 2.7 | 3.2 | 3.1 | Current | 9.6 | 4.1 | 2.7 | 3.1 | 2.6 | 3.5 |
| 1.5 | 1.9 | 1.9 | | 1.6 | 1.9 | 1.9 | 2.1 | 1.8 | 1.8 |
| 1.2 | 1.2 | 1.3 | | .5 | 1.4 | 1.5 | 1.4 | 1.3 | 1.2 |
| 1.0 | 1.2 | 1.2 | Quick | 4.5 | 1.5 | 1.2 | 1.2 | 1.1 | 1.3 |
| .6 | .7 | .7 | | .4 | .5 | .8 | 1.0 | .8 | .7 |
| .3 | .3 | .4 | | .1 | .2 | .3 | .5 | .4 | .4 |
| 20  18.6 | 16  23.1 | 19  18.9 | Sales/Receivables | 0  UND | 10  35.8 | 17  21.2 | 18  20.1 | 21  17.7 | 27  13.4 |
| 34  10.8 | 32  11.3 | 36  10.1 | | 25  14.5 | 32  11.3 | 27  13.5 | 38  9.7 | 36  10.1 | 41  8.9 |
| 55  6.6 | 52  7.0 | 51  7.2 | | 33  11.1 | 42  8.7 | 54  6.7 | 53  6.9 | 47  7.8 | 56  6.5 |
| 43  8.5 | 40  9.0 | 44  8.3 | Cost of Sales/Inventory | 13  29.0 | 31  11.6 | 72  5.1 | 42  8.7 | 41  9.0 | 55  6.6 |
| 99  3.7 | 88  4.1 | 99  3.7 | | 76  4.8 | 104  3.5 | 101  3.6 | 85  4.3 | 94  3.9 | 107  3.4 |
| 199  1.8 | 174  2.1 | 166  2.2 | | 203  1.8 | 174  2.1 | 174  2.1 | 140  2.6 | 182  2.0 | 166  2.2 |
| 16  23.5 | 18  20.8 | 19  19.6 | Cost of Sales/Payables | 0  UND | 18  19.9 | 20  18.6 | 25  14.7 | 19 | 17  21.0 |
| 30  12.0 | 29  12.7 | 32  11.4 | | 16  23.2 | 27  13.3 | 35  10.5 | 38  9.6 | 30  12.1 | 32  11.5 |
| 50  7.3 | 46  8.0 | 47  7.8 | | 43  8.5 | 42  8.6 | 54  6.8 | 56  6.5 | 46  7.9 | 52  7.0 |
| 4.2 | 3.7 | 3.9 | Sales/Working Capital | 4.5 | 4.0 | 5.5 | 3.5 | 4.6 | 3.3 |
| 7.5 | 6.5 | 6.9 | | 8.8 | 6.2 | 6.5 | 6.6 | 7.8 | 6.3 |
| 40.3 | 18.9 | 18.2 | | -17.6 | 15.1 | 10.4 | 16.4 | 17.8 | 21.7 |
| 10.2 | 20.7 | 26.9 | EBIT/Interest | | 18.5 | 17.1 | 36.9 | 25.0 | 28.1 |
| (171)  3.2 | (179)  5.7 | (180)  7.6 | | | (22)  5.3 | (13)  9.5 | (31)  12.1 | (42)  7.5 | (65)  9.5 |
| 1.1 | 1.5 | 2.8 | | | .3 | 2.0 | 2.7 | 3.5 | 2.9 |
| 7.4 | 13.1 | 13.3 | Net Profit + Depr., Dep., Amort./Cur. Mat. L/T/D | | | | | | 19.1 |
| (33)  2.8 | (42)  4.5 | (35)  5.0 | | | | | | | (19)  5.7 |
| 1.3 | .9 | 2.9 | | | | | | | 1.1 |
| .1 | .0 | .0 | Fixed/Worth | .0 | .0 | .0 | .0 | .0 | .0 |
| .3 | .2 | .2 | | .5 | .1 | .2 | .1 | .2 | .2 |
| 1.0 | .7 | .5 | | NM | .7 | .3 | .4 | .8 | .5 |
| .8 | .6 | .7 | Debt/Worth | .7 | .7 | .6 | .6 | .6 | .8 |
| 2.0 | 1.5 | 1.5 | | 9.7 | 1.4 | 1.1 | 1.4 | 1.7 | 1.7 |
| 4.1 | 4.0 | 3.8 | | -2.1 | 5.3 | 1.9 | 3.1 | 3.0 | 4.4 |
| 33.1 | 42.6 | 53.4 | % Profit Before Taxes/Tangible Net Worth | | 74.2 | 35.5 | 54.0 | 46.8 | 56.5 |
| (167)  14.7 | (189)  18.6 | (191)  24.7 | | | (22)  13.0 | 19.7 | (31)  22.7 | (42)  28.4 | (72)  33.8 |
| 3.4 | 5.2 | 9.7 | | | -4.4 | 4.1 | 9.7 | 10.1 | 14.2 |
| 12.7 | 15.6 | 18.7 | % Profit Before Taxes/Total Assets | 10.5 | 37.8 | 18.4 | 17.3 | 16.4 | 19.7 |
| 3.7 | 7.5 | 8.9 | | 3.9 | 13.0 | 8.8 | 7.3 | 11.5 | 11.2 |
| .3 | 1.9 | 2.6 | | -18.2 | -1.2 | 1.3 | 4.1 | 3.9 | 3.9 |
| 113.9 | 122.0 | 202.7 | Sales/Net Fixed Assets | UND | UND | 120.5 | 266.2 | 196.2 | 96.4 |
| 30.1 | 37.7 | 48.3 | | 13.8 | 235.0 | 33.9 | 77.0 | 37.5 | 35.0 |
| 9.9 | 11.7 | 14.0 | | 7.3 | 26.2 | 12.2 | 32.7 | 6.8 | 15.4 |
| 3.2 | 3.2 | 3.4 | Sales/Total Assets | 5.9 | 3.9 | 3.7 | 3.2 | 3.6 | 3.1 |
| 2.1 | 2.3 | 2.3 | | 1.8 | 2.7 | 2.4 | 2.4 | 2.5 | 1.9 |
| 1.3 | 1.4 | 1.5 | | .6 | 2.0 | 1.4 | 1.8 | 1.6 | 1.4 |
| .3 | .3 | .3 | % Depr., Dep., Amort./Sales | | .3 | | .2 | .2 | .3 |
| (154)  .7 | (161)  .7 | (151)  .7 | | | (13)  .4 | | (25)  .5 | (33)  .6 | (62)  .7 |
| 1.4 | 1.7 | 1.8 | | | 1.3 | | 1.6 | 2.0 | 1.7 |
| 1.9 | 2.1 | 1.7 | % Officers', Directors' Owners' Comp/Sales | | .6 | | .2 | 1.6 | .7 |
| (56)  3.3 | (60)  4.4 | (76)  4.8 | | | (12)  11.6 | | (21)  3.1 | (18)  2.3 | (13)  1.0 |
| 7.5 | 7.1 | 7.9 | | | 12.9 | | 6.1 | 5.5 | 5.0 |
| 5394444M | 5486799M | 7005784M | Net Sales ($) | 5975M | 53506M | 65407M | 272048M | 695886M | 5912962M |
| 3235022M | 2914793M | 3762554M | Total Assets ($) | 5966M | 41440M | 31015M | 166612M | 394109M | 3123412M |

M = $ thousand   MM = $ million
See Pages 9 through 22 for Explanation of Ratios and Data

## Current Data Sorted by Assets                                    ## Comparative Historical Data

| | 0-500M | 500M-2MM | 2-10MM | 10-50MM | 50-100MM | 100-250MM | Type of Statement | 4/1/07-3/31/08 ALL | 4/1/08-3/31/09 ALL |
|---|---|---|---|---|---|---|---|---|---|
| | | | 8 | 24 | 9 | 8 | Unqualified | 43 | 60 |
| | | 6 | 54 | 24 | 3 | | Reviewed | 80 | 82 |
| | 5 | 15 | 26 | | | | Compiled | 40 | 54 |
| | 19 | 32 | 21 | 3 | | | Tax Returns | 40 | 60 |
| | 9 | 31 | 58 | 39 | 8 | 5 | Other | 133 | 138 |
| | | 67 (4/1-9/30/11) | | 340 (10/1/11-3/31/12) | | | | | |
| **NUMBER OF STATEMENTS** | 33 | 84 | 167 | 90 | 20 | 13 | | 336 | 394 |
| | % | % | % | % | % | % | **ASSETS** | % | % |
| Cash & Equivalents | 21.8 | 14.5 | 8.1 | 6.4 | 5.0 | 4.4 | | 8.3 | 8.1 |
| Trade Receivables (net) | 26.2 | 24.2 | 24.2 | 26.6 | 32.9 | 28.6 | | 26.6 | 24.0 |
| Inventory | 37.0 | 39.2 | 47.5 | 41.9 | 40.1 | 35.3 | | 42.9 | 45.3 |
| All Other Current | 1.0 | 2.6 | 2.5 | 3.1 | 2.9 | 3.7 | | 3.0 | 2.7 |
| Total Current | 86.1 | 80.5 | 82.3 | 78.1 | 80.9 | 72.0 | | 80.8 | 80.0 |
| Fixed Assets (net) | 8.2 | 9.1 | 9.0 | 9.3 | 13.4 | 6.4 | | 8.6 | 9.6 |
| Intangibles (net) | 3.4 | 4.0 | 3.4 | 7.1 | .8 | 15.6 | | 5.3 | 5.8 |
| All Other Non-Current | 2.2 | 6.5 | 5.2 | 5.6 | 4.9 | 6.0 | | 5.3 | 4.6 |
| Total | 100.0 | 100.0 | 100.0 | 100.0 | 100.0 | 100.0 | | 100.0 | 100.0 |
| | | | | | | | **LIABILITIES** | | |
| Notes Payable-Short Term | 16.8 | 16.9 | 14.0 | 19.1 | 11.9 | 13.5 | | 18.0 | 18.4 |
| Cur. Mat.-L.T.D. | 2.8 | 1.7 | 1.6 | 1.3 | 3.9 | .3 | | 2.0 | 2.3 |
| Trade Payables | 23.2 | 23.2 | 20.6 | 16.5 | 20.8 | 16.5 | | 20.7 | 19.2 |
| Income Taxes Payable | .1 | .1 | .2 | .2 | .1 | .4 | | .2 | .1 |
| All Other Current | 8.5 | 11.4 | 9.8 | 9.1 | 11.0 | 9.1 | | 8.4 | 9.1 |
| Total Current | 51.4 | 53.3 | 46.2 | 46.1 | 47.6 | 40.0 | | 49.2 | 49.1 |
| Long-Term Debt | 15.3 | 7.4 | 6.1 | 10.3 | 5.9 | 15.0 | | 7.6 | 8.4 |
| Deferred Taxes | .0 | .1 | .1 | .2 | .2 | 2.7 | | .2 | .2 |
| All Other Non-Current | 21.9 | 5.3 | 8.8 | 3.2 | 4.2 | 2.9 | | 6.3 | 6.0 |
| Net Worth | 11.3 | 33.9 | 38.7 | 40.1 | 42.1 | 39.5 | | 36.7 | 36.3 |
| Total Liabilties & Net Worth | 100.0 | 100.0 | 100.0 | 100.0 | 100.0 | 100.0 | | 100.0 | 100.0 |
| | | | | | | | **INCOME DATA** | | |
| Net Sales | 100.0 | 100.0 | 100.0 | 100.0 | 100.0 | 100.0 | | 100.0 | 100.0 |
| Gross Profit | 37.8 | 36.5 | 30.5 | 28.3 | 26.8 | 26.6 | | 31.7 | 31.6 |
| Operating Expenses | 36.9 | 32.4 | 26.5 | 24.1 | 19.3 | 20.6 | | 27.2 | 28.0 |
| Operating Profit | .9 | 4.1 | 4.0 | 4.2 | 7.4 | 6.0 | | 4.5 | 3.6 |
| All Other Expenses (net) | -.1 | .2 | .4 | .7 | .0 | 1.5 | | 1.2 | .8 |
| Profit Before Taxes | 1.0 | 3.9 | 3.6 | 3.5 | 7.5 | 4.5 | | 3.4 | 2.8 |
| | | | | | | | **RATIOS** | | |
| Current | 6.5 | 2.8 | 2.9 | 2.9 | 3.6 | 2.8 | | 2.6 | 2.7 |
| | 2.1 | 1.8 | 1.7 | 1.7 | 1.6 | 2.0 | | 1.7 | 1.7 |
| | 1.1 | 1.1 | 1.3 | 1.2 | 1.2 | 1.3 | | 1.2 | 1.2 |
| Quick | 3.4 | 1.5 | 1.2 | 1.1 | 1.3 | 1.6 | | 1.2 | 1.2 |
| | 1.3 | .7 | .7 | .7 | .9 | .9 | (335) | .7 | .6 |
| | .4 | .3 | .4 | .4 | .4 | .5 | | .4 | .4 |
| Sales/Receivables | 3 140.2 | 9 40.2 | 20 18.3 | 27 13.4 | 32 11.5 | 42 8.7 | 19 | 19.4 / 19 | 19.1 |
| | 26 14.2 | 25 14.7 | 31 11.8 | 42 8.6 | 44 8.3 | 70 5.2 | 36 | 10.2 / 36 | 10.2 |
| | 42 8.7 | 42 8.6 | 52 7.0 | 68 5.4 | 66 5.5 | 79 4.6 | 54 | 6.7 / 53 | 6.9 |
| Cost of Sales/Inventory | 7 54.4 | 35 10.3 | 63 5.8 | 70 5.2 | 85 4.3 | 83 4.4 | 53 | 6.9 / 58 | 6.3 |
| | 69 5.3 | 74 4.9 | 101 3.6 | 114 3.2 | 96 3.8 | 104 3.5 | 101 | 3.6 / 100 | 3.6 |
| | 182 2.0 | 135 2.7 | 159 2.3 | 159 2.3 | 126 2.9 | 135 2.7 | 147 | 2.5 / 159 | 2.3 |
| Cost of Sales/Payables | 0 UND | 14 25.6 | 15 24.0 | 18 20.2 | 16 22.9 | 27 13.4 | 15 | 24.8 / 14 | 27.0 |
| | 17 22.1 | 40 9.1 | 30 12.3 | 34 10.8 | 28 12.9 | 41 8.9 | 32 | 11.3 / 31 | 11.9 |
| | 51 7.1 | 61 6.0 | 63 5.8 | 61 6.0 | 72 5.1 | 56 6.5 | 56 | 6.5 / 55 | 6.6 |
| Sales/Working Capital | 4.5 | 5.5 | 4.1 | 3.7 | 4.2 | 2.6 | | 4.5 | 4.7 |
| | 8.0 | 9.1 | 7.1 | 6.7 | 5.8 | 4.6 | | 8.5 | 7.9 |
| | 27.9 | 47.0 | 14.2 | 11.9 | 11.1 | 13.9 | | 20.0 | 19.9 |
| EBIT/Interest | 18.0 | 20.9 | 16.4 | 14.1 | 82.0 | 150.2 | | 9.7 | 9.4 |
| | (11) 1.3 | (62) 3.8 | (153) 5.2 | (86) 3.6 | (17) 9.4 | 10.9 | (303) | 2.9 / (357) | 3.0 |
| | -5.9 | 1.6 | 2.0 | 1.3 | 4.1 | 3.1 | | 1.3 | 1.1 |
| Net Profit + Depr., Dep., Amort./Cur. Mat. L/T/D | | | 13.3 | 5.2 | | | | 9.3 | 8.9 |
| | | | (26) 3.5 | (22) 2.0 | | | (59) | 2.8 / (76) | 3.6 |
| | | | 1.2 | .3 | | | | .9 | 1.1 |
| Fixed/Worth | .0 | .0 | .1 | .0 | .1 | .1 | | .1 | .1 |
| | .1 | .1 | .2 | .1 | .3 | .2 | | .2 | .2 |
| | 1.5 | 2.3 | .5 | .5 | .8 | NM | | .7 | .9 |
| Debt/Worth | 1.0 | .6 | .7 | .8 | .5 | .6 | | .8 | .8 |
| | 2.0 | 1.3 | 1.9 | 2.4 | 1.9 | 1.8 | | 1.8 | 1.9 |
| | -29.4 | 12.5 | 4.6 | 5.5 | 4.4 | NM | | 6.2 | 7.4 |
| % Profit Before Taxes/Tangible Net Worth | 81.1 | 71.8 | 44.8 | 37.5 | 49.6 | 29.0 | | 43.5 | 41.4 |
| | (22) 22.3 | (68) 27.8 | (151) 22.9 | (81) 16.3 | 27.4 | (10) 14.8 | (292) | 20.7 / (340) | 14.1 |
| | .9 | 6.7 | 7.8 | 3.9 | 15.7 | 8.0 | | 5.1 | 3.3 |
| % Profit Before Taxes/Total Assets | 25.5 | 22.7 | 13.3 | 13.0 | 22.9 | 8.5 | | 15.6 | 13.1 |
| | 5.3 | 7.3 | 6.8 | 3.9 | 12.3 | 5.4 | | 6.6 | 4.5 |
| | -.7 | 1.1 | 2.0 | .7 | 7.2 | 4.2 | | 1.0 | .3 |
| Sales/Net Fixed Assets | UND | 188.2 | 170.4 | 110.2 | 97.2 | 79.3 | | 157.3 | 134.3 |
| | 173.7 | 88.4 | 53.9 | 49.6 | 26.7 | 15.0 | | 52.7 | 53.2 |
| | 29.8 | 26.2 | 22.4 | 18.7 | 10.4 | 11.4 | | 22.6 | 19.9 |
| Sales/Total Assets | 6.0 | 4.3 | 3.3 | 2.4 | 2.9 | 2.4 | | 3.4 | 3.4 |
| | 3.5 | 3.0 | 2.4 | 1.9 | 2.0 | 1.4 | | 2.5 | 2.3 |
| | 1.9 | 2.2 | 1.7 | 1.4 | 1.5 | 1.1 | | 1.7 | 1.7 |
| % Depr., Dep., Amort./Sales | .9 | .2 | .3 | .3 | .3 | .4 | | .3 | .3 |
| | (11) 1.0 | (48) .5 | (123) .5 | (72) .6 | (18) .7 | .8 | (254) | .6 / (294) | .6 |
| | 1.7 | 1.2 | 1.0 | 1.3 | 1.6 | 2.0 | | 1.1 | 1.1 |
| % Officers', Directors' Owners' Comp/Sales | 3.6 | 2.4 | 1.2 | 1.0 | | | | 1.4 | 1.4 |
| | (15) 6.0 | (48) 4.3 | (69) 2.3 | (21) 1.4 | | | (143) | 3.0 / (154) | 3.1 |
| | 10.1 | 6.3 | 4.7 | 5.5 | | | | 5.7 | 6.0 |
| Net Sales ($) | 32163M | 321344M | 2195963M | 4077528M | 3161028M | 4101936M | | 12932831M | 14160930M |
| Total Assets ($) | 7417M | 100319M | 825432M | 2052571M | 1270671M | 2101698M | | 5776951M | 6490458M |

M = $ thousand    MM = $ million
See Pages 9 through 22 for Explanation of Ratios and Data

## Comparative Historical Data | | Current Data Sorted by Sales

| 4/1/09-3/31/10 ALL | 4/1/10-3/31/11 ALL | 4/1/11-3/31/12 ALL | Type of Statement | 0-1MM | 1-3MM | 3-5MM | 5-10MM | 10-25MM | 25MM & OVER |
|---|---|---|---|---|---|---|---|---|---|
| | | | | | 67 (4/1-9/30/11) | | 340 (10/1/11-3/31/12) | | |
| 62 | 41 | 49 | Unqualified | | | | 2 | 7 | 40 |
| 92 | 78 | 87 | Reviewed | | 3 | | 15 | 38 | 24 |
| 42 | 46 | 46 | Compiled | 4 | 6 | 9 | 18 | 5 | 4 |
| 71 | 80 | 75 | Tax Returns | 13 | 18 | 18 | 17 | 7 | 2 |
| 155 | 169 | 150 | Other | 8 | 23 | 9 | 27 | 39 | 44 |
| 422 | 414 | 407 | **NUMBER OF STATEMENTS** | 25 | 50 | 43 | 79 | 96 | 114 |
| % | % | % | **ASSETS** | % | % | % | % | % | % |
| 9.4 | 9.6 | 9.9 | Cash & Equivalents | 18.9 | 12.3 | 19.0 | 10.9 | 6.5 | 5.7 |
| 26.9 | 26.0 | 25.5 | Trade Receivables (net) | 20.6 | 25.6 | 21.8 | 21.6 | 25.7 | 30.3 |
| 40.8 | 41.6 | 43.0 | Inventory | 41.8 | 41.8 | 38.7 | 45.2 | 44.8 | 42.3 |
| 2.3 | 2.2 | 2.6 | All Other Current | .4 | 2.0 | 2.0 | 2.7 | 3.0 | 3.1 |
| 79.4 | 79.5 | 80.9 | Total Current | 81.8 | 81.6 | 81.5 | 80.4 | 80.0 | 81.4 |
| 10.0 | 9.2 | 9.1 | Fixed Assets (net) | 9.4 | 9.4 | 8.2 | 10.8 | 9.6 | 7.8 |
| 5.4 | 5.3 | 4.6 | Intangibles (net) | 7.2 | 3.4 | 3.4 | 3.7 | 3.5 | 6.6 |
| 5.1 | 5.9 | 5.3 | All Other Non-Current | 1.6 | 5.6 | 6.9 | 5.2 | 6.9 | 4.3 |
| 100.0 | 100.0 | 100.0 | Total | 100.0 | 100.0 | 100.0 | 100.0 | 100.0 | 100.0 |
| | | | **LIABILITIES** | | | | | | |
| 18.7 | 16.0 | 15.8 | Notes Payable-Short Term | 17.5 | 17.1 | 14.4 | 13.4 | 17.2 | 16.0 |
| 2.2 | 2.0 | 1.7 | Cur. Mat.-L.T.D. | 3.7 | 1.7 | 2.7 | 1.0 | 1.7 | 1.5 |
| 20.3 | 20.1 | 20.3 | Trade Payables | 17.1 | 21.9 | 20.8 | 20.4 | 20.9 | 19.6 |
| .2 | .2 | .2 | Income Taxes Payable | .2 | .0 | .1 | .2 | .2 | .2 |
| 9.7 | 11.2 | 9.9 | All Other Current | 10.9 | 9.4 | 9.3 | 8.9 | 11.3 | 9.6 |
| 51.1 | 49.5 | 48.0 | Total Current | 49.3 | 50.0 | 47.2 | 44.0 | 51.4 | 46.8 |
| 10.3 | 8.2 | 8.3 | Long-Term Debt | 15.8 | 10.2 | 5.8 | 8.0 | 6.9 | 8.2 |
| .2 | .2 | .2 | Deferred Taxes | .0 | .0 | .1 | .1 | .3 | .4 |
| 7.1 | 6.8 | 7.5 | All Other Non-Current | 15.2 | 13.9 | 6.0 | 8.8 | 5.1 | 4.7 |
| 31.3 | 35.3 | 36.0 | Net Worth | 19.5 | 25.8 | 40.9 | 39.1 | 36.3 | 39.9 |
| 100.0 | 100.0 | 100.0 | Total Liabilities & Net Worth | 100.0 | 100.0 | 100.0 | 100.0 | 100.0 | 100.0 |
| | | | **INCOME DATA** | | | | | | |
| 100.0 | 100.0 | 100.0 | Net Sales | 100.0 | 100.0 | 100.0 | 100.0 | 100.0 | 100.0 |
| 31.9 | 31.8 | 31.6 | Gross Profit | 37.9 | 37.9 | 39.0 | 32.7 | 29.2 | 25.7 |
| 28.3 | 27.5 | 27.5 | Operating Expenses | 37.4 | 35.9 | 32.4 | 28.8 | 25.1 | 20.8 |
| 3.7 | 4.2 | 4.1 | Operating Profit | .5 | 2.0 | 6.5 | 3.9 | 4.1 | 4.9 |
| 1.0 | .5 | .4 | All Other Expenses (net) | .4 | .2 | .6 | .3 | .4 | .6 |
| 2.7 | 3.7 | 3.7 | Profit Before Taxes | .1 | 1.9 | 5.9 | 3.6 | 3.7 | 4.3 |
| | | | **RATIOS** | | | | | | |
| 2.8 | 2.8 | 3.0 | Current | 6.1 | 4.7 | 3.9 | 2.7 | 2.5 | 2.9 |
| 1.6 | 1.6 | 1.8 | | 2.0 | 2.1 | 2.1 | 2.0 | 1.5 | 1.9 |
| 1.2 | 1.2 | 1.2 | | 1.1 | 1.0 | 1.3 | 1.4 | 1.2 | 1.2 |
| 1.3 | 1.2 | 1.3 | Quick | 2.8 | 1.9 | 2.1 | 1.3 | 1.0 | 1.2 |
| .7 | .7 | .7 | | 1.0 | .9 | 1.0 | .7 | .6 | .7 |
| .4 | .4 | .4 | | .2 | .3 | .5 | .4 | .4 | .4 |
| 19  19.1 | 19  19.0 | 20  18.7 | Sales/Receivables | 5  76.5 | 10  35.1 | 14  26.8 | 19  19.0 | 19  19.6 | 28  13.0 |
| 37  9.8 | 33  10.9 | 33  10.9 | | 22  16.7 | 31  11.6 | 25  14.4 | 29  12.8 | 31  11.7 | 41  8.8 |
| 59  6.2 | 59  6.2 | 55  6.6 | | 43  8.4 | 58  6.3 | 49  7.5 | 47  7.8 | 57  6.4 | 65  5.6 |
| 52  7.0 | 51  7.1 | 53  6.9 | Cost of Sales/Inventory | 42  8.7 | 25  14.5 | 46  8.0 | 40  9.1 | 66  5.5 | 63  5.8 |
| 89  4.1 | 100  3.7 | 96  3.8 | | 146  2.5 | 89  4.1 | 107  3.4 | 104  3.5 | 99  3.7 | 94  3.9 |
| 142  2.6 | 153  2.4 | 159  2.3 | | 228  1.6 | 203  1.8 | 152  2.4 | 159  2.3 | 159  2.3 | 135  2.7 |
| 14  26.2 | 15  24.5 | 15  24.0 | Cost of Sales/Payables | 0  UND | 7  50.1 | 13  27.8 | 14  26.7 | 15  24.0 | 20  18.6 |
| 31  11.8 | 35  10.3 | 32  11.4 | | 19  19.0 | 30  12.0 | 43  8.5 | 35  10.4 | 29  12.7 | 33  11.2 |
| 55  6.7 | 59  6.2 | 60  6.1 | | 54  6.7 | 69  5.3 | 74  4.9 | 59  6.2 | 64  5.7 | 50  7.3 |
| 4.3 | 4.4 | 4.2 | Sales/Working Capital | 4.5 | 3.5 | 3.3 | 4.1 | 5.4 | 3.9 |
| 8.7 | 8.4 | 7.4 | | 5.9 | 7.3 | 7.6 | 6.7 | 8.9 | 6.8 |
| 33.1 | 22.2 | 15.9 | | 19.0 | 284.0 | 16.4 | 11.6 | 17.3 | 14.1 |
| 12.6 | 15.1 | 18.7 | EBIT/Interest | 16.5 | 24.0 | 11.5 | 13.7 | 19.8 | 29.2 |
| (386)  3.3 | (368)  4.2 | (342)  4.9 | | (10)  2.2 | (31)  3.0 | (35)  4.8 | (68)  4.1 | (90)  4.9 | (108)  5.9 |
| 1.2 | 1.5 | 1.7 | | -2.5 | -1.5 | 1.7 | 2.1 | 1.6 | 2.1 |
| 9.4 | 13.2 | 10.0 | Net Profit + Depr., Dep., Amort./Cur. Mat. L/T/D | | | | | 9.4 | 11.3 |
| (72)  2.9 | (62)  3.3 | (61)  3.4 | | | | | | (18)  3.6 | (29)  3.6 |
| .7 | 1.2 | 1.1 | | | | | | .6 | 1.5 |
| .0 | .0 | .0 | Fixed/Worth | .0 | .0 | .0 | .1 | .1 | .1 |
| .2 | .2 | .2 | | .1 | .1 | .1 | .2 | .2 | .2 |
| .9 | .7 | .6 | | -2.8 | 1.2 | .5 | .9 | .5 | .4 |
| .7 | .7 | .7 | Debt/Worth | 1.0 | .6 | .6 | .8 | 1.0 | .7 |
| 2.2 | 2.2 | 1.9 | | 3.0 | 1.4 | 1.1 | 1.8 | 2.1 | 2.4 |
| 8.9 | 6.0 | 5.9 | | -6.3 | NM | 2.9 | 4.2 | 5.9 | 5.0 |
| 48.1 | 48.7 | 49.2 | % Profit Before Taxes/Tangible Net Worth | 78.0 | 60.4 | 52.2 | 40.4 | 53.3 | 42.9 |
| (359)  19.7 | (362)  20.2 | (352)  22.2 | | (15)  7.5 | (38)  25.6 | (37)  15.7 | (68)  15.7 | (90)  25.9 | (104)  22.9 |
| 4.1 | 5.1 | 6.7 | | .0 | 6.0 | 5.5 | 5.7 | 3.8 | 10.4 |
| 15.5 | 14.8 | 15.6 | % Profit Before Taxes/Total Assets | 17.6 | 22.3 | 15.7 | 14.5 | 14.3 | 15.5 |
| 5.5 | 6.3 | 6.7 | | 1.9 | 7.4 | 6.5 | 5.9 | 6.6 | 7.3 |
| .6 | 1.1 | 1.4 | | -.7 | -3.0 | 2.4 | 1.6 | 1.1 | 2.7 |
| 173.5 | 139.2 | 173.7 | Sales/Net Fixed Assets | UND | 193.1 | 188.7 | 152.8 | 164.4 | 153.2 |
| 56.9 | 50.6 | 55.4 | | 57.7 | 80.0 | 64.8 | 52.6 | 54.4 | 54.3 |
| 18.4 | 20.6 | 20.1 | | 24.0 | 27.3 | 19.3 | 16.1 | 20.5 | 17.7 |
| 3.3 | 3.4 | 3.3 | Sales/Total Assets | 3.5 | 4.1 | 3.7 | 3.4 | 3.3 | 3.0 |
| 2.3 | 2.3 | 2.3 | | 2.1 | 2.6 | 2.5 | 2.4 | 2.4 | 2.2 |
| 1.7 | 1.6 | 1.6 | | 1.4 | 1.5 | 1.6 | 1.7 | 1.7 | 1.6 |
| .3 | .3 | .3 | % Depr., Dep., Amort./Sales | | .4 | .3 | .2 | .3 | .3 |
| (305)  .6 | (303)  .6 | (285)  .6 | | | (26)  .8 | (28)  .6 | (49)  .5 | (76)  .6 | (97)  .5 |
| 1.3 | 1.2 | 1.2 | | | 1.4 | 1.3 | 1.0 | 1.1 | 1.1 |
| 1.6 | 1.6 | 1.5 | % Officers', Directors' Owners' Comp/Sales | | 2.9 | 2.0 | 1.9 | 1.2 | .7 |
| (158)  3.4 | (168)  3.2 | (156)  3.3 | | | (24)  5.0 | (27)  3.7 | (41)  2.9 | (35)  2.1 | (20)  1.1 |
| 5.9 | 5.6 | 5.7 | | | 8.3 | 7.3 | 4.6 | 6.0 | 1.6 |
| 19238299M | 15476778M | 13889962M | Net Sales ($) | 13052M | 102235M | 172779M | 576313M | 1599375M | 11426208M |
| 7647073M | 7270866M | 6358108M | Total Assets ($) | 7785M | 51862M | 81254M | 276943M | 776257M | 5164007M |

© RMA 2012

M = $ thousand    MM = $ million
See Pages 9 through 22 for Explanation of Ratios and Data

# WHOLESALE—Toy and Hobby Goods and Supplies Merchant Wholesalers  NAICS 423920

**Current Data Sorted by Assets**  **Comparative Historical Data**

| 0-500M | 500M-2MM | 2-10MM | 10-50MM | 50-100MM | 100-250MM | Type of Statement | 4/1/07-3/31/08 ALL | 4/1/08-3/31/09 ALL |
|---|---|---|---|---|---|---|---|---|
| | | 4 | 7 | 2 | 5 | Unqualified | 21 | 23 |
| 1 | 1 | 17 | 7 | | | Reviewed | 22 | 26 |
| | 9 | 8 | 1 | | | Compiled | 7 | 15 |
| 3 | 13 | 9 | | | | Tax Returns | 19 | 24 |
| 3 | 14 | 20 | 16 | 1 | 5 | Other | 60 | 61 |
| | 30 (4/1-9/30/11) | | 116 (10/1/11-3/31/12) | | | | | |
| 7 | 37 | 58 | 31 | 3 | 10 | **NUMBER OF STATEMENTS** | 129 | 149 |
| % | % | % | % | % | % | **ASSETS** | % | % |
| | 8.1 | 8.0 | 6.3 | | 9.4 | Cash & Equivalents | 8.8 | 9.3 |
| | 30.5 | 28.1 | 27.7 | | 24.4 | Trade Receivables (net) | 25.7 | 25.4 |
| | 41.9 | 44.2 | 43.9 | | 25.7 | Inventory | 40.3 | 40.4 |
| | 5.5 | 3.4 | 3.1 | | 1.0 | All Other Current | 5.0 | 4.3 |
| | 86.0 | 83.7 | 81.0 | | 60.5 | Total Current | 79.7 | 79.5 |
| | 5.2 | 7.8 | 10.2 | | 24.5 | Fixed Assets (net) | 12.0 | 12.5 |
| | 4.4 | 2.8 | 2.8 | | 12.0 | Intangibles (net) | 3.0 | 3.5 |
| | 4.4 | 5.7 | 6.0 | | 2.9 | All Other Non-Current | 5.2 | 4.5 |
| | 100.0 | 100.0 | 100.0 | | 100.0 | Total | 100.0 | 100.0 |
| | | | | | | **LIABILITIES** | | |
| | 20.4 | 16.8 | 16.5 | | 10.2 | Notes Payable-Short Term | 20.4 | 18.2 |
| | .6 | 3.3 | .7 | | 3.6 | Cur. Mat.-L.T.D. | 2.2 | 3.1 |
| | 15.8 | 21.2 | 21.7 | | 18.6 | Trade Payables | 17.8 | 20.0 |
| | .3 | .1 | .0 | | .1 | Income Taxes Payable | .7 | .1 |
| | 8.8 | 6.4 | 7.6 | | 5.1 | All Other Current | 8.2 | 6.9 |
| | 45.9 | 47.9 | 46.6 | | 37.6 | Total Current | 49.2 | 48.2 |
| | 7.5 | 7.4 | 4.5 | | 21.2 | Long-Term Debt | 10.3 | 9.2 |
| | .0 | .1 | .1 | | .0 | Deferred Taxes | .1 | .1 |
| | 13.1 | 5.0 | 16.8 | | 7.0 | All Other Non-Current | 7.5 | 9.0 |
| | 33.5 | 39.7 | 32.0 | | 34.2 | Net Worth | 32.9 | 33.6 |
| | 100.0 | 100.0 | 100.0 | | 100.0 | Total Liabilities & Net Worth | 100.0 | 100.0 |
| | | | | | | **INCOME DATA** | | |
| | 100.0 | 100.0 | 100.0 | | 100.0 | Net Sales | 100.0 | 100.0 |
| | 32.8 | 33.3 | 31.0 | | 40.3 | Gross Profit | 35.6 | 33.1 |
| | 29.8 | 28.6 | 26.4 | | 33.6 | Operating Expenses | 31.7 | 30.9 |
| | 3.0 | 4.7 | 4.6 | | 6.7 | Operating Profit | 3.9 | 2.2 |
| | .5 | .5 | .7 | | 2.4 | All Other Expenses (net) | 1.4 | 1.2 |
| | 2.5 | 4.2 | 3.9 | | 4.4 | Profit Before Taxes | 2.5 | 1.0 |
| | | | | | | **RATIOS** | | |
| | 3.1 | 3.0 | 3.3 | | 3.0 | | 2.8 | 2.9 |
| | 2.1 | 1.7 | 1.5 | | 1.5 | Current | 1.7 | 1.8 |
| | 1.3 | 1.3 | 1.4 | | .8 | | 1.2 | 1.2 |
| | 1.3 | 1.5 | 1.2 | | 1.9 | | 1.1 | 1.3 |
| | 1.0 | .8 | .6 | | .7 | Quick | .6 | .7 |
| | .5 | .2 | .4 | | .3 | | .4 | .4 |
| | 17 21.9 | 18 20.2 | 27 13.6 | | 16 23.2 | | 21 17.2 | 20 18.7 |
| | 26 13.9 | 35 10.5 | 43 8.5 | | 34 10.6 | Sales/Receivables | 34 10.6 | 36 10.2 |
| | 55 6.6 | 56 6.5 | 63 5.8 | | 79 4.6 | | 55 6.7 | 56 6.5 |
| | 26 14.1 | 46 8.0 | 73 5.0 | | 32 11.4 | | 48 7.7 | 43 8.5 |
| | 96 3.8 | 101 3.6 | 122 3.0 | | 114 3.2 | Cost of Sales/Inventory | 109 3.4 | 108 3.4 |
| | 166 2.2 | 215 1.7 | 166 2.2 | | 182 2.0 | | 163 2.2 | 168 2.2 |
| | 5 77.9 | 14 26.1 | 24 15.3 | | 26 14.0 | | 19 19.3 | 16 22.2 |
| | 21 17.6 | 34 10.6 | 38 9.6 | | 55 6.6 | Cost of Sales/Payables | 32 11.5 | 32 11.2 |
| | 37 9.8 | 62 5.9 | 61 6.0 | | 87 4.2 | | 67 5.5 | 60 6.1 |
| | 4.1 | 4.1 | 3.9 | | 4.0 | | 4.5 | 4.6 |
| | 6.9 | 8.1 | 6.6 | | 9.8 | Sales/Working Capital | 7.6 | 8.2 |
| | 16.0 | 14.3 | -13.8 | | -15.3 | | 21.9 | 22.8 |
| | 10.9 | 15.4 | 27.8 | | | | 6.4 | 6.9 |
| | (29) 4.4 | (51) 4.1 | (27) 4.7 | | | EBIT/Interest | (115) 2.1 | (127) 2.1 |
| | 2.0 | 1.5 | 1.3 | | | | 1.0 | .8 |
| | | | | | | | 18.3 | 6.2 |
| | | | | | | Net Profit + Depr., Dep., Amort./Cur. Mat. L/T/D | (22) 3.0 | (20) 2.2 |
| | | | | | | | .6 | 1.0 |
| | .0 | .0 | .0 | | .2 | | .0 | .0 |
| | .1 | .1 | .2 | | 1.0 | Fixed/Worth | .2 | .2 |
| | .7 | .5 | 1.2 | | NM | | 1.2 | .8 |
| | 1.1 | .6 | 1.1 | | 1.2 | | .8 | .7 |
| | 2.5 | 1.7 | 1.9 | | 2.0 | Debt/Worth | 1.9 | 1.9 |
| | 16.3 | 3.5 | 6.1 | | NM | | 6.7 | 4.3 |
| | 50.5 | 46.3 | 52.5 | | | | 41.6 | 32.1 |
| | (33) 29.1 | (52) 12.5 | (27) 29.8 | | | % Profit Before Taxes/Tangible Net Worth | (110) 14.2 | (135) 9.0 |
| | 11.1 | 3.4 | 11.8 | | | | 1.7 | .2 |
| | 15.0 | 17.1 | 19.9 | | 10.7 | | 13.4 | 10.8 |
| | 9.4 | 4.5 | 7.2 | | 6.3 | % Profit Before Taxes/Total Assets | 3.6 | 2.6 |
| | 1.9 | .7 | 1.0 | | 4.4 | | .2 | -1.2 |
| | 478.7 | 455.9 | 199.8 | | 113.6 | | 126.7 | 287.1 |
| | 88.1 | 59.7 | 40.2 | | 15.5 | Sales/Net Fixed Assets | 40.1 | 49.6 |
| | 44.2 | 18.2 | 18.7 | | 1.4 | | 14.2 | 11.7 |
| | 4.9 | 3.5 | 2.6 | | 2.6 | | 3.1 | 3.6 |
| | 2.5 | 2.5 | 2.1 | | 1.4 | Sales/Total Assets | 2.2 | 2.2 |
| | 2.0 | 1.5 | 1.4 | | .9 | | 1.6 | 1.5 |
| | .2 | .3 | .3 | | .2 | | .3 | .3 |
| | (21) .3 | (39) .5 | (25) .7 | | 1.6 | % Depr., Dep., Amort./Sales | (99) .8 | (109) .7 |
| | .9 | 1.4 | 1.2 | | 5.1 | | 1.9 | 2.0 |
| | 1.9 | .8 | | | | | 1.7 | 1.8 |
| | (15) 3.7 | (28) 2.1 | | | | % Officers', Directors', Owners' Comp/Sales | (50) 4.0 | (60) 3.7 |
| | 4.0 | 3.8 | | | | | 7.4 | 6.1 |
| 9588M | 149961M | 748748M | 1717373M | 568017M | 2544954M | Net Sales ($) | 4843369M | 5719380M |
| 1975M | 43628M | 279444M | 707759M | 253074M | 1361643M | Total Assets ($) | 2383819M | 2740491M |

© RMA 2012

M = $ thousand    MM = $ million
See Pages 9 through 22 for Explanation of Ratios and Data

## Comparative Historical Data | Current Data Sorted by Sales

| | | | Type of Statement | | | | | | |
|---|---|---|---|---|---|---|---|---|---|
| 14 | 23 | 18 | Unqualified | | | | 1 | 2 | 15 |
| 23 | 32 | 26 | Reviewed | | 3 | 1 | 4 | 14 | 4 |
| 15 | 28 | 18 | Compiled | 1 | 4 | 4 | 6 | 3 | |
| 26 | 29 | 25 | Tax Returns | 1 | 8 | 5 | 8 | 2 | 1 |
| 60 | 53 | 59 | Other | 2 | 8 | 6 | 11 | 11 | 21 |
| 4/1/09-3/31/10 ALL | 4/1/10-3/31/11 ALL | 4/1/11-3/31/12 ALL | | | 30 (4/1-9/30/11) | | 116 (10/1/11-3/31/12) | | |
| | | | | 0-1MM | 1-3MM | 3-5MM | 5-10MM | 10-25MM | 25MM & OVER |
| 138 | 165 | 146 | NUMBER OF STATEMENTS | 4 | 23 | 16 | 30 | 32 | 41 |
| % | % | % | ASSETS | % | % | % | % | % | % |
| 9.5 | 8.7 | 8.9 | Cash & Equivalents | | 15.2 | 4.8 | 7.1 | 8.0 | 8.8 |
| 26.2 | 27.8 | 27.5 | Trade Receivables (net) | | 23.1 | 20.8 | 21.0 | 38.8 | 31.1 |
| 39.7 | 38.8 | 42.1 | Inventory | | 46.0 | 48.5 | 47.3 | 37.1 | 36.3 |
| 3.0 | 4.2 | 4.1 | All Other Current | | 4.9 | .9 | 5.4 | 3.1 | 2.5 |
| 78.4 | 79.5 | 82.7 | Total Current | | 89.2 | 75.1 | 80.8 | 87.0 | 78.7 |
| 12.0 | 10.1 | 8.6 | Fixed Assets (net) | | 5.3 | 9.6 | 8.5 | 6.4 | 12.2 |
| 3.2 | 4.1 | 3.7 | Intangibles (net) | | 1.1 | 9.2 | 3.5 | 1.8 | 5.2 |
| 6.5 | 6.3 | 5.0 | All Other Non-Current | | 4.4 | 6.2 | 7.2 | 4.9 | 3.9 |
| 100.0 | 100.0 | 100.0 | Total | | 100.0 | 100.0 | 100.0 | 100.0 | 100.0 |
| | | | LIABILITIES | | | | | | |
| 16.1 | 17.1 | 17.5 | Notes Payable-Short Term | | 25.4 | 23.8 | 17.0 | 16.3 | 12.5 |
| 2.6 | 2.3 | 2.5 | Cur. Mat.-L.T.D. | | .4 | 1.1 | 4.5 | 1.8 | 1.3 |
| 16.8 | 19.0 | 20.2 | Trade Payables | | 17.4 | 21.0 | 19.0 | 22.4 | 22.2 |
| .3 | .1 | .2 | Income Taxes Payable | | .2 | .4 | .1 | .1 | .1 |
| 6.9 | 9.4 | 7.6 | All Other Current | | 3.9 | 4.1 | 8.2 | 6.9 | 8.4 |
| 42.7 | 47.9 | 47.9 | Total Current | | 47.4 | 50.4 | 48.8 | 47.6 | 44.6 |
| 7.9 | 7.4 | 7.6 | Long-Term Debt | | 10.5 | 12.5 | 7.5 | 1.5 | 8.7 |
| .1 | .1 | .0 | Deferred Taxes | | .0 | .0 | .0 | .2 | .0 |
| 7.6 | 9.2 | 9.4 | All Other Non-Current | | 11.2 | 6.9 | 10.8 | 5.8 | 12.1 |
| 41.7 | 35.4 | 35.1 | Net Worth | | 30.8 | 30.3 | 33.0 | 44.9 | 34.6 |
| 100.0 | 100.0 | 100.0 | Total Liabilties & Net Worth | | 100.0 | 100.0 | 100.0 | 100.0 | 100.0 |
| | | | INCOME DATA | | | | | | |
| 100.0 | 100.0 | 100.0 | Net Sales | | 100.0 | 100.0 | 100.0 | 100.0 | 100.0 |
| 34.7 | 33.6 | 32.9 | Gross Profit | | 41.7 | 32.6 | 33.9 | 31.6 | 29.3 |
| 30.7 | 28.9 | 28.7 | Operating Expenses | | 36.5 | 30.1 | 32.2 | 24.4 | 25.3 |
| 4.0 | 4.7 | 4.3 | Operating Profit | | 5.3 | 2.6 | 1.7 | 7.2 | 4.0 |
| .6 | .7 | .7 | All Other Expenses (net) | | .8 | 1.1 | .3 | .3 | 1.0 |
| 3.5 | 4.0 | 3.6 | Profit Before Taxes | | 4.5 | 1.5 | 1.4 | 6.9 | 3.0 |
| | | | RATIOS | | | | | | |
| 3.0 | 3.1 | 2.9 | Current | | 3.6 | 2.3 | 3.1 | 2.5 | 3.2 |
| 1.9 | 1.7 | 1.8 | | | 2.3 | 1.7 | 1.5 | 1.7 | 1.5 |
| 1.3 | 1.2 | 1.3 | | | 1.8 | .9 | 1.2 | 1.4 | 1.3 |
| 1.5 | 1.3 | 1.3 | Quick | | 1.3 | 1.0 | 1.2 | 1.5 | 1.6 |
| .9 | .8 | .8 | | | .9 | .5 | .6 | .9 | .8 |
| .4 | .4 | .4 | | | .5 | .2 | .3 | .6 | .5 |
| 18 20.5 | 14 26.7 | 17 20.9 | Sales/Receivables | | 13 28.6 | 18 20.7 | 9 38.7 | 28 13.0 | 18 20.0 |
| 36 10.0 | 35 10.6 | 35 10.5 | | | 45 8.1 | 22 16.6 | 24 15.1 | 45 8.1 | 40 9.1 |
| 57 6.4 | 54 6.8 | 60 6.1 | | | 68 5.4 | 42 8.6 | 44 8.3 | 62 5.9 | 73 5.0 |
| 44 8.3 | 40 9.1 | 43 8.4 | Cost of Sales/Inventory | | 85 4.3 | 89 4.1 | 49 7.4 | 29 12.6 | 34 10.7 |
| 101 3.6 | 97 3.8 | 104 3.5 | | | 140 2.6 | 96 3.8 | 146 2.5 | 72 5.1 | 99 3.7 |
| 168 2.2 | 161 2.3 | 182 2.0 | | | 243 1.5 | 203 1.8 | 228 1.6 | 140 2.6 | 166 2.2 |
| 16 23.0 | 13 28.5 | 16 22.9 | Cost of Sales/Payables | | 0 UND | 4 97.9 | 16 22.6 | 16 22.5 | 24 15.4 |
| 31 11.8 | 31 11.6 | 32 11.3 | | | 33 11.1 | 22 16.4 | 27 13.4 | 34 10.7 | 40 9.1 |
| 51 7.2 | 64 5.7 | 54 6.7 | | | 69 5.3 | 45 8.2 | 53 6.9 | 56 6.5 | 60 6.1 |
| 4.0 | 4.0 | 4.1 | Sales/Working Capital | | 2.5 | 5.7 | 4.1 | 4.2 | 4.3 |
| 6.9 | 8.7 | 7.3 | | | 4.1 | 9.2 | 9.2 | 7.1 | 8.2 |
| 14.7 | 24.8 | 14.5 | | | 9.7 | NM | 39.8 | 12.6 | 14.7 |
| 18.7 | 16.4 | 15.5 | EBIT/Interest | | 7.7 | 7.1 | 11.3 | 23.2 | 26.2 |
| (122) 5.3 | (139) 4.8 | (125) 4.4 | | (20) 4.5 | (14) 3.7 | (25) 3.5 | (27) 6.1 | (35) 5.4 | |
| 1.7 | 2.1 | 1.5 | | | 1.4 | .0 | 1.1 | 1.8 | 1.8 |
| 3.7 | 6.8 | 7.6 | Net Profit + Depr., Dep., Amort./Cur. Mat. L/T/D | | | | | | |
| (16) 1.8 | (23) 3.5 | (13) 2.1 | | | | | | | |
| 1.4 | 1.2 | .7 | | | | | | | |
| .0 | .0 | .0 | Fixed/Worth | | .0 | .0 | .0 | .0 | .0 |
| .1 | .2 | .1 | | | .3 | .1 | .2 | .1 | .2 |
| .6 | .7 | .6 | | | .8 | NM | .7 | .2 | 1.6 |
| .7 | .9 | .8 | Debt/Worth | | .8 | .9 | 1.0 | .6 | .8 |
| 1.3 | 2.0 | 1.8 | | | 1.7 | 2.4 | 2.1 | 1.5 | 1.9 |
| 3.4 | 6.6 | 4.6 | | | 4.9 | NM | 5.1 | 3.4 | 5.4 |
| 43.8 | 60.2 | 50.2 | % Profit Before Taxes/Tangible Net Worth | | 51.5 | 42.3 | 29.9 | 80.9 | 52.9 |
| (127) 22.7 | (142) 22.6 | (128) 22.0 | | (20) 24.9 | (12) 26.7 | (26) 12.0 | 28.8 | (35) 32.1 | |
| 3.7 | 7.4 | 7.9 | | | 10.3 | 9.9 | -1.7 | 6.4 | 11.8 |
| 16.7 | 17.6 | 16.7 | % Profit Before Taxes/Total Assets | | 15.5 | 14.0 | 11.0 | 27.4 | 18.9 |
| 7.6 | 6.5 | 6.5 | | | 8.1 | 8.8 | 4.1 | 8.2 | 6.7 |
| 1.1 | 2.3 | 1.5 | | | 1.7 | -2.5 | -.9 | 1.7 | 2.6 |
| 229.2 | 247.2 | 339.2 | Sales/Net Fixed Assets | | 287.9 | 276.6 | 637.3 | 783.6 | 278.0 |
| 47.1 | 55.8 | 72.2 | | | 76.6 | 60.4 | 65.7 | 91.0 | 45.5 |
| 14.6 | 15.1 | 21.1 | | | 35.2 | 13.7 | 12.7 | 39.5 | 18.2 |
| 3.2 | 3.5 | 3.6 | Sales/Total Assets | | 2.7 | 3.6 | 4.0 | 3.6 | 3.5 |
| 2.2 | 2.3 | 2.4 | | | 2.2 | 2.1 | 2.2 | 3.0 | 2.3 |
| 1.4 | 1.5 | 1.5 | | | 1.7 | 1.6 | 1.3 | 2.1 | 1.4 |
| .4 | .2 | .2 | % Depr., Dep., Amort./Sales | | .1 | | .3 | .1 | .2 |
| (88) .9 | (115) .6 | (101) .5 | | (17) .4 | (20) .6 | (23) .3 | (32) .8 | | |
| 1.6 | 1.5 | 1.1 | | | .7 | 2.1 | .6 | 2.0 | |
| 1.9 | 1.4 | 1.0 | % Officers', Directors' Owners' Comp/Sales | | 1.9 | 2.4 | .8 | .7 | .2 |
| (56) 3.9 | (65) 2.7 | (55) 2.3 | | (11) 3.7 | (10) 3.5 | (13) 2.0 | (11) 3.7 | (10) .8 | |
| 7.5 | 5.2 | 3.9 | | | 3.9 | 4.5 | 3.0 | 7.8 | 1.5 |
| 5319086M | 6457695M | 5738641M | Net Sales ($) | 3170M | 46651M | 63236M | 224210M | 545417M | 4855957M |
| 2607094M | 3275644M | 2647523M | Total Assets ($) | 2127M | 29541M | 30481M | 112502M | 210386M | 2262486M |

© RMA 2012

M = $ thousand    MM = $ million
See Pages 9 through 22 for Explanation of Ratios and Data

**Current Data Sorted by Assets**      **Comparative Historical Data**

### Type of Statement

| Type of Statement | 0-500M | 500M-2MM | 2-10MM | 10-50MM | 50-100MM | 100-250MM | 4/1/07-3/31/08 ALL | 4/1/08-3/31/09 ALL |
|---|---|---|---|---|---|---|---|---|
| Unqualified |  | 6 | 6 | 20 | 5 | 6 | 39 | 41 |
| Reviewed | 7 | 14 | 39 | 48 | 4 |  | 85 | 86 |
| Compiled | 14 | 47 | 26 | 8 |  | 2 | 61 | 56 |
| Tax Returns | 9 | 40 | 24 | 4 | 12 | 10 | 65 | 60 |
| Other |  |  | 67 | 67 |  |  | 156 | 184 |
|  |  | 66 (4/1-9/30/11) | 419 (10/1/11-3/31/12) |  |  |  |  |  |
| **NUMBER OF STATEMENTS** | 30 | 107 | 162 | 147 | 21 | 18 | 406 | 427 |

### ASSETS (%)

| Item | 0-500M | 500M-2MM | 2-10MM | 10-50MM | 50-100MM | 100-250MM | 4/1/07-3/31/08 ALL | 4/1/08-3/31/09 ALL |
|---|---|---|---|---|---|---|---|---|
| Cash & Equivalents | 30.5 | 16.3 | 9.7 | 8.3 | 4.7 | 5.1 | 11.1 | 13.2 |
| Trade Receivables (net) | 13.8 | 18.0 | 25.1 | 28.7 | 32.8 | 30.7 | 29.6 | 22.8 |
| Inventory | 16.9 | 16.5 | 22.9 | 22.3 | 19.8 | 22.3 | 18.5 | 15.8 |
| All Other Current | 1.5 | 2.8 | 3.3 | 2.6 | 2.2 | 5.5 | 2.5 | 3.6 |
| Total Current | 62.7 | 53.7 | 61.1 | 61.8 | 59.6 | 63.5 | 61.7 | 55.4 |
| Fixed Assets (net) | 27.8 | 32.3 | 30.1 | 27.9 | 27.4 | 23.1 | 28.4 | 31.8 |
| Intangibles (net) | 2.3 | 5.0 | 3.1 | 3.0 | 8.3 | 9.5 | 3.1 | 4.0 |
| All Other Non-Current | 7.3 | 9.0 | 5.7 | 7.2 | 4.7 | 3.9 | 6.7 | 8.8 |
| Total | 100.0 | 100.0 | 100.0 | 100.0 | 100.0 | 100.0 | 100.0 | 100.0 |

### LIABILITIES

| Item | 0-500M | 500M-2MM | 2-10MM | 10-50MM | 50-100MM | 100-250MM | 4/1/07-3/31/08 ALL | 4/1/08-3/31/09 ALL |
|---|---|---|---|---|---|---|---|---|
| Notes Payable-Short Term | 21.3 | 9.8 | 11.4 | 12.7 | 11.7 | 12.1 | 11.0 | 12.3 |
| Cur. Mat.-L.T.D. | 1.8 | 5.2 | 3.8 | 3.0 | 4.4 | 2.5 | 4.0 | 3.8 |
| Trade Payables | 22.5 | 16.1 | 15.9 | 16.1 | 16.0 | 17.0 | 17.9 | 15.6 |
| Income Taxes Payable | .2 | .1 | .2 | .2 | .0 | .0 | .3 | .3 |
| All Other Current | 19.7 | 10.3 | 7.4 | 8.7 | 7.8 | 9.0 | 8.5 | 7.3 |
| Total Current | 65.5 | 41.5 | 38.7 | 40.7 | 39.9 | 40.6 | 41.6 | 39.3 |
| Long-Term Debt | 22.3 | 23.6 | 15.7 | 13.6 | 11.7 | 17.9 | 15.1 | 17.4 |
| Deferred Taxes | .0 | .2 | .2 | .7 | .6 | .9 | .3 | .3 |
| All Other Non-Current | 12.8 | 9.3 | 5.8 | 4.6 | 8.3 | 1.5 | 4.7 | 5.3 |
| Net Worth | -.6 | 25.4 | 39.7 | 41.4 | 39.5 | 39.1 | 38.2 | 37.6 |
| Total Liabilities & Net Worth | 100.0 | 100.0 | 100.0 | 100.0 | 100.0 | 100.0 | 100.0 | 100.0 |

### INCOME DATA

| Item | 0-500M | 500M-2MM | 2-10MM | 10-50MM | 50-100MM | 100-250MM | 4/1/07-3/31/08 ALL | 4/1/08-3/31/09 ALL |
|---|---|---|---|---|---|---|---|---|
| Net Sales | 100.0 | 100.0 | 100.0 | 100.0 | 100.0 | 100.0 | 100.0 | 100.0 |
| Gross Profit | 31.4 | 28.1 | 21.4 | 17.3 | 10.6 | 10.7 | 24.4 | 20.7 |
| Operating Expenses | 28.3 | 24.4 | 16.9 | 13.4 | 8.0 | 6.9 | 18.0 | 16.6 |
| Operating Profit | 3.0 | 3.8 | 4.5 | 3.9 | 2.6 | 3.8 | 6.4 | 4.1 |
| All Other Expenses (net) | .6 | .7 | .2 | .2 | .6 | .6 | .5 | .4 |
| Profit Before Taxes | 2.4 | 3.1 | 4.4 | 3.7 | 2.0 | 3.3 | 5.8 | 3.7 |

### RATIOS

| Ratio | 0-500M | 500M-2MM | 2-10MM | 10-50MM | 50-100MM | 100-250MM | 4/1/07-3/31/08 ALL | 4/1/08-3/31/09 ALL |
|---|---|---|---|---|---|---|---|---|
| Current | 9.0 | 3.4 | 2.7 | 2.3 | 2.7 | 2.4 | 2.6 | 2.6 |
|  | 1.3 | 1.4 | 1.5 | 1.4 | 1.4 | 1.6 | 1.5 | 1.5 |
|  | .5 | .8 | 1.0 | 1.1 | 1.1 | 1.2 | 1.1 | .9 |
| Quick | 5.7 | 2.4 | 1.7 | 1.5 | 1.3 | 1.4 | 1.8 | 1.8 |
|  | .9 | .9 | .9 | .9 | 1.1 | .9 | (405) 1.1 | .9 |
|  | .2 | .4 | .5 | .5 | .7 | .7 | .6 | .5 |
| Sales/Receivables | 0 UND | 0 UND | 10 37.5 | 19 18.9 | 26 13.8 | 26 13.9 | 15 24.3 | 6 62.0 |
|  | 2 233.7 | 6 56.9 | 20 18.2 | 28 13.1 | 30 12.1 | 32 11.5 | 29 12.5 | 16 23.4 |
|  | 13 28.4 | 21 17.2 | 31 11.6 | 37 9.8 | 40 9.2 | 40 9.2 | 41 8.8 | 28 13.2 |
| Cost of Sales/Inventory | 0 UND | 0 UND | 7 52.2 | 12 31.3 | 11 34.7 | 10 36.1 | 5 79.0 | 3 114.6 |
|  | 0 UND | 7 52.1 | 17 22.0 | 26 14.0 | 17 21.4 | 22 16.6 | 14 26.1 | 10 35.6 |
|  | 9 42.2 | 17 21.0 | 39 9.4 | 42 8.7 | 32 11.5 | 37 9.9 | 34 10.7 | 22 16.4 |
| Cost of Sales/Payables | 0 UND | 0 999.8 | 5 72.9 | 8 46.8 | 11 33.3 | 13 27.4 | 7 50.3 | 4 90.2 |
|  | 2 180.8 | 8 45.4 | 13 27.9 | 17 21.0 | 18 20.2 | 15 24.1 | 19 19.1 | 11 33.3 |
|  | 14 26.3 | 31 11.7 | 28 13.1 | 29 12.6 | 24 15.2 | 29 12.8 | 35 10.3 | 24 15.1 |
| Sales/Working Capital | 16.2 | 14.4 | 9.4 | 9.0 | 10.7 | 9.7 | 9.1 | 12.1 |
|  | 218.4 | 48.1 | 24.5 | 20.2 | 20.0 | 20.8 | 21.4 | 33.0 |
|  | -23.1 | -64.1 | 234.8 | 55.4 | 57.8 | 33.9 | 86.8 | -131.0 |
| EBIT/Interest | 21.4 | 27.7 | 23.0 | 16.9 | 19.9 | 18.8 | 24.3 | 19.8 |
|  | (24) 5.2 | (89) 4.6 | (150) 8.6 | (138) 7.6 | 5.4 | (17) 8.5 | (379) 8.3 | (393) 6.0 |
|  | -.4 | 1.1 | 3.2 | 2.4 | 1.5 | 4.3 | 2.8 | 1.8 |
| Net Profit + Depr., Dep., Amort./Cur. Mat. L/T/D |  |  | 14.0 | 10.3 |  |  | 10.9 | 12.0 |
|  |  |  | (25) 4.3 | (32) 3.4 |  |  | (87) 4.0 | (87) 4.2 |
|  |  |  | 1.6 | 1.7 |  |  | 1.4 | 1.7 |
| Fixed/Worth | .0 | .3 | .2 | .3 | .4 | .2 | .2 | .3 |
|  | 1.3 | 1.2 | .8 | .7 | 1.0 | .9 | .6 | .9 |
|  | -3.1 | -546.0 | 2.2 | 1.4 | 2.5 | 1.4 | 1.7 | 2.6 |
| Debt/Worth | .2 | .6 | .7 | .7 | .8 | 1.0 | .7 | .7 |
|  | 2.7 | 2.8 | 1.8 | 1.8 | 1.4 | 1.6 | 1.7 | 1.8 |
|  | -4.1 | -58.6 | 5.5 | 3.6 | 7.6 | 6.5 | 4.4 | 4.9 |
| % Profit Before Taxes/Tangible Net Worth | 109.3 | 81.8 | 69.1 | 44.7 | 39.8 | 67.9 | 78.8 | 71.6 |
|  | (18) 57.8 | (79) 33.0 | (151) 31.3 | (139) 26.7 | (18) 20.5 | (17) 25.3 | (377) 43.8 | (372) 36.8 |
|  | 1.3 | 10.3 | 10.8 | 10.7 | -4.1 | 16.0 | 21.6 | 9.9 |
| % Profit Before Taxes/Total Assets | 64.5 | 29.9 | 22.6 | 16.3 | 15.6 | 14.0 | 31.2 | 27.0 |
|  | 15.3 | 11.3 | 11.0 | 8.9 | 7.5 | 8.2 | 15.4 | 12.7 |
|  | -1.3 | .4 | 3.6 | 2.7 | .6 | 7.0 | 5.4 | 1.9 |
| Sales/Net Fixed Assets | UND | 131.5 | 48.2 | 42.1 | 20.8 | 42.0 | 41.1 | 46.1 |
|  | 53.8 | 23.5 | 15.4 | 14.0 | 17.0 | 16.4 | 16.9 | 17.9 |
|  | 17.7 | 10.0 | 6.6 | 6.2 | 8.6 | 9.4 | 7.0 | 7.9 |
| Sales/Total Assets | 16.2 | 11.1 | 6.2 | 5.0 | 4.6 | 4.3 | 5.3 | 6.8 |
|  | 10.6 | 6.0 | 3.9 | 3.3 | 3.4 | 3.4 | 3.7 | 4.5 |
|  | 4.9 | 3.0 | 2.6 | 2.1 | 2.7 | 3.1 | 2.4 | 2.6 |
| % Depr., Dep., Amort./Sales | .3 | .6 | .6 | .5 | 1.0 | .5 | .6 | .6 |
|  | (13) .9 | (64) 1.3 | (128) 1.5 | (135) 1.2 | (18) 1.2 | (14) 1.1 | (362) 1.6 | (357) 1.5 |
|  | 3.7 | 2.9 | 3.0 | 2.2 | 1.6 | 1.3 | 2.9 | 3.0 |
| % Officers', Directors' Owners' Comp/Sales | 3.2 | .8 | .8 | .3 |  |  | .9 | 1.0 |
|  | (11) 7.8 | (53) 1.5 | (64) 1.6 | (45) 1.2 |  |  | (169) 2.0 | (162) 2.3 |
|  | 11.6 | 3.4 | 3.0 | 2.1 |  |  | 4.8 | 4.1 |
| Net Sales ($) | 107696M | 1007674M | 3815330M | 12833568M | 5814014M | 9382551M | 26482551M | 33145394M |
| Total Assets ($) | 7930M | 126703M | 821425M | 3277111M | 1532108M | 2444200M | 7369954M | 7846744M |

M = $ thousand     MM = $ million

See Pages 9 through 22 for Explanation of Ratios and Data

## Comparative Historical Data | Current Data Sorted by Sales

| Type of Statement | | | | | | | | |
|---|---|---|---|---|---|---|---|---|
| Unqualified | 39 | 42 | 37 | | | | | 5 | 32 |
| Reviewed | 81 | 92 | 97 | | 2 | 2 | 7 | 23 | 63 |
| Compiled | 51 | 67 | 57 | 2 | 4 | 5 | 10 | 20 | 16 |
| Tax Returns | 75 | 87 | 89 | 5 | 10 | 11 | 21 | 31 | 11 |
| Other | 173 | 207 | 205 | 6 | 15 | 9 | 27 | 45 | 103 |
| | 4/1/09-3/31/10 ALL | 4/1/10-3/31/11 ALL | 4/1/11-3/31/12 ALL | 66 (4/1-9/30/11) | | | 419 (10/1/11-3/31/12) | | |
| | | | | 0-1MM | 1-3MM | 3-5MM | 5-10MM | 10-25MM | 25MM & OVER |
| NUMBER OF STATEMENTS | 419 | 495 | 485 | 13 | 31 | 27 | 65 | 124 | 225 |
| | % | % | % | % | % | % | % | % | % |
| **ASSETS** | | | | | | | | | |
| Cash & Equivalents | 10.9 | 9.5 | 11.6 | 11.3 | 17.8 | 14.7 | 16.2 | 14.0 | 7.8 |
| Trade Receivables (net) | 24.0 | 25.3 | 24.5 | 12.9 | 20.0 | 14.1 | 19.7 | 19.8 | 30.9 |
| Inventory | 17.7 | 21.0 | 20.8 | 15.3 | 14.4 | 17.0 | 17.6 | 20.6 | 23.5 |
| All Other Current | 3.8 | 2.7 | 2.9 | .1 | 4.1 | 3.2 | 2.0 | 2.6 | 3.3 |
| Total Current | 56.3 | 58.5 | 59.8 | 39.6 | 56.3 | 49.0 | 55.6 | 57.1 | 65.5 |
| Fixed Assets (net) | 33.7 | 30.5 | 29.4 | 43.3 | 30.5 | 31.9 | 33.8 | 33.0 | 24.9 |
| Intangibles (net) | 3.4 | 3.9 | 3.9 | 5.2 | 5.4 | 4.6 | 2.9 | 4.1 | 3.7 |
| All Other Non-Current | 6.6 | 7.1 | 6.9 | 11.9 | 7.9 | 14.6 | 7.8 | 5.8 | 5.9 |
| Total | 100.0 | 100.0 | 100.0 | 100.0 | 100.0 | 100.0 | 100.0 | 100.0 | 100.0 |
| **LIABILITIES** | | | | | | | | | |
| Notes Payable-Short Term | 11.3 | 11.3 | 12.1 | 19.8 | 19.4 | 7.5 | 8.3 | 10.9 | 13.0 |
| Cur. Mat.-L.T.D. | 4.2 | 4.1 | 3.7 | .2 | 2.1 | 7.3 | 4.1 | 3.7 | 3.7 |
| Trade Payables | 14.8 | 16.6 | 16.4 | 24.8 | 15.9 | 12.9 | 11.9 | 16.1 | 18.0 |
| Income Taxes Payable | .3 | .2 | .2 | .0 | .0 | .2 | .3 | .2 | .1 |
| All Other Current | 7.5 | 8.7 | 9.2 | 15.9 | 11.4 | 11.1 | 11.5 | 6.7 | 9.1 |
| Total Current | 38.1 | 40.9 | 41.7 | 60.8 | 48.9 | 39.0 | 36.1 | 37.5 | 43.9 |
| Long-Term Debt | 16.4 | 15.9 | 17.1 | 24.0 | 31.2 | 20.0 | 19.2 | 17.7 | 13.5 |
| Deferred Taxes | .4 | .4 | .4 | .0 | .0 | .0 | .5 | .2 | .6 |
| All Other Non-Current | 6.2 | 6.9 | 6.3 | 23.4 | 17.2 | 1.6 | 10.2 | 5.1 | 3.9 |
| Net Worth | 38.9 | 35.9 | 34.5 | -8.2 | 2.8 | 39.4 | 34.0 | 39.5 | 38.2 |
| Total Liabilities & Net Worth | 100.0 | 100.0 | 100.0 | 100.0 | 100.0 | 100.0 | 100.0 | 100.0 | 100.0 |
| **INCOME DATA** | | | | | | | | | |
| Net Sales | 100.0 | 100.0 | 100.0 | 100.0 | 100.0 | 100.0 | 100.0 | 100.0 | 100.0 |
| Gross Profit | 24.7 | 24.1 | 21.4 | 57.9 | 37.1 | 31.7 | 29.6 | 21.9 | 13.2 |
| Operating Expenses | 22.7 | 19.5 | 17.4 | 50.9 | 28.3 | 27.0 | 26.3 | 17.6 | 10.2 |
| Operating Profit | 2.1 | 4.6 | 4.0 | 7.0 | 8.8 | 4.8 | 3.3 | 4.2 | 3.1 |
| All Other Expenses (net) | .6 | .3 | .4 | 2.7 | 2.0 | .2 | .1 | .2 | .2 |
| Profit Before Taxes | 1.5 | 4.3 | 3.6 | 4.3 | 6.9 | 4.6 | 3.3 | 4.0 | 2.9 |
| **RATIOS** | | | | | | | | | |
| Current | 3.0 | 2.7 | 2.7 | 12.3 | 6.0 | 3.0 | 3.5 | 3.3 | 2.3 |
| | 1.6 | 1.5 | 1.5 | 1.5 | 1.2 | 1.2 | 1.8 | 1.6 | 1.4 |
| | 1.0 | 1.0 | 1.0 | .5 | .6 | .7 | 1.1 | 1.0 | 1.1 |
| Quick | 2.0 | 1.6 | 1.7 | 4.4 | 2.4 | 1.8 | 2.1 | 2.0 | 1.4 |
| | (418) .9 | .9 | 1.0 | 1.2 | .7 | .6 | 1.0 | 1.0 | .9 |
| | .5 | .5 | .5 | .2 | .5 | .2 | .4 | .5 | .5 |
| Sales/Receivables | 16 23.1 | 11 34.5 | 8 47.2 | 3 120.3 | 1 296.9 | 0 UND | 1 697.4 | 6 66.3 | 15 23.7 |
| | 32 11.3 | 27 13.5 | 21 17.3 | 17 22.1 | 18 20.5 | 10 34.8 | 13 28.4 | 18 20.6 | 27 13.7 |
| | 48 7.6 | 40 9.0 | 33 10.9 | 43 8.4 | 30 12.2 | 33 11.1 | 31 11.6 | 29 12.7 | 35 10.5 |
| Cost of Sales/Inventory | 8 43.5 | 7 54.9 | 5 74.0 | 0 UND | 0 UND | 1 255.8 | 1 378.7 | 4 85.5 | 9 40.1 |
| | 26 14.1 | 21 17.8 | 16 22.8 | 0 UND | 5 78.7 | 12 31.6 | 14 25.2 | 14 25.7 | 19 19.7 |
| | 53 6.9 | 42 8.6 | 36 10.2 | 126 2.9 | 48 7.6 | 30 12.1 | 38 9.6 | 37 9.8 | 35 10.5 |
| Cost of Sales/Payables | 10 36.8 | 7 53.0 | 5 79.0 | 0 UND | 1 287.3 | 1 300.8 | 2 218.8 | 3 115.5 | 7 55.0 |
| | 22 16.9 | 18 20.7 | 14 26.8 | 36 10.2 | 10 36.4 | 16 22.9 | 8 45.0 | 12 30.4 | 15 25.1 |
| | 41 9.0 | 32 11.4 | 28 13.2 | 74 4.9 | 41 8.9 | 31 11.7 | 33 11.0 | 29 12.8 | 24 14.9 |
| Sales/Working Capital | 6.7 | 8.8 | 10.5 | 1.9 | 9.1 | 9.1 | 9.6 | 10.0 | 11.1 |
| | 14.4 | 21.8 | 27.2 | 14.4 | 127.7 | 69.8 | 27.3 | 34.6 | 24.0 |
| | 999.8 | 999.8 | 342.4 | -7.9 | -27.5 | -49.8 | NM | -247.3 | 75.2 |
| EBIT/Interest | 11.9 | 21.1 | 21.9 | 3.2 | 15.0 | 18.3 | 36.9 | 29.0 | 16.5 |
| | (376) 3.4 | (441) 7.3 | (439) 7.6 | (10) .7 | (26) 4.6 | (23) 4.3 | (61) 9.5 | (108) 9.6 | (211) 7.6 |
| | -.3 | 2.7 | 2.4 | -4.8 | 1.1 | 1.8 | 1.8 | 2.8 | 2.6 |
| Net Profit + Depr., Dep., Amort./Cur. Mat. L/T/D | 2.9 | 8.9 | 12.3 | | | | | 6.4 | 12.0 |
| | (62) 1.2 | (84) 2.7 | (71) 3.7 | | | | | (19) 2.1 | (45) 3.7 |
| | -.1 | 1.0 | 1.8 | | | | | 1.3 | 1.8 |
| Fixed/Worth | .3 | .3 | .3 | .3 | .4 | .3 | .2 | .3 | .2 |
| | .8 | .8 | .8 | .9 | 2.1 | .8 | 1.1 | 1.0 | .7 |
| | 2.5 | 2.1 | 2.2 | NM | -1.1 | 4.7 | 4.6 | 3.6 | 1.4 |
| Debt/Worth | .5 | .7 | .7 | .2 | 1.8 | .4 | .6 | .5 | .9 |
| | 1.6 | 1.6 | 2.0 | 2.5 | 8.6 | 1.8 | 2.0 | 1.6 | 1.8 |
| | 4.7 | 6.0 | 6.1 | -13.4 | -4.4 | 21.0 | 9.3 | 6.2 | 4.1 |
| % Profit Before Taxes/Tangible Net Worth | 32.5 | 56.3 | 61.3 | | 51.9 | 94.0 | 79.9 | 64.0 | 53.7 |
| | (367) 12.1 | (428) 28.3 | (422) 29.0 | (19) 31.4 | (22) 28.6 | (57) 42.2 | (107) 30.3 | (209) 26.8 | |
| | -3.8 | 10.9 | 10.8 | | 2.7 | 16.0 | 10.3 | 11.1 | 11.4 |
| % Profit Before Taxes/Total Assets | 12.3 | 20.2 | 20.6 | 6.8 | 24.8 | 19.2 | 33.5 | 23.9 | 17.7 |
| | 4.2 | 10.0 | 9.5 | -.8 | 10.8 | 12.6 | 14.5 | 12.6 | 8.8 |
| | -2.8 | 3.3 | 2.5 | -5.0 | .1 | 4.7 | 1.8 | 3.0 | 3.1 |
| Sales/Net Fixed Assets | 24.6 | 37.9 | 54.7 | 49.5 | 83.3 | 31.6 | 97.0 | 49.9 | 61.3 |
| | 9.0 | 13.5 | 17.2 | 3.4 | 16.2 | 13.6 | 16.5 | 15.0 | 19.0 |
| | 3.8 | 5.8 | 7.3 | 1.4 | 4.8 | 6.5 | 7.6 | 6.5 | 8.6 |
| Sales/Total Assets | 3.6 | 5.1 | 6.7 | 4.2 | 7.1 | 6.0 | 7.8 | 7.3 | 6.5 |
| | 2.4 | 3.3 | 4.1 | 1.4 | 3.2 | 3.2 | 4.4 | 3.9 | 4.3 |
| | 1.6 | 2.2 | 2.6 | .7 | 2.0 | 2.6 | 2.7 | 2.5 | 3.0 |
| % Depr., Dep., Amort./Sales | 1.1 | .8 | .6 | | .6 | 1.0 | .7 | .8 | .5 |
| | (357) 2.8 | (408) 1.7 | (372) 1.3 | (22) 1.4 | (20) 2.5 | (37) 1.9 | (91) 1.7 | (196) 1.0 | |
| | 5.1 | 3.3 | 2.6 | | 5.3 | 3.6 | 3.2 | 3.2 | 1.8 |
| % Officers', Directors' Owners' Comp/Sales | 1.2 | .7 | .7 | | | | 1.4 | .8 | .3 |
| | (163) 2.7 | (185) 1.8 | (174) 1.5 | | | | (33) 2.7 | (57) 1.4 | (65) 1.0 |
| | 4.6 | 3.6 | 3.0 | | | | 5.6 | 2.9 | 1.7 |
| Net Sales ($) | 15348257M | 30927431M | 32960833M | 7931M | 66252M | 103725M | 489645M | 2125272M | 30168008M |
| Total Assets ($) | 6942041M | 9240525M | 8209477M | 7098M | 40698M | 34623M | 149797M | 654144M | 7323117M |

© RMA 2012

M = $ thousand    MM = $ million
See Pages 9 through 22 for Explanation of Ratios and Data

## Current Data Sorted by Assets | Comparative Historical Data

| Type of Statement | 0-500M | 500M-2MM | 2-10MM | 10-50MM | 50-100MM | 100-250MM | | 4/1/07-3/31/08 ALL | 4/1/08-3/31/09 ALL |
|---|---|---|---|---|---|---|---|---|---|
| Unqualified | | | | 6 | 3 | 2 | | 24 | 22 |
| Reviewed | | 7 | 30 | 11 | 1 | 1 | | 62 | 68 |
| Compiled | 4 | 5 | 15 | 1 | | | | 33 | 25 |
| Tax Returns | 7 | 28 | 32 | 2 | | | | 31 | 32 |
| Other | 5 | 12 | 19 | 13 | 1 | | | 45 | 76 |
| | 33 (4/1-9/30/11) | | | 172 (10/1/11-3/31/12) | | | | | |
| NUMBER OF STATEMENTS | 16 | 52 | 96 | 33 | 5 | 3 | | 195 | 223 |
| | % | % | % | % | % | % | ASSETS | % | % |
| Cash & Equivalents | 20.6 | 11.7 | 10.0 | 8.7 | | | | 7.1 | 5.8 |
| Trade Receivables (net) | 4.9 | 24.9 | 25.6 | 30.4 | | | | 28.6 | 25.3 |
| Inventory | 42.3 | 47.3 | 49.0 | 42.5 | | | | 49.7 | 53.8 |
| All Other Current | 4.8 | 3.5 | 3.2 | 4.0 | | | | 2.7 | 2.7 |
| Total Current | 72.5 | 87.4 | 87.9 | 85.6 | | | | 88.1 | 87.7 |
| Fixed Assets (net) | 9.5 | 7.2 | 5.7 | 6.1 | | | | 6.2 | 6.1 |
| Intangibles (net) | 6.4 | 1.3 | 1.2 | 5.1 | | | | 1.8 | 1.4 |
| All Other Non-Current | 11.6 | 4.1 | 5.2 | 3.2 | | | | 3.8 | 4.8 |
| Total | 100.0 | 100.0 | 100.0 | 100.0 | | | | 100.0 | 100.0 |
| | | | | | | | LIABILITIES | | |
| Notes Payable-Short Term | 7.9 | 10.9 | 12.2 | 17.3 | | | | 20.2 | 20.1 |
| Cur. Mat.-L.T.D. | 1.8 | 1.3 | 1.8 | 1.5 | | | | 1.9 | 1.9 |
| Trade Payables | 8.0 | 34.5 | 25.0 | 24.4 | | | | 22.6 | 22.1 |
| Income Taxes Payable | .0 | .0 | .1 | .0 | | | | .2 | .1 |
| All Other Current | 19.3 | 3.4 | 4.9 | 5.7 | | | | 9.1 | 11.3 |
| Total Current | 37.1 | 50.2 | 43.9 | 49.0 | | | | 54.0 | 55.4 |
| Long-Term Debt | 4.4 | 7.0 | 6.9 | 7.3 | | | | 7.1 | 6.5 |
| Deferred Taxes | .0 | .0 | .0 | .2 | | | | .1 | .1 |
| All Other Non-Current | 21.2 | 13.1 | 6.7 | 7.9 | | | | 4.9 | 5.4 |
| Net Worth | 37.3 | 29.8 | 42.5 | 35.6 | | | | 33.8 | 32.6 |
| Total Liabilities & Net Worth | 100.0 | 100.0 | 100.0 | 100.0 | | | | 100.0 | 100.0 |
| | | | | | | | INCOME DATA | | |
| Net Sales | 100.0 | 100.0 | 100.0 | 100.0 | | | | 100.0 | 100.0 |
| Gross Profit | 37.9 | 32.9 | 26.2 | 25.3 | | | | 25.0 | 26.4 |
| Operating Expenses | 33.9 | 31.2 | 21.7 | 19.9 | | | | 20.8 | 24.0 |
| Operating Profit | 4.1 | 1.6 | 4.5 | 5.4 | | | | 4.3 | 2.4 |
| All Other Expenses (net) | -.6 | .2 | .6 | .5 | | | | 1.2 | 1.2 |
| Profit Before Taxes | 4.7 | 1.5 | 4.0 | 4.9 | | | | 3.1 | 1.2 |
| | | | | | | | RATIOS | | |
| Current | 7.3 | 3.0 | 3.8 | 2.6 | | | | 2.4 | 2.2 |
| | 2.2 | 2.0 | 2.0 | 1.6 | | | | 1.6 | 1.5 |
| | .9 | 1.2 | 1.3 | 1.3 | | | | 1.2 | 1.3 |
| Quick | 1.1 | 1.3 | 1.6 | 1.0 | | | | 1.0 | .9 |
| | .8 | .8 | .8 | .7 | | | (193) | .6 | .5 |
| | .4 | .4 | .5 | .4 | | | | .4 | .3 |
| Sales/Receivables | 0 UND | 16 22.3 | 15 24.8 | 26 14.2 | | | 20 | 18.3 | 18 20.7 |
| | 0 UND | 35 10.3 | 39 9.4 | 43 8.5 | | | 49 | 7.4 | 42 8.7 |
| | 6 62.3 | 54 6.7 | 70 5.2 | 69 5.3 | | | 84 | 4.3 | 68 5.4 |
| Cost of Sales/Inventory | 1 288.3 | 41 8.8 | 46 7.9 | 30 12.0 | | | 56 | 6.6 | 65 5.6 |
| | 52 7.0 | 83 4.4 | 104 3.5 | 87 4.2 | | | 114 | 3.2 | 133 2.7 |
| | 91 4.0 | 228 1.6 | 243 1.5 | 140 2.6 | | | 196 | 1.9 | 247 1.5 |
| Cost of Sales/Payables | 0 UND | 13 28.7 | 12 30.3 | 17 20.9 | | | 14 | 26.4 | 14 26.4 |
| | 0 UND | 50 7.3 | 43 8.4 | 32 11.5 | | | 43 | 8.5 | 43 8.5 |
| | 16 23.1 | 94 3.9 | 99 3.7 | 66 5.5 | | | 91 | 4.0 | 90 4.1 |
| Sales/Working Capital | 7.5 | 3.3 | 2.7 | 4.4 | | | | 3.8 | 3.7 |
| | 14.3 | 7.6 | 6.6 | 7.8 | | | | 7.0 | 6.2 |
| | NM | 25.7 | 14.9 | 19.9 | | | | 15.3 | 17.3 |
| EBIT/Interest | | 16.2 | 21.9 | 42.5 | | | | 6.1 | 5.2 |
| | (40) | 3.9 (81) | 5.9 (30) | 10.3 | | | (178) | 2.3 (201) | 2.1 |
| | | 1.5 | 2.6 | 5.7 | | | | 1.2 | 1.0 |
| Net Profit + Depr., Dep., Amort./Cur. Mat. L/T/D | | | | | | | | 5.0 | 20.5 |
| | | | | | | | (20) | 2.2 (18) | 1.6 |
| | | | | | | | | .4 | .1 |
| Fixed/Worth | .0 | .0 | .0 | .0 | | | | .0 | .0 |
| | .1 | .1 | .0 | .1 | | | | .1 | .1 |
| | NM | .8 | .2 | .6 | | | | .4 | .3 |
| Debt/Worth | .2 | .9 | .5 | 1.0 | | | | 1.0 | 1.1 |
| | .6 | 2.5 | 1.8 | 1.7 | | | | 2.2 | 2.3 |
| | NM | 8.8 | 4.3 | 5.5 | | | | 4.5 | 4.4 |
| % Profit Before Taxes/Tangible Net Worth | 103.0 | 46.3 | 47.2 | 54.4 | | | | 27.9 | 26.8 |
| | (12) 32.5 | (44) 19.8 | (95) 20.1 | (30) 31.4 | | | (176) | 14.0 (204) | 6.6 |
| | -9.6 | 5.1 | 6.3 | 12.8 | | | | 3.6 | .4 |
| % Profit Before Taxes/Total Assets | 39.8 | 10.8 | 15.8 | 19.7 | | | | 10.3 | 7.9 |
| | 14.1 | 5.8 | 6.2 | 9.2 | | | | 3.5 | 2.1 |
| | -9.1 | .8 | 1.6 | 4.8 | | | | .8 | .1 |
| Sales/Net Fixed Assets | UND | 994.4 | 999.8 | 600.7 | | | | 539.5 | 462.4 |
| | 365.9 | 133.0 | 207.1 | 74.5 | | | | 113.5 | 120.4 |
| | 58.9 | 36.7 | 41.9 | 18.1 | | | | 28.5 | 30.3 |
| Sales/Total Assets | 8.0 | 4.0 | 3.4 | 3.4 | | | | 3.1 | 3.0 |
| | 5.1 | 2.2 | 2.2 | 2.5 | | | | 2.0 | 1.9 |
| | 3.0 | 1.3 | 1.2 | 1.6 | | | | 1.3 | 1.2 |
| % Depr., Dep., Amort./Sales | | .1 | .1 | .1 | | | | .1 | .1 |
| | (32) | .3 (58) | .2 (26) | .4 | | | (146) | .2 (174) | .3 |
| | | .6 | 1.0 | .8 | | | | .7 | .7 |
| % Officers', Directors' Owners' Comp/Sales | | 1.8 | 1.3 | .4 | | | | .8 | 1.1 |
| | (28) | 4.7 (67) | 2.7 (17) | 1.6 | | | (114) | 2.1 (127) | 2.4 |
| | | 9.4 | 4.8 | 2.9 | | | | 4.6 | 5.1 |
| Net Sales ($) | 48793M | 394763M | 1777633M | 4016195M | 633251M | 632375M | | 11996294M | 16616821M |
| Total Assets ($) | 4368M | 61354M | 468348M | 722617M | 398327M | 552807M | | 4168621M | 4933873M |

© RMA 2012

M = $ thousand   MM = $ million
See Pages 9 through 22 for Explanation of Ratios and Data

| Comparative Historical Data | | | | Current Data Sorted by Sales | | | | | |
|---|---|---|---|---|---|---|---|---|---|
| | | | **Type of Statement** | | | | | 1 | 10 |
| 16 | 12 | 11 | Unqualified | | | | | 1 | 10 |
| 57 | 44 | 49 | Reviewed | 1 | 5 | 3 | 12 | 14 | 14 |
| 30 | 30 | 25 | Compiled | 1 | 4 | 4 | 7 | 5 | 4 |
| 48 | 51 | 69 | Tax Returns | 7 | 15 | 16 | 12 | 10 | 9 |
| 62 | 56 | 51 | Other | 5 | 11 | 3 | 5 | 15 | 12 |
| 4/1/09-3/31/10 ALL | 4/1/10-3/31/11 ALL | 4/1/11-3/31/12 ALL | | 0-1MM | 33 (4/1-9/30/11) 1-3MM | 3-5MM | 172 (10/1/11-3/31/12) 5-10MM | 10-25MM | 25MM & OVER |
| 213 | 193 | 205 | **NUMBER OF STATEMENTS** | 14 | 35 | 26 | 36 | 45 | 49 |
| % | % | % | **ASSETS** | % | % | % | % | % | % |
| 9.7 | 11.1 | 11.1 | Cash & Equivalents | 14.0 | 11.0 | 11.0 | 6.5 | 10.9 | 14.1 |
| 28.4 | 26.2 | 24.4 | Trade Receivables (net) | 10.9 | 18.6 | 27.6 | 25.3 | 32.5 | 22.5 |
| 47.5 | 47.6 | 46.7 | Inventory | 52.3 | 47.8 | 46.7 | 52.4 | 41.7 | 44.9 |
| 1.6 | 2.0 | 3.7 | All Other Current | .4 | 6.6 | 1.2 | 1.7 | 3.2 | 5.7 |
| 87.2 | 87.0 | 85.9 | Total Current | 77.5 | 84.0 | 86.5 | 85.9 | 88.3 | 87.2 |
| 5.5 | 5.9 | 6.4 | Fixed Assets (net) | 3.4 | 11.0 | 5.8 | 5.4 | 6.2 | 5.2 |
| 1.5 | 2.1 | 2.5 | Intangibles (net) | 1.6 | 1.7 | 4.4 | 1.1 | 2.8 | 3.2 |
| 5.8 | 5.0 | 5.1 | All Other Non-Current | 17.5 | 3.2 | 3.3 | 7.6 | 2.7 | 4.4 |
| 100.0 | 100.0 | 100.0 | Total | 100.0 | 100.0 | 100.0 | 100.0 | 100.0 | 100.0 |
| | | | **LIABILITIES** | | | | | | |
| 17.2 | 14.0 | 12.2 | Notes Payable-Short Term | 13.0 | 11.0 | 5.5 | 11.0 | 15.1 | 14.8 |
| 1.5 | 1.4 | 1.6 | Cur. Mat.-L.T.D. | 2.3 | 1.4 | 1.5 | 1.4 | 1.4 | 2.0 |
| 25.7 | 26.1 | 25.9 | Trade Payables | 15.3 | 27.0 | 29.0 | 25.0 | 25.2 | 27.9 |
| .2 | .2 | .1 | Income Taxes Payable | .0 | .0 | .0 | .1 | .0 | .1 |
| 8.4 | 8.6 | 6.0 | All Other Current | 14.1 | 4.3 | 5.1 | 4.9 | 5.4 | 6.6 |
| 52.9 | 50.3 | 45.8 | Total Current | 44.7 | 43.6 | 41.2 | 42.5 | 47.2 | 51.4 |
| 5.7 | 5.2 | 6.8 | Long-Term Debt | 8.1 | 9.5 | 9.0 | 5.9 | 4.4 | 6.4 |
| .1 | .2 | .1 | Deferred Taxes | .0 | .0 | .0 | .0 | .0 | .3 |
| 7.7 | 6.3 | 9.4 | All Other Non-Current | 24.1 | 12.5 | 7.1 | 6.4 | 6.3 | 9.4 |
| 33.7 | 37.9 | 37.8 | Net Worth | 23.1 | 34.4 | 42.7 | 45.2 | 42.1 | 32.5 |
| 100.0 | 100.0 | 100.0 | Total Liabilities & Net Worth | 100.0 | 100.0 | 100.0 | 100.0 | 100.0 | 100.0 |
| | | | **INCOME DATA** | | | | | | |
| 100.0 | 100.0 | 100.0 | Net Sales | 100.0 | 100.0 | 100.0 | 100.0 | 100.0 | 100.0 |
| 25.3 | 27.2 | 29.2 | Gross Profit | 47.3 | 35.9 | 33.2 | 28.5 | 24.7 | 21.9 |
| 22.3 | 23.8 | 25.3 | Operating Expenses | 48.6 | 33.1 | 28.4 | 24.3 | 19.3 | 17.6 |
| 3.0 | 3.4 | 4.0 | Operating Profit | -1.3 | 2.8 | 4.8 | 4.2 | 5.4 | 4.3 |
| .9 | .6 | .3 | All Other Expenses (net) | -.4 | .3 | .6 | .5 | .2 | .3 |
| 2.1 | 2.8 | 3.6 | Profit Before Taxes | -.9 | 2.5 | 4.3 | 3.7 | 5.2 | 4.0 |
| | | | **RATIOS** | | | | | | |
| 2.5 | 3.0 | 3.1 | | 9.6 | 4.2 | 4.2 | 3.7 | 2.8 | 2.7 |
| 1.6 | 1.8 | 2.0 | Current | 2.1 | 2.1 | 2.1 | 2.1 | 1.6 | 1.8 |
| 1.3 | 1.2 | 1.3 | | 1.0 | 1.1 | 1.4 | 1.6 | 1.3 | 1.3 |
| 1.1 | 1.4 | 1.3 | | 1.0 | 1.3 | 1.9 | 1.2 | 2.0 | 1.5 |
| .7 | .7 | .8 | Quick | .5 | .8 | .9 | .7 | .8 | .7 |
| .4 | .4 | .4 | | .1 | .4 | .6 | .4 | .6 | .4 |
| 11 34.3 | 8 45.2 | 10 38.2 | | 0 UND | 12 29.8 | 25 14.7 | 16 22.6 | 26 13.8 | 2 154.4 |
| 48 7.7 | 33 11.1 | 34 10.6 | Sales/Receivables | 11 32.6 | 33 11.1 | 39 9.4 | 36 10.0 | 57 6.4 | 20 18.7 |
| 77 4.7 | 64 5.7 | 61 6.0 | | 57 6.4 | 70 5.2 | 78 4.7 | 60 6.1 | 81 4.5 | 46 8.0 |
| 45 8.1 | 37 9.8 | 41 8.9 | | 0 UND | 66 5.5 | 45 8.2 | 59 6.2 | 38 9.5 | 13 27.1 |
| 108 3.4 | 92 4.0 | 96 3.8 | Cost of Sales/Inventory | 243 1.5 | 174 2.1 | 101 3.6 | 101 3.6 | 78 4.7 | 55 6.6 |
| 213 1.7 | 173 2.1 | 203 1.8 | | 912 .4 | 304 1.2 | 281 1.3 | 243 1.5 | 126 2.9 | 122 3.0 |
| 13 28.6 | 12 29.4 | 11 33.4 | | 0 UND | 10 34.9 | 26 14.0 | 12 31.1 | 13 29.0 | 3 121.7 |
| 45 8.2 | 38 9.6 | 38 9.5 | Cost of Sales/Payables | 0 UND | 70 5.2 | 63 5.8 | 40 9.1 | 44 8.3 | 24 15.4 |
| 89 4.1 | 83 4.4 | 85 4.3 | | 74 4.9 | 174 2.1 | 107 3.4 | 104 3.5 | 83 4.4 | 47 7.7 |
| 3.0 | 3.9 | 3.4 | | 2.1 | 1.5 | 2.3 | 3.1 | 3.8 | 6.1 |
| 6.3 | 6.9 | 7.2 | Sales/Working Capital | 4.8 | 5.8 | 5.0 | 5.6 | 7.2 | 15.6 |
| 18.0 | 29.1 | 17.4 | | -120.4 | 15.3 | 11.9 | 10.8 | 15.4 | 48.6 |
| 9.2 | 19.5 | 20.2 | | | 12.8 | 16.4 | 20.6 | 20.8 | 45.2 |
| (175) 2.9 | (153) 5.5 | (163) 6.2 | EBIT/Interest | (27) 3.1 | (19) 4.6 | (29) 3.9 | (38) 8.1 | (43) 12.5 |
| 1.3 | 1.8 | 2.5 | | | 1.1 | 2.5 | 2.1 | 4.3 | 6.2 |
| 52.7 | 17.3 | 15.4 | Net Profit + Depr., Dep., | | | | | | |
| (14) 6.4 | (15) 8.3 | (13) 5.4 | Amort./Cur. Mat. L/T/D | | | | | | |
| .1 | .8 | 1.6 | | | | | | | |
| .0 | .0 | .0 | | .0 | .0 | .0 | .0 | .0 | .0 |
| .1 | .1 | .1 | Fixed/Worth | .1 | .0 | .1 | .0 | .1 | .1 |
| .2 | .2 | .3 | | -3.1 | 1.1 | .6 | .2 | .3 | .3 |
| .9 | .7 | .6 | | .2 | .5 | .7 | .5 | .6 | .8 |
| 2.1 | 1.7 | 1.8 | Debt/Worth | 2.6 | 2.0 | 1.9 | 1.4 | 1.9 | 1.6 |
| 5.4 | 5.5 | 5.3 | | -64.9 | 8.1 | 4.3 | 3.7 | 4.1 | 7.5 |
| 36.0 | 48.9 | 47.2 | | 63.4 | 50.4 | 45.8 | 33.1 | 45.4 | 92.8 |
| (196) 11.5 | (176) 17.6 | (187) 20.7 | % Profit Before Taxes/Tangible Net Worth | (10) -4.3 | (30) 9.5 | (24) 20.5 | (35) 12.9 | 25.9 | (43) 38.1 |
| 2.3 | 4.0 | 6.7 | | -11.3 | 1.5 | 4.9 | 5.6 | 13.8 | 12.0 |
| 11.5 | 15.9 | 16.8 | | 11.8 | 8.9 | 16.3 | 11.8 | 13.3 | 25.9 |
| 2.9 | 5.2 | 7.0 | % Profit Before Taxes/Total Assets | -3.3 | 3.0 | 6.5 | 3.1 | 7.8 | 13.2 |
| .6 | 1.0 | 1.7 | | -9.7 | .3 | 2.5 | 1.2 | 3.7 | 4.7 |
| 721.5 | 999.8 | 999.8 | | UND | UND | 999.8 | 999.8 | 803.4 | 999.8 |
| 126.9 | 134.1 | 134.0 | Sales/Net Fixed Assets | 162.2 | 115.6 | 69.4 | 169.0 | 127.6 | 204.9 |
| 36.4 | 38.8 | 36.4 | | 60.7 | 16.8 | 24.5 | 42.0 | 35.7 | 37.4 |
| 3.2 | 4.0 | 4.0 | | 3.6 | 3.0 | 4.1 | 3.3 | 3.6 | 11.3 |
| 2.0 | 2.4 | 2.3 | Sales/Total Assets | 1.2 | 1.5 | 2.1 | 2.1 | 2.4 | 3.5 |
| 1.2 | 1.5 | 1.4 | | .8 | .9 | 1.4 | 1.2 | 1.7 | 2.2 |
| .1 | .1 | .1 | | | .2 | .2 | .1 | .1 | .0 |
| (159) .2 | (118) .4 | (127) .3 | % Depr., Dep., Amort./Sales | (20) .4 | (14) .4 | (23) .4 | (31) .2 | (35) .2 | .2 |
| .7 | .9 | .9 | | | .9 | 1.2 | 1.0 | .5 | 1.1 |
| 1.4 | 1.3 | 1.3 | | | 2.8 | 2.0 | 1.7 | .9 | .4 |
| (127) 2.8 | (109) 2.8 | (119) 2.8 | % Officers', Directors', Owners' Comp/Sales | (17) 6.9 | (18) 4.0 | (28) 2.7 | (31) 2.2 | (22) .9 |
| 5.1 | 5.7 | 5.2 | | | 9.5 | 5.8 | 4.8 | 3.7 | 2.5 |
| 21525980M | 20440338M | 7503010M | Net Sales ($) | 7933M | 68466M | 101833M | 253340M | 716489M | 6354949M |
| 3793394M | 2563995M | 2207821M | Total Assets ($) | 7014M | 54198M | 56901M | 142517M | 538199M | 1408992M |

## Current Data Sorted by Assets                    Comparative Historical Data

| Type of Statement | 0-500M | 500M-2MM | 2-10MM | 10-50MM | 50-100MM | 100-250MM | | 4/1/07-3/31/08 ALL | 4/1/08-3/31/09 ALL |
|---|---|---|---|---|---|---|---|---|---|
| Unqualified | | 1 | 12 | 33 | 13 | 6 | | 50 | 54 |
| Reviewed | 2 | 11 | 72 | 28 | 1 | | | 109 | 118 |
| Compiled | 11 | 44 | 50 | 7 | | | | 90 | 114 |
| Tax Returns | 65 | 127 | 96 | 6 | 2 | | | 143 | 188 |
| Other | 36 | 95 | 116 | 43 | 8 | 9 | | 209 | 257 |
| | | 110 (4/1-9/30/11) | | | 784 (10/1/11-3/31/12) | | | | |
| **NUMBER OF STATEMENTS** | 114 | 278 | 346 | 117 | 24 | 15 | | 601 | 731 |
| **ASSETS** | % | % | % | % | % | % | | % | % |
| Cash & Equivalents | 22.5 | 12.5 | 9.5 | 7.1 | 4.8 | 1.7 | | 8.6 | 9.3 |
| Trade Receivables (net) | 24.8 | 28.1 | 30.9 | 29.5 | 27.5 | 19.7 | | 30.4 | 28.8 |
| Inventory | 28.0 | 37.9 | 37.4 | 38.7 | 37.7 | 35.9 | | 37.1 | 38.1 |
| All Other Current | 1.1 | 1.8 | 2.4 | 3.1 | 1.8 | 3.4 | | 2.5 | 2.7 |
| Total Current | 76.4 | 80.4 | 80.2 | 78.5 | 71.9 | 60.7 | | 78.6 | 78.9 |
| Fixed Assets (net) | 9.9 | 9.7 | 10.3 | 10.6 | 13.3 | 11.7 | | 11.2 | 12.1 |
| Intangibles (net) | 5.6 | 3.6 | 3.4 | 4.2 | 10.0 | 14.5 | | 4.3 | 3.8 |
| All Other Non-Current | 8.1 | 6.2 | 6.1 | 6.7 | 4.8 | 13.1 | | 5.9 | 5.2 |
| Total | 100.0 | 100.0 | 100.0 | 100.0 | 100.0 | 100.0 | | 100.0 | 100.0 |
| **LIABILITIES** | | | | | | | | | |
| Notes Payable-Short Term | 21.9 | 13.6 | 12.3 | 15.5 | 18.1 | 11.2 | | 17.2 | 18.3 |
| Cur. Mat.-L.T.D. | 2.3 | 2.4 | 1.9 | 1.7 | 4.5 | 1.0 | | 3.1 | 2.9 |
| Trade Payables | 23.4 | 19.9 | 22.1 | 18.2 | 17.3 | 12.9 | | 22.6 | 21.0 |
| Income Taxes Payable | .2 | .1 | .1 | .1 | .1 | .1 | | .1 | .1 |
| All Other Current | 13.2 | 8.7 | 10.1 | 10.5 | 7.5 | 9.3 | | 10.4 | 9.7 |
| Total Current | 61.0 | 44.7 | 46.6 | 46.1 | 47.5 | 34.5 | | 53.4 | 52.0 |
| Long-Term Debt | 13.4 | 10.8 | 9.1 | 10.2 | 16.9 | 13.0 | | 10.0 | 10.5 |
| Deferred Taxes | .0 | .1 | .2 | .0 | .3 | 1.3 | | .1 | .1 |
| All Other Non-Current | 7.3 | 12.0 | 6.3 | 5.8 | 2.4 | 10.7 | | 6.9 | 5.9 |
| Net Worth | 18.2 | 32.4 | 37.9 | 37.8 | 32.8 | 40.4 | | 29.6 | 31.4 |
| Total Liabilities & Net Worth | 100.0 | 100.0 | 100.0 | 100.0 | 100.0 | 100.0 | | 100.0 | 100.0 |
| **INCOME DATA** | | | | | | | | | |
| Net Sales | 100.0 | 100.0 | 100.0 | 100.0 | 100.0 | 100.0 | | 100.0 | 100.0 |
| Gross Profit | 36.1 | 33.9 | 30.7 | 27.2 | 28.3 | 30.0 | | 33.0 | 31.9 |
| Operating Expenses | 31.7 | 29.9 | 26.3 | 23.3 | 22.6 | 27.5 | | 28.3 | 27.8 |
| Operating Profit | 4.4 | 3.9 | 4.4 | 3.9 | 5.7 | 2.5 | | 4.7 | 4.1 |
| All Other Expenses (net) | .0 | .4 | .5 | .6 | 1.4 | 1.9 | | .9 | .8 |
| Profit Before Taxes | 4.3 | 3.5 | 3.9 | 3.3 | 4.3 | .6 | | 3.7 | 3.3 |
| **RATIOS** | | | | | | | | | |
| Current | 3.5 | 3.6 | 3.0 | 2.5 | 2.0 | 3.0 | | 2.4 | 2.5 |
| | 1.5 | 1.9 | 1.7 | 1.8 | 1.5 | 1.8 | | 1.5 | 1.6 |
| | 1.0 | 1.3 | 1.2 | 1.3 | 1.2 | 1.2 | | 1.1 | 1.1 |
| Quick | 2.3 | 1.7 | 1.6 | 1.3 | 1.0 | 1.2 | | 1.3 | 1.3 |
| | .8 | (277) .9 | .9 | .8 | .7 | .8 | | .8 | .7 |
| | .4 | .5 | .6 | .5 | .4 | .4 | | .5 | .4 |
| Sales/Receivables | 0 UND | 17  21.9 | 26  14.1 | 32  11.5 | 11  32.0 | 30  12.1 | | 24  15.5 | 20  18.7 |
| | 17  21.3 | 31  11.8 | 39  9.4 | 41  8.8 | 40  9.1 | 37  9.9 | | 37  10.0 | 34  10.9 |
| | 37  9.9 | 47  7.7 | 55  6.6 | 55  6.6 | 68  5.4 | 57  6.4 | | 52  7.0 | 48  7.6 |
| Cost of Sales/Inventory | 0 UND | 27  13.4 | 32  11.4 | 51  7.2 | 33  10.9 | 66  5.5 | | 30  12.1 | 29  12.4 |
| | 20  18.4 | 63  5.8 | 68  5.4 | 81  4.5 | 81  4.5 | 74  4.9 | | 67  5.4 | 66  5.5 |
| | 78  4.7 | 130  2.8 | 122  3.0 | 135  2.7 | 135  2.7 | 146  2.5 | | 117  3.1 | 129  2.8 |
| Cost of Sales/Payables | 0 UND | 8  45.4 | 19  19.6 | 20  18.7 | 12  31.3 | 27  13.5 | | 16  22.6 | 13  28.1 |
| | 19  19.5 | 26  14.2 | 35  10.5 | 30  12.1 | 32  11.3 | 35  10.4 | | 33  11.1 | 28  13.2 |
| | 50  7.3 | 49  7.4 | 61  6.0 | 51  7.1 | 60  6.1 | 53  6.9 | | 56  6.6 | 52  7.0 |
| Sales/Working Capital | 7.5 | 4.7 | 4.7 | 4.1 | 6.6 | 4.1 | | 5.6 | 5.2 |
| | 26.9 | 9.1 | 9.0 | 7.7 | 12.5 | 6.0 | | 11.4 | 10.2 |
| | -353.4 | 24.0 | 20.5 | 17.9 | 23.6 | 18.9 | | 49.2 | 46.1 |
| EBIT/Interest | 21.2 | 15.9 | 22.3 | 18.2 | 9.7 | 6.9 | | 11.1 | 9.9 |
| | (73) 3.8 | (221) 4.4 | (301) 6.7 | (105) 6.4 | (23) 5.0 | (14) 1.6 | | (533) 3.8 | (651) 3.5 |
| | 1.0 | 1.5 | 2.4 | 2.0 | 1.9 | -2.1 | | 1.5 | 1.2 |
| Net Profit + Depr., Dep., Amort./Cur. Mat. L/T/D | | 11.3 | 18.0 | 12.2 | | | | 8.2 | 6.6 |
| | | (12) 3.3 | (37) 3.5 | (17) 3.4 | | | | (75) 2.7 | (102) 2.9 |
| | | 1.8 | 1.3 | 1.6 | | | | .6 | .9 |
| Fixed/Worth | .0 | .0 | .0 | .1 | .1 | .1 | | .1 | .1 |
| | .2 | .2 | .1 | .2 | .4 | .4 | | .2 | .2 |
| | 3.3 | .8 | .6 | .5 | .9 | 9.1 | | 1.3 | 1.1 |
| Debt/Worth | .8 | .8 | .8 | .8 | .8 | .8 | | 1.1 | .9 |
| | 3.1 | 1.8 | 1.8 | 1.9 | 2.0 | 2.3 | | 2.5 | 2.4 |
| | -10.4 | 7.0 | 5.6 | 3.6 | 12.7 | 61.1 | | 9.5 | 9.7 |
| % Profit Before Taxes/Tangible Net Worth | 127.9 | 60.8 | 52.8 | 44.4 | 56.4 | 43.3 | | 62.8 | 53.6 |
| | (82) 48.8 | (235) 23.7 | (318) 22.3 | (107) 20.5 | (20) 29.7 | (12) 16.0 | | (502) 28.7 | (612) 23.0 |
| | 10.6 | 5.0 | 8.2 | 6.7 | 8.9 | -12.5 | | 9.2 | 4.0 |
| % Profit Before Taxes/Total Assets | 38.1 | 19.6 | 16.1 | 14.1 | 19.5 | 7.1 | | 18.1 | 16.3 |
| | 13.0 | 7.6 | 6.8 | 6.2 | 5.8 | 1.5 | | 6.9 | 5.3 |
| | .4 | 1.3 | 1.9 | 2.2 | 2.2 | -5.6 | | 1.6 | .6 |
| Sales/Net Fixed Assets | UND | 503.6 | 257.7 | 103.0 | 93.1 | 71.5 | | 159.2 | 200.6 |
| | 149.7 | 83.9 | 69.6 | 42.7 | 37.8 | 49.9 | | 50.0 | 53.9 |
| | 35.6 | 27.7 | 20.9 | 14.1 | 11.0 | 12.8 | | 20.7 | 18.0 |
| Sales/Total Assets | 8.9 | 4.3 | 3.7 | 3.1 | 3.3 | 2.4 | | 3.9 | 4.1 |
| | 4.4 | 3.1 | 2.6 | 2.2 | 2.3 | 1.8 | | 2.9 | 2.9 |
| | 2.6 | 2.1 | 1.8 | 1.7 | 1.6 | 1.1 | | 2.1 | 1.9 |
| % Depr., Dep., Amort./Sales | .2 | .2 | .2 | .3 | .3 | .3 | | .2 | .3 |
| | (47) .6 | (159) .6 | (250) .5 | (95) .6 | (21) .7 | (10) 1.5 | | (452) .6 | (542) .7 |
| | 1.8 | 1.2 | 1.2 | 1.3 | 2.5 | 2.8 | | 1.4 | 1.4 |
| % Officers', Directors' Owners' Comp/Sales | 4.2 | 2.1 | 1.5 | .9 | | | | 2.0 | 1.9 |
| | (60) 5.8 | (159) 4.2 | (190) 2.7 | (21) 1.9 | | | | (282) 3.7 | (309) 3.4 |
| | 9.9 | 7.0 | 5.3 | 3.4 | | | | 7.0 | 6.6 |
| Net Sales ($) | 221052M | 1189834M | 4758875M | 6673367M | 5097121M | 4129166M | | 14313178M | 15047492M |
| Total Assets ($) | 32900M | 332443M | 1583043M | 2567868M | 1603422M | 2358570M | | 5106697M | 6243671M |

© RMA 2012

M = $ thousand    MM = $ million
See Pages 9 through 22 for Explanation of Ratios and Data

## Comparative Historical Data / Current Data Sorted by Sales

| | | | Type of Statement | 0-1MM | 1-3MM | 3-5MM | 5-10MM | 10-25MM | 25MM & OVER |
|---|---|---|---|---|---|---|---|---|---|
| 63 | 52 | 65 | Unqualified | | 1 | | 3 | 11 | 50 |
| 102 | 110 | 114 | Reviewed | 1 | 2 | 10 | 30 | 39 | 32 |
| 97 | 98 | 112 | Compiled | 6 | 19 | 21 | 24 | 34 | 8 |
| 212 | 222 | 296 | Tax Returns | 34 | 81 | 55 | 73 | 42 | 11 |
| 251 | 275 | 307 | Other | 17 | 67 | 37 | 62 | 63 | 61 |
| 4/1/09-3/31/10 ALL | 4/1/10-3/31/11 ALL | 4/1/11-3/31/12 ALL | | 110 (4/1-9/30/11) | | | 784 (10/1/11-3/31/12) | | |
| 725 | 757 | 894 | **NUMBER OF STATEMENTS** | 58 | 170 | 123 | 192 | 189 | 162 |
| % | % | % | **ASSETS** | % | % | % | % | % | % |
| 11.1 | 12.1 | 11.5 | Cash & Equivalents | 16.5 | 13.0 | 14.0 | 12.5 | 10.0 | 7.0 |
| 30.9 | 29.4 | 28.8 | Trade Receivables (net) | 21.5 | 24.5 | 27.2 | 30.7 | 32.6 | 30.5 |
| 34.7 | 34.7 | 36.5 | Inventory | 34.5 | 35.4 | 38.0 | 36.5 | 35.8 | 38.1 |
| 2.9 | 2.5 | 2.2 | All Other Current | .7 | 1.9 | 1.9 | 1.9 | 2.7 | 2.8 |
| 79.6 | 78.6 | 79.0 | Total Current | 73.2 | 74.7 | 81.1 | 81.7 | 81.1 | 78.4 |
| 10.9 | 11.2 | 10.2 | Fixed Assets (net) | 10.4 | 12.2 | 10.2 | 8.8 | 9.6 | 10.5 |
| 4.1 | 4.6 | 4.2 | Intangibles (net) | 7.8 | 6.1 | 3.7 | 2.9 | 2.3 | 5.0 |
| 5.4 | 5.6 | 6.6 | All Other Non-Current | 8.6 | 7.0 | 5.0 | 6.6 | 7.0 | 6.1 |
| 100.0 | 100.0 | 100.0 | Total | 100.0 | 100.0 | 100.0 | 100.0 | 100.0 | 100.0 |
| | | | **LIABILITIES** | | | | | | |
| 16.4 | 15.0 | 14.5 | Notes Payable-Short Term | 22.0 | 15.3 | 13.2 | 13.5 | 13.0 | 15.0 |
| 2.5 | 1.9 | 2.1 | Cur. Mat.-L.T.D. | 1.9 | 2.9 | 1.5 | 2.3 | 1.9 | 2.1 |
| 22.0 | 21.6 | 20.8 | Trade Payables | 20.2 | 17.8 | 20.4 | 21.6 | 23.2 | 20.5 |
| .1 | .2 | .1 | Income Taxes Payable | .1 | .2 | .1 | .1 | .1 | .2 |
| 9.9 | 8.3 | 10.0 | All Other Current | 13.1 | 8.7 | 8.7 | 10.7 | 10.1 | 10.3 |
| 51.0 | 47.0 | 47.6 | Total Current | 57.2 | 44.9 | 43.9 | 48.1 | 48.4 | 48.1 |
| 10.3 | 10.6 | 10.6 | Long-Term Debt | 14.4 | 16.5 | 9.7 | 7.5 | 7.9 | 10.7 |
| .1 | .1 | .2 | Deferred Taxes | .1 | .0 | .2 | .1 | .2 | .2 |
| 6.6 | 7.3 | 8.1 | All Other Non-Current | 4.5 | 15.7 | 9.3 | 5.0 | 5.3 | 7.5 |
| 32.0 | 35.0 | 33.5 | Net Worth | 23.8 | 22.9 | 36.9 | 39.2 | 38.2 | 33.5 |
| 100.0 | 100.0 | 100.0 | Total Liabilities & Net Worth | 100.0 | 100.0 | 100.0 | 100.0 | 100.0 | 100.0 |
| | | | **INCOME DATA** | | | | | | |
| 100.0 | 100.0 | 100.0 | Net Sales | 100.0 | 100.0 | 100.0 | 100.0 | 100.0 | 100.0 |
| 32.0 | 32.7 | 31.8 | Gross Profit | 39.3 | 39.6 | 33.1 | 31.9 | 27.5 | 25.1 |
| 28.5 | 28.3 | 27.6 | Operating Expenses | 36.1 | 34.7 | 29.2 | 27.6 | 23.3 | 21.2 |
| 3.5 | 4.4 | 4.2 | Operating Profit | 3.2 | 4.9 | 3.9 | 4.3 | 4.1 | 4.0 |
| .7 | .6 | .5 | All Other Expenses (net) | -.1 | .8 | .4 | .3 | .4 | .7 |
| 2.8 | 3.8 | 3.7 | Profit Before Taxes | 3.3 | 4.2 | 3.5 | 3.9 | 3.7 | 3.2 |
| | | | **RATIOS** | | | | | | |
| 2.8 | 3.1 | 3.0 | | 3.5 | 4.6 | 4.1 | 3.1 | 2.7 | 2.4 |
| 1.7 | 1.7 | 1.8 | Current | 1.4 | 1.9 | 1.9 | 1.8 | 1.8 | 1.7 |
| 1.1 | 1.2 | 1.2 | | 1.0 | 1.1 | 1.3 | 1.2 | 1.2 | 1.2 |
| 1.4 | 1.6 | 1.6 | | 1.5 | 2.1 | 1.8 | 1.7 | 1.6 | 1.2 |
| .8 | .9 (893) | .9 | Quick | .8 (169) | .9 | .9 | .9 | .9 | .8 |
| .3 | .5 | .5 | | .3 | .4 | .6 | .6 | .5 | .5 |
| 23 15.8 | 22 16.9 | 21 17.3 | | 0 UND | 17 22.1 | 20 18.6 | 24 14.9 | 22 16.3 | 22 16.3 |
| 37 9.9 | 37 9.7 | 35 10.4 | Sales/Receivables | 23 16.2 | 33 11.1 | 33 11.0 | 40 9.1 | 35 10.4 | 37 9.8 |
| 54 6.8 | 54 6.7 | 51 7.1 | | 53 6.9 | 48 7.6 | 52 7.0 | 55 6.6 | 52 7.0 | 50 7.3 |
| 26 14.0 | 27 13.7 | 26 13.8 | | 0 UND | 22 16.8 | 22 16.9 | 29 12.7 | 24 15.0 | 38 9.5 |
| 64 5.7 | 62 5.9 | 64 5.7 | Cost of Sales/Inventory | 73 5.0 | 85 4.3 | 68 5.4 | 62 5.9 | 56 6.5 | 68 5.4 |
| 119 3.1 | 123 3.0 | 122 3.0 | | 203 1.8 | 146 2.5 | 146 2.5 | 107 3.4 | 101 3.6 | 107 3.4 |
| 15 25.0 | 15 24.7 | 13 27.1 | | 4 82.0 | 6 65.6 | 9 39.2 | 16 22.2 | 17 21.5 | 18 20.3 |
| 31 11.8 | 31 11.9 | 29 12.4 | Cost of Sales/Payables | 22 16.4 | 26 14.0 | 33 11.0 | 30 12.3 | 30 12.3 | 30 12.3 |
| 54 6.8 | 55 6.6 | 53 6.9 | | 72 5.1 | 58 6.3 | 51 7.2 | 57 6.4 | 50 7.3 | 49 7.5 |
| 5.1 | 4.8 | 4.9 | | 3.6 | 4.1 | 4.7 | 4.3 | 5.6 | 5.4 |
| 9.9 | 8.8 | 9.5 | Sales/Working Capital | 15.3 | 9.3 | 8.0 | 9.1 | 11.1 | 10.0 |
| 34.9 | 26.6 | 26.5 | | 418.0 | 53.9 | 17.4 | 28.2 | 26.4 | 21.3 |
| 12.8 | 17.3 | 20.0 | | 12.9 | 13.5 | 23.1 | 20.4 | 26.2 | 21.0 |
| (638) 4.3 | (646) 4.9 | (737) 5.0 | EBIT/Interest | (37) 3.8 | (131) 2.7 | (104) 4.2 | (151) 5.3 | (168) 7.8 | (146) 6.3 |
| 1.2 | 1.7 | 1.8 | | -2.1 | 1.0 | 1.8 | 1.8 | 2.8 | 2.1 |
| 6.5 | 15.1 | 13.8 | Net Profit + Depr., Dep., | | | | 23.9 | 15.3 | 13.8 |
| (98) 2.9 | (92) 4.8 | (79) 3.6 | Amort./Cur. Mat. L/T/D | | | | (12) 3.1 | (29) 3.6 | (27) 4.3 |
| .7 | 1.5 | 1.6 | | | | | 1.5 | 1.5 | 1.7 |
| .0 | .0 | .0 | | .0 | .0 | .0 | .0 | .0 | .1 |
| .2 | .2 | .2 | Fixed/Worth | .2 | .2 | .2 | .1 | .1 | .2 |
| 1.1 | .8 | .7 | | 1.0 | -5.7 | 1.6 | .5 | .6 | .7 |
| .8 | .7 | .8 | | .8 | .7 | .6 | .8 | .8 | .9 |
| 2.1 | 1.8 | 1.9 | Debt/Worth | 3.2 | 2.3 | 1.6 | 1.5 | 1.8 | 2.2 |
| 8.9 | 7.1 | 6.4 | | 43.0 | -14.9 | 6.8 | 4.2 | 4.3 | 6.1 |
| 54.2 | 54.8 | 59.1 | % Profit Before Taxes/Tangible | 75.5 | 60.6 | 68.3 | 55.8 | 59.1 | 52.3 |
| (609) 19.3 | (640) 23.8 | (774) 24.7 | Net Worth | (46) 18.0 | (124) 27.3 | (104) 26.8 | (177) 19.5 | (178) 25.4 | (145) 26.8 |
| 2.9 | 7.1 | 7.4 | | 2.9 | 2.9 | 4.9 | 6.8 | 10.6 | 9.2 |
| 15.5 | 18.4 | 18.5 | % Profit Before Taxes/Total | 23.2 | 20.5 | 21.5 | 18.0 | 17.8 | 15.3 |
| 5.5 | 7.6 | 7.1 | Assets | 5.0 | 8.0 | 6.8 | 6.0 | 8.0 | 6.7 |
| .4 | 1.4 | 1.6 | | -4.5 | .4 | 1.5 | 1.8 | 2.9 | 2.2 |
| 233.1 | 251.7 | 315.0 | | UND | 545.3 | 373.5 | 300.3 | 325.0 | 128.5 |
| 61.4 | 58.6 | 69.4 | Sales/Net Fixed Assets | 59.6 | 66.7 | 93.8 | 79.5 | 76.5 | 47.8 |
| 18.5 | 19.2 | 21.9 | | 13.6 | 17.4 | 26.8 | 25.3 | 29.4 | 18.4 |
| 4.0 | 4.0 | 4.1 | | 3.6 | 3.9 | 4.2 | 3.9 | 4.6 | 4.1 |
| 2.7 | 2.7 | 2.8 | Sales/Total Assets | 2.2 | 2.6 | 2.9 | 2.7 | 3.2 | 2.7 |
| 1.9 | 1.8 | 1.9 | | 1.3 | 1.8 | 1.8 | 1.9 | 2.2 | 2.0 |
| .2 | .2 | .2 | | .3 | .4 | .2 | .2 | .2 | .2 |
| (522) .6 | (525) .6 | (582) .6 | % Depr., Dep., Amort./Sales | (25) 1.0 | (87) .9 | (75) .6 | (124) .5 | (139) .4 | (132) .6 |
| 1.3 | 1.3 | 1.3 | | 2.3 | 2.0 | 1.5 | 1.2 | 1.0 | 1.2 |
| 2.0 | 1.6 | 1.9 | % Officers', Directors' | 4.6 | 2.8 | 2.2 | 1.9 | 1.0 | .9 |
| (329) 3.8 | (358) 3.3 | (433) 3.7 | Owners' Comp/Sales | (27) 9.7 | (90) 5.0 | (72) 4.7 | (115) 3.3 | (102) 2.2 | (27) 1.8 |
| 6.7 | 5.8 | 6.5 | | 16.4 | 7.9 | 7.3 | 5.8 | 4.4 | 3.6 |
| 16563935M | 17088766M | 22069415M | Net Sales ($) | 33317M | 346505M | 498116M | 1374314M | 3024314M | 16792849M |
| 6687697M | 6862419M | 8478246M | Total Assets ($) | 20412M | 155292M | 221563M | 598539M | 1129157M | 6353283M |

## Current Data Sorted by Assets   |   Comparative Historical Data

| | 0-500M | 500M-2MM | 2-10MM | 10-50MM | 50-100MM | 100-250MM | | 4/1/07-3/31/08 ALL | 4/1/08-3/31/09 ALL |
|---|---|---|---|---|---|---|---|---|---|
| **Type of Statement** | | | | | | | | | |
| Unqualified | | | 4 | 11 | 2 | 2 | | 22 | 26 |
| Reviewed | 1 | 3 | 10 | 7 | 1 | | | 22 | 30 |
| Compiled | 1 | 6 | 11 | | | | | 9 | 11 |
| Tax Returns | 8 | 5 | 6 | 3 | | | | 11 | 27 |
| Other | 6 | 6 | 13 | 14 | 3 | 4 | | 35 | 31 |
| | 18 (4/1-9/30/11) | | 109 (10/1/11-3/31/12) | | | | | | |
| **NUMBER OF STATEMENTS** | 16 | 20 | 44 | 35 | 6 | 6 | | 99 | 125 |
| | % | % | % | % | % | % | | % | % |
| **ASSETS** | | | | | | | | | |
| Cash & Equivalents | 26.2 | 9.2 | 8.6 | 4.7 | | | | 5.5 | 6.3 |
| Trade Receivables (net) | 33.5 | 41.2 | 42.6 | 40.9 | | | | 40.7 | 37.3 |
| Inventory | 6.3 | 22.3 | 28.4 | 27.0 | | | | 29.5 | 27.7 |
| All Other Current | 7.9 | 5.8 | 1.7 | 1.5 | | | | 2.2 | 3.1 |
| Total Current | 74.0 | 78.6 | 81.2 | 74.0 | | | | 77.9 | 74.4 |
| Fixed Assets (net) | 18.3 | 11.9 | 12.0 | 14.3 | | | | 11.9 | 13.7 |
| Intangibles (net) | 2.1 | 4.2 | 1.5 | 5.4 | | | | 4.1 | 3.4 |
| All Other Non-Current | 5.6 | 5.3 | 5.2 | 6.3 | | | | 6.2 | 8.6 |
| Total | 100.0 | 100.0 | 100.0 | 100.0 | | | | 100.0 | 100.0 |
| **LIABILITIES** | | | | | | | | | |
| Notes Payable-Short Term | 36.8 | 14.5 | 16.1 | 15.6 | | | | 18.3 | 23.7 |
| Cur. Mat.-L.T.D. | 5.6 | .9 | 1.3 | 2.8 | | | | 1.7 | 3.3 |
| Trade Payables | 18.5 | 25.9 | 26.0 | 19.2 | | | | 25.4 | 20.4 |
| Income Taxes Payable | .0 | .0 | .2 | .0 | | | | .1 | .2 |
| All Other Current | 27.1 | 6.5 | 7.4 | 11.3 | | | | 8.0 | 9.3 |
| Total Current | 88.0 | 47.9 | 50.9 | 48.9 | | | | 53.5 | 56.9 |
| Long-Term Debt | 8.5 | 8.8 | 9.8 | 16.6 | | | | 9.4 | 11.9 |
| Deferred Taxes | .0 | .1 | .1 | .2 | | | | .2 | .2 |
| All Other Non-Current | 5.4 | 3.7 | 4.4 | 3.9 | | | | 3.1 | 4.0 |
| Net Worth | -1.8 | 39.5 | 34.9 | 30.5 | | | | 33.9 | 27.1 |
| Total Liabilties & Net Worth | 100.0 | 100.0 | 100.0 | 100.0 | | | | 100.0 | 100.0 |
| **INCOME DATA** | | | | | | | | | |
| Net Sales | 100.0 | 100.0 | 100.0 | 100.0 | | | | 100.0 | 100.0 |
| Gross Profit | 33.4 | 23.9 | 20.5 | 19.7 | | | | 22.0 | 21.5 |
| Operating Expenses | 33.4 | 20.6 | 19.2 | 17.9 | | | | 20.2 | 19.4 |
| Operating Profit | .0 | 3.3 | 1.3 | 1.8 | | | | 1.8 | 2.1 |
| All Other Expenses (net) | .9 | -.2 | .0 | 1.5 | | | | .4 | .6 |
| Profit Before Taxes | -.9 | 3.5 | 1.3 | .4 | | | | 1.4 | 1.4 |
| **RATIOS** | | | | | | | | | |
| Current | 2.4 | 3.0 | 3.0 | 2.0 | | | | 1.9 | 2.2 |
| | 1.2 | 1.4 | 1.5 | 1.4 | | | | 1.4 | 1.4 |
| | .6 | 1.2 | 1.1 | 1.1 | | | | 1.2 | 1.0 |
| Quick | 2.3 | 1.8 | 1.5 | 1.0 | | | | 1.2 | 1.3 |
| | 1.1 | 1.0 | 1.0 | .9 | | | | .9 | .8 |
| | .4 | .7 | .6 | .7 | | | | .6 | .6 |
| Sales/Receivables | 0 UND | 27 13.3 | 30 12.3 | 35 10.5 | | | | 30 12.1 | 27 13.6 |
| | 17 20.9 | 35 10.3 | 41 8.8 | 41 9.0 | | | | 40 9.2 | 34 10.6 |
| | 36 10.1 | 44 8.3 | 46 7.9 | 51 7.2 | | | | 49 7.4 | 43 8.5 |
| Cost of Sales/Inventory | 0 UND | 6 65.5 | 14 27.0 | 16 23.4 | | | | 17 21.2 | 16 23.5 |
| | 1 277.3 | 22 16.9 | 28 12.9 | 40 9.2 | | | | 36 10.1 | 32 11.4 |
| | 9 42.9 | 45 8.1 | 58 6.3 | 51 7.2 | | | | 60 6.1 | 53 6.9 |
| Cost of Sales/Payables | 0 UND | 13 28.8 | 16 23.0 | 12 30.8 | | | | 18 20.7 | 13 27.2 |
| | 4 83.0 | 27 13.7 | 29 12.8 | 19 19.3 | | | | 28 13.0 | 22 16.4 |
| | 30 12.1 | 51 7.2 | 38 9.5 | 35 10.4 | | | | 40 9.1 | 37 10.0 |
| Sales/Working Capital | 7.2 | 6.7 | 7.2 | 8.9 | | | | 9.0 | 8.4 |
| | 77.0 | 22.6 | 16.3 | 12.4 | | | | 16.6 | 18.1 |
| | -25.6 | 51.6 | 45.0 | 44.4 | | | | 48.5 | 151.6 |
| EBIT/Interest | 15.8 | 27.7 | 16.9 | 13.3 | | | | 9.0 | 8.1 |
| | (11) 2.7 | (18) 6.1 | (41) 3.8 | 4.0 | | | | (91) 2.5 | (120) 2.3 |
| | -2.0 | 2.3 | 1.3 | 1.5 | | | | 1.2 | 1.1 |
| Net Profit + Depr., Dep., Amort./Cur. Mat. L/T/D | | | | 9.5 | | | | 6.2 | 4.0 |
| | | | | (11) 3.5 | | | | (23) 1.4 | (24) 1.1 |
| | | | | 1.0 | | | | .6 | .0 |
| Fixed/Worth | .0 | .1 | .0 | .0 | | | | .1 | .1 |
| | .7 | .2 | .1 | .3 | | | | .3 | .4 |
| | -.7 | .9 | .9 | .9 | | | | .8 | 1.2 |
| Debt/Worth | .8 | 1.1 | .8 | 1.5 | | | | 1.1 | 1.1 |
| | 3.5 | 1.5 | 2.1 | 3.1 | | | | 2.3 | 2.7 |
| | -3.7 | 3.9 | 8.8 | 5.8 | | | | 6.0 | 14.1 |
| % Profit Before Taxes/Tangible Net Worth | 71.5 | 152.2 | 29.5 | 25.9 | | | | 32.8 | 31.3 |
| | (11) 33.8 | (19) 38.1 | (40) 10.4 | (31) 16.8 | | | | (92) 14.1 | (104) 15.9 |
| | -48.0 | 5.5 | 1.6 | 5.2 | | | | 3.1 | 4.4 |
| % Profit Before Taxes/Total Assets | 21.5 | 25.1 | 8.3 | 10.3 | | | | 9.6 | 8.8 |
| | 5.3 | 9.3 | 4.1 | 3.9 | | | | 3.6 | 3.3 |
| | -28.0 | 1.9 | .6 | .6 | | | | .5 | .2 |
| Sales/Net Fixed Assets | UND | 407.6 | 368.0 | 345.6 | | | | 183.4 | 203.6 |
| | 98.9 | 62.1 | 115.1 | 49.5 | | | | 57.9 | 69.4 |
| | 16.5 | 18.9 | 15.2 | 14.1 | | | | 18.6 | 15.7 |
| Sales/Total Assets | 10.2 | 5.8 | 4.9 | 4.2 | | | | 4.9 | 4.7 |
| | 5.4 | 4.4 | 3.7 | 3.4 | | | | 3.9 | 3.9 |
| | 4.2 | 2.7 | 2.8 | 2.8 | | | | 2.8 | 2.7 |
| % Depr., Dep., Amort./Sales | | .1 | .1 | .1 | | | | .1 | .2 |
| | | (10) .4 | (34) .2 | (31) .3 | | | | (83) .5 | (99) .4 |
| | | 1.3 | .5 | .6 | | | | .9 | 1.1 |
| % Officers', Directors' Owners' Comp/Sales | | 2.5 | 1.1 | .6 | | | | .9 | 1.1 |
| | | (12) 4.0 | (26) 2.1 | (11) 1.0 | | | | (39) 2.8 | (52) 2.7 |
| | | 4.8 | 4.2 | 1.5 | | | | 5.2 | 4.7 |
| Net Sales ($) | 17939M | 96052M | 893808M | 2636642M | 1511407M | 2721301M | | 8427830M | 8392298M |
| Total Assets ($) | 3075M | 22879M | 229809M | 743519M | 413200M | 962250M | | 2172061M | 2415288M |

© RMA 2012

M = $ thousand   MM = $ million
See Pages 9 through 22 for Explanation of Ratios and Data

## Comparative Historical Data     Current Data Sorted by Sales

| | | | Type of Statement | | | | | | |
|---|---|---|---|---|---|---|---|---|---|
| 17 | 18 | 19 | Unqualified | | 1 | | 3 | 3 | 15 |
| 24 | 24 | 22 | Reviewed | 2 | 1 | | 3 | 6 | 10 |
| 18 | 12 | 18 | Compiled | | 3 | 3 | 2 | 5 | 5 |
| 28 | 14 | 22 | Tax Returns | 5 | 2 | 4 | 4 | 3 | 4 |
| 39 | 38 | 46 | Other | 2 | 5 | 3 | 7 | 7 | 22 |
| 4/1/09-3/31/10 ALL | 4/1/10-3/31/11 ALL | 4/1/11-3/31/12 ALL | | | 18 (4/1-9/30/11) | | 109 (10/1/11-3/31/12) | | |
| | | | | 0-1MM | 1-3MM | 3-5MM | 5-10MM | 10-25MM | 25MM & OVER |
| 126 | 106 | 127 | **NUMBER OF STATEMENTS** | 9 | 12 | 10 | 16 | 24 | 56 |
| % | % | % | **ASSETS** | % | % | % | % | % | % |
| 7.7 | 7.8 | 9.7 | Cash & Equivalents | | 6.5 | 24.9 | 4.9 | 9.3 | 5.5 |
| 39.9 | 41.1 | 40.3 | Trade Receivables (net) | | 32.0 | 37.3 | 39.5 | 39.9 | 44.3 |
| 27.3 | 26.5 | 24.3 | Inventory | | 13.8 | 16.8 | 26.6 | 29.3 | 28.3 |
| 2.3 | 3.4 | 3.4 | All Other Current | | 9.6 | .4 | .9 | 1.8 | 2.0 |
| 77.1 | 78.9 | 77.7 | Total Current | | 62.0 | 79.5 | 71.8 | 80.3 | 80.1 |
| 12.9 | 11.9 | 13.6 | Fixed Assets (net) | | 23.1 | 13.2 | 23.0 | 14.2 | 9.3 |
| 3.7 | 3.0 | 3.3 | Intangibles (net) | | 5.1 | 1.9 | 2.3 | 1.2 | 4.4 |
| 6.3 | 6.2 | 5.3 | All Other Non-Current | | 9.8 | 5.5 | 2.9 | 4.3 | 6.2 |
| 100.0 | 100.0 | 100.0 | Total | | 100.0 | 100.0 | 100.0 | 100.0 | 100.0 |
| | | | **LIABILITIES** | | | | | | |
| 18.1 | 20.3 | 17.7 | Notes Payable-Short Term | | 35.6 | 13.9 | 14.6 | 19.5 | 14.9 |
| 2.2 | 1.9 | 2.1 | Cur. Mat.-L.T.D. | | 7.6 | .7 | 1.3 | 1.6 | 1.8 |
| 23.5 | 25.3 | 23.4 | Trade Payables | | 17.0 | 28.1 | 22.3 | 21.2 | 25.3 |
| .1 | .1 | .1 | Income Taxes Payable | | .0 | .0 | .5 | .0 | .0 |
| 9.0 | 9.8 | 10.7 | All Other Current | | 30.1 | 14.4 | 5.9 | 6.2 | 9.9 |
| 52.8 | 57.4 | 54.0 | Total Current | | 90.2 | 57.1 | 44.5 | 48.6 | 52.0 |
| 13.6 | 9.5 | 11.4 | Long-Term Debt | | 17.3 | 7.9 | 15.6 | 13.8 | 9.8 |
| .1 | .1 | .3 | Deferred Taxes | | .0 | .0 | .2 | .1 | .5 |
| 6.3 | 9.3 | 4.5 | All Other Non-Current | | 3.5 | 2.5 | 5.2 | 1.8 | 5.5 |
| 27.2 | 23.7 | 30.0 | Net Worth | | -11.0 | 32.5 | 34.5 | 35.8 | 32.2 |
| 100.0 | 100.0 | 100.0 | Total Liabilities & Net Worth | | 100.0 | 100.0 | 100.0 | 100.0 | 100.0 |
| | | | **INCOME DATA** | | | | | | |
| 100.0 | 100.0 | 100.0 | Net Sales | | 100.0 | 100.0 | 100.0 | 100.0 | 100.0 |
| 21.8 | 20.9 | 21.8 | Gross Profit | | 31.4 | 28.6 | 24.9 | 20.3 | 16.2 |
| 19.9 | 18.7 | 20.1 | Operating Expenses | | 32.5 | 26.9 | 21.1 | 19.0 | 14.5 |
| 2.0 | 2.2 | 1.7 | Operating Profit | | -1.1 | 1.6 | 3.9 | 1.3 | 1.7 |
| .5 | .3 | .5 | All Other Expenses (net) | | .5 | -1.5 | .4 | .4 | .8 |
| 1.4 | 1.9 | 1.2 | Profit Before Taxes | | -1.6 | 3.2 | 3.5 | .9 | .9 |
| | | | **RATIOS** | | | | | | |
| 2.7 | 2.3 | 2.7 | Current | | 1.7 | 3.4 | 2.7 | 3.4 | 2.3 |
| 1.6 | 1.4 | 1.5 | | | .9 | 1.4 | 1.5 | 1.5 | 1.6 |
| 1.1 | 1.1 | 1.1 | | | .7 | 1.0 | 1.3 | 1.1 | 1.1 |
| 1.5 | 1.3 | 1.5 | Quick | | 1.1 | 2.9 | 1.4 | 2.1 | 1.3 |
| 1.0 | .9 | 1.0 | | | .7 | 1.2 | 1.0 | .9 | 1.0 |
| .6 | .6 | .7 | | | .3 | .7 | .8 | .6 | .7 |
| 29  12.6 | 29  12.4 | 28  13.1 | Sales/Receivables | | 16  22.3 | 24  15.2 | 31  11.6 | 29  12.5 | 31  11.7 |
| 40  9.2 | 39  9.4 | 38  9.6 | | | 28  13.0 | 33  11.0 | 38  9.7 | 39  9.3 | 39  9.4 |
| 52  7.0 | 48  7.7 | 46  7.9 | | | 47  7.8 | 44  8.3 | 46  7.9 | 54  6.7 | 46  8.0 |
| 15  23.9 | 13  27.1 | 10  37.2 | Cost of Sales/Inventory | | 1  273.0 | 2  189.1 | 14  26.5 | 18  20.3 | 15  23.9 |
| 35  10.4 | 32  11.3 | 27  13.6 | | | 10  35.5 | 18  20.0 | 28  13.1 | 35  10.5 | 33  11.0 |
| 58  6.3 | 53  6.9 | 49  7.5 | | | 29  12.4 | 53  6.9 | 45  8.1 | 76  4.8 | 50  7.3 |
| 15  24.4 | 16  23.0 | 13  27.7 | Cost of Sales/Payables | | 3  112.3 | 6  57.6 | 18  20.5 | 16  23.4 | 13  27.6 |
| 26  14.3 | 25  14.4 | 25  14.7 | | | 26  14.2 | 47  7.7 | 31  11.9 | 29  12.8 | 23  15.9 |
| 43  8.5 | 39  9.4 | 38  9.5 | | | 39  9.3 | 73  5.0 | 49  7.4 | 36  10.2 | 31  11.6 |
| 6.8 | 7.7 | 7.4 | Sales/Working Capital | | 22.2 | 5.8 | 8.9 | 5.4 | 7.7 |
| 12.0 | 15.4 | 16.2 | | | -45.2 | 24.8 | 14.4 | 14.8 | 15.3 |
| 45.1 | 82.5 | 55.1 | | | -22.8 | NM | 30.0 | 40.8 | 45.9 |
| 11.6 | 11.0 | 15.5 | EBIT/Interest | | 14.7 | | 21.6 | 18.2 | 14.3 |
| (113) 3.0 | (95) 3.9 | (115) 4.5 | | | 2.1 | | (15) 6.2 | (23) 2.7 | (53) 4.5 |
| 1.1 | 1.5 | 1.4 | | | -1.8 | | 2.0 | 1.1 | 1.8 |
| 4.0 | 6.9 | 9.7 | Net Profit + Depr., Dep., Amort./Cur. Mat. L/T/D | | | | | | 11.0 |
| (20) 1.9 | (15) 3.4 | (18) 2.4 | | | | | | | (13) 4.7 |
| -.2 | 1.9 | 1.0 | | | | | | | 1.2 |
| .1 | .0 | .0 | Fixed/Worth | | .3 | .0 | .1 | .0 | .0 |
| .2 | .2 | .2 | | | 4.1 | .1 | .6 | .1 | .2 |
| 1.3 | .8 | 1.0 | | | -.7 | 1.3 | 3.8 | 1.3 | .7 |
| .8 | 1.1 | .9 | Debt/Worth | | 1.4 | .8 | 1.0 | .4 | 1.2 |
| 2.3 | 2.8 | 2.7 | | | 7.1 | 2.1 | 2.0 | 2.7 | 2.7 |
| 8.9 | 9.7 | 7.6 | | | -5.4 | 127.2 | 5.4 | -15.9 | 4.8 |
| 35.1 | 35.4 | 34.2 | % Profit Before Taxes/Tangible Net Worth | | | | 69.1 | 30.7 | 25.9 |
| (110) 14.6 | (92) 18.3 | (112) 14.7 | | | | | (15) 31.0 | (21) 9.4 | (51) 15.4 |
| 1.5 | 6.4 | 4.3 | | | | | 5.5 | 1.5 | 5.7 |
| 11.5 | 11.2 | 10.5 | % Profit Before Taxes/Total Assets | | 23.1 | 18.8 | 19.9 | 7.5 | 9.7 |
| 3.4 | 4.2 | 4.6 | | | 5.3 | 8.1 | 7.5 | 2.9 | 4.4 |
| .4 | 1.4 | .6 | | | -10.2 | 3.3 | 1.1 | .4 | 1.2 |
| 288.6 | 398.3 | 375.2 | Sales/Net Fixed Assets | | 54.1 | 412.1 | 122.3 | 295.7 | 461.6 |
| 77.2 | 82.3 | 61.1 | | | 24.6 | 90.3 | 22.4 | 103.6 | 73.2 |
| 14.9 | 22.6 | 19.9 | | | 12.9 | 13.2 | 9.4 | 15.2 | 31.9 |
| 4.7 | 5.1 | 5.0 | Sales/Total Assets | | 6.2 | 6.7 | 5.4 | 4.4 | 5.0 |
| 3.3 | 3.6 | 3.8 | | | 4.7 | 4.4 | 3.8 | 3.3 | 3.7 |
| 2.6 | 2.8 | 2.7 | | | 2.5 | 2.2 | 2.4 | 2.7 | 3.0 |
| .2 | .1 | .1 | % Depr., Dep., Amort./Sales | | | | .5 | .1 | .1 |
| (98) .4 | (88) .3 | (93) .3 | | | | | (10) .7 | (19) .2 | (49) .3 |
| .9 | .8 | .7 | | | | | 4.4 | .7 | .4 |
| 1.3 | 1.0 | 1.1 | % Officers', Directors' Owners' Comp/Sales | | | | 1.9 | 1.1 | .3 |
| (56) 2.5 | (44) 1.9 | (59) 2.5 | | | | | (11) 3.7 | (13) 1.6 | (17) .7 |
| 5.3 | 6.2 | 4.9 | | | | | 4.9 | 3.0 | 2.7 |
| 7797035M | 8356629M | 7887149M | Net Sales ($) | 4094M | 23813M | 38315M | 126878M | 433858M | 7250191M |
| 2260557M | 2516631M | 2374732M | Total Assets ($) | 1389M | 8578M | 11972M | 47204M | 154432M | 2151157M |

© RMA 2012

M = $ thousand    MM = $ million
See Pages 9 through 22 for Explanation of Ratios and Data

**Current Data Sorted by Assets** — 27 (4/1-9/30/11); 114 (10/1/11-3/31/12)

**Comparative Historical Data**

| Type of Statement | 0-500M | 500M-2MM | 2-10MM | 10-50MM | 50-100MM | 100-250MM | | 4/1/07-3/31/08 ALL | 4/1/08-3/31/09 ALL |
|---|---|---|---|---|---|---|---|---|---|
| Unqualified | 1 | 5 | 3 | 3 | 3 | 1 | | 12 | 12 |
| Reviewed | | | 25 | 4 | 1 | | | 33 | 44 |
| Compiled | 2 | 5 | 11 | 1 | | | | 18 | 22 |
| Tax Returns | 8 | 10 | 3 | 2 | | | | 13 | 22 |
| Other | 4 | 19 | 15 | 11 | 1 | 3 | | 38 | 45 |
| **NUMBER OF STATEMENTS** | **15** | **39** | **57** | **21** | **5** | **4** | | **114** | **145** |
| **ASSETS** | % | % | % | % | % | % | | % | % |
| Cash & Equivalents | 10.4 | 10.3 | 9.8 | 2.6 | | | | 6.8 | 6.6 |
| Trade Receivables (net) | 41.6 | 39.9 | 31.5 | 32.8 | | | | 38.4 | 39.7 |
| Inventory | 25.4 | 23.8 | 30.9 | 27.5 | | | | 29.0 | 29.6 |
| All Other Current | 3.2 | 2.3 | 4.6 | 7.2 | | | | 3.0 | 2.5 |
| Total Current | 80.7 | 76.3 | 76.8 | 70.0 | | | | 77.1 | 78.3 |
| Fixed Assets (net) | 8.9 | 9.6 | 12.1 | 11.0 | | | | 11.1 | 12.0 |
| Intangibles (net) | .6 | 8.0 | 4.0 | 15.3 | | | | 6.2 | 5.1 |
| All Other Non-Current | 9.8 | 6.1 | 7.1 | 3.7 | | | | 5.6 | 4.6 |
| Total | 100.0 | 100.0 | 100.0 | 100.0 | | | | 100.0 | 100.0 |
| **LIABILITIES** | | | | | | | | | |
| Notes Payable-Short Term | 16.8 | 12.8 | 15.7 | 12.1 | | | | 20.6 | 19.1 |
| Cur. Mat.-L.T.D. | 1.8 | 2.8 | 1.5 | 5.0 | | | | 2.7 | 3.7 |
| Trade Payables | 45.7 | 30.1 | 20.7 | 18.5 | | | | 23.5 | 23.3 |
| Income Taxes Payable | .0 | .1 | .1 | .1 | | | | .2 | .3 |
| All Other Current | 10.0 | 12.7 | 12.6 | 13.0 | | | | 11.4 | 8.8 |
| Total Current | 74.3 | 58.3 | 50.6 | 48.7 | | | | 58.3 | 55.1 |
| Long-Term Debt | 11.9 | 9.2 | 9.5 | 15.3 | | | | 11.0 | 10.5 |
| Deferred Taxes | .0 | .2 | .3 | .9 | | | | .2 | .3 |
| All Other Non-Current | 17.7 | 6.8 | 4.0 | 12.5 | | | | 5.8 | 8.0 |
| Net Worth | -3.9 | 25.5 | 35.6 | 22.6 | | | | 24.6 | 26.1 |
| Total Liabilities & Net Worth | 100.0 | 100.0 | 100.0 | 100.0 | | | | 100.0 | 100.0 |
| **INCOME DATA** | | | | | | | | | |
| Net Sales | 100.0 | 100.0 | 100.0 | 100.0 | | | | 100.0 | 100.0 |
| Gross Profit | 28.6 | 32.9 | 33.9 | 36.0 | | | | 31.3 | 30.3 |
| Operating Expenses | 26.9 | 30.6 | 31.0 | 33.4 | | | | 28.6 | 27.9 |
| Operating Profit | 1.8 | 2.3 | 2.9 | 2.6 | | | | 2.7 | 2.5 |
| All Other Expenses (net) | .1 | .5 | .5 | 1.0 | | | | .9 | .9 |
| Profit Before Taxes | 1.7 | 1.8 | 2.4 | 1.5 | | | | 1.8 | 1.6 |
| **RATIOS** | | | | | | | | | |
| Current | 2.7 / 1.5 / .6 | 2.6 / 1.6 / .9 | 2.3 / 1.5 / 1.2 | 3.0 / 1.4 / 1.0 | | | | 2.2 / 1.4 / 1.1 | 2.0 / 1.4 / 1.1 |
| Quick | 1.3 / .7 / .3 | 1.5 / 1.1 / .5 | 1.4 / .8 / .5 | 1.7 / .7 / .4 | | | | 1.4 / .8 / .6 | 1.3 / .8 / .6 |
| Sales/Receivables | 13 27.2 / 27 13.7 / 41 8.8 | 27 13.6 / 36 10.2 / 47 7.7 | 27 13.6 / 34 10.7 / 42 8.6 | 29 12.4 / 38 9.6 / 56 6.5 | | | | 28 13.2 / 39 9.5 / 49 7.5 | 28 12.9 / 38 9.5 / 48 7.6 |
| Cost of Sales/Inventory | 0 UND / 18 20.4 / 50 7.3 | 11 32.4 / 24 14.9 / 74 4.9 | 20 18.4 / 53 6.9 / 118 3.1 | 16 22.2 / 52 7.0 / 118 3.1 | | | | 20 18.4 / 39 9.4 / 80 4.6 | 18 20.8 / 35 10.5 / 84 4.4 |
| Cost of Sales/Payables | 16 23.2 / 36 10.1 / 54 6.7 | 17 21.7 / 30 12.2 / 54 6.7 | 22 16.4 / 31 11.7 / 43 8.4 | 25 14.6 / 33 11.1 / 50 7.3 | | | | 18 19.9 / 28 12.9 / 44 8.4 | 18 20.3 / 29 12.8 / 45 8.2 |
| Sales/Working Capital | 9.1 / 18.3 / -19.2 | 7.3 / 18.9 / -851.6 | 7.4 / 14.2 / 36.5 | 9.0 / 13.9 / NM | | | | 8.5 / 16.3 / 120.3 | 8.9 / 15.5 / 48.9 |
| EBIT/Interest | 18.0 / / .6 | (35) 5.8 | 8.0 / (49) 3.1 / 1.5 | 7.4 / (20) 2.9 / 1.0 | | | | 7.4 / (104) 2.4 / 1.1 | 6.0 / (134) 2.7 / 1.0 |
| Net Profit + Depr., Dep., Amort./Cur. Mat. L/T/D | | | 14.8 / (12) 2.6 / 1.7 | | | | | 6.5 / (30) 2.6 / 1.3 | 6.0 / (33) 2.4 / 1.1 |
| Fixed/Worth | .0 / .7 / -.3 | .0 / .2 / 1.3 | .0 / .2 / .7 | .3 / .8 / -.5 | | | | .1 / .4 / 1.3 | .1 / .4 / 1.7 |
| Debt/Worth | .7 / 4.1 / -3.7 | .9 / 2.1 / -16.0 | .9 / 2.0 / 8.4 | 1.3 / 14.0 / -4.2 | | | | 1.2 / 2.9 / 15.8 | 1.3 / 3.0 / 18.3 |
| % Profit Before Taxes/Tangible Net Worth | 37.0 / / -8.8 | (29) 11.5 | 35.0 / (50) 13.0 / 1.9 | 35.2 / (12) 16.8 / 6.5 | | | | 45.2 / (91) 23.6 / 7.7 | 42.6 / (119) 14.5 / 1.9 |
| % Profit Before Taxes/Total Assets | 27.5 / 13.2 / -8.1 | 10.8 / 3.0 / -2.7 | 9.6 / 3.8 / 1.1 | 7.0 / 3.5 / .1 | | | | 13.4 / 4.2 / .4 | 12.1 / 3.7 / .3 |
| Sales/Net Fixed Assets | UND / 83.5 / 38.9 | 638.7 / 71.9 / 22.5 | 259.3 / 67.4 / 16.8 | 109.1 / 34.7 / 22.0 | | | | 139.3 / 53.5 / 21.8 | 97.0 / 44.3 / 20.9 |
| Sales/Total Assets | 8.0 / 5.1 / 3.6 | 5.8 / 4.2 / 2.9 | 4.1 / 2.9 / 2.2 | 4.5 / 3.2 / 1.6 | | | | 4.8 / 3.9 / 2.5 | 5.0 / 3.7 / 2.5 |
| % Depr., Dep., Amort./Sales | .3 / (10) .4 / 1.0 | .2 / (22) .6 / 1.2 | .3 / (42) .7 / 1.3 | .6 / (19) 1.0 / 1.2 | | | | .3 / (88) .7 / 1.5 | .3 / (117) .6 / 1.3 |
| % Officers', Directors', Owners' Comp/Sales | 2.4 / (10) 4.2 / 5.7 | 2.4 / (24) 4.2 / 8.3 | 1.0 / (33) 2.8 / 4.1 | | | | | 1.6 / (51) 3.4 / 6.2 | 1.4 / (59) 3.2 / 6.9 |
| Net Sales ($) | 26029M | 226020M | 988767M | 1236074M | 1052895M | 887242M | | 5511059M | 5843959M |
| Total Assets ($) | 4479M | 47553M | 289104M | 396148M | 363070M | 516882M | | 1673556M | 1851895M |

M = $ thousand    MM = $ million
See Pages 9 through 22 for Explanation of Ratios and Data

**Comparative Historical Data** | **Current Data Sorted by Sales**

**Type of Statement**

| 4/1/09-3/31/10 ALL | 4/1/10-3/31/11 ALL | 4/1/11-3/31/12 ALL | Type of Statement | 0-1MM | 1-3MM | 3-5MM | 5-10MM | 10-25MM | 25MM & OVER |
|---|---|---|---|---|---|---|---|---|---|
| 9 | 9 | 10 | Unqualified | | | | 1 | | 9 |
| 47 | 40 | 36 | Reviewed | | | 4 | 7 | 17 | 8 |
| 22 | 27 | 19 | Compiled | | 2 | 3 | 4 | 5 | 5 |
| 12 | 15 | 23 | Tax Returns | 3 | 7 | 3 | 6 | 2 | 2 |
| 47 | 48 | 53 | Other | 4 | 7 | 5 | 12 | 9 | 16 |

Current period groupings: **27 (4/1-9/30/11)**  **114 (10/1/11-3/31/12)**

| 137 | 139 | 141 | **NUMBER OF STATEMENTS** | 7 | 16 | 15 | 30 | 33 | 40 |
|---|---|---|---|---|---|---|---|---|---|
| % | % | % | **ASSETS** | % | % | % | % | % | % |
| 7.4 | 8.6 | 8.7 | Cash & Equivalents | | 9.3 | 12.7 | 6.4 | 11.7 | 5.8 |
| 37.2 | 36.6 | 34.8 | Trade Receivables (net) | | 32.9 | 37.3 | 34.7 | 32.9 | 36.7 |
| 28.7 | 26.0 | 27.9 | Inventory | | 31.1 | 24.9 | 33.0 | 26.2 | 27.2 |
| 3.9 | 4.4 | 4.1 | All Other Current | | .0 | 3.0 | 2.7 | 4.5 | 6.3 |
| 77.1 | 75.6 | 75.5 | Total Current | | 73.2 | 77.9 | 76.8 | 75.2 | 76.1 |
| 11.6 | 11.8 | 11.0 | Fixed Assets (net) | | 11.0 | 12.3 | 12.0 | 11.5 | 9.9 |
| 6.4 | 6.1 | 6.6 | Intangibles (net) | | 7.7 | 5.4 | 5.4 | 6.8 | 8.0 |
| 4.9 | 6.5 | 6.8 | All Other Non-Current | | 8.1 | 4.5 | 5.8 | 6.5 | 6.0 |
| 100.0 | 100.0 | 100.0 | Total | | 100.0 | 100.0 | 100.0 | 100.0 | 100.0 |
| | | | **LIABILITIES** | | | | | | |
| 17.8 | 16.0 | 14.2 | Notes Payable-Short Term | | 15.9 | 11.3 | 18.1 | 13.2 | 13.9 |
| 3.5 | 3.0 | 2.8 | Cur. Mat.-L.T.D. | | 5.8 | 2.2 | .9 | 2.1 | 4.4 |
| 26.5 | 25.8 | 25.3 | Trade Payables | | 31.1 | 36.0 | 23.4 | 24.4 | 23.4 |
| .2 | .1 | .1 | Income Taxes Payable | | .0 | .0 | .1 | .1 | .2 |
| 9.7 | 11.7 | 12.3 | All Other Current | | 9.6 | 6.4 | 13.4 | 15.1 | 13.4 |
| 57.6 | 56.6 | 54.8 | Total Current | | 62.4 | 55.9 | 56.0 | 54.9 | 55.2 |
| 9.9 | 8.4 | 11.1 | Long-Term Debt | | 21.9 | 7.7 | 10.4 | 9.1 | 11.3 |
| .3 | .3 | .3 | Deferred Taxes | | .0 | .0 | .5 | .2 | .5 |
| 5.9 | 8.6 | 7.4 | All Other Non-Current | | 10.6 | 7.4 | 4.8 | 4.7 | 7.7 |
| 26.3 | 26.2 | 26.4 | Net Worth | | 5.1 | 29.0 | 28.4 | 31.1 | 25.2 |
| 100.0 | 100.0 | 100.0 | Total Liabilities & Net Worth | | 100.0 | 100.0 | 100.0 | 100.0 | 100.0 |
| | | | **INCOME DATA** | | | | | | |
| 100.0 | 100.0 | 100.0 | Net Sales | | 100.0 | 100.0 | 100.0 | 100.0 | 100.0 |
| 32.6 | 32.0 | 33.3 | Gross Profit | | 35.0 | 31.0 | 34.6 | 34.3 | 30.2 |
| 31.0 | 30.0 | 30.7 | Operating Expenses | | 32.7 | 28.7 | 32.4 | 31.3 | 27.9 |
| 1.6 | 2.0 | 2.6 | Operating Profit | | 2.3 | 2.3 | 2.2 | 3.0 | 2.3 |
| .6 | .5 | .6 | All Other Expenses (net) | | .5 | 1.0 | .5 | .3 | .6 |
| 1.0 | 1.5 | 2.0 | Profit Before Taxes | | 1.8 | 1.3 | 1.7 | 2.6 | 1.6 |
| | | | **RATIOS** | | | | | | |
| 2.0 | 2.4 | 2.4 | | | 2.9 | 3.0 | 2.3 | 1.8 | 1.9 |
| 1.5 | 1.5 | 1.5 | Current | | 1.9 | 1.7 | 1.5 | 1.4 | 1.4 |
| 1.0 | 1.0 | 1.0 | | | .8 | .8 | 1.1 | 1.0 | 1.1 |
| 1.2 | 1.5 | 1.5 | | | 1.6 | 2.0 | 1.3 | 1.5 | 1.3 |
| .7 | .9 | .8 | Quick | | .9 | 1.1 | .8 | .8 | .7 |
| .6 | .5 | .5 | | | .5 | .5 | .5 | .5 | .5 |
| 27  13.7 | 28  13.2 | 27  13.7 | | | 21  17.5 | 26  13.8 | 29  12.7 | 22  16.3 | 29  12.7 |
| 38  9.5 | 37  9.8 | 35  10.4 | Sales/Receivables | | 28  12.9 | 31  11.9 | 38  9.7 | 36  10.2 | 36  10.2 |
| 47  7.8 | 48  7.6 | 47  7.7 | | | 45  8.2 | 47  7.7 | 42  8.7 | 46  8.0 | 52  7.0 |
| 16  22.6 | 16  22.4 | 17  22.0 | | | 17  21.0 | 13  28.3 | 24  15.4 | 14  25.6 | 17  21.2 |
| 43  8.5 | 33  10.9 | 42  8.7 | Cost of Sales/Inventory | | 47  7.7 | 26  14.3 | 49  7.5 | 42  8.7 | 41  8.8 |
| 83  4.4 | 79  4.6 | 99  3.7 | | | 89  4.1 | 76  4.8 | 111  3.3 | 74  4.9 | 104  3.5 |
| 20  18.5 | 22  16.2 | 21  17.6 | | | 12  29.8 | 17  21.1 | 21  17.8 | 22  16.6 | 24  15.1 |
| 34  10.9 | 35  10.5 | 33  11.2 | Cost of Sales/Payables | | 33  11.2 | 29  12.4 | 35  10.3 | 30  12.3 | 33  11.0 |
| 49  7.4 | 51  7.2 | 48  7.6 | | | 61  6.0 | 54  6.7 | 46  7.9 | 42  8.6 | 46  7.9 |
| 7.4 | 7.4 | 7.4 | | | 5.8 | 6.4 | 6.9 | 8.1 | 9.2 |
| 14.2 | 13.9 | 14.2 | Sales/Working Capital | | 13.5 | 11.9 | 17.6 | 21.1 | 14.2 |
| 251.0 | 207.3 | 141.0 | | | -26.2 | -31.4 | 169.2 | UND | 141.6 |
| 5.6 | 9.4 | 8.1 | | | 10.1 | 14.2 | 6.2 | 8.0 | 8.1 |
| (121) 2.7 | (130) 3.3 | (122) 3.2 | EBIT/Interest | | (11) .6 | (13) 5.1 | (26) 3.0 | (29) 3.2 | (38) 4.4 |
| -.2 | .9 | .8 | | | -4.4 | 1.7 | .5 | 1.5 | 1.3 |
| 3.7 | 5.3 | 8.0 | | | | | | | 16.9 | 5.7 |
| (41) 2.0 | (35) 1.9 | (25) 3.4 | Net Profit + Depr., Dep., Amort./Cur. Mat. L/T/D | | | | | (10) 2.9 | (12) 3.3 |
| .6 | .9 | 1.5 | | | | | | | 1.6 | 1.1 |
| .1 | .1 | .0 | | | .0 | .1 | .0 | .0 | .1 |
| .4 | .3 | .3 | Fixed/Worth | | .4 | .4 | .2 | .3 | .3 |
| 2.4 | .9 | 2.3 | | | NM | 12.2 | 1.5 | 1.6 | -8.6 |
| 1.1 | 1.1 | 1.0 | | | .8 | .6 | 1.2 | 1.1 | 1.3 |
| 2.8 | 2.6 | 2.5 | Debt/Worth | | 3.1 | 2.9 | 2.6 | 2.0 | 3.2 |
| 23.5 | 13.2 | NM | | | -3.2 | -16.0 | 7.6 | 30.1 | -82.3 |
| 31.4 | 35.6 | 34.8 | | | 70.0 | 34.7 | 18.7 | 56.8 | 28.4 |
| (106) 11.4 | (112) 15.4 | (106) 12.9 | % Profit Before Taxes/Tangible Net Worth | | (11) 4.7 | (11) 21.4 | (24) 5.9 | (26) 16.6 | (29) 15.6 |
| -.1 | 1.5 | 1.4 | | | -48.1 | -3.1 | -3.3 | 3.1 | 5.6 |
| 10.0 | 9.9 | 10.6 | | | 29.7 | 12.8 | 7.9 | 12.9 | 8.3 |
| 2.7 | 3.6 | 3.8 | % Profit Before Taxes/Total Assets | | 2.2 | 3.7 | 2.1 | 5.0 | 3.9 |
| -1.8 | .1 | -.2 | | | -8.4 | .4 | -1.5 | 1.3 | .4 |
| 165.6 | 152.9 | 259.3 | | | 603.3 | 116.5 | 729.0 | 334.1 | 125.8 |
| 43.4 | 56.0 | 57.0 | Sales/Net Fixed Assets | | 42.3 | 57.0 | 86.4 | 70.2 | 43.7 |
| 18.1 | 18.5 | 19.8 | | | 24.0 | 20.3 | 18.8 | 15.0 | 20.4 |
| 4.8 | 4.8 | 4.9 | | | 6.6 | 6.3 | 4.9 | 4.7 | 4.9 |
| 3.4 | 3.5 | 3.4 | Sales/Total Assets | | 3.8 | 3.9 | 3.7 | 3.0 | 3.4 |
| 2.3 | 2.2 | 2.2 | | | 1.9 | 2.2 | 2.1 | 2.5 | 1.9 |
| .4 | .3 | .3 | | | | .3 | .3 | .4 | .4 |
| (106) .7 | (114) .6 | (101) .7 | % Depr., Dep., Amort./Sales | | | (12) .6 | (19) .9 | (21) .7 | (36) .9 |
| 1.3 | 1.1 | 1.3 | | | | .7 | 1.6 | 1.2 | 1.3 |
| 1.3 | 1.4 | 1.9 | | | 3.5 | 2.3 | 2.5 | 1.0 | |
| (61) 3.3 | (64) 3.1 | (71) 3.3 | % Officers', Directors' Owners' Comp/Sales | | (10) 4.6 | (11) 4.0 | (23) 3.5 | (17) 2.2 | |
| 6.3 | 5.2 | 5.7 | | | 7.9 | 8.5 | 5.7 | 5.7 | |
| 4692606M | 6403806M | 4417027M | Net Sales ($) | 3426M | 29497M | 61085M | 216375M | 519150M | 3587494M |
| 1515748M | 1979770M | 1617236M | Total Assets ($) | 3095M | 12343M | 20614M | 79338M | 165807M | 1336039M |

M = $ thousand    MM = $ million
See Pages 9 through 22 for Explanation of Ratios and Data

## Current Data Sorted by Assets         Comparative Historical Data

| 0-500M | 500M-2MM | 2-10MM | 10-50MM | 50-100MM | 100-250MM | | 4/1/07-3/31/08 ALL | 4/1/08-3/31/09 ALL |
|---|---|---|---|---|---|---|---|---|
| | | | | | | **Type of Statement** | | |
| | | 4 | 9 | 4 | 3 | Unqualified | 24 | 23 |
| | 3 | 40 | 25 | | 2 | Reviewed | 60 | 66 |
| 2 | 8 | 20 | 2 | | 2 | Compiled | 26 | 31 |
| 2 | 10 | 10 | 1 | | | Tax Returns | 20 | 24 |
| 1 | 15 | 16 | 21 | 4 | 5 | Other | 75 | 84 |
| | 38 (4/1-9/30/11) | | 169 (10/1/11-3/31/12) | | | | | |
| 5 | 36 | 90 | 58 | 8 | 10 | **NUMBER OF STATEMENTS** | 205 | 228 |
| % | % | % | % | % | % | **ASSETS** | % | % |
| | 8.5 | 7.3 | 5.3 | | 2.0 | Cash & Equivalents | 5.6 | 4.7 |
| | 40.4 | 38.4 | 36.4 | | 41.0 | Trade Receivables (net) | 40.8 | 39.4 |
| | 33.5 | 31.8 | 31.9 | | 25.3 | Inventory | 29.9 | 30.8 |
| | 1.4 | 1.9 | 4.3 | | 3.0 | All Other Current | 2.3 | 2.9 |
| | 83.8 | 79.4 | 77.9 | | 71.4 | Total Current | 78.7 | 77.8 |
| | 10.2 | 12.5 | 13.1 | | 15.8 | Fixed Assets (net) | 13.6 | 13.9 |
| | 1.8 | 2.1 | 3.7 | | 6.3 | Intangibles (net) | 2.5 | 3.2 |
| | 4.3 | 5.9 | 5.3 | | 6.5 | All Other Non-Current | 5.2 | 5.0 |
| | 100.0 | 100.0 | 100.0 | | 100.0 | Total | 100.0 | 100.0 |
| | | | | | | **LIABILITIES** | | |
| | 16.5 | 14.3 | 19.7 | | 11.2 | Notes Payable-Short Term | 18.3 | 19.3 |
| | 2.1 | 2.0 | 1.5 | | 1.4 | Cur. Mat.-L.T.D. | 2.7 | 3.0 |
| | 30.1 | 24.5 | 21.6 | | 24.2 | Trade Payables | 28.7 | 25.2 |
| | .1 | .2 | .1 | | .0 | Income Taxes Payable | .2 | .1 |
| | 5.2 | 5.5 | 8.6 | | 7.9 | All Other Current | 8.1 | 7.3 |
| | 54.0 | 46.5 | 51.4 | | 44.8 | Total Current | 58.0 | 54.9 |
| | 5.8 | 7.9 | 8.6 | | 17.7 | Long-Term Debt | 11.3 | 11.5 |
| | .0 | .6 | .4 | | .8 | Deferred Taxes | .2 | .3 |
| | 6.1 | 4.5 | 5.2 | | 1.4 | All Other Non-Current | 3.3 | 5.8 |
| | 34.0 | 40.5 | 34.4 | | 35.3 | Net Worth | 27.2 | 27.5 |
| | 100.0 | 100.0 | 100.0 | | 100.0 | Total Liabilities & Net Worth | 100.0 | 100.0 |
| | | | | | | **INCOME DATA** | | |
| | 100.0 | 100.0 | 100.0 | | 100.0 | Net Sales | 100.0 | 100.0 |
| | 27.5 | 22.1 | 22.6 | | 17.0 | Gross Profit | 23.3 | 23.7 |
| | 26.3 | 19.8 | 20.0 | | 13.7 | Operating Expenses | 20.8 | 21.3 |
| | 1.2 | 2.3 | 2.6 | | 3.2 | Operating Profit | 2.6 | 2.4 |
| | -.3 | .0 | .4 | | .5 | All Other Expenses (net) | .5 | .5 |
| | 1.5 | 2.3 | 2.3 | | 2.8 | Profit Before Taxes | 2.0 | 2.0 |
| | | | | | | **RATIOS** | | |
| | 2.2 | 2.7 | 2.1 | | 3.0 | | 2.0 | 2.0 |
| | 1.5 | 1.6 | 1.5 | | 1.8 | Current | 1.4 | 1.4 |
| | 1.1 | 1.2 | 1.2 | | 1.1 | | 1.1 | 1.1 |
| | 1.4 | 1.5 | 1.3 | | 1.4 | | 1.3 | 1.2 |
| | .8 | .9 | .8 | | 1.0 | Quick | .8 | .8 |
| | .6 | .6 | .6 | | .7 | | .6 | .5 |
| | **26** 14.2 | **27** 13.4 | **32** 11.3 | | **43** 8.5 | | **29** 12.5 | **28** 13.0 |
| | **31** 11.6 | **34** 10.7 | **39** 9.4 | | **46** 8.0 | Sales/Receivables | **37** 9.9 | **34** 10.6 |
| | **44** 8.3 | **45** 8.2 | **44** 8.3 | | **47** 7.7 | | **47** 7.8 | **42** 8.7 |
| | **24** 15.1 | **26** 14.0 | **33** 11.0 | | **3** 112.3 | | **25** 14.9 | **24** 15.2 |
| | **40** 9.2 | **42** 8.7 | **45** 8.1 | | **48** 7.6 | Cost of Sales/Inventory | **39** 9.3 | **39** 9.4 |
| | **57** 6.4 | **60** 6.1 | **56** 6.5 | | **89** 4.1 | | **57** 6.4 | **55** 6.6 |
| | **19** 19.0 | **16** 23.1 | **16** 22.7 | | **22** 16.7 | | **20** 18.3 | **17** 22.0 |
| | **32** 11.5 | **25** 14.6 | **21** 17.4 | | **25** 14.8 | Cost of Sales/Payables | **30** 12.1 | **27** 13.5 |
| | **53** 6.9 | **37** 9.8 | **37** 9.9 | | **45** 8.2 | | **44** 8.3 | **40** 9.1 |
| | 8.8 | 7.3 | 8.4 | | 5.6 | | 9.1 | 8.8 |
| | 13.5 | 13.3 | 14.3 | | 8.3 | Sales/Working Capital | 18.2 | 17.9 |
| | 73.8 | 29.7 | 27.3 | | 73.9 | | 61.8 | 49.1 |
| | 20.3 | 14.3 | 18.6 | | | | 6.9 | 7.2 |
| | (32) 5.8 | (80) 4.3 | (56) 5.3 | | | EBIT/Interest | (198) 2.3 | (212) 3.1 |
| | 1.2 | 1.4 | 2.1 | | | | 1.2 | 1.3 |
| | | 4.9 | 11.1 | | | Net Profit + Depr., Dep., | 3.9 | 4.7 |
| | | (11) 2.0 | (22) 4.6 | | | Amort./Cur. Mat. L/T/D | (54) 2.5 | (55) 2.1 |
| | | .9 | 1.5 | | | | 1.2 | 1.0 |
| | .1 | .0 | .1 | | .1 | | .1 | .1 |
| | .3 | .2 | .3 | | .5 | Fixed/Worth | .4 | .4 |
| | .8 | .7 | .9 | | NM | | 1.0 | 1.2 |
| | .8 | .7 | 1.0 | | 1.1 | | 1.2 | 1.2 |
| | 2.7 | 1.6 | 2.3 | | 1.6 | Debt/Worth | 3.0 | 2.8 |
| | 9.0 | 3.2 | 4.3 | | NM | | 7.4 | 8.0 |
| | 59.9 | 27.4 | 33.7 | | | % Profit Before Taxes/Tangible | 36.8 | 32.6 |
| | (32) 14.9 | (83) 10.7 | (53) 17.9 | | | Net Worth | (182) 17.8 | (195) 16.4 |
| | 3.6 | 2.9 | 5.3 | | | | 4.6 | 4.8 |
| | 15.6 | 11.7 | 9.9 | | 9.4 | % Profit Before Taxes/Total | 11.7 | 10.4 |
| | 4.5 | 4.4 | 5.5 | | 7.5 | Assets | 4.0 | 4.5 |
| | .8 | 1.0 | 1.8 | | 3.8 | | .7 | .8 |
| | 193.6 | 231.2 | 130.7 | | 350.8 | | 142.0 | 180.5 |
| | 111.1 | 62.5 | 40.9 | | 41.4 | Sales/Net Fixed Assets | 51.1 | 52.4 |
| | 29.8 | 17.4 | 12.8 | | 7.8 | | 21.4 | 17.7 |
| | 5.5 | 4.8 | 4.1 | | 3.7 | | 5.0 | 5.2 |
| | 4.4 | 3.5 | 3.5 | | 2.3 | Sales/Total Assets | 3.9 | 3.8 |
| | 3.5 | 2.9 | 2.5 | | 2.1 | | 2.7 | 2.8 |
| | .2 | .2 | .2 | | | | .2 | .2 |
| | (25) .5 | (79) .5 | (55) .5 | | | % Depr., Dep., Amort./Sales | (180) .5 | (179) .6 |
| | 1.1 | .8 | 1.0 | | | | 1.0 | 1.1 |
| | 1.5 | 1.2 | .9 | | | % Officers', Directors' | 1.3 | 1.2 |
| | (25) 3.2 | (48) 2.2 | (15) 1.7 | | | Owners' Comp/Sales | (91) 2.5 | (87) 2.5 |
| | 4.4 | 3.5 | 2.3 | | | | 4.8 | 3.9 |
| 3155M | 219703M | 1589650M | 3980426M | 1945562M | 3850440M | Net Sales ($) | 14037694M | 14529538M |
| 1245M | 44962M | 432637M | 1202005M | 600914M | 1340145M | Total Assets ($) | 3802187M | 3458210M |

M = $ thousand     MM = $ million
See Pages 9 through 22 for Explanation of Ratios and Data

## Comparative Historical Data | Current Data Sorted by Sales

| Type of Statement | | | | | | | | | |
|---|---|---|---|---|---|---|---|---|---|
| 25 | 26 | 20 | Unqualified | | | | 1 | 3 | 16 |
| 65 | 69 | 70 | Reviewed | | | 1 | 4 | 31 | 34 |
| 35 | 35 | 32 | Compiled | 1 | 2 | 2 | 7 | 17 | 3 |
| 28 | 24 | 23 | Tax Returns | 2 | 2 | 1 | 7 | 9 | 2 |
| 67 | 53 | 62 | Other | 2 | 4 | 3 | 9 | 12 | 32 |
| 4/1/09-3/31/10 ALL | 4/1/10-3/31/11 ALL | 4/1/11-3/31/12 ALL | | 0-1MM | 1-3MM | 3-5MM | 5-10MM | 10-25MM | 25MM & OVER |
| | | | | | 38 (4/1-9/30/11) | | 169 (10/1/11-3/31/12) | | |
| 220 | 207 | 207 | **NUMBER OF STATEMENTS** | 5 | 8 | 7 | 28 | 72 | 87 |
| % | % | % | **ASSETS** | % | % | % | % | % | % |
| 7.0 | 6.5 | 6.6 | Cash & Equivalents | | | | 9.6 | 7.9 | 4.7 |
| 36.1 | 37.7 | 38.2 | Trade Receivables (net) | | | | 37.2 | 37.8 | 38.6 |
| 30.0 | 33.4 | 31.4 | Inventory | | | | 36.0 | 31.8 | 31.2 |
| 3.4 | 2.8 | 2.6 | All Other Current | | | | 2.4 | 2.1 | 3.7 |
| 76.6 | 80.4 | 78.7 | Total Current | | | | 85.1 | 79.6 | 78.2 |
| 14.4 | 12.0 | 13.0 | Fixed Assets (net) | | | | 9.4 | 13.1 | 13.0 |
| 3.9 | 2.7 | 3.0 | Intangibles (net) | | | | 1.5 | 2.3 | 3.5 |
| 5.2 | 4.8 | 5.3 | All Other Non-Current | | | | 3.9 | 5.0 | 5.3 |
| 100.0 | 100.0 | 100.0 | Total | | | | 100.0 | 100.0 | 100.0 |
| | | | **LIABILITIES** | | | | | | |
| 16.5 | 16.7 | 16.5 | Notes Payable-Short Term | | | | 15.2 | 13.2 | 19.6 |
| 2.4 | 1.7 | 1.8 | Cur. Mat.-L.T.D. | | | | 2.5 | 2.3 | 1.3 |
| 24.4 | 24.1 | 25.2 | Trade Payables | | | | 27.0 | 25.6 | 21.3 |
| .2 | .2 | .1 | Income Taxes Payable | | | | .3 | .1 | .1 |
| 7.8 | 7.1 | 6.7 | All Other Current | | | | 5.6 | 5.4 | 8.9 |
| 51.3 | 49.7 | 50.3 | Total Current | | | | 50.6 | 46.6 | 51.3 |
| 10.0 | 8.0 | 8.4 | Long-Term Debt | | | | 5.4 | 8.3 | 9.1 |
| .3 | .3 | .4 | Deferred Taxes | | | | .6 | .2 | .3 |
| 5.0 | 4.8 | 4.6 | All Other Non-Current | | | | 7.0 | 3.8 | 4.5 |
| 33.5 | 37.1 | 36.3 | Net Worth | | | | 36.4 | 41.1 | 34.8 |
| 100.0 | 100.0 | 100.0 | Total Liabilities & Net Worth | | | | 100.0 | 100.0 | 100.0 |
| | | | **INCOME DATA** | | | | | | |
| 100.0 | 100.0 | 100.0 | Net Sales | | | | 100.0 | 100.0 | 100.0 |
| 23.9 | 23.5 | 23.6 | Gross Profit | | | | 27.1 | 22.2 | 21.0 |
| 21.7 | 21.1 | 21.3 | Operating Expenses | | | | 24.4 | 19.9 | 18.6 |
| 2.2 | 2.5 | 2.3 | Operating Profit | | | | 2.7 | 2.3 | 2.4 |
| .5 | .3 | .1 | All Other Expenses (net) | | | | -.3 | .1 | .3 |
| 1.6 | 2.1 | 2.2 | Profit Before Taxes | | | | 3.0 | 2.2 | 2.1 |
| | | | **RATIOS** | | | | | | |
| 2.3 | 2.6 | 2.4 | | | | | 2.7 | 2.6 | 2.3 |
| 1.5 | 1.6 | 1.6 | Current | | | | 1.5 | 1.7 | 1.5 |
| 1.1 | 1.2 | 1.2 | | | | | 1.2 | 1.2 | 1.2 |
| 1.4 | 1.4 | 1.3 | | | | | 1.4 | 1.6 | 1.3 |
| .8 | .9 | .8 | Quick | | | | .8 | 1.0 | .8 |
| .6 | .6 | .6 | | | | | .6 | .6 | .6 |
| 28  13.2 | 29  12.8 | 29  12.5 | | | | | 26  14.2 | 27  13.6 | 31  11.8 |
| 35  10.4 | 35  10.4 | 36  10.2 | Sales/Receivables | | | | 33  11.1 | 34  10.6 | 38  9.5 |
| 45  8.2 | 44  8.4 | 46  8.0 | | | | | 40  9.2 | 46  7.9 | 45  8.1 |
| 26  14.2 | 32  11.4 | 27  13.3 | | | | | 33  11.2 | 26  14.2 | 33  11.0 |
| 39  9.5 | 41  8.8 | 43  8.5 | Cost of Sales/Inventory | | | | 49  7.5 | 41  8.9 | 43  8.5 |
| 61  6.0 | 61  6.0 | 59  6.2 | | | | | 66  5.5 | 56  6.5 | 56  6.5 |
| 17  21.5 | 17  22.0 | 18  20.3 | | | | | 18  19.9 | 16  22.8 | 17  21.7 |
| 28  13.2 | 28  12.9 | 25  14.7 | Cost of Sales/Payables | | | | 29  12.4 | 26  14.0 | 22  16.7 |
| 46  7.9 | 44  8.3 | 41  8.9 | | | | | 51  7.1 | 38  9.5 | 33  10.9 |
| 8.0 | 7.2 | 8.0 | | | | | 7.6 | 7.2 | 8.2 |
| 13.9 | 12.8 | 13.4 | Sales/Working Capital | | | | 13.3 | 13.0 | 14.5 |
| 47.0 | 31.7 | 31.9 | | | | | 31.4 | 31.0 | 29.6 |
| 10.1 | 11.4 | 15.5 | | | | | 16.3 | 16.3 | 15.8 |
| (203)  3.3 | (185)  4.1 | (188)  5.2 | EBIT/Interest | | | | (23)  7.3 | (65)  4.9 | (83)  5.3 |
| 1.2 | 1.6 | 1.8 | | | | | 1.3 | 2.1 | 2.1 |
| 5.2 | 7.6 | 7.8 | Net Profit + Depr., Dep., | | | | | | 10.9 |
| (55)  1.9 | (53)  3.3 | (44)  4.2 | Amort./Cur. Mat. L/T/D | | | | | (26) | 4.9 |
| .3 | 1.0 | 1.7 | | | | | | | 2.4 |
| .1 | .1 | .1 | | | | | .1 | .1 | .1 |
| .3 | .2 | .3 | Fixed/Worth | | | | .2 | .2 | .3 |
| 1.0 | .8 | .8 | | | | | .5 | .8 | .8 |
| 1.0 | .8 | .9 | | | | | .9 | .6 | 1.0 |
| 2.2 | 1.9 | 2.0 | Debt/Worth | | | | 2.3 | 1.3 | 2.1 |
| 5.9 | 4.2 | 4.8 | | | | | 5.4 | 3.9 | 4.4 |
| 32.9 | 34.0 | 37.2 | % Profit Before Taxes/Tangible | | | | 69.9 | 27.4 | 33.8 |
| (196)  14.7 | (188)  15.2 | (187)  15.8 | Net Worth | | | | (25)  16.6 | (67)  10.7 | (79)  18.5 |
| 3.1 | 3.5 | 5.3 | | | | | 5.3 | 4.1 | 8.5 |
| 10.1 | 9.5 | 10.9 | % Profit Before Taxes/Total | | | | 21.3 | 11.8 | 9.7 |
| 3.5 | 4.8 | 5.2 | Assets | | | | 9.0 | 4.4 | 5.8 |
| .4 | 1.1 | 1.2 | | | | | 1.6 | 1.1 | 2.0 |
| 143.2 | 173.9 | 165.7 | | | | | 193.6 | 193.0 | 167.9 |
| 47.2 | 58.5 | 57.9 | Sales/Net Fixed Assets | | | | 98.5 | 65.3 | 52.9 |
| 16.3 | 17.0 | 15.0 | | | | | 26.0 | 13.4 | 14.5 |
| 4.5 | 4.5 | 4.6 | | | | | 5.5 | 4.9 | 4.2 |
| 3.5 | 3.5 | 3.6 | Sales/Total Assets | | | | 4.0 | 3.6 | 3.5 |
| 2.5 | 2.7 | 2.6 | | | | | 3.0 | 2.8 | 2.6 |
| .3 | .3 | .2 | | | | | .3 | .2 | .2 |
| (182)  .6 | (165)  .6 | (179)  .5 | % Depr., Dep., Amort./Sales | | | | (22)  .5 | (64)  .4 | (79)  .5 |
| 1.3 | 1.0 | 1.1 | | | | | .9 | .7 | 1.0 |
| 1.2 | 1.3 | 1.2 | % Officers', Directors' | | | | 1.8 | 1.2 | .9 |
| (98)  2.5 | (92)  2.3 | (97)  2.3 | Owners' Comp/Sales | | | | (17)  3.2 | (41)  2.4 | (28)  1.3 |
| 4.0 | 4.6 | 4.0 | | | | | 4.5 | 3.5 | 2.1 |
| 12497523M | 10299975M | 11588936M | Net Sales ($) | 1843M | 16861M | 29164M | 205625M | 1137719M | 10197724M |
| 3641056M | 2926728M | 3621908M | Total Assets ($) | 1504M | 5849M | 10908M | 57237M | 350160M | 3196250M |

© RMA 2012

M = $ thousand    MM = $ million
See Pages 9 through 22 for Explanation of Ratios and Data

## Current Data Sorted by Assets   |   Comparative Historical Data

| Type of Statement | 0-500M | 500M-2MM | 2-10MM | 10-50MM | 50-100MM | 100-250MM | 4/1/07-3/31/08 ALL | 4/1/08-3/31/09 ALL |
|---|---|---|---|---|---|---|---|---|
| Unqualified | | 2 | 6 | 21 | 7 | 11 | 27 | 53 |
| Reviewed | | 10 | 27 | 16 | 1 | | 37 | 47 |
| Compiled | 1 | 19 | 14 | 5 | | | 22 | 21 |
| Tax Returns | 10 | 22 | 23 | 2 | 1 | | 28 | 37 |
| Other | 4 | | 42 | 36 | 12 | 14 | 108 | 101 |
| | | 51 (4/1-9/30/11) | | 255 (10/1/11-3/31/12) | | | | |
| **NUMBER OF STATEMENTS** | 15 | 53 | 112 | 80 | 21 | 25 | 222 | 259 |
| **ASSETS** | % | % | % | % | % | % | % | % |
| Cash & Equivalents | 22.2 | 14.5 | 10.5 | 6.9 | 3.3 | 9.7 | 9.0 | 10.1 |
| Trade Receivables (net) | 19.0 | 30.8 | 33.7 | 33.1 | 27.2 | 25.5 | 30.8 | 30.6 |
| Inventory | 35.7 | 28.8 | 33.9 | 31.9 | 30.8 | 23.1 | 32.8 | 31.8 |
| All Other Current | .9 | 2.6 | 3.6 | 3.1 | 4.1 | 3.6 | 3.2 | 3.7 |
| Total Current | 77.8 | 76.7 | 81.7 | 75.0 | 65.3 | 62.0 | 75.9 | 76.2 |
| Fixed Assets (net) | 8.4 | 12.9 | 8.4 | 7.9 | 13.4 | 11.9 | 11.0 | 9.7 |
| Intangibles (net) | 2.1 | 4.4 | 3.7 | 10.8 | 18.1 | 20.9 | 7.5 | 8.2 |
| All Other Non-Current | 11.7 | 6.0 | 6.1 | 6.3 | 3.1 | 5.3 | 5.6 | 5.9 |
| Total | 100.0 | 100.0 | 100.0 | 100.0 | 100.0 | 100.0 | 100.0 | 100.0 |
| **LIABILITIES** | | | | | | | | |
| Notes Payable-Short Term | 14.6 | 14.1 | 13.2 | 12.0 | 7.9 | 7.1 | 15.6 | 15.5 |
| Cur. Mat.-L.T.D. | .7 | 1.3 | 1.3 | 1.4 | 3.1 | 3.3 | 2.1 | 2.4 |
| Trade Payables | 12.4 | 19.6 | 23.9 | 26.7 | 20.4 | 20.3 | 24.2 | 24.3 |
| Income Taxes Payable | .3 | .0 | .1 | .2 | .7 | .3 | .2 | .2 |
| All Other Current | 13.0 | 11.4 | 11.5 | 9.1 | 9.5 | 7.8 | 9.1 | 8.6 |
| Total Current | 40.9 | 46.3 | 50.0 | 49.5 | 41.6 | 38.7 | 51.1 | 50.9 |
| Long-Term Debt | 9.5 | 9.3 | 6.4 | 5.2 | 11.1 | 14.4 | 11.5 | 12.3 |
| Deferred Taxes | .0 | .0 | .1 | .6 | .7 | .9 | .2 | .5 |
| All Other Non-Current | 21.7 | 14.3 | 10.2 | 4.9 | 9.5 | 6.3 | 5.0 | 5.0 |
| Net Worth | 27.9 | 30.1 | 33.2 | 39.8 | 37.1 | 39.7 | 32.2 | 31.4 |
| Total Liabilities & Net Worth | 100.0 | 100.0 | 100.0 | 100.0 | 100.0 | 100.0 | 100.0 | 100.0 |
| **INCOME DATA** | | | | | | | | |
| Net Sales | 100.0 | 100.0 | 100.0 | 100.0 | 100.0 | 100.0 | 100.0 | 100.0 |
| Gross Profit | 42.6 | 31.3 | 32.5 | 25.2 | 32.1 | 34.1 | 33.3 | 31.3 |
| Operating Expenses | 39.4 | 26.6 | 27.0 | 20.4 | 26.5 | 27.7 | 27.4 | 26.0 |
| Operating Profit | 3.2 | 4.7 | 5.6 | 4.8 | 5.6 | 6.4 | 5.9 | 5.2 |
| All Other Expenses (net) | -.2 | .7 | .6 | .8 | 1.5 | 2.7 | .8 | 1.0 |
| Profit Before Taxes | 3.4 | 4.0 | 4.9 | 4.0 | 4.1 | 3.7 | 5.1 | 4.2 |
| **RATIOS** | | | | | | | | |
| Current | 6.7 | 3.4 | 2.5 | 2.1 | 3.0 | 2.4 | 2.3 | 2.3 |
| | 2.7 | 1.8 | 1.7 | 1.5 | 1.6 | 1.5 | 1.5 | 1.5 |
| | 1.5 | 1.1 | 1.3 | 1.2 | 1.1 | 1.2 | 1.2 | 1.1 |
| Quick | 4.6 | 2.1 | 1.4 | 1.1 | 1.3 | 1.5 | 1.2 | 1.3 |
| | 1.4 | 1.0 | .9 | .8 | .7 | .8 | .7 | .8 |
| | .7 | .5 | .6 | .5 | .5 | .5 | .5 | .5 |
| Sales/Receivables | 0 UND | 16  22.9 | 23  15.6 | 29  12.6 | 34  10.7 | 29  12.8 | 22  16.4 | 25  14.7 |
| | 13  28.6 | 26  13.8 | 39  9.3 | 36  10.2 | 45  8.2 | 43  8.4 | 35  10.4 | 38  9.5 |
| | 30  12.2 | 42  8.6 | 52  7.0 | 52  7.0 | 69  5.3 | 62  5.9 | 49  7.4 | 50  7.3 |
| Cost of Sales/Inventory | 4  100.7 | 7  52.7 | 24  14.9 | 27  13.6 | 21  17.1 | 20  18.4 | 27  13.5 | 23  16.0 |
| | 20  18.0 | 37  9.9 | 51  7.1 | 53  6.9 | 91  4.0 | 91  4.0 | 53  6.9 | 52  7.1 |
| | 130  2.8 | 64  5.7 | 126  2.9 | 99  3.7 | 159  2.3 | 159  2.3 | 104  3.5 | 112  3.2 |
| Cost of Sales/Payables | 0 UND | 7  56.0 | 16  22.7 | 26  13.9 | 19  18.8 | 28  13.0 | 20  18.3 | 21  17.3 |
| | 0  999.8 | 26  14.3 | 31  11.8 | 41  8.9 | 31  11.8 | 35  10.3 | 39  9.4 | 37  9.9 |
| | 63  5.8 | 51  7.1 | 66  5.5 | 59  6.2 | 54  6.8 | 78  4.7 | 58  6.3 | 57  6.4 |
| Sales/Working Capital | 7.1 | 6.6 | 5.6 | 6.0 | 4.4 | 4.6 | 6.4 | 5.7 |
| | 19.6 | 9.5 | 10.4 | 11.1 | 7.8 | 8.0 | 13.5 | 12.6 |
| | 43.7 | 84.2 | 25.4 | 27.6 | 56.2 | 22.0 | 34.1 | 41.8 |
| EBIT/Interest | | 20.8 | 30.3 | 42.6 | 21.8 | 7.7 | 13.9 | 22.1 |
| | | (41) 6.5 | (91) 11.4 | (67) 8.3 | (19) 6.1 | (21) 3.4 | (194) 4.6 | (236) 6.0 |
| | | 1.8 | 4.1 | 3.0 | 1.9 | 1.3 | 2.0 | 2.3 |
| Net Profit + Depr., Dep., Amort./Cur. Mat. L/T/D | | | 22.3 | 22.7 | | 4.3 | 14.8 | 11.1 |
| | | | (14) 7.1 | (19) 10.1 | | (12) 2.1 | (43) 5.0 | (40) 1.5 |
| | | | 2.0 | 1.6 | | .6 | 1.7 | .2 |
| Fixed/Worth | .0 | .0 | .0 | .0 | .2 | .1 | .1 | .0 |
| | .0 | .2 | .1 | .1 | 1.0 | .7 | .3 | .3 |
| | UND | 1.0 | .4 | .5 | NM | 3.0 | 1.2 | 1.0 |
| Debt/Worth | .7 | .6 | .8 | 1.0 | .8 | 1.5 | 1.1 | 1.1 |
| | 2.1 | 1.7 | 1.6 | 2.0 | 2.9 | 3.8 | 2.5 | 2.9 |
| | -14.4 | 10.3 | 4.0 | 6.8 | NM | 19.8 | 10.3 | 12.1 |
| % Profit Before Taxes/Tangible Net Worth | 122.3 | 94.2 | 66.3 | 52.0 | 41.9 | 53.7 | 76.6 | 78.9 |
| | (11) 70.9 | (44) 27.7 | (102) 34.7 | (70) 26.7 | (16) 23.8 | (20) 9.6 | (188) 36.4 | (213) 35.4 |
| | 1.4 | 12.4 | 11.5 | 11.7 | 14.1 | 6.7 | 11.3 | 10.4 |
| % Profit Before Taxes/Total Assets | 60.6 | 21.1 | 21.5 | 14.7 | 13.1 | 7.9 | 25.0 | 18.1 |
| | 3.8 | 10.6 | 10.4 | 6.8 | 5.0 | 2.7 | 9.6 | 7.5 |
| | .8 | 3.4 | 3.9 | 2.5 | 1.6 | .8 | 2.6 | 1.9 |
| Sales/Net Fixed Assets | UND | 512.1 | 300.9 | 301.5 | 55.7 | 139.2 | 204.5 | 245.5 |
| | 999.8 | 72.7 | 79.0 | 82.1 | 30.2 | 33.1 | 54.9 | 68.8 |
| | 283.5 | 18.7 | 31.3 | 31.2 | 11.8 | 12.4 | 22.4 | 23.1 |
| Sales/Total Assets | 18.7 | 5.2 | 4.4 | 3.7 | 3.1 | 4.2 | 4.4 | 4.3 |
| | 8.1 | 3.7 | 3.0 | 3.0 | 1.6 | 1.5 | 3.2 | 3.0 |
| | 2.5 | 2.6 | 2.1 | 1.9 | 1.0 | .9 | 1.9 | 1.8 |
| % Depr., Dep., Amort./Sales | | .2 | .1 | .1 | .2 | .1 | .2 | .2 |
| | | (32) .5 | (86) .4 | (63) .3 | (16) 1.0 | (19) 1.1 | (166) .6 | (187) .5 |
| | | 1.6 | .9 | .9 | 2.0 | 2.1 | 1.1 | 1.4 |
| % Officers', Directors' Owners' Comp/Sales | | 1.6 | 1.2 | .5 | | | 1.0 | 1.1 |
| | | (25) 3.5 | (52) 2.3 | (19) 1.8 | | | (78) 2.4 | (88) 2.1 |
| | | 4.7 | 4.0 | 3.6 | | | 6.3 | 4.4 |
| Net Sales ($) | 36325M | 271721M | 2025516M | 5311706M | 3174495M | 8545801M | 13324737M | 16340606M |
| Total Assets ($) | 4419M | 63756M | 578605M | 1785970M | 1410789M | 3705809M | 5057294M | 6330924M |

M = $ thousand    MM = $ million
See Pages 9 through 22 for Explanation of Ratios and Data

## Comparative Historical Data | | | | Current Data Sorted by Sales

| | | | Type of Statement | 0-1MM | 1-3MM | 3-5MM | 5-10MM | 10-25MM | 25MM & OVER |
|---|---|---|---|---|---|---|---|---|---|
| 55 | 58 | 45 | Unqualified | | | 2 | 6 | | 37 |
| 56 | 44 | 46 | Reviewed | 1 | | 2 | 11 | 13 | 19 |
| 19 | 20 | 30 | Compiled | | 3 | 2 | 8 | 10 | 7 |
| 38 | 36 | 55 | Tax Returns | 5 | 8 | 8 | 12 | 16 | 6 |
| 97 | 106 | 130 | Other | 1 | 12 | 9 | 13 | 21 | 74 |
| 4/1/09-3/31/10 ALL | 4/1/10-3/31/11 ALL | 4/1/11-3/31/12 ALL | | | 51 (4/1-9/30/11) | | 255 (10/1/11-3/31/12) | | |
| 265 | 264 | 306 | NUMBER OF STATEMENTS | 7 | 23 | 21 | 46 | 66 | 143 |
| % | % | % | **ASSETS** | % | % | % | % | % | % |
| 10.6 | 10.9 | 10.3 | Cash & Equivalents | | 14.0 | 18.2 | 12.2 | 11.0 | 7.4 |
| 29.4 | 30.7 | 31.2 | Trade Receivables (net) | | 23.0 | 26.8 | 28.5 | 32.7 | 34.0 |
| 32.1 | 32.1 | 31.5 | Inventory | | 29.7 | 35.4 | 33.2 | 31.8 | 30.2 |
| 3.6 | 2.8 | 3.2 | All Other Current | | 1.8 | 2.5 | 5.3 | 2.7 | 3.2 |
| 75.7 | 76.5 | 76.2 | Total Current | | 68.4 | 83.0 | 79.2 | 78.3 | 74.8 |
| 10.0 | 10.0 | 9.7 | Fixed Assets (net) | | 14.1 | 10.3 | 8.5 | 8.0 | 9.5 |
| 8.5 | 9.3 | 8.0 | Intangibles (net) | | 6.1 | 3.0 | 5.7 | 6.7 | 10.4 |
| 5.8 | 4.2 | 6.2 | All Other Non-Current | | 11.3 | 3.7 | 6.6 | 7.0 | 5.3 |
| 100.0 | 100.0 | 100.0 | Total | | 100.0 | 100.0 | 100.0 | 100.0 | 100.0 |
| | | | **LIABILITIES** | | | | | | |
| 13.3 | 12.5 | 12.2 | Notes Payable-Short Term | | 12.8 | 8.2 | 15.3 | 14.3 | 10.9 |
| 2.4 | 1.6 | 1.6 | Cur. Mat.-L.T.D. | | 2.2 | .7 | 1.0 | 1.3 | 1.8 |
| 22.8 | 25.6 | 22.8 | Trade Payables | | 12.6 | 21.2 | 20.7 | 21.1 | 26.5 |
| .2 | .2 | .2 | Income Taxes Payable | | .2 | .0 | .1 | .0 | .3 |
| 10.4 | 8.9 | 10.5 | All Other Current | | 17.4 | 6.9 | 12.6 | 11.6 | 9.3 |
| 49.1 | 48.8 | 47.3 | Total Current | | 45.0 | 36.9 | 49.8 | 48.3 | 48.8 |
| 8.3 | 7.8 | 7.7 | Long-Term Debt | | 12.8 | 9.7 | 6.0 | 6.8 | 7.1 |
| .3 | .3 | .3 | Deferred Taxes | | .0 | .0 | .0 | .2 | .6 |
| 7.5 | 6.4 | 9.7 | All Other Non-Current | | 26.5 | 10.1 | 20.7 | 3.6 | 5.5 |
| 34.8 | 36.6 | 34.9 | Net Worth | | 15.7 | 43.3 | 23.5 | 41.2 | 38.0 |
| 100.0 | 100.0 | 100.0 | Total Liabilities & Net Worth | | 100.0 | 100.0 | 100.0 | 100.0 | 100.0 |
| | | | **INCOME DATA** | | | | | | |
| 100.0 | 100.0 | 100.0 | Net Sales | | 100.0 | 100.0 | 100.0 | 100.0 | 100.0 |
| 31.7 | 31.8 | 31.0 | Gross Profit | | 40.1 | 29.7 | 34.7 | 33.3 | 26.3 |
| 26.8 | 26.3 | 25.8 | Operating Expenses | | 36.3 | 24.0 | 29.4 | 27.5 | 20.9 |
| 5.0 | 5.5 | 5.2 | Operating Profit | | 3.8 | 5.7 | 5.3 | 5.7 | 5.5 |
| .8 | 1.0 | .9 | All Other Expenses (net) | | 1.2 | .4 | 1.2 | .3 | 1.1 |
| 4.1 | 4.5 | 4.3 | Profit Before Taxes | | 2.6 | 5.3 | 4.1 | 5.4 | 4.4 |
| | | | **RATIOS** | | | | | | |
| 2.3 | 2.3 | 2.7 | | | 3.4 | 4.6 | 3.5 | 2.7 | 2.3 |
| 1.5 | 1.6 | 1.7 | Current | | 1.7 | 2.9 | 1.7 | 1.7 | 1.6 |
| 1.2 | 1.2 | 1.2 | | | .8 | 1.7 | 1.1 | 1.2 | 1.2 |
| 1.2 | 1.4 | 1.4 | | | 1.9 | 2.5 | 1.8 | 1.3 | 1.2 |
| .8 | .8 | .9 | Quick | | .8 | 1.0 | .9 | .9 | .9 |
| .5 | .5 | .6 | | | .4 | .4 | .5 | .6 | .5 |
| 25 14.7 | 26 14.0 | 24 15.5 | | | 13 28.6 | 5 73.1 | 18 20.3 | 22 16.9 | 28 13.1 |
| 38 9.6 | 37 9.9 | 36 10.1 | Sales/Receivables | | 27 13.4 | 24 15.3 | 38 9.5 | 40 9.1 | 37 9.9 |
| 51 7.2 | 53 6.9 | 50 7.3 | | | 47 7.8 | 43 8.4 | 50 7.3 | 55 6.6 | 51 7.2 |
| 28 13.3 | 27 13.3 | 20 18.3 | | 0 UND | 19 18.9 | 20 18.4 | 23 15.6 | 20 18.5 | |
| 61 6.0 | 58 6.3 | 51 7.1 | Cost of Sales/Inventory | 62 5.9 | 51 7.2 | 63 5.8 | 61 6.0 | 47 7.8 | |
| 119 3.1 | 107 3.4 | 114 3.2 | | 159 2.3 | 91 4.0 | 182 2.0 | 122 3.0 | 94 3.9 | |
| 20 18.2 | 22 16.9 | 18 20.3 | | 0 UND | 10 36.8 | 14 26.0 | 11 32.6 | 24 14.9 | |
| 34 10.6 | 36 10.0 | 33 11.0 | Cost of Sales/Payables | 26 14.3 | 28 12.9 | 42 8.7 | 28 13.0 | 35 10.5 | |
| 59 6.2 | 60 6.1 | 58 6.3 | | 69 5.3 | 54 6.7 | 73 5.0 | 56 6.5 | 51 7.2 | |
| 6.1 | 6.1 | 5.8 | | | 6.6 | 6.0 | 5.8 | 5.4 | 6.6 |
| 11.6 | 11.0 | 10.7 | Sales/Working Capital | | 13.6 | 8.0 | 8.0 | 10.6 | 11.5 |
| 26.5 | 29.4 | 30.6 | | | -28.4 | 12.3 | 33.4 | 26.7 | 30.6 |
| 18.6 | 26.0 | 27.0 | | | 18.8 | 27.5 | 24.8 | 22.6 | 39.8 |
| (227) 5.8 | (214) 6.2 | (246) 6.8 | EBIT/Interest | | (18) 4.8 | (14) 6.2 | (37) 6.0 | (54) 11.5 | (120) 7.8 |
| 2.2 | 2.3 | 2.4 | | | 1.4 | 2.6 | 1.0 | 4.3 | 2.9 |
| 11.3 | 16.4 | 20.4 | Net Profit + Depr., Dep., | | | | | | 21.4 |
| (49) 3.5 | (42) 2.6 | (54) 5.1 | Amort./Cur. Mat. L/T/D | | | | | (40) 4.1 | |
| 1.0 | 1.1 | 1.4 | | | | | | | 1.5 |
| .0 | .0 | .0 | | | .0 | .0 | .0 | .0 | .1 |
| .2 | .2 | .2 | Fixed/Worth | | .2 | .0 | .1 | .1 | .2 |
| .9 | .9 | .8 | | | .9 | .9 | .5 | .4 | 1.0 |
| 1.0 | .9 | .9 | | | 1.1 | .3 | .8 | .8 | .9 |
| 2.3 | 2.1 | 1.9 | Debt/Worth | | 2.1 | 1.2 | 1.8 | 1.6 | 2.1 |
| 5.4 | 7.7 | 7.4 | | | 15.2 | 7.6 | 4.2 | 4.3 | 8.7 |
| 62.5 | 61.2 | 65.4 | % Profit Before Taxes/Tangible | | 80.6 | 43.0 | 50.7 | 76.7 | 64.1 |
| (233) 27.3 | (222) 26.8 | (263) 29.6 | Net Worth | (19) 46.8 | (18) 23.1 | (39) 22.2 | (59) 34.2 | (124) 29.1 | |
| 11.1 | 10.2 | 10.9 | | | 13.5 | 11.1 | 4.0 | 12.1 | 11.8 |
| 16.4 | 19.1 | 19.0 | % Profit Before Taxes/Total | | 30.0 | 16.7 | 16.1 | 21.5 | 19.0 |
| 6.8 | 7.4 | 8.3 | Assets | | 11.7 | 10.6 | 6.7 | 10.4 | 7.7 |
| 2.5 | 2.2 | 2.2 | | | 1.2 | 4.0 | .9 | 4.2 | 2.4 |
| 275.0 | 236.5 | 324.2 | | | UND | 999.8 | 395.1 | 554.8 | 208.6 |
| 66.5 | 80.9 | 75.8 | Sales/Net Fixed Assets | | 60.7 | 209.1 | 88.1 | 113.6 | 55.8 |
| 19.4 | 23.8 | 27.6 | | | 12.8 | 31.5 | 39.1 | 33.4 | 23.4 |
| 4.0 | 4.2 | 4.4 | | | 3.7 | 4.7 | 3.9 | 4.4 | 4.4 |
| 2.8 | 3.0 | 3.0 | Sales/Total Assets | | 2.4 | 3.6 | 2.8 | 3.0 | 3.1 |
| 1.9 | 1.8 | 1.9 | | | 1.8 | 2.5 | 1.9 | 2.2 | 1.9 |
| .2 | .2 | .1 | | | | | .1 | .1 | .2 |
| (176) .5 | (192) .4 | (219) .4 | % Depr., Dep., Amort./Sales | | | (35) | (47) .3 | (117) .4 | .4 |
| 1.5 | 1.0 | 1.0 | | | | | 1.0 | .8 | 1.1 |
| 1.0 | 1.0 | 1.0 | | | 1.0 | 1.6 | 1.2 | 1.2 | .5 |
| (95) 2.2 | (99) 2.1 | (108) 2.5 | % Officers', Directors' Owners' Comp/Sales | (10) 3.9 | (10) 3.2 | (20) 2.7 | (29) 2.9 | (37) 1.5 | |
| 4.3 | 3.7 | 4.3 | | | 4.6 | 8.0 | 4.7 | 4.9 | 2.6 |
| 17515127M | 16373464M | 19365564M | Net Sales ($) | 5424M | 47693M | 84401M | 321815M | 1049092M | 17857139M |
| 6158936M | 6527525M | 7549348M | Total Assets ($) | 4197M | 19089M | 28545M | 149975M | 508359M | 6839183M |

M = $ thousand     MM = $ million
See Pages 9 through 22 for Explanation of Ratios and Data

## Current Data Sorted by Assets        Comparative Historical Data

| 0-500M | 500M-2MM | 2-10MM | 10-50MM | 50-100MM | 100-250MM | Type of Statement | 4/1/07-3/31/08 ALL | 4/1/08-3/31/09 ALL |
|---|---|---|---|---|---|---|---|---|
| 1 | | 3 | 10 | 4 | | Unqualified | 15 | 18 |
| 1 | 10 | 28 | 17 | 1 | | Reviewed | 51 | 55 |
| | 7 | 16 | 4 | | | Compiled | 30 | 30 |
| 12 | 21 | 11 | 3 | | | Tax Returns | 26 | 25 |
| 2 | 17 | 24 | 11 | 4 | | Other | 46 | 52 |
| 37 (4/1-9/30/11) | | | 170 (10/1/11-3/31/12) | | | | | |
| 16 | 55 | 82 | 45 | 9 | | NUMBER OF STATEMENTS | 168 | 180 |
| % | % | % | % | % | % | ASSETS | % | % |
| 21.1 | 14.5 | 7.8 | 5.8 | | | Cash & Equivalents | 7.9 | 10.0 |
| 19.5 | 26.0 | 31.1 | 30.0 | | | Trade Receivables (net) | 30.5 | 27.1 |
| 29.5 | 35.9 | 45.5 | 45.8 | | | Inventory | 39.7 | 42.7 |
| 4.4 | 3.3 | 4.2 | 4.5 | | | All Other Current | 3.0 | 3.3 |
| 74.5 | 79.7 | 88.6 | 86.1 | | | Total Current | 81.2 | 83.2 |
| 11.2 | 8.7 | 5.4 | 6.2 | | DATA | Fixed Assets (net) | 8.6 | 8.4 |
| 6.8 | 4.8 | 1.5 | 1.0 | | NOT | Intangibles (net) | 3.1 | 2.4 |
| 7.1 | 6.8 | 4.5 | 6.8 | | AVAILABLE | All Other Non-Current | 7.1 | 6.0 |
| 100.0 | 100.0 | 100.0 | 100.0 | | | Total | 100.0 | 100.0 |
| | | | | | | **LIABILITIES** | | |
| 27.6 | 13.0 | 16.2 | 16.0 | | | Notes Payable-Short Term | 17.1 | 18.9 |
| 2.7 | 3.0 | 1.0 | .9 | | | Cur. Mat.-L.T.D. | 1.6 | 2.2 |
| 26.6 | 26.9 | 24.8 | 20.7 | | | Trade Payables | 19.3 | 17.2 |
| .2 | .2 | .3 | .2 | | | Income Taxes Payable | .1 | .1 |
| 24.4 | 7.6 | 7.5 | 8.7 | | | All Other Current | 7.0 | 9.2 |
| 81.5 | 50.7 | 49.8 | 46.5 | | | Total Current | 45.1 | 47.7 |
| 20.1 | 11.9 | 2.6 | 10.3 | | | Long-Term Debt | 6.4 | 7.8 |
| .0 | .0 | .2 | .2 | | | Deferred Taxes | .2 | .1 |
| 8.4 | 6.7 | 6.7 | 5.3 | | | All Other Non-Current | 7.2 | 5.6 |
| -10.5 | 30.7 | 40.8 | 37.8 | | | Net Worth | 41.1 | 38.9 |
| 100.0 | 100.0 | 100.0 | 100.0 | | | Total Liabilties & Net Worth | 100.0 | 100.0 |
| | | | | | | **INCOME DATA** | | |
| 100.0 | 100.0 | 100.0 | 100.0 | | | Net Sales | 100.0 | 100.0 |
| 37.1 | 37.1 | 28.5 | 26.1 | | | Gross Profit | 30.4 | 32.0 |
| 31.1 | 32.2 | 23.9 | 21.8 | | | Operating Expenses | 26.6 | 28.9 |
| 6.0 | 4.8 | 4.5 | 4.3 | | | Operating Profit | 3.8 | 3.2 |
| 1.6 | .5 | .2 | .2 | | | All Other Expenses (net) | .9 | .9 |
| 4.4 | 4.4 | 4.3 | 4.1 | | | Profit Before Taxes | 2.8 | 2.3 |
| | | | | | | **RATIOS** | | |
| 2.3 | 3.6 | 3.1 | 4.2 | | | | 2.9 | 2.8 |
| .9 | 1.7 | 1.8 | 1.7 | | | Current | 1.6 | 1.7 |
| .6 | 1.2 | 1.3 | 1.3 | | | | 1.3 | 1.3 |
| 1.1 | 1.6 | 1.1 | 1.4 | | | | 1.3 | 1.2 |
| .6 | .8 | .7 | .8 | | | Quick | .9 | .7 |
| .2 | .5 | .5 | .5 | | | | .5 | .4 |
| 0 UND | 12 30.2 | 19 19.5 | 28 13.0 | | | | 26 14.0 | 22 16.6 |
| 8 47.3 | 28 13.0 | 43 8.5 | 51 7.2 | | | Sales/Receivables | 41 8.8 | 40 9.2 |
| 24 15.3 | 43 8.5 | 65 5.6 | 66 5.5 | | | | 57 6.4 | 59 6.2 |
| 0 UND | 28 12.9 | 42 8.7 | 55 6.6 | | | | 42 8.6 | 47 7.8 |
| 16 22.6 | 52 7.0 | 94 3.9 | 104 3.5 | | | Cost of Sales/Inventory | 86 4.2 | 101 3.6 |
| 62 5.9 | 140 2.6 | 152 2.4 | 171 2.1 | | | | 149 2.4 | 157 2.3 |
| 0 UND | 10 36.5 | 20 17.9 | 16 23.2 | | | | 16 22.7 | 15 25.0 |
| 16 23.4 | 31 11.8 | 42 8.7 | 38 9.6 | | | Cost of Sales/Payables | 33 11.0 | 29 12.6 |
| 42 8.6 | 69 5.3 | 66 5.5 | 69 5.3 | | | | 55 6.6 | 51 7.2 |
| 33.8 | 5.3 | 3.9 | 3.1 | | | | 4.0 | 3.8 |
| -102.6 | 8.6 | 7.9 | 6.1 | | | Sales/Working Capital | 7.1 | 7.3 |
| -15.5 | 34.9 | 19.3 | 11.4 | | | | 18.3 | 15.5 |
| 15.2 | 17.5 | 18.0 | 17.0 | | | | 7.0 | 6.3 |
| (12) 6.2 | (43) 4.1 | (71) 7.2 | (40) 4.9 | | | EBIT/Interest | (145) 2.8 | (153) 2.8 |
| 1.5 | 1.8 | 2.7 | 2.2 | | | | 1.2 | .6 |
| | | * | 14.4 | | | | 21.2 | 7.3 |
| | | | (10) 6.2 | | | Net Profit + Depr., Dep., Amort./Cur. Mat. L/T/D | (17) 3.0 | (22) 2.5 |
| | | | 2.1 | | | | 2.1 | .4 |
| .0 | .0 | .0 | .0 | | | | .0 | .0 |
| 1.0 | .1 | .1 | .1 | | | Fixed/Worth | .1 | .1 |
| -.7 | 1.4 | .2 | .3 | | | | .4 | .4 |
| 2.4 | 1.2 | .7 | .8 | | | | .5 | .8 |
| -38.3 | 2.1 | 1.6 | 1.8 | | | Debt/Worth | 1.7 | 1.8 |
| -2.1 | 15.3 | 4.1 | 4.7 | | | | 4.5 | 3.6 |
| | 65.9 | 57.7 | 38.6 | | | % Profit Before Taxes/Tangible Net Worth | 33.7 | 33.3 |
| | (44) 29.4 | (76) 25.3 | (43) 18.2 | | | | (153) 14.1 | (165) 13.5 |
| | 15.2 | 9.2 | 8.8 | | | | 2.2 | 1.6 |
| 29.6 | 19.2 | 19.6 | 13.8 | | | | 13.1 | 10.5 |
| 15.5 | 7.5 | 8.7 | 4.5 | | | % Profit Before Taxes/Total Assets | 5.0 | 4.4 |
| -1.0 | 2.6 | 2.1 | 2.0 | | | | .9 | .3 |
| UND | 999.8 | 600.2 | 275.6 | | | | 302.7 | 365.5 |
| 158.9 | 157.0 | 127.7 | 82.1 | | | Sales/Net Fixed Assets | 68.8 | 74.3 |
| 33.5 | 32.1 | 47.7 | 34.0 | | | | 23.2 | 20.4 |
| 10.0 | 4.6 | 3.2 | 2.5 | | | | 3.3 | 3.1 |
| 5.2 | 3.4 | 2.6 | 2.0 | | | Sales/Total Assets | 2.4 | 2.3 |
| 3.1 | 1.8 | 2.1 | 1.6 | | | | 1.7 | 1.6 |
| | .1 | .1 | .2 | | | | .2 | .2 |
| | (29) .3 | (53) .2 | (35) .3 | | | % Depr., Dep., Amort./Sales | (116) .4 | (133) .4 |
| | 1.1 | .6 | .7 | | | | 1.1 | .9 |
| | 1.7 | 1.5 | 1.1 | | | | 2.2 | 1.7 |
| | (33) 3.6 | (43) 2.2 | (19) 2.0 | | | % Officers', Directors' Owners' Comp/Sales | (90) 4.0 | (93) 3.4 |
| | 6.8 | 4.4 | 2.8 | | | | 6.5 | 6.9 |
| 21216M | 254679M | 1152282M | 2099925M | 1561122M | | Net Sales ($) | 6295508M | 4951055M |
| 3376M | 64194M | 401986M | 978315M | 673114M | | Total Assets ($) | 2559889M | 1976343M |

© RMA 2012

M = $ thousand    MM = $ million
See Pages 9 through 22 for Explanation of Ratios and Data

## Comparative Historical Data | | | | Current Data Sorted by Sales

| | | | Type of Statement | | | | | | |
|---|---|---|---|---|---|---|---|---|---|
| | | | | | 37 (4/1-9/30/11) | | 170 (10/1/11-3/31/12) | | |
| 22 | 13 | 18 | Unqualified | | 1 | | | 1 | 16 |
| 44 | 61 | 57 | Reviewed | | 3 | 5 | 11 | 23 | 15 |
| 24 | 30 | 27 | Compiled | | 6 | 3 | 9 | 7 | 2 |
| 37 | 38 | 47 | Tax Returns | 7 | 13 | 5 | 9 | 8 | 5 |
| 48 | 66 | 58 | Other | 3 | 7 | 7 | 10 | 15 | 16 |
| 4/1/09-3/31/10 ALL | 4/1/10-3/31/11 ALL | 4/1/11-3/31/12 ALL | | 0-1MM | 1-3MM | 3-5MM | 5-10MM | 10-25MM | 25MM & OVER |
| 175 | 208 | 207 | **NUMBER OF STATEMENTS** | 10 | 30 | 20 | 39 | 54 | 54 |
| % | % | % | **ASSETS** | % | % | % | % | % | % |
| 9.9 | 8.9 | 10.0 | Cash & Equivalents | 18.1 | 15.3 | 13.6 | 7.8 | 8.6 | 7.3 |
| 29.8 | 28.3 | 28.3 | Trade Receivables (net) | 11.4 | 23.5 | 22.3 | 31.1 | 29.3 | 33.3 |
| 41.2 | 40.2 | 41.6 | Inventory | 28.4 | 37.5 | 44.3 | 42.5 | 45.7 | 40.4 |
| 3.5 | 4.3 | 4.0 | All Other Current | .6 | 3.3 | 4.8 | 3.4 | 5.2 | 4.1 |
| 84.4 | 81.7 | 83.9 | Total Current | 58.5 | 79.6 | 84.9 | 84.8 | 88.8 | 85.1 |
| 6.6 | 8.4 | 6.9 | Fixed Assets (net) | 18.7 | 11.2 | 5.8 | 6.5 | 5.4 | 4.8 |
| 3.4 | 4.3 | 3.3 | Intangibles (net) | 11.0 | .8 | 5.2 | 4.8 | 1.3 | 3.4 |
| 5.6 | 5.7 | 5.8 | All Other Non-Current | 11.1 | 8.4 | 4.1 | 3.9 | 4.5 | 6.7 |
| 100.0 | 100.0 | 100.0 | Total | 100.0 | 100.0 | 100.0 | 100.0 | 100.0 | 100.0 |
| | | | **LIABILITIES** | | | | | | |
| 17.6 | 15.6 | 16.4 | Notes Payable-Short Term | 32.3 | 14.2 | 13.2 | 18.3 | 15.4 | 15.4 |
| 3.1 | 2.8 | 1.7 | Cur. Mat.-L.T.D. | .0 | 6.3 | .9 | .8 | 1.2 | .7 |
| 20.1 | 21.3 | 24.5 | Trade Payables | 16.7 | 24.9 | 21.4 | 25.8 | 23.7 | 26.7 |
| .1 | .2 | .3 | Income Taxes Payable | .3 | .0 | .3 | .3 | .3 | .3 |
| 9.3 | 7.4 | 9.0 | All Other Current | 21.2 | 11.3 | 3.3 | 6.7 | 11.3 | 7.0 |
| 50.2 | 47.3 | 51.8 | Total Current | 70.5 | 56.7 | 39.1 | 51.8 | 51.9 | 50.2 |
| 7.6 | 8.7 | 8.6 | Long-Term Debt | 32.5 | 15.1 | 5.8 | 6.0 | 2.2 | 9.8 |
| .2 | .1 | .1 | Deferred Taxes | .0 | .0 | .0 | .0 | .3 | .1 |
| 8.8 | 7.5 | 6.4 | All Other Non-Current | 8.7 | 9.0 | 8.1 | 8.1 | 4.0 | 5.1 |
| 33.2 | 36.3 | 33.1 | Net Worth | -12.6 | 19.2 | 47.0 | 34.0 | 41.5 | 34.9 |
| 100.0 | 100.0 | 100.0 | Total Liabilities & Net Worth | 100.0 | 100.0 | 100.0 | 100.0 | 100.0 | 100.0 |
| | | | **INCOME DATA** | | | | | | |
| 100.0 | 100.0 | 100.0 | Net Sales | 100.0 | 100.0 | 100.0 | 100.0 | 100.0 | 100.0 |
| 31.7 | 31.1 | 30.8 | Gross Profit | 50.3 | 43.0 | 35.7 | 26.5 | 30.3 | 22.1 |
| 27.9 | 26.7 | 26.2 | Operating Expenses | 40.5 | 37.3 | 30.8 | 23.0 | 25.5 | 18.5 |
| 3.8 | 4.4 | 4.6 | Operating Profit | 9.8 | 5.7 | 4.8 | 3.4 | 4.8 | 3.6 |
| .7 | .5 | .4 | All Other Expenses (net) | 2.6 | .7 | .7 | .0 | .4 | .0 |
| 3.0 | 3.9 | 4.2 | Profit Before Taxes | 7.2 | 5.0 | 4.1 | 3.5 | 4.4 | 3.5 |
| | | | **RATIOS** | | | | | | |
| 3.0 | 3.2 | 3.1 | | 2.6 | 3.0 | 4.7 | 3.0 | 2.5 | 3.5 |
| 1.7 | 1.7 | 1.7 | Current | 1.6 | 1.6 | 2.7 | 1.5 | 1.7 | 1.6 |
| 1.2 | 1.2 | 1.2 | | .5 | .9 | 1.5 | 1.2 | 1.2 | 1.3 |
| 1.4 | 1.4 | 1.2 | | 1.2 | 1.4 | 2.3 | 1.1 | 1.1 | 1.5 |
| .8 | .7 | .7 | Quick | .6 | .9 | .9 | .7 | .7 | .8 |
| .4 | .4 | .5 | | .3 | .3 | .5 | .5 | .5 | .5 |
| 26  14.2 | 19  18.8 | 17  21.4 | | 3  133.7 | 10  37.7 | 16  22.6 | 11  32.2 | 17  21.2 | 25  14.4 |
| 40  9.1 | 37  9.9 | 36  10.1 | Sales/Receivables | 21  17.6 | 31  11.6 | 25  14.4 | 37  9.8 | 32  11.4 | 45  8.2 |
| 62  5.9 | 58  6.3 | 57  6.4 | | 38  9.5 | 46  8.0 | 50  7.3 | 52  7.0 | 59  6.2 | 65  5.6 |
| 48  7.5 | 37  9.8 | 40  9.2 | | 0  UND | 22  16.5 | 43  8.4 | 28  13.1 | 43  8.4 | 46  8.0 |
| 94  3.9 | 86  4.2 | 83  4.4 | Cost of Sales/Inventory | 56  6.5 | 81  4.5 | 94  3.9 | 65  5.6 | 99  3.7 | 79  4.6 |
| 147  2.5 | 135  2.7 | 146  2.5 | | 192  1.9 | 228  1.6 | 192  1.9 | 118  3.1 | 166  2.2 | 122  3.0 |
| 18  20.8 | 16  22.6 | 15  25.1 | | 5  80.3 | 7  49.6 | 11  33.7 | 11  32.1 | 20  18.5 | 20  18.4 |
| 34  10.9 | 31  11.8 | 36  10.2 | Cost of Sales/Payables | 28  13.0 | 30  12.3 | 35  10.4 | 31  11.6 | 36  10.2 | 38  9.6 |
| 53  6.9 | 57  6.4 | 65  5.6 | | 87  4.2 | 87  4.2 | 60  6.1 | 58  6.3 | 66  5.5 | 61  6.0 |
| 3.9 | 4.2 | 4.2 | | 5.1 | 5.3 | 3.6 | 4.0 | 4.4 | 4.0 |
| 7.1 | 7.9 | 8.5 | Sales/Working Capital | 19.3 | 8.9 | 4.8 | 9.1 | 7.9 | 8.8 |
| 16.5 | 24.6 | 21.9 | | -4.7 | -40.7 | 9.7 | 25.0 | 20.5 | 17.6 |
| 13.4 | 19.7 | 16.6 | | | 9.9 | 20.1 | 20.4 | 17.4 | 13.0 |
| (151)  2.8 | (184)  5.0 | (175)  5.3 | EBIT/Interest | | (24)  3.8 | (17)  3.3 | (33)  6.9 | (48)  5.9 | (47)  5.2 |
| 1.3 | 1.9 | 2.4 | | | 1.6 | 1.0 | 1.3 | 2.6 | 2.5 |
| 2.6 | 14.0 | 18.5 | Net Profit + Depr., Dep., | | | | | | |
| (19)  1.7 | (22)  3.0 | (23)  6.7 | Amort./Cur. Mat. L/T/D | | | | | | |
| -.3 | 1.0 | 2.1 | | | | | | | |
| .0 | .0 | .0 | | .1 | .0 | .0 | .0 | .0 | .0 |
| .1 | .1 | .1 | Fixed/Worth | 6.6 | .4 | .1 | .1 | .1 | .1 |
| .4 | .5 | .4 | | .0 | -2.1 | .5 | .2 | .2 | .3 |
| .8 | .9 | .9 | | 2.1 | 1.3 | .4 | .9 | .7 | 1.3 |
| 2.0 | 1.9 | 2.0 | Debt/Worth | -7.6 | 2.5 | 1.5 | 2.2 | 1.5 | 2.5 |
| 4.7 | 4.7 | 6.1 | | -2.0 | -15.0 | 4.0 | 5.6 | 3.7 | 5.9 |
| 39.8 | 47.3 | 54.2 | % Profit Before Taxes/Tangible | | 78.9 | 53.7 | 57.9 | 51.8 | 52.7 |
| (153)  15.3 | (181)  22.3 | (176)  24.7 | Net Worth | | (20)  23.8 | (18)  26.5 | (33)  29.1 | (52)  24.2 | (49)  21.7 |
| 2.3 | 10.2 | 9.3 | | | 10.4 | 1.7 | 14.2 | 9.3 | 10.6 |
| 13.5 | 17.3 | 17.5 | % Profit Before Taxes/Total | 32.9 | 17.6 | 23.9 | 19.6 | 19.4 | 13.4 |
| 4.3 | 7.7 | 7.3 | Assets | 7.2 | 7.9 | 5.7 | 9.5 | 7.1 | 5.7 |
| .8 | 2.2 | 2.1 | | 2.1 | 2.4 | .3 | 1.3 | 3.0 | 2.1 |
| 440.0 | 433.3 | 583.9 | | UND | 804.6 | 999.8 | 769.9 | 331.5 | 591.5 |
| 76.9 | 108.4 | 118.1 | Sales/Net Fixed Assets | 87.6 | 119.1 | 147.6 | 174.6 | 94.0 | 121.3 |
| 32.0 | 29.3 | 39.1 | | 4.1 | 15.4 | 15.1 | 53.3 | 53.9 | 38.7 |
| 3.2 | 3.5 | 3.6 | | 3.9 | 4.4 | 3.6 | 3.6 | 3.2 | 3.6 |
| 2.2 | 2.4 | 2.6 | Sales/Total Assets | 2.3 | 2.6 | 2.6 | 2.7 | 2.5 | 2.4 |
| 1.7 | 1.8 | 1.9 | | 1.1 | 1.7 | 1.5 | 2.3 | 1.9 | 1.8 |
| .2 | .1 | .1 | | | .2 | | .1 | .1 | .1 |
| (129)  .4 | (136)  .4 | (131)  .3 | % Depr., Dep., Amort./Sales | | (17)  .6 | (22)  .2 | (36)  .3 | (42)  .3 | |
| 1.0 | .8 | .7 | | | 2.3 | | .6 | .6 | .6 |
| 1.6 | 1.3 | 1.5 | % Officers', Directors' | | 4.1 | 3.3 | 1.6 | .9 | 1.1 |
| (89)  3.4 | (97)  2.5 | (104)  2.8 | Owners' Comp/Sales | | (17)  6.8 | (14)  4.3 | (20)  2.2 | (30)  1.5 | (19)  1.7 |
| 7.0 | 6.3 | 5.7 | | | 10.1 | 5.9 | 4.4 | 3.3 | 2.8 |
| 4640146M | 4965890M | 5089224M | Net Sales ($) | 5636M | 56465M | 76983M | 267914M | 871915M | 3810311M |
| 1971063M | 1994236M | 2120985M | Total Assets ($) | 4888M | 22365M | 38447M | 95787M | 370670M | 1588828M |

© RMA 2012

M = $ thousand    MM = $ million
See Pages 9 through 22 for Explanation of Ratios and Data

## Current Data Sorted by Assets      Comparative Historical Data

| 0-500M | 500M-2MM | 2-10MM | 10-50MM | 50-100MM | 100-250MM | Type of Statement | 4/1/07-3/31/08 ALL | 4/1/08-3/31/09 ALL |
|---|---|---|---|---|---|---|---|---|
| | 1 | 6 | 20 | 4 | 4 | Unqualified | 26 | 32 |
| | 2 | 27 | 11 | 2 | | Reviewed | 36 | 51 |
| | 4 | 3 | 2 | 1 | | Compiled | 9 | 16 |
| 3 | 11 | 4 | 1 | | | Tax Returns | 8 | 15 |
| 3 | 10 | 23 | 19 | 4 | 3 | Other | 42 | 50 |
| | 21 (4/1-9/30/11) | | 147 (10/1/11-3/31/12) | | | | | |
| 6 | 28 | 63 | 53 | 11 | 7 | NUMBER OF STATEMENTS | 121 | 164 |
| % | % | % | % | % | % | ASSETS | % | % |
| | 9.6 | 9.5 | 7.1 | 12.7 | | Cash & Equivalents | 8.5 | 8.6 |
| | 29.5 | 31.0 | 26.3 | 24.8 | | Trade Receivables (net) | 32.7 | 30.0 |
| | 43.4 | 40.0 | 44.9 | 44.0 | | Inventory | 39.6 | 43.2 |
| | 2.0 | 3.9 | 2.6 | 2.3 | | All Other Current | 4.4 | 3.1 |
| | 84.5 | 84.3 | 80.9 | 83.9 | | Total Current | 85.2 | 84.9 |
| | 7.6 | 9.3 | 7.3 | 2.5 | | Fixed Assets (net) | 7.1 | 7.2 |
| | 4.6 | 2.4 | 6.0 | 8.8 | | Intangibles (net) | 2.8 | 2.7 |
| | 3.4 | 4.1 | 5.8 | 4.8 | | All Other Non-Current | 4.9 | 5.2 |
| | 100.0 | 100.0 | 100.0 | 100.0 | | Total | 100.0 | 100.0 |
| | | | | | | LIABILITIES | | |
| | 11.4 | 16.9 | 20.9 | 14.1 | | Notes Payable-Short Term | 20.7 | 18.7 |
| | 3.4 | .6 | 2.1 | .2 | | Cur. Mat.-L.T.D. | 2.1 | 2.2 |
| | 29.8 | 14.0 | 16.8 | 12.6 | | Trade Payables | 17.1 | 17.0 |
| | .1 | .2 | .3 | 1.1 | | Income Taxes Payable | .2 | .1 |
| | 10.5 | 14.5 | 8.7 | 6.8 | | All Other Current | 7.6 | 8.4 |
| | 55.2 | 46.2 | 48.8 | 34.8 | | Total Current | 47.6 | 46.4 |
| | 10.7 | 4.1 | 5.7 | 3.8 | | Long-Term Debt | 5.4 | 4.9 |
| | .0 | .1 | .0 | .1 | | Deferred Taxes | .1 | .2 |
| | 6.6 | 8.9 | 5.2 | 6.0 | | All Other Non-Current | 6.2 | 6.1 |
| | 27.5 | 40.7 | 40.3 | 55.3 | | Net Worth | 40.7 | 42.4 |
| | 100.0 | 100.0 | 100.0 | 100.0 | | Total Liabilities & Net Worth | 100.0 | 100.0 |
| | | | | | | INCOME DATA | | |
| | 100.0 | 100.0 | 100.0 | 100.0 | | Net Sales | 100.0 | 100.0 |
| | 37.4 | 29.9 | 33.6 | 28.4 | | Gross Profit | 30.0 | 30.6 |
| | 34.6 | 25.4 | 28.3 | 20.8 | | Operating Expenses | 26.3 | 27.2 |
| | 2.8 | 4.4 | 5.2 | 7.6 | | Operating Profit | 3.8 | 3.5 |
| | .3 | .7 | 1.4 | .3 | | All Other Expenses (net) | 1.0 | .5 |
| | 2.5 | 3.7 | 3.8 | 7.3 | | Profit Before Taxes | 2.8 | 3.0 |
| | | | | | | RATIOS | | |
| | 2.7 | 3.4 | 2.6 | 5.7 | | | 3.2 | 3.5 |
| | 1.5 | 2.0 | 1.7 | 4.0 | | Current | 1.8 | 1.9 |
| | 1.1 | 1.5 | 1.3 | 1.4 | | | 1.3 | 1.4 |
| | 1.0 | 1.5 | 1.1 | 3.4 | | | 1.5 | 1.5 |
| | .8 | 1.0 | .6 | 1.7 | | Quick | .9 | .8 |
| | .3 | .5 | .4 | .5 | | | .5 | .5 |
| | 11   34.0 | 22   16.6 | 27   13.4 | 29   12.4 | | | 30   12.1 | 24   15.1 |
| | 33   11.1 | 41   9.0 | 46   8.0 | 52   7.0 | | Sales/Receivables | 39   9.3 | 41   8.9 |
| | 55   6.6 | 53   6.9 | 65   5.6 | 66   5.5 | | | 68   5.4 | 61   6.0 |
| | 43   8.5 | 34   10.6 | 94   3.9 | 69   5.3 | | | 44   8.2 | 51   7.1 |
| | 96   3.8 | 74   4.9 | 130   2.8 | 122   3.0 | | Cost of Sales/Inventory | 97   3.7 | 102   3.6 |
| | 152   2.4 | 140   2.6 | 192   1.9 | 203   1.8 | | | 146   2.5 | 160   2.3 |
| | 19   18.9 | 8   44.1 | 21   17.3 | 17   21.7 | | | 11   32.9 | 10   35.8 |
| | 39   9.3 | 19   19.2 | 38   9.7 | 27   13.5 | | Cost of Sales/Payables | 23   16.2 | 23   15.6 |
| | 81   4.5 | 49   7.5 | 55   6.6 | 49   7.5 | | | 53   6.9 | 46   7.9 |
| | 4.6 | 3.6 | 4.1 | 2.1 | | | 3.8 | 3.3 |
| | 10.1 | 6.5 | 6.0 | 3.6 | | Sales/Working Capital | 7.2 | 7.0 |
| | 36.6 | 11.2 | 12.4 | 14.5 | | | 13.2 | 14.2 |
| | 7.7 | 24.9 | 14.9 | | | | 6.3 | 8.9 |
| | (22) 3.3 | (54) 3.7 | (49) 6.8 | | | EBIT/Interest | (110) 2.5 | (142) 4.0 |
| | -1.1 | 2.0 | 1.7 | | | | 1.3 | 1.3 |
| | | 7.8 | 88.5 | | | Net Profit + Depr., Dep., | 12.5 | 26.4 |
| | (10) 3.8 | (10) 5.7 | | | | Amort./Cur. Mat. L/T/D | (19) 8.5 | (24) 8.7 |
| | | .9 | .0 | | | | 1.4 | 2.5 |
| | .0 | .0 | .0 | .0 | | | .0 | .0 |
| | .2 | .1 | .1 | .1 | | Fixed/Worth | .1 | .1 |
| | 3.1 | .4 | .4 | -.5 | | | .4 | .3 |
| | .7 | .5 | .8 | .3 | | | .5 | .6 |
| | 3.3 | 1.0 | 1.6 | .5 | | Debt/Worth | 1.5 | 1.5 |
| | 24.7 | 3.1 | 3.7 | -13.5 | | | 4.1 | 3.6 |
| | 56.4 | 51.4 | 38.1 | | | % Profit Before Taxes/Tangible | 34.1 | 41.8 |
| | (23) 9.9 | (59) 18.7 | (47) 21.9 | | | Net Worth | (109) 13.6 | (151) 15.5 |
| | -30.6 | 5.1 | 8.1 | | | | 1.5 | 2.8 |
| | 14.8 | 17.7 | 14.2 | 17.0 | | % Profit Before Taxes/Total | 14.2 | 13.6 |
| | 3.9 | 7.5 | 9.2 | 8.8 | | Assets | 5.4 | 5.1 |
| | -3.3 | 1.9 | 1.7 | 6.0 | | | .4 | .8 |
| | 361.8 | 999.8 | 171.6 | 172.2 | | | 167.6 | 225.6 |
| | 82.0 | 82.5 | 41.1 | 80.4 | | Sales/Net Fixed Assets | 88.9 | 70.0 |
| | 25.8 | 20.0 | 18.5 | 58.0 | | | 28.0 | 25.7 |
| | 4.3 | 3.2 | 2.6 | 2.4 | | | 3.1 | 3.4 |
| | 3.2 | 2.4 | 1.9 | 2.1 | | Sales/Total Assets | 2.3 | 2.3 |
| | 1.9 | 1.9 | 1.5 | 1.1 | | | 1.8 | 1.6 |
| | .1 | .2 | .2 | .2 | | | .2 | .2 |
| | (15) .3 | (45) .4 | (45) .6 | (10) .3 | | % Depr., Dep., Amort./Sales | (98) .4 | (128) .4 |
| | 1.1 | .9 | 1.4 | .7 | | | .8 | 1.0 |
| | 1.9 | 1.5 | | | | % Officers', Directors' | 1.6 | 1.7 |
| | (17) 3.2 | (25) 2.1 | | | | Owners' Comp/Sales | (54) 3.1 | (69) 3.0 |
| | 5.3 | 4.8 | | | | | 5.1 | 5.0 |
| 19234M | 109710M | 795374M | 2789465M | 1574957M | 1607057M | Net Sales ($) | 6052756M | 6184835M |
| 2301M | 32797M | 308866M | 1308606M | 860640M | 927993M | Total Assets ($) | 2790167M | 2668616M |

M = $ thousand    MM = $ million
See Pages 9 through 22 for Explanation of Ratios and Data

## Comparative Historical Data / Current Data Sorted by Sales

| 4/1/09-3/31/10 ALL | 4/1/10-3/31/11 ALL | 4/1/11-3/31/12 ALL | Type of Statement | 0-1MM | 1-3MM | 3-5MM | 5-10MM | 10-25MM | 25MM & OVER |
|---|---|---|---|---|---|---|---|---|---|
| 34 | 33 | 35 | Unqualified | | | 1 | | 10 | 24 |
| 52 | 47 | 42 | Reviewed | | 1 | 4 | 10 | 15 | 12 |
| 11 | 15 | 10 | Compiled | | 3 | 2 | 2 | 1 | 2 |
| 17 | 21 | 19 | Tax Returns | 1 | 6 | 3 | 6 | 3 | |
| 46 | 65 | 62 | Other | 2 | 5 | 6 | 10 | 16 | 23 |
| 4/1/09-3/31/10 ALL | 4/1/10-3/31/11 ALL | 4/1/11-3/31/12 ALL | | | 21 (4/1-9/30/11) | | 147 (10/1/11-3/31/12) | | |
| 160 | 181 | 168 | NUMBER OF STATEMENTS | 3 | 15 | 16 | 28 | 45 | 61 |
| % | % | % | **ASSETS** | % | % | % | % | % | % |
| 11.3 | 7.9 | 9.5 | Cash & Equivalents | | 20.1 | 6.6 | 9.2 | 11.7 | 6.4 |
| 29.8 | 31.3 | 28.5 | Trade Receivables (net) | | 23.7 | 36.0 | 27.1 | 29.5 | 28.6 |
| 36.3 | 39.4 | 41.9 | Inventory | | 43.5 | 34.1 | 39.6 | 40.6 | 44.9 |
| 4.4 | 5.0 | 2.8 | All Other Current | | 1.7 | 2.3 | 3.1 | 3.7 | 2.6 |
| 81.8 | 83.6 | 82.7 | Total Current | | 89.1 | 79.0 | 79.1 | 85.6 | 82.4 |
| 8.9 | 7.6 | 7.6 | Fixed Assets (net) | | 8.1 | 8.8 | 11.4 | 6.5 | 6.2 |
| 3.0 | 4.2 | 5.2 | Intangibles (net) | | 1.8 | 4.6 | 4.9 | 3.7 | 6.3 |
| 6.3 | 4.6 | 4.5 | All Other Non-Current | | 1.0 | 7.6 | 4.6 | 4.2 | 5.0 |
| 100.0 | 100.0 | 100.0 | Total | | 100.0 | 100.0 | 100.0 | 100.0 | 100.0 |
| | | | **LIABILITIES** | | | | | | |
| 16.7 | 16.6 | 17.9 | Notes Payable-Short Term | | 15.0 | 13.1 | 14.4 | 17.5 | 20.8 |
| 1.8 | 2.1 | 1.6 | Cur. Mat.-L.T.D. | | 2.6 | 2.7 | 1.0 | 2.1 | 1.2 |
| 16.7 | 17.5 | 17.5 | Trade Payables | | 29.2 | 18.5 | 16.9 | 17.0 | 15.5 |
| .1 | .4 | .3 | Income Taxes Payable | | .2 | .0 | .1 | .4 | .4 |
| 10.8 | 14.9 | 10.9 | All Other Current | | 4.3 | 11.9 | 11.7 | 14.2 | 8.9 |
| 46.2 | 51.5 | 48.2 | Total Current | | 51.4 | 46.1 | 44.0 | 51.2 | 46.7 |
| 5.4 | 4.4 | 6.1 | Long-Term Debt | | 7.3 | 12.7 | 7.4 | 2.5 | 5.7 |
| .1 | .2 | .1 | Deferred Taxes | | .0 | .4 | .0 | .0 | .1 |
| 6.6 | 12.2 | 7.3 | All Other Non-Current | | 6.2 | 7.9 | 9.3 | 7.0 | 6.4 |
| 41.6 | 31.7 | 38.3 | Net Worth | | 35.0 | 32.9 | 39.3 | 39.3 | 41.1 |
| 100.0 | 100.0 | 100.0 | Total Liabilties & Net Worth | | 100.0 | 100.0 | 100.0 | 100.0 | 100.0 |
| | | | **INCOME DATA** | | | | | | |
| 100.0 | 100.0 | 100.0 | Net Sales | | 100.0 | 100.0 | 100.0 | 100.0 | 100.0 |
| 33.5 | 31.8 | 32.0 | Gross Profit | | 35.9 | 32.5 | 31.9 | 30.2 | 31.9 |
| 29.2 | 27.0 | 27.5 | Operating Expenses | | 33.4 | 32.8 | 27.6 | 25.2 | 25.4 |
| 4.3 | 4.8 | 4.6 | Operating Profit | | 2.5 | -.2 | 4.3 | 5.0 | 6.5 |
| .6 | .8 | .9 | All Other Expenses (net) | | -.2 | .4 | .8 | .9 | 1.4 |
| 3.7 | 4.0 | 3.7 | Profit Before Taxes | | 2.7 | -.6 | 3.5 | 4.1 | 5.1 |
| | | | **RATIOS** | | | | | | |
| 4.3 | 3.2 | 3.0 | | | 4.2 | 3.8 | 2.8 | 2.8 | 3.2 |
| 1.9 | 1.8 | 1.9 | Current | | 1.7 | 1.7 | 2.0 | 1.9 | 1.7 |
| 1.3 | 1.3 | 1.3 | | | 1.1 | .9 | 1.5 | 1.3 | 1.3 |
| 1.8 | 1.5 | 1.4 | | | 1.7 | 2.7 | 1.4 | 1.4 | 1.3 |
| .9 | .8 | .8 | Quick | | .8 | .8 | .9 | .8 | .7 |
| .4 | .5 | .5 | | | .4 | .5 | .6 | .5 | .5 |
| 25  14.6 | 25  14.5 | 22  16.9 | | | 7  51.9 | 23  15.8 | 21  17.6 | 17  21.2 | 28  12.9 |
| 43  8.5 | 45  8.1 | 42  8.6 | Sales/Receivables | | 34  10.6 | 47  7.8 | 36  10.0 | 40  9.2 | 46  7.9 |
| 63  5.8 | 65  5.6 | 61  6.0 | | | 57  6.4 | 91  4.0 | 55  6.6 | 53  6.9 | 64  5.7 |
| 41  8.9 | 43  8.5 | 56  6.5 | | | 45  8.1 | 22  16.3 | 43  8.5 | 33  11.2 | 76  4.8 |
| 88  4.2 | 104  3.5 | 104  3.5 | Cost of Sales/Inventory | | 114  3.2 | 91  4.0 | 72  5.1 | 83  4.4 | 118  3.1 |
| 138  2.6 | 156  2.3 | 152  2.4 | | | 243  1.5 | 192  1.9 | 166  2.2 | 140  2.6 | 152  2.4 |
| 12  31.0 | 11  32.7 | 14  26.8 | | | 21  17.0 | 6  57.4 | 12  29.5 | 7  51.1 | 19  19.5 |
| 26  14.0 | 29  12.4 | 30  12.2 | Cost of Sales/Payables | | 42  8.6 | 33  11.2 | 24  15.4 | 23  15.7 | 31  11.8 |
| 54  6.8 | 55  6.6 | 51  7.1 | | | 91  4.0 | 70  5.2 | 49  7.4 | 51  7.2 | 49  7.5 |
| 3.8 | 3.7 | 3.8 | | | 2.3 | 3.1 | 3.8 | 4.2 | 3.6 |
| 6.9 | 7.1 | 6.7 | Sales/Working Capital | | 8.0 | 8.8 | 6.5 | 6.7 | 6.0 |
| 14.9 | 18.3 | 14.3 | | | 36.6 | NM | 15.3 | 12.9 | 12.8 |
| 18.3 | 18.3 | 20.1 | | | 5.0 | 6.1 | 12.7 | 32.6 | 25.8 |
| (137) 5.8 | (147) 6.4 | (143) 4.7 | EBIT/Interest | (10) 1.9 | (15) 1.4 | (22) 4.3 | (38) 4.8 | (56) 9.4 | |
| 1.6 | 1.9 | 1.4 | | | -5.5 | -1.6 | 2.5 | 2.6 | 2.1 |
| 17.5 | 33.4 | 23.2 | Net Profit + Depr., Dep., Amort./Cur. Mat. L/T/D | | | | | | |
| (19) 7.0 | (26) 7.0 | (22) 3.8 | | | | | | | |
| 1.7 | 4.2 | .9 | | | | | | | |
| .0 | .0 | .0 | | | .0 | .0 | .0 | .0 | .0 |
| .1 | .1 | .1 | Fixed/Worth | | .1 | .2 | .1 | .1 | .1 |
| .3 | .4 | .7 | | | 2.0 | 2.6 | 1.5 | .3 | .7 |
| .4 | .6 | .5 | | | .3 | .3 | .6 | .5 | .7 |
| 1.1 | 1.5 | 1.6 | Debt/Worth | | 3.0 | 2.4 | 1.5 | 1.2 | 1.6 |
| 3.5 | 5.2 | 5.6 | | | 7.3 | 111.0 | 21.3 | 2.9 | 4.0 |
| 37.9 | 54.2 | 44.9 | | | 88.7 | 28.7 | 31.1 | 62.7 | 39.2 |
| (146) 15.5 | (158) 25.3 | (146) 20.4 | % Profit Before Taxes/Tangible Net Worth | (14) 5.6 | (13) 4.5 | (23) 13.7 | (44) 25.5 | (51) 26.3 | |
| 3.0 | 7.3 | 5.0 | | | -31.6 | -18.1 | 6.9 | 7.3 | 12.5 |
| 16.5 | 18.9 | 15.6 | | | 21.0 | 9.2 | 11.3 | 28.5 | 15.9 |
| 6.6 | 8.7 | 8.3 | % Profit Before Taxes/Total Assets | | 7.9 | .9 | 7.3 | 8.2 | 10.8 |
| 1.1 | 1.7 | 1.3 | | | -3.7 | -5.2 | 1.9 | 3.0 | 3.1 |
| 200.2 | 313.0 | 257.3 | | | UND | 420.9 | 283.7 | 483.1 | 180.3 |
| 61.0 | 91.2 | 79.5 | Sales/Net Fixed Assets | | 48.0 | 46.3 | 86.8 | 82.5 | 78.7 |
| 23.4 | 27.6 | 20.4 | | | 17.8 | 25.1 | 21.1 | 19.6 | 25.2 |
| 3.2 | 3.2 | 3.2 | | | 4.4 | 3.2 | 3.0 | 4.2 | 2.6 |
| 2.4 | 2.2 | 2.3 | Sales/Total Assets | | 2.5 | 2.3 | 2.3 | 2.4 | 2.1 |
| 1.7 | 1.7 | 1.7 | | | 1.6 | 1.7 | 1.6 | 1.7 | 1.6 |
| .3 | .2 | .2 | | | | | .2 | .2 | .2 |
| (124) .5 | (126) .4 | (120) .5 | % Depr., Dep., Amort./Sales | | | | (22) .3 | (33) .4 | (50) .5 |
| 1.0 | 1.3 | 1.1 | | | | | .9 | .8 | 1.1 |
| 1.5 | 1.2 | 1.3 | | | 2.0 | | 1.5 | 1.1 | |
| (61) 3.3 | (54) 2.5 | (55) 2.2 | % Officers', Directors' Owners' Comp/Sales | | (10) 3.4 | | (17) 2.2 | (11) 2.1 | |
| 6.6 | 4.8 | 4.0 | | | 9.9 | | 6.0 | 4.0 | |
| 6017797M | 6688652M | 6895797M | Net Sales ($) | 2434M | 31848M | 63205M | 207060M | 758753M | 5832497M |
| 2782683M | 3141166M | 3441203M | Total Assets ($) | 1441M | 22186M | 56760M | 103866M | 322836M | 2934114M |

M = $ thousand    MM = $ million
See Pages 9 through 22 for Explanation of Ratios and Data

## Current Data Sorted by Assets / Comparative Historical Data

| 0-500M | 500M-2MM | 2-10MM | 10-50MM | 50-100MM | 100-250MM | | 4/1/07-3/31/08 ALL | 4/1/08-3/31/09 ALL |
|---|---|---|---|---|---|---|---|---|
| | | | | | | **Type of Statement** | | |
| | 2 | 12 | 29 | 4 | 3 | Unqualified | 26 | 28 |
| 1 | 8 | 30 | 21 | 2 | | Reviewed | 31 | 31 |
| 2 | 8 | 10 | 1 | | | Compiled | 13 | 14 |
| 2 | 22 | 7 | 2 | | | Tax Returns | 31 | 19 |
| 4 | 18 | 41 | 39 | 7 | 4 | Other | 68 | 69 |
| | 24 (4/1-9/30/11) | | 255 (10/1/11-3/31/12) | | | | | |
| 9 | 58 | 100 | 92 | 13 | 7 | **NUMBER OF STATEMENTS** | 169 | 161 |
| % | % | % | % | % | % | **ASSETS** | % | % |
| | 10.1 | 9.4 | 8.2 | 1.8 | | Cash & Equivalents | 9.5 | 10.6 |
| | 30.4 | 31.0 | 33.8 | 30.2 | | Trade Receivables (net) | 32.6 | 30.2 |
| | 39.5 | 36.3 | 36.9 | 45.7 | | Inventory | 37.4 | 36.8 |
| | 7.3 | 6.6 | 4.5 | 7.0 | | All Other Current | 4.5 | 4.1 |
| | 87.3 | 83.3 | 83.4 | 84.8 | | Total Current | 84.0 | 81.7 |
| | 4.3 | 7.0 | 7.8 | 6.5 | | Fixed Assets (net) | 8.0 | 7.0 |
| | 1.9 | 1.9 | 2.4 | 2.5 | | Intangibles (net) | 2.3 | 4.0 |
| | 6.4 | 7.8 | 6.4 | 6.2 | | All Other Non-Current | 5.6 | 7.2 |
| | 100.0 | 100.0 | 100.0 | 100.0 | | Total | 100.0 | 100.0 |
| | | | | | | **LIABILITIES** | | |
| | 15.5 | 17.2 | 20.7 | 16.4 | | Notes Payable-Short Term | 22.9 | 20.7 |
| | .9 | .6 | 2.0 | 10.5 | | Cur. Mat.-L.T.D. | 1.0 | 1.4 |
| | 25.9 | 22.5 | 18.4 | 28.3 | | Trade Payables | 18.7 | 18.6 |
| | .0 | .1 | .1 | .1 | | Income Taxes Payable | .2 | .1 |
| | 9.7 | 12.2 | 8.7 | 9.5 | | All Other Current | 8.6 | 9.6 |
| | 52.1 | 52.6 | 49.8 | 64.9 | | Total Current | 51.4 | 50.4 |
| | 5.2 | 5.5 | 7.9 | 4.7 | | Long-Term Debt | 7.4 | 6.9 |
| | .0 | .0 | .1 | .0 | | Deferred Taxes | .1 | .2 |
| | 6.9 | 7.7 | 5.6 | 3.3 | | All Other Non-Current | 5.1 | 7.6 |
| | 35.8 | 34.2 | 36.6 | 27.1 | | Net Worth | 36.0 | 34.9 |
| | 100.0 | 100.0 | 100.0 | 100.0 | | Total Liabilities & Net Worth | 100.0 | 100.0 |
| | | | | | | **INCOME DATA** | | |
| | 100.0 | 100.0 | 100.0 | 100.0 | | Net Sales | 100.0 | 100.0 |
| | 36.6 | 32.1 | 31.1 | 30.0 | | Gross Profit | 34.0 | 32.7 |
| | 32.6 | 27.5 | 25.6 | 26.0 | | Operating Expenses | 28.5 | 28.6 |
| | 4.0 | 4.6 | 5.6 | 3.9 | | Operating Profit | 5.5 | 4.1 |
| | .7 | 1.1 | 1.5 | 3.0 | | All Other Expenses (net) | 1.3 | 1.3 |
| | 3.3 | 3.4 | 4.0 | .9 | | Profit Before Taxes | 4.1 | 2.7 |
| | | | | | | **RATIOS** | | |
| | 2.8 | 2.4 | 3.1 | 1.7 | | | 3.0 | 2.6 |
| | 1.9 | 1.6 | 1.7 | 1.2 | | Current | 1.8 | 1.7 |
| | 1.4 | 1.3 | 1.2 | 1.1 | | | 1.3 | 1.2 |
| | 1.3 | 1.2 | 1.4 | .9 | | | 1.4 | 1.6 |
| | .9 | .7 | .8 | .5 | | Quick | .9 | .8 |
| | .5 | .4 | .5 | .4 | | | .5 | .5 |
| | (16) 22.9 | (19) 18.8 | (34) 10.8 | (34) 10.8 | | | (24) 15.5 | (24) 15.3 |
| | (31) 11.6 | (38) 9.7 | (49) 7.4 | (54) 6.7 | | Sales/Receivables | (46) 7.9 | (41) 9.0 |
| | (49) 7.4 | (56) 6.5 | (72) 5.1 | (76) 4.8 | | | (68) 5.4 | (56) 6.5 |
| | (37) 9.8 | (24) 15.2 | (45) 8.1 | (85) 4.3 | | | (46) 7.9 | (38) 9.6 |
| | (60) 6.1 | (65) 5.6 | (74) 4.9 | (96) 3.8 | | Cost of Sales/Inventory | (81) 4.5 | (75) 4.8 |
| | (118) 3.1 | (126) 2.9 | (122) 3.0 | (114) 3.2 | | | (140) 2.6 | (131) 2.8 |
| | (10) 36.7 | (17) 21.0 | (13) 28.3 | (39) 9.3 | | | (16) 23.2 | (13) 28.9 |
| | (31) 11.9 | (33) 11.0 | (34) 10.8 | (56) 6.5 | | Cost of Sales/Payables | (32) 11.3 | (30) 12.2 |
| | (69) 5.3 | (57) 6.4 | (49) 7.4 | (104) 3.5 | | | (50) 7.3 | (55) 6.6 |
| | 4.8 | 5.6 | 4.3 | 7.5 | | | 4.3 | 4.9 |
| | 9.1 | 10.5 | 7.9 | 11.3 | | Sales/Working Capital | 6.9 | 8.2 |
| | 17.1 | 22.1 | 20.6 | 31.0 | | | 16.2 | 18.9 |
| | 16.9 | 11.2 | 23.4 | 25.4 | | | 9.3 | 8.1 |
| | (51) 6.7 | (79) 2.8 | (83) 3.5 | 2.7 | | EBIT/Interest | (148) 3.7 | (141) 2.8 |
| | 1.4 | 1.5 | 1.4 | .5 | | | 1.5 | .9 |
| | | | 34.6 | | | | 60.6 | 6.5 |
| | | (15) 7.2 | | | | Net Profit + Depr., Dep., Amort./Cur. Mat. L/T/D | (25) 9.5 | (21) 1.7 |
| | | | 1.7 | | | | 1.0 | .0 |
| | .0 | .0 | .0 | .1 | | | .0 | .0 |
| | .1 | .1 | .1 | .3 | | Fixed/Worth | .1 | .1 |
| | .3 | .3 | .4 | .7 | | | .3 | .4 |
| | .8 | .9 | .6 | 1.7 | | | .7 | .6 |
| | 1.6 | 1.8 | 1.7 | 3.9 | | Debt/Worth | 1.6 | 1.7 |
| | 6.4 | 3.8 | 5.5 | 8.1 | | | 5.3 | 5.0 |
| | 61.8 | 56.3 | 66.4 | 36.7 | | | 57.4 | 52.1 |
| | (53) 28.9 | (89) 22.0 | (81) 22.3 | (11) 16.6 | | % Profit Before Taxes/Tangible Net Worth | (152) 23.2 | (142) 18.4 |
| | 9.2 | 5.3 | 4.0 | -7.1 | | | 5.7 | 1.3 |
| | 26.8 | 16.0 | 17.8 | 10.2 | | | 18.6 | 16.9 |
| | 8.0 | 5.3 | 5.4 | 3.1 | | % Profit Before Taxes/Total Assets | 6.4 | 5.2 |
| | 1.0 | 1.6 | .9 | -1.0 | | | 1.3 | -.2 |
| | UND | 712.5 | 238.4 | 113.4 | | | 269.6 | 191.4 |
| | 227.3 | 153.2 | 89.1 | 80.9 | | Sales/Net Fixed Assets | 85.5 | 73.1 |
| | 53.1 | 43.5 | 29.8 | 18.9 | | | 29.0 | 30.2 |
| | 4.9 | 4.3 | 3.5 | 2.7 | | | 3.2 | 3.8 |
| | 3.2 | 2.9 | 2.5 | 2.5 | | Sales/Total Assets | 2.4 | 2.6 |
| | 2.2 | 1.9 | 1.8 | 2.1 | | | 1.7 | 1.8 |
| | .1 | .1 | .2 | .1 | | | .2 | .2 |
| | (30) .2 | (59) .3 | (72) .4 | (11) .5 | | % Depr., Dep., Amort./Sales | (127) .4 | (111) .4 |
| | .4 | .8 | .8 | .8 | | | .8 | 1.0 |
| | 1.7 | 2.2 | .5 | | | | 1.8 | 1.4 |
| | (31) 3.0 | (40) 3.4 | (28) 2.0 | | | % Officers', Directors' Owners' Comp/Sales | (82) 3.0 | (65) 3.1 |
| | 5.0 | 5.5 | 3.4 | | | | 5.0 | 5.4 |
| 12371M | 266377M | 1734249M | 5897763M | 2049077M | 1557267M | Net Sales ($) | 7515694M | 7810144M |
| 3005M | 71580M | 529722M | 2197065M | 883912M | 1003408M | Total Assets ($) | 3452492M | 3518063M |

M = $ thousand    MM = $ million
See Pages 9 through 22 for Explanation of Ratios and Data

## Comparative Historical Data · Current Data Sorted by Sales

| 4/1/09-3/31/10 ALL | 4/1/10-3/31/11 ALL | 4/1/11-3/31/12 ALL | Type of Statement | 0-1MM | 1-3MM | 3-5MM | 5-10MM | 10-25MM | 25MM & OVER |
|---|---|---|---|---|---|---|---|---|---|
| 47 | 49 | 50 | Unqualified | | | | 4 | 11 | 35 |
| 57 | 65 | 62 | Reviewed | | 3 | 2 | 13 | 20 | 24 |
| 11 | 17 | 21 | Compiled | 2 | 3 | 4 | 4 | 6 | 2 |
| 43 | 25 | 33 | Tax Returns | 4 | 6 | 7 | 10 | 3 | 3 |
| 60 | 104 | 113 | Other | 3 | 12 | 7 | 11 | 23 | 57 |
| | | | | | 24 (4/1-9/30/11) | | 255 (10/1/11-3/31/12) | | |
| 218 | 260 | 279 | **NUMBER OF STATEMENTS** | 9 | 24 | 20 | 42 | 63 | 121 |
| % | % | % | **ASSETS** | % | % | % | % | % | % |
| 12.2 | 10.8 | 8.6 | Cash & Equivalents | | 12.9 | 3.9 | 11.8 | 9.7 | 7.3 |
| 33.3 | 30.5 | 31.1 | Trade Receivables (net) | | 24.9 | 32.9 | 25.8 | 31.8 | 34.6 |
| 33.0 | 35.1 | 38.1 | Inventory | | 33.6 | 40.2 | 41.7 | 36.1 | 37.2 |
| 5.1 | 5.8 | 6.1 | All Other Current | | 8.9 | 11.1 | 4.7 | 6.1 | 5.2 |
| 83.6 | 82.2 | 83.9 | Total Current | | 80.3 | 88.1 | 84.1 | 83.6 | 84.3 |
| 7.2 | 7.5 | 6.7 | Fixed Assets (net) | | 6.6 | 4.5 | 9.9 | 5.3 | 6.0 |
| 3.7 | 3.8 | 2.6 | Intangibles (net) | | 1.4 | 2.5 | 2.7 | 1.7 | 3.4 |
| 5.5 | 6.5 | 6.8 | All Other Non-Current | | 11.7 | 4.9 | 3.3 | 9.4 | 6.3 |
| 100.0 | 100.0 | 100.0 | Total | | 100.0 | 100.0 | 100.0 | 100.0 | 100.0 |
| | | | **LIABILITIES** | | | | | | |
| 20.6 | 20.5 | 18.9 | Notes Payable-Short Term | | 13.7 | 18.9 | 19.6 | 17.7 | 18.8 |
| 2.0 | 2.4 | 1.6 | Cur. Mat.-L.T.D. | | .7 | .9 | 1.1 | .7 | 2.6 |
| 22.0 | 21.8 | 21.2 | Trade Payables | | 19.3 | 29.7 | 19.3 | 21.3 | 21.7 |
| .1 | .2 | .1 | Income Taxes Payable | | .0 | .0 | .0 | .2 | .1 |
| 8.9 | 11.2 | 10.1 | All Other Current | | 13.2 | 7.8 | 11.8 | 8.3 | 9.9 |
| 53.6 | 56.1 | 52.0 | Total Current | | 47.0 | 57.2 | 51.9 | 48.2 | 53.1 |
| 5.0 | 6.1 | 6.4 | Long-Term Debt | | 9.0 | 9.8 | 5.5 | 3.7 | 6.8 |
| .2 | .2 | .1 | Deferred Taxes | | .0 | .0 | .0 | .0 | .2 |
| 10.1 | 9.2 | 7.0 | All Other Non-Current | | 10.4 | 8.0 | 9.0 | 5.2 | 5.7 |
| 31.1 | 28.3 | 34.5 | Net Worth | | 33.6 | 25.0 | 33.6 | 42.9 | 34.1 |
| 100.0 | 100.0 | 100.0 | Total Liabilties & Net Worth | | 100.0 | 100.0 | 100.0 | 100.0 | 100.0 |
| | | | **INCOME DATA** | | | | | | |
| 100.0 | 100.0 | 100.0 | Net Sales | | 100.0 | 100.0 | 100.0 | 100.0 | 100.0 |
| 31.7 | 32.1 | 33.2 | Gross Profit | | 40.0 | 29.8 | 36.6 | 33.8 | 29.8 |
| 27.0 | 27.2 | 28.4 | Operating Expenses | | 34.1 | 29.0 | 33.2 | 28.9 | 24.6 |
| 4.7 | 4.9 | 4.8 | Operating Profit | | 5.9 | .7 | 3.4 | 4.9 | 5.2 |
| 1.2 | .9 | 1.3 | All Other Expenses (net) | | 1.1 | .8 | 1.0 | 1.0 | 1.4 |
| 3.5 | 4.0 | 3.5 | Profit Before Taxes | | 4.8 | -.1 | 2.4 | 3.9 | 3.8 |
| | | | **RATIOS** | | | | | | |
| 2.8 | 2.6 | 2.7 | | | 2.7 | 2.9 | 2.6 | 2.8 | 2.5 |
| 1.7 | 1.5 | 1.7 | Current | | 1.8 | 2.1 | 1.8 | 1.7 | 1.6 |
| 1.2 | 1.2 | 1.3 | | | 1.4 | 1.5 | 1.3 | 1.3 | 1.2 |
| 1.6 | 1.2 | 1.3 | | | 1.2 | 1.7 | 1.2 | 1.5 | 1.2 |
| .8 | (259) .7 | .8 | Quick | | .9 | .8 | .6 | .8 | .8 |
| .6 | .5 | .5 | | | .4 | .4 | .4 | .5 | .5 |
| 22 16.2 | 19 19.3 | 21 17.3 | | | 11 31.8 | 16 22.4 | 17 21.1 | 19 19.1 | 31 11.7 |
| 41 8.8 | 41 8.8 | 41 8.8 | Sales/Receivables | | 38 9.6 | 41 8.9 | 30 12.0 | 38 9.6 | 46 7.9 |
| 63 5.8 | 60 6.1 | 59 6.2 | | | 55 6.6 | 60 6.1 | 51 7.1 | 63 5.8 | 62 5.9 |
| 30 12.1 | 33 11.1 | 39 9.4 | | | 29 12.8 | 31 11.6 | 42 8.6 | 34 10.6 | 41 9.0 |
| 57 6.4 | 65 5.6 | 73 5.0 | Cost of Sales/Inventory | | 72 5.0 | 66 5.5 | 94 3.9 | 64 5.7 | 72 5.1 |
| 91 4.0 | 111 3.3 | 122 3.0 | | | 166 2.2 | 111 3.3 | 130 2.8 | 135 2.7 | 107 3.4 |
| 15 24.4 | 18 20.6 | 14 26.9 | | | 0 UND | 18 20.1 | 14 25.3 | 14 25.2 | 19 18.8 |
| 31 11.9 | 33 11.2 | 34 10.8 | Cost of Sales/Payables | | 30 12.0 | 26 14.1 | 30 12.3 | 34 10.7 | 36 10.2 |
| 57 6.4 | 56 6.5 | 56 6.5 | | | 99 3.7 | 65 5.6 | 68 5.4 | 58 6.3 | 52 7.0 |
| 5.2 | 5.7 | 4.9 | | | 3.6 | 4.4 | 4.1 | 5.4 | 5.5 |
| 8.9 | 9.8 | 9.1 | Sales/Working Capital | | 6.5 | 6.7 | 8.6 | 9.9 | 10.2 |
| 24.4 | 31.9 | 20.4 | | | 11.8 | 17.4 | 14.6 | 19.0 | 26.1 |
| 15.2 | 14.9 | 17.2 | | | 15.2 | 14.1 | 13.2 | 13.6 | 23.7 |
| (188) 4.4 | (213) 4.2 | (238) 3.7 | EBIT/Interest | | (18) 6.2 | (18) 4.2 | (37) 3.9 | (50) 2.1 | (107) 3.9 |
| 1.8 | 1.7 | 1.4 | | | 1.4 | 1.2 | 1.7 | 1.0 | 1.5 |
| 22.4 | 19.4 | 22.0 | Net Profit + Depr., Dep., | | | | | | 32.0 |
| (28) 2.7 | (36) 3.5 | (32) 5.6 | Amort./Cur. Mat. L/T/D | | | | | | (22) 4.4 |
| .3 | .7 | 1.1 | | | | | | | 1.1 |
| .0 | .0 | .0 | | | .0 | .0 | .0 | .0 | .0 |
| .1 | .1 | .1 | Fixed/Worth | | .1 | .1 | .1 | .0 | .1 |
| .4 | .6 | .4 | | | .4 | .4 | .4 | .2 | .4 |
| .7 | .9 | .8 | | | 1.0 | 1.2 | .7 | .6 | .8 |
| 1.9 | 2.4 | 1.8 | Debt/Worth | | 2.2 | 1.6 | 2.0 | 1.4 | 2.2 |
| 5.7 | 8.1 | 4.8 | | | 9.4 | 6.4 | 4.9 | 3.4 | 5.5 |
| 62.8 | 61.1 | 61.5 | % Profit Before Taxes/Tangible | | 66.8 | 38.0 | 33.2 | 54.6 | 76.9 |
| (191) 27.0 | (215) 29.2 | (245) 23.3 | Net Worth | | (22) 31.0 | (17) 10.4 | (37) 16.9 | (58) 20.0 | (106) 30.8 |
| 8.4 | 7.7 | 5.2 | | | 8.0 | 2.8 | 8.6 | 3.9 | 4.4 |
| 20.4 | 19.1 | 18.1 | % Profit Before Taxes/Total | | 29.9 | 11.9 | 10.9 | 25.6 | 20.3 |
| 7.8 | 7.0 | 6.0 | Assets | | 7.9 | 3.8 | 6.8 | 5.0 | 6.3 |
| 1.7 | 1.9 | .9 | | | 1.4 | .3 | 1.6 | .9 | .8 |
| 438.7 | 279.8 | 435.7 | | | UND | 488.3 | 282.9 | 729.4 | 270.7 |
| 114.8 | 85.8 | 111.2 | Sales/Net Fixed Assets | | 155.1 | 158.3 | 86.2 | 154.2 | 110.6 |
| 40.9 | 34.1 | 35.3 | | | 28.9 | 61.8 | 27.4 | 43.6 | 44.2 |
| 3.9 | 3.8 | 3.9 | | | 3.3 | 3.8 | 3.9 | 4.3 | 3.9 |
| 2.8 | 2.7 | 2.7 | Sales/Total Assets | | 2.2 | 3.3 | 2.6 | 3.0 | 2.7 |
| 1.9 | 1.9 | 1.9 | | | 1.7 | 2.3 | 1.8 | 1.9 | 2.0 |
| .2 | .2 | .1 | | | .1 | .1 | .1 | .1 | .1 |
| (143) .4 | (165) .4 | (181) .3 | % Depr., Dep., Amort./Sales | | | (12) .1 | (30) .4 | (33) .3 | (93) .3 |
| .8 | .8 | .8 | | | | .2 | 1.3 | .8 | .8 |
| 1.0 | 1.2 | 1.3 | | | | 1.1 | 2.2 | 2.3 | .7 |
| (107) 2.5 | (85) 2.4 | (111) 3.0 | % Officers', Directors' Owners' Comp/Sales | | | (14) 3.5 | (24) 3.3 | (22) 3.1 | (40) 1.4 |
| 5.0 | 4.0 | 5.4 | | | | 6.4 | 6.5 | 4.9 | 4.2 |
| 9115726M | 12760262M | 11517104M | Net Sales ($) | 6559M | 52728M | 76006M | 314627M | 1026817M | 10040367M |
| 3625124M | 5853432M | 4688692M | Total Assets ($) | 9104M | 25231M | 28318M | 145178M | 392337M | 4088524M |

© RMA 2012    M = $ thousand    MM = $ million
See Pages 9 through 22 for Explanation of Ratios and Data

## Current Data Sorted by Assets      Comparative Historical Data

| 0-500M | 500M-2MM | 2-10MM | 10-50MM | 50-100MM | 100-250MM | Type of Statement | 4/1/07-3/31/08 ALL | 4/1/08-3/31/09 ALL |
|---|---|---|---|---|---|---|---|---|
| | 1 | 3 | 11 | 7 | 3 | Unqualified | 10 | 11 |
| 1 | 4 | 15 | 11 | | | Reviewed | 27 | 17 |
| | 4 | 4 | 1 | 1 | | Compiled | 9 | 7 |
| 1 | 5 | 5 | | | | Tax Returns | 6 | 11 |
| | 1 | 11 | 16 | 3 | 4 | Other | 41 | 52 |
| | 22 (4/1-9/30/11) | | 90 (10/1/11-3/31/12) | | | | | |
| 2 | 15 | 38 | 39 | 11 | 7 | **NUMBER OF STATEMENTS** | 93 | 98 |
| % | % | % | % | % | % | **ASSETS** | % | % |
| | 9.4 | 9.3 | 7.1 | 15.6 | | Cash & Equivalents | 7.3 | 7.7 |
| | 24.8 | 30.6 | 30.6 | 25.1 | | Trade Receivables (net) | 33.0 | 28.7 |
| | 48.4 | 44.8 | 43.9 | 28.5 | | Inventory | 39.4 | 43.3 |
| | 1.4 | 3.2 | 3.2 | 4.5 | | All Other Current | 2.9 | 4.1 |
| | 83.9 | 87.9 | 84.9 | 73.8 | | Total Current | 82.6 | 83.8 |
| | 5.5 | 5.7 | 5.8 | 8.2 | | Fixed Assets (net) | 7.1 | 7.1 |
| | 1.4 | 1.1 | 3.7 | 12.9 | | Intangibles (net) | 4.1 | 4.7 |
| | 9.1 | 5.3 | 5.6 | 5.1 | | All Other Non-Current | 6.1 | 4.4 |
| | 100.0 | 100.0 | 100.0 | 100.0 | | Total | 100.0 | 100.0 |
| | | | | | | **LIABILITIES** | | |
| | 12.3 | 21.3 | 24.1 | 3.8 | | Notes Payable-Short Term | 20.0 | 18.7 |
| | 3.5 | 1.2 | .6 | .4 | | Cur. Mat.-L.T.D. | 1.0 | 1.6 |
| | 12.6 | 25.8 | 18.8 | 18.5 | | Trade Payables | 15.9 | 17.1 |
| | .1 | .3 | .0 | .1 | | Income Taxes Payable | .2 | .1 |
| | 3.7 | 7.5 | 10.2 | 20.4 | | All Other Current | 8.6 | 7.8 |
| | 32.1 | 56.1 | 53.9 | 43.2 | | Total Current | 45.7 | 45.3 |
| | 11.1 | 4.8 | 4.7 | 1.3 | | Long-Term Debt | 4.5 | 5.5 |
| | .0 | .0 | .1 | .7 | | Deferred Taxes | .1 | .2 |
| | 10.3 | 5.7 | 4.5 | 8.8 | | All Other Non-Current | 4.2 | 10.5 |
| | 46.5 | 33.3 | 36.8 | 45.9 | | Net Worth | 45.6 | 38.5 |
| | 100.0 | 100.0 | 100.0 | 100.0 | | Total Liabilities & Net Worth | 100.0 | 100.0 |
| | | | | | | **INCOME DATA** | | |
| | 100.0 | 100.0 | 100.0 | 100.0 | | Net Sales | 100.0 | 100.0 |
| | 28.6 | 35.3 | 31.3 | 34.2 | | Gross Profit | 34.1 | 32.8 |
| | 27.4 | 31.1 | 28.9 | 29.9 | | Operating Expenses | 29.6 | 30.1 |
| | 1.2 | 4.2 | 2.4 | 4.4 | | Operating Profit | 4.5 | 2.7 |
| | .6 | 1.2 | 1.0 | 1.1 | | All Other Expenses (net) | 1.0 | 1.0 |
| | .5 | 3.0 | 1.4 | 3.2 | | Profit Before Taxes | 3.5 | 1.7 |
| | | | | | | **RATIOS** | | |
| | 6.7 | 2.5 | 2.3 | 3.6 | | | 2.8 | 3.2 |
| | 2.5 | 1.5 | 1.6 | 1.6 | | Current | 1.8 | 1.9 |
| | 1.5 | 1.1 | 1.2 | .9 | | | 1.3 | 1.4 |
| | 2.3 | 1.3 | 1.2 | 3.3 | | | 1.5 | 1.4 |
| | 1.4 | .7 | .8 | .8 | | Quick | .9 | .8 |
| | .3 | .4 | .5 | .5 | | | .6 | .6 |
| | 3   137.0 | 25   14.6 | 37   9.9 | 37   9.8 | | | 38   9.6 | 30   12.2 |
| | 29   12.5 | 43   8.5 | 50   7.3 | 49   7.4 | | Sales/Receivables | 53   6.9 | 50   7.3 |
| | 49   7.4 | 58   6.3 | 60   6.1 | 54   6.8 | | | 75   4.9 | 65   5.6 |
| | 42   8.6 | 61   6.0 | 66   5.5 | 33   11.2 | | | 59   6.2 | 71   5.2 |
| | 99   3.7 | 104   3.5 | 96   3.8 | 111   3.3 | | Cost of Sales/Inventory | 95   3.9 | 103   3.6 |
| | 182   2.0 | 166   2.2 | 166   2.2 | 126   2.9 | | | 157   2.3 | 167   2.2 |
| | 0   999.8 | 21   17.2 | 11   33.7 | 19   19.6 | | | 13   29.0 | 10   36.7 |
| | 9   39.5 | 46   8.0 | 31   11.7 | 68   5.4 | | Cost of Sales/Payables | 34   10.8 | 28   12.8 |
| | 42   8.7 | 76   4.8 | 59   6.2 | 83   4.4 | | | 58   6.3 | 57   6.4 |
| | 2.8 | 4.7 | 4.3 | 2.1 | | | 3.8 | 3.6 |
| | 6.8 | 8.2 | 8.0 | 7.2 | | Sales/Working Capital | 6.3 | 6.0 |
| | 15.6 | 21.4 | 17.4 | -36.4 | | | 10.9 | 10.8 |
| | | 13.2 | 11.0 | | | | 7.4 | 7.1 |
| | (35)   5.0 | (37)   3.7 | | | | EBIT/Interest | (85)   3.0 | (85)   2.6 |
| | 1.3 | 1.8 | | | | | 1.3 | 1.5 |
| | | | | | | | 75.5 | 11.7 |
| | | | | | | Net Profit + Depr., Dep., Amort./Cur. Mat. L/T/D | (14)   8.1 | (18)   4.1 |
| | | | | | | | 2.2 | 1.6 |
| | .0 | .0 | .1 | .1 | | | .0 | .1 |
| | .1 | .1 | .1 | .4 | | Fixed/Worth | .1 | .1 |
| | .2 | .3 | .3 | -2.1 | | | .3 | .5 |
| | .3 | .8 | 1.1 | .4 | | | .5 | .7 |
| | 1.1 | 2.0 | 2.2 | 1.5 | | Debt/Worth | 1.3 | 1.9 |
| | 5.7 | 5.2 | 3.8 | -25.3 | | | 3.0 | 4.5 |
| | 47.9 | 51.2 | 27.2 | | | | 36.7 | 34.2 |
| | (14)   11.5 | (35)   17.4 | (38)   13.6 | | | % Profit Before Taxes/Tangible Net Worth | (89)   12.9 | (87)   14.4 |
| | -5.3 | 6.1 | 8.0 | | | | 4.1 | 3.6 |
| | 16.0 | 17.9 | 11.8 | 8.3 | | | 14.1 | 10.6 |
| | 7.1 | 7.5 | 5.0 | 7.1 | | % Profit Before Taxes/Total Assets | 5.3 | 4.0 |
| | -1.3 | .7 | 1.9 | 2.3 | | | .9 | .4 |
| | 623.7 | 448.7 | 115.5 | 55.0 | | | 181.4 | 100.6 |
| | 101.9 | 83.8 | 58.8 | 29.6 | | Sales/Net Fixed Assets | 63.8 | 47.9 |
| | 63.4 | 37.0 | 25.7 | 17.0 | | | 25.4 | 26.7 |
| | 4.7 | 3.6 | 2.9 | 2.6 | | | 3.1 | 3.1 |
| | 2.4 | 2.3 | 2.2 | 1.5 | | Sales/Total Assets | 2.1 | 2.1 |
| | 2.2 | 1.9 | 1.7 | 1.4 | | | 1.6 | 1.6 |
| | | .1 | .2 | | | | .2 | .3 |
| | (27)   .4 | (36)   .5 | | | | % Depr., Dep., Amort./Sales | (69)   .5 | (78)   .5 |
| | | 1.0 | .9 | | | | 1.1 | .9 |
| | | 1.9 | | | | | 1.1 | .8 |
| | (16)   3.3 | | | | | % Officers', Directors' Owners' Comp/Sales | (38)   2.6 | (37)   2.1 |
| | | 7.2 | | | | | 6.8 | 4.8 |
| 5975M | 65698M | 579803M | 1704454M | 1526890M | 1408938M | Net Sales ($) | 3731593M | 4485191M |
| 543M | 18760M | 214866M | 750914M | 794241M | 882746M | Total Assets ($) | 2056942M | 2223321M |

M = $ thousand   MM = $ million
See Pages 9 through 22 for Explanation of Ratios and Data

## Comparative Historical Data | Current Data Sorted by Sales

| | | | Type of Statement | 0-1MM | 1-3MM | 3-5MM | 5-10MM | 10-25MM | 25MM & OVER |
|---|---|---|---|---|---|---|---|---|---|
| 18 | 17 | 25 | Unqualified | | | 1 | | 4 | 20 |
| 31 | 35 | 31 | Reviewed | 1 | 2 | 3 | 5 | 11 | 9 |
| 11 | 11 | 10 | Compiled | | | 3 | | 6 | 1 |
| 7 | 10 | 11 | Tax Returns | | 3 | | 5 | 3 | |
| 35 | 37 | 35 | Other | | 1 | | 3 | 6 | 25 |
| 4/1/09-3/31/10 ALL | 4/1/10-3/31/11 ALL | 4/1/11-3/31/12 ALL | | | 22 (4/1-9/30/11) | | | 90 (10/1/11-3/31/12) | |
| 102 | 110 | 112 | **NUMBER OF STATEMENTS** | 1 | 6 | 7 | 13 | 30 | 55 |
| % | % | % | **ASSETS** | % | % | % | % | % | % |
| 11.9 | 10.1 | 9.9 | Cash & Equivalents | | | | 17.2 | 5.0 | 10.0 |
| 32.7 | 29.0 | 28.4 | Trade Receivables (net) | | | | 34.0 | 26.9 | 30.2 |
| 35.9 | 43.0 | 42.6 | Inventory | | | | 33.8 | 51.9 | 37.2 |
| 4.1 | 4.5 | 2.9 | All Other Current | | | | 3.6 | 2.4 | 3.5 |
| 84.5 | 86.7 | 83.8 | Total Current | | | | 88.5 | 86.1 | 80.9 |
| 6.6 | 6.2 | 6.3 | Fixed Assets (net) | | | | 3.9 | 7.1 | 6.3 |
| 4.2 | 2.2 | 4.2 | Intangibles (net) | | | | .2 | 1.2 | 7.5 |
| 4.7 | 4.9 | 5.7 | All Other Non-Current | | | | 7.4 | 5.6 | 5.3 |
| 100.0 | 100.0 | 100.0 | Total | | | | 100.0 | 100.0 | 100.0 |
| | | | **LIABILITIES** | | | | | | |
| 16.4 | 17.1 | 18.6 | Notes Payable-Short Term | | | | 20.5 | 22.8 | 16.5 |
| 1.6 | 1.2 | 1.2 | Cur. Mat.-L.T.D. | | | | .0 | 1.9 | .5 |
| 17.5 | 22.0 | 20.1 | Trade Payables | | | | 20.7 | 22.5 | 20.9 |
| .3 | .2 | .1 | Income Taxes Payable | | | | .4 | .2 | .1 |
| 11.8 | 8.8 | 9.7 | All Other Current | | | | 5.4 | 6.7 | 13.3 |
| 47.7 | 49.3 | 49.8 | Total Current | | | | 47.1 | 54.2 | 51.3 |
| 5.3 | 5.5 | 5.4 | Long-Term Debt | | | | 1.0 | 6.8 | 4.2 |
| .2 | .2 | .2 | Deferred Taxes | | | | .1 | .0 | .4 |
| 5.6 | 6.4 | 6.1 | All Other Non-Current | | | | 17.0 | 5.7 | 4.1 |
| 41.1 | 38.6 | 38.5 | Net Worth | | | | 34.8 | 33.2 | 40.0 |
| 100.0 | 100.0 | 100.0 | Total Liabilities & Net Worth | | | | 100.0 | 100.0 | 100.0 |
| | | | **INCOME DATA** | | | | | | |
| 100.0 | 100.0 | 100.0 | Net Sales | | | | 100.0 | 100.0 | 100.0 |
| 31.6 | 32.8 | 33.2 | Gross Profit | | | | 36.4 | 32.6 | 32.7 |
| 27.8 | 28.3 | 29.6 | Operating Expenses | | | | 30.6 | 28.7 | 28.8 |
| 3.8 | 4.4 | 3.6 | Operating Profit | | | | 5.8 | 3.9 | 3.8 |
| .4 | .6 | 1.0 | All Other Expenses (net) | | | | 2.4 | .5 | 1.0 |
| 3.4 | 3.9 | 2.6 | Profit Before Taxes | | | | 3.4 | 3.4 | 2.9 |
| | | | **RATIOS** | | | | | | |
| 2.9 | 3.1 | 3.1 | Current | | | | 4.0 | 2.5 | 2.5 |
| 1.8 | 1.8 | 1.7 | | | | | 2.1 | 1.4 | 1.6 |
| 1.4 | 1.3 | 1.2 | | | | | 1.3 | 1.1 | 1.2 |
| 1.8 | 1.4 | 1.6 | Quick | | | | 1.7 | 1.4 | 1.3 |
| 1.0 | .8 | .8 | | | | | 1.1 | .6 | .9 |
| .5 | .4 | .5 | | | | | .6 | .3 | .5 |
| 33  11.0 | 22  16.8 | 27  13.7 | Sales/Receivables | | | | 5  79.7 | 26  14.0 | 37  9.9 |
| 50  7.3 | 44  8.3 | 46  7.9 | | | | | 54  6.7 | 41  8.8 | 49  7.5 |
| 69  5.3 | 61  6.0 | 58  6.3 | | | | | 76  4.8 | 54  6.8 | 59  6.2 |
| 44  8.3 | 58  6.3 | 61  6.0 | Cost of Sales/Inventory | | | | 4  102.0 | 79  4.6 | 59  6.2 |
| 91  4.0 | 92  4.0 | 107  3.4 | | | | | 76  4.8 | 140  2.6 | 96  3.8 |
| 142  2.6 | 153  2.4 | 166  2.2 | | | | | 140  2.6 | 192  1.9 | 140  2.6 |
| 11  31.9 | 16  22.7 | 12  30.7 | Cost of Sales/Payables | | | | 4  85.6 | 18  20.0 | 15  25.0 |
| 30  12.4 | 38  9.6 | 39  9.4 | | | | | 42  8.7 | 43  8.4 | 39  9.4 |
| 55  6.7 | 74  4.9 | 72  5.1 | | | | | 85  4.3 | 74  4.9 | 74  4.9 |
| 3.8 | 3.8 | 3.9 | Sales/Working Capital | | | | 4.1 | 4.7 | 4.2 |
| 6.2 | 7.4 | 8.0 | | | | | 7.8 | 7.7 | 8.9 |
| 15.1 | 16.1 | 18.8 | | | | | 22.1 | 21.4 | 17.7 |
| 11.2 | 17.0 | 13.2 | EBIT/Interest | | | | | 13.4 | 20.4 |
| (88) 4.1 | (96) 6.2 | (98) 3.9 | | | | | | (29) 4.6 | (49) 4.5 |
| 1.5 | 1.8 | 1.5 | | | | | | 1.9 | 1.9 |
| 12.2 | 21.8 | 4.3 | Net Profit + Depr., Dep., | | | | | | |
| (20) 5.3 | (18) 5.7 | (15) 1.0 | Amort./Cur. Mat. L/T/D | | | | | | |
| 2.3 | 1.5 | -1.8 | | | | | | | |
| .0 | .0 | .0 | Fixed/Worth | | | | .0 | .0 | .1 |
| .1 | .1 | .1 | | | | | .1 | .1 | .2 |
| .4 | .2 | .3 | | | | | .3 | .4 | .3 |
| .6 | .7 | .8 | Debt/Worth | | | | .8 | .8 | 1.0 |
| 1.4 | 1.5 | 2.0 | | | | | 1.3 | 2.0 | 2.0 |
| 4.2 | 4.5 | 5.0 | | | | | 12.2 | 4.5 | 4.1 |
| 32.5 | 53.1 | 43.0 | % Profit Before Taxes/Tangible | | | | 50.8 | 49.5 | 44.3 |
| (92) 16.6 | (102) 19.8 | (102) 15.4 | Net Worth | | | (12) 14.3 | (28) 19.5 | (49) 17.4 |
| 4.1 | 6.2 | 6.8 | | | | | -.6 | 8.4 | 8.2 |
| 14.3 | 17.1 | 12.7 | % Profit Before Taxes/Total | | | | 19.8 | 18.8 | 12.0 |
| 5.0 | 7.6 | 5.8 | Assets | | | | 9.0 | 5.9 | 6.3 |
| .6 | 1.8 | 1.9 | | | | | -.5 | 1.9 | 2.5 |
| 209.5 | 199.3 | 175.0 | Sales/Net Fixed Assets | | | | 811.8 | 350.2 | 127.3 |
| 63.9 | 60.6 | 68.3 | | | | | 80.4 | 50.8 | 55.0 |
| 29.1 | 27.0 | 25.3 | | | | | 72.9 | 22.2 | 24.6 |
| 3.1 | 3.3 | 3.2 | Sales/Total Assets | | | | 3.9 | 3.6 | 2.9 |
| 2.3 | 2.4 | 2.3 | | | | | 2.6 | 2.2 | 2.2 |
| 1.7 | 1.9 | 1.7 | | | | | 1.9 | 1.7 | 1.5 |
| .2 | .3 | .2 | % Depr., Dep., Amort./Sales | | | | | .2 | .3 |
| (81) .5 | (78) .6 | (87) .5 | | | | | | (23) .5 | (48) .6 |
| 1.1 | 1.0 | 1.0 | | | | | | 1.0 | 1.1 |
| 1.3 | 1.0 | 1.2 | % Officers', Directors' | | | | | 1.0 | 1.1 |
| (34) 2.4 | (31) 2.1 | (36) 2.3 | Owners' Comp/Sales | | | | | (14) 1.9 | (10) 1.8 |
| 5.3 | 5.9 | 6.2 | | | | | | 4.9 | 4.5 |
| 4569900M | 4738392M | 5291758M | Net Sales ($) | 888M | 11502M | 29501M | 93526M | 490450M | 4665891M |
| 2469810M | 2151027M | 2662070M | Total Assets ($) | 61M | 6532M | 12762M | 44943M | 224658M | 2373114M |

## Current Data Sorted by Assets

## Comparative Historical Data

| | | | | | | Type of Statement | | |
|---|---|---|---|---|---|---|---|---|
| 1 | | 4 | 34 | 18 | 28 | Unqualified | 79 | 82 |
| 2 | 1 | 42 | 41 | 1 | | Reviewed | 71 | 90 |
| 6 | 12 | 47 | 4 | | | Compiled | 56 | 44 |
| 14 | 48 | 57 | 1 | | 1 | Tax Returns | 50 | 73 |
| 12 | 25 | 64 | 54 | 12 | 9 | Other | 128 | 132 |
| | 107 (4/1-9/30/11) | | 431 (10/1/11-3/31/12) | | | | 4/1/07-3/31/08 | 4/1/08-3/31/09 |
| 0-500M | 500M-2MM | 2-10MM | 10-50MM | 50-100MM | 100-250MM | | ALL | ALL |
| 35 | 86 | 214 | 134 | 31 | 38 | NUMBER OF STATEMENTS | 384 | 421 |
| % | % | % | % | % | % | ASSETS | % | % |
| 22.1 | 11.1 | 7.5 | 7.4 | 7.6 | 7.7 | Cash & Equivalents | 7.7 | 7.1 |
| 19.8 | 27.0 | 35.0 | 31.5 | 29.5 | 25.2 | Trade Receivables (net) | 29.9 | 31.9 |
| 31.9 | 32.0 | 32.5 | 33.3 | 26.2 | 31.0 | Inventory | 31.0 | 32.6 |
| 5.3 | 3.3 | 2.2 | 2.3 | 4.1 | 2.0 | All Other Current | 3.8 | 3.2 |
| 79.1 | 73.4 | 77.2 | 74.5 | 67.3 | 65.9 | Total Current | 72.5 | 74.8 |
| 15.4 | 12.3 | 13.1 | 18.3 | 25.2 | 23.2 | Fixed Assets (net) | 18.8 | 17.4 |
| 2.2 | 7.6 | 3.9 | 2.1 | 2.4 | 5.3 | Intangibles (net) | 2.9 | 2.8 |
| 3.3 | 6.7 | 5.8 | 5.2 | 5.2 | 5.5 | All Other Non-Current | 5.8 | 5.1 |
| 100.0 | 100.0 | 100.0 | 100.0 | 100.0 | 100.0 | Total | 100.0 | 100.0 |
| | | | | | | LIABILITIES | | |
| 4.9 | 6.7 | 12.8 | 18.7 | 13.0 | 10.8 | Notes Payable-Short Term | 15.0 | 15.1 |
| 4.1 | 2.5 | 1.3 | 2.5 | 2.0 | 1.4 | Cur. Mat.-L.T.D. | 2.9 | 2.7 |
| 25.3 | 26.9 | 26.9 | 21.7 | 22.3 | 21.2 | Trade Payables | 23.8 | 24.0 |
| .4 | .1 | .2 | .1 | .3 | .4 | Income Taxes Payable | .3 | .2 |
| 9.9 | 10.0 | 8.1 | 7.7 | 6.8 | 10.3 | All Other Current | 8.3 | 9.1 |
| 44.7 | 46.1 | 49.2 | 50.7 | 44.4 | 44.1 | Total Current | 50.4 | 51.1 |
| 18.9 | 11.9 | 10.7 | 10.6 | 15.2 | 17.8 | Long-Term Debt | 13.0 | 12.7 |
| .1 | .0 | .3 | .3 | .8 | .7 | Deferred Taxes | .2 | .3 |
| 10.2 | 6.5 | 4.0 | 4.7 | 4.4 | 4.6 | All Other Non-Current | 5.6 | 4.4 |
| 26.2 | 35.5 | 35.8 | 33.6 | 35.3 | 32.9 | Net Worth | 30.8 | 31.4 |
| 100.0 | 100.0 | 100.0 | 100.0 | 100.0 | 100.0 | Total Liabilties & Net Worth | 100.0 | 100.0 |
| | | | | | | INCOME DATA | | |
| 100.0 | 100.0 | 100.0 | 100.0 | 100.0 | 100.0 | Net Sales | 100.0 | 100.0 |
| 26.5 | 22.8 | 17.0 | 16.0 | 15.0 | 15.2 | Gross Profit | 18.6 | 17.4 |
| 22.3 | 20.1 | 14.9 | 13.5 | 12.5 | 13.1 | Operating Expenses | 16.5 | 15.5 |
| 4.2 | 2.7 | 2.1 | 2.5 | 2.5 | 2.1 | Operating Profit | 2.0 | 1.9 |
| -.3 | .0 | .2 | .3 | .3 | .5 | All Other Expenses (net) | .4 | .3 |
| 4.5 | 2.7 | 1.9 | 2.1 | 2.3 | 1.7 | Profit Before Taxes | 1.7 | 1.5 |
| | | | | | | RATIOS | | |
| 5.9 | 3.4 | 2.3 | 2.1 | 2.4 | 2.1 | | 2.2 | 2.1 |
| 1.9 | 1.6 | 1.5 | 1.3 | 1.4 | 1.4 | Current | 1.4 | 1.4 |
| 1.2 | 1.1 | 1.2 | 1.1 | 1.2 | 1.2 | | 1.1 | 1.1 |
| 2.4 | 1.9 | 1.3 | 1.1 | 1.4 | 1.3 | | 1.1 | 1.1 |
| 1.1 | .8 | .8 | .7 | .8 | .7 | Quick | .7 | .7 |
| .4 | .5 | .6 | .5 | .6 | .5 | | .5 | .5 |

| | | | | | | | | | | | | | | | | |
|---|---|---|---|---|---|---|---|---|---|---|---|---|---|---|---|---|
| 0 | UND | 1 | 453.8 | 17 | 21.2 | 16 | 23.2 | 14 | 25.3 | 11 | 34.2 | Sales/Receivables | 13 | 27.6 | 15 | 24.0 |
| 5 | 75.8 | 16 | 23.1 | 25 | 14.7 | 24 | 14.9 | 21 | 17.5 | 17 | 22.1 | | 23 | 16.1 | 24 | 15.2 |
| 25 | 14.4 | 27 | 13.6 | 35 | 10.3 | 35 | 10.5 | 32 | 11.3 | 25 | 14.7 | | 33 | 11.0 | 35 | 10.4 |
| 12 | 30.9 | 9 | 40.7 | 14 | 25.7 | 17 | 21.6 | 14 | 25.7 | 18 | 20.8 | Cost of Sales/Inventory | 16 | 22.9 | 16 | 23.3 |
| 20 | 18.1 | 21 | 17.0 | 26 | 13.8 | 28 | 13.0 | 19 | 19.6 | 26 | 14.0 | | 27 | 13.5 | 27 | 13.6 |
| 38 | 9.7 | 39 | 9.3 | 49 | 7.4 | 49 | 7.4 | 23 | 15.8 | 30 | 12.0 | | 43 | 8.5 | 44 | 8.3 |
| 0 | 765.0 | 8 | 44.8 | 11 | 32.4 | 12 | 31.4 | 12 | 29.3 | 13 | 27.9 | Cost of Sales/Payables | 10 | 35.3 | 10 | 37.2 |
| 10 | 35.3 | 14 | 26.3 | 20 | 18.3 | 18 | 20.1 | 18 | 20.3 | 18 | 20.8 | | 19 | 19.2 | 19 | 19.7 |
| 35 | 10.3 | 33 | 11.2 | 33 | 11.2 | 29 | 12.8 | 30 | 12.0 | 21 | 17.5 | | 34 | 10.7 | 30 | 12.2 |
| | 8.6 | | 12.8 | | 9.7 | | 13.1 | | 8.9 | | 14.0 | Sales/Working Capital | | 11.6 | | 11.0 |
| | 19.6 | | 23.4 | | 19.9 | | 23.6 | | 39.7 | | 26.4 | | | 25.7 | | 25.1 |
| | 163.8 | | 108.3 | | 41.8 | | 63.8 | | 88.2 | | 89.8 | | | 62.4 | | 80.8 |
| | 19.7 | | 12.3 | | 15.3 | | 14.8 | | 10.2 | | 7.8 | EBIT/Interest | | 8.5 | | 9.0 |
| (21) | 6.8 | (61) | 5.8 | (189) | 4.5 | (125) | 4.4 | (29) | 5.0 | (34) | 3.9 | | (346) | 2.9 | (380) | 3.6 |
| | 2.7 | | 2.1 | | 1.4 | | 1.9 | | 2.3 | | 2.4 | | | 1.4 | | 1.7 |
| | | | | | 8.4 | | 16.9 | | 8.7 | | 20.4 | Net Profit + Depr., Dep., Amort./Cur. Mat. L/T/D | | 7.6 | | 7.0 |
| | | (38) | 3.8 | (33) | 4.8 | (15) | 2.6 | (19) | 3.9 | | | (100) | 2.4 | (95) | 3.7 |
| | | | | | 1.7 | | 1.7 | | 1.7 | | 2.0 | | | .9 | | 1.5 |
| | .0 | | .0 | | .1 | | .1 | | .2 | | .4 | Fixed/Worth | | .1 | | .1 |
| | .3 | | .2 | | .2 | | .4 | | .7 | | .9 | | | .5 | | .4 |
| | .7 | | 2.0 | | .9 | | 1.3 | | 2.1 | | 3.0 | | | 1.6 | | 1.4 |
| | .7 | | .7 | | 1.0 | | 1.1 | | 1.1 | | 1.2 | Debt/Worth | | 1.1 | | 1.3 |
| | 2.3 | | 2.4 | | 2.2 | | 2.9 | | 3.0 | | 3.6 | | | 2.7 | | 2.7 |
| | 4.9 | | 9.1 | | 4.5 | | 5.7 | | 4.8 | | 7.5 | | | 6.7 | | 6.1 |
| | 83.1 | | 50.1 | | 37.6 | | 43.7 | | 26.1 | | 29.3 | % Profit Before Taxes/Tangible Net Worth | | 41.1 | | 42.3 |
| (29) | 44.7 | (72) | 28.3 | (192) | 17.0 | (130) | 25.1 | | 19.5 | (33) | 14.3 | | (344) | 18.5 | (378) | 19.3 |
| | 14.4 | | 9.9 | | 4.6 | | 8.2 | | 6.2 | | 9.4 | | | 6.3 | | 7.2 |
| | 40.3 | | 21.0 | | 10.8 | | 13.7 | | 9.0 | | 11.4 | % Profit Before Taxes/Total Assets | | 11.0 | | 11.3 |
| | 13.2 | | 9.1 | | 5.2 | | 6.0 | | 5.0 | | 5.4 | | | 5.2 | | 5.8 |
| | 4.7 | | 3.5 | | .9 | | 2.3 | | 2.0 | | 2.2 | | | 1.1 | | 1.6 |
| | 572.0 | | 999.8 | | 264.3 | | 156.6 | | 68.6 | | 104.5 | Sales/Net Fixed Assets | | 113.6 | | 152.2 |
| | 93.4 | | 140.8 | | 77.3 | | 36.5 | | 18.9 | | 23.0 | | | 39.5 | | 50.5 |
| | 35.2 | | 39.8 | | 24.1 | | 14.9 | | 11.5 | | 12.2 | | | 13.7 | | 16.7 |
| | 9.6 | | 9.8 | | 7.0 | | 6.6 | | 8.2 | | 6.5 | Sales/Total Assets | | 6.7 | | 6.9 |
| | 6.8 | | 5.5 | | 4.9 | | 4.9 | | 4.9 | | 4.8 | | | 4.7 | | 5.0 |
| | 3.9 | | 3.7 | | 3.4 | | 2.9 | | 3.0 | | 4.0 | | | 3.1 | | 3.2 |
| | .1 | | .1 | | .1 | | .2 | | .2 | | .3 | % Depr., Dep., Amort./Sales | | .2 | | .2 |
| (18) | .3 | (56) | .4 | (170) | .3 | (122) | .5 | (29) | .7 | (32) | .4 | | (329) | .5 | (348) | .5 |
| | 1.1 | | .8 | | .8 | | .9 | | 1.2 | | .9 | | | 1.0 | | .9 |
| | 1.3 | | .6 | | .8 | | .6 | | | | | | % Officers', Directors' Owners' Comp/Sales | | .6 | | .8 |
| (14) | 2.4 | (56) | 1.9 | (104) | 1.4 | (32) | 1.0 | | | | | | (134) | 1.4 | (144) | 1.6 |
| | 3.4 | | 4.8 | | 2.8 | | 2.0 | | | | | | | | 2.8 | | 2.8 |
| 87972M | 697858M | 5716153M | 15490668M | 11495367M | 34379465M | Net Sales ($) | 44906671M | 47154033M |
| 10565M | 100654M | 1022860M | 2851102M | 2147835M | 6188818M | Total Assets ($) | 9537092M | 9534459M |

M = $ thousand    MM = $ million
See Pages 9 through 22 for Explanation of Ratios and Data

## Comparative Historical Data  |  Current Data Sorted by Sales

Current data groupings: **107 (4/1-9/30/11)** covers 0-1MM and 1-3MM; **431 (10/1/11-3/31/12)** covers 3-5MM, 5-10MM, 10-25MM, 25MM & OVER.

| 4/1/09-3/31/10 ALL | 4/1/10-3/31/11 ALL | 4/1/11-3/31/12 ALL | Type of Statement | 0-1MM | 1-3MM | 3-5MM | 5-10MM | 10-25MM | 25MM & OVER |
|---|---|---|---|---|---|---|---|---|---|
| 82 | 79 | 85 | Unqualified | 1 | | | | 4 | 80 |
| 86 | 78 | 87 | Reviewed | | 1 | 1 | 3 | 17 | 65 |
| 67 | 64 | 69 | Compiled | 5 | 3 | 3 | 11 | 23 | 24 |
| 85 | 94 | 121 | Tax Returns | 3 | 15 | 21 | 18 | 45 | 19 |
| 136 | 168 | 176 | Other | 4 | 8 | 13 | 20 | 36 | 95 |
| 456 | 483 | 538 | **NUMBER OF STATEMENTS** | 13 | 27 | 38 | 52 | 125 | 283 |
| % | % | % | **ASSETS** | % | % | % | % | % | % |
| 8.9 | 8.3 | 9.0 | Cash & Equivalents | 22.5 | 16.0 | 7.2 | 12.2 | 11.5 | 6.3 |
| 30.1 | 29.7 | 30.9 | Trade Receivables (net) | 22.2 | 19.8 | 20.8 | 28.1 | 34.1 | 32.7 |
| 30.5 | 32.3 | 32.1 | Inventory | 24.0 | 28.2 | 35.8 | 33.8 | 30.6 | 32.7 |
| 3.4 | 3.5 | 2.7 | All Other Current | 3.8 | 6.8 | .9 | 2.7 | 2.1 | 2.7 |
| 72.9 | 73.8 | 74.7 | Total Current | 72.5 | 70.8 | 64.7 | 76.8 | 78.3 | 74.5 |
| 18.7 | 17.5 | 15.8 | Fixed Assets (net) | 24.1 | 15.1 | 20.4 | 13.2 | 12.8 | 16.7 |
| 3.1 | 2.8 | 3.9 | Intangibles (net) | .8 | 5.3 | 8.9 | 4.6 | 3.4 | 3.4 |
| 5.3 | 5.9 | 5.6 | All Other Non-Current | 2.5 | 8.8 | 6.0 | 5.4 | 5.5 | 5.4 |
| 100.0 | 100.0 | 100.0 | Total | 100.0 | 100.0 | 100.0 | 100.0 | 100.0 | 100.0 |
| | | | **LIABILITIES** | | | | | | |
| 13.6 | 12.7 | 12.6 | Notes Payable-Short Term | 2.1 | 6.3 | 7.8 | 9.5 | 9.9 | 16.1 |
| 3.0 | 1.9 | 2.0 | Cur. Mat.-L.T.D. | 1.4 | .2 | 6.0 | 1.9 | 1.2 | 2.1 |
| 24.0 | 24.3 | 24.8 | Trade Payables | 19.3 | 18.5 | 27.2 | 24.5 | 27.3 | 24.3 |
| .3 | .2 | .2 | Income Taxes Payable | .7 | .2 | .1 | .2 | .1 | .2 |
| 9.6 | 9.6 | 8.5 | All Other Current | 6.4 | 13.0 | 5.9 | 9.0 | 9.5 | 8.0 |
| 50.4 | 48.6 | 48.2 | Total Current | 29.8 | 38.3 | 47.0 | 45.3 | 48.0 | 50.7 |
| 12.7 | 11.6 | 12.2 | Long-Term Debt | 20.2 | 19.1 | 23.4 | 12.3 | 8.7 | 11.1 |
| .3 | .3 | .3 | Deferred Taxes | .0 | .1 | .0 | .0 | .3 | .4 |
| 4.9 | 5.9 | 5.0 | All Other Non-Current | 11.3 | 9.8 | 6.6 | 7.2 | 4.2 | 4.0 |
| 31.7 | 33.6 | 34.4 | Net Worth | 38.8 | 32.7 | 23.1 | 35.2 | 38.8 | 33.7 |
| 100.0 | 100.0 | 100.0 | Total Liabilities & Net Worth | 100.0 | 100.0 | 100.0 | 100.0 | 100.0 | 100.0 |
| | | | **INCOME DATA** | | | | | | |
| 100.0 | 100.0 | 100.0 | Net Sales | 100.0 | 100.0 | 100.0 | 100.0 | 100.0 | 100.0 |
| 19.0 | 18.5 | 18.1 | Gross Profit | 37.4 | 32.3 | 25.9 | 20.7 | 17.5 | 14.5 |
| 17.0 | 16.5 | 15.6 | Operating Expenses | 26.7 | 28.4 | 22.1 | 18.0 | 15.6 | 12.6 |
| 2.0 | 2.0 | 2.5 | Operating Profit | 10.7 | 4.0 | 3.7 | 2.7 | 1.9 | 1.9 |
| .3 | .3 | .2 | All Other Expenses (net) | 1.0 | -.6 | .2 | .4 | .1 | .2 |
| 1.7 | 1.7 | 2.3 | Profit Before Taxes | 9.7 | 4.6 | 3.5 | 2.3 | 1.8 | 1.7 |
| | | | **RATIOS** | | | | | | |
| 2.3 | 2.4 | 2.4 | Current | 21.0 | 5.4 | 2.2 | 2.6 | 2.6 | 2.0 |
| 1.5 | 1.5 | 1.5 | | 2.7 | 2.5 | 1.5 | 1.6 | 1.6 | 1.4 |
| 1.1 | 1.2 | 1.2 | | 1.3 | 1.0 | 1.1 | 1.2 | 1.2 | 1.2 |
| 1.3 | 1.3 | 1.3 | Quick | 13.4 | 2.2 | 1.2 | 1.5 | 1.6 | 1.1 |
| .8 | (482) .8 | .8 | | 1.7 | 1.1 | .7 | .8 | .9 | .7 |
| .5 | .5 | .5 | | .7 | .3 | .4 | .5 | .6 | .5 |
| 12  30.2 | 11  31.8 | 12  29.5 | Sales/Receivables | 0  UND | 0  UND | 0  886.6 | 2  155.6 | 17  21.6 | 12  29.3 |
| 23  15.7 | 23  15.9 | 23  15.7 | | 2  188.0 | 18  20.1 | 20  18.2 | 26  13.9 | 25  14.7 | 22  16.3 |
| 34  10.7 | 33  10.9 | 32  11.4 | | 62  5.9 | 30  12.2 | 35  10.4 | 41  8.8 | 37  9.8 | 30  12.2 |
| 15  24.5 | 15  23.7 | 14  25.7 | Cost of Sales/Inventory | 13  27.4 | 5  72.7 | 21  17.6 | 15  24.9 | 13  28.8 | 14  25.7 |
| 26  14.1 | 26  13.8 | 25  14.6 | | 33  11.2 | 24  15.3 | 38  9.6 | 29  12.7 | 26  14.3 | 24  15.3 |
| 44  8.4 | 44  8.2 | 43  8.4 | | 63  5.8 | 66  5.5 | 70  5.2 | 58  6.3 | 49  7.4 | 38  9.7 |
| 10  35.6 | 10  36.0 | 10  36.0 | Cost of Sales/Payables | 0  UND | 7  55.9 | 8  44.2 | 10  37.3 | 11  33.5 | 11  34.7 |
| 18  19.8 | 19  19.4 | 18  20.2 | | 12  31.7 | 16  22.6 | 20  18.5 | 20  18.3 | 20  18.4 | 17  21.0 |
| 32  11.5 | 31  11.7 | 30  12.0 | | 56  6.5 | 43  8.5 | 49  7.4 | 36  10.0 | 33  11.2 | 26  14.2 |
| 10.0 | 10.2 | 11.0 | Sales/Working Capital | 4.3 | 5.5 | 7.6 | 7.5 | 9.5 | 14.6 |
| 22.4 | 22.1 | 21.7 | | 9.2 | 12.5 | 16.2 | 17.2 | 16.5 | 27.9 |
| 72.9 | 65.0 | 62.6 | | 15.5 | 94.8 | 183.0 | 45.7 | 42.2 | 66.4 |
| 12.8 | 12.5 | 14.4 | EBIT/Interest | | 17.6 | 16.1 | 12.4 | 23.5 | 13.5 |
| (400) 4.6 | (414) 4.1 | (459) 4.8 | | | (16) 3.3 | (32) 5.1 | (40) 5.6 | (102) 4.8 | (262) 4.4 |
| 1.9 | 1.6 | 1.9 | | | 1.3 | 1.6 | 2.2 | 1.5 | 2.0 |
| 8.9 | 10.6 | 9.9 | Net Profit + Depr., Dep., Amort./Cur. Mat. L/T/D | | | | | 8.4 | 13.1 |
| (98) 3.2 | (107) 3.9 | (107) 3.9 | | | | | | (21) 3.8 | (80) 4.0 |
| 1.5 | 1.9 | 1.7 | | | | | | 1.4 | 1.7 |
| .1 | .1 | .1 | Fixed/Worth | .0 | .0 | .1 | .0 | .0 | .1 |
| .4 | .4 | .3 | | .1 | .3 | .5 | .2 | .2 | .4 |
| 1.5 | 1.4 | 1.4 | | 2.1 | 3.7 | 4.8 | 1.0 | .8 | 1.5 |
| 1.1 | .9 | 1.0 | Debt/Worth | .5 | .7 | 1.0 | .9 | .8 | 1.2 |
| 2.4 | 2.4 | 2.5 | | 2.9 | 1.0 | 3.3 | 2.5 | 1.8 | 2.9 |
| 6.0 | 5.2 | 5.3 | | 6.1 | 6.9 | NM | 5.4 | 4.0 | 5.6 |
| 42.2 | 36.6 | 40.7 | % Profit Before Taxes/Tangible Net Worth | 75.5 | 49.1 | 58.6 | 63.3 | 32.9 | 37.3 |
| (407) 22.0 | (437) 19.2 | (487) 21.1 | | (12) 48.6 | (22) 29.1 | (29) 32.7 | (46) 26.8 | (113) 15.8 | (265) 21.0 |
| 8.3 | 5.8 | 7.2 | | 19.3 | 5.2 | 11.6 | 10.6 | 4.4 | 8.0 |
| 13.4 | 11.4 | 13.1 | % Profit Before Taxes/Total Assets | 41.1 | 27.6 | 21.8 | 16.0 | 11.2 | 11.5 |
| 6.1 | 5.3 | 6.0 | | 14.8 | 8.7 | 10.3 | 8.5 | 5.2 | 5.6 |
| 2.0 | 1.5 | 2.0 | | 7.2 | 1.4 | 3.9 | 3.3 | 1.5 | 1.9 |
| 153.8 | 171.9 | 205.5 | Sales/Net Fixed Assets | UND | 166.3 | 161.8 | 231.7 | 471.7 | 183.1 |
| 47.5 | 51.0 | 66.2 | | 78.0 | 88.4 | 38.9 | 75.7 | 83.6 | 59.0 |
| 14.8 | 17.0 | 19.2 | | 18.7 | 19.5 | 14.2 | 31.0 | 21.6 | 18.3 |
| 6.9 | 7.2 | 7.4 | Sales/Total Assets | 5.5 | 6.8 | 6.2 | 6.6 | 7.1 | 8.0 |
| 4.7 | 5.1 | 5.0 | | 2.3 | 3.9 | 3.9 | 4.4 | 4.8 | 5.5 |
| 3.0 | 3.1 | 3.3 | | 1.2 | 2.5 | 2.3 | 3.0 | 3.2 | 4.0 |
| .2 | .2 | .2 | % Depr., Dep., Amort./Sales | | .2 | .3 | .1 | .1 | .2 |
| (371) .5 | (399) .5 | (427) .4 | | | (16) .7 | (27) .7 | (38) .5 | (94) .5 | (246) .4 |
| 1.0 | .9 | .9 | | | 2.5 | 1.7 | .8 | .9 | .4 |
| .6 | .6 | .7 | % Officers', Directors' Owners' Comp/Sales | | 2.3 | .8 | .8 | .8 | .5 |
| (169) 1.4 | (190) 1.1 | (210) 1.3 | | | (12) 2.9 | (23) 2.7 | (29) 2.0 | (70) 1.2 | (75) 1.0 |
| 3.2 | 2.6 | 2.7 | | | 6.3 | 5.0 | 3.5 | 2.7 | 2.2 |
| 49142349M | 63463342M | 67867483M | Net Sales ($) | 8136M | 52474M | 151420M | 392784M | 2091697M | 65170972M |
| 10066495M | 11282507M | 12321834M | Total Assets ($) | 4907M | 19544M | 47357M | 110638M | 516184M | 11623204M |

© RMA 2012     M = $ thousand     MM = $ million
See Pages 9 through 22 for Explanation of Ratios and Data

## Current Data Sorted by Assets / Comparative Historical Data

| | 0-500M | 500M-2MM | 2-10MM | 10-50MM | 50-100MM | 100-250MM | | 4/1/07-3/31/08 ALL | 4/1/08-3/31/09 ALL |
|---|---|---|---|---|---|---|---|---|---|
| **Type of Statement** | | | | | | | | | |
| Unqualified | | | 5 | 15 | 7 | 1 | | 30 | 45 |
| Reviewed | 1 | | 18 | 12 | | | | 20 | 30 |
| Compiled | | 4 | 10 | 3 | | | | 12 | 18 |
| Tax Returns | | 8 | 6 | 2 | | | | 11 | 20 |
| Other | 6 | 6 | 23 | 29 | 7 | 6 | | 53 | 50 |
| | | 32 (4/1-9/30/11) | | 137 (10/1/11-3/31/12) | | | | | |
| NUMBER OF STATEMENTS | 7 | 18 | 62 | 61 | 14 | 7 | | 126 | 163 |
| | % | % | % | % | % | % | | % | % |
| **ASSETS** | | | | | | | | | |
| Cash & Equivalents | | 11.0 | 7.5 | 4.2 | 3.0 | | | 6.7 | 7.0 |
| Trade Receivables (net) | | 42.8 | 37.5 | 30.7 | 31.5 | | | 34.5 | 32.3 |
| Inventory | | 21.1 | 30.1 | 33.2 | 35.3 | | | 30.4 | 32.1 |
| All Other Current | | 2.2 | 3.0 | 3.0 | 4.2 | | | 2.9 | 3.1 |
| Total Current | | 77.0 | 78.1 | 71.0 | 74.0 | | | 74.6 | 74.5 |
| Fixed Assets (net) | | 11.9 | 13.7 | 17.3 | 19.1 | | | 17.9 | 16.4 |
| Intangibles (net) | | 7.6 | 2.5 | 7.5 | 2.5 | | | 2.1 | 2.6 |
| All Other Non-Current | | 3.4 | 5.7 | 4.2 | 4.4 | | | 5.4 | 6.5 |
| Total | | 100.0 | 100.0 | 100.0 | 100.0 | | | 100.0 | 100.0 |
| **LIABILITIES** | | | | | | | | | |
| Notes Payable-Short Term | | 10.3 | 18.5 | 18.0 | 21.2 | | | 20.6 | 21.5 |
| Cur. Mat.-L.T.D. | | 3.3 | 2.6 | 4.2 | 1.7 | | | 2.1 | 2.4 |
| Trade Payables | | 47.5 | 27.8 | 16.8 | 21.0 | | | 24.4 | 22.8 |
| Income Taxes Payable | | .0 | .0 | .2 | .2 | | | .1 | .1 |
| All Other Current | | 4.0 | 7.6 | 8.6 | 6.2 | | | 8.7 | 7.9 |
| Total Current | | 65.1 | 56.5 | 47.7 | 50.4 | | | 56.0 | 54.7 |
| Long-Term Debt | | 9.2 | 5.7 | 10.5 | 13.4 | | | 12.9 | 10.1 |
| Deferred Taxes | | .0 | .2 | .1 | .5 | | | .2 | .3 |
| All Other Non-Current | | 3.3 | 5.8 | 8.0 | 4.0 | | | 8.4 | 4.5 |
| Net Worth | | 22.4 | 31.7 | 33.7 | 31.7 | | | 22.5 | 30.4 |
| Total Liabilities & Net Worth | | 100.0 | 100.0 | 100.0 | 100.0 | | | 100.0 | 100.0 |
| **INCOME DATA** | | | | | | | | | |
| Net Sales | | 100.0 | 100.0 | 100.0 | 100.0 | | | 100.0 | 100.0 |
| Gross Profit | | 24.0 | 15.9 | 16.0 | 13.4 | | | 19.5 | 17.2 |
| Operating Expenses | | 20.7 | 13.6 | 13.7 | 11.2 | | | 16.3 | 14.6 |
| Operating Profit | | 3.2 | 2.4 | 2.3 | 2.2 | | | 3.2 | 2.6 |
| All Other Expenses (net) | | .0 | .3 | .5 | .6 | | | .8 | .5 |
| Profit Before Taxes | | 3.2 | 2.0 | 1.8 | 1.6 | | | 2.4 | 2.2 |
| **RATIOS** | | | | | | | | | |
| Current | | 2.1 | 2.3 | 2.1 | 2.2 | | | 2.1 | 1.8 |
| | | 1.2 | 1.3 | 1.4 | 1.4 | | | 1.3 | 1.3 |
| | | 1.1 | 1.0 | 1.2 | 1.1 | | | 1.0 | 1.1 |
| Quick | | 1.6 | 1.2 | 1.2 | 1.2 | | | 1.2 | 1.1 |
| | | .9 | .7 | .7 | .6 | | | .7 | .6 |
| | | .6 | .5 | .4 | .4 | | | .4 | .4 |
| Sales/Receivables | | 11  33.5 | 21  17.6 | 19  18.9 | 20  18.4 | | | 19  18.8 | 17  21.5 |
| | | 20  18.5 | 30  12.0 | 26  13.8 | 26  14.0 | | | 27  13.6 | 27  13.7 |
| | | 35  10.5 | 37  9.9 | 38  9.7 | 38  9.5 | | | 40  9.1 | 36  10.2 |
| Cost of Sales/Inventory | | 5  69.8 | 16  23.5 | 20  18.7 | 18  20.3 | | | 16  22.4 | 18  20.6 |
| | | 15  25.1 | 27  13.3 | 33  11.1 | 37  9.9 | | | 29  12.5 | 29  12.4 |
| | | 21  17.0 | 42  8.6 | 74  4.9 | 68  5.4 | | | 53  6.9 | 53  6.9 |
| Cost of Sales/Payables | | 14  26.4 | 16  23.3 | 10  35.6 | 15  24.9 | | | 14  25.2 | 13  29.0 |
| | | 35  10.4 | 23  15.6 | 18  20.4 | 19  19.4 | | | 22  16.5 | 20  18.0 |
| | | 52  7.0 | 36  10.1 | 28  13.1 | 28  13.0 | | | 37  9.8 | 30  12.1 |
| Sales/Working Capital | | 25.1 | 8.8 | 9.4 | 8.4 | | | 11.3 | 11.7 |
| | | 42.2 | 24.3 | 17.1 | 15.2 | | | 27.1 | 25.3 |
| | | 152.1 | 470.8 | 48.9 | 228.3 | | | 106.6 | 112.2 |
| EBIT/Interest | | 45.1 | 10.8 | 11.2 | 7.8 | | | 7.2 | 7.9 |
| | (15) 3.6 | (56) 2.9 | (58) 3.7 | 2.9 | | | | (118) 2.7 | (155) 2.8 |
| | | .9 | 1.7 | 1.5 | 1.8 | | | 1.3 | 1.4 |
| Net Profit + Depr., Dep., Amort./Cur. Mat. L/T/D | | | | 8.8 | | | | 10.7 | 5.3 |
| | | | (18) 2.3 | | | | | (32) 3.6 | (45) 2.2 |
| | | | | .4 | | | | 1.3 | 1.0 |
| Fixed/Worth | | .0 | .1 | .1 | .3 | | | .1 | .1 |
| | | .2 | .2 | .4 | .4 | | | .5 | .4 |
| | | -11.0 | 1.0 | 1.7 | 1.1 | | | 1.5 | 1.2 |
| Debt/Worth | | .9 | .8 | 1.5 | 1.1 | | | 1.5 | 1.5 |
| | | 9.4 | 3.0 | 3.2 | 2.5 | | | 3.2 | 3.0 |
| | | -15.1 | 8.0 | 8.0 | 8.1 | | | 7.0 | 7.1 |
| % Profit Before Taxes/Tangible Net Worth | | 62.2 | 42.0 | 35.1 | 26.8 | | | 50.1 | 50.3 |
| | (12) 36.1 | (56) 28.7 | (53) 20.2 | (13) 16.8 | | | | (109) 22.1 | (149) 18.1 |
| | | 9.0 | 9.0 | 4.7 | 9.6 | | | 8.6 | 7.1 |
| % Profit Before Taxes/Total Assets | | 26.9 | 10.6 | 9.2 | 7.5 | | | 12.2 | 11.2 |
| | | 4.8 | 4.8 | 4.2 | 3.3 | | | 4.1 | 4.3 |
| | | .2 | 2.0 | 1.6 | 1.4 | | | 1.5 | 1.4 |
| Sales/Net Fixed Assets | | UND | 255.8 | 259.8 | 93.4 | | | 146.2 | 252.4 |
| | | 417.4 | 98.0 | 34.6 | 41.1 | | | 35.4 | 45.3 |
| | | 24.8 | 24.7 | 10.5 | 6.5 | | | 14.7 | 16.9 |
| Sales/Total Assets | | 10.1 | 6.6 | 5.9 | 7.4 | | | 5.7 | 6.3 |
| | | 8.2 | 4.5 | 3.7 | 3.2 | | | 4.1 | 4.6 |
| | | 4.3 | 3.2 | 2.0 | 2.2 | | | 2.6 | 2.4 |
| % Depr., Dep., Amort./Sales | | .1 | .1 | .1 | .2 | | | .3 | .2 |
| | (10) .6 | (48) .3 | (52) .6 | (13) .5 | | | | (97) .5 | (139) .5 |
| | | 1.4 | .9 | 1.4 | 1.6 | | | 1.1 | .9 |
| % Officers', Directors' Owners' Comp/Sales | | | .6 | .5 | | | | 1.1 | .8 |
| | | (25) .9 | (15) 1.0 | | | | | (39) 1.8 | (52) 1.6 |
| | | | 2.2 | 2.3 | | | | 3.2 | 2.4 |
| Net Sales ($) | 19927M | 188755M | 1614604M | 6069290M | 4716940M | 4334753M | | 13864858M | 18021918M |
| Total Assets ($) | 2461M | 24216M | 325046M | 1313501M | 1042534M | 942445M | | 3550459M | 3751837M |

M = $ thousand    MM = $ million
See Pages 9 through 22 for Explanation of Ratios and Data

## Comparative Historical Data                    Current Data Sorted by Sales

| | | | Type of Statement | 0-1MM | 1-3MM | 3-5MM | 5-10MM | 10-25MM | 25MM & OVER |
|---|---|---|---|---|---|---|---|---|---|
| 29 | 33 | 28 | Unqualified | | | | 1 | 2 | 25 |
| 27 | 25 | 31 | Reviewed | | 1 | | 3 | 10 | 17 |
| 21 | 15 | 17 | Compiled | 1 | 1 | | 3 | 4 | 8 |
| 19 | 23 | 16 | Tax Returns | 1 | 2 | | 3 | 9 | 2 |
| 59 | 55 | 77 | Other | 4 | 2 | | 8 | 10 | 53 |
| 4/1/09-3/31/10 ALL | 4/1/10-3/31/11 ALL | 4/1/11-3/31/12 ALL | | 32 (4/1-9/30/11) | | | 137 (10/1/11-3/31/12) | | |
| 155 | 151 | 169 | **NUMBER OF STATEMENTS** | | 5 | 6 | 18 | 35 | 105 |
| % | % | % | **ASSETS** | % | % | % | % | % | % |
| 6.9 | 7.1 | 6.4 | Cash & Equivalents | | | | 17.9 | 7.6 | 3.5 |
| 33.4 | 32.2 | 34.5 | Trade Receivables (net) | | | | 32.5 | 36.6 | 33.9 |
| 30.5 | 32.6 | 30.2 | Inventory | | | | 23.0 | 24.4 | 34.7 |
| 2.9 | 2.5 | 2.9 | All Other Current | | | | 2.8 | 3.6 | 2.9 |
| 73.7 | 74.5 | 74.0 | Total Current | | | | 76.1 | 72.3 | 75.0 |
| 17.1 | 16.0 | 16.3 | Fixed Assets (net) | | | | 16.3 | 17.0 | 15.4 |
| 4.7 | 5.7 | 5.1 | Intangibles (net) | | | | 3.8 | 4.6 | 5.1 |
| 4.5 | 3.8 | 4.6 | All Other Non-Current | | | | 3.7 | 6.1 | 4.4 |
| 100.0 | 100.0 | 100.0 | Total | | | | 100.0 | 100.0 | 100.0 |
| | | | **LIABILITIES** | | | | | | |
| 17.1 | 18.2 | 17.2 | Notes Payable-Short Term | | | | 7.1 | 18.3 | 19.1 |
| 2.3 | 2.6 | 3.0 | Cur. Mat.-L.T.D. | | | | .9 | 5.7 | 2.4 |
| 22.2 | 25.2 | 26.3 | Trade Payables | | | | 22.3 | 35.1 | 21.5 |
| .2 | .1 | .1 | Income Taxes Payable | | | | .1 | .1 | .1 |
| 7.6 | 6.8 | 7.2 | All Other Current | | | | 4.4 | 7.0 | 8.3 |
| 49.4 | 52.8 | 53.9 | Total Current | | | | 34.8 | 66.2 | 51.5 |
| 12.6 | 10.3 | 9.2 | Long-Term Debt | | | | 7.4 | 6.7 | 10.3 |
| .2 | .2 | .2 | Deferred Taxes | | | | .0 | .2 | .2 |
| 4.5 | 5.8 | 5.8 | All Other Non-Current | | | | 5.9 | 7.4 | 5.8 |
| 33.3 | 30.8 | 30.9 | Net Worth | | | | 51.8 | 19.6 | 32.2 |
| 100.0 | 100.0 | 100.0 | Total Liabilities & Net Worth | | | | 100.0 | 100.0 | 100.0 |
| | | | **INCOME DATA** | | | | | | |
| 100.0 | 100.0 | 100.0 | Net Sales | | | | 100.0 | 100.0 | 100.0 |
| 18.3 | 18.3 | 16.7 | Gross Profit | | | | 24.5 | 16.6 | 14.3 |
| 15.5 | 16.1 | 14.3 | Operating Expenses | | | | 19.5 | 15.5 | 12.1 |
| 2.8 | 2.1 | 2.4 | Operating Profit | | | | 5.1 | 1.1 | 2.2 |
| .6 | .3 | .5 | All Other Expenses (net) | | | | .6 | .0 | .5 |
| 2.2 | 1.8 | 2.0 | Profit Before Taxes | | | | 4.5 | 1.0 | 1.7 |
| | | | **RATIOS** | | | | | | |
| 2.1 | 2.0 | 2.2 | | | | | 4.2 | 1.6 | 2.1 |
| 1.4 | 1.4 | 1.4 | Current | | | | 2.5 | 1.2 | 1.4 |
| 1.2 | 1.1 | 1.1 | | | | | 1.5 | .9 | 1.1 |
| 1.2 | 1.2 | 1.2 | | | | | 3.1 | 1.0 | 1.1 |
| .7 | .7 | .7 | Quick | | | | 1.7 | .6 | .7 |
| .5 | .4 | .5 | | | | | .8 | .4 | .5 |
| 18  19.8 | 17  21.1 | 18  19.9 | | | | | 23  16.2 | 18  20.7 | 20  18.5 |
| 27  13.4 | 27  13.7 | 26  13.8 | Sales/Receivables | | | | 31  11.7 | 26  14.1 | 26  14.1 |
| 36  10.1 | 36  10.2 | 36  10.0 | | | | | 37  9.8 | 33  11.0 | 37  9.9 |
| 19  18.8 | 19  19.1 | 16  23.4 | | | | | 6  56.8 | 11  34.2 | 19  18.9 |
| 29  12.4 | 31  11.6 | 27  13.7 | Cost of Sales/Inventory | | | | 23  16.1 | 20  18.6 | 30  12.2 |
| 54  6.8 | 64  5.7 | 46  8.0 | | | | | 60  6.1 | 38  9.6 | 53  6.9 |
| 11  31.9 | 12  30.6 | 13  28.8 | | | | | 8  46.5 | 17  21.9 | 12  30.1 |
| 21  17.7 | 20  18.0 | 21  17.6 | Cost of Sales/Payables | | | | 29  12.7 | 30  12.2 | 19  19.4 |
| 30  12.0 | 34  10.6 | 34  10.8 | | | | | 48  7.6 | 38  9.7 | 27  13.4 |
| 9.6 | 9.4 | 9.5 | | | | | 4.3 | 16.5 | 10.7 |
| 19.1 | 21.4 | 20.6 | Sales/Working Capital | | | | 8.2 | 34.9 | 20.3 |
| 65.0 | 63.2 | 112.4 | | | | | 29.8 | -103.5 | 57.7 |
| 8.4 | 9.3 | 9.7 | | | | | 8.1 | 11.1 | 9.7 |
| (144)  3.7 | (140)  3.2 | (157)  3.1 | EBIT/Interest | | | | (13)  2.7 | (32)  2.1 | (101)  3.5 |
| 1.8 | 1.9 | 1.6 | | | | | 1.4 | .8 | 1.8 |
| 8.2 | 6.7 | 7.2 | Net Profit + Depr., Dep., | | | | | | 7.8 |
| (35)  2.6 | (37)  2.3 | (37)  2.2 | Amort./Cur. Mat. L/T/D | | | | | | (30)  4.2 |
| 1.7 | 1.1 | .9 | | | | | | | .9 |
| .1 | .1 | .1 | | | | | .1 | .0 | .1 |
| .5 | .5 | .4 | Fixed/Worth | | | | .3 | .2 | .4 |
| 1.6 | 2.0 | 1.5 | | | | | 1.1 | 5.9 | 1.2 |
| 1.0 | 1.5 | 1.2 | | | | | .3 | 1.8 | 1.3 |
| 2.9 | 3.2 | 3.2 | Debt/Worth | | | | .6 | 4.4 | 3.2 |
| 5.7 | 9.9 | 9.0 | | | | | 5.5 | 37.1 | 8.0 |
| 52.0 | 36.6 | 36.9 | % Profit Before Taxes/Tangible | | | | 37.0 | 46.1 | 36.5 |
| (138)  22.1 | (127)  23.4 | (145)  19.1 | Net Worth | | | (16)  16.3 | | (29)  31.3 | (95)  18.8 |
| 6.5 | 10.3 | 8.2 | | | | | 6.8 | 6.3 | 8.5 |
| 12.7 | 10.8 | 10.2 | % Profit Before Taxes/Total | | | | 16.3 | 9.0 | 10.1 |
| 6.0 | 4.7 | 4.2 | Assets | | | | 5.6 | 3.7 | 4.2 |
| 1.9 | 1.9 | 1.5 | | | | | 3.0 | .4 | 1.8 |
| 184.7 | 280.0 | 295.7 | | | | | 191.7 | 618.0 | 250.8 |
| 34.3 | 42.9 | 53.9 | Sales/Net Fixed Assets | | | | 44.4 | 116.4 | 53.9 |
| 15.1 | 16.2 | 13.4 | | | | | 8.1 | 13.2 | 14.0 |
| 6.3 | 5.8 | 6.8 | | | | | 4.8 | 9.0 | 6.4 |
| 4.2 | 3.9 | 4.3 | Sales/Total Assets | | | | 3.3 | 5.2 | 4.5 |
| 2.4 | 2.5 | 2.6 | | | | | 2.7 | 2.6 | 2.5 |
| .2 | .2 | .1 | | | | | .1 | .1 | .1 |
| (126)  .6 | (123)  .5 | (133)  .5 | % Depr., Dep., Amort./Sales | | | (13)  .8 | | (24)  .5 | (90)  .4 |
| 1.1 | 1.1 | 1.3 | | | | | 1.7 | 2.1 | 1.1 |
| 1.2 | .6 | .6 | % Officers', Directors' | | | | | .5 | .7 |
| (48)  1.9 | (54)  1.6 | (52)  1.1 | Owners' Comp/Sales | | | | | (15)  .8 | (27)  1.0 |
| 2.9 | 3.3 | 2.9 | | | | | | 2.4 | 2.6 |
| 16552126M | 14610582M | 16944269M | Net Sales ($) | | 8662M | 25564M | 129801M | 640655M | 16139587M |
| 3614234M | 3506782M | 3650203M | Total Assets ($) | | 2676M | 4351M | 40041M | 205128M | 3398007M |

Note: For the three smallest current-data columns (0-1MM, 1-3MM, 3-5MM) the Assets, Liabilities, Income Data and upper Ratio figures are marked **DATA NOT AVAILABLE**.

M = $ thousand    MM = $ million
See Pages 9 through 22 for Explanation of Ratios and Data

## Current Data Sorted by Assets | Comparative Historical Data

| 0-500M | 500M-2MM | 2-10MM | 10-50MM | 50-100MM | 100-250MM | Type of Statement | 4/1/07-3/31/08 ALL | 4/1/08-3/31/09 ALL |
|---|---|---|---|---|---|---|---|---|
|  | 1 | 3 | 8 |  | 5 | Unqualified | 17 | 16 |
|  |  | 21 | 12 |  |  | Reviewed | 27 | 32 |
|  | 3 | 3 | 3 | 1 |  | Compiled | 12 | 14 |
| 5 | 5 | 3 | 3 |  |  | Tax Returns | 7 | 13 |
| 1 | 4 | 9 | 14 | 1 | 1 | Other | 31 | 24 |
|  | 21 (4/1-9/30/11) |  | 85 (10/1/11-3/31/12) |  |  |  |  |  |
| 6 | 13 | 39 | 40 | 2 | 6 | NUMBER OF STATEMENTS | 94 | 99 |
| % | % | % | % | % | % | ASSETS | % | % |
|  | 16.7 | 8.6 | 8.2 |  |  | Cash & Equivalents | 8.1 | 12.3 |
|  | 33.8 | 34.6 | 36.8 |  |  | Trade Receivables (net) | 37.6 | 35.3 |
|  | 14.0 | 21.2 | 24.6 |  |  | Inventory | 20.8 | 21.0 |
|  | 2.9 | 1.9 | 2.8 |  |  | All Other Current | 2.0 | 2.7 |
|  | 67.3 | 66.3 | 72.4 |  |  | Total Current | 68.5 | 71.3 |
|  | 27.3 | 26.0 | 14.5 |  |  | Fixed Assets (net) | 22.2 | 20.6 |
|  | 1.9 | 2.1 | 8.4 |  |  | Intangibles (net) | 3.6 | 3.8 |
|  | 3.5 | 5.7 | 4.7 |  |  | All Other Non-Current | 5.7 | 4.3 |
|  | 100.0 | 100.0 | 100.0 |  |  | Total | 100.0 | 100.0 |
|  |  |  |  |  |  | **LIABILITIES** |  |  |
|  | 9.1 | 12.1 | 12.8 |  |  | Notes Payable-Short Term | 11.0 | 16.1 |
|  | 1.2 | 4.1 | 1.8 |  |  | Cur. Mat.-L.T.D. | 3.5 | 2.3 |
|  | 29.4 | 29.5 | 38.2 |  |  | Trade Payables | 37.8 | 29.7 |
|  | .1 | .1 | .1 |  |  | Income Taxes Payable | .1 | .1 |
|  | 5.7 | 9.0 | 6.9 |  |  | All Other Current | 9.1 | 9.0 |
|  | 45.5 | 54.8 | 59.9 |  |  | Total Current | 61.5 | 57.2 |
|  | 19.2 | 9.7 | 8.7 |  |  | Long-Term Debt | 11.4 | 10.0 |
|  | .6 | .7 | .3 |  |  | Deferred Taxes | .5 | .3 |
|  | 3.6 | 7.0 | 2.8 |  |  | All Other Non-Current | 3.5 | 4.1 |
|  | 31.1 | 27.8 | 28.2 |  |  | Net Worth | 23.0 | 28.4 |
|  | 100.0 | 100.0 | 100.0 |  |  | Total Liabilities & Net Worth | 100.0 | 100.0 |
|  |  |  |  |  |  | **INCOME DATA** |  |  |
|  | 100.0 | 100.0 | 100.0 |  |  | Net Sales | 100.0 | 100.0 |
|  | 20.2 | 20.8 | 16.2 |  |  | Gross Profit | 15.9 | 17.1 |
|  | 14.5 | 19.7 | 14.1 |  |  | Operating Expenses | 14.3 | 15.7 |
|  | 5.7 | 1.1 | 2.1 |  |  | Operating Profit | 1.6 | 1.4 |
|  | 3.3 | .2 | .3 |  |  | All Other Expenses (net) | .3 | .4 |
|  | 2.4 | .9 | 1.8 |  |  | Profit Before Taxes | 1.2 | 1.0 |
|  |  |  |  |  |  | **RATIOS** |  |  |
|  | 3.3 | 1.6 | 1.6 |  |  | Current | 1.5 | 1.9 |
|  | 1.2 | 1.4 | 1.2 |  |  |  | 1.1 | 1.3 |
|  | 1.0 | .9 | 1.0 |  |  |  | .9 | 1.0 |
|  | 3.0 | 1.2 | .9 |  |  | Quick | 1.0 | 1.3 |
|  | 1.0 | .8 | .8 |  |  |  | .7 | .8 |
|  | .4 | .5 | .6 |  |  |  | .5 | .6 |
|  | 1 669.4 | 18 20.8 | 22 16.5 |  |  | Sales/Receivables | 18 19.9 | 16 22.6 |
|  | 15 23.6 | 27 13.5 | 27 13.6 |  |  |  | 27 13.7 | 22 16.3 |
|  | 29 12.6 | 33 11.1 | 32 11.5 |  |  |  | 37 9.8 | 30 12.0 |
|  | 0 UND | 11 32.1 | 8 45.8 |  |  | Cost of Sales/Inventory | 7 48.8 | 8 46.0 |
|  | 9 42.0 | 19 19.5 | 18 19.8 |  |  |  | 16 22.6 | 15 23.8 |
|  | 26 14.3 | 30 12.0 | 35 10.5 |  |  |  | 34 10.6 | 28 13.0 |
|  | 0 UND | 14 25.2 | 20 18.4 |  |  | Cost of Sales/Payables | 21 17.8 | 14 26.9 |
|  | 19 18.9 | 24 15.2 | 31 11.9 |  |  |  | 29 12.6 | 19 19.6 |
|  | 27 13.6 | 34 10.6 | 49 7.5 |  |  |  | 44 8.4 | 29 12.7 |
|  | 19.8 | 17.9 | 16.4 |  |  | Sales/Working Capital | 17.5 | 13.8 |
|  | 42.4 | 27.6 | 34.7 |  |  |  | 121.6 | 39.0 |
|  | 461.6 | -67.3 | -216.7 |  |  |  | -90.3 | 966.6 |
|  |  | 13.5 | 23.5 |  |  | EBIT/Interest | 8.8 | 12.5 |
|  |  | (33) 3.1 | (39) 5.0 |  |  |  | (85) 3.2 | (88) 4.9 |
|  |  | .9 | 2.6 |  |  |  | 1.3 | 1.6 |
|  |  |  | 4.8 |  |  | Net Profit + Depr., Dep., | 3.6 | 3.6 |
|  |  | (15) 3.3 |  |  |  | Amort./Cur. Mat. L/T/D | (23) 2.0 | (19) 2.4 |
|  |  |  | 1.1 |  |  |  | .7 | 1.4 |
|  | .1 | .2 | .2 |  |  | Fixed/Worth | .2 | .1 |
|  | .4 | .9 | .5 |  |  |  | 1.0 | .6 |
|  | NM | 3.0 | 2.5 |  |  |  | 5.0 | 2.0 |
|  | .7 | 1.6 | 1.9 |  |  | Debt/Worth | 1.7 | 1.0 |
|  | 1.8 | 2.9 | 3.6 |  |  |  | 4.6 | 2.4 |
|  | NM | 12.1 | 14.8 |  |  |  | 13.0 | 6.4 |
|  | 25.0 | 44.2 | 58.4 |  |  | % Profit Before Taxes/Tangible | 49.2 | 44.8 |
|  | (10) 12.4 | (31) 10.0 | (35) 31.8 |  |  | Net Worth | (80) 22.0 | (85) 19.7 |
|  | 1.2 | -.7 | 4.3 |  |  |  | 6.0 | 7.0 |
|  | 7.7 | 11.1 | 11.8 |  |  | % Profit Before Taxes/Total | 10.2 | 12.2 |
|  | 4.9 | 3.8 | 4.1 |  |  | Assets | 4.2 | 6.3 |
|  | .5 | -.5 | 2.0 |  |  |  | .7 | 1.9 |
|  | 712.5 | 288.3 | 131.4 |  |  | Sales/Net Fixed Assets | 222.4 | 270.8 |
|  | 28.9 | 20.2 | 43.0 |  |  |  | 30.0 | 31.7 |
|  | 14.9 | 7.8 | 20.1 |  |  |  | 9.7 | 12.4 |
|  | 12.5 | 6.7 | 7.0 |  |  | Sales/Total Assets | 6.4 | 7.2 |
|  | 7.4 | 4.2 | 5.2 |  |  |  | 4.7 | 5.3 |
|  | 2.9 | 3.3 | 3.2 |  |  |  | 2.7 | 3.4 |
|  | .1 | .3 | .2 |  |  | % Depr., Dep., Amort./Sales | .3 | .2 |
|  | (10) .5 | (34) 1.1 | (38) .5 |  |  |  | (79) .8 | (80) .6 |
|  | 2.7 | 2.3 | 1.5 |  |  |  | 1.6 | 1.7 |
|  |  | .6 | .2 |  |  | % Officers', Directors', | .7 | 1.1 |
|  |  | (17) 1.5 | (11) 1.7 |  |  | Owners' Comp/Sales | (32) 1.2 | (47) 1.7 |
|  |  | 2.2 | 2.7 |  |  |  | 1.6 | 3.0 |
| 13960M | 138066M | 991140M | 4881003M | 600580M | 5222062M | Net Sales ($) | 11461123M | 9245984M |
| 1065M | 17400M | 201156M | 905644M | 151323M | 1020153M | Total Assets ($) | 2643801M | 2162218M |

M = $ thousand   MM = $ million
See Pages 9 through 22 for Explanation of Ratios and Data

## Comparative Historical Data / Current Data Sorted by Sales

| 4/1/09-3/31/10 ALL | 4/1/10-3/31/11 ALL | 4/1/11-3/31/12 ALL | Type of Statement | 0-1MM | 1-3MM | 3-5MM | 5-10MM | 10-25MM | 25MM & OVER |
|---|---|---|---|---|---|---|---|---|---|
| 24 | 20 | 17 | Unqualified | | | | 1 | | 16 |
| 23 | 21 | 33 | Reviewed | | | | 2 | 14 | 17 |
| 15 | 12 | 10 | Compiled | | | | 1 | 4 | 5 |
| 7 | 10 | 16 | Tax Returns | 2 | | | 2 | 6 | 4 |
| 30 | 30 | 30 | Other | 2 | 1 | 6 | | 5 | 18 |
| | | | | 21 (4/1-9/30/11) | | | 85 (10/1/11-3/31/12) | | |
| 99 | 93 | 106 | NUMBER OF STATEMENTS | 4 | 1 | 6 | 6 | 29 | 60 |
| % | % | % | ASSETS | % | % | % | % | % | % |
| 9.0 | 10.0 | 11.6 | Cash & Equivalents | | | | | 13.2 | 8.7 |
| 35.0 | 34.0 | 33.8 | Trade Receivables (net) | | | | | 36.8 | 37.2 |
| 24.0 | 23.8 | 22.1 | Inventory | | | | | 17.1 | 22.3 |
| 3.1 | 3.5 | 2.4 | All Other Current | | | | | 2.0 | 2.9 |
| 71.1 | 71.3 | 69.9 | Total Current | | | | | 69.2 | 71.1 |
| 20.3 | 20.9 | 21.0 | Fixed Assets (net) | | | | | 25.6 | 17.9 |
| 3.0 | 3.5 | 4.3 | Intangibles (net) | | | | | .9 | 6.4 |
| 5.6 | 4.3 | 4.7 | All Other Non-Current | | | | | 4.3 | 4.6 |
| 100.0 | 100.0 | 100.0 | Total | | | | | 100.0 | 100.0 |
| | | | LIABILITIES | | | | | | |
| 15.7 | 15.4 | 12.8 | Notes Payable-Short Term | | | | | 8.5 | 12.2 |
| 2.7 | 3.7 | 2.8 | Cur. Mat.-L.T.D. | | | | | 3.2 | 2.2 |
| 30.2 | 31.0 | 32.6 | Trade Payables | | | | | 33.3 | 34.6 |
| .2 | .1 | .1 | Income Taxes Payable | | | | | .1 | .1 |
| 8.5 | 10.5 | 8.1 | All Other Current | | | | | 5.6 | 9.3 |
| 57.3 | 60.6 | 56.4 | Total Current | | | | | 50.8 | 58.4 |
| 10.9 | 11.8 | 11.0 | Long-Term Debt | | | | | 8.9 | 9.8 |
| .3 | .3 | .5 | Deferred Taxes | | | | | .5 | .4 |
| 5.1 | 4.9 | 5.5 | All Other Non-Current | | | | | 8.5 | 2.6 |
| 26.4 | 22.5 | 26.6 | Net Worth | | | | | 31.2 | 28.8 |
| 100.0 | 100.0 | 100.0 | Total Liabilities & Net Worth | | | | | 100.0 | 100.0 |
| | | | INCOME DATA | | | | | | |
| 100.0 | 100.0 | 100.0 | Net Sales | | | | | 100.0 | 100.0 |
| 19.8 | 19.7 | 19.1 | Gross Profit | | | | | 20.7 | 15.8 |
| 16.8 | 16.7 | 16.8 | Operating Expenses | | | | | 18.4 | 14.1 |
| 3.0 | 3.0 | 2.4 | Operating Profit | | | | | 2.3 | 1.7 |
| .5 | .4 | .6 | All Other Expenses (net) | | | | | .0 | .2 |
| 2.6 | 2.6 | 1.7 | Profit Before Taxes | | | | | 2.3 | 1.5 |
| | | | RATIOS | | | | | | |
| 1.7 | 1.7 | 1.6 | Current | | | | | 2.3 | 1.5 |
| 1.3 | 1.3 | 1.3 | | | | | | 1.5 | 1.2 |
| 1.1 | 1.0 | 1.0 | | | | | | 1.0 | 1.0 |
| 1.1 | 1.1 | 1.1 | Quick | | | | | 1.5 | 1.0 |
| .8 | .8 | .8 | | | | | | 1.1 | .8 |
| .6 | .5 | .5 | | | | | | .7 | .6 |
| 18  20.3 | 19  19.6 | 18  20.3 | Sales/Receivables | | | | | 15  23.6 | 20  18.7 |
| 27  13.6 | 25  14.6 | 26  14.3 | | | | | | 27  13.7 | 26  14.1 |
| 37  9.9 | 33  11.2 | 31  11.6 | | | | | | 34  10.7 | 31  11.9 |
| 9  41.9 | 9  39.4 | 8  45.5 | Cost of Sales/Inventory | | | | | 7  49.0 | 7  52.9 |
| 15  23.7 | 21  17.7 | 18  20.6 | | | | | | 14  26.8 | 17  21.7 |
| 48  7.6 | 35  10.3 | 30  12.0 | | | | | | 23  15.9 | 28  12.9 |
| 14  26.6 | 15  23.6 | 16  23.4 | Cost of Sales/Payables | | | | | 13  27.9 | 16  22.4 |
| 25  14.7 | 25  14.7 | 25  14.5 | | | | | | 21  17.1 | 27  13.6 |
| 37  9.9 | 35  10.4 | 35  10.3 | | | | | | 34  10.7 | 36  10.0 |
| 12.6 | 15.3 | 17.2 | Sales/Working Capital | | | | | 14.0 | 18.3 |
| 29.7 | 34.8 | 35.1 | | | | | | 24.4 | 48.9 |
| 236.7 | -353.9 | -451.3 | | | | | | 461.6 | -309.6 |
| 15.0 | 22.7 | 18.8 | EBIT/Interest | | | | | 18.4 | 21.3 |
| (89) 6.0 | (80) 5.6 | (93) 5.0 | | | | | | (23) 6.0 | (57) 6.9 |
| 2.2 | 1.5 | 1.8 | | | | | | .6 | 2.1 |
| 8.0 | 5.0 | 3.8 | Net Profit + Depr., Dep., Amort./Cur. Mat. L/T/D | | | | | | 3.9 |
| (26) 3.5 | (25) 3.0 | (27) 2.7 | | | | | | | (19) 3.3 |
| 2.0 | 1.6 | 1.1 | | | | | | | 1.1 |
| .0 | .1 | .2 | Fixed/Worth | | | | | .1 | .2 |
| .7 | .8 | .7 | | | | | | .7 | .5 |
| 2.1 | 1.9 | 2.6 | | | | | | 2.3 | 2.1 |
| 1.0 | 1.2 | 1.3 | Debt/Worth | | | | | .7 | 1.8 |
| 2.7 | 2.7 | 3.0 | | | | | | 2.3 | 3.3 |
| 6.4 | 6.8 | 16.4 | | | | | | 15.4 | 8.3 |
| 50.6 | 48.6 | 44.2 | % Profit Before Taxes/Tangible Net Worth | | | | | 47.7 | 43.0 |
| (85) 24.5 | (80) 21.2 | (87) 16.7 | | | | | | (26) 18.7 | (53) 18.8 |
| 8.5 | 8.4 | 3.2 | | | | | | -.2 | 4.2 |
| 13.8 | 14.9 | 10.6 | % Profit Before Taxes/Total Assets | | | | | 13.6 | 9.8 |
| 7.4 | 7.0 | 4.5 | | | | | | 5.1 | 4.1 |
| 1.9 | 1.4 | 1.1 | | | | | | -.2 | 1.4 |
| 377.3 | 225.9 | 293.8 | Sales/Net Fixed Assets | | | | | 548.7 | 131.4 |
| 29.1 | 29.9 | 33.5 | | | | | | 31.4 | 35.4 |
| 11.5 | 12.8 | 14.3 | | | | | | 8.3 | 16.1 |
| 6.1 | 7.0 | 7.2 | Sales/Total Assets | | | | | 7.9 | 7.1 |
| 4.3 | 4.4 | 5.0 | | | | | | 4.4 | 5.3 |
| 2.8 | 3.0 | 3.3 | | | | | | 3.4 | 4.0 |
| .4 | .4 | .2 | % Depr., Dep., Amort./Sales | | | | | .2 | .2 |
| (78) .8 | (72) .9 | (93) .7 | | | | | | (25) .9 | (57) .6 |
| 2.0 | 2.0 | 1.8 | | | | | | 2.1 | 1.5 |
| .9 | .6 | .7 | % Officers', Directors' Owners' Comp/Sales | | | | | 1.2 | .1 |
| (34) 2.1 | (34) 1.6 | (38) 1.6 | | | | | | (13) 1.6 | (20) 1.5 |
| 4.6 | 2.3 | 2.5 | | | | | | 2.4 | 2.6 |
| 11366407M | 10090059M | 11846811M | Net Sales ($) | 1820M | 2848M | 26212M | 41867M | 482725M | 11291339M |
| 2453572M | 2433724M | 2296741M | Total Assets ($) | 2329M | 91M | 19921M | 14912M | 99098M | 2160390M |

M = $ thousand    MM = $ million
See Pages 9 through 22 for Explanation of Ratios and Data

## Current Data Sorted by Assets

## Comparative Historical Data

| 0-500M | 500M-2MM | 2-10MM | 10-50MM | 50-100MM | 100-250MM | Type of Statement | 12 | 13 |
|---|---|---|---|---|---|---|---|---|
| | | 1 | 3 | 1 | 1 | Unqualified | 12 | 13 |
| | 3 | 7 | 4 | | | Reviewed | 9 | 14 |
| 1 | 4 | 4 | | | | Compiled | 9 | 9 |
| 4 | 5 | 4 | 2 | | | Tax Returns | 2 | 2 |
| 2 | 4 | 8 | 4 | 4 | | Other | 17 | 19 |
| | 12 (4/1-9/30/11) | | 54 (10/1/11-3/31/12) | | | | 4/1/07- 3/31/08 ALL | 4/1/08- 3/31/09 ALL |
| 7 | 16 | 24 | 13 | 5 | 1 | **NUMBER OF STATEMENTS** | 49 | 57 |
| % | % | % | % | % | % | **ASSETS** | % | % |
| | 8.6 | 6.4 | 9.6 | | | Cash & Equivalents | 5.9 | 7.7 |
| | 56.7 | 43.7 | 35.0 | | | Trade Receivables (net) | 43.2 | 40.3 |
| | 22.3 | 15.2 | 15.0 | | | Inventory | 20.4 | 22.5 |
| | .8 | 2.3 | 1.4 | | | All Other Current | 3.1 | 3.6 |
| | 88.4 | 67.6 | 61.0 | | | Total Current | 72.6 | 74.2 |
| | 6.5 | 12.6 | 28.0 | | | Fixed Assets (net) | 19.7 | 18.9 |
| | 2.2 | 5.3 | 2.4 | | | Intangibles (net) | 2.6 | 2.3 |
| | 2.9 | 14.5 | 8.6 | | | All Other Non-Current | 5.0 | 4.6 |
| | 100.0 | 100.0 | 100.0 | | | Total | 100.0 | 100.0 |
| | | | | | | **LIABILITIES** | | |
| | 18.9 | 20.4 | 10.7 | | | Notes Payable-Short Term | 15.1 | 21.1 |
| | 2.7 | 1.0 | 1.4 | | | Cur. Mat.-L.T.D. | 3.4 | 2.4 |
| | 38.5 | 28.8 | 26.9 | | | Trade Payables | 24.8 | 24.7 |
| | .0 | .1 | 1.8 | | | Income Taxes Payable | .1 | .4 |
| | 5.1 | 6.1 | 7.0 | | | All Other Current | 6.5 | 6.2 |
| | 65.2 | 56.4 | 47.8 | | | Total Current | 49.9 | 54.8 |
| | 7.3 | 5.5 | 7.9 | | | Long-Term Debt | 11.1 | 10.2 |
| | .0 | .2 | .0 | | | Deferred Taxes | .0 | .1 |
| | 6.6 | 7.3 | 1.4 | | | All Other Non-Current | 2.7 | 1.8 |
| | 20.9 | 30.7 | 42.8 | | | Net Worth | 36.3 | 33.1 |
| | 100.0 | 100.0 | 100.0 | | | Total Liabilities & Net Worth | 100.0 | 100.0 |
| | | | | | | **INCOME DATA** | | |
| | 100.0 | 100.0 | 100.0 | | | Net Sales | 100.0 | 100.0 |
| | 16.1 | 13.6 | 15.0 | | | Gross Profit | 15.8 | 13.3 |
| | 15.6 | 12.0 | 10.5 | | | Operating Expenses | 13.0 | 11.3 |
| | .5 | 1.6 | 4.5 | | | Operating Profit | 2.8 | 2.0 |
| | -.4 | .1 | -.1 | | | All Other Expenses (net) | .2 | .2 |
| | .8 | 1.5 | 4.6 | | | Profit Before Taxes | 2.6 | 1.8 |
| | | | | | | **RATIOS** | | |
| | 1.7 | 1.6 | 3.2 | | | | 1.9 | 2.0 |
| | 1.3 | 1.2 | 1.1 | | | Current | 1.4 | 1.2 |
| | 1.1 | 1.0 | .9 | | | | 1.1 | 1.0 |
| | 1.5 | 1.3 | 1.1 | | | | 1.5 | 1.3 |
| | 1.0 | .9 | .7 | | | Quick | 1.0 | .8 |
| | .8 | .7 | .6 | | | | .7 | .7 |
| | 15 23.8 | 15 24.3 | 18 20.5 | | | | 15 24.0 | 15 23.6 |
| | 22 16.9 | 24 14.9 | 21 17.4 | | | Sales/Receivables | 21 17.3 | 21 17.4 |
| | 27 13.3 | 36 10.0 | 30 12.1 | | | | 29 12.5 | 29 12.6 |
| | 3 142.5 | 2 192.3 | 7 51.2 | | | | 6 65.5 | 6 62.3 |
| | 9 38.6 | 8 48.3 | 13 28.5 | | | Cost of Sales/Inventory | 10 35.2 | 14 26.4 |
| | 14 25.5 | 16 23.2 | 26 13.9 | | | | 23 15.8 | 22 16.4 |
| | 10 36.9 | 13 27.8 | 9 42.2 | | | | 9 42.4 | 8 45.9 |
| | 22 16.6 | 19 19.6 | 14 25.9 | | | Cost of Sales/Payables | 13 27.4 | 13 28.1 |
| | 26 13.8 | 29 12.8 | 21 17.0 | | | | 21 17.4 | 19 18.9 |
| | 24.6 | 30.7 | 10.9 | | | | 21.5 | 21.3 |
| | 45.5 | 62.7 | 100.5 | | | Sales/Working Capital | 35.7 | 36.6 |
| | 122.5 | NM | -91.7 | | | | 97.2 | 254.3 |
| | 11.4 | 21.4 | 41.4 | | | | 9.5 | 8.3 |
| | (15) 1.4 | (23) 6.6 | (11) 6.6 | | | EBIT/Interest | (46) 3.8 | (53) 4.9 |
| | -3.9 | 2.2 | 3.0 | | | | 1.7 | 1.8 |
| | | | | | | | | 24.3 |
| | | | | | | Net Profit + Depr., Dep., Amort./Cur. Mat. L/T/D | | (12) 9.4 |
| | | | | | | | | 3.9 |
| | .0 | .1 | .1 | | | | .1 | .1 |
| | .4 | .3 | 1.2 | | | Fixed/Worth | .3 | .4 |
| | 1.0 | 1.1 | 1.6 | | | | 1.6 | 1.4 |
| | 2.3 | 1.2 | .5 | | | | 1.1 | 1.1 |
| | 4.6 | 3.4 | 2.6 | | | Debt/Worth | 2.1 | 2.3 |
| | 14.5 | 7.3 | 3.8 | | | | 4.2 | 4.6 |
| | 118.6 | 67.7 | 41.4 | | | | 55.2 | 43.3 |
| | (13) 11.8 | (21) 23.6 | 27.4 | | | % Profit Before Taxes/Tangible Net Worth | (47) 24.1 | (51) 24.7 |
| | -41.9 | 12.7 | 17.0 | | | | 8.9 | 8.3 |
| | 19.4 | 13.5 | 21.0 | | | | 18.1 | 15.4 |
| | 2.3 | 9.4 | 7.3 | | | % Profit Before Taxes/Total Assets | 8.2 | 5.9 |
| | -13.2 | 2.2 | 3.2 | | | | 2.9 | 1.2 |
| | 999.8 | 469.3 | 110.0 | | | | 690.3 | 668.2 |
| | 138.5 | 75.2 | 18.7 | | | Sales/Net Fixed Assets | 66.7 | 61.7 |
| | 89.9 | 32.9 | 10.5 | | | | 12.3 | 18.8 |
| | 10.8 | 8.7 | 8.3 | | | | 10.0 | 9.7 |
| | 9.4 | 6.2 | 5.6 | | | Sales/Total Assets | 6.9 | 7.2 |
| | 7.5 | 4.4 | 2.3 | | | | 4.6 | 5.0 |
| | .1 | .1 | .1 | | | | .1 | .1 |
| | (11) .2 | (22) .4 | (11) .3 | | | % Depr., Dep., Amort./Sales | (34) .5 | (45) .3 |
| | .5 | .8 | 1.0 | | | | 1.7 | .7 |
| | | | | | | | .3 | .4 |
| | | | | | | % Officers', Directors' Owners' Comp/Sales | (15) 1.4 | (14) .9 |
| | | | | | | | 2.8 | 1.9 |
| 21477M | 181424M | 714332M | 1571939M | 2254970M | 172088M | Net Sales ($) | 4143212M | 6232383M |
| 1843M | 19022M | 115946M | 261945M | 339391M | 128425M | Total Assets ($) | 990984M | 1228841M |

M = $ thousand   MM = $ million
See Pages 9 through 22 for Explanation of Ratios and Data

## Comparative Historical Data | | | | Current Data Sorted by Sales

| | | | Type of Statement | | | | | | |
|---|---|---|---|---|---|---|---|---|---|
| 9 | 14 | 6 | Unqualified | | | | 1 | | 5 |
| 13 | 11 | 14 | Reviewed | | | | 3 | 4 | 7 |
| 7 | 8 | 9 | Compiled | | | | 1 | 5 | 2 |
| 7 | 9 | 15 | Tax Returns | 1 | | | 3 | 6 | 3 |
| 20 | 28 | 22 | Other | 2 | 1 | | 2 | 5 | 13 |
| 4/1/09- | 4/1/10- | 4/1/11- | | 1 | 1 | | | | |
| 3/31/10 | 3/31/11 | 3/31/12 | | | 12 (4/1-9/30/11) | | 54 (10/1/11-3/31/12) | | |
| ALL | ALL | ALL | | 0-1MM | 1-3MM | 3-5MM | 5-10MM | 10-25MM | 25MM & OVER |
| 56 | 70 | 66 | **NUMBER OF STATEMENTS** | 4 | 2 | | 10 | 20 | 30 |
| % | % | % | **ASSETS** | % | % | % | % | % | % |
| 6.5 | 7.6 | 8.1 | Cash & Equivalents | | | | 8.2 | 7.7 | 6.7 |
| 39.9 | 36.8 | 41.5 | Trade Receivables (net) | | | | 40.1 | 51.3 | 41.7 |
| 20.2 | 23.2 | 19.4 | Inventory | | | | 30.0 | 14.8 | 20.7 |
| 4.9 | 2.7 | 2.0 | All Other Current | | | | .7 | 1.9 | 2.1 |
| 71.5 | 70.3 | 71.0 | Total Current | | | | 79.0 | 75.6 | 71.2 |
| 18.1 | 20.6 | 17.5 | Fixed Assets (net) | | | | 11.0 | 16.1 | 17.3 |
| 2.0 | 3.0 | 3.0 | Intangibles (net) | | | | 3.6 | 1.7 | 4.3 |
| 8.5 | 6.1 | 8.5 | All Other Non-Current | | | | 6.4 | 6.5 | 7.2 |
| 100.0 | 100.0 | 100.0 | Total | | | | 100.0 | 100.0 | 100.0 |
| | | | **LIABILITIES** | | | | | | |
| 16.3 | 17.3 | 17.2 | Notes Payable-Short Term | | | | 24.6 | 17.2 | 16.6 |
| 2.9 | 4.7 | 2.5 | Cur. Mat.-L.T.D. | | | | 5.7 | 1.2 | 2.0 |
| 26.7 | 26.0 | 30.5 | Trade Payables | | | | 26.3 | 34.9 | 30.1 |
| .2 | .1 | .4 | Income Taxes Payable | | | | .0 | .1 | .9 |
| 8.3 | 7.9 | 6.0 | All Other Current | | | | 7.6 | 4.8 | 6.7 |
| 54.4 | 56.0 | 56.6 | Total Current | | | | 64.3 | 58.0 | 56.2 |
| 10.4 | 12.5 | 9.5 | Long-Term Debt | | | | 14.3 | 9.2 | 7.1 |
| .3 | .4 | .1 | Deferred Taxes | | | | .0 | .2 | .0 |
| 3.8 | 3.8 | 5.8 | All Other Non-Current | | | | 7.2 | 3.9 | 2.7 |
| 31.1 | 27.3 | 28.1 | Net Worth | | | | 14.1 | 28.7 | 34.0 |
| 100.0 | 100.0 | 100.0 | Total Liabilties & Net Worth | | | | 100.0 | 100.0 | 100.0 |
| | | | **INCOME DATA** | | | | | | |
| 100.0 | 100.0 | 100.0 | Net Sales | | | | 100.0 | 100.0 | 100.0 |
| 13.9 | 16.6 | 15.7 | Gross Profit | | | | 25.6 | 13.0 | 11.6 |
| 11.8 | 14.6 | 13.6 | Operating Expenses | | | | 24.9 | 10.8 | 9.3 |
| 2.1 | 2.1 | 2.2 | Operating Profit | | | | .7 | 2.3 | 2.2 |
| .2 | .6 | .0 | All Other Expenses (net) | | | | -.4 | -.1 | .2 |
| 1.9 | 1.5 | 2.1 | Profit Before Taxes | | | | 1.1 | 2.3 | 2.0 |
| | | | **RATIOS** | | | | | | |
| 2.2 | 2.1 | 1.7 | | | | | 1.6 | 3.0 | 1.6 |
| 1.3 | 1.4 | 1.3 | Current | | | | 1.2 | 1.3 | 1.3 |
| 1.0 | 1.0 | 1.0 | | | | | 1.0 | 1.0 | 1.0 |
| 1.3 | 1.3 | 1.3 | | | | | 1.0 | 1.3 | 1.1 |
| .8 | .8 | .9 | Quick | | | | .8 | 1.1 | .8 |
| .5 | .5 | .6 | | | | | .4 | .8 | .6 |

| Hist ALL (days) | Hist ALL (days) | Hist ALL (days) | Ratio | 5-10MM | 10-25MM | 25MM & OVER |
|---|---|---|---|---|---|---|
| 13 / 29.0 | 15 / 23.7 | 13 / 27.3 | **Sales/Receivables** | 19 / 19.7 | 14 / 26.9 | 16 / 22.7 |
| 20 / 18.2 | 23 / 16.0 | 22 / 16.9 | | 25 / 14.7 | 23 / 16.2 | 23 / 16.1 |
| 29 / 12.7 | 30 / 12.2 | 29 / 12.7 | | 33 / 11.1 | 31 / 11.8 | 31 / 11.7 |
| 5 / 71.8 | 7 / 51.9 | 3 / 111.6 | **Cost of Sales/Inventory** | 7 / 53.2 | 2 / 192.1 | 6 / 62.5 |
| 10 / 37.0 | 13 / 28.0 | 10 / 34.9 | | 12 / 30.8 | 9 / 40.5 | 13 / 27.6 |
| 25 / 14.8 | 32 / 11.3 | 19 / 19.3 | | 29 / 12.5 | 14 / 25.4 | 21 / 17.8 |
| 10 / 35.0 | 10 / 38.3 | 9 / 39.8 | **Cost of Sales/Payables** | 9 / 41.8 | 7 / 50.8 | 12 / 31.5 |
| 14 / 25.9 | 16 / 22.4 | 17 / 22.0 | | 21 / 17.8 | 17 / 21.4 | 17 / 22.0 |
| 24 / 15.4 | 30 / 12.0 | 24 / 15.0 | | 27 / 13.6 | 26 / 13.9 | 24 / 15.4 |
| 14.5 | 13.6 | 23.4 | **Sales/Working Capital** | 20.1 | 25.7 | 19.5 |
| 37.0 | 32.2 | 47.8 | | 52.3 | 51.0 | 39.6 |
| 271.7 | 247.8 | 388.7 | | NM | 833.5 | NM |
| 22.6 | 14.6 | 21.6 | **EBIT/Interest** | | 22.7 | 36.7 |
| (49) 6.3 | (63) 2.8 | (58) 4.5 | | | 4.9 | (28) 6.2 |
| 1.2 | .6 | 1.8 | | | .5 | 2.8 |
| | | | **Net Profit + Depr., Dep., Amort./Cur. Mat. L/T/D** | | | |
| .0 | .1 | .1 | **Fixed/Worth** | .0 | .1 | .1 |
| .4 | .5 | .4 | | .6 | .5 | .4 |
| 1.8 | 1.8 | 1.2 | | -1.1 | 1.2 | 1.4 |
| .9 | 1.0 | 1.4 | **Debt/Worth** | 1.3 | 1.6 | 1.5 |
| 3.1 | 2.7 | 3.3 | | 7.7 | 3.2 | 2.9 |
| 6.8 | 6.8 | 7.1 | | -12.0 | 5.4 | 5.3 |
| 57.6 | 38.2 | 62.4 | **% Profit Before Taxes/Tangible Net Worth** | | 92.3 | 47.6 |
| (49) 33.6 | (61) 16.4 | (58) 25.8 | | (18) | 25.8 | (28) 25.5 |
| 10.8 | .0 | 13.0 | | | 3.0 | 16.6 |
| 19.3 | 14.3 | 15.3 | **% Profit Before Taxes/Total Assets** | 5.5 | 18.8 | 14.4 |
| 9.0 | 5.5 | 6.8 | | 4.4 | 7.9 | 8.4 |
| 1.3 | -.9 | 1.8 | | -4.4 | -.6 | 3.1 |
| 736.2 | 352.7 | 334.3 | **Sales/Net Fixed Assets** | 999.8 | 273.3 | 249.5 |
| 64.0 | 48.5 | 88.4 | | 92.4 | 95.3 | 75.2 |
| 16.4 | 12.2 | 25.5 | | 31.2 | 37.3 | 15.9 |
| 10.5 | 9.1 | 9.5 | **Sales/Total Assets** | 9.7 | 10.6 | 8.9 |
| 7.0 | 6.2 | 6.9 | | 6.9 | 8.4 | 6.4 |
| 4.7 | 2.9 | 4.8 | | 4.7 | 5.2 | 4.8 |
| .0 | .2 | .1 | **% Depr., Dep., Amort./Sales** | | .1 | .1 |
| (44) .2 | (54) .5 | (50) .3 | | (16) | .2 | (26) .3 |
| 1.1 | 1.2 | .8 | | | .6 | .9 |
| .3 | .4 | .7 | **% Officers', Directors' Owners' Comp/Sales** | | | |
| (18) 1.1 | (11) 1.9 | (23) 1.5 | | | | |
| 3.2 | 3.3 | 3.9 | | | | |
| 6366833M | 7285664M | 4916230M | Net Sales ($) | 2819M | 4242M | | 74786M | 329776M | 4504607M |
| 1358847M | 1844891M | 866572M | Total Assets ($) | 4400M | 576M | | 15096M | 67957M | 778543M |

© RMA 2012    M = $ thousand    MM = $ million
See Pages 9 through 22 for Explanation of Ratios and Data

## Current Data Sorted by Assets      Comparative Historical Data

### Type of Statement

| | 0-500M | 500M-2MM | 2-10MM | 10-50MM | 50-100MM | 100-250MM | | 4/1/07-3/31/08 ALL | 4/1/08-3/31/09 ALL |
|---|---|---|---|---|---|---|---|---|---|
| Unqualified | | | 1 | 5 | 2 | | | 7 | 8 |
| Reviewed | | 2 | 10 | 11 | | | | 18 | 16 |
| Compiled | | 3 | 10 | | | | | 15 | 17 |
| Tax Returns | 1 | 7 | 3 | | | 1 | | 12 | 9 |
| Other | 1 | 5 | 9 | 7 | 3 | 1 | | 21 | 27 |
| | 2 | | | | | | | | |
| | 22 (4/1-9/30/11) | | | 62 (10/1/11-3/31/12) | | | | | |
| NUMBER OF STATEMENTS | 4 | 17 | 33 | 24 | 5 | 1 | | 73 | 77 |

| | 0-500M | 500M-2MM | 2-10MM | 10-50MM | 50-100MM | 100-250MM | | 07-08 ALL | 08-09 ALL |
|---|---|---|---|---|---|---|---|---|---|
| | % | % | % | % | % | % | | % | % |
| **ASSETS** | | | | | | | | | |
| Cash & Equivalents | | 12.0 | 7.9 | 3.2 | | | | 7.4 | 6.7 |
| Trade Receivables (net) | | 27.9 | 32.3 | 30.0 | | | | 27.3 | 29.8 |
| Inventory | | 26.8 | 35.7 | 38.0 | | | | 37.3 | 36.4 |
| All Other Current | | 1.7 | 2.0 | 1.8 | | | | 3.0 | 3.4 |
| Total Current | | 68.4 | 77.9 | 73.1 | | | | 75.0 | 76.3 |
| Fixed Assets (net) | | 15.6 | 13.3 | 18.8 | | | | 18.2 | 16.3 |
| Intangibles (net) | | 6.9 | 5.2 | 3.5 | | | | 2.3 | 3.2 |
| All Other Non-Current | | 9.1 | 3.6 | 4.7 | | | | 4.5 | 4.2 |
| Total | | 100.0 | 100.0 | 100.0 | | | | 100.0 | 100.0 |
| **LIABILITIES** | | | | | | | | | |
| Notes Payable-Short Term | | 12.9 | 12.8 | 17.4 | | | | 15.7 | 16.9 |
| Cur. Mat.-L.T.D. | | 1.6 | 1.8 | 2.0 | | | | 3.4 | 1.2 |
| Trade Payables | | 20.1 | 29.0 | 22.7 | | | | 18.3 | 19.9 |
| Income Taxes Payable | | .3 | .0 | .0 | | | | .1 | .1 |
| All Other Current | | 11.3 | 7.8 | 5.4 | | | | 12.8 | 10.2 |
| Total Current | | 46.2 | 51.4 | 47.5 | | | | 50.1 | 48.3 |
| Long-Term Debt | | 13.9 | 10.1 | 11.2 | | | | 13.0 | 9.5 |
| Deferred Taxes | | .0 | .0 | .3 | | | | .4 | .2 |
| All Other Non-Current | | 13.2 | 6.7 | 2.3 | | | | 12.1 | 3.1 |
| Net Worth | | 26.7 | 31.9 | 38.6 | | | | 24.4 | 38.9 |
| Total Liabilities & Net Worth | | 100.0 | 100.0 | 100.0 | | | | 100.0 | 100.0 |
| **INCOME DATA** | | | | | | | | | |
| Net Sales | | 100.0 | 100.0 | 100.0 | | | | 100.0 | 100.0 |
| Gross Profit | | 32.0 | 19.5 | 17.6 | | | | 27.1 | 22.2 |
| Operating Expenses | | 28.0 | 18.3 | 15.2 | | | | 24.4 | 19.3 |
| Operating Profit | | 4.0 | 1.2 | 2.4 | | | | 2.7 | 3.0 |
| All Other Expenses (net) | | .0 | .6 | .1 | | | | .6 | .3 |
| Profit Before Taxes | | 4.0 | .6 | 2.3 | | | | 2.2 | 2.7 |
| **RATIOS** | | | | | | | | | |
| Current | | 2.3 | 2.1 | 2.0 | | | | 3.1 | 2.7 |
| | | 1.5 | 1.5 | 1.3 | | | | 1.5 | 1.5 |
| | | 1.1 | 1.2 | 1.2 | | | | 1.1 | 1.2 |
| Quick | | 1.2 | 1.3 | 1.0 | | | | 1.1 | 1.2 |
| | | .8 | .8 | .7 | | | | .6 | .7 |
| | | .5 | .5 | .5 | | | | .4 | .5 |
| Sales/Receivables | 12  — | 30.3 | 17  21.1 | 20  18.0 | | | 16 | 22.5 | 18  19.9 |
| | 22 | 16.7 | 29  12.8 | 27  13.6 | | | 25 | 14.3 | 27  13.7 |
| | 38 | 9.7 | 41  9.0 | 35  10.3 | | | 36 | 10.1 | 34  10.8 |
| Cost of Sales/Inventory | 7 | 49.1 | 24  15.2 | 28  12.9 | | | 29 | 12.8 | 27  13.7 |
| | 33 | 11.2 | 35  10.3 | 47  7.7 | | | 53 | 6.9 | 48  7.7 |
| | 49 | 7.4 | 60  6.1 | 63  5.8 | | | 73 | 5.0 | 70  5.2 |
| Cost of Sales/Payables | 0 | UND | 12  31.1 | 13  27.3 | | | 9 | 38.6 | 9  42.5 |
| | 17 | 20.9 | 31  11.8 | 22  16.7 | | | 22 | 16.8 | 19  19.7 |
| | 41 | 9.0 | 58  6.3 | 36  10.0 | | | 41 | 9.0 | 36  10.0 |
| Sales/Working Capital | | 7.2 | 11.4 | 11.2 | | | | 8.3 | 8.3 |
| | | 20.0 | 16.5 | 21.5 | | | | 15.4 | 15.0 |
| | | 181.9 | 40.0 | 38.9 | | | | 36.0 | 31.2 |
| EBIT/Interest | | 13.1 | 40.6 | 15.0 | | | | 9.2 | 9.0 |
| | (13) | 7.9 | (31) 6.0 | (21) 5.8 | | | (68) | 2.6 | (72) 3.8 |
| | | 2.0 | 1.5 | 3.5 | | | | 1.2 | 1.5 |
| Net Profit + Depr., Dep., Amort./Cur. Mat. L/T/D | | | | | | | | 4.0 | 2.9 |
| | | | | | | | (17) | 2.0 | (15) 2.0 |
| | | | | | | | | 1.2 | .5 |
| Fixed/Worth | | .0 | .1 | .1 | | | | .1 | .1 |
| | | .2 | .2 | .5 | | | | .4 | .4 |
| | | .8 | .6 | 1.4 | | | | 2.0 | .8 |
| Debt/Worth | | 1.5 | 1.1 | 1.0 | | | | .8 | .7 |
| | | 2.6 | 2.3 | 2.2 | | | | 2.2 | 1.8 |
| | | 4.6 | 5.4 | 4.0 | | | | 9.8 | 4.7 |
| % Profit Before Taxes/Tangible Net Worth | | 37.7 | 59.3 | 29.4 | | | | 40.7 | 43.3 |
| | (14) | 32.0 | (30) 23.9 | (23) 19.7 | | | (60) | 14.0 | (71) 15.3 |
| | | 10.2 | 6.9 | 15.4 | | | | 5.3 | 5.0 |
| % Profit Before Taxes/Total Assets | | 17.6 | 17.2 | 11.3 | | | | 14.2 | 14.8 |
| | | 9.4 | 5.5 | 8.1 | | | | 4.1 | 6.5 |
| | | 5.3 | .8 | 4.8 | | | | .6 | 1.0 |
| Sales/Net Fixed Assets | | 878.9 | 251.4 | 127.2 | | | | 93.9 | 165.8 |
| | | 49.4 | 106.9 | 21.3 | | | | 46.1 | 40.6 |
| | | 15.5 | 26.5 | 10.2 | | | | 10.8 | 13.0 |
| Sales/Total Assets | | 4.7 | 6.2 | 4.5 | | | | 5.2 | 5.0 |
| | | 3.7 | 4.4 | 3.3 | | | | 3.5 | 3.7 |
| | | 2.7 | 2.6 | 2.5 | | | | 2.4 | 2.5 |
| % Depr., Dep., Amort./Sales | | .4 | .1 | .1 | | | | .3 | .2 |
| | (10) | .9 | (28) .3 | (22) .6 | | | (62) | .6 | (69) .6 |
| | | 3.3 | 1.7 | 1.5 | | | | 2.0 | 1.3 |
| % Officers', Directors', Owners' Comp/Sales | | 2.2 | .6 | .6 | | | | 1.4 | 1.0 |
| | (11) | 2.8 | (18) 1.0 | (12) .6 | | | (33) | 2.4 | (31) 2.2 |
| | | 4.8 | 2.2 | 2.4 | | | | 4.8 | 4.2 |
| Net Sales ($) | 14533M | 82144M | 609543M | 2281555M | 766027M | 387884M | | 2147674M | 3159738M |
| Total Assets ($) | 1322M | 21315M | 152359M | 561422M | 365079M | 198195M | | 661605M | 998253M |

© RMA 2012

M = $ thousand     MM = $ million
See Pages 9 through 22 for Explanation of Ratios and Data

## Comparative Historical Data / Current Data Sorted by Sales

| 4/1/09-3/31/10 ALL | 4/1/10-3/31/11 ALL | 4/1/11-3/31/12 ALL | | 0-1MM | 1-3MM | 3-5MM | 5-10MM | 10-25MM | 25MM & OVER |
|---|---|---|---|---|---|---|---|---|---|
| | | | **Type of Statement** | | | | | | |
| 11 | 7 | 8 | Unqualified | | | | | | 8 |
| 20 | 24 | 23 | Reviewed | | | 2 | 2 | 5 | 14 |
| 17 | 10 | 14 | Compiled | | 3 | 1 | 2 | 7 | 1 |
| 13 | 12 | 12 | Tax Returns | | 2 | 3 | 3 | 3 | 1 |
| 16 | 25 | 27 | Other | | 1 | 4 | 2 | 8 | 12 |
| | | | | | 22 (4/1-9/30/11) | | 62 (10/1/11-3/31/12) | | |
| 77 | 78 | 84 | **NUMBER OF STATEMENTS** | | 6 | 10 | 9 | 23 | 36 |
| % | % | % | **ASSETS** | % | % | % | % | % | % |
| 6.6 | 6.9 | 8.4 | Cash & Equivalents | | | 17.8 | | 8.1 | 3.7 |
| 27.3 | 28.3 | 28.7 | Trade Receivables (net) | | | 17.0 | | 33.5 | 29.5 |
| 33.7 | 34.0 | 34.8 | Inventory | | | 30.2 | | 36.8 | 39.4 |
| 3.0 | 2.2 | 2.5 | All Other Current | | | 1.0 | | .5 | 2.6 |
| 70.7 | 71.4 | 74.4 | Total Current | | | 66.1 | | 78.9 | 75.2 |
| 21.2 | 21.2 | 15.8 | Fixed Assets (net) | | | 23.9 | | 16.0 | 16.5 |
| 3.2 | 2.5 | 5.2 | Intangibles (net) | | | 7.0 | | 1.8 | 4.7 |
| 4.9 | 4.8 | 4.6 | All Other Non-Current | | | 3.0 | | 3.3 | 3.7 |
| 100.0 | 100.0 | 100.0 | Total | | | 100.0 | | 100.0 | 100.0 |
| | | | **LIABILITIES** | | | | | | |
| 18.2 | 14.1 | 14.1 | Notes Payable-Short Term | | | 7.5 | | 11.2 | 16.5 |
| 2.0 | 1.8 | 1.7 | Cur. Mat.-L.T.D. | | | 2.1 | | 2.1 | 1.4 |
| 18.8 | 21.4 | 24.0 | Trade Payables | | | 17.4 | | 27.1 | 24.7 |
| .2 | .2 | .2 | Income Taxes Payable | | | .3 | | .0 | .3 |
| 8.8 | 6.9 | 7.8 | All Other Current | | | 13.0 | | 8.7 | 6.7 |
| 47.9 | 44.5 | 47.7 | Total Current | | | 40.3 | | 49.1 | 49.5 |
| 12.5 | 13.9 | 11.2 | Long-Term Debt | | | 27.1 | | 6.6 | 8.7 |
| .2 | .0 | .1 | Deferred Taxes | | | .0 | | .0 | .3 |
| 6.5 | 5.5 | 7.7 | All Other Non-Current | | | 15.1 | | 7.2 | 3.6 |
| 32.8 | 36.0 | 33.2 | Net Worth | | | 17.5 | | 37.1 | 37.9 |
| 100.0 | 100.0 | 100.0 | Total Liabilities & Net Worth | | | 100.0 | | 100.0 | 100.0 |
| | | | **INCOME DATA** | | | | | | |
| 100.0 | 100.0 | 100.0 | Net Sales | | | 100.0 | | 100.0 | 100.0 |
| 23.1 | 24.6 | 22.3 | Gross Profit | | | 37.8 | | 21.4 | 17.6 |
| 20.8 | 21.9 | 19.5 | Operating Expenses | | | 35.4 | | 19.3 | 14.1 |
| 2.3 | 2.7 | 2.7 | Operating Profit | | | 2.4 | | 2.2 | 3.5 |
| .5 | .8 | .4 | All Other Expenses (net) | | | .3 | | .0 | .2 |
| 1.8 | 1.9 | 2.4 | Profit Before Taxes | | | 2.2 | | 2.1 | 3.3 |
| | | | **RATIOS** | | | | | | |
| 2.6 | 2.1 | 2.1 | | | | 3.9 | | 2.9 | 1.9 |
| 1.6 | 1.5 | 1.5 | Current | | | 2.1 | | 1.5 | 1.4 |
| 1.2 | 1.2 | 1.2 | | | | 1.0 | | 1.2 | 1.2 |
| 1.2 | 1.1 | 1.2 | | | | 2.7 | | 1.3 | 1.0 |
| .8 | .8 | .7 | Quick | | | .8 | | .8 | .6 |
| .5 | .5 | .5 | | | | .4 | | .5 | .5 |
| 17 21.3 | 18 20.6 | 18 20.7 | | | | 1 276.4 | | 15 23.9 | 20 18.0 |
| 27 13.7 | 26 13.8 | 27 13.6 | Sales/Receivables | | | 21 17.7 | | 24 15.5 | 32 11.5 |
| 37 9.9 | 38 9.5 | 36 10.0 | | | | 31 11.9 | | 39 9.3 | 36 10.0 |
| 25 14.8 | 25 14.4 | 24 14.9 | | | | 24 15.4 | | 23 15.8 | 28 13.0 |
| 46 7.9 | 47 7.8 | 40 9.2 | Cost of Sales/Inventory | | | 36 10.0 | | 35 10.3 | 45 8.2 |
| 66 5.5 | 65 5.6 | 64 5.7 | | | | 107 3.4 | | 59 6.2 | 70 5.2 |
| 10 36.8 | 13 28.2 | 11 33.0 | | | | 0 UND | | 10 35.7 | 16 22.9 |
| 22 16.9 | 24 15.5 | 23 16.2 | Cost of Sales/Payables | | | 14 26.4 | | 26 14.2 | 23 15.6 |
| 37 9.8 | 48 7.6 | 45 8.1 | | | | 104 3.5 | | 39 9.3 | 44 8.3 |
| 8.4 | 9.5 | 10.1 | | | | | | 10.8 | 10.6 |
| 16.7 | 18.3 | 18.1 | Sales/Working Capital | | | 17.6 | | 15.7 | 19.0 |
| 41.7 | 29.5 | 42.3 | | | | NM | | 26.4 | 38.6 |
| 9.6 | 9.5 | 20.4 | | | | | | 36.0 | 23.7 |
| (74) 4.0 | (76) 4.0 | (75) 6.2 | EBIT/Interest | | | | | (21) 4.6 | (33) 7.4 |
| 1.3 | 1.5 | 2.7 | | | | | | 1.7 | 3.9 |
| 15.1 | 5.4 | 19.8 | | | | | | | 8.2 |
| (17) 3.2 | (18) 2.6 | (18) 3.6 | Net Profit + Depr., Dep., Amort./Cur. Mat. L/T/D | | | | | | (11) 3.6 |
| 1.0 | 1.4 | 1.8 | | | | | | | 1.4 |
| .1 | .2 | .1 | | | | .1 | | .1 | .1 |
| .4 | .5 | .4 | Fixed/Worth | | | .4 | | .3 | .5 |
| 1.3 | 1.3 | 1.0 | | | | NM | | .5 | 1.2 |
| .9 | .9 | 1.2 | | | | .7 | | 1.0 | 1.2 |
| 1.9 | 1.7 | 2.5 | Debt/Worth | | | 2.3 | | 1.9 | 1.8 |
| 4.9 | 3.9 | 4.4 | | | | -10.4 | | 3.3 | 3.8 |
| 34.8 | 38.1 | 43.4 | | | | | | 59.3 | 44.3 |
| (68) 17.5 | (69) 19.0 | (75) 28.5 | % Profit Before Taxes/Tangible Net Worth | | | | | (34) 20.1 | 28.7 |
| 5.7 | 5.4 | 9.0 | | | | | | 4.5 | 16.0 |
| 12.1 | 13.5 | 15.2 | | | | 37.8 | | 17.0 | 15.0 |
| 6.3 | 5.4 | 8.3 | % Profit Before Taxes/Total Assets | | | 12.2 | | 6.1 | 8.9 |
| .9 | 1.3 | 2.3 | | | | .5 | | .8 | 4.8 |
| 106.9 | 88.7 | 198.9 | | | | UND | | 135.6 | 173.3 |
| 30.1 | 29.7 | 52.6 | Sales/Net Fixed Assets | | | 31.7 | | 55.7 | 29.1 |
| 9.3 | 8.2 | 12.4 | | | | 8.3 | | 18.9 | 10.2 |
| 4.6 | 4.5 | 5.0 | | | | 4.3 | | 6.5 | 4.6 |
| 3.3 | 3.6 | 3.7 | Sales/Total Assets | | | 3.4 | | 4.4 | 3.3 |
| 2.4 | 2.4 | 2.5 | | | | 2.2 | | 2.7 | 2.4 |
| .2 | .3 | .2 | | | | | | .2 | .1 |
| (67) .6 | (69) .9 | (67) .6 | % Depr., Dep., Amort./Sales | | | | | (20) .4 | (33) .6 |
| 1.6 | 2.0 | 1.6 | | | | | | 1.9 | 1.4 |
| 1.1 | .8 | .6 | | | | | | .6 | .6 |
| (45) 2.2 | (37) 1.5 | (43) 1.3 | % Officers', Directors' Owners' Comp/Sales | | | | | (15) 1.3 | (15) .9 |
| 4.8 | 2.8 | 2.8 | | | | | | 2.6 | 1.7 |
| 2902395M | 3282551M | 4141686M | Net Sales ($) | 10920M | 39282M | 61510M | | 382126M | 3647848M |
| 894387M | 942002M | 1299692M | Total Assets ($) | 7017M | 13163M | 16479M | | 95496M | 1167537M |

*(Note: in the ASSETS, LIABILITIES, INCOME DATA and related sections, "DATA NOT AVAILABLE" is printed across the 0-1MM and 1-3MM columns.)*

M = $ thousand    MM = $ million
See Pages 9 through 22 for Explanation of Ratios and Data

## Current Data Sorted by Assets        Comparative Historical Data

| 0-500M | 500M-2MM | 2-10MM | 10-50MM | 50-100MM | 100-250MM | Type of Statement | 4/1/07-3/31/08 | 4/1/08-3/31/09 |
|---|---|---|---|---|---|---|---|---|
|  |  | 5 | 21 | 7 | 2 | Unqualified | 40 | 42 |
| 2 | 2 | 34 | 18 |  |  | Reviewed | 47 | 59 |
| 2 | 4 | 24 | 1 |  |  | Compiled | 30 | 31 |
| 3 | 21 | 21 | 30 | 10 | 11 | Tax Returns | 21 | 33 |
| 6 | 14 | 31 |  |  |  | Other | 104 | 112 |
| | 42 (4/1-9/30/11) | | 227 (10/1/11-3/31/12) | | | | ALL | ALL |
| 13 | 41 | 115 | 70 | 17 | 13 | NUMBER OF STATEMENTS | 242 | 277 |
| % | % | % | % | % | % | ASSETS | % | % |
| 18.6 | 22.1 | 8.2 | 4.7 | 3.4 | 5.5 | Cash & Equivalents | 6.2 | 8.0 |
| 40.4 | 26.8 | 36.7 | 29.7 | 27.9 | 23.4 | Trade Receivables (net) | 36.3 | 32.8 |
| 10.6 | 22.1 | 34.7 | 42.5 | 43.0 | 44.8 | Inventory | 35.7 | 34.4 |
| 6.5 | 3.4 | 3.2 | 1.9 | 3.9 | 4.4 | All Other Current | 2.8 | 2.4 |
| 76.1 | 74.4 | 82.7 | 78.7 | 78.2 | 78.1 | Total Current | 81.1 | 77.6 |
| 18.4 | 16.7 | 12.0 | 13.2 | 15.5 | 14.4 | Fixed Assets (net) | 13.1 | 15.3 |
| 2.8 | .3 | 1.0 | 3.1 | 2.5 | 3.7 | Intangibles (net) | 2.2 | 2.7 |
| 2.7 | 8.6 | 4.3 | 4.9 | 3.8 | 3.8 | All Other Non-Current | 3.6 | 4.4 |
| 100.0 | 100.0 | 100.0 | 100.0 | 100.0 | 100.0 | Total | 100.0 | 100.0 |
|  |  |  |  |  |  | LIABILITIES |  |  |
| 9.7 | 9.5 | 17.0 | 29.7 | 30.7 | 27.3 | Notes Payable-Short Term | 24.3 | 24.0 |
| 4.8 | 2.7 | 1.9 | 1.0 | .8 | 1.8 | Cur. Mat.-L.T.D. | 2.8 | 2.0 |
| 37.3 | 21.9 | 27.2 | 19.9 | 20.6 | 17.2 | Trade Payables | 25.1 | 23.0 |
| .0 | .0 | .3 | .1 | .7 | .1 | Income Taxes Payable | .1 | .1 |
| 1.5 | 8.1 | 6.7 | 5.3 | 3.4 | 13.0 | All Other Current | 8.0 | 8.4 |
| 53.3 | 42.3 | 53.1 | 56.1 | 56.2 | 59.3 | Total Current | 60.3 | 57.5 |
| 10.9 | 10.6 | 6.9 | 8.4 | 6.5 | 6.8 | Long-Term Debt | 7.2 | 9.1 |
| .4 | .0 | .2 | .2 | .0 | .2 | Deferred Taxes | .3 | .2 |
| 9.9 | 7.5 | 6.4 | 5.2 | 1.8 | 1.0 | All Other Non-Current | 5.8 | 4.5 |
| 25.4 | 39.6 | 33.4 | 30.1 | 35.4 | 32.9 | Net Worth | 26.4 | 28.7 |
| 100.0 | 100.0 | 100.0 | 100.0 | 100.0 | 100.0 | Total Liabilities & Net Worth | 100.0 | 100.0 |
|  |  |  |  |  |  | INCOME DATA |  |  |
| 100.0 | 100.0 | 100.0 | 100.0 | 100.0 | 100.0 | Net Sales | 100.0 | 100.0 |
| 18.9 | 17.3 | 12.8 | 13.6 | 16.9 | 12.9 | Gross Profit | 14.6 | 15.2 |
| 17.2 | 15.4 | 10.5 | 10.1 | 12.5 | 10.7 | Operating Expenses | 12.4 | 13.1 |
| 1.7 | 1.9 | 2.3 | 3.5 | 4.4 | 2.2 | Operating Profit | 2.2 | 2.1 |
| .6 | .0 | .3 | .6 | .1 | .2 | All Other Expenses (net) | .8 | .6 |
| 1.1 | 1.9 | 2.1 | 2.9 | 4.3 | 2.1 | Profit Before Taxes | 1.4 | 1.5 |
|  |  |  |  |  |  | RATIOS |  |  |
| 2.6 | 4.1 | 2.3 | 1.9 | 1.6 | 1.6 | Current | 1.8 | 1.8 |
| 1.2 | 1.6 | 1.5 | 1.3 | 1.4 | 1.4 |  | 1.3 | 1.4 |
| 1.0 | 1.2 | 1.2 | 1.2 | 1.2 | 1.2 |  | 1.1 | 1.1 |
| 2.1 | 1.8 | 1.3 | .8 | .8 | .8 | Quick | 1.0 | 1.0 |
| 1.0 | 1.0 | .8 | .6 | .6 | .5 |  | .6 | .7 |
| .8 | .7 | .5 | .4 | .4 | .4 |  | .5 | .5 |
| 4 88.9 | 8 46.8 | 21 17.6 | 25 14.6 | 23 16.1 | 30 12.2 | Sales/Receivables | 23 16.0 | 22 16.9 |
| 21 17.0 | 18 20.2 | 29 12.4 | 32 11.4 | 33 10.9 | 36 10.2 |  | 31 11.6 | 29 12.8 |
| 27 13.4 | 30 12.1 | 35 10.4 | 41 9.0 | 38 9.5 | 39 9.4 |  | 40 9.1 | 37 9.7 |
| 0 UND | 2 221.2 | 11 32.7 | 31 11.7 | 37 9.9 | 44 8.3 | Cost of Sales/Inventory | 14 25.3 | 14 25.3 |
| 1 461.5 | 14 26.0 | 31 11.8 | 54 6.8 | 55 6.6 | 78 4.7 |  | 37 9.8 | 35 10.5 |
| 7 51.3 | 40 9.1 | 55 6.6 | 91 4.0 | 83 4.4 | 104 3.5 |  | 66 5.5 | 59 6.2 |
| 3 107.8 | 3 135.0 | 13 29.0 | 13 28.7 | 14 25.5 | 19 18.9 | Cost of Sales/Payables | 13 29.1 | 12 29.5 |
| 6 57.7 | 21 17.5 | 22 16.8 | 24 15.2 | 26 13.8 | 24 15.1 |  | 23 15.7 | 22 17.0 |
| 35 10.4 | 33 11.2 | 33 11.2 | 35 10.3 | 34 10.8 | 43 8.4 |  | 36 10.0 | 31 11.9 |
| 21.9 | 9.6 | 9.5 | 7.8 | 6.6 | 9.6 | Sales/Working Capital | 10.7 | 10.6 |
| 66.6 | 19.6 | 15.4 | 17.1 | 18.8 | 11.7 |  | 21.2 | 18.9 |
| UND | 76.0 | 39.7 | 30.2 | 51.2 | 15.8 |  | 70.0 | 57.0 |
|  | 16.8 | 16.4 | 9.6 | 22.6 | 5.2 | EBIT/Interest | 5.6 | 6.4 |
| (32) 3.5 | (104) 6.1 | (69) 4.9 | 4.5 | (12) 3.9 |  |  | (228) 2.6 | (257) 2.5 |
| 1.6 | 2.6 | 2.4 | 2.1 | 3.1 |  |  | 1.4 | 1.2 |
|  |  | 9.8 | 12.1 |  |  | Net Profit + Depr., Dep., Amort./Cur. Mat. L/T/D | 8.5 | 12.4 |
|  | (12) 2.3 | (22) 4.9 |  |  |  |  | (57) 4.9 | (70) 2.9 |
|  | 1.4 | 3.5 |  |  |  |  | 1.6 | 1.5 |
| .0 | .1 | .0 | .0 | .0 | .1 | Fixed/Worth | .1 | .1 |
| .8 | .2 | .2 | .2 | .3 | .5 |  | .3 | .3 |
| UND | .8 | .7 | .9 | .8 | .8 |  | .9 | 1.1 |
| 1.0 | .6 | 1.1 | 1.6 | 1.5 | 1.3 | Debt/Worth | 1.5 | 1.3 |
| 2.0 | 1.9 | 2.5 | 3.1 | 2.4 | 2.3 |  | 3.4 | 2.7 |
| -82.4 | 4.9 | 5.8 | 6.5 | 4.3 | 5.1 |  | 7.7 | 7.5 |
|  | 38.8 | 56.7 | 47.2 | 44.1 | 27.4 | % Profit Before Taxes/Tangible Net Worth | 35.5 | 38.8 |
| (39) 18.9 | (111) 21.4 | (66) 25.3 | 22.8 | (12) 14.2 |  |  | (218) 19.4 | (250) 14.9 |
|  | 6.3 | 7.9 | 11.8 | 8.8 | 8.7 |  | 7.6 | 5.0 |
| 12.6 | 12.8 | 12.5 | 12.5 | 16.8 | 7.1 | % Profit Before Taxes/Total Assets | 10.1 | 10.2 |
| 1.3 | 6.9 | 6.3 | 6.7 | 4.8 | 4.9 |  | 4.1 | 3.9 |
| -1.4 | 1.6 | 2.4 | 2.8 | 2.0 | 3.0 |  | 1.4 | 1.1 |
| UND | 198.3 | 943.4 | 556.4 | 403.3 | 671.7 | Sales/Net Fixed Assets | 339.4 | 315.4 |
| 126.5 | 81.1 | 140.2 | 52.1 | 107.8 | 29.7 |  | 74.7 | 64.3 |
| 35.0 | 15.5 | 32.1 | 17.5 | 9.3 | 8.9 |  | 24.6 | 18.2 |
| 15.6 | 8.4 | 5.9 | 4.8 | 4.2 | 2.9 | Sales/Total Assets | 5.6 | 5.5 |
| 9.8 | 4.7 | 4.3 | 3.0 | 3.3 | 2.4 |  | 4.0 | 3.9 |
| 4.9 | 3.3 | 3.4 | 2.1 | 1.7 | 2.0 |  | 2.9 | 2.8 |
|  | .3 | .1 | .1 | .1 | .2 | % Depr., Dep., Amort./Sales | .1 | .1 |
| (22) .6 | (81) .3 | (60) .5 | (15) .2 | (11) .4 |  |  | (203) .3 | (231) .4 |
|  | 1.4 | .6 | .9 | 1.2 | 1.4 |  | 1.0 | 1.0 |
|  | .9 | .6 | .6 |  |  | % Officers', Directors' Owners' Comp/Sales | .7 | .8 |
| (25) 1.8 | (57) 1.2 | (17) .8 |  |  |  |  | (89) 1.5 | (108) 1.5 |
|  | 3.6 | 2.5 | 2.0 |  |  |  | 3.9 | 2.9 |
| 47508M | 282504M | 2556086M | 5517389M | 3825904M | 4984748M | Net Sales ($) | 12960161M | 16806383M |
| 3395M | 46647M | 562403M | 1683871M | 1203993M | 2015017M | Total Assets ($) | 3992636M | 5148197M |

M = $ thousand    MM = $ million
See Pages 9 through 22 for Explanation of Ratios and Data

## Comparative Historical Data / Current Data Sorted by Sales

| | | | | | Type of Statement / Sales | | | | |
|---|---|---|---|---|---|---|---|---|---|
| 35 | 32 | 35 | Unqualified | | | | 1 | 1 | 33 |
| 62 | 64 | 56 | Reviewed | 1 | | | 6 | 16 | 33 |
| 30 | 23 | 30 | Compiled | | 4 | 2 | 2 | 13 | 9 |
| 35 | 37 | 46 | Tax Returns | 1 | 4 | 7 | 10 | 18 | 6 |
| 95 | 88 | 102 | Other | 3 | 4 | 4 | 10 | 23 | 58 |
| 4/1/09- 3/31/10 ALL | 4/1/10- 3/31/11 ALL | 4/1/11- 3/31/12 ALL | | | 42 (4/1-9/30/11) | | 227 (10/1/11-3/31/12) | | |
| | | | | 0-1MM | 1-3MM | 3-5MM | 5-10MM | 10-25MM | 25MM & OVER |
| 257 | 244 | 269 | NUMBER OF STATEMENTS | 5 | 12 | 13 | 29 | 71 | 139 |
| % | % | % | **ASSETS** | % | % | % | % | % | % |
| 6.2 | 7.4 | 9.5 | Cash & Equivalents | | 24.8 | 11.6 | 17.8 | 10.6 | 5.5 |
| 35.3 | 34.8 | 32.3 | Trade Receivables (net) | | 26.7 | 16.7 | 28.3 | 38.9 | 31.8 |
| 35.0 | 32.7 | 34.7 | Inventory | | 14.3 | 32.2 | 28.3 | 29.5 | 41.2 |
| 2.0 | 2.6 | 3.1 | All Other Current | | 8.0 | .9 | 4.8 | 3.2 | 2.5 |
| 78.5 | 77.6 | 79.6 | Total Current | | 73.8 | 61.4 | 79.3 | 82.1 | 81.1 |
| 14.0 | 14.5 | 13.7 | Fixed Assets (net) | | 20.2 | 27.1 | 16.1 | 10.8 | 12.5 |
| 2.9 | 2.9 | 1.7 | Intangibles (net) | | .2 | .2 | .3 | 1.8 | 2.0 |
| 4.6 | 5.0 | 5.0 | All Other Non-Current | | 5.8 | 11.3 | 4.3 | 5.2 | 4.4 |
| 100.0 | 100.0 | 100.0 | Total | | 100.0 | 100.0 | 100.0 | 100.0 | 100.0 |
| | | | **LIABILITIES** | | | | | | |
| 22.1 | 21.2 | 20.2 | Notes Payable-Short Term | | 12.8 | 8.0 | 5.2 | 14.8 | 28.0 |
| 3.1 | 1.7 | 1.9 | Cur. Mat.-L.T.D. | | 5.1 | 3.5 | 4.0 | 1.8 | 1.0 |
| 23.7 | 25.1 | 24.1 | Trade Payables | | 17.1 | 9.0 | 25.0 | 28.8 | 23.1 |
| .1 | .2 | .2 | Income Taxes Payable | | .0 | .1 | .0 | .4 | .2 |
| 6.2 | 7.0 | 6.4 | All Other Current | | 10.4 | 8.5 | 6.6 | 6.3 | 6.0 |
| 55.1 | 55.2 | 52.7 | Total Current | | 45.4 | 29.0 | 40.9 | 52.1 | 58.4 |
| 9.8 | 7.5 | 8.0 | Long-Term Debt | | 4.6 | 24.2 | 10.7 | 7.0 | 6.1 |
| .2 | .2 | .2 | Deferred Taxes | | .0 | .0 | .5 | .1 | .1 |
| 5.5 | 5.6 | 5.9 | All Other Non-Current | | 6.0 | 11.0 | 8.3 | 7.5 | 4.1 |
| 29.4 | 31.5 | 33.2 | Net Worth | | 43.9 | 35.8 | 39.6 | 33.2 | 31.2 |
| 100.0 | 100.0 | 100.0 | Total Liabilities & Net Worth | | 100.0 | 100.0 | 100.0 | 100.0 | 100.0 |
| | | | **INCOME DATA** | | | | | | |
| 100.0 | 100.0 | 100.0 | Net Sales | | 100.0 | 100.0 | 100.0 | 100.0 | 100.0 |
| 14.5 | 14.4 | 14.2 | Gross Profit | | 21.1 | 25.3 | 16.6 | 13.5 | 12.2 |
| 12.5 | 12.5 | 11.6 | Operating Expenses | | 18.8 | 20.6 | 14.6 | 11.2 | 9.4 |
| 2.0 | 2.0 | 2.7 | Operating Profit | | 2.3 | 4.7 | 2.0 | 2.3 | 2.8 |
| .5 | .4 | .3 | All Other Expenses (net) | | -.3 | .1 | .6 | .1 | .4 |
| 1.5 | 1.5 | 2.4 | Profit Before Taxes | | 2.7 | 4.5 | 1.4 | 2.2 | 2.4 |
| | | | **RATIOS** | | | | | | |
| 1.8 | 1.9 | 2.0 | Current | | 4.1 | 2.8 | 4.1 | 2.3 | 1.7 |
| 1.4 | 1.4 | 1.4 | | | 1.3 | 1.7 | 1.8 | 1.6 | 1.3 |
| 1.1 | 1.1 | 1.2 | | | .8 | 1.6 | 1.2 | 1.2 | 1.2 |
| 1.1 | 1.1 | 1.2 | Quick | | 3.7 | 1.4 | 2.4 | 1.4 | .8 |
| .7 | .7 | .7 | | | 1.0 | .9 | 1.2 | .9 | .6 |
| .5 | .5 | .5 | | | .6 | .6 | .6 | .6 | .4 |
| 23  15.8 | 21  17.0 | 20  18.2 | Sales/Receivables | 8  43.0 | 6  57.8 | 10  35.5 | 23  15.6 | 23  15.8 |
| 29  12.4 | 30  12.0 | 29  12.4 | | | 22  16.8 | 17  20.9 | 23  16.0 | 31  11.8 | 31  11.9 |
| 39  9.4 | 39  9.3 | 37  9.9 | | | 35  10.4 | 24  14.9 | 33  11.2 | 37  9.8 | 38  9.7 |
| 16  22.7 | 12  31.3 | 12  29.3 | Cost of Sales/Inventory | 0  UND | 10  36.5 | 2  174.3 | 8  44.9 | 26  14.2 |
| 39  9.5 | 34  10.8 | 35  10.3 | | | 14  26.7 | 39  9.4 | 32  11.3 | 26  13.8 | 46  8.0 |
| 58  6.3 | 65  5.6 | 64  5.7 | | | 42  8.7 | 59  6.2 | 51  7.1 | 53  6.9 | 78  4.7 |
| 13  27.8 | 12  29.6 | 12  31.4 | Cost of Sales/Payables | 5  79.4 | 3  121.4 | 3  144.5 | 14  25.8 | 14  27.0 |
| 22  16.3 | 23  16.1 | 23  16.2 | | | 10  37.9 | 12  31.5 | 15  25.1 | 23  15.7 | 24  15.3 |
| 33  11.0 | 34  10.7 | 33  10.9 | | | 37  9.8 | 35  10.3 | 30  12.2 | 37  9.9 | 33  10.9 |
| 10.3 | 10.3 | 9.4 | Sales/Working Capital | | 6.1 | 8.6 | 5.0 | 10.0 | 9.7 |
| 17.5 | 19.2 | 16.5 | | | 24.7 | 12.8 | 10.4 | 17.2 | 17.1 |
| 56.4 | 70.0 | 39.8 | | | NM | 24.2 | 91.1 | 41.7 | 34.1 |
| 7.8 | 10.2 | 12.9 | EBIT/Interest | | | 18.4 | 5.4 | 20.6 | 10.1 |
| (243) 3.1 | (219) 4.4 | (243) 4.8 | | | | (12) 6.5 | (21) 3.0 | (63) 6.5 | (135) 4.9 |
| 1.3 | 1.8 | 2.3 | | | | 1.5 | .4 | 2.6 | 2.5 |
| 7.5 | 10.2 | 11.7 | Net Profit + Depr., Dep., Amort./Cur. Mat. L/T/D | | | | | | 11.8 |
| (64) 3.9 | (53) 4.3 | (49) 4.3 | | | | | | (40) | 4.4 |
| 1.0 | 1.7 | 1.8 | | | | | | | 2.4 |
| .0 | .0 | .0 | Fixed/Worth | | .1 | .1 | .0 | .0 | .0 |
| .3 | .3 | .2 | | | .4 | .5 | .1 | .2 | .3 |
| 1.0 | 1.0 | .8 | | | 1.2 | 1.9 | .8 | .7 | .8 |
| 1.4 | 1.2 | 1.2 | Debt/Worth | | .4 | .7 | .5 | 1.2 | 1.5 |
| 2.9 | 2.6 | 2.6 | | | 1.7 | 1.3 | 1.5 | 2.7 | 2.8 |
| 7.7 | 6.0 | 5.8 | | | 3.9 | 6.2 | 4.9 | 6.0 | 5.8 |
| 39.3 | 44.8 | 47.1 | % Profit Before Taxes/Tangible Net Worth | | 65.7 | 57.3 | 21.9 | 60.4 | 46.5 |
| (232) 15.3 | (221) 21.6 | (254) 21.8 | | | (11) 16.9 | 15.5 | (25) 15.9 | (69) 27.2 | (133) 23.6 |
| 4.5 | 7.5 | 9.1 | | | 6.6 | 6.5 | 4.6 | 5.7 | 10.9 |
| 10.4 | 11.6 | 12.0 | % Profit Before Taxes/Total Assets | | 15.8 | 17.7 | 9.5 | 13.9 | 10.9 |
| 3.8 | 4.3 | 6.2 | | | 5.9 | 6.9 | 5.1 | 7.9 | 5.7 |
| .9 | 1.7 | 2.4 | | | 1.6 | 1.4 | -.7 | 2.4 | 2.6 |
| 385.6 | 422.9 | 617.5 | Sales/Net Fixed Assets | | 107.0 | 120.2 | 216.9 | 706.9 | 789.2 |
| 79.9 | 88.1 | 85.4 | | | 18.7 | 17.3 | 104.7 | 141.1 | 85.4 |
| 20.8 | 17.7 | 20.7 | | | 9.3 | 8.4 | 21.6 | 32.6 | 18.5 |
| 5.3 | 5.6 | 5.5 | Sales/Total Assets | | 4.9 | 4.9 | 6.9 | 6.1 | 5.2 |
| 4.1 | 3.9 | 4.0 | | | 3.0 | 3.9 | 3.8 | 4.7 | 3.7 |
| 2.7 | 2.8 | 2.7 | | | 2.1 | 2.5 | 2.9 | 3.6 | 2.6 |
| .1 | .1 | .1 | % Depr., Dep., Amort./Sales | | | | .1 | .1 | .1 |
| (212) .4 | (191) .4 | (195) .4 | | | | | (20) .3 | (44) .3 | (115) .4 |
| .9 | 1.0 | .9 | | | | | .9 | .8 | .9 |
| .8 | .8 | .7 | % Officers', Directors' Owners' Comp/Sales | | | | 1.2 | .6 | .6 |
| (110) 1.3 | (105) 1.5 | (107) 1.4 | | | | | (18) 1.8 | (36) 1.0 | (39) 1.0 |
| 2.4 | 2.7 | 2.6 | | | | | 3.1 | 1.8 | 2.5 |
| 15630556M | 16377187M | 17214139M | Net Sales ($) | 2550M | 25992M | 49874M | 209843M | 1172296M | 15753584M |
| 5174124M | 4964324M | 5515326M | Total Assets ($) | 628M | 8732M | 17029M | 60124M | 286321M | 5142492M |

M = $ thousand    MM = $ million
See Pages 9 through 22 for Explanation of Ratios and Data

# WHOLESALE—Meat and Meat Product Merchant Wholesalers  NAICS 424470

## Current Data Sorted by Assets | Comparative Historical Data

| Type of Statement | 0-500M | 500M-2MM | 2-10MM | 10-50MM | 50-100MM | 100-250MM | 4/1/07-3/31/08 ALL | 4/1/08-3/31/09 ALL |
|---|---|---|---|---|---|---|---|---|
| Unqualified | | | 4 | 13 | 3 | 5 | 25 | 32 |
| Reviewed | | 3 | 25 | 13 | 1 | | 52 | 53 |
| Compiled | 1 | 13 | 20 | 3 | 1 | | 29 | 35 |
| Tax Returns | 4 | 14 | 7 | 1 | | | 18 | 27 |
| Other | 2 | 20 | 29 | 25 | 9 | 7 | 52 | 60 |
| | | 32 (4/1-9/30/11) | 191 (10/1/11-3/31/12) | | | | | |
| **NUMBER OF STATEMENTS** | 7 | 50 | 85 | 55 | 14 | 12 | 176 | 207 |
| | % | % | % | % | % | % | % | % |
| **ASSETS** | | | | | | | | |
| Cash & Equivalents | | 9.3 | 5.5 | 6.9 | 3.6 | 3.7 | 6.9 | 7.7 |
| Trade Receivables (net) | | 40.0 | 39.5 | 38.3 | 39.5 | 41.6 | 37.5 | 38.1 |
| Inventory | | 22.3 | 28.4 | 28.7 | 30.6 | 25.5 | 25.7 | 26.8 |
| All Other Current | | 1.6 | 1.6 | 5.1 | 2.1 | 2.6 | 2.4 | 2.4 |
| Total Current | | 73.2 | 75.1 | 79.0 | 75.7 | 73.4 | 72.6 | 75.0 |
| Fixed Assets (net) | | 15.8 | 16.4 | 14.3 | 15.2 | 16.6 | 18.0 | 16.7 |
| Intangibles (net) | | 6.2 | 4.2 | 2.6 | 6.2 | 8.0 | 5.0 | 3.5 |
| All Other Non-Current | | 4.8 | 4.4 | 4.0 | 2.9 | 2.0 | 4.4 | 4.9 |
| Total | | 100.0 | 100.0 | 100.0 | 100.0 | 100.0 | 100.0 | 100.0 |
| **LIABILITIES** | | | | | | | | |
| Notes Payable-Short Term | | 15.1 | 20.6 | 20.7 | 21.0 | 16.0 | 18.6 | 18.0 |
| Cur. Mat.-L.T.D. | | 2.4 | 1.3 | 2.9 | 1.3 | .7 | 2.6 | 1.9 |
| Trade Payables | | 28.7 | 21.9 | 20.5 | 24.9 | 29.1 | 21.4 | 21.1 |
| Income Taxes Payable | | .0 | .1 | .1 | .0 | .0 | .1 | .1 |
| All Other Current | | 6.9 | 5.3 | 8.5 | 5.9 | 8.7 | 7.5 | 7.5 |
| Total Current | | 53.1 | 49.2 | 52.7 | 53.2 | 54.5 | 50.1 | 48.7 |
| Long-Term Debt | | 15.9 | 11.8 | 9.2 | 19.1 | 5.9 | 12.5 | 10.3 |
| Deferred Taxes | | .0 | .2 | .2 | .4 | 2.2 | .1 | .1 |
| All Other Non-Current | | 13.7 | 5.1 | 4.5 | 3.3 | 1.5 | 5.2 | 6.0 |
| Net Worth | | 17.3 | 33.6 | 33.4 | 24.0 | 35.9 | 32.2 | 34.9 |
| Total Liabilities & Net Worth | | 100.0 | 100.0 | 100.0 | 100.0 | 100.0 | 100.0 | 100.0 |
| **INCOME DATA** | | | | | | | | |
| Net Sales | | 100.0 | 100.0 | 100.0 | 100.0 | 100.0 | 100.0 | 100.0 |
| Gross Profit | | 15.4 | 14.1 | 11.7 | 11.5 | 9.9 | 14.0 | 14.6 |
| Operating Expenses | | 13.6 | 12.2 | 9.8 | 9.3 | 7.8 | 11.7 | 12.4 |
| Operating Profit | | 1.8 | 1.9 | 1.8 | 2.2 | 2.2 | 2.3 | 2.2 |
| All Other Expenses (net) | | .0 | .2 | .3 | .7 | .2 | .7 | .4 |
| Profit Before Taxes | | 1.7 | 1.6 | 1.5 | 1.5 | 1.9 | 1.6 | 1.8 |
| **RATIOS** | | | | | | | | |
| Current | | 1.8 | 2.0 | 2.2 | 1.9 | 2.1 | 2.1 | 2.3 |
| | | 1.4 | 1.5 | 1.4 | 1.4 | 1.3 | 1.4 | 1.5 |
| | | 1.0 | 1.2 | 1.2 | 1.1 | 1.1 | 1.1 | 1.2 |
| Quick | | 1.4 | 1.3 | 1.2 | 1.1 | 1.2 | 1.3 | 1.5 |
| | | .8 | .9 | .9 | .7 | .7 | .9 | .9 |
| | | .6 | .6 | .5 | .5 | .6 | .6 | .6 |
| Sales/Receivables | | 11  33.8 | 17  21.3 | 16  22.7 | 21  17.1 | 16  23.0 | 15  24.0 | 14  26.4 |
| | | 18  20.6 | 21  17.7 | 20  18.5 | 26  14.3 | 19  18.8 | 20  18.5 | 19  19.0 |
| | | 29  12.7 | 32  11.4 | 26  13.8 | 35  10.4 | 23  16.1 | 27  13.7 | 27  13.6 |
| Cost of Sales/Inventory | | 6  60.3 | 10  38.0 | 7  55.1 | 15  23.6 | 11  33.4 | 8  45.1 | 8  48.0 |
| | | 13  27.5 | 19  19.1 | 18  20.5 | 22  16.6 | 15  24.1 | 16  22.9 | 16  22.4 |
| | | 20  18.7 | 30  12.1 | 40  9.2 | 54  6.7 | 26  14.3 | 28  12.9 | 30  12.3 |
| Cost of Sales/Payables | | 9  41.9 | 8  44.7 | 9  41.0 | 13  28.8 | 11  32.9 | 8  48.3 | 7  53.3 |
| | | 14  25.5 | 15  25.0 | 13  27.6 | 15  24.5 | 15  24.3 | 13  28.3 | 12  31.4 |
| | | 25  14.6 | 20  18.3 | 19  19.1 | 20  18.4 | 20  18.1 | 18  19.8 | 20  18.4 |
| Sales/Working Capital | | 21.6 | 14.1 | 13.7 | 9.8 | 13.3 | 15.9 | 15.0 |
| | | 44.4 | 25.1 | 24.4 | 27.7 | 40.5 | 28.0 | 30.1 |
| | | -788.9 | 49.7 | 55.1 | 86.9 | 154.9 | 100.8 | 74.8 |
| EBIT/Interest | | 17.4 | 10.3 | 11.2 | 9.1 | | 6.4 | 9.3 |
| | | (45) 4.6 | (76) 4.5 | (53) 3.2 | (13) 3.0 | | (158) 2.7 | (185) 3.7 |
| | | 1.3 | 1.7 | 1.6 | 2.2 | | 1.4 | 1.5 |
| Net Profit + Depr., Dep., Amort./Cur. Mat. L/T/D | | | 7.0 | 10.0 | | | 15.5 | 5.9 |
| | | | (17) 3.2 | (16) 6.3 | | | (35) 3.9 | (35) 2.8 |
| | | | 1.9 | 1.7 | | | 1.2 | 1.0 |
| Fixed/Worth | | .1 | .1 | .1 | .2 | .2 | .1 | .1 |
| | | .6 | .3 | .4 | .5 | .4 | .4 | .4 |
| | | 7.1 | 1.4 | .9 | NM | 1.2 | 1.4 | 1.0 |
| Debt/Worth | | 1.2 | 1.3 | 1.1 | 2.2 | 1.1 | 1.2 | 1.0 |
| | | 4.4 | 2.4 | 2.2 | 5.7 | 3.1 | 2.8 | 2.2 |
| | | NM | 4.7 | 6.0 | NM | 7.3 | 5.4 | 4.5 |
| % Profit Before Taxes/Tangible Net Worth | | 73.7 | 40.0 | 42.8 | 46.0 | 43.1 | 41.3 | 47.2 |
| | | (38) 42.8 | (78) 22.7 | (50) 13.3 | (11) 20.8 | 28.7 | (160) 20.1 | (191) 23.4 |
| | | 5.3 | 8.9 | 4.5 | 14.6 | 23.0 | 7.0 | 7.1 |
| % Profit Before Taxes/Total Assets | | 19.9 | 13.2 | 9.4 | 8.2 | 10.2 | 10.5 | 14.2 |
| | | 6.6 | 5.4 | 4.5 | 4.3 | 6.4 | 5.0 | 6.2 |
| | | .3 | 2.2 | 1.0 | 2.1 | 4.0 | 1.4 | 2.1 |
| Sales/Net Fixed Assets | | 325.0 | 295.3 | 513.6 | 270.5 | 312.1 | 238.8 | 316.7 |
| | | 75.0 | 77.7 | 82.6 | 59.8 | 106.8 | 64.1 | 81.0 |
| | | 28.6 | 22.2 | 15.9 | 8.0 | 16.7 | 18.9 | 21.8 |
| Sales/Total Assets | | 10.5 | 7.9 | 9.1 | 6.9 | 9.1 | 8.4 | 9.4 |
| | | 7.6 | 5.9 | 5.7 | 4.7 | 7.5 | 6.0 | 6.2 |
| | | 5.3 | 4.3 | 3.8 | 2.1 | 4.9 | 3.9 | 4.2 |
| % Depr., Dep., Amort./Sales | | .1 | .1 | .1 | .2 | .1 | .1 | .1 |
| | | (32) .3 | (72) .3 | (46) .4 | (12) .5 | (10) .2 | (148) .4 | (167) .4 |
| | | .7 | .8 | .8 | 1.2 | 1.7 | .8 | .9 |
| % Officers', Directors' Owners' Comp/Sales | | .8 | .6 | .3 | | | .5 | .5 |
| | | (27) 1.3 | (47) 1.1 | (12) .6 | | | (74) 1.2 | (93) 1.0 |
| | | 2.2 | 2.2 | | | | 2.2 | 2.1 |
| Net Sales ($) | 22172M | 537072M | 2484879M | 7746222M | 4558726M | 10846185M | 16572918M | 19013536M |
| Total Assets ($) | 1706M | 65893M | 407414M | 1240827M | 940755M | 1625018M | 3163148M | 3607430M |

© RMA 2012

M = $ thousand     MM = $ million
See Pages 9 through 22 for Explanation of Ratios and Data

## Comparative Historical Data | | Current Data Sorted by Sales

| 4/1/09-3/31/10 ALL | 4/1/10-3/31/11 ALL | 4/1/11-3/31/12 ALL | Type of Statement | 0-1MM | 1-3MM | 3-5MM | 5-10MM | 10-25MM | 25MM & OVER |
|---|---|---|---|---|---|---|---|---|---|
| 32 | 32 | 25 | Unqualified | | | | 1 | 2 | 22 |
| 52 | 49 | 42 | Reviewed | | | | 3 | 12 | 27 |
| 45 | 46 | 38 | Compiled | 1 | 2 | 3 | 3 | 16 | 13 |
| 20 | 27 | 26 | Tax Returns | 1 | 2 | 3 | 6 | 10 | 4 |
| 69 | 73 | 92 | Other | 1 | 2 | 1 | 8 | 22 | 58 |
| | | | | 32 (4/1-9/30/11) | | | 191 (10/1/11-3/31/12) | | |
| 218 | 227 | 223 | **NUMBER OF STATEMENTS** | 3 | 6 | 7 | 21 | 62 | 124 |
| % | % | % | **ASSETS** | % | % | % | % | % | % |
| 8.4 | 7.3 | 7.0 | Cash & Equivalents | | | | 8.4 | 8.8 | 4.9 |
| 37.0 | 37.8 | 39.2 | Trade Receivables (net) | | | | 30.4 | 36.7 | 43.4 |
| 25.7 | 27.1 | 26.7 | Inventory | | | | 25.2 | 25.6 | 28.9 |
| 2.8 | 2.4 | 2.6 | All Other Current | | | | 1.9 | 3.6 | 2.4 |
| 73.9 | 74.5 | 75.4 | Total Current | | | | 66.0 | 74.7 | 79.6 |
| 17.3 | 16.9 | 15.4 | Fixed Assets (net) | | | | 21.0 | 16.1 | 13.0 |
| 4.9 | 4.2 | 5.1 | Intangibles (net) | | | | 11.0 | 4.3 | 3.7 |
| 4.0 | 4.4 | 4.1 | All Other Non-Current | | | | 2.0 | 4.9 | 3.7 |
| 100.0 | 100.0 | 100.0 | Total | | | | 100.0 | 100.0 | 100.0 |
| | | | **LIABILITIES** | | | | | | |
| 17.4 | 15.9 | 18.7 | Notes Payable-Short Term | | | | 14.4 | 14.4 | 22.7 |
| 1.8 | 2.9 | 2.1 | Cur. Mat.-L.T.D. | | | | 2.9 | 1.3 | 2.0 |
| 18.7 | 21.0 | 24.3 | Trade Payables | | | | 24.6 | 24.0 | 23.3 |
| .2 | .1 | .1 | Income Taxes Payable | | | | .1 | .1 | .1 |
| 7.6 | 7.3 | 6.5 | All Other Current | | | | 4.6 | 5.9 | 7.7 |
| 45.7 | 47.3 | 51.7 | Total Current | | | | 46.7 | 45.7 | 55.7 |
| 11.7 | 10.3 | 12.3 | Long-Term Debt | | | | 18.5 | 12.5 | 10.0 |
| .1 | .2 | .3 | Deferred Taxes | | | | .2 | .2 | .3 |
| 9.8 | 6.8 | 6.6 | All Other Non-Current | | | | 22.0 | 4.7 | 4.1 |
| 32.7 | 35.5 | 29.1 | Net Worth | | | | 12.7 | 36.9 | 29.9 |
| 100.0 | 100.0 | 100.0 | Total Liabilities & Net Worth | | | | 100.0 | 100.0 | 100.0 |
| | | | **INCOME DATA** | | | | | | |
| 100.0 | 100.0 | 100.0 | Net Sales | | | | 100.0 | 100.0 | 100.0 |
| 16.5 | 14.5 | 13.8 | Gross Profit | | | | 20.6 | 14.3 | 10.9 |
| 13.9 | 12.5 | 11.8 | Operating Expenses | | | | 19.8 | 12.0 | 9.2 |
| 2.6 | 2.1 | 2.0 | Operating Profit | | | | .8 | 2.3 | 1.7 |
| .3 | .4 | .3 | All Other Expenses (net) | | | | .5 | .0 | .3 |
| 2.3 | 1.7 | 1.7 | Profit Before Taxes | | | | .3 | 2.3 | 1.4 |
| | | | **RATIOS** | | | | | | |
| 2.8 | 2.4 | 2.1 | | | | | 2.4 | 2.2 | 1.9 |
| 1.6 | 1.6 | 1.4 | Current | | | | 1.3 | 1.5 | 1.4 |
| 1.2 | 1.2 | 1.1 | | | | | .8 | 1.2 | 1.2 |
| 1.6 | 1.6 | 1.3 | | | | | 1.5 | 1.5 | 1.2 |
| .9 | .9 | .9 | Quick | | | | .8 | .8 | .9 |
| .6 | .6 | .6 | | | | | .5 | .6 | .6 |
| 15  24.8 | 15  25.0 | 15  23.8 | | | | | 11  32.2 | 11  31.8 | 17  21.2 |
| 21  17.5 | 21  17.5 | 20  17.9 | Sales/Receivables | | | | 28  12.9 | 19  19.4 | 21  17.5 |
| 29  12.8 | 28  12.8 | 28  12.9 | | | | | 34  10.8 | 25  14.4 | 28  13.0 |
| 8  43.6 | 8  43.7 | 8  48.0 | | | | | 7  51.9 | 7  56.1 | 8  44.4 |
| 18  20.4 | 18  19.9 | 17  21.2 | Cost of Sales/Inventory | | | | 25  14.5 | 18  20.3 | 17  21.2 |
| 31  11.6 | 31  11.9 | 29  12.8 | | | | | 42  8.6 | 25  14.4 | 30  12.2 |
| 7  49.4 | 7  51.7 | 9  41.0 | | | | | 12  29.2 | 8  48.5 | 9  40.8 |
| 12  31.0 | 13  28.0 | 15  25.1 | Cost of Sales/Payables | | | | 25  14.8 | 13  27.5 | 14  25.8 |
| 18  20.0 | 20  18.4 | 21  17.3 | | | | | 33  11.0 | 21  17.3 | 18  20.6 |
| 11.2 | 11.6 | 14.8 | | | | | 9.4 | 14.2 | 16.2 |
| 23.2 | 23.3 | 26.8 | Sales/Working Capital | | | | 32.5 | 27.2 | 26.5 |
| 68.2 | 57.6 | 83.4 | | | | | -66.8 | 75.0 | 62.6 |
| 16.5 | 15.7 | 12.9 | | | | | 9.8 | 23.6 | 10.7 |
| (195)  5.2 | (199)  5.0 | (201)  4.4 | EBIT/Interest | | | (20)  2.4 | | (53)  6.5 | (116)  3.9 |
| 2.0 | 1.9 | 1.7 | | | | | .6 | 3.0 | 1.8 |
| 15.5 | 14.4 | 8.1 | | | | | | | 10.0 |
| (39)  4.7 | (39)  5.1 | (40)  3.8 | Net Profit + Depr., Dep., Amort./Cur. Mat. L/T/D | | | | | (32) | 4.7 |
| 1.5 | 1.4 | 1.8 | | | | | | | 1.8 |
| .1 | .1 | .1 | | | | | .1 | .1 | .1 |
| .4 | .4 | .4 | Fixed/Worth | | | | 1.4 | .4 | .3 |
| 1.7 | 1.0 | 1.5 | | | | | NM | 1.5 | .9 |
| .8 | 1.0 | 1.3 | | | | | 1.9 | 1.0 | 1.3 |
| 2.2 | 2.1 | 2.7 | Debt/Worth | | | | 3.2 | 2.3 | 2.7 |
| 7.1 | 4.6 | 7.2 | | | | | NM | 6.7 | 6.6 |
| 55.1 | 43.3 | 47.7 | | | | | 42.6 | 59.5 | 45.2 |
| (188)  27.9 | (203)  23.3 | (192)  23.3 | % Profit Before Taxes/Tangible Net Worth | | | (16)  9.3 | | (56)  25.3 | (111)  24.3 |
| 12.3 | 7.1 | 7.8 | | | | | -3.0 | 11.6 | 8.2 |
| 18.2 | 15.3 | 13.8 | | | | | 10.1 | 17.1 | 11.0 |
| 8.2 | 6.9 | 5.5 | % Profit Before Taxes/Total Assets | | | | 2.3 | 7.6 | 5.2 |
| 2.5 | 2.0 | 2.1 | | | | | -1.4 | 3.7 | 2.1 |
| 234.6 | 315.3 | 383.4 | | | | | 167.9 | 391.9 | 440.2 |
| 67.9 | 70.4 | 82.6 | Sales/Net Fixed Assets | | | | 50.4 | 69.4 | 101.1 |
| 15.6 | 16.3 | 21.1 | | | | | 11.0 | 22.4 | 34.8 |
| 8.1 | 8.7 | 9.1 | | | | | 6.2 | 9.9 | 9.1 |
| 5.6 | 5.8 | 6.1 | Sales/Total Assets | | | | 4.6 | 6.4 | 6.5 |
| 3.7 | 4.0 | 4.2 | | | | | 2.7 | 4.5 | 4.8 |
| .1 | .1 | .1 | | | | | .1 | .2 | .1 |
| (176)  .4 | (180)  .5 | (174)  .3 | % Depr., Dep., Amort./Sales | | | (16)  .3 | | (43)  .4 | (105)  .3 |
| .8 | 1.0 | .8 | | | | | 1.4 | .8 | .8 |
| .7 | .5 | .5 | | | | | 1.4 | .7 | .3 |
| (86)  1.6 | (94)  1.1 | (92)  1.1 | % Officers', Directors', Owners' Comp/Sales | | | (12)  1.8 | | (38)  1.1 | (35)  .8 |
| 3.0 | 2.5 | 2.0 | | | | | 2.3 | 2.1 | 1.1 |
| 20612883M | 23073269M | 26195256M | Net Sales ($) | 1822M | 13446M | 25117M | 157349M | 1000986M | 24996536M |
| 3994373M | 4178882M | 4281613M | Total Assets ($) | 2252M | 3673M | 6122M | 71375M | 183061M | 4015130M |

M = $ thousand     MM = $ million
See Pages 9 through 22 for Explanation of Ratios and Data

## Current Data Sorted by Assets　　　　　Comparative Historical Data

| 0-500M | 500M-2MM | 2-10MM | 10-50MM | 50-100MM | 100-250MM | Type of Statement | 4/1/07-3/31/08 ALL | 4/1/08-3/31/09 ALL |
|---|---|---|---|---|---|---|---|---|
|  | 4 | 5 | 23 | 2 | 5 | Unqualified | 36 | 38 |
| 1 | 9 | 35 | 31 | 5 | 1 | Reviewed | 70 | 73 |
| 2 | 19 | 38 | 11 | 2 |  | Compiled | 75 | 67 |
| 5 | 20 | 26 | 1 |  |  | Tax Returns | 22 | 40 |
| 2 | 20 | 41 | 33 | 11 | 5 | Other | 85 | 93 |
|  | 89 (4/1-9/30/11) |  | 268 (10/1/11-3/31/12) |  |  |  |  |  |
| 10 | 72 | 145 | 99 | 20 | 11 | **NUMBER OF STATEMENTS** | 288 | 311 |
| % | % | % | % | % | % | **ASSETS** | % | % |
| 10.8 | 15.0 | 10.9 | 9.7 | 14.3 | 4.2 | Cash & Equivalents | 10.1 | 9.7 |
| 31.5 | 45.6 | 46.1 | 36.0 | 21.7 | 26.5 | Trade Receivables (net) | 41.6 | 40.6 |
| 12.8 | 10.4 | 8.8 | 10.0 | 12.7 | 11.3 | Inventory | 8.1 | 10.0 |
| 10.0 | 3.8 | 6.3 | 4.6 | 4.1 | 6.6 | All Other Current | 5.9 | 5.7 |
| 65.2 | 74.8 | 72.1 | 60.2 | 52.8 | 48.7 | Total Current | 65.7 | 66.0 |
| 30.2 | 15.8 | 17.4 | 29.0 | 32.4 | 39.9 | Fixed Assets (net) | 23.8 | 22.7 |
| .6 | 2.8 | 2.3 | 5.9 | 4.9 | 1.0 | Intangibles (net) | 3.0 | 3.0 |
| 4.0 | 6.6 | 8.2 | 4.8 | 9.9 | 10.4 | All Other Non-Current | 7.6 | 8.3 |
| 100.0 | 100.0 | 100.0 | 100.0 | 100.0 | 100.0 | Total | 100.0 | 100.0 |
|  |  |  |  |  |  | **LIABILITIES** |  |  |
| 15.5 | 11.2 | 10.2 | 5.5 | 5.5 | 5.7 | Notes Payable-Short Term | 10.3 | 9.6 |
| 6.9 | 1.3 | 1.9 | 3.0 | 3.3 | 3.0 | Cur. Mat.-L.T.D. | 2.4 | 2.2 |
| 41.7 | 33.1 | 35.9 | 28.3 | 16.1 | 24.6 | Trade Payables | 31.2 | 32.7 |
| .0 | .2 | .1 | .3 | .2 | .2 | Income Taxes Payable | .2 | .2 |
| 8.5 | 11.5 | 7.9 | 9.8 | 10.0 | 7.8 | All Other Current | 9.0 | 9.3 |
| 72.6 | 57.4 | 56.0 | 47.0 | 35.2 | 41.3 | Total Current | 53.1 | 53.9 |
| 40.6 | 9.9 | 9.4 | 15.9 | 22.6 | 18.9 | Long-Term Debt | 12.0 | 12.8 |
| .0 | .0 | .4 | .6 | 1.2 | 2.2 | Deferred Taxes | .4 | .4 |
| 4.9 | 5.2 | 3.3 | 2.8 | 3.4 | 4.9 | All Other Non-Current | 3.2 | 5.4 |
| -18.1 | 27.5 | 30.8 | 33.8 | 37.6 | 32.7 | Net Worth | 31.4 | 27.5 |
| 100.0 | 100.0 | 100.0 | 100.0 | 100.0 | 100.0 | Total Liabilties & Net Worth | 100.0 | 100.0 |
|  |  |  |  |  |  | **INCOME DATA** |  |  |
| 100.0 | 100.0 | 100.0 | 100.0 | 100.0 | 100.0 | Net Sales | 100.0 | 100.0 |
| 15.2 | 17.1 | 19.5 | 23.6 | 29.4 | 20.6 | Gross Profit | 20.0 | 20.0 |
| 14.0 | 14.5 | 15.9 | 18.6 | 19.1 | 9.4 | Operating Expenses | 16.3 | 17.1 |
| 1.3 | 2.5 | 3.6 | 4.9 | 10.3 | 11.2 | Operating Profit | 3.7 | 2.9 |
| .2 | .8 | .1 | .2 | -.1 | .5 | All Other Expenses (net) | .3 | .4 |
| 1.1 | 1.7 | 3.5 | 4.8 | 10.4 | 10.6 | Profit Before Taxes | 3.4 | 2.6 |
|  |  |  |  |  |  | **RATIOS** |  |  |
| 2.0 | 2.1 | 1.7 | 1.8 | 2.1 | 1.4 | Current | 1.7 | 1.6 |
| 1.0 | 1.3 | 1.2 | 1.2 | 1.6 | 1.2 |  | 1.2 | 1.2 |
| .3 | 1.0 | 1.0 | 1.0 | 1.2 | 1.0 |  | 1.0 | 1.0 |
| 1.9 | 1.7 | 1.4 | 1.3 | 1.8 | 1.1 | Quick | 1.3 | 1.3 |
| .5 | 1.1 | 1.0 | .9 | 1.0 | .8 |  | .9 | .9 |
| .2 | .7 | .8 | .7 | .7 | .4 |  | .7 | .7 |
| 0　UND | 15　24.2 | 21　17.3 | 24　14.9 | 26　14.0 | 27　13.7 | Sales/Receivables | 20　18.2 | 20　18.0 |
| 15　24.6 | 26　14.2 | 27　13.6 | 29　12.5 | 29　12.7 | 29　12.5 |  | 28　13.1 | 28　13.2 |
| 24　14.9 | 43　8.5 | 38　9.7 | 38　9.6 | 35　10.5 | 43　8.4 |  | 39　9.4 | 37　9.9 |
| 0　UND | 0　UND | 1　378.8 | 4　94.1 | 5　75.2 | 7　53.9 | Cost of Sales/Inventory | 1　506.6 | 2　214.3 |
| 2　222.4 | 2　183.7 | 5　71.4 | 7　51.2 | 8　47.3 | 41　9.0 |  | 5　76.4 | 6　66.3 |
| 11　32.6 | 12　31.1 | 9　39.9 | 15　23.9 | 56　6.5 | 101　3.6 |  | 10　37.3 | 12　31.6 |
| 0　UND | 6　62.6 | 14　26.1 | 19　18.8 | 17　21.0 | 18　19.8 | Cost of Sales/Payables | 15　23.7 | 15　24.7 |
| 11　34.0 | 21　17.0 | 26　14.2 | 29　12.7 | 22　16.6 | 32　11.4 |  | 25　14.7 | 25　14.7 |
| 45　8.1 | 35　10.3 | 35　10.4 | 46　7.9 | 58　6.3 | 140　2.6 |  | 36　10.2 | 36　10.1 |
| 69.2 | 13.9 | 17.2 | 12.6 | 4.4 | 13.3 | Sales/Working Capital | 18.8 | 19.9 |
| NM | 40.0 | 45.8 | 36.1 | 16.5 | 52.3 |  | 53.8 | 43.2 |
| -27.5 | -244.5 | 677.9 | 521.5 | 31.2 | 87.3 |  | -999.8 | 999.8 |
|  | 28.7 | 29.3 | 18.3 | 8.8 | 18.0 | EBIT/Interest | 14.2 | 14.3 |
| (58)　4.5 | (130)　7.4 | (93)　8.9 | (16)　4.7 | (10)　6.9 |  |  | (258)　5.0 | (283)　4.4 |
| .9 | 2.7 | 2.7 | 3.1 | 3.4 |  |  | 1.8 | 1.8 |
|  |  | 17.5 | 6.2 |  |  | Net Profit + Depr., Dep., Amort./Cur. Mat. L/T/D | 10.5 | 6.6 |
|  | (32)　5.1 | (38)　3.0 |  |  |  |  | (70)　3.4 | (76)　2.8 |
|  | 1.6 | 1.8 |  |  |  |  | 1.7 | 1.5 |
| .3 | .0 | .1 | .4 | .5 | .6 | Fixed/Worth | .2 | .2 |
| 53.1 | .3 | .5 | .9 | 1.1 | 1.2 |  | .6 | .6 |
| -.4 | 2.5 | 1.4 | 1.9 | 1.8 | 1.7 |  | 2.0 | 1.8 |
| 3.5 | .1 | 1.2 | 1.2 | 1.0 | 1.3 | Debt/Worth | 1.3 | 1.3 |
| 111.7 | 2.6 | 2.7 | 2.3 | 1.8 | 2.1 |  | 2.4 | 2.7 |
| -2.8 | 37.0 | 6.5 | 5.2 | 3.1 | 2.5 |  | 5.0 | 7.1 |
|  | 60.6 | 64.1 | 53.6 | 31.4 | 44.7 | % Profit Before Taxes/Tangible Net Worth | 50.7 | 50.7 |
| (56)　23.3 | (131)　18.7 | (88)　23.7 | (18)　19.7 | 23.6 |  |  | (257)　20.0 | (274)　20.0 |
| .7 | 6.9 | 13.8 | 14.1 | 14.1 |  |  | 8.2 | 4.9 |
| 30.0 | 17.7 | 14.5 | 12.3 | 11.8 | 13.3 | % Profit Before Taxes/Total Assets | 16.0 | 13.5 |
| 11.1 | 5.7 | 5.8 | 7.7 | 5.0 | 7.7 |  | 6.0 | 5.5 |
| -.8 | -.9 | 1.7 | 2.8 | 4.0 | .3 |  | 1.4 | 1.0 |
| 201.2 | 441.2 | 255.4 | 38.6 | 22.0 | 15.6 | Sales/Net Fixed Assets | 119.4 | 120.4 |
| 92.6 | 83.4 | 58.1 | 13.8 | 11.3 | 10.9 |  | 29.7 | 35.3 |
| 31.7 | 22.5 | 19.5 | 5.6 | 2.7 | 1.3 |  | 10.6 | 12.0 |
| 18.8 | 9.4 | 8.1 | 6.4 | 4.2 | 3.6 | Sales/Total Assets | 7.9 | 7.7 |
| 9.9 | 6.2 | 6.2 | 3.7 | 2.6 | 2.4 |  | 5.2 | 5.6 |
| 4.5 | 3.8 | 3.7 | 1.9 | .8 | .7 |  | 2.7 | 3.0 |
|  | .2 | .2 | .5 | .9 | .8 | % Depr., Dep., Amort./Sales | .2 | .2 |
| (55)　.4 | (116)　.4 | (95)　1.1 | (19)　2.0 | 1.0 |  |  | (255)　.7 | (263)　.6 |
| 1.0 | 1.1 | 3.0 | 3.8 | 7.0 |  |  | 1.4 | 1.4 |
|  | 1.1 | .8 | .5 |  |  | % Officers', Directors' Owners' Comp/Sales | .6 | .6 |
| (35)　1.9 | (68)　1.6 | (28)　.9 |  |  |  |  | (110)　1.7 | (118)　1.5 |
| 2.7 | 2.3 |  |  |  |  |  | 2.6 | 2.6 |
| 38396M | 605126M | 4433861M | 8376237M | 3716600M | 3686514M | Net Sales ($) | 20524342M | 19652929M |
| 2991M | 90106M | 737669M | 2130097M | 1363975M | 1580657M | Total Assets ($) | 4886626M | 5352042M |

M = $ thousand　　MM = $ million
See Pages 9 through 22 for Explanation of Ratios and Data

| Comparative Historical Data | | | | Current Data Sorted by Sales | | | | | |
|---|---|---|---|---|---|---|---|---|---|
| | | | **Type of Statement** | | | | | | |
| 42 | 40 | 39 | Unqualified | 1 | 1 | | 3 | 6 | 28 |
| 76 | 72 | 82 | Reviewed | 1 | | 6 | 18 | 56 | |
| 76 | 63 | 72 | Compiled | 1 | 3 | 7 | 12 | 18 | 31 |
| 43 | 39 | 52 | Tax Returns | 2 | 2 | 2 | 19 | 16 | 11 |
| 101 | 106 | 112 | Other | 2 | 7 | 4 | 13 | 24 | 62 |
| 4/1/09-3/31/10 ALL | 4/1/10-3/31/11 ALL | 4/1/11-3/31/12 ALL | | 89 (4/1-9/30/11) | | | 268 (10/1/11-3/31/12) | | |
| | | | | 0-1MM | 1-3MM | 3-5MM | 5-10MM | 10-25MM | 25MM & OVER |
| 338 | 320 | 357 | **NUMBER OF STATEMENTS** | 7 | 13 | 14 | 53 | 82 | 188 |
| % | % | % | **ASSETS** | % | % | % | % | % | % |
| 11.3 | 10.7 | 11.4 | Cash & Equivalents | 11.3 | 20.5 | 14.6 | 12.2 | 9.3 | |
| 41.2 | 40.0 | 40.8 | Trade Receivables (net) | 39.2 | 32.0 | 36.5 | 45.3 | 42.0 | |
| 9.5 | 11.6 | 9.8 | Inventory | 9.2 | 7.9 | 10.8 | 9.5 | 9.9 | |
| 5.3 | 4.4 | 5.3 | All Other Current | 9.1 | 19.4 | 4.3 | 4.4 | 4.8 | |
| 67.3 | 66.8 | 67.4 | Total Current | 68.7 | 79.8 | 66.1 | 71.3 | 66.1 | |
| 22.0 | 23.9 | 22.2 | Fixed Assets (net) | 22.9 | 14.5 | 22.5 | 18.7 | 23.4 | |
| 2.7 | 3.2 | 3.5 | Intangibles (net) | .6 | .1 | 4.5 | 2.2 | 4.3 | |
| 8.0 | 6.1 | 7.0 | All Other Non-Current | 7.8 | 5.6 | 6.9 | 7.8 | 6.2 | |
| 100.0 | 100.0 | 100.0 | Total | 100.0 | 100.0 | 100.0 | 100.0 | 100.0 | |
| | | | **LIABILITIES** | | | | | | |
| 9.3 | 8.0 | 8.8 | Notes Payable-Short Term | 23.6 | 24.9 | 9.4 | 9.3 | 6.4 | |
| 2.5 | 2.3 | 2.3 | Cur. Mat.-L.T.D. | 3.1 | .8 | 2.2 | 2.0 | 2.4 | |
| 31.8 | 31.3 | 32.0 | Trade Payables | 31.1 | 18.0 | 29.5 | 32.0 | 33.9 | |
| .2 | .2 | .2 | Income Taxes Payable | .7 | .6 | .1 | .2 | .2 | |
| 8.9 | 9.3 | 9.3 | All Other Current | 11.3 | 7.5 | 10.5 | 8.7 | 9.1 | |
| 52.5 | 51.1 | 52.6 | Total Current | 69.8 | 51.8 | 51.8 | 52.3 | 52.0 | |
| 12.6 | 12.2 | 13.2 | Long-Term Debt | 22.3 | 10.7 | 16.1 | 9.6 | 12.9 | |
| .3 | .4 | .5 | Deferred Taxes | .1 | .1 | .4 | .3 | .6 | |
| 3.8 | 3.8 | 3.7 | All Other Non-Current | 3.0 | 5.3 | 3.7 | 5.4 | 2.4 | |
| 30.8 | 32.5 | 30.1 | Net Worth | 4.8 | 32.1 | 28.0 | 32.4 | 32.2 | |
| 100.0 | 100.0 | 100.0 | Total Liabilities & Net Worth | 100.0 | 100.0 | 100.0 | 100.0 | 100.0 | |
| | | | **INCOME DATA** | | | | | | |
| 100.0 | 100.0 | 100.0 | Net Sales | 100.0 | 100.0 | 100.0 | 100.0 | 100.0 | |
| 19.1 | 20.3 | 20.6 | Gross Profit | 33.3 | 47.4 | 25.1 | 18.7 | 16.4 | |
| 16.3 | 16.2 | 16.3 | Operating Expenses | 27.5 | 38.4 | 20.5 | 14.5 | 13.1 | |
| 2.9 | 4.1 | 4.3 | Operating Profit | 5.9 | 9.0 | 4.6 | 4.2 | 3.3 | |
| .2 | .3 | .3 | All Other Expenses (net) | .7 | .2 | .1 | .0 | .1 | |
| 2.7 | 3.8 | 4.0 | Profit Before Taxes | 5.2 | 8.8 | 4.5 | 4.2 | 3.2 | |
| | | | **RATIOS** | | | | | | |
| 1.9 | 1.8 | 1.8 | Current | 2.2 | 3.4 | 2.3 | 2.2 | 1.7 | |
| 1.3 | 1.3 | 1.2 | | 1.3 | 1.3 | 1.4 | 1.3 | 1.2 | |
| 1.0 | 1.0 | 1.0 | | .6 | 1.0 | 1.0 | 1.0 | 1.0 | |
| 1.4 | 1.4 | 1.4 | Quick | 1.8 | 2.7 | 1.4 | 1.7 | 1.3 | |
| 1.0 | 1.0 | 1.0 | | .8 | .9 | 1.0 | 1.1 | 1.0 | |
| .7 | .7 | .7 | | .3 | .5 | .7 | .8 | .7 | |
| 21  17.7 | 23  16.2 | 21  17.2 | Sales/Receivables | 21  17.2 | 15  25.1 | 16  22.4 | 21  17.4 | 22  16.8 | |
| 29  12.6 | 29  12.7 | 28  13.1 | | 64  5.7 | 38  9.7 | 29  12.5 | 28  12.9 | 28  13.2 | |
| 37  9.7 | 37  9.8 | 38  9.7 | | 96  3.8 | 135  2.7 | 49  7.4 | 41  9.0 | 33  11.1 | |
| 2  199.3 | 3  138.3 | 1  259.2 | Cost of Sales/Inventory | 0  UND | 0  UND | 0  740.8 | 0  UND | 6  142.8 | |
| 6  61.8 | 6  56.9 | 6  63.3 | | 0  UND | 6  62.5 | 8  48.6 | 5  66.9 | 6  60.7 | |
| 11  34.3 | 15  24.5 | 12  30.0 | | 19  18.8 | 38  9.7 | 18  20.8 | 14  26.7 | 10  37.7 | |
| 15  24.3 | 17  21.6 | 15  24.2 | Cost of Sales/Payables | 7  52.9 | 1  269.3 | 9  39.7 | 14  26.2 | 17  21.7 | |
| 25  14.8 | 27  13.3 | 26  14.3 | | 43  8.5 | 30  12.1 | 26  13.8 | 24  15.4 | 26  14.1 | |
| 37  9.8 | 41  9.0 | 39  9.3 | | 215  1.7 | 261  1.4 | 44  8.3 | 36  10.0 | 35  10.5 | |
| 14.7 | 13.7 | 15.7 | Sales/Working Capital | 4.3 | 4.6 | 8.2 | 15.9 | 18.5 | |
| 35.3 | 34.8 | 40.1 | | 11.9 | 14.2 | 25.4 | 39.6 | 48.3 | |
| 725.5 | 228.6 | 702.6 | | -36.0 | 85.0 | -195.4 | 888.0 | 261.6 | |
| 16.2 | 21.6 | 21.5 | EBIT/Interest | | | 73.3 | 23.0 | 21.1 | 23.5 |
| (298) 6.1 | (282) 6.9 | (315) 7.3 | | | | (13) 7.9 | (45) 7.4 | (70) 7.8 | (173) 8.1 |
| 1.7 | 2.7 | 2.6 | | | | 3.9 | 2.4 | 1.6 | 3.2 |
| 8.8 | 7.7 | 7.2 | Net Profit + Depr., Dep., Amort./Cur. Mat. L/T/D | | | | | 17.0 | 6.6 |
| (82) 3.0 | (86) 3.4 | (89) 2.8 | | | | | | (16) 5.8 | (65) 2.7 |
| 1.4 | 2.2 | 1.6 | | | | | | 1.5 | 1.7 |
| .2 | .2 | .2 | Fixed/Worth | .1 | .0 | .2 | .1 | .3 | |
| .6 | .7 | .6 | | .7 | .4 | .6 | .4 | .8 | |
| 1.8 | 1.6 | 1.8 | | -1.3 | 1.3 | 3.2 | 1.4 | 1.6 | |
| 1.0 | 1.1 | 1.1 | Debt/Worth | 1.6 | .8 | 1.0 | 1.0 | 1.2 | |
| 2.4 | 2.3 | 2.5 | | 9.2 | 2.2 | 2.4 | 2.6 | 2.4 | |
| 6.0 | 5.2 | 7.3 | | -11.0 | 12.1 | 10.2 | 6.6 | 5.5 | |
| 50.1 | 52.3 | 54.5 | % Profit Before Taxes/Tangible Net Worth | | | 48.8 | 47.4 | 68.0 | 55.7 |
| (303) 20.3 | (292) 26.6 | (310) 22.4 | | | | (12) 36.6 | (42) 25.3 | (75) 18.7 | (169) 22.3 |
| 5.1 | 8.1 | 8.4 | | | | 11.3 | 2.8 | 4.8 | 9.5 |
| 15.2 | 14.9 | 14.5 | % Profit Before Taxes/Total Assets | 5.4 | 24.7 | 15.0 | 18.2 | 14.2 | |
| 5.0 | 6.8 | 6.7 | | 2.5 | 8.6 | 8.3 | 6.4 | 7.1 | |
| 1.4 | 1.9 | 1.8 | | -5.7 | .8 | 1.7 | 1.4 | 2.4 | |
| 161.0 | 119.1 | 165.9 | Sales/Net Fixed Assets | 67.8 | 171.1 | 138.3 | 306.5 | 133.2 | |
| 34.9 | 28.4 | 35.1 | | 22.7 | 57.1 | 42.9 | 40.6 | 31.8 | |
| 10.2 | 9.1 | 10.3 | | 6.3 | 10.5 | 9.3 | 10.2 | 11.2 | |
| 7.5 | 7.3 | 7.7 | Sales/Total Assets | 3.9 | 4.1 | 7.6 | 8.4 | 7.8 | |
| 5.3 | 5.3 | 5.2 | | 2.6 | 2.1 | 4.9 | 5.8 | 5.6 | |
| 3.0 | 2.6 | 2.6 | | 1.3 | .7 | 2.1 | 2.9 | 3.5 | |
| .2 | .3 | .2 | % Depr., Dep., Amort./Sales | | | .2 | .4 | .1 | .2 |
| (278) .7 | (269) .6 | (300) .7 | | | | (11) .8 | (42) 1.0 | (69) .6 | (164) .6 |
| 1.6 | 1.7 | 1.6 | | | | 3.0 | 4.0 | 1.7 | 1.3 |
| .8 | .7 | .8 | % Officers', Directors' Owners' Comp/Sales | | | | .9 | 1.1 | .6 |
| (125) 1.7 | (121) 1.4 | (140) 1.4 | | | | | (27) 1.8 | (38) 2.0 | (63) 1.0 |
| 3.1 | 2.6 | 2.3 | | | | | 2.8 | 2.4 | 1.5 |
| 21831021M | 19768438M | 20856734M | Net Sales ($) | 4008M | 27280M | 55665M | 396904M | 1379461M | 18993416M |
| 5676819M | 5522450M | 5905495M | Total Assets ($) | 7222M | 86639M | 47254M | 229108M | 459495M | 5075777M |

## Current Data Sorted by Assets                                    Comparative Historical Data

| | | | | | | | Type of Statement | | |
|---|---|---|---|---|---|---|---|---|---|
| | | 1 | 16 | 33 | 12 | 5 | Unqualified | 78 | 63 |
| | 4 | 7 | 49 | 46 | 1 | 1 | Reviewed | 65 | 90 |
| | 19 | 21 | 38 | 3 | | | Compiled | 51 | 51 |
| | 11 | 29 | 37 | 2 | | 1 | Tax Returns | 47 | 54 |
| | | 26 | 47 | 50 | 20 | 5 | Other | 115 | 150 |
| | | 95 (4/1-9/30/11) | | 389 (10/1/11-3/31/12) | | | | 4/1/07-3/31/08 | 4/1/08-3/31/09 |
| | 0-500M | 500M-2MM | 2-10MM | 10-50MM | 50-100MM | 100-250MM | | ALL | ALL |
| | 34 | 84 | 187 | 134 | 33 | 12 | NUMBER OF STATEMENTS | 356 | 408 |
| | % | % | % | % | % | % | ASSETS | % | % |
| | 15.0 | 10.7 | 7.7 | 7.1 | 4.1 | 7.0 | Cash & Equivalents | 7.9 | 7.1 |
| | 23.4 | 34.4 | 30.2 | 28.3 | 23.7 | 25.3 | Trade Receivables (net) | 28.3 | 29.2 |
| | 24.3 | 32.2 | 33.1 | 33.9 | 26.6 | 27.3 | Inventory | 29.9 | 31.5 |
| | 2.1 | 2.6 | 1.9 | 4.4 | 4.2 | 2.8 | All Other Current | 3.5 | 4.0 |
| | 64.9 | 79.9 | 73.0 | 73.7 | 58.5 | 62.4 | Total Current | 69.6 | 71.8 |
| | 21.2 | 13.7 | 16.6 | 16.2 | 22.5 | 18.8 | Fixed Assets (net) | 19.4 | 18.0 |
| | 5.2 | 2.8 | 4.8 | 4.7 | 13.4 | 16.4 | Intangibles (net) | 4.4 | 4.2 |
| | 9.0 | 3.6 | 5.7 | 5.5 | 5.6 | 2.4 | All Other Non-Current | 6.6 | 6.1 |
| | 100.0 | 100.0 | 100.0 | 100.0 | 100.0 | 100.0 | Total | 100.0 | 100.0 |
| | | | | | | | LIABILITIES | | |
| | 10.1 | 12.8 | 12.4 | 13.1 | 11.2 | 20.1 | Notes Payable-Short Term | 17.0 | 17.4 |
| | 2.3 | 4.3 | 2.6 | 1.8 | 2.8 | .9 | Cur. Mat.-L.T.D. | 2.5 | 2.9 |
| | 16.6 | 29.5 | 27.4 | 22.7 | 17.9 | 18.9 | Trade Payables | 22.2 | 21.9 |
| | .4 | .4 | .2 | .1 | .5 | .2 | Income Taxes Payable | .2 | .2 |
| | 17.9 | 4.7 | 7.2 | 9.6 | 7.3 | 12.4 | All Other Current | 8.9 | 9.0 |
| | 47.3 | 51.7 | 49.9 | 47.3 | 39.7 | 52.4 | Total Current | 50.9 | 51.3 |
| | 19.8 | 15.4 | 10.1 | 8.3 | 16.4 | 16.8 | Long-Term Debt | 15.7 | 12.5 |
| | .1 | .0 | .4 | .4 | 1.5 | 1.0 | Deferred Taxes | .2 | .3 |
| | 7.7 | 5.9 | 5.7 | 5.3 | 7.1 | 1.0 | All Other Non-Current | 4.8 | 4.0 |
| | 24.8 | 27.0 | 34.0 | 38.8 | 35.3 | 28.8 | Net Worth | 28.4 | 31.9 |
| | 100.0 | 100.0 | 100.0 | 100.0 | 100.0 | 100.0 | Total Liabilities & Net Worth | 100.0 | 100.0 |
| | | | | | | | INCOME DATA | | |
| | 100.0 | 100.0 | 100.0 | 100.0 | 100.0 | 100.0 | Net Sales | 100.0 | 100.0 |
| | 32.6 | 26.0 | 22.4 | 21.1 | 20.1 | 24.9 | Gross Profit | 24.6 | 22.9 |
| | 27.8 | 23.7 | 19.7 | 16.4 | 15.5 | 16.8 | Operating Expenses | 21.4 | 20.1 |
| | 4.8 | 2.2 | 2.7 | 4.7 | 4.5 | 8.1 | Operating Profit | 3.2 | 2.8 |
| | .8 | .2 | .3 | 1.4 | .8 | .7 | All Other Expenses (net) | .7 | .7 |
| | 4.0 | 2.0 | 2.4 | 3.4 | 3.8 | 7.5 | Profit Before Taxes | 2.5 | 2.1 |
| | | | | | | | RATIOS | | |
| | 4.9 | 3.3 | 2.1 | 2.1 | 2.3 | 2.3 | | 2.2 | 2.2 |
| | 1.9 | 1.7 | 1.5 | 1.5 | 1.3 | 1.3 | Current | 1.4 | 1.4 |
| | 1.1 | 1.2 | 1.1 | 1.2 | 1.1 | .9 | | 1.1 | 1.1 |
| | 3.3 | 1.6 | 1.1 | 1.0 | 1.3 | 1.1 | | 1.3 | 1.2 |
| | .9 | 1.0 | .8 | .7 | .7 | .8 | Quick (355) | .7 | .7 |
| | .5 | .5 | .5 | .5 | .5 | .4 | | .4 | .5 |
| | 2  222.4 | 18  20.6 | 19  19.3 | 20  18.0 | 20  18.0 | 15  24.9 | | 18  20.7 | 18  20.0 |
| | 16  22.4 | 25  14.6 | 27  13.6 | 29  12.8 | 27  13.3 | 30  12.2 | Sales/Receivables | 26  13.9 | 27  13.5 |
| | 27  13.4 | 33  11.0 | 37  9.8 | 39  9.4 | 40  9.2 | 43  8.5 | | 37  9.8 | 37  9.8 |
| | 5  74.9 | 16  23.1 | 20  18.7 | 20  18.1 | 26  14.0 | 11  32.4 | | 18  20.5 | 19  19.5 |
| | 28  12.9 | 33  11.0 | 37  9.8 | 41  8.9 | 45  8.1 | 26  14.2 | Cost of Sales/Inventory | 34  10.8 | 33  11.2 |
| | 54  6.7 | 53  6.9 | 72  5.1 | 87  4.2 | 68  5.4 | 85  4.3 | | 62  5.9 | 63  5.8 |
| | 1  567.6 | 12  30.6 | 15  23.8 | 15  24.2 | 18  20.4 | 17  21.4 | | 13  28.7 | 14  26.7 |
| | 12  29.5 | 25  14.7 | 27  13.3 | 27  13.7 | 26  14.0 | 23  15.6 | Cost of Sales/Payables | 25  14.5 | 23  15.9 |
| | 31  11.7 | 36  10.0 | 45  8.2 | 39  9.3 | 36  10.2 | 35  10.3 | | 37  10.0 | 36  10.2 |
| | 10.9 | 8.7 | 9.5 | 6.8 | 7.7 | 15.4 | | 9.7 | 9.0 |
| | 22.4 | 15.4 | 16.7 | 13.8 | 19.9 | 34.3 | Sales/Working Capital | 19.8 | 18.9 |
| | 174.3 | 53.5 | 52.4 | 36.3 | 62.8 | -58.7 | | 79.7 | 65.2 |
| | 17.7 | 14.4 | 12.6 | 32.4 | 7.0 | 25.7 | | 10.7 | 11.5 |
| | (25)  4.3 | (69)  6.2 | (170)  4.8 | (124)  8.1 | (30)  3.7 | (11)  7.2 | EBIT/Interest (320) | 3.2 | (376)  3.6 |
| | .4 | 1.9 | 1.5 | 3.2 | 1.9 | 2.4 | | 1.4 | 1.4 |
| | | | 8.1 | 20.8 | 10.6 | | | 17.6 | 11.7 |
| | | (35)  3.9 | (37)  4.5 | (16)  4.1 | | | Net Profit + Depr., Dep., Amort./Cur. Mat. L/T/D (85) | 6.0 | (91)  5.0 |
| | | 1.5 | 2.5 | 1.4 | | | | 2.0 | 1.7 |
| | .0 | .1 | .1 | .1 | .4 | .5 | | .1 | .1 |
| | .3 | .3 | .3 | .3 | 1.2 | 1.4 | Fixed/Worth | .5 | .4 |
| | -14.9 | 1.5 | 1.3 | 1.0 | NM | 3.4 | | 1.7 | 1.5 |
| | .5 | .7 | 1.1 | 1.0 | 1.0 | 1.5 | | 1.1 | 1.0 |
| | 1.1 | 3.0 | 2.3 | 2.0 | 2.4 | 3.7 | Debt/Worth | 2.4 | 2.5 |
| | -8.6 | 21.1 | 5.6 | 4.5 | NM | 30.1 | | 8.1 | 6.9 |
| | 83.9 | 51.6 | 43.2 | 44.8 | 38.6 | 53.3 | | 45.1 | 41.2 |
| | (23)  33.2 | (67)  24.7 | (172)  21.0 | (127)  25.2 | (25)  22.1 | (10)  38.2 | % Profit Before Taxes/Tangible Net Worth (308) | 21.6 | (352)  19.7 |
| | 5.5 | 6.3 | 6.0 | 12.8 | 16.9 | 29.0 | | 7.8 | 6.6 |
| | 26.5 | 19.9 | 12.2 | 13.5 | 11.1 | 11.8 | | 14.0 | 13.0 |
| | 8.5 | 8.3 | 5.9 | 7.1 | 6.6 | 9.2 | % Profit Before Taxes/Total Assets | 6.2 | 6.1 |
| | 1.9 | 1.9 | 1.0 | 3.5 | 2.4 | 3.0 | | 1.3 | 1.1 |
| | UND | 354.6 | 204.3 | 200.5 | 63.4 | 68.2 | | 140.7 | 188.5 |
| | 65.9 | 82.3 | 48.8 | 32.9 | 13.2 | 19.6 | Sales/Net Fixed Assets | 34.6 | 41.0 |
| | 14.0 | 20.8 | 15.0 | 12.4 | 6.3 | 7.3 | | 11.7 | 11.6 |
| | 11.3 | 6.7 | 5.2 | 4.7 | 4.4 | 5.9 | | 5.3 | 5.1 |
| | 4.1 | 5.1 | 3.6 | 3.1 | 2.4 | 3.4 | Sales/Total Assets | 3.5 | 3.5 |
| | 2.6 | 3.4 | 2.6 | 2.1 | 1.6 | 1.0 | | 2.6 | 2.5 |
| | .3 | .2 | .2 | .2 | .2 | .6 | | .3 | .2 |
| | (19)  1.5 | (55)  .5 | (148)  .6 | (108)  .5 | (27)  1.4 | | % Depr., Dep., Amort./Sales (288) | .7 | (324)  .6 |
| | 4.5 | 1.4 | 1.4 | 1.4 | 2.5 | | | 1.5 | 1.5 |
| | 2.3 | 1.2 | 1.0 | .8 | | | | .9 | .9 |
| | (16)  5.7 | (46)  2.3 | (89)  1.8 | (33)  1.9 | | | % Officers', Directors' Owners' Comp/Sales (137) | 1.8 | (145)  1.5 |
| | 8.1 | 3.4 | 3.0 | 3.1 | | | | 4.4 | 3.2 |
| | 60095M | 565696M | 3819734M | 11129662M | 6647516M | 6027165M | Net Sales ($) | 25557364M | 32108238M |
| | 9623M | 104186M | 910697M | 3000509M | 2222803M | 1609105M | Total Assets ($) | 7713201M | 8755269M |

M = $ thousand   MM = $ million
See Pages 9 through 22 for Explanation of Ratios and Data

## Comparative Historical Data      Current Data Sorted by Sales

| | | | Type of Statement | | | | | | |
|---|---|---|---|---|---|---|---|---|---|
| 80 | 80 | 67 | Unqualified | | 1 | 1 | 2 | 5 | 58 |
| 100 | 107 | 104 | Reviewed | 2 | 1 | 1 | 7 | 32 | 61 |
| 49 | 63 | 66 | Compiled | 2 | 5 | 2 | 24 | 24 | 9 |
| 66 | 69 | 88 | Tax Returns | 6 | 15 | 13 | 25 | 20 | 9 |
| 157 | 165 | 159 | Other | 6 | 12 | 9 | 18 | 30 | 84 |
| 4/1/09-3/31/10 | 4/1/10-3/31/11 | 4/1/11-3/31/12 | | | 95 (4/1-9/30/11) | | | 389 (10/1/11-3/31/12) | |
| ALL | ALL | ALL | | 0-1MM | 1-3MM | 3-5MM | 5-10MM | 10-25MM | 25MM & OVER |
| 452 | 484 | 484 | **NUMBER OF STATEMENTS** | 16 | 34 | 26 | 76 | 111 | 221 |
| % | % | % | **ASSETS** | % | % | % | % | % | % |
| 7.9 | 8.1 | 8.3 | Cash & Equivalents | 12.2 | 16.3 | 10.6 | 8.4 | 9.1 | 6.1 |
| 30.2 | 30.9 | 29.4 | Trade Receivables (net) | 17.2 | 17.7 | 32.2 | 30.4 | 30.0 | 31.0 |
| 30.9 | 31.8 | 32.0 | Inventory | 18.5 | 27.7 | 33.8 | 34.2 | 32.1 | 32.5 |
| 3.1 | 3.2 | 2.9 | All Other Current | 1.2 | 2.4 | 2.6 | 1.5 | 3.3 | 3.4 |
| 72.0 | 73.9 | 72.6 | Total Current | 49.2 | 64.1 | 79.1 | 74.6 | 74.5 | 73.1 |
| 17.8 | 16.4 | 16.7 | Fixed Assets (net) | 31.6 | 24.9 | 11.7 | 15.4 | 15.4 | 16.1 |
| 4.8 | 4.7 | 5.3 | Intangibles (net) | 15.4 | 2.8 | 4.9 | 4.5 | 4.9 | 5.6 |
| 5.4 | 5.0 | 5.4 | All Other Non-Current | 4.3 | 8.2 | 4.4 | 5.5 | 5.2 | 5.2 |
| 100.0 | 100.0 | 100.0 | Total | 100.0 | 100.0 | 100.0 | 100.0 | 100.0 | 100.0 |
| | | | **LIABILITIES** | | | | | | |
| 15.8 | 15.7 | 12.6 | Notes Payable-Short Term | 6.2 | 10.8 | 19.1 | 12.4 | 11.3 | 13.4 |
| 2.8 | 2.2 | 2.6 | Cur. Mat.-L.T.D. | 1.7 | 4.2 | 4.5 | 3.7 | 2.0 | 2.2 |
| 22.8 | 25.6 | 24.8 | Trade Payables | 8.0 | 16.5 | 27.4 | 25.9 | 28.8 | 24.7 |
| .3 | .2 | .2 | Income Taxes Payable | .8 | .0 | .0 | .5 | .1 | .2 |
| 9.0 | 8.1 | 8.3 | All Other Current | 33.2 | 6.4 | 5.5 | 8.5 | 5.6 | 8.5 |
| 50.7 | 51.8 | 48.7 | Total Current | 49.9 | 37.9 | 56.5 | 51.0 | 47.8 | 48.9 |
| 12.3 | 10.8 | 11.8 | Long-Term Debt | 38.3 | 14.1 | 17.4 | 14.1 | 8.1 | 9.9 |
| .3 | .3 | .4 | Deferred Taxes | .3 | .0 | .0 | .1 | .5 | .6 |
| 4.5 | 4.4 | 5.7 | All Other Non-Current | 7.9 | 8.5 | 8.6 | 4.2 | 6.8 | 4.8 |
| 32.2 | 32.8 | 33.4 | Net Worth | 3.2 | 39.5 | 17.6 | 30.7 | 36.8 | 35.8 |
| 100.0 | 100.0 | 100.0 | Total Liabilities & Net Worth | 100.0 | 100.0 | 100.0 | 100.0 | 100.0 | 100.0 |
| | | | **INCOME DATA** | | | | | | |
| 100.0 | 100.0 | 100.0 | Net Sales | 100.0 | 100.0 | 100.0 | 100.0 | 100.0 | 100.0 |
| 23.5 | 22.4 | 23.3 | Gross Profit | 38.7 | 34.6 | 30.9 | 27.0 | 22.3 | 18.7 |
| 19.9 | 18.8 | 19.7 | Operating Expenses | 32.4 | 32.1 | 25.4 | 22.9 | 19.8 | 15.0 |
| 3.6 | 3.6 | 3.6 | Operating Profit | 6.4 | 2.6 | 5.5 | 4.1 | 2.5 | 3.7 |
| .4 | .3 | .7 | All Other Expenses (net) | 1.5 | .8 | 3.8 | 1.3 | .0 | .3 |
| 3.2 | 3.2 | 2.9 | Profit Before Taxes | 4.9 | 1.8 | 1.7 | 2.8 | 2.5 | 3.4 |
| | | | **RATIOS** | | | | | | |
| 2.1 | 2.1 | 2.3 | | 7.7 | 5.4 | 2.9 | 2.1 | 2.2 | 2.1 |
| 1.5 | 1.4 | 1.5 | Current | 1.6 | 1.8 | 1.6 | 1.5 | 1.5 | 1.5 |
| 1.1 | 1.1 | 1.1 | | 1.0 | 1.1 | 1.1 | 1.2 | 1.2 | 1.1 |
| 1.1 | 1.1 | 1.2 | | 3.6 | 3.2 | 1.5 | 1.2 | 1.2 | 1.1 |
| .8 | .7 | .8 | Quick | .8 | .8 | .9 | .7 | .9 | .8 |
| .5 | .5 | .5 | | .4 | .4 | .4 | .4 | .5 | .5 |
| 19   19.1 | 20   18.3 | 18   19.8 | | 0   UND | 10   36.7 | 15   25.0 | 20   18.0 | 17   22.1 | 20   18.6 |
| 27   13.3 | 28   13.0 | 27   13.6 | Sales/Receivables | 24   15.1 | 23   16.0 | 24   15.1 | 27   13.4 | 26   14.1 | 28   13.1 |
| 38   9.6 | 38   9.5 | 37   9.9 | | 43   8.5 | 29   12.5 | 36   10.0 | 38   9.7 | 37   9.8 | 37   9.8 |
| 19   19.5 | 19   19.4 | 19   19.4 | | 1   664.8 | 9   38.7 | 23   15.7 | 26   14.0 | 19   19.0 | 17   20.9 |
| 37   9.9 | 36   10.2 | 37   9.8 | Cost of Sales/Inventory | 35   10.4 | 41   9.0 | 37   9.9 | 51   7.2 | 34   10.6 | 33   11.1 |
| 62   5.9 | 68   5.3 | 70   5.2 | | 104   3.5 | 69   5.3 | 69   5.3 | 78   4.7 | 70   5.2 | 65   5.6 |
| 15   24.7 | 14   25.5 | 15   25.0 | | 1   329.1 | 4   102.4 | 19   19.0 | 14   25.2 | 16   22.7 | 15   24.8 |
| 24   15.2 | 26   14.1 | 26   14.1 | Cost of Sales/Payables | 22   16.4 | 21   17.0 | 33   11.2 | 26   14.1 | 27   13.3 | 25   14.5 |
| 38   9.7 | 45   8.1 | 41   9.0 | | 43   8.4 | 47   7.7 | 50   7.3 | 48   7.6 | 46   8.0 | 36   10.2 |
| 8.9 | 8.9 | 8.4 | | 3.6 | 6.4 | 7.4 | 8.5 | 8.5 | 8.9 |
| 17.6 | 17.8 | 16.1 | Sales/Working Capital | 23.5 | 15.8 | 14.2 | 15.9 | 14.6 | 17.2 |
| 69.6 | 64.6 | 54.1 | | NM | NM | UND | 42.7 | 39.1 | 62.6 |
| 16.4 | 14.8 | 15.9 | | 4.9 | 15.8 | 14.4 | 9.3 | 14.5 | 28.0 |
| (416) 5.2 | (431) 5.6 | (429) 5.4 | EBIT/Interest | (12) 1.5 | (28) 3.9 | (21) 3.3 | (63) 5.0 | (104) 4.7 | (201) 7.2 |
| 2.0 | 2.3 | 2.0 | | -.8 | -.5 | 1.2 | 1.1 | 1.6 | 2.8 |
| 9.6 | 9.5 | 10.8 | | | | | 4.1 | 12.3 | 12.5 |
| (112) 4.0 | (111) 3.3 | (98) 4.3 | Net Profit + Depr., Dep., Amort./Cur. Mat. L/T/D | | | (11) 2.8 | (23) 3.9 | (62) 4.5 | |
| 1.8 | 1.8 | 2.1 | | | | | .1 | 1.9 | 2.4 |
| .1 | .1 | .1 | | .0 | .1 | .0 | .0 | .1 | .1 |
| .4 | .4 | .4 | Fixed/Worth | 11.5 | .4 | .3 | .3 | .3 | .4 |
| 1.7 | 1.5 | 1.5 | | -1.4 | NM | NM | 2.0 | 1.0 | 1.3 |
| 1.0 | 1.0 | .9 | | .5 | .5 | .9 | 1.2 | .8 | 1.0 |
| 2.4 | 2.6 | 2.4 | Debt/Worth | NM | .9 | 5.5 | 2.7 | 2.3 | 2.0 |
| 6.4 | 6.8 | 6.6 | | -4.1 | NM | -52.9 | 5.1 | 6.5 | 5.3 |
| 45.3 | 51.9 | 44.8 | | | 38.7 | 61.4 | 58.2 | 43.7 | 45.4 |
| (397) 25.1 | (434) 23.8 | (424) 24.6 | % Profit Before Taxes/Tangible Net Worth | (26) 22.2 | (19) 20.7 | (66) 24.5 | (104) 17.3 | (201) 26.8 | |
| 11.1 | 9.5 | 9.0 | | 1.4 | 2.9 | 8.9 | 4.4 | 16.0 | |
| 14.9 | 15.2 | 15.0 | | 23.7 | 18.5 | 20.8 | 17.4 | 11.9 | 15.3 |
| 7.2 | 6.8 | 6.9 | % Profit Before Taxes/Total Assets | 4.7 | 5.3 | 6.7 | 7.5 | 5.8 | 7.5 |
| 2.5 | 2.6 | 2.2 | | -2.2 | -1.5 | .3 | 2.4 | 1.0 | 3.4 |
| 162.0 | 232.2 | 221.3 | | UND | 125.1 | 796.7 | 285.0 | 204.4 | 208.0 |
| 39.5 | 47.7 | 45.4 | Sales/Net Fixed Assets | 8.3 | 18.9 | 233.1 | 61.1 | 43.7 | 45.1 |
| 11.6 | 13.8 | 12.7 | | 3.0 | 5.9 | 22.2 | 18.2 | 13.6 | 13.3 |
| 5.4 | 5.4 | 5.5 | | 2.8 | 4.7 | 5.9 | 5.1 | 5.6 | 5.7 |
| 3.5 | 3.5 | 3.6 | Sales/Total Assets | 1.9 | 3.3 | 4.0 | 3.4 | 3.6 | 4.0 |
| 2.4 | 2.4 | 2.4 | | 1.0 | 1.9 | 2.8 | 2.4 | 2.6 | 2.5 |
| .2 | .2 | .2 | | 2.6 | .3 | .1 | .2 | .2 | .2 |
| (364) .7 | (371) .6 | (366) .6 | % Depr., Dep., Amort./Sales | (11) 4.5 | (20) 1.6 | (13) .3 | (51) .7 | (89) .6 | (182) .5 |
| 1.6 | 1.5 | 1.6 | | 7.4 | 2.7 | 1.7 | 1.6 | 1.5 | 1.4 |
| .8 | 1.1 | 1.0 | | | 3.2 | 1.7 | 1.1 | 1.0 | .7 |
| (170) 1.8 | (182) 2.0 | (192) 2.0 | % Officers', Directors' Owners' Comp/Sales | (19) 5.8 | (17) 2.4 | (41) 2.4 | (55) 1.6 | (56) 1.3 | |
| 3.7 | 3.5 | 3.7 | | 8.9 | 4.8 | 3.4 | 2.8 | 2.3 | |
| 34063970M | 33925884M | 28249868M | Net Sales ($) | 8520M | 67007M | 104538M | 561585M | 1729668M | 25778550M |
| 9107496M | 8948939M | 7856923M | Total Assets ($) | 5717M | 31230M | 42065M | 203673M | 621375M | 6952863M |

**M = $ thousand    MM = $ million**
See Pages 9 through 22 for Explanation of Ratios and Data

## Current Data Sorted by Assets      Comparative Historical Data

| | | | | | | Type of Statement | | |
|---|---|---|---|---|---|---|---|---|
| 1 | 2 | 36 | 78 | 25 | 35 | Unqualified | 220 | 174 |
| | 10 | 45 | 25 | 1 | | Reviewed | 92 | 73 |
| 1 | 4 | 8 | 6 | | | Compiled | 17 | 17 |
| 5 | 2 | 10 | 3 | | | Tax Returns | 11 | 18 |
| 1 | 3 | 23 | 22 | 10 | 7 | Other | 79 | 76 |
| | 211 (4/1-9/30/11) | | 152 (10/1/11-3/31/12) | | | | 4/1/07-3/31/08 | 4/1/08-3/31/09 |
| 0-500M | 500M-2MM | 2-10MM | 10-50MM | 50-100MM | 100-250MM | | ALL | ALL |
| 8 | 21 | 122 | 134 | 36 | 42 | NUMBER OF STATEMENTS | 419 | 358 |
| % | % | % | % | % | % | ASSETS | % | % |
| | 15.6 | 13.5 | 6.9 | 5.7 | 5.9 | Cash & Equivalents | 7.3 | 8.1 |
| | 24.0 | 20.0 | 12.3 | 17.2 | 18.0 | Trade Receivables (net) | 17.8 | 19.0 |
| | 25.4 | 28.3 | 42.8 | 39.6 | 45.0 | Inventory | 38.9 | 39.1 |
| | 8.2 | 7.7 | 11.3 | 11.7 | 10.4 | All Other Current | 8.1 | 9.8 |
| | 73.3 | 69.5 | 73.3 | 74.3 | 79.4 | Total Current | 72.2 | 76.1 |
| | 18.5 | 23.5 | 22.4 | 17.8 | 14.6 | Fixed Assets (net) | 21.2 | 17.8 |
| | 1.4 | 1.0 | .4 | 2.5 | .9 | Intangibles (net) | .4 | .5 |
| | 6.8 | 6.0 | 4.0 | 5.3 | 5.1 | All Other Non-Current | 6.1 | 5.6 |
| | 100.0 | 100.0 | 100.0 | 100.0 | 100.0 | Total | 100.0 | 100.0 |
| | | | | | | LIABILITIES | | |
| | 11.6 | 14.1 | 24.0 | 27.5 | 31.1 | Notes Payable-Short Term | 27.1 | 26.0 |
| | 1.5 | 2.1 | 1.5 | 1.1 | .8 | Cur. Mat.-L.T.D. | 1.6 | 2.2 |
| | 19.2 | 21.6 | 17.2 | 15.8 | 17.6 | Trade Payables | 16.2 | 17.6 |
| | .1 | .4 | .2 | .2 | .2 | Income Taxes Payable | .3 | .4 |
| | 3.1 | 11.1 | 11.9 | 9.2 | 10.9 | All Other Current | 10.0 | 12.5 |
| | 35.4 | 49.4 | 54.8 | 53.8 | 60.7 | Total Current | 55.4 | 58.6 |
| | 10.0 | 8.5 | 10.3 | 9.6 | 5.2 | Long-Term Debt | 9.1 | 7.9 |
| | .7 | 1.6 | 1.6 | 1.2 | 1.0 | Deferred Taxes | 1.1 | .8 |
| | 4.4 | 5.3 | 1.4 | 1.5 | 2.1 | All Other Non-Current | 1.2 | 1.6 |
| | 49.4 | 35.3 | 31.9 | 33.9 | 31.0 | Net Worth | 33.2 | 31.0 |
| | 100.0 | 100.0 | 100.0 | 100.0 | 100.0 | Total Liabilities & Net Worth | 100.0 | 100.0 |
| | | | | | | INCOME DATA | | |
| | 100.0 | 100.0 | 100.0 | 100.0 | 100.0 | Net Sales | 100.0 | 100.0 |
| | 13.6 | 12.2 | 9.6 | 9.5 | 7.2 | Gross Profit | 10.9 | 10.1 |
| | 11.9 | 9.2 | 6.1 | 6.6 | 4.4 | Operating Expenses | 7.9 | 7.1 |
| | 1.7 | 3.0 | 3.5 | 3.0 | 2.8 | Operating Profit | 3.0 | 3.1 |
| | .0 | .4 | .4 | .4 | .1 | All Other Expenses (net) | .6 | .4 |
| | 1.6 | 2.6 | 3.1 | 2.6 | 2.7 | Profit Before Taxes | 2.5 | 2.6 |
| | | | | | | RATIOS | | |
| | 3.7 | 2.0 | 1.5 | 1.5 | 1.4 | | 1.6 | 1.6 |
| | 2.1 | 1.5 | 1.3 | 1.3 | 1.3 | Current | 1.2 | 1.2 |
| | 1.4 | 1.2 | 1.2 | 1.2 | 1.2 | | 1.1 | 1.1 |
| | 2.4 | 1.1 | .5 | .6 | .6 | | .8 | .8 |
| | 1.1 | .7 | .3 | .3 | .3 | Quick | .4 | .4 |
| | .6 | .3 | .1 | .1 | .2 | | .2 | .2 |

| | | | | | | | | | | | | | | |
|---|---|---|---|---|---|---|---|---|---|---|---|---|---|---|
| 5 | 68.8 | 6 | 58.0 | 5 | 67.9 | 7 | 55.3 | 8 | 46.4 | Sales/Receivables | 7 | 51.1 | 6 | 57.4 |
| 14 | 27.0 | 15 | 24.8 | 12 | 30.1 | 15 | 23.9 | 12 | 29.2 | | 17 | 21.5 | 15 | 24.0 |
| 28 | 13.2 | 25 | 14.4 | 25 | 14.7 | 36 | 10.0 | 31 | 11.6 | | 33 | 11.2 | 31 | 11.8 |
| 2 | 204.4 | 7 | 49.4 | 31 | 11.7 | 39 | 9.4 | 30 | 12.1 | Cost of Sales/Inventory | 29 | 12.4 | 24 | 15.3 |
| 14 | 26.5 | 30 | 12.1 | 63 | 5.8 | 64 | 5.7 | 60 | 6.1 | | 55 | 6.6 | 49 | 7.4 |
| 55 | 6.6 | 55 | 6.6 | 111 | 3.3 | 85 | 4.3 | 94 | 3.9 | | 92 | 4.0 | 87 | 4.2 |
| 2 | 198.6 | 5 | 78.7 | 6 | 65.5 | 9 | 41.9 | 11 | 32.3 | Cost of Sales/Payables | 7 | 54.6 | 5 | 74.5 |
| 9 | 40.6 | 14 | 25.5 | 18 | 20.1 | 19 | 19.1 | 19 | 18.9 | | 16 | 23.5 | 13 | 28.8 |
| 18 | 19.9 | 33 | 11.1 | 38 | 9.6 | 42 | 8.7 | 28 | 13.1 | | 34 | 10.9 | 31 | 11.9 |

| | | | | | | | | | | | | | | |
|---|---|---|---|---|---|---|---|---|---|---|---|---|---|---|
| | 8.0 | | 9.9 | | 10.7 | | 10.1 | | 12.5 | Sales/Working Capital | | 12.2 | | 12.7 |
| | 14.4 | | 20.6 | | 16.6 | | 15.6 | | 20.1 | | | 20.7 | | 23.1 |
| | 34.1 | | 43.5 | | 28.3 | | 21.9 | | 31.0 | | | 37.8 | | 51.4 |
| | 10.6 | | 9.3 | | 7.0 | | 9.2 | | 10.9 | EBIT/Interest | | 3.9 | | 6.4 |
| (18) | 2.6 | (114) | 4.0 | (130) | 4.0 | (35) | 5.8 | (41) | 4.2 | | (400) | 2.4 | (343) | 2.7 |
| | .9 | | 1.8 | | 2.4 | | 2.3 | | 3.1 | | | 1.5 | | 1.6 |
| | | | 10.2 | | 6.8 | | 9.1 | | 19.2 | Net Profit + Depr., Dep., Amort./Cur. Mat. L/T/D | | 6.7 | | 9.6 |
| | | (43) | 4.5 | (60) | 4.3 | (11) | 6.1 | (16) | 7.5 | | (148) | 4.2 | (144) | 4.4 |
| | | | 2.2 | | 2.5 | | 2.6 | | 2.2 | | | 2.4 | | 2.5 |

| | | | | | | | | | |
|---|---|---|---|---|---|---|---|---|---|
| | .1 | .3 | .4 | .3 | .2 | Fixed/Worth | .4 | .3 |
| | .2 | .6 | .7 | .6 | .5 | | .7 | .6 |
| | .7 | 1.0 | .9 | .9 | .7 | | 1.1 | 1.0 |
| | .5 | .9 | 1.6 | 1.7 | 1.7 | Debt/Worth | 1.2 | 1.5 |
| | 1.1 | 1.7 | 2.4 | 2.9 | 2.8 | | 2.3 | 2.7 |
| | 2.6 | 3.1 | 3.4 | 4.0 | 4.4 | | 5.0 | 5.1 |

| | | | | | | | | | | | | | | |
|---|---|---|---|---|---|---|---|---|---|---|---|---|---|---|
| | 26.8 | | 24.8 | | 30.8 | | 30.4 | | 31.6 | % Profit Before Taxes/Tangible Net Worth | | 25.1 | | 34.4 |
| | 8.1 | (117) | 15.6 | | 20.4 | | 21.8 | | 22.0 | | (411) | 14.8 | (349) | 21.0 |
| | .4 | | 8.8 | | 11.1 | | 10.7 | | 13.3 | | | 7.6 | | 9.1 |
| | 11.3 | | 9.9 | | 10.0 | | 8.6 | | 11.6 | % Profit Before Taxes/Total Assets | | 7.1 | | 10.3 |
| | 3.5 | | 5.8 | | 5.5 | | 5.7 | | 5.3 | | | 4.1 | | 5.3 |
| | -.3 | | 2.4 | | 2.4 | | 2.2 | | 2.9 | | | 1.8 | | 2.0 |
| | 215.1 | | 42.2 | | 19.9 | | 26.0 | | 77.5 | Sales/Net Fixed Assets | | 28.2 | | 45.8 |
| | 49.9 | | 15.9 | | 12.4 | | 15.1 | | 21.1 | | | 14.1 | | 18.2 |
| | 13.7 | | 9.5 | | 9.4 | | 8.6 | | 11.2 | | | 9.2 | | 10.9 |

| | | | | | | | | | |
|---|---|---|---|---|---|---|---|---|---|
| | 7.4 | 5.1 | 3.8 | 3.5 | 4.3 | Sales/Total Assets | 3.9 | 4.5 |
| | 5.2 | 3.7 | 2.7 | 2.6 | 2.7 | | 2.7 | 3.1 |
| | 3.7 | 2.5 | 1.9 | 1.8 | 2.2 | | 1.9 | 2.1 |

| | | | | | | | | | | | | | | |
|---|---|---|---|---|---|---|---|---|---|---|---|---|---|---|
| | .2 | | .4 | | .5 | | .5 | | .2 | % Depr., Dep., Amort./Sales | | .6 | | .4 |
| (16) | .6 | (111) | .8 | (133) | .8 | (33) | .8 | (39) | .6 | | (394) | 1.0 | (326) | .7 |
| | 1.5 | | 1.3 | | 1.3 | | 1.4 | | 1.0 | | | 1.4 | | 1.0 |
| | | | .5 | | .2 | | | | | % Officers', Directors' Owners' Comp/Sales | | .5 | | .3 |
| | | (27) | 1.1 | (17) | .8 | | | | | | (57) | 1.4 | (60) | 1.0 |
| | | | 2.1 | | 1.8 | | | | | | | 3.1 | | 1.7 |

| | | | | | | | | | |
|---|---|---|---|---|---|---|---|---|---|
| 9979M | 173255M | 2529413M | 9074136M | 7623093M | 24095533M | Net Sales ($) | 28552463M | 49371391M |
| 1928M | 26027M | 643701M | 3165461M | 2621567M | 6501979M | Total Assets ($) | 11187017M | 12476073M |

M = $ thousand     MM = $ million
See Pages 9 through 22 for Explanation of Ratios and Data

## Comparative Historical Data / Current Data Sorted by Sales

| | | | Type of Statement | | | | | | |
|---|---|---|---|---|---|---|---|---|---|
| 171 | 185 | 177 | Unqualified | 1 | 1 | 1 | 4 | 25 | 145 |
| 65 | 69 | 81 | Reviewed | 1 | 2 | 4 | 11 | 31 | 32 |
| 11 | 18 | 19 | Compiled | 1 | 2 | 2 | 5 | 4 | 5 |
| 19 | 26 | 20 | Tax Returns | 2 | 3 | 1 | 3 | 5 | 6 |
| 50 | 74 | 66 | Other | 1 | 4 | 4 | 5 | 13 | 42 |
| 4/1/09-3/31/10 ALL | 4/1/10-3/31/11 ALL | 4/1/11-3/31/12 ALL | | **211 (4/1-9/30/11)** | | **152 (10/1/11-3/31/12)** | | | |
| | | | | 0-1MM | 1-3MM | 3-5MM | 5-10MM | 10-25MM | 25MM & OVER |
| 316 | 372 | 363 | **NUMBER OF STATEMENTS** | 6 | 9 | 12 | 28 | 78 | 230 |
| % | % | % | **ASSETS** | % | % | % | % | % | % |
| 10.1 | 10.1 | 9.6 | Cash & Equivalents | | | 11.8 | 15.3 | 14.2 | 7.0 |
| 19.2 | 19.0 | 16.6 | Trade Receivables (net) | | | 13.9 | 22.7 | 16.5 | 16.2 |
| 34.4 | 35.2 | 36.3 | Inventory | | | 35.3 | 25.0 | 33.5 | 39.9 |
| 4.9 | 7.1 | 9.7 | All Other Current | | | 3.8 | 6.9 | 7.7 | 11.5 |
| 68.7 | 71.4 | 72.2 | Total Current | | | 64.8 | 69.9 | 71.9 | 74.5 |
| 23.8 | 21.7 | 21.5 | Fixed Assets (net) | | | 21.4 | 21.5 | 22.1 | 20.3 |
| .4 | .8 | 1.0 | Intangibles (net) | | | 3.9 | 1.6 | .6 | .8 |
| 7.1 | 6.1 | 5.4 | All Other Non-Current | | | 10.0 | 7.0 | 5.4 | 4.4 |
| 100.0 | 100.0 | 100.0 | Total | | | 100.0 | 100.0 | 100.0 | 100.0 |
| | | | **LIABILITIES** | | | | | | |
| 13.6 | 17.2 | 20.9 | Notes Payable-Short Term | | | 21.0 | 10.7 | 17.5 | 23.9 |
| 2.2 | 1.9 | 1.6 | Cur. Mat.-L.T.D. | | | .6 | 2.2 | 2.1 | 1.4 |
| 19.2 | 19.2 | 18.6 | Trade Payables | | | 6.4 | 20.8 | 22.1 | 18.0 |
| .4 | .3 | .2 | Income Taxes Payable | | | .1 | .1 | .3 | .3 |
| 11.8 | 12.2 | 10.6 | All Other Current | | | 6.5 | 7.5 | 9.7 | 11.1 |
| 47.2 | 50.8 | 51.9 | Total Current | | | 34.6 | 41.3 | 51.7 | 54.6 |
| 11.6 | 9.5 | 9.1 | Long-Term Debt | | | 6.3 | 10.9 | 9.2 | 8.5 |
| 1.3 | 1.2 | 1.4 | Deferred Taxes | | | 1.2 | .6 | 1.3 | 1.6 |
| 2.1 | 3.7 | 3.0 | All Other Non-Current | | | 1.0 | 3.7 | .7 | 2.2 |
| 37.8 | 34.8 | 34.6 | Net Worth | | | 56.9 | 43.4 | 37.1 | 33.2 |
| 100.0 | 100.0 | 100.0 | Total Liabilities & Net Worth | | | 100.0 | 100.0 | 100.0 | 100.0 |
| | | | **INCOME DATA** | | | | | | |
| 100.0 | 100.0 | 100.0 | Net Sales | | | 100.0 | 100.0 | 100.0 | 100.0 |
| 10.6 | 12.0 | 11.0 | Gross Profit | | | 25.9 | 18.4 | 12.7 | 7.9 |
| 7.7 | 8.8 | 7.9 | Operating Expenses | | | 18.7 | 11.6 | 9.7 | 5.4 |
| 3.0 | 3.2 | 3.1 | Operating Profit | | | 7.2 | 6.8 | 3.1 | 2.6 |
| -.1 | -.1 | .3 | All Other Expenses (net) | | | .0 | .6 | .5 | .2 |
| 3.1 | 3.2 | 2.8 | Profit Before Taxes | | | 7.2 | 6.2 | 2.6 | 2.3 |
| | | | **RATIOS** | | | | | | |
| 1.9 | 1.8 | 1.7 | Current | | | 3.8 | 3.3 | 1.8 | 1.5 |
| 1.4 | 1.3 | 1.3 | | | | 2.0 | 1.9 | 1.4 | 1.3 |
| 1.2 | 1.1 | 1.2 | | | | 1.5 | 1.2 | 1.2 | 1.2 |
| 1.0 | 1.0 | .8 | Quick | | | 1.8 | 2.1 | .9 | .6 |
| (315) .6 | (371) .5 | .4 | | | | 1.0 | .9 | .6 | .3 |
| .3 | .2 | .2 | | | | .3 | .3 | .3 | .2 |
| 6 60.6 | 7 48.7 | 6 56.3 | Sales/Receivables | | | 5 69.4 | 10 38.4 | 7 56.0 | 6 56.7 |
| 13 27.3 | 17 22.0 | 14 26.5 | | | | 16 22.4 | 15 24.9 | 16 23.4 | 11 32.1 |
| 28 13.1 | 31 11.6 | 27 13.7 | | | | 35 10.3 | 30 12.2 | 29 12.7 | 26 13.9 |
| 16 22.4 | 22 16.7 | 19 19.3 | Cost of Sales/Inventory | | | 3 130.5 | 3 110.0 | 14 27.0 | 24 15.5 |
| 37 9.9 | 44 8.2 | 47 7.7 | | | | 79 4.6 | 30 12.1 | 45 8.2 | 49 7.4 |
| 67 5.5 | 87 4.2 | 85 4.3 | | | | 104 3.5 | 64 5.7 | 94 3.9 | 83 4.4 |
| 6 60.6 | 7 54.7 | 5 66.9 | Cost of Sales/Payables | | | 2 190.5 | 2 236.1 | 6 60.9 | 6 58.0 |
| 16 22.4 | 18 20.5 | 17 22.0 | | | | 7 49.2 | 16 23.0 | 22 16.5 | 16 22.7 |
| 30 12.3 | 37 9.8 | 34 10.7 | | | | 20 18.2 | 55 6.6 | 45 8.2 | 29 12.7 |
| 10.5 | 9.5 | 10.5 | Sales/Working Capital | | | 2.9 | 7.3 | 7.7 | 12.2 |
| 19.4 | 16.4 | 18.3 | | | | 7.0 | 14.3 | 18.2 | 18.8 |
| 37.4 | 32.1 | 29.4 | | | | 17.8 | 31.3 | 29.1 | 29.4 |
| 13.6 | 16.9 | 8.4 | EBIT/Interest | | | 27.6 | 72.8 | 8.7 | 7.5 |
| (295) 5.5 | (349) 6.6 | (343) 4.1 | | (10) 4.7 | (24) 6.6 | | | (73) 3.9 | (224) 4.1 |
| 2.7 | 2.9 | 2.3 | | | | 2.2 | 3.2 | 1.6 | 2.4 |
| 9.9 | 8.8 | 8.1 | Net Profit + Depr., Dep., Amort./Cur. Mat. L/T/D | | | | | 6.6 | 8.4 |
| (107) 5.9 | (133) 4.8 | (133) 4.5 | | | | | (24) 4.5 | (100) 4.7 | |
| 2.8 | 2.5 | 2.4 | | | | | | 2.0 | 2.5 |
| .3 | .3 | .3 | Fixed/Worth | | | .2 | .1 | .2 | .4 |
| .6 | .6 | .6 | | | | .3 | .4 | .5 | .6 |
| 1.0 | .9 | .9 | | | | .7 | 1.1 | 1.0 | .9 |
| 1.0 | 1.1 | 1.2 | Debt/Worth | | | .3 | .6 | 1.1 | 1.5 |
| 1.7 | 2.0 | 2.2 | | | | .9 | 1.8 | 1.9 | 2.4 |
| 3.4 | 3.7 | 3.4 | | | | 2.1 | 3.1 | 3.1 | 3.5 |
| 37.1 | 31.8 | 29.2 | % Profit Before Taxes/Tangible Net Worth | | | 23.5 | 42.7 | 25.6 | 29.2 |
| (309) 23.2 | (362) 22.1 | (357) 17.9 | | | | 15.2 | 22.9 | (77) 13.9 | (228) 20.4 |
| 10.1 | 11.3 | 9.4 | | | | 6.1 | 8.8 | 6.2 | 11.0 |
| 14.4 | 12.3 | 10.2 | % Profit Before Taxes/Total Assets | | | 13.6 | 15.0 | 10.0 | 9.6 |
| 7.8 | 7.0 | 5.5 | | | | 10.5 | 7.5 | 5.5 | 5.4 |
| 3.3 | 3.2 | 2.3 | | | | 2.3 | 2.8 | 1.5 | 2.6 |
| 32.3 | 35.7 | 32.8 | Sales/Net Fixed Assets | | | 22.1 | 87.2 | 31.7 | 31.0 |
| 15.6 | 14.9 | 14.9 | | | | 12.7 | 16.1 | 13.8 | 15.8 |
| 9.3 | 8.3 | 9.6 | | | | 5.1 | 9.0 | 9.3 | 10.5 |
| 4.9 | 4.3 | 4.6 | Sales/Total Assets | | | 3.1 | 5.2 | 4.8 | 4.5 |
| 3.4 | 2.9 | 3.1 | | | | 2.0 | 3.2 | 3.2 | 3.1 |
| 2.5 | 1.9 | 2.1 | | | | 1.4 | 1.7 | 2.0 | 2.3 |
| .4 | .5 | .4 | % Depr., Dep., Amort./Sales | | | .6 | .6 | .6 | .4 |
| (294) .8 | (334) .9 | (337) .8 | | (11) 1.3 | (22) 1.3 | | | (71) .9 | (222) .7 |
| 1.2 | 1.3 | 1.3 | | | | 4.4 | 2.2 | 1.6 | 1.0 |
| .3 | .7 | .5 | % Officers', Directors' Owners' Comp/Sales | | | | | .5 | .2 |
| (55) .8 | (63) 1.4 | (54) 1.1 | | | | | | (17) 1.1 | (25) .9 |
| 2.4 | 2.4 | 2.4 | | | | | | 2.4 | 2.0 |
| 39026495M | 37795281M | 43505409M | Net Sales ($) | 2713M | 22410M | 47901M | 206922M | 1396891M | 41828572M |
| 10341080M | 12328064M | 12960663M | Total Assets ($) | 1626M | 21591M | 37806M | 90220M | 585648M | 12223772M |

**M = $ thousand   MM = $ million**
See Pages 9 through 22 for Explanation of Ratios and Data

**Current Data Sorted by Assets**  **Comparative Historical Data**

| 0-500M | 500M-2MM | 2-10MM | 10-50MM | 50-100MM | 100-250MM | Type of Statement | 4/1/07-3/31/08 ALL | 4/1/08-3/31/09 ALL |
|---|---|---|---|---|---|---|---|---|
| | | | 1 | 1 | 1 | Unqualified | 3 | 9 |
| | 1 | 4 | 1 | | | Reviewed | 3 | 3 |
| | 2 | 2 | | | | Compiled | 2 | 4 |
| 1 | 3 | 2 | | | | Tax Returns | 9 | 5 |
| 1 | | 4 | 2 | | | Other | 17 | 8 |
| | 7 (4/1-9/30/11) | | 19 (10/1/11-3/31/12) | | | | | |
| 2 | 6 | 12 | 4 | 1 | 1 | **NUMBER OF STATEMENTS** | 34 | 29 |
| % | % | % | % | % | % | | % | % |
| | | | | | | **ASSETS** | | |
| | | -5.6 | | | | Cash & Equivalents | 13.1 | 10.2 |
| | | 23.4 | | | | Trade Receivables (net) | 23.7 | 24.0 |
| | | 29.9 | | | | Inventory | 20.1 | 25.7 |
| | | 7.6 | | | | All Other Current | 7.3 | 4.4 |
| | | 55.2 | | | | Total Current | 64.2 | 64.3 |
| | | 28.1 | | | | Fixed Assets (net) | 23.8 | 24.4 |
| | | 5.4 | | | | Intangibles (net) | .2 | 3.2 |
| | | 11.2 | | | | All Other Non-Current | 11.7 | 8.1 |
| | | 100.0 | | | | Total | 100.0 | 100.0 |
| | | | | | | **LIABILITIES** | | |
| | | 22.7 | | | | Notes Payable-Short Term | 23.8 | 24.6 |
| | | 3.0 | | | | Cur. Mat.-L.T.D. | 2.1 | 2.7 |
| | | 9.1 | | | | Trade Payables | 11.5 | 9.6 |
| | | .6 | | | | Income Taxes Payable | .1 | .9 |
| | | 16.3 | | | | All Other Current | 12.8 | 16.7 |
| | | 51.7 | | | | Total Current | 50.2 | 54.4 |
| | | 22.6 | | | | Long-Term Debt | 21.2 | 12.3 |
| | | .4 | | | | Deferred Taxes | .1 | .0 |
| | | 1.0 | | | | All Other Non-Current | 1.2 | 3.6 |
| | | 24.4 | | | | Net Worth | 27.3 | 29.7 |
| | | 100.0 | | | | Total Liabilities & Net Worth | 100.0 | 100.0 |
| | | | | | | **INCOME DATA** | | |
| | | 100.0 | | | | Net Sales | 100.0 | 100.0 |
| | | 21.4 | | | | Gross Profit | 19.2 | 23.6 |
| | | 18.7 | | | | Operating Expenses | 19.5 | 21.5 |
| | | 2.7 | | | | Operating Profit | -.3 | 2.1 |
| | | .7 | | | | All Other Expenses (net) | -.5 | -.2 |
| | | 2.0 | | | | Profit Before Taxes | .2 | 2.4 |
| | | | | | | **RATIOS** | | |
| | | 1.7 | | | | | 2.2 | 2.1 |
| | | 1.2 | | | | Current | 1.1 | 1.3 |
| | | .8 | | | | | .9 | .9 |
| | | .7 | | | | | 1.7 | 1.2 |
| | (11) | .6 | | | | Quick | .9 | .6 |
| | | .3 | | | | | .3 | .3 |
| | 4 | 102.2 | | | | | 0 UND | 1 486.4 |
| | 13 | 27.6 | | | | Sales/Receivables | 6 58.6 | 9 40.0 |
| | 24 | 15.5 | | | | | 18 20.7 | 21 17.3 |
| | 1 | 501.5 | | | | | 1 459.4 | 2 156.3 |
| | 16 | 23.1 | | | | Cost of Sales/Inventory | 4 87.2 | 19 19.1 |
| | 63 | 5.8 | | | | | 28 12.9 | 46 7.9 |
| | 3 | 127.8 | | | | | 0 UND | 1 505.2 |
| | 5 | 72.9 | | | | Cost of Sales/Payables | 3 126.5 | 4 103.0 |
| | 17 | 21.6 | | | | | 14 26.5 | 21 17.5 |
| | | 27.1 | | | | | 22.3 | 18.3 |
| | | 171.6 | | | | Sales/Working Capital | 127.3 | 63.6 |
| | | -16.6 | | | | | -130.1 | NM |
| | | 16.9 | | | | | 11.2 | 12.6 |
| | | 4.3 | | | | EBIT/Interest | (30) 2.2 | (23) 1.9 |
| | | .9 | | | | | 1.0 | .8 |
| | | | | | | Net Profit + Depr., Dep., Amort./Cur. Mat. L/T/D | | |
| | | .4 | | | | | .3 | .3 |
| | | 1.0 | | | | Fixed/Worth | .9 | .8 |
| | | 2.8 | | | | | 1.8 | 3.1 |
| | | 1.3 | | | | | 1.0 | .7 |
| | | 2.5 | | | | Debt/Worth | 3.8 | 3.2 |
| | | NM | | | | | 12.0 | 11.9 |
| | | | | | | % Profit Before Taxes/Tangible Net Worth | 64.9 | 51.6 |
| | | | | | | | (30) 20.7 | (24) 22.4 |
| | | | | | | | -.1 | 2.7 |
| | | 13.5 | | | | | 14.0 | 28.4 |
| | | 8.6 | | | | % Profit Before Taxes/Total Assets | 2.5 | 4.9 |
| | | .6 | | | | | -.2 | .5 |
| | | 159.6 | | | | | 175.6 | 173.8 |
| | | 41.0 | | | | Sales/Net Fixed Assets | 35.5 | 35.6 |
| | | 10.1 | | | | | 14.9 | 17.8 |
| | | 9.5 | | | | | 15.3 | 12.4 |
| | | 5.9 | | | | Sales/Total Assets | 7.2 | 6.5 |
| | | 1.9 | | | | | 3.9 | 3.9 |
| | | .2 | | | | | .2 | .3 |
| | (10) | 1.0 | | | | % Depr., Dep., Amort./Sales | (32) .5 | (26) .5 |
| | | 1.7 | | | | | .8 | 1.7 |
| | | | | | | % Officers', Directors' Owners' Comp/Sales | .3 | |
| | | | | | | | (13) 1.1 | |
| | | | | | | | 2.2 | |
| 2142M | 52644M | 308395M | 851407M | 188787M | 691602M | Net Sales ($) | 906105M | 1094056M |
| 537M | 5692M | 55511M | 110460M | 94002M | 151095M | Total Assets ($) | 146092M | 201868M |

M = $ thousand    MM = $ million
See Pages 9 through 22 for Explanation of Ratios and Data

## Comparative Historical Data | Current Data Sorted by Sales

| Type of Statement | 4/1/09-3/31/10 ALL | 4/1/10-3/31/11 ALL | 4/1/11-3/31/12 ALL | 0-1MM | 1-3MM | 3-5MM | 5-10MM | 10-25MM | 25MM & OVER |
|---|---|---|---|---|---|---|---|---|---|
| | | | | | 7 (4/1-9/30/11) | | | 19 (10/1/11-3/31/12) | |
| Unqualified | | | | | | | | | 3 |
| Reviewed | 4 | 5 | 3 | | 1 | | 1 | 1 | 3 |
| Compiled | 4 | 7 | 6 | | 3 | | | 1 | . |
| Tax Returns | 4 | 5 | 4 | | 2 | | | 4 | . |
| Other | 11 | 5 | 6 | 1 | | | 1 | | 5 |
| **NUMBER OF STATEMENTS** | 30 | 28 | 26 | 1 | 6 | | 2 | 6 | 11 |
| | % | % | % | % | % | % | % | % | % |
| **ASSETS** | | | | | | | | | |
| Cash & Equivalents | 12.4 | 6.2 | 3.3 | | | | | | -4.1 |
| Trade Receivables (net) | 27.0 | 22.4 | 18.9 | | | | | | 28.7 |
| Inventory | 24.9 | 28.0 | 26.7 | | | | | | 20.5 |
| All Other Current | 3.6 | 5.2 | 6.5 | | | | | | 9.5 |
| Total Current | 67.9 | 61.9 | 55.4 | | | | | | 54.6 |
| Fixed Assets (net) | 21.6 | 27.4 | 33.0 | | | | | | 33.6 |
| Intangibles (net) | 1.4 | 2.0 | 2.7 | | | | | | .2 |
| All Other Non-Current | 9.1 | 8.7 | 9.0 | | | | | | 11.6 |
| Total | 100.0 | 100.0 | 100.0 | | | | | | 100.0 |
| **LIABILITIES** | | | | | | | | | |
| Notes Payable-Short Term | 16.5 | 16.7 | 18.3 | | | | | | 15.8 |
| Cur. Mat.-L.T.D. | 4.3 | 4.8 | 4.1 | | | | | | 3.4 |
| Trade Payables | 13.0 | 17.5 | 9.2 | | | | | | 13.8 |
| Income Taxes Payable | .2 | .1 | .3 | | | | | | .5 |
| All Other Current | 21.5 | 11.4 | 11.4 | | | | | | 11.2 |
| Total Current | 55.5 | 50.5 | 43.3 | | | | | | 44.7 |
| Long-Term Debt | 15.5 | 21.9 | 21.9 | | | | | | 17.1 |
| Deferred Taxes | .0 | .1 | .2 | | | | | | .4 |
| All Other Non-Current | 2.4 | 8.2 | 1.1 | | | | | | 1.4 |
| Net Worth | 26.6 | 19.3 | 33.5 | | | | | | 36.4 |
| Total Liabilities & Net Worth | 100.0 | 100.0 | 100.0 | | | | | | 100.0 |
| **INCOME DATA** | | | | | | | | | |
| Net Sales | 100.0 | 100.0 | 100.0 | | | | | | 100.0 |
| Gross Profit | 26.5 | 23.6 | 27.4 | | | | | | 9.1 |
| Operating Expenses | 25.3 | 21.5 | 25.0 | | | | | | 7.3 |
| Operating Profit | 1.3 | 2.1 | 2.4 | | | | | | 1.7 |
| All Other Expenses (net) | -.5 | 1.0 | .3 | | | | | | .0 |
| Profit Before Taxes | 1.7 | 1.1 | 2.1 | | | | | | 1.7 |
| **RATIOS** | | | | | | | | | |
| Current | 2.1 | 2.0 | 3.1 | | | | | | 1.9 |
| | 1.4 | 1.4 | 1.3 | | | | | | 1.2 |
| | 1.0 | 1.0 | 1.0 | | | | | | 1.0 |
| Quick | 1.0 | 1.4 | 1.0 | | | | | | .9 |
| | .8 | (25) .7 | .6 | | | | | | (10) .7 |
| | .5 | .3 | .3 | | | | | | .5 |
| Sales/Receivables | 4  88.7 | 10  36.0 | 0  UND | | | | | | 9  39.1 |
| | 15  23.6 | 16  23.0 | 11  33.8 | | | | | | 12  29.4 |
| | 23  15.9 | 29  12.5 | 27  13.7 | | | | | | 15  24.8 |
| Cost of Sales/Inventory | 3  140.7 | 3  138.6 | 2  174.7 | | | | | | 1  613.4 |
| | 18  20.4 | 30  12.2 | 16  23.2 | | | | | | 3  107.3 |
| | 62  5.9 | 80  4.6 | 66  5.5 | | | | | | 19  19.2 |
| Cost of Sales/Payables | 0  UND | 1  254.1 | 0  761.9 | | | | | | 2  201.3 |
| | 9  42.3 | 9  42.4 | 7  49.6 | | | | | | 4  91.2 |
| | 19  18.9 | 46  7.9 | 20  18.2 | | | | | | 17  21.1 |
| Sales/Working Capital | 13.7 | 13.0 | 19.1 | | | | | | 24.2 |
| | 35.7 | 24.0 | 37.7 | | | | | | 147.7 |
| | -573.5 | NM | -274.1 | | | | | | -999.8 |
| EBIT/Interest | 13.1 | 7.4 | 20.3 | | | | | | 41.9 |
| | (26) 3.5 | (26) 2.6 | (25) 5.8 | | | | | | 9.4 |
| | 1.3 | 1.2 | 1.6 | | | | | | 3.5 |
| Net Profit + Depr., Dep., Amort./Cur. Mat. L/T/D | | | | | | | | | |
| Fixed/Worth | .1 | .4 | .3 | | | | | | .5 |
| | .8 | 1.0 | .9 | | | | | | 1.0 |
| | 2.5 | 3.7 | 2.7 | | | | | | 1.5 |
| Debt/Worth | 1.1 | 1.0 | .9 | | | | | | .8 |
| | 3.9 | 4.6 | 2.2 | | | | | | 1.7 |
| | 18.9 | 11.3 | 9.5 | | | | | | 4.4 |
| % Profit Before Taxes/Tangible Net Worth | 57.6 | 55.4 | 37.2 | | | | | | 51.2 |
| | (27) 17.0 | (25) 24.9 | (22) 25.6 | | | | | | (10) 30.8 |
| | 7.1 | 3.8 | 7.3 | | | | | | 10.9 |
| % Profit Before Taxes/Total Assets | 13.0 | 11.6 | 14.2 | | | | | | 20.6 |
| | 4.8 | 4.8 | 8.2 | | | | | | 9.4 |
| | .9 | .5 | 1.2 | | | | | | 4.8 |
| Sales/Net Fixed Assets | 249.0 | 57.2 | 89.0 | | | | | | 94.2 |
| | 28.1 | 18.2 | 18.0 | | | | | | 19.3 |
| | 11.8 | 8.0 | 7.0 | | | | | | 9.4 |
| Sales/Total Assets | 11.7 | 8.2 | 9.4 | | | | | | 10.9 |
| | 5.2 | 4.0 | 4.6 | | | | | | 6.8 |
| | 3.3 | 2.1 | 2.0 | | | | | | 4.6 |
| % Depr., Dep., Amort./Sales | .2 | .3 | .3 | | | | | | .2 |
| | (26) .7 | (24) 1.1 | (22) 1.2 | | | | | | (10) 1.0 |
| | 2.5 | 3.1 | 1.8 | | | | | | 1.3 |
| % Officers', Directors' Owners' Comp/Sales | .3 | .4 | | | | | | | |
| | (12) 1.1 | (11) 2.8 | | | | | | | |
| | 5.4 | 4.1 | | | | | | | |
| Net Sales ($) | 3650854M | 2454230M | 2094977M | 995M | 10446M | | 17795M | 114942M | 1950799M |
| Total Assets ($) | 345547M | 622234M | 417297M | 139M | 6580M | | 12055M | 24997M | 373526M |

*Note: For the current-data middle columns (0-1MM, 1-3MM, 3-5MM and 5-10MM, 10-25MM) the asset/liability/income/ratio detail is marked "DATA NOT AVAILABLE."*

M = $ thousand   MM = $ million
See Pages 9 through 22 for Explanation of Ratios and Data

## Current Data Sorted by Assets      Comparative Historical Data

| | 0-500M | 500M-2MM | 2-10MM | 10-50MM | 50-100MM | 100-250MM | Type of Statement | 4/1/07-3/31/08 ALL | 4/1/08-3/31/09 ALL |
|---|---|---|---|---|---|---|---|---|---|
| | | | 3 | 5 | 3 | 10 | Unqualified | 29 | 25 |
| | | 2 | 9 | 9 | 3 | 2 | Reviewed | 21 | 26 |
| | | 4 | 8 | 3 | 1 | | Compiled | 16 | 19 |
| | | 6 | 10 | 3 | | | Tax Returns | 11 | 21 |
| | | 3 | 5 | 13 | 6 | 6 | Other | 51 | 45 |
| | | 44 (4/1-9/30/11) | | 70 (10/1/11-3/31/12) | | | | | |
| | | **15** | **35** | **33** | **13** | **18** | **NUMBER OF STATEMENTS** | **128** | **136** |
| | % | % | % | % | % | % | **ASSETS** | % | % |
| D | | 14.0 | 9.5 | 7.3 | 4.9 | 1.8 | Cash & Equivalents | 7.4 | 8.7 |
| A | | 42.2 | 39.9 | 29.4 | 30.1 | 17.4 | Trade Receivables (net) | 34.6 | 34.5 |
| T | | 17.7 | 26.1 | 31.5 | 31.3 | 47.8 | Inventory | 32.5 | 30.5 |
| A | | 6.6 | 6.8 | 3.4 | 7.7 | 7.8 | All Other Current | 5.9 | 5.6 |
| | | 80.5 | 82.3 | 71.7 | 74.1 | 75.0 | Total Current | 80.4 | 79.4 |
| N | | 9.3 | 12.1 | 14.2 | 11.3 | 13.7 | Fixed Assets (net) | 14.2 | 14.2 |
| O | | 6.4 | 1.6 | 2.5 | 10.5 | 4.8 | Intangibles (net) | 1.3 | 1.5 |
| T | | 3.8 | 4.0 | 11.7 | 4.1 | 6.6 | All Other Non-Current | 4.2 | 4.8 |
| | | 100.0 | 100.0 | 100.0 | 100.0 | 100.0 | Total | 100.0 | 100.0 |
| A | | | | | | | **LIABILITIES** | | |
| V | | 8.7 | 12.6 | 17.7 | 13.1 | 30.7 | Notes Payable-Short Term | 23.5 | 24.2 |
| A | | .4 | 2.3 | 1.5 | 1.5 | .9 | Cur. Mat.-L.T.D. | 1.3 | 1.6 |
| I | | 26.9 | 34.8 | 24.5 | 19.6 | 16.6 | Trade Payables | 20.5 | 23.4 |
| L | | .2 | .1 | .1 | .3 | .1 | Income Taxes Payable | .1 | .2 |
| A | | 13.3 | 10.3 | 15.2 | 22.2 | 11.7 | All Other Current | 11.5 | 8.8 |
| B | | 49.5 | 60.2 | 58.9 | 56.7 | 60.0 | Total Current | 56.9 | 58.1 |
| L | | 1.7 | 4.6 | 11.0 | 12.9 | 5.7 | Long-Term Debt | 7.4 | 6.7 |
| E | | .1 | .2 | .2 | .1 | .5 | Deferred Taxes | .2 | .1 |
| | | 3.2 | 2.6 | 2.2 | 4.3 | 2.0 | All Other Non-Current | 4.4 | 2.8 |
| | | 45.5 | 32.5 | 27.8 | 26.0 | 31.7 | Net Worth | 31.2 | 32.2 |
| | | 100.0 | 100.0 | 100.0 | 100.0 | 100.0 | Total Liabilities & Net Worth | 100.0 | 100.0 |
| | | | | | | | **INCOME DATA** | | |
| | | 100.0 | 100.0 | 100.0 | 100.0 | 100.0 | Net Sales | 100.0 | 100.0 |
| | | 14.3 | 16.2 | 13.9 | 16.8 | 16.5 | Gross Profit | 16.5 | 16.2 |
| | | 12.6 | 12.4 | 9.9 | 10.7 | 12.6 | Operating Expenses | 12.5 | 13.0 |
| | | 1.6 | 3.8 | 4.0 | 6.1 | 3.9 | Operating Profit | 3.9 | 3.2 |
| | | -.4 | .5 | 1.5 | .3 | .7 | All Other Expenses (net) | 1.1 | .9 |
| | | 2.0 | 3.3 | 2.5 | 5.8 | 3.2 | Profit Before Taxes | 2.8 | 2.4 |
| | | | | | | | **RATIOS** | | |
| | | 2.4 | 1.8 | 1.5 | 2.1 | 1.7 | | 1.9 | 1.9 |
| | | 1.8 | 1.4 | 1.3 | 1.1 | 1.2 | Current | 1.3 | 1.3 |
| | | 1.2 | 1.1 | 1.1 | 1.0 | 1.1 | | 1.1 | 1.1 |
| | | 1.8 | 1.3 | 1.0 | 1.2 | .6 | | 1.1 | 1.2 |
| | | 1.0 | .8 | .6 | .4 | .3 | Quick | .8 | .8 |
| | | .7 | .4 | .4 | .3 | .1 | | .5 | .4 |
| | | 12 30.1 | 14 25.6 | 21 17.7 | 31 11.7 | 14 26.2 | | 17 21.2 | 19 19.2 |
| | | 16 22.3 | 36 10.2 | 31 11.6 | 38 9.5 | 26 14.2 | Sales/Receivables | 34 10.8 | 30 12.1 |
| | | 41 8.8 | 54 6.7 | 47 7.7 | 73 5.0 | 34 10.8 | | 45 8.0 | 47 7.8 |
| | | 0 UND | 1 505.5 | 9 39.9 | 27 13.7 | 43 8.4 | | 9 40.7 | 8 48.2 |
| | | 7 55.4 | 18 20.4 | 41 8.8 | 65 5.6 | 72 5.1 | Cost of Sales/Inventory | 42 8.7 | 34 10.6 |
| | | 37 9.8 | 76 4.8 | 101 3.6 | 146 2.5 | 182 2.0 | | 90 4.0 | 86 4.2 |
| | | 4 93.7 | 13 28.6 | 14 25.7 | 5 81.0 | 12 31.7 | | 9 41.3 | 9 39.7 |
| | | 16 23.1 | 31 11.6 | 24 15.0 | 16 23.3 | 23 15.8 | Cost of Sales/Payables | 21 17.5 | 23 15.8 |
| | | 27 13.5 | 78 4.7 | 41 8.8 | 79 4.6 | 35 10.3 | | 42 8.7 | 51 7.1 |
| | | 5.8 | 11.0 | 9.4 | 4.2 | 10.2 | | 10.2 | 10.1 |
| | | 17.3 | 21.9 | 31.0 | 27.3 | 14.0 | Sales/Working Capital | 18.9 | 21.2 |
| | | 129.1 | 48.1 | 187.3 | NM | 33.0 | | 37.7 | 44.4 |
| | | 50.5 | 29.9 | 14.2 | 23.4 | 17.8 | | 7.3 | 7.8 |
| | (12) | 6.6 | (29) 3.6 | (31) 5.5 | (12) 6.8 | (17) 3.8 | EBIT/Interest | (122) 2.8 | (129) 3.5 |
| | | 5.8 | 1.1 | 2.9 | 2.9 | 1.9 | | 1.6 | 1.3 |
| | | | | | | | Net Profit + Depr., Dep., | 16.0 | 7.9 |
| | | | | | | | Amort./Cur. Mat. L/T/D | (27) 5.4 | (22) 4.0 |
| | | | | | | | | 2.1 | 2.2 |
| | | .0 | .0 | .1 | .1 | .3 | | .0 | .1 |
| | | .2 | .2 | .5 | .7 | .4 | Fixed/Worth | .2 | .3 |
| | | .4 | 1.0 | 1.8 | 2.2 | .7 | | .7 | 1.0 |
| | | .6 | 1.3 | 1.4 | 1.8 | 1.5 | | 1.3 | 1.1 |
| | | 1.1 | 2.5 | 3.4 | 5.5 | 2.5 | Debt/Worth | 2.7 | 2.6 |
| | | 6.8 | 6.7 | 10.2 | 14.8 | 5.5 | | 5.2 | 5.6 |
| | | 40.9 | 64.6 | 42.0 | 71.3 | 33.1 | % Profit Before Taxes/Tangible | 37.8 | 39.1 |
| | (14) | 23.8 | (34) 15.4 | (29) 27.4 | (11) 45.4 | 21.7 | Net Worth | (122) 16.8 | (127) 18.1 |
| | | 13.8 | 2.8 | 15.3 | 21.0 | 17.5 | | 6.2 | 2.6 |
| | | 17.1 | 13.1 | 10.0 | 16.1 | 9.8 | % Profit Before Taxes/Total | 10.4 | 11.5 |
| | | 10.0 | 6.8 | 6.8 | 4.9 | 6.1 | Assets | 4.4 | 5.0 |
| | | 1.8 | .4 | 3.2 | 1.9 | 2.7 | | 1.7 | .5 |
| | | 999.8 | 336.9 | 203.3 | 384.6 | 73.7 | | 410.3 | 286.1 |
| | | 180.7 | 126.2 | 27.7 | 49.5 | 26.4 | Sales/Net Fixed Assets | 46.6 | 47.6 |
| | | 34.6 | 14.7 | 11.3 | 7.0 | 9.7 | | 11.1 | 11.2 |
| | | 10.2 | 5.3 | 4.3 | 3.0 | 3.1 | | 4.8 | 5.3 |
| | | 5.3 | 3.4 | 2.7 | 1.9 | 2.1 | Sales/Total Assets | 3.3 | 3.3 |
| | | 3.3 | 2.3 | 1.8 | 1.5 | 1.8 | | 2.1 | 2.0 |
| | | .2 | .1 | .2 | .0 | .2 | | .1 | .2 |
| | (11) | .5 | (25) .6 | (26) .7 | (12) .4 | (14) .4 | % Depr., Dep., Amort./Sales | (103) .5 | (106) .6 |
| | | .9 | 1.6 | 1.0 | 2.3 | 1.1 | | 1.5 | 1.9 |
| | | | .9 | | | | % Officers', Directors', | | .6 | .4 |
| | | | (10) 1.9 | | | | Owners' Comp/Sales | (36) 1.4 | (40) .9 |
| | | | 2.5 | | | | | 3.3 | 3.1 |
| | | 140096M | 754203M | 2626461M | 2016517M | 7082843M | Net Sales ($) | 9391871M | 9129058M |
| | | 18515M | 180229M | 786520M | 870856M | 2742243M | Total Assets ($) | 3135412M | 2867251M |

M = $ thousand    MM = $ million
See Pages 9 through 22 for Explanation of Ratios and Data

## Comparative Historical Data | Current Data Sorted by Sales

| | | | Type of Statement | 0-1MM | 1-3MM | 3-5MM | 5-10MM | 10-25MM | 25MM & OVER |
|---|---|---|---|---|---|---|---|---|---|
| 22 | 25 | 21 | Unqualified | | | 1 | | 2 | 18 |
| 27 | 20 | 25 | Reviewed | 1 | | 1 | 1 | 4 | 19 |
| 14 | 23 | 15 | Compiled | 3 | | 2 | 2 | 6 | 4 |
| 15 | 17 | 20 | Tax Returns | 1 | 1 | 3 | | 9 | 6 |
| 33 | 29 | 33 | Other | 2 | | | | 8 | 23 |
| 4/1/09-3/31/10 ALL | 4/1/10-3/31/11 ALL | 4/1/11-3/31/12 ALL | | | 44 (4/1-9/30/11) | | 70 (10/1/11-3/31/12) | | |
| 111 | 114 | 114 | NUMBER OF STATEMENTS | | 7 | 2 | 6 | 29 | 70 |
| % | % | % | **ASSETS** | % | % | % | % | % | % |
| 9.7 | 12.6 | 7.7 | Cash & Equivalents | | | | | 9.8 | 6.7 |
| 37.5 | 34.1 | 32.5 | Trade Receivables (net) | | | | | 37.1 | 30.5 |
| 29.7 | 27.8 | 30.6 | Inventory | | | | | 29.6 | 31.3 |
| 5.0 | 6.1 | 6.1 | All Other Current | | | | | 3.4 | 7.0 |
| 81.8 | 80.6 | 76.9 | Total Current | | | | | 79.8 | 75.4 |
| 12.9 | 13.4 | 12.5 | Fixed Assets (net) | | | | | 15.5 | 12.0 |
| .8 | 2.2 | 4.0 | Intangibles (net) | | | | | 2.1 | 4.4 |
| 4.6 | 3.8 | 6.6 | All Other Non-Current | | | | | 2.6 | 8.2 |
| 100.0 | 100.0 | 100.0 | Total | | | | | 100.0 | 100.0 |
| | | | **LIABILITIES** | | | | | | |
| 19.8 | 13.4 | 16.5 | Notes Payable-Short Term | | | | | 12.7 | 19.7 |
| 1.0 | 1.8 | 1.5 | Cur. Mat.-L.T.D. | | | | | 1.7 | 1.1 |
| 22.6 | 26.3 | 26.2 | Trade Payables | | | | | 31.0 | 23.5 |
| .2 | .1 | .1 | Income Taxes Payable | | | | | .2 | .1 |
| 13.1 | 12.4 | 13.7 | All Other Current | | | | | 18.0 | 13.3 |
| 56.7 | 54.1 | 58.0 | Total Current | | | | | 63.6 | 57.8 |
| 6.8 | 5.9 | 7.2 | Long-Term Debt | | | | | 6.0 | 8.8 |
| .2 | .2 | .2 | Deferred Taxes | | | | | .2 | .3 |
| 2.8 | 5.1 | 2.7 | All Other Non-Current | | | | | 2.0 | 2.5 |
| 33.4 | 34.7 | 32.0 | Net Worth | | | | | 28.2 | 30.7 |
| 100.0 | 100.0 | 100.0 | Total Liabilties & Net Worth | | | | | 100.0 | 100.0 |
| | | | **INCOME DATA** | | | | | | |
| 100.0 | 100.0 | 100.0 | Net Sales | | | | | 100.0 | 100.0 |
| 16.4 | 17.1 | 15.4 | Gross Profit | | | | | 14.6 | 13.8 |
| 12.4 | 13.0 | 11.5 | Operating Expenses | | | | | 12.6 | 9.6 |
| 4.0 | 4.0 | 3.9 | Operating Profit | | | | | 2.0 | 4.2 |
| .8 | 1.2 | .7 | All Other Expenses (net) | | | | | .3 | .9 |
| 3.2 | 2.9 | 3.2 | Profit Before Taxes | | | | | 1.7 | 3.3 |
| | | | **RATIOS** | | | | | | |
| 1.9 | 2.0 | 1.8 | | | | | | 1.6 | 1.6 |
| 1.3 | 1.5 | 1.3 | Current | | | | | 1.3 | 1.3 |
| 1.1 | 1.1 | 1.1 | | | | | | 1.1 | 1.1 |
| 1.2 | 1.3 | 1.1 | | | | | | 1.2 | 1.0 |
| .8 | .8 | .7 | Quick | | | | | .8 | .6 |
| .5 | .5 | .3 | | | | | | .3 | .3 |
| 23  15.8 | 17  21.9 | 16  23.2 | | | | | | 14  25.9 | 19  19.7 |
| 37  9.9 | 35  10.5 | 30  12.0 | Sales/Receivables | | | | | 30  12.2 | 30  12.1 |
| 59  6.2 | 50  7.3 | 47  7.7 | | | | | | 51  7.1 | 45  8.1 |
| 3  140.5 | 3  117.3 | 6  56.6 | | | | | | 3  114.1 | 13  28.3 |
| 33  11.2 | 39  9.2 | 39  9.3 | Cost of Sales/Inventory | | | | | 20  18.6 | 42  8.6 |
| 86  4.2 | 93  3.9 | 94  3.9 | | | | | | 114  3.2 | 94  3.9 |
| 9  40.8 | 12  29.8 | 12  29.9 | | | | | | 9  40.5 | 13  28.7 |
| 27  13.5 | 24  15.1 | 24  15.3 | Cost of Sales/Payables | | | | | 23  15.6 | 22  16.4 |
| 49  7.5 | 55  6.7 | 47  7.8 | | | | | | 64  5.7 | 34  10.7 |
| 7.8 | 7.0 | 9.5 | | | | | | 10.6 | 10.5 |
| 16.1 | 13.2 | 21.7 | Sales/Working Capital | | | | | 25.7 | 22.9 |
| 37.9 | 34.0 | 66.9 | | | | | | 103.0 | 63.0 |
| 24.8 | 18.3 | 19.0 | | | | | | 11.6 | 19.8 |
| (105)  6.2 | (107)  6.5 | (101)  5.9 | EBIT/Interest | | | | | (24)  4.6 | (64)  6.1 |
| 1.7 | 1.7 | 1.9 | | | | | | 1.6 | 2.7 |
| 9.5 | 16.5 | 11.8 | | | | | | | 11.9 |
| (19)  4.5 | (16)  3.5 | (22)  5.2 | Net Profit + Depr., Dep., Amort./Cur. Mat. L/T/D | | | | | | (18)  6.5 |
| 1.8 | .2 | 1.3 | | | | | | | 1.3 |
| .0 | .0 | .1 | | | | | | .2 | .1 |
| .2 | .3 | .3 | Fixed/Worth | | | | | .5 | .3 |
| .8 | .9 | .8 | | | | | | 1.0 | .8 |
| 1.2 | 1.0 | 1.2 | | | | | | 1.8 | 1.4 |
| 2.4 | 2.6 | 2.8 | Debt/Worth | | | | | 3.8 | 3.1 |
| 4.9 | 5.4 | 6.8 | | | | | | 6.8 | 6.9 |
| 60.7 | 51.2 | 45.1 | | | | | | 42.4 | 45.2 |
| (104)  25.1 | (108)  19.2 | (106)  23.9 | % Profit Before Taxes/Tangible Net Worth | | | | | (28)  16.7 | (65)  25.7 |
| 7.6 | 4.6 | 14.3 | | | | | | 10.0 | 17.1 |
| 15.2 | 12.3 | 11.3 | | | | | | 12.5 | 10.0 |
| 7.8 | 6.4 | 6.6 | % Profit Before Taxes/Total Assets | | | | | 6.8 | 6.6 |
| 1.5 | 1.3 | 2.1 | | | | | | 1.0 | 3.1 |
| 574.0 | 341.8 | 263.0 | | | | | | 370.0 | 247.3 |
| 38.6 | 32.8 | 42.0 | Sales/Net Fixed Assets | | | | | 48.5 | 40.4 |
| 11.5 | 10.6 | 12.3 | | | | | | 13.6 | 11.7 |
| 4.6 | 4.5 | 4.7 | | | | | | 5.4 | 4.7 |
| 3.0 | 2.9 | 2.9 | Sales/Total Assets | | | | | 3.4 | 2.8 |
| 1.9 | 1.8 | 1.9 | | | | | | 2.5 | 1.9 |
| .3 | .1 | .1 | | | | | | .4 | .1 |
| (82)  .8 | (91)  .7 | (88)  .6 | % Depr., Dep., Amort./Sales | | | | | (20)  1.2 | (57)  .5 |
| 1.6 | 1.4 | 1.4 | | | | | | 1.9 | |
| .6 | .7 | .4 | | | | | | | .3 |
| (31)  1.5 | (29)  1.7 | (28)  1.0 | % Officers', Directors' Owners' Comp/Sales | | | | | | (16)  .6 |
| 2.4 | 3.5 | 2.3 | | | | | | | 2.0 |
| 6705988M | 8827823M | 12620120M | Net Sales ($) | | 17361M | 6722M | 42202M | 482521M | 12071314M |
| 2501937M | 3310686M | 4598363M | Total Assets ($) | | 12402M | 8052M | 19174M | 167776M | 4390959M |

© RMA 2012

M = $ thousand    MM = $ million

See Pages 9 through 22 for Explanation of Ratios and Data

## Current Data Sorted by Assets

## Comparative Historical Data

| 0-500M | 500M-2MM | 2-10MM | 10-50MM | 50-100MM | 100-250MM | | 4/1/07-3/31/08 ALL | 4/1/08-3/31/09 ALL |
|---|---|---|---|---|---|---|---|---|
| | | 7 | 12 | 6 | 2 | Type of Statement — Unqualified | 20 | 25 |
| | 2 | 17 | 10 | 1 | | Reviewed | 35 | 31 |
| | 9 | 15 | 1 | | | Compiled | 25 | 10 |
| 10 | 17 | 9 | 2 | | | Tax Returns | 18 | 17 |
| 4 | 6 | 27 | 20 | 1 | 6 | Other | 62 | 49 |
| | 19 (4/1-9/30/11) | | 165 (10/1/11-3/31/12) | | | | | |
| 14 | 34 | 75 | 45 | 8 | 8 | NUMBER OF STATEMENTS | 160 | 132 |
| % | % | % | % | % | % | ASSETS | % | % |
| 14.2 | 18.8 | 6.1 | 9.2 | | | Cash & Equivalents | 6.4 | 7.6 |
| 24.3 | 35.4 | 36.7 | 40.5 | | | Trade Receivables (net) | 40.1 | 40.1 |
| 23.9 | 25.6 | 31.3 | 31.8 | | | Inventory | 30.4 | 30.0 |
| 6.0 | .7 | 2.7 | 1.5 | | | All Other Current | 2.5 | 2.3 |
| 68.4 | 80.6 | 76.8 | 83.0 | | | Total Current | 79.5 | 80.0 |
| 8.2 | 11.5 | 13.4 | 12.2 | | | Fixed Assets (net) | 11.7 | 11.4 |
| 5.2 | .5 | 4.1 | 2.5 | | | Intangibles (net) | 2.4 | 2.3 |
| 18.2 | 7.5 | 5.7 | 2.3 | | | All Other Non-Current | 6.4 | 6.4 |
| 100.0 | 100.0 | 100.0 | 100.0 | | | Total | 100.0 | 100.0 |
| | | | | | | LIABILITIES | | |
| 24.1 | 12.0 | 13.2 | 21.1 | | | Notes Payable-Short Term | 17.2 | 21.4 |
| .3 | .9 | 1.6 | 1.0 | | | Cur. Mat.-L.T.D. | 2.4 | 1.9 |
| 24.7 | 29.5 | 23.7 | 24.9 | | | Trade Payables | 27.8 | 24.7 |
| .0 | .1 | .5 | .0 | | | Income Taxes Payable | .1 | .1 |
| 14.0 | 6.8 | 7.4 | 6.4 | | | All Other Current | 9.2 | 7.9 |
| 63.0 | 49.3 | 46.4 | 53.4 | | | Total Current | 56.7 | 56.0 |
| 5.3 | 9.6 | 9.8 | 4.7 | | | Long-Term Debt | 8.6 | 8.5 |
| .0 | .1 | .2 | .2 | | | Deferred Taxes | .2 | .1 |
| 14.2 | 7.0 | 9.4 | 3.7 | | | All Other Non-Current | 4.6 | 6.8 |
| 17.5 | 34.1 | 34.2 | 37.9 | | | Net Worth | 29.8 | 28.6 |
| 100.0 | 100.0 | 100.0 | 100.0 | | | Total Liabilities & Net Worth | 100.0 | 100.0 |
| | | | | | | INCOME DATA | | |
| 100.0 | 100.0 | 100.0 | 100.0 | | | Net Sales | 100.0 | 100.0 |
| 27.5 | 27.5 | 23.3 | 18.0 | | | Gross Profit | 23.0 | 22.0 |
| 30.1 | 23.6 | 18.4 | 13.9 | | | Operating Expenses | 19.0 | 20.1 |
| -2.6 | 3.8 | 4.8 | 4.1 | | | Operating Profit | 4.0 | 1.9 |
| -.2 | .2 | .8 | .2 | | | All Other Expenses (net) | .8 | .8 |
| -2.3 | 3.6 | 4.1 | 3.9 | | | Profit Before Taxes | 3.1 | 1.1 |
| | | | | | | RATIOS | | |
| 1.3 | 3.2 | 2.5 | 2.4 | | | Current | 2.0 | 2.1 |
| 1.1 | 1.8 | 1.6 | 1.4 | | | | 1.4 | 1.4 |
| .7 | 1.0 | 1.2 | 1.1 | | | | 1.1 | 1.1 |
| 1.2 | 2.0 | 1.4 | 1.5 | | | Quick | 1.2 | 1.2 |
| .5 | 1.0 | .9 | .9 | | | | .8 | .8 |
| .1 | .7 | .6 | .6 | | | | .6 | .5 |
| 0 UND | 17 21.0 | 29 12.7 | 37 9.8 | | | Sales/Receivables | 33 11.2 | 31 11.8 |
| 12 30.0 | 32 11.5 | 41 8.8 | 46 8.0 | | | | 43 8.4 | 37 9.8 |
| 29 12.6 | 43 8.4 | 49 7.4 | 63 5.8 | | | | 56 6.6 | 51 7.2 |
| 0 UND | 5 69.7 | 20 18.5 | 31 11.7 | | | Cost of Sales/Inventory | 23 16.1 | 16 23.4 |
| 15 24.5 | 34 10.8 | 39 9.4 | 51 7.1 | | | | 48 7.6 | 40 9.1 |
| 59 6.2 | 68 5.4 | 74 4.9 | 69 5.3 | | | | 85 4.3 | 77 4.7 |
| 0 UND | 14 26.5 | 17 20.9 | 25 14.5 | | | Cost of Sales/Payables | 25 14.4 | 17 21.6 |
| 24 15.4 | 29 12.6 | 34 10.8 | 40 9.1 | | | | 39 9.4 | 31 11.7 |
| 38 9.6 | 52 7.0 | 46 7.9 | 48 7.6 | | | | 55 6.6 | 41 8.8 |
| 26.2 | 6.7 | 6.3 | 6.9 | | | Sales/Working Capital | 7.9 | 8.2 |
| UND | 11.0 | 13.6 | 10.3 | | | | 12.8 | 15.0 |
| -81.2 | 134.4 | 31.4 | 26.7 | | | | 34.6 | 67.3 |
| | 38.6 | 21.8 | 18.3 | | | EBIT/Interest | 9.7 | 7.9 |
| | (26) 6.1 | (67) 7.2 | (39) 5.4 | | | | (143) 2.9 | (119) 3.3 |
| | 1.6 | 3.3 | 2.3 | | | | 1.6 | 1.1 |
| | | 15.3 | 36.4 | | | Net Profit + Depr., Dep., | 7.3 | 9.0 |
| | | (16) 2.7 | (12) 3.2 | | | Amort./Cur. Mat. L/T/D | (30) 4.0 | (26) 3.2 |
| | | 1.3 | 1.7 | | | | 1.6 | 1.4 |
| .0 | .0 | .0 | .0 | | | Fixed/Worth | .0 | .0 |
| .2 | .1 | .2 | .1 | | | | .2 | .2 |
| -1.0 | .6 | .8 | .5 | | | | .9 | 1.0 |
| .9 | .6 | .8 | .7 | | | Debt/Worth | 1.1 | 1.2 |
| 11.2 | 2.2 | 2.3 | 2.3 | | | | 2.8 | 2.7 |
| -6.1 | 11.0 | 6.2 | 4.6 | | | | 7.6 | 7.0 |
| | 51.9 | 70.2 | 32.1 | | | % Profit Before Taxes/Tangible | 42.7 | 39.5 |
| | (31) 14.4 | (69) 28.3 | 20.0 | | | Net Worth | (139) 25.5 | (115) 19.0 |
| | 4.5 | 10.7 | 11.9 | | | | 9.4 | 4.9 |
| 27.9 | 23.8 | 15.3 | 12.4 | | | % Profit Before Taxes/Total | 14.7 | 11.0 |
| -.5 | 9.4 | 8.2 | 5.4 | | | Assets | 6.0 | 5.5 |
| -18.5 | 1.0 | 3.6 | 2.6 | | | | 2.2 | .7 |
| UND | 829.0 | 163.1 | 969.2 | | | Sales/Net Fixed Assets | 298.8 | 517.3 |
| 233.9 | 151.9 | 44.0 | 143.8 | | | | 68.8 | 82.0 |
| 161.2 | 33.9 | 13.9 | 14.4 | | | | 14.7 | 18.5 |
| 7.1 | 4.8 | 4.3 | 3.5 | | | Sales/Total Assets | 3.9 | 4.4 |
| 5.0 | 3.9 | 3.1 | 2.9 | | | | 3.0 | 3.4 |
| 3.1 | 3.1 | 2.4 | 2.3 | | | | 2.3 | 2.6 |
| | .1 | .2 | .1 | | | % Depr., Dep., Amort./Sales | .2 | .1 |
| | (21) .5 | (58) .7 | (33) .6 | | | | (123) .6 | (105) .5 |
| | 1.4 | 1.7 | 1.5 | | | | 1.3 | 1.3 |
| | 2.0 | .8 | .5 | | | % Officers', Directors' | .9 | 1.0 |
| | (24) 4.4 | (28) 1.2 | (11) 1.0 | | | Owners' Comp/Sales | (73) 2.6 | (60) 2.6 |
| | 6.4 | 2.5 | 2.4 | | | | 5.4 | 5.3 |
| 30085M | 169565M | 1266771M | 2716015M | 1619841M | 4725680M | Net Sales ($) | 6421253M | 8024058M |
| 3776M | 42739M | 387012M | 957186M | 533790M | 1391802M | Total Assets ($) | 2296577M | 2233752M |

M = $ thousand   MM = $ million
See Pages 9 through 22 for Explanation of Ratios and Data

## Comparative Historical Data | Current Data Sorted by Sales

| Type of Statement | 4/1/09-3/31/10 ALL | 4/1/10-3/31/11 ALL | 4/1/11-3/31/12 ALL | 0-1MM | 1-3MM | 3-5MM | 5-10MM | 10-25MM | 25MM & OVER |
|---|---|---|---|---|---|---|---|---|---|
| Unqualified | 26 | 26 | 27 | 1 | 1 | | | 6 | 19 |
| Reviewed | 33 | 33 | 30 | | | 2 | 4 | 11 | 13 |
| Compiled | 16 | 22 | 25 | | 2 | 5 | 8 | 7 | 3 |
| Tax Returns | 26 | 22 | 38 | 4 | 4 | 10 | 12 | 5 | 3 |
| Other | 63 | 62 | 64 | 1 | 4 | 4 | 9 | 13 | 33 |
| | | | | 19 (4/1-9/30/11) | | 165 (10/1/11-3/31/12) | | | |
| NUMBER OF STATEMENTS | 164 | 165 | 184 | 6 | 11 | 21 | 33 | 42 | 71 |

| | % | % | % | % | % | % | % | % | % |
|---|---|---|---|---|---|---|---|---|---|
| **ASSETS** | | | | | | | | | |
| Cash & Equivalents | 8.3 | 9.3 | 9.5 | | 23.1 | 9.2 | 15.1 | 6.0 | 7.5 |
| Trade Receivables (net) | 40.2 | 39.9 | 37.1 | | 29.7 | 32.7 | 29.7 | 38.5 | 44.1 |
| Inventory | 28.4 | 29.7 | 30.3 | | 19.3 | 30.4 | 25.7 | 32.3 | 32.7 |
| All Other Current | 1.9 | 1.8 | 2.2 | | .8 | 4.2 | 4.3 | 1.5 | 1.5 |
| Total Current | 78.8 | 80.7 | 79.1 | | 72.9 | 76.5 | 74.8 | 78.3 | 85.9 |
| Fixed Assets (net) | 11.1 | 11.7 | 12.1 | | 9.5 | 13.0 | 13.1 | 13.4 | 9.6 |
| Intangibles (net) | 3.2 | 2.6 | 3.0 | | 3.2 | .7 | 5.7 | 3.3 | 2.0 |
| All Other Non-Current | 6.9 | 5.0 | 5.8 | | 14.4 | 9.8 | 6.4 | 5.0 | 2.6 |
| Total | 100.0 | 100.0 | 100.0 | | 100.0 | 100.0 | 100.0 | 100.0 | 100.0 |
| **LIABILITIES** | | | | | | | | | |
| Notes Payable-Short Term | 17.4 | 15.2 | 16.3 | | 7.5 | 13.9 | 16.5 | 13.0 | 20.0 |
| Cur. Mat.-L.T.D. | 1.6 | 1.4 | 1.2 | | .5 | 1.5 | 1.5 | 1.6 | .9 |
| Trade Payables | 28.0 | 28.0 | 25.5 | | 27.6 | 21.6 | 27.7 | 23.1 | 27.7 |
| Income Taxes Payable | .2 | .2 | .3 | | .0 | .1 | .8 | .3 | .1 |
| All Other Current | 6.4 | 8.2 | 7.4 | | 8.5 | 5.0 | 8.3 | 7.4 | 6.5 |
| Total Current | 53.6 | 53.0 | 50.6 | | 44.0 | 42.1 | 54.8 | 45.4 | 55.1 |
| Long-Term Debt | 9.3 | 7.4 | 8.2 | | 7.7 | 12.7 | 8.1 | 9.2 | 5.3 |
| Deferred Taxes | .3 | .2 | .2 | | .2 | .0 | .2 | .2 | .2 |
| All Other Non-Current | 6.3 | 4.2 | 7.2 | | 15.7 | 1.6 | 15.4 | 6.2 | 3.4 |
| Net Worth | 30.5 | 35.1 | 33.8 | | 32.5 | 43.6 | 21.4 | 39.0 | 36.1 |
| Total Liabilities & Net Worth | 100.0 | 100.0 | 100.0 | | 100.0 | 100.0 | 100.0 | 100.0 | 100.0 |
| **INCOME DATA** | | | | | | | | | |
| Net Sales | 100.0 | 100.0 | 100.0 | | 100.0 | 100.0 | 100.0 | 100.0 | 100.0 |
| Gross Profit | 21.5 | 23.3 | 21.9 | | 33.3 | 28.7 | 25.8 | 22.1 | 15.4 |
| Operating Expenses | 18.1 | 19.4 | 18.2 | | 32.1 | 25.4 | 21.4 | 17.8 | 11.7 |
| Operating Profit | 3.4 | 3.8 | 3.8 | | 1.2 | 3.4 | 4.4 | 4.2 | 3.6 |
| All Other Expenses (net) | .6 | .4 | .4 | | .1 | -.3 | .2 | .4 | .2 |
| Profit Before Taxes | 2.8 | 3.5 | 3.3 | | 1.1 | 3.7 | 4.1 | 3.9 | 3.4 |
| **RATIOS** | | | | | | | | | |
| Current | 2.4 | 2.5 | 2.3 | | 3.1 | 4.1 | 2.0 | 2.6 | 2.5 |
| | 1.5 | 1.5 | 1.5 | | 1.6 | 1.9 | 1.3 | 1.7 | 1.4 |
| | 1.1 | 1.1 | 1.1 | | 1.1 | 1.2 | .9 | 1.2 | 1.1 |
| Quick | 1.4 | 1.5 | 1.5 | | 2.1 | 1.9 | 1.0 | 1.5 | 1.5 |
| | .9 | .9 | .9 | | 1.2 | 1.3 | .8 | .9 | .9 |
| | .6 | .6 | .6 | | .7 | .7 | .5 | .6 | .6 |
| Sales/Receivables | 35  10.6 | 31  11.6 | 29  12.8 | | 10  38.1 | 26  14.3 | 9  40.6 | 34  10.7 | 36  10.0 |
| | 44  8.3 | 44  8.3 | 41  8.8 | | 30  12.1 | 32  11.5 | 39  9.3 | 43  8.5 | 43  8.5 |
| | 58  6.3 | 56  6.5 | 51  7.2 | | 61  6.0 | 41  8.8 | 51  7.1 | 51  7.2 | 54  6.8 |
| Cost of Sales/Inventory | 17  21.4 | 22  16.6 | 22  16.9 | | 12  30.9 | 21  17.1 | 5  78.9 | 24  15.3 | 30  12.0 |
| | 47  7.8 | 45  8.2 | 42  8.7 | | 37  9.8 | 49  7.5 | 37  9.8 | 45  8.1 | 43  8.5 |
| | 75  4.9 | 76  4.8 | 68  5.4 | | 58  6.3 | 76  4.8 | 76  4.8 | 81  4.5 | 63  5.8 |
| Cost of Sales/Payables | 21  17.6 | 23  15.6 | 19  19.2 | | 15  23.9 | 17  21.5 | 14  25.6 | 18  20.6 | 25  14.8 |
| | 37  9.8 | 36  10.0 | 34  10.7 | | 35  10.3 | 28  13.0 | 38  9.6 | 32  11.4 | 37  9.9 |
| | 55  6.7 | 51  7.1 | 46  7.9 | | 64  5.7 | 45  8.1 | 58  6.3 | 46  8.0 | 45  8.1 |
| Sales/Working Capital | 6.2 | 5.9 | 6.7 | | 5.2 | 6.0 | 8.2 | 6.3 | 6.6 |
| | 12.7 | 11.9 | 12.6 | | 25.6 | 7.8 | 15.5 | 11.4 | 11.9 |
| | 40.6 | 35.4 | 39.4 | | 87.1 | 49.9 | -143.8 | 24.9 | 30.5 |
| EBIT/Interest | 16.1 | 26.8 | 22.2 | | | 68.4 | 27.6 | 23.8 | 21.9 |
| | (146) 6.0 | (143) 6.4 | (153) 6.6 | | | (18) 9.1 | (28) 5.8 | (36) 8.0 | (65) 6.1 |
| | 1.6 | 2.6 | 2.9 | | | 1.1 | 1.9 | 3.2 | 3.4 |
| Net Profit + Depr., Dep., Amort./Cur. Mat. L/T/D | 5.3 | 13.1 | 16.0 | | | | | 22.5 | 35.9 |
| | (32) 2.5 | (31) 4.4 | (35) 3.1 | | | | | (10) 4.0 | (17) 3.5 |
| | 1.1 | 2.1 | 1.4 | | | | | 1.6 | 2.0 |
| Fixed/Worth | .0 | .0 | .0 | | .0 | .0 | .1 | .0 | .0 |
| | .2 | .1 | .1 | | .1 | .1 | .3 | .2 | .0 |
| | 1.0 | .6 | .6 | | 1.3 | .5 | 3.3 | .5 | .4 |
| Debt/Worth | 1.1 | .8 | .8 | | .9 | .4 | 1.1 | .8 | .7 |
| | 2.6 | 2.0 | 2.4 | | 2.7 | 1.1 | 6.1 | 2.1 | 2.4 |
| | 7.3 | 5.6 | 6.1 | | 16.7 | 4.0 | 53.4 | 4.0 | 4.7 |
| % Profit Before Taxes/Tangible Net Worth | 53.6 | 47.3 | 50.6 | | | 51.8 | 60.5 | 69.4 | 47.2 |
| | (146) 27.4 | (151) 23.2 | (170) 21.8 | | | (20) 13.1 | (27) 25.9 | (40) 28.3 | (70) 20.5 |
| | 5.8 | 9.3 | 10.5 | | | 4.9 | 6.6 | 12.0 | 12.9 |
| % Profit Before Taxes/Total Assets | 15.3 | 16.3 | 15.1 | | 11.3 | 20.0 | 26.6 | 17.1 | 12.6 |
| | 6.0 | 6.9 | 7.4 | | 1.2 | 7.1 | 8.2 | 8.4 | 7.4 |
| | 1.2 | 3.0 | 2.7 | | -7.4 | 1.2 | 1.9 | 5.5 | 3.4 |
| Sales/Net Fixed Assets | 548.2 | 499.0 | 665.7 | | 748.7 | 223.8 | 271.0 | 175.8 | 999.8 |
| | 85.4 | 62.3 | 118.0 | | 205.4 | 90.1 | 50.9 | 55.7 | 219.2 |
| | 14.5 | 14.9 | 16.8 | | 7.3 | 13.8 | 17.0 | 13.5 | 28.1 |
| Sales/Total Assets | 3.9 | 4.2 | 4.3 | | 5.8 | 4.5 | 4.8 | 4.7 | 3.8 |
| | 2.9 | 3.0 | 3.2 | | 3.2 | 3.4 | 3.2 | 3.0 | 3.3 |
| | 2.2 | 2.3 | 2.4 | | 1.8 | 2.5 | 2.5 | 2.4 | 2.5 |
| % Depr., Dep., Amort./Sales | .1 | .2 | .1 | | | .1 | .1 | .2 | .0 |
| | (111) .7 | (120) .7 | (135) .5 | | | (15) .5 | (23) 1.2 | (33) .6 | (57) .3 |
| | 2.0 | 1.7 | 1.3 | | | 1.5 | 2.6 | 1.1 | .9 |
| % Officers', Directors' Owners' Comp/Sales | .6 | .8 | 1.0 | | | 3.9 | 1.2 | .9 | .5 |
| | (67) 1.7 | (72) 2.2 | (70) 2.1 | | | (16) 5.3 | (17) 2.0 | (14) 1.2 | (18) .9 |
| | 4.5 | 4.3 | 5.2 | | | 7.3 | 3.5 | 2.7 | 1.7 |
| Net Sales ($) | 6745514M | 8300926M | 10527957M | 2529M | 23436M | 85628M | 250016M | 741863M | 9424485M |
| Total Assets ($) | 2361354M | 2776305M | 3316305M | 6752M | 8582M | 28929M | 91400M | 252497M | 2928145M |

© RMA 2012   M = $ thousand   MM = $ million
See Pages 9 through 22 for Explanation of Ratios and Data

## Current Data Sorted by Assets      Comparative Historical Data

| 0-500M | 500M-2MM | 2-10MM | 10-50MM | 50-100MM | 100-250MM | Type of Statement | 4/1/07-3/31/08 ALL | 4/1/08-3/31/09 ALL |
|---|---|---|---|---|---|---|---|---|
| 1 | 1 | 14 | 41 | 13 | 14 | Unqualified | 69 | 71 |
| 1 | 5 | 47 | 38 | 2 | 1 | Reviewed | 84 | 84 |
| 4 | 20 | 29 | 6 | | 2 | Compiled | 48 | 47 |
| 11 | 24 | 26 | 1 | | | Tax Returns | 37 | 52 |
| 13 | 27 | 48 | 57 | 13 | 9 | Other | 110 | 156 |
| | 78 (4/1-9/30/11) | | 389 (10/1/11-3/31/12) | | | | | |
| 29 | 77 | 164 | 143 | 28 | 26 | NUMBER OF STATEMENTS | 348 | 410 |
| % | % | % | % | % | % | **ASSETS** | % | % |
| 16.4 | 10.9 | 8.5 | 6.9 | 4.2 | 4.5 | Cash & Equivalents | 8.2 | 7.8 |
| 20.8 | 36.7 | 38.1 | 36.4 | 31.8 | 33.0 | Trade Receivables (net) | 37.2 | 37.5 |
| 35.0 | 29.5 | 33.7 | 32.3 | 29.4 | 22.9 | Inventory | 27.8 | 31.4 |
| 7.2 | 1.4 | 1.9 | 2.6 | 3.8 | 3.8 | All Other Current | 2.3 | 2.3 |
| 79.4 | 78.4 | 82.2 | 78.2 | 69.3 | 64.3 | Total Current | 75.4 | 78.9 |
| 9.7 | 8.9 | 11.3 | 13.8 | 19.4 | 20.8 | Fixed Assets (net) | 16.1 | 13.6 |
| 6.9 | 5.0 | 2.0 | 4.7 | 8.5 | 10.4 | Intangibles (net) | 3.0 | 2.7 |
| 3.9 | 7.6 | 4.5 | 3.4 | 2.8 | 4.5 | All Other Non-Current | 5.5 | 4.8 |
| 100.0 | 100.0 | 100.0 | 100.0 | 100.0 | 100.0 | Total | 100.0 | 100.0 |
| | | | | | | **LIABILITIES** | | |
| 14.8 | 13.6 | 14.3 | 16.4 | 13.9 | 8.4 | Notes Payable-Short Term | 16.9 | 17.6 |
| .9 | 2.0 | 1.6 | 2.1 | 1.3 | .7 | Cur. Mat.-L.T.D. | 3.2 | 2.2 |
| 20.2 | 25.3 | 25.6 | 22.9 | 21.2 | 20.0 | Trade Payables | 25.2 | 24.4 |
| .0 | .2 | .2 | .2 | .2 | .6 | Income Taxes Payable | .2 | .2 |
| 35.8 | 6.1 | 6.3 | 7.4 | 8.9 | 13.5 | All Other Current | 8.7 | 8.3 |
| 71.7 | 47.2 | 47.9 | 49.0 | 45.6 | 43.2 | Total Current | 54.3 | 52.7 |
| 12.0 | 11.0 | 5.9 | 7.0 | 11.1 | 9.8 | Long-Term Debt | 10.3 | 8.8 |
| .0 | .0 | .2 | .5 | 1.0 | 1.1 | Deferred Taxes | .3 | .3 |
| 5.7 | 12.9 | 4.2 | 1.8 | 3.8 | 6.5 | All Other Non-Current | 3.8 | 3.7 |
| 10.6 | 28.8 | 41.8 | 41.7 | 38.5 | 39.4 | Net Worth | 31.4 | 34.5 |
| 100.0 | 100.0 | 100.0 | 100.0 | 100.0 | 100.0 | Total Liabilities & Net Worth | 100.0 | 100.0 |
| | | | | | | **INCOME DATA** | | |
| 100.0 | 100.0 | 100.0 | 100.0 | 100.0 | 100.0 | Net Sales | 100.0 | 100.0 |
| 36.6 | 29.9 | 22.8 | 20.5 | 19.1 | 21.1 | Gross Profit | 25.4 | 24.1 |
| 26.7 | 27.2 | 18.3 | 15.8 | 12.9 | 15.7 | Operating Expenses | 20.9 | 19.4 |
| 9.9 | 2.6 | 4.5 | 4.8 | 6.3 | 5.4 | Operating Profit | 4.4 | 4.7 |
| 1.2 | .0 | .3 | .3 | .6 | .6 | All Other Expenses (net) | .6 | .5 |
| 8.7 | 2.7 | 4.2 | 4.5 | 5.7 | 4.8 | Profit Before Taxes | 3.9 | 4.2 |
| | | | | | | **RATIOS** | | |
| 3.6 | 2.8 | 2.5 | 2.3 | 2.3 | 2.2 | | 2.0 | 2.1 |
| 1.5 | 1.8 | 1.7 | 1.5 | 1.5 | 1.4 | Current | 1.4 | 1.5 |
| .8 | 1.1 | 1.3 | 1.2 | 1.2 | 1.2 | | 1.1 | 1.2 |
| 1.2 | 1.9 | 1.6 | 1.3 | 1.2 | 1.2 | | 1.2 | 1.3 |
| .7 | 1.0 | .9 | .9 | .9 | .9 | Quick | (347) .8 | .8 |
| .2 | .6 | .7 | .6 | .5 | .6 | | .6 | .6 |
| 5   66.8 | 27   13.6 | 32   11.3 | 35   10.3 | 33   10.9 | 32   11.3 | | 33   11.0 | 30   12.1 |
| 26   14.1 | 32   11.4 | 40   9.1 | 42   8.6 | 43   8.5 | 40   9.1 | Sales/Receivables | 43   8.5 | 39   9.3 |
| 38   9.6 | 44   8.3 | 52   7.0 | 49   7.4 | 51   7.1 | 53   6.9 | | 52   7.0 | 50   7.2 |
| 15   23.6 | 8   43.2 | 28   13.0 | 31   11.9 | 28   12.9 | 21   17.8 | | 24   15.3 | 22   16.4 |
| 53   6.9 | 37   9.9 | 52   7.0 | 51   7.1 | 55   6.6 | 38   9.7 | Cost of Sales/Inventory | 45   8.2 | 47   7.8 |
| 104   3.5 | 69   5.3 | 78   4.7 | 76   4.8 | 85   4.3 | 54   6.7 | | 65   5.6 | 76   4.8 |
| 8   47.1 | 17   20.9 | 21   17.3 | 23   16.1 | 22   16.3 | 20   17.9 | | 24   15.5 | 18   20.4 |
| 27   13.4 | 29   12.4 | 32   11.5 | 31   11.8 | 31   11.7 | 27   13.5 | Cost of Sales/Payables | 36   10.2 | 28   12.8 |
| 48   7.6 | 46   8.0 | 51   7.1 | 43   8.4 | 46   8.0 | 46   7.9 | | 54   6.8 | 47   7.8 |
| 5.3 | 6.0 | 6.4 | 6.1 | 5.0 | 6.2 | | 8.3 | 7.4 |
| 20.2 | 12.6 | 9.6 | 10.8 | 11.7 | 9.4 | Sales/Working Capital | 15.2 | 12.6 |
| -141.9 | 42.9 | 16.0 | 21.9 | 22.7 | 31.3 | | 41.9 | 31.9 |
| 34.0 | 18.6 | 22.9 | 25.2 | 23.4 | 35.0 | | 9.3 | 13.3 |
| (17) 9.3 | (63) 5.0 | (140) 7.4 | (124) 10.7 | 10.8 | (22) 6.6 | EBIT/Interest | (313) 3.8 | (363) 5.7 |
| 3.2 | 1.9 | 2.9 | 3.7 | 4.2 | 1.5 | | 2.0 | 2.0 |
| | | 13.5 | 8.5 | | 143.6 | | 7.1 | 12.6 |
| | (31) 3.3 | (47) 5.0 | | | (10) 18.2 | Net Profit + Depr., Dep., Amort./Cur. Mat. L/T/D | (97) 3.2 | (93) 4.1 |
| | | 1.6 | 2.6 | | 7.5 | | 1.2 | 1.7 |
| .0 | .0 | .0 | .0 | .1 | .2 | | .1 | .0 |
| .0 | .1 | .1 | .1 | .3 | .5 | Fixed/Worth | .3 | .2 |
| 11.0 | .9 | .5 | .6 | 1.1 | 1.4 | | 1.1 | .8 |
| .5 | .9 | .6 | .9 | .8 | .9 | | 1.1 | .9 |
| 3.4 | 2.0 | 1.5 | 1.9 | 3.0 | 2.1 | Debt/Worth | 2.5 | 2.4 |
| -13.4 | 10.7 | 3.5 | 3.7 | 9.9 | 4.7 | | 6.9 | 5.0 |
| 136.3 | 53.8 | 43.5 | 46.9 | 67.2 | 57.6 | | 53.6 | 55.0 |
| (21) 46.5 | (65) 21.1 | (158) 24.6 | (138) 28.1 | (26) 32.0 | (24) 28.9 | % Profit Before Taxes/Tangible Net Worth | (312) 28.5 | (375) 28.7 |
| 24.3 | 5.9 | 8.9 | 19.6 | 20.0 | 11.2 | | 10.3 | 9.3 |
| 35.7 | 17.0 | 19.2 | 16.0 | 18.1 | 15.3 | | 15.4 | 17.3 |
| 13.6 | 5.5 | 7.3 | 8.6 | 9.2 | 11.4 | % Profit Before Taxes/Total Assets | 8.6 | 8.7 |
| 2.5 | 1.8 | 3.3 | 5.1 | 5.7 | 1.1 | | 2.9 | 2.5 |
| UND | 389.9 | 327.5 | 285.4 | 273.1 | 81.3 | | 138.4 | 284.7 |
| 665.0 | 86.7 | 66.9 | 32.9 | 17.6 | 14.8 | Sales/Net Fixed Assets | 39.1 | 50.7 |
| 40.4 | 46.4 | 17.4 | 12.5 | 7.1 | 4.4 | | 11.1 | 14.7 |
| 4.9 | 5.1 | 4.1 | 3.8 | 3.5 | 3.6 | | 4.0 | 4.4 |
| 3.5 | 3.4 | 3.1 | 2.9 | 2.6 | 1.8 | Sales/Total Assets | 3.1 | 3.3 |
| 2.4 | 2.6 | 2.3 | 2.1 | 1.6 | 1.5 | | 2.1 | 2.3 |
| | .2 | .2 | .2 | .3 | .2 | | .3 | .2 |
| | (49) .4 | (130) .5 | (116) .6 | (23) 1.1 | (20) .9 | % Depr., Dep., Amort./Sales | (291) .7 | (333) .5 |
| | 1.1 | 1.0 | 1.2 | 2.7 | 2.0 | | 1.8 | 1.4 |
| 1.6 | 2.8 | 1.6 | .7 | | | | 1.5 | 1.2 |
| (10) 6.0 | (38) 4.5 | (73) 2.2 | (35) 1.4 | | | % Officers', Directors' Owners' Comp/Sales | (119) 2.9 | (149) 3.0 |
| 6.9 | 8.6 | 4.2 | 3.7 | | | | 5.7 | 5.6 |
| 41013M | 387001M | 2818979M | 10994708M | 4712881M | 15862585M | Net Sales ($) | 17186747M | 25017181M |
| 7713M | 96863M | 842845M | 3283692M | 1940378M | 4222892M | Total Assets ($) | 6129167M | 7669498M |

## Comparative Historical Data / Current Data Sorted by Sales

| | | | Type of Statement | 0-1MM | 1-3MM | 3-5MM | 5-10MM | 10-25MM | 25MM & OVER |
|---|---|---|---|---|---|---|---|---|---|
| 73 | 62 | 83 | Unqualified | | | 3 | 3 | 11 | 66 |
| 89 | 82 | 94 | Reviewed | 1 | | 1 | 15 | 29 | 48 |
| 47 | 57 | 61 | Compiled | 2 | 5 | 9 | 19 | 16 | 10 |
| 53 | 63 | 62 | Tax Returns | 7 | 10 | 8 | 16 | 18 | 3 |
| 152 | 173 | 167 | Other | 8 | 13 | 12 | 18 | 36 | 80 |
| 4/1/09-3/31/10 ALL | 4/1/10-3/31/11 ALL | 4/1/11-3/31/12 ALL | | 78 (4/1-9/30/11) | | | 389 (10/1/11-3/31/12) | | |
| 414 | 437 | 467 | NUMBER OF STATEMENTS | 18 | 28 | 33 | 71 | 110 | 207 |
| % | % | % | **ASSETS** | % | % | % | % | % | % |
| 10.2 | 7.8 | 8.4 | Cash & Equivalents | 19.9 | 9.9 | 9.1 | 10.2 | 9.5 | 5.9 |
| 34.0 | 36.3 | 35.6 | Trade Receivables (net) | 13.0 | 26.1 | 31.4 | 38.0 | 37.0 | 38.0 |
| 29.1 | 30.4 | 31.8 | Inventory | 23.9 | 40.1 | 30.6 | 29.7 | 34.8 | 30.7 |
| 2.8 | 2.5 | 2.6 | All Other Current | 6.8 | .5 | 2.0 | 2.1 | 2.4 | 2.8 |
| 76.0 | 77.1 | 78.4 | Total Current | 63.7 | 76.6 | 73.2 | 80.1 | 83.8 | 77.4 |
| 15.1 | 13.5 | 12.6 | Fixed Assets (net) | 22.6 | 9.3 | 10.9 | 12.2 | 9.7 | 14.1 |
| 3.9 | 4.5 | 4.4 | Intangibles (net) | 10.1 | 4.0 | 6.1 | 4.3 | 1.9 | 5.2 |
| 5.0 | 4.9 | 4.5 | All Other Non-Current | 3.6 | 10.1 | 9.9 | 3.4 | 4.6 | 3.3 |
| 100.0 | 100.0 | 100.0 | Total | 100.0 | 100.0 | 100.0 | 100.0 | 100.0 | 100.0 |
| | | | **LIABILITIES** | | | | | | |
| 14.1 | 13.6 | 14.5 | Notes Payable-Short Term | 5.4 | 12.5 | 21.3 | 10.3 | 15.8 | 15.3 |
| 2.2 | 2.0 | 1.7 | Cur. Mat.-L.T.D. | 1.0 | 1.5 | 2.1 | 1.8 | 1.8 | 1.7 |
| 22.3 | 24.5 | 23.8 | Trade Payables | 15.5 | 24.0 | 20.6 | 23.8 | 26.8 | 23.4 |
| .3 | .2 | .2 | Income Taxes Payable | .0 | .2 | .1 | .2 | .2 | .3 |
| 8.5 | 6.9 | 9.0 | All Other Current | 46.5 | 7.7 | 5.3 | 7.2 | 6.2 | 8.6 |
| 47.3 | 47.2 | 49.2 | Total Current | 68.4 | 45.9 | 49.3 | 43.3 | 50.8 | 49.2 |
| 9.6 | 9.3 | 8.0 | Long-Term Debt | 22.6 | 19.4 | 7.8 | 8.6 | 4.3 | 7.0 |
| .4 | .4 | .3 | Deferred Taxes | .0 | .0 | .3 | .1 | .2 | .6 |
| 3.0 | 4.3 | 5.1 | All Other Non-Current | 8.0 | 19.4 | 11.5 | 3.5 | 4.5 | 2.7 |
| 39.7 | 38.8 | 37.4 | Net Worth | 1.0 | 15.3 | 31.1 | 44.5 | 40.3 | 40.5 |
| 100.0 | 100.0 | 100.0 | Total Liabilities & Net Worth | 100.0 | 100.0 | 100.0 | 100.0 | 100.0 | 100.0 |
| | | | **INCOME DATA** | | | | | | |
| 100.0 | 100.0 | 100.0 | Net Sales | 100.0 | 100.0 | 100.0 | 100.0 | 100.0 | 100.0 |
| 26.4 | 26.1 | 23.8 | Gross Profit | 48.5 | 36.7 | 28.2 | 27.3 | 22.2 | 18.9 |
| 21.9 | 21.7 | 19.1 | Operating Expenses | 33.5 | 34.3 | 25.9 | 21.6 | 18.6 | 14.0 |
| 4.4 | 4.4 | 4.8 | Operating Profit | 15.0 | 2.4 | 2.3 | 5.7 | 3.6 | 4.9 |
| .4 | .4 | .3 | All Other Expenses (net) | 2.5 | -.8 | .9 | .1 | .3 | .3 |
| 4.1 | 4.0 | 4.4 | Profit Before Taxes | 12.5 | 3.2 | 1.4 | 5.6 | 3.3 | 4.6 |
| | | | **RATIOS** | | | | | | |
| 2.5 | 2.5 | 2.5 | Current | 5.7 | 4.2 | 2.2 | 3.4 | 2.2 | 2.2 |
| 1.6 | 1.7 | 1.6 | | 2.8 | 1.9 | 1.6 | 2.0 | 1.6 | 1.5 |
| 1.2 | 1.3 | 1.2 | | .6 | 1.1 | 1.0 | 1.4 | 1.3 | 1.2 |
| 1.6 | 1.4 | 1.4 | Quick | 2.9 | 1.4 | 1.3 | 2.2 | 1.3 | 1.3 |
| 1.0 | .9 | .9 | | .8 | .8 | .8 | 1.2 | .9 | .9 |
| .6 | .6 | .6 | | .2 | .4 | .4 | .7 | .6 | .6 |
| 32  11.4 | 32  11.3 | 30  12.0 | Sales/Receivables | 0  UND | 25  14.5 | 27  13.4 | 29  12.6 | 32  11.4 | 34  10.8 |
| 41  8.8 | 41  8.9 | 40  9.1 | | 24  15.0 | 31  11.7 | 32  11.3 | 44  8.3 | 40  9.2 | 41  8.8 |
| 53  6.9 | 52  7.0 | 50  7.3 | | 33  10.9 | 42  8.6 | 45  8.1 | 61  6.0 | 50  7.3 | 50  7.3 |
| 26  14.0 | 26  13.9 | 26  14.2 | Cost of Sales/Inventory | 0  UND | 32  11.5 | 24  15.3 | 22  16.5 | 28  13.0 | 26  13.8 |
| 48  7.6 | 48  7.6 | 48  7.6 | | 38  9.5 | 66  5.5 | 46  8.0 | 49  7.4 | 54  6.7 | 43  8.4 |
| 82  4.4 | 77  4.7 | 78  4.7 | | 118  3.1 | 152  2.4 | 79  4.6 | 79  4.6 | 79  4.6 | 72  5.1 |
| 23  16.1 | 23  15.8 | 20  17.9 | Cost of Sales/Payables | 7  55.4 | 20  18.3 | 16  23.5 | 18  20.7 | 22  16.8 | 22  16.8 |
| 33  11.0 | 35  10.5 | 31  11.9 | | 19  18.9 | 31  11.9 | 28  13.1 | 34  10.8 | 36  10.2 | 30  12.1 |
| 48  7.6 | 49  7.4 | 46  7.9 | | 54  6.7 | 62  5.9 | 44  8.3 | 49  7.4 | 53  6.9 | 43  8.5 |
| 6.1 | 6.5 | 6.1 | Sales/Working Capital | 3.6 | 3.5 | 7.5 | 5.0 | 6.7 | 6.5 |
| 10.5 | 10.5 | 10.8 | | 6.8 | 9.5 | 13.5 | 8.6 | 10.8 | 11.6 |
| 21.3 | 21.3 | 22.7 | | -20.9 | 42.3 | -142.7 | 15.1 | 16.8 | 24.4 |
| 16.3 | 23.8 | 23.0 | EBIT/Interest | | 7.5 | 15.2 | 49.8 | 22.9 | 25.5 |
| (369)  4.8 | (381)  7.9 | (394)  8.3 | | | (22)  3.6 | (29)  2.4 | (60)  8.1 | (92)  5.7 | (182)  11.1 |
| 2.1 | 2.6 | 2.9 | | | 1.9 | .4 | 2.9 | 2.9 | 4.0 |
| 9.0 | 12.5 | 13.5 | Net Profit + Depr., Dep., Amort./Cur. Mat. L/T/D | | | | 5.2 | 13.4 | 13.5 |
| (95)  3.2 | (96)  4.7 | (102)  5.0 | | | | (11)  2.1 | (26)  3.6 | (61)  6.0 |
| 1.4 | 2.5 | 2.2 | | | | | .5 | 1.4 | 3.1 |
| .0 | .0 | .0 | Fixed/Worth | .0 | .0 | .0 | .0 | .0 | .0 |
| .2 | .2 | .2 | | .0 | .2 | .2 | .2 | .1 | .3 |
| .9 | .7 | .7 | | 12.5 | -1.0 | 4.2 | .6 | .5 | .7 |
| .8 | .8 | .8 | Debt/Worth | .3 | .6 | 1.1 | .5 | .7 | .9 |
| 1.8 | 1.8 | 1.8 | | 5.2 | 2.0 | 3.6 | 1.3 | 1.6 | 2.0 |
| 3.9 | 4.2 | 4.8 | | -7.6 | -12.3 | 18.9 | 3.7 | 3.5 | 4.3 |
| 49.2 | 48.5 | 50.3 | % Profit Before Taxes/Tangible Net Worth | 123.1 | 31.9 | 38.3 | 60.9 | 43.3 | 50.4 |
| (387)  24.7 | (400)  25.2 | (432)  28.3 | | (13)  46.5 | (20)  14.3 | (27)  20.0 | (66)  28.5 | (107)  25.1 | (199)  29.4 |
| 8.4 | 11.3 | 11.5 | | 26.2 | 3.8 | .5 | 8.1 | 8.9 | 19.7 |
| 17.1 | 16.7 | 17.9 | % Profit Before Taxes/Total Assets | 34.8 | 15.3 | 10.9 | 25.7 | 17.9 | 16.4 |
| 7.2 | 8.5 | 8.0 | | 15.9 | 6.1 | 3.9 | 7.9 | 6.8 | 9.8 |
| 2.3 | 2.9 | 3.5 | | 2.3 | .8 | -.6 | 3.7 | 3.1 | 4.7 |
| 189.2 | 286.2 | 351.7 | Sales/Net Fixed Assets | UND | 486.9 | 424.5 | 186.1 | 471.5 | 306.1 |
| 40.7 | 50.5 | 57.7 | | UND | 78.6 | 68.2 | 60.4 | 73.5 | 36.3 |
| 11.7 | 13.7 | 13.9 | | 3.0 | 20.6 | 24.9 | 12.2 | 22.3 | 12.1 |
| 3.8 | 4.0 | 4.1 | Sales/Total Assets | 3.8 | 3.4 | 4.7 | 4.2 | 4.2 | 4.1 |
| 2.8 | 3.0 | 3.1 | | 1.8 | 2.6 | 3.1 | 3.1 | 3.1 | 3.1 |
| 2.1 | 2.2 | 2.2 | | .6 | 1.3 | 2.2 | 2.3 | 2.3 | 2.1 |
| .3 | .2 | .2 | % Depr., Dep., Amort./Sales | | | .2 | .3 | .2 | .1 |
| (323)  .8 | (333)  .6 | (342)  .5 | | | | (24)  .8 | (49)  .6 | (86)  .5 | (169)  .5 |
| 2.0 | 1.6 | 1.3 | | | | 2.0 | 1.3 | 1.0 | 1.4 |
| 1.6 | 1.4 | 1.4 | % Officers', Directors' Owners' Comp/Sales | | 1.6 | 2.5 | 1.5 | 1.6 | .7 |
| (148)  3.3 | (161)  2.6 | (160)  2.6 | | | (11)  6.2 | (14)  4.6 | (35)  3.3 | (52)  2.1 | (43)  1.4 |
| 6.0 | 5.2 | 5.0 | | | 14.3 | 8.3 | 6.2 | 4.3 | 2.6 |
| 21351752M | 19694343M | 34817167M | Net Sales ($) | 6317M | 49745M | 133263M | 529327M | 1883533M | 32214982M |
| 7775832M | 7127929M | 10394383M | Total Assets ($) | 5131M | 23173M | 51143M | 210450M | 644707M | 9459779M |

© RMA 2012

M = $ thousand     MM = $ million
See Pages 9 through 22 for Explanation of Ratios and Data

## Current Data Sorted by Assets  |  Comparative Historical Data

| 0-500M | 500M-2MM | 2-10MM | 10-50MM | 50-100MM | 100-250MM | Type of Statement | 4/1/07-3/31/08 ALL | 4/1/08-3/31/09 ALL |
|---|---|---|---|---|---|---|---|---|
|  | 1 | 9 | 23 | 11 | 10 | Unqualified | 57 | 41 |
|  | 2 | 36 | 47 | 3 |  | Reviewed | 68 | 87 |
| 8 | 18 | 32 | 13 | 1 | 2 | Compiled | 83 | 48 |
| 3 | 17 | 15 | 6 |  |  | Tax Returns | 26 | 28 |
| 3 | 8 | 27 | 44 | 10 | 6 | Other | 86 | 97 |
| | 116 (4/1-9/30/11) | | 239 (10/1/11-3/31/12) | | | | | |
| 14 | 46 | 119 | 133 | 25 | 18 | NUMBER OF STATEMENTS | 320 | 301 |
| % | % | % | % | % | % | **ASSETS** | % | % |
| 12.5 | 10.1 | 11.4 | 8.0 | 6.3 | 2.3 | Cash & Equivalents | 8.2 | 10.2 |
| 26.3 | 37.1 | 34.5 | 30.9 | 35.2 | 31.0 | Trade Receivables (net) | 35.3 | 30.2 |
| 14.3 | 16.5 | 15.9 | 12.2 | 12.5 | 16.3 | Inventory | 14.5 | 14.1 |
| 2.9 | 1.4 | 1.7 | 2.5 | 3.5 | 4.0 | All Other Current | 2.9 | 3.4 |
| 55.9 | 65.0 | 63.4 | 53.6 | 57.5 | 53.6 | Total Current | 60.9 | 57.8 |
| 28.2 | 22.8 | 26.0 | 32.9 | 30.6 | 37.2 | Fixed Assets (net) | 30.3 | 33.3 |
| 3.0 | 4.2 | 2.8 | 3.6 | 3.7 | 4.1 | Intangibles (net) | 3.2 | 3.2 |
| 12.9 | 8.0 | 7.8 | 9.9 | 8.1 | 5.1 | All Other Non-Current | 5.6 | 5.8 |
| 100.0 | 100.0 | 100.0 | 100.0 | 100.0 | 100.0 | Total | 100.0 | 100.0 |
|  |  |  |  |  |  | **LIABILITIES** |  |  |
| 16.1 | 15.3 | 9.7 | 12.6 | 20.0 | 12.2 | Notes Payable-Short Term | 12.9 | 10.5 |
| 11.2 | 2.5 | 3.5 | 3.3 | 3.1 | 2.9 | Cur. Mat.-L.T.D. | 3.8 | 3.9 |
| 47.2 | 28.2 | 28.2 | 24.4 | 25.4 | 19.4 | Trade Payables | 27.4 | 23.1 |
| .0 | .2 | .1 | .1 | .2 | .2 | Income Taxes Payable | .1 | .2 |
| 6.2 | 8.6 | 8.0 | 6.9 | 4.7 | 7.5 | All Other Current | 6.1 | 7.3 |
| 80.7 | 54.8 | 49.5 | 47.3 | 53.5 | 42.1 | Total Current | 50.3 | 44.9 |
| 27.6 | 16.8 | 13.6 | 14.4 | 12.0 | 25.9 | Long-Term Debt | 17.1 | 17.0 |
| .0 | .1 | .5 | 1.0 | 1.3 | .5 | Deferred Taxes | .8 | .6 |
| 18.8 | 3.5 | 5.3 | 2.6 | 2.1 | 3.4 | All Other Non-Current | 3.3 | 3.0 |
| -27.2 | 24.7 | 31.1 | 34.6 | 31.2 | 28.1 | Net Worth | 28.5 | 34.5 |
| 100.0 | 100.0 | 100.0 | 100.0 | 100.0 | 100.0 | Total Liabilities & Net Worth | 100.0 | 100.0 |
|  |  |  |  |  |  | **INCOME DATA** |  |  |
| 100.0 | 100.0 | 100.0 | 100.0 | 100.0 | 100.0 | Net Sales | 100.0 | 100.0 |
| 18.1 | 18.1 | 10.0 | 8.4 | 7.3 | 11.3 | Gross Profit | 10.7 | 9.2 |
| 17.7 | 16.8 | 9.3 | 7.5 | 6.7 | 8.6 | Operating Expenses | 9.6 | 8.0 |
| .4 | 1.3 | .7 | 1.0 | .7 | 2.8 | Operating Profit | 1.1 | 1.2 |
| -.2 | .1 | .1 | -.1 | .1 | .6 | All Other Expenses (net) | .1 | .1 |
| .6 | 1.2 | .6 | 1.0 | .5 | 2.2 | Profit Before Taxes | 1.0 | 1.1 |
|  |  |  |  |  |  | **RATIOS** |  |  |
| 1.6 | 2.0 | 1.7 | 1.4 | 1.2 | 1.8 | Current | 1.6 | 1.7 |
| .9 | 1.2 | 1.3 | 1.1 | 1.1 | 1.4 |  | 1.2 | 1.3 |
| .5 | .8 | 1.0 | .9 | 1.0 | .8 |  | 1.0 | 1.0 |
| 1.0 | 1.5 | 1.2 | 1.1 | 1.0 | 1.1 | Quick | 1.1 | 1.3 |
| .6 | .8 | .9 | .9 | .8 | .8 |  | .9 | .8 |
| .3 | .5 | .6 | .6 | .6 | .4 |  | .7 | .6 |
| 0 UND | 13 27.8 | 9 38.6 | 8 46.8 | 9 42.4 | 6 58.7 | Sales/Receivables | 11 33.2 | 6 63.1 |
| 8 46.5 | 22 16.3 | 15 23.6 | 13 27.2 | 19 19.6 | 17 21.2 |  | 18 20.5 | 11 33.1 |
| 22 16.3 | 31 11.7 | 26 14.0 | 25 14.7 | 24 15.3 | 31 11.6 |  | 28 13.0 | 20 18.1 |
| 0 UND | 3 118.9 | 3 105.6 | 3 126.9 | 3 129.4 | 3 106.9 | Cost of Sales/Inventory | 3 116.1 | 2 152.9 |
| 5 70.3 | 11 32.2 | 7 50.9 | 6 63.6 | 6 63.9 | 7 48.9 |  | 7 53.9 | 5 72.0 |
| 12 30.6 | 21 17.6 | 14 26.6 | 10 35.3 | 15 25.1 | 19 19.3 |  | 13 27.8 | 10 37.9 |
| 0 UND | 8 44.0 | 8 43.0 | 9 40.0 | 10 37.4 | 6 56.2 | Cost of Sales/Payables | 11 34.1 | 6 61.3 |
| 8 45.4 | 11 33.2 | 12 30.7 | 12 29.6 | 12 29.7 | 10 36.1 |  | 14 26.5 | 9 40.9 |
| 30 12.1 | 22 16.3 | 17 21.2 | 15 24.0 | 16 23.0 | 18 20.0 |  | 20 18.5 | 14 26.5 |
| 59.4 | 17.0 | 30.1 | 44.2 | 41.9 | 17.9 | Sales/Working Capital | 27.2 | 32.1 |
| -574.7 | 50.8 | 55.2 | 126.9 | 274.8 | 53.1 |  | 82.1 | 81.1 |
| -11.3 | -51.1 | 999.8 | -133.1 | -624.5 | -50.7 |  | -999.8 | -999.8 |
|  | 5.6 | 6.9 | 10.3 | 9.2 | 8.6 | EBIT/Interest | 5.0 | 7.1 |
|  | (42) 2.2 | (107) 2.7 | (126) 3.4 | (24) 4.0 | 3.3 |  | (302) 2.5 | (290) 3.3 |
|  | .5 | 1.1 | 1.5 | 1.1 | 1.6 |  | 1.3 | 1.6 |
|  |  | 4.2 | 4.4 | 8.5 |  | Net Profit + Depr., Dep., Amort./Cur. Mat. L/T/D | 4.3 | 5.1 |
|  |  | (27) 2.0 | (54) 2.1 | (11) 4.4 |  |  | (109) 1.9 | (107) 2.5 |
|  |  | 1.0 | 1.3 | 1.2 |  |  | 1.0 | 1.4 |
| .3 | .2 | .4 | .6 | .6 | .5 | Fixed/Worth | .5 | .5 |
| 3.9 | .6 | .8 | 1.1 | 1.0 | 1.3 |  | 1.2 | 1.0 |
| -2.7 | 8.4 | 1.6 | 1.9 | 2.8 | 3.0 |  | 2.3 | 2.0 |
| 1.0 | 1.1 | 1.3 | 1.1 | 1.7 | 2.3 | Debt/Worth | 1.5 | 1.1 |
| NM | 2.8 | 2.6 | 2.6 | 2.3 | 2.8 |  | 3.3 | 2.5 |
| -5.0 | 79.9 | 5.6 | 4.4 | 6.1 | 14.5 |  | 6.4 | 4.8 |
|  | 33.0 | 34.2 | 29.1 | 28.2 | 41.1 | % Profit Before Taxes/Tangible Net Worth | 33.0 | 36.7 |
|  | (36) 12.6 | (111) 11.7 | (125) 15.8 | (24) 15.7 | 20.6 |  | (291) 13.7 | (281) 19.4 |
|  | 2.0 | 1.3 | 4.7 | 4.2 | 6.9 |  | 4.3 | 5.9 |
| 27.7 | 9.7 | 7.1 | 7.9 | 8.7 | 7.6 | % Profit Before Taxes/Total Assets | 8.0 | 11.3 |
| 8.1 | 1.8 | 2.8 | 4.4 | 3.6 | 4.0 |  | 3.2 | 4.7 |
| -30.5 | -.6 | .4 | 1.0 | .3 | 1.3 |  | .9 | 1.5 |
| 305.5 | 122.1 | 92.5 | 63.0 | 51.2 | 73.1 | Sales/Net Fixed Assets | 63.2 | 77.2 |
| 37.3 | 59.1 | 42.7 | 26.9 | 27.3 | 19.0 |  | 27.8 | 31.1 |
| 14.3 | 9.7 | 17.3 | 12.2 | 14.8 | 5.7 |  | 12.4 | 13.5 |
| 21.3 | 9.2 | 11.4 | 9.9 | 9.3 | 7.8 | Sales/Total Assets | 9.8 | 12.7 |
| 8.1 | 5.7 | 7.1 | 7.3 | 7.5 | 6.0 |  | 6.8 | 8.7 |
| 4.5 | 3.0 | 4.4 | 4.4 | 5.6 | 3.4 |  | 4.5 | 5.6 |
|  | .3 | .3 | .3 | .4 | .2 | % Depr., Dep., Amort./Sales | .4 | .3 |
|  | (34) .7 | (104) .5 | (128) .6 | (24) .6 | (14) .7 |  | (291) .5 | (280) .5 |
|  | 2.7 | .9 | 1.0 | .9 | 1.3 |  | 1.2 | 1.0 |
|  | .4 | .2 | .1 |  |  | % Officers', Directors' Owners' Comp/Sales | .2 | .2 |
|  | (31) 1.0 | (40) .4 | (30) .4 |  |  |  | (112) .6 | (98) .4 |
|  | 2.9 | .6 | .7 |  |  |  | 1.2 | .9 |
| 54059M | 494001M | 6128220M | 24376129M | 14720010M | 16782901M | Net Sales ($) | 58700713M | 66936986M |
| 4154M | 61094M | 689081M | 3083385M | 1745729M | 2640278M | Total Assets ($) | 7566895M | 6682355M |

M = $ thousand    MM = $ million
See Pages 9 through 22 for Explanation of Ratios and Data

## Comparative Historical Data      Current Data Sorted by Sales

Current Data columns: **116 (4/1-9/30/11)** spans 0-1MM, 1-3MM, 3-5MM; **239 (10/1/11-3/31/12)** spans 5-10MM, 10-25MM, 25MM & OVER.

| 4/1/09-3/31/10 ALL | 4/1/10-3/31/11 ALL | 4/1/11-3/31/12 ALL | Item | 0-1MM | 1-3MM | 3-5MM | 5-10MM | 10-25MM | 25MM & OVER |
|---|---|---|---|---|---|---|---|---|---|
| | | | **Type of Statement** | | | | | | |
| 56 | 67 | 54 | Unqualified | 1 | | 1 | | 6 | 46 |
| 96 | 104 | 88 | Reviewed | | | | 2 | 10 | 76 |
| 63 | 69 | 74 | Compiled | 2 | 3 | 6 | 7 | 17 | 39 |
| 38 | 49 | 41 | Tax Returns | 2 | 3 | 6 | 7 | 5 | 18 |
| 98 | 104 | 98 | Other | | 5 | 1 | 5 | 7 | 80 |
| 351 | 393 | 355 | **NUMBER OF STATEMENTS** | 5 | 11 | 14 | 21 | 45 | 259 |
| % | % | % | **ASSETS** | % | % | % | % | % | % |
| 10.8 | 9.7 | 9.2 | Cash & Equivalents | | 16.7 | 11.7 | 10.3 | 8.2 | 8.6 |
| 28.6 | 30.8 | 33.0 | Trade Receivables (net) | | 23.6 | 20.1 | 30.5 | 32.1 | 34.8 |
| 14.0 | 14.4 | 14.3 | Inventory | | 13.3 | 16.0 | 17.3 | 17.4 | 13.5 |
| 2.6 | 3.4 | 2.2 | All Other Current | | .5 | 2.6 | 1.4 | 1.4 | 2.5 |
| 56.1 | 58.3 | 58.7 | Total Current | | 54.0 | 50.5 | 59.6 | 59.2 | 59.3 |
| 32.0 | 30.1 | 29.2 | Fixed Assets (net) | | 34.6 | 40.9 | 21.1 | 29.0 | 29.2 |
| 4.1 | 3.7 | 3.4 | Intangibles (net) | | 7.5 | 1.1 | 4.2 | 4.8 | 3.0 |
| 7.9 | 7.8 | 8.7 | All Other Non-Current | | 4.0 | 7.5 | 15.1 | 7.0 | 8.5 |
| 100.0 | 100.0 | 100.0 | Total | | 100.0 | 100.0 | 100.0 | 100.0 | 100.0 |
| | | | **LIABILITIES** | | | | | | |
| 9.0 | 10.3 | 12.6 | Notes Payable-Short Term | | 9.9 | 14.8 | 12.3 | 13.3 | 12.7 |
| 3.8 | 3.3 | 3.5 | Cur. Mat.-L.T.D. | | 10.5 | 3.3 | 1.6 | 4.1 | 3.3 |
| 24.0 | 25.9 | 26.9 | Trade Payables | | 43.3 | 24.2 | 20.1 | 23.8 | 27.3 |
| .2 | .3 | .1 | Income Taxes Payable | | .0 | .2 | .1 | .0 | .1 |
| 9.6 | 9.1 | 7.4 | All Other Current | | 9.5 | 7.9 | 11.3 | 7.7 | 7.0 |
| 46.6 | 48.9 | 50.5 | Total Current | | 73.2 | 50.5 | 45.4 | 49.1 | 50.4 |
| 19.1 | 15.9 | 15.4 | Long-Term Debt | | 22.8 | 26.9 | 19.5 | 17.7 | 13.6 |
| .6 | .6 | .7 | Deferred Taxes | | .0 | .3 | .0 | .4 | .8 |
| 2.8 | 3.8 | 4.3 | All Other Non-Current | | 13.6 | 2.7 | 10.9 | 3.5 | 3.6 |
| 30.8 | 30.8 | 29.1 | Net Worth | | -9.6 | 19.5 | 24.1 | 29.4 | 31.6 |
| 100.0 | 100.0 | 100.0 | Total Liabilties & Net Worth | | 100.0 | 100.0 | 100.0 | 100.0 | 100.0 |
| | | | **INCOME DATA** | | | | | | |
| 100.0 | 100.0 | 100.0 | Net Sales | | 100.0 | 100.0 | 100.0 | 100.0 | 100.0 |
| 12.2 | 11.8 | 10.6 | Gross Profit | | 30.3 | 22.2 | 18.1 | 16.7 | 7.0 |
| 10.8 | 10.3 | 9.7 | Operating Expenses | | 32.7 | 19.3 | 16.3 | 14.6 | 6.3 |
| 1.4 | 1.5 | 1.0 | Operating Profit | | -2.4 | 2.9 | 1.8 | 2.0 | .6 |
| .0 | .0 | .0 | All Other Expenses (net) | | .9 | .6 | -.2 | .1 | -.1 |
| 1.4 | 1.5 | .9 | Profit Before Taxes | | -3.3 | 2.3 | 2.0 | 1.9 | .7 |
| | | | **RATIOS** | | | | | | |
| 1.7 | 1.6 | 1.6 | Current | | 3.5 | 1.4 | 3.1 | 1.8 | 1.5 |
| 1.2 | 1.2 | 1.2 | | | 1.1 | 1.0 | 1.1 | 1.3 | 1.2 |
| .9 | .9 | .9 | | | .4 | .7 | .9 | 1.1 | .9 |
| 1.2 | 1.2 | 1.1 | Quick | | 3.5 | 1.0 | 2.8 | 1.5 | 1.1 |
| .8 | .8 | .9 | | | .5 | .6 | .8 | .9 | .9 |
| .6 | .6 | .6 | | | .3 | .4 | .3 | .5 | .6 |
| 8  45.3 | 8  45.3 | 9  41.3 | Sales/Receivables | | 15  23.9 | 0  UND | 3  130.5 | 15  25.0 | 8  46.1 |
| 15  24.2 | 15  24.0 | 15  23.6 | | | 23  15.6 | 18  19.9 | 25  14.7 | 23  15.7 | 13  27.2 |
| 25  14.7 | 26  14.0 | 26  14.3 | | | 33  11.0 | 26  14.3 | 31  11.7 | 30  12.1 | 23  15.8 |
| 3  113.4 | 3  120.9 | 3  123.1 | Cost of Sales/Inventory | | 0  UND | 2  207.3 | 5  76.9 | 7  52.9 | 2  151.8 |
| 7  51.7 | 7  50.7 | 7  53.0 | | | 12  30.1 | 16  22.3 | 10  35.4 | 12  31.2 | 6  65.3 |
| 15  23.6 | 15  23.8 | 13  27.4 | | | 21  17.5 | 28  12.9 | 23  16.2 | 23  15.9 | 10  37.3 |
| 10  36.5 | 9  39.7 | 9  41.8 | Cost of Sales/Payables | | 5  71.2 | 7  54.0 | 8  46.3 | 10  35.6 | 9  41.8 |
| 13  27.4 | 13  27.6 | 12  29.9 | | | 11  34.0 | 21  17.6 | 10  35.1 | 17  22.0 | 12  30.7 |
| 20  18.3 | 18  20.4 | 17  21.4 | | | 34  10.6 | 37  9.8 | 31  11.9 | 37  9.9 | 15  24.2 |
| 24.3 | 24.5 | 31.3 | Sales/Working Capital | | 3.8 | 25.8 | 14.9 | 18.7 | 40.6 |
| 70.6 | 73.4 | 92.1 | | | 148.2 | NM | 91.3 | 36.9 | 113.6 |
| -172.6 | -257.7 | -154.0 | | | -5.9 | -29.0 | -515.0 | 195.8 | -193.3 |
| 8.0 | 8.4 | 8.2 | EBIT/Interest | | | | 5.0 | 9.3 | 4.7 | 8.7 |
| (329) 3.0 | (351) 2.9 | (326) 3.0 | | | | (12) 2.6 | (18) 5.1 | (43) 2.4 | (243) 3.2 |
| 1.5 | 1.5 | 1.2 | | | | .9 | -.2 | .8 | 1.4 |
| 5.5 | 4.1 | 4.5 | Net Profit + Depr., Dep., Amort./Cur. Mat. L/T/D | | | | | 3.3 | 4.6 |
| (108) 2.4 | (112) 2.1 | (104) 2.1 | | | | | (12) 2.1 | (90) 2.1 |
| 1.4 | 1.2 | 1.2 | | | | | | .6 | 1.3 |
| .5 | .5 | .5 | Fixed/Worth | | .2 | .5 | .2 | .3 | .5 |
| 1.2 | 1.0 | 1.0 | | | 7.9 | 3.0 | .6 | .7 | 1.0 |
| 2.7 | 2.3 | 2.1 | | | -3.0 | 8.0 | NM | 1.8 | 1.9 |
| 1.3 | 1.3 | 1.2 | Debt/Worth | | .6 | 2.5 | .8 | .9 | 1.3 |
| 2.6 | 2.5 | 2.6 | | | 9.0 | 6.7 | 2.9 | 1.9 | 2.6 |
| 6.9 | 5.9 | 6.3 | | | -10.0 | 12.9 | NM | 4.6 | 5.5 |
| 37.7 | 30.7 | 32.4 | % Profit Before Taxes/Tangible Net Worth | | | 84.2 | 66.2 | 25.8 | 31.6 |
| (317) 16.6 | (358) 13.9 | (321) 14.6 | | | | (12) 30.8 | (16) 28.1 | (39) 8.6 | (245) 15.0 |
| 4.6 | 4.4 | 3.2 | | | | 10.3 | 9.0 | 1.1 | 3.7 |
| 8.7 | 7.9 | 8.0 | % Profit Before Taxes/Total Assets | | 7.6 | 15.6 | 19.8 | 6.5 | 7.4 |
| 4.2 | 3.5 | 3.6 | | | 1.9 | 7.5 | 6.8 | 1.6 | 3.9 |
| 1.1 | 1.1 | .5 | | | -24.9 | .8 | -1.5 | -.2 | .9 |
| 58.6 | 81.8 | 80.5 | Sales/Net Fixed Assets | | 38.8 | 88.2 | 101.1 | 104.1 | 80.1 |
| 24.4 | 29.2 | 33.4 | | | 11.7 | 11.1 | 56.7 | 27.9 | 34.7 |
| 9.8 | 11.1 | 12.5 | | | 4.4 | 4.3 | 20.3 | 7.0 | 15.5 |
| 9.0 | 9.9 | 10.4 | Sales/Total Assets | | 5.4 | 5.6 | 8.9 | 7.9 | 11.2 |
| 6.1 | 6.5 | 7.1 | | | 2.8 | 3.4 | 6.1 | 4.8 | 7.9 |
| 3.6 | 4.3 | 4.3 | | | 1.0 | 2.8 | 3.0 | 2.8 | 5.9 |
| .5 | .4 | .3 | % Depr., Dep., Amort./Sales | | 1.0 | 1.2 | .2 | .3 | .3 |
| (318) .8 | (345) .7 | (313) .6 | | | (10) 2.1 | (11) 2.4 | (14) .6 | (40) .9 | (235) .5 |
| 1.4 | 1.1 | 1.1 | | | 6.8 | 3.6 | 2.3 | 2.3 | .9 |
| .3 | .3 | .2 | % Officers', Directors' Owners' Comp/Sales | | | | .6 | .3 | .2 |
| (114) .6 | (133) .4 | (111) .5 | | | | | (11) 1.0 | (16) .8 | (73) .4 |
| 1.3 | 1.0 | 1.0 | | | | | 2.9 | 1.5 | .7 |
| 43368505M | 62359123M | 62555320M | Net Sales ($) | 3058M | 22024M | 53234M | 144822M | 775612M | 61556570M |
| 7795804M | 8765040M | 8223721M | Total Assets ($) | 9755M | 16684M | 14303M | 37990M | 336439M | 7808550M |

© RMA 2012

**M = $ thousand    MM = $ million**
See Pages 9 through 22 for Explanation of Ratios and Data

**Current Data Sorted by Assets**                                          **Comparative Historical Data**

| | | | | | | Type of Statement | | |
|---|---|---|---|---|---|---|---|---|
| | 3 | 7 | 44 | 27 | 23 | Unqualified | 95 | 109 |
| | 7 | 85 | 83 | 4 | | Reviewed | 180 | 197 |
| 3 | 25 | 59 | 18 | 1 | | Compiled | 127 | 112 |
| 6 | 26 | 24 | 6 | | | Tax Returns | 44 | 50 |
| 8 | 20 | 78 | 93 | 25 | 29 | Other | 198 | 232 |
| | 183 (4/1-9/30/11) | | 521 (10/1/11-3/31/12) | | | | 4/1/07-3/31/08 ALL | 4/1/08-3/31/09 ALL |
| 0-500M | 500M-2MM | 2-10MM | 10-50MM | 50-100MM | 100-250MM | | | |
| 17 | 81 | 253 | 244 | 57 | 52 | NUMBER OF STATEMENTS | 644 | 700 |
| % | % | % | % | % | % | ASSETS | % | % |
| 18.4 | 14.6 | 12.3 | 8.3 | 6.4 | 5.2 | Cash & Equivalents | 8.4 | 11.3 |
| 27.7 | 34.5 | 37.7 | 35.3 | 34.1 | 30.0 | Trade Receivables (net) | 37.9 | 33.0 |
| 22.5 | 15.7 | 15.6 | 13.6 | 15.4 | 18.6 | Inventory | 13.9 | 13.5 |
| 3.7 | 2.2 | 2.7 | 3.1 | 4.6 | 4.1 | All Other Current | 3.2 | 3.5 |
| 72.3 | 66.9 | 68.4 | 60.4 | 60.4 | 57.9 | Total Current | 63.4 | 61.4 |
| 19.5 | 18.6 | 20.3 | 26.7 | 29.9 | 31.4 | Fixed Assets (net) | 26.5 | 27.1 |
| 3.3 | 4.5 | 3.6 | 4.7 | 3.9 | 4.2 | Intangibles (net) | 2.7 | 3.6 |
| 4.7 | 10.0 | 7.8 | 8.2 | 5.9 | 6.5 | All Other Non-Current | 7.3 | 7.9 |
| 100.0 | 100.0 | 100.0 | 100.0 | 100.0 | 100.0 | Total | 100.0 | 100.0 |
| | | | | | | LIABILITIES | | |
| 10.2 | 11.1 | 11.0 | 11.9 | 14.5 | 11.4 | Notes Payable-Short Term | 12.8 | 11.2 |
| 3.9 | 3.5 | 2.5 | 3.0 | 2.8 | 1.6 | Cur. Mat.-L.T.D. | 3.1 | 3.5 |
| 36.9 | 31.2 | 32.2 | 30.4 | 25.2 | 24.3 | Trade Payables | 29.5 | 26.4 |
| .2 | .1 | .2 | .2 | .4 | .2 | Income Taxes Payable | .3 | .2 |
| 5.5 | 14.2 | 6.7 | 6.4 | 8.6 | 5.0 | All Other Current | 7.3 | 8.3 |
| 56.7 | 60.3 | 52.5 | 51.9 | 51.6 | 42.6 | Total Current | 52.9 | 49.7 |
| 14.7 | 12.9 | 10.3 | 12.6 | 16.5 | 20.7 | Long-Term Debt | 15.6 | 16.0 |
| .6 | .0 | .3 | .8 | .6 | .4 | Deferred Taxes | .6 | .6 |
| 1.7 | 4.5 | 3.4 | 2.9 | 2.9 | 2.9 | All Other Non-Current | 3.7 | 3.5 |
| 26.2 | 22.3 | 33.4 | 31.9 | 28.3 | 33.4 | Net Worth | 27.2 | 30.3 |
| 100.0 | 100.0 | 100.0 | 100.0 | 100.0 | 100.0 | Total Liabilities & Net Worth | 100.0 | 100.0 |
| | | | | | | INCOME DATA | | |
| 100.0 | 100.0 | 100.0 | 100.0 | 100.0 | 100.0 | Net Sales | 100.0 | 100.0 |
| 15.3 | 14.7 | 9.6 | 8.1 | 7.0 | 7.2 | Gross Profit | 9.7 | 9.1 |
| 15.1 | 12.8 | 8.6 | 7.2 | 5.9 | 4.8 | Operating Expenses | 8.6 | 8.0 |
| .2 | 1.9 | 1.0 | .9 | 1.2 | 2.4 | Operating Profit | 1.1 | 1.2 |
| .2 | .2 | -.1 | .0 | .0 | .4 | All Other Expenses (net) | .1 | .0 |
| .0 | 1.7 | 1.1 | .9 | 1.2 | 2.0 | Profit Before Taxes | 1.0 | 1.2 |
| | | | | | | RATIOS | | |
| 3.5 | 2.1 | 1.7 | 1.4 | 1.3 | 1.8 | | 1.5 | 1.6 |
| 1.2 | 1.2 | 1.3 | 1.2 | 1.1 | 1.3 | Current | 1.2 | 1.2 |
| 1.0 | .8 | 1.0 | .9 | 1.0 | 1.0 | | 1.0 | 1.0 |
| 1.8 | 1.6 | 1.2 | 1.1 | 1.0 | 1.1 | | 1.1 | 1.2 |
| 1.0 | .9 | .9 | .8 | .8 | .8 | Quick | (643) .9 | .9 |
| .4 | .4 | .6 | .6 | .6 | .5 | | .6 | .6 |
| 0 UND | 6 58.3 | 9 41.1 | 8 45.3 | 11 34.3 | 6 62.0 | | 10 36.3 | 5 66.5 |
| 3 105.9 | 15 23.9 | 17 22.1 | 14 25.4 | 17 21.6 | 13 28.5 | Sales/Receivables | 18 20.0 | 12 30.4 |
| 29 12.4 | 27 13.3 | 27 13.3 | 25 14.5 | 24 15.4 | 21 17.7 | | 30 12.1 | 23 16.0 |
| 0 UND | 2 232.5 | 2 196.7 | 2 217.3 | 3 124.0 | 3 117.6 | | 2 167.7 | 1 246.7 |
| 9 40.3 | 6 62.0 | 6 62.9 | 5 78.4 | 6 62.5 | 6 61.7 | Cost of Sales/Inventory | 6 61.3 | 4 85.1 |
| 19 19.0 | 18 20.8 | 15 25.0 | 11 33.1 | 13 28.8 | 12 29.2 | | 12 29.4 | 10 36.9 |
| 2 153.8 | 6 63.0 | 9 40.3 | 9 38.8 | 10 37.2 | 8 45.7 | | 10 36.6 | 6 59.8 |
| 8 45.2 | 11 33.1 | 12 29.8 | 12 29.4 | 14 26.9 | 12 31.4 | Cost of Sales/Payables | 14 26.9 | 9 39.5 |
| 27 13.4 | 28 13.1 | 20 18.5 | 18 20.8 | 17 21.1 | 19 19.5 | | 21 17.5 | 16 23.0 |
| 23.0 | 18.8 | 19.3 | 39.8 | 44.8 | 19.0 | | 29.9 | 32.2 |
| 112.7 | 89.1 | 64.7 | 118.5 | 152.7 | 67.2 | Sales/Working Capital | 86.4 | 107.6 |
| UND | -107.1 | 650.6 | -255.8 | -234.6 | 411.7 | | -306.4 | -421.8 |
| | 12.9 | 14.3 | 11.1 | 14.6 | 11.7 | | 5.8 | 7.2 |
| | (63) 4.6 | (229) 4.0 | (233) 4.6 | (54) 6.4 | (51) 4.7 | EBIT/Interest | (606) 2.6 | (666) 3.4 |
| | 1.5 | 1.3 | 2.3 | 3.0 | 1.6 | | 1.4 | 1.7 |
| | | 9.8 | 5.7 | 8.7 | 6.7 | | 4.5 | 5.9 |
| | (57) 3.7 | (76) 2.9 | (22) 3.7 | (12) 3.0 | | Net Profit + Depr., Dep., Amort./Cur. Mat. L/T/D | (208) 2.4 | (225) 2.6 |
| | 1.7 | 1.8 | 1.9 | 1.7 | | | 1.3 | 1.6 |
| .1 | .1 | .2 | .4 | .5 | .2 | | .4 | .4 |
| .6 | .5 | .6 | .9 | 1.3 | .9 | Fixed/Worth | 1.0 | 1.0 |
| UND | 5.2 | 1.3 | 2.0 | 2.5 | 2.9 | | 2.2 | 2.3 |
| .6 | 1.0 | 1.3 | 1.5 | 1.7 | 1.8 | | 1.7 | 1.4 |
| 4.5 | 2.9 | 2.5 | 2.6 | 2.9 | 2.6 | Debt/Worth | 3.4 | 3.0 |
| -12.2 | 22.2 | 4.8 | 5.6 | 6.8 | 6.5 | | 6.6 | 6.4 |
| 93.7 | 46.4 | 35.0 | 32.9 | 45.5 | 37.9 | | 34.8 | 41.4 |
| (12) 46.0 | (63) 14.8 | (232) 11.9 | (225) 18.7 | (54) 23.8 | (50) 22.5 | % Profit Before Taxes/Tangible Net Worth | (582) 17.4 | (640) 21.3 |
| 6.7 | 3.2 | 3.0 | 9.7 | 11.7 | 5.8 | | 6.1 | 8.3 |
| 26.0 | 14.7 | 9.4 | 8.9 | 10.8 | 8.8 | | 8.2 | 11.0 |
| 12.7 | 5.2 | 4.0 | 4.8 | 6.2 | 5.5 | % Profit Before Taxes/Total Assets | 3.9 | 5.4 |
| -2.1 | .2 | .8 | 2.6 | 2.7 | 2.3 | | 1.2 | 1.6 |
| UND | 297.2 | 151.1 | 100.2 | 85.6 | 242.2 | | 85.2 | 117.1 |
| 163.4 | 84.1 | 50.8 | 39.2 | 29.5 | 24.8 | Sales/Net Fixed Assets | 35.2 | 42.5 |
| 23.7 | 22.0 | 22.9 | 14.6 | 13.2 | 8.9 | | 14.9 | 16.2 |
| 27.8 | 12.9 | 13.7 | 12.3 | 9.6 | 10.9 | | 10.5 | 13.9 |
| 9.5 | 7.5 | 7.7 | 8.3 | 7.5 | 6.2 | Sales/Total Assets | 7.0 | 8.8 |
| 4.5 | 3.9 | 4.9 | 4.9 | 4.7 | 3.8 | | 4.6 | 5.0 |
| | .2 | .2 | .2 | .3 | .2 | | .3 | .2 |
| | (55) .5 | (213) .4 | (227) .5 | (56) .5 | (37) .5 | % Depr., Dep., Amort./Sales | (573) .5 | (627) .5 |
| | 1.2 | .8 | 1.0 | .9 | 1.1 | | .9 | .9 |
| | .6 | .2 | .1 | | | | .2 | .2 |
| | (34) 1.1 | (97) .5 | (71) .3 | | | % Officers', Directors' Owners' Comp/Sales | (216) .5 | (200) .5 |
| | 2.2 | 1.0 | .6 | | | | 1.0 | 1.2 |
| 101427M | 1005757M | 14190266M | 50458557M | 31363379M | 65623365M | Net Sales ($) | 126804496M | 182793373M |
| 4927M | 103347M | 1395668M | 5659679M | 3977682M | 8352772M | Total Assets ($) | 16476615M | 18605472M |

© RMA 2012

M = $ thousand   MM = $ million
See Pages 9 through 22 for Explanation of Ratios and Data

## Comparative Historical Data | Current Data Sorted by Sales

| | | | Type of Statement | 0-1MM | 1-3MM | 3-5MM | 5-10MM | 10-25MM | 25MM & OVER |
|---|---|---|---|---|---|---|---|---|---|
| 107 | 98 | 104 | Unqualified | | | 2 | 3 | 2 | 97 |
| 184 | 171 | 179 | Reviewed | 1 | 1 | 1 | 6 | 20 | 150 |
| 107 | 111 | 106 | Compiled | 1 | 4 | 5 | 11 | 28 | 57 |
| 59 | 55 | 62 | Tax Returns | 1 | 4 | 3 | 8 | 17 | 29 |
| 250 | 242 | 253 | Other | 2 | 6 | 6 | 10 | 39 | 190 |
| 4/1/09-3/31/10 ALL | 4/1/10-3/31/11 ALL | 4/1/11-3/31/12 ALL | | | 183 (4/1-9/30/11) | | | 521 (10/1/11-3/31/12) | |
| 707 | 677 | 704 | NUMBER OF STATEMENTS | 5 | 15 | 17 | 38 | 106 | 523 |
| % | % | % | ASSETS | % | % | % | % | % | % |
| 11.5 | 10.8 | 10.3 | Cash & Equivalents | | 10.4 | 11.9 | 10.5 | 12.2 | 10.0 |
| 31.8 | 33.2 | 35.4 | Trade Receivables (net) | | 22.1 | 16.7 | 28.1 | 34.5 | 37.2 |
| 13.9 | 15.3 | 15.3 | Inventory | | 13.8 | 23.0 | 18.3 | 19.5 | 14.0 |
| 3.7 | 3.4 | 3.1 | All Other Current | | 1.2 | 1.0 | 4.0 | 1.8 | 3.4 |
| 60.8 | 62.7 | 64.1 | Total Current | | 47.5 | 52.6 | 60.8 | 68.0 | 64.6 |
| 27.8 | 25.5 | 23.9 | Fixed Assets (net) | | 22.6 | 37.6 | 23.5 | 20.0 | 24.1 |
| 3.8 | 3.6 | 4.1 | Intangibles (net) | | 13.0 | 3.7 | 6.3 | 3.1 | 4.0 |
| 7.6 | 8.2 | 7.8 | All Other Non-Current | | 16.8 | 6.1 | 9.5 | 8.9 | 7.4 |
| 100.0 | 100.0 | 100.0 | Total | | 100.0 | 100.0 | 100.0 | 100.0 | 100.0 |
| | | | LIABILITIES | | | | | | |
| 9.4 | 12.0 | 11.6 | Notes Payable-Short Term | | 11.9 | 8.5 | 7.0 | 12.6 | 11.9 |
| 3.0 | 2.6 | 2.8 | Cur. Mat.-L.T.D. | | .4 | 5.1 | 5.1 | 2.2 | 2.6 |
| 27.0 | 28.1 | 30.4 | Trade Payables | | 23.0 | 17.5 | 24.2 | 29.6 | 31.6 |
| .2 | .2 | .2 | Income Taxes Payable | | .4 | .1 | .1 | .3 | .2 |
| 8.0 | 7.2 | 7.5 | All Other Current | | 5.0 | 12.3 | 11.8 | 6.6 | 6.9 |
| 47.7 | 50.2 | 52.5 | Total Current | | 40.6 | 43.5 | 48.3 | 51.3 | 53.3 |
| 16.7 | 13.6 | 12.8 | Long-Term Debt | | 21.4 | 15.7 | 18.4 | 8.7 | 12.7 |
| .5 | .6 | .5 | Deferred Taxes | | 1.0 | .1 | .0 | .5 | .5 |
| 3.4 | 3.6 | 3.2 | All Other Non-Current | | 8.8 | 3.9 | 5.9 | 3.1 | 2.9 |
| 31.7 | 31.9 | 31.0 | Net Worth | | 28.2 | 36.7 | 27.4 | 36.3 | 30.6 |
| 100.0 | 100.0 | 100.0 | Total Liabilities & Net Worth | | 100.0 | 100.0 | 100.0 | 100.0 | 100.0 |
| | | | INCOME DATA | | | | | | |
| 100.0 | 100.0 | 100.0 | Net Sales | | 100.0 | 100.0 | 100.0 | 100.0 | 100.0 |
| 11.5 | 10.6 | 9.4 | Gross Profit | | 29.8 | 34.2 | 20.6 | 12.2 | 6.5 |
| 10.2 | 9.5 | 8.3 | Operating Expenses | | 26.5 | 32.7 | 19.0 | 10.7 | 5.5 |
| 1.3 | 1.1 | 1.2 | Operating Profit | | 3.3 | 1.6 | 1.6 | 1.5 | .9 |
| -.1 | .0 | .0 | All Other Expenses (net) | | -.2 | .1 | -.4 | .0 | .0 |
| 1.4 | 1.1 | 1.1 | Profit Before Taxes | | 3.5 | 1.5 | 1.9 | 1.5 | .9 |
| | | | RATIOS | | | | | | |
| 1.6 | 1.6 | 1.6 | | | 3.3 | 2.0 | 2.2 | 2.1 | 1.4 |
| 1.2 | 1.2 | 1.2 | Current | | 1.0 | 1.1 | 1.4 | 1.4 | 1.2 |
| 1.0 | 1.0 | 1.0 | | | .5 | .6 | .9 | 1.0 | 1.0 |
| 1.2 | 1.2 | 1.2 | | | 2.0 | 1.6 | 1.3 | 1.5 | 1.1 |
| .9 | .9 | .8 | Quick | | .8 | .5 | .9 | .9 | .8 |
| .6 | .6 | .6 | | | .1 | .3 | .4 | .6 | .6 |
| 9 42.9 | 8 43.9 | 8 45.6 | | 1 348.8 | 1 571.0 | 10 36.2 | 12 30.7 | | 8 47.5 |
| 16 23.1 | 16 22.4 | 16 23.3 | Sales/Receivables | 25 14.4 | 20 18.3 | 19 19.4 | 21 17.2 | | 14 26.6 |
| 28 13.1 | 29 12.7 | 26 13.9 | | 43 8.4 | 35 10.5 | 36 10.2 | 33 10.9 | | 23 16.2 |
| 2 165.3 | 2 148.5 | 2 196.0 | | 0 UND | 4 93.4 | 5 70.6 | 5 78.4 | | 2 217.0 |
| 6 56.9 | 7 54.4 | 6 64.7 | Cost of Sales/Inventory | 16 23.3 | 22 16.5 | 13 28.6 | 10 36.1 | | 5 76.7 |
| 15 25.2 | 16 23.4 | 13 28.3 | | 52 7.0 | 63 5.8 | 36 10.0 | 30 12.3 | | 10 36.6 |
| 10 36.8 | 10 36.9 | 9 41.5 | | 19 18.8 | 6 57.6 | 3 106.6 | 9 39.8 | | 9 41.5 |
| 14 26.5 | 13 27.3 | 12 29.7 | Cost of Sales/Payables | 40 9.2 | 29 12.7 | 14 26.4 | 14 25.6 | | 12 31.1 |
| 21 17.6 | 20 18.0 | 19 19.4 | | 72 5.1 | 56 6.5 | 38 9.7 | 33 11.2 | | 16 23.0 |
| 22.5 | 21.8 | 25.6 | | | 11.2 | 7.6 | 15.2 | 13.8 | 39.7 |
| 67.8 | 63.6 | 92.7 | Sales/Working Capital | | -478.0 | 23.0 | 32.7 | 32.3 | 107.4 |
| -999.8 | -415.1 | -577.5 | | | -8.5 | -16.7 | -716.9 | 240.1 | -619.8 |
| 9.8 | 10.4 | 12.8 | | | 13.1 | 6.4 | 29.4 | 13.8 | 12.9 |
| (657) 3.5 | (614) 3.8 | (639) 4.5 | EBIT/Interest | | (10) 5.3 | (13) 3.3 | (30) 3.0 | (94) 4.5 | (489) 4.8 |
| 1.7 | 1.7 | 1.9 | | | .7 | -2.2 | 1.1 | 1.4 | 2.2 |
| 5.9 | 6.5 | 7.2 | Net Profit + Depr., Dep., | | | | | 7.3 | 7.1 |
| (208) 2.5 | (185) 2.7 | (173) 3.3 | Amort./Cur. Mat. L/T/D | | | | | (21) 2.4 | (145) 3.4 |
| 1.3 | 1.5 | 1.8 | | | | | | 1.4 | 1.8 |
| .3 | .3 | .3 | | | .1 | .6 | .3 | .1 | .3 |
| .9 | .8 | .8 | Fixed/Worth | | 1.1 | 1.5 | .8 | .4 | .8 |
| 2.3 | 1.8 | 2.0 | | | -3.7 | 12.4 | -1.4 | 1.0 | 1.9 |
| 1.3 | 1.2 | 1.3 | | | .4 | .5 | 1.0 | .9 | 1.7 |
| 2.5 | 2.5 | 2.6 | Debt/Worth | | 3.1 | 3.7 | 3.1 | 1.6 | 2.8 |
| 6.3 | 5.6 | 6.0 | | | -9.0 | 17.5 | -9.5 | 3.7 | 5.6 |
| 37.4 | 31.9 | 35.9 | % Profit Before Taxes/Tangible | | 98.5 | 26.4 | 35.7 | 34.0 | 36.0 |
| (645) 17.3 | (625) 15.8 | (636) 17.8 | Net Worth | | (10) 44.7 | (14) 3.8 | (27) 11.9 | (96) 12.2 | (486) 18.7 |
| 5.3 | 6.4 | 6.2 | | | -4.9 | -3.3 | 5.0 | 2.4 | 7.6 |
| 10.0 | 8.5 | 9.4 | % Profit Before Taxes/Total | | 25.8 | 17.1 | 12.9 | 10.6 | 9.0 |
| 4.5 | 4.2 | 4.9 | Assets | | 12.7 | 4.9 | 4.6 | 4.9 | 4.9 |
| 1.3 | 1.4 | 1.3 | | | -4.2 | -.9 | .1 | .4 | 1.9 |
| 85.7 | 94.6 | 146.1 | | | 158.2 | 52.5 | 155.2 | 150.9 | 146.4 |
| 29.9 | 35.8 | 45.2 | Sales/Net Fixed Assets | | 19.1 | 10.6 | 50.6 | 42.9 | 47.3 |
| 11.9 | 14.0 | 16.9 | | | 6.6 | 3.4 | 8.7 | 14.4 | 20.4 |
| 9.7 | 10.2 | 12.5 | | | 4.3 | 4.5 | 9.2 | 8.3 | 13.7 |
| 6.1 | 6.7 | 7.7 | Sales/Total Assets | | 2.8 | 2.5 | 4.4 | 5.5 | 9.0 |
| 3.9 | 4.1 | 4.5 | | | 1.6 | 1.7 | 2.3 | 3.6 | 5.5 |
| .3 | .3 | .2 | | | .4 | 1.1 | .4 | .2 | .2 |
| (620) .7 | (593) .6 | (596) .5 | % Depr., Dep., Amort./Sales | | (10) .7 | (14) 1.7 | (27) .7 | (81) .5 | (461) .4 |
| 1.2 | 1.1 | .9 | | | 2.2 | 4.2 | 3.7 | 1.1 | .8 |
| .2 | .2 | .2 | | | | | 1.3 | .5 | .1 |
| (222) .5 | (186) .5 | (221) .5 | % Officers', Directors' Owners' Comp/Sales | | | | (16) 2.3 | (50) .9 | (148) .3 |
| 1.1 | 1.1 | 1.0 | | | | | 4.6 | 1.8 | .6 |
| 123954917M | 116925557M | 162742751M | Net Sales ($) | 481M | 30444M | 64924M | 263727M | 1812049M | 160571126M |
| 18554210M | 16981003M | 19494075M | Total Assets ($) | 1020M | 13442M | 68988M | 80113M | 457376M | 18873136M |

M = $ thousand     MM = $ million
See Pages 9 through 22 for Explanation of Ratios and Data

**Current Data Sorted by Assets**      **Comparative Historical Data**

| 0-500M | 500M-2MM | 2-10MM | 10-50MM | 50-100MM | 100-250MM | Type of Statement | 4/1/07-3/31/08 ALL | 4/1/08-3/31/09 ALL |
|---|---|---|---|---|---|---|---|---|
| | | 10 | 48 | 21 | 12 | Unqualified | 108 | 100 |
| | 4 | 46 | 44 | 1 | 2 | Reviewed | 110 | 129 |
| 2 | 8 | 28 | 14 | 1 | | Compiled | 56 | 64 |
| 3 | 5 | 16 | 4 | 1 | | Tax Returns | 18 | 22 |
| 2 | 13 | 48 | 79 | 24 | 20 | Other | 157 | 185 |
| | 50 (4/1-9/30/11) | | 405 (10/1/11-3/31/12) | | | | | |
| 7 | 30 | 148 | 189 | 47 | 34 | **NUMBER OF STATEMENTS** | 449 | 500 |
| % | % | % | % | % | % | **ASSETS** | % | % |
| | 15.0 | 12.8 | 9.4 | 3.0 | 4.9 | Cash & Equivalents | 10.8 | 10.4 |
| | 9.4 | 10.5 | 9.5 | 6.3 | 4.8 | Trade Receivables (net) | 9.7 | 9.3 |
| | 41.4 | 29.8 | 18.4 | 10.7 | 14.0 | Inventory | 20.3 | 19.2 |
| | 2.0 | 2.2 | 2.1 | 1.7 | 2.1 | All Other Current | 3.1 | 2.6 |
| | 67.8 | 55.2 | 39.3 | 21.7 | 25.8 | Total Current | 43.8 | 41.5 |
| | 18.4 | 19.7 | 18.8 | 20.5 | 11.9 | Fixed Assets (net) | 21.7 | 20.7 |
| | 8.2 | 16.4 | 34.2 | 53.8 | 57.0 | Intangibles (net) | 25.8 | 29.1 |
| | 5.7 | 8.7 | 7.6 | 4.1 | 5.2 | All Other Non-Current | 8.7 | 8.8 |
| | 100.0 | 100.0 | 100.0 | 100.0 | 100.0 | Total | 100.0 | 100.0 |
| | | | | | | **LIABILITIES** | | |
| | 10.0 | 7.0 | 5.9 | 2.0 | 3.6 | Notes Payable-Short Term | 7.0 | 6.8 |
| | 3.8 | 4.7 | 3.5 | 3.1 | 2.3 | Cur. Mat.-L.T.D. | 3.6 | 3.6 |
| | 17.3 | 12.9 | 8.5 | 6.0 | 5.7 | Trade Payables | 10.7 | 9.5 |
| | .2 | .1 | .3 | .0 | .0 | Income Taxes Payable | .1 | .1 |
| | 8.0 | 8.8 | 7.7 | 4.7 | 4.1 | All Other Current | 7.2 | 6.2 |
| | 39.2 | 33.5 | 25.9 | 15.8 | 15.8 | Total Current | 28.6 | 26.2 |
| | 13.8 | 12.2 | 24.2 | 38.4 | 34.0 | Long-Term Debt | 24.9 | 26.8 |
| | .1 | .4 | .5 | .3 | .2 | Deferred Taxes | .4 | .4 |
| | 6.4 | 2.5 | 6.5 | 6.5 | 4.2 | All Other Non-Current | 4.6 | 3.9 |
| | 40.6 | 51.3 | 42.9 | 39.0 | 45.8 | Net Worth | 41.5 | 42.8 |
| | 100.0 | 100.0 | 100.0 | 100.0 | 100.0 | Total Liabilities & Net Worth | 100.0 | 100.0 |
| | | | | | | **INCOME DATA** | | |
| | 100.0 | 100.0 | 100.0 | 100.0 | 100.0 | Net Sales | 100.0 | 100.0 |
| | 24.7 | 26.1 | 25.5 | 25.9 | 25.5 | Gross Profit | 25.3 | 25.3 |
| | 21.8 | 22.3 | 20.8 | 20.0 | 19.5 | Operating Expenses | 21.3 | 21.1 |
| | 3.0 | 3.8 | 4.6 | 5.8 | 6.0 | Operating Profit | 4.1 | 4.2 |
| | .6 | .0 | .6 | .7 | 1.0 | All Other Expenses (net) | .2 | .4 |
| | 2.4 | 3.8 | 4.0 | 5.2 | 5.0 | Profit Before Taxes | 3.8 | 3.8 |
| | | | | | | **RATIOS** | | |
| | 3.3 | 3.4 | 2.6 | 1.8 | 2.5 | | 2.5 | 2.5 |
| | 1.7 | 1.8 | 1.6 | 1.4 | 1.7 | Current | 1.4 | 1.6 |
| | 1.3 | 1.2 | 1.0 | 1.0 | 1.2 | | 1.0 | 1.1 |
| | 1.6 | 1.4 | 1.3 | .7 | 1.0 | | 1.3 | 1.3 |
| | .6 | .6 | .7 | .5 | .5 | Quick | .6 | .7 |
| | .3 | .3 | .3 | .3 | .3 | | .3 | .3 |
| | 0 UND | 1 269.6 | 2 157.4 | 3 116.7 | 2 149.7 | | 2 209.5 | 2 222.8 |
| | 3 138.9 | 5 72.3 | 5 75.4 | 7 52.3 | 4 92.7 | Sales/Receivables | 5 71.5 | 5 79.3 |
| | 13 29.0 | 17 21.2 | 20 18.1 | 16 22.7 | 13 27.4 | | 18 20.5 | 18 20.8 |
| | 23 15.7 | 24 15.0 | 22 16.9 | 22 16.7 | 24 15.1 | | 16 22.7 | 18 20.6 |
| | 31 11.9 | 29 12.8 | 26 14.2 | 27 13.3 | 26 13.9 | Cost of Sales/Inventory | 24 15.1 | 24 15.0 |
| | 42 8.6 | 39 9.4 | 31 11.6 | 30 12.0 | 31 11.6 | | 32 11.4 | 32 11.5 |
| | 3 139.3 | 6 62.8 | 6 58.0 | 9 40.3 | 8 48.6 | | 7 54.4 | 7 51.9 |
| | 13 29.1 | 12 30.7 | 12 29.3 | 13 27.7 | 12 30.5 | Cost of Sales/Payables | 13 29.1 | 12 30.4 |
| | 26 13.8 | 18 20.8 | 17 21.3 | 18 20.4 | 19 19.1 | | 19 19.3 | 18 20.7 |
| | 12.5 | 11.1 | 12.2 | 18.7 | 12.8 | | 12.5 | 12.9 |
| | 21.8 | 21.1 | 23.3 | 35.4 | 23.8 | Sales/Working Capital | 27.7 | 24.1 |
| | 42.4 | 52.7 | 388.4 | 268.4 | 64.1 | | 562.1 | 116.9 |
| | 34.1 | 29.2 | 13.8 | 9.1 | 11.6 | | 10.9 | 12.2 |
| | (27) 5.1 | (127) 8.1 | (176) 6.4 | (45) 4.9 | (31) 5.0 | EBIT/Interest | (404) 4.7 | (457) 4.8 |
| | .9 | 2.5 | 3.2 | 3.3 | 3.2 | | 2.3 | 2.5 |
| | | 6.2 | 7.3 | 13.7 | | Net Profit + Depr., Dep., | 6.6 | 7.9 |
| | | (28) 2.4 | (42) 2.8 | (12) 3.4 | | Amort./Cur. Mat. L/T/D | (100) 3.0 | (115) 2.6 |
| | | 1.1 | 1.3 | 1.6 | | | 2.0 | 1.6 |
| | .1 | .2 | .4 | 2.0 | .7 | | .4 | .3 |
| | .4 | .5 | 1.4 | -1.0 | -4.9 | Fixed/Worth | 1.2 | 1.4 |
| | 1.5 | 1.4 | -.8 | -.2 | -.2 | | -1.5 | -1.1 |
| | .3 | .5 | .8 | 3.9 | 3.7 | | .9 | .8 |
| | 1.6 | 1.4 | 4.4 | -3.4 | -15.5 | Debt/Worth | 3.0 | 3.1 |
| | 7.7 | 5.7 | -3.3 | -1.8 | -1.6 | | -6.0 | -4.0 |
| | 50.6 | 52.9 | 58.2 | 77.5 | 393.6 | | 65.3 | 67.6 |
| | (25) 27.5 | (128) 27.4 | (112) 33.1 | (14) 57.0 | (16) 71.4 | % Profit Before Taxes/Tangible Net Worth | (302) 33.9 | (325) 32.5 |
| | 11.7 | 12.6 | 19.3 | 22.0 | 43.9 | | 18.5 | 13.9 |
| | 26.7 | 18.7 | 15.4 | 11.9 | 12.9 | | 18.1 | 16.4 |
| | 10.1 | 10.7 | 10.3 | 8.7 | 8.6 | % Profit Before Taxes/Total Assets | 10.5 | 9.5 |
| | .4 | 3.0 | 5.5 | 6.3 | 5.5 | | 5.5 | 4.6 |
| | 94.1 | 71.9 | 47.5 | 30.3 | 42.9 | | 44.0 | 43.3 |
| | 39.2 | 29.9 | 23.7 | 11.5 | 18.0 | Sales/Net Fixed Assets | 20.9 | 21.5 |
| | 18.6 | 12.7 | 10.1 | 6.0 | 12.3 | | 10.4 | 10.1 |
| | 7.8 | 5.8 | 3.8 | 2.4 | 2.5 | | 4.6 | 4.5 |
| | 5.7 | 3.8 | 2.9 | 1.8 | 2.1 | Sales/Total Assets | 3.3 | 3.1 |
| | 3.9 | 2.8 | 2.1 | 1.5 | 1.5 | | 2.5 | 2.3 |
| | .3 | .6 | .7 | .7 | .7 | | .7 | .7 |
| | (23) 1.0 | (131) .9 | (167) .9 | (45) 1.1 | (25) 1.0 | % Depr., Dep., Amort./Sales | (399) 1.1 | (437) 1.1 |
| | 1.3 | 1.3 | 1.3 | 1.5 | 1.2 | | 1.6 | 1.6 |
| | 1.3 | 1.3 | .5 | | | | .8 | .9 |
| | (13) 2.1 | (67) 2.1 | (44) .8 | | | % Officers', Directors' Owners' Comp/Sales | (140) 1.5 | (132) 1.6 |
| | 3.6 | 4.0 | 1.6 | | | | 2.9 | 3.0 |
| 7924M | 250286M | 3283139M | 12994776M | 6383144M | 11022341M | Net Sales ($) | 30407156M | 32256216M |
| 1491M | 38397M | 796831M | 4406771M | 3219653M | 5192853M | Total Assets ($) | 10654488M | 12604666M |

M = $ thousand    MM = $ million
See Pages 9 through 22 for Explanation of Ratios and Data

## Comparative Historical Data       Current Data Sorted by Sales

| | | | Type of Statement | 0-1MM | 1-3MM | 3-5MM | 5-10MM | 10-25MM | 25MM & OVER |
|---|---|---|---|---|---|---|---|---|---|
| 118 | 93 | 91 | Unqualified | | | | 1 | 9 | 81 |
| 106 | 119 | 97 | Reviewed | | 1 | 1 | 4 | 36 | 55 |
| 52 | 45 | 53 | Compiled | | 2 | 2 | 8 | 15 | 26 |
| 22 | 29 | 28 | Tax Returns | 4 | | 2 | 6 | 9 | 7 |
| 195 | 192 | 186 | Other | 1 | 4 | 4 | 7 | 23 | 147 |
| 4/1/09- 3/31/10 | 4/1/10- 3/31/11 | 4/1/11- 3/31/12 | | 50 (4/1-9/30/11) | | | 405 (10/1/11-3/31/12) | | |
| ALL | ALL | ALL | | | | | | | |
| 493 | 478 | 455 | **NUMBER OF STATEMENTS** | 5 | 7 | 9 | 26 | 92 | 316 |
| % | % | % | **ASSETS** | % | % | % | % | % | % |
| 10.1 | 9.7 | 10.1 | Cash & Equivalents | | | | 14.3 | 13.5 | 8.5 |
| 8.5 | 8.9 | 9.1 | Trade Receivables (net) | | | | 13.9 | 9.1 | 8.5 |
| 19.9 | 21.8 | 22.8 | Inventory | | | | 35.1 | 27.3 | 19.5 |
| 2.3 | 2.1 | 2.0 | All Other Current | | | | 2.1 | 1.7 | 2.2 |
| 40.8 | 42.5 | 44.0 | Total Current | | | | 65.4 | 51.6 | 38.7 |
| 19.9 | 18.6 | 18.6 | Fixed Assets (net) | | | | 16.7 | 20.6 | 18.2 |
| 29.3 | 30.1 | 30.1 | Intangibles (net) | | | | 10.9 | 19.5 | 36.2 |
| 10.0 | 8.9 | 7.3 | All Other Non-Current | | | | 7.0 | 8.2 | 6.9 |
| 100.0 | 100.0 | 100.0 | Total | | | | 100.0 | 100.0 | 100.0 |
| | | | **LIABILITIES** | | | | | | |
| 6.1 | 6.2 | 6.0 | Notes Payable-Short Term | | | | 7.9 | 7.2 | 5.3 |
| 3.4 | 3.8 | 3.8 | Cur. Mat.-L.T.D. | | | | 3.3 | 6.4 | 3.1 |
| 8.9 | 10.0 | 10.1 | Trade Payables | | | | 20.2 | 11.7 | 8.4 |
| .1 | .1 | .2 | Income Taxes Payable | | | | .0 | .2 | .2 |
| 7.0 | 7.3 | 7.5 | All Other Current | | | | 5.5 | 6.8 | 7.7 |
| 25.5 | 27.5 | 27.6 | Total Current | | | | 37.0 | 32.4 | 24.7 |
| 25.6 | 22.8 | 22.0 | Long-Term Debt | | | | 13.7 | 15.6 | 24.7 |
| .4 | .4 | .4 | Deferred Taxes | | | | .4 | .3 | .4 |
| 5.6 | 5.4 | 5.2 | All Other Non-Current | | | | 5.4 | 2.4 | 5.7 |
| 42.8 | 43.9 | 44.8 | Net Worth | | | | 43.6 | 49.3 | 44.5 |
| 100.0 | 100.0 | 100.0 | Total Liabilities & Net Worth | | | | 100.0 | 100.0 | 100.0 |
| | | | **INCOME DATA** | | | | | | |
| 100.0 | 100.0 | 100.0 | Net Sales | | | | 100.0 | 100.0 | 100.0 |
| 25.1 | 25.6 | 25.7 | Gross Profit | | | | 27.7 | 25.3 | 25.4 |
| 20.5 | 20.9 | 21.2 | Operating Expenses | | | | 23.0 | 21.9 | 20.7 |
| 4.7 | 4.7 | 4.5 | Operating Profit | | | | 4.7 | 3.4 | 4.6 |
| .4 | .6 | .4 | All Other Expenses (net) | | | | .5 | -.2 | .6 |
| 4.3 | 4.1 | 4.0 | Profit Before Taxes | | | | 4.2 | 3.6 | 4.0 |
| | | | **RATIOS** | | | | | | |
| 2.8 | 2.7 | 2.7 | | | | | 3.0 | 3.6 | 2.5 |
| 1.6 | 1.6 | 1.6 | Current | | | | 1.9 | 1.7 | 1.6 |
| 1.1 | 1.0 | 1.1 | | | | | 1.2 | 1.2 | 1.1 |
| 1.2 | 1.2 | 1.2 | | | | | 1.6 | 1.8 | 1.1 |
| .7 | .6 | .6 | Quick | | | | .6 | .7 | .6 |
| .3 | .3 | .3 | | | | | .4 | .4 | .3 |
| 1   273.0 | 2   196.7 | 2   185.9 | | | | | 1   642.1 | 1   421.8 | 2   164.2 |
| 4   101.5 | 5   76.5 | 5   78.0 | Sales/Receivables | | | | 8   48.1 | 4   93.5 | 5   78.0 |
| 17   21.3 | 17   21.4 | 18   20.5 | | | | | 33   10.9 | 17   21.4 | 17   21.4 |
| 19   19.0 | 22   16.6 | 23   16.2 | | | | | 30   12.3 | 23   16.0 | 22   16.6 |
| 23   15.8 | 26   13.8 | 27   13.3 | Cost of Sales/Inventory | | | | 38   9.6 | 28   13.0 | 26   14.0 |
| 31   11.6 | 33   11.1 | 33   11.0 | | | | | 91   4.0 | 37   9.9 | 31   11.7 |
| 6   62.1 | 6   58.0 | 6   57.7 | | | | | 13   27.4 | 6   69.0 | 6   57.4 |
| 11   32.8 | 12   30.2 | 12   29.5 | Cost of Sales/Payables | | | | 22   16.8 | 11   32.9 | 12   29.9 |
| 16   22.7 | 18   20.4 | 18   20.6 | | | | | 49   7.5 | 15   23.9 | 17   21.7 |
| 13.1 | 12.9 | 12.4 | | | | | 7.6 | 11.3 | 13.3 |
| 25.1 | 24.8 | 23.5 | Sales/Working Capital | | | | 12.6 | 22.7 | 25.6 |
| 181.1 | 224.2 | 95.0 | | | | | NM | 53.1 | 142.3 |
| 14.1 | 16.4 | 16.0 | | | | | 28.2 | 22.5 | 14.7 |
| (445) 6.3 | (440) 6.6 | (411) 5.7 | EBIT/Interest | | | | (25) 4.6 | (80) 6.4 | (289) 5.8 |
| 3.3 | 3.4 | 2.9 | | | | | 1.0 | 2.8 | 3.2 |
| 8.7 | 8.5 | 7.3 | | | | | | 7.3 | 7.8 |
| (94) 3.3 | (95) 3.3 | (88) 2.6 | Net Profit + Depr., Dep., Amort./Cur. Mat. L/T/D | | | | | (18) 3.4 | (66) 2.6 |
| 1.9 | 1.5 | 1.3 | | | | | | 1.3 | 1.4 |
| .3 | .3 | .3 | | | | | .1 | .2 | .4 |
| 1.4 | 1.4 | 1.1 | Fixed/Worth | | | | .4 | .8 | 1.6 |
| -1.1 | -.8 | -1.3 | | | | | 1.5 | 3.1 | -.6 |
| .8 | .8 | .7 | | | | | .5 | .4 | .8 |
| 3.1 | 4.1 | 3.4 | Debt/Worth | | | | 1.9 | 1.7 | 4.7 |
| -4.3 | -4.0 | -4.0 | | | | | 5.5 | 15.4 | -3.1 |
| 67.7 | 61.3 | 60.6 | | | | | 78.0 | 51.0 | 75.0 |
| (312) 38.7 | (300) 35.2 | (298) 32.7 | % Profit Before Taxes/Tangible Net Worth | | | | (24) 31.0 | (72) 27.4 | (186) 35.1 |
| 20.9 | 20.2 | 17.7 | | | | | 9.0 | 16.2 | 19.3 |
| 17.6 | 16.8 | 16.2 | | | | | 20.3 | 19.5 | 15.5 |
| 11.7 | 10.2 | 9.6 | % Profit Before Taxes/Total Assets | | | | 6.8 | 10.3 | 9.9 |
| 6.6 | 5.6 | 4.8 | | | | | .5 | 4.0 | 5.6 |
| 51.1 | 55.7 | 53.3 | | | | | 109.1 | 64.6 | 44.5 |
| 22.5 | 25.7 | 25.0 | Sales/Net Fixed Assets | | | | 32.0 | 30.6 | 23.7 |
| 10.4 | 11.2 | 11.0 | | | | | 9.3 | 10.4 | 11.0 |
| 4.5 | 4.5 | 4.4 | | | | | 5.2 | 5.3 | 4.0 |
| 3.0 | 3.0 | 3.0 | Sales/Total Assets | | | | 3.6 | 3.6 | 2.8 |
| 2.2 | 2.2 | 2.1 | | | | | 1.8 | 2.6 | 2.0 |
| .7 | .6 | .6 | | | | | .4 | .6 | .7 |
| (423) 1.0 | (405) 1.0 | (395) .9 | % Depr., Dep., Amort./Sales | | | | (21) 1.0 | (78) 1.0 | (281) .9 |
| 1.4 | 1.4 | 1.3 | | | | | 1.7 | 1.4 | 1.3 |
| .8 | .7 | .8 | | | | | 1.4 | 1.5 | .5 |
| (135) 1.6 | (134) 1.6 | (129) 1.6 | % Officers', Directors' Owners' Comp/Sales | | | | (16) 1.9 | (41) 2.2 | (64) 1.1 |
| 2.9 | 2.8 | 3.2 | | | | | 2.9 | 4.1 | 2.0 |
| 36717361M | 36195543M | 33941610M | Net Sales ($) | 2752M | 12125M | 38704M | 187289M | 1577479M | 32123261M |
| 14725305M | 14526789M | 13655996M | Total Assets ($) | 1226M | 8963M | 14896M | 71158M | 475262M | 13084491M |

M = $ thousand    MM = $ million
See Pages 9 through 22 for Explanation of Ratios and Data

## Current Data Sorted by Assets      Comparative Historical Data

| | | | | | | Type of Statement | | |
|---|---|---|---|---|---|---|---|---|
| 2 | | 4 | 12 | 5 | 15 | Unqualified | 46 | 54 |
| | 10 | | 7 | 1 | 2 | Reviewed | 18 | 24 |
| | 5 | 16 | 4 | | | Compiled | 17 | 24 |
| 5 | 11 | 8 | 4 | | | Tax Returns | 25 | 22 |
| 3 | 11 | 22 | 17 | 8 | 23 | Other | 63 | 68 |
| | 31 (4/1-9/30/11) | | | 164 (10/1/11-3/31/12) | | | 4/1/07-3/31/08 | 4/1/08-3/31/09 |
| 0-500M | 500M-2MM | 2-10MM | 10-50MM | 50-100MM | 100-250MM | | ALL | ALL |
| 10 | 27 | 60 | 44 | 14 | 40 | **NUMBER OF STATEMENTS** | 169 | 192 |
| % | % | % | % | % | % | **ASSETS** | % | % |
| 11.1 | 10.3 | 6.3 | 5.8 | 6.7 | 4.4 | Cash & Equivalents | 6.5 | 6.8 |
| 17.2 | 24.2 | 27.9 | 24.0 | 19.8 | 20.5 | Trade Receivables (net) | 22.0 | 21.2 |
| 35.9 | 48.0 | 42.3 | 38.6 | 37.1 | 32.2 | Inventory | 42.5 | 41.8 |
| 9.7 | 1.6 | 1.4 | 5.0 | 7.5 | 3.7 | All Other Current | 3.4 | 2.9 |
| 73.9 | 84.2 | 77.9 | 73.4 | 71.2 | 60.7 | Total Current | 74.5 | 72.8 |
| 23.2 | 10.1 | 11.5 | 9.2 | 7.0 | 10.7 | Fixed Assets (net) | 9.9 | 11.3 |
| .6 | .4 | 5.9 | 10.0 | 18.8 | 16.6 | Intangibles (net) | 9.9 | 10.9 |
| 2.3 | 5.3 | 4.7 | 7.5 | 3.0 | 12.0 | All Other Non-Current | 5.8 | 5.1 |
| 100.0 | 100.0 | 100.0 | 100.0 | 100.0 | 100.0 | Total | 100.0 | 100.0 |
| | | | | | | **LIABILITIES** | | |
| 21.5 | 17.1 | 12.6 | 12.6 | 14.9 | 4.9 | Notes Payable-Short Term | 13.7 | 15.4 |
| .3 | 3.3 | 2.3 | 1.2 | 2.8 | 2.1 | Cur. Mat.-L.T.D. | 1.7 | 2.0 |
| 46.9 | 30.0 | 30.0 | 22.3 | 16.9 | 18.0 | Trade Payables | 24.4 | 23.5 |
| .0 | .0 | .3 | .1 | .4 | .0 | Income Taxes Payable | .1 | .2 |
| 18.2 | 8.3 | 7.1 | 10.4 | 11.6 | 10.5 | All Other Current | 9.9 | 9.4 |
| 86.9 | 58.7 | 52.2 | 46.7 | 46.6 | 35.5 | Total Current | 49.8 | 50.6 |
| 48.5 | 14.1 | 5.5 | 8.8 | 12.3 | 20.0 | Long-Term Debt | 11.7 | 11.8 |
| .0 | .0 | .0 | .1 | .4 | .8 | Deferred Taxes | .4 | .3 |
| 41.8 | 6.5 | 4.7 | 6.2 | 2.2 | 4.6 | All Other Non-Current | 5.9 | 4.0 |
| -77.3 | 20.8 | 37.5 | 38.3 | 38.5 | 39.1 | Net Worth | 32.1 | 33.2 |
| 100.0 | 100.0 | 100.0 | 100.0 | 100.0 | 100.0 | Total Liabilities & Net Worth | 100.0 | 100.0 |
| | | | | | | **INCOME DATA** | | |
| 100.0 | 100.0 | 100.0 | 100.0 | 100.0 | 100.0 | Net Sales | 100.0 | 100.0 |
| 28.2 | 31.9 | 28.1 | 25.8 | 23.1 | 24.6 | Gross Profit | 26.8 | 27.1 |
| 27.2 | 28.6 | 23.6 | 22.0 | 18.8 | 20.5 | Operating Expenses | 22.6 | 24.1 |
| 1.0 | 3.2 | 4.5 | 3.8 | 4.3 | 4.1 | Operating Profit | 4.1 | 3.0 |
| .3 | 1.3 | .6 | .7 | .3 | .6 | All Other Expenses (net) | .5 | .5 |
| .7 | 1.9 | 3.9 | 3.1 | 4.0 | 3.5 | Profit Before Taxes | 3.6 | 2.6 |
| | | | | | | **RATIOS** | | |
| 4.5 | 2.0 | 2.0 | 2.4 | 2.7 | 2.4 | | 2.1 | 2.2 |
| 1.6 | 1.4 | 1.6 | 1.5 | 1.6 | 1.9 | Current | 1.5 | 1.5 |
| .5 | 1.0 | 1.2 | 1.2 | 1.2 | 1.3 | | 1.2 | 1.1 |
| .9 | .8 | 1.0 | .9 | .8 | 1.0 | | .9 | .9 |
| .6 | .5 | .7 | .5 | .6 | .7 | Quick | .6 | .6 |
| .1 | .3 | .4 | .4 | .3 | .5 | | .4 | .4 |
| 0   UND | 18   20.0 | 15   25.0 | 18   19.9 | 11   33.8 | 20   17.9 | | 9   40.0 | 10   37.2 |
| 0   UND | 33   11.0 | 36   10.0 | 39   9.4 | 34   10.7 | 30   12.1 | Sales/Receivables | 31   11.7 | 31   11.8 |
| 33   11.1 | 56   6.5 | 60   6.1 | 49   7.5 | 38   9.6 | 42   8.6 | | 45   8.1 | 43   8.6 |
| 0   UND | 27   13.6 | 47   7.7 | 42   8.7 | 49   7.5 | 41   8.9 | | 41   9.0 | 41   8.9 |
| 61   6.0 | 83   4.4 | 76   4.8 | 74   4.9 | 62   5.9 | 63   5.8 | Cost of Sales/Inventory | 60   6.1 | 67   5.5 |
| 83   4.4 | 215   1.7 | 118   3.1 | 101   3.6 | 70   5.2 | 79   4.6 | | 101   3.6 | 100   3.6 |
| 0   UND | 8   43.3 | 31   11.8 | 23   16.1 | 23   16.1 | 22   16.6 | | 21   17.0 | 21   17.4 |
| 25   14.5 | 43   8.5 | 47   7.8 | 39   9.4 | 28   13.1 | 33   11.1 | Cost of Sales/Payables | 35   10.5 | 34   10.9 |
| 159   2.3 | 63   5.8 | 79   4.6 | 70   5.2 | 38   9.5 | 43   8.4 | | 66   5.6 | 60   6.1 |
| 7.9 | 4.4 | 6.3 | 5.4 | 5.7 | 6.8 | | 6.8 | 7.0 |
| 12.1 | 19.5 | 11.2 | 11.0 | 12.6 | 9.9 | Sales/Working Capital | 13.5 | 12.7 |
| -4.7 | 124.4 | 20.8 | 24.6 | 22.5 | 18.1 | | 36.3 | 49.4 |
| | 12.7 | 22.0 | 19.9 | 28.7 | 26.0 | | 15.0 | 9.3 |
| | (21) 2.7 | (54) 8.2 | (41) 6.4 | (13) 12.1 | (39) 7.6 | EBIT/Interest | (158) 4.9 | (169) 3.7 |
| | .3 | 2.6 | 1.5 | 2.2 | 2.7 | | 2.0 | 1.2 |
| | | | | | 121.2 | | 10.9 | 8.1 |
| | | | | (13) | 16.8 | Net Profit + Depr., Dep., Amort./Cur. Mat. L/T/D | (33) 4.5 | (42) 3.5 |
| | | | | | 4.2 | | 1.7 | 1.1 |
| .0 | .0 | .0 | .1 | .2 | .2 | | .1 | .1 |
| .4 | .2 | .1 | .1 | .4 | .5 | Fixed/Worth | .3 | .3 |
| NM | .8 | .7 | 1.1 | NM | 24.6 | | 1.8 | 2.6 |
| .9 | 1.3 | .8 | .9 | 1.3 | 1.2 | | 1.4 | 1.2 |
| NM | 2.6 | 2.4 | 2.2 | 3.4 | 2.5 | Debt/Worth | 2.9 | 3.4 |
| -1.8 | 8.3 | 7.1 | 5.8 | NM | 85.9 | | 15.4 | 23.0 |
| | 98.3 | 63.4 | 33.9 | 70.5 | 47.3 | | 82.5 | 45.6 |
| | (23) 35.8 | (54) 25.6 | (38) 18.7 | (11) 27.9 | (31) 36.6 | % Profit Before Taxes/Tangible Net Worth | (141) 28.9 | (149) 22.0 |
| | 3.0 | 13.5 | 5.0 | 1.5 | 17.6 | | 10.3 | 5.2 |
| 28.3 | 19.4 | 16.5 | 13.8 | 15.4 | 13.7 | | 15.5 | 13.4 |
| 2.8 | 2.3 | 8.1 | 6.7 | 8.2 | 9.5 | % Profit Before Taxes/Total Assets | 8.5 | 6.1 |
| -18.6 | -1.6 | 2.2 | 1.5 | 1.4 | 4.3 | | 2.7 | .8 |
| UND | 703.9 | 406.3 | 204.3 | 87.6 | 89.3 | | 171.3 | 116.6 |
| 18.9 | 65.3 | 94.9 | 119.0 | 61.1 | 28.1 | Sales/Net Fixed Assets | 57.0 | 55.0 |
| 11.6 | 17.3 | 27.4 | 36.0 | 30.8 | 14.7 | | 22.3 | 19.5 |
| 5.5 | 4.4 | 3.8 | 3.2 | 3.7 | 3.3 | | 4.1 | 3.7 |
| 3.8 | 2.6 | 2.9 | 2.5 | 3.0 | 2.6 | Sales/Total Assets | 2.9 | 2.9 |
| 1.8 | 1.3 | 1.8 | 1.7 | 1.3 | 1.4 | | 2.1 | 2.0 |
| | .1 | .2 | .2 | .3 | .4 | | .3 | .3 |
| | (16) .4 | (38) .4 | (33) .5 | (12) .6 | (30) .8 | % Depr., Dep., Amort./Sales | (130) .5 | (154) .6 |
| | 2.3 | 1.5 | .8 | 1.0 | 1.4 | | 1.0 | 1.3 |
| | 1.9 | 1.0 | 1.0 | | | | 1.5 | 1.3 |
| | (12) 3.7 | (23) 1.9 | (16) 1.3 | | | % Officers', Directors' Owners' Comp/Sales | (45) 2.7 | (42) 2.6 |
| | 5.0 | 2.8 | 3.1 | | | | 4.4 | 4.7 |
| 8956M | 99784M | 911432M | 3093304M | 2765221M | 16466482M | Net Sales ($) | 16833017M | 22478097M |
| 2135M | 28517M | 320331M | 1102082M | 994645M | 6726860M | Total Assets ($) | 6474514M | 8649454M |

**M = $ thousand    MM = $ million**
See Pages 9 through 22 for Explanation of Ratios and Data

## Comparative Historical Data | Current Data Sorted by Sales

| | | | Type of Statement | | | | | | |
|---|---|---|---|---|---|---|---|---|---|
| 51 | 49 | 38 | Unqualified | 1 | 1 | 1 | 1 | 3 | 31 |
| 35 | 21 | 20 | Reviewed | | | | 1 | 5 | 14 |
| 18 | 17 | 25 | Compiled | | 4 | 1 | 4 | 12 | 4 |
| 17 | 29 | 28 | Tax Returns | 7 | 3 | 4 | 5 | 3 | 6 |
| 67 | 79 | 84 | Other | 8 | 1 | 5 | 11 | 13 | 46 |
| 4/1/09-<br>3/31/10<br>ALL | 4/1/10-<br>3/31/11<br>ALL | 4/1/11-<br>3/31/12<br>ALL | | 31 (4/1-9/30/11) | | 164 (10/1/11-3/31/12) | | | |
| | | | | 0-1MM | 1-3MM | 3-5MM | 5-10MM | 10-25MM | 25MM & OVER |
| 188 | 195 | 195 | NUMBER OF STATEMENTS | 16 | 9 | 11 | 22 | 36 | 101 |
| % | % | % | ASSETS | % | % | % | % | % | % |
| 6.5 | 5.4 | 6.6 | Cash & Equivalents | 7.0 | | 3.6 | 8.2 | 6.8 | 5.4 |
| 21.7 | 23.7 | 23.9 | Trade Receivables (net) | 14.3 | | 28.4 | 24.0 | 28.9 | 23.3 |
| 41.5 | 42.2 | 39.5 | Inventory | 49.5 | | 37.2 | 44.0 | 42.6 | 36.3 |
| 2.7 | 2.7 | 3.6 | All Other Current | 6.0 | | .8 | .8 | 3.6 | 4.2 |
| 72.4 | 73.9 | 73.6 | Total Current | 76.9 | | 70.0 | 77.0 | 81.9 | 69.2 |
| 11.2 | 10.1 | 10.9 | Fixed Assets (net) | 17.6 | | 18.4 | 13.6 | 8.7 | 9.0 |
| 9.9 | 9.4 | 8.9 | Intangibles (net) | 3.6 | | 3.3 | 5.1 | 3.9 | 13.7 |
| 6.5 | 6.6 | 6.6 | All Other Non-Current | 1.9 | | 8.3 | 4.3 | 5.5 | 8.1 |
| 100.0 | 100.0 | 100.0 | Total | 100.0 | | 100.0 | 100.0 | 100.0 | 100.0 |
| | | | LIABILITIES | | | | | | |
| 13.8 | 13.7 | 12.3 | Notes Payable-Short Term | 21.4 | | 9.0 | 12.6 | 12.7 | 10.0 |
| 1.6 | 2.6 | 2.1 | Cur. Mat.-L.T.D. | 5.1 | | 1.6 | 3.4 | 1.4 | 1.8 |
| 23.1 | 25.6 | 25.7 | Trade Payables | 28.5 | | 40.5 | 29.8 | 30.3 | 21.6 |
| .1 | .1 | .2 | Income Taxes Payable | .0 | | .0 | .0 | .5 | .1 |
| 9.5 | 9.8 | 9.6 | All Other Current | 4.2 | | 16.8 | 7.0 | 8.5 | 9.7 |
| 48.2 | 51.9 | 49.8 | Total Current | 59.2 | | 67.8 | 52.7 | 53.4 | 43.2 |
| 14.5 | 12.6 | 13.1 | Long-Term Debt | 21.2 | | 14.1 | 7.9 | 6.0 | 12.6 |
| .3 | .2 | .2 | Deferred Taxes | .0 | | .0 | .0 | .0 | .4 |
| 4.0 | 4.4 | 7.0 | All Other Non-Current | 10.1 | | 2.6 | 5.3 | 4.3 | 4.2 |
| 33.1 | 31.0 | 29.9 | Net Worth | 9.6 | | 15.5 | 34.1 | 36.3 | 39.7 |
| 100.0 | 100.0 | 100.0 | Total Liabilties & Net Worth | 100.0 | | 100.0 | 100.0 | 100.0 | 100.0 |
| | | | INCOME DATA | | | | | | |
| 100.0 | 100.0 | 100.0 | Net Sales | 100.0 | | 100.0 | 100.0 | 100.0 | 100.0 |
| 26.6 | 27.4 | 27.0 | Gross Profit | 29.0 | | 34.9 | 33.2 | 25.4 | 24.6 |
| 23.2 | 23.7 | 23.2 | Operating Expenses | 29.3 | | 31.3 | 26.3 | 21.5 | 20.8 |
| 3.4 | 3.7 | 3.9 | Operating Profit | -.3 | | 3.6 | 6.9 | 3.9 | 3.8 |
| .5 | .6 | .7 | All Other Expenses (net) | 1.6 | | 1.1 | .9 | .6 | .4 |
| 2.9 | 3.1 | 3.2 | Profit Before Taxes | -1.9 | | 2.5 | 6.0 | 3.3 | 3.4 |
| | | | RATIOS | | | | | | |
| 2.1 | 2.2 | 2.2 | | 4.4 | | 1.7 | 2.1 | 1.9 | 2.3 |
| 1.5 | 1.5 | 1.6 | Current | 1.5 | | 1.0 | 1.5 | 1.6 | 1.6 |
| 1.2 | 1.2 | 1.2 | | .8 | | .8 | 1.2 | 1.2 | 1.3 |
| .9 | .9 | 1.0 | | .8 | | .7 | 1.0 | .9 | 1.0 |
| .6 (194) | .6 | .6 | Quick | .4 | | .5 | .6 | .7 | .6 |
| .4 | .4 | .4 | | .2 | | .3 | .3 | .4 | .4 |
| 10 35.2 | 13 28.2 | 16 23.1 | | 0 UND | 9 39.8 | 7 53.9 | 19 19.5 | 17 21.2 | |
| 30 12.4 | 31 11.7 | 33 11.1 | Sales/Receivables | 26 13.9 | 45 8.1 | 34 10.8 | 40 9.2 | 31 11.7 | |
| 44 8.3 | 47 7.8 | 49 7.5 | | 63 5.8 | 61 6.0 | 72 5.1 | 57 6.4 | 42 8.7 | |
| 39 9.4 | 45 8.1 | 45 8.2 | | 57 6.4 | 27 13.6 | 59 6.2 | 38 9.5 | 42 8.6 | |
| 67 5.5 | 67 5.5 | 69 5.3 | Cost of Sales/Inventory | 140 2.6 | 52 7.0 | 96 3.8 | 66 5.5 | 63 5.8 | |
| 102 3.6 | 110 3.3 | 104 3.5 | | 365 1.0 | 135 2.7 | 130 2.8 | 126 2.9 | 81 4.5 | |
| 18 20.3 | 23 16.1 | 22 16.5 | | 0 UND | 42 8.6 | 34 10.6 | 18 20.1 | 23 15.6 | |
| 32 11.3 | 38 9.5 | 38 9.7 | Cost of Sales/Payables | 8 47.2 | 55 6.6 | 57 6.4 | 43 8.5 | 34 10.7 | |
| 56 6.5 | 62 5.9 | 60 6.1 | | 166 2.2 | 94 3.9 | 94 3.9 | 74 4.9 | 49 7.4 | |
| 6.5 | 6.6 | 6.1 | | 3.6 | | 6.3 | 6.1 | 5.5 | 6.7 |
| 11.3 | 12.7 | 11.0 | Sales/Working Capital | 8.0 | | 54.6 | 11.6 | 12.3 | 10.9 |
| 32.3 | 30.9 | 25.3 | | -6.2 | | -40.3 | 19.9 | 25.0 | 22.3 |
| 18.9 | 18.8 | 21.5 | | | | | 15.8 | 22.7 | 23.8 |
| (164) 5.9 | (185) 6.4 | (172) 7.6 | EBIT/Interest | | | (20) 11.1 | (34) 7.6 | (94) 8.3 | |
| 1.8 | 2.6 | 1.9 | | | | 1.7 | 2.7 | 2.6 | |
| 7.5 | 11.4 | 17.7 | | | | | | | 18.8 |
| (41) 2.9 | (42) 6.2 | (32) 5.5 | Net Profit + Depr., Dep.,<br>Amort./Cur. Mat. L/T/D | | | | | (27) 4.5 | |
| 1.3 | 2.7 | 1.9 | | | | | | 1.8 | |
| .1 | .1 | .1 | | .2 | | .0 | .1 | .0 | .1 |
| .3 | .3 | .2 | Fixed/Worth | .6 | | .5 | .1 | .1 | .3 |
| 1.9 | 2.1 | 1.1 | | -.4 | | 2.0 | .9 | .5 | 1.2 |
| 1.0 | 1.2 | 1.0 | | 1.6 | | 1.0 | 1.2 | .9 | .9 |
| 2.3 | 3.2 | 2.5 | Debt/Worth | 2.7 | | 4.6 | 3.0 | 2.4 | 2.2 |
| 20.2 | 29.3 | 8.7 | | -4.1 | | 17.6 | 6.3 | 5.7 | 10.6 |
| 51.2 | 50.3 | 53.3 | | 91.3 | | 69.1 | 68.2 | 46.5 | |
| (148) 22.6 | (153) 29.8 | (162) 25.6 | % Profit Before Taxes/Tangible<br>Net Worth | (10) 2.9 | | (21) 41.0 | (33) 22.2 | (83) 26.4 | |
| 5.5 | 10.7 | 8.1 | | -20.5 | | 17.0 | 9.9 | 11.1 | |
| 15.3 | 14.3 | 14.3 | | 3.8 | | 18.0 | 15.5 | 16.8 | 14.1 |
| 7.5 | 6.9 | 6.8 | % Profit Before Taxes/Total<br>Assets | -2.4 | | 6.7 | 12.3 | 5.6 | 9.0 |
| 2.0 | 3.0 | 1.8 | | -14.3 | | 1.5 | 1.8 | 3.0 | 2.0 |
| 154.2 | 196.6 | 199.1 | | 29.4 | | 999.8 | 402.5 | 718.5 | 147.3 |
| 58.6 | 72.9 | 76.3 | Sales/Net Fixed Assets | 15.4 | | 79.4 | 114.6 | 192.4 | 71.4 |
| 22.6 | 20.8 | 18.4 | | 9.8 | | 18.4 | 50.8 | 31.2 | 20.1 |
| 3.8 | 3.7 | 3.7 | | 2.0 | | 6.1 | 4.0 | 3.8 | 3.6 |
| 3.0 | 2.8 | 2.8 | Sales/Total Assets | 1.3 | | 3.0 | 2.3 | 3.0 | 2.9 |
| 1.9 | 1.9 | 1.7 | | .8 | | 1.9 | 1.4 | 1.6 | 1.9 |
| .3 | .2 | .3 | | | | | .2 | .1 | .3 |
| (151) .6 | (154) .5 | (133) .5 | % Depr., Dep., Amort./Sales | | | (12) .3 | (23) .2 | (78) .6 | |
| 1.3 | 1.2 | 1.1 | | | | | 2.2 | .8 | 1.0 |
| 1.2 | 2.3 | 1.0 | | | | | | 1.0 | .8 |
| (47) 2.1 | (59) 3.5 | (58) 1.9 | % Officers', Directors'<br>Owners' Comp/Sales | | | | (18) 1.8 | (17) 1.1 | |
| 4.6 | 6.2 | 3.5 | | | | | | 3.4 | 2.9 |
| 22779131M | 24716295M | 23345179M | Net Sales ($) | 8160M | 19234M | 44286M | 163700M | 590242M | 22519557M |
| 8700126M | 8971951M | 9174570M | Total Assets ($) | 9519M | 19192M | 15513M | 83931M | 275504M | 8770911M |

© RMA 2012

M = $ thousand    MM = $ million
See Pages 9 through 22 for Explanation of Ratios and Data

## Current Data Sorted by Assets | Comparative Historical Data

| Type of Statement | 0-500M | 500M-2MM | 2-10MM | 10-50MM | 50-100MM | 100-250MM | | 4/1/07-3/31/08 ALL | 4/1/08-3/31/09 ALL |
|---|---|---|---|---|---|---|---|---|---|
| Unqualified | | 22 | 164 | 248 | 71 | 55 | | 587 | 519 |
| Reviewed | 1 | 4 | 55 | 20 | 3 | | | 74 | 81 |
| Compiled | 1 | 17 | 32 | 7 | | | | 65 | 71 |
| Tax Returns | 10 | 17 | 13 | 4 | | | | 44 | 33 |
| Other | 4 | 15 | 52 | 53 | 9 | 9 | | 120 | 148 |
| | 377 (4/1-9/30/11) | | | 509 (10/1/11-3/31/12) | | | | | |
| NUMBER OF STATEMENTS | 16 | 75 | 316 | 332 | 83 | 64 | | 890 | 852 |
| | % | % | % | % | % | % | **ASSETS** | % | % |
| | 13.4 | 12.3 | 8.0 | 6.0 | 3.7 | 3.7 | Cash & Equivalents | 6.9 | 6.6 |
| | 19.8 | 23.6 | 23.5 | 21.0 | 17.2 | 17.1 | Trade Receivables (net) | 22.2 | 21.6 |
| | 32.5 | 31.2 | 31.6 | 33.0 | 35.0 | 37.6 | Inventory | 32.3 | 34.4 |
| | 1.2 | 3.3 | 3.8 | 7.9 | 12.4 | 12.9 | All Other Current | 5.9 | 7.0 |
| | 66.9 | 70.5 | 66.8 | 68.0 | 68.4 | 71.4 | Total Current | 67.3 | 69.6 |
| | 20.0 | 16.9 | 20.3 | 19.2 | 18.8 | 17.3 | Fixed Assets (net) | 19.8 | 18.8 |
| | 10.5 | 1.6 | .5 | 1.1 | 2.7 | 1.6 | Intangibles (net) | .7 | .8 |
| | 2.6 | 10.9 | 12.5 | 11.7 | 10.0 | 9.7 | All Other Non-Current | 12.3 | 10.8 |
| | 100.0 | 100.0 | 100.0 | 100.0 | 100.0 | 100.0 | Total | 100.0 | 100.0 |
| | | | | | | | **LIABILITIES** | | |
| | 37.7 | 13.6 | 13.9 | 17.2 | 19.4 | 23.0 | Notes Payable-Short Term | 20.6 | 18.5 |
| | 3.3 | 2.8 | 1.7 | 1.7 | 1.4 | 1.1 | Cur. Mat.-L.T.D. | 1.9 | 1.9 |
| | 27.1 | 14.0 | 19.3 | 22.5 | 23.0 | 20.1 | Trade Payables | 17.7 | 20.0 |
| | .0 | .1 | .2 | .4 | .3 | .3 | Income Taxes Payable | .6 | .5 |
| | 1.0 | 8.7 | 8.2 | 7.6 | 9.5 | 9.4 | All Other Current | 7.9 | 9.1 |
| | 69.2 | 39.1 | 43.3 | 49.4 | 53.6 | 53.9 | Total Current | 48.7 | 50.0 |
| | 19.4 | 6.4 | 5.9 | 7.1 | 10.2 | 9.8 | Long-Term Debt | 8.0 | 7.9 |
| | .0 | .1 | .3 | .6 | .7 | .6 | Deferred Taxes | .3 | .3 |
| | 2.2 | 5.3 | 1.2 | 2.0 | 2.3 | 2.8 | All Other Non-Current | 2.0 | 1.7 |
| | 9.3 | 49.0 | 49.3 | 41.0 | 33.2 | 32.8 | Net Worth | 41.0 | 40.1 |
| | 100.0 | 100.0 | 100.0 | 100.0 | 100.0 | 100.0 | Total Liabilities & Net Worth | 100.0 | 100.0 |
| | | | | | | | **INCOME DATA** | | |
| | 100.0 | 100.0 | 100.0 | 100.0 | 100.0 | 100.0 | Net Sales | 100.0 | 100.0 |
| | 25.8 | 22.6 | 17.3 | 12.7 | 11.5 | 10.8 | Gross Profit | 15.6 | 15.5 |
| | 25.8 | 21.2 | 15.1 | 9.9 | 9.0 | 8.1 | Operating Expenses | 13.3 | 12.4 |
| | .0 | 1.4 | 2.2 | 2.8 | 2.6 | 2.6 | Operating Profit | 2.3 | 3.1 |
| | .7 | -.3 | -.9 | -.7 | -.2 | -.1 | All Other Expenses (net) | -.6 | -.6 |
| | -.7 | 1.7 | 3.1 | 3.5 | 2.8 | 2.7 | Profit Before Taxes | 2.9 | 3.7 |
| | | | | | | | **RATIOS** | | |
| | 4.6 | 3.1 | 2.1 | 1.6 | 1.4 | 1.4 | | 1.7 | 1.7 |
| | 1.3 | 1.8 | 1.5 | 1.3 | 1.3 | 1.3 | Current | 1.3 | 1.3 |
| | .8 | 1.2 | 1.2 | 1.2 | 1.2 | 1.2 | | 1.1 | 1.2 |
| | 2.7 | 1.6 | 1.1 | .8 | .6 | .6 | | .9 | .9 |
| | .4 | 1.0 | (315) .8 | .6 | .4 | .3 | Quick | .6 (851) .5 | |
| | .2 | .5 | .4 | .3 | .2 | .2 | | .4 | .3 |
| | 4 81.7 | 9 39.1 | 17 21.0 | 17 21.9 | 13 28.8 | 14 26.7 | | 19 19.5 | 16 23.0 |
| | 15 24.4 | 20 18.1 | 29 12.6 | 26 14.1 | 25 14.7 | 22 16.6 | Sales/Receivables | 30 12.2 | 26 14.2 |
| | 23 16.0 | 30 12.3 | 41 8.8 | 41 8.9 | 39 9.3 | 38 9.6 | | 45 8.2 | 39 9.4 |
| | 10 35.2 | 19 18.9 | 31 11.8 | 36 10.1 | 45 8.1 | 38 9.5 | | 36 10.1 | 34 10.8 |
| | 51 7.1 | 41 8.9 | 56 6.5 | 55 6.6 | 59 6.2 | 68 5.4 | Cost of Sales/Inventory | 58 6.3 | 57 6.5 |
| | 87 4.2 | 79 4.6 | 85 4.3 | 85 4.3 | 87 4.2 | 94 3.9 | | 85 4.3 | 85 4.3 |
| | 0 UND | 5 79.2 | 15 24.0 | 19 18.9 | 24 15.4 | 21 17.5 | | 15 23.9 | 15 23.7 |
| | 17 22.0 | 16 22.9 | 27 13.5 | 32 11.5 | 37 9.8 | 30 12.3 | Cost of Sales/Payables | 28 13.0 | 28 13.1 |
| | 53 6.9 | 27 13.7 | 46 7.9 | 54 6.7 | 56 6.5 | 48 7.6 | | 47 7.8 | 46 8.0 |
| | 9.0 | 6.0 | 6.5 | 9.4 | 10.9 | 11.2 | | 8.5 | 9.5 |
| | 19.1 | 13.4 | 12.5 | 15.2 | 16.7 | 15.3 | Sales/Working Capital | 15.1 | 16.3 |
| | NM | 43.4 | 24.9 | 23.2 | 23.5 | 21.4 | | 28.4 | 27.7 |
| | 14.8 | 13.7 | 16.9 | 15.2 | 9.1 | 8.0 | | 6.4 | 10.1 |
| | (13) 1.0 | (60) 3.8 | (293) 6.1 | (321) 7.2 | (81) 6.1 | (63) 4.2 | EBIT/Interest | (833) 3.4 | (794) 5.1 |
| | -5.0 | .6 | 2.7 | 4.0 | 4.0 | 3.0 | | 2.1 | 2.8 |
| | | | 8.9 | 11.0 | 12.2 | 12.6 | | 9.9 | 12.7 |
| | | (95) 4.6 | (186) 6.6 | (48) 7.5 | (40) 7.2 | | Net Profit + Depr., Dep., Amort./Cur. Mat. L/T/D | (427) 5.8 | (383) 6.6 |
| | | | 2.6 | 3.4 | 4.7 | 3.7 | | 3.5 | 3.8 |
| | .0 | .1 | .2 | .3 | .4 | .4 | | .3 | .3 |
| | .4 | .3 | .4 | .5 | .5 | .6 | Fixed/Worth | .5 | .4 |
| | -.4 | .7 | .7 | .7 | .8 | .7 | | .7 | .7 |
| | .5 | .3 | .5 | .9 | 1.5 | 1.4 | | .8 | .8 |
| | 4.5 | 1.0 | 1.0 | 1.5 | 2.1 | 2.3 | Debt/Worth | 1.5 | 1.7 |
| | -2.7 | 5.3 | 2.0 | 2.6 | 3.1 | 3.1 | | 2.9 | 3.0 |
| | 24.9 | 28.9 | 20.9 | 25.0 | 31.0 | 26.7 | | 23.9 | 34.3 |
| | (10) 5.0 | (67) 8.1 | (314) 11.0 | (328) 18.0 | (80) 20.6 | (63) 19.7 | % Profit Before Taxes/Tangible Net Worth | (868) 15.3 | (834) 22.0 |
| | -22.3 | .5 | 6.2 | 11.4 | 15.4 | 13.5 | | 8.7 | 12.0 |
| | 7.9 | 11.2 | 9.8 | 10.7 | 9.6 | 8.3 | | 9.6 | 12.5 |
| | .3 | 3.6 | 6.0 | 6.9 | 6.7 | 5.9 | % Profit Before Taxes/Total Assets | 5.9 | 7.8 |
| | -9.5 | -.3 | 2.2 | 4.4 | 4.9 | 4.1 | | 3.3 | 4.5 |
| | UND | 71.3 | 27.6 | 20.4 | 19.0 | 18.3 | | 21.1 | 27.0 |
| | 33.8 | 26.8 | 14.0 | 12.9 | 13.3 | 13.7 | Sales/Net Fixed Assets | 13.0 | 15.6 |
| | 15.5 | 13.6 | 8.1 | 8.7 | 8.8 | 11.1 | | 8.4 | 10.2 |
| | 6.0 | 4.9 | 3.3 | 3.1 | 2.6 | 2.8 | | 2.9 | 3.4 |
| | 4.2 | 3.3 | 2.4 | 2.4 | 2.2 | 2.3 | Sales/Total Assets | 2.3 | 2.5 |
| | 1.7 | 2.2 | 1.9 | 1.8 | 1.8 | 1.9 | | 1.7 | 1.9 |
| | | .6 | .7 | .7 | .8 | .6 | | .8 | .7 |
| | | (54) .9 | (293) 1.1 | (318) 1.2 | (78) 1.1 | (61) 1.0 | % Depr., Dep., Amort./Sales | (844) 1.2 | (803) 1.0 |
| | | 2.0 | 1.8 | 1.6 | 1.5 | 1.2 | | 1.7 | 1.5 |
| | | 1.4 | 1.1 | .4 | | | | 1.1 | 1.0 |
| | | (25) 2.4 | (50) 2.3 | (15) 1.6 | | | % Officers', Directors' Owners' Comp/Sales | (107) 2.2 | (105) 2.1 |
| | | 3.9 | 3.3 | 2.6 | | | | 4.8 | 4.0 |
| | 28928M | 418879M | 4727413M | 20275218M | 13493842M | 24855001M | Net Sales ($) | 46797126M | 62130173M |
| | 5869M | 100270M | 1703145M | 7802098M | 5807275M | 10141516M | Total Assets ($) | 20583502M | 22981696M |

M = $ thousand    MM = $ million
See Pages 9 through 22 for Explanation of Ratios and Data

## Comparative Historical Data | Current Data Sorted by Sales

| Type of Statement | 4/1/09-3/31/10 ALL | 4/1/10-3/31/11 ALL | 4/1/11-3/31/12 ALL | | 0-1MM | 1-3MM | 3-5MM | 5-10MM | 10-25MM | 25MM & OVER |
|---|---|---|---|---|---|---|---|---|---|---|
| Unqualified | 526 | 539 | 560 | | | 10 | 16 | 48 | 127 | 359 |
| Reviewed | 88 | 80 | 83 | | | 5 | 4 | 17 | 29 | 28 |
| Compiled | 60 | 47 | 57 | | 1 | 5 | 6 | 20 | 14 | 11 |
| Tax Returns | 30 | 38 | 44 | | 2 | 12 | 8 | 5 | 13 | 4 |
| Other | 142 | 133 | 142 | | 3 | 6 | 9 | 21 | 35 | 68 |
| | | | | | 377 (4/1-9/30/11) | | | 509 (10/1/11-3/31/12) | | |
| **NUMBER OF STATEMENTS** | 846 | 837 | 886 | | 6 | 38 | 43 | 111 | 218 | 470 |
| **ASSETS** | % | % | % | | % | % | % | % | % | % |
| Cash & Equivalents | 7.7 | 6.9 | 7.0 | | | 16.3 | 10.3 | 9.1 | 7.1 | 5.4 |
| Trade Receivables (net) | 21.7 | 20.6 | 21.5 | | | 17.3 | 21.9 | 20.3 | 23.2 | 21.4 |
| Inventory | 30.9 | 31.8 | 32.8 | | | 30.4 | 33.3 | 33.0 | 31.1 | 33.7 |
| All Other Current | 5.0 | 6.2 | 6.7 | | | 1.4 | 4.1 | 3.5 | 5.0 | 9.0 |
| Total Current | 65.4 | 65.5 | 68.0 | | | 65.4 | 69.6 | 65.9 | 66.4 | 69.5 |
| Fixed Assets (net) | 20.8 | 21.0 | 19.2 | | | 19.9 | 17.6 | 19.8 | 20.3 | 18.7 |
| Intangibles (net) | .9 | 1.0 | 1.3 | | | 3.2 | .1 | 1.1 | 1.1 | 1.2 |
| All Other Non-Current | 12.9 | 12.5 | 11.4 | | | 11.5 | 12.7 | 13.2 | 12.2 | 10.6 |
| Total | 100.0 | 100.0 | 100.0 | | | 100.0 | 100.0 | 100.0 | 100.0 | 100.0 |
| **LIABILITIES** | | | | | | | | | | |
| Notes Payable-Short Term | 14.8 | 15.5 | 16.7 | | | 19.4 | 15.2 | 13.4 | 13.9 | 18.2 |
| Cur. Mat.-L.T.D. | 1.7 | 2.1 | 1.7 | | | 3.6 | 2.3 | 1.7 | 1.8 | 1.5 |
| Trade Payables | 19.9 | 19.6 | 20.6 | | | 12.7 | 15.6 | 14.5 | 20.5 | 23.3 |
| Income Taxes Payable | .3 | .3 | .3 | | | .1 | .1 | .2 | .2 | .4 |
| All Other Current | 7.9 | 7.9 | 8.1 | | | 5.6 | 8.9 | 8.3 | 8.0 | 8.3 |
| Total Current | 44.6 | 45.4 | 47.4 | | | 41.4 | 42.0 | 38.1 | 44.5 | 51.7 |
| Long-Term Debt | 7.8 | 8.4 | 7.3 | | | 9.9 | 6.7 | 7.0 | 6.1 | 7.7 |
| Deferred Taxes | .4 | .4 | .4 | | | .1 | .1 | .1 | .4 | .6 |
| All Other Non-Current | 2.2 | 2.0 | 2.1 | | | 2.6 | 2.4 | 2.8 | .9 | 2.2 |
| Net Worth | 44.9 | 43.8 | 42.7 | | | 46.1 | 48.7 | 52.0 | 48.0 | 37.8 |
| Total Liabilities & Net Worth | 100.0 | 100.0 | 100.0 | | | 100.0 | 100.0 | 100.0 | 100.0 | 100.0 |
| **INCOME DATA** | | | | | | | | | | |
| Net Sales | 100.0 | 100.0 | 100.0 | | | 100.0 | 100.0 | 100.0 | 100.0 | 100.0 |
| Gross Profit | 15.1 | 16.0 | 15.2 | | | 26.8 | 22.8 | 20.8 | 16.5 | 11.4 |
| Operating Expenses | 13.2 | 13.7 | 12.8 | | | 26.1 | 21.1 | 18.2 | 13.9 | 9.0 |
| Operating Profit | 1.9 | 2.3 | 2.4 | | | .6 | 1.6 | 2.6 | 2.6 | 2.4 |
| All Other Expenses (net) | -.9 | -.8 | -.6 | | | -.5 | -.5 | -.9 | -.8 | -.5 |
| Profit Before Taxes | 2.8 | 3.1 | 3.0 | | | 1.2 | 2.1 | 3.5 | 3.5 | 2.9 |
| **RATIOS** | | | | | | | | | | |
| Current | 1.9 | 1.8 | 1.8 | | | 3.6 | 3.9 | 2.6 | 1.9 | 1.5 |
| | 1.4 | 1.4 | 1.4 | | | 1.8 | 1.7 | 1.7 | 1.5 | 1.3 |
| | 1.2 | 1.2 | 1.2 | | | 1.1 | 1.2 | 1.3 | 1.2 | 1.2 |
| Quick | 1.0 | .9 | .9 | | | 1.8 | 2.2 | 1.3 | 1.0 | .8 |
| | .6 | .6 | (885) .6 | | | .9 | .7 | .8 (217) | .7 | .5 |
| | .4 | .4 | .3 | | | .3 | .5 | .4 | .4 | .3 |
| Sales/Receivables | 17 21.3 | 17 22.0 | 15 24.2 | | 7 49.8 | 21 17.3 | 12 30.5 | 17 21.1 | 15 24.6 | |
| | 26 13.9 | 27 13.5 | 26 14.2 | | 20 18.7 | 30 12.3 | 26 13.9 | 29 12.4 | 24 15.1 | |
| | 40 9.2 | 42 8.7 | 40 9.2 | | 50 7.3 | 45 8.2 | 41 9.0 | 41 8.8 | 36 10.0 | |
| Cost of Sales/Inventory | 29 12.7 | 34 10.7 | 34 10.8 | | 24 15.1 | 41 8.9 | 37 9.8 | 34 10.8 | 33 11.2 | |
| | 49 7.5 | 57 6.4 | 55 6.6 | | 81 4.5 | 65 5.6 | 65 5.6 | 54 6.7 | 52 7.0 | |
| | 81 4.5 | 90 4.1 | 85 4.3 | | 118 3.1 | 87 4.2 | 101 3.6 | 85 4.3 | 79 4.6 | |
| Cost of Sales/Payables | 15 24.0 | 17 21.3 | 17 21.8 | | 6 57.1 | 12 31.0 | 10 36.8 | 18 19.9 | 19 19.2 | |
| | 26 14.0 | 29 12.4 | 28 12.9 | | 20 18.1 | 23 15.8 | 24 15.5 | 32 11.5 | 29 12.4 | |
| | 47 7.8 | 51 7.1 | 49 7.5 | | 34 10.6 | 34 10.7 | 44 8.3 | 53 6.9 | 49 7.4 | |
| Sales/Working Capital | 8.1 | 7.9 | 8.5 | | | 3.7 | 3.7 | 5.8 | 7.3 | 11.3 |
| | 13.7 | 13.5 | 14.6 | | | 6.9 | 8.8 | 9.6 | 12.2 | 16.6 |
| | 24.8 | 22.5 | 23.9 | | | 239.4 | 32.5 | 17.2 | 20.4 | 25.5 |
| EBIT/Interest | 13.5 | 15.9 | 13.6 | | | 7.6 | 16.4 | 18.1 | 17.2 | 11.9 |
| | (793) 6.0 | (791) 7.1 | (831) 5.9 | | (30) 1.3 | (38) 3.0 | (102) 8.1 | (202) 6.7 | (455) 5.9 | |
| | 2.4 | 3.0 | 3.0 | | | -1.5 | .6 | 2.9 | 3.2 | 3.5 |
| Net Profit + Depr., Dep., Amort./Cur. Mat. L/T/D | 10.9 | 10.7 | 10.9 | | | | | 8.7 | 8.8 | 11.2 |
| | (384) 6.0 | (379) 5.6 | (375) 5.9 | | | | (23) 4.4 | (83) 5.2 | (260) 6.6 | |
| | 3.0 | 3.4 | 3.4 | | | | | 3.0 | 2.4 | 3.5 |
| Fixed/Worth | .3 | .3 | .3 | | | .1 | .1 | .2 | .2 | .3 |
| | .4 | .5 | .4 | | | .3 | .2 | .3 | .4 | .5 |
| | .7 | .7 | .7 | | | .9 | .8 | .7 | .6 | .7 |
| Debt/Worth | .6 | .7 | .7 | | | .3 | .3 | .4 | .6 | 1.2 |
| | 1.2 | 1.3 | 1.5 | | | 1.0 | .8 | 1.0 | 1.1 | 1.8 |
| | 2.3 | 2.6 | 2.6 | | | 2.4 | 4.2 | 1.8 | 2.1 | 2.8 |
| % Profit Before Taxes/Tangible Net Worth | 25.9 | 24.2 | 24.9 | | | 24.0 | 20.6 | 27.1 | 21.1 | 27.2 |
| | (818) 16.4 | (812) 16.1 | (862) 16.1 | | (32) 1.6 | (39) 8.7 | (109) 11.1 | (216) 12.7 | (462) 18.5 | |
| | 6.6 | 8.1 | 8.1 | | | -2.9 | .9 | 4.6 | 7.2 | 12.8 |
| % Profit Before Taxes/Total Assets | 11.5 | 10.1 | 9.9 | | | 6.5 | 9.3 | 11.8 | 9.8 | 9.9 |
| | 6.9 | 6.3 | 6.4 | | | .8 | 2.6 | 6.3 | 6.5 | 6.6 |
| | 2.5 | 3.2 | 3.1 | | | -3.6 | -.8 | 2.4 | 2.9 | 4.2 |
| Sales/Net Fixed Assets | 22.8 | 19.3 | 24.3 | | | 46.3 | 38.6 | 32.4 | 24.6 | 21.7 |
| | 13.2 | 11.8 | 14.1 | | | 20.4 | 15.7 | 13.6 | 12.5 | 14.4 |
| | 8.7 | 7.6 | 8.9 | | | 6.2 | 7.3 | 8.1 | 7.7 | 9.8 |
| Sales/Total Assets | 3.3 | 3.0 | 3.2 | | | 3.7 | 3.3 | 3.1 | 3.1 | 3.2 |
| | 2.5 | 2.2 | 2.4 | | | 2.5 | 2.0 | 2.3 | 2.2 | 2.5 |
| | 1.9 | 1.6 | 1.8 | | | 1.2 | 1.6 | 1.8 | 1.7 | 2.0 |
| % Depr., Dep., Amort./Sales | .8 | .8 | .7 | | | .7 | .7 | .6 | .8 | .7 |
| | (800) 1.1 | (778) 1.3 | (813) 1.1 | | (31) 1.3 | (35) 1.1 | (101) 1.2 | (198) 1.3 | (445) 1.0 | |
| | 1.7 | 1.8 | 1.6 | | | 2.5 | 2.4 | 1.9 | 1.9 | 1.4 |
| % Officers', Directors' Owners' Comp/Sales | 1.0 | .9 | 1.1 | | | 2.5 | 1.5 | 1.3 | .9 | .4 |
| | (100) 2.0 | (105) 2.1 | (102) 2.3 | | (11) 3.4 | (11) 2.4 | (28) 2.3 | (31) 1.7 | (20) 1.3 | |
| | 1.7 | 1.8 | 3.3 | | | 7.7 | 3.7 | 5.3 | 2.7 | 2.5 |
| Net Sales ($) | 54874862M | 51029011M | 63799281M | | 2871M | 79981M | 171902M | 812850M | 3650384M | 59081293M |
| Total Assets ($) | 20463262M | 22125447M | 25560173M | | 3248M | 47859M | 113138M | 370471M | 1733975M | 23291482M |

© RMA 2012

M = $ thousand    MM = $ million
See Pages 9 through 22 for Explanation of Ratios and Data

## Current Data Sorted by Assets     Comparative Historical Data

| 0-500M | 500M-2MM | 2-10MM | 10-50MM | 50-100MM | 100-250MM | Type of Statement | 4/1/07-3/31/08 ALL | 4/1/08-3/31/09 ALL |
|---|---|---|---|---|---|---|---|---|
| | | 2 | 6 | | | Unqualified | 9 | 9 |
| | 1 | 6 | 4 | | | Reviewed | 9 | 7 |
| 1 | 3 | 4 | 1 | 1 | | Compiled | 6 | 8 |
| 4 | 4 | 5 | | | | Tax Returns | 8 | 13 |
| 3 | 5 | 3 | 7 | 1 | 2 | Other | 22 | 23 |
| | | | | | | | ALL | ALL |
| **12 (4/1-9/30/11)** | | | **51 (10/1/11-3/31/12)** | | | | | |
| 8 | 13 | 20 | 18 | 2 | 2 | **NUMBER OF STATEMENTS** | 54 | 60 |
| % | % | % | % | % | % | **ASSETS** | % | % |
| | 8.9 | 6.0 | 4.2 | | | Cash & Equivalents | 8.7 | 10.3 |
| | 21.0 | 27.6 | 31.3 | | | Trade Receivables (net) | 28.9 | 28.5 |
| | 38.2 | 42.5 | 36.7 | | | Inventory | 32.4 | 31.3 |
| | 2.1 | 2.1 | 3.3 | | | All Other Current | 4.1 | 4.7 |
| | 70.2 | 78.1 | 75.6 | | | Total Current | 74.0 | 74.8 |
| | 19.9 | 12.6 | 18.2 | | | Fixed Assets (net) | 12.1 | 15.0 |
| | 4.4 | 3.5 | 1.9 | | | Intangibles (net) | 3.7 | 4.1 |
| | 5.6 | 5.8 | 4.4 | | | All Other Non-Current | 10.1 | 6.1 |
| | 100.0 | 100.0 | 100.0 | | | Total | 100.0 | 100.0 |
| | | | | | | **LIABILITIES** | | |
| | 13.3 | 8.7 | 9.0 | | | Notes Payable-Short Term | 15.2 | 13.9 |
| | 1.6 | 3.5 | 1.0 | | | Cur. Mat.-L.T.D. | 1.7 | 3.2 |
| | 30.3 | 32.9 | 33.2 | | | Trade Payables | 33.2 | 32.8 |
| | .2 | .0 | .2 | | | Income Taxes Payable | .3 | .2 |
| | 8.1 | 4.3 | 10.7 | | | All Other Current | 11.8 | 14.1 |
| | 53.5 | 49.5 | 54.1 | | | Total Current | 62.2 | 64.3 |
| | 9.1 | 10.7 | 7.2 | | | Long-Term Debt | 8.6 | 9.8 |
| | .0 | .0 | .3 | | | Deferred Taxes | .0 | .0 |
| | .3 | 5.3 | 3.6 | | | All Other Non-Current | 3.8 | 5.7 |
| | 37.1 | 34.5 | 34.7 | | | Net Worth | 25.4 | 20.2 |
| | 100.0 | 100.0 | 100.0 | | | Total Liabilities & Net Worth | 100.0 | 100.0 |
| | | | | | | **INCOME DATA** | | |
| | 100.0 | 100.0 | 100.0 | | | Net Sales | 100.0 | 100.0 |
| | 45.9 | 33.1 | 39.9 | | | Gross Profit | 33.6 | 36.7 |
| | 41.4 | 27.5 | 38.6 | | | Operating Expenses | 31.2 | 34.1 |
| | 4.4 | 5.6 | 1.3 | | | Operating Profit | 2.4 | 2.6 |
| | -.3 | 1.6 | .0 | | | All Other Expenses (net) | .6 | .2 |
| | 4.7 | 4.0 | 1.3 | | | Profit Before Taxes | 1.8 | 2.4 |
| | | | | | | **RATIOS** | | |
| | 4.8 | 3.0 | 1.9 | | | Current | 2.0 | 1.8 |
| | 1.2 | 1.9 | 1.2 | | | | 1.2 | 1.2 |
| | .8 | 1.2 | 1.0 | | | | 1.0 | 1.0 |
| | 1.0 | 1.0 | .9 | | | Quick | 1.0 | .9 |
| | .7 | .6 | .6 | | | | .6 (59) | .6 |
| | .4 | .4 | .4 | | | | .4 | .4 |
| | 5   67.2 | 13   28.9 | 26   14.1 | | | Sales/Receivables | 21   17.6 | 18   19.9 |
| | 23   15.8 | 27   13.5 | 49   7.5 | | | | 43   8.6 | 37   9.9 |
| | 58   6.3 | 53   6.9 | 54   6.7 | | | | 62   5.9 | 65   5.6 |
| | 20   18.5 | 24   15.0 | 57   6.4 | | | Cost of Sales/Inventory | 34   10.9 | 19   19.4 |
| | 72   5.1 | 89   4.1 | 78   4.7 | | | | 59   6.1 | 56   6.5 |
| | 146   2.5 | 166   2.2 | 140   2.6 | | | | 152   2.4 | 127   2.9 |
| | 7   55.5 | 17   21.3 | 51   7.1 | | | Cost of Sales/Payables | 25   14.5 | 19   19.4 |
| | 64   5.7 | 35   10.3 | 69   5.3 | | | | 60   6.0 | 67   5.5 |
| | 76   4.8 | 74   4.9 | 107   3.4 | | | | 104   3.5 | 103   3.5 |
| | 5.0 | 4.7 | 5.2 | | | Sales/Working Capital | 6.4 | 6.6 |
| | 29.9 | 9.3 | 18.2 | | | | 20.6 | 23.8 |
| | -88.3 | 44.4 | 59.5 | | | | -98.8 | -162.8 |
| | 9.0 | 22.4 | 19.2 | | | EBIT/Interest | 11.8 | 11.2 |
| | (11) 4.1 | 8.2 | (16) 6.6 | | | | (47) 3.7 | (49) 4.2 |
| | 1.3 | 1.0 | -2.9 | | | | 1.1 | .8 |
| | | | | | | Net Profit + Depr., Dep., Amort./Cur. Mat. L/T/D | 35.8 (10) 7.2 1.3 | |
| | .1 | .1 | .1 | | | Fixed/Worth | .2 | .1 |
| | .6 | .3 | .4 | | | | .4 | .5 |
| | 4.2 | 6.1 | .8 | | | | 2.1 | 3.5 |
| | .6 | .7 | 1.2 | | | Debt/Worth | 1.1 | 1.3 |
| | 1.8 | 1.6 | 2.2 | | | | 4.0 | 3.3 |
| | 18.0 | 15.7 | 4.4 | | | | 17.6 | 28.3 |
| | 92.7 | 55.0 | 28.7 | | | % Profit Before Taxes/Tangible Net Worth | 54.0 | 48.8 |
| | (12) 10.1 | (16) 19.2 | (17) 21.4 | | | | (44) 14.1 | (47) 15.7 |
| | 2.1 | 5.8 | -2.1 | | | | 3.7 | 1.3 |
| | 14.1 | 18.9 | 12.6 | | | % Profit Before Taxes/Total Assets | 11.1 | 13.1 |
| | 5.2 | 5.9 | 2.2 | | | | 3.4 | 4.4 |
| | .9 | .2 | -1.6 | | | | .2 | -.8 |
| | 295.1 | 127.6 | 72.8 | | | Sales/Net Fixed Assets | 175.2 | 95.0 |
| | 22.1 | 57.1 | 24.6 | | | | 30.7 | 39.2 |
| | 9.1 | 13.3 | 9.4 | | | | 15.1 | 15.9 |
| | 4.9 | 3.7 | 3.1 | | | Sales/Total Assets | 4.1 | 4.1 |
| | 3.3 | 2.5 | 2.5 | | | | 2.4 | 2.5 |
| | 2.2 | 2.0 | 1.9 | | | | 1.5 | 1.6 |
| | | .5 | .3 | | | % Depr., Dep., Amort./Sales | .4 | .5 |
| | | (14) 1.1 | (17) .6 | | | | (40) .9 | (44) .9 |
| | | 1.8 | 2.3 | | | | 1.6 | 1.4 |
| | | | | | | % Officers', Directors' Owners' Comp/Sales | 1.3 | 1.8 |
| | | | | | | | (16) 2.6 | (21) 2.4 |
| | | | | | | | 6.2 | 3.6 |
| 10339M | 51141M | 283888M | 941582M | 335656M | 809829M | Net Sales ($) | 2418762M | 2138924M |
| 2368M | 14786M | 93031M | 390443M | 108825M | 366439M | Total Assets ($) | 1199469M | 1069132M |

M = $ thousand     MM = $ million
See Pages 9 through 22 for Explanation of Ratios and Data

## Comparative Historical Data

## Current Data Sorted by Sales

| | | | | Type of Statement | | | | | | |
|---|---|---|---|---|---|---|---|---|---|---|
| 7 | | 8 | | 8 | Unqualified | | | 1 | 3 | 4 |
| 11 | | 11 | | 11 | Reviewed | | 1 | 2 | 3 | 5 |
| 9 | | 7 | | 10 | Compiled | | 3 | 2 | 2 | 2 |
| 13 | | 6 | | 13 | Tax Returns | 1 | 1 | 3 | 3 | |
| 28 | | 25 | | 21 | Other | 2 | 4 | 3 | 3 | 8 |
| | | | | | 3 | 3 | | | | |
| 4/1/09- | | 4/1/10- | | 4/1/11- | | | 12 (4/1-9/30/11) | | 51 (10/1/11-3/31/12) | |
| 3/31/10 | | 3/31/11 | | 3/31/12 | | 0-1MM | 1-3MM | 3-5MM | 5-10MM | 10-25MM | 25MM & OVER |
| ALL | | ALL | | ALL | | | | | | |
| 68 | | 57 | | 63 | NUMBER OF STATEMENTS | 5 | 8 | 7 | 11 | 13 | 19 |
| % | | % | | % | ASSETS | % | % | % | % | % | % |
| 10.0 | | 7.8 | | 6.8 | Cash & Equivalents | | | | 10.5 | 5.4 | 2.1 |
| 26.5 | | 26.0 | | 27.9 | Trade Receivables (net) | | | | 22.2 | 22.2 | 37.6 |
| 33.1 | | 34.1 | | 38.5 | Inventory | | | | 50.3 | 40.7 | 36.6 |
| 4.2 | | 2.8 | | 2.7 | All Other Current | | | | 1.5 | 1.0 | 5.3 |
| 73.7 | | 70.7 | | 75.9 | Total Current | | | | 84.5 | 69.3 | 81.7 |
| 14.0 | | 14.9 | | 14.6 | Fixed Assets (net) | | | | 10.1 | 18.6 | 11.9 |
| 4.0 | | 5.6 | | 4.1 | Intangibles (net) | | | | .7 | 4.7 | 3.1 |
| 8.3 | | 8.8 | | 5.5 | All Other Non-Current | | | | 4.7 | 7.4 | 3.3 |
| 100.0 | | 100.0 | | 100.0 | Total | | | | 100.0 | 100.0 | 100.0 |
| | | | | | LIABILITIES | | | | | | |
| 9.5 | | 10.1 | | 12.5 | Notes Payable-Short Term | | | | 7.1 | 10.8 | 9.0 |
| 4.6 | | 2.3 | | 2.1 | Cur. Mat.-L.T.D. | | | | 3.2 | 2.3 | .5 |
| 28.7 | | 28.9 | | 32.7 | Trade Payables | | | | 47.8 | 21.8 | 43.0 |
| .1 | | .1 | | .1 | Income Taxes Payable | | | | .2 | .2 | .1 |
| 12.5 | | 8.5 | | 7.7 | All Other Current | | | | 2.8 | 4.3 | 11.2 |
| 55.5 | | 49.8 | | 55.1 | Total Current | | | | 61.1 | 39.3 | 63.8 |
| 11.6 | | 12.4 | | 8.7 | Long-Term Debt | | | | 10.3 | 10.7 | 5.3 |
| .1 | | .1 | | .1 | Deferred Taxes | | | | .0 | .1 | .2 |
| 4.6 | | 4.5 | | 7.4 | All Other Non-Current | | | | 5.0 | 4.0 | 3.5 |
| 28.3 | | 33.2 | | 28.7 | Net Worth | | | | 23.6 | 45.9 | 27.2 |
| 100.0 | | 100.0 | | 100.0 | Total Liabilties & Net Worth | | | | 100.0 | 100.0 | 100.0 |
| | | | | | INCOME DATA | | | | | | |
| 100.0 | | 100.0 | | 100.0 | Net Sales | | | | 100.0 | 100.0 | 100.0 |
| 36.0 | | 35.0 | | 38.9 | Gross Profit | | | | 36.3 | 40.9 | 29.2 |
| 32.3 | | 31.4 | | 35.5 | Operating Expenses | | | | 30.1 | 39.5 | 27.0 |
| 3.7 | | 3.6 | | 3.5 | Operating Profit | | | | 6.3 | 1.4 | 2.3 |
| .5 | | 1.2 | | .6 | All Other Expenses (net) | | | | 2.9 | .2 | .0 |
| 3.2 | | 2.4 | | 2.9 | Profit Before Taxes | | | | 3.4 | 1.2 | 2.3 |
| | | | | | RATIOS | | | | | | |
| 2.3 | | 2.4 | | 2.7 | | | | | 5.4 | 3.5 | 1.7 |
| 1.3 | | 1.5 | | 1.2 | Current | | | | 1.9 | 1.8 | 1.2 |
| 1.0 | | 1.1 | | 1.0 | | | | | 1.0 | 1.1 | 1.1 |
| 1.1 | | 1.2 | | 1.0 | | | | | 2.5 | 1.2 | .9 |
| .6 | | .7 | | .6 | Quick | | | | .6 | .5 | .6 |
| .3 | | .4 | | .4 | | | | | .3 | .4 | .4 |
| 17 21.7 | 20 18.2 | 10 36.2 | | | Sales/Receivables | 7 50.8 | 13 27.9 | 33 11.1 |
| 34 10.6 | 35 10.5 | 29 12.5 | | | | 15 23.7 | 27 13.3 | 49 7.5 |
| 59 6.2 | 61 6.0 | 52 7.0 | | | | 56 6.5 | 45 8.2 | 52 7.0 |
| 18 20.1 | 32 11.5 | 37 9.9 | | | Cost of Sales/Inventory | 46 8.0 | 10 36.8 | 43 8.5 |
| 74 4.9 | 69 5.3 | 83 4.4 | | | | 83 4.4 | 130 2.8 | 66 5.5 |
| 152 2.4 | 122 3.0 | 146 2.5 | | | | 146 2.5 | 203 1.8 | 96 3.8 |
| 28 13.0 | 21 17.6 | 19 19.0 | | | Cost of Sales/Payables | 15 24.4 | 29 12.6 | 34 10.7 |
| 53 6.8 | 45 8.1 | 56 6.5 | | | | 54 6.7 | 43 8.4 | 69 5.3 |
| 88 4.1 | 90 4.0 | 91 4.0 | | | | 76 4.8 | 70 5.2 | 122 3.0 |
| 3.9 | 5.6 | 5.2 | | | Sales/Working Capital | | | 4.7 | 3.3 | 9.8 |
| 13.0 | 13.4 | 16.9 | | | | | | 8.1 | 8.9 | 23.4 |
| NM | 114.8 | 62.0 | | | | | | 111.4 | 55.1 | 62.0 |
| 19.6 | 25.4 | 15.0 | | | EBIT/Interest | | | 13.3 | 29.6 | 29.3 |
| (54) 3.7 | (52) 3.5 | (56) 4.5 | | | | | | 4.3 | (12) 4.6 | (18) 12.1 |
| 1.2 | 1.3 | .7 | | | | | | -3.7 | .7 | -1.3 |
| | | | | | Net Profit + Depr., Dep., Amort./Cur. Mat. L/T/D | | | | | | |
| .1 | .2 | .1 | | | Fixed/Worth | | | .0 | .1 | .1 |
| .5 | .4 | .4 | | | | | | .3 | .4 | .4 |
| 2.3 | 1.8 | 2.3 | | | | | | -.7 | 1.6 | 1.2 |
| 1.5 | .9 | 1.1 | | | Debt/Worth | | | .6 | .3 | 1.7 |
| 3.1 | 2.4 | 2.5 | | | | | | 1.3 | 1.2 | 3.2 |
| 17.1 | 7.1 | 24.1 | | | | | | -10.9 | 5.5 | 12.0 |
| 44.9 | 43.4 | 54.2 | | | % Profit Before Taxes/Tangible Net Worth | | | | 28.3 | 61.7 |
| (56) 20.3 | (48) 17.3 | (51) 19.3 | | | | | | (11) 7.1 | (16) 22.8 |
| 2.7 | 2.4 | 3.8 | | | | | | -.3 | 9.8 |
| 14.2 | 11.8 | 12.0 | | | % Profit Before Taxes/Total Assets | | | 12.0 | 10.1 | 15.4 |
| 3.5 | 4.6 | 3.9 | | | | | | 1.6 | 3.0 | 3.9 |
| .0 | -.1 | .0 | | | | | | -3.1 | -.1 | -.5 |
| 102.0 | 83.3 | 138.7 | | | Sales/Net Fixed Assets | | | 189.3 | 85.8 | 65.6 |
| 31.8 | 31.3 | 41.8 | | | | | | 91.4 | 22.8 | 41.8 |
| 14.4 | 11.4 | 12.5 | | | | | | 21.6 | 6.5 | 17.5 |
| 3.8 | 3.6 | 3.7 | | | Sales/Total Assets | | | 4.7 | 3.4 | 3.5 |
| 2.4 | 2.6 | 2.6 | | | | | | 2.6 | 1.9 | 2.8 |
| 1.6 | 1.7 | 2.0 | | | | | | 2.2 | 1.4 | 2.4 |
| .6 | .4 | .4 | | | % Depr., Dep., Amort./Sales | | | | .5 | .4 |
| (52) 1.1 | (49) 1.0 | (47) .8 | | | | | | (10) 1.4 | .7 |
| 1.7 | 1.7 | 1.6 | | | | | | 2.8 | 1.2 |
| 1.8 | 2.3 | 2.2 | | | % Officers', Directors' Owners' Comp/Sales | | | | | |
| (21) 2.6 | (14) 3.9 | (20) 3.6 | | | | | | | | |
| 4.4 | 7.4 | 10.4 | | | | | | | | |
| 1771196M | 1920452M | 2432435M | | | Net Sales ($) | 1870M | 16458M | 28000M | 87869M | 221182M | 2077056M |
| 710370M | 761656M | 975892M | | | Total Assets ($) | 1820M | 5233M | 10415M | 30505M | 133089M | 794830M |

© RMA 2012        M = $ thousand    MM = $ million
See Pages 9 through 22 for Explanation of Ratios and Data

## Current Data Sorted by Assets          Comparative Historical Data

| 0-500M | 500M-2MM | 2-10MM | 10-50MM | 50-100MM | 100-250MM | Type of Statement | 4/1/07-3/31/08 ALL | 4/1/08-3/31/09 ALL |
|---|---|---|---|---|---|---|---|---|
| | | 2 | 4 | | 1 | Unqualified | 13 | 9 |
| | 1 | 19 | 5 | 1 | | Reviewed | 34 | 34 |
| 6 | 5 | 12 | 2 | | | Compiled | 31 | 28 |
| 8 | 14 | 10 | | | | Tax Returns | 16 | 23 |
| 9 | 17 | 12 | 13 | 1 | | Other | 40 | 50 |
| | 41 (4/1-9/30/11) | | 101 (10/1/11-3/31/12) | | | | | |
| 23 | 37 | 55 | 24 | 2 | 1 | **NUMBER OF STATEMENTS** | 134 | 144 |
| % | % | % | % | % | % | **ASSETS** | % | % |
| 20.5 | 6.6 | 8.0 | 9.3 | | | Cash & Equivalents | 7.9 | 6.0 |
| 17.3 | 32.5 | 23.2 | 27.7 | | | Trade Receivables (net) | 25.1 | 26.4 |
| 23.7 | 30.4 | 28.5 | 23.8 | | | Inventory | 28.2 | 27.5 |
| 4.4 | .8 | 2.4 | 3.8 | | | All Other Current | 4.0 | 4.5 |
| 65.9 | 70.3 | 62.2 | 64.6 | | | Total Current | 65.1 | 64.4 |
| 27.0 | 21.7 | 27.0 | 23.5 | | | Fixed Assets (net) | 21.9 | 24.8 |
| 1.1 | .7 | 2.2 | 4.9 | | | Intangibles (net) | 4.7 | 3.4 |
| 6.0 | 7.3 | 8.6 | 7.1 | | | All Other Non-Current | 8.2 | 7.5 |
| 100.0 | 100.0 | 100.0 | 100.0 | | | Total | 100.0 | 100.0 |
| | | | | | | **LIABILITIES** | | |
| 18.8 | 12.3 | 8.8 | 14.2 | | | Notes Payable-Short Term | 14.4 | 15.7 |
| 6.2 | 6.8 | 4.6 | 1.2 | | | Cur. Mat.-L.T.D. | 3.6 | 3.7 |
| 25.4 | 25.5 | 17.5 | 15.3 | | | Trade Payables | 17.0 | 16.4 |
| .1 | .0 | .4 | .3 | | | Income Taxes Payable | .6 | .3 |
| 8.1 | 4.3 | 4.3 | 5.5 | | | All Other Current | 7.4 | 7.4 |
| 58.7 | 48.9 | 35.5 | 36.4 | | | Total Current | 43.0 | 43.4 |
| 34.0 | 26.2 | 18.2 | 10.4 | | | Long-Term Debt | 12.3 | 14.8 |
| .6 | .0 | .6 | .1 | | | Deferred Taxes | .4 | .2 |
| 5.6 | 13.5 | 6.2 | 4.2 | | | All Other Non-Current | 7.6 | 8.4 |
| 1.3 | 11.3 | 39.5 | 48.9 | | | Net Worth | 36.6 | 33.3 |
| 100.0 | 100.0 | 100.0 | 100.0 | | | Total Liabilities & Net Worth | 100.0 | 100.0 |
| | | | | | | **INCOME DATA** | | |
| 100.0 | 100.0 | 100.0 | 100.0 | | | Net Sales | 100.0 | 100.0 |
| 46.4 | 41.0 | 36.4 | 25.2 | | | Gross Profit | 33.6 | 36.8 |
| 43.2 | 40.5 | 33.8 | 23.0 | | | Operating Expenses | 30.4 | 35.1 |
| 3.1 | .4 | 2.6 | 2.1 | | | Operating Profit | 3.2 | 1.8 |
| 1.3 | .6 | .7 | .1 | | | All Other Expenses (net) | 1.0 | .9 |
| 1.9 | -.2 | 1.9 | 2.0 | | | Profit Before Taxes | 2.2 | .9 |
| | | | | | | **RATIOS** | | |
| 3.7 | 3.0 | 3.1 | 3.2 | | | Current | 3.1 | 2.9 |
| 1.2 | 1.8 | 1.7 | 1.7 | | | | 1.6 | 1.5 |
| .6 | 1.2 | 1.1 | 1.2 | | | | 1.1 | 1.0 |
| 2.0 | 1.9 | 1.3 | 2.1 | | | Quick | 1.3 | 1.4 |
| .7 | 1.0 | .8 | 1.0 | | | | .8 | .8 |
| .2 | .4 | .5 | .6 | | | | .4 | .4 |
| 0 UND | 16 23.2 | 11 34.5 | 23 15.9 | | | Sales/Receivables | 13 27.2 | 17 21.6 |
| 4 92.4 | 32 11.3 | 26 13.8 | 36 10.0 | | | | 27 13.5 | 29 12.8 |
| 21 17.2 | 47 7.7 | 41 8.8 | 69 5.3 | | | | 43 8.4 | 44 8.3 |
| 0 UND | 4 95.7 | 12 29.5 | 15 25.1 | | | Cost of Sales/Inventory | 15 25.0 | 13 29.0 |
| 16 23.5 | 73 5.0 | 50 7.3 | 47 7.8 | | | | 47 7.8 | 43 8.5 |
| 51 7.1 | 111 3.3 | 152 2.4 | 135 2.7 | | | | 108 3.4 | 127 2.9 |
| 0 UND | 9 39.1 | 11 33.0 | 15 23.8 | | | Cost of Sales/Payables | 12 29.2 | 11 33.8 |
| 15 25.0 | 34 10.8 | 33 11.2 | 29 12.7 | | | | 26 14.2 | 24 15.3 |
| 44 8.3 | 73 5.0 | 49 7.4 | 40 9.1 | | | | 46 8.0 | 41 8.9 |
| 10.1 | 6.1 | 4.2 | 5.3 | | | Sales/Working Capital | 4.6 | 5.0 |
| 63.2 | 8.7 | 15.6 | 7.9 | | | | 13.1 | 15.8 |
| -20.5 | 41.1 | 102.7 | 24.4 | | | | 75.2 | 146.9 |
| 13.2 | 4.2 | 14.4 | 16.1 | | | EBIT/Interest | 7.5 | 6.0 |
| (14) 3.5 | (32) 1.2 | (50) 2.9 | 3.2 | | | | (124) 2.0 | (132) 1.7 |
| -.6 | -.1 | .1 | 1.5 | | | | 1.0 | -.4 |
| | | | | | | Net Profit + Depr., Dep., Amort./Cur. Mat. L/T/D | 5.1 | 4.1 |
| | | | | | | | (33) 2.9 | (38) 1.9 |
| | | | | | | | 1.0 | .7 |
| .0 | .2 | .1 | .2 | | | Fixed/Worth | .2 | .2 |
| .4 | 1.5 | .7 | .4 | | | | .6 | .6 |
| -1.2 | -.9 | 2.2 | .8 | | | | 1.9 | 3.0 |
| .3 | 1.5 | .6 | .6 | | | Debt/Worth | .8 | .8 |
| 3.0 | 7.2 | 1.3 | 1.1 | | | | 1.8 | 1.9 |
| -3.9 | -15.6 | 3.8 | 2.3 | | | | 6.9 | 9.2 |
| 118.5 | 20.1 | 25.5 | 27.9 | | | % Profit Before Taxes/Tangible Net Worth | 32.1 | 25.9 |
| (14) 16.9 | (23) 3.6 | (47) 9.2 | (23) 6.5 | | | | (115) 11.1 | (117) 7.8 |
| -27.8 | 1.2 | -1.7 | 1.9 | | | | 1.6 | -1.6 |
| 30.9 | 3.5 | 9.4 | 11.8 | | | % Profit Before Taxes/Total Assets | 10.6 | 7.9 |
| 12.1 | .9 | 3.7 | 3.1 | | | | 3.7 | 2.0 |
| -7.2 | -6.0 | -1.1 | .4 | | | | -.2 | -3.5 |
| 301.7 | 59.2 | 64.3 | 36.4 | | | Sales/Net Fixed Assets | 48.8 | 50.3 |
| 34.9 | 29.2 | 11.4 | 10.7 | | | | 22.5 | 17.5 |
| 12.9 | 6.0 | 3.8 | 5.2 | | | | 6.1 | 7.0 |
| 8.5 | 4.1 | 4.2 | 3.0 | | | Sales/Total Assets | 3.9 | 4.1 |
| 5.3 | 2.8 | 2.6 | 2.2 | | | | 2.7 | 2.8 |
| 3.1 | 1.9 | 1.6 | 1.5 | | | | 1.7 | 1.9 |
| .6 | .2 | .7 | .6 | | | % Depr., Dep., Amort./Sales | .5 | .6 |
| (14) 1.2 | (29) 1.1 | (48) 1.4 | 1.0 | | | | (123) 1.1 | (127) 1.2 |
| 2.4 | 1.8 | 2.8 | 3.9 | | | | 2.2 | 2.6 |
| 1.8 | .7 | 1.3 | | | | % Officers', Directors' Owners' Comp/Sales | 2.1 | 2.2 |
| (11) 3.2 | (20) 4.2 | (24) 2.8 | | | | | (51) 3.5 | (55) 3.2 |
| 12.1 | 7.1 | 4.8 | | | | | 5.6 | 6.9 |
| 33985M | 153417M | 724004M | 1258167M | 102266M | 146245M | Net Sales ($) | 2508432M | 2974366M |
| 5660M | 45951M | 252020M | 569325M | 121563M | 144874M | Total Assets ($) | 1091134M | 1236129M |

© RMA 2012

M = $ thousand     MM = $ million
See Pages 9 through 22 for Explanation of Ratios and Data

### Comparative Historical Data      Current Data Sorted by Sales

| | | | | Type of Statement | | | | | | |
|---|---|---|---|---|---|---|---|---|---|---|
| 14 | 9 | 7 | | Unqualified | | | 2 | 11 | 2 | 5 |
| 26 | 33 | 26 | | Reviewed | | | 8 | 6 | 8 | 5 |
| 27 | 25 | 25 | | Compiled | 3 | 7 | 2 | 6 | 6 | 1 |
| 29 | 36 | 32 | | Tax Returns | 6 | 8 | 11 | 4 | 2 | 1 |
| 47 | 36 | 52 | | Other | 5 | 9 | 7 | 8 | 9 | 14 |
| 4/1/09-3/31/10 ALL | 4/1/10-3/31/11 ALL | 4/1/11-3/31/12 ALL | | | 41 (4/1-9/30/11) | | | 101 (10/1/11-3/31/12) | | |
| | | | | | 0-1MM | 1-3MM | 3-5MM | 5-10MM | 10-25MM | 25MM & OVER |
| 143 | 139 | 142 | | **NUMBER OF STATEMENTS** | 14 | 24 | 22 | 29 | 27 | 26 |
| % | % | % | | **ASSETS** | % | % | % | % | % | % |
| 8.7 | 7.7 | 9.7 | | Cash & Equivalents | 4.1 | 18.0 | 10.5 | 4.7 | 11.8 | 7.9 |
| 24.1 | 25.0 | 25.3 | | Trade Receivables (net) | 18.4 | 17.2 | 19.9 | 28.6 | 30.7 | 31.9 |
| 29.2 | 26.1 | 27.3 | | Inventory | 32.0 | 33.2 | 26.7 | 30.4 | 24.9 | 18.7 |
| 3.1 | 4.1 | 2.5 | | All Other Current | 7.2 | .2 | 1.4 | 1.0 | 3.2 | 4.0 |
| 65.1 | 62.9 | 64.9 | | Total Current | 61.7 | 68.7 | 58.5 | 64.8 | 70.6 | 62.5 |
| 24.5 | 25.2 | 25.3 | | Fixed Assets (net) | 30.4 | 18.7 | 33.9 | 25.5 | 21.9 | 24.9 |
| 3.7 | 3.4 | 2.4 | | Intangibles (net) | .8 | .9 | 2.3 | 2.9 | .9 | 5.9 |
| 6.7 | 8.5 | 7.4 | | All Other Non-Current | 7.0 | 11.7 | 5.3 | 6.8 | 6.6 | 6.8 |
| 100.0 | 100.0 | 100.0 | | Total | 100.0 | 100.0 | 100.0 | 100.0 | 100.0 | 100.0 |
| | | | | **LIABILITIES** | | | | | | |
| 12.6 | 15.0 | 12.4 | | Notes Payable-Short Term | 16.9 | 20.5 | 7.9 | 8.8 | 11.5 | 11.3 |
| 3.7 | 3.6 | 4.8 | | Cur. Mat.-L.T.D. | 2.2 | 13.1 | 6.4 | 3.9 | 1.5 | 1.6 |
| 16.2 | 20.6 | 20.3 | | Trade Payables | 37.9 | 15.5 | 11.8 | 21.7 | 21.9 | 19.4 |
| .3 | .3 | .2 | | Income Taxes Payable | .2 | .0 | .0 | .2 | .6 | .3 |
| 5.8 | 8.6 | 5.1 | | All Other Current | 11.4 | 5.2 | 3.7 | 2.8 | 4.9 | 5.4 |
| 38.7 | 48.1 | 42.9 | | Total Current | 68.6 | 54.4 | 29.9 | 37.5 | 40.4 | 38.1 |
| 18.1 | 18.7 | 21.8 | | Long-Term Debt | 47.5 | 16.7 | 36.8 | 21.5 | 9.5 | 13.2 |
| .1 | .6 | .4 | | Deferred Taxes | .9 | .9 | .1 | .2 | .1 | .2 |
| 9.5 | 12.5 | 7.6 | | All Other Non-Current | 4.2 | 12.8 | 5.4 | 11.8 | 7.3 | 1.9 |
| 33.6 | 20.2 | 27.4 | | Net Worth | -20.9 | 15.3 | 27.8 | 29.0 | 42.7 | 46.6 |
| 100.0 | 100.0 | 100.0 | | Total Liabilities & Net Worth | 100.0 | 100.0 | 100.0 | 100.0 | 100.0 | 100.0 |
| | | | | **INCOME DATA** | | | | | | |
| 100.0 | 100.0 | 100.0 | | Net Sales | 100.0 | 100.0 | 100.0 | 100.0 | 100.0 | 100.0 |
| 36.2 | 35.1 | 37.1 | | Gross Profit | 56.0 | 45.1 | 40.4 | 37.4 | 26.1 | 27.9 |
| 34.8 | 34.0 | 35.0 | | Operating Expenses | 53.5 | 43.3 | 38.7 | 35.7 | 23.5 | 25.6 |
| 1.5 | 1.0 | 2.1 | | Operating Profit | 2.5 | 1.8 | 1.7 | 1.7 | 2.6 | 2.3 |
| 1.4 | .8 | .8 | | All Other Expenses (net) | 2.5 | .6 | 1.2 | .8 | -.4 | .8 |
| .1 | .3 | 1.3 | | Profit Before Taxes | -.1 | 1.2 | .5 | .9 | 3.0 | 1.5 |
| | | | | **RATIOS** | | | | | | |
| 3.4 | 2.5 | 3.1 | | | 3.8 | 3.3 | 3.3 | 3.6 | 3.2 | 2.2 |
| 1.9 | 1.5 | 1.6 | | Current | 1.2 | 1.5 | 2.2 | 2.2 | 1.8 | 1.5 |
| 1.1 | 1.0 | 1.1 | | | .3 | .8 | 1.2 | .9 | 1.2 | 1.2 |
| 1.5 | 1.4 | 1.5 | | | 1.9 | 1.8 | 1.6 | 1.3 | 2.0 | 1.5 |
| .9 | .8 | .8 | | Quick | .3 | .6 | 1.0 | .7 | 1.1 | 1.0 |
| .4 | .4 | .4 | | | .1 | .3 | .2 | .5 | .6 | .6 |
| 12  30.4 | 9  42.6 | 8  48.1 | | | 0  UND | 0  UND | 6  57.1 | 17  21.0 | 13  28.3 | 28  13.2 |
| 29  12.4 | 26  13.9 | 27  13.5 | | Sales/Receivables | 6  58.8 | 16  22.3 | 27  13.7 | 29  12.7 | 23  15.7 | 39  9.4 |
| 40  9.0 | 46  7.9 | 42  8.6 | | | 32  11.4 | 39  9.4 | 47  7.7 | 42  8.6 | 40  9.1 | 64  5.7 |
| 12  31.4 | 6  59.0 | 10  36.3 | | | 0  UND | 9  38.7 | 31  11.8 | 3  108.0 | 2  235.6 | 12  29.5 |
| 48  7.6 | 48  7.7 | 49  7.4 | | Cost of Sales/Inventory | 38  9.5 | 51  7.2 | 89  4.1 | 43  8.5 | 31  11.9 | 35  10.3 |
| 156  2.3 | 121  3.0 | 135  2.7 | | | 215  1.7 | 228  1.6 | 203  1.8 | 166  2.2 | 130  2.8 | 63  5.8 |
| 10  38.1 | 13  29.0 | 11  33.0 | | | 0  UND | 0  UND | 10  38.4 | 11  33.0 | 10  36.5 | 19  18.9 |
| 23  15.6 | 31  11.8 | 30  12.2 | | Cost of Sales/Payables | 38  9.7 | 21  17.8 | 33  11.0 | 34  10.7 | 27  13.6 | 31  11.7 |
| 45  8.1 | 56  6.5 | 50  7.3 | | | 406  .9 | 46  7.9 | 85  4.3 | 54  6.7 | 38  9.7 | 41  8.8 |
| 5.0 | 6.1 | 5.6 | | | 7.1 | 6.0 | 4.1 | 4.0 | 5.6 | 5.9 |
| 10.2 | 17.1 | 12.5 | | Sales/Working Capital | 26.9 | 21.9 | 9.9 | 8.3 | 15.6 | 13.4 |
| 32.8 | 999.8 | 168.1 | | | -4.3 | -60.0 | 28.7 | NM | 30.7 | 35.2 |
| 7.1 | 8.1 | 8.3 | | | | 8.3 | 6.3 | 4.6 | 29.4 | 16.1 |
| (131) 1.8 | (133) 1.8 | (123) 2.6 | | EBIT/Interest | (19) 1.3 | (19) .7 | (27) 2.3 | (25) 4.5 | | (24) 4.2 |
| .2 | .2 | .1 | | | -.1 | -.7 | .2 | .0 | | 1.5 |
| 4.2 | 5.6 | 8.8 | | Net Profit + Depr., Dep., | | | | | | 27.1 |
| (35) 1.7 | (25) 2.2 | (21) 2.6 | | Amort./Cur. Mat. L/T/D | | | | | | (10) 2.7 |
| .9 | .6 | 1.6 | | | | | | | | 1.6 |
| .2 | .2 | .1 | | | .1 | .1 | .1 | .2 | .1 | .2 |
| .6 | .6 | .6 | | Fixed/Worth | .8 | 4.3 | 1.1 | .8 | .3 | .6 |
| 3.3 | -19.0 | 7.5 | | | -.6 | -1.7 | NM | -11.2 | 1.0 | 1.1 |
| .7 | .9 | .7 | | | 1.6 | 1.0 | .5 | .6 | .5 | .7 |
| 1.6 | 2.0 | 1.7 | | Debt/Worth | 7.2 | 14.9 | 2.3 | 1.5 | 1.1 | 1.3 |
| 7.5 | -28.0 | 20.7 | | | -2.2 | -28.3 | NM | -35.5 | 2.6 | 2.3 |
| 27.4 | 31.6 | 27.8 | | % Profit Before Taxes/Tangible | | 56.7 | 16.7 | 11.9 | 34.5 | 27.8 |
| (116) 8.8 | (101) 8.7 | (109) 6.7 | | Net Worth | (14) 20.4 | (17) 1.2 | (20) 4.3 | (24) 10.9 | (25) 10.1 | |
| -.9 | .2 | -.1 | | | 1.8 | -12.5 | 1.2 | 4.3 | 2.3 | |
| 10.1 | 7.6 | 9.8 | | % Profit Before Taxes/Total | 16.8 | 14.4 | 8.2 | 6.1 | 19.2 | 11.4 |
| 2.6 | 1.7 | 2.3 | | Assets | .1 | 1.5 | -.2 | 2.0 | 4.1 | 5.1 |
| -2.4 | -1.8 | -3.3 | | | -14.3 | -.4 | -6.0 | -2.2 | -3.4 | .5 |
| 56.4 | 63.1 | 70.3 | | | 172.1 | 150.6 | 92.8 | 48.0 | 103.8 | 50.5 |
| 15.6 | 19.1 | 16.9 | | Sales/Net Fixed Assets | 19.2 | 21.3 | 5.2 | 19.0 | 20.4 | 13.0 |
| 5.2 | 6.3 | 5.5 | | | 3.9 | 6.9 | 2.8 | 5.7 | 6.3 | 7.1 |
| 4.2 | 4.1 | 4.4 | | | 4.9 | 5.8 | 3.0 | 4.3 | 5.4 | 4.0 |
| 2.5 | 2.7 | 2.6 | | Sales/Total Assets | 2.8 | 2.7 | 2.2 | 2.6 | 3.3 | 2.6 |
| 1.7 | 1.8 | 1.7 | | | 1.0 | 1.2 | 1.2 | 1.8 | 2.2 | 1.9 |
| .7 | .7 | .6 | | | .7 | .4 | .4 | .5 | .4 | .6 |
| (126) 1.4 | (124) 1.4 | (118) 1.2 | | % Depr., Dep., Amort./Sales | (10) 1.5 | (16) 1.7 | (19) 1.5 | (25) 1.0 | (24) .9 | (24) 1.0 |
| 3.5 | 2.9 | 2.5 | | | 5.1 | 3.6 | 3.0 | 2.2 | 2.7 | 3.3 |
| 1.8 | 1.9 | 1.6 | | % Officers', Directors' | | 3.2 | 2.1 | 1.6 | | |
| (59) 2.9 | (70) 2.9 | (60) 3.2 | | Owners' Comp/Sales | (15) 4.4 | (14) 3.7 | (11) 2.5 | | | |
| 6.4 | 4.8 | 6.0 | | | | 11.6 | 5.3 | 4.2 | | |
| 2864066M | 2274555M | 2418084M | | Net Sales ($) | 7176M | 46806M | 86484M | 215700M | 480773M | 1581145M |
| 1374721M | 853644M | 1139393M | | Total Assets ($) | 4989M | 21980M | 56875M | 92983M | 184561M | 778005M |

## Current Data Sorted by Assets      Comparative Historical Data

| 0-500M | 500M-2MM | 2-10MM | 10-50MM | 50-100MM | 100-250MM | Type of Statement | 4/1/07-3/31/08 ALL | 4/1/08-3/31/09 ALL |
|---|---|---|---|---|---|---|---|---|
| | | 4 | 8 | 6 | 1 | Unqualified | 27 | 25 |
| | 3 | 28 | 9 | | | Reviewed | 36 | 35 |
| 2 | 3 | 9 | 2 | | | Compiled | 9 | 14 |
| 3 | 7 | 9 | | | | Tax Returns | 10 | 17 |
| 1 | 4 | 9 | 14 | 1 | 3 | Other | 26 | 29 |
| | 19 (4/1-9/30/11) | | 107 (10/1/11-3/31/12) | | | | | |
| 6 | 17 | 59 | 33 | 7 | 4 | NUMBER OF STATEMENTS | 108 | 120 |
| % | % | % | % | % | % | **ASSETS** | % | % |
| | 7.8 | 11.0 | 9.0 | | | Cash & Equivalents | 8.2 | 8.4 |
| | 17.7 | 29.9 | 31.4 | | | Trade Receivables (net) | 31.5 | 31.1 |
| | 49.4 | 40.8 | 30.1 | | | Inventory | 36.9 | 37.3 |
| | 2.6 | 2.2 | 3.6 | | | All Other Current | 2.9 | 2.8 |
| | 77.5 | 83.9 | 74.1 | | | Total Current | 79.4 | 79.5 |
| | 13.4 | 8.1 | 14.6 | | | Fixed Assets (net) | 11.1 | 12.8 |
| | .2 | .9 | 2.1 | | | Intangibles (net) | 1.6 | 1.4 |
| | 8.8 | 7.1 | 9.1 | | | All Other Non-Current | 7.9 | 6.3 |
| | 100.0 | 100.0 | 100.0 | | | Total | 100.0 | 100.0 |
| | | | | | | **LIABILITIES** | | |
| | 19.3 | 18.1 | 24.5 | | | Notes Payable-Short Term | 23.5 | 20.2 |
| | 1.6 | 1.3 | 1.3 | | | Cur. Mat.-L.T.D. | 1.8 | 2.5 |
| | 18.3 | 21.6 | 13.3 | | | Trade Payables | 17.5 | 20.2 |
| | .0 | .1 | .1 | | | Income Taxes Payable | .2 | .1 |
| | 8.5 | 7.3 | 10.0 | | | All Other Current | 6.6 | 7.3 |
| | 47.7 | 48.3 | 49.2 | | | Total Current | 49.5 | 50.5 |
| | 15.4 | 4.3 | 7.1 | | | Long-Term Debt | 9.6 | 11.1 |
| | .0 | .3 | .2 | | | Deferred Taxes | .2 | .1 |
| | 10.6 | 3.2 | 2.5 | | | All Other Non-Current | 3.5 | 3.5 |
| | 26.3 | 43.9 | 41.2 | | | Net Worth | 37.2 | 34.9 |
| | 100.0 | 100.0 | 100.0 | | | Total Liabilities & Net Worth | 100.0 | 100.0 |
| | | | | | | **INCOME DATA** | | |
| | 100.0 | 100.0 | 100.0 | | | Net Sales | 100.0 | 100.0 |
| | 17.9 | 9.7 | 12.3 | | | Gross Profit | 9.6 | 11.1 |
| | 14.8 | 8.5 | 10.0 | | | Operating Expenses | 7.9 | 10.2 |
| | 3.1 | 1.2 | 2.4 | | | Operating Profit | 1.7 | .9 |
| | .0 | -.1 | .2 | | | All Other Expenses (net) | -.1 | .4 |
| | 3.1 | 1.4 | 2.2 | | | Profit Before Taxes | 1.8 | .5 |
| | | | | | | **RATIOS** | | |
| | 3.6 | 2.2 | 2.5 | | | | 2.5 | 2.7 |
| | 2.4 | 1.7 | 1.4 | | | Current | 1.5 | 1.6 |
| | 1.3 | 1.3 | 1.2 | | | | 1.1 | 1.2 |
| | 2.1 | 1.2 | 1.2 | | | | 1.3 | 1.4 |
| | (16) .8 | .8 | .8 | | | Quick | .7 | .8 |
| | .2 | .5 | .7 | | | | .5 | .5 |
| | 2 192.6 | 6 57.1 | 8 43.7 | | | | 9 42.2 | 9 40.8 |
| | 6 62.5 | 12 31.4 | 13 27.1 | | | Sales/Receivables | 15 24.6 | 15 25.0 |
| | 14 25.2 | 18 19.8 | 19 19.7 | | | | 21 17.4 | 22 16.5 |
| | 17 21.4 | 11 32.9 | 7 49.9 | | | | 11 33.1 | 11 34.3 |
| | 28 13.1 | 19 19.4 | 12 29.4 | | | Cost of Sales/Inventory | 18 20.3 | 16 23.5 |
| | 68 5.4 | 29 12.4 | 23 15.9 | | | | 27 13.3 | 30 12.0 |
| | 3 123.9 | 3 129.9 | 4 104.1 | | | | 4 102.9 | 4 84.4 |
| | 7 51.7 | 9 41.4 | 5 69.5 | | | Cost of Sales/Payables | 8 45.1 | 9 42.3 |
| | 21 17.8 | 15 24.5 | 11 33.9 | | | | 15 23.7 | 16 22.7 |
| | 7.3 | 14.9 | 15.2 | | | | 14.4 | 14.6 |
| | 24.7 | 23.5 | 39.2 | | | Sales/Working Capital | 32.3 | 32.2 |
| | 104.8 | 43.3 | 64.3 | | | | 92.9 | 99.1 |
| | 10.3 | 10.9 | 20.3 | | | | 6.5 | 7.0 |
| | (15) 4.0 | (49) 2.8 | (32) 3.9 | | | EBIT/Interest | (102) 2.5 | (110) 2.6 |
| | .5 | 1.6 | 3.3 | | | | 1.5 | 1.4 |
| | | 11.9 | 14.5 | | | | 5.8 | 6.0 |
| | | (14) 3.9 | (10) 4.2 | | | Net Profit + Depr., Dep., Amort./Cur. Mat. L/T/D | (35) 2.9 | (28) 2.0 |
| | | 1.5 | 2.9 | | | | 1.4 | .3 |
| | .1 | .0 | .1 | | | | .1 | .1 |
| | .2 | .1 | .3 | | | Fixed/Worth | .2 | .3 |
| | 1.1 | .3 | .7 | | | | .8 | .8 |
| | .8 | .7 | .6 | | | | .8 | .8 |
| | 1.9 | 1.7 | 1.9 | | | Debt/Worth | 2.4 | 2.2 |
| | 11.7 | 2.9 | 3.5 | | | | 4.9 | 4.8 |
| | 77.1 | 24.0 | 32.8 | | | | 26.2 | 25.8 |
| | (16) 41.5 | 10.6 | 21.3 | | | % Profit Before Taxes/Tangible Net Worth | (102) 12.4 | (111) 14.2 |
| | 4.4 | 3.7 | 10.0 | | | | 4.3 | 3.8 |
| | 20.1 | 10.5 | 13.4 | | | | 7.7 | 9.1 |
| | 10.5 | 3.6 | 6.4 | | | % Profit Before Taxes/Total Assets | 3.9 | 3.4 |
| | -.1 | 1.3 | 3.2 | | | | 1.6 | 1.1 |
| | 203.2 | 684.8 | 176.1 | | | | 229.6 | 243.1 |
| | 96.5 | 202.3 | 54.1 | | | Sales/Net Fixed Assets | 120.7 | 95.5 |
| | 40.3 | 76.6 | 30.5 | | | | 47.3 | 41.5 |
| | 14.0 | 12.0 | 12.2 | | | | 9.5 | 10.3 |
| | 7.4 | 8.3 | 9.2 | | | Sales/Total Assets | 7.9 | 8.3 |
| | 3.0 | 6.4 | 4.0 | | | | 5.4 | 5.4 |
| | .2 | .1 | .1 | | | | .1 | .1 |
| | (14) .3 | (45) .2 | (31) .3 | | | % Depr., Dep., Amort./Sales | (100) .2 | (105) .2 |
| | .6 | .3 | .5 | | | | .4 | .4 |
| | | .3 | | | | | .3 | .4 |
| | | (35) .7 | (10) 1.2 | | | % Officers', Directors' Owners' Comp/Sales | (37) .8 | (51) .8 |
| | | 1.1 | 3.7 | | | | 1.8 | 1.4 |
| 15299M | 156308M | 2613462M | 5885076M | 4079315M | 4432082M | Net Sales ($) | 19840027M | 14055654M |
| 1298M | 19624M | 295017M | 718880M | 518972M | 533477M | Total Assets ($) | 2550502M | 1868636M |

M = $ thousand     MM = $ million
See Pages 9 through 22 for Explanation of Ratios and Data

## Comparative Historical Data | Current Data Sorted by Sales

| | | | Type of Statement | 0-1MM | 1-3MM | 3-5MM | 5-10MM | 10-25MM | 25MM & OVER |
|---|---|---|---|---|---|---|---|---|---|
| 27 | 21 | 19 | Unqualified | | | | | 2 | 17 |
| 45 | 35 | 40 | Reviewed | | | | 1 | 10 | 29 |
| 22 | 17 | 16 | Compiled | | 2 | 1 | 2 | 2 | 9 |
| 20 | 21 | 19 | Tax Returns | | 5 | 2 | 1 | 4 | 7 |
| 37 | 36 | 32 | Other | 1 | 1 | 1 | | 6 | 23 |
| 4/1/09-3/31/10 ALL | 4/1/10-3/31/11 ALL | 4/1/11-3/31/12 ALL | | 19 (4/1-9/30/11) | | | 107 (10/1/11-3/31/12) | | |
| 151 | 130 | 126 | **NUMBER OF STATEMENTS** | 1 | 8 | 4 | 4 | 24 | 85 |
| % | % | % | **ASSETS** | % | % | % | % | % | % |
| 9.0 | 12.2 | 10.7 | Cash & Equivalents | | | | | 8.1 | 10.1 |
| 32.0 | 29.0 | 28.3 | Trade Receivables (net) | | | | | 22.6 | 32.2 |
| 37.7 | 36.8 | 37.4 | Inventory | | | | | 46.7 | 33.8 |
| 2.7 | 2.3 | 3.0 | All Other Current | | | | | 2.8 | 3.4 |
| 81.5 | 80.3 | 79.3 | Total Current | | | | | 80.2 | 79.5 |
| 10.3 | 11.7 | 11.0 | Fixed Assets (net) | | | | | 10.5 | 10.9 |
| 1.6 | 2.1 | 1.2 | Intangibles (net) | | | | | .6 | 1.5 |
| 6.6 | 5.9 | 8.5 | All Other Non-Current | | | | | 8.6 | 8.1 |
| 100.0 | 100.0 | 100.0 | Total | | | | | 100.0 | 100.0 |
| | | | **LIABILITIES** | | | | | | |
| 18.4 | 15.5 | 18.9 | Notes Payable-Short Term | | | | | 19.6 | 20.5 |
| 2.0 | 1.4 | 1.3 | Cur. Mat.-L.T.D. | | | | | 1.4 | 1.3 |
| 19.2 | 19.9 | 18.9 | Trade Payables | | | | | 18.2 | 18.4 |
| .4 | .3 | .1 | Income Taxes Payable | | | | | .1 | .2 |
| 8.4 | 7.4 | 8.1 | All Other Current | | | | | 11.4 | 7.7 |
| 48.4 | 44.5 | 47.3 | Total Current | | | | | 50.7 | 48.0 |
| 7.2 | 8.8 | 7.5 | Long-Term Debt | | | | | 6.9 | 6.6 |
| .1 | .2 | .2 | Deferred Taxes | | | | | .0 | .3 |
| 4.6 | 4.3 | 3.7 | All Other Non-Current | | | | | 5.6 | 2.9 |
| 39.7 | 42.2 | 41.3 | Net Worth | | | | | 36.8 | 42.3 |
| 100.0 | 100.0 | 100.0 | Total Liabilities & Net Worth | | | | | 100.0 | 100.0 |
| | | | **INCOME DATA** | | | | | | |
| 100.0 | 100.0 | 100.0 | Net Sales | | | | | 100.0 | 100.0 |
| 10.3 | 10.1 | 11.8 | Gross Profit | | | | | 12.7 | 9.0 |
| 8.2 | 8.8 | 9.8 | Operating Expenses | | | | | 11.5 | 7.5 |
| 2.1 | 1.3 | 2.0 | Operating Profit | | | | | 1.2 | 1.5 |
| .0 | .1 | .0 | All Other Expenses (net) | | | | | .6 | .0 |
| 2.1 | 1.2 | 2.0 | Profit Before Taxes | | | | | .6 | 1.4 |
| | | | **RATIOS** | | | | | | |
| 2.6 | 2.7 | 2.7 | Current | | | | | 3.1 | 2.5 |
| 1.7 | 1.8 | 1.7 | | | | | | 1.9 | 1.6 |
| 1.2 | 1.2 | 1.3 | | | | | | 1.3 | 1.3 |
| 1.5 | 1.6 | 1.3 | Quick | | | | | 1.2 | 1.2 |
| .8 (129) | .9 (125) | .8 | | | | | | .8 | .8 |
| .5 | .6 | .5 | | | | | | .2 | .6 |
| 8  44.3 | 7  51.6 | 6  56.4 | Sales/Receivables | | | | | 2  148.3 | 8  48.3 |
| 14  25.7 | 12  29.3 | 12  30.8 | | | | | | 12  31.0 | 12  30.3 |
| 19  19.0 | 18  20.7 | 17  20.9 | | | | | | 35  10.4 | 16  22.3 |
| 11  32.6 | 10  35.3 | 11  34.2 | Cost of Sales/Inventory | | | | | 19  19.2 | 9  40.3 |
| 17  21.3 | 16  22.2 | 16  22.5 | | | | | | 24  15.5 | 13  28.1 |
| 29  12.7 | 29  12.8 | 29  12.5 | | | | | | 51  7.2 | 21  17.8 |
| 3  126.1 | 3  113.7 | 4  102.9 | Cost of Sales/Payables | | | | | 3  107.4 | 3  108.5 |
| 8  47.2 | 8  47.5 | 8  46.9 | | | | | | 11  34.2 | 6  56.9 |
| 14  26.2 | 14  25.8 | 14  25.9 | | | | | | 20  18.3 | 12  31.3 |
| 14.6 | 16.1 | 14.8 | Sales/Working Capital | | | | | 12.0 | 19.3 |
| 28.5 | 28.2 | 27.6 | | | | | | 17.6 | 30.9 |
| 64.2 | 53.2 | 55.6 | | | | | | 27.7 | 57.8 |
| 17.9 | 12.1 | 11.6 | EBIT/Interest | | | | | 10.4 | 11.8 |
| (136) 5.9 | (106) 4.7 | (108) 3.9 | | | | | | (22) 3.7 | (75) 3.8 |
| 2.6 | 2.0 | 1.9 | | | | | | .4 | 2.1 |
| 15.8 | 15.8 | 15.0 | Net Profit + Depr., Dep., Amort./Cur. Mat. L/T/D | | | | | | 17.9 |
| (35) 6.7 | (29) 8.1 | (30) 5.0 | | | | | | | (26) 5.0 |
| 2.9 | 2.6 | 2.1 | | | | | | | 2.1 |
| .1 | .1 | .1 | Fixed/Worth | | | | | .1 | .1 |
| .2 | .2 | .2 | | | | | | .2 | .2 |
| .6 | .5 | .5 | | | | | | .5 | .5 |
| .7 | .6 | .7 | Debt/Worth | | | | | .6 | .7 |
| 1.8 | 1.8 | 1.7 | | | | | | 1.1 | 1.8 |
| 4.3 | 3.9 | 3.4 | | | | | | 4.5 | 3.4 |
| 44.5 | 35.4 | 38.9 | % Profit Before Taxes/Tangible Net Worth | | | | | 39.8 | 29.1 |
| (145) 20.2 | (127) 18.5 | (125) 15.8 | | | | | | (23) 3.4 | 15.8 |
| 9.3 | 7.5 | 6.0 | | | | | | -.5 | 8.0 |
| 14.3 | 13.9 | 12.7 | % Profit Before Taxes/Total Assets | | | | | 9.9 | 12.0 |
| 7.2 | 6.4 | 4.9 | | | | | | 2.0 | 4.8 |
| 3.3 | 2.5 | 1.7 | | | | | | -.6 | 2.4 |
| 386.3 | 370.3 | 379.5 | Sales/Net Fixed Assets | | | | | 237.6 | 359.8 |
| 130.4 | 113.0 | 119.2 | | | | | | 105.2 | 128.3 |
| 55.2 | 46.3 | 47.8 | | | | | | 40.4 | 49.3 |
| 11.5 | 11.6 | 12.0 | Sales/Total Assets | | | | | 10.6 | 12.2 |
| 8.4 | 8.6 | 9.0 | | | | | | 7.3 | 9.4 |
| 5.7 | 5.6 | 5.5 | | | | | | 2.5 | 6.8 |
| .1 | .1 | .1 | % Depr., Dep., Amort./Sales | | | | | .1 | .1 |
| (125) .2 | (108) .2 | (104) .2 | | | | | | (22) .3 | (71) .2 |
| .4 | .4 | .4 | | | | | | .5 | .3 |
| .3 | .3 | .3 | % Officers', Directors' Owners' Comp/Sales | | | | | .4 | .3 |
| (68) .6 | (55) .8 | (54) .8 | | | | | | (11) .7 | (37) .5 |
| 1.3 | 1.3 | 1.3 | | | | | | 1.3 | 1.1 |
| 19811176M | 17958672M | 17181542M | Net Sales ($) | 696M | 17925M | 17184M | 35815M | 412494M | 16697428M |
| 2973422M | 2197317M | 2087268M | Total Assets ($) | 326M | 5732M | 3671M | 8533M | 156508M | 1912498M |

M = $ thousand     MM = $ million
See Pages 9 through 22 for Explanation of Ratios and Data

## Current Data Sorted by Assets       Comparative Historical Data

|  |  |  |  |  |  | Type of Statement |  |  |
|---|---|---|---|---|---|---|---|---|
|  |  |  | 2 | 1 |  | Unqualified | 9 | 7 |
|  | 1 |  | 1 |  |  | Reviewed | 9 | 10 |
|  |  | 8 | 1 |  |  | Compiled | 5 | 9 |
| 3 | 3 | 3 |  |  |  | Tax Returns | 14 | 12 |
|  | 6 | 3 |  |  |  | Other | 17 | 19 |
| 1 | 1 | 5 |  |  | 1 |  | 4/1/07- | 4/1/08- |
|  | 5 (4/1-9/30/11) |  | 40 (10/1/11-3/31/12) |  |  |  | 3/31/08 | 3/31/09 |
| 0-500M | 500M-2MM | 2-10MM | 10-50MM | 50-100MM | 100-250MM |  | ALL | ALL |
| 4 | 11 | 19 | 9 | 1 | 1 | NUMBER OF STATEMENTS | 54 | 57 |
| % | % | % | % | % | % | ASSETS | % | % |
|  | 4.0 | 7.6 |  |  |  | Cash & Equivalents | 5.8 | 4.5 |
|  | 28.4 | 32.0 |  |  |  | Trade Receivables (net) | 30.9 | 30.6 |
|  | 45.8 | 35.7 |  |  |  | Inventory | 38.4 | 40.4 |
|  | 2.6 | 2.1 |  |  |  | All Other Current | 4.1 | 3.6 |
|  | 80.8 | 77.4 |  |  |  | Total Current | 79.2 | 79.1 |
|  | 13.4 | 14.3 |  |  |  | Fixed Assets (net) | 10.9 | 11.0 |
|  | 3.7 | 4.4 |  |  |  | Intangibles (net) | 3.1 | 4.2 |
|  | 2.1 | 4.0 |  |  |  | All Other Non-Current | 6.8 | 5.6 |
|  | 100.0 | 100.0 |  |  |  | Total | 100.0 | 100.0 |
|  |  |  |  |  |  | LIABILITIES |  |  |
|  | 20.1 | 10.7 |  |  |  | Notes Payable-Short Term | 14.3 | 16.8 |
|  | 3.7 | 2.0 |  |  |  | Cur. Mat.-L.T.D. | 2.3 | 2.8 |
|  | 35.0 | 23.0 |  |  |  | Trade Payables | 28.1 | 27.0 |
|  | .0 | .0 |  |  |  | Income Taxes Payable | .2 | .1 |
|  | 11.5 | 4.8 |  |  |  | All Other Current | 9.9 | 7.0 |
|  | 70.3 | 40.7 |  |  |  | Total Current | 54.9 | 53.7 |
|  | 17.5 | 10.7 |  |  |  | Long-Term Debt | 11.6 | 11.6 |
|  | .0 | .5 |  |  |  | Deferred Taxes | .3 | .2 |
|  | 3.2 | 7.6 |  |  |  | All Other Non-Current | 5.6 | 7.0 |
|  | 9.0 | 40.5 |  |  |  | Net Worth | 27.6 | 27.5 |
|  | 100.0 | 100.0 |  |  |  | Total Liabilties & Net Worth | 100.0 | 100.0 |
|  |  |  |  |  |  | INCOME DATA |  |  |
|  | 100.0 | 100.0 |  |  |  | Net Sales | 100.0 | 100.0 |
|  | 34.7 | 31.3 |  |  |  | Gross Profit | 30.2 | 31.4 |
|  | 32.6 | 26.5 |  |  |  | Operating Expenses | 27.2 | 29.3 |
|  | 2.1 | 4.7 |  |  |  | Operating Profit | 3.1 | 2.1 |
|  | -1.0 | .1 |  |  |  | All Other Expenses (net) | .3 | .7 |
|  | 3.0 | 4.7 |  |  |  | Profit Before Taxes | 2.8 | 1.4 |
|  |  |  |  |  |  | RATIOS |  |  |
|  | 1.7 | 2.7 |  |  |  |  | 2.0 | 2.2 |
|  | 1.2 | 2.0 |  |  |  | Current | 1.4 | 1.4 |
|  | .8 | 1.5 |  |  |  |  | 1.1 | 1.2 |
|  | .7 | 1.4 |  |  |  |  | .9 | .9 |
|  | .5 | .8 |  |  |  | Quick | .6 | .6 |
|  | .3 | .7 |  |  |  |  | .4 | .5 |
| 25 | 14.4 | 29 | 12.6 |  |  | Sales/Receivables | 28   13.0 | 32   11.4 |
| 42 | 8.7 | 43 | 8.5 |  |  |  | 36   10.0 | 41   8.9 |
| 44 | 8.3 | 51 | 7.2 |  |  |  | 49   7.4 | 51   7.1 |
| 45 | 8.1 | 38 | 9.7 |  |  | Cost of Sales/Inventory | 51   7.1 | 54   6.8 |
| 114 | 3.2 | 69 | 5.3 |  |  |  | 66   5.5 | 85   4.3 |
| 166 | 2.2 | 111 | 3.3 |  |  |  | 111   3.3 | 114   3.2 |
| 14 | 27.0 | 36 | 10.2 |  |  | Cost of Sales/Payables | 26   14.1 | 27   13.5 |
| 76 | 4.8 | 44 | 8.3 |  |  |  | 39   9.5 | 44   8.2 |
| 126 | 2.9 | 56 | 6.5 |  |  |  | 76   4.8 | 76   4.8 |
|  | 7.8 | 5.4 |  |  |  | Sales/Working Capital | 6.9 | 6.6 |
|  | 102.0 | 7.8 |  |  |  |  | 12.3 | 11.2 |
|  | -23.4 | 10.8 |  |  |  |  | 29.9 | 24.8 |
|  | 13.0 | 21.2 |  |  |  | EBIT/Interest | 9.6 | 6.6 |
|  | 5.6 | (17) | 7.7 |  |  |  | (52)   3.3 | (53)   1.6 |
|  | 2.0 | 2.7 |  |  |  |  | 1.5 | -.3 |
|  |  |  |  |  |  | Net Profit + Depr., Dep., | 13.6 | 7.1 |
|  |  |  |  |  |  | Amort./Cur. Mat. L/T/D | (15)   3.9 | (15)   2.3 |
|  |  |  |  |  |  |  | 1.7 | 1.3 |
|  | .2 | .1 |  |  |  | Fixed/Worth | .1 | .2 |
|  | 3.3 | .3 |  |  |  |  | .3 | .4 |
|  | -.3 | 1.3 |  |  |  |  | 1.8 | 1.3 |
|  | 1.6 | .7 |  |  |  | Debt/Worth | 1.2 | 1.5 |
|  | 4.9 | 1.9 |  |  |  |  | 3.0 | 3.4 |
|  | -4.1 | 3.8 |  |  |  |  | 11.5 | 13.6 |
|  |  | 42.9 |  |  |  | % Profit Before Taxes/Tangible | 38.3 | 44.0 |
|  | (18) | 25.2 |  |  |  | Net Worth | (44)   23.1 | (47)   14.0 |
|  |  | 10.1 |  |  |  |  | 11.0 | .7 |
|  | 8.7 | 22.2 |  |  |  | % Profit Before Taxes/Total | 12.2 | 11.4 |
|  | 4.1 | 8.1 |  |  |  | Assets | 5.5 | 2.6 |
|  | 1.3 | 2.7 |  |  |  |  | 1.4 | -3.3 |
|  | 50.5 | 62.9 |  |  |  | Sales/Net Fixed Assets | 117.9 | 65.2 |
|  | 41.0 | 32.3 |  |  |  |  | 41.8 | 31.5 |
|  | 17.0 | 12.4 |  |  |  |  | 17.9 | 19.3 |
|  | 4.2 | 3.5 |  |  |  | Sales/Total Assets | 3.4 | 3.5 |
|  | 2.5 | 3.0 |  |  |  |  | 2.9 | 2.5 |
|  | 2.1 | 1.8 |  |  |  |  | 2.3 | 2.0 |
|  |  | .4 |  |  |  | % Depr., Dep., Amort./Sales | .4 | .5 |
|  | (15) | .6 |  |  |  |  | (48)   .6 | (52)   1.0 |
|  |  | 1.5 |  |  |  |  | 1.0 | 1.4 |
|  |  | 1.7 |  |  |  | % Officers', Directors' | 1.7 | 1.7 |
|  | (10) | 2.7 |  |  |  | Owners' Comp/Sales | (25)   3.4 | (25)   3.0 |
|  |  | 6.2 |  |  |  |  | 5.7 | 3.7 |
| 3306M | 37006M | 261186M | 557848M | 76739M | 199850M | Net Sales ($) | 2141153M | 1486125M |
| 984M | 12188M | 94420M | 247918M | 56160M | 178451M | Total Assets ($) | 847571M | 609115M |

M = $ thousand     MM = $ million
See Pages 9 through 22 for Explanation of Ratios and Data

## Comparative Historical Data      Current Data Sorted by Sales

**Type of Statement**

| Type of Statement | 4/1/09-3/31/10 ALL | 4/1/10-3/31/11 ALL | 4/1/11-3/31/12 ALL | 0-1MM | 1-3MM | 3-5MM | 5-10MM | 10-25MM | 25MM & OVER |
|---|---|---|---|---|---|---|---|---|---|
| Unqualified | 5 | 5 | 4 | | | | | 1 | 3 |
| Reviewed | 11 | 9 | 9 | | 1 | | 1 | 7 | 1 |
| Compiled | 13 | 7 | 10 | 2 | 2 | | 2 | 2 | 2 |
| Tax Returns | 6 | 9 | 9 | | 3 | 2 | 3 | 1 | |
| Other | 22 | 20 | 13 | 1 | | 2 | 2 | 2 | 5 |
| | | | | 3 | 6 | 4 | 8 | 13 | 11 |
| **NUMBER OF STATEMENTS** | 57 | 50 | 45 | 3 | 6 | 4 | 8 | 13 | 11 |

(Historical periods: 4/1/09-3/31/10 ALL, 4/1/10-3/31/11 ALL, 4/1/11-3/31/12 ALL. Current data: 5 (4/1-9/30/11) and 40 (10/1/11-3/31/12).)

**ASSETS (%)**

| | H1 | H2 | H3 | 10-25MM | 25MM & OVER |
|---|---|---|---|---|---|
| Cash & Equivalents | 6.1 | 7.3 | 5.6 | 7.9 | 4.9 |
| Trade Receivables (net) | 31.4 | 31.3 | 28.9 | 34.3 | 24.0 |
| Inventory | 39.5 | 36.8 | 40.5 | 35.5 | 38.7 |
| All Other Current | 3.9 | 3.6 | 3.4 | 3.8 | 6.4 |
| Total Current | 80.9 | 79.0 | 78.5 | 81.6 | 74.1 |
| Fixed Assets (net) | 10.0 | 11.0 | 12.8 | 7.9 | 12.8 |
| Intangibles (net) | 4.5 | 5.3 | 5.0 | 6.3 | 7.7 |
| All Other Non-Current | 4.6 | 4.7 | 3.7 | 4.3 | 5.5 |
| Total | 100.0 | 100.0 | 100.0 | 100.0 | 100.0 |

**LIABILITIES**

| | H1 | H2 | H3 | 10-25MM | 25MM & OVER |
|---|---|---|---|---|---|
| Notes Payable-Short Term | 15.5 | 14.9 | 13.5 | 11.6 | 7.8 |
| Cur. Mat.-L.T.D. | 2.2 | 2.1 | 2.4 | 2.6 | 1.2 |
| Trade Payables | 28.6 | 28.7 | 25.7 | 24.4 | 20.2 |
| Income Taxes Payable | .1 | .3 | .0 | .0 | .1 |
| All Other Current | 4.4 | 5.6 | 6.8 | 4.5 | 6.0 |
| Total Current | 50.8 | 51.6 | 48.4 | 43.0 | 35.3 |
| Long-Term Debt | 14.8 | 13.0 | 13.0 | 4.8 | 9.4 |
| Deferred Taxes | .3 | .3 | .6 | .5 | 1.7 |
| All Other Non-Current | 5.3 | 8.2 | 7.1 | 7.7 | 10.6 |
| Net Worth | 28.8 | 26.8 | 30.9 | 44.0 | 42.9 |
| Total Liabilities & Net Worth | 100.0 | 100.0 | 100.0 | 100.0 | 100.0 |

**INCOME DATA**

| | H1 | H2 | H3 | 10-25MM | 25MM & OVER |
|---|---|---|---|---|---|
| Net Sales | 100.0 | 100.0 | 100.0 | 100.0 | 100.0 |
| Gross Profit | 31.8 | 32.2 | 33.0 | 34.1 | 32.3 |
| Operating Expenses | 29.7 | 28.9 | 29.0 | 27.5 | 27.7 |
| Operating Profit | 2.1 | 3.4 | 4.1 | 6.6 | 4.6 |
| All Other Expenses (net) | .0 | .5 | .0 | .5 | -.5 |
| Profit Before Taxes | 2.1 | 2.9 | 4.1 | 6.1 | 5.1 |

**RATIOS**

| | H1 | H2 | H3 | 10-25MM | 25MM & OVER |
|---|---|---|---|---|---|
| Current | 2.5 | 2.6 | 2.5 | 3.0 | 3.7 |
| | 1.6 | 1.7 | 1.7 | 2.2 | 2.4 |
| | 1.2 | 1.2 | 1.3 | 1.5 | 1.7 |
| Quick | 1.4 | 1.3 | 1.2 | 1.6 | 1.4 |
| | .7 | .7 | .7 | .8 | .9 |
| | .5 | .5 | .5 | .7 | .5 |
| Sales/Receivables | 32  11.6 | 33  10.9 | 30  12.3 | 39  9.4 | 30  12.3 |
| | 39  9.5 | 43  8.5 | 41  8.8 | 45  8.2 | 36  10.1 |
| | 52  7.1 | 59  6.2 | 51  7.2 | 56  6.5 | 53  6.9 |
| Cost of Sales/Inventory | 60  6.1 | 48  7.6 | 52  7.0 | 33  11.1 | 57  6.4 |
| | 80  4.6 | 80  4.5 | 96  3.8 | 76  4.8 | 94  3.9 |
| | 127  2.9 | 112  3.2 | 130  2.8 | 114  3.2 | 140  2.6 |
| Cost of Sales/Payables | 28  13.0 | 28  13.2 | 21  17.4 | 22  16.9 | 18  20.3 |
| | 57  6.4 | 52  7.1 | 44  8.3 | 50  7.3 | 35  10.3 |
| | 78  4.7 | 83  4.4 | 78  4.7 | 78  4.7 | 62  5.9 |
| Sales/Working Capital | 5.8 | 5.1 | 5.4 | 4.5 | 3.6 |
| | 8.5 | 10.6 | 8.4 | 7.5 | 5.9 |
| | 19.3 | 33.3 | 15.7 | 10.8 | 8.9 |
| EBIT/Interest | 10.9 | 10.3 | 15.5 | 94.2 | 119.9 |
| | (49) 2.6 | (46) 3.1 | (42) 4.7 | (12) 16.8 | (10) 5.9 |
| | .6 | 1.2 | 2.5 | 3.9 | 3.5 |
| Net Profit + Depr., Dep., Amort./Cur. Mat. L/T/D | | 25.6 | 14.2 | | |
| | (10) 1.9 | (11) 4.2 | | | |
| | .9 | 1.5 | | | |
| Fixed/Worth | .1 | .2 | .2 | .1 | .1 |
| | .3 | .5 | .4 | .2 | .4 |
| | 1.2 | -3.7 | 3.4 | .3 | 2.4 |
| Debt/Worth | 1.4 | 1.0 | .9 | .6 | .3 |
| | 3.4 | 3.7 | 2.7 | 1.5 | 1.1 |
| | 10.2 | -46.0 | 62.7 | 3.3 | 107.2 |
| % Profit Before Taxes/Tangible Net Worth | 49.8 | 34.6 | 42.0 | 59.9 | |
| | (49) 14.9 | (36) 12.9 | (35) 17.9 | (12) 30.6 | |
| | -.7 | 3.7 | 8.3 | 17.5 | |
| % Profit Before Taxes/Total Assets | 10.2 | 10.4 | 13.1 | 24.5 | 14.2 |
| | 4.0 | 5.1 | 7.3 | 11.2 | 8.3 |
| | -1.6 | .5 | 3.1 | 6.9 | 5.3 |
| Sales/Net Fixed Assets | 78.8 | 82.2 | 57.4 | 104.1 | 51.9 |
| | 29.9 | 29.4 | 27.7 | 43.7 | 23.3 |
| | 16.1 | 17.0 | 15.0 | 24.7 | 14.0 |
| Sales/Total Assets | 3.6 | 3.2 | 3.5 | 3.7 | 2.8 |
| | 2.3 | 2.5 | 2.5 | 2.7 | 2.3 |
| | 1.9 | 1.9 | 2.0 | 1.8 | 2.0 |
| % Depr., Dep., Amort./Sales | .5 | .4 | .4 | .4 | .6 |
| | (44) .9 | (37) .7 | (34) .7 | (10) .5 | (10) 1.2 |
| | 1.7 | 1.6 | 1.8 | 2.0 | 2.1 |
| % Officers', Directors' Owners' Comp/Sales | 2.4 | 1.2 | 2.0 | | |
| | (23) 3.3 | (25) 2.7 | (17) 2.8 | | |
| | 5.2 | 4.5 | 6.5 | | |

| | H1 | H2 | H3 | 0-1MM | 1-3MM | 3-5MM | 5-10MM | 10-25MM | 25MM & OVER |
|---|---|---|---|---|---|---|---|---|---|
| Net Sales ($) | 1414806M | 1029163M | 1135935M | 2209M | 11486M | 14623M | 55451M | 211682M | 840484M |
| Total Assets ($) | 713208M | 554749M | 590121M | 587M | 5140M | 6551M | 21099M | 87033M | 469711M |

M = $ thousand     MM = $ million
See Pages 9 through 22 for Explanation of Ratios and Data

## Current Data Sorted by Assets      Comparative Historical Data

| 0-500M | 500M-2MM | 2-10MM | 10-50MM | 50-100MM | 100-250MM | Type of Statement | 4/1/07-3/31/08 ALL | 4/1/08-3/31/09 ALL |
|---|---|---|---|---|---|---|---|---|
| 1 | | 11 | 21 | 14 | 5 | Unqualified | 80 | 55 |
| 2 | 18 | 87 | 36 | 2 | 1 | Reviewed | 116 | 138 |
| 6 | 28 | 69 | 8 | | | Compiled | 107 | 103 |
| 50 | 123 | 79 | 6 | | 1 | Tax Returns | 138 | 162 |
| 27 | 64 | 120 | 63 | 10 | 8 | Other | 224 | 233 |
| | 122 (4/1-9/30/11) | | 738 (10/1/11-3/31/12) | | | | | |
| 86 | 233 | 366 | 134 | 26 | 15 | **NUMBER OF STATEMENTS** | 665 | 691 |
| % | % | % | % | % | % | **ASSETS** | % | % |
| 17.4 | 11.4 | 9.6 | 6.0 | 11.5 | 13.4 | Cash & Equivalents | 9.7 | 9.1 |
| 22.4 | 29.8 | 31.5 | 27.3 | 23.8 | 12.0 | Trade Receivables (net) | 30.9 | 29.8 |
| 31.9 | 35.1 | 36.2 | 37.5 | 28.9 | 20.4 | Inventory | 33.8 | 36.3 |
| .7 | 1.9 | 1.9 | 2.3 | 2.6 | 3.2 | All Other Current | 2.8 | 3.2 |
| 72.4 | 78.1 | 79.3 | 73.0 | 66.8 | 49.0 | Total Current | 77.1 | 78.3 |
| 13.7 | 12.4 | 11.8 | 13.1 | 10.2 | 17.3 | Fixed Assets (net) | 13.1 | 12.1 |
| 6.0 | 2.8 | 3.6 | 7.3 | 19.7 | 27.7 | Intangibles (net) | 4.0 | 4.2 |
| 7.9 | 6.7 | 5.4 | 6.6 | 3.2 | 6.0 | All Other Non-Current | 5.8 | 5.4 |
| 100.0 | 100.0 | 100.0 | 100.0 | 100.0 | 100.0 | Total | 100.0 | 100.0 |
| | | | | | | **LIABILITIES** | | |
| 19.4 | 12.5 | 13.4 | 18.4 | 10.1 | 14.4 | Notes Payable-Short Term | 16.5 | 18.2 |
| 3.0 | 2.8 | 1.7 | 2.0 | 1.9 | 1.8 | Cur. Mat.-L.T.D. | 2.5 | 2.7 |
| 17.5 | 24.9 | 25.1 | 19.3 | 14.0 | 10.3 | Trade Payables | 21.4 | 21.0 |
| .1 | .0 | .2 | .1 | .2 | .0 | Income Taxes Payable | .3 | .2 |
| 16.4 | 8.4 | 7.4 | 6.3 | 12.1 | 38.8 | All Other Current | 9.1 | 9.6 |
| 56.5 | 48.7 | 47.8 | 46.0 | 38.2 | 65.4 | Total Current | 49.9 | 51.7 |
| 30.5 | 11.8 | 8.4 | 10.1 | 10.1 | 17.1 | Long-Term Debt | 10.7 | 9.4 |
| .0 | .0 | .1 | .3 | 1.1 | .4 | Deferred Taxes | .1 | .2 |
| 13.5 | 10.8 | 6.2 | 6.9 | 5.8 | 13.4 | All Other Non-Current | 6.0 | 6.9 |
| -.5 | 28.6 | 37.5 | 36.6 | 44.8 | 3.7 | Net Worth | 33.3 | 31.9 |
| 100.0 | 100.0 | 100.0 | 100.0 | 100.0 | 100.0 | Total Liabilities & Net Worth | 100.0 | 100.0 |
| | | | | | | **INCOME DATA** | | |
| 100.0 | 100.0 | 100.0 | 100.0 | 100.0 | 100.0 | Net Sales | 100.0 | 100.0 |
| 38.9 | 32.0 | 28.8 | 28.4 | 31.5 | 41.0 | Gross Profit | 32.5 | 30.7 |
| 33.5 | 28.7 | 24.8 | 23.5 | 23.8 | 37.4 | Operating Expenses | 28.7 | 27.5 |
| 5.3 | 3.3 | 4.0 | 5.0 | 7.7 | 3.6 | Operating Profit | 3.9 | 3.3 |
| .9 | .2 | .4 | .8 | 1.3 | 2.5 | All Other Expenses (net) | .9 | .8 |
| 4.4 | 3.1 | 3.6 | 4.2 | 6.5 | 1.1 | Profit Before Taxes | 2.9 | 2.4 |
| | | | | | | **RATIOS** | | |
| 6.3 | 3.1 | 2.6 | 2.2 | 2.4 | 4.1 | Current | 2.7 | 2.5 |
| 1.6 | 1.8 | 1.6 | 1.5 | 1.8 | 1.7 | | 1.5 | 1.5 |
| .8 | 1.2 | 1.2 | 1.1 | 1.4 | .7 | | 1.2 | 1.2 |
| 2.9 | 1.7 | 1.4 | 1.1 | 1.6 | 1.3 | Quick | 1.4 | 1.3 |
| .8 | .9 | .8 | .7 | .9 | 1.0 | | .8 | .7 |
| .4 | .5 | .5 | .5 | .5 | .3 | | .5 | .5 |
| 1   674.5 | 14   26.5 | 23   15.6 | 27   13.6 | 20   18.4 | 5   78.0 | Sales/Receivables | 22   16.5 | 20   17.9 |
| 14   26.2 | 29   12.5 | 37   9.8 | 39   9.3 | 45   8.2 | 26   13.9 | | 37   9.9 | 33   10.9 |
| 36   10.1 | 43   8.5 | 53   6.9 | 56   6.5 | 56   6.5 | 49   7.5 | | 53   6.9 | 48   7.6 |
| 10   35.5 | 20   18.5 | 33   11.2 | 33   11.2 | 26   14.1 | 18   19.9 | Cost of Sales/Inventory | 27   13.3 | 25   14.7 |
| 43   8.4 | 48   7.6 | 63   5.8 | 85   4.3 | 68   5.4 | 107   3.4 | | 58   6.3 | 63   5.8 |
| 104   3.5 | 101   3.6 | 114   3.2 | 130   2.8 | 111   3.3 | 126   2.9 | | 115   3.2 | 119   3.1 |
| 0   UND | 11   33.7 | 18   19.9 | 18   20.7 | 16   23.5 | 14   25.5 | Cost of Sales/Payables | 15   24.6 | 13   27.8 |
| 11   33.9 | 27   13.4 | 35   10.3 | 33   11.1 | 33   11.0 | 27   13.4 | | 30   12.0 | 28   12.9 |
| 39   9.3 | 51   7.2 | 65   5.6 | 49   7.4 | 49   7.5 | 55   6.6 | | 53   6.8 | 51   7.2 |
| 6.1 | 5.6 | 4.9 | 4.9 | 6.1 | 3.8 | Sales/Working Capital | 5.4 | 5.8 |
| 26.0 | 9.6 | 11.1 | 10.5 | 8.2 | 4.8 | | 11.6 | 11.8 |
| -32.9 | 57.7 | 32.6 | 36.6 | 17.7 | -11.4 | | 34.9 | 32.3 |
| 11.2 | 18.7 | 22.0 | 19.4 | 56.6 | 30.7 | EBIT/Interest | 8.3 | 9.4 |
| (54) 3.2 | (194) 5.2 | (313) 5.1 | (126) 6.5 | (23) 10.2 | (14) 2.5 | | (577) 3.0 | (603) 3.0 |
| -1.3 | 1.7 | 2.1 | 2.8 | 2.0 | -5.8 | | 1.3 | 1.2 |
| | | 6.1 | 20.4 | | | Net Profit + Depr., Dep., Amort./Cur. Mat. L/T/D | 8.5 | 6.1 |
| | (45) 2.8 | (25) 5.5 | | | | | (103) 3.4 | (109) 2.8 |
| | .6 | 1.7 | | | | | .9 | 1.3 |
| .0 | .0 | .0 | .1 | .1 | .3 | Fixed/Worth | .1 | .1 |
| .3 | .2 | .2 | .3 | .4 | 9.1 | | .2 | .2 |
| -7.6 | 1.0 | .7 | 1.2 | -.3 | -.1 | | .9 | 1.0 |
| .5 | .9 | .8 | .9 | .9 | .9 | Debt/Worth | .9 | 1.0 |
| 2.7 | 2.2 | 2.0 | 2.1 | 1.5 | 61.1 | | 2.3 | 2.2 |
| -8.0 | 7.3 | 5.9 | 5.6 | -7.1 | -2.0 | | 6.7 | 6.4 |
| 115.3 | 62.8 | 54.5 | 46.7 | 51.7 | | % Profit Before Taxes/Tangible Net Worth | 46.3 | 41.7 |
| (57) 46.5 | (199) 28.3 | (336) 19.8 | (119) 24.6 | (19) 33.4 | | | (575) 18.0 | (595) 16.8 |
| 6.0 | 4.8 | 7.4 | 11.8 | 21.5 | | | 4.4 | 2.8 |
| 34.9 | 20.0 | 15.0 | 14.3 | 20.7 | 16.8 | % Profit Before Taxes/Total Assets | 14.6 | 12.6 |
| 13.8 | 7.0 | 5.6 | 7.7 | 12.1 | 4.3 | | 5.5 | 4.7 |
| -2.4 | 1.5 | 2.0 | 2.8 | 4.5 | -5.3 | | .9 | .5 |
| 800.1 | 583.1 | 236.1 | 120.7 | 240.7 | 112.0 | Sales/Net Fixed Assets | 142.9 | 198.8 |
| 86.6 | 89.3 | 74.4 | 39.8 | 42.2 | 20.1 | | 51.1 | 58.1 |
| 24.7 | 26.4 | 20.1 | 11.4 | 16.1 | 9.9 | | 16.5 | 18.8 |
| 7.0 | 4.8 | 4.0 | 3.1 | 3.0 | 2.2 | Sales/Total Assets | 4.0 | 4.3 |
| 4.3 | 3.4 | 2.7 | 2.1 | 2.2 | 1.9 | | 2.8 | 2.9 |
| 2.6 | 2.2 | 1.9 | 1.5 | 1.3 | .8 | | 1.9 | 2.0 |
| .3 | .1 | .2 | .3 | .3 | | % Depr., Dep., Amort./Sales | .3 | .2 |
| (38) .5 | (151) .4 | (271) .5 | (113) .6 | (19) 1.1 | | | (516) .6 | (527) .6 |
| 1.8 | 1.2 | 1.1 | 1.2 | 2.1 | | | 1.4 | 1.4 |
| 3.1 | 1.7 | 1.3 | .9 | | | % Officers', Directors' Owners' Comp/Sales | 1.6 | 1.3 |
| (50) 5.5 | (157) 3.2 | (193) 2.4 | (43) 1.9 | | | | (313) 3.0 | (322) 2.8 |
| 9.4 | 5.9 | 4.1 | 6.2 | | | | | 5.3 |
| 113495M | 1140868M | 5571539M | 7612592M | 5092019M | 4772009M | Net Sales ($) | 19693554M | 22453908M |
| 23110M | 286165M | 1677520M | 2627701M | 1945973M | 2409283M | Total Assets ($) | 7432726M | 7840976M |

**Comparative Historical Data**  —  **Current Data Sorted by Sales**

| 4/1/09-3/31/10 ALL | 4/1/10-3/31/11 ALL | 4/1/11-3/31/12 ALL | Type of Statement | 0-1MM | 1-3MM | 3-5MM | 5-10MM | 10-25MM | 25MM & OVER |
|---|---|---|---|---|---|---|---|---|---|
| 55 | 53 | 52 | Unqualified | | 1 | | 2 | 13 | 36 |
| 156 | 136 | 146 | Reviewed | 2 | 6 | 16 | 24 | 60 | 38 |
| 102 | 105 | 111 | Compiled | 7 | 16 | 13 | 30 | 33 | 12 |
| 199 | 194 | 259 | Tax Returns | 27 | 63 | 55 | 56 | 46 | 12 |
| 269 | 259 | 292 | Other | 15 | 27 | 35 | 58 | 77 | 80 |
| | | | | | **122 (4/1-9/30/11)** | | **738 (10/1/11-3/31/12)** | | |
| 781 | 747 | 860 | **NUMBER OF STATEMENTS** | 51 | 113 | 119 | 170 | 229 | 178 |
| % | % | % | **ASSETS** | % | % | % | % | % | % |
| 10.2 | 10.5 | 10.5 | Cash & Equivalents | 12.7 | 13.4 | 12.7 | 12.3 | 8.2 | 7.6 |
| 30.8 | 29.2 | 28.9 | Trade Receivables (net) | 18.5 | 22.4 | 27.4 | 28.0 | 34.6 | 30.4 |
| 32.1 | 35.8 | 35.2 | Inventory | 35.9 | 34.3 | 33.4 | 37.6 | 35.8 | 33.7 |
| 3.2 | 2.7 | 1.9 | All Other Current | .8 | 1.3 | 1.9 | 1.7 | 1.6 | 3.0 |
| 76.2 | 78.2 | 76.4 | Total Current | 68.0 | 71.5 | 75.4 | 79.6 | 80.1 | 74.7 |
| 12.6 | 11.4 | 12.4 | Fixed Assets (net) | 17.8 | 16.7 | 13.6 | 12.0 | 10.0 | 11.0 |
| 4.8 | 4.9 | 5.1 | Intangibles (net) | 8.0 | 4.0 | 3.6 | 2.7 | 4.4 | 9.0 |
| 6.4 | 5.5 | 6.1 | All Other Non-Current | 6.3 | 7.9 | 7.3 | 5.7 | 5.5 | 5.3 |
| 100.0 | 100.0 | 100.0 | Total | 100.0 | 100.0 | 100.0 | 100.0 | 100.0 | 100.0 |
| | | | **LIABILITIES** | | | | | | |
| 15.5 | 15.8 | 14.4 | Notes Payable-Short Term | 14.1 | 17.5 | 12.6 | 11.1 | 15.2 | 16.0 |
| 2.8 | 2.4 | 2.2 | Cur. Mat.-L.T.D. | 2.3 | 2.3 | 3.0 | 2.0 | 1.8 | 2.2 |
| 22.5 | 22.7 | 22.8 | Trade Payables | 10.7 | 19.1 | 24.5 | 24.0 | 25.4 | 22.9 |
| .2 | .1 | .1 | Income Taxes Payable | .1 | .1 | .0 | .0 | .2 | .2 |
| 8.2 | 8.4 | 9.1 | All Other Current | 19.6 | 7.8 | 8.5 | 8.4 | 6.6 | 11.3 |
| 49.2 | 49.3 | 48.7 | Total Current | 46.8 | 46.8 | 48.7 | 45.4 | 49.3 | 52.6 |
| 10.9 | 10.9 | 12.0 | Long-Term Debt | 36.5 | 19.0 | 14.7 | 8.0 | 7.3 | 8.5 |
| .2 | .2 | .1 | Deferred Taxes | .0 | .0 | .1 | .0 | .2 | .3 |
| 6.8 | 6.6 | 8.4 | All Other Non-Current | 16.9 | 16.6 | 8.1 | 7.9 | 4.2 | 6.9 |
| 32.9 | 33.1 | 30.8 | Net Worth | -.2 | 17.6 | 28.4 | 38.6 | 39.1 | 31.6 |
| 100.0 | 100.0 | 100.0 | Total Liabilties & Net Worth | 100.0 | 100.0 | 100.0 | 100.0 | 100.0 | 100.0 |
| | | | **INCOME DATA** | | | | | | |
| 100.0 | 100.0 | 100.0 | Net Sales | 100.0 | 100.0 | 100.0 | 100.0 | 100.0 | 100.0 |
| 31.6 | 32.7 | 30.9 | Gross Profit | 45.4 | 38.3 | 31.9 | 31.8 | 27.1 | 25.5 |
| 27.5 | 28.3 | 26.7 | Operating Expenses | 37.2 | 35.2 | 29.2 | 27.8 | 22.4 | 21.1 |
| 4.1 | 4.4 | 4.2 | Operating Profit | 8.2 | 3.1 | 2.7 | 4.0 | 4.6 | 4.4 |
| .8 | .6 | .5 | All Other Expenses (net) | 1.9 | .6 | .3 | .1 | .5 | .8 |
| 3.3 | 3.8 | 3.7 | Profit Before Taxes | 6.3 | 2.6 | 2.4 | 3.9 | 4.2 | 3.7 |
| | | | **RATIOS** | | | | | | |
| 2.6 | 2.8 | 2.8 | Current | 6.5 | 4.5 | 2.7 | 3.2 | 2.5 | 2.1 |
| 1.5 | 1.6 | 1.6 | | 1.8 | 1.9 | 1.8 | 1.9 | 1.5 | 1.5 |
| 1.2 | 1.2 | 1.1 | | .9 | 1.1 | 1.1 | 1.2 | 1.1 | 1.2 |
| 1.4 | 1.5 | 1.5 | Quick | 3.7 | 1.9 | 1.5 | 1.6 | 1.5 | 1.2 |
| .8 | .8 | .8 | | .8 | .8 | .8 | .8 | .8 | .7 |
| .5 | .5 | .5 | | .4 | .4 | .5 | .5 | .5 | .5 |
| 22  16.7 | 21  17.5 | 18  19.8 | Sales/Receivables | 1  336.0 | 9  41.0 | 19  19.7 | 21  17.2 | 27  13.3 | 18  20.0 |
| 36  10.0 | 36  10.2 | 34  10.7 | | 33  11.0 | 28  13.2 | 30  12.2 | 34  10.8 | 39  9.3 | 34  10.8 |
| 53  6.9 | 51  7.2 | 51  7.2 | | 49  7.5 | 52  7.0 | 47  7.7 | 47  7.8 | 53  6.9 | 49  7.4 |
| 24  15.2 | 28  13.0 | 26  14.0 | Cost of Sales/Inventory | 41  9.0 | 24  14.9 | 20  18.5 | 32  11.3 | 27  13.7 | 17  22.1 |
| 56  6.5 | 63  5.8 | 59  6.2 | | 91  4.0 | 65  5.6 | 59  6.2 | 64  5.7 | 54  6.7 | 55  6.6 |
| 108  3.4 | 116  3.1 | 114  3.2 | | 203  1.8 | 159  2.3 | 114  3.2 | 118  3.1 | 99  3.7 | 104  3.5 |
| 15  24.6 | 15  24.8 | 13  29.1 | Cost of Sales/Payables | 0  UND | 5  79.7 | 19  19.7 | 13  27.1 | 18  20.3 | 12  30.5 |
| 31  11.8 | 33  11.1 | 30  12.2 | | 16  22.5 | 26  14.1 | 36  10.1 | 32  11.3 | 34  10.7 | 28  13.2 |
| 56  6.6 | 57  6.4 | 56  6.5 | | 53  6.9 | 58  6.3 | 70  5.2 | 57  6.4 | 58  6.3 | 46  8.0 |
| 5.4 | 5.1 | 5.1 | Sales/Working Capital | 3.2 | 4.4 | 4.9 | 5.0 | 5.4 | 6.3 |
| 11.6 | 11.0 | 10.9 | | 7.6 | 8.5 | 8.4 | 8.3 | 12.6 | 15.1 |
| 38.4 | 30.4 | 42.8 | | -95.3 | 112.1 | 37.5 | 23.0 | 45.2 | 39.7 |
| 14.4 | 16.6 | 19.9 | EBIT/Interest | 8.1 | 11.9 | 13.8 | 22.8 | 26.3 | 25.8 |
| (677) 4.3 | (641) 5.4 | (724) 5.3 | | (35) 1.8 | (89) 2.9 | (98) 4.2 | (143) 6.3 | (195) 6.1 | (164) 7.0 |
| 1.4 | 2.0 | 2.0 | | .2 | .8 | 1.2 | 2.3 | 2.7 | 2.5 |
| 7.3 | 9.2 | 12.2 | Net Profit + Depr., Dep., Amort./Cur. Mat. L/T/D | | | | 5.1 | 8.4 | 25.8 |
| (125) 2.6 | (106) 3.3 | (85) 3.4 | | | | | (15) 2.7 | (31) 2.8 | (29) 6.0 |
| .8 | 1.4 | 1.0 | | | | | .7 | 1.2 | 1.3 |
| .1 | .0 | .0 | Fixed/Worth | .0 | .0 | .0 | .0 | .0 | .1 |
| .3 | .2 | .2 | | .3 | .3 | .1 | .2 | .2 | .3 |
| 1.2 | 1.0 | 1.1 | | -8.7 | 3.2 | 1.2 | .6 | .8 | 1.3 |
| .8 | .8 | .8 | Debt/Worth | .6 | .6 | 1.0 | .6 | .8 | 1.1 |
| 2.2 | 2.1 | 2.1 | | 3.3 | 1.8 | 2.7 | 1.9 | 1.9 | 2.3 |
| 7.4 | 7.8 | 7.3 | | -4.2 | 32.4 | 11.6 | 5.0 | 5.5 | 9.9 |
| 50.0 | 53.6 | 59.0 | % Profit Before Taxes/Tangible Net Worth | 92.7 | 59.4 | 50.2 | 58.9 | 54.9 | 67.1 |
| (666) 20.0 | (635) 21.8 | (738) 23.8 | | (32) 33.0 | (90) 19.3 | (102) 19.7 | (155) 19.9 | (210) 23.6 | (149) 30.7 |
| 5.1 | 8.1 | 8.0 | | 3.8 | 3.7 | 3.8 | 5.8 | 9.0 | 15.5 |
| 16.2 | 16.8 | 18.3 | % Profit Before Taxes/Total Assets | 21.8 | 22.0 | 14.6 | 19.4 | 18.1 | 17.4 |
| 5.9 | 6.8 | 6.9 | | 8.0 | 4.1 | 5.4 | 5.9 | 7.4 | 8.5 |
| 1.1 | 2.1 | 1.9 | | -.6 | .2 | .7 | 2.1 | 3.0 | 3.6 |
| 177.8 | 257.7 | 258.5 | Sales/Net Fixed Assets | 833.0 | 321.0 | 220.7 | 206.1 | 235.1 | 335.2 |
| 53.7 | 63.4 | 67.8 | | 48.9 | 48.1 | 73.5 | 68.9 | 80.9 | 65.4 |
| 16.7 | 19.8 | 18.2 | | 11.5 | 13.1 | 14.5 | 19.5 | 27.8 | 17.4 |
| 4.2 | 4.1 | 4.3 | Sales/Total Assets | 3.5 | 4.7 | 4.0 | 4.0 | 4.4 | 5.2 |
| 2.8 | 2.8 | 2.8 | | 2.0 | 2.7 | 2.8 | 3.0 | 3.0 | 2.9 |
| 1.9 | 1.8 | 1.9 | | 1.0 | 1.5 | 1.9 | 2.1 | 2.0 | 2.0 |
| .3 | .2 | .2 | % Depr., Dep., Amort./Sales | .4 | .3 | .2 | .2 | .2 | .2 |
| (568) .6 | (537) .5 | (600) .5 | | (26) 1.1 | (68) .8 | (78) .5 | (121) .5 | (167) .4 | (140) .5 |
| 1.5 | 1.4 | 1.2 | | 2.5 | 2.0 | 1.4 | 1.2 | .8 | 1.2 |
| 1.3 | 1.6 | 1.4 | % Officers', Directors' Owners' Comp/Sales | 2.9 | 2.9 | 2.1 | 1.6 | 1.1 | .6 |
| (350) 2.9 | (361) 2.9 | (448) 2.8 | | (26) 7.1 | (67) 5.4 | (79) 3.3 | (106) 2.7 | (122) 2.1 | (48) 1.3 |
| 5.2 | 5.2 | 5.2 | | 9.6 | 8.3 | 5.4 | 5.3 | 3.5 | 2.7 |
| 21871028M | 21932786M | 24302522M | Net Sales ($) | 29640M | 210995M | 467863M | 1222575M | 3639656M | 18731793M |
| 8281865M | 8350045M | 8969752M | Total Assets ($) | 20500M | 116340M | 223050M | 477799M | 1425214M | 6706849M |

M = $ thousand    MM = $ million
See Pages 9 through 22 for Explanation of Ratios and Data

## Current Data Sorted by Assets      Comparative Historical Data

| 0-500M | 500M-2MM | 2-10MM | 10-50MM | 50-100MM | 100-250MM | Type of Statement | 6<br>4/1/07-<br>3/31/08<br>ALL | 5<br>4/1/08-<br>3/31/09<br>ALL |
|---|---|---|---|---|---|---|---|---|
| | | 1 | 3 | 2 | 2 | Unqualified | 6 | 5 |
| | 4 | 11 | 4 | | | Reviewed | 13 | 3 |
| | 2 | 2 | 2 | | | Compiled | 2 | 4 |
| 2 | 4 | 2 | 1 | | | Tax Returns | 6 | 2 |
| 5 | 7 | 16 | 7 | | 2 | Other | 20 | 17 |
| | 6 (4/1-9/30/11) | | 73 (10/1/11-3/31/12) | | | | | |
| 7 | 17 | 32 | 17 | 2 | 4 | NUMBER OF STATEMENTS | 47 | 31 |
| % | % | % | % | % | % | ASSETS | % | % |
| | 22.7 | 11.7 | 10.2 | | | Cash & Equivalents | 14.3 | 12.0 |
| | 25.6 | 35.3 | 40.0 | | | Trade Receivables (net) | 43.2 | 29.5 |
| | 21.0 | 26.7 | 27.3 | | | Inventory | 17.9 | 29.4 |
| | 5.4 | 4.5 | 5.8 | | | All Other Current | 6.4 | 5.9 |
| | 74.7 | 78.3 | 83.3 | | | Total Current | 81.9 | 76.8 |
| | 11.4 | 7.9 | 7.2 | | | Fixed Assets (net) | 9.4 | 12.7 |
| | 2.4 | 5.8 | 6.6 | | | Intangibles (net) | 5.3 | 5.6 |
| | 11.6 | 8.1 | 2.9 | | | All Other Non-Current | 3.5 | 5.0 |
| | 100.0 | 100.0 | 100.0 | | | Total | 100.0 | 100.0 |
| | | | | | | **LIABILITIES** | | |
| | 10.8 | 10.1 | 9.4 | | | Notes Payable-Short Term | 9.9 | 23.6 |
| | 1.2 | 1.2 | .4 | | | Cur. Mat.-L.T.D. | 1.7 | 1.1 |
| | 19.9 | 27.3 | 27.4 | | | Trade Payables | 28.7 | 24.9 |
| | .1 | .1 | .3 | | | Income Taxes Payable | .2 | .3 |
| | 13.9 | 10.7 | 10.4 | | | All Other Current | 16.6 | 8.4 |
| | 46.0 | 49.4 | 47.9 | | | Total Current | 57.0 | 58.3 |
| | 14.4 | 6.6 | 4.3 | | | Long-Term Debt | 4.6 | 7.0 |
| | .0 | .0 | .5 | | | Deferred Taxes | .1 | .3 |
| | 3.1 | 4.1 | 5.0 | | | All Other Non-Current | 3.6 | 3.1 |
| | 36.5 | 39.9 | 42.3 | | | Net Worth | 34.6 | 31.2 |
| | 100.0 | 100.0 | 100.0 | | | Total Liabilities & Net Worth | 100.0 | 100.0 |
| | | | | | | **INCOME DATA** | | |
| | 100.0 | 100.0 | 100.0 | | | Net Sales | 100.0 | 100.0 |
| | 35.7 | 29.8 | 25.8 | | | Gross Profit | 32.4 | 33.2 |
| | 31.6 | 25.5 | 19.3 | | | Operating Expenses | 29.4 | 32.2 |
| | 4.2 | 4.2 | 6.5 | | | Operating Profit | 2.9 | 1.0 |
| | .2 | .2 | .2 | | | All Other Expenses (net) | .3 | .5 |
| | 4.0 | 4.1 | 6.4 | | | Profit Before Taxes | 2.6 | .5 |
| | | | | | | **RATIOS** | | |
| | 4.4 | 2.3 | 2.8 | | | | 2.0 | 2.1 |
| | 1.7 | 1.5 | 1.5 | | | Current | 1.7 | 1.4 |
| | 1.0 | 1.1 | 1.2 | | | | 1.1 | 1.1 |
| | 2.3 | 1.4 | 1.5 | | | | 1.6 | 1.2 |
| | 1.1 | 1.0 | 1.0 | | | Quick | 1.1 | .7 |
| | .3 | .7 | .8 | | | | .8 | .4 |
| | (1) 513.1 | (17) 21.3 | (33) 11.1 | | | | (26) 14.3 | (18) 20.3 |
| | (23) 15.6 | (43) 8.4 | (46) 8.0 | | | Sales/Receivables | (49) 7.5 | (37) 9.8 |
| | (42) 8.7 | (53) 6.9 | (57) 6.4 | | | | (65) 5.6 | (50) 7.3 |
| | (0) UND | (7) 55.8 | (18) 20.6 | | | | (4) 96.8 | (16) 22.9 |
| | (9) 40.2 | (45) 8.2 | (38) 9.6 | | | Cost of Sales/Inventory | (24) 15.2 | (54) 6.8 |
| | (76) 4.8 | (104) 3.5 | (70) 5.2 | | | | (58) 6.3 | (89) 4.1 |
| | (1) 423.4 | (12) 29.3 | (22) 16.8 | | | | (15) 24.9 | (11) 34.3 |
| | (21) 17.7 | (31) 11.6 | (37) 9.9 | | | Cost of Sales/Payables | (38) 9.6 | (37) 10.0 |
| | (44) 8.3 | (58) 6.3 | (54) 6.8 | | | | (67) 5.5 | (76) 4.8 |
| | 6.2 | 5.4 | 5.1 | | | | 5.9 | 6.0 |
| | 16.7 | 14.6 | 10.8 | | | Sales/Working Capital | 10.1 | 15.4 |
| | 489.3 | 62.0 | 32.0 | | | | 33.3 | 81.5 |
| | 104.1 | 38.5 | 80.0 | | | | 15.8 | 18.4 |
| | (15) 19.3 | (29) 12.6 | (15) 44.9 | | | EBIT/Interest | (40) 7.0 | (28) 4.3 |
| | 1.7 | 3.2 | 11.6 | | | | 2.4 | 1.8 |
| | | | | | | Net Profit + Depr., Dep., | 6.6 | |
| | | | | | | Amort./Cur. Mat. L/T/D | (11) 3.6 | |
| | | | | | | | 1.5 | |
| | .0 | .1 | .1 | | | | .1 | .1 |
| | .1 | .2 | .1 | | | Fixed/Worth | .3 | .4 |
| | 1.2 | .5 | .3 | | | | .6 | 1.3 |
| | .5 | .9 | .9 | | | | 1.0 | 1.1 |
| | 2.7 | 1.6 | 2.6 | | | Debt/Worth | 2.0 | 3.2 |
| | 7.2 | 7.3 | 4.1 | | | | 6.7 | 9.6 |
| | 114.4 | 65.3 | 114.3 | | | % Profit Before Taxes/Tangible | 44.3 | 70.0 |
| | (15) 48.1 | (30) 29.9 | (16) 40.5 | | | Net Worth | (42) 22.4 | (26) 11.3 |
| | 11.4 | 8.6 | 18.5 | | | | 7.1 | 3.9 |
| | 30.0 | 22.8 | 25.2 | | | % Profit Before Taxes/Total | 18.5 | 18.5 |
| | 21.3 | 9.4 | 12.9 | | | Assets | 8.9 | 4.4 |
| | 1.9 | 1.8 | 6.4 | | | | 3.7 | 1.4 |
| | 828.9 | 108.0 | 223.2 | | | | 93.8 | 85.9 |
| | 98.4 | 80.1 | 84.1 | | | Sales/Net Fixed Assets | 57.3 | 34.7 |
| | 30.4 | 33.1 | 32.8 | | | | 19.7 | 18.6 |
| | 6.3 | 4.5 | 4.6 | | | | 4.3 | 4.3 |
| | 4.6 | 3.2 | 3.1 | | | Sales/Total Assets | 3.3 | 3.0 |
| | 2.9 | 1.9 | 2.1 | | | | 2.5 | 1.9 |
| | .1 | .3 | .1 | | | | .2 | .2 |
| | (12) .3 | (26) .5 | (14) .3 | | | % Depr., Dep., Amort./Sales | (38) .7 | (23) .6 |
| | .9 | .9 | .7 | | | | 1.2 | 1.7 |
| | 1.7 | 1.3 | | | | % Officers', Directors' | 2.9 | |
| | (10) 5.7 | (13) 4.0 | | | | Owners' Comp/Sales | (13) 6.4 | |
| | 11.7 | 6.4 | | | | | 11.1 | |
| 20929M | 143817M | 632248M | 1713394M | 424146M | 275228M | Net Sales ($) | 2020937M | 1001021M |
| 2506M | 22107M | 173411M | 418923M | 110820M | 607760M | Total Assets ($) | 677858M | 343230M |

© RMA 2012

M = $ thousand    MM = $ million
See Pages 9 through 22 for Explanation of Ratios and Data

## Comparative Historical Data | Current Data Sorted by Sales

| 4/1/09-3/31/10 ALL | 4/1/10-3/31/11 ALL | 4/1/11-3/31/12 ALL | Type of Statement | 0-1MM | 1-3MM | 3-5MM | 5-10MM | 10-25MM | 25MM & OVER |
|---|---|---|---|---|---|---|---|---|---|
| 3 | 2 | 8 | Unqualified | | | | 1 | 1 | 6 |
| 3 | 5 | 19 | Reviewed | | 1 | | 6 | 3 | 9 |
| 3 | 3 | 6 | Compiled | | | | | 2 | 3 |
| 6 | 12 | 9 | Tax Returns | 1 | 2 | 2 | 1 | 2 | 1 |
| 14 | 19 | 37 | Other | 1 | 3 | 6 | 1 | 5 | 14 |
| | | | | | 6 (4/1-9/30/11) | | 73 (10/1/11-3/31/12) | | |
| 29 | 41 | 79 | **NUMBER OF STATEMENTS** | 2 | 6 | 9 | 16 | 13 | 33 |
| % | % | % | **ASSETS** | % | % | % | % | % | % |
| 15.5 | 16.9 | 14.8 | Cash & Equivalents | | | | 20.7 | 11.3 | 10.2 |
| 33.1 | 34.1 | 30.6 | Trade Receivables (net) | | | | 24.8 | 29.8 | 38.3 |
| 28.8 | 25.3 | 24.3 | Inventory | | | | 22.5 | 32.0 | 18.0 |
| 3.5 | 4.8 | 5.1 | All Other Current | | | | 1.9 | 7.9 | 7.0 |
| 80.9 | 81.1 | 74.8 | Total Current | | | | 69.8 | 80.9 | 73.4 |
| 9.6 | 10.0 | 8.9 | Fixed Assets (net) | | | | 10.2 | 4.4 | 8.5 |
| 4.9 | 5.4 | 6.9 | Intangibles (net) | | | | 7.1 | 8.9 | 7.8 |
| 4.6 | 3.5 | 9.4 | All Other Non-Current | | | | 12.8 | 5.7 | 10.4 |
| 100.0 | 100.0 | 100.0 | Total | | | | 100.0 | 100.0 | 100.0 |
| | | | **LIABILITIES** | | | | | | |
| 11.8 | 10.2 | 10.3 | Notes Payable-Short Term | | | | 13.4 | 7.2 | 9.2 |
| 3.4 | 7.0 | 1.2 | Cur. Mat.-L.T.D. | | | | 1.7 | 1.5 | 1.1 |
| 23.6 | 25.3 | 22.9 | Trade Payables | | | | 17.1 | 27.0 | 27.9 |
| .4 | .3 | .3 | Income Taxes Payable | | | | .0 | .0 | .6 |
| 11.5 | 14.6 | 10.1 | All Other Current | | | | 5.9 | 13.3 | 13.0 |
| 50.6 | 57.4 | 44.9 | Total Current | | | | 38.1 | 49.1 | 51.8 |
| 2.7 | 13.4 | 8.8 | Long-Term Debt | | | | 11.1 | 6.0 | 8.2 |
| .0 | .0 | .1 | Deferred Taxes | | | | .0 | .0 | .3 |
| 5.4 | 2.8 | 4.6 | All Other Non-Current | | | | 6.0 | 1.1 | 3.9 |
| 41.2 | 26.3 | 41.6 | Net Worth | | | | 44.7 | 43.8 | 35.8 |
| 100.0 | 100.0 | 100.0 | Total Liabilities & Net Worth | | | | 100.0 | 100.0 | 100.0 |
| | | | **INCOME DATA** | | | | | | |
| 100.0 | 100.0 | 100.0 | Net Sales | | | | 100.0 | 100.0 | 100.0 |
| 33.2 | 36.2 | 31.1 | Gross Profit | | | | 36.2 | 27.5 | 25.3 |
| 30.5 | 31.0 | 26.1 | Operating Expenses | | | | 32.1 | 20.9 | 20.4 |
| 2.7 | 5.3 | 5.0 | Operating Profit | | | | 4.1 | 6.7 | 4.8 |
| .7 | 1.4 | .5 | All Other Expenses (net) | | | | .2 | .3 | .9 |
| 2.0 | 3.8 | 4.5 | Profit Before Taxes | | | | 3.9 | 6.3 | 3.9 |
| | | | **RATIOS** | | | | | | |
| 3.0 | 3.5 | 3.0 | Current | | | | 2.8 | 3.9 | 2.0 |
| 1.5 | 1.6 | 1.5 | | | | | 1.9 | 1.5 | 1.3 |
| 1.2 | 1.0 | 1.1 | | | | | 1.1 | 1.1 | 1.0 |
| 1.6 | 2.3 | 1.7 | Quick | | | | 1.9 | 1.2 | 1.2 |
| .8 | 1.0 | 1.0 | | | | | 1.0 | .9 | 1.0 |
| .5 | .5 | .7 | | | | | .6 | .6 | .7 |
| 20 18.4 | 17 21.6 | 14 26.4 | Sales/Receivables | | | | 0 UND | 14 25.3 | 17 21.4 |
| 35 10.5 | 45 8.1 | 33 11.0 | | | | | 28 13.2 | 29 12.6 | 39 9.3 |
| 49 7.5 | 56 6.5 | 52 7.0 | | | | | 66 5.5 | 50 7.3 | 53 6.9 |
| 12 31.6 | 5 68.8 | 1 285.6 | Cost of Sales/Inventory | | | | 5 69.3 | 2 149.0 | 0 999.8 |
| 56 6.5 | 36 10.0 | 35 10.4 | | | | | 23 15.7 | 50 7.3 | 14 25.3 |
| 144 2.5 | 90 4.0 | 78 4.7 | | | | | 94 3.9 | 85 4.3 | 64 5.7 |
| 11 32.8 | 14 26.3 | 8 45.5 | Cost of Sales/Payables | | | | 1 364.1 | 13 28.2 | 14 26.1 |
| 31 11.9 | 28 12.8 | 26 14.0 | | | | | 10 36.7 | 34 10.6 | 29 12.5 |
| 49 7.4 | 48 7.6 | 54 6.8 | | | | | 51 7.2 | 47 7.8 | 58 6.3 |
| 4.8 | 5.2 | 5.8 | Sales/Working Capital | | | | 6.3 | 5.1 | 7.3 |
| 11.2 | 10.7 | 14.0 | | | | | 7.4 | 21.9 | 23.5 |
| 68.2 | 58.8 | 67.7 | | | | | 520.4 | 67.2 | 366.6 |
| 34.2 | 16.8 | 59.1 | EBIT/Interest | | | | 34.2 | 47.8 | 79.4 |
| (24) 5.2 | (34) 5.2 | (67) 13.1 | | | | | (12) 17.8 | (12) 15.6 | (30) 22.8 |
| -1.2 | 1.4 | 3.5 | | | | | 3.5 | 7.3 | 3.6 |
| | | | Net Profit + Depr., Dep., Amort./Cur. Mat. L/T/D | | | | | | |
| .1 | .1 | .1 | Fixed/Worth | | | | .1 | .1 | .1 |
| .2 | .2 | .2 | | | | | .1 | .2 | .2 |
| .7 | .8 | .5 | | | | | .5 | .9 | .5 |
| .7 | .7 | .8 | Debt/Worth | | | | .5 | .4 | 1.3 |
| 1.9 | 1.4 | 1.7 | | | | | 1.3 | 1.5 | 2.5 |
| 5.2 | 6.6 | 6.4 | | | | | 7.0 | 11.4 | 8.4 |
| 47.0 | 79.1 | 77.7 | % Profit Before Taxes/Tangible Net Worth | | | | 69.6 | 99.1 | 101.5 |
| (25) 6.1 | (37) 30.1 | (70) 32.3 | | | | | (14) 28.5 | (11) 39.5 | (29) 38.1 |
| -7.0 | 7.1 | 10.5 | | | | | 2.7 | 15.4 | 13.7 |
| 14.2 | 30.7 | 24.7 | % Profit Before Taxes/Total Assets | | | | 24.3 | 30.4 | 21.9 |
| 3.6 | 9.4 | 11.9 | | | | | 13.2 | 15.4 | 9.9 |
| -2.7 | 1.9 | 3.2 | | | | | 2.1 | 6.2 | 3.7 |
| 211.3 | 243.5 | 170.1 | Sales/Net Fixed Assets | | | | 168.2 | 210.8 | 141.9 |
| 47.2 | 44.7 | 83.1 | | | | | 70.6 | 86.5 | 84.1 |
| 20.1 | 24.1 | 29.3 | | | | | 31.4 | 50.1 | 28.7 |
| 5.2 | 5.5 | 5.1 | Sales/Total Assets | | | | 5.1 | 4.7 | 5.7 |
| 3.2 | 3.2 | 3.2 | | | | | 2.9 | 3.9 | 3.9 |
| 2.2 | 2.4 | 2.2 | | | | | 1.9 | 2.4 | 2.4 |
| .4 | .5 | .2 | % Depr., Dep., Amort./Sales | | | | .0 | .1 | .1 |
| (18) 1.3 | (29) .9 | (57) .4 | | | | | (12) .7 | (10) .3 | (26) .3 |
| 2.0 | 1.3 | .8 | | | | | .8 | 1.0 | .7 |
| .6 | 1.4 | 1.3 | % Officers', Directors' Owners' Comp/Sales | | | | | | .4 |
| (11) 4.2 | (19) 3.0 | (32) 4.3 | | | | | | | (11) .7 |
| 5.3 | 6.5 | 8.6 | | | | | | | 4.3 |
| 601557M | 1368426M | 3209762M | Net Sales ($) | 1354M | 13316M | 35043M | 117509M | 227622M | 2814918M |
| 179131M | 423903M | 1335527M | Total Assets ($) | 1198M | 2585M | 15252M | 46100M | 75156M | 1195236M |

© RMA 2012

M = $ thousand    MM = $ million
See Pages 9 through 22 for Explanation of Ratios and Data

## Current Data Sorted by Assets　　　　　　　　　　Comparative Historical Data

| 0-500M | 500M-2MM | 2-10MM | 10-50MM | 50-100MM | 100-250MM | Type of Statement | 4/1/07-3/31/08 ALL | 4/1/08-3/31/09 ALL |
|---|---|---|---|---|---|---|---|---|
| | | 5 | 10 | 1 | 2 | Unqualified | 17 | 15 |
| | 1 | 12 | 9 | | | Reviewed | 31 | 36 |
| 1 | 19 | 20 | 2 | | | Compiled | 27 | 24 |
| 11 | 20 | 19 | 1 | | | Tax Returns | 30 | 47 |
| 7 | 24 | 25 | 10 | 1 | 3 | Other | 55 | 57 |
| | 31 (4/1-9/30/11) | | 172 (10/1/11-3/31/12) | | | | | |
| 19 | 64 | 81 | 32 | 2 | 5 | NUMBER OF STATEMENTS | 160 | 179 |
| % | % | % | % | % | % | ASSETS | % | % |
| 33.3 | 17.2 | 9.1 | 13.7 | | | Cash & Equivalents | 9.0 | 12.0 |
| 19.5 | 30.5 | 40.1 | 32.9 | | | Trade Receivables (net) | 37.3 | 38.1 |
| 11.6 | 26.1 | 24.8 | 25.1 | | | Inventory | 28.8 | 24.2 |
| 5.3 | 1.4 | 4.9 | 5.3 | | | All Other Current | 3.4 | 4.4 |
| 69.7 | 75.1 | 79.0 | 77.0 | | | Total Current | 78.5 | 78.8 |
| 12.6 | 9.8 | 11.2 | 14.2 | | | Fixed Assets (net) | 12.8 | 10.8 |
| 2.7 | 3.9 | 2.8 | 1.8 | | | Intangibles (net) | 2.6 | 2.6 |
| 14.9 | 11.1 | 6.9 | 7.0 | | | All Other Non-Current | 6.2 | 7.9 |
| 100.0 | 100.0 | 100.0 | 100.0 | | | Total | 100.0 | 100.0 |
| | | | | | | **LIABILITIES** | | |
| 13.2 | 11.1 | 13.5 | 14.3 | | | Notes Payable-Short Term | 19.1 | 17.8 |
| 5.1 | 4.5 | 2.4 | 3.4 | | | Cur. Mat.-L.T.D. | 1.8 | 3.9 |
| 9.5 | 21.3 | 27.2 | 21.9 | | | Trade Payables | 22.5 | 24.4 |
| .0 | .1 | .0 | .1 | | | Income Taxes Payable | .1 | .1 |
| 29.9 | 8.1 | 9.5 | 8.9 | | | All Other Current | 8.4 | 11.2 |
| 57.6 | 45.1 | 52.7 | 48.5 | | | Total Current | 51.9 | 57.4 |
| 5.9 | 14.0 | 11.8 | 8.1 | | | Long-Term Debt | 11.4 | 7.9 |
| .0 | .0 | .1 | .1 | | | Deferred Taxes | .1 | .1 |
| 5.2 | 8.3 | 3.8 | 6.4 | | | All Other Non-Current | 4.4 | 3.5 |
| 31.3 | 32.7 | 31.6 | 36.9 | | | Net Worth | 32.2 | 31.1 |
| 100.0 | 100.0 | 100.0 | 100.0 | | | Total Liabilities & Net Worth | 100.0 | 100.0 |
| | | | | | | **INCOME DATA** | | |
| 100.0 | 100.0 | 100.0 | 100.0 | | | Net Sales | 100.0 | 100.0 |
| 29.5 | 33.9 | 22.8 | 20.8 | | | Gross Profit | 24.2 | 23.3 |
| 26.1 | 27.7 | 19.8 | 15.8 | | | Operating Expenses | 19.8 | 20.1 |
| 3.4 | 6.2 | 3.0 | 5.1 | | | Operating Profit | 4.4 | 3.2 |
| -.4 | .9 | .2 | .4 | | | All Other Expenses (net) | 1.0 | .4 |
| 3.8 | 5.3 | 2.8 | 4.7 | | | Profit Before Taxes | 3.4 | 2.8 |
| | | | | | | **RATIOS** | | |
| 2.7 | 2.8 | 2.3 | 2.2 | | | | 2.3 | 2.2 |
| 1.4 | 1.7 | 1.5 | 1.7 | | | Current | 1.5 | 1.4 |
| 1.0 | 1.2 | 1.1 | 1.2 | | | | 1.2 | 1.1 |
| 1.7 | 1.7 | 1.5 | 1.5 | | | | 1.5 | 1.4 |
| 1.1 | 1.0 | .9 | .9 | | | Quick | .9 | .9 |
| .2 | .6 | .7 | .6 | | | | .5 | .6 |
| 0 UND | 8 46.8 | 21 17.4 | 18 20.6 | | | | 18 20.7 | 18 20.4 |
| 0 UND | 20 18.7 | 34 10.6 | 45 8.2 | | | Sales/Receivables | 34 10.8 | 33 11.0 |
| 23 15.9 | 41 9.0 | 53 6.9 | 63 5.8 | | | | 51 7.2 | 52 7.0 |
| 0 UND | 0 UND | 3 117.1 | 0 UND | | | | 7 50.4 | 0 999.8 |
| 0 UND | 21 17.0 | 32 11.4 | 30 12.0 | | | Cost of Sales/Inventory | 31 11.8 | 18 19.8 |
| 16 22.6 | 72 5.1 | 78 4.7 | 65 5.6 | | | | 76 4.8 | 64 5.7 |
| 0 UND | 5 71.3 | 17 22.0 | 11 33.8 | | | | 8 44.7 | 10 36.5 |
| 2 174.9 | 24 15.4 | 30 12.0 | 29 12.5 | | | Cost of Sales/Payables | 24 15.0 | 24 15.0 |
| 19 19.2 | 47 7.8 | 49 7.4 | 56 6.5 | | | | 46 7.9 | 44 8.3 |
| 15.6 | 6.8 | 7.6 | 4.9 | | | | 7.5 | 8.4 |
| 26.5 | 16.7 | 15.3 | 12.6 | | | Sales/Working Capital | 16.3 | 19.1 |
| 999.8 | 67.5 | 52.0 | 39.7 | | | | 49.7 | 97.7 |
| 37.1 | 46.1 | 19.6 | 42.7 | | | | 10.2 | 16.5 |
| (12) 13.3 | (57) 8.9 | (73) 4.7 | (27) 6.4 | | | EBIT/Interest | (140) 3.7 | (148) 4.5 |
| 5.0 | 2.4 | 1.6 | 4.3 | | | | 1.5 | 1.6 |
| | | 16.0 | 7.5 | | | | 9.5 | 8.3 |
| | (10) 3.3 | | (10) 2.9 | | | Net Profit + Depr., Dep., Amort./Cur. Mat. L/T/D | (30) 3.7 | (24) 2.9 |
| | | 1.2 | 2.4 | | | | 1.3 | 1.7 |
| .0 | .0 | .0 | .0 | | | | .1 | .0 |
| .1 | .1 | .1 | .2 | | | Fixed/Worth | .2 | .2 |
| 1.5 | .6 | 1.2 | 1.2 | | | | .8 | .6 |
| .6 | .6 | 1.0 | 1.0 | | | | 1.0 | .9 |
| 1.5 | 1.9 | 2.3 | 1.5 | | | Debt/Worth | 2.6 | 2.2 |
| UND | 10.8 | 7.8 | 2.9 | | | | 7.2 | 6.7 |
| 309.7 | 84.4 | 53.1 | 52.0 | | | | 62.9 | 58.4 |
| (15) 62.1 | (53) 28.2 | (72) 24.9 | (29) 23.2 | | | % Profit Before Taxes/Tangible Net Worth | (141) 24.2 | (154) 20.0 |
| 17.8 | 5.4 | 5.3 | 14.9 | | | | 6.6 | 8.9 |
| 49.3 | 33.5 | 17.5 | 13.8 | | | | 19.3 | 16.0 |
| 20.0 | 10.1 | 6.3 | 9.3 | | | % Profit Before Taxes/Total Assets | 7.6 | 6.7 |
| 2.4 | 2.0 | 1.1 | 5.1 | | | | 1.7 | 1.4 |
| UND | 999.8 | 999.8 | 414.3 | | | | 290.5 | 759.5 |
| 366.6 | 123.5 | 156.2 | 90.4 | | | Sales/Net Fixed Assets | 66.2 | 74.9 |
| 52.0 | 36.7 | 24.4 | 11.4 | | | | 20.6 | 22.1 |
| 16.3 | 5.8 | 6.9 | 4.9 | | | | 6.2 | 5.9 |
| 9.6 | 3.9 | 3.6 | 2.7 | | | Sales/Total Assets | 3.6 | 3.6 |
| 7.0 | 2.4 | 2.2 | 1.3 | | | | 2.4 | 2.3 |
| | | .1 | .1 | .1 | | | .1 | .2 |
| | (31) .5 | (52) .3 | (30) .3 | | | % Depr., Dep., Amort./Sales | (121) .4 | (121) .4 |
| | 1.0 | 1.0 | 2.1 | | | | 1.1 | 1.0 |
| | | 1.2 | .8 | | | | 1.0 | 1.0 |
| | (35) 3.8 | (41) 1.8 | | | | % Officers', Directors' Owners' Comp/Sales | (71) 2.4 | (90) 3.1 |
| | 6.8 | 3.6 | | | | | 3.6 | 6.0 |
| 68527M | 384992M | 1751477M | 2321747M | 237347M | 2937172M | Net Sales ($) | 11016257M | 9055793M |
| 4792M | 70098M | 367228M | 618151M | 144034M | 667303M | Total Assets ($) | 2604440M | 2169101M |

M = $ thousand　　MM = $ million
See Pages 9 through 22 for Explanation of Ratios and Data

## Comparative Historical Data                                   Current Data Sorted by Sales

**Type of Statement**

| Type of Statement | 4/1/09-3/31/10 | 4/1/10-3/31/11 | 4/1/11-3/31/12 | 0-1MM | 1-3MM | 3-5MM | 5-10MM | 10-25MM | 25MM & OVER |
|---|---|---|---|---|---|---|---|---|---|
| Unqualified | 19 | 14 | 18 | | 1 | 1 | 4 | 2 | 16 |
| Reviewed | 23 | 24 | 22 | | 7 | 7 | 11 | 6 | 10 |
| Compiled | 29 | 25 | 42 | 1 | 9 | 8 | 12 | 9 | 7 |
| Tax Returns | 40 | 65 | 51 | 5 | | | | 12 | 5 |
| Other | 64 | 69 | 70 | 2 | 14 | 9 | 11 | 15 | 19 |
| | ALL | ALL | ALL | | 31 (4/1-9/30/11) | | 172 (10/1/11-3/31/12) | | |
| **NUMBER OF STATEMENTS** | 175 | 197 | 203 | 8 | 31 | 25 | 38 | 44 | 57 |

| | % | % | % | | % | % | % | % | % |
|---|---|---|---|---|---|---|---|---|---|
| **ASSETS** | | | | | | | | | |
| Cash & Equivalents | 12.2 | 15.1 | 14.6 | | 16.6 | 22.7 | 16.0 | 12.8 | 10.5 |
| Trade Receivables (net) | 36.0 | 34.0 | 33.9 | | 22.3 | 19.7 | 29.3 | 39.8 | 46.8 |
| Inventory | 25.2 | 25.4 | 24.3 | | 31.3 | 26.6 | 24.8 | 22.3 | 22.8 |
| All Other Current | 5.1 | 3.3 | 3.8 | | 2.1 | 4.3 | 1.7 | 7.6 | 3.2 |
| Total Current | 78.5 | 77.7 | 76.5 | | 72.3 | 73.3 | 71.9 | 82.5 | 83.3 |
| Fixed Assets (net) | 10.7 | 10.8 | 11.4 | | 17.1 | 8.1 | 13.9 | 9.2 | 9.1 |
| Intangibles (net) | 2.3 | 3.5 | 3.1 | | 3.4 | 4.3 | 1.9 | 1.6 | 2.7 |
| All Other Non-Current | 8.5 | 8.0 | 8.9 | | 7.2 | 14.3 | 12.3 | 6.7 | 4.9 |
| Total | 100.0 | 100.0 | 100.0 | | 100.0 | 100.0 | 100.0 | 100.0 | 100.0 |
| **LIABILITIES** | | | | | | | | | |
| Notes Payable-Short Term | 16.7 | 16.9 | 13.1 | | 8.0 | 20.2 | 8.7 | 11.9 | 17.0 |
| Cur. Mat.-L.T.D. | 3.8 | 2.6 | 3.5 | | 6.2 | 3.8 | 4.3 | 3.8 | 1.1 |
| Trade Payables | 24.5 | 22.8 | 22.6 | | 11.5 | 16.9 | 20.9 | 27.6 | 29.8 |
| Income Taxes Payable | .1 | .1 | .0 | | .0 | .1 | .1 | .0 | .0 |
| All Other Current | 10.5 | 11.8 | 10.9 | | 13.9 | 9.6 | 8.8 | 13.1 | 7.5 |
| Total Current | 55.6 | 54.1 | 50.1 | | 39.5 | 50.6 | 42.8 | 56.5 | 55.4 |
| Long-Term Debt | 8.8 | 8.9 | 11.2 | | 15.2 | 12.4 | 16.1 | 7.9 | 7.5 |
| Deferred Taxes | .1 | .1 | .1 | | .0 | .0 | .0 | .1 | .1 |
| All Other Non-Current | 4.6 | 7.6 | 5.7 | | 6.6 | 8.2 | 5.1 | 5.5 | 4.6 |
| Net Worth | 31.0 | 29.2 | 33.0 | | 38.7 | 28.8 | 36.1 | 30.0 | 32.4 |
| Total Liabilities & Net Worth | 100.0 | 100.0 | 100.0 | | 100.0 | 100.0 | 100.0 | 100.0 | 100.0 |
| **INCOME DATA** | | | | | | | | | |
| Net Sales | 100.0 | 100.0 | 100.0 | | 100.0 | 100.0 | 100.0 | 100.0 | 100.0 |
| Gross Profit | 26.4 | 26.5 | 26.7 | | 39.4 | 32.1 | 31.6 | 20.9 | 14.9 |
| Operating Expenses | 22.7 | 22.2 | 22.3 | | 32.4 | 27.5 | 28.0 | 16.7 | 12.3 |
| Operating Profit | 3.8 | 4.4 | 4.4 | | 7.1 | 4.6 | 3.6 | 4.2 | 2.6 |
| All Other Expenses (net) | .6 | .4 | .4 | | .7 | 1.6 | .1 | .5 | -.1 |
| Profit Before Taxes | 3.2 | 4.0 | 4.0 | | 6.4 | 2.9 | 3.5 | 3.7 | 2.7 |
| **RATIOS** | | | | | | | | | |
| Current | 2.3 | 2.5 | 2.3 | | 3.6 | 3.2 | 2.5 | 2.1 | 2.2 |
| | 1.5 | 1.6 | 1.6 | | 2.0 | 1.7 | 1.6 | 1.3 | 1.6 |
| | 1.1 | 1.1 | 1.1 | | 1.3 | 1.0 | 1.2 | 1.1 | 1.2 |
| Quick | 1.6 | 1.6 | 1.6 | | 1.7 | 1.7 | 1.4 | 1.3 | 1.6 |
| | .9 | 1.0 | 1.0 | | 1.0 | 1.1 | 1.0 | .9 | 1.0 |
| | .6 | .5 | .6 | | .3 | .6 | .7 | .6 | .7 |
| Sales/Receivables | 14  25.3 | 11  32.4 | 12  30.8 | | 5  79.9 | 0  884.8 | 16  22.9 | 18  20.8 | 17  21.5 |
| | 35  10.5 | 32  11.3 | 28  13.1 | | 20  18.2 | 18  20.1 | 37  9.9 | 32  11.4 | 30  12.3 |
| | 59  6.2 | 54  6.8 | 51  7.2 | | 51  7.2 | 36  10.0 | 60  6.1 | 51  7.1 | 46  7.9 |
| Cost of Sales/Inventory | 2  240.2 | 1  343.6 | 0  999.8 | | 4  100.6 | 0  UND | 7  55.4 | 0  UND | 1  541.1 |
| | 28  13.2 | 27  13.3 | 21  17.4 | | 52  7.0 | 40  9.2 | 43  8.4 | 15  24.9 | 16  23.2 |
| | 69  5.3 | 78  4.7 | 70  5.2 | | 203  1.8 | 70  5.2 | 89  4.1 | 70  5.2 | 41  8.8 |
| Cost of Sales/Payables | 9  39.4 | 7  53.7 | 8  45.6 | | 0  UND | 8  47.6 | 23  16.2 | 8  46.4 | 9  40.0 |
| | 25  14.5 | 24  15.4 | 25  14.5 | | 12  30.1 | 24  14.9 | 34  10.6 | 29  12.6 | 20  18.2 |
| | 51  7.1 | 49  7.4 | 49  7.4 | | 30  12.0 | 50  7.3 | 60  6.1 | 51  7.1 | 41  9.0 |
| Sales/Working Capital | 6.5 | 6.1 | 7.4 | | 4.8 | 7.9 | 5.2 | 8.0 | 11.3 |
| | 15.0 | 14.7 | 16.6 | | 11.4 | 16.1 | 17.6 | 16.5 | 19.4 |
| | 77.8 | 71.9 | 60.8 | | 34.7 | NM | 41.9 | 66.1 | 73.1 |
| EBIT/Interest | 13.5 | 16.4 | 32.2 | | 43.4 | 30.3 | 15.9 | 36.9 | 38.5 |
| | (145) 4.3 | (159) 5.4 | (176) 6.5 | | (27) 6.0 | (21) 6.5 | (32) 5.2 | (40) 6.2 | (52) 7.5 |
| | 1.8 | 2.0 | 2.4 | | .9 | 1.9 | 1.5 | 1.8 | 4.4 |
| Net Profit + Depr., Dep., Amort./Cur. Mat. L/T/D | 4.3 | 10.1 | 11.3 | | | | | 21.0 | 11.0 |
| | (20) 1.7 | (24) 2.5 | (27) 3.3 | | | | | (10) 4.6 | (11) 3.4 |
| | .7 | .6 | 2.1 | | | | | 2.0 | 2.7 |
| Fixed/Worth | .0 | .0 | .0 | | .0 | .0 | .0 | .0 | .0 |
| | .2 | .2 | .1 | | .2 | .1 | .1 | .1 | .1 |
| | .9 | 1.0 | .9 | | 1.3 | .3 | .9 | 1.1 | .8 |
| Debt/Worth | .9 | 1.0 | .9 | | .6 | .4 | .7 | 1.2 | 1.0 |
| | 2.4 | 2.3 | 1.7 | | 1.5 | 1.6 | 2.1 | 2.1 | 1.6 |
| | 6.2 | 8.5 | 6.6 | | 15.3 | 7.8 | 5.3 | 6.8 | 7.3 |
| % Profit Before Taxes/Tangible Net Worth | 56.1 | 80.3 | 62.0 | | 54.4 | 59.0 | 65.2 | 49.8 | 70.3 |
| | (157) 18.9 | (164) 33.0 | (176) 27.2 | | (25) 15.0 | (20) 22.3 | (34) 20.2 | (39) 21.9 | (52) 37.7 |
| | 4.6 | 10.4 | 6.6 | | 1.3 | 2.4 | 3.4 | 5.9 | 19.7 |
| % Profit Before Taxes/Total Assets | 14.9 | 24.6 | 20.5 | | 32.4 | 14.4 | 28.1 | 19.5 | 17.7 |
| | 6.7 | 8.4 | 8.8 | | 10.0 | 8.0 | 6.0 | 7.7 | 9.7 |
| | 1.8 | 2.0 | 2.2 | | .7 | 1.5 | .8 | 1.3 | 5.1 |
| Sales/Net Fixed Assets | 420.0 | 706.1 | 999.8 | | 127.5 | UND | 825.7 | 984.4 | 999.8 |
| | 75.8 | 97.9 | 120.0 | | 36.8 | 302.7 | 101.4 | 182.2 | 248.0 |
| | 18.5 | 27.0 | 34.3 | | 12.6 | 54.7 | 12.9 | 39.1 | 50.8 |
| Sales/Total Assets | 6.1 | 6.5 | 7.0 | | 4.4 | 6.0 | 4.4 | 7.0 | 9.2 |
| | 3.3 | 3.4 | 3.9 | | 2.6 | 4.1 | 2.9 | 3.8 | 5.4 |
| | 2.0 | 2.1 | 2.3 | | 2.1 | 2.7 | 1.9 | 2.2 | 3.4 |
| % Depr., Dep., Amort./Sales | .1 | .1 | .1 | | .4 | | .2 | .1 | .0 |
| | (125) .5 | (127) .4 | (126) .4 | | (18) .7 | | (25) .4 | (29) .4 | (44) .2 |
| | 1.1 | 1.1 | 1.0 | | 3.5 | | 2.3 | .7 | .6 |
| % Officers', Directors' Owners' Comp/Sales | 1.2 | 1.1 | 1.0 | | 3.1 | 1.1 | 1.5 | .9 | .4 |
| | (78) 2.4 | (102) 2.2 | (92) 2.2 | | (14) 4.4 | (14) 3.7 | (17) 2.2 | (25) 1.6 | (19) .8 |
| | 5.1 | 4.7 | 4.9 | | 8.0 | 7.2 | 3.1 | 1.6 | 1.8 |
| Net Sales ($) | 12675131M | 6164022M | 7701262M | 5455M | 62923M | 103797M | 266973M | 747869M | 6514245M |
| Total Assets ($) | 1977019M | 1883801M | 1871606M | 7025M | 25687M | 30933M | 124755M | 255636M | 1427570M |

M = $ thousand    MM = $ million
See Pages 9 through 22 for Explanation of Ratios and Data

# RETAIL TRADE

### Current Data Sorted by Assets | | | | | | | Comparative Historical Data

| 0-500M | 500M-2MM | 2-10MM | 10-50MM | 50-100MM | 100-250MM | Type of Statement | 4/1/07-3/31/08 ALL | 4/1/08-3/31/09 ALL |
|---|---|---|---|---|---|---|---|---|
| 1 | | 26 | 37 | 13 | 14 | Unqualified | 91 | 86 |
| | 3 | 132 | 167 | 20 | 12 | Reviewed | 337 | 322 |
| 1 | 15 | 65 | 35 | 3 | 1 | Compiled | 118 | 126 |
| 3 | 23 | 187 | 89 | 4 | | Tax Returns | 230 | 265 |
| 8 | 56 | 870 | 700 | 39 | 16 | Other | 1699 | 1860 |
| | 112 (4/1-9/30/11) | | | 2,428 (10/1/11-3/31/12) | | | | |
| 13 | 97 | 1280 | 1028 | 79 | 43 | NUMBER OF STATEMENTS | 2475 | 2659 |
| % | % | % | % | % | % | **ASSETS** | % | % |
| 14.7 | 8.5 | 12.8 | 14.6 | 11.1 | 11.1 | Cash & Equivalents | 9.9 | 9.9 |
| 7.5 | 9.5 | 7.3 | 8.2 | 7.8 | 7.5 | Trade Receivables (net) | 7.0 | 6.6 |
| 64.8 | 65.1 | 61.9 | 52.0 | 44.8 | 40.8 | Inventory | 62.8 | 61.7 |
| 5.8 | 1.5 | 2.5 | 2.4 | 4.0 | 2.3 | All Other Current | 2.4 | 2.2 |
| 92.9 | 84.5 | 84.4 | 77.2 | 67.7 | 61.7 | Total Current | 82.1 | 80.3 |
| 3.4 | 8.2 | 7.5 | 11.2 | 18.6 | 23.4 | Fixed Assets (net) | 9.6 | 10.4 |
| 1.8 | 1.0 | 2.8 | 3.8 | 6.5 | 6.8 | Intangibles (net) | 2.7 | 3.1 |
| 1.2 | 6.3 | 5.3 | 7.9 | 7.2 | 8.2 | All Other Non-Current | 5.6 | 6.2 |
| 100.0 | 100.0 | 100.0 | 100.0 | 100.0 | 100.0 | Total | 100.0 | 100.0 |
| | | | | | | **LIABILITIES** | | |
| 40.1 | 37.6 | 49.9 | 47.7 | 39.9 | 34.2 | Notes Payable-Short Term | 50.9 | 51.7 |
| 1.8 | 1.2 | 1.7 | 1.5 | 2.8 | 3.5 | Cur. Mat.-L.T.D. | 2.3 | 1.9 |
| 10.9 | 12.0 | 5.0 | 4.2 | 5.1 | 6.4 | Trade Payables | 4.5 | 4.2 |
| .0 | .0 | .0 | .1 | .1 | .1 | Income Taxes Payable | .1 | .1 |
| 6.3 | 14.8 | 10.8 | 9.7 | 9.0 | 9.3 | All Other Current | 13.0 | 11.8 |
| 59.1 | 65.6 | 67.4 | 63.1 | 57.0 | 53.5 | Total Current | 70.7 | 69.8 |
| 41.4 | 9.1 | 6.0 | 7.7 | 11.7 | 15.3 | Long-Term Debt | 7.6 | 8.1 |
| .0 | .1 | .1 | .2 | .4 | .3 | Deferred Taxes | .1 | .1 |
| 39.5 | 8.6 | 4.2 | 3.3 | 3.4 | 2.4 | All Other Non-Current | 3.6 | 4.1 |
| -40.1 | 16.6 | 22.3 | 25.7 | 27.6 | 28.6 | Net Worth | 18.0 | 18.0 |
| 100.0 | 100.0 | 100.0 | 100.0 | 100.0 | 100.0 | Total Liabilities & Net Worth | 100.0 | 100.0 |
| | | | | | | **INCOME DATA** | | |
| 100.0 | 100.0 | 100.0 | 100.0 | 100.0 | 100.0 | Net Sales | 100.0 | 100.0 |
| 22.0 | 15.9 | 12.2 | 12.2 | 13.4 | 15.2 | Gross Profit | 13.1 | 13.4 |
| 20.0 | 17.7 | 12.1 | 11.5 | 11.4 | 12.8 | Operating Expenses | 12.9 | 14.2 |
| 2.0 | -1.8 | .1 | .7 | 2.0 | 2.4 | Operating Profit | .2 | -.8 |
| -.6 | -.8 | -1.2 | -1.2 | -.1 | -.2 | All Other Expenses (net) | -.4 | -.6 |
| 2.6 | -1.0 | 1.3 | 1.8 | 2.1 | 2.6 | Profit Before Taxes | .6 | -.2 |
| | | | | | | **RATIOS** | | |
| 3.7 | 1.8 | 1.4 | 1.4 | 1.4 | 1.3 | | 1.3 | 1.3 |
| 1.7 | 1.4 | 1.2 | 1.2 | 1.2 | 1.1 | Current | 1.1 | 1.1 |
| 1.2 | 1.0 | 1.1 | 1.1 | 1.0 | 1.0 | | 1.0 | 1.0 |
| 1.8 | .5 | .4 | .5 | .5 | .4 | | .3 | .3 |
| (12) .4 | .2 | .3 | .3 | .3 | .3 | Quick | (2472) .2 | (2657) .2 |
| .1 | .1 | .2 | .2 | .2 | .2 | | .1 | .1 |
| 0 UND | 2 243.3 | 3 129.8 | 4 90.8 | 4 93.3 | 5 66.7 | | 3 131.4 | 3 131.5 |
| 5 73.7 | 5 71.5 | 5 67.4 | 6 57.2 | 7 54.4 | 9 39.9 | Sales/Receivables | 5 70.3 | 5 68.1 |
| 8 46.0 | 10 36.1 | 9 40.0 | 10 35.0 | 13 28.3 | 14 26.3 | | 9 39.5 | 9 38.7 |
| 40 9.2 | 51 7.2 | 50 7.3 | 46 7.9 | 45 8.1 | 49 7.5 | | 57 6.4 | 60 6.0 |
| 62 5.9 | 83 4.4 | 66 5.5 | 60 6.1 | 59 6.2 | 56 6.5 | Cost of Sales/Inventory | 73 5.0 | 77 4.7 |
| 68 5.4 | 114 3.2 | 87 4.2 | 78 4.7 | 76 4.8 | 76 4.8 | | 93 3.9 | 99 3.7 |
| 0 UND | 2 215.1 | 2 177.0 | 2 157.0 | 3 113.0 | 4 93.7 | | 2 205.0 | 2 201.8 |
| 9 40.7 | 5 69.0 | 4 102.8 | 4 96.1 | 5 78.4 | 5 69.3 | Cost of Sales/Payables | 3 111.0 | 3 113.9 |
| 15 25.0 | 15 24.5 | 6 59.8 | 6 63.4 | 9 39.7 | 11 34.0 | | 6 66.2 | 6 66.1 |
| 9.5 | 8.7 | 14.8 | 15.8 | 15.7 | 21.1 | | 18.1 | 17.4 |
| 21.0 | 15.6 | 25.2 | 26.4 | 34.8 | 44.4 | Sales/Working Capital | 34.2 | 34.7 |
| 32.5 | 123.1 | 52.2 | 75.0 | 311.3 | 470.7 | | 129.1 | 230.1 |
| | 3.5 | 10.9 | 14.2 | 14.3 | 11.8 | | 3.7 | 3.2 |
| | (67) 1.6 | (804) 3.8 | (672) 5.4 | (70) 5.5 | (36) 4.9 | EBIT/Interest | (1933) 1.7 | (1975) 1.2 |
| | -1.1 | 1.6 | 2.4 | 2.7 | 3.1 | | .8 | -.4 |
| | | 7.8 | 5.7 | 3.4 | 4.5 | Net Profit + Depr., Dep., | 5.9 | 3.7 |
| | (42) 3.0 | (62) 2.2 | (14) 1.4 | (12) 2.4 | | Amort./Cur. Mat. L/T/D | (166) 2.0 | (145) 1.6 |
| | 1.1 | 1.0 | .7 | .6 | | | .6 | .4 |
| .0 | .1 | .1 | .1 | .4 | .6 | | .2 | .2 |
| .0 | .3 | .3 | .4 | .7 | 1.2 | Fixed/Worth | .5 | .5 |
| -.3 | 1.2 | .7 | 1.0 | 2.2 | 2.2 | | 1.7 | 2.2 |
| 1.8 | 1.3 | 2.3 | 2.1 | 2.2 | 2.1 | | 2.8 | 2.8 |
| 5.3 | 6.7 | 4.0 | 3.8 | 4.3 | 3.5 | Debt/Worth | 5.6 | 5.4 |
| -5.6 | 25.4 | 9.0 | 8.6 | 10.6 | 9.3 | | 16.9 | 18.4 |
| | 28.6 | 44.5 | 50.0 | 61.1 | 63.8 | % Profit Before Taxes/Tangible | 36.2 | 24.6 |
| | (79) 8.6 | (1139) 21.1 | (943) 29.0 | (75) 34.6 | (41) 33.0 | Net Worth | (2116) 15.7 | (2203) 6.2 |
| | -4.1 | 7.1 | 12.8 | 16.0 | 17.2 | | 1.5 | -9.3 |
| 18.2 | 4.6 | 8.8 | 10.2 | 8.4 | 8.6 | % Profit Before Taxes/Total | 6.0 | 4.0 |
| 5.3 | 1.2 | 4.3 | 5.7 | 6.2 | 6.0 | Assets | 2.1 | .5 |
| .9 | -4.6 | 1.2 | 2.5 | 2.9 | 3.5 | | -.7 | -3.2 |
| UND | 322.8 | 206.8 | 162.4 | 54.3 | 37.9 | | 142.4 | 129.0 |
| UND | 88.7 | 96.6 | 62.8 | 24.1 | 12.7 | Sales/Net Fixed Assets | 67.7 | 60.4 |
| 101.9 | 31.3 | 41.4 | 24.0 | 9.0 | 7.8 | | 28.9 | 25.4 |
| 7.1 | 5.1 | 4.7 | 4.4 | 3.8 | 3.8 | | 4.5 | 4.1 |
| 5.1 | 3.7 | 3.8 | 3.6 | 3.1 | 2.8 | Sales/Total Assets | 3.6 | 3.3 |
| 4.2 | 2.4 | 3.1 | 2.8 | 2.4 | 2.1 | | 2.8 | 2.6 |
| | .1 | .1 | .1 | .3 | .3 | | .1 | .2 |
| | (64) .3 | (1027) .2 | (933) .2 | (77) .5 | (38) .5 | % Depr., Dep., Amort./Sales | (2150) .2 | (2297) .3 |
| | .7 | .4 | .4 | 1.0 | .9 | | .4 | .5 |
| | .7 | .3 | .2 | | .1 | | .3 | .3 |
| | (43) 1.3 | (733) .6 | (592) .5 | (31) .3 | | % Officers', Directors' Owners' Comp/Sales | (1514) .5 | (1558) .5 |
| | 2.3 | 1.1 | .8 | | .6 | | 1.0 | 1.0 |
| 14462M | 526494M | 30383538M | 68292934M | 16809002M | 19348712M | Net Sales ($) | 126662900M | 118960218M |
| 2161M | 130372M | 7628404M | 19440197M | 5483393M | 6610340M | Total Assets ($) | 35620298M | 36681715M |

## Comparative Historical Data

## Current Data Sorted by Sales

**Type of Statement**

| 4/1/09-3/31/10 ALL | 4/1/10-3/31/11 ALL | 4/1/11-3/31/12 ALL | Type of Statement | 0-1MM | 1-3MM | 3-5MM | 5-10MM | 10-25MM | 25MM & OVER |
|---|---|---|---|---|---|---|---|---|---|
| 115 | 87 | 91 | Unqualified | 1 | | | 3 | 11 | 76 |
| 380 | 328 | 334 | Reviewed | | | 2 | 8 | 60 | 264 |
| 113 | 109 | 120 | Compiled | | 7 | 4 | 10 | 44 | 55 |
| 335 | 290 | 306 | Tax Returns | 2 | 9 | 10 | 29 | 104 | 152 |
| 1747 | 1671 | 1689 | Other | 8 | 26 | 21 | 101 | 464 | 1069 |

Current data center labels: 112 (4/1-9/30/11) spans 0-1MM and 1-3MM; 2,428 (10/1/11-3/31/12) spans 3-5MM through 25MM & OVER.

| Hist 4/1/09-3/31/10 | Hist 4/1/10-3/31/11 | Hist 4/1/11-3/31/12 | | 0-1MM | 1-3MM | 3-5MM | 5-10MM | 10-25MM | 25MM & OVER |
|---|---|---|---|---|---|---|---|---|---|
| 2690 | 2485 | 2540 | **NUMBER OF STATEMENTS** | 11 | 42 | 37 | 151 | 683 | 1616 |
| % | % | % | **ASSETS** | % | % | % | % | % | % |
| 12.3 | 12.2 | 13.3 | Cash & Equivalents | 25.4 | 10.1 | 4.9 | 11.3 | 11.4 | 14.4 |
| 7.7 | 7.3 | 7.8 | Trade Receivables (net) | 10.4 | 7.8 | 8.4 | 7.9 | 7.6 | 7.8 |
| 54.7 | 57.7 | 57.1 | Inventory | 51.0 | 57.1 | 65.6 | 61.7 | 62.0 | 54.5 |
| 2.4 | 2.5 | 2.5 | All Other Current | .6 | 2.2 | 2.4 | 1.8 | 2.3 | 2.6 |
| 77.1 | 79.7 | 80.6 | Total Current | 87.5 | 77.2 | 81.2 | 82.7 | 83.3 | 79.3 |
| 11.5 | 10.5 | 9.6 | Fixed Assets (net) | 3.4 | 15.6 | 7.2 | 8.7 | 8.4 | 10.2 |
| 3.9 | 3.3 | 3.3 | Intangibles (net) | 2.2 | 2.1 | 3.8 | 3.1 | 2.9 | 3.6 |
| 7.4 | 6.5 | 6.5 | All Other Non-Current | 6.1 | 5.1 | 7.8 | 5.5 | 5.4 | 7.0 |
| 100.0 | 100.0 | 100.0 | Total | 100.0 | 100.0 | 100.0 | 100.0 | 100.0 | 100.0 |
| | | | **LIABILITIES** | | | | | | |
| 46.0 | 48.8 | 47.9 | Notes Payable-Short Term | 37.3 | 41.5 | 39.1 | 41.0 | 49.2 | 48.5 |
| 1.8 | 1.7 | 1.7 | Cur. Mat.-L.T.D. | .9 | 1.2 | 3.1 | 3.9 | 1.8 | 1.4 |
| 5.1 | 5.0 | 5.0 | Trade Payables | 4.0 | 9.1 | 7.5 | 7.7 | 5.1 | 4.5 |
| .1 | .1 | .1 | Income Taxes Payable | .0 | .4 | .0 | .0 | .0 | .1 |
| 11.0 | 9.9 | 10.4 | All Other Current | 14.8 | 11.1 | 12.1 | 10.6 | 10.6 | 10.2 |
| 63.9 | 65.5 | 65.0 | Total Current | 57.0 | 63.3 | 61.8 | 63.3 | 66.8 | 64.6 |
| 9.3 | 7.9 | 7.3 | Long-Term Debt | 26.9 | 18.5 | 12.8 | 9.5 | 6.7 | 6.8 |
| .1 | .1 | .1 | Deferred Taxes | .0 | .2 | .0 | .1 | .1 | .1 |
| 4.8 | 4.5 | 4.1 | All Other Non-Current | .0 | 7.6 | 19.4 | 8.2 | 4.2 | 3.3 |
| 21.9 | 22.0 | 23.4 | Net Worth | 15.9 | 10.4 | 5.9 | 18.9 | 22.2 | 25.1 |
| 100.0 | 100.0 | 100.0 | Total Liabilities & Net Worth | 100.0 | 100.0 | 100.0 | 100.0 | 100.0 | 100.0 |
| | | | **INCOME DATA** | | | | | | |
| 100.0 | 100.0 | 100.0 | Net Sales | 100.0 | 100.0 | 100.0 | 100.0 | 100.0 | 100.0 |
| 14.0 | 13.1 | 12.5 | Gross Profit | 23.2 | 18.9 | 14.9 | 15.4 | 12.3 | 12.0 |
| 14.3 | 12.9 | 12.1 | Operating Expenses | 23.5 | 20.1 | 16.2 | 16.0 | 12.4 | 11.2 |
| -.3 | .3 | .4 | Operating Profit | -.2 | -1.2 | -1.3 | -.6 | -.1 | .7 |
| -.9 | -1.0 | -1.1 | All Other Expenses (net) | -2.1 | -1.2 | -.6 | -.7 | -1.3 | -1.1 |
| .6 | 1.3 | 1.5 | Profit Before Taxes | 1.9 | .0 | -.7 | .1 | 1.2 | 1.8 |
| | | | **RATIOS** | | | | | | |
| 1.4 | 1.4 | 1.4 | Current | 3.3 | 1.8 | 1.8 | 1.6 | 1.4 | 1.4 |
| 1.2 | 1.2 | 1.2 | Current | 1.3 | 1.3 | 1.3 | 1.3 | 1.2 | 1.2 |
| 1.1 | 1.1 | 1.1 | Current | 1.2 | 1.0 | 1.1 | 1.1 | 1.1 | 1.1 |
| .4 | .4 | .4 | Quick | 1.2 | .5 | .4 | .4 | .4 | .5 |
| (2688) .3 | (2478) .3 | (2539) .3 | Quick | .6 | .2 | (36) .2 | .2 | .2 | .3 |
| .2 | .2 | .2 | Quick | .3 | .1 | .1 | .1 | .2 | .2 |
| 3 114.4 | 3 118.5 | 3 112.0 | Sales/Receivables | 0 UND | 0 UND | 2 158.8 | 2 149.7 | 3 117.8 | 4 103.4 |
| 6 63.5 | 6 64.4 | 6 61.7 | Sales/Receivables | 7 53.0 | 10 37.2 | 6 58.0 | 6 59.9 | 6 60.2 | 6 62.3 |
| 10 36.1 | 10 37.4 | 10 37.4 | Sales/Receivables | 10 37.7 | 28 13.2 | 17 21.6 | 11 32.2 | 10 36.1 | 9 39.0 |
| 51 7.2 | 54 6.8 | 48 7.6 | Cost of Sales/Inventory | 42 8.7 | 70 5.2 | 79 4.6 | 61 6.0 | 57 6.4 | 45 8.2 |
| 66 5.6 | 68 5.4 | 64 5.7 | Cost of Sales/Inventory | 62 5.9 | 130 2.8 | 94 3.9 | 87 4.2 | 74 4.9 | 58 6.3 |
| 85 4.3 | 87 4.2 | 83 4.4 | Cost of Sales/Inventory | 228 1.6 | 304 1.2 | 159 2.3 | 122 3.0 | 94 3.9 | 73 5.0 |
| 2 165.4 | 2 163.2 | 2 166.6 | Cost of Sales/Payables | 0 UND | 2 224.9 | 4 97.3 | 2 164.7 | 2 170.5 | 2 163.6 |
| 4 95.6 | 4 94.1 | 4 97.2 | Cost of Sales/Payables | 2 239.0 | 8 45.6 | 7 55.0 | 5 78.8 | 4 97.3 | 4 99.8 |
| 7 56.0 | 6 57.6 | 6 59.3 | Cost of Sales/Payables | 20 18.2 | 34 10.8 | 14 25.7 | 10 35.1 | 6 56.2 | 6 64.2 |
| 14.0 | 14.7 | 14.9 | Sales/Working Capital | 3.5 | 3.0 | 5.5 | 9.5 | 14.1 | 17.5 |
| 26.8 | 26.9 | 25.8 | Sales/Working Capital | 21.0 | 10.4 | 11.7 | 15.1 | 23.9 | 28.6 |
| 99.1 | 69.5 | 61.0 | Sales/Working Capital | 38.0 | NM | 40.2 | 46.4 | 52.0 | 70.3 |
| 6.3 | 9.8 | 11.9 | EBIT/Interest | | 3.3 | 6.9 | 3.5 | 8.8 | 14.8 |
| (1830) 2.3 | (1650) 3.4 | (1654) 4.4 | EBIT/Interest | | (27) 1.6 | (26) 1.8 | (104) 1.6 | (447) 3.4 | (1048) 5.5 |
| .8 | 1.5 | 1.9 | EBIT/Interest | | .9 | -1.2 | -.2 | 1.5 | 2.5 |
| 4.3 | 8.6 | 5.7 | Net Profit + Depr., Dep., Amort./Cur. Mat. L/T/D | | | | | 7.8 | 5.5 |
| (157) 1.8 | (154) 3.0 | (131) 2.3 | Net Profit + Depr., Dep., Amort./Cur. Mat. L/T/D | | | | (22) 2.7 | (100) 2.7 | 2.2 |
| .5 | 1.2 | 1.0 | Net Profit + Depr., Dep., Amort./Cur. Mat. L/T/D | | | | | 1.0 | 1.0 |
| .1 | .1 | .1 | Fixed/Worth | .0 | .0 | .1 | .1 | .1 | .1 |
| .4 | .4 | .3 | Fixed/Worth | .0 | .3 | .3 | .3 | .3 | .3 |
| 1.8 | 1.2 | 1.0 | Fixed/Worth | .3 | 2.4 | 2.9 | 1.6 | 1.0 | .9 |
| 2.1 | 2.2 | 2.2 | Debt/Worth | 1.4 | 1.6 | 2.3 | 1.9 | 2.3 | 2.2 |
| 4.3 | 4.2 | 3.9 | Debt/Worth | 3.0 | 6.8 | 6.4 | 4.3 | 4.2 | 3.8 |
| 12.6 | 10.7 | 9.2 | Debt/Worth | -11.0 | 236.4 | 28.2 | 24.8 | 9.8 | 8.4 |
| 34.5 | 43.7 | 47.4 | % Profit Before Taxes/Tangible Net Worth | | 18.5 | 16.9 | 21.5 | 37.7 | 53.5 |
| (2283) 14.3 | (2174) 22.1 | (2285) 24.7 | % Profit Before Taxes/Tangible Net Worth | | (33) 5.5 | (30) 3.2 | (123) 8.6 | (601) 18.3 | (1490) 30.3 |
| 1.0 | 7.0 | 9.4 | % Profit Before Taxes/Tangible Net Worth | | -3.6 | -21.7 | -2.2 | 5.8 | 14.2 |
| 6.9 | 8.2 | 9.3 | % Profit Before Taxes/Total Assets | 12.0 | 2.6 | 4.0 | 4.6 | 7.3 | 10.7 |
| 2.7 | 4.2 | 4.9 | % Profit Before Taxes/Total Assets | 5.3 | .8 | .0 | 1.1 | 3.5 | 6.0 |
| -.4 | 1.1 | 1.7 | % Profit Before Taxes/Total Assets | -1.7 | -2.7 | -4.8 | -2.7 | 1.0 | 2.8 |
| 130.2 | 158.9 | 186.5 | Sales/Net Fixed Assets | UND | 233.7 | 127.5 | 220.9 | 187.2 | 181.5 |
| 57.4 | 65.1 | 77.7 | Sales/Net Fixed Assets | UND | 25.0 | 51.1 | 87.7 | 88.0 | 73.7 |
| 23.2 | 26.4 | 29.7 | Sales/Net Fixed Assets | 31.2 | 5.4 | 22.1 | 25.3 | 33.5 | 29.6 |
| 4.3 | 4.3 | 4.6 | Sales/Total Assets | 4.5 | 2.4 | 3.5 | 4.0 | 4.3 | 4.7 |
| 3.4 | 3.5 | 3.7 | Sales/Total Assets | 4.1 | 1.4 | 2.5 | 3.1 | 3.4 | 3.8 |
| 2.6 | 2.7 | 2.9 | Sales/Total Assets | .3 | .7 | 1.1 | 2.0 | 2.8 | 3.1 |
| .2 | .1 | .1 | % Depr., Dep., Amort./Sales | | .3 | .1 | .1 | .1 | .1 |
| (2319) .3 | (2099) .3 | (2142) .2 | % Depr., Dep., Amort./Sales | | (26) .6 | (26) .3 | (112) .2 | (550) .2 | (1427) .2 |
| .6 | .5 | .4 | % Depr., Dep., Amort./Sales | | 1.6 | .6 | .4 | .4 | .4 |
| .3 | .3 | .3 | % Officers', Directors' Owners' Comp/Sales | | 1.3 | .6 | .4 | .4 | .2 |
| (1541) .6 | (1468) .6 | (1407) .5 | % Officers', Directors' Owners' Comp/Sales | | (15) 2.0 | (15) 1.4 | (79) .8 | (404) .7 | (893) .5 |
| 1.2 | 1.1 | 1.1 | % Officers', Directors' Owners' Comp/Sales | | 4.3 | 2.7 | 1.5 | 1.2 | .8 |
| 107537821M | 112010036M | 135375142M | Net Sales ($) | 2983M | 80558M | 142106M | 1161542M | 12268407M | 121719546M |
| 34551873M | 34185159M | 39294867M | Total Assets ($) | 6505M | 87877M | 89778M | 550380M | 3844881M | 34715446M |

© RMA 2012

M = $ thousand    MM = $ million
See Pages 9 through 22 for Explanation of Ratios and Data

**Current Data Sorted by Assets**     **Comparative Historical Data**

| 0-500M | 500M-2MM | 2-10MM | 10-50MM | 50-100MM | 100-250MM | Type of Statement | 4/1/07-3/31/08 ALL | 4/1/08-3/31/09 ALL |
|---|---|---|---|---|---|---|---|---|
| | 1 | 10 | 8 | 3 | | Unqualified | 20 | 17 |
| 2 | 7 | 23 | 6 | 1 | | Reviewed | 25 | 27 |
| 16 | 39 | 34 | 4 | | | Compiled | 102 | 108 |
| 70 | 107 | 42 | 6 | | 1 | Tax Returns | 212 | 224 |
| 23 | 64 | 63 | 12 | 5 | 2 | Other | 189 | 192 |
| | 52 (4/1-9/30/11) | | 497 (10/1/11-3/31/12) | | | | | |
| 111 | 218 | 172 | 36 | 9 | 3 | **NUMBER OF STATEMENTS** | 548 | 568 |
| % | % | % | % | % | % | **ASSETS** | % | % |
| 13.5 | 7.6 | 6.6 | 4.6 | | | Cash & Equivalents | 7.5 | 7.7 |
| 5.4 | 10.3 | 19.5 | 42.2 | | | Trade Receivables (net) | 13.1 | 14.3 |
| 61.9 | 63.0 | 55.0 | 31.2 | | | Inventory | 59.1 | 56.8 |
| 2.6 | 1.7 | 2.9 | 4.2 | | | All Other Current | 3.8 | 2.6 |
| 83.4 | 82.6 | 84.0 | 82.3 | | | Total Current | 83.5 | 81.5 |
| 10.7 | 8.9 | 9.5 | 7.1 | | | Fixed Assets (net) | 10.6 | 11.8 |
| .8 | 1.5 | 1.2 | 1.7 | | | Intangibles (net) | .8 | 1.1 |
| 4.9 | 6.9 | 5.3 | 8.8 | | | All Other Non-Current | 5.1 | 5.7 |
| 100.0 | 100.0 | 100.0 | 100.0 | | | Total | 100.0 | 100.0 |
| | | | | | | **LIABILITIES** | | |
| 37.6 | 29.1 | 36.5 | 36.1 | | | Notes Payable-Short Term | 37.7 | 42.3 |
| 2.6 | 1.9 | 1.4 | 1.7 | | | Cur. Mat.-L.T.D. | 3.2 | 2.2 |
| 3.6 | 7.0 | 6.4 | 3.7 | | | Trade Payables | 5.6 | 5.0 |
| .1 | .1 | .1 | .0 | | | Income Taxes Payable | .1 | .1 |
| 25.9 | 14.7 | 12.1 | 9.1 | | | All Other Current | 10.8 | 12.3 |
| 69.7 | 52.8 | 56.4 | 50.5 | | | Total Current | 57.4 | 61.9 |
| 18.5 | 11.4 | 10.3 | 12.9 | | | Long-Term Debt | 11.7 | 11.7 |
| .0 | .0 | .1 | .0 | | | Deferred Taxes | .0 | .0 |
| 14.5 | 12.6 | 7.7 | 5.1 | | | All Other Non-Current | 8.2 | 8.5 |
| -2.6 | 23.1 | 25.5 | 31.5 | | | Net Worth | 22.7 | 17.9 |
| 100.0 | 100.0 | 100.0 | 100.0 | | | Total Liabilties & Net Worth | 100.0 | 100.0 |
| | | | | | | **INCOME DATA** | | |
| 100.0 | 100.0 | 100.0 | 100.0 | | | Net Sales | 100.0 | 100.0 |
| 20.3 | 20.0 | 20.1 | 32.7 | | | Gross Profit | 19.6 | 20.2 |
| 18.6 | 18.4 | 17.2 | 24.3 | | | Operating Expenses | 17.4 | 18.5 |
| 1.7 | 1.6 | 3.0 | 8.3 | | | Operating Profit | 2.2 | 1.7 |
| .5 | .4 | .8 | 2.7 | | | All Other Expenses (net) | .8 | .9 |
| 1.2 | 1.2 | 2.1 | 5.7 | | | Profit Before Taxes | 1.4 | .8 |
| | | | | | | **RATIOS** | | |
| 5.7 | 2.8 | 2.3 | 3.0 | | | | 2.3 | 2.1 |
| 1.5 | 1.6 | 1.5 | 1.4 | | | Current | 1.4 | 1.3 |
| 1.0 | 1.2 | 1.1 | 1.1 | | | | 1.1 | 1.0 |
| 1.0 | .7 | .9 | 1.5 | | | | .7 | .8 |
| (109) .2 | (216) .3 | .3 | 1.1 | | | Quick | (546) .2 | (566) .2 |
| .1 | .1 | .1 | .2 | | | | .1 | .1 |
| 0 UND | 0 UND | 1 257.6 | 7 49.1 | | | | 0 UND | 0 UND |
| 0 UND | 2 177.7 | 6 60.1 | 99 3.7 | | | Sales/Receivables | 3 117.3 | 3 138.4 |
| 3 116.0 | 11 32.8 | 23 15.9 | 332 1.1 | | | | 15 24.8 | 14 26.5 |
| 30 12.2 | 45 8.1 | 48 7.6 | 50 7.3 | | | | 41 8.9 | 40 9.0 |
| 61 6.0 | 66 5.5 | 73 5.0 | 64 5.7 | | | Cost of Sales/Inventory | 65 5.6 | 65 5.6 |
| 104 3.5 | 111 3.3 | 101 3.6 | 94 3.9 | | | | 97 3.8 | 101 3.6 |
| 0 UND | 0 UND | 1 468.7 | 2 146.1 | | | | 0 UND | 0 UND |
| 0 UND | 2 149.8 | 4 103.4 | 6 62.0 | | | Cost of Sales/Payables | 2 172.2 | 2 167.9 |
| 1 314.3 | 9 39.1 | 11 33.0 | 13 28.0 | | | | 7 49.2 | 7 53.2 |
| 6.5 | 7.4 | 5.0 | 2.5 | | | | 6.9 | 7.1 |
| 21.3 | 14.7 | 11.7 | 4.2 | | | Sales/Working Capital | 18.9 | 19.6 |
| -999.8 | 47.7 | 51.8 | 21.9 | | | | 77.1 | 214.4 |
| 7.3 | 6.7 | 6.1 | 6.1 | | | | 4.5 | 4.0 |
| (76) 3.1 | (186) 2.5 | (156) 2.7 | (34) 3.6 | | | EBIT/Interest | (485) 1.9 | (491) 1.5 |
| -.2 | 1.1 | 1.3 | 1.7 | | | | 1.0 | .1 |
| | | 19.7 | | | | | 11.8 | 14.1 |
| | | (10) 6.0 | | | | Net Profit + Depr., Dep., Amort./Cur. Mat. L/T/D | (16) 2.0 | (16) 3.1 |
| | | 1.2 | | | | | 1.0 | .9 |
| .0 | .0 | .0 | .0 | | | | .0 | .0 |
| .1 | .2 | .2 | .2 | | | Fixed/Worth | .2 | .3 |
| UND | 1.0 | 1.0 | .5 | | | | 1.4 | 3.8 |
| 1.0 | 1.2 | 1.3 | 1.1 | | | | 1.5 | 1.6 |
| 3.8 | 3.2 | 3.7 | 3.0 | | | Debt/Worth | 3.9 | 4.3 |
| -9.2 | 15.0 | 8.9 | 6.0 | | | | 16.0 | 33.7 |
| 93.0 | 50.1 | 46.8 | 40.0 | | | | 48.1 | 39.9 |
| (79) 37.9 | (182) 21.5 | (156) 19.6 | (35) 21.8 | | | % Profit Before Taxes/Tangible Net Worth | (461) 20.2 | (445) 13.9 |
| 5.5 | 4.4 | 8.5 | 14.3 | | | | 3.8 | -5.3 |
| 22.7 | 11.3 | 10.0 | 10.5 | | | | 12.2 | 8.9 |
| 5.7 | 5.2 | 4.8 | 5.9 | | | % Profit Before Taxes/Total Assets | 3.9 | 2.2 |
| -2.9 | .3 | 1.2 | 3.9 | | | | .1 | -4.0 |
| UND | 999.8 | 412.0 | 140.3 | | | | 526.3 | 408.0 |
| 219.6 | 151.1 | 111.9 | 58.5 | | | Sales/Net Fixed Assets | 97.5 | 79.5 |
| 34.6 | 42.9 | 28.1 | 21.7 | | | | 25.1 | 23.7 |
| 7.6 | 6.1 | 4.7 | 3.6 | | | | 5.9 | 5.5 |
| 4.4 | 3.9 | 3.2 | 1.2 | | | Sales/Total Assets | 3.8 | 3.5 |
| 2.6 | 2.5 | 1.8 | .8 | | | | 2.4 | 2.2 |
| .2 | .1 | .1 | .1 | | | | .1 | .1 |
| (53) .3 | (115) .2 | (112) .2 | (32) .3 | | | % Depr., Dep., Amort./Sales | (367) .3 | (383) .3 |
| .8 | .6 | .5 | .6 | | | | .5 | .6 |
| 1.2 | .8 | .8 | 1.1 | | | | .8 | .8 |
| (57) 2.1 | (128) 1.7 | (88) 1.2 | | | | % Officers', Directors' Owners' Comp/Sales | (301) 1.6 | (295) 1.7 |
| 4.1 | 3.0 | 2.2 | | | | | 3.0 | 3.5 |
| 174818M | 1110937M | 2491582M | 1369875M | 855081M | 2122533M | Net Sales ($) | 7942528M | 6177684M |
| 28326M | 241079M | 728378M | 792274M | 611460M | 548479M | Total Assets ($) | 2621151M | 2311390M |

M = $ thousand    MM = $ million
See Pages 9 through 22 for Explanation of Ratios and Data

## Comparative Historical Data / Current Data Sorted by Sales

| 4/1/09-3/31/10 ALL | 4/1/10-3/31/11 ALL | 4/1/11-3/31/12 ALL | Type of Statement | 0-1MM | 1-3MM | 3-5MM | 5-10MM | 10-25MM | 25MM & OVER |
|---|---|---|---|---|---|---|---|---|---|
| 25 | 14 | 22 | Unqualified |  | 1 |  | 5 | 4 | 12 |
| 35 | 34 | 39 | Reviewed | 2 | 2 |  | 9 | 16 | 10 |
| 99 | 105 | 93 | Compiled | 9 | 18 | 24 | 17 | 21 | 4 |
| 235 | 236 | 226 | Tax Returns | 39 | 60 | 35 | 53 | 28 | 11 |
| 147 | 157 | 169 | Other | 15 | 33 | 24 | 34 | 40 | 23 |
|  |  |  |  | *52 (4/1-9/30/11)* |  |  | *497 (10/1/11-3/31/12)* |  |  |
| 541 | 546 | 549 | **NUMBER OF STATEMENTS** | 65 | 114 | 83 | 118 | 109 | 60 |
| % | % | % | **ASSETS** | % | % | % | % | % | % |
| 8.3 | 7.8 | 8.3 | Cash & Equivalents | 8.7 | 10.4 | 6.3 | 8.7 | 7.9 | 6.4 |
| 15.1 | 13.3 | 14.9 | Trade Receivables (net) | 11.1 | 12.6 | 12.9 | 15.0 | 16.3 | 23.9 |
| 57.5 | 59.4 | 57.1 | Inventory | 55.1 | 58.3 | 62.2 | 58.5 | 57.4 | 46.8 |
| 2.6 | 2.2 | 2.5 | All Other Current | 3.8 | 2.7 | .8 | 1.6 | 3.1 | 3.7 |
| 83.6 | 82.7 | 82.8 | Total Current | 78.7 | 84.0 | 82.2 | 83.8 | 84.7 | 80.8 |
| 10.2 | 10.7 | 9.6 | Fixed Assets (net) | 11.8 | 8.2 | 12.0 | 7.9 | 9.3 | 9.9 |
| 1.2 | 1.1 | 1.4 | Intangibles (net) | 1.1 | 2.0 | 2.0 | .7 | .6 | 2.3 |
| 5.0 | 5.5 | 6.2 | All Other Non-Current | 8.2 | 5.8 | 3.8 | 7.7 | 5.4 | 7.0 |
| 100.0 | 100.0 | 100.0 | Total | 100.0 | 100.0 | 100.0 | 100.0 | 100.0 | 100.0 |
|  |  |  | **LIABILITIES** |  |  |  |  |  |  |
| 39.8 | 35.4 | 33.8 | Notes Payable-Short Term | 27.6 | 40.5 | 24.4 | 35.1 | 33.8 | 38.3 |
| 3.6 | 3.4 | 1.9 | Cur. Mat.-L.T.D. | 2.1 | 2.8 | .6 | 1.6 | 2.5 | .9 |
| 5.2 | 6.2 | 5.8 | Trade Payables | 2.4 | 4.3 | 6.4 | 6.8 | 7.0 | 7.1 |
| .1 | .1 | .1 | Income Taxes Payable | .0 | .2 | .0 | .0 | .2 | .0 |
| 12.7 | 12.3 | 15.6 | All Other Current | 33.7 | 9.8 | 16.4 | 14.9 | 12.6 | 13.0 |
| 61.3 | 57.5 | 57.2 | Total Current | 65.8 | 57.6 | 47.9 | 58.5 | 56.1 | 59.2 |
| 11.8 | 12.0 | 12.7 | Long-Term Debt | 20.0 | 17.1 | 14.2 | 7.0 | 10.0 | 10.6 |
| .1 | .0 | .0 | Deferred Taxes | .0 | .0 | .0 | .0 | .1 | .1 |
| 11.3 | 11.8 | 10.8 | All Other Non-Current | 26.8 | 10.4 | 9.6 | 9.6 | 7.0 | 5.6 |
| 15.6 | 18.7 | 19.3 | Net Worth | -12.4 | 14.9 | 28.2 | 25.0 | 26.8 | 24.4 |
| 100.0 | 100.0 | 100.0 | Total Liabilties & Net Worth | 100.0 | 100.0 | 100.0 | 100.0 | 100.0 | 100.0 |
|  |  |  | **INCOME DATA** |  |  |  |  |  |  |
| 100.0 | 100.0 | 100.0 | Net Sales | 100.0 | 100.0 | 100.0 | 100.0 | 100.0 | 100.0 |
| 20.2 | 20.4 | 21.3 | Gross Profit | 26.6 | 22.5 | 19.8 | 20.2 | 18.0 | 23.3 |
| 18.6 | 18.1 | 18.6 | Operating Expenses | 26.2 | 19.0 | 17.5 | 18.3 | 15.3 | 18.3 |
| 1.6 | 2.3 | 2.6 | Operating Profit | .4 | 3.6 | 2.3 | 2.0 | 2.7 | 5.1 |
| .8 | .5 | .7 | All Other Expenses (net) | .6 | 1.2 | .1 | .5 | .4 | 1.9 |
| .8 | 1.8 | 1.9 | Profit Before Taxes | -.2 | 2.3 | 2.2 | 1.4 | 2.3 | 3.2 |
|  |  |  | **RATIOS** |  |  |  |  |  |  |
| 2.4 | 2.5 | 2.7 | Current | 14.2 | 2.9 | 3.9 | 2.2 | 2.3 | 1.8 |
| 1.4 | 1.4 | 1.5 |  | 2.0 | 1.6 | 1.7 | 1.4 | 1.5 | 1.3 |
| 1.1 | 1.1 | 1.1 |  | 1.0 | 1.1 | 1.2 | 1.1 | 1.2 | 1.1 |
| .7 | .8 | 1.0 | Quick | 1.8 | 1.1 | 1.5 | .7 | .8 | 1.1 |
| (538) .3 | (538) .3 | (545) .3 |  | .3 | (111) .3 | (82) .2 | .3 | .3 | .4 |
| .1 | .1 | .1 |  | .1 | .1 | .1 | .1 | .1 | .1 |
| 0 UND | 0 UND | 0 UND | Sales/Receivables | 0 UND | 0 UND | 0 UND | 0 UND | 1 430.3 | 2 174.8 |
| 3 119.8 | 3 127.4 | 3 113.9 |  | 0 UND | 1 459.9 | 3 109.2 | 4 100.6 | 4 81.2 | 7 51.1 |
| 15 25.1 | 11 34.5 | 14 26.3 |  | 28 13.2 | 13 27.2 | 11 32.9 | 12 29.3 | 13 27.2 | 49 7.4 |
| 43 8.5 | 43 8.4 | 45 8.1 | Cost of Sales/Inventory | 60 6.1 | 53 6.9 | 49 7.5 | 43 8.4 | 37 9.8 | 40 9.1 |
| 65 5.6 | 63 5.8 | 66 5.5 |  | 114 3.2 | 83 4.4 | 76 4.8 | 60 6.1 | 57 6.4 | 59 6.2 |
| 100 3.6 | 97 3.8 | 104 3.5 |  | 215 1.7 | 122 3.0 | 114 3.2 | 81 4.5 | 91 4.0 | 72 5.1 |
| 0 UND | 0 UND | 0 UND | Cost of Sales/Payables | 0 UND | 0 UND | 0 UND | 0 UND | 0 733.1 | 3 143.3 |
| 2 181.9 | 2 154.2 | 2 153.2 |  | 0 UND | 1 676.1 | 2 180.1 | 5 70.8 | 2 168.0 | 6 61.3 |
| 7 52.0 | 7 49.5 | 9 41.0 |  | 4 96.2 | 7 54.8 | 7 52.7 | 11 32.2 | 6 61.3 | 12 29.3 |
| 6.7 | 7.3 | 5.4 | Sales/Working Capital | 2.4 | 5.3 | 5.1 | 7.9 | 6.6 | 5.8 |
| 15.9 | 15.9 | 13.6 |  | 6.1 | 11.1 | 11.5 | 18.3 | 18.7 | 15.8 |
| 102.0 | 58.2 | 56.7 |  | UND | 50.3 | 55.9 | 60.6 | 49.1 | 71.6 |
| 4.9 | 5.6 | 6.6 | EBIT/Interest | 5.3 | 6.6 | 7.9 | 6.1 | 5.5 | 7.5 |
| (472) 2.1 | (476) 2.6 | (464) 2.8 |  | (43) 2.0 | (92) 2.3 | (74) 3.0 | (107) 2.1 | (93) 3.4 | (55) 3.4 |
| .7 | 1.1 | 1.2 |  | -.7 | 1.0 | 1.1 | 1.0 | 1.8 | 1.7 |
| 6.4 | 9.9 | 21.7 | Net Profit + Depr., Dep., Amort./Cur. Mat. L/T/D |  |  |  |  | 31.4 |  |
| (21) 3.4 | (16) 2.8 | (26) 8.7 |  |  |  |  |  | (11) 19.4 |  |
| .5 | .5 | 1.3 |  |  |  |  |  | 1.2 |  |
| .0 | .0 | .0 | Fixed/Worth | .0 | .0 | .0 | .0 | .0 | .0 |
| .3 | .2 | .2 |  | .4 | .1 | .2 | .1 | .2 | .3 |
| 4.0 | 2.2 | 1.0 |  | -18.5 | 1.0 | 1.9 | .7 | .7 | .8 |
| 1.4 | 1.4 | 1.2 | Debt/Worth | .9 | 1.2 | 1.0 | 1.6 | 1.2 | 1.7 |
| 4.1 | 3.9 | 3.4 |  | 6.9 | 3.2 | 2.6 | 3.2 | 4.0 | 3.3 |
| 189.5 | 40.4 | 12.2 |  | -5.7 | 31.5 | 17.4 | 9.0 | 9.0 | 7.8 |
| 39.4 | 52.4 | 51.9 | % Profit Before Taxes/Tangible Net Worth | 100.0 | 50.8 | 54.4 | 37.8 | 57.0 | 48.5 |
| (414) 17.7 | (428) 23.0 | (463) 22.3 |  | (43) 15.7 | (90) 19.4 | (67) 20.8 | (106) 21.1 | (100) 25.6 | (57) 25.5 |
| 2.8 | 6.3 | 7.4 |  | 1.5 | 6.6 | 3.1 | 4.3 | 11.8 | 14.1 |
| 9.1 | 12.3 | 11.7 | % Profit Before Taxes/Total Assets | 10.3 | 13.5 | 13.0 | 11.0 | 11.3 | 11.9 |
| 3.9 | 4.8 | 5.3 |  | .7 | 4.2 | 5.8 | 4.4 | 6.6 | 6.1 |
| -.8 | .2 | .6 |  | -5.8 | .3 | .7 | .1 | 2.4 | 3.4 |
| 463.8 | 462.2 | 618.1 | Sales/Net Fixed Assets | UND | 999.8 | 999.8 | 476.5 | 506.4 | 276.7 |
| 90.7 | 96.9 | 121.8 |  | 73.0 | 194.1 | 98.0 | 168.6 | 105.2 | 64.4 |
| 26.1 | 27.2 | 32.1 |  | 18.8 | 39.6 | 21.9 | 52.1 | 32.4 | 21.1 |
| 5.3 | 5.8 | 5.5 | Sales/Total Assets | 3.1 | 4.7 | 5.1 | 6.0 | 7.5 | 5.4 |
| 3.6 | 4.0 | 3.6 |  | 2.0 | 3.2 | 3.5 | 4.2 | 4.2 | 4.1 |
| 2.1 | 2.3 | 2.0 |  | 1.0 | 1.9 | 2.3 | 2.5 | 2.7 | 1.1 |
| .1 | .1 | .1 | % Depr., Dep., Amort./Sales | .4 | .1 | .1 | .1 | .1 | .1 |
| (372) .3 | (362) .3 | (322) .3 |  | (29) .9 | (54) .3 | (46) .3 | (70) .2 | (73) .2 | (50) .2 |
| .7 | .6 | .6 |  | 1.4 | .5 | .8 | .5 | .6 | .5 |
| .9 | .8 | .8 | % Officers', Directors' Owners' Comp/Sales | 2.3 | 1.2 | .8 | 1.0 | .5 | .5 |
| (294) 1.8 | (292) 1.7 | (284) 1.7 |  | (24) 3.7 | (64) 2.2 | (51) 1.6 | (60) 1.6 | (60) .9 | (25) 1.0 |
| 3.2 | 3.2 | 2.9 |  | 6.9 | 4.2 | 2.5 | 2.2 | 2.0 | 2.1 |
| 9299312M | 7376818M | 8124826M | Net Sales ($) | 28655M | 212616M | 325513M | 838811M | 1655481M | 5063750M |
| 2945039M | 2351532M | 2949996M | Total Assets ($) | 22865M | 100078M | 110078M | 300002M | 551329M | 1865644M |

M = $ thousand    MM = $ million
See Pages 9 through 22 for Explanation of Ratios and Data

## Current Data Sorted by Assets

## Comparative Historical Data

| | | | | | | Type of Statement | | |
|---|---|---|---|---|---|---|---|---|
| | | 4 | 9 | 1 | | Unqualified | 9 | 11 |
| | 2 | 19 | 13 | 1 | | Reviewed | 52 | 52 |
| | 18 | 38 | 5 | | | Compiled | 96 | 106 |
| 4 | 23 | 27 | 8 | | | Tax Returns | 74 | 96 |
| 7 | 18 | 70 | 21 | 4 | 1 | Other | 123 | 158 |
| 2 | 32 (4/1-9/30/11) | | 263 (10/1/11-3/31/12) | | | | 4/1/07-3/31/08 ALL | 4/1/08-3/31/09 ALL |
| 0-500M | 500M-2MM | 2-10MM | 10-50MM | 50-100MM | 100-250MM | NUMBER OF STATEMENTS | 354 | 423 |
| 13 | 61 | 158 | 56 | 6 | 1 | | | |
| % | % | % | % | % | % | ASSETS | % | % |
| 16.3 | 8.4 | 7.5 | 10.9 | | | Cash & Equivalents | 6.0 | 6.3 |
| 1.9 | 2.9 | 3.0 | 3.3 | | | Trade Receivables (net) | 2.8 | 2.7 |
| 55.4 | 69.2 | 75.0 | 68.7 | | | Inventory | 77.4 | 75.8 |
| 3.4 | .7 | .8 | 1.0 | | | All Other Current | .8 | .5 |
| 77.1 | 81.3 | 86.3 | 83.8 | | | Total Current | 87.0 | 85.4 |
| 14.1 | 14.3 | 9.4 | 8.4 | | | Fixed Assets (net) | 8.9 | 10.0 |
| 1.1 | 1.7 | 2.5 | 5.4 | | | Intangibles (net) | 2.5 | 3.1 |
| 7.6 | 2.7 | 1.8 | 2.3 | | | All Other Non-Current | 1.6 | 1.6 |
| 100.0 | 100.0 | 100.0 | 100.0 | | | Total | 100.0 | 100.0 |
| | | | | | | LIABILITIES | | |
| 46.7 | 41.5 | 50.5 | 46.3 | | | Notes Payable-Short Term | 55.9 | 53.9 |
| 9.0 | 2.6 | 2.1 | 1.4 | | | Cur. Mat.-L.T.D. | 1.8 | 2.0 |
| 8.7 | 6.4 | 5.0 | 5.0 | | | Trade Payables | 6.5 | 4.9 |
| .0 | .0 | .1 | .1 | | | Income Taxes Payable | .1 | .1 |
| 9.4 | 10.5 | 6.6 | 6.7 | | | All Other Current | 5.9 | 7.9 |
| 73.8 | 61.1 | 64.3 | 59.6 | | | Total Current | 70.2 | 68.8 |
| 27.0 | 13.7 | 7.1 | 5.3 | | | Long-Term Debt | 6.9 | 9.2 |
| .0 | .0 | .1 | .1 | | | Deferred Taxes | .0 | .0 |
| 26.1 | 7.1 | 5.3 | 3.1 | | | All Other Non-Current | 3.0 | 2.9 |
| -26.9 | 18.1 | 23.3 | 31.9 | | | Net Worth | 20.0 | 19.0 |
| 100.0 | 100.0 | 100.0 | 100.0 | | | Total Liabilties & Net Worth | 100.0 | 100.0 |
| | | | | | | INCOME DATA | | |
| 100.0 | 100.0 | 100.0 | 100.0 | | | Net Sales | 100.0 | 100.0 |
| 18.5 | 22.7 | 20.8 | 19.0 | | | Gross Profit | 20.1 | 21.2 |
| 19.1 | 22.0 | 18.2 | 16.2 | | | Operating Expenses | 17.5 | 20.7 |
| -.6 | .7 | 2.6 | 2.8 | | | Operating Profit | 2.6 | .5 |
| 1.3 | 1.0 | .9 | -.1 | | | All Other Expenses (net) | 1.9 | 1.7 |
| -1.9 | -.3 | 1.7 | 2.9 | | | Profit Before Taxes | .8 | -1.2 |
| | | | | | | RATIOS | | |
| 1.9 | 2.2 | 1.5 | 1.5 | | | | 1.3 | 1.4 |
| .9 | 1.3 | 1.3 | 1.3 | | | Current | 1.2 | 1.2 |
| .7 | 1.0 | 1.2 | 1.2 | | | | 1.1 | 1.1 |
| .8 | .3 | .2 | .4 | | | | .2 | .2 |
| .1 | .2 | .1 | .2 | | | Quick | .1 (421) | .1 |
| .0 | .1 | .1 | .1 | | | | .0 | .0 |
| 0 UND | 0 UND | 1 435.9 | 1 400.0 | | | | 1 711.0 | 0 929.6 |
| 0 UND | 1 535.7 | 3 134.7 | 2 153.5 | | | Sales/Receivables | 2 172.3 | 2 164.1 |
| 2 213.4 | 4 102.4 | 6 59.6 | 8 47.6 | | | | 5 73.8 | 6 61.1 |
| 18 20.3 | 96 3.8 | 114 3.2 | 104 3.5 | | | | 117 3.1 | 121 3.0 |
| 107 3.4 | 122 3.0 | 152 2.4 | 135 2.7 | | | Cost of Sales/Inventory | 152 2.4 | 173 2.1 |
| 182 2.0 | 182 2.0 | 192 1.9 | 166 2.2 | | | | 195 1.9 | 236 1.5 |
| 0 UND | 1 664.5 | 2 229.5 | 2 190.6 | | | | 1 359.6 | 1 429.6 |
| 3 115.2 | 3 138.5 | 4 92.4 | 4 87.4 | | | Cost of Sales/Payables | 4 102.9 | 3 125.1 |
| 11 31.9 | 8 47.4 | 10 38.2 | 11 33.2 | | | | 8 43.3 | 8 46.9 |
| 5.4 | 5.4 | 7.1 | 7.9 | | | | 10.7 | 8.1 |
| -323.6 | 12.8 | 12.2 | 11.2 | | | Sales/Working Capital | 20.0 | 15.6 |
| -13.1 | 81.9 | 21.7 | 16.0 | | | | 43.9 | 48.1 |
| 4.5 | 3.0 | 4.4 | 6.4 | | | | 1.9 | 1.9 |
| (12) 2.7 | (56) 1.5 | (148) 2.3 | (54) 2.6 | | | EBIT/Interest | (339) 1.3 | (398) 1.1 |
| 1.0 | .7 | 1.3 | 1.8 | | | | .9 | -.1 |
| | | 11.2 | 32.5 | | | | 8.1 | 8.7 |
| | (11) | 2.9 | (10) 12.0 | | | Net Profit + Depr., Dep., Amort./Cur. Mat. L/T/D | (34) 2.2 | (27) 1.7 |
| | | 1.1 | 4.1 | | | | .1 | .0 |
| .1 | .1 | .1 | .1 | | | | .1 | .1 |
| -10.5 | .4 | .2 | .2 | | | Fixed/Worth | .3 | .3 |
| -.2 | 9.4 | .7 | .6 | | | | 1.1 | 1.6 |
| 4.1 | 1.3 | 2.1 | 1.9 | | | | 3.0 | 2.6 |
| -15.0 | 4.7 | 3.6 | 2.9 | | | Debt/Worth | 5.4 | 5.2 |
| -3.9 | -37.6 | 7.8 | 5.4 | | | | 13.3 | 15.5 |
| | 21.2 | 40.0 | 42.5 | | | | 28.9 | 18.4 |
| (43) 10.3 | (143) 21.2 | (52) 20.7 | | | % Profit Before Taxes/Tangible Net Worth | (318) 8.8 | (358) 3.2 |
| | -.2 | 6.5 | 8.8 | | | | -1.4 | -16.4 |
| 11.6 | 4.9 | 9.0 | 9.8 | | | | 4.2 | 3.1 |
| 4.9 | 1.8 | 3.7 | 4.4 | | | % Profit Before Taxes/Total Assets | 1.5 | .2 |
| -2.8 | -1.8 | .9 | 2.7 | | | | -.7 | -4.5 |
| 108.1 | 163.8 | 190.1 | 160.7 | | | | 137.0 | 142.5 |
| 39.2 | 35.2 | 70.9 | 72.2 | | | Sales/Net Fixed Assets | 56.3 | 52.5 |
| 12.5 | 11.5 | 24.2 | 19.2 | | | | 21.4 | 16.9 |
| 5.9 | 3.3 | 2.9 | 2.8 | | | | 2.9 | 2.7 |
| 2.3 | 2.6 | 2.5 | 2.3 | | | Sales/Total Assets | 2.4 | 2.1 |
| 1.9 | 1.6 | 1.9 | 1.8 | | | | 1.8 | 1.5 |
| .4 | .3 | .2 | .2 | | | | .2 | .2 |
| (10) .6 | (43) .7 | (113) .3 | (46) .3 | | | % Depr., Dep., Amort./Sales | (281) .4 | (323) .5 |
| 1.9 | 1.2 | .6 | .7 | | | | .7 | .9 |
| | 1.4 | .9 | .6 | | | | .9 | .8 |
| (35) 2.1 | (83) 1.5 | (27) 1.0 | | | % Officers', Directors' Owners' Comp/Sales | (197) 1.7 | (233) 1.6 |
| | 3.8 | 2.3 | 1.9 | | | | 3.0 | 2.8 |
| 17131M | 198882M | 1885672M | 2488496M | 1090462M | 395239M | Net Sales ($) | 7492176M | 7551120M |
| 4357M | 75084M | 761216M | 1032458M | 440165M | 152672M | Total Assets ($) | 3193218M | 3637674M |

M = $ thousand　　MM = $ million
See Pages 9 through 22 for Explanation of Ratios and Data

## Comparative Historical Data | Current Data Sorted by Sales

| 4/1/09-3/31/10 ALL | 4/1/10-3/31/11 ALL | 4/1/11-3/31/12 ALL | Type of Statement | 0-1MM | 1-3MM | 3-5MM | 5-10MM | 10-25MM | 25MM & OVER |
|---|---|---|---|---|---|---|---|---|---|
| 12 | 10 | 14 | Unqualified |  |  |  | 2 | 2 | 10 |
| 42 | 54 | 35 | Reviewed |  |  | 4 | 8 | 12 | 11 |
| 108 | 90 | 65 | Compiled | 4 | 10 | 10 | 16 | 17 | 8 |
| 81 | 105 | 65 | Tax Returns | 8 | 7 | 15 | 14 | 15 | 6 |
| 154 | 100 | 116 | Other | 3 | 11 | 15 | 25 | 38 | 24 |
|  |  |  |  | 32 (4/1-9/30/11) | | | 263 (10/1/11-3/31/12) | | |
| 397 | 359 | 295 | **NUMBER OF STATEMENTS** | 15 | 28 | 44 | 65 | 84 | 59 |
| % | % | % | **ASSETS** | % | % | % | % | % | % |
| 9.0 | 8.3 | 8.7 | Cash & Equivalents | 8.0 | 9.1 | 9.3 | 7.2 | 8.1 | 10.7 |
| 2.9 | 3.2 | 3.2 | Trade Receivables (net) | 4.4 | 2.7 | 2.0 | 3.2 | 2.8 | 4.5 |
| 71.3 | 72.0 | 71.4 | Inventory | 62.9 | 62.5 | 69.1 | 77.4 | 74.4 | 68.5 |
| .7 | .5 | .9 | All Other Current | .9 | 2.6 | .4 | .7 | 1.1 | .7 |
| 84.0 | 84.0 | 84.2 | Total Current | 76.2 | 76.8 | 80.8 | 88.4 | 86.4 | 84.4 |
| 10.8 | 10.8 | 10.4 | Fixed Assets (net) | 19.4 | 20.4 | 13.6 | 7.8 | 8.3 | 7.1 |
| 3.1 | 3.0 | 3.1 | Intangibles (net) | 1.7 | 1.1 | 1.5 | 2.3 | 3.1 | 6.3 |
| 2.1 | 2.2 | 2.3 | All Other Non-Current | 2.7 | 1.7 | 4.2 | 1.5 | 2.2 | 2.2 |
| 100.0 | 100.0 | 100.0 | Total | 100.0 | 100.0 | 100.0 | 100.0 | 100.0 | 100.0 |
|  |  |  | **LIABILITIES** |  |  |  |  |  |  |
| 45.8 | 46.4 | 47.4 | Notes Payable-Short Term | 52.5 | 41.8 | 47.3 | 44.0 | 51.5 | 46.8 |
| 3.2 | 2.5 | 2.4 | Cur. Mat.-L.T.D. | 2.7 | 4.9 | 3.6 | 2.1 | 1.7 | 1.4 |
| 6.3 | 6.6 | 5.6 | Trade Payables | 11.8 | 3.4 | 4.3 | 6.4 | 5.0 | 5.8 |
| .1 | .1 | .1 | Income Taxes Payable | .0 | .1 | .1 | .0 | .0 | .2 |
| 8.0 | 8.3 | 7.6 | All Other Current | 6.4 | 5.0 | 4.3 | 12.3 | 6.7 | 7.5 |
| 63.4 | 63.8 | 63.0 | Total Current | 73.3 | 55.3 | 59.7 | 64.9 | 65.0 | 61.7 |
| 9.7 | 8.3 | 8.9 | Long-Term Debt | 21.1 | 17.1 | 19.1 | 4.5 | 5.5 | 3.9 |
| .0 | .0 | .1 | Deferred Taxes | .0 | .0 | .0 | .0 | .1 | .2 |
| 4.5 | 6.3 | 6.5 | All Other Non-Current | 26.9 | 8.6 | 4.0 | 7.2 | 3.4 | 5.8 |
| 22.3 | 21.6 | 21.5 | Net Worth | -21.3 | 19.0 | 17.1 | 23.5 | 26.0 | 28.4 |
| 100.0 | 100.0 | 100.0 | Total Liabilities & Net Worth | 100.0 | 100.0 | 100.0 | 100.0 | 100.0 | 100.0 |
|  |  |  | **INCOME DATA** |  |  |  |  |  |  |
| 100.0 | 100.0 | 100.0 | Net Sales | 100.0 | 100.0 | 100.0 | 100.0 | 100.0 | 100.0 |
| 21.4 | 20.8 | 20.8 | Gross Profit | 28.3 | 22.1 | 21.2 | 20.4 | 20.2 | 19.5 |
| 20.9 | 18.7 | 18.8 | Operating Expenses | 31.3 | 20.2 | 19.1 | 19.0 | 17.1 | 16.7 |
| .4 | 2.1 | 2.1 | Operating Profit | -3.1 | 1.9 | 2.1 | 1.4 | 3.1 | 2.8 |
| 1.3 | .9 | .8 | All Other Expenses (net) | 2.1 | 1.9 | 1.4 | .3 | .4 | .5 |
| -.8 | 1.2 | 1.3 | Profit Before Taxes | -5.2 | .0 | .7 | 1.1 | 2.6 | 2.3 |
|  |  |  | **RATIOS** |  |  |  |  |  |  |
| 1.6 / 1.3 / 1.1 | 1.6 / 1.3 / 1.1 | 1.6 / 1.3 / 1.1 | Current | 3.6 / 1.2 / .7 | 1.8 / 1.4 / 1.1 | 1.7 / 1.4 / 1.1 | 1.6 / 1.3 / 1.2 | 1.4 / 1.3 / 1.1 | 1.5 / 1.3 / 1.2 |
| .3 / .1 / .1 | .3 / .1 / .1 | .3 / .1 / .1 | Quick | .7 / .2 / .0 | .3 / .1 / .1 | .3 / .2 / .1 | .2 / .1 / .0 | .2 / .1 / .1 | .4 / .2 / .1 |
| 0 999.8 / 2 172.9 / 6 64.8 | 0 999.8 / 2 185.6 / 5 67.1 | 0 841.0 / 2 191.1 / 6 61.9 | Sales/Receivables | 0 UND / 1 461.5 / 33 10.9 | 0 UND / 0 999.8 / 3 113.8 | 0 UND / 2 175.0 / 6 61.1 | 0 802.8 / 2 186.2 / 5 71.9 | 1 424.3 / 2 190.9 / 6 66.0 | 1 339.1 / 3 108.0 / 9 39.8 |
| 109 3.4 / 148 2.5 / 210 1.7 | 104 3.5 / 140 2.6 / 181 2.0 | 104 3.5 / 140 2.6 / 182 2.0 | Cost of Sales/Inventory | 107 3.4 / 192 1.9 / 332 1.1 | 118 3.1 / 159 2.3 / 243 1.5 | 96 3.8 / 159 2.3 / 228 1.6 | 107 3.4 / 152 2.4 / 192 1.9 | 107 3.4 / 140 2.6 / 166 2.2 | 101 3.6 / 118 3.1 / 146 2.5 |
| 1 319.8 / 4 100.8 / 11 34.1 | 1 262.5 / 4 95.9 / 10 35.8 | 1 264.5 / 4 93.2 / 10 37.1 | Cost of Sales/Payables | 0 UND / 6 61.4 / 33 11.0 | 0 UND / 2 221.1 / 8 48.5 | 1 258.3 / 5 75.1 / 13 27.5 | 1 307.2 / 3 130.8 / 7 52.2 | 2 207.1 / 4 92.2 / 9 39.2 | 2 188.2 / 5 72.9 / 11 32.0 |
| 6.3 / 12.5 / 30.0 | 7.3 / 13.2 / 32.9 | 7.1 / 12.1 / 24.1 | Sales/Working Capital | 2.1 / 10.6 / -12.9 | 4.3 / 11.3 / 85.6 | 5.5 / 8.9 / 22.1 | 7.1 / 11.0 / 22.0 | 9.6 / 14.6 / 25.1 | 8.9 / 12.3 / 19.2 |
| 2.7 / (377) 1.1 / .1 | 3.5 / (343) 1.8 / 1.0 | 4.4 / (277) 2.2 / 1.2 | EBIT/Interest | 2.7 / (13) 1.1 / .1 | 1.8 / (27) 1.5 / .4 | 4.5 / (40) 1.8 / 1.2 | 3.4 / (60) 2.1 / 1.3 | 5.5 / (78) 2.7 / 1.6 | 6.4 / 2.6 / 1.6 |
| 4.8 / (19) 1.4 / .0 | 3.7 / (19) 1.2 / -8.5 | 17.4 / (27) 7.0 / 1.1 | Net Profit + Depr., Dep., Amort./Cur. Mat. L/T/D |  |  |  |  | 31.0 / (12) 12.0 / 2.1 | |
| .1 / .3 / 1.5 | .1 / .3 / 1.5 | .1 / .2 / 1.0 | Fixed/Worth | .1 / 5.0 / -.3 | .3 / .6 / NM | .1 / .5 / 4.0 | .0 / .2 / .7 | .1 / .2 / .7 | .1 / .2 / .5 |
| 1.9 / 3.8 / 11.3 | 1.8 / 3.8 / 12.3 | 1.9 / 3.8 / 10.6 | Debt/Worth | 1.8 / 9.8 / -4.3 | 1.6 / 5.5 / -121.6 | 1.5 / 4.0 / NM | 1.6 / 3.5 / 9.4 | 2.1 / 3.6 / 6.7 | 2.1 / 3.1 / 7.5 |
| 23.2 / (332) 5.0 / -9.9 | 35.3 / (297) 13.8 / 1.6 | 37.5 / (248) 17.8 / 4.9 | % Profit Before Taxes/Tangible Net Worth |  | 17.5 / (20) 1.1 / -10.0 | 27.2 / (33) 10.9 / 3.1 | 28.0 / (53) 15.4 / 3.6 | 42.4 / (80) 23.9 / 11.1 | 50.1 / (54) 29.8 / 7.8 |
| 4.5 / .4 / -3.9 | 7.1 / 3.0 / .0 | 8.4 / 3.7 / .6 | % Profit Before Taxes/Total Assets | 5.9 / .3 / -7.5 | 4.2 / .6 / -1.6 | 6.3 / 2.8 / .7 | 5.5 / 2.5 / .5 | 10.6 / 5.1 / 2.1 | 10.3 / 4.7 / 1.8 |
| 132.9 / 42.3 / 13.6 | 138.3 / 49.5 / 20.0 | 175.6 / 60.5 / 17.2 | Sales/Net Fixed Assets | 46.2 / 13.8 / 7.9 | 49.6 / 16.9 / 3.8 | 197.3 / 80.6 / 12.6 | 213.4 / 65.0 / 33.2 | 198.9 / 79.6 / 24.6 | 160.9 / 79.7 / 25.6 |
| 2.9 / 2.2 / 1.6 | 3.0 / 2.4 / 1.9 | 2.9 / 2.4 / 1.8 | Sales/Total Assets | 2.3 / 1.8 / 1.2 | 2.5 / 1.7 / 1.3 | 2.8 / 2.1 / 1.4 | 2.9 / 2.5 / 2.0 | 3.1 / 2.5 / 2.0 | 3.2 / 2.5 / 2.1 |
| .3 / (300) .5 / 1.2 | .2 / (288) .4 / 1.0 | .2 / (219) .4 / .8 | % Depr., Dep., Amort./Sales | .7 / (12) 1.4 / 3.3 | .6 / (21) .9 / 2.0 | .2 / (28) .4 / .6 | .2 / (43) .4 / .7 | .2 / (65) .3 / .6 | .2 / (50) .3 / .6 |
| .9 / (228) 1.8 / 3.2 | .9 / (213) 1.6 / 2.9 | .9 / (156) 1.6 / 2.4 | % Officers', Directors' Owners' Comp/Sales |  | 1.5 / (17) 2.6 / 3.8 | 1.4 / (26) 2.2 / 2.7 | .9 / (33) 1.9 / 2.8 | .6 / (44) 1.0 / 1.6 | .6 / (28) 1.2 / 1.8 |
| 5583622M | 5371833M | 6075882M | Net Sales ($) | 10870M | 59838M | 167845M | 460331M | 1417999M | 3958999M |
| 2440040M | 2275240M | 2465952M | Total Assets ($) | 7677M | 39379M | 97864M | 195136M | 579808M | 1546088M |

© RMA 2012

M = $ thousand    MM = $ million
See Pages 9 through 22 for Explanation of Ratios and Data

## Current Data Sorted by Assets · Comparative Historical Data

| Type of Statement | 0-500M | 500M-2MM | 2-10MM | 10-50MM | 50-100MM | 100-250MM | | 10 | 9 |
|---|---|---|---|---|---|---|---|---|---|
| Unqualified | | | 4 | 3 | 3 | | | 10 | 9 |
| Reviewed | | 1 | 30 | 8 | | | | 43 | 35 |
| Compiled | 2 | 8 | 39 | 1 | | | | 57 | 79 |
| Tax Returns | 5 | 29 | 43 | 2 | | | | 86 | 100 |
| Other | 3 | 17 | 78 | 16 | | 1 | | 127 | 132 |
| | | 23 (4/1-9/30/11) | | 270 (10/1/11-3/31/12) | | | | 4/1/07-3/31/08 ALL | 4/1/08-3/31/09 ALL |
| NUMBER OF STATEMENTS | 10 | 55 | 194 | 30 | 3 | 1 | | 323 | 355 |
| **ASSETS** | % | % | % | % | % | % | | % | % |
| Cash & Equivalents | 3.7 | 5.7 | 8.9 | 8.4 | | | | 6.2 | 6.8 |
| Trade Receivables (net) | .6 | 3.8 | 3.9 | 3.2 | | | | 3.8 | 4.4 |
| Inventory | 65.1 | 72.0 | 59.7 | 31.9 | | | | 64.8 | 63.4 |
| All Other Current | .5 | .5 | 1.4 | 2.3 | | | | 1.5 | 1.3 |
| Total Current | 69.9 | 82.0 | 74.0 | 45.9 | | | | 76.3 | 75.8 |
| Fixed Assets (net) | 16.2 | 12.5 | 11.3 | 32.3 | | | | 13.8 | 14.9 |
| Intangibles (net) | 3.8 | 3.3 | 10.6 | 14.6 | | | | 7.1 | 6.0 |
| All Other Non-Current | 10.1 | 2.2 | 4.1 | 7.2 | | | | 2.8 | 3.2 |
| Total | 100.0 | 100.0 | 100.0 | 100.0 | | | | 100.0 | 100.0 |
| **LIABILITIES** | | | | | | | | | |
| Notes Payable-Short Term | 28.2 | 39.5 | 29.3 | 19.1 | | | | 33.6 | 31.3 |
| Cur. Mat.-L.T.D. | .0 | 1.9 | 3.4 | 3.5 | | | | 3.6 | 3.7 |
| Trade Payables | 3.3 | 13.6 | 9.7 | 6.2 | | | | 11.7 | 12.0 |
| Income Taxes Payable | .0 | .0 | .0 | .9 | | | | .1 | .1 |
| All Other Current | 20.3 | 15.6 | 10.8 | 7.6 | | | | 9.7 | 11.8 |
| Total Current | 51.9 | 70.6 | 53.3 | 37.3 | | | | 58.7 | 58.8 |
| Long-Term Debt | 16.1 | 14.2 | 9.1 | 18.3 | | | | 13.7 | 11.5 |
| Deferred Taxes | .0 | .0 | .0 | .5 | | | | .0 | .0 |
| All Other Non-Current | 4.8 | 9.8 | 5.7 | 2.7 | | | | 4.2 | 3.8 |
| Net Worth | 27.3 | 5.4 | 31.9 | 41.3 | | | | 23.4 | 25.8 |
| Total Liabilities & Net Worth | 100.0 | 100.0 | 100.0 | 100.0 | | | | 100.0 | 100.0 |
| **INCOME DATA** | | | | | | | | | |
| Net Sales | 100.0 | 100.0 | 100.0 | 100.0 | | | | 100.0 | 100.0 |
| Gross Profit | 27.0 | 23.6 | 23.9 | 27.4 | | | | 23.1 | 23.1 |
| Operating Expenses | 27.3 | 23.2 | 21.3 | 24.5 | | | | 21.0 | 21.7 |
| Operating Profit | -.3 | .4 | 2.5 | 3.0 | | | | 2.1 | 1.4 |
| All Other Expenses (net) | 1.1 | .7 | .3 | -1.0 | | | | .5 | .4 |
| Profit Before Taxes | -1.4 | -.3 | 2.3 | 4.0 | | | | 1.6 | 1.0 |
| **RATIOS** | | | | | | | | | |
| Current | 3.2 | 1.4 | 1.9 | 1.9 | | | | 1.6 | 1.7 |
| | 1.7 | 1.2 | 1.3 | 1.2 | | | | 1.3 | 1.3 |
| | .8 | .9 | 1.1 | .9 | | | | 1.1 | 1.0 |
| Quick | | .3 | .4 | .6 | | | | .3 | .3 |
| | | .1 | .2 | .3 | | | | (322) .1 | (354) .1 |
| | | .0 | .1 | .1 | | | | .1 | .1 |
| Sales/Receivables | 0 UND | 0 999.8 | 2 201.1 | 2 208.4 | | | | 2 213.4 | 1 282.9 |
| | 0 UND | 3 116.3 | 4 92.9 | 5 73.8 | | | | 4 95.4 | 4 97.9 |
| | 0 UND | 7 53.2 | 8 44.5 | 10 38.2 | | | | 7 51.6 | 8 44.7 |
| Cost of Sales/Inventory | 27 13.3 | 104 3.5 | 91 4.0 | 73 5.0 | | | | 94 3.9 | 94 3.9 |
| | 85 4.3 | 152 2.4 | 118 3.1 | 81 4.5 | | | | 124 2.9 | 120 3.0 |
| | 140 2.6 | 192 1.9 | 159 2.3 | 104 3.5 | | | | 159 2.3 | 163 2.2 |
| Cost of Sales/Payables | 0 UND | 4 96.4 | 6 57.8 | 5 66.4 | | | | 4 82.6 | 5 76.5 |
| | 0 UND | 8 45.1 | 11 34.0 | 9 39.4 | | | | 9 41.9 | 8 40.2 |
| | 0 758.6 | 29 12.7 | 20 18.4 | 16 22.9 | | | | 19 19.3 | 22 16.8 |
| Sales/Working Capital | 8.8 | 9.2 | 7.2 | 7.0 | | | | 8.5 | 8.1 |
| | 23.0 | 21.4 | 13.3 | 22.7 | | | | 15.0 | 16.5 |
| | -418.9 | -29.7 | 75.8 | -90.6 | | | | 44.8 | 78.5 |
| EBIT/Interest | | 2.2 | 7.8 | 14.6 | | | | 4.5 | 4.9 |
| | (47) 1.2 | (181) 2.7 | (28) 4.3 | | | | | (293) 1.6 | (328) 1.5 |
| | | .1 | 1.2 | 2.0 | | | | .8 | .4 |
| Net Profit + Depr., Dep., Amort./Cur. Mat. L/T/D | | | | | | | | 11.1 | 8.7 |
| | | | | | | | | (20) 1.5 | (27) 1.6 |
| | | | | | | | | .2 | .7 |
| Fixed/Worth | .0 | .1 | .1 | .3 | | | | .2 | .2 |
| | .3 | 1.8 | .5 | 1.2 | | | | .6 | .5 |
| | NM | -.5 | 2.9 | 3.8 | | | | 4.0 | 3.6 |
| Debt/Worth | .9 | 3.0 | 1.3 | 1.3 | | | | 2.0 | 1.5 |
| | 2.9 | 12.6 | 3.5 | 2.7 | | | | 4.5 | 3.8 |
| | -21.0 | -7.8 | 26.4 | 5.6 | | | | 21.6 | 20.2 |
| % Profit Before Taxes/Tangible Net Worth | | 47.7 | 47.3 | 53.2 | | | | 44.2 | 31.8 |
| | (31) 11.2 | (156) 15.7 | (27) 22.7 | | | | | (257) 15.7 | (286) 9.9 |
| | | -4.3 | 2.8 | 8.0 | | | | 1.2 | -2.1 |
| % Profit Before Taxes/Total Assets | 5.2 | 5.2 | 10.9 | 12.9 | | | | 10.1 | 7.6 |
| | -2.2 | 1.0 | 4.2 | 6.0 | | | | 2.7 | 1.8 |
| | -17.2 | -4.8 | .7 | 1.6 | | | | -.6 | -2.1 |
| Sales/Net Fixed Assets | UND | 172.9 | 90.8 | 33.9 | | | | 74.5 | 88.1 |
| | 100.9 | 55.4 | 34.0 | 6.2 | | | | 29.5 | 33.1 |
| | 26.5 | 24.9 | 17.8 | 2.8 | | | | 13.1 | 13.7 |
| Sales/Total Assets | 8.6 | 3.1 | 3.1 | 2.2 | | | | 3.2 | 3.1 |
| | 4.3 | 2.4 | 2.3 | 1.8 | | | | 2.5 | 2.4 |
| | 2.3 | 1.8 | 1.7 | 1.3 | | | | 1.7 | 1.8 |
| % Depr., Dep., Amort./Sales | | .3 | .4 | .7 | | | | .4 | .4 |
| | (43) .4 | (149) .7 | (28) 1.2 | | | | | (271) .7 | (278) .7 |
| | | .7 | 1.2 | 2.2 | | | | 1.3 | 1.2 |
| % Officers', Directors' Owners' Comp/Sales | | 1.1 | .7 | 1.1 | | | | .8 | 1.0 |
| | (29) 1.6 | (90) 1.2 | (16) 1.2 | | | | | (158) 1.4 | (193) 1.7 |
| | | 2.8 | 2.2 | 1.4 | | | | 2.9 | 2.8 |
| Net Sales ($) | 15093M | 202483M | 2191172M | 989201M | 364045M | 1320610M | | 4427901M | 5538136M |
| Total Assets ($) | 2683M | 74744M | 898935M | 575523M | 205009M | 249586M | | 2021485M | 2578095M |

M = $ thousand   MM = $ million

## Comparative Historical Data | | | Current Data Sorted by Sales

| | | | | | Type of Statement | | | | | | |
|---|---|---|---|---|---|---|---|---|---|---|---|
| | 6 | | 7 | | 10 | Unqualified | | | | 1 | 2 | 7 |
| | 51 | | 40 | | 39 | Reviewed | | | 1 | 10 | 20 | 8 |
| | 90 | | 65 | | 50 | Compiled | | 6 | 6 | 19 | 16 | 2 |
| | 68 | | 83 | | 79 | Tax Returns | 1 | 10 | 19 | 28 | 15 | 2 |
| | 110 | | 108 | | 115 | Other | 5 | 11 | 18 | 31 | 41 | 12 |
| | 4/1/09- | | 4/1/10- | | 4/1/11- | | 2 | | | | | |
| | 3/31/10 | | 3/31/11 | | 3/31/12 | | | 23 (4/1-9/30/11) | | 270 (10/1/11-3/31/12) | | |
| | ALL | | ALL | | ALL | | 0-1MM | 1-3MM | 3-5MM | 5-10MM | 10-25MM | 25MM & OVER |
| | 325 | | 303 | | 293 | NUMBER OF STATEMENTS | 8 | 27 | 44 | 89 | 94 | 31 |
| | % | | % | | % | ASSETS | % | % | % | % | % | % |
| | 7.3 | | 8.0 | | 8.0 | Cash & Equivalents | | 4.2 | 6.6 | 6.9 | 11.0 | 8.6 |
| | 3.7 | | 4.0 | | 3.7 | Trade Receivables (net) | | 2.9 | 4.0 | 3.2 | 3.7 | 6.7 |
| | 61.2 | | 58.9 | | 59.1 | Inventory | | 70.8 | 63.2 | 63.9 | 56.1 | 38.7 |
| | 1.7 | | 1.5 | | 1.4 | All Other Current | | .4 | 2.4 | .4 | 1.5 | 3.2 |
| | 73.9 | | 72.4 | | 72.2 | Total Current | | 78.3 | 76.1 | 74.4 | 72.3 | 57.2 |
| | 14.9 | | 14.7 | | 13.8 | Fixed Assets (net) | | 12.9 | 11.9 | 10.4 | 11.8 | 28.6 |
| | 6.9 | | 8.8 | | 9.8 | Intangibles (net) | | 5.1 | 7.7 | 11.6 | 10.6 | 10.3 |
| | 4.3 | | 4.1 | | 4.2 | All Other Non-Current | | 3.7 | 4.4 | 3.6 | 5.3 | 3.9 |
| | 100.0 | | 100.0 | | 100.0 | Total | | 100.0 | 100.0 | 100.0 | 100.0 | 100.0 |
| | | | | | | LIABILITIES | | | | | | |
| | 32.1 | | 31.1 | | 29.9 | Notes Payable-Short Term | | 35.5 | 37.0 | 35.1 | 24.4 | 19.2 |
| | 4.7 | | 3.6 | | 3.1 | Cur. Mat.-L.T.D. | | 2.6 | 1.1 | 2.7 | 4.5 | 4.0 |
| | 9.4 | | 10.6 | | 9.9 | Trade Payables | | 16.9 | 6.2 | 10.7 | 9.3 | 10.7 |
| | .0 | | .1 | | .1 | Income Taxes Payable | | .0 | .6 | .0 | .0 | .1 |
| | 11.1 | | 10.6 | | 11.7 | All Other Current | | 18.0 | 12.2 | 9.9 | 12.1 | 8.9 |
| | 57.3 | | 56.0 | | 54.6 | Total Current | | 73.0 | 57.1 | 58.5 | 50.3 | 42.9 |
| | 13.5 | | 11.8 | | 11.4 | Long-Term Debt | | 22.1 | 10.3 | 10.2 | 7.2 | 18.1 |
| | .0 | | .1 | | .1 | Deferred Taxes | | .0 | .0 | .0 | .0 | .6 |
| | 5.2 | | 6.1 | | 6.2 | All Other Non-Current | | 8.6 | 8.4 | 6.3 | 4.3 | 4.2 |
| | 24.0 | | 26.1 | | 27.7 | Net Worth | | -3.6 | 24.2 | 25.0 | 38.2 | 34.3 |
| | 100.0 | | 100.0 | | 100.0 | Total Liabilities & Net Worth | | 100.0 | 100.0 | 100.0 | 100.0 | 100.0 |
| | | | | | | INCOME DATA | | | | | | |
| | 100.0 | | 100.0 | | 100.0 | Net Sales | | 100.0 | 100.0 | 100.0 | 100.0 | 100.0 |
| | 23.8 | | 24.4 | | 24.3 | Gross Profit | | 24.2 | 24.4 | 22.6 | 24.6 | 24.6 |
| | 24.3 | | 23.7 | | 22.2 | Operating Expenses | | 23.6 | 23.1 | 21.0 | 21.6 | 21.1 |
| | -.5 | | .7 | | 2.1 | Operating Profit | | .6 | 1.3 | 1.6 | 3.0 | 3.5 |
| | .7 | | .4 | | .3 | All Other Expenses (net) | | 1.5 | .4 | .5 | -.2 | -.3 |
| | -1.2 | | .3 | | 1.8 | Profit Before Taxes | | -.9 | .9 | 1.1 | 3.2 | 3.8 |
| | | | | | | RATIOS | | | | | | |
| | 1.8 | | 1.8 | | 1.8 | | | 1.4 | 1.8 | 1.5 | 2.0 | 1.9 |
| | 1.2 | | 1.3 | | 1.3 | Current | | 1.2 | 1.3 | 1.2 | 1.5 | 1.4 |
| | 1.0 | | 1.0 | | 1.0 | | | .9 | 1.0 | 1.0 | 1.1 | 1.1 |
| | .3 | | .4 | | .4 | | | .2 | .3 | .3 | .5 | .6 |
| (324) | .1 | (302) | .1 | (292) | .2 | Quick | | .1 | .2 | .1 | .2 | .3 |
| | .1 | | .1 | | .1 | | | .0 | .1 | .1 | .1 | .2 |
| 1 | 360.7 | 1 | 327.0 | 1 | 257.2 | | 0 960.0 | 1 322.6 | 2 194.9 | 1 256.4 | 2 146.5 | |
| 3 | 119.2 | 4 | 96.5 | 4 | 97.3 | Sales/Receivables | 4 96.2 | 4 84.2 | 4 95.2 | 3 116.9 | 6 65.3 | |
| 7 | 50.8 | 8 | 46.0 | 8 | 46.8 | | 8 43.1 | 11 32.9 | 8 48.3 | 6 56.3 | 10 36.8 | |
| 92 | 4.0 | 88 | 4.1 | 83 | 4.4 | | 152 2.4 | 118 3.1 | 99 3.7 | 74 4.9 | 57 6.4 | |
| 127 | 2.9 | 120 | 3.0 | 114 | 3.2 | Cost of Sales/Inventory | 192 1.9 | 152 2.4 | 126 2.9 | 94 3.9 | 79 4.6 | |
| 186 | 2.1 | 175 | 2.1 | 166 | 2.2 | | 261 1.4 | 182 2.0 | 182 2.0 | 118 3.1 | 99 3.7 | |
| 5 | 79.7 | 5 | 70.6 | 5 | 68.0 | | 2 211.2 | 5 79.2 | 7 49.9 | 5 68.1 | 7 54.7 | |
| 9 | 39.1 | 10 | 37.8 | 10 | 35.9 | Cost of Sales/Payables | 11 33.3 | 8 45.6 | 11 33.9 | 10 38.0 | 11 33.4 | |
| 19 | 19.2 | 23 | 16.0 | 20 | 18.2 | | 53 6.9 | 20 18.1 | 20 18.4 | 17 21.3 | 20 18.7 | |
| | 6.8 | | 7.3 | | 7.3 | | | 6.0 | 5.6 | 8.4 | 7.4 | 7.7 |
| | 15.2 | | 13.7 | | 14.3 | Sales/Working Capital | | 19.8 | 12.7 | 19.1 | 12.2 | 19.6 |
| | 502.6 | | 81.8 | | 136.6 | | | -18.6 | -662.8 | 112.8 | 93.6 | 83.8 |
| | 2.6 | | 3.8 | | 6.2 | | | 1.8 | 2.2 | 3.8 | 22.1 | 16.4 |
| (295) | .6 | (278) | 1.4 | (265) | 2.3 | EBIT/Interest | (23) 1.1 | (36) 1.2 | (85) 1.7 | (86) 4.7 | (30) 4.5 | |
| | -1.0 | | .0 | | 1.0 | | | -.7 | .1 | .8 | 2.2 | 1.9 |
| | .5 | | 2.4 | | 5.3 | | | | | | | |
| (21) | .0 | (19) | 1.5 | (15) | 2.7 | Net Profit + Depr., Dep., Amort./Cur. Mat. L/T/D | | | | | | |
| | -1.0 | | .2 | | 1.1 | | | | | | | |
| | .2 | | .2 | | .1 | | | .1 | .1 | .1 | .1 | .3 |
| | .6 | | .8 | | .6 | Fixed/Worth | | .7 | .9 | .7 | .3 | .9 |
| | 5.2 | | 8.7 | | 10.8 | | | -.7 | -.8 | NM | 1.2 | 3.6 |
| | 1.5 | | 1.4 | | 1.5 | | | 2.9 | 1.8 | 2.9 | 1.0 | 1.7 |
| | 4.3 | | 4.2 | | 4.0 | Debt/Worth | | 12.6 | 6.0 | 5.9 | 2.1 | 3.1 |
| | 89.2 | | 162.8 | | 108.3 | | | -5.9 | -16.9 | NM | 6.2 | 5.9 |
| | 15.9 | | 23.0 | | 47.7 | % Profit Before Taxes/Tangible Net Worth | | 36.6 | 12.4 | 49.7 | 57.8 | 53.4 |
| (249) | -.2 | (230) | 6.4 | (223) | 15.6 | | (15) 4.9 | (27) 4.9 | (67) 6.5 | (79) 29.9 | (28) 38.9 | |
| | -19.5 | | -5.2 | | 2.1 | | | -5.4 | -3.6 | -.9 | 8.5 | 9.6 |
| | 3.8 | | 5.3 | | 9.1 | | | 4.6 | 4.4 | 5.6 | 14.7 | 14.2 |
| | -.9 | | 1.4 | | 3.5 | % Profit Before Taxes/Total Assets | | .5 | .5 | 2.1 | 7.2 | 6.4 |
| | -5.8 | | -3.1 | | -.1 | | | -4.2 | -3.0 | -.8 | 2.7 | 1.8 |
| | 77.7 | | 82.0 | | 94.7 | | | 172.9 | 110.4 | 107.9 | 78.4 | 39.5 |
| | 28.8 | | 30.2 | | 34.5 | Sales/Net Fixed Assets | | 29.7 | 51.7 | 37.3 | 35.8 | 13.2 |
| | 10.0 | | 12.2 | | 15.0 | | | 4.8 | 14.4 | 17.7 | 21.3 | 3.5 |
| | 2.9 | | 3.0 | | 3.1 | | | 2.3 | 2.7 | 2.9 | 3.6 | 3.1 |
| | 2.2 | | 2.1 | | 2.3 | Sales/Total Assets | | 1.9 | 2.1 | 2.1 | 2.6 | 2.1 |
| | 1.5 | | 1.6 | | 1.7 | | | 1.5 | 1.4 | 1.5 | 2.1 | 1.6 |
| | .4 | | .4 | | .4 | | | .2 | .3 | .3 | .4 | .6 |
| (266) | .8 | (243) | .7 | (227) | .7 | % Depr., Dep., Amort./Sales | (20) .5 | (29) .4 | (75) .7 | (73) .7 | (26) 1.1 | |
| | 1.5 | | 1.4 | | 1.2 | | | 1.0 | 1.4 | 1.2 | 1.1 | 2.1 |
| | 1.1 | | 1.1 | | .8 | | | 1.4 | .7 | .6 | .4 | |
| (153) | 2.0 | (150) | 1.7 | (142) | 1.2 | % Officers', Directors' Owners' Comp/Sales | (13) 2.3 | (24) 1.6 | (40) 1.3 | (47) 1.2 | (14) 1.1 | |
| | 3.9 | | 3.1 | | 2.3 | | | 3.6 | 2.5 | 2.2 | 2.1 | 1.3 |
| 4140936M | | 3330075M | | 5082604M | | Net Sales ($) | 4509M | 58244M | 177043M | 681983M | 1349240M | 2811585M |
| 1942958M | | 1654315M | | 2006480M | | Total Assets ($) | 2995M | 46468M | 122201M | 347935M | 531513M | 955368M |

M = $ thousand    MM = $ million
See Pages 9 through 22 for Explanation of Ratios and Data

## Current Data Sorted by Assets      Comparative Historical Data

| 0-500M | 500M-2MM | 2-10MM | 10-50MM | 50-100MM | 100-250MM | Type of Statement | 4/1/07-3/31/08 ALL | 4/1/08-3/31/09 ALL |
|---|---|---|---|---|---|---|---|---|
| 1 |  | 2 |  |  |  | Unqualified | 8 | 6 |
| 1 | 6 | 16 | 7 |  |  | Reviewed | 41 | 25 |
| 3 | 14 | 21 | 1 |  |  | Compiled | 63 | 73 |
| 14 | 23 | 16 | 12 |  |  | Tax Returns | 55 | 54 |
| 4 | 21 | 33 |  | 4 |  | Other | 94 | 97 |
|  | 32 (4/1-9/30/11) |  | 167 (10/1/11-3/31/12) |  |  |  |  |  |
| 23 | 64 | 88 | 20 | 4 |  | NUMBER OF STATEMENTS | 261 | 255 |
| % | % | % | % | % | % | ASSETS | % | % |
| 15.4 | 7.9 | 9.8 | 9.7 |  |  | Cash & Equivalents | 6.4 | 6.0 |
| 8.3 | 4.7 | 5.0 | 4.8 |  |  | Trade Receivables (net) | 4.3 | 4.3 |
| 56.2 | 67.6 | 59.5 | 49.7 |  |  | Inventory | 71.9 | 72.2 |
| .5 | 2.9 | 2.2 | 2.1 |  |  | All Other Current | 2.1 | .7 |
| 80.4 | 83.1 | 76.5 | 66.3 |  |  | Total Current | 84.8 | 83.3 |
| 15.8 | 11.1 | 17.9 | 23.7 |  |  | Fixed Assets (net) | 10.9 | 12.3 |
| .9 | 1.3 | 2.1 | 4.5 |  |  | Intangibles (net) | 1.9 | 1.9 |
| 2.9 | 4.5 | 3.5 | 5.5 |  |  | All Other Non-Current | 2.3 | 2.5 |
| 100.0 | 100.0 | 100.0 | 100.0 |  |  | Total | 100.0 | 100.0 |
|  |  |  |  | DATA NOT AVAILABLE |  | LIABILITIES |  |  |
| 45.5 | 40.7 | 37.5 | 36.2 |  |  | Notes Payable-Short Term | 42.9 | 47.3 |
| .4 | 3.1 | 4.0 | .7 |  |  | Cur. Mat.-L.T.D. | 5.0 | 3.1 |
| 9.1 | 5.3 | 6.4 | 4.3 |  |  | Trade Payables | 7.7 | 6.8 |
| .0 | .1 | .4 | .1 |  |  | Income Taxes Payable | .1 | .1 |
| 22.0 | 9.5 | 11.1 | 7.4 |  |  | All Other Current | 10.2 | 9.0 |
| 76.9 | 58.6 | 59.4 | 48.7 |  |  | Total Current | 65.9 | 66.3 |
| 11.5 | 17.2 | 13.6 | 13.8 |  |  | Long-Term Debt | 11.0 | 13.0 |
| .0 | .0 | .0 | .4 |  |  | Deferred Taxes | .1 | .0 |
| 13.3 | 7.6 | 3.4 | 2.7 |  |  | All Other Non-Current | 4.6 | 3.5 |
| -1.7 | 16.5 | 23.6 | 34.5 |  |  | Net Worth | 18.4 | 17.1 |
| 100.0 | 100.0 | 100.0 | 100.0 |  |  | Total Liabilities & Net Worth | 100.0 | 100.0 |
|  |  |  |  |  |  | INCOME DATA |  |  |
| 100.0 | 100.0 | 100.0 | 100.0 |  |  | Net Sales | 100.0 | 100.0 |
| 40.2 | 31.6 | 27.9 | 24.8 |  |  | Gross Profit | 22.7 | 24.2 |
| 35.9 | 27.6 | 24.9 | 19.8 |  |  | Operating Expenses | 20.2 | 23.4 |
| 4.4 | 4.0 | 3.0 | 5.0 |  |  | Operating Profit | 2.5 | .8 |
| .7 | .8 | .7 | 1.3 |  |  | All Other Expenses (net) | 1.7 | 1.8 |
| 3.7 | 3.2 | 2.2 | 3.6 |  |  | Profit Before Taxes | .8 | -.9 |
|  |  |  |  |  |  | RATIOS |  |  |
| 3.4 | 2.1 | 1.7 | 1.5 |  |  | Current | 1.5 | 1.5 |
| 1.4 | 1.4 | 1.3 | 1.2 |  |  | | 1.2 | 1.2 |
| .8 | 1.1 | 1.0 | 1.2 |  |  | | 1.0 | 1.0 |
| .9 | .4 | .4 | .4 |  |  | Quick | .3 | .3 |
| .2 | .1 | .2 | .2 |  |  | | (260) .1 | (254) .1 |
| .1 | .1 | .1 | .1 |  |  | | .0 | .0 |
| 0 UND | 1 261.0 | 1 388.9 | 6 63.2 |  |  | Sales/Receivables | 1 488.3 | 1 465.5 |
| 2 168.8 | 7 55.6 | 6 64.4 | 14 26.4 |  |  | | 4 95.8 | 4 91.0 |
| 15 24.2 | 12 31.3 | 14 26.5 | 21 17.7 |  |  | | 10 37.1 | 11 32.8 |
| 39 9.4 | 107 3.4 | 126 2.9 | 104 3.5 |  |  | Cost of Sales/Inventory | 133 2.7 | 146 2.5 |
| 111 3.3 | 182 2.0 | 166 2.2 | 203 1.8 |  |  | | 188 1.9 | 219 1.7 |
| 215 1.7 | 243 1.5 | 215 1.7 | 228 1.6 |  |  | | 253 1.4 | 312 1.2 |
| 0 UND | 1 256.4 | 2 205.1 | 3 107.7 |  |  | Cost of Sales/Payables | 1 383.6 | 1 371.9 |
| 5 80.9 | 5 76.4 | 7 54.0 | 11 32.4 |  |  | | 4 91.2 | 4 93.6 |
| 16 22.7 | 12 29.4 | 20 18.1 | 20 18.0 |  |  | | 15 24.8 | 12 29.3 |
| 7.6 | 4.7 | 5.7 | 6.2 |  |  | Sales/Working Capital | 6.5 | 5.8 |
| 26.7 | 8.8 | 9.7 | 9.0 |  |  | | 14.2 | 12.7 |
| -29.5 | 45.8 | 121.3 | 22.5 |  |  | | 48.6 | 56.8 |
| 7.5 | 4.6 | 5.2 | 4.7 |  |  | EBIT/Interest | 2.5 | 1.7 |
| (20) 2.6 | (59) 2.4 | (85) 2.4 | (19) 2.5 |  |  | | (252) 1.3 | (239) 1.0 |
| 1.5 | 1.1 | 1.2 | 1.1 |  |  | | .7 | -.1 |
|  |  | 4.0 |  |  |  | Net Profit + Depr., Dep., Amort./Cur. Mat. L/T/D | 4.4 | 2.3 |
|  |  | (14) 1.2 |  |  |  | | (33) 2.3 | (20) 1.3 |
|  |  | .2 |  |  |  | | .4 | .2 |
| .1 | .1 | .1 | .2 |  |  | Fixed/Worth | .1 | .1 |
| .6 | .4 | .4 | .7 |  |  | | .5 | .6 |
| -1.1 | -1.8 | 2.1 | 1.1 |  |  | | 2.4 | 3.5 |
| .9 | 1.4 | 1.6 | 1.3 |  |  | Debt/Worth | 2.4 | 2.6 |
| 2.8 | 4.0 | 3.8 | 3.0 |  |  | | 5.4 | 5.3 |
| -6.5 | -16.2 | 10.7 | 6.1 |  |  | | 24.8 | 30.3 |
| 81.1 | 34.5 | 45.1 | 20.4 |  |  | % Profit Before Taxes/Tangible Net Worth | 29.5 | 16.7 |
| (14) 11.0 | (44) 18.5 | (77) 17.8 | 14.5 |  |  | | (221) 9.6 | (206) 3.1 |
| 2.3 | 3.8 | 5.3 | 3.4 |  |  | | -3.0 | -13.5 |
| 24.1 | 10.7 | 7.0 | 5.6 |  |  | % Profit Before Taxes/Total Assets | 5.2 | 2.9 |
| 4.8 | 4.0 | 4.0 | 2.9 |  |  | | 1.4 | .3 |
| .6 | .4 | .7 | .7 |  |  | | -1.6 | -3.9 |
| 76.9 | 128.0 | 60.7 | 54.5 |  |  | Sales/Net Fixed Assets | 95.6 | 78.9 |
| 36.3 | 36.4 | 24.9 | 6.8 |  |  | | 36.3 | 29.8 |
| 10.9 | 11.9 | 5.2 | 2.4 |  |  | | 12.3 | 11.0 |
| 4.4 | 2.8 | 2.4 | 1.9 |  |  | Sales/Total Assets | 2.5 | 2.3 |
| 2.7 | 1.9 | 1.8 | 1.3 |  |  | | 1.8 | 1.6 |
| 2.0 | 1.6 | 1.3 | .9 |  |  | | 1.4 | 1.1 |
| .2 | .3 | .4 | .5 |  |  | % Depr., Dep., Amort./Sales | .3 | .4 |
| (12) .9 | (41) .8 | (71) .8 | (18) 1.2 |  |  | | (212) .5 | (205) .8 |
| 1.5 | 1.3 | 1.5 | 2.6 |  |  | | 1.0 | 1.3 |
| 2.9 | 1.8 | 1.1 | .9 |  |  | % Officers', Directors' Owners' Comp/Sales | 1.1 | 1.3 |
| (14) 5.1 | (39) 3.0 | (43) 1.6 | (10) 1.3 |  |  | | (119) 1.9 | (130) 2.4 |
| 9.1 | 5.5 | 3.3 | 2.1 |  |  | | 4.0 | 4.8 |
| 26852M | 169485M | 753143M | 499650M | 387137M |  | Net Sales ($) | 4211309M | 2783410M |
| 7244M | 76308M | 402373M | 347137M | 294868M |  | Total Assets ($) | 2278530M | 1804974M |

M = $ thousand    MM = $ million
See Pages 9 through 22 for Explanation of Ratios and Data

## Comparative Historical Data | Current Data Sorted by Sales

| | | | | Type of Statement | | | | | | |
|---|---|---|---|---|---|---|---|---|---|---|
| 6 | | | 3 | Unqualified | 1 | | | 1 | 1 | |
| 30 | | 33 | 30 | Reviewed | | 8 | 3 | 9 | 8 | 2 |
| 53 | | 44 | 39 | Compiled | 2 | 12 | 9 | 12 | 4 | 2 |
| 53 | | 51 | 53 | Tax Returns | 11 | 20 | 11 | 6 | 4 | 1 |
| 91 | | 86 | 74 | Other | 6 | 14 | 8 | 19 | 17 | 10 |
| | 4/1/09-3/31/10 | 4/1/10-3/31/11 | 4/1/11-3/31/12 | | | 32 (4/1-9/30/11) | | 167 (10/1/11-3/31/12) | | |
| | ALL | ALL | ALL | | 0-1MM | 1-3MM | 3-5MM | 5-10MM | 10-25MM | 25MM & OVER |
| | 233 | 214 | 199 | NUMBER OF STATEMENTS | 20 | 54 | 31 | 47 | 34 | 13 |

| Metric | ALL 4/1/09-3/31/10 | ALL 4/1/10-3/31/11 | ALL 4/1/11-3/31/12 | 0-1MM | 1-3MM | 3-5MM | 5-10MM | 10-25MM | 25MM & OVER |
|---|---|---|---|---|---|---|---|---|---|
| | % | % | % | % | % | % | % | % | % |
| **ASSETS** | | | | | | | | | |
| Cash & Equivalents | 8.5 | 9.3 | 9.8 | 6.5 | 10.0 | 8.3 | 12.2 | 9.5 | 9.2 |
| Trade Receivables (net) | 5.0 | 5.0 | 5.3 | 9.1 | 4.4 | 4.2 | 4.9 | 4.8 | 7.8 |
| Inventory | 62.5 | 59.7 | 60.3 | 56.6 | 61.7 | 64.6 | 64.3 | 52.6 | 56.1 |
| All Other Current | 1.4 | 1.6 | 2.4 | .1 | 2.0 | 4.6 | 1.3 | 3.1 | 3.7 |
| Total Current | 77.4 | 75.7 | 77.7 | 72.3 | 78.1 | 81.7 | 82.7 | 70.0 | 76.8 |
| Fixed Assets (net) | 16.8 | 18.4 | 16.2 | 20.5 | 16.3 | 13.2 | 12.1 | 23.0 | 13.2 |
| Intangibles (net) | 2.9 | 2.6 | 2.2 | 1.4 | 1.5 | 2.8 | 1.4 | 2.0 | 8.4 |
| All Other Non-Current | 2.8 | 3.4 | 3.9 | 5.8 | 4.2 | 2.3 | 3.8 | 5.0 | 1.6 |
| Total | 100.0 | 100.0 | 100.0 | 100.0 | 100.0 | 100.0 | 100.0 | 100.0 | 100.0 |
| **LIABILITIES** | | | | | | | | | |
| Notes Payable-Short Term | 39.0 | 36.3 | 39.1 | 54.6 | 34.4 | 41.9 | 37.5 | 37.0 | 39.0 |
| Cur. Mat.-L.T.D. | 3.0 | 2.5 | 2.9 | 5.0 | 2.4 | 1.4 | 5.4 | 1.2 | .1 |
| Trade Payables | 5.9 | 6.5 | 6.2 | 9.3 | 4.3 | 3.5 | 7.2 | 6.8 | 10.3 |
| Income Taxes Payable | .2 | .2 | .3 | .0 | .2 | .2 | .2 | .4 | 1.0 |
| All Other Current | 11.1 | 10.3 | 11.4 | 28.8 | 7.1 | 15.2 | 9.4 | 9.2 | 6.3 |
| Total Current | 59.3 | 55.7 | 59.7 | 97.6 | 48.3 | 62.1 | 59.6 | 54.6 | 56.8 |
| Long-Term Debt | 16.2 | 16.5 | 14.9 | 13.8 | 17.4 | 20.7 | 8.7 | 15.2 | 14.7 |
| Deferred Taxes | .1 | .1 | .1 | .0 | .0 | .1 | .0 | .2 | .0 |
| All Other Non-Current | 5.0 | 6.6 | 5.8 | 14.8 | 6.5 | 8.1 | 3.1 | 2.7 | 1.7 |
| Net Worth | 19.4 | 21.1 | 19.5 | -26.2 | 27.8 | 9.1 | 28.5 | 27.3 | 26.7 |
| Total Liabilities & Net Worth | 100.0 | 100.0 | 100.0 | 100.0 | 100.0 | 100.0 | 100.0 | 100.0 | 100.0 |
| **INCOME DATA** | | | | | | | | | |
| Net Sales | 100.0 | 100.0 | 100.0 | 100.0 | 100.0 | 100.0 | 100.0 | 100.0 | 100.0 |
| Gross Profit | 26.2 | 28.4 | 30.2 | 46.8 | 34.6 | 28.1 | 25.9 | 24.4 | 22.7 |
| Operating Expenses | 25.2 | 25.5 | 26.5 | 41.8 | 31.2 | 25.0 | 22.1 | 20.2 | 19.8 |
| Operating Profit | 1.0 | 2.9 | 3.7 | 5.0 | 3.4 | 3.1 | 3.8 | 4.2 | 2.9 |
| All Other Expenses (net) | 2.2 | 1.4 | .9 | 1.7 | 1.1 | .4 | .8 | .6 | .9 |
| Profit Before Taxes | -1.2 | 1.5 | 2.9 | 3.3 | 2.4 | 2.7 | 3.0 | 3.6 | 2.0 |
| **RATIOS** | | | | | | | | | |
| Current | 1.7 | 1.9 | 1.8 | 1.2 | 3.5 | 2.2 | 1.8 | 1.4 | 1.5 |
| | 1.3 | 1.3 | 1.3 | 1.0 | 1.5 | 1.3 | 1.4 | 1.2 | 1.3 |
| | 1.0 | 1.1 | 1.1 | .6 | 1.2 | 1.1 | 1.0 | 1.1 | 1.2 |
| Quick | .4 | .5 | .5 | .3 | .5 | .4 | .5 | .4 | .4 |
| | .2 | .2 | .2 | .1 | .2 | .1 | .2 | .2 | .3 |
| | .1 | .1 | .1 | .1 | .1 | .1 | .1 | .1 | .2 |
| Sales/Receivables | 1 415.0 | 1 526.1 | 1 321.8 | 0 UND | 1 251.4 | 1 411.3 | 0 999.8 | 2 196.2 | 3 127.6 |
| | 5 73.8 | 5 70.5 | 6 58.8 | 9 40.4 | 7 54.9 | 6 56.2 | 4 81.3 | 6 61.3 | 12 29.7 |
| | 12 29.8 | 13 28.1 | 15 24.9 | 39 9.3 | 12 29.6 | 15 24.4 | 13 28.9 | 14 26.5 | 22 16.5 |
| Cost of Sales/Inventory | 103 3.5 | 116 3.1 | 107 3.4 | 66 5.5 | 107 3.4 | 122 3.0 | 107 3.4 | 104 3.5 | 57 6.4 |
| | 189 1.9 | 167 2.2 | 174 2.1 | 228 1.6 | 182 2.0 | 192 1.9 | 152 2.4 | 159 2.3 | 215 1.7 |
| | 300 1.2 | 236 1.5 | 228 1.6 | 365 1.0 | 243 1.5 | 243 1.5 | 203 1.8 | 215 1.7 | 261 1.4 |
| Cost of Sales/Payables | 1 440.8 | 1 312.8 | 2 211.6 | 0 UND | 0 999.8 | 2 162.6 | 2 221.2 | 4 102.3 | 3 114.1 |
| | 5 71.4 | 7 56.0 | 6 59.0 | 6 61.5 | 4 84.8 | 7 51.2 | 5 71.0 | 11 33.7 | 23 15.7 |
| | 15 24.5 | 19 19.2 | 18 20.8 | 24 15.3 | 14 26.8 | 12 30.1 | 13 27.4 | 19 18.9 | 30 12.1 |
| Sales/Working Capital | 4.8 | 5.2 | 5.6 | 6.3 | 3.8 | 5.6 | 5.3 | 7.0 | 5.6 |
| | 9.4 | 9.7 | 9.7 | NM | 8.6 | 9.1 | 9.0 | 10.9 | 8.4 |
| | 77.4 | 50.6 | 56.8 | -4.2 | 25.2 | 24.6 | -127.0 | 46.9 | 19.7 |
| EBIT/Interest | 2.2 | 4.1 | 4.9 | 6.9 | 4.9 | 3.8 | 5.1 | 6.2 | 4.9 |
| | (221) 1.0 | (201) 1.6 | (187) 2.4 | (17) 1.7 | (51) 2.3 | (29) 2.1 | (45) 2.9 | (33) 2.5 | (12) 2.2 |
| | -.3 | .8 | 1.2 | 1.3 | .5 | 1.1 | 1.5 | 1.2 | 1.3 |
| Net Profit + Depr., Dep., Amort./Cur. Mat. L/T/D | 1.6 | 3.4 | 6.8 | | | | | | |
| | (30) .4 | (20) 1.5 | (24) 2.2 | | | | | | |
| | -1.0 | .8 | .5 | | | | | | |
| Fixed/Worth | .2 | .1 | .1 | .2 | .1 | .1 | .1 | .4 | .1 |
| | .8 | .6 | .5 | NM | .4 | .8 | .2 | .8 | .4 |
| | 5.9 | 3.9 | 3.6 | -.7 | NM | -2.1 | .9 | 1.7 | 3.2 |
| Debt/Worth | 1.7 | 1.5 | 1.5 | 3.7 | .9 | 1.8 | 1.3 | 1.8 | 2.1 |
| | 4.8 | 3.8 | 3.6 | -30.8 | 1.8 | 9.0 | 3.2 | 3.7 | 3.3 |
| | 36.4 | 22.3 | 21.7 | -5.3 | NM | -13.7 | 8.2 | 7.9 | 10.2 |
| % Profit Before Taxes/Tangible Net Worth | 18.5 | 33.8 | 38.1 | | 27.6 | 55.8 | 38.4 | 39.7 | 27.4 |
| | (186) 3.7 | (173) 13.3 | (158) 15.9 | | (41) 7.7 | (21) 25.6 | (43) 18.7 | (33) 17.0 | (12) 16.6 |
| | -16.1 | 1.1 | 4.7 | | 2.6 | 6.6 | 5.1 | 6.9 | 3.8 |
| % Profit Before Taxes/Total Assets | 4.3 | 7.5 | 8.6 | 15.2 | 10.3 | 8.5 | 7.8 | 9.9 | 7.0 |
| | .2 | 2.5 | 3.9 | 3.2 | 3.6 | 2.2 | 4.2 | 4.8 | 2.8 |
| | -4.9 | -1.0 | .7 | .7 | -.1 | .2 | 1.2 | .7 | .8 |
| Sales/Net Fixed Assets | 69.4 | 75.6 | 75.2 | 62.3 | 75.5 | 122.5 | 243.1 | 33.4 | 102.2 |
| | 20.9 | 22.2 | 26.1 | 12.0 | 25.9 | 31.2 | 47.6 | 9.5 | 41.2 |
| | 6.4 | 6.0 | 7.1 | 4.3 | 8.6 | 7.4 | 12.0 | 4.0 | 7.8 |
| Sales/Total Assets | 2.5 | 2.5 | 2.5 | 2.5 | 2.7 | 2.4 | 2.9 | 2.3 | 2.9 |
| | 1.7 | 1.8 | 1.9 | 1.8 | 1.8 | 1.8 | 2.0 | 1.7 | 1.9 |
| | 1.1 | 1.2 | 1.4 | 1.1 | 1.4 | 1.4 | 1.6 | 1.3 | 1.2 |
| % Depr., Dep., Amort./Sales | .5 | .5 | .4 | .4 | .4 | .6 | .3 | .7 | .5 |
| | (189) .9 | (161) .8 | (146) .8 | (10) 1.4 | (39) 1.0 | (22) .9 | (35) .5 | (29) .9 | (11) .6 |
| | 1.7 | 1.8 | 1.5 | 2.1 | 1.8 | 1.4 | 1.0 | 2.0 | .7 |
| % Officers', Directors' Owners' Comp/Sales | 1.4 | 1.1 | 1.2 | 3.1 | 2.1 | 1.8 | 1.0 | .9 | |
| | (115) 2.6 | (108) 2.3 | (107) 2.5 | (11) 4.3 | (28) 4.1 | (19) 2.9 | (26) 1.6 | (17) 1.3 | |
| | 4.7 | 4.1 | 5.0 | 12.8 | 5.6 | 5.6 | 2.5 | 3.3 | |
| Net Sales ($) | 1955981M | 1454600M | 1836267M | 12357M | 107243M | 119152M | 340118M | 513049M | 744348M |
| Total Assets ($) | 1288789M | 911798M | 1127930M | 10839M | 67410M | 75861M | 182781M | 328398M | 462641M |

© RMA 2012

M = $ thousand   MM = $ million
See Pages 9 through 22 for Explanation of Ratios and Data

## Current Data Sorted by Assets       Comparative Historical Data

| | | | | | | Type of Statement | | |
|---|---|---|---|---|---|---|---|---|
| | 1 | 6 | 17 | 8 | 4 | Unqualified | 42 | 37 |
| | 2 | 24 | 25 | 2 | 1 | Reviewed | 44 | 52 |
| 4 | 14 | 27 | 10 | 1 | | Compiled | 53 | 46 |
| 17 | 34 | 25 | 3 | | | Tax Returns | 71 | 56 |
| 5 | 23 | 35 | 34 | 8 | 10 | Other | 120 | 117 |
| | 59 (4/1-9/30/11) | | 281 (10/1/11-3/31/12) | | | | 4/1/07-3/31/08 | 4/1/08-3/31/09 |
| 0-500M | 500M-2MM | 2-10MM | 10-50MM | 50-100MM | 100-250MM | | ALL | ALL |
| 26 | 74 | 117 | 89 | 19 | 15 | NUMBER OF STATEMENTS | 330 | 308 |
| % | % | % | % | % | % | ASSETS | % | % |
| 11.0 | 10.8 | 11.2 | 10.5 | 4.1 | 2.8 | Cash & Equivalents | 7.9 | 7.8 |
| 12.5 | 9.8 | 14.3 | 11.6 | 18.5 | 12.0 | Trade Receivables (net) | 11.5 | 11.2 |
| 55.4 | 53.1 | 51.7 | 44.8 | 39.5 | 42.2 | Inventory | 52.2 | 52.5 |
| 1.5 | 1.0 | 1.8 | 1.9 | 5.1 | 3.4 | All Other Current | 3.0 | 2.1 |
| 80.5 | 74.8 | 79.0 | 68.8 | 67.2 | 60.3 | Total Current | 74.7 | 73.5 |
| 14.8 | 15.2 | 15.0 | 22.3 | 19.7 | 24.2 | Fixed Assets (net) | 17.7 | 18.0 |
| .4 | 4.3 | 1.3 | 2.4 | 5.6 | 3.2 | Intangibles (net) | 1.5 | 2.1 |
| 4.3 | 5.8 | 4.7 | 6.5 | 7.4 | 12.3 | All Other Non-Current | 6.0 | 6.4 |
| 100.0 | 100.0 | 100.0 | 100.0 | 100.0 | 100.0 | Total | 100.0 | 100.0 |
| | | | | | | LIABILITIES | | |
| 14.4 | 28.9 | 30.5 | 27.4 | 35.9 | 31.7 | Notes Payable-Short Term | 31.4 | 32.2 |
| 5.3 | 2.6 | 2.9 | 4.8 | 7.0 | 6.4 | Cur. Mat.-L.T.D. | 4.7 | 4.4 |
| 18.5 | 10.2 | 10.0 | 10.2 | 8.0 | 5.7 | Trade Payables | 10.4 | 8.6 |
| .0 | .0 | .1 | .1 | .0 | .5 | Income Taxes Payable | .1 | .1 |
| 13.0 | 9.4 | 9.3 | 9.8 | 5.5 | 7.4 | All Other Current | 10.4 | 9.4 |
| 51.3 | 51.2 | 52.7 | 52.3 | 56.4 | 51.7 | Total Current | 57.0 | 54.7 |
| 14.5 | 16.7 | 12.8 | 15.1 | 14.0 | 19.0 | Long-Term Debt | 14.1 | 15.4 |
| .0 | .0 | .2 | .9 | 1.0 | .7 | Deferred Taxes | .3 | .3 |
| 22.6 | 9.8 | 3.0 | 3.6 | 5.2 | 6.1 | All Other Non-Current | 3.5 | 5.0 |
| 11.6 | 22.4 | 31.3 | 28.1 | 23.4 | 22.5 | Net Worth | 25.1 | 24.5 |
| 100.0 | 100.0 | 100.0 | 100.0 | 100.0 | 100.0 | Total Liabilties & Net Worth | 100.0 | 100.0 |
| | | | | | | INCOME DATA | | |
| 100.0 | 100.0 | 100.0 | 100.0 | 100.0 | 100.0 | Net Sales | 100.0 | 100.0 |
| 30.4 | 29.0 | 23.2 | 21.1 | 18.1 | 21.8 | Gross Profit | 22.0 | 22.2 |
| 29.9 | 24.6 | 20.1 | 18.0 | 15.6 | 18.4 | Operating Expenses | 19.5 | 20.8 |
| .5 | 4.4 | 3.1 | 3.1 | 2.5 | 3.4 | Operating Profit | 2.5 | 1.4 |
| .8 | .6 | .4 | .5 | .2 | .7 | All Other Expenses (net) | .7 | .7 |
| -.3 | 3.8 | 2.6 | 2.7 | 2.3 | 2.6 | Profit Before Taxes | 1.8 | .7 |
| | | | | | | RATIOS | | |
| 3.9 | 3.3 | 2.0 | 1.7 | 1.4 | 1.5 | | 1.8 | 1.7 |
| 1.8 | 1.6 | 1.5 | 1.2 | 1.2 | 1.1 | Current | 1.3 | 1.3 |
| 1.2 | 1.0 | 1.2 | 1.1 | 1.1 | 1.0 | | 1.1 | 1.0 |
| 1.2 | 1.5 | .8 | .7 | .5 | .4 | | .6 | .6 |
| .5 | .3 | .4 | .4 | .3 | .2 | Quick | (327) .3 | .3 |
| .1 | .1 | .2 | .2 | .2 | .2 | | .1 | .1 |
| 0 UND | 0 UND | 6 58.8 | 8 43.9 | 12 31.7 | 16 23.0 | | 4 104.2 | 5 79.3 |
| 3 125.8 | 6 59.6 | 14 26.5 | 14 26.0 | 20 18.1 | 22 16.8 | Sales/Receivables | 11 32.7 | 12 29.8 |
| 9 41.4 | 19 19.5 | 26 14.3 | 23 16.1 | 32 11.4 | 33 11.0 | | 22 17.0 | 25 14.6 |
| 28 12.9 | 44 8.3 | 51 7.2 | 47 7.8 | 55 6.6 | 73 5.0 | | 50 7.3 | 53 6.8 |
| 66 5.5 | 94 3.9 | 83 4.4 | 74 4.9 | 72 5.1 | 114 3.2 | Cost of Sales/Inventory | 79 4.6 | 82 4.4 |
| 152 2.4 | 159 2.3 | 135 2.7 | 114 3.2 | 96 3.8 | 140 2.6 | | 124 2.9 | 135 2.7 |
| 0 UND | 0 UND | 5 69.6 | 7 55.9 | 6 61.6 | 9 40.5 | | 3 145.3 | 3 125.6 |
| 6 65.0 | 4 84.4 | 13 28.3 | 14 26.7 | 13 28.8 | 15 24.1 | Cost of Sales/Payables | 8 44.6 | 9 41.3 |
| 37 9.8 | 31 11.6 | 22 16.9 | 22 16.6 | 25 14.7 | 26 14.3 | | 19 19.2 | 19 18.9 |
| 5.0 | 5.9 | 6.0 | 8.3 | 10.0 | 8.6 | | 8.4 | 8.5 |
| 15.1 | 13.4 | 11.7 | 16.5 | 30.9 | 57.7 | Sales/Working Capital | 18.5 | 18.6 |
| 41.0 | 150.4 | 27.8 | 83.9 | 60.5 | 726.0 | | 80.3 | 128.3 |
| 10.0 | 15.4 | 8.7 | 8.3 | 8.6 | 4.9 | | 4.6 | 3.7 |
| (19) 1.8 | (63) 3.7 | (108) 3.4 | (82) 3.9 | 3.9 | 4.0 | EBIT/Interest | (302) 2.1 | (277) 1.7 |
| 1.0 | 1.3 | 1.6 | 2.0 | 2.4 | 1.7 | | 1.2 | .9 |
| | | 7.7 | 2.9 | | | | 7.0 | 3.9 |
| | (17) 3.1 | (20) 1.5 | | | | Net Profit + Depr., Dep., Amort./Cur. Mat. L/T/D | (48) 1.4 | (47) 1.5 |
| | 1.8 | 1.0 | | | | | .8 | .8 |
| .0 | .1 | .1 | .2 | .4 | 1.0 | | .2 | .2 |
| .3 | .3 | .3 | .7 | 1.0 | 1.5 | Fixed/Worth | .5 | .6 |
| 2.2 | 3.1 | 1.1 | 2.3 | 2.0 | 2.0 | | 1.6 | 2.5 |
| .9 | 1.1 | 1.2 | 1.7 | 3.1 | 1.8 | | 1.5 | 1.7 |
| 2.5 | 3.5 | 2.6 | 3.6 | 4.4 | 5.6 | Debt/Worth | 3.4 | 3.7 |
| 8.9 | 11.7 | 5.3 | 6.7 | 12.5 | 10.9 | | 8.7 | 11.9 |
| 42.3 | 61.3 | 41.1 | 33.5 | 65.4 | 53.1 | % Profit Before Taxes/Tangible Net Worth | 40.0 | 31.0 |
| (21) 14.4 | (59) 25.2 | (108) 21.8 | (83) 19.6 | 35.0 | 20.4 | | (294) 18.7 | (272) 11.0 |
| -2.0 | 5.8 | 6.6 | 8.4 | 10.9 | 13.9 | | 5.1 | .0 |
| 14.9 | 15.9 | 11.5 | 8.9 | 8.5 | 6.2 | % Profit Before Taxes/Total Assets | 9.8 | 7.8 |
| 4.0 | 6.0 | 4.6 | 5.1 | 4.2 | 3.9 | | 4.1 | 2.0 |
| -3.5 | 1.3 | 1.7 | 2.2 | 2.3 | 2.3 | | .5 | -.6 |
| 829.5 | 226.9 | 105.4 | 56.6 | 75.5 | 33.7 | | 84.4 | 67.1 |
| 112.4 | 49.7 | 47.1 | 14.8 | 12.0 | 10.4 | Sales/Net Fixed Assets | 27.8 | 28.6 |
| 31.5 | 12.7 | 12.8 | 5.5 | 8.5 | 4.8 | | 9.6 | 8.4 |
| 8.1 | 4.3 | 3.8 | 3.5 | 2.9 | 2.4 | | 3.6 | 3.5 |
| 4.0 | 3.0 | 2.9 | 2.3 | 2.3 | 1.7 | Sales/Total Assets | 2.7 | 2.5 |
| 2.1 | 1.6 | 1.9 | 1.6 | 1.9 | 1.2 | | 2.0 | 1.7 |
| .2 | .2 | .3 | .4 | .4 | | | .3 | .4 |
| (14) .3 | (44) .6 | (92) .6 | (80) 1.3 | (15) .6 | | % Depr., Dep., Amort./Sales | (275) .7 | (251) .9 |
| .8 | 1.2 | 1.6 | 3.5 | 1.9 | | | 2.0 | 2.6 |
| 1.5 | 1.0 | .7 | .4 | | | | .7 | 1.0 |
| (15) 3.4 | (42) 2.1 | (62) 1.6 | (22) .9 | | | % Officers', Directors' Owners' Comp/Sales | (120) 1.6 | (124) 1.8 |
| 5.5 | 6.4 | 2.4 | 2.3 | | | | 4.1 | 3.7 |
| 48920M | 296879M | 1856893M | 5024662M | 2891782M | 4414487M | Net Sales ($) | 11361900M | 9663951M |
| 7841M | 85016M | 604542M | 1992000M | 1222658M | 2477588M | Total Assets ($) | 4631918M | 4272693M |

M = $ thousand    MM = $ million
See Pages 9 through 22 for Explanation of Ratios and Data

**Comparative Historical Data** | | | | **Current Data Sorted by Sales** | | | | | |

### Type of Statement

| | | | Type of Statement | 0-1MM | 1-3MM | 3-5MM | 5-10MM | 10-25MM | 25MM & OVER |
|---|---|---|---|---|---|---|---|---|---|
| 34 | 41 | 36 | Unqualified | | 1 | 1 | | 4 | 30 |
| 66 | 70 | 54 | Reviewed | | | | 5 | 19 | 29 |
| 43 | 50 | 56 | Compiled | 2 | 10 | 5 | 12 | 18 | 9 |
| 77 | 81 | 79 | Tax Returns | 11 | 23 | 15 | 10 | 16 | 4 |
| 104 | 116 | 115 | Other | 5 | 12 | 10 | 15 | 20 | 53 |
| 4/1/09-3/31/10 ALL | 4/1/10-3/31/11 ALL | 4/1/11-3/31/12 ALL | | | 59 (4/1-9/30/11) | | 281 (10/1/11-3/31/12) | | |
| 324 | 358 | 340 | **NUMBER OF STATEMENTS** | 18 | 46 | 32 | 42 | 77 | 125 |
| % | % | % | **ASSETS** | % | % | % | % | % | % |
| 8.3 | 9.6 | 10.1 | Cash & Equivalents | 5.4 | 9.7 | 11.7 | 11.6 | 10.8 | 9.7 |
| 12.4 | 13.0 | 12.6 | Trade Receivables (net) | 6.5 | 11.3 | 8.1 | 15.9 | 12.9 | 13.8 |
| 51.7 | 50.7 | 49.4 | Inventory | 61.9 | 45.9 | 58.0 | 51.9 | 50.3 | 45.3 |
| 2.4 | 2.0 | 1.9 | All Other Current | 1.6 | .8 | 1.9 | 1.4 | 1.7 | 2.6 |
| 74.8 | 75.2 | 74.0 | Total Current | 75.4 | 67.7 | 79.7 | 80.8 | 75.7 | 71.5 |
| 17.3 | 16.6 | 17.6 | Fixed Assets (net) | 18.3 | 21.0 | 15.7 | 13.1 | 16.8 | 18.8 |
| 2.0 | 1.7 | 2.5 | Intangibles (net) | .2 | 4.2 | 2.1 | 2.1 | 1.8 | 2.9 |
| 5.9 | 6.5 | 5.8 | All Other Non-Current | 6.0 | 7.1 | 2.5 | 4.0 | 5.7 | 6.9 |
| 100.0 | 100.0 | 100.0 | Total | 100.0 | 100.0 | 100.0 | 100.0 | 100.0 | 100.0 |
| | | | **LIABILITIES** | | | | | | |
| 34.0 | 31.4 | 28.5 | Notes Payable-Short Term | 23.6 | 24.9 | 32.0 | 26.7 | 25.5 | 32.0 |
| 4.2 | 4.4 | 3.9 | Cur. Mat.-L.T.D. | 2.0 | 4.3 | 4.2 | 2.7 | 3.4 | 4.7 |
| 10.1 | 12.3 | 10.4 | Trade Payables | 5.1 | 13.8 | 5.2 | 12.8 | 10.0 | 10.8 |
| .0 | .1 | .1 | Income Taxes Payable | .1 | .0 | .0 | .0 | .1 | .1 |
| 9.8 | 8.7 | 9.4 | All Other Current | 17.7 | 5.8 | 6.3 | 12.8 | 9.4 | 9.2 |
| 58.2 | 57.0 | 52.3 | Total Current | 48.5 | 48.8 | 47.8 | 55.0 | 48.5 | 56.8 |
| 13.5 | 11.2 | 14.7 | Long-Term Debt | 20.5 | 20.2 | 16.2 | 11.2 | 15.9 | 12.0 |
| .2 | .4 | .4 | Deferred Taxes | .0 | .0 | .0 | .0 | .3 | .9 |
| 8.8 | 7.7 | 6.4 | All Other Non-Current | 29.1 | 8.9 | 11.5 | 1.8 | 5.2 | 3.1 |
| 19.3 | 23.6 | 26.2 | Net Worth | 2.0 | 22.1 | 24.5 | 32.0 | 30.0 | 27.3 |
| 100.0 | 100.0 | 100.0 | Total Liabilities & Net Worth | 100.0 | 100.0 | 100.0 | 100.0 | 100.0 | 100.0 |
| | | | **INCOME DATA** | | | | | | |
| 100.0 | 100.0 | 100.0 | Net Sales | 100.0 | 100.0 | 100.0 | 100.0 | 100.0 | 100.0 |
| 23.4 | 23.2 | 24.1 | Gross Profit | 43.7 | 32.0 | 27.7 | 22.2 | 22.2 | 19.3 |
| 22.3 | 21.0 | 20.9 | Operating Expenses | 42.0 | 26.8 | 23.7 | 19.2 | 19.6 | 16.5 |
| 1.1 | 2.2 | 3.2 | Operating Profit | 1.7 | 5.2 | 3.9 | 3.0 | 2.6 | 2.8 |
| .8 | .5 | .5 | All Other Expenses (net) | .9 | 1.3 | .4 | .4 | .3 | .3 |
| .3 | 1.7 | 2.7 | Profit Before Taxes | .8 | 3.9 | 3.5 | 2.6 | 2.3 | 2.5 |
| | | | **RATIOS** | | | | | | |
| 1.8 | 1.9 | 2.0 | Current | 69.6 | 3.1 | 4.6 | 2.2 | 2.3 | 1.5 |
| 1.3 | 1.3 | 1.4 | | 2.0 | 1.4 | 1.8 | 1.4 | 1.5 | 1.2 |
| 1.1 | 1.1 | 1.1 | | 1.1 | 1.0 | 1.2 | 1.1 | 1.2 | 1.0 |
| .7 | .7 | .8 | Quick | 5.7 | 1.3 | 1.0 | .9 | .8 | .6 |
| .3 | .4 | .4 | | .3 | .4 | .2 | .5 | .4 | .3 |
| .1 | .2 | .2 | | .0 | .1 | .1 | .2 | .2 | .2 |
| 5 77.5 | 4 82.7 | 5 76.4 | Sales/Receivables | 0 UND | 0 UND | 0 UND | 4 81.3 | 7 54.3 | 9 42.2 |
| 14 25.4 | 14 26.4 | 12 29.4 | | 3 125.8 | 9 41.8 | 6 62.7 | 12 29.5 | 14 25.4 | 16 23.0 |
| 27 13.8 | 25 14.5 | 23 15.8 | | 8 47.1 | 27 13.7 | 17 22.0 | 29 12.7 | 23 16.1 | 25 14.5 |
| 51 7.2 | 49 7.5 | 49 7.5 | Cost of Sales/Inventory | 146 2.5 | 32 11.5 | 50 7.3 | 52 7.0 | 49 7.4 | 47 7.7 |
| 86 4.3 | 82 4.5 | 81 4.5 | | 281 1.3 | 91 4.0 | 107 3.4 | 79 4.6 | 78 4.7 | 72 5.1 |
| 145 2.5 | 131 2.8 | 126 2.9 | | 456 .8 | 174 2.1 | 159 2.3 | 111 3.3 | 140 2.6 | 107 3.4 |
| 4 85.4 | 4 84.8 | 4 88.8 | Cost of Sales/Payables | 0 UND | 0 UND | 0 UND | 3 112.2 | 5 69.6 | 7 55.9 |
| 12 30.3 | 13 27.2 | 12 30.3 | | 1 509.5 | 11 33.6 | 3 140.3 | 12 29.9 | 11 32.6 | 14 26.7 |
| 24 15.3 | 25 14.6 | 24 15.1 | | 23 15.9 | 53 6.9 | 18 20.4 | 27 13.7 | 20 18.7 | 22 16.6 |
| 7.1 | 7.4 | 6.9 | Sales/Working Capital | 2.0 | 4.6 | 4.3 | 6.8 | 6.6 | 11.1 |
| 17.2 | 16.1 | 14.1 | | 4.9 | 17.6 | 8.4 | 11.9 | 11.5 | 20.6 |
| 88.1 | 78.3 | 63.8 | | 20.5 | NM | 21.5 | 29.8 | 25.6 | 90.3 |
| 3.8 | 7.1 | 8.3 | EBIT/Interest | 3.1 | 7.7 | 17.8 | 13.6 | 9.2 | 8.6 |
| (286) 1.7 | (326) 2.7 | (306) 3.7 | | (11) 1.2 | (38) 3.0 | (30) 3.3 | (38) 3.9 | (74) 3.1 | (115) 4.0 |
| .4 | 1.2 | 1.6 | | .4 | 1.2 | 1.4 | 1.6 | 1.4 | 2.5 |
| 3.5 | 3.0 | 5.2 | Net Profit + Depr., Dep., Amort./Cur. Mat. L/T/D | | | | | 17.9 | 2.9 |
| (47) 1.2 | (56) 1.4 | (48) 2.3 | | | | | | (14) 3.2 | (28) 1.4 |
| .7 | .9 | 1.2 | | | | | | 1.5 | 1.0 |
| .1 | .1 | .1 | Fixed/Worth | .0 | .1 | .1 | .1 | .1 | .2 |
| .5 | .4 | .5 | | .2 | .5 | .4 | .2 | .5 | .6 |
| 2.1 | 2.0 | 1.9 | | NM | 5.9 | 4.0 | .9 | 1.8 | 1.8 |
| 1.6 | 1.3 | 1.5 | Debt/Worth | .8 | 1.8 | 1.0 | 1.1 | 1.3 | 1.8 |
| 3.2 | 3.0 | 3.1 | | 3.5 | 3.2 | 2.7 | 2.7 | 2.9 | 3.6 |
| 10.9 | 7.1 | 8.6 | | -4.0 | 10.9 | NM | 5.5 | 8.8 | 7.1 |
| 27.0 | 34.5 | 45.0 | % Profit Before Taxes/Tangible Net Worth | 18.9 | 44.3 | 47.3 | 55.3 | 38.5 | 47.6 |
| (278) 9.6 | (310) 17.1 | (305) 21.5 | | (13) .0 | (38) 22.7 | (24) 22.7 | (39) 22.1 | (71) 17.4 | (120) 24.0 |
| -5.0 | 4.3 | 7.0 | | -13.1 | 6.2 | 9.5 | 5.3 | 5.9 | 13.3 |
| 6.5 | 10.0 | 10.7 | % Profit Before Taxes/Total Assets | 5.5 | 12.9 | 16.0 | 13.5 | 10.9 | 8.9 |
| 2.0 | 3.8 | 4.8 | | .3 | 5.9 | 5.2 | 4.7 | 3.5 | 5.4 |
| -1.8 | .6 | 1.7 | | -5.1 | 1.2 | 2.0 | 1.7 | 1.4 | 2.7 |
| 79.8 | 86.1 | 105.7 | Sales/Net Fixed Assets | 342.9 | 163.6 | 130.5 | 254.8 | 87.8 | 85.5 |
| 27.3 | 34.7 | 35.5 | | 57.5 | 30.8 | 39.0 | 54.4 | 32.8 | 31.2 |
| 8.1 | 10.4 | 8.7 | | 7.0 | 4.9 | 12.6 | 18.6 | 8.9 | 6.8 |
| 3.6 | 3.9 | 3.8 | Sales/Total Assets | 2.4 | 4.0 | 4.2 | 4.0 | 3.6 | 3.8 |
| 2.5 | 2.6 | 2.6 | | 1.5 | 2.4 | 2.7 | 3.2 | 2.8 | 2.6 |
| 1.6 | 1.7 | 1.7 | | .7 | 1.4 | 1.6 | 2.2 | 1.8 | 1.8 |
| .4 | .3 | .3 | % Depr., Dep., Amort./Sales | | .2 | .6 | .2 | .4 | .3 |
| (267) .8 | (288) .8 | (254) .7 | | | (32) .7 | (23) .7 | (27) .6 | (63) .7 | (101) .8 |
| 2.7 | 2.2 | 2.2 | | | 3.3 | 2.1 | 1.3 | 2.6 | 2.4 |
| 1.0 | 1.0 | .7 | % Officers', Directors' Owners' Comp/Sales | | 1.1 | 1.5 | 1.3 | .7 | .3 |
| (138) 2.1 | (149) 1.9 | (146) 1.6 | | | (32) 2.5 | (20) 2.2 | (22) 1.7 | (36) 1.1 | (31) .5 |
| 3.9 | 3.4 | 3.7 | | | 5.6 | 5.9 | 2.9 | 2.2 | 1.4 |
| 8485708M | 13248941M | 14533623M | Net Sales ($) | 11599M | 88869M | 127677M | 323746M | 1250920M | 12730812M |
| 3771432M | 5710759M | 6389645M | Total Assets ($) | 10704M | 49734M | 60206M | 122904M | 547337M | 5598760M |

## RETAIL—Automotive Parts and Accessories Stores   NAICS 441310

### Current Data Sorted by Assets

| Type of Statement | 0-500M | 500M-2MM | 2-10MM | 10-50MM | 50-100MM | 100-250MM |
|---|---|---|---|---|---|---|
| Unqualified | 1 |  | 7 | 11 | 3 | 5 |
| Reviewed |  | 11 | 34 | 15 | 3 |  |
| Compiled | 17 | 27 | 31 | 4 |  |  |
| Tax Returns | 69 | 73 | 35 | 5 |  |  |
| Other | 32 | 57 | 37 | 18 | 4 | 4 |
|  |  | 59 (4/1-9/30/11) |  | 444 (10/1/11-3/31/12) |  |  |

### Comparative Historical Data

| Type of Statement | 4/1/07-3/31/08 ALL | 4/1/08-3/31/09 ALL |
|---|---|---|
| Unqualified | 15 | 20 |
| Reviewed | 29 | 45 |
| Compiled | 74 | 80 |
| Tax Returns | 113 | 133 |
| Other | 106 | 98 |

| 0-500M | 500M-2MM | 2-10MM | 10-50MM | 50-100MM | 100-250MM | | 4/1/07-3/31/08 ALL | 4/1/08-3/31/09 ALL |
|---|---|---|---|---|---|---|---|---|
| 119 | 168 | 144 | 53 | 10 | 9 | **NUMBER OF STATEMENTS** | 337 | 376 |
| % | % | % | % | % | % | **ASSETS** | % | % |
| 16.5 | 9.1 | 5.5 | 4.6 | 5.7 | | Cash & Equivalents | 6.8 | 6.7 |
| 10.5 | 13.8 | 17.7 | 15.3 | 16.0 | | Trade Receivables (net) | 15.4 | 16.7 |
| 43.2 | 47.1 | 51.0 | 48.2 | 40.0 | | Inventory | 48.2 | 48.2 |
| 1.6 | 1.9 | 1.2 | 2.2 | 2.0 | | All Other Current | 2.7 | 1.8 |
| 71.8 | 71.8 | 75.3 | 70.3 | 63.7 | | Total Current | 73.1 | 73.4 |
| 18.0 | 18.7 | 16.1 | 19.4 | 19.1 | | Fixed Assets (net) | 17.7 | 17.8 |
| 3.5 | 3.3 | 3.2 | 4.4 | 11.9 | | Intangibles (net) | 3.3 | 3.0 |
| 6.8 | 6.1 | 5.3 | 5.9 | 5.3 | | All Other Non-Current | 5.9 | 5.8 |
| 100.0 | 100.0 | 100.0 | 100.0 | 100.0 | | Total | 100.0 | 100.0 |
| | | | | | | **LIABILITIES** | | |
| 9.2 | 9.5 | 10.5 | 15.3 | 8.0 | | Notes Payable-Short Term | 10.4 | 11.2 |
| 4.0 | 2.4 | 3.0 | 1.9 | 2.4 | | Cur. Mat.-L.T.D. | 4.2 | 3.2 |
| 20.1 | 17.1 | 21.2 | 23.0 | 18.7 | | Trade Payables | 18.8 | 20.8 |
| .2 | .1 | .1 | .1 | .0 | | Income Taxes Payable | .1 | .1 |
| 16.9 | 9.9 | 8.6 | 5.5 | 8.9 | | All Other Current | 8.6 | 10.5 |
| 50.3 | 38.9 | 43.5 | 45.9 | 38.1 | | Total Current | 42.1 | 45.8 |
| 20.6 | 19.9 | 16.5 | 11.1 | 8.3 | | Long-Term Debt | 21.5 | 19.9 |
| .0 | .1 | .1 | .7 | .6 | | Deferred Taxes | .1 | .2 |
| 16.0 | 6.8 | 5.1 | 6.3 | 13.7 | | All Other Non-Current | 7.0 | 5.4 |
| 13.0 | 34.3 | 34.7 | 36.1 | 39.2 | | Net Worth | 29.3 | 28.6 |
| 100.0 | 100.0 | 100.0 | 100.0 | 100.0 | | Total Liabilities & Net Worth | 100.0 | 100.0 |
| | | | | | | **INCOME DATA** | | |
| 100.0 | 100.0 | 100.0 | 100.0 | 100.0 | | Net Sales | 100.0 | 100.0 |
| 42.0 | 39.1 | 32.9 | 33.6 | 33.1 | | Gross Profit | 37.0 | 36.5 |
| 37.4 | 35.3 | 29.5 | 28.7 | 28.5 | | Operating Expenses | 34.1 | 33.8 |
| 4.6 | 3.8 | 3.4 | 4.9 | 4.6 | | Operating Profit | 2.9 | 2.6 |
| 1.4 | .5 | .3 | .8 | 1.5 | | All Other Expenses (net) | .6 | .9 |
| 3.2 | 3.3 | 3.1 | 4.1 | 3.2 | | Profit Before Taxes | 2.3 | 1.8 |
| | | | | | | **RATIOS** | | |
| 5.3 | 3.7 | 2.8 | 2.5 | 2.3 | | | 3.1 | 3.1 |
| 1.8 | 2.1 | 1.7 | 1.5 | 1.5 | | Current | 1.9 | 1.8 |
| 1.1 | 1.2 | 1.2 | 1.1 | 1.3 | | | 1.2 | 1.2 |
| 1.4 | 1.3 | 1.0 | .7 | 1.1 | | | 1.0 | 1.0 |
| .6 | .5 | .5 | .4 | .5 | | Quick | .5 | .5 |
| .2 | .3 | .3 | .2 | .1 | | | .3 | .3 |
| 0 UND | 4 90.3 | 14 25.3 | 8 44.8 | 4 102.1 | | | 8 48.5 | 8 48.0 |
| 5 76.8 | 16 23.5 | 26 14.2 | 24 15.2 | 21 17.8 | | Sales/Receivables | 22 16.8 | 21 17.2 |
| 16 23.1 | 30 12.2 | 35 10.4 | 34 10.6 | 54 6.7 | | | 32 11.3 | 33 11.1 |
| 23 15.8 | 52 7.0 | 68 5.4 | 72 5.1 | 72 5.1 | | | 62 5.9 | 53 6.9 |
| 48 7.6 | 104 3.5 | 107 3.4 | 111 3.3 | 114 3.2 | | Cost of Sales/Inventory | 104 3.5 | 97 3.8 |
| 140 2.6 | 174 2.1 | 166 2.2 | 203 1.8 | 152 2.4 | | | 168 2.2 | 172 2.1 |
| 0 UND | 10 35.6 | 24 15.2 | 27 13.6 | 31 11.9 | | | 17 21.5 | 19 19.4 |
| 19 19.1 | 30 12.2 | 39 9.3 | 57 6.4 | 33 10.9 | | Cost of Sales/Payables | 34 10.6 | 35 10.4 |
| 38 9.7 | 59 6.2 | 68 5.4 | 81 4.5 | 69 5.3 | | | 61 6.0 | 57 6.4 |
| 5.5 | 4.0 | 4.4 | 3.8 | 5.3 | | | 4.0 | 4.2 |
| 18.3 | 8.2 | 8.4 | 9.9 | 9.5 | | Sales/Working Capital | 8.3 | 9.1 |
| 135.2 | 34.7 | 21.6 | 60.1 | 31.2 | | | 25.6 | 31.4 |
| 11.5 | 12.5 | 9.8 | 13.8 | | | | 5.8 | 7.7 |
| (81) 3.1 | (139) 3.0 | (134) 3.9 | (51) 6.7 | | | EBIT/Interest | (300) 2.3 | (339) 2.9 |
| .0 | 1.0 | 1.9 | 2.2 | | | | 1.1 | 1.0 |
| | | 4.9 | 4.5 | | | | 4.4 | 5.2 |
| | (29) 2.5 | (13) 3.2 | | | | Net Profit + Depr., Dep., Amort./Cur. Mat. L/T/D | (55) 1.5 | (64) 2.0 |
| | | .7 | 1.3 | | | | .5 | .8 |
| .1 | .1 | .1 | .2 | .2 | | | .1 | .1 |
| .4 | .3 | .3 | .4 | .6 | | Fixed/Worth | .4 | .4 |
| -1.5 | 2.6 | 1.1 | 1.8 | NM | | | 1.7 | 1.7 |
| .6 | .7 | .9 | .8 | .8 | | | .9 | .9 |
| 1.8 | 2.0 | 2.0 | 2.7 | 2.6 | | Debt/Worth | 2.2 | 2.3 |
| -6.4 | 8.4 | 4.8 | 9.4 | NM | | | 8.8 | 8.2 |
| 90.0 | 39.2 | 34.9 | 39.0 | | | % Profit Before Taxes/Tangible Net Worth | 42.2 | 34.5 |
| (80) 29.1 | (137) 18.1 | (131) 18.2 | (47) 23.3 | | | | (285) 15.5 | (312) 13.9 |
| 5.8 | 8.4 | 6.9 | 9.5 | | | | 4.4 | 2.3 |
| 30.1 | 15.1 | 11.1 | 11.8 | 10.3 | | % Profit Before Taxes/Total Assets | 11.6 | 11.0 |
| 8.9 | 6.8 | 5.0 | 6.0 | 7.5 | | | 4.3 | 4.2 |
| -1.2 | .8 | 2.0 | 2.8 | -2.5 | | | .6 | .0 |
| 114.6 | 105.3 | 74.5 | 74.4 | 69.9 | | Sales/Net Fixed Assets | 60.2 | 67.2 |
| 38.4 | 30.2 | 31.6 | 19.7 | 14.2 | | | 24.8 | 26.9 |
| 16.3 | 11.8 | 13.4 | 8.5 | 4.6 | | | 11.7 | 12.3 |
| 7.1 | 3.6 | 3.4 | 2.6 | 2.9 | | Sales/Total Assets | 3.6 | 3.8 |
| 4.7 | 2.4 | 2.5 | 2.2 | 1.8 | | | 2.5 | 2.6 |
| 2.6 | 1.8 | 1.9 | 1.5 | 1.2 | | | 1.8 | 1.9 |
| .5 | .3 | .4 | .6 | .5 | | | .5 | .5 |
| (67) 1.2 | (118) .9 | (116) .8 | (47) 1.1 | 1.6 | | % Depr., Dep., Amort./Sales | (272) 1.0 | (307) 1.0 |
| 2.2 | 1.7 | 1.5 | 1.7 | 2.4 | | | 1.7 | 1.9 |
| 2.8 | 1.8 | 1.4 | 1.6 | | | | 1.5 | 1.6 |
| (56) 5.2 | (89) 3.1 | (80) 2.1 | (13) 2.1 | | | % Officers', Directors' Owners' Comp/Sales | (185) 3.3 | (183) 3.1 |
| 9.3 | 5.2 | 3.2 | 3.5 | | | | 5.9 | 5.6 |
| 165549M | 592264M | 1608295M | 2975329M | 1730716M | 3282030M | Net Sales ($) | 6929065M | 9273020M |
| 31084M | 188629M | 610389M | 1274998M | 772320M | 1325112M | Total Assets ($) | 3011706M | 3884791M |

© RMA 2012

M = $ thousand    MM = $ million
See Pages 9 through 22 for Explanation of Ratios and Data

## Comparative Historical Data | | | | Current Data Sorted by Sales

| Hist 1 | Hist 2 | Hist 3 | Type of Statement | 0-1MM | 1-3MM | 3-5MM | 5-10MM | 10-25MM | 25MM & OVER |
|---|---|---|---|---|---|---|---|---|---|
| 20 | 18 | 27 | Unqualified |  | 1 |  | 1 | 9 | 16 |
| 55 | 53 | 63 | Reviewed |  | 4 | 5 | 12 | 19 | 23 |
| 77 | 78 | 79 | Compiled | 13 | 25 | 9 | 17 | 11 | 4 |
| 158 | 173 | 182 | Tax Returns | 44 | 65 | 23 | 31 | 14 | 5 |
| 116 | 144 | 152 | Other | 19 | 41 | 26 | 23 | 19 | 24 |
| 4/1/09-3/31/10 ALL | 4/1/10-3/31/11 ALL | 4/1/11-3/31/12 ALL | | 59 (4/1-9/30/11) | | | 444 (10/1/11-3/31/12) | | |
| 426 | 466 | 503 | **NUMBER OF STATEMENTS** | 76 | 136 | 63 | 84 | 72 | 72 |
| % | % | % | **ASSETS** | % | % | % | % | % | % |
| 7.5 | 8.8 | 9.2 | Cash & Equivalents | 11.1 | 12.0 | 11.6 | 7.4 | 6.3 | 5.0 |
| 14.1 | 14.5 | 14.5 | Trade Receivables (net) | 9.6 | 12.5 | 15.0 | 15.0 | 19.2 | 17.5 |
| 46.2 | 47.4 | 47.1 | Inventory | 45.2 | 46.4 | 45.9 | 50.9 | 46.6 | 47.5 |
| 1.9 | 1.6 | 1.7 | All Other Current | .4 | 2.3 | 1.9 | 1.5 | 1.1 | 2.4 |
| 69.7 | 72.3 | 72.5 | Total Current | 66.4 | 73.2 | 74.3 | 74.9 | 73.1 | 72.4 |
| 19.6 | 17.1 | 17.8 | Fixed Assets (net) | 22.5 | 17.1 | 16.3 | 17.9 | 15.1 | 18.2 |
| 4.6 | 4.2 | 3.7 | Intangibles (net) | 4.7 | 3.6 | 2.5 | 2.9 | 4.0 | 4.5 |
| 6.1 | 6.3 | 6.0 | All Other Non-Current | 6.4 | 6.1 | 6.9 | 4.4 | 7.8 | 4.9 |
| 100.0 | 100.0 | 100.0 | Total | 100.0 | 100.0 | 100.0 | 100.0 | 100.0 | 100.0 |
| | | | **LIABILITIES** | | | | | | |
| 12.1 | 9.7 | 10.2 | Notes Payable-Short Term | 10.8 | 6.7 | 9.4 | 10.6 | 12.7 | 14.1 |
| 3.0 | 2.8 | 2.9 | Cur. Mat.-L.T.D. | 2.9 | 3.1 | 3.1 | 3.0 | 3.0 | 1.8 |
| 20.1 | 20.3 | 19.8 | Trade Payables | 13.4 | 18.1 | 22.1 | 19.9 | 23.6 | 24.0 |
| .1 | .1 | .1 | Income Taxes Payable | .0 | .2 | .1 | .1 | .2 | .2 |
| 8.9 | 10.2 | 10.8 | All Other Current | 12.0 | 15.8 | 5.9 | 8.1 | 10.5 | 7.5 |
| 44.2 | 43.1 | 43.8 | Total Current | 39.1 | 43.9 | 40.6 | 41.7 | 50.0 | 47.6 |
| 21.6 | 18.8 | 17.8 | Long-Term Debt | 31.6 | 18.4 | 19.4 | 15.8 | 10.8 | 10.1 |
| .1 | .1 | .2 | Deferred Taxes | .0 | .0 | .0 | .2 | .3 | .5 |
| 7.1 | 9.2 | 8.6 | All Other Non-Current | 20.5 | 8.4 | 7.4 | 4.0 | 7.2 | 3.9 |
| 27.0 | 28.8 | 29.7 | Net Worth | 8.8 | 29.3 | 32.6 | 38.3 | 31.7 | 37.9 |
| 100.0 | 100.0 | 100.0 | Total Liabilities & Net Worth | 100.0 | 100.0 | 100.0 | 100.0 | 100.0 | 100.0 |
| | | | **INCOME DATA** | | | | | | |
| 100.0 | 100.0 | 100.0 | Net Sales | 100.0 | 100.0 | 100.0 | 100.0 | 100.0 | 100.0 |
| 37.3 | 37.7 | 37.3 | Gross Profit | 45.9 | 40.9 | 35.3 | 35.3 | 29.9 | 32.9 |
| 34.9 | 33.9 | 33.3 | Operating Expenses | 39.4 | 37.2 | 31.4 | 32.7 | 26.9 | 28.2 |
| 2.4 | 3.8 | 4.0 | Operating Profit | 6.5 | 3.8 | 3.9 | 2.5 | 3.0 | 4.8 |
| .8 | .9 | .7 | All Other Expenses (net) | 2.5 | .4 | .4 | -.1 | .7 | .6 |
| 1.6 | 2.9 | 3.3 | Profit Before Taxes | 4.0 | 3.3 | 3.5 | 2.6 | 2.3 | 4.2 |
| | | | **RATIOS** | | | | | | |
| 3.3 / 1.7 / 1.1 | 3.4 / 1.8 / 1.2 | 3.4 / 1.8 / 1.2 | Current | 6.3 / 2.3 / 1.1 | 3.8 / 1.9 / 1.2 | 4.1 / 2.3 / 1.3 | 3.4 / 1.9 / 1.3 | 2.1 / 1.5 / 1.0 | 2.1 / 1.4 / 1.1 |
| 1.0 / .5 / .3 | 1.0 / .5 / .3 | 1.0 / .5 / .3 | Quick | 1.2 / .6 / .2 | 1.3 / .5 / .3 | 1.4 / .7 / .4 | 1.2 / .5 / .3 | .8 / .4 / .3 | .7 / .4 / .3 |
| 6  60.4 / 20  18.2 / 33  11.2 | 5  68.7 / 19  18.9 / 31  11.8 | 4  86.2 / 17  21.5 / 30  12.1 | Sales/Receivables | 0  UND / 9  40.7 / 22  16.8 | 3  128.0 / 15  24.0 / 27  13.3 | 4  84.0 / 16  23.3 / 32  11.5 | 5  76.1 / 21  17.2 / 30  12.2 | 9  39.6 / 23  15.8 / 33  11.1 | 8  47.5 / 24  14.9 / 39  9.4 |
| 55  6.7 / 104  3.5 / 187  2.0 | 52  7.0 / 98  3.7 / 172  2.1 | 48  7.6 / 96  3.8 / 166  2.2 | Cost of Sales/Inventory | 26  13.9 / 122  3.0 / 243  1.5 | 41  8.9 / 94  3.9 / 174  2.1 | 51  7.1 / 94  3.9 / 159  2.3 | 50  7.3 / 104  3.5 / 159  2.3 | 39  9.3 / 87  4.2 / 135  2.7 | 60  6.1 / 91  4.0 / 159  2.3 |
| 21  17.2 / 37  9.7 / 59  6.2 | 18  20.5 / 35  10.5 / 59  6.2 | 16  22.3 / 32  11.3 / 62  5.9 | Cost of Sales/Payables | 0  UND / 20  18.6 / 62  5.9 | 13  28.5 / 29  12.5 / 56  6.5 | 18  20.5 / 31  11.9 / 59  6.2 | 18  20.4 / 38  9.7 / 62  5.9 | 19  19.7 / 34  10.8 / 59  6.2 | 29  12.5 / 51  7.2 / 73  5.0 |
| 4.2 / 8.0 / 39.4 | 4.2 / 8.4 / 37.0 | 4.3 / 9.4 / 43.7 | Sales/Working Capital | 3.5 / 7.3 / 82.8 | 4.4 / 8.5 / 33.6 | 3.6 / 7.3 / 25.6 | 4.4 / 8.7 / 24.3 | 7.1 / 11.7 / 141.6 | 6.1 / 13.9 / 47.9 |
| (381) 6.1 / 2.6 / 1.0 | (403) 11.8 / 3.7 / 1.2 | (421) 12.8 / 3.9 / 1.4 | EBIT/Interest | (56) 5.6 / 2.3 / .0 | (105) 12.6 / 2.7 / .9 | (55) 11.1 / 4.7 / 1.5 | (74) 16.1 / 3.7 / 1.9 | (66) 11.6 / 4.0 / 1.7 | (65) 16.9 / 7.5 / 2.3 |
| (62) 4.8 / 2.1 / .6 | (72) 4.7 / 2.5 / .8 | (61) 4.9 / 2.6 / .9 | Net Profit + Depr., Dep., Amort./Cur. Mat. L/T/D | | | | (10) 4.4 / 2.7 / .7 | (20) 8.3 / 2.3 / .6 | (23) 5.3 / 3.0 / 1.7 |
| .1 / .4 / 3.3 | .1 / .3 / 1.9 | .1 / .4 / 2.5 | Fixed/Worth | .1 / 1.1 / -1.0 | .1 / .3 / 2.8 | .0 / .2 / 2.4 | .1 / .3 / 1.5 | .2 / .4 / 1.3 | .2 / .4 / 1.1 |
| 1.0 / 2.3 / 13.8 | .8 / 1.8 / 9.0 | .8 / 2.0 / 9.6 | Debt/Worth | .8 / 4.5 / -5.5 | .6 / 1.8 / 13.9 | .8 / 1.9 / 8.8 | .8 / 1.6 / 5.1 | 1.4 / 2.2 / 5.0 | .9 / 2.4 / 5.2 |
| (343) 30.8 / 11.4 / .4 | (383) 39.8 / 17.2 / 4.4 | (411) 42.4 / 19.6 / 7.5 | % Profit Before Taxes/Tangible Net Worth | (45) 59.5 / 15.5 / 4.8 | (106) 47.5 / 21.8 / 8.1 | (54) 46.3 / 20.8 / 10.9 | (77) 34.6 / 18.2 / 6.0 | (64) 43.4 / 17.7 / 7.8 | (65) 42.4 / 22.8 / 10.9 |
| 9.9 / 3.5 / -.2 | 13.2 / 5.4 / .6 | 14.3 / 6.1 / 1.4 | % Profit Before Taxes/Total Assets | 13.3 / 6.4 / -3.0 | 17.0 / 7.2 / .1 | 18.5 / 8.4 / 1.3 | 12.1 / 5.1 / 1.5 | 11.3 / 5.2 / 1.6 | 13.7 / 7.4 / 3.5 |
| 65.1 / 23.6 / 8.9 | 81.6 / 32.7 / 12.3 | 87.1 / 31.3 / 12.1 | Sales/Net Fixed Assets | 60.5 / 25.9 / 8.0 | 104.0 / 35.0 / 15.4 | 159.3 / 54.3 / 14.5 | 91.7 / 31.3 / 12.5 | 91.0 / 31.0 / 16.1 | 74.3 / 21.8 / 9.6 |
| 3.4 / 2.4 / 1.7 | 3.9 / 2.6 / 1.8 | 4.0 / 2.6 / 1.9 | Sales/Total Assets | 4.9 / 2.4 / 1.3 | 5.2 / 2.5 / 1.9 | 4.1 / 2.6 / 1.9 | 3.9 / 2.8 / 2.1 | 4.1 / 2.9 / 2.0 | 3.4 / 2.4 / 1.8 |
| (342) .6 / 1.1 / 1.8 | (350) .5 / 1.0 / 1.8 | (366) .4 / .9 / 1.7 | % Depr., Dep., Amort./Sales | (52) .5 / 1.3 / 2.4 | (81) .5 / 1.0 / 1.8 | (43) .2 / .7 / 1.6 | (62) .5 / .9 / 1.8 | (63) .3 / .7 / 1.4 | (65) .6 / 1.1 / 1.6 |
| (222) 1.8 / 3.2 / 6.2 | (240) 1.8 / 3.3 / 5.3 | (240) 1.6 / 2.8 / 5.3 | % Officers', Directors' Owners' Comp/Sales | (34) 5.0 / 6.4 / 12.5 | (67) 2.1 / 3.4 / 5.5 | (38) 1.9 / 3.0 / 4.4 | (54) 1.1 / 2.0 / 3.3 | (29) 1.4 / 1.9 / 2.9 | (18) .8 / 2.0 / 3.0 |
| 7950722M | 8602754M | 10354183M | Net Sales ($) | 47914M | 256994M | 241496M | 603972M | 1137134M | 8066673M |
| 3851618M | 4167823M | 4202532M | Total Assets ($) | 25140M | 108072M | 97382M | 234488M | 468900M | 3268550M |

## Current Data Sorted by Assets      Comparative Historical Data

Type of Statement — counts

| 0-500M | 500M-2MM | 2-10MM | 10-50MM | 50-100MM | 100-250MM | Type of Statement | 15 | 16 |
|---|---|---|---|---|---|---|---|---|
| 5 | 5 | 25 | 7 | 5 | 7 | Unqualified | 15 | 16 |
|  | 15 | 20 | 15 | 2 | 1 | Reviewed | 40 | 46 |
| 21 | 19 | 10 | 5 | 2 | 2 | Compiled | 42 | 37 |
| 24 | 13 | 15 | 2 | 3 |  | Tax Returns | 42 | 32 |
|  |  |  | 16 |  |  | Other | 33 | 44 |
|  | 40 (4/1-9/30/11) |  | 199 (10/1/11-3/31/12) |  |  |  | 4/1/07-3/31/08 ALL | 4/1/08-3/31/09 ALL |
| 50 | 52 | 70 | 45 | 12 | 10 | NUMBER OF STATEMENTS | 172 | 175 |

| 0-500M | 500M-2MM | 2-10MM | 10-50MM | 50-100MM | 100-250MM | | 4/1/07-3/31/08 ALL | 4/1/08-3/31/09 ALL |
|---|---|---|---|---|---|---|---|---|
| % | % | % | % | % | % | **ASSETS** | % | % |
| 9.8 | 9.7 | 10.7 | 9.5 | 11.4 | 6.8 | Cash & Equivalents | 7.9 | 7.2 |
| 12.0 | 16.1 | 17.7 | 16.9 | 16.3 | 12.0 | Trade Receivables (net) | 20.4 | 19.4 |
| 34.8 | 36.7 | 39.4 | 41.4 | 45.7 | 33.4 | Inventory | 38.0 | 42.0 |
| 2.1 | 2.6 | 2.3 | 2.7 | 1.5 | .9 | All Other Current | 2.5 | 3.1 |
| 58.8 | 65.1 | 70.1 | 70.5 | 74.8 | 53.2 | Total Current | 68.8 | 71.7 |
| 25.9 | 22.4 | 21.9 | 20.3 | 17.3 | 31.6 | Fixed Assets (net) | 23.9 | 20.3 |
| 6.4 | 7.3 | 1.8 | 5.5 | 2.7 | 5.1 | Intangibles (net) | .9 | 2.2 |
| 9.0 | 5.2 | 6.2 | 3.6 | 5.2 | 10.1 | All Other Non-Current | 6.5 | 5.8 |
| 100.0 | 100.0 | 100.0 | 100.0 | 100.0 | 100.0 | Total | 100.0 | 100.0 |
|  |  |  |  |  |  | **LIABILITIES** |  |  |
| 8.6 | 4.9 | 6.6 | 8.3 | 10.8 | 3.9 | Notes Payable-Short Term | 9.2 | 10.4 |
| 2.0 | 4.0 | 2.0 | 2.1 | 1.2 | 1.8 | Cur. Mat.-L.T.D. | 4.0 | 3.3 |
| 26.3 | 27.4 | 29.0 | 33.3 | 32.8 | 18.0 | Trade Payables | 33.2 | 30.0 |
| .0 | .0 | .0 | .4 | .2 | .1 | Income Taxes Payable | .2 | .1 |
| 13.1 | 7.8 | 6.5 | 9.7 | 15.2 | 7.5 | All Other Current | 8.3 | 8.9 |
| 50.1 | 44.1 | 44.2 | 53.8 | 60.2 | 31.4 | Total Current | 54.9 | 52.7 |
| 29.3 | 22.9 | 10.2 | 10.2 | 5.4 | 36.1 | Long-Term Debt | 17.9 | 11.3 |
| .0 | .0 | .2 | .4 | .5 | .5 | Deferred Taxes | .2 | .3 |
| 9.5 | 7.7 | 3.6 | 2.4 | .6 | 7.3 | All Other Non-Current | 5.9 | 6.9 |
| 11.1 | 25.3 | 41.9 | 33.3 | 33.3 | 24.7 | Net Worth | 20.9 | 28.8 |
| 100.0 | 100.0 | 100.0 | 100.0 | 100.0 | 100.0 | Total Liabilities & Net Worth | 100.0 | 100.0 |
|  |  |  |  |  |  | **INCOME DATA** |  |  |
| 100.0 | 100.0 | 100.0 | 100.0 | 100.0 | 100.0 | Net Sales | 100.0 | 100.0 |
| 44.0 | 39.9 | 34.9 | 31.1 | 26.7 | 29.6 | Gross Profit | 34.5 | 33.5 |
| 40.8 | 37.3 | 30.3 | 27.7 | 24.7 | 25.4 | Operating Expenses | 31.6 | 31.0 |
| 3.3 | 2.6 | 4.6 | 3.3 | 2.0 | 4.2 | Operating Profit | 2.9 | 2.5 |
| 1.0 | 1.1 | .3 | .2 | -.5 | -.2 | All Other Expenses (net) | .3 | .0 |
| 2.3 | 1.5 | 4.3 | 3.2 | 2.5 | 4.4 | Profit Before Taxes | 2.7 | 2.4 |
|  |  |  |  |  |  | **RATIOS** |  |  |
| 2.6 | 2.3 | 2.0 | 1.7 | 1.6 | 1.9 |  | 2.0 | 2.1 |
| 1.5 | 1.5 | 1.6 | 1.3 | 1.2 | 1.5 | Current | 1.4 | 1.4 |
| .8 | 1.0 | 1.3 | 1.1 | 1.0 | 1.2 |  | 1.0 | 1.1 |
| 1.0 | .9 | 1.0 | .7 | .5 | .8 |  | .8 | .7 |
| (49) .4 | (51) .6 | .6 | .5 | .4 | .5 | Quick | .5 | .5 |
| .2 | .4 | .4 | .3 | .2 | .2 |  | .3 | .3 |
| 2 227.1 | 5 76.5 | 10 38.4 | 8 47.6 | 6 58.7 | 6 60.4 |  | 9 38.7 | 10 37.8 |
| 5 69.6 | 16 22.9 | 21 17.4 | 22 16.7 | 17 20.9 | 11 34.6 | Sales/Receivables | 20 18.2 | 19 18.8 |
| 11 32.3 | 27 13.7 | 34 10.7 | 33 10.9 | 25 14.8 | 32 11.3 |  | 34 10.8 | 33 11.1 |
| 30 12.1 | 39 9.3 | 54 6.8 | 52 7.0 | 45 8.1 | 68 5.4 |  | 43 8.5 | 48 7.6 |
| 41 8.8 | 64 5.7 | 72 5.1 | 76 4.8 | 72 5.1 | 74 4.9 | Cost of Sales/Inventory | 65 5.6 | 68 5.4 |
| 59 6.2 | 104 3.5 | 107 3.4 | 96 3.8 | 99 3.7 | 85 4.3 |  | 90 4.1 | 100 3.6 |
| 15 23.8 | 34 10.7 | 33 10.9 | 45 8.2 | 29 12.8 | 20 18.2 |  | 32 11.4 | 33 11.1 |
| 26 13.8 | 49 7.4 | 51 7.2 | 61 6.0 | 36 10.1 | 47 7.8 | Cost of Sales/Payables | 49 7.4 | 49 7.5 |
| 46 7.9 | 74 4.9 | 76 4.8 | 81 4.5 | 59 6.2 | 69 5.3 |  | 69 5.3 | 66 5.5 |
| 12.5 | 6.6 | 7.4 | 9.4 | 14.0 | 7.0 |  | 8.4 | 8.5 |
| 28.7 | 16.1 | 11.6 | 17.6 | 25.1 | 14.0 | Sales/Working Capital | 19.4 | 16.7 |
| -42.6 | 86.1 | 23.1 | 52.4 | NM | 63.8 |  | 75.8 | 77.8 |
| 21.4 | 9.8 | 25.0 | 20.5 | 27.8 | 11.2 |  | 8.3 | 10.2 |
| (35) 2.0 | (46) 3.5 | (62) 7.0 | (43) 10.4 | (11) 9.0 | 6.4 | EBIT/Interest | (153) 3.5 | (157) 4.7 |
| -.7 | 1.0 | 2.5 | 3.3 | 4.1 | 3.7 |  | 1.9 | 1.8 |
|  |  | 14.2 | 5.8 |  |  |  | 9.4 | 7.6 |
|  | (15) 4.9 | (16) 3.3 |  |  |  | Net Profit + Depr., Dep., Amort./Cur. Mat. L/T/D | (34) 4.1 | (42) 2.8 |
|  |  | 2.9 | 1.6 |  |  |  | 2.2 | 1.3 |
| .4 | .2 | .2 | .2 | .3 | .2 |  | .2 | .2 |
| 4.4 | .8 | .4 | .7 | .7 | 1.5 | Fixed/Worth | .7 | .6 |
| -.8 | -4.3 | .9 | 1.8 | 1.3 | 3.8 |  | 2.0 | 1.5 |
| .5 | 1.0 | .7 | 1.2 | 1.1 | 1.3 |  | 1.0 | 1.1 |
| 7.7 | 3.6 | 1.5 | 2.5 | 2.6 | 4.1 | Debt/Worth | 2.1 | 2.2 |
| -4.4 | -27.3 | 2.2 | 5.3 | 3.7 | 5.5 |  | 7.2 | 5.2 |
| 91.0 | 35.5 | 41.3 | 50.4 | 33.2 |  |  | 37.3 | 33.0 |
| (30) 32.2 | (36) 15.3 | (66) 20.2 | (41) 32.6 | (11) 19.5 |  | % Profit Before Taxes/Tangible Net Worth | (146) 20.9 | (150) 16.1 |
| 10.0 | .2 | 7.4 | 17.1 | 1.3 |  |  | 8.7 | 4.8 |
| 27.4 | 11.8 | 13.9 | 15.1 | 10.5 | 10.4 |  | 13.0 | 12.2 |
| 6.2 | 4.2 | 5.7 | 8.2 | 7.0 | 6.1 | % Profit Before Taxes/Total Assets | 5.5 | 5.3 |
| -4.0 | -.4 | 2.9 | 4.0 | 1.6 | 3.4 |  | 2.2 | 1.5 |
| 95.7 | 74.6 | 38.9 | 40.5 | 30.0 | 65.2 |  | 46.9 | 44.2 |
| 26.2 | 28.5 | 23.3 | 20.6 | 23.0 | 8.3 | Sales/Net Fixed Assets | 19.3 | 20.6 |
| 12.0 | 8.6 | 10.2 | 9.7 | 10.3 | 2.9 |  | 9.7 | 11.8 |
| 6.9 | 4.0 | 3.6 | 3.6 | 5.4 | 2.5 |  | 4.4 | 4.2 |
| 5.2 | 3.0 | 2.9 | 2.8 | 3.6 | 2.1 | Sales/Total Assets | 3.3 | 3.2 |
| 3.1 | 2.1 | 2.1 | 2.1 | 2.4 | 1.5 |  | 2.4 | 2.5 |
| .4 | .5 | .7 | .8 | .8 | .3 |  | .7 | .7 |
| (30) .8 | (36) .8 | (64) 1.2 | (41) 1.1 | (11) .8 | 1.8 | % Depr., Dep., Amort./Sales | (155) 1.2 | (157) 1.2 |
| 1.6 | 1.3 | 1.8 | 1.7 | 2.0 | 2.5 |  | 1.9 | 1.8 |
| 2.3 | 2.3 | 1.2 | .8 |  |  |  | 1.2 | .7 |
| (24) 4.3 | (26) 3.9 | (29) 2.1 | (12) 1.4 |  |  | % Officers', Directors' Owners' Comp/Sales | (94) 3.1 | (67) 1.7 |
| 7.6 | 4.9 | 4.1 | 2.8 |  |  |  | 5.9 | 5.3 |
| 67915M | 171741M | 1028258M | 2924257M | 2837643M | 3569813M | Net Sales ($) | 6816057M | 7102577M |
| 13808M | 56044M | 341901M | 992088M | 723846M | 1531940M | Total Assets ($) | 2124796M | 2255184M |

## Comparative Historical Data | Current Data Sorted by Sales

| | | | Type of Statement | 0-1MM | 1-3MM | 3-5MM | 5-10MM | 10-25MM | 25MM & OVER |
|---|---|---|---|---|---|---|---|---|---|
| 17 | 15 | 19 | Unqualified | | | | | | 19 |
| 33 | 46 | 47 | Reviewed | | 2 | 2 | 6 | 19 | 18 |
| 32 | 41 | 46 | Compiled | 2 | 11 | 2 | 10 | 11 | 10 |
| 49 | 50 | 52 | Tax Returns | 12 | 16 | 7 | 12 | 3 | 2 |
| 39 | 65 | 75 | Other | 10 | 26 | 4 | 4 | 9 | 22 |
| 4/1/09-3/31/10 | 4/1/10-3/31/11 | 4/1/11-3/31/12 | | 40 (4/1-9/30/11) | | | 199 (10/1/11-3/31/12) | | |
| ALL | ALL | ALL | | 0-1MM | 1-3MM | 3-5MM | 5-10MM | 10-25MM | 25MM & OVER |
| 170 | 217 | 239 | **NUMBER OF STATEMENTS** | 24 | 55 | 15 | 32 | 42 | 71 |
| % | % | % | **ASSETS** | % | % | % | % | % | % |
| 9.1 | 11.5 | 9.9 | Cash & Equivalents | 6.2 | 9.9 | 8.8 | 13.7 | 10.6 | 9.4 |
| 18.7 | 16.3 | 15.7 | Trade Receivables (net) | 5.3 | 16.1 | 15.9 | 17.5 | 18.3 | 16.5 |
| 38.7 | 37.3 | 38.3 | Inventory | 25.1 | 36.9 | 37.0 | 34.0 | 44.7 | 42.2 |
| 2.7 | 2.5 | 2.3 | All Other Current | 1.6 | 2.8 | 3.0 | 3.3 | 2.4 | 1.6 |
| 69.3 | 67.7 | 66.3 | Total Current | 38.2 | 65.7 | 64.6 | 68.6 | 76.1 | 69.7 |
| 20.4 | 22.1 | 22.7 | Fixed Assets (net) | 41.2 | 20.9 | 23.2 | 21.9 | 18.3 | 20.8 |
| 4.2 | 4.4 | 4.8 | Intangibles (net) | 9.2 | 7.9 | 1.0 | 3.3 | 1.2 | 4.6 |
| 6.0 | 5.8 | 6.2 | All Other Non-Current | 11.4 | 5.6 | 11.1 | 6.1 | 4.5 | 4.9 |
| 100.0 | 100.0 | 100.0 | Total | 100.0 | 100.0 | 100.0 | 100.0 | 100.0 | 100.0 |
| | | | **LIABILITIES** | | | | | | |
| 9.8 | 8.2 | 7.1 | Notes Payable-Short Term | 6.1 | 7.3 | 5.8 | 4.4 | 9.7 | 7.3 |
| 3.1 | 3.2 | 2.4 | Cur. Mat.-L.T.D. | 2.0 | 3.6 | 2.5 | 3.5 | 1.0 | 1.9 |
| 32.2 | 29.7 | 28.6 | Trade Payables | 12.7 | 25.8 | 39.0 | 31.3 | 30.4 | 31.8 |
| .1 | .1 | .1 | Income Taxes Payable | .0 | .0 | .1 | .0 | .2 | .2 |
| 7.2 | 11.0 | 9.2 | All Other Current | 15.8 | 9.7 | 5.9 | 4.6 | 8.9 | 9.7 |
| 52.3 | 52.1 | 47.5 | Total Current | 36.6 | 46.3 | 53.3 | 43.9 | 50.2 | 50.9 |
| 17.4 | 16.5 | 17.8 | Long-Term Debt | 58.7 | 19.7 | 13.7 | 15.3 | 5.8 | 11.6 |
| .2 | .1 | .2 | Deferred Taxes | .0 | .0 | .0 | .0 | .3 | .4 |
| 3.0 | 3.3 | 5.5 | All Other Non-Current | 11.0 | 9.5 | 4.0 | 3.9 | 3.6 | 2.7 |
| 27.1 | 28.0 | 29.1 | Net Worth | -6.3 | 24.5 | 29.0 | 37.0 | 40.1 | 34.5 |
| 100.0 | 100.0 | 100.0 | Total Liabilities & Net Worth | 100.0 | 100.0 | 100.0 | 100.0 | 100.0 | 100.0 |
| | | | **INCOME DATA** | | | | | | |
| 100.0 | 100.0 | 100.0 | Net Sales | 100.0 | 100.0 | 100.0 | 100.0 | 100.0 | 100.0 |
| 34.9 | 36.4 | 36.5 | Gross Profit | 50.8 | 42.1 | 40.3 | 35.5 | 30.9 | 30.4 |
| 32.4 | 33.2 | 33.0 | Operating Expenses | 46.3 | 38.4 | 37.5 | 32.2 | 27.2 | 27.3 |
| 2.5 | 3.2 | 3.5 | Operating Profit | 4.6 | 3.7 | 2.8 | 3.3 | 3.7 | 3.1 |
| .2 | .3 | .5 | All Other Expenses (net) | 3.4 | .9 | -.1 | .3 | -.3 | .0 |
| 2.3 | 2.9 | 3.0 | Profit Before Taxes | 1.2 | 2.8 | 2.8 | 3.1 | 4.0 | 3.1 |
| | | | **RATIOS** | | | | | | |
| 1.9 | 1.9 | 2.1 | | 2.1 | 2.8 | 1.6 | 2.1 | 2.0 | 1.7 |
| 1.4 | 1.4 | 1.4 | Current | 1.3 | 1.8 | 1.2 | 1.5 | 1.5 | 1.4 |
| 1.0 | 1.0 | 1.1 | | .5 | 1.1 | .9 | 1.2 | 1.2 | 1.1 |
| .9 | .9 | .8 | | 1.0 | 1.2 | .6 | 1.0 | 1.0 | .7 |
| (169) .5 | (216) .5 | (237) .6 | Quick | .3 | (53) .7 | .4 | .7 | .5 | .5 |
| .3 | .3 | .3 | | .1 | .3 | .3 | .5 | .3 | .3 |
| 7 51.5 | 6 66.3 | 5 75.7 | | 0 UND | 4 103.9 | 5 78.7 | 9 40.4 | 11 32.1 | 6 59.1 |
| 18 20.8 | 15 24.7 | 14 26.7 | Sales/Receivables | 2 188.5 | 9 39.5 | 11 34.1 | 18 20.6 | 24 15.5 | 16 23.0 |
| 33 11.1 | 32 11.4 | 28 13.0 | | 16 23.0 | 22 16.4 | 27 13.4 | 30 12.3 | 34 10.6 | 31 11.6 |
| 45 8.1 | 44 8.4 | 43 8.5 | | 29 12.4 | 31 11.8 | 46 7.9 | 38 9.5 | 54 6.8 | 53 6.9 |
| 65 5.6 | 64 5.7 | 63 5.8 | Cost of Sales/Inventory | 45 8.1 | 47 7.7 | 66 5.5 | 63 5.8 | 87 4.2 | 74 4.9 |
| 94 3.9 | 93 3.9 | 94 3.9 | | 74 4.9 | 81 4.5 | 96 3.8 | 94 3.9 | 122 3.0 | 91 4.0 |
| 35 10.4 | 29 12.4 | 29 12.8 | | 3 111.6 | 19 19.3 | 36 10.0 | 36 10.2 | 33 11.2 | 35 10.3 |
| 49 7.4 | 48 7.6 | 46 8.0 | Cost of Sales/Payables | 29 12.8 | 36 10.1 | 66 5.5 | 46 8.0 | 52 7.0 | 54 6.8 |
| 66 5.5 | 67 5.4 | 69 5.3 | | 47 7.8 | 55 6.6 | 78 4.7 | 74 4.9 | 81 4.5 | 69 5.3 |
| 9.3 | 8.2 | 8.1 | | 17.5 | 7.1 | 11.4 | 6.8 | 7.4 | 9.7 |
| 15.6 | 18.4 | 17.3 | Sales/Working Capital | 43.9 | 17.3 | 22.9 | 13.1 | 10.9 | 17.7 |
| 221.5 | 273.2 | 73.2 | | -16.2 | 87.7 | -40.6 | 44.3 | 25.1 | 51.3 |
| 10.7 | 13.5 | 18.6 | | 1.9 | 14.4 | 40.8 | 39.3 | 19.4 | 21.1 |
| (147) 4.1 | (191) 4.6 | (207) 5.8 | EBIT/Interest | (16) 1.1 | (44) 3.8 | (13) 5.9 | (30) 6.3 | (37) 9.7 | (67) 9.7 |
| 1.4 | 1.6 | 1.9 | | -5.1 | .9 | 1.5 | 1.1 | 3.3 | 3.9 |
| 5.0 | 9.1 | 6.1 | | | | | | | 5.9 |
| (37) 2.8 | (37) 4.7 | (42) 3.5 | Net Profit + Depr., Dep., Amort./Cur. Mat. L/T/D | | | | | (25) | 3.1 |
| 1.8 | 2.8 | 1.8 | | | | | | | 1.6 |
| .2 | .2 | .2 | | .9 | .2 | .2 | .2 | .2 | .2 |
| .6 | .7 | .7 | Fixed/Worth | 147.3 | .8 | .6 | .7 | .4 | .6 |
| 1.5 | 2.8 | 5.2 | | -.8 | -1.0 | 6.2 | 1.9 | .8 | 1.4 |
| 1.0 | 1.0 | .9 | | 2.0 | .6 | 1.5 | .7 | .8 | 1.1 |
| 2.1 | 2.4 | 2.2 | Debt/Worth | 223.5 | 7.0 | 2.0 | 1.3 | 1.7 | 2.5 |
| 5.3 | 9.8 | 13.9 | | -2.9 | -9.2 | 13.9 | 7.1 | 3.8 | 4.4 |
| 35.8 | 34.1 | 46.8 | | 69.6 | 88.0 | 47.4 | 32.6 | 47.5 | 42.2 |
| (144) 15.5 | (176) 20.3 | (193) 22.5 | % Profit Before Taxes/Tangible Net Worth | (13) 37.6 | (35) 23.8 | (12) 21.0 | (27) 9.2 | (41) 22.4 | (65) 25.0 |
| 6.1 | 5.3 | 8.0 | | -1.0 | 4.8 | 13.7 | .8 | 10.0 | 12.0 |
| 11.8 | 13.4 | 14.0 | | 10.2 | 17.4 | 15.5 | 13.0 | 12.3 | 14.9 |
| 5.1 | 6.0 | 6.3 | % Profit Before Taxes/Total Assets | 1.5 | 7.2 | 9.7 | 3.8 | 6.2 | 7.2 |
| .6 | 1.3 | 1.6 | | -16.1 | -.3 | 1.6 | .0 | 3.2 | 3.6 |
| 56.6 | 54.7 | 48.5 | | 60.9 | 114.7 | 40.6 | 44.4 | 40.5 | 41.2 |
| 20.3 | 22.2 | 23.7 | Sales/Net Fixed Assets | 8.0 | 30.7 | 20.5 | 24.4 | 23.3 | 22.6 |
| 10.2 | 9.7 | 9.8 | | 1.3 | 12.1 | 9.3 | 8.3 | 12.2 | 9.8 |
| 4.2 | 4.5 | 4.2 | | 4.8 | 6.4 | 4.1 | 4.5 | 3.5 | 3.9 |
| 3.2 | 3.2 | 3.1 | Sales/Total Assets | 2.6 | 3.9 | 3.5 | 2.9 | 2.8 | 3.2 |
| 2.2 | 2.1 | 2.2 | | 1.0 | 2.2 | 2.5 | 2.0 | 2.2 | 2.2 |
| .7 | .8 | .6 | | .9 | .4 | .4 | .6 | .7 | .7 |
| (143) 1.2 | (185) 1.3 | (192) 1.1 | % Depr., Dep., Amort./Sales | (15) 1.8 | (35) .9 | (11) .6 | (26) 1.3 | (38) 1.1 | (67) 1.0 |
| 1.8 | 1.8 | 1.7 | | 4.3 | 1.7 | 1.2 | 2.1 | 1.4 | 1.7 |
| 1.2 | 1.6 | 1.3 | | 6.0 | 2.3 | | 1.3 | .9 | .8 |
| (79) 3.0 | (81) 2.8 | (95) 2.8 | % Officers', Directors' Owners' Comp/Sales | (10) 7.1 | (26) 3.8 | | (22) 2.3 | (14) 1.5 | (15) 1.3 |
| 6.3 | 5.6 | 4.9 | | 10.5 | | | 4.2 | 2.1 | 3.2 |
| 6316932M | 7269888M | 10599627M | Net Sales ($) | 15230M | 103416M | 57257M | 214640M | 665057M | 9544027M |
| 2256498M | 2825544M | 3659627M | Total Assets ($) | 11021M | 34501M | 18473M | 82781M | 335051M | 3177800M |

M = $ thousand    MM = $ million
See Pages 9 through 22 for Explanation of Ratios and Data

## Current Data Sorted by Assets / Comparative Historical Data

| | | | | | | Type of Statement | | |
|---|---|---|---|---|---|---|---|---|
| | 2 | 6 | 12 | 11 | 6 | Unqualified | 52 | 46 |
| 2 | 11 | 43 | 35 | | | Reviewed | 90 | 83 |
| 15 | 48 | 46 | 11 | 1 | 1 | Compiled | 132 | 126 |
| 59 | 86 | 42 | | | 1 | Tax Returns | 164 | 163 |
| 29 | 64 | 80 | 42 | 6 | 11 | Other | 198 | 238 |
| | 141 (4/1-9/30/11) | | 529 (10/1/11-3/31/12) | | | | 4/1/07-3/31/08 | 4/1/08-3/31/09 |
| 0-500M | 500M-2MM | 2-10MM | 10-50MM | 50-100MM | 100-250MM | | ALL | ALL |
| 105 | 211 | 217 | 100 | 18 | 19 | NUMBER OF STATEMENTS | 636 | 656 |
| % | % | % | % | % | % | ASSETS | % | % |
| 15.7 | 11.6 | 9.4 | 8.0 | 8.0 | 7.5 | Cash & Equivalents | 9.2 | 9.3 |
| 8.3 | 11.7 | 12.9 | 14.7 | 15.8 | 8.7 | Trade Receivables (net) | 12.5 | 12.4 |
| 53.3 | 51.0 | 46.5 | 38.0 | 30.6 | 24.5 | Inventory | 47.5 | 45.0 |
| 1.8 | 1.0 | 2.3 | 3.6 | 4.4 | 1.5 | All Other Current | 2.7 | 2.8 |
| 79.2 | 75.3 | 71.0 | 64.3 | 58.8 | 42.3 | Total Current | 71.8 | 69.5 |
| 13.0 | 15.6 | 18.6 | 27.5 | 31.3 | 51.1 | Fixed Assets (net) | 20.3 | 22.1 |
| 1.7 | 2.4 | 3.2 | 3.2 | 2.5 | 2.5 | Intangibles (net) | 1.9 | 3.1 |
| 6.2 | 6.7 | 7.2 | 5.0 | 7.4 | 4.1 | All Other Non-Current | 5.9 | 5.3 |
| 100.0 | 100.0 | 100.0 | 100.0 | 100.0 | 100.0 | Total | 100.0 | 100.0 |
| | | | | | | LIABILITIES | | |
| 18.5 | 10.8 | 8.5 | 7.4 | 5.3 | 4.7 | Notes Payable-Short Term | 11.7 | 13.8 |
| 2.1 | 2.7 | 2.3 | 2.2 | 1.7 | 4.5 | Cur. Mat.-L.T.D. | 2.5 | 3.3 |
| 15.3 | 18.8 | 19.6 | 15.3 | 9.9 | 8.3 | Trade Payables | 18.3 | 16.3 |
| .1 | .3 | .2 | .2 | .2 | .3 | Income Taxes Payable | .2 | .2 |
| 17.7 | 19.2 | 17.3 | 18.2 | 16.1 | 10.4 | All Other Current | 18.7 | 16.7 |
| 53.9 | 51.9 | 47.9 | 43.3 | 33.3 | 28.2 | Total Current | 51.4 | 50.4 |
| 19.2 | 14.9 | 12.1 | 15.2 | 17.0 | 23.1 | Long-Term Debt | 14.5 | 17.1 |
| .0 | .0 | .1 | .2 | .1 | .3 | Deferred Taxes | .0 | .1 |
| 13.4 | 12.2 | 5.6 | 4.8 | 6.8 | 7.3 | All Other Non-Current | 6.7 | 7.0 |
| 13.6 | 21.0 | 34.4 | 36.5 | 42.8 | 41.1 | Net Worth | 27.3 | 25.5 |
| 100.0 | 100.0 | 100.0 | 100.0 | 100.0 | 100.0 | Total Liabilties & Net Worth | 100.0 | 100.0 |
| | | | | | | INCOME DATA | | |
| 100.0 | 100.0 | 100.0 | 100.0 | 100.0 | 100.0 | Net Sales | 100.0 | 100.0 |
| 45.0 | 42.7 | 41.5 | 42.2 | 49.3 | 43.5 | Gross Profit | 42.5 | 42.4 |
| 41.8 | 40.0 | 39.1 | 38.4 | 44.1 | 39.4 | Operating Expenses | 40.4 | 41.3 |
| 3.2 | 2.7 | 2.4 | 3.9 | 5.1 | 4.1 | Operating Profit | 2.1 | 1.1 |
| 1.0 | .4 | -.1 | .6 | -.6 | .8 | All Other Expenses (net) | .5 | .6 |
| 2.2 | 2.3 | 2.5 | 3.2 | 5.7 | 3.3 | Profit Before Taxes | 1.7 | .5 |
| | | | | | | RATIOS | | |
| 5.2 | 3.2 | 2.5 | 1.9 | 4.2 | 2.4 | | 2.3 | 2.4 |
| 1.6 | 1.8 | 1.6 | 1.4 | 2.0 | 1.3 | Current | 1.4 | 1.4 |
| 1.0 | 1.1 | 1.1 | 1.1 | 1.1 | 1.1 | | 1.0 | 1.0 |
| 1.7 | 1.1 | .8 | .8 | 2.1 | 1.0 | | .9 | .8 |
| .4 | .4 | (216) .3 | .3 | .3 | .3 | Quick | (632) .3 | (654) .3 |
| .1 | .1 | .1 | .1 | .0 | .1 | | .1 | .1 |
| 0 UND | 0 UND | 0 787.7 | 1 284.2 | 1 551.9 | 1 257.1 | | 0 999.8 | 0 999.8 |
| 0 UND | 4 91.0 | 3 106.1 | 5 80.7 | 2 212.6 | 4 90.6 | Sales/Receivables | 4 99.5 | 3 110.6 |
| 12 30.7 | 20 17.9 | 23 15.9 | 29 12.8 | 14 27.0 | 18 19.8 | | 19 19.1 | 19 19.6 |
| 47 7.7 | 63 5.8 | 61 6.0 | 59 6.2 | 96 3.8 | 69 5.3 | | 65 5.6 | 56 6.5 |
| 99 3.7 | 122 3.0 | 114 3.2 | 104 3.5 | 122 3.0 | 87 4.2 | Cost of Sales/Inventory | 104 3.5 | 101 3.6 |
| 166 2.2 | 203 1.8 | 192 1.9 | 130 2.8 | 140 2.6 | 114 3.2 | | 156 2.3 | 154 2.4 |
| 0 UND | 12 29.9 | 20 18.7 | 21 17.2 | 21 17.2 | 19 19.0 | | 17 22.1 | 14 26.0 |
| 11 32.3 | 29 12.6 | 36 10.1 | 31 11.7 | 32 11.3 | 27 13.6 | Cost of Sales/Payables | 32 11.3 | 28 13.0 |
| 36 10.2 | 51 7.1 | 59 6.2 | 46 7.9 | 47 7.7 | 38 9.5 | | 51 7.2 | 49 7.5 |
| 6.3 | 4.8 | 5.1 | 5.8 | 2.4 | 6.2 | | 5.9 | 6.4 |
| 16.6 | 9.5 | 10.6 | 15.8 | 6.2 | 21.7 | Sales/Working Capital | 16.0 | 15.7 |
| -105.3 | 53.3 | 81.6 | 64.3 | 279.0 | 41.6 | | -446.3 | 114.4 |
| 8.0 | 9.3 | 13.0 | 14.5 | 28.4 | 10.7 | | 6.4 | 5.8 |
| (71) 2.5 | (168) 2.9 | (187) 3.9 | (81) 5.1 | (15) 7.6 | 3.3 | EBIT/Interest | (524) 2.4 | (560) 1.6 |
| .2 | .5 | 1.2 | 1.5 | 2.0 | 2.2 | | .3 | -.5 |
| | | 6.5 | 10.3 | | | | 8.1 | 5.0 |
| | (29) 3.1 | (25) 5.0 | | | | Net Profit + Depr., Dep., Amort./Cur. Mat. L/T/D | (87) 2.6 | (86) 2.0 |
| | .2 | 1.7 | | | | | .4 | .2 |
| .0 | .1 | .1 | .3 | .3 | .7 | | .2 | .2 |
| .2 | .4 | .5 | .8 | .5 | 1.7 | Fixed/Worth | .7 | .8 |
| -4.7 | 4.0 | 1.5 | 2.7 | 2.2 | 2.3 | | 3.4 | 5.2 |
| .6 | 1.0 | .8 | .8 | .6 | .8 | | 1.0 | 1.0 |
| 2.3 | 2.6 | 1.9 | 2.0 | 1.8 | 1.6 | Debt/Worth | 2.7 | 2.9 |
| -6.5 | 52.1 | 7.0 | 6.1 | 3.5 | 3.3 | | 12.5 | 17.0 |
| 85.4 | 51.3 | 35.9 | 38.8 | 44.4 | 18.4 | | 40.7 | 31.8 |
| (70) 25.1 | (165) 19.9 | (191) 14.3 | (94) 19.1 | (17) 21.3 | (18) 11.7 | % Profit Before Taxes/Tangible Net Worth | (516) 14.1 | (522) 7.3 |
| 6.4 | 3.3 | 3.2 | 4.9 | 6.8 | 4.4 | | 1.3 | -5.0 |
| 24.0 | 15.2 | 11.4 | 12.9 | 14.8 | 8.9 | | 12.2 | 9.0 |
| 6.8 | 4.4 | 4.2 | 5.4 | 7.5 | 5.9 | % Profit Before Taxes/Total Assets | 4.0 | 1.6 |
| -2.4 | -.9 | .9 | 1.5 | 3.2 | 2.5 | | -1.6 | -4.2 |
| 225.5 | 103.2 | 63.1 | 36.0 | 17.1 | 4.6 | | 60.1 | 57.0 |
| 66.4 | 37.2 | 25.2 | 15.2 | 8.6 | 2.9 | Sales/Net Fixed Assets | 22.4 | 20.9 |
| 20.4 | 13.4 | 11.0 | 5.6 | 2.5 | 2.2 | | 9.1 | 8.4 |
| 5.9 | 3.9 | 3.8 | 4.0 | 3.1 | 2.0 | | 4.0 | 4.3 |
| 3.7 | 2.8 | 2.6 | 2.5 | 1.5 | 1.6 | Sales/Total Assets | 2.9 | 2.8 |
| 2.3 | 1.7 | 1.8 | 1.2 | 1.0 | 1.2 | | 1.9 | 1.8 |
| .3 | .3 | .4 | .5 | 1.1 | 1.4 | | .4 | .4 |
| (63) .6 | (152) .7 | (168) .8 | (90) 1.0 | (14) 2.0 | (13) 2.3 | % Depr., Dep., Amort./Sales | (505) .8 | (520) 1.0 |
| 1.2 | 1.2 | 1.3 | 1.7 | 2.7 | 3.5 | | 1.5 | 1.6 |
| 2.2 | 1.6 | 1.3 | .5 | | | | 1.6 | 1.6 |
| (62) 4.8 | (139) 3.2 | (91) 2.3 | (16) 1.2 | | | % Officers', Directors' Owners' Comp/Sales | (280) 3.5 | (292) 3.1 |
| 7.7 | 5.4 | 3.9 | 2.3 | | | | 5.9 | 5.5 |
| 115618M | 728231M | 2963387M | 5068368M | 2456131M | 5305721M | Net Sales ($) | 21887143M | 21661544M |
| 29388M | 236997M | 994541M | 1992908M | 1343675M | 3102394M | Total Assets ($) | 8771758M | 9445744M |

© RMA 2012

M = $ thousand    MM = $ million
See Pages 9 through 22 for Explanation of Ratios and Data

## Comparative Historical Data / Current Data Sorted by Sales

| | | | Type of Statement | 0-1MM | 1-3MM | 3-5MM | 5-10MM | 10-25MM | 25MM & OVER |
|---|---|---|---|---|---|---|---|---|---|
| 70 | 47 | 37 | Unqualified | | 3 | | 1 | 6 | 27 |
| 105 | 79 | 91 | Reviewed | | 9 | 8 | 12 | 24 | 38 |
| 148 | 111 | 122 | Compiled | 11 | 37 | 18 | 23 | 20 | 13 |
| 176 | 157 | 188 | Tax Returns | 43 | 71 | 26 | 30 | 15 | 3 |
| 230 | 215 | 232 | Other | 23 | 40 | 26 | 33 | 50 | 60 |
| 4/1/09-3/31/10 ALL | 4/1/10-3/31/11 ALL | 4/1/11-3/31/12 ALL | | 141 (4/1-9/30/11) | | | 529 (10/1/11-3/31/12) | | |
| 729 | 609 | 670 | **NUMBER OF STATEMENTS** | 77 | 160 | 78 | 99 | 115 | 141 |
| % | % | % | **ASSETS** | % | % | % | % | % | % |
| 9.6 | 10.0 | 10.8 | Cash & Equivalents | 15.2 | 10.4 | 11.2 | 10.1 | 10.7 | 9.1 |
| 11.8 | 12.3 | 12.0 | Trade Receivables (net) | 6.1 | 10.5 | 11.7 | 13.6 | 16.1 | 12.7 |
| 45.1 | 45.9 | 46.7 | Inventory | 51.5 | 52.2 | 47.5 | 52.9 | 38.3 | 39.7 |
| 2.2 | 2.0 | 2.0 | All Other Current | 1.4 | 1.1 | 1.3 | 1.3 | 3.6 | 3.0 |
| 68.7 | 70.2 | 71.5 | Total Current | 74.2 | 74.3 | 71.7 | 77.8 | 68.7 | 64.6 |
| 22.2 | 21.0 | 19.4 | Fixed Assets (net) | 16.8 | 17.1 | 18.9 | 13.7 | 19.8 | 27.3 |
| 3.1 | 2.1 | 2.7 | Intangibles (net) | 2.0 | 1.8 | 2.0 | 2.6 | 4.6 | 2.9 |
| 6.0 | 6.7 | 6.5 | All Other Non-Current | 7.1 | 6.8 | 7.5 | 5.9 | 6.9 | 5.2 |
| 100.0 | 100.0 | 100.0 | Total | 100.0 | 100.0 | 100.0 | 100.0 | 100.0 | 100.0 |
| | | | **LIABILITIES** | | | | | | |
| 11.2 | 10.9 | 10.5 | Notes Payable-Short Term | 22.7 | 10.4 | 10.2 | 8.0 | 7.8 | 8.0 |
| 2.7 | 2.3 | 2.4 | Cur. Mat.-L.T.D. | 2.1 | 3.0 | 2.8 | 1.9 | 2.6 | 2.1 |
| 18.4 | 17.7 | 17.4 | Trade Payables | 8.6 | 15.9 | 17.9 | 19.9 | 22.6 | 17.9 |
| .2 | .2 | .2 | Income Taxes Payable | .0 | .4 | .1 | .1 | .3 | .2 |
| 19.8 | 19.0 | 17.9 | All Other Current | 12.8 | 17.8 | 17.4 | 18.6 | 20.5 | 18.4 |
| 52.2 | 50.1 | 48.5 | Total Current | 46.1 | 47.4 | 48.4 | 48.5 | 53.8 | 46.5 |
| 15.0 | 15.8 | 15.0 | Long-Term Debt | 23.5 | 18.6 | 12.6 | 11.8 | 11.0 | 13.0 |
| .1 | .1 | .1 | Deferred Taxes | .0 | .0 | .0 | .0 | .1 | .2 |
| 7.1 | 9.1 | 8.9 | All Other Non-Current | 15.1 | 14.0 | 8.9 | 5.9 | 4.8 | 4.9 |
| 25.6 | 24.9 | 27.6 | Net Worth | 15.4 | 20.0 | 30.0 | 33.7 | 30.3 | 35.3 |
| 100.0 | 100.0 | 100.0 | Total Liabilities & Net Worth | 100.0 | 100.0 | 100.0 | 100.0 | 100.0 | 100.0 |
| | | | **INCOME DATA** | | | | | | |
| 100.0 | 100.0 | 100.0 | Net Sales | 100.0 | 100.0 | 100.0 | 100.0 | 100.0 | 100.0 |
| 42.1 | 42.4 | 42.8 | Gross Profit | 47.6 | 44.6 | 42.2 | 41.3 | 39.9 | 41.8 |
| 41.0 | 40.1 | 39.8 | Operating Expenses | 44.0 | 41.2 | 40.5 | 38.7 | 37.5 | 38.4 |
| 1.1 | 2.3 | 3.0 | Operating Profit | 3.6 | 3.4 | 1.7 | 2.6 | 2.4 | 3.5 |
| .5 | .4 | .4 | All Other Expenses (net) | 2.1 | .6 | -.1 | -.2 | -.1 | .2 |
| .6 | 1.9 | 2.6 | Profit Before Taxes | 1.5 | 2.8 | 1.8 | 2.8 | 2.5 | 3.3 |
| | | | **RATIOS** | | | | | | |
| 2.3 | 2.5 | 2.7 | | 7.4 | 3.6 | 2.7 | 2.8 | 1.9 | 2.0 |
| 1.4 | 1.5 | 1.6 | Current | 1.9 | 1.9 | 1.8 | 1.7 | 1.4 | 1.3 |
| 1.0 | 1.1 | 1.1 | | 1.0 | 1.1 | 1.1 | 1.1 | 1.0 | 1.1 |
| .8 | .9 | 1.0 | | 1.7 | 1.3 | 1.1 | 1.0 | .9 | .8 |
| (724) .3 | (608) .3 | (669) .4 | Quick | .4 | .3 | .4 | .3 | .4 (140) | .3 |
| .1 | .1 | .1 | | .1 | .1 | .1 | .1 | .2 | .1 |
| 0 UND | 0 999.8 | 0 UND | | 0 UND | 0 UND | 0 UND | 1 471.6 | 1 479.5 | 1 393.3 |
| 3 118.6 | 3 113.2 | 3 109.7 | Sales/Receivables | 0 UND | 3 109.0 | 2 199.5 | 5 75.5 | 4 94.5 | 4 95.9 |
| 20 18.4 | 20 18.4 | 20 18.5 | | 21 17.1 | 19 18.9 | 17 21.0 | 20 17.9 | 26 13.8 | 10 37.8 |
| 59 6.2 | 62 5.9 | 63 5.8 | | 69 5.3 | 79 4.6 | 87 4.2 | 66 5.5 | 36 10.2 | 60 6.1 |
| 102 3.6 | 108 3.4 | 107 3.4 | Cost of Sales/Inventory | 182 2.0 | 135 2.7 | 126 2.9 | 118 3.1 | 85 4.3 | 89 4.1 |
| 150 2.4 | 173 2.1 | 174 2.1 | | 332 1.1 | 215 1.7 | 166 2.2 | 192 1.9 | 130 2.8 | 122 3.0 |
| 17 21.1 | 16 22.7 | 15 23.7 | | 0 UND | 8 45.6 | 21 17.5 | 18 20.2 | 20 18.7 | 21 17.7 |
| 33 11.2 | 32 11.5 | 30 12.3 | Cost of Sales/Payables | 8 46.1 | 26 14.0 | 33 11.2 | 36 10.1 | 33 11.2 | 31 11.9 |
| 53 6.9 | 51 7.1 | 49 7.4 | | 37 9.8 | 51 7.1 | 53 6.9 | 58 6.3 | 54 6.7 | 46 7.9 |
| 6.6 | 5.4 | 5.2 | | 2.6 | 3.8 | 5.2 | 5.4 | 6.9 | 7.3 |
| 16.5 | 12.5 | 12.1 | Sales/Working Capital | 9.4 | 9.4 | 8.4 | 9.0 | 16.4 | 20.6 |
| UND | 66.6 | 73.6 | | -523.5 | 34.6 | 46.3 | 49.1 | -802.7 | 102.5 |
| 7.1 | 13.4 | 12.1 | | 4.2 | 7.4 | 8.4 | 12.5 | 22.6 | 16.4 |
| (611) 2.1 | (499) 2.5 | (541) 3.3 | EBIT/Interest | (52) 1.5 | (126) 2.3 | (64) 2.2 | (85) 4.1 | (96) 7.6 | (118) 5.8 |
| -.5 | .6 | 1.1 | | .2 | .4 | .4 | 1.5 | 1.4 | 2.0 |
| 5.6 | 7.2 | 7.4 | | | | | 8.0 | 6.7 | 8.7 |
| (104) 2.1 | (74) 2.7 | (70) 3.5 | Net Profit + Depr., Dep., Amort./Cur. Mat. L/T/D | | | (13) 3.3 | (13) 4.6 | | (30) 4.0 |
| .4 | .4 | .8 | | | | .2 | .5 | | 1.4 |
| .2 | .2 | .1 | | .0 | .1 | .2 | .1 | .1 | .3 |
| .8 | .5 | .5 | Fixed/Worth | .3 | .4 | .5 | .3 | .5 | .8 |
| 5.5 | 2.9 | 2.6 | | 42.3 | 11.7 | 1.6 | 1.8 | 1.4 | 2.5 |
| 1.0 | .8 | .9 | | .8 | .8 | .8 | .7 | 1.1 | .9 |
| 2.6 | 2.3 | 2.1 | Debt/Worth | 3.7 | 2.0 | 2.3 | 1.9 | 2.0 | 2.0 |
| 21.3 | 10.1 | 12.1 | | -11.7 | 83.8 | 7.7 | 24.4 | 6.5 | 5.5 |
| 32.7 | 42.1 | 43.2 | | 83.9 | 46.9 | 27.7 | 45.3 | 51.4 | 39.1 |
| (572) 10.6 | (497) 14.3 | (555) 17.9 | % Profit Before Taxes/Tangible Net Worth | (53) 20.0 | (121) 17.1 | (68) 8.0 | (83) 18.5 | (101) 23.6 | (129) 19.3 |
| -.8 | .7 | 4.2 | | .6 | 2.5 | -1.2 | 5.5 | 5.6 | 7.3 |
| 9.4 | 13.3 | 13.5 | | 17.0 | 13.9 | 8.3 | 13.1 | 15.1 | 13.5 |
| 2.7 | 4.1 | 4.9 | % Profit Before Taxes/Total Assets | 3.5 | 4.5 | 2.9 | 5.5 | 5.6 | 6.2 |
| -4.0 | -.7 | .5 | | -2.6 | -.8 | -1.5 | 1.5 | 1.4 | 2.3 |
| 58.7 | 64.4 | 77.7 | | 277.3 | 83.8 | 58.5 | 98.6 | 73.8 | 41.0 |
| 22.4 | 24.1 | 27.1 | Sales/Net Fixed Assets | 60.1 | 31.7 | 29.0 | 41.2 | 24.9 | 16.3 |
| 8.0 | 8.2 | 9.8 | | 11.4 | 11.2 | 8.2 | 17.2 | 10.9 | 5.1 |
| 4.3 | 3.9 | 4.1 | | 3.6 | 3.9 | 3.8 | 4.0 | 4.4 | 4.4 |
| 2.8 | 2.6 | 2.7 | Sales/Total Assets | 2.2 | 2.5 | 2.6 | 2.8 | 3.1 | 2.9 |
| 1.7 | 1.6 | 1.7 | | 1.2 | 1.6 | 1.8 | 2.0 | 2.0 | 1.7 |
| .5 | .4 | .4 | | .4 | .3 | .3 | .4 | .4 | .5 |
| (594) 1.0 | (493) .9 | (500) .8 | % Depr., Dep., Amort./Sales | (42) .8 | (124) .8 | (57) .7 | (76) .6 | (82) .8 | (119) 1.1 |
| 1.7 | 1.6 | 1.4 | | 1.6 | 1.4 | 1.3 | 1.2 | 1.3 | 1.8 |
| 1.6 | 1.5 | 1.4 | | 2.5 | 2.1 | 2.2 | 1.3 | 1.0 | .4 |
| (308) 3.0 | (265) 3.0 | (314) 2.8 | % Officers', Directors' Owners' Comp/Sales | (41) 5.4 | (105) 4.1 | (48) 3.1 | (50) 2.2 | (38) 1.6 | (32) 1.1 |
| 5.4 | 5.3 | 5.4 | | 8.6 | 6.1 | 4.0 | 4.0 | 3.0 | 2.2 |
| 24075403M | 17551637M | 16637456M | Net Sales ($) | 46443M | 305174M | 314500M | 712811M | 1741474M | 13517054M |
| 10598271M | 8432478M | 7699903M | Total Assets ($) | 31472M | 159590M | 159735M | 305628M | 705963M | 6337515M |

© RMA 2012

M = $ thousand    MM = $ million
See Pages 9 through 22 for Explanation of Ratios and Data

## RETAIL—Floor Covering Stores  NAICS 442210

### Current Data Sorted by Assets | Comparative Historical Data

| | | | | | | Type of Statement | | |
|---|---|---|---|---|---|---|---|---|
| | | | | 1 | | Unqualified | 13 | 11 |
| 1 | 7 | 3 | 3 | | | Reviewed | 52 | 49 |
| 19 | 24 | 24 | 5 | | | Compiled | 70 | 78 |
| 60 | 60 | 16 | 1 | | 1 | Tax Returns | 88 | 110 |
| 23 | 55 | 23 | 2 | | 2 | Other | 114 | 118 |
| | | 35 | 9 | | | | 4/1/07- 3/31/08 | 4/1/08- 3/31/09 |
| | 49 (4/1-9/30/11) | | 325 (10/1/11-3/31/12) | | | | ALL | ALL |
| 0-500M | 500M-2MM | 2-10MM | 10-50MM | 50-100MM | 100-250MM | | | |
| 103 | 146 | 101 | 20 | 1 | 3 | NUMBER OF STATEMENTS | 337 | 366 |
| % | % | % | % | % | % | ASSETS | % | % |
| 13.3 | 8.3 | 8.5 | 5.8 | | | Cash & Equivalents | 9.4 | 8.3 |
| 15.8 | 27.7 | 25.8 | 21.5 | | | Trade Receivables (net) | 28.7 | 25.2 |
| 39.9 | 35.4 | 33.6 | 38.6 | | | Inventory | 31.9 | 34.4 |
| 3.8 | 3.7 | 5.6 | 2.9 | | | All Other Current | 4.0 | 2.8 |
| 72.8 | 75.1 | 73.5 | 68.7 | | | Total Current | 73.9 | 70.7 |
| 18.5 | 15.8 | 16.6 | 19.8 | | | Fixed Assets (net) | 16.9 | 17.6 |
| 4.0 | 1.6 | 2.7 | 5.1 | | | Intangibles (net) | 2.4 | 3.9 |
| 4.8 | 7.5 | 7.1 | 6.4 | | | All Other Non-Current | 6.8 | 7.8 |
| 100.0 | 100.0 | 100.0 | 100.0 | | | Total | 100.0 | 100.0 |
| | | | | | | LIABILITIES | | |
| 21.8 | 14.0 | 11.6 | 12.3 | | | Notes Payable-Short Term | 14.4 | 15.6 |
| 8.4 | 2.9 | 1.6 | 3.0 | | | Cur. Mat.-L.T.D. | 3.0 | 4.7 |
| 19.5 | 18.8 | 17.0 | 23.3 | | | Trade Payables | 19.4 | 19.4 |
| .1 | .0 | .3 | .2 | | | Income Taxes Payable | .3 | .1 |
| 19.6 | 14.7 | 12.6 | 11.5 | | | All Other Current | 14.7 | 17.3 |
| 69.4 | 50.5 | 43.2 | 50.2 | | | Total Current | 51.8 | 57.1 |
| 19.8 | 11.3 | 13.2 | 10.0 | | | Long-Term Debt | 14.5 | 13.0 |
| .0 | .0 | .1 | .3 | | | Deferred Taxes | .1 | .1 |
| 18.5 | 10.2 | 5.6 | 4.3 | | | All Other Non-Current | 5.3 | 6.8 |
| -7.8 | 28.0 | 37.9 | 35.1 | | | Net Worth | 28.3 | 23.0 |
| 100.0 | 100.0 | 100.0 | 100.0 | | | Total Liabilities & Net Worth | 100.0 | 100.0 |
| | | | | | | INCOME DATA | | |
| 100.0 | 100.0 | 100.0 | 100.0 | | | Net Sales | 100.0 | 100.0 |
| 38.7 | 35.2 | 32.4 | 33.3 | | | Gross Profit | 35.3 | 34.7 |
| 38.9 | 33.4 | 31.1 | 32.5 | | | Operating Expenses | 32.7 | 34.0 |
| -.2 | 1.7 | 1.3 | .8 | | | Operating Profit | 2.6 | .8 |
| .3 | .3 | .4 | .4 | | | All Other Expenses (net) | .4 | .4 |
| -.5 | 1.4 | .9 | .5 | | | Profit Before Taxes | 2.2 | .4 |
| | | | | | | RATIOS | | |
| 2.5 | 2.4 | 2.7 | 2.3 | | | | 2.5 | 2.2 |
| 1.4 | 1.5 | 1.6 | 1.3 | | | Current | 1.5 | 1.4 |
| .7 | 1.1 | 1.2 | 1.1 | | | | 1.1 | 1.0 |
| 1.0 | 1.2 | 1.3 | .8 | | | | 1.3 | 1.2 |
| .5 | .7 | .8 | .6 | | | Quick | .7 (365) | .6 |
| .2 | .4 | .4 | .3 | | | | .4 | .3 |
| 0 UND | 14 26.8 | 12 30.6 | 9 40.6 | | | | 11 33.1 | 8 48.4 |
| 8 43.1 | 23 16.2 | 31 11.7 | 26 14.3 | | | Sales/Receivables | 25 14.4 | 23 15.6 |
| 26 14.2 | 46 8.0 | 42 8.6 | 36 10.1 | | | | 43 8.5 | 39 9.4 |
| 17 20.9 | 24 15.0 | 29 12.6 | 33 10.9 | | | | 19 19.3 | 22 16.8 |
| 49 7.4 | 49 7.5 | 51 7.2 | 69 5.3 | | | Cost of Sales/Inventory | 41 8.9 | 45 8.1 |
| 83 4.4 | 96 3.8 | 91 4.0 | 152 2.4 | | | | 76 4.8 | 94 3.9 |
| 7 51.3 | 15 24.3 | 17 21.9 | 18 20.3 | | | | 13 27.3 | 13 27.8 |
| 19 19.3 | 26 14.0 | 28 13.0 | 30 12.0 | | | Cost of Sales/Payables | 24 15.4 | 23 15.9 |
| 38 9.6 | 41 8.9 | 47 7.7 | 42 8.6 | | | | 43 8.5 | 40 9.0 |
| 9.4 | 7.2 | 5.8 | 6.7 | | | | 7.5 | 8.4 |
| 24.8 | 14.6 | 10.0 | 14.5 | | | Sales/Working Capital | 14.4 | 18.5 |
| -19.1 | 102.7 | 28.0 | 133.2 | | | | 109.4 | -230.7 |
| 10.6 | 8.0 | 5.8 | 6.1 | | | | 11.0 | 6.4 |
| (75) 2.3 | (116) 2.4 | (90) 2.3 | (18) 1.8 | | | EBIT/Interest | (293) 3.3 | (315) 1.8 |
| -3.1 | 1.1 | -.3 | .4 | | | | 1.2 | -.7 |
| | | 5.6 | | | | Net Profit + Depr., Dep., | 4.4 | 4.7 |
| | (13) 2.1 | | | | | Amort./Cur. Mat. L/T/D | (41) 1.8 | (44) 1.5 |
| | | .8 | | | | | .6 | -.2 |
| .1 | .1 | .1 | .2 | | | | .1 | .2 |
| 1.2 | .3 | .3 | .4 | | | Fixed/Worth | .4 | .5 |
| -.4 | 3.1 | 1.0 | 1.5 | | | | 1.4 | 6.3 |
| 1.1 | .9 | .9 | .8 | | | | 1.0 | .9 |
| 17.8 | 2.0 | 1.9 | 2.6 | | | Debt/Worth | 2.3 | 2.5 |
| -2.8 | 9.6 | 3.3 | 17.1 | | | | 7.2 | 26.5 |
| 64.2 | 38.3 | 22.4 | 31.7 | | | % Profit Before Taxes/Tangible Net Worth | 52.2 | 36.5 |
| (56) 12.1 | (117) 10.6 | (91) 8.4 | (17) 8.4 | | | | (288) 21.5 | (292) 12.2 |
| -9.1 | 1.5 | -1.9 | -.5 | | | | 4.4 | -5.6 |
| 21.7 | 8.9 | 8.7 | 5.8 | | | % Profit Before Taxes/Total Assets | 16.3 | 9.2 |
| .8 | 3.4 | 2.5 | 2.2 | | | | 5.8 | 2.3 |
| -15.0 | .2 | -1.9 | -1.2 | | | | .6 | -4.2 |
| 132.0 | 95.6 | 93.8 | 74.3 | | | | 86.5 | 76.8 |
| 33.7 | 40.0 | 33.4 | 26.7 | | | Sales/Net Fixed Assets | 33.1 | 32.4 |
| 15.6 | 17.1 | 8.7 | 8.1 | | | | 15.3 | 15.4 |
| 6.4 | 4.6 | 3.6 | 3.7 | | | | 4.8 | 5.1 |
| 4.6 | 3.5 | 2.9 | 2.6 | | | Sales/Total Assets | 3.7 | 3.6 |
| 2.8 | 2.4 | 1.9 | 1.6 | | | | 2.5 | 2.3 |
| .5 | .4 | .3 | .4 | | | | .4 | .4 |
| (63) .8 | (102) .7 | (82) .6 | (16) .9 | | | % Depr., Dep., Amort./Sales | (274) .7 | (288) .7 |
| 1.4 | 1.2 | 1.1 | 1.3 | | | | 1.2 | 1.2 |
| 2.6 | 1.9 | 1.2 | | | | % Officers', Directors' | 1.9 | 1.7 |
| (51) 5.8 | (88) 3.2 | (61) 2.6 | | | | Owners' Comp/Sales | (202) 3.6 | (210) 3.3 |
| 8.2 | 5.7 | 4.3 | | | | | 6.6 | 6.3 |
| 126594M | 571380M | 1131445M | 1464101M | 578106M | 1008010M | Net Sales ($) | 5731901M | 5396098M |
| 27652M | 157643M | 411312M | 380592M | 98014M | 414980M | Total Assets ($) | 1653845M | 1749744M |

M = $ thousand    MM = $ million

See Pages 9 through 22 for Explanation of Ratios and Data

## Comparative Historical Data / Current Data Sorted by Sales

| | | | Type of Statement | | | | | | |
|---|---|---|---|---|---|---|---|---|---|
| 9 | 10 | 7 | Unqualified | 1 | 4 | 1 | 8 | 16 | 4 |
| 52 | 49 | 37 | Reviewed | 9 | 17 | 13 | 14 | 5 | 7 |
| 53 | 47 | 60 | Compiled | 31 | 53 | 24 | 25 | 11 | 2 |
| 121 | 107 | 146 | Tax Returns | 20 | 30 | 23 | 23 | 18 | 2 |
| 124 | 111 | 124 | Other | | | | | | 10 |
| 4/1/09-3/31/10 ALL | 4/1/10-3/31/11 ALL | 4/1/11-3/31/12 ALL | | 49 (4/1-9/30/11) | | 325 (10/1/11-3/31/12) | | | |
| | | | | 0-1MM | 1-3MM | 3-5MM | 5-10MM | 10-25MM | 25MM & OVER |
| 359 | 324 | 374 | NUMBER OF STATEMENTS | 61 | 104 | 61 | 71 | 52 | 25 |

| Hist 1 % | Hist 2 % | Hist 3 % | Item | 0-1MM % | 1-3MM % | 3-5MM % | 5-10MM % | 10-25MM % | 25MM&Over % |
|---|---|---|---|---|---|---|---|---|---|
| | | | **ASSETS** | | | | | | |
| 10.3 | 10.8 | 9.6 | Cash & Equivalents | 9.2 | 11.6 | 9.9 | 8.2 | 8.8 | 6.6 |
| 21.1 | 22.8 | 23.4 | Trade Receivables (net) | 12.1 | 19.6 | 24.2 | 34.7 | 28.7 | 21.4 |
| 33.7 | 34.4 | 36.4 | Inventory | 41.1 | 39.7 | 32.2 | 31.4 | 32.5 | 43.7 |
| 3.6 | 2.8 | 4.2 | All Other Current | 3.5 | 3.4 | 5.5 | 3.5 | 6.4 | 4.0 |
| 68.8 | 70.9 | 73.6 | Total Current | 66.0 | 74.3 | 71.8 | 77.8 | 76.5 | 75.8 |
| 18.3 | 18.4 | 17.1 | Fixed Assets (net) | 24.2 | 17.7 | 14.3 | 13.0 | 17.2 | 15.2 |
| 4.2 | 3.2 | 2.8 | Intangibles (net) | 5.5 | 1.4 | 4.7 | 1.5 | .6 | 5.3 |
| 8.8 | 7.5 | 6.6 | All Other Non-Current | 4.3 | 6.6 | 9.2 | 7.7 | 5.8 | 3.7 |
| 100.0 | 100.0 | 100.0 | Total | 100.0 | 100.0 | 100.0 | 100.0 | 100.0 | 100.0 |
| | | | **LIABILITIES** | | | | | | |
| 15.2 | 15.8 | 15.3 | Notes Payable-Short Term | 17.3 | 17.9 | 12.8 | 15.2 | 12.7 | 10.9 |
| 4.1 | 4.0 | 4.0 | Cur. Mat.-L.T.D. | 7.6 | 6.4 | 2.6 | 1.1 | 1.8 | 2.2 |
| 19.4 | 19.9 | 18.8 | Trade Payables | 14.9 | 18.4 | 17.5 | 18.9 | 23.5 | 23.1 |
| .3 | .1 | .2 | Income Taxes Payable | .0 | .1 | .1 | .5 | .0 | .4 |
| 17.7 | 21.2 | 15.4 | All Other Current | 17.7 | 18.0 | 12.8 | 13.3 | 12.9 | 15.7 |
| 56.7 | 61.0 | 53.7 | Total Current | 57.6 | 60.8 | 45.8 | 49.0 | 51.0 | 52.3 |
| 14.7 | 11.5 | 14.5 | Long-Term Debt | 18.4 | 19.2 | 16.0 | 6.6 | 11.1 | 11.1 |
| -.1 | .1 | .1 | Deferred Taxes | .0 | .0 | .0 | .1 | .2 | .3 |
| 9.5 | 8.2 | 10.9 | All Other Non-Current | 27.5 | 11.2 | 5.8 | 6.2 | 6.0 | 4.2 |
| 19.0 | 19.2 | 20.9 | Net Worth | -3.5 | 8.8 | 32.3 | 38.1 | 31.7 | 32.0 |
| 100.0 | 100.0 | 100.0 | Total Liabilities & Net Worth | 100.0 | 100.0 | 100.0 | 100.0 | 100.0 | 100.0 |
| | | | **INCOME DATA** | | | | | | |
| 100.0 | 100.0 | 100.0 | Net Sales | 100.0 | 100.0 | 100.0 | 100.0 | 100.0 | 100.0 |
| 37.5 | 36.1 | 35.5 | Gross Profit | 43.4 | 38.4 | 34.4 | 30.4 | 28.2 | 36.6 |
| 37.6 | 34.5 | 34.4 | Operating Expenses | 45.2 | 37.0 | 31.9 | 29.4 | 26.1 | 34.5 |
| -.1 | 1.6 | 1.1 | Operating Profit | -1.8 | 1.4 | 2.6 | 1.0 | 2.1 | 2.0 |
| .6 | .6 | .4 | All Other Expenses (net) | 1.2 | .5 | .3 | -.3 | .2 | .0 |
| -.7 | 1.0 | .8 | Profit Before Taxes | -3.0 | .9 | 2.3 | 1.3 | 2.0 | 2.0 |
| | | | **RATIOS** | | | | | | |
| 2.4 | 2.5 | 2.4 | Current | 3.0 | 2.7 | 3.3 | 2.2 | 2.2 | 2.3 |
| 1.4 | 1.3 | 1.5 | | 1.6 | 1.5 | 1.4 | 1.6 | 1.4 | 1.2 |
| .9 | .9 | 1.0 | | .7 | .9 | 1.1 | 1.2 | 1.2 | 1.1 |
| 1.2 | 1.2 | 1.2 | Quick | 1.0 | 1.1 | 1.3 | 1.4 | 1.2 | .8 |
| (358) .6 | .6 | .6 | | .4 | .5 | .7 | .8 | .7 | .5 |
| .2 | .3 | .3 | | .1 | .3 | .4 | .5 | .4 | .3 |
| 6  57.0 | 6  56.7 | 7  49.4 | Sales/Receivables | 0 UND | 5  70.5 | 7  50.5 | 21  17.7 | 10  36.9 | 7  54.5 |
| 20  18.5 | 21  17.5 | 22  16.9 | | 8  45.1 | 15  24.3 | 21  17.2 | 32  11.4 | 28  12.9 | 23  15.9 |
| 32  11.3 | 39  9.4 | 37  9.8 | | 28  13.0 | 28  13.2 | 44  8.3 | 42  8.0 | 34  8.6 | 34  10.8 |
| 24  15.4 | 23  16.2 | 26  14.2 | Cost of Sales/Inventory | 36  10.0 | 24  15.4 | 14  26.0 | 27  13.7 | 23  15.7 | 38  9.7 |
| 49  7.4 | 51  7.2 | 51  7.2 | | 101  3.6 | 54  6.7 | 40  9.1 | 39  9.3 | 49  7.5 | 65  5.6 |
| 92  4.0 | 97  3.8 | 96  3.8 | | 243  1.5 | 91  4.0 | 85  4.3 | 61  6.0 | 72  5.1 | 146  2.5 |
| 14  26.9 | 15  24.8 | 15  25.1 | Cost of Sales/Payables | 7  53.1 | 13  27.4 | 13  28.5 | 15  24.2 | 17  21.7 | 21  21.7 |
| 25  14.8 | 25  14.5 | 26  14.1 | | 30  12.1 | 26  14.1 | 21  17.2 | 23  16.2 | 28  13.1 | 34  10.7 |
| 43  8.5 | 45  8.2 | 42  8.6 | | 61  6.0 | 45  8.2 | 41  9.0 | 33  11.2 | 42  8.7 | 65  5.6 |
| 6.7 | 6.7 | 7.2 | Sales/Working Capital | 3.7 | 6.0 | 8.0 | 8.1 | 6.9 | 6.1 |
| 17.2 | 19.5 | 14.1 | | 13.8 | 14.6 | 15.9 | 12.3 | 14.0 | 17.3 |
| -50.2 | -93.4 | 140.4 | | -16.1 | -45.4 | 74.1 | 33.6 | 35.6 | 131.2 |
| 5.3 | 7.8 | 7.8 | EBIT/Interest | 4.0 | 9.1 | 11.0 | 8.1 | 7.6 | 8.0 |
| (299) 1.0 | (275) 2.1 | (303) 2.3 | | (46) .8 | (78) 2.7 | (47) 2.2 | (63) 3.0 | (46) 2.4 | (23) 3.8 |
| -4.1 | -.5 | -.1 | | -6.0 | -.4 | .8 | .7 | .8 | 1.4 |
| 3.9 | 3.2 | 4.6 | Net Profit + Depr., Dep., Amort./Cur. Mat. L/T/D | | | | | | |
| (37) 1.7 | (25) 2.0 | (28) 2.2 | | | | | | | |
| -.2 | .7 | .7 | | | | | | | |
| .2 | .1 | .1 | Fixed/Worth | .1 | .2 | .1 | .1 | .1 | .3 |
| .6 | .6 | .4 | | 3.5 | .5 | .2 | .2 | .3 | .5 |
| 165.0 | 4.8 | 4.5 | | -.5 | -1.4 | 1.9 | .7 | 1.0 | 1.0 |
| .8 | .8 | .9 | Debt/Worth | .8 | 1.1 | .9 | .9 | 1.0 | .7 |
| 2.4 | 2.3 | 2.2 | | 17.8 | 2.8 | 1.9 | 1.5 | 1.8 | 2.8 |
| -70.7 | UND | 45.7 | | -2.8 | -9.4 | 7.1 | 3.1 | 3.6 | 9.0 |
| 26.1 | 39.2 | 35.0 | % Profit Before Taxes/Tangible Net Worth | 39.2 | 43.0 | 42.5 | 26.3 | 31.7 | 37.3 |
| (268) 5.6 | (243) 9.7 | (284) 9.9 | | (32) 1.9 | (69) 8.6 | (50) 13.3 | (65) 10.0 | (46) 13.0 | (22) 9.0 |
| -12.7 | -.9 | .0 | | -9.1 | -4.3 | 2.1 | .1 | 3.2 | 3.4 |
| 8.6 | 10.6 | 10.1 | % Profit Before Taxes/Total Assets | 6.3 | 14.2 | 10.6 | 9.1 | 10.2 | 9.8 |
| .9 | 2.7 | 2.5 | | -.8 | 2.6 | 4.5 | 4.0 | 3.5 | 2.5 |
| -9.3 | -2.9 | -2.6 | | -14.2 | -5.2 | .4 | -.1 | .0 | 1.2 |
| 65.7 | 72.3 | 96.3 | Sales/Net Fixed Assets | 41.6 | 85.7 | 159.4 | 134.3 | 79.5 | 74.1 |
| 28.1 | 29.9 | 35.7 | | 17.6 | 30.3 | 64.3 | 51.4 | 48.3 | 30.5 |
| 12.0 | 11.4 | 13.8 | | 8.3 | 14.1 | 16.6 | 25.9 | 12.7 | 10.4 |
| 4.7 | 4.7 | 4.8 | Sales/Total Assets | 4.1 | 5.5 | 4.5 | 4.9 | 4.0 | 4.4 |
| 3.3 | 3.2 | 3.4 | | 2.0 | 4.0 | 3.2 | 3.9 | 3.2 | 3.1 |
| 2.1 | 2.1 | 2.2 | | 1.1 | 2.4 | 2.5 | 2.9 | 2.7 | 2.0 |
| .4 | .4 | .4 | % Depr., Dep., Amort./Sales | .7 | .5 | .3 | .3 | .3 | .4 |
| (280) .9 | (258) .7 | (267) .7 | | (33) 1.2 | (71) .8 | (34) .7 | (61) .5 | (46) .5 | (22) .9 |
| 1.6 | 1.3 | 1.2 | | 2.5 | 1.4 | 1.3 | 1.0 | 1.0 | 1.1 |
| 2.1 | 1.6 | 1.7 | % Officers', Directors' Owners' Comp/Sales | 2.6 | 2.5 | 1.9 | 1.6 | .9 | |
| (193) 3.9 | (191) 3.5 | (206) 3.1 | | (27) 6.1 | (57) 5.7 | (35) 3.5 | (50) 2.6 | (30) 1.4 | |
| 7.2 | 6.6 | 6.1 | | 8.5 | 8.8 | 4.9 | 5.6 | 2.9 | |
| 7966895M | 5062112M | 4879636M | Net Sales ($) | 38341M | 192530M | 228220M | 503072M | 766750M | 3150723M |
| 2342391M | 1543894M | 1490193M | Total Assets ($) | 26726M | 72152M | 82402M | 160671M | 258902M | 889340M |

M = $ thousand    MM = $ million
See Pages 9 through 22 for Explanation of Ratios and Data

## Current Data Sorted by Assets | Comparative Historical Data

| 0-500M | 500M-2MM | 2-10MM | 10-50MM | 50-100MM | 100-250MM | | 4/1/07-3/31/08 ALL | 4/1/08-3/31/09 ALL |
|---|---|---|---|---|---|---|---|---|
| | | | **Type of Statement** | | | | | |
| | | | 5 | 1 | 4 | Unqualified | 12 | 7 |
| 1 | 1 | 9 | 3 | | | Reviewed | 14 | 15 |
| 5 | 14 | 7 | 1 | | | Compiled | 24 | 32 |
| 33 | 33 | 15 | | | | Tax Returns | 69 | 65 |
| 19 | 27 | 23 | 9 | 2 | 1 | Other | 49 | 67 |
| | 30 (4/1-9/30/11) | | 183 (10/1/11-3/31/12) | | | | | |
| 58 | 75 | 54 | 18 | 3 | 5 | **NUMBER OF STATEMENTS** | 168 | 186 |
| % | % | % | % | % | % | **ASSETS** | % | % |
| 18.6 | 10.7 | 6.7 | 15.7 | | | Cash & Equivalents | 8.7 | 9.2 |
| 9.1 | 12.8 | 11.8 | 11.4 | | | Trade Receivables (net) | 9.2 | 11.7 |
| 48.3 | 46.3 | 49.9 | 40.0 | | | Inventory | 53.6 | 49.6 |
| .4 | 2.3 | 1.8 | 5.4 | | | All Other Current | 1.9 | 3.5 |
| 76.3 | 72.2 | 70.1 | 72.5 | | | Total Current | 73.3 | 73.9 |
| 15.1 | 14.6 | 22.6 | 18.9 | | | Fixed Assets (net) | 19.1 | 17.7 |
| 3.5 | 6.3 | 2.0 | 1.8 | | | Intangibles (net) | 3.1 | 3.5 |
| 5.1 | 6.9 | 5.3 | 6.9 | | | All Other Non-Current | 4.6 | 4.9 |
| 100.0 | 100.0 | 100.0 | 100.0 | | | Total | 100.0 | 100.0 |
| | | | | | | **LIABILITIES** | | |
| 12.7 | 11.4 | 7.5 | 4.8 | | | Notes Payable-Short Term | 14.0 | 13.1 |
| 2.8 | 2.8 | 1.8 | 2.5 | | | Cur. Mat.-L.T.D. | 4.4 | 3.2 |
| 18.0 | 19.0 | 20.6 | 15.2 | | | Trade Payables | 20.0 | 21.1 |
| .0 | .0 | .1 | .0 | | | Income Taxes Payable | .3 | .1 |
| 14.1 | 10.1 | 16.3 | 13.9 | | | All Other Current | 16.3 | 15.9 |
| 47.5 | 43.4 | 46.3 | 36.5 | | | Total Current | 55.1 | 53.3 |
| 33.5 | 15.2 | 12.2 | 13.0 | | | Long-Term Debt | 15.1 | 19.7 |
| .0 | .0 | .1 | .5 | | | Deferred Taxes | .1 | .1 |
| 23.4 | 11.3 | 7.0 | 3.8 | | | All Other Non-Current | 9.1 | 12.4 |
| -4.4 | 30.1 | 34.5 | 46.2 | | | Net Worth | 20.8 | 14.6 |
| 100.0 | 100.0 | 100.0 | 100.0 | | | Total Liabilites & Net Worth | 100.0 | 100.0 |
| | | | | | | **INCOME DATA** | | |
| 100.0 | 100.0 | 100.0 | 100.0 | | | Net Sales | 100.0 | 100.0 |
| 43.4 | 42.8 | 43.2 | 42.2 | | | Gross Profit | 44.7 | 43.2 |
| 40.1 | 38.6 | 40.3 | 37.3 | | | Operating Expenses | 41.4 | 41.7 |
| 3.3 | 4.2 | 3.0 | 4.9 | | | Operating Profit | 3.3 | 1.5 |
| .8 | 1.1 | -.2 | -.3 | | | All Other Expenses (net) | 1.1 | .5 |
| 2.5 | 3.1 | 3.2 | 5.2 | | | Profit Before Taxes | 2.2 | 1.0 |
| | | | | | | **RATIOS** | | |
| 4.3 | 3.1 | 2.6 | 3.9 | | | Current | 2.3 | 2.6 |
| 2.1 | 1.9 | 1.6 | 1.9 | | | | 1.4 | 1.5 |
| 1.1 | 1.2 | 1.1 | 1.2 | | | | .9 | 1.0 |
| 1.7 | 1.0 | .7 | 1.4 | | | Quick | .6 | .9 |
| .5 | .4 | .3 | .6 | | | | (166) .3 | (184) .4 |
| .2 | .2 | .2 | .3 | | | | .1 | .1 |
| 0 UND | 0 UND | 1 498.6 | 1 620.0 | | | Sales/Receivables | 0 UND | 0 UND |
| 1 334.3 | 10 38.3 | 7 53.3 | 6 57.9 | | | | 4 103.2 | 5 80.9 |
| 11 34.0 | 26 14.3 | 21 17.5 | 42 8.6 | | | | 19 19.5 | 21 17.7 |
| 33 10.9 | 50 7.3 | 65 5.6 | 72 5.1 | | | Cost of Sales/Inventory | 70 5.2 | 54 6.8 |
| 79 4.6 | 122 3.0 | 126 2.9 | 126 2.9 | | | | 111 3.3 | 114 3.2 |
| 166 2.2 | 192 1.9 | 203 1.8 | 203 1.8 | | | | 171 2.1 | 193 1.9 |
| 0 UND | 12 30.7 | 19 19.0 | 19 19.7 | | | Cost of Sales/Payables | 20 17.9 | 16 22.7 |
| 21 17.8 | 36 10.2 | 37 9.8 | 38 9.7 | | | | 40 9.1 | 34 10.7 |
| 45 8.1 | 63 5.8 | 59 6.2 | 78 4.7 | | | | 63 5.8 | 64 5.7 |
| 5.0 | 3.9 | 4.4 | 3.1 | | | Sales/Working Capital | 6.5 | 5.2 |
| 11.4 | 8.1 | 10.4 | 8.8 | | | | 15.3 | 11.4 |
| 92.3 | 52.7 | 72.2 | 19.0 | | | | -87.4 | -104.1 |
| 6.3 | 13.9 | 12.6 | 32.8 | | | EBIT/Interest | 6.8 | 7.5 |
| (39) 2.0 | (59) 2.7 | (50) 6.3 | (15) 6.8 | | | | (146) 2.6 | (158) 2.5 |
| .0 | .7 | 2.0 | 3.8 | | | | .8 | -.7 |
| | | | | | | Net Profit + Depr., Dep., Amort./Cur. Mat. L/T/D | 43.8 | 6.7 |
| | | | | | | | (18) 6.1 | (14) 1.2 |
| | | | | | | | 1.8 | -.3 |
| .1 | .1 | .2 | .2 | | | Fixed/Worth | .2 | .2 |
| .5 | .3 | .6 | .4 | | | | .6 | .7 |
| -.6 | 3.1 | 1.4 | 1.2 | | | | 10.3 | 11.3 |
| .9 | .7 | .8 | .6 | | | Debt/Worth | 1.3 | 1.1 |
| 3.1 | 2.3 | 2.0 | 1.1 | | | | 2.7 | 2.9 |
| -3.8 | 50.9 | 4.9 | 3.1 | | | | 31.0 | NM |
| 74.3 | 42.8 | 48.1 | 37.7 | | | % Profit Before Taxes/Tangible Net Worth | 57.9 | 45.9 |
| (36) 37.5 | (58) 20.3 | (48) 11.9 | (17) 17.6 | | | | (130) 18.0 | (140) 12.1 |
| 4.9 | 3.0 | 2.6 | 5.6 | | | | 1.5 | -.5 |
| 27.8 | 15.8 | 13.8 | 25.5 | | | % Profit Before Taxes/Total Assets | 17.2 | 11.6 |
| 8.4 | 6.0 | 5.9 | 7.8 | | | | 4.7 | 2.8 |
| -3.4 | .1 | 1.0 | 4.1 | | | | -.8 | -5.2 |
| 238.0 | 123.5 | 42.5 | 26.4 | | | Sales/Net Fixed Assets | 63.1 | 67.7 |
| 51.5 | 42.0 | 16.7 | 15.4 | | | | 25.0 | 26.9 |
| 16.7 | 10.8 | 6.1 | 10.4 | | | | 12.5 | 9.7 |
| 4.8 | 3.8 | 3.1 | 2.8 | | | Sales/Total Assets | 4.1 | 3.9 |
| 3.4 | 2.5 | 2.3 | 2.0 | | | | 2.9 | 2.7 |
| 2.5 | 1.6 | 1.9 | 1.6 | | | | 2.0 | 1.9 |
| .2 | .3 | .6 | .4 | | | % Depr., Dep., Amort./Sales | .4 | .5 |
| (29) .6 | (53) .6 | (44) .9 | (16) 1.1 | | | | (130) .9 | (132) 1.1 |
| 1.6 | 1.9 | 1.5 | 1.9 | | | | 1.6 | 1.8 |
| 2.9 | 3.0 | 1.4 | | | | % Officers', Directors' Owners' Comp/Sales | 2.2 | 1.8 |
| (32) 5.4 | (41) 5.3 | (28) 3.3 | | | | | (80) 4.0 | (87) 3.7 |
| 8.5 | 9.1 | 6.8 | | | | | 6.4 | 7.3 |
| 62618M | 223714M | 628746M | 817136M | 400627M | 1834310M | Net Sales ($) | 4483701M | 5787317M |
| 15679M | 81592M | 235445M | 355988M | 235834M | 727103M | Total Assets ($) | 1645637M | 2293305M |

M = $ thousand    MM = $ million
See Pages 9 through 22 for Explanation of Ratios and Data

## Comparative Historical Data / Current Data Sorted by Sales

| | 12 / 14 / 28 / 63 / 69 | 14 / 10 / 24 / 58 / 60 | 10 / 14 / 27 / 81 / 81 | Type of Statement | 0-1MM | 1-3MM | 3-5MM | 5-10MM | 10-25MM | 25MM & OVER |
|---|---|---|---|---|---|---|---|---|---|---|
| | | | | Unqualified | | | | 3 | 7 | 10 |
| | | | | Reviewed | 1 | 12 | 5 | 4 | 2 | 3 |
| | | | | Compiled | 3 | 27 | 15 | 10 | 3 | 1 |
| | | | | Tax Returns | 25 | 22 | | 11 | 3 | 1 |
| | | | | Other | 14 | | 7 | | 15 | 12 |
| | 4/1/09-3/31/10 ALL | 4/1/10-3/31/11 ALL | 4/1/11-3/31/12 ALL | | 30 (4/1-9/30/11) | | | 183 (10/1/11-3/31/12) | | |
| NUMBER OF STATEMENTS | 186 | 166 | 213 | | 43 | 61 | 27 | 28 | 27 | 27 |

### ASSETS (%)

| Item | H1 | H2 | H3 | 0-1MM | 1-3MM | 3-5MM | 5-10MM | 10-25MM | 25MM & OVER |
|---|---|---|---|---|---|---|---|---|---|
| Cash & Equivalents | 13.0 | 12.7 | 12.9 | 15.2 | 13.8 | 8.7 | 11.9 | 6.0 | 19.3 |
| Trade Receivables (net) | 11.1 | 11.8 | 11.1 | 8.9 | 9.1 | 11.3 | 19.0 | 14.2 | 7.3 |
| Inventory | 44.5 | 43.4 | 46.7 | 46.7 | 45.6 | 58.9 | 42.7 | 48.1 | 39.9 |
| All Other Current | 3.0 | 2.9 | 2.0 | 2.1 | 1.2 | .9 | 1.5 | 2.9 | 4.4 |
| Total Current | 71.6 | 70.7 | 72.7 | 72.9 | 69.7 | 79.8 | 75.2 | 71.2 | 71.0 |
| Fixed Assets (net) | 16.7 | 16.7 | 17.4 | 16.6 | 17.1 | 12.6 | 18.9 | 18.8 | 20.9 |
| Intangibles (net) | 3.6 | 3.9 | 4.1 | 5.1 | 5.3 | 2.2 | 4.0 | 2.3 | 3.3 |
| All Other Non-Current | 8.2 | 8.6 | 5.9 | 5.3 | 7.9 | 5.3 | 2.0 | 7.7 | 4.8 |
| Total | 100.0 | 100.0 | 100.0 | 100.0 | 100.0 | 100.0 | 100.0 | 100.0 | 100.0 |

### LIABILITIES

| Item | H1 | H2 | H3 | 0-1MM | 1-3MM | 3-5MM | 5-10MM | 10-25MM | 25MM & OVER |
|---|---|---|---|---|---|---|---|---|---|
| Notes Payable-Short Term | 13.9 | 13.0 | 9.9 | 12.4 | 12.4 | 6.8 | 9.0 | 10.2 | 3.6 |
| Cur. Mat.-L.T.D. | 2.9 | 2.0 | 2.4 | 3.1 | 2.7 | 1.8 | 2.4 | 1.9 | 1.8 |
| Trade Payables | 17.7 | 18.7 | 18.9 | 13.2 | 18.6 | 19.5 | 21.8 | 19.5 | 24.1 |
| Income Taxes Payable | .2 | .2 | .1 | .0 | .0 | .0 | .2 | .1 | .2 |
| All Other Current | 16.8 | 15.2 | 13.3 | 11.1 | 14.4 | 9.2 | 11.5 | 17.3 | 16.2 |
| Total Current | 51.4 | 49.0 | 44.5 | 39.9 | 48.1 | 37.3 | 44.9 | 49.0 | 45.8 |
| Long-Term Debt | 17.1 | 13.9 | 18.7 | 30.1 | 21.5 | 21.6 | 9.5 | 11.7 | 7.8 |
| Deferred Taxes | .2 | .1 | .1 | .0 | .0 | .0 | .0 | .0 | .7 |
| All Other Non-Current | 8.9 | 6.6 | 12.8 | 28.7 | 10.8 | 10.1 | 10.4 | 1.4 | 8.6 |
| Net Worth | 22.4 | 30.4 | 23.9 | 1.3 | 19.6 | 31.0 | 35.2 | 37.7 | 37.1 |
| Total Liabilities & Net Worth | 100.0 | 100.0 | 100.0 | 100.0 | 100.0 | 100.0 | 100.0 | 100.0 | 100.0 |

### INCOME DATA

| Item | H1 | H2 | H3 | 0-1MM | 1-3MM | 3-5MM | 5-10MM | 10-25MM | 25MM & OVER |
|---|---|---|---|---|---|---|---|---|---|
| Net Sales | 100.0 | 100.0 | 100.0 | 100.0 | 100.0 | 100.0 | 100.0 | 100.0 | 100.0 |
| Gross Profit | 44.0 | 43.9 | 42.9 | 45.2 | 43.9 | 42.6 | 38.2 | 43.9 | 41.5 |
| Operating Expenses | 41.5 | 41.2 | 39.3 | 41.9 | 40.2 | 39.2 | 34.3 | 39.7 | 38.0 |
| Operating Profit | 2.6 | 2.7 | 3.7 | 3.4 | 3.7 | 3.3 | 3.9 | 4.3 | 3.5 |
| All Other Expenses (net) | .6 | .5 | .5 | 1.7 | .7 | -.1 | .1 | -.5 | .1 |
| Profit Before Taxes | 1.9 | 2.2 | 3.1 | 1.6 | 3.0 | 3.4 | 3.8 | 4.7 | 3.4 |

### RATIOS

| Ratio | H1 | H2 | H3 | 0-1MM | 1-3MM | 3-5MM | 5-10MM | 10-25MM | 25MM & OVER |
|---|---|---|---|---|---|---|---|---|---|
| Current | 2.8 | 2.9 | 3.0 | 4.6 | 3.1 | 3.5 | 2.9 | 2.6 | 3.0 |
| | 1.6 | 1.6 | 1.9 | 2.5 | 1.8 | 2.2 | 1.6 | 1.5 | 1.8 |
| | 1.0 | 1.0 | 1.1 | 1.2 | 1.0 | 1.3 | 1.0 | 1.1 | 1.2 |
| Quick | 1.1 | 1.1 | 1.1 | 2.0 | 1.2 | .8 | 1.0 | .5 | 1.3 |
| | .4 | (165) .4 | .5 | .5 | .4 | .5 | .6 | .3 | .7 |
| | .1 | .2 | .2 | .2 | .1 | .2 | .2 | .3 | .3 |
| Sales/Receivables | 0 UND | 0 UND | 0 UND | 0 UND | 0 UND | 0 UND | 3 129.5 | 1 498.7 | 0 846.6 |
| | 6 58.9 | 7 56.1 | 5 69.2 | 0 UND | 3 107.2 | 7 51.4 | 13 29.1 | 11 33.0 | 4 98.9 |
| | 23 15.7 | 22 16.4 | 20 17.9 | 20 18.0 | 18 20.8 | 25 14.8 | 29 12.7 | 27 13.3 | 13 28.5 |
| Cost of Sales/Inventory | 63 5.8 | 49 7.5 | 53 6.9 | 57 6.4 | 42 8.7 | 85 4.3 | 16 23.3 | 78 4.7 | 54 6.7 |
| | 119 3.1 | 110 3.3 | 107 3.4 | 107 3.4 | 114 3.2 | 135 2.7 | 91 4.0 | 130 2.8 | 87 4.2 |
| | 188 1.9 | 189 1.9 | 182 2.0 | 192 1.9 | 192 1.9 | 228 1.6 | 166 2.2 | 182 2.0 | 159 2.3 |
| Cost of Sales/Payables | 17 21.5 | 18 20.8 | 14 26.4 | 0 UND | 12 31.0 | 19 19.1 | 11 33.8 | 27 13.6 | 29 12.8 |
| | 34 10.8 | 36 10.3 | 34 10.6 | 17 21.6 | 35 10.5 | 39 9.3 | 30 12.0 | 39 9.3 | 35 10.3 |
| | 61 6.0 | 63 5.8 | 54 6.7 | 54 6.8 | 69 5.3 | 53 6.9 | 54 6.8 | 54 6.7 | 78 4.7 |
| Sales/Working Capital | 5.0 | 4.7 | 4.4 | 4.0 | 4.4 | 3.9 | 4.7 | 5.3 | 4.4 |
| | 11.4 | 10.1 | 8.7 | 7.3 | 10.9 | 6.6 | 12.6 | 17.7 | 10.5 |
| | -119.1 | NM | 51.5 | 28.3 | NM | 20.4 | NM | 41.8 | 41.5 |
| EBIT/Interest | 7.6 | 10.1 | 12.7 | 6.5 | 7.3 | 41.5 | 20.4 | 14.2 | 24.7 |
| | (149) 2.8 | (127) 4.1 | (171) 3.7 | (30) 1.7 | (48) 2.1 | (18) 4.4 | (26) 6.7 | (25) 6.7 | (24) 5.7 |
| | .3 | 1.1 | 1.1 | -.5 | -.7 | 2.5 | 2.3 | 2.2 | 1.4 |
| Net Profit + Depr., Dep., Amort./Cur. Mat. L/T/D | 17.3 | 32.2 | 16.7 | | | | | | |
| | (21) 2.1 | (19) 2.7 | (12) 2.9 | | | | | | |
| | .0 | .8 | 1.3 | | | | | | |
| Fixed/Worth | .1 | .1 | .1 | .1 | .1 | .0 | .1 | .2 | .2 |
| | .6 | .4 | .4 | .8 | .5 | .2 | .6 | .5 | .5 |
| | UND | 1.8 | 2.8 | -.6 | -2.5 | .4 | 1.2 | .9 | 2.1 |
| Debt/Worth | .9 | .7 | .8 | 1.0 | .5 | .6 | .8 | 1.0 | .8 |
| | 2.4 | 2.3 | 2.1 | 5.5 | 2.8 | .9 | 2.2 | 1.7 | 1.2 |
| | -52.2 | 10.5 | 19.5 | -3.8 | -6.8 | 3.6 | 11.3 | 4.5 | 3.9 |
| % Profit Before Taxes/Tangible Net Worth | 46.1 | 45.1 | 49.6 | 65.0 | 54.9 | 41.4 | 83.7 | 61.9 | 32.3 |
| | (138) 14.7 | (134) 15.9 | (167) 17.9 | (27) 31.8 | (43) 19.5 | (25) 14.9 | (24) 10.9 | (24) 26.4 | (24) 14.5 |
| | 1.2 | 2.3 | 3.1 | 4.5 | -2.9 | 11.0 | 2.6 | 2.6 | 2.8 |
| % Profit Before Taxes/Total Assets | 15.4 | 13.4 | 17.1 | 22.9 | 16.6 | 14.1 | 13.4 | 21.0 | 15.1 |
| | 4.0 | 4.9 | 6.8 | 2.7 | 5.6 | 9.2 | 5.5 | 12.5 | 6.4 |
| | -2.6 | .0 | .6 | -7.5 | -2.9 | 2.1 | 1.2 | 1.4 | 1.4 |
| Sales/Net Fixed Assets | 69.2 | 89.1 | 85.1 | 148.2 | 98.0 | 94.9 | 118.4 | 45.3 | 41.6 |
| | 24.4 | 24.6 | 29.6 | 44.3 | 29.6 | 37.9 | 41.2 | 16.1 | 15.7 |
| | 8.3 | 9.8 | 9.9 | 8.3 | 11.4 | 16.1 | 10.1 | 7.3 | 7.9 |
| Sales/Total Assets | 3.7 | 3.7 | 3.8 | 3.7 | 3.8 | 3.8 | 4.8 | 3.3 | 3.9 |
| | 2.5 | 2.6 | 2.6 | 2.6 | 2.3 | 2.8 | 2.8 | 2.5 | 2.5 |
| | 1.8 | 1.8 | 1.9 | 1.3 | 1.6 | 2.0 | 2.2 | 1.9 | 1.7 |
| % Depr., Dep., Amort./Sales | .5 | .5 | .4 | .2 | .4 | .2 | .5 | .7 | .5 |
| | (137) 1.0 | (117) 1.0 | (148) .9 | (24) .6 | (37) .9 | (22) .5 | (20) .8 | (22) 1.0 | (23) 1.1 |
| | 2.0 | 1.8 | 1.7 | 1.6 | 2.2 | .9 | 1.9 | 1.6 | 2.0 |
| % Officers', Directors' Owners' Comp/Sales | 2.0 | 2.0 | 2.6 | 4.1 | 2.9 | 2.8 | 1.8 | .9 | |
| | (96) 4.6 | (91) 4.1 | (107) 4.7 | (22) 7.1 | (32) 5.0 | (18) 5.5 | (17) 3.0 | (13) 2.7 | |
| | 7.4 | 7.6 | 8.4 | 9.8 | 8.4 | 9.5 | 5.4 | 4.7 | |
| Net Sales ($) | 5084226M | 5569529M | 3967151M | 25478M | 106185M | 106167M | 200982M | 399462M | 3128877M |
| Total Assets ($) | 2198927M | 2420665M | 1651641M | 13114M | 52286M | 41788M | 73771M | 167191M | 1303491M |

© RMA 2012

M = $ thousand    MM = $ million
See Pages 9 through 22 for Explanation of Ratios and Data

## Current Data Sorted by Assets

## Comparative Historical Data

| 0-500M | 500M-2MM | 2-10MM | 10-50MM | 50-100MM | 100-250MM | Type of Statement | | 6 / 4/1/07- 3/31/08 ALL | 6 / 4/1/08- 3/31/09 ALL |
|---|---|---|---|---|---|---|---|---|---|
| 1 | | 9 | 7 | 1 | 2 | Unqualified | | | |
| | 4 | 10 | 8 | 1 | | Reviewed | | 13 | 18 |
| 1 | 9 | 4 | 2 | | | Compiled | | 29 | 29 |
| 13 | 25 | | | | | Tax Returns | | 29 | 40 |
| 5 | 9 | 13 | 5 | | 2 | Other | | 41 | 39 |
| | 16 (4/1-9/30/11) | | 115 (10/1/11-3/31/12) | | | | | | |
| 20 | 47 | 36 | 22 | 2 | 4 | **NUMBER OF STATEMENTS** | | 118 | 132 |
| % | % | % | % | % | % | **ASSETS** | | % | % |
| 11.8 | 9.2 | 8.9 | 9.6 | | | Cash & Equivalents | | 12.6 | 10.5 |
| 11.8 | 15.5 | 13.8 | 10.6 | | | Trade Receivables (net) | | 17.9 | 13.7 |
| 45.5 | 53.5 | 50.3 | 49.6 | | | Inventory | | 44.6 | 48.2 |
| .7 | 1.6 | 2.1 | 2.8 | | | All Other Current | | 2.4 | 2.3 |
| 69.7 | 79.9 | 75.1 | 72.6 | | | Total Current | | 77.5 | 74.6 |
| 18.7 | 9.9 | 15.7 | 22.0 | | | Fixed Assets (net) | | 14.1 | 18.0 |
| 3.5 | 3.9 | 2.6 | 2.5 | | | Intangibles (net) | | 3.0 | 2.2 |
| 8.1 | 6.3 | 6.6 | 2.9 | | | All Other Non-Current | | 5.5 | 5.1 |
| 100.0 | 100.0 | 100.0 | 100.0 | | | Total | | 100.0 | 100.0 |
| | | | | | | **LIABILITIES** | | | |
| 26.5 | 15.8 | 10.7 | 14.5 | | | Notes Payable-Short Term | | 13.4 | 15.1 |
| 11.5 | 1.8 | 1.3 | .7 | | | Cur. Mat.-L.T.D. | | 3.1 | 4.3 |
| 24.1 | 23.0 | 15.2 | 21.5 | | | Trade Payables | | 19.6 | 18.9 |
| .3 | .0 | .2 | .2 | | | Income Taxes Payable | | .1 | .1 |
| 19.9 | 12.1 | 15.7 | 17.0 | | | All Other Current | | 14.2 | 14.9 |
| 82.4 | 52.7 | 43.1 | 53.9 | | | Total Current | | 50.5 | 53.3 |
| 32.9 | 15.2 | 10.6 | 7.7 | | | Long-Term Debt | | 13.7 | 15.8 |
| .1 | .0 | .0 | .1 | | | Deferred Taxes | | .0 | .0 |
| 20.4 | 10.1 | 8.5 | 3.3 | | | All Other Non-Current | | 6.4 | 4.1 |
| -35.9 | 21.9 | 37.8 | 34.9 | | | Net Worth | | 29.3 | 26.9 |
| 100.0 | 100.0 | 100.0 | 100.0 | | | Total Liabilities & Net Worth | | 100.0 | 100.0 |
| | | | | | | **INCOME DATA** | | | |
| 100.0 | 100.0 | 100.0 | 100.0 | | | Net Sales | | 100.0 | 100.0 |
| 46.1 | 31.0 | 31.4 | 33.2 | | | Gross Profit | | 32.9 | 35.0 |
| 44.5 | 29.3 | 30.2 | 30.9 | | | Operating Expenses | | 29.6 | 33.2 |
| 1.6 | 1.7 | 1.2 | 2.3 | | | Operating Profit | | 3.2 | 1.8 |
| .6 | 1.0 | -.3 | .4 | | | All Other Expenses (net) | | .5 | .2 |
| 1.0 | .8 | 1.5 | 2.0 | | | Profit Before Taxes | | 2.7 | 1.6 |
| | | | | | | **RATIOS** | | | |
| 2.0 | 2.4 | 2.8 | 2.4 | | | | | 2.5 | 2.6 |
| 1.1 | 1.5 | 1.8 | 1.4 | | | Current | | 1.4 | 1.5 |
| .5 | 1.2 | 1.2 | 1.1 | | | | | 1.1 | 1.1 |
| .7 | .9 | .8 | .7 | | | | | 1.1 | .9 |
| .3 | .4 | .4 | .3 | | | Quick | | .6 | .4 |
| .1 | .2 | .3 | .2 | | | | | .2 | .2 |
| 0 UND | 4 101.4 | 6 65.9 | 6 57.0 | | | | 5 72.5 | 3 107.9 | |
| 6 58.5 | 11 34.1 | 15 24.8 | 13 29.0 | | | Sales/Receivables | 14 25.2 | 9 39.8 | |
| 17 21.5 | 23 16.1 | 25 14.6 | 20 18.7 | | | | 31 11.9 | 22 16.4 | |
| 14 25.3 | 46 8.0 | 57 6.4 | 73 5.0 | | | | 45 8.1 | 53 6.9 | |
| 55 6.6 | 74 4.9 | 94 3.9 | 94 3.9 | | | Cost of Sales/Inventory | 69 5.3 | 76 4.8 | |
| 135 2.7 | 140 2.6 | 104 3.5 | 111 3.3 | | | | 105 3.5 | 114 3.2 | |
| 0 UND | 16 22.6 | 17 21.1 | 18 20.0 | | | | 12 29.9 | 14 27.0 | |
| 19 19.0 | 36 10.1 | 26 14.3 | 30 12.3 | | | Cost of Sales/Payables | 27 13.6 | 28 13.2 | |
| 53 6.9 | 56 6.5 | 33 10.9 | 49 7.5 | | | | 49 7.4 | 44 8.3 | |
| 8.2 | 5.9 | 4.8 | 6.6 | | | | | 6.6 | 7.3 |
| 149.0 | 12.0 | 8.7 | 18.0 | | | Sales/Working Capital | | 13.8 | 12.6 |
| -10.7 | 25.0 | 32.3 | NM | | | | | 67.7 | 89.8 |
| 4.8 | 8.8 | 10.5 | 30.1 | | | | 7.0 | 9.0 | |
| (16) 1.1 | (42) 1.7 | (29) 3.5 | (19) 6.4 | | | EBIT/Interest | (99) 3.2 | (109) 2.6 | |
| -9.0 | -1.2 | 1.2 | -.2 | | | | 1.5 | .7 | |
| | | | | | | Net Profit + Depr., Dep., Amort./Cur. Mat. L/T/D | 5.7 | 3.2 | |
| | | | | | | | (16) 2.5 | (15) 1.1 | |
| | | | | | | | .4 | .4 | |
| .1 | .0 | .2 | .2 | | | | | .1 | .2 |
| NM | .2 | .4 | .6 | | | Fixed/Worth | | .4 | .5 |
| -.3 | .6 | 1.7 | 1.3 | | | | | 1.5 | 4.4 |
| 2.9 | 1.4 | .7 | 1.1 | | | | | .9 | .8 |
| -6.9 | 2.7 | 1.4 | 2.7 | | | Debt/Worth | | 2.3 | 2.0 |
| -2.5 | 17.8 | 9.0 | 3.9 | | | | | 12.0 | 26.2 |
| | 27.6 | 28.8 | 44.6 | | | % Profit Before Taxes/Tangible Net Worth | | 48.1 | 36.6 |
| (37) 11.2 | (34) 11.4 | (20) 17.4 | | | | (96) 26.5 | (106) 16.4 | | |
| | .0 | 3.1 | -9.4 | | | | | 8.5 | 5.8 |
| 14.5 | 8.2 | 8.2 | 12.8 | | | % Profit Before Taxes/Total Assets | | 16.1 | 13.3 |
| 1.3 | 2.4 | 3.1 | 6.2 | | | | | 6.9 | 4.4 |
| -12.8 | -2.3 | 1.1 | -3.1 | | | | | 1.7 | -.5 |
| 256.1 | 434.1 | 37.5 | 52.7 | | | Sales/Net Fixed Assets | | 87.9 | 68.9 |
| 25.9 | 76.1 | 27.8 | 16.5 | | | | | 34.9 | 25.8 |
| 10.9 | 28.9 | 15.4 | 7.8 | | | | | 15.3 | 12.3 |
| 7.0 | 4.6 | 3.5 | 3.5 | | | Sales/Total Assets | | 4.7 | 4.5 |
| 3.8 | 3.4 | 3.0 | 2.7 | | | | | 3.5 | 3.3 |
| 2.6 | 2.4 | 1.9 | 2.2 | | | | | 2.4 | 2.3 |
| .4 | .2 | .3 | .5 | | | | | .3 | .4 |
| (10) 1.4 | (27) .5 | (34) .7 | (21) 1.1 | | | % Depr., Dep., Amort./Sales | (91) .7 | (107) .6 | |
| 4.2 | 1.0 | 1.4 | 1.3 | | | | | 1.2 | 1.2 |
| 3.1 | 1.7 | 1.4 | | | | % Officers', Directors' Owners' Comp/Sales | | 1.6 | 1.5 |
| (12) 6.2 | (31) 3.3 | (17) 2.1 | | | | (56) 2.8 | (74) 3.1 | | |
| 17.2 | 4.2 | 2.8 | | | | | | 4.2 | 5.3 |
| 16951M | 182074M | 503708M | 1110268M | 495451M | 777418M | Net Sales ($) | | 2348291M | 3979457M |
| 4074M | 52658M | 174258M | 404052M | 147134M | 450043M | Total Assets ($) | | 738055M | 1060507M |

M = $ thousand    MM = $ million
See Pages 9 through 22 for Explanation of Ratios and Data

## Comparative Historical Data | | | | Current Data Sorted by Sales

| | | | Type of Statement | | | | | | |
|---|---|---|---|---|---|---|---|---|---|
| | | | Unqualified | 1 | | | | 1 | 9 |
| | | | Reviewed | | 1 | 3 | 1 | 8 | 9 |
| | | | Compiled | 1 | 2 | 3 | 7 | 7 | 2 |
| | | | Tax Returns | 11 | 13 | 10 | 6 | 2 | |
| | | | Other | 5 | 7 | 2 | 6 | | 9 |
| 5 17 23 45 42 | 6 10 31 32 41 | 11 22 22 42 34 | | | 16 (4/1-9/30/11) | | 115 (10/1/11-3/31/12) | | |
| 4/1/09-3/31/10 ALL | 4/1/10-3/31/11 ALL | 4/1/11-3/31/12 ALL | | 0-1MM | 1-3MM | 3-5MM | 5-10MM | 10-25MM | 25MM & OVER |
| 132 | 120 | 131 | NUMBER OF STATEMENTS | 18 | 23 | 18 | 19 | 24 | 29 |
| % | % | % | **ASSETS** | % | % | % | % | % | % |
| 10.9 | 10.7 | 9.6 | Cash & Equivalents | 11.0 | 7.5 | 10.6 | 10.0 | 8.2 | 10.8 |
| 13.4 | 13.3 | 13.6 | Trade Receivables (net) | 11.5 | 11.1 | 17.6 | 16.0 | 15.2 | 11.5 |
| 45.1 | 49.2 | 50.0 | Inventory | 37.3 | 58.0 | 56.2 | 44.9 | 54.5 | 47.2 |
| 2.3 | 2.7 | 1.8 | All Other Current | .7 | 1.1 | 1.3 | 2.2 | 3.1 | 2.2 |
| 71.7 | 75.9 | 75.0 | Total Current | 60.5 | 77.7 | 85.6 | 73.1 | 81.0 | 71.7 |
| 18.7 | 18.6 | 15.4 | Fixed Assets (net) | 24.7 | 10.9 | 7.0 | 14.1 | 12.2 | 21.8 |
| 3.6 | 2.7 | 3.5 | Intangibles (net) | 5.2 | 6.0 | 1.6 | 3.2 | 2.0 | 3.2 |
| 6.0 | 2.8 | 6.1 | All Other Non-Current | 9.5 | 5.3 | 5.8 | 9.7 | 4.8 | 3.4 |
| 100.0 | 100.0 | 100.0 | Total | 100.0 | 100.0 | 100.0 | 100.0 | 100.0 | 100.0 |
| | | | **LIABILITIES** | | | | | | |
| 15.3 | 17.5 | 15.9 | Notes Payable-Short Term | 25.9 | 16.9 | 13.7 | 13.1 | 12.7 | 14.8 |
| 4.1 | 3.0 | 3.0 | Cur. Mat.-L.T.D. | 6.3 | 7.3 | .9 | 1.9 | 1.1 | 1.2 |
| 21.1 | 20.3 | 20.3 | Trade Payables | 22.6 | 22.1 | 20.3 | 20.9 | 16.6 | 20.1 |
| .1 | .1 | .1 | Income Taxes Payable | .4 | .0 | .1 | .0 | .2 | .1 |
| 16.8 | 15.9 | 15.5 | All Other Current | 7.3 | 20.9 | 14.9 | 8.7 | 18.9 | 18.2 |
| 57.3 | 56.8 | 54.9 | Total Current | 62.5 | 67.2 | 49.9 | 44.6 | 49.6 | 54.4 |
| 16.0 | 11.1 | 15.0 | Long-Term Debt | 30.1 | 24.1 | 12.0 | 16.3 | 5.8 | 6.8 |
| .1 | .2 | .2 | Deferred Taxes | .1 | .0 | .0 | .0 | .0 | .6 |
| 8.2 | 6.8 | 9.7 | All Other Non-Current | 12.1 | 20.4 | 7.8 | 8.8 | 8.1 | 3.0 |
| 18.4 | 25.2 | 20.3 | Net Worth | -4.9 | -11.7 | 30.2 | 30.3 | 36.3 | 35.2 |
| 100.0 | 100.0 | 100.0 | Total Liabilities & Net Worth | 100.0 | 100.0 | 100.0 | 100.0 | 100.0 | 100.0 |
| | | | **INCOME DATA** | | | | | | |
| 100.0 | 100.0 | 100.0 | Net Sales | 100.0 | 100.0 | 100.0 | 100.0 | 100.0 | 100.0 |
| 33.5 | 32.1 | 34.3 | Gross Profit | 49.0 | 34.8 | 28.8 | 32.3 | 29.0 | 34.1 |
| 32.1 | 30.9 | 32.7 | Operating Expenses | 45.1 | 35.5 | 27.2 | 30.0 | 27.7 | 32.0 |
| 1.4 | 1.2 | 1.7 | Operating Profit | 3.9 | -.8 | 1.5 | 2.3 | 1.4 | 2.1 |
| .4 | .2 | .5 | All Other Expenses (net) | 1.8 | .5 | .1 | -.2 | .0 | .6 |
| 1.0 | 1.0 | 1.2 | Profit Before Taxes | 2.1 | -1.3 | 1.4 | 2.5 | 1.4 | 1.5 |
| | | | **RATIOS** | | | | | | |
| 2.0 | 2.5 | 2.4 | | 2.3 | 2.6 | 3.4 | 2.4 | 2.8 | 1.7 |
| 1.4 | 1.4 | 1.5 | Current | 1.2 | 1.3 | 1.6 | 2.1 | 1.7 | 1.4 |
| 1.0 | 1.0 | 1.1 | | .4 | .7 | 1.4 | 1.4 | 1.1 | 1.0 |
| .8 | .9 | .7 | | .7 | .6 | 1.1 | 1.3 | .7 | .6 |
| .4 | (118) .5 | .4 | Quick | .4 | .2 | .6 | .6 | .4 | .3 |
| .2 | .2 | .2 | | .1 | .1 | .2 | .3 | .3 | .2 |
| 4 85.4 | 4 86.5 | 5 67.9 | | 0 UND | 3 130.0 | 6 65.5 | 4 94.7 | 9 42.4 | 6 63.6 |
| 10 35.5 | 10 37.7 | 11 34.1 | Sales/Receivables | 8 47.0 | 7 53.6 | 15 24.6 | 12 30.4 | 15 23.8 | 11 34.3 |
| 20 17.9 | 20 17.8 | 21 17.3 | | 24 14.9 | 17 21.7 | 27 13.7 | 38 9.7 | 25 14.6 | 16 22.2 |
| 46 8.0 | 55 6.6 | 53 6.9 | | 19 19.5 | 46 8.0 | 65 5.6 | 25 14.4 | 66 5.5 | 69 5.3 |
| 76 4.8 | 81 4.5 | 85 4.3 | Cost of Sales/Inventory | 59 6.2 | 96 3.8 | 74 4.9 | 59 6.2 | 94 3.9 | 85 4.3 |
| 111 3.3 | 114 3.2 | 122 3.0 | | 192 1.9 | 192 1.9 | 114 3.2 | 107 3.4 | 107 3.4 | 101 3.6 |
| 16 23.5 | 13 28.3 | 17 21.6 | | 0 UND | 21 17.8 | 16 23.4 | 17 21.6 | 13 27.1 | 23 16.1 |
| 30 12.0 | 23 15.8 | 29 12.7 | Cost of Sales/Payables | 14 25.8 | 39 9.3 | 23 16.2 | 29 12.7 | 25 14.6 | 31 11.6 |
| 55 6.6 | 53 6.9 | 49 7.5 | | 70 5.2 | 54 6.8 | 58 6.3 | 47 7.8 | 33 10.9 | 45 8.1 |
| 7.4 | 6.7 | 6.2 | | 5.9 | 4.8 | 5.7 | 6.2 | 6.4 | 6.5 |
| 18.2 | 14.2 | 13.9 | Sales/Working Capital | 29.1 | 15.2 | 10.3 | 10.8 | 10.4 | 19.3 |
| 810.3 | 105.9 | 63.6 | | -9.3 | -16.7 | 15.4 | 26.2 | 36.8 | NM |
| 8.9 | 9.2 | 9.3 | | 5.3 | 3.5 | 7.2 | 16.0 | 9.8 | 36.2 |
| (117) 2.5 | (100) 2.3 | (112) 2.8 | EBIT/Interest | (14) 2.1 | (22) 1.1 | (14) 1.7 | (17) 8.6 | (20) 3.3 | (25) 6.0 |
| .4 | .9 | -.4 | | -2.0 | -3.8 | .1 | .6 | 1.1 | -1.6 |
| 12.2 | 17.9 | 21.6 | Net Profit + Depr., Dep., | | | | | | |
| (25) 3.1 | (20) 2.7 | (16) 6.0 | Amort./Cur. Mat. L/T/D | | | | | | |
| 1.1 | .8 | .3 | | | | | | | |
| .2 | .2 | .1 | | .2 | .1 | .0 | .0 | .2 | .2 |
| .6 | .5 | .4 | Fixed/Worth | 3.9 | .4 | .1 | .2 | .4 | .6 |
| 5.0 | 1.6 | 2.1 | | -.6 | -.3 | .4 | .5 | 1.7 | 1.3 |
| 1.3 | 1.0 | 1.1 | | 2.8 | 1.4 | .8 | 1.1 | .6 | 1.2 |
| 3.0 | 2.5 | 2.8 | Debt/Worth | -63.1 | 15.1 | 2.0 | 2.3 | 2.1 | 2.5 |
| 48.3 | 7.6 | 17.8 | | -4.4 | -3.1 | 6.9 | 5.7 | 11.7 | 3.8 |
| 37.2 | 27.1 | 28.6 | % Profit Before Taxes/Tangible | | 24.5 | 20.4 | 52.9 | 24.8 | 33.9 |
| (101) 13.5 | (101) 9.7 | (104) 11.1 | Net Worth | (13) 8.0 | (16) 9.6 | (18) 17.5 | (23) 12.2 | | (26) 18.4 |
| 1.8 | 1.8 | -2.4 | | -34.0 | -3.8 | 1.6 | 5.4 | | -11.3 |
| 10.5 | 8.1 | 9.0 | % Profit Before Taxes/Total | 17.2 | 9.0 | 8.0 | 12.5 | 7.5 | 12.3 |
| 2.6 | 2.6 | 3.0 | Assets | 2.1 | .2 | 2.3 | 3.4 | 3.1 | 5.1 |
| -1.1 | -.6 | -2.6 | | -8.5 | -11.0 | -1.2 | .1 | 1.2 | -4.8 |
| 73.9 | 62.4 | 92.5 | | 176.8 | 172.4 | 999.8 | 434.1 | 41.6 | 43.9 |
| 27.1 | 28.3 | 32.4 | Sales/Net Fixed Assets | 16.6 | 58.0 | 72.1 | 39.7 | 31.0 | 17.6 |
| 11.8 | 12.9 | 13.8 | | 5.7 | 24.7 | 27.8 | 15.0 | 19.6 | 8.1 |
| 4.3 | 4.3 | 4.1 | | 3.7 | 4.9 | 4.0 | 5.2 | 3.8 | 3.7 |
| 3.1 | 3.1 | 3.2 | Sales/Total Assets | 2.7 | 3.8 | 3.3 | 3.2 | 3.2 | 2.7 |
| 2.3 | 2.2 | 2.1 | | 1.3 | 2.0 | 2.8 | 1.9 | 2.4 | 2.2 |
| .4 | .3 | .3 | | .4 | .2 | .2 | .3 | .3 | .6 |
| (102) .8 | (99) .7 | (98) .7 | % Depr., Dep., Amort./Sales | (11) 1.4 | (13) .5 | (11) .4 | (12) .6 | .7 | (27) 1.1 |
| 1.3 | 1.2 | 1.3 | | 5.5 | 1.3 | .7 | 1.9 | 1.1 | 1.5 |
| 1.4 | 1.6 | 1.7 | | 4.0 | 2.4 | 1.7 | 1.3 | 1.3 | |
| (61) 2.8 | (49) 2.6 | (64) 3.0 | % Officers', Directors' Owners' Comp/Sales | (10) 7.4 | (13) 3.5 | (13) 3.1 | (13) 1.9 | (11) 2.4 | |
| 4.9 | 4.3 | 4.3 | | 20.1 | 7.0 | 4.2 | 3.1 | 2.7 | |
| 2669531M | 3341086M | 3085870M | Net Sales ($) | 9191M | 48470M | 74893M | 134629M | 399681M | 2419006M |
| 939433M | 1249544M | 1232219M | Total Assets ($) | 6028M | 18660M | 24997M | 47881M | 151519M | 983134M |

M = $ thousand    MM = $ million
See Pages 9 through 22 for Explanation of Ratios and Data

**Current Data Sorted by Assets**      **Comparative Historical Data**

| 0-500M | 500M-2MM | 2-10MM | 10-50MM | 50-100MM | 100-250MM | Type of Statement | 4/1/07-3/31/08 ALL | 4/1/08-3/31/09 ALL |
|---|---|---|---|---|---|---|---|---|
| | | 4 | 5 | 3 | 1 | Unqualified | 20 | 13 |
| 1 | | 10 | 5 | | | Reviewed | 20 | 29 |
| | 6 | 6 | 1 | | | Compiled | 18 | 21 |
| 14 | 27 | 6 | 1 | | 1 | Tax Returns | 30 | 33 |
| 9 | 19 | 23 | 13 | 3 | 3 | Other | 53 | 59 |
| | 28 (4/1-9/30/11) | | | 133 (10/1/11-3/31/12) | | | | |
| 23 | 53 | 49 | 25 | 6 | 5 | NUMBER OF STATEMENTS | 141 | 155 |
| % | % | % | % | % | % | **ASSETS** | % | % |
| 16.9 | 13.0 | 12.2 | 13.4 | | | Cash & Equivalents | 12.4 | 12.2 |
| 16.7 | 23.4 | 26.6 | 29.0 | | | Trade Receivables (net) | 23.9 | 20.7 |
| 27.9 | 37.0 | 30.3 | 26.5 | | | Inventory | 36.6 | 37.3 |
| 3.2 | 1.9 | 4.2 | 5.4 | | | All Other Current | 3.7 | 3.9 |
| 64.7 | 75.2 | 73.4 | 74.4 | | | Total Current | 76.6 | 74.1 |
| 21.4 | 11.7 | 14.6 | 13.8 | | | Fixed Assets (net) | 14.8 | 15.4 |
| 5.0 | 4.6 | 4.9 | 7.2 | | | Intangibles (net) | 3.4 | 3.5 |
| 8.8 | 8.4 | 7.1 | 4.7 | | | All Other Non-Current | 5.3 | 6.9 |
| 100.0 | 100.0 | 100.0 | 100.0 | | | Total | 100.0 | 100.0 |
| | | | | | | **LIABILITIES** | | |
| 44.1 | 9.5 | 9.0 | 5.3 | | | Notes Payable-Short Term | 14.2 | 11.9 |
| 7.1 | 1.7 | 1.4 | 2.3 | | | Cur. Mat.-L.T.D. | 1.4 | 2.4 |
| 22.7 | 28.2 | 29.5 | 30.5 | | | Trade Payables | 25.1 | 27.6 |
| .0 | .0 | .2 | .2 | | | Income Taxes Payable | .1 | .1 |
| 15.8 | 15.6 | 8.8 | 11.7 | | | All Other Current | 14.9 | 14.2 |
| 89.7 | 55.0 | 48.8 | 49.9 | | | Total Current | 55.7 | 56.1 |
| 17.3 | 10.2 | 5.9 | 8.5 | | | Long-Term Debt | 9.7 | 9.4 |
| .0 | .0 | .1 | .5 | | | Deferred Taxes | .1 | .1 |
| 5.9 | 9.4 | 3.9 | 3.3 | | | All Other Non-Current | 7.9 | 7.7 |
| -12.9 | 25.3 | 41.3 | 37.8 | | | Net Worth | 26.6 | 26.6 |
| 100.0 | 100.0 | 100.0 | 100.0 | | | Total Liabilties & Net Worth | 100.0 | 100.0 |
| | | | | | | **INCOME DATA** | | |
| 100.0 | 100.0 | 100.0 | 100.0 | | | Net Sales | 100.0 | 100.0 |
| 39.9 | 36.6 | 32.0 | 37.6 | | | Gross Profit | 34.9 | 36.3 |
| 37.5 | 34.5 | 28.3 | 31.2 | | | Operating Expenses | 32.5 | 33.7 |
| 2.5 | 2.0 | 3.7 | 6.4 | | | Operating Profit | 2.3 | 2.7 |
| .4 | .0 | .1 | .8 | | | All Other Expenses (net) | .6 | .6 |
| 2.0 | 2.0 | 3.6 | 5.6 | | | Profit Before Taxes | 1.8 | 2.1 |
| | | | | | | **RATIOS** | | |
| 1.4 | 2.0 | 2.7 | 2.1 | | | | 2.4 | 1.9 |
| 1.0 | 1.4 | 1.4 | 1.5 | | | Current | 1.4 | 1.4 |
| .6 | 1.1 | 1.1 | 1.1 | | | | 1.0 | 1.0 |
| .8 | 1.1 | 1.4 | 1.6 | | | | 1.3 | 1.0 |
| .5 | .8 | (48) .8 | .7 | | | Quick | .7 | .6 |
| .2 | .4 | .4 | .6 | | | | .3 | .3 |
| 0 UND | 2 148.7 | 10 36.7 | 19 19.1 | | | | 6 57.9 | 6 59.0 |
| 8 45.1 | 23 16.2 | 30 12.2 | 28 13.0 | | | Sales/Receivables | 22 16.9 | 16 22.2 |
| 27 13.4 | 51 7.1 | 44 8.3 | 48 7.6 | | | | 40 9.1 | 34 10.6 |
| 0 UND | 34 10.8 | 22 16.7 | 27 13.6 | | | | 27 13.8 | 26 13.9 |
| 26 14.0 | 51 7.1 | 38 9.5 | 38 9.7 | | | Cost of Sales/Inventory | 48 7.6 | 61 6.0 |
| 72 5.1 | 118 3.1 | 81 4.5 | 54 6.8 | | | | 94 3.9 | 93 3.9 |
| 0 UND | 21 17.4 | 26 14.3 | 30 12.0 | | | | 17 21.4 | 20 18.6 |
| 14 25.9 | 45 8.1 | 38 9.7 | 46 8.0 | | | Cost of Sales/Payables | 32 11.5 | 37 9.9 |
| 49 7.4 | 81 4.5 | 60 6.1 | 78 4.7 | | | | 61 6.0 | 61 6.0 |
| 23.3 | 7.2 | 6.7 | 8.4 | | | | 7.0 | 8.8 |
| -235.8 | 15.1 | 17.0 | 14.0 | | | Sales/Working Capital | 20.1 | 20.0 |
| -13.3 | 61.2 | 48.6 | 75.8 | | | | 204.6 | -284.6 |
| 5.6 | 7.5 | 52.9 | 285.5 | | | | 10.3 | 10.8 |
| (14) -.1 | (38) 3.7 | (41) 8.9 | (22) 11.6 | | | EBIT/Interest | (109) 3.5 | (123) 3.7 |
| -4.7 | 1.5 | 2.7 | 8.3 | | | | 1.4 | .9 |
| | | | | | | | 12.9 | 10.2 |
| | | | | | | Net Profit + Depr., Dep., Amort./Cur. Mat. L/T/D | (19) 7.6 | (27) 2.4 |
| | | | | | | | 1.8 | 1.0 |
| .3 | .0 | .1 | .2 | | | | .2 | .1 |
| 1.5 | .5 | .3 | .4 | | | Fixed/Worth | .5 | .5 |
| -.4 | 1.8 | .9 | 2.7 | | | | 2.1 | 2.0 |
| 1.7 | 1.2 | .7 | .8 | | | | 1.0 | 1.2 |
| 24.7 | 3.6 | 2.0 | 2.3 | | | Debt/Worth | 2.7 | 3.5 |
| -5.6 | NM | 4.4 | 20.1 | | | | 13.9 | 10.8 |
| 140.5 | 52.9 | 52.8 | 111.9 | | | | 57.8 | 70.0 |
| (15) 75.0 | (40) 22.9 | (44) 27.3 | (22) 41.6 | | | % Profit Before Taxes/Tangible Net Worth | (111) 26.7 | (124) 21.5 |
| -115.9 | 5.0 | 8.6 | 16.9 | | | | 6.1 | 3.5 |
| 25.0 | 14.6 | 18.4 | 26.4 | | | | 16.1 | 17.6 |
| 2.8 | 4.9 | 7.4 | 16.0 | | | % Profit Before Taxes/Total Assets | 5.7 | 5.6 |
| -15.6 | 1.2 | 2.7 | 6.9 | | | | .5 | -.6 |
| 188.5 | 453.0 | 77.2 | 54.3 | | | | 89.9 | 97.5 |
| 53.6 | 30.6 | 40.9 | 27.3 | | | Sales/Net Fixed Assets | 34.1 | 37.3 |
| 16.1 | 16.3 | 15.8 | 13.7 | | | | 17.3 | 16.9 |
| 9.2 | 4.1 | 4.6 | 4.4 | | | | 4.9 | 5.0 |
| 5.7 | 3.2 | 3.3 | 3.6 | | | Sales/Total Assets | 3.4 | 3.5 |
| 3.7 | 2.2 | 2.4 | 2.5 | | | | 2.6 | 2.6 |
| .2 | .4 | .2 | .4 | | | | .4 | .4 |
| (16) .5 | (28) .8 | (39) .5 | (23) .9 | | | % Depr., Dep., Amort./Sales | (116) .6 | (116) .7 |
| .7 | 1.6 | 1.4 | 2.3 | | | | 1.4 | 1.3 |
| 1.9 | 1.8 | .8 | | | | | 1.5 | 1.1 |
| (13) 3.4 | (35) 4.1 | (15) 1.3 | | | | % Officers', Directors' Owners' Comp/Sales | (60) 3.8 | (64) 2.6 |
| 6.1 | 7.7 | 2.3 | | | | | 6.7 | 5.4 |
| 30582M | 225406M | 821896M | 2039172M | 1677670M | 3955470M | Net Sales ($) | 6068803M | 7083331M |
| 5162M | 66481M | 225473M | 562362M | 483083M | 899579M | Total Assets ($) | 1752022M | 1918894M |

© RMA 2012

M = $ thousand     MM = $ million
See Pages 9 through 22 for Explanation of Ratios and Data

## Comparative Historical Data | | | | Current Data Sorted by Sales

| Hist. '09-10 | Hist. '10-11 | Hist. '11-12 | Type of Statement | 0-1MM | 1-3MM | 3-5MM | 5-10MM | 10-25MM | 25MM & OVER |
|---|---|---|---|---|---|---|---|---|---|
| 15 | 14 | 13 | Unqualified | | | | | 5 | 8 |
| 20 | 16 | 16 | Reviewed | | | 2 | 2 | 5 | 7 |
| 25 | 15 | 13 | Compiled | | 2 | 2 | 5 | 2 | 2 |
| 39 | 53 | 49 | Tax Returns | 5 | 17 | 10 | 10 | 5 | 2 |
| 59 | 61 | 70 | Other | 6 | 9 | 9 | 12 | 10 | 24 |
| 4/1/09-3/31/10 ALL | 4/1/10-3/31/11 ALL | 4/1/11-3/31/12 ALL | | 28 (4/1-9/30/11) | | 133 (10/1/11-3/31/12) | | | |
| 158 | 159 | 161 | **NUMBER OF STATEMENTS** | 11 | 28 | 23 | 29 | 27 | 43 |
| % | % | % | **ASSETS** | % | % | % | % | % | % |
| 13.7 | 14.1 | 12.9 | Cash & Equivalents | 13.1 | 11.7 | 17.8 | 14.7 | 10.0 | 11.8 |
| 21.0 | 20.8 | 24.3 | Trade Receivables (net) | 22.1 | 19.6 | 21.5 | 26.5 | 24.9 | 27.5 |
| 36.3 | 34.2 | 32.3 | Inventory | 16.0 | 35.4 | 32.5 | 32.5 | 35.4 | 32.2 |
| 2.9 | 4.4 | 3.5 | All Other Current | 3.5 | 2.0 | 2.3 | 2.8 | 5.8 | 4.1 |
| 73.9 | 73.4 | 73.0 | Total Current | 54.7 | 68.7 | 74.1 | 76.4 | 76.1 | 75.6 |
| 16.8 | 14.7 | 14.6 | Fixed Assets (net) | 19.1 | 19.5 | 12.3 | 12.3 | 12.6 | 14.4 |
| 3.2 | 5.2 | 5.3 | Intangibles (net) | 13.5 | 3.1 | 1.7 | 7.0 | 7.5 | 3.9 |
| 6.1 | 6.8 | 7.1 | All Other Non-Current | 12.5 | 8.7 | 11.9 | 4.3 | 3.8 | 6.1 |
| 100.0 | 100.0 | 100.0 | Total | 100.0 | 100.0 | 100.0 | 100.0 | 100.0 | 100.0 |
| | | | **LIABILITIES** | | | | | | |
| 13.7 | 8.3 | 13.9 | Notes Payable-Short Term | 13.1 | 36.0 | 15.4 | 7.9 | 7.0 | 7.4 |
| 3.1 | 1.5 | 2.4 | Cur. Mat.-L.T.D. | 4.1 | 4.9 | 1.5 | 1.6 | 2.1 | 1.6 |
| 24.9 | 25.7 | 28.3 | Trade Payables | 16.5 | 24.2 | 24.3 | 33.6 | 29.7 | 31.7 |
| .3 | .2 | .1 | Income Taxes Payable | .0 | .0 | .0 | .0 | .2 | .2 |
| 15.1 | 11.5 | 12.8 | All Other Current | 15.3 | 13.0 | 15.7 | 16.0 | 8.9 | 10.7 |
| 57.2 | 47.1 | 57.5 | Total Current | 49.1 | 78.1 | 56.9 | 59.2 | 47.9 | 51.6 |
| 15.9 | 10.7 | 9.4 | Long-Term Debt | 29.7 | 8.1 | 11.6 | 8.3 | 3.9 | 7.9 |
| .1 | .1 | .1 | Deferred Taxes | .0 | .0 | .1 | .5 | .0 | .0 |
| 6.2 | 5.6 | 5.7 | All Other Non-Current | 15.1 | 6.7 | 6.2 | 5.2 | 5.9 | 2.8 |
| 20.7 | 36.5 | 27.3 | Net Worth | 6.2 | 7.2 | 25.2 | 26.8 | 42.3 | 37.7 |
| 100.0 | 100.0 | 100.0 | Total Liabilities & Net Worth | 100.0 | 100.0 | 100.0 | 100.0 | 100.0 | 100.0 |
| | | | **INCOME DATA** | | | | | | |
| 100.0 | 100.0 | 100.0 | Net Sales | 100.0 | 100.0 | 100.0 | 100.0 | 100.0 | 100.0 |
| 35.7 | 36.1 | 35.0 | Gross Profit | 44.5 | 37.7 | 39.3 | 34.1 | 31.6 | 31.1 |
| 32.5 | 31.6 | 31.7 | Operating Expenses | 39.3 | 38.1 | 37.1 | 30.6 | 26.4 | 26.8 |
| 3.3 | 4.5 | 3.3 | Operating Profit | 5.3 | -.4 | 2.2 | 3.6 | 5.2 | 4.3 |
| .2 | .2 | .3 | All Other Expenses (net) | .2 | -.3 | .7 | .5 | .1 | .4 |
| 3.1 | 4.3 | 3.0 | Profit Before Taxes | 5.0 | -.1 | 1.5 | 3.1 | 5.1 | 3.9 |
| | | | **RATIOS** | | | | | | |
| 2.3 | 2.7 | 2.1 | Current | 2.5 | 1.9 | 2.0 | 2.0 | 2.9 | 2.4 |
| 1.4 | 1.6 | 1.3 | | 1.4 | 1.2 | 1.2 | 1.3 | 1.4 | 1.5 |
| 1.0 | 1.1 | 1.0 | | .7 | .6 | .9 | .9 | 1.2 | 1.2 |
| 1.1 | 1.2 | 1.1 | Quick | 1.7 | 1.0 | 1.1 | 1.2 | 1.1 | 1.5 |
| .6 | .7 (160) | .7 | | .5 | .6 | .8 | .6 (26) | .8 | .7 |
| .2 | .4 | .4 | | .4 | .1 | .3 | .5 | .4 | .4 |
| 5  72.3 | 3  107.2 | 5  75.6 | Sales/Receivables | 0  UND | 1  251.8 | 5  66.7 | 8  44.1 | 5  77.8 | 6  60.9 |
| 20  18.2 | 16  22.1 | 24  15.5 | | 21  17.4 | 20  18.1 | 25  14.6 | 25  14.6 | 28  12.9 | 24  15.5 |
| 37  9.8 | 37  10.0 | 44  8.3 | | 49  7.5 | 51  7.1 | 55  6.6 | 41  8.9 | 43  8.4 | 38  9.6 |
| 25  14.4 | 22  16.6 | 23  15.6 | Cost of Sales/Inventory | 0  UND | 20  18.0 | 30  12.1 | 22  16.9 | 29  12.8 | 25  14.7 |
| 56  6.5 | 44  8.3 | 44  8.3 | | 21  17.4 | 59  6.2 | 7  7.3 | 44  8.3 | 45  8.2 | 36  10.2 |
| 98  3.7 | 90  4.0 | 78  4.7 | | 111  3.3 | 152  2.4 | 111  3.3 | 61  6.0 | 87  4.2 | 60  6.1 |
| 19  18.8 | 15  24.3 | 19  19.3 | Cost of Sales/Payables | 4  87.2 | 3  143.1 | 17  22.0 | 29  12.7 | 27  13.7 | 19  18.9 |
| 34  10.8 | 33  10.9 | 38  9.7 | | 21  17.4 | 39  9.4 | 42  8.6 | 41  8.9 | 38  9.7 | 34  10.6 |
| 57  6.4 | 56  6.5 | 69  5.3 | | 76  4.8 | 74  4.9 | 69  5.3 | 87  4.2 | 78  4.7 | 68  5.4 |
| 7.2 | 6.1 | 8.3 | Sales/Working Capital | 3.9 | 8.0 | 7.7 | 9.8 | 6.4 | 9.6 |
| 17.7 | 15.1 | 17.7 | | 36.1 | 27.1 | 16.2 | 26.1 | 17.2 | 16.5 |
| -158.6 | 68.5 | NM | | -24.3 | -17.6 | -76.9 | -65.2 | 37.3 | 52.1 |
| 14.6 | 18.2 | 26.5 | EBIT/Interest | | 4.9 | 4.7 | 14.3 | 90.8 | 56.7 |
| (129) 4.8 | (121) 6.0 | (126) 5.5 | | | (21) 1.1 | (16) 1.9 | (24) 6.7 | (22) 27.9 | (39) 10.5 |
| 1.2 | 1.3 | 1.7 | | | -5.5 | -.3 | 3.4 | 4.8 | 2.9 |
| 9.7 | 12.5 | 5.4 | Net Profit + Depr., Dep., Amort./Cur. Mat. L/T/D | | | | | | |
| (23) 2.4 | (18) 2.4 | (18) 3.2 | | | | | | | |
| 1.0 | .7 | 1.0 | | | | | | | |
| .1 | .1 | .1 | Fixed/Worth | .4 | .2 | .1 | .1 | .1 | .1 |
| .5 | .3 | .4 | | 1.2 | .8 | .4 | .5 | .3 | .3 |
| 2.5 | 1.1 | 1.6 | | -.2 | UND | 2.1 | NM | 1.0 | 1.0 |
| 1.1 | .8 | 1.0 | Debt/Worth | 1.0 | 1.1 | 1.3 | 1.3 | .8 | .8 |
| 2.7 | 1.8 | 2.9 | | 3.1 | 6.7 | 3.6 | 3.4 | 1.7 | 2.3 |
| 27.9 | 7.7 | 12.9 | | -1.8 | -41.2 | 13.2 | NM | 4.5 | 4.9 |
| 94.4 | 73.8 | 66.7 | % Profit Before Taxes/Tangible Net Worth | | 74.6 | 52.4 | 48.6 | 83.3 | 85.5 |
| (127) 27.8 | (136) 31.5 | (131) 29.2 | | | (20) 3.3 | (18) 16.5 | (22) 27.5 | (24) 36.7 | (39) 36.5 |
| 4.5 | 3.8 | 6.5 | | | -96.0 | 4.6 | 13.1 | 10.9 | 14.4 |
| 19.6 | 22.8 | 19.1 | % Profit Before Taxes/Total Assets | 21.0 | 7.2 | 11.1 | 17.4 | 28.8 | 22.5 |
| 8.0 | 10.3 | 7.5 | | 10.4 | .5 | 4.8 | 9.1 | 16.2 | 13.6 |
| .6 | 1.0 | 1.7 | | 2.2 | -15.3 | .3 | 2.5 | 4.0 | 3.9 |
| 89.7 | 139.2 | 120.5 | Sales/Net Fixed Assets | 188.5 | 119.6 | 241.2 | 275.6 | 97.0 | 76.8 |
| 27.2 | 40.9 | 40.4 | | 15.2 | 28.6 | 34.8 | 32.5 | 50.0 | 43.0 |
| 13.2 | 14.0 | 15.6 | | 7.3 | 15.7 | 17.1 | 16.6 | 15.4 | 17.0 |
| 4.5 | 5.2 | 4.6 | Sales/Total Assets | 6.3 | 5.6 | 3.8 | 4.5 | 4.9 | 4.8 |
| 3.3 | 3.5 | 3.5 | | 3.9 | 3.1 | 2.9 | 3.6 | 3.3 | 3.8 |
| 2.4 | 2.4 | 2.5 | | 1.6 | 2.1 | 2.1 | 2.8 | 2.4 | 3.0 |
| .4 | .3 | .3 | % Depr., Dep., Amort./Sales | | .4 | .6 | .2 | .2 | .4 |
| (117) .8 | (102) .7 | (113) .7 | | | (20) .6 | (10) 1.0 | (20) .7 | (20) .5 | (36) .7 |
| 1.4 | 1.5 | 1.4 | | | 1.3 | 2.5 | 1.9 | 1.0 | 1.1 |
| 1.4 | 1.4 | 1.3 | % Officers', Directors', Owners' Comp/Sales | | 2.8 | 1.5 | 1.3 | | .6 |
| (64) 3.0 | (74) 3.6 | (73) 3.3 | | | (13) 5.3 | (15) 4.1 | (19) 2.2 | | (12) 1.6 |
| 6.5 | 6.5 | 5.9 | | | 7.0 | 9.0 | 5.4 | | 15.5 |
| 7755080M | 9456672M | 8750196M | Net Sales ($) | 6204M | 50994M | 89437M | 207795M | 445262M | 7950504M |
| 2214872M | 2648757M | 2242140M | Total Assets ($) | 3674M | 20367M | 33597M | 66246M | 145580M | 1972676M |

M = $ thousand    MM = $ million
See Pages 9 through 22 for Explanation of Ratios and Data

## Current Data Sorted by Assets       Comparative Historical Data

| 0-500M | 500M-2MM | 2-10MM | 10-50MM | 50-100MM | 100-250MM | Type of Statement | 4/1/07-3/31/08 ALL | 4/1/08-3/31/09 ALL |
|---|---|---|---|---|---|---|---|---|
| | | 2 | 4 | 3 | 1 | Unqualified | 10 | 8 |
| | | 2 | 10 | 3 | | Reviewed | 8 | 12 |
| | 2 | 3 | 6 | 1 | | Compiled | 5 | 14 |
| 13 | 14 | 7 | | | | Tax Returns | 24 | 35 |
| 9 | 20 | 17 | 11 | 3 | 1 | Other | 43 | 48 |
| | 17 (4/1-9/30/11) | | 115 (10/1/11-3/31/12) | | | | | |
| 24 | 41 | 44 | 18 | 3 | 2 | **NUMBER OF STATEMENTS** | 90 | 117 |
| % | % | % | % | % | % | **ASSETS** | % | % |
| 23.7 | 18.1 | 16.9 | 8.1 | | | Cash & Equivalents | 14.0 | 13.8 |
| 22.0 | 31.8 | 42.7 | 34.6 | | | Trade Receivables (net) | 36.0 | 35.8 |
| 16.1 | 23.6 | 18.4 | 19.6 | | | Inventory | 18.2 | 18.0 |
| 2.8 | 1.8 | 1.7 | 2.7 | | | All Other Current | 3.4 | 2.6 |
| 64.6 | 75.2 | 79.7 | 65.0 | | | Total Current | 71.6 | 70.2 |
| 24.4 | 13.5 | 10.1 | 15.1 | | | Fixed Assets (net) | 13.6 | 17.0 |
| 4.0 | 1.4 | 2.5 | 9.0 | | | Intangibles (net) | 8.5 | 6.2 |
| 7.1 | 9.9 | 7.7 | 10.9 | | | All Other Non-Current | 6.3 | 6.6 |
| 100.0 | 100.0 | 100.0 | 100.0 | | | Total | 100.0 | 100.0 |
| | | | | | | **LIABILITIES** | | |
| 17.5 | 12.2 | 5.3 | 15.8 | | | Notes Payable-Short Term | 13.0 | 13.8 |
| 2.7 | 1.4 | 1.2 | .5 | | | Cur. Mat.-L.T.D. | 3.6 | 2.9 |
| 22.7 | 27.8 | 35.1 | 25.4 | | | Trade Payables | 27.0 | 27.3 |
| .1 | .0 | .2 | .1 | | | Income Taxes Payable | .2 | .9 |
| 28.9 | 10.6 | 9.9 | 13.0 | | | All Other Current | 19.0 | 13.8 |
| 71.9 | 52.0 | 51.6 | 54.7 | | | Total Current | 62.8 | 58.7 |
| 14.0 | 11.6 | 5.6 | 5.9 | | | Long-Term Debt | 11.3 | 10.3 |
| .0 | .1 | .7 | .1 | | | Deferred Taxes | .3 | .4 |
| 10.3 | 7.8 | 11.1 | 6.6 | | | All Other Non-Current | 4.2 | 7.1 |
| 3.8 | 28.5 | 31.0 | 32.6 | | | Net Worth | 21.5 | 23.6 |
| 100.0 | 100.0 | 100.0 | 100.0 | | | Total Liabilties & Net Worth | 100.0 | 100.0 |
| | | | | | | **INCOME DATA** | | |
| 100.0 | 100.0 | 100.0 | 100.0 | | | Net Sales | 100.0 | 100.0 |
| 53.5 | 36.0 | 30.6 | 29.2 | | | Gross Profit | 39.2 | 38.4 |
| 51.1 | 31.2 | 25.8 | 25.0 | | | Operating Expenses | 35.6 | 35.6 |
| 2.4 | 4.7 | 4.8 | 4.2 | | | Operating Profit | 3.7 | 2.8 |
| .4 | .6 | .1 | .4 | | | All Other Expenses (net) | .8 | 1.2 |
| 2.0 | 4.1 | 4.7 | 3.8 | | | Profit Before Taxes | 2.9 | 1.6 |
| | | | | | | **RATIOS** | | |
| 2.6 | 3.0 | 2.5 | 1.8 | | | | 2.0 | 2.0 |
| 1.0 | 1.6 | 1.7 | 1.1 | | | Current | 1.2 | 1.3 |
| .7 | 1.0 | 1.1 | .9 | | | | .9 | .9 |
| 1.7 | 1.7 | 1.9 | 1.1 | | | | 1.3 | 1.3 |
| .7 | 1.0 | 1.2 | .8 | | | Quick | .9 | .8 |
| .4 | .6 | .7 | .6 | | | | .6 | .6 |
| 0 UND | 8 46.5 | 17 21.1 | 29 12.4 | | | | 19 19.3 | 12 31.0 |
| 10 36.8 | 26 14.3 | 39 9.4 | 39 9.4 | | | Sales/Receivables | 37 9.8 | 27 13.3 |
| 22 16.9 | 41 8.8 | 61 6.0 | 61 6.0 | | | | 58 6.3 | 48 7.7 |
| 0 UND | 2 188.9 | 0 UND | 20 UND | | | | 0 964.7 | 1 585.8 |
| 10 36.9 | 18 20.0 | 10 35.0 | 20 18.1 | | | Cost of Sales/Inventory | 18 20.7 | 15 24.1 |
| 26 14.2 | 68 5.4 | 24 15.3 | 39 9.3 | | | | 47 7.8 | 44 8.2 |
| 0 UND | 9 42.1 | 20 18.3 | 25 14.6 | | | | 21 17.5 | 15 25.0 |
| 26 14.0 | 30 12.3 | 36 10.2 | 37 9.9 | | | Cost of Sales/Payables | 37 10.0 | 32 11.4 |
| 35 10.4 | 45 8.1 | 56 6.5 | 50 7.3 | | | | 57 6.4 | 55 6.6 |
| 13.8 | 7.1 | 7.5 | 13.2 | | | | 8.8 | 12.0 |
| UND | 14.9 | 14.6 | 54.1 | | | Sales/Working Capital | 24.5 | 32.0 |
| -33.3 | 139.7 | 50.7 | -41.6 | | | | -55.1 | -62.2 |
| 22.2 | 28.2 | 67.7 | 27.1 | | | | 10.1 | 13.1 |
| (17) 4.5 | (34) 9.8 | (38) 16.3 | (16) 5.4 | | | EBIT/Interest | (75) 3.6 | (99) 4.2 |
| .1 | 2.2 | 6.3 | 2.1 | | | | 1.8 | .8 |
| | | | | | | Net Profit + Depr., Dep., | 3.1 | 3.7 |
| | | | | | | Amort./Cur. Mat. L/T/D | (12) 1.6 | (11) 1.8 |
| | | | | | | | .8 | .4 |
| .0 | .0 | .0 | .1 | | | | .2 | .1 |
| .8 | .3 | .2 | .5 | | | Fixed/Worth | .5 | .4 |
| -.7 | 1.0 | .7 | 3.2 | | | | 3.1 | 2.3 |
| .4 | .8 | .9 | 1.0 | | | | 1.3 | 1.4 |
| 1.4 | 3.3 | 2.1 | 4.5 | | | Debt/Worth | 4.1 | 3.4 |
| -4.1 | 10.5 | 8.3 | 17.8 | | | | NM | 14.9 |
| 100.0 | 101.9 | 78.1 | 47.2 | | | % Profit Before Taxes/Tangible | 81.8 | 74.8 |
| (15) 41.3 | (34) 32.0 | (40) 35.2 | (15) 30.4 | | | Net Worth | (68) 34.4 | (93) 27.8 |
| 12.2 | 13.3 | 9.5 | 12.9 | | | | 13.6 | 2.2 |
| 42.9 | 30.0 | 17.7 | 9.5 | | | % Profit Before Taxes/Total | 18.0 | 14.9 |
| 8.1 | 15.6 | 11.6 | 6.3 | | | Assets | 7.9 | 6.2 |
| 5.7 | 3.6 | 4.4 | 2.3 | | | | 1.9 | -1.2 |
| 483.9 | 684.5 | 376.6 | 84.3 | | | | 106.0 | 174.8 |
| 50.7 | 103.1 | 85.2 | 44.6 | | | Sales/Net Fixed Assets | 39.8 | 47.1 |
| 17.1 | 22.0 | 23.0 | 16.0 | | | | 16.5 | 16.8 |
| 7.9 | 6.7 | 5.9 | 4.7 | | | | 5.1 | 6.0 |
| 5.1 | 4.4 | 3.8 | 3.4 | | | Sales/Total Assets | 3.6 | 4.1 |
| 4.2 | 2.7 | 2.4 | 1.9 | | | | 2.0 | 2.8 |
| .3 | .2 | .1 | .2 | | | | .4 | .3 |
| (10) .9 | (24) .4 | (32) .4 | (17) .4 | | | % Depr., Dep., Amort./Sales | (61) .7 | (84) .7 |
| 2.0 | 1.3 | .9 | .7 | | | | 1.8 | 1.5 |
| 4.5 | 1.4 | .9 | | | | | 1.6 | 2.8 |
| (16) 8.8 | (22) 3.9 | (15) 1.4 | | | | % Officers', Directors', Owners' Comp/Sales | (39) 4.0 | (49) 4.2 |
| 19.7 | 6.4 | 8.9 | | | | | 9.2 | 7.0 |
| 34779M | 265681M | 934272M | 1207203M | 453231M | 1729880M | Net Sales ($) | 2568355M | 3206435M |
| 5923M | 51580M | 210108M | 365364M | 222290M | 390774M | Total Assets ($) | 1153130M | 1037608M |

M = $ thousand     MM = $ million
See Pages 9 through 22 for Explanation of Ratios and Data

## Comparative Historical Data | Current Data Sorted by Sales

| | Comparative Historical Data | | Type of Statement | Current Data Sorted by Sales | | | | | |
|---|---|---|---|---|---|---|---|---|---|
| | | | | 0-1MM | 1-3MM | 3-5MM | 5-10MM | 10-25MM | 25MM & OVER |
| 11 | 11 | 10 | Unqualified | | | 1 | 2 | 2 | 5 |
| 14 | 14 | 15 | Reviewed | | | 1 | 3 | 5 | 6 |
| 11 | 14 | 12 | Compiled | | 2 | 1 | 4 | 2 | 3 |
| 36 | 31 | 34 | Tax Returns | 5 | 11 | 5 | 4 | 8 | 1 |
| 52 | 48 | 61 | Other | 3 | 11 | 7 | 12 | 13 | 15 |
| 4/1/09-3/31/10 ALL | 4/1/10-3/31/11 ALL | 4/1/11-3/31/12 ALL | | | 17 (4/1-9/30/11) | | 115 (10/1/11-3/31/12) | | |
| 124 | 118 | 132 | **NUMBER OF STATEMENTS** | 8 | 24 | 15 | 25 | 30 | 30 |
| % | % | % | **ASSETS** | % | % | % | % | % | % |
| 15.8 | 16.4 | 17.0 | Cash & Equivalents | | 19.5 | 20.5 | 14.7 | 19.3 | 12.2 |
| 35.5 | 32.9 | 34.4 | Trade Receivables (net) | | 16.0 | 31.1 | 37.3 | 47.9 | 36.9 |
| 20.3 | 19.7 | 19.8 | Inventory | | 20.3 | 21.6 | 18.6 | 16.0 | 24.9 |
| 2.8 | 3.1 | 2.1 | All Other Current | | 2.1 | 1.4 | 1.1 | 2.7 | 2.5 |
| 74.4 | 72.0 | 73.2 | Total Current | | 57.8 | 74.5 | 71.7 | 85.8 | 76.5 |
| 12.5 | 12.9 | 14.3 | Fixed Assets (net) | | 30.3 | 12.0 | 13.4 | 7.4 | 8.1 |
| 5.6 | 6.8 | 3.9 | Intangibles (net) | | 1.2 | .1 | 2.6 | 4.4 | 5.7 |
| 7.5 | 8.3 | 8.6 | All Other Non-Current | | 10.7 | 13.4 | 12.2 | 2.4 | 9.8 |
| 100.0 | 100.0 | 100.0 | Total | | 100.0 | 100.0 | 100.0 | 100.0 | 100.0 |
| | | | **LIABILITIES** | | | | | | |
| 9.7 | 16.3 | 11.1 | Notes Payable-Short Term | | 14.5 | 15.7 | 12.7 | 3.6 | 12.2 |
| 3.1 | 2.3 | 1.5 | Cur. Mat.-L.T.D. | | 2.1 | 2.4 | .7 | 1.2 | .7 |
| 28.3 | 24.5 | 28.9 | Trade Payables | | 14.0 | 26.3 | 28.8 | 40.1 | 33.6 |
| .5 | .2 | .1 | Income Taxes Payable | | .1 | .1 | .0 | .2 | .1 |
| 14.3 | 20.2 | 14.2 | All Other Current | | 26.9 | 14.8 | 9.9 | 10.7 | 11.5 |
| 55.8 | 63.4 | 55.8 | Total Current | | 57.5 | 59.3 | 52.1 | 55.7 | 58.1 |
| 10.9 | 11.6 | 9.0 | Long-Term Debt | | 16.0 | 11.6 | 5.5 | 6.3 | 3.0 |
| .1 | .2 | .3 | Deferred Taxes | | .1 | .0 | .3 | .7 | .1 |
| 7.4 | 6.1 | 9.1 | All Other Non-Current | | 12.1 | 7.6 | 11.8 | 9.8 | 6.0 |
| 25.8 | 18.7 | 25.9 | Net Worth | | 14.3 | 21.4 | 30.3 | 27.5 | 32.8 |
| 100.0 | 100.0 | 100.0 | Total Liabilties & Net Worth | | 100.0 | 100.0 | 100.0 | 100.0 | 100.0 |
| | | | **INCOME DATA** | | | | | | |
| 100.0 | 100.0 | 100.0 | Net Sales | | 100.0 | 100.0 | 100.0 | 100.0 | 100.0 |
| 36.4 | 39.8 | 36.3 | Gross Profit | | 49.8 | 43.9 | 39.8 | 29.7 | 19.6 |
| 31.9 | 36.2 | 32.0 | Operating Expenses | | 44.7 | 39.6 | 34.0 | 23.2 | 17.7 |
| 4.5 | 3.6 | 4.3 | Operating Profit | | 5.1 | 4.2 | 5.8 | 6.5 | 2.0 |
| .7 | .4 | .4 | All Other Expenses (net) | | 1.1 | .3 | .4 | .0 | .1 |
| 3.8 | 3.1 | 4.0 | Profit Before Taxes | | 4.0 | 3.9 | 5.4 | 6.4 | 1.8 |
| | | | **RATIOS** | | | | | | |
| 2.1 / 1.2 / 1.0 | 2.5 / 1.4 / .9 | 2.4 / 1.4 / 1.0 | Current | | 3.6 / 1.9 / .7 | 2.0 / 1.5 / .8 | 3.1 / 1.3 / 1.2 | 2.8 / 1.8 / 1.2 | 1.9 / 1.2 / 1.0 |
| 1.5 / .9 / .5 | 1.5 / 1.0 / .5 | 1.7 / 1.0 / .6 | Quick | | 1.8 / .8 | 1.6 / 1.0 / .8 | 1.5 / 1.0 / .8 | 2.2 / 1.2 / .9 | 1.2 / .8 / .5 |
| 11 32.4 / 34 10.8 / 55 6.6 | 15 24.8 / 32 11.6 / 52 7.0 | 9 40.0 / 30 12.3 / 54 6.8 | Sales/Receivables | | 0 UND / 12 30.1 / 22 16.9 | 8 46.8 / 32 11.3 / 56 6.5 | 28 13.2 / 37 9.9 / 51 7.2 | 15 23.7 / 45 8.1 / 62 5.9 | 9 42.8 / 35 10.4 / 54 6.7 |
| 0 848.8 / 18 20.1 / 55 6.7 | 2 207.6 / 17 21.2 / 53 6.8 | 1 562.9 / 13 28.9 / 42 8.6 | Cost of Sales/Inventory | | 3 125.1 / 17 21.0 / 50 7.3 | 0 UND / 25 14.8 / 69 5.3 | 1 432.2 / 13 28.5 / 56 6.5 | 0 UND / 8 45.4 / 17 21.0 | 5 80.7 / 17 22.0 / 39 9.3 |
| 18 20.6 / 38 9.6 / 57 6.4 | 14 26.0 / 34 10.8 / 53 6.9 | 16 22.3 / 31 11.8 / 47 7.7 | Cost of Sales/Payables | | 0 UND / 19 19.4 / 43 8.4 | 4 90.8 / 34 10.8 / 47 7.8 | 10 36.5 / 30 12.3 / 61 6.0 | 27 13.4 / 36 10.2 / 62 5.9 | 21 17.6 / 31 11.7 / 43 8.5 |
| 8.4 / 25.1 / 442.9 | 8.1 / 23.0 / -80.8 | 8.1 / 21.5 / -883.0 | Sales/Working Capital | | 7.4 / 25.4 / -33.3 | 9.2 / 21.1 / -32.4 | 8.2 / 19.7 / -632.9 | 6.1 / 11.5 / 43.9 | 14.0 / 35.8 / -733.1 |
| 27.9 / (102) 6.0 / 2.0 | 30.8 / (98) 5.2 / 1.1 | 37.7 / (110) 9.8 / 2.7 | EBIT/Interest | | 34.4 / (18) 3.4 / 1.5 | 28.7 / 12.7 / 1.7 | 13.4 / (20) 7.8 / 1.2 | 60.6 / (26) 14.6 / 7.8 | 60.3 / (26) 15.5 / 4.5 |
| | 13.5 / (17) 3.0 / .9 | 51.9 / (12) 9.6 / 2.1 | Net Profit + Depr., Dep., Amort./Cur. Mat. L/T/D | | | | | | |
| .1 / .4 / 2.7 | .1 / .3 / NM | .1 / .3 / 1.2 | Fixed/Worth | | .1 / .5 / 2.4 | .1 / .6 / 1.1 | .1 / .3 / 1.1 | .0 / .1 / .6 | .1 / .3 / .8 |
| 1.2 / 3.6 / 25.1 | 1.0 / 3.4 / -22.8 | .8 / 3.1 / 14.7 | Debt/Worth | | .4 / 1.4 / 10.5 | .9 / 5.3 / -18.0 | 1.0 / 3.3 / 11.2 | .8 / 2.1 / 34.4 | 1.0 / 4.1 / 11.4 |
| 63.5 / (97) 31.4 / 11.4 | 72.2 / (86) 38.9 / 8.0 | 76.2 / (108) 34.3 / 12.6 | % Profit Before Taxes/Tangible Net Worth | | 94.6 / (20) 40.7 / 14.1 | 100.3 / (11) 28.7 / 12.5 | 113.0 / (21) 28.2 / 4.3 | 86.3 / (25) 43.3 / 26.8 | 67.7 / (27) 36.1 / 20.6 |
| 17.6 / 7.9 / 1.4 | 28.1 / 8.6 / .4 | 22.0 / 10.3 / 4.4 | % Profit Before Taxes/Total Assets | | 35.1 / 8.1 / 4.6 | 30.6 / 16.1 / 1.4 | 33.0 / 11.9 / 1.3 | 19.2 / 12.7 / 8.3 | 14.2 / 6.9 / 5.7 |
| 226.1 / 66.7 / 18.4 | 188.7 / 52.6 / 22.7 | 341.8 / 66.0 / 20.7 | Sales/Net Fixed Assets | | 178.2 / 50.7 / 4.7 | 244.1 / 65.6 / 18.8 | 355.9 / 44.5 / 20.4 | 703.0 / 120.1 / 28.6 | 398.3 / 68.6 / 25.7 |
| 5.2 / 3.6 / 2.6 | 5.2 / 3.6 / 2.5 | 6.2 / 4.1 / 2.7 | Sales/Total Assets | | 7.0 / 4.6 / 2.0 | 6.4 / 4.4 / 2.6 | 5.9 / 3.6 / 2.7 | 6.6 / 3.9 / 2.2 | 5.9 / 4.3 / 3.4 |
| .2 / (76) .6 / 1.3 | .5 / (74) .8 / 1.6 | .1 / (87) .5 / 1.0 | % Depr., Dep., Amort./Sales | | .3 / (11) .8 / 1.9 | | .4 / (16) .9 / 1.6 | .1 / (20) .3 / .7 | .0 / (27) .4 / .6 |
| 2.4 / (50) 4.2 / 7.8 | 2.2 / (58) 4.9 / 8.9 | 1.4 / (58) 4.2 / | % Officers', Directors' Owners' Comp/Sales | | 4.2 / (16) 7.4 / 11.4 | | | .7 / (12) 1.6 / 6.5 | |
| 4059757M | 3451504M | 4625046M | Net Sales ($) | 4993M | 45077M | 59773M | 176043M | 491846M | 3847314M |
| 1300659M | 990237M | 1246039M | Total Assets ($) | 1624M | 16546M | 16633M | 76729M | 145324M | 989183M |

M = $ thousand    MM = $ million
See Pages 9 through 22 for Explanation of Ratios and Data

## Current Data Sorted by Assets / Comparative Historical Data

| | | | | | | Type of Statement | | |
|---|---|---|---|---|---|---|---|---|
| | | | | | 1 | Unqualified | 1 | 1 |
| | 2 | 3 | 1 | | | Reviewed | 3 | 7 |
| | | 4 | | | | Compiled | 3 | 2 |
| 1 | 1 | | | | | Tax Returns | 6 | 9 |
| 1 | 2 | 4 | 2 | 1 | | Other | 13 | 17 |
| | 6 (4/1-9/30/11) | | 17 (10/1/11-3/31/12) | | | | 4/1/07-3/31/08 | 4/1/08-3/31/09 |
| 0-500M | 500M-2MM | 2-10MM | 10-50MM | 50-100MM | 100-250MM | | ALL | ALL |
| 2 | 5 | 11 | 3 | 2 | | NUMBER OF STATEMENTS | 26 | 36 |
| % | % | % | % | % | % | ASSETS | % | % |
| | | 14.9 | | | | Cash & Equivalents | 12.0 | 11.4 |
| | | 13.1 | | | | Trade Receivables (net) | 5.5 | 12.1 |
| | | 45.4 | | | | Inventory | 46.4 | 38.6 |
| | | 2.8 | | | | All Other Current | 1.6 | 4.2 |
| | | 76.2 | | | | Total Current | 65.5 | 66.3 |
| | | 17.9 | | | | Fixed Assets (net) | 22.9 | 22.4 |
| | | 1.6 | | | | Intangibles (net) | 5.5 | 4.1 |
| | | 4.3 | | | | All Other Non-Current | 6.0 | 7.2 |
| | | 100.0 | | | | Total | 100.0 | 100.0 |
| | | | | | | LIABILITIES | | |
| | | 6.9 | | | | Notes Payable-Short Term | 10.7 | 13.0 |
| | | 1.7 | | | | Cur. Mat.-L.T.D. | 3.4 | 4.2 |
| | | 21.6 | | | | Trade Payables | 25.6 | 19.4 |
| | | .0 | | | | Income Taxes Payable | .4 | .2 |
| | | 6.4 | | | | All Other Current | 12.3 | 6.7 |
| | | 36.7 | | | | Total Current | 52.3 | 43.6 |
| | | 6.9 | | | | Long-Term Debt | 25.3 | 21.8 |
| | | .0 | | | | Deferred Taxes | .0 | .0 |
| | | 2.9 | | | | All Other Non-Current | 3.7 | 7.2 |
| | | 53.5 | | | | Net Worth | 18.7 | 27.4 |
| | | 100.0 | | | | Total Liabilities & Net Worth | 100.0 | 100.0 |
| | | | | | | INCOME DATA | | |
| | | 100.0 | | | | Net Sales | 100.0 | 100.0 |
| | | 31.6 | | | | Gross Profit | 37.6 | 40.0 |
| | | 29.4 | | | | Operating Expenses | 36.0 | 37.1 |
| | | 2.2 | | | | Operating Profit | 1.6 | 3.0 |
| | | -.6 | | | | All Other Expenses (net) | 1.2 | .7 |
| | | 2.8 | | | | Profit Before Taxes | .5 | 2.3 |
| | | | | | | RATIOS | | |
| | | 3.1 | | | | | 2.5 | 2.6 |
| | | 2.1 | | | | Current | 1.3 | 1.6 |
| | | 1.7 | | | | | .9 | 1.1 |
| | | 1.0 | | | | | .7 | .9 |
| | | .6 | | | | Quick | (25) .2 | .4 |
| | | .5 | | | | | .1 | .2 |
| | 1 | 362.7 | | | | | 0 UND | 2 148.3 |
| | 10 | 38.3 | | | | Sales/Receivables | 3 140.8 | 5 67.2 |
| | 22 | 16.9 | | | | | 6 59.2 | 16 22.3 |
| | 38 | 9.6 | | | | | 53 6.9 | 26 13.9 |
| | 57 | 6.4 | | | | Cost of Sales/Inventory | 73 5.0 | 65 5.6 |
| | 94 | 3.9 | | | | | 113 3.2 | 81 4.5 |
| | 11 | 33.4 | | | | | 9 39.7 | 9 40.5 |
| | 31 | 11.7 | | | | Cost of Sales/Payables | 30 12.0 | 26 14.1 |
| | 38 | 9.7 | | | | | 51 7.2 | 50 7.3 |
| | | 6.0 | | | | | 9.1 | 8.4 |
| | | 9.8 | | | | Sales/Working Capital | 26.5 | 15.3 |
| | | 16.1 | | | | | -98.8 | 96.5 |
| | | | | | | | 9.7 | 7.7 |
| | | | | | | EBIT/Interest | (22) 5.6 | (31) 2.3 |
| | | | | | | | .3 | .0 |
| | | | | | | Net Profit + Depr., Dep., Amort./Cur. Mat. L/T/D | | |
| | | .1 | | | | | .2 | .2 |
| | | .2 | | | | Fixed/Worth | .5 | .6 |
| | | .9 | | | | | 3.7 | 2.4 |
| | | .3 | | | | | .9 | .9 |
| | | .6 | | | | Debt/Worth | 3.6 | 2.3 |
| | | 3.0 | | | | | NM | 8.1 |
| | | 27.0 | | | | | 41.1 | 27.2 |
| | | 16.9 | | | | % Profit Before Taxes/Tangible Net Worth | (20) 17.0 | (32) 10.5 |
| | | 7.9 | | | | | -13.8 | -3.9 |
| | | 12.7 | | | | | 13.4 | 18.2 |
| | | 8.4 | | | | % Profit Before Taxes/Total Assets | 4.7 | 4.5 |
| | | 3.2 | | | | | -3.5 | -2.1 |
| | | 71.1 | | | | | 55.7 | 62.9 |
| | | 39.2 | | | | Sales/Net Fixed Assets | 25.8 | 22.0 |
| | | 9.4 | | | | | 6.5 | 10.6 |
| | | 6.9 | | | | | 4.9 | 4.6 |
| | | 3.9 | | | | Sales/Total Assets | 3.6 | 4.0 |
| | | 2.2 | | | | | 2.2 | 2.5 |
| | | | | | | | .5 | .6 |
| | | | | | | % Depr., Dep., Amort./Sales | (22) 1.3 | (30) 1.5 |
| | | | | | | | 3.2 | 3.9 |
| | | | | | | | .7 | 1.0 |
| | | | | | | % Officers', Directors' Owners' Comp/Sales | (12) 2.6 | (16) 4.2 |
| | | | | | | | 4.7 | 6.4 |
| 5917M | 23607M | 199916M | 128282M | 771179M | | Net Sales ($) | 598290M | 1393874M |
| 568M | 6260M | 51549M | 58319M | 136322M | | Total Assets ($) | 132632M | 455637M |

Note: The wide band down the left-center columns reads: **DATA NOT AVAILABLE**

## Comparative Historical Data | Current Data Sorted by Sales

| 4/1/09-3/31/10 ALL | 4/1/10-3/31/11 ALL | 4/1/11-3/31/12 ALL | Type of Statement | 0-1MM | 1-3MM | 3-5MM | 5-10MM | 10-25MM | 25MM & OVER |
|---|---|---|---|---|---|---|---|---|---|
| 1 | | 1 | Unqualified | | | | | | 1 |
| 5 | 6 | 6 | Reviewed | | | 1 | 3 | 2 | 1 |
| 5 | 8 | 4 | Compiled | | | 1 | 2 | 1 | |
| 2 | 2 | 2 | Tax Returns | | 1 | | | | |
| 6 | 7 | 10 | Other | 2 | 1 | | | | 3 |
| 4/1/09-3/31/10 ALL | 4/1/10-3/31/11 ALL | 4/1/11-3/31/12 ALL | | | 6 (4/1-9/30/11) | | 17 (10/1/11-3/31/12) | | |
| 19 | 23 | 23 | NUMBER OF STATEMENTS | 2 | 1 | 2 | 4 | 9 | 5 |
| % | % | % | **ASSETS** | % | % | % | % | % | % |
| 7.7 | 9.4 | 16.2 | Cash & Equivalents | | | | | | |
| 15.0 | 13.8 | 10.8 | Trade Receivables (net) | | | | | | |
| 43.9 | 49.9 | 47.5 | Inventory | | | | | | |
| 3.7 | 1.3 | 1.9 | All Other Current | | | | | | |
| 70.3 | 74.3 | 76.4 | Total Current | | | | | | |
| 20.2 | 16.2 | 18.6 | Fixed Assets (net) | | | | | | |
| 3.2 | 2.6 | 1.2 | Intangibles (net) | | | | | | |
| 6.3 | 6.9 | 3.7 | All Other Non-Current | | | | | | |
| 100.0 | 100.0 | 100.0 | Total | | | | | | |
| | | | **LIABILITIES** | | | | | | |
| 30.1 | 7.3 | 9.3 | Notes Payable-Short Term | | | | | | |
| 4.2 | 4.1 | 1.8 | Cur. Mat.-L.T.D. | | | | | | |
| 19.3 | 21.0 | 17.5 | Trade Payables | | | | | | |
| 1.0 | .6 | .0 | Income Taxes Payable | | | | | | |
| 11.6 | 9.0 | 11.8 | All Other Current | | | | | | |
| 66.2 | 42.0 | 40.5 | Total Current | | | | | | |
| 19.8 | 5.6 | 16.1 | Long-Term Debt | | | | | | |
| .0 | .0 | .0 | Deferred Taxes | | | | | | |
| 4.1 | 4.5 | 3.6 | All Other Non-Current | | | | | | |
| 9.8 | 47.8 | 39.8 | Net Worth | | | | | | |
| 100.0 | 100.0 | 100.0 | Total Liabilties & Net Worth | | | | | | |
| | | | **INCOME DATA** | | | | | | |
| 100.0 | 100.0 | 100.0 | Net Sales | | | | | | |
| 38.0 | 30.7 | 33.7 | Gross Profit | | | | | | |
| 35.3 | 28.7 | 32.9 | Operating Expenses | | | | | | |
| 2.7 | 2.0 | .8 | Operating Profit | | | | | | |
| .6 | -.4 | .8 | All Other Expenses (net) | | | | | | |
| 2.1 | 2.3 | .0 | Profit Before Taxes | | | | | | |
| | | | **RATIOS** | | | | | | |
| 2.9 | 2.4 | 3.1 | | | | | | | |
| 1.6 | 1.6 | 1.8 | Current | | | | | | |
| 1.1 | 1.2 | 1.6 | | | | | | | |
| .9 | .7 | .9 | | | | | | | |
| .4 | .5 | .6 | Quick | | | | | | |
| .2 | .3 | .5 | | | | | | | |
| 5  79.3 | 2  211.2 | 2  154.1 | | | | | | | |
| 9  40.3 | 7  53.0 | 8  45.2 | Sales/Receivables | | | | | | |
| 24  15.1 | 28  13.2 | 21  17.2 | | | | | | | |
| 45  8.1 | 41  8.8 | 39  9.4 | | | | | | | |
| 68  5.4 | 58  6.3 | 83  4.4 | Cost of Sales/Inventory | | | | | | |
| 92  4.0 | 89  4.1 | 111  3.3 | | | | | | | |
| 7  50.6 | 14  26.5 | 9  40.4 | | | | | | | |
| 24  15.4 | 28  13.2 | 23  15.9 | Cost of Sales/Payables | | | | | | |
| 62  5.9 | 42  8.7 | 36  10.0 | | | | | | | |
| 8.8 | 6.3 | 6.0 | | | | | | | |
| 13.9 | 14.9 | 9.8 | Sales/Working Capital | | | | | | |
| 97.3 | 34.4 | 25.0 | | | | | | | |
| 13.7 | 82.1 | 8.0 | | | | | | | |
| 5.0 | 8.1 | (19) 3.6 | EBIT/Interest | | | | | | |
| 1.3 | 1.5 | .9 | | | | | | | |
| | | | Net Profit + Depr., Dep., Amort./Cur. Mat. L/T/D | | | | | | |
| .2 | .1 | .2 | | | | | | | |
| .6 | .2 | .4 | Fixed/Worth | | | | | | |
| .9 | .9 | 1.0 | | | | | | | |
| .5 | .6 | .5 | | | | | | | |
| 1.7 | 1.0 | 1.9 | Debt/Worth | | | | | | |
| 5.8 | 3.1 | 4.2 | | | | | | | |
| 35.3 | 40.9 | 27.2 | | | | | | | |
| (17) 21.4 | 20.5 | (22) 16.7 | % Profit Before Taxes/Tangible Net Worth | | | | | | |
| .9 | 1.6 | 1.4 | | | | | | | |
| 15.9 | 18.0 | 11.0 | | | | | | | |
| 6.8 | 8.9 | 5.6 | % Profit Before Taxes/Total Assets | | | | | | |
| .5 | 1.1 | .4 | | | | | | | |
| 48.0 | 60.3 | 71.1 | | | | | | | |
| 24.4 | 37.7 | 30.6 | Sales/Net Fixed Assets | | | | | | |
| 8.5 | 16.4 | 9.4 | | | | | | | |
| 6.0 | 6.0 | 6.7 | | | | | | | |
| 3.9 | 3.7 | 3.9 | Sales/Total Assets | | | | | | |
| 2.8 | 2.8 | 2.2 | | | | | | | |
| .6 | .5 | .2 | | | | | | | |
| (15) 1.2 | (19) 1.0 | (19) 1.1 | % Depr., Dep., Amort./Sales | | | | | | |
| 3.2 | 2.5 | 2.2 | | | | | | | |
| | | .7 | | | | | | | |
| | (12) | 2.1 | % Officers', Directors' Owners' Comp/Sales | | | | | | |
| | | 7.0 | | | | | | | |
| 249969M | 553461M | 1128901M | Net Sales ($) | 1429M | 1331M | 9423M | 31967M | 141225M | 943526M |
| 75568M | 156082M | 253018M | Total Assets ($) | 1457M | 193M | 1852M | 24729M | 36976M | 187811M |

© RMA 2012

M = $ thousand    MM = $ million
See Pages 9 through 22 for Explanation of Ratios and Data

## Current Data Sorted by Assets          Comparative Historical Data

| 0-500M | 500M-2MM | 2-10MM | 10-50MM | 50-100MM | 100-250MM | | 4/1/07-3/31/08 ALL | 4/1/08-3/31/09 ALL |
|---|---|---|---|---|---|---|---|---|
| | | | | | | **Type of Statement** | | |
| | 2 | 9 | 20 | 2 | 2 | Unqualified | 56 | 39 |
| | 7 | 53 | 18 | 1 | 1 | Reviewed | 118 | 114 |
| 1 | 27 | 30 | 5 | | | Compiled | 92 | 69 |
| 6 | 23 | 15 | 1 | | | Tax Returns | 49 | 44 |
| 7 | 11 | 48 | 34 | 4 | 2 | Other | 117 | 102 |
| | 40 (4/1-9/30/11) | | 289 (10/1/11-3/31/12) | | | | | |
| 14 | 70 | 155 | 78 | 7 | 5 | **NUMBER OF STATEMENTS** | 432 | 368 |
| % | % | % | % | % | % | **ASSETS** | % | % |
| 7.8 | 8.5 | 8.4 | 5.0 | | | Cash & Equivalents | 7.1 | 7.3 |
| 22.1 | 20.2 | 22.3 | 19.7 | | | Trade Receivables (net) | 27.0 | 23.9 |
| 26.2 | 44.2 | 39.9 | 33.8 | | | Inventory | 33.6 | 33.7 |
| .9 | 1.5 | 1.5 | 3.4 | | | All Other Current | 2.6 | 2.4 |
| 57.1 | 74.4 | 72.1 | 61.9 | | | Total Current | 70.3 | 67.4 |
| 25.0 | 17.1 | 19.7 | 25.3 | | | Fixed Assets (net) | 21.1 | 21.8 |
| .5 | .5 | 1.3 | 4.3 | | | Intangibles (net) | 1.9 | 2.3 |
| 17.5 | 8.0 | 6.9 | 8.5 | | | All Other Non-Current | 6.7 | 8.6 |
| 100.0 | 100.0 | 100.0 | 100.0 | | | Total | 100.0 | 100.0 |
| | | | | | | **LIABILITIES** | | |
| 32.4 | 12.8 | 17.7 | 22.1 | | | Notes Payable-Short Term | 12.9 | 14.7 |
| 12.2 | 1.3 | 2.4 | 3.0 | | | Cur. Mat.-L.T.D. | 3.5 | 3.4 |
| 15.5 | 14.5 | 12.4 | 10.2 | | | Trade Payables | 13.9 | 12.3 |
| .0 | .0 | .1 | .0 | | | Income Taxes Payable | .1 | .1 |
| 58.0 | 9.1 | 7.4 | 5.7 | | | All Other Current | 7.0 | 7.0 |
| 118.1 | 37.7 | 40.0 | 41.0 | | | Total Current | 37.4 | 37.5 |
| 15.6 | 16.3 | 10.2 | 14.3 | | | Long-Term Debt | 14.2 | 14.8 |
| .0 | .1 | .4 | .5 | | | Deferred Taxes | .2 | .3 |
| 14.3 | 5.4 | 5.3 | 7.0 | | | All Other Non-Current | 4.4 | 6.1 |
| -48.0 | 40.5 | 44.1 | 37.2 | | | Net Worth | 43.9 | 41.3 |
| 100.0 | 100.0 | 100.0 | 100.0 | | | Total Liabilities & Net Worth | 100.0 | 100.0 |
| | | | | | | **INCOME DATA** | | |
| 100.0 | 100.0 | 100.0 | 100.0 | | | Net Sales | 100.0 | 100.0 |
| 40.6 | 31.0 | 25.0 | 24.4 | | | Gross Profit | 27.4 | 27.7 |
| 38.8 | 30.5 | 24.8 | 23.6 | | | Operating Expenses | 25.5 | 27.7 |
| 1.7 | .5 | .2 | .7 | | | Operating Profit | 1.9 | .1 |
| .2 | .1 | -.4 | .6 | | | All Other Expenses (net) | .1 | .2 |
| 1.6 | .4 | .6 | .2 | | | Profit Before Taxes | 1.7 | -.2 |
| | | | | | | **RATIOS** | | |
| 1.5 | 3.5 | 3.0 | 2.4 | | | Current | 3.4 | 3.5 |
| .9 | 2.3 | 1.9 | 1.4 | | | | 2.0 | 2.0 |
| .2 | 1.6 | 1.3 | 1.1 | | | | 1.4 | 1.3 |
| .6 | 1.5 | 1.6 | 1.2 | | | Quick | 1.7 | 1.6 |
| .2 | .7 | .8 | .6 | | | | .9 | .8 |
| .1 | .4 | .4 | .3 | | | | .5 | .5 |
| 0 UND | 10 38.0 | 20 18.3 | 13 28.6 | | | Sales/Receivables | 24 15.5 | 21 17.5 |
| 12 30.7 | 28 13.0 | 33 11.2 | 33 11.0 | | | | 33 10.9 | 31 11.8 |
| 32 11.3 | 41 8.8 | 46 8.0 | 47 7.8 | | | | 46 7.9 | 44 8.2 |
| 0 UND | 53 6.9 | 48 7.6 | 47 7.8 | | | Cost of Sales/Inventory | 39 9.3 | 42 8.7 |
| 22 16.8 | 81 4.5 | 70 5.2 | 65 5.6 | | | | 58 6.3 | 64 5.7 |
| 83 4.4 | 126 2.9 | 107 3.4 | 94 3.9 | | | | 84 4.3 | 91 4.0 |
| 0 UND | 13 27.8 | 11 32.9 | 14 26.5 | | | Cost of Sales/Payables | 13 28.1 | 11 34.6 |
| 21 17.7 | 22 16.5 | 23 16.0 | 23 15.8 | | | | 20 18.3 | 17 21.2 |
| 41 9.0 | 39 9.4 | 36 10.2 | 31 11.6 | | | | 31 11.9 | 30 12.1 |
| 18.0 | 4.8 | 4.9 | 6.5 | | | Sales/Working Capital | 5.3 | 4.9 |
| -57.6 | 7.1 | 7.3 | 11.1 | | | | 8.3 | 8.1 |
| -9.0 | 15.2 | 20.7 | 52.4 | | | | 15.7 | 18.5 |
| 16.9 | 5.8 | 4.5 | 3.4 | | | EBIT/Interest | 6.5 | 4.0 |
| (11) 1.0 | (57) 1.9 | (130) 1.8 | (67) 1.7 | | | | (404) 2.2 | (347) 1.5 |
| -.1 | .2 | .3 | .5 | | | | .8 | -.9 |
| | | 5.5 | 5.1 | | | Net Profit + Depr., Dep., Amort./Cur. Mat. L/T/D | 7.7 | 3.4 |
| | (40) 1.6 | (18) 2.7 | | | | | (121) 2.0 | (101) 1.7 |
| | | .6 | .9 | | | | .9 | .3 |
| .2 | .1 | .2 | .3 | | | Fixed/Worth | .2 | .2 |
| 3.5 | .3 | .3 | .8 | | | | .4 | .5 |
| -.4 | .8 | .9 | 1.7 | | | | 1.1 | 1.1 |
| 2.7 | .5 | .5 | .7 | | | Debt/Worth | .6 | .5 |
| 53.9 | 1.3 | 1.3 | 2.0 | | | | 1.3 | 1.4 |
| -1.8 | 3.9 | 3.5 | 5.4 | | | | 2.7 | 3.4 |
| | 17.8 | 13.5 | 15.1 | | | % Profit Before Taxes/Tangible Net Worth | 24.4 | 12.3 |
| | (64) 3.3 | (150) 3.7 | (68) 4.4 | | | | (398) 9.4 | (328) 3.0 |
| | -1.9 | -1.7 | -.4 | | | | -.3 | -8.3 |
| 46.2 | 7.8 | 4.9 | 4.3 | | | % Profit Before Taxes/Total Assets | 9.7 | 5.6 |
| 2.4 | 1.6 | 1.6 | 2.1 | | | | 3.1 | 1.1 |
| -7.3 | -2.5 | -.8 | -.6 | | | | -.6 | -4.9 |
| 55.7 | 121.7 | 44.7 | 38.0 | | | Sales/Net Fixed Assets | 31.9 | 28.7 |
| 22.7 | 21.3 | 17.3 | 8.9 | | | | 14.7 | 14.3 |
| 12.2 | 9.1 | 7.2 | 5.4 | | | | 7.5 | 7.5 |
| 8.0 | 3.5 | 3.3 | 2.9 | | | Sales/Total Assets | 3.5 | 3.3 |
| 3.7 | 2.7 | 2.5 | 2.2 | | | | 2.7 | 2.5 |
| 3.0 | 2.1 | 1.8 | 1.6 | | | | 2.0 | 1.9 |
| | .4 | .5 | .6 | | | % Depr., Dep., Amort./Sales | .7 | .8 |
| | (53) .8 | (140) 1.0 | (75) 1.0 | | | | (398) 1.2 | (329) 1.4 |
| | 1.6 | 1.6 | 2.1 | | | | 1.8 | 2.1 |
| | 1.6 | 1.0 | .4 | | | % Officers', Directors' Owners' Comp/Sales | 1.3 | 1.4 |
| | (45) 3.4 | (73) 1.8 | (27) .9 | | | | (174) 2.3 | (156) 2.3 |
| | 4.5 | 3.2 | 2.1 | | | | 4.3 | 4.5 |
| 27915M | 256943M | 1925816M | 3966542M | 964700M | 1420027M | Net Sales ($) | 14652606M | 11505635M |
| 4517M | 84337M | 731922M | 1704139M | 514575M | 642430M | Total Assets ($) | 5602496M | 4524109M |

M = $ thousand    MM = $ million
See Pages 9 through 22 for Explanation of Ratios and Data

## Comparative Historical Data | | | Type of Statement | Current Data Sorted by Sales | | | | | |

| | | | Type of Statement | | | | | | |
|---|---|---|---|---|---|---|---|---|---|
| 33 | 40 | 35 | Unqualified | | | 2 | 2 | 10 | 21 |
| 102 | 81 | 80 | Reviewed | | 5 | 7 | 24 | 25 | 19 |
| 75 | 76 | 63 | Compiled | 2 | 14 | 13 | 20 | 10 | 4 |
| 45 | 43 | 45 | Tax Returns | 2 | 19 | 6 | 12 | 6 | |
| 102 | 115 | 106 | Other | 4 | 8 | 5 | 17 | 31 | 41 |
| 4/1/09-3/31/10 ALL | 4/1/10-3/31/11 ALL | 4/1/11-3/31/12 ALL | | | 40 (4/1-9/30/11) | | 289 (10/1/11-3/31/12) | | |
| | | | | 0-1MM | 1-3MM | 3-5MM | 5-10MM | 10-25MM | 25MM & OVER |
| 357 | 355 | 329 | NUMBER OF STATEMENTS | 8 | 46 | 33 | 75 | 82 | 85 |
| % | % | % | ASSETS | % | % | % | % | % | % |
| 7.6 | 8.3 | 7.6 | Cash & Equivalents | | 5.1 | 8.4 | 9.6 | 9.3 | 5.8 |
| 21.8 | 20.9 | 21.0 | Trade Receivables (net) | | 18.9 | 19.5 | 23.4 | 22.5 | 19.8 |
| 33.3 | 36.9 | 38.5 | Inventory | | 45.2 | 41.7 | 36.7 | 36.5 | 37.9 |
| 2.3 | 2.3 | 2.1 | All Other Current | | .7 | 1.8 | 1.2 | 2.1 | 3.8 |
| 65.1 | 68.4 | 69.2 | Total Current | | 70.0 | 71.3 | 70.9 | 70.3 | 67.3 |
| 22.8 | 21.5 | 21.1 | Fixed Assets (net) | | 19.8 | 22.8 | 20.7 | 19.1 | 22.2 |
| 2.2 | 2.5 | 1.8 | Intangibles (net) | | .1 | .9 | 1.1 | 2.1 | 3.4 |
| 10.0 | 7.6 | 7.9 | All Other Non-Current | | 10.0 | 5.0 | 7.4 | 8.4 | 7.1 |
| 100.0 | 100.0 | 100.0 | Total | | 100.0 | 100.0 | 100.0 | 100.0 | 100.0 |
| | | | LIABILITIES | | | | | | |
| 12.6 | 17.2 | 18.1 | Notes Payable-Short Term | | 18.3 | 12.2 | 12.8 | 17.8 | 25.9 |
| 3.2 | 2.9 | 2.8 | Cur. Mat.-L.T.D. | | 3.5 | 1.4 | 2.2 | 3.0 | 2.7 |
| 12.7 | 11.9 | 12.4 | Trade Payables | | 13.0 | 14.6 | 12.5 | 12.4 | 10.6 |
| .1 | .1 | .0 | Income Taxes Payable | | .1 | .0 | .0 | .0 | .0 |
| 6.0 | 7.7 | 9.5 | All Other Current | | 10.9 | 7.6 | 7.7 | 8.3 | 6.0 |
| 34.6 | 39.8 | 42.8 | Total Current | | 45.8 | 35.8 | 35.4 | 41.5 | 45.2 |
| 16.0 | 14.0 | 12.9 | Long-Term Debt | | 18.1 | 16.1 | 11.8 | 9.4 | 11.6 |
| .3 | .3 | .4 | Deferred Taxes | | .1 | .1 | .4 | .5 | .5 |
| 5.8 | 5.7 | 6.0 | All Other Non-Current | | 8.6 | 5.3 | 6.2 | 4.6 | 6.2 |
| 43.3 | 40.1 | 37.9 | Net Worth | | 27.4 | 42.8 | 46.3 | 44.0 | 36.5 |
| 100.0 | 100.0 | 100.0 | Total Liabilities & Net Worth | | 100.0 | 100.0 | 100.0 | 100.0 | 100.0 |
| | | | INCOME DATA | | | | | | |
| 100.0 | 100.0 | 100.0 | Net Sales | | 100.0 | 100.0 | 100.0 | 100.0 | 100.0 |
| 28.5 | 26.2 | 26.7 | Gross Profit | | 32.6 | 30.0 | 27.4 | 24.5 | 22.3 |
| 29.5 | 26.2 | 26.2 | Operating Expenses | | 32.6 | 28.9 | 26.9 | 24.1 | 21.3 |
| -1.0 | .0 | .5 | Operating Profit | | .0 | 1.1 | .5 | .4 | .9 |
| .0 | .0 | .0 | All Other Expenses (net) | | .2 | .0 | -.1 | -.3 | .2 |
| -1.1 | .1 | .5 | Profit Before Taxes | | -.2 | 1.2 | .6 | .7 | .7 |
| | | | RATIOS | | | | | | |
| 3.5 | 3.5 | 3.0 | Current | | 3.4 | 3.7 | 3.6 | 3.0 | 2.4 |
| 2.1 | 1.9 | 1.8 | | | 2.0 | 2.3 | 2.1 | 1.9 | 1.5 |
| 1.3 | 1.2 | 1.2 | | | 1.4 | 1.3 | 1.5 | 1.2 | 1.1 |
| 1.6 | 1.6 | 1.4 | Quick | | 1.4 | 1.5 | 1.6 | 1.7 | 1.0 |
| .9 | .7 | .7 | | | .7 | .6 | 1.0 | .7 | .5 |
| .5 | .4 | .4 | | | .3 | .4 | .6 | .4 | .3 |
| 23  15.8 | 16  22.9 | 15  24.9 | Sales/Receivables | 14  26.3 | 20  18.2 | 19  18.9 | 19  19.0 | 11  32.3 | |
| 34  10.8 | 30  12.2 | 31  11.6 | | 30  12.0 | 34  10.7 | 33  11.0 | 31  11.8 | 28  13.2 | |
| 47  7.8 | 43  8.5 | 45  8.2 | | 41  9.0 | 46  7.9 | 50  7.3 | 46  8.0 | 42  8.6 | |
| 49  7.4 | 47  7.8 | 47  7.8 | Cost of Sales/Inventory | 68  5.4 | 59  6.2 | 44  8.3 | 45  8.1 | 46  8.0 | |
| 70  5.3 | 68  5.4 | 70  5.2 | | 99  3.7 | 85  4.3 | 66  5.5 | 66  5.5 | 65  5.6 | |
| 101  3.6 | 97  3.8 | 104  3.5 | | 140  2.6 | 146  2.5 | 101  3.6 | 99  3.7 | 89  4.1 | |
| 14  25.9 | 11  34.7 | 13  28.6 | Cost of Sales/Payables | 10  37.0 | 14  26.2 | 15  24.3 | 12  30.3 | 8  43.4 | |
| 22  16.6 | 20  17.9 | 23  16.2 | | 22  16.6 | 31  11.6 | 24  14.9 | 21  17.0 | 22  16.6 | |
| 35  10.5 | 31  11.8 | 36  10.2 | | 39  9.4 | 45  8.1 | 36  10.2 | 30  12.2 | 32  11.3 | |
| 4.5 | 4.8 | 5.1 | Sales/Working Capital | | 4.6 | 4.1 | 4.8 | 5.3 | 7.4 |
| 7.0 | 8.6 | 7.9 | | | 7.1 | 6.1 | 6.9 | 8.4 | 12.1 |
| 16.4 | 28.0 | 25.2 | | | 21.0 | 17.2 | 14.1 | 26.5 | 34.3 |
| 3.0 | 4.7 | 4.6 | EBIT/Interest | (38) 2.6 | (29) 6.1 | (65) 4.2 | (68) 4.6 | (70) 4.9 | |
| (323) .8 | (307) 1.4 | (277) 1.8 | | 1.1 | 2.3 | 1.5 | 2.2 | 2.0 | |
| -2.8 | -.7 | .4 | | -1.9 | .2 | -.2 | 1.0 | .7 | |
| 3.2 | 3.2 | 4.7 | Net Profit + Depr., Dep., Amort./Cur. Mat. L/T/D | | | (15) 3.0 | (22) 8.6 | (23) 5.5 | |
| (85) 1.2 | (79) 1.4 | (68) 1.7 | | | | 1.3 | 1.7 | 2.1 | |
| -.4 | .0 | .6 | | | | .7 | .4 | .9 | |
| .2 | .2 | .2 | Fixed/Worth | | .1 | .1 | .1 | .2 | .3 |
| .5 | .5 | .4 | | | .5 | .5 | .3 | .3 | .5 |
| 1.2 | 1.2 | 1.2 | | | 2.6 | 1.7 | .9 | .8 | 1.5 |
| .4 | .6 | .6 | Debt/Worth | | .7 | .5 | .5 | .5 | .7 |
| 1.2 | 1.5 | 1.5 | | | 1.7 | 1.2 | 1.2 | 1.2 | 2.0 |
| 3.6 | 4.9 | 4.2 | | | 10.0 | 3.5 | 2.7 | 4.0 | 6.0 |
| 7.0 | 17.1 | 14.6 | % Profit Before Taxes/Tangible Net Worth | (39) 9.1 | (31) 18.4 | (72) 14.8 | (77) 11.2 | (78) 18.8 | |
| (319) -.7 | (316) 3.7 | (302) 3.9 | | 2.6 | 4.8 | 2.4 | 4.1 | 6.4 | |
| -13.3 | -5.2 | -1.2 | | -5.8 | -2.8 | -3.7 | 1.4 | -.6 | |
| 3.1 | 5.8 | 5.2 | % Profit Before Taxes/Total Assets | | 2.8 | 8.2 | 5.3 | 4.7 | 5.6 |
| -.5 | 1.4 | 1.7 | | | .4 | 1.9 | 1.1 | 1.9 | 3.0 |
| -6.9 | -2.7 | -.8 | | | -5.1 | -2.7 | -1.9 | .3 | -.2 |
| 24.9 | 38.4 | 44.6 | Sales/Net Fixed Assets | | 55.1 | 28.0 | 36.3 | 51.0 | 43.8 |
| 11.0 | 15.1 | 16.7 | | | 18.1 | 14.7 | 18.1 | 16.8 | 13.4 |
| 6.0 | 6.7 | 6.7 | | | 6.3 | 5.4 | 7.5 | 6.8 | 6.7 |
| 2.9 | 3.2 | 3.4 | Sales/Total Assets | | 3.2 | 3.0 | 3.1 | 3.5 | 3.6 |
| 2.2 | 2.5 | 2.5 | | | 2.5 | 2.0 | 2.3 | 2.7 | 2.6 |
| 1.6 | 1.8 | 1.7 | | | 1.7 | 1.5 | 1.8 | 1.9 | 1.8 |
| 1.0 | .6 | .5 | % Depr., Dep., Amort./Sales | (38) .4 | (28) .6 | (64) .5 | (71) .6 | (81) .4 | |
| (318) 1.5 | (310) 1.2 | (287) 1.0 | | 1.0 | 1.0 | 1.0 | 1.1 | .8 | |
| 2.4 | 2.0 | 1.8 | | 2.1 | 2.5 | 1.9 | 1.6 | 1.5 | |
| 1.5 | .8 | 1.0 | % Officers', Directors' Owners' Comp/Sales | (32) 2.3 | (20) 2.1 | (40) 1.4 | (34) .8 | (28) .3 | |
| (156) 2.8 | (176) 2.0 | (156) 2.1 | | 3.9 | 2.9 | 1.9 | 1.2 | .6 | |
| 4.4 | 4.2 | 3.8 | | 4.8 | 4.2 | 3.5 | 2.5 | 2.1 | |
| 8133858M | 9548637M | 8561943M | Net Sales ($) | 3983M | 97527M | 128917M | 545835M | 1385696M | 6399985M |
| 3971953M | 4166891M | 3681920M | Total Assets ($) | 3878M | 49326M | 64255M | 252304M | 608455M | 2703702M |

M = $ thousand    MM = $ million
See Pages 9 through 22 for Explanation of Ratios and Data

## Current Data Sorted by Assets | Comparative Historical Data

Type of Statement counts and period breakdowns: current period split **4 (4/1–9/30/11)** and **33 (10/1/11–3/31/12)**.

| 0-500M | 500M-2MM | 2-10MM | 10-50MM | 50-100MM | 100-250MM | Type of Statement | 4/1/07-3/31/08 ALL | 4/1/08-3/31/09 ALL |
|---|---|---|---|---|---|---|---|---|
| | | | | | | Unqualified | 4 | 3 |
| 2 | 2 | 2 | | | | Reviewed | 8 | 11 |
| | | 1 | | | | Compiled | 7 | 6 |
| 4 | 17 | 5 | | | | Tax Returns | 15 | 11 |
| 1 | 2 | 1 | | | | Other | 9 | 6 |
| 7 | 21 | 9 | | | | NUMBER OF STATEMENTS | 43 | 37 |
| % | % | % | % | % | % | **ASSETS** | % | % |
| | 9.2 | | | | | Cash & Equivalents | 8.7 | 10.0 |
| | 25.3 | | D | D | D | Trade Receivables (net) | 26.9 | 26.3 |
| | 36.6 | | A | A | A | Inventory | 38.2 | 37.2 |
| | 1.2 | | T | T | T | All Other Current | 1.0 | 2.0 |
| | 72.4 | | A | A | A | Total Current | 74.8 | 75.4 |
| | 12.7 | | | | | Fixed Assets (net) | 17.9 | 16.9 |
| | 3.0 | | N | N | N | Intangibles (net) | 1.6 | 3.1 |
| | 11.8 | | O | O | O | All Other Non-Current | 5.7 | 4.6 |
| | 100.0 | | T | T | T | Total | 100.0 | 100.0 |
| | | | | | | **LIABILITIES** | | |
| | 9.9 | | A | A | A | Notes Payable-Short Term | 12.4 | 11.2 |
| | 2.4 | | V | V | V | Cur. Mat.-L.T.D. | 2.8 | 1.2 |
| | 26.9 | | A | A | A | Trade Payables | 19.7 | 18.5 |
| | .1 | | I | I | I | Income Taxes Payable | .0 | .0 |
| | 6.9 | | L | L | L | All Other Current | 9.0 | 6.8 |
| | 46.2 | | A | A | A | Total Current | 43.9 | 37.7 |
| | 30.2 | | B | B | B | Long-Term Debt | 19.5 | 14.6 |
| | .0 | | L | L | L | Deferred Taxes | .0 | .1 |
| | 4.9 | | E | E | E | All Other Non-Current | 7.8 | 9.6 |
| | 18.6 | | | | | Net Worth | 28.8 | 38.0 |
| | 100.0 | | | | | Total Liabilities & Net Worth | 100.0 | 100.0 |
| | | | | | | **INCOME DATA** | | |
| | 100.0 | | | | | Net Sales | 100.0 | 100.0 |
| | 35.3 | | | | | Gross Profit | 34.7 | 38.1 |
| | 32.0 | | | | | Operating Expenses | 31.9 | 36.9 |
| | 3.3 | | | | | Operating Profit | 2.8 | 1.2 |
| | .5 | | | | | All Other Expenses (net) | -.4 | .0 |
| | 2.8 | | | | | Profit Before Taxes | 3.3 | 1.2 |
| | | | | | | **RATIOS** | | |
| | 3.2 | | | | | Current | 3.1 | 3.9 |
| | 2.1 | | | | | | 1.7 | 2.4 |
| | 1.3 | | | | | | 1.2 | 1.4 |
| | 1.6 | | | | | Quick | 1.2 | 2.0 |
| | 1.1 | | | | | | .7 | 1.0 |
| | .5 | | | | | | .4 | .5 |
| | 24  14.9 | | | | | Sales/Receivables | 17  21.9 | 12  29.7 |
| | 32  11.5 | | | | | | 25  14.3 | 25  14.6 |
| | 43  8.5 | | | | | | 42  8.6 | 44  8.4 |
| | 50  7.3 | | | | | Cost of Sales/Inventory | 36  10.1 | 36  10.1 |
| | 66  5.5 | | | | | | 60  6.0 | 62  5.9 |
| | 99  3.7 | | | | | | 102  3.6 | 112  3.3 |
| | 21  17.7 | | | | | Cost of Sales/Payables | 17  21.8 | 16  22.7 |
| | 31  11.6 | | | | | | 33  10.9 | 22  16.8 |
| | 87  4.2 | | | | | | 49  7.5 | 57  6.4 |
| | 5.4 | | | | | Sales/Working Capital | 6.3 | 5.7 |
| | 7.8 | | | | | | 10.4 | 7.4 |
| | 25.0 | | | | | | 32.2 | 17.7 |
| | 12.8 | | | | | EBIT/Interest | 18.1 | 7.1 |
| | (19) 4.4 | | | | | | (39) 4.7 | (32) 3.0 |
| | 1.5 | | | | | | .9 | 1.0 |
| | | | | | | Net Profit + Depr., Dep., Amort./Cur. Mat. L/T/D | 12.6 | |
| | | | | | | | (10) 2.3 | |
| | | | | | | | -.6 | |
| | .2 | | | | | Fixed/Worth | .1 | .1 |
| | .6 | | | | | | .4 | .3 |
| | -.8 | | | | | | 1.8 | 1.7 |
| | 1.1 | | | | | Debt/Worth | .8 | .5 |
| | 6.5 | | | | | | 2.4 | 1.9 |
| | -10.4 | | | | | | 5.4 | 5.3 |
| | 77.9 | | | | | % Profit Before Taxes/Tangible Net Worth | 83.5 | 36.3 |
| | (14) 12.8 | | | | | | (37) 30.9 | (31) 12.0 |
| | -1.3 | | | | | | 2.9 | -.5 |
| | 15.8 | | | | | % Profit Before Taxes/Total Assets | 22.3 | 11.8 |
| | 5.7 | | | | | | 6.8 | 2.8 |
| | 1.4 | | | | | | -.9 | -.3 |
| | 101.8 | | | | | Sales/Net Fixed Assets | 86.2 | 50.5 |
| | 56.6 | | | | | | 19.6 | 23.6 |
| | 31.0 | | | | | | 11.8 | 15.1 |
| | 3.6 | | | | | Sales/Total Assets | 3.8 | 3.8 |
| | 2.6 | | | | | | 3.2 | 3.3 |
| | 2.1 | | | | | | 2.7 | 2.9 |
| | .3 | | | | | % Depr., Dep., Amort./Sales | .4 | .6 |
| | (13) .6 | | | | | | (35) 1.0 | (32) 1.0 |
| | .9 | | | | | | 1.4 | 1.5 |
| | 2.0 | | | | | % Officers', Directors' Owners' Comp/Sales | .8 | 1.7 |
| | (16) 3.5 | | | | | | (20) 2.9 | (19) 3.5 |
| | 5.3 | | | | | | 5.3 | 7.6 |
| 4740M | 62570M | 107251M | | | | Net Sales ($) | 1170240M | 335637M |
| 1242M | 22188M | 35879M | | | | Total Assets ($) | 329700M | 132593M |

M = $ thousand    MM = $ million
See Pages 9 through 22 for Explanation of Ratios and Data

## Comparative Historical Data     Current Data Sorted by Sales

| Type of Statement | 4/1/09-3/31/10 ALL | 4/1/10-3/31/11 ALL | 4/1/11-3/31/12 ALL | 0-1MM | 1-3MM | 3-5MM | 5-10MM | 10-25MM | 25MM & OVER |
|---|---|---|---|---|---|---|---|---|---|
| Unqualified | | | | | | | | | |
| Reviewed | 4 | 1 | | | | | 1 | 1 | |
| Compiled | 5 | 1 | 2 | 2 | 2 | 1 | | | |
| Tax Returns | 9 | 6 | 9 | 5 | 8 | 6 | 3 | 3 | 1 |
| Other | 10 | 16 | 22 | 1 | 1 | | 2 | | |
| | 6 | 7 | 4 | | 4 (4/1-9/30/11) | | 33 (10/1/11-3/31/12) | | |
| **NUMBER OF STATEMENTS** | 34 | 31 | 37 | 8 | 11 | 7 | 6 | 4 | 1 |
| **ASSETS** | % | % | % | % | % | % | % | % | % |
| Cash & Equivalents | 7.7 | 8.6 | 7.3 | | 9.7 | | | | |
| Trade Receivables (net) | 21.2 | 27.8 | 25.7 | | 23.3 | | | | |
| Inventory | 38.8 | 37.6 | 38.9 | | 34.5 | | | | |
| All Other Current | 2.9 | 1.1 | 1.8 | | 2.2 | | | | |
| Total Current | 70.6 | 75.1 | 73.7 | | 69.7 | | | | |
| Fixed Assets (net) | 18.1 | 17.1 | 13.2 | | 14.9 | | | | |
| Intangibles (net) | 5.1 | 3.0 | 4.3 | | 2.1 | | | | |
| All Other Non-Current | 6.2 | 4.7 | 8.8 | | 13.3 | | | | |
| Total | 100.0 | 100.0 | 100.0 | | 100.0 | | | | |
| **LIABILITIES** | | | | | | | | | |
| Notes Payable-Short Term | 12.7 | 11.6 | 10.1 | | 4.7 | | | | |
| Cur. Mat.-L.T.D. | 3.9 | 3.5 | 3.8 | | 2.4 | | | | |
| Trade Payables | 17.0 | 29.1 | 24.8 | | 23.5 | | | | |
| Income Taxes Payable | .2 | .0 | .1 | | .2 | | | | |
| All Other Current | 8.5 | 9.1 | 7.1 | | 9.5 | | | | |
| Total Current | 42.3 | 53.4 | 45.9 | | 40.3 | | | | |
| Long-Term Debt | 27.9 | 24.9 | 37.8 | | 33.4 | | | | |
| Deferred Taxes | .3 | .1 | .0 | | .0 | | | | |
| All Other Non-Current | 3.0 | 9.9 | 3.9 | | 2.5 | | | | |
| Net Worth | 26.6 | 11.7 | 12.4 | | 23.9 | | | | |
| Total Liabilities & Net Worth | 100.0 | 100.0 | 100.0 | | 100.0 | | | | |
| **INCOME DATA** | | | | | | | | | |
| Net Sales | 100.0 | 100.0 | 100.0 | | 100.0 | | | | |
| Gross Profit | 34.4 | 35.7 | 34.0 | | 35.2 | | | | |
| Operating Expenses | 36.6 | 34.1 | 31.2 | | 31.6 | | | | |
| Operating Profit | -2.2 | 1.7 | 2.7 | | 3.6 | | | | |
| All Other Expenses (net) | .3 | 1.4 | .6 | | .6 | | | | |
| Profit Before Taxes | -2.5 | .2 | 2.2 | | 3.0 | | | | |
| **RATIOS** | | | | | | | | | |
| Current | 2.4 | 2.9 | 2.5 | | 2.6 | | | | |
| Current | 1.8 | 1.9 | 1.9 | | 2.2 | | | | |
| Current | 1.3 | 1.1 | 1.4 | | 1.5 | | | | |
| Quick | 1.1 | 1.7 | 1.4 | | 1.4 | | | | |
| Quick | .7 | 1.0 | .7 | | 1.1 | | | | |
| Quick | .3 | .4 | .5 | | .4 | | | | |
| Sales/Receivables | 15   24.3 | 16   22.5 | 19   19.1 | | 24   15.0 | | | | |
| Sales/Receivables | 26   14.2 | 34   10.8 | 30   12.1 | | 34   10.8 | | | | |
| Sales/Receivables | 44   8.3 | 53   6.9 | 43   8.4 | | 45   8.2 | | | | |
| Cost of Sales/Inventory | 53   6.9 | 35   10.4 | 42   8.6 | | 39   9.3 | | | | |
| Cost of Sales/Inventory | 79   4.6 | 56   6.5 | 62   5.9 | | 51   7.1 | | | | |
| Cost of Sales/Inventory | 122   3.0 | 116   3.1 | 99   3.7 | | 152   2.4 | | | | |
| Cost of Sales/Payables | 17   21.3 | 30   12.4 | 20   18.0 | | 26   14.3 | | | | |
| Cost of Sales/Payables | 33   11.1 | 41   9.0 | 33   11.1 | | 31   11.6 | | | | |
| Cost of Sales/Payables | 57   6.4 | 59   6.2 | 54   6.7 | | 99   3.7 | | | | |
| Sales/Working Capital | 4.9 | 4.7 | 6.2 | | 4.9 | | | | |
| Sales/Working Capital | 9.2 | 8.1 | 8.6 | | 7.8 | | | | |
| Sales/Working Capital | 21.2 | 35.9 | 17.5 | | 11.6 | | | | |
| EBIT/Interest | 4.1 | 6.0 | 11.4 | | 12.8 | | | | |
| EBIT/Interest | (32)   .8 | (28)   1.6 | (33)   4.4 | | (10)   4.4 | | | | |
| EBIT/Interest | -4.0 | -1.8 | 1.1 | | 1.7 | | | | |
| Net Profit + Depr., Dep., Amort./Cur. Mat. L/T/D | | | | | | | | | |
| Fixed/Worth | .1 | .1 | .2 | | .0 | | | | |
| Fixed/Worth | .4 | .4 | .6 | | .3 | | | | |
| Fixed/Worth | 3.4 | UND | -.9 | | -.8 | | | | |
| Debt/Worth | .8 | 1.2 | 1.1 | | 1.1 | | | | |
| Debt/Worth | 2.0 | 2.5 | 4.0 | | 6.5 | | | | |
| Debt/Worth | 7.1 | UND | -7.4 | | -13.2 | | | | |
| % Profit Before Taxes/Tangible Net Worth | 13.6 | 23.2 | 57.3 | | | | | | |
| % Profit Before Taxes/Tangible Net Worth | (27)   .6 | (24)   2.5 | (25)   18.1 | | | | | | |
| % Profit Before Taxes/Tangible Net Worth | -14.2 | -14.7 | 3.2 | | | | | | |
| % Profit Before Taxes/Total Assets | 2.2 | 7.2 | 15.8 | | 9.3 | | | | |
| % Profit Before Taxes/Total Assets | -.6 | 1.2 | 5.7 | | 5.7 | | | | |
| % Profit Before Taxes/Total Assets | -12.1 | -8.1 | .4 | | 2.2 | | | | |
| Sales/Net Fixed Assets | 72.6 | 73.6 | 86.7 | | 87.7 | | | | |
| Sales/Net Fixed Assets | 22.4 | 25.7 | 51.1 | | 48.1 | | | | |
| Sales/Net Fixed Assets | 9.9 | 14.1 | 22.9 | | 17.0 | | | | |
| Sales/Total Assets | 3.4 | 3.5 | 3.7 | | 3.4 | | | | |
| Sales/Total Assets | 2.5 | 2.7 | 2.7 | | 2.4 | | | | |
| Sales/Total Assets | 1.9 | 2.1 | 2.3 | | 2.0 | | | | |
| % Depr., Dep., Amort./Sales | .8 | .6 | .3 | | | | | | |
| % Depr., Dep., Amort./Sales | (30)   1.4 | (25)   1.3 | (27)   .7 | | | | | | |
| % Depr., Dep., Amort./Sales | 2.2 | 2.0 | 1.1 | | | | | | |
| % Officers', Directors' Owners' Comp/Sales | 1.8 | .7 | 1.2 | | | | | | |
| % Officers', Directors' Owners' Comp/Sales | (20)   2.9 | (22)   2.3 | (27)   3.2 | | | | | | |
| % Officers', Directors' Owners' Comp/Sales | 5.9 | | 7.7 | | | | | | |
| Net Sales ($) | 263109M | 180603M | 174561M | 5560M | 21346M | 27219M | 38867M | 54952M | 26617M |
| Total Assets ($) | 120147M | 83122M | 59309M | 1804M | 9327M | 9798M | 11830M | 18511M | 8039M |

M = $ thousand    MM = $ million

See Pages 9 through 22 for Explanation of Ratios and Data

## Current Data Sorted by Assets | Comparative Historical Data

| Type of Statement | 0-500M | 500M-2MM | 2-10MM | 10-50MM | 50-100MM | 100-250MM | | 4/1/07-3/31/08 ALL | 4/1/08-3/31/09 ALL |
|---|---|---|---|---|---|---|---|---|---|
| Unqualified | 1 | 1 | 1 | 5 | | 1 | | 10 | 12 |
| Reviewed | 8 | 5 | 15 | 13 | 1 | | | 47 | 33 |
| Compiled | 26 | 42 | 26 | 3 | | | | 90 | 83 |
| Tax Returns | 11 | 80 | 29 | | | | | 69 | 106 |
| Other | | 46 | 35 | 10 | 2 | 3 | | 89 | 103 |
| | | 40 (4/1-9/30/11) | | | 324 (10/1/11-3/31/12) | | | | |
| NUMBER OF STATEMENTS | 46 | 174 | 106 | 31 | 3 | 4 | | 305 | 337 |
| | % | % | % | % | % | % | | % | % |
| **ASSETS** | | | | | | | | | |
| Cash & Equivalents | 10.0 | 7.4 | 6.3 | 4.9 | | | | 6.4 | 6.4 |
| Trade Receivables (net) | 9.1 | 7.7 | 12.5 | 11.9 | | | | 12.8 | 10.3 |
| Inventory | 52.0 | 54.6 | 49.9 | 49.1 | | | | 51.0 | 53.7 |
| All Other Current | 1.8 | 2.4 | 1.9 | 2.5 | | | | 2.2 | 2.6 |
| Total Current | 72.9 | 72.1 | 70.6 | 68.3 | | | | 72.4 | 73.0 |
| Fixed Assets (net) | 12.5 | 13.2 | 15.6 | 21.0 | | | | 16.3 | 14.4 |
| Intangibles (net) | 3.1 | 3.7 | 3.3 | 4.0 | | | | 1.8 | 2.3 |
| All Other Non-Current | 11.5 | 10.9 | 10.6 | 6.7 | | | | 9.6 | 10.2 |
| Total | 100.0 | 100.0 | 100.0 | 100.0 | | | | 100.0 | 100.0 |
| **LIABILITIES** | | | | | | | | | |
| Notes Payable-Short Term | 10.9 | 6.1 | 8.7 | 11.5 | | | | 10.3 | 12.1 |
| Cur. Mat.-L.T.D. | 2.6 | 2.4 | 2.7 | 1.4 | | | | 3.4 | 3.0 |
| Trade Payables | 18.1 | 10.3 | 11.9 | 16.9 | | | | 13.8 | 13.2 |
| Income Taxes Payable | .1 | .1 | .0 | .1 | | | | .2 | .1 |
| All Other Current | 11.7 | 7.6 | 6.0 | 5.2 | | | | 7.5 | 7.0 |
| Total Current | 43.5 | 26.5 | 29.2 | 35.1 | | | | 35.2 | 35.4 |
| Long-Term Debt | 20.2 | 23.0 | 17.0 | 10.7 | | | | 21.0 | 19.8 |
| Deferred Taxes | .0 | .0 | .2 | .3 | | | | .1 | .1 |
| All Other Non-Current | 24.2 | 12.4 | 8.0 | 6.3 | | | | 6.6 | 7.8 |
| Net Worth | 12.0 | 38.1 | 45.5 | 47.6 | | | | 37.1 | 36.9 |
| Total Liabilities & Net Worth | 100.0 | 100.0 | 100.0 | 100.0 | | | | 100.0 | 100.0 |
| **INCOME DATA** | | | | | | | | | |
| Net Sales | 100.0 | 100.0 | 100.0 | 100.0 | | | | 100.0 | 100.0 |
| Gross Profit | 41.2 | 38.8 | 36.1 | 35.9 | | | | 36.7 | 36.4 |
| Operating Expenses | 40.2 | 36.9 | 34.6 | 32.4 | | | | 34.4 | 34.7 |
| Operating Profit | 1.0 | 1.9 | 1.5 | 3.4 | | | | 2.3 | 1.7 |
| All Other Expenses (net) | -.4 | -.3 | -.2 | .1 | | | | .2 | .0 |
| Profit Before Taxes | 1.4 | 2.2 | 1.7 | 3.3 | | | | 2.0 | 1.7 |
| **RATIOS** | | | | | | | | | |
| Current | 5.5 | 5.9 | 4.8 | 3.3 | | | | 4.1 | 4.2 |
| | 2.5 | 3.6 | 2.7 | 1.8 | | | | 2.4 | 2.6 |
| | 1.2 | 1.9 | 1.7 | 1.5 | | | | 1.5 | 1.6 |
| Quick | 1.4 | 1.1 | 1.2 | 1.0 | | | | 1.1 | 1.0 |
| | (45) .7 | .5 | .7 | .4 | | | | (304) .5 | .5 |
| | .2 | .3 | .2 | .2 | | | | .3 | .2 |
| Sales/Receivables | 4 90.2 | 3 112.8 | 4 89.1 | 5 78.6 | | | | 6 56.4 | 4 81.5 |
| | 9 41.2 | 8 46.9 | 10 36.0 | 15 23.9 | | | | 12 29.3 | 9 39.4 |
| | 16 23.3 | 15 24.2 | 28 12.9 | 36 10.1 | | | | 29 12.6 | 22 16.4 |
| Cost of Sales/Inventory | 79 4.6 | 107 3.4 | 89 4.1 | 111 3.3 | | | | 85 4.3 | 94 3.9 |
| | 118 3.1 | 152 2.4 | 135 2.7 | 135 2.7 | | | | 126 2.9 | 138 2.7 |
| | 174 2.1 | 203 1.8 | 182 2.0 | 166 2.2 | | | | 173 2.1 | 185 2.0 |
| Cost of Sales/Payables | 9 41.1 | 11 34.6 | 15 23.8 | 26 14.2 | | | | 15 24.3 | 14 26.4 |
| | 22 16.3 | 22 16.7 | 24 15.4 | 37 9.9 | | | | 26 14.3 | 24 15.0 |
| | 37 9.9 | 38 9.7 | 38 9.6 | 48 7.6 | | | | 42 8.6 | 38 9.5 |
| Sales/Working Capital | 4.3 | 3.4 | 3.7 | 4.2 | | | | 4.2 | 3.8 |
| | 7.3 | 4.7 | 5.2 | 6.8 | | | | 5.9 | 5.6 |
| | NM | 7.8 | 8.3 | 9.8 | | | | 11.7 | 10.5 |
| EBIT/Interest | 7.3 | 9.4 | 8.9 | 12.5 | | | | 5.2 | 6.5 |
| | (32) 1.5 | (156) 3.0 | (95) 2.9 | (28) 6.6 | | | | (281) 2.4 | (306) 2.4 |
| | -1.3 | .9 | 1.2 | 1.2 | | | | 1.0 | .9 |
| Net Profit + Depr., Dep., Amort./Cur. Mat. L/T/D | | 10.0 | 15.1 | 25.2 | | | | 4.3 | 4.1 |
| | | (10) 1.5 | (16) 2.5 | (10) 5.5 | | | | (61) 1.9 | (54) 1.7 |
| | | .1 | .9 | .5 | | | | .7 | .4 |
| Fixed/Worth | .0 | .1 | .1 | .1 | | | | .1 | .1 |
| | .3 | .2 | .3 | .4 | | | | .4 | .3 |
| | NM | 1.2 | .7 | 1.1 | | | | 1.0 | 1.1 |
| Debt/Worth | .6 | .5 | .5 | .5 | | | | .7 | .6 |
| | 1.9 | 1.5 | 1.1 | 1.1 | | | | 1.6 | 1.6 |
| | -6.7 | 11.9 | 3.3 | 2.7 | | | | 4.7 | 4.6 |
| % Profit Before Taxes/Tangible Net Worth | 35.2 | 30.5 | 22.1 | 25.8 | | | | 25.1 | 25.4 |
| | (33) 19.1 | (141) 11.8 | (98) 8.3 | (28) 16.2 | | | | (269) 9.7 | (289) 12.2 |
| | 1.7 | 2.6 | 1.5 | 2.8 | | | | 1.6 | 1.5 |
| % Profit Before Taxes/Total Assets | 13.9 | 11.0 | 8.8 | 11.3 | | | | 9.0 | 9.8 |
| | 3.4 | 3.9 | 3.0 | 6.6 | | | | 3.5 | 4.2 |
| | -4.3 | .0 | .6 | .9 | | | | .3 | -.2 |
| Sales/Net Fixed Assets | 180.4 | 87.7 | 52.2 | 46.2 | | | | 53.3 | 73.0 |
| | 43.3 | 33.2 | 24.3 | 15.9 | | | | 23.1 | 26.0 |
| | 15.5 | 14.2 | 9.0 | 6.4 | | | | 10.2 | 10.2 |
| Sales/Total Assets | 3.9 | 3.0 | 2.8 | 2.7 | | | | 2.9 | 3.0 |
| | 2.8 | 2.3 | 2.2 | 2.1 | | | | 2.4 | 2.4 |
| | 1.9 | 1.6 | 1.8 | 1.6 | | | | 1.8 | 1.8 |
| % Depr., Dep., Amort./Sales | .6 | .5 | .7 | .4 | | | | .5 | .6 |
| | (26) 1.1 | (122) .9 | (90) 1.0 | (28) 1.2 | | | | (256) 1.2 | (269) 1.2 |
| | 1.8 | 1.9 | 1.6 | 1.7 | | | | 1.8 | 2.0 |
| % Officers', Directors' Owners' Comp/Sales | 3.2 | 2.3 | 1.4 | | | | | 2.3 | 1.7 |
| | (27) 6.3 | (107) 3.5 | (62) 2.7 | | | | | (172) 4.0 | (197) 3.1 |
| | 8.1 | 5.7 | 3.9 | | | | | 6.4 | 5.4 |
| Net Sales ($) | 40268M | 441337M | 986026M | 1470258M | 381781M | 1484927M | | 4482123M | 5286386M |
| Total Assets ($) | 13382M | 181933M | 427140M | 690205M | 234268M | 743505M | | 1909677M | 2072674M |

M = $ thousand   MM = $ million
See Pages 9 through 22 for Explanation of Ratios and Data

## Comparative Historical Data     Current Data Sorted by Sales

| | | | Type of Statement | | | | | | |
|---|---|---|---|---|---|---|---|---|---|
| 6 | 10 | 8 | Unqualified | 1 | 5 | 1 2 | 1 4 | 9 | 6 14 |
| 48 | 33 | 35 | Reviewed | 1 | 5 | 2 | 4 | 9 | 14 |
| 64 | 88 | 79 | Compiled | 7 | 28 | 10 | 21 | 10 | 3 |
| 121 | 134 | 135 | Tax Returns | 32 | 55 | 16 | 24 | 8 | |
| 98 | 104 | 107 | Other | 11 | 38 | 11 | 23 | 10 | 14 |
| 4/1/09- 3/31/10 ALL | 4/1/10- 3/31/11 ALL | 4/1/11- 3/31/12 ALL | | | 40 (4/1-9/30/11) | | 324 (10/1/11-3/31/12) | | |
| | | | | 0-1MM | 1-3MM | 3-5MM | 5-10MM | 10-25MM | 25MM & OVER |
| 337 | 369 | 364 | NUMBER OF STATEMENTS | 51 | 126 | 40 | 73 | 37 | 37 |
| % | % | % | ASSETS | % | % | % | % | % | % |
| 7.2 | 6.8 | 7.1 | Cash & Equivalents | 7.2 | 6.7 | 11.4 | 7.1 | 5.9 | 4.9 |
| 10.0 | 8.5 | 9.7 | Trade Receivables (net) | 6.4 | 6.5 | 10.7 | 13.7 | 14.7 | 11.4 |
| 51.0 | 53.1 | 52.2 | Inventory | 52.1 | 56.2 | 48.1 | 51.1 | 48.2 | 48.9 |
| 1.7 | 2.1 | 2.2 | All Other Current | 2.5 | 2.2 | 1.7 | 2.1 | 2.0 | 2.2 |
| 69.9 | 70.4 | 71.1 | Total Current | 68.2 | 71.5 | 72.0 | 74.0 | 71.0 | 67.4 |
| 15.3 | 15.0 | 14.8 | Fixed Assets (net) | 14.7 | 13.3 | 16.4 | 12.0 | 16.8 | 21.3 |
| 3.9 | 2.7 | 3.7 | Intangibles (net) | 4.8 | 3.7 | 3.0 | 3.4 | 2.9 | 4.4 |
| 10.9 | 11.8 | 10.4 | All Other Non-Current | 12.2 | 11.5 | 8.6 | 10.5 | 9.4 | 6.9 |
| 100.0 | 100.0 | 100.0 | Total | 100.0 | 100.0 | 100.0 | 100.0 | 100.0 | 100.0 |
| | | | LIABILITIES | | | | | | |
| 8.9 | 8.4 | 7.9 | Notes Payable-Short Term | 7.9 | 7.2 | 8.9 | 6.8 | 8.9 | 10.6 |
| 3.5 | 2.8 | 2.4 | Cur. Mat.-L.T.D. | 2.6 | 2.6 | 1.4 | 3.2 | 2.1 | 1.3 |
| 12.0 | 12.9 | 12.3 | Trade Payables | 10.6 | 10.8 | 11.5 | 13.9 | 13.1 | 17.1 |
| .2 | .1 | .1 | Income Taxes Payable | .1 | .1 | .0 | .0 | .1 | .1 |
| 6.5 | 6.9 | 7.5 | All Other Current | 9.3 | 8.1 | 7.6 | 4.9 | 8.5 | 6.8 |
| 30.9 | 31.2 | 30.2 | Total Current | 30.5 | 28.8 | 29.5 | 28.9 | 32.7 | 35.7 |
| 22.7 | 21.0 | 19.8 | Long-Term Debt | 30.1 | 22.7 | 17.5 | 17.3 | 11.3 | 11.1 |
| .1 | .1 | .1 | Deferred Taxes | .0 | .0 | .1 | .0 | .4 | .7 |
| 9.5 | 11.5 | 12.0 | All Other Non-Current | 22.6 | 14.8 | 6.8 | 7.2 | 7.6 | 7.6 |
| 36.7 | 36.1 | 37.8 | Net Worth | 16.7 | 33.7 | 46.1 | 46.6 | 48.0 | 44.9 |
| 100.0 | 100.0 | 100.0 | Total Liabilties & Net Worth | 100.0 | 100.0 | 100.0 | 100.0 | 100.0 | 100.0 |
| | | | INCOME DATA | | | | | | |
| 100.0 | 100.0 | 100.0 | Net Sales | 100.0 | 100.0 | 100.0 | 100.0 | 100.0 | 100.0 |
| 38.9 | 38.0 | 38.1 | Gross Profit | 42.3 | 40.0 | 36.3 | 35.5 | 34.7 | 36.2 |
| 37.2 | 36.4 | 36.3 | Operating Expenses | 42.0 | 38.2 | 33.5 | 33.8 | 32.6 | 33.3 |
| 1.7 | 1.6 | 1.8 | Operating Profit | .4 | 1.8 | 2.8 | 1.7 | 2.1 | 2.9 |
| .0 | -.2 | -.2 | All Other Expenses (net) | -.1 | -.4 | -.1 | -.3 | -.1 | .0 |
| 1.8 | 1.8 | 2.0 | Profit Before Taxes | .5 | 2.1 | 2.8 | 2.0 | 2.2 | 2.9 |
| | | | RATIOS | | | | | | |
| 4.9 | 4.5 | 5.3 | | 5.5 | 6.1 | 6.1 | 4.9 | 4.3 | 3.0 |
| 2.8 | 2.8 | 3.0 | Current | 3.2 | 3.6 | 3.6 | 3.0 | 2.3 | 1.8 |
| 1.6 | 1.6 | 1.8 | | 1.7 | 2.2 | 1.5 | 1.9 | 1.6 | 1.4 |
| 1.1 | 1.0 | 1.1 | | 1.1 | 1.1 | 2.4 | 1.5 | 1.0 | .8 |
| .5 | .5 (363) | .5 | Quick | (50) .4 | .5 | .6 | .8 | .7 | .4 |
| .2 | .2 | .2 | | .2 | .2 | .3 | .3 | .2 | .2 |
| 5   78.7 | 4   98.1 | 4   98.7 | | 4   87.5 | 3   117.9 | 4   96.9 | 5   73.2 | 4   86.2 | 3   134.0 |
| 10   36.7 | 8   45.6 | 9   41.2 | Sales/Receivables | 9   39.4 | 7   53.4 | 11   34.7 | 11   32.2 | 9   38.5 | 15   24.4 |
| 20   18.0 | 18   19.9 | 18   20.0 | | 16   23.4 | 14   26.0 | 21   17.6 | 28   13.2 | 31   11.8 | 38   9.7 |
| 95   3.8 | 100   3.6 | 99   3.7 | | 114   3.2 | 122   3.0 | 69   5.3 | 83   4.4 | 62   5.9 | 99   3.7 |
| 141   2.6 | 141   2.6 | 140   2.6 | Cost of Sales/Inventory | 215   1.7 | 166   2.2 | 122   3.0 | 118   3.1 | 101   3.6 | 135   2.7 |
| 200   1.8 | 187   1.9 | 192   1.9 | | 304   1.2 | 203   1.8 | 159   2.3 | 174   2.1 | 166   2.2 | 159   2.3 |
| 14   26.6 | 15   24.2 | 13   27.2 | | 14   26.3 | 9   41.9 | 12   30.6 | 17   21.3 | 15   24.0 | 25   14.6 |
| 24   15.4 | 26   13.9 | 25   14.6 | Cost of Sales/Payables | 30   12.3 | 20   18.2 | 20   18.3 | 26   13.9 | 22   16.7 | 36   10.0 |
| 37   9.8 | 43   8.4 | 39   9.4 | | 45   8.1 | 34   10.6 | 41   9.0 | 40   9.2 | 35   10.4 | 50   7.3 |
| 3.7 | 3.7 | 3.7 | | 2.5 | 3.6 | 3.7 | 3.9 | 4.5 | 5.0 |
| 5.5 | 5.4 | 5.1 | Sales/Working Capital | 4.7 | 4.5 | 5.5 | 5.3 | 6.4 | 7.6 |
| 9.2 | 10.1 | 9.1 | | 9.9 | 7.0 | 14.5 | 7.8 | 13.4 | 14.2 |
| 6.7 | 6.6 | 9.1 | | 4.4 | 8.2 | 16.2 | 10.0 | 9.6 | 13.4 |
| (295) 2.6 | (336) 3.0 | (318) 2.9 | EBIT/Interest | (39) 1.8 | (110) 2.4 | (36) 3.8 | (65) 3.4 | (34) 4.8 | (34) 4.4 |
| .5 | 1.0 | 1.0 | | -1.2 | .6 | .6 | 1.2 | 2.0 | 1.4 |
| 4.2 | 5.5 | 10.6 | | | | | | 14.9 | 20.5 |
| (50) 1.6 | (44) 1.6 | (39) 2.4 | Net Profit + Depr., Dep., Amort./Cur. Mat. L/T/D | | | | (12) 3.7 | (12) 4.9 |
| .5 | .4 | .6 | | | | | | 1.0 | 1.0 |
| .1 | .1 | .1 | | .0 | .1 | .1 | .1 | .1 | .3 |
| .3 | .3 | .3 | Fixed/Worth | .3 | .2 | .3 | .2 | .3 | .4 |
| 1.6 | 1.1 | 1.0 | | -12.9 | 2.5 | .9 | .5 | .6 | 1.2 |
| .6 | .6 | .5 | | .8 | .4 | .3 | .5 | .6 | .6 |
| 1.7 | 1.5 | 1.4 | Debt/Worth | 3.0 | 1.4 | 1.0 | 1.0 | 1.1 | 1.2 |
| 7.3 | 5.6 | 5.5 | | -7.4 | 13.2 | 2.9 | 3.7 | 2.8 | 3.4 |
| 26.9 | 23.9 | 28.3 | | 40.3 | 28.1 | 29.9 | 26.3 | 27.7 | 26.3 |
| (280) 11.0 | (311) 11.2 | (306) 10.7 | % Profit Before Taxes/Tangible Net Worth | (35) 18.1 | (99) 9.8 | (35) 8.0 | (67) 10.6 | 9.8 | (33) 13.7 |
| 1.9 | 2.1 | 2.3 | | .6 | 2.7 | 2.3 | 1.4 | 2.6 | 6.6 |
| 9.9 | 9.9 | 10.3 | | 7.9 | 9.8 | 16.5 | 9.1 | 10.6 | 10.3 |
| 4.1 | 4.1 | 3.8 | % Profit Before Taxes/Total Assets | 1.4 | 3.9 | 3.0 | 3.9 | 5.1 | 5.8 |
| -.5 | .0 | .2 | | -5.2 | -.1 | .2 | .6 | 1.2 | 1.3 |
| 56.5 | 64.1 | 71.7 | | 396.5 | 72.3 | 67.3 | 92.0 | 60.5 | 32.4 |
| 24.4 | 25.3 | 28.6 | Sales/Net Fixed Assets | 32.5 | 29.6 | 32.7 | 35.3 | 27.0 | 15.7 |
| 9.7 | 9.8 | 11.3 | | 11.1 | 13.7 | 7.0 | 17.0 | 8.3 | 6.2 |
| 2.9 | 2.8 | 2.9 | | 2.5 | 2.8 | 3.2 | 3.0 | 3.5 | 2.9 |
| 2.2 | 2.3 | 2.3 | Sales/Total Assets | 1.7 | 2.2 | 2.4 | 2.4 | 2.5 | 2.4 |
| 1.7 | 1.7 | 1.7 | | 1.2 | 1.7 | 1.9 | 1.9 | 1.8 | 1.6 |
| .6 | .7 | .5 | | .7 | .5 | .5 | .5 | .5 | .5 |
| (270) 1.3 | (283) 1.2 | (272) 1.0 | % Depr., Dep., Amort./Sales | (27) 1.4 | (87) 1.1 | (34) .8 | (59) .9 | (33) .8 | (32) 1.3 |
| 2.2 | 2.1 | 1.8 | | 2.3 | 2.2 | 1.7 | 1.4 | 1.1 | 1.8 |
| 1.9 | 1.6 | 2.0 | | 3.2 | 2.3 | 2.1 | 2.2 | .9 | |
| (201) 3.5 | (220) 3.4 | (205) 3.2 | % Officers', Directors' Owners' Comp/Sales | (26) 6.6 | (80) 3.9 | (23) 2.8 | (47) 3.0 | (20) 1.6 | |
| 5.6 | 5.6 | 5.4 | | 7.9 | 5.7 | 4.4 | 4.9 | 3.3 | |
| 3234499M | 3274629M | 4804597M | Net Sales ($) | 33610M | 238419M | 155485M | 487906M | 549460M | 3339717M |
| 1496318M | 1464549M | 2290433M | Total Assets ($) | 21758M | 114718M | 68940M | 214233M | 246080M | 1624704M |

## Current Data Sorted by Assets  |  Comparative Historical Data

| 0-500M | 500M-2MM | 2-10MM | 10-50MM | 50-100MM | 100-250MM | Type of Statement | 4/1/07-3/31/08 ALL | 4/1/08-3/31/09 ALL |
|---|---|---|---|---|---|---|---|---|
| | | 9 | 14 | 7 | 1 | Unqualified | 30 | 38 |
| 3 | 17 | 52 | 30 | 2 | 1 | Reviewed | 87 | 110 |
| 8 | 24 | 33 | 3 | | | Compiled | 80 | 66 |
| 42 | 60 | 36 | 2 | | | Tax Returns | 133 | 130 |
| 23 | 59 | 58 | 20 | 7 | 5 | Other | 144 | 147 |
| 47 (4/1-9/30/11) | | | 469 (10/1/11-3/31/12) | | | | | |
| 76 | 160 | 188 | 69 | 16 | 7 | NUMBER OF STATEMENTS | 474 | 491 |
| % | % | % | % | % | % | ASSETS | % | % |
| 15.7 | 10.1 | 7.4 | 5.3 | 3.0 | | Cash & Equivalents | 7.8 | 8.2 |
| 25.6 | 26.9 | 28.6 | 28.2 | 20.9 | | Trade Receivables (net) | 27.6 | 26.0 |
| 24.9 | 35.2 | 34.8 | 32.1 | 25.7 | | Inventory | 32.1 | 34.5 |
| 3.0 | 3.2 | 2.6 | 2.3 | 2.4 | | All Other Current | 3.0 | 2.3 |
| 69.2 | 75.5 | 73.3 | 67.9 | 52.0 | | Total Current | 70.4 | 70.9 |
| 13.1 | 14.9 | 16.5 | 23.2 | 32.8 | | Fixed Assets (net) | 19.3 | 19.1 |
| 6.2 | 2.1 | 3.4 | 2.5 | 10.8 | | Intangibles (net) | 3.4 | 2.3 |
| 11.5 | 7.6 | 6.8 | 6.4 | 4.4 | | All Other Non-Current | 6.9 | 7.7 |
| 100.0 | 100.0 | 100.0 | 100.0 | 100.0 | | Total | 100.0 | 100.0 |
| | | | | | | LIABILITIES | | |
| 22.8 | 10.4 | 11.9 | 12.4 | 6.5 | | Notes Payable-Short Term | 12.3 | 18.0 |
| 4.2 | 2.7 | 2.7 | 4.2 | 3.1 | | Cur. Mat.-L.T.D. | 4.1 | 3.6 |
| 19.7 | 21.4 | 16.9 | 15.8 | 10.8 | | Trade Payables | 17.5 | 15.9 |
| .1 | .1 | .1 | .1 | .1 | | Income Taxes Payable | .1 | .2 |
| 21.7 | 10.3 | 8.4 | 6.5 | 5.5 | | All Other Current | 10.8 | 10.4 |
| 68.5 | 44.9 | 40.0 | 38.9 | 26.1 | | Total Current | 44.9 | 48.2 |
| 14.1 | 20.1 | 10.5 | 16.4 | 16.8 | | Long-Term Debt | 16.2 | 17.2 |
| .0 | .1 | .1 | .5 | .7 | | Deferred Taxes | .2 | .3 |
| 13.6 | 11.8 | 4.9 | 5.1 | 4.8 | | All Other Non-Current | 8.1 | 5.9 |
| 3.8 | 23.1 | 44.5 | 39.0 | 51.6 | | Net Worth | 30.6 | 28.4 |
| 100.0 | 100.0 | 100.0 | 100.0 | 100.0 | | Total Liabilities & Net Worth | 100.0 | 100.0 |
| | | | | | | INCOME DATA | | |
| 100.0 | 100.0 | 100.0 | 100.0 | 100.0 | | Net Sales | 100.0 | 100.0 |
| 36.8 | 35.0 | 29.0 | 28.1 | 26.7 | | Gross Profit | 31.1 | 30.0 |
| 34.9 | 32.6 | 27.4 | 25.1 | 24.4 | | Operating Expenses | 28.5 | 29.2 |
| 1.9 | 2.4 | 1.7 | 3.0 | 2.4 | | Operating Profit | 2.6 | .8 |
| .7 | .6 | -.1 | .3 | .3 | | All Other Expenses (net) | .7 | .5 |
| 1.2 | 1.8 | 1.7 | 2.7 | 2.1 | | Profit Before Taxes | 2.0 | .3 |
| | | | | | | RATIOS | | |
| 3.2 | 3.8 | 3.2 | 3.1 | 3.5 | | Current | 2.9 | 2.9 |
| 1.2 | 1.9 | 2.0 | 1.8 | 2.1 | | | 1.7 | 1.8 |
| .6 | 1.2 | 1.3 | 1.3 | 1.2 | | | 1.1 | 1.1 |
| 1.9 | 1.6 | 1.6 | 1.5 | 1.8 | | Quick | 1.5 | 1.5 |
| .7 | .9 | .9 | .9 | 1.0 | | | .8 | .8 |
| .3 | .4 | .5 | .5 | .5 | | | .5 | .4 |
| 0 UND | 17 21.6 | 23 15.6 | 33 10.9 | 31 11.8 | | Sales/Receivables | 21 17.2 | 16 22.5 |
| 16 22.5 | 31 11.7 | 38 9.7 | 46 8.0 | 43 8.5 | | | 31 11.7 | 30 12.2 |
| 38 9.7 | 50 7.3 | 56 6.5 | 63 5.8 | 49 7.4 | | | 46 7.9 | 44 8.3 |
| 0 UND | 28 12.9 | 38 9.6 | 48 7.6 | 41 8.9 | | Cost of Sales/Inventory | 26 14.3 | 30 12.3 |
| 14 26.5 | 65 5.6 | 66 5.5 | 64 5.7 | 60 6.1 | | | 53 6.8 | 56 6.5 |
| 74 4.9 | 118 3.1 | 107 3.4 | 94 3.9 | 87 4.2 | | | 86 4.2 | 92 4.0 |
| 0 UND | 18 20.6 | 18 20.8 | 22 16.9 | 16 23.0 | | Cost of Sales/Payables | 14 26.6 | 11 34.0 |
| 17 21.9 | 36 10.2 | 29 12.4 | 32 11.5 | 24 15.0 | | | 25 14.6 | 21 17.5 |
| 48 7.6 | 51 7.1 | 47 7.7 | 47 7.7 | 33 10.9 | | | 42 8.7 | 37 9.8 |
| 7.4 | 4.4 | 4.9 | 4.7 | 5.2 | | Sales/Working Capital | 5.9 | 5.9 |
| 57.2 | 8.7 | 7.6 | 7.3 | 7.1 | | | 10.3 | 10.8 |
| -13.6 | 24.5 | 15.0 | 19.1 | 26.0 | | | 43.5 | 69.4 |
| 5.2 | 6.9 | 9.4 | 9.9 | 9.9 | | EBIT/Interest | 7.3 | 6.6 |
| (50) 1.2 | (131) 2.2 | (167) 3.2 | (66) 3.1 | 3.6 | | | (431) 2.5 | (443) 2.0 |
| -1.4 | .2 | 1.1 | 1.3 | 1.7 | | | .4 | -.5 |
| | 9.1 | 4.5 | 4.7 | | | Net Profit + Depr., Dep., Amort./Cur. Mat. L/T/D | 4.4 | 5.7 |
| | (12) 2.6 | (33) 1.9 | (23) 2.8 | | | | (78) 1.5 | (83) 1.7 |
| | .8 | .8 | 1.2 | | | | .3 | .2 |
| .0 | .1 | .1 | .2 | .3 | | Fixed/Worth | .2 | .2 |
| .3 | .4 | .3 | .5 | .9 | | | .5 | .5 |
| -6.5 | NM | .8 | 1.3 | 1.6 | | | 1.9 | 1.7 |
| .7 | .7 | .6 | .5 | .4 | | Debt/Worth | .9 | .7 |
| 5.8 | 2.3 | 1.4 | 1.6 | 1.5 | | | 1.9 | 2.0 |
| -5.3 | -103.4 | 3.0 | 3.7 | 1.8 | | | 8.4 | 8.4 |
| 71.4 | 32.9 | 25.1 | 17.2 | 20.6 | | % Profit Before Taxes/Tangible Net Worth | 36.4 | 27.2 |
| (47) 14.3 | (118) 9.9 | (176) 7.3 | (65) 8.4 | (15) 7.5 | | | (388) 13.9 | (402) 7.9 |
| -9.4 | .2 | .8 | 2.1 | 4.5 | | | .7 | -4.2 |
| 21.3 | 11.7 | 9.6 | 8.4 | 5.6 | | % Profit Before Taxes/Total Assets | 12.4 | 10.5 |
| 3.9 | 3.5 | 3.3 | 2.8 | 3.6 | | | 4.5 | 2.6 |
| -5.9 | -1.6 | .2 | .2 | 1.6 | | | -1.7 | -4.3 |
| UND | 116.9 | 54.8 | 26.1 | 20.2 | | Sales/Net Fixed Assets | 52.7 | 55.6 |
| 95.6 | 30.5 | 22.7 | 13.0 | 5.3 | | | 21.9 | 24.0 |
| 23.8 | 13.0 | 10.8 | 5.0 | 2.0 | | | 9.6 | 10.1 |
| 5.8 | 3.7 | 3.2 | 2.7 | 2.6 | | Sales/Total Assets | 4.0 | 4.0 |
| 4.1 | 2.8 | 2.4 | 2.3 | 1.8 | | | 2.8 | 2.9 |
| 2.9 | 1.9 | 1.9 | 1.5 | 1.0 | | | 2.1 | 2.1 |
| .3 | .4 | .5 | .7 | .8 | | % Depr., Dep., Amort./Sales | .6 | .6 |
| (33) 1.2 | (110) 1.0 | (155) .9 | (62) 1.1 | (15) 1.9 | | | (395) 1.1 | (395) 1.1 |
| 2.1 | 1.6 | 1.8 | 2.1 | 2.4 | | | 2.0 | 2.1 |
| 5.0 | 2.1 | 1.3 | .4 | | | % Officers', Directors' Owners' Comp/Sales | 1.8 | 1.7 |
| (38) 6.9 | (80) 3.7 | (87) 2.4 | (25) 1.5 | | | | (238) 3.2 | (225) 3.2 |
| 10.5 | 5.3 | 4.4 | 2.5 | | | | 5.7 | 5.8 |
| 83357M | 515593M | 2181385M | 2977812M | 2047375M | 1707530M | Net Sales ($) | 9650983M | 10117302M |
| 17480M | 179040M | 856753M | 1373925M | 1045866M | 957234M | Total Assets ($) | 3663549M | 4200071M |

M = $ thousand    MM = $ million
See Pages 9 through 22 for Explanation of Ratios and Data

## Comparative Historical Data | Current Data Sorted by Sales

| 37 | 38 | 31 | Type of Statement Unqualified | | | 1 | 1 | 7 | 22 |
|---|---|---|---|---|---|---|---|---|---|
| 94 | 89 | 105 | Reviewed | 3 | 7 | 10 | 23 | 33 | 29 |
| 74 | 65 | 68 | Compiled | 3 | 16 | 15 | 18 | 13 | 3 |
| 135 | 153 | 140 | Tax Returns | 26 | 46 | 26 | 20 | 20 | 2 |
| 143 | 134 | 172 | Other | 21 | 34 | 25 | 32 | 34 | 26 |
| 4/1/09-3/31/10 ALL | 4/1/10-3/31/11 ALL | 4/1/11-3/31/12 ALL | | 47 (4/1-9/30/11) | | 469 (10/1/11-3/31/12) | | | |
| | | | | 0-1MM | 1-3MM | 3-5MM | 5-10MM | 10-25MM | 25MM & OVER |
| 483 | 479 | 516 | NUMBER OF STATEMENTS | 53 | 103 | 77 | 94 | 107 | 82 |
| % | % | % | ASSETS | % | % | % | % | % | % |
| 8.9 | 8.7 | 9.0 | Cash & Equivalents | 18.3 | 8.3 | 11.2 | 9.4 | 5.8 | 5.5 |
| 25.1 | 25.2 | 27.1 | Trade Receivables (net) | 22.7 | 23.6 | 26.9 | 27.7 | 30.7 | 29.4 |
| 33.0 | 34.0 | 32.7 | Inventory | 24.0 | 36.1 | 31.5 | 35.4 | 34.1 | 30.4 |
| 2.4 | 2.3 | 2.8 | All Other Current | 2.9 | 3.4 | 2.7 | 2.5 | 2.5 | 2.8 |
| 69.5 | 70.2 | 71.7 | Total Current | 67.9 | 71.4 | 72.2 | 75.0 | 73.1 | 68.2 |
| 19.0 | 19.1 | 17.2 | Fixed Assets (net) | 12.9 | 15.6 | 17.4 | 14.7 | 18.4 | 23.0 |
| 3.4 | 3.1 | 3.6 | Intangibles (net) | 5.6 | 4.2 | 2.9 | 3.4 | 2.1 | 4.2 |
| 8.1 | 7.6 | 7.6 | All Other Non-Current | 13.6 | 8.8 | 7.5 | 7.0 | 6.4 | 4.6 |
| 100.0 | 100.0 | 100.0 | Total | 100.0 | 100.0 | 100.0 | 100.0 | 100.0 | 100.0 |
| | | | LIABILITIES | | | | | | |
| 14.1 | 13.2 | 12.8 | Notes Payable-Short Term | 17.4 | 16.4 | 9.0 | 9.7 | 14.2 | 10.6 |
| 3.5 | 3.4 | 3.1 | Cur. Mat.-L.T.D. | 3.0 | 3.4 | 3.1 | 2.2 | 4.1 | 2.7 |
| 17.6 | 18.5 | 18.3 | Trade Payables | 15.1 | 20.7 | 19.0 | 20.0 | 17.0 | 16.2 |
| .1 | .1 | .1 | Income Taxes Payable | .1 | .2 | .0 | .1 | .0 | .1 |
| 11.3 | 11.1 | 10.6 | All Other Current | 25.5 | 9.7 | 12.1 | 8.6 | 7.2 | 7.3 |
| 46.6 | 46.3 | 44.9 | Total Current | 61.1 | 50.3 | 43.2 | 40.7 | 42.6 | 36.8 |
| 17.2 | 15.6 | 15.0 | Long-Term Debt | 12.7 | 24.8 | 14.2 | 12.5 | 9.8 | 14.8 |
| .3 | .2 | .2 | Deferred Taxes | .0 | .1 | .0 | .2 | .1 | .6 |
| 8.7 | 8.9 | 8.4 | All Other Non-Current | 16.9 | 10.0 | 12.6 | 5.4 | 5.0 | 4.6 |
| 27.3 | 29.1 | 31.6 | Net Worth | 9.3 | 14.9 | 29.9 | 41.2 | 42.6 | 43.1 |
| 100.0 | 100.0 | 100.0 | Total Liabilities & Net Worth | 100.0 | 100.0 | 100.0 | 100.0 | 100.0 | 100.0 |
| | | | INCOME DATA | | | | | | |
| 100.0 | 100.0 | 100.0 | Net Sales | 100.0 | 100.0 | 100.0 | 100.0 | 100.0 | 100.0 |
| 30.7 | 31.0 | 31.9 | Gross Profit | 39.8 | 36.2 | 34.4 | 30.0 | 26.6 | 28.2 |
| 30.6 | 30.6 | 29.7 | Operating Expenses | 37.2 | 34.0 | 32.5 | 28.0 | 24.7 | 25.1 |
| .1 | .4 | 2.2 | Operating Profit | 2.6 | 2.2 | 1.9 | 1.9 | 1.8 | 3.1 |
| .4 | .2 | .3 | All Other Expenses (net) | 1.3 | .8 | -.1 | .0 | .1 | .0 |
| -.3 | .2 | 1.9 | Profit Before Taxes | 1.4 | 1.4 | 2.0 | 1.9 | 1.7 | 3.1 |
| | | | RATIOS | | | | | | |
| 3.1 | 3.1 | 3.3 | Current | 5.2 | 3.5 | 3.4 | 3.4 | 2.8 | 3.3 |
| 1.7 | 1.8 | 1.9 | | 1.9 | 1.9 | 1.9 | 1.8 | 1.9 | 2.1 |
| 1.1 | 1.2 | 1.2 | | .7 | 1.0 | 1.2 | 1.4 | 1.3 | 1.3 |
| 1.5 | 1.4 | 1.6 | Quick | 2.5 | 1.4 | 1.9 | 1.7 | 1.4 | 1.6 |
| (482) .8 | .8 | .9 | | .9 | .7 | .9 | 1.0 | .8 | 1.0 |
| .4 | .4 | .5 | | .3 | .3 | .4 | .5 | .6 | .6 |
| 19 19.5 | 19 19.5 | 19 19.2 | Sales/Receivables | 0 UND | 11 32.4 | 16 22.8 | 16 22.2 | 29 12.7 | 30 12.2 |
| 31 11.8 | 31 11.7 | 34 10.6 | | 19 19.6 | 28 12.9 | 30 12.0 | 33 11.0 | 40 9.2 | 42 8.6 |
| 44 8.3 | 45 8.1 | 52 7.0 | | 52 7.0 | 49 7.4 | 52 7.0 | 56 7.2 | 56 6.5 | 56 6.5 |
| 32 11.2 | 32 11.4 | 29 12.5 | Cost of Sales/Inventory | 0 UND | 25 14.6 | 25 14.8 | 37 9.8 | 38 9.7 | 42 8.6 |
| 61 6.0 | 64 5.7 | 62 5.9 | | 19 19.0 | 89 4.1 | 64 5.7 | 61 6.0 | 60 6.1 | 61 6.0 |
| 101 3.6 | 102 3.6 | 104 3.5 | | 94 3.9 | 146 2.5 | 118 3.1 | 101 3.6 | 104 3.5 | 83 4.4 |
| 15 25.2 | 14 26.3 | 16 22.3 | Cost of Sales/Payables | 0 UND | 16 22.2 | 16 23.5 | 16 22.5 | 19 19.6 | 18 19.9 |
| 25 14.4 | 28 13.2 | 30 12.0 | | 17 21.1 | 34 10.6 | 33 11.2 | 31 11.7 | 28 13.1 | 29 12.7 |
| 42 8.6 | 47 7.8 | 48 7.6 | | 43 8.4 | 55 6.6 | 56 6.5 | 49 7.5 | 42 8.7 | 46 8.0 |
| 4.9 | 5.1 | 5.0 | Sales/Working Capital | 4.0 | 4.1 | 4.5 | 5.2 | 5.3 | 5.1 |
| 9.5 | 8.7 | 8.4 | | 22.5 | 8.8 | 9.1 | 7.6 | 8.1 | 7.6 |
| 39.5 | 43.6 | 26.9 | | -12.8 | -999.8 | -25.7 | 15.0 | 20.0 | 18.0 |
| 5.9 | 6.4 | 8.8 | EBIT/Interest | 3.2 | 6.4 | 6.4 | 10.3 | 8.8 | 18.9 |
| (415) 1.6 | (424) 1.8 | (437) 2.6 | | (33) 1.0 | (78) 1.4 | (65) 2.6 | (84) 2.9 | (99) 3.1 | (78) 4.2 |
| -1.6 | -.6 | .7 | | -1.2 | -1.1 | .5 | .9 | 1.2 | 1.7 |
| 3.1 | 4.8 | 4.7 | Net Profit + Depr., Dep., Amort./Cur. Mat. L/T/D | | | | 3.0 | 4.5 | 9.2 |
| (73) 1.7 | (74) 2.0 | (76) 2.4 | | | | | (18) 1.6 | (21) 2.8 | (24) 3.4 |
| .0 | .4 | .8 | | | | | .7 | 1.2 | 1.2 |
| .1 | .1 | .1 | Fixed/Worth | .0 | .0 | .1 | .1 | .1 | .2 |
| .4 | .5 | .4 | | .7 | .3 | .6 | .3 | .3 | .5 |
| 2.0 | 1.8 | 1.5 | | -3.2 | 9.1 | 7.1 | .8 | 1.1 | .9 |
| .7 | .7 | .6 | Debt/Worth | .3 | .7 | .7 | .6 | .6 | .5 |
| 1.9 | 1.7 | 1.7 | | 3.0 | 4.0 | 2.0 | 1.6 | 1.5 | 1.5 |
| 13.9 | 8.6 | 7.2 | | -10.8 | -16.0 | 41.3 | -4.8 | 2.9 | 3.0 |
| 23.9 | 18.2 | 29.7 | % Profit Before Taxes/Tangible Net Worth | 35.3 | 38.1 | 31.7 | 39.5 | 22.6 | 22.0 |
| (388) 4.7 | (394) 4.9 | (428) 8.8 | | (33) 7.7 | (72) 8.7 | (59) 7.2 | (84) 6.5 | (103) 8.4 | (77) 10.1 |
| -8.7 | -4.7 | 1.2 | | -21.4 | -2.9 | 1.2 | .7 | 1.3 | 3.2 |
| 7.7 | 7.7 | 10.5 | % Profit Before Taxes/Total Assets | 15.7 | 12.2 | 12.2 | 13.0 | 8.1 | 9.0 |
| 1.4 | 1.6 | 3.4 | | 2.7 | 3.0 | 3.6 | 2.6 | 3.6 | 3.7 |
| -7.1 | -3.2 | -.2 | | -5.7 | -3.3 | .2 | -.5 | .5 | 1.6 |
| 56.9 | 64.8 | 78.6 | Sales/Net Fixed Assets | UND | 242.4 | 72.1 | 79.0 | 61.0 | 42.1 |
| 23.1 | 22.3 | 24.6 | | 43.4 | 33.1 | 26.5 | 26.7 | 22.1 | 15.6 |
| 9.7 | 9.1 | 10.3 | | 14.0 | 11.2 | 9.8 | 13.8 | 8.7 | 4.4 |
| 3.7 | 3.8 | 3.7 | Sales/Total Assets | 4.5 | 3.5 | 3.9 | 3.5 | 3.7 | 3.0 |
| 2.7 | 2.7 | 2.6 | | 3.1 | 2.5 | 2.6 | 2.7 | 2.7 | 2.5 |
| 1.8 | 1.8 | 1.9 | | 1.6 | 1.8 | 1.8 | 2.1 | 1.9 | 1.7 |
| .6 | .6 | .5 | % Depr., Dep., Amort./Sales | .4 | .5 | .4 | .5 | .5 | .6 |
| (399) 1.2 | (366) 1.1 | (381) 1.0 | | (24) 1.1 | (67) 1.1 | (52) 1.1 | (72) 1.0 | (92) 1.0 | (74) 1.0 |
| 2.2 | 2.1 | 1.9 | | 1.8 | 2.0 | 1.9 | 1.8 | 1.7 | 2.0 |
| 1.9 | 1.8 | 1.6 | % Officers', Directors' Owners' Comp/Sales | 6.4 | 2.4 | 2.4 | 1.6 | 1.0 | .5 |
| (224) 3.2 | (237) 3.2 | (232) 3.1 | | (25) 8.2 | (50) 4.7 | (44) 3.9 | (40) 2.7 | (49) 1.7 | (24) 1.2 |
| 6.1 | 6.0 | 5.8 | | 12.7 | 7.1 | 5.2 | 5.1 | 2.6 | 2.2 |
| 8998197M | 9257751M | 9513052M | Net Sales ($) | 28673M | 193065M | 301411M | 657355M | 1695560M | 6636988M |
| 4110696M | 4379547M | 4430298M | Total Assets ($) | 12877M | 86083M | 140212M | 268726M | 745405M | 3176995M |

© RMA 2012

M = $ thousand      MM = $ million
See Pages 9 through 22 for Explanation of Ratios and Data

## Current Data Sorted by Assets

## Comparative Historical Data

| 3 11 7 | 2 8 17 11 | 7 10 13 10 | 1 7 1 2 5 | 1 | 1 1 | Type of Statement Unqualified Reviewed Compiled Tax Returns Other | | 1 6 22 22 29 | 3 10 21 24 25 |
|---|---|---|---|---|---|---|---|---|---|
| | 18 (4/1-9/30/11) | | 100 (10/1/11-3/31/12) | | | | | 4/1/07-3/31/08 | 4/1/08-3/31/09 |
| 0-500M | 500M-2MM | 2-10MM | 10-50MM | 50-100MM | 100-250MM | | | ALL | ALL |
| 21 | 38 | 40 | 16 | | 3 | NUMBER OF STATEMENTS | | 80 | 83 |
| % | % | % | % | % | % | ASSETS | | % | % |
| 11.3 | 9.8 | 4.9 | 3.7 | | | Cash & Equivalents | | 5.3 | 6.4 |
| 7.7 | 12.1 | 9.4 | 13.9 | D | | Trade Receivables (net) | | 10.3 | 10.6 |
| 53.9 | 54.8 | 64.5 | 64.0 | A | | Inventory | | 61.7 | 61.6 |
| 2.8 | .7 | 1.3 | .7 | T | | All Other Current | | 1.3 | .6 |
| 75.7 | 77.4 | 80.0 | 82.3 | A | | Total Current | | 78.6 | 79.2 |
| 16.9 | 13.7 | 14.3 | 14.7 | | | Fixed Assets (net) | | 17.2 | 14.4 |
| 3.2 | 2.2 | 1.0 | 1.6 | N | | Intangibles (net) | | 1.7 | 1.5 |
| 4.0 | 6.7 | 4.7 | 1.4 | O | | All Other Non-Current | | 2.6 | 4.9 |
| 100.0 | 100.0 | 100.0 | 100.0 | T | | Total | | 100.0 | 100.0 |
| | | | | A | | LIABILITIES | | | |
| 23.8 | 10.2 | 27.0 | 26.9 | V | | Notes Payable-Short Term | | 19.8 | 23.6 |
| 2.0 | 4.2 | 1.1 | 1.2 | A | | Cur. Mat.-L.T.D. | | 4.8 | 2.4 |
| 20.7 | 22.2 | 15.5 | 24.1 | I | | Trade Payables | | 24.3 | 19.5 |
| .0 | .1 | .0 | .2 | L | | Income Taxes Payable | | .1 | .3 |
| 13.9 | 10.6 | 11.8 | 8.2 | A | | All Other Current | | 11.3 | 10.5 |
| 60.4 | 47.5 | 55.5 | 60.5 | B | | Total Current | | 60.4 | 56.3 |
| 12.6 | 16.1 | 9.6 | 7.1 | L | | Long-Term Debt | | 16.1 | 12.9 |
| .0 | .0 | .2 | .1 | E | | Deferred Taxes | | .4 | .2 |
| 21.7 | 7.1 | 5.5 | 1.1 | | | All Other Non-Current | | 4.7 | 3.4 |
| 5.3 | 29.3 | 29.3 | 31.1 | | | Net Worth | | 18.5 | 27.2 |
| 100.0 | 100.0 | 100.0 | 100.0 | | | Total Liabilities & Net Worth | | 100.0 | 100.0 |
| | | | | | | INCOME DATA | | | |
| 100.0 | 100.0 | 100.0 | 100.0 | | | Net Sales | | 100.0 | 100.0 |
| 36.8 | 34.3 | 26.2 | 29.4 | | | Gross Profit | | 28.3 | 28.6 |
| 33.9 | 28.6 | 24.8 | 27.6 | | | Operating Expenses | | 26.5 | 26.5 |
| 3.0 | 5.7 | 1.4 | 1.8 | | | Operating Profit | | 1.8 | 2.0 |
| .7 | .9 | .2 | -.5 | | | All Other Expenses (net) | | .9 | 1.2 |
| 2.3 | 4.8 | 1.2 | 2.3 | | | Profit Before Taxes | | .9 | .8 |
| | | | | | | RATIOS | | | |
| 3.7 | 3.3 | 1.9 | 1.6 | | | | | 1.6 | 2.2 |
| 1.7 | 1.7 | 1.4 | 1.3 | | | Current | | 1.3 | 1.5 |
| 1.1 | 1.1 | 1.2 | 1.1 | | | | | 1.1 | 1.1 |
| .6 | 1.1 | .4 | .5 | | | | | .4 | .6 |
| .2 | .3 | .3 | .2 | | | Quick | | .2 | .2 |
| .1 | .1 | .1 | .1 | | | | (79) | .1 (82) | .1 |
| 1 323.6 | 3 108.0 | 4 81.9 | 2 183.2 | | | | 3 | 138.1 | 4 95.9 |
| 7 54.1 | 10 36.9 | 10 36.6 | 16 23.3 | | | Sales/Receivables | 9 | 42.4 | 10 37.9 |
| 17 21.4 | 23 15.8 | 23 15.8 | 38 9.5 | | | | 21 | 17.4 | 23 16.0 |
| 26 13.8 | 60 6.1 | 81 4.5 | 101 3.6 | | | | 78 | 4.7 | 81 4.5 |
| 96 3.8 | 122 3.0 | 146 2.5 | 130 2.8 | | | Cost of Sales/Inventory | 118 | 3.1 | 129 2.8 |
| 215 1.7 | 192 1.9 | 215 1.7 | 174 2.1 | | | | 203 | 1.8 | 213 1.7 |
| 0 UND | 11 32.9 | 6 61.4 | 12 29.5 | | | | 12 | 30.0 | 8 48.4 |
| 23 16.1 | 38 9.6 | 15 23.6 | 40 9.2 | | | Cost of Sales/Payables | 29 | 12.7 | 23 15.5 |
| 81 4.5 | 72 5.1 | 58 6.3 | 91 4.0 | | | | 72 | 5.1 | 63 5.8 |
| 5.4 | 4.3 | 5.8 | 6.9 | | | | | 8.4 | 5.5 |
| 9.6 | 9.8 | 9.3 | 11.8 | | | Sales/Working Capital | | 14.5 | 10.6 |
| 49.4 | 29.2 | 20.5 | 28.5 | | | | | 80.7 | 20.9 |
| 18.3 | 13.2 | 8.0 | 22.7 | | | | | 5.1 | 4.5 |
| (17) 3.3 | (36) 5.5 | 3.4 | (15) 3.4 | | | EBIT/Interest | (78) | 1.6 (74) | 2.0 |
| -3.0 | 1.4 | 1.4 | 1.7 | | | | | .9 | .9 |
| | | | | | | Net Profit + Depr., Dep., Amort./Cur. Mat. L/T/D | | 8.0 | 16.1 |
| | | | | | | | (14) | 1.8 (13) | 6.5 |
| | | | | | | | | 1.2 | 2.5 |
| .3 | .0 | .1 | .1 | | | | | .2 | .1 |
| .9 | .2 | .4 | .2 | | | Fixed/Worth | | .5 | .3 |
| -.7 | 1.7 | 2.0 | .7 | | | | | 3.4 | 1.7 |
| 1.7 | 1.2 | 1.4 | 1.6 | | | | | 1.9 | 1.3 |
| 4.3 | 2.4 | 2.2 | 2.4 | | | Debt/Worth | | 3.7 | 2.5 |
| -3.6 | 8.0 | 8.2 | 5.4 | | | | | 13.8 | 9.5 |
| 68.1 | 48.4 | 22.6 | 36.3 | | | | | 34.7 | 34.4 |
| (14) 16.8 | (32) 13.9 | (36) 12.6 | 18.1 | | | % Profit Before Taxes/Tangible Net Worth | (67) | 10.5 (73) | 10.2 |
| 5.4 | 4.2 | 3.0 | 9.4 | | | | | 1.8 | 2.1 |
| 13.5 | 11.3 | 9.0 | 7.5 | | | | | 6.9 | 6.6 |
| 4.3 | 3.9 | 3.2 | 5.0 | | | % Profit Before Taxes/Total Assets | | 1.6 | 2.8 |
| -2.1 | .6 | .6 | 1.9 | | | | | -.7 | .0 |
| 78.4 | 121.0 | 75.0 | 71.9 | | | | | 77.7 | 89.2 |
| 30.0 | 40.7 | 35.2 | 33.9 | | | Sales/Net Fixed Assets | | 27.4 | 35.6 |
| 10.7 | 15.6 | 16.0 | 15.7 | | | | | 10.7 | 11.4 |
| 4.2 | 4.0 | 3.2 | 2.9 | | | | | 3.8 | 3.3 |
| 2.9 | 2.5 | 2.2 | 2.5 | | | Sales/Total Assets | | 2.6 | 2.3 |
| 1.8 | 1.7 | 1.4 | 1.8 | | | | | 1.7 | 1.6 |
| | .4 | .5 | .4 | | | | | .5 | .5 |
| (23) .8 | (32) .8 | (12) .7 | | | % Depr., Dep., Amort./Sales | (65) | 1.0 (60) | .9 |
| 1.6 | 1.3 | 1.2 | | | | | 1.7 | 2.1 |
| 3.3 | 1.4 | 1.2 | | | | | 1.0 | 1.3 |
| (11) 5.7 | (20) 2.7 | (24) 2.2 | | | % Officers', Directors' Owners' Comp/Sales | (46) | 2.4 (46) | 2.4 |
| 6.3 | 5.0 | 2.9 | | | | | 3.6 | 4.6 |
| 17531M | 112054M | 378097M | 647927M | 1523862M | | Net Sales ($) | | 1033121M | 1400995M |
| 5607M | 39787M | 161230M | 280192M | 591029M | | Total Assets ($) | | 419118M | 597394M |

M = $ thousand    MM = $ million
See Pages 9 through 22 for Explanation of Ratios and Data

## Comparative Historical Data / Current Data Sorted by Sales

| | 4/1/09-3/31/10 ALL | 4/1/10-3/31/11 ALL | 4/1/11-3/31/12 ALL | 0-1MM | 1-3MM | 3-5MM | 5-10MM | 10-25MM | 25MM & OVER |
|---|---|---|---|---|---|---|---|---|---|
| **Type of Statement** | | | | 18 (4/1-9/30/11) | | | 100 (10/1/11-3/31/12) | | |
| Unqualified | 3 | 4 | 2 | | 1 | 2 | 3 | 3 | 2 |
| Reviewed | 17 | 13 | 16 | | | | 8 | 4 | 7 |
| Compiled | 26 | 21 | 22 | 3 | 3 | 3 | 9 | 3 | 1 |
| Tax Returns | 35 | 37 | 44 | 8 | 15 | 6 | 4 | 3 | 3 |
| Other | 22 | 33 | 34 | 6 | 10 | 6 | 4 | 4 | 4 |
| **NUMBER OF STATEMENTS** | 103 | 108 | 118 | 17 | 29 | 17 | 24 | 14 | 17 |
| | % | % | % | % | % | % | % | % | % |
| **ASSETS** | | | | | | | | | |
| Cash & Equivalents | 6.9 | 8.5 | 7.4 | 7.1 | 9.0 | 8.6 | 7.9 | 6.0 | 4.0 |
| Trade Receivables (net) | 12.0 | 11.5 | 10.7 | 6.1 | 9.4 | 16.2 | 8.5 | 10.3 | 15.7 |
| Inventory | 59.2 | 57.4 | 58.9 | 48.2 | 64.4 | 55.2 | 58.2 | 66.7 | 58.8 |
| All Other Current | 1.0 | 1.5 | 1.3 | 3.5 | .3 | 1.7 | 1.3 | .9 | .6 |
| Total Current | 79.1 | 78.9 | 78.3 | 64.9 | 83.1 | 81.7 | 75.9 | 83.9 | 79.1 |
| Fixed Assets (net) | 14.8 | 14.9 | 14.9 | 21.6 | 11.5 | 13.8 | 16.5 | 9.7 | 17.1 |
| Intangibles (net) | 1.5 | 2.5 | 2.0 | 6.9 | .5 | 1.9 | .7 | 1.8 | 1.8 |
| All Other Non-Current | 4.6 | 3.7 | 4.7 | 6.3 | 4.9 | 2.6 | 6.9 | 4.6 | 2.1 |
| Total | 100.0 | 100.0 | 100.0 | 100.0 | 100.0 | 100.0 | 100.0 | 100.0 | 100.0 |
| **LIABILITIES** | | | | | | | | | |
| Notes Payable-Short Term | 19.0 | 23.7 | 20.6 | 23.7 | 15.7 | 20.9 | 22.8 | 15.4 | 26.5 |
| Cur. Mat.-L.T.D. | 3.5 | 2.1 | 2.3 | 1.6 | 3.1 | 1.3 | 4.0 | .9 | 1.2 |
| Trade Payables | 21.9 | 21.4 | 20.3 | 14.3 | 19.8 | 23.1 | 21.2 | 20.5 | 22.8 |
| Income Taxes Payable | .1 | .1 | .1 | .0 | .0 | .3 | .0 | .2 | .0 |
| All Other Current | 11.1 | 11.5 | 11.3 | 4.3 | 18.3 | 7.8 | 7.7 | 16.8 | 10.4 |
| Total Current | 55.6 | 58.7 | 54.5 | 44.0 | 56.9 | 53.4 | 55.8 | 53.8 | 60.9 |
| Long-Term Debt | 13.3 | 11.8 | 11.8 | 16.7 | 16.6 | 11.3 | 11.6 | 1.8 | 7.9 |
| Deferred Taxes | .1 | .2 | .1 | .0 | .0 | .0 | .0 | .5 | .1 |
| All Other Non-Current | 5.9 | 5.5 | 8.4 | 14.7 | 14.5 | 9.7 | 4.5 | .1 | 2.7 |
| Net Worth | 25.1 | 23.7 | 25.1 | 24.5 | 11.9 | 25.5 | 28.1 | 43.9 | 28.4 |
| Total Liabilities & Net Worth | 100.0 | 100.0 | 100.0 | 100.0 | 100.0 | 100.0 | 100.0 | 100.0 | 100.0 |
| **INCOME DATA** | | | | | | | | | |
| Net Sales | 100.0 | 100.0 | 100.0 | 100.0 | 100.0 | 100.0 | 100.0 | 100.0 | 100.0 |
| Gross Profit | 28.6 | 27.6 | 31.3 | 43.7 | 32.3 | 29.8 | 28.6 | 23.1 | 29.1 |
| Operating Expenses | 28.3 | 26.3 | 28.1 | 33.9 | 29.3 | 26.5 | 28.3 | 21.3 | 27.1 |
| Operating Profit | .4 | 1.3 | 3.2 | 9.8 | 2.9 | 3.3 | .4 | 1.8 | 2.0 |
| All Other Expenses (net) | .7 | .3 | .4 | 1.8 | .6 | .8 | .0 | -.6 | -.2 |
| Profit Before Taxes | -.3 | 1.0 | 2.7 | 7.9 | 2.3 | 2.5 | .4 | 2.4 | 2.2 |
| **RATIOS** | | | | | | | | | |
| Current | 2.3 | 1.9 | 2.1 | 3.4 | 4.0 | 5.6 | 1.8 | 2.3 | 1.5 |
| | 1.5 | 1.4 | 1.5 | 1.7 | 1.7 | 1.5 | 1.4 | 1.5 | 1.2 |
| | 1.1 | 1.1 | 1.1 | 1.2 | 1.2 | 1.0 | 1.1 | 1.3 | 1.1 |
| Quick | .5 | .6 | .5 | .8 | .6 | 1.3 | .5 | .4 | .5 |
| | .2 | .3 | .3 | .2 | .3 | .3 | .2 | .3 | .4 |
| | .1 | .1 | .1 | .1 | .1 | .1 | .1 | .2 | .1 |
| Sales/Receivables | 5  77.3 | 5  78.7 | 4  101.2 | 0  UND | 4  103.3 | 3  109.1 | 3  111.6 | 7  52.3 | 7  54.1 |
| | 11  32.7 | 11  32.0 | 9  38.9 | 7  54.1 | 9  40.7 | 6  60.7 | 9  38.8 | 10  37.8 | 18  20.3 |
| | 26  14.3 | 25  14.5 | 22  16.3 | 20  18.2 | 23  16.1 | 32  11.4 | 22  16.4 | 19  19.4 | 40  9.2 |
| Cost of Sales/Inventory | 79  4.6 | 63  5.8 | 72  5.1 | 24  14.9 | 89  4.1 | 28  13.0 | 73  5.0 | 73  5.0 | 73  5.0 |
| | 126  2.9 | 121  3.0 | 130  2.8 | 146  2.5 | 140  2.6 | 111  3.3 | 140  2.6 | 107  3.4 | 118  3.1 |
| | 201  1.8 | 179  2.0 | 192  1.9 | 228  1.6 | 228  1.6 | 182  2.0 | 203  1.8 | 166  2.2 | 140  2.6 |
| Cost of Sales/Payables | 12  29.3 | 12  31.7 | 8  44.6 | 0  UND | 14  26.9 | 0  UND | 8  45.8 | 11  32.7 | 11  31.9 |
| | 38  9.5 | 33  10.9 | 27  13.4 | 16  23.3 | 37  9.9 | 17  21.1 | 33  11.1 | 17  21.9 | 38  9.6 |
| | 70  5.2 | 65  5.6 | 72  5.1 | 87  4.2 | 72  5.1 | 70  5.2 | 65  5.6 | 59  6.2 | 83  4.4 |
| Sales/Working Capital | 5.8 | 6.0 | 5.2 | 4.8 | 3.6 | 6.5 | 5.8 | 5.7 | 10.4 |
| | 10.1 | 11.7 | 10.2 | 7.1 | 7.0 | 10.5 | 13.4 | 9.3 | 17.4 |
| | 18.5 | 28.6 | 30.8 | 32.1 | 14.6 | NM | 51.4 | 18.9 | 58.9 |
| EBIT/Interest | 4.4 | 8.2 | 12.3 | 14.4 | 9.6 | 22.8 | 7.7 | 26.5 | 13.0 |
| | (98) 2.1 | (97) 3.0 | (111) 3.6 | (14) 5.4 | (27) 2.7 | (16) 4.1 | 2.9 | 7.4 | (16) 3.2 |
| | 1.1 | 1.0 | 1.4 | 1.3 | 1.3 | 1.4 | .8 | 4.2 | 1.6 |
| Net Profit + Depr., Dep., Amort./Cur. Mat. L/T/D | 5.5 | 5.3 | 8.5 | | | | | | |
| | (15) 2.9 | (17) 2.8 | (18) 4.7 | | | | | | |
| | 1.1 | 1.0 | 1.9 | | | | | | |
| Fixed/Worth | .1 | .1 | .1 | .2 | .1 | .1 | .1 | .2 | .1 |
| | .4 | .3 | .4 | .9 | .4 | 1.4 | .5 | .2 | .4 |
| | 1.8 | 1.3 | 1.7 | -1.7 | NM | NM | 1.5 | .4 | 1.2 |
| Debt/Worth | 1.3 | 1.3 | 1.3 | 1.2 | 1.1 | 1.2 | 1.7 | .7 | 1.6 |
| | 2.9 | 2.9 | 2.5 | 4.3 | 4.3 | 4.7 | 2.2 | 1.8 | 3.0 |
| | 12.0 | 10.0 | 7.7 | -15.4 | NM | NM | 4.9 | 2.2 | 5.7 |
| % Profit Before Taxes/Tangible Net Worth | 21.4 | 31.2 | 36.3 | 44.8 | 59.7 | 74.8 | 28.4 | 19.8 | 38.4 |
| | (86) 9.7 | (91) 14.2 | (100) 13.8 | (12) 14.4 | (22) 10.6 | (13) 20.0 | (23) 11.6 | 13.3 | (16) 19.4 |
| | 2.2 | 2.7 | 5.3 | 7.0 | 3.6 | 5.7 | -.4 | 8.6 | 9.5 |
| % Profit Before Taxes/Total Assets | 4.9 | 8.8 | 9.3 | 14.8 | 9.2 | 12.7 | 7.5 | 10.0 | 9.3 |
| | 2.4 | 2.8 | 3.9 | 4.8 | 3.8 | 1.6 | | 5.3 | 5.2 |
| | .1 | .0 | .9 | .9 | .7 | .3 | -.3 | 2.9 | 2.0 |
| Sales/Net Fixed Assets | 78.6 | 68.6 | 80.2 | 56.9 | 89.9 | 115.0 | 90.3 | 39.8 | 102.3 |
| | 33.3 | 29.4 | 33.2 | 14.2 | 42.0 | 41.8 | 63.5 | 30.8 | 34.7 |
| | 11.6 | 11.9 | 13.5 | 6.1 | 17.0 | 19.0 | 5.8 | 18.7 | 13.1 |
| Sales/Total Assets | 3.2 | 3.3 | 3.4 | 2.9 | 3.6 | 4.1 | 3.3 | 3.6 | 3.2 |
| | 2.3 | 2.4 | 2.4 | 1.8 | 2.4 | 2.4 | 2.3 | 3.1 | 2.7 |
| | 1.6 | 1.7 | 1.7 | 1.2 | 1.5 | 1.7 | 1.5 | 2.0 | 2.0 |
| % Depr., Dep., Amort./Sales | .5 | .4 | .5 | | .5 | | .3 | .6 | .4 |
| | (87) .9 | (74) 1.1 | (78) .8 | | (20) .8 | | (20) .7 | (12) .8 | (11) .9 |
| | 1.9 | 2.2 | 1.5 | | 1.6 | | 2.6 | 1.2 | 1.9 |
| % Officers', Directors' Owners' Comp/Sales | 1.2 | .9 | 1.2 | | 2.1 | | 1.2 | | |
| | (53) 2.3 | (45) 2.5 | (62) 2.7 | | (16) 3.1 | | (15) 2.4 | | |
| | 5.6 | 5.4 | 4.2 | | 5.9 | | 2.9 | | |
| Net Sales ($) | 1505132M | 2254456M | 2679471M | 9316M | 53111M | 67785M | 170168M | 229835M | 2149256M |
| Total Assets ($) | 734842M | 882786M | 1077845M | 5149M | 26643M | 29346M | 81794M | 90657M | 844256M |

© RMA 2012

M = $ thousand   MM = $ million
See Pages 9 through 22 for Explanation of Ratios and Data

## Current Data Sorted by Assets

## Comparative Historical Data

| 1 | 6 | 4 | 6 | 1 | 2 | Type of Statement | 19 | 16 |
|---|---|---|---|---|---|---|---|---|
| | | 17 | 10 | | | Unqualified | | |
| 3 | 33 | 14 | 2 | | | Reviewed | 37 | 46 |
| 24 | 39 | 9 | | | | Compiled | 69 | 60 |
| 8 | 21 | 14 | 14 | | | Tax Returns | 49 | 54 |
| | 32 (4/1-9/30/11) | | 13 | 3 | | Other | 70 | 62 |
| | | | 198 (10/1/11-3/31/12) | | | | 4/1/07-3/31/08 | 4/1/08-3/31/09 |
| 0-500M | 500M-2MM | 2-10MM | 10-50MM | 50-100MM | 100-250MM | | ALL | ALL |
| 36 | 99 | 58 | 31 | 4 | 2 | NUMBER OF STATEMENTS | 244 | 238 |
| % | % | % | % | % | % | ASSETS | % | % |
| 13.4 | 8.0 | 6.8 | 2.4 | | | Cash & Equivalents | 8.0 | 8.1 |
| 9.3 | 10.7 | 13.1 | 10.2 | | | Trade Receivables (net) | 14.7 | 12.5 |
| 42.3 | 41.8 | 37.9 | 40.7 | | | Inventory | 35.9 | 36.7 |
| .9 | 1.2 | 1.7 | .7 | | | All Other Current | 2.3 | 1.9 |
| 65.9 | 61.6 | 59.5 | 54.0 | | | Total Current | 60.9 | 59.3 |
| 27.7 | 28.7 | 34.0 | 33.9 | | | Fixed Assets (net) | 30.2 | 31.9 |
| 2.1 | 4.1 | 1.2 | 3.5 | | | Intangibles (net) | 2.7 | 2.0 |
| 4.2 | 5.6 | 5.3 | 8.6 | | | All Other Non-Current | 6.2 | 6.9 |
| 100.0 | 100.0 | 100.0 | 100.0 | | | Total | 100.0 | 100.0 |
| | | | | | | LIABILITIES | | |
| 23.4 | 17.4 | 9.0 | 15.8 | | | Notes Payable-Short Term | 15.3 | 14.7 |
| 3.9 | 4.7 | 4.8 | 2.5 | | | Cur. Mat.-L.T.D. | 5.0 | 4.8 |
| 19.7 | 15.4 | 15.5 | 19.1 | | | Trade Payables | 14.1 | 15.2 |
| .3 | .1 | .1 | .8 | | | Income Taxes Payable | .2 | .4 |
| 14.7 | 8.6 | 12.4 | 8.1 | | | All Other Current | 7.9 | 9.2 |
| 62.0 | 46.2 | 41.8 | 46.3 | | | Total Current | 42.6 | 44.3 |
| 31.2 | 25.7 | 17.2 | 16.9 | | | Long-Term Debt | 21.7 | 22.8 |
| .0 | .2 | .3 | 1.3 | | | Deferred Taxes | .4 | .4 |
| 19.8 | 8.4 | 6.9 | 4.4 | | | All Other Non-Current | 6.0 | 6.0 |
| -13.0 | 19.5 | 33.9 | 31.1 | | | Net Worth | 29.2 | 26.5 |
| 100.0 | 100.0 | 100.0 | 100.0 | | | Total Liabilties & Net Worth | 100.0 | 100.0 |
| | | | | | | INCOME DATA | | |
| 100.0 | 100.0 | 100.0 | 100.0 | | | Net Sales | 100.0 | 100.0 |
| 42.4 | 39.2 | 35.0 | 32.5 | | | Gross Profit | 38.0 | 37.6 |
| 41.4 | 37.9 | 33.1 | 28.5 | | | Operating Expenses | 35.1 | 35.9 |
| 1.1 | 1.3 | 1.9 | 4.0 | | | Operating Profit | 3.0 | 1.7 |
| .4 | .7 | 1.1 | .5 | | | All Other Expenses (net) | .9 | .9 |
| .7 | .6 | .8 | 3.5 | | | Profit Before Taxes | 2.0 | .8 |
| | | | | | | RATIOS | | |
| 4.9 | 2.5 | 2.2 | 1.6 | | | | 2.6 | 2.3 |
| 1.6 | 1.4 | 1.4 | 1.1 | | | Current | 1.4 | 1.4 |
| .8 | .9 | 1.1 | .9 | | | | 1.0 | 1.0 |
| 1.3 | 1.0 | 1.0 | .4 | | | | 1.1 | .9 |
| .4 | .4 | .4 | .2 | | | Quick | .4 (237) | .4 |
| .1 | .1 | .2 | .1 | | | | .2 | .1 |
| 0 UND | 0 999.8 | 5 79.9 | 2 177.5 | | | | 3 104.9 | 2 150.6 |
| 4 99.6 | 8 46.1 | 14 25.9 | 7 51.6 | | | Sales/Receivables | 13 28.4 | 10 36.8 |
| 12 30.7 | 21 17.2 | 28 13.2 | 30 12.2 | | | | 30 12.1 | 25 14.5 |
| 3 107.9 | 37 9.8 | 49 7.4 | 65 5.6 | | | | 39 9.3 | 39 9.4 |
| 47 7.7 | 83 4.4 | 79 4.6 | 101 3.6 | | | Cost of Sales/Inventory | 75 4.9 | 75 4.9 |
| 111 3.3 | 152 2.4 | 146 2.5 | 166 2.2 | | | | 136 2.7 | 138 2.6 |
| 0 UND | 5 75.4 | 14 26.0 | 29 12.8 | | | | 9 39.7 | 10 36.5 |
| 11 34.0 | 26 14.2 | 29 12.5 | 46 8.0 | | | Cost of Sales/Payables | 26 14.3 | 24 15.1 |
| 35 10.5 | 41 8.8 | 53 6.9 | 68 5.4 | | | | 49 7.4 | 50 7.3 |
| 8.5 | 6.5 | 6.1 | 8.6 | | | | 6.1 | 7.5 |
| 24.6 | 13.5 | 13.7 | 29.6 | | | Sales/Working Capital | 14.5 | 17.1 |
| -29.3 | -131.6 | 79.5 | -60.4 | | | | 999.8 | -901.5 |
| 6.3 | 6.1 | 8.6 | 7.9 | | | | 5.8 | 5.6 |
| (32) 1.7 | (94) 1.8 | (54) 2.5 | (30) 3.4 | | | EBIT/Interest | (228) 2.0 | (220) 1.9 |
| -1.0 | .4 | 1.0 | 2.1 | | | | .9 | .3 |
| 3.7 | 3.3 | 6.2 | | | | 3.7 | 4.6 |
| | (11) 1.7 | (11) 1.3 | (16) 2.9 | | | Net Profit + Depr., Dep., Amort./Cur. Mat. L/T/D | (37) 2.1 | (54) 1.8 |
| | .2 | .2 | 1.9 | | | | 1.0 | .4 |
| .3 | .4 | .3 | .7 | | | | .3 | .4 |
| NM | 1.1 | .9 | 1.2 | | | Fixed/Worth | .9 | 1.0 |
| -.6 | -30.1 | 1.9 | 3.3 | | | | 3.2 | 3.2 |
| 1.0 | 1.1 | 1.0 | 1.4 | | | | .9 | 1.0 |
| NM | 2.9 | 2.2 | 2.8 | | | Debt/Worth | 2.7 | 2.7 |
| -2.4 | -111.1 | 3.7 | 10.0 | | | | 7.4 | 6.9 |
| 37.3 | 38.5 | 25.3 | 34.5 | | | | 34.8 | 28.2 |
| (18) 7.8 | (71) 13.7 | (53) 10.8 | (28) 22.4 | | | % Profit Before Taxes/Tangible Net Worth | (206) 12.7 | (197) 9.5 |
| -1.2 | .4 | 2.2 | 6.9 | | | | .7 | -4.8 |
| 13.4 | 8.7 | 10.2 | 8.4 | | | | 10.5 | 7.8 |
| 4.9 | 2.4 | 2.7 | 6.9 | | | % Profit Before Taxes/Total Assets | 3.1 | 2.5 |
| -8.7 | -1.8 | .2 | 2.5 | | | | -.4 | -2.8 |
| 73.6 | 30.9 | 28.8 | 13.1 | | | | 27.6 | 26.0 |
| 25.9 | 14.1 | 8.2 | 7.3 | | | Sales/Net Fixed Assets | 10.6 | 9.9 |
| 9.6 | 4.7 | 4.5 | 3.7 | | | | 4.8 | 4.6 |
| 6.5 | 3.6 | 3.4 | 2.9 | | | | 3.6 | 3.7 |
| 4.7 | 2.8 | 2.2 | 1.9 | | | Sales/Total Assets | 2.5 | 2.6 |
| 2.8 | 1.7 | 1.4 | 1.6 | | | | 1.6 | 1.8 |
| .5 | .8 | .6 | .9 | | | | .9 | .8 |
| (30) 1.4 | (83) 1.7 | (52) 1.6 | 1.7 | | | % Depr., Dep., Amort./Sales | (212) 1.6 | (206) 1.5 |
| 2.9 | 2.8 | 3.9 | 3.3 | | | | 3.1 | 3.6 |
| 4.0 | 2.1 | .7 | | | | | 1.6 | 1.9 |
| (17) 5.8 | (61) 3.4 | (25) 1.7 | | | | % Officers', Directors' Owners' Comp/Sales | (116) 3.4 | (116) 3.5 |
| 9.4 | 5.2 | 3.1 | | | | | 5.7 | 6.9 |
| 45203M | 336971M | 662631M | 1337846M | 656006M | 660679M | Net Sales ($) | 2626085M | 4104721M |
| 10074M | 111685M | 254323M | 625492M | 309176M | 370493M | Total Assets ($) | 1140757M | 1832240M |

M = $ thousand    MM = $ million
See Pages 9 through 22 for Explanation of Ratios and Data

## Comparative Historical Data                                   Current Data Sorted by Sales

| | | | Type of Statement | | | | | | |
|---|---|---|---|---|---|---|---|---|---|
| 17 | 11 | 13 | Unqualified | | | 1 | 9 | 5 | 7 |
| 33 | 35 | 34 | Reviewed | | 4 | 5 | 10 | 10 | 6 |
| 48 | 59 | 52 | Compiled | 5 | 16 | 13 | 10 | 6 | 2 |
| 60 | 77 | 72 | Tax Returns | 17 | 29 | 11 | 12 | 2 | 1 |
| 64 | 65 | 59 | Other | 5 | 14 | 9 | 9 | 5 | 17 |
| 4/1/09-3/31/10 ALL | 4/1/10-3/31/11 ALL | 4/1/11-3/31/12 ALL | | | 32 (4/1-9/30/11) | | 198 (10/1/11-3/31/12) | | |
| | | | | 0-1MM | 1-3MM | 3-5MM | 5-10MM | 10-25MM | 25MM & OVER |
| 222 | 247 | 230 | NUMBER OF STATEMENTS | 27 | 63 | 39 | 40 | 28 | 33 |
| % | % | % | **ASSETS** | % | % | % | % | % | % |
| 7.7 | 7.9 | 7.6 | Cash & Equivalents | 6.8 | 10.1 | 9.9 | 7.5 | 5.3 | 3.2 |
| 11.3 | 11.5 | 11.2 | Trade Receivables (net) | 6.7 | 8.5 | 13.1 | 13.8 | 14.3 | 12.0 |
| 37.9 | 38.9 | 40.6 | Inventory | 46.1 | 36.7 | 37.2 | 46.0 | 41.7 | 40.0 |
| 1.8 | 1.7 | 1.2 | All Other Current | .7 | .9 | .6 | 2.1 | 1.7 | 1.4 |
| 58.7 | 60.0 | 60.7 | Total Current | 60.3 | 56.2 | 60.7 | 69.4 | 63.0 | 56.7 |
| 32.4 | 29.6 | 30.3 | Fixed Assets (net) | 32.6 | 33.8 | 31.4 | 22.8 | 30.9 | 29.1 |
| 2.9 | 3.7 | 3.2 | Intangibles (net) | 2.4 | 5.3 | 2.1 | .8 | 1.9 | 5.0 |
| 6.1 | 6.6 | 5.9 | All Other Non-Current | 4.7 | 4.7 | 5.7 | 7.0 | 4.2 | 9.3 |
| 100.0 | 100.0 | 100.0 | Total | 100.0 | 100.0 | 100.0 | 100.0 | 100.0 | 100.0 |
| | | | **LIABILITIES** | | | | | | |
| 14.5 | 15.2 | 15.9 | Notes Payable-Short Term | 26.2 | 15.2 | 14.7 | 13.8 | 13.9 | 14.1 |
| 4.7 | 4.2 | 4.5 | Cur. Mat.-L.T.D. | 6.5 | 3.0 | 3.0 | 7.9 | 3.8 | 3.9 |
| 16.6 | 15.2 | 16.7 | Trade Payables | 28.2 | 10.3 | 12.0 | 15.5 | 25.6 | 19.0 |
| .1 | .3 | .2 | Income Taxes Payable | .0 | .2 | .1 | .2 | .8 | .1 |
| 14.8 | 13.0 | 10.4 | All Other Current | 8.8 | 9.2 | 10.6 | 13.1 | 11.8 | 9.3 |
| 50.8 | 47.9 | 47.7 | Total Current | 69.7 | 38.0 | 40.3 | 50.6 | 56.0 | 46.4 |
| 21.3 | 23.7 | 22.9 | Long-Term Debt | 39.0 | 34.2 | 16.6 | 13.8 | 14.2 | 14.2 |
| .4 | .4 | .3 | Deferred Taxes | .0 | .3 | .1 | .1 | .7 | .9 |
| 7.3 | 7.0 | 9.1 | All Other Non-Current | 21.0 | 10.0 | 8.1 | 9.6 | 1.2 | 5.0 |
| 20.2 | 21.0 | 19.9 | Net Worth | -29.6 | 17.5 | 34.9 | 25.9 | 27.9 | 33.4 |
| 100.0 | 100.0 | 100.0 | Total Liabilities & Net Worth | 100.0 | 100.0 | 100.0 | 100.0 | 100.0 | 100.0 |
| | | | **INCOME DATA** | | | | | | |
| 100.0 | 100.0 | 100.0 | Net Sales | 100.0 | 100.0 | 100.0 | 100.0 | 100.0 | 100.0 |
| 37.8 | 39.9 | 37.4 | Gross Profit | 46.2 | 43.3 | 34.3 | 32.4 | 35.2 | 30.2 |
| 36.8 | 37.4 | 35.5 | Operating Expenses | 46.3 | 42.3 | 31.2 | 30.7 | 32.4 | 27.1 |
| .9 | 2.5 | 1.8 | Operating Profit | -.1 | 1.0 | 3.1 | 1.7 | 2.7 | 3.1 |
| .7 | 1.0 | .7 | All Other Expenses (net) | 1.1 | 1.3 | .4 | .6 | -.1 | .7 |
| .2 | 1.6 | 1.1 | Profit Before Taxes | -1.2 | -.4 | 2.7 | 1.1 | 2.8 | 2.4 |
| | | | **RATIOS** | | | | | | |
| 2.3 | 2.7 | 2.5 | | 2.5 | 3.9 | 2.5 | 1.9 | 1.6 | 2.0 |
| 1.4 | 1.4 | 1.4 | Current | 1.1 | 1.8 | 1.7 | 1.4 | 1.2 | 1.2 |
| .9 | .9 | .9 | | .7 | .8 | 1.1 | 1.0 | .9 | 1.0 |
| .8 | .9 | .9 | | .8 | 1.3 | 1.3 | .9 | .7 | .5 |
| .4 | .4 | .3 | Quick | .1 | .4 | .7 | .3 | .2 | .2 |
| .1 | .1 | .1 | | .1 | .1 | .2 | .1 | .1 | .1 |
| 2 166.8 | 2 222.0 | 1 265.8 | | 0 UND | 1 720.5 | 2 209.2 | 2 186.8 | 2 214.4 | 2 172.7 |
| 9 41.7 | 10 35.6 | 10 36.7 | Sales/Receivables | 3 130.1 | 6 58.9 | 16 22.7 | 14 26.4 | 10 37.3 | 10 35.7 |
| 24 15.0 | 28 13.2 | 23 15.8 | | 16 22.4 | 21 17.2 | 23 15.8 | 23 15.9 | 26 13.9 | 34 10.6 |
| 44 8.4 | 43 8.4 | 37 9.8 | | 37 9.9 | 22 16.3 | 49 7.5 | 41 9.0 | 59 6.2 | 49 7.4 |
| 72 5.1 | 83 4.4 | 81 4.5 | Cost of Sales/Inventory | 122 3.0 | 68 5.4 | 72 5.1 | 78 4.7 | 91 4.0 | 81 4.5 |
| 128 2.8 | 150 2.4 | 140 2.6 | | 281 1.3 | 174 2.1 | 111 3.3 | 122 3.0 | 159 2.3 | 130 2.8 |
| 9 41.3 | 9 42.5 | 9 39.6 | | 0 UND | 4 101.4 | 4 93.0 | 11 33.1 | 23 15.9 | 24 15.5 |
| 23 15.8 | 27 13.8 | 28 13.0 | Cost of Sales/Payables | 29 12.4 | 18 20.2 | 20 18.2 | 30 12.3 | 49 7.4 | 38 9.5 |
| 51 7.2 | 53 6.9 | 51 7.1 | | 146 2.5 | 40 9.2 | 35 10.5 | 41 8.8 | 70 5.2 | 52 7.0 |
| 7.1 | 5.9 | 6.8 | | 4.3 | 4.7 | 6.5 | 10.0 | 9.3 | 9.1 |
| 15.6 | 17.1 | 16.5 | Sales/Working Capital | 46.2 | 13.2 | 10.7 | 17.6 | 18.7 | 25.1 |
| -64.6 | -45.0 | -104.0 | | -10.1 | -74.9 | 45.1 | 97.6 | -25.1 | -219.1 |
| 5.7 | 5.2 | 7.4 | | 4.4 | 4.3 | 8.6 | 7.9 | 9.1 | 10.5 |
| (206) 1.8 | (225) 1.8 | (216) 2.4 | EBIT/Interest | (26) .2 | (56) 1.4 | (38) 2.9 | (39) 3.0 | (26) 3.3 | (31) 3.2 |
| .1 | .0 | .7 | | -2.6 | -.2 | 1.0 | 1.4 | 1.5 | 1.2 |
| 5.7 | 6.8 | 4.8 | Net Profit + Depr., Dep., | | | | | | 23.1 |
| (37) 2.9 | (42) 2.8 | (39) 1.9 | Amort./Cur. Mat. L/T/D | | | | | | (13) 4.8 |
| .4 | .9 | 1.1 | | | | | | | 2.1 |
| .4 | .3 | .4 | | 1.0 | .2 | .4 | .3 | .7 | .3 |
| 1.2 | 1.0 | 1.1 | Fixed/Worth | -3.8 | 1.2 | .9 | .7 | .9 | 1.2 |
| 14.9 | 7.4 | 48.4 | | -.2 | -3.2 | 1.9 | 5.3 | 3.0 | 2.5 |
| .9 | .9 | 1.1 | | 1.2 | 1.1 | .8 | 1.3 | 1.6 | .9 |
| 2.2 | 2.9 | 2.4 | Debt/Worth | -9.0 | 3.4 | 2.0 | 2.3 | 2.3 | 2.7 |
| 38.0 | 43.2 | 165.9 | | -2.3 | -14.6 | 3.9 | 10.2 | 3.8 | 5.3 |
| 25.2 | 37.5 | 32.7 | % Profit Before Taxes/Tangible | 12.2 | 33.6 | 38.7 | 31.1 | 43.0 | 34.4 |
| (173) 8.4 | (194) 11.5 | (175) 14.1 | Net Worth | (11) -.8 | (44) 6.9 | (34) 14.7 | (33) 16.3 | (24) 21.1 | (29) 14.1 |
| -4.1 | -3.7 | 2.3 | | -9.5 | -.9 | 1.8 | 5.5 | 7.0 | 5.1 |
| 8.3 | 10.7 | 9.9 | % Profit Before Taxes/Total | 7.7 | 6.9 | 10.5 | 10.2 | 10.1 | 9.3 |
| 1.6 | 2.5 | 3.4 | Assets | -1.6 | 1.9 | 5.1 | 4.6 | 3.7 | 6.6 |
| -2.2 | -2.9 | -.6 | | -13.1 | -3.3 | -.1 | .8 | .9 | .9 |
| 25.0 | 31.4 | 31.4 | | 45.6 | 48.0 | 31.0 | 35.5 | 26.4 | 20.4 |
| 10.1 | 11.1 | 12.8 | Sales/Net Fixed Assets | 6.7 | 14.1 | 12.3 | 17.8 | 8.4 | 10.4 |
| 4.7 | 4.5 | 4.8 | | 3.7 | 3.7 | 5.6 | 6.9 | 5.2 | 4.6 |
| 3.6 | 3.5 | 3.8 | | 3.7 | 4.6 | 3.6 | 4.3 | 4.6 | 3.2 |
| 2.4 | 2.3 | 2.6 | Sales/Total Assets | 2.0 | 2.6 | 2.9 | 3.2 | 2.5 | 2.4 |
| 1.7 | 1.6 | 1.7 | | 1.2 | 1.5 | 2.0 | 1.9 | 1.6 | 1.8 |
| 1.0 | 1.0 | .7 | | .9 | .6 | 1.0 | .6 | .7 | .8 |
| (195) 1.8 | (202) 1.7 | (201) 1.5 | % Depr., Dep., Amort./Sales | (24) 1.8 | (51) 2.1 | (34) 1.8 | (34) 1.2 | (26) 1.5 | (32) 1.3 |
| 3.6 | 3.4 | 3.1 | | 2.8 | 5.3 | 3.0 | 2.4 | 2.7 | 2.5 |
| 1.5 | 2.4 | 1.9 | % Officers', Directors' | 5.2 | 3.0 | 1.8 | 1.2 | | |
| (114) 3.3 | (120) 4.2 | (107) 3.3 | Owners' Comp/Sales | (13) | (32) 4.1 | (28) 2.6 | (23) 2.2 | | |
| 6.2 | 7.1 | 5.5 | | 10.9 | 7.4 | 3.9 | 3.7 | | |
| 3348207M | 3829889M | 3699336M | Net Sales ($) | 19846M | 116596M | 144507M | 288128M | 455241M | 2675018M |
| 1429329M | 1568762M | 1681243M | Total Assets ($) | 11619M | 58911M | 61443M | 116706M | 208751M | 1223813M |

M = $ thousand    MM = $ million
See Pages 9 through 22 for Explanation of Ratios and Data

## Current Data Sorted by Assets            Comparative Historical Data

| Type of Statement | 0-500M | 500M-2MM | 2-10MM | 10-50MM | 50-100MM | 100-250MM | | 4/1/07-3/31/08 ALL | 4/1/08-3/31/09 ALL |
|---|---|---|---|---|---|---|---|---|---|
| Unqualified | | 3 | 11 | 30 | 17 | 22 | | 78 | 77 |
| Reviewed | 2 | 7 | 39 | 36 | 5 | | | 93 | 93 |
| Compiled | 10 | 63 | 84 | 19 | 1 | | | 161 | 136 |
| Tax Returns | 65 | 178 | 64 | 6 | 1 | | | 185 | 254 |
| Other | 14 | 94 | 106 | 36 | 23 | 26 | | 284 | 279 |
| | | 163 (4/1-9/30/11) | | | 799 (10/1/11-3/31/12) | | | | |
| NUMBER OF STATEMENTS | 91 | 345 | 304 | 127 | 47 | 48 | | 801 | 839 |

| | 0-500M % | 500M-2MM % | 2-10MM % | 10-50MM % | 50-100MM % | 100-250MM % | ASSETS | ALL % | ALL % |
|---|---|---|---|---|---|---|---|---|---|
| | 17.1 | 14.5 | 15.3 | 13.1 | 12.0 | 9.3 | Cash & Equivalents | 13.8 | 13.9 |
| | 1.7 | 3.2 | 3.3 | 3.8 | 3.6 | 4.5 | Trade Receivables (net) | 4.1 | 4.2 |
| | 46.7 | 38.6 | 26.0 | 24.0 | 19.4 | 19.6 | Inventory | 30.6 | 29.8 |
| | 4.2 | 2.4 | 3.0 | 3.6 | 4.2 | 3.8 | All Other Current | 3.2 | 3.2 |
| | 69.8 | 58.7 | 47.8 | 44.4 | 39.3 | 37.1 | Total Current | 51.7 | 51.1 |
| | 16.5 | 26.9 | 33.9 | 39.1 | 46.4 | 45.6 | Fixed Assets (net) | 35.5 | 34.0 |
| | 4.9 | 5.4 | 7.0 | 7.2 | 6.8 | 8.8 | Intangibles (net) | 4.9 | 4.9 |
| | 8.8 | 8.9 | 11.4 | 9.3 | 7.6 | 8.5 | All Other Non-Current | 7.8 | 10.0 |
| | 100.0 | 100.0 | 100.0 | 100.0 | 100.0 | 100.0 | Total | 100.0 | 100.0 |
| | | | | | | | **LIABILITIES** | | |
| | 6.2 | 5.5 | 3.1 | 2.7 | 3.2 | 2.4 | Notes Payable-Short Term | 4.0 | 4.9 |
| | 2.5 | 2.7 | 3.9 | 3.7 | 3.1 | 3.4 | Cur. Mat.-L.T.D. | 3.7 | 3.1 |
| | 15.1 | 20.1 | 18.5 | 19.8 | 17.1 | 15.3 | Trade Payables | 18.8 | 18.1 |
| | .0 | .1 | .1 | .1 | .1 | .2 | Income Taxes Payable | .2 | .1 |
| | 8.1 | 12.4 | 10.0 | 8.9 | 9.5 | 10.7 | All Other Current | 10.2 | 11.2 |
| | 31.9 | 40.8 | 35.5 | 35.3 | 33.1 | 31.9 | Total Current | 36.9 | 37.4 |
| | 16.1 | 23.9 | 22.4 | 21.3 | 18.5 | 20.2 | Long-Term Debt | 24.4 | 24.0 |
| | .0 | .1 | .1 | .5 | .8 | 1.4 | Deferred Taxes | .2 | .2 |
| | 11.2 | 11.9 | 8.2 | 8.0 | 7.0 | 9.7 | All Other Non-Current | 8.4 | 8.3 |
| | 40.7 | 23.2 | 33.7 | 34.9 | 40.6 | 36.8 | Net Worth | 30.1 | 30.2 |
| | 100.0 | 100.0 | 100.0 | 100.0 | 100.0 | 100.0 | Total Liabilities & Net Worth | 100.0 | 100.0 |
| | | | | | | | **INCOME DATA** | | |
| | 100.0 | 100.0 | 100.0 | 100.0 | 100.0 | 100.0 | Net Sales | 100.0 | 100.0 |
| | 25.3 | 25.0 | 27.2 | 26.4 | 24.2 | 29.3 | Gross Profit | 25.3 | 25.4 |
| | 23.9 | 24.5 | 25.7 | 25.1 | 22.5 | 27.5 | Operating Expenses | 24.0 | 24.2 |
| | 1.4 | .5 | 1.4 | 1.2 | 1.7 | 1.8 | Operating Profit | 1.3 | 1.2 |
| | -.7 | -.5 | -.4 | .0 | .1 | .6 | All Other Expenses (net) | -.2 | -.3 |
| | 2.1 | .9 | 1.8 | 1.2 | 1.5 | 1.3 | Profit Before Taxes | 1.5 | 1.5 |

### RATIOS

| | 0-500M | 500M-2MM | 2-10MM | 10-50MM | 50-100MM | 100-250MM | Ratio | ALL | ALL |
|---|---|---|---|---|---|---|---|---|---|
| | 7.9 | 3.4 | 2.5 | 2.1 | 1.6 | 1.6 | | 2.5 | 2.4 |
| | 3.1 | 1.8 | 1.5 | 1.2 | 1.2 | 1.1 | Current | 1.4 | 1.4 |
| | 1.3 | 1.1 | .9 | .8 | .8 | .8 | | 1.0 | .9 |
| | 2.0 | 1.1 | 1.1 | .9 | .6 | .7 | | .9 | .9 |
| | .6 | (344) .4 | .5 | .4 | .4 | .3 | Quick | (799) .4 | (837) .4 |
| | .1 | .1 | .2 | .2 | .2 | .2 | | .2 | .2 |
| | 0 UND | 0 UND | 0 999.8 | 1 662.7 | 1 515.5 | 2 182.4 | | 0 UND | 0 999.8 |
| | 0 UND | 0 921.0 | 1 387.1 | 2 184.1 | 3 134.6 | 4 99.4 | Sales/Receivables | 1 326.2 | 0 344.0 |
| | 1 521.6 | 2 195.5 | 2 146.6 | 4 100.4 | 4 93.1 | 6 59.1 | | 3 128.8 | 3 117.2 |
| | 14 26.0 | 19 18.9 | 18 20.1 | 17 21.1 | 17 21.6 | 21 17.4 | | 17 22.1 | 17 21.2 |
| | 29 12.4 | 27 13.7 | 24 15.5 | 24 15.4 | 22 16.5 | 26 13.9 | Cost of Sales/Inventory | 24 15.4 | 24 15.2 |
| | 49 7.4 | 36 10.0 | 33 11.0 | 31 11.6 | 28 13.0 | 34 10.6 | | 33 11.1 | 34 10.8 |
| | 0 UND | 5 74.5 | 10 37.5 | 12 29.7 | 15 24.4 | 16 23.5 | | 7 53.2 | 7 52.5 |
| | 6 59.1 | 11 33.9 | 15 23.9 | 20 18.4 | 18 19.8 | 20 18.3 | Cost of Sales/Payables | 14 25.8 | 14 26.1 |
| | 15 24.6 | 19 19.6 | 23 15.8 | 26 13.9 | 24 14.9 | 28 13.1 | | 22 16.9 | 22 16.9 |
| | 9.5 | 13.7 | 15.3 | 18.2 | 26.6 | 20.7 | | 17.1 | 16.9 |
| | 18.8 | 30.9 | 37.6 | 55.0 | 52.8 | 119.4 | Sales/Working Capital | 40.1 | 41.9 |
| | 67.0 | 273.8 | -234.8 | -76.8 | -130.2 | -54.3 | | -436.9 | -293.1 |
| | 19.3 | 18.1 | 12.4 | 8.3 | 18.1 | 11.9 | | 9.8 | 10.7 |
| | (57) 6.5 | (269) 3.8 | (256) 4.2 | (119) 3.8 | (45) 5.8 | (46) 5.2 | EBIT/Interest | (663) 3.7 | (691) 3.6 |
| | 1.7 | .5 | 1.3 | 1.5 | 1.8 | 1.8 | | 1.1 | 1.3 |
| | | 10.1 | 4.9 | 3.2 | 5.8 | 11.3 | | 4.9 | 4.7 |
| | | (12) 4.4 | (50) 2.4 | (42) 2.1 | (16) 3.1 | (16) 3.4 | Net Profit + Depr., Dep., Amort./Cur. Mat. L/T/D | (119) 2.3 | (123) 2.4 |
| | | 2.7 | 1.3 | 1.1 | 1.2 | 1.9 | | 1.4 | 1.3 |
| | .1 | .3 | .4 | .8 | .8 | .9 | | .5 | .5 |
| | .3 | 1.1 | 1.1 | 1.3 | 1.3 | 1.6 | Fixed/Worth | 1.3 | 1.3 |
| | 1.8 | -6.4 | 6.7 | 4.1 | 3.2 | 4.8 | | 9.4 | 5.9 |
| | .3 | .8 | .7 | 1.1 | .9 | 1.2 | | .8 | .8 |
| | 1.8 | 2.7 | 1.8 | 2.3 | 1.5 | 2.5 | Debt/Worth | 2.3 | 2.4 |
| | 8.3 | -13.2 | 17.8 | 7.7 | 3.8 | 7.1 | | 19.5 | 14.7 |
| | 104.3 | 57.3 | 53.4 | 32.7 | 37.5 | 32.7 | | 44.9 | 55.2 |
| | (79) 37.5 | (248) 26.4 | (243) 18.7 | (106) 17.1 | (45) 16.9 | (42) 19.4 | % Profit Before Taxes/Tangible Net Worth | (625) 21.2 | (669) 24.8 |
| | 8.8 | 5.9 | 4.6 | 7.5 | 8.9 | 9.5 | | 6.7 | 7.6 |
| | 25.9 | 18.7 | 13.0 | 10.3 | 11.3 | 8.5 | | 15.7 | 16.0 |
| | 11.7 | 6.2 | 6.8 | 5.2 | 6.2 | 6.5 | % Profit Before Taxes/Total Assets | 6.7 | 6.4 |
| | 3.3 | -.8 | .9 | 1.5 | 1.9 | 2.5 | | .6 | 1.0 |
| | 340.7 | 102.7 | 38.0 | 23.8 | 14.0 | 12.3 | | 47.8 | 47.1 |
| | 75.4 | 36.1 | 16.1 | 12.4 | 9.3 | 7.9 | Sales/Net Fixed Assets | 17.8 | 17.3 |
| | 27.0 | 13.2 | 8.7 | 8.4 | 6.3 | 5.6 | | 8.5 | 8.1 |
| | 10.8 | 9.2 | 7.0 | 6.1 | 5.0 | 4.5 | | 7.8 | 7.8 |
| | 7.3 | 6.7 | 4.7 | 4.8 | 4.4 | 4.0 | Sales/Total Assets | 5.3 | 5.1 |
| | 4.9 | 4.2 | 3.4 | 3.1 | 3.5 | 2.7 | | 3.6 | 3.7 |
| | .3 | .4 | .6 | .8 | 1.0 | 1.1 | | .6 | .6 |
| | (62) .6 | (282) .7 | (277) .9 | (123) 1.1 | (45) 1.3 | (28) 1.5 | % Depr., Dep., Amort./Sales | (683) 1.0 | (719) 1.0 |
| | 1.2 | 1.4 | 1.6 | 1.8 | 1.7 | 1.9 | | 1.6 | 1.6 |
| | 1.3 | .7 | .6 | .4 | | | | .8 | .7 |
| | (60) 2.4 | (187) 1.3 | (116) 1.2 | (28) 1.0 | | | % Officers', Directors', Owners' Comp/Sales | (313) 1.4 | (331) 1.3 |
| | 3.4 | 2.4 | 2.3 | 1.9 | | | | 2.4 | 2.4 |
| | 253028M | 2700549M | 7227355M | 13799888M | 14388886M | 27538419M | Net Sales ($) | 71166362M | 74780490M |
| | 28520M | 380881M | 1409025M | 2884502M | 3288586M | 7179029M | Total Assets ($) | 15402235M | 16330138M |

M = $ thousand    MM = $ million
See Pages 9 through 22 for Explanation of Ratios and Data

## Comparative Historical Data | Current Data Sorted by Sales

| | | | Type of Statement | | | | | | |
|---|---|---|---|---|---|---|---|---|---|
| 75 | 85 | 83 | Unqualified | | | 2 | 3 | 3 | 75 |
| 93 | 69 | 89 | Reviewed | | | 3 | 8 | 19 | 59 |
| 161 | 150 | 177 | Compiled | 2 | 4 | 12 | 42 | 59 | 58 |
| 242 | 232 | 314 | Tax Returns | 12 | 65 | 51 | 91 | 71 | 24 |
| 287 | 270 | 299 | Other | 3 | 22 | 33 | 44 | 73 | 124 |
| 4/1/09-3/31/10 ALL | 4/1/10-3/31/11 ALL | 4/1/11-3/31/12 ALL | | 163 (4/1-9/30/11) | | | 799 (10/1/11-3/31/12) | | |
| | | | | 0-1MM | 1-3MM | 3-5MM | 5-10MM | 10-25MM | 25MM & OVER |
| 858 | 806 | 962 | NUMBER OF STATEMENTS | 17 | 91 | 101 | 188 | 225 | 340 |
| % | % | % | ASSETS | % | % | % | % | % | % |
| 14.0 | 12.8 | 14.5 | Cash & Equivalents | 10.1 | 12.9 | 16.2 | 15.2 | 15.2 | 13.7 |
| 3.8 | 4.0 | 3.3 | Trade Receivables (net) | .1 | 1.9 | 2.4 | 3.1 | 3.8 | 3.8 |
| 30.9 | 30.4 | 31.6 | Inventory | 41.7 | 35.3 | 37.0 | 33.8 | 35.2 | 24.8 |
| 2.9 | 3.7 | 3.1 | All Other Current | .2 | 4.4 | 3.6 | 2.7 | 2.6 | 3.3 |
| 51.6 | 50.9 | 52.4 | Total Current | 52.1 | 54.4 | 59.3 | 54.8 | 56.7 | 45.6 |
| 33.5 | 33.0 | 31.6 | Fixed Assets (net) | 38.9 | 28.5 | 27.0 | 26.5 | 28.7 | 38.3 |
| 5.6 | 6.1 | 6.3 | Intangibles (net) | 7.1 | 7.6 | 5.9 | 6.3 | 5.0 | 7.0 |
| 9.3 | 10.0 | 9.6 | All Other Non-Current | 1.9 | 9.4 | 7.8 | 12.5 | 9.6 | 9.1 |
| 100.0 | 100.0 | 100.0 | Total | 100.0 | 100.0 | 100.0 | 100.0 | 100.0 | 100.0 |
| | | | LIABILITIES | | | | | | |
| 5.0 | 4.6 | 4.2 | Notes Payable-Short Term | 1.0 | 5.4 | 8.5 | 3.1 | 5.1 | 2.7 |
| 3.9 | 4.4 | 3.3 | Cur. Mat.-L.T.D. | .5 | 2.2 | 2.8 | 3.0 | 3.3 | 3.9 |
| 19.2 | 18.2 | 18.7 | Trade Payables | 3.4 | 11.6 | 15.2 | 17.2 | 23.3 | 20.1 |
| .1 | .1 | .1 | Income Taxes Payable | .0 | .0 | .0 | .1 | .1 | .1 |
| 10.4 | 10.6 | 10.5 | All Other Current | 9.5 | 6.9 | 12.0 | 10.0 | 12.0 | 10.5 |
| 38.6 | 37.9 | 36.7 | Total Current | 14.4 | 26.2 | 38.5 | 33.4 | 43.9 | 37.3 |
| 24.3 | 23.7 | 21.9 | Long-Term Debt | 26.3 | 26.3 | 31.6 | 20.4 | 19.6 | 20.0 |
| .2 | .2 | .3 | Deferred Taxes | .0 | .0 | .2 | .1 | .1 | .5 |
| 8.3 | 9.2 | 9.8 | All Other Non-Current | 15.7 | 11.8 | 7.1 | 12.7 | 11.4 | 7.1 |
| 28.5 | 28.9 | 31.3 | Net Worth | 43.6 | 35.6 | 22.6 | 33.4 | 24.9 | 35.1 |
| 100.0 | 100.0 | 100.0 | Total Liabilities & Net Worth | 100.0 | 100.0 | 100.0 | 100.0 | 100.0 | 100.0 |
| | | | INCOME DATA | | | | | | |
| 100.0 | 100.0 | 100.0 | Net Sales | 100.0 | 100.0 | 100.0 | 100.0 | 100.0 | 100.0 |
| 26.6 | 26.3 | 26.1 | Gross Profit | 27.9 | 29.8 | 24.5 | 25.2 | 25.6 | 26.3 |
| 24.9 | 24.9 | 25.0 | Operating Expenses | 28.1 | 29.5 | 23.2 | 24.2 | 24.6 | 24.9 |
| 1.7 | 1.4 | 1.1 | Operating Profit | -.2 | .3 | 1.3 | 1.1 | 1.0 | 1.4 |
| -.3 | -.2 | -.3 | All Other Expenses (net) | -.5 | -.5 | -.3 | -.5 | -.5 | .0 |
| 2.0 | 1.6 | 1.4 | Profit Before Taxes | .3 | .9 | 1.5 | 1.5 | 1.5 | 1.4 |
| | | | RATIOS | | | | | | |
| 2.6 | 2.5 | 2.9 | | 18.9 | 6.6 | 4.2 | 3.3 | 2.4 | 1.9 |
| 1.4 | 1.4 | 1.5 | Current | 10.7 | 2.4 | 2.4 | 1.9 | 1.4 | 1.2 |
| .9 | .9 | .9 | | 3.8 | 1.2 | 1.2 | 1.1 | .9 | .9 |
| 1.0 | .9 | 1.0 | | 4.3 | 1.8 | 2.0 | 1.1 | 1.1 | .8 |
| (855) .4 | (803) .4 | (961) .4 | Quick | 1.0 | .5 | (100) .6 | .4 | .4 | .4 |
| .2 | .2 | .2 | | .0 | .1 | .2 | .2 | .1 | .2 |
| 0 999.8 | 0 999.8 | 0 UND | | 0 UND | 0 UND | 0 UND | 0 UND | 0 999.8 | 1 711.5 |
| 1 307.2 | 1 310.3 | 1 438.4 | Sales/Receivables | 0 UND | 0 UND | 0 999.8 | 1 729.7 | 1 508.2 | 2 186.8 |
| 3 122.0 | 3 106.9 | 3 128.8 | | 0 UND | 2 225.0 | 2 182.0 | 2 154.8 | 2 181.5 | 2 98.5 |
| 17 20.9 | 18 20.7 | 18 20.1 | | 34 10.6 | 22 16.7 | 20 18.5 | 20 18.2 | 18 20.1 | 17 21.3 |
| 24 15.0 | 25 14.5 | 25 14.7 | Cost of Sales/Inventory | 52 7.0 | 35 10.3 | 29 12.4 | 27 13.5 | 23 15.6 | 23 15.9 |
| 34 10.8 | 35 10.6 | 35 10.5 | | 89 4.1 | 54 6.8 | 41 8.9 | 37 9.8 | 31 11.9 | 29 12.5 |
| 7 50.5 | 8 48.2 | 8 47.4 | | 0 UND | 0 UND | 3 112.9 | 6 60.0 | 8 46.7 | 12 30.2 |
| 14 26.5 | 14 27.0 | 14 26.2 | Cost of Sales/Payables | 3 138.3 | 9 40.8 | 9 39.2 | 11 31.9 | 14 26.8 | 18 20.4 |
| 22 16.5 | 22 16.9 | 22 16.4 | | 7 52.5 | 17 20.9 | 18 20.1 | 19 19.5 | 23 15.8 | 24 14.9 |
| 16.7 | 16.6 | 14.5 | | 4.8 | 8.8 | 12.2 | 13.3 | 16.8 | 24.0 |
| 40.8 | 40.7 | 37.5 | Sales/Working Capital | 10.2 | 13.5 | 19.5 | 26.7 | 46.3 | 60.5 |
| -204.5 | -243.4 | -273.7 | | 47.6 | 101.6 | 70.1 | 147.0 | -151.3 | -92.2 |
| 12.9 | 12.1 | 13.3 | | | 9.0 | 11.3 | 16.8 | 17.9 | 11.9 |
| (717) 4.6 | (684) 3.5 | (792) 4.2 | EBIT/Interest | (67) 2.0 | (81) 4.4 | (149) 4.0 | (176) 4.2 | (311) 4.8 | |
| 1.6 | 1.2 | 1.3 | | | .5 | 1.2 | .7 | 1.3 | 1.8 |
| 6.8 | 5.7 | 5.1 | Net Profit + Depr., Dep., | | | | 6.9 | 5.2 | 4.8 |
| (150) 2.8 | (125) 2.1 | (137) 2.6 | Amort./Cur. Mat. L/T/D | | | (12) 3.0 | (24) 2.6 | (94) 2.6 | |
| 1.3 | 1.1 | 1.3 | | | | | .6 | 1.3 | 1.3 |
| .4 | .4 | .4 | | .1 | .1 | .3 | .2 | .4 | .7 |
| 1.3 | 1.2 | 1.1 | Fixed/Worth | 1.7 | 1.1 | 1.3 | .7 | 1.0 | 1.3 |
| 15.3 | 15.2 | 6.6 | | NM | 12.0 | -7.3 | 7.1 | -21.6 | 3.5 |
| .8 | .8 | .8 | | .1 | .6 | .7 | .4 | .9 | 1.0 |
| 2.3 | 2.3 | 2.1 | Debt/Worth | 2.0 | 2.4 | 2.7 | 1.7 | 2.3 | 2.2 |
| 64.9 | 48.9 | 18.1 | | NM | 29.3 | -12.0 | 18.6 | -40.5 | 6.1 |
| 55.2 | 51.9 | 52.0 | % Profit Before Taxes/Tangible | 29.9 | 49.5 | 56.2 | 46.5 | 88.0 | 41.3 |
| (657) 23.1 | (618) 20.0 | (763) 20.9 | Net Worth | (13) 9.7 | (75) 17.6 | (72) 26.2 | (145) 19.3 | (166) 29.2 | (292) 19.2 |
| 9.0 | 5.8 | 6.6 | | -1.9 | 1.8 | 6.4 | 4.6 | 10.6 | 9.2 |
| 16.9 | 13.9 | 14.3 | % Profit Before Taxes/Total | 16.5 | 12.9 | 16.5 | 15.8 | 21.5 | 12.0 |
| 7.6 | 5.5 | 6.6 | Assets | 3.7 | 4.6 | 7.1 | 6.8 | 8.0 | 6.7 |
| 2.0 | .6 | 1.0 | | -2.5 | -1.0 | .4 | .2 | 1.1 | 2.3 |
| 47.2 | 47.0 | 56.5 | | 36.2 | 86.7 | 104.4 | 101.0 | 87.5 | 26.5 |
| 19.5 | 18.8 | 20.0 | Sales/Net Fixed Assets | 11.4 | 20.3 | 35.5 | 28.8 | 26.8 | 13.6 |
| 8.6 | 8.5 | 9.2 | | 1.8 | 6.9 | 10.0 | 12.1 | 12.1 | 8.1 |
| 7.7 | 7.4 | 7.7 | | 5.7 | 6.1 | 8.1 | 7.9 | 9.6 | 6.6 |
| 5.5 | 5.0 | 5.2 | Sales/Total Assets | 2.7 | 4.2 | 5.5 | 5.9 | 6.5 | 5.0 |
| 3.7 | 3.6 | 3.6 | | 1.2 | 2.6 | 3.7 | 3.6 | 4.2 | 3.7 |
| .6 | .6 | .5 | | 1.0 | .5 | .4 | .4 | .5 | .7 |
| (727) 1.0 | (683) 1.0 | (817) .9 | % Depr., Dep., Amort./Sales | (14) 2.2 | (70) 1.2 | (83) .7 | (155) .7 | (189) .8 | (306) 1.1 |
| 1.5 | 1.6 | 1.6 | | 3.7 | 2.1 | 1.7 | 1.5 | 1.4 | 1.6 |
| .6 | .7 | .7 | | | 1.2 | 1.1 | .8 | .6 | .4 |
| (322) 1.2 | (292) 1.2 | (401) 1.4 | % Officers', Directors' Owners' Comp/Sales | (55) 2.8 | (55) 1.6 | (103) 1.3 | (104) 1.0 | (76) .8 | |
| 2.5 | 2.3 | 2.6 | | 4.3 | 2.7 | 2.2 | 2.3 | 1.8 | |
| 70072922M | 68768480M | 65908125M | Net Sales ($) | 11566M | 177824M | 406271M | 1361487M | 3581246M | 60369731M |
| 15304591M | 15281343M | 15170543M | Total Assets ($) | 6909M | 60837M | 92730M | 303727M | 665672M | 14040668M |

© RMA 2012

M = $ thousand    MM = $ million
See Pages 9 through 22 for Explanation of Ratios and Data

## Current Data Sorted by Assets        Comparative Historical Data

| 0-500M | 500M-2MM | 2-10MM | 10-50MM | 50-100MM | 100-250MM | Type of Statement | 4/1/07-3/31/08 ALL | 4/1/08-3/31/09 ALL |
|---|---|---|---|---|---|---|---|---|
| 1 | | 1 | 4 | 3 | | Unqualified | 19 | 16 |
| 2 | 2 | 3 | 6 | 2 | | Reviewed | 11 | 20 |
| 9 | 8 | 6 | 2 | | | Compiled | 27 | 20 |
| 109 | 63 | 13 | 1 | 1 | 2 | Tax Returns | 122 | 152 |
| 31 | 31 | 12 | 7 | 4 | 3 | Other | 56 | 57 |
| 25 (4/1-9/30/11) | | | 301 (10/1/11-3/31/12) | | | | | |
| 152 | 104 | 35 | 20 | 10 | 5 | NUMBER OF STATEMENTS | 235 | 265 |
| % | % | % | % | % | % | **ASSETS** | % | % |
| 16.3 | 10.5 | 10.8 | 10.9 | 7.6 | | Cash & Equivalents | 12.4 | 12.8 |
| 1.9 | 2.1 | 9.1 | 7.6 | 3.9 | | Trade Receivables (net) | 4.0 | 3.8 |
| 44.3 | 18.5 | 15.0 | 14.8 | 11.4 | | Inventory | 27.9 | 26.4 |
| .9 | .7 | .7 | 1.0 | .3 | | All Other Current | 1.8 | 1.6 |
| 63.5 | 31.8 | 35.5 | 34.3 | 23.1 | | Total Current | 46.1 | 44.6 |
| 20.5 | 53.3 | 49.3 | 51.2 | 69.9 | | Fixed Assets (net) | 39.1 | 39.4 |
| 11.1 | 8.1 | 4.3 | 6.3 | 4.3 | | Intangibles (net) | 8.9 | 10.4 |
| 5.0 | 6.8 | 10.9 | 8.2 | 2.7 | | All Other Non-Current | 6.0 | 5.7 |
| 100.0 | 100.0 | 100.0 | 100.0 | 100.0 | | Total | 100.0 | 100.0 |
| | | | | | | **LIABILITIES** | | |
| 7.1 | 3.6 | 2.7 | 6.2 | 3.0 | | Notes Payable-Short Term | 4.8 | 2.9 |
| 2.3 | 2.1 | 2.9 | 4.3 | 3.9 | | Cur. Mat.-L.T.D. | 3.0 | 2.8 |
| 9.3 | 8.4 | 12.4 | 16.8 | 13.7 | | Trade Payables | 12.2 | 10.5 |
| .1 | .0 | .1 | .2 | .0 | | Income Taxes Payable | .1 | .0 |
| 19.8 | 8.5 | 8.2 | 10.4 | 5.0 | | All Other Current | 12.5 | 11.4 |
| 38.6 | 22.6 | 26.3 | 37.8 | 25.6 | | Total Current | 32.7 | 27.5 |
| 18.8 | 47.3 | 39.1 | 29.6 | 47.8 | | Long-Term Debt | 31.9 | 36.3 |
| .0 | .0 | .3 | 1.3 | .1 | | Deferred Taxes | .2 | .2 |
| 21.0 | 5.1 | 9.0 | 2.1 | 6.6 | | All Other Non-Current | 11.1 | 12.1 |
| 21.6 | 25.1 | 25.4 | 29.1 | 20.0 | | Net Worth | 24.2 | 23.8 |
| 100.0 | 100.0 | 100.0 | 100.0 | 100.0 | | Total Liabilities & Net Worth | 100.0 | 100.0 |
| | | | | | | **INCOME DATA** | | |
| 100.0 | 100.0 | 100.0 | 100.0 | 100.0 | | Net Sales | 100.0 | 100.0 |
| 20.6 | 17.2 | 14.9 | 12.5 | 14.5 | | Gross Profit | 19.4 | 19.0 |
| 20.1 | 15.9 | 13.4 | 12.2 | 13.0 | | Operating Expenses | 17.3 | 17.8 |
| .4 | 1.2 | 1.5 | .3 | 1.5 | | Operating Profit | 2.1 | 1.2 |
| -1.0 | .0 | -.2 | -.2 | .1 | | All Other Expenses (net) | -.2 | -.3 |
| 1.4 | 1.2 | 1.7 | .6 | 1.4 | | Profit Before Taxes | 2.3 | 1.5 |
| | | | | | | **RATIOS** | | |
| 10.6 | 3.5 | 2.5 | 1.4 | 1.2 | | | 4.0 | 4.9 |
| 3.2 | 1.7 | 1.8 | .9 | 1.1 | | Current | 1.6 | 1.9 |
| 1.3 | .9 | .9 | .6 | .6 | | | .8 | .9 |
| 2.4 | 1.4 | 1.9 | .8 | .6 | | | 1.4 | 1.7 |
| (149) .7 | .5 | .9 | .4 | .5 | | Quick | (232) .5 | (261) .6 |
| .2 | .1 | .3 | .2 | .4 | | | .2 | .2 |
| 0 UND | 0 UND | 0 UND | 1 287.1 | 2 223.4 | | | 0 UND | 0 UND |
| 0 UND | 0 UND | 2 172.5 | 3 120.5 | 3 126.0 | | Sales/Receivables | 0 999.8 | 0 UND |
| 0 UND | 1 694.9 | 4 82.1 | 5 48.2 | 6 64.1 | | | 3 117.4 | 2 212.7 |
| 12 29.8 | 8 46.9 | 8 47.0 | 5 79.2 | 6 57.0 | | | 9 39.1 | 7 50.6 |
| 21 17.2 | 12 29.3 | 11 32.6 | 10 36.3 | 11 32.9 | | Cost of Sales/Inventory | 15 24.1 | 13 27.3 |
| 41 8.9 | 34 10.8 | 21 17.4 | 12 31.4 | 16 23.3 | | | 34 10.8 | 34 10.8 |
| 0 UND | 0 UND | 3 144.9 | 8 43.1 | 11 33.9 | | | 0 UND | 0 UND |
| 0 UND | 3 136.7 | 7 50.6 | 11 32.0 | 12 30.9 | | Cost of Sales/Payables | 4 101.9 | 3 119.5 |
| 5 69.7 | 8 43.3 | 13 28.4 | 15 24.0 | 17 21.9 | | | 12 29.8 | 10 38.3 |
| 11.3 | 16.8 | 18.0 | 59.0 | 99.9 | | | 13.7 | 15.5 |
| 24.4 | 45.9 | 46.5 | -211.5 | 201.8 | | Sales/Working Capital | 48.3 | 45.1 |
| 95.5 | -205.2 | -118.8 | -33.0 | -41.3 | | | -106.6 | -418.2 |
| 7.4 | 5.4 | 9.6 | 6.5 | 6.8 | | | 5.1 | 6.0 |
| (65) 3.5 | (89) 2.4 | (31) 2.3 | (19) 2.2 | 2.0 | | EBIT/Interest | (170) 2.4 | (191) 2.4 |
| 1.0 | 1.1 | 1.1 | 1.3 | 1.5 | | | 1.0 | 1.1 |
| | | | | | | Net Profit + Depr., Dep., | 4.3 | 5.4 |
| | | | | | | Amort./Cur. Mat. L/T/D | (20) 2.4 | (17) 2.4 |
| | | | | | | | 1.4 | 1.3 |
| .0 | 1.0 | .8 | 1.0 | 1.7 | | | .3 | .4 |
| .5 | 3.0 | 3.5 | 1.8 | 4.0 | | Fixed/Worth | 2.3 | 2.5 |
| -7.5 | -19.2 | -94.8 | 5.5 | NM | | | -22.7 | -50.9 |
| .4 | .9 | 1.0 | 1.1 | 1.8 | | | 1.0 | 1.0 |
| 2.6 | 4.4 | 4.5 | 2.6 | 3.7 | | Debt/Worth | 3.9 | 4.3 |
| -9.2 | -23.6 | -110.2 | 6.9 | NM | | | -24.1 | -42.0 |
| 70.5 | 43.2 | 41.6 | 26.8 | | | | 67.7 | 73.6 |
| (103) 26.8 | (76) 18.1 | (26) 22.6 | (17) 14.4 | | | % Profit Before Taxes/Tangible Net Worth | (166) 33.7 | (194) 31.4 |
| 4.7 | 5.1 | 6.4 | -3.0 | | | | 11.3 | 8.8 |
| 23.9 | 11.3 | 10.6 | 7.9 | 7.0 | | | 16.7 | 16.5 |
| 11.3 | 3.7 | 3.9 | 4.5 | 3.1 | | % Profit Before Taxes/Total Assets | 7.4 | 6.8 |
| -1.7 | .0 | 1.0 | -.3 | 1.7 | | | .7 | 1.0 |
| 847.5 | 29.0 | 22.9 | 20.4 | 10.4 | | | 64.1 | 86.0 |
| 81.1 | 6.9 | 9.4 | 10.2 | 5.6 | | Sales/Net Fixed Assets | 16.0 | 17.0 |
| 22.8 | 3.3 | 3.1 | 5.3 | 4.9 | | | 6.3 | 5.9 |
| 15.6 | 6.9 | 7.0 | 8.0 | 6.4 | | | 10.1 | 9.5 |
| 8.1 | 3.4 | 4.2 | 5.5 | 4.2 | | Sales/Total Assets | 4.9 | 5.1 |
| 4.0 | 2.0 | 2.2 | 3.2 | 3.8 | | | 2.5 | 2.8 |
| .5 | .6 | .6 | .8 | | | | .5 | .4 |
| (86) .9 | (87) 1.3 | (33) 1.0 | (17) .9 | | | % Depr., Dep., Amort./Sales | (173) 1.0 | (195) .9 |
| 1.9 | 1.7 | 1.7 | 1.2 | | | | 1.7 | 1.9 |
| 1.0 | .6 | .3 | | | | | 1.0 | .7 |
| (75) 2.0 | (45) 1.0 | (15) .7 | | | | % Officers', Directors' Owners' Comp/Sales | 2.0 | (111) 1.6 |
| 4.4 | 2.1 | 1.3 | | | | | (95) 4.7 | 3.0 |
| 320150M | 479332M | 953169M | 2513860M | 3295373M | 4373277M | Net Sales ($) | 20740848M | 14585502M |
| 34382M | 93691M | 143537M | 402371M | 685005M | 754642M | Total Assets ($) | 2501821M | 2680062M |

© RMA 2012

M = $ thousand     MM = $ million
See Pages 9 through 22 for Explanation of Ratios and Data

## Comparative Historical Data | Current Data Sorted by Sales

### Type of Statement

| Type of Statement | 4/1/09-3/31/10 | 4/1/10-3/31/11 | 4/1/11-3/31/12 | 0-1MM | 1-3MM | 3-5MM | 5-10MM | 10-25MM | 25MM & OVER |
|---|---|---|---|---|---|---|---|---|---|
| Unqualified | 9 | 8 | 9 | 1 | | 2 | | 2 | 8 |
| Reviewed | 15 | 10 | 15 | | 1 | | 2 | | 8 |
| Compiled | 30 | 31 | 25 | 6 | 8 | | 5 | 2 | 4 |
| Tax Returns | 184 | 151 | 189 | 46 | 70 | 29 | 22 | 15 | 7 |
| Other | 70 | 87 | 88 | 11 | 29 | 18 | 6 | 7 | 17 |
| | ALL | ALL | ALL | 25 (4/1-9/30/11) | | | 301 (10/1/11-3/31/12) | | |

### Data

| | 4/1/09-3/31/10 ALL | 4/1/10-3/31/11 ALL | 4/1/11-3/31/12 ALL | 0-1MM | 1-3MM | 3-5MM | 5-10MM | 10-25MM | 25MM & OVER |
|---|---|---|---|---|---|---|---|---|---|
| **NUMBER OF STATEMENTS** | 308 | 287 | 326 | 64 | 108 | 49 | 35 | 26 | 44 |
| | % | % | % | % | % | % | % | % | % |
| **ASSETS** | | | | | | | | | |
| Cash & Equivalents | 11.7 | 12.9 | 13.1 | 11.7 | 12.4 | 13.2 | 17.7 | 18.7 | 9.6 |
| Trade Receivables (net) | 2.8 | 3.8 | 3.2 | 1.3 | 2.1 | 2.4 | 3.6 | 5.2 | 7.6 |
| Inventory | 29.2 | 26.0 | 29.7 | 36.9 | 33.9 | 24.2 | 29.0 | 26.4 | 17.8 |
| All Other Current | 1.5 | 1.5 | .8 | .5 | .7 | .9 | 1.8 | .3 | 1.0 |
| Total Current | 45.2 | 44.2 | 46.8 | 50.4 | 49.1 | 40.8 | 52.2 | 50.6 | 36.0 |
| Fixed Assets (net) | 40.1 | 41.2 | 38.1 | 29.2 | 36.0 | 43.4 | 38.1 | 36.7 | 50.8 |
| Intangibles (net) | 8.2 | 7.6 | 8.9 | 14.8 | 10.1 | 7.8 | 4.5 | 3.0 | 5.6 |
| All Other Non-Current | 6.5 | 7.0 | 6.3 | 5.6 | 4.8 | 8.1 | 5.3 | 9.8 | 7.6 |
| Total | 100.0 | 100.0 | 100.0 | 100.0 | 100.0 | 100.0 | 100.0 | 100.0 | 100.0 |
| **LIABILITIES** | | | | | | | | | |
| Notes Payable-Short Term | 6.5 | 5.0 | 5.2 | 10.7 | 4.5 | 1.3 | 6.3 | 3.5 | 3.7 |
| Cur. Mat.-L.T.D. | 2.5 | 2.7 | 2.6 | 2.5 | 2.0 | 1.9 | 2.9 | 2.8 | 4.7 |
| Trade Payables | 11.0 | 10.7 | 10.0 | 3.7 | 7.2 | 6.9 | 18.3 | 18.2 | 17.8 |
| Income Taxes Payable | .1 | .1 | .1 | .1 | .0 | .0 | .2 | .0 | .1 |
| All Other Current | 12.2 | 12.0 | 13.8 | 18.7 | 10.3 | 24.8 | 5.5 | 10.2 | 11.8 |
| Total Current | 32.3 | 30.4 | 31.7 | 35.7 | 24.1 | 34.9 | 33.3 | 34.7 | 38.1 |
| Long-Term Debt | 35.8 | 33.5 | 31.7 | 28.5 | 29.0 | 39.7 | 40.5 | 25.0 | 31.1 |
| Deferred Taxes | .2 | .3 | .2 | .0 | .0 | .2 | .0 | .0 | 1.1 |
| All Other Non-Current | 9.5 | 11.3 | 12.8 | 24.1 | 14.1 | 7.7 | 11.4 | 2.0 | 5.9 |
| Net Worth | 22.2 | 24.6 | 23.6 | 11.7 | 32.7 | 17.4 | 14.9 | 38.3 | 23.8 |
| Total Liabilities & Net Worth | 100.0 | 100.0 | 100.0 | 100.0 | 100.0 | 100.0 | 100.0 | 100.0 | 100.0 |
| **INCOME DATA** | | | | | | | | | |
| Net Sales | 100.0 | 100.0 | 100.0 | 100.0 | 100.0 | 100.0 | 100.0 | 100.0 | 100.0 |
| Gross Profit | 20.2 | 21.4 | 18.1 | 27.5 | 19.5 | 13.8 | 14.4 | 12.9 | 12.0 |
| Operating Expenses | 18.6 | 19.8 | 17.3 | 28.4 | 17.9 | 12.4 | 13.5 | 11.6 | 11.1 |
| Operating Profit | 1.6 | 1.6 | .9 | -.9 | 1.6 | 1.4 | .8 | 1.3 | 1.0 |
| All Other Expenses (net) | -.5 | -.3 | -.5 | -1.1 | -.6 | -.2 | -.1 | .0 | -.1 |
| Profit Before Taxes | 2.2 | 1.9 | 1.3 | .2 | 2.2 | 1.6 | .9 | 1.3 | 1.1 |
| **RATIOS** | | | | | | | | | |
| Current | 4.9 | 5.3 | 5.0 | 15.5 | 10.4 | 4.9 | 2.3 | 3.5 | 1.3 |
| | 1.7 | 1.8 | 1.9 | 2.7 | 2.5 | 2.4 | 1.7 | 1.4 | .9 |
| | .9 | .9 | .9 | 1.0 | 1.2 | 1.0 | 1.0 | .8 | .6 |
| Quick | 1.8 | 1.9 | 1.6 | 2.1 | 2.0 | 1.6 | 1.4 | 1.7 | .7 |
| | (307) .5 | (285) .6 | (323) .6 | (61) .5 | .7 | .8 | .4 | .6 | .4 |
| | .2 | .2 | .2 | .1 | .1 | .2 | .2 | .2 | .2 |
| Sales/Receivables | 0 UND | 0 UND | 0 UND | 0 UND | 0 UND | 0 UND | 0 UND | 0 UND | 1 263.3 |
| | 0 UND | 0 UND | 0 UND | 0 UND | 0 UND | 0 UND | 0 856.3 | 0 864.0 | 3 143.4 |
| | 2 230.3 | 2 180.1 | 1 291.2 | 0 UND | 0 UND | 1 472.1 | 1 278.5 | 3 136.9 | 5 77.0 |
| Cost of Sales/Inventory | 10 37.2 | 9 40.0 | 9 42.4 | 24 15.5 | 11 32.0 | 8 45.8 | 7 55.7 | 4 88.4 | 5 67.6 |
| | 18 20.1 | 16 23.4 | 16 23.3 | 43 8.4 | 21 17.8 | 11 31.8 | 10 35.8 | 10 35.2 | 10 36.3 |
| | 35 10.3 | 28 13.1 | 31 11.9 | 74 4.9 | 34 10.6 | 17 22.1 | 18 20.2 | 17 21.0 | 12 30.5 |
| Cost of Sales/Payables | 0 UND | 0 UND | 0 UND | 0 UND | 0 UND | 0 UND | 1 478.6 | 1 412.6 | 6 59.5 |
| | 4 103.2 | 2 180.3 | 3 125.2 | 0 UND | 2 237.1 | 2 202.4 | 6 57.3 | 6 59.9 | 11 32.5 |
| | 13 29.0 | 10 37.4 | 9 39.6 | 3 122.1 | 7 55.5 | 7 55.1 | 13 29.1 | 12 31.2 | 14 27.0 |
| Sales/Working Capital | 14.5 | 15.2 | 16.6 | 5.8 | 13.7 | 19.2 | 27.2 | 30.2 | 69.1 |
| | 42.6 | 38.0 | 41.4 | 15.3 | 25.9 | 41.1 | 50.2 | 67.6 | -228.3 |
| | -256.6 | -240.1 | -313.2 | -247.8 | 114.6 | NM | -631.4 | -261.5 | -43.7 |
| EBIT/Interest | 6.6 | 7.1 | 7.3 | 3.2 | 5.2 | 7.8 | 16.1 | 13.6 | 8.0 |
| | (233) 2.7 | (217) 2.7 | (218) 2.6 | (28) 1.1 | (67) 2.5 | (36) 3.9 | (29) 4.4 | (18) 2.9 | (40) 2.3 |
| | 1.1 | 1.1 | 1.1 | -.6 | 1.0 | 1.4 | .1 | 1.4 | 1.5 |
| Net Profit + Depr., Dep., Amort./Cur. Mat. L/T/D | 4.2 | 3.7 | 6.2 | | | | | | |
| | (20) 2.0 | (19) 2.2 | (14) 2.2 | | | | | | |
| | 1.4 | 1.1 | 1.2 | | | | | | |
| Fixed/Worth | .3 | .4 | .3 | .1 | .1 | .4 | .5 | .3 | 1.3 |
| | 2.1 | 1.8 | 1.7 | 1.8 | 1.3 | 1.9 | 3.6 | .8 | 2.2 |
| | 195.4 | 46.0 | -37.1 | -.7 | 21.4 | -7.6 | -1.6 | 5.0 | 5.8 |
| Debt/Worth | 1.1 | .9 | .8 | .4 | .6 | .9 | .7 | .6 | 1.6 |
| | 3.9 | 3.9 | 3.6 | 7.6 | 2.0 | 3.9 | 6.9 | 2.3 | 3.7 |
| | -66.7 | -27.0 | -19.0 | -3.5 | 99.9 | -8.0 | -5.7 | 9.0 | 11.4 |
| % Profit Before Taxes/Tangible Net Worth | 75.3 | 54.0 | 49.7 | 37.3 | 72.8 | 46.6 | 42.3 | 50.4 | 31.1 |
| | (224) 29.8 | (208) 25.8 | (235) 20.8 | (36) 8.9 | (84) 28.4 | (33) 20.5 | (23) 23.2 | (23) 18.4 | (36) 15.6 |
| | 11.3 | 5.7 | 5.2 | -18.6 | 7.1 | 11.1 | 3.0 | 1.6 | 6.5 |
| % Profit Before Taxes/Total Assets | 15.2 | 16.6 | 15.3 | 11.5 | 22.4 | 15.4 | 17.4 | 14.9 | 10.1 |
| | 6.4 | 6.1 | 6.1 | 2.7 | 9.4 | 7.6 | 8.8 | 4.7 | 4.5 |
| | .7 | .4 | .0 | -6.9 | .8 | 1.6 | -4.2 | 1.1 | 1.4 |
| Sales/Net Fixed Assets | 71.1 | 93.8 | 106.6 | 364.6 | 115.2 | 102.6 | 115.1 | 103.1 | 22.5 |
| | 15.3 | 16.0 | 21.0 | 25.3 | 23.2 | 12.4 | 34.5 | 27.6 | 10.9 |
| | 4.8 | 5.1 | 5.7 | 4.7 | 4.0 | 5.4 | 7.9 | 13.6 | 6.6 |
| Sales/Total Assets | 9.1 | 9.6 | 11.1 | 6.8 | 10.2 | 12.2 | 17.3 | 17.9 | 8.0 |
| | 4.4 | 4.8 | 5.4 | 2.8 | 4.5 | 6.0 | 9.2 | 9.7 | 6.2 |
| | 2.4 | 2.7 | 2.8 | 1.7 | 2.4 | 3.5 | 4.3 | 4.3 | 4.4 |
| % Depr., Dep., Amort./Sales | .5 | .5 | .6 | .9 | .7 | .6 | .4 | .4 | .7 |
| | (223) 1.1 | (208) 1.1 | (233) 1.0 | (36) 1.9 | (74) 1.2 | (37) 1.3 | (28) .6 | (21) .6 | (37) .9 |
| | 2.0 | 1.9 | 1.7 | 3.4 | 1.9 | 1.8 | 1.3 | 1.0 | 1.2 |
| % Officers', Directors' Owners' Comp/Sales | .8 | .7 | .6 | 2.1 | 1.1 | .5 | .4 | .3 | .2 |
| | (149) 1.7 | (130) 1.7 | (144) 1.2 | (32) 3.8 | (50) 2.0 | (19) .7 | (18) .6 | (12) .7 | (13) .3 |
| | 3.6 | 3.5 | 2.9 | 6.2 | 3.0 | 1.2 | 1.4 | 1.0 | .7 |
| Net Sales ($) | 14852356M | 10555281M | 11935161M | 38413M | 197362M | 191282M | 241776M | 386677M | 10879651M |
| Total Assets ($) | 3010621M | 1966001M | 2113628M | 16819M | 57231M | 42374M | 51539M | 65472M | 1880193M |

© RMA 2012

M = $ thousand    MM = $ million
See Pages 9 through 22 for Explanation of Ratios and Data

## Current Data Sorted by Assets

## Comparative Historical Data

| | | | | | | | Type of Statement | | |
|---|---|---|---|---|---|---|---|---|---|
| | 1 | 1 | | | | | Unqualified | 4 | 4 |
| | 1 | 5 | 1 | | | | Reviewed | 3 | 4 |
| 4 | 1 | 1 | | | | | Compiled | 5 | 9 |
| 13 | 13 | 1 | | | | | Tax Returns | 24 | 17 |
| 4 | 4 | 4 | | 3 | | | Other | 20 | 20 |
| | 6 (4/1-9/30/11) | | | 49 (10/1/11-3/31/12) | | | | 4/1/07-3/31/08 | 4/1/08-3/31/09 |
| 0-500M | 500M-2MM | 2-10MM | 10-50MM | 50-100MM | 100-250MM | | | ALL | ALL |
| 21 | 19 | 11 | 4 | | | | NUMBER OF STATEMENTS | 56 | 54 |
| % | % | % | % | % | % | | ASSETS | % | % |
| 10.5 | 10.6 | 6.5 | | | | | Cash & Equivalents | 12.4 | 12.8 |
| 5.2 | 13.2 | 9.7 | D | D | | | Trade Receivables (net) | 7.8 | 9.6 |
| 15.4 | 16.8 | 14.0 | A | A | | | Inventory | 25.1 | 21.2 |
| 3.3 | .1 | 1.1 | T | T | | | All Other Current | 1.0 | 3.1 |
| 34.5 | 40.7 | 31.3 | A | A | | | Total Current | 46.3 | 46.7 |
| 54.6 | 43.8 | 56.6 | | | | | Fixed Assets (net) | 37.9 | 36.8 |
| 3.2 | 5.6 | .9 | N | N | | | Intangibles (net) | 9.5 | 10.4 |
| 7.5 | 9.9 | 11.2 | O | O | | | All Other Non-Current | 6.3 | 6.0 |
| 100.0 | 100.0 | 100.0 | T | T | | | Total | 100.0 | 100.0 |
| | | | | | | | LIABILITIES | | |
| 24.6 | 9.8 | 4.7 | A | A | | | Notes Payable-Short Term | 5.4 | 10.4 |
| 1.9 | 2.8 | 3.6 | V | V | | | Cur. Mat.-L.T.D. | 3.8 | 4.8 |
| 8.2 | 9.1 | 8.2 | A | A | | | Trade Payables | 12.3 | 14.0 |
| .0 | .0 | .1 | I | I | | | Income Taxes Payable | .1 | .0 |
| 13.3 | 6.6 | 5.8 | L | L | | | All Other Current | 13.6 | 9.1 |
| 47.9 | 28.4 | 22.4 | A | A | | | Total Current | 35.2 | 38.5 |
| 41.0 | 36.3 | 43.0 | B | B | | | Long-Term Debt | 26.9 | 20.2 |
| .0 | .0 | .0 | L | L | | | Deferred Taxes | .1 | .1 |
| 32.0 | 9.2 | 2.7 | E | E | | | All Other Non-Current | 11.6 | 9.1 |
| -20.9 | 26.1 | 31.9 | | | | | Net Worth | 26.2 | 32.2 |
| 100.0 | 100.0 | 100.0 | | | | | Total Liabilities & Net Worth | 100.0 | 100.0 |
| | | | | | | | INCOME DATA | | |
| 100.0 | 100.0 | 100.0 | | | | | Net Sales | 100.0 | 100.0 |
| 35.1 | 31.9 | 34.3 | | | | | Gross Profit | 36.1 | 33.4 |
| 32.6 | 27.5 | 30.6 | | | | | Operating Expenses | 35.5 | 30.7 |
| 2.5 | 4.3 | 3.7 | | | | | Operating Profit | .6 | 2.7 |
| .9 | .9 | 1.4 | | | | | All Other Expenses (net) | 1.1 | .5 |
| 1.6 | 3.4 | 2.3 | | | | | Profit Before Taxes | -.5 | 2.2 |
| | | | | | | | RATIOS | | |
| 3.3 | 2.3 | 1.9 | | | | | | 3.5 | 2.6 |
| 1.0 | 1.6 | 1.3 | | | | | Current | 1.7 | 1.5 |
| .4 | 1.0 | .8 | | | | | | .6 | .7 |
| 1.7 | 1.9 | 1.0 | | | | | | 1.7 | 1.4 |
| .4 | 1.0 | .8 | | | | | Quick | (55) .5 | .5 |
| .2 | .2 | .4 | | | | | | .1 | .2 |
| 0 UND | 0 UND | 2 210.1 | | | | | | 0 UND | 0 UND |
| 0 UND | 0 999.8 | 6 64.0 | | | | | Sales/Receivables | 2 189.0 | 1 666.9 |
| 5 80.7 | 14 25.8 | 18 20.4 | | | | | | 8 43.7 | 15 24.1 |
| 3 140.9 | 8 44.2 | 10 36.8 | | | | | | 14 26.6 | 8 47.6 |
| 14 26.1 | 12 31.6 | 13 27.9 | | | | | Cost of Sales/Inventory | 20 18.6 | 20 18.0 |
| 23 15.7 | 24 15.3 | 23 15.7 | | | | | | 44 8.4 | 40 9.1 |
| 0 UND | 0 UND | 7 55.0 | | | | | | 3 107.0 | 1 605.1 |
| 1 442.5 | 7 50.2 | 13 27.8 | | | | | Cost of Sales/Payables | 14 26.3 | 10 36.4 |
| 20 18.5 | 15 25.0 | 19 18.8 | | | | | | 24 15.4 | 30 12.0 |
| 16.5 | 17.4 | 14.9 | | | | | | 11.7 | 14.5 |
| -437.0 | 36.9 | 31.4 | | | | | Sales/Working Capital | 55.7 | 48.7 |
| -25.1 | 459.3 | -55.8 | | | | | | -22.7 | -34.1 |
| 8.7 | 12.0 | 5.7 | | | | | | 6.9 | 10.1 |
| (20) 2.0 | (14) 3.4 | 1.7 | | | | | EBIT/Interest | (42) 1.4 | (45) 3.7 |
| .1 | 2.4 | 1.2 | | | | | | -.9 | .3 |
| | | | | | | | Net Profit + Depr., Dep., Amort./Cur. Mat. L/T/D | | |
| 1.1 | .6 | 1.1 | | | | | | | |
| 17.1 | 1.2 | 1.4 | | | | | Fixed/Worth | .2 | .3 |
| -.9 | 48.2 | 5.4 | | | | | | 1.3 | 1.6 |
| | | | | | | | | -5.3 | UND |
| 1.5 | 1.7 | 1.1 | | | | | | .7 | .8 |
| 24.2 | 3.6 | 1.5 | | | | | Debt/Worth | 2.5 | 3.0 |
| -2.3 | 49.8 | 6.3 | | | | | | -7.7 | -34.0 |
| 121.1 | 125.0 | | | | | | | 42.8 | 42.2 |
| (11) 13.9 | (15) 49.2 | | | | | | % Profit Before Taxes/Tangible Net Worth | (39) 14.3 | (39) 9.2 |
| 1.9 | 16.5 | | | | | | | -2.4 | -3.7 |
| 18.9 | 19.7 | 11.3 | | | | | | 19.7 | 19.5 |
| 3.8 | 5.3 | 3.7 | | | | | % Profit Before Taxes/Total Assets | 2.3 | 4.9 |
| -3.4 | 4.3 | .4 | | | | | | -4.6 | -1.9 |
| 24.3 | 29.5 | 11.2 | | | | | | 73.1 | 64.6 |
| 11.2 | 10.8 | 4.2 | | | | | Sales/Net Fixed Assets | 16.0 | 16.1 |
| 5.3 | 3.6 | 2.2 | | | | | | 4.0 | 5.3 |
| 7.9 | 5.9 | 4.5 | | | | | | 6.8 | 7.5 |
| 5.7 | 3.1 | 2.3 | | | | | Sales/Total Assets | 4.9 | 5.0 |
| 3.3 | 2.6 | 1.6 | | | | | | 2.3 | 1.9 |
| .9 | .3 | | | | | | | .6 | .5 |
| (20) 1.7 | (17) .8 | | | | | | % Depr., Dep., Amort./Sales | (42) 1.8 | (42) 1.2 |
| 2.0 | 2.9 | | | | | | | 4.4 | 2.9 |
| 1.8 | 1.3 | | | | | | | 1.4 | 1.0 |
| (15) 3.2 | (16) 3.1 | | | | | | % Officers', Directors' Owners' Comp/Sales | (30) 3.3 | (26) 2.7 |
| 5.9 | 5.2 | | | | | | | 5.7 | 5.5 |
| 26542M | 80190M | 123138M | 367329M | | | | Net Sales ($) | 1098310M | 998220M |
| 5274M | 20718M | 39292M | 94241M | | | | Total Assets ($) | 457387M | 401978M |

M = $ thousand     MM = $ million
See Pages 9 through 22 for Explanation of Ratios and Data

## Comparative Historical Data

## Current Data Sorted by Sales

| | | | Type of Statement | | | | | | |
|---|---|---|---|---|---|---|---|---|---|
| 1 | 1 | 1 | Unqualified | | | | | | 1 |
| 4 | 3 | 2 | Reviewed | | 1 | | 1 | 1 | |
| 11 | 7 | 10 | Compiled | 3 | 2 | 1 | 2 | 2 | |
| 23 | 19 | 27 | Tax Returns | 5 | 14 | 3 | 4 | 1 | |
| 27 | 18 | 15 | Other | 2 | 3 | 3 | 2 | 1 | 4 |
| 4/1/09-3/31/10 ALL | 4/1/10-3/31/11 ALL | 4/1/11-3/31/12 ALL | | 0-1MM | 6 (4/1-9/30/11) 1-3MM | 3-5MM | 49 (10/1/11-3/31/12) 5-10MM | 10-25MM | 25MM & OVER |
| 66 | 48 | 55 | NUMBER OF STATEMENTS | 10 | 19 | 8 | 8 | 5 | 5 |
| % | % | % | ASSETS | % | % | % | % | % | % |
| 11.9 | 18.1 | 9.2 | Cash & Equivalents | 6.3 | 10.8 | | | | |
| 7.4 | 7.3 | 9.7 | Trade Receivables (net) | 3.1 | 9.9 | | | | |
| 21.8 | 18.1 | 16.8 | Inventory | 12.6 | 17.1 | | | | |
| 1.6 | 1.2 | 1.5 | All Other Current | 5.9 | .6 | | | | |
| 42.8 | 44.6 | 37.3 | Total Current | 27.9 | 38.5 | | | | |
| 38.7 | 39.1 | 49.5 | Fixed Assets (net) | 60.3 | 51.7 | | | | |
| 11.0 | 5.2 | 3.9 | Intangibles (net) | 2.1 | 3.0 | | | | |
| 7.5 | 11.1 | 9.2 | All Other Non-Current | 9.4 | 6.8 | | | | |
| 100.0 | 100.0 | 100.0 | Total | 100.0 | 100.0 | | | | |
| | | | LIABILITIES | | | | | | |
| 7.5 | 10.7 | 14.6 | Notes Payable-Short Term | 44.4 | 11.4 | | | | |
| 3.0 | 5.7 | 2.8 | Cur. Mat.-L.T.D. | .0 | 3.5 | | | | |
| 16.6 | 13.2 | 8.5 | Trade Payables | 4.1 | 8.6 | | | | |
| .1 | .1 | .0 | Income Taxes Payable | .0 | .0 | | | | |
| 14.0 | 6.1 | 9.3 | All Other Current | 14.6 | 10.5 | | | | |
| 41.2 | 35.9 | 35.2 | Total Current | 63.1 | 34.0 | | | | |
| 29.3 | 35.1 | 38.8 | Long-Term Debt | 37.9 | 41.6 | | | | |
| .0 | .0 | .0 | Deferred Taxes | .0 | .0 | | | | |
| 15.9 | 10.8 | 16.1 | All Other Non-Current | 26.0 | 26.8 | | | | |
| 13.6 | 18.1 | 10.0 | Net Worth | -27.0 | -2.4 | | | | |
| 100.0 | 100.0 | 100.0 | Total Liabilities & Net Worth | 100.0 | 100.0 | | | | |
| | | | INCOME DATA | | | | | | |
| 100.0 | 100.0 | 100.0 | Net Sales | 100.0 | 100.0 | | | | |
| 35.2 | 37.6 | 32.9 | Gross Profit | 38.0 | 36.3 | | | | |
| 31.9 | 33.3 | 29.3 | Operating Expenses | 35.6 | 32.7 | | | | |
| 3.3 | 4.3 | 3.6 | Operating Profit | 2.4 | 3.6 | | | | |
| .6 | .9 | 1.0 | All Other Expenses (net) | .9 | 1.0 | | | | |
| 2.7 | 3.4 | 2.6 | Profit Before Taxes | 1.4 | 2.5 | | | | |
| | | | RATIOS | | | | | | |
| 2.4 | 3.6 | 2.3 | | 1.9 | 3.2 | | | | |
| 1.3 | 1.6 | 1.3 | Current | .8 | 1.1 | | | | |
| .7 | .7 | .7 | | .3 | .7 | | | | |
| 1.1 | 2.6 | 1.6 | | .9 | 2.1 | | | | |
| (65) .5 | .6 | .8 | Quick | .3 | .8 | | | | |
| .1 | .3 | .2 | | .1 | .1 | | | | |
| 0 UND | 0 UND | 0 UND | | 0 UND | 0 UND | | | | |
| 1 382.9 | 2 158.0 | 2 242.3 | Sales/Receivables | 0 UND | 0 UND | | | | |
| 8 47.7 | 10 37.4 | 13 28.2 | | 0 UND | 12 30.0 | | | | |
| 6 59.7 | 5 71.2 | 8 48.6 | | 3 123.1 | 9 40.8 | | | | |
| 20 18.2 | 14 25.3 | 13 27.9 | Cost of Sales/Inventory | 14 26.3 | 16 23.5 | | | | |
| 32 11.5 | 34 10.9 | 26 14.0 | | 19 19.3 | 26 14.0 | | | | |
| 2 187.7 | 0 UND | 0 UND | | 0 UND | 0 UND | | | | |
| 16 23.5 | 9 40.0 | 8 43.7 | Cost of Sales/Payables | 0 UND | 1 383.0 | | | | |
| 28 13.0 | 22 16.8 | 19 19.7 | | 14 25.7 | 20 18.4 | | | | |
| 16.8 | 15.1 | 16.7 | | 85.5 | 16.6 | | | | |
| 69.6 | 38.9 | 71.6 | Sales/Working Capital | -74.4 | 71.6 | | | | |
| -48.5 | -40.3 | -55.8 | | -10.0 | -30.3 | | | | |
| 8.5 | 13.2 | 6.7 | | 12.0 | 8.7 | | | | |
| (52) 3.1 | (36) 3.5 | (49) 3.0 | EBIT/Interest | 1.4 (17) | 3.1 | | | | |
| .2 | 1.4 | 1.7 | | -.1 | 2.0 | | | | |
| | | | Net Profit + Depr., Dep., Amort./Cur. Mat. L/T/D | | | | | | |
| .5 | .4 | .8 | | .6 | .9 | | | | |
| 1.8 | 1.9 | 2.1 | Fixed/Worth | -2.2 | 3.2 | | | | |
| -3.2 | NM | -88.1 | | -.6 | -15.6 | | | | |
| 1.2 | 1.0 | 1.3 | | .2 | 2.2 | | | | |
| 4.5 | 2.9 | 4.0 | Debt/Worth | -3.8 | 4.2 | | | | |
| -5.0 | NM | -121.4 | | -1.9 | -22.5 | | | | |
| 82.7 | 74.9 | 62.5 | % Profit Before Taxes/Tangible Net Worth | | 100.8 | | | | |
| (45) 21.0 | (36) 32.6 | (39) 23.8 | | (13) | 55.0 | | | | |
| -6.0 | 7.8 | 10.5 | | | 18.4 | | | | |
| 19.0 | 21.3 | 15.5 | % Profit Before Taxes/Total Assets | 22.1 | 16.1 | | | | |
| 7.5 | 9.5 | 4.8 | | .8 | 5.3 | | | | |
| -3.3 | 1.5 | 1.7 | | -6.7 | 3.1 | | | | |
| 61.1 | 75.6 | 21.1 | Sales/Net Fixed Assets | 17.9 | 20.2 | | | | |
| 16.3 | 12.4 | 10.5 | | 10.4 | 10.1 | | | | |
| 5.2 | 3.7 | 3.6 | | 3.3 | 3.8 | | | | |
| 8.8 | 7.7 | 6.3 | Sales/Total Assets | 6.9 | 6.0 | | | | |
| 4.6 | 4.0 | 4.1 | | 5.6 | 3.8 | | | | |
| 2.3 | 2.3 | 2.6 | | 2.8 | 2.9 | | | | |
| .6 | .7 | .5 | % Depr., Dep., Amort./Sales | .9 | .9 | | | | |
| (50) 1.6 | (39) 2.0 | (50) 1.5 | | 1.7 (17) | 2.0 | | | | |
| 3.3 | 3.0 | 2.4 | | 1.8 | 2.9 | | | | |
| 1.3 | .8 | 1.3 | % Officers', Directors' Owners' Comp/Sales | | 1.7 | | | | |
| (36) 3.2 | (26) 3.3 | (38) 3.1 | | (14) | 3.1 | | | | |
| 6.9 | 5.8 | 5.6 | | | 6.1 | | | | |
| 1144166M | 524442M | 597199M | Net Sales ($) | 8191M | 33900M | 29862M | 54834M | 64477M | 405935M |
| 342653M | 124766M | 159525M | Total Assets ($) | 2085M | 10846M | 13565M | 16205M | 26659M | 90165M |

© RMA 2012

M = $ thousand    MM = $ million
See Pages 9 through 22 for Explanation of Ratios and Data

## RETAIL—Fruit and Vegetable Markets  NAICS 445230

### Current Data Sorted by Assets  |  Comparative Historical Data

Type of Statement counts (Current Data, by asset size):

| | 0-500M | 500M-2MM | 2-10MM |
|---|---|---|---|
| | 1 | 1 | 3 |
| | 4 | 5 | 5 |
| | 2 | 5 | 1 |
| | | 4 | 4 |

Current Data periods: 5 (4/1-9/30/11) · 26 (10/1/11-3/31/12)

| 0-500M | 500M-2MM | 2-10MM | 10-50MM | 50-100MM | 100-250MM | Type of Statement | 1 / 4/1/07-3/31/08 ALL | 2 / 4/1/08-3/31/09 ALL |
|---|---|---|---|---|---|---|---|---|
| | | | | | | Unqualified | 1 | 2 |
| | | | | | | Reviewed | 1 | 2 |
| | | | | | | Compiled | 13 | 9 |
| | | | | | | Tax Returns | 13 | 8 |
| | | | | | | Other | 5 | 4 |
| 7 | 10 | 13 | | | 1 | **NUMBER OF STATEMENTS** | 33 | 25 |
| % | % | % | % | % | % | **ASSETS** | % | % |
| | 6.2 | 16.1 | | | | Cash & Equivalents | 14.5 | 11.3 |
| | 23.9 | 12.1 | | | | Trade Receivables (net) | 11.8 | 15.8 |
| | 11.8 | 15.3 | | | | Inventory | 21.5 | 17.1 |
| | 2.8 | 1.4 | | | | All Other Current | 2.5 | 1.5 |
| | 44.7 | 44.9 | | | | Total Current | 50.3 | 45.7 |
| | 41.8 | 35.3 | | | | Fixed Assets (net) | 36.3 | 30.8 |
| | 10.8 | 8.7 | | | | Intangibles (net) | 8.1 | 12.6 |
| | 2.7 | 11.2 | | | | All Other Non-Current | 5.3 | 10.9 |
| | 100.0 | 100.0 | | | | Total | 100.0 | 100.0 |
| | | | | | | **LIABILITIES** | | |
| | 4.1 | 5.4 | | | | Notes Payable-Short Term | 8.6 | 7.2 |
| | .9 | 5.8 | | | | Cur. Mat.-L.T.D. | 2.1 | 4.9 |
| | 27.9 | 19.9 | | | | Trade Payables | 29.8 | 24.8 |
| | .0 | .5 | | | | Income Taxes Payable | .7 | .1 |
| | 30.2 | 19.2 | | | | All Other Current | 16.2 | 28.2 |
| | 63.1 | 50.8 | | | | Total Current | 57.4 | 65.1 |
| | 47.3 | 31.0 | | | | Long-Term Debt | 20.2 | 21.1 |
| | .3 | .5 | | | | Deferred Taxes | .0 | .0 |
| | 2.2 | 8.1 | | | | All Other Non-Current | 2.6 | 4.2 |
| | -12.9 | 9.5 | | | | Net Worth | 19.7 | 9.5 |
| | 100.0 | 100.0 | | | | Total Liabilities & Net Worth | 100.0 | 100.0 |
| | | | | | | **INCOME DATA** | | |
| | 100.0 | 100.0 | | | | Net Sales | 100.0 | 100.0 |
| | 25.8 | 29.4 | | | | Gross Profit | 29.4 | 30.2 |
| | 23.7 | 28.1 | | | | Operating Expenses | 28.0 | 28.9 |
| | 2.1 | 1.3 | | | | Operating Profit | 1.4 | 1.3 |
| | .7 | .0 | | | | All Other Expenses (net) | .6 | .1 |
| | 1.5 | 1.3 | | | | Profit Before Taxes | .9 | 1.2 |
| | | | | | | **RATIOS** | | |
| | 1.9 | 1.6 | | | | | 1.9 | 1.6 |
| | 1.1 | .7 | | | | Current | 1.1 | .8 |
| | .4 | .4 | | | | | .5 | .3 |
| | | 1.2 | | | | | 1.2 | 1.0 |
| | | .2 | | | | Quick | (32) .5 | .4 |
| | | .1 | | | | | .1 | .1 |
| | 0 UND | 0 UND | | | | | 0 UND | 0 UND |
| | 2 199.9 | 1 396.2 | | | | Sales/Receivables | 0 999.8 | 6 64.5 |
| | 25 14.8 | 4 85.1 | | | | | 9 41.0 | 20 17.9 |
| | 7 55.2 | 7 51.5 | | | | | 5 66.8 | 5 77.6 |
| | 8 43.0 | 14 25.7 | | | | Cost of Sales/Inventory | 9 42.4 | 9 40.5 |
| | 14 25.9 | 23 16.2 | | | | | 22 16.6 | 20 18.6 |
| | 7 51.4 | 7 50.3 | | | | | 3 125.6 | 0 UND |
| | 22 16.7 | 22 16.5 | | | | Cost of Sales/Payables | 23 16.0 | 17 21.4 |
| | 25 14.8 | 32 11.5 | | | | | 41 9.0 | 38 9.5 |
| | 18.4 | 27.8 | | | | | 28.9 | 46.6 |
| | NM | -30.7 | | | | Sales/Working Capital | 116.9 | -57.1 |
| | -26.1 | -15.2 | | | | | -23.4 | -7.6 |
| | | 20.2 | | | | | 26.2 | 14.5 |
| | | (10) 3.1 | | | | EBIT/Interest | (26) 5.5 | (19) 1.6 |
| | | -.6 | | | | | .2 | -.2 |
| | | | | | | | | |
| | | | | | | Net Profit + Depr., Dep., Amort./Cur. Mat. L/T/D | | |
| | | | | | | | | |
| | .9 | .2 | | | | | .4 | .5 |
| | 5.7 | 2.7 | | | | Fixed/Worth | 1.0 | 1.4 |
| | -.4 | -1.0 | | | | | -.9 | -2.4 |
| | 2.4 | 1.5 | | | | | .6 | 1.6 |
| | 22.3 | 4.7 | | | | Debt/Worth | 3.6 | 7.8 |
| | -1.8 | -3.0 | | | | | -16.5 | -5.8 |
| | | | | | | | 47.8 | 37.2 |
| | | | | | | % Profit Before Taxes/Tangible Net Worth | (23) 23.7 | (16) 9.1 |
| | | | | | | | 10.2 | -28.4 |
| | 25.0 | 19.3 | | | | | 19.9 | 23.3 |
| | 10.9 | 5.6 | | | | % Profit Before Taxes/Total Assets | 9.5 | 7.2 |
| | 1.0 | -1.0 | | | | | -.6 | -1.9 |
| | 94.4 | 97.2 | | | | | 66.9 | 74.3 |
| | 17.9 | 14.4 | | | | Sales/Net Fixed Assets | 22.3 | 28.3 |
| | 4.2 | 8.1 | | | | | 8.3 | 8.6 |
| | 8.6 | 7.8 | | | | | 9.7 | 10.8 |
| | 5.9 | 4.2 | | | | Sales/Total Assets | 5.7 | 5.2 |
| | 3.2 | 2.8 | | | | | 3.8 | 3.5 |
| | | .2 | | | | | .3 | .5 |
| | (12) | 1.2 | | | | % Depr., Dep., Amort./Sales | (26) 1.2 | (21) .9 |
| | | 3.0 | | | | | 3.2 | 2.7 |
| | | | | | | | 1.3 | 1.7 |
| | | | | | | % Officers', Directors', Owners' Comp/Sales | (15) 2.0 | (14) 2.5 |
| | | | | | | | 5.9 | 3.7 |
| 14709M | 60199M | 343033M | | 317995M | | Net Sales ($) | 560644M | 421864M |
| 1598M | 10009M | 56920M | | 70082M | | Total Assets ($) | 93666M | 76698M |

Columns 10-50MM, 50-100MM, and 100-250MM: DATA NOT AVAILABLE.

© RMA 2012

M = $ thousand   MM = $ million
See Pages 9 through 22 for Explanation of Ratios and Data

## Comparative Historical Data

## Current Data Sorted by Sales

| | | | Type of Statement | | | | | | |
|---|---|---|---|---|---|---|---|---|---|
| 2 | 3 | | Unqualified | | | | 1 | 1 | 1 |
| 4 | 3 | 3 | Reviewed | | | | 2 | 3 | 2 |
| 12 | 12 | 7 | Compiled | | | | 2 | 2 | 2 |
| 16 | 5 | 10 | Tax Returns | 3 | 2 | 1 | 2 | 2 | |
| 10 | 5 | 11 | Other | 1 | 4 | | 2 | 2 | 2 |
| 4/1/09-3/31/10 | 4/1/10-3/31/11 | 4/1/11-3/31/12 | | 5 (4/1-9/30/11) | | | 26 (10/1/11-3/31/12) | | |
| ALL | ALL | ALL | | 0-1MM | 1-3MM | 3-5MM | 5-10MM | 10-25MM | 25MM & OVER |
| 44 | 28 | 31 | NUMBER OF STATEMENTS | 4 | 6 | 1 | 7 | 8 | 5 |
| % | % | % | | % | % | % | % | % | % |
| | | | ASSETS | | | | | | |
| 17.0 | 16.6 | 11.3 | Cash & Equivalents | | | | | | |
| 19.0 | 13.7 | 15.5 | Trade Receivables (net) | | | | | | |
| 17.2 | 14.4 | 14.9 | Inventory | | | | | | |
| .9 | 2.1 | 2.2 | All Other Current | | | | | | |
| 54.0 | 46.8 | 43.9 | Total Current | | | | | | |
| 34.0 | 33.5 | 39.0 | Fixed Assets (net) | | | | | | |
| 5.3 | 8.5 | 10.9 | Intangibles (net) | | | | | | |
| 6.7 | 11.2 | 6.2 | All Other Non-Current | | | | | | |
| 100.0 | 100.0 | 100.0 | Total | | | | | | |
| | | | LIABILITIES | | | | | | |
| 6.1 | 7.8 | 4.9 | Notes Payable-Short Term | | | | | | |
| 5.7 | 6.4 | 3.2 | Cur. Mat.-L.T.D. | | | | | | |
| 29.5 | 27.3 | 26.2 | Trade Payables | | | | | | |
| .6 | .1 | .2 | Income Taxes Payable | | | | | | |
| 11.9 | 8.8 | 19.2 | All Other Current | | | | | | |
| 53.8 | 50.4 | 53.6 | Total Current | | | | | | |
| 16.4 | 32.0 | 35.4 | Long-Term Debt | | | | | | |
| .0 | .1 | .3 | Deferred Taxes | | | | | | |
| 6.9 | 3.8 | 12.3 | All Other Non-Current | | | | | | |
| 22.8 | 13.6 | -1.5 | Net Worth | | | | | | |
| 100.0 | 100.0 | 100.0 | Total Liabilities & Net Worth | | | | | | |
| | | | INCOME DATA | | | | | | |
| 100.0 | 100.0 | 100.0 | Net Sales | | | | | | |
| 29.2 | 26.7 | 29.1 | Gross Profit | | | | | | |
| 26.9 | 23.9 | 27.3 | Operating Expenses | | | | | | |
| 2.3 | 2.8 | 1.8 | Operating Profit | | | | | | |
| .2 | .4 | .3 | All Other Expenses (net) | | | | | | |
| 2.1 | 2.3 | 1.5 | Profit Before Taxes | | | | | | |
| | | | RATIOS | | | | | | |
| 2.2 | 1.4 | 1.5 | | | | | | | |
| 1.1 | .9 | .7 | Current | | | | | | |
| .6 | .7 | .4 | | | | | | | |
| 2.0 | 1.1 | 1.2 | | | | | | | |
| (43) .9 | .5 | (29) .5 | Quick | | | | | | |
| .3 | .2 | .1 | | | | | | | |
| 0 UND | 0 UND | 0 UND | | | | | | | |
| 3 135.5 | 1 653.3 | 1 463.7 | Sales/Receivables | | | | | | |
| 27 13.3 | 29 12.7 | 22 16.7 | | | | | | | |
| 4 83.7 | 3 112.1 | 6 65.2 | | | | | | | |
| 8 44.9 | 10 37.0 | 11 32.5 | Cost of Sales/Inventory | | | | | | |
| 22 16.9 | 17 21.3 | 20 18.3 | | | | | | | |
| 3 106.8 | 9 40.6 | 6 56.4 | | | | | | | |
| 18 20.4 | 25 14.8 | 18 20.5 | Cost of Sales/Payables | | | | | | |
| 40 9.1 | 43 8.5 | 27 13.6 | | | | | | | |
| 17.4 | 49.9 | 33.1 | | | | | | | |
| 127.2 | -207.6 | -89.6 | Sales/Working Capital | | | | | | |
| -24.0 | -25.7 | -22.8 | | | | | | | |
| 5.7 | 15.5 | 15.7 | | | | | | | |
| (29) 3.4 | (23) 4.4 | (23) 4.0 | EBIT/Interest | | | | | | |
| .7 | 2.1 | .0 | | | | | | | |
| | | | Net Profit + Depr., Dep., Amort./Cur. Mat. L/T/D | | | | | | |
| .3 | .2 | .5 | | | | | | | |
| 1.4 | 1.2 | 5.8 | Fixed/Worth | | | | | | |
| 15.6 | 3.1 | -1.0 | | | | | | | |
| .8 | 1.2 | 1.8 | | | | | | | |
| 2.6 | 4.1 | 37.6 | Debt/Worth | | | | | | |
| NM | 36.2 | -2.7 | | | | | | | |
| 92.4 | 59.4 | 98.0 | | | | | | | |
| (33) 29.5 | (22) 28.1 | (16) 26.2 | % Profit Before Taxes/Tangible Net Worth | | | | | | |
| 11.7 | 11.0 | 7.3 | | | | | | | |
| 15.5 | 21.3 | 20.8 | | | | | | | |
| 8.8 | 6.1 | 7.3 | % Profit Before Taxes/Total Assets | | | | | | |
| 3.3 | 2.8 | -2.5 | | | | | | | |
| 76.9 | 84.6 | 87.2 | | | | | | | |
| 26.6 | 19.4 | 14.4 | Sales/Net Fixed Assets | | | | | | |
| 6.3 | 5.7 | 6.1 | | | | | | | |
| 9.3 | 7.9 | 8.2 | | | | | | | |
| 4.5 | 4.6 | 4.5 | Sales/Total Assets | | | | | | |
| 2.6 | 2.6 | 3.3 | | | | | | | |
| .5 | .3 | .4 | | | | | | | |
| (39) 1.1 | (24) 1.1 | (25) 1.1 | % Depr., Dep., Amort./Sales | | | | | | |
| 2.5 | 2.0 | 2.9 | | | | | | | |
| 1.2 | 1.6 | 1.3 | | | | | | | |
| (21) 2.1 | (13) 2.7 | (10) 4.3 | % Officers', Directors' Owners' Comp/Sales | | | | | | |
| 4.1 | 4.2 | 7.1 | | | | | | | |
| 1145425M | 875468M | 735936M | Net Sales ($) | 3066M | 12690M | 3668M | 56680M | 138028M | 521804M |
| 299020M | 229310M | 138609M | Total Assets ($) | 601M | 4028M | 1163M | 12284M | 32544M | 87989M |

© RMA 2012

**M = $ thousand    MM = $ million**

See Pages 9 through 22 for Explanation of Ratios and Data

## Current Data Sorted by Assets       Comparative Historical Data

| 0-500M | 500M-2MM | 2-10MM | 10-50MM | 50-100MM | 100-250MM | Type of Statement | 1 | 2 |
|---|---|---|---|---|---|---|---|---|
| | | | | | | Unqualified | | |
| | | | | | | Reviewed | | |
| | 3 | 3 | | | | Compiled | 4 | 11 |
| 26 | 14 | 3 | | | | Tax Returns | 18 | 23 |
| 7 | 9 | 6 | | | 1 | Other | 7 | 9 |
| 4 (4/1-9/30/11) | | | 69 (10/1/11-3/31/12) | | | | 4/1/07-3/31/08 ALL | 4/1/08-3/31/09 ALL |
| **33** | **26** | **12** | **1** | | **1** | **NUMBER OF STATEMENTS** | **30** | **45** |
| % | % | % | % | % | % | **ASSETS** | % | % |
| 16.0 | 9.3 | 11.2 | | | | Cash & Equivalents | 9.0 | 6.7 |
| 3.4 | 5.0 | 7.4 | | | | Trade Receivables (net) | 3.7 | 6.6 |
| 6.1 | 3.6 | 9.9 | | | | Inventory | 5.1 | 3.9 |
| 7.8 | 16.6 | 3.7 | | | | All Other Current | 3.7 | 5.7 |
| 33.3 | 34.4 | 32.2 | | | | Total Current | 21.5 | 22.9 |
| 44.0 | 46.5 | 47.6 | | | | Fixed Assets (net) | 55.3 | 50.5 |
| 16.1 | 10.8 | 8.6 | | | | Intangibles (net) | 13.2 | 11.9 |
| 6.6 | 8.4 | 11.6 | | | | All Other Non-Current | 10.0 | 14.8 |
| 100.0 | 100.0 | 100.0 | | | | Total | 100.0 | 100.0 |
| | | | | | | **LIABILITIES** | | |
| 15.2 | 2.8 | 3.6 | | | | Notes Payable-Short Term | 2.8 | 3.7 |
| 3.3 | 2.4 | 3.8 | | | | Cur. Mat.-L.T.D. | 4.6 | 3.6 |
| 9.4 | 6.0 | 13.8 | | | | Trade Payables | 5.6 | 7.9 |
| .0 | .0 | .0 | | | | Income Taxes Payable | .1 | .0 |
| 45.0 | 24.7 | 9.6 | | | | All Other Current | 11.1 | 21.0 |
| 73.0 | 35.9 | 30.8 | | | | Total Current | 24.2 | 36.3 |
| 33.8 | 25.3 | 23.6 | | | | Long-Term Debt | 57.8 | 39.5 |
| .0 | .0 | .0 | | | | Deferred Taxes | .2 | .1 |
| 28.6 | 14.4 | 7.4 | | | | All Other Non-Current | 13.5 | 14.9 |
| -35.3 | 24.4 | 38.2 | | | | Net Worth | 4.3 | 9.2 |
| 100.0 | 100.0 | 100.0 | | | | Total Liabilities & Net Worth | 100.0 | 100.0 |
| | | | | | | **INCOME DATA** | | |
| 100.0 | 100.0 | 100.0 | | | | Net Sales | 100.0 | 100.0 |
| 59.8 | 52.1 | 52.4 | | | | Gross Profit | 54.5 | 53.7 |
| 56.2 | 46.9 | 42.5 | | | | Operating Expenses | 52.1 | 49.6 |
| 3.6 | 5.1 | 9.9 | | | | Operating Profit | 2.4 | 4.1 |
| .3 | .6 | 1.1 | | | | All Other Expenses (net) | 2.6 | 3.2 |
| 3.4 | 4.6 | 8.8 | | | | Profit Before Taxes | -.2 | .8 |
| | | | | | | **RATIOS** | | |
| 1.9 | 5.2 | 1.8 | | | | | 2.6 | 1.3 |
| .4 | 1.2 | 1.2 | | | | Current | .5 | .6 |
| .2 | .5 | .6 | | | | | .3 | .2 |
| 1.0 | 2.2 | 1.4 | | | | | 1.7 | .7 |
| .3 | .4 | .5 | | | | Quick | .4 | .4 |
| .1 | .1 | .3 | | | | | .2 | .1 |
| 0 UND | 0 UND | 0 UND | | | | | 0 UND | 0 UND |
| 0 UND | 0 UND | 1 277.5 | | | | Sales/Receivables | 0 UND | 0 UND |
| 0 UND | 5 69.1 | 8 46.5 | | | | | 0 UND | 4 83.2 |
| 2 185.6 | 4 91.2 | 5 66.4 | | | | | 3 128.8 | 3 124.2 |
| 7 56.0 | 6 61.3 | 14 25.2 | | | | Cost of Sales/Inventory | 7 48.8 | 5 71.8 |
| 11 33.2 | 11 32.4 | 24 15.1 | | | | | 15 23.6 | 10 38.0 |
| 0 UND | 0 UND | 4 95.0 | | | | | 0 UND | 0 UND |
| 3 112.5 | 7 54.6 | 15 24.9 | | | | Cost of Sales/Payables | 17 21.7 | 12 29.4 |
| 29 12.7 | 26 13.9 | 54 6.8 | | | | | 34 10.6 | 36 10.0 |
| 23.6 | 5.6 | 18.7 | | | | | 33.2 | 64.7 |
| -38.4 | 218.2 | 80.7 | | | | Sales/Working Capital | -29.0 | -41.3 |
| -5.3 | -21.5 | -52.8 | | | | | -11.0 | -15.3 |
| 7.6 | 11.6 | 30.6 | | | | | 4.2 | 4.4 |
| (18) 1.3 | (19) 4.2 | (11) 19.4 | | | | EBIT/Interest | (28) 2.1 | (36) 2.1 |
| -.1 | 1.7 | 2.9 | | | | | .3 | .6 |
| | | | | | | Net Profit + Depr., Dep., Amort./Cur. Mat. L/T/D | | |
| 1.5 | .6 | .8 | | | | | 2.5 | 1.5 |
| -1.3 | 3.3 | 1.3 | | | | Fixed/Worth | NM | 8.8 |
| -.4 | -1.9 | NM | | | | | -2.1 | -2.3 |
| 2.9 | .8 | .6 | | | | | 2.5 | 2.1 |
| -3.5 | 2.9 | 1.2 | | | | Debt/Worth | NM | 269.0 |
| -1.6 | -5.7 | NM | | | | | -3.6 | -3.5 |
| 115.4 | 41.8 | | | | | | 151.1 | 73.8 |
| (11) 41.7 | (15) 27.6 | | | | | % Profit Before Taxes/Tangible Net Worth | (15) 47.8 | (23) 42.0 |
| 21.6 | 6.1 | | | | | | 2.4 | 6.1 |
| 37.0 | 19.9 | 50.9 | | | | | 14.7 | 15.0 |
| 3.9 | 11.7 | 26.9 | | | | % Profit Before Taxes/Total Assets | 2.8 | 5.0 |
| -1.4 | 1.3 | 5.2 | | | | | -8.2 | -1.9 |
| 17.6 | 9.4 | 11.5 | | | | | 7.4 | 9.3 |
| 10.4 | 6.8 | 6.7 | | | | Sales/Net Fixed Assets | 3.7 | 4.9 |
| 4.5 | 4.1 | 4.9 | | | | | 2.0 | 3.0 |
| 5.2 | 3.5 | 5.2 | | | | | 3.5 | 4.0 |
| 3.8 | 2.6 | 3.5 | | | | Sales/Total Assets | 1.9 | 2.1 |
| 2.2 | 1.3 | 2.2 | | | | | 1.1 | 1.6 |
| 1.4 | 2.0 | .9 | | | | | 2.3 | 1.8 |
| (24) 3.2 | (19) 2.5 | (11) 2.4 | | | | % Depr., Dep., Amort./Sales | (29) 5.2 | (44) 3.2 |
| 7.3 | 4.0 | 3.5 | | | | | 7.8 | 5.1 |
| | | | | | | | 1.5 | 3.1 |
| | | | | | | % Officers', Directors' Owners' Comp/Sales | (10) 3.7 | (14) 4.7 |
| | | | | | | | 5.0 | 8.1 |
| 34029M | 72830M | 130654M | 32030M | | 1466186M | Net Sales ($) | 125132M | 1635888M |
| 8112M | 25597M | 34763M | 12998M | | 109377M | Total Assets ($) | 43793M | 361438M |

(Columns 10-50MM, 50-100MM, and 100-250MM for the Assets, Liabilities, Income Data and Ratios sections are marked "DATA NOT AVAILABLE".)

© RMA 2012

M = $ thousand    MM = $ million
See Pages 9 through 22 for Explanation of Ratios and Data

## Comparative Historical Data | Current Data Sorted by Sales

| | | | Type of Statement | | | | | | |
|---|---|---|---|---|---|---|---|---|---|
| 2 | 1 | 1 | Unqualified | | | | | | 1 |
| | | | Reviewed | | | | 2 | 1 | 1 |
| 2 | 2 | 6 | Compiled | | 3 | | 1 | 1 | 1 |
| 36 | 22 | 44 | Tax Returns | 17 | 22 | 2 | 4 | 3 | |
| 9 | 10 | 22 | Other | 4 | 6 | 4 | | | |
| 4/1/09- | 4/1/10- | 4/1/11- | | | | 4 (4/1-9/30/11) | 69 (10/1/11-3/31/12) | | |
| 3/31/10 | 3/31/11 | 3/31/12 | | | | | | | |
| ALL | ALL | ALL | | 0-1MM | 1-3MM | 3-5MM | 5-10MM | 10-25MM | 25MM & OVER |
| 49 | 35 | 73 | NUMBER OF STATEMENTS | 21 | 31 | 6 | 7 | 5 | 3 |
| % | % | % | **ASSETS** | % | % | % | % | % | % |
| 7.9 | 11.4 | 13.4 | Cash & Equivalents | 17.9 | 10.5 | | | | |
| 5.7 | 1.7 | 4.8 | Trade Receivables (net) | .7 | 4.9 | | | | |
| 5.2 | 4.4 | 6.1 | Inventory | 4.1 | 4.5 | | | | |
| 1.6 | 13.5 | 10.0 | All Other Current | 8.6 | 12.6 | | | | |
| 20.4 | 31.1 | 34.3 | Total Current | 31.3 | 32.4 | | | | |
| 41.2 | 44.9 | 45.0 | Fixed Assets (net) | 50.9 | 37.7 | | | | |
| 22.0 | 12.6 | 12.7 | Intangibles (net) | 12.9 | 17.7 | | | | |
| 16.4 | 11.5 | 8.0 | All Other Non-Current | 4.9 | 12.2 | | | | |
| 100.0 | 100.0 | 100.0 | Total | 100.0 | 100.0 | | | | |
| | | | **LIABILITIES** | | | | | | |
| 2.7 | 5.6 | 8.5 | Notes Payable-Short Term | 4.0 | 13.5 | | | | |
| 2.8 | 3.7 | 3.0 | Cur. Mat.-L.T.D. | 2.3 | 2.7 | | | | |
| 10.1 | 7.3 | 9.2 | Trade Payables | 6.0 | 8.1 | | | | |
| .1 | .0 | .0 | Income Taxes Payable | .0 | .0 | | | | |
| 28.5 | 25.9 | 30.8 | All Other Current | 49.9 | 27.7 | | | | |
| 44.3 | 42.5 | 51.4 | Total Current | 62.2 | 52.1 | | | | |
| 50.9 | 44.0 | 28.5 | Long-Term Debt | 36.9 | 33.3 | | | | |
| .1 | .0 | .0 | Deferred Taxes | .0 | .0 | | | | |
| 24.3 | 10.7 | 19.7 | All Other Non-Current | 21.6 | 27.5 | | | | |
| -19.6 | 2.8 | .5 | Net Worth | -20.6 | -12.9 | | | | |
| 100.0 | 100.0 | 100.0 | Total Liabilities & Net Worth | 100.0 | 100.0 | | | | |
| | | | **INCOME DATA** | | | | | | |
| 100.0 | 100.0 | 100.0 | Net Sales | 100.0 | 100.0 | | | | |
| 57.7 | 57.0 | 55.4 | Gross Profit | 63.2 | 57.1 | | | | |
| 54.4 | 52.1 | 50.0 | Operating Expenses | 58.2 | 52.9 | | | | |
| 3.3 | 4.9 | 5.4 | Operating Profit | 5.0 | 4.1 | | | | |
| 2.0 | 1.3 | .5 | All Other Expenses (net) | .8 | .2 | | | | |
| 1.4 | 3.6 | 4.9 | Profit Before Taxes | 4.3 | 4.0 | | | | |
| | | | **RATIOS** | | | | | | |
| 1.1 | 2.1 | 2.3 | | 2.3 | 3.3 | | | | |
| .5 | .6 | .9 | Current | .4 | 1.0 | | | | |
| .2 | .3 | .4 | | .1 | .4 | | | | |
| .7 | .8 | 1.4 | | 1.7 | 1.4 | | | | |
| .3 | .3 | .4 | Quick | .3 | .4 | | | | |
| .1 | .1 | .1 | | .0 | .1 | | | | |
| 0 UND | 0 UND | 0 UND | | 0 UND | 0 UND | | | | |
| 0 UND | 0 UND | 0 UND | Sales/Receivables | 0 UND | 0 UND | | | | |
| 3 129.4 | 0 UND | 2 187.3 | | 0 UND | 1 298.8 | | | | |
| 3 123.8 | 2 149.4 | 3 116.7 | | 1 291.5 | 3 130.7 | | | | |
| 6 63.7 | 5 70.2 | 7 52.2 | Cost of Sales/Inventory | 8 46.1 | 5 75.9 | | | | |
| 10 34.9 | 10 37.0 | 14 25.6 | | 11 32.1 | 10 37.1 | | | | |
| 0 UND | 3 110.4 | 0 UND | | 0 UND | 0 UND | | | | |
| 15 23.8 | 22 16.8 | 7 54.1 | Cost of Sales/Payables | 0 UND | 6 59.5 | | | | |
| 33 10.9 | 26 13.9 | 29 12.7 | | 29 12.4 | 28 12.9 | | | | |
| 137.2 | 20.3 | 17.8 | | 15.7 | 17.6 | | | | |
| -31.0 | -41.2 | -297.5 | Sales/Working Capital | -38.4 | 931.0 | | | | |
| -7.6 | -14.2 | -14.8 | | -3.1 | -23.1 | | | | |
| 4.8 | 10.2 | 19.4 | | 5.7 | 10.1 | | | | |
| (40) 1.7 | (25) 3.4 | (50) 4.4 | EBIT/Interest | (11) 2.3 | (22) 3.0 | | | | |
| .8 | 1.4 | 1.2 | | -.4 | .8 | | | | |
| | | | Net Profit + Depr., Dep., Amort./Cur. Mat. L/T/D | | | | | | |
| 1.0 | .9 | .8 | | 1.3 | .8 | | | | |
| -4.1 | UND | 14.0 | Fixed/Worth | -1.9 | -2.4 | | | | |
| -.3 | -.8 | -.7 | | -.6 | -.2 | | | | |
| 6.0 | 1.8 | .8 | | 2.3 | 1.8 | | | | |
| -5.0 | UND | 14.4 | Debt/Worth | -4.4 | -6.2 | | | | |
| -1.6 | -2.3 | -2.3 | | -1.9 | -1.6 | | | | |
| 87.3 | 146.7 | 89.1 | | | 41.2 | | | | |
| (15) 28.7 | (18) 45.7 | (37) 39.7 | % Profit Before Taxes/Tangible Net Worth | | (12) 18.8 | | | | |
| 2.6 | 10.8 | 14.1 | | | 1.3 | | | | |
| 28.8 | 31.4 | 29.1 | | 28.7 | 19.4 | | | | |
| 5.6 | 10.1 | 13.2 | % Profit Before Taxes/Total Assets | 13.2 | 4.5 | | | | |
| -.7 | 3.8 | 1.3 | | -1.6 | -.2 | | | | |
| 18.2 | 24.4 | 15.7 | | 14.3 | 14.1 | | | | |
| 7.9 | 6.7 | 8.5 | Sales/Net Fixed Assets | 7.1 | 9.3 | | | | |
| 4.1 | 4.5 | 4.8 | | 3.1 | 5.6 | | | | |
| 4.2 | 6.1 | 4.9 | | 4.0 | 3.9 | | | | |
| 2.5 | 3.3 | 3.2 | Sales/Total Assets | 2.7 | 2.6 | | | | |
| 1.6 | 1.9 | 2.1 | | 2.0 | 1.3 | | | | |
| 1.5 | 1.3 | 1.5 | | 1.5 | 1.6 | | | | |
| (37) 5.0 | (30) 2.9 | (55) 2.6 | % Depr., Dep., Amort./Sales | (16) 4.2 | (24) 3.0 | | | | |
| 7.9 | 5.1 | 5.3 | | 7.9 | 6.4 | | | | |
| 2.7 | 3.4 | 1.9 | | | 1.4 | | | | |
| (14) 4.2 | (13) 6.8 | (24) 5.8 | % Officers', Directors' Owners' Comp/Sales | | (11) 8.5 | | | | |
| 6.4 | 13.4 | 9.2 | | | 9.2 | | | | |
| 3176672M | 121272M | 1735729M | Net Sales ($) | 12468M | 49565M | 22733M | 46221M | 75788M | 1528954M |
| 457986M | 45558M | 190847M | Total Assets ($) | 4886M | 24812M | 5500M | 14260M | 13358M | 128031M |

M = $ thousand    MM = $ million
See Pages 9 through 22 for Explanation of Ratios and Data

**Current Data Sorted by Assets**       **Comparative Historical Data**

### Type of Statement

| | 0-500M | 500M-2MM | 2-10MM | 10-50MM | 50-100MM | 100-250MM | Type of Statement | 4/1/07-3/31/08 ALL | 4/1/08-3/31/09 ALL |
|---|---|---|---|---|---|---|---|---|---|
| Unqualified | 1 | | 1 | | | | Unqualified | 3 | 2 |
| Reviewed | 5 | 3 | 2 | | | | Reviewed | 4 | 4 |
| Compiled | 7 | 2 | 2 | | | | Compiled | 7 | 7 |
| Tax Returns | 4 | 5 | 1 | | | | Tax Returns | 9 | 17 |
| Other | | | | 2 | 1 | | Other | 5 | 8 |
| | 7 (4/1-9/30/11) | | | 29 (10/1/11-3/31/12) | | | | | |
| **Number of Statements** | **17** | **10** | **6** | **2** | **1** | | **NUMBER OF STATEMENTS** | **28** | **38** |

*Columns 2-10MM, 10-50MM, 50-100MM, 100-250MM marked "DATA NOT AVAILABLE".*

### Assets (%)

| 0-500M | 500M-2MM | | 4/1/07-3/31/08 ALL | 4/1/08-3/31/09 ALL |
|---|---|---|---|---|
| 22.9 | 26.3 | Cash & Equivalents | 15.3 | 10.9 |
| 3.7 | 6.6 | Trade Receivables (net) | 6.8 | 7.1 |
| 11.1 | 23.6 | Inventory | 25.8 | 23.9 |
| .5 | 1.5 | All Other Current | 1.9 | 3.4 |
| 38.2 | 58.0 | Total Current | 49.8 | 45.3 |
| 33.9 | 34.4 | Fixed Assets (net) | 34.5 | 38.0 |
| 10.5 | 1.3 | Intangibles (net) | 9.6 | 9.1 |
| 17.3 | 6.4 | All Other Non-Current | 6.1 | 7.6 |
| 100.0 | 100.0 | Total | 100.0 | 100.0 |

### Liabilities

| 0-500M | 500M-2MM | | 4/1/07-3/31/08 ALL | 4/1/08-3/31/09 ALL |
|---|---|---|---|---|
| 17.5 | 4.0 | Notes Payable-Short Term | 19.0 | 6.4 |
| 3.6 | 2.4 | Cur. Mat.-L.T.D. | 8.2 | 4.4 |
| 8.2 | 17.1 | Trade Payables | 11.3 | 13.2 |
| .1 | .4 | Income Taxes Payable | .4 | .1 |
| 14.0 | 4.8 | All Other Current | 12.5 | 14.0 |
| 43.3 | 28.8 | Total Current | 51.5 | 38.1 |
| 26.9 | 49.3 | Long-Term Debt | 23.8 | 32.1 |
| .0 | .0 | Deferred Taxes | .1 | .1 |
| 1.7 | 9.7 | All Other Non-Current | 1.6 | 22.1 |
| 28.0 | 12.3 | Net Worth | 23.0 | 7.6 |
| 100.0 | 100.0 | Total Liabilities & Net Worth | 100.0 | 100.0 |

### Income Data

| 0-500M | 500M-2MM | | 4/1/07-3/31/08 ALL | 4/1/08-3/31/09 ALL |
|---|---|---|---|---|
| 100.0 | 100.0 | Net Sales | 100.0 | 100.0 |
| 60.0 | 49.1 | Gross Profit | 47.4 | 55.0 |
| 54.9 | 45.1 | Operating Expenses | 42.2 | 52.1 |
| 5.2 | 4.0 | Operating Profit | 5.2 | 3.0 |
| 1.1 | 1.9 | All Other Expenses (net) | 1.9 | 1.6 |
| 4.1 | 2.1 | Profit Before Taxes | 3.3 | 1.4 |

### Ratios

| 0-500M | 500M-2MM | | 4/1/07-3/31/08 ALL | 4/1/08-3/31/09 ALL |
|---|---|---|---|---|
| 1.7 | 5.5 | Current | 2.9 | 2.7 |
| .8 | 2.6 | | 1.1 | 1.3 |
| .3 | 1.5 | | .5 | .7 |
| .8 | 4.4 | Quick | 1.4 | 1.1 |
| .5 | 1.2 | | .4 | .5 |
| .3 | .1 | | .2 | .1 |
| 0 UND | 0 UND | Sales/Receivables | 0 UND | 0 UND |
| 0 UND | 0 UND | | 0 999.8 | 1 370.1 |
| 2 208.8 | 9 40.9 | | 11 33.6 | 17 21.0 |
| 0 UND | 13 28.1 | Cost of Sales/Inventory | 33 11.0 | 13 27.6 |
| 17 21.8 | 35 10.3 | | 71 5.1 | 44 8.3 |
| 33 10.9 | 79 4.6 | | 114 3.2 | 76 4.8 |
| 0 UND | 0 UND | Cost of Sales/Payables | 4 103.5 | 0 UND |
| 0 UND | 15 24.6 | | 16 22.5 | 10 35.0 |
| 29 12.8 | 29 12.5 | | 56 6.5 | 42 8.6 |
| 13.7 | 4.8 | Sales/Working Capital | 7.5 | 13.2 |
| -68.8 | 10.3 | | 143.8 | 25.6 |
| -8.7 | 23.8 | | -11.7 | -23.7 |
| 17.3 | | EBIT/Interest | 10.6 | 6.1 |
| (11) 1.6 | | | (26) 2.6 | (32) 2.2 |
| .0 | | | .8 | -1.5 |
| | | Net Profit + Depr., Dep., Amort./Cur. Mat. L/T/D | | |
| .4 | .4 | Fixed/Worth | .5 | .6 |
| 1.2 | 1.1 | | 1.6 | 2.0 |
| -1.2 | -2.3 | | -.8 | -2.5 |
| .8 | .6 | Debt/Worth | .3 | 1.7 |
| 1.5 | 3.4 | | 3.4 | 4.9 |
| -3.7 | -5.3 | | -4.0 | -5.2 |
| 91.3 | | % Profit Before Taxes/Tangible Net Worth | 30.3 | 75.7 |
| (11) 20.0 | | | (20) 24.0 | (25) 20.4 |
| 13.6 | | | 1.3 | -2.5 |
| 36.1 | 22.7 | % Profit Before Taxes/Total Assets | 18.5 | 18.0 |
| 11.1 | 1.2 | | 5.5 | 3.0 |
| -.8 | -5.6 | | -1.1 | -6.3 |
| 172.7 | 28.7 | Sales/Net Fixed Assets | 25.5 | 27.5 |
| 8.7 | 8.8 | | 8.6 | 7.0 |
| 5.1 | 4.5 | | 3.1 | 3.4 |
| 4.8 | 4.1 | Sales/Total Assets | 3.7 | 4.2 |
| 3.3 | 3.2 | | 2.3 | 2.3 |
| 1.9 | 1.8 | | 1.5 | 1.5 |
| 1.0 | | % Depr., Dep., Amort./Sales | 1.3 | 1.1 |
| (10) 2.2 | | | (22) 1.9 | (32) 2.2 |
| 5.7 | | | 3.6 | 4.6 |
| 4.5 | | % Officers', Directors' Owners' Comp/Sales | 2.4 | 2.7 |
| (10) 5.9 | | | (12) 3.8 | (17) 3.8 |
| 6.7 | | | 9.0 | 11.3 |

### Net Sales / Total Assets

| 0-500M | 500M-2MM | 2-10MM | 10-50MM | 50-100MM | | 4/1/07-3/31/08 ALL | 4/1/08-3/31/09 ALL |
|---|---|---|---|---|---|---|---|
| 12791M | 25797M | 60682M | 93635M | 199774M | Net Sales ($) | 529913M | 300326M |
| 3796M | 8868M | 29917M | 47417M | 56457M | Total Assets ($) | 252936M | 119602M |

M = $ thousand    MM = $ million

See Pages 9 through 22 for Explanation of Ratios and Data

## Comparative Historical Data | Current Data Sorted by Sales

| Type of Statement | | | | | | | | | |
|---|---|---|---|---|---|---|---|---|---|
| Unqualified | 6 | 3 | 1 | 1 | | | | | |
| Reviewed | | 2 | 1 | | | | 1 | 1 | |
| Compiled | 13 | 12 | 10 | 3 | 3 | 1 | 3 | | |
| Tax Returns | 21 | 11 | 11 | 6 | 3 | | | 2 | |
| Other | 6 | 11 | 13 | 5 | 3 | 1 | | | 3 |
| | 4/1/09-3/31/10 ALL | 4/1/10-3/31/11 ALL | 4/1/11-3/31/12 ALL | 0-1MM | 1-3MM | 3-5MM | 5-10MM | 10-25MM | 25MM & OVER |
| | | | | 7 (4/1-9/30/11) | | | 29 (10/1/11-3/31/12) | | |
| **NUMBER OF STATEMENTS** | 46 | 39 | 36 | 15 | 9 | 2 | 4 | 3 | 3 |
| | % | % | % | % | % | % | % | % | % |
| **ASSETS** | | | | | | | | | |
| Cash & Equivalents | 17.6 | 15.2 | 20.5 | 18.1 | | | | | |
| Trade Receivables (net) | 9.2 | 7.7 | 7.3 | 3.2 | | | | | |
| Inventory | 16.4 | 24.1 | 19.5 | 12.2 | | | | | |
| All Other Current | 2.3 | 1.5 | 1.0 | 1.0 | | | | | |
| Total Current | 45.4 | 48.6 | 48.3 | 34.5 | | | | | |
| Fixed Assets (net) | 36.5 | 35.1 | 33.6 | 38.2 | | | | | |
| Intangibles (net) | 4.1 | 3.9 | 5.5 | 11.1 | | | | | |
| All Other Non-Current | 13.9 | 12.4 | 12.5 | 16.1 | | | | | |
| Total | 100.0 | 100.0 | 100.0 | 100.0 | | | | | |
| **LIABILITIES** | | | | | | | | | |
| Notes Payable-Short Term | 3.4 | 10.1 | 11.8 | 19.1 | | | | | |
| Cur. Mat.-L.T.D. | 3.0 | 2.3 | 3.2 | 4.1 | | | | | |
| Trade Payables | 9.5 | 10.3 | 11.4 | 4.3 | | | | | |
| Income Taxes Payable | .4 | .1 | .2 | .0 | | | | | |
| All Other Current | 16.7 | 11.2 | 9.9 | 14.2 | | | | | |
| Total Current | 33.1 | 34.1 | 36.5 | 41.7 | | | | | |
| Long-Term Debt | 36.4 | 24.8 | 32.5 | 32.8 | | | | | |
| Deferred Taxes | .1 | .1 | .1 | .0 | | | | | |
| All Other Non-Current | 13.2 | 8.0 | 7.3 | 2.5 | | | | | |
| Net Worth | 17.2 | 33.1 | 23.5 | 22.9 | | | | | |
| Total Liabilties & Net Worth | 100.0 | 100.0 | 100.0 | 100.0 | | | | | |
| **INCOME DATA** | | | | | | | | | |
| Net Sales | 100.0 | 100.0 | 100.0 | 100.0 | | | | | |
| Gross Profit | 54.5 | 50.8 | 50.2 | 58.9 | | | | | |
| Operating Expenses | 49.1 | 46.7 | 46.2 | 54.2 | | | | | |
| Operating Profit | 5.4 | 4.1 | 3.9 | 4.7 | | | | | |
| All Other Expenses (net) | 1.7 | .5 | 1.6 | 1.4 | | | | | |
| Profit Before Taxes | 3.8 | 3.7 | 2.3 | 3.3 | | | | | |
| **RATIOS** | | | | | | | | | |
| Current | 4.3 | 3.0 | 2.9 | 2.0 | | | | | |
| | 1.6 | 1.5 | 1.3 | .8 | | | | | |
| | .6 | 1.2 | .7 | .3 | | | | | |
| Quick | 2.3 | 1.6 | 1.3 | .7 | | | | | |
| | .7 | .7 | .6 | .4 | | | | | |
| | .2 | .2 | .3 | .2 | | | | | |
| Sales/Receivables | 0 UND | 0 UND | 0 UND | 0 UND | | | | | |
| | 1 595.6 | 0 999.8 | 1 425.3 | 0 UND | | | | | |
| | 12 30.4 | 18 20.8 | 14 26.6 | 1 469.0 | | | | | |
| Cost of Sales/Inventory | 9 40.3 | 22 16.4 | 8 45.9 | 0 UND | | | | | |
| | 35 10.5 | 49 7.4 | 33 11.0 | 17 21.8 | | | | | |
| | 68 5.4 | 88 4.1 | 68 5.4 | 64 5.7 | | | | | |
| Cost of Sales/Payables | 0 UND | 1 464.7 | 0 UND | 0 UND | | | | | |
| | 13 27.6 | 14 26.7 | 16 22.5 | 0 UND | | | | | |
| | 31 11.9 | 31 11.6 | 30 12.3 | 21 17.3 | | | | | |
| Sales/Working Capital | 5.9 | 9.5 | 8.3 | 12.7 | | | | | |
| | 18.6 | 16.2 | 19.9 | -68.8 | | | | | |
| | -17.1 | 56.0 | -17.5 | -7.1 | | | | | |
| EBIT/Interest | 8.9 | 11.8 | 13.9 | 4.0 | | | | | |
| | (35) 3.8 | (32) 3.2 | (26) 1.5 | (11) 1.2 | | | | | |
| | 1.3 | .8 | -.3 | .0 | | | | | |
| Net Profit + Depr., Dep., Amort./Cur. Mat. L/T/D | | | | | | | | | |
| Fixed/Worth | .3 | .4 | .5 | .5 | | | | | |
| | .9 | 1.0 | 1.2 | 1.7 | | | | | |
| | -2.9 | 4.4 | -2.2 | -1.2 | | | | | |
| Debt/Worth | .6 | .6 | .8 | .8 | | | | | |
| | 2.4 | 1.6 | 1.5 | 1.5 | | | | | |
| | -5.3 | 7.7 | -5.1 | -2.9 | | | | | |
| % Profit Before Taxes/Tangible Net Worth | 47.9 | 54.9 | 51.6 | | | | | | |
| | (30) 26.6 | (31) 25.4 | (25) 20.0 | | | | | | |
| | 2.8 | -1.0 | -5.4 | | | | | | |
| % Profit Before Taxes/Total Assets | 20.4 | 25.7 | 20.0 | 35.5 | | | | | |
| | 7.7 | 8.4 | 4.3 | 7.7 | | | | | |
| | .7 | -.5 | -3.8 | -3.0 | | | | | |
| Sales/Net Fixed Assets | 17.8 | 19.7 | 50.0 | 158.8 | | | | | |
| | 5.8 | 8.3 | 8.4 | 8.0 | | | | | |
| | 3.9 | 4.6 | 4.2 | 3.6 | | | | | |
| Sales/Total Assets | 3.9 | 4.9 | 4.1 | 4.2 | | | | | |
| | 2.5 | 2.7 | 2.8 | 2.5 | | | | | |
| | 1.6 | 1.9 | 1.8 | 1.8 | | | | | |
| % Depr., Dep., Amort./Sales | 1.1 | .5 | .7 | | | | | | |
| | (35) 2.0 | (31) 1.8 | (23) 2.1 | | | | | | |
| | 4.8 | 4.3 | 3.6 | | | | | | |
| % Officers', Directors' Owners' Comp/Sales | 3.0 | 1.5 | 1.4 | | | | | | |
| | (18) 5.2 | (19) 2.8 | (19) 5.3 | | | | | | |
| | 7.3 | 6.2 | 6.9 | | | | | | |
| Net Sales ($) | 714404M | 1157013M | 392679M | 8006M | 17085M | 7988M | 25652M | 40539M | 293409M |
| Total Assets ($) | 358976M | 384287M | 146455M | 3285M | 6368M | 1497M | 14304M | 17127M | 103874M |

M = $ thousand    MM = $ million
See Pages 9 through 22 for Explanation of Ratios and Data

## Current Data Sorted by Assets                                         Comparative Historical Data

| 0-500M | 500M-2MM | 2-10MM | 10-50MM | 50-100MM | 100-250MM | Type of Statement | 4/1/07-3/31/08 ALL | 4/1/08-3/31/09 ALL |
|---|---|---|---|---|---|---|---|---|
|  |  | 1 | 5 |  | 2 | Unqualified | 14 | 20 |
|  | 2 | 11 | 3 |  |  | Reviewed | 15 | 20 |
| 9 | 10 | 7 |  |  |  | Compiled | 20 | 26 |
| 74 | 31 | 10 |  |  |  | Tax Returns | 107 | 120 |
| 21 | 19 | 17 | 5 | 4 | 1 | Other | 55 | 56 |
|  | 26 (4/1-9/30/11) |  | 206 (10/1/11-3/31/12) |  |  |  |  |  |
| 104 | 62 | 46 | 13 | 4 | 3 | NUMBER OF STATEMENTS | 211 | 242 |
| % | % | % | % | % | % | ASSETS | % | % |
| 15.2 | 10.1 | 13.6 | 11.2 |  |  | Cash & Equivalents | 11.1 | 12.2 |
| 1.2 | 6.6 | 13.9 | 14.2 |  |  | Trade Receivables (net) | 7.6 | 7.7 |
| 19.0 | 16.0 | 25.7 | 27.7 |  |  | Inventory | 16.2 | 16.6 |
| 4.0 | 1.0 | 4.3 | 1.6 |  |  | All Other Current | 3.4 | 3.2 |
| 39.3 | 33.7 | 57.4 | 54.6 |  |  | Total Current | 38.3 | 39.6 |
| 40.3 | 41.9 | 29.5 | 28.0 |  |  | Fixed Assets (net) | 39.3 | 40.6 |
| 12.3 | 10.9 | 6.3 | 6.5 |  |  | Intangibles (net) | 13.1 | 13.5 |
| 8.1 | 13.6 | 6.8 | 10.8 |  |  | All Other Non-Current | 9.3 | 6.3 |
| 100.0 | 100.0 | 100.0 | 100.0 |  |  | Total | 100.0 | 100.0 |
|  |  |  |  |  |  | LIABILITIES |  |  |
| 5.7 | 6.2 | 8.5 | 30.0 |  |  | Notes Payable-Short Term | 7.0 | 9.0 |
| 4.1 | 3.0 | 6.5 | 2.2 |  |  | Cur. Mat.-L.T.D. | 4.9 | 3.5 |
| 10.9 | 14.4 | 17.2 | 21.5 |  |  | Trade Payables | 12.2 | 12.9 |
| .1 | .2 | .4 | .3 |  |  | Income Taxes Payable | .1 | .1 |
| 32.2 | 9.3 | 11.8 | 25.5 |  |  | All Other Current | 12.8 | 13.0 |
| 53.0 | 33.0 | 44.5 | 79.6 |  |  | Total Current | 37.0 | 38.5 |
| 26.2 | 34.5 | 16.4 | 16.6 |  |  | Long-Term Debt | 28.8 | 32.4 |
| .0 | .0 | .2 | .5 |  |  | Deferred Taxes | .1 | .1 |
| 24.8 | 8.9 | 7.9 | 17.7 |  |  | All Other Non-Current | 10.0 | 9.4 |
| -4.0 | 23.6 | 31.1 | -14.3 |  |  | Net Worth | 24.1 | 19.6 |
| 100.0 | 100.0 | 100.0 | 100.0 |  |  | Total Liabilities & Net Worth | 100.0 | 100.0 |
|  |  |  |  |  |  | INCOME DATA |  |  |
| 100.0 | 100.0 | 100.0 | 100.0 |  |  | Net Sales | 100.0 | 100.0 |
| 53.0 | 44.4 | 36.9 | 35.1 |  |  | Gross Profit | 48.7 | 47.5 |
| 51.4 | 40.7 | 32.6 | 31.8 |  |  | Operating Expenses | 45.1 | 43.5 |
| 1.6 | 3.6 | 4.2 | 3.3 |  |  | Operating Profit | 3.6 | 4.1 |
| .3 | .8 | .7 | .4 |  |  | All Other Expenses (net) | 1.1 | 1.4 |
| 1.3 | 2.8 | 3.5 | 2.9 |  |  | Profit Before Taxes | 2.4 | 2.6 |
|  |  |  |  |  |  | RATIOS |  |  |
| 4.3 | 2.3 | 2.1 | 1.6 |  |  | Current | 2.4 | 2.4 |
| 1.3 | 1.1 | 1.4 | 1.0 |  |  |  | 1.2 | 1.2 |
| .4 | .5 | .9 | .3 |  |  |  | .6 | .5 |
| 1.7 | 1.5 | 1.1 | 1.1 |  |  | Quick | 1.5 | 1.2 |
| (103) .4 | (61) .4 | .5 | .3 |  |  |  | (210) .4 | .5 |
| .1 | .1 |  | .1 |  |  |  | .2 | .2 |
| 0 UND | 0 UND | 0 999.8 | 6 64.8 |  |  | Sales/Receivables | 0 UND | 0 UND |
| 0 UND | 0 UND | 10 36.4 | 7 52.7 |  |  |  | 0 UND | 0 999.8 |
| 0 UND | 3 115.1 | 31 11.8 | 38 9.7 |  |  |  | 8 45.8 | 10 36.0 |
| 3 110.4 | 7 52.0 | 10 38.1 | 21 17.3 |  |  | Cost of Sales/Inventory | 7 52.5 | 7 53.9 |
| 9 39.5 | 13 28.2 | 37 9.9 | 36 10.2 |  |  |  | 14 25.5 | 16 23.5 |
| 39 9.4 | 34 10.6 | 79 4.6 | 91 4.0 |  |  |  | 43 8.6 | 37 9.7 |
| 0 UND | 6 56.6 | 10 38.3 | 28 13.2 |  |  | Cost of Sales/Payables | 0 UND | 1 597.1 |
| 6 63.1 | 19 19.7 | 24 15.2 | 39 9.3 |  |  |  | 14 25.2 | 18 20.4 |
| 21 17.8 | 33 11.2 | 56 6.5 | 61 6.0 |  |  |  | 35 10.5 | 38 9.7 |
| 18.5 | 15.0 | 7.9 | 13.7 |  |  | Sales/Working Capital | 15.4 | 14.3 |
| 133.1 | 96.7 | 17.8 | 999.8 |  |  |  | 82.2 | 70.6 |
| -15.1 | -17.5 | -36.5 | -6.9 |  |  |  | -27.0 | -29.6 |
| 9.1 | 14.5 | 15.8 | 14.3 |  |  | EBIT/Interest | 5.6 | 8.5 |
| (65) 2.4 | (53) 4.4 | (41) 6.5 | 6.6 |  |  |  | (161) 2.1 | (186) 2.4 |
| -1.1 | 1.1 | 1.6 | -.1 |  |  |  | .8 | .7 |
|  |  |  |  |  |  | Net Profit + Depr., Dep., Amort./Cur. Mat. L/T/D | 6.1 | 9.2 |
|  |  |  |  |  |  |  | (20) 4.0 | (22) 2.5 |
|  |  |  |  |  |  |  | 1.2 | 1.8 |
| .5 | .5 | .2 | .2 |  |  | Fixed/Worth | .7 | .6 |
| 3.0 | 2.1 | .8 | 1.1 |  |  |  | 1.9 | 2.3 |
| -1.1 | -2.3 | 5.8 | 2.7 |  |  |  | -3.4 | -3.4 |
| .7 | 1.1 | .9 | 1.5 |  |  | Debt/Worth | 1.1 | 1.1 |
| 11.2 | 4.7 | 2.1 | 3.3 |  |  |  | 3.5 | 4.5 |
| -2.5 | -4.7 | 16.9 | 6.4 |  |  |  | -8.8 | -5.1 |
| 92.5 | 58.9 | 46.9 | 99.0 |  |  | % Profit Before Taxes/Tangible Net Worth | 95.4 | 84.7 |
| (54) 30.9 | (40) 26.4 | (36) 18.6 | (11) 16.5 |  |  |  | (143) 25.5 | (154) 27.1 |
| -2.0 | 6.9 | 10.9 | -2.0 |  |  |  | .7 | 6.7 |
| 31.9 | 20.1 | 13.8 | 16.8 |  |  | % Profit Before Taxes/Total Assets | 21.9 | 20.7 |
| 8.0 | 6.4 | 8.6 | 5.2 |  |  |  | 5.1 | 6.9 |
| -8.0 | .4 | 2.7 | -3.5 |  |  |  | -1.3 | -.9 |
| 56.4 | 29.3 | 41.0 | 45.5 |  |  | Sales/Net Fixed Assets | 30.8 | 32.3 |
| 13.5 | 7.6 | 14.3 | 12.6 |  |  |  | 14.4 | 10.5 |
| 5.0 | 3.2 | 5.9 | 9.4 |  |  |  | 4.5 | 4.3 |
| 6.5 | 5.0 | 4.1 | 4.5 |  |  | Sales/Total Assets | 6.5 | 5.5 |
| 4.2 | 3.0 | 2.8 | 2.6 |  |  |  | 3.7 | 2.9 |
| 2.6 | 1.7 | 2.2 | 1.7 |  |  |  | 1.8 | 1.8 |
| 1.0 | .9 | .6 | 1.2 |  |  | % Depr., Dep., Amort./Sales | .9 | 1.2 |
| (75) 3.0 | (46) 2.8 | (40) 1.1 | (12) 1.6 |  |  |  | (177) 1.8 | (197) 2.5 |
| 4.7 | 4.6 | 2.3 | 2.4 |  |  |  | 3.4 | 4.5 |
| 3.3 | 1.7 | .7 |  |  |  | % Officers', Directors' Owners' Comp/Sales | 1.6 | 1.6 |
| (51) 5.4 | (32) 2.9 | (18) 1.9 |  |  |  |  | (85) 2.7 | (106) 2.9 |
| 7.2 | 4.8 | 3.6 |  |  |  |  |  | 6.1 |
| 100579M | 227377M | 707784M | 714015M | 1431536M | 1644234M | Net Sales ($) | 5016147M | 5038173M |
| 22200M | 62252M | 217499M | 243034M | 316445M | 478241M | Total Assets ($) | 1769575M | 1505936M |

M = $ thousand   MM = $ million
See Pages 9 through 22 for Explanation of Ratios and Data

## Comparative Historical Data                              Current Data Sorted by Sales

| Hist 1 | Hist 2 | Hist 3 | Type of Statement | 0-1MM | 1-3MM | 3-5MM | 5-10MM | 10-25MM | 25MM & OVER |
|---|---|---|---|---|---|---|---|---|---|
| 20 | 14 | 8 | Unqualified | | 1 | | | 1 | 7 |
| 26 | 9 | 16 | Reviewed | | 6 | 2 | 4 | 6 | 3 |
| 22 | 23 | 26 | Compiled | 7 | 6 | 5 | 4 | 4 | |
| 124 | 93 | 115 | Tax Returns | 56 | 37 | 5 | 8 | 7 | 2 |
| 63 | 86 | 67 | Other | 16 | 14 | 6 | 9 | 11 | 11 |
| 4/1/09-3/31/10 ALL | 4/1/10-3/31/11 ALL | 4/1/11-3/31/12 ALL | | 26 (4/1-9/30/11) | | | 206 (10/1/11-3/31/12) | | |
| 255 | 225 | 232 | NUMBER OF STATEMENTS | 79 | 58 | 18 | 25 | 29 | 23 |
| % | % | % | **ASSETS** | % | % | % | % | % | % |
| 15.5 | 14.4 | 13.5 | Cash & Equivalents | 15.3 | 9.6 | 20.3 | 14.6 | 13.7 | 10.4 |
| 7.2 | 8.6 | 6.3 | Trade Receivables (net) | 1.8 | 3.6 | 4.8 | 11.6 | 14.1 | 14.3 |
| 18.4 | 16.0 | 20.1 | Inventory | 16.4 | 15.7 | 22.3 | 26.2 | 26.6 | 27.1 |
| 2.5 | 2.5 | 3.2 | All Other Current | 3.5 | 2.8 | .3 | 3.7 | 3.7 | 3.7 |
| 43.6 | 41.5 | 43.0 | Total Current | 36.9 | 31.6 | 47.6 | 56.1 | 58.1 | 55.6 |
| 36.5 | 38.9 | 37.5 | Fixed Assets (net) | 43.5 | 41.9 | 32.1 | 32.9 | 27.7 | 27.5 |
| 12.2 | 12.3 | 10.0 | Intangibles (net) | 14.3 | 10.4 | 11.4 | 4.0 | 5.9 | 5.3 |
| 7.7 | 7.3 | 9.4 | All Other Non-Current | 5.2 | 16.0 | 9.0 | 7.0 | 8.2 | 11.6 |
| 100.0 | 100.0 | 100.0 | Total | 100.0 | 100.0 | 100.0 | 100.0 | 100.0 | 100.0 |
| | | | **LIABILITIES** | | | | | | |
| 7.6 | 7.4 | 7.7 | Notes Payable-Short Term | 4.4 | 7.0 | 6.5 | 11.8 | 7.2 | 17.9 |
| 4.8 | 3.9 | 4.1 | Cur. Mat.-L.T.D. | 3.0 | 4.3 | 3.1 | 10.5 | 3.3 | 2.1 |
| 11.7 | 12.4 | 13.8 | Trade Payables | 9.5 | 9.5 | 16.6 | 23.3 | 21.7 | 17.2 |
| .1 | .2 | .2 | Income Taxes Payable | .1 | .2 | .0 | .4 | .6 | .2 |
| 15.2 | 15.9 | 21.1 | All Other Current | 37.1 | 12.9 | 10.2 | 9.9 | 9.0 | 22.4 |
| 39.4 | 39.8 | 46.9 | Total Current | 54.1 | 34.0 | 36.3 | 55.8 | 41.7 | 59.7 |
| 29.1 | 28.3 | 26.6 | Long-Term Debt | 28.7 | 35.6 | 23.3 | 18.0 | 14.4 | 23.9 |
| .1 | .1 | .1 | Deferred Taxes | .0 | .0 | .0 | .0 | .3 | .7 |
| 8.3 | 12.5 | 17.3 | All Other Non-Current | 23.2 | 17.6 | 11.7 | 7.2 | 7.3 | 24.0 |
| 23.2 | 19.2 | 9.1 | Net Worth | -6.0 | 12.8 | 28.7 | 18.9 | 36.3 | -8.4 |
| 100.0 | 100.0 | 100.0 | Total Liabilties & Net Worth | 100.0 | 100.0 | 100.0 | 100.0 | 100.0 | 100.0 |
| | | | **INCOME DATA** | | | | | | |
| 100.0 | 100.0 | 100.0 | Net Sales | 100.0 | 100.0 | 100.0 | 100.0 | 100.0 | 100.0 |
| 46.6 | 48.4 | 45.9 | Gross Profit | 54.1 | 49.8 | 43.0 | 41.8 | 32.2 | 32.5 |
| 42.8 | 43.6 | 43.0 | Operating Expenses | 53.4 | 45.1 | 38.6 | 38.5 | 29.0 | 27.9 |
| 3.8 | 4.8 | 2.9 | Operating Profit | .6 | 4.6 | 4.4 | 3.3 | 3.2 | 4.7 |
| .8 | 1.0 | .6 | All Other Expenses (net) | .5 | .7 | 2.2 | -.5 | .4 | .5 |
| 3.0 | 3.8 | 2.4 | Profit Before Taxes | .1 | 4.0 | 2.2 | 3.8 | 2.8 | 4.2 |
| | | | **RATIOS** | | | | | | |
| 2.7 | 3.0 | 2.7 | | 4.6 | 2.5 | 2.3 | 1.9 | 2.4 | 2.6 |
| 1.3 | 1.3 | 1.3 | Current | 1.3 | 1.3 | 1.3 | 1.1 | 1.4 | 1.3 |
| .7 | .6 | .5 | | .5 | .3 | .7 | .4 | .8 | .5 |
| 1.7 | 1.7 | 1.4 | | 2.4 | 1.3 | 1.4 | 1.2 | 1.2 | 1.1 |
| .6 | .7 (230) | .4 | Quick | (78) .4 | .3 | .7 | (24) .4 | .6 | .3 |
| .2 | .2 | .1 | | .1 | .1 | .2 | .2 | .2 | .2 |
| 0 UND | 0 UND | 0 UND | | 0 UND | 0 UND | 0 UND | 0 999.8 | 0 999.8 | 2 169.1 |
| 0 UND | 0 999.8 | 0 UND | Sales/Receivables | 0 UND | 0 UND | 0 733.8 | 12 30.9 | 6 65.0 | 7 54.8 |
| 6 58.1 | 9 39.0 | 5 72.5 | | 0 UND | 0 999.8 | 3 113.3 | 27 13.6 | 42 8.7 | 29 12.7 |
| 7 51.4 | 7 54.9 | 6 65.2 | | 3 111.3 | 5 80.2 | 10 36.1 | 10 34.8 | 11 32.9 | 19 19.3 |
| 17 20.9 | 15 23.8 | 16 22.2 | Cost of Sales/Inventory | 10 35.4 | 9 42.3 | 28 13.1 | 21 17.8 | 20 18.2 | 27 13.6 |
| 47 7.7 | 39 9.5 | 53 6.9 | | 46 7.9 | 37 9.8 | 40 9.2 | 89 4.1 | 73 5.0 | 99 3.7 |
| 0 UND | 0 UND | 4 98.5 | | 0 UND | 0 UND | 15 23.7 | 17 21.8 | 12 30.9 | 15 24.3 |
| 15 24.3 | 14 26.3 | 15 23.6 | Cost of Sales/Payables | 6 57.3 | 7 51.5 | 29 12.7 | 33 10.9 | 26 14.2 | 23 15.6 |
| 32 11.4 | 31 11.9 | 34 10.8 | | 22 16.9 | 23 15.7 | 44 8.3 | 54 6.8 | 53 6.9 | 39 9.3 |
| 12.8 | 12.7 | 12.6 | | 13.3 | 18.0 | 13.1 | 6.9 | 8.4 | 11.5 |
| 32.9 | 54.4 | 49.0 | Sales/Working Capital | 107.5 | 246.6 | 50.0 | 49.6 | 18.2 | 29.1 |
| -38.7 | -31.0 | -17.2 | | -10.4 | -19.3 | -14.4 | -20.6 | -74.7 | -24.1 |
| 13.9 | 13.2 | 12.8 | | 6.9 | 12.4 | 20.0 | 25.4 | 12.9 | 16.1 |
| (200) 3.7 | (182) 5.1 | (177) 4.1 | EBIT/Interest | (49) 2.3 | (44) 2.5 | (16) 7.8 | (23) 7.7 | (26) 4.6 | (19) 7.0 |
| 1.1 | 1.8 | .6 | | -.6 | .4 | 1.0 | 4.4 | 1.5 | 1.2 |
| 5.0 | 4.3 | 18.0 | Net Profit + Depr., Dep., | | | | | | |
| (33) 1.6 | (22) 2.8 | (17) 6.6 | Amort./Cur. Mat. L/T/D | | | | | | |
| .8 | 1.8 | 1.5 | | | | | | | |
| .5 | .6 | .4 | | .5 | .5 | .5 | .2 | .2 | .3 |
| 1.4 | 1.9 | 1.6 | Fixed/Worth | -12.0 | 1.9 | 1.0 | 1.7 | .5 | .7 |
| -4.6 | -2.7 | -2.4 | | -1.0 | -2.2 | NM | -9.2 | 3.7 | 1.3 |
| .8 | .9 | .9 | | .9 | 1.0 | .9 | 1.2 | .8 | .7 |
| 2.8 | 4.1 | 3.5 | Debt/Worth | -19.0 | 4.5 | 1.5 | 3.3 | 1.4 | 2.7 |
| -5.1 | -5.1 | -4.3 | | -2.3 | -4.1 | NM | -7.6 | 6.1 | 4.6 |
| 75.3 | 124.4 | 59.3 | % Profit Before Taxes/Tangible | 52.8 | 93.3 | 57.9 | 76.0 | 41.6 | 45.2 |
| (171) 30.0 | (152) 41.1 | (147) 21.9 | Net Worth | (36) 24.1 | (36) 33.9 | (14) 31.2 | (17) 27.6 | (24) 14.3 | (20) 18.7 |
| 10.5 | 14.9 | 6.3 | | -24.1 | 5.5 | 7.6 | 15.9 | 9.0 | 12.7 |
| 24.4 | 27.5 | 21.5 | % Profit Before Taxes/Total | 19.0 | 29.9 | 27.5 | 23.8 | 11.4 | 23.2 |
| 9.0 | 10.1 | 7.8 | Assets | 4.4 | 7.7 | 7.0 | 10.1 | 5.5 | 8.2 |
| .7 | 2.6 | -1.4 | | -10.6 | .2 | 1.4 | 5.7 | 1.5 | .5 |
| 32.8 | 33.6 | 41.3 | | 41.6 | 28.6 | 35.1 | 49.5 | 82.9 | 31.4 |
| 11.9 | 11.5 | 12.0 | Sales/Net Fixed Assets | 10.3 | 9.2 | 13.2 | 18.8 | 18.7 | 12.5 |
| 5.0 | 5.1 | 4.9 | | 4.2 | 3.5 | 5.3 | 6.4 | 6.2 | 8.1 |
| 5.5 | 5.8 | 5.3 | | 4.7 | 5.8 | 4.9 | 5.3 | 4.7 | 5.8 |
| 3.4 | 3.3 | 3.3 | Sales/Total Assets | 3.3 | 3.3 | 3.4 | 3.5 | 3.3 | 3.3 |
| 2.0 | 2.3 | 2.3 | | 2.3 | 1.9 | 2.0 | 2.6 | 2.3 | 2.3 |
| .9 | .9 | .8 | | 1.9 | .7 | .8 | .7 | .3 | 1.1 |
| (208) 1.8 | (172) 1.8 | (176) 1.9 | % Depr., Dep., Amort./Sales | (57) 4.0 | (45) 1.9 | (15) 1.1 | (16) .9 | (26) .8 | (17) 1.2 |
| 3.5 | 3.9 | 4.3 | | 5.8 | 4.4 | 3.0 | 2.8 | 1.8 | 2.1 |
| .9 | 1.9 | 1.8 | % Officers', Directors' | 3.7 | 2.3 | | 1.0 | .6 | |
| (116) 3.3 | (106) 3.3 | (101) 3.7 | Owners' Comp/Sales | (33) 5.5 | (30) 3.8 | | (15) 2.0 | (10) 2.0 | |
| 5.7 | 6.8 | 6.2 | | 6.7 | 7.4 | | 4.7 | 6.5 | |
| 8919875M | 4106904M | 4825525M | Net Sales ($) | 48664M | 99437M | 73763M | 178117M | 449325M | 3976219M |
| 2455672M | 1620071M | 1339671M | Total Assets ($) | 17294M | 34830M | 25556M | 57252M | 153287M | 1051452M |

© RMA 2012    M = $ thousand   MM = $ million
See Pages 9 through 22 for Explanation of Ratios and Data

## Current Data Sorted by Assets      Comparative Historical Data

| 0-500M | 500M-2MM | 2-10MM | 10-50MM | 50-100MM | 100-250MM | Type of Statement | 4/1/07-3/31/08 ALL | 4/1/08-3/31/09 ALL |
|---|---|---|---|---|---|---|---|---|
| 1 | 2 | 5 | 4 | | 2 | Unqualified | 12 | 17 |
| 1 | 4 | 17 | 5 | | | Reviewed | 25 | 29 |
| 7 | 18 | 16 | 2 | | | Compiled | 69 | 49 |
| 117 | 87 | 26 | 1 | | | Tax Returns | 194 | 171 |
| 24 | 36 | 17 | 9 | 2 | 4 | Other | 59 | 63 |
| | 39 (4/1-9/30/11) | | | 368 (10/1/11-3/31/12) | | | | |
| 150 | 147 | 81 | 21 | 2 | 6 | NUMBER OF STATEMENTS | 359 | 329 |
| % | % | % | % | % | % | ASSETS | % | % |
| 10.0 | 12.8 | 14.4 | 8.8 | | | Cash & Equivalents | 11.4 | 11.0 |
| 1.3 | 1.0 | 2.0 | 4.6 | | | Trade Receivables (net) | 2.3 | 1.0 |
| 54.6 | 46.3 | 44.0 | 42.3 | | | Inventory | 45.5 | 45.8 |
| 1.7 | 1.4 | 1.5 | 1.4 | | | All Other Current | 2.4 | 1.5 |
| 67.6 | 61.5 | 61.9 | 57.1 | | | Total Current | 61.6 | 59.3 |
| 14.3 | 17.4 | 24.2 | 19.1 | | | Fixed Assets (net) | 19.1 | 18.2 |
| 14.5 | 15.1 | 10.0 | 15.5 | | | Intangibles (net) | 13.8 | 15.4 |
| 3.6 | 6.0 | 3.9 | 8.3 | | | All Other Non-Current | 5.6 | 7.0 |
| 100.0 | 100.0 | 100.0 | 100.0 | | | Total | 100.0 | 100.0 |
| | | | | | | LIABILITIES | | |
| 7.4 | 3.6 | 8.1 | 4.7 | | | Notes Payable-Short Term | 6.7 | 8.5 |
| 3.3 | 1.7 | 1.6 | 4.7 | | | Cur. Mat.-L.T.D. | 2.0 | 4.4 |
| 12.7 | 19.6 | 24.2 | 19.1 | | | Trade Payables | 15.5 | 12.7 |
| .1 | .1 | .1 | .0 | | | Income Taxes Payable | .1 | .0 |
| 13.1 | 8.4 | 7.1 | 6.2 | | | All Other Current | 9.8 | 10.9 |
| 36.7 | 33.2 | 41.1 | 34.7 | | | Total Current | 34.1 | 36.5 |
| 22.3 | 25.5 | 22.7 | 14.9 | | | Long-Term Debt | 23.0 | 25.2 |
| .0 | .0 | .0 | .0 | | | Deferred Taxes | .0 | .0 |
| 29.4 | 13.8 | 9.1 | 5.9 | | | All Other Non-Current | 14.0 | 11.7 |
| 11.7 | 27.5 | 27.0 | 44.5 | | | Net Worth | 28.9 | 26.5 |
| 100.0 | 100.0 | 100.0 | 100.0 | | | Total Liabilities & Net Worth | 100.0 | 100.0 |
| | | | | | | INCOME DATA | | |
| 100.0 | 100.0 | 100.0 | 100.0 | | | Net Sales | 100.0 | 100.0 |
| 24.9 | 23.6 | 21.7 | 25.1 | | | Gross Profit | 23.5 | 23.9 |
| 25.6 | 22.3 | 19.1 | 20.7 | | | Operating Expenses | 21.6 | 21.8 |
| -.7 | 1.2 | 2.6 | 4.3 | | | Operating Profit | 1.9 | 2.1 |
| -.9 | .0 | .6 | .0 | | | All Other Expenses (net) | -.6 | -.2 |
| .2 | 1.3 | 2.0 | 4.4 | | | Profit Before Taxes | 2.5 | 2.2 |
| | | | | | | RATIOS | | |
| 10.1 | 5.6 | 2.2 | 3.1 | | | | 5.5 | 6.0 |
| 3.2 | 2.2 | 1.4 | 1.7 | | | Current | 2.2 | 2.0 |
| 1.4 | 1.3 | 1.1 | 1.1 | | | | 1.2 | 1.1 |
| 1.4 | 1.0 | .7 | .6 | | | | .9 | 1.2 |
| (147) .5 | .4 | (80) .4 | .2 | | | Quick | (354) .4 | (325) .3 |
| .1 | .1 | .1 | .1 | | | | .1 | .1 |
| 0 UND | 0 UND | 0 UND | 0 UND | | | | 0 UND | 0 UND |
| 0 UND | 0 UND | 0 UND | 3 115.2 | | | Sales/Receivables | 0 UND | 0 UND |
| 0 UND | 0 UND | 1 341.6 | 7 50.0 | | | | 1 547.4 | 0 759.0 |
| 40 9.2 | 46 7.9 | 45 8.2 | 51 7.2 | | | | 37 10.0 | 38 9.7 |
| 62 5.9 | 74 4.9 | 63 5.8 | 76 4.8 | | | Cost of Sales/Inventory | 60 6.1 | 62 5.9 |
| 91 4.0 | 104 3.5 | 89 4.1 | 146 2.5 | | | | 86 4.3 | 93 3.9 |
| 0 UND | 0 UND | 15 24.3 | 14 26.1 | | | | 0 UND | 0 UND |
| 2 151.0 | 23 15.6 | 35 10.3 | 34 10.8 | | | Cost of Sales/Payables | 15 25.2 | 11 32.2 |
| 21 17.3 | 42 8.7 | 54 6.7 | 53 6.9 | | | | 34 10.7 | 28 13.0 |
| 5.6 | 5.2 | 7.6 | 4.2 | | | | 6.6 | 6.4 |
| 10.6 | 9.7 | 18.4 | 13.6 | | | Sales/Working Capital | 12.7 | 14.6 |
| 36.2 | 24.3 | 74.0 | 94.3 | | | | 43.5 | 106.0 |
| 6.5 | 10.0 | 9.0 | 13.1 | | | | 7.5 | 8.6 |
| (90) 2.3 | (103) 2.6 | (70) 4.6 | (17) 6.4 | | | EBIT/Interest | (284) 3.4 | (264) 3.6 |
| -.6 | 1.0 | 1.7 | 3.3 | | | | 1.5 | 1.1 |
| | | | | | | | 13.9 | 5.7 |
| | | | | | | Net Profit + Depr., Dep., Amort./Cur. Mat. L/T/D | (20) 6.8 | (19) 1.4 |
| | | | | | | | 1.8 | .1 |
| .1 | .1 | .3 | .1 | | | | .2 | .1 |
| .9 | 1.0 | .8 | .6 | | | Fixed/Worth | .9 | .9 |
| -.3 | -1.2 | NM | 3.3 | | | | -1.8 | -1.3 |
| .8 | .9 | 1.9 | .4 | | | | .9 | .9 |
| UND | 5.6 | 4.1 | 2.7 | | | Debt/Worth | 4.3 | 4.7 |
| -3.2 | -6.4 | -46.0 | 22.8 | | | | -6.4 | -4.7 |
| 61.8 | 47.7 | 48.4 | 43.3 | | | | 60.9 | 57.1 |
| (77) 23.3 | (96) 17.6 | (57) 15.3 | (17) 27.0 | | | % Profit Before Taxes/Tangible Net Worth | (243) 28.4 | (215) 25.5 |
| 5.2 | 8.6 | 5.8 | 9.7 | | | | 10.2 | 9.8 |
| 12.6 | 13.2 | 10.1 | 13.6 | | | | 14.0 | 15.5 |
| 3.9 | 5.2 | 4.5 | 9.9 | | | % Profit Before Taxes/Total Assets | 7.0 | 6.7 |
| -4.7 | 1.0 | 1.3 | 3.7 | | | | 2.1 | .4 |
| 194.0 | 100.8 | 45.7 | 51.6 | | | | 108.7 | 126.0 |
| 62.5 | 36.1 | 17.0 | 29.8 | | | Sales/Net Fixed Assets | 35.8 | 33.0 |
| 23.1 | 11.4 | 6.5 | 9.4 | | | | 11.5 | 10.6 |
| 6.3 | 4.3 | 3.9 | 3.7 | | | | 5.0 | 4.8 |
| 4.1 | 2.8 | 2.7 | 2.8 | | | Sales/Total Assets | 3.4 | 3.4 |
| 2.8 | 1.8 | 1.8 | 1.5 | | | | 2.2 | 2.1 |
| .3 | .3 | .3 | .4 | | | | .3 | .4 |
| (82) .9 | (106) .8 | (66) .8 | (20) .7 | | | % Depr., Dep., Amort./Sales | (273) .8 | (223) .9 |
| 1.9 | 1.9 | 1.3 | 1.2 | | | | 1.7 | 1.9 |
| 2.1 | 1.3 | .9 | | | | | 1.5 | 1.5 |
| (88) 3.1 | (88) 2.4 | (35) 1.5 | | | | % Officers', Directors' Owners' Comp/Sales | (208) 2.7 | (175) 2.9 |
| 5.4 | 5.4 | 2.4 | | | | | 4.3 | 5.0 |
| 186477M | 512157M | 958602M | 1006989M | 372990M | 2533977M | Net Sales ($) | 6588970M | 6774982M |
| 41419M | 151972M | 335475M | 387749M | 151108M | 839068M | Total Assets ($) | 1912616M | 1957276M |

M = $ thousand    MM = $ million
See Pages 9 through 22 for Explanation of Ratios and Data

| Comparative Historical Data | | | | Current Data Sorted by Sales | | | | | |
|---|---|---|---|---|---|---|---|---|---|

**Type of Statement**

| | | | | | | 39 (4/1-9/30/11) | 368 (10/1/11-3/31/12) | | |
|---|---|---|---|---|---|---|---|---|---|
| | | | | | 0-1MM | 1-3MM | 3-5MM | 5-10MM | 10-25MM | 25MM & OVER |

| Hist 4/1/09-3/31/10 ALL | Hist 4/1/10-3/31/11 ALL | Hist 4/1/11-3/31/12 ALL | | 0-1MM | 1-3MM | 3-5MM | 5-10MM | 10-25MM | 25MM & OVER |
|---|---|---|---|---|---|---|---|---|---|
| 15 | 11 | 14 | Unqualified | 1 | 2 | | 1 | 3 | 7 |
| 20 | 24 | 27 | Reviewed | 1 | | | 10 | 8 | 8 |
| 60 | 48 | 43 | Compiled | 4 | 10 | 6 | 11 | 10 | 2 |
| 224 | 211 | 231 | Tax Returns | 67 | 102 | 27 | 21 | 14 | |
| 57 | 70 | 92 | Other | 22 | 21 | 10 | 16 | 11 | 12 |
| 376 | 364 | 407 | **NUMBER OF STATEMENTS** | 95 | 135 | 43 | 59 | 46 | 29 |
| % | % | % | **ASSETS** | % | % | % | % | % | % |
| 11.4 | 12.5 | 11.7 | Cash & Equivalents | 8.4 | 11.8 | 11.0 | 15.7 | 16.4 | 7.5 |
| 1.7 | 1.6 | 1.5 | Trade Receivables (net) | 1.1 | 1.3 | 1.2 | 1.3 | 1.4 | 4.6 |
| 46.8 | 47.1 | 48.7 | Inventory | 47.3 | 51.6 | 42.6 | 53.7 | 45.6 | 44.4 |
| 2.0 | 2.2 | 1.5 | All Other Current | 2.1 | .5 | 2.0 | 2.7 | 1.5 | 1.5 |
| 61.9 | 63.4 | 63.5 | Total Current | 58.9 | 65.2 | 56.8 | 73.5 | 65.0 | 58.0 |
| 17.6 | 18.0 | 18.0 | Fixed Assets (net) | 19.1 | 14.8 | 22.5 | 14.5 | 21.8 | 23.7 |
| 15.0 | 13.4 | 13.8 | Intangibles (net) | 17.9 | 15.2 | 14.5 | 7.8 | 7.9 | 14.3 |
| 5.5 | 5.2 | 4.7 | All Other Non-Current | 4.2 | 4.8 | 6.3 | 4.2 | 5.4 | 4.0 |
| 100.0 | 100.0 | 100.0 | Total | 100.0 | 100.0 | 100.0 | 100.0 | 100.0 | 100.0 |
| | | | **LIABILITIES** | | | | | | |
| 6.6 | 7.6 | 6.1 | Notes Payable-Short Term | 5.9 | 6.0 | 3.7 | 7.9 | 5.4 | 8.6 |
| 3.0 | 2.8 | 2.4 | Cur. Mat.-L.T.D. | 3.6 | 2.0 | 2.0 | 1.5 | 1.5 | 4.5 |
| 14.6 | 16.1 | 17.9 | Trade Payables | 6.6 | 15.3 | 21.6 | 28.7 | 30.6 | 20.0 |
| .1 | .1 | .1 | Income Taxes Payable | .1 | .1 | .0 | .2 | .0 | .0 |
| 10.3 | 9.4 | 9.7 | All Other Current | 13.1 | 9.9 | 4.7 | 10.2 | 7.5 | 7.5 |
| 34.6 | 36.1 | 36.3 | Total Current | 29.3 | 33.3 | 32.0 | 48.5 | 45.0 | 40.6 |
| 23.6 | 22.6 | 23.2 | Long-Term Debt | 25.1 | 25.6 | 31.3 | 18.1 | 14.2 | 18.6 |
| .0 | .0 | .0 | Deferred Taxes | .0 | .0 | .0 | .0 | .1 | .0 |
| 12.5 | 14.6 | 18.1 | All Other Non-Current | 32.4 | 21.5 | 10.8 | 7.0 | 8.0 | 5.0 |
| 29.3 | 26.7 | 22.4 | Net Worth | 13.3 | 19.5 | 25.9 | 26.4 | 32.8 | 35.8 |
| 100.0 | 100.0 | 100.0 | Total Liabilities & Net Worth | 100.0 | 100.0 | 100.0 | 100.0 | 100.0 | 100.0 |
| | | | **INCOME DATA** | | | | | | |
| 100.0 | 100.0 | 100.0 | Net Sales | 100.0 | 100.0 | 100.0 | 100.0 | 100.0 | 100.0 |
| 23.0 | 24.0 | 23.7 | Gross Profit | 26.0 | 24.6 | 20.3 | 21.5 | 23.1 | 23.0 |
| 21.2 | 22.2 | 22.7 | Operating Expenses | 27.6 | 23.7 | 18.1 | 19.6 | 20.0 | 19.7 |
| 1.9 | 1.9 | 1.0 | Operating Profit | -1.6 | .9 | 2.2 | 1.9 | 3.1 | 3.3 |
| -.5 | -.1 | -.2 | All Other Expenses (net) | -1.0 | -.3 | .7 | .1 | .1 | .4 |
| 2.3 | 2.0 | 1.2 | Profit Before Taxes | -.6 | 1.2 | 1.5 | 1.7 | 3.0 | 2.9 |
| | | | **RATIOS** | | | | | | |
| 5.3 | 4.7 | 5.1 | Current | 14.3 | 7.4 | 5.0 | 2.7 | 2.3 | 1.8 |
| 2.1 | 2.0 | 2.1 | | 3.9 | 2.7 | 1.8 | 1.6 | 1.4 | 1.4 |
| 1.2 | 1.2 | 1.2 | | 1.4 | 1.3 | 1.2 | 1.2 | 1.0 | 1.1 |
| 1.2 | 1.0 | 1.0 | Quick | 2.0 | 1.2 | .8 | .7 | .7 | .5 |
| (370) .4 | (360) .3 | (403) .4 | | (94) .5 | (134) .3 | (42) .4 | (58) .4 | .3 | .2 |
| .1 | .1 | .1 | | .1 | .1 | .2 | .1 | .1 | .1 |
| 0 UND | 0 UND | 0 UND | Sales/Receivables | 0 UND | 0 UND | 0 UND | 0 UND | 0 UND | 1 320.5 |
| 0 UND | 0 UND | 0 UND | | 0 UND | 0 UND | 0 UND | 0 UND | 0 UND | 3 115.2 |
| 1 552.4 | 0 999.8 | 0 999.8 | | 0 UND | 0 UND | 0 UND | 0 999.8 | 0 814.0 | 7 53.3 |
| 40 9.2 | 37 10.0 | 44 8.3 | Cost of Sales/Inventory | 45 8.1 | 47 7.7 | 41 8.8 | 41 8.9 | 42 8.6 | 51 7.2 |
| 63 5.8 | 61 6.0 | 66 5.5 | | 76 4.8 | 74 4.9 | 66 5.5 | 58 6.3 | 52 7.0 | 72 5.1 |
| 88 4.1 | 93 3.9 | 96 3.8 | | 107 3.4 | 111 3.3 | 81 4.5 | 83 4.4 | 70 5.2 | 101 3.6 |
| 0 UND | 0 UND | 0 UND | Cost of Sales/Payables | 0 UND | 0 UND | 0 UND | 9 39.9 | 21 17.3 | 14 26.9 |
| 12 30.1 | 17 21.0 | 17 21.3 | | 1 349.0 | 12 30.1 | 23 15.7 | 32 11.5 | 38 9.6 | 29 12.8 |
| 33 11.0 | 34 10.7 | 40 9.1 | | 16 22.3 | 31 11.8 | 49 7.4 | 43 8.4 | 51 7.1 | 45 8.1 |
| 5.8 | 6.5 | 5.6 | Sales/Working Capital | 4.7 | 5.2 | 6.7 | 9.2 | 10.4 | 9.0 |
| 12.1 | 12.6 | 11.9 | | 7.5 | 9.1 | 14.6 | 16.5 | 22.7 | 19.3 |
| 32.9 | 48.1 | 40.3 | | 28.3 | 21.8 | 66.0 | 82.0 | 212.6 | 192.4 |
| 8.0 | 9.3 | 8.4 | EBIT/Interest | 4.1 | 6.5 | 3.8 | 13.1 | 16.7 | 9.7 |
| (276) 3.2 | (275) 3.2 | (288) 3.1 | | (50) 1.2 | (93) 2.0 | (32) 2.0 | (47) 6.1 | (39) 6.1 | (27) 6.4 |
| 1.1 | 1.1 | 1.1 | | -3.4 | .6 | .7 | 2.3 | 2.9 | 3.0 |
| 7.5 | 5.1 | 5.7 | Net Profit + Depr., Dep., Amort./Cur. Mat. L/T/D | | | | | | |
| (21) 2.2 | (14) 1.7 | (17) 2.0 | | | | | | | |
| 1.0 | .4 | 1.4 | | | | | | | |
| .1 | .1 | .1 | Fixed/Worth | .1 | .1 | .2 | .1 | .2 | .5 |
| .9 | .9 | .8 | | UND | 1.0 | 1.6 | .5 | .7 | .8 |
| -1.7 | -1.2 | -1.7 | | -.3 | -.4 | -3.4 | -22.5 | 3.3 | 10.8 |
| .8 | .9 | 1.1 | Debt/Worth | .8 | .6 | 1.8 | 1.2 | 1.3 | 1.2 |
| 3.8 | 4.3 | 5.6 | | -30.5 | 6.4 | 7.4 | 2.1 | 3.0 | 3.5 |
| -7.4 | -5.6 | -6.0 | | -3.0 | -3.3 | -7.8 | -34.2 | 16.2 | 31.1 |
| 63.5 | 50.2 | 50.8 | % Profit Before Taxes/Tangible Net Worth | 44.9 | 48.7 | 60.9 | 53.3 | 46.0 | 55.8 |
| (249) 22.7 | (233) 23.1 | (254) 20.0 | | (44) 18.8 | (80) 21.4 | (28) 15.4 | (41) 18.3 | (38) 15.3 | (23) 30.2 |
| 9.3 | 7.9 | 6.9 | | 4.4 | 7.8 | 1.8 | 8.5 | 6.5 | 19.4 |
| 14.1 | 13.3 | 12.1 | % Profit Before Taxes/Total Assets | 8.7 | 12.6 | 12.8 | 15.3 | 13.0 | 12.3 |
| 6.1 | 5.9 | 4.9 | | 2.3 | 3.7 | 4.1 | 6.7 | 6.1 | 7.0 |
| .8 | .6 | .3 | | -9.5 | -1.1 | .2 | 2.9 | 1.9 | 3.7 |
| 127.8 | 150.9 | 127.3 | Sales/Net Fixed Assets | 151.8 | 167.8 | 89.7 | 294.7 | 109.5 | 35.3 |
| 37.1 | 39.7 | 36.8 | | 32.4 | 53.3 | 31.4 | 63.8 | 26.7 | 17.9 |
| 11.6 | 11.9 | 11.4 | | 9.0 | 13.9 | 7.5 | 24.7 | 9.6 | 7.7 |
| 4.8 | 5.3 | 4.7 | Sales/Total Assets | 4.4 | 4.9 | 4.2 | 5.6 | 4.6 | 3.9 |
| 3.1 | 3.3 | 3.2 | | 2.8 | 3.3 | 2.8 | 4.1 | 3.4 | 3.2 |
| 2.1 | 2.3 | 2.1 | | 1.6 | 2.1 | 1.7 | 2.8 | 2.5 | 2.1 |
| .4 | .3 | .3 | % Depr., Dep., Amort./Sales | .7 | .3 | .4 | .2 | .2 | .5 |
| (261) .8 | (255) .7 | (282) .8 | | (51) 1.6 | (86) 1.0 | (36) 1.0 | (44) .4 | (37) .5 | (28) .8 |
| 1.9 | 1.7 | 1.7 | | 2.5 | 2.1 | 1.9 | .8 | 1.0 | 1.1 |
| 1.3 | 1.5 | 1.5 | % Officers', Directors' Owners' Comp/Sales | 2.5 | 1.8 | .8 | 1.3 | .9 | |
| (199) 2.5 | (197) 2.7 | (217) 2.5 | | (39) 4.7 | (96) 2.9 | (24) 1.5 | (35) 2.0 | (18) 1.6 | |
| 4.1 | 4.6 | 4.7 | | 7.1 | 5.1 | 2.9 | 3.1 | 2.0 | |
| 4940075M | 9465836M | 5571192M | Net Sales ($) | 63601M | 237695M | 156365M | 413775M | 695095M | 4004661M |
| 1589747M | 2163357M | 1906791M | Total Assets ($) | 28103M | 104547M | 67509M | 116648M | 245024M | 1344960M |

© RMA 2012     M = $ thousand     MM = $ million
See Pages 9 through 22 for Explanation of Ratios and Data

## Current Data Sorted by Assets        Comparative Historical Data

| | | | | | | Type of Statement | | |
|---|---|---|---|---|---|---|---|---|
| 2 | | 4 | 15 | 3 | 3 | Unqualified | 21 | 22 |
| 1 | 10 | 17 | 2 | | | Reviewed | 30 | 27 |
| 12 | 35 | 23 | 2 | 1 | | Compiled | 59 | 78 |
| 58 | 111 | 36 | 1 | | | Tax Returns | 116 | 165 |
| 12 | 36 | 23 | 13 | 7 | 4 | Other | 91 | 97 |
| | 62 (4/1-9/30/11) | | 369 (10/1/11-3/31/12) | | | | 4/1/07-3/31/08 | 4/1/08-3/31/09 |
| 0-500M | 500M-2MM | 2-10MM | 10-50MM | 50-100MM | 100-250MM | | ALL | ALL |
| 85 | 192 | 103 | 33 | 11 | 7 | NUMBER OF STATEMENTS | 317 | 389 |
| % | % | % | % | % | % | ASSETS | % | % |
| 17.7 | 14.4 | 11.4 | 7.2 | 4.1 | | Cash & Equivalents | 10.9 | 12.1 |
| 14.7 | 22.6 | 28.5 | 34.3 | 28.8 | | Trade Receivables (net) | 24.8 | 25.0 |
| 44.8 | 35.8 | 24.8 | 22.1 | 18.2 | | Inventory | 34.1 | 33.3 |
| 1.4 | 1.2 | 1.9 | 3.9 | 6.2 | | All Other Current | 2.0 | 2.1 |
| 78.6 | 74.0 | 66.6 | 67.4 | 57.4 | | Total Current | 71.8 | 72.5 |
| 11.2 | 10.1 | 12.9 | 12.8 | 12.6 | | Fixed Assets (net) | 14.5 | 12.9 |
| 2.8 | 8.6 | 13.9 | 13.0 | 26.4 | | Intangibles (net) | 7.1 | 7.5 |
| 7.4 | 7.4 | 6.6 | 6.7 | 3.6 | | All Other Non-Current | 6.6 | 7.2 |
| 100.0 | 100.0 | 100.0 | 100.0 | 100.0 | | Total | 100.0 | 100.0 |
| | | | | | | **LIABILITIES** | | |
| 21.2 | 7.5 | 9.0 | 9.8 | 12.5 | | Notes Payable-Short Term | 12.1 | 9.8 |
| 2.6 | 2.2 | 4.0 | 3.2 | 1.3 | | Cur. Mat.-L.T.D. | 4.4 | 4.5 |
| 22.9 | 26.8 | 25.9 | 19.4 | 18.6 | | Trade Payables | 23.4 | 25.3 |
| .3 | .2 | .0 | .1 | .2 | | Income Taxes Payable | .1 | .1 |
| 15.6 | 7.7 | 7.7 | 6.9 | 7.8 | | All Other Current | 8.3 | 9.5 |
| 62.5 | 44.4 | 46.7 | 39.5 | 40.3 | | Total Current | 48.2 | 49.2 |
| 17.7 | 16.2 | 17.4 | 16.0 | 15.9 | | Long-Term Debt | 16.4 | 16.7 |
| .0 | .0 | .0 | .2 | 1.0 | | Deferred Taxes | .1 | .1 |
| 10.5 | 4.4 | 4.3 | 5.8 | 9.5 | | All Other Non-Current | 6.2 | 4.5 |
| 9.2 | 35.0 | 31.6 | 38.5 | 33.3 | | Net Worth | 29.0 | 29.6 |
| 100.0 | 100.0 | 100.0 | 100.0 | 100.0 | | Total Liabilities & Net Worth | 100.0 | 100.0 |
| | | | | | | **INCOME DATA** | | |
| 100.0 | 100.0 | 100.0 | 100.0 | 100.0 | | Net Sales | 100.0 | 100.0 |
| 27.9 | 23.7 | 27.0 | 28.7 | 35.2 | | Gross Profit | 26.0 | 25.2 |
| 25.5 | 21.0 | 23.8 | 25.2 | 29.2 | | Operating Expenses | 23.9 | 22.7 |
| 2.4 | 2.8 | 3.2 | 3.6 | 6.0 | | Operating Profit | 2.1 | 2.4 |
| .3 | .0 | .1 | .1 | 1.0 | | All Other Expenses (net) | .3 | .2 |
| 2.1 | 2.8 | 3.1 | 3.4 | 5.1 | | Profit Before Taxes | 1.7 | 2.2 |
| | | | | | | **RATIOS** | | |
| 4.1 | 3.4 | 2.2 | 2.8 | 2.6 | | Current | 2.5 | 2.7 |
| 1.8 | 1.8 | 1.5 | 1.7 | 1.9 | | | 1.6 | 1.6 |
| 1.1 | 1.2 | 1.1 | 1.2 | 1.3 | | | 1.1 | 1.1 |
| 1.6 | 1.8 | 1.3 | 1.8 | 1.7 | | Quick | 1.2 | 1.5 |
| (84) .7 | .9 | .9 | 1.2 | 1.1 | | | (316) .8 | .8 |
| .3 | .5 | .5 | .6 | .4 | | | .5 | .5 |
| 0 UND | 6 61.4 | 15 23.7 | 20 18.4 | 33 11.2 | | Sales/Receivables | 11 34.0 | 9 40.7 |
| 4 88.7 | 15 24.2 | 22 16.3 | 30 12.3 | 47 7.7 | | | 19 18.8 | 19 18.9 |
| 18 20.5 | 23 16.1 | 33 11.0 | 54 6.7 | 58 6.3 | | | 28 13.0 | 27 13.4 |
| 17 21.7 | 20 18.3 | 19 19.6 | 14 26.2 | 14 25.9 | | Cost of Sales/Inventory | 22 16.2 | 21 17.5 |
| 32 11.3 | 30 12.3 | 31 11.9 | 30 12.3 | 24 15.2 | | | 33 11.1 | 31 11.9 |
| 51 7.1 | 41 8.8 | 43 8.4 | 47 7.8 | 58 6.3 | | | 47 7.7 | 42 8.7 |
| 0 845.4 | 10 37.8 | 16 23.1 | 18 20.8 | 26 14.0 | | Cost of Sales/Payables | 14 26.1 | 14 25.9 |
| 14 26.8 | 19 19.7 | 29 12.4 | 29 12.5 | 31 11.6 | | | 21 17.5 | 21 17.4 |
| 24 15.0 | 32 11.5 | 46 8.0 | 35 10.3 | 45 8.1 | | | 35 10.3 | 35 10.5 |
| 12.6 | 9.8 | 10.7 | 6.8 | 6.3 | | Sales/Working Capital | 11.0 | 10.2 |
| 22.4 | 16.7 | 20.7 | 13.5 | 8.2 | | | 19.4 | 20.0 |
| 79.0 | 54.9 | 57.1 | 53.2 | 35.6 | | | 93.3 | 71.6 |
| 29.2 | 16.1 | 22.0 | 33.8 | 22.4 | | EBIT/Interest | 9.9 | 13.2 |
| (43) 5.0 | (136) 3.8 | (90) 5.5 | (32) 5.7 | (10) 5.7 | | | (269) 3.5 | (317) 4.3 |
| 1.7 | 1.2 | 1.6 | 1.8 | 3.3 | | | 1.1 | 1.1 |
| | | 4.9 | | | | Net Profit + Depr., Dep., Amort./Cur. Mat. L/T/D | 6.2 | 4.8 |
| | | (11) 2.0 | | | | | (48) 1.8 | (44) 1.4 |
| | | .7 | | | | | .5 | .4 |
| .0 | .0 | .2 | .2 | .6 | | Fixed/Worth | .2 | .1 |
| .3 | .2 | .6 | .4 | 2.5 | | | .5 | .5 |
| -15.7 | 3.2 | UND | 1.7 | -.2 | | | 3.4 | 6.0 |
| .5 | .7 | 1.1 | .9 | 1.5 | | Debt/Worth | .9 | .9 |
| 5.3 | 2.7 | 4.1 | 2.5 | 7.7 | | | 2.4 | 2.5 |
| -17.2 | 44.9 | -39.0 | 6.7 | -4.2 | | | 22.9 | 257.1 |
| 212.5 | 72.1 | 79.7 | 69.9 | | | % Profit Before Taxes/Tangible Net Worth | 57.1 | 64.8 |
| (59) 64.4 | (147) 26.2 | (77) 39.0 | (28) 22.4 | | | | (252) 22.4 | (296) 27.0 |
| 19.4 | 2.4 | 10.0 | 4.8 | | | | 5.9 | 7.8 |
| 31.3 | 21.1 | 18.9 | 22.8 | 20.3 | | % Profit Before Taxes/Total Assets | 18.2 | 19.9 |
| 13.7 | 9.0 | 8.0 | 7.2 | 6.7 | | | 5.6 | 7.6 |
| .9 | 1.5 | 1.3 | 1.0 | 2.7 | | | .7 | .9 |
| 428.4 | 476.8 | 150.7 | 96.1 | 75.2 | | Sales/Net Fixed Assets | 121.7 | 149.5 |
| 117.4 | 104.6 | 62.5 | 35.7 | 28.5 | | | 48.6 | 59.4 |
| 39.0 | 38.6 | 25.1 | 19.6 | 9.3 | | | 21.0 | 27.4 |
| 10.2 | 7.4 | 5.4 | 4.1 | 3.8 | | Sales/Total Assets | 6.4 | 6.7 |
| 7.1 | 5.3 | 4.2 | 3.4 | 2.7 | | | 4.7 | 4.8 |
| 4.6 | 3.8 | 2.9 | 2.8 | 1.0 | | | 3.3 | 3.4 |
| .2 | .1 | .3 | .4 | | | % Depr., Dep., Amort./Sales | .3 | .3 |
| (45) .5 | (122) .3 | (77) .6 | (27) .6 | | | | (261) .6 | (297) .6 |
| 1.2 | .9 | 1.3 | 1.0 | | | | 1.2 | 1.1 |
| 2.3 | 1.6 | 1.0 | | | | % Officers', Directors' Owners' Comp/Sales | 1.6 | 1.7 |
| (56) 4.3 | (130) 3.2 | (47) 2.1 | | | | | (162) 3.0 | (210) 3.1 |
| 7.3 | 5.7 | 3.2 | | | | | 5.1 | 5.3 |
| 201020M | 1168093M | 1755739M | 2318637M | 2096416M | 3752132M | Net Sales ($) | 9487431M | 10579641M |
| 24099M | 207087M | 419557M | 692490M | 773342M | 1210106M | Total Assets ($) | 2354203M | 2839091M |

M = $ thousand     MM = $ million
See Pages 9 through 22 for Explanation of Ratios and Data

## Comparative Historical Data

## Current Data Sorted by Sales

| | | | Type of Statement | 0-1MM | 1-3MM | 3-5MM | 5-10MM | 10-25MM | 25MM & OVER |
|---|---|---|---|---|---|---|---|---|---|
| 19 | 29 | 27 | Unqualified | 2 | | | 2 | 3 | 20 |
| 32 | 35 | 30 | Reviewed | 1 | 1 | 2 | 7 | 11 | 8 |
| 73 | 69 | 73 | Compiled | 4 | 14 | 10 | 23 | 16 | 6 |
| 160 | 146 | 206 | Tax Returns | 11 | 48 | 41 | 61 | 39 | 6 |
| 114 | 118 | 95 | Other | | 18 | 17 | 14 | 15 | 31 |
| 4/1/09-3/31/10 ALL | 4/1/10-3/31/11 ALL | 4/1/11-3/31/12 ALL | | 62 (4/1-9/30/11) | | | 369 (10/1/11-3/31/12) | | |
| 398 | 397 | 431 | **NUMBER OF STATEMENTS** | 18 | 81 | 70 | 107 | 84 | 71 |
| % | % | % | **ASSETS** | % | % | % | % | % | % |
| 11.9 | 10.6 | 13.4 | Cash & Equivalents | 21.5 | 14.2 | 14.4 | 14.2 | 13.8 | 7.7 |
| 24.8 | 25.0 | 23.4 | Trade Receivables (net) | 11.0 | 17.9 | 17.5 | 20.3 | 30.9 | 34.4 |
| 32.6 | 34.1 | 33.5 | Inventory | 42.6 | 36.6 | 38.6 | 34.8 | 30.3 | 24.6 |
| 1.4 | 2.0 | 1.8 | All Other Current | 1.6 | 1.1 | .9 | 1.9 | 1.6 | 3.3 |
| 70.7 | 71.8 | 72.1 | Total Current | 76.8 | 69.7 | 71.5 | 71.2 | 76.6 | 70.1 |
| 12.4 | 12.7 | 11.4 | Fixed Assets (net) | 12.7 | 12.1 | 11.8 | 10.8 | 10.6 | 11.5 |
| 7.6 | 8.3 | 9.6 | Intangibles (net) | 3.8 | 11.5 | 10.6 | 7.8 | 7.2 | 13.4 |
| 9.4 | 7.2 | 7.0 | All Other Non-Current | 6.4 | 6.8 | 6.0 | 10.2 | 5.6 | 5.0 |
| 100.0 | 100.0 | 100.0 | Total | 100.0 | 100.0 | 100.0 | 100.0 | 100.0 | 100.0 |
| | | | **LIABILITIES** | | | | | | |
| 11.2 | 9.4 | 10.9 | Notes Payable-Short Term | 37.6 | 14.9 | 9.4 | 7.7 | 6.1 | 11.5 |
| 3.4 | 4.0 | 2.8 | Cur. Mat.-L.T.D. | 3.9 | 2.8 | 1.8 | 3.3 | 2.6 | 2.8 |
| 27.0 | 24.8 | 25.0 | Trade Payables | 14.4 | 18.3 | 23.2 | 27.4 | 31.6 | 25.6 |
| .1 | .1 | .2 | Income Taxes Payable | .0 | .3 | .0 | .3 | .0 | .1 |
| 9.1 | 9.4 | 9.2 | All Other Current | 32.0 | 10.0 | 7.9 | 8.1 | 8.0 | 6.8 |
| 50.9 | 47.7 | 48.0 | Total Current | 87.9 | 46.4 | 42.4 | 46.7 | 48.4 | 46.9 |
| 15.1 | 15.3 | 16.7 | Long-Term Debt | 28.6 | 24.3 | 17.1 | 13.4 | 12.1 | 14.9 |
| .1 | .1 | .1 | Deferred Taxes | .0 | .0 | .0 | .0 | .0 | .2 |
| 5.7 | 5.6 | 6.0 | All Other Non-Current | 10.5 | 9.2 | 5.3 | 4.8 | 4.0 | 6.1 |
| 28.2 | 31.3 | 29.3 | Net Worth | -27.0 | 20.1 | 35.2 | 35.1 | 35.4 | 31.9 |
| 100.0 | 100.0 | 100.0 | Total Liabilities & Net Worth | 100.0 | 100.0 | 100.0 | 100.0 | 100.0 | 100.0 |
| | | | **INCOME DATA** | | | | | | |
| 100.0 | 100.0 | 100.0 | Net Sales | 100.0 | 100.0 | 100.0 | 100.0 | 100.0 | 100.0 |
| 26.8 | 26.0 | 26.1 | Gross Profit | 35.1 | 30.3 | 24.4 | 24.1 | 23.9 | 26.3 |
| 23.7 | 23.5 | 23.2 | Operating Expenses | 29.9 | 27.1 | 21.6 | 21.8 | 21.4 | 22.9 |
| 3.1 | 2.4 | 2.9 | Operating Profit | 5.2 | 3.2 | 2.9 | 2.3 | 2.5 | 3.4 |
| .2 | .2 | .1 | All Other Expenses (net) | 1.3 | .5 | .0 | .1 | -.4 | .2 |
| 2.9 | 2.2 | 2.8 | Profit Before Taxes | 3.9 | 2.7 | 2.9 | 2.2 | 2.8 | 3.2 |
| | | | **RATIOS** | | | | | | |
| 2.6 | 2.6 | 3.0 | | 3.9 | 4.6 | 3.7 | 3.0 | 2.4 | 2.4 |
| 1.6 | 1.6 | 1.7 | Current | 1.8 | 1.8 | 2.1 | 1.7 | 1.6 | 1.5 |
| 1.1 | 1.1 | 1.2 | | 1.2 | 1.2 | 1.1 | 1.1 | 1.2 | 1.1 |
| 1.4 | 1.3 | 1.6 | | 1.4 | 2.5 | 1.7 | 1.5 | 1.4 | 1.5 |
| .8 (395) | .8 (430) | .9 | Quick | .8 (80) | .8 | .9 | .8 | 1.0 | .9 |
| .5 | .5 | .5 | | .3 | .3 | .4 | .4 | .6 | .6 |
| 8 46.2 | 9 42.2 | 7 55.9 | | 0 UND | 0 763.3 | 3 141.9 | 4 89.3 | 13 27.5 | 18 19.8 |
| 19 18.7 | 19 19.3 | 17 21.4 | Sales/Receivables | 3 105.8 | 13 27.4 | 13 28.1 | 14 25.4 | 18 20.3 | 28 13.0 |
| 28 12.8 | 29 12.8 | 27 13.6 | | 20 18.0 | 25 14.5 | 23 15.8 | 22 16.5 | 29 12.7 | 45 8.1 |
| 20 18.0 | 21 17.5 | 19 19.1 | | 41 8.9 | 26 14.1 | 21 17.2 | 18 20.1 | 17 21.3 | 12 30.9 |
| 31 11.9 | 32 11.3 | 32 11.9 | Cost of Sales/Inventory | 54 6.8 | 37 9.9 | 31 11.7 | 28 13.0 | 25 14.6 | 30 12.2 |
| 45 8.1 | 47 7.8 | 44 8.3 | | 94 3.9 | 53 6.9 | 41 9.0 | 38 9.6 | 34 10.6 | 50 7.3 |
| 13 27.1 | 13 28.7 | 11 32.9 | | 0 UND | 2 185.1 | 8 46.9 | 11 32.9 | 16 23.3 | 18 20.7 |
| 23 15.6 | 23 16.0 | 21 17.6 | Cost of Sales/Payables | 17 21.9 | 17 21.0 | 17 21.8 | 19 19.1 | 25 14.5 | 31 11.8 |
| 41 8.9 | 36 10.1 | 34 10.8 | | 30 12.2 | 29 12.7 | 30 12.0 | 33 11.1 | 35 10.3 | 37 9.8 |
| 10.3 | 10.2 | 9.8 | | 7.5 | 8.1 | 9.6 | 10.1 | 12.7 | 8.2 |
| 20.8 | 18.6 | 18.8 | Sales/Working Capital | 13.6 | 19.8 | 14.0 | 21.5 | 20.4 | 18.2 |
| 111.4 | 82.7 | 56.1 | | 43.8 | 59.9 | 61.6 | 221.9 | 38.6 | 55.9 |
| 18.5 | 17.3 | 19.3 | | | 15.4 | 13.6 | 17.2 | 32.1 | 25.9 |
| (319) 4.9 | (317) 4.3 | (318) 4.5 | EBIT/Interest | | (57) 3.0 | (51) 5.5 | (68) 3.5 | (67) 8.6 | (68) 5.5 |
| 1.4 | 1.3 | 1.5 | | | 1.4 | 1.5 | 1.1 | 2.2 | 1.7 |
| 4.6 | 4.3 | 4.8 | | | | | | | 6.9 |
| (45) 1.4 | (48) 1.3 | (27) 1.1 | Net Profit + Depr., Dep., Amort./Cur. Mat. L/T/D | | | | | (13) 2.5 | |
| .7 | .3 | .3 | | | | | | | .2 |
| .1 | .1 | .1 | | .1 | .0 | .1 | .0 | .1 | .2 |
| .4 | .4 | .4 | Fixed/Worth | .6 | .6 | .3 | .2 | .3 | .7 |
| 3.9 | 3.0 | 5.1 | | -.5 | -1.5 | 3.7 | 1.6 | 1.1 | -6.5 |
| .9 | .9 | .8 | | .9 | .6 | .6 | .7 | .8 | 1.4 |
| 2.8 | 2.7 | 3.1 | Debt/Worth | 13.1 | 6.1 | 3.1 | 2.5 | 2.6 | 4.5 |
| 44.6 | 27.5 | -69.7 | | -2.0 | -6.7 | -59.2 | 9.2 | 9.2 | -39.0 |
| 88.1 | 82.8 | 83.8 | | 234.4 | 171.7 | 69.5 | 60.4 | 92.8 | 76.5 |
| (305) 33.5 | (314) 27.1 | (321) 32.7 | % Profit Before Taxes/Tangible Net Worth | (10) 98.0 | (51) 48.9 | (52) 28.7 | (84) 24.5 | (73) 40.6 | (51) 27.7 |
| 10.6 | 4.2 | 5.4 | | 53.0 | 8.1 | .7 | 2.7 | 5.8 | 7.2 |
| 22.6 | 19.9 | 22.0 | | 37.1 | 28.1 | 21.3 | 18.9 | 25.0 | 20.1 |
| 9.3 | 7.8 | 8.2 | % Profit Before Taxes/Total Assets | 14.3 | 7.4 | 9.9 | 7.4 | 11.7 | 6.7 |
| 1.3 | .5 | 1.2 | | -5.7 | 1.4 | .2 | 1.5 | 1.7 | 1.2 |
| 180.2 | 200.1 | 305.2 | | 355.8 | 345.2 | 387.7 | 556.0 | 265.3 | 107.3 |
| 58.0 | 59.5 | 78.7 | Sales/Net Fixed Assets | 69.3 | 79.8 | 84.5 | 126.8 | 78.8 | 38.5 |
| 25.3 | 23.9 | 28.5 | | 35.8 | 23.8 | 34.3 | 34.1 | 30.5 | 21.3 |
| 6.5 | 6.8 | 7.0 | | 7.8 | 6.7 | 7.1 | 7.7 | 7.6 | 5.0 |
| 4.6 | 4.6 | 4.8 | Sales/Total Assets | 4.3 | 4.2 | 5.4 | 5.3 | 5.4 | 3.9 |
| 3.5 | 3.4 | 3.4 | | 2.7 | 3.0 | 3.4 | 4.1 | 4.0 | 2.9 |
| .2 | .2 | .2 | | .1 | .3 | .2 | .2 | .2 | .4 |
| (288) .6 | (275) .5 | (283) .5 | % Depr., Dep., Amort./Sales | (10) .4 | (42) .9 | (42) .4 | (66) .4 | (67) .4 | (56) .7 |
| 1.1 | 1.0 | 1.1 | | .9 | 1.9 | .9 | 1.3 | .9 | 1.0 |
| 1.5 | 1.7 | 1.6 | | | 2.5 | 2.0 | 1.4 | 1.3 | .4 |
| (218) 2.8 | (188) 3.1 | (235) 3.0 | % Officers', Directors' Owners' Comp/Sales | | (48) 4.5 | (50) 3.3 | (72) 3.0 | (47) 2.1 | (12) .6 |
| 4.3 | 5.7 | 5.6 | | | 7.4 | 6.4 | 5.6 | 3.2 | 1.0 |
| 8741307M | 13061035M | 11292037M | Net Sales ($) | 11284M | 167107M | 276053M | 721354M | 1226233M | 8890006M |
| 2596477M | 3912816M | 3326681M | Total Assets ($) | 2642M | 45579M | 62787M | 180161M | 255140M | 2780372M |

© RMA 2012

M = $ thousand    MM = $ million
See Pages 9 through 22 for Explanation of Ratios and Data

## Current Data Sorted by Assets       Comparative Historical Data

| | | | | | | Type of Statement | | |
|---|---|---|---|---|---|---|---|---|
| | | | 2 | 2 | 1 | Unqualified | 7 | 7 |
| | | | 3 | 1 | | Reviewed | 8 | 6 |
| | | 5 | 6 | | | Compiled | 6 | 12 |
| 13 | 12 | 5 | 2 | | | Tax Returns | 12 | 19 |
| 3 | 11 | 6 | 6 | 4 | 1 | Other | 16 | 24 |
| | 9 (4/1-9/30/11) | | 74 (10/1/11-3/31/12) | | | | 4/1/07-3/31/08 | 4/1/08-3/31/09 |
| 0-500M | 500M-2MM | 2-10MM | 10-50MM | 50-100MM | 100-250MM | | ALL | ALL |
| 16 | 28 | 22 | 11 | 5 | 1 | NUMBER OF STATEMENTS | 49 | 68 |
| % | % | % | % | % | % | ASSETS | % | % |
| 12.3 | 10.9 | 11.2 | 24.9 | | | Cash & Equivalents | 11.0 | 11.5 |
| 5.1 | 10.4 | 14.8 | 11.1 | | | Trade Receivables (net) | 16.8 | 13.4 |
| 63.7 | 48.7 | 53.7 | 23.5 | | | Inventory | 46.9 | 44.6 |
| .2 | .4 | 2.9 | 9.0 | | | All Other Current | 2.6 | 2.8 |
| 81.4 | 70.5 | 82.6 | 68.6 | | | Total Current | 77.3 | 72.4 |
| 14.4 | 15.7 | 10.2 | 24.4 | | | Fixed Assets (net) | 10.7 | 16.6 |
| 1.6 | 8.1 | 3.9 | 3.4 | | | Intangibles (net) | 4.0 | 6.5 |
| 2.7 | 5.7 | 3.3 | 3.6 | | | All Other Non-Current | 8.0 | 4.5 |
| 100.0 | 100.0 | 100.0 | 100.0 | | | Total | 100.0 | 100.0 |
| | | | | | | LIABILITIES | | |
| 22.2 | 12.1 | 4.0 | 6.5 | | | Notes Payable-Short Term | 14.3 | 16.6 |
| .0 | .8 | 3.3 | 4.3 | | | Cur. Mat.-L.T.D. | 1.2 | 1.5 |
| 16.3 | 15.8 | 22.2 | 17.0 | | | Trade Payables | 20.4 | 18.3 |
| .0 | .0 | .0 | .2 | | | Income Taxes Payable | .1 | .0 |
| 15.5 | 6.0 | 3.1 | 9.8 | | | All Other Current | 16.4 | 10.1 |
| 54.0 | 34.7 | 32.6 | 37.7 | | | Total Current | 52.3 | 46.6 |
| 5.4 | 8.0 | 11.0 | 23.6 | | | Long-Term Debt | 11.7 | 19.3 |
| .0 | .0 | .0 | .1 | | | Deferred Taxes | .3 | .2 |
| 11.4 | 3.6 | 10.8 | 12.6 | | | All Other Non-Current | 8.0 | 16.0 |
| 29.2 | 53.8 | 45.6 | 26.0 | | | Net Worth | 27.8 | 17.7 |
| 100.0 | 100.0 | 100.0 | 100.0 | | | Total Liabilities & Net Worth | 100.0 | 100.0 |
| | | | | | | INCOME DATA | | |
| 100.0 | 100.0 | 100.0 | 100.0 | | | Net Sales | 100.0 | 100.0 |
| 45.1 | 38.4 | 41.7 | 41.5 | | | Gross Profit | 45.3 | 43.7 |
| 38.5 | 33.1 | 34.8 | 37.9 | | | Operating Expenses | 40.1 | 38.5 |
| 6.6 | 5.3 | 6.9 | 3.6 | | | Operating Profit | 5.2 | 5.2 |
| -.7 | .3 | .6 | -.8 | | | All Other Expenses (net) | .6 | 1.4 |
| 7.3 | 5.0 | 6.4 | 4.3 | | | Profit Before Taxes | 4.6 | 3.8 |
| | | | | | | RATIOS | | |
| 3.5 | 4.6 | 5.7 | 1.9 | | | Current | 3.5 | 3.6 |
| 2.1 | 2.9 | 3.3 | 1.5 | | | | 1.8 | 1.8 |
| 1.3 | 1.1 | 1.8 | 1.1 | | | | 1.0 | 1.1 |
| .5 | 1.2 | 2.0 | 1.3 | | | Quick | 1.6 | 1.3 |
| .3 | .6 | .8 | .7 | | | | .5 | .4 |
| .2 | .2 | .4 | .2 | | | | .3 | .2 |
| 0 UND | 0 UND | 2 229.6 | 1 259.7 | | | Sales/Receivables | 2 241.7 | 2 153.9 |
| 0 UND | 2 158.9 | 16 23.0 | 11 33.7 | | | | 21 17.7 | 12 31.0 |
| 0 UND | 21 17.1 | 33 11.2 | 47 7.8 | | | | 47 7.8 | 28 13.1 |
| 59 6.2 | 42 8.7 | 87 4.2 | 60 6.1 | | | Cost of Sales/Inventory | 78 4.7 | 63 5.8 |
| 152 2.4 | 89 4.1 | 146 2.5 | 76 4.8 | | | | 134 2.7 | 117 3.1 |
| 228 1.6 | 159 2.3 | 203 1.8 | 96 3.8 | | | | 201 1.8 | 202 1.8 |
| 0 UND | 4 93.0 | 12 29.9 | 9 40.7 | | | Cost of Sales/Payables | 22 16.3 | 15 24.7 |
| 23 15.6 | 33 11.0 | 35 10.3 | 28 13.1 | | | | 46 7.9 | 34 10.6 |
| 76 4.8 | 45 8.1 | 74 4.9 | 66 5.5 | | | | 79 4.6 | 61 6.0 |
| 3.2 | 3.8 | 3.2 | 2.7 | | | Sales/Working Capital | 4.2 | 4.0 |
| 12.8 | 6.8 | 4.8 | 9.5 | | | | 7.1 | 7.0 |
| 35.2 | 63.0 | 12.2 | 76.5 | | | | 289.9 | 41.3 |
| | 20.7 | 15.8 | | | | EBIT/Interest | 19.7 | 6.7 |
| | (17) 3.2 | (17) 4.1 | | | | | (43) 6.0 | (55) 2.3 |
| | -2.0 | .9 | | | | | 1.7 | -1.6 |
| | | | | | | Net Profit + Depr., Dep., Amort./Cur. Mat. L/T/D | | |
| .0 | .0 | .0 | .1 | | | Fixed/Worth | .1 | .0 |
| .2 | .3 | .1 | 1.5 | | | | .3 | .3 |
| .8 | .5 | .4 | -1.5 | | | | 1.0 | 3.1 |
| .7 | .3 | .4 | 1.1 | | | Debt/Worth | .7 | .8 |
| 1.3 | .8 | 1.0 | 2.1 | | | | 2.5 | 2.1 |
| 4.8 | 4.1 | 5.1 | -8.3 | | | | 39.4 | 19.5 |
| 156.1 | 64.6 | 61.8 | | | | % Profit Before Taxes/Tangible Net Worth | 57.7 | 39.5 |
| (15) 31.0 | (27) 16.9 | (20) 27.8 | | | | | (38) 31.0 | (53) 13.6 |
| 26.9 | 1.1 | 8.0 | | | | | 14.3 | -1.6 |
| 34.5 | 18.6 | 23.0 | 15.0 | | | % Profit Before Taxes/Total Assets | 22.2 | 14.5 |
| 17.0 | 8.3 | 8.5 | 3.5 | | | | 9.8 | 4.9 |
| 6.7 | .6 | 1.4 | -2.4 | | | | 1.1 | -4.8 |
| 113.8 | 157.9 | 507.0 | 35.8 | | | Sales/Net Fixed Assets | 120.6 | 150.3 |
| 51.4 | 37.7 | 64.1 | 9.9 | | | | 43.4 | 39.3 |
| 19.5 | 12.4 | 16.9 | 6.4 | | | | 13.7 | 10.6 |
| 4.3 | 3.7 | 3.5 | 3.2 | | | Sales/Total Assets | 3.2 | 3.7 |
| 3.0 | 3.1 | 2.5 | 1.9 | | | | 2.5 | 2.4 |
| 2.1 | 2.1 | 1.9 | 1.1 | | | | 1.6 | 1.6 |
| .1 | .2 | .4 | 1.3 | | | % Depr., Dep., Amort./Sales | .3 | .3 |
| (10) .5 | (19) .8 | (10) 1.0 | (10) 2.7 | | | | (39) .8 | (50) 1.1 |
| 1.5 | 1.7 | 2.4 | 4.1 | | | | 1.4 | 2.1 |
| 1.8 | 1.2 | | | | | % Officers', Directors' Owners' Comp/Sales | 1.8 | 1.5 |
| (12) 6.1 | (13) 2.8 | | | | | | (21) 2.7 | (30) 2.9 |
| 9.4 | 6.9 | | | | | | 8.4 | 5.7 |
| 21659M | 96561M | 266225M | 509960M | 838380M | 20733M | Net Sales ($) | 1216371M | 1431678M |
| 5201M | 28910M | 99869M | 219948M | 425189M | 142715M | Total Assets ($) | 605558M | 751535M |

M = $ thousand    MM = $ million
See Pages 9 through 22 for Explanation of Ratios and Data

**Comparative Historical Data**  |  **Current Data Sorted by Sales**

| 10 stmt¹ | | | Type of Statement | | | | | | |
|---|---|---|---|---|---|---|---|---|---|
| 4/1/09-3/31/10 ALL | 4/1/10-3/31/11 ALL | 4/1/11-3/31/12 ALL | | 0-1MM | 1-3MM | 3-5MM | 5-10MM | 10-25MM | 25MM & OVER |
| 10 | 7 | 5 | Unqualified | | | | 2 | | 3 |
| 5 | 4 | 4 | Reviewed | | | | | 4 | |
| 12 | 5 | 11 | Compiled | 1 | 3 | 1 | 3 | 3 | |
| 20 | 25 | 32 | Tax Returns | 7 | 9 | 8 | 3 | 3 | 2 |
| 25 | 28 | 31 | Other | 1 | 8 | 3 | 3 | 3 | 8 |
| | | | | | 9 (4/1-9/30/11) | | 74 (10/1/11-3/31/12) | | |
| 72 | 69 | 83 | **NUMBER OF STATEMENTS** | 9 | 20 | 12 | 11 | 18 | 13 |
| % | % | % | **ASSETS** | % | % | % | % | % | % |
| 12.6 | 14.4 | 12.9 | Cash & Equivalents | | 14.9 | 10.0 | 9.7 | 18.6 | 12.0 |
| 13.1 | 11.5 | 10.8 | Trade Receivables (net) | | 4.7 | 15.0 | 21.9 | 11.8 | 13.2 |
| 44.4 | 41.4 | 47.9 | Inventory | | 54.9 | 52.3 | 45.5 | 41.7 | 29.1 |
| 3.4 | 3.0 | 2.5 | All Other Current | | .4 | .1 | 1.0 | 3.8 | 8.8 |
| 73.5 | 70.4 | 74.2 | Total Current | | 74.9 | 77.4 | 78.0 | 75.9 | 63.1 |
| 16.9 | 16.7 | 14.8 | Fixed Assets (net) | | 15.1 | 14.5 | 13.4 | 11.1 | 20.8 |
| 3.8 | 9.0 | 6.9 | Intangibles (net) | | 6.0 | 5.1 | 2.4 | 8.1 | 11.0 |
| 5.8 | 3.9 | 4.2 | All Other Non-Current | | 4.0 | 3.0 | 6.1 | 4.9 | 5.1 |
| 100.0 | 100.0 | 100.0 | Total | | 100.0 | 100.0 | 100.0 | 100.0 | 100.0 |
| | | | **LIABILITIES** | | | | | | |
| 11.0 | 11.5 | 10.4 | Notes Payable-Short Term | | 16.3 | 20.1 | 11.3 | 2.6 | 6.1 |
| 2.2 | 3.5 | 1.9 | Cur. Mat.-L.T.D. | | .4 | 1.1 | 3.8 | 2.7 | 3.3 |
| 19.9 | 20.2 | 17.3 | Trade Payables | | 18.9 | 15.4 | 25.3 | 15.6 | 18.6 |
| .1 | .2 | .1 | Income Taxes Payable | | .0 | .0 | .0 | .0 | .4 |
| 12.4 | 7.5 | 8.4 | All Other Current | | 6.6 | 8.3 | 2.2 | 4.7 | 14.5 |
| 45.7 | 42.9 | 38.0 | Total Current | | 42.3 | 44.9 | 42.7 | 25.6 | 43.0 |
| 14.3 | 14.0 | 11.3 | Long-Term Debt | | 6.3 | 12.4 | 12.1 | 9.2 | 26.0 |
| .2 | .1 | .2 | Deferred Taxes | | .0 | .0 | .0 | .7 | .4 |
| 8.1 | 6.4 | 8.4 | All Other Non-Current | | 9.3 | 3.5 | 4.9 | 8.6 | 8.6 |
| 31.7 | 36.5 | 42.1 | Net Worth | | 42.2 | 39.3 | 40.2 | 55.9 | 22.0 |
| 100.0 | 100.0 | 100.0 | Total Liabilities & Net Worth | | 100.0 | 100.0 | 100.0 | 100.0 | 100.0 |
| | | | **INCOME DATA** | | | | | | |
| 100.0 | 100.0 | 100.0 | Net Sales | | 100.0 | 100.0 | 100.0 | 100.0 | 100.0 |
| 47.7 | 47.7 | 42.0 | Gross Profit | | 43.1 | 36.0 | 44.0 | 41.0 | 45.2 |
| 43.5 | 41.0 | 35.8 | Operating Expenses | | 36.7 | 31.2 | 36.0 | 35.5 | 38.1 |
| 4.1 | 6.7 | 6.2 | Operating Profit | | 6.4 | 4.8 | 7.9 | 5.5 | 7.1 |
| .8 | 1.0 | .5 | All Other Expenses (net) | | .5 | -.2 | -.1 | 2.2 | -.1 |
| 3.3 | 5.7 | 5.7 | Profit Before Taxes | | 5.9 | 5.0 | 8.1 | 3.3 | 7.2 |
| | | | **RATIOS** | | | | | | |
| 4.1 | 3.4 | 4.5 | | | 4.3 | 7.6 | 5.1 | 7.0 | 1.7 |
| 1.7 | 1.9 | 2.1 | Current | | 2.2 | 3.1 | 1.8 | 3.3 | 1.5 |
| 1.1 | 1.1 | 1.4 | | | 1.1 | 1.7 | 1.1 | 1.9 | 1.2 |
| 1.3 | 1.2 | 1.2 | | | .8 | 1.7 | 1.8 | 2.6 | .8 |
| .6 | .5 | .6 | Quick | | .5 | .9 | .7 | 1.1 | .5 |
| .2 | .2 | .3 | | | .2 | .4 | .5 | .5 | .3 |
| 0 UND | 1 391.1 | 0 UND | | | 0 UND | 8 43.9 | 1 492.8 | 5 78.2 | |
| 7 54.1 | 10 35.3 | 5 67.1 | Sales/Receivables | | 0 UND | 6 59.3 | 28 12.9 | 15 24.7 | 13 27.2 |
| 32 11.3 | 30 12.1 | 28 13.0 | | | 6 62.0 | 31 11.7 | 37 9.9 | 32 11.3 | 35 10.3 |
| 68 5.3 | 69 5.3 | 61 6.0 | | | 78 4.7 | 32 11.3 | 36 10.0 | 72 5.1 | 53 6.9 |
| 112 3.3 | 112 3.3 | 122 3.0 | Cost of Sales/Inventory | | 146 2.5 | 83 4.4 | 122 3.0 | 118 3.1 | 76 4.8 |
| 165 2.2 | 176 2.1 | 182 2.0 | | | 182 2.0 | 159 2.3 | 243 1.5 | 182 2.0 | 140 2.6 |
| 26 14.2 | 15 24.1 | 11 33.4 | | | 4 88.4 | 0 UND | 31 11.6 | 5 75.4 | 17 21.4 |
| 34 10.7 | 32 11.5 | 33 10.9 | Cost of Sales/Payables | | 44 8.3 | 14 25.5 | 41 9.0 | 17 21.7 | 51 7.2 |
| 56 6.5 | 68 5.3 | 64 5.7 | | | 61 6.0 | 33 10.9 | 72 5.1 | 72 5.1 | 64 5.7 |
| 4.0 | 4.5 | 3.4 | | | 3.4 | 3.6 | 3.8 | 3.0 | 9.0 |
| 9.9 | 9.8 | 7.3 | Sales/Working Capital | | 6.8 | 7.6 | 9.9 | 3.8 | 11.9 |
| 56.0 | 77.3 | 25.4 | | | 84.1 | 22.8 | 72.4 | 6.9 | 49.6 |
| 10.9 | 20.1 | 34.5 | | | | | 11.9 | 86.8 | 139.5 |
| (53) 3.2 | (48) 4.8 | (53) 4.1 | EBIT/Interest | | | | (10) 4.0 | (15) 2.6 | (10) 1.8 |
| -.4 | .6 | .1 | | | | | -3.0 | -.6 | -.2 |
| | 24.4 | | Net Profit + Depr., Dep., | | | | | | |
| | (10) 5.2 | | Amort./Cur. Mat. L/T/D | | | | | | |
| | 1.9 | | | | | | | | |
| .0 | .0 | .0 | | | .0 | .0 | .0 | .0 | .4 |
| .3 | .3 | .3 | Fixed/Worth | | .2 | .4 | .2 | .1 | .8 |
| 1.3 | 3.5 | .9 | | | .4 | 1.1 | .9 | .6 | -4.2 |
| .6 | .5 | .5 | | | .4 | .3 | .8 | .3 | 1.7 |
| 1.6 | 1.8 | 1.1 | Debt/Worth | | 1.4 | .8 | 2.4 | .8 | 6.0 |
| 8.2 | 25.6 | 6.6 | | | 10.4 | 4.4 | 6.8 | 2.2 | -17.7 |
| 54.3 | 87.3 | 80.2 | | | 113.5 | 79.7 | 99.2 | 48.5 | |
| (57) 16.7 | (53) 29.6 | (74) 26.4 | % Profit Before Taxes/Tangible Net Worth | | (18) 19.9 | (11) 24.5 | 46.3 | (16) 14.9 | |
| .5 | 7.7 | 5.7 | | | 3.0 | 13.8 | -3.0 | 1.4 | |
| 19.9 | 24.2 | 24.5 | | | 35.6 | 34.5 | 21.6 | 30.3 | 37.9 |
| 5.3 | 7.5 | 9.6 | % Profit Before Taxes/Total Assets | | 6.3 | 16.8 | 6.5 | 8.4 | 4.4 |
| -4.2 | .4 | 1.1 | | | .6 | 5.4 | -1.6 | -1.6 | -.2 |
| 179.8 | 273.2 | 118.8 | | | 125.5 | 262.8 | 999.8 | 221.6 | 44.4 |
| 44.0 | 31.9 | 35.8 | Sales/Net Fixed Assets | | 44.5 | 53.3 | 71.3 | 33.1 | 13.8 |
| 7.0 | 9.0 | 12.4 | | | 13.4 | 17.4 | 10.2 | 10.1 | 6.9 |
| 3.5 | 3.6 | 3.5 | | | 3.3 | 7.2 | 4.0 | 3.5 | 3.4 |
| 2.7 | 2.5 | 2.8 | Sales/Total Assets | | 2.9 | 3.4 | 2.9 | 2.2 | 2.8 |
| 1.9 | 1.5 | 1.8 | | | 1.9 | 2.7 | 2.0 | 1.2 | 1.7 |
| .2 | .3 | .4 | | | .3 | | | | .7 |
| (46) 1.3 | (45) 1.5 | (55) 1.0 | % Depr., Dep., Amort./Sales | | (12) .6 | | | | 1.5 |
| 3.2 | 3.0 | 2.2 | | | 1.5 | | | | 2.9 |
| 1.3 | 1.3 | 1.4 | % Officers', Directors' | | | | | | |
| (26) 3.4 | (28) 2.4 | (36) 2.5 | Owners' Comp/Sales | | | | | | |
| 7.7 | 5.1 | 7.0 | | | | | | | |
| 1714207M | 1663577M | 1753518M | Net Sales ($) | 4764M | 36103M | 44776M | 81490M | 261970M | 1324415M |
| 765714M | 932739M | 921832M | Total Assets ($) | 2759M | 15763M | 13517M | 31621M | 261366M | 596806M |

M = $ thousand    MM = $ million
See Pages 9 through 22 for Explanation of Ratios and Data

## Current Data Sorted by Assets      Comparative Historical Data

**Type of Statement**

| | 0-500M | 500M-2MM | 2-10MM | 10-50MM | 50-100MM | 100-250MM | | 4/1/07-3/31/08 ALL | 4/1/08-3/31/09 ALL |
|---|---|---|---|---|---|---|---|---|---|
| Unqualified | | | | 2 | 1 | | | | 1 |
| Reviewed | | | 1 | 3 | | | | 3 | 5 |
| Compiled | 5 | 3 | 2 | 1 | | | | 7 | 3 |
| Tax Returns | 15 | 10 | 3 | 1 | | 1 | | 20 | 12 |
| Other | 9 | 3 | 1 | | 2 | | | 13 | 15 |

Date groupings: 7 (4/1-9/30/11) — 53 (10/1/11-3/31/12)

| | 0-500M | 500M-2MM | 2-10MM | 10-50MM | 50-100MM | 100-250MM | | 4/1/07-3/31/08 ALL | 4/1/08-3/31/09 ALL |
|---|---|---|---|---|---|---|---|---|---|
| **NUMBER OF STATEMENTS** | 29 | 13 | 7 | 7 | 3 | 1 | | 43 | 36 |
| | % | % | % | % | % | % | **ASSETS** | % | % |
| | 22.7 | 10.1 | | | | | Cash & Equivalents | 11.9 | 13.2 |
| | 7.7 | 15.2 | | | | | Trade Receivables (net) | 14.4 | 15.5 |
| | 29.4 | 25.5 | | | | | Inventory | 25.3 | 26.1 |
| | 2.2 | .7 | | | | | All Other Current | 3.1 | 2.5 |
| | 61.9 | 51.5 | | | | | Total Current | 54.6 | 57.3 |
| | 23.2 | 16.8 | | | | | Fixed Assets (net) | 25.4 | 25.9 |
| | 10.7 | 13.8 | | | | | Intangibles (net) | 11.0 | 8.4 |
| | 4.2 | 17.9 | | | | | All Other Non-Current | 8.9 | 8.4 |
| | 100.0 | 100.0 | | | | | Total | 100.0 | 100.0 |
| | | | | | | | **LIABILITIES** | | |
| | 4.9 | 3.2 | | | | | Notes Payable-Short Term | 13.1 | 8.5 |
| | 4.8 | 3.9 | | | | | Cur. Mat.-L.T.D. | 5.5 | 6.1 |
| | 6.7 | 19.2 | | | | | Trade Payables | 25.6 | 15.2 |
| | .0 | .0 | | | | | Income Taxes Payable | .0 | .2 |
| | 12.1 | 18.7 | | | | | All Other Current | 13.9 | 19.1 |
| | 28.5 | 44.9 | | | | | Total Current | 58.2 | 49.1 |
| | 29.3 | 17.2 | | | | | Long-Term Debt | 22.4 | 21.9 |
| | .0 | .3 | | | | | Deferred Taxes | .0 | .0 |
| | 21.2 | 22.6 | | | | | All Other Non-Current | 9.1 | 10.6 |
| | 21.0 | 14.9 | | | | | Net Worth | 10.3 | 18.4 |
| | 100.0 | 100.0 | | | | | Total Liabilities & Net Worth | 100.0 | 100.0 |
| | | | | | | | **INCOME DATA** | | |
| | 100.0 | 100.0 | | | | | Net Sales | 100.0 | 100.0 |
| | 63.3 | 48.0 | | | | | Gross Profit | 58.9 | 56.1 |
| | 56.3 | 44.5 | | | | | Operating Expenses | 52.8 | 49.3 |
| | 7.0 | 3.5 | | | | | Operating Profit | 6.1 | 6.8 |
| | .3 | .4 | | | | | All Other Expenses (net) | 1.3 | 1.7 |
| | 6.7 | 3.1 | | | | | Profit Before Taxes | 4.8 | 5.1 |
| | | | | | | | **RATIOS** | | |
| | 10.1 | 2.3 | | | | | | 2.2 | 2.7 |
| | 3.6 | 1.2 | | | | | Current | 1.1 | 1.2 |
| | 1.1 | .4 | | | | | | .6 | .8 |
| | 5.6 | 1.0 | | | | | | 1.3 | 1.1 |
| | 1.5 | .4 | | | | | Quick | .6 | .6 |
| | .3 | .2 | | | | | | .1 | .2 |
| | 0 UND | 0 UND | | | | | | 0 UND | 1 495.8 |
| | 0 UND | 4 82.3 | | | | | Sales/Receivables | 9 39.6 | 12 31.4 |
| | 7 53.1 | 25 14.8 | | | | | | 21 17.5 | 22 16.9 |
| | 24 14.9 | 40 9.1 | | | | | | 22 16.6 | 32 11.3 |
| | 70 5.2 | 48 7.6 | | | | | Cost of Sales/Inventory | 63 5.8 | 76 4.8 |
| | 111 3.3 | 79 4.6 | | | | | | 107 3.4 | 128 2.9 |
| | 0 UND | 0 UND | | | | | | 15 24.7 | 2 189.7 |
| | 0 UND | 28 13.2 | | | | | Cost of Sales/Payables | 36 10.0 | 28 13.2 |
| | 21 17.8 | 87 4.2 | | | | | | 70 5.3 | 46 7.9 |
| | 5.4 | 10.6 | | | | | | 12.7 | 11.6 |
| | 19.1 | 46.8 | | | | | Sales/Working Capital | 82.0 | 31.3 |
| | NM | -13.8 | | | | | | -22.0 | -27.8 |
| | 14.3 | 15.8 | | | | | | 11.5 | 12.1 |
| (18) | 7.7 | (10) 3.2 | | | | | EBIT/Interest | (33) 3.3 | (28) 3.4 |
| | .9 | -1.3 | | | | | | 1.0 | 1.5 |
| | | | | | | | Net Profit + Depr., Dep., Amort./Cur. Mat. L/T/D | | |
| | .1 | .0 | | | | | | .3 | .3 |
| | .7 | .5 | | | | | Fixed/Worth | 1.4 | .9 |
| | -2.6 | -.6 | | | | | | -.8 | -1.7 |
| | .2 | .7 | | | | | | 1.1 | .7 |
| | .8 | 1.8 | | | | | Debt/Worth | 3.4 | 6.4 |
| | -6.0 | -3.3 | | | | | | -3.0 | -5.2 |
| | 97.4 | | | | | | | 72.6 | 77.8 |
| (18) | 51.9 | | | | | | % Profit Before Taxes/Tangible Net Worth | (28) 24.8 | (23) 47.6 |
| | 22.0 | | | | | | | 2.0 | 7.3 |
| | 64.8 | 17.7 | | | | | | 33.3 | 31.4 |
| | 22.3 | 8.0 | | | | | % Profit Before Taxes/Total Assets | 9.5 | 10.2 |
| | 5.9 | -4.6 | | | | | | .0 | 2.7 |
| | 237.3 | UND | | | | | | 101.4 | 70.3 |
| | 32.7 | 35.4 | | | | | Sales/Net Fixed Assets | 21.8 | 16.7 |
| | 14.7 | 15.0 | | | | | | 8.8 | 6.8 |
| | 8.3 | 5.0 | | | | | | 6.1 | 5.6 |
| | 3.8 | 2.4 | | | | | Sales/Total Assets | 3.6 | 2.6 |
| | 2.8 | 1.7 | | | | | | 2.4 | 1.8 |
| | .8 | | | | | | | .4 | .5 |
| (18) | 1.1 | | | | | | % Depr., Dep., Amort./Sales | (29) 1.3 | (25) 1.9 |
| | 1.9 | | | | | | | 2.4 | 5.1 |
| | 2.0 | | | | | | | 1.9 | 7.0 |
| (15) | 10.3 | | | | | | % Officers', Directors' Owners' Comp/Sales | (21) 4.5 | (13) 9.6 |
| | 17.3 | | | | | | | 7.0 | 12.4 |
| | 38048M | 50829M | 90240M | 302095M | 397435M | 261871M | Net Sales ($) | 747487M | 629321M |
| | 6944M | 13877M | 27482M | 107937M | 193300M | 242096M | Total Assets ($) | 406937M | 285235M |

M = $ thousand     MM = $ million
See Pages 9 through 22 for Explanation of Ratios and Data

## Comparative Historical Data | Current Data Sorted by Sales

| | | | Type of Statement | | | | | | |
|---|---|---|---|---|---|---|---|---|---|
| 2 | 3 | 3 | Unqualified | | | | | | 3 |
| 2 | 3 | 4 | Reviewed | | | | 2 | 2 | |
| 5 | 4 | 8 | Compiled | 3 | 2 | 1 | 2 | 1 | 1 |
| 22 | 25 | 29 | Tax Returns | 7 | 11 | 5 | 2 | 3 | 1 |
| 21 | 10 | 16 | Other | 7 | 3 | | 2 | 1 | 3 |
| 4/1/09-<br>3/31/10<br>ALL | 4/1/10-<br>3/31/11<br>ALL | 4/1/11-<br>3/31/12<br>ALL | | 0-1MM | 7 (4/1-9/30/11)<br>1-3MM | 3-5MM | 53 (10/1/11-3/31/12)<br>5-10MM | 10-25MM | 25MM & OVER |
| 52 | 45 | 60 | NUMBER OF STATEMENTS | 17 | 16 | 6 | 6 | 7 | 8 |
| % | % | % | ASSETS | % | % | % | % | % | % |
| 13.4 | 14.4 | 16.7 | Cash & Equivalents | 23.1 | 13.4 | | | | |
| 9.1 | 12.9 | 10.1 | Trade Receivables (net) | 5.8 | 15.7 | | | | |
| 26.3 | 28.1 | 26.6 | Inventory | 27.0 | 30.5 | | | | |
| 2.5 | 1.8 | 2.4 | All Other Current | 3.3 | .4 | | | | |
| 51.3 | 57.2 | 55.8 | Total Current | 59.2 | 60.0 | | | | |
| 25.7 | 25.0 | 23.3 | Fixed Assets (net) | 27.1 | 11.6 | | | | |
| 10.3 | 11.9 | 12.8 | Intangibles (net) | 9.4 | 19.0 | | | | |
| 12.6 | 5.9 | 8.1 | All Other Non-Current | 4.3 | 9.4 | | | | |
| 100.0 | 100.0 | 100.0 | Total | 100.0 | 100.0 | | | | |
| | | | LIABILITIES | | | | | | |
| 5.8 | 8.5 | 4.4 | Notes Payable-Short Term | 6.3 | 2.9 | | | | |
| 7.1 | 5.5 | 4.5 | Cur. Mat.-L.T.D. | 3.4 | 4.9 | | | | |
| 19.9 | 18.0 | 12.3 | Trade Payables | 6.0 | 14.5 | | | | |
| .0 | .2 | .0 | Income Taxes Payable | .0 | .0 | | | | |
| 21.8 | 11.9 | 13.6 | All Other Current | 15.9 | 16.2 | | | | |
| 54.7 | 44.1 | 34.9 | Total Current | 31.6 | 38.5 | | | | |
| 17.3 | 24.1 | 23.7 | Long-Term Debt | 27.5 | 26.8 | | | | |
| .1 | .0 | .2 | Deferred Taxes | .0 | .0 | | | | |
| 8.6 | 9.8 | 16.0 | All Other Non-Current | 33.8 | 3.4 | | | | |
| 19.3 | 22.0 | 25.2 | Net Worth | 7.2 | 31.3 | | | | |
| 100.0 | 100.0 | 100.0 | Total Liabilties & Net Worth | 100.0 | 100.0 | | | | |
| | | | INCOME DATA | | | | | | |
| 100.0 | 100.0 | 100.0 | Net Sales | 100.0 | 100.0 | | | | |
| 58.5 | 61.2 | 58.1 | Gross Profit | 62.1 | 56.5 | | | | |
| 52.9 | 54.9 | 52.0 | Operating Expenses | 53.9 | 50.8 | | | | |
| 5.6 | 6.3 | 6.1 | Operating Profit | 8.2 | 5.7 | | | | |
| .5 | .6 | .3 | All Other Expenses (net) | .5 | .8 | | | | |
| 5.1 | 5.7 | 5.8 | Profit Before Taxes | 7.8 | 4.9 | | | | |
| | | | RATIOS | | | | | | |
| 2.2 | 2.4 | 3.8 | | 14.2 | 5.9 | | | | |
| 1.3 | 1.4 | 1.4 | Current | 3.7 | 1.3 | | | | |
| .9 | .9 | 1.0 | | .9 | .9 | | | | |
| .8 | 1.1 | 1.7 | | 5.6 | 2.3 | | | | |
| .4 | .6 | .7 | Quick | .8 | .7 | | | | |
| .1 | .3 | .3 | | .1 | .3 | | | | |
| 0 UND | 0 UND | 0 UND | | 0 UND | 0 UND | | | | |
| 1 404.6 | 10 35.1 | 2 169.5 | Sales/Receivables | 0 UND | 0 UND | | | | |
| 16 23.2 | 20 18.3 | 18 20.7 | | 7 53.1 | 37 9.9 | | | | |
| 35 10.5 | 52 7.1 | 40 9.1 | | 38 9.5 | 40 9.2 | | | | |
| 90 4.0 | 80 4.6 | 74 4.9 | Cost of Sales/Inventory | 74 4.9 | 69 5.3 | | | | |
| 183 2.0 | 117 3.1 | 122 3.0 | | 182 2.0 | 101 3.6 | | | | |
| 21 17.4 | 22 16.7 | 0 UND | | 0 UND | 0 UND | | | | |
| 46 8.0 | 41 9.0 | 19 19.3 | Cost of Sales/Payables | 0 UND | 18 20.7 | | | | |
| 122 3.0 | 61 6.0 | 66 5.5 | | 21 17.8 | 58 6.3 | | | | |
| 12.6 | 12.4 | 7.4 | | 5.2 | 5.2 | | | | |
| 30.3 | 22.3 | 21.3 | Sales/Working Capital | 10.7 | 41.9 | | | | |
| -38.8 | -50.9 | -148.9 | | -83.7 | -57.1 | | | | |
| 27.6 | 20.7 | 17.9 | | 24.0 | 4.1 | | | | |
| (36) 4.4 | (35) 6.8 | (43) 7.0 | EBIT/Interest | (11) 9.9 | (10) 2.7 | | | | |
| 2.3 | 2.5 | 1.2 | | 4.7 | -4.4 | | | | |
| | | | Net Profit + Depr., Dep.,<br>Amort./Cur. Mat. L/T/D | | | | | | |
| .3 | .3 | .1 | | .1 | .0 | | | | |
| .8 | .7 | .8 | Fixed/Worth | .6 | .6 | | | | |
| NM | -2.6 | -5.6 | | -4.3 | -.5 | | | | |
| .8 | .7 | .5 | | .1 | .6 | | | | |
| 3.3 | 2.3 | 1.8 | Debt/Worth | .8 | 3.7 | | | | |
| -11.6 | -7.5 | -6.4 | | -5.3 | -3.3 | | | | |
| 145.1 | 110.9 | 84.6 | % Profit Before Taxes/Tangible<br>Net Worth | 87.8 | | | | | |
| (38) 66.4 | (32) 56.7 | (41) 44.3 | | (11) 66.2 | | | | | |
| 30.5 | 19.7 | 14.5 | | 23.9 | | | | | |
| 30.0 | 36.6 | 34.2 | % Profit Before Taxes/Total<br>Assets | 66.1 | 29.0 | | | | |
| 9.3 | 13.0 | 13.0 | | 24.3 | 10.8 | | | | |
| 1.6 | 4.5 | 4.2 | | 5.9 | 1.0 | | | | |
| 69.5 | 43.8 | 89.7 | | 322.7 | 485.2 | | | | |
| 13.2 | 17.0 | 24.6 | Sales/Net Fixed Assets | 27.1 | 54.8 | | | | |
| 5.5 | 8.4 | 10.9 | | 4.0 | 18.6 | | | | |
| 3.8 | 5.0 | 5.0 | | 6.1 | 4.1 | | | | |
| 2.5 | 3.4 | 3.5 | Sales/Total Assets | 3.1 | 3.6 | | | | |
| 1.7 | 2.4 | 2.1 | | 2.1 | 1.9 | | | | |
| .5 | .6 | .8 | | .8 | | | | | |
| (30) 1.2 | (39) 1.6 | (43) 1.4 | % Depr., Dep., Amort./Sales | (12) 1.1 | | | | | |
| 2.7 | 3.1 | 2.6 | | 4.4 | | | | | |
| 2.7 | 2.1 | 1.9 | % Officers', Directors'<br>Owners' Comp/Sales | | | | | | |
| (23) 6.9 | (18) 6.0 | (27) 7.4 | | | | | | | |
| 12.3 | 11.1 | 15.3 | | | | | | | |
| 727408M | 925626M | 1140518M | Net Sales ($) | 9743M | 25272M | 23110M | 46922M | 121466M | 914005M |
| 248819M | 367736M | 591636M | Total Assets ($) | 3457M | 9117M | 8087M | 17905M | 50060M | 503010M |

M = $ thousand    MM = $ million
See Pages 9 through 22 for Explanation of Ratios and Data

## Current Data Sorted by Assets      Comparative Historical Data

Date ranges: 3 (4/1-9/30/11)  ·  52 (10/1/11-3/31/12)

Note: Columns 50-100MM (and most of 10-50MM and 100-250MM) show **DATA NOT AVAILABLE**.

| 0-500M | 500M-2MM | 2-10MM | 10-50MM | 50-100MM | 100-250MM | | 4/1/07-3/31/08 ALL | 4/1/08-3/31/09 ALL |
|---|---|---|---|---|---|---|---|---|
| | | | | | | **Type of Statement** | | |
| | | 1 | | | 2 | Unqualified | 3 | 5 |
| | | 4 | 1 | | | Reviewed | 2 | 2 |
| | 1 | 1 | 1 | | | Compiled | 1 | 2 |
| 10 | 2 | 4 | | | 1 | Tax Returns | 6 | 3 |
| 4 | 7 | 10 | 6 | | | Other | 4 | 10 |
| 14 | 10 | 20 | 8 | | 3 | **NUMBER OF STATEMENTS** | 16 | 22 |
| % | % | % | | | | **ASSETS** | % | % |
| 22.8 | 11.3 | 6.5 | | | | Cash & Equivalents | 10.8 | 11.9 |
| 12.9 | 24.7 | 21.5 | | | | Trade Receivables (net) | 10.1 | 13.8 |
| 40.5 | 24.2 | 34.4 | | | | Inventory | 33.6 | 31.5 |
| .0 | .3 | 5.1 | | | | All Other Current | 6.1 | 12.3 |
| 76.2 | 60.5 | 67.5 | | | | Total Current | 60.6 | 69.6 |
| 14.4 | 9.1 | 15.6 | | | | Fixed Assets (net) | 19.9 | 21.7 |
| 4.9 | 2.1 | 5.0 | | | | Intangibles (net) | 6.7 | 5.6 |
| 4.3 | 28.2 | 11.9 | | | | All Other Non-Current | 12.8 | 3.1 |
| 100.0 | 100.0 | 100.0 | | | | Total | 100.0 | 100.0 |
| | | | | | | **LIABILITIES** | | |
| 18.3 | 14.7 | 8.9 | | | | Notes Payable-Short Term | 12.6 | 11.4 |
| 2.9 | 3.3 | 1.8 | | | | Cur. Mat.-L.T.D. | .9 | 3.1 |
| 22.2 | 30.9 | 31.4 | | | | Trade Payables | 17.3 | 18.0 |
| .0 | .0 | .0 | | | | Income Taxes Payable | .2 | .8 |
| 9.4 | 6.5 | 14.4 | | | | All Other Current | 9.8 | 18.8 |
| 52.9 | 55.4 | 56.5 | | | | Total Current | 40.8 | 52.1 |
| 15.1 | 14.1 | 9.4 | | | | Long-Term Debt | 25.4 | 35.7 |
| .0 | .0 | .0 | | | | Deferred Taxes | .0 | .3 |
| 8.0 | 28.4 | 20.6 | | | | All Other Non-Current | 26.1 | 15.8 |
| 24.1 | 2.1 | 13.5 | | | | Net Worth | 7.7 | -3.8 |
| 100.0 | 100.0 | 100.0 | | | | Total Liabilities & Net Worth | 100.0 | 100.0 |
| | | | | | | **INCOME DATA** | | |
| 100.0 | 100.0 | 100.0 | | | | Net Sales | 100.0 | 100.0 |
| 52.0 | 41.4 | 35.5 | | | | Gross Profit | 51.3 | 48.5 |
| 44.6 | 38.8 | 33.0 | | | | Operating Expenses | 50.5 | 41.1 |
| 7.5 | 2.6 | 2.5 | | | | Operating Profit | .8 | 7.4 |
| .4 | .9 | .3 | | | | All Other Expenses (net) | 1.7 | 1.3 |
| 7.0 | 1.7 | 2.2 | | | | Profit Before Taxes | -.9 | 6.1 |
| | | | | | | **RATIOS** | | |
| 6.6 | 2.1 | 1.6 | | | | | 3.1 | 2.2 |
| 2.1 | .9 | 1.2 | | | | Current | 1.5 | 1.4 |
| 1.2 | .5 | .9 | | | | | 1.0 | .9 |
| 2.7 | 1.4 | .9 | | | | | 1.0 | 1.2 |
| .9 | .5 | .4 | | | | Quick | .3 | .4 |
| .4 | .2 | .1 | | | | | .1 | .1 |
| 0 UND | 6 57.8 | 2 167.5 | | | | | 0 UND | 1 561.1 |
| 0 UND | 19 19.5 | 19 19.1 | | | | Sales/Receivables | 2 165.7 | 8 45.1 |
| 29 12.8 | 38 9.5 | 44 8.3 | | | | | 19 18.8 | 47 7.8 |
| 45 8.1 | 13 28.6 | 27 13.7 | | | | | 25 14.4 | 47 7.7 |
| 61 6.0 | 36 10.0 | 54 6.8 | | | | Cost of Sales/Inventory | 73 5.0 | 81 4.5 |
| 126 2.9 | 69 5.3 | 78 4.7 | | | | | 153 2.4 | 101 3.6 |
| 0 UND | 15 25.1 | 32 11.5 | | | | | 21 17.0 | 11 32.6 |
| 38 9.6 | 34 10.8 | 46 7.9 | | | | Cost of Sales/Payables | 34 10.6 | 32 11.4 |
| 70 5.2 | 114 3.2 | 85 4.3 | | | | | 60 6.1 | 62 5.9 |
| 6.9 | 7.2 | 10.8 | | | | | 5.4 | 6.2 |
| 10.3 | NM | 52.7 | | | | Sales/Working Capital | 19.5 | 18.0 |
| NM | -6.9 | -39.3 | | | | | NM | -70.3 |
| | 24.1 | 25.1 | | | | | 7.3 | 19.1 |
| | 2.8 | 7.8 | | | | EBIT/Interest | (14) 1.6 | (15) 4.8 |
| | -1.5 | -1.9 | | | | | -9.6 | .6 |
| | | | | | | Net Profit + Depr., Dep., Amort./Cur. Mat. L/T/D | | |
| .2 | .0 | .2 | | | | | .2 | .2 |
| .6 | .6 | 30.4 | | | | Fixed/Worth | .4 | 1.3 |
| -1.3 | -1.4 | -.5 | | | | | NM | -.8 |
| .6 | 3.8 | 1.9 | | | | | 1.0 | 1.3 |
| 1.9 | 15.0 | 165.1 | | | | Debt/Worth | 4.0 | 1.7 |
| -8.1 | -7.4 | -8.3 | | | | | NM | -4.7 |
| | | 98.3 | | | | | 248.7 | 112.8 |
| | (11) | 36.3 | | | | % Profit Before Taxes/Tangible Net Worth | (12) 31.0 | (13) 50.7 |
| | | 24.6 | | | | | -7.4 | 21.8 |
| 57.7 | 14.2 | 23.2 | | | | | 21.4 | 39.4 |
| 35.9 | 4.3 | 5.9 | | | | % Profit Before Taxes/Total Assets | 3.6 | 17.2 |
| 5.4 | -6.9 | -3.3 | | | | | -10.9 | 1.7 |
| 68.2 | UND | 144.8 | | | | | 73.3 | 95.1 |
| 42.4 | 303.8 | 48.7 | | | | Sales/Net Fixed Assets | 24.8 | 13.3 |
| 17.9 | 24.2 | 16.6 | | | | | 6.6 | 7.9 |
| 7.1 | 5.8 | 4.6 | | | | | 4.9 | 5.1 |
| 4.4 | 3.8 | 3.6 | | | | Sales/Total Assets | 2.6 | 3.2 |
| 3.2 | 2.3 | 2.7 | | | | | 1.2 | 2.3 |
| | | .1 | | | | | .3 | .4 |
| | (19) | .7 | | | | % Depr., Dep., Amort./Sales | (12) 1.1 | (16) 1.0 |
| | | 1.1 | | | | | 2.9 | 2.5 |
| | | | | | | % Officers', Directors' Owners' Comp/Sales | | |
| 13699M | 48387M | 339329M | 509621M | | 674853M | Net Sales ($) | 710699M | 2716142M |
| 2970M | 11320M | 80871M | 149055M | | 383782M | Total Assets ($) | 341564M | 963324M |

## Comparative Historical Data      Current Data Sorted by Sales

| H1 | H2 | H3 | Type of Statement | 0-1MM | 1-3MM | 3-5MM | 5-10MM | 10-25MM | 25MM & OVER |
|---|---|---|---|---|---|---|---|---|---|
| 5 | 5 | 4 | Unqualified | | | | | 1 | 3 |
| 2 | 1 | 5 | Reviewed | | | | | 3 | 2 |
| 3 | 6 | 2 | Compiled | | | | 1 | 1 | |
| 14 | 10 | 16 | Tax Returns | | | | 2 | 3 | |
| 16 | 16 | 28 | Other | 6 | 3 | 2 | 2 | 5 | 8 |
| | | | | 2 | 7 | | 4 | | |
| 4/1/09-3/31/10 ALL | 4/1/10-3/31/11 ALL | 4/1/11-3/31/12 ALL | | 3 (4/1-9/30/11) | | | 52 (10/1/11-3/31/12) | | |
| 40 | 38 | 55 | **NUMBER OF STATEMENTS** | 8 | 10 | 6 | 6 | 12 | 13 |
| % | % | % | **ASSETS** | % | % | % | % | % | % |
| 13.3 | 17.5 | 15.2 | Cash & Equivalents | | 12.1 | | | 6.8 | 22.5 |
| 12.5 | 12.2 | 18.0 | Trade Receivables (net) | | 16.2 | | | 22.7 | 11.9 |
| 27.5 | 27.1 | 31.8 | Inventory | | 30.5 | | | 39.8 | 27.7 |
| 7.0 | 5.6 | 3.3 | All Other Current | | .0 | | | 3.0 | 6.5 |
| 60.3 | 62.4 | 68.3 | Total Current | | 58.8 | | | 72.4 | 68.6 |
| 20.7 | 19.2 | 14.1 | Fixed Assets (net) | | 4.9 | | | 16.5 | 18.4 |
| 9.2 | 9.8 | 4.8 | Intangibles (net) | | 2.3 | | | 9.2 | 1.1 |
| 9.8 | 8.6 | 12.8 | All Other Non-Current | | 34.1 | | | 2.0 | 11.9 |
| 100.0 | 100.0 | 100.0 | Total | | 100.0 | | | 100.0 | 100.0 |
| | | | **LIABILITIES** | | | | | | |
| 9.2 | 8.8 | 10.7 | Notes Payable-Short Term | | 1.0 | | | 11.4 | 3.2 |
| 5.5 | 3.8 | 3.3 | Cur. Mat.-L.T.D. | | 2.2 | | | 2.6 | 6.0 |
| 23.7 | 17.7 | 25.2 | Trade Payables | | 39.8 | | | 33.0 | 14.3 |
| .0 | .1 | .0 | Income Taxes Payable | | .0 | | | .0 | .1 |
| 15.8 | 13.2 | 10.8 | All Other Current | | 6.7 | | | 12.3 | 13.1 |
| 54.3 | 43.6 | 50.0 | Total Current | | 49.7 | | | 59.2 | 36.7 |
| 21.1 | 34.1 | 16.2 | Long-Term Debt | | 15.1 | | | 7.7 | 28.4 |
| .0 | .2 | .0 | Deferred Taxes | | .0 | | | .0 | .0 |
| 17.3 | 11.1 | 15.2 | All Other Non-Current | | 14.9 | | | 15.8 | 2.8 |
| 7.3 | 11.1 | 18.6 | Net Worth | | 20.3 | | | 17.2 | 32.0 |
| 100.0 | 100.0 | 100.0 | Total Liabilities & Net Worth | | 100.0 | | | 100.0 | 100.0 |
| | | | **INCOME DATA** | | | | | | |
| 100.0 | 100.0 | 100.0 | Net Sales | | 100.0 | | | 100.0 | 100.0 |
| 54.7 | 52.1 | 44.4 | Gross Profit | | 41.7 | | | 37.4 | 48.1 |
| 48.7 | 47.6 | 38.2 | Operating Expenses | | 36.8 | | | 36.0 | 34.4 |
| 6.1 | 4.6 | 6.2 | Operating Profit | | 5.0 | | | 1.4 | 13.7 |
| 1.2 | .2 | .3 | All Other Expenses (net) | | .6 | | | .3 | -.2 |
| 4.9 | 4.4 | 5.8 | Profit Before Taxes | | 4.3 | | | 1.1 | 13.9 |
| | | | **RATIOS** | | | | | | |
| 3.0 | 2.9 | 2.9 | | | 2.7 | | | 1.5 | 3.8 |
| 1.5 | 1.8 | 1.5 | Current | | 1.3 | | | 1.3 | 2.7 |
| .9 | 1.0 | .8 | | | .4 | | | .9 | .9 |
| 1.5 | 1.8 | 1.4 | | | 1.2 | | | 1.0 | 2.7 |
| .5 (37) | .7 (54) | .6 | Quick | | .3 | | | .4 (12) | .9 |
| .1 | .1 | .3 | | | .3 | | | .1 | .4 |
| 0 UND | 0 999.8 | 0 999.8 | | 0 UND | | | 2 171.6 | 0 999.8 | |
| 3 136.8 | 5 70.7 | 16 23.3 | Sales/Receivables | 18 20.1 | | | 8 47.2 | 17 21.8 | |
| 17 21.0 | 23 15.8 | 34 10.7 | | 38 9.7 | | | 36 10.1 | 29 12.6 | |
| 26 13.9 | 26 14.2 | 32 11.3 | | 32 11.3 | | | 27 13.7 | 28 13.2 | |
| 59 6.2 | 51 7.1 | 54 6.7 | Cost of Sales/Inventory | 59 6.2 | | | 52 7.0 | 54 6.7 | |
| 104 3.5 | 84 4.4 | 99 3.7 | | 107 3.4 | | | 96 3.8 | 114 3.2 | |
| 4 103.1 | 10 35.0 | 16 22.7 | | 45 8.2 | | | 23 16.2 | 9 42.8 | |
| 24 15.2 | 31 11.7 | 40 9.1 | Cost of Sales/Payables | 83 4.4 | | | 37 9.8 | 35 10.4 | |
| 60 6.1 | 52 7.0 | 79 4.6 | | 111 3.3 | | | 70 5.2 | 52 7.0 | |
| 11.2 | 5.7 | 7.1 | | 6.2 | | | 15.0 | 3.8 | |
| 27.2 | 14.2 | 19.0 | Sales/Working Capital | NM | | | 26.5 | 7.4 | |
| -48.1 | NM | -46.3 | | -5.2 | | | -105.0 | -162.4 | |
| 20.0 | 9.4 | 22.4 | | | | | 24.6 | | |
| (30) 3.6 | (29) 3.3 | (43) 8.6 | EBIT/Interest | | | | 2.5 | | |
| 1.2 | 1.5 | 1.1 | | | | | -.4 | | |
| | | | Net Profit + Depr., Dep., Amort./Cur. Mat. L/T/D | | | | | | |
| .2 | .2 | .2 | | | .1 | | | .4 | .1 |
| 1.0 | .7 | .7 | Fixed/Worth | | .2 | | | NM | .2 |
| -.5 | -.3 | -1.4 | | | -.1 | | | -.5 | 1.7 |
| .9 | .5 | 1.1 | | | 1.1 | | | 2.1 | .3 |
| 2.5 | 3.2 | 3.7 | Debt/Worth | | 5.7 | | | NM | .7 |
| -2.3 | -2.7 | -9.4 | | | -7.4 | | | -8.3 | 2.4 |
| 105.3 | 89.1 | 98.3 | | | | | | | 94.6 |
| (25) 45.0 | (23) 27.0 | (35) 55.6 | % Profit Before Taxes/Tangible Net Worth | | | | | (11) | 48.1 |
| 18.7 | 8.4 | 24.6 | | | | | | | 29.9 |
| 32.7 | 35.0 | 37.3 | % Profit Before Taxes/Total Assets | | 32.2 | | | 20.1 | 70.7 |
| 16.8 | 11.5 | 13.9 | | | 12.7 | | | 2.6 | 35.8 |
| .6 | 1.6 | 1.2 | | | 4.5 | | | -2.6 | 14.1 |
| 104.0 | 74.5 | 155.3 | | | UND | | | 144.8 | 123.2 |
| 25.9 | 21.7 | 50.9 | Sales/Net Fixed Assets | | 303.8 | | | 56.3 | 36.9 |
| 10.5 | 12.9 | 18.2 | | | 38.7 | | | 23.5 | 13.3 |
| 7.1 | 5.5 | 5.1 | | | 4.4 | | | 5.8 | 6.1 |
| 4.0 | 3.8 | 3.4 | Sales/Total Assets | | 2.5 | | | 4.0 | 2.6 |
| 2.4 | 2.2 | 2.4 | | | 1.7 | | | 3.4 | 2.1 |
| .5 | .6 | .3 | | | | | | .1 | .3 |
| (26) 1.0 | (26) 1.2 | (40) .7 | % Depr., Dep., Amort./Sales | | | | | .2 (10) | .6 |
| 2.3 | 1.7 | 1.2 | | | | | | .8 | 1.1 |
| 2.7 | 2.7 | 1.2 | | | | | | | |
| (14) 9.8 | (14) 9.3 | (18) 3.9 | % Officers', Directors' Owners' Comp/Sales | | | | | | |
| 14.6 | 19.5 | 7.3 | | | | | | | |
| 1355877M | 1581069M | 1585889M | Net Sales ($) | 4054M | 16562M | 24772M | 41932M | 172963M | 1325606M |
| 444400M | 541408M | 627998M | Total Assets ($) | 1030M | 8296M | 12284M | 13699M | 45264M | 547425M |

M = $ thousand    MM = $ million
See Pages 9 through 22 for Explanation of Ratios and Data

## Current Data Sorted by Assets     Comparative Historical Data

| 1 10 7 | 3 4 9 | 2 3 3 3 5 | 5 | 2 | | Type of Statement | 2 1 6 2 11 | 6 1 5 8 12 |
|---|---|---|---|---|---|---|---|---|
| | 7 (4/1-9/30/11) | | 52 (10/1/11-3/31/12) | | | Unqualified / Reviewed / Compiled / Tax Returns / Other | 4/1/07-3/31/08 ALL | 4/1/08-3/31/09 ALL |
| 0-500M | 500M-2MM | 2-10MM | 10-50MM | 50-100MM | 100-250MM | | | |
| 18 | 16 | 16 | 5 | 4 | | NUMBER OF STATEMENTS | 22 | 32 |
| % | % | % | % | % | % | **ASSETS** | % | % |
| 17.1 | 7.3 | 8.3 | | | | Cash & Equivalents | 7.5 | 7.7 |
| 23.6 | 36.1 | 36.7 | | | | Trade Receivables (net) | 33.5 | 28.8 |
| 18.5 | 23.8 | 28.3 | | | | Inventory | 20.5 | 17.9 |
| .1 | .3 | 2.3 | | | | All Other Current | 2.7 | 4.6 |
| 59.4 | 67.6 | 75.6 | | | | Total Current | 64.2 | 59.0 |
| 31.1 | 14.3 | 16.2 | | | | Fixed Assets (net) | 18.9 | 16.8 |
| 3.0 | 15.1 | 3.0 | | | | Intangibles (net) | 9.6 | 17.0 |
| 6.5 | 3.0 | 5.1 | | | | All Other Non-Current | 7.3 | 7.2 |
| 100.0 | 100.0 | 100.0 | | | | Total | 100.0 | 100.0 |
| | | | | | | **LIABILITIES** | | |
| 7.3 | 10.8 | 13.1 | | | | Notes Payable-Short Term | 25.7 | 13.0 |
| 5.5 | 2.9 | 3.3 | | | | Cur. Mat.-L.T.D. | 4.1 | 3.4 |
| 11.3 | 26.6 | 21.4 | | | | Trade Payables | 20.3 | 21.0 |
| .0 | .0 | .0 | | | | Income Taxes Payable | 1.1 | 1.0 |
| 4.3 | 7.6 | 8.8 | | | | All Other Current | 9.5 | 9.2 |
| 28.4 | 47.9 | 46.6 | | | | Total Current | 60.7 | 47.5 |
| 51.9 | 30.9 | 8.5 | | | | Long-Term Debt | 12.1 | 11.2 |
| .0 | .0 | .7 | | | | Deferred Taxes | .4 | .6 |
| 6.5 | 3.6 | 2.6 | | | | All Other Non-Current | 5.2 | 3.5 |
| 13.2 | 17.6 | 41.6 | | | | Net Worth | 21.6 | 37.1 |
| 100.0 | 100.0 | 100.0 | | | | Total Liabilities & Net Worth | 100.0 | 100.0 |
| | | | | | | **INCOME DATA** | | |
| 100.0 | 100.0 | 100.0 | | | | Net Sales | 100.0 | 100.0 |
| 63.2 | 50.9 | 52.5 | | | | Gross Profit | 53.9 | 54.9 |
| 54.0 | 44.2 | 45.1 | | | | Operating Expenses | 50.4 | 49.2 |
| 9.3 | 6.7 | 7.4 | | | | Operating Profit | 3.5 | 5.7 |
| .9 | 1.2 | .1 | | | | All Other Expenses (net) | 1.5 | 1.0 |
| 8.3 | 5.5 | 7.3 | | | | Profit Before Taxes | 1.9 | 4.7 |
| | | | | | | **RATIOS** | | |
| 8.7 | 3.9 | 3.0 | | | | | 2.4 | 1.7 |
| 3.7 | 2.3 | 1.5 | | | | Current | 1.1 | 1.2 |
| 1.1 | 1.0 | 1.3 | | | | | .9 | .9 |
| 4.8 | 2.3 | 1.9 | | | | | 1.3 | 1.3 |
| 2.7 | 1.2 | 1.0 | | | | Quick | .9 | .9 |
| .7 | .6 | .6 | | | | | .4 | .5 |
| 0 UND | 15 24.4 | 20 18.7 | | | | | 22 16.8 | 12 30.2 |
| 14 26.7 | 40 9.2 | 40 9.1 | | | | Sales/Receivables | 37 9.9 | 42 8.7 |
| 59 6.2 | 49 7.5 | 104 3.5 | | | | | 71 5.1 | 56 6.5 |
| 0 UND | 6 63.5 | 31 11.6 | | | | | 26 13.8 | 20 18.3 |
| 20 18.3 | 32 11.3 | 89 4.1 | | | | Cost of Sales/Inventory | 37 9.7 | 40 9.0 |
| 66 5.5 | 62 5.9 | 122 3.0 | | | | | 81 4.5 | 55 6.7 |
| 0 UND | 4 95.2 | 24 15.5 | | | | | 24 14.9 | 27 13.6 |
| 17 22.0 | 31 11.8 | 47 7.8 | | | | Cost of Sales/Payables | 57 6.5 | 60 6.1 |
| 54 6.8 | 81 4.5 | 89 4.1 | | | | | 107 3.4 | 81 4.5 |
| 6.3 | 6.4 | 4.2 | | | | | 8.1 | 9.1 |
| 8.7 | 11.8 | 10.6 | | | | Sales/Working Capital | 68.6 | 24.0 |
| 77.0 | NM | 33.2 | | | | | -76.5 | -48.0 |
| 32.3 | 74.9 | 64.0 | | | | | 22.6 | 34.0 |
| (15) 10.5 | (13) 7.3 | (14) 15.7 | | | | EBIT/Interest | (21) 4.8 | (27) 5.9 |
| 5.2 | 1.1 | 7.2 | | | | | -.5 | 2.1 |
| | | | | | | Net Profit + Depr., Dep., Amort./Cur. Mat. L/T/D | | |
| .3 | .3 | .1 | | | | | .3 | .3 |
| 1.3 | 1.1 | .4 | | | | Fixed/Worth | .8 | .8 |
| NM | -.4 | .9 | | | | | NM | -.9 |
| .9 | .9 | .5 | | | | | 1.1 | 1.0 |
| 2.6 | 2.1 | 1.4 | | | | Debt/Worth | 3.0 | 2.6 |
| NM | -3.5 | 2.6 | | | | | NM | -11.7 |
| 158.3 | | 79.0 | | | | | 57.2 | 90.6 |
| (14) 57.2 | | (14) 50.3 | | | | % Profit Before Taxes/Tangible Net Worth | (17) 40.8 | (23) 28.7 |
| 18.1 | | 14.6 | | | | | -8.9 | 15.6 |
| 65.6 | 23.4 | 30.5 | | | | | 20.5 | 24.7 |
| 24.6 | 15.2 | 18.2 | | | | % Profit Before Taxes/Total Assets | 5.2 | 7.7 |
| 3.9 | 2.6 | 3.7 | | | | | -5.6 | 2.6 |
| 40.0 | 166.2 | 156.9 | | | | | 52.0 | 97.9 |
| 23.4 | 24.3 | 60.4 | | | | Sales/Net Fixed Assets | 18.3 | 26.3 |
| 7.8 | 15.2 | 6.4 | | | | | 9.0 | 9.3 |
| 5.8 | 5.3 | 4.5 | | | | | 4.0 | 3.8 |
| 4.2 | 3.6 | 3.3 | | | | Sales/Total Assets | 2.9 | 2.7 |
| 2.9 | 2.4 | 1.8 | | | | | 2.0 | 2.0 |
| .3 | | .3 | | | | | .7 | .7 |
| (11) 1.3 | | (12) 2.0 | | | | % Depr., Dep., Amort./Sales | (19) 1.5 | (21) 1.1 |
| 2.1 | | 3.7 | | | | | 4.0 | 4.0 |
| | | | | | | | | 2.3 |
| | | | | | | % Officers', Directors' Owners' Comp/Sales | (16) 7.0 | |
| | | | | | | | 18.8 | |
| 17236M | 60645M | 224590M | 282446M | 396394M | | Net Sales ($) | 331576M | 1014568M |
| 4477M | 16177M | 75148M | 127807M | 283069M | | Total Assets ($) | 171495M | 422442M |

Note: In columns 10-50MM, 50-100MM, and 100-250MM the notation "DATA NOT AVAILABLE" appears across the ASSETS, LIABILITIES, INCOME DATA and RATIOS sections.

## Comparative Historical Data | Current Data Sorted by Sales

| | | | Type of Statement | | | | | | |
|---|---|---|---|---|---|---|---|---|---|
| 4 | 3 | 4 | Unqualified | | | | 1 | 1 | 2 |
| 2 | 4 | 3 | Reviewed | | | 1 | 1 | | 1 |
| 5 | 8 | 7 | Compiled | | 2 | | 3 | 1 | 1 |
| 9 | 13 | 17 | Tax Returns | 7 | 5 | 2 | 1 | 2 | |
| 11 | 25 | 28 | Other | 6 | 4 | 6 | 1 | 4 | 6 |
| 4/1/09- | 4/1/10- | 4/1/11- | | | 7 (4/1-9/30/11) | | 52 (10/1/11-3/31/12) | | |
| 3/31/10 | 3/31/11 | 3/31/12 | | | | | | | |
| ALL | ALL | ALL | | 0-1MM | 1-3MM | 3-5MM | 5-10MM | 10-25MM | 25MM & OVER |
| 31 | 53 | 59 | NUMBER OF STATEMENTS | 13 | 11 | 9 | 8 | 8 | 10 |
| % | % | % | ASSETS | % | % | % | % | % | % |
| 8.6 | 15.8 | 11.5 | Cash & Equivalents | 14.6 | 18.5 | | | | 12.1 |
| 32.5 | 20.6 | 30.3 | Trade Receivables (net) | 17.4 | 30.9 | | | | 30.4 |
| 22.8 | 22.8 | 22.6 | Inventory | 20.1 | 19.1 | | | | 18.1 |
| 6.2 | 2.8 | 1.1 | All Other Current | .1 | .0 | | | | 2.0 |
| 70.1 | 61.9 | 65.6 | Total Current | 52.2 | 68.5 | | | | 62.6 |
| 18.8 | 20.9 | 20.1 | Fixed Assets (net) | 30.3 | 21.8 | | | | 12.1 |
| 5.2 | 13.2 | 9.0 | Intangibles (net) | 9.6 | 7.9 | | | | 18.8 |
| 5.9 | 4.0 | 5.3 | All Other Non-Current | 7.9 | 1.8 | | | | 6.5 |
| 100.0 | 100.0 | 100.0 | Total | 100.0 | 100.0 | | | | 100.0 |
| | | | LIABILITIES | | | | | | |
| 7.9 | 15.8 | 9.4 | Notes Payable-Short Term | 9.0 | 1.5 | | | | 7.7 |
| 3.9 | 4.2 | 3.7 | Cur. Mat.-L.T.D. | 7.6 | 2.4 | | | | 1.5 |
| 29.2 | 19.1 | 19.6 | Trade Payables | 9.0 | 14.9 | | | | 25.1 |
| 1.5 | 1.3 | .1 | Income Taxes Payable | .0 | .0 | | | | .6 |
| 17.4 | 14.7 | 7.0 | All Other Current | 3.0 | 9.4 | | | | 9.1 |
| 59.8 | 55.1 | 39.9 | Total Current | 28.6 | 28.2 | | | | 44.0 |
| 17.1 | 20.2 | 27.6 | Long-Term Debt | 58.8 | 35.4 | | | | 6.1 |
| .3 | .7 | .3 | Deferred Taxes | .0 | .0 | | | | .4 |
| 6.0 | 3.7 | 7.5 | All Other Non-Current | 8.5 | 5.9 | | | | 9.3 |
| 16.8 | 20.3 | 24.8 | Net Worth | 4.1 | 30.6 | | | | 40.3 |
| 100.0 | 100.0 | 100.0 | Total Liabilities & Net Worth | 100.0 | 100.0 | | | | 100.0 |
| | | | INCOME DATA | | | | | | |
| 100.0 | 100.0 | 100.0 | Net Sales | 100.0 | 100.0 | | | | 100.0 |
| 52.9 | 52.6 | 53.3 | Gross Profit | 62.9 | 62.0 | | | | 40.1 |
| 47.6 | 47.2 | 45.5 | Operating Expenses | 51.2 | 55.7 | | | | 33.5 |
| 5.2 | 5.4 | 7.8 | Operating Profit | 11.7 | 6.3 | | | | 6.6 |
| 1.6 | 1.5 | 1.2 | All Other Expenses (net) | 1.7 | .4 | | | | 3.0 |
| 3.7 | 3.9 | 6.6 | Profit Before Taxes | 9.9 | 5.9 | | | | 3.6 |
| | | | RATIOS | | | | | | |
| 2.3 | 2.5 | 4.0 | | 10.1 | 4.9 | | | | 1.8 |
| 1.4 | 1.5 | 2.2 | Current | 3.4 | 4.0 | | | | 1.4 |
| 1.0 | .8 | 1.3 | | .9 | 1.5 | | | | 1.3 |
| 1.2 | 1.5 | 2.6 | | 4.5 | 4.8 | | | | 1.5 |
| (30) .8 | .9 | 1.3 | Quick | 2.5 | 2.3 | | | | 1.1 |
| .5 | .4 | .7 | | .5 | 1.1 | | | | .8 |
| 15 24.3 | 0 UND | 5 68.3 | | 0 UND | 0 999.8 | | | | 36 10.1 |
| 52 7.0 | 24 15.0 | 39 9.4 | Sales/Receivables | 2 218.7 | 23 16.2 | | | | 51 7.1 |
| 61 5.9 | 45 8.1 | 58 6.3 | | 63 5.8 | 46 8.0 | | | | 76 4.8 |
| 14 26.6 | 19 19.5 | 7 55.3 | | 0 UND | 0 UND | | | | 6 63.4 |
| 43 8.5 | 40 9.2 | 38 9.5 | Cost of Sales/Inventory | 22 16.5 | 26 14.2 | | | | 24 15.0 |
| 63 5.8 | 80 4.6 | 79 4.6 | | 74 4.9 | 60 6.1 | | | | 81 4.5 |
| 26 14.1 | 12 30.9 | 10 36.9 | | 0 UND | 10 36.9 | | | | 33 11.0 |
| 50 7.3 | 37 9.9 | 35 10.3 | Cost of Sales/Payables | 0 UND | 36 10.1 | | | | 47 7.8 |
| 99 3.7 | 68 5.3 | 74 4.9 | | 48 7.6 | 52 7.0 | | | | 73 5.0 |
| 7.9 | 6.5 | 6.2 | | 6.3 | 5.7 | | | | 6.7 |
| 17.4 | 20.0 | 10.2 | Sales/Working Capital | 11.7 | 7.3 | | | | 11.4 |
| -135.8 | -39.0 | 38.9 | | NM | 15.5 | | | | 34.7 |
| 14.9 | 13.6 | 38.7 | | 16.0 | | | | | |
| (25) 4.1 | (43) 4.5 | (50) 9.8 | EBIT/Interest | (11) 9.5 | | | | | |
| 1.7 | .9 | 1.8 | | 1.4 | | | | | |
| | | | Net Profit + Depr., Dep., Amort./Cur. Mat. L/T/D | | | | | | |
| .2 | .2 | .2 | | .4 | .2 | | | | .2 |
| .9 | .8 | .7 | Fixed/Worth | 4.8 | 1.3 | | | | .8 |
| -3.0 | NM | -1.3 | | -1.2 | -7.0 | | | | -.4 |
| 1.3 | .9 | .8 | | 1.3 | .9 | | | | .6 |
| 4.3 | 2.1 | 1.9 | Debt/Worth | 5.5 | 1.8 | | | | 2.2 |
| -13.8 | -4.2 | -10.7 | | -6.9 | -341.0 | | | | -9.3 |
| 95.8 | 76.1 | 77.7 | % Profit Before Taxes/Tangible | | | | | | |
| (21) 36.5 | (38) 24.6 | (42) 42.5 | Net Worth | | | | | | |
| 13.4 | .6 | 14.5 | | | | | | | |
| 23.3 | 26.4 | 29.8 | % Profit Before Taxes/Total | 65.9 | 36.0 | | | | 27.6 |
| 8.9 | 7.4 | 17.7 | Assets | 27.7 | 12.4 | | | | 5.8 |
| .4 | -.9 | 2.9 | | 9.5 | 2.4 | | | | 2.0 |
| 82.3 | 113.6 | 78.5 | | 28.1 | 68.2 | | | | 133.8 |
| 26.6 | 24.4 | 24.2 | Sales/Net Fixed Assets | 22.6 | 17.2 | | | | 20.1 |
| 13.3 | 8.4 | 9.3 | | 9.0 | 7.4 | | | | 8.3 |
| 4.5 | 5.7 | 4.9 | | 5.6 | 5.4 | | | | 4.6 |
| 3.4 | 3.5 | 3.2 | Sales/Total Assets | 4.1 | 2.9 | | | | 2.1 |
| 2.0 | 1.8 | 2.1 | | 2.7 | 2.7 | | | | 1.1 |
| .6 | .6 | .3 | | | | | | | |
| (23) 1.2 | (37) 1.5 | (38) 1.0 | % Depr., Dep., Amort./Sales | | | | | | |
| 5.8 | 3.3 | 2.9 | | | | | | | |
| 3.7 | 3.0 | 2.1 | % Officers', Directors' | | | | | | |
| (16) 5.7 | (25) 5.0 | (23) 5.5 | Owners' Comp/Sales | | | | | | |
| 11.9 | 10.6 | 8.3 | | | | | | | |
| 1066570M | 1085754M | 981311M | Net Sales ($) | 8044M | 20633M | 31754M | 62153M | 142292M | 716435M |
| 405311M | 766636M | 506678M | Total Assets ($) | 3260M | 5749M | 20713M | 20063M | 46835M | 410058M |

© RMA 2012                     M = $ thousand   MM = $ million
See Pages 9 through 22 for Explanation of Ratios and Data

## Current Data Sorted by Assets      Comparative Historical Data

| | | | | | | Type of Statement | | |
|---|---|---|---|---|---|---|---|---|
| 1 | 2 | 5 | 41 | 28 | 24 | Unqualified | 72 | 108 |
| 2 | 12 | 35 | 54 | 6 | | Reviewed | 75 | 130 |
| 38 | 69 | 67 | 18 | 1 | | Compiled | 170 | 189 |
| 298 | 257 | 100 | 4 | | 1 | Tax Returns | 366 | 433 |
| 106 | 164 | 115 | 73 | 26 | 34 | Other | 286 | 362 |
| | 188 (4/1-9/30/11) | | 1,393 (10/1/11-3/31/12) | | | | 4/1/07-3/31/08 | 4/1/08-3/31/09 |
| 0-500M | 500M-2MM | 2-10MM | 10-50MM | 50-100MM | 100-250MM | | ALL | ALL |
| 445 | 504 | 322 | 190 | 61 | 59 | NUMBER OF STATEMENTS | 969 | 1222 |
| % | % | % | % | % | % | ASSETS | % | % |
| 18.3 | 10.7 | 9.0 | 11.2 | 10.8 | 6.1 | Cash & Equivalents | 11.1 | 12.6 |
| 4.1 | 3.9 | 7.4 | 10.2 | 9.3 | 7.4 | Trade Receivables (net) | 7.1 | 6.5 |
| 41.7 | 14.4 | 12.1 | 12.5 | 9.2 | 10.0 | Inventory | 19.8 | 17.4 |
| 1.5 | 1.9 | 1.5 | 2.6 | 1.2 | 1.7 | All Other Current | 2.0 | 2.4 |
| 65.5 | 30.8 | 29.9 | 36.5 | 30.6 | 25.2 | Total Current | 40.0 | 38.9 |
| 17.9 | 52.7 | 57.0 | 50.7 | 59.7 | 60.4 | Fixed Assets (net) | 47.0 | 47.2 |
| 10.1 | 9.0 | 6.2 | 4.3 | 4.2 | 6.1 | Intangibles (net) | 6.5 | 6.7 |
| 6.5 | 7.4 | 6.9 | 8.5 | 5.6 | 8.3 | All Other Non-Current | 6.5 | 7.2 |
| 100.0 | 100.0 | 100.0 | 100.0 | 100.0 | 100.0 | Total | 100.0 | 100.0 |
| | | | | | | LIABILITIES | | |
| 8.6 | 3.3 | 2.4 | 3.6 | 2.4 | 1.9 | Notes Payable-Short Term | 4.7 | 4.4 |
| 2.1 | 2.9 | 4.1 | 4.1 | 5.2 | 4.0 | Cur. Mat.-L.T.D. | 3.2 | 3.3 |
| 21.2 | 12.0 | 14.6 | 20.3 | 16.5 | 16.5 | Trade Payables | 18.2 | 14.7 |
| .1 | .1 | .0 | .2 | .0 | .1 | Income Taxes Payable | .2 | .1 |
| 18.5 | 9.4 | 6.6 | 6.7 | 6.4 | 6.3 | All Other Current | 8.8 | 10.2 |
| 50.5 | 27.6 | 27.8 | 34.8 | 30.6 | 28.9 | Total Current | 35.1 | 32.8 |
| 19.1 | 50.5 | 44.8 | 28.8 | 33.5 | 30.9 | Long-Term Debt | 38.0 | 37.4 |
| .0 | .0 | .2 | .7 | 1.0 | .6 | Deferred Taxes | .2 | .2 |
| 22.8 | 8.6 | 5.9 | 3.7 | 3.9 | 5.4 | All Other Non-Current | 11.0 | 9.0 |
| 7.5 | 13.3 | 21.4 | 32.0 | 31.0 | 34.1 | Net Worth | 15.6 | 20.7 |
| 100.0 | 100.0 | 100.0 | 100.0 | 100.0 | 100.0 | Total Liabilties & Net Worth | 100.0 | 100.0 |
| | | | | | | INCOME DATA | | |
| 100.0 | 100.0 | 100.0 | 100.0 | 100.0 | 100.0 | Net Sales | 100.0 | 100.0 |
| 12.6 | 12.2 | 12.1 | 10.3 | 10.9 | 8.6 | Gross Profit | 12.7 | 12.3 |
| 12.5 | 10.9 | 11.0 | 9.6 | 8.8 | 7.3 | Operating Expenses | 11.8 | 10.8 |
| .1 | 1.2 | 1.1 | .7 | 2.1 | 1.3 | Operating Profit | .9 | 1.4 |
| -.4 | .4 | .3 | -.1 | .5 | .0 | All Other Expenses (net) | .3 | .4 |
| .5 | .8 | .9 | .8 | 1.5 | 1.3 | Profit Before Taxes | .6 | 1.1 |
| | | | | | | RATIOS | | |
| 6.9 | 3.5 | 2.3 | 1.6 | 1.3 | 1.1 | | 2.2 | 2.5 |
| 2.1 | 1.6 | 1.2 | 1.1 | .9 | .9 | Current | 1.2 | 1.2 |
| 1.0 | .7 | .7 | .8 | .8 | .6 | | .8 | .8 |
| 1.7 | 1.4 | 1.3 | 1.0 | .9 | .8 | | 1.0 | 1.2 |
| (440) .7 | (501) .6 | .6 | .6 | .6 | .4 | Quick | (967) .5 | (1219) .6 |
| .2 | .2 | .3 | .4 | .4 | .2 | | .2 | .2 |
| 0 UND | 0 UND | 0 UND | 2 160.3 | 3 143.0 | 2 148.1 | | 0 UND | 0 UND |
| 0 UND | 0 UND | 1 315.3 | 4 92.9 | 4 101.0 | 4 98.0 | Sales/Receivables | 1 299.5 | 1 371.5 |
| 1 442.2 | 2 241.5 | 5 80.8 | 7 54.0 | 6 63.0 | 7 55.2 | | 5 80.1 | 3 107.8 |
| 5 73.5 | 5 74.7 | 4 82.1 | 4 81.5 | 3 106.0 | 4 101.6 | | 5 69.2 | 4 89.8 |
| 8 44.4 | 8 46.7 | 7 52.3 | 7 50.9 | 6 59.0 | 6 60.6 | Cost of Sales/Inventory | 8 45.1 | 7 56.1 |
| 14 26.9 | 12 30.0 | 11 34.0 | 10 36.3 | 9 42.6 | 11 34.6 | | 12 29.3 | 10 35.7 |
| 0 UND | 0 UND | 2 186.0 | 8 46.0 | 8 46.3 | 10 38.4 | | 2 227.7 | 1 308.5 |
| 2 157.0 | 4 102.6 | 6 59.3 | 12 31.5 | 11 33.7 | 12 31.5 | Cost of Sales/Payables | 7 49.8 | 5 71.9 |
| 7 51.9 | 8 44.5 | 11 31.8 | 14 25.7 | 13 27.6 | 15 24.1 | | 13 28.6 | 9 38.9 |
| 31.0 | 33.3 | 39.0 | 46.2 | 79.2 | 259.2 | | 40.1 | 40.2 |
| 68.0 | 85.9 | 126.5 | 389.7 | -329.2 | -177.4 | Sales/Working Capital | 154.4 | 150.3 |
| -719.8 | -98.6 | -82.2 | -88.2 | -74.7 | -52.3 | | -83.3 | -100.9 |
| 10.4 | 4.0 | 4.7 | 7.3 | 6.1 | 9.6 | | 3.6 | 5.7 |
| (179) 2.4 | (415) 1.8 | (297) 2.1 | (180) 2.7 | (60) 3.5 | (58) 4.6 | EBIT/Interest | (776) 1.7 | (999) 2.4 |
| -.5 | .9 | 1.0 | 1.5 | 2.0 | 1.9 | | .7 | 1.1 |
| | 2.8 | 3.5 | 3.1 | 4.3 | 6.0 | | 5.3 | 4.3 |
| | (16) 1.5 | (32) 2.0 | (57) 2.1 | (24) 1.9 | (12) 2.8 | Net Profit + Depr., Dep., Amort./Cur. Mat. L/T/D | (118) 2.6 | (151) 2.4 |
| | 1.1 | 1.1 | 1.2 | 1.0 | 1.0 | | 1.3 | 1.3 |
| .0 | 1.5 | 1.4 | .9 | 1.5 | 1.6 | | .9 | .8 |
| .4 | 7.2 | 3.6 | 2.0 | 2.4 | 2.1 | Fixed/Worth | 3.4 | 2.6 |
| -2.4 | -3.9 | -21.2 | 4.8 | 3.1 | 3.2 | | -14.1 | UND |
| .6 | 2.2 | 1.6 | 1.1 | 1.5 | 1.5 | | 1.7 | 1.4 |
| 3.2 | 9.8 | 4.7 | 2.7 | 2.9 | 2.3 | Debt/Worth | 5.5 | 3.9 |
| -5.5 | -6.5 | -31.2 | 7.4 | -5.3 | 4.1 | | -18.6 | -80.2 |
| 82.3 | 58.3 | 35.5 | 23.7 | 30.2 | 35.7 | | 44.2 | 56.5 |
| (288) 33.6 | (309) 22.3 | (231) 16.5 | (170) 13.2 | (56) 16.8 | (55) 21.2 | % Profit Before Taxes/Tangible Net Worth | (678) 18.7 | (903) 23.8 |
| 10.5 | 6.4 | 4.2 | 5.6 | 11.1 | 12.0 | | 4.7 | 7.3 |
| 22.9 | 9.7 | 8.4 | 7.0 | 7.8 | 10.0 | | 9.1 | 13.2 |
| 9.7 | 3.8 | 3.3 | 3.6 | 5.3 | 6.8 | % Profit Before Taxes/Total Assets | 3.0 | 5.1 |
| -1.6 | -.2 | .1 | 1.4 | 2.3 | 2.6 | | -.9 | .3 |
| 999.8 | 48.2 | 25.7 | 24.2 | 14.8 | 12.3 | | 70.6 | 65.9 |
| 283.1 | 10.2 | 8.8 | 11.4 | 9.5 | 8.2 | Sales/Net Fixed Assets | 13.8 | 15.6 |
| 69.9 | 4.4 | 3.7 | 6.9 | 5.3 | 5.5 | | 5.5 | 6.2 |
| 29.3 | 10.3 | 9.0 | 9.8 | 7.9 | 6.9 | | 12.3 | 13.0 |
| 18.2 | 5.3 | 4.6 | 6.5 | 5.7 | 5.5 | Sales/Total Assets | 6.4 | 7.2 |
| 9.9 | 3.0 | 2.8 | 4.2 | 3.7 | 3.5 | | 3.5 | 3.9 |
| .1 | .4 | .5 | .5 | .6 | .6 | | .5 | .4 |
| (236) .3 | (415) .9 | (282) 1.0 | (183) .8 | (59) .9 | (42) .8 | % Depr., Dep., Amort./Sales | (801) .9 | (981) .8 |
| .7 | 1.5 | 1.7 | 1.1 | 1.3 | 1.2 | | 1.5 | 1.4 |
| .5 | .4 | .3 | .1 | | | | .3 | .3 |
| (216) .8 | (224) .7 | (121) .5 | (37) .2 | | | % Officers', Directors' Owners' Comp/Sales | (389) .7 | (467) .6 |
| 1.5 | 1.4 | 1.1 | .4 | | | | 1.6 | 1.3 |
| 2022328M | 3926606M | 9952025M | 34130390M | 25929734M | 55341922M | Net Sales ($) | 67922918M | 125639612M |
| 108987M | 558274M | 1381120M | 4489094M | 4169468M | 9823809M | Total Assets ($) | 11583578M | 17069698M |

© RMA 2012

**M = $ thousand   MM = $ million**
See Pages 9 through 22 for Explanation of Ratios and Data

| Comparative Historical Data | | | Type of Statement | Current Data Sorted by Sales | | | | | |
|---|---|---|---|---|---|---|---|---|---|
| 93 | 93 | 101 | Unqualified | | 2 | 2 | 1 | 4 | 92 |
| 122 | 109 | 109 | Reviewed | | 1 | 3 | 7 | 11 | 87 |
| 175 | 201 | 193 | Compiled | 2 | 25 | 39 | 36 | 39 | 52 |
| 603 | 513 | 660 | Tax Returns | 24 | 157 | 157 | 179 | 104 | 39 |
| 322 | 390 | 518 | Other | 15 | 66 | 60 | 114 | 87 | 176 |
| 4/1/09-3/31/10 ALL | 4/1/10-3/31/11 ALL | 4/1/11-3/31/12 ALL | | 188 (4/1-9/30/11) | | | 1,393 (10/1/11-3/31/12) | | |
| | | | | 0-1MM | 1-3MM | 3-5MM | 5-10MM | 10-25MM | 25MM & OVER |
| 1315 | 1306 | 1581 | NUMBER OF STATEMENTS | 41 | 251 | 261 | 337 | 245 | 446 |
| % | % | % | ASSETS | % | % | % | % | % | % |
| 12.0 | 11.7 | 12.4 | Cash & Equivalents | 11.7 | 11.3 | 12.6 | 13.0 | 14.7 | 11.1 |
| 5.4 | 5.9 | 5.8 | Trade Receivables (net) | 3.0 | 2.4 | 2.8 | 3.6 | 5.6 | 11.3 |
| 20.8 | 20.2 | 21.0 | Inventory | 21.0 | 27.8 | 28.2 | 20.0 | 18.4 | 15.1 |
| 2.0 | 1.8 | 1.7 | All Other Current | .9 | 1.4 | 1.5 | 1.7 | 1.9 | 2.0 |
| 40.3 | 39.6 | 40.8 | Total Current | 36.6 | 42.9 | 45.1 | 38.4 | 40.7 | 39.5 |
| 44.6 | 45.6 | 44.1 | Fixed Assets (net) | 52.0 | 42.8 | 39.0 | 43.1 | 45.5 | 47.1 |
| 7.4 | 7.1 | 7.9 | Intangibles (net) | 8.9 | 9.5 | 8.8 | 10.2 | 7.0 | 5.1 |
| 7.7 | 7.7 | 7.2 | All Other Non-Current | 2.5 | 4.8 | 7.1 | 8.3 | 6.8 | 8.3 |
| 100.0 | 100.0 | 100.0 | Total | 100.0 | 100.0 | 100.0 | 100.0 | 100.0 | 100.0 |
| | | | LIABILITIES | | | | | | |
| 4.4 | 3.8 | 4.6 | Notes Payable-Short Term | 5.3 | 5.2 | 7.8 | 3.7 | 3.9 | 3.3 |
| 2.9 | 3.8 | 3.2 | Cur. Mat.-L.T.D. | 3.2 | 2.7 | 2.8 | 2.3 | 3.5 | 4.3 |
| 15.8 | 15.7 | 16.4 | Trade Payables | 14.6 | 11.5 | 11.7 | 15.1 | 16.2 | 23.4 |
| .1 | .1 | .1 | Income Taxes Payable | .0 | .0 | .0 | .1 | .1 | .1 |
| 10.8 | 9.4 | 10.8 | All Other Current | 14.9 | 10.1 | 15.9 | 10.7 | 10.9 | 8.0 |
| 34.0 | 32.8 | 35.1 | Total Current | 38.0 | 29.5 | 38.2 | 31.8 | 34.5 | 39.0 |
| 35.9 | 36.9 | 36.5 | Long-Term Debt | 52.4 | 41.0 | 36.2 | 42.3 | 38.1 | 27.4 |
| .3 | .2 | .2 | Deferred Taxes | .0 | .0 | .0 | .1 | .0 | .6 |
| 10.9 | 10.0 | 11.2 | All Other Non-Current | 22.5 | 19.4 | 15.1 | 12.7 | 7.4 | 4.2 |
| 18.9 | 20.1 | 17.0 | Net Worth | -13.0 | 10.2 | 10.5 | 13.1 | 20.0 | 28.8 |
| 100.0 | 100.0 | 100.0 | Total Liabilities & Net Worth | 100.0 | 100.0 | 100.0 | 100.0 | 100.0 | 100.0 |
| | | | INCOME DATA | | | | | | |
| 100.0 | 100.0 | 100.0 | Net Sales | 100.0 | 100.0 | 100.0 | 100.0 | 100.0 | 100.0 |
| 13.5 | 12.8 | 11.9 | Gross Profit | 38.9 | 15.9 | 11.3 | 10.5 | 10.8 | 9.1 |
| 12.7 | 11.7 | 11.0 | Operating Expenses | 37.5 | 15.0 | 10.6 | 9.5 | 9.8 | 8.4 |
| .8 | 1.1 | .9 | Operating Profit | 1.4 | 1.0 | .7 | 1.1 | 1.0 | .7 |
| .1 | .1 | .1 | All Other Expenses (net) | .9 | .2 | -.1 | .2 | .0 | -.1 |
| .8 | 1.0 | .8 | Profit Before Taxes | .5 | .8 | .7 | .8 | 1.0 | .7 |
| | | | RATIOS | | | | | | |
| 2.5 | 2.8 | 2.9 | | 8.3 | 6.2 | 4.1 | 4.3 | 2.3 | 1.5 |
| 1.3 | 1.3 | 1.3 | Current | 1.3 | 1.9 | 2.0 | 1.7 | 1.3 | 1.0 |
| .8 | .8 | .8 | | .4 | .9 | .9 | .8 | .8 | .7 |
| 1.1 | 1.1 | 1.3 | | 1.0 | 1.9 | 1.6 | 1.8 | 1.2 | .9 |
| (1313) .5 | (1300) .5 | (1573) .6 | Quick | (40) .3 | (247) .5 | (259) .6 | (336) .7 | .6 | .5 |
| .2 | .2 | .2 | | .1 | .2 | .2 | .3 | .3 | .3 |
| 0 UND | 0 UND | 0 UND | | 0 UND | 0 UND | 0 UND | 0 UND | 0 UND | 2 188.4 |
| 1 478.2 | 1 420.9 | 1 695.1 | Sales/Receivables | 0 UND | 0 UND | 0 UND | 0 UND | 0 UND | 4 101.9 |
| 3 105.5 | 4 101.1 | 3 107.4 | | 0 UND | 1 414.7 | 1 420.0 | 1 289.0 | 3 113.4 | 6 56.3 |
| 6 65.3 | 5 67.4 | 5 78.4 | | 0 UND | 9 42.5 | 7 53.8 | 4 83.5 | 4 99.5 | 4 95.3 |
| 9 40.0 | 9 42.6 | 8 48.5 | Cost of Sales/Inventory | 21 17.3 | 13 28.5 | 9 39.1 | 6 61.5 | 6 63.7 | 7 56.1 |
| 14 26.1 | 13 28.9 | 12 31.0 | | 49 7.4 | 20 18.2 | 13 28.8 | 9 42.7 | 8 43.7 | 10 37.3 |
| 1 406.0 | 1 488.7 | 1 572.4 | | 0 UND | 0 UND | 0 UND | 0 999.8 | 1 295.0 | 7 54.9 |
| 6 59.1 | 6 61.2 | 5 71.1 | Cost of Sales/Payables | 4 90.5 | 1 245.9 | 2 196.8 | 3 124.1 | 5 72.4 | 11 33.9 |
| 12 29.3 | 12 30.2 | 11 32.9 | | 31 11.8 | 8 48.2 | 6 56.6 | 8 47.6 | 10 35.8 | 14 26.3 |
| 32.2 | 34.8 | 35.0 | | 10.0 | 18.9 | 31.3 | 41.9 | 43.5 | 55.6 |
| 109.2 | 115.6 | 105.2 | Sales/Working Capital | 40.7 | 42.9 | 58.3 | 88.0 | 143.2 | 999.8 |
| -77.9 | -81.6 | -106.5 | | -8.0 | -146.8 | -219.4 | -187.2 | -130.8 | -79.0 |
| 4.7 | 5.3 | 5.2 | | 2.4 | 3.0 | 3.6 | 4.2 | 7.1 | 7.6 |
| (1006) 2.0 | (1023) 2.2 | (1189) 2.2 | EBIT/Interest | (20) 1.3 | (155) 1.5 | (162) 1.7 | (245) 1.9 | (194) 2.8 | (413) 3.3 |
| .9 | 1.0 | 1.0 | | -.5 | .3 | 1.0 | .7 | 1.0 | 1.6 |
| 3.4 | 3.9 | 3.2 | | | | | 2.5 | 3.2 | 3.5 |
| (150) 2.0 | (144) 1.9 | (141) 2.0 | Net Profit + Depr., Dep., Amort./Cur. Mat. L/T/D | | | (10) 1.3 | (20) 2.0 | (107) 2.1 |
| 1.3 | 1.2 | 1.2 | | | | | .8 | 1.4 | 1.2 |
| .7 | .7 | .7 | | .2 | .2 | .2 | .6 | .7 | .9 |
| 2.7 | 2.9 | 2.7 | Fixed/Worth | 5.7 | 3.5 | 3.4 | 5.7 | 2.7 | 2.0 |
| -15.3 | -21.8 | -13.9 | | -4.1 | -9.4 | -5.1 | -2.2 | -5.5 | 4.8 |
| 1.3 | 1.4 | 1.2 | | 2.4 | 1.6 | 1.2 | 1.1 | 1.2 | 1.2 |
| 4.1 | 4.2 | 4.6 | Debt/Worth | -208.2 | 6.8 | 5.8 | 8.9 | 4.0 | 2.9 |
| -19.4 | -28.6 | -14.7 | | -3.3 | -11.2 | -9.7 | -5.1 | -10.0 | 8.6 |
| 47.8 | 47.4 | 46.5 | | 73.9 | 56.5 | 55.8 | 66.6 | 68.4 | 29.6 |
| (943) 20.9 | (937) 20.6 | (1109) 20.7 | % Profit Before Taxes/Tangible Net Worth | (20) 21.7 | (163) 26.3 | (172) 23.7 | (202) 26.0 | (172) 25.7 | (380) 16.3 |
| 4.9 | 5.6 | 6.8 | | .0 | 6.7 | 7.8 | 8.8 | 6.2 | 7.0 |
| 10.9 | 11.4 | 11.5 | | 7.9 | 13.9 | 13.7 | 13.7 | 14.6 | 8.5 |
| 3.9 | 4.6 | 4.5 | % Profit Before Taxes/Total Assets | 1.1 | 4.2 | 4.3 | 5.0 | 6.4 | 4.2 |
| .0 | .2 | .2 | | -6.3 | -2.6 | -.2 | -.5 | .1 | 1.5 |
| 84.6 | 81.0 | 125.6 | | 513.4 | 309.8 | 354.3 | 259.4 | 90.0 | 36.2 |
| 13.6 | 14.2 | 17.0 | Sales/Net Fixed Assets | 5.6 | 11.0 | 31.0 | 20.6 | 20.1 | 15.1 |
| 4.9 | 5.1 | 5.7 | | .6 | 3.1 | 5.0 | 5.3 | 6.7 | 8.3 |
| 12.2 | 12.7 | 14.6 | | 5.0 | 11.2 | 19.7 | 16.3 | 16.2 | 11.2 |
| 5.9 | 6.2 | 7.2 | Sales/Total Assets | 2.4 | 4.6 | 7.9 | 8.0 | 8.4 | 7.4 |
| 3.1 | 3.4 | 3.8 | | .5 | 2.2 | 3.2 | 3.9 | 4.5 | 4.8 |
| .5 | .5 | .4 | | .8 | .5 | .3 | .3 | .3 | .4 |
| (1037) 1.0 | (1041) 1.0 | (1217) .8 | % Depr., Dep., Amort./Sales | (27) 4.4 | (168) 1.3 | (184) .8 | (236) .8 | (207) .6 | (395) .7 |
| 1.8 | 1.6 | 1.3 | | 14.4 | 2.6 | 1.5 | 1.4 | 1.2 | 1.0 |
| .4 | .4 | .4 | | 2.1 | .7 | .5 | .4 | .3 | .1 |
| (572) .8 | (531) .7 | (611) .6 | % Officers', Directors' Owners' Comp/Sales | (10) 4.5 | (95) 1.3 | (119) .7 | (162) .6 | (114) .6 | (111) .3 |
| 1.6 | 1.4 | 1.3 | | 5.9 | 2.1 | 1.5 | 1.0 | 1.1 | .6 |
| 84856215M | 95228672M | 131303005M | Net Sales ($) | 24439M | 506914M | 1028475M | 2383000M | 3570098M | 123790079M |
| 15791819M | 16105062M | 20530752M | Total Assets ($) | 21156M | 159826M | 248498M | 468031M | 655860M | 18977381M |

M = $ thousand    MM = $ million
See Pages 9 through 22 for Explanation of Ratios and Data

## Current Data Sorted by Assets

## Comparative Historical Data

| 0-500M | 500M-2MM | 2-10MM | 10-50MM | 50-100MM | 100-250MM | Type of Statement | 4/1/07-3/31/08 ALL | 4/1/08-3/31/09 ALL |
|---|---|---|---|---|---|---|---|---|
| | 2 | 3 12 10 | 3 8 6 | 4 | 4 | Unqualified | 39 | 13 |
| 2 | 13 | | | | | Reviewed | 56 | 10 |
| 23 | 20 | 9 | | | 1 | Compiled | 47 | 20 |
| 7 | 19 | 17 | 16 | 7 | 6 | Tax Returns | 83 | 61 |
| | 35 (4/1-9/30/11) | | 157 (10/1/11-3/31/12) | | | Other | 82 | 38 |
| 32 | 54 | 51 | 33 | 11 | 11 | NUMBER OF STATEMENTS | 307 | 142 |
| % | % | % | % | % | % | ASSETS | % | % |
| 16.5 | 10.6 | 9.6 | 10.1 | 8.3 | 4.8 | Cash & Equivalents | 10.2 | 12.1 |
| 8.3 | 13.8 | 15.7 | 13.4 | 18.0 | 13.7 | Trade Receivables (net) | 12.4 | 10.1 |
| 33.0 | 14.6 | 10.8 | 13.7 | 12.2 | 11.5 | Inventory | 14.6 | 17.9 |
| 6.6 | 2.6 | 1.8 | 4.8 | 9.3 | 1.2 | All Other Current | 2.2 | 2.3 |
| 64.4 | 41.5 | 37.9 | 42.0 | 47.8 | 31.3 | Total Current | 39.4 | 42.4 |
| 26.0 | 44.6 | 47.3 | 48.4 | 43.1 | 60.7 | Fixed Assets (net) | 47.8 | 43.3 |
| 3.4 | 9.9 | 6.9 | 2.0 | 5.4 | 4.0 | Intangibles (net) | 5.7 | 5.0 |
| 6.1 | 3.9 | 7.8 | 7.6 | 3.7 | 4.0 | All Other Non-Current | 7.1 | 9.3 |
| 100.0 | 100.0 | 100.0 | 100.0 | 100.0 | 100.0 | Total | 100.0 | 100.0 |
| | | | | | | LIABILITIES | | |
| 4.2 | 4.3 | 5.1 | 5.0 | 3.9 | 6.2 | Notes Payable-Short Term | 4.2 | 6.6 |
| 2.8 | 2.9 | 3.3 | 3.8 | 1.9 | 2.3 | Cur. Mat.-L.T.D. | 3.5 | 3.8 |
| 17.8 | 19.6 | 15.4 | 22.3 | 22.4 | 13.6 | Trade Payables | 17.7 | 15.3 |
| .0 | .1 | .1 | .6 | .3 | .0 | Income Taxes Payable | .1 | .1 |
| 14.3 | 6.6 | 4.6 | 8.2 | 3.7 | 6.3 | All Other Current | 8.3 | 12.5 |
| 39.1 | 33.5 | 28.5 | 39.9 | 32.3 | 28.4 | Total Current | 33.9 | 38.1 |
| 18.4 | 41.0 | 36.8 | 23.0 | 25.0 | 29.1 | Long-Term Debt | 33.7 | 35.3 |
| .0 | .1 | .5 | 1.1 | .7 | .1 | Deferred Taxes | .2 | .1 |
| 16.4 | 4.9 | 4.5 | 3.7 | 2.3 | 3.5 | All Other Non-Current | 5.7 | 9.2 |
| 26.0 | 20.6 | 29.7 | 32.3 | 39.6 | 38.9 | Net Worth | 26.6 | 17.2 |
| 100.0 | 100.0 | 100.0 | 100.0 | 100.0 | 100.0 | Total Liabilities & Net Worth | 100.0 | 100.0 |
| | | | | | | INCOME DATA | | |
| 100.0 | 100.0 | 100.0 | 100.0 | 100.0 | 100.0 | Net Sales | 100.0 | 100.0 |
| 12.4 | 11.5 | 12.1 | 8.2 | 8.3 | 11.3 | Gross Profit | 12.2 | 12.8 |
| 12.3 | 10.7 | 10.5 | 7.6 | 6.9 | 9.3 | Operating Expenses | 10.6 | 11.7 |
| .1 | .7 | 1.6 | .6 | 1.4 | 1.9 | Operating Profit | 1.5 | 1.1 |
| -.2 | -.1 | .3 | .0 | .1 | .1 | All Other Expenses (net) | .3 | .3 |
| .3 | .8 | 1.4 | .6 | 1.3 | 1.8 | Profit Before Taxes | 1.3 | .7 |
| | | | | | | RATIOS | | |
| 5.2 | 3.1 | 2.7 | 1.4 | 1.9 | 1.4 | | 1.9 | 2.5 |
| 1.9 | 1.3 | 1.2 | 1.0 | 1.3 | 1.0 | Current | 1.1 | 1.2 |
| 1.0 | .8 | .8 | .9 | .9 | .6 | | .8 | .8 |
| 1.9 | 1.5 | 1.5 | .8 | 1.3 | .9 | | 1.0 | 1.4 |
| .7 | .7 | .9 | .6 | .7 | .6 | Quick | (306) .6 | .6 |
| .2 | .3 | .4 | .3 | .6 | .4 | | .3 | .3 |
| 0 UND | 0 999.8 | 1 427.1 | 2 154.3 | 4 103.2 | 4 89.9 | | 0 999.8 | 0 UND |
| 0 795.0 | 3 130.7 | 5 80.4 | 6 63.5 | 7 55.8 | 6 63.6 | Sales/Receivables | 3 104.3 | 2 216.7 |
| 4 101.8 | 7 54.4 | 12 30.6 | 9 41.2 | 17 21.7 | 7 51.6 | | 9 39.3 | 6 60.4 |
| 4 85.0 | 5 75.6 | 3 117.2 | 4 96.6 | 3 142.0 | 3 129.8 | | 4 91.5 | 4 99.4 |
| 6 56.5 | 8 45.6 | 6 60.6 | 6 56.4 | 5 73.9 | 8 48.4 | Cost of Sales/Inventory | 7 53.3 | 6 65.3 |
| 11 33.7 | 12 29.5 | 12 30.9 | 11 34.7 | 8 43.6 | 12 30.9 | | 10 35.4 | 10 35.6 |
| 0 UND | 3 138.3 | 3 117.4 | 8 45.2 | 11 34.2 | 11 44.3 | | 4 98.7 | 1 320.9 |
| 1 276.1 | 7 55.9 | 7 50.8 | 12 30.4 | 11 32.8 | 12 31.5 | Cost of Sales/Payables | 9 38.9 | 5 76.4 |
| 6 60.2 | 15 24.7 | 13 27.1 | 14 26.8 | 16 22.2 | 16 23.4 | | 14 26.0 | 10 38.2 |
| 22.7 | 26.7 | 24.9 | 63.7 | 18.6 | 54.9 | | 47.0 | 39.9 |
| 83.5 | 100.7 | 101.8 | 575.5 | 70.8 | -999.8 | Sales/Working Capital | 205.4 | 145.6 |
| NM | -82.0 | -114.6 | -162.5 | -212.3 | -39.0 | | -82.2 | -125.7 |
| 4.3 | 3.2 | 8.2 | 18.8 | 16.5 | 13.9 | | 4.9 | 7.0 |
| (14) 1.2 | (41) 1.5 | (49) 3.0 | (32) 4.5 | 3.6 | 4.1 | EBIT/Interest | (263) 2.1 | (121) 2.3 |
| -1.5 | .8 | 1.4 | 1.7 | 2.2 | 3.3 | | 1.2 | 1.2 |
| | | | 5.2 | | | | 4.4 | 12.6 |
| | | (13) 2.8 | | | | Net Profit + Depr., Dep., Amort./Cur. Mat. L/T/D | (53) 2.0 | (18) 5.6 |
| | | | 1.1 | | | | .9 | 2.3 |
| .1 | .7 | .6 | 1.0 | .3 | 1.3 | | .9 | .6 |
| .5 | 2.9 | 1.6 | 1.2 | 1.5 | 1.9 | Fixed/Worth | 2.2 | 1.9 |
| 6.6 | -4.7 | 9.9 | 2.6 | 2.8 | 3.0 | | 12.2 | 36.1 |
| .6 | 1.2 | 1.0 | 1.4 | .9 | 1.3 | | 1.4 | 1.1 |
| 2.3 | 4.4 | 2.0 | 2.2 | 2.1 | 1.5 | Debt/Worth | 3.4 | 4.1 |
| 12.6 | -5.2 | 14.9 | 5.1 | 3.3 | 3.4 | | 26.6 | 291.7 |
| 41.3 | 49.1 | 22.3 | 22.4 | 28.9 | 28.6 | | 39.7 | 54.3 |
| (26) 22.3 | (35) 14.7 | (40) 14.2 | (31) 14.0 | 14.5 | 26.1 | % Profit Before Taxes/Tangible Net Worth | (244) 17.7 | (109) 21.6 |
| -3.8 | .7 | 5.2 | 8.6 | 11.5 | 18.4 | | 6.0 | 7.9 |
| 13.7 | 9.0 | 7.8 | 6.6 | 8.2 | 11.4 | | 10.1 | 13.2 |
| 4.4 | 2.6 | 3.5 | 3.2 | 6.5 | 7.8 | % Profit Before Taxes/Total Assets | 4.6 | 5.2 |
| -7.6 | -.9 | 1.2 | 2.1 | 2.4 | 5.2 | | .7 | .9 |
| 564.9 | 59.3 | 30.3 | 28.5 | 28.8 | 15.3 | | 44.3 | 87.4 |
| 171.0 | 13.6 | 11.6 | 15.7 | 15.3 | 9.1 | Sales/Net Fixed Assets | 12.2 | 21.2 |
| 36.4 | 4.9 | 5.8 | 7.8 | 7.4 | 4.2 | | 5.3 | 6.9 |
| 26.4 | 10.1 | 8.8 | 11.4 | 9.9 | 6.6 | | 11.0 | 15.4 |
| 17.2 | 5.3 | 6.0 | 7.2 | 7.1 | 5.7 | Sales/Total Assets | 6.4 | 7.5 |
| 10.8 | 3.2 | 3.1 | 4.6 | 3.8 | 3.3 | | 3.7 | 4.3 |
| .1 | .2 | .5 | .5 | .3 | | | .4 | .4 |
| (16) .4 | (44) .5 | (45) .8 | .6 | .7 | | % Depr., Dep., Amort./Sales | (265) .9 | (120) .7 |
| 1.1 | 1.2 | 1.4 | 1.0 | 1.2 | | | 1.3 | 1.3 |
| .4 | .4 | .3 | .2 | | | | .3 | .3 |
| (16) .7 | (27) .8 | (23) .5 | (11) .4 | | | % Officers', Directors' Owners' Comp/Sales | (116) .7 | (55) .6 |
| 2.2 | 1.3 | 1.1 | .8 | | | | 1.2 | 1.0 |
| 134120M | 547034M | 1679838M | 5908639M | 5760553M | 9800933M | Net Sales ($) | 36904497M | 17696951M |
| 7790M | 62436M | 229139M | 706122M | 812010M | 1679662M | Total Assets ($) | 5883973M | 2383327M |

M = $ thousand   MM = $ million
See Pages 9 through 22 for Explanation of Ratios and Data

## Comparative Historical Data

## Current Data Sorted by Sales

| | | | | Type of Statement | | | | | | |
|---|---|---|---|---|---|---|---|---|---|---|
| | | | | | | | | | 1 | 13 |
| 25 | | 22 | 14 | Unqualified | | | 2 | 1 | 3 | 16 |
| 31 | | 27 | 22 | Reviewed | | 2 | 5 | 5 | 6 | 13 |
| 44 | | 44 | 31 | Compiled | | 9 | 11 | 12 | 11 | 6 |
| 67 | | 51 | 53 | Tax Returns | 4 | 3 | 10 | 13 | 8 | 36 |
| 107 | | 101 | 72 | Other | 2 | | | | | |
| 4/1/09-3/31/10 | | 4/1/10-3/31/11 | 4/1/11-3/31/12 | | | 35 (4/1-9/30/11) | | 157 (10/1/11-3/31/12) | | |
| ALL | | ALL | ALL | | 0-1MM | 1-3MM | 3-5MM | 5-10MM | 10-25MM | 25MM & OVER |
| 274 | | 245 | 192 | **NUMBER OF STATEMENTS** | 6 | 14 | 28 | 31 | 29 | 84 |
| % | | % | % | **ASSETS** | % | % | % | % | % | % |
| 11.5 | | 10.7 | 10.8 | Cash & Equivalents | 14.3 | 12.8 | 9.7 | 10.2 | 10.3 | |
| 9.8 | | 10.6 | 13.6 | Trade Receivables (net) | 8.0 | 7.3 | 6.6 | 18.8 | 18.0 | |
| 14.2 | | 14.4 | 16.2 | Inventory | 20.2 | 16.8 | 17.6 | 18.1 | 13.3 | |
| 2.9 | | 4.8 | 3.7 | All Other Current | 3.3 | 2.8 | 5.0 | .6 | 4.0 | |
| 38.4 | | 40.6 | 44.2 | Total Current | 45.8 | 39.8 | 38.9 | 47.8 | 45.6 | |
| 46.3 | | 46.3 | 43.7 | Fixed Assets (net) | 43.2 | 45.2 | 44.3 | 42.0 | 43.7 | |
| 6.8 | | 5.5 | 6.1 | Intangibles (net) | 7.6 | 10.7 | 10.8 | 4.6 | 3.5 | |
| 8.5 | | 7.6 | 6.0 | All Other Non-Current | 3.4 | 4.3 | 6.1 | 5.6 | 7.2 | |
| 100.0 | | 100.0 | 100.0 | Total | 100.0 | 100.0 | 100.0 | 100.0 | 100.0 | |
| | | | | **LIABILITIES** | | | | | | |
| 4.3 | | 3.9 | 4.7 | Notes Payable-Short Term | 5.7 | 5.5 | 2.0 | 5.7 | 5.3 | |
| 4.0 | | 3.2 | 3.0 | Cur. Mat.-L.T.D. | 1.6 | 2.7 | 3.4 | 3.1 | 2.8 | |
| 14.3 | | 17.8 | 18.5 | Trade Payables | 11.7 | 6.5 | 14.5 | 23.8 | 22.9 | |
| .1 | | .1 | .2 | Income Taxes Payable | .0 | .0 | .1 | .1 | .3 | |
| 9.7 | | 8.3 | 7.5 | All Other Current | 7.2 | 6.5 | 9.3 | 9.0 | 6.4 | |
| 32.3 | | 33.3 | 33.8 | Total Current | 26.1 | 21.1 | 29.3 | 41.6 | 37.7 | |
| 35.5 | | 33.9 | 31.4 | Long-Term Debt | 37.3 | 40.4 | 40.6 | 37.1 | 22.3 | |
| .7 | | .3 | .4 | Deferred Taxes | .0 | .0 | .0 | .4 | .8 | |
| 7.1 | | 6.4 | 6.3 | All Other Non-Current | 9.2 | 5.0 | 5.7 | 6.3 | 3.5 | |
| 24.3 | | 26.2 | 28.1 | Net Worth | 27.4 | 33.5 | 24.3 | 14.6 | 35.8 | |
| 100.0 | | 100.0 | 100.0 | Total Liabilties & Net Worth | 100.0 | 100.0 | 100.0 | 100.0 | 100.0 | |
| | | | | **INCOME DATA** | | | | | | |
| 100.0 | | 100.0 | 100.0 | Net Sales | 100.0 | 100.0 | 100.0 | 100.0 | 100.0 | |
| 14.1 | | 12.7 | 11.0 | Gross Profit | 15.2 | 12.7 | 14.0 | 9.2 | 8.4 | |
| 12.4 | | 11.1 | 10.1 | Operating Expenses | 15.1 | 11.1 | 12.3 | 8.8 | 7.5 | |
| 1.7 | | 1.6 | .9 | Operating Profit | .1 | 1.6 | 1.7 | .4 | .9 | |
| .3 | | .4 | .0 | All Other Expenses (net) | -1.0 | .2 | .2 | .1 | .0 | |
| 1.3 | | 1.2 | .9 | Profit Before Taxes | 1.2 | 1.4 | 1.5 | .3 | .9 | |
| | | | | **RATIOS** | | | | | | |
| 2.2 | | 2.4 | 2.4 | | 9.5 | 4.0 | 4.4 | 2.3 | 1.6 | |
| 1.2 | | 1.3 | 1.3 | Current | 2.3 | 1.8 | 1.3 | 1.2 | 1.2 | |
| .7 | | .9 | .8 | | .6 | 1.0 | .8 | .8 | .9 | |
| 1.3 | | 1.2 | 1.3 | | 5.7 | 1.8 | 1.1 | 1.1 | 1.1 | |
| .6 | (243) | .7 | .7 | Quick | .6 | .8 | .4 | .7 | .7 | |
| .3 | | .4 | .3 | | .3 | .2 | .1 | .4 | .4 | |
| 0 | 734.2 | 0 | UND | 1 | 604.2 | | Sales/Receivables | 0 | UND | 0 | UND | 0 | UND | 1 | 270.5 | 3 | 135.8 |

| | | | | | | | | | | | | | | | | | | |
|---|---|---|---|---|---|---|---|---|---|---|---|---|---|---|---|---|---|---|
| 0 | 734.2 | 0 | UND | 1 | 604.2 | Sales/Receivables | 0 | UND | 0 | UND | 0 | UND | 1 | 270.5 | 3 | 135.8 |
| 3 | 137.8 | 3 | 123.8 | 3 | 104.3 | | 0 | 957.1 | 2 | 217.4 | 1 | 606.8 | 3 | 113.8 | 6 | 63.5 |
| 7 | 51.6 | 7 | 51.9 | 8 | 45.8 | | 6 | 58.9 | 6 | 58.5 | 3 | 113.5 | 16 | 23.2 | 10 | 36.3 |
| 5 | 75.6 | 4 | 95.6 | 4 | 98.5 | Cost of Sales/Inventory | 5 | 67.6 | 5 | 79.6 | 4 | 86.8 | 4 | 90.5 | 3 | 119.3 |
| 8 | 46.7 | 7 | 51.3 | 7 | 51.1 | | 8 | 47.1 | 9 | 42.2 | 7 | 50.7 | 8 | 48.6 | 5 | 69.0 |
| 12 | 29.8 | 11 | 33.0 | 11 | 32.4 | | 23 | 16.2 | 14 | 25.5 | 12 | 29.8 | 11 | 32.8 | 10 | 37.8 |
| 2 | 198.4 | 2 | 186.4 | 3 | 130.3 | Cost of Sales/Payables | 1 | 507.7 | 0 | UND | 0 | 999.8 | 4 | 86.8 | 7 | 53.9 |
| 9 | 41.6 | 9 | 39.4 | 8 | 44.4 | | 4 | 100.5 | 3 | 112.5 | 5 | 75.4 | 7 | 50.7 | 11 | 33.2 |
| 14 | 26.4 | 13 | 27.1 | 13 | 27.1 | | 14 | 26.1 | 7 | 53.4 | 13 | 27.6 | 14 | 26.9 | 14 | 26.8 |
| | 30.4 | | 30.2 | | 29.7 | Sales/Working Capital | | 24.1 | | 16.9 | | 27.2 | | 29.0 | | 47.3 |
| | 132.1 | | 93.5 | | 109.1 | | | 44.3 | | 28.0 | | 101.4 | | 156.0 | | 201.5 |
| | -73.6 | | -171.3 | | -128.0 | | | -84.7 | | -831.6 | | -90.5 | | -116.2 | | -197.7 |
| | 5.8 | | 7.3 | | 8.1 | EBIT/Interest | | 3.0 | | 5.8 | | 3.8 | | 2.7 | | 13.7 |
| (243) | 2.6 | (209) | 2.6 | (158) | 2.5 | | (11) | 1.3 | (19) | 2.0 | (22) | 1.7 | (23) | 1.5 | (80) | 5.0 |
| | 1.1 | | 1.5 | | 1.1 | | | .8 | | .9 | | .8 | | .7 | | 2.1 |
| | 3.6 | | 4.8 | | 5.4 | Net Profit + Depr., Dep., Amort./Cur. Mat. L/T/D | | | | | | | | | | 5.3 |
| (39) | 2.2 | (37) | 3.1 | (32) | 3.8 | | | | | | | | | | (29) | 3.6 |
| | 1.5 | | 1.2 | | 2.1 | | | | | | | | | | | 2.2 |
| | .9 | | .7 | | .6 | Fixed/Worth | | .2 | | .4 | | .4 | | .8 | | .7 |
| | 2.1 | | 1.7 | | 1.6 | | | 4.9 | | 1.7 | | 2.4 | | 3.3 | | 1.3 |
| | 21.9 | | 7.6 | | 7.2 | | | -6.6 | | NM | | -3.0 | | -4.2 | | 2.3 |
| | 1.4 | | 1.3 | | 1.2 | Debt/Worth | | .9 | | .8 | | 1.2 | | 1.2 | | 1.2 |
| | 3.0 | | 2.6 | | 2.5 | | | 8.4 | | 2.6 | | 3.7 | | 3.9 | | 2.0 |
| | 34.6 | | 12.7 | | 14.8 | | | -11.4 | | -16.5 | | -7.3 | | -13.8 | | 3.8 |
| | 39.6 | | 34.1 | | 28.6 | % Profit Before Taxes/Tangible Net Worth | | | | 43.2 | | 58.3 | | 15.7 | | 28.1 |
| (217) | 16.0 | (200) | 17.9 | (154) | 15.4 | | | | (20) | 21.5 | (22) | 24.8 | (20) | 10.6 | (80) | 16.1 |
| | 4.3 | | 5.9 | | 6.7 | | | | | | 3.0 | | 3.4 | | -.6 | | 10.2 |
| | 8.7 | | 9.6 | | 8.6 | % Profit Before Taxes/Total Assets | | 11.1 | | 13.5 | | 13.5 | | 5.4 | | 8.6 |
| | 3.9 | | 4.6 | | 3.8 | | | 1.6 | | 5.5 | | 2.7 | | 2.3 | | 5.1 |
| | .0 | | 1.3 | | .6 | | | -1.7 | | -.7 | | .1 | | -.6 | | 2.4 |
| | 40.3 | | 44.5 | | 56.4 | Sales/Net Fixed Assets | | 195.9 | | 101.0 | | 161.0 | | 55.5 | | 39.6 |
| | 10.9 | | 13.0 | | 15.7 | | | 6.6 | | 12.3 | | 13.7 | | 16.6 | | 17.8 |
| | 5.7 | | 5.5 | | 6.8 | | | 3.3 | | 4.2 | | 4.0 | | 8.8 | | 9.5 |
| | 9.5 | | 10.4 | | 11.9 | Sales/Total Assets | | 17.4 | | 11.0 | | 15.7 | | 12.2 | | 11.6 |
| | 5.4 | | 6.0 | | 7.0 | | | 4.9 | | 4.9 | | 5.5 | | 7.3 | | 7.3 |
| | 3.1 | | 3.3 | | 4.0 | | | 2.2 | | 2.7 | | 3.2 | | 4.1 | | 5.6 |
| | .6 | | .4 | | .3 | % Depr., Dep., Amort./Sales | | .2 | | .4 | | .3 | | .4 |
| (218) | 1.0 | (191) | .8 | (157) | .7 | | (17) | .5 | (25) | .8 | (26) | .7 | (77) | .6 |
| | 1.6 | | 1.4 | | 1.2 | | | .8 | | 1.9 | | 1.4 | | 1.0 |
| | .4 | | .3 | | .3 | % Officers', Directors' Owners' Comp/Sales | | .5 | | .4 | | .3 | | .1 |
| (99) | .8 | (88) | .6 | (83) | .6 | | (17) | .6 | (13) | .9 | (18) | .8 | (29) | .3 |
| | 2.0 | | 1.2 | | 1.2 | | | 1.0 | | 1.5 | | 1.6 | | .7 |
| 27193363M | | 32673472M | 23831117M | Net Sales ($) | 3219M | 32147M | 110049M | 217043M | 433952M | 23034707M |
| 5501208M | | 5639583M | 3497159M | Total Assets ($) | 1215M | 8737M | 27597M | 52604M | 69144M | 3337862M |

© RMA 2012

**M = $ thousand    MM = $ million**
See Pages 9 through 22 for Explanation of Ratios and Data

## Current Data Sorted by Assets      Comparative Historical Data

| 0-500M | 500M-2MM | 2-10MM | 10-50MM | 50-100MM | 100-250MM | Type of Statement | 4/1/07-3/31/08 ALL | 4/1/08-3/31/09 ALL |
|---|---|---|---|---|---|---|---|---|
| | | | 1 | 1 | 1 | Unqualified | 6 | 10 |
| | 1 | 4 | 2 | | | Reviewed | 12 | 9 |
| 6 | 3 | | 1 | | | Compiled | 10 | 10 |
| 9 | 7 | 2 | | | | Tax Returns | 11 | 16 |
| 1 | 13 | 5 | 4 | 1 | 1 | Other | 18 | 21 |
| | 17 (4/1-9/30/11) | | 46 (10/1/11-3/31/12) | | | | | |
| 16 | 24 | 11 | 8 | 2 | 2 | NUMBER OF STATEMENTS | 57 | 66 |
| % | % | % | % | % | % | ASSETS | % | % |
| 12.1 | 17.1 | 3.2 | | | | Cash & Equivalents | 12.0 | 11.1 |
| 4.5 | 9.6 | 10.4 | | | | Trade Receivables (net) | 6.8 | 7.1 |
| 68.9 | 46.5 | 38.7 | | | | Inventory | 53.2 | 47.2 |
| 1.6 | 1.2 | 1.0 | | | | All Other Current | 2.8 | 2.6 |
| 87.1 | 74.4 | 53.4 | | | | Total Current | 74.7 | 68.0 |
| 6.4 | 11.0 | 19.7 | | | | Fixed Assets (net) | 18.7 | 19.5 |
| 2.3 | .6 | 2.5 | | | | Intangibles (net) | 1.4 | 3.7 |
| 4.3 | 14.0 | 24.5 | | | | All Other Non-Current | 5.2 | 8.8 |
| 100.0 | 100.0 | 100.0 | | | | Total | 100.0 | 100.0 |
| | | | | | | LIABILITIES | | |
| 33.7 | 11.8 | 8.6 | | | | Notes Payable-Short Term | 10.5 | 8.7 |
| 1.3 | .5 | 2.0 | | | | Cur. Mat.-L.T.D. | 2.4 | 2.3 |
| 22.2 | 25.0 | 8.8 | | | | Trade Payables | 26.1 | 24.2 |
| .0 | .0 | .0 | | | | Income Taxes Payable | 1.2 | .2 |
| 32.1 | 6.7 | 11.9 | | | | All Other Current | 10.1 | 10.8 |
| 89.3 | 44.0 | 31.3 | | | | Total Current | 50.4 | 46.2 |
| 4.3 | 13.0 | 14.0 | | | | Long-Term Debt | 16.7 | 20.2 |
| .0 | .0 | .0 | | | | Deferred Taxes | .1 | .0 |
| 3.1 | 2.6 | 3.3 | | | | All Other Non-Current | 9.3 | 6.0 |
| 3.5 | 40.4 | 51.4 | | | | Net Worth | 23.6 | 27.6 |
| 100.0 | 100.0 | 100.0 | | | | Total Liabilities & Net Worth | 100.0 | 100.0 |
| | | | | | | INCOME DATA | | |
| 100.0 | 100.0 | 100.0 | | | | Net Sales | 100.0 | 100.0 |
| 45.8 | 53.7 | 37.3 | | | | Gross Profit | 46.0 | 48.2 |
| 44.0 | 47.5 | 33.0 | | | | Operating Expenses | 44.0 | 45.5 |
| 1.8 | 6.2 | 4.3 | | | | Operating Profit | 2.0 | 2.7 |
| .4 | .3 | 1.7 | | | | All Other Expenses (net) | 1.1 | .7 |
| 1.4 | 6.0 | 2.6 | | | | Profit Before Taxes | .9 | 2.0 |
| | | | | | | RATIOS | | |
| 3.1 | 3.0 | 2.8 | | | | | 2.2 | 2.5 |
| 1.0 | 1.6 | 1.9 | | | | Current | 1.5 | 1.8 |
| .7 | 1.2 | 1.4 | | | | | 1.1 | 1.1 |
| .4 | 1.2 | .8 | | | | | .6 | .8 |
| .2 | .6 | .4 | | | | Quick | .2 | .3 |
| .1 | .2 | .1 | | | | | .1 | .1 |
| 0 UND | 0 UND | 0 UND | | | | | 0 UND | 0 UND |
| 0 UND | 0 941.2 | 2 155.7 | | | | Sales/Receivables | 2 186.3 | 1 250.7 |
| 7 50.6 | 11 33.7 | 41 8.8 | | | | | 16 22.4 | 12 30.1 |
| 101 3.6 | 126 2.9 | 107 3.4 | | | | | 96 3.8 | 85 4.3 |
| 152 2.4 | 152 2.4 | 203 1.8 | | | | Cost of Sales/Inventory | 137 2.7 | 138 2.6 |
| 261 1.4 | 203 1.8 | 304 1.2 | | | | | 196 1.9 | 204 1.8 |
| 13 28.7 | 35 10.3 | 8 45.1 | | | | | 40 9.2 | 33 11.0 |
| 28 13.1 | 72 5.1 | 36 10.0 | | | | Cost of Sales/Payables | 61 6.0 | 59 6.2 |
| 65 5.6 | 152 2.4 | 74 4.9 | | | | | 97 3.8 | 103 3.5 |
| 4.9 | 3.7 | 4.2 | | | | | 6.1 | 4.5 |
| NM | 9.1 | 6.1 | | | | Sales/Working Capital | 11.2 | 9.4 |
| -10.6 | 58.9 | 11.4 | | | | | 125.9 | 24.2 |
| 5.2 | 25.6 | 7.2 | | | | | 4.9 | 5.7 |
| (10) 2.5 | (15) 4.0 | (10) 2.9 | | | | EBIT/Interest | (45) 2.0 | (55) 2.1 |
| -2.6 | .7 | -4.3 | | | | | .0 | -.5 |
| | | | | | | Net Profit + Depr., Dep., Amort./Cur. Mat. L/T/D | | |
| .0 | .0 | .0 | | | | | .1 | .1 |
| .1 | .2 | .1 | | | | Fixed/Worth | .5 | .6 |
| -2.6 | .6 | 1.7 | | | | | 2.2 | 2.6 |
| .6 | .4 | .2 | | | | | 1.1 | .8 |
| 4.4 | .8 | 1.0 | | | | Debt/Worth | 1.6 | 2.0 |
| -5.6 | 5.8 | 5.9 | | | | | 20.3 | 30.3 |
| 83.4 | 50.0 | | | | | | 25.5 | 33.6 |
| (10) 6.6 | (22) 13.6 | | | | | % Profit Before Taxes/Tangible Net Worth | (44) 9.4 | (51) 12.0 |
| -.1 | 4.8 | | | | | | .5 | -2.2 |
| 13.4 | 14.8 | 11.7 | | | | | 12.0 | 10.1 |
| 2.0 | 6.9 | .9 | | | | % Profit Before Taxes/Total Assets | 3.1 | 4.5 |
| -4.6 | .7 | -.4 | | | | | -.3 | -4.5 |
| 805.0 | 302.3 | 43.7 | | | | | 72.0 | 44.6 |
| 113.9 | 37.2 | 20.7 | | | | Sales/Net Fixed Assets | 19.9 | 14.7 |
| 63.7 | 17.1 | 1.9 | | | | | 7.9 | 7.7 |
| 4.4 | 3.3 | 2.0 | | | | | 3.8 | 3.0 |
| 2.8 | 2.4 | .9 | | | | Sales/Total Assets | 2.6 | 2.2 |
| 1.9 | 1.9 | .5 | | | | | 2.0 | 1.7 |
| .2 | .3 | | | | | | .3 | .4 |
| (10) .3 | (17) .8 | | | | | % Depr., Dep., Amort./Sales | (42) 1.0 | (58) 1.0 |
| .9 | 1.7 | | | | | | 1.6 | 1.9 |
| | | | | | | | 1.6 | 3.0 |
| | | | | | | % Officers', Directors' Owners' Comp/Sales | (25) 5.4 | (25) 6.3 |
| | | | | | | | 7.9 | 12.7 |
| 12965M | 71876M | 47207M | 257398M | 343007M | 639956M | Net Sales ($) | 3671737M | 4100298M |
| 4130M | 24998M | 37721M | 130880M | 106344M | 388941M | Total Assets ($) | 1204920M | 1725007M |

M = $ thousand    MM = $ million
See Pages 9 through 22 for Explanation of Ratios and Data

## Comparative Historical Data  |  Current Data Sorted by Sales

| 4/1/09-3/31/10 ALL | 4/1/10-3/31/11 ALL | 4/1/11-3/31/12 ALL | Type of Statement | 0-1MM | 1-3MM | 3-5MM | 5-10MM | 10-25MM | 25MM & OVER |
|---|---|---|---|---|---|---|---|---|---|
| | | | Unqualified | | | | | | |
| 4 | 2 | 3 | Reviewed | 1 | 1 | 2 | 2 | | 3 |
| 7 | 9 | 7 | Compiled | 3 | 3 | 2 | 1 | | 1 |
| 10 | 13 | 10 | Tax Returns | 9 | 6 | 1 | 1 | | 1 |
| 15 | 11 | 18 | Other | 2 | 13 | 1 | 1 | 1 | 4 |
| 18 | 24 | 25 | | | | | | | |
| | | | | 17 (4/1-9/30/11) | | 46 (10/1/11-3/31/12) | | | |
| 54 | 59 | 63 | **NUMBER OF STATEMENTS** | 15 | 23 | 7 | 6 | 3 | 9 |
| % | % | % | **ASSETS** | % | % | % | % | % | % |
| 12.4 | 13.5 | 11.3 | Cash & Equivalents | 11.0 | 18.1 | | | | |
| 6.4 | 7.6 | 7.4 | Trade Receivables (net) | 5.7 | 3.3 | | | | |
| 50.1 | 45.1 | 49.8 | Inventory | 64.0 | 45.1 | | | | |
| 2.6 | 1.9 | 1.9 | All Other Current | 1.5 | .8 | | | | |
| 71.5 | 68.1 | 70.3 | Total Current | 82.3 | 67.3 | | | | |
| 17.4 | 15.7 | 14.6 | Fixed Assets (net) | 9.2 | 12.6 | | | | |
| 3.0 | 3.0 | 2.8 | Intangibles (net) | 2.4 | .4 | | | | |
| 8.1 | 13.2 | 12.3 | All Other Non-Current | 6.1 | 19.7 | | | | |
| 100.0 | 100.0 | 100.0 | Total | 100.0 | 100.0 | | | | |
| | | | **LIABILITIES** | | | | | | |
| 8.4 | 9.1 | 15.9 | Notes Payable-Short Term | 37.0 | 6.9 | | | | |
| 3.0 | 2.0 | 2.0 | Cur. Mat.-L.T.D. | 1.3 | .7 | | | | |
| 23.6 | 22.0 | 21.1 | Trade Payables | 18.1 | 21.6 | | | | |
| .2 | .1 | .1 | Income Taxes Payable | .0 | .0 | | | | |
| 13.8 | 15.1 | 14.2 | All Other Current | 16.2 | 17.5 | | | | |
| 49.0 | 48.3 | 53.3 | Total Current | 72.7 | 46.7 | | | | |
| 15.1 | 9.3 | 11.1 | Long-Term Debt | 2.5 | 19.0 | | | | |
| .1 | .0 | .1 | Deferred Taxes | .0 | .0 | | | | |
| 2.9 | 5.5 | 3.9 | All Other Non-Current | 3.6 | 1.5 | | | | |
| 32.8 | 37.0 | 31.7 | Net Worth | 21.1 | 32.8 | | | | |
| 100.0 | 100.0 | 100.0 | Total Liabilities & Net Worth | 100.0 | 100.0 | | | | |
| | | | **INCOME DATA** | | | | | | |
| 100.0 | 100.0 | 100.0 | Net Sales | 100.0 | 100.0 | | | | |
| 44.6 | 51.0 | 48.3 | Gross Profit | 51.0 | 49.7 | | | | |
| 42.6 | 45.0 | 43.7 | Operating Expenses | 47.1 | 43.8 | | | | |
| 1.9 | 6.0 | 4.6 | Operating Profit | 3.9 | 6.0 | | | | |
| .5 | .5 | .8 | All Other Expenses (net) | .3 | .7 | | | | |
| 1.4 | 5.5 | 3.8 | Profit Before Taxes | 3.6 | 5.2 | | | | |
| | | | **RATIOS** | | | | | | |
| 3.0 | 3.0 | 2.7 | Current | 3.2 | 3.3 | | | | |
| 1.7 | 1.9 | 1.6 | | 1.1 | 2.5 | | | | |
| 1.1 | 1.1 | 1.0 | | .7 | 1.4 | | | | |
| .8 | 1.2 | .7 | Quick | .7 | 1.1 | | | | |
| .3 | .3 | .3 | | .2 | .5 | | | | |
| .1 | .1 | .1 | | .2 | .1 | | | | |
| 0 UND | 0 UND | 0 UND | Sales/Receivables | 0 UND | 0 UND | | | | |
| 3 118.0 | 1 262.0 | 1 451.5 | | 0 UND | 0 999.8 | | | | |
| 12 30.0 | 15 24.9 | 11 33.9 | | 19 19.0 | 2 155.7 | | | | |
| 83 4.4 | 114 3.2 | 114 3.2 | Cost of Sales/Inventory | 152 2.4 | 126 2.9 | | | | |
| 143 2.5 | 148 2.5 | 152 2.4 | | 192 1.9 | 152 2.4 | | | | |
| 229 1.6 | 225 1.6 | 203 1.8 | | 456 .8 | 203 1.8 | | | | |
| 32 11.2 | 34 10.6 | 26 13.8 | Cost of Sales/Payables | 0 UND | 26 13.8 | | | | |
| 49 7.5 | 60 6.1 | 58 6.3 | | 31 11.9 | 70 5.2 | | | | |
| 89 4.1 | 147 2.5 | 114 3.2 | | 130 2.8 | 159 2.3 | | | | |
| 4.3 | 4.2 | 4.8 | Sales/Working Capital | 2.4 | 4.2 | | | | |
| 9.0 | 7.2 | 9.2 | | 44.1 | 6.3 | | | | |
| 35.6 | 43.9 | -639.6 | | -10.4 | 16.8 | | | | |
| 6.1 | 21.6 | 9.1 | EBIT/Interest | | 13.0 | | | | |
| (45) 3.0 | (42) 4.9 | (46) 2.9 | | | (14) 1.9 | | | | |
| -.6 | .7 | .6 | | | -1.0 | | | | |
| | | | Net Profit + Depr., Dep., Amort./Cur. Mat. L/T/D | | | | | | |
| .1 | .1 | .1 | Fixed/Worth | .0 | .0 | | | | |
| .5 | .4 | .3 | | .3 | .1 | | | | |
| UND | 2.2 | 1.5 | | -4.8 | .4 | | | | |
| .7 | .4 | .5 | Debt/Worth | .7 | .3 | | | | |
| 1.4 | 1.0 | 1.5 | | 4.1 | .7 | | | | |
| UND | 14.8 | 14.5 | | -16.5 | 3.2 | | | | |
| 24.5 | 59.0 | 36.5 | % Profit Before Taxes/Tangible Net Worth | 98.6 | 29.5 | | | | |
| (41) 13.0 | (47) 15.9 | (49) 10.9 | | (11) 10.9 | (19) 11.8 | | | | |
| .6 | 5.9 | 1.2 | | 2.3 | 1.1 | | | | |
| 9.8 | 15.2 | 12.6 | % Profit Before Taxes/Total Assets | 13.7 | 13.1 | | | | |
| 4.4 | 6.1 | 4.4 | | 2.2 | 5.0 | | | | |
| -4.6 | .8 | -.4 | | 1.0 | -1.1 | | | | |
| 53.3 | 64.0 | 110.4 | Sales/Net Fixed Assets | UND | 120.6 | | | | |
| 17.8 | 27.6 | 34.2 | | 88.5 | 34.2 | | | | |
| 7.4 | 10.1 | 10.1 | | 14.0 | 9.2 | | | | |
| 3.2 | 3.1 | 3.0 | Sales/Total Assets | 2.8 | 2.8 | | | | |
| 2.3 | 2.0 | 2.2 | | 2.1 | 2.2 | | | | |
| 1.5 | 1.3 | 1.4 | | 1.1 | .9 | | | | |
| .4 | .3 | .4 | % Depr., Dep., Amort./Sales | .2 | .3 | | | | |
| (43) .7 | (43) .9 | (47) 1.0 | | (10) .6 | (17) .6 | | | | |
| 1.9 | 1.6 | 1.9 | | 2.0 | 2.1 | | | | |
| 1.9 | 3.4 | 3.3 | % Officers', Directors' Owners' Comp/Sales | | | | | | |
| (21) 5.0 | (23) 6.6 | (19) 8.4 | | | | | | | |
| 7.7 | 11.3 | 11.4 | | | | | | | |
| 2597531M | 1234385M | 1372409M | Net Sales ($) | 8613M | 43777M | 24398M | 41359M | 51882M | 1202380M |
| 1084817M | 641330M | 693014M | Total Assets ($) | 5582M | 32956M | 11148M | 39245M | 24564M | 579519M |

M = $ thousand    MM = $ million
See Pages 9 through 22 for Explanation of Ratios and Data

## Current Data Sorted by Assets | Comparative Historical Data

| 0-500M | 500M-2MM | 2-10MM | 10-50MM | 50-100MM | 100-250MM | Type of Statement | 4/1/07-3/31/08 ALL | 4/1/08-3/31/09 ALL |
|---|---|---|---|---|---|---|---|---|
| | 2 | 4 | 6 | 2 | 5 | Unqualified | 15 | 19 |
| | 2 | 5 | 3 | | | Reviewed | 12 | 15 |
| 4 | 10 | 2 | | | | Compiled | 12 | 15 |
| 21 | 11 | 6 | | | 1 | Tax Returns | 14 | 23 |
| 16 | 17 | 6 | 5 | 2 | 6 | Other | 31 | 31 |
| **0-500M** | **500M-2MM** 16 (4/1-9/30/11) | **2-10MM** | **10-50MM** 120 (10/1/11-3/31/12) | **50-100MM** | **100-250MM** | | | |
| 41 | 42 | 23 | 14 | 4 | 12 | NUMBER OF STATEMENTS | 84 | 103 |
| % | % | % | % | % | % | **ASSETS** | % | % |
| 19.8 | 17.4 | 15.1 | 13.1 | | 10.7 | Cash & Equivalents | 12.8 | 11.7 |
| 5.8 | 7.7 | 6.7 | 5.7 | | 1.3 | Trade Receivables (net) | 6.5 | 8.2 |
| 46.9 | 45.8 | 39.5 | 36.6 | | 34.4 | Inventory | 51.2 | 42.0 |
| 1.9 | .6 | 7.7 | 2.3 | | 3.5 | All Other Current | 3.4 | 4.1 |
| 74.3 | 71.5 | 69.0 | 57.7 | | 49.9 | Total Current | 73.9 | 66.1 |
| 19.4 | 15.4 | 19.5 | 29.2 | | 30.7 | Fixed Assets (net) | 17.9 | 21.7 |
| 1.9 | 2.2 | .7 | 2.0 | | 14.6 | Intangibles (net) | 2.9 | 3.4 |
| 4.4 | 10.8 | 10.8 | 11.1 | | 4.7 | All Other Non-Current | 5.3 | 8.8 |
| 100.0 | 100.0 | 100.0 | 100.0 | | 100.0 | Total | 100.0 | 100.0 |
| | | | | | | **LIABILITIES** | | |
| 9.9 | 4.9 | 5.7 | 4.7 | | 4.4 | Notes Payable-Short Term | 12.4 | 13.0 |
| 4.2 | 1.2 | 1.4 | 1.0 | | 3.4 | Cur. Mat.-L.T.D. | 6.4 | 3.6 |
| 8.4 | 21.7 | 26.1 | 24.4 | | 18.4 | Trade Payables | 19.6 | 15.5 |
| .2 | .2 | .0 | .1 | | .6 | Income Taxes Payable | .4 | .4 |
| 32.6 | 7.7 | 10.4 | 13.0 | | 12.8 | All Other Current | 12.4 | 12.0 |
| 55.3 | 35.7 | 43.6 | 43.2 | | 39.6 | Total Current | 51.3 | 44.6 |
| 23.6 | 9.0 | 7.3 | 9.5 | | 21.2 | Long-Term Debt | 14.0 | 13.3 |
| .0 | .0 | .0 | .4 | | .6 | Deferred Taxes | .1 | .3 |
| 20.3 | 21.3 | 2.2 | 12.1 | | 7.8 | All Other Non-Current | 7.9 | 6.2 |
| .8 | 34.0 | 46.8 | 34.9 | | 30.8 | Net Worth | 26.7 | 35.6 |
| 100.0 | 100.0 | 100.0 | 100.0 | | 100.0 | Total Liabilities & Net Worth | 100.0 | 100.0 |
| | | | | | | **INCOME DATA** | | |
| 100.0 | 100.0 | 100.0 | 100.0 | | 100.0 | Net Sales | 100.0 | 100.0 |
| 50.3 | 47.1 | 49.9 | 44.1 | | 45.4 | Gross Profit | 44.3 | 46.7 |
| 45.9 | 42.0 | 46.9 | 41.7 | | 45.3 | Operating Expenses | 41.8 | 44.5 |
| 4.4 | 5.1 | 3.0 | 2.4 | | .0 | Operating Profit | 2.5 | 2.2 |
| .5 | -.1 | -.2 | .9 | | 1.7 | All Other Expenses (net) | .9 | .8 |
| 3.9 | 5.3 | 3.2 | 1.5 | | -1.7 | Profit Before Taxes | 1.6 | 1.4 |
| | | | | | | **RATIOS** | | |
| 12.0 | 5.6 | 2.9 | 1.8 | | 1.9 | | 2.5 | 3.3 |
| 3.4 | 2.1 | 1.7 | 1.5 | | 1.3 | Current | 1.5 | 1.7 |
| 1.0 | 1.4 | 1.1 | 1.2 | | .9 | | 1.2 | 1.0 |
| 5.0 | 1.9 | .9 | .9 | | .5 | | .8 | 1.0 |
| .8 | (41) .7 | .4 | .5 | | .3 | Quick | .3 | (101) .4 |
| .1 | .3 | .2 | .2 | | .1 | | .1 | .1 |
| 0 UND | 0 UND | 0 UND | 0 UND | | 0 UND | | 0 UND | 0 UND |
| 0 UND | 0 UND | 0 UND | 2 163.6 | | 1 293.0 | Sales/Receivables | 2 199.9 | 1 479.8 |
| 0 UND | 17 21.6 | 9 40.6 | 8 46.2 | | 3 121.7 | | 8 47.4 | 15 24.3 |
| 63 5.8 | 48 7.6 | 54 6.7 | 52 7.0 | | 42 8.6 | | 76 4.8 | 56 6.5 |
| 126 2.9 | 118 3.1 | 107 3.4 | 69 5.3 | | 85 4.3 | Cost of Sales/Inventory | 112 3.3 | 98 3.7 |
| 203 1.8 | 243 1.5 | 166 2.2 | 91 4.0 | | 122 3.0 | | 184 2.0 | 173 2.1 |
| 0 UND | 10 38.3 | 29 12.8 | 31 11.9 | | 30 12.0 | | 21 17.1 | 9 38.7 |
| 2 167.5 | 33 11.1 | 64 5.7 | 38 9.6 | | 39 9.4 | Cost of Sales/Payables | 36 10.0 | 31 11.8 |
| 33 11.1 | 78 4.7 | 76 4.8 | 49 7.4 | | 54 6.8 | | 69 5.3 | 53 6.9 |
| 3.7 | 3.0 | 5.4 | 11.3 | | 9.7 | | 6.0 | 5.4 |
| 7.7 | 8.2 | 8.5 | 19.2 | | 31.4 | Sales/Working Capital | 13.7 | 13.1 |
| NM | 24.0 | 86.1 | 45.9 | | NM | | 32.5 | 304.4 |
| 10.5 | 26.4 | 18.9 | 7.9 | | | | 7.7 | 4.9 |
| (17) 5.3 | (27) 5.5 | (17) 2.4 | (13) 1.8 | | | EBIT/Interest | (73) 1.8 | (78) 1.2 |
| 1.2 | 2.0 | 1.1 | -.7 | | | | -1.2 | -1.1 |
| | | | | | | | 19.4 | 6.2 |
| | | | | | | Net Profit + Depr., Dep., Amort./Cur. Mat. L/T/D | (12) 2.6 | (15) 1.4 |
| | | | | | | | 1.6 | .8 |
| .1 | .1 | .1 | .5 | | .6 | | .2 | .1 |
| .4 | .4 | .4 | 1.1 | | 2.8 | Fixed/Worth | .6 | .6 |
| -1.3 | NM | .8 | 1.9 | | -3.7 | | 1.6 | 2.5 |
| .6 | .5 | .8 | .9 | | 1.0 | | .9 | .5 |
| 2.0 | 1.6 | 1.1 | 1.7 | | 6.2 | Debt/Worth | 2.0 | 1.2 |
| -5.1 | NM | 3.9 | 4.1 | | -11.0 | | 10.8 | 10.3 |
| 56.7 | 54.6 | 51.3 | 30.4 | | | | 47.3 | 29.3 |
| (27) 25.5 | (32) 20.9 | 10.9 | (13) 17.2 | | | % Profit Before Taxes/Tangible Net Worth | (67) 16.0 | (80) 8.5 |
| 8.3 | 6.3 | 2.3 | -.4 | | | | -.6 | -4.8 |
| 27.4 | 27.1 | 17.6 | 10.9 | | 21.2 | | 19.0 | 14.2 |
| 9.9 | 7.3 | 5.4 | 4.9 | | 3.8 | % Profit Before Taxes/Total Assets | 3.5 | 1.7 |
| .8 | 1.1 | 1.0 | -.7 | | -18.5 | | -3.6 | -4.5 |
| 129.0 | 124.2 | 50.7 | 32.5 | | 11.4 | | 51.0 | 42.0 |
| 24.2 | 24.9 | 12.1 | 14.3 | | 9.9 | Sales/Net Fixed Assets | 21.0 | 16.0 |
| 10.2 | 11.1 | 6.4 | 7.9 | | 8.1 | | 9.4 | 7.4 |
| 4.6 | 4.2 | 4.2 | 4.6 | | 3.1 | | 4.2 | 4.1 |
| 2.7 | 2.8 | 3.0 | 3.8 | | 2.7 | Sales/Total Assets | 2.7 | 2.8 |
| 1.9 | 1.9 | 1.4 | 2.6 | | 2.3 | | 2.0 | 1.8 |
| .5 | .2 | .6 | .7 | | | | .5 | .4 |
| (23) 1.1 | (29) .5 | (20) 1.2 | 1.7 | | | % Depr., Dep., Amort./Sales | (58) 1.2 | (74) 1.1 |
| 2.5 | 1.2 | 1.7 | 2.4 | | | | 2.1 | 2.0 |
| 4.4 | 2.1 | 1.8 | | | | | 1.7 | 2.0 |
| (19) 5.4 | (27) 4.2 | (12) 3.3 | | | | % Officers', Directors' Owners' Comp/Sales | (30) 3.6 | (43) 3.0 |
| 6.6 | 7.2 | 5.0 | | | | | 5.4 | 5.2 |
| 32470M | 148096M | 325504M | 1225159M | 783327M | 5035553M | Net Sales ($) | 4032536M | 5455843M |
| 10496M | 44074M | 110488M | 336948M | 296657M | 1806922M | Total Assets ($) | 1531599M | 2384260M |

M = $ thousand   MM = $ million
See Pages 9 through 22 for Explanation of Ratios and Data

## Comparative Historical Data | | Type of Statement | Current Data Sorted by Sales

| | | | Type of Statement | | | | | | |
|---|---|---|---|---|---|---|---|---|---|
| 16 | 14 | 19 | Unqualified | | 1 | 2 | 3 | 13 | |
| 11 | 11 | 10 | Reviewed | | 1 | 2 | 2 | 5 | |
| 9 | 14 | 16 | Compiled | | 2 | 3 | 1 | | |
| 38 | 25 | 39 | Tax Returns | 17 | 13 | 2 | 2 | 4 | 1 |
| 35 | 35 | 52 | Other | 18 | 10 | 5 | 3 | 4 | 12 |
| 4/1/09-3/31/10 ALL | 4/1/10-3/31/11 ALL | 4/1/11-3/31/12 ALL | | 16 (4/1-9/30/11) | | | 120 (10/1/11-3/31/12) | | |
| | | | | 0-1MM | 1-3MM | 3-5MM | 5-10MM | 10-25MM | 25MM & OVER |
| 109 | 99 | 136 | NUMBER OF STATEMENTS | 36 | 32 | 11 | 12 | 14 | 31 |
| % | % | % | ASSETS | % | % | % | % | % | % |
| 14.5 | 16.5 | 17.0 | Cash & Equivalents | 18.0 | 16.3 | 16.6 | 16.7 | 22.0 | 14.5 |
| 4.9 | 8.9 | 6.0 | Trade Receivables (net) | 6.8 | 6.4 | 2.3 | 8.5 | 9.5 | 3.5 |
| 41.3 | 38.8 | 42.6 | Inventory | 46.8 | 49.4 | 49.9 | 32.2 | 33.9 | 36.1 |
| 5.5 | 5.3 | 2.7 | All Other Current | 1.9 | 1.9 | .9 | 5.7 | 4.8 | 3.1 |
| 66.3 | 69.5 | 68.3 | Total Current | 73.5 | 74.0 | 69.7 | 63.2 | 70.2 | 57.1 |
| 23.9 | 19.0 | 20.2 | Fixed Assets (net) | 19.8 | 16.0 | 16.0 | 15.6 | 19.6 | 28.6 |
| 3.9 | 4.2 | 3.0 | Intangibles (net) | 2.6 | 1.8 | 1.5 | .6 | .5 | 7.5 |
| 5.9 | 7.3 | 8.4 | All Other Non-Current | 4.0 | 8.3 | 12.8 | 20.7 | 9.8 | 6.7 |
| 100.0 | 100.0 | 100.0 | Total | 100.0 | 100.0 | 100.0 | 100.0 | 100.0 | 100.0 |
| | | | LIABILITIES | | | | | | |
| 8.8 | 12.6 | 6.3 | Notes Payable-Short Term | 10.1 | 5.6 | 8.3 | 7.3 | 1.5 | 3.9 |
| 4.8 | 4.2 | 2.3 | Cur. Mat.-L.T.D. | 4.1 | 1.0 | 1.9 | 2.8 | 1.2 | 1.8 |
| 13.7 | 18.9 | 18.3 | Trade Payables | 9.4 | 13.4 | 18.3 | 21.6 | 40.5 | 22.3 |
| .1 | .3 | .2 | Income Taxes Payable | .4 | .0 | .2 | .0 | .0 | .3 |
| 15.1 | 13.4 | 16.9 | All Other Current | 32.9 | 8.5 | 19.4 | 7.9 | 9.2 | 13.1 |
| 42.6 | 49.3 | 44.0 | Total Current | 56.9 | 28.5 | 48.2 | 39.6 | 52.4 | 41.4 |
| 15.9 | 12.1 | 14.1 | Long-Term Debt | 23.5 | 15.6 | 3.7 | 3.1 | 6.5 | 13.2 |
| .5 | .3 | .1 | Deferred Taxes | .0 | .0 | .1 | .0 | .0 | .4 |
| 8.0 | 8.8 | 15.3 | All Other Non-Current | 23.8 | 14.3 | 24.7 | 13.2 | 3.1 | 9.3 |
| 33.0 | 29.5 | 26.5 | Net Worth | -4.3 | 41.6 | 23.3 | 44.1 | 38.0 | 35.7 |
| 100.0 | 100.0 | 100.0 | Total Liabilities & Net Worth | 100.0 | 100.0 | 100.0 | 100.0 | 100.0 | 100.0 |
| | | | INCOME DATA | | | | | | |
| 100.0 | 100.0 | 100.0 | Net Sales | 100.0 | 100.0 | 100.0 | 100.0 | 100.0 | 100.0 |
| 46.4 | 46.4 | 48.1 | Gross Profit | 52.4 | 48.0 | 46.0 | 52.4 | 42.1 | 45.1 |
| 44.8 | 41.5 | 44.4 | Operating Expenses | 47.5 | 42.9 | 44.5 | 47.3 | 38.8 | 43.9 |
| 1.6 | 4.9 | 3.7 | Operating Profit | 4.9 | 5.1 | 1.5 | 5.1 | 3.3 | 1.2 |
| .9 | 1.0 | .3 | All Other Expenses (net) | .6 | -.1 | .0 | .2 | -.9 | 1.1 |
| .7 | 3.9 | 3.3 | Profit Before Taxes | 4.3 | 5.2 | 1.5 | 4.9 | 4.2 | .1 |
| | | | RATIOS | | | | | | |
| 3.6 | 3.0 | 4.9 | | 13.4 | 9.9 | 2.4 | 2.7 | 3.1 | 1.9 |
| 1.7 | 1.7 | 1.8 | Current | 4.1 | 2.7 | 1.7 | 1.6 | 1.8 | 1.5 |
| 1.1 | 1.0 | 1.2 | | 1.0 | 1.6 | .8 | 1.0 | .9 | 1.2 |
| 1.0 | 1.2 | 1.5 | | 5.3 | 2.0 | 1.1 | 1.4 | 1.2 | 1.0 |
| .4 (98) | .5 (135) | .6 | Quick | 1.0 (31) | .7 | .2 | .4 | .8 | .5 |
| .2 | .1 | .2 | | .1 | .3 | .1 | .3 | .2 | .1 |
| 0 UND | 0 UND | 0 UND | | 0 UND | 0 UND | 0 UND | 0 UND | 0 UND | 0 UND |
| 0 999.8 | 1 446.5 | 0 UND | Sales/Receivables | 0 UND | 0 UND | 0 UND | 2 214.2 | 0 UND | 2 166.4 |
| 4 94.9 | 9 39.4 | 5 72.4 | | 0 UND | 8 46.7 | 1 380.9 | 22 16.8 | 9 38.7 | 4 89.0 |
| 50 7.2 | 49 7.5 | 54 6.7 | | 85 4.3 | 74 4.9 | 46 8.0 | 8 47.5 | 33 11.2 | 45 8.2 |
| 84 4.3 | 86 4.3 | 101 3.6 | Cost of Sales/Inventory | 159 2.3 | 126 2.9 | 126 2.9 | 65 5.6 | 78 4.7 | 79 4.6 |
| 148 2.5 | 141 2.6 | 174 2.1 | | 281 1.3 | 243 1.5 | 228 1.6 | 114 3.2 | 111 3.3 | 94 3.9 |
| 8 43.6 | 16 22.9 | 7 49.4 | | 0 UND | 0 UND | 20 18.3 | 13 29.1 | 32 11.5 | 32 11.4 |
| 22 17.0 | 36 10.0 | 33 11.0 | Cost of Sales/Payables | 3 143.6 | 15 23.6 | 54 6.7 | 33 11.2 | 52 7.0 | 39 9.3 |
| 53 6.9 | 61 6.0 | 58 6.3 | | 43 8.4 | 51 7.2 | 94 3.9 | 65 5.6 | 76 4.8 | 51 7.1 |
| 5.6 | 5.5 | 5.2 | | 2.6 | 3.1 | 6.5 | 9.3 | 6.5 | 9.7 |
| 12.4 | 13.1 | 9.7 | Sales/Working Capital | 5.5 | 7.3 | 8.5 | 19.3 | 11.3 | 20.6 |
| 58.2 | 136.1 | 45.1 | | -106.3 | 15.3 | -56.6 | 520.1 | -58.3 | 50.2 |
| 8.8 | 18.6 | 16.9 | | 5.8 | 14.3 | | 38.6 | 79.0 | 15.1 |
| (81) 1.4 | (81) 4.4 | (86) 4.1 | EBIT/Interest | (13) 4.2 | (21) 5.5 | | (10) 17.3 | (11) 6.0 | (24) 2.4 |
| -5.1 | 1.2 | 1.2 | | .6 | 1.8 | | 2.1 | 1.4 | -.3 |
| 22.3 | 12.7 | | Net Profit + Depr., Dep., | | | | | | |
| (14) 1.9 | (13) 4.1 | | Amort./Cur. Mat. L/T/D | | | | | | |
| -.3 | 1.3 | | | | | | | | |
| .2 | .1 | .2 | | .1 | .1 | .0 | .1 | .1 | .5 |
| .6 | .5 | .6 | Fixed/Worth | .5 | .3 | .5 | .5 | .4 | .7 |
| 2.0 | 1.6 | 4.7 | | -1.0 | 1.0 | -.9 | 1.2 | 2.2 | 2.9 |
| .5 | .5 | .7 | | .7 | .3 | .9 | .5 | .5 | .9 |
| 1.5 | 1.6 | 1.5 | Debt/Worth | 10.7 | .9 | 5.1 | 1.2 | 1.8 | 1.6 |
| 8.0 | 14.2 | 48.7 | | -4.4 | 2.8 | -7.8 | 3.0 | 5.4 | 10.8 |
| 33.5 | 69.2 | 49.9 | % Profit Before Taxes/Tangible | 47.3 | 49.6 | | 74.8 | 82.2 | 35.7 |
| (90) 12.0 | (79) 25.0 | (106) 18.4 | Net Worth | (22) 26.8 | (27) 17.9 | | 18.1 | (13) 39.8 | (25) 14.4 |
| -7.2 | 3.1 | | | 8.5 | 3.2 | | 9.2 | 1.9 | -1.5 |
| 13.8 | 22.0 | 18.3 | % Profit Before Taxes/Total | 19.4 | 26.5 | 8.1 | 35.9 | 42.8 | 12.3 |
| 3.2 | 11.3 | 6.0 | Assets | 7.4 | 7.3 | 4.9 | 9.3 | 10.3 | 4.3 |
| -6.9 | .9 | .1 | | -2.6 | 1.3 | -7.2 | 2.7 | 1.9 | -1.5 |
| 44.9 | 82.4 | 74.8 | | 117.8 | 92.7 | 147.4 | 95.3 | 155.9 | 16.0 |
| 15.1 | 16.7 | 16.6 | Sales/Net Fixed Assets | 18.2 | 28.7 | 18.4 | 36.7 | 21.6 | 11.8 |
| 7.3 | 9.1 | 9.5 | | 8.8 | 8.9 | 7.8 | 11.7 | 9.7 | 8.8 |
| 3.9 | 4.2 | 4.3 | | 3.0 | 4.0 | 5.8 | 5.1 | 5.6 | 4.4 |
| 2.8 | 2.9 | 2.9 | Sales/Total Assets | 2.1 | 2.8 | 2.7 | 3.7 | 3.7 | 3.1 |
| 2.1 | 2.2 | 2.0 | | 1.4 | 1.9 | 1.9 | 3.0 | 2.3 | 2.6 |
| .6 | .5 | .4 | | .5 | .2 | | .3 | .2 | .8 |
| (80) 1.5 | (72) 1.3 | (94) 1.1 | % Depr., Dep., Amort./Sales | (19) 1.7 | (20) .5 | | (10) .5 | (13) .9 | (23) 1.8 |
| 2.6 | 2.5 | 2.1 | | 2.6 | 1.9 | | 1.0 | 2.0 | 2.8 |
| 1.8 | 1.8 | 2.5 | % Officers', Directors' | 4.6 | 3.2 | | | | |
| (43) 4.0 | (38) 3.6 | (62) 4.6 | Owners' Comp/Sales | (19) 6.4 | (14) 6.0 | | | | |
| 6.1 | 7.1 | 6.6 | | 8.0 | 9.8 | | | | |
| 8363772M | 6814175M | 7550109M | Net Sales ($) | 20774M | 57585M | 45079M | 84732M | 221071M | 7120868M |
| 3128948M | 2403813M | 2605585M | Total Assets ($) | 11429M | 27549M | 17152M | 29574M | 75804M | 2444077M |

M = $ thousand    MM = $ million
See Pages 9 through 22 for Explanation of Ratios and Data

## Current Data Sorted by Assets      Comparative Historical Data

| | 1 | | 1 | 3 | 4 | 2 | Type of Statement | 9 | 10 |
|---|---|---|---|---|---|---|---|---|---|
| | | 1 | 10 | 2 | | 1 | Unqualified | 10 | 10 |
| | 1 | 5 | 9 | | | | Reviewed | 6 | 11 |
| | 11 | 14 | 10 | | | | Compiled | 16 | 27 |
| | 7 | 7 | 5 | | 4 | 5 | Tax Returns / Other | 31 | 35 |
| | | 19 (4/1-9/30/11) | | 1 | 85 (10/1/11-3/31/12) | | | 4/1/07-3/31/08 | 4/1/08-3/31/09 |
| | 0-500M | 500M-2MM | 2-10MM | 10-50MM | 50-100MM | 100-250MM | | ALL | ALL |
| NUMBER OF STATEMENTS | 20 | 27 | 35 | 6 | 8 | 8 | | 72 | 93 |
| | % | % | % | % | % | % | ASSETS | % | % |
| | 22.3 | 10.3 | 12.7 | | | | Cash & Equivalents | 10.6 | 11.0 |
| | 2.4 | 5.4 | 10.3 | | | | Trade Receivables (net) | 7.1 | 9.0 |
| | 56.8 | 59.5 | 46.2 | | | | Inventory | 49.2 | 46.0 |
| | .9 | 1.9 | 2.5 | | | | All Other Current | 2.5 | 3.0 |
| | 82.4 | 77.1 | 71.8 | | | | Total Current | 69.3 | 69.0 |
| | 9.3 | 12.7 | 19.1 | | | | Fixed Assets (net) | 20.8 | 20.3 |
| | 1.3 | 1.5 | .6 | | | | Intangibles (net) | 3.0 | 1.9 |
| | 7.0 | 8.7 | 8.4 | | | | All Other Non-Current | 6.9 | 8.8 |
| | 100.0 | 100.0 | 100.0 | | | | Total | 100.0 | 100.0 |
| | | | | | | | **LIABILITIES** | | |
| | 23.5 | 7.8 | 5.0 | | | | Notes Payable-Short Term | 8.5 | 7.9 |
| | 5.2 | 3.1 | 1.0 | | | | Cur. Mat.-L.T.D. | 3.0 | 2.5 |
| | 15.1 | 16.8 | 25.5 | | | | Trade Payables | 17.2 | 19.0 |
| | .1 | .1 | .3 | | | | Income Taxes Payable | .3 | .2 |
| | 10.3 | 8.9 | 8.7 | | | | All Other Current | 12.3 | 13.0 |
| | 54.2 | 36.7 | 40.5 | | | | Total Current | 41.2 | 42.6 |
| | 12.6 | 10.0 | 10.7 | | | | Long-Term Debt | 15.5 | 12.6 |
| | .0 | .0 | .0 | | | | Deferred Taxes | .4 | .0 |
| | 6.0 | 13.7 | 11.1 | | | | All Other Non-Current | 7.2 | 6.9 |
| | 27.2 | 39.7 | 37.7 | | | | Net Worth | 35.8 | 37.9 |
| | 100.0 | 100.0 | 100.0 | | | | Total Liabilties & Net Worth | 100.0 | 100.0 |
| | | | | | | | **INCOME DATA** | | |
| | 100.0 | 100.0 | 100.0 | | | | Net Sales | 100.0 | 100.0 |
| | 45.6 | 44.2 | 39.7 | | | | Gross Profit | 43.5 | 44.3 |
| | 41.3 | 38.6 | 37.1 | | | | Operating Expenses | 40.2 | 41.1 |
| | 4.3 | 5.7 | 2.5 | | | | Operating Profit | 3.3 | 3.2 |
| | .4 | 1.2 | -1.4 | | | | All Other Expenses (net) | .8 | .7 |
| | 4.0 | 4.4 | 3.9 | | | | Profit Before Taxes | 2.4 | 2.6 |
| | | | | | | | **RATIOS** | | |
| | 3.8 | 3.1 | 3.7 | | | | | 3.0 | 3.2 |
| | 2.0 | 2.3 | 1.9 | | | | Current | 1.7 | 1.8 |
| | 1.2 | 1.6 | 1.2 | | | | | 1.3 | 1.1 |
| | 1.3 | .8 | 1.3 | | | | | .9 | 1.0 |
| | .3 | (26) .4 | .5 | | | | Quick | .3 | .5 |
| | .1 | .1 | .1 | | | | | .1 | .1 |
| | 0 UND | 0 UND | 0 UND | | | | | 0 UND | 0 UND |
| | 0 UND | 0 UND | 3 114.3 | | | | Sales/Receivables | 1 271.7 | 1 280.9 |
| | 2 149.5 | 7 55.2 | 14 25.7 | | | | | 10 35.3 | 12 29.7 |
| | 35 10.5 | 104 3.5 | 76 4.8 | | | | | 64 5.7 | 60 6.0 |
| | 122 3.0 | 146 2.5 | 111 3.3 | | | | Cost of Sales/Inventory | 114 3.2 | 105 3.5 |
| | 174 2.1 | 332 1.1 | 152 2.4 | | | | | 154 2.4 | 164 2.2 |
| | 0 UND | 9 40.3 | 14 26.2 | | | | | 14 25.6 | 21 17.4 |
| | 23 15.9 | 32 11.5 | 53 6.9 | | | | Cost of Sales/Payables | 36 10.2 | 38 9.7 |
| | 39 9.3 | 65 5.6 | 87 4.2 | | | | | 66 5.5 | 62 5.9 |
| | 3.5 | 3.5 | 5.7 | | | | | 6.0 | 6.0 |
| | 12.6 | 7.4 | 9.6 | | | | Sales/Working Capital | 10.6 | 12.4 |
| | 53.8 | 10.2 | 29.8 | | | | | 26.7 | 45.2 |
| | 13.9 | 35.3 | 30.0 | | | | | 4.7 | 12.4 |
| | (14) 7.3 | (22) 4.7 | (28) 2.8 | | | | EBIT/Interest | (60) 1.8 | (75) 3.3 |
| | .7 | .0 | 1.3 | | | | | .4 | .6 |
| | | | | | | | | 2.5 | 14.1 |
| | | | | | | | Net Profit + Depr., Dep., Amort./Cur. Mat. L/T/D | (15) .2 | (10) 2.3 |
| | | | | | | | | -1.3 | -1.0 |
| | .1 | .1 | .1 | | | | | .3 | .1 |
| | .3 | .1 | .5 | | | | Fixed/Worth | .5 | .4 |
| | 1.5 | .3 | 1.9 | | | | | 1.9 | 1.0 |
| | .6 | .5 | .6 | | | | | .8 | .7 |
| | 2.0 | 1.5 | 1.5 | | | | Debt/Worth | 1.7 | 1.4 |
| | 18.8 | 3.5 | 6.3 | | | | | 7.2 | 2.6 |
| | 111.4 | 63.9 | 48.1 | | | | | 32.9 | 53.2 |
| | (16) 35.3 | (24) 19.0 | (30) 18.8 | | | | % Profit Before Taxes/Tangible Net Worth | (62) 7.9 | (83) 13.5 |
| | 7.0 | 1.8 | 3.6 | | | | | 1.0 | 1.1 |
| | 25.1 | 26.6 | 17.8 | | | | | 9.6 | 18.7 |
| | 13.9 | 6.0 | 6.3 | | | | % Profit Before Taxes/Total Assets | 2.8 | 5.8 |
| | 2.7 | -1.1 | 1.1 | | | | | -3.0 | -.3 |
| | 200.1 | 184.7 | 102.2 | | | | | 31.8 | 55.5 |
| | 65.6 | 40.1 | 22.8 | | | | Sales/Net Fixed Assets | 15.3 | 18.3 |
| | 25.2 | 18.4 | 8.3 | | | | | 8.7 | 9.0 |
| | 6.2 | 3.6 | 4.1 | | | | | 3.9 | 4.1 |
| | 4.1 | 2.3 | 3.1 | | | | Sales/Total Assets | 2.7 | 2.6 |
| | 2.2 | 1.7 | 2.0 | | | | | 2.0 | 2.0 |
| | .4 | .2 | .4 | | | | | .6 | .6 |
| | (13) .5 | (18) .5 | (30) .7 | | | | % Depr., Dep., Amort./Sales | (60) 1.0 | (66) 1.2 |
| | 1.0 | 1.1 | 2.0 | | | | | 2.0 | 2.2 |
| | 3.3 | 2.0 | .7 | | | | | 2.2 | 2.1 |
| | (13) 5.7 | (18) 4.1 | (15) 1.7 | | | | % Officers', Directors' Owners' Comp/Sales | (26) 3.3 | (40) 4.1 |
| | 9.7 | 8.9 | 3.0 | | | | | 6.4 | 7.7 |
| | 22484M | 69249M | 649512M | 392420M | 1411698M | 2722425M | Net Sales ($) | 5269706M | 5043540M |
| | 5497M | 27414M | 169601M | 114402M | 588709M | 1172438M | Total Assets ($) | 1986777M | 1671505M |

M = $ thousand    MM = $ million
See Pages 9 through 22 for Explanation of Ratios and Data

## Comparative Historical Data | Current Data Sorted by Sales

### Type of Statement

| | | | | | 0-1MM | 1-3MM | 3-5MM | 5-10MM | 10-25MM | 25MM & OVER |
|---|---|---|---|---|---|---|---|---|---|---|
| 11 | 10 | 11 | Unqualified | | | 1 | | | | 10 |
| 20 | 9 | 14 | Reviewed | | | 2 | 2 | 1 | 4 | 5 |
| 13 | 13 | 15 | Compiled | | | 4 | 2 | 5 | 1 | 3 |
| 24 | 25 | 35 | Tax Returns | | 9 | 16 | 2 | 4 | 2 | 2 |
| 30 | 35 | 29 | Other | | 3 | 7 | 3 | 3 | 2 | 11 |
| 4/1/09-3/31/10 ALL | 4/1/10-3/31/11 ALL | 4/1/11-3/31/12 ALL | | | | 19 (4/1-9/30/11) | | 85 (10/1/11-3/31/12) | | |
| 98 | 92 | 104 | NUMBER OF STATEMENTS | | 12 | 30 | 9 | 13 | 9 | 31 |
| % | % | % | ASSETS | | % | % | % | % | % | % |
| 14.8 | 11.9 | 15.2 | Cash & Equivalents | | 17.5 | 12.6 | | 17.2 | | 16.0 |
| 8.2 | 7.3 | 5.9 | Trade Receivables (net) | | 1.2 | 5.0 | | 7.5 | | 7.6 |
| 46.5 | 54.1 | 50.9 | Inventory | | 62.4 | 51.0 | | 55.4 | | 42.6 |
| 2.4 | 2.4 | 2.4 | All Other Current | | 1.6 | 1.3 | | 4.3 | | 3.8 |
| 71.9 | 75.7 | 74.4 | Total Current | | 82.7 | 70.0 | | 84.4 | | 70.0 |
| 17.2 | 17.1 | 15.8 | Fixed Assets (net) | | 11.8 | 16.8 | | 12.2 | | 20.3 |
| 3.3 | 2.3 | 2.0 | Intangibles (net) | | 1.4 | 1.6 | | .2 | | 4.1 |
| 7.6 | 4.9 | 7.8 | All Other Non-Current | | 4.1 | 11.5 | | 3.3 | | 5.7 |
| 100.0 | 100.0 | 100.0 | Total | | 100.0 | 100.0 | | 100.0 | | 100.0 |
| | | | LIABILITIES | | | | | | | |
| 7.4 | 8.8 | 8.4 | Notes Payable-Short Term | | 12.8 | 17.1 | | 8.5 | | 1.8 |
| 2.9 | 3.5 | 2.3 | Cur. Mat.-L.T.D. | | 9.5 | 2.2 | | 1.2 | | .9 |
| 16.3 | 22.0 | 20.7 | Trade Payables | | 5.3 | 14.9 | | 34.9 | | 23.7 |
| .3 | .3 | .2 | Income Taxes Payable | | .1 | .1 | | .6 | | .1 |
| 13.4 | 9.2 | 10.3 | All Other Current | | 9.5 | 9.9 | | 4.7 | | 14.1 |
| 40.3 | 43.6 | 41.9 | Total Current | | 37.2 | 44.2 | | 49.9 | | 40.6 |
| 14.3 | 10.8 | 10.2 | Long-Term Debt | | 23.4 | 12.3 | | 6.5 | | 7.3 |
| .1 | .1 | .1 | Deferred Taxes | | .0 | .0 | | .0 | | .3 |
| 6.2 | 6.4 | 9.5 | All Other Non-Current | | 10.8 | 11.5 | | 14.3 | | 6.4 |
| 39.2 | 39.1 | 38.3 | Net Worth | | 28.6 | 32.0 | | 29.3 | | 45.3 |
| 100.0 | 100.0 | 100.0 | Total Liabilities & Net Worth | | 100.0 | 100.0 | | 100.0 | | 100.0 |
| | | | INCOME DATA | | | | | | | |
| 100.0 | 100.0 | 100.0 | Net Sales | | 100.0 | 100.0 | | 100.0 | | 100.0 |
| 44.0 | 42.3 | 42.6 | Gross Profit | | 43.1 | 49.1 | | 36.3 | | 40.7 |
| 40.9 | 38.3 | 38.1 | Operating Expenses | | 36.2 | 44.0 | | 36.4 | | 35.2 |
| 3.1 | 4.0 | 4.4 | Operating Profit | | 6.9 | 5.1 | | -.2 | | 5.5 |
| .2 | .2 | .2 | All Other Expenses (net) | | 1.3 | -.2 | | -1.5 | | .8 |
| 2.8 | 3.8 | 4.3 | Profit Before Taxes | | 5.6 | 5.4 | | 1.4 | | 4.7 |
| | | | RATIOS | | | | | | | |
| 4.3 | 3.2 | 3.1 | | | 3.8 | 4.2 | | 2.8 | | 3.0 |
| 2.0 | 2.0 | 2.0 | Current | | 2.4 | 2.0 | | 2.2 | | 1.9 |
| 1.2 | 1.3 | 1.2 | | | 1.3 | 1.5 | | 1.1 | | 1.2 |
| 1.2 | 1.1 | 1.2 | | | 1.2 | 1.0 | | 1.4 | | 1.3 |
| .6 | .3 (103) | .4 | Quick | | .3 | (29) .4 | | .4 | | .4 |
| .2 | .1 | .1 | | | .0 | .1 | | .1 | | .1 |
| 0 UND | 0 UND | 0 UND | | | 0 UND | 0 UND | | 0 UND | | 0 999.8 |
| 0 973.0 | 1 325.1 | 1 329.4 | Sales/Receivables | | 0 UND | 0 UND | | 1 277.1 | | 2 237.9 |
| 13 28.1 | 6 58.7 | 6 57.9 | | | 2 152.0 | 9 42.8 | | 10 35.3 | | 6 65.9 |
| 73 5.0 | 72 5.1 | 81 4.5 | | | 146 2.5 | 104 3.5 | | 87 4.2 | | 59 6.2 |
| 109 3.4 | 120 3.1 | 114 3.2 | Cost of Sales/Inventory | | 243 1.5 | 126 2.9 | | 99 3.7 | | 87 4.2 |
| 179 2.0 | 210 1.7 | 166 2.2 | | | 406 .9 | 243 1.5 | | 146 2.5 | | 130 2.8 |
| 11 32.7 | 17 22.0 | 14 25.3 | | | 0 UND | 4 88.4 | | 36 10.1 | | 29 12.4 |
| 34 10.8 | 41 9.0 | 39 9.3 | Cost of Sales/Payables | | 22 16.6 | 23 16.0 | | 64 5.7 | | 43 8.5 |
| 53 6.9 | 69 5.3 | 66 5.5 | | | 36 10.1 | 59 6.2 | | 89 4.1 | | 62 5.9 |
| 4.3 | 4.0 | 4.6 | | | 2.7 | 3.5 | | 4.7 | | 5.1 |
| 9.0 | 8.9 | 9.0 | Sales/Working Capital | | 3.7 | 8.4 | | 6.7 | | 11.1 |
| 29.8 | 30.8 | 27.1 | | | 11.0 | 25.9 | | 60.0 | | 32.9 |
| 12.7 | 20.2 | 21.2 | | | 22.0 | 10.3 | | | | 26.3 |
| (73) 4.0 | (71) 6.0 | (80) 5.3 | EBIT/Interest | | (11) 3.8 | (21) 2.3 | | | (24) | 9.0 |
| 1.2 | 1.4 | 1.5 | | | .7 | .4 | | | | 2.2 |
| 8.3 | 10.4 | 9.8 | Net Profit + Depr., Dep., | | | | | | | |
| (12) 1.5 | (13) 2.2 | (13) 2.2 | Amort./Cur. Mat. L/T/D | | | | | | | |
| -3.9 | .3 | .8 | | | | | | | | |
| .1 | .1 | .1 | | | .1 | .1 | | .1 | | .2 |
| .4 | .3 | .3 | Fixed/Worth | | .2 | .3 | | .2 | | .5 |
| 1.1 | 1.4 | 1.2 | | | 1.5 | 2.1 | | NM | | 1.1 |
| .5 | .5 | .5 | | | 1.4 | .6 | | .7 | | .5 |
| 1.2 | 1.5 | 1.5 | Debt/Worth | | 3.7 | 1.4 | | 1.6 | | 1.4 |
| 5.4 | 5.2 | 5.3 | | | 12.7 | 4.7 | | NM | | 3.9 |
| 58.0 | 50.6 | 60.1 | % Profit Before Taxes/Tangible | | 102.8 | 71.2 | | 32.7 | | 54.2 |
| (84) 15.2 | (82) 22.5 | (91) 24.9 | Net Worth | | (11) 33.1 | (24) 28.5 | | (10) 14.6 | (28) | 28.8 |
| 4.0 | 3.7 | 4.8 | | | 5.5 | 3.0 | | 1.6 | | 17.5 |
| 16.7 | 19.4 | 21.9 | % Profit Before Taxes/Total | | 30.2 | 26.7 | | 8.8 | | 16.3 |
| 5.4 | 7.5 | 8.6 | Assets | | 12.3 | 9.0 | | 6.0 | | 9.4 |
| .7 | 1.2 | 1.8 | | | .2 | -.1 | | .3 | | 4.3 |
| 114.0 | 92.8 | 95.3 | | | 208.6 | 121.6 | | 89.2 | | 29.3 |
| 21.1 | 24.9 | 28.5 | Sales/Net Fixed Assets | | 89.7 | 34.0 | | 28.5 | | 17.7 |
| 10.5 | 10.2 | 13.6 | | | 20.2 | 15.9 | | 15.1 | | 8.8 |
| 4.2 | 4.4 | 4.2 | | | 4.0 | 4.0 | | 3.8 | | 4.3 |
| 2.8 | 2.6 | 2.9 | Sales/Total Assets | | 2.0 | 2.4 | | 2.8 | | 3.2 |
| 1.7 | 1.7 | 1.8 | | | 1.0 | 1.7 | | 2.1 | | 1.7 |
| .5 | .4 | .4 | | | | .4 | | .5 | | .7 |
| (68) 1.1 | (67) .7 | (81) .8 | % Depr., Dep., Amort./Sales | | | (25) .6 | | (10) .9 | | (27) 1.0 |
| 1.6 | 1.5 | 1.5 | | | | | | 1.4 | | 1.8 |
| 1.3 | 1.1 | 1.0 | % Officers', Directors' | | | 2.2 | | | | |
| (37) 3.8 | (30) 2.6 | (49) 3.0 | Owners' Comp/Sales | | | (20) 3.7 | | | | |
| 6.7 | 5.6 | 6.1 | | | | 8.5 | | | | |
| 3894911M | 5987829M | 5267788M | Net Sales ($) | | 8070M | 54363M | 34483M | 96614M | 144387M | 4929871M |
| 1358963M | 2138977M | 2078061M | Total Assets ($) | | 5242M | 37030M | 11030M | 35252M | 43555M | 1945952M |

M = $ thousand     MM = $ million
See Pages 9 through 22 for Explanation of Ratios and Data

## Current Data Sorted by Assets | Comparative Historical Data

| | 0-500M | 500M-2MM | 2-10MM | 10-50MM | 50-100MM | 100-250MM | Type of Statement | 4/1/07-3/31/08 ALL | 4/1/08-3/31/09 ALL |
|---|---|---|---|---|---|---|---|---|---|
| | | | 4 | 2 | 3 | 1 | Unqualified | 11 | 5 |
| | | 2 | 4 | | | | Reviewed | 7 | 7 |
| | 2 | 3 | 4 | 1 | | | Compiled | 7 | 7 |
| | 10 | 16 | 4 | | | | Tax Returns | 18 | 17 |
| | 7 | | 5 | 2 | 1 | 2 | Other | 9 | 20 |
| | | 10 (4/1-9/30/11) | | 70 (10/1/11-3/31/12) | | | | | |
| NUMBER OF STATEMENTS | 19 | 28 | 21 | | 4 | 3 | | 52 | 56 |
| | % | % | % | % | % | % | **ASSETS** | % | % |
| | 17.2 | 15.4 | 11.3 | | | | Cash & Equivalents | 13.4 | 12.9 |
| | 5.7 | 8.0 | 16.7 | | | | Trade Receivables (net) | 14.3 | 10.7 |
| | 44.7 | 45.4 | 47.6 | | | | Inventory | 44.1 | 42.3 |
| | 4.2 | 2.7 | 1.7 | | | | All Other Current | 1.9 | 3.7 |
| | 71.7 | 71.4 | 77.3 | | | | Total Current | 73.7 | 69.6 |
| | 13.3 | 14.3 | 11.5 | | | | Fixed Assets (net) | 14.3 | 17.4 |
| | 3.3 | 1.3 | 3.6 | | | | Intangibles (net) | 5.9 | 3.7 |
| | 11.7 | 13.0 | 7.7 | | | | All Other Non-Current | 6.2 | 9.4 |
| | 100.0 | 100.0 | 100.0 | | | | Total | 100.0 | 100.0 |
| | | | | | | | **LIABILITIES** | | |
| | 10.5 | 6.5 | 11.6 | | | | Notes Payable-Short Term | 9.5 | 8.7 |
| | 1.1 | 1.1 | 3.9 | | | | Cur. Mat.-L.T.D. | 2.2 | 2.2 |
| | 9.8 | 17.0 | 28.2 | | | | Trade Payables | 22.2 | 16.3 |
| | .1 | .2 | .1 | | | | Income Taxes Payable | .5 | .1 |
| | 8.9 | 7.0 | 13.4 | | | | All Other Current | 10.0 | 9.6 |
| | 30.3 | 31.8 | 57.1 | | | | Total Current | 44.4 | 36.9 |
| | 13.9 | 19.7 | 7.1 | | | | Long-Term Debt | 10.6 | 12.9 |
| | .0 | .1 | .1 | | | | Deferred Taxes | .3 | .2 |
| | 21.8 | 14.6 | 7.5 | | | | All Other Non-Current | 7.0 | 8.1 |
| | 34.0 | 33.8 | 28.2 | | | | Net Worth | 37.7 | 42.0 |
| | 100.0 | 100.0 | 100.0 | | | | Total Liabilties & Net Worth | 100.0 | 100.0 |
| | | | | | | | **INCOME DATA** | | |
| | 100.0 | 100.0 | 100.0 | | | | Net Sales | 100.0 | 100.0 |
| | 47.2 | 48.3 | 44.5 | | | | Gross Profit | 45.7 | 48.9 |
| | 44.8 | 45.3 | 40.1 | | | | Operating Expenses | 40.7 | 47.1 |
| | 2.4 | 3.0 | 4.4 | | | | Operating Profit | 5.1 | 1.7 |
| | .7 | 1.1 | .0 | | | | All Other Expenses (net) | 1.0 | .5 |
| | 1.7 | 1.9 | 4.3 | | | | Profit Before Taxes | 4.1 | 1.3 |
| | | | | | | | **RATIOS** | | |
| | 6.8 | 4.1 | 1.9 | | | | | 2.8 | 4.4 |
| | 3.0 | 2.3 | 1.5 | | | | Current | 1.9 | 2.3 |
| | 1.7 | 1.2 | 1.0 | | | | | 1.2 | 1.2 |
| | 2.7 | 2.0 | .9 | | | | | 1.2 | 1.0 |
| | 1.1 | .7 | .3 | | | | Quick | .5 | .5 |
| | .1 | .2 | .1 | | | | | .2 | .2 |
| | 0 UND | 0 UND | 0 UND | | | | | 0 UND | 0 UND |
| | 0 UND | 2 197.6 | 3 115.5 | | | | Sales/Receivables | 7 49.3 | 4 85.5 |
| | 2 194.0 | 11 33.4 | 48 7.6 | | | | | 32 11.5 | 28 13.2 |
| | 47 7.8 | 47 7.7 | 59 6.2 | | | | | 74 5.0 | 80 4.6 |
| | 72 5.1 | 107 3.4 | 140 2.6 | | | | Cost of Sales/Inventory | 110 3.3 | 119 3.1 |
| | 159 2.3 | 243 1.5 | 182 2.0 | | | | | 190 1.9 | 197 1.9 |
| | 0 UND | 19 19.7 | 17 21.8 | | | | | 17 21.7 | 7 54.5 |
| | 5 78.7 | 31 11.6 | 51 7.2 | | | | Cost of Sales/Payables | 54 6.8 | 24 15.3 |
| | 33 11.1 | 63 5.8 | 87 4.2 | | | | | 69 5.3 | 55 6.7 |
| | 5.6 | 4.0 | 7.3 | | | | | 4.7 | 4.4 |
| | 7.6 | 8.3 | 12.1 | | | | Sales/Working Capital | 9.2 | 6.9 |
| | 20.1 | 35.1 | 332.7 | | | | | 19.6 | 50.1 |
| | 19.6 | 21.0 | 21.0 | | | | | 13.9 | 17.4 |
| | (11) 5.0 | (23) 7.1 | (16) 9.4 | | | | EBIT/Interest | (44) 4.1 | (43) 2.1 |
| | -3.9 | -1.3 | 4.3 | | | | | 1.5 | -2.1 |
| | | | | | | | Net Profit + Depr., Dep., Amort./Cur. Mat. L/T/D | | |
| | .0 | .1 | .1 | | | | | .1 | .1 |
| | .1 | .3 | .4 | | | | Fixed/Worth | .3 | .4 |
| | -2.5 | .8 | 1.4 | | | | | 2.4 | 1.0 |
| | .4 | .5 | 1.4 | | | | | .5 | .4 |
| | 1.8 | 1.6 | 3.1 | | | | Debt/Worth | 1.8 | 1.0 |
| | -37.9 | 9.0 | 9.8 | | | | | 10.6 | 12.9 |
| | 116.8 | 75.5 | 48.3 | | | | % Profit Before Taxes/Tangible Net Worth | 57.3 | 47.5 |
| | (14) 39.5 | (23) 22.7 | (18) 19.6 | | | | | (44) 17.5 | (47) 22.2 |
| | 14.5 | 6.0 | 6.0 | | | | | 5.6 | -13.3 |
| | 45.8 | 16.6 | 18.8 | | | | % Profit Before Taxes/Total Assets | 22.9 | 26.1 |
| | 12.1 | 10.3 | 7.1 | | | | | 6.6 | 3.6 |
| | -9.8 | 1.6 | 2.5 | | | | | 1.3 | -7.7 |
| | 999.8 | 142.9 | 94.5 | | | | | 72.8 | 60.8 |
| | 85.2 | 45.3 | 32.1 | | | | Sales/Net Fixed Assets | 26.0 | 17.6 |
| | 9.8 | 15.3 | 17.9 | | | | | 12.2 | 9.1 |
| | 5.8 | 3.9 | 3.6 | | | | | 3.7 | 3.7 |
| | 3.9 | 2.7 | 2.6 | | | | Sales/Total Assets | 2.6 | 2.4 |
| | 1.8 | 1.8 | 2.2 | | | | | 1.8 | 1.7 |
| | .4 | .2 | .6 | | | | | .6 | .3 |
| | (12) 1.4 | (17) 1.0 | (16) 1.1 | | | | % Depr., Dep., Amort./Sales | (39) .9 | (42) 1.5 |
| | 3.1 | 1.4 | 1.7 | | | | | 2.1 | 2.9 |
| | | | 1.8 | | | | | 2.2 | 2.0 |
| | | (15) 3.1 | 3.1 | | | | % Officers', Directors' Owners' Comp/Sales | (17) 3.1 | (22) 3.5 |
| | | | 6.0 | | | | | 7.6 | 5.5 |
| | 19854M | 102445M | 286374M | 401769M | 586655M | 796587M | Net Sales ($) | 1541693M | 1746798M |
| | 5181M | 33407M | 93205M | 130059M | 302807M | 551509M | Total Assets ($) | 740768M | 1001515M |

M = $ thousand    MM = $ million
See Pages 9 through 22 for Explanation of Ratios and Data

## Comparative Historical Data | Current Data Sorted by Sales

| | Comparative Historical Data | | | | Current Data Sorted by Sales (10 (4/1-9/30/11) / 70 (10/1/11-3/31/12)) | | | | | |
|---|---|---|---|---|---|---|---|---|---|---|
| **Type of Statement** | 4/1/09-3/31/10 ALL | 4/1/10-3/31/11 ALL | 4/1/11-3/31/12 ALL | | 0-1MM | 1-3MM | 3-5MM | 5-10MM | 10-25MM | 25MM & OVER |
| Unqualified | 4 | 5 | 10 | | | | | | 4 | 6 |
| Reviewed | 6 | 8 | 6 | | 2 | | 1 | 1 | 3 | 1 |
| Compiled | 3 | 9 | 10 | | | | 3 | 3 | 1 | 1 |
| Tax Returns | 35 | 25 | 30 | | 5 | 12 | 4 | 7 | 2 | |
| Other | 22 | 26 | 24 | | 6 | 6 | 3 | 3 | 1 | 5 |
| **NUMBER OF STATEMENTS** | 70 | 73 | 80 | | 13 | 18 | 11 | 14 | 11 | 13 |
| **ASSETS** | % | % | % | | % | % | % | % | % | % |
| Cash & Equivalents | 12.0 | 11.3 | 13.9 | | 10.1 | 23.2 | 14.8 | 7.4 | 16.1 | 9.2 |
| Trade Receivables (net) | 11.0 | 12.7 | 9.0 | | 6.1 | 6.4 | 6.9 | 22.1 | 9.1 | 2.9 |
| Inventory | 48.1 | 45.2 | 44.3 | | 51.6 | 33.9 | 54.3 | 47.9 | 46.2 | 37.2 |
| All Other Current | 2.4 | 1.7 | 2.9 | | .6 | 6.6 | 2.5 | .0 | 3.2 | 3.3 |
| Total Current | 73.4 | 71.0 | 70.0 | | 68.4 | 70.2 | 78.5 | 77.4 | 74.6 | 52.7 |
| Fixed Assets (net) | 14.7 | 17.8 | 15.5 | | 15.8 | 13.8 | 12.7 | 10.8 | 12.3 | 27.6 |
| Intangibles (net) | 4.3 | 3.5 | 4.4 | | 4.8 | .0 | 4.5 | .6 | 3.4 | 15.1 |
| All Other Non-Current | 7.6 | 7.8 | 10.1 | | 11.1 | 16.0 | 4.4 | 11.2 | 9.7 | 4.7 |
| Total | 100.0 | 100.0 | 100.0 | | 100.0 | 100.0 | 100.0 | 100.0 | 100.0 | 100.0 |
| **LIABILITIES** | | | | | | | | | | |
| Notes Payable-Short Term | 14.1 | 6.4 | 8.5 | | 13.3 | 9.9 | 2.3 | 12.0 | 6.8 | 4.4 |
| Cur. Mat.-L.T.D. | 2.6 | 3.1 | 2.0 | | 2.0 | .1 | 1.5 | .3 | 7.0 | 2.4 |
| Trade Payables | 24.3 | 18.2 | 17.9 | | 4.4 | 13.3 | 18.4 | 23.4 | 34.8 | 17.0 |
| Income Taxes Payable | .3 | .4 | .4 | | .1 | .0 | .2 | .3 | .2 | 1.7 |
| All Other Current | 8.7 | 9.3 | 10.1 | | 4.6 | 10.5 | 5.3 | 14.9 | 11.2 | 12.9 |
| Total Current | 50.1 | 37.5 | 38.8 | | 24.3 | 33.9 | 27.7 | 50.8 | 59.9 | 38.4 |
| Long-Term Debt | 13.3 | 22.1 | 14.5 | | 30.0 | 5.4 | 21.9 | 11.2 | 6.3 | 15.7 |
| Deferred Taxes | .3 | .3 | .2 | | .0 | .0 | .0 | .2 | .0 | 1.3 |
| All Other Non-Current | 10.5 | 12.1 | 14.4 | | 26.7 | 23.9 | 3.5 | 5.0 | 8.5 | 13.2 |
| Net Worth | 25.8 | 28.1 | 32.1 | | 19.0 | 36.8 | 46.8 | 32.8 | 25.2 | 31.4 |
| Total Liabilities & Net Worth | 100.0 | 100.0 | 100.0 | | 100.0 | 100.0 | 100.0 | 100.0 | 100.0 | 100.0 |
| **INCOME DATA** | | | | | | | | | | |
| Net Sales | 100.0 | 100.0 | 100.0 | | 100.0 | 100.0 | 100.0 | 100.0 | 100.0 | 100.0 |
| Gross Profit | 48.0 | 46.8 | 46.6 | | 57.9 | 46.8 | 45.1 | 36.7 | 48.4 | 45.2 |
| Operating Expenses | 45.7 | 42.4 | 42.8 | | 59.2 | 42.9 | 38.8 | 33.7 | 43.2 | 39.0 |
| Operating Profit | 2.4 | 4.4 | 3.8 | | -1.3 | 3.9 | 6.2 | 3.0 | 5.1 | 6.2 |
| All Other Expenses (net) | .7 | .9 | .9 | | 1.3 | 1.1 | -.2 | .1 | .6 | 2.3 |
| Profit Before Taxes | 1.6 | 3.5 | 2.8 | | -2.6 | 2.7 | 6.4 | 2.9 | 4.5 | 3.9 |
| **RATIOS** | | | | | | | | | | |
| Current | 3.4 | 4.7 | 3.6 | | 12.1 | 4.3 | 15.1 | 2.9 | 1.8 | 2.3 |
| | 1.7 | 1.9 | 1.9 | | 4.9 | 2.1 | 2.9 | 1.4 | 1.6 | 1.4 |
| | .9 | 1.2 | 1.1 | | 2.0 | 1.1 | 1.4 | 1.0 | .7 | 1.0 |
| Quick | .9 | 1.3 | 1.4 | | 2.8 | 1.8 | 3.1 | 1.1 | .8 | .6 |
| | (69) .4 | .5 | .6 | | 1.0 | 1.1 | .7 | .6 | .3 | .2 |
| | .1 | .2 | .1 | | .1 | .3 | .0 | .1 | .2 | .1 |
| Sales/Receivables | 0 UND | 0 UND | 0 UND | | 0 UND | 0 UND | 0 UND | 2 193.9 | 0 UND | 1 341.9 |
| | 2 152.9 | 3 104.7 | 2 182.6 | | 0 UND | 0 UND | 0 999.8 | 11 32.7 | 0 999.8 | 4 89.0 |
| | 20 18.6 | 23 15.6 | 13 27.4 | | 6 58.0 | 4 96.2 | 14 26.2 | 42 8.6 | 16 23.1 | 8 48.1 |
| Cost of Sales/Inventory | 61 6.0 | 72 5.1 | 55 6.6 | | 96 3.8 | 29 12.5 | 64 5.7 | 26 14.2 | 41 9.0 | 66 5.5 |
| | 124 2.9 | 114 3.2 | 99 3.7 | | 174 2.1 | 68 5.4 | 135 2.7 | 81 4.5 | 96 3.8 | 99 3.7 |
| | 268 1.4 | 182 2.0 | 174 2.1 | | 456 .8 | 166 2.2 | 166 2.2 | 146 2.5 | 182 2.0 | 122 3.0 |
| Cost of Sales/Payables | 11 33.0 | 8 44.3 | 11 32.2 | | 1 410.0 | 0 UND | 11 33.1 | 20 18.3 | 35 10.5 | 26 13.8 |
| | 38 9.5 | 41 9.0 | 30 12.1 | | 9 40.3 | 20 18.6 | 26 13.9 | 28 12.9 | 56 6.5 | 32 11.3 |
| | 76 4.8 | 67 5.5 | 58 6.3 | | 45 8.2 | 49 7.4 | 54 6.7 | 59 6.2 | 91 4.0 | 56 6.5 |
| Sales/Working Capital | 3.6 | 4.3 | 5.8 | | 2.0 | 6.0 | 3.0 | 7.2 | 8.2 | 8.3 |
| | 8.5 | 7.6 | 9.9 | | 5.6 | 8.5 | 6.4 | 16.1 | 12.1 | 11.7 |
| | -82.0 | 27.3 | 38.7 | | 18.1 | NM | 18.6 | NM | -28.1 | 398.4 |
| EBIT/Interest | 10.1 | 16.3 | 19.9 | | 16.2 | 21.0 | | 118.2 | | 21.1 |
| | (53) 3.1 | (54) 5.4 | (62) 7.2 | | (11) 1.6 | (11) 7.1 | | (12) 13.6 | | 5.5 |
| | -.6 | .3 | 1.5 | | -3.9 | -1.2 | | 3.2 | | 1.2 |
| Net Profit + Depr., Dep., Amort./Cur. Mat. L/T/D | | | | | | | | | | |
| Fixed/Worth | .1 | .1 | .1 | | .1 | .0 | .0 | .0 | .2 | .6 |
| | .4 | .5 | .4 | | .9 | .1 | .2 | .2 | .4 | 2.0 |
| | NM | NM | 2.2 | | -.8 | 1.4 | 2.0 | .7 | 1.1 | NM |
| Debt/Worth | .5 | .6 | .8 | | 1.3 | .4 | .1 | .8 | 1.6 | 1.4 |
| | 2.2 | 2.4 | 1.8 | | 2.6 | 1.1 | 1.2 | 1.7 | 2.3 | 3.3 |
| | NM | NM | 10.8 | | -5.1 | 8.7 | 8.0 | 9.7 | 5.3 | NM |
| % Profit Before Taxes/Tangible Net Worth | 57.2 | 47.3 | 66.1 | | | 92.6 | | 57.0 | 48.3 | 106.2 |
| | (53) 20.0 | (55) 23.0 | (64) 24.4 | | | (15) 29.1 | | (12) 21.7 | (10) 22.3 | (10) 26.7 |
| | -4.7 | 9.2 | 6.2 | | | 13.9 | | 5.8 | 11.1 | -.4 |
| % Profit Before Taxes/Total Assets | 24.6 | 19.4 | 18.9 | | 16.5 | 28.1 | 24.7 | 16.3 | 19.6 | 10.9 |
| | 6.5 | 7.8 | 7.8 | | 1.7 | 11.9 | 16.8 | 6.8 | 8.1 | 5.5 |
| | -3.6 | .0 | 1.1 | | -17.3 | 3.5 | 5.8 | 1.4 | 4.1 | .0 |
| Sales/Net Fixed Assets | 103.1 | 89.9 | 128.0 | | 249.8 | 489.5 | 145.7 | 271.7 | 77.7 | 23.0 |
| | 30.9 | 22.7 | 31.4 | | 13.5 | 93.3 | 37.2 | 46.2 | 39.9 | 11.8 |
| | 11.8 | 8.1 | 11.7 | | 6.9 | 17.2 | 18.3 | 19.4 | 14.2 | 5.6 |
| Sales/Total Assets | 4.1 | 3.8 | 3.9 | | 3.3 | 4.5 | 3.6 | 4.3 | 4.1 | 3.4 |
| | 2.4 | 2.5 | 2.7 | | 1.6 | 3.2 | 2.8 | 3.8 | 2.6 | 2.6 |
| | 1.7 | 1.7 | 2.0 | | 1.3 | 2.0 | 2.1 | 2.5 | 2.5 | 1.4 |
| % Depr., Dep., Amort./Sales | .4 | .3 | .5 | | | | .3 | | | 1.5 |
| | (52) .7 | (52) 1.2 | (54) 1.1 | | | (12) .7 | | | (10) | 1.8 |
| | 1.9 | 2.3 | 2.1 | | | | 1.8 | | | 3.0 |
| % Officers', Directors' Owners' Comp/Sales | 1.9 | 2.3 | 1.7 | | | | 1.4 | | | |
| | (30) 5.0 | (31) 3.4 | (31) 4.8 | | | (10) 5.0 | | | | |
| | 10.3 | 6.8 | 6.6 | | | | 6.4 | | | |
| Net Sales ($) | 916192M | 1408739M | 2193684M | | 7724M | 27958M | 45092M | 103066M | 176148M | 1833696M |
| Total Assets ($) | 526226M | 834658M | 1116168M | | 4269M | 11572M | 16597M | 31912M | 59010M | 992808M |

M = $ thousand     MM = $ million
See Pages 9 through 22 for Explanation of Ratios and Data

## Current Data Sorted by Assets | Comparative Historical Data

| Type of Statement | 0-500M | 500M-2MM | 2-10MM | 10-50MM | 50-100MM | 100-250MM | | 4/1/07-3/31/08 ALL | 4/1/08-3/31/09 ALL |
|---|---|---|---|---|---|---|---|---|---|
| Unqualified | | 2 | 2 | 5 | | | | 11 | 16 |
| Reviewed | | 2 | 15 | 2 | | | | 17 | 21 |
| Compiled | 1 | 9 | 9 | 3 | | | | 20 | 17 |
| Tax Returns | 26 | 21 | 10 | | | | | 45 | 34 |
| Other | 15 | 21 | 27 | 8 | 4 | | | 56 | 42 |
| | | 26 (4/1-9/30/11) | | 156 (10/1/11-3/31/12) | | | | | |
| NUMBER OF STATEMENTS | 42 | 55 | 63 | 18 | 4 | | | 149 | 130 |
| | % | % | % | % | % | % | ASSETS | % | % |
| Cash & Equivalents | 17.3 | 9.6 | 9.8 | 6.9 | | | | 8.7 | 8.4 |
| Trade Receivables (net) | 5.5 | 8.1 | 11.3 | 11.6 | | | | 10.3 | 12.7 |
| Inventory | 43.5 | 54.1 | 44.8 | 45.2 | | | | 48.7 | 46.4 |
| All Other Current | 2.1 | 1.9 | 1.8 | 2.4 | | | | 2.8 | 2.4 |
| Total Current | 68.3 | 73.7 | 67.6 | 66.1 | | | | 70.5 | 69.9 |
| Fixed Assets (net) | 18.8 | 18.2 | 20.1 | 19.8 | | | | 18.8 | 19.3 |
| Intangibles (net) | 5.0 | 1.2 | 3.4 | 8.7 | | | | 4.8 | 4.6 |
| All Other Non-Current | 7.9 | 6.9 | 8.8 | 5.4 | | | | 6.0 | 6.2 |
| Total | 100.0 | 100.0 | 100.0 | 100.0 | | | | 100.0 | 100.0 |
| | | | | | | | LIABILITIES | | |
| Notes Payable-Short Term | 19.8 | 8.7 | 10.0 | 14.6 | | | | 14.6 | 13.6 |
| Cur. Mat.-L.T.D. | .7 | 2.3 | 1.0 | 6.0 | | | | 3.5 | 3.6 |
| Trade Payables | 16.0 | 20.4 | 18.6 | 14.2 | | | | 16.7 | 21.5 |
| Income Taxes Payable | .1 | .1 | .1 | .0 | | | | .1 | .1 |
| All Other Current | 16.6 | 7.5 | 9.4 | 14.8 | | | | 11.9 | 11.8 |
| Total Current | 53.2 | 39.0 | 39.1 | 49.6 | | | | 46.8 | 50.6 |
| Long-Term Debt | 21.3 | 15.3 | 11.1 | 10.1 | | | | 16.3 | 14.3 |
| Deferred Taxes | .0 | .0 | .0 | .1 | | | | .3 | .1 |
| All Other Non-Current | 9.4 | 6.2 | 6.6 | 7.8 | | | | 8.7 | 7.5 |
| Net Worth | 16.1 | 39.5 | 43.2 | 32.5 | | | | 27.9 | 27.5 |
| Total Liabilities & Net Worth | 100.0 | 100.0 | 100.0 | 100.0 | | | | 100.0 | 100.0 |
| | | | | | | | INCOME DATA | | |
| Net Sales | 100.0 | 100.0 | 100.0 | 100.0 | | | | 100.0 | 100.0 |
| Gross Profit | 50.5 | 48.1 | 46.3 | 50.1 | | | | 45.7 | 45.0 |
| Operating Expenses | 44.7 | 42.8 | 42.1 | 43.5 | | | | 42.1 | 42.4 |
| Operating Profit | 5.8 | 5.3 | 4.2 | 6.6 | | | | 3.6 | 2.6 |
| All Other Expenses (net) | 1.2 | 1.4 | 1.1 | 1.7 | | | | 1.4 | 1.5 |
| Profit Before Taxes | 4.6 | 3.9 | 3.1 | 4.8 | | | | 2.2 | 1.1 |

(Columns 50-100MM and 100-250MM indicate "DATA NOT AVAILABLE")

### RATIOS

| Ratio | 0-500M | 500M-2MM | 2-10MM | 10-50MM | | 4/1/07-3/31/08 ALL | 4/1/08-3/31/09 ALL |
|---|---|---|---|---|---|---|---|
| Current | 5.8 | 4.6 | 3.2 | 2.5 | | 3.0 | 2.5 |
| | 2.2 | 2.4 | 1.7 | 1.4 | | 1.7 | 1.5 |
| | .8 | 1.2 | 1.3 | 1.2 | | 1.1 | 1.0 |
| Quick | 1.5 | 1.1 | 1.3 | .7 | | .8 | .8 |
| | .7 | .5 | .4 | .3 | (148) | .3 | .3 |
| | .2 | .2 | .1 | .0 | | .1 | .1 |
| Sales/Receivables | 0 UND | 0 UND | 0 999.8 | 1 422.1 | 0 UND | 0 UND | |
| | 0 UND | 1 531.5 | 6 62.0 | 8 45.1 | 2 155.9 | 5 66.9 | |
| | 6 58.3 | 18 20.0 | 40 9.2 | 31 11.6 | 28 13.2 | 32 11.5 | |
| Cost of Sales/Inventory | 43 8.4 | 73 5.0 | 81 4.5 | 126 2.9 | 81 4.5 | 77 4.7 | |
| | 101 3.6 | 159 2.3 | 126 2.9 | 182 2.0 | 139 2.6 | 113 3.2 | |
| | 182 2.0 | 304 1.2 | 192 1.9 | 281 1.3 | 222 1.6 | 215 1.7 | |
| Cost of Sales/Payables | 0 UND | 10 37.5 | 22 16.7 | 34 10.7 | 14 26.4 | 20 18.0 | |
| | 18 20.2 | 35 10.5 | 38 9.7 | 47 7.7 | 36 10.1 | 42 8.6 | |
| | 39 9.4 | 73 5.0 | 87 4.2 | 107 3.4 | 68 5.4 | 77 4.7 | |
| Sales/Working Capital | 4.6 | 3.3 | 4.5 | 4.6 | | 4.9 | 5.8 |
| | 17.5 | 6.2 | 9.0 | 10.2 | | 10.0 | 11.7 |
| | -19.2 | 22.6 | 20.0 | 24.2 | | 65.7 | 140.6 |
| EBIT/Interest | 15.3 | 21.4 | 17.6 | 16.3 | | 8.0 | 6.7 |
| | (26) 2.3 | (41) 4.5 | (51) 2.7 | (17) 7.8 | (132) 2.4 | (108) 2.2 | |
| | -.8 | 1.4 | 1.3 | 2.6 | | .8 | -.4 |
| Net Profit + Depr., Dep., Amort./Cur. Mat. L/T/D | | | | | | 10.9 | 6.2 |
| | | | | | (24) 2.4 | (14) 2.8 | |
| | | | | | | 1.2 | .7 |
| Fixed/Worth | .0 | .1 | .1 | .1 | | .2 | .1 |
| | .5 | .3 | .4 | .4 | | .6 | .6 |
| | -1.7 | 1.9 | 1.8 | 1.6 | | 10.5 | 3.4 |
| Debt/Worth | .5 | .3 | .5 | 1.2 | | .8 | 1.0 |
| | 1.8 | 1.4 | 1.1 | 2.3 | | 3.1 | 2.5 |
| | -3.1 | 10.4 | 3.6 | 4.7 | | 59.1 | 11.8 |
| % Profit Before Taxes/Tangible Net Worth | 99.2 | 44.3 | 25.4 | 54.3 | | 54.1 | 43.1 |
| | (28) 37.5 | (45) 23.3 | (56) 12.4 | (15) 18.0 | (118) 21.0 | (105) 14.1 | |
| | 12.5 | 5.0 | 2.1 | 9.4 | | 3.1 | .2 |
| % Profit Before Taxes/Total Assets | 31.2 | 19.2 | 9.4 | 14.2 | | 15.7 | 14.8 |
| | 12.7 | 9.0 | 3.3 | 5.2 | | 6.5 | 3.4 |
| | -3.8 | 1.2 | .5 | 4.2 | | -.7 | -3.9 |
| Sales/Net Fixed Assets | 304.2 | 87.5 | 42.4 | 40.6 | | 44.6 | 60.4 |
| | 35.2 | 29.3 | 16.1 | 18.9 | | 19.7 | 19.6 |
| | 8.8 | 8.9 | 7.0 | 7.6 | | 8.7 | 8.6 |
| Sales/Total Assets | 4.4 | 3.4 | 2.9 | 2.7 | | 3.5 | 3.6 |
| | 3.3 | 2.4 | 2.1 | 1.9 | | 2.5 | 2.4 |
| | 1.9 | 1.5 | 1.5 | 1.1 | | 1.7 | 1.7 |
| % Depr., Dep., Amort./Sales | .5 | .3 | .5 | .9 | | .5 | .6 |
| | (24) 1.4 | (32) .6 | (50) .9 | (16) 1.2 | (115) 1.0 | (101) 1.2 | |
| | 2.5 | 1.2 | 1.8 | 3.9 | | 1.8 | 2.1 |
| % Officers', Directors' Owners' Comp/Sales | 4.3 | 2.0 | 2.1 | | | 2.3 | 2.0 |
| | (20) 6.3 | (32) 3.9 | (28) 3.4 | | (78) 4.0 | (63) 3.2 | |
| | 11.8 | 7.3 | 5.2 | | | 6.7 | 6.2 |

| | 0-500M | 500M-2MM | 2-10MM | 10-50MM | 50-100MM | | 4/1/07-3/31/08 ALL | 4/1/08-3/31/09 ALL |
|---|---|---|---|---|---|---|---|---|
| Net Sales ($) | 37137M | 185725M | 665911M | 757124M | 495231M | | 3091418M | 3048118M |
| Total Assets ($) | 9650M | 67142M | 298450M | 403807M | 342296M | | 1344396M | 1584245M |

M = $ thousand   MM = $ million
See Pages 9 through 22 for Explanation of Ratios and Data

## Comparative Historical Data

## Current Data Sorted by Sales

| Type of Statement | 4/1/09-3/31/10 ALL | 4/1/10-3/31/11 ALL | 4/1/11-3/31/12 ALL | | 0-1MM | 1-3MM | 3-5MM | 5-10MM | 10-25MM | 25MM & OVER |
|---|---|---|---|---|---|---|---|---|---|---|
| Unqualified | 19 | 9 | 9 | | | 1 | | 1 | 2 | 5 |
| Reviewed | 19 | 25 | 19 | | | 1 | 3 | 5 | 9 | 1 |
| Compiled | 22 | 17 | 22 | | 1 | 6 | 3 | 8 | 3 | 1 |
| Tax Returns | 54 | 52 | 57 | | 23 | 14 | 9 | 7 | 3 | 1 |
| Other | 55 | 56 | 75 | | 12 | 18 | 6 | 15 | 12 | 12 |
| | | | | | 26 (4/1-9/30/11) | | | 156 (10/1/11-3/31/12) | | |
| NUMBER OF STATEMENTS | 169 | 159 | 182 | | 36 | 40 | 21 | 36 | 29 | 20 |
| **ASSETS** | % | % | % | | % | % | % | % | % | % |
| Cash & Equivalents | 11.1 | 10.4 | 11.0 | | 12.0 | 10.8 | 17.1 | 8.0 | 11.0 | 8.8 |
| Trade Receivables (net) | 10.9 | 10.9 | 8.9 | | 6.6 | 4.8 | 8.1 | 15.6 | 8.8 | 10.6 |
| Inventory | 44.2 | 47.7 | 47.3 | | 45.9 | 50.9 | 50.7 | 44.3 | 45.4 | 47.1 |
| All Other Current | 2.0 | 2.3 | 1.9 | | 2.0 | 1.8 | 2.0 | 1.1 | 2.8 | 2.3 |
| Total Current | 68.2 | 71.3 | 69.2 | | 66.5 | 68.3 | 77.9 | 69.0 | 67.9 | 68.8 |
| Fixed Assets (net) | 19.9 | 17.3 | 19.7 | | 22.0 | 21.4 | 9.8 | 18.0 | 22.3 | 21.5 |
| Intangibles (net) | 5.0 | 5.1 | 3.6 | | 4.5 | 2.1 | 5.3 | 1.3 | 4.6 | 6.0 |
| All Other Non-Current | 6.8 | 6.2 | 7.5 | | 6.9 | 8.2 | 7.1 | 11.7 | 5.2 | 3.6 |
| Total | 100.0 | 100.0 | 100.0 | | 100.0 | 100.0 | 100.0 | 100.0 | 100.0 | 100.0 |
| **LIABILITIES** | | | | | | | | | | |
| Notes Payable-Short Term | 13.6 | 11.7 | 12.4 | | 20.9 | 8.5 | 11.0 | 11.4 | 10.9 | 10.4 |
| Cur. Mat.-L.T.D. | 3.5 | 2.7 | 1.9 | | 1.0 | 2.4 | 1.0 | 2.2 | 1.7 | 2.9 |
| Trade Payables | 19.1 | 21.3 | 18.1 | | 11.5 | 14.7 | 22.2 | 23.5 | 21.3 | 18.0 |
| Income Taxes Payable | .1 | .1 | .1 | | .1 | .0 | .0 | .3 | .1 | .0 |
| All Other Current | 9.4 | 8.7 | 10.9 | | 11.9 | 12.5 | 6.7 | 11.7 | 7.4 | 13.7 |
| Total Current | 45.7 | 44.6 | 43.4 | | 45.5 | 38.1 | 41.0 | 49.1 | 41.5 | 45.1 |
| Long-Term Debt | 17.8 | 12.4 | 15.0 | | 24.8 | 18.8 | 11.5 | 9.9 | 7.9 | 12.9 |
| Deferred Taxes | .1 | .1 | .0 | | .0 | .0 | .0 | .1 | .0 | .0 |
| All Other Non-Current | 12.7 | 8.8 | 7.1 | | 11.1 | 6.5 | 4.3 | 5.1 | 7.4 | 7.1 |
| Net Worth | 23.6 | 34.2 | 34.5 | | 18.6 | 36.6 | 43.2 | 35.9 | 43.2 | 34.9 |
| Total Liabilities & Net Worth | 100.0 | 100.0 | 100.0 | | 100.0 | 100.0 | 100.0 | 100.0 | 100.0 | 100.0 |
| **INCOME DATA** | | | | | | | | | | |
| Net Sales | 100.0 | 100.0 | 100.0 | | 100.0 | 100.0 | 100.0 | 100.0 | 100.0 | 100.0 |
| Gross Profit | 46.2 | 47.7 | 48.1 | | 50.5 | 50.6 | 47.0 | 45.0 | 45.6 | 49.0 |
| Operating Expenses | 42.7 | 42.9 | 42.8 | | 43.8 | 44.5 | 42.9 | 39.9 | 43.1 | 42.1 |
| Operating Profit | 3.6 | 4.8 | 5.3 | | 6.7 | 6.1 | 4.1 | 5.1 | 2.5 | 7.0 |
| All Other Expenses (net) | 1.2 | .9 | 1.3 | | 2.5 | .9 | .2 | 1.5 | .6 | 1.7 |
| Profit Before Taxes | 2.4 | 3.9 | 4.0 | | 4.2 | 5.2 | 3.9 | 3.5 | 1.9 | 5.3 |
| **RATIOS** | | | | | | | | | | |
| Current | 2.5 | 2.9 | 3.5 | | 7.1 | 5.3 | 2.8 | 3.6 | 2.6 | 2.8 |
| | 1.7 | 1.8 | 1.8 | | 2.8 | 2.7 | 2.1 | 1.4 | 1.5 | 1.5 |
| | 1.1 | 1.1 | 1.2 | | .9 | 1.4 | 1.5 | 1.0 | 1.2 | 1.2 |
| Quick | 1.1 | 1.0 | 1.2 | | 1.6 | 1.2 | 1.3 | 1.2 | 1.0 | .9 |
| | (168) .4 | .4 | .4 | | .6 | .6 | .5 | .4 | .3 | .3 |
| | .1 | .1 | .1 | | .1 | .2 | .1 | .1 | .1 | .0 |
| Sales/Receivables | 0 UND | 0 UND | 0 UND | | 0 UND | 0 UND | 0 UND | 0 UND | 0 999.8 | 0 UND |
| | 4 94.4 | 3 128.3 | 1 257.6 | | 0 UND | 0 UND | 6 58.7 | 6 59.1 | 4 88.6 | 1 336.8 |
| | 29 12.8 | 26 14.2 | 25 14.4 | | 13 28.2 | 11 33.3 | 27 13.4 | 42 8.7 | 21 17.8 | 30 12.3 |
| Cost of Sales/Inventory | 74 4.9 | 73 5.0 | 72 5.1 | | 65 5.6 | 69 5.3 | 74 4.9 | 66 5.5 | 73 5.0 | 118 3.1 |
| | 120 3.0 | 132 2.8 | 135 2.7 | | 146 2.5 | 140 2.6 | 159 2.3 | 118 3.1 | 111 3.3 | 166 2.2 |
| | 200 1.8 | 204 1.8 | 228 1.6 | | 228 1.6 | 304 1.2 | 261 1.4 | 192 1.9 | 166 2.2 | 261 1.4 |
| Cost of Sales/Payables | 17 21.5 | 20 18.5 | 17 21.1 | | 0 UND | 4 101.1 | 26 13.9 | 21 17.5 | 25 14.4 | 35 10.3 |
| | 42 8.8 | 44 8.3 | 35 10.3 | | 18 20.2 | 23 16.2 | 54 6.7 | 47 7.8 | 38 9.7 | 47 7.7 |
| | 75 4.9 | 85 4.3 | 73 5.0 | | 38 9.6 | 64 5.7 | 107 3.4 | 96 3.8 | 66 5.5 | 104 3.5 |
| Sales/Working Capital | 4.7 | 5.0 | 4.4 | | 3.1 | 2.8 | 4.2 | 5.7 | 6.9 | 4.3 |
| | 10.1 | 8.6 | 8.8 | | 7.7 | 5.8 | 6.9 | 11.7 | 12.3 | 9.7 |
| | 64.2 | 43.5 | 38.8 | | -174.2 | 32.3 | 20.7 | NM | 19.8 | 38.1 |
| EBIT/Interest | 8.9 | 13.7 | 16.0 | | 3.6 | 14.0 | 44.7 | 23.8 | 7.3 | 24.6 |
| | (136) 3.3 | (131) 3.3 | (139) 3.3 | | (27) 1.7 | (23) 4.5 | (17) 3.9 | (30) 4.2 | (24) 2.5 | (18) 9.1 |
| | .6 | 1.0 | 1.3 | | -.8 | 1.0 | .3 | 2.1 | 1.3 | 3.5 |
| Net Profit + Depr., Dep., Amort./Cur. Mat. L/T/D | 11.2 | 16.8 | 44.5 | | | | | | | |
| | (19) 2.7 | (14) 4.0 | (12) 2.9 | | | | | | | |
| | 1.1 | 1.3 | 1.3 | | | | | | | |
| Fixed/Worth | .1 | .1 | .1 | | .0 | .1 | .1 | .2 | .2 | .1 |
| | .5 | .4 | .4 | | .5 | .3 | .2 | .5 | .5 | .4 |
| | 9.9 | 1.9 | 2.5 | | UND | 3.6 | .5 | 2.9 | 1.6 | 1.2 |
| Debt/Worth | .7 | .7 | .5 | | .4 | .3 | .5 | .5 | .7 | .8 |
| | 2.3 | 2.0 | 1.6 | | 2.2 | 1.1 | 1.1 | 2.4 | 1.2 | 2.2 |
| | 45.9 | 10.8 | 8.8 | | -4.7 | 21.2 | 4.2 | 21.0 | 3.4 | 3.2 |
| % Profit Before Taxes/Tangible Net Worth | 45.7 | 53.9 | 44.9 | | 51.2 | 59.6 | 49.6 | 41.4 | 23.8 | 60.2 |
| | (130) 15.5 | (131) 18.6 | (148) 20.3 | | (24) 21.4 | (31) 23.2 | (19) 22.2 | (30) 19.5 | (26) 12.5 | (18) 34.0 |
| | 1.2 | 4.4 | 5.9 | | 4.5 | 5.3 | 1.4 | 6.4 | 1.2 | 11.9 |
| % Profit Before Taxes/Total Assets | 16.5 | 15.4 | 18.7 | | 23.1 | 24.2 | 19.8 | 15.0 | 8.4 | 17.4 |
| | 5.5 | 4.6 | 5.6 | | 6.2 | 10.1 | 7.0 | 4.1 | 3.3 | 10.1 |
| | -1.3 | .6 | 1.1 | | -4.8 | 5.3 | 1.6 | 1.6 | .5 | 5.2 |
| Sales/Net Fixed Assets | 86.9 | 81.5 | 68.1 | | UND | 77.1 | 71.5 | 159.7 | 42.9 | 40.2 |
| | 21.7 | 21.5 | 22.6 | | 27.7 | 22.9 | 34.8 | 22.9 | 16.1 | 18.9 |
| | 8.0 | 9.9 | 8.6 | | 5.5 | 8.6 | 14.0 | 7.8 | 9.5 | 8.0 |
| Sales/Total Assets | 3.5 | 3.6 | 3.6 | | 4.0 | 3.4 | 2.9 | 3.6 | 4.5 | 3.0 |
| | 2.4 | 2.6 | 2.4 | | 2.1 | 2.3 | 2.2 | 2.4 | 2.5 | 2.2 |
| | 1.6 | 1.7 | 1.5 | | 1.4 | 1.4 | 1.8 | 1.5 | 2.0 | 1.3 |
| % Depr., Dep., Amort./Sales | .4 | .5 | .4 | | 1.2 | .3 | .4 | .4 | .5 | 1.0 |
| | (122) 1.0 | (111) 1.0 | (126) .9 | | (20) 2.2 | (25) .4 | (13) .8 | (24) .7 | (25) .9 | (19) 1.2 |
| | 2.1 | 2.3 | 2.1 | | 2.9 | .8 | 1.5 | 1.3 | 2.0 | 3.6 |
| % Officers', Directors' Owners' Comp/Sales | 2.4 | 2.1 | 2.2 | | 4.2 | 3.2 | 1.9 | 1.6 | 2.3 | |
| | (90) 4.0 | (80) 3.7 | (88) 3.9 | | (18) 5.7 | (17) 5.8 | (13) 3.5 | (22) 2.6 | (11) 3.2 | |
| | 6.5 | 5.8 | 6.5 | | 12.3 | 9.3 | 7.6 | 4.7 | 5.3 | |
| Net Sales ($) | 3789332M | 2988057M | 2141128M | | 18579M | 72448M | 84959M | 263742M | 436939M | 1264461M |
| Total Assets ($) | 1544098M | 1405791M | 1121345M | | 10691M | 40388M | 47693M | 144993M | 169892M | 707688M |

M = $ thousand    MM = $ million
See Pages 9 through 22 for Explanation of Ratios and Data

## Current Data Sorted by Assets   Comparative Historical Data

| | | | | | | | | Type of Statement | | |
|---|---|---|---|---|---|---|---|---|---|---|
| | | | | 2 | 1 | | | Unqualified | 6 | 7 |
| | 1 | 9 | 8 | | | | | Reviewed | 12 | 9 |
| 1 | 3 | 4 | 3 | | | | | Compiled | 16 | 14 |
| 14 | 16 | 4 | | | | | | Tax Returns | 22 | 29 |
| 6 | 8 | 14 | 6 | | | | | Other | 29 | 31 |
| | 16 (4/1-9/30/11) | | 84 (10/1/11-3/31/12) | | | | | | 4/1/07-3/31/08 | 4/1/08-3/31/09 |
| 0-500M | 500M-2MM | 2-10MM | 10-50MM | 50-100MM | 100-250MM | | | | ALL | ALL |
| 21 | 28 | 31 | 19 | | 1 | | | NUMBER OF STATEMENTS | 85 | 90 |
| % | % | % | % | % | % | | | ASSETS | % | % |
| 13.6 | 8.8 | 7.7 | 14.7 | | | | | Cash & Equivalents | 9.3 | 13.3 |
| 1.7 | 4.0 | 3.2 | 5.2 | | | D | | Trade Receivables (net) | 5.3 | 4.3 |
| 66.6 | 70.4 | 57.9 | 47.3 | | | A | | Inventory | 61.1 | 58.0 |
| .9 | .1 | .8 | 1.9 | | | T | | All Other Current | 2.4 | 2.2 |
| 82.9 | 83.2 | 69.6 | 69.0 | | | A | | Total Current | 78.1 | 77.9 |
| 8.1 | 12.1 | 17.6 | 24.3 | | | | | Fixed Assets (net) | 14.7 | 14.5 |
| 2.4 | 1.4 | 5.6 | 1.5 | | | N | | Intangibles (net) | 1.3 | 2.8 |
| 6.6 | 3.3 | 7.2 | 5.1 | | | O | | All Other Non-Current | 5.9 | 4.8 |
| 100.0 | 100.0 | 100.0 | 100.0 | | | T | | Total | 100.0 | 100.0 |
| | | | | | | | | LIABILITIES | | |
| 10.3 | 10.1 | 9.5 | 9.1 | | | A | | Notes Payable-Short Term | 9.9 | 11.5 |
| 1.5 | .8 | .8 | 2.5 | | | V | | Cur. Mat.-L.T.D. | 3.7 | 3.3 |
| 20.7 | 22.3 | 23.6 | 24.8 | | | A | | Trade Payables | 23.0 | 22.7 |
| .2 | .0 | .1 | .1 | | | I | | Income Taxes Payable | .0 | .1 |
| 21.9 | 10.3 | 15.2 | 9.3 | | | L | | All Other Current | 10.4 | 9.4 |
| 54.7 | 43.4 | 49.3 | 45.8 | | | A | | Total Current | 47.0 | 47.0 |
| 10.6 | 16.5 | 8.4 | 8.7 | | | B | | Long-Term Debt | 7.0 | 14.5 |
| .0 | .0 | .2 | .1 | | | L | | Deferred Taxes | .0 | .0 |
| 10.9 | 5.5 | 7.1 | 4.0 | | | E | | All Other Non-Current | 5.7 | 6.0 |
| 23.8 | 34.6 | 35.0 | 41.3 | | | | | Net Worth | 40.2 | 32.4 |
| 100.0 | 100.0 | 100.0 | 100.0 | | | | | Total Liabilities & Net Worth | 100.0 | 100.0 |
| | | | | | | | | INCOME DATA | | |
| 100.0 | 100.0 | 100.0 | 100.0 | | | | | Net Sales | 100.0 | 100.0 |
| 38.9 | 44.3 | 43.5 | 40.7 | | | | | Gross Profit | 43.1 | 41.9 |
| 35.1 | 38.9 | 39.0 | 37.1 | | | | | Operating Expenses | 39.6 | 39.2 |
| 3.8 | 5.4 | 4.4 | 3.6 | | | | | Operating Profit | 3.4 | 2.7 |
| .7 | .3 | .5 | -.7 | | | | | All Other Expenses (net) | .8 | .8 |
| 3.1 | 5.0 | 3.9 | 4.3 | | | | | Profit Before Taxes | 2.7 | 1.9 |
| | | | | | | | | RATIOS | | |
| 5.6 | 4.1 | 3.1 | 2.4 | | | | | | 3.5 | 3.2 |
| 3.0 | 2.1 | 1.8 | 1.6 | | | | | Current | 1.7 | 1.7 |
| 1.3 | 1.3 | 1.2 | 1.1 | | | | | | 1.2 | 1.2 |
| .9 | .5 | .4 | 1.0 | | | | | | .7 | .9 |
| .2 | .2 | .2 | .3 | | | | | Quick | .3 | .2 |
| .1 | .1 | .1 | .2 | | | | | | .1 | .1 |

| | | | | | | | | | | | | | | | |
|---|---|---|---|---|---|---|---|---|---|---|---|---|---|---|---|
| 0 | UND | 0 | UND | 0 | UND | 0 | UND | | | Sales/Receivables | 0 | UND | 0 | UND | |
| 0 | UND | 0 | 787.0 | 1 | 666.2 | 1 | 254.1 | | | | 1 | 389.0 | 0 | UND | |
| 0 | UND | 6 | 62.3 | 4 | 84.1 | 14 | 25.5 | | | | 6 | 60.2 | 4 | 95.0 | |
| 76 | 4.8 | 104 | 3.5 | 122 | 3.0 | 64 | 5.7 | | | Cost of Sales/Inventory | 98 | 3.7 | 81 | 4.5 | |
| 96 | 3.8 | 174 | 2.1 | 146 | 2.5 | 107 | 3.4 | | | | 167 | 2.2 | 159 | 2.3 | |
| 192 | 1.9 | 243 | 1.5 | 203 | 1.8 | 166 | 2.0 | | | | 219 | 1.7 | 232 | 1.6 | |
| 0 | UND | 24 | 15.5 | 43 | 8.5 | 28 | 13.1 | | | Cost of Sales/Payables | 22 | 16.7 | 22 | 17.0 | |
| 23 | 15.6 | 43 | 8.5 | 59 | 6.2 | 46 | 7.9 | | | | 42 | 8.6 | 40 | 9.0 | |
| 39 | 9.4 | 69 | 5.3 | 79 | 4.6 | 85 | 4.3 | | | | 82 | 4.4 | 76 | 4.8 | |

| | | | | | | | | | | | | | | | |
|---|---|---|---|---|---|---|---|---|---|---|---|---|---|---|---|
| | 4.2 | | 3.9 | | 4.3 | | 4.4 | | | Sales/Working Capital | | 4.0 | | 3.9 | |
| | 7.7 | | 6.3 | | 6.9 | | 12.9 | | | | | 7.2 | | 7.6 | |
| | 21.5 | | 16.8 | | 19.8 | | 48.7 | | | | | 21.2 | | 41.0 | |
| | 12.9 | | 15.9 | | 15.7 | | 36.7 | | | EBIT/Interest | | 9.6 | | 11.6 | |
| (14) | 2.3 | (24) | 5.8 | (28) | 5.4 | (18) | 6.3 | | | | (66) 2.9 | | (76) 3.0 | | |
| | -.4 | | 2.1 | | 2.3 | | 2.0 | | | | | .8 | | .2 | |
| | | | | | | | | | | Net Profit + Depr., Dep., Amort./Cur. Mat. L/T/D | | 2.5 | | 1.9 | |
| | | | | | | | | | | | (14) .7 | | (14) 1.4 | | |
| | | | | | | | | | | | | -22.3 | | .0 | |
| | .0 | | .0 | | .2 | | .3 | | | Fixed/Worth | | .1 | | .1 | |
| | .2 | | .2 | | .3 | | .7 | | | | | .3 | | .3 | |
| | UND | | 1.7 | | 1.8 | | 1.1 | | | | | .9 | | 1.7 | |
| | .3 | | .6 | | .7 | | .5 | | | Debt/Worth | | .6 | | .6 | |
| | 1.2 | | 2.4 | | 1.3 | | 1.4 | | | | | 1.5 | | 1.7 | |
| | UND | | 7.5 | | 5.3 | | 6.8 | | | | | 5.2 | | 8.1 | |
| | 74.3 | | 108.1 | | 33.8 | | 32.3 | | | % Profit Before Taxes/Tangible Net Worth | | 39.1 | | 46.0 | |
| (16) | 19.9 | (25) | 21.7 | (25) | 15.5 | (18) | 20.2 | | | | (78) 17.5 | | (74) 15.5 | | |
| | 1.4 | | 4.0 | | 8.2 | | 12.0 | | | | | .7 | | 2.0 | |
| | 21.8 | | 18.8 | | 13.4 | | 14.7 | | | % Profit Before Taxes/Total Assets | | 14.5 | | 13.6 | |
| | 4.5 | | 7.2 | | 6.8 | | 7.9 | | | | | 5.2 | | 4.1 | |
| | -.2 | | 1.8 | | 2.1 | | 1.6 | | | | | -1.1 | | -2.3 | |
| | UND | | 230.7 | | 35.9 | | 19.1 | | | Sales/Net Fixed Assets | | 79.5 | | 71.7 | |
| | 61.1 | | 37.8 | | 21.1 | | 14.7 | | | | | 25.6 | | 26.9 | |
| | 24.3 | | 19.7 | | 11.2 | | 7.0 | | | | | 11.8 | | 11.4 | |
| | 5.0 | | 4.1 | | 2.9 | | 3.6 | | | Sales/Total Assets | | 3.6 | | 3.5 | |
| | 4.0 | | 2.7 | | 2.6 | | 2.7 | | | | | 2.5 | | 2.4 | |
| | 2.6 | | 1.9 | | 2.0 | | 1.9 | | | | | 1.9 | | 1.8 | |
| | .3 | | .2 | | .5 | | .8 | | | % Depr., Dep., Amort./Sales | | .5 | | .5 | |
| (13) | .4 | (20) | .4 | (25) | .9 | (16) | 1.3 | | | | (68) .9 | | (71) .9 | | |
| | 1.5 | | 1.0 | | 1.6 | | 2.3 | | | | | 1.8 | | 1.9 | |
| | 3.4 | | 2.0 | | 1.7 | | | | | % Officers', Directors' Owners' Comp/Sales | | 1.6 | | 1.7 | |
| (15) | 7.3 | (19) | 3.2 | (13) | 2.8 | | | | | | (39) 3.4 | | (47) 4.3 | | |
| | 9.1 | | 5.6 | | 6.3 | | | | | | | 7.3 | | 7.4 | |

| | | | | | | | |
|---|---|---|---|---|---|---|---|
| 20567M | 80457M | 363385M | 1250953M | | 478944M | Net Sales ($) | 4221032M | 1950471M |
| 5730M | 27424M | 149375M | 445866M | | 249818M | Total Assets ($) | 1726681M | 951869M |

M = $ thousand MM = $ million
See Pages 9 through 22 for Explanation of Ratios and Data

## Comparative Historical Data | Current Data Sorted by Sales

| 4/1/09-3/31/10 ALL | 4/1/10-3/31/11 ALL | 4/1/11-3/31/12 ALL | | 0-1MM | 1-3MM | 3-5MM | 5-10MM | 10-25MM | 25MM & OVER |
|---|---|---|---|---|---|---|---|---|---|
| | | | **Type of Statement** | | | | | | |
| 4 | 8 | 3 | Unqualified | | 1 | | 3 | 6 | 3 |
| 8 | 15 | 18 | Reviewed | | 1 | | 3 | 2 | 8 |
| 17 | 9 | 11 | Compiled | | | 3 | 3 | | 2 |
| 31 | 37 | 34 | Tax Returns | 10 | 12 | 7 | 5 | | |
| 38 | 26 | 34 | Other | 3 | 10 | 2 | 5 | 8 | 6 |
| | | | | | 16 (4/1-9/30/11) | | 84 (10/1/11-3/31/12) | | |
| 98 | 95 | 100 | **NUMBER OF STATEMENTS** | 13 | 24 | 12 | 16 | 16 | 19 |
| % | % | % | **ASSETS** | % | % | % | % | % | % |
| 11.0 | 10.0 | 10.7 | Cash & Equivalents | 7.4 | 10.9 | 9.8 | 13.4 | 7.2 | 14.1 |
| 5.3 | 4.1 | 3.6 | Trade Receivables (net) | 2.9 | 2.9 | 2.7 | 2.8 | 4.0 | 6.0 |
| 58.7 | 58.4 | 60.8 | Inventory | 75.1 | 66.4 | 64.9 | 59.9 | 54.0 | 47.7 |
| 2.3 | 1.8 | .8 | All Other Current | .1 | .8 | .2 | .5 | 1.3 | 1.8 |
| 77.3 | 74.3 | 76.0 | Total Current | 85.5 | 81.1 | 77.6 | 76.6 | 66.4 | 69.7 |
| 13.1 | 14.7 | 15.3 | Fixed Assets (net) | 5.8 | 12.7 | 19.2 | 9.8 | 18.7 | 24.5 |
| 3.5 | 3.1 | 3.0 | Intangibles (net) | 1.7 | 1.6 | 2.6 | 3.1 | 7.7 | 1.7 |
| 6.2 | 7.8 | 5.7 | All Other Non-Current | 7.0 | 4.6 | .7 | 10.5 | 7.2 | 4.1 |
| 100.0 | 100.0 | 100.0 | Total | 100.0 | 100.0 | 100.0 | 100.0 | 100.0 | 100.0 |
| | | | **LIABILITIES** | | | | | | |
| 10.1 | 9.2 | 9.7 | Notes Payable-Short Term | 15.2 | 9.0 | 6.9 | 5.9 | 12.7 | 9.1 |
| 3.9 | 1.3 | 1.3 | Cur. Mat.-L.T.D. | .8 | 1.3 | 1.1 | .7 | 1.1 | 2.3 |
| 18.6 | 20.8 | 22.8 | Trade Payables | 14.1 | 22.3 | 23.3 | 26.4 | 23.8 | 25.3 |
| .2 | .0 | .1 | Income Taxes Payable | .0 | .2 | .0 | .2 | .0 | .1 |
| 21.5 | 8.2 | 14.0 | All Other Current | 28.6 | 12.4 | 6.3 | 22.3 | 8.1 | 8.9 |
| 54.3 | 39.6 | 47.9 | Total Current | 58.7 | 45.2 | 37.6 | 55.5 | 45.7 | 45.7 |
| 12.1 | 13.1 | 11.1 | Long-Term Debt | 10.9 | 14.6 | 21.4 | 6.5 | 7.6 | 7.1 |
| .0 | .1 | .1 | Deferred Taxes | .0 | .0 | .0 | .0 | .4 | .1 |
| 2.5 | 11.0 | 7.0 | All Other Non-Current | 10.1 | 10.0 | 6.1 | 4.0 | 5.8 | 5.1 |
| 31.0 | 36.2 | 34.0 | Net Worth | 20.3 | 30.2 | 34.9 | 34.0 | 40.5 | 42.1 |
| 100.0 | 100.0 | 100.0 | Total Liabilities & Net Worth | 100.0 | 100.0 | 100.0 | 100.0 | 100.0 | 100.0 |
| | | | **INCOME DATA** | | | | | | |
| 100.0 | 100.0 | 100.0 | Net Sales | 100.0 | 100.0 | 100.0 | 100.0 | 100.0 | 100.0 |
| 45.0 | 42.3 | 42.2 | Gross Profit | 44.6 | 40.9 | 40.6 | 44.5 | 43.5 | 40.1 |
| 41.9 | 38.0 | 37.8 | Operating Expenses | 37.8 | 36.7 | 36.4 | 39.3 | 39.5 | 37.3 |
| 3.1 | 4.3 | 4.4 | Operating Profit | 6.8 | 4.1 | 4.2 | 5.3 | 4.0 | 2.8 |
| 1.5 | .6 | .3 | All Other Expenses (net) | .9 | .6 | .4 | -.3 | .7 | -.3 |
| 1.6 | 3.7 | 4.1 | Profit Before Taxes | 5.9 | 3.5 | 3.8 | 5.6 | 3.3 | 3.0 |
| | | | **RATIOS** | | | | | | |
| 3.0 | 3.4 | 3.6 | Current | 6.1 | 4.5 | 4.5 | 3.5 | 2.7 | 2.5 |
| 1.8 | 2.1 | 1.9 | | 3.4 | 1.7 | 2.7 | 2.0 | 1.5 | 1.6 |
| 1.2 | 1.5 | 1.2 | | 1.5 | 1.2 | 1.5 | 1.3 | .9 | 1.1 |
| .8 | .7 | .6 | Quick | .8 | .6 | 1.0 | .6 | .5 | 1.0 |
| .2 | .3 | .2 | | .2 | .2 | .2 | .3 | .2 | .3 |
| .0 | .0 | .1 | | .0 | .1 | .1 | .2 | .1 | .2 |
| 0 UND | 0 UND | 0 UND | Sales/Receivables | 0 UND | 0 UND | 0 UND | 0 UND | 0 UND | 0 UND |
| 0 999.8 | 1 544.2 | 0 999.8 | | 0 UND | 0 UND | 0 787.0 | 1 516.9 | 1 554.2 | 1 254.1 |
| 6 56.5 | 5 76.8 | 5 73.3 | | 17 21.0 | 1 515.8 | 3 125.3 | 5 68.0 | 4 83.9 | 14 25.5 |
| 88 4.2 | 95 3.8 | 89 4.1 | Cost of Sales/Inventory | 85 4.3 | 87 4.2 | 89 4.1 | 114 3.2 | 96 3.8 | 60 6.1 |
| 163 2.2 | 144 2.5 | 140 2.6 | | 243 1.5 | 126 2.7 | 135 2.7 | 174 2.1 | 126 2.9 | 99 3.7 |
| 255 1.4 | 213 1.7 | 215 1.7 | | 521 .7 | 228 1.6 | 192 1.9 | 215 1.7 | 174 2.1 | 166 2.2 |
| 15 24.6 | 27 13.4 | 26 14.1 | Cost of Sales/Payables | 19 19.4 | 0 UND | 22 16.4 | 44 8.3 | 41 8.8 | 28 13.1 |
| 40 9.2 | 42 8.8 | 44 8.3 | | 31 11.6 | 28 13.1 | 36 10.2 | 63 5.8 | 58 6.3 | 46 7.9 |
| 75 4.9 | 59 6.1 | 72 5.1 | | 55 6.6 | 58 6.3 | 69 5.3 | 94 3.9 | 78 4.7 | 76 4.8 |
| 3.6 | 3.9 | 4.2 | Sales/Working Capital | 2.7 | 5.6 | 3.9 | 3.7 | 5.6 | 4.6 |
| 8.3 | 7.4 | 7.3 | | 4.0 | 8.1 | 6.2 | 5.8 | 12.0 | 12.9 |
| 24.2 | 18.4 | 20.6 | | 6.4 | 30.3 | 13.1 | 18.7 | NM | 48.7 |
| 23.3 | 12.8 | 16.3 | EBIT/Interest | 20.2 | 11.8 | 15.2 | 41.1 | 12.6 | 36.7 |
| (76) 4.2 | (77) 2.9 | (85) 5.5 | | (10) 3.9 | (19) 6.0 | (10) 3.3 | (13) 7.3 | (15) 3.1 | (18) 6.0 |
| .6 | 1.3 | 1.9 | | .9 | 1.1 | .6 | 4.6 | 2.3 | 1.0 |
| 3.9 | 9.4 | | Net Profit + Depr., Dep., Amort./Cur. Mat. L/T/D | | | | | | |
| (13) 2.1 | (13) 2.7 | | | | | | | | |
| 1.2 | .8 | | | | | | | | |
| .1 | .1 | .1 | Fixed/Worth | .0 | .0 | .1 | .1 | .2 | .3 |
| .3 | .3 | .3 | | .0 | .3 | .2 | .2 | .4 | .7 |
| 1.2 | 2.0 | 1.3 | | .1 | 59.5 | 2.3 | .3 | NM | 1.1 |
| .5 | .7 | .5 | Debt/Worth | .3 | .4 | .6 | .5 | .7 | .5 |
| 1.6 | 1.7 | 1.4 | | .9 | 2.3 | 2.6 | 1.0 | 1.7 | 1.4 |
| 6.9 | 5.6 | 7.5 | | NM | 248.0 | 8.7 | 1.8 | NM | 6.8 |
| 36.8 | 36.7 | 47.2 | % Profit Before Taxes/Tangible Net Worth | 83.6 | 113.6 | 54.7 | 54.7 | 37.0 | 32.3 |
| (79) 16.7 | (82) 20.7 | (85) 17.0 | | (10) 18.7 | (20) 25.6 | (11) 15.0 | (14) 16.1 | (12) 15.0 | (18) 19.8 |
| .2 | 7.3 | 5.0 | | 1.0 | 8.4 | -.4 | 7.5 | 5.1 | 5.1 |
| 17.6 | 17.6 | 15.0 | % Profit Before Taxes/Total Assets | 21.8 | 17.8 | 33.3 | 14.0 | 14.7 | 14.7 |
| 5.5 | 6.7 | 7.1 | | 5.6 | 8.9 | 4.7 | 7.2 | 6.6 | 7.5 |
| -1.6 | 2.1 | 1.6 | | .5 | 2.2 | .2 | 4.1 | 1.9 | 1.3 |
| 93.7 | 71.4 | 83.5 | Sales/Net Fixed Assets | UND | 268.5 | 127.6 | 198.1 | 31.0 | 19.1 |
| 25.6 | 29.4 | 24.3 | | 120.3 | 36.0 | 22.2 | 29.4 | 18.9 | 14.7 |
| 11.6 | 11.3 | 14.8 | | 44.3 | 17.0 | 19.7 | 15.4 | 9.9 | 8.5 |
| 3.4 | 3.5 | 3.7 | Sales/Total Assets | 3.7 | 4.2 | 4.6 | 3.0 | 3.0 | 3.6 |
| 2.4 | 2.4 | 2.7 | | 2.1 | 3.2 | 3.1 | 2.6 | 2.6 | 2.7 |
| 1.7 | 1.9 | 2.0 | | 1.1 | 2.3 | 2.2 | 2.0 | 2.2 | 1.9 |
| .4 | .6 | .4 | % Depr., Dep., Amort./Sales | | .2 | | .4 | .6 | .8 |
| (73) .7 | (76) .9 | (75) .8 | | | (18) .4 | | (12) .6 | (13) .9 | (16) 1.3 |
| 1.5 | 1.8 | 1.5 | | | 1.2 | | 1.0 | 2.0 | 2.2 |
| 2.1 | 2.1 | 2.0 | % Officers', Directors' Owners' Comp/Sales | | 3.2 | | 2.5 | | |
| (56) 4.1 | (51) 3.6 | (55) 3.1 | | | (16) 5.0 | | (10) 2.9 | | |
| 7.9 | 6.6 | 7.3 | | | 8.5 | | 7.4 | | |
| 2235573M | 2311244M | 2194306M | Net Sales ($) | 8020M | 40364M | 45028M | 122943M | 255445M | 1722506M |
| 1011578M | 1238903M | 878213M | Total Assets ($) | 4406M | 14534M | 19672M | 61325M | 99036M | 679240M |

M = $ thousand    MM = $ million
See Pages 9 through 22 for Explanation of Ratios and Data

## Current Data Sorted by Assets      Comparative Historical Data

| | | | | | | | Type of Statement | | |
|---|---|---|---|---|---|---|---|---|---|
| 1 | | 1 | 10 | 3 | 1 | | Unqualified | 14 | 12 |
| | 3 | 22 | 15 | | | | Reviewed | 45 | 36 |
| 3 | 19 | 28 | 3 | | | | Compiled | 55 | 73 |
| 18 | 40 | 17 | 3 | | | | Tax Returns | 73 | 68 |
| 7 | 17 | 31 | 14 | 5 | 3 | | Other | 89 | 90 |
| | 62 (4/1-9/30/11) | | 202 (10/1/11-3/31/12) | | | | | 4/1/07-3/31/08 | 4/1/08-3/31/09 |
| 0-500M | 500M-2MM | 2-10MM | 10-50MM | 50-100MM | 100-250MM | | | ALL | ALL |
| 29 | 79 | 99 | 45 | 8 | 4 | NUMBER OF STATEMENTS | | 276 | 279 |
| % | % | % | % | % | % | ASSETS | | % | % |
| 19.3 | 11.9 | 7.0 | 4.7 | | | Cash & Equivalents | | 5.8 | 5.6 |
| 5.1 | 4.3 | 7.6 | 9.9 | | | Trade Receivables (net) | | 8.1 | 7.3 |
| 58.7 | 68.8 | 64.0 | 60.3 | | | Inventory | | 68.7 | 68.6 |
| .0 | 1.0 | 2.6 | 2.5 | | | All Other Current | | 1.5 | 1.5 |
| 83.0 | 86.0 | 81.2 | 77.4 | | | Total Current | | 84.1 | 83.0 |
| 8.9 | 6.8 | 10.4 | 12.1 | | | Fixed Assets (net) | | 10.2 | 10.1 |
| 4.5 | 2.3 | 1.8 | 2.5 | | | Intangibles (net) | | 1.6 | 2.0 |
| 3.6 | 4.8 | 6.5 | 8.1 | | | All Other Non-Current | | 4.1 | 4.9 |
| 100.0 | 100.0 | 100.0 | 100.0 | | | Total | | 100.0 | 100.0 |
| | | | | | | LIABILITIES | | | |
| 8.7 | 7.6 | 10.5 | 11.9 | | | Notes Payable-Short Term | | 15.1 | 15.1 |
| 2.3 | 2.2 | 2.0 | 2.3 | | | Cur. Mat.-L.T.D. | | 2.3 | 3.7 |
| 10.8 | 15.9 | 17.9 | 16.5 | | | Trade Payables | | 20.9 | 19.1 |
| .0 | .2 | .1 | .5 | | | Income Taxes Payable | | .1 | .1 |
| 7.8 | 7.7 | 7.8 | 12.2 | | | All Other Current | | 9.1 | 8.8 |
| 29.5 | 33.7 | 38.4 | 43.3 | | | Total Current | | 47.4 | 46.8 |
| 19.2 | 12.1 | 8.2 | 8.1 | | | Long-Term Debt | | 13.5 | 12.8 |
| .0 | .0 | .0 | .1 | | | Deferred Taxes | | .1 | .1 |
| 10.7 | 7.2 | 7.0 | 5.2 | | | All Other Non-Current | | 7.9 | 8.7 |
| 40.5 | 47.0 | 46.4 | 43.2 | | | Net Worth | | 31.1 | 31.6 |
| 100.0 | 100.0 | 100.0 | 100.0 | | | Total Liabilities & Net Worth | | 100.0 | 100.0 |
| | | | | | | INCOME DATA | | | |
| 100.0 | 100.0 | 100.0 | 100.0 | | | Net Sales | | 100.0 | 100.0 |
| 45.6 | 44.8 | 39.9 | 40.1 | | | Gross Profit | | 43.1 | 43.6 |
| 38.0 | 36.9 | 34.1 | 35.2 | | | Operating Expenses | | 39.0 | 40.7 |
| 7.6 | 7.9 | 5.8 | 4.9 | | | Operating Profit | | 4.1 | 3.0 |
| 1.5 | .8 | 1.5 | .7 | | | All Other Expenses (net) | | 1.9 | 1.5 |
| 6.2 | 7.1 | 4.3 | 4.2 | | | Profit Before Taxes | | 2.2 | 1.5 |
| | | | | | | RATIOS | | | |
| 12.8 | 5.6 | 3.6 | 3.0 | | | | | 2.9 | 3.1 |
| 3.2 | 3.3 | 2.0 | 1.9 | | | Current | | 1.9 | 1.9 |
| 1.5 | 1.8 | 1.5 | 1.3 | | | | | 1.3 | 1.4 |
| 2.2 | 1.1 | .7 | .8 | | | | | .6 | .5 |
| .7 | (77) .4 | .2 | .2 | | | Quick | | .2 (277) | .2 |
| .3 | .1 | .1 | .1 | | | | | .1 | .1 |
| 0 UND | 0 UND | 0 999.8 | 2 215.8 | | | | 0 UND | 0 UND | |
| 0 UND | 2 197.3 | 6 63.7 | 12 30.2 | | | Sales/Receivables | 6 60.5 | 5 68.4 | |
| 1 298.5 | 9 39.8 | 16 23.2 | 39 9.4 | | | | 20 18.2 | 18 20.2 | |
| 42 8.7 | 182 2.0 | 146 2.5 | 146 2.5 | | | | 189 1.9 | 193 1.9 | |
| 152 2.4 | 281 1.3 | 243 1.5 | 261 1.4 | | | Cost of Sales/Inventory | 304 1.2 | 312 1.2 | |
| 281 1.3 | 406 .9 | 332 1.1 | 406 .9 | | | | 438 .8 | 479 .8 | |
| 0 UND | 20 17.9 | 31 11.9 | 31 11.7 | | | | 30 12.2 | 28 12.8 | |
| 16 22.8 | 49 7.5 | 50 7.3 | 53 6.9 | | | Cost of Sales/Payables | 68 5.4 | 58 6.3 | |
| 47 7.7 | 76 4.8 | 91 4.0 | 76 4.8 | | | | 126 2.9 | 118 3.1 | |
| 3.3 | 2.0 | 2.2 | 2.0 | | | | | 2.5 | 2.5 |
| 5.9 | 3.1 | 4.5 | 4.4 | | | Sales/Working Capital | | 4.4 | 4.4 |
| 19.8 | 6.3 | 7.4 | 12.6 | | | | | 7.6 | 8.7 |
| 17.0 | 40.4 | 11.8 | 19.4 | | | | | 5.3 | 5.9 |
| (19) 8.0 | (68) 8.0 | (92) 3.4 | (42) 5.3 | | | EBIT/Interest | (258) 2.1 | (261) 1.7 | |
| 2.5 | 1.9 | 1.3 | 1.5 | | | | | 1.0 | .5 |
| | | 10.6 | 12.0 | | | | | 4.7 | 1.9 |
| | (13) 1.7 | (14) 3.1 | | | | Net Profit + Depr., Dep., Amort./Cur. Mat. L/T/D | (50) 1.7 | (47) .7 | |
| | | .2 | .8 | | | | | .4 | .0 |
| .0 | .0 | .0 | .1 | | | | | .1 | .1 |
| .1 | .1 | .2 | .3 | | | Fixed/Worth | | .2 | .2 |
| .5 | .3 | .3 | .6 | | | | | .7 | .7 |
| .2 | .4 | .4 | .5 | | | | | .9 | .8 |
| .9 | 1.0 | 1.4 | 1.0 | | | Debt/Worth | | 2.0 | 1.9 |
| 7.5 | 2.4 | 2.4 | 3.4 | | | | | 5.9 | 5.6 |
| 104.0 | 47.7 | 35.2 | 31.0 | | | % Profit Before Taxes/Tangible Net Worth | | 26.2 | 22.1 |
| (25) 31.0 | (74) 19.5 | (96) 14.1 | (40) 14.1 | | | | (237) 9.2 | (243) 7.6 | |
| 11.2 | 5.0 | 2.2 | 4.6 | | | | | 1.2 | -.7 |
| 36.2 | 18.5 | 12.9 | 15.1 | | | % Profit Before Taxes/Total Assets | | 8.4 | 7.2 |
| 13.0 | 8.4 | 6.2 | 6.1 | | | | | 2.9 | 1.9 |
| 1.8 | 2.6 | 1.1 | 1.4 | | | | | -.2 | -1.6 |
| 999.8 | 136.6 | 107.3 | 32.3 | | | | | 79.9 | 80.4 |
| 41.5 | 50.4 | 33.5 | 18.2 | | | Sales/Net Fixed Assets | | 23.7 | 25.4 |
| 16.6 | 15.4 | 12.5 | 9.6 | | | | | 10.4 | 10.1 |
| 5.0 | 2.4 | 2.4 | 2.0 | | | | | 2.0 | 2.1 |
| 2.6 | 1.7 | 1.7 | 1.5 | | | Sales/Total Assets | | 1.5 | 1.5 |
| 1.9 | 1.3 | 1.1 | 1.2 | | | | | 1.2 | 1.1 |
| .4 | .3 | .3 | .4 | | | | | .4 | .3 |
| (16) .8 | (52) .8 | (76) .6 | (39) 1.0 | | | % Depr., Dep., Amort./Sales | (217) .9 | (212) .9 | |
| 1.2 | 1.5 | 1.1 | 1.5 | | | | | 1.7 | 1.9 |
| 2.7 | 4.5 | 1.8 | 1.0 | | | | | 2.9 | 3.1 |
| (21) 5.0 | (52) 6.7 | (50) 4.3 | (13) 2.3 | | | % Officers', Directors' Owners' Comp/Sales | (147) 5.2 | (138) 5.5 | |
| 8.8 | 10.2 | 5.4 | 3.3 | | | | | 8.5 | 9.7 |
| 30130M | 233598M | 838018M | 1879631M | 1380008M | 1100974M | Net Sales ($) | | 7046532M | 5279892M |
| 8111M | 87042M | 475584M | 1052321M | 554329M | 605225M | Total Assets ($) | | 3982732M | 3232773M |

M = $ thousand    MM = $ million
See Pages 9 through 22 for Explanation of Ratios and Data

## Comparative Historical Data | Current Data Sorted by Sales

| Type of Statement | | | | | | | | | |
|---|---|---|---|---|---|---|---|---|---|
| Unqualified | 16 | 15 | 16 | 1 | 2 | | | 2 | 11 |
| Reviewed | 31 | 34 | 40 | 1 | 4 | 3 | 6 | 15 | 11 |
| Compiled | 56 | 64 | 53 | 4 | 19 | 7 | 12 | 9 | 2 |
| Tax Returns | 92 | 81 | 78 | 16 | 39 | 7 | 11 | 4 | 1 |
| Other | 81 | 74 | 77 | 5 | 17 | 11 | 12 | 15 | 17 |
| | 4/1/09-3/31/10 ALL | 4/1/10-3/31/11 ALL | 4/1/11-3/31/12 ALL | 62 (4/1-9/30/11) | | | 202 (10/1/11-3/31/12) | | |
| | | | | 0-1MM | 1-3MM | 3-5MM | 5-10MM | 10-25MM | 25MM & OVER |
| NUMBER OF STATEMENTS | 276 | 268 | 264 | 27 | 81 | 28 | 41 | 45 | 42 |
| ASSETS | % | % | % | % | % | % | % | % | % |
| Cash & Equivalents | 7.8 | 8.0 | 9.7 | 12.9 | 10.3 | 6.2 | 10.7 | 8.6 | 8.8 |
| Trade Receivables (net) | 7.4 | 6.3 | 6.6 | 8.7 | 3.5 | 5.8 | 9.1 | 5.8 | 10.6 |
| Inventory | 65.5 | 66.9 | 64.1 | 63.5 | 67.5 | 66.6 | 61.3 | 63.9 | 59.4 |
| All Other Current | 1.7 | 1.7 | 1.8 | 1.2 | .9 | 1.2 | .5 | 4.0 | 3.3 |
| Total Current | 82.4 | 82.9 | 82.3 | 86.3 | 82.2 | 79.7 | 81.5 | 82.3 | 82.2 |
| Fixed Assets (net) | 10.5 | 10.5 | 9.6 | 5.6 | 9.1 | 9.9 | 10.0 | 11.0 | 11.3 |
| Intangibles (net) | 2.3 | 1.9 | 2.3 | 5.6 | 3.0 | 1.8 | 1.0 | .7 | 2.4 |
| All Other Non-Current | 4.9 | 4.6 | 5.8 | 2.5 | 5.7 | 8.7 | 7.5 | 6.0 | 4.1 |
| Total | 100.0 | 100.0 | 100.0 | 100.0 | 100.0 | 100.0 | 100.0 | 100.0 | 100.0 |
| LIABILITIES | | | | | | | | | |
| Notes Payable-Short Term | 14.5 | 14.8 | 9.7 | 9.8 | 8.6 | 10.5 | 9.1 | 11.3 | 10.3 |
| Cur. Mat.-L.T.D. | 2.4 | 2.4 | 2.2 | 2.2 | 2.5 | 3.4 | 1.6 | 1.0 | 2.7 |
| Trade Payables | 17.7 | 18.0 | 16.4 | 11.0 | 13.8 | 16.3 | 17.3 | 18.9 | 21.5 |
| Income Taxes Payable | .2 | .2 | .2 | .1 | .2 | .0 | .1 | .1 | .6 |
| All Other Current | 9.0 | 9.9 | 8.8 | 7.2 | 5.8 | 9.8 | 8.9 | 10.4 | 12.7 |
| Total Current | 43.8 | 45.2 | 37.3 | 30.2 | 30.9 | 40.0 | 37.2 | 41.7 | 47.8 |
| Long-Term Debt | 12.4 | 11.5 | 11.2 | 19.8 | 14.5 | 10.5 | 6.5 | 4.3 | 11.9 |
| Deferred Taxes | .1 | .2 | .1 | .0 | .0 | .0 | .0 | .2 | .2 |
| All Other Non-Current | 8.3 | 9.4 | 7.1 | 12.5 | 7.2 | 6.4 | 9.5 | 4.7 | 4.2 |
| Net Worth | 35.4 | 33.8 | 44.3 | 37.5 | 47.3 | 43.0 | 46.8 | 49.1 | 35.9 |
| Total Liabilities & Net Worth | 100.0 | 100.0 | 100.0 | 100.0 | 100.0 | 100.0 | 100.0 | 100.0 | 100.0 |
| INCOME DATA | | | | | | | | | |
| Net Sales | 100.0 | 100.0 | 100.0 | 100.0 | 100.0 | 100.0 | 100.0 | 100.0 | 100.0 |
| Gross Profit | 42.7 | 43.8 | 42.2 | 50.9 | 43.2 | 45.6 | 38.2 | 38.9 | 39.7 |
| Operating Expenses | 39.4 | 39.1 | 35.8 | 41.4 | 36.5 | 38.3 | 32.9 | 33.8 | 34.0 |
| Operating Profit | 3.3 | 4.7 | 6.4 | 9.5 | 6.7 | 7.3 | 5.3 | 5.1 | 5.7 |
| All Other Expenses (net) | 1.3 | 1.3 | 1.1 | 2.2 | 1.2 | 1.9 | 1.1 | .4 | .5 |
| Profit Before Taxes | 2.1 | 3.3 | 5.3 | 7.3 | 5.5 | 5.3 | 4.2 | 4.7 | 5.2 |
| RATIOS | | | | | | | | | |
| Current | 3.4 | 3.7 | 4.4 | 9.0 | 5.6 | 4.2 | 3.8 | 3.5 | 2.8 |
| | 2.0 | 2.0 | 2.3 | 4.2 | 2.7 | 1.9 | 2.0 | 1.9 | 1.7 |
| | 1.4 | 1.4 | 1.5 | 1.8 | 1.8 | 1.5 | 1.5 | 1.5 | 1.3 |
| Quick | .6 | .7 | 1.0 | 2.3 | 1.0 | .9 | 1.3 | .7 | .7 |
| | .3 | .2 | (262) .3 | .7 | (80) .3 | (27) .3 | .3 | .3 | .2 |
| | .1 | .1 | .1 | .3 | .1 | .1 | .1 | .1 | .1 |
| Sales/Receivables | 0 UND | 0 UND | 0 UND | 0 UND | 0 UND | 0 UND | 0 UND | 1 423.4 | 2 214.7 |
| | 5 68.2 | 4 102.0 | 3 110.0 | 1 435.5 | 1 443.8 | 4 90.2 | 5 66.5 | 6 61.3 | 8 45.5 |
| | 18 20.2 | 15 24.2 | 14 26.2 | 24 15.4 | 8 45.2 | 22 16.6 | 14 25.2 | 16 23.4 | 22 16.9 |
| Cost of Sales/Inventory | 185 2.0 | 183 2.0 | 140 2.6 | 146 2.5 | 174 2.1 | 228 1.6 | 126 2.9 | 122 3.0 | 118 3.1 |
| | 308 1.2 | 291 1.3 | 243 1.5 | 304 1.2 | 281 1.3 | 304 1.2 | 192 1.9 | 215 1.7 | 182 2.0 |
| | 496 .7 | 456 .8 | 365 1.0 | 912 .4 | 406 .9 | 365 1.0 | 304 1.2 | 332 1.1 | 332 1.1 |
| Cost of Sales/Payables | 24 14.9 | 28 13.2 | 22 16.4 | 5 78.9 | 16 22.9 | 24 15.4 | 27 13.5 | 33 11.0 | 28 13.2 |
| | 54 6.7 | 56 6.5 | 46 8.0 | 31 11.6 | 49 7.5 | 44 8.3 | 46 7.9 | 49 7.4 | 45 8.2 |
| | 102 3.6 | 104 3.5 | 79 4.6 | 94 3.9 | 76 3.6 | 101 3.6 | 74 4.9 | 79 4.6 | 76 4.8 |
| Sales/Working Capital | 2.0 | 2.3 | 2.3 | 1.2 | 2.2 | 2.2 | 2.4 | 3.3 | 3.4 |
| | 3.9 | 4.0 | 4.2 | 2.4 | 3.5 | 4.0 | 5.0 | 5.0 | 6.0 |
| | 8.4 | 8.3 | 8.4 | 10.6 | 6.3 | 7.3 | 8.1 | 9.6 | 14.8 |
| EBIT/Interest | 8.1 | 7.7 | 15.8 | 14.4 | 32.9 | 21.8 | 10.8 | 46.7 | 14.4 |
| | (249) 2.8 | (249) 3.1 | (232) 5.1 | (20) 7.5 | (72) 4.3 | (24) 4.2 | (37) 3.8 | (41) 8.6 | (38) 5.7 |
| | 1.0 | 1.0 | 1.5 | 2.5 | 1.4 | 1.3 | 1.3 | 2.1 | 1.5 |
| Net Profit + Depr., Dep., Amort./Cur. Mat. L/T/D | 6.8 | 4.2 | 11.6 | | | | | 11.4 | 27.6 |
| | (36) 1.4 | (39) 1.6 | (38) 2.3 | | | | | (11) 4.0 | (14) 3.1 |
| | .7 | .2 | .5 | | | | | .4 | 1.4 |
| Fixed/Worth | .0 | .1 | .0 | .0 | .0 | .0 | .0 | .0 | .1 |
| | .2 | .2 | .2 | .1 | .1 | .2 | .2 | .2 | .2 |
| | .6 | .6 | .4 | .2 | .4 | .4 | .4 | .3 | .6 |
| Debt/Worth | .7 | .7 | .5 | .2 | .5 | .5 | .6 | .4 | .6 |
| | 1.8 | 1.6 | 1.2 | .9 | 1.0 | 1.5 | 1.3 | 1.1 | 1.5 |
| | 5.9 | 3.9 | 2.7 | 12.8 | 2.4 | 4.1 | 2.0 | 2.4 | 5.9 |
| % Profit Before Taxes/Tangible Net Worth | 20.7 | 25.9 | 38.5 | 92.4 | 40.1 | 40.3 | 29.5 | 37.9 | 33.1 |
| | (237) 8.2 | (235) 10.0 | (244) 17.0 | (23) 18.6 | (75) 18.9 | (27) 19.5 | (40) 10.2 | (44) 16.6 | (35) 20.0 |
| | 1.7 | 1.4 | 3.7 | 6.6 | 2.4 | .7 | 2.4 | 4.0 | 5.9 |
| % Profit Before Taxes/Total Assets | 8.1 | 9.6 | 16.0 | 27.6 | 19.1 | 17.0 | 12.0 | 13.2 | 15.5 |
| | 2.8 | 3.6 | 6.9 | 9.9 | 6.0 | 8.9 | 6.2 | 6.5 | 7.4 |
| | -.2 | .1 | 1.5 | .4 | 1.4 | .5 | .9 | 2.0 | 1.5 |
| Sales/Net Fixed Assets | 68.2 | 63.6 | 103.1 | UND | 115.4 | 149.8 | 85.1 | 105.2 | 36.3 |
| | 21.2 | 23.5 | 30.2 | 41.8 | 41.0 | 41.3 | 33.5 | 23.1 | 18.7 |
| | 8.5 | 10.5 | 12.9 | 14.5 | 12.6 | 13.6 | 9.2 | 12.8 | 13.1 |
| Sales/Total Assets | 2.0 | 2.2 | 2.5 | 2.4 | 2.4 | 2.2 | 2.5 | 2.8 | 2.8 |
| | 1.4 | 1.5 | 1.8 | 1.6 | 1.6 | 1.5 | 1.9 | 1.8 | 1.8 |
| | 1.0 | 1.0 | 1.2 | .8 | 1.2 | 1.1 | 1.2 | 1.3 | 1.5 |
| % Depr., Dep., Amort./Sales | .5 | .4 | .3 | .5 | .5 | .2 | .2 | .3 | .4 |
| | (207) 1.1 | (213) .9 | (193) .8 | (14) .9 | (55) .9 | (17) .7 | (37) .5 | (34) .9 | (36) .9 |
| | 2.0 | 1.9 | 1.3 | 1.8 | 1.6 | 1.6 | .9 | 1.3 | 1.5 |
| % Officers', Directors', Owners' Comp/Sales | 2.7 | 2.6 | 2.4 | 4.9 | 3.8 | 3.1 | 2.1 | 1.2 | .6 |
| | (124) 5.3 | (140) 4.9 | (138) 4.8 | (16) 7.4 | (56) 6.1 | (15) 5.1 | (18) 4.2 | (23) 2.4 | (10) 1.0 |
| | 9.3 | 8.4 | 7.5 | 9.0 | 9.3 | 10.3 | 6.1 | 4.7 | 2.5 |
| Net Sales ($) | 4469390M | 4919053M | 5462359M | 15334M | 149621M | 103895M | 299591M | 717013M | 4176905M |
| Total Assets ($) | 2776435M | 2936651M | 2782612M | 12488M | 131826M | 86474M | 187807M | 438317M | 1925700M |

© RMA 2012

M = $ thousand    MM = $ million
See Pages 9 through 22 for Explanation of Ratios and Data

## Current Data Sorted by Assets      Comparative Historical Data

| 0-500M | 500M-2MM | 2-10MM | 10-50MM | 50-100MM | 100-250MM | Type of Statement | 4/1/07-3/31/08 ALL | 4/1/08-3/31/09 ALL |
|---|---|---|---|---|---|---|---|---|
| | | 3 | 7 | 2 | 4 | Unqualified | 14 | 23 |
| | 7 | 20 | 5 | | | Reviewed | 34 | 24 |
| 6 | 29 | 25 | 4 | 1 | | Compiled | 65 | 59 |
| 49 | 70 | 27 | | | | Tax Returns | 101 | 106 |
| 26 | 44 | 54 | 14 | 6 | 4 | Other | 94 | 111 |
| | 62 (4/1-9/30/11) | | 345 (10/1/11-3/31/12) | | | | | |
| 81 | 150 | 129 | 30 | 9 | 8 | NUMBER OF STATEMENTS | 308 | 323 |
| % | % | % | % | % | % | ASSETS | % | % |
| 14.2 | 11.3 | 7.8 | 5.2 | | | Cash & Equivalents | 9.8 | 8.8 |
| 8.2 | 5.9 | 5.0 | 2.4 | | | Trade Receivables (net) | 6.2 | 6.2 |
| 56.8 | 57.7 | 60.1 | 56.3 | | | Inventory | 57.3 | 59.5 |
| 1.5 | 1.3 | 2.4 | 4.0 | | | All Other Current | 2.0 | 1.8 |
| 80.7 | 76.2 | 75.2 | 67.9 | | | Total Current | 75.3 | 76.3 |
| 13.0 | 15.4 | 14.9 | 23.6 | | | Fixed Assets (net) | 16.3 | 15.3 |
| 3.7 | 3.7 | 2.1 | 2.6 | | | Intangibles (net) | 3.5 | 3.3 |
| 2.6 | 4.7 | 7.7 | 5.9 | | | All Other Non-Current | 4.9 | 5.1 |
| 100.0 | 100.0 | 100.0 | 100.0 | | | Total | 100.0 | 100.0 |
| | | | | | | LIABILITIES | | |
| 21.2 | 12.8 | 11.3 | 8.2 | | | Notes Payable-Short Term | 13.7 | 14.5 |
| 3.2 | 3.6 | 2.3 | 1.7 | | | Cur. Mat.-L.T.D. | 2.0 | 2.5 |
| 27.3 | 24.8 | 27.0 | 23.6 | | | Trade Payables | 23.7 | 24.4 |
| .0 | .1 | .1 | .2 | | | Income Taxes Payable | .1 | .2 |
| 10.6 | 6.9 | 8.7 | 9.6 | | | All Other Current | 12.1 | 11.2 |
| 62.3 | 48.2 | 49.3 | 43.4 | | | Total Current | 51.6 | 52.8 |
| 19.3 | 15.6 | 11.4 | 17.5 | | | Long-Term Debt | 15.4 | 15.9 |
| .0 | .0 | .2 | .3 | | | Deferred Taxes | .0 | .0 |
| 15.1 | 9.5 | 3.6 | 2.8 | | | All Other Non-Current | 9.3 | 6.3 |
| 3.3 | 26.7 | 35.5 | 35.9 | | | Net Worth | 23.7 | 25.0 |
| 100.0 | 100.0 | 100.0 | 100.0 | | | Total Liabilities & Net Worth | 100.0 | 100.0 |
| | | | | | | INCOME DATA | | |
| 100.0 | 100.0 | 100.0 | 100.0 | | | Net Sales | 100.0 | 100.0 |
| 38.3 | 37.4 | 36.4 | 38.6 | | | Gross Profit | 38.5 | 37.6 |
| 35.6 | 34.4 | 32.8 | 32.4 | | | Operating Expenses | 35.7 | 35.7 |
| 2.7 | 2.9 | 3.6 | 6.2 | | | Operating Profit | 2.9 | 1.9 |
| 1.1 | .9 | .5 | 1.1 | | | All Other Expenses (net) | 1.4 | 1.1 |
| 1.6 | 2.1 | 3.1 | 5.1 | | | Profit Before Taxes | 1.5 | .8 |
| | | | | | | RATIOS | | |
| 3.6 | 3.3 | 2.5 | 2.1 | | | | 2.3 | 2.4 |
| 1.4 | 1.7 | 1.5 | 1.5 | | | Current | 1.6 | 1.6 |
| .9 | 1.1 | 1.2 | 1.2 | | | | 1.1 | 1.0 |
| 1.1 | .7 | .4 | .3 | | | | .6 | .6 |
| .2 | (148) .3 | .2 | .1 | | | Quick | (305) .2 | (320) .2 |
| .1 | .1 | .1 | .0 | | | | .1 | .1 |
| 0 UND | 0 UND | 0 UND | 0 UND | | | | 0 UND | 0 UND |
| 0 UND | 0 999.8 | 2 196.3 | 2 216.5 | | | Sales/Receivables | 2 222.5 | 1 309.4 |
| 7 56.0 | 8 46.2 | 8 43.4 | 6 61.9 | | | | 11 34.5 | 9 39.3 |
| 55 6.6 | 94 3.9 | 101 3.6 | 130 2.8 | | | | 87 4.2 | 91 4.0 |
| 111 3.3 | 140 2.6 | 152 2.4 | 166 2.2 | | | Cost of Sales/Inventory | 146 2.5 | 136 2.7 |
| 192 1.9 | 203 1.8 | 215 1.7 | 228 1.6 | | | | 205 1.8 | 199 1.8 |
| 3 139.4 | 25 14.4 | 33 10.9 | 49 7.5 | | | | 27 13.5 | 23 16.1 |
| 37 9.8 | 45 8.2 | 57 6.4 | 58 6.3 | | | Cost of Sales/Payables | 50 7.3 | 46 7.9 |
| 87 4.2 | 87 4.2 | 91 4.0 | 78 4.7 | | | | 79 4.6 | 79 4.6 |
| 5.8 | 4.0 | 5.2 | 5.2 | | | | 5.6 | 5.6 |
| 17.1 | 8.8 | 8.4 | 9.9 | | | Sales/Working Capital | 9.3 | 11.0 |
| -40.1 | 28.7 | 28.6 | 24.6 | | | | 44.7 | 154.8 |
| 6.7 | 12.3 | 11.8 | 17.0 | | | | 5.6 | 6.7 |
| (59) 1.4 | (128) 4.4 | (118) 5.1 | (29) 5.6 | | | EBIT/Interest | (267) 2.2 | (275) 2.2 |
| .1 | .2 | 1.8 | 3.4 | | | | .7 | -.3 |
| | 12.0 | 5.8 | 12.5 | | | | 7.7 | 10.0 |
| | (13) 1.3 | (19) 3.3 | (10) 3.8 | | | Net Profit + Depr., Dep., Amort./Cur. Mat. L/T/D | (36) 1.9 | (38) 2.0 |
| | .3 | .9 | 2.1 | | | | .6 | .5 |
| .1 | .1 | .1 | .2 | | | | .1 | .1 |
| .4 | .3 | .3 | .6 | | | Fixed/Worth | .5 | .5 |
| -.9 | 4.8 | .8 | 1.5 | | | | 4.1 | 3.6 |
| 1.6 | .8 | .9 | 1.2 | | | | 1.1 | 1.1 |
| 8.7 | 2.4 | 2.0 | 2.4 | | | Debt/Worth | 2.8 | 3.2 |
| -4.6 | 57.1 | 4.5 | 3.4 | | | | 20.0 | 21.4 |
| 94.4 | 41.4 | 37.1 | 43.3 | | | | 40.9 | 36.7 |
| (49) 27.3 | (116) 18.6 | (121) 17.8 | (29) 25.3 | | | % Profit Before Taxes/Tangible Net Worth | (247) 16.1 | (259) 13.8 |
| 1.9 | .6 | 4.4 | 15.8 | | | | .8 | -3.8 |
| 14.6 | 14.9 | 11.5 | 12.2 | | | | 9.5 | 10.8 |
| 3.4 | 5.4 | 5.6 | 8.8 | | | % Profit Before Taxes/Total Assets | 3.4 | 3.0 |
| -3.1 | -1.4 | 1.4 | 4.6 | | | | -1.5 | -3.2 |
| 342.3 | 132.1 | 63.9 | 48.4 | | | | 86.1 | 85.7 |
| 52.7 | 35.7 | 26.8 | 13.5 | | | Sales/Net Fixed Assets | 29.4 | 29.5 |
| 18.1 | 11.7 | 11.2 | 5.8 | | | | 10.7 | 12.2 |
| 4.4 | 3.1 | 3.1 | 2.6 | | | | 3.3 | 3.4 |
| 3.2 | 2.4 | 2.2 | 2.1 | | | Sales/Total Assets | 2.4 | 2.5 |
| 2.3 | 1.8 | 1.6 | 1.4 | | | | 1.7 | 1.8 |
| .5 | .3 | .4 | .5 | | | | .5 | .4 |
| (44) .9 | (103) .6 | (101) .9 | (25) 1.0 | | | % Depr., Dep., Amort./Sales | (218) .9 | (232) .8 |
| 1.8 | 1.9 | 1.3 | 2.6 | | | | 2.0 | 1.5 |
| 2.9 | 2.4 | .9 | | | | | 2.1 | 2.0 |
| (43) 4.6 | (91) 3.9 | (62) 2.6 | | | | % Officers', Directors' Owners' Comp/Sales | (144) 4.1 | (141) 3.5 |
| 7.8 | 6.4 | 3.8 | | | | | 6.9 | 6.1 |
| 74720M | 417682M | 1373781M | 1273356M | 1265804M | 2931903M | Net Sales ($) | 6858998M | 8895047M |
| 20939M | 162676M | 568656M | 660825M | 649494M | 1147303M | Total Assets ($) | 3188658M | 3554149M |

M = $ thousand     MM = $ million
See Pages 9 through 22 for Explanation of Ratios and Data

## Comparative Historical Data | Current Data Sorted by Sales

### Type of Statement

| | | | Type of Statement | 0-1MM | 1-3MM | 3-5MM | 5-10MM | 10-25MM | 25MM & OVER |
|---|---|---|---|---|---|---|---|---|---|
| 20 | 19 | 16 | Unqualified | 1 | 3 | 7 | 8 | 2 | 14 |
| 34 | 31 | 32 | Reviewed | 4 | 22 | 10 | 16 | 9 | 4 |
| 65 | 51 | 65 | Compiled | 43 | 52 | 25 | 16 | 8 | 5 |
| 101 | 122 | 146 | Tax Returns | 22 | 35 | 23 | 15 | 10 | |
| 125 | 129 | 148 | Other | | | | | 29 | 24 |
| 4/1/09-3/31/10 ALL | 4/1/10-3/31/11 ALL | 4/1/11-3/31/12 ALL | | 62 (4/1-9/30/11) | | | 345 (10/1/11-3/31/12) | | |

### Data

| 20 | 19 | 16 | | 0-1MM | 1-3MM | 3-5MM | 5-10MM | 10-25MM | 25MM & OVER |
|---|---|---|---|---|---|---|---|---|---|
| 345 | 352 | 407 | NUMBER OF STATEMENTS | 70 | 112 | 65 | 55 | 58 | 47 |
| % | % | % | ASSETS | % | % | % | % | % | % |
| 9.6 | 9.6 | 9.9 | Cash & Equivalents | 12.1 | 11.0 | 13.6 | 8.2 | 7.8 | 3.7 |
| 5.5 | 5.8 | 5.8 | Trade Receivables (net) | 5.1 | 6.9 | 5.0 | 5.9 | 6.6 | 4.1 |
| 58.0 | 56.7 | 58.2 | Inventory | 55.0 | 58.1 | 53.4 | 63.5 | 59.5 | 62.6 |
| 2.1 | 1.8 | 1.9 | All Other Current | 1.6 | .9 | 2.5 | 1.4 | 3.5 | 2.7 |
| 75.2 | 73.9 | 75.9 | Total Current | 73.8 | 76.9 | 74.5 | 78.9 | 77.4 | 73.1 |
| 16.0 | 16.4 | 15.4 | Fixed Assets (net) | 18.3 | 14.1 | 16.0 | 13.6 | 14.6 | 16.5 |
| 4.5 | 4.4 | 3.4 | Intangibles (net) | 4.4 | 3.7 | 2.8 | 2.1 | 1.9 | 5.0 |
| 4.3 | 5.3 | 5.4 | All Other Non-Current | 3.5 | 5.3 | 6.7 | 5.3 | 6.1 | 5.4 |
| 100.0 | 100.0 | 100.0 | Total | 100.0 | 100.0 | 100.0 | 100.0 | 100.0 | 100.0 |
| | | | LIABILITIES | | | | | | |
| 12.8 | 12.1 | 13.7 | Notes Payable-Short Term | 22.2 | 13.5 | 9.5 | 9.7 | 14.3 | 11.3 |
| 3.8 | 3.1 | 3.0 | Cur. Mat.-L.T.D. | 2.4 | 4.8 | 1.9 | 1.1 | 3.6 | 2.8 |
| 25.4 | 23.7 | 25.8 | Trade Payables | 22.6 | 26.9 | 26.7 | 25.2 | 26.7 | 26.7 |
| .2 | .1 | .1 | Income Taxes Payable | .0 | .1 | .1 | .2 | .2 | .2 |
| 12.3 | 10.0 | 8.8 | All Other Current | 10.6 | 7.7 | 5.1 | 8.2 | 10.8 | 11.6 |
| 54.6 | 49.0 | 51.4 | Total Current | 57.7 | 53.0 | 43.3 | 44.3 | 55.5 | 52.6 |
| 14.4 | 17.1 | 15.1 | Long-Term Debt | 24.0 | 16.1 | 13.4 | 9.9 | 10.6 | 13.4 |
| .1 | .1 | .1 | Deferred Taxes | .0 | .0 | .2 | .0 | .2 | .4 |
| 6.2 | 8.6 | 8.4 | All Other Non-Current | 21.0 | 7.1 | 7.4 | 3.0 | 2.6 | 7.4 |
| 24.8 | 25.2 | 25.0 | Net Worth | -2.6 | 23.7 | 35.7 | 42.8 | 31.2 | 26.2 |
| 100.0 | 100.0 | 100.0 | Total Liabilities & Net Worth | 100.0 | 100.0 | 100.0 | 100.0 | 100.0 | 100.0 |
| | | | INCOME DATA | | | | | | |
| 100.0 | 100.0 | 100.0 | Net Sales | 100.0 | 100.0 | 100.0 | 100.0 | 100.0 | 100.0 |
| 36.9 | 37.6 | 37.3 | Gross Profit | 40.2 | 37.0 | 37.6 | 36.0 | 36.6 | 36.1 |
| 34.8 | 34.5 | 34.0 | Operating Expenses | 38.1 | 34.0 | 33.3 | 32.2 | 33.1 | 31.9 |
| 2.1 | 3.2 | 3.4 | Operating Profit | 2.1 | 3.0 | 4.2 | 3.7 | 3.4 | 4.2 |
| .8 | 1.2 | .8 | All Other Expenses (net) | 1.8 | .9 | .5 | -.1 | .7 | 1.2 |
| 1.2 | 2.0 | 2.5 | Profit Before Taxes | .3 | 2.2 | 3.7 | 3.8 | 2.7 | 3.0 |
| | | | RATIOS | | | | | | |
| 2.6 | 2.5 | 2.8 | Current | 3.3 | 3.2 | 2.4 | 3.4 | 2.3 | 1.8 |
| 1.5 | 1.6 | 1.6 | | 1.7 | 1.6 | 1.6 | 1.6 | 1.6 | 1.4 |
| 1.1 | 1.1 | 1.1 | | .9 | 1.1 | 1.2 | 1.3 | 1.1 | 1.1 |
| .6 | .7 | .6 | Quick | .7 | .8 | .7 | 1.0 | .5 | .2 |
| (343) .2 | .2 | (405) .2 | | .2 | (110) .2 | .3 | .2 | .2 | .1 |
| .1 | .1 | .1 | | .1 | .1 | .1 | .1 | .1 | .0 |
| 0 UND | 0 UND | 0 UND | Sales/Receivables | 0 UND | 0 UND | 0 UND | 0 UND | 0 UND | 1 353.5 |
| 2 219.6 | 1 302.5 | 1 343.1 | | 0 UND | 0 784.2 | 0 999.8 | 0 999.8 | 3 121.8 | 3 145.1 |
| 8 43.6 | 7 50.2 | 8 46.3 | | 6 57.7 | 8 45.9 | 4 91.6 | 9 40.1 | 8 45.7 | 9 40.3 |
| 91 4.0 | 93 3.9 | 91 4.0 | Cost of Sales/Inventory | 76 4.8 | 87 4.2 | 87 4.2 | 101 3.6 | 87 4.2 | 126 2.9 |
| 144 2.5 | 140 2.6 | 146 2.6 | | 182 2.0 | 146 2.5 | 130 2.8 | 146 2.5 | 122 3.0 | 146 2.5 |
| 209 1.7 | 201 1.8 | 203 1.8 | | 304 1.2 | 182 2.0 | 203 1.8 | 192 1.9 | 174 2.1 | 192 1.9 |
| 25 14.8 | 23 15.6 | 25 14.4 | Cost of Sales/Payables | 7 52.4 | 23 15.6 | 27 13.7 | 25 14.7 | 33 10.9 | 41 8.8 |
| 48 7.5 | 47 7.8 | 53 6.9 | | 42 8.7 | 47 7.7 | 55 6.6 | 47 7.7 | 49 7.5 | 59 6.2 |
| 84 4.4 | 87 4.2 | 87 4.2 | | 114 3.2 | 89 4.1 | 101 3.6 | 72 5.1 | 73 5.0 | 76 4.8 |
| 4.9 | 5.3 | 4.8 | Sales/Working Capital | 3.1 | 4.3 | 5.1 | 4.7 | 6.5 | 7.0 |
| 10.1 | 9.4 | 9.7 | | 7.9 | 9.6 | 11.1 | 7.0 | 12.4 | 11.9 |
| 51.1 | 45.4 | 42.7 | | -26.6 | 127.2 | 29.3 | 16.8 | 32.5 | 35.0 |
| 7.1 | 10.1 | 11.0 | EBIT/Interest | 5.2 | 11.0 | 12.5 | 15.7 | 11.8 | 16.1 |
| (301) 2.1 | (301) 3.2 | (349) 4.1 | | (53) 1.4 | (95) 2.1 | (52) 4.1 | (50) 6.6 | (57) 6.7 | (42) 4.7 |
| .1 | .7 | 1.0 | | .1 | -.1 | .9 | 2.0 | 3.0 | 2.4 |
| 8.1 | 6.6 | 7.8 | Net Profit + Depr., Dep., Amort./Cur. Mat. L/T/D | | | | | | 10.2 |
| (47) 1.6 | (42) 2.5 | (50) 3.4 | | | | | | (18) | 3.8 |
| .3 | .3 | .8 | | | | | | | 2.1 |
| .1 | .1 | .1 | Fixed/Worth | .1 | .0 | .1 | .1 | .2 | .2 |
| .4 | .4 | .3 | | .9 | .4 | .3 | .2 | .4 | .6 |
| 6.3 | 2.9 | 2.4 | | -1.9 | -9.8 | 1.4 | .6 | 1.0 | 1.6 |
| 1.0 | 1.1 | .9 | Debt/Worth | 1.9 | .9 | .7 | .7 | .9 | 1.6 |
| 2.9 | 2.7 | 2.5 | | 12.4 | 2.9 | 1.9 | 1.7 | 2.2 | 2.7 |
| 26.3 | 24.8 | 13.7 | | -4.1 | -78.2 | 5.4 | 3.9 | 5.5 | 5.7 |
| 31.3 | 44.9 | 43.4 | % Profit Before Taxes/Tangible Net Worth | 82.4 | 27.4 | 43.2 | 45.3 | 44.9 | 43.7 |
| (264) 12.7 | (273) 19.0 | (326) 19.8 | | (41) 22.2 | (82) 16.1 | (55) 14.6 | (54) 21.0 | (55) 24.6 | (39) 29.4 |
| -.3 | 4.3 | 4.1 | | -.5 | 2.0 | .5 | 5.4 | 8.1 | 8.7 |
| 9.3 | 12.6 | 13.1 | % Profit Before Taxes/Total Assets | 11.6 | 12.7 | 16.2 | 14.1 | 12.0 | 13.5 |
| 3.4 | 5.0 | 5.4 | | 2.6 | 4.1 | 5.1 | 7.0 | 7.5 | 7.3 |
| -2.3 | -.3 | .1 | | -4.9 | -2.6 | .0 | 2.4 | 2.7 | 1.8 |
| 80.3 | 88.8 | 104.1 | Sales/Net Fixed Assets | 174.0 | 185.3 | 115.2 | 112.2 | 60.9 | 48.1 |
| 27.2 | 28.7 | 29.9 | | 35.3 | 43.4 | 23.7 | 30.0 | 29.6 | 17.6 |
| 10.8 | 11.0 | 11.5 | | 7.4 | 12.3 | 9.6 | 14.5 | 12.5 | 10.2 |
| 3.2 | 3.3 | 3.2 | Sales/Total Assets | 3.3 | 3.2 | 3.2 | 3.2 | 3.6 | 3.0 |
| 2.3 | 2.4 | 2.4 | | 2.2 | 2.5 | 2.3 | 2.6 | 2.9 | 2.3 |
| 1.7 | 1.6 | 1.8 | | 1.0 | 1.8 | 1.7 | 1.9 | 2.0 | 1.9 |
| .4 | .4 | .4 | % Depr., Dep., Amort./Sales | .6 | .4 | .3 | .3 | .4 | .6 |
| (256) .8 | (253) .8 | (287) .9 | | (38) 1.4 | (76) .8 | (45) .8 | (40) .7 | (49) .9 | (39) 1.2 |
| 1.7 | 1.7 | 1.7 | | 2.7 | 1.7 | 1.5 | 1.3 | 1.3 | 2.6 |
| 1.8 | 1.6 | 2.1 | % Officers', Directors' Owners' Comp/Sales | 3.7 | 2.7 | 1.6 | 1.2 | 1.1 | |
| (166) 3.3 | (168) 3.5 | (200) 3.5 | | (31) 6.5 | (67) 4.0 | (38) 3.0 | (35) 2.4 | (22) 2.8 | |
| 6.2 | 6.5 | 5.8 | | 11.0 | 5.7 | 6.1 | 4.2 | 3.9 | |
| 9031200M | 6882605M | 7337246M | Net Sales ($) | 37964M | 210326M | 257246M | 388238M | 870308M | 5573164M |
| 3416877M | 2961101M | 3209893M | Total Assets ($) | 25573M | 97831M | 127217M | 179291M | 357458M | 2422523M |

## Current Data Sorted by Assets       Comparative Historical Data

| | | | | | | Type of Statement | | |
|---|---|---|---|---|---|---|---|---|
| | | 1 | 1 | 1 | 2 | Unqualified | 4 | 4 |
| | 1 | 1 | 1 | | | Reviewed | 4 | 6 |
| 2 | 3 | 4 | 1 | | | Compiled | 10 | 6 |
| 10 | 7 | 4 | | | | Tax Returns | 23 | 18 |
| 13 | 4 | 3 | 1 | | 1 | Other | 18 | 8 |
| | 8 (4/1-9/30/11) | | 53 (10/1/11-3/31/12) | | | | 4/1/07-3/31/08 | 4/1/08-3/31/09 |
| 0-500M | 500M-2MM | 2-10MM | 10-50MM | 50-100MM | 100-250MM | | ALL | ALL |
| 25 | 15 | 13 | 4 | 1 | 3 | **NUMBER OF STATEMENTS** | 59 | 42 |
| % | % | % | % | % | % | **ASSETS** | % | % |
| 17.0 | 17.3 | 10.3 | | | | Cash & Equivalents | 11.4 | 8.8 |
| 2.3 | 8.7 | 6.8 | | | | Trade Receivables (net) | 5.8 | 6.3 |
| 60.4 | 54.8 | 58.9 | | | | Inventory | 54.2 | 62.3 |
| 1.6 | .4 | 1.9 | | | | All Other Current | 3.0 | 1.4 |
| 81.2 | 81.4 | 77.9 | | | | Total Current | 74.3 | 78.8 |
| 10.1 | 9.4 | 6.9 | | | | Fixed Assets (net) | 16.6 | 11.4 |
| 3.6 | 3.3 | 9.1 | | | | Intangibles (net) | 2.3 | 4.0 |
| 5.1 | 5.9 | 6.0 | | | | All Other Non-Current | 6.8 | 5.8 |
| 100.0 | 100.0 | 100.0 | | | | Total | 100.0 | 100.0 |
| | | | | | | **LIABILITIES** | | |
| 19.1 | 21.3 | 12.5 | | | | Notes Payable-Short Term | 13.3 | 13.5 |
| 1.6 | 3.7 | 3.9 | | | | Cur. Mat.-L.T.D. | 4.1 | 2.1 |
| 14.8 | 16.0 | 17.7 | | | | Trade Payables | 17.5 | 15.8 |
| .0 | .0 | .0 | | | | Income Taxes Payable | .2 | .0 |
| 18.9 | 14.6 | 16.2 | | | | All Other Current | 10.4 | 11.7 |
| 54.5 | 55.5 | 50.3 | | | | Total Current | 45.5 | 43.1 |
| 26.1 | 8.5 | 15.4 | | | | Long-Term Debt | 18.2 | 24.7 |
| .0 | .0 | .0 | | | | Deferred Taxes | .2 | .3 |
| 10.4 | 11.1 | 3.5 | | | | All Other Non-Current | 6.0 | 7.1 |
| 9.0 | 24.9 | 30.8 | | | | Net Worth | 30.1 | 24.8 |
| 100.0 | 100.0 | 100.0 | | | | Total Liabilities & Net Worth | 100.0 | 100.0 |
| | | | | | | **INCOME DATA** | | |
| 100.0 | 100.0 | 100.0 | | | | Net Sales | 100.0 | 100.0 |
| 44.3 | 40.9 | 35.9 | | | | Gross Profit | 41.4 | 42.4 |
| 39.9 | 36.7 | 34.0 | | | | Operating Expenses | 37.6 | 39.9 |
| 4.3 | 4.2 | 2.0 | | | | Operating Profit | 3.8 | 2.5 |
| 1.8 | .5 | 1.0 | | | | All Other Expenses (net) | 1.7 | 1.5 |
| 2.6 | 3.7 | 1.0 | | | | Profit Before Taxes | 2.1 | 1.0 |
| | | | | | | **RATIOS** | | |
| 10.2 | 4.2 | 2.7 | | | | | 3.6 | 3.9 |
| 2.6 | 2.1 | 1.6 | | | | Current | 1.8 | 2.3 |
| 1.0 | 1.3 | 1.0 | | | | | 1.1 | 1.3 |
| 2.0 | 1.7 | .6 | | | | | .6 | .8 |
| (24) .4 | .4 | .3 | | | | Quick | .3 | .3 |
| .0 | .1 | .1 | | | | | .1 | .1 |
| 0 UND | 0 UND | 0 828.7 | | | | | 0 UND | 0 UND |
| 0 UND | 1 373.0 | 4 95.5 | | | | Sales/Receivables | 0 910.5 | 1 388.9 |
| 2 165.1 | 20 18.4 | 23 15.7 | | | | | 7 53.9 | 17 22.1 |
| 50 7.3 | 87 4.2 | 55 6.6 | | | | | 90 4.1 | 88 4.2 |
| 114 3.2 | 135 2.7 | 101 3.6 | | | | Cost of Sales/Inventory | 126 2.9 | 164 2.2 |
| 261 1.4 | 261 1.4 | 228 1.6 | | | | | 180 2.0 | 229 1.6 |
| 0 UND | 23 16.2 | 13 27.6 | | | | | 14 25.4 | 14 25.7 |
| 14 26.5 | 31 11.6 | 51 7.2 | | | | Cost of Sales/Payables | 32 11.6 | 25 14.5 |
| 62 5.9 | 54 6.7 | 63 5.8 | | | | | 52 7.0 | 45 8.2 |
| 5.3 | 3.9 | 4.7 | | | | | 4.6 | 4.2 |
| 11.6 | 7.8 | 10.2 | | | | Sales/Working Capital | 10.3 | 5.8 |
| NM | 17.7 | NM | | | | | 82.2 | 21.8 |
| 17.0 | 12.1 | 25.5 | | | | | 7.0 | 7.3 |
| (18) 3.1 | (11) 3.0 | (12) 5.2 | | | | EBIT/Interest | (45) 2.4 | (40) 2.5 |
| .3 | .1 | 1.5 | | | | | .7 | -.5 |
| | | | | | | Net Profit + Depr., Dep., Amort./Cur. Mat. L/T/D | | |
| .0 | .0 | .0 | | | | | .1 | .1 |
| .3 | .4 | .2 | | | | Fixed/Worth | .3 | .2 |
| -.9 | -.8 | 2.3 | | | | | 3.5 | 4.8 |
| .5 | .5 | 1.2 | | | | | .6 | .7 |
| 22.2 | 1.7 | 3.3 | | | | Debt/Worth | 2.0 | 2.4 |
| -6.0 | -5.7 | 21.5 | | | | | 15.2 | -16.8 |
| 62.2 | 68.1 | 87.0 | | | | | 45.7 | 40.1 |
| (14) 26.5 | (11) 25.9 | (11) 15.9 | | | | % Profit Before Taxes/Tangible Net Worth | (50) 15.2 | (31) 12.5 |
| -55.3 | 4.6 | 2.9 | | | | | -4.8 | -6.7 |
| 33.5 | 25.3 | 14.9 | | | | | 15.4 | 14.1 |
| 8.5 | 10.3 | 2.3 | | | | % Profit Before Taxes/Total Assets | 4.6 | 3.4 |
| -3.5 | -1.1 | -.5 | | | | | -1.1 | -5.2 |
| UND | 225.0 | 549.5 | | | | | 111.0 | 119.7 |
| 164.0 | 21.7 | 191.3 | | | | Sales/Net Fixed Assets | 48.0 | 40.9 |
| 12.8 | 17.6 | 19.6 | | | | | 11.5 | 21.2 |
| 5.8 | 3.3 | 3.9 | | | | | 4.2 | 3.1 |
| 4.2 | 2.4 | 3.3 | | | | Sales/Total Assets | 2.7 | 2.3 |
| 1.9 | 1.7 | 1.5 | | | | | 1.6 | 2.0 |
| .3 | | | | | | | .4 | .5 |
| (11) .5 | | | | | | % Depr., Dep., Amort./Sales | (42) .8 | (29) .9 |
| 2.2 | | | | | | | 2.5 | 1.6 |
| 1.5 | 1.8 | 1.1 | | | | | 2.3 | 2.0 |
| (10) 4.2 | (11) 3.4 | (10) 2.2 | | | | % Officers', Directors' Owners' Comp/Sales | (33) 3.7 | (20) 2.8 |
| 8.5 | 4.5 | 6.7 | | | | | 5.8 | 5.3 |
| 27557M | 47162M | 244206M | 282188M | 96299M | 948520M | Net Sales ($) | 505075M | 789892M |
| 6358M | 16387M | 61113M | 119185M | 63389M | 523000M | Total Assets ($) | 246125M | 351167M |

© RMA 2012

M = $ thousand    MM = $ million
See Pages 9 through 22 for Explanation of Ratios and Data

## Comparative Historical Data | Current Data Sorted by Sales

### Type of Statement

| Type of Statement | 4/1/09-3/31/10 ALL | 4/1/10-3/31/11 ALL | 4/1/11-3/31/12 ALL | 0-1MM | 1-3MM | 3-5MM | 5-10MM | 10-25MM | 25MM & OVER |
|---|---|---|---|---|---|---|---|---|---|
| Unqualified | 6 | 8 | 5 | | | 1 | | | 4 |
| Reviewed | 4 | 2 | 3 | | | 1 | | | 2 |
| Compiled | 4 | 7 | 10 | 1 | 3 | 1 | 2 | | 3 |
| Tax Returns | 27 | 19 | 21 | 8 | 8 | 2 | 2 | 1 | |
| Other | 19 | 26 | 22 | 9 | 5 | 3 | | 2 | 3 |
| | | | | 8 (4/1-9/30/11) | | 53 (10/1/11-3/31/12) | | | |
| NUMBER OF STATEMENTS | 60 | 62 | 61 | 18 | 16 | 8 | 4 | 3 | 12 |

### ASSETS (%)

| | 4/1/09-3/31/10 | 4/1/10-3/31/11 | 4/1/11-3/31/12 | 0-1MM | 1-3MM | 3-5MM | 5-10MM | 10-25MM | 25MM & OVER |
|---|---|---|---|---|---|---|---|---|---|
| Cash & Equivalents | 9.0 | 12.5 | 15.3 | 11.8 | 18.9 | | | | 16.1 |
| Trade Receivables (net) | 6.7 | 7.9 | 5.2 | 1.9 | 6.0 | | | | 5.8 |
| Inventory | 57.9 | 53.8 | 56.9 | 64.9 | 56.9 | | | | 47.0 |
| All Other Current | 2.1 | 1.9 | 1.6 | 2.2 | .3 | | | | 2.6 |
| Total Current | 75.7 | 76.1 | 79.0 | 80.8 | 82.0 | | | | 71.5 |
| Fixed Assets (net) | 14.0 | 13.6 | 11.0 | 11.7 | 6.3 | | | | 18.2 |
| Intangibles (net) | 6.3 | 5.3 | 4.7 | 4.2 | 2.3 | | | | 6.5 |
| All Other Non-Current | 4.0 | 5.0 | 5.2 | 3.1 | 9.4 | | | | 3.8 |
| Total | 100.0 | 100.0 | 100.0 | 100.0 | 100.0 | | | | 100.0 |

### LIABILITIES

| | 4/1/09-3/31/10 | 4/1/10-3/31/11 | 4/1/11-3/31/12 | 0-1MM | 1-3MM | 3-5MM | 5-10MM | 10-25MM | 25MM & OVER |
|---|---|---|---|---|---|---|---|---|---|
| Notes Payable-Short Term | 8.9 | 14.3 | 15.9 | 25.5 | 21.9 | | | | 2.3 |
| Cur. Mat.-L.T.D. | 2.0 | 1.9 | 2.8 | 1.9 | 2.2 | | | | 3.5 |
| Trade Payables | 15.4 | 16.9 | 16.2 | 10.7 | 17.8 | | | | 19.8 |
| Income Taxes Payable | .1 | .1 | .2 | .0 | .0 | | | | 1.0 |
| All Other Current | 11.9 | 14.8 | 15.9 | 23.3 | 13.2 | | | | 15.5 |
| Total Current | 38.2 | 48.0 | 51.1 | 61.4 | 55.2 | | | | 42.1 |
| Long-Term Debt | 26.1 | 21.9 | 17.4 | 28.5 | 13.9 | | | | 9.5 |
| Deferred Taxes | .1 | .2 | .0 | .0 | .0 | | | | .2 |
| All Other Non-Current | 5.0 | 10.8 | 9.5 | 10.6 | 10.8 | | | | 11.4 |
| Net Worth | 30.6 | 19.1 | 22.0 | -.6 | 20.1 | | | | 36.9 |
| Total Liabilities & Net Worth | 100.0 | 100.0 | 100.0 | 100.0 | 100.0 | | | | 100.0 |

### INCOME DATA

| | 4/1/09-3/31/10 | 4/1/10-3/31/11 | 4/1/11-3/31/12 | 0-1MM | 1-3MM | 3-5MM | 5-10MM | 10-25MM | 25MM & OVER |
|---|---|---|---|---|---|---|---|---|---|
| Net Sales | 100.0 | 100.0 | 100.0 | 100.0 | 100.0 | | | | 100.0 |
| Gross Profit | 45.3 | 42.7 | 41.2 | 48.4 | 42.2 | | | | 38.2 |
| Operating Expenses | 41.8 | 39.6 | 37.3 | 44.9 | 37.1 | | | | 33.4 |
| Operating Profit | 3.5 | 3.1 | 3.9 | 3.6 | 5.1 | | | | 4.9 |
| All Other Expenses (net) | 1.3 | 1.7 | 1.1 | 2.4 | .4 | | | | .4 |
| Profit Before Taxes | 2.2 | 1.4 | 2.8 | 1.1 | 4.7 | | | | 4.5 |

### RATIOS

| | 4/1/09-3/31/10 | 4/1/10-3/31/11 | 4/1/11-3/31/12 | 0-1MM | 1-3MM | 3-5MM | 5-10MM | 10-25MM | 25MM & OVER |
|---|---|---|---|---|---|---|---|---|---|
| Current | 4.3 | 2.6 | 4.2 | 5.4 | 4.8 | | | | 3.8 |
| | 2.2 | 1.8 | 1.8 | 1.7 | 2.3 | | | | 1.8 |
| | 1.4 | 1.3 | 1.2 | .9 | 1.2 | | | | 1.2 |
| Quick | 1.1 | .9 | 1.1 | 1.0 | 1.6 | | | | 1.0 |
| | (59) .3 | (60) .4 | .4 | (17) .3 | .4 | | | | .4 |
| | .2 | .1 | .1 | .0 | .1 | | | | .2 |
| Sales/Receivables | 0 UND | 0 UND | 0 UND | 0 UND | 0 UND | | | | 0 781.7 |
| | 2 216.8 | 1 245.2 | 1 475.0 | 0 UND | 0 UND | | | | 4 83.1 |
| | 15 23.9 | 13 29.1 | 9 39.5 | 3 134.7 | 17 20.9 | | | | 10 35.1 |
| Cost of Sales/Inventory | 96 3.8 | 75 4.9 | 66 5.5 | 89 4.1 | 49 7.4 | | | | 53 6.9 |
| | 168 2.2 | 107 3.4 | 118 3.1 | 140 2.6 | 126 2.9 | | | | 91 4.0 |
| | 243 1.5 | 199 1.8 | 243 1.5 | 281 1.3 | 281 1.3 | | | | 174 2.1 |
| Cost of Sales/Payables | 23 15.9 | 15 24.0 | 10 36.7 | 0 UND | 5 68.5 | | | | 25 14.4 |
| | 37 9.8 | 35 10.5 | 30 12.2 | 22 16.9 | 31 11.8 | | | | 45 8.1 |
| | 57 6.5 | 56 6.5 | 59 6.2 | 66 5.5 | 47 7.7 | | | | 56 6.5 |
| Sales/Working Capital | 3.1 | 6.3 | 5.0 | 5.0 | 4.2 | | | | 4.1 |
| | 5.9 | 9.2 | 8.7 | 7.3 | 7.4 | | | | 8.6 |
| | 16.4 | 25.9 | 63.8 | -62.5 | 46.5 | | | | 72.0 |
| EBIT/Interest | 10.0 | 9.0 | 16.8 | 5.7 | 12.1 | | | | 28.6 |
| | (53) 3.2 | (55) 2.4 | (48) 3.9 | (13) 1.1 | (11) 3.0 | | | | (11) 9.2 |
| | -.1 | -.3 | .5 | -.8 | 1.4 | | | | -.8 |
| Net Profit + Depr., Dep., Amort./Cur. Mat. L/T/D | | | | | | | | | |
| Fixed/Worth | .1 | .1 | .0 | .0 | .0 | | | | .2 |
| | .3 | .5 | .3 | .3 | .3 | | | | .7 |
| | 2.0 | -1.0 | 86.1 | -19.4 | -.1 | | | | 2.7 |
| Debt/Worth | .6 | 1.1 | .6 | .6 | .4 | | | | 1.1 |
| | 2.3 | 3.9 | 2.4 | 144.6 | 2.5 | | | | 2.4 |
| | 10.4 | -6.2 | -21.8 | -6.1 | -3.9 | | | | 11.5 |
| % Profit Before Taxes/Tangible Net Worth | 71.2 | 69.9 | 61.9 | 45.1 | 111.4 | | | | 87.0 |
| | (50) 17.5 | (42) 23.3 | (44) 24.7 | (10) 19.4 | (10) 25.6 | | | | (11) 25.5 |
| | -5.2 | 3.5 | -.3 | -68.7 | 3.1 | | | | -2.3 |
| % Profit Before Taxes/Total Assets | 12.2 | 14.2 | 24.6 | 18.5 | 28.7 | | | | 22.3 |
| | 6.3 | 4.0 | 7.3 | 8.2 | 8.8 | | | | 5.2 |
| | -3.8 | -2.4 | -1.1 | -5.1 | -.4 | | | | -1.0 |
| Sales/Net Fixed Assets | 112.9 | 124.3 | 329.0 | UND | 749.6 | | | | 32.8 |
| | 31.7 | 32.2 | 40.3 | 129.3 | 118.1 | | | | 16.2 |
| | 9.7 | 11.0 | 12.8 | 10.1 | 19.2 | | | | 6.8 |
| Sales/Total Assets | 3.0 | 4.7 | 4.3 | 4.5 | 4.7 | | | | 4.2 |
| | 2.1 | 2.5 | 2.8 | 2.7 | 3.1 | | | | 2.4 |
| | 1.5 | 1.9 | 1.8 | 1.6 | 1.5 | | | | 1.7 |
| % Depr., Dep., Amort./Sales | .5 | .4 | .5 | .3 | | | | | |
| | (42) .8 | (42) .9 | (35) 1.0 | (10) 1.2 | | | | | |
| | 2.7 | 2.1 | 2.1 | 2.3 | | | | | |
| % Officers', Directors' Owners' Comp/Sales | 1.3 | 1.8 | 1.3 | | 2.0 | | | | |
| | (31) 3.1 | (26) 5.1 | (33) 3.2 | | (10) 3.5 | | | | |
| | 6.5 | 8.9 | 5.0 | | 4.7 | | | | |
| Net Sales ($) | 1343624M | 2375856M | 1645932M | 10140M | 31380M | 31390M | 27865M | 40089M | 1505068M |
| Total Assets ($) | 779602M | 984614M | 789432M | 4116M | 13441M | 16912M | 10204M | 11231M | 733528M |

M = $ thousand     MM = $ million
See Pages 9 through 22 for Explanation of Ratios and Data

## Current Data Sorted by Assets      Comparative Historical Data

| | 0-500M | 500M-2MM | 2-10MM | 10-50MM | 50-100MM | 100-250MM | Type of Statement | 4/1/07-3/31/08 ALL | 4/1/08-3/31/09 ALL |
|---|---|---|---|---|---|---|---|---|---|
| | | | | | | 1 | Unqualified | | |
| | 2 | 9 | 1 | | | | Reviewed | 13 | 13 |
| 1 | 11 | 11 | 1 | | | | Compiled | 22 | 19 |
| 7 | 10 | 2 | 1 | | | | Tax Returns | 16 | 21 |
| 5 | 8 | 9 | 3 | 2 | | | Other | 23 | 22 |
| | 23 (4/1-9/30/11) | | | 61 (10/1/11-3/31/12) | | | | | |
| 13 | 31 | 31 | 6 | 2 | 1 | | **NUMBER OF STATEMENTS** | 74 | 77 |
| % | % | % | % | % | % | | **ASSETS** | % | % |
| 9.7 | 8.8 | 5.8 | | | | | Cash & Equivalents | 6.7 | 7.5 |
| 2.8 | 9.3 | 11.1 | | | | | Trade Receivables (net) | 13.0 | 12.0 |
| 67.0 | 55.6 | 58.6 | | | | | Inventory | 55.7 | 60.7 |
| .3 | .3 | 4.8 | | | | | All Other Current | 1.8 | 1.7 |
| 79.7 | 74.0 | 80.3 | | | | | Total Current | 77.2 | 81.9 |
| 15.8 | 17.0 | 10.6 | | | | | Fixed Assets (net) | 14.4 | 13.5 |
| 1.2 | 1.3 | 3.1 | | | | | Intangibles (net) | 2.1 | .9 |
| 3.2 | 7.7 | 6.0 | | | | | All Other Non-Current | 6.3 | 3.7 |
| 100.0 | 100.0 | 100.0 | | | | | Total | 100.0 | 100.0 |
| | | | | | | | **LIABILITIES** | | |
| 13.3 | 9.6 | 18.7 | | | | | Notes Payable-Short Term | 19.4 | 17.0 |
| 2.4 | 7.2 | 5.2 | | | | | Cur. Mat.-L.T.D. | 4.1 | 3.7 |
| 10.8 | 21.7 | 17.3 | | | | | Trade Payables | 17.2 | 18.6 |
| .0 | .0 | .1 | | | | | Income Taxes Payable | .3 | .5 |
| 15.9 | 9.8 | 8.7 | | | | | All Other Current | 7.3 | 8.7 |
| 42.5 | 48.3 | 50.0 | | | | | Total Current | 48.2 | 48.4 |
| 14.7 | 14.5 | 9.7 | | | | | Long-Term Debt | 17.4 | 14.4 |
| .0 | .0 | .1 | | | | | Deferred Taxes | .1 | .1 |
| 12.8 | 6.9 | 8.3 | | | | | All Other Non-Current | 5.6 | 4.0 |
| 30.0 | 30.3 | 31.9 | | | | | Net Worth | 28.7 | 33.1 |
| 100.0 | 100.0 | 100.0 | | | | | Total Liabilities & Net Worth | 100.0 | 100.0 |
| | | | | | | | **INCOME DATA** | | |
| 100.0 | 100.0 | 100.0 | | | | | Net Sales | 100.0 | 100.0 |
| 50.9 | 43.4 | 43.7 | | | | | Gross Profit | 41.8 | 41.9 |
| 49.0 | 42.3 | 41.1 | | | | | Operating Expenses | 37.9 | 39.8 |
| 1.9 | 1.1 | 2.6 | | | | | Operating Profit | 3.9 | 2.1 |
| .3 | .1 | .4 | | | | | All Other Expenses (net) | 1.6 | 1.0 |
| 1.6 | .9 | 2.3 | | | | | Profit Before Taxes | 2.4 | 1.1 |
| | | | | | | | **RATIOS** | | |
| 3.5 | 3.1 | 2.4 | | | | | | 2.0 | 2.7 |
| 2.0 | 1.4 | 1.6 | | | | | Current | 1.6 | 1.8 |
| 1.4 | 1.0 | 1.1 | | | | | | 1.2 | 1.3 |
| .5 | .7 | .5 | | | | | | .7 | .8 |
| .3 | .3 | .3 | | | | | Quick | .3 | .3 |
| .1 | .2 | .1 | | | | | | .1 | .1 |
| 0 UND | 2 174.1 | 7 53.8 | | | | | | 2 146.4 | 1 282.8 |
| 0 UND | 12 30.4 | 11 32.1 | | | | | Sales/Receivables | 11 32.4 | 11 32.6 |
| 11 33.3 | 21 17.6 | 35 10.3 | | | | | | 31 11.9 | 26 14.0 |
| 159 2.3 | 99 3.7 | 140 2.6 | | | | | | 105 3.5 | 119 3.1 |
| 281 1.3 | 192 1.9 | 215 1.7 | | | | | Cost of Sales/Inventory | 181 2.0 | 190 1.9 |
| 456 .8 | 243 1.5 | 332 1.1 | | | | | | 270 1.4 | 310 1.2 |
| 0 UND | 20 18.6 | 32 11.5 | | | | | | 16 23.0 | 15 23.7 |
| 16 22.2 | 37 9.8 | 54 6.8 | | | | | Cost of Sales/Payables | 37 9.8 | 40 9.1 |
| 58 6.3 | 76 4.8 | 79 4.6 | | | | | | 85 4.3 | 76 4.8 |
| 3.0 | 3.9 | 3.6 | | | | | | 3.6 | 4.0 |
| 5.0 | 7.8 | 6.2 | | | | | Sales/Working Capital | 8.8 | 6.8 |
| 24.8 | 189.6 | 40.2 | | | | | | 22.8 | 14.4 |
| 5.4 | 4.3 | 4.9 | | | | | | 3.1 | 5.1 |
| 1.6 | (27) 1.7 | (28) 3.0 | | | | | EBIT/Interest | (69) 1.8 | (69) 2.0 |
| .6 | -2.1 | 1.5 | | | | | | 1.2 | .4 |
| | | | | | | | Net Profit + Depr., Dep., | 13.9 | 17.7 |
| | | | | | | | Amort./Cur. Mat. L/T/D | (15) 3.3 | (19) 4.0 |
| | | | | | | | | 1.6 | .5 |
| .0 | .1 | .1 | | | | | | .1 | .1 |
| .3 | .3 | .2 | | | | | Fixed/Worth | .3 | .2 |
| NM | 7.4 | 1.9 | | | | | | 1.7 | .8 |
| .8 | .8 | 1.0 | | | | | | 1.1 | .8 |
| 1.5 | 3.1 | 2.1 | | | | | Debt/Worth | 2.3 | 1.8 |
| NM | 32.0 | 10.9 | | | | | | 7.8 | 4.5 |
| 28.7 | 29.5 | 42.9 | | | | | % Profit Before Taxes/Tangible | 30.6 | 18.3 |
| (10) 2.1 | (24) 8.4 | (27) 9.9 | | | | | Net Worth | (62) 8.6 | (70) 4.8 |
| -5.8 | -4.5 | 1.6 | | | | | | 1.2 | -4.1 |
| 13.2 | 6.3 | 5.3 | | | | | % Profit Before Taxes/Total | 8.3 | 6.6 |
| 1.5 | 1.7 | 2.6 | | | | | Assets | 2.9 | 2.1 |
| -1.5 | -6.0 | .8 | | | | | | .5 | -1.9 |
| 375.0 | 127.0 | 88.6 | | | | | | 57.4 | 73.5 |
| 20.0 | 22.0 | 40.4 | | | | | Sales/Net Fixed Assets | 24.6 | 26.3 |
| 8.8 | 6.5 | 15.5 | | | | | | 10.6 | 10.1 |
| 3.0 | 2.8 | 2.3 | | | | | | 3.0 | 2.9 |
| 2.3 | 2.2 | 1.6 | | | | | Sales/Total Assets | 1.9 | 2.1 |
| 1.3 | 1.5 | 1.3 | | | | | | 1.4 | 1.4 |
| | .5 | .3 | | | | | | .4 | .6 |
| (23) | .7 (25) | .8 | | | | | % Depr., Dep., Amort./Sales | (60) .9 (62) | 1.1 |
| | 3.6 | 3.9 | | | | | | 1.9 | 2.1 |
| | 3.7 | 1.2 | | | | | | 2.0 | 2.5 |
| (17) | 4.5 (10) | 1.5 | | | | | % Officers', Directors' | (38) 4.5 (35) | 3.7 |
| | 7.0 | 4.3 | | | | | Owners' Comp/Sales | 6.2 | 6.4 |
| 10437M | 87224M | 254943M | 169660M | 227736M | 330787M | | Net Sales ($) | 604247M | 1043948M |
| 4621M | 37867M | 136699M | 107655M | 144637M | 128317M | | Total Assets ($) | 377513M | 543393M |

M = $ thousand    MM = $ million
See Pages 9 through 22 for Explanation of Ratios and Data

## Comparative Historical Data

## Current Data Sorted by Sales

| | | | Type of Statement | | | | | | |
|---|---|---|---|---|---|---|---|---|---|
| 6 | 4 | 2 | Unqualified | | 2 | 3 | 4 | 2 | 2 |
| 12 | 9 | 12 | Reviewed | | 6 | | 7 | 4 | 1 |
| 20 | 21 | 24 | Compiled | 2 | 6 | 4 | 7 | | 1 |
| 25 | 27 | 19 | Tax Returns | 4 | 8 | 4 | 3 | | 1 |
| 12 | 34 | 27 | Other | 5 | 8 | | 7 | 4 | 3 |
| 4/1/09-3/31/10 ALL | 4/1/10-3/31/11 ALL | 4/1/11-3/31/12 ALL | | 23 (4/1-9/30/11) | | | 61 (10/1/11-3/31/12) | | |
| | | | | 0-1MM | 1-3MM | 3-5MM | 5-10MM | 10-25MM | 25MM & OVER |
| 75 | 95 | 84 | NUMBER OF STATEMENTS | 11 | 24 | 11 | 21 | 10 | 7 |

| % | % | % | ASSETS | % | % | % | % | % | % |
|---|---|---|---|---|---|---|---|---|---|
| 6.3 | 6.0 | 7.0 | Cash & Equivalents | 8.1 | 9.2 | 7.6 | 6.2 | 5.5 | |
| 10.9 | 12.7 | 12.5 | Trade Receivables (net) | 3.6 | 6.4 | 12.2 | 10.8 | 19.9 | |
| 62.2 | 57.9 | 56.4 | Inventory | 61.5 | 54.4 | 60.8 | 58.2 | 61.6 | |
| 2.4 | 2.4 | 2.1 | All Other Current | .3 | 1.9 | 4.4 | 2.7 | 1.5 | |
| 81.8 | 79.0 | 78.0 | Total Current | 73.5 | 71.9 | 85.0 | 78.1 | 88.5 | |
| 12.3 | 12.7 | 13.8 | Fixed Assets (net) | 22.6 | 18.3 | 9.9 | 11.1 | 4.9 | |
| 1.9 | 2.4 | 2.0 | Intangibles (net) | 1.3 | 1.5 | .1 | 2.7 | 4.4 | |
| 4.0 | 5.8 | 6.2 | All Other Non-Current | 2.7 | 8.4 | 5.0 | 8.1 | 2.2 | |
| 100.0 | 100.0 | 100.0 | Total | 100.0 | 100.0 | 100.0 | 100.0 | 100.0 | |

| | | | LIABILITIES | | | | | | |
|---|---|---|---|---|---|---|---|---|---|
| 17.2 | 16.7 | 14.0 | Notes Payable-Short Term | 16.1 | 8.5 | 16.3 | 18.9 | 16.5 | |
| 2.8 | 2.4 | 5.0 | Cur. Mat.-L.T.D. | 1.1 | 8.0 | 5.8 | 3.0 | 8.3 | |
| 14.8 | 16.0 | 18.3 | Trade Payables | 6.9 | 23.2 | 6.2 | 22.2 | 19.9 | |
| .1 | .1 | .1 | Income Taxes Payable | .0 | .0 | .3 | .1 | .0 | |
| 7.5 | 10.9 | 10.4 | All Other Current | 10.3 | 10.5 | 17.3 | 5.7 | 12.0 | |
| 42.4 | 46.0 | 47.8 | Total Current | 34.4 | 50.1 | 45.8 | 49.9 | 56.7 | |
| 12.0 | 14.8 | 13.1 | Long-Term Debt | 23.4 | 14.8 | 7.5 | 10.2 | 3.7 | |
| .1 | .1 | .0 | Deferred Taxes | .0 | .0 | .0 | .1 | .0 | |
| 9.3 | 8.0 | 8.8 | All Other Non-Current | 7.8 | 9.7 | 7.5 | 11.4 | .9 | |
| 36.1 | 31.1 | 30.3 | Net Worth | 34.4 | 25.3 | 39.1 | 28.4 | 38.7 | |
| 100.0 | 100.0 | 100.0 | Total Liabilities & Net Worth | 100.0 | 100.0 | 100.0 | 100.0 | 100.0 | |

| | | | INCOME DATA | | | | | | |
|---|---|---|---|---|---|---|---|---|---|
| 100.0 | 100.0 | 100.0 | Net Sales | 100.0 | 100.0 | 100.0 | 100.0 | 100.0 | |
| 43.5 | 43.8 | 43.8 | Gross Profit | 53.1 | 47.1 | 46.6 | 41.7 | 34.3 | |
| 42.0 | 40.2 | 41.7 | Operating Expenses | 53.9 | 42.5 | 48.9 | 40.6 | 29.7 | |
| 1.5 | 3.6 | 2.2 | Operating Profit | -.8 | 4.6 | -2.3 | 1.1 | 4.6 | |
| .5 | 1.9 | .4 | All Other Expenses (net) | -1.0 | .9 | .3 | .1 | .4 | |
| 1.0 | 1.7 | 1.7 | Profit Before Taxes | .2 | 3.7 | -2.6 | 1.0 | 4.2 | |

| | | | RATIOS | | | | | | |
|---|---|---|---|---|---|---|---|---|---|
| 3.5 | 3.0 | 2.9 | Current | 4.5 | 3.4 | 3.4 | 2.9 | 1.8 | |
| 1.9 | 1.7 | 1.6 | | 2.1 | 1.4 | 2.1 | 1.4 | 1.6 | |
| 1.3 | 1.2 | 1.1 | | 1.3 | 1.0 | 1.4 | 1.1 | 1.4 | |
| .7 | .6 | .6 | Quick | .5 | .4 | 1.0 | .6 | .5 | |
| .3 | .3 | .3 | | .3 | .2 | .5 | .3 | .4 | |
| .1 | .1 | .2 | | .2 | .1 | .1 | .1 | .2 | |
| 2  147.7 | 2  174.0 | 3  127.9 | Sales/Receivables | 0  UND | 1  533.6 | 8  44.1 | 4  84.1 | 5  75.8 | |
| 11  32.2 | 10  37.9 | 12  31.2 | | 9  42.0 | 8  48.1 | 16  22.4 | 11  32.8 | 24  14.9 | |
| 24  15.5 | 29  12.4 | 25  14.4 | | 16  22.6 | 19  19.5 | 25  14.8 | 24  15.5 | 40  9.2 | |
| 142  2.6 | 124  2.9 | 135  2.7 | Cost of Sales/Inventory | 281  1.3 | 135  2.7 | 159  2.3 | 111  3.3 | 91  4.0 | |
| 227  1.6 | 196  1.9 | 192  1.9 | | 365  1.0 | 203  1.8 | 174  2.1 | 192  1.9 | 152  2.4 | |
| 321  1.1 | 348  1.0 | 281  1.3 | | 521  .7 | 261  1.4 | 281  1.3 | 304  1.2 | 192  1.9 | |
| 16  22.8 | 22  16.4 | 24  15.0 | Cost of Sales/Payables | 0  UND | 27  13.3 | 4  103.3 | 32  11.4 | 16  23.5 | |
| 36  10.2 | 39  9.2 | 43  8.4 | | 17  21.9 | 47  7.8 | 25  14.6 | 51  7.1 | 44  8.3 | |
| 55  6.7 | 68  5.3 | 72  5.1 | | 70  5.2 | 111  3.3 | 51  7.2 | 85  4.3 | 54  6.8 | |
| 2.8 | 3.0 | 3.5 | Sales/Working Capital | 1.5 | 4.1 | 3.3 | 4.4 | 5.3 | |
| 5.0 | 5.3 | 6.7 | | 3.4 | 9.4 | 4.8 | 7.1 | 6.6 | |
| 11.1 | 22.1 | 41.1 | | 8.2 | NM | 7.8 | 73.5 | 17.8 | |
| 5.3 | 5.2 | 5.1 | EBIT/Interest | 1.9 | 4.3 | | 4.1 | 13.7 | |
| (70)  1.5 | (84)  2.1 | (77)  2.0 | | 1.4 | (23)  1.9 | | (17)  2.7 | 5.7 | |
| .6 | 1.1 | .9 | | -8.0 | .9 | | 1.4 | 3.4 | |
| 29.6 | 5.3 | 2.4 | Net Profit + Depr., Dep., Amort./Cur. Mat. L/T/D | | | | | | |
| (15)  5.5 | (11)  1.7 | (12)  1.1 | | | | | | | |
| .4 | .7 | .3 | | | | | | | |
| .1 | .1 | .1 | Fixed/Worth | .0 | .1 | .1 | .1 | .1 | |
| .2 | .3 | .3 | | .3 | .5 | .1 | .5 | .1 | |
| 1.1 | 1.7 | 3.2 | | 4.8 | -1.5 | .3 | 23.5 | .2 | |
| .9 | 1.0 | 1.0 | Debt/Worth | .9 | 1.2 | .8 | .7 | 1.1 | |
| 2.1 | 2.6 | 2.2 | | 1.5 | 4.3 | 1.3 | 3.3 | 2.0 | |
| 4.2 | 9.1 | 10.5 | | 6.5 | -15.9 | 2.2 | 69.8 | 3.4 | |
| 19.2 | 34.3 | 31.0 | % Profit Before Taxes/Tangible Net Worth | 7.4 | 60.6 | 9.0 | 28.6 | 60.1 | |
| (68)  4.4 | (83)  10.6 | (70)  9.7 | | (10)  -.9 | (16)  17.5 | (10)  -1.5 | (17)  9.5 | 34.1 | |
| -3.6 | .7 | -1.0 | | -6.7 | -.3 | -21.9 | 1.1 | 14.8 | |
| 5.8 | 8.8 | 7.0 | % Profit Before Taxes/Total Assets | 3.5 | 16.3 | 1.8 | 4.6 | 19.6 | |
| 1.3 | 2.5 | 1.9 | | .7 | 2.7 | -2.4 | 1.9 | 7.0 | |
| -1.7 | .0 | -.6 | | -1.1 | -.4 | -15.1 | .3 | 4.2 | |
| 87.6 | 96.7 | 88.6 | Sales/Net Fixed Assets | 84.0 | 110.7 | 63.3 | 88.5 | 110.7 | |
| 26.1 | 26.7 | 28.0 | | 9.5 | 19.0 | 47.8 | 27.7 | 78.0 | |
| 12.1 | 9.6 | 11.6 | | 3.9 | 5.2 | 17.0 | 15.9 | 34.1 | |
| 2.7 | 2.6 | 2.5 | Sales/Total Assets | 1.8 | 2.7 | 2.7 | 2.6 | 3.8 | |
| 1.8 | 1.7 | 1.9 | | 1.2 | 2.2 | 2.0 | 1.6 | 2.3 | |
| 1.3 | 1.3 | 1.3 | | .9 | 1.3 | 1.3 | 1.6 | 1.9 | |
| .5 | .4 | .5 | % Depr., Dep., Amort./Sales | | .6 | | .3 | | |
| (63)  1.0 | (64)  .9 | (63)  .8 | | | (17)  2.6 | | (19)  .8 | | |
| 2.1 | 2.1 | 3.5 | | | 4.9 | | 3.7 | | |
| 2.2 | 2.2 | 1.6 | % Officers', Directors' Owners' Comp/Sales | | 3.8 | | | | |
| (38)  4.5 | (44)  3.9 | (36)  4.2 | | | (11)  4.5 | | | | |
| 8.2 | 7.5 | 7.1 | | | 7.0 | | | | |
| 1215551M | 1104638M | 1080787M | Net Sales ($) | 6077M | 43562M | 43512M | 138031M | 152858M | 696747M |
| 613180M | 640896M | 559796M | Total Assets ($) | 6033M | 25561M | 24214M | 78417M | 67915M | 357656M |

© RMA 2012

M = $ thousand    MM = $ million
See Pages 9 through 22 for Explanation of Ratios and Data

## Current Data Sorted by Assets     Comparative Historical Data

**Type of Statement**

| Type of Statement | 0-500M | 500M-2MM | 2-10MM | 10-50MM | 50-100MM | 100-250MM | | 14 / 4/1/07-3/31/08 ALL | 13 / 4/1/08-3/31/09 ALL |
|---|---|---|---|---|---|---|---|---|---|
| Unqualified | | | | 7 | 1 | | | 14 | 13 |
| Reviewed | | | 1 | 2 | | | | 4 | 3 |
| Compiled | | 4 | 3 | 2 | | | | 9 | 10 |
| Tax Returns | 8 | 7 | 6 | | | | | 13 | 16 |
| Other | 2 | 3 | 8 | 3 | | 1 | | 17 | 17 |
| | 0-500M | 17 (4/1-9/30/11)<br>500M-2MM | 2-10MM | 41 (10/1/11-3/31/12)<br>10-50MM | 50-100MM | 100-250MM | | | |
| **NUMBER OF STATEMENTS** | 10 | 14 | 18 | 14 | 1 | 1 | | 57 | 59 |
| | % | % | % | % | % | % | | % | % |
| **ASSETS** | | | | | | | | | |
| Cash & Equivalents | 9.7 | 8.0 | 15.0 | 13.3 | | | | 14.5 | 13.3 |
| Trade Receivables (net) | 2.6 | 7.2 | 7.3 | 4.6 | | | | 6.4 | 6.7 |
| Inventory | 65.3 | 54.8 | 47.7 | 38.0 | | | | 50.6 | 44.9 |
| All Other Current | 1.6 | .5 | 3.0 | 1.6 | | | | 1.7 | 2.4 |
| Total Current | 79.2 | 70.5 | 73.0 | 57.5 | | | | 73.2 | 67.2 |
| Fixed Assets (net) | 18.4 | 16.0 | 12.3 | 34.4 | | | | 19.5 | 23.3 |
| Intangibles (net) | .3 | 5.7 | 8.8 | 1.0 | | | | 2.7 | 1.7 |
| All Other Non-Current | 1.3 | 7.7 | 6.0 | 7.1 | | | | 4.6 | 7.8 |
| Total | 100.0 | 100.0 | 100.0 | 100.0 | | | | 100.0 | 100.0 |
| **LIABILITIES** | | | | | | | | | |
| Notes Payable-Short Term | 17.0 | 23.4 | 9.1 | 4.3 | | | | 15.8 | 9.7 |
| Cur. Mat.-L.T.D. | 1.0 | 1.4 | 1.9 | .8 | | | | 2.3 | 1.8 |
| Trade Payables | 28.0 | 36.6 | 19.7 | 11.7 | | | | 28.6 | 28.6 |
| Income Taxes Payable | .0 | .0 | .0 | .0 | | | | 2.1 | .7 |
| All Other Current | 63.4 | 10.3 | 8.8 | 15.6 | | | | 14.4 | 21.2 |
| Total Current | 109.4 | 71.7 | 39.6 | 32.3 | | | | 63.1 | 62.1 |
| Long-Term Debt | 8.9 | 3.7 | 7.2 | 8.2 | | | | 10.6 | 11.1 |
| Deferred Taxes | .0 | .0 | .2 | .3 | | | | .2 | .1 |
| All Other Non-Current | 38.8 | 5.5 | 4.9 | 5.7 | | | | 4.9 | 11.0 |
| Net Worth | -57.0 | 19.1 | 48.1 | 53.4 | | | | 21.2 | 15.6 |
| Total Liabilities & Net Worth | 100.0 | 100.0 | 100.0 | 100.0 | | | | 100.0 | 100.0 |
| **INCOME DATA** | | | | | | | | | |
| Net Sales | 100.0 | 100.0 | 100.0 | 100.0 | | | | 100.0 | 100.0 |
| Gross Profit | 46.0 | 41.8 | 43.5 | 43.7 | | | | 37.6 | 43.5 |
| Operating Expenses | 44.4 | 42.9 | 39.5 | 42.5 | | | | 36.2 | 40.9 |
| Operating Profit | 1.7 | -1.1 | 4.0 | 1.2 | | | | 1.4 | 2.6 |
| All Other Expenses (net) | .0 | .3 | -.2 | .7 | | | | 1.1 | .9 |
| Profit Before Taxes | 1.7 | -1.4 | 4.2 | .5 | | | | .4 | 1.7 |
| **RATIOS** | | | | | | | | | |
| Current | 3.9 | 1.4 | 2.5 | 3.4 | | | | 2.6 | 2.4 |
| | .9 | 1.0 | 1.7 | 2.1 | | | | 1.5 | 1.5 |
| | .4 | .7 | 1.3 | 1.2 | | | | .8 | .9 |
| Quick | .3 | .3 | 1.0 | 1.4 | | | | .8 | .9 |
| | .1 | .2 | .5 | .4 | | | | .3 | .4 |
| | .0 | .0 | .2 | .2 | | | | .1 | .1 |
| Sales/Receivables | 0 UND | 1 653.4 | 2 174.0 | 2 163.9 | | | | 1 477.1 | 0 754.0 |
| | 0 UND | 3 144.8 | 7 49.8 | 8 47.0 | | | | 3 107.2 | 2 166.8 |
| | 4 97.3 | 15 24.7 | 25 14.8 | 13 28.6 | | | | 14 25.2 | 11 32.6 |
| Cost of Sales/Inventory | 62 5.9 | 78 4.7 | 56 6.5 | 87 4.2 | | | | 77 4.7 | 70 5.2 |
| | 101 3.6 | 101 3.6 | 111 3.3 | 104 3.5 | | | | 115 3.2 | 113 3.2 |
| | 159 2.3 | 182 2.0 | 243 1.5 | 159 2.3 | | | | 146 2.5 | 153 2.4 |
| Cost of Sales/Payables | 13 28.3 | 53 6.9 | 16 22.4 | 20 18.1 | | | | 27 13.4 | 26 14.1 |
| | 26 13.8 | 72 5.1 | 56 6.5 | 29 12.8 | | | | 44 8.2 | 53 6.9 |
| | 72 5.1 | 122 3.0 | 99 3.7 | 47 7.7 | | | | 78 4.7 | 98 3.7 |
| Sales/Working Capital | 9.9 | 13.3 | 4.5 | 5.1 | | | | 6.5 | 6.4 |
| | -57.5 | -341.3 | 8.2 | 6.6 | | | | 14.4 | 12.0 |
| | -3.3 | -12.6 | 16.1 | 272.8 | | | | -22.3 | -23.1 |
| EBIT/Interest | | 7.9 | 17.1 | 110.6 | | | | 10.3 | 12.7 |
| | | 1.5 | (16) 4.1 | (13) 1.9 | | | | (48) 1.8 | (51) 3.2 |
| | | -3.4 | 1.4 | -3.8 | | | | .5 | -.1 |
| Net Profit + Depr., Dep., Amort./Cur. Mat. L/T/D | | | | | | | | | |
| Fixed/Worth | .2 | .3 | .1 | .3 | | | | .2 | .2 |
| | -1.6 | 1.0 | .2 | .5 | | | | .6 | .5 |
| | -.1 | -2.4 | .6 | 1.4 | | | | -1.0 | -5.7 |
| Debt/Worth | .9 | 2.4 | .8 | .3 | | | | .5 | .6 |
| | -5.5 | 7.7 | 1.2 | .9 | | | | 3.3 | 2.1 |
| | -1.5 | -8.8 | 2.3 | 2.0 | | | | -5.4 | -12.5 |
| % Profit Before Taxes/Tangible Net Worth | | 30.9 | 57.3 | 24.5 | | | | 14.4 | 38.7 |
| | | (10) 7.0 | (17) 7.2 | 3.8 | | | | (40) 5.7 | (42) 13.2 |
| | | -31.3 | 1.5 | -9.7 | | | | -1.3 | 1.0 |
| % Profit Before Taxes/Total Assets | 7.2 | 3.7 | 21.2 | 9.2 | | | | 7.9 | 13.1 |
| | 4.0 | 1.0 | 4.0 | 2.5 | | | | 1.7 | 6.8 |
| | -7.9 | -7.1 | .8 | -4.4 | | | | -2.1 | -2.3 |
| Sales/Net Fixed Assets | 62.8 | 84.2 | 52.0 | 20.0 | | | | 55.2 | 51.5 |
| | 24.7 | 39.9 | 30.5 | 5.9 | | | | 15.2 | 13.0 |
| | 11.6 | 15.8 | 11.7 | 3.1 | | | | 7.6 | 7.7 |
| Sales/Total Assets | 5.6 | 3.7 | 3.1 | 2.5 | | | | 3.6 | 3.3 |
| | 4.8 | 3.0 | 2.4 | 2.1 | | | | 2.6 | 2.6 |
| | 2.8 | 1.9 | 1.4 | 1.4 | | | | 1.7 | 2.2 |
| % Depr., Dep., Amort./Sales | | .4 | .5 | 1.3 | | | | .8 | .7 |
| | | (10) .9 | (15) .8 | (12) 1.6 | | | | (46) 1.4 | (47) 1.1 |
| | | 1.3 | 1.0 | 3.1 | | | | 1.9 | 1.9 |
| % Officers', Directors' Owners' Comp/Sales | | | | | | | | 2.2 | 1.8 |
| | | | | | | | | (12) 4.2 | (22) 3.0 |
| | | | | | | | | 8.1 | 3.8 |
| Net Sales ($) | 14808M | 34858M | 197882M | 625882M | 261981M | 234285M | | 2483349M | 1265366M |
| Total Assets ($) | 2739M | 13163M | 81086M | 318852M | 87693M | 108885M | | 948334M | 538209M |

M = $ thousand    MM = $ million
See Pages 9 through 22 for Explanation of Ratios and Data

## Comparative Historical Data
## Current Data Sorted by Sales

| Hist 1 | Hist 2 | Hist 3 | Type of Statement | 0-1MM | 1-3MM | 3-5MM | 5-10MM | 10-25MM | 25MM & OVER |
|---|---|---|---|---|---|---|---|---|---|
| 8 | 11 | 8 | Unqualified | | | | | 2 | 6 |
| 4 | 8 | 3 | Reviewed | | | | | 1 | 2 |
| 7 | 10 | 9 | Compiled | | 3 | 1 | | 3 | 2 |
| 22 | 17 | 21 | Tax Returns | 4 | 7 | 4 | 5 | 1 | |
| 18 | 28 | 17 | Other | 3 | 4 | 2 | | 3 | 5 |
| 4/1/09-3/31/10 ALL | 4/1/10-3/31/11 ALL | 4/1/11-3/31/12 ALL | | 17 (4/1-9/30/11) | | | 41 (10/1/11-3/31/12) | | |
| 59 | 74 | 58 | NUMBER OF STATEMENTS | 7 | 14 | 7 | 5 | 10 | 15 |
| % | % | % | **ASSETS** | % | % | % | % | % | % |
| 14.0 | 10.6 | 12.0 | Cash & Equivalents | | 7.7 | | | 15.9 | 11.2 |
| 5.0 | 9.9 | 5.6 | Trade Receivables (net) | | 7.9 | | | 6.0 | 5.4 |
| 50.7 | 46.0 | 50.0 | Inventory | | 48.2 | | | 46.0 | 42.2 |
| 2.2 | 2.7 | 2.0 | All Other Current | | .9 | | | 4.3 | 3.5 |
| 71.9 | 69.1 | 69.6 | Total Current | | 64.7 | | | 72.2 | 62.3 |
| 17.6 | 18.4 | 20.1 | Fixed Assets (net) | | 15.0 | | | 22.7 | 30.4 |
| 2.8 | 3.4 | 4.4 | Intangibles (net) | | 12.3 | | | .6 | 1.0 |
| 7.7 | 9.1 | 5.7 | All Other Non-Current | | 8.0 | | | 4.4 | 6.3 |
| 100.0 | 100.0 | 100.0 | Total | | 100.0 | | | 100.0 | 100.0 |
| | | | **LIABILITIES** | | | | | | |
| 14.8 | 18.7 | 12.5 | Notes Payable-Short Term | | 22.2 | | | 11.1 | 4.1 |
| 2.9 | 1.6 | 1.4 | Cur. Mat.-L.T.D. | | 2.2 | | | 1.5 | 1.0 |
| 22.0 | 23.5 | 23.5 | Trade Payables | | 38.5 | | | 10.5 | 15.0 |
| .6 | .6 | .0 | Income Taxes Payable | | .0 | | | .1 | .0 |
| 14.7 | 12.0 | 20.2 | All Other Current | | 38.7 | | | 14.0 | 15.4 |
| 55.1 | 56.4 | 57.6 | Total Current | | 101.5 | | | 37.1 | 35.6 |
| 17.6 | 12.2 | 6.6 | Long-Term Debt | | 8.0 | | | 4.2 | 5.7 |
| .3 | .1 | .1 | Deferred Taxes | | .0 | | | .0 | .4 |
| 3.9 | 7.5 | 13.2 | All Other Non-Current | | 19.6 | | | 2.4 | 13.1 |
| 23.1 | 23.7 | 22.5 | Net Worth | | -29.1 | | | 56.3 | 45.2 |
| 100.0 | 100.0 | 100.0 | Total Liabilities & Net Worth | | 100.0 | | | 100.0 | 100.0 |
| | | | **INCOME DATA** | | | | | | |
| 100.0 | 100.0 | 100.0 | Net Sales | | 100.0 | | | 100.0 | 100.0 |
| 41.3 | 40.1 | 44.1 | Gross Profit | | 35.8 | | | 43.0 | 47.9 |
| 37.9 | 38.2 | 42.4 | Operating Expenses | | 35.8 | | | 40.3 | 45.8 |
| 3.4 | 1.9 | 1.7 | Operating Profit | | .0 | | | 2.8 | 2.0 |
| .9 | .8 | .3 | All Other Expenses (net) | | 1.1 | | | -.6 | 1.4 |
| 2.6 | 1.1 | 1.4 | Profit Before Taxes | | -1.1 | | | 3.4 | .7 |
| | | | **RATIOS** | | | | | | |
| 2.8 | 2.5 | 2.4 | Current | | 1.0 | | | 4.2 | 3.3 |
| 1.8 | 1.5 | 1.4 | | | .8 | | | 1.8 | 2.0 |
| 1.0 | 1.0 | .9 | | | .7 | | | 1.3 | 1.1 |
| 1.0 | .9 | .8 | Quick | | .4 | | | 1.8 | 1.0 |
| .4 (73) | .4 | .3 | | | .1 | | | .5 | .4 |
| .2 | .1 | .1 | | | .0 | | | .2 | .2 |
| 0 UND | 1 679.0 | 1 321.3 | Sales/Receivables | 0 UND | | | | 3 130.9 | 2 156.7 |
| 3 142.9 | 3 111.5 | 4 101.4 | | 3 144.8 | | | | 8 43.2 | 6 60.7 |
| 17 21.2 | 20 18.3 | 12 29.3 | | 28 13.0 | | | | 13 28.2 | 14 25.7 |
| 92 4.0 | 67 5.4 | 76 4.8 | Cost of Sales/Inventory | 73 5.0 | | | | 42 8.7 | 89 4.1 |
| 123 3.0 | 112 3.2 | 104 3.5 | | 85 4.3 | | | | 89 4.1 | 135 2.7 |
| 161 2.3 | 168 2.2 | 166 2.2 | | 114 3.2 | | | | 159 2.3 | 152 2.4 |
| 21 17.5 | 24 15.3 | 22 16.6 | Cost of Sales/Payables | 53 6.9 | | | | 3 116.8 | 21 17.8 |
| 47 7.8 | 57 6.5 | 46 8.0 | | 99 3.7 | | | | 27 13.5 | 30 12.1 |
| 79 4.6 | 82 4.4 | 96 3.8 | | 118 3.1 | | | | 44 8.3 | 73 5.0 |
| 4.8 | 5.3 | 5.5 | Sales/Working Capital | NM | | | | 3.1 | 5.2 |
| 9.0 | 12.4 | 12.8 | | -27.9 | | | | 7.7 | 6.7 |
| 474.7 | 120.9 | -68.0 | | -10.8 | | | | 39.1 | 43.1 |
| 15.7 | 14.2 | 10.6 | EBIT/Interest | 3.8 | | | | 166.9 | 15.6 |
| (46) 3.9 | (59) 5.1 | (50) 2.2 | | (13) 1.3 | | | | 11.0 | (12) 1.3 |
| .7 | -.8 | -1.4 | | -6.0 | | | | 1.3 | -4.6 |
| | | | Net Profit + Depr., Dep., Amort./Cur. Mat. L/T/D | | | | | | |
| .1 | .1 | .2 | Fixed/Worth | | .3 | | | .1 | .2 |
| .4 | .4 | .5 | | | -2.5 | | | .5 | .4 |
| 1.8 | 1.4 | 1.5 | | | -.3 | | | .8 | 1.5 |
| .5 | .7 | .8 | Debt/Worth | | 8.6 | | | .2 | .3 |
| 1.7 | 2.0 | 1.6 | | | -7.8 | | | 1.0 | .9 |
| 64.1 | 11.0 | 11.0 | | | -2.6 | | | 1.3 | 3.0 |
| 38.9 | 46.9 | 33.0 | % Profit Before Taxes/Tangible Net Worth | | | | | 58.7 | 24.5 |
| (46) 9.3 | (58) 14.7 | (46) 7.2 | | | | | | 7.4 | (14) 7.2 |
| .8 | .8 | -5.5 | | | | | | -1.3 | -6.3 |
| 14.9 | 14.3 | 7.3 | % Profit Before Taxes/Total Assets | | 3.4 | | | 23.4 | 9.7 |
| 3.2 | 4.2 | 2.6 | | | .9 | | | 6.2 | 4.8 |
| .2 | -2.7 | -3.6 | | | -14.8 | | | -.5 | -3.5 |
| 139.7 | 110.0 | 50.1 | Sales/Net Fixed Assets | | 61.8 | | | 52.0 | 29.2 |
| 20.8 | 24.8 | 25.4 | | | 32.6 | | | 19.2 | 7.7 |
| 8.7 | 7.6 | 7.2 | | | 12.4 | | | 7.5 | 3.4 |
| 3.3 | 3.3 | 3.5 | Sales/Total Assets | | 4.7 | | | 3.5 | 3.0 |
| 2.5 | 2.5 | 2.5 | | | 3.2 | | | 2.4 | 2.3 |
| 1.7 | 1.7 | 1.6 | | | 1.9 | | | 1.6 | 1.7 |
| .7 | .8 | .6 | % Depr., Dep., Amort./Sales | | .5 | | | | 1.2 |
| (39) 1.3 | (55) 1.4 | (46) 1.0 | | | (10) .8 | | | | (13) 1.5 |
| 2.2 | 2.1 | 1.5 | | | 1.1 | | | | 2.6 |
| 2.8 | 1.8 | 2.3 | % Officers', Directors' Owners' Comp/Sales | | | | | | |
| (22) 4.6 | (18) 3.5 | (19) 3.2 | | | | | | | |
| 8.2 | 6.2 | 4.8 | | | | | | | |
| 1644900M | 1690271M | 1369696M | Net Sales ($) | 3261M | 27891M | 30365M | 36686M | 163914M | 1107579M |
| 739325M | 831403M | 612418M | Total Assets ($) | 2758M | 12835M | 12622M | 15589M | 73421M | 495193M |

M = $ thousand   MM = $ million
See Pages 9 through 22 for Explanation of Ratios and Data

## Current Data Sorted by Assets | Comparative Historical Data

| 0-500M | 500M-2MM | 2-10MM | 10-50MM | 50-100MM | 100-250MM | Type of Statement | 4/1/07-3/31/08 ALL | 4/1/08-3/31/09 ALL |
|---|---|---|---|---|---|---|---|---|
| | | | 3 | | 1 | Unqualified | 6 | 13 |
| | | | 6 | | | Reviewed | 4 | 4 |
| 1 | 3 | 1 | | | | Compiled | 3 | 4 |
| 2 | 3 | 2 | | | | Tax Returns | 9 | 8 |
| | 2 | 2 | | 1 | 1 | Other | 17 | 6 |
| | 2 (4/1-9/30/11) | | 29 (10/1/11-3/31/12) | | | | | |
| 3 | 8 | 5 | 12 | 1 | 2 | NUMBER OF STATEMENTS | 39 | 35 |
| % | % | % | % | % | % | | % | % |
| | | | 23.0 | | | **ASSETS** Cash & Equivalents | 7.1 | 9.8 |
| | | | 1.6 | | | Trade Receivables (net) | 9.5 | 5.4 |
| | | | 38.1 | | | Inventory | 48.2 | 50.4 |
| | | | 2.9 | | | All Other Current | 2.7 | 1.1 |
| | | | 65.7 | | | Total Current | 67.6 | 66.7 |
| | | | 26.6 | | | Fixed Assets (net) | 21.7 | 24.5 |
| | | | 1.9 | | | Intangibles (net) | 3.3 | 2.5 |
| | | | 5.8 | | | All Other Non-Current | 7.4 | 6.4 |
| | | | 100.0 | | | Total | 100.0 | 100.0 |
| | | | .6 | | | **LIABILITIES** Notes Payable-Short Term | 7.1 | 9.7 |
| | | | .7 | | | Cur. Mat.-L.T.D. | 2.1 | 1.7 |
| | | | 18.8 | | | Trade Payables | 16.5 | 13.8 |
| | | | .2 | | | Income Taxes Payable | .1 | .1 |
| | | | 9.4 | | | All Other Current | 8.8 | 9.9 |
| | | | 29.7 | | | Total Current | 34.6 | 35.3 |
| | | | 16.3 | | | Long-Term Debt | 16.3 | 17.7 |
| | | | .3 | | | Deferred Taxes | .4 | .5 |
| | | | 7.1 | | | All Other Non-Current | 5.2 | 8.2 |
| | | | 46.6 | | | Net Worth | 43.5 | 38.3 |
| | | | 100.0 | | | Total Liabilties & Net Worth | 100.0 | 100.0 |
| | | | 100.0 | | | **INCOME DATA** Net Sales | 100.0 | 100.0 |
| | | | 30.9 | | | Gross Profit | 40.1 | 42.7 |
| | | | 28.6 | | | Operating Expenses | 36.5 | 38.1 |
| | | | 2.3 | | | Operating Profit | 3.6 | 4.6 |
| | | | -1.2 | | | All Other Expenses (net) | .7 | 1.7 |
| | | | 3.5 | | | Profit Before Taxes | 2.9 | 3.0 |
| | | | 3.4 | | | **RATIOS** Current | 3.5 | 3.8 |
| | | | 2.1 | | | | 2.4 | 2.1 |
| | | | 1.5 | | | | 1.5 | 1.3 |
| | | | 1.8 | | | Quick | 1.3 | 1.2 |
| | | | .8 | | | | .4 | .3 |
| | | | .2 | | | | .1 | .1 |
| | | | 0 UND | | | Sales/Receivables | 0 UND | 0 UND |
| | | | 1 693.2 | | | | 4 93.2 | 2 228.1 |
| | | | 2 159.8 | | | | 18 20.2 | 15 24.8 |
| | | | 43 8.4 | | | Cost of Sales/Inventory | 56 6.6 | 94 3.9 |
| | | | 59 6.2 | | | | 118 3.1 | 124 2.9 |
| | | | 130 2.8 | | | | 200 1.8 | 215 1.7 |
| | | | 12 29.5 | | | Cost of Sales/Payables | 14 25.4 | 12 30.9 |
| | | | 34 10.7 | | | | 29 12.8 | 29 12.7 |
| | | | 50 7.3 | | | | 53 6.8 | 54 6.8 |
| | | | 3.6 | | | Sales/Working Capital | 3.6 | 3.9 |
| | | | 9.0 | | | | 6.3 | 6.2 |
| | | | 20.6 | | | | 14.3 | 18.3 |
| | | | 136.2 | | | EBIT/Interest | 8.3 | 8.7 |
| | | | (10) 11.9 | | | | (34) 3.1 | (34) 1.9 |
| | | | 1.9 | | | | 1.3 | -.2 |
| | | | | | | Net Profit + Depr., Dep., Amort./Cur. Mat. L/T/D | 3.5 | |
| | | | | | | | (10) 1.9 | |
| | | | | | | | .6 | |
| | | | .2 | | | Fixed/Worth | .1 | .2 |
| | | | .5 | | | | .4 | .5 |
| | | | 9.1 | | | | 1.1 | 1.7 |
| | | | .4 | | | Debt/Worth | .4 | .7 |
| | | | .8 | | | | 1.2 | 2.0 |
| | | | 23.1 | | | | 2.9 | 3.7 |
| | | | 29.1 | | | % Profit Before Taxes/Tangible Net Worth | 15.2 | 34.2 |
| | | | (10) 16.0 | | | | (34) 5.5 | (32) 7.8 |
| | | | 3.3 | | | | 1.0 | -7.4 |
| | | | 14.8 | | | % Profit Before Taxes/Total Assets | 8.8 | 9.1 |
| | | | 5.7 | | | | 3.1 | 3.5 |
| | | | 1.6 | | | | .3 | -2.4 |
| | | | 52.0 | | | Sales/Net Fixed Assets | 71.8 | 37.8 |
| | | | 12.3 | | | | 16.4 | 12.9 |
| | | | 4.7 | | | | 5.8 | 5.0 |
| | | | 3.8 | | | Sales/Total Assets | 3.6 | 3.1 |
| | | | 2.3 | | | | 2.3 | 2.3 |
| | | | 2.0 | | | | 1.5 | 1.5 |
| | | | .6 | | | % Depr., Dep., Amort./Sales | .4 | .6 |
| | | | (11) 1.2 | | | | (30) 1.2 | (27) 1.5 |
| | | | 2.1 | | | | 3.4 | 2.3 |
| | | | | | | % Officers', Directors' Owners' Comp/Sales | 1.4 | 1.1 |
| | | | | | | | (10) 2.8 | (11) 4.1 |
| | | | | | | | 8.5 | 7.3 |
| 5478M | 29525M | 93178M | 848016M | 57811M | 854646M | Net Sales ($) | 3396186M | 2906528M |
| 805M | 11113M | 23196M | 283956M | 54061M | 292843M | Total Assets ($) | 1426787M | 1277213M |

© RMA 2012

M = $ thousand   MM = $ million
See Pages 9 through 22 for Explanation of Ratios and Data

## Comparative Historical Data / Current Data Sorted by Sales

| | | | Type of Statement | 0-1MM | 1-3MM | 3-5MM | 5-10MM | 10-25MM | 25MM & OVER |
|---|---|---|---|---|---|---|---|---|---|
| 10 | 7 | 4 | Unqualified | | | | | | 4 |
| 9 | 7 | 6 | Reviewed | | | | | 1 | 5 |
| 9 | 5 | 5 | Compiled | | 2 | 1 | 1 | | 1 |
| 9 | 5 | 8 | Tax Returns | | 2 | 2 | 2 | 1 | 1 |
| 16 | 7 | 8 | Other | | 2 | | 1 | 1 | 4 |
| 4/1/09-3/31/10 ALL | 4/1/10-3/31/11 ALL | 4/1/11-3/31/12 ALL | | | 2 (4/1-9/30/11) | | 29 (10/1/11-3/31/12) | | |
| 53 | 31 | 31 | NUMBER OF STATEMENTS | 6 | 3 | 4 | 3 | 15 | |
| % | % | % | **ASSETS** | % | % | % | % | % | % |
| 15.0 | 14.2 | 20.7 | Cash & Equivalents | | | | | | 24.1 |
| 9.2 | 9.9 | 5.7 | Trade Receivables (net) | | | | | | 5.8 |
| 45.0 | 47.9 | 43.4 | Inventory | | | | | | 36.3 |
| 1.7 | 1.8 | 1.4 | All Other Current | | | | | | 2.8 |
| 71.0 | 73.8 | 71.3 | Total Current | | | | | | 69.0 |
| 21.6 | 17.1 | 19.2 | Fixed Assets (net) | | | | | | 22.6 |
| 2.4 | 1.7 | 2.4 | Intangibles (net) | | | | | | 3.3 |
| 5.0 | 7.4 | 7.1 | All Other Non-Current | | | | | | 5.1 |
| 100.0 | 100.0 | 100.0 | Total | | | | | | 100.0 |
| | | | **LIABILITIES** | | | | | | |
| 10.3 | 9.3 | 5.7 | Notes Payable-Short Term | | | | | | 2.4 |
| 2.1 | 1.9 | .7 | Cur. Mat.-L.T.D. | | | | | | .4 |
| 16.4 | 18.8 | 16.9 | Trade Payables | | | | | | 21.1 |
| .5 | .1 | .3 | Income Taxes Payable | | | | | | .5 |
| 7.9 | 8.7 | 8.2 | All Other Current | | | | | | 10.5 |
| 37.2 | 38.8 | 31.8 | Total Current | | | | | | 35.0 |
| 14.5 | 12.2 | 12.5 | Long-Term Debt | | | | | | 12.7 |
| .5 | .3 | .2 | Deferred Taxes | | | | | | .5 |
| 9.3 | 6.0 | 8.8 | All Other Non-Current | | | | | | 6.7 |
| 38.6 | 42.6 | 46.7 | Net Worth | | | | | | 45.2 |
| 100.0 | 100.0 | 100.0 | Total Liabilities & Net Worth | | | | | | 100.0 |
| | | | **INCOME DATA** | | | | | | |
| 100.0 | 100.0 | 100.0 | Net Sales | | | | | | 100.0 |
| 41.1 | 39.4 | 36.6 | Gross Profit | | | | | | 34.7 |
| 35.9 | 34.0 | 32.3 | Operating Expenses | | | | | | 31.1 |
| 5.2 | 5.4 | 4.3 | Operating Profit | | | | | | 3.5 |
| 2.5 | .1 | -.3 | All Other Expenses (net) | | | | | | .1 |
| 2.7 | 5.3 | 4.6 | Profit Before Taxes | | | | | | 3.4 |
| | | | **RATIOS** | | | | | | |
| 3.1 | 2.9 | 3.5 | Current | | | | | | 3.3 |
| 2.1 | 1.9 | 2.2 | | | | | | | 1.9 |
| 1.3 | 1.3 | 1.5 | | | | | | | 1.5 |
| 1.2 | 1.2 | 1.5 | Quick | | | | | | 1.5 |
| .8 | .6 | .7 | | | | | | | .8 |
| .2 | .2 | .3 | | | | | | | .4 |
| 0 UND | 0 999.8 | 0 UND | Sales/Receivables | | | | | | 0 UND |
| 2 216.7 | 2 167.5 | 2 234.6 | | | | | | | 2 234.6 |
| 15 24.1 | 15 24.3 | 9 39.2 | | | | | | | 9 39.2 |
| 54 6.8 | 54 6.8 | 43 8.4 | Cost of Sales/Inventory | | | | | | 43 8.4 |
| 104 3.5 | 106 3.4 | 79 4.6 | | | | | | | 65 5.6 |
| 155 2.4 | 136 2.7 | 114 3.2 | | | | | | | 126 2.9 |
| 8 43.0 | 14 26.9 | 10 35.3 | Cost of Sales/Payables | | | | | | 31 11.7 |
| 26 14.2 | 36 10.1 | 34 10.7 | | | | | | | 35 10.3 |
| 42 8.7 | 50 7.3 | 44 8.3 | | | | | | | 50 7.3 |
| 5.4 | 3.8 | 3.7 | Sales/Working Capital | | | | | | 3.5 |
| 7.7 | 8.1 | 8.5 | | | | | | | 9.5 |
| 19.3 | 17.7 | 20.3 | | | | | | | 20.3 |
| 25.9 | 28.6 | 46.2 | EBIT/Interest | | | | | | 88.0 |
| (44) 5.3 | (28) 4.3 | (25) 5.7 | | | | | | (12) | 19.3 |
| 1.8 | 1.4 | 1.6 | | | | | | | 2.0 |
| 8.9 | | | Net Profit + Depr., Dep., Amort./Cur. Mat. L/T/D | | | | | | |
| (18) 3.4 | | | | | | | | | |
| .1 | | | | | | | | | |
| .1 | .1 | .1 | Fixed/Worth | | | | | | .2 |
| .4 | .4 | .3 | | | | | | | .5 |
| 1.2 | .8 | 1.2 | | | | | | | 1.0 |
| .5 | .6 | .4 | Debt/Worth | | | | | | .4 |
| 1.6 | 1.5 | 1.1 | | | | | | | 1.1 |
| 6.3 | 2.7 | 2.7 | | | | | | | 3.2 |
| 41.6 | 46.1 | 43.5 | % Profit Before Taxes/Tangible Net Worth | | | | | | 48.2 |
| (46) 17.5 | (29) 17.4 | (28) 20.2 | | | | | | (13) | 26.0 |
| 5.7 | 4.3 | 4.4 | | | | | | | 5.2 |
| 16.6 | 20.2 | 23.9 | % Profit Before Taxes/Total Assets | | | | | | 24.2 |
| 8.0 | 4.7 | 6.6 | | | | | | | 7.4 |
| 1.7 | .9 | 2.1 | | | | | | | 2.1 |
| 88.3 | 149.3 | 90.6 | Sales/Net Fixed Assets | | | | | | 31.8 |
| 24.3 | 28.7 | 29.0 | | | | | | | 13.4 |
| 7.9 | 11.6 | 11.9 | | | | | | | 5.2 |
| 4.2 | 4.2 | 4.2 | Sales/Total Assets | | | | | | 3.8 |
| 2.7 | 2.9 | 2.8 | | | | | | | 2.3 |
| 1.8 | 1.8 | 1.9 | | | | | | | 2.1 |
| .3 | .5 | .3 | % Depr., Dep., Amort./Sales | | | | | | .5 |
| (46) .9 | (24) .7 | (24) .7 | | | | | | (14) | 1.1 |
| 2.0 | 1.5 | 1.7 | | | | | | | 1.8 |
| 1.8 | .8 | .8 | % Officers', Directors' Owners' Comp/Sales | | | | | | |
| (24) 3.3 | (10) 2.1 | (12) 2.2 | | | | | | | |
| 5.5 | 5.7 | 6.2 | | | | | | | |
| 3072976M | 2501446M | 1888654M | Net Sales ($) | | 10375M | 11532M | 29722M | 44298M | 1792727M |
| 1193591M | 875007M | 665974M | Total Assets ($) | | 4854M | 3971M | 8877M | 28615M | 619657M |

Note: For the right-hand size groups 0-1MM through 10-25MM, the ASSETS and LIABILITIES sections are marked "DATA NOT AVAILABLE."

© RMA 2012

M = $ thousand     MM = $ million
See Pages 9 through 22 for Explanation of Ratios and Data

## Current Data Sorted by Assets            Comparative Historical Data

| 0-500M | 500M-2MM | 2-10MM | 10-50MM | 50-100MM | 100-250MM | Type of Statement | 4/1/07-3/31/08 ALL | 4/1/08-3/31/09 ALL |
|---|---|---|---|---|---|---|---|---|
| | | 3 | 3 | 1 | 5 | Unqualified | 10 | 12 |
| | | 3 | 8 | 1 | | Reviewed | 18 | 17 |
| 5 | 13 | 9 | 1 | | | Compiled | 25 | 15 |
| 35 | 24 | 12 | 1 | | | Tax Returns | 42 | 49 |
| 11 | 11 | 14 | 10 | | 3 | Other | 44 | 45 |
| | 22 (4/1-9/30/11) | | 151 (10/1/11-3/31/12) | | | | | |
| 51 | 48 | 41 | 23 | 2 | 8 | NUMBER OF STATEMENTS | 139 | 138 |
| % | % | % | % | % | % | **ASSETS** | % | % |
| 19.6 | 8.7 | 9.2 | 10.7 | | | Cash & Equivalents | 10.9 | 11.0 |
| 6.6 | 8.4 | 13.8 | 8.0 | | | Trade Receivables (net) | 9.5 | 8.7 |
| 48.8 | 48.0 | 38.5 | 50.6 | | | Inventory | 43.9 | 47.9 |
| 3.9 | 1.9 | 2.4 | 5.9 | | | All Other Current | 3.2 | 5.1 |
| 78.9 | 67.0 | 63.9 | 75.1 | | | Total Current | 67.4 | 72.6 |
| 14.5 | 21.9 | 21.7 | 18.0 | | | Fixed Assets (net) | 21.4 | 16.2 |
| 3.3 | 3.9 | 5.5 | 3.8 | | | Intangibles (net) | 4.8 | 4.3 |
| 3.3 | 7.2 | 8.8 | 3.1 | | | All Other Non-Current | 6.3 | 6.9 |
| 100.0 | 100.0 | 100.0 | 100.0 | | | Total | 100.0 | 100.0 |
| | | | | | | **LIABILITIES** | | |
| 19.1 | 11.0 | 10.0 | 11.6 | | | Notes Payable-Short Term | 8.6 | 10.9 |
| 3.2 | 1.2 | 2.2 | 2.5 | | | Cur. Mat.-L.T.D. | 2.4 | 3.5 |
| 18.5 | 17.4 | 14.6 | 18.2 | | | Trade Payables | 16.7 | 15.2 |
| .0 | .2 | .0 | .1 | | | Income Taxes Payable | .2 | .1 |
| 14.6 | 13.3 | 12.3 | 15.8 | | | All Other Current | 8.0 | 11.3 |
| 55.4 | 43.2 | 39.0 | 48.3 | | | Total Current | 35.9 | 40.9 |
| 12.3 | 17.5 | 14.2 | 7.9 | | | Long-Term Debt | 20.7 | 16.1 |
| .0 | .1 | .3 | .3 | | | Deferred Taxes | .1 | .1 |
| 18.6 | 8.9 | 9.1 | 1.7 | | | All Other Non-Current | 9.5 | 10.2 |
| 13.7 | 30.3 | 37.4 | 41.8 | | | Net Worth | 33.9 | 32.7 |
| 100.0 | 100.0 | 100.0 | 100.0 | | | Total Liabilities & Net Worth | 100.0 | 100.0 |
| | | | | | | **INCOME DATA** | | |
| 100.0 | 100.0 | 100.0 | 100.0 | | | Net Sales | 100.0 | 100.0 |
| 48.4 | 38.5 | 33.3 | 33.1 | | | Gross Profit | 41.5 | 39.4 |
| 41.8 | 36.1 | 29.1 | 27.9 | | | Operating Expenses | 37.7 | 35.3 |
| 6.5 | 2.3 | 4.2 | 5.2 | | | Operating Profit | 3.8 | 4.1 |
| -.2 | .4 | .1 | .3 | | | All Other Expenses (net) | .9 | 1.2 |
| 6.7 | 2.0 | 4.1 | 4.8 | | | Profit Before Taxes | 2.8 | 2.8 |
| | | | | | | **RATIOS** | | |
| 8.0 | 3.6 | 4.9 | 3.3 | | | | 3.6 | 4.0 |
| 1.9 | 2.1 | 1.5 | 1.4 | | | Current | 2.0 | 2.0 |
| 1.0 | 1.3 | 1.1 | 1.1 | | | | 1.3 | 1.3 |
| 2.1 | 1.0 | 1.2 | .8 | | | | 1.2 | 1.1 |
| .4 | .4 | .5 | (22) .4 | | | Quick | .4 (137) | .4 |
| .1 | .1 | .1 | .1 | | | | .1 | .1 |
| 0 UND | 0 UND | 0 UND | 1 647.4 | | | | 0 UND | 0 UND |
| 0 UND | 1 591.4 | 10 36.8 | 2 198.4 | | | Sales/Receivables | 2 178.4 | 2 183.7 |
| 10 35.2 | 13 27.6 | 34 10.6 | 7 49.3 | | | | 17 21.0 | 18 20.5 |
| 34 10.6 | 37 9.9 | 27 13.5 | 96 3.8 | | | | 41 9.0 | 47 7.7 |
| 83 4.4 | 96 3.8 | 81 4.5 | 135 2.7 | | | Cost of Sales/Inventory | 103 3.6 | 96 3.8 |
| 152 2.4 | 192 1.9 | 135 2.7 | 182 2.0 | | | | 167 2.2 | 166 2.2 |
| 0 UND | 5 73.2 | 8 45.6 | 17 21.7 | | | | 9 41.0 | 4 94.5 |
| 5 70.4 | 15 24.4 | 18 20.1 | 32 11.4 | | | Cost of Sales/Payables | 27 13.3 | 22 16.8 |
| 34 10.7 | 32 11.3 | 40 9.2 | 49 7.4 | | | | 52 7.1 | 42 8.7 |
| 3.8 | 4.7 | 3.9 | 4.0 | | | | 4.2 | 4.4 |
| 12.6 | 11.2 | 11.1 | 8.7 | | | Sales/Working Capital | 9.2 | 8.6 |
| 126.2 | 29.8 | 69.0 | 53.7 | | | | 28.3 | 28.7 |
| 18.8 | 14.5 | 15.1 | 20.1 | | | | 8.0 | 12.9 |
| (29) 4.5 | (44) 6.0 | (36) 4.0 | (21) 10.0 | | | EBIT/Interest | (119) 2.5 | (118) 3.7 |
| 1.5 | 1.3 | 1.5 | 4.6 | | | | 1.2 | .7 |
| | | | | | | Net Profit + Depr., Dep., | 18.9 | 16.9 |
| | | | | | | Amort./Cur. Mat. L/T/D | (23) 3.1 (18) | 3.0 |
| | | | | | | | 1.2 | 1.5 |
| .0 | .1 | .1 | .2 | | | | .2 | .1 |
| .3 | .4 | .4 | .5 | | | Fixed/Worth | .7 | .4 |
| -3.2 | -7.0 | 3.0 | 1.0 | | | | 8.4 | 1.9 |
| .5 | .6 | .8 | .6 | | | | .6 | .7 |
| 2.3 | 2.2 | 2.0 | 1.6 | | | Debt/Worth | 2.0 | 1.6 |
| -14.2 | -25.8 | 5.5 | 4.0 | | | | 17.4 | 7.3 |
| 101.9 | 61.1 | 39.7 | 61.1 | | | | 38.1 | 48.9 |
| (36) 51.9 | (35) 20.6 | (35) 14.3 | (21) 30.4 | | | % Profit Before Taxes/Tangible Net Worth | (107) 14.5 | (115) 13.7 |
| 9.3 | 6.8 | 6.2 | 11.0 | | | | 3.8 | 2.0 |
| 37.5 | 14.5 | 18.3 | 21.1 | | | | 13.3 | 18.7 |
| 17.3 | 8.0 | 3.7 | 9.6 | | | % Profit Before Taxes/Total Assets | 4.3 | 4.5 |
| 2.4 | 1.7 | 1.8 | 5.2 | | | | .8 | -.8 |
| 140.8 | 80.1 | 57.5 | 27.7 | | | | 45.7 | 71.6 |
| 62.2 | 29.5 | 20.2 | 21.3 | | | Sales/Net Fixed Assets | 21.4 | 29.6 |
| 20.4 | 8.1 | 7.8 | 11.6 | | | | 7.5 | 12.4 |
| 6.8 | 5.0 | 2.9 | 2.9 | | | | 3.8 | 4.4 |
| 3.8 | 3.1 | 2.5 | 2.4 | | | Sales/Total Assets | 2.4 | 2.8 |
| 2.3 | 1.8 | 1.6 | 1.9 | | | | 1.4 | 2.0 |
| .4 | .3 | .5 | .7 | | | | .6 | .4 |
| (32) .8 | (39) .7 | (33) .8 | (22) .8 | | | % Depr., Dep., Amort./Sales | (110) 1.2 (101) | .9 |
| 1.2 | 2.2 | 1.9 | 1.3 | | | | 2.0 | 1.6 |
| 4.7 | 2.2 | 1.3 | | | | | 2.0 | 1.9 |
| (29) 5.5 | (31) 3.5 | (17) 1.9 | | | | % Officers', Directors' Owners' Comp/Sales | (64) 3.6 (59) | 4.0 |
| 10.1 | 7.6 | 4.7 | | | | | 9.5 | 8.9 |
| 60334M | 206481M | 473318M | 1468975M | 89026M | 4211534M | Net Sales ($) | 5651576M | 5301191M |
| 13556M | 52329M | 181973M | 564007M | 117799M | 1431314M | Total Assets ($) | 2374406M | 1992501M |

M = $ thousand     MM = $ million
See Pages 9 through 22 for Explanation of Ratios and Data

## Comparative Historical Data | Current Data Sorted by Sales

| Comparative Historical Data | | | Type of Statement | | | | | | |
|---|---|---|---|---|---|---|---|---|---|
| 20 | 15 | 12 | Unqualified | | | | 1 | 2 | 10 |
| 19 | 18 | 12 | Reviewed | | | | 3 | 8 | 8 |
| 15 | 29 | 28 | Compiled | 4 | 5 | 1 | 10 | 6 | 2 |
| 61 | 52 | 72 | Tax Returns | 22 | 27 | 7 | 9 | 6 | 1 |
| 62 | 49 | 49 | Other | 9 | 8 | 6 | 7 | 8 | 11 |
| 4/1/09- | 4/1/10- | 4/1/11- | | | 22 (4/1-9/30/11) | | 151 (10/1/11-3/31/12) | | |
| 3/31/10 | 3/31/11 | 3/31/12 | | | | | | | |
| ALL | ALL | ALL | | 0-1MM | 1-3MM | 3-5MM | 5-10MM | 10-25MM | 25MM & OVER |
| 177 | 163 | 173 | NUMBER OF STATEMENTS | 35 | 40 | 14 | 27 | 25 | 32 |
| % | % | % | ASSETS | % | % | % | % | % | % |
| 12.3 | 11.1 | 12.3 | Cash & Equivalents | 17.6 | 12.7 | 10.5 | 10.0 | 10.6 | 9.9 |
| 8.8 | 7.2 | 9.0 | Trade Receivables (net) | 5.6 | 5.0 | 9.0 | 14.7 | 14.8 | 8.1 |
| 43.9 | 48.4 | 45.9 | Inventory | 50.5 | 44.5 | 44.4 | 45.1 | 41.6 | 47.0 |
| 2.8 | 2.3 | 3.1 | All Other Current | 2.9 | 2.8 | 3.0 | 1.3 | 5.3 | 3.7 |
| 67.8 | 69.0 | 70.2 | Total Current | 76.6 | 65.0 | 67.0 | 71.1 | 72.3 | 68.7 |
| 20.0 | 19.1 | 19.6 | Fixed Assets (net) | 14.7 | 26.0 | 25.6 | 15.9 | 13.6 | 22.0 |
| 6.1 | 5.0 | 4.2 | Intangibles (net) | 4.7 | 2.4 | 5.1 | 5.0 | 5.0 | 4.3 |
| 6.1 | 6.9 | 6.0 | All Other Non-Current | 4.0 | 6.5 | 2.3 | 8.0 | 9.0 | 5.1 |
| 100.0 | 100.0 | 100.0 | Total | 100.0 | 100.0 | 100.0 | 100.0 | 100.0 | 100.0 |
| | | | LIABILITIES | | | | | | |
| 9.9 | 9.3 | 12.6 | Notes Payable-Short Term | 17.1 | 12.7 | 17.2 | 11.7 | 9.5 | 8.8 |
| 2.6 | 2.9 | 2.4 | Cur. Mat.-L.T.D. | 2.7 | 1.0 | 6.9 | 2.4 | .7 | 3.1 |
| 14.9 | 16.4 | 17.1 | Trade Payables | 9.1 | 18.8 | 19.0 | 18.6 | 21.7 | 17.9 |
| .1 | .1 | .1 | Income Taxes Payable | .0 | .0 | .0 | .3 | .1 | .1 |
| 10.6 | 9.2 | 13.9 | All Other Current | 10.7 | 15.3 | 9.0 | 16.2 | 13.6 | 15.9 |
| 38.2 | 37.8 | 46.0 | Total Current | 39.6 | 47.7 | 52.1 | 49.2 | 45.6 | 45.8 |
| 20.0 | 20.3 | 15.1 | Long-Term Debt | 15.4 | 20.4 | 16.3 | 12.1 | 5.8 | 17.2 |
| .1 | .2 | .2 | Deferred Taxes | .0 | .0 | .0 | .3 | .4 | .4 |
| 11.1 | 9.0 | 10.6 | All Other Non-Current | 22.2 | 7.3 | 25.0 | 6.5 | 5.9 | 3.1 |
| 30.5 | 32.7 | 28.1 | Net Worth | 22.9 | 24.5 | 6.6 | 31.9 | 42.3 | 33.5 |
| 100.0 | 100.0 | 100.0 | Total Liabilities & Net Worth | 100.0 | 100.0 | 100.0 | 100.0 | 100.0 | 100.0 |
| | | | INCOME DATA | | | | | | |
| 100.0 | 100.0 | 100.0 | Net Sales | 100.0 | 100.0 | 100.0 | 100.0 | 100.0 | 100.0 |
| 40.1 | 36.7 | 39.7 | Gross Profit | 50.5 | 43.7 | 39.4 | 33.0 | 32.5 | 34.1 |
| 37.0 | 32.4 | 34.9 | Operating Expenses | 42.6 | 40.5 | 36.1 | 29.7 | 28.8 | 28.3 |
| 3.1 | 4.4 | 4.7 | Operating Profit | 7.8 | 3.2 | 3.4 | 3.3 | 3.6 | 5.8 |
| .8 | .8 | .3 | All Other Expenses (net) | .0 | .0 | .9 | .1 | .1 | 1.0 |
| 2.3 | 3.6 | 4.5 | Profit Before Taxes | 7.8 | 3.2 | 2.5 | 3.3 | 3.6 | 4.9 |
| | | | RATIOS | | | | | | |
| 4.1 | 3.8 | 3.8 | | 11.7 | 3.4 | 4.4 | 2.4 | 5.9 | 2.5 |
| 2.1 | 1.8 | 1.8 | Current | 2.9 | 1.9 | 2.0 | 1.5 | 1.5 | 1.5 |
| 1.2 | 1.2 | 1.1 | | 1.3 | 1.1 | .9 | 1.1 | 1.0 | 1.1 |
| 1.2 | 1.0 | 1.0 | | 2.9 | 1.0 | .9 | 1.0 | 1.2 | .8 |
| (176) .4 | (161) .4 | (172) .4 | Quick | .4 | .4 | .5 | .4 | (31) .7 | .3 |
| .1 | .2 | .1 | | .1 | .1 | .1 | .1 | .1 | .1 |
| 0 UND | 0 UND | 0 UND | | 0 UND | 0 UND | 0 UND | 0 UND | 0 999.8 | 0 944.3 |
| 2 184.8 | 2 153.7 | 1 474.7 | Sales/Receivables | 0 UND | 0 999.8 | 1 544.4 | 6 66.2 | 7 49.3 | 2 176.2 |
| 12 29.4 | 13 27.1 | 15 24.2 | | 10 35.0 | 11 33.6 | 16 22.8 | 34 10.7 | 26 14.0 | 13 27.9 |
| 36 10.2 | 51 7.2 | 38 9.7 | | 64 5.7 | 41 9.0 | 10 37.4 | 26 14.3 | 30 12.0 | 40 9.1 |
| 99 3.7 | 110 3.3 | 91 4.0 | Cost of Sales/Inventory | 126 2.9 | 83 4.4 | 65 5.6 | 78 4.7 | 79 4.6 | 111 3.3 |
| 181 2.0 | 164 2.2 | 159 2.3 | | 332 1.1 | 192 1.9 | 118 3.1 | 130 2.8 | 130 2.8 | 159 2.3 |
| 6 56.4 | 7 48.8 | 4 86.2 | | 0 UND | 3 124.8 | 7 49.0 | 9 41.8 | 10 35.2 | 19 19.3 |
| 23 15.7 | 27 13.5 | 18 20.0 | Cost of Sales/Payables | 6 64.8 | 10 36.1 | 23 15.8 | 15 24.4 | 29 12.6 | 31 11.7 |
| 48 7.7 | 48 7.6 | 42 8.6 | | 34 10.7 | 54 6.7 | 29 12.6 | 34 10.6 | 39 9.3 | 55 6.6 |
| 4.5 | 4.1 | 4.5 | | 2.1 | 4.4 | 5.6 | 7.8 | 4.8 | 5.9 |
| 8.0 | 10.3 | 11.4 | Sales/Working Capital | 5.6 | 13.3 | 14.4 | 14.6 | 10.6 | 12.1 |
| 31.1 | 35.0 | 38.6 | | 22.5 | 35.1 | -118.2 | 55.4 | NM | 77.9 |
| 15.9 | 10.7 | 15.4 | | 16.3 | 23.0 | 13.0 | 13.2 | 19.5 | 19.6 |
| (144) 3.9 | (136) 3.0 | (139) 5.5 | EBIT/Interest | (19) 3.8 | (31) 3.2 | (13) 9.1 | (25) 5.5 | (21) 7.3 | (30) 9.0 |
| .6 | 1.2 | 1.6 | | 1.9 | .5 | 1.2 | 1.6 | 2.7 | 3.4 |
| 9.0 | 12.9 | 7.3 | Net Profit + Depr., Dep., | | | | | | |
| (25) 3.7 | (17) 4.8 | (22) 4.2 | Amort./Cur. Mat. L/T/D | | | | | | |
| 2.2 | 2.4 | 1.8 | | | | | | | |
| .1 | .1 | .1 | | .0 | .1 | .2 | .1 | .1 | .3 |
| .5 | .6 | .4 | Fixed/Worth | .1 | .5 | NM | .2 | .3 | .6 |
| 2.7 | 4.5 | 3.4 | | UND | 6.0 | -.9 | 3.1 | .7 | 2.1 |
| .7 | .7 | .6 | | .3 | .5 | 1.8 | .7 | .7 | 1.1 |
| 2.1 | 2.3 | 2.1 | Debt/Worth | 1.5 | 2.4 | NM | 2.1 | 1.4 | 2.1 |
| 8.5 | 26.7 | 12.6 | | -31.4 | 23.3 | -6.2 | 5.3 | 6.0 | 6.9 |
| 50.9 | 58.2 | 56.8 | % Profit Before Taxes/Tangible | 65.7 | 77.4 | | 51.2 | 43.8 | 52.9 |
| (143) 19.5 | (130) 19.7 | (135) 24.7 | Net Worth | (26) 32.7 | (31) 25.2 | | (21) 14.3 | (22) 19.0 | (28) 30.8 |
| 4.4 | 4.1 | 7.1 | | 6.7 | 3.2 | | 6.0 | 10.0 | 13.3 |
| 16.3 | 15.0 | 20.2 | % Profit Before Taxes/Total | 35.9 | 31.5 | 19.4 | 16.7 | 19.8 | 16.5 |
| 6.1 | 5.2 | 8.9 | Assets | 10.2 | 8.7 | 6.9 | 4.9 | 9.4 | 9.5 |
| -.9 | .6 | 2.1 | | 2.1 | .5 | 1.0 | 2.0 | 1.4 | 4.1 |
| 56.2 | 83.2 | 79.8 | | 139.0 | 93.4 | 76.3 | 82.5 | 131.4 | 27.1 |
| 21.4 | 21.6 | 26.6 | Sales/Net Fixed Assets | 38.6 | 22.4 | 28.4 | 42.7 | 28.3 | 19.3 |
| 8.6 | 8.8 | 10.7 | | 9.0 | 5.7 | 6.8 | 20.2 | 12.0 | 12.0 |
| 3.8 | 3.8 | 4.4 | | 4.5 | 4.4 | 8.3 | 5.2 | 4.4 | 3.6 |
| 2.5 | 2.6 | 2.7 | Sales/Total Assets | 2.3 | 2.8 | 4.4 | 2.9 | 2.8 | 2.4 |
| 1.8 | 1.8 | 1.9 | | 1.3 | 1.7 | 2.3 | 2.3 | 2.1 | 2.0 |
| .7 | .6 | .5 | | .6 | .4 | .3 | .3 | .4 | .6 |
| (133) 1.2 | (123) .9 | (134) .8 | % Depr., Dep., Amort./Sales | (24) 1.1 | (30) .8 | (10) .8 | (22) .5 | (19) .8 | (29) .8 |
| 2.0 | 1.9 | 1.7 | | 3.0 | 2.5 | 1.2 | 1.7 | 1.6 | 1.5 |
| 1.8 | 1.8 | 1.8 | | 4.9 | 3.4 | | 1.1 | .9 | |
| (70) 3.9 | (61) 3.8 | (83) 4.5 | % Officers', Directors' Owners' Comp/Sales | (20) 8.5 | (22) 5.1 | | (15) 1.9 | (14) 1.7 | |
| 6.9 | 6.8 | 7.5 | | 12.5 | 7.5 | | 6.6 | 2.6 | |
| 8503183M | 7323733M | 6509668M | Net Sales ($) | 20310M | 70108M | 54858M | 189585M | 387433M | 5787374M |
| 3142103M | 2743407M | 2360978M | Total Assets ($) | 10638M | 38757M | 19270M | 64336M | 173957M | 2054020M |

© RMA 2012

M = $ thousand    MM = $ million
See Pages 9 through 22 for Explanation of Ratios and Data

## Current Data Sorted by Assets      Comparative Historical Data

| | | | | | | Type of Statement | | |
|---|---|---|---|---|---|---|---|---|
| | | | | | | Unqualified | | |
| 1 | | 1 | 1 | | | Reviewed | 2 | 1 |
| 2 | 3 | 7 | | | | Compiled | 3 | 4 |
| 19 | 4 | 2 | | | | Tax Returns | 13 | 18 |
| 9 | 5 | 3 | | | | Other | 31 | 30 |
| | 13 (4/1-9/30/11) | | 2 | 46 (10/1/11-3/31/12) | | | 22 | 8 |
| | | | | | | | 4/1/07-3/31/08 | 4/1/08-3/31/09 |
| 0-500M | 500M-2MM | 2-10MM | 10-50MM | 50-100MM | 100-250MM | | ALL | ALL |
| 31 | 12 | 13 | 3 | | | NUMBER OF STATEMENTS | 71 | 61 |
| % | % | % | % | % | % | ASSETS | % | % |
| 13.2 | 8.1 | 15.7 | | | | Cash & Equivalents | 10.2 | 7.7 |
| 11.2 | 14.0 | 11.6 | D | D | | Trade Receivables (net) | 15.8 | 13.5 |
| 23.1 | 25.4 | 23.2 | A | A | | Inventory | 23.2 | 23.0 |
| 2.4 | 10.5 | .7 | T | T | | All Other Current | 2.6 | 2.0 |
| 50.0 | 57.9 | 51.2 | A | A | | Total Current | 51.8 | 46.3 |
| 30.6 | 35.7 | 27.8 | | | | Fixed Assets (net) | 34.7 | 32.9 |
| 11.4 | 1.7 | 12.8 | N | N | | Intangibles (net) | 6.8 | 13.4 |
| 7.9 | 4.7 | 8.2 | O | O | | All Other Non-Current | 6.7 | 7.5 |
| 100.0 | 100.0 | 100.0 | T | T | | Total | 100.0 | 100.0 |
| | | | | | | LIABILITIES | | |
| 30.9 | 13.3 | 20.4 | A | A | | Notes Payable-Short Term | 17.4 | 12.3 |
| 6.5 | 2.1 | 1.4 | V | V | | Cur. Mat.-L.T.D. | 5.3 | 4.7 |
| 24.5 | 16.1 | 16.5 | A | A | | Trade Payables | 19.5 | 13.6 |
| .3 | .0 | .0 | I | I | | Income Taxes Payable | .1 | .0 |
| 19.8 | 20.4 | 14.1 | L | L | | All Other Current | 11.7 | 11.2 |
| 81.9 | 52.0 | 52.5 | A | A | | Total Current | 53.9 | 41.8 |
| 26.7 | 14.5 | 20.1 | B | B | | Long-Term Debt | 42.9 | 34.6 |
| .0 | .6 | .0 | L | L | | Deferred Taxes | .1 | .2 |
| 15.5 | 18.7 | 4.7 | E | E | | All Other Non-Current | 12.8 | 9.8 |
| -24.1 | 14.3 | 22.7 | | | | Net Worth | -9.8 | 13.6 |
| 100.0 | 100.0 | 100.0 | | | | Total Liabilties & Net Worth | 100.0 | 100.0 |
| | | | | | | INCOME DATA | | |
| 100.0 | 100.0 | 100.0 | | | | Net Sales | 100.0 | 100.0 |
| 56.1 | 54.8 | 47.2 | | | | Gross Profit | 53.7 | 53.4 |
| 52.0 | 56.1 | 47.4 | | | | Operating Expenses | 52.3 | 52.4 |
| 4.1 | -1.3 | -.2 | | | | Operating Profit | 1.4 | 1.0 |
| 1.5 | -.7 | -.9 | | | | All Other Expenses (net) | 1.2 | .4 |
| 2.6 | -.6 | .7 | | | | Profit Before Taxes | .2 | .6 |
| | | | | | | RATIOS | | |
| 2.1 | 2.9 | 1.9 | | | | | 2.6 | 2.1 |
| .9 | 1.4 | 1.1 | | | | Current | 1.3 | 1.2 |
| .4 | .9 | .7 | | | | | .8 | .7 |
| 1.0 | 1.4 | 1.3 | | | | | 1.3 | 1.0 |
| .5 | .5 | .6 | | | | Quick | .6 | .6 |
| .2 | .2 | .3 | | | | | .2 | .2 |
| 0 UND | 5 76.6 | 3 127.7 | | | | | 5 77.2 | 4 88.3 |
| 7 50.6 | 11 33.2 | 16 23.5 | | | | Sales/Receivables | 13 28.8 | 12 30.7 |
| 11 33.1 | 22 16.5 | 21 17.5 | | | | | 26 14.2 | 20 18.6 |
| 13 27.5 | 24 14.9 | 26 14.1 | | | | | 21 17.1 | 19 19.5 |
| 33 11.1 | 43 8.5 | 51 7.1 | | | | Cost of Sales/Inventory | 53 6.9 | 36 10.2 |
| 73 5.0 | 89 4.1 | 69 5.3 | | | | | 90 4.0 | 93 3.9 |
| 0 UND | 16 22.2 | 15 24.9 | | | | | 8 47.8 | 10 35.8 |
| 37 9.8 | 34 10.7 | 36 10.0 | | | | Cost of Sales/Payables | 34 10.9 | 34 10.8 |
| 51 7.1 | 45 8.1 | 63 5.8 | | | | | 58 6.3 | 53 6.8 |
| 16.6 | 6.4 | 6.7 | | | | | 9.7 | 10.1 |
| -49.5 | 37.3 | 105.7 | | | | Sales/Working Capital | 34.6 | 66.8 |
| -7.7 | -229.8 | -20.4 | | | | | -22.6 | -33.5 |
| 6.2 | | 4.8 | | | | | 5.8 | 4.6 |
| (24) 2.1 | (11) 2.3 | | | | | EBIT/Interest | (58) 1.5 | (57) 1.8 |
| .6 | | -2.3 | | | | | .0 | -.1 |
| | | | | | | Net Profit + Depr., Dep., Amort./Cur. Mat. L/T/D | | |
| 1.7 | .4 | .2 | | | | | .4 | .5 |
| -.8 | 1.6 | 1.9 | | | | Fixed/Worth | 2.0 | 1.9 |
| -.3 | -2.3 | -3.9 | | | | | -.8 | -1.3 |
| 1.4 | .6 | 1.1 | | | | | .8 | 1.6 |
| -4.1 | 3.1 | 2.8 | | | | Debt/Worth | 4.0 | 6.6 |
| -2.0 | -4.6 | -19.1 | | | | | -2.9 | -3.7 |
| 71.4 | | | | | | | 58.9 | 46.9 |
| (10) 28.2 | | | | | | % Profit Before Taxes/Tangible Net Worth | (41) 22.9 | (38) 9.6 |
| -.5 | | | | | | | 1.1 | -5.2 |
| 18.3 | 5.8 | 5.6 | | | | | 13.1 | 9.1 |
| 2.2 | -3.4 | 2.8 | | | | % Profit Before Taxes/Total Assets | 1.7 | 3.0 |
| -2.0 | -11.1 | -2.5 | | | | | -3.8 | -4.7 |
| 52.2 | 26.7 | 74.0 | | | | | 31.8 | 64.0 |
| 19.6 | 9.9 | 16.3 | | | | Sales/Net Fixed Assets | 10.1 | 12.9 |
| 7.7 | 7.1 | 4.2 | | | | | 5.5 | 5.1 |
| 9.0 | 4.7 | 4.2 | | | | | 4.9 | 4.9 |
| 4.0 | 3.9 | 2.4 | | | | Sales/Total Assets | 3.0 | 2.8 |
| 2.1 | 2.4 | 1.3 | | | | | 1.8 | 1.9 |
| .5 | 1.4 | .5 | | | | | 1.1 | 1.1 |
| (21) 1.4 | (11) 2.1 | (12) 1.0 | | | | % Depr., Dep., Amort./Sales | (55) 2.0 | (52) 1.9 |
| 3.4 | 2.3 | 4.0 | | | | | 3.4 | 3.2 |
| 4.2 | | | | | | | 3.5 | 3.0 |
| (14) 6.3 | | | | | | % Officers', Directors' Owners' Comp/Sales | (46) 6.0 | (35) 5.3 |
| 8.5 | | | | | | | 10.3 | 8.6 |
| 29189M | 44255M | 139488M | 80639M | | | Net Sales ($) | 449284M | 798579M |
| 6264M | 10839M | 47041M | 59876M | | | Total Assets ($) | 195675M | 169612M |

M = $ thousand    MM = $ million
See Pages 9 through 22 for Explanation of Ratios and Data

## Comparative Historical Data | Current Data Sorted by Sales

| 4/1/09-3/31/10 ALL | 4/1/10-3/31/11 ALL | 4/1/11-3/31/12 ALL | Type of Statement | 0-1MM | 1-3MM | 3-5MM | 5-10MM | 10-25MM | 25MM & OVER |
|---|---|---|---|---|---|---|---|---|---|
| 2 | 1 | 1 | Unqualified | | | | | | 1 |
| 3 | 4 | 2 | Reviewed | | 1 | 1 | | | |
| 7 | 11 | 12 | Compiled | 1 | 4 | 3 | 2 | 1 | 1 |
| 25 | 25 | 25 | Tax Returns | 14 | 7 | 1 | 3 | | |
| 15 | 12 | 19 | Other | 5 | 7 | | 2 | 4 | 1 |
| 4/1/09-3/31/10 ALL | 4/1/10-3/31/11 ALL | 4/1/11-3/31/12 ALL | | 13 (4/1-9/30/11) | | | 46 (10/1/11-3/31/12) | | |
| **52** | **53** | **59** | **NUMBER OF STATEMENTS** | **20** | **19** | **5** | **7** | **5** | **3** |
| % | % | % | **ASSETS** | % | % | % | % | % | % |
| 11.7 | 15.1 | 12.3 | Cash & Equivalents | 12.9 | 10.0 | | | | |
| 14.9 | 12.1 | 11.4 | Trade Receivables (net) | 6.0 | 17.9 | | | | |
| 20.6 | 27.6 | 23.0 | Inventory | 15.4 | 33.5 | | | | |
| 3.6 | 2.8 | 3.6 | All Other Current | 7.1 | .7 | | | | |
| 50.8 | 57.7 | 50.3 | Total Current | 41.5 | 62.3 | | | | |
| 36.2 | 27.0 | 32.4 | Fixed Assets (net) | 35.2 | 29.2 | | | | |
| 6.8 | 6.6 | 9.2 | Intangibles (net) | 13.1 | 5.4 | | | | |
| 6.2 | 8.8 | 8.0 | All Other Non-Current | 10.1 | 3.2 | | | | |
| 100.0 | 100.0 | 100.0 | Total | 100.0 | 100.0 | | | | |
| | | | **LIABILITIES** | | | | | | |
| 10.8 | 10.2 | 23.6 | Notes Payable-Short Term | 19.4 | 31.3 | | | | |
| 4.7 | 4.8 | 4.3 | Cur. Mat.-L.T.D. | 3.7 | 6.8 | | | | |
| 27.9 | 18.5 | 20.3 | Trade Payables | 15.5 | 28.4 | | | | |
| .1 | .1 | .2 | Income Taxes Payable | .0 | .5 | | | | |
| 17.9 | 11.7 | 17.7 | All Other Current | 16.6 | 20.0 | | | | |
| 61.3 | 45.4 | 66.1 | Total Current | 55.2 | 86.9 | | | | |
| 40.8 | 22.4 | 24.5 | Long-Term Debt | 29.6 | 20.2 | | | | |
| .0 | .0 | .1 | Deferred Taxes | .0 | .0 | | | | |
| 14.6 | 16.9 | 13.0 | All Other Non-Current | 10.1 | 26.4 | | | | |
| -16.6 | 15.3 | -3.7 | Net Worth | 5.1 | -33.6 | | | | |
| 100.0 | 100.0 | 100.0 | Total Liabilties & Net Worth | 100.0 | 100.0 | | | | |
| | | | **INCOME DATA** | | | | | | |
| 100.0 | 100.0 | 100.0 | Net Sales | 100.0 | 100.0 | | | | |
| 54.4 | 55.5 | 53.2 | Gross Profit | 56.2 | 55.8 | | | | |
| 53.3 | 54.8 | 51.2 | Operating Expenses | 51.6 | 55.4 | | | | |
| 1.1 | .6 | 2.0 | Operating Profit | 4.6 | .4 | | | | |
| .4 | -.1 | .5 | All Other Expenses (net) | 1.7 | -.2 | | | | |
| .7 | .8 | 1.5 | Profit Before Taxes | 2.9 | .6 | | | | |
| | | | **RATIOS** | | | | | | |
| 1.8 | 3.5 | 2.1 | Current | 2.7 | 2.5 | | | | |
| 1.2 | 1.1 | 1.0 | | 1.0 | 1.1 | | | | |
| .8 | .7 | .6 | | .4 | .6 | | | | |
| .9 | 1.4 | 1.0 | Quick | 1.3 | .9 | | | | |
| .5 | .6 | .5 | | .5 | .5 | | | | |
| .3 | .3 | .2 | | .2 | .2 | | | | |
| 7  49.4 | 2  161.6 | 2  195.5 | Sales/Receivables | 0  UND | 7  51.7 | | | | |
| 13  27.6 | 10  37.6 | 10  37.2 | | 3  137.7 | 10  35.4 | | | | |
| 22  16.6 | 22  16.6 | 17  22.1 | | 11  32.1 | 14  26.8 | | | | |
| 22  16.2 | 24  15.2 | 20  18.5 | Cost of Sales/Inventory | 9  42.1 | 31  11.9 | | | | |
| 38  9.6 | 59  6.2 | 39  9.3 | | 22  16.3 | 46  8.0 | | | | |
| 104  3.5 | 112  3.3 | 74  4.9 | | 70  5.2 | 89  4.1 | | | | |
| 9  39.7 | 16  22.8 | 13  27.7 | Cost of Sales/Payables | 0  UND | 24  14.9 | | | | |
| 42  8.7 | 41  8.9 | 37  9.9 | | 30  12.3 | 43  8.5 | | | | |
| 66  5.5 | 78  4.7 | 51  7.1 | | 51  7.1 | 47  7.7 | | | | |
| 11.0 | 8.4 | 10.2 | Sales/Working Capital | 9.0 | 9.0 | | | | |
| 50.6 | 44.3 | 999.8 | | NM | 107.5 | | | | |
| -25.7 | -25.6 | -19.3 | | -8.5 | -23.2 | | | | |
| 5.6 | 3.7 | 3.3 | EBIT/Interest | 7.8 | 2.6 | | | | |
| (45)  1.4 | (37)  .8 | (46)  1.7 | | (15)  2.7 | (14)  1.4 | | | | |
| -.4 | -3.3 | -.1 | | .4 | -.7 | | | | |
| | | | Net Profit + Depr., Dep., Amort./Cur. Mat. L/T/D | | | | | | |
| .6 | .2 | .8 | Fixed/Worth | 1.1 | .9 | | | | |
| 7.2 | 1.4 | 10.9 | | -1.7 | -1.7 | | | | |
| -1.7 | -1.5 | -.5 | | -.5 | -.1 | | | | |
| 3.1 | .5 | 1.1 | Debt/Worth | 1.1 | 1.1 | | | | |
| 15.3 | 3.0 | 34.5 | | -6.5 | -4.1 | | | | |
| -3.5 | -5.0 | -2.7 | | -2.3 | -2.0 | | | | |
| 135.2 | 25.2 | 28.4 | % Profit Before Taxes/Tangible Net Worth | | | | | | |
| (31)  28.9 | (35)  -1.6 | (30)  9.6 | | | | | | | |
| 2.6 | -12.8 | .3 | | | | | | | |
| 16.7 | 6.1 | 11.4 | % Profit Before Taxes/Total Assets | 19.0 | 7.0 | | | | |
| 1.6 | .0 | 2.1 | | 1.3 | 1.3 | | | | |
| -7.2 | -6.2 | -3.2 | | -5.1 | -6.9 | | | | |
| 29.7 | 98.2 | 45.7 | Sales/Net Fixed Assets | 47.8 | 165.3 | | | | |
| 13.2 | 15.5 | 15.2 | | 11.8 | 20.3 | | | | |
| 3.3 | 6.5 | 5.6 | | 3.5 | 7.7 | | | | |
| 4.7 | 5.6 | 5.0 | Sales/Total Assets | 4.3 | 9.0 | | | | |
| 2.7 | 3.4 | 3.5 | | 2.9 | 4.3 | | | | |
| 1.7 | 2.3 | 1.9 | | 1.4 | 2.7 | | | | |
| 1.2 | .5 | .7 | % Depr., Dep., Amort./Sales | .4 | .8 | | | | |
| (40)  2.2 | (45)  1.6 | (47)  1.6 | | (15)  1.7 | (13)  1.7 | | | | |
| 3.8 | 2.7 | 3.1 | | 3.8 | 2.5 | | | | |
| 2.4 | 3.1 | 2.8 | % Officers', Directors' Owners' Comp/Sales | 4.2 | | | | | |
| (30)  5.4 | (27)  6.0 | (25)  5.4 | | (10)  6.0 | | | | | |
| 7.2 | 9.2 | 7.0 | | 8.9 | | | | | |
| 157394M | 1065344M | 293571M | Net Sales ($) | 9481M | 32173M | 19328M | 42739M | 82647M | 107203M |
| 69580M | 304262M | 124020M | Total Assets ($) | 3791M | 10368M | 13760M | 12465M | 46226M | 37410M |

© RMA 2012

**M = $ thousand    MM = $ million**
See Pages 9 through 22 for Explanation of Ratios and Data

## Current Data Sorted by Assets      Comparative Historical Data

| | | | | | | Type of Statement | | |
|---|---|---|---|---|---|---|---|---|
| 1 | 5 | 2<br>8 | 1<br>2 | 1 | | Unqualified | 7 | 3 |
| 3 | 11 | 7 | | | | Reviewed | 15 | 14 |
| 12 | 15 | 8 | | | | Compiled | 28 | 30 |
| 5 | 11 | 13 | | | | Tax Returns | 20 | 29 |
| | 26 (4/1-9/30/11) | | 86 (10/1/11-3/31/12) | | | Other | 37 | 40 |
| | | | | | | | 4/1/07-<br>3/31/08 | 4/1/08-<br>3/31/09 |
| 0-500M | 500M-2MM | 2-10MM | 10-50MM | 50-100MM | 100-250MM | | ALL | ALL |
| 21 | 42 | 38 | 7 | 3 | 1 | NUMBER OF STATEMENTS | 107 | 116 |
| % | % | % | % | % | % | ASSETS | % | % |
| 18.0 | 9.5 | 9.1 | | | | Cash & Equivalents | 9.8 | 10.0 |
| 13.7 | 36.7 | 31.3 | | | | Trade Receivables (net) | 29.8 | 29.4 |
| 32.7 | 30.4 | 22.2 | | | | Inventory | 32.1 | 29.2 |
| 1.6 | 2.2 | 2.8 | | | | All Other Current | 2.5 | 1.5 |
| 66.0 | 78.9 | 65.3 | | | | Total Current | 74.2 | 70.2 |
| 20.7 | 9.3 | 18.6 | | | | Fixed Assets (net) | 13.4 | 17.6 |
| 7.2 | 4.2 | 7.5 | | | | Intangibles (net) | 6.0 | 4.9 |
| 6.1 | 7.6 | 8.6 | | | | All Other Non-Current | 6.4 | 7.3 |
| 100.0 | 100.0 | 100.0 | | | | Total | 100.0 | 100.0 |
| | | | | | | LIABILITIES | | |
| 26.4 | 16.7 | 10.7 | | | | Notes Payable-Short Term | 13.2 | 17.3 |
| 7.7 | 3.5 | 3.5 | | | | Cur. Mat.-L.T.D. | 4.9 | 5.1 |
| 13.6 | 22.0 | 17.8 | | | | Trade Payables | 27.2 | 26.0 |
| .0 | .1 | .0 | | | | Income Taxes Payable | .1 | .2 |
| 13.0 | 12.5 | 10.5 | | | | All Other Current | 13.9 | 12.1 |
| 60.8 | 54.9 | 42.5 | | | | Total Current | 59.3 | 60.7 |
| 37.0 | 13.1 | 11.3 | | | | Long-Term Debt | 16.3 | 15.2 |
| .0 | .1 | .1 | | | | Deferred Taxes | .1 | .1 |
| 22.5 | 4.7 | 6.4 | | | | All Other Non-Current | 6.0 | 3.8 |
| -20.3 | 27.2 | 39.7 | | | | Net Worth | 18.4 | 20.3 |
| 100.0 | 100.0 | 100.0 | | | | Total Liabilities & Net Worth | 100.0 | 100.0 |
| | | | | | | INCOME DATA | | |
| 100.0 | 100.0 | 100.0 | | | | Net Sales | 100.0 | 100.0 |
| 51.4 | 35.5 | 37.0 | | | | Gross Profit | 37.7 | 38.7 |
| 44.3 | 34.5 | 33.3 | | | | Operating Expenses | 35.8 | 37.1 |
| 7.0 | .9 | 3.7 | | | | Operating Profit | 1.9 | 1.7 |
| 1.2 | .3 | .1 | | | | All Other Expenses (net) | .4 | .4 |
| 5.9 | .7 | 3.5 | | | | Profit Before Taxes | 1.5 | 1.2 |
| | | | | | | RATIOS | | |
| 5.5 | 2.1 | 2.5 | | | | | 2.1 | 1.9 |
| 2.0 | 1.5 | 1.6 | | | | Current | 1.5 | 1.2 |
| .9 | 1.0 | 1.2 | | | | | 1.0 | .8 |
| 2.5 | 1.2 | 1.4 | | | | | 1.2 | 1.1 |
| .9 | .7 | .9 | | | | Quick | .7 | .7 |
| .2 | .6 | .7 | | | | | .4 | .4 |
| 0 UND | 25 14.5 | 21 17.2 | | | | | 11 32.1 | 15 24.1 |
| 3 107.2 | 30 12.3 | 31 11.6 | | | | Sales/Receivables | 28 12.9 | 28 12.9 |
| 26 14.1 | 44 8.3 | 41 9.0 | | | | | 37 9.7 | 39 9.3 |
| 3 141.5 | 21 17.4 | 12 30.4 | | | | | 24 14.9 | 19 18.7 |
| 56 6.5 | 39 9.3 | 39 9.4 | | | | Cost of Sales/Inventory | 50 7.3 | 40 9.1 |
| 83 4.4 | 83 4.4 | 62 5.9 | | | | | 95 3.8 | 106 3.4 |
| 0 UND | 16 23.5 | 11 33.7 | | | | | 19 18.7 | 18 20.7 |
| 9 39.8 | 26 14.3 | 25 14.4 | | | | Cost of Sales/Payables | 30 12.2 | 34 10.7 |
| 37 9.9 | 33 10.9 | 39 9.4 | | | | | 53 6.9 | 54 6.7 |
| 6.5 | 8.9 | 7.1 | | | | | 9.2 | 12.0 |
| 16.1 | 16.7 | 14.9 | | | | Sales/Working Capital | 16.2 | 40.8 |
| UND | NM | 43.5 | | | | | 200.6 | -26.3 |
| 16.9 | 5.9 | 7.2 | | | | | 6.9 | 5.8 |
| (14) 2.7 | (37) 1.8 | (37) 4.2 | | | | EBIT/Interest | (97) 2.3 | (107) 1.8 |
| .1 | -1.8 | 1.2 | | | | | .7 | -.6 |
| | | | | | | Net Profit + Depr., Dep., | 6.3 | 5.0 |
| | | | | | | Amort./Cur. Mat. L/T/D | (18) 2.9 | (15) 2.1 |
| | | | | | | | 1.6 | 1.7 |
| .3 | .1 | .2 | | | | | .1 | .2 |
| 1.5 | .3 | .5 | | | | Fixed/Worth | .4 | .8 |
| -.3 | 1.3 | 1.9 | | | | | -4.0 | -8.9 |
| .7 | 1.4 | .8 | | | | | .8 | 1.3 |
| 10.4 | 2.0 | 2.4 | | | | Debt/Worth | 2.4 | 3.5 |
| -1.9 | 8.8 | 5.0 | | | | | -22.6 | -13.4 |
| 299.0 | 28.8 | 34.6 | | | | | 32.0 | 43.1 |
| (12) 72.7 | (33) 4.9 | (32) 14.9 | | | | % Profit Before Taxes/Tangible<br>Net Worth | (76) 13.2 | (84) 14.3 |
| 18.3 | -12.2 | 1.0 | | | | | 2.4 | -6.2 |
| 62.7 | 6.6 | 14.2 | | | | | 13.0 | 13.3 |
| 17.4 | 1.1 | 4.9 | | | | % Profit Before Taxes/Total<br>Assets | 3.4 | 1.9 |
| 2.3 | -4.1 | .3 | | | | | -.3 | -3.9 |
| 108.2 | 163.8 | 61.3 | | | | | 90.6 | 71.5 |
| 44.7 | 45.9 | 31.6 | | | | Sales/Net Fixed Assets | 40.4 | 34.7 |
| 23.0 | 21.7 | 10.4 | | | | | 18.5 | 13.0 |
| 7.3 | 4.8 | 4.7 | | | | | 5.3 | 5.2 |
| 3.7 | 3.9 | 3.3 | | | | Sales/Total Assets | 3.4 | 3.4 |
| 2.0 | 3.1 | 2.3 | | | | | 2.5 | 2.3 |
| .5 | .2 | .6 | | | | | .4 | .4 |
| (13) 1.4 | (32) .6 | (31) .9 | | | | % Depr., Dep., Amort./Sales | (82) .7 | (96) .8 |
| 2.1 | 1.2 | 1.8 | | | | | 1.6 | 1.7 |
| 4.9 | 2.6 | 2.2 | | | | | 2.0 | 1.7 |
| (14) 6.6 | (21) 4.6 | (15) 3.7 | | | | % Officers', Directors'<br>Owners' Comp/Sales | (47) 3.3 | (52) 2.9 |
| 13.7 | 6.0 | 6.1 | | | | | 6.4 | 8.3 |
| 23332M | 196005M | 593496M | 380472M | 432649M | 160804M | Net Sales ($) | 1449974M | 2184617M |
| 4890M | 48854M | 166243M | 112905M | 166325M | 151427M | Total Assets ($) | 569719M | 689537M |

© RMA 2012

M = $ thousand    MM = $ million
See Pages 9 through 22 for Explanation of Ratios and Data

## Comparative Historical Data | Current Data Sorted by Sales

Historical columns: **4/1/09-3/31/10 ALL**, **4/1/10-3/31/11 ALL**, **4/1/11-3/31/12 ALL**
Current columns span: **26 (4/1-9/30/11)** for 0-1MM / 1-3MM / 3-5MM and **86 (10/1/11-3/31/12)** for 5-10MM / 10-25MM / 25MM & OVER.

| | 4/1/09-3/31/10 ALL | 4/1/10-3/31/11 ALL | 4/1/11-3/31/12 ALL | 0-1MM | 1-3MM | 3-5MM | 5-10MM | 10-25MM | 25MM & OVER |
|---|---|---|---|---|---|---|---|---|---|
| **Type of Statement** | | | | | | | | | |
| Unqualified | 7 | 6 | 4 | | | | 2 | 2 | 2 |
| Reviewed | 12 | 18 | 16 | 1 | 2 | 3 | 2 | 5 | 3 |
| Compiled | 24 | 17 | 21 | 1 | 2 | 6 | 6 | 3 | 3 |
| Tax Returns | 33 | 23 | 35 | 11 | 9 | 4 | 6 | 5 | |
| Other | 37 | 42 | 36 | 2 | 7 | 3 | 11 | 5 | 8 |
| **NUMBER OF STATEMENTS** | 113 | 106 | 112 | 15 | 20 | 16 | 25 | 20 | 16 |
| | % | % | % | % | % | % | % | % | % |
| **ASSETS** | | | | | | | | | |
| Cash & Equivalents | 8.7 | 11.0 | 10.2 | 16.2 | 8.7 | 10.2 | 16.1 | 5.4 | 3.6 |
| Trade Receivables (net) | 29.2 | 25.9 | 30.4 | 7.3 | 31.7 | 33.6 | 31.4 | 35.7 | 38.7 |
| Inventory | 27.8 | 26.5 | 26.9 | 32.5 | 28.4 | 35.0 | 26.4 | 22.7 | 17.6 |
| All Other Current | 3.1 | 4.2 | 2.5 | .6 | 1.7 | 2.1 | 3.9 | 2.4 | 3.5 |
| Total Current | 68.8 | 67.5 | 70.0 | 56.7 | 70.6 | 80.9 | 77.8 | 66.1 | 63.3 |
| Fixed Assets (net) | 17.4 | 13.7 | 15.2 | 25.5 | 12.5 | 11.4 | 12.5 | 15.1 | 16.8 |
| Intangibles (net) | 5.8 | 9.3 | 7.5 | 9.7 | 4.9 | 1.2 | 4.6 | 10.1 | 16.2 |
| All Other Non-Current | 8.0 | 9.4 | 7.4 | 8.1 | 12.1 | 6.5 | 5.1 | 8.6 | 3.7 |
| Total | 100.0 | 100.0 | 100.0 | 100.0 | 100.0 | 100.0 | 100.0 | 100.0 | 100.0 |
| **LIABILITIES** | | | | | | | | | |
| Notes Payable-Short Term | 16.0 | 13.5 | 16.7 | 34.3 | 13.0 | 12.8 | 16.3 | 11.3 | 15.9 |
| Cur. Mat.-L.T.D. | 3.4 | 4.2 | 4.2 | 9.5 | 4.1 | 5.4 | 2.0 | 3.7 | 2.1 |
| Trade Payables | 22.4 | 22.7 | 18.7 | 12.5 | 20.2 | 16.6 | 18.6 | 21.2 | 22.0 |
| Income Taxes Payable | .1 | .3 | .1 | .0 | .0 | .1 | .0 | .1 | .2 |
| All Other Current | 10.5 | 11.3 | 12.3 | 16.5 | 6.8 | 17.0 | 10.3 | 12.1 | 14.1 |
| Total Current | 52.4 | 52.0 | 52.0 | 72.8 | 44.0 | 51.8 | 47.3 | 48.3 | 54.3 |
| Long-Term Debt | 14.2 | 14.6 | 16.6 | 39.6 | 26.5 | 11.5 | 9.9 | 7.7 | 9.4 |
| Deferred Taxes | .1 | .1 | .2 | .0 | .0 | .0 | .3 | .1 | .7 |
| All Other Non-Current | 5.2 | 6.8 | 8.8 | 30.9 | 3.2 | 6.6 | 6.0 | 5.3 | 5.9 |
| Net Worth | 28.0 | 26.4 | 22.5 | -43.2 | 26.3 | 30.1 | 36.6 | 38.6 | 29.7 |
| Total Liabilities & Net Worth | 100.0 | 100.0 | 100.0 | 100.0 | 100.0 | 100.0 | 100.0 | 100.0 | 100.0 |
| **INCOME DATA** | | | | | | | | | |
| Net Sales | 100.0 | 100.0 | 100.0 | 100.0 | 100.0 | 100.0 | 100.0 | 100.0 | 100.0 |
| Gross Profit | 38.7 | 38.9 | 39.4 | 50.0 | 42.3 | 39.7 | 37.7 | 33.5 | 35.3 |
| Operating Expenses | 37.3 | 36.7 | 36.2 | 43.5 | 37.4 | 37.4 | 35.2 | 32.0 | 33.8 |
| Operating Profit | 1.3 | 2.2 | 3.1 | 6.5 | 4.9 | 2.3 | 2.5 | 1.5 | 1.6 |
| All Other Expenses (net) | .3 | .5 | .4 | 1.0 | 1.3 | .8 | -.4 | .2 | -.2 |
| Profit Before Taxes | 1.0 | 1.7 | 2.7 | 5.5 | 3.7 | 1.5 | 2.9 | 1.3 | 1.7 |
| **RATIOS** | | | | | | | | | |
| Current | 2.0 | 2.1 | 2.3 | 5.3 | 3.0 | 2.3 | 2.9 | 2.3 | 1.4 |
| | 1.3 | 1.3 | 1.5 | 1.2 | 1.8 | 1.6 | 1.7 | 1.3 | 1.1 |
| | 1.0 | 1.0 | 1.0 | .6 | 1.2 | 1.3 | 1.1 | 1.0 | 1.0 |
| Quick | 1.2 | 1.3 | 1.3 | 1.8 | 2.0 | 1.3 | 1.6 | 1.3 | 1.0 |
| | .8 | .8 | .8 | .4 | .9 | .7 | 1.0 | .9 | .8 |
| | .4 | .4 | .5 | .1 | .7 | .5 | .6 | .7 | .7 |
| Sales/Receivables | 21  17.6 | 12  30.6 | 19  18.8 | 0  UND | 29  12.7 | 25  14.8 | 20  18.5 | 26  14.0 | 28  12.9 |
| | 29  12.4 | 29  12.7 | 30  12.1 | 1  529.0 | 37  9.8 | 28  12.9 | 27  13.5 | 31  11.6 | 37  9.8 |
| | 40  9.1 | 36  10.1 | 42  8.7 | 19  19.7 | 49  7.4 | 41  9.0 | 41  8.8 | 38  9.6 | 47  7.7 |
| Cost of Sales/Inventory | 16  23.0 | 18  20.1 | 17  20.9 | 2  198.0 | 20  18.4 | 32  11.5 | 21  17.2 | 9  40.7 | 13  27.2 |
| | 39  9.4 | 40  9.2 | 39  9.3 | 41  8.8 | 63  5.8 | 54  6.7 | 38  9.7 | 39  9.4 | 25  14.7 |
| | 93  3.9 | 74  4.9 | 76  4.8 | 243  1.5 | 94  3.9 | 94  3.9 | 52  7.0 | 55  6.6 | 37  9.9 |
| Cost of Sales/Payables | 20  18.7 | 18  19.8 | 11  32.5 | 0  UND | 19  19.4 | 11  32.5 | 12  29.6 | 12  31.1 | 21  17.4 |
| | 34  10.8 | 28  13.1 | 25  14.6 | 0  UND | 32  11.3 | 22  16.8 | 26  14.1 | 25  14.4 | 30  12.3 |
| | 49  7.4 | 49  7.4 | 35  10.3 | 29  12.4 | 61  6.0 | 34  10.6 | 32  11.3 | 33  11.1 | 42  8.7 |
| Sales/Working Capital | 9.7 | 9.1 | 8.0 | 6.4 | 4.9 | 9.4 | 7.7 | 7.7 | 18.6 |
| | 22.4 | 21.0 | 17.3 | 19.7 | 11.1 | 14.8 | 13.2 | 25.7 | 46.8 |
| | -165.8 | -122.3 | 129.0 | -90.2 | 34.8 | 22.7 | 63.0 | -491.8 | -419.4 |
| EBIT/Interest | 7.6 | 9.7 | 7.3 | 16.9 | 4.1 | 3.1 | 14.9 | 7.3 | 10.0 |
| | (104) 1.9 | (97) 2.9 | (99) 2.8 | (10) 2.7 | (16) 1.7 | (14) 1.7 | (24) 2.5 | (19) 4.2 | 5.8 |
| | .0 | 1.0 | .7 | -3.7 | .8 | -2.8 | -1.2 | 1.2 | 1.9 |
| Net Profit + Depr., Dep., Amort./Cur. Mat. L/T/D | 5.7 | 6.2 | 4.4 | | | | | | |
| | (18) 2.4 | (15) 2.5 | (19) 3.2 | | | | | | |
| | -.6 | 1.3 | .6 | | | | | | |
| Fixed/Worth | .2 | .1 | .2 | .5 | .2 | .1 | .1 | .2 | .4 |
| | .7 | .6 | .5 | -9.0 | .6 | .3 | .3 | .8 | 1.1 |
| | 4.8 | 4.8 | UND | -.2 | -.6 | .8 | .7 | NM | -2.0 |
| Debt/Worth | 1.0 | 1.3 | 1.2 | .9 | .6 | 1.1 | 1.4 | .9 | 1.9 |
| | 2.6 | 2.6 | 2.5 | -105.0 | 2.5 | 1.5 | 2.4 | 1.8 | 4.7 |
| | 33.1 | NM | UND | -1.7 | -9.9 | 2.8 | 4.1 | NM | -17.7 |
| % Profit Before Taxes/Tangible Net Worth | 35.7 | 38.3 | 49.1 | | 56.2 | 20.1 | 68.1 | 35.2 | 50.4 |
| | (87) 5.8 | (80) 10.2 | (84) 14.8 | | (14)* 11.0 | (14) 6.3 | (23) 8.7 | (15) 10.9 | (11) 32.6 |
| | -1.7 | .3 | 1.0 | | 1.0 | -4.8 | -15.9 | 1.1 | 13.4 |
| % Profit Before Taxes/Total Assets | 11.6 | 10.8 | 12.0 | 66.4 | 10.0 | 5.4 | 16.2 | 12.1 | 10.3 |
| | 2.3 | 3.5 | 3.9 | 17.4 | 1.6 | 1.5 | 2.9 | 3.6 | 4.7 |
| | -1.8 | -.2 | -.4 | 3.7 | -.3 | -9.3 | -2.9 | .4 | 1.4 |
| Sales/Net Fixed Assets | 75.4 | 100.8 | 90.5 | 50.1 | 113.0 | 179.4 | 136.5 | 68.5 | 68.1 |
| | 35.2 | 35.7 | 37.9 | 29.4 | 37.2 | 39.9 | 49.0 | 35.7 | 29.2 |
| | 10.7 | 17.1 | 19.0 | 14.5 | 19.3 | 26.7 | 19.8 | 15.0 | 13.5 |
| Sales/Total Assets | 4.8 | 4.9 | 4.8 | 7.6 | 4.0 | 5.7 | 4.8 | 5.4 | 5.4 |
| | 3.4 | 3.4 | 3.7 | 3.1 | 3.4 | 3.8 | 3.9 | 3.7 | 4.2 |
| | 2.2 | 2.3 | 2.6 | 1.8 | 1.5 | 3.0 | 3.2 | 2.6 | 2.8 |
| % Depr., Dep., Amort./Sales | .5 | .5 | .4 | .5 | .2 | .4 | .3 | .5 | .4 |
| | (91) 1.1 | (79) 1.0 | (86) .8 | (10) 1.7 | (15) .9 | (12) .7 | (18) .6 | (16) .8 | (15) 1.1 |
| | 2.2 | 1.5 | 1.7 | 2.5 | 2.5 | 1.4 | 1.0 | 1.7 | 2.7 |
| % Officers', Directors' Owners' Comp/Sales | 1.8 | 1.4 | 2.6 | 4.9 | 3.8 | | 2.6 | | |
| | (54) 3.3 | (45) 4.1 | (52) 4.9 | (11) 7.1 | (15) 5.1 | | (11) 3.8 | | |
| | 6.5 | 6.9 | 6.7 | 14.7 | 6.1 | | 5.0 | | |
| Net Sales ($) | 2282500M | 1645639M | 1786758M | 8349M | 42144M | 59762M | 183713M | 321305M | 1171485M |
| Total Assets ($) | 721321M | 517817M | 650644M | 2557M | 22889M | 18140M | 48954M | 94014M | 464090M |

## Current Data Sorted by Assets

## Comparative Historical Data

| Type of Statement | 0-500M | 500M-2MM | 2-10MM | 10-50MM | 50-100MM | 100-250MM | | 4/1/07-3/31/08 ALL | 4/1/08-3/31/09 ALL |
|---|---|---|---|---|---|---|---|---|---|
| Unqualified | 1 | 1 | 1 | 2 | | | | 8 | 11 |
| Reviewed | 10 | 13 | 12 | 4 | | | | 20 | 21 |
| Compiled | 41 | 32 | 8 | 1 | | | | 29 | 30 |
| Tax Returns | 25 | 26 | 22 | | | | | 77 | 83 |
| Other | | | 21 | 9 | 1 | 3 | | 57 | 49 |
| | | 26 (4/1-9/30/11) | | 210 (10/1/11-3/31/12) | | | | | |
| NUMBER OF STATEMENTS | 77 | 72 | 64 | 16 | 4 | 3 | | 191 | 194 |
| **ASSETS** | % | % | % | % | % | % | | % | % |
| Cash & Equivalents | 19.4 | 13.9 | 12.6 | 16.5 | | | | 14.4 | 12.3 |
| Trade Receivables (net) | 4.2 | 7.6 | 10.0 | 12.7 | | | | 6.5 | 5.8 |
| Inventory | 46.6 | 46.0 | 37.0 | 23.8 | | | | 46.3 | 47.8 |
| All Other Current | 1.8 | 3.7 | 2.4 | 3.4 | | | | 3.4 | 2.9 |
| Total Current | 72.0 | 71.1 | 62.1 | 56.5 | | | | 70.6 | 68.8 |
| Fixed Assets (net) | 17.4 | 17.8 | 25.4 | 29.2 | | | | 21.2 | 22.6 |
| Intangibles (net) | 4.9 | -2.1 | 2.8 | 8.5 | | | | 2.8 | 2.7 |
| All Other Non-Current | 5.7 | 9.0 | 9.7 | 5.8 | | | | 5.4 | 5.9 |
| Total | 100.0 | 100.0 | 100.0 | 100.0 | | | | 100.0 | 100.0 |
| **LIABILITIES** | | | | | | | | | |
| Notes Payable-Short Term | 12.0 | 12.7 | 7.9 | 5.8 | | | | 9.3 | 9.9 |
| Cur. Mat.-L.T.D. | 2.4 | 2.3 | 4.5 | 1.3 | | | | 2.5 | 3.6 |
| Trade Payables | 22.4 | 13.4 | 14.1 | 16.3 | | | | 18.1 | 17.1 |
| Income Taxes Payable | .1 | .1 | .0 | .2 | | | | .2 | .1 |
| All Other Current | 7.2 | 12.2 | 8.6 | 4.7 | | | | 9.7 | 8.8 |
| Total Current | 44.1 | 40.7 | 35.1 | 28.3 | | | | 39.8 | 39.4 |
| Long-Term Debt | 12.0 | 13.4 | 16.6 | 17.5 | | | | 21.6 | 18.4 |
| Deferred Taxes | .0 | .0 | .0 | .0 | | | | .0 | .1 |
| All Other Non-Current | 22.8 | 7.1 | 5.8 | 4.1 | | | | 9.1 | 10.5 |
| Net Worth | 21.1 | 38.8 | 42.5 | 50.2 | | | | 29.5 | 31.7 |
| Total Liabilties & Net Worth | 100.0 | 100.0 | 100.0 | 100.0 | | | | 100.0 | 100.0 |
| **INCOME DATA** | | | | | | | | | |
| Net Sales | 100.0 | 100.0 | 100.0 | 100.0 | | | | 100.0 | 100.0 |
| Gross Profit | 48.9 | 48.5 | 47.6 | 46.3 | | | | 48.6 | 47.9 |
| Operating Expenses | 45.2 | 45.1 | 41.9 | 40.1 | | | | 43.7 | 45.1 |
| Operating Profit | 3.7 | 3.5 | 5.7 | 6.2 | | | | 4.9 | 2.8 |
| All Other Expenses (net) | .9 | .5 | 1.4 | 1.0 | | | | 1.3 | 1.5 |
| Profit Before Taxes | 2.8 | 2.9 | 4.2 | 5.1 | | | | 3.6 | 1.3 |

### RATIOS

| Ratio | 0-500M | 500M-2MM | 2-10MM | 10-50MM | 50-100MM | 100-250MM | | 4/1/07-3/31/08 ALL | 4/1/08-3/31/09 ALL |
|---|---|---|---|---|---|---|---|---|---|
| Current | 6.2 | 3.9 | 4.4 | 2.9 | | | | 3.6 | 3.9 |
| | 2.2 | 2.0 | 2.2 | 1.8 | | | | 1.8 | 1.9 |
| | 1.1 | 1.2 | 1.0 | 1.4 | | | | 1.2 | 1.2 |
| Quick | 1.9 | 1.3 | 1.5 | 2.3 | | | | 1.1 | 1.0 |
| | (76) .6 | .5 | .4 | 1.0 | | | | (188) .5 | (192) .4 |
| | .2 | .2 | .1 | .3 | | | | .2 | .1 |
| Sales/Receivables | 0 UND | 0 UND | 0 UND | 0 UND | | | | 0 UND | 0 UND |
| | 0 UND | 0 UND | 1 587.5 | 3 124.0 | | | | 0 UND | 0 UND |
| | 0 806.5 | 6 59.2 | 21 17.5 | 25 14.6 | | | | 5 74.1 | 8 47.1 |
| Cost of Sales/Inventory | 38 9.5 | 49 7.5 | 54 6.7 | 19 19.0 | | | | 66 5.5 | 61 6.0 |
| | 107 3.4 | 126 2.9 | 118 3.1 | 65 5.6 | | | | 126 2.9 | 130 2.8 |
| | 192 1.9 | 215 1.7 | 203 1.8 | 135 2.7 | | | | 201 1.8 | 211 1.7 |
| Cost of Sales/Payables | 0 UND | 4 89.6 | 8 43.1 | 24 15.3 | | | | 5 72.4 | 7 51.8 |
| | 19 19.7 | 25 14.4 | 31 11.6 | 43 8.4 | | | | 31 11.8 | 28 12.9 |
| | 51 7.1 | 62 5.9 | 74 4.9 | 64 5.7 | | | | 67 5.5 | 63 5.8 |
| Sales/Working Capital | 4.3 | 5.1 | 4.3 | 4.4 | | | | 4.7 | 4.8 |
| | 10.4 | 9.3 | 8.2 | 7.0 | | | | 8.4 | 8.9 |
| | 121.2 | 50.9 | NM | 20.8 | | | | 26.0 | 38.1 |
| EBIT/Interest | 13.1 | 15.0 | 11.1 | 38.0 | | | | 10.6 | 8.3 |
| | (50) 3.2 | (60) 4.6 | (56) 2.9 | (13) 8.8 | | | | (151) 3.1 | (158) 2.5 |
| | -.3 | 1.0 | 1.1 | 2.1 | | | | .8 | -.1 |
| Net Profit + Depr., Dep., Amort./Cur. Mat. L/T/D | | | | | | | | 8.8 | 6.0 |
| | | | | | | | | (17) 3.6 | (15) 2.5 |
| | | | | | | | | .7 | .9 |
| Fixed/Worth | .1 | .1 | .1 | .2 | | | | .1 | .2 |
| | .5 | .3 | .3 | .6 | | | | .5 | .5 |
| | -13.0 | 1.7 | 1.5 | 3.0 | | | | 2.3 | 2.3 |
| Debt/Worth | .2 | .5 | .4 | .3 | | | | .8 | .6 |
| | 2.5 | 1.4 | 1.7 | 1.8 | | | | 2.0 | 2.5 |
| | -9.0 | 7.9 | 4.7 | 3.6 | | | | 9.3 | 6.9 |
| % Profit Before Taxes/Tangible Net Worth | 44.9 | 52.7 | 41.7 | 57.1 | | | | 50.4 | 40.4 |
| | (54) 23.6 | (59) 20.6 | (58) 14.4 | (14) 17.7 | | | | (156) 26.8 | (166) 20.0 |
| | 4.4 | 1.7 | 2.3 | 11.2 | | | | 1.9 | .1 |
| % Profit Before Taxes/Total Assets | 22.7 | 19.2 | 13.6 | 18.9 | | | | 19.9 | 15.9 |
| | 11.3 | 3.8 | 4.5 | 10.6 | | | | 7.3 | 4.4 |
| | -6.8 | -1.0 | 1.1 | 3.8 | | | | -.3 | -3.4 |
| Sales/Net Fixed Assets | 223.8 | 169.3 | 69.0 | 46.7 | | | | 65.5 | 49.4 |
| | 24.6 | 30.0 | 20.5 | 11.6 | | | | 21.1 | 17.7 |
| | 11.6 | 11.7 | 5.3 | 3.5 | | | | 8.7 | 7.4 |
| Sales/Total Assets | 4.9 | 4.1 | 3.0 | 3.7 | | | | 3.7 | 3.8 |
| | 2.8 | 2.6 | 2.0 | 1.9 | | | | 2.6 | 2.6 |
| | 2.0 | 1.6 | 1.1 | 1.0 | | | | 1.7 | 1.6 |
| % Depr., Dep., Amort./Sales | .7 | .4 | .7 | 1.4 | | | | .6 | .7 |
| | (42) 1.6 | (51) 1.0 | (52) 1.5 | (14) 2.0 | | | | (147) 1.1 | (156) 1.2 |
| | 2.7 | 2.1 | 2.4 | 3.2 | | | | 2.1 | 2.5 |
| % Officers', Directors' Owners' Comp/Sales | 2.9 | 1.4 | 1.2 | | | | | 2.5 | 2.1 |
| | (41) 5.6 | (45) 3.6 | (33) 2.4 | | | | | (95) 4.8 | (88) 3.9 |
| | 8.4 | 6.0 | 3.7 | | | | | 7.1 | 7.0 |
| Net Sales ($) | 64537M | 263932M | 665118M | 750943M | 936161M | 1024750M | | 4223496M | 3462194M |
| Total Assets ($) | 19410M | 71840M | 285081M | 306381M | 369854M | 514988M | | 1770342M | 1400336M |

M = $ thousand    MM = $ million
See Pages 9 through 22 for Explanation of Ratios and Data

## Comparative Historical Data

## Current Data Sorted by Sales

| 4/1/09-3/31/10 ALL | 4/1/10-3/31/11 ALL | 4/1/11-3/31/12 ALL | Type of Statement | 0-1MM | 1-3MM | 3-5MM | 5-10MM | 10-25MM | 25MM & OVER |
|---|---|---|---|---|---|---|---|---|---|
| 11 | 9 | 3 | Unqualified | 1 |  | 1 | 5 | 7 | 3 |
| 8 | 23 | 18 | Reviewed |  |  |  |  |  | 4 |
| 37 | 40 | 32 | Compiled | 10 | 11 | 4 | 1 | 4 | 2 |
| 100 | 98 | 96 | Tax Returns | 34 | 29 | 12 | 13 | 7 | 1 |
| 81 | 77 | 87 | Other | 24 | 20 | 10 | 8 | 12 | 13 |
|  |  |  |  | 26 (4/1-9/30/11) | | 210 (10/1/11-3/31/12) | | | |
| 237 | 247 | 236 | NUMBER OF STATEMENTS | 69 | 60 | 27 | 27 | 30 | 23 |
| % | % | % | ASSETS | % | % | % | % | % | % |
| 14.2 | 14.1 | 15.3 | Cash & Equivalents | 16.8 | 15.4 | 14.2 | 12.9 | 13.3 | 17.0 |
| 5.8 | 6.3 | 7.4 | Trade Receivables (net) | 4.2 | 4.6 | 9.6 | 10.1 | 12.9 | 11.4 |
| 45.1 | 45.8 | 41.8 | Inventory | 41.2 | 50.1 | 36.9 | 44.8 | 37.7 | 29.5 |
| 3.9 | 2.4 | 2.6 | All Other Current | 2.3 | 2.9 | 4.1 | 2.3 | 2.4 | 1.9 |
| 68.9 | 68.6 | 67.1 | Total Current | 64.5 | 73.0 | 64.8 | 70.1 | 66.2 | 59.8 |
| 21.7 | 21.2 | 21.1 | Fixed Assets (net) | 23.2 | 17.2 | 22.7 | 22.8 | 19.1 | 24.5 |
| 2.9 | 3.4 | 4.0 | Intangibles (net) | 4.9 | 2.9 | 4.3 | 1.6 | 1.1 | 10.8 |
| 6.4 | 6.7 | 7.7 | All Other Non-Current | 7.5 | 6.9 | 8.3 | 5.6 | 13.5 | 4.9 |
| 100.0 | 100.0 | 100.0 | Total | 100.0 | 100.0 | 100.0 | 100.0 | 100.0 | 100.0 |
|  |  |  | LIABILITIES |  |  |  |  |  |  |
| 17.2 | 10.2 | 10.6 | Notes Payable-Short Term | 13.8 | 10.1 | 6.3 | 8.8 | 11.3 | 8.6 |
| 3.0 | 3.7 | 2.9 | Cur. Mat.-L.T.D. | 2.2 | 2.5 | 2.9 | 3.7 | 5.0 | 2.3 |
| 17.4 | 22.0 | 16.8 | Trade Payables | 18.7 | 15.0 | 14.8 | 17.7 | 16.6 | 17.2 |
| .1 | .1 | .1 | Income Taxes Payable | .1 | .1 | .1 | .0 | .0 | .2 |
| 11.7 | 12.3 | 9.0 | All Other Current | 7.7 | 7.8 | 17.9 | 6.4 | 10.4 | 6.7 |
| 49.5 | 48.2 | 39.3 | Total Current | 42.6 | 35.4 | 41.9 | 36.6 | 43.3 | 35.0 |
| 18.5 | 20.7 | 15.2 | Long-Term Debt | 18.9 | 12.9 | 12.0 | 14.2 | 10.4 | 21.3 |
| .1 | .1 | .1 | Deferred Taxes | .0 | .0 | .0 | .0 | .1 | .9 |
| 12.7 | 9.2 | 11.6 | All Other Non-Current | 22.9 | 10.2 | 4.2 | 7.9 | 4.8 | 3.6 |
| 19.3 | 21.7 | 33.7 | Net Worth | 15.7 | 41.5 | 41.8 | 41.3 | 41.4 | 39.3 |
| 100.0 | 100.0 | 100.0 | Total Liabilities & Net Worth | 100.0 | 100.0 | 100.0 | 100.0 | 100.0 | 100.0 |
|  |  |  | INCOME DATA |  |  |  |  |  |  |
| 100.0 | 100.0 | 100.0 | Net Sales | 100.0 | 100.0 | 100.0 | 100.0 | 100.0 | 100.0 |
| 49.3 | 48.6 | 48.6 | Gross Profit | 53.0 | 47.4 | 49.6 | 46.9 | 41.2 | 49.0 |
| 45.8 | 44.1 | 44.1 | Operating Expenses | 49.0 | 42.3 | 44.4 | 42.3 | 39.2 | 42.2 |
| 3.5 | 4.6 | 4.5 | Operating Profit | 4.0 | 5.0 | 5.1 | 4.5 | 2.0 | 6.8 |
| 1.1 | 1.6 | 1.0 | All Other Expenses (net) | 1.8 | .9 | .2 | .8 | .2 | 1.1 |
| 2.5 | 2.9 | 3.4 | Profit Before Taxes | 2.2 | 4.1 | 4.9 | 3.7 | 1.8 | 5.7 |
|  |  |  | RATIOS |  |  |  |  |  |  |
| 3.2 | 3.8 | 4.4 |  | 5.1 | 5.0 | 4.7 | 3.8 | 2.8 | 2.8 |
| 1.7 | 1.8 | 2.0 | Current | 1.5 | 2.8 | 2.3 | 2.3 | 1.4 | 1.9 |
| 1.0 | 1.0 | 1.1 |  | .9 | 1.2 | 1.1 | 1.2 | 1.0 | 1.1 |
| .9 | 1.2 | 1.6 |  | 1.4 | 1.8 | 1.9 | 1.3 | .9 | 2.0 |
| .4 (243) | .4 (235) | .5 | Quick | (68) .5 | .5 | .5 | .3 | .4 | .7 |
| .1 | .1 | .2 |  | .2 | .2 | .2 | .1 | .2 | .2 |
| 0 UND | 0 UND | 0 UND |  | 0 UND | 0 UND | 0 UND | 0 UND | 0 UND | 0 UND |
| 0 UND | 0 999.8 | 0 UND | Sales/Receivables | 0 UND | 0 UND | 1 549.0 | 1 514.8 | 1 382.8 | 2 156.5 |
| 4 99.7 | 5 74.3 | 7 50.5 |  | 2 212.1 | 1 246.2 | 22 16.3 | 12 30.1 | 29 12.5 | 22 16.3 |
| 70 5.2 | 55 6.7 | 51 7.2 |  | 69 5.3 | 40 9.2 | 41 8.8 | 74 4.9 | 37 9.8 | 16 23.0 |
| 136 2.7 | 116 3.1 | 114 3.2 | Cost of Sales/Inventory | 166 2.2 | 130 2.8 | 96 3.8 | 126 2.9 | 87 4.2 | 62 5.9 |
| 217 1.7 | 198 1.8 | 203 1.8 |  | 261 1.4 | 243 1.5 | 174 2.1 | 215 1.7 | 126 2.9 | 159 2.3 |
| 9 39.0 | 8 45.8 | 4 92.8 |  | 0 UND | 5 70.1 | 4 92.5 | 18 20.7 | 8 45.9 | 22 16.3 |
| 35 10.4 | 31 11.7 | 28 13.0 | Cost of Sales/Payables | 13 27.9 | 26 13.8 | 32 11.5 | 29 12.8 | 30 12.2 | 51 7.2 |
| 74 4.9 | 80 4.6 | 66 5.5 |  | 87 4.2 | 60 6.1 | 51 7.1 | 72 5.1 | 70 5.2 | 74 4.9 |
| 5.0 | 5.0 | 4.5 |  | 3.6 | 3.4 | 5.1 | 4.8 | 6.7 | 6.3 |
| 10.6 | 10.5 | 9.6 | Sales/Working Capital | 9.6 | 9.0 | 8.0 | 7.8 | 14.4 | 17.8 |
| NM | 153.0 | 98.2 |  | -29.5 | 21.6 | 139.2 | 56.3 | 191.1 | 49.0 |
| 10.4 | 9.2 | 13.3 |  | 11.5 | 12.9 | 16.9 | 12.3 | 25.4 | 38.6 |
| (185) 3.2 | (198) 2.6 | (186) 3.5 | EBIT/Interest | (47) 2.0 | (46) 3.7 | (23) 4.8 | (24) 3.0 | (26) 3.4 | (20) 7.7 |
| .4 | .4 | 1.0 |  | -.3 | .6 | 1.0 | 1.1 | 1.2 | 2.7 |
| 3.8 | 16.1 | 6.2 |  |  |  |  |  |  |  |
| (19) 2.2 | (17) 2.2 | (11) 1.3 | Net Profit + Depr., Dep., Amort./Cur. Mat. L/T/D |  |  |  |  |  |  |
| -.2 | 1.0 | .1 |  |  |  |  |  |  |  |
| .1 | .1 | .1 |  | .1 | .1 | .1 | .1 | .2 | .2 |
| .6 | .5 | .5 | Fixed/Worth | .7 | .3 | .9 | .3 | .3 | -.8 |
| 23.2 | 4.7 | 3.6 |  | -13.3 | 1.8 | 1.5 | 1.6 | 1.0 | -6.8 |
| .8 | .6 | .4 |  | .6 | .3 | .6 | .4 | .3 | .5 |
| 2.3 | 2.4 | 2.0 | Debt/Worth | 3.9 | .7 | 1.4 | 2.1 | 2.0 | 2.6 |
| UND | 60.9 | 13.8 |  | -7.2 | 11.5 | 4.8 | 5.2 | 3.9 | -11.3 |
| 50.3 | 53.0 | 45.3 |  | 41.8 | 35.9 | 58.2 | 45.8 | 51.0 | 74.9 |
| (178) 22.7 | (192) 19.1 | (188) 19.4 | % Profit Before Taxes/Tangible Net Worth | (47) 15.7 | (47) 21.3 | (25) 27.4 | (25) 13.9 | (28) 16.8 | (16) 41.2 |
| 2.4 | 2.9 | 4.7 |  | .0 | 5.4 | 2.9 | 1.3 | .3 | 16.1 |
| 19.2 | 16.8 | 19.1 |  | 18.9 | 22.5 | 24.6 | 14.2 | 15.8 | 19.2 |
| 5.1 | 5.1 | 5.5 | % Profit Before Taxes/Total Assets | 3.3 | 6.8 | 7.8 | 4.3 | 3.7 | 11.1 |
| -1.1 | -1.1 | -.1 |  | -8.6 | -.2 | .2 | .8 | -1.2 | 9.2 |
| 76.3 | 96.7 | 103.8 |  | 119.3 | 117.6 | 106.9 | 69.3 | 133.3 | 55.6 |
| 22.1 | 24.8 | 23.0 | Sales/Net Fixed Assets | 21.2 | 28.6 | 22.3 | 33.2 | 35.7 | 12.1 |
| 8.1 | 8.0 | 8.9 |  | 8.3 | 14.7 | 9.6 | 5.3 | 8.2 | 6.9 |
| 3.7 | 3.9 | 4.2 |  | 3.4 | 4.3 | 4.1 | 3.8 | 5.4 | 4.8 |
| 2.4 | 2.5 | 2.5 | Sales/Total Assets | 2.1 | 2.6 | 2.5 | 2.2 | 2.9 | 2.6 |
| 1.6 | 1.5 | 1.6 |  | 1.2 | 1.6 | 1.7 | 1.5 | 2.0 | 1.7 |
| .5 | .5 | .6 |  | .7 | .5 | .4 | .5 | .2 | .9 |
| (186) 1.3 | (173) 1.2 | (162) 1.3 | % Depr., Dep., Amort./Sales | (43) 1.9 | (37) 1.3 | (21) 1.0 | (21) 1.4 | (24) .8 | (16) 1.6 |
| 2.4 | 2.7 | 2.6 |  | 3.2 | 2.4 | 2.4 | 2.6 | 1.7 | 3.0 |
| 2.1 | 2.1 | 1.8 |  | 2.4 | 2.3 | 1.5 | 1.4 | 2.2 |  |
| (101) 3.8 | (117) 4.0 | (122) 3.5 | % Officers', Directors' Owners' Comp/Sales | (32) 5.9 | (36) 5.0 | (20) 3.3 | (14) 3.0 | (16) 2.2 |  |
| 6.9 | 6.9 | 6.5 |  | 8.6 | 7.0 | 5.3 | 3.5 | 3.5 |  |
| 3921186M | 4796041M | 3705441M | Net Sales ($) | 38820M | 106293M | 105310M | 198187M | 459826M | 2797005M |
| 1793172M | 1851574M | 1567554M | Total Assets ($) | 27715M | 52124M | 49862M | 112114M | 176012M | 1149727M |

M = $ thousand    MM = $ million
See Pages 9 through 22 for Explanation of Ratios and Data

## Current Data Sorted by Assets      Comparative Historical Data

| Type of Statement | 0-500M | 500M-2MM | 2-10MM | 10-50MM | 50-100MM | 100-250MM | | 4/1/07-3/31/08 | 4/1/08-3/31/09 |
|---|---|---|---|---|---|---|---|---|---|
| Unqualified | | | 1 | 8 | | | | 10 | 9 |
| Reviewed | | | 1 | 2 | | | | 3 | 6 |
| Compiled | 4 | 5 | 1 | 1 | | | | 11 | 8 |
| Tax Returns | 12 | 17 | 6 | 1 | | | | 34 | 39 |
| Other | 4 | 8 | 10 | 5 | | | | 31 | 24 |
| | 23 (4/1-9/30/11) | | 62 (10/1/11-3/31/12) | | | | | ALL | ALL |
| NUMBER OF STATEMENTS | 20 | 30 | 19 | 16 | | | | 89 | 86 |

Columns 50-100MM and 100-250MM: **DATA NOT AVAILABLE**

| | 0-500M | 500M-2MM | 2-10MM | 10-50MM | | 4/1/07-3/31/08 | 4/1/08-3/31/09 |
|---|---|---|---|---|---|---|---|
| | % | % | % | % | **ASSETS** | % | % |
| Cash & Equivalents | 25.8 | 10.8 | 13.5 | 15.3 | | 11.9 | 14.5 |
| Trade Receivables (net) | 6.1 | 15.5 | 15.6 | 14.4 | | 13.4 | 11.2 |
| Inventory | 28.9 | 38.2 | 37.0 | 21.2 | | 40.0 | 34.4 |
| All Other Current | 3.6 | 5.9 | 4.7 | 1.6 | | 3.3 | 5.5 |
| Total Current | 64.3 | 70.4 | 70.9 | 52.6 | | 68.6 | 65.5 |
| Fixed Assets (net) | 26.1 | 20.2 | 15.4 | 32.5 | | 21.9 | 23.0 |
| Intangibles (net) | 1.2 | 3.0 | 3.9 | 9.3 | | 3.5 | 3.8 |
| All Other Non-Current | 8.4 | 6.4 | 9.8 | 5.7 | | 6.0 | 7.7 |
| Total | 100.0 | 100.0 | 100.0 | 100.0 | | 100.0 | 100.0 |
| | | | | | **LIABILITIES** | | |
| Notes Payable-Short Term | 33.7 | 16.3 | 6.8 | 5.4 | | 13.3 | 13.3 |
| Cur. Mat.-L.T.D. | 3.6 | .5 | 2.4 | 2.1 | | 3.3 | 3.0 |
| Trade Payables | 6.5 | 5.4 | 8.6 | 8.3 | | 9.3 | 11.8 |
| Income Taxes Payable | .2 | .7 | .1 | .0 | | .1 | .1 |
| All Other Current | 34.8 | 11.8 | 9.7 | 12.8 | | 7.9 | 14.1 |
| Total Current | 78.7 | 34.7 | 27.6 | 28.5 | | 33.9 | 42.3 |
| Long-Term Debt | 17.4 | 8.1 | 5.0 | 18.5 | | 17.0 | 16.6 |
| Deferred Taxes | .0 | .0 | .0 | .2 | | .1 | .0 |
| All Other Non-Current | 15.3 | 5.5 | 20.2 | 5.7 | | 13.5 | 10.6 |
| Net Worth | -11.4 | 51.7 | 47.2 | 47.1 | | 35.5 | 30.5 |
| Total Liabilities & Net Worth | 100.0 | 100.0 | 100.0 | 100.0 | | 100.0 | 100.0 |
| | | | | | **INCOME DATA** | | |
| Net Sales | 100.0 | 100.0 | 100.0 | 100.0 | | 100.0 | 100.0 |
| Gross Profit | 57.4 | 58.4 | 65.5 | 53.7 | | 52.3 | 56.2 |
| Operating Expenses | 52.4 | 52.7 | 56.0 | 45.4 | | 47.6 | 51.5 |
| Operating Profit | 5.0 | 5.7 | 9.6 | 8.3 | | 4.7 | 4.7 |
| All Other Expenses (net) | .1 | .7 | .7 | .6 | | 1.0 | .8 |
| Profit Before Taxes | 4.9 | 5.0 | 8.9 | 7.7 | | 3.7 | 3.9 |

### RATIOS

| | 0-500M | 500M-2MM | 2-10MM | 10-50MM | | 4/1/07-3/31/08 | 4/1/08-3/31/09 |
|---|---|---|---|---|---|---|---|
| | 7.2 | 5.8 | 7.9 | 3.5 | | 6.0 | 8.8 |
| Current | 2.1 | 3.3 | 2.5 | 1.7 | | 2.5 | 2.3 |
| | .7 | 1.1 | 1.7 | 1.3 | | 1.2 | 1.2 |
| | 2.0 | 2.2 | 4.3 | 1.4 | | 1.8 | 2.4 |
| Quick | .9 | .7 | (18) .9 | 1.1 | | (88) .8 | .7 |
| | .1 | .2 | .6 | .7 | | .2 | .2 |
| | 0 UND | 0 UND | 0 UND | 2 162.8 | | 0 UND | 0 UND |
| Sales/Receivables | 0 UND | 4 82.9 | 3 116.3 | 8 45.1 | | 7 52.9 | 1 333.5 |
| | 0 UND | 45 8.1 | 41 8.8 | 23 15.7 | | 58 6.3 | 35 10.5 |
| | 15 25.0 | 32 11.5 | 34 10.6 | 29 12.8 | | 34 10.7 | 26 14.3 |
| Cost of Sales/Inventory | 41 8.8 | 114 3.2 | 146 2.5 | 83 4.4 | | 119 3.1 | 97 3.8 |
| | 73 5.0 | 281 1.3 | 730 .5 | 152 2.4 | | 314 1.2 | 225 1.6 |
| | 0 UND | 0 UND | 0 UND | 8 47.8 | | 0 UND | 0 UND |
| Cost of Sales/Payables | 0 UND | 6 62.7 | 9 41.7 | 21 17.2 | | 9 40.3 | 8 43.0 |
| | 31 11.8 | 37 9.8 | 107 3.4 | 94 3.9 | | 42 8.7 | 30 12.2 |
| | 8.7 | 2.3 | 1.9 | 4.0 | | 2.4 | 3.2 |
| Sales/Working Capital | 20.7 | 7.6 | 7.7 | 17.1 | | 6.3 | 9.3 |
| | -52.5 | 74.7 | 23.0 | 28.2 | | 37.8 | 59.2 |
| | 27.7 | 53.1 | 28.2 | 41.0 | | 10.5 | 15.2 |
| EBIT/Interest | (13) 8.3 | (23) 10.3 | (15) 15.6 | (14) 10.9 | | (77) 3.7 | (71) 4.8 |
| | 5.5 | 2.7 | 4.5 | 4.6 | | .7 | 1.1 |
| | | | | | Net Profit + Depr., Dep., Amort./Cur. Mat. L/T/D | | |
| | .2 | .1 | .0 | .3 | | .0 | .1 |
| Fixed/Worth | .4 | .2 | .2 | .8 | | .4 | .3 |
| | NM | .7 | 1.0 | 1.8 | | 2.6 | 2.4 |
| | .5 | .4 | .4 | .5 | | .5 | .4 |
| Debt/Worth | 1.1 | .9 | 1.0 | 1.0 | | 1.2 | 1.0 |
| | -2.3 | 2.9 | 4.3 | 6.3 | | 9.7 | 15.4 |
| | 120.2 | 52.9 | 69.8 | 72.7 | | 52.7 | 48.6 |
| % Profit Before Taxes/Tangible Net Worth | (14) 55.5 | 21.5 | (17) 21.6 | (13) 34.7 | | (72) 19.4 | (68) 17.1 |
| | 15.2 | 5.6 | 4.1 | 18.6 | | 3.2 | -1.3 |
| | 58.4 | 22.9 | 31.1 | 28.1 | | 21.4 | 23.5 |
| % Profit Before Taxes/Total Assets | 32.0 | 7.9 | 13.4 | 12.0 | | 6.8 | 5.4 |
| | 12.5 | 2.9 | 5.6 | 8.0 | | -.5 | -4.1 |
| | 136.1 | 164.1 | 116.9 | 88.0 | | 95.3 | 96.8 |
| Sales/Net Fixed Assets | 44.7 | 33.2 | 35.2 | 12.5 | | 23.3 | 22.0 |
| | 18.4 | 11.6 | 11.3 | 3.4 | | 6.1 | 9.8 |
| | 12.7 | 4.7 | 4.4 | 2.9 | | 3.7 | 5.0 |
| Sales/Total Assets | 5.4 | 2.1 | 2.2 | 2.1 | | 1.8 | 2.6 |
| | 3.9 | 1.2 | 1.2 | 1.6 | | 1.1 | 1.5 |
| | .3 | .3 | .2 | .6 | | .4 | .5 |
| % Depr., Dep., Amort./Sales | (16) .6 | (23) .9 | (13) 1.1 | (12) 1.9 | | (58) 1.1 | (62) 1.2 |
| | 1.1 | 1.4 | 2.4 | 3.1 | | 2.0 | 2.6 |
| | 1.7 | 1.3 | 2.3 | | | 2.4 | 2.0 |
| % Officers', Directors' Owners' Comp/Sales | (11) 4.1 | (18) 4.7 | (10) 3.9 | | | (47) 4.2 | (41) 3.2 |
| | 5.2 | 5.7 | 6.1 | | | 11.1 | 8.4 |
| Net Sales ($) | 35832M | 122977M | 235924M | 767301M | | 1750442M | 1199473M |
| Total Assets ($) | 5125M | 35110M | 89166M | 326821M | | 653642M | 565723M |

M = $ thousand     MM = $ million
See Pages 9 through 22 for Explanation of Ratios and Data

| | Comparative Historical Data | | | Current Data Sorted by Sales | | | | | |
|---|---|---|---|---|---|---|---|---|---|
| Type of Statement | | | | | | | | | |
| Unqualified | | | | | | | | 1 | 8 |
| Reviewed | | | | | | | 2 | 2 | 1 |
| Compiled | | | | 2 | 5 | | | 1 | |
| Tax Returns | | | | 8 | 15 | 8 | 4 | 1 | |
| Other | | | | 3 | 3 | 2 | 6 | 8 | 5 |
| | 10 / 10 / 10 / 33 / 20 | 7 / 13 / 11 / 38 / 27 | 9 / 3 / 10 / 36 / 27 | | 23 (4/1-9/30/11) | | 62 (10/1/11-3/31/12) | | |
| | 4/1/09-3/31/10 ALL | 4/1/10-3/31/11 ALL | 4/1/11-3/31/12 ALL | 0-1MM | 1-3MM | 3-5MM | 5-10MM | 10-25MM | 25MM & OVER |
| NUMBER OF STATEMENTS | 83 | 96 | 85 | 13 | 23 | 10 | 12 | 13 | 14 |
| | % | % | % | % | % | % | % | % | % |
| **ASSETS** | | | | | | | | | |
| Cash & Equivalents | 14.5 | 16.0 | 15.8 | 8.8 | 22.0 | 17.2 | 10.0 | 14.1 | 17.6 |
| Trade Receivables (net) | 13.2 | 16.4 | 13.1 | 11.7 | 9.8 | 13.5 | 24.5 | 12.9 | 10.1 |
| Inventory | 35.4 | 29.0 | 32.5 | 40.0 | 36.4 | 43.6 | 20.8 | 31.4 | 22.5 |
| All Other Current | 5.4 | 5.7 | 4.3 | 2.9 | 2.6 | 5.1 | 9.3 | 5.2 | 2.5 |
| Total Current | 68.5 | 67.1 | 65.7 | 63.3 | 70.7 | 79.5 | 64.7 | 63.6 | 52.8 |
| Fixed Assets (net) | 21.3 | 21.6 | 22.8 | 27.4 | 18.1 | 17.8 | 15.5 | 26.9 | 32.4 |
| Intangibles (net) | 3.0 | 5.0 | 4.0 | .6 | 4.0 | .3 | 6.9 | 9.0 | 10.5 |
| All Other Non-Current | 7.2 | 6.3 | 7.5 | 8.7 | 7.2 | 2.5 | 12.9 | 9.0 | 4.3 |
| Total | 100.0 | 100.0 | 100.0 | 100.0 | 100.0 | 100.0 | 100.0 | 100.0 | 100.0 |
| **LIABILITIES** | | | | | | | | | |
| Notes Payable-Short Term | 15.4 | 15.3 | 16.2 | 13.6 | 14.2 | 22.0 | 46.2 | 4.9 | 2.6 |
| Cur. Mat.-L.T.D. | 4.9 | 4.0 | 2.0 | .6 | 3.2 | .6 | 3.4 | .6 | 2.2 |
| Trade Payables | 6.7 | 6.4 | 6.9 | 6.0 | 4.1 | 2.8 | 16.6 | 3.9 | 9.9 |
| Income Taxes Payable | .1 | .4 | .3 | .0 | .6 | .0 | .9 | .1 | .0 |
| All Other Current | 13.4 | 15.9 | 16.9 | 7.2 | 23.1 | 16.9 | 15.1 | 19.2 | 15.2 |
| Total Current | 40.4 | 42.0 | 42.3 | 27.4 | 45.2 | 42.2 | 82.1 | 28.7 | 29.9 |
| Long-Term Debt | 12.1 | 10.6 | 11.6 | 15.1 | 16.3 | 1.7 | 4.2 | 8.7 | 16.5 |
| Deferred Taxes | .0 | .0 | .0 | .0 | .0 | .0 | .0 | .1 | .2 |
| All Other Non-Current | 5.4 | 5.3 | 11.1 | 16.9 | 9.2 | 4.7 | 7.3 | 20.4 | 8.2 |
| Net Worth | 42.1 | 42.0 | 35.0 | 40.7 | 29.3 | 51.4 | 6.4 | 42.1 | 45.2 |
| Total Liabilties & Net Worth | 100.0 | 100.0 | 100.0 | 100.0 | 100.0 | 100.0 | 100.0 | 100.0 | 100.0 |
| **INCOME DATA** | | | | | | | | | |
| Net Sales | 100.0 | 100.0 | 100.0 | 100.0 | 100.0 | 100.0 | 100.0 | 100.0 | 100.0 |
| Gross Profit | 58.7 | 59.6 | 58.9 | 60.5 | 55.1 | 57.0 | 75.3 | 55.5 | 53.9 |
| Operating Expenses | 52.7 | 52.9 | 52.0 | 54.7 | 48.6 | 48.4 | 66.9 | 50.0 | 46.6 |
| Operating Profit | 6.0 | 6.7 | 6.9 | 5.7 | 6.5 | 8.6 | 8.4 | 5.4 | 7.3 |
| All Other Expenses (net) | .6 | .7 | .5 | 1.1 | .4 | .3 | .7 | .3 | .6 |
| Profit Before Taxes | 5.3 | 6.0 | 6.3 | 4.6 | 6.1 | 8.4 | 7.8 | 5.1 | 6.8 |
| **RATIOS** | | | | | | | | | |
| Current | 5.7 | 6.4 | 5.7 | 12.1 | 4.3 | 3.8 | 7.2 | 6.0 | 3.0 |
| | 2.1 | 2.4 | 2.1 | 7.6 | 2.2 | 2.9 | 1.4 | 2.2 | 1.8 |
| | 1.4 | 1.4 | 1.1 | 1.8 | 1.0 | 1.1 | .6 | 1.6 | 1.3 |
| Quick | 2.2 | 3.0 | 2.1 | 5.4 | 2.0 | 2.3 | 2.8 | 2.5 | 1.3 |
| | .8 | (84) 1.2 | .9 | 1.7 | .9 | (11) .6 | .7 | 1.0 | 1.0 |
| | .3 | .5 | .3 | .1 | .1 | .3 | .4 | .6 | .5 |
| Sales/Receivables | 0 UND | 0 UND | 0 UND | 0 UND | 0 UND | 0 UND | 0 UND | 0 UND | 2 168.9 |
| | 3 113.7 | 2 190.1 | 3 116.3 | 0 UND | 0 UND | 3 107.7 | 11 34.5 | 1 527.4 | 7 55.7 |
| | 45 8.1 | 68 5.4 | 20 18.0 | 56 6.5 | 7 50.6 | 76 4.8 | 50 7.3 | 19 18.9 | 10 35.2 |
| Cost of Sales/Inventory | 46 8.0 | 27 13.3 | 28 13.0 | 85 4.3 | 19 19.7 | 46 8.0 | 13 28.1 | 13 28.2 | 22 16.8 |
| | 124 2.9 | 95 3.9 | 81 4.5 | 261 1.4 | 58 6.3 | 87 4.2 | 66 5.5 | 111 3.3 | 38 9.6 |
| | 254 1.4 | 179 2.0 | 243 1.5 | 1217 .3 | 174 2.1 | 228 1.6 | 261 1.4 | 203 1.8 | 91 4.0 |
| Cost of Sales/Payables | 0 UND | 2 178.7 | 0 UND | 0 UND | 0 UND | 0 UND | 0 UND | 0 UND | 12 29.3 |
| | 14 25.9 | 13 27.1 | 9 42.8 | 0 UND | 5 79.4 | 1 257.4 | 50 7.3 | 3 120.3 | 21 17.2 |
| | 36 10.1 | 34 10.7 | 45 8.1 | 83 4.4 | 35 10.3 | 16 23.0 | 130 2.8 | 31 11.9 | 101 3.6 |
| Sales/Working Capital | 2.6 | 3.1 | 3.4 | 1.4 | 5.0 | 1.8 | 5.6 | 5.0 | 6.5 |
| | 6.2 | 8.7 | 13.2 | 2.6 | 13.2 | 7.1 | 35.0 | 14.2 | 20.4 |
| | 22.6 | 23.4 | 68.5 | 46.5 | 123.8 | 66.2 | -29.1 | 32.7 | 29.2 |
| EBIT/Interest | 31.8 | 41.3 | 36.3 | 11.3 | 30.2 | | 83.5 | 69.5 | 24.0 |
| | (64) 6.0 | (72) 8.2 | (65) 11.8 | (10) 3.2 | (16) 11.1 | | (10) 21.9 | (10) 17.2 | (11) 10.0 |
| | 1.2 | 1.4 | 4.4 | .3 | 3.7 | | 6.0 | 4.0 | 4.7 |
| Net Profit + Depr., Dep., Amort./Cur. Mat. L/T/D | | | | | | | | | |
| Fixed/Worth | .0 | .1 | .1 | .0 | .1 | .0 | .2 | .2 | .3 |
| | .2 | .3 | .4 | .1 | .2 | .2 | .3 | .7 | .8 |
| | 1.0 | .9 | 1.0 | 1.9 | .7 | .8 | 1.3 | 3.4 | NM |
| Debt/Worth | .3 | .3 | .5 | .2 | .6 | .3 | .8 | .2 | .6 |
| | .9 | .8 | 1.0 | .5 | 1.0 | .5 | 2.3 | 1.6 | 1.0 |
| | 2.7 | 3.0 | 4.5 | 3.1 | 3.2 | 2.1 | 7.1 | 9.6 | NM |
| % Profit Before Taxes/Tangible Net Worth | 49.3 | 54.8 | 65.7 | 15.8 | 64.3 | | 186.6 | 187.2 | 81.5 |
| | (72) 20.1 | (85) 30.1 | (74) 29.3 | (11) 6.8 | (21) 38.5 | (11) 42.1 | (11) 25.7 | (11) 58.0 | |
| | 4.6 | 8.7 | 8.3 | 1.6 | 12.6 | | 14.2 | 8.5 | 19.7 |
| % Profit Before Taxes/Total Assets | 28.6 | 31.6 | 35.3 | 13.6 | 51.3 | 36.5 | 32.3 | 32.9 | 35.1 |
| | 9.5 | 11.6 | 13.4 | 4.0 | 22.3 | 16.3 | 14.8 | 13.4 | 13.3 |
| | 1.8 | 2.8 | 5.5 | -3.3 | 3.4 | 6.2 | 7.0 | 6.9 | 9.9 |
| Sales/Net Fixed Assets | 118.6 | 110.8 | 121.4 | 80.0 | 200.8 | 118.7 | 127.1 | 73.7 | 148.9 |
| | 24.4 | 29.1 | 30.7 | 17.0 | 42.3 | 68.4 | 27.8 | 44.4 | 13.3 |
| | 10.4 | 10.9 | 11.6 | 2.8 | 15.8 | 13.3 | 12.0 | 8.9 | 3.6 |
| Sales/Total Assets | 4.5 | 5.5 | 5.3 | 3.3 | 5.4 | 5.5 | 4.3 | 17.0 | 4.7 |
| | 2.0 | 2.4 | 2.6 | .9 | 3.2 | 3.7 | 2.5 | 4.4 | 2.5 |
| | 1.2 | 1.4 | 1.4 | .4 | 1.5 | 1.3 | 1.6 | 2.0 | 1.9 |
| % Depr., Dep., Amort./Sales | .3 | .4 | .3 | | | | .3 | .3 | .5 |
| | (64) 1.0 | (74) 1.0 | (64) .9 | | (18) .6 | | | (11) .9 | (10) 1.8 |
| | 2.0 | 1.8 | 2.1 | | 1.0 | | | 2.1 | 2.8 |
| % Officers', Directors' Owners' Comp/Sales | 1.2 | 1.2 | 1.7 | | 2.9 | | | | |
| | (43) 3.4 | (42) 2.6 | (43) 4.0 | | (14) 4.9 | | | | |
| | 7.0 | 6.0 | 5.2 | | 5.7 | | | | |
| Net Sales ($) | 813923M | 895251M | 1162034M | 7891M | 45591M | 40385M | 90288M | 216378M | 761501M |
| Total Assets ($) | 471343M | 397257M | 456222M | 10694M | 17545M | 16126M | 42097M | 80118M | 289642M |

© RMA 2012

M = $ thousand    MM = $ million
See Pages 9 through 22 for Explanation of Ratios and Data

## Current Data Sorted by Assets

## Comparative Historical Data

| | | | | | | Type of Statement | | |
|---|---|---|---|---|---|---|---|---|
| | | | | | | Unqualified | 3 | 3 |
| 2 | 1 | 5 | | 1 | 2 | Reviewed | 4 | 6 |
| 1 | 2 | 2 | 3 | | | Compiled | 6 | 5 |
| 10 | 11 | 5 | 1 | | | Tax Returns | 10 | 14 |
| 5 | 9 | 8 | | | | Other | 12 | 12 |
| | 7 (4/1-9/30/11) | | 65 (10/1/11-3/31/12) | | | | 4/1/07- 3/31/08 | 4/1/08- 3/31/09 |
| 0-500M | 500M-2MM | 2-10MM | 10-50MM | 50-100MM | 100-250MM | | ALL | ALL |
| 18 | 23 | 20 | 7 | 2 | 2 | NUMBER OF STATEMENTS | 35 | 40 |
| % | % | % | % | % | % | ASSETS | % | % |
| 20.2 | 10.3 | 8.9 | | | | Cash & Equivalents | 9.4 | 11.1 |
| 1.2 | 11.4 | 10.5 | | | | Trade Receivables (net) | 14.6 | 9.9 |
| 43.3 | 43.9 | 41.9 | | | | Inventory | 45.2 | 47.1 |
| .3 | 2.4 | 2.3 | | | | All Other Current | 4.2 | 1.6 |
| 64.9 | 68.0 | 63.5 | | | | Total Current | 73.4 | 69.7 |
| 23.4 | 23.2 | 24.1 | | | | Fixed Assets (net) | 17.4 | 22.4 |
| 1.8 | 3.4 | 5.3 | | | | Intangibles (net) | 4.1 | 2.9 |
| 9.9 | 5.4 | 7.1 | | | | All Other Non-Current | 5.2 | 5.0 |
| 100.0 | 100.0 | 100.0 | | | | Total | 100.0 | 100.0 |
| | | | | | | LIABILITIES | | |
| 6.7 | 6.6 | 7.9 | | | | Notes Payable-Short Term | 19.8 | 12.2 |
| 2.8 | 4.4 | 3.3 | | | | Cur. Mat.-L.T.D. | 2.2 | 1.9 |
| 10.8 | 11.8 | 14.9 | | | | Trade Payables | 19.2 | 17.3 |
| .2 | .1 | .0 | | | | Income Taxes Payable | .0 | .1 |
| 4.4 | 18.4 | 7.4 | | | | All Other Current | 11.2 | 7.4 |
| 25.0 | 41.4 | 33.5 | | | | Total Current | 52.3 | 38.8 |
| 25.9 | 24.1 | 18.8 | | | | Long-Term Debt | 15.9 | 20.3 |
| .0 | .0 | .1 | | | | Deferred Taxes | .0 | .1 |
| 13.0 | 5.7 | 2.0 | | | | All Other Non-Current | 7.7 | 9.1 |
| 36.1 | 28.8 | 45.6 | | | | Net Worth | 24.1 | 31.7 |
| 100.0 | 100.0 | 100.0 | | | | Total Liabilities & Net Worth | 100.0 | 100.0 |
| | | | | | | INCOME DATA | | |
| 100.0 | 100.0 | 100.0 | | | | Net Sales | 100.0 | 100.0 |
| 51.6 | 36.4 | 40.7 | | | | Gross Profit | 37.0 | 38.3 |
| 47.9 | 34.1 | 35.1 | | | | Operating Expenses | 34.0 | 33.9 |
| 3.7 | 2.4 | 5.5 | | | | Operating Profit | 3.0 | 4.3 |
| -.1 | .9 | .4 | | | | All Other Expenses (net) | .8 | .6 |
| 3.8 | 1.4 | 5.1 | | | | Profit Before Taxes | 2.3 | 3.8 |
| | | | | | | RATIOS | | |
| 8.8 | 3.2 | 2.7 | | | | | 2.7 | 2.7 |
| 3.1 | 1.6 | 1.7 | | | | Current | 1.7 | 1.9 |
| 1.3 | 1.3 | 1.5 | | | | | 1.2 | 1.3 |
| 4.1 | 1.2 | .9 | | | | | .9 | 1.1 |
| 1.2 | .4 | .4 | | | | Quick | .4 | .4 |
| .1 | .1 | .2 | | | | | .2 | .1 |
| 0 UND | 0 UND | 1 537.9 | | | | | 0 999.8 | 0 UND |
| 0 UND | 0 999.8 | 3 114.3 | | | | Sales/Receivables | 4 102.6 | 3 138.1 |
| 2 198.1 | 17 21.4 | 17 21.5 | | | | | 24 15.2 | 19 19.2 |
| 46 7.9 | 35 10.5 | 45 8.2 | | | | | 37 9.9 | 49 7.5 |
| 66 5.5 | 70 5.2 | 54 6.7 | | | | Cost of Sales/Inventory | 56 6.6 | 67 5.4 |
| 122 3.0 | 107 3.4 | 76 4.8 | | | | | 102 3.6 | 106 3.4 |
| 0 UND | 4 94.7 | 13 28.9 | | | | | 4 103.6 | 12 29.6 |
| 4 104.0 | 12 30.0 | 20 17.9 | | | | Cost of Sales/Payables | 23 15.7 | 21 17.2 |
| 32 11.3 | 24 14.9 | 42 8.7 | | | | | 46 8.0 | 39 9.4 |
| 7.3 | 7.1 | 5.3 | | | | | 8.5 | 5.6 |
| 12.1 | 12.7 | 16.2 | | | | Sales/Working Capital | 12.8 | 13.7 |
| 47.5 | 28.3 | 25.9 | | | | | 62.0 | 24.7 |
| | 7.4 | 10.8 | | | | | 13.9 | 11.6 |
| (19) .9 | (19) 4.6 | | | | EBIT/Interest | (27) 2.5 | (34) 2.8 |
| | -1.4 | 2.1 | | | | | 1.1 | .7 |
| | | | | | | Net Profit + Depr., Dep., Amort./Cur. Mat. L/T/D | | |
| .0 | .2 | .3 | | | | | .1 | .2 |
| .5 | .6 | .5 | | | | Fixed/Worth | .6 | .7 |
| NM | 13.3 | .9 | | | | | 1.3 | 2.5 |
| .1 | 1.0 | .5 | | | | | 1.0 | 1.0 |
| .9 | 2.8 | 1.4 | | | | Debt/Worth | 2.8 | 2.6 |
| NM | 22.9 | 5.6 | | | | | 8.0 | 6.2 |
| 64.6 | 43.7 | 53.5 | | | | | 48.3 | 70.2 |
| (14) 34.7 | (18) 13.9 | (19) 16.1 | | | | % Profit Before Taxes/Tangible Net Worth | (28) 20.8 | (37) 27.8 |
| 9.0 | -27.0 | 6.2 | | | | | 2.7 | 1.1 |
| 41.7 | 20.2 | 17.8 | | | | | 18.1 | 17.5 |
| 13.3 | 3.0 | 7.2 | | | | % Profit Before Taxes/Total Assets | 3.7 | 8.7 |
| -1.0 | -5.4 | 1.6 | | | | | .2 | .1 |
| 251.6 | 48.1 | 51.6 | | | | | 112.3 | 44.9 |
| 41.2 | 31.9 | 20.8 | | | | Sales/Net Fixed Assets | 35.9 | 29.9 |
| 12.9 | 10.6 | 9.2 | | | | | 12.7 | 10.0 |
| 5.3 | 4.4 | 4.1 | | | | | 5.4 | 5.6 |
| 3.8 | 3.2 | 3.3 | | | | Sales/Total Assets | 3.7 | 3.9 |
| 2.5 | 2.3 | 2.2 | | | | | 2.6 | 2.3 |
| .4 | .6 | .5 | | | | | .4 | .5 |
| (10) .8 | (18) 1.3 | (16) .9 | | | | % Depr., Dep., Amort./Sales | (26) .9 | (31) 1.0 |
| 3.4 | 2.1 | 1.3 | | | | | 1.7 | 2.0 |
| 2.7 | 2.0 | | | | | | 2.3 | 1.3 |
| (11) 7.6 | (12) 3.3 | | | | | % Officers', Directors' Owners' Comp/Sales | (17) 3.4 | (18) 3.0 |
| 10.7 | 5.1 | | | | | | 5.7 | 5.4 |
| 16996M | 97394M | 342791M | 377320M | 450003M | 401868M | Net Sales ($) | 608088M | 981931M |
| 4156M | 27352M | 88956M | 128264M | 163721M | 332602M | Total Assets ($) | 170063M | 314951M |

© RMA 2012

M = $ thousand    MM = $ million
See Pages 9 through 22 for Explanation of Ratios and Data

## Comparative Historical Data | | | Type of Statement | Current Data Sorted by Sales

| 4/1/09-3/31/10 ALL | 4/1/10-3/31/11 ALL | 4/1/11-3/31/12 ALL | Type of Statement | 0-1MM | 1-3MM | 3-5MM | 5-10MM | 10-25MM | 25MM & OVER |
|---|---|---|---|---|---|---|---|---|---|
| | | | | 7 (4/1-9/30/11) | | | 65 (10/1/11-3/31/12) | | |
| 6 | 4 | 3 | Unqualified | 1 | 1 | 1 | 2 | 3 | 3 |
| 8 | 3 | 11 | Reviewed | | | | | 3 | 3 |
| 10 | 9 | 6 | Compiled | 2 | | | 2 | 1 | 1 |
| 28 | 27 | 26 | Tax Returns | 6 | 6 | 8 | 2 | 3 | 1 |
| 19 | 21 | 26 | Other | 4 | 5 | 5 | 1 | 2 | 6 |
| 71 | 64 | 72 | **NUMBER OF STATEMENTS** | 13 | 12 | 14 | 7 | 12 | 14 |
| % | % | % | **ASSETS** | % | % | % | % | % | % |
| 9.7 | 7.6 | 13.1 | Cash & Equivalents | 15.0 | 17.0 | 14.4 | | 12.5 | 10.7 |
| 7.7 | 6.2 | 9.3 | Trade Receivables (net) | 1.1 | 2.8 | 12.6 | | 12.6 | 11.4 |
| 46.5 | 46.3 | 40.5 | Inventory | 40.0 | 37.1 | 52.4 | | 36.8 | 36.6 |
| 2.2 | 3.4 | 2.0 | All Other Current | .0 | .7 | 3.6 | | 1.3 | 3.9 |
| 66.2 | 63.5 | 64.8 | Total Current | 56.1 | 57.5 | 83.0 | | 63.2 | 62.6 |
| 23.7 | 24.8 | 24.2 | Fixed Assets (net) | 28.4 | 33.5 | 11.7 | | 23.9 | 25.7 |
| 4.8 | 6.2 | 4.5 | Intangibles (net) | 2.6 | 4.3 | 1.8 | | 8.4 | 7.9 |
| 5.4 | 5.4 | 6.5 | All Other Non-Current | 12.9 | 4.7 | 3.6 | | 4.5 | 3.8 |
| 100.0 | 100.0 | 100.0 | Total | 100.0 | 100.0 | 100.0 | | 100.0 | 100.0 |
| | | | **LIABILITIES** | | | | | | |
| 13.3 | 17.5 | 8.2 | Notes Payable-Short Term | 6.7 | 3.4 | 8.5 | | 7.1 | 14.0 |
| 1.5 | 6.7 | 3.3 | Cur. Mat.-L.T.D. | 1.7 | 3.0 | 3.6 | | 2.3 | 1.1 |
| 17.2 | 17.4 | 12.6 | Trade Payables | 10.4 | 9.5 | 13.1 | | 15.4 | 15.3 |
| .1 | .1 | .1 | Income Taxes Payable | .3 | .0 | .2 | | .0 | .2 |
| 9.3 | 10.3 | 10.2 | All Other Current | 3.5 | 10.7 | 21.1 | | 9.2 | 9.1 |
| 41.4 | 52.0 | 34.3 | Total Current | 22.7 | 26.6 | 46.5 | | 34.1 | 39.8 |
| 24.3 | 16.2 | 21.0 | Long-Term Debt | 36.4 | 21.9 | 21.7 | | 12.1 | 11.2 |
| .1 | .1 | .1 | Deferred Taxes | .0 | .0 | .0 | | .0 | .5 |
| 6.9 | 11.7 | 6.1 | All Other Non-Current | 16.8 | 10.8 | .7 | | 1.3 | 4.3 |
| 27.3 | 19.9 | 38.4 | Net Worth | 24.1 | 40.7 | 31.1 | | 52.6 | 44.3 |
| 100.0 | 100.0 | 100.0 | Total Liabilities & Net Worth | 100.0 | 100.0 | 100.0 | | 100.0 | 100.0 |
| | | | **INCOME DATA** | | | | | | |
| 100.0 | 100.0 | 100.0 | Net Sales | 100.0 | 100.0 | 100.0 | | 100.0 | 100.0 |
| 36.7 | 42.5 | 41.7 | Gross Profit | 56.5 | 40.5 | 39.2 | | 34.6 | 36.5 |
| 34.2 | 38.7 | 37.8 | Operating Expenses | 52.6 | 37.6 | 35.0 | | 33.6 | 31.9 |
| 2.5 | 3.8 | 4.0 | Operating Profit | 4.0 | 2.9 | 4.2 | | 1.0 | 4.5 |
| .7 | .5 | .5 | All Other Expenses (net) | 1.1 | .3 | .9 | | -.7 | .4 |
| 1.9 | 3.3 | 3.5 | Profit Before Taxes | 2.9 | 2.7 | 3.3 | | 1.7 | 4.2 |
| | | | **RATIOS** | | | | | | |
| 2.9 | 3.1 | 4.2 | | 9.7 | 7.2 | 6.1 | | 3.1 | 2.4 |
| 1.6 | 1.7 | 1.8 | Current | 2.6 | 1.5 | 1.9 | | 2.0 | 1.7 |
| 1.1 | .9 | 1.3 | | 1.1 | 1.0 | 1.5 | | 1.3 | 1.3 |
| .8 | .7 | 1.6 | | 4.5 | 3.4 | 1.7 | | 1.0 | 1.1 |
| (70) .4 | .3 | .6 | Quick | .9 | .5 | .6 | | .5 | .3 |
| .1 | .0 | .2 | | .1 | .1 | .2 | | .3 | .1 |
| 0 UND | 0 UND | 0 UND | | 0 UND | 0 UND | 0 UND | | 0 UND | 1 667.0 |
| 1 601.5 | 0 UND | 2 219.3 | Sales/Receivables | 0 UND | 0 UND | 4 94.0 | | 2 158.6 | 3 134.5 |
| 8 46.9 | 7 52.1 | 9 40.0 | | 2 164.2 | 3 141.2 | 18 20.8 | | 30 12.3 | 13 29.1 |
| 48 7.6 | 44 8.3 | 45 8.2 | | 30 12.2 | 36 10.2 | 46 7.9 | | 30 12.2 | 45 8.2 |
| 62 5.9 | 61 6.0 | 61 6.0 | Cost of Sales/Inventory | 70 5.2 | 57 6.4 | 85 4.3 | | 47 7.7 | 57 6.4 |
| 95 3.8 | 109 3.3 | 87 4.2 | | 146 2.5 | 104 3.5 | 182 2.0 | | 68 5.4 | 64 5.7 |
| 12 30.8 | 7 52.5 | 4 88.8 | | 0 UND | 0 UND | 6 65.4 | | 13 28.9 | 14 26.7 |
| 24 14.9 | 23 15.8 | 15 23.9 | Cost of Sales/Payables | 3 128.5 | 6 56.2 | 14 26.7 | | 16 23.3 | 20 18.5 |
| 41 8.9 | 36 10.2 | 39 9.3 | | 24 15.4 | 27 13.5 | 47 7.8 | | 35 10.3 | 43 8.4 |
| 8.6 | 10.0 | 7.1 | | 5.9 | 7.7 | 4.5 | | 11.8 | 7.2 |
| 15.6 | 16.8 | 13.8 | Sales/Working Capital | 20.9 | 15.6 | 9.6 | | 16.5 | 17.8 |
| 125.8 | -180.0 | 35.2 | | NM | NM | 13.3 | | 21.2 | 40.8 |
| 16.2 | 13.3 | 12.2 | | | | 13.4 | | 10.7 | 16.6 |
| (65) 4.0 | (55) 7.0 | (55) 3.4 | EBIT/Interest | | | (13) .9 | | (10) 6.6 | (12) 4.9 |
| .9 | 1.2 | .9 | | | | -1.7 | | 1.8 | 3.3 |
| | | 7.8 | Net Profit + Depr., Dep., Amort./Cur. Mat. L/T/D | | | | | | |
| | (12) 4.4 | 4.4 | | | | | | | |
| | | .8 | | | | | | | |
| .2 | .3 | .1 | | .1 | .1 | .1 | | .3 | .1 |
| .8 | 1.0 | .5 | Fixed/Worth | 1.1 | 1.3 | .4 | | .5 | .7 |
| 4.0 | NM | 3.6 | | -3.7 | 11.3 | NM | | .9 | 3.1 |
| 1.1 | 1.1 | .5 | | .1 | .5 | .7 | | .3 | 1.1 |
| 2.9 | 2.1 | 1.4 | Debt/Worth | 1.2 | 3.9 | 1.3 | | 1.0 | 1.5 |
| 10.9 | NM | 9.4 | | -8.3 | 11.7 | NM | | 6.1 | 5.7 |
| 61.4 | 65.8 | 52.2 | | | 60.7 | 48.4 | | 45.4 | 42.2 |
| (58) 33.5 | (48) 32.7 | (60) 21.7 | % Profit Before Taxes/Tangible Net Worth | (10) 22.5 | (11) 6.2 | | 14.2 | (12) 29.5 | |
| 9.1 | 12.0 | 5.1 | | | 5.2 | -40.9 | | 2.7 | 11.1 |
| 18.8 | 20.7 | 20.3 | | 37.0 | 33.9 | 28.3 | | 10.0 | 12.9 |
| 9.6 | 8.7 | 7.4 | % Profit Before Taxes/Total Assets | 2.3 | 8.7 | 2.3 | | 7.2 | 8.4 |
| -.1 | .9 | .4 | | -3.4 | -.2 | -12.0 | | 1.0 | 5.0 |
| 66.6 | 58.0 | 53.0 | | 188.2 | 140.3 | 69.9 | | 52.1 | 32.9 |
| 26.3 | 28.6 | 24.5 | Sales/Net Fixed Assets | 31.4 | 11.8 | 38.6 | | 21.1 | 20.6 |
| 8.1 | 9.0 | 9.2 | | 9.8 | 3.7 | 29.7 | | 7.0 | 7.4 |
| 5.1 | 6.3 | 4.2 | | 4.2 | 5.7 | 4.6 | | 6.4 | 4.2 |
| 3.5 | 4.1 | 3.4 | Sales/Total Assets | 3.5 | 3.3 | 3.4 | | 3.5 | 3.3 |
| 2.3 | 2.2 | 2.3 | | 1.9 | 2.1 | 2.7 | | 2.7 | 2.4 |
| .4 | .5 | .6 | | | | .7 | | .4 | .8 |
| (52) 1.0 | (46) 1.0 | (55) 1.1 | % Depr., Dep., Amort./Sales | | | (10) 1.3 | | (10) .7 | (13) 1.1 |
| 1.7 | 1.8 | 1.8 | | | | 1.8 | | 2.3 | 1.4 |
| 2.3 | 2.1 | 1.8 | | | | | | | |
| (31) 3.6 | (26) 3.3 | (34) 3.3 | % Officers', Directors' Owners' Comp/Sales | | | | | | |
| 6.4 | 6.6 | 7.6 | | | | | | | |
| 1951133M | 1375586M | 1686372M | Net Sales ($) | 7500M | 20396M | 57681M | 46579M | 176214M | 1378002M |
| 689655M | 544913M | 745051M | Total Assets ($) | 4274M | 7233M | 20214M | 21420M | 52899M | 639011M |

M = $ thousand    MM = $ million
See Pages 9 through 22 for Explanation of Ratios and Data

## Current Data Sorted by Assets　　　　　　　　Comparative Historical Data

| | | | | | | Type of Statement | | |
|---|---|---|---|---|---|---|---|---|
| | | 1 | 2 | | | Unqualified | 2 | 4 |
| | | 3 | 2 | | | Reviewed | 7 | 6 |
| | 1 | 2 | 1 | 1 | | Compiled | 4 | 3 |
| 3 | 10 | 4 | | | | Tax Returns | 10 | 11 |
| 4 | 5 | 7 | | | | Other | 10 | 16 |
| | 10 (4/1-9/30/11) | | 40 (10/1/11-3/31/12) | | | | 4/1/07-3/31/08 | 4/1/08-3/31/09 |
| 0-500M | 500M-2MM | 2-10MM | 10-50MM | 50-100MM | 100-250MM | | ALL | ALL |
| 7 | 16 | 17 | 6 | 3 | 1 | NUMBER OF STATEMENTS | 33 | 40 |
| % | % | % | % | % | % | ASSETS | % | % |
| | 18.3 | 13.6 | | | | Cash & Equivalents | 14.4 | 6.4 |
| | 15.5 | 8.0 | | | | Trade Receivables (net) | 10.4 | 10.7 |
| | 44.8 | 53.1 | | | | Inventory | 53.4 | 47.2 |
| | 5.0 | .7 | | | | All Other Current | 3.9 | .8 |
| | 83.5 | 75.4 | | | | Total Current | 82.0 | 65.1 |
| | 10.7 | 9.6 | | | | Fixed Assets (net) | 9.9 | 22.1 |
| | 1.5 | 3.3 | | | | Intangibles (net) | 2.4 | 3.3 |
| | 4.2 | 11.7 | | | | All Other Non-Current | 5.7 | 9.4 |
| | 100.0 | 100.0 | | | | Total | 100.0 | 100.0 |
| | | | | | | LIABILITIES | | |
| | 13.4 | 11.7 | | | | Notes Payable-Short Term | 12.3 | 9.7 |
| | .8 | .1 | | | | Cur. Mat.-L.T.D. | 5.2 | 2.2 |
| | 11.3 | 16.9 | | | | Trade Payables | 17.9 | 20.3 |
| | .0 | .1 | | | | Income Taxes Payable | .0 | .0 |
| | 9.6 | 8.9 | | | | All Other Current | 7.8 | 11.5 |
| | 35.1 | 37.6 | | | | Total Current | 43.2 | 43.6 |
| | 6.9 | 6.9 | | | | Long-Term Debt | 13.7 | 17.3 |
| | .0 | .0 | | | | Deferred Taxes | .0 | .0 |
| | 10.3 | 27.3 | | | | All Other Non-Current | 7.8 | 20.0 |
| | 47.7 | 28.2 | | | | Net Worth | 35.2 | 19.0 |
| | 100.0 | 100.0 | | | | Total Liabilties & Net Worth | 100.0 | 100.0 |
| | | | | | | INCOME DATA | | |
| | 100.0 | 100.0 | | | | Net Sales | 100.0 | 100.0 |
| | 46.9 | 45.5 | | | | Gross Profit | 45.0 | 45.8 |
| | 37.7 | 34.3 | | | | Operating Expenses | 37.0 | 40.0 |
| | 9.3 | 11.2 | | | | Operating Profit | 7.9 | 5.8 |
| | -.3 | 3.4 | | | | All Other Expenses (net) | -.3 | 3.2 |
| | 9.6 | 7.8 | | | | Profit Before Taxes | 8.2 | 2.6 |
| | | | | | | RATIOS | | |
| | 11.4 | 4.4 | | | | | 3.5 | 4.5 |
| | 2.5 | 2.3 | | | | Current | 2.3 | 2.1 |
| | 1.5 | 1.3 | | | | | 1.2 | 1.0 |
| | 2.2 | .9 | | | | | 1.1 | 1.4 |
| | .7 | .5 | | | | Quick | .6 | .4 |
| | .2 | .3 | | | | | .2 | .1 |
| 0 | UND | 0 | UND | | | | 0 | UND | 0 | UND |
| 9 | 39.9 | 9 | 39.9 | | | Sales/Receivables | 15 | 24.2 | 12 | 31.1 |
| 43 | 8.5 | 46 | 7.9 | | | | 36 | 10.2 | 52 | 7.1 |
| 35 | 10.3 | 111 | 3.3 | | | | 69 | 5.3 | 96 | 3.8 |
| 182 | 2.0 | 215 | 1.7 | | | Cost of Sales/Inventory | 170 | 2.2 | 222 | 1.6 |
| 730 | .5 | 365 | 1.0 | | | | 607 | .6 | 443 | .8 |
| 3 | 104.9 | 5 | 75.8 | | | | 1 | 402.6 | 5 | 75.8 |
| 10 | 35.4 | 73 | 5.0 | | | Cost of Sales/Payables | 58 | 6.3 | 31 | 11.9 |
| 42 | 8.6 | 114 | 3.2 | | | | 99 | 3.7 | 79 | 4.6 |
| | 1.6 | 1.9 | | | | | 1.9 | 2.2 |
| | 4.2 | 4.5 | | | | Sales/Working Capital | 5.0 | 3.4 |
| | 13.7 | 13.2 | | | | | 21.9 | 313.3 |
| | | 22.4 | | | | | 6.1 | 9.0 |
| | (16) | 9.8 | | | | EBIT/Interest | (21) | 3.7 | (31) | 3.4 |
| | | 1.9 | | | | | 1.5 | 1.2 |
| | | | | | | Net Profit + Depr., Dep., Amort./Cur. Mat. L/T/D | | |
| | .0 | .1 | | | | | .0 | .1 |
| | .3 | .1 | | | | Fixed/Worth | .1 | 1.2 |
| | .9 | 11.2 | | | | | UND | 12.0 |
| | .3 | .7 | | | | | .6 | .5 |
| | .8 | 1.7 | | | | Debt/Worth | 1.6 | 2.2 |
| | 7.3 | 63.0 | | | | | UND | 79.2 |
| | 53.9 | 69.6 | | | | | 45.2 | 31.3 |
| (13) | 6.0 | (15) | 24.1 | | | % Profit Before Taxes/Tangible Net Worth | (26) | 26.1 | (31) | 8.9 |
| | 5.1 | 1.6 | | | | | 6.0 | 2.0 |
| | 14.9 | 24.4 | | | | | 21.5 | 10.3 |
| | 4.2 | 8.6 | | | | % Profit Before Taxes/Total Assets | 10.3 | 3.3 |
| | .7 | .7 | | | | | 2.9 | -1.5 |
| | 40.6 | 64.9 | | | | | 289.7 | 47.2 |
| | 25.2 | 26.4 | | | | Sales/Net Fixed Assets | 48.0 | 16.1 |
| | 14.1 | 7.9 | | | | | 14.5 | 4.1 |
| | 2.9 | 2.4 | | | | | 3.0 | 2.5 |
| | 1.9 | 1.4 | | | | Sales/Total Assets | 1.8 | 1.5 |
| | .6 | .7 | | | | | .9 | .8 |
| | | .1 | | | | | .3 | .5 |
| | (11) | .4 | | | | % Depr., Dep., Amort./Sales | (23) | .6 | (30) | 1.2 |
| | | 1.1 | | | | | 1.4 | 2.1 |
| | 4.6 | 2.1 | | | | | 2.1 | 2.8 |
| (11) | 6.8 | (13) | 3.8 | | | % Officers', Directors' Owners' Comp/Sales | (20) | 4.9 | (18) | 4.7 |
| | 11.9 | 9.2 | | | | | 12.4 | 8.0 |
| 4910M | 40756M | 110139M | 73671M | 235608M | 30776M | Net Sales ($) | 944104M | 662825M |
| 1595M | 18890M | 76799M | 103063M | 231642M | 212648M | Total Assets ($) | 744445M | 744966M |

M = $ thousand　　MM = $ million
See Pages 9 through 22 for Explanation of Ratios and Data

## Comparative Historical Data | Current Data Sorted by Sales

Historical columns: 4/1/09-3/31/10 ALL · 4/1/10-3/31/11 ALL · 4/1/11-3/31/12 ALL
Current columns period: 10 (4/1-9/30/11) · 40 (10/1/11-3/31/12)

| | 4/1/09-3/31/10 ALL | 4/1/10-3/31/11 ALL | 4/1/11-3/31/12 ALL | 0-1MM | 1-3MM | 3-5MM | 5-10MM | 10-25MM | 25MM & OVER |
|---|---|---|---|---|---|---|---|---|---|
| **Type of Statement** | | | | | | | | | |
| Unqualified | 4 | 2 | 3 | | 2 | | 3 | 2 | 1 |
| Reviewed | 7 | 9 | 6 | | | | 1 | | |
| Compiled | 6 | 1 | 4 | | 1 | | 2 | 1 | |
| Tax Returns | 12 | 18 | 17 | 6 | 6 | 2 | 3 | | |
| Other | 16 | 17 | 20 | 3 | 6 | | 6 | 2 | 3 |
| **NUMBER OF STATEMENTS** | 45 | 47 | 50 | 9 | 15 | 2 | 15 | 5 | 4 |
| | % | % | % | % | % | % | % | % | % |
| **ASSETS** | | | | | | | | | |
| Cash & Equivalents | 16.3 | 12.1 | 16.0 | | 15.2 | | 19.2 | | |
| Trade Receivables (net) | 8.8 | 9.0 | 9.9 | | 14.7 | | 9.5 | | |
| Inventory | 49.2 | 53.2 | 49.0 | | 47.7 | | 54.0 | | |
| All Other Current | 1.2 | 1.6 | 3.1 | | 1.5 | | .6 | | |
| Total Current | 75.5 | 76.0 | 78.0 | | 79.1 | | 83.3 | | |
| Fixed Assets (net) | 14.1 | 15.6 | 10.3 | | 11.4 | | 8.7 | | |
| Intangibles (net) | 2.3 | 2.3 | 2.0 | | 2.0 | | 1.8 | | |
| All Other Non-Current | 8.1 | 6.1 | 9.7 | | 7.5 | | 6.2 | | |
| Total | 100.0 | 100.0 | 100.0 | | 100.0 | | 100.0 | | |
| **LIABILITIES** | | | | | | | | | |
| Notes Payable-Short Term | 13.5 | 16.6 | 14.5 | | 13.1 | | 18.2 | | |
| Cur. Mat.-L.T.D. | .9 | 1.9 | .7 | | 1.3 | | .4 | | |
| Trade Payables | 9.3 | 17.7 | 14.2 | | 11.7 | | 16.4 | | |
| Income Taxes Payable | .3 | .0 | .0 | | .0 | | .0 | | |
| All Other Current | 9.8 | 13.5 | 9.8 | | 15.4 | | 6.4 | | |
| Total Current | 33.7 | 49.6 | 39.3 | | 41.5 | | 41.3 | | |
| Long-Term Debt | 12.8 | 5.9 | 9.3 | | 8.0 | | 4.1 | | |
| Deferred Taxes | .0 | .0 | .0 | | .0 | | .0 | | |
| All Other Non-Current | 9.5 | 9.7 | 29.1 | | 9.3 | | 19.0 | | |
| Net Worth | 43.9 | 34.7 | 22.2 | | 41.2 | | 35.6 | | |
| Total Liabilities & Net Worth | 100.0 | 100.0 | 100.0 | | 100.0 | | 100.0 | | |
| **INCOME DATA** | | | | | | | | | |
| Net Sales | 100.0 | 100.0 | 100.0 | | 100.0 | | 100.0 | | |
| Gross Profit | 42.1 | 46.5 | 46.2 | | 49.7 | | 38.5 | | |
| Operating Expenses | 36.1 | 39.8 | 35.9 | | 41.8 | | 29.6 | | |
| Operating Profit | 6.0 | 6.7 | 10.3 | | 7.9 | | 8.9 | | |
| All Other Expenses (net) | 1.6 | 2.7 | 1.7 | | .9 | | 5.2 | | |
| Profit Before Taxes | 4.4 | 4.0 | 8.6 | | 7.1 | | 3.7 | | |
| **RATIOS** | | | | | | | | | |
| Current | 5.0 / 2.4 / 1.4 | 5.2 / 1.6 / .9 | 5.0 / 2.2 / 1.3 | | 5.1 / 1.9 / 1.2 | | 3.3 / 2.2 / 1.5 | | |
| Quick | 2.1 / .6 / .2 | 1.1 / .4 / .1 | 1.0 / .5 / .2 | | 1.7 / .6 / .3 | | 1.1 / .5 / .2 | | |
| Sales/Receivables | 0 UND / 13 27.6 / 49 7.4 | 0 UND / 6 58.4 / 40 9.0 | 0 UND / 10 36.2 / 45 8.1 | | 7 50.6 / 28 13.0 / 50 7.3 | | 0 UND / 9 39.9 / 47 7.8 | | |
| Cost of Sales/Inventory | 69 5.3 / 247 1.5 / 655 .6 | 80 4.5 / 209 1.7 / 795 .5 | 89 4.1 / 203 1.8 / 608 .6 | | 52 7.0 / 182 2.0 / 912 .4 | | 73 5.0 / 228 1.6 / 456 .8 | | |
| Cost of Sales/Payables | 2 167.1 / 25 14.5 / 77 4.8 | 8 48.2 / 42 8.6 / 105 3.5 | 5 78.0 / 37 9.8 / 104 3.5 | | 7 51.0 / 36 10.0 / 89 4.1 | | 16 23.0 / 65 5.6 / 85 4.3 | | |
| Sales/Working Capital | 1.5 / 4.3 / 20.0 | 1.1 / 6.4 / -15.9 | 2.0 / 4.8 / 15.7 | | 3.1 / 5.6 / 17.7 | | 2.1 / 5.0 / 15.5 | | |
| EBIT/Interest | (35) 14.2 / 4.1 / 1.6 | (37) 15.7 / 4.0 / .8 | (38) 20.3 / 6.2 / 1.6 | | (13) 21.7 / 4.0 / 1.5 | | (11) 15.2 / 3.1 / -.4 | | |
| Net Profit + Depr., Dep., Amort./Cur. Mat. L/T/D | | | | | | | | | |
| Fixed/Worth | .0 / .2 / 2.0 | .1 / .4 / 4.7 | .1 / .2 / 5.4 | | .0 / .2 / 1.0 | | .1 / .2 / 10.9 | | |
| Debt/Worth | .4 / 1.6 / 6.8 | .4 / 2.3 / 49.5 | .7 / 2.2 / 25.5 | | .5 / 1.7 / 8.8 | | 1.0 / 1.4 / 51.2 | | |
| % Profit Before Taxes/Tangible Net Worth | (41) 49.2 / 14.7 / 4.6 | (39) 77.0 / 17.4 / .5 | (41) 65.6 / 20.0 / 5.4 | | (13) 106.9 / 17.0 / 1.5 | | (13) 65.6 / 20.3 / 3.9 | | |
| % Profit Before Taxes/Total Assets | 11.0 / 5.8 / .6 | 19.7 / 6.4 / -.3 | 15.5 / 5.5 / 1.1 | | 15.4 / 5.8 / .6 | | 33.3 / 3.3 / -.5 | | |
| Sales/Net Fixed Assets | 98.0 / 22.0 / 9.5 | 84.2 / 24.2 / 7.8 | 62.8 / 26.4 / 10.8 | | 34.3 / 21.6 / 8.0 | | 69.3 / 15.9 / 9.0 | | |
| Sales/Total Assets | 2.5 / 1.6 / .5 | 4.5 / 1.2 / .5 | 2.4 / 1.7 / .6 | | 2.4 / 1.8 / .6 | | 2.8 / 1.7 / .6 | | |
| % Depr., Dep., Amort./Sales | (28) .2 / 1.2 / 1.9 | (33) .3 / .7 / 1.6 | (31) .2 / .6 / 1.4 | | | | .3 / .7 / 1.4 | (10) | |
| % Officers', Directors', Owners' Comp/Sales | (25) 2.0 / 3.2 / 7.5 | (29) 2.6 / 6.0 / 10.1 | (34) 2.1 / 5.4 / 8.1 | | (10) 3.5 / 6.1 / 10.0 | | (12) 2.0 / 3.1 / 8.9 | | |
| Net Sales ($) | 870265M | 557806M | 495860M | 2408M | 29582M | 8985M | 105091M | 83410M | 266384M |
| Total Assets ($) | 689616M | 687830M | 644637M | 5803M | 27345M | 3959M | 117415M | 45825M | 444290M |

M = $ thousand    MM = $ million
See Pages 9 through 22 for Explanation of Ratios and Data

## Current Data Sorted by Assets

## Comparative Historical Data

| | | | | | | | Type of Statement | | | |
|---|---|---|---|---|---|---|---|---|---|---|
| | | 1 | 3 | | | | Unqualified | | 4 | 9 |
| | 2 | 1 | 4 | | | | Reviewed | | 4 | 16 |
| | 16 | 9 | 1 | | | | Compiled | | 44 | 33 |
| 6 | 14 | 5 | 1 | | | | Tax Returns | | 39 | 45 |
| 1 | 14 | 5 | 4 | 1 | | | Other | | 24 | 36 |
| | 18 (4/1-9/30/11) | | 70 (10/1/11-3/31/12) | | | | | | 4/1/07-3/31/08 | 4/1/08-3/31/09 |
| 0-500M | 500M-2MM | 2-10MM | 10-50MM | 50-100MM | 100-250MM | | | | ALL | ALL |
| 7 | 46 | 21 | 13 | 1 | | | NUMBER OF STATEMENTS | | 115 | 139 |
| % | % | % | % | % | % | | ASSETS | | % | % |
| | 11.0 | 12.4 | 6.3 | | | D | Cash & Equivalents | | 7.6 | 9.8 |
| | 9.2 | 11.3 | 9.3 | | | A | Trade Receivables (net) | | 8.4 | 7.8 |
| | 53.4 | 43.8 | 24.8 | | | T | Inventory | | 56.5 | 53.9 |
| | 3.4 | 3.8 | .9 | | | A | All Other Current | | 4.2 | 3.4 |
| | 77.1 | 71.2 | 41.2 | | | | Total Current | | 76.8 | 74.9 |
| | 14.4 | 20.4 | 37.8 | | | N | Fixed Assets (net) | | 14.7 | 16.7 |
| | 1.9 | .7 | .9 | | | O | Intangibles (net) | | 1.3 | 1.6 |
| | 6.6 | 7.7 | 20.0 | | | T | All Other Non-Current | | 7.2 | 6.8 |
| | 100.0 | 100.0 | 100.0 | | | | Total | | 100.0 | 100.0 |
| | | | | | | A | LIABILITIES | | | |
| | 35.9 | 15.4 | 15.0 | | | V | Notes Payable-Short Term | | 36.4 | 33.6 |
| | 3.4 | 1.5 | 1.4 | | | A | Cur. Mat.-L.T.D. | | 3.0 | 4.8 |
| | 4.3 | 6.5 | 5.4 | | | I | Trade Payables | | 8.7 | 5.1 |
| | .1 | .0 | .0 | | | L | Income Taxes Payable | | .0 | .1 |
| | 11.3 | 17.1 | 13.0 | | | A | All Other Current | | 11.9 | 13.6 |
| | 55.0 | 40.5 | 34.8 | | | B | Total Current | | 60.1 | 57.1 |
| | 15.5 | 16.4 | 11.8 | | | L | Long-Term Debt | | 9.9 | 14.8 |
| | .0 | .0 | .0 | | | E | Deferred Taxes | | .0 | .0 |
| | 9.6 | 5.7 | 3.1 | | | | All Other Non-Current | | 5.1 | 5.8 |
| | 20.0 | 37.4 | 50.3 | | | | Net Worth | | 24.9 | 22.3 |
| | 100.0 | 100.0 | 100.0 | | | | Total Liabilities & Net Worth | | 100.0 | 100.0 |
| | | | | | | | INCOME DATA | | | |
| | 100.0 | 100.0 | 100.0 | | | | Net Sales | | 100.0 | 100.0 |
| | 27.6 | 30.8 | 31.5 | | | | Gross Profit | | 22.9 | 25.3 |
| | 25.1 | 27.0 | 29.7 | | | | Operating Expenses | | 21.0 | 22.7 |
| | 2.5 | 3.7 | 1.8 | | | | Operating Profit | | 1.8 | 2.6 |
| | 1.7 | .5 | .0 | | | | All Other Expenses (net) | | 1.1 | 1.2 |
| | .8 | 3.3 | 1.8 | | | | Profit Before Taxes | | .7 | 1.4 |
| | | | | | | | RATIOS | | | |
| | 2.9 | 2.7 | 2.8 | | | | | | 2.0 | 2.4 |
| | 1.4 | 1.7 | 1.3 | | | | Current | | 1.2 | 1.3 |
| | .9 | 1.3 | .4 | | | | | | 1.0 | 1.0 |
| | .6 | 1.2 | 1.0 | | | | | | .6 | .7 |
| | .3 | .5 | .4 | | | | Quick | (113) | .2 | .3 |
| | .2 | .1 | .2 | | | | | | .1 | .1 |

| | | | | | 2 | 237.1 | | 0 | 999.8 | 0 | UND |
|---|---|---|---|---|---|---|---|---|---|---|---|
| 0 | UND | 0 | UND | | | | | | | | |
| 6 | 61.0 | 3 | 104.3 | 10 | 36.4 | Sales/Receivables | 6 | 58.5 | 5 | 78.6 |
| 25 | 14.5 | 31 | 11.7 | 39 | 9.4 | | 19 | 19.4 | 22 | 16.6 |
| 118 | 3.1 | 81 | 4.5 | 6 | 62.0 | | 96 | 3.8 | 83 | 4.4 |
| 166 | 2.2 | 146 | 2.5 | 126 | 2.9 | Cost of Sales/Inventory | 141 | 2.6 | 141 | 2.6 |
| 228 | 1.6 | 365 | 1.0 | 174 | 2.1 | | 201 | 1.8 | 226 | 1.6 |
| 0 | UND | 3 | 130.8 | 9 | 40.8 | | 1 | 633.2 | 0 | UND |
| 4 | 85.1 | 8 | 44.7 | 20 | 18.6 | Cost of Sales/Payables | 4 | 81.3 | 4 | 82.9 |
| 19 | 19.5 | 38 | 9.7 | 25 | 14.6 | | 15 | 24.2 | 15 | 24.3 |

| | | | | | | | | | | |
|---|---|---|---|---|---|---|---|---|---|---|
| | 4.1 | 2.2 | 4.3 | | | | | | 4.8 | 3.9 |
| | 8.3 | 5.6 | 17.0 | | | Sales/Working Capital | | | 11.8 | 13.2 |
| | -39.8 | 11.5 | -16.2 | | | | | | UND | -73.6 |
| | 3.1 | 10.8 | 16.3 | | | | | | 3.8 | 3.5 |
| (45) | 1.6 | (19) 2.6 | 3.9 | | | EBIT/Interest | (109) | | 1.4 | (132) 1.4 |
| | .8 | -.1 | -1.6 | | | | | | .6 | .0 |
| | | | | | | | | | | 6.3 |
| | | | | | | Net Profit + Depr., Dep., Amort./Cur. Mat. L/T/D | (18) | | | 2.5 |
| | | | | | | | | | | .0 |
| | .1 | .1 | .4 | | | | | | .1 | .1 |
| | .5 | .3 | .9 | | | Fixed/Worth | | | .5 | .5 |
| | -8.6 | 1.0 | 1.3 | | | | | | 3.4 | 2.6 |
| | 1.8 | .8 | .5 | | | | | | 1.2 | 1.2 |
| | 4.9 | 1.6 | 1.1 | | | Debt/Worth | | | 3.7 | 3.9 |
| | -65.0 | 5.3 | 2.1 | | | | | | 44.0 | 17.4 |
| | 30.9 | 43.1 | 22.4 | | | | | | 36.8 | 25.9 |
| (32) | 9.6 | (19) 8.7 | 6.3 | | | % Profit Before Taxes/Tangible Net Worth | (94) | | 12.3 | (112) 8.9 |
| | 1.1 | .3 | -4.9 | | | | | | -2.5 | -5.8 |
| | 8.3 | 11.1 | 10.3 | | | | | | 8.8 | 7.3 |
| | 2.5 | 3.5 | 5.0 | | | % Profit Before Taxes/Total Assets | | | 2.3 | 1.5 |
| | -1.8 | -2.4 | -3.0 | | | | | | -2.9 | -4.1 |
| | 61.4 | 50.2 | 11.3 | | | | | | 67.7 | 76.0 |
| | 17.4 | 11.6 | 7.0 | | | Sales/Net Fixed Assets | | | 24.4 | 27.3 |
| | 7.4 | 3.7 | 2.0 | | | | | | 9.2 | 7.1 |
| | 2.6 | 1.8 | 2.5 | | | | | | 2.9 | 2.9 |
| | 1.7 | 1.2 | 1.9 | | | Sales/Total Assets | | | 2.1 | 1.8 |
| | 1.1 | .8 | 1.0 | | | | | | 1.4 | 1.1 |
| | .5 | .6 | .7 | | | | | | .4 | .3 |
| (27) | 1.1 | (19) 1.5 | (11) 2.0 | | | % Depr., Dep., Amort./Sales | (94) | | .7 | (110) .7 |
| | 2.5 | 4.3 | 2.5 | | | | | | 1.4 | 1.7 |
| | 1.8 | | | | | | | | 1.4 | 1.5 |
| (20) | 3.4 | | | | | % Officers', Directors' Owners' Comp/Sales | (52) | | 2.6 | (65) 2.4 |
| | 6.5 | | | | | | | | 3.8 | 4.1 |

| 5986M | 90622M | 125479M | 584544M | 307822M | | Net Sales ($) | | 891560M | 1751751M |
|---|---|---|---|---|---|---|---|---|---|
| 1837M | 49218M | 98119M | 302272M | 85770M | | Total Assets ($) | | 448878M | 873106M |

M = $ thousand    MM = $ million
See Pages 9 through 22 for Explanation of Ratios and Data

## Comparative Historical Data | Current Data Sorted by Sales

| 6 15 26 28 31 (4/1/09-3/31/10 ALL) | 5 10 34 24 32 (4/1/10-3/31/11 ALL) | 4 7 26 26 25 (4/1/11-3/31/12 ALL) | Type of Statement | 18 (4/1-9/30/11) 0-1MM | 1-3MM | 70 (10/1/11-3/31/12) 3-5MM | 5-10MM | 10-25MM | 25MM & OVER |
|---|---|---|---|---|---|---|---|---|---|
| 6 | 5 | 4 | Unqualified | | | 1 | | | 3 |
| 15 | 10 | 7 | Reviewed | | | 3 | | 3 | 1 |
| 26 | 34 | 26 | Compiled | 7 | 8 | 5 | 4 | 1 | 1 |
| 28 | 24 | 26 | Tax Returns | 9 | 10 | 2 | 3 | 2 | |
| 31 | 32 | 25 | Other | 6 | 8 | 3 | 3 | 2 | 3 |
| 106 | 105 | 88 | **NUMBER OF STATEMENTS** | 22 | 26 | 14 | 10 | 8 | 8 |
| % | % | % | **ASSETS** | % | % | % | % | % | % |
| 8.9 | 13.9 | 10.7 | Cash & Equivalents | 8.3 | 10.7 | 13.2 | 19.6 | | |
| 8.6 | 11.1 | 10.6 | Trade Receivables (net) | 12.4 | 6.8 | 10.5 | 16.6 | | |
| 49.7 | 40.6 | 45.4 | Inventory | 46.8 | 54.4 | 44.6 | 43.3 | | |
| 4.9 | 3.6 | 2.9 | All Other Current | 5.1 | 1.6 | 1.9 | 6.1 | | |
| 72.1 | 69.2 | 69.6 | Total Current | 72.6 | 73.4 | 70.3 | 85.6 | | |
| 18.1 | 18.8 | 20.1 | Fixed Assets (net) | 19.0 | 19.5 | 17.8 | 11.2 | | |
| 1.3 | 1.3 | 1.5 | Intangibles (net) | .6 | 2.8 | .1 | 1.4 | | |
| 8.5 | 10.7 | 8.8 | All Other Non-Current | 7.8 | 4.2 | 11.9 | 1.8 | | |
| 100.0 | 100.0 | 100.0 | Total | 100.0 | 100.0 | 100.0 | 100.0 | | |
| | | | **LIABILITIES** | | | | | | |
| 37.6 | 29.3 | 27.4 | Notes Payable-Short Term | 30.4 | 31.7 | 22.9 | 31.3 | | |
| 3.9 | 4.6 | 3.1 | Cur. Mat.-L.T.D. | 5.9 | 3.8 | .9 | .8 | | |
| 5.3 | 5.6 | 5.2 | Trade Payables | 5.4 | 2.3 | 5.9 | 6.8 | | |
| .1 | .2 | .0 | Income Taxes Payable | .0 | .1 | .0 | .0 | | |
| 13.2 | 11.5 | 12.5 | All Other Current | 11.2 | 15.1 | 13.8 | 10.4 | | |
| 60.1 | 51.3 | 48.3 | Total Current | 53.0 | 53.1 | 43.6 | 49.2 | | |
| 16.4 | 13.5 | 15.6 | Long-Term Debt | 26.3 | 12.4 | 5.8 | 18.5 | | |
| .0 | .0 | .0 | Deferred Taxes | .0 | .0 | .1 | .0 | | |
| 9.0 | 13.8 | 10.0 | All Other Non-Current | 21.6 | 8.6 | 6.4 | 3.4 | | |
| 14.4 | 21.4 | 26.1 | Net Worth | -.9 | 25.9 | 44.1 | 28.9 | | |
| 100.0 | 100.0 | 100.0 | Total Liabilities & Net Worth | 100.0 | 100.0 | 100.0 | 100.0 | | |
| | | | **INCOME DATA** | | | | | | |
| 100.0 | 100.0 | 100.0 | Net Sales | 100.0 | 100.0 | 100.0 | 100.0 | | |
| 27.7 | 28.5 | 29.0 | Gross Profit | 30.8 | 33.8 | 26.7 | 18.1 | | |
| 26.4 | 25.8 | 26.2 | Operating Expenses | 30.0 | 30.1 | 22.8 | 15.6 | | |
| 1.2 | 2.7 | 2.8 | Operating Profit | .8 | 3.7 | 3.8 | 2.6 | | |
| 1.2 | .2 | 1.1 | All Other Expenses (net) | 2.0 | 1.4 | .9 | 1.1 | | |
| .1 | 2.5 | 1.6 | Profit Before Taxes | -1.1 | 2.3 | 2.9 | 1.5 | | |
| | | | **RATIOS** | | | | | | |
| 2.2 | 2.5 | 2.7 | Current | 7.0 | 2.8 | 2.7 | 3.2 | | |
| 1.3 | 1.6 | 1.4 | | 1.5 | 1.4 | 1.6 | 1.8 | | |
| .9 | 1.0 | .9 | | .8 | .9 | 1.1 | 1.3 | | |
| .6 | 1.1 | .9 | Quick | .7 | .8 | 1.3 | 1.6 | | |
| (105) .2 | .5 | .3 | | .3 | .3 | .5 | .6 | | |
| .1 | .2 | .2 | | .1 | .1 | .2 | .2 | | |
| 0 UND | 0 UND | 0 UND | Sales/Receivables | 0 UND | 0 UND | 0 UND | 0 UND | | |
| 5 79.4 | 6 60.6 | 6 56.6 | | 3 114.0 | 5 78.8 | 5 66.7 | 5 74.3 | | |
| 20 18.5 | 29 12.8 | 25 14.7 | | 55 6.6 | 27 13.7 | 23 15.6 | 31 11.6 | | |
| 73 5.0 | 60 6.1 | 94 3.9 | Cost of Sales/Inventory | 140 2.6 | 130 2.8 | 74 4.9 | 31 11.9 | | |
| 159 2.3 | 117 3.1 | 140 2.6 | | 243 1.5 | 166 2.2 | 101 3.6 | 78 4.7 | | |
| 271 1.3 | 176 2.1 | 203 1.8 | | 608 .6 | 203 1.8 | 130 2.8 | 192 1.9 | | |
| 0 UND | 0 UND | 1 549.0 | Cost of Sales/Payables | 2 161.8 | 0 UND | 2 203.5 | 0 UND | | |
| 6 64.8 | 8 45.7 | 6 57.5 | | 9 41.8 | 0 UND | 6 58.8 | 3 108.0 | | |
| 18 20.4 | 21 17.6 | 23 15.7 | | 73 5.0 | 9 42.4 | 25 14.6 | 12 31.0 | | |
| 4.1 | 3.5 | 3.9 | Sales/Working Capital | 1.4 | 4.8 | 5.0 | 2.0 | | |
| 17.1 | 8.1 | 8.3 | | 6.6 | 7.9 | 7.2 | 5.3 | | |
| -32.7 | -595.5 | -40.0 | | -11.0 | -33.1 | NM | 11.8 | | |
| 3.8 | 8.7 | 4.5 | EBIT/Interest | 3.0 | 3.2 | 6.6 | 10.8 | | |
| (104) 1.3 | (98) 2.7 | (83) 2.4 | | (20) .8 | 1.8 | (11) 2.4 | 3.5 | | |
| -.5 | .9 | .5 | | -.9 | .6 | 1.5 | .3 | | |
| 6.2 | | | Net Profit + Depr., Dep., Amort./Cur. Mat. L/T/D | | | | | | |
| (11) 3.5 | | | | | | | | | |
| -3.2 | | | | | | | | | |
| .2 | .1 | .1 | Fixed/Worth | .2 | .1 | .0 | .0 | | |
| .7 | .4 | .5 | | 2.2 | .8 | .4 | .1 | | |
| -4.4 | 1.6 | 3.5 | | -1.8 | -65.9 | .7 | 1.2 | | |
| 1.8 | .8 | 1.1 | Debt/Worth | 2.5 | 1.3 | .6 | 1.3 | | |
| 4.4 | 2.4 | 2.8 | | 11.1 | 3.5 | 1.2 | 2.5 | | |
| -23.2 | 8.4 | 13.2 | | -9.9 | -162.0 | 3.5 | 8.3 | | |
| 34.3 | 24.7 | 40.0 | % Profit Before Taxes/Tangible Net Worth | 55.2 | 75.1 | 24.5 | | | |
| (76) 10.0 | (87) 11.4 | (70) 8.6 | | (12) -.4 | (19) 10.8 | 10.9 | | | |
| -7.9 | 1.0 | -.2 | | -15.2 | 1.6 | 3.2 | | | |
| 7.0 | 8.8 | 9.6 | % Profit Before Taxes/Total Assets | 6.8 | 9.9 | 11.1 | 13.7 | | |
| 1.4 | 3.6 | 3.1 | | -.1 | 2.5 | 4.9 | 5.9 | | |
| -5.4 | -.5 | -2.2 | | -4.5 | -.9 | .9 | -2.4 | | |
| 46.8 | 42.7 | 47.3 | Sales/Net Fixed Assets | 53.2 | 27.7 | 295.7 | 320.9 | | |
| 14.3 | 14.6 | 13.5 | | 12.3 | 12.0 | 26.1 | 101.1 | | |
| 5.1 | 5.1 | 5.1 | | 2.0 | 7.5 | 7.9 | 18.3 | | |
| 2.3 | 2.5 | 2.5 | Sales/Total Assets | 1.7 | 2.3 | 3.0 | 2.9 | | |
| 1.7 | 1.8 | 1.6 | | 1.1 | 1.8 | 2.1 | 1.7 | | |
| 1.1 | 1.0 | 1.0 | | .4 | 1.1 | 1.3 | 1.0 | | |
| .6 | .6 | .5 | % Depr., Dep., Amort./Sales | .4 | .8 | .6 | | | |
| (80) .9 | (78) .9 | (63) 1.4 | | (13) 1.1 | (18) 1.4 | (10) 1.2 | | | |
| 1.9 | 2.0 | 2.5 | | 4.1 | 2.9 | 4.4 | | | |
| 1.3 | 1.7 | 1.4 | % Officers', Directors' Owners' Comp/Sales | | 1.8 | | | | |
| (43) 2.5 | (42) 2.8 | (31) 2.9 | | | (11) 5.1 | | | | |
| 4.3 | 5.5 | 6.1 | | | 7.7 | | | | |
| 1333561M | 2179177M | 1114453M | Net Sales ($) | 13953M | 47537M | 50744M | 69671M | 108658M | 823890M |
| 682865M | 990069M | 537216M | Total Assets ($) | 39520M | 32937M | 34878M | 54142M | 78973M | 296766M |

© RMA 2012

M = $ thousand    MM = $ million
See Pages 9 through 22 for Explanation of Ratios and Data

## Current Data Sorted by Assets         Comparative Historical Data

**Type of Statement**

| Type of Statement | 0-500M | 500M-2MM | 2-10MM | 10-50MM | 50-100MM | 100-250MM | | 4/1/07-3/31/08 ALL | 4/1/08-3/31/09 ALL |
|---|---|---|---|---|---|---|---|---|---|
| Unqualified | 1 | | 7 | | | 1 | | 1 | |
| Reviewed | 1 | 2 | 2 | | | 1 | | 2 | 3 |
| Compiled | | 17 | 10 | 1 | | | | 4 | 9 |
| Tax Returns | 23 | 9 | 8 | 3 | | | | 3 | 3 |
| Other | 5 | | | | | | | 6 | 7 |
| | 9 (4/1-9/30/11) | | 82 (10/1/11-3/31/12) | | | | | | |

| 0-500M | 500M-2MM | 2-10MM | 10-50MM | 50-100MM | 100-250MM | | 4/1/07-3/31/08 ALL | 4/1/08-3/31/09 ALL |
|---|---|---|---|---|---|---|---|---|
| **30** | **28** | **27** | **4** | | **2** | **NUMBER OF STATEMENTS** | **16** | **22** |
| % | % | % | % | % | % | **ASSETS** | % | % |
| 14.6 | 10.7 | 12.3 | | | | Cash & Equivalents | 16.7 | 12.8 |
| 2.9 | 10.0 | 14.1 | | | | Trade Receivables (net) | 7.2 | 9.8 |
| 58.7 | 45.4 | 35.5 | | | | Inventory | 44.9 | 45.3 |
| .7 | .3 | 1.1 | | | | All Other Current | 6.1 | 5.0 |
| 76.9 | 66.2 | 63.1 | | | | Total Current | 74.7 | 72.9 |
| 13.1 | 21.9 | 24.7 | | | | Fixed Assets (net) | 14.2 | 15.6 |
| 1.1 | 2.0 | 2.2 | | | | Intangibles (net) | 5.0 | 2.5 |
| 8.9 | 9.9 | 10.0 | | | | All Other Non-Current | 6.0 | 9.0 |
| 100.0 | 100.0 | 100.0 | | | | Total | 100.0 | 100.0 |
| | | | | | | **LIABILITIES** | | |
| 13.3 | 6.4 | 10.7 | | | | Notes Payable-Short Term | 6.7 | 23.2 |
| 1.3 | 5.4 | 2.4 | | | | Cur. Mat.-L.T.D. | 1.3 | 1.1 |
| 14.9 | 14.8 | 21.6 | | | | Trade Payables | 18.8 | 15.0 |
| .0 | .0 | .0 | | | | Income Taxes Payable | .1 | .0 |
| 20.8 | 15.9 | 10.6 | | | | All Other Current | 9.9 | 6.6 |
| 50.3 | 42.5 | 45.3 | | | | Total Current | 36.8 | 46.0 |
| 8.2 | 24.5 | 16.5 | | | | Long-Term Debt | 5.6 | 11.8 |
| .0 | .0 | .0 | | | | Deferred Taxes | .0 | .0 |
| 16.2 | 4.4 | 4.2 | | | | All Other Non-Current | 3.4 | 3.7 |
| 25.1 | 28.6 | 34.0 | | | | Net Worth | 54.2 | 38.6 |
| 100.0 | 100.0 | 100.0 | | | | Total Liabilities & Net Worth | 100.0 | 100.0 |
| | | | | | | **INCOME DATA** | | |
| 100.0 | 100.0 | 100.0 | | | | Net Sales | 100.0 | 100.0 |
| 38.0 | 37.5 | 26.2 | | | | Gross Profit | 15.9 | 17.5 |
| 36.6 | 33.4 | 23.9 | | | | Operating Expenses | 13.1 | 16.1 |
| 1.4 | 4.0 | 2.3 | | | | Operating Profit | 2.9 | 1.4 |
| -.3 | .9 | .3 | | | | All Other Expenses (net) | .0 | .2 |
| 1.7 | 3.1 | 2.1 | | | | Profit Before Taxes | 2.8 | 1.3 |
| | | | | | | **RATIOS** | | |
| 3.8 | 2.1 | 2.2 | | | | | 7.5 | 3.0 |
| 2.1 | 1.6 | 1.3 | | | | Current | 2.8 | 1.6 |
| 1.1 | 1.1 | .9 | | | | | 1.2 | 1.1 |
| .8 | 1.1 | 1.0 | | | | | 2.3 | .8 |
| .3 | .2 | .5 | | | | Quick | .8 (21) | .5 |
| .1 | .1 | .3 | | | | | .1 | .2 |
| 0 UND | 0 UND | 1 335.4 | | | | | 0 UND | 1 535.2 |
| 0 UND | 1 303.7 | 5 70.5 | | | | Sales/Receivables | 1 250.9 | 4 87.3 |
| 0 798.1 | 7 51.7 | 35 10.5 | | | | | 4 94.8 | 8 45.7 |
| 22 16.7 | 52 7.0 | 18 20.2 | | | | | 16 23.2 | 21 17.5 |
| 70 5.2 | 114 3.2 | 41 8.8 | | | | Cost of Sales/Inventory | 26 14.3 | 28 13.1 |
| 174 2.1 | 174 2.1 | 72 5.1 | | | | | 43 8.4 | 55 6.6 |
| 0 UND | 1 448.0 | 10 37.9 | | | | | 2 240.8 | 3 118.1 |
| 7 49.2 | 7 50.3 | 21 17.3 | | | | Cost of Sales/Payables | 11 32.2 | 11 34.0 |
| 40 9.1 | 53 6.9 | 66 5.5 | | | | | 21 17.0 | 17 22.0 |
| 6.2 | 5.5 | 8.1 | | | | | 10.4 | 18.0 |
| 21.9 | 10.4 | 30.7 | | | | Sales/Working Capital | 23.4 | 27.5 |
| NM | 203.4 | -44.7 | | | | | 70.5 | 115.4 |
| 41.0 | 19.1 | 23.3 | | | | | 73.1 | 13.2 |
| (19) 6.2 | (21) 3.4 | (23) 3.3 | | | | EBIT/Interest | (12) 4.4 | (18) 2.0 |
| -1.0 | 1.9 | 1.9 | | | | | .8 | .0 |
| | | | | | | Net Profit + Depr., Dep., Amort./Cur. Mat. L/T/D | | |
| .0 | .1 | .1 | | | | | .0 | .1 |
| .3 | .5 | .4 | | | | Fixed/Worth | .2 | .3 |
| 1.1 | NM | 2.3 | | | | | .6 | .8 |
| .6 | .7 | 1.1 | | | | | .1 | .5 |
| 2.0 | 3.1 | 3.0 | | | | Debt/Worth | .9 | 2.6 |
| 18.0 | NM | 7.1 | | | | | 5.3 | 8.6 |
| 65.8 | 65.3 | 62.9 | | | | | 53.3 | 35.8 |
| (26) 31.5 | (21) 38.2 | (24) 31.2 | | | | % Profit Before Taxes/Tangible Net Worth | (13) 36.6 | (19) 16.4 |
| -1.3 | 8.4 | 3.5 | | | | | 4.2 | 4.2 |
| 40.8 | 15.1 | 16.8 | | | | | 32.5 | 18.2 |
| 11.2 | 5.3 | 5.5 | | | | % Profit Before Taxes/Total Assets | 17.0 | 2.9 |
| -1.8 | 1.6 | 1.6 | | | | | -.2 | -2.4 |
| UND | 64.6 | 162.7 | | | | | 333.5 | 152.1 |
| 97.8 | 21.1 | 23.3 | | | | Sales/Net Fixed Assets | 94.6 | 70.9 |
| 28.2 | 8.3 | 6.2 | | | | | 26.7 | 23.2 |
| 11.2 | 3.4 | 5.2 | | | | | 9.9 | 7.5 |
| 5.4 | 2.4 | 2.8 | | | | Sales/Total Assets | 7.1 | 5.6 |
| 2.3 | 1.4 | 2.2 | | | | | 5.7 | 4.9 |
| .2 | .9 | .4 | | | | | .1 | .1 |
| (12) 1.2 | (16) 1.6 | (18) .9 | | | | % Depr., Dep., Amort./Sales | (12) .3 | (18) .3 |
| 2.5 | 3.0 | 1.9 | | | | | .6 | .5 |
| 1.7 | 2.6 | .7 | | | | | | |
| (18) 5.5 | (14) 5.1 | (14) 1.8 | | | | % Officers', Directors' Owners' Comp/Sales | | |
| 8.7 | 7.2 | 5.0 | | | | | | |
| 46720M | 103027M | 526123M | 332118M | | 1066827M | Net Sales ($) | 644183M | 235669M |
| 7345M | 27500M | 124793M | 65807M | | 373950M | Total Assets ($) | 163413M | 43994M |

M = $ thousand     MM = $ million
See Pages 9 through 22 for Explanation of Ratios and Data

## Comparative Historical Data | Current Data Sorted by Sales

| | | | Type of Statement | | | | | | |
|---|---|---|---|---|---|---|---|---|---|
| 1 | 3 | 2 | Unqualified | | 1 | | | | 1 |
| 7 | 7 | 8 | Reviewed | | | | | | 6 |
| 4 | 4 | 5 | Compiled | 1 | 1 | | 1 | 1 | 1 |
| 33 | 30 | 51 | Tax Returns | 15 | 15 | 6 | 7 | 5 | 3 |
| 23 | 13 | 25 | Other | 5 | 8 | 2 | 4 | 3 | 3 |
| 4/1/09-3/31/10 ALL | 4/1/10-3/31/11 ALL | 4/1/11-3/31/12 ALL | | 9 (4/1-9/30/11) | | | 82 (10/1/11-3/31/12) | | |
| | | | | 0-1MM | 1-3MM | 3-5MM | 5-10MM | 10-25MM | 25MM & OVER |
| 68 | 57 | 91 | NUMBER OF STATEMENTS | 21 | 25 | 8 | 12 | 11 | 14 |
| % | % | % | ASSETS | % | % | % | % | % | % |
| 10.0 | 10.0 | 12.7 | Cash & Equivalents | 10.5 | 10.7 | | 17.4 | 10.5 | 12.5 |
| 10.9 | 15.0 | 9.8 | Trade Receivables (net) | 6.7 | 3.0 | | 9.8 | 21.5 | 12.7 |
| 39.7 | 38.8 | 45.6 | Inventory | 54.5 | 49.8 | | 35.9 | 38.5 | 42.6 |
| 2.6 | 2.4 | 1.3 | All Other Current | .3 | .6 | | 1.5 | 5.0 | 1.5 |
| 63.2 | 66.1 | 69.4 | Total Current | 72.1 | 64.1 | | 64.6 | 75.5 | 69.4 |
| 21.7 | 20.1 | 19.2 | Fixed Assets (net) | 17.8 | 24.6 | | 20.7 | 18.4 | 16.8 |
| 5.2 | 4.2 | 1.8 | Intangibles (net) | .1 | 3.3 | | .6 | .1 | 4.6 |
| 9.8 | 9.6 | 9.6 | All Other Non-Current | 10.0 | 7.9 | | 14.0 | 6.0 | 9.2 |
| 100.0 | 100.0 | 100.0 | Total | 100.0 | 100.0 | | 100.0 | 100.0 | 100.0 |
| | | | LIABILITIES | | | | | | |
| 12.1 | 12.8 | 9.6 | Notes Payable-Short Term | 11.9 | 10.3 | | 8.6 | 8.6 | 11.3 |
| 2.5 | 3.0 | 2.9 | Cur. Mat.-L.T.D. | 2.8 | 2.3 | | 3.9 | .0 | 3.0 |
| 18.3 | 19.0 | 16.9 | Trade Payables | 14.7 | 15.1 | | 12.1 | 23.9 | 21.2 |
| .1 | .4 | .0 | Income Taxes Payable | .0 | .0 | | .0 | .0 | .0 |
| 10.1 | 14.0 | 15.8 | All Other Current | 17.8 | 14.3 | | 21.9 | 18.4 | 6.7 |
| 43.0 | 49.2 | 45.3 | Total Current | 47.1 | 42.0 | | 46.4 | 50.9 | 42.2 |
| 19.7 | 18.8 | 15.7 | Long-Term Debt | 11.5 | 28.4 | | 10.9 | 13.4 | 8.4 |
| .0 | .0 | .0 | Deferred Taxes | .0 | .0 | | .0 | .0 | .0 |
| 17.4 | 17.1 | 8.2 | All Other Non-Current | 15.7 | 8.5 | | 10.4 | 3.4 | 2.8 |
| 19.9 | 14.9 | 30.7 | Net Worth | 25.6 | 21.0 | | 32.3 | 32.3 | 46.5 |
| 100.0 | 100.0 | 100.0 | Total Liabilities & Net Worth | 100.0 | 100.0 | | 100.0 | 100.0 | 100.0 |
| | | | INCOME DATA | | | | | | |
| 100.0 | 100.0 | 100.0 | Net Sales | 100.0 | 100.0 | | 100.0 | 100.0 | 100.0 |
| 35.5 | 35.8 | 33.9 | Gross Profit | 40.0 | 45.1 | | 25.8 | 21.4 | 22.6 |
| 35.6 | 33.3 | 31.2 | Operating Expenses | 41.1 | 39.2 | | 22.3 | 19.7 | 19.8 |
| -.1 | 2.5 | 2.7 | Operating Profit | -1.1 | 5.9 | | 3.5 | 1.7 | 2.7 |
| .5 | .9 | .2 | All Other Expenses (net) | .5 | .9 | | .0 | -1.1 | -.2 |
| -.6 | 1.6 | 2.5 | Profit Before Taxes | -1.6 | 5.0 | | 3.5 | 2.9 | 3.0 |
| | | | RATIOS | | | | | | |
| 2.9 | -2.2 | 2.7 | | 6.3 | 2.5 | | 3.1 | 1.9 | 2.7 |
| 1.4 | 1.4 | 1.6 | Current | 1.5 | 1.7 | | 1.4 | 1.3 | 1.9 |
| 1.1 | 1.0 | 1.1 | | .9 | .9 | | .7 | 1.2 | 1.2 |
| 1.0 | .9 | 1.0 | | 1.2 | .7 | | 1.1 | 1.0 | 1.3 |
| .3 | .4 | .4 | Quick | .4 | .2 | | .7 | .8 | .5 |
| .1 | .2 | .1 | | .1 | .1 | | .1 | .2 | .3 |
| 0 823.1 | 0 UND | 0 UND | | 0 UND | 0 UND | | 0 UND | 0 999.8 | 2 196.9 |
| 3 122.2 | 3 130.4 | 1 254.8 | Sales/Receivables | 0 UND | 0 UND | | 1 540.1 | 3 126.8 | 3 110.6 |
| 21 17.2 | 24 15.2 | 9 39.8 | | 7 56.1 | 3 128.6 | | 41 8.8 | 49 7.5 | 9 40.7 |
| 16 23.0 | 11 33.8 | 24 15.0 | | 70 5.2 | 33 11.2 | | 20 17.9 | 0 999.8 | 22 16.9 |
| 42 8.8 | 40 9.2 | 57 6.4 | Cost of Sales/Inventory | 146 2.5 | 85 4.3 | | 46 8.0 | 17 22.0 | 31 11.7 |
| 134 2.7 | 117 3.1 | 135 2.7 | | 365 1.0 | 174 2.1 | | 87 4.2 | 111 3.3 | 49 7.4 |
| 8 47.1 | 0 UND | 1 289.6 | | 0 UND | 0 UND | | 0 UND | 6 61.1 | 10 36.0 |
| 21 17.5 | 19 19.3 | 15 23.6 | Cost of Sales/Payables | 17 21.2 | 13 27.2 | | 2 174.5 | 23 15.9 | 15 23.8 |
| 57 6.3 | 53 6.9 | 53 6.9 | | 58 6.3 | 94 3.9 | | 57 6.4 | 47 7.8 | 21 17.4 |
| 6.7 | 7.1 | 6.2 | | 2.6 | 5.6 | | 7.2 | 9.6 | 7.2 |
| 19.1 | 30.3 | 22.1 | Sales/Working Capital | 6.8 | 19.9 | | 31.9 | 22.1 | 33.5 |
| 106.9 | -248.8 | 106.1 | | NM | -216.2 | | -18.4 | 241.9 | 60.6 |
| 13.3 | 13.7 | 31.4 | | 7.0 | 51.9 | | 33.1 | | 40.2 |
| (50) 3.3 | (44) 4.2 | (68) 5.1 | EBIT/Interest | (12) 1.2 | (18) 5.3 | | (11) 3.6 | | (13) 20.5 |
| .2 | 1.2 | 1.9 | | -4.0 | 1.6 | | 1.2 | | 5.2 |
| | | | Net Profit + Depr., Dep., Amort./Cur. Mat. L/T/D | | | | | | |
| .2 | .1 | .0 | | .0 | .2 | | .2 | .0 | .2 |
| .7 | .7 | .4 | Fixed/Worth | .3 | .5 | | .5 | .2 | .3 |
| 14.5 | -7.1 | 2.7 | | 2.7 | -26.8 | | 3.4 | 1.2 | .9 |
| 1.2 | 1.1 | .7 | | .8 | .6 | | .6 | 1.2 | .6 |
| 3.0 | 4.1 | 2.5 | Debt/Worth | 2.8 | 4.4 | | 3.8 | 2.7 | 1.3 |
| UND | -13.3 | 11.7 | | 33.5 | -113.6 | | 10.3 | 6.1 | 3.0 |
| 71.5 | 57.5 | 63.8 | | 37.9 | 362.9 | | 65.4 | 63.9 | 70.8 |
| (52) 25.4 | (40) 24.5 | (77) 33.5 | % Profit Before Taxes/Tangible Net Worth | (18) 6.5 | (18) 55.4 | | (11) 43.4 | (10) 24.8 | (13) 40.1 |
| 2.1 | 6.9 | 5.9 | | -3.7 | 19.2 | | 14.5 | 6.6 | 16.9 |
| 20.4 | 16.5 | 21.4 | | 9.6 | 43.5 | | 17.0 | 11.3 | 25.1 |
| 3.2 | 5.4 | 9.2 | % Profit Before Taxes/Total Assets | .5 | 12.7 | | 7.4 | 6.9 | 16.4 |
| -4.8 | .0 | 1.2 | | -6.1 | 2.8 | | 1.1 | 1.7 | 5.6 |
| 101.4 | 245.6 | 277.9 | | UND | 152.8 | | 108.1 | 999.8 | 118.1 |
| 30.0 | 36.5 | 36.8 | Sales/Net Fixed Assets | 34.7 | 30.4 | | 14.9 | 72.2 | 38.9 |
| 9.5 | 12.8 | 10.4 | | 5.4 | 8.5 | | 8.7 | 10.4 | 22.7 |
| 5.4 | 7.0 | 6.4 | | 3.5 | 8.5 | | 5.2 | 6.4 | 9.1 |
| 2.9 | 3.3 | 2.9 | Sales/Total Assets | 1.5 | 2.9 | | 2.7 | 2.8 | 5.9 |
| 1.9 | 1.8 | 1.9 | | 1.1 | 1.9 | | 1.9 | 2.2 | 4.3 |
| .3 | .4 | .4 | | | 1.0 | | | | .4 |
| (51) 1.0 | (44) 1.1 | (50) 1.2 | % Depr., Dep., Amort./Sales | | (11) 1.6 | | | | (11) .5 |
| 3.1 | 2.7 | 2.0 | | | 3.5 | | | | .9 |
| 1.7 | 1.2 | 1.5 | | 5.8 | 2.7 | | | | |
| (26) 3.8 | (25) 4.5 | (48) 3.4 | % Officers', Directors' Owners' Comp/Sales | (11) 7.6 | (14) 4.3 | | | | |
| 7.2 | 6.9 | 6.9 | | 11.8 | 6.7 | | | | |
| 2697543M | 2717725M | 2074815M | Net Sales ($) | 11494M | 40765M | 29848M | 87959M | 161650M | 1743099M |
| 748514M | 622411M | 599395M | Total Assets ($) | 7985M | 20658M | 8029M | 30433M | 58083M | 474207M |

M = $ thousand    MM = $ million
See Pages 9 through 22 for Explanation of Ratios and Data

## Current Data Sorted by Assets      Comparative Historical Data

| | | | | | | | | |
|---|---|---|---|---|---|---|---|---|
| **Type of Statement** | | | | | | | | |
| 4 | 4 | 8 | 10 | | | Unqualified | 42 | 51 |
| 8 | 9 | 26 | 11 | | | Reviewed | 51 | 72 |
| | 23 | 23 | 2 | | | Compiled | 76 | 66 |
| 75 | 91 | 33 | 2 | 1 | 2 | Tax Returns | 128 | 184 |
| 39 | 50 | 61 | 21 | 3 | 4 | Other | 179 | 215 |
| | 66 (4/1-9/30/11) | | 457 (10/1/11-3/31/12) | | | | 4/1/07-3/31/08 ALL | 4/1/08-3/31/09 ALL |
| **0-500M** | **500M-2MM** | **2-10MM** | **10-50MM** | **50-100MM** | **100-250MM** | | | |
| 126 | 177 | 151 | 46 | 10 | 13 | **NUMBER OF STATEMENTS** | 476 | 588 |
| % | % | % | % | % | % | **ASSETS** | % | % |
| 16.5 | 11.4 | 8.4 | 9.9 | 17.3 | 12.4 | Cash & Equivalents | 9.7 | 10.2 |
| 10.2 | 13.8 | 15.1 | 15.5 | 14.6 | 13.0 | Trade Receivables (net) | 18.6 | 17.0 |
| 42.4 | 41.0 | 36.3 | 35.6 | 29.4 | 35.2 | Inventory | 37.9 | 38.5 |
| 1.4 | 2.1 | 3.4 | 4.0 | 3.2 | 6.8 | All Other Current | 3.5 | 3.1 |
| 70.6 | 68.3 | 63.3 | 65.0 | 64.4 | 67.4 | Total Current | 69.8 | 68.7 |
| 17.3 | 17.4 | 24.4 | 18.4 | 15.1 | 19.5 | Fixed Assets (net) | 19.1 | 20.8 |
| 6.7 | 7.7 | 5.3 | 12.4 | 16.4 | 8.3 | Intangibles (net) | 5.1 | 4.9 |
| 5.5 | 6.6 | 7.0 | 4.2 | 4.1 | 4.7 | All Other Non-Current | 6.0 | 5.6 |
| 100.0 | 100.0 | 100.0 | 100.0 | 100.0 | 100.0 | Total | 100.0 | 100.0 |
| | | | | | | **LIABILITIES** | | |
| 12.8 | 10.4 | 12.0 | 9.7 | 7.9 | 5.7 | Notes Payable-Short Term | 13.8 | 17.3 |
| 2.2 | 2.8 | 3.9 | 5.0 | 1.4 | 1.0 | Cur. Mat.-L.T.D. | 3.5 | 3.7 |
| 14.8 | 17.4 | 17.0 | 16.2 | 25.6 | 14.6 | Trade Payables | 21.5 | 17.8 |
| .1 | .0 | .1 | .1 | .0 | .7 | Income Taxes Payable | .4 | .2 |
| 19.5 | 10.7 | 12.0 | 10.5 | 11.5 | 12.1 | All Other Current | 12.1 | 11.6 |
| 49.4 | 41.5 | 45.0 | 41.5 | 46.4 | 34.2 | Total Current | 51.3 | 50.5 |
| 21.9 | 18.8 | 16.6 | 11.3 | 10.3 | 29.4 | Long-Term Debt | 17.4 | 18.4 |
| .0 | .1 | .0 | .5 | .8 | .1 | Deferred Taxes | .2 | .3 |
| 13.6 | 7.8 | 5.9 | 4.6 | 10.3 | 14.5 | All Other Non-Current | 8.5 | 7.8 |
| 15.1 | 31.8 | 32.5 | 42.1 | 32.2 | 21.8 | Net Worth | 22.6 | 23.0 |
| 100.0 | 100.0 | 100.0 | 100.0 | 100.0 | 100.0 | Total Liabilities & Net Worth | 100.0 | 100.0 |
| | | | | | | **INCOME DATA** | | |
| 100.0 | 100.0 | 100.0 | 100.0 | 100.0 | 100.0 | Net Sales | 100.0 | 100.0 |
| 48.1 | 42.2 | 37.9 | 39.6 | 34.8 | 42.6 | Gross Profit | 37.5 | 38.8 |
| 43.2 | 38.0 | 34.4 | 33.4 | 32.6 | 36.4 | Operating Expenses | 33.8 | 35.1 |
| 4.9 | 4.2 | 3.5 | 6.2 | 2.2 | 6.1 | Operating Profit | 3.7 | 3.7 |
| .5 | .4 | 1.2 | .7 | 1.0 | 1.3 | All Other Expenses (net) | 1.0 | 1.0 |
| 4.4 | 3.8 | 2.3 | 5.5 | 1.2 | 4.8 | Profit Before Taxes | 2.7 | 2.7 |
| | | | | | | **RATIOS** | | |
| 4.5 | 3.8 | 2.3 | 2.8 | 1.8 | 3.0 | | 2.3 | 2.6 |
| 1.7 | 1.9 | 1.5 | 1.5 | 1.5 | 2.0 | Current | 1.5 | 1.5 |
| .9 | 1.0 | 1.0 | 1.1 | 1.3 | 1.3 | | 1.0 | 1.1 |
| 1.5 | 1.6 | .9 | 1.0 | 1.4 | 1.8 | | 1.1 | 1.1 |
| .5 | .6 | .5 | .5 | .6 | .8 | Quick | (474) .6 | (587) .5 |
| .2 | .2 | .2 | .2 | .3 | .4 | | .2 | .2 |
| 0   UND | 0   UND | 0   999.8 | 4   94.9 | 8   46.0 | 10   34.9 | | 2   206.1 | 2   228.6 |
| 2   167.1 | 8   46.9 | 10   38.1 | 12   29.3 | 16   22.5 | 16   22.3 | Sales/Receivables | 15   23.8 | 14   26.9 |
| 15   24.8 | 23   16.0 | 34   10.7 | 41   8.9 | 35   10.4 | 27   13.3 | | 39   9.4 | 35   10.5 |
| 24   15.0 | 46   7.9 | 18   19.9 | 32   11.3 | 15   24.5 | 43   8.5 | | 24   15.0 | 26   14.2 |
| 66   5.5 | 87   4.2 | 68   5.4 | 81   4.5 | 49   7.4 | 87   4.2 | Cost of Sales/Inventory | 70   5.2 | 75   4.9 |
| 152   2.4 | 146   2.5 | 146   2.5 | 152   2.4 | 89   4.1 | 203   1.8 | | 137   2.7 | 150   2.4 |
| 0   UND | 9   38.7 | 10   35.9 | 19   18.9 | 40   9.2 | 16   22.4 | | 16   23.4 | 9   39.8 |
| 10   36.2 | 29   12.8 | 32   11.4 | 37   9.8 | 54   6.8 | 32   11.4 | Cost of Sales/Payables | 34   10.6 | 30   12.0 |
| 39   9.3 | 55   6.6 | 62   5.9 | 64   5.7 | 94   3.9 | 79   4.6 | | 60   6.0 | 56   6.5 |
| 5.4 | 5.4 | 6.4 | 5.4 | 7.9 | 3.9 | | 6.2 | 6.0 |
| 21.6 | 10.2 | 17.5 | 14.1 | 11.3 | 5.6 | Sales/Working Capital | 13.9 | 14.1 |
| -190.6 | 92.3 | 297.6 | 107.7 | 16.9 | 23.7 | | 106.1 | 96.5 |
| 8.8 | 15.6 | 9.5 | 25.0 | | 59.1 | | 11.0 | 7.1 |
| (86) 2.8 | (150) 3.9 | (135) 4.2 | (43) 7.4 | | (12) 4.4 | EBIT/Interest | (414) 3.1 | (510) 2.8 |
| -.9 | .5 | 1.4 | 2.1 | | 2.0 | | 1.0 | .7 |
| | | 7.9 | 12.2 | | | | 10.8 | 7.2 |
| | (18) 2.2 | (15) 3.2 | | | | Net Profit + Depr., Dep., Amort./Cur. Mat. L/T/D | (90) 2.9 | (89) 2.5 |
| | | .9 | .4 | | | | 1.1 | 1.2 |
| .0 | .1 | .2 | .1 | .1 | .2 | | .2 | .2 |
| .7 | .5 | .7 | .6 | .4 | .7 | Fixed/Worth | .5 | .6 |
| -7.7 | 3.2 | 2.8 | 1.9 | 1.7 | -1.2 | | 2.5 | 4.1 |
| .5 | 1.0 | 1.1 | .8 | 1.4 | .6 | | 1.1 | 1.0 |
| 3.2 | 2.5 | 2.9 | 2.2 | 2.3 | 2.2 | Debt/Worth | 2.9 | 2.8 |
| -11.1 | 7.7 | 15.7 | 10.9 | 3.9 | -9.2 | | 11.9 | 24.8 |
| 85.7 | 58.6 | 57.0 | 64.7 | | | | 50.7 | 49.5 |
| (87) 38.6 | (142) 23.7 | (128) 19.4 | (39) 25.7 | | | % Profit Before Taxes/Tangible Net Worth | (394) 22.2 | (464) 18.9 |
| 1.7 | 3.5 | 5.2 | 13.0 | | | | 4.1 | 2.0 |
| 28.8 | 20.6 | 13.6 | 16.9 | 7.1 | 16.5 | | 15.7 | 14.8 |
| 11.8 | 7.9 | 5.8 | 11.1 | 2.4 | 8.4 | % Profit Before Taxes/Total Assets | 5.3 | 4.6 |
| -2.5 | -.1 | 1.1 | 2.6 | -5.1 | 3.3 | | -.1 | -.5 |
| 345.3 | 174.8 | 58.4 | 51.5 | 136.7 | 31.1 | | 73.5 | 77.3 |
| 54.9 | 41.7 | 23.0 | 26.6 | 17.7 | 11.0 | Sales/Net Fixed Assets | 26.4 | 22.2 |
| 17.0 | 11.5 | 5.6 | 8.3 | 8.8 | 7.3 | | 9.5 | 7.5 |
| 6.3 | 4.2 | 3.7 | 3.1 | 3.3 | 2.6 | | 4.2 | 4.2 |
| 3.7 | 2.7 | 2.6 | 2.2 | 2.0 | 2.1 | Sales/Total Assets | 2.7 | 2.6 |
| 2.5 | 2.0 | 1.7 | 1.4 | 1.5 | 1.5 | | 1.9 | 1.7 |
| .3 | .3 | .4 | .5 | | | | .4 | .5 |
| (65) 1.3 | (120) 1.0 | (124) .9 | (39) 1.4 | | | % Depr., Dep., Amort./Sales | (361) 1.1 | (452) 1.1 |
| 2.6 | 2.0 | 2.4 | 2.3 | | | | 2.3 | 2.4 |
| 3.3 | 2.1 | 1.3 | | | | | 1.7 | 1.8 |
| (71) 7.0 | (97) 3.6 | (68) 2.5 | | | | % Officers', Directors' Owners' Comp/Sales | (188) 3.7 | (222) 3.4 |
| 9.5 | 7.1 | 4.4 | | | | | 6.7 | 5.9 |
| 133171M | 690541M | 2190549M | 2604939M | 1564947M | 5135095M | Net Sales ($) | 16083622M | 18080077M |
| 30044M | 194878M | 698466M | 1074409M | 736304M | 2295135M | Total Assets ($) | 7452913M | 8120300M |

© RMA 2012

M = $ thousand    MM = $ million
See Pages 9 through 22 for Explanation of Ratios and Data

## Comparative Historical Data | Current Data Sorted by Sales

| | Hist 1 | Hist 2 | Hist 3 | Item | 0-1MM | 1-3MM | 3-5MM | 5-10MM | 10-25MM | 25MM & OVER |
|---|---|---|---|---|---|---|---|---|---|---|
| Type of Statement | | | | | | | | | | |
| Unqualified | 45 | 35 | 35 | | | 2 | 3 | 1 | 5 | 24 |
| Reviewed | 69 | 42 | 50 | | | 9 | 3 | 10 | 16 | 12 |
| Compiled | 82 | 82 | 56 | | 4 | 9 | 12 | 11 | 14 | 6 |
| Tax Returns | 187 | 164 | 204 | | 64 | 63 | 28 | 30 | 12 | 7 |
| Other | 205 | 182 | 178 | | 27 | 42 | 26 | 21 | 32 | 30 |
| | 4/1/09-3/31/10 ALL | 4/1/10-3/31/11 ALL | 4/1/11-3/31/12 ALL | | 66 (4/1-9/30/11) | | | 457 (10/1/11-3/31/12) | | |
| NUMBER OF STATEMENTS | 588 | 505 | 523 | | 95 | 125 | 72 | 73 | 79 | 79 |
| | % | % | % | ASSETS | % | % | % | % | % | % |
| | 11.7 | 11.2 | 11.8 | Cash & Equivalents | 14.2 | 12.2 | 10.7 | 10.1 | 10.7 | 11.7 |
| | 14.9 | 14.3 | 13.5 | Trade Receivables (net) | 5.5 | 13.3 | 13.5 | 16.8 | 19.0 | 14.8 |
| | 37.3 | 38.1 | 39.2 | Inventory | 40.3 | 39.6 | 38.8 | 39.8 | 39.8 | 36.2 |
| | 2.7 | 3.0 | 2.6 | All Other Current | 1.6 | 1.2 | 4.0 | 2.3 | 2.7 | 5.1 |
| | 66.6 | 66.6 | 67.0 | Total Current | 61.6 | 66.3 | 67.0 | 69.0 | 72.2 | 67.6 |
| | 20.2 | 21.7 | 19.5 | Fixed Assets (net) | 23.2 | 20.0 | 17.7 | 18.6 | 19.1 | 17.1 |
| | 5.8 | 4.9 | 7.4 | Intangibles (net) | 11.0 | 6.0 | 8.4 | 5.2 | 3.3 | 10.2 |
| | 7.3 | 6.9 | 6.1 | All Other Non-Current | 4.2 | 7.7 | 6.9 | 7.2 | 5.4 | 5.1 |
| | 100.0 | 100.0 | 100.0 | Total | 100.0 | 100.0 | 100.0 | 100.0 | 100.0 | 100.0 |
| | | | | LIABILITIES | | | | | | |
| | 13.0 | 14.2 | 11.2 | Notes Payable-Short Term | 13.5 | 11.1 | 10.7 | 10.4 | 12.1 | 9.1 |
| | 3.7 | 3.3 | 3.1 | Cur. Mat.-L.T.D. | 2.4 | 3.0 | 3.2 | 3.8 | 2.9 | 3.6 |
| | 18.6 | 17.4 | 16.6 | Trade Payables | 10.9 | 16.7 | 16.0 | 17.6 | 19.7 | 20.0 |
| | .2 | .1 | .1 | Income Taxes Payable | .2 | .0 | .1 | .0 | .1 | .4 |
| | 14.3 | 15.5 | 13.3 | All Other Current | 15.8 | 15.1 | 11.7 | 12.2 | 11.7 | 11.4 |
| | 49.9 | 50.5 | 44.3 | Total Current | 42.6 | 45.9 | 41.7 | 44.0 | 46.6 | 44.4 |
| | 17.9 | 16.1 | 18.4 | Long-Term Debt | 25.3 | 23.7 | 14.9 | 15.7 | 12.5 | 12.9 |
| | .3 | .1 | .1 | Deferred Taxes | .0 | .1 | .1 | .0 | .0 | .4 |
| | 9.3 | 9.6 | 8.6 | All Other Non-Current | 16.7 | 7.0 | 8.0 | 4.8 | 6.7 | 7.2 |
| | 22.5 | 23.7 | 28.6 | Net Worth | 15.4 | 23.3 | 35.3 | 35.6 | 34.2 | 35.1 |
| | 100.0 | 100.0 | 100.0 | Total Liabilities & Net Worth | 100.0 | 100.0 | 100.0 | 100.0 | 100.0 | 100.0 |
| | | | | INCOME DATA | | | | | | |
| | 100.0 | 100.0 | 100.0 | Net Sales | 100.0 | 100.0 | 100.0 | 100.0 | 100.0 | 100.0 |
| | 39.6 | 41.4 | 42.0 | Gross Profit | 50.7 | 45.6 | 40.6 | 41.1 | 36.5 | 33.5 |
| | 36.4 | 37.8 | 37.7 | Operating Expenses | 46.5 | 40.5 | 37.4 | 36.9 | 31.2 | 29.9 |
| | 3.2 | 3.6 | 4.4 | Operating Profit | 4.2 | 5.2 | 3.2 | 4.2 | 5.3 | 3.5 |
| | .9 | 1.2 | .7 | All Other Expenses (net) | .6 | 1.3 | 1.0 | .0 | .4 | .6 |
| | 2.2 | 2.4 | 3.6 | Profit Before Taxes | 3.6 | 3.8 | 2.2 | 4.2 | 4.9 | 2.9 |
| | | | | RATIOS | | | | | | |
| | 2.6 | 2.7 | 3.2 | Current | 4.7 | 4.8 | 2.9 | 3.1 | 2.6 | 2.3 |
| | 1.5 | 1.5 | 1.7 | | 1.8 | 1.8 | 1.8 | 1.8 | 1.6 | 1.5 |
| | 1.0 | 1.0 | 1.0 | | .8 | .9 | 1.1 | 1.2 | 1.1 | 1.2 |
| | 1.1 | 1.0 | 1.2 | Quick | 1.2 | 1.8 | 1.2 | 1.4 | 1.0 | 1.0 |
| (587) | .5 | .5 | .5 | | .5 | .6 | .6 | .6 | .6 | .5 |
| | .2 | .2 | .2 | | .2 | .2 | .2 | .2 | .2 | .3 |
| | 1 507.0 | 0 999.8 | 0 UND | Sales/Receivables | 0 UND | 0 UND | 0 UND | 0 999.8 | 1 615.2 | 4 97.6 |
| | 10 35.7 | 10 36.4 | 8 46.9 | | 0 840.0 | 8 43.9 | 8 46.7 | 11 34.3 | 17 21.4 | 10 35.3 |
| | 36 10.1 | 33 11.2 | 26 14.3 | | 9 41.0 | 23 15.7 | 27 13.4 | 28 13.0 | 41 8.9 | 29 12.4 |
| | 28 13.0 | 30 12.0 | 30 12.1 | Cost of Sales/Inventory | 43 8.5 | 39 9.3 | 36 10.1 | 18 20.5 | 21 17.4 | 21 17.1 |
| | 70 5.2 | 69 5.3 | 76 4.8 | | 107 3.4 | 87 4.2 | 72 5.1 | 72 5.1 | 81 4.5 | 54 6.7 |
| | 139 2.6 | 137 2.7 | 146 2.5 | | 228 1.6 | 159 2.3 | 122 3.0 | 122 3.0 | 140 2.6 | 99 3.7 |
| | 12 31.7 | 8 43.5 | 7 55.0 | Cost of Sales/Payables | 0 UND | 8 44.4 | 15 25.0 | 6 65.7 | 11 33.4 | 14 25.3 |
| | 29 12.4 | 28 13.1 | 28 13.2 | | 13 27.5 | 29 12.7 | 29 12.8 | 23 15.7 | 31 11.7 | 36 10.2 |
| | 57 6.5 | 56 6.6 | 55 6.6 | | 47 7.7 | 66 5.5 | 52 7.0 | 56 6.5 | 49 7.5 | 63 5.8 |
| | 6.2 | 6.0 | 5.7 | Sales/Working Capital | 5.2 | 4.2 | 6.0 | 6.0 | 6.3 | 7.2 |
| | 14.5 | 15.0 | 13.9 | | 16.7 | 13.5 | 12.5 | 9.5 | 18.0 | 16.9 |
| | -155.8 | -168.1 | 198.1 | | -39.4 | -50.9 | 77.1 | 37.4 | 172.0 | 77.5 |
| | 9.5 | 10.1 | 12.2 | EBIT/Interest | 6.8 | 10.5 | 11.0 | 12.6 | 18.1 | 22.2 |
| (507) 2.8 | (414) 3.2 | (435) 3.9 | | (66) 2.6 | (103) 2.4 | (60) 2.8 | (65) 3.3 | (69) 5.0 | (72) 5.7 | |
| | .6 | .7 | 1.1 | | -1.1 | -.6 | -.1 | 1.6 | 2.8 | 2.2 |
| | 5.7 | 6.3 | 6.9 | Net Profit + Depr., Dep., Amort./Cur. Mat. L/T/D | | | | | 7.3 | 9.7 |
| (108) 2.3 | (60) 2.1 | (47) 2.4 | | | | | | (15) 2.4 | (18) 3.4 | |
| | .6 | .7 | .5 | | | | | | 1.1 | .3 |
| | .2 | .1 | .1 | Fixed/Worth | .1 | .1 | .1 | .1 | .1 | .1 |
| | .7 | .6 | .6 | | 1.1 | .7 | .4 | .5 | .7 | .5 |
| | 13.4 | 3.6 | 4.3 | | -8.3 | -51.9 | 2.1 | 1.3 | 2.2 | 1.8 |
| | .9 | .9 | .9 | Debt/Worth | .9 | .9 | 1.0 | .8 | .8 | 1.1 |
| | 2.8 | 2.4 | 2.6 | | 5.3 | 2.8 | 2.7 | 2.0 | 2.2 | 2.3 |
| | 100.8 | 19.6 | 24.0 | | -9.6 | -19.8 | 7.1 | 6.3 | 8.3 | 8.1 |
| | 53.3 | 50.1 | 58.8 | % Profit Before Taxes/Tangible Net Worth | 78.4 | 62.3 | 44.4 | 61.0 | 59.4 | 56.4 |
| (452) 16.5 | (403) 19.0 | (414) 24.4 | | (64) 29.9 | (91) 23.0 | (59) 19.3 | (65) 15.9 | (70) 27.5 | (65) 24.6 | |
| | 1.9 | 3.4 | 5.2 | | -3.3 | -3.7 | 4.8 | 4.4 | 12.1 | 9.8 |
| | 14.0 | 15.6 | 18.6 | % Profit Before Taxes/Total Assets | 24.1 | 21.5 | 16.3 | 15.3 | 17.6 | 15.6 |
| | 4.8 | 5.5 | 7.6 | | 9.5 | 8.0 | 5.2 | 5.2 | 9.8 | 8.4 |
| | -.7 | -.4 | .6 | | -1.6 | -3.0 | -1.0 | 1.3 | 3.7 | 2.4 |
| | 80.1 | 106.3 | 117.7 | Sales/Net Fixed Assets | 210.0 | 119.5 | 120.5 | 159.0 | 77.7 | 81.9 |
| | 21.9 | 26.4 | 31.6 | | 31.4 | 36.5 | 37.1 | 34.4 | 26.8 | 28.0 |
| | 7.1 | 7.9 | 10.0 | | 6.4 | 9.9 | 12.1 | 10.4 | 11.3 | 11.7 |
| | 4.0 | 4.2 | 4.3 | Sales/Total Assets | 3.9 | 4.2 | 4.4 | 4.2 | 4.5 | 4.0 |
| | 2.7 | 2.7 | 2.7 | | 2.6 | 2.5 | 2.7 | 2.9 | 2.9 | 2.9 |
| | 1.7 | 1.8 | 1.9 | | 1.5 | 1.8 | 2.1 | 2.1 | 2.3 | 2.1 |
| | .5 | .4 | .4 | % Depr., Dep., Amort./Sales | .8 | .4 | .3 | .5 | .3 | .3 |
| (447) 1.1 | (374) 1.1 | (363) 1.0 | | (52) 2.0 | (74) 1.0 | (48) .8 | (56) 1.1 | (69) .8 | (64) .9 | |
| | 2.4 | 2.4 | 2.2 | | 5.6 | 2.4 | 1.9 | 1.7 | 1.7 | 1.9 |
| | 1.8 | 1.6 | 2.0 | % Officers', Directors' Owners' Comp/Sales | 5.1 | 2.3 | 2.0 | 1.8 | .9 | .5 |
| (238) 3.8 | (232) 4.2 | (245) 3.8 | | (53) 7.8 | (62) 3.9 | (42) 3.5 | (37) 3.4 | (30) 2.3 | (21) 1.0 | |
| | 6.5 | 7.9 | 7.4 | | 10.4 | 7.2 | 7.2 | 5.0 | 3.9 | 3.6 |
| | 14869721M | 14317661M | 12319242M | Net Sales ($) | 54666M | 223893M | 276813M | 515172M | 1264639M | 9984059M |
| | 7178099M | 5435881M | 5029236M | Total Assets ($) | 32152M | 110398M | 120116M | 207758M | 528776M | 4030036M |

M = $ thousand    MM = $ million
See Pages 9 through 22 for Explanation of Ratios and Data

## Current Data Sorted by Assets

## Comparative Historical Data

| | | | | | | Type of Statement | | |
|---|---|---|---|---|---|---|---|---|
| | | 3 | 15 | 2 | 4 | Unqualified | | |
| | 1 | 4 | 4 | | | Reviewed | 8 | 15 |
| 2 | 5 | 4 | 1 | | | Compiled | 4 | 5 |
| 8 | 7 | 5 | | | | Tax Returns | 5 | 6 |
| 3 | 16 | 22 | 19 | 6 | 6 | Other | 11 | 14 |
| | 12 (4/1-9/30/11) | | 125 (10/1/11-3/31/12) | | | | 30 | 40 |
| | | | | | | | 4/1/07- | 4/1/08- |
| | | | | | | | 3/31/08 | 3/31/09 |
| 0-500M | 500M-2MM | 2-10MM | 10-50MM | 50-100MM | 100-250MM | | ALL | ALL |
| 13 | 29 | 38 | 39 | 8 | 10 | NUMBER OF STATEMENTS | 58 | 80 |
| % | % | % | % | % | % | ASSETS | % | % |
| 22.0 | 12.4 | 15.7 | 14.1 | | 23.0 | Cash & Equivalents | 19.2 | 15.0 |
| 11.3 | 13.1 | 8.6 | 12.1 | | 13.3 | Trade Receivables (net) | 13.3 | 10.6 |
| 24.0 | 51.3 | 44.6 | 36.1 | | 28.6 | Inventory | 39.4 | 37.7 |
| 3.1 | 3.1 | 3.6 | 9.0 | | 4.4 | All Other Current | 5.4 | 7.4 |
| 60.4 | 79.9 | 72.4 | 71.3 | | 69.3 | Total Current | 77.3 | 70.8 |
| 6.5 | 5.9 | 11.1 | 14.8 | | 14.9 | Fixed Assets (net) | 13.0 | 14.4 |
| 11.3 | 6.2 | 11.0 | 10.6 | | 11.2 | Intangibles (net) | 5.9 | 8.6 |
| 21.8 | 8.1 | 5.5 | 3.3 | | 4.7 | All Other Non-Current | 3.8 | 6.2 |
| 100.0 | 100.0 | 100.0 | 100.0 | | 100.0 | Total | 100.0 | 100.0 |
| | | | | | | LIABILITIES | | |
| 25.1 | 12.1 | 9.5 | 6.2 | | 2.2 | Notes Payable-Short Term | 15.6 | 16.2 |
| 6.2 | 1.1 | 1.9 | 2.4 | | .8 | Cur. Mat.-L.T.D. | 2.9 | 2.4 |
| 43.9 | 26.7 | 28.6 | 23.0 | | 24.7 | Trade Payables | 22.5 | 25.6 |
| .3 | .3 | 1.1 | .3 | | .2 | Income Taxes Payable | .1 | .4 |
| 13.7 | 8.9 | 11.5 | 13.0 | | 13.5 | All Other Current | 16.4 | 15.0 |
| 89.2 | 49.0 | 52.7 | 45.0 | | 41.4 | Total Current | 57.5 | 59.7 |
| 17.3 | 9.7 | 14.2 | 8.7 | | 6.8 | Long-Term Debt | 9.5 | 11.2 |
| .0 | .2 | .1 | .2 | | .7 | Deferred Taxes | .3 | .2 |
| .8 | 1.4 | 10.1 | 3.1 | | 5.5 | All Other Non-Current | 10.1 | 6.6 |
| -7.2 | 39.7 | 23.0 | 43.0 | | 45.6 | Net Worth | 22.7 | 22.4 |
| 100.0 | 100.0 | 100.0 | 100.0 | | 100.0 | Total Liabilities & Net Worth | 100.0 | 100.0 |
| | | | | | | INCOME DATA | | |
| 100.0 | 100.0 | 100.0 | 100.0 | | 100.0 | Net Sales | 100.0 | 100.0 |
| 39.1 | 34.5 | 37.0 | 39.3 | | 33.9 | Gross Profit | 38.6 | 40.6 |
| 33.9 | 28.6 | 34.5 | 35.5 | | 33.5 | Operating Expenses | 33.4 | 37.5 |
| 5.2 | 5.9 | 2.5 | 3.8 | | .4 | Operating Profit | 5.2 | 3.1 |
| .2 | .8 | .7 | .6 | | 1.1 | All Other Expenses (net) | .6 | 1.5 |
| 5.0 | 5.1 | 1.8 | 3.2 | | -.7 | Profit Before Taxes | 4.6 | 1.6 |
| | | | | | | RATIOS | | |
| 1.6 | 2.1 | 2.3 | 2.6 | | 2.0 | | 2.2 | 2.1 |
| 1.1 | 1.6 | 1.3 | 1.4 | | 1.6 | Current | 1.6 | 1.5 |
| .2 | 1.2 | .9 | 1.1 | | 1.3 | | 1.0 | 1.0 |
| .8 | .8 | .8 | 1.0 | | 1.3 | | 1.1 | 1.0 |
| .4 | .5 | .4 | .4 | | 1.2 | Quick | .5 | .4 |
| .1 | .2 | .2 | .1 | | .3 | | .2 | .1 |

| | | | | | | | | | | | | | | |
|---|---|---|---|---|---|---|---|---|---|---|---|---|---|---|
| 0 | UND | 0 | UND | 0 | 733.5 | 1 | 340.1 | | 1 | 443.8 | | 2 | 234.3 | 1 | 592.4 |

(Sales/Receivables and subsequent ratio rows below)

| | | | | | | | | | | | Sales/Receivables | | |
|---|---|---|---|---|---|---|---|---|---|---|---|---|---|
| 0 | UND | 0 | UND | 0 | 733.5 | 1 | 340.1 | 1 | 443.8 | | 2 | 234.3 | 1 | 592.4 |
| 1 | 609.2 | 3 | 105.6 | 3 | 122.7 | 4 | 104.2 | 3 | 112.2 | | 6 | 62.9 | 4 | 83.5 |
| 12 | 31.6 | 11 | 34.3 | 15 | 23.9 | 19 | 19.5 | 26 | 13.9 | | 14 | 25.2 | 13 | 27.3 |
| 0 | UND | 23 | 15.7 | 31 | 11.8 | 10 | 35.3 | 46 | 8.0 | Cost of Sales/Inventory | 31 | 12.0 | 24 | 15.2 |
| 8 | 45.3 | 54 | 6.8 | 64 | 5.7 | 79 | 4.6 | 66 | 5.5 | | 71 | 5.2 | 68 | 5.4 |
| 23 | 16.2 | 87 | 4.2 | 104 | 3.5 | 135 | 2.7 | 91 | 4.0 | | 123 | 3.0 | 132 | 2.8 |
| 11 | 33.8 | 5 | 75.0 | 16 | 23.0 | 26 | 14.1 | 32 | 11.4 | Cost of Sales/Payables | 17 | 21.4 | 16 | 22.8 |
| 16 | 23.3 | 26 | 13.8 | 35 | 10.3 | 43 | 8.4 | 49 | 7.5 | | 25 | 14.3 | 32 | 11.3 |
| 45 | 8.2 | 66 | 5.5 | 64 | 5.7 | 63 | 5.8 | 63 | 5.8 | | 53 | 6.9 | 56 | 6.5 |

| | | | | | | | | |
|---|---|---|---|---|---|---|---|---|
| 27.5 | 8.7 | 6.4 | 5.6 | | 5.8 | Sales/Working Capital | 7.4 | 8.4 |
| 165.9 | 16.8 | 23.5 | 15.2 | | 8.5 | | 13.6 | 18.9 |
| -12.8 | 50.7 | -49.2 | 78.0 | | 21.6 | | 207.5 | 193.4 |

| | | | | | | | | | | |
|---|---|---|---|---|---|---|---|---|---|---|
| | | | 101.0 | | 62.5 | | 58.1 | | 36.9 | | | | 14.5 | | 13.5 |
| | (23) | 18.4 | (33) | 6.7 | (31) | 18.6 | | 5.4 | EBIT/Interest | (47) | 4.7 | (61) | 3.8 |
| | | 3.5 | | .2 | | 2.0 | | -14.4 | | | 1.6 | | -.5 |

| | | | | | | |
|---|---|---|---|---|---|---|
| | | | | | Net Profit + Depr., Dep., | 44.5 | |
| | | | | | Amort./Cur. Mat. L/T/D | (11) 9.2 | |
| | | | | | | 1.6 | |

| | | | | | | | | |
|---|---|---|---|---|---|---|---|---|
| .0 | .0 | .0 | .1 | | .2 | Fixed/Worth | .1 | .2 |
| .2 | .0 | .2 | .4 | | .4 | | .5 | .4 |
| .4 | .2 | -1.0 | 1.2 | | 1.6 | | 2.3 | UND |
| 1.1 | 1.0 | 1.2 | .6 | | .9 | Debt/Worth | 1.1 | .8 |
| 8.7 | 1.8 | 3.9 | 2.0 | | 1.4 | | 2.4 | 2.7 |
| -6.6 | 3.8 | -7.3 | 5.7 | | 6.3 | | 8.5 | UND |

| | | | | | | | | | |
|---|---|---|---|---|---|---|---|---|---|
| | | 97.5 | 121.4 | 79.5 | | | % Profit Before Taxes/Tangible | 71.1 | 65.4 |
| | (25) | 48.3 | (26) 49.1 | (34) 32.2 | | | Net Worth | (50) 38.7 | (60) 34.7 |
| | | 23.8 | 18.2 | 3.1 | | | | -.2 | 7.7 |
| 142.4 | 37.9 | 26.2 | 24.0 | | 12.7 | % Profit Before Taxes/Total | 21.0 | 21.5 |
| 36.5 | 19.2 | 9.3 | 7.7 | | 6.1 | Assets | 11.1 | 7.5 |
| 4.2 | 8.6 | -.6 | -.5 | | -20.8 | | -.1 | -3.5 |
| UND | UND | 502.0 | 63.9 | | 21.8 | Sales/Net Fixed Assets | 144.9 | 98.5 |
| 518.4 | 234.3 | 55.2 | 33.3 | | 16.9 | | 40.9 | 32.6 |
| 57.6 | 72.1 | 23.8 | 16.9 | | 11.9 | | 15.2 | 14.7 |
| 22.7 | 7.2 | 5.4 | 3.8 | | 2.8 | Sales/Total Assets | 4.9 | 4.9 |
| 10.0 | 4.2 | 3.8 | 2.7 | | 1.9 | | 3.6 | 3.2 |
| 5.5 | 3.0 | 2.6 | 2.1 | | 1.7 | | 2.5 | 2.2 |

| | | | | | | | | |
|---|---|---|---|---|---|---|---|---|
| | .3 | .3 | .4 | | | % Depr., Dep., Amort./Sales | .3 | .4 |
| (11) | .4 | (23) .9 | (34) .8 | | | | (40) .8 | (50) .7 |
| | .6 | 2.7 | 2.1 | | | | 1.9 | 1.9 |

| | | | | | | | |
|---|---|---|---|---|---|---|---|
| | 1.3 | .4 | | | % Officers', Directors' | .6 | 1.3 |
| (13) | 1.7 | (11) 2.5 | | | Owners' Comp/Sales | (18) 3.3 | (15) 5.7 |
| | 5.2 | 3.5 | | | | 7.6 | 9.4 |

| | | | | | | | | |
|---|---|---|---|---|---|---|---|---|
| 50209M | 174537M | 695915M | 2733231M | 1673095M | 4405511M | Net Sales ($) | 6637379M | 7315087M |
| 3644M | 32040M | 177302M | 850679M | 573788M | 1734311M | Total Assets ($) | 2219788M | 2432713M |

© RMA 2012

M = $ thousand　　MM = $ million
See Pages 9 through 22 for Explanation of Ratios and Data

## Comparative Historical Data    Current Data Sorted by Sales

Current Data period headers: **12 (4/1-9/30/11)** covers columns 0-1MM, 1-3MM, 3-5MM; **125 (10/1/11-3/31/12)** covers columns 5-10MM, 10-25MM, 25MM & OVER.

| | 4/1/09-3/31/10 ALL | 4/1/10-3/31/11 ALL | 4/1/11-3/31/12 ALL | 0-1MM | 1-3MM | 3-5MM | 5-10MM | 10-25MM | 25MM & OVER |
|---|---|---|---|---|---|---|---|---|---|
| **Type of Statement** | | | | | | | | | |
| Unqualified | 13 | 20 | 24 | | | 1 | | 2 | 21 |
| Reviewed | 4 | 11 | 9 | | | | 1 | 2 | 6 |
| Compiled | 4 | 8 | 12 | | 2 | 3 | 3 | 2 | 2 |
| Tax Returns | 15 | 27 | 20 | 2 | 4 | 5 | 4 | 5 | |
| Other | 46 | 49 | 72 | 1 | 7 | 6 | 8 | 16 | 34 |
| **NUMBER OF STATEMENTS** | 82 | 115 | 137 | 3 | 13 | 15 | 16 | 27 | 63 |
| **ASSETS** | % | % | % | % | % | % | % | % | % |
| Cash & Equivalents | 16.9 | 20.0 | 15.9 | | 6.3 | 13.1 | 11.9 | 19.1 | 17.1 |
| Trade Receivables (net) | 10.5 | 10.6 | 11.2 | | 12.8 | 15.1 | 6.7 | 10.0 | 11.3 |
| Inventory | 36.3 | 36.3 | 39.8 | | 20.7 | 44.5 | 63.4 | 41.7 | 36.6 |
| All Other Current | 4.9 | 4.9 | 5.2 | | 7.1 | 3.3 | 1.7 | 4.2 | 6.7 |
| Total Current | 68.6 | 71.9 | 72.1 | | 46.9 | 76.0 | 83.7 | 75.1 | 71.7 |
| Fixed Assets (net) | 15.4 | 12.5 | 11.1 | | 8.0 | 7.2 | 4.3 | 12.7 | 14.2 |
| Intangibles (net) | 10.3 | 9.1 | 10.1 | | 25.0 | 12.4 | 2.3 | 6.1 | 10.5 |
| All Other Non-Current | 5.7 | 6.5 | 6.7 | | 20.1 | 4.5 | 9.7 | 6.2 | 3.6 |
| Total | 100.0 | 100.0 | 100.0 | | 100.0 | 100.0 | 100.0 | 100.0 | 100.0 |
| **LIABILITIES** | | | | | | | | | |
| Notes Payable-Short Term | 9.4 | 9.6 | 9.7 | | 24.1 | 18.6 | 11.6 | 8.5 | 5.0 |
| Cur. Mat.-L.T.D. | 2.0 | 1.7 | 2.5 | | 7.2 | .2 | .9 | 1.5 | 3.1 |
| Trade Payables | 22.1 | 25.1 | 27.5 | | 31.7 | 20.5 | 34.0 | 21.9 | 28.1 |
| Income Taxes Payable | .4 | .3 | .5 | | .7 | .2 | .4 | 1.3 | .3 |
| All Other Current | 13.6 | 10.5 | 12.2 | | 15.0 | 3.5 | 8.5 | 12.1 | 14.5 |
| Total Current | 47.5 | 47.2 | 52.4 | | 78.7 | 42.9 | 55.4 | 45.3 | 51.0 |
| Long-Term Debt | 11.8 | 9.6 | 11.6 | | 37.8 | 12.9 | 3.8 | 10.9 | 8.7 |
| Deferred Taxes | .4 | .4 | .2 | | .3 | .0 | .1 | .1 | .4 |
| All Other Non-Current | 5.0 | 2.8 | 4.5 | | 1.2 | 7.0 | 3.4 | 8.6 | 3.2 |
| Net Worth | 35.3 | 40.0 | 31.3 | | -18.0 | 37.1 | 37.3 | 35.2 | 36.8 |
| Total Liabilities & Net Worth | 100.0 | 100.0 | 100.0 | | 100.0 | 100.0 | 100.0 | 100.0 | 100.0 |
| **INCOME DATA** | | | | | | | | | |
| Net Sales | 100.0 | 100.0 | 100.0 | | 100.0 | 100.0 | 100.0 | 100.0 | 100.0 |
| Gross Profit | 39.2 | 37.7 | 37.2 | | 44.2 | 38.3 | 32.2 | 38.4 | 36.1 |
| Operating Expenses | 34.8 | 34.4 | 33.9 | | 36.0 | 37.4 | 28.2 | 35.0 | 33.6 |
| Operating Profit | 4.5 | 3.3 | 3.4 | | 8.2 | .8 | 4.0 | 3.4 | 2.6 |
| All Other Expenses (net) | .8 | .4 | .7 | | 1.3 | 1.6 | .2 | .4 | .5 |
| Profit Before Taxes | 3.6 | 2.9 | 2.7 | | 6.9 | -.7 | 3.8 | 3.0 | 2.0 |
| **RATIOS** | | | | | | | | | |
| Current | 2.3 | 2.5 | 2.3 | | 1.6 | 3.3 | 2.2 | 2.6 | 2.3 |
| | 1.5 | 1.5 | 1.5 | | .9 | 1.7 | 1.7 | 1.5 | 1.4 |
| | 1.1 | 1.1 | 1.1 | | .2 | 1.1 | 1.0 | 1.1 | 1.1 |
| Quick | 1.1 | 1.1 | .9 | | .8 | 1.5 | .5 | 1.1 | 1.1 |
| | .6 | .5 | .4 | | .4 | .5 | .2 | .7 | .4 |
| | .2 | .3 | .2 | | .1 | .2 | .1 | .3 | .1 |
| Sales/Receivables | 0 999.8 | 0 999.8 | 0 757.2 | | 0 UND | 1 709.6 | 0 UND | 1 530.5 | 1 567.0 |
| | 3 117.9 | 3 134.8 | 3 111.5 | | 2 215.2 | 7 51.4 | 1 708.1 | 3 105.6 | 3 129.6 |
| | 14 25.7 | 14 26.4 | 15 25.0 | | 17 22.0 | 41 8.9 | 8 47.5 | 15 25.1 | 13 28.6 |
| Cost of Sales/Inventory | 30 12.3 | 17 21.5 | 18 20.8 | | 0 UND | 31 11.7 | 37 9.8 | 26 14.2 | 21 17.3 |
| | 61 6.0 | 59 6.2 | 59 6.2 | | 10 35.5 | 54 6.8 | 65 5.6 | 54 6.7 | 65 5.6 |
| | 107 3.4 | 102 3.6 | 107 3.4 | | 83 4.4 | 114 3.2 | 135 2.7 | 114 3.2 | 107 3.4 |
| Cost of Sales/Payables | 20 18.0 | 20 18.7 | 16 22.6 | | 18 20.7 | 2 155.5 | 12 31.4 | 12 29.6 | 26 14.1 |
| | 34 10.7 | 35 10.3 | 35 10.5 | | 45 8.1 | 18 20.5 | 28 13.1 | 25 14.8 | 47 7.8 |
| | 53 6.9 | 56 6.5 | 61 6.0 | | 94 3.9 | 101 3.6 | 57 6.4 | 59 6.2 | 60 6.1 |
| Sales/Working Capital | 7.7 | 7.2 | 7.1 | | 10.9 | 7.3 | 9.6 | 6.6 | 6.4 |
| | 17.3 | 15.9 | 17.2 | | -34.5 | 21.8 | 17.0 | 21.9 | 15.7 |
| | 158.1 | 143.0 | 191.5 | | -12.8 | 58.1 | NM | 136.9 | 78.0 |
| EBIT/Interest | 56.2 | 23.5 | 56.6 | | 14.8 | -43.5 | 140.1 | 256.0 | 52.6 |
| | (65) 9.3 | (93) 7.6 | (108) 7.7 | | (11) 7.4 | (12) .8 | (10) 17.4 | (19) 11.1 | (56) 8.0 |
| | 1.7 | 1.5 | .4 | | .7 | -10.8 | 6.2 | 2.0 | -.3 |
| Net Profit + Depr., Dep., Amort./Cur. Mat. L/T/D | 146.8 | 17.1 | 26.7 | | | | | | 31.3 |
| | (13) 25.1 | (15) 8.3 | (16) 1.6 | | | | | | (12) 1.6 |
| | 2.8 | 2.9 | -.7 | | | | | | .6 |
| Fixed/Worth | .1 | .1 | .0 | | .0 | .0 | .0 | .1 | .1 |
| | .4 | .3 | .2 | | .4 | .1 | .0 | .2 | .4 |
| | 2.1 | 1.5 | 1.2 | | -1.9 | .3 | .2 | 1.0 | 1.6 |
| Debt/Worth | .8 | .9 | .9 | | 2.0 | .5 | 1.2 | .6 | .9 |
| | 1.9 | 2.2 | 2.2 | | -28.8 | 1.8 | 1.7 | 2.3 | 2.0 |
| | 7.9 | 8.1 | 21.4 | | -1.3 | 164.2 | 4.2 | 11.9 | 16.3 |
| % Profit Before Taxes/Tangible Net Worth | 76.4 | 75.7 | 91.9 | | | 113.6 | 120.7 | 138.8 | 56.0 |
| | (70) 39.9 | (96) 40.5 | (106) 33.9 | | | (12) 34.0 | (14) 63.0 | (23) 59.1 | (50) 25.3 |
| | 15.6 | 11.8 | 10.5 | | | -28.7 | 23.9 | 25.3 | -2.0 |
| % Profit Before Taxes/Total Assets | 27.2 | 30.4 | 29.1 | | 26.8 | 39.7 | 37.1 | 37.1 | 19.8 |
| | 11.8 | 9.7 | 10.2 | | 14.3 | 2.9 | 18.4 | 13.6 | 7.7 |
| | 2.1 | 1.2 | -.2 | | 3.4 | -12.1 | 8.6 | 2.1 | -.8 |
| Sales/Net Fixed Assets | 110.0 | 241.0 | 320.6 | | UND | UND | UND | 110.0 | 96.7 |
| | 31.3 | 45.4 | 52.8 | | 68.3 | 263.7 | 618.2 | 50.4 | 26.9 |
| | 16.3 | 20.0 | 20.1 | | 33.1 | 46.9 | 77.0 | 19.5 | 16.9 |
| Sales/Total Assets | 5.5 | 5.4 | 5.2 | | 5.5 | 5.8 | 8.1 | 5.9 | 4.5 |
| | 3.4 | 3.4 | 3.6 | | 3.5 | 3.0 | 4.3 | 3.8 | 3.1 |
| | 2.4 | 2.2 | 2.2 | | 2.0 | 1.7 | 3.7 | 2.7 | 2.1 |
| % Depr., Dep., Amort./Sales | .5 | .4 | .4 | | | | | .5 | .4 |
| | (53) 1.2 | (77) .9 | (83) .7 | | | | | (19) .9 | (48) .8 |
| | 2.5 | 2.1 | 2.0 | | | | | 2.1 | 2.0 |
| % Officers', Directors' Owners' Comp/Sales | 1.0 | 1.0 | .8 | | | | | | |
| | (21) 2.6 | (35) 2.0 | (35) 2.5 | | | | | | |
| | 7.6 | 4.6 | 4.3 | | | | | | |
| Net Sales ($) | 6007468M | 9475805M | 9732498M | 1642M | 25692M | 63572M | 111928M | 439658M | 9090006M |
| Total Assets ($) | 2497632M | 3439207M | 3371764M | 281M | 10886M | 27238M | 22226M | 146790M | 3164343M |

## Current Data Sorted by Assets        Comparative Historical Data

| 0-500M | 500M-2MM | 2-10MM | 10-50MM | 50-100MM | 100-250MM | Type of Statement | 4/1/07-3/31/08 ALL | 4/1/08-3/31/09 ALL |
|---|---|---|---|---|---|---|---|---|
| | | 2 | 12 | 2 | 9 | Unqualified | 34 | 30 |
| | | 10 | 3 | | | Reviewed | 19 | 11 |
| 1 | 1 | 6 | 1 | | | Compiled | 16 | 15 |
| 2 | 6 | 1 | 1 | 1 | | Tax Returns | 24 | 19 |
| 1 | 9 | 14 | 15 | 6 | 1 | Other | 53 | 62 |
| | 17 (4/1-9/30/11) | | 87 (10/1/11-3/31/12) | | | | | |
| 4 | 16 | 33 | 32 | 9 | 10 | NUMBER OF STATEMENTS | 146 | 137 |
| % | % | % | % | % | % | ASSETS | % | % |
| | 13.1 | 10.7 | 15.0 | | 11.9 | Cash & Equivalents | 16.1 | 11.6 |
| | 10.4 | 15.6 | 12.6 | | 6.7 | Trade Receivables (net) | 11.1 | 11.4 |
| | 46.7 | 43.6 | 37.5 | | 37.5 | Inventory | 38.0 | 40.8 |
| | 2.4 | 2.2 | 5.8 | | 4.9 | All Other Current | 4.8 | 4.4 |
| | 72.6 | 72.1 | 70.9 | | 60.9 | Total Current | 69.9 | 68.1 |
| | 15.0 | 13.6 | 12.0 | | 20.5 | Fixed Assets (net) | 12.8 | 16.3 |
| | 2.9 | 5.7 | 10.6 | | 12.6 | Intangibles (net) | 9.5 | 8.0 |
| | 9.5 | 8.6 | 6.4 | | 6.0 | All Other Non-Current | 7.8 | 7.7 |
| | 100.0 | 100.0 | 100.0 | | 100.0 | Total | 100.0 | 100.0 |
| | | | | | | LIABILITIES | | |
| | 17.2 | 11.9 | 6.7 | | 7.7 | Notes Payable-Short Term | 11.6 | 15.4 |
| | 1.9 | 1.8 | 1.1 | | .9 | Cur. Mat.-L.T.D. | 3.1 | 3.0 |
| | 22.9 | 28.5 | 19.9 | | 20.8 | Trade Payables | 22.5 | 21.5 |
| | .0 | .1 | .4 | | .1 | Income Taxes Payable | .3 | .3 |
| | 12.9 | 8.2 | 11.2 | | 18.2 | All Other Current | 12.7 | 12.5 |
| | 54.9 | 50.5 | 39.3 | | 47.8 | Total Current | 50.2 | 52.6 |
| | 24.1 | 7.0 | 6.0 | | 10.6 | Long-Term Debt | 11.8 | 11.8 |
| | .0 | .1 | 1.4 | | .2 | Deferred Taxes | .6 | .4 |
| | 19.1 | 12.9 | 8.2 | | 14.1 | All Other Non-Current | 6.9 | 8.4 |
| | 1.9 | 29.5 | 45.0 | | 27.3 | Net Worth | 30.6 | 26.7 |
| | 100.0 | 100.0 | 100.0 | | 100.0 | Total Liabilties & Net Worth | 100.0 | 100.0 |
| | | | | | | INCOME DATA | | |
| | 100.0 | 100.0 | 100.0 | | 100.0 | Net Sales | 100.0 | 100.0 |
| | 36.6 | 43.3 | 47.0 | | 35.0 | Gross Profit | 43.1 | 44.2 |
| | 32.6 | 38.3 | 41.5 | | 33.2 | Operating Expenses | 39.5 | 41.9 |
| | 3.9 | 5.0 | 5.6 | | 1.8 | Operating Profit | 3.7 | 2.4 |
| | .3 | .6 | .9 | | 2.5 | All Other Expenses (net) | .8 | .9 |
| | 3.7 | 4.4 | 4.6 | | -.7 | Profit Before Taxes | 2.9 | 1.5 |
| | | | | | | RATIOS | | |
| | 2.6 | 3.1 | 3.0 | | 2.2 | | 2.8 | 2.4 |
| | 1.2 | 1.8 | 1.8 | | 1.2 | Current | 1.5 | 1.5 |
| | .7 | .9 | 1.2 | | .9 | | 1.1 | .9 |
| | .8 | 1.5 | 1.1 | | 1.0 | | 1.2 | 1.0 |
| | .2 | .4 | .7 | | .5 | Quick | .4 | .4 |
| | .1 | .1 | .3 | | .1 | | .1 | .1 |
| 0 999.8 | 1 271.3 | 2 198.6 | 1 273.0 | | | | 1 445.0 | 2 201.3 |
| 4 100.7 | 6 56.6 | 5 79.6 | 5 75.4 | | | Sales/Receivables | 5 67.6 | 6 59.6 |
| 12 29.3 | 26 13.8 | 25 14.6 | 26 14.1 | | | | 15 24.4 | 19 19.3 |
| 12 29.2 | 29 12.7 | 46 7.9 | 60 6.1 | | | | 39 9.3 | 35 10.4 |
| 55 6.6 | 72 5.1 | 96 3.8 | 94 3.9 | | | Cost of Sales/Inventory | 78 4.7 | 79 4.6 |
| 140 2.6 | 118 3.1 | 135 2.7 | 135 2.2 | | | | 116 3.1 | 140 2.6 |
| 7 48.9 | 21 17.6 | 22 16.8 | 23 16.2 | | | | 18 19.9 | 20 18.4 |
| 24 15.5 | 29 12.7 | 36 10.2 | 43 8.4 | | | Cost of Sales/Payables | 34 10.6 | 37 9.9 |
| 50 7.3 | 61 6.0 | 68 5.4 | 51 7.1 | | | | 63 5.8 | 60 6.1 |
| | 7.8 | 7.4 | 5.6 | | 7.5 | | 6.8 | 7.0 |
| | 40.9 | 13.0 | 8.4 | | 41.5 | Sales/Working Capital | 13.7 | 14.9 |
| | -23.3 | -87.5 | 26.8 | | -61.7 | | 54.0 | -77.9 |
| | 17.2 | 26.5 | 60.4 | | 37.7 | | 15.9 | 10.0 |
| | (13) 1.9 | (30) 5.7 | (26) 22.8 | | 6.9 | EBIT/Interest | (114) 3.9 | (118) 3.5 |
| | -.3 | 1.8 | 1.1 | | -5.0 | | 1.4 | -1.3 |
| | | | | | | Net Profit + Depr., Dep., Amort./Cur. Mat. L/T/D | 21.2 | 21.4 |
| | | | | | | | (21) 3.8 | (27) 6.2 |
| | | | | | | | 2.3 | 1.5 |
| | .0 | .1 | .1 | | .4 | | .1 | .2 |
| | 5.1 | .2 | .3 | | 1.6 | Fixed/Worth | .3 | .5 |
| | -1.0 | 2.0 | .9 | | NM | | 2.0 | 3.7 |
| | 1.1 | .8 | .4 | | .8 | | .7 | .9 |
| | 47.3 | 1.6 | 2.3 | | 6.4 | Debt/Worth | 1.7 | 2.2 |
| | -6.2 | 10.7 | 3.3 | | NM | | 19.5 | 27.6 |
| | | 52.9 | 74.2 | | | | 60.9 | 71.6 |
| | | (27) 24.3 | (28) 31.2 | | | % Profit Before Taxes/Tangible Net Worth | (115) 31.1 | (107) 20.5 |
| | | 8.7 | 16.9 | | | | 9.4 | 2.8 |
| | 28.8 | 16.7 | 24.0 | | 12.0 | | 20.5 | 13.6 |
| | 15.2 | 8.9 | 15.3 | | 7.1 | % Profit Before Taxes/Total Assets | 8.1 | 6.5 |
| | -3.8 | 2.0 | .4 | | -13.8 | | 1.1 | -2.2 |
| | 898.7 | 176.5 | 63.8 | | 30.8 | | 121.9 | 84.5 |
| | 64.1 | 60.1 | 23.9 | | 12.0 | Sales/Net Fixed Assets | 37.6 | 30.9 |
| | 27.2 | 20.2 | 15.5 | | 7.2 | | 14.9 | 11.3 |
| | 6.6 | 5.6 | 3.9 | | 3.0 | | 4.5 | 4.4 |
| | 5.2 | 3.8 | 2.5 | | 1.8 | Sales/Total Assets | 3.2 | 3.1 |
| | 1.8 | 2.7 | 1.9 | | 1.7 | | 2.2 | 2.2 |
| | .0 | .2 | .4 | | | | .4 | .6 |
| | (11) .7 | (28) .7 | (26) .9 | | | % Depr., Dep., Amort./Sales | (103) .8 | (102) 1.0 |
| | 1.8 | 1.3 | 1.3 | | | | 1.6 | 1.7 |
| | | .5 | | | | | 1.2 | 1.9 |
| | | (11) 2.2 | | | | % Officers', Directors' Owners' Comp/Sales | (37) 3.0 | (35) 2.7 |
| | | 4.1 | | | | | 7.4 | 6.2 |
| 5587M | 105301M | 768474M | 2494973M | 1662242M | 4134261M | Net Sales ($) | 12385152M | 11992022M |
| 1117M | 20383M | 174284M | 838269M | 631840M | 1597523M | Total Assets ($) | 5015679M | 3847815M |

## Comparative Historical Data | Current Data Sorted by Sales

### Type of Statement

| | 4/1/09-3/31/10 ALL | 4/1/10-3/31/11 ALL | 4/1/11-3/31/12 ALL | | 0-1MM | 1-3MM | 3-5MM | 5-10MM | 10-25MM | 25MM & OVER |
|---|---|---|---|---|---|---|---|---|---|---|
| Unqualified | 31 | 31 | 25 | | | | | | 2 | 23 |
| Reviewed | 13 | 10 | 13 | | | | 1 | | 5 | 7 |
| Compiled | 10 | 10 | 9 | | | 1 | | 2 | 3 | 3 |
| Tax Returns | 12 | 9 | 11 | | 2 | 3 | | 2 | 2 | 2 |
| Other | 58 | 60 | 46 | | 2 | 2 | 3 | 2 | 10 | 27 |
| | | | | | 17 (4/1-9/30/11) | | | 87 (10/1/11-3/31/12) | | |
| NUMBER OF STATEMENTS | 124 | 120 | 104 | | 4 | 6 | 4 | 6 | 22 | 62 |

### ASSETS (%)

| | ALL | ALL | ALL | 10-25MM | 25MM & OVER |
|---|---|---|---|---|---|
| Cash & Equivalents | 13.3 | 16.5 | 12.9 | 14.6 | 15.1 |
| Trade Receivables (net) | 12.8 | 11.1 | 13.2 | 15.5 | 11.8 |
| Inventory | 37.0 | 38.1 | 40.3 | 43.0 | 39.2 |
| All Other Current | 4.4 | 4.3 | 3.5 | 2.7 | 4.2 |
| Total Current | 67.5 | 70.1 | 69.9 | 75.9 | 70.3 |
| Fixed Assets (net) | 16.4 | 14.5 | 14.7 | 11.8 | 13.2 |
| Intangibles (net) | 8.4 | 9.5 | 7.8 | 5.6 | 8.7 |
| All Other Non-Current | 7.7 | 5.9 | 7.6 | 6.7 | 7.8 |
| Total | 100.0 | 100.0 | 100.0 | 100.0 | 100.0 |

### LIABILITIES

| | ALL | ALL | ALL | 10-25MM | 25MM & OVER |
|---|---|---|---|---|---|
| Notes Payable-Short Term | 10.0 | 10.4 | 10.7 | 14.4 | 5.9 |
| Cur. Mat.-L.T.D. | 2.0 | 2.1 | 1.9 | 1.3 | 1.5 |
| Trade Payables | 21.2 | 19.6 | 23.3 | 24.1 | 24.2 |
| Income Taxes Payable | .3 | .3 | .2 | .1 | .3 |
| All Other Current | 10.6 | 10.4 | 11.5 | 10.1 | 12.0 |
| Total Current | 44.1 | 42.8 | 47.6 | 49.9 | 43.9 |
| Long-Term Debt | 11.8 | 10.1 | 11.0 | 2.9 | 6.8 |
| Deferred Taxes | .8 | .6 | .5 | .1 | .9 |
| All Other Non-Current | 15.0 | 7.9 | 11.4 | 6.1 | 12.1 |
| Net Worth | 28.3 | 38.7 | 29.5 | 41.0 | 36.3 |
| Total Liabilities & Net Worth | 100.0 | 100.0 | 100.0 | 100.0 | 100.0 |

### INCOME DATA

| | ALL | ALL | ALL | 10-25MM | 25MM & OVER |
|---|---|---|---|---|---|
| Net Sales | 100.0 | 100.0 | 100.0 | 100.0 | 100.0 |
| Gross Profit | 43.4 | 44.1 | 42.9 | 35.8 | 45.0 |
| Operating Expenses | 39.3 | 39.1 | 38.6 | 32.4 | 40.6 |
| Operating Profit | 4.1 | 5.0 | 4.3 | 3.4 | 4.4 |
| All Other Expenses (net) | 1.0 | .9 | .9 | .2 | 1.1 |
| Profit Before Taxes | 3.1 | 4.1 | 3.4 | 3.2 | 3.3 |

### RATIOS

| | ALL | ALL | ALL | 10-25MM | 25MM & OVER |
|---|---|---|---|---|---|
| Current | 2.8 | 2.9 | 3.0 | 2.9 | 3.0 |
| | 1.7 | 1.6 | 1.6 | 1.9 | 1.7 |
| | 1.1 | 1.1 | 1.0 | .9 | 1.2 |
| Quick | 1.2 | 1.1 | 1.1 | 1.5 | 1.2 |
| | .6 | .6 | (103) .5 | .6 | .6 |
| | .2 | .2 | .1 | .2 | .1 |
| Sales/Receivables | 2  171.4 | 2  182.1 | 1  271.1 | 4  95.9 | 1  277.5 |
| | 7  55.9 | 5  78.3 | 5  77.8 | 8  45.0 | 5  80.7 |
| | 21  17.4 | 20  18.1 | 23  15.9 | 23  16.1 | 23  16.1 |
| Cost of Sales/Inventory | 45  8.0 | 46  7.9 | 40  9.1 | 21  17.0 | 46  8.0 |
| | 82  4.5 | 81  4.5 | 78  4.7 | 69  5.3 | 85  4.3 |
| | 124  2.9 | 128  2.8 | 130  2.8 | 140  2.6 | 130  2.8 |
| Cost of Sales/Payables | 19  19.4 | 20  18.6 | 21  17.7 | 19  18.9 | 22  16.4 |
| | 35  10.3 | 35  10.4 | 35  10.4 | 29  12.8 | 39  9.3 |
| | 53  6.9 | 59  6.2 | 58  6.3 | 51  7.1 | 63  5.8 |
| Sales/Working Capital | 5.8 | 6.1 | 6.5 | 7.3 | 5.9 |
| | 11.6 | 12.1 | 12.9 | 12.3 | 12.2 |
| | 76.7 | 75.3 | -320.0 | -77.6 | 47.0 |
| EBIT/Interest | 20.5 | 23.8 | 28.8 | 26.0 | 56.3 |
| | (102) 5.1 | (99) 7.6 | (88) 5.6 | (20) 11.8 | (50) 17.3 |
| | 1.1 | 2.3 | .1 | 2.0 | .6 |
| Net Profit + Depr., Dep., Amort./Cur. Mat. L/T/D | 20.4 | 24.4 | 24.4 | | 24.7 |
| | (26) 3.6 | (23) 5.4 | (15) 7.5 | | (14) 10.1 |
| | .9 | 1.7 | .5 | | 1.0 |
| Fixed/Worth | .1 | .1 | .1 | .1 | .1 |
| | .4 | .4 | .3 | .2 | .3 |
| | 1.9 | 1.7 | 3.2 | 2.2 | 1.3 |
| Debt/Worth | .6 | .5 | .6 | .7 | .4 |
| | 1.7 | 2.0 | 2.4 | 1.2 | 2.4 |
| | 7.5 | 9.0 | 15.8 | 8.3 | 5.1 |
| % Profit Before Taxes/Tangible Net Worth | 55.8 | 66.0 | 56.3 | 52.9 | 67.8 |
| | (98) 24.6 | (97) 29.0 | (82) 26.1 | (19) 24.3 | (53) 31.6 |
| | 10.3 | 7.2 | 5.7 | 9.6 | 14.7 |
| % Profit Before Taxes/Total Assets | 17.4 | 16.1 | 21.1 | 19.6 | 22.4 |
| | 9.1 | 10.2 | 10.2 | 13.7 | 12.6 |
| | 1.3 | 2.5 | -1.2 | 2.6 | .1 |
| Sales/Net Fixed Assets | 69.0 | 109.5 | 99.4 | 302.2 | 73.4 |
| | 28.6 | 31.7 | 39.0 | 55.0 | 28.5 |
| | 13.3 | 13.5 | 14.5 | 22.1 | 15.2 |
| Sales/Total Assets | 4.8 | 4.1 | 4.9 | 5.7 | 4.4 |
| | 3.1 | 3.1 | 3.2 | 3.6 | 2.8 |
| | 1.9 | 2.1 | 2.0 | 2.6 | 1.9 |
| % Depr., Dep., Amort./Sales | .5 | .4 | .4 | .1 | .5 |
| | (90) .8 | (88) 1.0 | (82) .9 | (20) .5 | (49) 1.0 |
| | 1.6 | 1.5 | 1.6 | .8 | 1.6 |
| % Officers', Directors' Owners' Comp/Sales | 1.1 | 2.0 | 1.4 | | |
| | (21) 3.0 | (26) 3.2 | (27) 2.5 | | |
| | 5.6 | 7.8 | 5.6 | | |

| | ALL | ALL | ALL | 0-1MM | 1-3MM | 3-5MM | 5-10MM | 10-25MM | 25MM & OVER |
|---|---|---|---|---|---|---|---|---|---|
| Net Sales ($) | 11333065M | 11359707M | 9170838M | 2414M | 12197M | 15803M | 48626M | 360473M | 8731325M |
| Total Assets ($) | 4602199M | 3892078M | 3263416M | 4345M | 5643M | 4839M | 12761M | 102336M | 3133492M |

M = $ thousand    MM = $ million
See Pages 9 through 22 for Explanation of Ratios and Data

## Current Data Sorted by Assets      Comparative Historical Data

| Type of Statement | 0-500M | 500M-2MM | 2-10MM | 10-50MM | 50-100MM | 100-250MM | 4/1/07-3/31/08 ALL | 4/1/08-3/31/09 ALL |
|---|---|---|---|---|---|---|---|---|
| Unqualified | | | 1 | 4 | | | 4 | 6 |
| Reviewed | | 1 | 9 | 3 | | | 17 | 24 |
| Compiled | 2 | 5 | 8 | 2 | | | 17 | 23 |
| Tax Returns | 3 | 12 | 8 | 2 | | | 17 | 17 |
| Other | 2 | 10 | 12 | 5 | | 1 | 31 | 32 |
| | 16 (4/1-9/30/11) | | | 72 (10/1/11-3/31/12) | | | | |
| **NUMBER OF STATEMENTS** | 7 | 28 | 38 | 14 | | 1 | 86 | 102 |

| | 0-500M % | 500M-2MM % | 2-10MM % | 10-50MM % | 50-100MM % | 100-250MM % | ASSETS | 4/1/07-3/31/08 ALL % | 4/1/08-3/31/09 ALL % |
|---|---|---|---|---|---|---|---|---|---|
| | | 20.5 | 12.7 | 10.1 | | | Cash & Equivalents | 9.5 | 9.1 |
| | | 4.2 | 7.4 | 12.2 | | | Trade Receivables (net) | 6.5 | 8.6 |
| | | 16.6 | 15.7 | 14.9 | | | Inventory | 15.6 | 17.7 |
| | | 5.0 | 5.2 | .6 | | | All Other Current | 2.7 | 2.4 |
| | | 46.3 | 41.0 | 37.8 | | | Total Current | 34.4 | 37.9 |
| | | 32.5 | 43.7 | 40.1 | | | Fixed Assets (net) | 51.9 | 47.8 |
| | | 11.1 | 8.4 | 15.3 | | | Intangibles (net) | 8.3 | 6.7 |
| | | 10.1 | 7.0 | 6.8 | | | All Other Non-Current | 5.4 | 7.6 |
| | | 100.0 | 100.0 | 100.0 | | | Total | 100.0 | 100.0 |
| | | | | | | | **LIABILITIES** | | |
| | | 9.1 | 6.2 | 5.0 | | | Notes Payable-Short Term | 8.2 | 7.9 |
| | | 5.1 | 7.0 | 7.4 | | | Cur. Mat.-L.T.D. | 7.3 | 8.3 |
| | | 13.6 | 13.8 | 12.1 | | | Trade Payables | 14.1 | 15.5 |
| | | .0 | .0 | .0 | | | Income Taxes Payable | .1 | .1 |
| | | 13.5 | 6.8 | 11.9 | | | All Other Current | 8.8 | 10.2 |
| | | 41.4 | 33.7 | 36.5 | | | Total Current | 38.5 | 42.1 |
| | | 34.1 | 29.1 | 13.3 | | | Long-Term Debt | 29.4 | 30.0 |
| | | .0 | .3 | 1.0 | | | Deferred Taxes | .4 | .5 |
| | | 5.6 | 10.3 | 13.1 | | | All Other Non-Current | 10.5 | 8.9 |
| | | 18.9 | 26.6 | 36.1 | | | Net Worth | 21.1 | 18.6 |
| | | 100.0 | 100.0 | 100.0 | | | Total Liabilities & Net Worth | 100.0 | 100.0 |
| | | | | | | | **INCOME DATA** | | |
| | | 100.0 | 100.0 | 100.0 | | | Net Sales | 100.0 | 100.0 |
| | | 49.4 | 48.8 | 43.6 | | | Gross Profit | 46.8 | 43.0 |
| | | 47.1 | 46.5 | 37.9 | | | Operating Expenses | 45.0 | 41.5 |
| | | 2.3 | 2.3 | 5.7 | | | Operating Profit | 1.8 | 1.5 |
| | | .6 | .0 | .6 | | | All Other Expenses (net) | 1.1 | .7 |
| | | 1.7 | 2.3 | 5.1 | | | Profit Before Taxes | .7 | .8 |

*(Columns 0-500M, 50-100MM, 100-250MM: DATA NOT AVAILABLE)*

### RATIOS

| | 0-500M | 500M-2MM | 2-10MM | 10-50MM | 50-100MM | 100-250MM | Ratio | 4/1/07-3/31/08 ALL | 4/1/08-3/31/09 ALL |
|---|---|---|---|---|---|---|---|---|---|
| | | 2.4 | 2.3 | 1.7 | | | Current | 1.3 | 1.5 |
| | | 1.2 | 1.2 | 1.0 | | | | .9 | 1.0 |
| | | .6 | .7 | .7 | | | | .6 | .6 |
| | | 1.0 | 1.0 | 1.2 | | | Quick | .6 | .8 |
| | | .5 | .5 | .5 | | | | .4 | .4 |
| | | .3 | .3 | .4 | | | | .2 | .2 |
| | 0 UND | | 2 190.6 | 7 56.1 | | | Sales/Receivables | 1 391.2 | 2 231.5 |
| | 3 133.0 | | 5 75.4 | 14 26.6 | | | | 5 79.9 | 6 62.1 |
| | 6 61.3 | | 16 23.0 | 26 14.2 | | | | 11 32.1 | 14 26.4 |
| | 15 24.6 | | 23 16.1 | 26 14.0 | | | Cost of Sales/Inventory | 22 16.5 | 17 21.7 |
| | 29 12.6 | | 34 10.6 | 38 9.7 | | | | 32 11.3 | 31 11.6 |
| | 45 8.1 | | 56 6.5 | 61 6.0 | | | | 43 8.5 | 45 8.0 |
| | 14 26.8 | | 14 25.9 | 21 17.8 | | | Cost of Sales/Payables | 13 27.1 | 11 33.5 |
| | 26 13.8 | | 29 12.7 | 25 14.4 | | | | 29 12.7 | 24 15.1 |
| | 45 8.2 | | 53 6.9 | 47 7.7 | | | | 44 8.2 | 42 8.6 |
| | | 11.9 | 11.6 | 14.5 | | | Sales/Working Capital | 36.4 | 26.8 |
| | | 100.9 | 57.7 | NM | | | | -73.1 | -139.7 |
| | | -16.7 | -24.3 | -32.7 | | | | -18.9 | -15.3 |
| | | 9.2 | 4.9 | 20.5 | | | EBIT/Interest | 4.1 | 3.6 |
| | (22) | .9 | (36) 1.8 | (13) 15.4 | | | | (82) 1.6 | (99) 1.6 |
| | | -3.9 | .1 | 3.8 | | | | .5 | .5 |
| | | | | | | | Net Profit + Depr., Dep., | 3.5 | 5.2 |
| | | | | | | | Amort./Cur. Mat. L/T/D | (12) 1.9 | (18) 2.0 |
| | | | | | | | | 1.3 | 1.2 |
| | | .7 | 1.2 | .9 | | | Fixed/Worth | 1.2 | 1.3 |
| | | 2.5 | 2.8 | 2.4 | | | | 2.9 | 2.6 |
| | | -3.7 | -3.3 | 5.6 | | | | -63.5 | -11.3 |
| | | .7 | 1.5 | 1.0 | | | Debt/Worth | 1.5 | 1.5 |
| | | 5.6 | 3.5 | 3.0 | | | | 4.3 | 4.4 |
| | | -9.1 | -15.4 | 8.5 | | | | -90.8 | -15.9 |
| | | 66.8 | 53.2 | 183.7 | | | % Profit Before Taxes/Tangible Net Worth | 37.0 | 32.9 |
| | (19) | -14.3 | (28) 9.3 | (13) 34.2 | | | | (64) 16.8 | (70) 16.4 |
| | | -36.8 | -2.9 | 24.7 | | | | -1.9 | -4.7 |
| | | 12.1 | 8.6 | 17.7 | | | % Profit Before Taxes/Total Assets | 9.6 | 8.5 |
| | | .2 | 2.5 | 11.3 | | | | 2.2 | 2.7 |
| | | -13.6 | -1.5 | 3.3 | | | | -1.5 | -3.0 |
| | | 17.4 | 17.9 | 9.1 | | | Sales/Net Fixed Assets | 8.9 | 13.5 |
| | | 12.0 | 5.6 | 6.9 | | | | 6.1 | 6.9 |
| | | 5.9 | 3.1 | 4.3 | | | | 3.6 | 5.0 |
| | | 4.6 | 3.3 | 3.7 | | | Sales/Total Assets | 3.9 | 5.0 |
| | | 2.9 | 2.6 | 2.9 | | | | 2.9 | 3.3 |
| | | 1.9 | 1.7 | 1.8 | | | | 2.1 | 2.4 |
| | | 2.4 | 3.3 | 3.0 | | | % Depr., Dep., Amort./Sales | 3.3 | 2.9 |
| | (22) | 3.7 | (31) 4.8 | (13) 4.0 | | | | (79) 4.3 | (92) 4.3 |
| | | 12.8 | 6.8 | 7.9 | | | | 6.5 | 5.7 |
| | | 2.0 | 1.0 | | | | % Officers', Directors' Owners' Comp/Sales | 1.3 | 1.2 |
| | (15) | 3.3 | (20) 2.0 | | | | | (34) 2.8 | (43) 2.6 |
| | | 7.3 | 3.8 | | | | | 6.2 | 4.1 |
| | 8359M | 93630M | 438706M | 814583M | | 470177M | Net Sales ($) | 1703879M | 1921358M |
| | 1950M | 28432M | 162621M | 312504M | | 248539M | Total Assets ($) | 677679M | 668637M |

M = $ thousand    MM = $ million
See Pages 9 through 22 for Explanation of Ratios and Data

## Comparative Historical Data | Current Data Sorted by Sales

| | | | | Type of Statement | | | | | | |
|---|---|---|---|---|---|---|---|---|---|---|
| 6 | 8 | 5 | | Unqualified | | | | | 1 | 4 |
| 14 | 17 | 13 | | Reviewed | | 1 | | 3 | 5 | 4 |
| 15 | 17 | 15 | | Compiled | | 3 | 5 | 4 | 3 | |
| 17 | 20 | 25 | | Tax Returns | 3 | 6 | 3 | 7 | 5 | 1 |
| 39 | 32 | 30 | | Other | 3 | 7 | 5 | 2 | 5 | 8 |
| 4/1/09-3/31/10 | 4/1/10-3/31/11 | 4/1/11-3/31/12 | | | | 16 (4/1-9/30/11) | | 72 (10/1/11-3/31/12) | | |
| ALL | ALL | ALL | | | 0-1MM | 1-3MM | 3-5MM | 5-10MM | 10-25MM | 25MM & OVER |
| 91 | 94 | 88 | | NUMBER OF STATEMENTS | 6 | 17 | 13 | 16 | 19 | 17 |
| % | % | % | | ASSETS | % | % | % | % | % | % |
| 12.8 | 15.0 | 14.5 | | Cash & Equivalents | | 12.6 | 24.5 | 16.8 | 11.6 | 11.0 |
| 9.0 | 7.6 | 6.6 | | Trade Receivables (net) | | 3.3 | 3.0 | 4.4 | 9.5 | 12.4 |
| 14.9 | 15.6 | 17.3 | | Inventory | | 20.5 | 15.9 | 16.5 | 19.0 | 16.6 |
| 1.9 | 3.8 | 3.9 | | All Other Current | | 12.4 | 1.7 | .7 | 4.5 | .9 |
| 38.6 | 41.9 | 42.3 | | Total Current | | 48.8 | 45.2 | 38.4 | 44.6 | 41.0 |
| 45.3 | 42.1 | 39.0 | | Fixed Assets (net) | | 30.2 | 46.4 | 42.2 | 38.6 | 41.1 |
| 10.1 | 8.2 | 10.7 | | Intangibles (net) | | 12.7 | 1.9 | 11.5 | 9.6 | 12.9 |
| 6.0 | 7.7 | 8.0 | | All Other Non-Current | | 8.3 | 6.5 | 7.8 | 7.2 | 5.0 |
| 100.0 | 100.0 | 100.0 | | Total | | 100.0 | 100.0 | 100.0 | 100.0 | 100.0 |
| | | | | LIABILITIES | | | | | | |
| 7.2 | 8.7 | 7.4 | | Notes Payable-Short Term | | 9.6 | 11.9 | 1.8 | 7.8 | 8.5 |
| 8.5 | 6.3 | 8.1 | | Cur. Mat.-L.T.D. | | 3.8 | 3.2 | 10.4 | 7.8 | 6.7 |
| 11.5 | 15.4 | 16.5 | | Trade Payables | | 11.0 | 14.2 | 8.1 | 15.7 | 18.3 |
| .1 | .1 | .0 | | Income Taxes Payable | | .0 | .0 | .0 | .0 | .0 |
| 7.4 | 9.5 | 9.5 | | All Other Current | | 6.4 | 14.8 | 9.2 | 7.7 | 12.4 |
| 34.7 | 40.0 | 41.5 | | Total Current | | 30.7 | 44.1 | 29.5 | 39.0 | 45.9 |
| 29.7 | 27.1 | 37.4 | | Long-Term Debt | | 47.7 | 39.1 | 23.7 | 29.7 | 36.7 |
| .3 | .3 | .3 | | Deferred Taxes | | .0 | .0 | .2 | .5 | .8 |
| 10.6 | 9.0 | 9.1 | | All Other Non-Current | | 7.2 | 11.3 | 6.1 | 10.4 | 13.5 |
| 24.7 | 23.6 | 11.7 | | Net Worth | | 14.3 | 5.6 | 40.5 | 20.5 | 3.1 |
| 100.0 | 100.0 | 100.0 | | Total Liabilties & Net Worth | | 100.0 | 100.0 | 100.0 | 100.0 | 100.0 |
| | | | | INCOME DATA | | | | | | |
| 100.0 | 100.0 | 100.0 | | Net Sales | | 100.0 | 100.0 | 100.0 | 100.0 | 100.0 |
| 45.4 | 44.8 | 48.5 | | Gross Profit | | 52.3 | 54.9 | 48.6 | 43.7 | 42.4 |
| 41.4 | 41.2 | 45.0 | | Operating Expenses | | 50.2 | 52.0 | 43.8 | 42.9 | 39.5 |
| 4.0 | 3.6 | 3.5 | | Operating Profit | | 2.1 | 2.9 | 4.8 | .7 | 2.9 |
| .8 | .2 | .8 | | All Other Expenses (net) | | .0 | .3 | .3 | -.9 | 1.1 |
| 3.2 | 3.4 | 2.7 | | Profit Before Taxes | | 2.0 | 2.6 | 4.5 | 1.7 | 1.8 |
| | | | | RATIOS | | | | | | |
| 1.8 | 2.0 | 2.0 | | | | 3.3 | 2.3 | 2.8 | 2.0 | 1.2 |
| 1.1 | 1.1 | 1.1 | | Current | | 1.8 | 1.2 | 1.1 | 1.4 | .8 |
| .6 | .7 | .7 | | | | .8 | .6 | .7 | .8 | .7 |
| 1.2 | 1.1 | 1.0 | | | | 1.4 | 1.9 | 2.1 | 1.0 | .8 |
| (90) .5 | .5 | .5 | | Quick | | .6 | .5 | .5 | .6 | .5 |
| .2 | .3 | .3 | | | | .2 | .3 | .3 | .3 | .3 |
| 0  999.8 | 0  867.5 | 1  653.9 | | | 0  UND | 1  646.1 | 2  214.0 | 2  190.3 | 4  93.5 | |
| 3  106.3 | 4  86.5 | 4  84.7 | | Sales/Receivables | 0  774.3 | 4  101.5 | 3  109.7 | 6  58.1 | 13  29.0 | |
| 12  30.0 | 13  28.5 | 12  29.2 | | | 8  44.2 | 5  72.3 | 12  30.7 | 18  20.7 | 20  18.5 | |
| 14  25.9 | 15  23.9 | 22  16.6 | | | 8  46.1 | 21  17.6 | 29  12.4 | 22  16.3 | 28  13.2 | |
| 32  11.3 | 34  10.8 | 35  10.5 | | Cost of Sales/Inventory | 45  8.1 | 35  10.4 | 36  10.2 | 38  9.5 | 32  11.3 | |
| 47  7.8 | 49  7.5 | 55  6.6 | | | 96  3.8 | 63  5.8 | 72  5.1 | 52  7.0 | 47  7.8 | |
| 7  53.7 | 10  37.4 | 14  25.4 | | | 15  24.4 | 15  25.0 | 4  97.9 | 15  25.1 | 22  16.4 | |
| 17  21.3 | 27  13.7 | 26  13.9 | | Cost of Sales/Payables | 26  14.2 | 28  13.1 | 22  16.3 | 26  13.8 | 36  10.2 | |
| 37  9.9 | 42  8.6 | 49  7.5 | | | 44  8.3 | 63  5.8 | 37  9.9 | 51  7.1 | 54  6.8 | |
| 16.5 | 18.4 | 12.4 | | | 5.7 | 9.9 | 10.4 | 12.0 | 45.0 | |
| 133.0 | 81.5 | 185.0 | | Sales/Working Capital | 15.5 | 123.1 | 161.1 | 34.5 | -45.4 | |
| -20.7 | -25.1 | -21.0 | | | -25.6 | -19.9 | -31.5 | -38.6 | -16.3 | |
| 6.1 | 7.3 | 9.3 | | | 6.7 | 7.4 | 8.0 | 7.1 | 18.4 | |
| (84) 2.3 | (83) 2.5 | (77) 2.0 | | EBIT/Interest | (15) 1.1 | (10) .5 | (14) 2.2 | 2.2 | (16) 3.8 | |
| .8 | .9 | .2 | | | -2.0 | -4.6 | .5 | .3 | -.9 | |
| 2.7 | 5.6 | 3.9 | | Net Profit + Depr., Dep., | | | | | | |
| (13) 2.1 | (16) 2.9 | (10) 2.5 | | Amort./Cur. Mat. L/T/D | | | | | | |
| 1.4 | 1.2 | .9 | | | | | | | | |
| 1.0 | .7 | .9 | | | .4 | 1.0 | .5 | 1.9 | 1.3 | |
| 2.8 | 1.9 | 2.9 | | Fixed/Worth | 3.6 | 2.9 | 1.6 | 2.7 | 5.0 | |
| -13.3 | -8.9 | -3.2 | | | -1.1 | NM | 11.7 | -1.6 | NM | |
| 1.3 | .7 | 1.1 | | | .5 | .8 | .6 | 2.6 | 2.2 | |
| 4.4 | 3.4 | 4.5 | | Debt/Worth | 10.9 | 2.9 | 2.0 | 4.2 | 7.4 | |
| -24.2 | -19.1 | -9.4 | | | -5.2 | NM | 15.6 | -4.6 | NM | |
| 71.5 | 49.8 | 61.0 | | % Profit Before Taxes/Tangible | 60.3 | 57.6 | 63.8 | 53.3 | 183.7 | |
| (66) 19.0 | (69) 19.7 | (62) 10.9 | | Net Worth | (11) -2.2 | (10) 7.9 | (14) 9.6 | (12) 25.8 | (13) 34.2 | |
| .9 | 1.4 | -11.2 | | | -20.0 | -58.2 | -2.5 | 3.9 | -43.7 | |
| 11.9 | 11.9 | 14.1 | | % Profit Before Taxes/Total | 13.7 | 11.8 | 17.8 | 10.9 | 15.4 | |
| 3.6 | 5.4 | 3.2 | | Assets | .4 | 2.7 | 4.3 | 3.8 | 6.9 | |
| -.8 | -.1 | -2.2 | | | -4.1 | -9.5 | -.6 | -1.3 | -6.7 | |
| 12.4 | 15.7 | 15.5 | | | 50.8 | 15.0 | 39.8 | 34.2 | 10.6 | |
| 6.4 | 7.3 | 7.2 | | Sales/Net Fixed Assets | 11.8 | 9.1 | 5.9 | 7.5 | 6.9 | |
| 3.6 | 4.1 | 4.0 | | | 5.7 | 2.2 | 3.1 | 4.5 | 5.2 | |
| 4.1 | 4.0 | 4.2 | | | 3.5 | 5.4 | 4.3 | 4.4 | 3.9 | |
| 2.8 | 2.9 | 2.8 | | Sales/Total Assets | 2.7 | 2.5 | 2.7 | 2.9 | 2.9 | |
| 1.7 | 2.0 | 1.8 | | | 1.8 | 1.3 | 1.6 | 2.3 | 2.4 | |
| 3.0 | 2.3 | 2.7 | | | 1.2 | 3.2 | 3.7 | 2.1 | 2.7 | |
| (68) 5.0 | (76) 4.1 | (72) 4.1 | | % Depr., Dep., Amort./Sales | (15) 3.8 | (10) 4.9 | (13) 4.8 | (15) 3.7 | (15) 3.7 | |
| 6.6 | 6.3 | 7.4 | | | 12.8 | 10.6 | 9.0 | 5.5 | 5.7 | |
| 1.5 | .9 | 1.1 | | | | | | 1.1 | .8 | |
| (31) 3.2 | (30) 3.0 | (40) 2.6 | | % Officers', Directors' Owners' Comp/Sales | | | (11) 2.7 | (10) 1.1 | | |
| 5.8 | 4.6 | 4.3 | | | | | 3.5 | 2.7 | | |
| 1389197M | 1573453M | 1825455M | | Net Sales ($) | 2973M | 35023M | 49805M | 112777M | 250176M | 1374701M |
| 493798M | 668006M | 754046M | | Total Assets ($) | 2276M | 15831M | 22890M | 80784M | 87085M | 545180M |

M = $ thousand    MM = $ million
See Pages 9 through 22 for Explanation of Ratios and Data

# RETAIL—Heating Oil Dealers  NAICS 454311

**Current Data Sorted by Assets**     **Comparative Historical Data**

| 0-500M | 500M-2MM | 2-10MM | 10-50MM | 50-100MM | 100-250MM | Type of Statement | ALL | ALL |
|---|---|---|---|---|---|---|---|---|
|  | 2 | 5 | 12 | 7 | 2 | Unqualified | 29 | 28 |
|  | 10 | 61 | 23 | 2 |  | Reviewed | 117 | 93 |
| 2 | 21 | 23 | 1 |  | 1 | Compiled | 73 | 63 |
| 8 | 31 | 4 |  |  | 2 | Tax Returns | 37 | 31 |
|  | 9 | 16 | 9 |  | 7 | Other | 58 | 46 |
|  | 120 (4/1-9/30/11) |  | 138 (10/1/11-3/31/12) |  |  |  | 4/1/07-3/31/08 | 4/1/08-3/31/09 |
| 10 | 73 | 109 | 45 | 9 | 12 | **NUMBER OF STATEMENTS** | 314 | 261 |
| % | % | % | % | % | % | **ASSETS** | % | % |
| 22.3 | 15.5 | 13.3 | 12.3 |  | 15.8 | Cash & Equivalents | 13.9 | 18.0 |
| 40.2 | 32.0 | 35.1 | 31.3 |  | 23.7 | Trade Receivables (net) | 31.1 | 27.8 |
| 8.2 | 13.7 | 11.4 | 12.8 |  | 9.9 | Inventory | 11.3 | 10.3 |
| .0 | 2.4 | 2.3 | 2.4 |  | 4.0 | All Other Current | 2.6 | 2.8 |
| 70.8 | 63.5 | 62.1 | 58.8 |  | 53.5 | Total Current | 58.9 | 58.8 |
| 23.4 | 20.7 | 22.4 | 26.8 |  | 26.5 | Fixed Assets (net) | 25.8 | 24.4 |
| 4.5 | 6.3 | 8.5 | 7.6 |  | 13.3 | Intangibles (net) | 8.0 | 8.4 |
| 1.3 | 9.5 | 7.0 | 6.7 |  | 6.7 | All Other Non-Current | 7.3 | 8.4 |
| 100.0 | 100.0 | 100.0 | 100.0 |  | 100.0 | Total | 100.0 | 100.0 |
|  |  |  |  |  |  | **LIABILITIES** |  |  |
| 31.0 | 15.7 | 12.5 | 9.1 |  | 27.1 | Notes Payable-Short Term | 13.2 | 13.3 |
| 2.4 | 3.9 | 2.2 | 2.6 |  | 2.7 | Cur. Mat.-L.T.D. | 4.0 | 3.4 |
| 21.3 | 19.7 | 19.1 | 22.4 |  | 11.5 | Trade Payables | 19.0 | 16.9 |
| .0 | .1 | .5 | .1 |  | .2 | Income Taxes Payable | .2 | .3 |
| 25.9 | 14.4 | 16.8 | 13.1 |  | 10.9 | All Other Current | 20.7 | 17.5 |
| 80.7 | 53.8 | 51.2 | 47.4 |  | 52.4 | Total Current | 57.1 | 51.4 |
| 14.1 | 17.3 | 9.9 | 11.9 |  | 23.9 | Long-Term Debt | 15.6 | 15.3 |
| .0 | .1 | .6 | 1.0 |  | 1.5 | Deferred Taxes | .4 | .4 |
| 16.6 | 8.6 | 4.1 | 3.7 |  | 8.6 | All Other Non-Current | 5.1 | 7.9 |
| -11.4 | 20.2 | 34.3 | 36.0 |  | 13.5 | Net Worth | 21.8 | 24.9 |
| 100.0 | 100.0 | 100.0 | 100.0 |  | 100.0 | Total Liabilities & Net Worth | 100.0 | 100.0 |
|  |  |  |  |  |  | **INCOME DATA** |  |  |
| 100.0 | 100.0 | 100.0 | 100.0 |  | 100.0 | Net Sales | 100.0 | 100.0 |
| 18.4 | 16.1 | 16.4 | 13.8 |  | 12.0 | Gross Profit | 16.5 | 14.1 |
| 17.9 | 15.2 | 15.3 | 12.0 |  | 10.8 | Operating Expenses | 15.4 | 13.2 |
| .5 | 1.0 | 1.1 | 1.8 |  | 1.1 | Operating Profit | 1.1 | .9 |
| .3 | .3 | .0 | .3 |  | .6 | All Other Expenses (net) | .2 | .0 |
| .2 | .6 | 1.1 | 1.5 |  | .5 | Profit Before Taxes | .9 | .9 |
|  |  |  |  |  |  | **RATIOS** |  |  |
| 2.8 | 1.8 | 1.7 | 1.6 |  | 2.0 | Current | 1.4 | 1.6 |
| 1.2 | 1.2 | 1.2 | 1.2 |  | 1.4 |  | 1.0 | 1.1 |
| .6 | .8 | 1.0 | .9 |  | .9 |  | .8 | .8 |
| 1.8 | 1.4 | 1.3 | 1.2 |  | 1.4 | Quick | 1.1 | 1.3 |
| 1.1 | .8 | 1.0 | 1.0 |  | .9 |  | .8 | .9 |
| .6 | .5 | .7 | .6 |  | .6 |  | .5 | .6 |
| 0 UND | 11 32.3 | 15 25.1 | 12 30.0 |  | 5 80.3 | Sales/Receivables | 11 31.7 | 9 39.5 |
| 16 23.0 | 20 18.0 | 23 15.8 | 21 17.2 |  | 24 15.1 |  | 20 18.2 | 16 22.6 |
| 33 11.1 | 26 13.8 | 33 11.1 | 29 12.5 |  | 40 9.2 |  | 33 11.0 | 26 13.9 |
| 0 UND | 2 152.9 | 3 130.8 | 3 106.4 |  | 2 220.8 | Cost of Sales/Inventory | 4 103.0 | 2 161.4 |
| 2 179.8 | 6 57.3 | 8 45.8 | 9 39.8 |  | 8 43.1 |  | 9 42.5 | 6 60.4 |
| 3 122.9 | 16 23.4 | 18 20.7 | 20 18.3 |  | 20 18.3 |  | 14 25.6 | 12 29.4 |
| 0 UND | 7 48.9 | 9 39.9 | 3 42.6 |  | 5 71.2 | Cost of Sales/Payables | 9 42.0 | 7 52.3 |
| 12 30.1 | 14 26.9 | 13 28.3 | 13 28.4 |  | 11 32.6 |  | 14 26.7 | 11 34.4 |
| 17 22.0 | 20 18.6 | 19 19.3 | 20 18.0 |  | 20 18.7 |  | 21 17.4 | 16 23.4 |
| 24.8 | 18.0 | 18.9 | 17.4 |  | 10.8 | Sales/Working Capital | 22.8 | 22.4 |
| 132.2 | 49.1 | 54.1 | 77.6 |  | 29.5 |  | 214.7 | 124.6 |
| -15.5 | -36.1 | -159.8 | -68.0 |  | -112.9 |  | -38.6 | -63.6 |
|  | 5.9 | 7.5 | 10.3 |  | 4.2 | EBIT/Interest | 5.1 | 5.7 |
|  | (68) 2.6 | (96) 3.1 | (40) 3.9 |  | 2.4 |  | (292) 2.2 | (246) 2.2 |
|  | 1.1 | 1.3 | 1.8 |  | .7 |  | .9 | 1.1 |
|  | 3.6 | 6.0 | 7.3 |  |  | Net Profit + Depr., Dep., Amort./Cur. Mat. L/T/D | 3.2 | 3.8 |
|  | (10) 2.3 | (33) 3.1 | (18) 2.0 |  |  |  | (99) 2.0 | (85) 2.1 |
|  | .9 | 2.0 | 1.3 |  |  |  | 1.2 | 1.1 |
| .1 | .2 | .3 | .3 |  | .5 | Fixed/Worth | .6 | .5 |
| 2.9 | 1.0 | .8 | 1.1 |  | 2.6 |  | 1.5 | 1.2 |
| -.2 | -3.5 | 4.2 | 2.4 |  | -2.8 |  | -7.1 | 9.5 |
| 1.7 | 1.5 | 1.1 | 1.2 |  | 1.7 | Debt/Worth | 1.6 | 1.4 |
| 5.1 | 3.9 | 2.9 | 2.0 |  | 4.9 |  | 4.6 | 3.8 |
| -1.9 | -11.9 | 11.7 | 8.1 |  | -15.1 |  | -27.2 | 48.5 |
|  | 33.7 | 31.0 | 35.7 |  |  | % Profit Before Taxes/Tangible Net Worth | 31.2 | 37.7 |
|  | (50) 16.2 | (93) 14.6 | (38) 14.5 |  |  |  | (226) 14.6 | (199) 16.8 |
|  | 2.1 | 4.3 | 4.8 |  |  |  | 2.6 | 4.1 |
| 23.8 | 7.9 | 8.2 | 8.1 |  | 6.2 | % Profit Before Taxes/Total Assets | 7.8 | 8.3 |
| .4 | 4.6 | 3.8 | 4.1 |  | 3.4 |  | 3.2 | 3.3 |
| -4.7 | .3 | .7 | 1.7 |  | .4 |  | .0 | .5 |
| UND | 79.8 | 58.2 | 46.1 |  | 33.7 | Sales/Net Fixed Assets | 52.5 | 62.8 |
| 108.9 | 35.8 | 21.7 | 21.1 |  | 25.2 |  | 22.5 | 27.3 |
| 22.6 | 16.7 | 12.9 | 10.9 |  | 17.3 |  | 12.2 | 15.3 |
| 12.3 | 7.0 | 7.3 | 7.7 |  | 8.3 | Sales/Total Assets | 6.8 | 7.9 |
| 9.0 | 5.3 | 4.6 | 4.4 |  | 3.8 |  | 4.7 | 5.4 |
| 7.0 | 4.1 | 3.3 | 3.3 |  | 2.9 |  | 3.4 | 3.8 |
|  | .4 | .6 | .5 |  | .4 | % Depr., Dep., Amort./Sales | .6 | .5 |
|  | (63) .7 | (102) 1.1 | (41) .8 |  | (10) .6 |  | (281) 1.1 | (233) .9 |
|  | 1.4 | 1.7 | 1.5 |  | 1.6 |  | 1.7 | 1.5 |
|  | 1.0 | 1.0 | .3 |  |  | % Officers', Directors' Owners' Comp/Sales | .9 | .7 |
|  | (51) 2.2 | (58) 1.4 | (16) .9 |  |  |  | (154) 1.7 | (139) 1.3 |
|  | 3.5 | 2.9 | 1.9 |  |  |  | 3.0 | 2.7 |
| 30340M | 511072M | 2880759M | 5498451M | 3503096M | 9818432M | Net Sales ($) | 19437758M | 19228617M |
| 3049M | 87515M | 517948M | 934229M | 616517M | 1671692M | Total Assets ($) | 3997671M | 3468379M |

M = $ thousand    MM = $ million
See Pages 9 through 22 for Explanation of Ratios and Data

## Comparative Historical Data | Current Data Sorted by Sales

| 26 | 26 | 28 | Type of Statement |  |  |  |  |  |  |
|---|---|---|---|---|---|---|---|---|---|
| 26 | 26 | 28 | Unqualified |  |  | 2 |  | 4 | 22 |
| 97 | 79 | 96 | Reviewed |  | 1 | 5 | 5 | 35 | 50 |
| 60 | 60 | 48 | Compiled | 1 | 1 | 7 | 10 | 17 | 12 |
| 36 | 34 | 45 | Tax Returns |  | 10 | 9 | 17 | 5 | 4 |
| 54 | 55 | 41 | Other |  |  | 5 | 10 | 7 | 19 |

| 4/1/09-3/31/10 ALL | 4/1/10-3/31/11 ALL | 4/1/11-3/31/12 ALL |  | 0-1MM | 1-3MM | 3-5MM | 5-10MM | 10-25MM | 25MM & OVER |
|---|---|---|---|---|---|---|---|---|---|
|  |  |  |  |  | 120 (4/1-9/30/11) |  | 138 (10/1/11-3/31/12) |  |  |
| **273** | **254** | **258** | **NUMBER OF STATEMENTS** | 1 | 12 | 28 | 42 | 68 | 107 |
| % | % | % | **ASSETS** | % | % | % | % | % | % |
| 18.0 | 14.9 | 14.2 | Cash & Equivalents |  | 12.9 | 14.5 | 14.0 | 13.7 | 14.5 |
| 24.8 | 29.8 | 32.9 | Trade Receivables (net) |  | 32.9 | 26.2 | 31.6 | 35.5 | 33.3 |
| 10.9 | 11.9 | 12.2 | Inventory |  | 11.5 | 15.9 | 12.3 | 12.6 | 11.1 |
| 3.6 | 2.4 | 2.3 | All Other Current |  | .1 | 1.7 | 3.8 | 1.1 | 3.0 |
| 57.3 | 59.0 | 61.7 | Total Current |  | 57.5 | 58.3 | 61.6 | 62.9 | 62.0 |
| 25.6 | 24.9 | 23.2 | Fixed Assets (net) |  | 22.9 | 20.9 | 22.8 | 24.6 | 23.4 |
| 7.8 | 7.1 | 7.6 | Intangibles (net) |  | .8 | 11.3 | 6.3 | 7.4 | 8.1 |
| 9.2 | 9.0 | 7.5 | All Other Non-Current |  | 18.8 | 9.4 | 9.3 | 5.2 | 6.5 |
| 100.0 | 100.0 | 100.0 | Total |  | 100.0 | 100.0 | 100.0 | 100.0 | 100.0 |
|  |  |  | **LIABILITIES** |  |  |  |  |  |  |
| 9.8 | 12.1 | 14.0 | Notes Payable-Short Term |  | 29.3 | 20.2 | 15.2 | 11.6 | 11.7 |
| 4.2 | 2.9 | 2.8 | Cur. Mat.-L.T.D. |  | 3.1 | 2.8 | 4.0 | 3.1 | 2.1 |
| 17.8 | 18.2 | 19.6 | Trade Payables |  | 25.4 | 13.2 | 19.1 | 16.8 | 22.5 |
| .2 | .1 | .3 | Income Taxes Payable |  | .0 | .1 | .1 | .2 | .5 |
| 20.2 | 15.8 | 15.7 | All Other Current |  | 29.2 | 18.1 | 16.4 | 15.5 | 13.6 |
| 52.3 | 49.2 | 52.3 | Total Current |  | 87.0 | 54.4 | 54.7 | 47.3 | 50.4 |
| 15.1 | 15.3 | 13.5 | Long-Term Debt |  | 8.0 | 17.3 | 18.4 | 12.8 | 11.7 |
| .5 | .5 | .5 | Deferred Taxes |  | .0 | .1 | .2 | .4 | 1.0 |
| 6.9 | 6.9 | 6.0 | All Other Non-Current |  | 11.6 | 9.6 | 11.8 | 3.1 | 4.0 |
| 25.2 | 28.1 | 27.7 | Net Worth |  | -6.5 | 18.7 | 14.9 | 36.4 | 32.9 |
| 100.0 | 100.0 | 100.0 | Total Liabilities & Net Worth |  | 100.0 | 100.0 | 100.0 | 100.0 | 100.0 |
|  |  |  | **INCOME DATA** |  |  |  |  |  |  |
| 100.0 | 100.0 | 100.0 | Net Sales |  | 100.0 | 100.0 | 100.0 | 100.0 | 100.0 |
| 19.8 | 18.4 | 15.7 | Gross Profit |  | 26.5 | 17.4 | 17.5 | 17.8 | 12.0 |
| 17.8 | 17.0 | 14.5 | Operating Expenses |  | 27.2 | 15.8 | 16.3 | 16.4 | 10.9 |
| 2.1 | 1.5 | 1.2 | Operating Profit |  | -.7 | 1.5 | 1.1 | 1.4 | 1.1 |
| .1 | .1 | .2 | All Other Expenses (net) |  | .7 | .2 | .3 | .3 | .0 |
| 2.0 | 1.3 | 1.0 | Profit Before Taxes |  | -1.5 | 1.3 | .8 | 1.1 | 1.1 |
|  |  |  | **RATIOS** |  |  |  |  |  |  |
| 1.7 | 1.8 | 1.7 | Current |  | 1.7 | 1.8 | 1.5 | 1.9 | 1.7 |
| 1.1 | 1.2 | 1.2 |  |  | .6 | 1.1 | 1.1 | 1.3 | 1.2 |
| .8 | .9 | .9 |  |  | .3 | .6 | .8 | 1.0 | 1.0 |
| 1.3 | 1.4 | 1.3 | Quick |  | 1.3 | 1.6 | 1.2 | 1.4 | 1.2 |
| .8 | .9 | .9 |  |  | .5 | .7 | .8 | 1.0 | 1.0 |
| .5 | .6 | .6 |  |  | .2 | .3 | .5 | .6 | .7 |
| 8  43.4 | 11  33.6 | 13  28.9 | Sales/Receivables |  | 7  50.6 | 13  28.2 | 13  28.1 | 16  23.3 | 10  36.5 |
| 16  23.0 | 21  17.8 | 21  17.0 |  |  | 23  15.9 | 22  16.8 | 21  17.5 | 25  14.5 | 19  19.1 |
| 28  12.9 | 32  11.5 | 31  11.6 |  |  | 34  10.6 | 32  11.4 | 29  11.1 | 33  11.1 | 29  12.5 |
| 4  102.2 | 4  97.2 | 3  142.7 | Cost of Sales/Inventory |  | 0  UND | 3  135.5 | 2  162.9 | 4  86.5 | 2  170.1 |
| 8  43.1 | 9  42.0 | 8  48.2 |  |  | 4  87.2 | 13  28.5 | 8  46.8 | 10  37.8 | 6  57.5 |
| 16  23.3 | 19  19.7 | 17  21.9 |  |  | 30  12.0 | 29  12.7 | 17  21.5 | 19  19.1 | 13  28.5 |
| 8  43.0 | 9  39.3 | 8  43.0 | Cost of Sales/Payables |  | 12  30.8 | 7  53.2 | 9  42.1 | 8  43.4 | 9  41.5 |
| 14  26.2 | 14  25.4 | 13  28.3 |  |  | 22  16.8 | 14  26.1 | 16  22.7 | 12  30.3 | 12  29.2 |
| 24  15.3 | 23  16.1 | 20  18.5 |  |  | 66  5.5 | 21  17.8 | 23  15.8 | 17  21.6 | 18  20.5 |
| 19.7 | 14.5 | 18.3 | Sales/Working Capital |  | 20.6 | 16.4 | 20.1 | 17.2 | 20.4 |
| 72.1 | 73.3 | 56.8 |  |  | -14.8 | 116.2 | 63.5 | 39.6 | 55.2 |
| -59.1 | -66.5 | -90.0 |  |  | -8.0 | -12.9 | -37.6 | -124.2 | -222.0 |
| 12.3 | 9.5 | 7.0 | EBIT/Interest |  | 8.1 | 4.6 | 3.9 | 9.6 | 9.9 |
| (247) 3.9 | (224) 2.9 | (234) 3.1 |  | (10) 1.2 | (25) 1.7 | (41) 2.0 | (61) 2.9 | (97) 4.4 |
| 1.5 | 1.2 | 1.3 |  |  | -.3 | .8 | 1.1 | 1.1 | 2.2 |
| 6.8 | 4.1 | 5.6 | Net Profit + Depr., Dep., Amort./Cur. Mat. L/T/D |  |  |  |  | 5.4 | 7.1 |
| (82) 2.8 | (73) 2.1 | (70) 2.7 |  |  |  |  | (24) 3.6 | (40) 2.5 |
| 1.3 | 1.3 | 1.7 |  |  |  |  |  | 1.4 | 1.7 |
| .4 | .4 | .3 | Fixed/Worth |  | .1 | .2 | .4 | .3 | .3 |
| 1.1 | 1.0 | .9 |  |  | 2.3 | 3.2 | 1.6 | .9 | .8 |
| 17.4 | 9.1 | 7.0 |  |  | -.7 | -1.6 | -3.5 | 2.3 | 2.5 |
| 1.2 | 1.1 | 1.2 | Debt/Worth |  | 2.0 | 1.7 | 2.2 | .9 | 1.2 |
| 3.2 | 3.2 | 3.0 |  |  | 5.8 | 7.5 | 4.9 | 2.5 | 2.2 |
| 324.7 | 19.1 | 24.4 |  |  | -4.0 | -11.8 | -9.5 | 6.5 | 9.5 |
| 55.3 | 38.6 | 33.6 | % Profit Before Taxes/Tangible Net Worth |  |  | 16.9 | 33.7 | 30.2 | 37.0 |
| (206) 21.7 | (201) 15.6 | (203) 15.0 |  |  | (16) 4.7 | (29) 12.1 | (59) 14.5 | (91) 17.1 |
| 8.2 | 2.5 | 4.1 |  |  |  | -1.4 | 1.5 | 2.8 | 6.7 |
| 13.8 | 9.5 | 8.1 | % Profit Before Taxes/Total Assets |  | 12.5 | 5.0 | 6.1 | 9.1 | 8.3 |
| 5.9 | 4.4 | 4.0 |  |  | .6 | 2.2 | 2.8 | 4.4 | 4.5 |
| 1.5 | .5 | .7 |  |  | -13.0 | -.4 | .3 | .4 | 1.8 |
| 54.7 | 54.3 | 75.0 | Sales/Net Fixed Assets |  | 119.1 | 73.3 | 61.8 | 45.1 | 94.0 |
| 19.9 | 23.5 | 25.6 |  |  | 43.9 | 18.5 | 33.2 | 19.4 | 27.5 |
| 11.7 | 12.4 | 13.2 |  |  | 10.9 | 10.5 | 13.1 | 13.1 | 15.6 |
| 6.5 | 6.7 | 7.6 | Sales/Total Assets |  | 6.7 | 5.7 | 6.7 | 7.3 | 8.8 |
| 4.3 | 4.4 | 4.9 |  |  | 4.1 | 4.3 | 5.3 | 4.7 | 5.4 |
| 3.2 | 3.2 | 3.5 |  |  | 2.6 | 2.2 | 3.5 | 3.3 | 4.0 |
| .6 | .6 | .5 | % Depr., Dep., Amort./Sales |  |  | .4 | .5 | .6 | .4 |
| (234) 1.2 | (227) .9 | (231) .9 |  |  | (26) 1.0 | (34) 1.2 | (65) 1.0 | (97) .7 |
| 1.9 | 1.8 | 1.6 |  |  |  | 2.0 | 1.9 | 1.6 | 1.3 |
| 1.2 | .9 | 1.0 | % Officers', Directors' Owners' Comp/Sales |  | 2.5 | 1.8 | 1.0 | .9 | .3 |
| (145) 2.0 | (141) 1.7 | (136) 1.6 |  | (10) 4.8 | (14) 2.5 | (30) 1.6 | (44) 1.2 | (38) 1.2 |
| 4.0 | 3.4 | 3.0 |  |  | 7.6 | 3.7 | 4.4 | 2.3 | 2.2 |
| 17798414M | 19870430M | 22242150M | Net Sales ($) | 910M | 24188M | 110271M | 294514M | 1139707M | 20672560M |
| 3552805M | 3697620M | 3830950M | Total Assets ($) | 140M | 6512M | 35561M | 71900M | 287375M | 3429462M |

M = $ thousand    MM = $ million
See Pages 9 through 22 for Explanation of Ratios and Data

## Current Data Sorted by Assets

## Comparative Historical Data

| | | | | | | | Type of Statement | | | |
|---|---|---|---|---|---|---|---|---|---|---|
| | | 2 | | 6 | 4 | | Unqualified | | 18 | 22 |
| | 2 | 8 | | 2 | | | Reviewed | | 17 | 17 |
| | 5 | 6 | | | | 1 | Compiled | | 18 | 22 |
| 5 | 17 | 5 | | | | | Tax Returns | | 18 | 22 |
| | 8 | 6 | | | 5 | | Other | | 35 | 23 |
| | 29 (4/1-9/30/11) | | | 53 (10/1/11-3/31/12) | | | | | 4/1/07- 3/31/08 | 4/1/08- 3/31/09 |
| 0-500M | 500M-2MM | 2-10MM | 10-50MM | 50-100MM | 100-250MM | | | | ALL | ALL |
| 5 | 32 | 27 | 8 | 9 | 1 | | NUMBER OF STATEMENTS | | 106 | 106 |
| % | % | % | % | % | % | | ASSETS | | % | % |
| | 12.1 | 9.2 | | | | | Cash & Equivalents | | 8.1 | 11.0 |
| | 22.7 | 23.9 | | | | | Trade Receivables (net) | | 24.5 | 23.1 |
| | 7.6 | 14.3 | | | | | Inventory | | 12.0 | 10.2 |
| | 10.7 | 2.5 | | | | | All Other Current | | 3.6 | 3.7 |
| | 53.1 | 49.8 | | | | | Total Current | | 48.2 | 48.0 |
| | 34.7 | 37.0 | | | | | Fixed Assets (net) | | 40.2 | 38.7 |
| | 3.2 | 7.7 | | | | | Intangibles (net) | | 4.2 | 5.7 |
| | 8.9 | 5.4 | | | | | All Other Non-Current | | 7.4 | 7.5 |
| | 100.0 | 100.0 | | | | | Total | | 100.0 | 100.0 |
| | | | | | | | LIABILITIES | | | |
| | 7.5 | 5.7 | | | | | Notes Payable-Short Term | | 7.9 | 5.3 |
| | 5.3 | 5.4 | | | | | Cur. Mat.-L.T.D. | | 4.7 | 7.1 |
| | 24.1 | 13.3 | | | | | Trade Payables | | 18.4 | 16.5 |
| | .2 | .8 | | | | | Income Taxes Payable | | .4 | .1 |
| | 11.6 | 7.9 | | | | | All Other Current | | 12.2 | 12.2 |
| | 48.7 | 33.1 | | | | | Total Current | | 43.6 | 41.3 |
| | 33.2 | 11.5 | | | | | Long-Term Debt | | 26.2 | 24.4 |
| | .0 | .3 | | | | | Deferred Taxes | | 1.2 | 1.0 |
| | 23.6 | 9.0 | | | | | All Other Non-Current | | 5.5 | 5.4 |
| | -5.5 | 46.2 | | | | | Net Worth | | 23.5 | 28.0 |
| | 100.0 | 100.0 | | | | | Total Liabilties & Net Worth | | 100.0 | 100.0 |
| | | | | | | | INCOME DATA | | | |
| | 100.0 | 100.0 | | | | | Net Sales | | 100.0 | 100.0 |
| | 26.8 | 27.2 | | | | | Gross Profit | | 27.4 | 25.6 |
| | 25.7 | 23.4 | | | | | Operating Expenses | | 24.9 | 23.0 |
| | 1.1 | 3.9 | | | | | Operating Profit | | 2.5 | 2.6 |
| | -1.0 | .3 | | | | | All Other Expenses (net) | | 1.0 | .7 |
| | 2.1 | 3.5 | | | | | Profit Before Taxes | | 1.5 | 1.8 |
| | | | | | | | RATIOS | | | |
| | 3.1 | 2.5 | | | | | | | 1.8 | 2.0 |
| | 1.1 | 1.7 | | | | | Current | | 1.2 | 1.2 |
| | .6 | .8 | | | | | | | .8 | .7 |
| | 2.1 | 1.9 | | | | | | | 1.3 | 1.4 |
| | .8 | .9 | | | | | Quick | | .8 | .8 |
| | .3 | .5 | | | | | | | .5 | .5 |
| | 13   27.2 | 15   24.1 | | | | | | 18   19.8 | 14   25.6 |
| | 21   17.0 | 27   13.3 | | | | | Sales/Receivables | 30   12.4 | 27   13.7 |
| | 34   10.8 | 39   9.3 | | | | | | 38   9.6 | 35   10.4 |
| | 5   69.8 | 11   34.2 | | | | | | 8   47.0 | 6   61.0 |
| | 11   33.8 | 18   20.1 | | | | | Cost of Sales/Inventory | 16   22.4 | 14   27.0 |
| | 18   20.0 | 36   10.1 | | | | | | 29   12.6 | 30   12.3 |
| | 9   41.0 | 13   27.6 | | | | | | 14   25.9 | 9   41.2 |
| | 18   20.6 | 19   19.4 | | | | | Cost of Sales/Payables | 23   16.1 | 17   21.0 |
| | 46   7.9 | 26   14.2 | | | | | | 36   10.2 | 30   12.0 |
| | 10.0 | 7.8 | | | | | | | 14.8 | 12.6 |
| | 80.0 | 15.7 | | | | | Sales/Working Capital | | 45.5 | 58.4 |
| | -21.0 | -46.6 | | | | | | | -34.4 | -28.9 |
| | 7.0 | 9.2 | | | | | | | 5.9 | 9.3 |
| | (28) 2.7 | (24) 5.1 | | | | | EBIT/Interest | (100) 2.4 | (100) 3.0 |
| | .4 | 1.6 | | | | | | | 1.1 | 1.1 |
| | | | | | | | Net Profit + Depr., Dep., | | 6.0 | 5.3 |
| | | | | | | | Amort./Cur. Mat. L/T/D | (33) 2.0 | (23) 3.1 |
| | | | | | | | | | 1.3 | 1.1 |
| | .7 | .4 | | | | | | | .6 | .6 |
| | 3.1 | .8 | | | | | Fixed/Worth | | 1.7 | 1.8 |
| | -1.9 | 1.9 | | | | | | | 35.1 | 5.9 |
| | 1.1 | .6 | | | | | | | 1.2 | 1.0 |
| | 15.8 | 1.2 | | | | | Debt/Worth | | 2.7 | 2.6 |
| | -5.0 | 2.3 | | | | | | | 110.3 | 13.3 |
| | 101.6 | 29.8 | | | | | % Profit Before Taxes/Tangible | 33.4 | 46.4 |
| | (18) 21.6 | (24) 12.4 | | | | | Net Worth | (81) 17.2 | (87) 23.1 |
| | -.3 | 3.6 | | | | | | | 4.1 | 6.9 |
| | 10.4 | 13.6 | | | | | % Profit Before Taxes/Total | 10.3 | 13.9 |
| | 3.0 | 5.7 | | | | | Assets | | 4.9 | 4.6 |
| | -1.7 | 1.8 | | | | | | | .3 | 1.4 |
| | 36.3 | 18.1 | | | | | | | 15.7 | 18.7 |
| | 10.3 | 9.2 | | | | | Sales/Net Fixed Assets | | 7.3 | 8.3 |
| | 4.2 | 4.6 | | | | | | | 3.3 | 3.6 |
| | 5.8 | 4.1 | | | | | | | 4.7 | 4.7 |
| | 3.2 | 3.0 | | | | | Sales/Total Assets | | 2.6 | 2.9 |
| | 1.8 | 2.1 | | | | | | | 1.9 | 1.8 |
| | 1.2 | 1.8 | | | | | | | 1.6 | 1.4 |
| | (24) 3.0 | (24) 3.3 | | | | | % Depr., Dep., Amort./Sales | (96) 3.2 | (97) 3.0 |
| | 4.5 | 4.2 | | | | | | | 4.6 | 4.7 |
| | 2.0 | .9 | | | | | | | 1.6 | 1.0 |
| | (23) 3.4 | (10) 1.9 | | | | | % Officers', Directors' | (46) 3.1 | (40) 2.1 |
| | 5.0 | 3.9 | | | | | Owners' Comp/Sales | | 6.1 | 4.3 |
| 11324M | 130565M | 408431M | 388419M | 3925452M | 809939M | | Net Sales ($) | | 4180002M | 5726298M |
| 2043M | 33486M | 115028M | 154507M | 649903M | 160118M | | Total Assets ($) | | 1492095M | 1900396M |

M = $ thousand    MM = $ million
See Pages 9 through 22 for Explanation of Ratios and Data

## Comparative Historical Data | Current Data Sorted by Sales

| 4/1/09-3/31/10 ALL | 4/1/10-3/31/11 ALL | 4/1/11-3/31/12 ALL | Type of Statement | 0-1MM | 1-3MM | 3-5MM | 5-10MM | 10-25MM | 25MM & OVER |
|---|---|---|---|---|---|---|---|---|---|
| 15 | 14 | 12 | Unqualified | | | 1 | 3 | 3 | 8 |
| 18 | 15 | 12 | Reviewed | | 1 | | 3 | 6 | 2 |
| 13 | 18 | 12 | Compiled | | 1 | 2 | 4 | 2 | 3 |
| 27 | 18 | 27 | Tax Returns | | 17 | 4 | 4 | 1 | 1 |
| 31 | 22 | 19 | Other | 1 | 2 | 1 | 6 | 3 | 6 |
| | | | | | 29 (4/1-9/30/11) | | 53 (10/1/11-3/31/12) | | |
| 104 | 87 | 82 | NUMBER OF STATEMENTS | 1 | 21 | 8 | 17 | 15 | 20 |
| % | % | % | ASSETS | % | % | % | % | % | % |
| 11.6 | 10.1 | 9.8 | Cash & Equivalents | | 8.5 | | 9.3 | 13.5 | 7.0 |
| 20.4 | 22.8 | 22.3 | Trade Receivables (net) | | 17.3 | | 19.3 | 25.5 | 29.3 |
| 10.7 | 12.7 | 11.6 | Inventory | | 8.3 | | 12.5 | 13.5 | 13.1 |
| 3.8 | 3.0 | 6.9 | All Other Current | | 16.7 | | 1.4 | 5.8 | 3.2 |
| 46.5 | 48.6 | 50.6 | Total Current | | 50.8 | | 42.6 | 58.2 | 52.5 |
| 40.3 | 38.8 | 36.8 | Fixed Assets (net) | | 40.7 | | 38.0 | 33.1 | 35.0 |
| 6.9 | 5.4 | 5.5 | Intangibles (net) | | 1.2 | | 10.8 | 3.4 | 4.8 |
| 6.2 | 7.1 | 7.1 | All Other Non-Current | | 7.4 | | 8.6 | 5.3 | 7.6 |
| 100.0 | 100.0 | 100.0 | Total | | 100.0 | | 100.0 | 100.0 | 100.0 |
| | | | LIABILITIES | | | | | | |
| 6.6 | 5.4 | 6.4 | Notes Payable-Short Term | | 5.4 | | 6.4 | 7.2 | 6.7 |
| 6.9 | 4.8 | 5.6 | Cur. Mat.-L.T.D. | | 5.9 | | 6.0 | 3.9 | 6.0 |
| 13.3 | 17.0 | 18.6 | Trade Payables | | 18.9 | | 16.8 | 14.3 | 21.1 |
| .2 | .4 | .4 | Income Taxes Payable | | .0 | | 1.5 | .1 | .1 |
| 11.8 | 12.2 | 9.0 | All Other Current | | 4.8 | | 11.4 | 14.6 | 7.5 |
| 38.7 | 39.8 | 40.0 | Total Current | | 35.1 | | 42.1 | 40.1 | 41.4 |
| 24.7 | 20.6 | 21.4 | Long-Term Debt | | 45.1 | | 19.3 | 10.0 | 11.1 |
| 1.4 | 1.3 | .7 | Deferred Taxes | | .0 | | .0 | .4 | 2.4 |
| 3.0 | 4.1 | 13.0 | All Other Non-Current | | 24.3 | | 17.5 | 1.5 | 4.2 |
| 32.3 | 34.1 | 24.9 | Net Worth | | -4.5 | | 21.1 | 48.0 | 40.8 |
| 100.0 | 100.0 | 100.0 | Total Liabilities & Net Worth | | 100.0 | | 100.0 | 100.0 | 100.0 |
| | | | INCOME DATA | | | | | | |
| 100.0 | 100.0 | 100.0 | Net Sales | | 100.0 | | 100.0 | 100.0 | 100.0 |
| 33.2 | 28.9 | 25.8 | Gross Profit | | 27.2 | | 32.2 | 27.2 | 18.4 |
| 28.4 | 25.5 | 23.4 | Operating Expenses | | 26.4 | | 29.7 | 20.8 | 17.1 |
| 4.9 | 3.4 | 2.5 | Operating Profit | | .8 | | 2.5 | 6.3 | 1.3 |
| .4 | .4 | -.2 | All Other Expenses (net) | | -1.4 | | .8 | -.5 | .4 |
| 4.4 | 3.0 | 2.7 | Profit Before Taxes | | 2.2 | | 1.7 | 6.8 | .9 |
| | | | RATIOS | | | | | | |
| 2.2 | 2.4 | 2.5 | Current | | 4.1 | | 2.5 | 3.3 | 2.0 |
| 1.3 | 1.2 | 1.3 | | | 1.5 | | 1.1 | 1.5 | 1.3 |
| .8 | .8 | .8 | | | .8 | | .6 | 1.1 | .9 |
| 1.9 | 1.7 | 1.6 | Quick | | 2.8 | | 1.7 | 2.1 | 1.2 |
| .9 | .8 | .8 | | | .8 | | .7 | .8 | .8 |
| .4 | .5 | .4 | | | .3 | | .2 | .6 | .6 |
| 15 25.1 | 16 23.3 | 14 26.2 | Sales/Receivables | | 11 32.8 | | 12 29.3 | 17 21.0 | 18 20.6 |
| 26 14.2 | 29 12.6 | 22 16.3 | | | 19 19.7 | | 20 18.0 | 25 14.5 | 24 15.1 |
| 35 10.4 | 40 9.2 | 33 11.0 | | | 36 10.0 | | 33 10.9 | 36 10.2 | 31 11.7 |
| 9 40.8 | 10 37.4 | 8 48.0 | Cost of Sales/Inventory | | 5 80.9 | | 8 46.7 | 7 54.9 | 8 45.6 |
| 18 20.0 | 18 20.3 | 15 24.8 | | | 15 23.8 | | 18 20.1 | 13 27.4 | 17 22.1 |
| 37 9.8 | 35 10.4 | 32 11.5 | | | 29 12.5 | | 40 9.1 | 35 10.4 | 35 10.3 |
| 10 38.4 | 14 25.8 | 11 33.2 | Cost of Sales/Payables | | 5 80.6 | | 15 23.8 | 2 168.9 | 13 27.3 |
| 19 19.5 | 22 16.9 | 19 19.6 | | | 24 14.9 | | 21 17.3 | 16 23.4 | 18 20.3 |
| 34 10.8 | 36 10.2 | 29 12.6 | | | 39 9.3 | | 26 13.9 | 27 13.7 | 26 14.2 |
| 8.6 | 8.8 | 9.1 | Sales/Working Capital | | 7.5 | | 7.8 | 5.0 | 11.1 |
| 31.0 | 33.5 | 32.5 | | | 15.4 | | 106.0 | 15.7 | 32.6 |
| -33.4 | -29.7 | -35.7 | | | -34.3 | | -12.7 | 275.3 | NM |
| 17.7 | 16.5 | 11.0 | EBIT/Interest | | 11.7 | | 6.2 | 19.4 | 11.2 |
| (95) 3.5 | (82) 2.7 | (74) 3.6 | | (18) 2.0 | | (15) 3.7 | | (13) 7.5 | 3.6 |
| 1.4 | .7 | 1.1 | | | -.3 | | 1.0 | 2.0 | 1.5 |
| 21.7 | 15.7 | 6.3 | Net Profit + Depr., Dep., Amort./Cur. Mat. L/T/D | | | | | | |
| (22) 3.8 | (17) 3.0 | (11) 2.8 | | | | | | | |
| 1.5 | 1.3 | .8 | | | | | | | |
| .6 | .6 | .5 | Fixed/Worth | | .5 | | 1.0 | .3 | .4 |
| 1.3 | 1.3 | 1.1 | | | 2.6 | | 1.9 | .8 | .8 |
| 3.4 | 3.1 | 12.4 | | | -7.1 | | -.9 | 1.1 | 2.4 |
| .8 | .7 | .7 | Debt/Worth | | .7 | | 1.0 | .4 | 1.0 |
| 2.0 | 1.8 | 2.1 | | | 7.2 | | 14.4 | 1.0 | 1.6 |
| 6.0 | 7.7 | 83.8 | | | -9.2 | | -7.1 | 2.9 | 3.4 |
| 56.6 | 37.1 | 35.3 | % Profit Before Taxes/Tangible Net Worth | | 61.4 | | 41.3 | 51.6 | 21.7 |
| (85) 23.1 | (73) 18.5 | (63) 13.1 | | (13) 28.8 | | (11) 5.6 | | (14) 25.7 | (19) 8.4 |
| 5.1 | 5.0 | 3.0 | | | 1.2 | | 3.2 | 10.1 | 1.9 |
| 17.0 | 14.2 | 12.9 | % Profit Before Taxes/Total Assets | | 11.5 | | 14.1 | 21.6 | 6.1 |
| 6.3 | 4.1 | 3.5 | | | 3.2 | | 3.4 | 10.4 | 2.8 |
| 1.2 | -.1 | .1 | | | -1.7 | | -.9 | 3.0 | .5 |
| 18.3 | 18.1 | 26.4 | Sales/Net Fixed Assets | | 12.5 | | 28.3 | 36.9 | 38.4 |
| 6.8 | 7.2 | 9.1 | | | 6.5 | | 7.9 | 11.4 | 12.0 |
| 3.4 | 3.7 | 4.2 | | | 3.4 | | 4.3 | 5.5 | 5.0 |
| 3.8 | 3.9 | 5.0 | Sales/Total Assets | | 4.1 | | 4.1 | 6.4 | 5.8 |
| 2.6 | 2.7 | 3.1 | | | 2.7 | | 3.0 | 3.2 | 4.0 |
| 1.7 | 1.9 | 1.9 | | | 1.6 | | 1.9 | 2.4 | 2.1 |
| 2.1 | 1.9 | 1.5 | % Depr., Dep., Amort./Sales | | 3.0 | | 2.2 | 1.4 | .9 |
| (85) 3.2 | (79) 3.4 | (68) 3.0 | | (17) 4.4 | | (13) 3.7 | | (14) 2.8 | (18) 1.7 |
| 5.9 | 4.7 | 4.6 | | | 6.2 | | 6.0 | 4.7 | 2.7 |
| 1.5 | 1.6 | 1.6 | % Officers', Directors', Owners' Comp/Sales | | 2.1 | | | | |
| (30) 3.0 | (29) 2.6 | (37) 2.4 | | (14) 3.4 | | | | | |
| 6.5 | 4.9 | 4.5 | | | 6.1 | | | | |
| 4043586M | 3176582M | 5674130M | Net Sales ($) | 843M | 41841M | 33178M | 117050M | 237525M | 5243693M |
| 1324791M | 1211193M | 1115085M | Total Assets ($) | 568M | 17916M | 11118M | 48776M | 92442M | 944265M |

M = $ thousand    MM = $ million
See Pages 9 through 22 for Explanation of Ratios and Data

## Current Data Sorted by Assets　　　　　　　　　　Comparative Historical Data

| Type of Statement | 0-500M | 500M-2MM | 2-10MM | 10-50MM | 50-100MM | 100-250MM | | 4/1/07-3/31/08 ALL | 4/1/08-3/31/09 ALL |
|---|---|---|---|---|---|---|---|---|---|
| Unqualified | 1 | 1 | 1 | 9 | 6 | 8 | | 12 | 18 |
| Reviewed | | 2 | 12 | 5 | 1 | | | 10 | 11 |
| Compiled | 7 | 15 | 12 | | 1 | | | 23 | 24 |
| Tax Returns | 52 | 60 | 19 | 2 | | | | 80 | 86 |
| Other | 24 | 38 | 38 | 18 | 5 | 9 | | 75 | 88 |
| | 32 (4/1-9/30/11) | | | 314 (10/1/11-3/31/12) | | | | | |
| **NUMBER OF STATEMENTS** | 84 | 116 | 82 | 34 | 13 | 17 | | 200 | 227 |
| **ASSETS** | % | % | % | % | % | % | | % | % |
| Cash & Equivalents | 27.4 | 16.2 | 14.5 | 12.9 | 19.7 | 11.7 | | 16.5 | 11.8 |
| Trade Receivables (net) | 15.9 | 24.1 | 25.6 | 22.3 | 13.0 | 17.3 | | 21.9 | 22.8 |
| Inventory | 24.5 | 29.4 | 29.7 | 31.0 | 25.3 | 26.5 | | 28.2 | 30.3 |
| All Other Current | 5.3 | 2.7 | 2.7 | 3.0 | 6.0 | 4.5 | | 3.5 | 2.7 |
| Total Current | 73.1 | 72.4 | 72.5 | 69.2 | 64.0 | 60.1 | | 70.1 | 67.6 |
| Fixed Assets (net) | 11.1 | 17.1 | 13.6 | 15.0 | 25.6 | 18.1 | | 17.8 | 18.5 |
| Intangibles (net) | 7.3 | 3.8 | 3.5 | 6.1 | 4.0 | 11.7 | | 5.0 | 5.7 |
| All Other Non-Current | 8.6 | 6.7 | 10.4 | 9.7 | 6.4 | 10.1 | | 7.2 | 8.1 |
| Total | 100.0 | 100.0 | 100.0 | 100.0 | 100.0 | 100.0 | | 100.0 | 100.0 |
| **LIABILITIES** | | | | | | | | | |
| Notes Payable-Short Term | 21.5 | 14.2 | 11.1 | 9.5 | 3.2 | 7.5 | | 13.3 | 17.2 |
| Cur. Mat.-L.T.D. | 2.2 | 3.1 | 2.4 | 2.4 | 4.0 | 1.7 | | 4.0 | 4.0 |
| Trade Payables | 19.8 | 17.9 | 20.9 | 13.0 | 11.9 | 13.6 | | 20.0 | 17.7 |
| Income Taxes Payable | .0 | .1 | .1 | .6 | .5 | .2 | | .3 | .2 |
| All Other Current | 16.8 | 12.6 | 15.7 | 13.0 | 23.2 | 16.6 | | 16.3 | 17.3 |
| Total Current | 60.4 | 48.0 | 50.2 | 38.4 | 42.8 | 39.6 | | 54.0 | 56.5 |
| Long-Term Debt | 8.6 | 18.8 | 9.5 | 10.1 | 13.7 | 20.1 | | 21.3 | 22.3 |
| Deferred Taxes | .2 | .0 | .1 | .2 | .6 | 1.0 | | .2 | .2 |
| All Other Non-Current | 9.4 | 8.8 | 5.7 | 4.6 | 6.2 | 5.8 | | 5.7 | 8.9 |
| Net Worth | 21.5 | 24.4 | 34.6 | 46.8 | 36.6 | 33.5 | | 18.8 | 12.2 |
| Total Liabilities & Net Worth | 100.0 | 100.0 | 100.0 | 100.0 | 100.0 | 100.0 | | 100.0 | 100.0 |
| **INCOME DATA** | | | | | | | | | |
| Net Sales | 100.0 | 100.0 | 100.0 | 100.0 | 100.0 | 100.0 | | 100.0 | 100.0 |
| Gross Profit | 42.8 | 45.6 | 39.3 | 42.8 | 58.4 | 50.8 | | 42.6 | 40.1 |
| Operating Expenses | 36.1 | 40.1 | 32.7 | 33.2 | 51.0 | 39.8 | | 36.0 | 35.6 |
| Operating Profit | 6.7 | 5.4 | 6.6 | 9.6 | 7.4 | 11.0 | | 6.6 | 4.6 |
| All Other Expenses (net) | .2 | .5 | .5 | .2 | 1.1 | 1.3 | | .9 | 1.3 |
| Profit Before Taxes | 6.6 | 4.9 | 6.1 | 9.4 | 6.3 | 9.7 | | 5.7 | 3.3 |
| **RATIOS** | | | | | | | | | |
| Current | 6.0 | 3.1 | 2.7 | 3.4 | 3.3 | 2.2 | | 3.0 | 2.0 |
| | 1.3 | 1.6 | 1.5 | 2.0 | 1.7 | 1.8 | | 1.5 | 1.2 |
| | .8 | 1.0 | 1.0 | 1.2 | .8 | 1.1 | | 1.0 | .8 |
| Quick | 3.1 | 1.7 | 1.4 | 1.9 | 1.7 | 1.3 | | 1.6 | 1.1 |
| | (83) .8 | .9 | .7 | 1.0 | .8 | .8 | | .8 | (226) .6 |
| | .3 | .4 | .4 | .4 | .2 | .4 | | .3 | .3 |
| Sales/Receivables | 0 UND | 2 165.3 | 7 50.0 | 8 45.7 | 1 444.3 | 4 94.3 | | 1 374.3 | 3 127.8 |
| | 1 298.2 | 21 17.3 | 25 14.5 | 33 10.9 | 3 115.0 | 22 16.8 | | 18 20.2 | 22 16.6 |
| | 22 16.7 | 43 8.4 | 52 7.0 | 55 6.6 | 49 7.4 | 50 7.3 | | 41 8.9 | 39 9.4 |
| Cost of Sales/Inventory | 0 UND | 8 48.1 | 21 17.1 | 30 12.2 | 54 6.8 | 72 5.1 | | 5 66.6 | 11 34.5 |
| | 12 29.8 | 41 8.9 | 43 8.4 | 76 4.8 | 91 4.0 | 94 3.9 | | 38 9.6 | 43 8.4 |
| | 56 6.5 | 101 3.6 | 104 3.5 | 166 2.2 | 140 2.6 | 152 2.4 | | 89 4.1 | 102 3.6 |
| Cost of Sales/Payables | 0 UND | 3 144.7 | 15 23.9 | 19 19.6 | 18 20.2 | 29 12.5 | | 8 46.7 | 9 38.8 |
| | 2 158.3 | 28 12.9 | 30 12.2 | 27 13.5 | 44 8.3 | 46 7.9 | | 26 14.1 | 24 15.4 |
| | 35 10.3 | 55 6.6 | 56 6.5 | 66 5.5 | 70 5.2 | 65 5.6 | | 52 7.0 | 45 8.1 |
| Sales/Working Capital | 9.2 | 6.5 | 6.0 | 4.2 | 3.3 | 3.7 | | 6.7 | 8.6 |
| | 44.2 | 14.8 | 13.4 | 7.8 | 16.6 | 9.1 | | 13.7 | 23.8 |
| | -48.7 | -341.3 | NM | 26.9 | -22.6 | 48.9 | | NM | -43.6 |
| EBIT/Interest | 30.3 | 22.2 | 50.1 | 23.9 | 15.1 | 213.3 | | 14.9 | 13.4 |
| | (50) 7.4 | (93) 4.1 | (68) 8.3 | (28) 11.9 | (11) 5.8 | (15) 8.7 | | (168) 5.2 | (190) 3.5 |
| | .2 | 1.4 | 1.6 | 4.6 | 3.1 | 2.5 | | 1.5 | 1.2 |
| Net Profit + Depr., Dep., Amort./Cur. Mat. L/T/D | | | | | | | | 10.5 | 5.6 |
| | | | | | | | | (19) 2.3 | (23) 1.3 |
| | | | | | | | | .9 | .7 |
| Fixed/Worth | .0 | .1 | .1 | .1 | .2 | .1 | | .1 | .1 |
| | .2 | .5 | .3 | .2 | .6 | .6 | | .6 | .9 |
| | 3.4 | 77.3 | 2.4 | 1.0 | NM | NM | | UND | -4.2 |
| Debt/Worth | .5 | .8 | .7 | .6 | .4 | .7 | | 1.0 | 1.4 |
| | 2.4 | 3.6 | 2.0 | 1.0 | 1.2 | 2.6 | | 4.0 | 5.5 |
| | -6.3 | -44.4 | 10.7 | 3.8 | NM | NM | | UND | -11.8 |
| % Profit Before Taxes/Tangible Net Worth | 122.3 | 102.5 | 77.0 | 73.9 | 94.7 | 85.2 | | 107.3 | 92.3 |
| | (56) 73.1 | (86) 44.4 | (70) 30.0 | (31) 45.4 | (10) 20.5 | (13) 38.1 | | (150) 45.9 | (160) 29.3 |
| | 20.1 | 13.4 | 7.9 | 19.8 | 14.3 | 28.5 | | 18.6 | 5.7 |
| % Profit Before Taxes/Total Assets | 61.6 | 32.6 | 29.0 | 24.0 | 30.5 | 23.5 | | 29.7 | 23.6 |
| | 21.7 | 11.3 | 9.7 | 14.2 | 14.4 | 11.9 | | 11.5 | 7.2 |
| | .4 | 2.6 | 2.1 | 6.8 | .9 | 5.8 | | 2.2 | .1 |
| Sales/Net Fixed Assets | UND | 237.2 | 123.8 | 193.4 | 24.0 | 36.4 | | 126.1 | 109.2 |
| | 151.9 | 47.8 | 50.1 | 33.9 | 10.1 | 23.6 | | 38.4 | 31.6 |
| | 43.8 | 12.9 | 14.4 | 8.9 | 5.8 | 9.0 | | 14.2 | 12.5 |
| Sales/Total Assets | 11.5 | 5.0 | 4.3 | 2.8 | 3.4 | 2.8 | | 5.1 | 5.2 |
| | 6.1 | 3.6 | 2.8 | 2.4 | 2.1 | 1.8 | | 3.2 | 3.2 |
| | 3.2 | 2.1 | 2.0 | 1.6 | 1.4 | 1.3 | | 2.0 | 2.0 |
| % Depr., Dep., Amort./Sales | .3 | .4 | .4 | .5 | .6 | .7 | | .4 | .5 |
| | (30) .8 | (66) 1.2 | (54) .7 | (24) 1.1 | (12) 2.1 | (12) 1.4 | | (140) .9 | (145) 1.1 |
| | 1.3 | 2.3 | 1.9 | 2.5 | 4.9 | 2.6 | | 1.8 | 2.3 |
| % Officers', Directors' Owners' Comp/Sales | 3.4 | 1.7 | 1.3 | | | | | 2.4 | 1.6 |
| | (39) 6.3 | (66) 3.5 | (31) 2.2 | | | | | (98) 4.5 | (94) 3.3 |
| | 11.3 | 5.8 | 3.5 | | | | | 7.9 | 7.4 |
| Net Sales ($) | 164070M | 557969M | 1103681M | 1648217M | 2132617M | 5957201M | | 6204997M | 9205659M |
| Total Assets ($) | 20078M | 130614M | 336641M | 712070M | 902596M | 3007398M | | 2412357M | 3162562M |

© RMA 2012

M = $ thousand　　MM = $ million
See Pages 9 through 22 for Explanation of Ratios and Data

## Comparative Historical Data

## Current Data Sorted by Sales

| | | | Type of Statement | | | | | | |
|---|---|---|---|---|---|---|---|---|---|
| 23 | 28 | 26 | Unqualified | 1 | 1 | | 1 | 1 | 22 |
| 23 | 10 | 20 | Reviewed | | 2 | 1 | 4 | 8 | 5 |
| 23 | 32 | 35 | Compiled | 2 | 10 | 4 | 10 | 6 | 3 |
| 92 | 94 | 133 | Tax Returns | 29 | 30 | 34 | 24 | 14 | 2 |
| 92 | 105 | 132 | Other | 18 | 22 | 12 | 20 | 23 | 37 |
| 4/1/09-<br>3/31/10<br>ALL | 4/1/10-<br>3/31/11<br>ALL | 4/1/11-<br>3/31/12<br>ALL | | 0-1MM | 32 (4/1-9/30/11)<br>1-3MM | 3-5MM | 314 (10/1/11-3/31/12)<br>5-10MM | 10-25MM | 25MM & OVER |
| 253 | 269 | 346 | NUMBER OF STATEMENTS | 50 | 65 | 51 | 59 | 52 | 69 |
| % | % | % | ASSETS | % | % | % | % | % | % |
| 15.0 | 16.8 | 18.1 | Cash & Equivalents | 27.7 | 17.1 | 14.9 | 15.2 | 20.5 | 15.0 |
| 21.6 | 19.8 | 21.5 | Trade Receivables (net) | 13.6 | 24.3 | 20.4 | 24.2 | 26.8 | 19.4 |
| 27.9 | 28.8 | 28.2 | Inventory | 28.6 | 23.8 | 35.2 | 27.6 | 24.8 | 29.8 |
| 3.2 | 3.1 | 3.6 | All Other Current | 3.4 | 4.1 | 2.6 | 4.1 | 2.3 | 4.5 |
| 67.7 | 68.5 | 71.3 | Total Current | 73.2 | 69.4 | 73.0 | 71.1 | 74.3 | 68.6 |
| 17.8 | 15.7 | 15.0 | Fixed Assets (net) | 11.3 | 19.3 | 15.3 | 13.5 | 12.3 | 16.7 |
| 6.9 | 7.1 | 5.2 | Intangibles (net) | 5.4 | 6.3 | 4.1 | 5.8 | 2.4 | 6.4 |
| 7.6 | 8.8 | 8.5 | All Other Non-Current | 10.1 | 5.0 | 7.6 | 9.7 | 11.0 | 8.3 |
| 100.0 | 100.0 | 100.0 | Total | 100.0 | 100.0 | 100.0 | 100.0 | 100.0 | 100.0 |
| | | | LIABILITIES | | | | | | |
| 14.2 | 12.3 | 14.0 | Notes Payable-Short Term | 28.0 | 18.8 | 11.2 | 10.4 | 10.1 | 7.6 |
| 3.4 | 3.9 | 2.6 | Cur. Mat.-L.T.D. | 2.0 | 1.8 | 3.3 | 3.3 | 3.3 | 2.3 |
| 17.2 | 20.2 | 18.2 | Trade Payables | 15.3 | 14.8 | 22.1 | 18.5 | 23.6 | 16.1 |
| .2 | .3 | .1 | Income Taxes Payable | .0 | .1 | .0 | .1 | .1 | .4 |
| 16.0 | 21.3 | 15.0 | All Other Current | 22.2 | 10.0 | 8.7 | 15.8 | 11.9 | 20.8 |
| 51.0 | 58.0 | 50.0 | Total Current | 67.4 | 45.6 | 45.3 | 48.1 | 49.0 | 47.2 |
| 19.2 | 14.3 | 13.1 | Long-Term Debt | 9.4 | 18.5 | 17.7 | 10.6 | 8.1 | 13.3 |
| .1 | .3 | .2 | Deferred Taxes | .0 | .0 | .0 | .4 | .0 | .5 |
| 6.1 | 9.0 | 7.6 | All Other Non-Current | 5.8 | 14.1 | 8.6 | 7.1 | 3.7 | 5.2 |
| 23.6 | 18.4 | 29.2 | Net Worth | 17.3 | 21.9 | 28.4 | 33.7 | 39.1 | 33.9 |
| 100.0 | 100.0 | 100.0 | Total Liabilities & Net Worth | 100.0 | 100.0 | 100.0 | 100.0 | 100.0 | 100.0 |
| | | | INCOME DATA | | | | | | |
| 100.0 | 100.0 | 100.0 | Net Sales | 100.0 | 100.0 | 100.0 | 100.0 | 100.0 | 100.0 |
| 42.0 | 43.5 | 43.9 | Gross Profit | 50.0 | 48.8 | 42.5 | 41.0 | 34.5 | 45.3 |
| 36.9 | 39.1 | 37.1 | Operating Expenses | 43.3 | 40.0 | 37.2 | 36.4 | 27.7 | 37.5 |
| 5.1 | 4.5 | 6.8 | Operating Profit | 6.8 | 8.8 | 5.3 | 4.6 | 6.9 | 7.8 |
| 1.0 | .7 | .5 | All Other Expenses (net) | .7 | .4 | .4 | .5 | .2 | .6 |
| 4.1 | 3.8 | 6.3 | Profit Before Taxes | 6.1 | 8.3 | 4.9 | 4.2 | 6.6 | 7.2 |
| | | | RATIOS | | | | | | |
| 2.7 | 2.2 | 3.1 | | 6.1 | 4.8 | 2.7 | 2.9 | 3.2 | 2.7 |
| 1.5 | 1.5 | 1.6 | Current | 1.4 | 1.6 | 1.8 | 1.5 | 1.6 | 1.7 |
| 1.0 | .8 | 1.0 | | .6 | .9 | 1.0 | 1.0 | 1.0 | 1.1 |
| 1.6 | 1.3 | 1.8 | | 2.7 | 3.1 | 1.5 | 1.3 | 2.1 | 1.3 |
| (251) .8 | (345) .7 | .8 | Quick | (49) .7 | .9 | .7 | .8 | .9 | .8 |
| .3 | .4 | .4 | | .2 | .4 | .4 | .4 | .6 | .4 |
| 1 343.1 | 1 636.6 | 1 310.5 | | 0 UND | 7 51.6 | 0 999.8 | 0 748.2 | 5 69.9 | 3 129.6 |
| 15 24.8 | 14 26.3 | 19 19.5 | Sales/Receivables | 1 267.6 | 24 15.1 | 13 28.6 | 20 18.5 | 25 14.5 | 16 23.0 |
| 39 9.4 | 40 9.1 | 43 8.5 | | 32 11.5 | 40 9.1 | 32 11.5 | 41 8.9 | 57 6.4 | 47 7.7 |
| 8 45.4 | 9 41.2 | 11 33.0 | | 0 UND | 0 UND | 14 26.0 | 12 29.9 | 5 76.3 | 34 10.6 |
| 40 9.1 | 47 7.7 | 42 8.7 | Cost of Sales/Inventory | 44 8.3 | 39 9.3 | 41 8.9 | 40 9.2 | 27 13.7 | 78 4.7 |
| 92 4.0 | 109 3.3 | 101 3.6 | | 166 2.2 | 99 3.7 | 83 4.4 | 70 5.2 | 60 6.1 | 130 2.8 |
| 6 58.2 | 10 38.2 | 5 69.6 | | 0 UND | 0 UND | 5 67.7 | 7 55.3 | 9 41.8 | 19 19.0 |
| 24 15.5 | 29 12.6 | 26 13.9 | Cost of Sales/Payables | 22 16.4 | 22 16.3 | 24 15.2 | 24 15.3 | 20 17.9 | 30 12.2 |
| 49 7.5 | 57 6.4 | 54 6.7 | | 74 4.9 | 55 6.6 | 44 8.3 | 54 6.7 | 59 6.2 | 59 6.2 |
| 6.7 | 7.3 | 5.9 | | 3.7 | 4.8 | 7.2 | 8.7 | 9.0 | 4.4 |
| 21.2 | 17.5 | 16.0 | Sales/Working Capital | 34.6 | 12.2 | 19.0 | 19.2 | 16.2 | 10.9 |
| -150.5 | -63.5 | -501.9 | | -15.4 | -80.6 | 478.0 | -999.8 | 122.2 | 61.1 |
| 18.5 | 21.4 | 28.6 | | 8.8 | 22.9 | 28.9 | 27.6 | 123.1 | 24.8 |
| (201) 4.3 | (212) 4.3 | (265) 7.4 | EBIT/Interest | (27) 1.7 | (51) 3.4 | (40) 4.1 | (49) 6.6 | (41) 25.2 | (57) 10.0 |
| 1.2 | 1.1 | 1.6 | | -3.8 | 1.1 | 2.0 | 1.6 | 4.6 | 4.0 |
| 13.9 | 11.9 | 15.9 | Net Profit + Depr., Dep., | | | | | | 25.6 |
| (21) 3.2 | (26) 2.9 | (31) 3.1 | Amort./Cur. Mat. L/T/D | | | | | | (22) 4.1 |
| 1.2 | 1.0 | .6 | | | | | | | 1.5 |
| .1 | .1 | .1 | | .0 | .1 | .0 | .1 | .1 | .1 |
| .6 | .5 | .3 | Fixed/Worth | .1 | .4 | .4 | .4 | .2 | .4 |
| 44.8 | 14.9 | 3.4 | | NM | -1.4 | 3.8 | 5.1 | 1.0 | 5.4 |
| .8 | 1.0 | .6 | | .3 | .6 | .9 | .6 | .6 | .6 |
| 3.8 | 3.5 | 2.4 | Debt/Worth | 3.4 | 2.5 | 3.2 | 3.0 | 1.7 | 2.2 |
| UND | -25.5 | 155.2 | | -6.3 | -7.9 | UND | 46.7 | 8.3 | 11.6 |
| 102.9 | 97.0 | 100.0 | % Profit Before Taxes/Tangible | 110.4 | 101.9 | 100.0 | 82.0 | 111.3 | 79.4 |
| (190) 31.2 | (196) 36.4 | (266) 44.7 | Net Worth | (33) 67.0 | (44) 43.6 | (39) 41.7 | (47) 31.2 | (48) 57.3 | (55) 38.1 |
| 9.5 | 8.9 | 14.0 | | 12.8 | 9.5 | 15.0 | 13.5 | 14.1 | 19.8 |
| 28.1 | 24.7 | 35.1 | % Profit Before Taxes/Total | 40.6 | 42.5 | 32.3 | 36.2 | 44.5 | 25.2 |
| 9.4 | 9.2 | 11.8 | Assets | 11.6 | 12.0 | 12.3 | 7.7 | 12.5 | 13.5 |
| .9 | .2 | 2.7 | | -2.2 | 1.6 | 2.5 | 2.3 | 6.2 | 6.6 |
| 115.5 | 187.7 | 237.6 | | UND | 185.5 | 560.9 | 139.7 | 312.6 | 90.5 |
| 33.3 | 44.5 | 51.0 | Sales/Net Fixed Assets | 163.7 | 36.2 | 56.8 | 51.3 | 74.5 | 30.0 |
| 11.6 | 15.6 | 15.1 | | 27.6 | 10.2 | 12.0 | 24.5 | 28.6 | 9.0 |
| 5.5 | 5.0 | 5.4 | | 6.5 | 5.1 | 5.8 | 6.2 | 6.4 | 3.5 |
| 3.1 | 3.2 | 3.1 | Sales/Total Assets | 2.5 | 3.0 | 3.9 | 3.5 | 3.9 | 2.5 |
| 2.0 | 2.0 | 2.0 | | 1.4 | 1.7 | 2.4 | 2.4 | 2.5 | 1.8 |
| .4 | .4 | .4 | | .6 | .4 | .5 | .4 | .1 | .5 |
| (162) 1.3 | (175) 1.0 | (198) .9 | % Depr., Dep., Amort./Sales | (17) .9 | (35) 1.1 | (28) 1.3 | (37) .8 | (30) 1.0 | (51) .8 |
| 2.4 | 2.0 | 2.1 | | 2.3 | 3.1 | 1.9 | 1.6 | 2.0 | 2.4 |
| 1.8 | 1.8 | 1.8 | | 3.8 | 3.4 | 2.0 | 1.8 | .5 | |
| (103) 3.7 | (116) 3.6 | (142) 3.4 | % Officers', Directors' Owners' Comp/Sales | (22) 8.0 | (30) 5.2 | (30) 3.2 | (32) 2.8 | (19) 1.9 | |
| 7.5 | 9.2 | 7.7 | | 16.4 | 9.3 | 5.9 | 4.8 | 3.2 | |
| 11173401M<br>4100067M | 10219906M<br>3882267M | 11563755M<br>5109397M | Net Sales ($)<br>Total Assets ($) | 26242M<br>14640M | 124060M<br>50091M | 198988M<br>62548M | 419561M<br>135644M | 749208M<br>260633M | 10045696M<br>4585841M |

M = $ thousand    MM = $ million
See Pages 9 through 22 for Explanation of Ratios and Data

# TRANSPORTATION AND
# WAREHOUSING

## Current Data Sorted by Assets | Comparative Historical Data

| Type of Statement | 0-500M | 500M-2MM | 2-10MM | 10-50MM | 50-100MM | 100-250MM | 4/1/07-3/31/08 ALL | 4/1/08-3/31/09 ALL |
|---|---|---|---|---|---|---|---|---|
| Unqualified | | | 1 | 7 | 3 | 3 | 12 | 11 |
| Reviewed | | | 4 | 4 | | | 2 | 2 |
| Compiled | | | 1 | 1 | | | 1 | 5 |
| Tax Returns | 1 | 1 | 2 | 1 | | | 8 | 5 |
| Other | 4 | 3 | 10 | 6 | | 1 | 28 | 30 |

10 (4/1-9/30/11)   44 (10/1/11-3/31/12)

| | 0-500M | 500M-2MM | 2-10MM | 10-50MM | 50-100MM | 100-250MM | | 4/1/07-3/31/08 ALL | 4/1/08-3/31/09 ALL |
|---|---|---|---|---|---|---|---|---|---|
| NUMBER OF STATEMENTS | 5 | 5 | 18 | 19 | 3 | 4 | | 51 | 53 |
| | % | % | % | % | % | % | **ASSETS** | % | % |
| | | | 14.1 | 8.8 | | | Cash & Equivalents | 17.6 | 13.1 |
| | | | 16.5 | 13.2 | | | Trade Receivables (net) | 16.4 | 18.2 |
| | | | 12.0 | 7.6 | | | Inventory | 6.5 | 6.1 |
| | | | 5.2 | 3.6 | | | All Other Current | 3.3 | 5.6 |
| | | | 47.8 | 33.2 | | | Total Current | 43.8 | 43.0 |
| | | | 40.6 | 54.4 | | | Fixed Assets (net) | 42.9 | 40.2 |
| | | | 1.0 | 6.4 | | | Intangibles (net) | 4.1 | 3.7 |
| | | | 10.6 | 6.0 | | | All Other Non-Current | 9.2 | 13.0 |
| | | | 100.0 | 100.0 | | | Total | 100.0 | 100.0 |
| | | | | | | | **LIABILITIES** | | |
| | | | 7.3 | 9.5 | | | Notes Payable-Short Term | 7.0 | 8.0 |
| | | | 5.7 | 3.5 | | | Cur. Mat.-L.T.D. | 5.6 | 3.8 |
| | | | 14.3 | 8.9 | | | Trade Payables | 13.7 | 11.1 |
| | | | .1 | .1 | | | Income Taxes Payable | .1 | .2 |
| | | | 17.7 | 15.7 | | | All Other Current | 15.0 | 20.3 |
| | | | 45.2 | 37.7 | | | Total Current | 41.4 | 43.3 |
| | | | 38.8 | 20.7 | | | Long-Term Debt | 31.2 | 37.9 |
| | | | .1 | 1.6 | | | Deferred Taxes | .5 | .1 |
| | | | 4.5 | 6.1 | | | All Other Non-Current | 13.8 | 4.6 |
| | | | 11.4 | 33.9 | | | Net Worth | 13.2 | 14.1 |
| | | | 100.0 | 100.0 | | | Total Liabilities & Net Worth | 100.0 | 100.0 |
| | | | | | | | **INCOME DATA** | | |
| | | | 100.0 | 100.0 | | | Net Sales | 100.0 | 100.0 |
| | | | | | | | Gross Profit | | |
| | | | 90.7 | 88.0 | | | Operating Expenses | 92.3 | 95.6 |
| | | | 9.3 | 12.0 | | | Operating Profit | 7.7 | 4.4 |
| | | | 1.7 | 2.3 | | | All Other Expenses (net) | 1.6 | 3.2 |
| | | | 7.6 | 9.7 | | | Profit Before Taxes | 6.1 | 1.3 |
| | | | | | | | **RATIOS** | | |
| | | | 4.4 | 1.8 | | | | 2.0 | 1.9 |
| | | | 1.7 | 1.2 | | | Current | 1.3 | 1.1 |
| | | | .8 | .7 | | | | .8 | .7 |
| | | | 2.5 | 1.0 | | | | 1.5 | 1.4 |
| | | | 1.4 | .8 | | | Quick | .8 | .7 |
| | | | .5 | .4 | | | | .5 | .5 |
| | | 0 | UND | 7 | 51.4 | | | 10 | 36.9 | 8 | 45.2 |
| | | 17 | 22.0 | 18 | 19.9 | | Sales/Receivables | 23 | 15.9 | 24 | 15.5 |
| | | 25 | 14.6 | 26 | 13.9 | | | 39 | 9.3 | 34 | 10.8 |
| | | | | | | | Cost of Sales/Inventory | | |
| | | | | | | | Cost of Sales/Payables | | |
| | | | 4.3 | 7.8 | | | | 10.2 | 9.8 |
| | | | 12.3 | 33.2 | | | Sales/Working Capital | 27.9 | 46.1 |
| | | | -22.2 | -26.9 | | | | -19.0 | -20.2 |
| | | | 10.1 | 9.4 | | | | 5.1 | 7.2 |
| | | (17) | 4.2 | (18) | 5.8 | | EBIT/Interest | (43) | 3.1 | (44) | 1.8 |
| | | | 1.1 | 1.9 | | | | 1.4 | .1 |
| | | | | | | | Net Profit + Depr., Dep., Amort./Cur. Mat. L/T/D | 6.3 | |
| | | | | | | | | (13) 1.7 | |
| | | | | | | | | .6 | |
| | | | 1.0 | 1.0 | | | | 1.1 | .7 |
| | | | 2.2 | 1.3 | | | Fixed/Worth | 2.5 | 1.6 |
| | | | -4.9 | 19.5 | | | | 30.3 | NM |
| | | | 1.2 | .8 | | | | 1.4 | 1.4 |
| | | | 2.3 | 1.5 | | | Debt/Worth | 4.3 | 4.0 |
| | | | -26.5 | 74.7 | | | | 47.7 | -42.8 |
| | | | 37.1 | 60.1 | | | % Profit Before Taxes/Tangible Net Worth | 56.2 | 48.5 |
| | | (13) | 9.3 | (15) | 35.9 | | | (40) | 31.2 | (39) | 22.4 |
| | | | -2.0 | 22.4 | | | | 8.7 | -3.0 |
| | | | 12.6 | 18.2 | | | % Profit Before Taxes/Total Assets | 18.8 | 11.9 |
| | | | 4.9 | 11.1 | | | | 7.5 | 2.7 |
| | | | -.2 | 2.2 | | | | 1.7 | -3.8 |
| | | | 38.3 | 7.6 | | | Sales/Net Fixed Assets | 16.3 | 45.1 |
| | | | 6.9 | 2.3 | | | | 5.6 | 6.0 |
| | | | 2.2 | 1.4 | | | | 2.4 | 1.9 |
| | | | 4.5 | 2.9 | | | Sales/Total Assets | 3.4 | 4.3 |
| | | | 2.7 | 1.2 | | | | 2.5 | 2.2 |
| | | | .9 | .8 | | | | 1.4 | 1.0 |
| | | | 1.0 | 1.9 | | | % Depr., Dep., Amort./Sales | 1.5 | 1.1 |
| | | (14) | 3.1 | | 4.2 | | | (46) | 3.7 | (44) | 4.0 |
| | | | 6.9 | 8.4 | | | | 6.6 | 7.7 |
| | | | | | | | % Officers', Directors' Owners' Comp/Sales | 1.0 | 1.2 |
| | | | | | | | | (15) 1.4 | (15) 1.6 |
| | | | | | | | | 11.6 | 6.5 |
| Net Sales ($) | 2014M | 17684M | 206430M | 1014711M | 189004M | 677237M | | 3787906M | 5109112M |
| Total Assets ($) | 966M | 6557M | 79615M | 487363M | 231234M | 589069M | | 1701582M | 2144300M |

M = $ thousand   MM = $ million
See Pages 9 through 22 for Explanation of Ratios and Data

## Comparative Historical Data | | | Type of Statement | Current Data Sorted by Sales

| | | | | Type of Statement | | | | | | |
|---|---|---|---|---|---|---|---|---|---|---|
| 13 | | 11 | 14 | Unqualified | | 1 | | | 2 | 11 |
| 6 | | 6 | 8 | Reviewed | | | 1 | | 3 | 4 |
| 1 | | 5 | 3 | Compiled | | | 1 | | 2 | |
| 15 | | 9 | 5 | Tax Returns | | | 1 | 2 | 1 | |
| 31 | | 39 | 24 | Other | 2 | 2 | 2 | 2 | 6 | 4 |
| 4/1/09-3/31/10 ALL | | 4/1/10-3/31/11 ALL | 4/1/11-3/31/12 ALL | | 8 | 10 (4/1-9/30/11) | | 44 (10/1/11-3/31/12) | | |
| | | | | | 0-1MM | 1-3MM | 3-5MM | 5-10MM | 10-25MM | 25MM & OVER |
| 66 | | 70 | 54 | NUMBER OF STATEMENTS | 10 | 2 | 3 | 6 | 14 | 19 |
| % | | % | % | ASSETS | % | % | % | % | % | % |
| 12.5 | | 12.5 | 11.5 | Cash & Equivalents | 15.8 | | | | 13.2 | 10.1 |
| 16.7 | | 18.1 | 14.7 | Trade Receivables (net) | 1.0 | | | | 22.7 | 15.1 |
| 6.4 | | 5.6 | 7.2 | Inventory | 1.3 | | | | 13.3 | 5.7 |
| 4.6 | | 4.6 | 3.6 | All Other Current | 3.2 | | | | 4.7 | 3.3 |
| 40.3 | | 40.8 | 37.1 | Total Current | 21.4 | | | | 53.8 | 34.1 |
| 41.4 | | 41.7 | 51.5 | Fixed Assets (net) | 72.4 | | | | 39.3 | 47.1 |
| 5.0 | | 3.5 | 3.1 | Intangibles (net) | .5 | | | | 1.4 | 6.3 |
| 13.2 | | 14.0 | 8.4 | All Other Non-Current | 5.7 | | | | 5.5 | 12.4 |
| 100.0 | | 100.0 | 100.0 | Total | 100.0 | | | | 100.0 | 100.0 |
| | | | | LIABILITIES | | | | | | |
| 7.9 | | 4.3 | 7.5 | Notes Payable-Short Term | 7.8 | | | | 5.8 | 6.1 |
| 4.9 | | 4.6 | 4.1 | Cur. Mat.-L.T.D. | 3.5 | | | | 3.5 | 3.2 |
| 12.4 | | 13.7 | 10.1 | Trade Payables | 3.9 | | | | 12.0 | 12.8 |
| .1 | | .1 | .1 | Income Taxes Payable | .0 | | | | .1 | .1 |
| 14.5 | | 13.7 | 15.9 | All Other Current | 11.3 | | | | 11.3 | 21.6 |
| 39.8 | | 36.5 | 37.6 | Total Current | 26.5 | | | | 32.8 | 43.7 |
| 27.7 | | 29.5 | 36.6 | Long-Term Debt | 75.4 | | | | 42.1 | 21.4 |
| .9 | | .7 | 1.0 | Deferred Taxes | .0 | | | | .8 | 2.0 |
| 5.3 | | 4.2 | 3.9 | All Other Non-Current | 4.7 | | | | 1.4 | 7.1 |
| 26.4 | | 29.0 | 21.0 | Net Worth | -6.4 | | | | 22.9 | 25.9 |
| 100.0 | | 100.0 | 100.0 | Total Liabilities & Net Worth | 100.0 | | | | 100.0 | 100.0 |
| | | | | INCOME DATA | | | | | | |
| 100.0 | | 100.0 | 100.0 | Net Sales | 100.0 | | | | 100.0 | 100.0 |
| | | | | Gross Profit | | | | | | |
| 94.6 | | 91.5 | 89.6 | Operating Expenses | 71.9 | | | | 92.7 | 95.8 |
| 5.4 | | 8.5 | 10.4 | Operating Profit | 28.1 | | | | 7.3 | 4.2 |
| 1.8 | | 2.7 | 2.2 | All Other Expenses (net) | 6.5 | | | | .9 | .5 |
| 3.6 | | 5.8 | 8.2 | Profit Before Taxes | 21.7 | | | | 6.4 | 3.7 |
| | | | | RATIOS | | | | | | |
| 2.5 | | 2.5 | 2.4 | | 29.7 | | | | 3.2 | 1.3 |
| 1.3 | | 1.3 | 1.5 | Current | 3.0 | | | | 2.1 | 1.0 |
| .7 | | .6 | .7 | | .2 | | | | 1.5 | .6 |
| 1.7 | | 1.8 | 2.0 | | 29.4 | | | | 2.4 | .9 |
| .8 | | .8 | .8 | Quick | 2.2 | | | | 1.3 | .7 |
| .5 | | .4 | .3 | | .1 | | | | .5 | .4 |
| 10  35.7 | 9  38.6 | 5  67.9 | | Sales/Receivables | 0  UND | | | 9  40.6 | 7  51.5 |
| 23  15.7 | 24  15.5 | 17  21.1 | | | 0  UND | | | 21  17.8 | 18  19.9 |
| 44  8.2 | 40  9.0 | 27  13.5 | | | 5  74.4 | | | 36  10.2 | 29  12.5 |
| | | | | Cost of Sales/Inventory | | | | | | |
| | | | | Cost of Sales/Payables | | | | | | |
| 6.0 | | 6.9 | 6.3 | | .9 | | | | 6.3 | 31.0 |
| 22.0 | | 24.5 | 23.2 | Sales/Working Capital | 14.2 | | | | 8.6 | -103.2 |
| -17.1 | | -15.3 | -18.9 | | -2.4 | | | | 57.5 | -11.6 |
| 8.0 | | 16.9 | 8.3 | | | | | | 9.9 | 10.2 |
| (56)  3.3 | (58)  3.9 | (49)  3.9 | EBIT/Interest | | | | (13)  4.8 | (17)  5.5 |
| .4 | | 1.3 | 1.5 | | | | | | 2.1 | 1.9 |
| 4.3 | | 4.3 | 4.8 | Net Profit + Depr., Dep., | | | | | | |
| (13)  2.0 | (14)  1.7 | (10)  1.8 | Amort./Cur. Mat. L/T/D | | | | | | |
| .9 | | .9 | 1.1 | | | | | | | |
| .9 | | .4 | 1.0 | | .9 | | | | .6 | 1.0 |
| 1.4 | | 1.5 | 1.4 | Fixed/Worth | 2.8 | | | | 1.3 | 1.5 |
| 6.0 | | 4.2 | 9.0 | | NM | | | | NM | 12.9 |
| .9 | | .7 | .9 | | .9 | | | | .9 | 1.3 |
| 3.1 | | 2.5 | 2.0 | Debt/Worth | 2.2 | | | | 1.3 | 2.5 |
| 9.4 | | 9.3 | 14.3 | | NM | | | | NM | 15.8 |
| 45.1 | | 44.8 | 43.6 | % Profit Before Taxes/Tangible | | | | | 38.2 | 58.3 |
| (54)  23.7 | (56)  26.5 | (43)  22.0 | Net Worth | | | | (11)  22.0 | (16)  33.2 |
| 5.0 | | 4.7 | 2.3 | | | | | | 7.7 | 5.9 |
| 13.3 | | 19.0 | 17.2 | % Profit Before Taxes/Total | 18.5 | | | | 19.9 | 17.0 |
| 5.2 | | 8.7 | 5.3 | Assets | 5.2 | | | | 9.6 | 6.4 |
| -1.2 | | .5 | .9 | | -2.1 | | | | 2.7 | 1.8 |
| 19.7 | | 23.6 | 12.3 | | 2.0 | | | | 41.4 | 16.5 |
| 4.2 | | 4.5 | 2.7 | Sales/Net Fixed Assets | .6 | | | | 6.0 | 4.4 |
| 1.8 | | 1.6 | .8 | | .3 | | | | 2.1 | 2.0 |
| 2.8 | | 3.1 | 3.3 | | 1.1 | | | | 4.8 | 3.8 |
| 1.8 | | 1.7 | 1.6 | Sales/Total Assets | .4 | | | | 2.8 | 2.3 |
| 1.0 | | .9 | .6 | | .2 | | | | 1.1 | 1.2 |
| 1.2 | | 1.2 | 1.6 | | | | | | 1.5 | 1.4 |
| (58)  4.1 | (58)  3.6 | (44)  4.1 | % Depr., Dep., Amort./Sales | | | | (12)  4.1 | (16)  2.2 |
| 9.0 | | 7.7 | 9.7 | | | | | | 9.3 | 4.3 |
| 1.5 | | 1.4 | | % Officers', Directors' | | | | | | |
| (12)  3.7 | (12)  2.0 | | Owners' Comp/Sales | | | | | | |
| 9.3 | | 4.7 | | | | | | | | |
| 2422050M | | 3720189M | 2107080M | Net Sales ($) | 5095M | 2187M | 10360M | 37231M | 232564M | 1819643M |
| 1443375M | | 2226601M | 1394804M | Total Assets ($) | 20497M | 7364M | 85506M | 44956M | 135202M | 1101279M |

**M = $ thousand    MM = $ million**
See Pages 9 through 22 for Explanation of Ratios and Data

## Current Data Sorted by Assets        Comparative Historical Data

| 0-500M | 500M-2MM | 2-10MM | 10-50MM | 50-100MM | 100-250MM | | 4/1/07-3/31/08 ALL | 4/1/08-3/31/09 ALL |
|---|---|---|---|---|---|---|---|---|
| | | 2 | 4 | 1 | 1 | **Type of Statement** Unqualified | 22 | 11 |
| | 1 | 3 | 2 | | | Reviewed | 6 | 6 |
| | 3 | 6 | 3 | | | Compiled | 12 | 12 |
| 1 | 6 | 3 | | | | Tax Returns | 12 | 9 |
| 1 | 9 | 12 | 17 | 1 | 3 | Other | 50 | 46 |
| | 13 (4/1-9/30/11) | | 66 (10/1/11-3/31/12) | | | | | |
| 2 | 19 | 26 | 26 | 2 | 4 | **NUMBER OF STATEMENTS** | 102 | 84 |
| % | % | % | % | % | % | **ASSETS** | % | % |
| | 10.5 | 10.3 | 9.9 | | | Cash & Equivalents | 9.7 | 11.0 |
| | 30.8 | 14.6 | 12.7 | | | Trade Receivables (net) | 22.3 | 15.0 |
| | 2.7 | 10.9 | 8.3 | | | Inventory | 7.6 | 8.2 |
| | 6.0 | 6.7 | 3.7 | | | All Other Current | 5.3 | 5.2 |
| | 50.0 | 42.5 | 34.7 | | | Total Current | 44.9 | 39.4 |
| | 35.8 | 43.1 | 50.5 | | | Fixed Assets (net) | 43.7 | 46.0 |
| | 3.8 | 4.4 | 5.9 | | | Intangibles (net) | 2.4 | 4.4 |
| | 10.4 | 10.1 | 8.9 | | | All Other Non-Current | 9.0 | 10.2 |
| | 100.0 | 100.0 | 100.0 | | | Total | 100.0 | 100.0 |
| | | | | | | **LIABILITIES** | | |
| | 4.8 | 26.5 | 3.5 | | | Notes Payable-Short Term | 7.6 | 11.1 |
| | 5.4 | 3.5 | 5.2 | | | Cur. Mat.-L.T.D. | 4.7 | 5.4 |
| | 21.9 | 7.9 | 9.0 | | | Trade Payables | 16.0 | 10.0 |
| | .0 | .5 | .5 | | | Income Taxes Payable | .7 | .5 |
| | 14.7 | 9.5 | 11.2 | | | All Other Current | 11.8 | 10.5 |
| | 46.8 | 47.8 | 29.4 | | | Total Current | 40.8 | 37.5 |
| | 54.3 | 36.5 | 40.1 | | | Long-Term Debt | 44.3 | 44.6 |
| | .0 | .8 | .5 | | | Deferred Taxes | .4 | .7 |
| | 11.2 | 15.7 | 4.7 | | | All Other Non-Current | 6.4 | 5.7 |
| | -12.3 | -.8 | 25.3 | | | Net Worth | 8.1 | 11.5 |
| | 100.0 | 100.0 | 100.0 | | | Total Liabilities & Net Worth | 100.0 | 100.0 |
| | | | | | | **INCOME DATA** | | |
| | 100.0 | 100.0 | 100.0 | | | Net Sales | 100.0 | 100.0 |
| | | | | | | Gross Profit | | |
| | 90.9 | 98.1 | 92.9 | | | Operating Expenses | 95.2 | 98.3 |
| | 9.1 | 1.9 | 7.1 | | | Operating Profit | 4.8 | 1.7 |
| | 5.5 | 2.2 | 2.2 | | | All Other Expenses (net) | 3.3 | 2.9 |
| | 3.6 | -.3 | 4.9 | | | Profit Before Taxes | 1.5 | -1.2 |
| | | | | | | **RATIOS** | | |
| | 1.9 | 3.2 | 2.1 | | | Current | 1.9 | 1.8 |
| | .8 | 1.4 | 1.3 | | | | 1.1 | 1.1 |
| | .6 | .8 | .8 | | | | .8 | .7 |
| | 1.2 | 2.2 | 1.8 | | | Quick | 1.3 | 1.4 |
| | .8 | .8 | .8 | | | | .7 | .6 |
| | .5 | .3 | .4 | | | | .3 | .3 |
| | 19   18.9 | 11   33.3 | 14   26.3 | | | Sales/Receivables | 16   22.3 | 5   69.7 |
| | 31   11.9 | 20   17.9 | 26   14.2 | | | | 27   13.4 | 19   19.5 |
| | 45   8.1 | 31   11.6 | 38   9.5 | | | | 48   7.6 | 37   9.9 |
| | | | | | | Cost of Sales/Inventory | | |
| | | | | | | Cost of Sales/Payables | | |
| | 10.2 | 7.1 | 8.5 | | | Sales/Working Capital | 10.8 | 12.1 |
| | -44.2 | 27.4 | 21.6 | | | | 58.4 | 83.9 |
| | -11.1 | -23.0 | -25.8 | | | | -13.5 | -18.1 |
| | 10.8 | 4.4 | 9.2 | | | EBIT/Interest | 7.5 | 4.6 |
| | (15)   4.2 | (23)   1.0 | (22)   2.3 | | | | (90)   3.1 | (75)   1.4 |
| | -.8 | -.1 | 1.1 | | | | .5 | -1.2 |
| | | | | | | Net Profit + Depr., Dep., Amort./Cur. Mat. L/T/D | 3.8 | 8.8 |
| | | | | | | | (18)   1.4 | (22)   2.7 |
| | | | | | | | .9 | .9 |
| | .4 | .8 | .9 | | | Fixed/Worth | .6 | .9 |
| | 8.1 | 16.2 | 2.1 | | | | 2.5 | 3.1 |
| | -.9 | -2.0 | 46.9 | | | | -4.8 | -4.5 |
| | 1.7 | 1.3 | 1.1 | | | Debt/Worth | 1.7 | 1.2 |
| | 76.2 | 42.8 | 2.7 | | | | 4.9 | 4.4 |
| | -3.3 | -4.1 | 76.8 | | | | -11.7 | -9.6 |
| | 399.2 | 17.8 | 54.1 | | | % Profit Before Taxes/Tangible Net Worth | 55.6 | 42.9 |
| | (10)   91.3 | (14)   7.0 | (21)   23.1 | | | | (71)   30.1 | (58)   15.1 |
| | 30.0 | -7.2 | .7 | | | | 10.1 | -3.9 |
| | 20.8 | 4.8 | 15.0 | | | % Profit Before Taxes/Total Assets | 12.7 | 9.7 |
| | 13.3 | .5 | 4.9 | | | | 6.0 | 1.7 |
| | -12.3 | -3.8 | -.3 | | | | -2.2 | -7.5 |
| | 80.7 | 12.4 | 10.5 | | | Sales/Net Fixed Assets | 15.9 | 17.6 |
| | 23.7 | 4.6 | 2.6 | | | | 4.2 | 4.3 |
| | 1.1 | 2.7 | 1.2 | | | | 1.7 | 1.8 |
| | 4.4 | 2.3 | 2.2 | | | Sales/Total Assets | 3.1 | 3.6 |
| | 3.0 | 1.8 | 1.5 | | | | 1.7 | 2.0 |
| | 1.0 | 1.0 | .8 | | | | 1.0 | 1.0 |
| | .7 | 1.2 | 2.1 | | | % Depr., Dep., Amort./Sales | 1.2 | 1.8 |
| | (12)   2.3 | (22)   3.6 | (25)   5.0 | | | | (80)   3.9 | (69)   3.9 |
| | 12.2 | 8.6 | 12.8 | | | | 9.0 | 9.4 |
| | | | | | | % Officers', Directors' Owners' Comp/Sales | 1.5 | 1.6 |
| | | | | | | | (19)   3.4 | (16)   3.8 |
| | | | | | | | 6.6 | 7.6 |
| 16352M | 78848M | 238608M | 784070M | 324260M | 671224M | Net Sales ($) | 3023799M | 2609380M |
| 800M | 22097M | 130432M | 442736M | 128793M | 663126M | Total Assets ($) | 2430649M | 1932324M |

M = $ thousand     MM = $ million
See Pages 9 through 22 for Explanation of Ratios and Data

## Comparative Historical Data | Current Data Sorted by Sales

**Type of Statement**

| 4/1/09-3/31/10 ALL | 4/1/10-3/31/11 ALL | 4/1/11-3/31/12 ALL | Type of Statement | 0-1MM | 1-3MM | 3-5MM | 5-10MM | 10-25MM | 25MM & OVER |
|---|---|---|---|---|---|---|---|---|---|
| 16 | 13 | 8 | Unqualified | | | 1 | | 1 | 6 |
| 12 | 14 | 6 | Reviewed | | 1 | | 1 | 3 | 1 |
| 11 | 9 | 12 | Compiled | | 3 | 2 | 3 | 3 | 1 |
| 7 | 11 | 10 | Tax Returns | 3 | 1 | 2 | 3 | 1 | |
| 45 | 47 | 43 | Other | 2 | 4 | 4 | 10 | 10 | 13 |
| | | | | 13 (4/1-9/30/11) | | | 66 (10/1/11-3/31/12) | | |
| 91 | 94 | 79 | **NUMBER OF STATEMENTS** | 5 | 9 | 9 | 17 | 18 | 21 |

**ASSETS**

| % | % | % | | % | % | % | % | % | % |
|---|---|---|---|---|---|---|---|---|---|
| 9.9 | 10.8 | 11.1 | Cash & Equivalents | | | | 11.1 | 12.6 | 11.2 |
| 15.1 | 16.0 | 18.0 | Trade Receivables (net) | | | | 16.7 | 23.4 | 18.5 |
| 8.5 | 7.0 | 7.5 | Inventory | | | | 10.9 | 5.4 | 11.4 |
| 5.1 | 6.0 | 5.2 | All Other Current | | | | 3.6 | 5.6 | 8.5 |
| 38.6 | 39.8 | 41.8 | Total Current | | | | 42.3 | 47.0 | 49.5 |
| 45.7 | 45.8 | 43.2 | Fixed Assets (net) | | | | 48.1 | 36.2 | 36.3 |
| 4.6 | 4.8 | 5.4 | Intangibles (net) | | | | 1.9 | 3.6 | 7.7 |
| 11.1 | 9.6 | 9.7 | All Other Non-Current | | | | 7.8 | 13.2 | 6.5 |
| 100.0 | 100.0 | 100.0 | Total | | | | 100.0 | 100.0 | 100.0 |

**LIABILITIES**

| H1 | H2 | H3 | | 0-1MM | 1-3MM | 3-5MM | 5-10MM | 10-25MM | 25MM & OVER |
|---|---|---|---|---|---|---|---|---|---|
| 11.4 | 6.5 | 12.0 | Notes Payable-Short Term | | | | 6.8 | 9.3 | 5.5 |
| 6.2 | 5.8 | 4.5 | Cur. Mat.-L.T.D. | | | | 3.3 | 3.4 | 4.8 |
| 13.6 | 10.5 | 12.6 | Trade Payables | | | | 10.3 | 16.1 | 12.8 |
| .2 | .4 | .3 | Income Taxes Payable | | | | .0 | 1.5 | .0 |
| 12.5 | 14.1 | 12.5 | All Other Current | | | | 13.6 | 11.1 | 15.7 |
| 43.9 | 37.3 | 42.0 | Total Current | | | | 33.9 | 41.4 | 38.9 |
| 38.5 | 41.2 | 40.0 | Long-Term Debt | | | | 38.1 | 32.4 | 25.9 |
| .9 | .9 | .5 | Deferred Taxes | | | | .0 | 1.0 | .4 |
| 7.1 | 15.1 | 9.6 | All Other Non-Current | | | | 14.1 | 15.3 | 5.0 |
| 9.5 | 5.5 | 7.9 | Net Worth | | | | 14.0 | 10.0 | 29.8 |
| 100.0 | 100.0 | 100.0 | Total Liabilities & Net Worth | | | | 100.0 | 100.0 | 100.0 |

**INCOME DATA**

| H1 | H2 | H3 | | 0-1MM | 1-3MM | 3-5MM | 5-10MM | 10-25MM | 25MM & OVER |
|---|---|---|---|---|---|---|---|---|---|
| 100.0 | 100.0 | 100.0 | Net Sales | | | | 100.0 | 100.0 | 100.0 |
| | | | Gross Profit | | | | | | |
| 98.7 | 93.3 | 94.2 | Operating Expenses | | | | 93.5 | 96.7 | 95.2 |
| 1.3 | 6.7 | 5.8 | Operating Profit | | | | 6.5 | 3.3 | 4.8 |
| 2.8 | 4.0 | 2.9 | All Other Expenses (net) | | | | 2.7 | .3 | .6 |
| -1.5 | 2.6 | 3.0 | Profit Before Taxes | | | | 3.8 | 3.0 | 4.2 |

**RATIOS**

| H1 | H2 | H3 | | 0-1MM | 1-3MM | 3-5MM | 5-10MM | 10-25MM | 25MM & OVER |
|---|---|---|---|---|---|---|---|---|---|
| 1.7 | 1.7 | 2.0 | Current | | | | 2.8 | 1.8 | 2.0 |
| 1.0 | 1.1 | 1.3 | | | | | 1.3 | 1.0 | 1.6 |
| .5 | .6 | .7 | | | | | .9 | .8 | 1.0 |
| 1.1 | 1.3 | 1.5 | Quick | | | | 1.9 | 1.6 | 1.4 |
| .6 | .7 | .8 | | | | | 1.1 | .8 | .8 |
| .2 | .3 | .4 | | | | | .6 | .5 | .5 |
| 13  27.4 | 14  26.4 | 15  24.6 | Sales/Receivables | | | | 11  32.1 | 18  20.6 | 17  21.3 |
| 25  14.4 | 26  14.3 | 26  14.2 | | | | | 19  19.3 | 32  11.5 | 30  12.1 |
| 43  8.5 | 42  8.7 | 38  9.5 | | | | | 29  12.4 | 46  7.9 | 41  8.9 |
| | | | Cost of Sales/Inventory | | | | | | |
| | | | Cost of Sales/Payables | | | | | | |
| 10.8 | 9.3 | 9.0 | Sales/Working Capital | | | | 9.3 | 8.3 | 7.8 |
| 256.1 | 118.0 | 30.1 | | | | | 25.6 | NM | 12.5 |
| -7.4 | -11.5 | -22.8 | | | | | NM | -30.7 | 376.0 |
| 4.5 | 6.1 | 7.4 | EBIT/Interest | | | | 7.4 | 10.0 | 8.4 |
| (79) .7 | (86) 2.7 | (67) 2.5 | | | | (15) 1.8 | 3.0 | (19) 3.3 | |
| -.1 | .2 | .4 | | | | | -.1 | -.8 | .9 |
| 2.6 | 1.5 | 6.1 | Net Profit + Depr., Dep., Amort./Cur. Mat. L/T/D | | | | | | |
| (22) 1.2 | (17) .6 | (15) 1.9 | | | | | | | |
| .4 | .0 | 1.0 | | | | | | | |
| .9 | 1.2 | .8 | Fixed/Worth | | | | .9 | .5 | .8 |
| 3.3 | 2.5 | 2.9 | | | | | 3.5 | 1.9 | 1.4 |
| -3.8 | -2.7 | -3.6 | | | | | -3.2 | -5.0 | 88.5 |
| 1.3 | 1.1 | 1.5 | Debt/Worth | | | | 1.6 | 1.3 | 1.0 |
| 6.4 | 4.3 | 4.4 | | | | | 3.0 | 3.0 | 3.8 |
| -9.2 | -5.5 | -6.8 | | | | | -6.0 | -7.5 | 140.5 |
| 30.3 | 40.2 | 60.0 | % Profit Before Taxes/Tangible Net Worth | | | | 58.6 | 49.9 | 60.6 |
| (59) 5.3 | (63) 13.3 | (51) 23.1 | | | | (12) 43.0 | (12) 12.8 | (17) 24.1 | |
| -8.3 | .6 | 6.8 | | | | | 6.0 | 4.8 | 8.8 |
| 7.2 | 11.8 | 13.9 | % Profit Before Taxes/Total Assets | | | | 20.3 | 11.6 | 13.8 |
| -.9 | 3.2 | 4.8 | | | | | 4.4 | 3.2 | 6.5 |
| -5.8 | -2.9 | -2.2 | | | | | -3.0 | -4.8 | -.1 |
| 9.1 | 12.4 | 23.6 | Sales/Net Fixed Assets | | | | 24.9 | 37.1 | 24.2 |
| 3.1 | 3.7 | 3.8 | | | | | 2.8 | 5.1 | 9.0 |
| 1.5 | 1.4 | 1.4 | | | | | 1.6 | 1.8 | 2.7 |
| 2.2 | 2.4 | 3.2 | Sales/Total Assets | | | | 3.6 | 3.7 | 3.3 |
| 1.4 | 1.4 | 1.8 | | | | | 1.9 | 1.8 | 1.9 |
| .9 | .8 | .9 | | | | | .8 | 1.0 | 1.5 |
| 2.1 | 2.5 | 1.4 | % Depr., Dep., Amort./Sales | | | | 1.2 | .9 | 1.0 |
| (68) 5.2 | (70) 5.3 | (65) 3.7 | | | | (15) 3.7 | (16) 3.3 | (19) 2.6 | |
| 10.3 | 10.7 | 10.8 | | | | | 8.4 | 10.8 | 3.8 |
| 1.8 | 1.8 | 1.6 | % Officers', Directors' Owners' Comp/Sales | | | | | | |
| (16) 2.9 | (20) 2.9 | (23) 3.5 | | | | | | | |
| 5.8 | 6.1 | 4.9 | | | | | | | |
| 2667953M | 2667132M | 2113362M | Net Sales ($) | 2331M | 16773M | 34578M | 122172M | 246912M | 1690596M |
| 2309377M | 2022992M | 1387984M | Total Assets ($) | 7813M | 46729M | 23409M | 94862M | 163740M | 1051431M |

M = $ thousand   MM = $ million
See Pages 9 through 22 for Explanation of Ratios and Data

## Current Data Sorted by Assets      Comparative Historical Data

| 0-500M | 500M-2MM | 2-10MM | 10-50MM | 50-100MM | 100-250MM | Type of Statement | 4/1/07-3/31/08 ALL | 4/1/08-3/31/09 ALL |
|---|---|---|---|---|---|---|---|---|
|  | 1 |  | 4 | 3 | 2 | Unqualified | 12 | 10 |
|  | 1 |  | 2 |  |  | Reviewed | 11 | 3 |
|  | 4 | 1 | 1 |  |  | Compiled | 4 | 5 |
|  |  | 1 |  |  |  | Tax Returns | 7 | 5 |
| 5 | 2 | 12 | 5 | 3 | 1 | Other | 21 | 27 |
|  | 9 (4/1-9/30/11) |  | 39 (10/1/11-3/31/12) |  |  |  |  |  |
| 5 | 8 | 14 | 12 | 6 | 3 | **NUMBER OF STATEMENTS** | 55 | 50 |
| % | % | % | % | % | % | **ASSETS** | % | % |
|  |  | 12.4 | 12.7 |  |  | Cash & Equivalents | 7.8 | 10.3 |
|  |  | 10.1 | 13.1 |  |  | Trade Receivables (net) | 17.6 | 17.9 |
|  |  | 9.5 | 6.4 |  |  | Inventory | 8.3 | 5.2 |
|  |  | 9.4 | 3.6 |  |  | All Other Current | 1.6 | 3.4 |
|  |  | 41.4 | 35.7 |  |  | Total Current | 35.3 | 36.7 |
|  |  | 43.1 | 46.3 |  |  | Fixed Assets (net) | 47.7 | 47.9 |
|  |  | 4.3 | .6 |  |  | Intangibles (net) | 1.9 | 5.7 |
|  |  | 11.2 | 17.4 |  |  | All Other Non-Current | 15.1 | 9.7 |
|  |  | 100.0 | 100.0 |  |  | Total | 100.0 | 100.0 |
|  |  |  |  |  |  | **LIABILITIES** |  |  |
|  |  | 1.6 | 1.9 |  |  | Notes Payable-Short Term | 8.8 | 7.0 |
|  |  | 6.0 | 8.3 |  |  | Cur. Mat.-L.T.D. | 5.5 | 7.8 |
|  |  | 7.0 | 8.0 |  |  | Trade Payables | 10.5 | 9.3 |
|  |  | .4 | .0 |  |  | Income Taxes Payable | .2 | .1 |
|  |  | 26.7 | 13.1 |  |  | All Other Current | 17.3 | 11.4 |
|  |  | 41.7 | 31.2 |  |  | Total Current | 42.3 | 35.6 |
|  |  | 50.4 | 27.2 |  |  | Long-Term Debt | 39.4 | 43.4 |
|  |  | .0 | 1.8 |  |  | Deferred Taxes | .2 | .6 |
|  |  | 8.8 | 4.9 |  |  | All Other Non-Current | 16.2 | 6.1 |
|  |  | -.9 | 34.9 |  |  | Net Worth | 2.0 | 14.3 |
|  |  | 100.0 | 100.0 |  |  | Total Liabilities & Net Worth | 100.0 | 100.0 |
|  |  |  |  |  |  | **INCOME DATA** |  |  |
|  |  | 100.0 | 100.0 |  |  | Net Sales | 100.0 | 100.0 |
|  |  |  |  |  |  | Gross Profit |  |  |
|  |  | 90.7 | 95.6 |  |  | Operating Expenses | 89.1 | 88.9 |
|  |  | 9.3 | 4.4 |  |  | Operating Profit | 10.9 | 11.1 |
|  |  | 6.9 | .9 |  |  | All Other Expenses (net) | 3.1 | 7.4 |
|  |  | 2.4 | 3.6 |  |  | Profit Before Taxes | 7.8 | 3.8 |
|  |  |  |  |  |  | **RATIOS** |  |  |
|  |  | 5.7 | 1.8 |  |  |  | 1.6 | 2.2 |
|  |  | 1.3 | 1.3 |  |  | Current | 1.0 | 1.1 |
|  |  | .5 | 1.0 |  |  |  | .4 | .5 |
|  |  | 1.4 | 1.4 |  |  |  | 1.1 | 1.7 |
|  |  | .5 | 1.1 |  |  | Quick | .5 | .7 |
|  |  | .1 | .5 |  |  |  | .2 | .3 |
|  |  | 0 UND | 4 86.3 |  |  |  | 9 42.6 | 7 49.7 |
|  |  | 18 20.4 | 19 19.2 |  |  | Sales/Receivables | 22 16.6 | 26 13.9 |
|  |  | 39 9.3 | 34 10.8 |  |  |  | 35 10.5 | 43 8.6 |
|  |  |  |  |  |  | Cost of Sales/Inventory |  |  |
|  |  |  |  |  |  | Cost of Sales/Payables |  |  |
|  |  | 4.1 | 8.9 |  |  |  | 16.1 | 9.8 |
|  |  | 27.8 | 22.0 |  |  | Sales/Working Capital | -298.1 | 133.0 |
|  |  | -3.1 | NM |  |  |  | -7.6 | -7.4 |
|  |  |  | 7.2 |  |  |  | 8.8 | 9.2 |
|  |  |  | 5.4 |  |  | EBIT/Interest | (46) 2.2 | (37) 2.7 |
|  |  |  | 1.5 |  |  |  | .1 | .5 |
|  |  |  |  |  |  |  |  | 2.6 |
|  |  |  |  |  |  | Net Profit + Depr., Dep., Amort./Cur. Mat. L/T/D |  | (11) 1.6 |
|  |  |  |  |  |  |  |  | .1 |
|  |  | .3 | .6 |  |  |  | .5 | .5 |
|  |  | 1.5 | 1.1 |  |  | Fixed/Worth | 2.1 | 1.9 |
|  |  | -.9 | 1.6 |  |  |  | -224.1 | -6.4 |
|  |  | 1.4 | .7 |  |  |  | 1.1 | 1.0 |
|  |  | NM | .9 |  |  | Debt/Worth | 4.6 | 4.3 |
|  |  | -2.9 | 6.6 |  |  |  | -311.0 | -9.7 |
|  |  |  | 49.7 |  |  |  | 40.8 | 75.5 |
|  |  | (11) | 23.0 |  |  | % Profit Before Taxes/Tangible Net Worth | (41) 21.8 | (35) 24.7 |
|  |  |  | 6.3 |  |  |  | 7.8 | -3.0 |
|  |  | 12.1 | 15.1 |  |  |  | 13.5 | 15.2 |
|  |  | 5.2 | 5.4 |  |  | % Profit Before Taxes/Total Assets | 6.5 | 5.6 |
|  |  | -6.9 | .9 |  |  |  | -.6 | -1.5 |
|  |  | 116.2 | 51.5 |  |  |  | 15.4 | 28.8 |
|  |  | 1.4 | 2.3 |  |  | Sales/Net Fixed Assets | 3.2 | 3.4 |
|  |  | .6 | 1.5 |  |  |  | 1.7 | 1.0 |
|  |  | 2.2 | 3.1 |  |  |  | 2.6 | 2.7 |
|  |  | .8 | 1.3 |  |  | Sales/Total Assets | 1.4 | 1.4 |
|  |  | .3 | .9 |  |  |  | 1.1 | .8 |
|  |  | 2.7 | 3.0 |  |  |  | 2.1 | 1.1 |
|  |  | (10) 17.2 | (10) 7.6 |  |  | % Depr., Dep., Amort./Sales | (44) 4.7 | (43) 6.5 |
|  |  | 64.6 | 15.2 |  |  |  | 10.3 | 14.4 |
|  |  |  |  |  |  |  |  | 1.9 |
|  |  |  |  |  |  | % Officers', Directors' Owners' Comp/Sales | (13) 4.5 |  |
|  |  |  |  |  |  |  | 8.2 |  |
| 4715M | 38932M | 90252M | 407513M | 727585M | 741664M | Net Sales ($) | 1494790M | 1627505M |
| 1378M | 11520M | 68343M | 212698M | 428376M | 349098M | Total Assets ($) | 811656M | 1056612M |

M = $ thousand    MM = $ million
See Pages 9 through 22 for Explanation of Ratios and Data

## Comparative Historical Data | Current Data Sorted by Sales

| | | | Type of Statement | 0-1MM | 1-3MM | 3-5MM | 5-10MM | 10-25MM | 25MM & OVER |
|---|---|---|---|---|---|---|---|---|---|
| 12 | 11 | 10 | Unqualified | 1 | | | | 4 | 5 |
| 5 | 4 | 3 | Reviewed | | 1 | | | 1 | 1 |
| 5 | 5 | 6 | Compiled | | 2 | | 3 | 1 | |
| 4 | 7 | 1 | Tax Returns | | | | | 1 | |
| 25 | 25 | 28 | Other | 6 | 5 | 4 | 2 | 5 | 6 |
| 4/1/09-3/31/10 ALL | 4/1/10-3/31/11 ALL | 4/1/11-3/31/12 ALL | | | 9 (4/1-9/30/11) | | | 39 (10/1/11-3/31/12) | |
| 51 | 52 | 48 | **NUMBER OF STATEMENTS** | 7 | 8 | 4 | 5 | 12 | 12 |
| % | % | % | **ASSETS** | % | % | % | % | % | % |
| 8.3 | 10.7 | 13.0 | Cash & Equivalents | | | | | 22.8 | 11.9 |
| 13.2 | 12.7 | 12.3 | Trade Receivables (net) | | | | | 12.6 | 24.3 |
| 6.3 | 6.3 | 7.2 | Inventory | | | | | 3.4 | 5.8 |
| 3.6 | 3.0 | 7.3 | All Other Current | | | | | 1.0 | 8.9 |
| 31.4 | 32.7 | 39.8 | Total Current | | | | | 39.8 | 51.0 |
| 51.1 | 54.2 | 46.6 | Fixed Assets (net) | | | | | 46.0 | 30.1 |
| 5.9 | 3.0 | 2.0 | Intangibles (net) | | | | | 3.6 | 2.5 |
| 11.6 | 10.0 | 11.6 | All Other Non-Current | | | | | 10.6 | 16.4 |
| 100.0 | 100.0 | 100.0 | Total | | | | | 100.0 | 100.0 |
| | | | **LIABILITIES** | | | | | | |
| 8.3 | 10.7 | 2.8 | Notes Payable-Short Term | | | | | .7 | 3.1 |
| 4.7 | 6.0 | 8.5 | Cur. Mat.-L.T.D. | | | | | 6.7 | 4.5 |
| 12.4 | 5.9 | 7.9 | Trade Payables | | | | | 11.1 | 14.7 |
| .2 | .0 | .4 | Income Taxes Payable | | | | | .4 | .0 |
| 14.1 | 6.2 | 20.7 | All Other Current | | | | | 12.7 | 27.6 |
| 39.7 | 28.9 | 40.2 | Total Current | | | | | 31.6 | 50.0 |
| 40.1 | 40.7 | 43.8 | Long-Term Debt | | | | | 36.3 | 19.2 |
| .8 | 1.2 | .5 | Deferred Taxes | | | | | .9 | 1.0 |
| 5.2 | 4.1 | 6.7 | All Other Non-Current | | | | | 2.6 | 8.7 |
| 14.2 | 25.2 | 8.8 | Net Worth | | | | | 28.6 | 21.1 |
| 100.0 | 100.0 | 100.0 | Total Liabilities & Net Worth | | | | | 100.0 | 100.0 |
| | | | **INCOME DATA** | | | | | | |
| 100.0 | 100.0 | 100.0 | Net Sales | | | | | 100.0 | 100.0 |
| | | | Gross Profit | | | | | | |
| 87.8 | 87.9 | 91.5 | Operating Expenses | | | | | 92.0 | 95.4 |
| 12.2 | 12.1 | 8.5 | Operating Profit | | | | | 8.0 | 4.6 |
| 7.1 | 7.1 | 3.7 | All Other Expenses (net) | | | | | -.1 | 1.3 |
| 5.1 | 5.0 | 4.8 | Profit Before Taxes | | | | | 8.1 | 3.3 |
| | | | **RATIOS** | | | | | | |
| 1.6 | 3.2 | 1.9 | | | | | | 2.0 | 1.5 |
| .9 | 1.2 | 1.2 | Current | | | | | 1.4 | 1.2 |
| .5 | .4 | .5 | | | | | | .7 | .5 |
| 1.0 | 2.3 | 1.3 | | | | | | 1.5 | 1.2 |
| .6 | .8 | .6 | Quick | | | | | 1.2 | .8 |
| .3 | .3 | .2 | | | | | | .6 | .3 |
| 0 999.8 | 0 UND | 2 205.6 | | | | | | 0 UND | 18 20.5 |
| 25 14.7 | 23 16.0 | 19 19.7 | Sales/Receivables | | | | | 19 19.2 | 30 12.3 |
| 44 8.3 | 40 9.1 | 31 11.8 | | | | | | 27 13.5 | 38 9.6 |
| | | | Cost of Sales/Inventory | | | | | | |
| | | | Cost of Sales/Payables | | | | | | |
| 12.6 | 8.6 | 11.5 | | | | | | 8.3 | 14.5 |
| -56.8 | 20.1 | 37.3 | Sales/Working Capital | | | | | 15.3 | 29.8 |
| -6.6 | -11.1 | -9.9 | | | | | | -157.8 | -23.8 |
| 4.7 | 14.2 | 10.2 | | | | | | 8.9 | 371.2 |
| (39) 2.0 | (41) 4.3 | (37) 3.9 | EBIT/Interest | | | | (10) 3.0 | (11) 5.7 |  |
| -.3 | .0 | .8 | | | | | | -3.4 | .7 |
| 12.5 | 9.5 | | | | | | | | |
| (10) 2.7 | (11) 2.8 | | Net Profit + Depr., Dep., Amort./Cur. Mat. L/T/D | | | | | | |
| .4 | 2.2 | | | | | | | | |
| .8 | .6 | .9 | | | | | | .4 | .5 |
| 2.3 | 1.6 | 1.6 | Fixed/Worth | | | | | 1.2 | 1.3 |
| -6.5 | 19.2 | -3.4 | | | | | | NM | NM |
| 1.3 | .7 | .8 | | | | | | .7 | .8 |
| 3.6 | 2.1 | 5.6 | Debt/Worth | | | | | 1.5 | 6.9 |
| -7.3 | NM | -7.9 | | | | | | NM | NM |
| 26.1 | 56.7 | 53.5 | % Profit Before Taxes/Tangible Net Worth | | | | | | |
| (35) 8.9 | (39) 9.5 | (32) 22.4 | | | | | | | |
| -4.8 | 1.8 | -.1 | | | | | | | |
| 7.8 | 16.0 | 16.6 | % Profit Before Taxes/Total Assets | | | | | 19.9 | 18.3 |
| 3.3 | 3.5 | 5.4 | | | | | | 6.4 | 5.2 |
| -3.0 | -3.3 | -4.0 | | | | | | -3.3 | .4 |
| 12.4 | 8.7 | 17.5 | | | | | | 290.0 | 123.7 |
| 1.6 | 2.3 | 2.9 | Sales/Net Fixed Assets | | | | | 2.3 | 11.7 |
| .9 | .9 | 1.1 | | | | | | 1.3 | 3.5 |
| 1.9 | 2.1 | 3.6 | | | | | | 5.3 | 4.5 |
| 1.0 | 1.1 | 1.3 | Sales/Total Assets | | | | | 1.4 | 2.7 |
| .5 | .6 | .7 | | | | | | .9 | 1.4 |
| 3.2 | 2.9 | 1.0 | | | | | | 1.1 | .6 |
| (42) 7.1 | (41) 6.6 | (37) 3.8 | % Depr., Dep., Amort./Sales | | | | | (11) 3.9 | (10) 1.9 |
| 12.3 | 18.5 | 18.4 | | | | | | 18.3 | 4.9 |
| | 1.0 | | | | | | | | |
| | (12) 1.8 | | % Officers', Directors' Owners' Comp/Sales | | | | | | |
| | 8.9 | | | | | | | | |
| 1194015M | 1494587M | 2010661M | Net Sales ($) | 4546M | 13109M | 15326M | 38395M | 220023M | 1719262M |
| 936038M | 1406432M | 1071413M | Total Assets ($) | 11914M | 23011M | 20971M | 131585M | 216208M | 667724M |

M = $ thousand   MM = $ million
See Pages 9 through 22 for Explanation of Ratios and Data

## Current Data Sorted by Assets      Comparative Historical Data

| 0-500M | 500M-2MM | 2-10MM | 10-50MM | 50-100MM | 100-250MM | Type of Statement | 4/1/07-3/31/08 ALL | 4/1/08-3/31/09 ALL |
|---|---|---|---|---|---|---|---|---|
| | 1 | 3 | 7 | 1 | 6 | Unqualified | 20 | 19 |
| | | 7 | 4 | | | Reviewed | 14 | 12 |
| | | 1 | 1 | | | Compiled | 4 | 9 |
| 2 | | 1 | | | | Tax Returns | 5 | 5 |
| 2 | 3 | 6 | 11 | 2 | 4 | Other | 28 | 33 |
| | 8 (4/1-9/30/11) | | 54 (10/1/11-3/31/12) | | | | | |
| 4 | 4 | 18 | 23 | 3 | 10 | NUMBER OF STATEMENTS | 71 | 78 |
| % | % | % | % | % | % | ASSETS | % | % |
| | | 11.7 | 13.5 | | 8.9 | Cash & Equivalents | 9.6 | 7.2 |
| | | 24.8 | 15.8 | | 13.1 | Trade Receivables (net) | 15.8 | 16.4 |
| | | 1.6 | 1.7 | | 8.1 | Inventory | 3.9 | 2.1 |
| | | 7.9 | 1.8 | | 1.4 | All Other Current | 4.9 | 3.5 |
| | | 46.1 | 32.8 | | 31.5 | Total Current | 34.2 | 29.2 |
| | | 41.3 | 60.2 | | 59.0 | Fixed Assets (net) | 54.2 | 56.2 |
| | | 1.4 | .5 | | 5.6 | Intangibles (net) | 1.6 | 2.2 |
| | | 11.2 | 6.5 | | 3.8 | All Other Non-Current | 10.0 | 12.4 |
| | | 100.0 | 100.0 | | 100.0 | Total | 100.0 | 100.0 |
| | | | | | | LIABILITIES | | |
| | | 4.4 | 4.4 | | 3.9 | Notes Payable-Short Term | 3.2 | 5.7 |
| | | 8.0 | 4.0 | | 2.2 | Cur. Mat.-L.T.D. | 3.6 | 4.8 |
| | | 11.8 | 7.4 | | 3.1 | Trade Payables | 11.1 | 8.6 |
| | | .8 | .1 | | .2 | Income Taxes Payable | .2 | 1.0 |
| | | 9.9 | 6.8 | | 9.0 | All Other Current | 7.8 | 12.4 |
| | | 34.8 | 22.6 | | 18.3 | Total Current | 25.9 | 32.5 |
| | | 15.5 | 20.6 | | 17.5 | Long-Term Debt | 26.3 | 27.4 |
| | | .6 | 3.7 | | 4.7 | Deferred Taxes | 1.7 | 1.9 |
| | | 6.5 | 8.9 | | 8.5 | All Other Non-Current | 4.1 | 4.1 |
| | | 42.7 | 44.2 | | 51.0 | Net Worth | 42.2 | 34.1 |
| | | 100.0 | 100.0 | | 100.0 | Total Liabilities & Net Worth | 100.0 | 100.0 |
| | | | | | | INCOME DATA | | |
| | | 100.0 | 100.0 | | 100.0 | Net Sales | 100.0 | 100.0 |
| | | | | | | Gross Profit | | |
| | | 90.4 | 86.0 | | 81.9 | Operating Expenses | 80.9 | 82.9 |
| | | 9.6 | 14.0 | | 18.1 | Operating Profit | 19.1 | 17.1 |
| | | .5 | -.5 | | -.7 | All Other Expenses (net) | 1.5 | 1.7 |
| | | 9.1 | 14.5 | | 18.8 | Profit Before Taxes | 17.6 | 15.4 |
| | | | | | | RATIOS | | |
| | | 3.8 | 2.1 | | 2.9 | | 2.4 | 1.9 |
| | | 1.6 | 1.5 | | 1.7 | Current | 1.4 | 1.1 |
| | | .8 | 1.1 | | 1.1 | | .9 | .6 |
| | | 2.3 | 1.8 | | 2.8 | | 1.7 | 1.7 |
| | | 1.1 | 1.2 | | 1.4 | Quick | 1.0 | .7 |
| | | .6 | .8 | | .4 | | .5 | .4 |
| | | 24   14.9 | 29   12.7 | | 36   10.0 | | 26   14.3 | 18   20.7 |
| | | 41   9.0 | 36   10.1 | | 48   7.6 | Sales/Receivables | 44   8.3 | 36   10.2 |
| | | 49   7.4 | 66   5.5 | | 78   4.7 | | 58   6.3 | 55   6.6 |
| | | | | | | Cost of Sales/Inventory | | |
| | | | | | | Cost of Sales/Payables | | |
| | | 3.6 | 5.4 | | 2.6 | | 5.1 | 7.6 |
| | | 21.6 | 18.5 | | 10.2 | Sales/Working Capital | 12.4 | 67.1 |
| | | -33.9 | 75.7 | | NM | | -30.4 | -10.9 |
| | | 16.2 | 15.4 | | | | 17.2 | 10.1 |
| | | (17) 6.3 | (22) 5.7 | | | EBIT/Interest | (60) 7.5 | (68) 3.8 |
| | | .7 | 2.7 | | | | 3.8 | 2.1 |
| | | | 8.6 | | | Net Profit + Depr., Dep., | 14.7 | 9.2 |
| | | | (14) 4.5 | | | Amort./Cur. Mat. L/T/D | (23) 2.4 | (24) 3.9 |
| | | | 2.3 | | | | 1.7 | 1.3 |
| | | .2 | .8 | | .8 | | .8 | .9 |
| | | 1.0 | 1.5 | | 1.3 | Fixed/Worth | 1.3 | 1.7 |
| | | 2.7 | 2.5 | | 2.2 | | 3.2 | 3.9 |
| | | .3 | .7 | | .6 | | .6 | .7 |
| | | 1.6 | 1.3 | | 1.0 | Debt/Worth | 1.4 | 2.1 |
| | | 5.5 | 2.7 | | 2.5 | | 3.3 | 6.2 |
| | | 48.3 | 30.1 | | 35.0 | % Profit Before Taxes/Tangible | 56.7 | 64.3 |
| | | (17) 22.3 | 19.6 | | 22.4 | Net Worth | (66) 30.3 | (71) 30.3 |
| | | -.3 | 12.8 | | 14.9 | | 13.0 | 10.1 |
| | | 17.4 | 12.4 | | 15.7 | % Profit Before Taxes/Total | 19.4 | 14.6 |
| | | 12.5 | 8.0 | | 10.2 | Assets | 11.3 | 7.6 |
| | | .4 | 4.2 | | 7.2 | | 5.5 | 2.9 |
| | | 17.3 | 2.5 | | 3.8 | | 5.1 | 7.3 |
| | | 4.0 | 1.3 | | 1.0 | Sales/Net Fixed Assets | 1.5 | 1.7 |
| | | 1.9 | .8 | | .7 | | .7 | .6 |
| | | 2.9 | 1.7 | | 1.1 | | 1.8 | 2.3 |
| | | 1.7 | .8 | | .6 | Sales/Total Assets | .8 | .9 |
| | | .6 | .6 | | .5 | | .5 | .5 |
| | | 1.9 | 4.6 | | | | 2.9 | 2.2 |
| | | (16) 5.7 | (21) 8.0 | | | % Depr., Dep., Amort./Sales | (63) 6.2 | (69) 6.7 |
| | | 8.6 | 10.2 | | | | 9.6 | 9.1 |
| | | | | | | % Officers', Directors' Owners' Comp/Sales | | |
| 3365M | 4945M | 171345M | 848992M | 708657M | 1382383M | Net Sales ($) | 2088264M | 2528706M |
| 741M | 3862M | 98227M | 598364M | 263959M | 1666142M | Total Assets ($) | 2039450M | 2882789M |

M = $ thousand    MM = $ million
See Pages 9 through 22 for Explanation of Ratios and Data

| Comparative Historical Data | | | | | | | Current Data Sorted by Sales | | | | |
|---|---|---|---|---|---|---|---|---|---|---|---|

## Type of Statement

| | | | | Type of Statement | | | | | | | |
|---|---|---|---|---|---|---|---|---|---|---|---|
| 22 | 21 | 17 | | Unqualified | | 1 | | | 6 | 10 | |
| 8 | 7 | 12 | | Reviewed | | 2 | 1 | 4 | 2 | 3 | |
| 6 | 6 | 2 | | Compiled | | | | 1 | 1 | | |
| 8 | 5 | 3 | | Tax Returns | | | | | 1 | | |
| 33 | 35 | 28 | | Other | 1 | 1 | | 4 | 9 | 8 | |
| 4/1/09-3/31/10 | 4/1/10-3/31/11 | 4/1/11-3/31/12 | | | 4 | 2 | 1 | 4 | | | |
| ALL | ALL | ALL | | | | 8 (4/1-9/30/11) | | | 54 (10/1/11-3/31/12) | | |
| | | | | | 0-1MM | 1-3MM | 3-5MM | 5-10MM | 10-25MM | 25MM & OVER | |
| 77 | 74 | 62 | | NUMBER OF STATEMENTS | 5 | 6 | 2 | 9 | 19 | 21 | |

| % | % | % | | ASSETS | % | % | % | % | % | % |
|---|---|---|---|---|---|---|---|---|---|---|
| 9.5 | 12.2 | 12.7 | | Cash & Equivalents | | | | | 11.5 | 10.5 |
| 16.0 | 15.9 | 19.6 | | Trade Receivables (net) | | | | | 21.0 | 20.3 |
| 2.0 | 2.8 | 3.1 | | Inventory | | | | | 1.5 | 6.7 |
| 3.5 | 3.4 | 3.5 | | All Other Current | | | | | 2.4 | 1.7 |
| 30.9 | 34.2 | 38.9 | | Total Current | | | | | 36.4 | 39.2 |
| 52.3 | 53.9 | 49.0 | | Fixed Assets (net) | | | | | 55.4 | 51.2 |
| 2.9 | 2.0 | 2.1 | | Intangibles (net) | | | | | 2.2 | 3.9 |
| 13.9 | 9.9 | 9.9 | | All Other Non-Current | | | | | 5.9 | 5.7 |
| 100.0 | 100.0 | 100.0 | | Total | | | | | 100.0 | 100.0 |

## LIABILITIES

| | | | | LIABILITIES | | | | | | |
|---|---|---|---|---|---|---|---|---|---|---|
| 2.6 | 4.0 | 4.5 | | Notes Payable-Short Term | | | | | 2.9 | 5.7 |
| 6.0 | 5.1 | 4.5 | | Cur. Mat.-L.T.D. | | | | | 5.8 | 2.9 |
| 9.0 | 8.5 | 8.1 | | Trade Payables | | | | | 10.5 | 9.0 |
| .4 | .2 | .3 | | Income Taxes Payable | | | | | .2 | .1 |
| 27.1 | 9.5 | 14.7 | | All Other Current | | | | | 6.0 | 9.2 |
| 45.0 | 27.3 | 32.1 | | Total Current | | | | | 25.4 | 26.8 |
| 29.4 | 22.5 | 17.6 | | Long-Term Debt | | | | | 18.1 | 16.7 |
| 2.3 | 3.5 | 2.6 | | Deferred Taxes | | | | | 4.3 | 3.4 |
| 3.2 | 6.7 | 7.2 | | All Other Non-Current | | | | | 8.6 | 9.4 |
| 20.2 | 39.9 | 40.5 | | Net Worth | | | | | 43.6 | 43.6 |
| 100.0 | 100.0 | 100.0 | | Total Liabilties & Net Worth | | | | | 100.0 | 100.0 |

## INCOME DATA

| | | | | INCOME DATA | | | | | | |
|---|---|---|---|---|---|---|---|---|---|---|
| 100.0 | 100.0 | 100.0 | | Net Sales | | | | | 100.0 | 100.0 |
| | | | | Gross Profit | | | | | | |
| 88.9 | 86.1 | 87.1 | | Operating Expenses | | | | | 85.4 | 88.4 |
| 11.1 | 13.9 | 12.9 | | Operating Profit | | | | | 14.6 | 11.6 |
| 2.0 | 1.0 | .5 | | All Other Expenses (net) | | | | | .7 | -.8 |
| 9.1 | 12.9 | 12.4 | | Profit Before Taxes | | | | | 13.9 | 12.4 |

## RATIOS

| | | | | | | RATIOS | | | | | | | |
|---|---|---|---|---|---|---|---|---|---|---|---|---|---|
| | 2.3 | | 2.1 | | 2.3 | | | | | | | 2.1 | 2.0 |
| | 1.1 | | 1.4 | | 1.5 | Current | | | | | | 1.5 | 1.5 |
| | .6 | | .7 | | .9 | | | | | | | 1.2 | 1.1 |
| | 1.8 | | 1.8 | | 1.9 | | | | | | | 1.8 | 1.7 |
| | .8 | | 1.1 | | 1.2 | Quick | | | | | | 1.2 | 1.2 |
| | .4 | | .6 | | .7 | | | | | | | .8 | .8 |
| 15 | 24.9 | 23 | 16.2 | 25 | 14.5 | | | | | | 33 | 11.1 | 26 | 13.8 |
| 38 | 9.5 | 40 | 9.2 | 39 | 9.3 | Sales/Receivables | | | | | 41 | 8.9 | 39 | 9.4 |
| 57 | 6.4 | 58 | 6.3 | 59 | 6.2 | | | | | | 63 | 5.8 | 54 | 6.7 |
| | | | | | | Cost of Sales/Inventory | | | | | | | |
| | | | | | | Cost of Sales/Payables | | | | | | | |
| | 6.2 | | 5.4 | | 4.2 | | | | | | | 4.3 | 4.8 |
| | 74.0 | | 22.2 | | 17.2 | Sales/Working Capital | | | | | | 20.3 | 16.0 |
| | -8.4 | | -23.1 | | -58.6 | | | | | | | 31.6 | NM |
| | 8.7 | | 14.9 | | 17.1 | | | | | | | 11.8 | 27.6 |
| (69) | 2.8 | (63) | 4.8 | (54) | 7.4 | EBIT/Interest | | | | (18) | 7.3 | (20) | 11.0 |
| | 1.2 | | 2.6 | | 2.7 | | | | | | | 4.3 | 3.1 |
| | 5.6 | | 5.5 | | 14.5 | Net Profit + Depr., Dep., | | | | | | 6.7 | 27.7 |
| (28) | 1.9 | (23) | 1.8 | (30) | 6.3 | Amort./Cur. Mat. L/T/D | | | | (11) | 4.4 | (13) | 11.2 |
| | 1.4 | | .7 | | 2.8 | | | | | | | 1.5 | 2.5 |
| | .8 | | .6 | | .6 | | | | | | | .7 | .6 |
| | 1.5 | | 1.6 | | 1.2 | Fixed/Worth | | | | | | 1.5 | 1.0 |
| | 4.7 | | 3.1 | | 2.5 | | | | | | | 2.5 | 2.4 |
| | .6 | | .8 | | .7 | | | | | | | .9 | .7 |
| | 1.8 | | 1.8 | | 1.5 | Debt/Worth | | | | | | 1.3 | 1.2 |
| | 7.2 | | 4.1 | | 2.9 | | | | | | | 2.2 | 2.7 |
| | 32.0 | | 50.3 | | 35.0 | % Profit Before Taxes/Tangible | | | | | | 37.2 | 39.1 |
| (66) | 15.2 | (70) | 21.5 | (58) | 22.1 | Net Worth | | | | (18) | 28.2 | | 21.8 |
| | 3.6 | | 6.3 | | 10.3 | | | | | | | 17.9 | 15.5 |
| | 12.8 | | 14.5 | | 14.3 | % Profit Before Taxes/Total | | | | | | 17.4 | 12.2 |
| | 6.3 | | 7.9 | | 8.6 | Assets | | | | | | 12.4 | 8.2 |
| | .8 | | 3.4 | | 1.9 | | | | | | | 7.5 | 5.3 |
| | 7.1 | | 5.7 | | 7.4 | | | | | | | 9.9 | 5.7 |
| | 1.7 | | 1.4 | | 2.0 | Sales/Net Fixed Assets | | | | | | 1.5 | 2.5 |
| | .7 | | .6 | | .9 | | | | | | | .8 | .9 |
| | 2.4 | | 2.0 | | 2.3 | | | | | | | 2.3 | 2.1 |
| | .9 | | .8 | | 1.0 | Sales/Total Assets | | | | | | .9 | 1.0 |
| | .4 | | .4 | | .5 | | | | | | | .6 | .6 |
| | 3.8 | | 2.5 | | 3.1 | | | | | | | 3.1 | 2.4 |
| (70) | 8.8 | (63) | 7.4 | (52) | 7.1 | % Depr., Dep., Amort./Sales | | | (17) | 7.8 | (18) | 4.9 |
| | 11.6 | | 11.4 | | 9.5 | | | | | | | 10.7 | 8.1 |
| | | | | | | % Officers', Directors' Owners' Comp/Sales | | | | | | | |

| 2172616M | 4421863M | 3119687M | | Net Sales ($) | 2114M | 11086M | 8169M | 63266M | 323357M | 2711695M |
|---|---|---|---|---|---|---|---|---|---|---|
| 2766320M | 2978835M | 2631295M | | Total Assets ($) | 3363M | 27386M | 10443M | 49706M | 422488M | 2117909M |

M = $ thousand    MM = $ million
See Pages 9 through 22 for Explanation of Ratios and Data

## Current Data Sorted by Assets        Comparative Historical Data

Current data periods: **3 (4/1-9/30/11)**    **43 (10/1/11-3/31/12)**

| Type of Statement | 0-500M | 500M-2MM | 2-10MM | 10-50MM | 50-100MM | 100-250MM | 4/1/07-3/31/08 ALL | 4/1/08-3/31/09 ALL |
|---|---|---|---|---|---|---|---|---|
| Unqualified |  |  |  | 5 | 2 | 6 | 5 | 7 |
| Reviewed |  | 1 |  | 4 |  |  | 1 |  |
| Compiled |  |  |  |  |  | 1 | 1 | 1 |
| Tax Returns |  |  |  |  |  |  | 1 |  |
| Other | 3 |  | 4 | 6 |  | 6 | 5 | 5 |
| **NUMBER OF STATEMENTS** | 4 | 4 | 7 | 15 | 3 | 13 | 13 | 13 |
| | % | % | % | % | % | % | % | % |
| **ASSETS** | | | | | | | | |
| Cash & Equivalents |  |  |  | 9.5 |  | 4.4 | 12.2 | 6.6 |
| Trade Receivables (net) |  |  |  | 15.8 |  | 12.0 | 12.6 | 10.7 |
| Inventory |  |  |  | 1.6 |  | 3.5 | .2 | .2 |
| All Other Current |  |  |  | 1.5 |  | 4.2 | 4.8 | 5.9 |
| Total Current |  |  |  | 28.4 |  | 24.1 | 29.8 | 23.4 |
| Fixed Assets (net) |  |  |  | 64.5 |  | 67.5 | 58.5 | 63.5 |
| Intangibles (net) |  |  |  | 2.7 |  | 5.0 | 5.0 | 3.5 |
| All Other Non-Current |  |  |  | 4.4 |  | 3.5 | 6.7 | 9.7 |
| Total |  |  |  | 100.0 |  | 100.0 | 100.0 | 100.0 |
| **LIABILITIES** | | | | | | | | |
| Notes Payable-Short Term |  |  |  | 2.9 |  | 5.4 | 2.2 | 1.1 |
| Cur. Mat.-L.T.D. |  |  |  | 3.6 |  | 5.0 | 3.8 | 2.7 |
| Trade Payables |  |  |  | 10.3 |  | 4.0 | 6.6 | 3.7 |
| Income Taxes Payable |  |  |  | .5 |  | .2 | .7 | .0 |
| All Other Current |  |  |  | 4.5 |  | 4.8 | 10.0 | 7.0 |
| Total Current |  |  |  | 21.9 |  | 19.3 | 23.3 | 14.6 |
| Long-Term Debt |  |  |  | 33.1 |  | 28.2 | 37.3 | 30.5 |
| Deferred Taxes |  |  |  | 1.6 |  | 3.6 | 2.2 | 1.1 |
| All Other Non-Current |  |  |  | 7.3 |  | 4.7 | 1.9 | 10.1 |
| Net Worth |  |  |  | 36.1 |  | 44.2 | 35.3 | 43.7 |
| Total Liabilties & Net Worth |  |  |  | 100.0 |  | 100.0 | 100.0 | 100.0 |
| **INCOME DATA** | | | | | | | | |
| Net Sales |  |  |  | 100.0 |  | 100.0 | 100.0 | 100.0 |
| Gross Profit |  |  |  |  |  |  |  |  |
| Operating Expenses |  |  |  | 81.7 |  | 89.9 | 82.5 | 79.3 |
| Operating Profit |  |  |  | 18.3 |  | 10.1 | 17.5 | 20.7 |
| All Other Expenses (net) |  |  |  | 6.1 |  | 1.4 | 2.9 | 6.2 |
| Profit Before Taxes |  |  |  | 12.2 |  | 8.7 | 14.6 | 14.5 |
| **RATIOS** | | | | | | | | |
| Current |  |  |  | 2.0 |  | 2.1 | 3.5 | 3.3 |
|  |  |  |  | 1.0 |  | 1.3 | 1.1 | 1.1 |
|  |  |  |  | .6 |  | .7 | .4 | .9 |
| Quick |  |  |  | 1.9 |  | 1.6 | 2.3 | 1.9 |
|  |  |  |  | 1.0 |  | .9 | 1.0 | 1.0 |
|  |  |  |  | .6 |  | .5 | .3 | .9 |
| Sales/Receivables |  |  |  | 20   17.9 |  | 33   11.2 | 14   26.6 | 23   16.1 |
|  |  |  |  | 40   9.2 |  | 50   7.3 | 30   12.3 | 30   12.0 |
|  |  |  |  | 62   5.9 |  | 72   5.1 | 61   6.0 | 81   4.5 |
| Cost of Sales/Inventory |  |  |  |  |  |  |  |  |
| Cost of Sales/Payables |  |  |  |  |  |  |  |  |
| Sales/Working Capital |  |  |  | 4.1 |  | 6.0 | 5.1 | 4.3 |
|  |  |  |  | 146.1 |  | 19.7 | 39.8 | 29.0 |
|  |  |  |  | -6.9 |  | -14.9 | -4.5 | -91.3 |
| EBIT/Interest |  |  |  | 7.7 |  | 8.7 | 12.0 | 6.4 |
|  |  |  |  | (11) 4.8 |  | 4.1 | 3.8 | (11) 4.0 |
|  |  |  |  | 2.1 |  | 2.2 | 2.3 | 2.6 |
| Net Profit + Depr., Dep., Amort./Cur. Mat. L/T/D |  |  |  |  |  |  |  |  |
| Fixed/Worth |  |  |  | 1.1 |  | 1.3 | .6 | .7 |
|  |  |  |  | 2.0 |  | 2.0 | 1.4 | 2.0 |
|  |  |  |  | 4.2 |  | 2.6 | NM | 2.6 |
| Debt/Worth |  |  |  | 1.0 |  | .8 | .8 | .5 |
|  |  |  |  | 2.6 |  | 1.7 | 1.1 | 1.6 |
|  |  |  |  | 4.5 |  | 2.4 | NM | 2.1 |
| % Profit Before Taxes/Tangible Net Worth |  |  |  | 47.7 |  | 24.8 | 36.8 | 32.2 |
|  |  |  |  | (14) 16.6 |  | (12) 20.9 | (10) 26.5 | (12) 21.8 |
|  |  |  |  | 1.0 |  | 4.1 | 10.5 | 9.1 |
| % Profit Before Taxes/Total Assets |  |  |  | 11.6 |  | 12.9 | 15.6 | 12.8 |
|  |  |  |  | 4.5 |  | 7.6 | 9.4 | 9.5 |
|  |  |  |  | 2.4 |  | 2.9 | 5.5 | 4.9 |
| Sales/Net Fixed Assets |  |  |  | 2.3 |  | 2.5 | 3.9 | 2.2 |
|  |  |  |  | 1.7 |  | .9 | 1.1 | .9 |
|  |  |  |  | .3 |  | .7 | .6 | .6 |
| Sales/Total Assets |  |  |  | 1.4 |  | 1.4 | 1.6 | 1.1 |
|  |  |  |  | .9 |  | .7 | .6 | .6 |
|  |  |  |  | .3 |  | .6 | .4 | .4 |
| % Depr., Dep., Amort./Sales |  |  |  | 3.2 |  |  | 3.6 | 3.2 |
|  |  |  |  | (14) 6.6 |  |  | (11) 4.7 | (10) 4.4 |
|  |  |  |  | 25.7 |  |  | 8.3 | 6.7 |
| % Officers', Directors' Owners' Comp/Sales |  |  |  |  |  |  |  |  |
| Net Sales ($) | 3827M | 13912M | 84391M | 475616M | 129530M | 2137043M | 826546M | 904061M |
| Total Assets ($) | 1232M | 6379M | 35694M | 446324M | 251592M | 2172617M | 1170225M | 1439483M |

**Comparative Historical Data** | **Current Data Sorted by Sales**

| | Comparative Historical Data | | | Current Data Sorted by Sales | | | | | |
|---|---|---|---|---|---|---|---|---|---|
| **Type of Statement** | | | | | | | 3 (4/1-9/30/11) | 43 (10/1/11-3/31/12) | |
| Unqualified | 13 | 9 | 14 | | 1 | | | | 13 |
| Reviewed | 3 | 2 | 7 | | | 2 | 1 | 2 | 2 |
| Compiled | 1 | 2 | 1 | | | | | | 1 |
| Tax Returns | 2 | 1 | 3 | 2 | | | 1 | | |
| Other | 12 | 7 | 21 | 1 | 2 | 5 | 1 | 3 | 9 |
| | 4/1/09-3/31/10 ALL | 4/1/10-3/31/11 ALL | 4/1/11-3/31/12 ALL | 0-1MM | 1-3MM | 3-5MM | 5-10MM | 10-25MM | 25MM & OVER |
| **NUMBER OF STATEMENTS** | 31 | 21 | 46 | 3 | 3 | 7 | 3 | 5 | 25 |
| | % | % | % | % | % | % | % | % | % |
| **ASSETS** | | | | | | | | | |
| Cash & Equivalents | 12.6 | 12.1 | 11.6 | | | | | | 9.2 |
| Trade Receivables (net) | 12.9 | 11.7 | 15.8 | | | | | | 15.7 |
| Inventory | 1.9 | .8 | 1.7 | | | | | | 2.0 |
| All Other Current | 5.6 | 3.4 | 3.2 | | | | | | 5.1 |
| Total Current | 33.0 | 28.0 | 32.2 | | | | | | 31.9 |
| Fixed Assets (net) | 55.0 | 64.6 | 61.4 | | | | | | 60.0 |
| Intangibles (net) | 2.5 | 2.7 | 2.4 | | | | | | 4.0 |
| All Other Non-Current | 9.5 | 4.7 | 4.0 | | | | | | 4.2 |
| Total | 100.0 | 100.0 | 100.0 | | | | | | 100.0 |
| **LIABILITIES** | | | | | | | | | |
| Notes Payable-Short Term | 5.8 | 6.4 | 7.2 | | | | | | 6.1 |
| Cur. Mat.-L.T.D. | 6.3 | 3.8 | 3.5 | | | | | | 3.6 |
| Trade Payables | 7.4 | 5.1 | 7.1 | | | | | | 8.4 |
| Income Taxes Payable | .1 | 1.0 | .7 | | | | | | 1.2 |
| All Other Current | 7.4 | 8.5 | 8.7 | | | | | | 9.4 |
| Total Current | 27.0 | 24.8 | 27.2 | | | | | | 28.6 |
| Long-Term Debt | 28.2 | 36.0 | 31.6 | | | | | | 22.8 |
| Deferred Taxes | 2.3 | .0 | 1.6 | | | | | | 2.9 |
| All Other Non-Current | 5.2 | 7.6 | 7.2 | | | | | | 6.0 |
| Net Worth | 37.3 | 31.5 | 32.4 | | | | | | 39.7 |
| Total Liabilities & Net Worth | 100.0 | 100.0 | 100.0 | | | | | | 100.0 |
| **INCOME DATA** | | | | | | | | | |
| Net Sales | 100.0 | 100.0 | 100.0 | | | | | | 100.0 |
| Gross Profit | | | | | | | | | |
| Operating Expenses | 86.8 | 85.8 | 88.6 | | | | | | 89.5 |
| Operating Profit | 13.2 | 14.2 | 11.4 | | | | | | 10.5 |
| All Other Expenses (net) | 1.9 | 5.4 | 2.9 | | | | | | 1.8 |
| Profit Before Taxes | 11.3 | 8.7 | 8.4 | | | | | | 8.7 |
| **RATIOS** | | | | | | | | | |
| Current | 2.2 | 2.0 | 2.1 | | | | | | 2.1 |
| | 1.2 | 1.1 | 1.1 | | | | | | 1.1 |
| | .7 | .6 | .6 | | | | | | .8 |
| Quick | 1.8 | 1.8 | 1.8 | | | | | | 1.8 |
| | 1.0 | 1.0 | .9 | | | | | | .9 |
| | .2 | .4 | .4 | | | | | | .6 |
| Sales/Receivables | 14   25.6 | 32   11.6 | 25   14.6 | | | | | | 31   11.7 |
| | 38   9.7 | 39   9.3 | 43   8.5 | | | | | | 45   8.2 |
| | 55   6.7 | 54   6.7 | 64   5.7 | | | | | | 68   5.4 |
| Cost of Sales/Inventory | | | | | | | | | |
| Cost of Sales/Payables | | | | | | | | | |
| Sales/Working Capital | 7.0 | 5.2 | 5.4 | | | | | | 6.0 |
| | 38.2 | 58.3 | 69.6 | | | | | | 61.6 |
| | -9.2 | -8.7 | -7.2 | | | | | | -31.1 |
| EBIT/Interest | 5.1 | 13.5 | 11.3 | | | | | | 10.7 |
| | (27) 1.8 | (20) 3.0 | (42) 4.2 | | | | | (24) | 4.9 |
| | 1.2 | .4 | 1.9 | | | | | | 2.5 |
| Net Profit + Depr., Dep., Amort./Cur. Mat. L/T/D | | | | | | | | | |
| Fixed/Worth | 1.1 | 1.2 | 1.2 | | | | | | 1.1 |
| | 1.6 | 2.0 | 2.1 | | | | | | 1.9 |
| | 4.4 | 7.5 | 4.3 | | | | | | 2.8 |
| Debt/Worth | .7 | 1.0 | 1.0 | | | | | | 1.0 |
| | 2.1 | 2.9 | 2.4 | | | | | | 2.0 |
| | 6.2 | 8.7 | 5.3 | | | | | | 3.4 |
| % Profit Before Taxes/Tangible Net Worth | 47.3 | 70.8 | 47.7 | | | | | | 32.7 |
| | (29) 15.3 | (18) 20.5 | (41) 20.5 | | | | | (24) | 23.3 |
| | 2.1 | -2.6 | 5.4 | | | | | | 14.3 |
| % Profit Before Taxes/Total Assets | 9.1 | 14.2 | 15.5 | | | | | | 15.0 |
| | 3.4 | 4.8 | 6.2 | | | | | | 7.6 |
| | 1.6 | -1.2 | 1.9 | | | | | | 3.6 |
| Sales/Net Fixed Assets | 10.5 | 2.1 | 4.1 | | | | | | 5.7 |
| | 1.1 | .7 | 1.8 | | | | | | 1.2 |
| | .5 | .4 | .7 | | | | | | .8 |
| Sales/Total Assets | 2.5 | 1.2 | 2.2 | | | | | | 2.1 |
| | .5 | .5 | 1.0 | | | | | | .8 |
| | .3 | .3 | .6 | | | | | | .6 |
| % Depr., Dep., Amort./Sales | 2.2 | 2.8 | 2.8 | | | | | | 1.6 |
| | (24) 5.5 | (17) 9.3 | (35) 4.0 | | | | | (17) | 3.6 |
| | 11.5 | 17.1 | 10.4 | | | | | | 7.1 |
| % Officers', Directors' Owners' Comp/Sales | | | | | | | | | |
| Net Sales ($) | 1469650M | 921202M | 2844319M | 1730M | 5005M | 27158M | 22648M | 79317M | 2708461M |
| Total Assets ($) | 1993348M | 1364144M | 2913838M | 870M | 5910M | 73884M | 86756M | 74221M | 2672197M |

M = $ thousand     MM = $ million
See Pages 9 through 22 for Explanation of Ratios and Data

| | | Current Data Sorted by Assets | | | | | Comparative Historical Data | |
|---|---|---|---|---|---|---|---|---|
| | | | | | | | **Type of Statement** | | |
| | | 1 | 11 | 3 | 10 | | Unqualified | 26 | 23 |
| | | 2 | 4 | 3 | | | Reviewed | 3 | 9 |
| 1 | 1 | 10 | 3 | | 1 | | Compiled | 8 | 8 |
| 7 | 3 | 3 | 1 | | | | Tax Returns | 7 | 11 |
| 3 | 7 | 12 | 13 | 5 | 12 | | Other | 39 | 59 |
| | 12 (4/1-9/30/11) | | 104 (10/1/11-3/31/12) | | | | | 4/1/07-3/31/08 ALL | 4/1/08-3/31/09 ALL |
| 0-500M | 500M-2MM | 2-10MM | 10-50MM | 50-100MM | 100-250MM | | | | |
| 11 | 11 | 28 | 32 | 11 | 23 | | **NUMBER OF STATEMENTS** | 83 | 110 |
| % | % | % | % | % | % | | **ASSETS** | % | % |
| 56.6 | 16.6 | 17.3 | 7.8 | 9.1 | 7.2 | | Cash & Equivalents | 10.5 | 10.1 |
| 17.4 | 30.4 | 20.6 | 16.0 | 7.9 | 7.8 | | Trade Receivables (net) | 12.1 | 12.8 |
| 1.4 | .2 | 1.7 | .7 | 1.0 | 1.6 | | Inventory | 1.2 | 4.0 |
| .5 | .6 | 4.9 | 6.2 | 1.6 | 2.0 | | All Other Current | 4.5 | 4.2 |
| 75.9 | 47.8 | 44.4 | 30.7 | 19.7 | 18.7 | | Total Current | 28.3 | 31.2 |
| 20.1 | 46.5 | 42.6 | 60.8 | 65.2 | 72.8 | | Fixed Assets (net) | 64.9 | 58.1 |
| 2.9 | 1.3 | .6 | 2.4 | 5.4 | 2.3 | | Intangibles (net) | 1.6 | 3.7 |
| 1.1 | 4.4 | 12.3 | 6.1 | 9.7 | 6.2 | | All Other Non-Current | 5.3 | 7.0 |
| 100.0 | 100.0 | 100.0 | 100.0 | 100.0 | 100.0 | | Total | 100.0 | 100.0 |
| | | | | | | | **LIABILITIES** | | |
| 2.0 | 2.5 | 3.6 | 4.9 | 8.4 | 1.1 | | Notes Payable-Short Term | 3.5 | 3.1 |
| 7.8 | 3.0 | 6.9 | 4.0 | 5.1 | 10.2 | | Cur. Mat.-L.T.D. | 4.0 | 4.5 |
| 4.4 | 8.2 | 7.3 | 8.0 | 4.5 | 4.7 | | Trade Payables | 4.7 | 7.8 |
| .0 | .0 | .0 | .3 | .1 | .3 | | Income Taxes Payable | .4 | .2 |
| 8.5 | 17.1 | 11.6 | 8.8 | 6.5 | 4.0 | | All Other Current | 6.6 | 7.9 |
| 22.7 | 30.7 | 29.3 | 26.0 | 24.5 | 20.3 | | Total Current | 19.1 | 23.6 |
| 34.1 | 26.0 | 25.6 | 30.7 | 34.4 | 37.6 | | Long-Term Debt | 37.3 | 36.0 |
| .0 | .0 | .0 | 1.7 | 4.2 | 6.1 | | Deferred Taxes | 2.5 | 1.7 |
| 22.6 | 5.2 | 2.9 | 4.8 | 3.2 | 2.7 | | All Other Non-Current | 2.6 | 3.3 |
| 20.6 | 38.0 | 42.1 | 36.9 | 33.7 | 33.3 | | Net Worth | 38.4 | 35.3 |
| 100.0 | 100.0 | 100.0 | 100.0 | 100.0 | 100.0 | | Total Liabilties & Net Worth | 100.0 | 100.0 |
| | | | | | | | **INCOME DATA** | | |
| 100.0 | 100.0 | 100.0 | 100.0 | 100.0 | 100.0 | | Net Sales | 100.0 | 100.0 |
| | | | | | | | Gross Profit | | |
| 79.2 | 90.0 | 84.0 | 85.1 | 86.7 | 88.5 | | Operating Expenses | 80.0 | 84.2 |
| 20.8 | 10.0 | 16.0 | 14.9 | 13.3 | 11.5 | | Operating Profit | 20.0 | 15.8 |
| 2.2 | 1.3 | 6.1 | 2.9 | 4.3 | 2.6 | | All Other Expenses (net) | 5.5 | 3.4 |
| 18.7 | 8.7 | 9.9 | 12.0 | 9.0 | 8.8 | | Profit Before Taxes | 14.5 | 12.4 |
| | | | | | | | **RATIOS** | | |
| 10.8 | 7.8 | 3.4 | 2.0 | 2.8 | 2.1 | | | 3.2 | 2.3 |
| 4.1 | 1.5 | 1.6 | 1.1 | 1.3 | 1.3 | | Current | 1.3 | 1.5 |
| 1.9 | .8 | .9 | .8 | .4 | .6 | | | .8 | .9 |
| 10.8 | 7.8 | 3.1 | 1.8 | 2.1 | 1.5 | | | 2.8 | 1.8 |
| 3.5 | 1.5 | 1.3 | 1.0 | .8 | .8 | | Quick | 1.1 | 1.2 |
| 1.9 | .8 | .7 | .8 | .3 | .4 | | | .6 | .4 |
| 0 UND | 14 25.9 | 0 UND | 31 11.9 | 24 15.3 | 27 13.3 | | | 23 16.2 | 16 23.1 |
| 17 21.8 | 32 11.3 | 34 10.7 | 42 8.7 | 41 8.8 | 45 8.2 | | Sales/Receivables | 38 9.5 | 34 10.9 |
| 33 11.0 | 114 3.2 | 68 5.4 | 51 7.1 | 51 7.1 | 53 6.9 | | | 55 6.6 | 47 7.8 |
| | | | | | | | Cost of Sales/Inventory | | |
| | | | | | | | Cost of Sales/Payables | | |
| 2.8 | 4.4 | 4.8 | 6.2 | 5.4 | 5.1 | | | 4.0 | 5.8 |
| 6.6 | 12.3 | 13.0 | 43.9 | 8.8 | 22.1 | | Sales/Working Capital | 20.7 | 14.9 |
| 13.9 | -27.3 | -72.0 | -23.0 | -4.7 | -6.0 | | | -28.7 | -165.4 |
| | | | 163.8 | 14.9 | 7.5 | | | 13.9 | 11.1 |
| | (23) | 8.3 | (31) 5.0 | | 3.6 | | EBIT/Interest | (67) 4.6 | (94) 4.6 |
| | | 2.8 | 1.5 | | 1.7 | | | 2.4 | 2.0 |
| | | | | | | | Net Profit + Depr., Dep., | 3.3 | 11.8 |
| | | | | | | | Amort./Cur. Mat. L/T/D | (18) 2.3 | (25) 3.9 |
| | | | | | | | | 1.5 | 2.4 |
| .0 | .5 | .4 | .8 | 1.2 | 1.6 | | | .9 | .9 |
| .1 | 1.5 | .9 | 2.0 | 2.2 | 2.1 | | Fixed/Worth | 1.9 | 2.0 |
| -1.3 | -12.0 | 2.5 | 4.2 | 8.8 | 3.6 | | | 4.7 | 5.0 |
| .1 | .3 | .4 | .9 | .7 | 1.2 | | | .7 | .8 |
| 1.0 | 1.5 | 1.6 | 2.5 | 2.0 | 1.8 | | Debt/Worth | 2.0 | 2.1 |
| -3.3 | -481.0 | 5.8 | 4.9 | 9.1 | 3.4 | | | 4.9 | 6.0 |
| | | 57.4 | 36.7 | | 25.7 | | % Profit Before Taxes/Tangible | 46.9 | 49.4 |
| | (25) | 32.3 | (30) 25.5 | | (21) 17.6 | | Net Worth | (78) 27.3 | (95) 28.5 |
| | | 5.4 | 3.5 | | 10.1 | | | 15.8 | 10.2 |
| 80.3 | 5.9 | 27.4 | 16.5 | 9.4 | 9.3 | | % Profit Before Taxes/Total | 18.4 | 16.9 |
| 37.5 | -.2 | 10.8 | 5.5 | 2.7 | 5.9 | | Assets | 9.5 | 8.7 |
| 2.0 | -3.5 | -.2 | 2.0 | .0 | 2.0 | | | 4.5 | 3.2 |
| UND | 273.6 | 13.7 | 2.2 | 1.5 | 1.0 | | | 2.6 | 3.7 |
| 38.4 | 4.0 | 4.0 | 1.5 | 1.0 | .8 | | Sales/Net Fixed Assets | 1.0 | 1.4 |
| 3.7 | .9 | 1.2 | .9 | .6 | .5 | | | .6 | .7 |
| 5.7 | 5.4 | 2.9 | 1.3 | .9 | .8 | | | 1.5 | 1.8 |
| 2.5 | 1.2 | 1.1 | 1.0 | .6 | .6 | | Sales/Total Assets | .7 | .9 |
| 1.4 | .7 | .7 | .7 | .4 | .4 | | | .5 | .5 |
| | .4 | 2.6 | 3.4 | 6.3 | 5.9 | | | 3.1 | 2.9 |
| | (10) 6.6 | (23) 5.2 | (31) 7.2 | 7.7 | (11) 8.5 | | % Depr., Dep., Amort./Sales | (69) 6.0 | (86) 5.9 |
| | | 16.4 | 11.3 | 12.4 | 11.5 | 10.7 | | 10.4 | 8.9 |
| | | 1.3 | | | | | % Officers', Directors' | .6 | .9 |
| | (10) | 4.4 | | | | | Owners' Comp/Sales | (17) 2.2 | (23) 1.3 |
| | | 13.8 | | | | | | 8.4 | 3.2 |
| 10647M | 37008M | 289877M | 1089026M | 848237M | 3230089M | | Net Sales ($) | 3859157M | 5518590M |
| 2862M | 13161M | 149160M | 712613M | 801374M | 3986404M | | Total Assets ($) | 4651107M | 5969113M |

M = $ thousand    MM = $ million
See Pages 9 through 22 for Explanation of Ratios and Data

## Comparative Historical Data | Current Data Sorted by Sales

| | | | | Type of Statement | | | | | | |
|---|---|---|---|---|---|---|---|---|---|---|
| 23 | 18 | 25 | | Unqualified | | | | 1 | 5 | 19 |
| 11 | 8 | 9 | | Reviewed | | | | 1 | 6 | 2 |
| 11 | 14 | 16 | | Compiled | 1 | 3 | 2 | 5 | 2 | 3 |
| 12 | 13 | 14 | | Tax Returns | 9 | 2 | | 1 | 2 | |
| 70 | 59 | 52 | | Other | 4 | 7 | 2 | 8 | 10 | 21 |
| 4/1/09-3/31/10 | 4/1/10-3/31/11 | 4/1/11-3/31/12 | | | | 12 (4/1-9/30/11) | | | 104 (10/1/11-3/31/12) | |
| ALL | ALL | ALL | | | 0-1MM | 1-3MM | 3-5MM | 5-10MM | 10-25MM | 25MM & OVER |
| 127 | 112 | 116 | | **NUMBER OF STATEMENTS** | 14 | 12 | 4 | 16 | 25 | 45 |
| % | % | % | | **ASSETS** | % | % | % | % | % | % |
| 12.3 | 15.3 | 15.6 | | Cash & Equivalents | 33.5 | 16.4 | | 28.0 | 8.1 | 9.0 |
| 12.1 | 14.7 | 16.2 | | Trade Receivables (net) | 9.9 | 15.1 | | 16.7 | 17.9 | 15.5 |
| .9 | 1.4 | 1.2 | | Inventory | 1.1 | 1.9 | | .2 | 1.2 | 1.4 |
| 3.8 | 4.4 | 3.5 | | All Other Current | .8 | .5 | | 5.2 | 5.5 | 3.8 |
| 29.1 | 35.8 | 36.5 | | Total Current | 45.3 | 33.9 | | 50.1 | 32.8 | 29.7 |
| 61.4 | 56.6 | 54.0 | | Fixed Assets (net) | 37.7 | 62.5 | | 31.8 | 60.3 | 63.6 |
| 2.5 | 1.6 | 2.2 | | Intangibles (net) | 2.3 | 1.2 | | 2.1 | 3.5 | 1.9 |
| 7.0 | 5.9 | 7.3 | | All Other Non-Current | 14.7 | 2.4 | | 15.9 | 3.5 | 4.8 |
| 100.0 | 100.0 | 100.0 | | Total | 100.0 | 100.0 | | 100.0 | 100.0 | 100.0 |
| | | | | **LIABILITIES** | | | | | | |
| 3.0 | 3.4 | 3.7 | | Notes Payable-Short Term | 2.2 | 11.5 | | 3.6 | 2.3 | 3.1 |
| 6.2 | 5.0 | 6.3 | | Cur. Mat.-L.T.D. | 7.7 | 4.8 | | 4.1 | 7.6 | 6.8 |
| 6.0 | 8.6 | 6.5 | | Trade Payables | 4.1 | 2.3 | | 11.1 | 6.5 | 7.0 |
| .2 | .1 | .1 | | Income Taxes Payable | .0 | .0 | | .0 | .3 | .2 |
| 10.3 | 9.5 | 9.1 | | All Other Current | 6.0 | 2.0 | | 22.1 | 6.2 | 8.6 |
| 25.6 | 26.6 | 25.7 | | Total Current | 20.0 | 20.6 | | 40.9 | 22.9 | 25.7 |
| 37.3 | 33.8 | 31.0 | | Long-Term Debt | 51.3 | 25.9 | | 17.1 | 33.5 | 30.5 |
| 1.3 | 1.5 | 2.1 | | Deferred Taxes | .0 | .1 | | .3 | 1.0 | 4.7 |
| 4.5 | 4.7 | 5.5 | | All Other Non-Current | 4.2 | 23.5 | | 5.0 | 4.0 | 2.6 |
| 31.3 | 33.4 | 35.7 | | Net Worth | 24.5 | 30.0 | | 36.8 | 38.6 | 36.4 |
| 100.0 | 100.0 | 100.0 | | Total Liabilities & Net Worth | 100.0 | 100.0 | | 100.0 | 100.0 | 100.0 |
| | | | | **INCOME DATA** | | | | | | |
| 100.0 | 100.0 | 100.0 | | Net Sales | 100.0 | 100.0 | | 100.0 | 100.0 | 100.0 |
| | | | | Gross Profit | | | | | | |
| 87.8 | 85.5 | 85.6 | | Operating Expenses | 65.3 | 85.0 | | 91.2 | 90.5 | 86.8 |
| 12.2 | 14.5 | 14.4 | | Operating Profit | 34.7 | 15.0 | | 8.8 | 9.5 | 13.2 |
| 5.1 | 4.0 | 3.5 | | All Other Expenses (net) | 13.1 | 3.4 | | 1.9 | 2.4 | 2.2 |
| 7.0 | 10.5 | 10.9 | | Profit Before Taxes | 21.6 | 11.6 | | 6.9 | 7.1 | 11.0 |
| | | | | **RATIOS** | | | | | | |
| 2.5 | 3.1 | 2.7 | | | 4.3 | 6.8 | | 3.1 | 3.0 | 2.0 |
| 1.4 | 1.4 | 1.4 | | Current | 1.6 | 1.1 | | 1.7 | 1.1 | 1.4 |
| .6 | .7 | .8 | | | .6 | .9 | | .9 | .8 | .8 |
| 2.1 | 2.5 | 2.4 | | | 3.7 | 6.8 | | 3.0 | 2.2 | 1.9 |
| 1.0 | 1.1 | 1.1 | | Quick | 1.6 | 1.0 | | 1.4 | .9 | 1.1 |
| .4 | .5 | .7 | | | .6 | .6 | | .6 | .6 | .6 |
| 5 66.7 | 12 30.4 | 17 21.1 | | | 0 UND | 0 UND | | 12 29.6 | 30 12.2 | 28 13.0 |
| 30 12.2 | 31 11.9 | 38 9.6 | | Sales/Receivables | 0 UND | 20 18.6 | | 50 7.3 | 41 8.9 | 41 8.8 |
| 47 7.7 | 47 7.8 | 52 7.0 | | | 35 10.5 | 62 5.9 | | 79 4.6 | 54 6.8 | 50 7.3 |
| | | | | Cost of Sales/Inventory | | | | | | |
| | | | | Cost of Sales/Payables | | | | | | |
| 5.6 | 5.4 | 5.1 | | | 2.9 | 4.7 | | 3.0 | 5.3 | 7.2 |
| 24.2 | 17.8 | 14.2 | | Sales/Working Capital | 16.9 | 27.8 | | 7.5 | 76.8 | 18.5 |
| -9.5 | -22.8 | -26.4 | | | -7.5 | -58.2 | | NM | -24.9 | -22.2 |
| 7.9 | 14.7 | 12.9 | | | | 8.7 | | 23.6 | 16.3 | 9.7 |
| (102) 2.9 | (93) 5.1 | (100) 3.9 | | EBIT/Interest | | (10) 3.8 | | (13) 2.8 | (24) 3.4 | (44) 4.5 |
| .4 | 2.2 | 1.5 | | | | -1.8 | | .7 | 1.1 | 2.3 |
| 4.6 | 3.9 | 4.6 | | | | | | | | 4.5 |
| (16) 3.3 | (13) 1.3 | (18) 1.9 | | Net Profit + Depr., Dep., Amort./Cur. Mat. L/T/D | | | | | (12) 1.9 | |
| 1.1 | 1.0 | 1.3 | | | | | | | | 1.4 |
| 1.0 | .7 | .7 | | | .0 | .8 | | .4 | 1.0 | 1.1 |
| 2.4 | 1.7 | 1.7 | | Fixed/Worth | 1.1 | 2.0 | | .9 | 2.3 | 2.0 |
| 10.6 | 5.0 | 3.7 | | | NM | 3.6 | | NM | 7.6 | 3.4 |
| .8 | .7 | .7 | | | .4 | .7 | | .3 | .8 | 1.0 |
| 2.1 | 2.2 | 1.8 | | Debt/Worth | 2.7 | 1.6 | | 2.3 | 2.4 | 1.8 |
| 12.9 | 5.7 | 4.9 | | | -8.2 | 3.3 | | NM | 7.9 | 3.3 |
| 49.0 | 46.8 | 40.4 | | | 83.7 | 31.3 | | 34.7 | 67.8 | 35.5 |
| (105) 16.4 | (98) 23.3 | (100) 21.8 | | % Profit Before Taxes/Tangible Net Worth | (10) 20.1 | (11) 12.6 | | (12) 29.8 | (23) 25.0 | (41) 22.8 |
| -1.6 | 11.8 | 4.2 | | | -.3 | -17.0 | | 4.6 | -4.4 | 10.7 |
| 11.1 | 15.2 | 16.4 | | | 46.0 | 17.0 | | 15.1 | 20.6 | 14.6 |
| 4.8 | 7.4 | 5.9 | | % Profit Before Taxes/Total Assets | 10.2 | 6.5 | | 3.1 | 5.4 | 6.6 |
| -2.2 | 3.1 | .5 | | | .2 | -5.5 | | -.2 | -.4 | 2.7 |
| 3.6 | 7.5 | 6.8 | | | UND | 8.8 | | 38.4 | 4.0 | 2.8 |
| 1.2 | 1.7 | 1.5 | | Sales/Net Fixed Assets | 3.1 | 1.0 | | 2.5 | 1.9 | 1.0 |
| .6 | .8 | .8 | | | .5 | .6 | | .9 | 1.3 | .7 |
| 1.6 | 2.3 | 1.9 | | | 2.1 | 1.8 | | 2.6 | 2.4 | 1.5 |
| .9 | 1.1 | .9 | | Sales/Total Assets | 1.1 | .8 | | 1.0 | 1.1 | .8 |
| .5 | .6 | .6 | | | .2 | .5 | | .5 | .9 | .6 |
| 4.0 | 2.6 | 3.4 | | | | 5.2 | | 3.7 | 3.7 | 2.3 |
| (97) 8.7 | (88) 6.9 | (90) 7.2 | | % Depr., Dep., Amort./Sales | (11) 7.0 | | (13) 7.2 | (24) 7.3 | (31) 6.3 |
| 18.4 | 12.8 | 11.5 | | | | 28.5 | | 12.1 | 11.2 | 9.0 |
| 1.3 | 1.2 | 1.5 | | | | | | | | |
| (17) 2.3 | (21) 2.6 | (18) 3.4 | | % Officers', Directors' Owners' Comp/Sales | | | | | | |
| 12.2 | 5.1 | 9.3 | | | | | | | | |
| 4402210M | 4646657M | 5504884M | | Net Sales ($) | 7049M | 18899M | 14974M | 112423M | 399572M | 4951967M |
| 5381805M | 4760202M | 5665574M | | Total Assets ($) | 31938M | 39280M | 12184M | 230708M | 357520M | 4993944M |

© RMA 2012

M = $ thousand    MM = $ million
See Pages 9 through 22 for Explanation of Ratios and Data

## Current Data Sorted by Assets      Comparative Historical Data

| Type of Statement | 0-500M | 500M-2MM | 2-10MM | 10-50MM | 50-100MM | 100-250MM | 4/1/07-3/31/08 ALL | 4/1/08-3/31/09 ALL |
|---|---|---|---|---|---|---|---|---|
| Unqualified | 2 | 2 | 7 | 33 | 15 | 11 | 63 | 56 |
| Reviewed | 4 | 26 | 85 | 45 | 1 | 1 | 195 | 180 |
| Compiled | 37 | 52 | 88 | 14 | 2 |  | 231 | 195 |
| Tax Returns | 116 | 127 | 56 | 4 | 1 | 1 | 245 | 233 |
| Other | 73 | 116 | 132 | 62 | 14 | 13 | 347 | 331 |
|  | 136 (4/1-9/30/11) | | | 1,004 (10/1/11-3/31/12) | | | | |
| NUMBER OF STATEMENTS | 232 | 323 | 368 | 158 | 33 | 26 | 1081 | 995 |
| **ASSETS** | % | % | % | % | % | % | % | % |
| Cash & Equivalents | 20.3 | 12.6 | 9.3 | 8.2 | 7.3 | 4.9 | 10.6 | 11.5 |
| Trade Receivables (net) | 18.8 | 31.3 | 32.0 | 26.8 | 24.0 | 22.7 | 26.7 | 25.4 |
| Inventory | 1.0 | 1.8 | 1.6 | 2.6 | 4.4 | .4 | 1.4 | 1.8 |
| All Other Current | 4.4 | 4.2 | 3.4 | 3.1 | 2.9 | 4.4 | 4.0 | 4.0 |
| Total Current | 44.6 | 50.0 | 46.2 | 40.7 | 38.5 | 32.4 | 42.7 | 42.6 |
| Fixed Assets (net) | 40.2 | 38.4 | 40.7 | 49.0 | 50.4 | 50.8 | 45.9 | 44.9 |
| Intangibles (net) | 3.9 | 2.6 | 3.2 | 3.1 | 6.5 | 8.2 | 3.2 | 3.0 |
| All Other Non-Current | 11.3 | 9.0 | 9.8 | 7.1 | 4.6 | 8.6 | 8.2 | 9.4 |
| Total | 100.0 | 100.0 | 100.0 | 100.0 | 100.0 | 100.0 | 100.0 | 100.0 |
| **LIABILITIES** | | | | | | | | |
| Notes Payable-Short Term | 16.9 | 10.5 | 7.9 | 8.5 | 8.3 | 2.2 | 8.8 | 10.8 |
| Cur. Mat.-L.T.D. | 9.8 | 6.4 | 6.4 | 7.8 | 11.1 | 11.1 | 9.2 | 9.0 |
| Trade Payables | 11.0 | 13.6 | 11.2 | 9.8 | 8.2 | 9.3 | 11.1 | 10.5 |
| Income Taxes Payable | .1 | .1 | .2 | .2 | .4 | .5 | .3 | .3 |
| All Other Current | 20.2 | 8.7 | 8.9 | 7.1 | 8.5 | 8.0 | 9.5 | 11.0 |
| Total Current | 58.0 | 39.2 | 34.6 | 33.4 | 36.6 | 31.0 | 38.9 | 41.6 |
| Long-Term Debt | 48.5 | 32.5 | 24.2 | 24.2 | 36.0 | 29.8 | 31.8 | 31.1 |
| Deferred Taxes | .1 | .2 | .9 | 2.0 | 2.1 | 2.5 | .8 | .7 |
| All Other Non-Current | 15.7 | 5.2 | 4.4 | 3.7 | 7.4 | 3.2 | 5.1 | 5.9 |
| Net Worth | -22.3 | 22.8 | 36.0 | 36.8 | 18.0 | 33.6 | 23.4 | 20.6 |
| Total Liabilties & Net Worth | 100.0 | 100.0 | 100.0 | 100.0 | 100.0 | 100.0 | 100.0 | 100.0 |
| **INCOME DATA** | | | | | | | | |
| Net Sales | 100.0 | 100.0 | 100.0 | 100.0 | 100.0 | 100.0 | 100.0 | 100.0 |
| Gross Profit | | | | | | | | |
| Operating Expenses | 96.0 | 94.1 | 93.4 | 94.8 | 94.5 | 94.6 | 95.5 | 95.7 |
| Operating Profit | 4.0 | 5.9 | 6.6 | 5.2 | 5.5 | 5.4 | 4.5 | 4.3 |
| All Other Expenses (net) | .5 | 1.8 | 1.6 | .9 | 1.3 | .9 | 1.2 | 1.5 |
| Profit Before Taxes | 3.5 | 4.1 | 4.9 | 4.3 | 4.2 | 4.5 | 3.2 | 2.9 |
| **RATIOS** | | | | | | | | |
| Current | 2.6 | 2.7 | 2.2 | 1.7 | 1.5 | 1.6 | 2.0 | 2.0 |
|  | 1.1 | 1.3 | 1.4 | 1.2 | 1.1 | 1.1 | 1.1 | 1.1 |
|  | .4 | .7 | .9 | .9 | .9 | .8 | .7 | .6 |
| Quick | 2.3 | 2.3 | 2.1 | 1.4 | 1.3 | 1.5 | 1.7 | 1.7 |
|  | (231) .9 | 1.1 | 1.3 | 1.0 | .9 | .9 | (1080) 1.0 | 1.0 |
|  | .3 | .5 | .7 | .7 | .6 | .5 | .6 | .5 |
| Sales/Receivables | 0 UND | 0 999.8 | 21 17.3 | 29 12.5 | 33 11.1 | 34 10.8 | 14 25.3 | 9 41.7 |
|  | 0 UND | 25 14.7 | 35 10.4 | 38 9.7 | 39 9.3 | 43 8.5 | 31 11.7 | 27 13.3 |
|  | 26 14.2 | 40 9.2 | 49 7.4 | 50 7.3 | 51 7.1 | 51 7.2 | 45 8.1 | 42 8.7 |
| Cost of Sales/Inventory | | | | | | | | |
| Cost of Sales/Payables | | | | | | | | |
| Sales/Working Capital | 21.5 | 11.0 | 10.1 | 14.2 | 17.3 | 14.0 | 13.3 | 13.7 |
|  | 189.9 | 47.4 | 26.5 | 28.7 | 60.1 | 81.7 | 76.2 | 92.0 |
|  | -19.7 | -28.4 | -58.6 | -41.2 | -53.7 | -14.1 | -24.9 | -17.8 |
| EBIT/Interest | 11.5 | 12.4 | 12.1 | 9.3 | 10.2 | 11.2 | 5.7 | 6.6 |
|  | (174) 3.4 | (276) 3.9 | (331) 4.1 | (152) 4.3 | (31) 4.3 | 4.8 | (961) 2.1 | (877) 2.3 |
|  | .2 | 1.2 | 1.5 | 1.9 | 2.0 | 2.8 | .7 | .5 |
| Net Profit + Depr., Dep., Amort./Cur. Mat. L/T/D |  | 9.1 | 3.9 | 2.7 | 3.0 |  | 2.6 | 2.4 |
|  |  | (22) 3.8 | (73) 1.7 | (54) 1.8 | (13) 1.5 |  | (212) 1.5 | (199) 1.5 |
|  |  | 1.1 | 1.2 | 1.2 | 1.1 |  | 1.0 | 1.0 |
| Fixed/Worth | .5 | .3 | .5 | .8 | 1.2 | 1.1 | .7 | .6 |
|  | 3.2 | 1.4 | 1.2 | 1.5 | 2.0 | 2.1 | 1.8 | 1.7 |
|  | -1.0 | 13.3 | 3.0 | 2.5 | 10.2 | 3.5 | 11.3 | 13.8 |
| Debt/Worth | 1.2 | .9 | .9 | 1.0 | 1.3 | 1.3 | 1.1 | 1.0 |
|  | 18.0 | 2.7 | 1.9 | 2.0 | 2.0 | 2.5 | 2.9 | 2.8 |
|  | -2.8 | 32.0 | 5.9 | 3.8 | 13.6 | 9.0 | 23.9 | 28.8 |
| % Profit Before Taxes/Tangible Net Worth | 103.9 | 72.6 | 51.2 | 39.3 | 45.8 | 38.2 | 47.6 | 47.1 |
|  | (126) 32.9 | (258) 26.2 | (322) 23.2 | (150) 19.8 | (26) 24.1 | (23) 21.0 | (855) 17.5 | (778) 19.4 |
|  | 7.2 | 5.1 | 7.0 | 6.7 | 16.4 | 16.5 | 1.6 | 2.7 |
| % Profit Before Taxes/Total Assets | 34.2 | 19.3 | 13.8 | 12.9 | 13.6 | 10.8 | 14.0 | 14.1 |
|  | 8.7 | 7.8 | 6.9 | 6.7 | 7.9 | 6.2 | 4.6 | 4.7 |
|  | -3.2 | .7 | 1.4 | 1.7 | 2.7 | 2.3 | -1.0 | -1.4 |
| Sales/Net Fixed Assets | 73.5 | 49.9 | 22.7 | 9.5 | 9.1 | 6.8 | 20.0 | 21.5 |
|  | 20.1 | 12.2 | 7.5 | 4.2 | 3.4 | 3.0 | 6.4 | 7.2 |
|  | 7.5 | 5.2 | 3.6 | 2.5 | 2.6 | 2.0 | 3.1 | 3.3 |
| Sales/Total Assets | 10.4 | 5.7 | 4.4 | 3.1 | 2.8 | 2.1 | 4.5 | 5.0 |
|  | 5.5 | 4.1 | 2.7 | 2.2 | 2.0 | 1.5 | 2.8 | 3.0 |
|  | 3.0 | 2.4 | 1.9 | 1.5 | 1.6 | 1.2 | 1.7 | 1.8 |
| % Depr., Dep., Amort./Sales | 1.3 | 1.1 | 1.3 | 2.3 | 2.3 |  | 1.9 | 1.9 |
|  | (117) 3.4 | (222) 3.2 | (318) 3.6 | (149) 4.7 | (26) 4.4 |  | (910) 4.6 | (811) 4.6 |
|  | 7.6 | 7.2 | 6.6 | 7.3 | 5.8 |  | 8.7 | 7.9 |
| % Officers', Directors' Owners' Comp/Sales | 2.0 | 1.5 | 1.0 | .4 |  |  | 1.3 | 1.5 |
|  | (97) 4.2 | (148) 2.7 | (144) 1.9 | (32) 1.0 |  |  | (396) 2.8 | (338) 2.7 |
|  | 6.7 | 5.0 | 4.2 | 3.3 |  |  | 5.9 | 5.7 |
| Net Sales ($) | 399520M | 1620465M | 5122243M | 9353316M | 6371341M | 8148299M | 22125752M | 20491156M |
| Total Assets ($) | 56172M | 370576M | 1680265M | 3574313M | 2326150M | 4490564M | 9801992M | 8263007M |

© RMA 2012

M = $ thousand    MM = $ million
See Pages 9 through 22 for Explanation of Ratios and Data

## Comparative Historical Data | Current Data Sorted by Sales

| | | | Type of Statement | | | | | | |
|---|---|---|---|---|---|---|---|---|---|
| 63 | 58 | 70 | Unqualified | 2 | | 1 | 3 | 8 | 56 |
| 173 | 153 | 162 | Reviewed | 2 | 13 | 11 | 27 | 58 | 51 |
| 191 | 202 | 193 | Compiled | 23 | 24 | 26 | 49 | 51 | 20 |
| 274 | 267 | 305 | Tax Returns | 64 | 94 | 44 | 59 | 35 | 9 |
| 349 | 380 | 410 | Other | 50 | 74 | 46 | 69 | 78 | 93 |
| 4/1/09-<br>3/31/10<br>ALL | 4/1/10-<br>3/31/11<br>ALL | 4/1/11-<br>3/31/12<br>ALL | | | 136 (4/1-9/30/11) | | | 1,004 (10/1/11-3/31/12) | |
| | | | | 0-1MM | 1-3MM | 3-5MM | 5-10MM | 10-25MM | 25MM & OVER |
| 1050 | 1060 | 1140 | NUMBER OF STATEMENTS | 141 | 205 | 128 | 207 | 230 | 229 |
| % | % | % | ASSETS | % | % | % | % | % | % |
| 11.1 | 12.0 | 12.2 | Cash & Equivalents | 13.1 | 18.0 | 14.5 | 11.6 | 9.8 | 8.0 |
| 25.3 | 28.2 | 28.0 | Trade Receivables (net) | 12.8 | 20.3 | 28.8 | 31.7 | 35.4 | 32.9 |
| 2.1 | 1.7 | 1.7 | Inventory | .6 | 1.3 | 1.3 | 2.3 | 2.0 | 2.3 |
| 4.4 | 4.1 | 3.8 | All Other Current | 2.2 | 4.6 | 3.2 | 4.3 | 3.7 | 4.1 |
| 42.8 | 46.0 | 45.7 | Total Current | 28.7 | 44.2 | 47.7 | 49.9 | 50.9 | 47.2 |
| 43.5 | 41.0 | 41.6 | Fixed Assets (net) | 58.3 | 42.5 | 37.6 | 37.3 | 37.9 | 40.5 |
| 4.0 | 3.2 | 3.4 | Intangibles (net) | 4.2 | 3.0 | 3.5 | 3.1 | 2.6 | 4.2 |
| 9.7 | 9.8 | 9.3 | All Other Non-Current | 8.9 | 10.3 | 11.1 | 9.7 | 8.7 | 8.1 |
| 100.0 | 100.0 | 100.0 | Total | 100.0 | 100.0 | 100.0 | 100.0 | 100.0 | 100.0 |
| | | | LIABILITIES | | | | | | |
| 11.0 | 10.3 | 10.5 | Notes Payable-Short Term | 11.9 | 10.6 | 11.1 | 8.7 | 12.2 | 8.9 |
| 9.5 | 8.3 | 7.5 | Cur. Mat.-L.T.D. | 10.2 | 6.5 | 9.7 | 5.8 | 6.3 | 8.3 |
| 10.5 | 10.9 | 11.5 | Trade Payables | 7.4 | 11.0 | 10.9 | 12.3 | 13.2 | 12.3 |
| .2 | .2 | .2 | Income Taxes Payable | .1 | .0 | .1 | .1 | .2 | .3 |
| 10.6 | 11.0 | 10.9 | All Other Current | 18.5 | 9.6 | 9.8 | 9.8 | 10.3 | 9.5 |
| 41.8 | 40.7 | 40.5 | Total Current | 48.0 | 37.9 | 41.5 | 36.8 | 42.1 | 39.3 |
| 30.2 | 28.6 | 32.0 | Long-Term Debt | 42.8 | 40.5 | 42.5 | 30.0 | 23.1 | 22.5 |
| .9 | .8 | .8 | Deferred Taxes | .1 | .2 | .3 | .6 | 1.3 | 1.5 |
| 7.1 | 6.4 | 6.9 | All Other Non-Current | 12.5 | 11.1 | 7.6 | 4.8 | 3.6 | 4.5 |
| 20.1 | 23.4 | 19.9 | Net Worth | -3.3 | 10.3 | 8.2 | 27.8 | 30.0 | 32.2 |
| 100.0 | 100.0 | 100.0 | Total Liabilties & Net Worth | 100.0 | 100.0 | 100.0 | 100.0 | 100.0 | 100.0 |
| | | | INCOME DATA | | | | | | |
| 100.0 | 100.0 | 100.0 | Net Sales | 100.0 | 100.0 | 100.0 | 100.0 | 100.0 | 100.0 |
| | | | Gross Profit | | | | | | |
| 96.7 | 95.7 | 94.4 | Operating Expenses | 81.8 | 95.5 | 96.8 | 96.9 | 95.9 | 96.1 |
| 3.3 | 4.3 | 5.6 | Operating Profit | 18.2 | 4.5 | 3.2 | 3.1 | 4.1 | 3.9 |
| 1.6 | .9 | 1.3 | All Other Expenses (net) | 8.1 | .3 | .0 | .1 | .6 | .6 |
| 1.6 | 3.4 | 4.3 | Profit Before Taxes | 10.1 | 4.2 | 3.2 | 3.0 | 3.5 | 3.3 |
| | | | RATIOS | | | | | | |
| 2.1 | 2.2 | 2.3 | | 1.8 | 3.6 | 2.7 | 2.6 | 2.2 | 1.7 |
| 1.1 | 1.2 | 1.3 | Current | .7 | 1.4 | 1.3 | 1.4 | 1.3 | 1.2 |
| .6 | .7 | .7 | | .1 | .6 | .7 | .8 | .9 | .9 |
| 1.8 | 2.0 | 2.0 | | 1.5 | 3.2 | 2.6 | 2.4 | 1.9 | 1.5 |
| .9 (1059) | 1.1 (1139) | 1.1 | Quick | (140) .5 | 1.1 | 1.2 | 1.2 | 1.2 | 1.1 |
| .5 | .6 | .6 | | .1 | .4 | .6 | .6 | .8 | .7 |
| 11 31.8 | 12 29.3 | 6 60.2 | | 0 UND | 0 UND | 1 403.7 | 14 26.1 | 23 15.7 | 29 12.4 |
| 32 11.6 | 32 11.5 | 29 12.4 | Sales/Receivables | 0 UND | 11 32.6 | 24 14.9 | 29 12.4 | 35 10.4 | 39 9.3 |
| 46 8.0 | 47 7.7 | 45 8.2 | | 26 14.3 | 34 10.8 | 49 7.5 | 43 8.4 | 47 7.7 | 48 7.6 |
| | | | Cost of Sales/Inventory | | | | | | |
| | | | Cost of Sales/Payables | | | | | | |
| 11.3 | 11.2 | 12.9 | | 17.2 | 12.1 | 10.0 | 10.9 | 13.2 | 15.4 |
| 82.4 | 46.3 | 42.7 | Sales/Working Capital | -23.9 | 44.9 | 57.4 | 28.3 | 30.1 | 37.4 |
| -16.6 | -27.4 | -30.5 | | -3.3 | -28.0 | -29.1 | -58.5 | -68.3 | -77.9 |
| 6.3 | 9.2 | 11.1 | | 9.8 | 11.6 | 10.8 | 10.7 | 13.5 | 10.7 |
| (927) 1.9 | (927) 3.2 | (990) 4.1 | EBIT/Interest | (84) 2.6 | (169) 4.0 | (111) 3.8 | (191) 3.9 | (220) 4.2 | (215) 4.7 |
| -.4 | 1.0 | 1.3 | | -.4 | .7 | 1.4 | 1.2 | 1.9 | 1.8 |
| 2.3 | 2.5 | 3.9 | | | | 12.8 | 5.0 | 4.7 | 2.9 |
| (188) 1.2 | (177) 1.7 | (168) 1.9 | Net Profit + Dep., Dep., | (12) 2.5 | (23) 1.6 | (52) 2.5 | (70) 1.7 | | |
| .7 | 1.1 | 1.2 | Amort./Cur. Mat. L/T/D | | | 1.1 | 1.2 | 1.3 | 1.1 |
| .6 | .5 | .5 | | 1.0 | .6 | .5 | .3 | .5 | .6 |
| 1.7 | 1.3 | 1.5 | Fixed/Worth | 3.5 | 2.0 | 2.4 | 1.1 | 1.3 | 1.3 |
| 25.5 | 6.6 | 6.7 | | -3.5 | -3.7 | -38.5 | 5.9 | 2.5 | 2.6 |
| .9 | .8 | 1.0 | | 1.3 | .9 | 1.0 | .8 | 1.0 | 1.1 |
| 2.7 | 2.2 | 2.4 | Debt/Worth | 5.9 | 2.7 | 3.6 | 2.1 | 2.1 | 2.2 |
| UND | 14.2 | 19.7 | | -4.7 | -8.0 | -43.0 | 10.8 | 5.1 | 5.6 |
| 33.8 | 46.5 | 57.2 | | 62.5 | 76.8 | 83.6 | 56.5 | 57.2 | 44.6 |
| (790) 10.6 | (854) 18.9 | (905) 23.8 | % Profit Before Taxes/Tangible | (88) 18.7 | (144) 24.3 | (93) 32.6 | (173) 25.7 | (202) 25.1 | (205) 21.9 |
| -5.5 | 2.5 | 7.0 | Net Worth | 2.9 | 4.8 | 10.8 | 5.1 | 7.9 | 10.1 |
| 11.4 | 16.7 | 17.2 | | 18.1 | 24.1 | 17.7 | 17.5 | 17.5 | 13.5 |
| 2.7 | 6.1 | 7.1 | % Profit Before Taxes/Total | 3.8 | 8.1 | 8.0 | 7.1 | 8.0 | 7.3 |
| -5.8 | .0 | .9 | Assets | -.1 | -1.6 | 1.4 | .6 | 1.9 | 1.8 |
| 22.3 | 28.8 | 32.7 | | 19.2 | 37.1 | 51.7 | 33.7 | 41.8 | 20.8 |
| 7.7 | 8.2 | 9.2 | Sales/Net Fixed Assets | 2.7 | 11.5 | 15.0 | 10.6 | 9.4 | 6.5 |
| 3.0 | 3.6 | 3.6 | | .4 | 4.6 | 4.9 | 5.0 | 4.0 | 3.3 |
| 4.8 | 5.0 | 5.3 | | 3.2 | 6.9 | 6.3 | 5.5 | 5.4 | 4.2 |
| 2.7 | 2.9 | 3.2 | Sales/Total Assets | 1.5 | 4.0 | 4.0 | 3.7 | 3.3 | 2.8 |
| 1.6 | 1.8 | 1.9 | | .3 | 2.2 | 2.2 | 2.4 | 2.2 | 1.9 |
| 1.8 | 1.7 | 1.4 | | 5.8 | 1.5 | 1.3 | 1.6 | .9 | 1.1 |
| (804) 5.0 | (821) 3.9 | (839) 3.7 | % Depr., Dep., Amort./Sales | (91) 13.9 | (135) 3.8 | (84) 3.4 | (150) 3.6 | (193) 3.3 | (186) 2.9 |
| 8.9 | 7.6 | 7.0 | | 26.0 | 7.4 | 5.9 | 6.2 | 6.2 | 5.6 |
| 1.6 | 1.5 | 1.3 | | 4.5 | 2.2 | 1.8 | 1.3 | .8 | .5 |
| (389) 3.4 | (395) 3.0 | (427) 2.6 | % Officers', Directors' | (35) 6.5 | (90) 3.7 | (62) 2.8 | (95) 2.1 | (94) 1.8 | (51) 1.0 |
| 6.2 | 5.4 | 5.2 | Owners' Comp/Sales | 16.4 | 5.8 | 5.3 | 4.1 | 3.2 | 3.3 |
| 24314987M | 31202397M | 31015184M | Net Sales ($) | 66386M | 391240M | 507355M | 1517641M | 3654495M | 24878067M |
| 11173569M | 10988437M | 12498040M | Total Assets ($) | 123733M | 173974M | 199522M | 500096M | 1554133M | 9946582M |

© RMA 2012

M = $ thousand    MM = $ million
See Pages 9 through 22 for Explanation of Ratios and Data

## Current Data Sorted by Assets      Comparative Historical Data

| | | | | | | Type of Statement | | |
|---|---|---|---|---|---|---|---|---|
| | 3 | 10 | 37 | 32 | 37 | Unqualified | 137 | 142 |
| 1 | 26 | 125 | 109 | 10 | 1 | Reviewed | 251 | 237 |
| 15 | 83 | 102 | 30 | 1 | 1 | Compiled | 268 | 255 |
| 73 | 69 | 51 | 6 | | | Tax Returns | 147 | 166 |
| 37 | 105 | 158 | 144 | 48 | 41 | Other | 477 | 490 |
| | 167 (4/1-9/30/11) | | 1,188 (10/1/11-3/31/12) | | | | 4/1/07-3/31/08 ALL | 4/1/08-3/31/09 ALL |
| 0-500M | 500M-2MM | 2-10MM | 10-50MM | 50-100MM | 100-250MM | | | |
| 126 | 286 | 446 | 326 | 91 | 80 | NUMBER OF STATEMENTS | 1280 | 1290 |
| % | % | % | % | % | % | ASSETS | % | % |
| 21.3 | 12.0 | 9.5 | 6.7 | 5.7 | 4.3 | Cash & Equivalents | 8.1 | 9.7 |
| 27.8 | 35.2 | 32.9 | 25.5 | 24.2 | 21.0 | Trade Receivables (net) | 28.1 | 26.8 |
| 1.3 | 1.0 | 1.2 | 1.9 | 1.7 | 1.3 | Inventory | 1.5 | 1.4 |
| 4.4 | 4.1 | 4.7 | 3.5 | 3.3 | 5.4 | All Other Current | 4.7 | 5.0 |
| 54.8 | 52.4 | 48.3 | 37.5 | 35.0 | 32.0 | Total Current | 42.3 | 42.9 |
| 32.4 | 35.8 | 40.2 | 52.6 | 52.9 | 52.9 | Fixed Assets (net) | 46.7 | 46.0 |
| 2.2 | 3.7 | 2.4 | 2.9 | 4.8 | 8.8 | Intangibles (net) | 2.3 | 2.2 |
| 10.5 | 8.1 | 9.1 | 7.0 | 7.3 | 6.4 | All Other Non-Current | 8.6 | 8.9 |
| 100.0 | 100.0 | 100.0 | 100.0 | 100.0 | 100.0 | Total | 100.0 | 100.0 |
| | | | | | | LIABILITIES | | |
| 9.8 | 8.4 | 8.1 | 6.4 | 5.1 | 2.6 | Notes Payable-Short Term | 8.4 | 8.4 |
| 7.9 | 7.5 | 8.4 | 10.4 | 9.6 | 11.9 | Cur. Mat.-L.T.D. | 9.8 | 10.2 |
| 19.4 | 13.3 | 10.7 | 7.6 | 9.2 | 6.8 | Trade Payables | 9.5 | 9.6 |
| .1 | .1 | .3 | .1 | .2 | .1 | Income Taxes Payable | .2 | .2 |
| 14.5 | 11.3 | 10.2 | 7.2 | 9.0 | 11.4 | All Other Current | 9.7 | 10.7 |
| 51.7 | 40.5 | 37.7 | 31.8 | 33.1 | 32.8 | Total Current | 37.6 | 39.1 |
| 35.3 | 26.9 | 22.5 | 27.7 | 31.8 | 31.4 | Long-Term Debt | 30.2 | 28.6 |
| .0 | .3 | 1.0 | 2.0 | 3.2 | 5.0 | Deferred Taxes | 1.4 | 1.3 |
| 16.0 | 9.9 | 3.7 | 3.3 | 4.3 | 5.3 | All Other Non-Current | 3.7 | 4.6 |
| -3.0 | 22.3 | 35.1 | 35.2 | 27.6 | 25.5 | Net Worth | 27.1 | 26.3 |
| 100.0 | 100.0 | 100.0 | 100.0 | 100.0 | 100.0 | Total Liabilities & Net Worth | 100.0 | 100.0 |
| | | | | | | INCOME DATA | | |
| 100.0 | 100.0 | 100.0 | 100.0 | 100.0 | 100.0 | Net Sales | 100.0 | 100.0 |
| | | | | | | Gross Profit | | |
| 95.6 | 96.4 | 94.5 | 94.8 | 95.6 | 96.5 | Operating Expenses | 96.2 | 95.9 |
| 4.4 | 3.6 | 5.5 | 5.2 | 4.4 | 3.5 | Operating Profit | 3.8 | 4.1 |
| .6 | .9 | .9 | 1.0 | .8 | 1.5 | All Other Expenses (net) | 1.1 | 1.3 |
| 3.8 | 2.8 | 4.6 | 4.2 | 3.5 | 2.1 | Profit Before Taxes | 2.7 | 2.8 |
| | | | | | | RATIOS | | |
| 3.3 | 3.0 | 2.0 | 1.6 | 1.6 | 1.5 | | 1.7 | 1.8 |
| 1.3 | 1.3 | 1.2 | 1.1 | 1.1 | 1.2 | Current | 1.1 | 1.1 |
| .6 | .7 | .8 | .8 | .8 | .8 | | .7 | .7 |
| 3.1 | 2.5 | 1.8 | 1.4 | 1.4 | 1.3 | | 1.5 | 1.5 |
| 1.1 | 1.2 | 1.1 | 1.0 | .9 | .9 | Quick | .9 | .9 |
| .5 | .6 | .7 | .7 | .6 | .6 | | .6 | .6 |
| 0 UND | 11 34.4 | 24 15.3 | 31 11.9 | 32 11.3 | 35 10.3 | | 23 16.0 | 18 19.8 |
| 8 47.5 | 27 13.4 | 33 11.0 | 36 10.0 | 40 9.1 | 41 9.0 | Sales/Receivables | 33 11.0 | 28 13.0 |
| 24 15.5 | 41 8.9 | 42 8.7 | 45 8.1 | 46 8.0 | 47 7.7 | | 44 8.4 | 38 9.7 |
| | | | | | | Cost of Sales/Inventory | | |
| | | | | | | Cost of Sales/Payables | | |
| 21.0 | 12.4 | 12.5 | 16.3 | 16.7 | 17.6 | | 16.4 | 16.0 |
| 94.0 | 39.3 | 44.9 | 63.3 | 70.4 | 50.2 | Sales/Working Capital | 70.1 | 72.4 |
| -38.5 | -46.8 | -37.7 | -42.2 | -35.1 | -21.9 | | -23.1 | -26.7 |
| 13.2 | 10.3 | 11.1 | 8.6 | 8.4 | 5.6 | | 4.5 | 4.9 |
| (90) 6.1 | (236) 3.2 | (402) 4.2 | (310) 3.9 | (88) 4.1 | (79) 2.6 | EBIT/Interest | (1173) 2.0 | (1173) 2.0 |
| 2.0 | .8 | 1.9 | 2.1 | 1.9 | 1.0 | | .7 | .7 |
| | 2.6 | 3.5 | 2.8 | 2.7 | 3.9 | | 2.3 | 2.2 |
| | (29) 1.6 | (100) 1.8 | (117) 1.5 | (36) 1.1 | (12) 1.4 | Net Profit + Depr., Dep., Amort./Cur. Mat. L/T/D | (336) 1.3 | (302) 1.3 |
| | .6 | 1.3 | 1.1 | .7 | .7 | | .9 | .9 |
| .0 | .3 | .5 | 1.0 | 1.2 | 1.7 | | .7 | .7 |
| .9 | 1.4 | 1.2 | 1.7 | 2.0 | 2.5 | Fixed/Worth | 1.8 | 1.8 |
| 109.0 | -49.0 | 3.0 | 2.9 | 4.7 | 6.6 | | 4.3 | 4.8 |
| 1.0 | .9 | .9 | 1.1 | 1.2 | 1.7 | | 1.2 | 1.1 |
| 3.5 | 3.0 | 2.0 | 2.0 | 2.3 | 3.2 | Debt/Worth | 2.7 | 2.5 |
| -5.8 | -34.0 | 5.7 | 4.4 | 6.9 | 9.0 | | 7.4 | 7.6 |
| 125.4 | 65.2 | 43.9 | 36.0 | 37.7 | 34.3 | | 33.3 | 32.9 |
| (86) 55.4 | (206) 24.6 | (401) 21.5 | (311) 20.0 | (81) 21.2 | (69) 24.6 | % Profit Before Taxes/Tangible Net Worth | (1108) 12.9 | (1088) 13.4 |
| 16.4 | 2.2 | 6.5 | 11.3 | -11.2 | 5.1 | | .0 | 1.3 |
| 33.6 | 16.7 | 14.7 | 11.4 | 10.7 | 8.7 | | 10.3 | 10.1 |
| 16.5 | 6.5 | 7.4 | 6.9 | 6.1 | 3.9 | % Profit Before Taxes/Total Assets | 3.5 | 3.5 |
| 1.4 | -.5 | 2.1 | 3.2 | 2.6 | -.3 | | -1.0 | -.8 |
| 709.7 | 70.3 | 29.9 | 6.7 | 5.9 | 5.7 | | 17.5 | 20.2 |
| 50.2 | 17.4 | 8.2 | 3.8 | 3.1 | 3.0 | Sales/Net Fixed Assets | 5.7 | 5.9 |
| 11.9 | 5.9 | 4.0 | 2.4 | 2.2 | 2.1 | | 2.8 | 3.1 |
| 12.4 | 6.7 | 4.6 | 3.1 | 2.5 | 2.3 | | 4.4 | 4.6 |
| 8.0 | 4.8 | 3.2 | 2.1 | 1.8 | 1.7 | Sales/Total Assets | 2.7 | 2.8 |
| 4.1 | 2.5 | 2.2 | 1.6 | 1.4 | 1.3 | | 1.7 | 1.8 |
| .4 | .5 | 1.4 | 3.0 | 3.2 | 1.3 | | 1.9 | 2.0 |
| (57) 2.1 | (200) 2.8 | (390) 3.5 | (313) 5.9 | (75) 5.1 | (21) 3.7 | % Depr., Dep., Amort./Sales | (1069) 4.9 | (1009) 5.0 |
| 5.3 | 6.4 | 6.3 | 8.6 | 6.8 | 5.4 | | 8.3 | 8.1 |
| 1.1 | 1.4 | 1.1 | .6 | .4 | | | 1.2 | 1.2 |
| (52) 2.6 | (109) 2.7 | (155) 1.8 | (67) 1.2 | (10) 1.1 | | % Officers', Directors' Owners' Comp/Sales | (392) 2.5 | (395) 2.6 |
| 5.6 | 4.8 | 4.0 | 3.6 | 1.4 | | | 5.4 | 5.4 |
| 316984M | 1735203M | 7640534M | 18477598M | 13884154M | 24202122M | Net Sales ($) | 55675103M | 65282580M |
| 32609M | 326873M | 2226856M | 7679185M | 6187099M | 12821464M | Total Assets ($) | 25058200M | 27427207M |

M = $ thousand    MM = $ million
See Pages 9 through 22 for Explanation of Ratios and Data

## Comparative Historical Data | Current Data Sorted by Sales

| | | | Type of Statement | | | | | | |
|---|---|---|---|---|---|---|---|---|---|
| 140 | 122 | 119 | Unqualified | | 1 | 2 | 1 | 7 | 108 |
| 231 | 251 | 272 | Reviewed | 2 | 11 | 7 | 32 | 96 | 124 |
| 214 | 245 | 232 | Compiled | 15 | 29 | 24 | 53 | 74 | 37 |
| 161 | 197 | 199 | Tax Returns | 34 | 36 | 33 | 45 | 41 | 10 |
| 463 | 533 | 533 | Other | 29 | 48 | 41 | 66 | 104 | 245 |
| 4/1/09-<br>3/31/10<br>ALL | 4/1/10-<br>3/31/11<br>ALL | 4/1/11-<br>3/31/12<br>ALL | | | 167 (4/1-9/30/11)<br>0-1MM | 3-5MM | 1,188 (10/1/11-3/31/12)<br>5-10MM | 10-25MM | 25MM & OVER |
| | | | | 0-1MM | 1-3MM | 3-5MM | 5-10MM | 10-25MM | 25MM & OVER |
| 1209 | 1348 | 1355 | NUMBER OF STATEMENTS | 80 | 125 | 107 | 197 | 322 | 524 |
| % | % | % | ASSETS | % | % | % | % | % | % |
| 9.6 | 9.5 | 9.9 | Cash & Equivalents | 14.1 | 14.4 | 13.5 | 11.5 | 10.0 | 6.7 |
| 26.8 | 29.2 | 29.8 | Trade Receivables (net) | 13.0 | 24.6 | 31.4 | 34.4 | 32.5 | 29.9 |
| 1.4 | 1.3 | 1.4 | Inventory | .6 | 1.3 | 1.1 | 1.3 | 1.1 | 1.8 |
| 5.5 | 5.1 | 4.2 | All Other Current | 5.9 | 4.5 | 4.2 | 3.4 | 4.2 | 4.2 |
| 43.3 | 45.2 | 45.3 | Total Current | 33.6 | 44.7 | 50.3 | 50.6 | 47.8 | 42.6 |
| 45.7 | 42.5 | 43.1 | Fixed Assets (net) | 56.1 | 40.6 | 37.5 | 38.8 | 40.7 | 46.0 |
| 2.8 | 2.8 | 3.3 | Intangibles (net) | .8 | 5.1 | 2.9 | 2.5 | 3.0 | 3.9 |
| 8.2 | 9.5 | 8.3 | All Other Non-Current | 9.4 | 9.5 | 9.3 | 8.1 | 8.5 | 7.5 |
| 100.0 | 100.0 | 100.0 | Total | 100.0 | 100.0 | 100.0 | 100.0 | 100.0 | 100.0 |
| | | | LIABILITIES | | | | | | |
| 10.5 | 8.9 | 7.4 | Notes Payable-Short Term | 6.6 | 6.8 | 9.0 | 7.4 | 7.7 | 7.2 |
| 10.2 | 9.0 | 8.9 | Cur. Mat.-L.T.D. | 6.8 | 7.8 | 10.2 | 7.8 | 9.0 | 9.6 |
| 9.7 | 10.9 | 11.0 | Trade Payables | 12.8 | 11.1 | 11.6 | 13.2 | 11.1 | 9.6 |
| .1 | .2 | .2 | Income Taxes Payable | .0 | .1 | .0 | .1 | .3 | .2 |
| 11.2 | 10.5 | 10.1 | All Other Current | 11.5 | 12.3 | 7.4 | 9.1 | 10.7 | 10.0 |
| 41.8 | 39.5 | 37.6 | Total Current | 37.7 | 38.0 | 38.2 | 37.6 | 38.8 | 36.6 |
| 26.8 | 25.8 | 27.0 | Long-Term Debt | 45.1 | 31.3 | 23.5 | 27.3 | 23.8 | 25.8 |
| 1.5 | 1.3 | 1.4 | Deferred Taxes | .2 | .2 | .4 | .6 | 1.2 | 2.5 |
| 5.1 | 5.2 | 6.2 | All Other Non-Current | 8.5 | 14.7 | 14.3 | 6.5 | 3.7 | 3.6 |
| 24.9 | 28.2 | 27.8 | Net Worth | 8.5 | 15.8 | 23.6 | 28.0 | 32.6 | 31.5 |
| 100.0 | 100.0 | 100.0 | Total Liabilities & Net Worth | 100.0 | 100.0 | 100.0 | 100.0 | 100.0 | 100.0 |
| | | | INCOME DATA | | | | | | |
| 100.0 | 100.0 | 100.0 | Net Sales | 100.0 | 100.0 | 100.0 | 100.0 | 100.0 | 100.0 |
| | | | Gross Profit | | | | | | |
| 96.6 | 94.8 | 95.2 | Operating Expenses | 81.2 | 92.8 | 96.1 | 96.1 | 96.6 | 96.6 |
| 3.4 | 5.2 | 4.8 | Operating Profit | 18.8 | 7.2 | 3.9 | 3.9 | 3.4 | 3.4 |
| 1.5 | 1.2 | .9 | All Other Expenses (net) | 7.3 | 1.5 | .6 | .4 | .2 | .5 |
| 1.9 | 3.9 | 3.8 | Profit Before Taxes | 11.5 | 5.7 | 3.3 | 3.5 | 3.2 | 2.8 |
| | | | RATIOS | | | | | | |
| 1.9 | 1.9 | 1.9 | | 2.7 | 3.1 | 3.3 | 3.1 | 1.9 | 1.6 |
| 1.1 | 1.2 | 1.2 | Current | .9 | 1.5 | 1.4 | 1.3 | 1.2 | 1.2 |
| .7 | .8 | .8 | | .4 | .5 | .9 | .8 | .8 | .9 |
| 1.6 | 1.6 | 1.7 | | 2.0 | 2.3 | 3.1 | 2.8 | 1.7 | 1.4 |
| .9 (1207) | 1.0 (1347) | 1.1 | Quick | .6 | 1.1 | 1.2 | 1.2 | 1.1 | 1.0 |
| .5 | .6 | .6 | | .2 | .4 | .7 | .6 | .7 | .7 |
| 21  17.4 | 21  17.2 | 21  17.6 | | 0  UND | 0  UND | 8  47.5 | 20  18.2 | 24  15.4 | 32  11.5 |
| 34  10.8 | 34  10.7 | 33  10.9 | Sales/Receivables | 0  UND | 20  18.1 | 26  14.3 | 30  12.3 | 33  11.2 | 38  9.7 |
| 44  8.4 | 44  8.3 | 43  8.4 | | 23  16.2 | 45  8.2 | 38  9.6 | 40  9.2 | 42  8.7 | 45  8.1 |
| | | | Cost of Sales/Inventory | | | | | | |
| | | | Cost of Sales/Payables | | | | | | |
| 13.5 | 14.1 | 14.2 | | 10.7 | 8.8 | 13.4 | 12.7 | 15.6 | 17.0 |
| 82.4 | 50.6 | 50.8 | Sales/Working Capital | -80.5 | 32.4 | 42.1 | 47.2 | 53.1 | 50.2 |
| -17.4 | -29.1 | -38.5 | | -6.6 | -18.0 | -60.2 | -35.2 | -49.1 | -46.4 |
| 4.9 | 7.8 | 9.9 | | 7.1 | 8.0 | 11.7 | 10.6 | 11.3 | 8.8 |
| 1.7 (1078) | 3.1 (1191) | 4.0 (1205) | EBIT/Interest | (50)  2.6 | (101)  4.2 | (85)  3.9 | (172)  3.5 | (296)  4.4 | (501)  4.1 |
| -.3 | 1.3 | 1.7 | | -.8 | 1.2 | 1.5 | 1.2 | 1.7 | 2.0 |
| 2.0 | 2.7 | 3.0 | | | | | 1.7 | 3.3 | 3.0 |
| 1.2 (273) | 1.5 (295) | 1.6 (296) | Net Profit + Depr., Dep., Amort./Cur. Mat. L/T/D | | (10)  1.3 | (30)  1.6 | (81)  1.7 | (163)  1.5 |
| .8 | 1.0 | 1.1 | | | .9 | .9 | 1.2 | 1.1 |
| .7 | .6 | .6 | | .8 | .2 | .3 | .3 | .5 | .9 |
| 1.7 | 1.5 | 1.5 | Fixed/Worth | 2.1 | 1.6 | 1.2 | 1.5 | 1.4 | 1.7 |
| 4.6 | 3.6 | 4.0 | | 154.7 | 49.8 | 4.0 | 7.3 | 3.3 | 3.1 |
| 1.0 | .9 | 1.0 | | 1.0 | 1.0 | .8 | .8 | 1.0 | 1.2 |
| 2.5 | 2.2 | 2.4 | Debt/Worth | 3.4 | 2.8 | 2.5 | 2.8 | 2.2 | 2.2 |
| 8.8 | 7.2 | 7.9 | | -209.8 | -18.7 | 34.6 | 26.2 | 6.5 | 5.4 |
| 28.7 | 40.0 | 46.6 | | 56.2 | 86.9 | 61.7 | 60.0 | 44.8 | 37.5 |
| 8.5 (1004) | 17.9 (1145) | 22.7 (1154) | % Profit Before Taxes/Tangible Net Worth | (59)  20.0 | (92)  27.0 | (86)  22.1 | (155)  25.2 | (276)  22.9 | (486)  21.6 |
| -6.3 | 4.4 | 8.1 | | 1.2 | 8.9 | 4.0 | 6.5 | 7.3 | 10.4 |
| 8.7 | 13.0 | 14.2 | | 16.7 | 18.2 | 18.3 | 17.9 | 15.3 | 11.2 |
| 2.2 | 5.7 | 7.0 | % Profit Before Taxes/Total Assets | 4.3 | 8.4 | 8.6 | 7.7 | 7.5 | 6.6 |
| -4.1 | .8 | 1.9 | | -.1 | 1.5 | .8 | .4 | 2.1 | 2.5 |
| 19.8 | 24.8 | 29.4 | | 16.2 | 49.5 | 70.9 | 55.7 | 30.0 | 13.7 |
| 5.7 | 6.4 | 6.7 | Sales/Net Fixed Assets | 1.5 | 10.1 | 14.1 | 14.0 | 8.0 | 5.0 |
| 2.7 | 3.2 | 3.2 | | .3 | 2.3 | 5.4 | 4.7 | 3.8 | 2.8 |
| 4.3 | 4.6 | 4.9 | | 3.4 | 5.5 | 7.1 | 6.4 | 4.9 | 3.8 |
| 2.6 | 2.8 | 3.0 | Sales/Total Assets | .9 | 3.0 | 4.9 | 4.2 | 3.2 | 2.4 |
| 1.6 | 1.8 | 1.9 | | .3 | 1.4 | 2.5 | 2.5 | 2.1 | 1.7 |
| 2.1 | 1.8 | 1.5 | | 7.5 | 1.2 | 1.2 | .9 | 1.3 | 1.7 |
| 5.7 (942) | 4.9 (1021) | 4.1 (1056) | % Depr., Dep., Amort./Sales | (49)  20.6 | (78)  3.6 | (70)  4.1 | (155)  3.6 | (283)  3.4 | (421)  4.1 |
| 9.8 | 8.0 | 7.3 | | 48.7 | 14.5 | 6.9 | 6.9 | 6.3 | 6.9 |
| 1.5 | 1.1 | 1.0 | | 1.5 | 1.7 | 1.4 | 1.3 | .8 | .6 |
| 2.8 (353) | 2.3 (417) | 2.1 (395) | % Officers', Directors' Owners' Comp/Sales | (15)  4.8 | (44)  3.4 | (44)  2.9 | (78)  2.2 | (117)  1.7 | (97)  1.2 |
| 6.0 | 4.5 | 4.5 | | 7.5 | 5.6 | 5.4 | 4.3 | 3.4 | 2.8 |
| 49389067M | 64588243M | 66256595M | Net Sales ($) | 39569M | 240128M | 414283M | 1450370M | 5349412M | 58762833M |
| 24328149M | 27350905M | 29274086M | Total Assets ($) | 77651M | 186358M | 178236M | 556388M | 2010275M | 26265178M |

M = $ thousand    MM = $ million
See Pages 9 through 22 for Explanation of Ratios and Data

| Current Data Sorted by Assets | | | | | | | Comparative Historical Data | |
|---|---|---|---|---|---|---|---|---|

### Type of Statement

| 0-500M | 500M-2MM | 2-10MM | 10-50MM | 50-100MM | 100-250MM | Type of Statement | 4/1/07-3/31/08 ALL | 4/1/08-3/31/09 ALL |
|---|---|---|---|---|---|---|---|---|
| 1 | | | 2 | 6 | 5 | Unqualified | 22 | 25 |
| | 1 | 7 | 5 | | 1 | Reviewed | 20 | 19 |
| 5 | 1 | 5 | 3 | | 1 | Compiled | 27 | 19 |
| 5 | 4 | 3 | | | | Tax Returns | 11 | 7 |
| 2 | 12 | 18 | 13 | 8 | 6 | Other | 44 | 49 |
| | | 13 (4/1-9/30/11) | | 101 (10/1/11-3/31/12) | | | | |
| 13 | 18 | 33 | 23 | 14 | 13 | NUMBER OF STATEMENTS | 124 | 119 |

| 0-500M % | 500M-2MM % | 2-10MM % | 10-50MM % | 50-100MM % | 100-250MM % |  | % | % |
|---|---|---|---|---|---|---|---|---|
| | | | | | | **ASSETS** | | |
| 22.8 | 6.5 | 9.8 | 7.0 | 3.8 | 3.8 | Cash & Equivalents | 7.4 | 8.0 |
| 16.3 | 51.2 | 35.2 | 22.4 | 24.0 | 20.0 | Trade Receivables (net) | 26.4 | 27.5 |
| .0 | .4 | 1.3 | 1.2 | .7 | 1.0 | Inventory | 2.1 | 2.1 |
| 12.6 | 2.5 | 4.9 | 6.6 | 7.3 | 5.7 | All Other Current | 5.7 | 4.3 |
| 51.7 | 60.7 | 51.2 | 37.3 | 35.7 | 30.4 | Total Current | 41.5 | 42.0 |
| 32.2 | 28.5 | 41.7 | 55.1 | 56.7 | 59.7 | Fixed Assets (net) | 47.8 | 45.6 |
| 3.8 | 3.4 | 1.5 | 2.0 | 2.7 | 4.3 | Intangibles (net) | 2.9 | 3.6 |
| 12.3 | 7.5 | 5.6 | 5.6 | 5.0 | 5.7 | All Other Non-Current | 7.8 | 8.7 |
| 100.0 | 100.0 | 100.0 | 100.0 | 100.0 | 100.0 | Total | 100.0 | 100.0 |
| | | | | | | **LIABILITIES** | | |
| 16.8 | 7.8 | 5.6 | 3.6 | 5.5 | .6 | Notes Payable-Short Term | 7.0 | 5.2 |
| 2.9 | 4.3 | 5.6 | 11.4 | 8.0 | 17.3 | Cur. Mat.-L.T.D. | 10.1 | 8.8 |
| 3.7 | 15.2 | 10.5 | 11.8 | 8.8 | 8.0 | Trade Payables | 11.5 | 8.8 |
| .1 | .1 | .0 | .2 | .1 | .1 | Income Taxes Payable | .2 | .2 |
| 50.4 | 21.6 | 10.2 | 4.6 | 13.7 | 9.0 | All Other Current | 10.8 | 11.5 |
| 74.0 | 48.9 | 32.0 | 31.5 | 36.2 | 35.0 | Total Current | 39.6 | 34.4 |
| 23.9 | 26.6 | 26.5 | 29.8 | 32.3 | 22.5 | Long-Term Debt | 30.4 | 28.0 |
| .0 | .0 | .3 | 3.1 | 1.5 | 2.3 | Deferred Taxes | 1.0 | 1.3 |
| 17.5 | 9.1 | 1.6 | .7 | 4.5 | 6.6 | All Other Non-Current | 4.3 | 3.5 |
| -15.3 | 15.4 | 39.6 | 34.9 | 25.5 | 33.6 | Net Worth | 24.7 | 32.8 |
| 100.0 | 100.0 | 100.0 | 100.0 | 100.0 | 100.0 | Total Liabilities & Net Worth | 100.0 | 100.0 |
| | | | | | | **INCOME DATA** | | |
| 100.0 | 100.0 | 100.0 | 100.0 | 100.0 | 100.0 | Net Sales | 100.0 | 100.0 |
| | | | | | | Gross Profit | | |
| 85.2 | 94.1 | 91.5 | 90.8 | 97.4 | 97.6 | Operating Expenses | 94.8 | 93.0 |
| 14.8 | 5.9 | 8.5 | 9.2 | 2.6 | 2.4 | Operating Profit | 5.2 | 7.0 |
| 1.4 | 3.5 | 2.4 | 1.8 | .5 | .6 | All Other Expenses (net) | 2.0 | 2.8 |
| 13.4 | 2.4 | 6.1 | 7.4 | 2.1 | 1.8 | Profit Before Taxes | 3.3 | 4.2 |
| | | | | | | **RATIOS** | | |
| 5.1 | 3.5 | 2.7 | 1.7 | 1.5 | 1.4 | Current | 1.5 | 1.7 |
| 1.1 | 1.3 | 1.7 | 1.4 | 1.0 | 1.1 | | 1.0 | 1.2 |
| .5 | .7 | .9 | .8 | .7 | .7 | | .7 | .7 |
| 4.0 | 3.2 | 2.6 | 1.6 | 1.2 | 1.3 | Quick | 1.2 | 1.5 |
| (12) 1.2 | 1.2 | 1.5 | 1.0 | .8 | .9 | | (123) .9 | 1.0 |
| .7 | .7 | .9 | .7 | .6 | .5 | | .6 | .6 |
| 0 UND | 21　17.5 | 18　19.9 | 17　20.9 | 34　10.8 | 33　10.9 | Sales/Receivables | 24　15.4 | 22　16.6 |
| 8　45.3 | 31　11.6 | 30　12.0 | 37　9.9 | 40　9.2 | 40　9.2 | | 34　10.7 | 30　12.3 |
| 38　9.5 | 37　9.9 | 43　8.4 | 43　8.4 | 43　8.5 | 42　8.7 | | 43　8.6 | 39　9.3 |
| | | | | | | Cost of Sales/Inventory | | |
| | | | | | | Cost of Sales/Payables | | |
| 8.4 | 11.8 | 10.1 | 12.2 | 16.7 | 23.7 | Sales/Working Capital | 21.8 | 16.9 |
| 142.2 | 87.0 | 24.9 | 24.9 | 598.5 | 64.0 | | 512.1 | 49.6 |
| -26.4 | -25.8 | -141.2 | -27.3 | -17.5 | -22.7 | | -20.9 | -23.1 |
| | 27.3 | 8.5 | 9.4 | 8.7 | 6.1 | EBIT/Interest | 6.4 | 6.8 |
| | (12) 7.4 | (30) 4.8 | (22) 3.9 | (13) 2.8 | 2.5 | | (112) 2.0 | (100) 2.7 |
| | 1.5 | 3.2 | 2.5 | .6 | .7 | | .6 | .9 |
| | | | | | | Net Profit + Depr., Dep., | 2.1 | 2.7 |
| | | | | | | Amort./Cur. Mat. L/T/D | (31) 1.3 | (33) 1.2 |
| | | | | | | | .9 | .9 |
| .1 | .2 | .7 | .8 | 1.2 | 1.3 | Fixed/Worth | .9 | .6 |
| .5 | .6 | 1.1 | 1.7 | 2.5 | 1.7 | | 1.9 | 1.8 |
| 4.4 | 4.8 | 2.8 | 3.1 | 4.9 | 3.6 | | 5.3 | 8.3 |
| 1.1 | .7 | 1.0 | .9 | 1.2 | 1.0 | Debt/Worth | 1.2 | 1.1 |
| 2.8 | 2.5 | 1.3 | 1.7 | 3.0 | 1.9 | | 2.7 | 2.0 |
| NM | NM | 6.3 | 3.5 | 6.4 | 4.9 | | 8.3 | 18.7 |
| 96.8 | 59.0 | 48.3 | 22.4 | 27.0 | 28.5 | % Profit Before Taxes/Tangible | 43.0 | 41.2 |
| (10) 11.5 | (14) 15.6 | (32) 20.7 | (20) 15.9 | (12) 20.2 | (12) 11.6 | Net Worth | (105) 15.6 | (98) 16.7 |
| -25.9 | 3.1 | 9.5 | 9.0 | 2.3 | .4 | | .7 | 3.1 |
| 25.9 | 27.2 | 14.5 | 8.5 | 7.4 | 8.6 | % Profit Before Taxes/Total | 9.8 | 11.0 |
| 10.0 | 6.4 | 8.3 | 6.5 | 4.2 | 4.0 | Assets | 3.8 | 4.8 |
| -6.6 | -1.8 | 4.0 | 3.7 | -2.4 | -2.2 | | -1.1 | -.3 |
| 170.5 | 97.3 | 18.8 | 6.1 | 5.3 | 5.5 | Sales/Net Fixed Assets | 13.3 | 22.3 |
| 10.7 | 34.6 | 10.1 | 3.1 | 3.9 | 3.4 | | 5.0 | 5.3 |
| 4.9 | 14.0 | 4.1 | 2.5 | 2.7 | 2.7 | | 2.7 | 2.6 |
| 6.0 | 8.1 | 5.4 | 3.4 | 2.6 | 2.5 | Sales/Total Assets | 3.5 | 4.5 |
| 2.7 | 6.4 | 3.3 | 1.9 | 2.1 | 2.3 | | 2.6 | 2.5 |
| 1.2 | 3.7 | 1.9 | 1.6 | 1.8 | 1.6 | | 1.7 | 1.7 |
| | .3 | 1.9 | 1.6 | 2.1 | | % Depr., Dep., Amort./Sales | 2.2 | 1.8 |
| | (15) .8 | (30) 3.6 | (22) 6.6 | (11) 4.7 | | | (99) 5.3 | (91) 4.4 |
| | 3.9 | 7.7 | 8.9 | 6.1 | | | 8.3 | 7.5 |
| | | .9 | | | | % Officers', Directors' | 1.4 | 1.4 |
| | | (12) 1.5 | | | | Owners' Comp/Sales | (32) 2.6 | (29) 2.2 |
| | | 3.5 | | | | | 4.9 | 2.9 |
| 6363M | 116909M | 543107M | 2035428M | 2072259M | 4851844M | Net Sales ($) | 8216990M | 8616177M |
| 2120M | 19961M | 159981M | 557013M | 957699M | 2266479M | Total Assets ($) | 3550159M | 3827601M |

**M = $ thousand　MM = $ million**
See Pages 9 through 22 for Explanation of Ratios and Data

## Comparative Historical Data / Current Data Sorted by Sales

| 4/1/09-3/31/10 ALL | 4/1/10-3/31/11 ALL | 4/1/11-3/31/12 ALL | Type of Statement | 0-1MM | 1-3MM | 3-5MM | 5-10MM | 10-25MM | 25MM & OVER |
|---|---|---|---|---|---|---|---|---|---|
| 19 | 19 | 14 | Unqualified | | | 1 | | | 13 |
| 16 | 25 | 14 | Reviewed | | 1 | 2 | 1 | | 10 |
| 16 | 19 | 15 | Compiled | 4 | 2 | 1 | | 3 | 5 |
| 13 | 10 | 12 | Tax Returns | 6 | | | 1 | 5 | |
| 36 | 50 | 59 | Other | 6 | 2 | 6 | 5 | 16 | 24 |
| | | | | | 13 (4/1-9/30/11) | | 101 (10/1/11-3/31/12) | | |
| 100 | 123 | 114 | **NUMBER OF STATEMENTS** | 16 | 5 | 9 | 8 | 24 | 52 |
| % | % | % | **ASSETS** | % | % | % | % | % | % |
| 8.2 | 9.1 | 8.8 | Cash & Equivalents | 18.0 | | | | 6.5 | 7.0 |
| 28.9 | 29.3 | 29.9 | Trade Receivables (net) | 7.7 | | | | 44.7 | 26.7 |
| 1.6 | 1.6 | .9 | Inventory | .0 | | | | 2.1 | 1.0 |
| 3.5 | 5.3 | 6.1 | All Other Current | 9.0 | | | | 2.2 | 6.5 |
| 42.2 | 45.2 | 45.7 | Total Current | 34.7 | | | | 55.5 | 41.2 |
| 47.6 | 46.0 | 45.1 | Fixed Assets (net) | 49.4 | | | | 37.1 | 51.0 |
| 2.4 | 1.9 | 2.6 | Intangibles (net) | 2.7 | | | | 3.0 | 2.4 |
| 7.8 | 6.9 | 6.6 | All Other Non-Current | 13.3 | | | | 4.4 | 5.4 |
| 100.0 | 100.0 | 100.0 | Total | 100.0 | | | | 100.0 | 100.0 |
| | | | **LIABILITIES** | | | | | | |
| 6.1 | 6.3 | 6.2 | Notes Payable-Short Term | 11.4 | | | | 4.1 | 4.6 |
| 9.3 | 9.5 | 7.9 | Cur. Mat.-L.T.D. | 3.9 | | | | 4.5 | 11.9 |
| 8.4 | 11.4 | 10.2 | Trade Payables | .5 | | | | 15.8 | 10.4 |
| .1 | .2 | .1 | Income Taxes Payable | .1 | | | | .0 | .1 |
| 11.9 | 10.4 | 15.8 | All Other Current | 39.8 | | | | 12.6 | 10.6 |
| 35.8 | 37.8 | 40.2 | Total Current | 55.7 | | | | 37.0 | 37.6 |
| 26.6 | 27.2 | 27.2 | Long-Term Debt | 37.6 | | | | 30.3 | 23.7 |
| 1.5 | 1.5 | 1.2 | Deferred Taxes | .0 | | | | .4 | 2.3 |
| 3.4 | 5.4 | 5.3 | All Other Non-Current | 15.3 | | | | .9 | 3.3 |
| 32.7 | 28.2 | 26.1 | Net Worth | -8.6 | | | | 31.5 | 33.1 |
| 100.0 | 100.0 | 100.0 | Total Liabilities & Net Worth | 100.0 | | | | 100.0 | 100.0 |
| | | | **INCOME DATA** | | | | | | |
| 100.0 | 100.0 | 100.0 | Net Sales | 100.0 | | | | 100.0 | 100.0 |
| | | | Gross Profit | | | | | | |
| 96.0 | 96.2 | 92.5 | Operating Expenses | 73.1 | | | | 97.4 | 97.2 |
| 4.0 | 3.8 | 7.5 | Operating Profit | 26.9 | | | | 2.6 | 2.8 |
| 2.8 | 1.8 | 1.9 | All Other Expenses (net) | 11.5 | | | | -.3 | .4 |
| 1.2 | 2.1 | 5.6 | Profit Before Taxes | 15.4 | | | | 2.9 | 2.4 |
| | | | **RATIOS** | | | | | | |
| 1.9 | 2.1 | 2.0 | Current | 7.0 | | | | 2.6 | 1.7 |
| 1.2 | 1.2 | 1.3 | | 1.0 | | | | 1.7 | 1.2 |
| .8 | .7 | .8 | | .2 | | | | 1.0 | .8 |
| 1.7 | 1.7 | 1.8 | Quick | 8.6 | | | | 2.5 | 1.5 |
| 1.0 | 1.1 | (113) 1.0 | | (15) 1.0 | | | | 1.5 | .9 |
| .6 | .6 | .7 | | .2 | | | | .9 | .7 |
| 31  11.7 | 26  14.3 | 23  16.1 | Sales/Receivables | 0  UND | | | | 26  14.0 | 32  11.5 |
| 37  9.9 | 38  9.6 | 35  10.4 | | 0  UND | | | | 36  10.0 | 39  9.4 |
| 47  7.7 | 44  8.3 | 42  8.7 | | 16  22.6 | | | | 48  7.6 | 42  8.7 |
| | | | Cost of Sales/Inventory | | | | | | |
| | | | Cost of Sales/Payables | | | | | | |
| 14.2 | 11.8 | 12.3 | Sales/Working Capital | 10.3 | | | | 11.4 | 16.5 |
| 37.1 | 46.4 | 38.8 | | UND | | | | 16.3 | 44.7 |
| -25.1 | -20.3 | -37.8 | | -2.8 | | | | NM | -31.4 |
| 3.6 | 7.0 | 9.3 | EBIT/Interest | | | | | 8.5 | 7.1 |
| (89) 1.4 | (109) 2.3 | (99) 3.7 | | | | | | (21) 4.8 | (51) 3.1 |
| -.2 | .3 | 1.7 | | | | | | 3.4 | 1.3 |
| 2.2 | 2.1 | 1.8 | Net Profit + Depr., Dep., Amort./Cur. Mat. L/T/D | | | | | | 1.7 |
| (29) 1.3 | (30) 1.3 | (22) 1.4 | | | | | | (13) | 1.1 |
| .8 | .7 | .9 | | | | | | | .5 |
| .6 | .5 | .6 | Fixed/Worth | .2 | | | | .4 | .8 |
| 1.6 | 1.5 | 1.5 | | 2.0 | | | | 1.3 | 1.8 |
| 3.1 | 6.6 | 3.2 | | 6.8 | | | | 2.6 | 3.3 |
| 1.0 | .8 | .9 | Debt/Worth | 1.3 | | | | 1.0 | 1.0 |
| 1.9 | 1.9 | 1.9 | | 3.0 | | | | 1.5 | 2.0 |
| 5.4 | 9.8 | 6.1 | | 137.1 | | | | 7.7 | 5.3 |
| 19.7 | 25.0 | 41.0 | % Profit Before Taxes/Tangible Net Worth | 82.6 | | | | 46.4 | 25.8 |
| (86) 6.4 | (100) 13.0 | (100) 17.4 | | (13) 9.0 | | | | (21) 27.3 | (47) 17.1 |
| -3.3 | .7 | 5.1 | | 2.7 | | | | 13.0 | 1.4 |
| 6.7 | 10.5 | 12.9 | % Profit Before Taxes/Total Assets | 17.8 | | | | 15.7 | 8.3 |
| 1.1 | 2.9 | 6.3 | | 6.0 | | | | 9.7 | 4.5 |
| -2.7 | -2.4 | .8 | | .3 | | | | 6.1 | .4 |
| 14.5 | 16.6 | 17.6 | Sales/Net Fixed Assets | 140.9 | | | | 26.4 | 9.4 |
| 5.5 | 5.7 | 5.3 | | 4.0 | | | | 10.4 | 4.4 |
| 2.4 | 3.1 | 3.0 | | .4 | | | | 4.5 | 2.9 |
| 3.9 | 4.4 | 4.8 | Sales/Total Assets | 2.8 | | | | 6.7 | 3.4 |
| 2.2 | 2.7 | 2.6 | | .8 | | | | 3.5 | 2.3 |
| 1.5 | 1.8 | 1.7 | | .2 | | | | 2.4 | 1.8 |
| 2.5 | 2.1 | 1.4 | % Depr., Dep., Amort./Sales | | | | | 1.0 | 2.0 |
| (73) 5.0 | (91) 4.3 | (84) 3.8 | | | | | | (21) 3.3 | (35) 4.4 |
| 8.3 | 7.4 | 7.7 | | | | | | 7.4 | 6.6 |
| 1.2 | 1.0 | 1.2 | % Officers', Directors' Owners' Comp/Sales | | | | | | .8 |
| (30) 2.5 | (27) 2.2 | (31) 2.9 | | | | | | (10) | 1.2 |
| 6.2 | 4.4 | 9.8 | | | | | | | 7.4 |
| 5623594M | 9222273M | 9625910M | Net Sales ($) | 5165M | 7877M | 39660M | 59966M | 401800M | 9111442M |
| 2974051M | 4485492M | 3963253M | Total Assets ($) | 11707M | 12923M | 10488M | 92678M | 124467M | 3710990M |

© RMA 2012

M = $ thousand    MM = $ million
See Pages 9 through 22 for Explanation of Ratios and Data

## Current Data Sorted by Assets      Comparative Historical Data

| Type of Statement | 0-500M | 500M-2MM | 2-10MM | 10-50MM | 50-100MM | 100-250MM | | 4/1/07-3/31/08 ALL | 4/1/08-3/31/09 ALL |
|---|---|---|---|---|---|---|---|---|---|
| Unqualified | | | | 3 | | 2 | | 7 | 9 |
| Reviewed | 7 | 10 | 24 | 9 | | | | 32 | 29 |
| Compiled | 22 | 15 | 8 | 3 | | 1 | | 18 | 31 |
| Tax Returns | 14 | 21 | 5 | 1 | | 3 | | 15 | 34 |
| Other | | 28 | 25 | 13 | 3 | | | 36 | 43 |
| | 18 (4/1-9/30/11) | | | 199 (10/1/11-3/31/12) | | | | | |
| NUMBER OF STATEMENTS | 43 | 74 | 62 | 29 | 3 | 6 | | 108 | 146 |
| | % | % | % | % | % | % | | % | % |
| **ASSETS** | | | | | | | | | |
| Cash & Equivalents | 14.9 | 14.4 | 11.6 | 11.1 | | | | 9.8 | 12.4 |
| Trade Receivables (net) | 16.2 | 28.8 | 30.8 | 30.7 | | | | 28.0 | 31.1 |
| Inventory | 1.8 | .7 | .3 | 3.6 | | | | 1.7 | 1.0 |
| All Other Current | 4.1 | 3.4 | 5.4 | 5.7 | | | | 6.7 | 5.4 |
| Total Current | 37.0 | 47.3 | 48.0 | 51.0 | | | | 46.1 | 50.0 |
| Fixed Assets (net) | 32.3 | 31.7 | 35.2 | 29.8 | | | | 38.4 | 31.5 |
| Intangibles (net) | 14.3 | 4.2 | 2.9 | 5.9 | | | | 3.6 | 3.5 |
| All Other Non-Current | 16.4 | 16.8 | 13.9 | 13.3 | | | | 11.9 | 15.0 |
| Total | 100.0 | 100.0 | 100.0 | 100.0 | | | | 100.0 | 100.0 |
| **LIABILITIES** | | | | | | | | | |
| Notes Payable-Short Term | 24.0 | 7.2 | 4.1 | 7.2 | | | | 8.5 | 8.1 |
| Cur. Mat.-L.T.D. | 5.1 | 9.2 | 4.3 | 2.8 | | | | 8.3 | 8.7 |
| Trade Payables | 9.4 | 9.7 | 9.0 | 12.9 | | | | 9.6 | 10.2 |
| Income Taxes Payable | .0 | .2 | .1 | .1 | | | | .1 | .1 |
| All Other Current | 39.5 | 15.8 | 10.3 | 13.5 | | | | 11.2 | 12.5 |
| Total Current | 78.0 | 42.1 | 27.8 | 36.6 | | | | 37.7 | 39.6 |
| Long-Term Debt | 28.1 | 31.4 | 23.2 | 18.3 | | | | 27.7 | 26.1 |
| Deferred Taxes | .0 | .2 | .8 | .6 | | | | .9 | .9 |
| All Other Non-Current | 14.9 | 5.3 | 4.0 | 2.5 | | | | 10.1 | 13.9 |
| Net Worth | -21.0 | 21.0 | 44.3 | 42.1 | | | | 23.6 | 19.4 |
| Total Liabilties & Net Worth | 100.0 | 100.0 | 100.0 | 100.0 | | | | 100.0 | 100.0 |
| **INCOME DATA** | | | | | | | | | |
| Net Sales | 100.0 | 100.0 | 100.0 | 100.0 | | | | 100.0 | 100.0 |
| Gross Profit | | | | | | | | | |
| Operating Expenses | 95.6 | 92.8 | 89.4 | 94.0 | | | | 98.1 | 97.7 |
| Operating Profit | 4.4 | 7.2 | 10.6 | 6.0 | | | | 1.9 | 2.3 |
| All Other Expenses (net) | 2.3 | 2.3 | 3.2 | .3 | | | | .9 | 1.3 |
| Profit Before Taxes | 2.1 | 4.9 | 7.5 | 5.8 | | | | 1.0 | 1.0 |
| **RATIOS** | | | | | | | | | |
| Current | 1.5 | 2.5 | 3.0 | 2.1 | | | | 2.0 | 2.3 |
| | .5 | 1.3 | 1.4 | 1.4 | | | | 1.3 | 1.3 |
| | .2 | .6 | 1.1 | 1.2 | | | | .8 | 1.0 |
| Quick | 1.3 | 2.1 | 3.0 | 1.7 | | | | 1.6 | 2.0 |
| | .4 | 1.3 | 1.3 | 1.3 | | | | 1.1 | 1.1 |
| | .1 | .6 | .9 | .8 | | | | .6 | .7 |
| Sales/Receivables | 0 UND | 11 33.2 | 17 21.2 | 37 9.8 | | | | 21 17.3 | 16 23.1 |
| | 1 364.0 | 26 14.3 | 35 10.5 | 49 7.4 | | | | 38 9.6 | 33 11.1 |
| | 19 18.8 | 48 7.6 | 58 6.3 | 59 6.2 | | | | 52 7.1 | 49 7.5 |
| Cost of Sales/Inventory | | | | | | | | | |
| Cost of Sales/Payables | | | | | | | | | |
| Sales/Working Capital | 32.3 | 9.6 | 6.3 | 7.5 | | | | 10.7 | 11.9 |
| | -51.2 | 31.6 | 16.8 | 17.1 | | | | 26.7 | 31.0 |
| | -4.4 | -25.0 | 51.9 | 28.8 | | | | -40.4 | -434.9 |
| EBIT/Interest | 18.3 | 8.1 | 29.7 | 31.2 | | | | 4.0 | 4.5 |
| | (29) 3.6 | (62) 3.9 | (49) 4.8 | (26) 5.4 | | | | (98) 2.1 | (129) 2.1 |
| | .4 | 1.1 | 1.5 | 3.0 | | | | .4 | -.4 |
| Net Profit + Depr., Dep., Amort./Cur. Mat. L/T/D | | | 3.2 | 9.9 | | | | 4.1 | 3.5 |
| | | (15) 1.8 | (10) 2.9 | | | | | (27) 1.8 | (44) 1.6 |
| | | | .8 | 1.8 | | | | .9 | .6 |
| Fixed/Worth | .3 | .2 | .2 | .3 | | | | .6 | .5 |
| | 6.9 | .7 | .7 | .6 | | | | 1.2 | 1.0 |
| | -.2 | 4.0 | 1.7 | 1.9 | | | | 5.1 | 3.1 |
| Debt/Worth | 1.9 | .7 | .5 | .7 | | | | 1.0 | .8 |
| | UND | 1.6 | 1.4 | 1.9 | | | | 2.2 | 2.0 |
| | -1.7 | 11.2 | 3.2 | 3.5 | | | | 10.0 | 6.8 |
| % Profit Before Taxes/Tangible Net Worth | 139.4 | 39.3 | 34.4 | 53.2 | | | | 36.0 | 34.7 |
| | (22) 48.5 | (58) 10.1 | (59) 12.5 | (27) 25.5 | | | | (89) 9.1 | (121) 8.5 |
| | 15.1 | 2.7 | 3.2 | 8.8 | | | | -1.6 | -1.2 |
| % Profit Before Taxes/Total Assets | 26.6 | 16.3 | 9.8 | 19.0 | | | | 9.8 | 9.8 |
| | 10.7 | 5.0 | 4.7 | 7.1 | | | | 3.6 | 2.6 |
| | -8.8 | .5 | 1.6 | 3.3 | | | | -3.0 | -2.0 |
| Sales/Net Fixed Assets | 75.7 | 35.9 | 31.2 | 29.5 | | | | 16.7 | 31.7 |
| | 37.4 | 16.7 | 10.5 | 13.3 | | | | 8.3 | 14.4 |
| | 11.4 | 5.7 | 2.9 | 3.0 | | | | 3.6 | 5.3 |
| Sales/Total Assets | 9.0 | 5.0 | 4.0 | 3.3 | | | | 3.7 | 5.0 |
| | 6.1 | 3.3 | 2.5 | 2.2 | | | | 2.6 | 3.4 |
| | 2.7 | 2.1 | 1.3 | 1.1 | | | | 1.7 | 2.1 |
| % Depr., Dep., Amort./Sales | .4 | .8 | 1.4 | .6 | | | | 1.6 | 1.1 |
| | (30) 1.6 | (63) 1.7 | (55) 2.6 | (23) 1.9 | | | | (94) 2.8 | (123) 2.5 |
| | 3.5 | 4.1 | 5.4 | 2.9 | | | | 4.4 | 4.0 |
| % Officers', Directors' Owners' Comp/Sales | 1.5 | 3.1 | .7 | | | | | 1.5 | 2.3 |
| | (22) 2.8 | (32) 4.1 | (15) 1.8 | | | | | (32) 4.3 | (52) 3.2 |
| | 5.6 | 7.5 | 5.1 | | | | | 9.3 | 6.8 |
| Net Sales ($) | 51380M | 285782M | 724263M | 1171841M | 225359M | 3204258M | | 2639031M | 4316329M |
| Total Assets ($) | 10088M | 83303M | 264128M | 530153M | 177807M | 1125464M | | 1289952M | 1633344M |

## Comparative Historical Data    ·    Current Data Sorted by Sales

| 4/1/09-3/31/10 ALL | 4/1/10-3/31/11 ALL | 4/1/11-3/31/12 ALL | Type of Statement | 0-1MM | 1-3MM | 3-5MM | 5-10MM | 10-25MM | 25MM & OVER |
|---|---|---|---|---|---|---|---|---|---|
| 8 | 14 | 5 | Unqualified | | | | | | 5 |
| 43 | 42 | 43 | Reviewed | 1 | 4 | 8 | 9 | 15 | 6 |
| 39 | 42 | 33 | Compiled | 6 | 5 | 7 | 9 | 5 | 1 |
| 34 | 49 | 50 | Tax Returns | 16 | 15 | 11 | 5 | 5 | 3 |
| 64 | 66 | 86 | Other | 12 | 25 | 9 | 5 | 12 | 19 |
| | | | | 18 (4/1-9/30/11) | | | 199 (10/1/11-3/31/12) | | |
| 188 | 213 | 217 | NUMBER OF STATEMENTS | 35 | 49 | 35 | 32 | 32 | 34 |
| % | % | % | ASSETS | % | % | % | % | % | % |
| 12.5 | 13.8 | 12.8 | Cash & Equivalents | 9.5 | 17.3 | 13.9 | 13.7 | 13.5 | 7.0 |
| 30.0 | 29.8 | 27.4 | Trade Receivables (net) | 6.6 | 25.6 | 24.5 | 32.3 | 38.1 | 39.6 |
| .5 | 1.5 | 1.1 | Inventory | 1.9 | .5 | .4 | .9 | .6 | 2.7 |
| 5.5 | 4.4 | 4.5 | All Other Current | .2 | 5.0 | 3.8 | 4.9 | 7.3 | 6.2 |
| 48.5 | 49.5 | 45.8 | Total Current | 18.3 | 48.4 | 42.5 | 51.7 | 59.6 | 55.5 |
| 33.9 | 34.4 | 33.1 | Fixed Assets (net) | 51.7 | 30.5 | 30.3 | 32.2 | 26.2 | 27.6 |
| 4.3 | 3.6 | 6.0 | Intangibles (net) | 13.2 | 4.5 | 7.6 | 1.2 | 3.7 | 5.9 |
| 13.4 | 12.5 | 15.1 | All Other Non-Current | 16.8 | 16.6 | 19.6 | 14.9 | 10.5 | 11.1 |
| 100.0 | 100.0 | 100.0 | Total | 100.0 | 100.0 | 100.0 | 100.0 | 100.0 | 100.0 |
| | | | LIABILITIES | | | | | | |
| 8.4 | 8.9 | 9.8 | Notes Payable-Short Term | 8.3 | 19.8 | 4.7 | 6.4 | 5.5 | 9.6 |
| 8.4 | 6.8 | 5.9 | Cur. Mat.-L.T.D. | 5.0 | 7.0 | 11.7 | 5.5 | 1.8 | 3.5 |
| 10.3 | 10.6 | 9.9 | Trade Payables | 4.6 | 9.3 | 6.8 | 14.2 | 9.3 | 16.1 |
| .3 | .2 | .1 | Income Taxes Payable | .0 | .1 | .3 | .1 | .1 | .2 |
| 16.7 | 14.9 | 18.4 | All Other Current | 25.3 | 23.1 | 14.2 | 17.2 | 15.5 | 12.8 |
| 44.1 | 41.4 | 44.2 | Total Current | 43.2 | 59.4 | 37.8 | 43.4 | 32.2 | 42.2 |
| 26.0 | 24.3 | 26.5 | Long-Term Debt | 46.5 | 25.9 | 24.6 | 28.7 | 12.7 | 19.9 |
| .3 | .8 | .4 | Deferred Taxes | .0 | .2 | .3 | .7 | .6 | .5 |
| 8.1 | 9.8 | 6.6 | All Other Non-Current | 7.2 | 11.0 | 4.1 | 7.0 | 2.2 | 6.2 |
| 21.4 | 23.8 | 22.2 | Net Worth | 3.1 | 3.5 | 33.2 | 20.2 | 52.2 | 31.1 |
| 100.0 | 100.0 | 100.0 | Total Liabilities & Net Worth | 100.0 | 100.0 | 100.0 | 100.0 | 100.0 | 100.0 |
| | | | INCOME DATA | | | | | | |
| 100.0 | 100.0 | 100.0 | Net Sales | 100.0 | 100.0 | 100.0 | 100.0 | 100.0 | 100.0 |
| | | | Gross Profit | | | | | | |
| 97.2 | 92.1 | 92.8 | Operating Expenses | 73.9 | 96.8 | 95.6 | 98.4 | 94.6 | 96.5 |
| 2.8 | 7.9 | 7.2 | Operating Profit | 26.1 | 3.2 | 4.4 | 1.6 | 5.4 | 3.5 |
| 2.0 | 2.3 | 2.2 | All Other Expenses (net) | 12.6 | .3 | .2 | .1 | .0 | .3 |
| .7 | 5.6 | 5.0 | Profit Before Taxes | 13.5 | 3.0 | 4.2 | 1.5 | 5.4 | 3.2 |
| | | | RATIOS | | | | | | |
| 2.9 | 2.5 | 2.2 | | 1.5 | 3.6 | 2.8 | 2.1 | 3.0 | 2.0 |
| 1.4 | 1.5 | 1.3 | Current | .5 | 1.2 | 1.3 | 1.3 | 1.9 | 1.3 |
| .7 | .7 | .6 | | .2 | .4 | .5 | 1.0 | 1.3 | 1.2 |
| 2.4 | 2.3 | 2.0 | | 1.5 | 3.4 | 2.1 | 1.9 | 3.0 | 1.4 |
| 1.2 | 1.2 | 1.2 | Quick | .5 | 1.2 | 1.2 | 1.2 | 1.5 | 1.2 |
| .6 | .7 | .6 | | .2 | .4 | .4 | .8 | 1.1 | .9 |
| 19 19.7 | 17 21.7 | 5 74.8 | | 0 UND | 1 323.7 | 9 40.9 | 22 16.8 | 31 11.7 | 38 9.7 |
| 38 9.7 | 35 10.3 | 31 11.6 | Sales/Receivables | 0 UND | 21 17.0 | 24 15.1 | 36 10.2 | 44 8.3 | 49 7.4 |
| 57 6.4 | 53 6.9 | 54 6.8 | | 8 44.4 | 54 6.7 | 46 8.0 | 54 6.7 | 68 5.4 | 57 6.4 |
| | | | Cost of Sales/Inventory | | | | | | |
| | | | Cost of Sales/Payables | | | | | | |
| 9.0 | 9.8 | 9.1 | | 23.8 | 8.1 | 9.5 | 9.1 | 6.5 | 11.9 |
| 26.1 | 21.2 | 30.9 | Sales/Working Capital | -10.7 | 39.6 | 20.6 | 39.3 | 13.7 | 24.5 |
| -23.3 | -28.8 | -30.0 | | -2.7 | -13.3 | -49.9 | -211.7 | 31.0 | 46.3 |
| 7.8 | 13.8 | 13.5 | | 8.6 | 10.0 | 13.8 | 10.0 | 74.9 | 10.0 |
| (158) 1.8 | (178) 3.3 | (175) 4.1 | EBIT/Interest | (20) 4.2 | (39) 3.4 | (29) 4.0 | (30) 2.8 | (25) 8.3 | (32) 3.3 |
| -2.0 | 1.1 | 1.5 | | 1.1 | 1.2 | 1.1 | .9 | 3.3 | 2.5 |
| 3.7 | 3.8 | 7.3 | Net Profit + Depr., Dep., | | | | | | 7.3 |
| (44) 1.7 | (56) 1.7 | (38) 2.9 | Amort./Cur. Mat. L/T/D | | | | | (15) 3.3 | |
| .1 | 1.0 | 1.6 | | | | | | | 1.9 |
| .4 | .4 | .3 | | 1.9 | .2 | .2 | .3 | .1 | .4 |
| .9 | 1.0 | .8 | Fixed/Worth | 6.9 | 1.5 | .6 | .8 | .4 | .7 |
| 4.0 | 5.1 | 4.9 | | -1.2 | -1.7 | 4.9 | 2.3 | .9 | 2.1 |
| .7 | .7 | .7 | | 1.6 | .5 | .5 | 1.0 | .4 | 1.3 |
| 1.7 | 2.1 | 2.0 | Debt/Worth | 12.3 | 2.6 | 1.0 | 2.1 | .8 | 2.0 |
| 10.1 | 9.9 | 11.4 | | -2.3 | -4.9 | 5.3 | 4.9 | 2.3 | 4.8 |
| 30.3 | 50.2 | 42.5 | % Profit Before Taxes/Tangible | 79.0 | 83.3 | 43.5 | 25.3 | 45.9 | 42.6 |
| (151) 7.0 | (173) 17.6 | (173) 16.4 | Net Worth | (21) 21.4 | (35) 23.7 | (28) 11.5 | (29) 5.0 | 22.9 | (28) 20.8 |
| -6.4 | 2.5 | 3.6 | | 2.9 | 3.3 | 1.0 | .5 | 8.4 | 8.1 |
| 10.1 | 17.8 | 18.2 | % Profit Before Taxes/Total | 21.1 | 24.6 | 19.7 | 8.6 | 18.8 | 17.1 |
| 1.7 | 5.2 | 5.9 | Assets | 7.3 | 6.0 | 7.3 | 2.1 | 7.7 | 5.7 |
| -5.3 | .4 | .8 | | .0 | -.2 | .4 | .0 | 3.4 | 2.8 |
| 28.2 | 32.4 | 38.3 | | 44.0 | 42.1 | 27.0 | 36.0 | 93.8 | 28.6 |
| 12.0 | 12.8 | 14.7 | Sales/Net Fixed Assets | 2.4 | 15.8 | 16.4 | 14.7 | 20.7 | 14.6 |
| 4.1 | 4.3 | 4.3 | | .2 | 10.2 | 8.7 | 4.1 | 5.5 | 6.4 |
| 4.3 | 4.5 | 4.7 | | 3.3 | 6.3 | 5.0 | 5.0 | 4.1 | 4.2 |
| 2.8 | 3.0 | 3.0 | Sales/Total Assets | .9 | 3.3 | 3.2 | 3.9 | 3.1 | 2.9 |
| 1.7 | 1.7 | 1.7 | | .2 | 2.2 | 2.2 | 1.8 | 1.9 | 1.8 |
| 1.6 | 1.5 | .8 | | 2.3 | .8 | .8 | 1.3 | .3 | 1.0 |
| (151) 2.9 | (174) 2.7 | (178) 2.2 | % Depr., Dep., Amort./Sales | (27) 14.1 | (37) 2.3 | (34) 1.3 | (27) 2.6 | (25) 1.6 | (28) 2.0 |
| 4.8 | 4.5 | 4.1 | | 22.1 | 3.7 | 2.8 | 4.1 | 2.4 | 3.3 |
| 2.2 | 2.2 | 1.8 | % Officers', Directors' | | 2.5 | 2.1 | 1.0 | | |
| (62) 4.9 | (71) 4.7 | (74) 3.5 | Owners' Comp/Sales | | (26) 4.0 | (19) 4.1 | (13) 3.5 | | |
| 9.0 | 9.0 | | | | 8.5 | 5.4 | 4.4 | | |
| 3010282M | 5107332M | 5662883M | Net Sales ($) | 17106M | 94113M | 141430M | 245733M | 512169M | 4652332M |
| 1258368M | 1963830M | 2190943M | Total Assets ($) | 39306M | 34307M | 61051M | 100667M | 227020M | 1728592M |

M = $ thousand    MM = $ million
See Pages 9 through 22 for Explanation of Ratios and Data

## Current Data Sorted by Assets | | Comparative Historical Data

| | | | | | | | Type of Statement | | | |
|---|---|---|---|---|---|---|---|---|---|---|
| | | 1 | 6 | 9 | 3 | 2 | Unqualified | | 12 | 11 |
| | 3 | 11 | 21 | 24 | 4 | | Reviewed | | 28 | 48 |
| | 13 | 19 | 19 | 2 | 1 | 1 | Compiled | | 36 | 46 |
| | 41 | 31 | 5 | 2 | | | Tax Returns | | 54 | 45 |
| | 11 | 22 | 32 | 24 | 3 | 1 | Other | | 73 | 86 |
| | | 39 (4/1-9/30/11) | | 272 (10/1/11-3/31/12) | | | | | 4/1/07-3/31/08 | 4/1/08-3/31/09 |
| | 0-500M | 500M-2MM | 2-10MM | 10-50MM | 50-100MM | 100-250MM | | | ALL | ALL |
| | 68 | 84 | 83 | 61 | 11 | 4 | NUMBER OF STATEMENTS | | 203 | 236 |
| | % | % | % | % | % | % | ASSETS | | % | % |
| | 22.2 | 12.8 | 12.2 | 7.9 | 4.7 | | Cash & Equivalents | | 9.9 | 10.8 |
| | 21.8 | 28.8 | 26.9 | 25.8 | 24.5 | | Trade Receivables (net) | | 26.2 | 23.7 |
| | .6 | 1.4 | 1.3 | 2.3 | 2.4 | | Inventory | | 2.4 | 1.7 |
| | 5.3 | 5.3 | 3.1 | 5.3 | 1.7 | | All Other Current | | 5.9 | 6.0 |
| | 50.0 | 48.3 | 43.5 | 41.3 | 33.4 | | Total Current | | 44.4 | 42.2 |
| | 31.3 | 39.0 | 47.9 | 46.7 | 49.3 | | Fixed Assets (net) | | 43.2 | 46.1 |
| | 6.9 | 3.9 | 3.2 | 4.6 | 9.2 | | Intangibles (net) | | 2.7 | 2.1 |
| | 11.8 | 8.8 | 5.4 | 7.4 | 8.2 | | All Other Non-Current | | 9.7 | 9.6 |
| | 100.0 | 100.0 | 100.0 | 100.0 | 100.0 | | Total | | 100.0 | 100.0 |
| | | | | | | | LIABILITIES | | | |
| | 16.4 | 14.7 | 5.1 | 4.4 | 6.7 | | Notes Payable-Short Term | | 11.1 | 11.7 |
| | 10.4 | 7.0 | 7.6 | 8.5 | 6.8 | | Cur. Mat.-L.T.D. | | 6.8 | 9.0 |
| | 14.8 | 12.7 | 8.9 | 8.3 | 6.7 | | Trade Payables | | 14.1 | 11.0 |
| | .0 | .4 | .5 | .1 | .1 | | Income Taxes Payable | | .2 | .3 |
| | 17.3 | 7.6 | 5.8 | 7.0 | 7.9 | | All Other Current | | 8.5 | 10.2 |
| | 58.9 | 42.4 | 27.9 | 28.3 | 28.1 | | Total Current | | 40.7 | 42.3 |
| | 53.3 | 27.2 | 24.2 | 23.9 | 26.3 | | Long-Term Debt | | 28.8 | 29.2 |
| | .0 | .3 | 1.4 | .8 | 3.2 | | Deferred Taxes | | .6 | .9 |
| | 12.2 | 4.3 | 6.2 | 2.3 | 4.6 | | All Other Non-Current | | 3.2 | 5.5 |
| | -24.5 | 25.8 | 40.3 | 44.7 | 37.8 | | Net Worth | | 26.7 | 22.2 |
| | 100.0 | 100.0 | 100.0 | 100.0 | 100.0 | | Total Liabilities & Net Worth | | 100.0 | 100.0 |
| | | | | | | | INCOME DATA | | | |
| | 100.0 | 100.0 | 100.0 | 100.0 | 100.0 | | Net Sales | | 100.0 | 100.0 |
| | | | | | | | Gross Profit | | | |
| | 94.6 | 92.9 | 91.8 | 92.7 | 92.1 | | Operating Expenses | | 96.2 | 95.3 |
| | 5.4 | 7.1 | 8.2 | 7.3 | 7.9 | | Operating Profit | | 3.8 | 4.7 |
| | .0 | .6 | .1 | .8 | 1.1 | | All Other Expenses (net) | | .5 | 1.3 |
| | 5.4 | 6.5 | 8.1 | 6.5 | 6.8 | | Profit Before Taxes | | 3.3 | 3.4 |
| | | | | | | | RATIOS | | | |
| | 2.6 | 2.8 | 2.3 | 2.2 | 1.7 | | | | 2.0 | 2.0 |
| | 1.2 | 1.4 | 1.5 | 1.4 | 1.3 | | Current | | 1.2 | 1.2 |
| | .2 | .8 | 1.0 | .9 | .9 | | | | .6 | .7 |
| | 2.3 | 2.4 | 2.0 | 2.0 | 1.4 | | | | 1.6 | 1.7 |
| (67) | 1.1 | 1.2 | 1.4 | 1.1 | 1.2 | | Quick | | .9 | .9 |
| | .2 | .6 | .8 | .7 | .7 | | | | .4 | .5 |
| 0 UND | 0 UND | 26 14.3 | 26 14.0 | 36 10.0 | | | | 10 36.2 | 10 37.8 | |
| 5 77.0 | 25 14.6 | 35 10.4 | 35 10.5 | 43 8.5 | | | Sales/Receivables | 28 13.2 | 25 14.5 | |
| 29 12.4 | 42 8.6 | 49 7.4 | 49 7.4 | 51 7.1 | | | | 42 8.7 | 39 9.4 | |
| | | | | | | | Cost of Sales/Inventory | | | |
| | | | | | | | Cost of Sales/Payables | | | |
| | 17.6 | 10.8 | 9.6 | 8.9 | 15.4 | | | | 12.7 | 13.7 |
| | 116.2 | 35.4 | 19.4 | 26.3 | 27.4 | | Sales/Working Capital | | 48.9 | 65.2 |
| | -20.7 | -69.8 | -323.3 | -72.3 | -41.3 | | | | -22.7 | -21.6 |
| | 10.4 | 11.3 | 15.5 | 20.7 | | | | | 7.7 | 7.8 |
| (55) | 3.7 (75) | 4.1 (76) | 5.2 (58) | 5.8 | | | EBIT/Interest | (179) | 2.7 (207) | 2.8 |
| | 1.0 | 1.5 | 1.7 | 2.4 | | | | | 1.1 | .9 |
| | | | 3.0 | 2.6 | | | | | 6.0 | 5.3 |
| | | (18) | 1.8 (16) | 1.6 | | | Net Profit + Depr., Dep., | (46) | 1.7 (51) | 1.9 |
| | | | 1.6 | 1.3 | | | Amort./Cur. Mat. L/T/D | | 1.1 | 1.0 |
| | .1 | .4 | .7 | .6 | 1.2 | | | | .6 | .6 |
| | 5.1 | 1.1 | 1.3 | 1.2 | 1.6 | | Fixed/Worth | | 1.5 | 1.5 |
| | -.7 | 14.0 | 2.2 | 2.5 | -2.4 | | | | 6.0 | 6.1 |
| | 1.8 | .8 | .8 | .7 | .8 | | | | 1.0 | .8 |
| | -24.0 | 3.1 | 1.7 | 1.4 | 1.5 | | Debt/Worth | | 3.0 | 2.4 |
| | -2.6 | 75.4 | 3.1 | 2.9 | -4.4 | | | | 11.3 | 9.5 |
| | 170.0 | 71.2 | 50.1 | 36.0 | | | % Profit Before Taxes/Tangible | | 59.0 | 51.8 |
| (32) | 37.0 (65) | 29.7 (77) | 29.1 (57) | 19.8 | | | Net Worth | (167) | 21.8 (195) | 20.1 |
| | 6.7 | 7.8 | 9.0 | 6.8 | | | | | 7.4 | 4.6 |
| | 43.2 | 20.0 | 19.2 | 16.8 | 21.6 | | % Profit Before Taxes/Total | | 15.5 | 15.6 |
| | 18.1 | 9.0 | 10.5 | 7.2 | 11.6 | | Assets | | 7.5 | 5.8 |
| | .1 | 1.9 | 2.2 | 3.1 | .7 | | | | .4 | -.7 |
| | 520.0 | 41.3 | 8.8 | 6.6 | 8.9 | | | | 20.8 | 18.4 |
| | 29.5 | 10.2 | 4.6 | 4.9 | 3.8 | | Sales/Net Fixed Assets | | 7.6 | 6.3 |
| | 10.8 | 5.5 | 3.0 | 3.2 | 2.7 | | | | 3.7 | 3.3 |
| | 10.6 | 5.4 | 3.4 | 3.0 | 2.6 | | | | 4.6 | 4.6 |
| | 6.7 | 3.7 | 2.2 | 2.3 | 2.1 | | Sales/Total Assets | | 2.9 | 2.6 |
| | 2.9 | 2.2 | 1.6 | 1.7 | 1.7 | | | | 2.0 | 1.9 |
| | 1.0 | 2.0 | 2.6 | 2.3 | 2.4 | | | | 1.8 | 1.6 |
| (32) | 3.8 (57) | 4.8 (74) | 5.5 (58) | 3.8 (10) | 4.0 | | % Depr., Dep., Amort./Sales | (168) | 4.9 (199) | 4.3 |
| | 8.8 | 8.0 | 8.5 | 7.1 | 5.8 | | | | 8.4 | 8.5 |
| | 2.4 | 1.3 | 1.1 | .3 | | | % Officers', Directors' | | 1.1 | 1.3 |
| (29) | 5.3 (39) | 3.3 (24) | 1.6 (13) | .9 | | | Owners' Comp/Sales | (81) | 2.8 (89) | 3.3 |
| | 9.7 | 7.0 | 4.2 | 1.6 | | | | | 6.4 | 6.9 |
| | 119101M | 403675M | 977286M | 2906330M | 1566327M | 729227M | Net Sales ($) | | 7040280M | 5836992M |
| | 16511M | 97468M | 394640M | 1206119M | 682497M | 611987M | Total Assets ($) | | 1289395M | 2303670M |

M = $ thousand   MM = $ million
See Pages 9 through 22 for Explanation of Ratios and Data

| Comparative Historical Data | | | Type of Statement | Current Data Sorted by Sales | | | | | |
|---|---|---|---|---|---|---|---|---|---|
| 7 | 12 | 21 | Unqualified | | 1 | 2 | 3 | | 15 |
| 49 | 69 | 63 | Reviewed | 1 | 5 | 8 | 7 | 16 | 26 |
| 39 | 46 | 55 | Compiled | 5 | 15 | 8 | 14 | 9 | 4 |
| 60 | 67 | 79 | Tax Returns | 26 | 19 | 16 | 13 | 2 | 3 |
| 94 | 94 | 93 | Other | 8 | 12 | 15 | 8 | 27 | 23 |
| 4/1/09-3/31/10 | 4/1/10-3/31/11 | 4/1/11-3/31/12 | | 39 (4/1-9/30/11) | | 272 (10/1/11-3/31/12) | | | |
| ALL | ALL | ALL | | 0-1MM | 1-3MM | 3-5MM | 5-10MM | 10-25MM | 25MM & OVER |
| 249 | 288 | 311 | **NUMBER OF STATEMENTS** | 40 | 52 | 49 | 45 | 54 | 71 |
| % | % | % | **ASSETS** | % | % | % | % | % | % |
| 12.0 | 13.2 | 13.3 | Cash & Equivalents | 18.8 | 18.8 | 10.7 | 15.2 | 11.9 | 8.0 |
| 23.1 | 24.6 | 25.9 | Trade Receivables (net) | 13.3 | 24.8 | 23.7 | 32.6 | 29.5 | 28.2 |
| 1.8 | 1.3 | 1.4 | Inventory | .3 | 1.0 | 1.9 | .9 | 1.7 | 2.3 |
| 4.5 | 5.0 | 4.5 | All Other Current | 3.6 | 3.1 | 8.8 | 3.9 | 2.6 | 5.1 |
| 41.3 | 44.1 | 45.2 | Total Current | 36.0 | 47.7 | 45.1 | 52.5 | 45.6 | 43.5 |
| 45.8 | 43.4 | 41.7 | Fixed Assets (net) | 45.5 | 36.2 | 40.1 | 40.3 | 46.6 | 41.7 |
| 2.7 | 4.1 | 5.0 | Intangibles (net) | 10.8 | 1.6 | 6.2 | 1.1 | 2.8 | 7.6 |
| 10.0 | 8.4 | 8.1 | All Other Non-Current | 7.7 | 14.5 | 8.5 | 6.1 | 5.0 | 7.2 |
| 100.0 | 100.0 | 100.0 | Total | 100.0 | 100.0 | 100.0 | 100.0 | 100.0 | 100.0 |
| | | | **LIABILITIES** | | | | | | |
| 6.9 | 10.1 | 10.0 | Notes Payable-Short Term | 12.8 | 12.7 | 10.8 | 16.3 | 6.2 | 4.9 |
| 9.6 | 8.9 | 8.1 | Cur. Mat.-L.T.D. | 12.0 | 6.2 | 10.6 | 6.2 | 8.1 | 6.9 |
| 10.7 | 10.6 | 11.0 | Trade Payables | 4.8 | 16.8 | 11.3 | 12.3 | 10.5 | 9.5 |
| .3 | .2 | .3 | Income Taxes Payable | .0 | .2 | .6 | .2 | .2 | .3 |
| 7.7 | 10.3 | 9.1 | All Other Current | 9.8 | 19.2 | 5.3 | 6.2 | 6.1 | 8.2 |
| 35.3 | 40.2 | 38.5 | Total Current | 39.3 | 55.0 | 38.5 | 41.3 | 31.2 | 29.8 |
| 33.8 | 29.6 | 31.6 | Long-Term Debt | 56.7 | 43.8 | 30.7 | 21.4 | 22.9 | 22.0 |
| .5 | .5 | .8 | Deferred Taxes | .3 | .3 | .1 | 1.6 | .6 | 1.6 |
| 4.7 | 5.0 | 6.2 | All Other Non-Current | 15.3 | 3.7 | 8.7 | 5.6 | 3.5 | 3.5 |
| 25.7 | 24.8 | 23.0 | Net Worth | -11.6 | -2.7 | 21.9 | 30.1 | 41.9 | 43.1 |
| 100.0 | 100.0 | 100.0 | Total Liabilities & Net Worth | 100.0 | 100.0 | 100.0 | 100.0 | 100.0 | 100.0 |
| | | | **INCOME DATA** | | | | | | |
| 100.0 | 100.0 | 100.0 | Net Sales | 100.0 | 100.0 | 100.0 | 100.0 | 100.0 | 100.0 |
| | | | Gross Profit | | | | | | |
| 95.8 | 94.1 | 92.9 | Operating Expenses | 81.2 | 96.1 | 93.6 | 94.9 | 94.2 | 94.3 |
| 4.2 | 5.9 | 7.1 | Operating Profit | 18.8 | 3.9 | 6.4 | 5.1 | 5.8 | 5.7 |
| 1.2 | .7 | .4 | All Other Expenses (net) | 2.8 | -.5 | .3 | -.4 | .3 | .5 |
| 3.0 | 5.2 | 6.7 | Profit Before Taxes | 16.1 | 4.3 | 6.0 | 5.5 | 5.4 | 5.2 |
| | | | **RATIOS** | | | | | | |
| 2.3 | 2.4 | 2.3 | | 4.2 | 2.9 | 1.9 | 3.4 | 2.2 | 2.1 |
| 1.2 | 1.3 | 1.4 | Current | 1.3 | 1.3 | 1.2 | 1.5 | 1.5 | 1.4 |
| .6 | .7 | .8 | | .1 | .4 | .7 | 1.1 | .9 | .9 |
| 2.0 | 2.1 | 2.1 | | 2.7 | 2.4 | 1.6 | 3.2 | 1.9 | 1.8 |
| 1.0 | 1.2 (310) | 1.2 | Quick | 1.1 | (51) 1.2 | .9 | 1.5 | 1.3 | 1.1 |
| .5 | .6 | .6 | | .1 | .3 | .4 | .8 | .8 | .8 |
| 11  32.5 | 14  26.7 | 9  42.0 | | 0  UND | 0  UND | 11  33.7 | 16  23.3 | 26  14.0 | 27  13.7 |
| 26  13.9 | 32  11.5 | 31  11.9 | Sales/Receivables | 0  UND | 8  47.1 | 28  13.2 | 31  11.7 | 35  10.5 | 35  10.3 |
| 43  8.5 | 47  7.8 | 45  8.2 | | 37  9.9 | 40  9.1 | 41  8.9 | 43  8.5 | 47  7.8 | 49  7.5 |
| | | | Cost of Sales/Inventory | | | | | | |
| | | | Cost of Sales/Payables | | | | | | |
| 12.4 | 11.2 | 11.2 | | 6.1 | 14.4 | 13.1 | 11.2 | 10.0 | 10.0 |
| 82.4 | 38.1 | 32.1 | Sales/Working Capital | 53.0 | 58.2 | 90.2 | 22.3 | 24.6 | 27.4 |
| -21.9 | -22.6 | -53.0 | | -9.0 | -42.9 | -25.0 | 212.8 | -208.5 | -93.0 |
| 7.8 | 11.0 | 13.2 | | 9.8 | 13.0 | 10.4 | 11.0 | 14.7 | 24.2 |
| (218) 2.8 | (253) 3.8 | (277) 4.9 | EBIT/Interest | (33) 3.4 | (43) 4.7 | (45) 3.8 | (40) 4.0 | (51) 6.6 | (65) 6.8 |
| .1 | .9 | 1.5 | | 1.3 | .5 | 2.0 | 1.4 | 2.2 | 2.2 |
| 2.4 | 3.0 | 3.3 | | | | | 3.0 | 2.8 | 3.3 |
| (52) 1.6 | (53) 1.9 | (49) 2.0 | Net Profit + Depr., Dep., Amort./Cur. Mat. L/T/D | | | (10) 1.8 | (12) 1.8 | (19) 2.3 | |
| .8 | .9 | 1.4 | | | | | 1.6 | 1.2 | 1.4 |
| .6 | .6 | .6 | | .8 | .3 | .4 | .4 | .7 | .6 |
| 1.4 | 1.6 | 1.3 | Fixed/Worth | 6.6 | 1.6 | 2.3 | 1.1 | 1.1 | 1.3 |
| 8.0 | 5.4 | 7.0 | | -.9 | -3.1 | -47.7 | 2.3 | 2.1 | 2.8 |
| .8 | .7 | .9 | | 1.1 | 1.1 | 1.3 | .7 | .7 | .8 |
| 2.3 | 2.2 | 2.1 | Debt/Worth | NM | 6.7 | 3.9 | 1.6 | 1.3 | 1.6 |
| 20.8 | 13.8 | 23.8 | | -2.6 | -6.3 | -65.8 | 4.9 | 2.7 | 3.5 |
| 45.0 | 60.8 | 63.7 | | 62.4 | 139.3 | 94.8 | 57.5 | 44.8 | 62.0 |
| (195) 15.9 | (232) 21.8 | (242) 28.5 | % Profit Before Taxes/Tangible Net Worth | (20) 32.1 | (35) 26.6 | (35) 36.0 | (37) 30.7 | (51) 24.8 | (64) 27.8 |
| .0 | 2.3 | 9.4 | | 11.0 | 2.3 | 10.9 | 2.6 | 7.9 | 11.4 |
| 17.6 | 23.0 | 22.5 | | 30.8 | 29.6 | 20.1 | 24.0 | 19.4 | 21.6 |
| 5.6 | 8.2 | 9.5 | % Profit Before Taxes/Total Assets | 9.7 | 10.6 | 9.5 | 10.0 | 11.1 | 9.0 |
| -2.3 | .1 | 2.0 | | 1.8 | -.5 | 2.3 | 1.5 | 2.9 | 2.8 |
| 18.1 | 25.1 | 31.7 | | 28.3 | 75.7 | 55.6 | 26.0 | 11.8 | 14.1 |
| 6.1 | 6.2 | 7.3 | Sales/Net Fixed Assets | 9.4 | 16.6 | 9.1 | 8.7 | 5.8 | 5.3 |
| 2.8 | 3.0 | 3.7 | | 1.4 | 5.7 | 4.0 | 4.3 | 3.4 | 3.7 |
| 4.5 | 4.4 | 5.0 | | 4.9 | 9.9 | 5.4 | 5.6 | 4.1 | 3.5 |
| 2.5 | 2.6 | 2.8 | Sales/Total Assets | 2.1 | 3.9 | 3.4 | 4.0 | 2.5 | 2.6 |
| 1.7 | 1.7 | 1.8 | | .7 | 1.8 | 2.1 | 2.0 | 1.8 | 2.0 |
| 2.1 | 2.6 | 2.1 | | 4.9 | 1.3 | 2.2 | 2.7 | 1.7 | 1.9 |
| (196) 5.1 | (216) 5.8 | (232) 4.6 | % Depr., Dep., Amort./Sales | (28) 10.4 | (30) 5.0 | (34) 5.4 | (31) 5.1 | (46) 4.8 | (63) 3.5 |
| 10.3 | 9.9 | 7.7 | | 26.9 | 11.3 | 7.9 | 7.4 | 7.2 | 5.0 |
| 1.3 | 1.5 | 1.1 | | 5.7 | 2.8 | 1.6 | .8 | 1.0 | .5 |
| (85) 3.1 | (96) 3.4 | (106) 2.7 | % Officers', Directors' Owners' Comp/Sales | (13) 5.7 | (21) 5.3 | (20) 2.8 | (18) 1.5 | (16) 1.5 | (18) .9 |
| 6.3 | 6.5 | 6.2 | | 14.1 | 9.8 | 6.1 | 4.5 | 3.3 | 1.5 |
| 3796516M | 5600418M | 6701946M | Net Sales ($) | 20969M | 105414M | 191511M | 317418M | 840234M | 5226400M |
| 1646024M | 2565694M | 3009222M | Total Assets ($) | 24190M | 45288M | 118572M | 105670M | 369256M | 2346246M |

© RMA 2012

**M = $ thousand    MM = $ million**
See Pages 9 through 22 for Explanation of Ratios and Data

## Current Data Sorted by Assets     Comparative Historical Data

| 0-500M | 500M-2MM | 2-10MM | 10-50MM | 50-100MM | 100-250MM | Type of Statement | 4/1/07-3/31/08 ALL | 4/1/08-3/31/09 ALL |
|---|---|---|---|---|---|---|---|---|
|  |  | 1 | 16 | 9 | 12 | Unqualified | 38 | 48 |
| 2 | 4 | 23 | 22 | 2 |  | Reviewed | 38 | 45 |
| 2 | 4 | 12 | 5 | 1 |  | Compiled | 21 | 26 |
| 9 | 17 | 4 | 1 |  |  | Tax Returns | 13 | 20 |
| 5 | 10 | 28 | 40 | 12 | 17 | Other | 53 | 75 |
| 32 (4/1-9/30/11) | | | 226 (10/1/11-3/31/12) | | | | | |
| 18 | 35 | 68 | 84 | 24 | 29 | **NUMBER OF STATEMENTS** | 163 | 214 |
| % | % | % | % | % | % | **ASSETS** | % | % |
| 16.5 | 14.7 | 8.7 | 7.0 | 4.1 | 6.7 | Cash & Equivalents | 8.0 | 9.7 |
| 18.8 | 32.4 | 32.4 | 22.1 | 19.7 | 19.0 | Trade Receivables (net) | 29.0 | 27.4 |
| 1.2 | 1.3 | .9 | 1.9 | 1.7 | .8 | Inventory | 1.3 | 1.4 |
| 5.6 | 3.7 | 6.9 | 4.0 | 2.4 | 2.5 | All Other Current | 3.9 | 4.2 |
| 42.1 | 52.0 | 48.9 | 35.0 | 27.9 | 28.9 | Total Current | 42.2 | 42.7 |
| 45.5 | 34.9 | 41.2 | 52.2 | 56.1 | 57.0 | Fixed Assets (net) | 47.8 | 45.7 |
| 2.8 | 3.3 | 3.0 | 6.4 | 9.1 | 10.4 | Intangibles (net) | 2.5 | 3.8 |
| 9.5 | 9.9 | 6.9 | 6.4 | 6.9 | 3.7 | All Other Non-Current | 7.6 | 7.8 |
| 100.0 | 100.0 | 100.0 | 100.0 | 100.0 | 100.0 | Total | 100.0 | 100.0 |
| | | | | | | **LIABILITIES** | | |
| 23.8 | 13.4 | 9.1 | 5.1 | 6.2 | 2.9 | Notes Payable-Short Term | 7.8 | 8.1 |
| 16.4 | 4.7 | 7.4 | 10.8 | 10.4 | 11.4 | Cur. Mat.-L.T.D. | 9.4 | 8.7 |
| 6.5 | 20.5 | 11.7 | 7.6 | 5.2 | 6.0 | Trade Payables | 9.9 | 9.5 |
| .0 | .2 | .5 | .5 | .1 | .1 | Income Taxes Payable | .3 | .1 |
| 1.9 | 10.7 | 8.4 | 7.1 | 5.8 | 7.7 | All Other Current | 9.2 | 10.6 |
| 48.6 | 49.6 | 37.2 | 31.1 | 27.7 | 28.1 | Total Current | 36.7 | 37.0 |
| 42.5 | 27.2 | 20.5 | 28.8 | 32.1 | 32.8 | Long-Term Debt | 27.9 | 28.3 |
| .0 | .4 | 1.0 | 1.9 | 3.9 | 4.5 | Deferred Taxes | 1.7 | 1.8 |
| 15.4 | 8.8 | 2.6 | 2.1 | 5.8 | 3.9 | All Other Non-Current | 2.5 | 4.6 |
| -6.4 | 14.0 | 38.7 | 36.1 | 30.5 | 30.8 | Net Worth | 31.2 | 28.3 |
| 100.0 | 100.0 | 100.0 | 100.0 | 100.0 | 100.0 | Total Liabilities & Net Worth | 100.0 | 100.0 |
| | | | | | | **INCOME DATA** | | |
| 100.0 | 100.0 | 100.0 | 100.0 | 100.0 | 100.0 | Net Sales | 100.0 | 100.0 |
| | | | | | | Gross Profit | | |
| 97.0 | 96.3 | 94.7 | 95.1 | 95.2 | 94.7 | Operating Expenses | 95.8 | 95.4 |
| 3.0 | 3.7 | 5.3 | 4.9 | 4.8 | 5.3 | Operating Profit | 4.2 | 4.6 |
| .9 | .6 | .3 | .9 | 1.6 | 1.3 | All Other Expenses (net) | 1.0 | .8 |
| 2.1 | 3.2 | 5.0 | 3.9 | 3.2 | 4.0 | Profit Before Taxes | 3.3 | 3.8 |
| | | | | | | **RATIOS** | | |
| 2.8 | 2.3 | 2.1 | 1.8 | 1.5 | 1.6 |  | 1.7 | 1.8 |
| .6 | 1.2 | 1.2 | 1.1 | 1.1 | 1.1 | Current | 1.1 | 1.1 |
| .5 | .6 | .9 | .6 | .7 | .7 |  | .8 | .8 |
| 2.1 | 1.9 | 1.9 | 1.5 | 1.3 | 1.5 |  | 1.5 | 1.6 |
| .6 | 1.2 | .9 | .9 | .9 | .9 | Quick | 1.0 | 1.0 |
| .4 | .6 | .7 | .6 | .6 | .6 |  | .6 | .6 |
| 0   UND | 4   99.8 | 24   15.4 | 26   13.9 | 36   10.2 | 35   10.5 |  | 26   14.0 | 20   17.9 |
| 1   594.4 | 25   14.8 | 34   10.7 | 36   10.1 | 46   7.9 | 41   8.8 | Sales/Receivables | 34   10.7 | 30   12.0 |
| 30   12.3 | 37   9.9 | 46   8.0 | 46   7.9 | 58   6.3 | 44   8.3 |  | 45   8.1 | 40   9.2 |
| | | | | | | Cost of Sales/Inventory | | |
| | | | | | | Cost of Sales/Payables | | |
| 19.2 | 13.4 | 10.8 | 12.3 | 17.9 | 12.9 |  | 14.4 | 15.7 |
| -197.1 | 27.5 | 51.3 | 136.7 | 175.0 | 93.1 | Sales/Working Capital | 82.5 | 74.6 |
| -19.6 | -16.6 | -89.9 | -17.9 | -16.0 | -16.9 |  | -26.2 | -37.1 |
| 13.7 | 8.0 | 12.3 | 10.9 | 8.5 | 6.4 |  | 5.6 | 6.8 |
| (10) 5.5 | (31) 3.9 | (65) 4.9 | (82) 3.6 | 4.0 | 2.9 | EBIT/Interest | (156) 2.6 | (199) 2.6 |
| 1.4 | .9 | 2.5 | 1.8 | 1.8 | 1.8 |  | 1.0 | 1.3 |
|  |  | 4.4 | 2.9 | 2.3 |  |  | 2.0 | 3.0 |
|  | (15) 1.8 | (39) 1.4 | (11) 1.2 |  |  | Net Profit + Depr., Dep., Amort./Cur. Mat. L/T/D | (60) 1.4 | (68) 1.5 |
|  |  | 1.2 | 1.2 | .9 |  |  | .9 | 1.0 |
| .1 | .6 | .4 | 1.0 | 1.6 | 1.6 |  | .7 | .7 |
| 2.3 | 1.6 | 1.3 | 2.0 | 2.3 | 2.7 | Fixed/Worth | 1.8 | 1.7 |
| -1.7 | -1.6 | 2.8 | 4.2 | 3.6 | 10.6 |  | 3.6 | 3.9 |
| 1.0 | 1.1 | .7 | 1.2 | 1.5 | 1.7 |  | 1.1 | 1.1 |
| 2.2 | 3.1 | 1.6 | 2.1 | 3.0 | 2.8 | Debt/Worth | 2.6 | 2.6 |
| -3.1 | -5.8 | 3.9 | 5.9 | 5.7 | 14.3 |  | 4.8 | 8.4 |
| 133.1 | 52.3 | 51.9 | 37.3 | 49.1 | 82.9 |  | 38.4 | 37.6 |
| (12) 31.6 | (24) 26.8 | (61) 24.2 | (76) 19.5 | (20) 24.5 | (26) 28.6 | % Profit Before Taxes/Tangible Net Worth | (152) 17.4 | (182) 20.4 |
| 14.1 | 11.9 | 6.1 | 9.5 | 13.9 | 12.9 |  | 2.4 | 4.7 |
| 31.6 | 16.9 | 16.3 | 12.2 | 12.4 | 10.4 |  | 14.7 | 12.7 |
| 13.7 | 6.0 | 7.8 | 5.8 | 6.0 | 5.7 | % Profit Before Taxes/Total Assets | 5.0 | 5.0 |
| 1.8 | .5 | 2.1 | 2.4 | 2.3 | 1.6 |  | .4 | 1.2 |
| UND | 46.1 | 21.8 | 6.7 | 3.9 | 4.7 |  | 12.7 | 17.5 |
| 18.6 | 19.4 | 7.8 | 3.5 | 3.0 | 2.7 | Sales/Net Fixed Assets | 4.7 | 6.1 |
| 5.9 | 4.8 | 3.7 | 2.5 | 2.2 | 2.0 |  | 2.6 | 3.1 |
| 19.4 | 6.6 | 4.3 | 2.6 | 2.0 | 2.1 |  | 3.8 | 4.6 |
| 6.6 | 4.9 | 3.2 | 1.8 | 1.6 | 1.6 | Sales/Total Assets | 2.5 | 2.6 |
| 3.0 | 2.5 | 1.9 | 1.6 | 1.2 | 1.3 |  | 1.6 | 1.8 |
| 1.0 | .8 | 1.7 | 2.8 | 4.6 |  |  | 2.4 | 2.2 |
| (10) 3.2 | (27) 2.2 | (59) 4.3 | (79) 6.3 | (22) 5.7 |  | % Depr., Dep., Amort./Sales | (132) 5.2 | (163) 4.7 |
| 8.8 | 5.7 | 7.3 | 9.1 | 6.8 |  |  | 7.8 | 7.1 |
|  | 1.7 | .8 | .5 |  |  |  | 1.1 | 1.0 |
|  | (16) 2.9 | (24) 2.2 | (12) 1.4 |  |  | % Officers', Directors' Owners' Comp/Sales | (52) 2.5 | (63) 2.2 |
|  | 5.4 | 3.7 | 1.9 |  |  |  | 5.8 | 5.1 |
| 28693M | 221932M | 1063674M | 4724886M | 2650219M | 7802859M | Net Sales ($) | 7476195M | 12059235M |
| 3216M | 43450M | 346232M | 2111796M | 1706086M | 4603704M | Total Assets ($) | 3783342M | 5474850M |

© RMA 2012

**M = $ thousand    MM = $ million**
See Pages 9 through 22 for Explanation of Ratios and Data

## Comparative Historical Data | Current Data Sorted by Sales

| H: 4/1/09-3/31/10 ALL | H: 4/1/10-3/31/11 ALL | H: 4/1/11-3/31/12 ALL | Type of Statement | 0-1MM | 1-3MM | 3-5MM | 5-10MM | 10-25MM | 25MM & OVER |
|---|---|---|---|---|---|---|---|---|---|
| 43 | 46 | 38 | Unqualified | | | | | 2 | 36 |
| 44 | 58 | 53 | Reviewed | 2 | 2 | 2 | 5 | 17 | 25 |
| 28 | 31 | 24 | Compiled | | | 3 | 6 | 9 | 6 |
| 22 | 26 | 31 | Tax Returns | 4 | 10 | 8 | 5 | 3 | 1 |
| 85 | 86 | 112 | Other | 4 | 5 | 3 | 10 | 25 | 65 |
| | | | | 32 (4/1-9/30/11) | | | 226 (10/1/11-3/31/12) | | |
| 222 | 247 | 258 | NUMBER OF STATEMENTS | 10 | 17 | 16 | 26 | 56 | 133 |
| % | % | % | **ASSETS** | % | % | % | % | % | % |
| 10.3 | 9.9 | 8.9 | Cash & Equivalents | 15.1 | 19.9 | 12.8 | 12.0 | 8.1 | 6.2 |
| 23.5 | 26.8 | 25.4 | Trade Receivables (net) | 16.6 | 15.8 | 25.5 | 24.3 | 32.3 | 24.6 |
| 1.9 | 1.4 | 1.4 | Inventory | .5 | 1.6 | 1.3 | .9 | .8 | 1.8 |
| 4.6 | 4.0 | 4.5 | All Other Current | .4 | 6.1 | 4.0 | 3.5 | 6.4 | 4.1 |
| 40.2 | 42.1 | 40.1 | Total Current | 32.6 | 43.5 | 43.6 | 40.7 | 47.6 | 36.6 |
| 47.2 | 45.4 | 47.4 | Fixed Assets (net) | 59.8 | 47.5 | 44.4 | 45.4 | 41.2 | 49.8 |
| 4.1 | 4.2 | 5.5 | Intangibles (net) | .2 | 2.9 | .9 | 7.6 | 2.6 | 7.6 |
| 8.4 | 8.3 | 7.0 | All Other Non-Current | 7.2 | 6.1 | 11.1 | 6.4 | 8.6 | 6.0 |
| 100.0 | 100.0 | 100.0 | Total | 100.0 | 100.0 | 100.0 | 100.0 | 100.0 | 100.0 |
| | | | **LIABILITIES** | | | | | | |
| 12.0 | 7.8 | 8.5 | Notes Payable-Short Term | 34.5 | 4.7 | 12.5 | 12.8 | 8.8 | 5.5 |
| 9.8 | 9.1 | 9.5 | Cur. Mat.-L.T.D. | 5.8 | 14.2 | 9.2 | 9.9 | 7.2 | 10.1 |
| 8.2 | 9.7 | 10.0 | Trade Payables | 6.4 | 5.6 | 23.3 | 10.6 | 11.9 | 8.2 |
| .3 | .2 | .3 | Income Taxes Payable | .0 | .5 | .0 | .7 | .3 | .3 |
| 10.9 | 8.6 | 7.5 | All Other Current | 4.8 | 10.8 | 5.3 | 3.8 | 9.3 | 7.5 |
| 41.2 | 35.4 | 35.8 | Total Current | 51.4 | 35.8 | 50.4 | 37.9 | 37.5 | 31.8 |
| 27.1 | 26.4 | 28.1 | Long-Term Debt | 35.7 | 37.1 | 33.5 | 32.2 | 19.6 | 28.4 |
| 1.8 | 2.0 | 1.8 | Deferred Taxes | .0 | 1.0 | .3 | .5 | .8 | 2.9 |
| 4.6 | 5.1 | 4.6 | All Other Non-Current | 29.3 | 5.0 | 9.6 | 3.4 | 2.6 | 3.2 |
| 25.3 | 31.0 | 29.7 | Net Worth | -16.3 | 21.0 | 6.2 | 25.9 | 39.5 | 33.8 |
| 100.0 | 100.0 | 100.0 | Total Liabilities & Net Worth | 100.0 | 100.0 | 100.0 | 100.0 | 100.0 | 100.0 |
| | | | **INCOME DATA** | | | | | | |
| 100.0 | 100.0 | 100.0 | Net Sales | 100.0 | 100.0 | 100.0 | 100.0 | 100.0 | 100.0 |
| | | | Gross Profit | | | | | | |
| 97.5 | 95.6 | 95.3 | Operating Expenses | 90.0 | 92.8 | 98.1 | 97.4 | 94.7 | 95.5 |
| 2.5 | 4.4 | 4.7 | Operating Profit | 10.0 | 7.2 | 1.9 | 2.6 | 5.3 | 4.5 |
| 1.0 | .9 | .8 | All Other Expenses (net) | 7.5 | .0 | .1 | -.4 | .3 | 1.0 |
| 1.5 | 3.5 | 3.9 | Profit Before Taxes | 2.5 | 7.3 | 1.9 | 3.0 | 5.1 | 3.6 |
| | | | **RATIOS** | | | | | | |
| 1.8 | 2.1 | 1.8 | | .9 | 5.4 | 1.9 | 1.8 | 2.2 | 1.7 |
| 1.1 | 1.2 | 1.1 | Current | .6 | 1.2 | 1.2 | 1.2 | 1.2 | 1.2 |
| .7 | .7 | .7 | | .4 | .5 | .6 | .5 | .9 | .7 |
| 1.6 | 1.8 | 1.6 | | .9 | 2.7 | 1.8 | 1.6 | 2.0 | 1.4 |
| .9 | 1.1 | .9 | Quick | .6 | .9 | 1.1 | 1.0 | .9 | .9 |
| .5 | .6 | .6 | | .4 | .5 | .5 | .5 | .6 | .6 |
| 20  18.6 | 26  14.3 | 22  16.5 | | 0 UND | 0 UND | 14  26.0 | 3  121.8 | 22  16.7 | 32  11.5 |
| 34  10.7 | 36  10.2 | 35  10.4 | Sales/Receivables | 0 UND | 4  99.8 | 24  15.0 | 30  12.2 | 34  10.7 | 38  9.5 |
| 44  8.4 | 47  7.8 | 45  8.2 | | 43  8.5 | 26  13.9 | 29  12.4 | 38  9.6 | 50  7.3 | 46  7.9 |
| | | | Cost of Sales/Inventory | | | | | | |
| | | | Cost of Sales/Payables | | | | | | |
| 15.9 | 12.5 | 13.1 | | NM | 8.1 | 14.5 | 12.1 | 10.8 | 14.9 |
| 98.7 | 48.2 | 68.5 | Sales/Working Capital | -11.6 | 81.8 | 51.5 | 41.2 | 43.0 | 86.1 |
| -16.9 | -26.4 | -20.6 | | -5.5 | -12.6 | -17.9 | -17.4 | -52.0 | -23.8 |
| 5.9 | 9.5 | 10.0 | | | 11.1 | 5.9 | 15.5 | 13.2 | 8.6 |
| (205) 2.3 | (231) 3.9 | (241) 4.1 | EBIT/Interest | | (12) 7.5 | (13) 1.8 | (24) 4.8 | (54) 4.6 | (132) 3.9 |
| .4 | 1.4 | 1.8 | | | 1.6 | .2 | 1.4 | 2.8 | 1.8 |
| 2.5 | 3.0 | 3.0 | | | | | | 7.6 | 2.8 |
| (74) 1.3 | (85) 1.5 | (74) 1.6 | Net Profit + Depr., Dep., Amort./Cur. Mat. L/T/D | | | | (11) 1.9 | (52) 1.4 | |
| .9 | 1.0 | 1.2 | | | | | | 1.5 | 1.1 |
| .7 | .6 | .8 | | 1.7 | .5 | 1.2 | .7 | .4 | 1.2 |
| 1.8 | 1.6 | 1.9 | Fixed/Worth | 5.1 | 1.1 | 2.3 | 1.6 | 1.4 | 2.1 |
| 3.9 | 6.0 | 4.5 | | -1.6 | 2.6 | -1.6 | -10.3 | 3.0 | 4.5 |
| 1.1 | 1.0 | 1.2 | | 2.2 | .5 | 1.9 | 1.1 | .7 | 1.4 |
| 2.6 | 2.4 | 2.2 | Debt/Worth | 8.5 | 1.3 | 3.4 | 1.8 | 1.6 | 2.4 |
| 7.4 | 11.5 | 6.6 | | -2.4 | 2.1 | -5.3 | -65.3 | 4.4 | 6.3 |
| 34.2 | 47.0 | 51.0 | | | 71.2 | 52.2 | 60.1 | 52.8 | 43.4 |
| (189) 13.5 | (210) 21.4 | (219) 24.2 | % Profit Before Taxes/Tangible Net Worth | | (14) 31.4 | (10) 28.0 | (19) 21.4 | (53) 24.2 | (117) 21.7 |
| -.4 | 6.2 | 9.6 | | | 10.1 | -5.4 | 10.4 | 7.4 | 11.1 |
| 10.1 | 16.4 | 13.7 | | 11.3 | 34.3 | 15.4 | 15.7 | 17.2 | 12.1 |
| 3.6 | 6.4 | 6.4 | % Profit Before Taxes/Total Assets | 2.0 | 16.9 | 6.0 | 6.1 | 7.7 | 6.0 |
| -1.9 | 1.3 | 2.0 | | -15.7 | 2.8 | -2.4 | 1.7 | 3.3 | 2.0 |
| 15.3 | 16.2 | 15.7 | | UND | 34.2 | 21.7 | 35.7 | 25.9 | 6.9 |
| 5.5 | 5.4 | 4.4 | Sales/Net Fixed Assets | 2.1 | 8.4 | 9.5 | 9.0 | 7.2 | 3.6 |
| 2.6 | 2.9 | 2.6 | | .9 | 2.1 | 2.7 | 3.6 | 3.5 | 2.5 |
| 4.1 | 4.2 | 3.9 | | 9.3 | 6.6 | 5.9 | 5.2 | 4.4 | 2.6 |
| 2.5 | 2.5 | 2.2 | Sales/Total Assets | 1.5 | 4.2 | 3.2 | 3.4 | 3.0 | 1.9 |
| 1.5 | 1.7 | 1.6 | | .5 | 1.3 | 1.9 | 1.9 | 1.8 | 1.5 |
| 2.3 | 1.9 | 2.0 | | | 2.1 | 1.3 | 1.3 | 1.6 | 2.4 |
| (180) 5.2 | (188) 4.0 | (201) 4.8 | % Depr., Dep., Amort./Sales | | (12) 4.9 | (12) 5.0 | (20) 2.5 | (49) 4.5 | (101) 4.8 |
| 8.7 | 7.4 | 8.1 | | | 11.9 | 9.3 | 7.9 | 7.3 | 7.9 |
| 1.0 | .9 | .9 | | | | | 1.1 | 1.2 | .4 |
| (68) 2.2 | (78) 1.6 | (70) 2.2 | % Officers', Directors' Owners' Comp/Sales | | | | (14) 1.8 | (20) 2.5 | (21) 1.03 |
| | | | | | | | 6.0 | 3.7 | 2.3 |
| 13484310M | 13688524M | 16492263M | Net Sales ($) | 3461M | 31028M | 66101M | 192660M | 889762M | 15309251M |
| 6123903M | 7145822M | 8814484M | Total Assets ($) | 4798M | 18174M | 36569M | 87065M | 395275M | 8272603M |

M = $ thousand   MM = $ million
See Pages 9 through 22 for Explanation of Ratios and Data

## Current Data Sorted by Assets      Comparative Historical Data

| Type of Statement | 0-500M | 500M-2MM | 2-10MM | 10-50MM | 50-100MM | 100-250MM | | 4/1/07-3/31/08 ALL | 4/1/08-3/31/09 ALL |
|---|---|---|---|---|---|---|---|---|---|
| Unqualified | | 1 | 3 | | | | | 2 | 10 |
| Reviewed | | | 1 | | | | | 3 | 4 |
| Compiled | 2 | 2 | 1 | | | | | 13 | 10 |
| Tax Returns | 9 | 6 | 3 | | | | | 9 | 10 |
| Other | 3 | 8 | 7 | 4 | 3 | | | 21 | 19 |
| | 7 (4/1-9/30/11) | | | 50 (10/1/11-3/31/12) | | | | | |
| NUMBER OF STATEMENTS | 14 | 17 | 14 | 9 | 3 | | | 48 | 53 |
| | % | % | % | % | % | % | | % | % |
| **ASSETS** | | | | | | | | | |
| Cash & Equivalents | 38.2 | 26.9 | 17.8 | | | | | 13.4 | 15.3 |
| Trade Receivables (net) | 19.8 | 23.9 | 19.0 | | | | | 17.8 | 13.5 |
| Inventory | .5 | 4.8 | .8 | | | | | .5 | 1.0 |
| All Other Current | 7.8 | 3.1 | 4.2 | | | | | 5.2 | 4.9 |
| Total Current | 66.2 | 58.7 | 41.8 | | | | | 36.9 | 34.7 |
| Fixed Assets (net) | 18.4 | 31.7 | 34.0 | | | | | 34.7 | 35.9 |
| Intangibles (net) | 5.9 | 6.6 | 16.6 | | | | | 16.3 | 13.1 |
| All Other Non-Current | 9.4 | 3.1 | 7.6 | | | | | 12.0 | 16.4 |
| Total | 100.0 | 100.0 | 100.0 | | | | | 100.0 | 100.0 |
| **LIABILITIES** | | | | | | | | | |
| Notes Payable-Short Term | 3.6 | .1 | 10.9 | | | | | 6.9 | 6.3 |
| Cur. Mat.-L.T.D. | 1.7 | 7.0 | 7.7 | | | | | 4.2 | 6.3 |
| Trade Payables | 12.7 | 8.9 | 7.1 | | | | | 6.1 | 8.1 |
| Income Taxes Payable | .0 | .4 | .2 | | | | | .2 | .0 |
| All Other Current | 32.5 | 25.4 | 5.8 | | | | | 12.3 | 15.0 |
| Total Current | 50.6 | 41.7 | 31.7 | | | | | 29.6 | 35.7 |
| Long-Term Debt | 31.3 | 21.0 | 20.6 | | | | | 35.5 | 27.7 |
| Deferred Taxes | .0 | .0 | .0 | | | | | .4 | 1.0 |
| All Other Non-Current | 5.2 | -15.5 | 5.6 | | | | | 9.5 | 14.8 |
| Net Worth | 13.0 | 21.8 | 42.1 | | | | | 25.0 | 20.8 |
| Total Liabilities & Net Worth | 100.0 | 100.0 | 100.0 | | | | | 100.0 | 100.0 |
| **INCOME DATA** | | | | | | | | | |
| Net Sales | 100.0 | 100.0 | 100.0 | | | | | 100.0 | 100.0 |
| Gross Profit | | | | | | | | | |
| Operating Expenses | 92.5 | 96.7 | 91.9 | | | | | 89.0 | 93.5 |
| Operating Profit | 7.5 | 3.3 | 8.1 | | | | | 11.0 | 6.5 |
| All Other Expenses (net) | 4.0 | .5 | .5 | | | | | 3.7 | 1.1 |
| Profit Before Taxes | 3.5 | 2.8 | 7.6 | | | | | 7.3 | 5.4 |
| **RATIOS** | | | | | | | | | |
| Current | 2.5 | 2.6 | 3.1 | | | | | 3.0 | 2.5 |
| | 1.4 | 1.5 | 1.1 | | | | | .9 | 1.2 |
| | .6 | .6 | .4 | | | | | .5 | .3 |
| Quick | 2.5 | 2.6 | 2.6 | | | | | 2.2 | 2.2 |
| | 1.0 | 1.5 | 1.0 | | | | | .9 (52) | .9 |
| | .5 | .5 | .4 | | | | | .4 | .3 |
| Sales/Receivables | 0 UND | 0 UND | 1 408.2 | | | | | 2 237.4 | 0 999.8 |
| | 6 62.6 | 23 15.6 | 34 10.7 | | | | | 16 22.7 | 10 36.1 |
| | 21 17.4 | 41 8.9 | 49 7.4 | | | | | 50 7.3 | 31 11.8 |
| Cost of Sales/Inventory | | | | | | | | | |
| Cost of Sales/Payables | | | | | | | | | |
| Sales/Working Capital | 10.3 | 9.0 | 6.9 | | | | | 8.1 | 16.7 |
| | 78.5 | 21.3 | 82.2 | | | | | -109.1 | 129.0 |
| | -17.1 | -12.1 | -7.4 | | | | | -16.4 | -12.1 |
| EBIT/Interest | | 12.9 | 36.7 | | | | | 12.8 | 10.1 |
| | | (11) 2.3 | 8.1 | | | | | (36) 6.1 | (38) 5.1 |
| | | -4.2 | 2.3 | | | | | .6 | 1.0 |
| Net Profit + Depr., Dep., Amort./Cur. Mat. L/T/D | | | | | | | | 6.3 | 16.2 |
| | | | | | | | | (10) 2.4 | (10) 2.5 |
| | | | | | | | | 1.6 | 1.3 |
| Fixed/Worth | .0 | .4 | .4 | | | | | .2 | .2 |
| | 4.6 | 3.9 | 1.3 | | | | | 1.7 | 1.7 |
| | -1.0 | -1.7 | -19.0 | | | | | -4.7 | -2.0 |
| Debt/Worth | .6 | .6 | .9 | | | | | .6 | .6 |
| | 101.3 | 4.5 | 1.7 | | | | | 2.0 | 2.2 |
| | -6.2 | -8.1 | -30.9 | | | | | -4.4 | -5.4 |
| % Profit Before Taxes/Tangible Net Worth | | 56.1 | 74.7 | | | | | 60.4 | 68.7 |
| | | (11) 26.7 | (10) 53.8 | | | | | (31) 31.9 | (37) 26.9 |
| | | 3.9 | 21.4 | | | | | 1.6 | 3.1 |
| % Profit Before Taxes/Total Assets | 61.9 | 19.0 | 28.6 | | | | | 31.8 | 21.4 |
| | 5.4 | 10.7 | 12.1 | | | | | 10.7 | 6.9 |
| | -.4 | -2.9 | 5.7 | | | | | -1.2 | .7 |
| Sales/Net Fixed Assets | UND | 529.2 | 29.4 | | | | | 84.9 | 42.2 |
| | 123.9 | 15.8 | 6.4 | | | | | 8.1 | 7.7 |
| | 18.0 | 4.1 | 4.8 | | | | | 3.6 | 4.0 |
| Sales/Total Assets | 8.6 | 5.3 | 3.6 | | | | | 3.9 | 4.2 |
| | 5.5 | 2.8 | 2.3 | | | | | 2.3 | 2.6 |
| | 4.6 | 1.8 | 1.5 | | | | | 1.2 | 1.4 |
| % Depr., Dep., Amort./Sales | | | 1.9 | | | | | 2.7 | 2.4 |
| | | (13) | 6.6 | | | | | (27) 4.8 | (36) 6.3 |
| | | | 9.3 | | | | | 7.8 | 10.0 |
| % Officers', Directors' Owners' Comp/Sales | | 1.3 | | | | | | 2.6 | 1.7 |
| | | (10) 3.7 | | | | | | (12) 4.5 | (17) 4.3 |
| | | 14.9 | | | | | | 9.1 | 9.3 |
| Net Sales ($) | 20222M | 88906M | 208306M | 411588M | 159890M | | | 1886509M | 840527M |
| Total Assets ($) | 2955M | 21378M | 85445M | 212546M | 197748M | | | 786526M | 529154M |

Note: Columns 10-50MM, 50-100MM, and 100-250MM show "DATA NOT AVAILABLE" for the detailed percentage and ratio sections.

## Comparative Historical Data    Current Data Sorted by Sales

| Type of Statement | | | | | 7 (4/1-9/30/11) | | | 50 (10/1/11-3/31/12) | | |
|---|---|---|---|---|---|---|---|---|---|---|
| Unqualified | 8 | 6 | 4 | | | 1 | | | 1 | 2 |
| Reviewed | 6 | 6 | 4 | | | 1 | 1 | 1 | 1 | 1 |
| Compiled | 7 | 6 | 6 | | | 2 | 1 | | 1 | 1 |
| Tax Returns | 9 | 21 | 18 | | 1 | 5 | 2 | 4 | 1 | 1 |
| Other | 22 | 28 | 25 | | 5 | 4 | 3 | 2 | 6 | 7 |
| | 4/1/09-3/31/10 ALL | 4/1/10-3/31/11 ALL | 4/1/11-3/31/12 ALL | | 0-1MM | 1-3MM | 3-5MM | 5-10MM | 10-25MM | 25MM & OVER |
| NUMBER OF STATEMENTS | 52 | 67 | 57 | | 9 | 12 | 8 | 7 | 10 | 11 |
| **ASSETS** | % | % | % | | % | % | % | % | % | % |
| Cash & Equivalents | 20.9 | 16.1 | 27.3 | | | 37.0 | | | 25.6 | 23.1 |
| Trade Receivables (net) | 16.3 | 13.2 | 17.9 | | | 16.5 | | | 9.0 | 14.6 |
| Inventory | .6 | .3 | 2.8 | | | .0 | | | 1.0 | 5.6 |
| All Other Current | 11.3 | 9.0 | 5.9 | | | 4.9 | | | 5.5 | 2.9 |
| Total Current | 49.2 | 38.6 | 53.8 | | | 58.3 | | | 41.1 | 46.1 |
| Fixed Assets (net) | 31.3 | 35.2 | 28.7 | | | 24.1 | | | 29.8 | 34.4 |
| Intangibles (net) | 8.0 | 9.4 | 11.2 | | | 5.8 | | | 23.6 | 13.9 |
| All Other Non-Current | 11.5 | 16.9 | 6.2 | | | 11.7 | | | 5.4 | 5.6 |
| Total | 100.0 | 100.0 | 100.0 | | | 100.0 | | | 100.0 | 100.0 |
| **LIABILITIES** | | | | | | | | | | |
| Notes Payable-Short Term | 10.0 | 12.9 | 5.1 | | | 5.2 | | | 5.5 | 11.4 |
| Cur. Mat.-L.T.D. | 6.2 | 4.9 | 5.0 | | | 4.6 | | | 4.4 | 3.2 |
| Trade Payables | 12.2 | 10.2 | 8.8 | | | 12.3 | | | 3.3 | 10.5 |
| Income Taxes Payable | .1 | .2 | .2 | | | .0 | | | .0 | .0 |
| All Other Current | 23.2 | 21.4 | 21.9 | | | 22.0 | | | 16.1 | 11.9 |
| Total Current | 51.6 | 49.6 | 41.0 | | | 44.1 | | | 29.4 | 36.9 |
| Long-Term Debt | 19.4 | 21.8 | 26.1 | | | 23.7 | | | 43.0 | 16.2 |
| Deferred Taxes | 1.1 | .3 | .1 | | | .0 | | | .5 | .0 |
| All Other Non-Current | 9.0 | 19.2 | 9.2 | | | 4.6 | | | 15.4 | 4.0 |
| Net Worth | 18.8 | 9.1 | 23.6 | | | 27.6 | | | 11.7 | 42.9 |
| Total Liabilities & Net Worth | 100.0 | 100.0 | 100.0 | | | 100.0 | | | 100.0 | 100.0 |
| **INCOME DATA** | | | | | | | | | | |
| Net Sales | 100.0 | 100.0 | 100.0 | | | 100.0 | | | 100.0 | 100.0 |
| Gross Profit | | | | | | | | | | |
| Operating Expenses | 88.8 | 89.2 | 90.6 | | | 89.2 | | | 93.4 | 92.1 |
| Operating Profit | 11.2 | 10.8 | 9.4 | | | 10.8 | | | 6.6 | 7.9 |
| All Other Expenses (net) | 3.9 | 4.4 | 3.8 | | | 6.3 | | | 3.1 | 1.6 |
| Profit Before Taxes | 7.3 | 6.4 | 5.6 | | | 4.5 | | | 3.6 | 6.4 |
| **RATIOS** | | | | | | | | | | |
| Current | 1.9 | 2.3 | 2.4 | | | 2.3 | | | 2.6 | 1.7 |
| | 1.1 | .8 | 1.3 | | | 1.4 | | | 1.2 | 1.1 |
| | .5 | .3 | .7 | | | .6 | | | .6 | 1.0 |
| Quick | 1.6 | 1.6 | 2.3 | | | 2.3 | | | 2.2 | 1.7 |
| | .7 | .6 | 1.0 | | | 1.3 | | | 1.0 | 1.0 |
| | .3 | .2 | .4 | | | .6 | | | .4 | .4 |
| Sales/Receivables | 0 744.1 | 0 UND | 0 UND | | | 0 UND | | | 0 UND | 5 77.1 |
| | 14 26.7 | 9 38.8 | 13 28.6 | | | 11 34.6 | | | 10 37.2 | 8 44.0 |
| | 32 11.3 | 29 12.5 | 36 10.0 | | | 19 19.5 | | | 33 10.9 | 31 11.6 |
| Cost of Sales/Inventory | | | | | | | | | | |
| Cost of Sales/Payables | | | | | | | | | | |
| Sales/Working Capital | 11.3 | 8.3 | 9.0 | | | 12.3 | | | 11.2 | 6.4 |
| | 76.4 | -84.8 | 60.5 | | | 57.5 | | | 53.4 | 66.5 |
| | -13.0 | -10.6 | -20.3 | | | -262.9 | | | -36.0 | 146.1 |
| EBIT/Interest | 18.3 | 13.5 | 12.9 | | | | | | | 23.6 |
| | (37) 5.9 | (47) 5.8 | (43) 4.8 | | | | | | (10) | 9.4 |
| | .8 | 1.2 | 1.6 | | | | | | | 1.9 |
| Net Profit + Depr., Dep., Amort./Cur. Mat. L/T/D | 6.9 | | | | | | | | | |
| | (10) 3.4 | | | | | | | | | |
| | 1.8 | | | | | | | | | |
| Fixed/Worth | .2 | .5 | .4 | | | .0 | | | .4 | .8 |
| | 1.5 | 2.3 | 2.3 | | | .5 | | | 8.0 | 1.2 |
| | -6.2 | -3.0 | -1.7 | | | -2.6 | | | -.4 | 2.3 |
| Debt/Worth | 1.3 | 1.4 | 1.0 | | | .6 | | | 1.2 | 1.0 |
| | 4.8 | 6.0 | 4.5 | | | 6.5 | | | 22.0 | 1.6 |
| | -14.7 | -5.7 | -6.7 | | | -7.1 | | | -1.8 | 8.8 |
| % Profit Before Taxes/Tangible Net Worth | 86.8 | 71.0 | 66.9 | | | | | | | |
| | (36) 50.4 | (43) 18.8 | (36) 36.1 | | | | | | | |
| | 15.5 | 7.2 | 17.5 | | | | | | | |
| % Profit Before Taxes/Total Assets | 30.0 | 17.5 | 21.3 | | | 15.9 | | | 26.6 | 27.9 |
| | 9.0 | 6.5 | 9.0 | | | 5.4 | | | 8.1 | 10.3 |
| | 1.4 | -1.8 | 1.3 | | | 1.2 | | | 1.8 | 5.3 |
| Sales/Net Fixed Assets | 78.5 | 63.6 | 117.3 | | | UND | | | 89.7 | 14.9 |
| | 11.1 | 11.9 | 14.9 | | | 20.1 | | | 18.3 | 7.2 |
| | 5.3 | 4.4 | 5.1 | | | 6.7 | | | 5.0 | 3.7 |
| Sales/Total Assets | 4.5 | 4.9 | 5.0 | | | 7.3 | | | 8.5 | 4.2 |
| | 2.5 | 2.3 | 2.8 | | | 4.5 | | | 2.6 | 2.3 |
| | 1.7 | 1.5 | 1.6 | | | 2.4 | | | 1.5 | 1.4 |
| % Depr., Dep., Amort./Sales | 3.1 | 3.2 | 1.1 | | | | | | | 1.0 |
| | (29) 5.9 | (42) 5.9 | (38) 5.6 | | | | | | | 4.9 |
| | 7.8 | 9.2 | 8.3 | | | | | | | 7.8 |
| % Officers', Directors' Owners' Comp/Sales | 1.0 | 1.8 | 2.6 | | | | | | | |
| | (12) 4.0 | (19) 4.2 | (20) 6.3 | | | | | | | |
| | 8.6 | 6.6 | 12.8 | | | | | | | |
| Net Sales ($) | 1251672M | 763498M | 888912M | | 5847M | 22454M | 29161M | 50805M | 162640M | 618005M |
| Total Assets ($) | 885993M | 495230M | 520072M | | 3763M | 11477M | 76101M | 21556M | 85205M | 321970M |

M = $ thousand    MM = $ million
See Pages 9 through 22 for Explanation of Ratios and Data

# TRANSPORTATION—Limousine Service NAICS 485320

| Current Data Sorted by Assets | | | | | | | Comparative Historical Data | |
|---|---|---|---|---|---|---|---|---|

| 0-500M | 500M-2MM | 2-10MM | 10-50MM | 50-100MM | 100-250MM | | 4/1/07-3/31/08 ALL | 4/1/08-3/31/09 ALL |
|---|---|---|---|---|---|---|---|---|
| | | 1 | | | | **Type of Statement** | | |
| | | | | | | Unqualified | 5 | 3 |
| | 1 | 5 | | | | Reviewed | 1 | 4 |
| 2 | 3 | 4 | | | 1 | Compiled | 6 | 5 |
| 8 | 4 | 5 | | | | Tax Returns | 20 | 13 |
| 2 | 6 | 13 | 6 | | | Other | 22 | 17 |
| 5 (4/1-9/30/11) | | | 57 (10/1/11-3/31/12) | | | | | |
| 12 | 14 | 27 | 8 | | 1 | **NUMBER OF STATEMENTS** | 54 | 42 |
| % | % | % | % | % | % | **ASSETS** | % | % |
| 16.5 | 16.6 | 8.6 | | | | Cash & Equivalents | 10.0 | 13.0 |
| 6.2 | 10.0 | 16.6 | | | | Trade Receivables (net) | 15.8 | 11.9 |
| 6.9 | .0 | .4 | | | | Inventory | 1.3 | .8 |
| 5.6 | 3.2 | 2.0 | | | | All Other Current | 5.5 | 4.5 |
| 35.2 | 29.8 | 27.6 | | | | Total Current | 32.7 | 30.1 |
| 60.0 | 48.8 | 59.9 | | | | Fixed Assets (net) | 54.4 | 52.4 |
| 3.6 | 6.4 | 3.8 | | | | Intangibles (net) | 5.9 | 8.0 |
| 1.1 | 15.0 | 8.8 | | | | All Other Non-Current | 7.0 | 9.5 |
| 100.0 | 100.0 | 100.0 | | | | Total | 100.0 | 100.0 |
| | | | | | | **LIABILITIES** | | |
| 19.8 | 6.6 | 5.0 | | | | Notes Payable-Short Term | 7.9 | 15.6 |
| 8.7 | 10.2 | 19.0 | | | | Cur. Mat.-L.T.D. | 8.2 | 9.9 |
| 12.7 | 4.2 | 6.8 | | | | Trade Payables | 6.8 | 4.8 |
| .0 | .0 | .0 | | | | Income Taxes Payable | .0 | .0 |
| 8.5 | 11.2 | 8.2 | | | | All Other Current | 13.8 | 22.7 |
| 49.7 | 32.3 | 39.1 | | | | Total Current | 36.7 | 52.9 |
| 74.3 | 43.2 | 33.9 | | | | Long-Term Debt | 39.9 | 44.7 |
| .0 | .0 | .2 | | | | Deferred Taxes | .5 | .4 |
| 5.8 | 15.4 | 7.4 | | | | All Other Non-Current | 6.0 | 5.5 |
| -29.8 | 9.1 | 19.3 | | | | Net Worth | 16.9 | -3.4 |
| 100.0 | 100.0 | 100.0 | | | | Total Liabilities & Net Worth | 100.0 | 100.0 |
| | | | | | | **INCOME DATA** | | |
| 100.0 | 100.0 | 100.0 | | | | Net Sales | 100.0 | 100.0 |
| | | | | | | Gross Profit | | |
| 96.7 | 91.0 | 91.9 | | | | Operating Expenses | 94.4 | 96.9 |
| 3.3 | 9.0 | 8.1 | | | | Operating Profit | 5.6 | 3.1 |
| 1.3 | 3.8 | 2.2 | | | | All Other Expenses (net) | 2.3 | 1.9 |
| 2.0 | 5.2 | 5.8 | | | | Profit Before Taxes | 3.2 | 1.2 |
| | | | | | | **RATIOS** | | |
| 1.5 | 2.9 | 1.4 | | | | | 1.7 | 1.8 |
| .7 | .9 | .6 | | | | Current | 1.0 | 1.0 |
| .2 | .4 | .3 | | | | | .6 | .5 |
| 1.2 | 2.9 | 1.3 | | | | | 1.2 | 1.3 |
| .5 | .9 | .6 | | | | Quick | .8 | .9 |
| .1 | .2 | .3 | | | | | .4 | .5 |
| 0 UND | 0 UND | 11 33.4 | | | | | 0 UND | 0 UND |
| 0 UND | 10 35.6 | 15 24.3 | | | | Sales/Receivables | 13 27.3 | 4 97.0 |
| 9 40.5 | 23 15.9 | 29 12.7 | | | | | 37 9.9 | 29 12.4 |
| | | | | | | Cost of Sales/Inventory | | |
| | | | | | | Cost of Sales/Payables | | |
| 42.1 | 9.1 | 29.1 | | | | | 22.9 | 20.0 |
| -41.5 | NM | -17.2 | | | | Sales/Working Capital | 412.7 | 452.3 |
| -11.2 | -8.0 | -9.2 | | | | | -27.8 | -18.0 |
| 11.4 | 8.5 | 10.2 | | | | | 4.7 | 5.5 |
| (10) 1.4 | (13) 3.4 | (25) 5.4 | | | | EBIT/Interest | (46) 2.1 | (35) 1.6 |
| -2.8 | .9 | 2.6 | | | | | .6 | -.3 |
| | | | | | | Net Profit + Depr., Dep., Amort./Cur. Mat. L/T/D | | |
| 1.2 | 1.2 | 1.5 | | | | | 1.1 | 1.1 |
| NM | 62.5 | 2.8 | | | | Fixed/Worth | 3.9 | 2.4 |
| -.8 | -.8 | -53.9 | | | | | -117.5 | -2.8 |
| 1.1 | 1.3 | 1.7 | | | | | 1.5 | 1.0 |
| NM | 115.3 | 4.4 | | | | Debt/Worth | 5.2 | 4.6 |
| -2.1 | -5.6 | -102.5 | | | | | -131.7 | -2.9 |
| | | 102.5 | | | | | 79.5 | 63.4 |
| | (20) 58.6 | | | | | % Profit Before Taxes/Tangible Net Worth | (40) 28.2 | (25) 43.3 |
| | 28.1 | | | | | | -.3 | -3.3 |
| 37.2 | 14.8 | 25.1 | | | | | 18.8 | 17.1 |
| 2.4 | 6.4 | 17.2 | | | | % Profit Before Taxes/Total Assets | 6.9 | 5.0 |
| -21.3 | -.3 | 2.8 | | | | | -1.0 | -7.7 |
| 31.6 | 21.2 | 6.1 | | | | | 9.9 | 9.3 |
| 8.7 | 3.8 | 4.2 | | | | Sales/Net Fixed Assets | 5.6 | 5.2 |
| 2.5 | 2.1 | 3.4 | | | | | 3.1 | 3.2 |
| 11.6 | 3.7 | 3.2 | | | | | 4.6 | 4.5 |
| 4.0 | 2.3 | 2.9 | | | | Sales/Total Assets | 2.8 | 2.4 |
| 2.0 | 1.2 | 2.4 | | | | | 1.8 | 1.7 |
| | 1.7 | 3.8 | | | | | 3.4 | 3.6 |
| (10) 7.8 | (26) 8.0 | | | | | % Depr., Dep., Amort./Sales | (51) 7.1 | (29) 9.6 |
| | 12.0 | 9.7 | | | | | 10.3 | 12.9 |
| | | | | | | | 2.9 | 2.5 |
| | | | | | | % Officers', Directors' Owners' Comp/Sales | (24) 4.3 | (14) 3.4 |
| | | | | | | | 8.6 | 4.7 |
| 20397M | 45777M | 366494M | 358320M | | 202380M | Net Sales ($) | 845007M | 1076300M |
| 3264M | 17452M | 120065M | 170391M | | 125262M | Total Assets ($) | 407383M | 506764M |

*(The 50-100MM column is marked "DATA NOT AVAILABLE".)*

M = $ thousand   MM = $ million
See Pages 9 through 22 for Explanation of Ratios and Data

## Comparative Historical Data  &  Current Data Sorted by Sales

### Type of Statement

| 3 | 3 | 1 | Type of Statement | 0-1MM | 1-3MM | 3-5MM | 5-10MM | 10-25MM | 25MM & OVER |
|---|---|---|---|---|---|---|---|---|---|
| | | | Unqualified | | | | 2 | 4 | 1 |
| 3 | 3 | 1 | Reviewed | 1 | 3 | 1 | 3 | 1 | 1 |
| 1 | 5 | 7 | Compiled | | | | | | |
| 10 | 12 | 9 | Tax Returns | 4 | 6 | 2 | 3 | 2 | |
| 14 | 19 | 17 | Other | 1 | 3 | 2 | 7 | 11 | 4 |
| 14 | 14 | 28 | | 5 (4/1-9/30/11) | | | 57 (10/1/11-3/31/12) | | |
| 4/1/09-3/31/10 ALL | 4/1/10-3/31/11 ALL | 4/1/11-3/31/12 ALL | | | | | | | |
| 42 | 53 | 62 | NUMBER OF STATEMENTS | 6 | 12 | 5 | 15 | 18 | 6 |

### Data

| 2010 ALL % | 2011 ALL % | 2012 ALL % | | 0-1MM % | 1-3MM % | 3-5MM % | 5-10MM % | 10-25MM % | 25MM % |
|---|---|---|---|---|---|---|---|---|---|
| | | | **ASSETS** | | | | | | |
| 9.9 | 12.8 | 12.7 | Cash & Equivalents | | 19.6 | | 12.9 | 8.5 | |
| 13.3 | 17.2 | 13.4 | Trade Receivables (net) | | 4.3 | | 14.2 | 17.5 | |
| 1.8 | 2.6 | 1.7 | Inventory | | 6.9 | | .1 | 1.0 | |
| 1.8 | 5.8 | 3.3 | All Other Current | | 5.9 | | 3.2 | 2.8 | |
| 26.7 | 38.3 | 31.1 | Total Current | | 36.7 | | 30.4 | 29.8 | |
| 47.3 | 51.1 | 54.7 | Fixed Assets (net) | | 47.6 | | 55.7 | 58.0 | |
| 14.1 | 5.3 | 5.2 | Intangibles (net) | | 8.2 | | 4.8 | 2.0 | |
| 12.0 | 5.2 | 8.9 | All Other Non-Current | | 7.4 | | 9.1 | 10.2 | |
| 100.0 | 100.0 | 100.0 | Total | | 100.0 | | 100.0 | 100.0 | |
| | | | **LIABILITIES** | | | | | | |
| 6.6 | 8.1 | 7.8 | Notes Payable-Short Term | | 8.9 | | 11.2 | 5.8 | |
| 10.1 | 12.2 | 13.7 | Cur. Mat.-L.T.D. | | 10.7 | | 15.7 | 20.6 | |
| 8.7 | 15.7 | 9.0 | Trade Payables | | 6.0 | | 7.7 | 11.5 | |
| .0 | .3 | .1 | Income Taxes Payable | | .0 | | .0 | .2 | |
| 9.1 | 8.0 | 9.2 | All Other Current | | 10.2 | | 5.9 | 9.5 | |
| 34.6 | 44.3 | 39.9 | Total Current | | 35.9 | | 40.6 | 47.7 | |
| 42.3 | 50.6 | 43.9 | Long-Term Debt | | 78.1 | | 46.7 | 27.7 | |
| .3 | .4 | .2 | Deferred Taxes | | .0 | | .0 | .6 | |
| 8.7 | 6.6 | 8.3 | All Other Non-Current | | 12.8 | | 9.5 | 7.1 | |
| 14.2 | -1.9 | 7.7 | Net Worth | | -26.9 | | 3.2 | 16.9 | |
| 100.0 | 100.0 | 100.0 | Total Liabilities & Net Worth | | 100.0 | | 100.0 | 100.0 | |
| | | | **INCOME DATA** | | | | | | |
| 100.0 | 100.0 | 100.0 | Net Sales | | 100.0 | | 100.0 | 100.0 | |
| | | | Gross Profit | | | | | | |
| 97.3 | 96.3 | 93.4 | Operating Expenses | | 97.4 | | 91.4 | 95.9 | |
| 2.7 | 3.7 | 6.6 | Operating Profit | | 2.6 | | 8.6 | 4.1 | |
| 1.7 | 1.4 | 2.4 | All Other Expenses (net) | | 1.8 | | 1.0 | .7 | |
| 1.0 | 2.2 | 4.3 | Profit Before Taxes | | .8 | | 7.6 | 3.4 | |
| | | | **RATIOS** | | | | | | |
| 2.2 / .8 / .3 | 2.0 / 1.2 / .3 | 1.5 / .7 / .3 | Current | | 3.3 / 1.6 / .4 | | 1.1 / .9 / .4 | 1.1 / .4 / .3 | |
| 2.2 / .7 / .2 | 1.8 / .8 / .3 | 1.3 / .7 / .3 | Quick | | 2.5 / .7 / .1 | | 1.1 / .8 / .3 | 1.0 / .4 / .3 | |
| 0 UND / 12 31.1 / 36 10.2 | 0 UND / 8 48.3 / 25 14.6 | 0 999.8 / 13 28.6 / 23 15.9 | Sales/Receivables | | 0 UND / 0 UND / 18 20.5 | | 0 809.3 / 15 24.3 / 29 12.7 | 9 40.2 / 16 22.6 / 43 8.5 | |
| | | | Cost of Sales/Inventory | | | | | | |
| | | | Cost of Sales/Payables | | | | | | |
| 23.8 / -65.6 / -9.7 | 17.0 / 145.9 / -11.6 | 27.0 / -41.5 / -8.7 | Sales/Working Capital | | 7.1 / 95.6 / -7.7 | | 104.1 / -130.5 / -17.2 | 256.2 / -10.6 / -7.8 | |
| 4.8 / (37) 1.5 / .0 | 8.5 / (48) 2.8 / .9 | 9.8 / (56) 4.8 / 1.2 | EBIT/Interest | | 3.4 / (11) 1.0 / -1.6 | | 11.3 / (14) 6.0 / 3.4 | 5.7 / (17) 4.1 / 1.3 | |
| | | 2.2 / (13) 1.5 / .9 | Net Profit + Depr., Dep., Amort./Cur. Mat. L/T/D | | | | | | |
| 1.3 / UND / -1.6 | .9 / 3.6 / -4.4 | 1.3 / 4.3 / -5.7 | Fixed/Worth | | 1.3 / -2.0 / -.7 | | 2.0 / 11.8 / -6.8 | 1.5 / 2.8 / -18.8 | |
| 1.8 / UND / -3.3 | 3.0 / 7.9 / -4.6 | 1.7 / 6.7 / -9.4 | Debt/Worth | | 2.8 / -5.7 / -1.9 | | 2.9 / 30.9 / -10.4 | 2.1 / 3.6 / -24.0 | |
| 66.8 / (22) 13.8 / -4.3 | 80.5 / (32) 28.1 / 2.1 | 102.5 / (40) 42.1 / 16.3 | % Profit Before Taxes/Tangible Net Worth | | | | | 84.1 / (13) 35.8 / 4.8 | |
| 10.9 / 1.5 / -3.8 | 19.6 / 6.6 / -.2 | 22.9 / 8.0 / .6 | % Profit Before Taxes/Total Assets | | 9.6 / .2 / -17.9 | | 44.8 / 21.6 / 10.3 | 22.3 / 6.9 / -.4 | |
| 18.1 / 5.8 / 2.7 | 24.0 / 6.0 / 3.3 | 11.4 / 4.4 / 3.1 | Sales/Net Fixed Assets | | 20.0 / 4.9 / 2.4 | | 6.1 / 5.1 / 4.0 | 8.7 / 4.2 / 3.1 | |
| 3.9 / 2.1 / 1.3 | 7.0 / 3.5 / 2.2 | 3.7 / 2.8 / 1.7 | Sales/Total Assets | | 4.8 / 2.7 / 1.4 | | 3.7 / 3.2 / 2.6 | 3.1 / 2.8 / 1.7 | |
| 2.3 / (36) 7.6 / 13.0 | 4.2 / (43) 6.8 / 11.2 | 3.9 / (51) 7.2 / 9.8 | % Depr., Dep., Amort./Sales | | | | 3.7 / (13) 6.8 / 10.5 | 4.4 / (17) 7.7 / 8.4 | |
| 3.1 / (20) 5.5 / 7.3 | 3.5 / (27) 4.5 / 8.1 | 2.9 / (22) 4.6 / 7.9 | % Officers', Directors' Owners' Comp/Sales | | | | | | |
| 389918M | 552980M | 993368M | Net Sales ($) | 1652M | 18183M | 18498M | 106438M | 307791M | 540806M |
| 163926M | 235594M | 436434M | Total Assets ($) | 4439M | 8073M | 6637M | 36883M | 157906M | 222496M |

© RMA 2012  
M = $ thousand    MM = $ million  
See Pages 9 through 22 for Explanation of Ratios and Data

## Current Data Sorted by Assets     Comparative Historical Data

| | | | | | | | Type of Statement | | |
|---|---|---|---|---|---|---|---|---|---|
| | 1 | 1 | 2 | 8 | 1 | 4 | Unqualified | 22 | 14 |
| 1 | | 7 | 30 | 12 | 1 | 2 | Reviewed | 48 | 36 |
| 2 | | 13 | 11 | 5 | | | Compiled | 32 | 32 |
| 13 | | 16 | 9 | 2 | | | Tax Returns | 16 | 28 |
| 4 | | 1 | 17 | 6 | 3 | 1 | Other | 29 | 31 |
| | 63 (4/1-9/30/11) | | | 109 (10/1/11-3/31/12) | | | | 4/1/07- 3/31/08 | 4/1/08- 3/31/09 |
| 0-500M | 500M-2MM | | 2-10MM | 10-50MM | 50-100MM | 100-250MM | | ALL | ALL |
| 20 | 38 | | 69 | 33 | 5 | 7 | NUMBER OF STATEMENTS | 147 | 141 |
| % | % | | % | % | % | % | ASSETS | % | % |
| 25.4 | 16.0 | | 10.4 | 12.8 | | | Cash & Equivalents | 12.0 | 13.8 |
| 9.2 | 11.1 | | 14.1 | 9.7 | | | Trade Receivables (net) | 11.0 | 10.5 |
| 4.1 | 2.8 | | 2.9 | 1.5 | | | Inventory | 2.3 | 2.2 |
| 1.3 | 2.1 | | 3.5 | 2.9 | | | All Other Current | 3.7 | 3.8 |
| 39.9 | 32.0 | | 30.9 | 26.9 | | | Total Current | 29.0 | 30.3 |
| 44.0 | 53.3 | | 57.0 | 60.4 | | | Fixed Assets (net) | 59.3 | 56.4 |
| 1.8 | 4.9 | | 4.8 | 3.4 | | | Intangibles (net) | 2.8 | 3.5 |
| 14.3 | 9.9 | | 7.3 | 9.3 | | | All Other Non-Current | 8.9 | 9.8 |
| 100.0 | 100.0 | | 100.0 | 100.0 | | | Total | 100.0 | 100.0 |
| | | | | | | | LIABILITIES | | |
| 5.5 | 7.5 | | 8.0 | 4.8 | | | Notes Payable-Short Term | 5.9 | 7.5 |
| 20.6 | 10.4 | | 12.3 | 10.8 | | | Cur. Mat.-L.T.D. | 12.7 | 10.7 |
| 2.0 | 5.0 | | 4.1 | 4.3 | | | Trade Payables | 3.4 | 3.5 |
| 1.0 | .1 | | .2 | .1 | | | Income Taxes Payable | .3 | .3 |
| 15.4 | 7.5 | | 7.7 | 12.5 | | | All Other Current | 5.9 | 6.8 |
| 44.5 | 30.5 | | 32.3 | 32.4 | | | Total Current | 28.2 | 28.8 |
| 42.9 | 45.9 | | 28.3 | 25.4 | | | Long-Term Debt | 35.0 | 33.4 |
| .0 | .3 | | 1.5 | 3.0 | | | Deferred Taxes | 1.4 | 1.1 |
| 5.5 | 5.1 | | 4.8 | 5.5 | | | All Other Non-Current | 3.8 | 4.6 |
| 7.1 | 18.2 | | 33.0 | 33.6 | | | Net Worth | 31.5 | 32.1 |
| 100.0 | 100.0 | | 100.0 | 100.0 | | | Total Liabilties & Net Worth | 100.0 | 100.0 |
| | | | | | | | INCOME DATA | | |
| 100.0 | 100.0 | | 100.0 | 100.0 | | | Net Sales | 100.0 | 100.0 |
| | | | | | | | Gross Profit | | |
| 91.7 | 95.3 | | 95.0 | 93.9 | | | Operating Expenses | 91.7 | 91.8 |
| 8.3 | 4.7 | | 5.0 | 6.1 | | | Operating Profit | 8.3 | 8.2 |
| .5 | 2.0 | | 1.4 | .9 | | | All Other Expenses (net) | 2.3 | 1.6 |
| 7.8 | 2.7 | | 3.6 | 5.2 | | | Profit Before Taxes | 6.0 | 6.6 |
| | | | | | | | RATIOS | | |
| 3.2 | 2.3 | | 2.1 | 2.2 | | | | 1.9 | 2.1 |
| 1.4 | 1.2 | | .9 | 1.1 | | | Current | 1.1 | 1.1 |
| .4 | .3 | | .5 | .5 | | | | .5 | .5 |
| 3.2 | 2.3 | | 1.7 | 2.2 | | | | 1.7 | 1.8 |
| 1.4 | .9 | | .7 | .9 | | | Quick | (146) .9 | .8 |
| .3 | .2 | | .4 | .4 | | | | .3 | .4 |
| 0 UND | 2 152.3 | 5 | 66.6 | 13 27.6 | | | | 3 138.6 | 1 255.6 |
| 0 UND | 9 42.9 | 29 | 12.6 | 27 13.7 | | | Sales/Receivables | 20 18.7 | 16 22.2 |
| 9 40.2 | 28 13.0 | 41 | 8.9 | 39 9.4 | | | | 33 11.1 | 31 11.8 |
| | | | | | | | Cost of Sales/Inventory | | |
| | | | | | | | Cost of Sales/Payables | | |
| 12.2 | 8.9 | | 8.6 | 7.6 | | | | 9.9 | 10.2 |
| 46.4 | 61.4 | | -75.2 | 114.3 | | | Sales/Working Capital | 90.4 | 183.2 |
| -12.2 | -9.4 | | -8.0 | -7.9 | | | | -11.0 | -12.6 |
| 7.2 | 8.1 | | 7.0 | 6.6 | | | | 6.3 | 7.6 |
| (13) 4.0 | (34) 2.4 | (68) | 2.2 | 3.2 | | | EBIT/Interest | (144) 3.0 | (132) 2.8 |
| .4 | -.2 | | 1.0 | 1.5 | | | | 1.3 | 1.3 |
| | | | 2.2 | 2.2 | | | | 1.9 | 2.3 |
| | | (27) | 1.2 | (16) 1.2 | | | Net Profit + Depr., Dep., Amort./Cur. Mat. L/T/D | (53) 1.5 | (40) 1.6 |
| | | | .7 | .9 | | | | 1.0 | 1.2 |
| .5 | .7 | | 1.0 | 1.2 | | | | .9 | 1.1 |
| 5.7 | 2.9 | | 1.9 | 1.4 | | | Fixed/Worth | 1.9 | 1.8 |
| -2.4 | -2.7 | | 5.6 | 5.1 | | | | 4.9 | 6.6 |
| .6 | .7 | | 1.0 | .8 | | | | .9 | .9 |
| 15.4 | 5.3 | | 2.3 | 2.0 | | | Debt/Worth | 1.9 | 1.8 |
| -5.7 | -4.6 | | 8.9 | 5.7 | | | | 5.2 | 8.2 |
| 298.1 | 87.6 | | 38.7 | 25.0 | | | | 43.4 | 43.3 |
| (13) 109.6 | (25) 29.0 | (59) | 15.4 | (28) 12.1 | | | % Profit Before Taxes/Tangible Net Worth | (130) 22.5 | (118) 22.3 |
| 25.3 | .9 | | 1.2 | 4.9 | | | | 7.2 | 5.4 |
| 52.1 | 18.3 | | 13.2 | 7.5 | | | | 13.7 | 15.7 |
| 27.2 | 3.8 | | 3.8 | .5.1 | | | % Profit Before Taxes/Total Assets | 7.4 | 6.7 |
| 2.6 | -7.2 | | .1 | 1.1 | | | | 1.2 | 1.3 |
| 57.8 | 7.6 | | 5.3 | 3.2 | | | | 4.8 | 5.5 |
| 6.8 | 4.4 | | 2.5 | 2.0 | | | Sales/Net Fixed Assets | 2.7 | 3.0 |
| 4.4 | 2.5 | | 1.6 | 1.3 | | | | 1.6 | 1.8 |
| 7.3 | 3.4 | | 2.3 | 1.6 | | | | 2.3 | 2.5 |
| 3.9 | 2.3 | | 1.6 | 1.2 | | | Sales/Total Assets | 1.6 | 1.8 |
| 2.4 | 1.6 | | 1.2 | .9 | | | | 1.1 | 1.2 |
| 3.6 | 5.8 | | 5.4 | 6.1 | | | | 6.5 | 6.1 |
| (11) 7.2 | (32) 8.6 | (65) | 9.9 | (31) 10.9 | | | % Depr., Dep., Amort./Sales | (141) 9.9 | (126) 9.4 |
| 9.3 | 14.0 | | 13.1 | 13.7 | | | | 13.4 | 13.5 |
| 4.1 | 3.3 | | 1.8 | .6 | | | | 2.1 | 1.2 |
| (10) 8.0 | (22) 5.4 | (29) | 3.8 | (14) 1.1 | | | % Officers', Directors' Owners' Comp/Sales | (71) 3.7 | (77) 3.5 |
| 14.1 | 8.0 | | 6.9 | 3.5 | | | | 7.5 | 5.9 |
| 25803M | 105364M | | 554940M | 1030311M | 505493M | 731396M | Net Sales ($) | 1834974M | 2046608M |
| 5754M | 43122M | | 337202M | 784679M | 310112M | 910435M | Total Assets ($) | 1196549M | 1471929M |

M = $ thousand    MM = $ million
See Pages 9 through 22 for Explanation of Ratios and Data

## Comparative Historical Data / Current Data Sorted by Sales

| | | | | | Type of Statement | | | 63 (4/1-9/30/11) | | 109 (10/1/11-3/31/12) | | |
|---|---|---|---|---|---|---|---|---|---|---|---|---|
| | 15 | | 17 | 16 | Unqualified | 1 | 1 | | | 4 | 10 | |
| | 40 | | 45 | 53 | Reviewed | | 8 | 3 | 16 | 20 | 6 | |
| | 31 | | 36 | 31 | Compiled | 1 | 6 | 7 | 11 | 1 | 5 | |
| | 31 | | 36 | 40 | Tax Returns | 8 | 22 | 2 | 4 | 3 | 1 | |
| | 31 | | 25 | 32 | Other | 3 | 3 | 1 | 11 | 6 | 8 | |
| | 4/1/09-3/31/10 ALL | | 4/1/10-3/31/11 ALL | 4/1/11-3/31/12 ALL | | 0-1MM | 1-3MM | 3-5MM | 5-10MM | 10-25MM | 25MM & OVER | |
| | 148 | | 159 | 172 | NUMBER OF STATEMENTS | 13 | 40 | 13 | 42 | 34 | 30 | |
| | % | | % | % | ASSETS | % | % | % | % | % | % | |
| | 14.1 | | 13.0 | 14.2 | Cash & Equivalents | 23.7 | 16.2 | 13.2 | 10.5 | 13.9 | 13.5 | |
| | 10.4 | | 10.8 | 12.0 | Trade Receivables (net) | 7.7 | 7.6 | 11.0 | 15.0 | 15.3 | 12.4 | |
| | 1.7 | | 3.0 | 2.7 | Inventory | .1 | 2.7 | 1.7 | 2.6 | 4.3 | 2.6 | |
| | 2.1 | | 3.0 | 2.7 | All Other Current | 2.7 | 1.5 | 3.2 | 3.4 | 3.2 | 2.6 | |
| | 28.3 | | 29.9 | 31.6 | Total Current | 34.2 | 27.9 | 29.1 | 31.5 | 36.7 | 31.1 | |
| | 59.5 | | 57.6 | 54.9 | Fixed Assets (net) | 50.3 | 58.9 | 49.5 | 59.0 | 50.9 | 52.3 | |
| | 4.3 | | 3.5 | 4.6 | Intangibles (net) | .6 | 5.9 | 4.6 | 3.7 | 4.6 | 5.9 | |
| | 8.0 | | 9.0 | 8.9 | All Other Non-Current | 14.9 | 7.3 | 16.8 | 5.9 | 7.8 | 10.7 | |
| | 100.0 | | 100.0 | 100.0 | Total | 100.0 | 100.0 | 100.0 | 100.0 | 100.0 | 100.0 | |
| | | | | | LIABILITIES | | | | | | | |
| | 5.7 | | 5.4 | 6.6 | Notes Payable-Short Term | 9.4 | 6.6 | 11.1 | 6.7 | 5.8 | 4.0 | |
| | 12.1 | | 12.4 | 12.1 | Cur. Mat.-L.T.D. | 3.3 | 16.8 | 14.1 | 13.3 | 10.3 | 9.2 | |
| | 2.9 | | 4.5 | 4.0 | Trade Payables | .9 | 4.4 | 3.2 | 4.8 | 4.6 | 3.6 | |
| | .4 | | .2 | .2 | Income Taxes Payable | .0 | .5 | .2 | .0 | .4 | .1 | |
| | 6.1 | | 4.8 | 9.5 | All Other Current | 8.2 | 12.3 | 7.2 | 7.2 | 8.1 | 12.2 | |
| | 27.1 | | 27.3 | 32.5 | Total Current | 21.9 | 40.6 | 35.7 | 32.1 | 29.2 | 29.1 | |
| | 33.9 | | 31.0 | 33.3 | Long-Term Debt | 33.0 | 52.5 | 29.0 | 29.1 | 23.7 | 26.7 | |
| | 1.7 | | 1.6 | 1.3 | Deferred Taxes | .0 | .3 | .7 | 1.5 | 2.5 | 1.8 | |
| | 4.3 | | 4.3 | 5.4 | All Other Non-Current | 5.8 | 4.6 | 3.5 | 4.3 | 7.0 | 7.0 | |
| | 32.9 | | 35.8 | 27.5 | Net Worth | 39.4 | 2.0 | 31.1 | 33.0 | 37.6 | 35.5 | |
| | 100.0 | | 100.0 | 100.0 | Total Liabilities & Net Worth | 100.0 | 100.0 | 100.0 | 100.0 | 100.0 | 100.0 | |
| | | | | | INCOME DATA | | | | | | | |
| | 100.0 | | 100.0 | 100.0 | Net Sales | 100.0 | 100.0 | 100.0 | 100.0 | 100.0 | 100.0 | |
| | | | | | Gross Profit | | | | | | | |
| | 91.8 | | 92.5 | 94.3 | Operating Expenses | 82.1 | 96.3 | 99.1 | 95.9 | 92.9 | 94.2 | |
| | 8.2 | | 7.5 | 5.7 | Operating Profit | 17.9 | 3.7 | .9 | 4.1 | 7.1 | 5.8 | |
| | 1.7 | | 1.5 | 1.4 | All Other Expenses (net) | 3.6 | 1.8 | -.2 | 1.3 | .7 | 1.8 | |
| | 6.5 | | 5.9 | 4.3 | Profit Before Taxes | 14.4 | 2.0 | 1.1 | 2.8 | 6.4 | 4.0 | |
| | | | | | RATIOS | | | | | | | |
| | 2.1 | | 2.1 | 2.3 | | 3.2 | 2.6 | 1.7 | 2.1 | 2.4 | 2.0 | |
| | 1.0 | | 1.1 | 1.1 | Current | 1.7 | .7 | 1.1 | .9 | 1.6 | 1.3 | |
| | .5 | | .5 | .5 | | .4 | .3 | .3 | .5 | .5 | .7 | |
| | 1.9 | | 1.8 | 2.0 | | 3.2 | 2.6 | 1.2 | 1.7 | 2.2 | 1.8 | |
| | .9 | | .9 | .8 | Quick | 1.7 | .5 | .6 | .6 | 1.1 | 1.1 | |
| | .4 | | .4 | .3 | | .4 | .2 | .2 | .4 | .5 | .5 | |
| 3 | 106.1 | 2 | 184.0 | 5 | 75.9 | | 0 | UND | 0 | UND | 3 | 119.5 | 5 | 68.5 | 13 | 27.4 | 22 | 16.8 |
| 18 | 20.1 | 15 | 23.7 | 23 | 16.2 | Sales/Receivables | 0 | UND | 8 | 48.3 | 15 | 24.4 | 23 | 16.0 | 27 | 13.4 | 33 | 10.9 |
| 34 | 10.8 | 35 | 10.3 | 38 | 9.5 | | 43 | 8.5 | 26 | 14.1 | 33 | 11.1 | 39 | 9.3 | 52 | 7.0 | 42 | 8.7 |
| | | | | | Cost of Sales/Inventory | | | | | | | |
| | | | | | Cost of Sales/Payables | | | | | | | |
| | 10.0 | | 9.4 | 8.6 | | 3.4 | 15.6 | 23.0 | 10.7 | 6.2 | 7.7 | |
| | 853.4 | | 107.0 | 68.0 | Sales/Working Capital | 11.8 | -32.0 | 74.0 | NM | 12.5 | 24.8 | |
| | -10.1 | | -10.8 | -9.2 | | -11.1 | -7.1 | -8.2 | -10.2 | -10.0 | -15.1 | |
| | 7.6 | | 8.3 | 7.1 | | | 6.7 | 9.3 | 5.0 | 11.2 | 6.1 | |
| (141) | 3.7 | (146) | 3.4 | (160) | 2.7 | EBIT/Interest | | (36) | 2.0 | (12) | 3.8 | (40) | 2.0 | (33) | 4.1 | 3.1 |
| | 2.0 | | 1.4 | 1.2 | | | -.5 | -6.7 | .7 | 1.7 | 1.8 | |
| | 2.5 | | 2.4 | 2.2 | | | | | 1.7 | 2.6 | 1.8 | |
| (57) | 1.9 | (46) | 1.7 | (56) | 1.2 | Net Profit + Depr., Dep., Amort./Cur. Mat. L/T/D | | | (18) | 1.1 | (15) | 2.1 | (13) | 1.2 |
| | 1.2 | | 1.1 | .9 | | | | | .6 | .9 | .9 | |
| | 1.1 | | .9 | 1.0 | | .4 | 1.1 | .7 | 1.1 | .6 | 1.1 | |
| | 2.0 | | 1.6 | 1.8 | Fixed/Worth | 1.0 | 39.7 | 3.9 | 1.7 | 1.5 | 1.4 | |
| | 5.7 | | 4.6 | 14.6 | | 26.9 | -1.9 | 12.3 | 4.3 | 5.4 | 3.2 | |
| | 1.0 | | .8 | .9 | | .6 | 1.4 | .7 | 1.1 | .8 | 1.3 | |
| | 2.1 | | 1.8 | 2.2 | Debt/Worth | 1.0 | 51.6 | 3.8 | 2.0 | 2.3 | 1.9 | |
| | 7.2 | | 6.9 | 25.9 | | 34.1 | -4.2 | 20.5 | 6.0 | 6.8 | 4.3 | |
| | 50.4 | | 46.5 | 42.6 | | 151.8 | 104.2 | 102.0 | 45.4 | 38.9 | 21.0 | |
| (123) | 26.8 | (139) | 22.7 | (135) | 17.1 | % Profit Before Taxes/Tangible Net Worth | (12) | 32.6 | (21) | 28.4 | (11) | 51.0 | (35) | 12.0 | (30) | 20.0 | (26) | 16.4 |
| | 13.0 | | 12.4 | 4.4 | | 4.6 | 1.8 | 1.4 | -3.4 | 7.0 | 6.0 | |
| | 13.9 | | 15.4 | 15.5 | | 20.8 | 23.5 | 22.0 | 12.6 | 15.0 | 7.2 | |
| | 8.1 | | 7.5 | 4.9 | % Profit Before Taxes/Total Assets | 17.3 | 3.6 | 7.0 | 3.3 | 6.5 | 4.6 | |
| | 2.7 | | 1.5 | .6 | | .7 | -6.8 | -13.9 | -1.2 | 2.6 | 1.9 | |
| | 4.9 | | 5.4 | 5.8 | | 6.0 | 6.5 | 11.4 | 4.5 | 7.2 | 4.8 | |
| | 2.7 | | 3.0 | 2.9 | Sales/Net Fixed Assets | 2.4 | 3.7 | 5.2 | 3.1 | 2.5 | 2.4 | |
| | 1.6 | | 1.8 | 1.7 | | 1.2 | 1.9 | 1.1 | 1.9 | 1.5 | 1.5 | |
| | 2.4 | | 2.5 | 2.5 | | 2.4 | 3.5 | 4.6 | 2.5 | 2.4 | 1.8 | |
| | 1.6 | | 1.6 | 1.6 | Sales/Total Assets | 1.1 | 2.3 | 2.4 | 1.6 | 1.4 | 1.3 | |
| | 1.1 | | 1.2 | 1.2 | | .4 | 1.3 | .7 | 1.3 | 1.1 | 1.0 | |
| | 6.3 | | 5.9 | 5.4 | | 7.4 | 6.6 | 5.6 | 5.5 | 4.1 | 4.5 | |
| (134) | 9.8 | (142) | 9.8 | (148) | 8.8 | % Depr., Dep., Amort./Sales | (11) | 8.7 | (32) | 10.9 | (10) | 8.2 | (38) | 9.2 | (33) | 8.9 | (24) | 7.4 |
| | 13.3 | | 14.6 | 13.1 | | 14.4 | 15.9 | 13.6 | 12.6 | 12.8 | 11.5 | |
| | 2.1 | | 1.3 | 2.0 | | | 4.1 | | 2.8 | .8 | .3 | |
| (76) | 3.9 | (82) | 4.3 | (78) | 4.1 | % Officers', Directors' Owners' Comp/Sales | | (24) | 5.7 | (17) | 4.0 | (16) | 2.4 | (10) | .6 |
| | 6.3 | | 7.0 | 7.5 | | | 9.0 | | 7.4 | 8.0 | 1.6 | |
| | 2983604M | | 3844294M | 2953307M | Net Sales ($) | 6622M | 80220M | 48213M | 294920M | 468482M | 2054850M | |
| | 1872455M | | 2192502M | 2391304M | Total Assets ($) | 8107M | 50800M | 36438M | 189029M | 349468M | 1757462M | |

M = $ thousand    MM = $ million
See Pages 9 through 22 for Explanation of Ratios and Data

## Current Data Sorted by Assets      Comparative Historical Data

| | 0-500M | 500M-2MM | 2-10MM | 10-50MM | 50-100MM | 100-250MM | | 4/1/07-3/31/08 ALL | 4/1/08-3/31/09 ALL |
|---|---|---|---|---|---|---|---|---|---|
| | | | 4 | 4 | | | Type of Statement | | |
| | | | 14 | 6 | | | Unqualified | 8 | 7 |
| | 1 | 9 | 5 | 5 | | | Reviewed | 25 | 20 |
| | 11 | 18 | 11 | 2 | | | Compiled | 29 | 26 |
| | 6 | 14 | 25 | 16 | | 1 | Tax Returns | 34 | 16 |
| | | 20 (4/1-9/30/11) | | 132 (10/1/11-3/31/12) | | | Other | 42 | 45 |
| | 18 | 41 | 59 | 33 | | 1 | NUMBER OF STATEMENTS | 138 | 114 |
| | % | % | % | % | % | % | ASSETS | % | % |
| | 33.6 | 15.9 | 8.6 | 8.8 | | | Cash & Equivalents | 10.2 | 8.9 |
| | 4.9 | 8.6 | 10.7 | 7.3 | | | Trade Receivables (net) | 7.8 | 9.4 |
| | .1 | .9 | 1.4 | 3.7 | | | Inventory | 1.8 | 1.8 |
| | 1.1 | 3.1 | 3.3 | 1.5 | | | All Other Current | 3.3 | 3.6 |
| | 39.7 | 28.5 | 24.0 | 21.3 | | | Total Current | 23.2 | 23.8 |
| | 39.1 | 57.3 | 63.2 | 67.0 | | | Fixed Assets (net) | 68.5 | 64.9 |
| | 2.2 | 4.0 | 4.5 | 4.4 | | | Intangibles (net) | 1.2 | 2.6 |
| | 19.0 | 10.3 | 8.3 | 7.2 | | | All Other Non-Current | 7.1 | 8.8 |
| | 100.0 | 100.0 | 100.0 | 100.0 | | | Total | 100.0 | 100.0 |
| | | | | | | | LIABILITIES | | |
| | 60.8 | 5.4 | 2.8 | 4.0 | | | Notes Payable-Short Term | 3.1 | 4.1 |
| | 16.7 | 16.7 | 16.2 | 9.3 | | | Cur. Mat.-L.T.D. | 12.1 | 12.1 |
| | 4.1 | 5.4 | 7.1 | 4.7 | | | Trade Payables | 5.3 | 4.5 |
| | .0 | .3 | .2 | .1 | | | Income Taxes Payable | .6 | .3 |
| | 16.3 | 10.7 | 6.0 | 4.4 | | | All Other Current | 6.9 | 11.0 |
| | 97.9 | 38.5 | 32.3 | 22.4 | | | Total Current | 28.0 | 31.9 |
| | 69.9 | 79.9 | 38.7 | 32.2 | | | Long-Term Debt | 51.7 | 45.4 |
| | .0 | .1 | 1.5 | 4.2 | | | Deferred Taxes | 1.7 | 1.1 |
| | 57.3 | 5.5 | 3.4 | 4.4 | | | All Other Non-Current | 8.0 | 4.9 |
| | -125.1 | -24.0 | 24.1 | 36.8 | | | Net Worth | 10.5 | 16.6 |
| | 100.0 | 100.0 | 100.0 | 100.0 | | | Total Liabilties & Net Worth | 100.0 | 100.0 |
| | | | | | | | INCOME DATA | | |
| | 100.0 | 100.0 | 100.0 | 100.0 | | | Net Sales | 100.0 | 100.0 |
| | | | | | | | Gross Profit | | |
| | 97.8 | 93.4 | 93.9 | 94.7 | | | Operating Expenses | 93.0 | 93.2 |
| | 2.2 | 6.6 | 6.1 | 5.3 | | | Operating Profit | 7.0 | 6.8 |
| | .8 | 2.9 | 1.9 | 2.2 | | | All Other Expenses (net) | 2.9 | 2.3 |
| | 1.4 | 3.7 | 4.2 | 3.0 | | | Profit Before Taxes | 4.1 | 4.5 |
| | | | | | | | RATIOS | | |
| | 2.0 | 1.8 | 1.5 | 1.7 | | | | 1.3 | 1.3 |
| | .6 | .9 | .7 | 1.0 | | | Current | .8 | .7 |
| | .2 | .3 | .4 | .4 | | | | .5 | .4 |
| | 2.0 | 1.6 | 1.1 | 1.2 | | | | 1.0 | .9 |
| | .4 | .7 | .6 | .6 | | | Quick | (137) .6 | .5 |
| | .2 | .2 | .3 | .3 | | | | .3 | .3 |
| | 0 UND | 0 UND | 3 118.3 | 10 38.2 | | | | 5 79.1 | 5 74.0 |
| | 0 UND | 8 43.5 | 16 22.3 | 23 16.0 | | | Sales/Receivables | 12 29.8 | 13 27.3 |
| | 0 UND | 19 19.1 | 25 14.6 | 34 10.8 | | | | 30 12.2 | 24 15.5 |
| | | | | | | | | | |
| | | | | | | | Cost of Sales/Inventory | | |
| | | | | | | | | | |
| | | | | | | | Cost of Sales/Payables | | |
| | 257.5 | 22.0 | 20.3 | 11.0 | | | | 40.4 | 30.7 |
| | -52.9 | -82.9 | -37.8 | -137.5 | | | Sales/Working Capital | -39.1 | -25.0 |
| | -10.8 | -9.1 | -6.9 | -8.1 | | | | -10.3 | -10.5 |
| | 9.6 | 4.4 | 5.5 | 4.6 | | | | 3.1 | 4.3 |
| | (14) 2.8 | (37) 1.5 | (57) 2.7 | (32) 2.9 | | | EBIT/Interest | (128) 1.9 | (105) 2.5 |
| | -.6 | .3 | 1.2 | 1.1 | | | | 1.0 | 1.2 |
| | | | 1.7 | 2.1 | | | | 1.9 | 2.0 |
| | | (20) 1.4 | (14) 1.5 | | | | Net Profit + Depr., Dep., Amort./Cur. Mat. L/T/D | (35) 1.5 | (39) 1.5 |
| | | | .9 | 1.1 | | | | 1.0 | 1.0 |
| | 1.2 | 1.7 | 1.5 | 1.3 | | | | 1.7 | 1.6 |
| | -.8 | -90.0 | 2.9 | 2.2 | | | Fixed/Worth | 5.4 | 3.0 |
| | -.2 | -.9 | 30.8 | 3.8 | | | | -11.1 | UND |
| | -7.7 | 2.1 | 1.2 | .9 | | | | 1.8 | 1.5 |
| | -2.3 | -93.6 | 3.3 | 1.9 | | | Debt/Worth | 5.9 | 3.4 |
| | -1.4 | -2.4 | 43.0 | 4.9 | | | | -14.9 | UND |
| | | 56.9 | 35.6 | 21.4 | | | | 33.2 | 37.6 |
| | (20) 11.2 | (47) 10.8 | (32) 13.0 | | | % Profit Before Taxes/Tangible Net Worth | (94) 16.5 | (86) 18.9 |
| | | -9.0 | 3.3 | -.4 | | | | 5.3 | 7.3 |
| | 59.3 | 18.9 | 12.4 | 7.1 | | | | 9.8 | 10.8 |
| | 12.6 | 2.0 | 4.1 | 4.6 | | | % Profit Before Taxes/Total Assets | 4.2 | 5.3 |
| | -11.4 | -5.4 | .7 | -.3 | | | | .1 | .7 |
| | 361.1 | 10.0 | 4.8 | 2.2 | | | | 4.3 | 5.1 |
| | 25.9 | 4.2 | 2.3 | 1.3 | | | Sales/Net Fixed Assets | 2.2 | 2.3 |
| | 10.0 | 2.4 | 1.5 | 1.0 | | | | 1.1 | 1.2 |
| | 17.3 | 4.2 | 2.6 | 1.3 | | | | 2.5 | 2.7 |
| | 12.5 | 2.7 | 1.6 | 1.0 | | | Sales/Total Assets | 1.5 | 1.5 |
| | 6.0 | 1.6 | 1.1 | .7 | | | | .9 | 1.0 |
| | | 6.5 | 5.2 | 7.3 | | | | 6.8 | 6.4 |
| | (28) 13.5 | (49) 9.0 | (31) 9.7 | | | % Depr., Dep., Amort./Sales | (125) 10.5 | (101) 9.2 |
| | | 18.0 | 13.4 | 13.2 | | | | 14.5 | 13.5 |
| | 3.6 | 1.7 | 1.4 | | | | | 2.0 | 1.3 |
| | (10) 4.3 | (20) 3.3 | (25) 3.6 | | | % Officers', Directors' Owners' Comp/Sales | (49) 3.2 | (40) 2.5 |
| | 7.0 | 6.2 | 5.0 | | | | | 5.7 | 4.9 |
| | 33850M | 140079M | 532891M | 766622M | | 140360M | Net Sales ($) | 1391293M | 2040455M |
| | 3771M | 48016M | 271967M | 699116M | | 124071M | Total Assets ($) | 1124561M | 1235336M |

*(The 50-100MM column is marked "DATA NOT AVAILABLE".)*

M = $ thousand    MM = $ million
See Pages 9 through 22 for Explanation of Ratios and Data

## Comparative Historical Data | Current Data Sorted by Sales

| | | | Type of Statement | | | | | | |
|---|---|---|---|---|---|---|---|---|---|
| 5 | 11 | 8 | Unqualified | | 1 | | | 6 | 1 |
| 21 | 27 | 20 | Reviewed | | | 4 | 8 | 5 | 3 |
| 24 | 17 | 20 | Compiled | 3 | 4 | 3 | 5 | 4 | 1 |
| 22 | 34 | 42 | Tax Returns | 6 | 14 | 12 | 5 | 4 | 1 |
| 50 | 68 | 62 | Other | 3 | 10 | 9 | 19 | 14 | 7 |
| 4/1/09-3/31/10 ALL | 4/1/10-3/31/11 ALL | 4/1/11-3/31/12 ALL | | 20 (4/1-9/30/11) | | | 132 (10/1/11-3/31/12) | | |
| | | | | 0-1MM | 1-3MM | 3-5MM | 5-10MM | 10-25MM | 25MM & OVER |
| 122 | 157 | 152 | NUMBER OF STATEMENTS | 12 | 29 | 28 | 37 | 33 | 13 |
| % | % | % | ASSETS | % | % | % | % | % | % |
| 10.7 | 9.3 | 13.6 | Cash & Equivalents | 23.6 | 15.3 | 12.4 | 13.7 | 9.9 | 12.0 |
| 8.4 | 8.7 | 8.7 | Trade Receivables (net) | 1.3 | 7.1 | 7.8 | 9.2 | 10.4 | 15.2 |
| 2.0 | 1.5 | 1.6 | Inventory | .0 | .5 | .8 | 1.7 | 1.8 | 6.5 |
| 4.3 | 4.1 | 2.6 | All Other Current | .0 | 1.6 | 2.6 | 4.6 | 2.2 | 2.7 |
| 25.4 | 23.6 | 26.5 | Total Current | 24.9 | 24.5 | 23.6 | 29.2 | 24.3 | 36.4 |
| 64.7 | 64.8 | 59.5 | Fixed Assets (net) | 71.3 | 51.3 | 67.6 | 55.6 | 61.5 | 56.0 |
| 2.4 | 2.8 | 4.1 | Intangibles (net) | .4 | 2.8 | 2.7 | 7.0 | 4.7 | 2.9 |
| 7.5 | 8.9 | 9.9 | All Other Non-Current | 3.3 | 21.3 | 6.1 | 8.1 | 9.5 | 4.7 |
| 100.0 | 100.0 | 100.0 | Total | 100.0 | 100.0 | 100.0 | 100.0 | 100.0 | 100.0 |
| | | | LIABILITIES | | | | | | |
| 4.9 | 6.5 | 10.7 | Notes Payable-Short Term | 1.2 | 40.5 | 4.8 | 3.8 | 2.8 | 5.0 |
| 12.4 | 11.8 | 14.8 | Cur. Mat.-L.T.D. | 14.4 | 13.7 | 15.5 | 21.2 | 10.8 | 8.3 |
| 5.1 | 5.1 | 5.8 | Trade Payables | .1 | 7.0 | 2.6 | 5.9 | 5.6 | 15.1 |
| .2 | .3 | .2 | Income Taxes Payable | .0 | .1 | .5 | .2 | .2 | .2 |
| 8.5 | 7.8 | 8.1 | All Other Current | 4.8 | 13.1 | 3.6 | 11.4 | 5.8 | 6.5 |
| 31.3 | 31.5 | 39.6 | Total Current | 20.5 | 74.4 | 27.0 | 42.4 | 25.2 | 35.0 |
| 49.2 | 47.7 | 52.0 | Long-Term Debt | 85.3 | 47.2 | 59.4 | 65.0 | 32.6 | 28.3 |
| 1.4 | 2.1 | 1.5 | Deferred Taxes | .0 | .5 | 2.0 | 1.1 | 2.1 | 4.2 |
| 7.1 | 7.1 | 10.6 | All Other Non-Current | 25.0 | 29.8 | 6.0 | 2.4 | 4.7 | 2.6 |
| 11.0 | 11.6 | -3.7 | Net Worth | -30.8 | -51.9 | 5.6 | -10.9 | 35.5 | 29.9 |
| 100.0 | 100.0 | 100.0 | Total Liabilities & Net Worth | 100.0 | 100.0 | 100.0 | 100.0 | 100.0 | 100.0 |
| | | | INCOME DATA | | | | | | |
| 100.0 | 100.0 | 100.0 | Net Sales | 100.0 | 100.0 | 100.0 | 100.0 | 100.0 | 100.0 |
| | | | Gross Profit | | | | | | |
| 94.4 | 93.5 | 94.4 | Operating Expenses | 83.0 | 96.7 | 97.3 | 93.3 | 94.5 | 96.6 |
| 5.6 | 6.5 | 5.6 | Operating Profit | 17.0 | 3.3 | 2.7 | 6.7 | 5.5 | 3.4 |
| 1.9 | 2.2 | 2.1 | All Other Expenses (net) | 7.0 | 1.9 | 1.5 | 1.4 | 1.7 | 2.0 |
| 3.7 | 4.3 | 3.5 | Profit Before Taxes | 10.0 | 1.4 | 1.2 | 5.2 | 3.9 | 1.4 |
| | | | RATIOS | | | | | | |
| 1.6 | 1.5 | 1.6 | | 2.8 | 1.2 | 1.9 | 1.4 | 1.5 | 1.8 |
| .8 | .7 | .9 | Current | .8 | .5 | .9 | .7 | 1.0 | 1.1 |
| .4 | .4 | .3 | | .2 | .2 | .3 | .3 | .6 | .5 |
| 1.2 | 1.0 | 1.2 | | 2.8 | .9 | 1.5 | 1.1 | 1.3 | 1.7 |
| .6 | .5 | .6 | Quick | .8 | .5 | .6 | .6 | .7 | .8 |
| .3 | .3 | .2 | | .2 | .2 | .2 | .2 | .5 | .4 |
| 5 75.8 | 5 69.2 | 0 UND | | 0 UND | 0 UND | 0 UND | 0 UND | 12 30.6 | 10 37.1 |
| 13 27.7 | 16 22.7 | 11 32.0 | Sales/Receivables | 0 UND | 4 85.0 | 10 35.9 | 9 42.7 | 23 16.2 | 33 11.2 |
| 27 13.4 | 25 14.3 | 25 14.7 | | 0 UND | 19 19.6 | 19 19.3 | 24 15.2 | 34 10.7 | 38 9.6 |
| | | | Cost of Sales/Inventory | | | | | | |
| | | | Cost of Sales/Payables | | | | | | |
| 15.8 | 17.7 | 20.2 | | 6.9 | 142.6 | 10.2 | 31.6 | 17.2 | 10.7 |
| -41.0 | -28.6 | -50.5 | Sales/Working Capital | NM | -14.5 | -82.8 | -30.8 | -137.5 | 65.2 |
| -9.1 | -7.4 | -9.0 | | -6.6 | -6.9 | -8.1 | -7.7 | -29.0 | -16.3 |
| 4.1 | 4.7 | 5.1 | | 4.7 | 4.2 | 4.0 | 5.9 | 5.6 | 5.0 |
| (114) 2.5 | (147) 2.2 | (141) 2.2 | EBIT/Interest | (10) 1.6 | (24) 1.5 | (27) 1.3 | (32) 3.6 | 3.2 | (11) 3.0 |
| 1.1 | .9 | 1.0 | | .7 | .4 | -.5 | 1.3 | 1.4 | -.7 |
| 2.2 | 1.8 | 1.7 | | | | | | 2.0 | |
| (34) 1.5 | (48) 1.3 | (36) 1.4 | Net Profit + Depr., Dep., Amort./Cur. Mat. L/T/D | | | | | (14) 1.4 | |
| 1.3 | 1.0 | 1.0 | | | | | | .9 | |
| 1.5 | 1.6 | 1.4 | | 1.1 | 1.7 | 1.6 | 1.6 | 1.3 | 1.1 |
| 3.2 | 3.1 | 3.1 | Fixed/Worth | 22.2 | 41.6 | 3.5 | 7.4 | 1.8 | 2.3 |
| -5.0 | -32.8 | -5.2 | | -2.0 | -.8 | -4.7 | -.9 | 3.9 | 6.5 |
| 1.5 | 1.5 | 1.4 | | 1.1 | 2.6 | 1.2 | 1.5 | 1.0 | 1.1 |
| 4.4 | 3.3 | 4.3 | Debt/Worth | NM | 194.3 | 3.5 | 11.4 | 2.0 | 1.9 |
| -7.2 | -44.8 | -8.0 | | -2.2 | -2.2 | -8.2 | -2.6 | 4.4 | 7.3 |
| 34.3 | 32.8 | 28.5 | | | 39.4 | 12.4 | 49.7 | 39.5 | 22.3 |
| (84) 18.6 | (115) 13.8 | (103) 12.0 | % Profit Before Taxes/Tangible Net Worth | (15) 6.3 | (17) 3.7 | (22) 19.1 | (31) 12.1 | (12) 14.8 |
| 5.7 | .4 | 1.4 | | | -22.6 | -2.8 | 8.5 | 6.2 | -60.2 |
| 10.6 | 10.8 | 12.7 | | 30.2 | 18.0 | 5.9 | 22.9 | 11.0 | 9.1 |
| 5.0 | 3.9 | 4.1 | % Profit Before Taxes/Total Assets | 2.6 | 2.0 | .9 | 7.0 | 4.1 | 5.4 |
| .7 | -.3 | -.2 | | -.5 | -3.3 | -1.3 | 1.1 | 1.8 | -7.0 |
| 4.3 | 4.1 | 7.4 | | 6.8 | 43.1 | 5.3 | 10.3 | 4.8 | 12.0 |
| 2.2 | 2.1 | 2.6 | Sales/Net Fixed Assets | 1.5 | 3.8 | 2.1 | 3.7 | 2.2 | 2.0 |
| 1.3 | 1.4 | 1.4 | | .7 | 2.3 | 1.1 | 2.0 | 1.3 | 1.4 |
| 2.4 | 2.4 | 3.7 | | 6.1 | 12.5 | 2.9 | 3.9 | 2.1 | 3.7 |
| 1.4 | 1.5 | 1.8 | Sales/Total Assets | 1.4 | 2.6 | 1.6 | 2.5 | 1.3 | 1.2 |
| 1.0 | 1.0 | 1.0 | | .4 | 1.4 | 1.0 | 1.5 | 1.0 | .9 |
| 5.7 | 6.7 | 5.8 | | 8.1 | 6.6 | 8.0 | 5.2 | 4.9 | 4.1 |
| (108) 10.3 | (131) 9.4 | (117) 9.9 | % Depr., Dep., Amort./Sales | (10) 12.3 | (21) 13.3 | (22) 13.6 | (25) 8.6 | (28) 7.7 | (11) 8.2 |
| 15.1 | 14.0 | 14.2 | | 31.7 | 18.5 | 17.0 | 10.9 | 11.1 | 13.1 |
| 1.5 | 1.5 | 1.5 | | | 3.1 | 2.1 | 2.0 | 1.2 | |
| (48) 2.8 | (59) 2.7 | (63) 3.3 | % Officers', Directors' Owners' Comp/Sales | (18) 5.0 | (13) 4.1 | (15) 3.0 | (11) 1.4 | |
| 4.8 | 4.6 | 5.2 | | | 7.9 | 4.8 | 4.7 | 1.7 | |
| 1383072M | 1844716M | 1613802M | Net Sales ($) | 8001M | 59140M | 110430M | 270684M | 534361M | 631186M |
| 1157546M | 1638653M | 1146941M | Total Assets ($) | 10704M | 31327M | 100494M | 161571M | 416286M | 426559M |

M = $ thousand    MM = $ million
See Pages 9 through 22 for Explanation of Ratios and Data

## Current Data Sorted by Assets      Comparative Historical Data

| Type of Statement | | | | | | | | |
|---|---|---|---|---|---|---|---|---|
| 0-500M | 500M-2MM | 2-10MM | 10-50MM | 50-100MM | 100-250MM | | 4/1/07-3/31/08 ALL | 4/1/08-3/31/09 ALL |
| 1 | | 3 | | | | Unqualified | 1 | 4 |
| | | 2 | 1 | | | Reviewed | | |
| | 2 | 1 | 1 | | | Compiled | | 2 |
| 3 | 1 | | | | | Tax Returns | 3 | |
| 2 | 3 | 9 | | | | Other | 1 | 6 |
| | 4 (4/1-9/30/11) | | 26 (10/1/11-3/31/12) | | | | | |
| **6** | **6** | **15** | **3** | | | **NUMBER OF STATEMENTS** | **6** | **12** |
| % | % | % | % | % | % | | % | % |
| | | 12.6 | D | D | | Cash & Equivalents | | 9.7 |
| | | 39.9 | A | A | | Trade Receivables (net) | | 25.6 |
| | | 4.2 | T | T | | Inventory | | 1.5 |
| | | 3.4 | A | A | | All Other Current | | 7.9 |
| | | 60.2 | | | | Total Current | | 44.7 |
| | | 34.2 | N | N | | Fixed Assets (net) | | 38.4 |
| | | 1.7 | O | O | | Intangibles (net) | | 4.9 |
| | | 4.0 | T | T | | All Other Non-Current | | 12.1 |
| | | 100.0 | | | | Total | | 100.0 |
| | | | A | A | | **LIABILITIES** | | |
| | | 7.3 | V | V | | Notes Payable-Short Term | | 4.9 |
| | | 3.2 | A | A | | Cur. Mat.-L.T.D. | | 6.1 |
| | | 10.8 | I | I | | Trade Payables | | 20.3 |
| | | .0 | L | L | | Income Taxes Payable | | .0 |
| | | 11.6 | A | A | | All Other Current | | 15.9 |
| | | 33.0 | B | B | | Total Current | | 47.2 |
| | | 14.8 | L | L | | Long-Term Debt | | 18.5 |
| | | 1.7 | E | E | | Deferred Taxes | | .0 |
| | | .2 | | | | All Other Non-Current | | 6.0 |
| | | 50.3 | | | | Net Worth | | 28.3 |
| | | 100.0 | | | | Total Liabilities & Net Worth | | 100.0 |
| | | | | | | **INCOME DATA** | | |
| | | 100.0 | | | | Net Sales | | 100.0 |
| | | | | | | Gross Profit | | |
| | | 91.2 | | | | Operating Expenses | | 92.4 |
| | | 8.8 | | | | Operating Profit | | 7.6 |
| | | 3.6 | | | | All Other Expenses (net) | | .6 |
| | | 5.2 | | | | Profit Before Taxes | | 7.0 |
| | | | | | | **RATIOS** | | |
| | | 10.7 | | | | | | 2.7 |
| | | 2.1 | | | | Current | | 1.1 |
| | | 1.1 | | | | | | .3 |
| | | 10.7 | | | | | | 2.1 |
| | | 2.1 | | | | Quick | | .8 |
| | | .9 | | | | | | .2 |
| | 43 | 8.5 | | | | | 0 | UND |
| | 48 | 7.6 | | | | Sales/Receivables | 25 | 14.7 |
| | 58 | 6.3 | | | | | 48 | 7.6 |
| | | | | | | Cost of Sales/Inventory | | |
| | | | | | | Cost of Sales/Payables | | |
| | | 5.1 | | | | | | 7.1 |
| | | 8.7 | | | | Sales/Working Capital | | NM |
| | | 64.5 | | | | | | -12.0 |
| | | 6.5 | | | | | | 12.8 |
| | (10) | 2.4 | | | | EBIT/Interest | (11) | 7.1 |
| | | -2.1 | | | | | | 2.4 |
| | | | | | | Net Profit + Depr., Dep., Amort./Cur. Mat. L/T/D | | |
| | | .3 | | | | | | .7 |
| | | .6 | | | | Fixed/Worth | | 1.8 |
| | | 3.1 | | | | | | NM |
| | | .1 | | | | | | .7 |
| | | 1.0 | | | | Debt/Worth | | 1.3 |
| | | 4.4 | | | | | | NM |
| | | 36.7 | | | | | | |
| | (13) | 11.6 | | | | % Profit Before Taxes/Tangible Net Worth | | |
| | | 1.1 | | | | | | |
| | | 13.5 | | | | | | 25.0 |
| | | 3.3 | | | | % Profit Before Taxes/Total Assets | | 7.2 |
| | | .5 | | | | | | 5.6 |
| | | 37.2 | | | | | | 28.5 |
| | | 5.2 | | | | Sales/Net Fixed Assets | | 7.4 |
| | | 2.6 | | | | | | 4.0 |
| | | 4.6 | | | | | | 3.8 |
| | | 2.4 | | | | Sales/Total Assets | | 3.2 |
| | | .8 | | | | | | 2.2 |
| | | .8 | | | | | | |
| | (14) | 4.6 | | | | % Depr., Dep., Amort./Sales | | |
| | | 10.9 | | | | | | |
| | | | | | | % Officers', Directors' Owners' Comp/Sales | | |
| 11686M | 22172M | 197084M | 169460M | | | Net Sales ($) | 123170M | 971029M |
| 1991M | 5067M | 67608M | 67224M | | | Total Assets ($) | 64210M | 283295M |

M = $ thousand    MM = $ million
See Pages 9 through 22 for Explanation of Ratios and Data

## Comparative Historical Data / Current Data Sorted by Sales

| | | | Type of Statement | 0-1MM | 1-3MM | 3-5MM | 5-10MM | 10-25MM | 25MM & OVER |
|---|---|---|---|---|---|---|---|---|---|
| 4 | 6 | 4 | Unqualified | | 1 | | 1 | 2 | 1 |
| 2 | 2 | 3 | Reviewed | | | | | 1 | |
| 4 | 7 | 3 | Compiled | | | 1 | 1 | | 1 |
| 7 | 6 | 5 | Tax Returns | | 1 | 2 | 2 | | 1 |
| 11 | 15 | 15 | Other | 2 | 5 | 1 | 2 | 2 | 3 |
| 4/1/09-3/31/10 ALL | 4/1/10-3/31/11 ALL | 4/1/11-3/31/12 ALL | | | 4 (4/1-9/30/11) | | | 26 (10/1/11-3/31/12) | |
| 28 | 36 | 30 | NUMBER OF STATEMENTS | 3 | 6 | 5 | 6 | 5 | 5 |
| % | % | % | | % | % | % | % | % | % |
| | | | **ASSETS** | | | | | | |
| 14.6 | 15.9 | 17.4 | Cash & Equivalents | | | | | | |
| 30.0 | 27.7 | 32.2 | Trade Receivables (net) | | | | | | |
| 1.4 | 1.5 | 2.6 | Inventory | | | | | | |
| 4.3 | 1.8 | 2.6 | All Other Current | | | | | | |
| 50.3 | 46.9 | 54.9 | Total Current | | | | | | |
| 43.8 | 38.8 | 31.0 | Fixed Assets (net) | | | | | | |
| 1.2 | 3.6 | 4.9 | Intangibles (net) | | | | | | |
| 4.7 | 10.8 | 9.2 | All Other Non-Current | | | | | | |
| 100.0 | 100.0 | 100.0 | Total | | | | | | |
| | | | **LIABILITIES** | | | | | | |
| 7.5 | 9.3 | 6.1 | Notes Payable-Short Term | | | | | | |
| 14.1 | 6.1 | 6.0 | Cur. Mat.-L.T.D. | | | | | | |
| 8.6 | 10.6 | 7.3 | Trade Payables | | | | | | |
| .9 | .7 | .2 | Income Taxes Payable | | | | | | |
| 11.3 | 14.1 | 10.3 | All Other Current | | | | | | |
| 42.5 | 40.9 | 29.8 | Total Current | | | | | | |
| 36.0 | 19.9 | 19.7 | Long-Term Debt | | | | | | |
| .3 | 1.1 | .9 | Deferred Taxes | | | | | | |
| 2.8 | 2.5 | .2 | All Other Non-Current | | | | | | |
| 18.4 | 35.6 | 49.4 | Net Worth | | | | | | |
| 100.0 | 100.0 | 100.0 | Total Liabilities & Net Worth | | | | | | |
| | | | **INCOME DATA** | | | | | | |
| 100.0 | 100.0 | 100.0 | Net Sales | | | | | | |
| | | | Gross Profit | | | | | | |
| 92.7 | 89.6 | 91.0 | Operating Expenses | | | | | | |
| 7.3 | 10.4 | 9.0 | Operating Profit | | | | | | |
| 1.9 | 2.0 | 2.0 | All Other Expenses (net) | | | | | | |
| 5.4 | 8.4 | 7.0 | Profit Before Taxes | | | | | | |
| | | | **RATIOS** | | | | | | |
| 4.8 | 3.3 | 5.6 | Current | | | | | | |
| 2.1 | 1.7 | 2.5 | | | | | | | |
| .6 | .6 | 1.0 | | | | | | | |
| 4.7 | 3.3 | 5.3 | Quick | | | | | | |
| 1.4 | 1.6 | 2.5 | | | | | | | |
| .4 | .5 | .9 | | | | | | | |
| 0 UND | 0 UND | 19 18.8 | Sales/Receivables | | | | | | |
| 32 11.3 | 38 9.6 | 45 8.2 | | | | | | | |
| 48 7.5 | 47 7.8 | 58 6.3 | | | | | | | |
| | | | Cost of Sales/Inventory | | | | | | |
| | | | Cost of Sales/Payables | | | | | | |
| 5.9 | 8.1 | 5.7 | Sales/Working Capital | | | | | | |
| 13.4 | 24.3 | 10.6 | | | | | | | |
| -13.8 | -14.5 | NM | | | | | | | |
| 13.4 | 17.9 | 23.6 | EBIT/Interest | | | | | | |
| (22) 4.4 | (28) 9.8 | (20) 3.8 | | | | | | | |
| 1.2 | 1.4 | -1.1 | | | | | | | |
| | | | Net Profit + Depr., Dep., Amort./Cur. Mat. L/T/D | | | | | | |
| .3 | .4 | .3 | Fixed/Worth | | | | | | |
| 1.6 | .8 | .7 | | | | | | | |
| -260.2 | 8.5 | 3.1 | | | | | | | |
| .5 | .6 | .4 | Debt/Worth | | | | | | |
| 1.3 | 2.0 | .8 | | | | | | | |
| -294.6 | 19.6 | 4.6 | | | | | | | |
| 84.9 | 84.3 | 49.2 | % Profit Before Taxes/Tangible Net Worth | | | | | | |
| (20) 53.6 | (30) 26.5 | (26) 22.7 | | | | | | | |
| 16.5 | 7.2 | 1.4 | | | | | | | |
| 53.7 | 32.9 | 29.2 | % Profit Before Taxes/Total Assets | | | | | | |
| 14.7 | 14.0 | 11.6 | | | | | | | |
| .0 | 4.5 | .6 | | | | | | | |
| 28.4 | 27.8 | 41.1 | Sales/Net Fixed Assets | | | | | | |
| 8.9 | 8.9 | 9.5 | | | | | | | |
| 4.1 | 4.2 | 4.6 | | | | | | | |
| 4.9 | 4.2 | 5.3 | Sales/Total Assets | | | | | | |
| 3.5 | 3.1 | 3.4 | | | | | | | |
| 1.8 | 2.2 | 1.8 | | | | | | | |
| 1.4 | 1.4 | 1.2 | % Depr., Dep., Amort./Sales | | | | | | |
| (24) 4.4 | (28) 3.0 | (25) 2.7 | | | | | | | |
| 11.1 | 7.8 | 7.7 | | | | | | | |
| 1.5 | 3.2 | | % Officers', Directors' Owners' Comp/Sales | | | | | | |
| (16) 4.1 | (13) 4.7 | | | | | | | | |
| 6.4 | 7.9 | | | | | | | | |
| 332268M | 441370M | 400402M | Net Sales ($) | 1164M | 11655M | 17003M | 42036M | 85624M | 242920M |
| 114373M | 143415M | 141890M | Total Assets ($) | 6355M | 5791M | 8764M | 21967M | 18366M | 80647M |

© RMA 2012

M = $ thousand    MM = $ million

See Pages 9 through 22 for Explanation of Ratios and Data

## Current Data Sorted by Assets                                  Comparative Historical Data

| | 0-500M | 500M-2MM | 2-10MM | 10-50MM | 50-100MM | 100-250MM | Type of Statement | 4/1/07-3/31/08 ALL | 4/1/08-3/31/09 ALL |
|---|---|---|---|---|---|---|---|---|---|
| | | 1 | 11 | 4 | 1 | 2 | Unqualified | 21 | 21 |
| | | 5 | 7 | 4 | | | Reviewed | 15 | 14 |
| | 1 | 5 | 7 | 2 | 1 | | Compiled | 9 | 12 |
| | 6 | 10 | 9 | 1 | | | Tax Returns | 16 | 16 |
| | 4 | 10 | 28 | 7 | 1 | 3 | Other | 26 | 41 |
| | | 23 (4/1-9/30/11) | | 107 (10/1/11-3/31/12) | | | | | |
| NUMBER OF STATEMENTS | 11 | 31 | 62 | 18 | 3 | 5 | | 87 | 104 |
| | % | % | % | % | % | % | **ASSETS** | % | % |
| Cash & Equivalents | 23.0 | 18.5 | 12.6 | 16.0 | | | | 10.8 | 10.4 |
| Trade Receivables (net) | 9.6 | 26.7 | 20.4 | 16.1 | | | | 22.7 | 22.2 |
| Inventory | .1 | .9 | 1.6 | 1.1 | | | | .6 | .6 |
| All Other Current | 10.2 | 4.2 | 1.8 | 4.6 | | | | 4.7 | 4.2 |
| Total Current | 42.8 | 50.3 | 36.4 | 38.0 | | | | 38.8 | 37.4 |
| Fixed Assets (net) | 37.0 | 36.3 | 45.8 | 47.5 | | | | 43.3 | 44.3 |
| Intangibles (net) | 5.0 | 6.5 | 5.4 | 6.0 | | | | 9.1 | 9.7 |
| All Other Non-Current | 15.2 | 7.0 | 12.4 | 8.6 | | | | 8.9 | 8.7 |
| Total | 100.0 | 100.0 | 100.0 | 100.0 | | | | 100.0 | 100.0 |
| | | | | | | | **LIABILITIES** | | |
| Notes Payable-Short Term | 32.9 | 5.8 | 6.5 | 4.4 | | | | 9.2 | 8.8 |
| Cur. Mat.-L.T.D. | 9.9 | 7.2 | 8.3 | 6.2 | | | | 11.3 | 7.3 |
| Trade Payables | 4.6 | 14.2 | 8.0 | 9.4 | | | | 10.9 | 6.3 |
| Income Taxes Payable | 1.3 | .0 | .1 | .1 | | | | .1 | .3 |
| All Other Current | 20.9 | 8.6 | 8.5 | 10.9 | | | | 10.6 | 12.5 |
| Total Current | 69.6 | 35.8 | 31.4 | 31.1 | | | | 42.1 | 35.2 |
| Long-Term Debt | 48.9 | 31.4 | 26.8 | 27.0 | | | | 30.0 | 25.9 |
| Deferred Taxes | .0 | .6 | .5 | .6 | | | | .4 | .7 |
| All Other Non-Current | 18.5 | 4.0 | 4.1 | 5.2 | | | | 6.6 | 7.1 |
| Net Worth | -37.0 | 28.2 | 37.2 | 36.1 | | | | 20.9 | 31.1 |
| Total Liabilities & Net Worth | 100.0 | 100.0 | 100.0 | 100.0 | | | | 100.0 | 100.0 |
| | | | | | | | **INCOME DATA** | | |
| Net Sales | 100.0 | 100.0 | 100.0 | 100.0 | | | | 100.0 | 100.0 |
| Gross Profit | | | | | | | | | |
| Operating Expenses | 93.4 | 94.4 | 93.5 | 95.5 | | | | 95.2 | 93.9 |
| Operating Profit | 6.6 | 5.6 | 6.5 | 4.5 | | | | 4.8 | 6.1 |
| All Other Expenses (net) | .4 | .1 | .7 | .4 | | | | 2.5 | 2.0 |
| Profit Before Taxes | 6.2 | 5.6 | 5.9 | 4.1 | | | | 2.3 | 4.1 |
| | | | | | | | **RATIOS** | | |
| Current | 1.6 | 2.7 | 2.2 | 3.1 | | | | 2.3 | 2.6 |
| | .7 | 1.4 | 1.2 | 1.6 | | | | .9 | 1.3 |
| | .3 | .7 | .5 | .8 | | | | .5 | .7 |
| Quick | 1.6 | 2.6 | 2.1 | 2.9 | | | | 1.9 | 2.3 |
| | .5 | 1.3 | .9 | 1.2 | | | | .8 | 1.1 |
| | .3 | .4 | .4 | .7 | | | | .3 | .6 |
| Sales/Receivables | 0 UND | 1 259.2 | 10 36.2 | 20 17.9 | | | | 11 33.6 | 4 86.1 |
| | 0 UND | 22 16.3 | 23 15.6 | 33 11.2 | | | | 30 12.2 | 27 13.6 |
| | 2 169.3 | 33 11.0 | 46 7.9 | 44 8.3 | | | | 57 6.4 | 57 6.4 |
| Cost of Sales/Inventory | | | | | | | | | |
| Cost of Sales/Payables | | | | | | | | | |
| Sales/Working Capital | 76.8 | 14.2 | 9.5 | 3.3 | | | | 8.5 | 8.3 |
| | -115.3 | 22.9 | 62.8 | 16.7 | | | | -106.6 | 45.1 |
| | -29.7 | -31.9 | -12.1 | -34.3 | | | | -12.7 | -20.6 |
| EBIT/Interest | | 33.2 | 14.4 | 9.1 | | | | 4.5 | 10.8 |
| | (26) | 7.2 (50) | 5.9 (15) | 2.6 | | | (74) | 2.0 (91) | 3.6 |
| | | -.1 | 2.3 | 1.1 | | | | .7 | .9 |
| Net Profit + Depr., Dep., Amort./Cur. Mat. L/T/D | | | | | | | | 2.0 | 3.1 |
| | | | | | | | (20) | 1.1 (19) | 1.5 |
| | | | | | | | | .4 | .4 |
| Fixed/Worth | 2.8 | .3 | .5 | .8 | | | | .7 | .7 |
| | -2.1 | 1.3 | 1.4 | 1.8 | | | | 3.4 | 1.7 |
| | -.3 | -6.8 | 6.4 | NM | | | | -2.4 | NM |
| Debt/Worth | 2.4 | .9 | .7 | .9 | | | | 1.5 | .8 |
| | -4.7 | 2.9 | 1.7 | 3.0 | | | | 4.9 | 2.2 |
| | -1.7 | -12.2 | 11.0 | NM | | | | -5.7 | NM |
| % Profit Before Taxes/Tangible Net Worth | | 122.8 | 91.2 | 43.3 | | | | 60.6 | 69.1 |
| | (22) | 53.3 (51) | 43.1 (14) | 9.8 | | | (58) | 20.8 (78) | 30.7 |
| | | 2.9 | 14.9 | 3.2 | | | | 5.8 | 3.7 |
| % Profit Before Taxes/Total Assets | 89.9 | 32.9 | 25.0 | 10.8 | | | | 12.2 | 20.5 |
| | 28.3 | 15.2 | 10.9 | 6.3 | | | | 4.4 | 6.5 |
| | 2.2 | -1.3 | 5.9 | .8 | | | | -1.3 | -.3 |
| Sales/Net Fixed Assets | 133.3 | 59.1 | 14.3 | 8.3 | | | | 15.5 | 16.1 |
| | 43.4 | 13.0 | 6.0 | 2.7 | | | | 6.3 | 6.9 |
| | 8.8 | 4.3 | 2.7 | 1.1 | | | | 2.9 | 2.9 |
| Sales/Total Assets | 22.4 | 6.2 | 4.0 | 2.7 | | | | 3.2 | 3.6 |
| | 5.7 | 5.3 | 2.4 | 1.7 | | | | 2.2 | 2.3 |
| | 4.2 | 2.7 | 1.5 | .6 | | | | 1.4 | 1.5 |
| % Depr., Dep., Amort./Sales | | .6 | 2.2 | 4.8 | | | | 2.5 | 2.6 |
| | (22) | 2.2 (55) | 4.2 (15) | 6.3 | | | (77) | 4.3 (80) | 4.2 |
| | | 5.9 | 8.9 | 13.1 | | | | 7.7 | 7.2 |
| % Officers', Directors', Owners' Comp/Sales | | .7 | 1.3 | | | | | 2.1 | 1.6 |
| | (11) | 6.0 (19) | 2.7 | | | | (25) | 3.6 (38) | 3.5 |
| | | 8.8 | 3.4 | | | | | 12.7 | 8.7 |
| Net Sales ($) | 17179M | 172141M | 835679M | 645587M | 354262M | 1854975M | | 1728676M | 3340932M |
| Total Assets ($) | 1772M | 36384M | 286729M | 376739M | 208082M | 1140373M | | 1193951M | 1695713M |

© RMA 2012

M = $ thousand   MM = $ million
See Pages 9 through 22 for Explanation of Ratios and Data

**Comparative Historical Data**  |  **Current Data Sorted by Sales**

| 4/1/09-3/31/10 ALL | 4/1/10-3/31/11 ALL | 4/1/11-3/31/12 ALL | Type of Statement | 0-1MM | 1-3MM | 3-5MM | 5-10MM | 10-25MM | 25MM & OVER |
|---|---|---|---|---|---|---|---|---|---|
| 19 | 15 | 19 | Unqualified | | 1 | 2 | 4 | 7 | 5 |
| 18 | 22 | 16 | Reviewed | | 2 | 1 | 4 | 5 | 4 |
| 23 | 18 | 16 | Compiled | | | 2 | 9 | 2 | 3 |
| 14 | 22 | 26 | Tax Returns | 4 | 6 | 3 | 9 | 9 | 4 |
| 36 | 38 | 53 | Other | 2 | 7 | 6 | 14 | 13 | 11 |
| | | | | 23 (4/1-9/30/11) | 107 (10/1/11-3/31/12) | | | | |
| 110 | 115 | 130 | NUMBER OF STATEMENTS | 6 | 16 | 14 | 40 | 31 | 23 |
| % | % | % | **ASSETS** | % | % | % | % | % | % |
| 12.7 | 12.6 | 14.9 | Cash & Equivalents | | 11.2 | 13.2 | 19.8 | 12.8 | 11.5 |
| 21.7 | 22.2 | 20.4 | Trade Receivables (net) | | 11.6 | 26.0 | 15.7 | 23.7 | 27.6 |
| .7 | .9 | 1.2 | Inventory | | 1.4 | .4 | .8 | .6 | 3.3 |
| 4.0 | 5.1 | 3.7 | All Other Current | | 8.1 | 2.8 | 2.1 | 4.6 | 3.5 |
| 39.1 | 40.7 | 40.2 | Total Current | | 32.3 | 42.4 | 38.4 | 41.8 | 45.8 |
| 40.7 | 40.4 | 42.2 | Fixed Assets (net) | | 58.4 | 39.6 | 42.8 | 41.1 | 32.4 |
| 7.1 | 9.3 | 7.2 | Intangibles (net) | | 2.4 | 5.2 | 7.4 | 5.6 | 12.4 |
| 13.1 | 9.6 | 10.5 | All Other Non-Current | | 6.9 | 12.8 | 11.3 | 11.5 | 9.4 |
| 100.0 | 100.0 | 100.0 | Total | | 100.0 | 100.0 | 100.0 | 100.0 | 100.0 |
| | | | **LIABILITIES** | | | | | | |
| 7.6 | 8.3 | 8.2 | Notes Payable-Short Term | | 10.7 | 22.5 | 6.5 | 5.9 | 5.9 |
| 9.0 | 10.6 | 7.6 | Cur. Mat.-L.T.D. | | 9.3 | 9.6 | 8.6 | 5.6 | 6.6 |
| 8.5 | 7.5 | 9.4 | Trade Payables | | 3.0 | 7.9 | 7.7 | 12.1 | 15.2 |
| | .4 | .2 | Income Taxes Payable | | .9 | .0 | .2 | .1 | .2 |
| 10.6 | 12.3 | 10.4 | All Other Current | | 13.1 | 6.3 | 7.3 | 13.5 | 9.7 |
| 35.9 | 39.1 | 35.8 | Total Current | | 36.9 | 46.3 | 30.3 | 37.1 | 37.5 |
| 26.8 | 27.4 | 29.9 | Long-Term Debt | | 45.6 | 24.6 | 33.0 | 18.4 | 26.5 |
| .5 | .2 | .7 | Deferred Taxes | | .0 | .0 | 1.2 | .4 | 1.3 |
| 4.2 | 6.4 | 5.9 | All Other Non-Current | | 4.7 | 1.9 | 7.0 | 2.2 | 5.6 |
| 32.6 | 26.9 | 27.7 | Net Worth | | 12.8 | 27.1 | 28.6 | 41.9 | 29.1 |
| 100.0 | 100.0 | 100.0 | Total Liabilities & Net Worth | | 100.0 | 100.0 | 100.0 | 100.0 | 100.0 |
| | | | **INCOME DATA** | | | | | | |
| 100.0 | 100.0 | 100.0 | Net Sales | | 100.0 | 100.0 | 100.0 | 100.0 | 100.0 |
| | | | Gross Profit | | | | | | |
| 94.9 | 94.5 | 93.7 | Operating Expenses | | 91.2 | 92.8 | 93.7 | 95.4 | 93.5 |
| 5.1 | 5.5 | 6.3 | Operating Profit | | 8.8 | 7.2 | 6.3 | 4.6 | 6.5 |
| 1.3 | 1.2 | .8 | All Other Expenses (net) | | .7 | .9 | .4 | .2 | 2.2 |
| 3.8 | 4.3 | 5.5 | Profit Before Taxes | | 8.0 | 6.3 | 5.8 | 4.3 | 4.3 |
| | | | **RATIOS** | | | | | | |
| 2.2 | 2.1 | 2.3 | Current | | 2.8 | 3.2 | 2.6 | 2.6 | 1.6 |
| 1.1 | 1.1 | 1.2 | | | .7 | 1.3 | 1.2 | 1.4 | 1.0 |
| .5 | .5 | .5 | | | .2 | .4 | .4 | .9 | .7 |
| 2.1 | 1.9 | 2.1 | Quick | | 2.3 | 3.1 | 2.6 | 2.4 | 1.2 |
| .9 | 1.0 | 1.0 | | | .4 | 1.3 | 1.0 | 1.2 | .8 |
| .4 | .4 | .5 | | | .1 | .4 | .4 | .7 | .6 |
| 4   93.6 | 2   158.2 | 5   66.9 | Sales/Receivables | 0   UND | 14   26.6 | 4   99.6 | 10   37.3 | 18   20.5 | |
| 26   13.9 | 22   16.3 | 23   15.9 | | 2   153.8 | 27   13.3 | 16   22.8 | 25   14.8 | 31   11.6 | |
| 52   7.0 | 44   8.3 | 42   8.7 | | 46   7.9 | 47   7.8 | 35   10.5 | 42   8.6 | 46   7.9 | |
| | | | Cost of Sales/Inventory | | | | | | |
| | | | Cost of Sales/Payables | | | | | | |
| 8.9 | 12.4 | 11.7 | Sales/Working Capital | | 9.7 | 10.1 | 12.2 | 9.1 | 15.7 |
| 74.3 | 178.4 | 64.1 | | | -499.7 | 24.2 | 57.6 | 30.3 | -138.6 |
| -16.1 | -15.6 | -23.0 | | | -8.8 | -16.7 | -12.1 | -185.8 | -23.4 |
| 11.9 | 11.8 | 15.6 | EBIT/Interest | | 25.4 | 2.1 | 28.3 | 10.9 | 15.6 |
| (99)  3.4 | (97)  4.9 | (106)  4.7 | | (12)  3.2 | (10)  .9 | (35)  9.3 | (23)  5.0 | 7.1 | |
| 1.3 | 1.1 | 1.5 | | | 1.8 | -1.1 | 1.9 | 2.8 | 1.5 |
| 2.3 | 3.4 | 2.9 | Net Profit + Depr., Dep., Amort./Cur. Mat. L/T/D | | | | | | |
| (24)  1.7 | (16)  2.0 | (20)  1.8 | | | | | | | |
| 1.2 | .7 | 1.4 | | | | | | | |
| .5 | .6 | .5 | Fixed/Worth | | .8 | .3 | .5 | .5 | .8 |
| 1.7 | 1.8 | 1.6 | | | 11.1 | .7 | 2.0 | 1.1 | 1.6 |
| 12.4 | -7.6 | -13.1 | | | -7.7 | NM | NM | 5.9 | 10.8 |
| .8 | 1.1 | .9 | Debt/Worth | | .9 | .3 | 1.2 | .4 | 1.4 |
| 2.6 | 2.8 | 3.0 | | | 13.1 | .9 | 3.0 | 1.1 | 3.6 |
| 157.5 | -19.0 | -20.8 | | | -13.7 | NM | NM | 25.0 | 14.3 |
| 58.7 | 84.4 | 90.5 | % Profit Before Taxes/Tangible Net Worth | | 249.1 | 77.8 | 122.8 | 72.0 | 104.9 |
| (84)  27.0 | (81)  41.6 | (95)  38.6 | | (10)  84.2 | (11)  4.1 | (30)  45.0 | (24)  25.6 | (18)  58.8 | |
| 4.5 | 5.1 | 9.4 | | | 18.4 | -39.0 | 19.7 | 9.3 | 16.0 |
| 19.0 | 26.0 | 24.5 | % Profit Before Taxes/Total Assets | | 50.3 | 18.0 | 24.2 | 18.7 | 26.1 |
| 6.9 | 7.8 | 10.4 | | | 9.1 | 2.2 | 14.8 | 8.3 | 11.0 |
| 1.1 | .1 | 2.3 | | | 3.9 | -9.7 | 3.3 | 5.6 | 2.2 |
| 16.8 | 30.8 | 25.3 | Sales/Net Fixed Assets | | 31.2 | 43.3 | 13.5 | 19.2 | 71.3 |
| 8.4 | 9.6 | 6.8 | | | 3.7 | 8.6 | 6.2 | 8.0 | 8.2 |
| 3.1 | 3.5 | 2.6 | | | 1.6 | 2.7 | 2.8 | 2.7 | 2.6 |
| 3.5 | 4.7 | 5.1 | Sales/Total Assets | | 5.0 | 5.8 | 5.0 | 4.8 | 5.2 |
| 2.4 | 2.9 | 2.7 | | | 2.2 | 2.3 | 2.8 | 2.6 | 2.8 |
| 1.6 | 1.7 | 1.6 | | | 1.0 | 1.6 | 1.5 | 1.6 | 1.7 |
| 2.3 | 2.1 | 2.0 | % Depr., Dep., Amort./Sales | | 2.8 | 1.9 | 2.2 | 1.1 | .5 |
| (90)  4.7 | (81)  4.6 | (99)  4.2 | | (10)  7.1 | (10)  3.8 | (33)  4.9 | (25)  4.2 | (18)  3.9 | |
| 9.1 | 7.8 | 9.1 | | | 14.3 | 10.9 | 8.5 | 8.0 | 5.7 |
| 1.7 | 2.5 | 1.3 | % Officers', Directors' Owners' Comp/Sales | | | | | .8 | 1.3 |
| (36)  4.8 | (37)  3.5 | (37)  2.8 | | | | (12) | (12)  2.8 | | |
| 12.4 | 6.3 | 6.6 | | | | | | 3.3 | 6.1 |
| 3163278M | 2999859M | 3879823M | Net Sales ($) | 3652M | 31927M | 57053M | 296766M | 488540M | 3001885M |
| 1712174M | 1489439M | 2050079M | Total Assets ($) | 1231M | 19457M | 25531M | 178515M | 246080M | 1579265M |

## Current Data Sorted by Assets                                           Comparative Historical Data

| 0-500M | 500M-2MM | 2-10MM | 10-50MM | 50-100MM | 100-250MM | Type of Statement | 4/1/07-3/31/08 ALL | 4/1/08-3/31/09 ALL |
|---|---|---|---|---|---|---|---|---|
|  |  | 1 | 2 |  | 1 | Unqualified | 1 | 4 |
|  | 1 | 1 | 1 |  |  | Reviewed | 4 | 5 |
|  | 1 | 3 |  |  |  | Compiled | 3 | 5 |
| 4 | 1 | 1 | 1 |  |  | Tax Returns | 4 | 4 |
| 5 | 3 | 4 | 2 |  |  | Other | 10 | 13 |
|  | 2 (4/1-9/30/11) |  | 30 (10/1/11-3/31/12) |  |  |  |  |  |
| 9 | 6 | 10 | 6 |  | 1 | **NUMBER OF STATEMENTS** | 22 | 31 |
| % | % | % | % | % | % | **ASSETS** | % | % |
|  |  | 16.3 |  |  |  | Cash & Equivalents | 20.5 | 15.6 |
|  |  | 12.6 |  |  |  | Trade Receivables (net) | 12.4 | 5.7 |
|  |  | 1.3 |  |  |  | Inventory | 5.4 | 2.6 |
|  |  | 4.6 |  |  |  | All Other Current | 2.0 | 1.9 |
|  |  | 34.9 |  |  |  | Total Current | 40.2 | 25.8 |
|  |  | 42.4 | D |  |  | Fixed Assets (net) | 46.6 | 53.2 |
|  |  | 14.6 | A |  |  | Intangibles (net) | .8 | 10.4 |
|  |  | 8.2 | T |  |  | All Other Non-Current | 12.4 | 10.5 |
|  |  | 100.0 | A | | | Total | 100.0 | 100.0 |
|  |  |  | N |  |  | **LIABILITIES** |  |  |
|  |  | .9 | O |  |  | Notes Payable-Short Term | 9.5 | 5.9 |
|  |  | 6.8 | T |  |  | Cur. Mat.-L.T.D. | 5.6 | 7.3 |
|  |  | 8.5 |  |  |  | Trade Payables | 14.0 | 6.3 |
|  |  | .0 | A |  |  | Income Taxes Payable | 2.2 | .0 |
|  |  | 15.8 | V |  |  | All Other Current | 14.7 | 18.3 |
|  |  | 32.1 | A |  |  | Total Current | 46.0 | 37.8 |
|  |  | 42.0 | I |  |  | Long-Term Debt | 51.1 | 50.4 |
|  |  | .0 | L |  |  | Deferred Taxes | .2 | .4 |
|  |  | 8.5 | A |  |  | All Other Non-Current | 8.6 | 9.6 |
|  |  | 17.4 | B |  |  | Net Worth | -5.9 | 1.8 |
|  |  | 100.0 | L |  |  | Total Liabilities & Net Worth | 100.0 | 100.0 |
|  |  |  | E |  |  | **INCOME DATA** |  |  |
|  |  | 100.0 |  |  |  | Net Sales | 100.0 | 100.0 |
|  |  |  |  |  |  | Gross Profit |  |  |
|  |  | 98.3 |  |  |  | Operating Expenses | 92.0 | 90.9 |
|  |  | 1.7 |  |  |  | Operating Profit | 8.0 | 9.1 |
|  |  | 1.8 |  |  |  | All Other Expenses (net) | 2.2 | 3.2 |
|  |  | -.1 |  |  |  | Profit Before Taxes | 5.8 | 5.8 |
|  |  |  |  |  |  | **RATIOS** |  |  |
|  |  | 1.7 |  |  |  |  | 1.8 | 2.4 |
|  |  | 1.4 |  |  |  | Current | 1.0 | 1.2 |
|  |  | .3 |  |  |  |  | .6 | .4 |
|  |  | 1.5 |  |  |  |  | 1.5 | 2.2 |
|  |  | .9 |  |  |  | Quick | .7 | .9 |
|  |  | .3 |  |  |  |  | .4 | .2 |
|  | 0 | UND |  |  |  |  | 0  872.0 | 0  UND |
|  | 1 | 319.4 |  |  |  | Sales/Receivables | 11  33.5 | 4  93.5 |
|  | 15 | 25.1 |  |  |  |  | 23  16.2 | 15  24.1 |
|  |  |  |  |  |  | Cost of Sales/Inventory |  |  |
|  |  |  |  |  |  | Cost of Sales/Payables |  |  |
|  |  | 11.1 |  |  |  |  | 10.2 | 9.3 |
|  |  | 25.5 |  |  |  | Sales/Working Capital | NM | 45.0 |
|  |  | -15.5 |  |  |  |  | -18.0 | -8.2 |
|  |  |  |  |  |  |  | 6.5 | 4.2 |
|  |  |  |  |  |  | EBIT/Interest | (18)  2.2 | (28)  2.3 |
|  |  |  |  |  |  |  | .9 | 1.0 |
|  |  |  |  |  |  | Net Profit + Depr., Dep., Amort./Cur. Mat. L/T/D |  |  |
|  |  | .4 |  |  |  |  | .8 | 1.4 |
|  |  | 5.1 |  |  |  | Fixed/Worth | 2.0 | 5.5 |
|  |  | -28.9 |  |  |  |  | NM | -3.0 |
|  |  | 1.5 |  |  |  |  | 1.4 | 1.0 |
|  |  | 11.3 |  |  |  | Debt/Worth | 3.8 | 5.7 |
|  |  | -50.3 |  |  |  |  | NM | -4.6 |
|  |  |  |  |  |  |  | 60.5 | 60.2 |
|  |  |  |  |  |  | % Profit Before Taxes/Tangible Net Worth | (17)  8.0 | (19)  27.8 |
|  |  |  |  |  |  |  | 2.5 | 10.6 |
|  |  | 7.4 |  |  |  |  | 23.0 | 12.0 |
|  |  | .5 |  |  |  | % Profit Before Taxes/Total Assets | 4.3 | 7.7 |
|  |  | -10.0 |  |  |  |  | -.1 | 1.5 |
|  |  | 15.3 |  |  |  |  | 13.7 | 5.8 |
|  |  | 3.1 |  |  |  | Sales/Net Fixed Assets | 7.5 | 2.1 |
|  |  | 1.6 |  |  |  |  | 1.4 | 1.4 |
|  |  | 2.6 |  |  |  |  | 3.7 | 1.9 |
|  |  | 1.5 |  |  |  | Sales/Total Assets | 2.2 | 1.2 |
|  |  | .9 |  |  |  |  | 1.0 | .9 |
|  |  |  |  |  |  |  | 1.3 | 3.6 |
|  |  |  |  |  |  | % Depr., Dep., Amort./Sales | (21)  4.7 | (26)  6.1 |
|  |  |  |  |  |  |  | 6.6 | 9.9 |
|  |  |  |  |  |  | % Officers', Directors' Owners' Comp/Sales |  |  |
| 7427M | 9556M | 95337M | 116119M |  | 95687M | Net Sales ($) | 381173M | 459023M |
| 2456M | 7016M | 45325M | 100944M |  | 108718M | Total Assets ($) | 243836M | 386319M |

M = $ thousand    MM = $ million
See Pages 9 through 22 for Explanation of Ratios and Data

## Comparative Historical Data | Current Data Sorted by Sales

| | | | Type of Statement | 0-1MM | 1-3MM | 3-5MM | 5-10MM | 10-25MM | 25MM & OVER |
|---|---|---|---|---|---|---|---|---|---|
| 5 | 4 | 5 | Unqualified | | 1 | | 1 | 1 | 2 |
| 1 | 4 | 2 | Reviewed | | | | | 1 | 1 |
| 3 | 4 | 4 | Compiled | 2 | | 1 | 1 | | |
| 3 | 5 | 7 | Tax Returns | 4 | | 1 | 1 | 1 | |
| 15 | 13 | 14 | Other | 3 | 6 | | 2 | 3 | |
| 4/1/09-3/31/10 ALL | 4/1/10-3/31/11 ALL | 4/1/11-3/31/12 ALL | | | 2 (4/1-9/30/11) | | 30 (10/1/11-3/31/12) | | |
| 27 | 30 | 32 | NUMBER OF STATEMENTS | 9 | 7 | 2 | 5 | 6 | 3 |
| % | % | % | ASSETS | % | % | % | % | % | % |
| 13.6 | 15.4 | 19.0 | Cash & Equivalents | | | | | | |
| 6.6 | 8.2 | 6.4 | Trade Receivables (net) | | | | | | |
| 1.8 | 3.4 | 2.2 | Inventory | | | | | | |
| 2.0 | 3.2 | 2.5 | All Other Current | | | | | | |
| 24.1 | 30.1 | 30.2 | Total Current | | | | | | |
| 56.5 | 50.7 | 48.7 | Fixed Assets (net) | | | | | | |
| 8.6 | 10.1 | 13.1 | Intangibles (net) | | | | | | |
| 10.8 | 9.2 | 8.0 | All Other Non-Current | | | | | | |
| 100.0 | 100.0 | 100.0 | Total | | | | | | |
| | | | LIABILITIES | | | | | | |
| 4.6 | 9.5 | 7.8 | Notes Payable-Short Term | | | | | | |
| 5.6 | 4.1 | 6.4 | Cur. Mat.-L.T.D. | | | | | | |
| 4.1 | 5.4 | 5.1 | Trade Payables | | | | | | |
| .0 | .0 | .3 | Income Taxes Payable | | | | | | |
| 23.9 | 9.8 | 8.2 | All Other Current | | | | | | |
| 38.2 | 29.0 | 27.8 | Total Current | | | | | | |
| 55.2 | 44.7 | 47.9 | Long-Term Debt | | | | | | |
| .5 | .3 | .5 | Deferred Taxes | | | | | | |
| 19.8 | 4.9 | 6.8 | All Other Non-Current | | | | | | |
| -13.7 | 21.1 | 16.9 | Net Worth | | | | | | |
| 100.0 | 100.0 | 100.0 | Total Liabilties & Net Worth | | | | | | |
| | | | INCOME DATA | | | | | | |
| 100.0 | 100.0 | 100.0 | Net Sales | | | | | | |
| | | | Gross Profit | | | | | | |
| 89.7 | 85.9 | 93.1 | Operating Expenses | | | | | | |
| 10.3 | 14.1 | 6.9 | Operating Profit | | | | | | |
| 5.1 | 2.9 | 1.5 | All Other Expenses (net) | | | | | | |
| 5.2 | 11.2 | 5.4 | Profit Before Taxes | | | | | | |
| | | | RATIOS | | | | | | |
| 2.4 | 2.0 | 2.1 | | | | | | | |
| .8 | 1.1 | 1.3 | Current | | | | | | |
| .3 | .7 | .4 | | | | | | | |
| 1.7 | 1.9 | 1.8 | | | | | | | |
| .5 | .9 | 1.1 | Quick | | | | | | |
| .2 | .3 | .3 | | | | | | | |
| 0  UND | 0  UND | 0  UND | | | | | | | |
| 1  305.1 | 4  97.6 | 2  206.9 | Sales/Receivables | | | | | | |
| 12  31.0 | 17  20.9 | 10  36.1 | | | | | | | |
| | | | Cost of Sales/Inventory | | | | | | |
| | | | Cost of Sales/Payables | | | | | | |
| 12.5 | 9.4 | 10.5 | | | | | | | |
| -48.2 | 293.4 | 26.4 | Sales/Working Capital | | | | | | |
| -6.2 | -12.5 | -12.9 | | | | | | | |
| 4.3 | 8.1 | 4.4 | | | | | | | |
| (22)  2.5 | (27)  3.6 | (27)  2.7 | EBIT/Interest | | | | | | |
| .4 | 1.5 | .8 | | | | | | | |
| | | | Net Profit + Depr., Dep., Amort./Cur. Mat. L/T/D | | | | | | |
| 1.7 | 1.5 | .7 | | | | | | | |
| 7.4 | 3.5 | 5.9 | Fixed/Worth | | | | | | |
| -1.3 | -4.5 | -2.8 | | | | | | | |
| 1.9 | 1.7 | .8 | | | | | | | |
| 11.9 | 3.9 | 15.1 | Debt/Worth | | | | | | |
| -3.2 | -9.1 | -3.9 | | | | | | | |
| 37.2 | 77.3 | 149.0 | % Profit Before Taxes/Tangible Net Worth | | | | | | |
| (14)  10.4 | (19)  24.6 | (20)  43.2 | | | | | | | |
| -20.6 | 12.2 | 6.9 | | | | | | | |
| 14.6 | 21.1 | 21.0 | % Profit Before Taxes/Total Assets | | | | | | |
| 3.5 | 7.1 | 3.8 | | | | | | | |
| -2.1 | 2.6 | -.1 | | | | | | | |
| 5.0 | 5.8 | 8.6 | Sales/Net Fixed Assets | | | | | | |
| 2.2 | 2.0 | 3.2 | | | | | | | |
| 1.2 | 1.4 | 1.6 | | | | | | | |
| 2.1 | 1.7 | 3.0 | Sales/Total Assets | | | | | | |
| 1.0 | 1.0 | 1.5 | | | | | | | |
| .7 | .8 | 1.0 | | | | | | | |
| 4.0 | 3.9 | 3.9 | % Depr., Dep., Amort./Sales | | | | | | |
| (24)  6.3 | (27)  6.2 | (25)  6.3 | | | | | | | |
| 11.6 | 9.6 | 7.9 | | | | | | | |
| | | 3.4 | % Officers', Directors' Owners' Comp/Sales | | | | | | |
| | (15) | 12.3 | | | | | | | |
| | | 22.3 | | | | | | | |
| 339159M | 458781M | 324126M | Net Sales ($) | 5172M | 10580M | 7342M | 35945M | 99697M | 165390M |
| 340968M | 404383M | 264459M | Total Assets ($) | 6837M | 6558M | 4327M | 24860M | 73142M | 148735M |

M = $ thousand   MM = $ million
See Pages 9 through 22 for Explanation of Ratios and Data

**Current Data Sorted by Assets**      **Comparative Historical Data**

| Type of Statement | 0-500M | 500M-2MM | 2-10MM | 10-50MM | 50-100MM | 100-250MM | | 4/1/07-3/31/08 ALL | 4/1/08-3/31/09 ALL |
|---|---|---|---|---|---|---|---|---|---|
| Unqualified | | | 2 | 5 | 6 | 4 | | 21 | 25 |
| Reviewed | 1 | 1 | 7 | 3 | | | | 12 | 15 |
| Compiled | 2 | 6 | 6 | 4 | | | | 10 | 9 |
| Tax Returns | 7 | 11 | 4 | | 1 | 1 | | 11 | 13 |
| Other | 3 | | 22 | 7 | | | | 35 | 38 |
| | | 13 (4/1-9/30/11) | | 90 (10/1/11-3/31/12) | | | | | |
| **NUMBER OF STATEMENTS** | 13 | 18 | 41 | 19 | 7 | 5 | | 89 | 100 |
| | % | % | % | % | % | % | **ASSETS** | % | % |
| Cash & Equivalents | 45.9 | 6.7 | 13.2 | 7.2 | | | | 10.0 | 12.9 |
| Trade Receivables (net) | 18.0 | 17.5 | 11.9 | 15.0 | | | | 15.3 | 17.5 |
| Inventory | 9.6 | 16.6 | 8.6 | 7.9 | | | | 10.2 | 9.5 |
| All Other Current | .6 | .7 | 3.6 | 2.7 | | | | 3.6 | 3.3 |
| Total Current | 74.2 | 41.4 | 37.3 | 32.8 | | | | 39.1 | 43.1 |
| Fixed Assets (net) | 23.8 | 44.9 | 54.3 | 43.0 | | | | 46.6 | 42.8 |
| Intangibles (net) | .6 | .4 | 3.9 | 14.0 | | | | 4.4 | 5.6 |
| All Other Non-Current | 1.4 | 13.2 | 4.6 | 10.1 | | | | 9.9 | 8.4 |
| Total | 100.0 | 100.0 | 100.0 | 100.0 | | | | 100.0 | 100.0 |
| | | | | | | | **LIABILITIES** | | |
| Notes Payable-Short Term | 10.7 | 5.9 | 1.9 | 5.4 | | | | 8.0 | 7.7 |
| Cur. Mat.-L.T.D. | 3.1 | 3.8 | 5.1 | 2.9 | | | | 4.4 | 3.7 |
| Trade Payables | 11.8 | 10.5 | 10.2 | 5.9 | | | | 10.9 | 11.8 |
| Income Taxes Payable | .0 | .6 | .0 | .4 | | | | .5 | .1 |
| All Other Current | 6.3 | 4.5 | 15.3 | 11.1 | | | | 14.3 | 13.6 |
| Total Current | 31.9 | 25.4 | 32.5 | 25.6 | | | | 38.1 | 37.0 |
| Long-Term Debt | 24.6 | 31.0 | 34.4 | 27.1 | | | | 30.7 | 31.8 |
| Deferred Taxes | .0 | .0 | .0 | .0 | | | | .3 | .3 |
| All Other Non-Current | .9 | 8.6 | 10.4 | 6.6 | | | | 5.5 | 7.7 |
| Net Worth | 42.6 | 35.0 | 22.7 | 40.8 | | | | 25.4 | 23.1 |
| Total Liabilities & Net Worth | 100.0 | 100.0 | 100.0 | 100.0 | | | | 100.0 | 100.0 |
| | | | | | | | **INCOME DATA** | | |
| Net Sales | 100.0 | 100.0 | 100.0 | 100.0 | | | | 100.0 | 100.0 |
| Gross Profit | | | | | | | | | |
| Operating Expenses | 81.9 | 88.8 | 94.6 | 88.9 | | | | 91.4 | 95.1 |
| Operating Profit | 18.1 | 11.2 | 5.4 | 11.1 | | | | 8.6 | 4.9 |
| All Other Expenses (net) | 2.5 | 3.8 | 2.3 | 3.6 | | | | 4.0 | 2.3 |
| Profit Before Taxes | 15.6 | 7.4 | 3.1 | 7.6 | | | | 4.6 | 2.6 |
| | | | | | | | **RATIOS** | | |
| Current | 19.2 | 3.0 | 2.8 | 2.5 | | | | 2.0 | 2.1 |
| | 2.5 | 1.4 | 1.2 | 1.0 | | | | 1.2 | 1.2 |
| | 1.1 | .5 | .7 | .5 | | | | .6 | .7 |
| Quick | 17.2 | 2.2 | 1.8 | 1.5 | | | | 1.3 | 1.3 |
| | 1.6 | .7 | .8 | .7 | | | | .8 | .9 |
| | 1.0 | .3 | .3 | .4 | | | | .3 | .4 |
| Sales/Receivables | 0 UND | 0 UND | 7 50.8 | 12 29.6 | | | | 10 35.9 | 9 42.2 |
| | 1 271.6 | 23 15.8 | 18 20.8 | 18 20.2 | | | | 26 14.3 | 19 19.3 |
| | 36 10.2 | 56 6.5 | 38 9.7 | 45 8.2 | | | | 42 8.6 | 44 8.4 |
| Cost of Sales/Inventory | | | | | | | | | |
| Cost of Sales/Payables | | | | | | | | | |
| Sales/Working Capital | 6.7 | 5.4 | 7.4 | 8.3 | | | | 10.1 | 8.9 |
| | 23.9 | 24.3 | 35.3 | -651.5 | | | | 36.8 | 32.6 |
| | NM | -15.0 | -14.6 | -7.9 | | | | -15.0 | -28.0 |
| EBIT/Interest | | 16.1 | 7.1 | 6.4 | | | | 4.7 | 8.7 |
| | | (17) 4.1 | (34) 2.6 | (17) 4.6 | | | | (70) 2.1 | (86) 2.5 |
| | | 2.8 | .1 | 1.9 | | | | .9 | .6 |
| Net Profit + Depr., Dep., Amort./Cur. Mat. L/T/D | | | | | | | | 7.7 | 25.6 |
| | | | | | | | | (15) 1.7 | (15) 4.9 |
| | | | | | | | | 1.1 | 1.3 |
| Fixed/Worth | .0 | .2 | 1.0 | .7 | | | | 1.0 | .8 |
| | .2 | 1.6 | 1.5 | 1.7 | | | | 2.1 | 1.5 |
| | 1.0 | 2.5 | NM | 8.8 | | | | 11.4 | -18.4 |
| Debt/Worth | .2 | .5 | .7 | 1.0 | | | | 1.0 | .7 |
| | 1.0 | 1.7 | 1.8 | 3.1 | | | | 3.1 | 2.8 |
| | 3.9 | 4.0 | NM | 23.0 | | | | 27.8 | -28.0 |
| % Profit Before Taxes/Tangible Net Worth | 433.3 | 37.5 | 21.7 | 38.5 | | | | 50.4 | 55.2 |
| | (11) 100.0 | (17) 15.6 | (31) 14.3 | (15) 12.1 | | | | (69) 20.4 | (71) 13.1 |
| | 15.5 | 6.1 | 3.3 | 3.3 | | | | 2.0 | .0 |
| % Profit Before Taxes/Total Assets | 91.9 | 14.8 | 10.2 | 9.3 | | | | 11.6 | 12.0 |
| | 42.6 | 6.1 | 4.2 | 5.3 | | | | 4.3 | 3.2 |
| | 11.9 | 2.4 | -2.8 | 1.5 | | | | -.3 | -1.0 |
| Sales/Net Fixed Assets | UND | 22.9 | 12.7 | 5.5 | | | | 19.2 | 45.0 |
| | 36.0 | 5.9 | 3.1 | 3.6 | | | | 4.3 | 5.3 |
| | 11.2 | 1.4 | 1.1 | 1.2 | | | | 1.2 | 1.6 |
| Sales/Total Assets | 7.8 | 2.6 | 2.9 | 2.8 | | | | 3.1 | 3.4 |
| | 4.2 | 2.3 | 1.5 | 1.2 | | | | 1.7 | 2.0 |
| | 1.6 | .8 | .7 | .3 | | | | .6 | 1.0 |
| % Depr., Dep., Amort./Sales | | 1.5 | 1.6 | .9 | | | | 1.0 | .7 |
| | | (13) 1.7 | (37) 3.4 | (18) 2.7 | | | | (77) 3.3 | (82) 1.9 |
| | | 12.8 | 7.8 | 4.8 | | | | 8.0 | 5.8 |
| % Officers', Directors' Owners' Comp/Sales | | | 1.2 | | | | | 1.9 | 1.7 |
| | | | (14) 3.4 | | | | | (21) 3.2 | (30) 2.9 |
| | | | 5.7 | | | | | 7.1 | 6.5 |
| Net Sales ($) | 18311M | 47620M | 365753M | 522169M | 1122584M | 652799M | | 3079264M | 4574897M |
| Total Assets ($) | 3555M | 22014M | 205376M | 383719M | 513385M | 784121M | | 2465041M | 2619653M |

M = $ thousand     MM = $ million
See Pages 9 through 22 for Explanation of Ratios and Data

## Comparative Historical Data | Current Data Sorted by Sales

| | 4/1/09-3/31/10 ALL | 4/1/10-3/31/11 ALL | 4/1/11-3/31/12 ALL | 0-1MM | 1-3MM | 3-5MM | 5-10MM | 10-25MM | 25MM & OVER |
|---|---|---|---|---|---|---|---|---|---|
| **Type of Statement** | | | | 13 (4/1-9/30/11) | | | 90 (10/1/11-3/31/12) | | |
| Unqualified | 28 | 21 | 17 | | 3 | 1 | 3 | 3 | 7 |
| Reviewed | 16 | 10 | 12 | | 1 | 2 | 3 | 3 | 3 |
| Compiled | 7 | 6 | 12 | 3 | 1 | | 3 | 3 | 2 |
| Tax Returns | 12 | 10 | 17 | 7 | 3 | 5 | 1 | | 1 |
| Other | 55 | 43 | 45 | 6 | 3 | 10 | 9 | 8 | 6 |
| **NUMBER OF STATEMENTS** | 118 | 90 | 103 | 16 | 14 | 18 | 19 | 17 | 19 |
| **ASSETS** | % | % | % | % | % | % | % | % | % |
| Cash & Equivalents | 10.9 | 10.7 | 14.3 | 26.7 | 10.2 | 15.0 | 15.6 | 7.5 | 11.0 |
| Trade Receivables (net) | 15.1 | 16.5 | 14.8 | 7.1 | 10.9 | 17.6 | 9.6 | 13.1 | 28.0 |
| Inventory | 7.7 | 7.3 | 9.4 | 4.7 | 11.9 | 10.9 | 10.9 | 11.8 | 6.6 |
| All Other Current | 4.6 | 6.5 | 2.4 | .2 | 2.6 | 1.3 | 2.2 | 3.1 | 4.5 |
| Total Current | 38.3 | 41.0 | 40.9 | 38.7 | 35.6 | 44.8 | 38.3 | 35.5 | 50.2 |
| Fixed Assets (net) | 47.3 | 46.6 | 46.5 | 56.4 | 56.3 | 48.0 | 47.9 | 44.5 | 30.2 |
| Intangibles (net) | 7.0 | 4.7 | 5.5 | .3 | .2 | .7 | 6.7 | 14.6 | 8.9 |
| All Other Non-Current | 7.4 | 7.7 | 7.1 | 4.6 | 7.9 | 6.5 | 7.1 | 5.4 | 10.7 |
| Total | 100.0 | 100.0 | 100.0 | 100.0 | 100.0 | 100.0 | 100.0 | 100.0 | 100.0 |
| **LIABILITIES** | | | | | | | | | |
| Notes Payable-Short Term | 10.7 | 7.6 | 4.8 | 9.8 | 3.2 | 3.9 | 2.1 | 3.2 | 6.6 |
| Cur. Mat.-L.T.D. | 3.4 | 3.6 | 3.9 | 4.0 | 3.8 | 4.5 | 2.9 | 4.3 | 4.1 |
| Trade Payables | 9.5 | 7.7 | 9.5 | 5.9 | 12.0 | 7.6 | 8.8 | 8.1 | 14.3 |
| Income Taxes Payable | .2 | .1 | .2 | .0 | .1 | .4 | .1 | .0 | .3 |
| All Other Current | 11.7 | 13.6 | 10.7 | 3.6 | 5.4 | 6.1 | 19.2 | 12.1 | 15.0 |
| Total Current | 35.5 | 32.6 | 29.0 | 23.3 | 24.5 | 22.6 | 33.1 | 27.7 | 40.4 |
| Long-Term Debt | 33.0 | 25.7 | 30.0 | 43.1 | 34.3 | 18.2 | 21.0 | 43.5 | 24.2 |
| Deferred Taxes | .4 | .3 | .0 | .0 | .0 | .0 | .0 | .0 | .0 |
| All Other Non-Current | 8.9 | 10.6 | 8.5 | 1.5 | 10.8 | 6.2 | 6.2 | 15.3 | 11.1 |
| Net Worth | 22.2 | 30.8 | 32.4 | 32.0 | 30.5 | 53.0 | 39.7 | 13.5 | 24.3 |
| Total Liabilties & Net Worth | 100.0 | 100.0 | 100.0 | 100.0 | 100.0 | 100.0 | 100.0 | 100.0 | 100.0 |
| **INCOME DATA** | | | | | | | | | |
| Net Sales | 100.0 | 100.0 | 100.0 | 100.0 | 100.0 | 100.0 | 100.0 | 100.0 | 100.0 |
| Gross Profit | | | | | | | | | |
| Operating Expenses | 95.4 | 93.7 | 91.7 | 75.2 | 90.3 | 98.3 | 95.7 | 93.2 | 94.8 |
| Operating Profit | 4.6 | 6.3 | 8.3 | 24.8 | 9.7 | 1.7 | 4.3 | 6.8 | 5.2 |
| All Other Expenses (net) | 3.3 | 2.2 | 3.2 | 9.1 | 2.7 | .5 | 1.5 | 2.0 | 4.0 |
| Profit Before Taxes | 1.3 | 4.1 | 5.1 | 15.7 | 7.0 | 1.2 | 2.8 | 4.7 | 1.2 |
| **RATIOS** | | | | | | | | | |
| Current | 2.0 | 2.4 | 2.8 | 11.3 | 3.8 | 4.4 | 4.8 | 1.6 | 2.0 |
| | 1.2 | 1.4 | 1.3 | .7 | 1.5 | 2.4 | 2.0 | 1.1 | 1.1 |
| | .6 | .9 | .8 | .3 | .9 | 1.1 | .6 | .8 | .9 |
| Quick | 1.3 | 1.8 | 2.0 | 10.3 | 1.7 | 3.2 | 3.4 | .9 | 1.9 |
| | .7 | 1.0 | .9 | .5 | .9 | 1.4 | 1.3 | .6 | .9 |
| | .4 | .5 | .4 | .2 | .2 | .7 | .4 | .4 | .7 |
| Sales/Receivables | 9  39.1 | 9  39.6 | 6  56.4 | 0  UND | 0  UND | 9  42.3 | 10  35.4 | 8  47.0 | 18  19.9 |
| | 22  16.9 | 24  15.4 | 19  19.3 | 0  UND | 6  56.4 | 16  22.9 | 20  18.6 | 18  20.2 | 32  11.4 |
| | 39  9.3 | 53  6.9 | 45  8.2 | 58  6.3 | 27  13.3 | 51  7.1 | 38  9.6 | 39  9.4 | 51  7.1 |
| Cost of Sales/Inventory | | | | | | | | | |
| Cost of Sales/Payables | | | | | | | | | |
| Sales/Working Capital | 8.3 | 5.8 | 7.0 | 7.2 | 4.4 | 5.0 | 4.2 | 15.9 | 10.8 |
| | 30.3 | 16.4 | 26.9 | -7.4 | 13.3 | 8.7 | 14.8 | 124.2 | 34.8 |
| | -16.1 | -84.1 | -44.1 | -3.0 | NM | 117.6 | -15.5 | -49.5 | -98.3 |
| EBIT/Interest | 7.8 | 9.4 | 8.6 | | 23.0 | 8.5 | 6.7 | 26.7 | 7.5 |
| | (101)  2.1 | (70)  3.5 | (84)  3.4 | (11)  3.0 | (16)  4.2 | (14)  2.0 | 4.6 | (18)  2.6 | |
| | -.8 | .6 | .9 | | .6 | 1.8 | .1 | 1.4 | .7 |
| Net Profit + Depr., Dep., Amort./Cur. Mat. L/T/D | 8.7 | 29.4 | 3.8 | | | | | | |
| | (20)  2.4 | (10)  2.5 | (12)  1.4 | | | | | | |
| | .5 | 1.2 | .8 | | | | | | |
| Fixed/Worth | .8 | .6 | .5 | .3 | .4 | .2 | .4 | 1.2 | .7 |
| | 1.7 | 1.3 | 1.3 | 1.9 | 1.4 | 1.1 | .9 | 4.6 | 2.0 |
| | -9.5 | 3.8 | 6.3 | 4.2 | -110.0 | 1.8 | 1.7 | -2.1 | -4.1 |
| Debt/Worth | .9 | .7 | .6 | .6 | .8 | .4 | .2 | 1.9 | 1.1 |
| | 2.7 | 1.6 | 1.7 | 1.6 | 1.9 | .9 | .6 | 7.8 | 5.5 |
| | -16.2 | 5.6 | 9.1 | 6.7 | -120.6 | 1.7 | 2.6 | -3.7 | -11.8 |
| % Profit Before Taxes/Tangible Net Worth | 46.8 | 35.4 | 41.9 | 109.2 | 54.3 | 28.6 | 29.3 | 78.6 | 42.1 |
| | (84)  14.1 | (74)  14.5 | (82)  15.6 | (14)  19.5 | (10)  10.6 | (17)  13.9 | (17)  11.3 | (11)  21.7 | (13)  22.3 |
| | -1.6 | .5 | 3.5 | 1.3 | -.7 | 5.3 | -.8 | 3.9 | 6.7 |
| % Profit Before Taxes/Total Assets | 10.3 | 13.0 | 11.9 | 36.3 | 26.0 | 12.0 | 11.6 | 10.2 | 10.6 |
| | 2.5 | 5.3 | 5.1 | 9.3 | 5.8 | 5.2 | 4.3 | 7.6 | 2.4 |
| | -4.1 | -.7 | -.1 | 2.4 | -1.2 | 1.5 | -1.3 | .7 | -1.1 |
| Sales/Net Fixed Assets | 13.1 | 12.6 | 19.7 | 41.0 | 23.6 | 19.6 | 23.8 | 13.9 | 60.1 |
| | 3.7 | 3.2 | 3.5 | 1.0 | 1.3 | 3.7 | 3.1 | 3.4 | 5.5 |
| | 1.3 | 1.1 | 1.2 | .2 | .2 | 2.2 | .9 | 2.2 | 3.6 |
| Sales/Total Assets | 2.9 | 2.4 | 3.0 | 3.3 | 3.4 | 2.5 | 2.8 | 3.4 | 5.1 |
| | 1.5 | 1.4 | 1.6 | .4 | 1.0 | 2.0 | 1.0 | 1.6 | 2.3 |
| | .7 | .7 | .6 | .2 | .2 | 1.4 | .5 | .9 | 1.3 |
| % Depr., Dep., Amort./Sales | 1.6 | 1.5 | 1.4 | | 1.6 | 1.5 | 1.1 | 1.0 | .8 |
| | (99)  3.9 | (73)  4.7 | (87)  3.1 | (13)  8.7 | (17)  3.2 | (14)  3.0 | (16)  2.5 | (18)  2.0 | |
| | 7.3 | 11.3 | 8.3 | | 20.8 | 6.3 | 11.1 | 4.4 | 4.8 |
| % Officers', Directors' Owners' Comp/Sales | 1.6 | 1.5 | 1.5 | | | | | | |
| | (25)  2.7 | (24)  2.1 | (33)  2.5 | | | | | | |
| | 9.7 | 6.8 | 4.6 | | | | | | |
| Net Sales ($) | 4543989M | 2542585M | 2729236M | 6253M | 24409M | 69413M | 136110M | 264068M | 2228983M |
| Total Assets ($) | 3542363M | 2386134M | 1912170M | 16337M | 125233M | 88208M | 325489M | 207831M | 1149072M |

**Current Data Sorted by Assets**  |  **Comparative Historical Data**

Current period counts: 22 (4/1-9/30/11) — covering 500M-2MM; 90 (10/1/11-3/31/12) — covering 10-50MM.
Historical periods: 28 (4/1/07-3/31/08 ALL); 32 (4/1/08-3/31/09 ALL).

| 0-500M | 500M-2MM | 2-10MM | 10-50MM | 50-100MM | 100-250MM | | 4/1/07-3/31/08 ALL | 4/1/08-3/31/09 ALL |
|---|---|---|---|---|---|---|---|---|
| | | | | | | **Type of Statement** | | |
| 1 | 1 | 4 | 15 | | 3 | Unqualified | 19 | 20 |
| 1 | 5 | 9 | 8 | | | Reviewed | 8 | 16 |
| 1 | 7 | 9 | | | | Compiled | 4 | 5 |
| 4 | 3 | 5 | 12 | 2 | 3 | Tax Returns | 7 | 6 |
| 3 | 3 | 17 | | | | Other | 28 | 32 |
| 9 | 16 | 44 | 35 | 2 | 6 | **NUMBER OF STATEMENTS** | 66 | 79 |
| % | % | % | % | % | % | **ASSETS** | % | % |
| | 21.1 | 9.4 | 12.5 | | | Cash & Equivalents | 9.9 | 10.7 |
| | 17.3 | 25.2 | 22.5 | | | Trade Receivables (net) | 19.7 | 17.2 |
| | 19.9 | 21.0 | 9.1 | | | Inventory | 13.7 | 17.2 |
| | .8 | 3.2 | 3.4 | | | All Other Current | 4.9 | 7.0 |
| | 59.1 | 58.8 | 47.5 | | | Total Current | 48.1 | 52.0 |
| | 30.0 | 29.5 | 33.9 | | | Fixed Assets (net) | 36.4 | 35.4 |
| | 3.1 | 4.5 | 9.0 | | | Intangibles (net) | 4.4 | 3.0 |
| | 7.8 | 7.2 | 9.6 | | | All Other Non-Current | 11.1 | 9.6 |
| | 100.0 | 100.0 | 100.0 | | | Total | 100.0 | 100.0 |
| | | | | | | **LIABILITIES** | | |
| | 7.3 | 9.5 | 6.1 | | | Notes Payable-Short Term | 7.4 | 9.3 |
| | 6.1 | 3.5 | 4.1 | | | Cur. Mat.-L.T.D. | 6.1 | 4.3 |
| | 19.4 | 13.2 | 9.5 | | | Trade Payables | 12.6 | 10.8 |
| | .1 | .1 | .2 | | | Income Taxes Payable | .6 | .2 |
| | 10.2 | 9.6 | 12.0 | | | All Other Current | 11.5 | 12.7 |
| | 43.1 | 36.0 | 31.7 | | | Total Current | 38.2 | 37.3 |
| | 18.7 | 22.1 | 23.7 | | | Long-Term Debt | 27.3 | 22.9 |
| | .0 | .0 | .4 | | | Deferred Taxes | .3 | .1 |
| | 2.0 | 3.5 | 5.4 | | | All Other Non-Current | 10.8 | 8.0 |
| | 36.1 | 38.4 | 38.7 | | | Net Worth | 23.5 | 31.7 |
| | 100.0 | 100.0 | 100.0 | | | Total Liabilities & Net Worth | 100.0 | 100.0 |
| | | | | | | **INCOME DATA** | | |
| | 100.0 | 100.0 | 100.0 | | | Net Sales | 100.0 | 100.0 |
| | | | | | | Gross Profit | | |
| | 91.8 | 90.8 | 92.9 | | | Operating Expenses | 94.8 | 93.7 |
| | 8.2 | 9.2 | 7.1 | | | Operating Profit | 5.2 | 6.3 |
| | 1.3 | 1.6 | 1.9 | | | All Other Expenses (net) | 1.4 | 1.7 |
| | 6.9 | 7.6 | 5.2 | | | Profit Before Taxes | 3.8 | 4.6 |
| | | | | | | **RATIOS** | | |
| | 3.6 | 3.0 | 2.4 | | | | 2.2 | 2.5 |
| | 1.3 | 1.6 | 1.4 | | | Current | 1.3 | 1.4 |
| | .8 | 1.0 | 1.0 | | | | .8 | .8 |
| | 3.3 | 1.6 | 2.0 | | | | 1.5 | 1.6 |
| | .7 | (43) .9 | 1.0 | | | Quick | .7 | .7 |
| | .4 | .7 | .6 | | | | .4 | .4 |
| | 10 37.5 | 24 14.9 | 14 26.4 | | | | 15 24.5 | 8 43.3 |
| | 17 21.9 | 35 10.3 | 41 8.9 | | | Sales/Receivables | 25 14.7 | 23 16.0 |
| | 38 9.5 | 54 6.8 | 55 6.6 | | | | 51 7.2 | 50 7.3 |
| | | | | | | Cost of Sales/Inventory | | |
| | | | | | | Cost of Sales/Payables | | |
| | 8.0 | 5.1 | 7.1 | | | | 6.1 | 7.0 |
| | 11.7 | 12.3 | 12.9 | | | Sales/Working Capital | 28.1 | 23.4 |
| | -33.9 | 470.3 | 143.7 | | | | -23.1 | -29.4 |
| | 31.8 | 26.1 | 9.9 | | | | 8.6 | 10.2 |
| | (12) 2.7 | (41) 4.4 | (32) 4.5 | | | EBIT/Interest | (60) 2.8 | (71) 3.4 |
| | 1.5 | 1.2 | .8 | | | | 1.4 | 1.2 |
| | | 5.1 | 4.1 | | | | 10.9 | 6.6 |
| | | (14) 2.0 | (15) 2.2 | | | Net Profit + Depr., Dep., Amort./Cur. Mat. L/T/D | (20) 2.9 | (19) 1.3 |
| | | 1.5 | 1.3 | | | | 1.7 | -.2 |
| | .3 | .3 | .4 | | | | .4 | .3 |
| | .7 | .9 | 1.3 | | | Fixed/Worth | 1.6 | 1.2 |
| | 4.0 | 3.0 | 2.7 | | | | NM | 8.0 |
| | 1.0 | .6 | 1.1 | | | | 1.2 | .7 |
| | 1.8 | 1.5 | 2.3 | | | Debt/Worth | 2.4 | 2.3 |
| | 10.9 | 5.4 | 6.4 | | | | NM | 20.4 |
| | 43.0 | 62.7 | 69.7 | | | | 56.1 | 58.8 |
| | (13) 30.0 | (37) 31.9 | (33) 13.6 | | | % Profit Before Taxes/Tangible Net Worth | (50) 28.0 | (63) 21.6 |
| | 7.7 | 11.5 | .5 | | | | 10.9 | 2.0 |
| | 26.4 | 27.1 | 18.0 | | | | 21.1 | 16.8 |
| | 11.3 | 8.9 | 5.5 | | | % Profit Before Taxes/Total Assets | 6.5 | 6.7 |
| | 3.1 | .9 | .2 | | | | -.5 | .2 |
| | 47.7 | 36.0 | 21.7 | | | | 15.7 | 21.3 |
| | 13.9 | 11.3 | 6.9 | | | Sales/Net Fixed Assets | 6.6 | 6.5 |
| | 4.6 | 3.6 | 2.1 | | | | 3.0 | 2.8 |
| | 6.3 | 3.3 | 2.9 | | | | 3.1 | 2.8 |
| | 2.1 | 2.6 | 1.7 | | | Sales/Total Assets | 1.9 | 1.9 |
| | 1.6 | 1.5 | 1.1 | | | | 1.2 | 1.2 |
| | 1.0 | .8 | 1.3 | | | | 1.4 | .9 |
| | (13) 1.8 | (39) 1.8 | (32) 1.8 | | | % Depr., Dep., Amort./Sales | (57) 2.8 | (70) 2.5 |
| | 3.6 | 4.8 | 6.7 | | | | 3.9 | 4.1 |
| | 3.1 | 1.8 | | | | | 4.3 | .9 |
| | (10) 3.8 | (19) 3.4 | | | | % Officers', Directors' Owners' Comp/Sales | (13) 6.2 | (17) 3.4 |
| | 5.3 | 5.9 | | | | | 16.5 | 7.0 |
| 9606M | 59977M | 490705M | 1451305M | 91198M | 1054031M | Net Sales ($) | 2809757M | 3916291M |
| 2050M | 17748M | 206479M | 801107M | 143100M | 1042245M | Total Assets ($) | 2000009M | 2533158M |

M = $ thousand    MM = $ million
See Pages 9 through 22 for Explanation of Ratios and Data

## Comparative Historical Data

## Current Data Sorted by Sales

| | | | Type of Statement | | 22 (4/1-9/30/11) | | 90 (10/1/11-3/31/12) | | |
|---|---|---|---|---|---|---|---|---|---|
| | | | | 0-1MM | 1-3MM | 3-5MM | 5-10MM | 10-25MM | 25MM & OVER |
| | | | **Unqualified** | | | | 1 | 7 | 14 |
| 15 | 19 | 22 | Reviewed | | 1 | 4 | 1 | 9 | 4 |
| 12 | 21 | 19 | Compiled | 2 | 4 | 3 | 3 | 3 | |
| 8 | 7 | 15 | Tax Returns | 2 | 6 | 2 | 3 | 3 | |
| 11 | 10 | 16 | Other | 2 | 2 | 2 | 10 | 12 | |
| 37 | 41 | 40 | | | | | | | 12 |
| 4/1/09-3/31/10 ALL | 4/1/10-3/31/11 ALL | 4/1/11-3/31/12 ALL | | | | | | | |
| 83 | 98 | 112 | **NUMBER OF STATEMENTS** | 6 | 13 | 11 | 18 | 34 | 30 |
| % | % | % | **ASSETS** | % | % | % | % | % | % |
| 14.3 | 12.4 | 13.1 | Cash & Equivalents | | 13.0 | 14.8 | 17.8 | 10.6 | 9.5 |
| 18.0 | 22.1 | 22.0 | Trade Receivables (net) | | 17.7 | 21.2 | 21.8 | 26.6 | 21.4 |
| 15.8 | 19.2 | 16.1 | Inventory | | 15.3 | 20.5 | 16.2 | 19.3 | 14.3 |
| 4.3 | 3.7 | 3.2 | All Other Current | | 3.0 | 2.2 | 3.4 | 2.4 | 5.1 |
| 52.4 | 57.4 | 54.5 | Total Current | | 49.0 | 58.7 | 59.2 | 58.8 | 50.3 |
| 36.6 | 31.3 | 29.8 | Fixed Assets (net) | | 31.4 | 32.7 | 25.6 | 28.3 | 26.7 |
| 4.9 | 3.7 | 6.4 | Intangibles (net) | | 5.1 | 2.4 | 7.5 | 5.5 | 10.1 |
| 6.0 | 7.6 | 9.3 | All Other Non-Current | | 14.4 | 6.3 | 7.7 | 7.4 | 13.0 |
| 100.0 | 100.0 | 100.0 | Total | | 100.0 | 100.0 | 100.0 | 100.0 | 100.0 |
| | | | **LIABILITIES** | | | | | | |
| 7.3 | 7.7 | 7.8 | Notes Payable-Short Term | | 6.2 | 8.0 | 5.5 | 10.1 | 8.2 |
| 4.1 | 3.8 | 4.0 | Cur. Mat.-L.T.D. | | 3.2 | 3.4 | 6.2 | 3.8 | 4.1 |
| 9.3 | 12.8 | 13.9 | Trade Payables | | 16.5 | 27.0 | 8.1 | 16.1 | 9.9 |
| .1 | .4 | .2 | Income Taxes Payable | | 1.0 | .1 | .0 | .3 | .1 |
| 11.3 | 12.4 | 12.8 | All Other Current | | 10.0 | 12.3 | 11.5 | 9.9 | 13.9 |
| 32.2 | 37.0 | 38.7 | Total Current | | 36.8 | 50.8 | 31.2 | 40.1 | 36.2 |
| 31.1 | 19.4 | 20.6 | Long-Term Debt | | 19.4 | 18.5 | 24.0 | 18.9 | 21.2 |
| .1 | .4 | .3 | Deferred Taxes | | .0 | .0 | .1 | .2 | .8 |
| 7.1 | 5.7 | 4.6 | All Other Non-Current | | 1.8 | 5.8 | 2.1 | 4.8 | 5.6 |
| 29.4 | 37.5 | 35.9 | Net Worth | | 42.0 | 24.9 | 42.6 | 36.0 | 36.2 |
| 100.0 | 100.0 | 100.0 | Total Liabilities & Net Worth | | 100.0 | 100.0 | 100.0 | 100.0 | 100.0 |
| | | | **INCOME DATA** | | | | | | |
| 100.0 | 100.0 | 100.0 | Net Sales | | 100.0 | 100.0 | 100.0 | 100.0 | 100.0 |
| | | | Gross Profit | | | | | | |
| 92.7 | 92.3 | 91.5 | Operating Expenses | | 87.6 | 94.3 | 90.0 | 93.5 | 93.9 |
| 7.3 | 7.7 | 8.5 | Operating Profit | | 12.4 | 5.7 | 10.0 | 6.5 | 6.1 |
| 1.9 | 2.4 | 1.6 | All Other Expenses (net) | | 1.9 | 1.0 | 1.7 | 1.0 | 1.6 |
| 5.3 | 5.3 | 6.8 | Profit Before Taxes | | 10.5 | 4.7 | 8.4 | 5.5 | 4.5 |
| | | | **RATIOS** | | | | | | |
| 2.6 | 2.5 | 2.6 | | | 2.9 | 3.4 | 3.6 | 2.5 | 2.3 |
| 1.7 | 1.6 | 1.4 | Current | | 1.0 | 1.4 | 2.1 | 1.4 | 1.4 |
| 1.0 | 1.2 | .9 | | | .8 | .8 | 1.1 | 1.0 | 1.0 |
| 1.6 | 1.5 | 1.6 | | | 2.0 | 2.9 | 2.5 | 1.5 | 1.5 |
| 1.0 | 1.0 (111) | .8 | Quick | | .8 | .5 | 1.1 (33) | 1.0 | .9 |
| .6 | .5 | .6 | | | .5 | .4 | .8 | .6 | .6 |
| 13  28.9 | 16  22.7 | 16  22.3 | | 13  28.2 | 13  28.2 | 23  15.6 | 25  14.5 | 14  26.2 | |
| 24  15.2 | 36  10.1 | 32  11.3 | Sales/Receivables | 34  10.8 | 24  15.1 | 30  12.0 | 37  9.8 | 41  9.0 | |
| 48  7.6 | 55  6.6 | 50  7.3 | | 47  7.7 | 41  9.0 | 51  7.1 | 59  6.2 | 51  7.1 | |
| | | | Cost of Sales/Inventory | | | | | | |
| | | | Cost of Sales/Payables | | | | | | |
| 6.1 | 5.0 | 6.1 | | | 6.0 | 8.4 | 5.1 | 5.3 | 6.8 |
| 13.8 | 10.1 | 12.9 | Sales/Working Capital | | UND | 12.2 | 11.4 | 13.6 | 15.7 |
| -297.7 | 37.2 | -74.0 | | | -25.8 | -46.9 | NM | NM | NM |
| 10.2 | 19.2 | 16.7 | | | | | 62.3 | 15.1 | 6.8 |
| (73) 3.6 | (82) 3.6 | (96) 3.8 | EBIT/Interest | | | | (15) 10.4 | (33) 4.4 | (29) 2.7 |
| 1.8 | 1.8 | 1.1 | | | | | .7 | 1.4 | .9 |
| 12.2 | 4.6 | 4.1 | | | | | | 4.2 | 4.3 |
| (14) 3.2 | (28) 2.3 | (34) 2.1 | Net Profit + Depr., Dep., Amort./Cur. Mat. L/T/D | | | | | (15) 2.0 | (12) 2.6 |
| 2.0 | .8 | 1.2 | | | | | | 1.6 | .9 |
| .4 | .3 | .3 | | | .0 | .2 | .1 | .3 | .4 |
| 1.3 | .7 | 1.0 | Fixed/Worth | | .6 | .8 | .5 | 1.2 | 1.3 |
| 9.6 | 2.1 | 3.0 | | | 2.3 | 3.0 | 52.6 | 2.9 | 2.4 |
| .8 | .8 | 1.0 | | | .7 | 1.0 | .5 | .8 | 1.4 |
| 2.4 | 1.7 | 2.2 | Debt/Worth | | 1.8 | 3.6 | 1.3 | 2.3 | 3.3 |
| 32.9 | 4.2 | 8.8 | | | 10.3 | -72.3 | 88.2 | 10.8 | 8.0 |
| 52.6 | 49.8 | 64.2 | | | 88.7 | | 132.3 | 48.4 | 69.9 |
| (69) 24.3 | (87) 17.8 | (96) 28.8 | % Profit Before Taxes/Tangible Net Worth | (12) 32.5 | | (15) 54.6 | (28) 28.8 | (28) 19.6 | |
| 3.6 | 4.3 | 4.7 | | | 3.7 | | 15.6 | 4.0 | .2 |
| 15.9 | 17.5 | 22.7 | | | 44.3 | 27.6 | 50.7 | 19.3 | 17.2 |
| 5.4 | 6.6 | 8.0 | % Profit Before Taxes/Total Assets | | 10.9 | 11.3 | 21.1 | 8.0 | 4.6 |
| 1.0 | 1.1 | 1.0 | | | 1.4 | 2.8 | .0 | 1.1 | .1 |
| 24.9 | 26.0 | 36.6 | | | 226.0 | 39.0 | 30.9 | 48.5 | 27.1 |
| 6.3 | 8.9 | 10.0 | Sales/Net Fixed Assets | | 7.8 | 6.4 | 14.9 | 10.7 | 7.1 |
| 1.8 | 3.8 | 3.0 | | | 2.6 | 2.3 | 6.1 | 4.5 | 2.6 |
| 3.3 | 2.9 | 3.4 | | | 3.6 | 6.6 | 3.3 | 3.3 | 3.1 |
| 1.7 | 2.0 | 2.1 | Sales/Total Assets | | 1.8 | 1.8 | 2.7 | 2.1 | 1.6 |
| 1.1 | 1.2 | 1.3 | | | 1.3 | 1.3 | 1.8 | 1.5 | .9 |
| 1.2 | .9 | 1.1 | | | | | .7 | .9 | 1.0 |
| (68) 2.3 | (75) 1.8 | (94) 1.8 | % Depr., Dep., Amort./Sales | | | | (13) 1.5 | (32) 1.7 | (27) 1.7 |
| 5.0 | 4.6 | 5.2 | | | | | 4.1 | 4.2 | 5.0 |
| 2.1 | 1.6 | 1.7 | | | | | | 1.2 | |
| (26) 4.1 | (24) 4.4 | (34) 3.4 | % Officers', Directors' Owners' Comp/Sales | | | | | (10) 3.2 | |
| 11.6 | 8.3 | 5.3 | | | | | | 6.1 | |
| 3003771M | 3022265M | 3156822M | Net Sales ($) | 2676M | 23592M | 39828M | 135848M | 593036M | 2361842M |
| 2034493M | 2108117M | 2212729M | Total Assets ($) | 4931M | 18871M | 20655M | 99302M | 308598M | 1760372M |

© RMA 2012

M = $ thousand    MM = $ million
See Pages 9 through 22 for Explanation of Ratios and Data

## Current Data Sorted by Assets

## Comparative Historical Data

| | | | | | | Type of Statement | | |
|---|---|---|---|---|---|---|---|---|
| | 1 | | | 3 | | | | |
| | | 1 | 3 | | | 3 | | |
| | 1 | 2 | | | 1 | Unqualified | 5 | 3 |
| 1 | 2 | 1 | | | | Reviewed | | 7 |
| | 2 | 5 | 5 | 1 | 3 | Compiled | 1 | 5 |
| | 2 (4/1-9/30/11) | | 30 (10/1/11-3/31/12) | | | Tax Returns | | |
| | | | | | | Other | 8 | 5 |
| 0-500M | 500M-2MM | 2-10MM | 10-50MM | 50-100MM | 100-250MM | | 4/1/07-3/31/08 ALL | 4/1/08-3/31/09 ALL |
| 1 | 6 | 9 | 8 | 1 | 7 | NUMBER OF STATEMENTS | 14 | 20 |
| % | % | % | % | % | % | ASSETS | % | % |
| | | | | | | Cash & Equivalents | 5.4 | 13.2 |
| | | | | | | Trade Receivables (net) | 31.7 | 32.7 |
| | | | | | | Inventory | 4.2 | 5.5 |
| | | | | | | All Other Current | 5.0 | 2.5 |
| | | | | | | Total Current | 46.3 | 53.9 |
| | | | | | | Fixed Assets (net) | 45.7 | 38.9 |
| | | | | | | Intangibles (net) | 4.1 | 3.8 |
| | | | | | | All Other Non-Current | 3.9 | 3.4 |
| | | | | | | Total | 100.0 | 100.0 |
| | | | | | | LIABILITIES | | |
| | | | | | | Notes Payable-Short Term | 2.8 | 8.5 |
| | | | | | | Cur. Mat.-L.T.D. | 3.8 | 3.6 |
| | | | | | | Trade Payables | 11.3 | 12.3 |
| | | | | | | Income Taxes Payable | .0 | .0 |
| | | | | | | All Other Current | 9.9 | 12.2 |
| | | | | | | Total Current | 27.8 | 36.6 |
| | | | | | | Long-Term Debt | 22.4 | 16.4 |
| | | | | | | Deferred Taxes | 2.3 | 2.3 |
| | | | | | | All Other Non-Current | 5.5 | 6.5 |
| | | | | | | Net Worth | 42.0 | 38.3 |
| | | | | | | Total Liabilties & Net Worth | 100.0 | 100.0 |
| | | | | | | INCOME DATA | | |
| | | | | | | Net Sales | 100.0 | 100.0 |
| | | | | | | Gross Profit | | |
| | | | | | | Operating Expenses | 88.5 | 89.9 |
| | | | | | | Operating Profit | 11.5 | 10.1 |
| | | | | | | All Other Expenses (net) | 1.3 | 1.5 |
| | | | | | | Profit Before Taxes | 10.3 | 8.6 |
| | | | | | | RATIOS | | |
| | | | | | | | 2.3 | 2.1 |
| | | | | | | Current | 1.4 | 1.4 |
| | | | | | | | 1.2 | 1.0 |
| | | | | | | | 1.9 | 2.0 |
| | | | | | | Quick | 1.1 | 1.2 |
| | | | | | | | .9 | .8 |
| | | | | | | | 33    11.0 | 36    10.2 |
| | | | | | | Sales/Receivables | 46    8.0 | 48    7.6 |
| | | | | | | | 74    5.0 | 69    5.3 |
| | | | | | | Cost of Sales/Inventory | | |
| | | | | | | Cost of Sales/Payables | | |
| | | | | | | | 5.0 | 5.6 |
| | | | | | | Sales/Working Capital | 12.4 | 13.2 |
| | | | | | | | 82.1 | NM |
| | | | | | | | 14.8 | 19.3 |
| | | | | | | EBIT/Interest | (11)    4.0 | (19)    6.8 |
| | | | | | | | 3.4 | 3.3 |
| | | | | | | Net Profit + Depr., Dep., Amort./Cur. Mat. L/T/D | | |
| | | | | | | | .4 | .6 |
| | | | | | | Fixed/Worth | 1.1 | 1.1 |
| | | | | | | | 2.5 | 2.8 |
| | | | | | | | .6 | .8 |
| | | | | | | Debt/Worth | 1.5 | 1.9 |
| | | | | | | | 5.0 | 2.9 |
| | | | | | | | 68.7 | 62.0 |
| | | | | | | % Profit Before Taxes/Tangible Net Worth | (13)    28.6 | (18)    22.6 |
| | | | | | | | 17.8 | 11.5 |
| | | | | | | | 23.5 | 15.7 |
| | | | | | | % Profit Before Taxes/Total Assets | 10.1 | 9.0 |
| | | | | | | | 6.8 | 3.4 |
| | | | | | | | 11.1 | 24.5 |
| | | | | | | Sales/Net Fixed Assets | 5.2 | 8.2 |
| | | | | | | | 1.6 | 1.8 |
| | | | | | | | 2.7 | 3.1 |
| | | | | | | Sales/Total Assets | 1.8 | 2.0 |
| | | | | | | | 1.2 | .8 |
| | | | | | | | 1.7 | .9 |
| | | | | | | % Depr., Dep., Amort./Sales | (11)    2.4 | (17)    3.1 |
| | | | | | | | 3.9 | 4.4 |
| | | | | | | % Officers', Directors' Owners' Comp/Sales | | |
| 661M | 16964M | 128329M | 269680M | 92564M | 2665138M | Net Sales ($) | 583319M | 648624M |
| 112M | 7921M | 53345M | 155019M | 66844M | 1116785M | Total Assets ($) | 583584M | 779458M |

© RMA 2012

M = $ thousand    MM = $ million
See Pages 9 through 22 for Explanation of Ratios and Data

## Comparative Historical Data · Current Data Sorted by Sales

| | | | | | 0-1MM | 1-3MM | 3-5MM | 5-10MM | 10-25MM | 25MM & OVER |
|---|---|---|---|---|---|---|---|---|---|---|
| 4 | 2 | 4 | | **Type of Statement** / Unqualified | | 1 | | | 4 | 3 |
| 2 | 6 | 4 | | Reviewed | | | | | 2 | 1 |
| 2 | 4 | 4 | | Compiled | | | 1 | | 1 | |
| 1 | 2 | 4 | | Tax Returns | | 2 | | | | |
| 9 | 11 | 16 | | Other | 1 | 2 | | 3 | 4 | 7 |
| 9 | 11 | 16 | | 2 (4/1-9/30/11) · 30 (10/1/11-3/31/12) | | | | | | |
| 4/1/09-3/31/10 ALL | 4/1/10-3/31/11 ALL | 4/1/11-3/31/12 ALL | | | | | | | | |
| 18 | 25 | 32 | | **NUMBER OF STATEMENTS** | 1 | 5 | 1 | 3 | 11 | 11 |
| % | % | % | | **ASSETS** | % | % | % | % | % | % |
| 9.1 | 12.0 | 15.9 | | Cash & Equivalents | | | | | 16.9 | 9.6 |
| 20.8 | 32.2 | 24.6 | | Trade Receivables (net) | | | | | 22.5 | 30.7 |
| 9.6 | 4.7 | 6.4 | | Inventory | | | | | 8.2 | 6.0 |
| 4.9 | 5.5 | 2.7 | | All Other Current | | | | | 2.6 | 4.0 |
| 44.3 | 54.4 | 49.6 | | Total Current | | | | | 50.3 | 50.2 |
| 45.0 | 38.3 | 41.3 | | Fixed Assets (net) | | | | | 38.8 | 40.8 |
| 3.7 | .4 | 2.8 | | Intangibles (net) | | | | | 6.0 | 2.2 |
| 6.9 | 6.9 | 6.3 | | All Other Non-Current | | | | | 5.0 | 6.8 |
| 100.0 | 100.0 | 100.0 | | Total | | | | | 100.0 | 100.0 |
| | | | | **LIABILITIES** | | | | | | |
| 7.6 | 4.4 | 4.1 | | Notes Payable-Short Term | | | | | 5.8 | .5 |
| 2.1 | 3.4 | 3.2 | | Cur. Mat.-L.T.D. | | | | | 4.7 | 2.0 |
| 7.1 | 11.2 | 10.0 | | Trade Payables | | | | | 11.6 | 11.5 |
| .4 | .3 | .1 | | Income Taxes Payable | | | | | .1 | .1 |
| 11.6 | 11.9 | 10.2 | | All Other Current | | | | | 12.5 | 15.2 |
| 28.8 | 31.2 | 27.6 | | Total Current | | | | | 34.7 | 29.2 |
| 23.7 | 19.2 | 21.2 | | Long-Term Debt | | | | | 19.6 | 20.6 |
| 2.3 | .7 | .8 | | Deferred Taxes | | | | | 1.0 | 1.3 |
| 9.5 | 9.1 | 6.6 | | All Other Non-Current | | | | | 1.4 | 6.1 |
| 35.7 | 39.9 | 43.8 | | Net Worth | | | | | 43.3 | 42.9 |
| 100.0 | 100.0 | 100.0 | | Total Liabilities & Net Worth | | | | | 100.0 | 100.0 |
| | | | | **INCOME DATA** | | | | | | |
| 100.0 | 100.0 | 100.0 | | Net Sales | | | | | 100.0 | 100.0 |
| | | | | Gross Profit | | | | | | |
| 89.0 | 89.3 | 87.8 | | Operating Expenses | | | | | 90.8 | 88.2 |
| 11.0 | 10.7 | 12.2 | | Operating Profit | | | | | 9.2 | 11.8 |
| 4.7 | 2.5 | 3.0 | | All Other Expenses (net) | | | | | 2.5 | .8 |
| 6.4 | 8.1 | 9.1 | | Profit Before Taxes | | | | | 6.7 | 11.0 |
| | | | | **RATIOS** | | | | | | |
| 2.3 | 3.7 | 2.9 | | Current | | | | | 2.5 | 2.2 |
| 1.5 | 1.6 | 1.8 | | | | | | | 1.2 | 1.5 |
| .8 | 1.0 | 1.1 | | | | | | | .9 | 1.3 |
| 1.5 | 3.3 | 2.5 | | Quick | | | | | 2.5 | 1.5 |
| .9 | 1.3 | 1.3 | | | | | | | 1.2 | 1.3 |
| .5 | .8 | .9 | | | | | | | .8 | 1.1 |
| 0 UND | 33 11.1 | 29 12.8 | | Sales/Receivables | | | | | 24 15.2 | 33 11.1 |
| 41 8.8 | 44 8.4 | 39 9.4 | | | | | | | 47 7.8 | 39 9.4 |
| 58 6.3 | 73 5.0 | 50 7.3 | | | | | | | 59 6.2 | 47 7.7 |
| | | | | Cost of Sales/Inventory | | | | | | |
| | | | | Cost of Sales/Payables | | | | | | |
| 5.8 | 5.0 | 4.3 | | Sales/Working Capital | | | | | 4.6 | 4.5 |
| 9.6 | 13.6 | 9.1 | | | | | | | 9.2 | 13.0 |
| -17.1 | NM | 65.5 | | | | | | | -50.4 | 39.7 |
| 12.1 | 194.4 | 24.6 | | EBIT/Interest | | | | | | |
| (16) 3.3 | (22) 18.7 | (26) 10.5 | | | | | | | | |
| 1.7 | 2.3 | 2.7 | | | | | | | | |
| | | | | Net Profit + Depr., Dep., Amort./Cur. Mat. L/T/D | | | | | | |
| .5 | .4 | .5 | | Fixed/Worth | | | | | .5 | .4 |
| 1.4 | .9 | 1.1 | | | | | | | 1.3 | .9 |
| 4.4 | 1.6 | 2.2 | | | | | | | 2.8 | 1.7 |
| .9 | .2 | .4 | | Debt/Worth | | | | | .4 | .4 |
| 2.3 | 1.1 | 1.3 | | | | | | | 2.8 | 1.1 |
| 5.6 | 5.7 | 4.2 | | | | | | | 5.6 | 4.4 |
| 34.8 | 91.7 | 54.4 | | % Profit Before Taxes/Tangible Net Worth | | | | | 47.8 | 186.6 |
| (16) 19.8 | (23) 23.6 | (29) 27.3 | | | | | | | (10) 21.9 | (10) 27.8 |
| 7.0 | 10.6 | 11.1 | | | | | | | .7 | 15.8 |
| 11.9 | 20.7 | 17.9 | | % Profit Before Taxes/Total Assets | | | | | 13.7 | 18.0 |
| 4.6 | 12.2 | 10.3 | | | | | | | 7.5 | 10.7 |
| 1.7 | 2.9 | 3.3 | | | | | | | 1.3 | 8.1 |
| 8.8 | 30.0 | 19.9 | | Sales/Net Fixed Assets | | | | | 20.4 | 50.6 |
| 3.7 | 4.9 | 4.2 | | | | | | | 4.0 | 4.3 |
| 1.0 | 2.7 | 2.5 | | | | | | | 2.5 | .9 |
| 2.3 | 4.2 | 3.2 | | Sales/Total Assets | | | | | 3.2 | 4.5 |
| 1.4 | 1.9 | 1.8 | | | | | | | 1.5 | 2.6 |
| .7 | 1.3 | 1.0 | | | | | | | .9 | .7 |
| 2.8 | .7 | .8 | | % Depr., Dep., Amort./Sales | | | | | 1.5 | |
| (16) 6.2 | (21) 3.4 | (28) 3.2 | | | | | | | 2.8 | |
| 11.3 | 8.1 | 6.2 | | | | | | | 6.8 | |
| | | | | % Officers', Directors' Owners' Comp/Sales | | | | | | |
| 1067846M | 2125761M | 3173336M | | Net Sales ($) | 661M | 9129M | 3815M | 19579M | 169913M | 2970239M |
| 835828M | 877955M | 1400026M | | Total Assets ($) | 112M | 18705M | 1172M | 10140M | 150232M | 1219665M |

## Current Data Sorted by Assets      Comparative Historical Data

| | | | | | 6 | | 4 | | 1 | | Type of Statement | | 5 | | 5 |
|---|---|---|---|---|---|---|---|---|---|---|---|---|---|---|---|
| | | 1 | | | 1 | | | | | | Unqualified | | | | |
| | | 1 | | 4 | | | | | | | Reviewed | | | | |
| 2 | | 2 | | 1 | | | | | | | Compiled | | 4 | | 1 |
| | | 3 | | 3 | | 2 | | | 1 | | Tax Returns | | 2 | | |
| | | 8 (4/1-9/30/11) | | | | 23 (10/1/11-3/31/12) | | | | | Other | | 10 | | 9 |
| 0-500M | 500M-2MM | 2-10MM | | 10-50MM | | 50-100MM | | 100-250MM | | | | | 4/1/07-3/31/08 | | 4/1/08-3/31/09 |
| 2 | 6 | 8 | | 9 | | 4 | | 2 | | NUMBER OF STATEMENTS | | 21 ALL | | 15 ALL |
| % | % | % | | % | | % | | % | | ASSETS | | % | | % |
| | | | | | | | | | | Cash & Equivalents | | 13.1 | | 7.8 |
| | | | | | | | | | | Trade Receivables (net) | | 11.0 | | 7.4 |
| | | | | | | | | | | Inventory | | 1.0 | | .4 |
| | | | | | | | | | | All Other Current | | 3.7 | | 1.0 |
| | | | | | | | | | | Total Current | | 28.8 | | 16.6 |
| | | | | | | | | | | Fixed Assets (net) | | 60.5 | | 74.6 |
| | | | | | | | | | | Intangibles (net) | | 6.1 | | 6.1 |
| | | | | | | | | | | All Other Non-Current | | 4.6 | | 2.7 |
| | | | | | | | | | | Total | | 100.0 | | 100.0 |
| | | | | | | | | | | LIABILITIES | | | | |
| | | | | | | | | | | Notes Payable-Short Term | | 2.6 | | 3.6 |
| | | | | | | | | | | Cur. Mat.-L.T.D. | | 7.4 | | 11.7 |
| | | | | | | | | | | Trade Payables | | 5.8 | | 2.6 |
| | | | | | | | | | | Income Taxes Payable | | .3 | | .0 |
| | | | | | | | | | | All Other Current | | 6.6 | | 5.7 |
| | | | | | | | | | | Total Current | | 22.7 | | 23.6 |
| | | | | | | | | | | Long-Term Debt | | 38.2 | | 34.5 |
| | | | | | | | | | | Deferred Taxes | | .7 | | .0 |
| | | | | | | | | | | All Other Non-Current | | 4.9 | | 7.9 |
| | | | | | | | | | | Net Worth | | 33.5 | | 34.1 |
| | | | | | | | | | | Total Liabilities & Net Worth | | 100.0 | | 100.0 |
| | | | | | | | | | | INCOME DATA | | | | |
| | | | | | | | | | | Net Sales | | 100.0 | | 100.0 |
| | | | | | | | | | | Gross Profit | | | | |
| | | | | | | | | | | Operating Expenses | | 69.4 | | 77.0 |
| | | | | | | | | | | Operating Profit | | 30.6 | | 23.0 |
| | | | | | | | | | | All Other Expenses (net) | | 6.6 | | 11.9 |
| | | | | | | | | | | Profit Before Taxes | | 24.0 | | 11.1 |
| | | | | | | | | | | RATIOS | | | | |
| | | | | | | | | | | Current | | 1.9 / 1.0 / .7 | | 1.5 / 1.1 / .2 |
| | | | | | | | | | | Quick | | 1.7 / 1.0 / .5 | | 1.5 / .8 / .2 |
| | | | | | | | | | | Sales/Receivables | | 0 UND / 31 11.7 / 44 8.3 | | 3 118.0 / 26 14.2 / 34 10.7 |
| | | | | | | | | | | Cost of Sales/Inventory | | | | |
| | | | | | | | | | | Cost of Sales/Payables | | | | |
| | | | | | | | | | | Sales/Working Capital | | 6.6 / 149.3 / -14.5 | | 12.7 / 49.6 / -2.4 |
| | | | | | | | | | | EBIT/Interest | | 13.4 / (15) 4.7 / 3.1 | | 14.0 / (11) 6.2 / 1.8 |
| | | | | | | | | | | Net Profit + Depr., Dep., Amort./Cur. Mat. L/T/D | | | | |
| | | | | | | | | | | Fixed/Worth | | 1.1 / 1.3 / 28.7 | | 1.1 / 1.8 / -16.4 |
| | | | | | | | | | | Debt/Worth | | .8 / 1.7 / NM | | .5 / 1.3 / -18.9 |
| | | | | | | | | | | % Profit Before Taxes/Tangible Net Worth | | 57.0 / (16) 29.7 / 12.2 | | 44.4 / (11) 14.8 / 8.4 |
| | | | | | | | | | | % Profit Before Taxes/Total Assets | | 17.6 / 6.7 / 5.0 | | 16.2 / 4.9 / -.2 |
| | | | | | | | | | | Sales/Net Fixed Assets | | 5.4 / 1.5 / .2 | | 4.0 / .7 / .2 |
| | | | | | | | | | | Sales/Total Assets | | 1.7 / .8 / .2 | | 1.9 / .6 / .2 |
| | | | | | | | | | | % Depr., Dep., Amort./Sales | | 4.9 / (18) 6.8 / 28.1 | | |
| | | | | | | | | | | % Officers', Directors' Owners' Comp/Sales | | | | |
| 4485M 662M | 12561M 6912M | 48721M 34567M | | 183490M 196761M | | 343243M 347756M | | 175077M 248975M | | Net Sales ($) Total Assets ($) | | 505026M 720569M | | 746656M 642058M |

## Comparative Historical Data | Current Data Sorted by Sales

| Type of Statement | | | | 0-1MM | 1-3MM | 3-5MM | 5-10MM | 10-25MM | 25MM & OVER |
|---|---|---|---|---|---|---|---|---|---|
| 6 | 7 | 11 | Unqualified | | | 1 | 1 | 4 | 5 |
| 1 | 1 | 1 | Reviewed | | | | | 1 | |
| 2 | 4 | 5 | Compiled | 1 | 1 | 1 | 1 | 1 | |
| 3 | 1 | 5 | Tax Returns | 3 | | 2 | | | |
| 8 | 11 | 9 | Other | 2 | 1 | | 1 | 4 | 1 |
| 4/1/09-3/31/10 ALL | 4/1/10-3/31/11 ALL | 4/1/11-3/31/12 ALL | | 8 (4/1-9/30/11) | | 23 (10/1/11-3/31/12) | | | |
| 20 | 24 | 31 | NUMBER OF STATEMENTS | 6 | 2 | 4 | 3 | 10 | 6 |
| % | % | % | ASSETS | % | % | % | % | % | % |
| 13.3 | 21.1 | 14.3 | Cash & Equivalents | | | | | 11.0 | |
| 14.2 | 10.0 | 9.9 | Trade Receivables (net) | | | | | 14.2 | |
| 1.7 | 1.6 | .4 | Inventory | | | | | .1 | |
| 5.5 | 1.6 | 4.8 | All Other Current | | | | | 4.6 | |
| 34.7 | 34.2 | 29.5 | Total Current | | | | | 29.9 | |
| 56.4 | 55.6 | 57.0 | Fixed Assets (net) | | | | | 59.5 | |
| 1.6 | 4.0 | 4.5 | Intangibles (net) | | | | | 1.3 | |
| 7.2 | 6.2 | 9.0 | All Other Non-Current | | | | | 9.3 | |
| 100.0 | 100.0 | 100.0 | Total | | | | | 100.0 | |
| | | | LIABILITIES | | | | | | |
| 4.6 | .7 | 2.3 | Notes Payable-Short Term | | | | | 2.9 | |
| 3.0 | 3.5 | 3.3 | Cur. Mat.-L.T.D. | | | | | 5.2 | |
| 8.7 | 8.4 | 4.4 | Trade Payables | | | | | 5.0 | |
| .1 | .1 | .0 | Income Taxes Payable | | | | | .1 | |
| 18.1 | 9.7 | 10.6 | All Other Current | | | | | 7.0 | |
| 34.5 | 22.4 | 20.6 | Total Current | | | | | 20.2 | |
| 43.8 | 36.2 | 35.1 | Long-Term Debt | | | | | 38.3 | |
| .5 | .6 | .5 | Deferred Taxes | | | | | .0 | |
| 3.1 | 6.4 | 5.2 | All Other Non-Current | | | | | 8.3 | |
| 18.1 | 34.5 | 38.6 | Net Worth | | | | | 33.1 | |
| 100.0 | 100.0 | 100.0 | Total Liabilties & Net Worth | | | | | 100.0 | |
| | | | INCOME DATA | | | | | | |
| 100.0 | 100.0 | 100.0 | Net Sales | | | | | 100.0 | |
| | | | Gross Profit | | | | | | |
| 92.5 | 89.5 | 81.1 | Operating Expenses | | | | | 82.5 | |
| 7.5 | 10.5 | 18.9 | Operating Profit | | | | | 17.5 | |
| 6.1 | 5.8 | 5.3 | All Other Expenses (net) | | | | | -.2 | |
| 1.5 | 4.6 | 13.7 | Profit Before Taxes | | | | | 17.7 | |
| | | | RATIOS | | | | | | |
| 2.3 | 2.7 | 2.7 | Current | | | | | 3.0 | |
| .9 | 1.5 | 1.4 | | | | | | 2.3 | |
| .6 | .8 | .7 | | | | | | .9 | |
| 1.7 | 2.7 | 2.7 | Quick | | | | | 2.9 | |
| .8 | 1.4 | .9 | | | | | | 2.2 | |
| .4 | .6 | .4 | | | | | | .6 | |
| 12  29.3 | 19  19.6 | 9  41.9 | Sales/Receivables | | | | | 27  13.7 | |
| 37  9.9 | 33  11.0 | 27  13.6 | | | | | | 37  9.9 | |
| 52  7.0 | 43  8.5 | 46  7.9 | | | | | | 47  7.7 | |
| | | | Cost of Sales/Inventory | | | | | | |
| | | | Cost of Sales/Payables | | | | | | |
| 6.3 | 4.2 | 4.6 | Sales/Working Capital | | | | | 4.0 | |
| -100.1 | 13.7 | 26.1 | | | | | | 11.1 | |
| -6.0 | -12.4 | -15.5 | | | | | | -751.5 | |
| 11.6 | 10.5 | 8.4 | EBIT/Interest | | | | | | |
| (18)  .3 | (15)  4.9 | (24)  3.9 | | | | | | | |
| -2.2 | .8 | 2.2 | | | | | | | |
| | | | Net Profit + Depr., Dep., Amort./Cur. Mat. L/T/D | | | | | | |
| .9 | .6 | .9 | Fixed/Worth | | | | | .9 | |
| 1.6 | 1.7 | 1.5 | | | | | | 1.7 | |
| 8.2 | -11.1 | 5.2 | | | | | | NM | |
| .6 | .7 | .3 | Debt/Worth | | | | | .3 | |
| 1.3 | 1.0 | .9 | | | | | | 1.8 | |
| 17.7 | -13.1 | 8.2 | | | | | | NM | |
| 14.1 | 79.9 | 53.7 | % Profit Before Taxes/Tangible Net Worth | | | | | | |
| (18)  -3.1 | (16)  13.5 | (25)  17.0 | | | | | | | |
| -17.3 | 4.0 | 4.2 | | | | | | | |
| 6.2 | 14.6 | 12.5 | % Profit Before Taxes/Total Assets | | | | | 23.7 | |
| -.6 | 3.0 | 5.3 | | | | | | 14.2 | |
| -5.7 | -1.1 | 1.9 | | | | | | 6.7 | |
| 18.8 | 10.1 | 4.2 | Sales/Net Fixed Assets | | | | | 4.0 | |
| 1.9 | 1.5 | 1.6 | | | | | | 2.2 | |
| .3 | .4 | .4 | | | | | | .6 | |
| 2.7 | 1.8 | 2.0 | Sales/Total Assets | | | | | 1.8 | |
| 1.2 | .9 | 1.0 | | | | | | 1.0 | |
| .3 | .2 | .2 | | | | | | .6 | |
| 1.4 | 2.7 | 3.5 | % Depr., Dep., Amort./Sales | | | | | | |
| (14)  10.6 | (19)  8.1 | (28)  8.2 | | | | | | | |
| 26.7 | 20.0 | 18.3 | | | | | | | |
| | | 2.6 | % Officers', Directors' Owners' Comp/Sales | | | | | | |
| | (10) | 7.1 | | | | | | | |
| | | 31.9 | | | | | | | |
| 802045M | 457858M | 767577M | Net Sales ($) | 3681M | 5376M | 17395M | 19324M | 131580M | 590221M |
| 610959M | 653050M | 835633M | Total Assets ($) | 11515M | 1886M | 47024M | 36624M | 261922M | 476662M |

M = $ thousand     MM = $ million
See Pages 9 through 22 for Explanation of Ratios and Data

## Current Data Sorted by Assets      Comparative Historical Data

| | | | | | | Type of Statement | | |
|---|---|---|---|---|---|---|---|---|
| | | 2 | 11 | 5 | 4 | Unqualified | 34 | 37 |
| | 2 | 4 | 8 | 2 | | Reviewed | 9 | 10 |
| | 1 | 5 | | | | Compiled | 8 | 3 |
| 3 | 1 | 3 | 2 | | | Tax Returns | 2 | 2 |
| 1 | 2 | 15 | 14 | 4 | 5 | Other | 30 | 33 |
| | 15 (4/1-9/30/11) | | 79 (10/1/11-3/31/12) | | | | 4/1/07-3/31/08 | 4/1/08-3/31/09 |
| 0-500M | 500M-2MM | 2-10MM | 10-50MM | 50-100MM | 100-250MM | | ALL | ALL |
| 4 | 6 | 29 | 35 | 11 | 9 | **NUMBER OF STATEMENTS** | 83 | 85 |
| % | % | % | % | % | % | **ASSETS** | % | % |
| | | 10.8 | 13.5 | 12.0 | | Cash & Equivalents | 11.0 | 10.7 |
| | | 28.9 | 15.1 | 19.7 | | Trade Receivables (net) | 22.6 | 21.9 |
| | | 1.4 | 2.1 | 1.6 | | Inventory | 1.8 | 1.7 |
| | | 5.0 | 5.3 | 2.6 | | All Other Current | 6.6 | 6.1 |
| | | 46.1 | 36.0 | 35.9 | | Total Current | 42.0 | 40.5 |
| | | 32.0 | 50.4 | 46.9 | | Fixed Assets (net) | 44.6 | 46.2 |
| | | 6.2 | 6.4 | 2.2 | | Intangibles (net) | 3.8 | 2.5 |
| | | 15.6 | 7.2 | 15.0 | | All Other Non-Current | 9.7 | 10.9 |
| | | 100.0 | 100.0 | 100.0 | | Total | 100.0 | 100.0 |
| | | | | | | **LIABILITIES** | | |
| | | 5.8 | 6.0 | .3 | | Notes Payable-Short Term | 4.5 | 7.2 |
| | | 3.2 | 4.1 | 5.5 | | Cur. Mat.-L.T.D. | 4.8 | 5.5 |
| | | 12.9 | 5.9 | 9.6 | | Trade Payables | 11.0 | 11.0 |
| | | .2 | .5 | .1 | | Income Taxes Payable | .7 | .2 |
| | | 12.6 | 9.7 | 8.3 | | All Other Current | 9.1 | 9.1 |
| | | 34.7 | 26.2 | 23.8 | | Total Current | 30.2 | 32.9 |
| | | 20.7 | 22.8 | 44.2 | | Long-Term Debt | 31.9 | 33.3 |
| | | .1 | 1.4 | .7 | | Deferred Taxes | 1.1 | .8 |
| | | 9.2 | 6.5 | 14.9 | | All Other Non-Current | 5.0 | 5.9 |
| | | 35.4 | 43.1 | 16.5 | | Net Worth | 31.8 | 27.0 |
| | | 100.0 | 100.0 | 100.0 | | Total Liabilities & Net Worth | 100.0 | 100.0 |
| | | | | | | **INCOME DATA** | | |
| | | 100.0 | 100.0 | 100.0 | | Net Sales | 100.0 | 100.0 |
| | | | | | | Gross Profit | | |
| | | 90.3 | 84.1 | 74.9 | | Operating Expenses | 90.0 | 87.9 |
| | | 9.7 | 15.9 | 25.1 | | Operating Profit | 10.0 | 12.1 |
| | | .3 | 2.8 | 2.1 | | All Other Expenses (net) | 1.8 | 1.2 |
| | | 9.4 | 13.1 | 23.0 | | Profit Before Taxes | 8.3 | 10.9 |
| | | | | | | **RATIOS** | | |
| | | 2.0 | 3.0 | 3.2 | | | 2.3 | 2.5 |
| | | 1.2 | 1.6 | 1.9 | | Current | 1.4 | 1.4 |
| | | .8 | .9 | 1.3 | | | .8 | .9 |
| | | 2.0 | 2.7 | 3.1 | | | 2.0 | 2.1 |
| | | 1.2 | 1.3 | 1.8 | | Quick | 1.0 | 1.0 |
| | | .6 | .5 | 1.3 | | | .6 | .6 |
| | | 17   21.7 | 20   18.3 | 28   13.1 | | | 28   13.1 | 24   15.2 |
| | | 43   8.5 | 37   9.9 | 38   9.6 | | Sales/Receivables | 43   8.5 | 38   9.6 |
| | | 68   5.4 | 51   7.2 | 47   7.7 | | | 59   6.2 | 60   6.0 |
| | | | | | | Cost of Sales/Inventory | | |
| | | | | | | Cost of Sales/Payables | | |
| | | 6.4 | 4.3 | 5.5 | | | 6.1 | 6.6 |
| | | 22.6 | 10.1 | 8.9 | | Sales/Working Capital | 15.3 | 14.1 |
| | | -33.7 | -75.4 | 29.2 | | | -28.8 | -52.1 |
| | | 24.0 | 33.7 | | | | 15.2 | 10.3 |
| | (24) | 6.0 | (32)   7.5 | | | EBIT/Interest | (71)   4.1 | (77)   4.9 |
| | | 2.0 | 2.8 | | | | 2.0 | 2.3 |
| | | | | | | Net Profit + Depr., Dep., | 5.6 | 8.9 |
| | | | | | | Amort./Cur. Mat. L/T/D | (22)   2.9 | (25)   3.7 |
| | | | | | | | 1.6 | 2.0 |
| | | .3 | .5 | .6 | | | .6 | .7 |
| | | .8 | 1.4 | 1.0 | | Fixed/Worth | 1.3 | 1.4 |
| | | 3.3 | 3.4 | 2.7 | | | 2.6 | 2.8 |
| | | 1.1 | .6 | .4 | | | .8 | .8 |
| | | 1.8 | 1.5 | .8 | | Debt/Worth | 1.7 | 2.2 |
| | | 5.8 | 4.4 | 2.6 | | | 4.8 | 4.0 |
| | | 86.8 | 36.3 | 66.7 | | % Profit Before Taxes/Tangible | 46.9 | 55.2 |
| | (25) | 36.9 | (30)   22.9 | (10)   35.5 | | Net Worth | (70)   29.1 | (77)   28.7 |
| | | 17.2 | 7.6 | 17.1 | | | 13.8 | 13.8 |
| | | 27.6 | 16.5 | 23.5 | | % Profit Before Taxes/Total | 17.4 | 17.3 |
| | | 7.6 | 8.0 | 16.6 | | Assets | 8.6 | 9.0 |
| | | 3.9 | 4.6 | 9.4 | | | 2.8 | 3.4 |
| | | 45.8 | 9.7 | 17.8 | | | 10.4 | 9.5 |
| | | 10.0 | 1.6 | 2.6 | | Sales/Net Fixed Assets | 3.4 | 3.3 |
| | | 2.9 | .8 | .6 | | | 1.5 | 1.3 |
| | | 3.8 | 1.9 | 2.9 | | | 2.2 | 2.4 |
| | | 2.0 | 1.0 | 1.4 | | Sales/Total Assets | 1.3 | 1.6 |
| | | 1.0 | .5 | .5 | | | .8 | .8 |
| | | .8 | 2.5 | | | | 2.1 | 2.0 |
| | (26) | 2.8 | (32)   6.7 | | | % Depr., Dep., Amort./Sales | (71)   4.8 | (72)   4.0 |
| | | 6.4 | 19.9 | | | | 7.4 | 8.4 |
| | | | | | | % Officers', Directors' | .5 | |
| | | | | | | Owners' Comp/Sales | (10)   3.6 | |
| | | | | | | | 9.1 | |
| 4898M | 26144M | 436720M | 980448M | 1615281M | 1557826M | Net Sales ($) | 5102525M | 5756588M |
| 976M | 7677M | 165884M | 808022M | 824095M | 1319921M | Total Assets ($) | 3113007M | 3167574M |

M = $ thousand    MM = $ million
See Pages 9 through 22 for Explanation of Ratios and Data

## Comparative Historical Data | Current Data Sorted by Sales

| 4/1/09-3/31/10 ALL | 4/1/10-3/31/11 ALL | 4/1/11-3/31/12 ALL | Type of Statement | 0-1MM | 1-3MM | 3-5MM | 5-10MM | 10-25MM | 25MM & OVER |
|---|---|---|---|---|---|---|---|---|---|
| 28 | 21 | 22 | Unqualified | | | 1 | 1 | 5 | 15 |
| 11 | 14 | 16 | Reviewed | 1 | 1 | 3 | 2 | 5 | 4 |
| 6 | 3 | 6 | Compiled | | 2 | | | 2 | |
| 10 | 6 | 9 | Tax Returns | 1 | 5 | | | 2 | 1 |
| 45 | 53 | 41 | Other | 1 | 2 | 3 | 9 | 4 | 22 |
| | | | | 15 (4/1-9/30/11) | | | 79 (10/1/11-3/31/12) | | |
| 100 | 97 | 94 | **NUMBER OF STATEMENTS** | 3 | 10 | 9 | 12 | 18 | 42 |
| % | % | % | **ASSETS** | % | % | % | % | % | % |
| 10.9 | 14.1 | 14.0 | Cash & Equivalents | | 25.8 | | 11.3 | 15.9 | 9.2 |
| 18.9 | 20.9 | 19.5 | Trade Receivables (net) | | 4.4 | | 18.5 | 29.5 | 22.9 |
| 1.5 | 1.7 | 1.8 | Inventory | | .1 | | 1.9 | 2.1 | 2.2 |
| 5.7 | 6.1 | 4.9 | All Other Current | | 1.1 | | 3.6 | 1.2 | 8.7 |
| 36.9 | 42.8 | 40.1 | Total Current | | 31.3 | | 35.3 | 48.7 | 43.0 |
| 47.1 | 42.3 | 44.6 | Fixed Assets (net) | | 56.1 | | 44.4 | 37.3 | 43.5 |
| 5.1 | 5.4 | 4.7 | Intangibles (net) | | .1 | | 6.5 | 4.4 | 5.6 |
| 10.9 | 9.5 | 10.6 | All Other Non-Current | | 12.5 | | 13.8 | 9.6 | 7.9 |
| 100.0 | 100.0 | 100.0 | Total | | 100.0 | | 100.0 | 100.0 | 100.0 |
| | | | **LIABILITIES** | | | | | | |
| 4.9 | 5.8 | 5.1 | Notes Payable-Short Term | | 5.6 | | 5.3 | 2.6 | 4.6 |
| 8.0 | 4.0 | 4.0 | Cur. Mat.-L.T.D. | | 4.1 | | 3.2 | 3.9 | 4.3 |
| 9.7 | 11.1 | 9.5 | Trade Payables | | 8.6 | | 7.6 | 13.8 | 9.8 |
| .2 | .6 | .4 | Income Taxes Payable | | .0 | | .0 | .1 | .4 |
| 11.4 | 9.6 | 10.0 | All Other Current | | 9.0 | | 11.7 | 10.5 | 10.3 |
| 34.2 | 31.2 | 29.0 | Total Current | | 27.3 | | 27.8 | 30.8 | 29.5 |
| 30.5 | 25.8 | 25.6 | Long-Term Debt | | 36.2 | | 22.2 | 20.4 | 26.1 |
| .7 | .7 | .8 | Deferred Taxes | | .0 | | .1 | .3 | 1.7 |
| 10.2 | 3.7 | 8.6 | All Other Non-Current | | 11.5 | | 9.6 | 13.1 | 7.2 |
| 24.3 | 38.6 | 36.0 | Net Worth | | 25.1 | | 40.2 | 35.3 | 35.5 |
| 100.0 | 100.0 | 100.0 | Total Liabilities & Net Worth | | 100.0 | | 100.0 | 100.0 | 100.0 |
| | | | **INCOME DATA** | | | | | | |
| 100.0 | 100.0 | 100.0 | Net Sales | | 100.0 | | 100.0 | 100.0 | 100.0 |
| | | | Gross Profit | | | | | | |
| 88.0 | 87.2 | 86.0 | Operating Expenses | | 73.4 | | 81.4 | 88.4 | 87.9 |
| 12.0 | 12.8 | 14.0 | Operating Profit | | 26.6 | | 18.6 | 11.6 | 12.1 |
| 2.7 | 3.7 | 1.8 | All Other Expenses (net) | | 6.5 | | 2.6 | .4 | .9 |
| 9.3 | 9.1 | 12.2 | Profit Before Taxes | | 20.0 | | 16.0 | 11.2 | 11.2 |
| | | | **RATIOS** | | | | | | |
| 2.2 | 3.1 | 2.8 | Current | | 8.2 | | 2.6 | 3.1 | 2.6 |
| 1.2 | 1.4 | 1.5 | | | 1.2 | | 1.6 | 1.6 | 1.6 |
| .7 | .8 | .9 | | | .5 | | .7 | .9 | 1.1 |
| 1.8 | 2.6 | 2.4 | Quick | | 8.2 | | 2.1 | 3.0 | 2.1 |
| .9 | 1.1 | 1.2 | | | 1.2 | | 1.3 | 1.5 | 1.2 |
| .5 | .7 | .7 | | | .5 | | .7 | .5 | .8 |
| 25  14.9 | 27  13.6 | 18  20.5 | Sales/Receivables | | 0  UND | | 12  29.8 | 31  11.6 | 31  11.6 |
| 39  9.3 | 41  8.8 | 40  9.2 | | | 0  UND | | 40  9.1 | 42  8.6 | 40  9.1 |
| 57  6.4 | 58  6.3 | 53  6.9 | | | 64  5.7 | | 74  4.9 | 53  6.9 | 54  6.8 |
| | | | Cost of Sales/Inventory | | | | | | |
| | | | Cost of Sales/Payables | | | | | | |
| 6.5 | 5.0 | 5.5 | Sales/Working Capital | | 3.6 | | 3.7 | 5.2 | 8.1 |
| 31.5 | 15.6 | 14.0 | | | 11.9 | | 8.3 | 21.5 | 12.4 |
| -10.6 | -30.2 | -68.7 | | | -9.3 | | -19.8 | -87.7 | 96.4 |
| 11.2 | 23.9 | 26.9 | EBIT/Interest | | | | 29.4 | 27.6 | 42.0 |
| (87)  3.7 | (74)  6.3 | (77)  7.4 | | | | | (10)  9.4 | (15)  7.4 | (37)  9.3 |
| .8 | 1.9 | 2.8 | | | | | 2.9 | 2.3 | 3.5 |
| 6.2 | 13.3 | 14.2 | Net Profit + Depr., Dep., Amort./Cur. Mat. L/T/D | | | | | | 23.7 |
| (27)  3.2 | (23)  4.9 | (22)  4.7 | | | | | | | (11)  4.9 |
| 2.4 | 2.6 | 3.3 | | | | | | | 3.4 |
| .8 | .5 | .5 | Fixed/Worth | | .1 | | 1.0 | .2 | .6 |
| 1.5 | 1.1 | 1.1 | | | 2.5 | | 1.4 | .7 | 1.0 |
| 2.7 | 2.4 | 3.3 | | | NM | | 3.6 | -34.3 | 2.6 |
| .7 | .5 | .6 | Debt/Worth | | .9 | | .6 | .4 | .8 |
| 1.8 | 1.6 | 1.8 | | | 3.3 | | 2.2 | 2.0 | 1.5 |
| 4.6 | 4.3 | 4.4 | | | NM | | 6.9 | -55.8 | 3.0 |
| 47.4 | 47.2 | 50.7 | % Profit Before Taxes/Tangible Net Worth | | | | 40.9 | 39.0 | 57.3 |
| (83)  17.1 | (86)  25.0 | (80)  27.0 | | | | | (10)  34.8 | (13)  21.2 | (40)  30.8 |
| 3.2 | 4.9 | 16.1 | | | | | 18.1 | 15.8 | 18.5 |
| 14.0 | 21.0 | 22.4 | % Profit Before Taxes/Total Assets | | 19.9 | | 26.2 | 20.0 | 23.5 |
| 5.3 | 8.8 | 9.9 | | | 7.8 | | 9.5 | 11.8 | 12.5 |
| .2 | 1.8 | 4.6 | | | 3.2 | | 3.8 | 4.8 | 6.0 |
| 10.0 | 12.7 | 18.0 | Sales/Net Fixed Assets | | 26.4 | | 9.6 | 72.0 | 19.9 |
| 2.7 | 3.5 | 4.2 | | | 1.8 | | 4.1 | 6.7 | 5.7 |
| 1.0 | 1.1 | 1.0 | | | .2 | | .7 | 1.5 | 1.6 |
| 2.0 | 2.6 | 2.9 | Sales/Total Assets | | 1.9 | | 2.3 | 4.1 | 3.1 |
| 1.3 | 1.3 | 1.4 | | | .5 | | 1.4 | 1.1 | 2.0 |
| .6 | .6 | .7 | | | .2 | | .4 | .9 | .9 |
| 3.1 | 3.1 | 1.5 | % Depr., Dep., Amort./Sales | | | | .7 | .7 | 1.6 |
| (85)  5.8 | (79)  6.6 | (83)  4.0 | | | | | 6.0 | 3.1 | (34)  3.4 |
| 10.4 | 10.2 | 10.2 | | | | | 17.9 | 7.4 | 8.7 |
| | | 1.5 | % Officers', Directors' Owners' Comp/Sales | | | | | | |
| | (16)  2.7 | | | | | | | | |
| | | 4.3 | | | | | | | |
| 4875476M | 4175898M | 4621317M | Net Sales ($) | 1591M | 19918M | 33807M | 87029M | 284147M | 4194825M |
| 3954039M | 3177608M | 3126575M | Total Assets ($) | 2027M | 75396M | 86811M | 152878M | 240415M | 2569048M |

**Current Data Sorted by Assets**  |  **Comparative Historical Data**

| 0-500M | 500M-2MM | 2-10MM | 10-50MM | 50-100MM | 100-250MM | Type of Statement | 4/1/07-3/31/08 ALL | 4/1/08-3/31/09 ALL |
|---|---|---|---|---|---|---|---|---|
| | | 4 | 3 | 5 | 2 | Unqualified | 9 | 10 |
| | 2 | 5 | 2 | | | Reviewed | 12 | 8 |
| | 10 | 4 | | | | Compiled | 8 | 16 |
| 1 | | 1 | | | | Tax Returns | 6 | 5 |
| 2 | 3 | 11 | 8 | 2 | 8 | Other | 21 | 22 |
| | 8 (4/1-9/30/11) | | 65 (10/1/11-3/31/12) | | | | | |
| 3 | 15 | 25 | 13 | 7 | 10 | NUMBER OF STATEMENTS | 56 | 61 |
| % | % | % | % | % | % | ASSETS | % | % |
| | 21.2 | 18.6 | 14.5 | | 5.4 | Cash & Equivalents | 15.8 | 12.0 |
| | 24.4 | 21.6 | 18.7 | | 9.2 | Trade Receivables (net) | 14.4 | 16.5 |
| | 1.2 | .7 | .8 | | 2.0 | Inventory | 3.5 | 1.4 |
| | 3.4 | 4.5 | 1.4 | | 3.0 | All Other Current | 3.7 | 3.2 |
| | 50.2 | 45.3 | 35.4 | | 19.7 | Total Current | 37.4 | 33.1 |
| | 35.0 | 44.5 | 52.8 | | 72.7 | Fixed Assets (net) | 46.7 | 56.1 |
| | 6.8 | 2.7 | 2.0 | | 1.1 | Intangibles (net) | 4.1 | 2.2 |
| | 8.0 | 7.4 | 9.8 | | 6.5 | All Other Non-Current | 11.8 | 8.7 |
| | 100.0 | 100.0 | 100.0 | | 100.0 | Total | 100.0 | 100.0 |
| | | | | | | LIABILITIES | | |
| | 3.1 | 5.6 | 1.1 | | 5.6 | Notes Payable-Short Term | 6.0 | 2.4 |
| | 4.4 | 3.8 | 2.3 | | 6.4 | Cur. Mat.-L.T.D. | 4.7 | 5.2 |
| | 8.6 | 2.8 | 9.9 | | 5.1 | Trade Payables | 6.6 | 5.8 |
| | .0 | .0 | .0 | | .0 | Income Taxes Payable | .4 | .3 |
| | 11.2 | 10.6 | 6.9 | | 4.5 | All Other Current | 6.3 | 5.4 |
| | 27.3 | 22.9 | 20.2 | | 21.8 | Total Current | 24.0 | 19.1 |
| | 29.7 | 30.0 | 32.8 | | 33.8 | Long-Term Debt | 28.4 | 31.5 |
| | .0 | .3 | 2.4 | | .8 | Deferred Taxes | 1.3 | 1.7 |
| | 7.7 | 3.4 | 8.2 | | 1.9 | All Other Non-Current | 4.2 | 4.2 |
| | 35.4 | 43.4 | 36.4 | | 41.7 | Net Worth | 42.1 | 43.6 |
| | 100.0 | 100.0 | 100.0 | | 100.0 | Total Liabilities & Net Worth | 100.0 | 100.0 |
| | | | | | | INCOME DATA | | |
| | 100.0 | 100.0 | 100.0 | | 100.0 | Net Sales | 100.0 | 100.0 |
| | | | | | | Gross Profit | | |
| | 84.9 | 72.3 | 82.3 | | 95.4 | Operating Expenses | 81.5 | 81.7 |
| | 15.1 | 27.7 | 17.7 | | 4.6 | Operating Profit | 18.5 | 18.3 |
| | 4.7 | 5.9 | 1.9 | | 3.1 | All Other Expenses (net) | 1.7 | 3.5 |
| | 10.4 | 21.8 | 15.8 | | 1.5 | Profit Before Taxes | 16.8 | 14.8 |
| | | | | | | RATIOS | | |
| | 6.1 | 5.9 | 3.1 | | 2.4 | | 3.4 | 2.4 |
| | 2.5 | 1.6 | 1.9 | | 1.1 | Current | 1.7 | 1.4 |
| | 1.0 | 1.0 | .9 | | .6 | | .7 | .8 |
| | 6.1 | 5.6 | 2.7 | | 1.7 | | 3.2 | 2.1 |
| | 2.3 | 1.6 | 1.5 | | .7 | Quick | 1.3 | 1.3 |
| | 1.0 | .8 | .9 | | .4 | | .5 | .6 |
| | 0 UND | 0 UND | 28 12.9 | | 28 13.1 | | 5 74.0 | 15 24.8 |
| | 13 28.2 | 34 10.6 | 44 8.3 | | 41 8.9 | Sales/Receivables | 37 10.0 | 36 10.2 |
| | 72 5.1 | 54 6.8 | 65 5.6 | | 85 4.3 | | 52 7.0 | 45 8.2 |
| | | | | | | Cost of Sales/Inventory | | |
| | | | | | | Cost of Sales/Payables | | |
| | 3.6 | 2.2 | 4.3 | | 5.1 | | 5.2 | 7.6 |
| | 15.9 | 13.1 | 10.7 | | NM | Sales/Working Capital | 15.6 | 20.5 |
| | 120.9 | NM | NM | | -7.8 | | -18.8 | -33.4 |
| | 40.4 | 21.5 | 43.1 | | 7.4 | | 16.8 | 18.6 |
| | (13) 4.5 | (16) 2.1 | (11) 3.7 | | 2.4 | EBIT/Interest | (49) 6.0 | (53) 5.9 |
| | .8 | 1.4 | 2.0 | | -.8 | | 2.2 | 2.3 |
| | | | | | | Net Profit + Depr., Dep., Amort./Cur. Mat. L/T/D | 9.4 | 8.4 |
| | | | | | | | (16) 2.9 | (17) 2.7 |
| | | | | | | | 1.6 | 1.3 |
| | .2 | .2 | .7 | | 1.3 | | .6 | .6 |
| | 1.0 | 1.1 | 1.7 | | 1.7 | Fixed/Worth | 1.3 | 1.5 |
| | -4.0 | 3.6 | 2.8 | | 4.3 | | 3.2 | 2.5 |
| | .5 | .4 | .9 | | .8 | | .7 | .7 |
| | 4.7 | 1.0 | 2.4 | | 1.3 | Debt/Worth | 1.9 | 1.5 |
| | -6.0 | 3.9 | 5.1 | | 4.9 | | 4.5 | 2.8 |
| | 87.4 | 80.7 | 127.1 | | 16.1 | % Profit Before Taxes/Tangible Net Worth | 64.3 | 50.5 |
| | (10) 29.1 | (22) 28.0 | (12) 13.8 | | 11.4 | | (52) 34.2 | (57) 28.2 |
| | -9.1 | 3.9 | 4.1 | | .6 | | 17.8 | 10.0 |
| | 20.6 | 33.1 | 50.5 | | 6.2 | % Profit Before Taxes/Total Assets | 28.5 | 20.7 |
| | 8.0 | 6.9 | 6.3 | | 3.7 | | 12.5 | 11.3 |
| | -.3 | 1.3 | 3.1 | | -.3 | | 4.7 | 4.2 |
| | 22.4 | 24.2 | 6.8 | | 1.7 | Sales/Net Fixed Assets | 8.9 | 7.8 |
| | 15.0 | 2.2 | 1.9 | | 1.0 | | 2.8 | 2.0 |
| | 2.4 | 1.2 | 1.4 | | .5 | | 1.1 | .9 |
| | 3.8 | 2.2 | 1.7 | | 1.1 | Sales/Total Assets | 2.3 | 2.5 |
| | 3.0 | 1.2 | 1.1 | | .7 | | 1.1 | 1.2 |
| | .9 | .7 | .8 | | .5 | | .7 | .6 |
| | 1.5 | 2.4 | 2.1 | | | % Depr., Dep., Amort./Sales | 1.7 | 2.7 |
| | (12) 3.6 | (20) 4.5 | (12) 5.7 | | | | (49) 6.0 | (50) 6.4 |
| | 15.3 | 11.8 | 11.5 | | | | 10.7 | 11.4 |
| | | | | | | % Officers', Directors' Owners' Comp/Sales | 3.9 | |
| | | | | | | | (15) 11.3 | |
| | | | | | | | 15.2 | |
| 3328M | 40994M | 234660M | 522244M | 460471M | 1104687M | Net Sales ($) | 1611756M | 2045891M |
| 1233M | 15568M | 125002M | 356184M | 521366M | 1609505M | Total Assets ($) | 1814615M | 2175498M |

M = $ thousand   MM = $ million
See Pages 9 through 22 for Explanation of Ratios and Data

## Comparative Historical Data     Current Data Sorted by Sales

| 4/1/09-3/31/10 ALL | 4/1/10-3/31/11 ALL | 4/1/11-3/31/12 ALL | Type of Statement | 0-1MM | 1-3MM | 3-5MM | 5-10MM | 10-25MM | 25MM & OVER |
|---|---|---|---|---|---|---|---|---|---|
| | | | | | 8 (4/1-9/30/11) | | | 65 (10/1/11-3/31/12) | |
| 12 | 7 | 14 | Unqualified | 2 | | 1 | | 3 | 8 |
| 7 | 11 | 7 | Reviewed | 1 | | 1 | | 3 | 2 |
| 13 | 10 | 6 | Compiled | | 1 | 3 | 1 | 1 | |
| 2 | 4 | 12 | Tax Returns | 3 | 6 | 1 | 2 | | |
| 30 | 31 | 34 | Other | 1 | 5 | 3 | 3 | 5 | 17 |
| 64 | 63 | 73 | **NUMBER OF STATEMENTS** | 7 | 12 | 9 | 6 | 12 | 27 |
| % | % | % | **ASSETS** | % | % | % | % | % | % |
| 12.3 | 12.1 | 15.2 | Cash & Equivalents | | 20.6 | | | 12.8 | 11.4 |
| 16.4 | 16.5 | 20.1 | Trade Receivables (net) | | 17.0 | | | 27.2 | 17.1 |
| 1.9 | 1.5 | 1.0 | Inventory | | .0 | | | .5 | 1.2 |
| 1.7 | 3.5 | 3.1 | All Other Current | | .3 | | | 3.5 | 2.6 |
| 32.3 | 33.6 | 39.4 | Total Current | | 37.9 | | | 44.1 | 32.4 |
| 54.1 | 56.2 | 50.3 | Fixed Assets (net) | | 43.1 | | | 41.7 | 60.1 |
| 2.1 | 2.1 | 2.9 | Intangibles (net) | | 8.4 | | | .6 | 1.3 |
| 11.5 | 8.1 | 7.4 | All Other Non-Current | | 10.6 | | | 13.6 | 6.3 |
| 100.0 | 100.0 | 100.0 | Total | | 100.0 | | | 100.0 | 100.0 |
| | | | **LIABILITIES** | | | | | | |
| 3.2 | 3.5 | 3.8 | Notes Payable-Short Term | | 3.6 | | | 6.8 | 4.3 |
| 5.1 | 4.0 | 3.8 | Cur. Mat.-L.T.D. | | 3.8 | | | 4.4 | 3.7 |
| 5.7 | 5.8 | 6.1 | Trade Payables | | 7.5 | | | 5.5 | 7.3 |
| .1 | .1 | .0 | Income Taxes Payable | | .0 | | | .1 | .0 |
| 8.6 | 5.8 | 9.1 | All Other Current | | 6.6 | | | 8.4 | 8.4 |
| 22.7 | 19.2 | 22.9 | Total Current | | 21.5 | | | 25.2 | 23.7 |
| 37.0 | 31.1 | 29.8 | Long-Term Debt | | 25.3 | | | 30.7 | 27.1 |
| 1.1 | 1.6 | .9 | Deferred Taxes | | .0 | | | .6 | 2.0 |
| 3.0 | 2.2 | 5.2 | All Other Non-Current | | 3.7 | | | 1.7 | 6.3 |
| 36.2 | 45.9 | 41.2 | Net Worth | | 49.6 | | | 41.8 | 40.9 |
| 100.0 | 100.0 | 100.0 | Total Liabilties & Net Worth | | 100.0 | | | 100.0 | 100.0 |
| | | | **INCOME DATA** | | | | | | |
| 100.0 | 100.0 | 100.0 | Net Sales | | 100.0 | | | 100.0 | 100.0 |
| | | | Gross Profit | | | | | | |
| 84.4 | 86.0 | 80.6 | Operating Expenses | | 88.2 | | | 74.8 | 86.1 |
| 15.6 | 14.0 | 19.4 | Operating Profit | | 11.8 | | | 25.2 | 13.9 |
| 3.0 | 2.6 | 4.1 | All Other Expenses (net) | | 1.0 | | | 3.6 | 1.9 |
| 12.6 | 11.4 | 15.3 | Profit Before Taxes | | 10.8 | | | 21.6 | 12.1 |
| | | | **RATIOS** | | | | | | |
| 2.8 | 2.9 | 4.0 | | | 27.1 | | | 3.2 | 2.6 |
| 1.4 | 1.5 | 1.8 | Current | | 2.4 | | | 1.5 | 1.6 |
| .9 | 1.0 | 1.0 | | | .7 | | | 1.2 | .8 |
| 1.9 | 2.3 | 3.5 | | | 27.1 | | | 3.2 | 2.2 |
| 1.3 | 1.2 | 1.5 | Quick | | 2.4 | | | 1.3 | 1.4 |
| .8 | .8 | .8 | | | .7 | | | .8 | .6 |
| 21   17.5 | 22   17.0 | 16   23.2 | | 0   UND | | | | 25   14.8 | 26   13.9 |
| 38   9.5 | 44   8.4 | 35   10.5 | Sales/Receivables | 28   13.2 | | | | 45   8.2 | 35   10.5 |
| 55   6.6 | 58   6.3 | 62   5.9 | | 65   5.6 | | | | 69   5.3 | 59   6.2 |
| | | | Cost of Sales/Inventory | | | | | | |
| | | | Cost of Sales/Payables | | | | | | |
| 6.3 | 4.8 | 4.2 | | | 5.9 | | | 4.6 | 5.4 |
| 22.0 | 13.3 | 13.1 | Sales/Working Capital | | 37.0 | | | 12.9 | 14.0 |
| -51.0 | -142.6 | UND | | | UND | | | 74.4 | -27.5 |
| 9.8 | 9.6 | 15.6 | | | 34.6 | | | 25.4 | 10.8 |
| (54)   3.7 | (57)   2.8 | (59)   3.8 | EBIT/Interest | (11)   11.3 | | | | (10)   2.7 | (24)   4.8 |
| 1.8 | 1.3 | 1.5 | | | 3.1 | | | 1.1 | 1.8 |
| 3.9 | 9.2 | 8.2 | Net Profit + Depr., Dep., | | | | | | |
| (12)   2.1 | (13)   2.3 | (13)   2.2 | Amort./Cur. Mat. L/T/D | | | | | | |
| 1.8 | 1.5 | 1.6 | | | | | | | |
| .7 | .6 | .6 | | | .6 | | | .2 | .8 |
| 1.5 | 1.3 | 1.4 | Fixed/Worth | | .9 | | | 1.1 | 1.6 |
| 3.4 | 3.3 | 3.6 | | | 3.1 | | | 2.7 | 2.8 |
| .8 | .5 | .5 | | | .5 | | | .4 | .6 |
| 1.6 | 1.0 | 1.4 | Debt/Worth | | 1.0 | | | 2.2 | 1.3 |
| 4.8 | 3.2 | 5.4 | | | 5.3 | | | 5.3 | 4.6 |
| 55.1 | 34.9 | 61.8 | % Profit Before Taxes/Tangible | | 58.5 | | | 268.9 | 52.3 |
| (57)   12.8 | (59)   19.1 | (64)   18.5 | Net Worth | (10)   28.5 | | | | (11)   11.4 | (26)   14.4 |
| 3.1 | 2.1 | 3.2 | | | 3.7 | | | 1.6 | 6.6 |
| 15.0 | 15.2 | 27.4 | % Profit Before Taxes/Total | | 32.4 | | | 61.8 | 28.0 |
| 7.5 | 5.1 | 6.8 | Assets | | 12.5 | | | 6.8 | 6.1 |
| 1.7 | .8 | 1.5 | | | 7.2 | | | .8 | 2.6 |
| 6.4 | 5.8 | 10.3 | | | 12.9 | | | 10.7 | 2.6 |
| 1.6 | 1.7 | 2.1 | Sales/Net Fixed Assets | | 4.7 | | | 3.3 | 1.6 |
| .9 | .9 | 1.1 | | | 2.4 | | | 1.5 | 1.0 |
| 1.7 | 1.8 | 2.6 | | | 3.3 | | | 2.5 | 1.4 |
| .9 | 1.0 | 1.2 | Sales/Total Assets | | 2.2 | | | 1.4 | .9 |
| .6 | .7 | .7 | | | .9 | | | .8 | .8 |
| 2.2 | 3.5 | 2.5 | | | 1.8 | | | 2.2 | 2.7 |
| (51)   5.8 | (56)   7.1 | (60)   5.2 | % Depr., Dep., Amort./Sales | (11)   5.0 | | | | (11)   6.4 | (21)   6.2 |
| 10.2 | 10.6 | 10.8 | | | 9.4 | | | 12.2 | 9.1 |
| 1.6 | 1.4 | 4.0 | % Officers', Directors' | | | | | | |
| (16)   8.1 | (11)   3.3 | (11)   6.3 | Owners' Comp/Sales | | | | | | |
| 17.8 | 14.1 | 12.3 | | | | | | | |
| 2437926M | 2128454M | 2366384M | Net Sales ($) | 3873M | 20277M | 38365M | 36099M | 183765M | 2084005M |
| 2924423M | 2678795M | 2628858M | Total Assets ($) | 19222M | 14428M | 32130M | 20521M | 175027M | 2367530M |

M = $ thousand    MM = $ million
See Pages 9 through 22 for Explanation of Ratios and Data

## Current Data Sorted by Assets       Comparative Historical Data

| | 0-500M | 500M-2MM | 2-10MM | 10-50MM | 50-100MM | 100-250MM | Type of Statement | 4/1/07-3/31/08 ALL | 4/1/08-3/31/09 ALL |
|---|---|---|---|---|---|---|---|---|---|
| | | | 4 | 4 | 1 | 3 | Unqualified | 21 | 11 |
| | | | 4 | 3 | | | Reviewed | 3 | 6 |
| | | | 1 | 2 | | | Compiled | 7 | 6 |
| | 3 | 2 | | | | | Tax Returns | 6 | 5 |
| | 2 | 2 | 4 | 7 | 3 | 1 | Other | 20 | 20 |
| | | | 6 (4/1-9/30/11) | 40 (10/1/11-3/31/12) | | | | | |
| NUMBER OF STATEMENTS | 5 | 4 | 13 | 16 | 4 | 4 | | 57 | 48 |
| | % | % | % | % | % | % | ASSETS | % | % |
| | | | 17.2 | 13.4 | | | Cash & Equivalents | 12.4 | 11.1 |
| | | | 18.8 | 12.9 | | | Trade Receivables (net) | 19.0 | 18.9 |
| | | | 1.6 | .7 | | | Inventory | 5.0 | 3.9 |
| | | | 1.5 | 7.3 | | | All Other Current | 4.9 | 6.0 |
| | | | 39.0 | 34.3 | | | Total Current | 41.4 | 39.9 |
| | | | 46.9 | 51.8 | | | Fixed Assets (net) | 49.7 | 50.3 |
| | | | 1.3 | 2.4 | | | Intangibles (net) | 1.4 | 2.6 |
| | | | 12.8 | 11.5 | | | All Other Non-Current | 7.5 | 7.2 |
| | | | 100.0 | 100.0 | | | Total | 100.0 | 100.0 |
| | | | | | | | **LIABILITIES** | | |
| | | | 1.2 | 2.8 | | | Notes Payable-Short Term | 6.9 | 5.0 |
| | | | 2.2 | 2.9 | | | Cur. Mat.-L.T.D. | 5.7 | 4.6 |
| | | | 10.5 | 7.9 | | | Trade Payables | 9.0 | 9.4 |
| | | | .0 | .0 | | | Income Taxes Payable | .1 | .0 |
| | | | 9.8 | 11.4 | | | All Other Current | 13.4 | 11.0 |
| | | | 23.8 | 25.0 | | | Total Current | 35.0 | 30.0 |
| | | | 42.5 | 22.6 | | | Long-Term Debt | 29.7 | 30.0 |
| | | | .1 | .5 | | | Deferred Taxes | .9 | 1.1 |
| | | | 12.0 | 7.9 | | | All Other Non-Current | 3.4 | 8.6 |
| | | | 21.6 | 44.0 | | | Net Worth | 31.0 | 30.3 |
| | | | 100.0 | 100.0 | | | Total Liabilities & Net Worth | 100.0 | 100.0 |
| | | | | | | | **INCOME DATA** | | |
| | | | 100.0 | 100.0 | | | Net Sales | 100.0 | 100.0 |
| | | | | | | | Gross Profit | | |
| | | | 85.7 | 90.9 | | | Operating Expenses | 81.7 | 87.7 |
| | | | 14.3 | 9.1 | | | Operating Profit | 18.3 | 12.3 |
| | | | 8.2 | 3.3 | | | All Other Expenses (net) | 4.2 | 4.1 |
| | | | 6.1 | 5.9 | | | Profit Before Taxes | 14.1 | 8.2 |
| | | | | | | | **RATIOS** | | |
| | | | 2.4 | 2.0 | | | Current | 2.6 | 2.4 |
| | | | 1.4 | 1.5 | | | | 1.4 | 1.4 |
| | | | .5 | 1.1 | | | | .9 | .9 |
| | | | 2.2 | 1.8 | | | Quick | 2.3 | 1.5 |
| | | | 1.2 | 1.2 | | | | 1.0 | 1.0 |
| | | | .3 | .8 | | | | .5 | .5 |
| | | | 0 UND | 20 18.6 | | | Sales/Receivables | 5 70.9 | 12 31.5 |
| | | | 26 13.8 | 38 9.6 | | | | 48 7.6 | 37 9.8 |
| | | | 53 6.9 | 59 6.2 | | | | 65 5.6 | 58 6.3 |
| | | | | | | | Cost of Sales/Inventory | | |
| | | | | | | | Cost of Sales/Payables | | |
| | | | 7.1 | 9.4 | | | Sales/Working Capital | 5.4 | 5.6 |
| | | | 11.2 | 10.9 | | | | 19.1 | 13.0 |
| | | | -20.8 | 53.9 | | | | -50.2 | -123.2 |
| | | | | 6.1 | | | EBIT/Interest | 13.2 | 13.7 |
| | | | (13) | 2.1 | | | | (46) 4.2 | (40) 4.3 |
| | | | | -.8 | | | | 1.4 | 1.6 |
| | | | | | | | Net Profit + Depr., Dep., | 5.3 | 3.1 |
| | | | | | | | Amort./Cur. Mat. L/T/D | (13) 2.6 | (12) 1.9 |
| | | | | | | | | 1.7 | 1.6 |
| | | | .0 | .6 | | | Fixed/Worth | .6 | .6 |
| | | | 1.5 | 1.1 | | | | 1.7 | 1.8 |
| | | | -5.1 | 2.5 | | | | 4.2 | 5.5 |
| | | | 1.0 | .8 | | | Debt/Worth | 1.0 | 1.1 |
| | | | 2.1 | 1.3 | | | | 2.1 | 2.2 |
| | | | -6.7 | 2.3 | | | | 5.4 | 8.9 |
| | | | | 20.5 | | | % Profit Before Taxes/Tangible | 64.1 | 63.0 |
| | | | (15) | 3.2 | | | Net Worth | (48) 29.0 | (41) 27.3 |
| | | | | -4.3 | | | | 16.8 | 4.1 |
| | | | 8.2 | 10.7 | | | % Profit Before Taxes/Total | 21.9 | 20.8 |
| | | | 3.1 | 2.6 | | | Assets | 9.0 | 7.5 |
| | | | -.8 | -1.9 | | | | 1.0 | .5 |
| | | | 158.2 | 4.9 | | | Sales/Net Fixed Assets | 10.4 | 13.1 |
| | | | 2.1 | 1.9 | | | | 2.8 | 3.1 |
| | | | .8 | 1.0 | | | | .8 | 1.1 |
| | | | 3.3 | 2.0 | | | Sales/Total Assets | 2.3 | 2.3 |
| | | | 1.2 | 1.0 | | | | 1.2 | 1.4 |
| | | | .5 | .7 | | | | .6 | .7 |
| | | | .6 | 3.3 | | | % Depr., Dep., Amort./Sales | 2.3 | 2.2 |
| | | | 4.7 | (14) 6.4 | | | | (46) 4.6 | (42) 5.7 |
| | | | 9.0 | 21.3 | | | | 9.3 | 10.8 |
| | | | | | | | % Officers', Directors' | 1.4 | 1.8 |
| | | | | | | | Owners' Comp/Sales | (17) 2.8 | (11) 2.6 |
| | | | | | | | | 8.6 | 8.4 |
| | 10771M | 69470M | 120930M | 456432M | 252170M | 493161M | Net Sales ($) | 2737819M | 1968024M |
| | 1443M | 4155M | 67432M | 375643M | 287386M | 575330M | Total Assets ($) | 2711292M | 1510684M |

M = $ thousand    MM = $ million
See Pages 9 through 22 for Explanation of Ratios and Data

## Comparative Historical Data / Current Data Sorted by Sales

| Type of Statement | 4/1/09-3/31/10 ALL | 4/1/10-3/31/11 ALL | 4/1/11-3/31/12 ALL | 0-1MM | 1-3MM | 3-5MM | 5-10MM | 10-25MM | 25MM & OVER |
|---|---|---|---|---|---|---|---|---|---|
| Unqualified | 8 | 8 | 8 | 1 | | | 1 | 1 | 5 |
| Reviewed | 4 | 7 | 7 | | | | 1 | 4 | 2 |
| Compiled | 6 | 5 | 4 | | 2 | 1 | | 1 | |
| Tax Returns | 4 | 4 | 8 | | 1 | 1 | | 1 | 2 |
| Other | 27 | 23 | 19 | 3 | 1 | 2 | 1 | 4 | 7 |
| | | | | 6 (4/1-9/30/11) | | | 40 (10/1/11-3/31/12) | | |
| **NUMBER OF STATEMENTS** | 49 | 47 | 46 | 4 | 8 | 4 | 3 | 11 | 16 |
| | % | % | % | % | % | % | % | % | % |
| **ASSETS** | | | | | | | | | |
| Cash & Equivalents | 12.2 | 9.1 | 17.9 | | | | | 23.0 | 18.8 |
| Trade Receivables (net) | 17.9 | 21.2 | 14.4 | | | | | 16.1 | 19.0 |
| Inventory | 2.4 | 4.0 | 3.6 | | | | | 1.6 | 1.7 |
| All Other Current | 6.0 | 4.8 | 4.6 | | | | | 1.5 | 8.3 |
| Total Current | 38.5 | 39.1 | 40.4 | | | | | 42.3 | 47.9 |
| Fixed Assets (net) | 48.9 | 50.2 | 46.1 | | | | | 47.1 | 39.4 |
| Intangibles (net) | 3.2 | 4.2 | 1.9 | | | | | 3.5 | .9 |
| All Other Non-Current | 9.4 | 6.6 | 11.5 | | | | | 7.2 | 11.8 |
| Total | 100.0 | 100.0 | 100.0 | | | | | 100.0 | 100.0 |
| **LIABILITIES** | | | | | | | | | |
| Notes Payable-Short Term | 4.6 | 5.5 | 3.4 | | | | | 3.2 | 5.7 |
| Cur. Mat.-L.T.D. | 3.9 | 4.4 | 4.2 | | | | | 2.8 | 2.6 |
| Trade Payables | 10.3 | 11.7 | 7.5 | | | | | 10.8 | 9.4 |
| Income Taxes Payable | .3 | .3 | .0 | | | | | .0 | .0 |
| All Other Current | 9.7 | 8.4 | 12.4 | | | | | 15.2 | 10.6 |
| Total Current | 28.7 | 30.4 | 27.5 | | | | | 32.1 | 28.3 |
| Long-Term Debt | 27.2 | 31.4 | 33.1 | | | | | 23.0 | 22.9 |
| Deferred Taxes | 1.4 | .6 | .2 | | | | | .6 | .2 |
| All Other Non-Current | 5.1 | 14.4 | 7.4 | | | | | 6.5 | 6.6 |
| Net Worth | 37.6 | 23.2 | 31.8 | | | | | 37.9 | 42.0 |
| Total Liabilties & Net Worth | 100.0 | 100.0 | 100.0 | | | | | 100.0 | 100.0 |
| **INCOME DATA** | | | | | | | | | |
| Net Sales | 100.0 | 100.0 | 100.0 | | | | | 100.0 | 100.0 |
| Gross Profit | | | | | | | | | |
| Operating Expenses | 89.5 | 89.9 | 86.9 | | | | | 94.9 | 88.9 |
| Operating Profit | 10.5 | 10.1 | 13.1 | | | | | 5.1 | 11.1 |
| All Other Expenses (net) | 4.7 | 3.4 | 4.6 | | | | | 2.2 | .5 |
| Profit Before Taxes | 5.9 | 6.8 | 8.6 | | | | | 2.9 | 10.6 |
| **RATIOS** | | | | | | | | | |
| Current | 2.8 | 2.5 | 2.3 | | | | | 1.9 | 2.6 |
| | 1.4 | 1.6 | 1.5 | | | | | 1.1 | 1.6 |
| | .8 | .8 | 1.0 | | | | | .8 | 1.5 |
| Quick | 2.3 | 1.9 | 2.1 | | | | | 1.8 | 2.4 |
| | 1.0 | 1.0 | 1.2 | | | | | 1.1 | 1.3 |
| | .4 | .6 | .8 | | | | | .8 | .9 |
| Sales/Receivables | 23  15.7 | 16  23.5 | 9  40.7 | | | | | 9  40.3 | 20  18.1 |
| | 38  9.6 | 35  10.4 | 25  14.8 | | | | | 37  9.9 | 41  9.0 |
| | 63  5.8 | 61  6.0 | 47  7.8 | | | | | 46  8.0 | 59  6.2 |
| Cost of Sales/Inventory | | | | | | | | | |
| Cost of Sales/Payables | | | | | | | | | |
| Sales/Working Capital | 4.7 | 5.9 | 8.2 | | | | | 8.8 | 6.1 |
| | 11.4 | 10.2 | 12.3 | | | | | 11.2 | 10.0 |
| | -26.2 | -26.7 | NM | | | | | -36.0 | 15.3 |
| EBIT/Interest | 25.6 | 9.7 | 11.0 | | | | | | 33.6 |
| | (35)  2.9 | (40)  2.2 | (37)  4.9 | | | | | (14)  6.1 | |
| | 1.5 | .8 | .8 | | | | | | 2.3 |
| Net Profit + Depr., Dep., Amort./Cur. Mat. L/T/D | 5.9 | 6.1 | 4.3 | | | | | | |
| | (10)  3.6 | (11)  1.7 | (10)  2.3 | | | | | | |
| | 1.5 | .9 | .2 | | | | | | |
| Fixed/Worth | .3 | .9 | .6 | | | | | .0 | .4 |
| | 1.5 | 2.1 | 1.1 | | | | | 1.5 | .8 |
| | 5.3 | -18.8 | 3.9 | | | | | 7.5 | 1.4 |
| Debt/Worth | .8 | 1.0 | .9 | | | | | .8 | .8 |
| | 1.9 | 2.8 | 1.7 | | | | | 1.2 | 1.2 |
| | 9.9 | -41.2 | 6.3 | | | | | 8.2 | 2.8 |
| % Profit Before Taxes/Tangible Net Worth | 42.4 | 43.7 | 43.0 | | | | | | 33.4 |
| | (41)  21.5 | (34)  14.9 | (39)  20.5 | | | | | | 22.9 |
| | 1.4 | 1.4 | .2 | | | | | | 10.3 |
| % Profit Before Taxes/Total Assets | 19.8 | 19.0 | 17.5 | | | | | 5.7 | 18.8 |
| | 4.8 | 3.9 | 6.4 | | | | | .2 | 11.7 |
| | .1 | -.1 | .0 | | | | | -3.7 | 3.2 |
| Sales/Net Fixed Assets | 13.3 | 5.8 | 22.6 | | | | | 278.0 | 24.0 |
| | 2.4 | 2.6 | 3.3 | | | | | 2.1 | 4.8 |
| | .9 | 1.2 | .9 | | | | | 1.0 | 1.8 |
| Sales/Total Assets | 1.9 | 2.1 | 3.0 | | | | | 2.8 | 2.4 |
| | .9 | 1.2 | 1.3 | | | | | 1.2 | 1.7 |
| | .5 | .7 | .6 | | | | | .9 | .8 |
| % Depr., Dep., Amort./Sales | 2.5 | 2.3 | 1.1 | | | | | .0 | 1.0 |
| | (39)  5.5 | (38)  5.0 | (39)  4.4 | | | | | (13)  5.3 | 3.6 |
| | 16.0 | 15.3 | 11.1 | | | | | 19.6 | 5.6 |
| % Officers', Directors' Owners' Comp/Sales | .9 | | 1.9 | | | | | | |
| | (12)  2.8 | | (16)  3.9 | | | | | | |
| | 5.9 | | 6.8 | | | | | | |
| Net Sales ($) | 1732681M | 1976337M | 1402934M | 3347M | 15710M | 17159M | 26899M | 177515M | 1162304M |
| Total Assets ($) | 1677439M | 1743365M | 1311389M | 16457M | 41212M | 6732M | 84962M | 254921M | 907105M |

M = $ thousand     MM = $ million

See Pages 9 through 22 for Explanation of Ratios and Data

## Current Data Sorted by Assets     Comparative Historical Data

| 0-500M | 500M-2MM | 2-10MM | 10-50MM | 50-100MM | 100-250MM | Type of Statement | 4/1/07-3/31/08 ALL | 4/1/08-3/31/09 ALL |
|---|---|---|---|---|---|---|---|---|
| 1 | | 4 | 1 | | | Unqualified | 4 | 3 |
| | 1 | 2 | 2 | 2 | | Reviewed | 5 | 1 |
| 6 | 3 | 6 | | 1 | | Compiled | 22 | 11 |
| 30 | 30 | 9 | | 1 | | Tax Returns | 45 | 48 |
| 10 | 12 | | 4 | | 2 | Other | 37 | 21 |
| | 20 (4/1-9/30/11) | | 107 (10/1/11-3/31/12) | | | | | |
| 47 | 46 | 21 | 7 | 4 | 2 | NUMBER OF STATEMENTS | 113 | 84 |

| 0-500M % | 500M-2MM % | 2-10MM % | 10-50MM % | 50-100MM % | 100-250MM % | | % | % |
|---|---|---|---|---|---|---|---|---|
| | | | | | | **ASSETS** | | |
| 21.9 | 15.8 | 7.5 | | | | Cash & Equivalents | 14.9 | 13.2 |
| 15.2 | 14.9 | 6.2 | | | | Trade Receivables (net) | 12.2 | 11.6 |
| 6.6 | 2.4 | 13.3 | | | | Inventory | 10.4 | 10.3 |
| 3.7 | 3.6 | .8 | | | | All Other Current | 3.5 | 3.7 |
| 47.4 | 36.6 | 27.8 | | | | Total Current | 41.0 | 38.7 |
| 32.6 | 43.5 | 59.0 | | | | Fixed Assets (net) | 44.3 | 49.3 |
| 9.6 | 6.8 | 8.6 | | | | Intangibles (net) | 7.7 | 4.2 |
| 10.5 | 13.1 | 4.6 | | | | All Other Non-Current | 7.1 | 7.8 |
| 100.0 | 100.0 | 100.0 | | | | Total | 100.0 | 100.0 |
| | | | | | | **LIABILITIES** | | |
| 12.0 | 10.2 | 7.7 | | | | Notes Payable-Short Term | 9.7 | 18.5 |
| 10.0 | 7.0 | 5.6 | | | | Cur. Mat.-L.T.D. | 8.6 | 11.2 |
| 15.2 | 5.6 | 7.0 | | | | Trade Payables | 9.6 | 9.3 |
| .0 | .0 | .1 | | | | Income Taxes Payable | .5 | .3 |
| 13.4 | 7.0 | 2.7 | | | | All Other Current | 6.8 | 7.9 |
| 50.7 | 29.7 | 23.0 | | | | Total Current | 35.2 | 47.3 |
| 50.9 | 44.9 | 40.4 | | | | Long-Term Debt | 39.4 | 41.7 |
| .1 | .2 | .4 | | | | Deferred Taxes | .2 | .2 |
| 11.8 | 7.0 | 2.0 | | | | All Other Non-Current | 7.5 | 4.8 |
| -13.6 | 18.1 | 34.1 | | | | Net Worth | 17.7 | 6.0 |
| 100.0 | 100.0 | 100.0 | | | | Total Liabilities & Net Worth | 100.0 | 100.0 |
| | | | | | | **INCOME DATA** | | |
| 100.0 | 100.0 | 100.0 | | | | Net Sales | 100.0 | 100.0 |
| | | | | | | Gross Profit | | |
| 93.9 | 94.4 | 96.4 | | | | Operating Expenses | 92.7 | 95.5 |
| 6.1 | 5.6 | 3.6 | | | | Operating Profit | 7.3 | 4.5 |
| 1.3 | 1.3 | 2.8 | | | | All Other Expenses (net) | 2.4 | 1.4 |
| 4.8 | 4.2 | .8 | | | | Profit Before Taxes | 5.0 | 3.1 |

### RATIOS

| 0-500M | 500M-2MM | 2-10MM | 10-50MM | 50-100MM | 100-250MM | | 4/1/07-3/31/08 | 4/1/08-3/31/09 |
|---|---|---|---|---|---|---|---|---|
| 2.5 | 3.3 | 1.3 | | | | | 2.5 | 2.8 |
| 1.0 | 1.9 | .9 | | | | Current | 1.2 | 1.1 |
| .5 | .6 | .6 | | | | | .7 | .5 |
| 2.0 | 3.2 | .9 | | | | | 1.6 | 1.4 |
| .7 | 1.6 | .6 | | | | Quick | .8 | .7 |
| .3 | .3 | .2 | | | | | .3 | .2 |
| 0 UND | 0 UND | 0 UND | | | | | 0 UND | 0 UND |
| 1 247.7 | 13 27.7 | 5 75.5 | | | | Sales/Receivables | 11 32.4 | 8 42.9 |
| 18 19.9 | 28 13.1 | 17 21.6 | | | | | 26 13.9 | 24 15.5 |
| | | | | | | Cost of Sales/Inventory | | |
| | | | | | | Cost of Sales/Payables | | |
| 15.3 | 8.4 | 40.6 | | | | | 10.6 | 13.1 |
| UND | 17.7 | -96.4 | | | | Sales/Working Capital | 77.5 | 110.4 |
| -16.4 | -36.0 | -40.4 | | | | | -20.2 | -12.4 |
| 8.2 | 11.5 | 5.5 | | | | | 5.8 | 7.1 |
| (36) 3.2 | (43) 2.0 | (20) 3.6 | | | | EBIT/Interest | (100) 2.4 | (72) 1.6 |
| .7 | .1 | 1.1 | | | | | 1.1 | -.2 |
| | | | | | | | 14.2 | |
| | | | | | | Net Profit + Depr., Dep., Amort./Cur. Mat. L/T/D | (15) 1.7 | |
| | | | | | | | 1.0 | |
| .2 | .6 | 1.1 | | | | | .6 | .7 |
| UND | 2.0 | 2.6 | | | | Fixed/Worth | 2.5 | 3.2 |
| -1.0 | -7.2 | 8.6 | | | | | -14.2 | -5.8 |
| 1.2 | .8 | 1.1 | | | | | 1.1 | 1.4 |
| UND | 2.8 | 2.8 | | | | Debt/Worth | 4.5 | 5.0 |
| -2.7 | -7.5 | 11.3 | | | | | -11.9 | -10.2 |
| 339.9 | 118.6 | 35.7 | | | | | 82.6 | 63.7 |
| (24) 45.6 | (31) 19.6 | (19) 29.6 | | | | % Profit Before Taxes/Tangible Net Worth | (78) 23.6 | (52) 22.9 |
| 7.4 | 2.5 | 8.5 | | | | | 7.8 | .1 |
| 38.9 | 30.2 | 11.0 | | | | | 18.0 | 24.6 |
| 10.5 | 3.8 | 4.5 | | | | % Profit Before Taxes/Total Assets | 6.4 | 5.1 |
| -.5 | -4.1 | -.3 | | | | | 1.9 | -4.6 |
| 123.2 | 18.7 | 5.6 | | | | | 29.5 | 16.2 |
| 17.9 | 7.0 | 4.3 | | | | Sales/Net Fixed Assets | 6.6 | 6.3 |
| 8.4 | 3.3 | 1.6 | | | | | 3.4 | 3.3 |
| 6.8 | 4.7 | 2.8 | | | | | 3.8 | 4.5 |
| 4.2 | 2.5 | 1.9 | | | | Sales/Total Assets | 2.7 | 3.0 |
| 3.3 | 1.5 | 1.4 | | | | | 1.7 | 1.8 |
| .9 | 3.0 | 3.4 | | | | | 1.9 | 2.1 |
| (26) 3.8 | (30) 5.4 | 5.2 | | | | % Depr., Dep., Amort./Sales | (93) 4.6 | (69) 5.1 |
| 6.8 | 11.4 | 8.9 | | | | | 7.9 | 10.2 |
| 2.3 | 2.0 | | | | | | 2.4 | 2.5 |
| (28) 6.0 | (30) 3.7 | | | | | % Officers', Directors' Owners' Comp/Sales | (59) 4.1 | (43) 4.2 |
| 9.9 | 7.0 | | | | | | 9.0 | 7.6 |
| 49320M | 149642M | 162086M | 207213M | 1232476M | 831591M | Net Sales ($) | 1320074M | 629495M |
| 10641M | 45805M | 74620M | 134986M | 342564M | 249879M | Total Assets ($) | 626677M | 339352M |

© RMA 2012

M = $ thousand    MM = $ million
See Pages 9 through 22 for Explanation of Ratios and Data

## Comparative Historical Data | Current Data Sorted by Sales

| | | | | 0-1MM | 1-3MM | 3-5MM | 5-10MM | 10-25MM | 25MM & OVER |
|---|---|---|---|---|---|---|---|---|---|
| | | | **Type of Statement** | | | | | | |
| 6 | 5 | 4 | Unqualified | 1 | | | 3 | | 3 |
| 6 | 3 | 7 | Reviewed | | 1 | 1 | 2 | 1 | 1 |
| 15 | 13 | 11 | Compiled | 4 | 4 | 1 | 5 | | |
| 60 | 71 | 67 | Tax Returns | 24 | 26 | 10 | 5 | 1 | 1 |
| 31 | 42 | 38 | Other | 7 | 10 | 5 | 6 | 6 | 4 |
| 4/1/09-3/31/10 ALL | 4/1/10-3/31/11 ALL | 4/1/11-3/31/12 ALL | | 20 (4/1-9/30/11) | | | 107 (10/1/11-3/31/12) | | |
| 118 | 134 | 127 | **NUMBER OF STATEMENTS** | 36 | 41 | 17 | 16 | 8 | 9 |
| % | % | % | **ASSETS** | % | % | % | % | % | % |
| 12.6 | 13.2 | 16.9 | Cash & Equivalents | 21.6 | 15.6 | 14.6 | 10.0 | | |
| 10.9 | 11.5 | 13.2 | Trade Receivables (net) | 13.0 | 14.6 | 7.3 | 15.5 | | |
| 7.0 | 6.8 | 6.1 | Inventory | 3.6 | 6.3 | 3.0 | 5.5 | | |
| 2.9 | 4.4 | 3.1 | All Other Current | 2.5 | 3.5 | 4.9 | 2.8 | | |
| 33.4 | 35.8 | 39.4 | Total Current | 40.8 | 39.9 | 29.8 | 33.9 | | |
| 47.5 | 46.7 | 42.1 | Fixed Assets (net) | 34.8 | 43.4 | 53.2 | 54.5 | | |
| 10.7 | 10.3 | 8.4 | Intangibles (net) | 11.8 | 5.9 | 7.7 | 5.7 | | |
| 8.4 | 7.1 | 10.2 | All Other Non-Current | 12.6 | 10.8 | 9.3 | 5.8 | | |
| 100.0 | 100.0 | 100.0 | Total | 100.0 | 100.0 | 100.0 | 100.0 | | |
| | | | **LIABILITIES** | | | | | | |
| 12.4 | 9.3 | 10.2 | Notes Payable-Short Term | 7.1 | 13.4 | 14.0 | 3.6 | | |
| 9.7 | 11.3 | 7.9 | Cur. Mat.-L.T.D. | 6.7 | 8.0 | 11.9 | 9.2 | | |
| 7.6 | 6.7 | 9.3 | Trade Payables | 12.5 | 9.1 | 3.3 | 6.5 | | |
| .3 | .2 | .1 | Income Taxes Payable | .0 | .0 | .0 | .1 | | |
| 10.4 | 7.9 | 8.7 | All Other Current | 14.9 | 4.6 | 11.2 | 3.8 | | |
| 40.5 | 35.4 | 36.2 | Total Current | 41.1 | 35.1 | 40.3 | 23.3 | | |
| 51.3 | 41.7 | 46.9 | Long-Term Debt | 55.6 | 45.5 | 48.9 | 36.9 | | |
| .3 | .2 | .2 | Deferred Taxes | .0 | .4 | .6 | .0 | | |
| 12.5 | 11.8 | 7.9 | All Other Non-Current | 9.3 | 8.6 | 1.7 | 1.7 | | |
| -4.6 | 10.9 | 8.8 | Net Worth | -6.1 | 10.4 | 8.6 | 38.1 | | |
| 100.0 | 100.0 | 100.0 | Total Liabilities & Net Worth | 100.0 | 100.0 | 100.0 | 100.0 | | |
| | | | **INCOME DATA** | | | | | | |
| 100.0 | 100.0 | 100.0 | Net Sales | 100.0 | 100.0 | 100.0 | 100.0 | | |
| | | | Gross Profit | | | | | | |
| 93.1 | 93.8 | 93.5 | Operating Expenses | 92.1 | 96.1 | 94.7 | 94.5 | | |
| 6.9 | 6.2 | 6.5 | Operating Profit | 7.9 | 3.9 | 5.3 | 5.5 | | |
| 3.1 | 1.1 | 1.6 | All Other Expenses (net) | 2.9 | 1.3 | .5 | 1.3 | | |
| 3.8 | 5.1 | 4.9 | Profit Before Taxes | 4.9 | 2.6 | 4.8 | 4.2 | | |
| | | | **RATIOS** | | | | | | |
| 1.9 | 2.0 | 2.6 | | 3.2 | 2.3 | 2.7 | 2.5 | | |
| 1.0 | 1.0 | 1.0 | Current | 1.0 | 1.4 | .7 | 1.1 | | |
| .3 | .5 | .6 | | .5 | .5 | .5 | .8 | | |
| 1.7 | 1.6 | 2.1 | | 3.2 | 2.1 | 2.1 | 1.8 | | |
| .6 | .6 | .8 | Quick | 1.0 | .8 | .6 | .8 | | |
| .4 | .3 | .3 | | .4 | .2 | .5 | .5 | | |
| 0 UND | 0 UND | 0 UND | | 0 UND | 0 UND | 0 UND | 3 127.5 | | |
| 8 48.3 | 8 43.5 | 8 43.7 | Sales/Receivables | 0 UND | 11 34.6 | 4 84.6 | 17 21.6 | | |
| 25 14.9 | 24 15.3 | 23 15.6 | | 23 16.0 | 27 13.5 | 14 25.3 | 33 11.1 | | |
| | | | Cost of Sales/Inventory | | | | | | |
| | | | Cost of Sales/Payables | | | | | | |
| 17.1 | 11.7 | 11.2 | | 11.2 | 8.9 | 18.0 | 10.2 | | |
| -807.8 | UND | 341.0 | Sales/Working Capital | UND | 33.5 | -46.6 | 218.3 | | |
| -9.6 | -24.1 | -30.6 | | -15.4 | -17.5 | -28.6 | -45.7 | | |
| 5.6 | 7.5 | 9.5 | | 9.0 | 6.4 | 40.2 | 12.4 | | |
| (103) 1.7 | (111) 3.3 | (110) 3.2 | EBIT/Interest | (27) 3.3 | (38) 2.2 | (15) 1.8 | (15) 2.5 | | |
| .3 | 1.2 | .6 | | 1.0 | -.5 | .5 | 1.0 | | |
| 16.7 | | | Net Profit + Depr., Dep., | | | | | | |
| (13) 1.7 | | | Amort./Cur. Mat. L/T/D | | | | | | |
| 1.0 | | | | | | | | | |
| 1.0 | .9 | .7 | | .2 | 1.0 | 1.5 | .8 | | |
| 4.8 | 2.8 | 2.6 | Fixed/Worth | 2.3 | 4.2 | 3.3 | 1.5 | | |
| -1.1 | -1.6 | -2.2 | | -1.3 | -1.6 | NM | 9.5 | | |
| 1.7 | 1.1 | 1.1 | | 1.1 | .9 | 1.4 | .6 | | |
| 9.9 | 5.2 | 5.1 | Debt/Worth | 6.9 | 9.0 | 4.0 | 1.4 | | |
| -2.9 | -4.0 | -4.6 | | -2.6 | -4.3 | NM | 12.1 | | |
| 100.0 | 73.2 | 97.5 | % Profit Before Taxes/Tangible | 272.4 | 253.3 | 109.9 | 46.2 | | |
| (71) 18.1 | (81) 25.1 | (82) 29.9 | Net Worth | (22) 22.0 | (23) 35.8 | (13) 51.8 | (14) 18.7 | | |
| -4.3 | 3.0 | 6.2 | | 3.0 | 6.4 | 4.0 | 8.8 | | |
| 19.2 | 27.8 | 28.0 | % Profit Before Taxes/Total | 36.2 | 26.7 | 34.5 | 17.4 | | |
| 4.6 | 7.2 | 7.1 | Assets | 8.1 | 3.4 | 3.9 | 4.9 | | |
| -2.4 | .5 | -.5 | | -.3 | -6.3 | -1.0 | .2 | | |
| 19.3 | 19.6 | 24.3 | | 128.6 | 19.9 | 19.6 | 12.3 | | |
| 6.0 | 6.3 | 9.3 | Sales/Net Fixed Assets | 10.3 | 10.0 | 7.3 | 4.4 | | |
| 3.0 | 3.4 | 3.7 | | 3.5 | 3.8 | 3.4 | 2.9 | | |
| 4.2 | 4.6 | 5.2 | | 5.9 | 5.3 | 5.6 | 3.4 | | |
| 2.4 | 2.9 | 2.9 | Sales/Total Assets | 3.2 | 2.9 | 3.9 | 2.6 | | |
| 1.5 | 1.9 | 1.8 | | 1.0 | 2.1 | 2.0 | 1.6 | | |
| 2.9 | 2.2 | 2.5 | | 2.8 | 2.2 | 3.8 | 4.1 | | |
| (87) 5.4 | (91) 5.4 | (85) 5.1 | % Depr., Dep., Amort./Sales | (23) 5.7 | (26) 4.1 | (12) 5.1 | (12) 6.8 | | |
| 12.5 | 9.5 | 8.6 | | 10.0 | 7.6 | 9.5 | 10.8 | | |
| 2.6 | 2.9 | 2.1 | % Officers', Directors' | 4.1 | 2.0 | 1.5 | | | |
| (57) 5.4 | (74) 4.5 | (68) 4.2 | Owners' Comp/Sales | (15) 8.8 | (31) 4.6 | (10) 3.0 | | | |
| 9.4 | 7.9 | 8.1 | | 12.0 | 8.1 | 5.2 | | | |
| 879655M | 1272914M | 2632328M | Net Sales ($) | 19904M | 74234M | 64677M | 118685M | 134987M | 2219841M |
| 534418M | 695799M | 858495M | Total Assets ($) | 13214M | 29949M | 21462M | 68868M | 48844M | 676158M |

© RMA 2012

M = $ thousand    MM = $ million

See Pages 9 through 22 for Explanation of Ratios and Data

## Current Data Sorted by Assets        Comparative Historical Data

| | | | | | | Type of Statement | | |
|---|---|---|---|---|---|---|---|---|
| | | | 2 | 2 | 3 | Unqualified | 5 | 7 |
| | | 12 | 6 | | | Reviewed | 16 | 6 |
| 2 | 2 | 6 | 1 | | | Compiled | 9 | 7 |
| 17 | 10 | 7 | | | | Tax Returns | 20 | 16 |
| 3 | 16 | 11 | 3 | | 1 | Other | 27 | 27 |
| | 12 (4/1-9/30/11) | | 92 (10/1/11-3/31/12) | | | | 4/1/07-3/31/08 | 4/1/08-3/31/09 |
| 0-500M | 500M-2MM | 2-10MM | 10-50MM | 50-100MM | 100-250MM | | ALL | ALL |
| 22 | 28 | 36 | 12 | 2 | 4 | NUMBER OF STATEMENTS | 77 | 63 |
| % | % | % | % | % | % | ASSETS | % | % |
| 29.3 | 10.8 | 7.8 | 9.8 | | | Cash & Equivalents | 12.3 | 12.6 |
| 18.5 | 33.0 | 29.8 | 22.4 | | | Trade Receivables (net) | 23.5 | 18.0 |
| 3.2 | 6.0 | 5.7 | 6.9 | | | Inventory | 7.4 | 5.6 |
| 6.2 | 2.8 | 4.3 | 1.2 | | | All Other Current | 5.2 | 6.2 |
| 57.2 | 52.6 | 47.6 | 40.3 | | | Total Current | 48.3 | 42.4 |
| 30.5 | 33.0 | 38.0 | 38.1 | | | Fixed Assets (net) | 39.2 | 43.3 |
| 2.9 | 3.0 | 8.4 | 8.3 | | | Intangibles (net) | 4.5 | 7.0 |
| 9.5 | 11.4 | 6.1 | 13.3 | | | All Other Non-Current | 8.1 | 7.3 |
| 100.0 | 100.0 | 100.0 | 100.0 | | | Total | 100.0 | 100.0 |
| | | | | | | LIABILITIES | | |
| 20.1 | 10.0 | 5.8 | .9 | | | Notes Payable-Short Term | 9.9 | 9.9 |
| 3.6 | 2.1 | 4.4 | 3.1 | | | Cur. Mat.-L.T.D. | 7.7 | 7.0 |
| 20.1 | 12.3 | 16.2 | 7.0 | | | Trade Payables | 8.8 | 8.4 |
| .0 | .0 | .3 | .0 | | | Income Taxes Payable | .2 | .2 |
| 12.0 | 8.5 | 8.0 | 13.5 | | | All Other Current | 11.2 | 11.8 |
| 55.9 | 32.9 | 34.7 | 24.6 | | | Total Current | 37.8 | 37.4 |
| 23.3 | 23.4 | 21.7 | 18.0 | | | Long-Term Debt | 26.0 | 27.5 |
| .5 | .0 | .3 | .0 | | | Deferred Taxes | .6 | .3 |
| 14.0 | 6.9 | 2.7 | 3.2 | | | All Other Non-Current | 12.0 | 4.9 |
| 6.3 | 36.9 | 40.6 | 54.2 | | | Net Worth | 23.5 | 29.9 |
| 100.0 | 100.0 | 100.0 | 100.0 | | | Total Liabilties & Net Worth | 100.0 | 100.0 |
| | | | | | | INCOME DATA | | |
| 100.0 | 100.0 | 100.0 | 100.0 | | | Net Sales | 100.0 | 100.0 |
| | | | | | | Gross Profit | | |
| 95.3 | 87.5 | 87.4 | 93.5 | | | Operating Expenses | 89.3 | 91.7 |
| 4.7 | 12.5 | 12.6 | 6.5 | | | Operating Profit | 10.7 | 8.3 |
| .9 | 3.7 | 4.2 | 1.6 | | | All Other Expenses (net) | 2.5 | 3.2 |
| 3.8 | 8.8 | 8.4 | 4.9 | | | Profit Before Taxes | 8.3 | 5.2 |
| | | | | | | RATIOS | | |
| 3.3 | 4.9 | 2.9 | 2.5 | | | | 2.8 | 2.2 |
| 1.6 | 1.8 | 1.6 | 1.6 | | | Current | 1.4 | 1.0 |
| .5 | .8 | .9 | 1.0 | | | | .7 | .5 |
| 2.3 | 3.6 | 2.0 | 2.5 | | | | 1.8 | 2.0 |
| 1.3 | 1.7 | 1.1 | 1.4 | | | Quick | 1.0 | .8 |
| .4 | .6 | .6 | 1.0 | | | | .4 | .4 |
| 0   UND | 2   233.2 | 13   27.2 | 25   14.4 | | | | 0   UND | 7   55.7 |
| 9   40.4 | 34   10.6 | 42   8.7 | 35   10.3 | | | Sales/Receivables | 28   13.2 | 29   12.7 |
| 38   9.6 | 47   7.7 | 55   6.6 | 45   8.2 | | | | 48   7.5 | 41   8.9 |
| | | | | | | Cost of Sales/Inventory | | |
| | | | | | | Cost of Sales/Payables | | |
| 12.5 | 5.8 | 7.3 | 7.4 | | | | 6.9 | 8.7 |
| 19.3 | 17.2 | 15.3 | 13.3 | | | Sales/Working Capital | 26.0 | 243.9 |
| -23.0 | -32.1 | -116.0 | NM | | | | -15.5 | -15.0 |
| 10.8 | 40.7 | 17.9 | | | | | 12.0 | 9.0 |
| (16)   6.9 | (22)   8.3 | (33)   4.5 | | | | EBIT/Interest | (60)   3.4 | (48)   4.1 |
| 1.3 | -1.0 | 2.2 | | | | | 1.0 | .0 |
| | | | | | | Net Profit + Depr., Dep., | 12.0 | |
| | | | | | | Amort./Cur. Mat. L/T/D | (11)   2.6 | |
| | | | | | | | 1.8 | |
| .0 | .1 | .2 | .2 | | | | .2 | .5 |
| .9 | .7 | 1.1 | 1.5 | | | Fixed/Worth | 1.5 | 1.6 |
| -2.1 | 10.2 | 3.1 | 2.3 | | | | 7.7 | 4.0 |
| .4 | .4 | .8 | .2 | | | | .9 | 1.1 |
| 3.2 | 1.4 | 1.9 | 1.8 | | | Debt/Worth | 2.4 | 2.2 |
| -6.0 | 19.7 | 5.5 | 3.0 | | | | 15.1 | 8.7 |
| 139.7 | 74.4 | 74.2 | 25.8 | | | % Profit Before Taxes/Tangible | 65.9 | 43.4 |
| (16)   42.6 | (23)   30.9 | (32)   32.2 | (11)   16.4 | | | Net Worth | (62)   26.1 | (53)   17.0 |
| 5.5 | 9.1 | 11.6 | 2.3 | | | | 2.9 | -5.6 |
| 26.9 | 25.3 | 18.7 | 13.7 | | | % Profit Before Taxes/Total | 19.7 | 16.1 |
| 15.2 | 10.3 | 7.9 | 5.8 | | | Assets | 8.8 | 5.5 |
| -.3 | .2 | 3.5 | .8 | | | | -.2 | -3.1 |
| 193.6 | 92.3 | 37.6 | 34.6 | | | | 57.1 | 41.1 |
| 18.9 | 16.5 | 6.2 | 4.0 | | | Sales/Net Fixed Assets | 11.1 | 5.9 |
| 9.3 | 2.8 | 1.3 | 2.5 | | | | 2.2 | 1.1 |
| 9.5 | 5.9 | 3.8 | 2.4 | | | | 4.5 | 3.6 |
| 5.5 | 3.3 | 2.0 | 2.1 | | | Sales/Total Assets | 2.5 | 2.3 |
| 2.3 | 1.5 | .8 | 1.2 | | | | .9 | .7 |
| .3 | .6 | .5 | .8 | | | | .8 | 1.2 |
| (11)   2.7 | (13)   2.0 | (28)   3.4 | (11)   4.8 | | | % Depr., Dep., Amort./Sales | (61)   3.8 | (49)   3.7 |
| 13.6 | 9.6 | 8.9 | 10.0 | | | | 10.9 | 11.0 |
| 3.3 | | | | | | | 2.0 | 2.5 |
| (14)   9.4 | | | | | | % Officers', Directors' | (26)   3.3 | (17)   4.0 |
| 13.4 | | | | | | Owners' Comp/Sales | 6.6 | 9.5 |
| 17637M | 114056M | 455817M | 802966M | 159102M | 565028M | Net Sales ($) | 856170M | 1791648M |
| 4445M | 30017M | 160004M | 344035M | 191064M | 579678M | Total Assets ($) | 491334M | 1264312M |

M = $ thousand    MM = $ million
See Pages 9 through 22 for Explanation of Ratios and Data

## Comparative Historical Data

## Current Data Sorted by Sales

| Type of Statement | | | | | | | | | |
|---|---|---|---|---|---|---|---|---|---|
| Unqualified | 5 | 10 | 7 | | 2 | 3 | 1 | 6 | 7 |
| Reviewed | 15 | 15 | 18 | 1 | 3 | 2 | 1 | 3 | 6 |
| Compiled | 12 | 11 | 11 | | | | | | 1 |
| Tax Returns | 23 | 15 | 34 | 17 | 9 | 2 | 2 | 3 | 1 |
| Other | 32 | 31 | 34 | 4 | 10 | 4 | 7 | 6 | 3 |
| | 4/1/09-3/31/10 ALL | 4/1/10-3/31/11 ALL | 4/1/11-3/31/12 ALL | 12 (4/1-9/30/11) | | | 92 (10/1/11-3/31/12) | | |
| | | | | 0-1MM | 1-3MM | 3-5MM | 5-10MM | 10-25MM | 25MM & OVER |
| NUMBER OF STATEMENTS | 87 | 82 | 104 | 22 | 24 | 11 | 11 | 18 | 18 |
| | % | % | % | % | % | % | % | % | % |
| **ASSETS** | | | | | | | | | |
| Cash & Equivalents | 18.0 | 13.0 | 14.7 | 23.1 | 13.3 | 8.6 | 15.6 | 5.2 | 18.8 |
| Trade Receivables (net) | 18.3 | 18.5 | 26.1 | 11.0 | 21.4 | 31.2 | 28.6 | 44.8 | 27.6 |
| Inventory | 5.5 | 6.0 | 5.1 | 3.2 | 3.0 | 10.7 | 2.7 | 10.5 | 2.9 |
| All Other Current | 5.1 | 5.5 | 3.8 | 6.1 | 3.4 | 7.0 | 1.2 | 3.2 | 1.6 |
| Total Current | 46.8 | 42.9 | 49.7 | 43.4 | 41.1 | 57.5 | 48.1 | 63.7 | 50.9 |
| Fixed Assets (net) | 36.0 | 38.8 | 35.0 | 44.2 | 43.3 | 25.1 | 35.5 | 23.1 | 30.6 |
| Intangibles (net) | 8.2 | 8.4 | 6.4 | .7 | 5.0 | 8.3 | 5.9 | 9.4 | 11.4 |
| All Other Non-Current | 8.9 | 9.8 | 8.9 | 11.7 | 10.6 | 9.1 | 10.5 | 3.7 | 7.2 |
| Total | 100.0 | 100.0 | 100.0 | 100.0 | 100.0 | 100.0 | 100.0 | 100.0 | 100.0 |
| **LIABILITIES** | | | | | | | | | |
| Notes Payable-Short Term | 6.0 | 12.5 | 9.1 | 18.0 | 10.0 | 3.9 | 14.1 | 3.2 | 2.8 |
| Cur. Mat.-L.T.D. | 7.9 | 3.5 | 3.4 | 4.5 | 2.3 | 7.2 | 1.0 | 2.7 | 3.3 |
| Trade Payables | 8.5 | 9.3 | 14.3 | 13.4 | 11.1 | 11.4 | 8.3 | 20.8 | 18.4 |
| Income Taxes Payable | .0 | .0 | .1 | .0 | .0 | .5 | .0 | .0 | .4 |
| All Other Current | 9.0 | 13.6 | 9.6 | 11.0 | 4.7 | 12.0 | 10.9 | 8.7 | 12.8 |
| Total Current | 31.5 | 38.8 | 36.4 | 46.9 | 28.1 | 35.1 | 34.3 | 35.4 | 37.7 |
| Long-Term Debt | 26.1 | 22.5 | 22.3 | 26.1 | 33.1 | 15.3 | 24.8 | 15.3 | 12.8 |
| Deferred Taxes | .1 | .2 | .3 | .0 | .6 | .0 | .0 | .3 | .4 |
| All Other Non-Current | 9.3 | 6.8 | 6.7 | 6.5 | 13.4 | 11.0 | .8 | .5 | 5.4 |
| Net Worth | 33.0 | 31.7 | 34.4 | 20.6 | 24.8 | 38.6 | 40.1 | 48.5 | 43.7 |
| Total Liabilities & Net Worth | 100.0 | 100.0 | 100.0 | 100.0 | 100.0 | 100.0 | 100.0 | 100.0 | 100.0 |
| **INCOME DATA** | | | | | | | | | |
| Net Sales | 100.0 | 100.0 | 100.0 | 100.0 | 100.0 | 100.0 | 100.0 | 100.0 | 100.0 |
| Gross Profit | | | | | | | | | |
| Operating Expenses | 87.8 | 89.0 | 90.2 | 79.1 | 90.8 | 90.7 | 97.4 | 92.9 | 95.6 |
| Operating Profit | 12.2 | 11.0 | 9.8 | 20.9 | 9.2 | 9.3 | 2.6 | 7.1 | 4.4 |
| All Other Expenses (net) | 3.2 | 2.5 | 2.9 | 7.1 | 3.4 | 2.3 | .4 | .7 | 1.3 |
| Profit Before Taxes | 9.0 | 8.5 | 6.9 | 13.8 | 5.8 | 7.0 | 2.1 | 6.4 | 3.1 |
| **RATIOS** | | | | | | | | | |
| Current | 2.8 | 3.3 | 3.3 | 3.3 | 6.4 | 2.7 | 4.6 | 4.3 | 2.5 |
| | 1.5 | 1.4 | 1.6 | 1.3 | 1.8 | 1.6 | 1.6 | 1.7 | 1.2 |
| | .8 | .7 | .9 | .1 | .8 | 1.1 | .6 | 1.3 | .9 |
| Quick | 2.4 | 2.5 | 2.7 | 2.3 | 5.2 | 1.8 | 3.5 | 3.0 | 2.4 |
| | 1.2 | 1.0 | 1.3 | .7 | 1.8 | 1.1 | 1.6 | 1.6 | 1.2 |
| | .6 | .6 | .7 | .1 | .4 | .5 | .6 | 1.0 | .9 |
| Sales/Receivables | 1  293.0 | 5  74.4 | 8  43.8 | 0  UND | 8  43.8 | 24  15.4 | 6  60.6 | 29  12.5 | 18  20.8 |
| | 22  16.7 | 26  14.1 | 34  10.8 | 3  114.4 | 32  11.4 | 45  8.1 | 30  12.1 | 46  7.9 | 33  11.0 |
| | 41  8.9 | 44  8.4 | 47  7.7 | 63  5.8 | 45  8.2 | 47  7.7 | 35  10.5 | 58  6.3 | 47  7.8 |
| Cost of Sales/Inventory | | | | | | | | | |
| Cost of Sales/Payables | | | | | | | | | |
| Sales/Working Capital | 5.9 | 5.3 | 7.3 | 7.3 | 4.9 | 5.5 | 8.4 | 7.2 | 6.6 |
| | 24.4 | 19.4 | 15.1 | 54.5 | 17.3 | 11.0 | 23.4 | 12.7 | 36.3 |
| | -37.4 | -19.4 | -101.7 | -5.1 | -42.6 | 45.9 | -28.7 | 64.4 | -116.1 |
| EBIT/Interest | 15.3 | 16.5 | 17.4 | 16.0 | 9.0 | | 55.3 | 103.7 | 91.0 |
| | (67) 3.6 | (63) 5.1 | (86) 6.4 | (12) 7.3 | (22) 3.5 | (10) 5.5 | 14.5 | (15) 8.7 | |
| | 1.2 | 2.1 | 1.9 | 4.8 | -1.9 | -1.6 | 4.2 | 2.2 | |
| Net Profit + Depr., Dep., Amort./Cur. Mat. L/T/D | | 2.8 | 4.8 | | | | | | |
| | | (13) 1.7 | (12) 2.5 | | | | | | |
| | | 1.3 | 1.7 | | | | | | |
| Fixed/Worth | .1 | .3 | .1 | .0 | .7 | .1 | .3 | .1 | .5 |
| | 1.0 | 1.2 | .9 | 1.6 | 1.6 | 1.5 | .8 | .2 | 1.0 |
| | 3.3 | 3.6 | 3.4 | 46.8 | NM | 3.4 | 17.6 | 2.1 | 2.0 |
| Debt/Worth | .5 | .6 | .5 | .4 | .9 | .7 | .4 | .4 | .5 |
| | 1.6 | 1.7 | 1.8 | 2.6 | 2.8 | 3.4 | 1.3 | 1.6 | 1.8 |
| | 8.8 | 5.3 | 14.2 | 49.2 | NM | 5.7 | 20.5 | 3.0 | 23.7 |
| % Profit Before Taxes/Tangible Net Worth | 58.3 | 51.6 | 67.0 | 77.1 | 78.8 | | | 69.1 | 32.3 |
| | (69) 27.0 | (68) 23.4 | (86) 30.0 | (18) 31.2 | (18) 40.2 | | (17) 38.9 | (15) 17.7 | |
| | 4.7 | 8.0 | 7.3 | 8.0 | -.1 | | | 23.8 | 5.9 |
| % Profit Before Taxes/Total Assets | 22.5 | 20.4 | 20.8 | 26.9 | 17.0 | 12.2 | 23.3 | 24.4 | 16.3 |
| | 7.4 | 6.4 | 6.9 | 9.7 | 7.9 | 4.6 | 3.9 | 12.3 | 5.8 |
| | .5 | 2.9 | 1.0 | 1.9 | -5.8 | 2.5 | -4.8 | 6.1 | 1.0 |
| Sales/Net Fixed Assets | 82.3 | 48.1 | 58.2 | 136.2 | 46.0 | 59.5 | 73.8 | 139.8 | 41.4 |
| | 8.7 | 5.7 | 11.1 | 10.4 | 4.8 | 23.1 | 18.5 | 29.8 | 5.4 |
| | 2.0 | 2.0 | 2.2 | 1.1 | 1.3 | 2.1 | 6.3 | 9.1 | 2.5 |
| Sales/Total Assets | 3.0 | 3.4 | 5.4 | 5.5 | 5.0 | 4.0 | 6.4 | 5.1 | 4.1 |
| | 1.8 | 1.8 | 2.4 | 1.4 | 1.9 | 1.3 | 5.1 | 3.1 | 2.1 |
| | .9 | .7 | 1.0 | .1 | .8 | .8 | 2.7 | 2.2 | 1.0 |
| % Depr., Dep., Amort./Sales | 1.0 | 1.5 | .7 | 3.0 | .8 | | | .4 | .7 |
| | (61) 4.1 | (61) 3.3 | (67) 3.5 | (12) 14.2 | (13) 4.2 | | (14) 1.1 | (15) 3.0 | |
| | 12.4 | 13.8 | 9.9 | 20.4 | 15.1 | | | 3.8 | 5.7 |
| % Officers', Directors' Owners' Comp/Sales | 1.7 | 1.7 | 2.6 | 2.6 | 4.7 | | | | |
| | (25) 2.8 | (21) 3.7 | (34) 5.6 | (10) 7.1 | (12) 6.8 | | | | |
| | 7.1 | 6.2 | 11.4 | 12.6 | 12.7 | | | | |
| Net Sales ($) | 1293595M | 1443560M | 2114606M | 10564M | 41210M | 43452M | 81592M | 289730M | 1648058M |
| Total Assets ($) | 841924M | 956031M | 1309243M | 16780M | 38676M | 40455M | 23372M | 135928M | 1054032M |

M = $ thousand     MM = $ million

See Pages 9 through 22 for Explanation of Ratios and Data

© RMA 2012

## Current Data Sorted by Assets | Comparative Historical Data

**Type of Statement** (number of statements)

| Type of Statement | 0-500M | 500M-2MM | 2-10MM | 10-50MM | 50-100MM | 100-250MM | 4/1/07-3/31/08 ALL | 4/1/08-3/31/09 ALL |
|---|---|---|---|---|---|---|---|---|
| Unqualified | | 1 | 9 | 25 | 11 | 5 | | |
| Reviewed | 2 | 10 | 45 | 29 | 1 | | 48 | 41 |
| Compiled | 9 | 28 | 35 | 4 | | | 92 | 77 |
| Tax Returns | 26 | 50 | 23 | 3 | | | 69 | 62 |
| Other | 27 | 61 | 83 | 54 | 10 | 17 | 73 | 67 |
| | | | | | | | 154 | 196 |

Period: 72 (4/1-9/30/11) ‖ 496 (10/1/11-3/31/12)

| 0-500M | 500M-2MM | 2-10MM | 10-50MM | 50-100MM | 100-250MM | | 4/1/07-3/31/08 ALL | 4/1/08-3/31/09 ALL |
|---|---|---|---|---|---|---|---|---|
| 64 | 150 | 195 | 115 | 22 | 22 | **NUMBER OF STATEMENTS** | 436 | 443 |
| % | % | % | % | % | % | **ASSETS** | % | % |
| 26.9 | 13.3 | 11.2 | 8.6 | 8.4 | 8.5 | Cash & Equivalents | 12.4 | 13.8 |
| 32.0 | 54.4 | 55.8 | 50.3 | 40.7 | 31.6 | Trade Receivables (net) | 51.0 | 48.2 |
| 1.2 | .4 | .8 | .9 | 2.3 | .1 | Inventory | .7 | .6 |
| 5.5 | 3.9 | 3.7 | 7.2 | 6.0 | 7.6 | All Other Current | 5.5 | 5.9 |
| 65.7 | 72.0 | 71.5 | 67.0 | 57.4 | 47.8 | Total Current | 69.6 | 68.6 |
| 17.7 | 13.3 | 15.3 | 18.7 | 13.8 | 21.9 | Fixed Assets (net) | 19.1 | 18.3 |
| 1.6 | 3.8 | 3.5 | 6.0 | 19.4 | 24.9 | Intangibles (net) | 4.0 | 4.5 |
| 15.0 | 10.9 | 9.7 | 8.2 | 9.5 | 5.4 | All Other Non-Current | 7.3 | 8.6 |
| 100.0 | 100.0 | 100.0 | 100.0 | 100.0 | 100.0 | Total | 100.0 | 100.0 |
| | | | | | | **LIABILITIES** | | |
| 11.4 | 9.6 | 9.8 | 8.8 | 8.0 | 3.7 | Notes Payable-Short Term | 10.8 | 12.6 |
| 4.7 | 1.9 | 2.4 | 3.3 | 2.5 | 6.5 | Cur. Mat.-L.T.D. | 3.9 | 3.8 |
| 20.3 | 26.3 | 30.6 | 25.0 | 21.3 | 15.4 | Trade Payables | 29.2 | 29.3 |
| .0 | .2 | .2 | .3 | .7 | .2 | Income Taxes Payable | .3 | .2 |
| 16.5 | 12.2 | 9.3 | 16.5 | 15.3 | 10.8 | All Other Current | 10.0 | 12.8 |
| 53.0 | 50.3 | 52.3 | 54.0 | 47.8 | 36.7 | Total Current | 54.1 | 58.8 |
| 18.1 | 9.8 | 7.4 | 13.9 | 8.6 | 22.0 | Long-Term Debt | 14.2 | 10.7 |
| .0 | .1 | .2 | .8 | .8 | 2.1 | Deferred Taxes | .3 | .4 |
| 11.8 | 4.7 | 3.7 | 3.5 | 5.8 | 4.2 | All Other Non-Current | 4.5 | 4.0 |
| 17.1 | 35.1 | 36.4 | 27.9 | 37.0 | 35.0 | Net Worth | 26.9 | 26.1 |
| 100.0 | 100.0 | 100.0 | 100.0 | 100.0 | 100.0 | Total Liabilities & Net Worth | 100.0 | 100.0 |
| | | | | | | **INCOME DATA** | | |
| 100.0 | 100.0 | 100.0 | 100.0 | 100.0 | 100.0 | Net Sales | 100.0 | 100.0 |
| | | | | | | Gross Profit | | |
| 92.5 | 93.9 | 94.7 | 95.2 | 96.3 | 93.3 | Operating Expenses | 94.9 | 95.2 |
| 7.5 | 6.1 | 5.3 | 4.8 | 3.7 | 6.7 | Operating Profit | 5.1 | 4.8 |
| 1.0 | 1.5 | .2 | .6 | .3 | 4.3 | All Other Expenses (net) | 1.1 | .8 |
| 6.5 | 4.6 | 5.0 | 4.2 | 3.4 | 2.4 | Profit Before Taxes | 4.0 | 4.0 |
| | | | | | | **RATIOS** | | |
| 3.7 | 2.6 | 2.0 | 1.7 | 1.5 | 1.9 | | 1.8 | 1.7 |
| 1.5 | 1.4 | 1.4 | 1.2 | 1.2 | 1.4 | Current | 1.3 | 1.3 |
| .8 | 1.0 | 1.0 | 1.1 | .9 | 1.1 | | 1.0 | .9 |
| 3.6 | 2.3 | 2.0 | 1.5 | 1.4 | 1.5 | | 1.6 | 1.6 |
| 1.5 | 1.3 | 1.3 | 1.2 | 1.0 | 1.1 | Quick | 1.2 | 1.1 |
| .5 | .9 | .9 | .8 | .8 | .9 | | .9 | .9 |
| 0 UND | 22 16.8 | 29 12.4 | 34 10.6 | 33 10.9 | 31 11.6 | | 28 12.9 | 23 16.2 |
| 12 30.2 | 35 10.3 | 40 9.1 | 44 8.3 | 44 8.3 | 47 7.8 | Sales/Receivables | 41 8.9 | 35 10.5 |
| 31 11.6 | 54 6.8 | 54 6.8 | 56 6.5 | 57 6.4 | 55 6.6 | | 57 6.4 | 52 7.0 |
| | | | | | | Cost of Sales/Inventory | | |
| | | | | | | Cost of Sales/Payables | | |
| 14.8 | 8.9 | 12.1 | 10.9 | 16.5 | 8.8 | | 12.0 | 14.8 |
| 42.6 | 27.8 | 24.5 | 32.9 | 50.1 | 15.9 | Sales/Working Capital | 30.0 | 36.3 |
| -88.5 | -356.5 | -774.3 | 132.5 | -118.1 | 47.0 | | -459.8 | -107.9 |
| 13.9 | 18.3 | 37.3 | 26.9 | 35.5 | 15.6 | | 15.8 | 19.0 |
| (33) 3.2 | (97) 6.9 | (146) 9.3 | (101) 7.1 | (19) 13.6 | (21) 4.0 | EBIT/Interest | (348) 4.9 | (360) 6.0 |
| -2.3 | 2.8 | 3.8 | 3.0 | 3.1 | 1.3 | | 1.5 | 1.6 |
| | | 17.0 | 19.5 | | | | 7.0 | 12.1 |
| | | (35) 5.6 | (39) 2.2 | | | Net Profit + Depr., Dep., Amort./Cur. Mat. L/T/D | (79) 2.6 | (89) 4.0 |
| | | 2.0 | 1.1 | | | | .8 | 1.4 |
| .0 | .0 | .0 | .1 | .2 | .3 | | .1 | .1 |
| .1 | .2 | .2 | .5 | .5 | 1.4 | Fixed/Worth | .4 | .4 |
| 9.2 | 1.4 | .9 | 1.8 | -4.1 | -.6 | | 2.1 | 1.7 |
| .5 | .7 | 1.0 | 1.3 | 1.1 | 1.1 | | 1.1 | 1.1 |
| 2.8 | 2.1 | 2.1 | 2.9 | 3.6 | 5.1 | Debt/Worth | 2.8 | 2.7 |
| -16.2 | 12.3 | 5.2 | 6.2 | -70.2 | -2.3 | | 11.2 | 10.1 |
| 251.5 | 75.6 | 68.6 | 74.5 | 79.9 | 68.8 | | 69.6 | 68.0 |
| (47) 83.1 | (130) 29.7 | (181) 40.4 | (105) 36.0 | (16) 25.4 | (15) 26.1 | % Profit Before Taxes/Tangible Net Worth | (371) 29.1 | (376) 25.7 |
| 8.6 | 10.5 | 17.6 | 18.2 | 2.8 | 21.1 | | 9.2 | 9.3 |
| 54.4 | 20.5 | 23.7 | 16.6 | 11.8 | 10.5 | | 18.5 | 17.3 |
| 22.8 | 8.6 | 11.7 | 9.6 | 6.8 | 5.6 | % Profit Before Taxes/Total Assets | 6.8 | 6.9 |
| -.6 | 2.3 | 4.4 | 4.0 | .9 | .8 | | 1.5 | 1.9 |
| UND | 685.4 | 391.9 | 199.8 | 132.6 | 81.3 | | 299.4 | 287.3 |
| 999.8 | 155.8 | 77.0 | 40.2 | 48.9 | 28.7 | Sales/Net Fixed Assets | 61.9 | 62.3 |
| 23.8 | 35.7 | 19.2 | 10.4 | 9.3 | 3.5 | | 11.1 | 15.0 |
| 13.8 | 7.7 | 6.8 | 5.4 | 5.3 | 3.1 | | 6.5 | 7.5 |
| 7.5 | 5.5 | 4.7 | 3.9 | 2.5 | 1.7 | Sales/Total Assets | 4.3 | 4.9 |
| 3.4 | 3.2 | 3.2 | 2.2 | 1.0 | .7 | | 2.3 | 2.6 |
| .1 | .1 | .1 | .2 | .3 | .3 | | .2 | .2 |
| (25) .5 | (87) .2 | (140) .4 | (93) .6 | (17) .6 | (12) 1.1 | % Depr., Dep., Amort./Sales | (307) .6 | (314) .6 |
| 2.4 | 1.3 | 1.3 | 1.7 | 3.5 | 3.1 | | 2.5 | 2.0 |
| 2.0 | 1.9 | 1.1 | .6 | | | | 1.3 | 1.3 |
| (27) 3.5 | (63) 2.7 | (62) 1.9 | (22) 1.1 | | | % Officers', Directors', Owners' Comp/Sales | (146) 2.5 | (133) 2.7 |
| 10.1 | 4.3 | 3.9 | 2.2 | | | | 5.3 | 6.3 |
| 135793M | 1030302M | 4462565M | 10630800M | 4987596M | 8248129M | Net Sales ($) | 19105539M | 21198825M |
| 15505M | 178712M | 876032M | 2550037M | 1642743M | 3694219M | Total Assets ($) | 6186957M | 6494826M |

M = $ thousand MM = $ million
See Pages 9 through 22 for Explanation of Ratios and Data

## Comparative Historical Data | Current Data Sorted by Sales

| | | | Type of Statement | | | | | | |
|---|---|---|---|---|---|---|---|---|---|
| 43 | 59 | .51 | Unqualified | | 2 | 1 | | 6 | 42 |
| 70 | 78 | 87 | Reviewed | 3 | 2 | 6 | 12 | 17 | 47 |
| 50 | 62 | 76 | Compiled | 5 | 16 | 5 | 19 | 23 | 8 |
| 56 | 90 | 102 | Tax Returns | 16 | 14 | 16 | 24 | 21 | 11 |
| 194 | 206 | 252 | Other | 15 | 24 | 20 | 31 | 56 | 106 |
| 4/1/09- | 4/1/10- | 4/1/11- | | | 72 (4/1-9/30/11) | | 496 (10/1/11-3/31/12) | | |
| 3/31/10 | 3/31/11 | 3/31/12 | | | | | | | |
| ALL | ALL | ALL | | 0-1MM | 1-3MM | 3-5MM | 5-10MM | 10-25MM | 25MM & OVER |
| 413 | 495 | 568 | NUMBER OF STATEMENTS | 39 | 58 | 48 | 86 | 123 | 214 |
| % | % | % | ASSETS | % | % | % | % | % | % |
| 13.5 | 14.2 | 12.8 | Cash & Equivalents | 17.1 | 21.6 | 17.3 | 12.7 | 11.7 | 9.3 |
| 48.1 | 48.5 | 50.1 | Trade Receivables (net) | 24.7 | 40.6 | 41.8 | 56.0 | 54.0 | 54.6 |
| .7 | .8 | .8 | Inventory | .0 | .5 | 2.2 | .2 | .6 | 1.0 |
| 7.1 | 5.4 | 4.9 | All Other Current | 6.9 | 5.1 | 2.2 | 3.2 | 4.8 | 5.9 |
| 69.4 | 68.9 | 68.6 | Total Current | 48.7 | 67.8 | 63.6 | 72.1 | 71.0 | 70.8 |
| 17.4 | 17.2 | 15.9 | Fixed Assets (net) | 35.6 | 14.4 | 18.7 | 15.0 | 14.4 | 13.4 |
| 4.4 | 4.5 | 5.3 | Intangibles (net) | 2.1 | 3.9 | 5.9 | 3.2 | 2.7 | 8.5 |
| 8.8 | 9.5 | 10.2 | All Other Non-Current | 13.6 | 13.8 | 11.8 | 9.7 | 11.9 | 7.4 |
| 100.0 | 100.0 | 100.0 | Total | 100.0 | 100.0 | 100.0 | 100.0 | 100.0 | 100.0 |
| | | | LIABILITIES | | | | | | |
| 11.9 | 11.3 | 9.4 | Notes Payable-Short Term | 3.9 | 9.1 | 14.1 | 7.7 | 12.0 | 8.7 |
| 3.2 | 3.2 | 2.9 | Cur. Mat.-L.T.D. | 4.6 | 4.0 | 2.3 | 2.6 | 2.1 | 3.0 |
| 27.1 | 27.8 | 26.2 | Trade Payables | 17.3 | 19.4 | 15.4 | 29.2 | 30.2 | 28.7 |
| .1 | .3 | .2 | Income Taxes Payable | .0 | .1 | .1 | .3 | .2 | .3 |
| 11.5 | 13.6 | 12.6 | All Other Current | 12.8 | 16.2 | 8.8 | 10.6 | 10.1 | 14.8 |
| 53.8 | 56.1 | 51.4 | Total Current | 38.6 | 48.8 | 40.7 | 50.3 | 54.5 | 55.5 |
| 11.6 | 11.2 | 11.2 | Long-Term Debt | 32.2 | 11.2 | 17.2 | 8.3 | 6.2 | 10.0 |
| .4 | .3 | .4 | Deferred Taxes | .0 | .0 | .8 | .2 | .2 | .6 |
| 4.3 | 5.2 | 4.9 | All Other Non-Current | 10.1 | 8.9 | 4.6 | 5.6 | 4.5 | 3.0 |
| 29.9 | 27.2 | 32.1 | Net Worth | 19.0 | 31.1 | 36.7 | 35.6 | 34.5 | 30.9 |
| 100.0 | 100.0 | 100.0 | Total Liabilties & Net Worth | 100.0 | 100.0 | 100.0 | 100.0 | 100.0 | 100.0 |
| | | | INCOME DATA | | | | | | |
| 100.0 | 100.0 | 100.0 | Net Sales | 100.0 | 100.0 | 100.0 | 100.0 | 100.0 | 100.0 |
| | | | Gross Profit | | | | | | |
| 96.4 | 94.7 | 94.4 | Operating Expenses | 74.3 | 93.4 | 94.8 | 96.4 | 96.3 | 96.2 |
| 3.6 | 5.3 | 5.6 | Operating Profit | 25.7 | 6.6 | 5.2 | 3.6 | 3.7 | 3.8 |
| 1.4 | .9 | .9 | All Other Expenses (net) | 7.7 | .4 | .2 | .0 | .3 | .6 |
| 2.1 | 4.4 | 4.7 | Profit Before Taxes | 18.0 | 6.1 | 5.0 | 3.6 | 3.4 | 3.1 |
| | | | RATIOS | | | | | | |
| 2.1 | 1.9 | 2.1 | | 2.9 | 3.5 | 3.0 | 2.7 | 2.0 | 1.7 |
| 1.3 | 1.3 | 1.3 | Current | 1.5 | 1.5 | 1.4 | 1.4 | 1.4 | 1.3 |
| 1.0 | .9 | 1.0 | | .4 | 1.0 | 1.0 | .9 | 1.0 | 1.0 |
| 1.8 | 1.7 | 1.9 | | 2.7 | 3.3 | 3.0 | 2.6 | 1.9 | 1.5 |
| 1.2 | 1.2 | 1.2 | Quick | 1.4 | 1.5 | 1.4 | 1.4 | 1.3 | 1.2 |
| .8 | .8 | .9 | | .3 | .9 | 1.0 | .9 | .8 | .9 |
| 28   12.8 | 25   14.5 | 25   14.4 | | 0   UND | 0   UND | 17   22.0 | 29   12.5 | 26   14.0 | 32   11.5 |
| 40   9.1 | 40   9.2 | 39   9.4 | Sales/Receivables | 0   UND | 35   10.3 | 39   9.4 | 41   8.8 | 35   10.5 | 41   8.8 |
| 61   6.0 | 56   6.5 | 53   6.9 | | 38   9.5 | 91   4.0 | 64   5.7 | 62   5.9 | 47   7.8 | 53   6.9 |
| | | | Cost of Sales/Inventory | | | | | | |
| | | | Cost of Sales/Payables | | | | | | |
| 9.9 | 11.1 | 11.3 | | 4.7 | 6.8 | 5.9 | 8.8 | 13.9 | 15.6 |
| 26.7 | 29.6 | 27.8 | Sales/Working Capital | 27.0 | 15.8 | 17.2 | 26.6 | 28.8 | 34.4 |
| -261.6 | -133.4 | -999.8 | | -6.7 | NM | 801.5 | -81.8 | -324.3 | 356.3 |
| 17.0 | 25.8 | 24.9 | | 5.6 | 31.0 | 11.3 | 11.9 | 28.5 | 33.3 |
| (321)   4.1 | (378)   8.2 | (417)   7.8 | EBIT/Interest | (14)   3.7 | (33)   7.4 | (36)   3.9 | (61)   5.0 | (92)   9.2 | (181)   10.2 |
| .5 | 2.2 | 2.9 | | -2.1 | 1.2 | 2.0 | 1.4 | 4.2 | 3.2 |
| 19.5 | 10.1 | 16.3 | | | | | 3.4 | 61.2 | 24.4 |
| (65)   3.5 | (87)   3.4 | (94)   2.8 | Net Profit + Depr., Dep., Amort./Cur. Mat. L/T/D | | | (12)   1.4 | (14)   6.5 | (58)   7.5 |
| .9 | 1.1 | 1.2 | | | | | 1.0 | 2.1 | 1.5 |
| .1 | .1 | .0 | | .0 | .0 | .0 | .0 | .0 | .1 |
| .3 | .4 | .3 | Fixed/Worth | .7 | .1 | .4 | .2 | .2 | .4 |
| 1.8 | 2.1 | 1.5 | | UND | 1.1 | 2.1 | 1.2 | .9 | 1.3 |
| 1.0 | 1.1 | 1.0 | | .5 | .3 | .6 | .7 | 1.1 | 1.1 |
| 2.6 | 2.8 | 2.4 | Debt/Worth | 2.0 | 2.1 | 2.2 | 2.7 | 2.3 | 2.6 |
| 8.3 | 10.7 | 7.9 | | UND | 12.2 | 8.8 | 8.0 | 5.3 | 8.1 |
| 52.4 | 76.9 | 76.7 | % Profit Before Taxes/Tangible Net Worth | 100.0 | 99.3 | 89.9 | 49.2 | 65.7 | 83.0 |
| (347)   18.1 | (418)   33.9 | (494)   35.8 | | (30)   20.7 | (48)   42.4 | (41)   24.3 | (76)   26.5 | (114)   41.7 | (185)   40.4 |
| 2.0 | 10.0 | 13.8 | | 8.4 | 10.1 | 8.6 | 10.3 | 17.5 | 21.1 |
| 15.8 | 21.2 | 22.3 | % Profit Before Taxes/Total Assets | 30.0 | 43.1 | 17.9 | 18.0 | 22.0 | 21.4 |
| 4.9 | 8.9 | 9.8 | | 9.7 | 12.1 | 7.7 | 7.8 | 11.6 | 9.7 |
| -1.3 | 1.8 | 3.2 | | .0 | 1.2 | 2.8 | 1.8 | 4.3 | 4.3 |
| 253.9 | 305.7 | 452.7 | Sales/Net Fixed Assets | UND | 999.8 | 850.0 | 354.1 | 706.9 | 244.1 |
| 50.8 | 63.8 | 88.5 | | 14.3 | 95.2 | 60.7 | 99.6 | 128.5 | 80.1 |
| 12.2 | 14.6 | 17.4 | | .6 | 14.9 | 12.4 | 22.6 | 19.5 | 21.2 |
| 6.3 | 7.1 | 7.1 | Sales/Total Assets | 3.7 | 6.8 | 6.9 | 7.3 | 7.6 | 6.8 |
| 3.9 | 4.7 | 4.7 | | 1.3 | 3.5 | 3.7 | 4.9 | 5.7 | 4.9 |
| 2.0 | 2.5 | 2.6 | | .2 | 2.1 | 1.6 | 3.1 | 3.9 | 2.9 |
| .3 | .2 | .1 | % Depr., Dep., Amort./Sales | 1.1 | .1 | .1 | .2 | .1 | .2 |
| (283)   .8 | (352)   .5 | (374)   .5 | | (20)   8.0 | (26)   .7 | (26)   .9 | (56)   .5 | (87)   .3 | (159)   .4 |
| 2.4 | 1.7 | 1.6 | | 24.5 | 2.7 | 2.9 | 2.1 | 1.1 | 1.2 |
| 1.3 | 1.4 | 1.4 | % Officers', Directors' Owners' Comp/Sales | | 2.4 | 2.3 | 1.9 | 1.3 | .6 |
| (125)   3.3 | (155)   2.8 | (179)   2.4 | | (19)   5.0 | (18)   4.0 | (37)   2.8 | (48)   2.1 | (49)   1.3 |
| 7.9 | 5.9 | 5.0 | | | 10.1 | 7.6 | 4.0 | 3.4 | 2.2 |
| 23691187M | 28925914M | 29495185M | Net Sales ($) | 16552M | 118630M | 195186M | 633521M | 1949431M | 26581865M |
| 6538872M | 8604907M | 8957248M | Total Assets ($) | 29147M | 73738M | 112992M | 212670M | 490288M | 8038413M |

M = $ thousand    MM = $ million
See Pages 9 through 22 for Explanation of Ratios and Data

## Current Data Sorted by Assets        Comparative Historical Data

| 0-500M | 500M-2MM | 2-10MM | 10-50MM | 50-100MM | 100-250MM | Type of Statement | 4/1/07-3/31/08 ALL | 4/1/08-3/31/09 ALL |
|---|---|---|---|---|---|---|---|---|
| 1 | | 2 | 3 | 2 | 1 | Unqualified | 11 | 8 |
| | 1 | 8 | 5 | | | Reviewed | 12 | 15 |
| 2 | 3 | 5 | | | | Compiled | 6 | 15 |
| 2 | 10 | 5 | | | | Tax Returns | 3 | 7 |
| 4 | 7 | 12 | 1 | 2 | | Other | 30 | 10 |
| | 7 (4/1-9/30/11) | | 69 (10/1/11-3/31/12) | | | | | |
| 9 | 21 | 32 | 9 | 4 | 1 | **NUMBER OF STATEMENTS** | 62 | 55 |
| % | % | % | % | % | % | **ASSETS** | % | % |
| | 19.8 | 12.5 | | | | Cash & Equivalents | 7.9 | 14.1 |
| | 37.6 | 27.9 | | | | Trade Receivables (net) | 37.6 | 31.3 |
| | 7.5 | 5.7 | | | | Inventory | 10.1 | 9.7 |
| | 2.9 | 1.9 | | | | All Other Current | 4.4 | 5.0 |
| | 67.8 | 48.1 | | | | Total Current | 59.9 | 60.0 |
| | 21.0 | 34.0 | | | | Fixed Assets (net) | 24.9 | 24.1 |
| | 4.0 | 3.5 | | | | Intangibles (net) | 6.3 | 3.9 |
| | 7.2 | 14.3 | | | | All Other Non-Current | 8.8 | 11.9 |
| | 100.0 | 100.0 | | | | Total | 100.0 | 100.0 |
| | | | | | | **LIABILITIES** | | |
| | 5.9 | 3.4 | | | | Notes Payable-Short Term | 9.1 | 9.6 |
| | 1.5 | 5.9 | | | | Cur. Mat.-L.T.D. | 2.9 | 2.1 |
| | 25.9 | 13.1 | | | | Trade Payables | 21.5 | 20.1 |
| | .0 | .1 | | | | Income Taxes Payable | .3 | .6 |
| | 12.1 | 13.1 | | | | All Other Current | 9.3 | 9.5 |
| | 45.4 | 35.5 | | | | Total Current | 43.1 | 41.9 |
| | 10.7 | 32.0 | | | | Long-Term Debt | 18.2 | 14.1 |
| | .0 | .0 | | | | Deferred Taxes | .2 | .3 |
| | 2.8 | 10.0 | | | | All Other Non-Current | 4.5 | 3.5 |
| | 41.1 | 22.5 | | | | Net Worth | 33.9 | 40.1 |
| | 100.0 | 100.0 | | | | Total Liabilities & Net Worth | 100.0 | 100.0 |
| | | | | | | **INCOME DATA** | | |
| | 100.0 | 100.0 | | | | Net Sales | 100.0 | 100.0 |
| | | | | | | Gross Profit | | |
| | 91.1 | 85.2 | | | | Operating Expenses | 92.9 | 92.7 |
| | 8.9 | 14.8 | | | | Operating Profit | 7.1 | 7.3 |
| | 1.4 | 3.8 | | | | All Other Expenses (net) | .8 | .8 |
| | 7.5 | 10.9 | | | | Profit Before Taxes | 6.2 | 6.5 |
| | | | | | | **RATIOS** | | |
| | 2.7 | 2.4 | | | | Current | 2.3 | 2.6 |
| | 2.0 | 1.4 | | | | | 1.4 | 1.6 |
| | .9 | .9 | | | | | 1.0 | 1.1 |
| | 2.4 | 2.1 | | | | Quick | 1.9 | 2.1 |
| | 1.7 | 1.1 | | | | | 1.0 | 1.3 |
| | .9 | .7 | | | | | .7 | .8 |
| | 1 543.6 | 21 17.1 | | | | Sales/Receivables | 34 10.8 | 23 15.9 |
| | 29 12.7 | 36 10.2 | | | | | 50 7.4 | 38 9.6 |
| | 66 5.5 | 58 6.3 | | | | | 63 5.8 | 55 6.6 |
| | | | | | | Cost of Sales/Inventory | | |
| | | | | | | Cost of Sales/Payables | | |
| | 9.6 | 8.2 | | | | Sales/Working Capital | 6.3 | 6.1 |
| | 19.3 | 23.0 | | | | | 15.6 | 12.6 |
| | NM | NM | | | | | NM | 249.1 |
| | 41.6 | 71.3 | | | | EBIT/Interest | 8.0 | 23.4 |
| | (12) 16.9 | (27) 11.4 | | | | | (48) 5.5 | (43) 5.6 |
| | 5.2 | 2.2 | | | | | 2.9 | 1.7 |
| | | | | | | Net Profit + Depr., Dep., Amort./Cur. Mat. L/T/D | 7.7 | 8.4 |
| | | | | | | | (10) 4.2 | (11) 3.9 |
| | | | | | | | 2.6 | 1.8 |
| | .0 | .2 | | | | Fixed/Worth | .2 | .1 |
| | .3 | 1.0 | | | | | .7 | .5 |
| | 2.4 | 4.5 | | | | | 2.6 | 1.4 |
| | .6 | .7 | | | | Debt/Worth | .7 | .6 |
| | 1.3 | 2.0 | | | | | 2.3 | 1.0 |
| | 30.6 | 6.8 | | | | | 9.0 | 2.7 |
| | 132.4 | 110.8 | | | | % Profit Before Taxes/Tangible Net Worth | 77.0 | 66.4 |
| | (18) 82.0 | (27) 35.0 | | | | | (53) 28.1 | (48) 30.5 |
| | 12.6 | 8.7 | | | | | 17.1 | 4.7 |
| | 38.8 | 34.0 | | | | % Profit Before Taxes/Total Assets | 20.9 | 30.8 |
| | 16.2 | 12.3 | | | | | 12.0 | 11.4 |
| | 3.9 | 4.6 | | | | | 4.5 | 2.1 |
| | UND | 29.6 | | | | Sales/Net Fixed Assets | 65.4 | 72.8 |
| | 37.8 | 9.4 | | | | | 14.9 | 16.9 |
| | 14.8 | 2.8 | | | | | 5.6 | 7.9 |
| | 5.1 | 4.0 | | | | Sales/Total Assets | 3.4 | 4.7 |
| | 4.0 | 2.4 | | | | | 2.7 | 2.9 |
| | 2.1 | 1.2 | | | | | 1.9 | 2.0 |
| | .4 | .7 | | | | % Depr., Dep., Amort./Sales | .5 | .6 |
| | (12) 1.2 | (27) 2.3 | | | | | (52) 1.0 | (44) 1.2 |
| | 2.9 | 4.7 | | | | | 2.8 | 2.6 |
| | 3.4 | | | | | % Officers', Directors' Owners' Comp/Sales | 1.5 | 1.9 |
| | (11) 4.7 | | | | | | (24) 2.8 | (26) 4.3 |
| | 7.2 | | | | | | 5.4 | 8.3 |
| 13140M | 129528M | 347283M | 414670M | 851811M | 80806M | Net Sales ($) | 3308363M | 2140662M |
| 1857M | 25208M | 134959M | 176382M | 280814M | 121929M | Total Assets ($) | 1367162M | 1009503M |

M = $ thousand    MM = $ million
See Pages 9 through 22 for Explanation of Ratios and Data

## Comparative Historical Data                    Current Data Sorted by Sales

| | | | Type of Statement | | | | | | |
|---|---|---|---|---|---|---|---|---|---|
| 4 | 8 | 9 | Unqualified | 1 | | 1 | | 1 | 6 |
| 15 | 9 | 14 | Reviewed | | | 3 | 3 | 4 | 4 |
| 11 | 10 | 10 | Compiled | | 4 | 2 | 2 | 1 | |
| 13 | 10 | 17 | Tax Returns | 1 | 2 | 2 | 5 | 2 | 1 |
| 33 | 21 | 26 | Other | 5 | 5 | 5 | 5 | 5 | 6 |
| 4/1/09- | 4/1/10- | 4/1/11- | | 2 | 3 | | | | |
| 3/31/10 | 3/31/11 | 3/31/12 | | | 7 (4/1-9/30/11) | | 69 (10/1/11-3/31/12) | | |
| ALL | ALL | ALL | | 0-1MM | 1-3MM | 3-5MM | 5-10MM | 10-25MM | 25MM & OVER |
| 76 | 58 | 76 | **NUMBER OF STATEMENTS** | 9 | 11 | 11 | 15 | 13 | 17 |
| % | % | % | **ASSETS** | % | % | % | % | % | % |
| 12.4 | 12.2 | 17.1 | Cash & Equivalents | 13.1 | 17.6 | 16.9 | 21.0 | 14.8 | |
| 29.7 | 32.0 | 31.3 | Trade Receivables (net) | 26.6 | 20.6 | 39.6 | 32.5 | 37.6 | |
| 11.4 | 8.4 | 9.5 | Inventory | 7.2 | 2.0 | 13.4 | 2.7 | 15.2 | |
| 2.6 | 4.3 | 2.2 | All Other Current | 3.5 | 3.6 | .4 | 2.2 | 3.1 | |
| 56.1 | 56.8 | 60.1 | Total Current | 50.4 | 43.8 | 70.3 | 58.5 | 70.7 | |
| 28.5 | 24.2 | 24.5 | Fixed Assets (net) | 24.0 | 32.5 | 21.7 | 25.9 | 14.9 | |
| 4.8 | 7.4 | 4.7 | Intangibles (net) | 1.8 | 8.8 | 1.9 | 1.3 | 8.1 | |
| 10.6 | 11.6 | 10.8 | All Other Non-Current | 23.8 | 14.9 | 6.1 | 14.3 | 6.3 | |
| 100.0 | 100.0 | 100.0 | Total | 100.0 | 100.0 | 100.0 | 100.0 | 100.0 | |
| | | | **LIABILITIES** | | | | | | |
| 16.9 | 8.8 | 5.9 | Notes Payable-Short Term | 6.0 | 4.4 | 7.7 | 1.9 | 10.3 | |
| 4.3 | 2.3 | 3.4 | Cur. Mat.-L.T.D. | 2.6 | 3.6 | 4.8 | 2.9 | 3.4 | |
| 14.8 | 12.8 | 17.0 | Trade Payables | 21.1 | 6.2 | 22.8 | 14.6 | 22.7 | |
| .1 | .1 | .0 | Income Taxes Payable | .0 | .0 | .1 | .0 | .0 | |
| 13.7 | 13.5 | 16.6 | All Other Current | 26.5 | 7.4 | 13.1 | 12.6 | 11.4 | |
| 49.8 | 37.3 | 42.9 | Total Current | 56.3 | 21.6 | 48.4 | 32.0 | 47.9 | |
| 14.9 | 17.4 | 19.0 | Long-Term Debt | 54.7 | 22.4 | 5.7 | 13.1 | 7.5 | |
| .3 | 1.0 | .1 | Deferred Taxes | .0 | .0 | .0 | .0 | .3 | |
| 2.9 | 8.0 | 6.8 | All Other Non-Current | 6.0 | 3.9 | 7.3 | 4.8 | 7.2 | |
| 32.2 | 36.2 | 31.2 | Net Worth | -17.1 | 52.2 | 38.6 | 50.2 | 37.1 | |
| 100.0 | 100.0 | 100.0 | Total Liabilities & Net Worth | 100.0 | 100.0 | 100.0 | 100.0 | 100.0 | |
| | | | **INCOME DATA** | | | | | | |
| 100.0 | 100.0 | 100.0 | Net Sales | 100.0 | 100.0 | 100.0 | 100.0 | 100.0 | |
| | | | Gross Profit | | | | | | |
| 90.6 | 91.1 | 89.1 | Operating Expenses | 84.5 | 91.8 | 93.4 | 92.8 | 92.9 | |
| 9.4 | 8.9 | 10.9 | Operating Profit | 15.5 | 8.2 | 6.6 | 7.2 | 7.1 | |
| 2.4 | 2.0 | 2.1 | All Other Expenses (net) | 3.8 | .6 | .7 | .4 | .2 | |
| 7.0 | 6.9 | 8.8 | Profit Before Taxes | 11.6 | 7.6 | 5.9 | 6.8 | 6.9 | |
| | | | **RATIOS** | | | | | | |
| 2.6 | 3.9 | 2.6 | | 3.1 | 3.0 | 2.7 | 3.1 | 2.1 | |
| 1.4 | 1.7 | 1.6 | Current | .9 | 2.1 | 1.7 | 1.6 | 1.5 | |
| .9 | 1.0 | 1.1 | | .6 | 1.2 | 1.3 | 1.2 | 1.1 | |
| 2.4 | 2.6 | 2.4 | | 2.4 | 2.5 | 2.4 | 2.8 | 1.5 | |
| 1.3 | 1.3 | 1.4 | Quick | .8 | 1.9 | 1.4 | 1.6 | 1.1 | |
| .6 | .5 | .7 | | .1 | .8 | .7 | 1.1 | .7 | |

| | | | | | | | | | | | | | Sales/Receivables | | | | | | | | | | | | | |
|---|---|---|---|---|---|---|---|---|---|---|---|---|---|---|---|---|---|---|---|---|---|---|---|---|---|---|

| | | | | | | | | | | | | | | |
|---|---|---|---|---|---|---|---|---|---|---|---|---|---|
| 29 | 12.7 | 24 | 14.9 | 13 | 27.3 | **Sales/Receivables** | 0 | UND | 0 | UND | 29 | 12.7 | 7 | 52.6 | 17 | 21.5 |
| 45 | 8.0 | 45 | 8.1 | 38 | 9.5 | | 25 | 14.7 | 58 | 6.3 | 45 | 8.1 | 36 | 10.0 | 45 | 8.1 |
| 61 | 6.0 | 62 | 5.9 | 58 | 6.3 | | 57 | 6.4 | 69 | 5.3 | 58 | 6.3 | 52 | 7.0 | 53 | 6.9 |

| | | | | | | | |
|---|---|---|---|---|---|---|---|
| | | | Cost of Sales/Inventory | | | | |
| | | | Cost of Sales/Payables | | | | |

| | | | | | | | |
|---|---|---|---|---|---|---|---|
| 6.3 | 6.9 | 6.3 | Sales/Working Capital | 11.0 | 5.2 | 7.4 | 9.7 | 7.7 |
| 15.5 | 14.5 | 15.0 | | -32.1 | 19.3 | 11.8 | 15.2 | 14.9 |
| -51.0 | NM | 185.7 | | -12.5 | 49.2 | 33.0 | 37.3 | 68.6 |

| | | | | | | | | | | | | | | |
|---|---|---|---|---|---|---|---|---|---|---|---|---|---|
| | 21.0 | | 19.4 | | 71.3 | | | | 132.1 | | 61.6 | | 38.2 | 57.7 |
| (59) | 5.0 | (42) | 5.2 | (55) | 11.4 | EBIT/Interest | (10) | 42.5 | (13) | 20.1 | (11) | 11.4 | (13) | 5.4 |
| | 1.3 | | .1 | | 2.2 | | | .1 | | 1.9 | | 2.8 | | 2.8 |

| | | | | | | | | | |
|---|---|---|---|---|---|---|---|---|---|
| | 4.2 | | | | 10.0 | Net Profit + Depr., Dep., | | | |
| (12) | 1.9 | | | (14) | 3.1 | Amort./Cur. Mat. L/T/D | | | |
| | 1.1 | | | | 2.3 | | | | |

| | | | | | | | | | | |
|---|---|---|---|---|---|---|---|---|---|---|
| .3 | .1 | .1 | | .0 | .1 | .2 | .1 | .1 | |
| .8 | .7 | .5 | Fixed/Worth | 3.7 | .9 | .6 | .7 | .4 | |
| 2.4 | 3.4 | 3.2 | | -.4 | 4.7 | 1.1 | 2.2 | 1.4 | |
| .7 | .8 | .5 | | .7 | .2 | .8 | .4 | .8 | |
| 1.9 | 1.9 | 1.6 | Debt/Worth | 28.6 | .8 | 1.4 | 1.1 | 2.1 | |
| 8.1 | 7.4 | 7.1 | | -5.9 | 7.1 | 2.6 | 2.8 | 14.0 | |

| | | | | | | | | | | | | |
|---|---|---|---|---|---|---|---|---|---|---|---|---|
| | 56.6 | | 65.6 | | 109.5 | % Profit Before Taxes/Tangible | | | 86.9 | 99.0 | 143.1 | |
| (64) | 27.5 | (46) | 19.2 | (65) | 43.3 | Net Worth | (13) | 47.1 | 35.0 | (16) | 54.8 | |
| | 7.8 | | 3.4 | | 13.5 | | | | 10.8 | 10.1 | 22.1 | |

| | | | | | | | | | |
|---|---|---|---|---|---|---|---|---|---|
| 19.4 | 24.9 | 34.9 | % Profit Before Taxes/Total | 28.7 | 38.5 | 39.1 | 46.8 | 26.9 | |
| 8.0 | 6.5 | 12.2 | Assets | 15.0 | 8.3 | 23.4 | 31.7 | 16.2 | |
| 2.2 | .4 | 4.0 | | 9.3 | .8 | 1.0 | 4.4 | 4.4 | |

| | | | | | | | | | |
|---|---|---|---|---|---|---|---|---|---|
| 31.7 | 48.4 | 74.4 | Sales/Net Fixed Assets | 999.8 | 35.6 | 37.8 | 61.7 | 93.4 | |
| 12.1 | 19.7 | 22.1 | | 51.9 | 9.7 | 21.8 | 9.9 | 33.0 | |
| 5.1 | 7.9 | 7.1 | | 7.4 | 2.6 | 11.8 | 5.5 | 13.9 | |

| | | | | | | | | | |
|---|---|---|---|---|---|---|---|---|---|
| 3.5 | 3.9 | 4.4 | Sales/Total Assets | 6.2 | 4.0 | 5.0 | 4.8 | 4.3 | |
| 2.5 | 2.8 | 2.9 | | 2.2 | 1.8 | 4.0 | 3.0 | 3.1 | |
| 1.3 | 1.7 | 1.8 | | 2.0 | 1.3 | 2.6 | 2.2 | 2.2 | |

| | | | | | | | | | | | | |
|---|---|---|---|---|---|---|---|---|---|---|---|---|
| | .9 | | .6 | | .6 | % Depr., Dep., Amort./Sales | | | .6 | .5 | .4 | |
| (58) | 2.1 | (42) | 1.6 | (53) | 1.3 | | (11) | 1.2 | (10) | 1.5 | (13) | .8 |
| | 3.8 | | 3.0 | | 3.7 | | | 1.4 | 4.0 | 2.2 | |

| | | | | | | | | |
|---|---|---|---|---|---|---|---|---|
| | 1.8 | | 1.8 | | 1.7 | % Officers', Directors' | | |
| (25) | 4.6 | (18) | 3.9 | (25) | 4.7 | Owners' Comp/Sales | | |
| | 7.2 | | 6.4 | | 6.8 | | | |

| | | | | | | | | | |
|---|---|---|---|---|---|---|---|---|---|
| 1577275M | 1495294M | 1837238M | Net Sales ($) | 4817M | 20534M | 41156M | 111178M | 204202M | 1455351M |
| 674622M | 629658M | 741149M | Total Assets ($) | 13743M | 10463M | 24279M | 43357M | 67825M | 581482M |

© RMA 2012                    **M = $ thousand    MM = $ million**
See Pages 9 through 22 for Explanation of Ratios and Data

## Current Data Sorted by Assets      Comparative Historical Data

| 0-500M | 500M-2MM | 2-10MM | 10-50MM | 50-100MM | 100-250MM | Type of Statement | 4/1/07-3/31/08 ALL | 4/1/08-3/31/09 ALL |
|---|---|---|---|---|---|---|---|---|
| | | 5 | 6 | 4 | 3 | Unqualified | 14 | 28 |
| | 2 | 12 | 4 | | | Reviewed | 15 | 20 |
| 1 | 4 | 15 | 1 | | | Compiled | 11 | 16 |
| 7 | 13 | 4 | | | 1 | Tax Returns | 10 | 28 |
| 7 | 13 | 20 | 8 | 4 | 2 | Other | 45 | 53 |
| | 12 (4/1-9/30/11) | | 124 (10/1/11-3/31/12) | | | | | |
| 15 | 32 | 56 | 19 | 8 | 6 | NUMBER OF STATEMENTS | 95 | 145 |
| % | % | % | % | % | % | ASSETS | % | % |
| 35.3 | 24.2 | 11.9 | 10.7 | | | Cash & Equivalents | 11.3 | 15.2 |
| 24.3 | 28.3 | 35.2 | 36.8 | | | Trade Receivables (net) | 29.5 | 26.8 |
| 3.2 | 4.0 | 6.8 | 7.8 | | | Inventory | 7.2 | 5.2 |
| 3.5 | 3.7 | 3.3 | 7.7 | | | All Other Current | 3.6 | 3.5 |
| 66.2 | 60.2 | 57.3 | 63.1 | | | Total Current | 51.5 | 50.7 |
| 25.0 | 29.4 | 27.0 | 27.9 | | | Fixed Assets (net) | 35.0 | 35.5 |
| 2.6 | 2.7 | 7.3 | 1.2 | | | Intangibles (net) | 6.7 | 6.8 |
| 6.2 | 7.7 | 8.4 | 7.8 | | | All Other Non-Current | 6.8 | 6.9 |
| 100.0 | 100.0 | 100.0 | 100.0 | | | Total | 100.0 | 100.0 |
| | | | | | | LIABILITIES | | |
| 21.0 | 6.4 | 9.4 | 12.0 | | | Notes Payable-Short Term | 8.5 | 12.9 |
| 8.5 | 2.5 | 3.8 | 2.5 | | | Cur. Mat.-L.T.D. | 6.0 | 6.3 |
| 10.1 | 15.7 | 16.8 | 15.7 | | | Trade Payables | 14.0 | 11.9 |
| .0 | .0 | .3 | .2 | | | Income Taxes Payable | .1 | .4 |
| 14.7 | 6.4 | 10.5 | 10.8 | | | All Other Current | 10.7 | 14.6 |
| 54.4 | 31.0 | 40.8 | 41.3 | | | Total Current | 39.3 | 46.1 |
| 21.1 | 23.7 | 16.7 | 13.8 | | | Long-Term Debt | 21.3 | 25.7 |
| .0 | .4 | .2 | .5 | | | Deferred Taxes | .9 | .2 |
| 18.9 | 7.2 | 3.2 | 5.1 | | | All Other Non-Current | 5.2 | 3.8 |
| 5.6 | 37.7 | 39.1 | 39.4 | | | Net Worth | 33.4 | 24.1 |
| 100.0 | 100.0 | 100.0 | 100.0 | | | Total Liabilities & Net Worth | 100.0 | 100.0 |
| | | | | | | INCOME DATA | | |
| 100.0 | 100.0 | 100.0 | 100.0 | | | Net Sales | 100.0 | 100.0 |
| | | | | | | Gross Profit | | |
| 89.6 | 95.7 | 90.3 | 89.4 | | | Operating Expenses | 91.7 | 94.6 |
| 10.4 | 4.3 | 9.7 | 10.6 | | | Operating Profit | 8.3 | 5.4 |
| .9 | .7 | 2.2 | 1.2 | | | All Other Expenses (net) | 1.5 | 1.8 |
| 9.5 | 3.6 | 7.6 | 9.4 | | | Profit Before Taxes | 6.7 | 3.6 |
| | | | | | | RATIOS | | |
| 7.8 | 10.4 | 2.7 | 2.2 | | | | 2.1 | 1.9 |
| 1.7 | 2.6 | 1.3 | 1.4 | | | Current | 1.2 | 1.2 |
| .4 | .8 | .8 | 1.1 | | | | .9 | .8 |
| 7.8 | 6.3 | 1.7 | 1.6 | | | | 1.7 | 1.7 |
| 1.7 | 2.1 | 1.0 | 1.2 | | | Quick | 1.0 | .9 |
| .4 | .5 | .6 | .8 | | | | .7 | .6 |
| 0 UND | 0 UND | 20 18.4 | 31 11.6 | | | | 16 22.7 | 9 42.3 |
| 0 UND | 27 13.3 | 39 9.3 | 51 7.2 | | | Sales/Receivables | 34 10.7 | 29 12.6 |
| 29 12.7 | 54 6.7 | 51 7.1 | 68 5.4 | | | | 48 7.5 | 47 7.8 |
| | | | | | | | | |
| | | | | | | Cost of Sales/Inventory | | |
| | | | | | | | | |
| | | | | | | | | |
| | | | | | | Cost of Sales/Payables | | |
| | | | | | | | | |
| 5.2 | 5.4 | 6.6 | 6.2 | | | | 10.3 | 13.3 |
| 17.9 | 9.6 | 32.4 | 12.8 | | | Sales/Working Capital | 49.0 | 43.2 |
| -14.5 | -176.3 | -40.4 | -57.8 | | | | -56.5 | -41.2 |
| | 10.4 | 24.0 | 71.1 | | | | 14.1 | 13.1 |
| | (22) 2.0 | (43) 7.5 | (17) 17.4 | | | EBIT/Interest | (79) 4.1 | (114) 3.3 |
| | -1.0 | 2.0 | 3.2 | | | | 1.7 | 1.2 |
| | | | | | | | 5.4 | 7.5 |
| | | | | | | Net Profit + Depr., Dep., Amort./Cur. Mat. L/T/D | (22) 2.1 | (21) 2.1 |
| | | | | | | | 1.5 | 1.4 |
| .0 | .1 | .1 | .1 | | | | .3 | .4 |
| 1.3 | .5 | .8 | .7 | | | Fixed/Worth | 1.2 | 1.5 |
| -.5 | 4.4 | 3.5 | 1.4 | | | | 5.9 | UND |
| .2 | .5 | 1.0 | .5 | | | | .8 | 1.1 |
| 7.8 | .9 | 2.3 | 2.0 | | | Debt/Worth | 2.5 | 2.9 |
| -2.8 | 7.3 | 7.6 | 6.2 | | | | 19.6 | UND |
| | 53.8 | 86.1 | 81.7 | | | | 58.6 | 61.8 |
| | (26) 25.0 | (49) 27.3 | (18) 26.1 | | | % Profit Before Taxes/Tangible Net Worth | (76) 32.0 | (109) 20.1 |
| | -2.0 | 5.1 | 21.8 | | | | 10.9 | 5.1 |
| 57.1 | 21.3 | 27.4 | 19.1 | | | | 19.4 | 14.4 |
| 20.7 | 10.7 | 10.8 | 11.6 | | | % Profit Before Taxes/Total Assets | 9.0 | 5.9 |
| -.4 | -1.5 | 1.7 | 6.2 | | | | 2.0 | .7 |
| 413.6 | 144.0 | 74.7 | 45.6 | | | | 72.3 | 77.3 |
| 17.7 | 34.0 | 21.2 | 20.8 | | | Sales/Net Fixed Assets | 8.5 | 12.3 |
| 7.7 | 6.3 | 4.8 | 3.3 | | | | 3.6 | 3.4 |
| 8.0 | 5.6 | 4.7 | 4.1 | | | | 4.7 | 5.8 |
| 3.9 | 3.7 | 2.9 | 2.0 | | | Sales/Total Assets | 2.4 | 2.6 |
| 2.1 | 2.0 | 1.5 | 1.0 | | | | 1.6 | 1.5 |
| | .3 | .7 | .2 | | | | .7 | .9 |
| | (19) .6 | (42) 1.5 | (18) .9 | | | % Depr., Dep., Amort./Sales | (77) 2.9 | (109) 2.7 |
| | 1.9 | 3.9 | 4.5 | | | | 6.1 | 7.4 |
| | 2.1 | 2.1 | | | | | 2.3 | 2.0 |
| | (15) 3.5 | (22) 2.6 | | | | % Officers', Directors' Owners' Comp/Sales | (22) 3.4 | (33) 3.9 |
| | 6.9 | 4.8 | | | | | 5.8 | 7.2 |
| 23277M | 152067M | 938480M | 1080596M | 1582754M | 1844985M | Net Sales ($) | 4052955M | 5323990M |
| 3493M | 36064M | 266316M | 453514M | 528167M | 915839M | Total Assets ($) | 1875802M | 2327227M |

## Comparative Historical Data | Current Data Sorted by Sales

| | Hist 1 | | Hist 2 | | Hist 3 | Type of Statement | | 0-1MM | | 1-3MM | 3-5MM | | 5-10MM | | 10-25MM | | 25MM & OVER |
|---|---|---|---|---|---|---|---|---|---|---|---|---|---|---|---|---|---|
| | 23 | | 15 | | 18 | Unqualified | | | | 1 | | | 1 | | 3 | | 13 |
| | 17 | | 16 | | 18 | Reviewed | | 1 | | 1 | 1 | | 3 | | 7 | | 5 |
| | 15 | | 13 | | 21 | Compiled | | 1 | | 3 | 1 | | 6 | | 8 | | 2 |
| | 27 | | 22 | | 25 | Tax Returns | | 6 | | 6 | 2 | | 7 | | 3 | | 1 |
| | 48 | | 62 | | 54 | Other | | 8 | | 8 | 5 | | 9 | | 9 | | 16 |
| | 4/1/09-3/31/10 ALL | | 4/1/10-3/31/11 ALL | | 4/1/11-3/31/12 ALL | | | 12 (4/1-9/30/11) | | | | 124 (10/1/11-3/31/12) | | | | | |
| | 130 | | 128 | | 136 | NUMBER OF STATEMENTS | | 16 | | 19 | 9 | | 25 | | 30 | | 37 |
| | % | | % | | % | ASSETS | | % | | % | % | | % | | % | | % |
| | 16.0 | | 15.3 | | 17.1 | Cash & Equivalents | | 19.8 | | 19.7 | | | 11.5 | | 17.2 | | 13.5 |
| | 29.3 | | 28.2 | | 32.1 | Trade Receivables (net) | | 18.7 | | 14.0 | | | 33.6 | | 41.4 | | 36.4 |
| | 5.6 | | 3.9 | | 5.3 | Inventory | | 3.0 | | 6.2 | | | 10.5 | | 4.5 | | 4.2 |
| | 5.0 | | 3.7 | | 4.0 | All Other Current | | 3.1 | | 5.7 | | | 1.8 | | 3.9 | | 6.2 |
| | 56.0 | | 51.2 | | 58.5 | Total Current | | 44.6 | | 45.6 | | | 57.4 | | 67.1 | | 60.3 |
| | 30.2 | | 34.2 | | 27.7 | Fixed Assets (net) | | 42.8 | | 39.5 | | | 27.0 | | 21.5 | | 24.2 |
| | 6.4 | | 6.9 | | 5.9 | Intangibles (net) | | 4.7 | | 2.7 | | | 7.1 | | 5.1 | | 8.0 |
| | 7.5 | | 7.8 | | 7.9 | All Other Non-Current | | 7.9 | | 12.2 | | | 8.5 | | 6.4 | | 7.5 |
| | 100.0 | | 100.0 | | 100.0 | Total | | 100.0 | | 100.0 | | | 100.0 | | 100.0 | | 100.0 |
| | | | | | | LIABILITIES | | | | | | | | | | | |
| | 6.5 | | 8.2 | | 9.7 | Notes Payable-Short Term | | 10.0 | | 11.8 | | | 11.7 | | 10.5 | | 7.4 |
| | 4.9 | | 4.8 | | 4.2 | Cur. Mat.-L.T.D. | | 4.9 | | 2.5 | | | 5.8 | | 4.3 | | 3.9 |
| | 14.8 | | 10.4 | | 15.2 | Trade Payables | | 8.9 | | 5.5 | | | 14.1 | | 20.4 | | 18.8 |
| | .2 | | .4 | | .2 | Income Taxes Payable | | .0 | | .0 | | | .0 | | .4 | | .3 |
| | 12.4 | | 11.8 | | 10.1 | All Other Current | | 4.4 | | 5.3 | | | 9.1 | | 11.8 | | 10.9 |
| | 38.7 | | 35.5 | | 39.3 | Total Current | | 28.2 | | 25.2 | | | 40.7 | | 47.5 | | 41.2 |
| | 23.1 | | 23.5 | | 19.3 | Long-Term Debt | | 35.3 | | 24.2 | | | 27.1 | | 10.3 | | 14.3 |
| | .4 | | .4 | | .4 | Deferred Taxes | | .0 | | .7 | | | .2 | | .2 | | .9 |
| | 7.7 | | 8.2 | | 6.9 | All Other Non-Current | | 15.0 | | 8.0 | | | 5.4 | | 6.8 | | 5.5 |
| | 30.1 | | 32.4 | | 34.1 | Net Worth | | 21.5 | | 42.0 | | | 26.6 | | 35.3 | | 38.0 |
| | 100.0 | | 100.0 | | 100.0 | Total Liabilities & Net Worth | | 100.0 | | 100.0 | | | 100.0 | | 100.0 | | 100.0 |
| | | | | | | INCOME DATA | | | | | | | | | | | |
| | 100.0 | | 100.0 | | 100.0 | Net Sales | | 100.0 | | 100.0 | | | 100.0 | | 100.0 | | 100.0 |
| | | | | | | Gross Profit | | | | | | | | | | | |
| | 92.0 | | 90.1 | | 91.1 | Operating Expenses | | 85.6 | | 92.0 | | | 93.9 | | 94.5 | | 88.9 |
| | 8.0 | | 9.9 | | 8.9 | Operating Profit | | 14.4 | | 8.0 | | | 6.1 | | 5.5 | | 11.1 |
| | 1.6 | | 2.1 | | 1.6 | All Other Expenses (net) | | 6.5 | | 2.1 | | | .6 | | .5 | | 1.0 |
| | 6.4 | | 7.8 | | 7.3 | Profit Before Taxes | | 7.8 | | 6.0 | | | 5.4 | | 5.0 | | 10.1 |
| | | | | | | RATIOS | | | | | | | | | | | |
| | 2.7 | | 2.5 | | 3.3 | Current | | 6.0 | | 12.5 | | | 3.3 | | 3.1 | | 2.2 |
| | 1.4 | | 1.4 | | 1.4 | | | 1.3 | | 2.4 | | | 1.5 | | 1.3 | | 1.4 |
| | .9 | | .9 | | .9 | | | .3 | | .2 | | | .8 | | 1.0 | | 1.1 |
| | 2.3 | | 2.1 | | 3.0 | Quick | | 6.0 | | 6.1 | | | 2.9 | | 2.9 | | 1.8 |
| | 1.2 | | 1.2 | | 1.2 | | | .8 | | 1.2 | | | 1.2 | | 1.2 | | 1.2 |
| | .7 | | .6 | | .6 | | | .1 | | .2 | | | .5 | | .7 | | .9 |
| 16 | 23.1 | 5 | 78.8 | 16 | 23.1 | Sales/Receivables | 0 | UND | 0 | UND | | 20 | 18.0 | 26 | 13.8 | 27 | 13.3 |
| 33 | 11.2 | 34 | 10.7 | 36 | 10.0 | | 0 | UND | 10 | 37.7 | | 36 | 10.0 | 40 | 9.1 | 45 | 8.1 |
| 53 | 6.9 | 60 | 6.1 | 55 | 6.6 | | 49 | 7.4 | 54 | 6.7 | | 69 | 5.3 | 51 | 7.1 | 57 | 6.4 |
| | | | | | | Cost of Sales/Inventory | | | | | | | | | | | |
| | | | | | | Cost of Sales/Payables | | | | | | | | | | | |
| | 7.8 | | 7.2 | | 6.5 | Sales/Working Capital | | 3.2 | | 3.5 | | | 8.5 | | 6.5 | | 8.4 |
| | 18.8 | | 26.4 | | 20.3 | | | 35.8 | | 6.5 | | | 14.9 | | 32.1 | | 25.8 |
| | -74.3 | | -161.5 | | -76.3 | | | -7.8 | | -8.4 | | | -41.6 | | -80.9 | | 93.1 |
| | 17.0 | | 22.4 | | 23.7 | EBIT/Interest | | | | 8.6 | | | 26.5 | | 23.1 | | 73.9 |
| (94) | 4.8 | (102) | 5.2 | (102) | 6.6 | | | | (14) 1.2 | | (23) | 6.9 | (24) | 6.8 | (28) | 17.3 |
| | 1.6 | | 1.7 | | 1.8 | | | | | -7.4 | | | 1.7 | | 3.0 | | 2.5 |
| | 7.7 | | 7.7 | | 7.6 | Net Profit + Depr., Dep., Amort./Cur. Mat. L/T/D | | | | | | | | | | | 7.4 |
| (18) | 3.2 | (11) | 3.8 | (24) | 2.5 | | | | | | | | | | (13) | 2.7 |
| | 1.4 | | 1.3 | | 1.5 | | | | | | | | | | | | 1.5 |
| | .2 | | .2 | | .1 | Fixed/Worth | | .2 | | .0 | | | .1 | | .1 | | .2 |
| | .9 | | 1.0 | | .7 | | | 1.8 | | .2 | | | .8 | | .8 | | .6 |
| | 3.6 | | 5.9 | | 4.1 | | | NM | | 10.6 | | | 3.7 | | 6.9 | | 1.1 |
| | .6 | | .7 | | .7 | Debt/Worth | | .7 | | .5 | | | .9 | | .9 | | .8 |
| | 1.9 | | 2.1 | | 2.1 | | | 5.8 | | 1.2 | | | 1.9 | | 2.7 | | 2.3 |
| | 42.1 | | 17.6 | | 11.1 | | | NM | | 10.1 | | | 15.3 | | 66.0 | | 7.2 |
| | 67.7 | | 62.6 | | 86.6 | % Profit Before Taxes/Tangible Net Worth | | 157.8 | | 35.1 | | | 77.9 | | 91.0 | | 130.6 |
| (101) | 23.1 | (102) | 23.7 | (111) | 28.0 | | (12) | 10.8 | (15) | 19.9 | | (20) | 25.2 | (26) | 37.0 | (31) | 31.2 |
| | 7.1 | | 4.3 | | 11.5 | | | -48.5 | | -7.8 | | | 10.2 | | 20.4 | | 17.0 |
| | 17.9 | | 20.7 | | 23.2 | % Profit Before Taxes/Total Assets | | 21.5 | | 17.2 | | | 18.8 | | 26.5 | | 27.7 |
| | 8.7 | | 9.5 | | 11.4 | | | 9.2 | | 4.3 | | | 8.9 | | 9.3 | | 11.6 |
| | 1.7 | | .9 | | 2.1 | | | -5.3 | | -4.6 | | | 2.3 | | 2.2 | | 3.8 |
| | 66.5 | | 64.3 | | 81.4 | Sales/Net Fixed Assets | | 16.7 | | 194.9 | | | 72.9 | | 123.1 | | 44.6 |
| | 13.9 | | 11.2 | | 22.4 | | | 6.8 | | 11.8 | | | 23.4 | | 43.1 | | 25.1 |
| | 3.7 | | 3.3 | | 5.4 | | | .5 | | 1.2 | | | 8.6 | | 7.5 | | 7.1 |
| | 4.8 | | 4.3 | | 4.9 | Sales/Total Assets | | 2.8 | | 3.7 | | | 5.7 | | 5.6 | | 5.0 |
| | 2.5 | | 2.4 | | 2.9 | | | 1.7 | | 2.0 | | | 3.7 | | 3.5 | | 3.9 |
| | 1.4 | | 1.3 | | 1.6 | | | .5 | | .7 | | | 1.6 | | 2.2 | | 1.7 |
| | .8 | | .8 | | .5 | % Depr., Dep., Amort./Sales | | .5 | | .1 | | | .7 | | .5 | | .5 |
| (91) | 2.2 | (86) | 2.9 | (99) | 1.6 | | (10) | 9.6 | (11) | 1.5 | | (18) | 1.7 | (24) | 1.4 | (34) | 1.4 |
| | 5.9 | | 8.5 | | 4.2 | | | 27.9 | | 5.2 | | | 2.5 | | 3.1 | | 5.3 |
| | 1.9 | | 1.6 | | 2.2 | % Officers', Directors' Owners' Comp/Sales | | | | | | | 2.0 | | 2.2 | | |
| (38) | 4.0 | (43) | 3.3 | (49) | 3.0 | | | | | | | (15) | 2.6 | (12) | 2.6 | | |
| | 6.7 | | 7.8 | | 8.0 | | | | | | | | 4.6 | | 4.0 | | |
| | 4528771M | | 3794736M | | 5622159M | Net Sales ($) | | 9242M | | 35967M | 32559M | | 194397M | | 473797M | | 4876197M |
| | 2196723M | | 1871289M | | 2203393M | Total Assets ($) | | 19201M | | 39139M | 10818M | | 84729M | | 158486M | | 1891020M |

© RMA 2012

M = $ thousand     MM = $ million

See Pages 9 through 22 for Explanation of Ratios and Data

## Current Data Sorted by Assets      Comparative Historical Data

| 0-500M | 500M-2MM | 2-10MM | 10-50MM | 50-100MM | 100-250MM | Type of Statement | 4/1/07-3/31/08 ALL | 4/1/08-3/31/09 ALL |
|---|---|---|---|---|---|---|---|---|
| | | 3 | 3 | 2 | 2 | Unqualified | 11 | 9 |
| | 4 | 8 | 2 | | | Reviewed | 12 | 12 |
| 4 | 4 | 5 | | | | Compiled | 16 | 11 |
| 15 | 12 | 4 | | | 1 | Tax Returns | 16 | 16 |
| 6 | 9 | 17 | 13 | 1 | 1 | Other | 35 | 20 |
| 0-500M | 8 (4/1-9/30/11) 500M-2MM | 2-10MM | 108 (10/1/11-3/31/12) 10-50MM | 50-100MM | 100-250MM | | | |
| 25 | 29 | 37 | 18 | 3 | 4 | NUMBER OF STATEMENTS | 90 | 68 |
| % | % | % | % | % | % | **ASSETS** | % | % |
| 13.7 | 14.5 | 6.1 | 10.6 | | | Cash & Equivalents | 9.9 | 8.7 |
| 20.9 | 38.4 | 43.4 | 33.7 | | | Trade Receivables (net) | 32.5 | 33.3 |
| .0 | 2.0 | 2.3 | .3 | | | Inventory | 2.8 | 1.5 |
| 4.7 | 1.8 | 9.9 | 4.2 | | | All Other Current | 4.6 | 6.3 |
| 39.3 | 56.8 | 61.7 | 48.8 | | | Total Current | 49.8 | 49.9 |
| 29.7 | 22.0 | 24.6 | 26.7 | | | Fixed Assets (net) | 28.1 | 29.6 |
| 9.0 | 8.8 | 7.6 | 16.1 | | | Intangibles (net) | 11.5 | 9.9 |
| 22.0 | 12.4 | 6.2 | 8.4 | | | All Other Non-Current | 10.6 | 10.7 |
| 100.0 | 100.0 | 100.0 | 100.0 | | | Total | 100.0 | 100.0 |
| | | | | | | **LIABILITIES** | | |
| 36.8 | 9.9 | 15.1 | 8.5 | | | Notes Payable-Short Term | 16.4 | 16.7 |
| 3.3 | 3.5 | 4.5 | 2.7 | | | Cur. Mat.-L.T.D. | 6.4 | 5.0 |
| 10.5 | 14.4 | 13.1 | 12.8 | | | Trade Payables | 15.8 | 9.8 |
| .4 | .1 | .4 | 1.0 | | | Income Taxes Payable | .2 | .1 |
| 20.4 | 14.5 | 9.4 | 10.4 | | | All Other Current | 14.1 | 13.8 |
| 71.5 | 42.4 | 42.5 | 35.4 | | | Total Current | 53.0 | 45.4 |
| 21.5 | 19.3 | 16.8 | 12.2 | | | Long-Term Debt | 20.3 | 18.2 |
| .0 | .1 | .6 | 1.5 | | | Deferred Taxes | .8 | .4 |
| 5.3 | 5.6 | 2.1 | 9.6 | | | All Other Non-Current | 4.3 | 5.5 |
| 1.8 | 32.7 | 38.0 | 41.3 | | | Net Worth | 21.6 | 30.6 |
| 100.0 | 100.0 | 100.0 | 100.0 | | | Total Liabilities & Net Worth | 100.0 | 100.0 |
| | | | | | | **INCOME DATA** | | |
| 100.0 | 100.0 | 100.0 | 100.0 | | | Net Sales | 100.0 | 100.0 |
| | | | | | | Gross Profit | | |
| 95.4 | 95.9 | 92.4 | 95.1 | | | Operating Expenses | 95.6 | 95.2 |
| 4.6 | 4.1 | 7.6 | 4.9 | | | Operating Profit | 4.4 | 4.8 |
| 1.6 | 1.4 | 4.4 | .8 | | | All Other Expenses (net) | .7 | 1.8 |
| 3.1 | 2.7 | 3.2 | 4.1 | | | Profit Before Taxes | 3.8 | 3.0 |
| | | | | | | **RATIOS** | | |
| 2.2 | 2.6 | 2.1 | 2.2 | | | | 1.7 | 1.8 |
| .8 | 1.6 | 1.4 | 1.3 | | | Current | 1.1 | 1.1 |
| .1 | .9 | 1.0 | 1.1 | | | | .7 | .8 |
| 1.9 | 2.5 | 1.8 | 2.0 | | | | 1.4 | 1.5 |
| .6 | 1.5 | 1.1 | 1.1 | | | Quick | .9 | .9 |
| .1 | .8 | .4 | 1.0 | | | | .5 | .6 |
| 0 UND | 0 UND | 24 15.0 | 31 11.6 | | | | 14 25.9 | 14 25.7 |
| 0 UND | 28 12.9 | 34 10.7 | 38 9.6 | | | Sales/Receivables | 32 11.5 | 31 11.7 |
| 25 14.7 | 42 8.7 | 43 8.4 | 46 8.0 | | | | 42 8.8 | 40 9.2 |
| | | | | | | Cost of Sales/Inventory | | |
| | | | | | | Cost of Sales/Payables | | |
| 18.0 | 12.4 | 11.9 | 8.9 | | | | 16.9 | 16.4 |
| -84.5 | 27.3 | 26.3 | 28.6 | | | Sales/Working Capital | 196.2 | 264.1 |
| -11.8 | -60.1 | -288.5 | 70.4 | | | | -27.6 | -39.0 |
| 15.3 | 45.2 | 33.9 | 35.7 | | | | 12.7 | 10.0 |
| (21) 5.7 | (26) 4.1 | (32) 9.0 | (16) 4.8 | | | EBIT/Interest | (84) 4.9 | (57) 3.7 |
| .5 | .4 | 1.3 | 1.5 | | | | 1.7 | 1.5 |
| | | | | | | Net Profit + Depr., Dep., | 5.1 | 3.9 |
| | | | | | | Amort./Cur. Mat. L/T/D | (17) 2.7 | (12) 2.5 |
| | | | | | | | .7 | 1.7 |
| .2 | .2 | .2 | .4 | | | | .3 | .6 |
| 1.6 | .6 | .8 | 1.2 | | | Fixed/Worth | 1.4 | 1.4 |
| -3.9 | -8.5 | 3.6 | NM | | | | 22.8 | UND |
| 1.8 | .6 | .7 | .9 | | | | 1.2 | .9 |
| 38.2 | 2.6 | 2.6 | 1.6 | | | Debt/Worth | 3.5 | 3.1 |
| -11.2 | -14.8 | 7.7 | NM | | | | NM | UND |
| 999.8 | 80.1 | 104.7 | 62.5 | | | % Profit Before Taxes/Tangible | 91.5 | 96.1 |
| (16) 126.9 | (20) 13.1 | (32) 53.9 | (14) 29.0 | | | Net Worth | (68) 40.2 | (52) 31.0 |
| 11.6 | 1.8 | 3.6 | 12.0 | | | | 15.8 | 3.0 |
| 69.5 | 18.1 | 33.6 | 26.8 | | | % Profit Before Taxes/Total | 21.7 | 19.3 |
| 13.8 | 5.7 | 14.9 | 9.8 | | | Assets | 12.5 | 7.4 |
| 2.3 | -.4 | .7 | 2.0 | | | | 2.5 | .0 |
| 199.0 | 294.8 | 104.3 | 31.5 | | | | 103.8 | 84.9 |
| 45.1 | 65.4 | 34.1 | 17.3 | | | Sales/Net Fixed Assets | 39.4 | 22.8 |
| 8.0 | 18.3 | 10.3 | 4.2 | | | | 6.3 | 5.3 |
| 12.3 | 8.0 | 7.1 | 5.1 | | | | 7.1 | 6.6 |
| 5.7 | 5.6 | 3.8 | 2.3 | | | Sales/Total Assets | 4.7 | 4.7 |
| 3.3 | 3.1 | 2.2 | 1.5 | | | | 2.2 | 2.5 |
| .7 | .3 | .3 | .9 | | | | .6 | .6 |
| (14) 2.3 | (20) .9 | (33) .8 | 2.7 | | | % Depr., Dep., Amort./Sales | (65) 1.3 | (48) 2.1 |
| 7.8 | 4.1 | 1.9 | 8.6 | | | | 3.5 | 4.0 |
| 2.8 | 1.4 | 1.9 | | | | | 1.2 | 2.5 |
| (19) 5.2 | (13) 4.3 | (13) 2.7 | | | | % Officers', Directors' | (35) 3.5 | (23) 4.9 |
| 8.7 | 8.0 | 7.7 | | | | Owners' Comp/Sales | 7.4 | 12.1 |
| 49701M | 192306M | 700377M | 1150219M | 950393M | 2579584M | Net Sales ($) | 2387107M | 2402521M |
| 5886M | 33871M | 149605M | 421984M | 259888M | 695357M | Total Assets ($) | 678283M | 638763M |

© RMA 2012

M = $ thousand    MM = $ million
See Pages 9 through 22 for Explanation of Ratios and Data

## Comparative Historical Data | Current Data Sorted by Sales

| Type of Statement | 4/1/09-3/31/10 ALL | 4/1/10-3/31/11 ALL | 4/1/11-3/31/12 ALL | | 0-1MM | 1-3MM | 3-5MM | 5-10MM | 10-25MM | 25MM & OVER |
|---|---|---|---|---|---|---|---|---|---|---|
| Unqualified | 12 | 16 | 10 | | | | | | 1 | 9 |
| Reviewed | 15 | 17 | 14 | | | 1 | | 2 | 3 | 8 |
| Compiled | 14 | 11 | 13 | | 3 | 1 | 1 | 3 | 3 | 2 |
| Tax Returns | 21 | 16 | 32 | | 8 | 10 | 2 | 6 | 5 | 1 |
| Other | 53 | 49 | 47 | | 3 | 4 | 4 | 7 | 7 | 15 |
| | | | | | 8 (4/1-9/30/11) | | | 108 (10/1/11-3/31/12) | | |
| **NUMBER OF STATEMENTS** | 115 | 109 | 116 | | 14 | 16 | 7 | 25 | 19 | 35 |
| | % | % | % | **ASSETS** | % | % | % | % | % | % |
| Cash & Equivalents | 12.9 | 11.9 | 11.3 | | 9.0 | 14.0 | | 12.7 | 12.3 | 10.7 |
| Trade Receivables (net) | 34.3 | 35.7 | 34.5 | | 13.4 | 15.1 | | 39.2 | 49.2 | 39.9 |
| Inventory | .7 | 1.3 | 1.3 | | .0 | .1 | | .6 | .2 | 2.4 |
| All Other Current | 5.1 | 5.7 | 5.5 | | 5.0 | 3.0 | | 6.7 | 7.8 | 3.7 |
| Total Current | 53.0 | 54.6 | 52.6 | | 27.4 | 32.1 | | 59.2 | 69.4 | 56.7 |
| Fixed Assets (net) | 26.9 | 24.1 | 24.2 | | 45.9 | 26.4 | | 22.8 | 19.5 | 17.3 |
| Intangibles (net) | 11.0 | 13.1 | 11.8 | | 11.8 | 15.4 | | 7.8 | 5.1 | 18.3 |
| All Other Non-Current | 9.1 | 8.2 | 11.3 | | 15.0 | 26.0 | | 10.2 | 5.9 | 7.7 |
| Total | 100.0 | 100.0 | 100.0 | | 100.0 | 100.0 | | 100.0 | 100.0 | 100.0 |
| | | | | **LIABILITIES** | | | | | | |
| Notes Payable-Short Term | 15.9 | 14.5 | 17.1 | | 15.1 | 27.1 | | 20.2 | 9.7 | 14.2 |
| Cur. Mat.-L.T.D. | 5.3 | 5.9 | 3.6 | | 1.3 | 4.6 | | 4.8 | 4.4 | 3.2 |
| Trade Payables | 11.5 | 12.3 | 12.8 | | 6.8 | 7.6 | | 14.5 | 12.2 | 15.3 |
| Income Taxes Payable | .2 | .3 | .4 | | .4 | .4 | | .2 | .8 | .6 |
| All Other Current | 14.5 | 11.0 | 13.2 | | 14.0 | 13.2 | | 8.7 | 15.8 | 11.8 |
| Total Current | 47.5 | 44.0 | 47.1 | | 37.6 | 52.9 | | 48.4 | 43.0 | 45.1 |
| Long-Term Debt | 21.2 | 23.1 | 18.1 | | 32.0 | 31.5 | | 16.0 | 8.5 | 11.4 |
| Deferred Taxes | .6 | .5 | .6 | | .0 | .0 | | 1.1 | .0 | 1.2 |
| All Other Non-Current | 5.6 | 5.7 | 6.1 | | 2.1 | 8.0 | | 4.0 | 2.0 | 10.4 |
| Net Worth | 25.1 | 26.6 | 28.1 | | 28.4 | 7.6 | | 30.7 | 46.5 | 31.9 |
| Total Liabilities & Net Worth | 100.0 | 100.0 | 100.0 | | 100.0 | 100.0 | | 100.0 | 100.0 | 100.0 |
| | | | | **INCOME DATA** | | | | | | |
| Net Sales | 100.0 | 100.0 | 100.0 | | 100.0 | 100.0 | | 100.0 | 100.0 | 100.0 |
| Gross Profit | | | | | | | | | | |
| Operating Expenses | 94.7 | 95.6 | 94.5 | | 83.6 | 96.1 | | 96.7 | 95.6 | 94.9 |
| Operating Profit | 5.3 | 4.4 | 5.5 | | 16.4 | 3.9 | | 3.3 | 4.4 | 5.1 |
| All Other Expenses (net) | 2.8 | 2.2 | 2.7 | | 13.2 | 1.2 | | .6 | -.1 | 2.1 |
| Profit Before Taxes | 2.6 | 2.2 | 2.8 | | 3.2 | 2.7 | | 2.7 | 4.5 | 3.0 |
| | | | | **RATIOS** | | | | | | |
| Current | 2.0 | 2.1 | 2.2 | | 2.6 | 2.0 | | 2.6 | 6.5 | 1.7 |
| | 1.3 | 1.3 | 1.4 | | .7 | .8 | | 1.7 | 1.7 | 1.2 |
| | .8 | .8 | .9 | | .1 | .2 | | 1.3 | .8 | 1.0 |
| Quick | 1.7 | 1.9 | 1.9 | | 2.2 | 1.9 | | 2.5 | 5.9 | 1.4 |
| | 1.0 | 1.2 | 1.1 | | .4 | .7 | | 1.5 | 1.3 | 1.1 |
| | .7 | .6 | .6 | | .1 | .1 | | 1.0 | .7 | 1.0 |
| Sales/Receivables | 14  25.8 | 16  22.6 | 11  32.9 | | 0  UND | 0  UND | | 22  16.3 | 22  16.4 | 29  12.8 |
| | 31  11.8 | 32  11.3 | 32  11.3 | | 0  UND | 0  UND | | 33  11.1 | 33  11.0 | 38  9.7 |
| | 42  8.8 | 43  8.5 | 42  8.6 | | 29  12.7 | 34  10.7 | | 44  8.3 | 45  8.2 | 43  8.5 |
| Cost of Sales/Inventory | | | | | | | | | | |
| Cost of Sales/Payables | | | | | | | | | | |
| Sales/Working Capital | 15.7 | 13.7 | 12.8 | | 9.3 | 30.3 | | 11.7 | 10.6 | 14.9 |
| | 51.8 | 49.8 | 31.6 | | NM | -79.6 | | 15.5 | 21.1 | 43.6 |
| | -47.8 | -50.9 | -68.2 | | -3.1 | -10.3 | | 49.7 | -51.1 | 642.1 |
| EBIT/Interest | 11.4 | 14.3 | 25.5 | | 19.5 | 10.2 | | 45.2 | 44.4 | 36.5 |
| | (99)  4.5 | (91)  4.3 | (101)  4.5 | | (10)  5.6 | (14)  3.0 | | (22)  4.4 | (17)  13.7 | (31)  6.8 |
| | 1.4 | .9 | .8 | | 1.4 | .2 | | 1.3 | -.4 | .7 |
| Net Profit + Depr., Dep., Amort./Cur. Mat. L/T/D | 7.1 | 4.2 | 13.3 | | | | | | | 14.4 |
| | (17)  2.8 | (20)  1.1 | (16)  3.1 | | | | | | | (11)  6.0 |
| | 1.4 | .0 | 1.0 | | | | | | | 1.6 |
| Fixed/Worth | .3 | .3 | .2 | | .2 | .4 | | .1 | .1 | .4 |
| | 1.2 | 1.1 | 1.0 | | 2.6 | 4.5 | | .5 | .2 | 1.0 |
| | 16.2 | -3.3 | -8.6 | | UND | -2.0 | | NM | 5.6 | 10.7 |
| Debt/Worth | 1.2 | 1.0 | .9 | | .5 | 1.4 | | .6 | .3 | 1.3 |
| | 3.3 | 3.3 | 3.6 | | 9.1 | 93.1 | | 2.0 | .9 | 2.6 |
| | -57.6 | -6.7 | -21.6 | | UND | -11.5 | | NM | 9.3 | 58.0 |
| % Profit Before Taxes/Tangible Net Worth | 70.3 | 81.7 | 117.1 | | 526.3 | | | 86.4 | 89.6 | 235.5 |
| | (84)  28.7 | (78)  20.1 | (85)  44.9 | | (11)  13.0 | | | (19)  17.4 | (17)  46.1 | (27)  59.6 |
| | 5.3 | 9.0 | 7.7 | | .2 | | | 4.9 | -1.1 | 16.7 |
| % Profit Before Taxes/Total Assets | 17.4 | 18.2 | 31.9 | | 34.0 | 36.0 | | 23.5 | 37.8 | 34.9 |
| | 9.1 | 7.1 | 9.8 | | 7.5 | 8.8 | | 10.1 | 13.6 | 10.2 |
| | 1.4 | .3 | .5 | | -.6 | -3.1 | | 1.2 | -.6 | .4 |
| Sales/Net Fixed Assets | 110.2 | 78.8 | 115.8 | | 142.1 | 281.3 | | 87.1 | 145.9 | 108.1 |
| | 28.5 | 34.3 | 37.6 | | 8.0 | 65.2 | | 43.1 | 51.4 | 32.0 |
| | 7.5 | 9.8 | 8.2 | | 2.3 | 7.6 | | 16.7 | 26.7 | 12.9 |
| Sales/Total Assets | 7.0 | 6.8 | 7.4 | | 3.8 | 10.0 | | 8.3 | 7.6 | 7.1 |
| | 4.5 | 4.8 | 4.9 | | 2.1 | 5.5 | | 5.0 | 6.0 | 3.6 |
| | 2.2 | 2.4 | 2.2 | | 1.2 | 2.9 | | 2.9 | 3.0 | 1.7 |
| % Depr., Dep., Amort./Sales | .7 | .5 | .3 | | | | | .3 | .3 | .4 |
| | (78)  1.7 | (82)  1.2 | (88)  1.1 | | | | | (22)  1.0 | (15)  .6 | (31)  1.2 |
| | 3.8 | 2.7 | 3.9 | | | | | 2.4 | 1.6 | 3.9 |
| % Officers', Directors' Owners' Comp/Sales | 2.8 | 1.7 | 2.0 | | | 2.0 | | 1.1 | | 1.8 |
| | (44)  4.3 | (40)  3.5 | (54)  3.8 | | | (12)  4.4 | | (12)  2.4 | | (11)  2.1 |
| | 9.2 | 6.6 | 6.9 | | | 8.2 | | 9.1 | | 3.2 |
| Net Sales ($) | 5504625M | 3777823M | 5622580M | | 5731M | 36651M | 28868M | 182968M | 285136M | 5083226M |
| Total Assets ($) | 1354402M | 1586222M | 1566591M | | 7272M | 9341M | 9829M | 56450M | 59773M | 1423926M |

© RMA 2012   M = $ thousand   MM = $ million
See Pages 9 through 22 for Explanation of Ratios and Data

## Current Data Sorted by Assets      Comparative Historical Data

| Type of Statement | 0-500M | 500M-2MM | 2-10MM | 10-50MM | 50-100MM | 100-250MM | | 4/1/07-3/31/08 ALL | 4/1/08-3/31/09 ALL |
|---|---|---|---|---|---|---|---|---|---|
| Unqualified | | 3 | 7 | 15 | 3 | 8 | | 31 | 32 |
| Reviewed | 2 | 8 | 30 | 20 | 1 | | | 45 | 62 |
| Compiled | 10 | 17 | 19 | 7 | 1 | | | 67 | 56 |
| Tax Returns | 31 | 57 | 39 | 3 | | | | 86 | 90 |
| Other | 14 | 44 | 64 | 41 | 9 | 8 | | 117 | 133 |
| | 0-500M | 500M-2MM | 44 (4/1-9/30/11) 2-10MM | 10-50MM | 417 (10/1/11-3/31/12) 50-100MM | 100-250MM | | | |
| **NUMBER OF STATEMENTS** | 57 | 129 | 159 | 86 | 14 | 16 | | 346 | 373 |
| **ASSETS** | % | % | % | % | % | % | | % | % |
| Cash & Equivalents | 22.2 | 10.0 | 9.7 | 12.6 | 12.4 | 10.7 | | 12.1 | 10.1 |
| Trade Receivables (net) | 25.4 | 17.9 | 17.1 | 14.7 | 20.1 | 21.1 | | 18.4 | 16.8 |
| Inventory | 2.4 | 3.0 | 2.2 | 1.5 | 3.3 | 15.5 | | 2.6 | 3.4 |
| All Other Current | 2.6 | 3.1 | 2.5 | 4.0 | 2.3 | 4.6 | | 3.6 | 3.9 |
| Total Current | 52.5 | 33.9 | 31.6 | 32.9 | 38.0 | 51.9 | | 36.7 | 34.2 |
| Fixed Assets (net) | 31.7 | 53.0 | 53.9 | 48.2 | 40.9 | 37.0 | | 49.5 | 52.6 |
| Intangibles (net) | 4.1 | 2.9 | 4.9 | 6.1 | 11.1 | 3.7 | | 3.3 | 4.6 |
| All Other Non-Current | 11.6 | 10.2 | 9.6 | 12.8 | 9.9 | 7.5 | | 10.4 | 8.5 |
| Total | 100.0 | 100.0 | 100.0 | 100.0 | 100.0 | 100.0 | | 100.0 | 100.0 |
| **LIABILITIES** | | | | | | | | | |
| Notes Payable-Short Term | 19.8 | 5.8 | 4.8 | 3.0 | 2.0 | 12.3 | | 7.6 | 6.3 |
| Cur. Mat.-L.T.D. | 4.7 | 5.8 | 3.5 | 4.2 | 2.8 | 2.1 | | 4.4 | 4.2 |
| Trade Payables | 15.9 | 9.0 | 6.5 | 6.7 | 4.8 | 8.9 | | 8.5 | 6.7 |
| Income Taxes Payable | .1 | .0 | .3 | .4 | .7 | .5 | | .2 | .1 |
| All Other Current | 26.3 | 13.7 | 6.9 | 8.9 | 8.0 | 9.0 | | 10.1 | 9.5 |
| Total Current | 66.7 | 34.4 | 22.0 | 23.1 | 18.1 | 32.7 | | 30.7 | 26.9 |
| Long-Term Debt | 19.9 | 49.6 | 42.9 | 28.2 | 29.7 | 21.2 | | 35.4 | 43.5 |
| Deferred Taxes | .0 | .0 | .3 | .9 | .4 | 1.3 | | .3 | .2 |
| All Other Non-Current | 5.7 | 9.9 | 5.2 | 7.2 | 5.8 | 6.2 | | 6.9 | 6.7 |
| Net Worth | 7.7 | 6.1 | 29.7 | 40.6 | 46.0 | 38.6 | | 26.7 | 22.7 |
| Total Liabilities & Net Worth | 100.0 | 100.0 | 100.0 | 100.0 | 100.0 | 100.0 | | 100.0 | 100.0 |
| **INCOME DATA** | | | | | | | | | |
| Net Sales | 100.0 | 100.0 | 100.0 | 100.0 | 100.0 | 100.0 | | 100.0 | 100.0 |
| Gross Profit | | | | | | | | | |
| Operating Expenses | 93.8 | 79.2 | 80.2 | 88.5 | 84.3 | 91.8 | | 84.9 | 83.1 |
| Operating Profit | 6.2 | 20.8 | 19.8 | 11.5 | 15.7 | 8.2 | | 15.1 | 16.9 |
| All Other Expenses (net) | .8 | 7.8 | 9.9 | 4.2 | 3.4 | 1.9 | | 6.8 | 8.0 |
| Profit Before Taxes | 5.5 | 13.0 | 10.0 | 7.3 | 12.3 | 6.3 | | 8.3 | 8.9 |
| **RATIOS** | | | | | | | | | |
| Current | 3.6 | 2.4 | 3.2 | 2.8 | 4.4 | 2.1 | | 2.3 | 2.4 |
| | 1.2 | 1.1 | 1.3 | 1.5 | 2.6 | 1.5 | | 1.3 | 1.3 |
| | .6 | .4 | .6 | 1.0 | 1.6 | 1.4 | | .7 | .6 |
| Quick | 3.5 | 2.1 | 3.1 | 2.5 | 4.2 | 1.9 | | 2.1 | 1.8 |
| | 1.0 | .8 | 1.1 | 1.3 | 2.4 | 1.3 | | 1.1 | .9 |
| | .5 | .3 | .5 | .9 | 1.3 | .6 | | .5 | .4 |
| Sales/Receivables | 0 UND | 0 UND | 0 UND | 21   17.8 | 28   13.1 | 42   8.7 | | 0   940.0 | 0 UND |
| | 13   27.7 | 15   24.3 | 27   13.3 | 36   10.0 | 44   8.3 | 50   7.3 | | 29   12.4 | 27   13.7 |
| | 35   10.4 | 37   9.9 | 47   7.8 | 47   7.8 | 56   6.5 | 73   5.0 | | 51   7.1 | 42   8.7 |
| Cost of Sales/Inventory | | | | | | | | | |
| Cost of Sales/Payables | | | | | | | | | |
| Sales/Working Capital | 17.8 | 9.4 | 5.3 | 4.6 | 3.9 | 2.2 | | 7.3 | 8.4 |
| | 132.5 | 109.8 | 23.5 | 11.6 | 6.2 | 8.4 | | 25.3 | 33.1 |
| | -20.9 | -9.9 | -14.3 | 122.2 | 12.0 | 14.2 | | -15.7 | -13.3 |
| EBIT/Interest | 24.0 | 8.9 | 11.3 | 13.5 | 25.5 | 14.3 | | 8.9 | 9.4 |
| | (33) 6.0 | (85) 3.4 | (114) 3.2 | (73) 5.8 | (13) 10.0 | (13) 6.9 | | (268) 2.7 | (266) 3.2 |
| | 1.4 | 1.4 | 1.2 | 2.5 | 3.1 | 3.5 | | 1.2 | 1.2 |
| Net Profit + Depr., Dep., Amort./Cur. Mat. L/T/D | | | 12.0 | 4.0 | | | | 5.0 | 4.7 |
| | | | (26) 3.8 | (34) 2.0 | | | | (52) 2.0 | (59) 2.4 |
| | | | 1.8 | 1.1 | | | | .8 | 1.0 |
| Fixed/Worth | .3 | .6 | .4 | .6 | .6 | .6 | | .6 | .7 |
| | .8 | 2.2 | 2.2 | 1.4 | 1.0 | 1.0 | | 1.8 | 2.2 |
| | 13.2 | -29.6 | 16.2 | 3.6 | 8.0 | 2.0 | | 6.1 | 28.2 |
| Debt/Worth | .5 | 1.0 | .9 | .7 | .5 | .9 | | 1.1 | 1.0 |
| | 3.5 | 3.0 | 2.5 | 1.7 | 2.4 | 2.0 | | 2.6 | 3.2 |
| | UND | -17.5 | 23.7 | 4.6 | 8.3 | 9.5 | | 10.8 | 43.4 |
| % Profit Before Taxes/Tangible Net Worth | 142.9 | 64.3 | 38.4 | 27.8 | 50.7 | 35.0 | | 48.4 | 49.4 |
| | (43) 42.2 | (92) 25.6 | (127) 18.0 | (73) 15.3 | (12) 23.6 | 21.9 | | (288) 20.1 | (286) 17.3 |
| | .0 | 9.8 | 5.1 | 7.7 | 15.4 | 14.5 | | 4.6 | 4.1 |
| % Profit Before Taxes/Total Assets | 32.1 | 22.6 | 11.4 | 11.3 | 14.0 | 9.1 | | 13.8 | 12.7 |
| | 11.7 | 6.8 | 4.8 | 6.0 | 9.3 | 6.1 | | 4.8 | 4.6 |
| | .0 | 1.7 | .8 | 1.4 | 6.3 | 2.9 | | .1 | .4 |
| Sales/Net Fixed Assets | 84.6 | 18.9 | 16.6 | 11.1 | 23.0 | 5.0 | | 14.1 | 16.6 |
| | 19.9 | 3.9 | 1.4 | 2.5 | 2.4 | 4.2 | | 4.1 | 2.7 |
| | 8.6 | .4 | .3 | .8 | .6 | 2.1 | | .6 | .5 |
| Sales/Total Assets | 10.4 | 3.5 | 2.5 | 1.9 | 1.8 | 2.1 | | 3.0 | 3.3 |
| | 4.7 | 1.5 | .8 | 1.0 | .9 | 1.5 | | 1.4 | 1.2 |
| | 3.1 | .3 | .2 | .5 | .4 | .5 | | .5 | .3 |
| % Depr., Dep., Amort./Sales | 1.0 | 2.0 | 1.9 | 1.9 | 2.1 | 2.3 | | 2.0 | 1.9 |
| | (35) 1.8 | (94) 7.1 | (140) 6.3 | (81) 4.6 | (13) 7.1 | (10) 3.1 | | (299) 4.2 | (328) 5.8 |
| | 5.7 | 14.9 | 15.0 | 8.8 | 12.5 | 6.4 | | 10.5 | 14.1 |
| % Officers', Directors' Owners' Comp/Sales | 3.2 | 3.0 | 1.0 | 3.2 | | | | 2.5 | 2.0 |
| | (27) 4.9 | (33) 4.8 | (36) 3.6 | (13) 7.5 | | | | (92) 5.2 | (91) 4.3 |
| | 9.2 | 10.0 | 7.8 | 8.5 | | | | 10.5 | 7.6 |
| Net Sales ($) | 91073M | 331194M | 1101591M | 2652455M | 1591463M | 3206366M | | 8755211M | 9295829M |
| Total Assets ($) | 13868M | 147135M | 725223M | 1911676M | 1007582M | 2410051M | | 4760011M | 4980000M |

## Comparative Historical Data | Current Data Sorted by Sales

| | | | Type of Statement | | | | | | |
|---|---|---|---|---|---|---|---|---|---|
| 33 | 32 | 36 | Unqualified | 3 | 4 | 1 | 4 | 5 | 19 |
| 59 | 59 | 61 | Reviewed | 6 | 12 | 2 | 13 | 18 | 10 |
| 47 | 55 | 54 | Compiled | 16 | 13 | 9 | 8 | 3 | 5 |
| 111 | 90 | 130 | Tax Returns | 64 | 37 | 13 | 11 | 5 | |
| 132 | 164 | 180 | Other | 36 | 40 | 15 | 20 | 27 | 42 |
| 4/1/09- | 4/1/10- | 4/1/11- | | | 44 (4/1-9/30/11) | | | 417 (10/1/11-3/31/12) | |
| 3/31/10 | 3/31/11 | 3/31/12 | | | | | | | |
| ALL | ALL | ALL | | 0-1MM | 1-3MM | 3-5MM | 5-10MM | 10-25MM | 25MM & OVER |
| 382 | 400 | 461 | **NUMBER OF STATEMENTS** | 125 | 106 | 40 | 56 | 58 | 76 |
| % | % | % | **ASSETS** | % | % | % | % | % | % |
| 10.8 | 12.2 | 12.0 | Cash & Equivalents | 9.7 | 14.0 | 11.5 | 11.7 | 14.4 | 11.6 |
| 18.1 | 19.5 | 18.1 | Trade Receivables (net) | 5.3 | 16.0 | 18.9 | 30.0 | 26.7 | 26.5 |
| 2.5 | 1.9 | 2.8 | Inventory | 1.3 | 2.3 | 2.8 | .9 | 3.1 | 7.2 |
| 3.5 | 3.1 | 3.0 | All Other Current | .8 | 1.8 | 2.9 | 7.0 | 4.8 | 4.2 |
| 34.9 | 36.7 | 36.0 | Total Current | 17.1 | 34.1 | 36.2 | 49.5 | 49.0 | 49.5 |
| 51.5 | 48.9 | 48.9 | Fixed Assets (net) | 71.9 | 50.3 | 48.0 | 30.5 | 37.5 | 31.7 |
| 4.4 | 5.0 | 4.6 | Intangibles (net) | 3.2 | 4.0 | 6.9 | 4.4 | 3.6 | 7.6 |
| 9.1 | 9.5 | 10.6 | All Other Non-Current | 7.8 | 11.6 | 8.9 | 15.7 | 9.9 | 11.3 |
| 100.0 | 100.0 | 100.0 | Total | 100.0 | 100.0 | 100.0 | 100.0 | 100.0 | 100.0 |
| | | | **LIABILITIES** | | | | | | |
| 8.4 | 7.6 | 6.8 | Notes Payable-Short Term | 8.4 | 7.2 | 5.4 | 4.0 | 6.2 | 6.7 |
| 5.7 | 4.0 | 4.3 | Cur. Mat.-L.T.D. | 3.5 | 5.7 | 6.8 | 4.1 | 3.4 | 3.4 |
| 7.4 | 8.0 | 8.4 | Trade Payables | 4.0 | 6.7 | 7.5 | 15.5 | 10.4 | 11.9 |
| .2 | .1 | .2 | Income Taxes Payable | .0 | .1 | .1 | .4 | .3 | .6 |
| 9.1 | 13.7 | 11.7 | All Other Current | 10.5 | 12.8 | 17.0 | 14.5 | 7.4 | 10.6 |
| 30.8 | 33.5 | 31.5 | Total Current | 26.4 | 32.4 | 36.9 | 38.5 | 27.8 | 33.2 |
| 38.4 | 35.9 | 38.0 | Long-Term Debt | 56.9 | 40.3 | 60.4 | 19.0 | 23.8 | 16.9 |
| .2 | .2 | .3 | Deferred Taxes | .0 | .1 | .2 | .6 | .5 | .9 |
| 6.8 | 6.4 | 7.0 | All Other Non-Current | 7.0 | 8.7 | 3.4 | 5.5 | 9.0 | 6.3 |
| 23.9 | 24.0 | 23.2 | Net Worth | 9.6 | 18.6 | -.9 | 36.5 | 39.0 | 42.7 |
| 100.0 | 100.0 | 100.0 | Total Liabilties & Net Worth | 100.0 | 100.0 | 100.0 | 100.0 | 100.0 | 100.0 |
| | | | **INCOME DATA** | | | | | | |
| 100.0 | 100.0 | 100.0 | Net Sales | 100.0 | 100.0 | 100.0 | 100.0 | 100.0 | 100.0 |
| | | | Gross Profit | | | | | | |
| 85.1 | 84.4 | 83.7 | Operating Expenses | 65.9 | 84.9 | 90.6 | 93.9 | 93.9 | 92.1 |
| 14.9 | 15.6 | 16.3 | Operating Profit | 34.1 | 15.1 | 9.4 | 6.1 | 6.1 | 7.9 |
| 7.7 | 7.7 | 6.6 | All Other Expenses (net) | 16.5 | 6.5 | 3.0 | .6 | 1.7 | .8 |
| 7.3 | 7.9 | 9.7 | Profit Before Taxes | 17.6 | 8.7 | 6.4 | 5.5 | 4.4 | 7.1 |
| | | | **RATIOS** | | | | | | |
| 2.4 | 2.7 | 3.0 | | 3.0 | 3.5 | 2.8 | 4.5 | 3.2 | 2.3 |
| 1.2 | 1.2 | 1.4 | Current | .8 | 1.2 | 1.2 | 1.6 | 1.8 | 1.5 |
| .6 | .6 | .7 | | .3 | .6 | .7 | .8 | 1.2 | 1.1 |
| 2.0 | 2.5 | 2.7 | | 3.0 | 2.9 | 2.8 | 4.5 | 2.8 | 2.0 |
| 1.0 | 1.1 | 1.1 | Quick | .8 | 1.0 | 1.1 | 1.2 | 1.5 | 1.2 |
| .5 | .4 | .6 | | .2 | .5 | .6 | .6 | 1.0 | .7 |
| 0 UND | 3 118.9 | 0 937.9 | | 0 UND | 1 528.3 | 10 37.1 | 24 15.2 | 27 13.3 | 34 10.8 |
| 28 13.0 | 30 12.2 | 27 13.3 | Sales/Receivables | 0 UND | 22 16.9 | 24 15.5 | 35 10.4 | 42 8.7 | 43 8.5 |
| 45 8.1 | 46 7.9 | 45 8.1 | | 14 26.2 | 38 9.5 | 40 9.1 | 49 7.5 | 51 7.2 | 53 6.9 |
| | | | Cost of Sales/Inventory | | | | | | |
| | | | Cost of Sales/Payables | | | | | | |
| 7.5 | 6.8 | 6.1 | | 6.0 | 6.9 | 10.1 | 4.9 | 5.0 | 6.4 |
| 41.4 | 36.4 | 28.0 | Sales/Working Capital | -28.2 | 59.8 | 36.9 | 17.2 | 8.3 | 17.8 |
| -12.9 | -12.7 | -20.3 | | -3.8 | -17.7 | -21.0 | -108.4 | 55.6 | 54.0 |
| 8.3 | 10.9 | 12.6 | | 6.7 | 7.4 | 5.1 | 18.2 | 14.1 | 33.9 |
| (285) 2.9 | (285) 3.5 | (331) 4.2 | EBIT/Interest | (56) 2.4 | (78) 3.1 | (31) 3.2 | (44) 5.6 | (51) 4.7 | (71) 7.6 |
| 1.0 | 1.4 | 1.7 | | 1.1 | 1.2 | 1.1 | 1.7 | 2.2 | 3.4 |
| 3.5 | 7.8 | 5.5 | Net Profit + Depr., Dep., | | | | 11.6 | 5.0 | 11.6 |
| (67) 2.0 | (62) 3.3 | (73) 3.0 | Amort./Cur. Mat. L/T/D | | | (12) 4.7 | (20) 2.8 | (24) 3.3 |
| 1.2 | 1.6 | 1.4 | | | | | 2.3 | .9 | 1.7 |
| .7 | .6 | .5 | | 1.4 | .5 | .8 | .3 | .4 | .4 |
| 2.1 | 1.7 | 1.6 | Fixed/Worth | 3.9 | 2.1 | 1.8 | .8 | .9 | .9 |
| 23.1 | 34.2 | 14.1 | | -55.5 | 55.1 | -2.9 | 2.5 | 2.7 | 2.0 |
| 1.0 | .8 | .8 | | 1.4 | .8 | .5 | .6 | .9 | .8 |
| 2.9 | 2.5 | 2.3 | Debt/Worth | 6.2 | 2.7 | 4.2 | 1.7 | 1.5 | 1.7 |
| 278.2 | 115.5 | 24.2 | | -28.7 | 231.1 | -4.8 | 8.3 | 4.4 | 4.6 |
| 42.5 | 51.3 | 45.3 | % Profit Before Taxes/Tangible | 39.1 | 62.2 | 56.8 | 55.2 | 37.5 | 40.1 |
| (288) 16.3 | (303) 17.5 | (363) 20.0 | Net Worth | (87) 15.0 | (81) 18.6 | (27) 14.3 | (47) 25.2 | (53) 18.4 | (68) 25.8 |
| 5.3 | 5.8 | 8.2 | | 6.0 | 5.2 | 4.8 | 11.5 | 6.1 | 14.5 |
| 11.2 | 13.9 | 13.5 | % Profit Before Taxes/Total | 9.3 | 12.8 | 24.7 | 24.7 | 14.3 | 14.4 |
| 4.7 | 5.4 | 6.4 | Assets | 4.2 | 6.9 | 5.1 | 7.1 | 6.9 | 9.3 |
| -.1 | .5 | 1.4 | | .3 | .9 | .6 | 1.9 | 1.8 | 4.6 |
| 15.1 | 21.7 | 18.8 | | 1.4 | 24.8 | 21.8 | 42.4 | 18.1 | 26.8 |
| 2.7 | 3.7 | 3.9 | Sales/Net Fixed Assets | .3 | 4.2 | 6.6 | 16.3 | 5.1 | 8.7 |
| .5 | .5 | .5 | | .2 | .6 | 1.3 | 2.3 | 1.7 | 2.8 |
| 2.8 | 3.1 | 3.2 | | .6 | 3.6 | 5.2 | 5.2 | 3.2 | 3.5 |
| 1.1 | 1.3 | 1.3 | Sales/Total Assets | .2 | 1.4 | 2.0 | 2.5 | 1.9 | 1.9 |
| .3 | .4 | .4 | | .1 | .4 | .8 | .9 | .8 | 1.3 |
| 2.0 | 2.1 | 1.8 | | 7.4 | 1.8 | 1.5 | 1.1 | 1.6 | 1.0 |
| (319) 5.1 | (317) 5.1 | (373) 4.7 | % Depr., Dep., Amort./Sales | (103) 14.0 | (78) 5.3 | (30) 5.2 | (44) 2.6 | (52) 2.4 | (66) 2.1 |
| 12.2 | 12.7 | 12.6 | | 23.5 | 13.2 | 8.9 | 5.0 | 5.4 | 5.4 |
| 2.6 | 2.8 | 2.7 | % Officers', Directors' | 4.7 | 3.5 | 1.7 | 1.9 | 1.0 | 2.8 |
| (99) 5.0 | (101) 4.7 | (114) 4.9 | Owners' Comp/Sales | (16) 5.7 | (38) 5.6 | (13) 3.2 | (13) 4.0 | (21) 1.8 | (13) 5.8 |
| 9.6 | 9.7 | 8.9 | | 10.5 | 11.1 | 11.4 | 8.1 | 5.8 | 9.3 |
| 7699245M | 7788967M | 8974142M | Net Sales ($) | 55611M | 199327M | 154402M | 403091M | 917958M | 7243753M |
| 4929404M | 4485268M | 6215535M | Total Assets ($) | 232637M | 345176M | 133730M | 296683M | 936903M | 4270406M |

**M = $ thousand    MM = $ million**
See Pages 9 through 22 for Explanation of Ratios and Data

## Current Data Sorted by Assets      Comparative Historical Data

### Type of Statement

| 0-500M | 500M-2MM | 2-10MM | 10-50MM | 50-100MM | 100-250MM | Type of Statement | 4/1/07-3/31/08 ALL | 4/1/08-3/31/09 ALL |
|---|---|---|---|---|---|---|---|---|
| | | 4 | 9 | 3 | 6 | Unqualified | 25 | 18 |
| 1 | 3 | 6 | 7 | | 1 | Reviewed | 15 | 11 |
| 4 | 4 | 6 | 8 | | 1 | Compiled | 17 | 20 |
| 3 | 8 | 3 | | | | Tax Returns | 9 | 18 |
| 5 | 15 | 18 | 11 | 2 | 4 | Other | 43 | 49 |
| 19 (4/1-9/30/11) | | | 113 (10/1/11-3/31/12) | | | | | |
| 13 | 30 | 37 | 35 | 5 | 12 | NUMBER OF STATEMENTS | 109 | 116 |
| % | % | % | % | % | % | **ASSETS** | % | % |
| 14.1 | 8.3 | 7.8 | 9.0 | | 8.8 | Cash & Equivalents | 7.8 | 9.0 |
| 45.3 | 19.3 | 15.4 | 7.2 | | 9.8 | Trade Receivables (net) | 15.1 | 13.2 |
| 1.5 | 3.0 | 8.1 | 7.8 | | 7.8 | Inventory | 5.4 | 4.7 |
| 3.6 | 3.4 | 1.9 | 2.0 | | 1.1 | All Other Current | 2.9 | 3.4 |
| 64.5 | 34.0 | 33.2 | 25.9 | | 27.5 | Total Current | 31.2 | 30.3 |
| 28.4 | 53.4 | 60.0 | 68.2 | | 50.5 | Fixed Assets (net) | 57.6 | 57.4 |
| .4 | 3.1 | 1.5 | 2.9 | | 20.1 | Intangibles (net) | 3.7 | 4.4 |
| 6.8 | 9.6 | 5.2 | 3.0 | | 2.0 | All Other Non-Current | 7.4 | 7.9 |
| 100.0 | 100.0 | 100.0 | 100.0 | | 100.0 | Total | 100.0 | 100.0 |
| | | | | | | **LIABILITIES** | | |
| 16.3 | 9.5 | 8.3 | 7.4 | | 3.4 | Notes Payable-Short Term | 13.6 | 10.6 |
| 8.4 | 9.1 | 3.1 | 3.9 | | 2.6 | Cur. Mat.-L.T.D. | 7.0 | 4.5 |
| 14.8 | 9.3 | 6.4 | 2.7 | | 4.2 | Trade Payables | 5.5 | 5.8 |
| .0 | .1 | .0 | .1 | | .0 | Income Taxes Payable | .1 | .1 |
| 22.0 | 14.1 | 5.8 | 5.9 | | 4.8 | All Other Current | 7.6 | 6.3 |
| 61.4 | 42.0 | 23.6 | 20.1 | | 15.1 | Total Current | 33.8 | 27.3 |
| 15.8 | 32.6 | 46.2 | 41.5 | | 24.7 | Long-Term Debt | 32.4 | 32.4 |
| .2 | .0 | .1 | 1.1 | | 1.9 | Deferred Taxes | .7 | 1.1 |
| 5.4 | 19.4 | 17.7 | 2.4 | | 10.4 | All Other Non-Current | 6.8 | 6.6 |
| 17.2 | 6.0 | 12.4 | 35.0 | | 48.0 | Net Worth | 26.3 | 32.6 |
| 100.0 | 100.0 | 100.0 | 100.0 | | 100.0 | Total Liabilities & Net Worth | 100.0 | 100.0 |
| | | | | | | **INCOME DATA** | | |
| 100.0 | 100.0 | 100.0 | 100.0 | | 100.0 | Net Sales | 100.0 | 100.0 |
| | | | | | | Gross Profit | | |
| 93.0 | 90.1 | 86.3 | 85.6 | | 88.1 | Operating Expenses | 86.7 | 88.0 |
| 7.0 | 9.9 | 13.7 | 14.4 | | 11.9 | Operating Profit | 13.3 | 12.0 |
| -.3 | 6.1 | 7.8 | 6.2 | | 6.0 | All Other Expenses (net) | 6.0 | 4.2 |
| 7.4 | 3.8 | 5.9 | 8.2 | | 5.8 | Profit Before Taxes | 7.3 | 7.9 |
| | | | | | | **RATIOS** | | |
| 2.4 | 2.1 | 2.2 | 1.9 | | 4.5 | Current | 2.2 | 2.4 |
| 1.4 | 1.0 | 1.4 | 1.1 | | 1.4 | | 1.2 | 1.2 |
| .7 | .2 | .8 | .6 | | 1.0 | | .7 | .7 |
| 2.4 | 1.8 | 2.1 | 1.7 | | 2.3 | Quick | 1.9 | 2.0 |
| 1.2 | .7 | .9 | .6 | | 1.2 | | .9 | .9 |
| .7 | .2 | .5 | .3 | | .8 | | .5 | .5 |
| 13   27.1 | 1   358.5 | 15   24.7 | 20   18.4 | | 35   10.4 | Sales/Receivables | 22   16.3 | 17   21.7 |
| 34   10.8 | 23   16.2 | 28   13.1 | 29   12.7 | | 47   7.8 | | 36   10.0 | 32   11.3 |
| 57   6.4 | 42   8.6 | 46   8.0 | 43   8.5 | | 57   6.4 | | 48   7.6 | 43   8.5 |
| | | | | | | Cost of Sales/Inventory | | |
| | | | | | | Cost of Sales/Payables | | |
| 9.9 | 12.5 | 8.2 | 4.8 | | 1.9 | Sales/Working Capital | 9.0 | 8.0 |
| 39.7 | NM | 25.0 | 14.5 | | 13.7 | | 28.0 | 34.2 |
| -16.4 | -6.3 | -43.6 | -13.3 | | 690.0 | | -16.2 | -16.6 |
| | 20.6 | 16.3 | 5.4 | | 3.7 | EBIT/Interest | 4.8 | 7.0 |
| | (24) 1.9 | (29) 4.0 | (32) 2.6 | | (10) -1.1 | | (91) 2.5 | (98) 2.9 |
| | .8 | 1.1 | 1.3 | | -11.4 | | 1.2 | 1.2 |
| | | | 3.3 | | | Net Profit + Depr., Dep., Amort./Cur. Mat. L/T/D | 7.8 | 5.7 |
| | | | (11) 2.2 | | | | (32) 3.4 | (26) 1.9 |
| | | | 1.1 | | | | 1.5 | 1.0 |
| .0 | .6 | .8 | 1.2 | | 1.2 | Fixed/Worth | .9 | .9 |
| .3 | 2.0 | 4.7 | 2.2 | | 2.3 | | 2.1 | 2.1 |
| 6.2 | -1.1 | 24.3 | 6.2 | | -14.0 | | 7.0 | 4.6 |
| .5 | .4 | 1.4 | .9 | | .8 | Debt/Worth | 1.0 | .8 |
| .9 | 2.6 | 5.5 | 2.3 | | 2.0 | | 2.2 | 1.8 |
| -10.6 | -2.5 | 52.3 | 6.8 | | -25.7 | | 11.5 | 7.2 |
| | 54.2 | 52.5 | 22.3 | | | % Profit Before Taxes/Tangible Net Worth | 39.4 | 37.4 |
| | (18) 20.9 | (29) 27.3 | (29) 9.7 | | | | (93) 17.5 | (103) 19.7 |
| | 5.8 | 8.3 | 2.8 | | | | 6.2 | 5.7 |
| 58.4 | 18.1 | 13.5 | 7.9 | | 7.8 | % Profit Before Taxes/Total Assets | 11.5 | 14.6 |
| -8.4 | 4.4 | 4.4 | 4.4 | | 2.1 | | 5.2 | 6.2 |
| -51.8 | -.3 | -.1 | .8 | | -9.0 | | .9 | 1.1 |
| UND | 22.3 | 7.3 | 1.3 | | 4.0 | Sales/Net Fixed Assets | 6.7 | 5.0 |
| 37.4 | 4.1 | 2.0 | .7 | | 1.2 | | 1.5 | 1.6 |
| 14.0 | .9 | .8 | .6 | | .6 | | .7 | .7 |
| 7.4 | 5.4 | 2.8 | .8 | | 1.0 | Sales/Total Assets | 2.6 | 2.0 |
| 6.1 | 2.6 | 1.2 | .6 | | .8 | | 1.0 | 1.0 |
| 3.8 | .5 | .6 | .3 | | .4 | | .5 | .5 |
| | 2.6 | 2.1 | 5.5 | | | % Depr., Dep., Amort./Sales | 3.0 | 3.4 |
| | (24) 5.9 | (33) 5.1 | 8.3 | | | | (99) 7.5 | (99) 7.4 |
| | 12.5 | 12.5 | 11.6 | | | | 10.7 | 10.5 |
| | | | | | | % Officers', Directors' Owners' Comp/Sales | 1.8 | 1.5 |
| | | | | | | | (32) 4.9 | (33) 4.8 |
| | | | | | | | 8.2 | 11.0 |
| 22127M | 88258M | 349144M | 559376M | 247505M | 1511861M | Net Sales ($) | 4079182M | 3142074M |
| 3567M | 33289M | 212880M | 761356M | 339508M | 1915673M | Total Assets ($) | 3254726M | 2686390M |

M = $ thousand    MM = $ million
See Pages 9 through 22 for Explanation of Ratios and Data

## Comparative Historical Data | Current Data Sorted by Sales

| | | | Type of Statement | | | | | | |
|---|---|---|---|---|---|---|---|---|---|
| 29 | 26 | 22 | Unqualified | | | 2 | 3 | 7 | 10 |
| 10 | 16 | 18 | Reviewed | 1 | 2 | 6 | 3 | 5 | 1 |
| 19 | 25 | 23 | Compiled | | 3 | 5 | 7 | 7 | 1 |
| 11 | 21 | 14 | Tax Returns | 5 | 4 | 2 | 3 | | |
| 45 | 58 | 55 | Other | 12 | 9 | 6 | 12 | 6 | 10 |
| 4/1/09-3/31/10 ALL | 4/1/10-3/31/11 ALL | 4/1/11-3/31/12 ALL | | | 19 (4/1-9/30/11) | | | 113 (10/1/11-3/31/12) | |
| | | | | 0-1MM | 1-3MM | 3-5MM | 5-10MM | 10-25MM | 25MM & OVER |
| 114 | 146 | 132 | **NUMBER OF STATEMENTS** | 18 | 18 | 21 | 28 | 25 | 22 |
| % | % | % | **ASSETS** | % | % | % | % | % | % |
| 10.2 | 9.4 | 9.0 | Cash & Equivalents | 8.2 | 10.0 | 5.9 | 8.6 | 10.3 | 10.6 |
| 12.2 | 13.4 | 16.3 | Trade Receivables (net) | 6.9 | 33.9 | 18.9 | 10.5 | 17.0 | 13.7 |
| 4.3 | 4.8 | 5.9 | Inventory | 7.0 | .6 | 1.4 | 9.5 | 6.5 | 8.2 |
| 2.2 | 2.4 | 2.3 | All Other Current | .1 | 4.5 | 3.1 | 3.3 | 1.7 | 1.1 |
| 28.8 | 29.9 | 33.5 | Total Current | 22.1 | 49.0 | 29.3 | 31.8 | 35.5 | 33.7 |
| 60.6 | 61.5 | 56.8 | Fixed Assets (net) | 65.3 | 45.8 | 56.5 | 63.0 | 57.7 | 49.9 |
| 4.3 | 2.4 | 3.8 | Intangibles (net) | 4.2 | 2.1 | 1.2 | .6 | 1.8 | 13.8 |
| 6.3 | 6.1 | 5.9 | All Other Non-Current | 8.3 | 3.1 | 12.9 | 4.5 | 4.9 | 2.6 |
| 100.0 | 100.0 | 100.0 | Total | 100.0 | 100.0 | 100.0 | 100.0 | 100.0 | 100.0 |
| | | | **LIABILITIES** | | | | | | |
| 6.6 | 5.1 | 8.4 | Notes Payable-Short Term | 7.5 | 14.2 | 3.6 | 14.4 | 4.9 | 5.1 |
| 5.8 | 3.5 | 5.3 | Cur. Mat.-L.T.D. | 2.0 | 16.0 | 5.5 | 4.0 | 3.7 | 2.3 |
| 4.6 | 5.0 | 6.6 | Trade Payables | 4.3 | 11.6 | 6.0 | 4.9 | 6.9 | 6.7 |
| .2 | .3 | .1 | Income Taxes Payable | .0 | .0 | .1 | .0 | .1 | .1 |
| 12.1 | 8.7 | 9.3 | All Other Current | 16.0 | 18.6 | 4.9 | 7.2 | 6.4 | 6.2 |
| 29.4 | 22.7 | 29.5 | Total Current | 29.7 | 60.4 | 20.2 | 30.4 | 22.0 | 20.6 |
| 36.9 | 39.1 | 36.1 | Long-Term Debt | 54.5 | 32.3 | 30.7 | 42.9 | 30.6 | 26.8 |
| .8 | .9 | .5 | Deferred Taxes | .0 | .1 | | .3 | .8 | 1.6 |
| 7.2 | 9.1 | 12.0 | All Other Non-Current | 5.3 | 19.7 | 11.8 | 22.9 | 4.1 | 6.2 |
| 25.8 | 28.2 | 21.9 | Net Worth | 10.5 | -12.5 | 37.3 | 3.5 | 42.6 | 44.9 |
| 100.0 | 100.0 | 100.0 | Total Liabilities & Net Worth | 100.0 | 100.0 | 100.0 | 100.0 | 100.0 | 100.0 |
| | | | **INCOME DATA** | | | | | | |
| 100.0 | 100.0 | 100.0 | Net Sales | 100.0 | 100.0 | 100.0 | 100.0 | 100.0 | 100.0 |
| | | | Gross Profit | | | | | | |
| 86.4 | 83.4 | 87.4 | Operating Expenses | 63.3 | 98.8 | 85.7 | 91.9 | 90.3 | 90.1 |
| 13.6 | 16.6 | 12.6 | Operating Profit | 36.7 | 1.2 | 14.3 | 8.1 | 9.7 | 9.9 |
| 5.3 | 6.5 | 6.1 | All Other Expenses (net) | 17.9 | 7.2 | 4.3 | 4.2 | 2.3 | 4.0 |
| 8.3 | 10.0 | 6.6 | Profit Before Taxes | 18.9 | -6.0 | 10.1 | 3.9 | 7.4 | 5.8 |
| | | | **RATIOS** | | | | | | |
| 2.5 | 2.7 | 2.1 | | 2.0 | 7.0 | 1.9 | 2.1 | 2.1 | 2.1 |
| 1.1 | 1.4 | 1.3 | Current | .7 | 1.1 | 1.0 | 1.1 | 1.6 | 1.4 |
| .5 | .7 | .6 | | .2 | .2 | .4 | .6 | .8 | .9 |
| 2.1 | 2.3 | 1.8 | | 1.5 | 5.5 | 1.7 | 1.7 | 1.8 | 2.0 |
| .9 | 1.1 | .9 | Quick | .6 | .7 | 1.0 | .6 | 1.4 | 1.1 |
| .4 | .5 | .4 | | .1 | .1 | .4 | .2 | .6 | .6 |
| 17 21.8 | 14 25.8 | 16 23.3 | | 0 UND | 12 29.8 | 9 40.0 | 16 23.3 | 21 17.5 | 24 15.5 |
| 29 12.5 | 32 11.5 | 28 12.9 | Sales/Receivables | 0 UND | 27 13.4 | 23 15.7 | 30 12.3 | 32 11.4 | 44 8.3 |
| 41 9.0 | 46 8.0 | 47 7.8 | | 43 8.4 | 53 6.9 | 38 9.6 | 46 7.9 | 47 7.7 | 57 6.4 |
| | | | Cost of Sales/Inventory | | | | | | |
| | | | Cost of Sales/Payables | | | | | | |
| 9.1 | 6.2 | 8.0 | | 13.8 | 6.9 | 14.8 | 7.5 | 6.8 | 6.3 |
| 40.7 | 26.5 | 33.7 | Sales/Working Capital | -8.4 | NM | -195.8 | 84.4 | 13.2 | 16.7 |
| -9.6 | -18.4 | -12.3 | | -4.9 | -6.1 | -12.7 | -13.8 | -103.7 | -174.5 |
| 7.1 | 11.0 | 9.0 | | 16.5 | 1.0 | 52.6 | 4.8 | 12.9 | 7.6 |
| (96) 2.9 | (114) 3.0 | (107) 2.6 | EBIT/Interest | (10) 1.9 | (12) -5.2 | (16) 9.3 | (26) 2.1 | (23) 4.8 | (20) 3.2 |
| 1.2 | 1.5 | 1.0 | | .9 | -13.5 | 1.3 | 1.0 | 2.2 | -3.0 |
| 6.3 | 5.5 | 5.3 | Net Profit + Depr., Dep., | | | | | | |
| (32) 2.1 | (30) 2.8 | (22) 2.8 | Amort./Cur. Mat. L/T/D | | | | | | |
| 1.4 | 2.0 | 1.2 | | | | | | | |
| 1.0 | .9 | .7 | | .9 | .1 | .6 | 1.3 | .6 | .7 |
| 2.3 | 2.3 | 2.1 | Fixed/Worth | 14.9 | NM | 1.3 | 2.4 | 1.4 | 2.1 |
| 8.1 | 17.4 | 40.3 | | -2.2 | -1.1 | 12.5 | 24.5 | 3.3 | -31.4 |
| .9 | .8 | .8 | | .7 | .8 | .4 | 1.4 | 1.0 | 1.1 |
| 2.2 | 2.9 | 2.3 | Debt/Worth | 19.9 | -7.6 | 1.7 | 4.4 | 1.4 | 1.7 |
| 11.0 | 22.9 | -42.1 | | -3.6 | -2.1 | 14.4 | 38.4 | 2.8 | -62.7 |
| 37.8 | 39.7 | 41.6 | % Profit Before Taxes/Tangible | 113.5 | | 54.0 | 27.6 | 40.8 | 24.0 |
| (98) 16.7 | (121) 20.0 | (98) 18.6 | Net Worth | (12) 34.3 | | (17) 24.3 | (22) 9.8 | (24) 21.6 | (16) 14.5 |
| 6.2 | 9.7 | 4.5 | | -1.6 | | 2.2 | 2.1 | 7.1 | 9.4 |
| 12.6 | 12.2 | 11.8 | % Profit Before Taxes/Total | 15.6 | 3.9 | 19.9 | 8.4 | 14.4 | 10.5 |
| 5.9 | 6.1 | 4.2 | Assets | 3.6 | -9.9 | 7.8 | 2.7 | 9.4 | 4.8 |
| .6 | .9 | -.1 | | .1 | -42.1 | .8 | .1 | 3.5 | -3.4 |
| 6.0 | 5.9 | 8.3 | | 1.2 | 59.4 | 20.3 | 6.8 | 8.0 | 4.9 |
| 1.3 | 1.2 | 1.6 | Sales/Net Fixed Assets | .6 | 7.7 | 1.3 | 1.5 | 3.4 | 1.8 |
| .6 | .6 | .7 | | .2 | 2.0 | .4 | .7 | .7 | .7 |
| 2.4 | 2.0 | 2.9 | | .6 | 5.7 | 3.4 | 1.8 | 3.2 | 1.7 |
| .8 | .8 | 1.0 | Sales/Total Assets | .2 | 2.8 | 1.0 | .8 | 1.4 | 1.0 |
| .5 | .4 | .5 | | .2 | 1.4 | .3 | .6 | .6 | .5 |
| 3.4 | 3.5 | 3.7 | | 7.8 | 3.0 | 3.2 | 2.5 | 2.3 | 4.5 |
| (101) 7.9 | (132) 7.6 | (111) 7.1 | % Depr., Dep., Amort./Sales | (13) 20.0 | (11) 9.7 | (19) 5.4 | (27) 5.4 | (24) 5.8 | (17) 6.4 |
| 11.0 | 13.6 | 11.6 | | 35.2 | 15.3 | 17.8 | 8.4 | 9.6 | 9.0 |
| 2.2 | 1.4 | 2.6 | % Officers', Directors' | | | | | | |
| (20) 4.8 | (27) 3.2 | (28) 4.0 | Owners' Comp/Sales | | | | | | |
| 7.0 | 9.3 | 5.4 | | | | | | | |
| 2512483M | 2351709M | 2778271M | Net Sales ($) | 7899M | 34488M | 83389M | 198905M | 404510M | 2049080M |
| 3024988M | 2939234M | 3266273M | Total Assets ($) | 40957M | 33680M | 194433M | 266600M | 415726M | 2314877M |

M = $ thousand    MM = $ million
See Pages 9 through 22 for Explanation of Ratios and Data

**Current Data Sorted by Assets**     **Comparative Historical Data**

| 0-500M | 500M-2MM | 2-10MM | 10-50MM | 50-100MM | 100-250MM | Type of Statement | 4/1/07-3/31/08 ALL | 4/1/08-3/31/09 ALL |
|---|---|---|---|---|---|---|---|---|
| 1 | 3 | 12 | 6 |  | 3 | Unqualified | 35 | 32 |
| 1 | 6 | 14 | 5 | 1 |  | Reviewed | 35 | 37 |
|  | 2 | 4 | 2 |  |  | Compiled | 14 | 4 |
|  | 5 | 6 |  |  |  | Tax Returns | 5 | 6 |
| 1 | 2 | 3 | 6 | 1 |  | Other | 18 | 15 |
|  | 47 (4/1-9/30/11) | | | 37 (10/1/11-3/31/12) | | | | |
| 3 | 18 | 39 | 19 | 2 | 3 | NUMBER OF STATEMENTS | 107 | 94 |
| % | % | % | % | % | % | ASSETS | % | % |
|  | 13.1 | 11.5 | 10.6 |  |  | Cash & Equivalents | 9.0 | 10.7 |
|  | 24.0 | 15.9 | 14.6 |  |  | Trade Receivables (net) | 16.1 | 16.3 |
|  | 14.1 | 23.2 | 19.1 |  |  | Inventory | 27.2 | 23.3 |
|  | 4.1 | 8.6 | 8.7 |  |  | All Other Current | 7.3 | 10.4 |
|  | 55.2 | 59.2 | 53.1 |  |  | Total Current | 59.5 | 60.8 |
|  | 38.0 | 35.6 | 37.3 |  |  | Fixed Assets (net) | 34.0 | 32.9 |
|  | .8 | .1 | 1.0 |  |  | Intangibles (net) | .6 | .8 |
|  | 5.9 | 5.2 | 8.6 |  |  | All Other Non-Current | 5.8 | 5.5 |
|  | 100.0 | 100.0 | 100.0 |  |  | Total | 100.0 | 100.0 |
|  |  |  |  |  |  | LIABILITIES | | |
|  | 6.6 | 15.3 | 13.2 |  |  | Notes Payable-Short Term | 21.5 | 18.3 |
|  | 2.9 | 2.1 | 3.0 |  |  | Cur. Mat.-L.T.D. | 3.7 | 3.7 |
|  | 13.5 | 12.7 | 10.5 |  |  | Trade Payables | 10.9 | 10.3 |
|  | .0 | .7 | .0 |  |  | Income Taxes Payable | .4 | .4 |
|  | 13.2 | 9.0 | 9.6 |  |  | All Other Current | 10.6 | 11.5 |
|  | 36.2 | 39.8 | 36.4 |  |  | Total Current | 47.1 | 44.2 |
|  | 13.1 | 11.2 | 15.8 |  |  | Long-Term Debt | 15.4 | 13.1 |
|  | .8 | 1.2 | .6 |  |  | Deferred Taxes | .8 | .7 |
|  | .8 | 1.4 | 2.6 |  |  | All Other Non-Current | 1.8 | 1.5 |
|  | 49.2 | 46.4 | 44.6 |  |  | Net Worth | 35.0 | 40.6 |
|  | 100.0 | 100.0 | 100.0 |  |  | Total Liabilities & Net Worth | 100.0 | 100.0 |
|  |  |  |  |  |  | INCOME DATA | | |
|  | 100.0 | 100.0 | 100.0 |  |  | Net Sales | 100.0 | 100.0 |
|  |  |  |  |  |  | Gross Profit | | |
|  | 90.1 | 95.0 | 95.9 |  |  | Operating Expenses | 90.7 | 89.5 |
|  | 9.9 | 5.0 | 4.1 |  |  | Operating Profit | 9.3 | 10.5 |
|  | 2.4 | .1 | -.6 |  |  | All Other Expenses (net) | 2.5 | 1.5 |
|  | 7.6 | 4.9 | 4.7 |  |  | Profit Before Taxes | 6.8 | 9.0 |
|  |  |  |  |  |  | RATIOS | | |
|  | 3.1 | 2.4 | 3.1 |  |  | Current | 1.7 | 2.1 |
|  | 1.8 | 1.6 | 1.5 |  |  | | 1.2 | 1.3 |
|  | .9 | 1.1 | 1.1 |  |  | | 1.0 | 1.0 |
|  | 2.7 | 1.5 | 1.6 |  |  | Quick | 1.1 | 1.1 |
|  | 1.0 | .8 | .5 |  |  | | .5 | .5 |
|  | .4 | .3 | .3 |  |  | | .2 | .2 |
| 0 737.6 | 6 65.9 | 8 45.0 |  |  |  | Sales/Receivables | 6 58.4 | 5 78.0 |
| 17 21.7 | 16 22.9 | 28 13.2 |  |  |  | | 18 19.8 | 14 26.5 |
| 26 14.3 | 33 10.9 | 35 10.4 |  |  |  | | 41 8.9 | 38 9.6 |
|  |  |  |  |  |  | Cost of Sales/Inventory | | |
|  |  |  |  |  |  | | | |
|  |  |  |  |  |  | Cost of Sales/Payables | | |
|  |  |  |  |  |  | | | |
|  | 6.8 | 8.2 | 5.0 |  |  | Sales/Working Capital | 8.7 | 6.0 |
|  | 28.3 | 15.4 | 18.9 |  |  | | 26.4 | 20.2 |
|  | -48.1 | 29.0 | 63.9 |  |  | | 252.7 | 54.2 |
|  | 13.8 | 11.2 | 8.8 |  |  | EBIT/Interest | 6.1 | 13.5 |
|  | (12) 6.4 | (36) 4.9 | (18) 3.5 |  |  | | (102) 2.3 | (90) 3.4 |
|  | 3.6 | 2.0 | 2.1 |  |  | | 1.4 | 2.0 |
|  |  |  |  |  |  | Net Profit + Depr., Dep., Amort./Cur. Mat. L/T/D | 6.2 | 9.7 |
|  |  |  |  |  |  | | (31) 3.6 | (31) 4.7 |
|  |  |  |  |  |  | | 1.2 | 2.2 |
|  | .1 | .4 | .4 |  |  | Fixed/Worth | .5 | .4 |
|  | .7 | .7 | .9 |  |  | | 1.0 | .7 |
|  | 3.0 | 1.3 | 1.3 |  |  | | 1.7 | 1.2 |
|  | .2 | .5 | .5 |  |  | Debt/Worth | .9 | .7 |
|  | .9 | 1.2 | 1.5 |  |  | | 2.3 | 1.9 |
|  | 5.9 | 2.4 | 5.3 |  |  | | 4.9 | 4.3 |
|  | 23.9 | 34.8 | 33.1 |  |  | % Profit Before Taxes/Tangible Net Worth | 34.5 | 40.4 |
|  | (16) 12.8 | (38) 15.6 | (18) 13.8 |  |  | | (102) 17.1 | (91) 22.8 |
|  | 3.4 | 6.7 | 4.2 |  |  | | 7.5 | 9.2 |
|  | 11.5 | 15.8 | 8.6 |  |  | % Profit Before Taxes/Total Assets | 9.4 | 14.6 |
|  | 6.2 | 6.3 | 5.3 |  |  | | 5.1 | 7.1 |
|  | 2.0 | 3.2 | 2.6 |  |  | | 1.7 | 3.4 |
|  | 84.0 | 29.2 | 12.7 |  |  | Sales/Net Fixed Assets | 20.8 | 28.3 |
|  | 19.6 | 11.8 | 5.3 |  |  | | 8.2 | 11.6 |
|  | 1.8 | 2.5 | 2.1 |  |  | | 2.7 | 2.1 |
|  | 6.6 | 4.5 | 2.8 |  |  | Sales/Total Assets | 3.2 | 3.7 |
|  | 3.8 | 2.4 | 1.7 |  |  | | 2.1 | 2.0 |
|  | 1.0 | 1.3 | .8 |  |  | | 1.1 | .9 |
|  | .5 | .5 | .6 |  |  | % Depr., Dep., Amort./Sales | .8 | .6 |
|  | (14) 1.8 | (37) 1.0 | (17) 1.7 |  |  | | (96) 1.6 | (87) 1.4 |
|  | 4.9 | 3.6 | 3.6 |  |  | | 2.8 | 3.8 |
|  |  | .3 |  |  |  | % Officers', Directors' Owners' Comp/Sales | .8 | .3 |
|  |  | (13) 1.2 |  |  |  | | (23) 2.1 | (16) 1.2 |
|  |  | 2.7 |  |  |  | | 3.1 | 2.6 |
| 16107M | 107951M | 701748M | 1117256M | 308729M | 4962398M | Net Sales ($) | 3484657M | 4662486M |
| 1015M | 22608M | 180891M | 426401M | 138158M | 494120M | Total Assets ($) | 1809747M | 1784822M |

M = $ thousand    MM = $ million
See Pages 9 through 22 for Explanation of Ratios and Data

## Comparative Historical Data                          Current Data Sorted by Sales

| Hist 1 | Hist 2 | Hist 3 | Type of Statement | 0-1MM | 1-3MM | 3-5MM | 5-10MM | 10-25MM | 25MM & OVER |
|---|---|---|---|---|---|---|---|---|---|
| 25 | 30 | 25 | Unqualified | 1 | 1 | 1 | 5 | 7 | 10 |
| 38 | 28 | 27 | Reviewed | 1 | 1 | 4 | 4 | 11 | 6 |
| 6 | 6 | 8 | Compiled | | | 2 | 1 | 3 | 1 |
| 9 | 11 | 11 | Tax Returns | | | 1 | 1 | 4 | |
| 15 | 19 | 13 | Other | 3 | 2 | 1 | 2 | 4 | 6 |
| | | | | 2 | 3 | | 1 | 1 | |
| 4/1/09-3/31/10 ALL | 4/1/10-3/31/11 ALL | 4/1/11-3/31/12 ALL | | 47 (4/1-9/30/11) | | | 37 (10/1/11-3/31/12) | | |
| 93 | 94 | 84 | **NUMBER OF STATEMENTS** | 7 | 8 | 7 | 13 | 26 | 23 |
| % | % | % | **ASSETS** | % | % | % | % | % | % |
| 10.2 | 9.1 | 12.8 | Cash & Equivalents | | | | 11.4 | 11.4 | 12.5 |
| 13.5 | 16.0 | 17.8 | Trade Receivables (net) | | | | 16.5 | 19.2 | 17.2 |
| 23.4 | 24.4 | 20.9 | Inventory | | | | 17.7 | 27.1 | 31.3 |
| 6.1 | 7.2 | 7.5 | All Other Current | | | | 3.5 | 12.3 | 7.2 |
| 53.3 | 56.7 | 58.9 | Total Current | | | | 49.1 | 70.0 | 68.1 |
| 37.2 | 34.4 | 34.3 | Fixed Assets (net) | | | | 46.0 | 23.5 | 25.4 |
| .7 | .6 | .4 | Intangibles (net) | | | | .1 | .1 | .8 |
| 8.8 | 8.4 | 6.3 | All Other Non-Current | | | | 4.9 | 6.4 | 5.7 |
| 100.0 | 100.0 | 100.0 | Total | | | | 100.0 | 100.0 | 100.0 |
| | | | **LIABILITIES** | | | | | | |
| 12.1 | 12.8 | 13.0 | Notes Payable-Short Term | | | | 16.8 | 10.7 | 21.5 |
| 3.1 | 3.3 | 2.3 | Cur. Mat.-L.T.D. | | | | 2.2 | 3.0 | 1.2 |
| 11.1 | 14.2 | 11.9 | Trade Payables | | | | 5.0 | 16.9 | 11.7 |
| .4 | .1 | .3 | Income Taxes Payable | | | | 1.1 | .2 | .3 |
| 10.1 | 11.1 | 11.0 | All Other Current | | | | 7.7 | 12.2 | 13.0 |
| 36.8 | 41.6 | 38.5 | Total Current | | | | 32.9 | 43.0 | 47.6 |
| 15.4 | 16.8 | 11.9 | Long-Term Debt | | | | 17.8 | 7.6 | 9.6 |
| 1.1 | 1.2 | .9 | Deferred Taxes | | | | .7 | .6 | 1.6 |
| 1.8 | 3.6 | 2.3 | All Other Non-Current | | | | 4.7 | .3 | .5 |
| 44.9 | 36.8 | 46.3 | Net Worth | | | | 43.9 | 48.6 | 40.7 |
| 100.0 | 100.0 | 100.0 | Total Liabilities & Net Worth | | | | 100.0 | 100.0 | 100.0 |
| | | | **INCOME DATA** | | | | | | |
| 100.0 | 100.0 | 100.0 | Net Sales | | | | 100.0 | 100.0 | 100.0 |
| | | | Gross Profit | | | | | | |
| 90.6 | 94.8 | 94.4 | Operating Expenses | | | | 94.7 | 98.0 | 96.4 |
| 9.4 | 5.2 | 5.6 | Operating Profit | | | | 5.3 | 2.0 | 3.6 |
| 1.2 | .7 | .4 | All Other Expenses (net) | | | | -.6 | .0 | -.2 |
| 8.3 | 4.5 | 5.2 | Profit Before Taxes | | | | 5.9 | 1.9 | 3.8 |
| | | | **RATIOS** | | | | | | |
| 2.3 | 2.1 | 2.8 | | | | | 2.8 | 2.4 | 3.1 |
| 1.4 | 1.5 | 1.6 | Current | | | | 1.5 | 1.7 | 1.2 |
| 1.0 | 1.1 | 1.1 | | | | | 1.1 | 1.2 | 1.1 |
| 1.1 | 1.3 | 1.6 | | | | | 1.7 | 1.4 | 1.2 |
| .6 | .7 | .8 | Quick | | | | 1.2 | .7 | .5 |
| .3 | .3 | .3 | | | | | .4 | .3 | .3 |
| 4  85.4 | 9  42.1 | 6  60.6 | | | | | 1  396.4 | 5  80.5 | 1  260.6 |
| 17  22.0 | 20  18.3 | 17  21.7 | Sales/Receivables | | | | 26  14.3 | 12  29.4 | 17  22.1 |
| 33  11.0 | 42  8.8 | 33  11.1 | | | | | 45  8.1 | 29  12.4 | 29  12.5 |
| | | | Cost of Sales/Inventory | | | | | | |
| | | | Cost of Sales/Payables | | | | | | |
| 8.0 | 7.8 | 7.2 | | | | | 4.3 | 10.4 | 10.3 |
| 18.7 | 17.4 | 17.4 | Sales/Working Capital | | | | 14.3 | 17.5 | 21.8 |
| 151.9 | 42.4 | 89.8 | | | | | 175.6 | 46.2 | 52.0 |
| 11.4 | 10.9 | 13.5 | | | | | 11.2 | 18.7 | 17.5 |
| (87)  5.0 | (89)  4.0 | (72)  5.5 | EBIT/Interest | | | | (12)  6.2 | (22)  5.7 | (22)  5.0 |
| 2.5 | 1.8 | 2.1 | | | | | 2.1 | 2.9 | 2.4 |
| 24.4 | 7.5 | 6.1 | Net Profit + Depr., Dep., | | | | | | |
| (29)  6.0 | (32)  3.5 | (19)  4.3 | Amort./Cur. Mat. L/T/D | | | | | | |
| 3.1 | 1.4 | 2.5 | | | | | | | |
| .4 | .4 | .4 | | | | | .5 | .2 | .4 |
| .8 | .8 | .7 | Fixed/Worth | | | | .8 | .4 | .7 |
| 1.3 | 1.3 | 1.3 | | | | | 1.7 | .8 | 1.3 |
| .6 | .7 | .5 | | | | | .5 | .7 | .6 |
| 1.4 | 1.5 | 1.2 | Debt/Worth | | | | 1.1 | 1.2 | 2.1 |
| 3.1 | 4.1 | 3.4 | | | | | 3.9 | 1.7 | 5.4 |
| 34.7 | 24.3 | 34.9 | % Profit Before Taxes/Tangible | | | | 31.0 | 23.9 | 42.7 |
| (91)  21.1 | (88)  15.7 | (80)  15.3 | Net Worth | | | | (12)  13.1 | (24)  14.2 | 23.7 |
| 10.2 | 6.5 | 5.6 | | | | | 4.4 | 5.0 | 11.7 |
| 15.5 | 10.8 | 12.1 | % Profit Before Taxes/Total | | | | 13.0 | 11.6 | 14.0 |
| 6.8 | 4.6 | 5.8 | Assets | | | | 4.6 | 6.3 | 7.4 |
| 2.9 | 1.6 | 2.6 | | | | | 2.9 | 2.4 | 3.8 |
| 21.4 | 23.2 | 30.9 | | | | | 12.1 | 47.9 | 30.8 |
| 9.6 | 10.7 | 11.7 | Sales/Net Fixed Assets | | | | 5.0 | 24.7 | 14.3 |
| 1.5 | 3.1 | 3.0 | | | | | 1.2 | 10.1 | 8.3 |
| 3.7 | 3.6 | 4.7 | | | | | 3.4 | 6.4 | 6.8 |
| 1.8 | 2.3 | 2.6 | Sales/Total Assets | | | | 1.9 | 3.7 | 3.1 |
| .8 | 1.0 | 1.1 | | | | | .6 | 2.3 | 2.0 |
| .7 | .6 | .5 | | | | | .8 | .4 | .4 |
| (85)  1.6 | (89)  1.2 | (74)  1.3 | % Depr., Dep., Amort./Sales | | | | 2.8 | (24)  .7 | (19)  .6 |
| 4.3 | 3.3 | 3.7 | | | | | 4.0 | 1.6 | 1.3 |
| .6 | .4 | .3 | % Officers', Directors' | | | | | | |
| (21)  2.0 | (23)  1.5 | (19)  1.2 | Owners' Comp/Sales | | | | | | |
| 2.6 | 2.8 | 2.8 | | | | | | | |
| 2226041M | 3498477M | 7214189M | Net Sales ($) | 4592M | 15952M | 27003M | 93169M | 444376M | 6629097M |
| 1168421M | 1380378M | 1263193M | Total Assets ($) | 9911M | 16475M | 20196M | 106229M | 156711M | 953671M |

M = $ thousand    MM = $ million
See Pages 9 through 22 for Explanation of Ratios and Data

**Current Data Sorted by Assets**      **Comparative Historical Data**

| 0-500M | 500M-2MM | 2-10MM | 10-50MM | 50-100MM | 100-250MM | Type of Statement | 4/1/07-3/31/08 ALL | 4/1/08-3/31/09 ALL |
|---|---|---|---|---|---|---|---|---|
| | | | 9 | 3 | 2 | Unqualified | 9 | 8 |
| | 1 | 8 | 5 | | | Reviewed | 20 | 22 |
| 1 | 6 | 7 | | 1 | | Compiled | 12 | 10 |
| 10 | 8 | 7 | | | | Tax Returns | 13 | 19 |
| 5 | 12 | 13 | 8 | 3 | 2 | Other | 39 | 42 |
| 10 (4/1-9/30/11) | | | 101 (10/1/11-3/31/12) | | | | | |
| 16 | 27 | 35 | 22 | 7 | 4 | **NUMBER OF STATEMENTS** | 93 | 101 |
| % | % | % | % | % | % | **ASSETS** | % | % |
| 18.7 | 9.2 | 11.1 | 13.0 | | | Cash & Equivalents | 12.6 | 12.4 |
| 14.2 | 18.2 | 15.2 | 19.5 | | | Trade Receivables (net) | 20.9 | 20.9 |
| .5 | 4.9 | 2.3 | 6.7 | | | Inventory | 3.2 | 3.5 |
| 5.1 | .7 | 3.2 | 3.0 | | | All Other Current | 2.8 | 4.1 |
| 38.5 | 33.0 | 32.0 | 42.2 | | | Total Current | 39.5 | 40.9 |
| 45.0 | 52.4 | 54.8 | 36.4 | | | Fixed Assets (net) | 45.7 | 47.2 |
| .8 | 10.0 | 5.5 | 7.8 | | | Intangibles (net) | 8.1 | 5.1 |
| 15.7 | 4.6 | 7.8 | 13.5 | | | All Other Non-Current | 6.8 | 6.7 |
| 100.0 | 100.0 | 100.0 | 100.0 | | | Total | 100.0 | 100.0 |
| | | | | | | **LIABILITIES** | | |
| 13.5 | 7.4 | 3.8 | 5.1 | | | Notes Payable-Short Term | 6.7 | 11.9 |
| 7.9 | 4.3 | 3.0 | 3.3 | | | Cur. Mat.-L.T.D. | 4.3 | 6.6 |
| 4.8 | 5.2 | 4.1 | 9.9 | | | Trade Payables | 14.2 | 8.2 |
| .0 | .5 | .1 | .3 | | | Income Taxes Payable | .2 | .2 |
| 10.6 | 4.2 | 7.9 | 6.7 | | | All Other Current | 7.8 | 9.9 |
| 36.8 | 21.6 | 18.9 | 25.3 | | | Total Current | 33.1 | 36.8 |
| 57.3 | 34.7 | 41.5 | 20.3 | | | Long-Term Debt | 33.9 | 33.5 |
| .0 | .1 | .1 | .8 | | | Deferred Taxes | .2 | .2 |
| 1.2 | 7.0 | 4.3 | 3.6 | | | All Other Non-Current | 5.2 | 4.6 |
| 4.7 | 36.5 | 35.3 | 50.1 | | | Net Worth | 27.5 | 25.0 |
| 100.0 | 100.0 | 100.0 | 100.0 | | | Total Liabilties & Net Worth | 100.0 | 100.0 |
| | | | | | | **INCOME DATA** | | |
| 100.0 | 100.0 | 100.0 | 100.0 | | | Net Sales | 100.0 | 100.0 |
| | | | | | | Gross Profit | | |
| 75.7 | 82.1 | 71.9 | 86.2 | | | Operating Expenses | 83.3 | 86.1 |
| 24.3 | 17.9 | 28.1 | 13.8 | | | Operating Profit | 16.7 | 13.9 |
| 4.6 | 7.7 | 10.3 | 2.9 | | | All Other Expenses (net) | 5.0 | 7.6 |
| 19.7 | 10.2 | 17.8 | 10.9 | | | Profit Before Taxes | 11.7 | 6.2 |
| | | | | | | **RATIOS** | | |
| 3.8 | 2.5 | 3.4 | 2.7 | | | | 3.1 | 3.5 |
| 1.0 | 1.8 | 1.4 | 1.2 | | | Current | 1.5 | 1.4 |
| .4 | .9 | .7 | .6 | | | | .9 | .9 |
| 3.8 | 2.5 | 2.8 | 2.0 | | | | 2.5 | 2.8 |
| 1.0 | 1.6 | .9 | 1.0 | | | Quick | 1.2 | 1.2 |
| .4 | .8 | .6 | .4 | | | | .7 | .7 |
| 0 UND | 0 UND | 0 UND | 31 11.6 | | | | 7 55.4 | 10 38.3 |
| 0 UND | 1 314.0 | 25 14.5 | 42 8.6 | | | Sales/Receivables | 36 10.2 | 33 11.1 |
| 5 73.1 | 47 7.8 | 45 8.1 | 50 7.3 | | | | 54 6.7 | 45 8.1 |
| | | | | | | Cost of Sales/Inventory | | |
| | | | | | | Cost of Sales/Payables | | |
| 8.6 | 7.9 | 4.9 | 4.8 | | | | 5.8 | 6.7 |
| UND | 21.8 | 13.3 | 24.3 | | | Sales/Working Capital | 17.5 | 18.8 |
| -10.2 | -84.5 | -15.4 | -10.5 | | | | -68.6 | -46.9 |
| 24.4 | 11.9 | 13.2 | 27.3 | | | | 9.3 | 8.1 |
| (10) 4.7 | (20) 3.9 | (26) 4.0 | (18) 4.1 | | | EBIT/Interest | (73) 4.9 | (76) 3.9 |
| 2.1 | 2.2 | 1.9 | 1.8 | | | | 2.0 | 1.5 |
| | | | 7.1 | | | | 7.0 | 10.7 |
| | | | (10) 1.9 | | | Net Profit + Depr., Dep., Amort./Cur. Mat. L/T/D | (21) 2.5 | (15) 3.5 |
| | | | 1.3 | | | | .8 | 1.2 |
| .5 | .4 | .6 | .3 | | | | .6 | .5 |
| 4.4 | 1.4 | 2.9 | .7 | | | Fixed/Worth | 1.7 | 1.5 |
| -1.4 | 5.0 | 7.6 | 3.8 | | | | 9.5 | 7.6 |
| .6 | 1.0 | .7 | .4 | | | | .7 | .8 |
| 4.2 | 2.1 | 3.7 | 1.3 | | | Debt/Worth | 2.3 | 3.2 |
| -11.1 | 4.1 | 9.2 | 3.2 | | | | 48.4 | 15.4 |
| 58.4 | 40.0 | 49.2 | 55.2 | | | | 47.5 | 54.4 |
| (11) 25.1 | (22) 17.6 | (29) 25.3 | 21.9 | | | % Profit Before Taxes/Tangible Net Worth | (71) 29.1 | (84) 22.5 |
| 2.2 | 2.2 | 10.9 | 3.5 | | | | 10.9 | 1.7 |
| 45.9 | 15.0 | 15.8 | 16.6 | | | | 15.8 | 12.9 |
| 12.9 | 5.6 | 6.1 | 5.7 | | | % Profit Before Taxes/Total Assets | 7.9 | 5.1 |
| 2.3 | 1.0 | 2.2 | 1.2 | | | | 2.6 | -.2 |
| 289.4 | 10.0 | 7.7 | 19.9 | | | | 11.8 | 16.0 |
| 12.0 | 3.9 | 1.2 | 4.2 | | | Sales/Net Fixed Assets | 4.3 | 4.7 |
| .5 | .3 | .3 | 2.2 | | | | .8 | .8 |
| 6.2 | 2.9 | 1.9 | 2.1 | | | | 2.7 | 3.3 |
| 3.5 | 1.4 | .9 | 1.2 | | | Sales/Total Assets | 1.7 | 1.6 |
| .4 | .3 | .2 | .4 | | | | .5 | .5 |
| | 2.0 | 1.7 | 1.6 | | | | 1.9 | 2.1 |
| | (23) 5.5 | (32) 7.2 | 4.7 | | | % Depr., Dep., Amort./Sales | (78) 4.4 | (84) 5.0 |
| | 13.9 | 16.7 | 6.7 | | | | 9.3 | 9.2 |
| | | | | | | | 3.3 | 2.4 |
| | | | | | | % Officers', Directors' Owners' Comp/Sales | (20) 4.7 | (25) 5.2 |
| | | | | | | | 13.4 | 8.0 |
| 25473M | 51035M | 228941M | 815841M | 445366M | 549525M | Net Sales ($) | 1923904M | 1458707M |
| 4487M | 29990M | 174245M | 588351M | 503441M | 722230M | Total Assets ($) | 1317907M | 1001471M |

M = $ thousand    MM = $ million
See Pages 9 through 22 for Explanation of Ratios and Data

## Comparative Historical Data | Current Data Sorted by Sales

| Hist 1 | Hist 2 | Hist 3 | Type of Statement | 0-1MM | 1-3MM | 3-5MM | 5-10MM | 10-25MM | 25MM & OVER |
|---|---|---|---|---|---|---|---|---|---|
| 7 | 6 | 14 | Unqualified | | | | 1 | 2 | 11 |
| 25 | 23 | 14 | Reviewed | 1 | 1 | | 3 | 6 | 3 |
| 13 | 13 | 15 | Compiled | 6 | 2 | 3 | 2 | 1 | 1 |
| 18 | 23 | 25 | Tax Returns | 13 | 5 | 4 | 1 | 2 | |
| 44 | 53 | 43 | Other | 11 | 11 | 4 | 3 | 5 | 9 |
| 4/1/09-3/31/10 ALL | 4/1/10-3/31/11 ALL | 4/1/11-3/31/12 ALL | | 10 (4/1-9/30/11) | | | 101 (10/1/11-3/31/12) | | |
| 107 | 118 | 111 | **NUMBER OF STATEMENTS** | 31 | 19 | 11 | 10 | 16 | 24 |
| % | % | % | **ASSETS** | % | % | % | % | % | % |
| 9.8 | 10.5 | 11.5 | Cash & Equivalents | 10.5 | 15.5 | 10.9 | 7.2 | 14.1 | 10.1 |
| 18.3 | 18.9 | 16.7 | Trade Receivables (net) | 1.6 | 24.5 | 18.0 | 27.6 | 15.2 | 26.0 |
| 3.7 | 6.8 | 3.4 | Inventory | .2 | .3 | 11.7 | 3.3 | 3.0 | 6.4 |
| 3.5 | 3.9 | 3.2 | All Other Current | 2.0 | 2.2 | .6 | 1.8 | 5.1 | 6.0 |
| 35.2 | 40.1 | 34.8 | Total Current | 14.3 | 42.5 | 41.1 | 40.0 | 37.3 | 48.6 |
| 49.3 | 47.6 | 48.3 | Fixed Assets (net) | 73.9 | 42.7 | 45.0 | 45.1 | 35.1 | 31.2 |
| 6.5 | 5.4 | 7.8 | Intangibles (net) | 4.3 | 10.0 | 4.9 | 4.0 | 8.7 | 13.1 |
| 8.9 | 6.9 | 9.1 | All Other Non-Current | 7.5 | 4.9 | 8.9 | 10.9 | 18.8 | 7.2 |
| 100.0 | 100.0 | 100.0 | Total | 100.0 | 100.0 | 100.0 | 100.0 | 100.0 | 100.0 |
| | | | **LIABILITIES** | | | | | | |
| 6.1 | 5.5 | 6.1 | Notes Payable-Short Term | 5.3 | 5.1 | 9.8 | 8.5 | 7.3 | 4.7 |
| 4.5 | 3.4 | 4.2 | Cur. Mat.-L.T.D. | 3.1 | 7.0 | 4.5 | 1.5 | 6.2 | 2.9 |
| 6.1 | 7.9 | 5.7 | Trade Payables | .7 | 6.5 | 9.2 | 4.3 | 5.3 | 10.6 |
| .1 | .0 | .2 | Income Taxes Payable | .0 | .0 | 1.3 | .1 | .1 | .2 |
| 6.3 | 7.0 | 7.4 | All Other Current | 6.5 | 7.1 | 4.1 | 9.0 | 7.3 | 9.5 |
| 23.1 | 23.9 | 23.5 | Total Current | 15.7 | 25.7 | 28.8 | 23.5 | 26.0 | 28.0 |
| 41.6 | 39.5 | 36.9 | Long-Term Debt | 51.5 | 55.4 | 27.0 | 31.4 | 24.5 | 18.6 |
| .2 | .1 | .3 | Deferred Taxes | .0 | .1 | .3 | .4 | .7 | .6 |
| 8.0 | 5.1 | 4.5 | All Other Non-Current | 4.7 | 3.8 | .7 | 4.6 | 3.7 | 6.8 |
| 27.1 | 31.4 | 34.7 | Net Worth | 28.1 | 14.9 | 43.2 | 40.2 | 45.0 | 46.1 |
| 100.0 | 100.0 | 100.0 | Total Liabilities & Net Worth | 100.0 | 100.0 | 100.0 | 100.0 | 100.0 | 100.0 |
| | | | **INCOME DATA** | | | | | | |
| 100.0 | 100.0 | 100.0 | Net Sales | 100.0 | 100.0 | 100.0 | 100.0 | 100.0 | 100.0 |
| | | | Gross Profit | | | | | | |
| 83.4 | 82.2 | 79.4 | Operating Expenses | 59.2 | 81.5 | 90.5 | 89.8 | 83.3 | 91.9 |
| 16.6 | 17.8 | 20.6 | Operating Profit | 40.8 | 18.5 | 9.5 | 10.2 | 16.7 | 8.1 |
| 7.1 | 7.5 | 7.0 | All Other Expenses (net) | 17.5 | 3.7 | 2.1 | 4.0 | 2.2 | 3.0 |
| 9.5 | 10.3 | 13.6 | Profit Before Taxes | 23.3 | 14.8 | 7.5 | 6.2 | 14.6 | 5.2 |
| | | | **RATIOS** | | | | | | |
| 2.3 | 2.8 | 2.7 | Current | 2.5 | 5.9 | 2.1 | 2.7 | 2.8 | 2.6 |
| 1.5 | 1.5 | 1.4 | | 1.0 | 1.9 | 1.4 | 1.6 | 1.0 | 1.6 |
| .8 | .9 | .7 | | .4 | .8 | .7 | .9 | .5 | 1.1 |
| 2.1 | 2.4 | 2.4 | Quick | 2.3 | 5.6 | 1.6 | 2.7 | 2.7 | 1.8 |
| 1.1 | 1.0 | 1.2 | | .8 | 1.9 | .9 | 1.3 | .8 | 1.2 |
| .6 | .6 | .5 | | .2 | .8 | .4 | .7 | .4 | .9 |
| 5  76.6 | 0  UND | 0  UND | Sales/Receivables | 0  UND | 0  UND | 1  414.3 | 42  8.7 | 23  16.2 | 38  9.5 |
| 38  9.7 | 32  11.4 | 34  10.8 | | 0  UND | 34  10.8 | 38  9.5 | 45  8.1 | 35  10.3 | 49  7.5 |
| 52  7.1 | 50  7.3 | 50  7.3 | | 0  UND | 52  7.0 | 46  7.9 | 55  6.6 | 54  6.7 | 63  5.8 |
| | | | Cost of Sales/Inventory | | | | | | |
| | | | Cost of Sales/Payables | | | | | | |
| 7.2 | 5.6 | 7.0 | Sales/Working Capital | 7.0 | 7.8 | 6.6 | 6.2 | 7.2 | 4.8 |
| 17.6 | 13.5 | 22.0 | | -312.0 | 12.1 | 25.9 | 14.2 | NM | 11.0 |
| -33.0 | -70.5 | -24.0 | | -7.5 | -46.5 | -84.5 | -50.0 | -10.2 | 35.0 |
| 15.2 | 13.1 | 12.6 | EBIT/Interest | 6.9 | 7.3 | 8.3 | | 50.1 | 14.3 |
| (79) 3.6 | (83) 4.4 | (83) 4.3 | | (16) 3.0 | (16) 4.7 | (10) 2.6 | | (14) 18.6 | (21) 6.1 |
| 1.1 | 1.3 | 2.0 | | 1.8 | 2.5 | 1.7 | | 2.0 | 1.7 |
| 9.4 | 13.0 | 4.6 | Net Profit + Depr., Dep., Amort./Cur. Mat. L/T/D | | | | | | |
| (27) 5.1 | (24) 3.5 | (23) 2.1 | | | | | | | |
| 1.6 | 1.9 | 1.5 | | | | | | | |
| .6 | .5 | .5 | Fixed/Worth | 1.5 | .2 | .4 | .3 | .3 | .5 |
| 1.6 | 1.4 | 1.6 | | 4.5 | 1.1 | 1.2 | 1.9 | .7 | 1.0 |
| 12.2 | 8.9 | 7.8 | | 12.9 | -2.6 | 1.8 | 6.5 | 5.0 | 4.8 |
| .8 | .7 | .7 | Debt/Worth | 1.6 | .5 | 1.0 | .8 | .4 | .8 |
| 2.4 | 2.2 | 2.0 | | 4.0 | 2.0 | 1.6 | 2.3 | .9 | 1.5 |
| 31.1 | 15.1 | 9.2 | | 12.6 | -4.8 | 2.7 | 6.8 | 7.1 | 5.5 |
| 59.6 | 45.3 | 46.6 | % Profit Before Taxes/Tangible Net Worth | 39.8 | 54.9 | 50.2 | | 61.5 | 42.9 |
| (82) 25.5 | (97) 16.9 | (92) 22.9 | | (26) 16.3 | (12) 23.5 | (10) 33.9 | | (14) 38.0 | (21) 21.2 |
| 8.0 | 3.3 | 4.6 | | 2.3 | 2.5 | 5.1 | | 9.3 | 9.1 |
| 16.0 | 15.8 | 16.5 | % Profit Before Taxes/Total Assets | 9.1 | 25.4 | 20.3 | 22.3 | 32.8 | 14.5 |
| 5.1 | 5.7 | 6.9 | | 3.5 | 12.2 | 7.1 | 5.0 | 12.9 | 7.1 |
| .4 | .6 | 1.9 | | .1 | 2.0 | 3.9 | 1.2 | 3.5 | 1.5 |
| 11.4 | 17.7 | 12.9 | Sales/Net Fixed Assets | .9 | 13.9 | 48.2 | 25.6 | 32.3 | 22.9 |
| 3.3 | 3.2 | 2.9 | | .3 | 5.4 | 9.5 | 5.8 | 6.5 | 4.2 |
| .5 | .5 | .4 | | .2 | .9 | 1.2 | 1.0 | 2.0 | 2.5 |
| 2.7 | 2.7 | 2.6 | Sales/Total Assets | .6 | 4.0 | 5.7 | 2.5 | 2.2 | 3.0 |
| 1.3 | 1.3 | 1.0 | | .2 | 1.9 | 2.9 | 1.5 | 1.2 | 1.5 |
| .4 | .3 | .3 | | .2 | .8 | .9 | .8 | .4 | .7 |
| 2.6 | 1.9 | 2.0 | % Depr., Dep., Amort./Sales | 9.7 | 3.0 | | | 1.3 | 1.5 |
| (96) 5.3 | (92) 4.2 | (94) 5.5 | | (26) 14.2 | (14) 5.0 | | | (15) 4.0 | (21) 2.5 |
| 10.5 | 12.0 | 11.7 | | 21.0 | 11.1 | | | 6.6 | 5.6 |
| 2.0 | 1.9 | 3.9 | % Officers', Directors' Owners' Comp/Sales | | | | | | |
| (18) 4.6 | (27) 4.6 | (26) 6.5 | | | | | | | |
| 9.0 | 7.4 | 13.1 | | | | | | | |
| 2312895M | 2468656M | 2116181M | Net Sales ($) | 13475M | 33576M | 41051M | 71277M | 237709M | 1719093M |
| 2118779M | 1662112M | 2022744M | Total Assets ($) | 58464M | 38020M | 26988M | 90893M | 317442M | 1490937M |

M = $ thousand    MM = $ million
See Pages 9 through 22 for Explanation of Ratios and Data

# INFORMATION

## Current Data Sorted by Assets      Comparative Historical Data

| | 0-500M | 500M-2MM | 2-10MM | 10-50MM | 50-100MM | 100-250MM | | 4/1/07-3/31/08 ALL | 4/1/08-3/31/09 ALL |
|---|---|---|---|---|---|---|---|---|---|
| **Type of Statement** | | | | | | | | | |
| Unqualified | 1 | 2 | 2 | 6 | 5 | 3 | | 20 | 12 |
| Reviewed | | | 4 | 1 | 2 | | | 13 | 11 |
| Compiled | | | 3 | 1 | | | | 4 | 3 |
| Tax Returns | 7 | 8 | 5 | 2 | | | | 13 | 12 |
| Other | 2 | 6 | 7 | 8 | 5 | 3 | | 31 | 36 |
| | | 16 (4/1-9/30/11) | | | 71 (10/1/11-3/31/12) | | | | |
| **NUMBER OF STATEMENTS** | 10 | 20 | 21 | 18 | 12 | 6 | | 81 | 74 |
| | % | % | % | % | % | % | | % | % |
| **ASSETS** | | | | | | | | | |
| Cash & Equivalents | 10.6 | 16.7 | 13.1 | 7.0 | 7.5 | | | 10.9 | 11.5 |
| Trade Receivables (net) | 40.1 | 27.1 | 18.3 | 13.9 | 10.1 | | | 24.8 | 26.6 |
| Inventory | 3.5 | 4.5 | 1.9 | 2.9 | 1.3 | | | 4.3 | 3.0 |
| All Other Current | 1.5 | 1.1 | 1.0 | 7.7 | 3.4 | | | 3.9 | 2.4 |
| Total Current | 55.7 | 49.5 | 34.3 | 31.6 | 22.3 | | | 43.9 | 43.4 |
| Fixed Assets (net) | 19.5 | 31.9 | 35.5 | 27.6 | 35.9 | | | 25.4 | 25.5 |
| Intangibles (net) | 17.2 | 15.5 | 16.9 | 23.8 | 30.1 | | | 19.7 | 19.2 |
| All Other Non-Current | 7.7 | 3.1 | 13.2 | 17.1 | 11.7 | | | 11.0 | 12.0 |
| Total | 100.0 | 100.0 | 100.0 | 100.0 | 100.0 | | | 100.0 | 100.0 |
| **LIABILITIES** | | | | | | | | | |
| Notes Payable-Short Term | 20.9 | 7.5 | 3.7 | 1.6 | .0 | | | 3.1 | 7.4 |
| Cur. Mat.-L.T.D. | 6.3 | 2.2 | 2.8 | 4.9 | 10.2 | | | 3.9 | 4.3 |
| Trade Payables | 17.8 | 10.4 | 6.4 | 4.0 | 2.6 | | | 8.3 | 13.4 |
| Income Taxes Payable | .0 | .0 | .0 | .0 | .0 | | | .1 | .3 |
| All Other Current | 9.3 | 36.5 | 12.0 | 11.9 | 11.0 | | | 12.7 | 11.5 |
| Total Current | 54.4 | 56.6 | 25.0 | 22.4 | 23.8 | | | 28.1 | 37.0 |
| Long-Term Debt | 19.6 | 17.2 | 27.7 | 21.8 | 31.6 | | | 22.1 | 25.3 |
| Deferred Taxes | .0 | .0 | .9 | .2 | 1.7 | | | .5 | .6 |
| All Other Non-Current | 7.8 | 10.3 | 6.7 | 7.9 | 5.3 | | | 13.9 | 12.0 |
| Net Worth | 18.0 | 15.9 | 39.7 | 47.7 | 37.6 | | | 35.3 | 25.2 |
| Total Liabilities & Net Worth | 100.0 | 100.0 | 100.0 | 100.0 | 100.0 | | | 100.0 | 100.0 |
| **INCOME DATA** | | | | | | | | | |
| Net Sales | 100.0 | 100.0 | 100.0 | 100.0 | 100.0 | | | 100.0 | 100.0 |
| Gross Profit | 50.0 | 53.8 | 47.6 | 47.8 | 54.3 | | | 47.6 | 53.6 |
| Operating Expenses | 47.1 | 50.4 | 44.9 | 43.6 | 45.9 | | | 39.9 | 49.7 |
| Operating Profit | 2.9 | 3.4 | 2.7 | 4.2 | 8.4 | | | 7.7 | 3.9 |
| All Other Expenses (net) | .8 | .9 | 1.7 | 1.2 | 4.7 | | | 1.5 | 2.4 |
| Profit Before Taxes | 2.1 | 2.5 | 1.0 | 3.0 | 3.7 | | | 6.2 | 1.5 |
| **RATIOS** | | | | | | | | | |
| Current | 4.5 | 5.3 | 4.4 | 3.4 | 2.0 | | | 2.6 | 2.6 |
| | 1.0 | 1.6 | 1.5 | .9 | 1.1 | | | 1.8 | 1.3 |
| | .5 | 1.0 | .6 | .8 | .7 | | | 1.1 | .8 |
| Quick | 4.2 | 5.2 | 4.2 | 1.9 | 1.0 | | | 2.2 | 2.3 |
| | .7 | 1.3 | 1.1 | .7 | .8 | | | 1.4 | 1.1 |
| | .3 | .7 | .5 | .6 | .5 | | | .8 | .7 |
| Sales/Receivables | 0 UND | 14 26.7 | 27 13.3 | 29 12.4 | 29 12.7 | | | 35 10.4 | 31 11.9 |
| | 36 10.0 | 28 13.0 | 40 9.2 | 32 11.3 | 33 11.1 | | | 39 9.3 | 38 9.7 |
| | 60 6.1 | 55 6.6 | 49 7.4 | 41 8.8 | 37 9.9 | | | 49 7.5 | 47 7.7 |
| Cost of Sales/Inventory | 0 UND | 0 UND | 0 UND | 7 54.3 | 4 92.9 | | | 0 UND | 0 UND |
| | 0 UND | 0 UND | 7 52.9 | 13 28.6 | 12 29.5 | | | 6 63.0 | 7 53.2 |
| | 40 9.1 | 14 27.0 | 16 23.0 | 22 16.9 | 19 19.4 | | | 18 20.5 | 24 15.1 |
| Cost of Sales/Payables | 0 UND | 14 26.7 | 9 42.9 | 8 47.8 | 9 42.9 | | | 12 30.9 | 13 29.1 |
| | 8 47.9 | 27 13.5 | 24 14.9 | 18 20.6 | 20 18.0 | | | 23 15.9 | 28 13.0 |
| | 46 7.9 | 43 8.4 | 49 7.5 | 47 7.8 | 37 9.8 | | | 42 8.7 | 53 6.9 |
| Sales/Working Capital | 28.4 | 6.9 | 5.8 | 6.4 | 16.5 | | | 6.6 | 7.0 |
| | -488.8 | 22.1 | 14.8 | -77.3 | 126.6 | | | 13.2 | 15.2 |
| | -25.1 | NM | -15.5 | -18.3 | -15.6 | | | 67.4 | -26.2 |
| EBIT/Interest | | 9.5 | 4.6 | 7.4 | 6.4 | | | 12.5 | 7.7 |
| | | (15) 1.9 | (17) 1.9 | (13) 2.5 | (10) 2.8 | | | (67) 4.5 | (61) 1.6 |
| | | -1.5 | -.1 | -1.3 | .6 | | | 1.4 | -.6 |
| Net Profit + Depr., Dep., Amort./Cur. Mat. L/T/D | | | | | | | | 8.3 | 3.3 |
| | | | | | | | | (12) 2.5 | (15) 1.1 |
| | | | | | | | | 1.0 | .3 |
| Fixed/Worth | .0 | .1 | .5 | .2 | .9 | | | .3 | .3 |
| | 1.0 | 1.1 | 1.4 | 1.2 | 7.1 | | | 1.2 | 1.3 |
| | -1.3 | 7.1 | NM | -8.9 | -1.7 | | | -1.5 | -2.2 |
| Debt/Worth | 2.4 | .8 | .6 | .4 | .8 | | | .7 | .7 |
| | NM | 1.4 | 2.4 | 1.6 | 9.1 | | | 2.6 | 3.5 |
| | -2.7 | 9.8 | NM | -9.6 | -3.5 | | | -4.4 | -4.4 |
| % Profit Before Taxes/Tangible Net Worth | | 65.4 | 22.6 | 28.0 | | | | 52.5 | 27.0 |
| | | (16) 3.2 | (16) 6.9 | (12) 2.6 | | | | (53) 20.9 | (50) 7.8 |
| | | -25.1 | -7.2 | -2.6 | | | | 9.9 | -5.5 |
| % Profit Before Taxes/Total Assets | 41.5 | 29.1 | 9.4 | 8.8 | 16.5 | | | 14.9 | 10.9 |
| | 3.9 | 2.0 | 2.9 | 1.9 | 7.1 | | | 7.8 | 3.6 |
| | -19.9 | -7.9 | -4.6 | -2.0 | -.4 | | | 1.7 | -4.2 |
| Sales/Net Fixed Assets | UND | 106.4 | 9.4 | 16.6 | 8.0 | | | 36.6 | 30.3 |
| | 79.4 | 16.4 | 4.9 | 4.3 | 3.5 | | | 8.3 | 8.2 |
| | 10.9 | 4.1 | 2.4 | 2.4 | 1.9 | | | 3.5 | 4.1 |
| Sales/Total Assets | 9.3 | 4.7 | 1.9 | 1.7 | 1.3 | | | 2.7 | 2.5 |
| | 4.8 | 3.2 | 1.4 | 1.0 | 1.1 | | | 1.6 | 1.6 |
| | 3.2 | 1.7 | 1.0 | .6 | .8 | | | 1.1 | 1.1 |
| % Depr., Dep., Amort./Sales | | .6 | 1.1 | 2.2 | | | | 1.2 | 1.0 |
| | | (15) 1.8 | (19) 2.3 | (16) 3.3 | | | | (67) 2.7 | (58) 2.7 |
| | | 4.5 | 5.2 | 5.2 | | | | 4.8 | 4.3 |
| % Officers', Directors' Owners' Comp/Sales | | 2.4 | | | | | | 1.6 | 1.1 |
| | | (10) 4.6 | | | | | | (19) 3.8 | (20) 3.3 |
| | | 7.6 | | | | | | 5.4 | 6.1 |
| Net Sales ($) | 9173M | 74926M | 158977M | 450761M | 909672M | 1109201M | | 2943685M | 1826852M |
| Total Assets ($) | 2043M | 23361M | 109574M | 391376M | 829979M | 944486M | | 2751466M | 1537891M |

M = $ thousand     MM = $ million
See Pages 9 through 22 for Explanation of Ratios and Data

## Comparative Historical Data | Current Data Sorted by Sales

| 4/1/09-3/31/10 ALL | 4/1/10-3/31/11 ALL | 4/1/11-3/31/12 ALL | Type of Statement | 0-1MM | 1-3MM | 3-5MM | 5-10MM | 10-25MM | 25MM & OVER |
|---|---|---|---|---|---|---|---|---|---|
| 20 | 11 | 19 | Unqualified | 2 | | | 2 | 5 | 10 |
| 6 | 9 | 7 | Reviewed | | 1 | 1 | 2 | 2 | 1 |
| 1 | 5 | 8 | Compiled | | 4 | | 2 | 2 | |
| 17 | 14 | 22 | Tax Returns | 4 | 7 | 6 | 4 | | 1 |
| 27 | 42 | 31 | Other | 2 | 1 | 4 | 9 | 3 | 12 |
| | | | | 16 (4/1-9/30/11) | | | 71 (10/1/11-3/31/12) | | |
| 71 | 81 | 87 | **NUMBER OF STATEMENTS** | 8 | 13 | 11 | 19 | 12 | 24 |
| % | % | % | **ASSETS** | % | % | % | % | % | % |
| 11.6 | 12.7 | 11.6 | Cash & Equivalents | 15.1 | 13.2 | 12.9 | 7.3 | | 11.4 |
| 23.0 | 21.9 | 20.2 | Trade Receivables (net) | 27.1 | 27.6 | 17.8 | 18.3 | | 13.7 |
| 3.3 | 4.0 | 2.8 | Inventory | 1.1 | 6.7 | 1.9 | 2.4 | | 2.7 |
| 2.8 | 3.1 | 3.0 | All Other Current | .8 | 1.0 | 5.6 | 1.6 | | 4.1 |
| 40.7 | 41.8 | 37.6 | Total Current | 44.1 | 48.5 | 38.2 | 29.6 | | 31.9 |
| 28.1 | 29.2 | 32.0 | Fixed Assets (net) | 30.8 | 25.8 | 32.4 | 29.0 | | 38.9 |
| 19.8 | 18.4 | 20.1 | Intangibles (net) | 6.0 | 21.1 | 21.5 | 23.0 | | 20.0 |
| 11.4 | 10.6 | 10.3 | All Other Non-Current | 19.1 | 4.6 | 7.9 | 18.3 | | 9.2 |
| 100.0 | 100.0 | 100.0 | Total | 100.0 | 100.0 | 100.0 | 100.0 | | 100.0 |
| | | | **LIABILITIES** | | | | | | |
| 6.8 | 6.7 | 5.5 | Notes Payable-Short Term | 7.6 | 5.1 | 4.9 | 3.7 | | 1.0 |
| 4.3 | 4.3 | 4.4 | Cur. Mat.-L.T.D. | 7.4 | 1.5 | 1.0 | 2.9 | | 7.8 |
| 9.6 | 8.8 | 7.4 | Trade Payables | 10.7 | 12.7 | 6.9 | 5.5 | | 3.7 |
| .2 | .1 | .0 | Income Taxes Payable | .0 | .0 | .0 | .0 | | .0 |
| 15.1 | 10.8 | 17.0 | All Other Current | 12.1 | 13.0 | 35.5 | 10.8 | | 13.1 |
| 36.0 | 30.8 | 34.4 | Total Current | 37.8 | 32.3 | 48.4 | 22.9 | | 25.6 |
| 24.4 | 24.3 | 24.4 | Long-Term Debt | 35.6 | 22.9 | 23.0 | 16.3 | | 28.8 |
| .4 | .4 | .5 | Deferred Taxes | .2 | .0 | .5 | .9 | | 1.0 |
| 17.6 | 6.8 | 8.8 | All Other Non-Current | 6.7 | 7.8 | 8.1 | 5.5 | | 10.7 |
| 21.6 | 37.7 | 32.0 | Net Worth | 19.7 | 37.0 | 20.1 | 54.3 | | 33.8 |
| 100.0 | 100.0 | 100.0 | Total Liabilities & Net Worth | 100.0 | 100.0 | 100.0 | 100.0 | | 100.0 |
| | | | **INCOME DATA** | | | | | | |
| 100.0 | 100.0 | 100.0 | Net Sales | 100.0 | 100.0 | 100.0 | 100.0 | | 100.0 |
| 50.0 | 55.6 | 51.2 | Gross Profit | 61.5 | 51.1 | 44.7 | 51.2 | | 51.9 |
| 46.9 | 49.7 | 46.9 | Operating Expenses | 58.3 | 49.9 | 41.6 | 47.7 | | 44.5 |
| 3.1 | 5.9 | 4.3 | Operating Profit | 3.2 | 1.2 | 3.1 | 3.6 | | 7.4 |
| 2.0 | 2.4 | 1.8 | All Other Expenses (net) | 2.3 | 1.7 | .6 | 2.3 | | 2.4 |
| 1.1 | 3.5 | 2.5 | Profit Before Taxes | .9 | -.5 | 2.5 | 1.3 | | 5.0 |
| | | | **RATIOS** | | | | | | |
| 2.5 | 2.9 | 3.3 | | 3.6 | 5.7 | 5.5 | 2.4 | | 2.6 |
| 1.4 | 1.4 | 1.2 | Current | 1.3 | 1.9 | 1.5 | 1.0 | | 1.1 |
| .8 | .9 | .8 | | .6 | .9 | .9 | .7 | | .8 |
| 1.9 | 2.3 | 2.4 | | 3.2 | 5.6 | 4.5 | 2.2 | | 2.0 |
| 1.1 | 1.0 | 1.0 | Quick | 1.3 | 1.7 | 1.1 | .7 | | .8 |
| .7 | .7 | .6 | | .5 | .6 | .7 | .6 | | .6 |
| 33  11.2 | 30  12.3 | 27  13.3 | | 18  20.3 | 25  14.5 | 21  17.4 | 29  12.5 | | 30  12.2 |
| 39  9.5 | 37  9.9 | 36  10.2 | Sales/Receivables | 38  9.5 | 41  9.0 | 33  11.2 | 38  9.6 | | 35  10.4 |
| 50  7.2 | 52  7.1 | 46  8.0 | | 61  6.0 | 53  6.9 | 46  7.9 | 56  6.5 | | 39  9.3 |
| 0  UND | 0  UND | 0  UND | | 0  UND | 0  UND | 0  UND | 7  54.6 | | 7  54.6 |
| 6  66.3 | 9  42.7 | 8  46.4 | Cost of Sales/Inventory | 0  UND | 10  36.6 | 3  140.5 | 14  26.0 | | 14  26.0 |
| 16  22.9 | 26  14.2 | 19  19.4 | | 16  23.1 | 79  4.6 | 12  29.8 | 19  18.8 | | 29  12.6 |
| 10  37.0 | 11  33.2 | 8  46.8 | | 6  59.3 | 20  18.6 | 3  108.2 | 12  31.2 | | 11  32.0 |
| 17  20.9 | 24  15.3 | 24  15.1 | Cost of Sales/Payables | 28  13.0 | 28  13.2 | 23  15.6 | 22  16.6 | | 23  15.9 |
| 44  8.4 | 55  6.6 | 42  8.6 | | 46  7.9 | 51  7.1 | 40  9.2 | 51  7.1 | | 41  8.9 |
| 7.7 | 7.1 | 6.4 | | 7.6 | 4.9 | 5.7 | 7.7 | | 5.3 |
| 31.5 | 22.4 | 68.0 | Sales/Working Capital | 26.1 | 9.5 | 49.7 | NM | | 126.6 |
| -24.2 | -35.4 | -27.5 | | -12.2 | -60.3 | -54.8 | -20.5 | | -29.2 |
| 4.4 | 6.4 | 6.7 | | 1.9 | | 4.6 | 7.8 | | 8.9 |
| (57) 1.0 | (66) 2.9 | (68) 2.3 | EBIT/Interest | (11) .5 | | (13) 3.5 | (10) 4.0 | | (19) 3.3 |
| -.9 | -.1 | -.3 | | -1.6 | | .3 | -1.9 | | .7 |
| | 4.2 | 3.3 | | | | | | | |
| (17) 2.0 | (14) 2.4 | | Net Profit + Depr., Dep., Amort./Cur. Mat. L/T/D | | | | | | |
| | .5 | .9 | | | | | | | |
| .5 | .3 | .4 | | .2 | .2 | .4 | .3 | | .4 |
| 2.9 | 1.2 | 1.4 | Fixed/Worth | 1.2 | 1.4 | .8 | 1.4 | | 3.6 |
| -1.2 | -4.9 | -5.5 | | -1.2 | -.3 | -6.1 | 3.3 | | -3.0 |
| .6 | .5 | .9 | | 1.0 | 1.0 | .4 | .7 | | .6 |
| 8.3 | 2.4 | 2.8 | Debt/Worth | 2.7 | 2.5 | 1.8 | 1.6 | | 5.8 |
| -2.8 | -6.7 | -7.9 | | -3.0 | -10.1 | -10.0 | 6.3 | | -6.1 |
| 25.6 | 49.2 | 45.7 | | | | | 26.5 | 35.6 | 51.9 |
| (40) 9.3 | (55) 13.6 | (59) 6.8 | % Profit Before Taxes/Tangible Net Worth | | | (14) 5.0 | (10) 11.0 | | (14) 13.1 |
| -7.6 | -5.1 | -7.8 | | | | -3.0 | -32.6 | | -2.4 |
| 8.1 | 12.3 | 11.5 | | 24.4 | 16.6 | 6.4 | 9.5 | | 15.7 |
| 1.9 | 5.0 | 2.9 | % Profit Before Taxes/Total Assets | -1.4 | 2.3 | 2.9 | 7.1 | | 5.0 |
| -5.0 | -2.5 | -4.4 | | -10.8 | -10.3 | -4.7 | -8.1 | | -.4 |
| 30.8 | 27.4 | 25.2 | | 239.7 | 59.7 | 32.2 | 19.3 | | 7.8 |
| 7.4 | 6.7 | 5.0 | Sales/Net Fixed Assets | 9.0 | 11.6 | 6.8 | 4.6 | | 3.3 |
| 2.9 | 2.5 | 2.5 | | 2.2 | 4.0 | 2.5 | 2.3 | | 2.4 |
| 2.6 | 2.6 | 2.9 | | 4.4 | 3.7 | 4.2 | 1.9 | | 1.8 |
| 1.4 | 1.7 | 1.6 | Sales/Total Assets | 1.8 | 2.0 | 1.6 | 1.2 | | 1.1 |
| 1.0 | .9 | .9 | | 1.0 | 1.4 | .8 | .6 | | .9 |
| 1.0 | 1.1 | 1.3 | | 1.0 | | .7 | 2.0 | | 3.0 |
| (57) 3.2 | (65) 3.0 | (66) 3.2 | % Depr., Dep., Amort./Sales | (10) 4.0 | | (17) 1.7 | (11) 2.8 | | (17) 4.2 |
| 4.8 | 5.3 | 5.2 | | 6.5 | | 4.6 | 3.6 | | 5.3 |
| 2.1 | 2.3 | 2.0 | | | | | | | |
| (13) 3.3 | (19) 7.3 | (24) 3.7 | % Officers', Directors', Owners' Comp/Sales | | | | | | |
| 15.7 | 9.2 | 7.5 | | | | | | | |
| 2236585M | 2256780M | 2712710M | Net Sales ($) | 3220M | 26286M | 42587M | 135548M | 215777M | 2289292M |
| 2043962M | 2187744M | 2300819M | Total Assets ($) | 2805M | 18159M | 26677M | 121376M | 244000M | 1887802M |

© RMA 2012    M = $ thousand    MM = $ million
See Pages 9 through 22 for Explanation of Ratios and Data

## Current Data Sorted by Assets / Comparative Historical Data

### Type of Statement

| Type of Statement | 0-500M | 500M-2MM | 2-10MM | 10-50MM | 50-100MM | 100-250MM | 4/1/07-3/31/08 ALL | 4/1/08-3/31/09 ALL |
|---|---|---|---|---|---|---|---|---|
| Unqualified | | 1 | 6 | 7 | 6 | 1 | 25 | 24 |
| Reviewed | | | 5 | 8 | | | 15 | 10 |
| Compiled | 1 | 6 | 5 | 1 | | | 9 | 8 |
| Tax Returns | 2 | 4 | 5 | 2 | | | 13 | 13 |
| Other | 5 | 7 | 17 | 16 | 5 | 3 | 37 | 53 |
| | | 20 (4/1-9/30/11) | | 93 (10/1/11-3/31/12) | | | | |
| NUMBER OF STATEMENTS | 8 | 18 | 38 | 34 | 11 | 4 | 99 | 108 |

### Financial Data

| 0-500M % | 500M-2MM % | 2-10MM % | 10-50MM % | 50-100MM % | 100-250MM % | | 4/1/07-3/31/08 ALL % | 4/1/08-3/31/09 ALL % |
|---|---|---|---|---|---|---|---|---|
| | | | | | | **ASSETS** | | |
| | 23.5 | 17.1 | 16.3 | 15.0 | | Cash & Equivalents | 13.8 | 13.9 |
| | 33.3 | 29.9 | 18.4 | 14.5 | | Trade Receivables (net) | 27.2 | 26.8 |
| | 12.2 | 6.0 | 5.7 | 1.7 | | Inventory | 6.0 | 5.2 |
| | 3.0 | 3.1 | 4.2 | .9 | | All Other Current | 4.4 | 4.7 |
| | 72.1 | 56.1 | 44.7 | 32.1 | | Total Current | 51.5 | 50.6 |
| | 15.6 | 17.8 | 11.9 | 7.9 | | Fixed Assets (net) | 18.5 | 14.0 |
| | 2.5 | 15.9 | 31.3 | 49.8 | | Intangibles (net) | 17.0 | 22.0 |
| | 9.9 | 10.2 | 12.0 | 10.3 | | All Other Non-Current | 13.0 | 13.4 |
| | 100.0 | 100.0 | 100.0 | 100.0 | | Total | 100.0 | 100.0 |
| | | | | | | **LIABILITIES** | | |
| | 18.4 | 5.9 | 1.4 | 1.8 | | Notes Payable-Short Term | 7.7 | 6.7 |
| | 4.3 | 10.8 | 4.0 | 2.6 | | Cur. Mat.-L.T.D. | 4.2 | 3.6 |
| | 16.8 | 11.9 | 9.0 | 5.2 | | Trade Payables | 12.5 | 14.0 |
| | .0 | .1 | .5 | .2 | | Income Taxes Payable | .2 | .8 |
| | 10.9 | 24.4 | 19.5 | 29.3 | | All Other Current | 21.9 | 17.7 |
| | 50.4 | 53.2 | 34.4 | 39.0 | | Total Current | 46.5 | 42.8 |
| | 9.5 | 18.9 | 17.9 | 21.6 | | Long-Term Debt | 24.0 | 26.4 |
| | .0 | .7 | .4 | .4 | | Deferred Taxes | .2 | .2 |
| | 7.7 | 14.5 | 18.2 | 7.9 | | All Other Non-Current | 19.5 | 20.0 |
| | 32.5 | 12.7 | 29.2 | 31.1 | | Net Worth | 9.8 | 10.5 |
| | 100.0 | 100.0 | 100.0 | 100.0 | | Total Liabilities & Net Worth | 100.0 | 100.0 |
| | | | | | | **INCOME DATA** | | |
| | 100.0 | 100.0 | 100.0 | 100.0 | | Net Sales | 100.0 | 100.0 |
| | 48.9 | 55.4 | 49.8 | 45.6 | | Gross Profit | 48.2 | 51.8 |
| | 44.5 | 50.2 | 43.5 | 34.1 | | Operating Expenses | 41.5 | 47.1 |
| | 4.3 | 5.2 | 6.3 | 11.4 | | Operating Profit | 6.8 | 4.7 |
| | .7 | 1.4 | 2.0 | 4.7 | | All Other Expenses (net) | 1.5 | 2.1 |
| | 3.6 | 3.8 | 4.2 | 6.7 | | Profit Before Taxes | 5.2 | 2.6 |
| | | | | | | **RATIOS** | | |
| | 2.4 | 2.5 | 2.9 | 1.0 | | Current | 2.1 | 2.3 |
| | 1.4 | 1.2 | 1.3 | .8 | | | 1.4 | 1.3 |
| | 1.1 | .7 | .7 | .7 | | | .8 | .7 |
| | 1.8 | 2.4 | 2.4 | .9 | | Quick | 1.6 | 2.0 |
| | 1.0 | 1.1 | 1.1 | .7 | | | (98) 1.1 | .9 |
| | .9 | .7 | .5 | .5 | | | .6 | .5 |
| | 12 30.3 | 26 14.0 | 26 14.0 | 12 29.6 | | Sales/Receivables | 30 12.0 | 23 15.9 |
| | 31 11.6 | 37 9.9 | 35 10.5 | 42 8.6 | | | 41 8.9 | 37 10.0 |
| | 49 7.4 | 61 6.0 | 60 6.1 | 66 5.5 | | | 61 6.0 | 56 6.5 |
| | 0 UND | 0 UND | 0 UND | 2 168.8 | | Cost of Sales/Inventory | 0 UND | 0 UND |
| | 0 UND | 0 UND | 8 45.1 | 4 94.3 | | | 5 68.1 | 5 74.5 |
| | 23 16.2 | 18 19.8 | 33 11.0 | 24 15.0 | | | 29 12.6 | 25 14.4 |
| | 3 116.0 | 16 23.5 | 18 20.7 | 9 42.4 | | Cost of Sales/Payables | 18 20.8 | 15 23.8 |
| | 13 27.6 | 37 9.8 | 33 11.1 | 27 13.5 | | | 29 12.6 | 32 11.5 |
| | 38 9.6 | 70 5.2 | 52 7.0 | 49 7.5 | | | 58 6.3 | 66 5.6 |
| | 6.1 | 6.5 | 4.7 | -999.8 | | Sales/Working Capital | 7.0 | 6.6 |
| | 19.1 | 21.3 | 19.5 | -13.1 | | | 18.2 | 25.4 |
| | 167.7 | -22.6 | -12.4 | -7.1 | | | -29.8 | -15.0 |
| | 6.7 | 23.2 | 25.4 | | | EBIT/Interest | 9.2 | 20.6 |
| | (13) 1.9 | (35) 2.7 | (27) 5.6 | | | | (84) 3.4 | (89) 3.0 |
| | -2.0 | .1 | 1.1 | | | | .8 | .1 |
| | | | | | | Net Profit + Depr., Dep., Amort./Cur. Mat. L/T/D | 24.8 | 5.1 |
| | | | | | | | (22) 3.3 | (23) 2.0 |
| | | | | | | | .4 | .3 |
| | .0 | .4 | .4 | 2.0 | | Fixed/Worth | .3 | .3 |
| | .4 | 2.8 | -1.0 | -.3 | | | 1.8 | -2.1 |
| | 1.8 | -.1 | -.1 | -.1 | | | -.4 | -.2 |
| | 1.2 | 1.3 | .9 | 16.7 | | Debt/Worth | 1.3 | 1.5 |
| | 2.1 | 6.3 | -9.2 | -3.2 | | | 5.9 | -14.2 |
| | 6.8 | -2.4 | -2.1 | -1.7 | | | -3.5 | -2.8 |
| | 115.5 | 77.7 | 51.1 | | | % Profit Before Taxes/Tangible Net Worth | 65.3 | 77.2 |
| | (15) 37.3 | (21) 35.4 | (15) 10.4 | | | | (62) 29.7 | (48) 33.3 |
| | 11.3 | 4.5 | 6.2 | | | | 1.2 | 2.5 |
| | 30.7 | 21.2 | 13.9 | 17.7 | | % Profit Before Taxes/Total Assets | 16.9 | 16.7 |
| | 9.8 | 7.2 | 7.0 | 8.0 | | | 7.8 | 4.7 |
| | -2.0 | -2.8 | .2 | -5.5 | | | -.9 | -3.6 |
| | 394.9 | 69.9 | 37.4 | 28.9 | | Sales/Net Fixed Assets | 45.5 | 60.8 |
| | 44.0 | 28.1 | 19.5 | 17.2 | | | 18.4 | 28.2 |
| | 14.3 | 8.1 | 8.2 | 11.0 | | | 8.2 | 10.5 |
| | 5.0 | 2.9 | 2.0 | 1.3 | | Sales/Total Assets | 3.0 | 3.5 |
| | 3.6 | 2.3 | 1.5 | .9 | | | 2.0 | 2.0 |
| | 2.4 | 1.6 | 1.1 | .7 | | | 1.2 | 1.2 |
| | .5 | .6 | 1.1 | | | % Depr., Dep., Amort./Sales | .6 | .8 |
| | (10) 1.2 | (26) 1.4 | (21) 1.7 | | | | (76) 1.4 | (64) 1.5 |
| | 2.0 | 2.4 | 2.8 | | | | 3.1 | 3.8 |
| | 4.7 | | | | | % Officers', Directors' Owners' Comp/Sales | 2.8 | 2.5 |
| | (10) 5.5 | | | | | | (29) 4.3 | (26) 4.3 |
| | 8.4 | | | | | | 6.4 | 7.0 |
| 13700M | 78121M | 445291M | 1300272M | 812333M | 821668M | Net Sales ($) | 2763068M | 3011835M |
| 2215M | 18772M | 202968M | 898899M | 769841M | 704385M | Total Assets ($) | 2196962M | 2852811M |

M = $ thousand    MM = $ million
See Pages 9 through 22 for Explanation of Ratios and Data

## Comparative Historical Data | Current Data Sorted by Sales

| | 4/1/09-3/31/10 ALL | 4/1/10-3/31/11 ALL | 4/1/11-3/31/12 ALL | 0-1MM | 1-3MM | 3-5MM | 5-10MM | 10-25MM | 25MM & OVER |
|---|---|---|---|---|---|---|---|---|---|
| **Type of Statement** | | | | | 20 (4/1-9/30/11) | | 93 (10/1/11-3/31/12) | | |
| Unqualified | 17 | 21 | 21 | | 1 | | 2 | 5 | 13 |
| Reviewed | 11 | 8 | 13 | | 4 | | 5 | | 4 |
| Compiled | 9 | 16 | 13 | 1 | 4 | 2 | 2 | 4 | |
| Tax Returns | 10 | 9 | 13 | | 3 | 1 | 6 | 3 | |
| Other | 58 | 54 | 53 | 2 | 4 | 4 | 5 | 19 | 19 |
| **NUMBER OF STATEMENTS** | 105 | 108 | 113 | 3 | 12 | 7 | 19 | 36 | 36 |
| | % | % | % | % | % | % | % | % | % |
| **ASSETS** | | | | | | | | | |
| Cash & Equivalents | 14.2 | 16.8 | 16.0 | | 18.2 | | 22.8 | 18.4 | 10.9 |
| Trade Receivables (net) | 25.6 | 26.4 | 26.3 | | 31.5 | | 29.7 | 26.8 | 17.6 |
| Inventory | 5.9 | 5.6 | 6.2 | | 15.2 | | 3.5 | 7.7 | 4.3 |
| All Other Current | 4.6 | 4.3 | 4.2 | | 2.3 | | 1.8 | 4.3 | 6.3 |
| Total Current | 50.3 | 53.1 | 52.8 | | 67.3 | | 57.8 | 57.2 | 39.1 |
| Fixed Assets (net) | 14.8 | 15.2 | 14.2 | | 23.9 | | 14.7 | 16.7 | 11.1 |
| Intangibles (net) | 25.8 | 22.5 | 22.6 | | 2.1 | | 13.6 | 17.0 | 39.4 |
| All Other Non-Current | 9.1 | 9.2 | 10.4 | | 6.8 | | 13.9 | 9.1 | 10.4 |
| Total | 100.0 | 100.0 | 100.0 | | 100.0 | | 100.0 | 100.0 | 100.0 |
| **LIABILITIES** | | | | | | | | | |
| Notes Payable-Short Term | 8.2 | 13.9 | 8.1 | | 27.7 | | 11.0 | 5.2 | 1.3 |
| Cur. Mat.-L.T.D. | 6.8 | 4.9 | 6.2 | | 4.1 | | 1.7 | 12.1 | 3.4 |
| Trade Payables | 12.9 | 10.2 | 14.3 | | 28.6 | | 14.7 | 11.2 | 8.9 |
| Income Taxes Payable | .3 | .2 | .2 | | .0 | | .0 | .5 | .1 |
| All Other Current | 21.8 | 20.0 | 21.9 | | 16.5 | | 18.6 | 24.5 | 25.8 |
| Total Current | 50.0 | 49.2 | 50.7 | | 76.9 | | 46.1 | 53.6 | 39.6 |
| Long-Term Debt | 26.1 | 24.8 | 17.9 | | 13.3 | | 6.6 | 18.9 | 24.7 |
| Deferred Taxes | .5 | .1 | .4 | | .0 | | .0 | .7 | .2 |
| All Other Non-Current | 19.1 | 15.1 | 13.1 | | 7.5 | | 13.8 | 11.1 | 18.0 |
| Net Worth | 4.4 | 10.7 | 17.8 | | 2.3 | | 33.5 | 15.7 | 17.6 |
| Total Liabilties & Net Worth | 100.0 | 100.0 | 100.0 | | 100.0 | | 100.0 | 100.0 | 100.0 |
| **INCOME DATA** | | | | | | | | | |
| Net Sales | 100.0 | 100.0 | 100.0 | | 100.0 | | 100.0 | 100.0 | 100.0 |
| Gross Profit | 47.9 | 54.0 | 50.3 | | 49.0 | | 51.2 | 63.5 | 46.1 |
| Operating Expenses | 44.4 | 48.9 | 44.8 | | 44.7 | | 46.3 | 49.3 | 38.2 |
| Operating Profit | 3.5 | 5.1 | 5.6 | | 4.3 | | 4.9 | 4.3 | 7.8 |
| All Other Expenses (net) | 3.4 | 2.0 | 1.7 | | .2 | | .5 | 1.3 | 3.5 |
| Profit Before Taxes | .0 | 3.1 | 3.8 | | 4.1 | | 4.4 | 3.0 | 4.3 |
| **RATIOS** | | | | | | | | | |
| Current | 2.0 | 2.3 | 2.2 | | 12.6 | | 2.6 | 2.6 | 1.8 |
| | 1.0 | 1.2 | 1.2 | | 1.5 | | 1.4 | 1.2 | 1.0 |
| | .6 | .7 | .7 | | 1.1 | | 1.0 | .6 | .7 |
| Quick | 1.5 | 1.9 | 1.8 | | 12.0 | | 2.6 | 2.2 | 1.2 |
| | .8 | 1.0 | 1.0 | | 1.3 | | 1.3 | 1.0 | .8 |
| | .4 | .5 | .6 | | .4 | | .8 | .5 | .5 |
| Sales/Receivables | 28  13.2 | 27  13.5 | 24  15.3 | | 14  25.9 | | 18  20.3 | 27  13.7 | 26  13.8 |
| | 39  9.4 | 41  8.8 | 36  10.2 | | 28  13.0 | | 30  12.1 | 36  10.1 | 39  9.4 |
| | 60  6.0 | 58  6.3 | 60  6.1 | | 51  7.1 | | 39  9.4 | 63  5.8 | 61  6.0 |
| Cost of Sales/Inventory | 0  UND | 0  UND | 0  UND | | 0  UND | | 0  UND | 0  UND | 0  UND |
| | 5  67.7 | 3  143.8 | 0  UND | | 0  UND | | 0  UND | 3  120.4 | 10  36.8 |
| | 23  15.6 | 23  15.5 | 21  17.5 | | 83  4.4 | | 0  UND | 23  16.0 | 30  12.3 |
| Cost of Sales/Payables | 15  24.6 | 12  29.5 | 12  31.1 | | 1  268.1 | | 12  31.4 | 18  20.2 | 11  31.9 |
| | 33  11.0 | 29  12.6 | 32  11.4 | | 17  20.9 | | 20  18.2 | 33  11.0 | 37  9.8 |
| | 84  4.3 | 54  6.7 | 64  5.7 | | 70  5.2 | | 43  8.5 | 59  6.2 | 61  6.0 |
| Sales/Working Capital | 8.3 | 6.4 | 7.1 | | 5.8 | | 5.4 | 6.5 | 8.8 |
| | 183.6 | 22.6 | 28.3 | | 10.5 | | 19.6 | 36.3 | -539.6 |
| | -8.1 | -11.4 | -14.6 | | 121.5 | | -997.9 | -9.3 | -10.8 |
| EBIT/Interest | 7.0 | 13.0 | 17.0 | | | | 44.9 | 17.2 | 20.2 |
| | (89)  1.6 | (89)  3.6 | (92)  3.4 | | | | (15)  2.6 | (31)  2.7 | (29)  5.4 |
| | -.9 | .6 | .6 | | | | -5.3 | .5 | .4 |
| Net Profit + Depr., Dep., Amort./Cur. Mat. L/T/D | 2.3 | 2.5 | 2.9 | | | | | | |
| | (18)  .6 | (12)  2.1 | (15)  2.7 | | | | | | |
| | -3.8 | .6 | -.6 | | | | | | |
| Fixed/Worth | .3 | .2 | .3 | | .2 | | .2 | .3 | 1.0 |
| | 49.0 | NM | 2.0 | | 1.2 | | .6 | -5.4 | -.8 |
| | -.1 | -.2 | -.2 | | 25.8 | | 1.2 | -.2 | .0 |
| Debt/Worth | 1.8 | 1.3 | 1.2 | | .2 | | 1.0 | .8 | 6.9 |
| | -8.0 | -15.7 | 16.7 | | .2 | | 2.7 | -31.0 | -3.8 |
| | -1.8 | -2.1 | -2.2 | | 345.3 | | 7.7 | -2.4 | -1.6 |
| % Profit Before Taxes/Tangible Net Worth | 55.7 | 70.9 | 66.9 | | 61.5 | | 101.4 | 63.4 | 95.4 |
| | (47)  10.1 | (48)  18.8 | (60)  28.8 | | (10)  33.7 | | (15)  35.4 | (17)  10.6 | (13)  35.0 |
| | -18.5 | 4.7 | 6.3 | | -19.4 | | 2.4 | 6.4 | 12.4 |
| % Profit Before Taxes/Total Assets | 9.7 | 16.0 | 16.1 | | 41.0 | | 20.8 | 20.1 | 13.0 |
| | 2.0 | 6.0 | 6.1 | | 11.1 | | 3.2 | 8.8 | 4.0 |
| | -8.1 | -1.6 | -.8 | | -3.0 | | -2.4 | -2.2 | -.1 |
| Sales/Net Fixed Assets | 66.0 | 71.6 | 70.7 | | 243.3 | | 69.8 | 60.2 | 43.5 |
| | 20.8 | 25.2 | 27.4 | | 18.9 | | 35.2 | 19.6 | 18.2 |
| | 10.2 | 9.9 | 11.1 | | 12.3 | | 27.4 | 7.1 | 10.0 |
| Sales/Total Assets | 3.0 | 3.0 | 3.0 | | 8.2 | | 3.9 | 2.7 | 2.0 |
| | 2.0 | 2.0 | 2.0 | | 2.9 | | 2.8 | 2.0 | 1.2 |
| | 1.0 | 1.3 | 1.2 | | 1.8 | | 2.3 | 1.4 | .9 |
| % Depr., Dep., Amort./Sales | .8 | .8 | .7 | | | | .5 | .7 | 1.7 |
| | (64)  1.4 | (64)  1.6 | (71)  1.5 | | | | (13)  1.4 | (26)  1.3 | (20)  2.6 |
| | 2.2 | 2.8 | 2.6 | | | | 1.9 | 2.6 | 4.1 |
| % Officers', Directors' Owners' Comp/Sales | 2.6 | 2.5 | 3.6 | | | | | | |
| | (29)  5.2 | (27)  5.3 | (28)  5.4 | | | | | | |
| | 10.5 | 9.5 | 7.8 | | | | | | |
| Net Sales ($) | 3000648M | 4518879M | 3471385M | 1493M | 22841M | 27140M | 143033M | 607249M | 2669629M |
| Total Assets ($) | 3007780M | 2833575M | 2597080M | 1413M | 9467M | 11470M | 58466M | 375005M | 2141259M |

© RMA 2012                M = $ thousand    MM = $ million
See Pages 9 through 22 for Explanation of Ratios and Data

## Current Data Sorted by Assets　　　　　Comparative Historical Data

| | 0-500M | 500M-2MM | 2-10MM | 10-50MM | 50-100MM | 100-250MM | | 4/1/07-3/31/08 ALL | 4/1/08-3/31/09 ALL |
|---|---|---|---|---|---|---|---|---|---|
| | | 20 (4/1-9/30/11) | | 75 (10/1/11-3/31/12) | | | | | |
| **Type of Statement** | | | | | | | | | |
| Unqualified | | | 3 | 6 | 3 | 4 | | 25 | 23 |
| Reviewed | | 1 | 9 | 5 | 1 | 1 | | 26 | 21 |
| Compiled | | | 4 | 2 | 1 | | | 5 | 3 |
| Tax Returns | | 5 | 4 | 1 | | | | 7 | 11 |
| Other | 1 | 9 | 10 | 10 | 9 | 6 | | 40 | 34 |
| **NUMBER OF STATEMENTS** | 1 | 15 | 30 | 24 | 14 | 11 | | 103 | 92 |
| | % | % | % | % | % | % | | % | % |
| **ASSETS** | | | | | | | | | |
| Cash & Equivalents | | 14.7 | 10.0 | 16.5 | 12.5 | 10.0 | | 9.9 | 11.0 |
| Trade Receivables (net) | | 26.6 | 28.4 | 17.3 | 17.7 | 20.4 | | 27.7 | 22.9 |
| Inventory | | 35.0 | 36.6 | 18.2 | 13.3 | 15.4 | | 29.4 | 29.3 |
| All Other Current | | 4.1 | 6.2 | 4.3 | 8.4 | 5.6 | | 3.6 | 4.9 |
| Total Current | | 80.4 | 81.2 | 56.4 | 51.9 | 51.3 | | 70.5 | 68.2 |
| Fixed Assets (net) | | 7.4 | 8.6 | 16.4 | 9.6 | 3.2 | | 12.1 | 12.4 |
| Intangibles (net) | | 4.3 | 5.0 | 14.7 | 30.4 | 34.9 | | 8.7 | 12.0 |
| All Other Non-Current | | 7.9 | 5.2 | 12.6 | 8.0 | 10.6 | | 8.7 | 7.4 |
| Total | | 100.0 | 100.0 | 100.0 | 100.0 | 100.0 | | 100.0 | 100.0 |
| **LIABILITIES** | | | | | | | | | |
| Notes Payable-Short Term | | 28.9 | 7.7 | 7.4 | 5.3 | 2.9 | | 8.4 | 9.2 |
| Cur. Mat.-L.T.D. | | 2.6 | 2.9 | 1.9 | 2.4 | 1.0 | | 2.6 | 1.7 |
| Trade Payables | | 14.4 | 13.1 | 12.6 | 7.8 | 11.3 | | 13.5 | 11.4 |
| Income Taxes Payable | | .0 | .1 | .5 | .2 | 1.0 | | .3 | .2 |
| All Other Current | | 22.2 | 13.7 | 10.9 | 17.1 | 7.2 | | 15.1 | 11.8 |
| Total Current | | 68.1 | 37.5 | 33.3 | 32.8 | 23.4 | | 40.0 | 34.3 |
| Long-Term Debt | | 4.4 | 9.8 | 10.3 | 11.1 | 17.7 | | 11.9 | 12.3 |
| Deferred Taxes | | .0 | .3 | .1 | 1.9 | 2.8 | | .2 | .3 |
| All Other Non-Current | | 23.7 | 15.2 | 5.6 | 5.4 | 6.2 | | 9.5 | 14.8 |
| Net Worth | | 3.8 | 37.2 | 50.7 | 48.8 | 49.9 | | 38.4 | 38.4 |
| Total Liabilities & Net Worth | | 100.0 | 100.0 | 100.0 | 100.0 | 100.0 | | 100.0 | 100.0 |
| **INCOME DATA** | | | | | | | | | |
| Net Sales | | 100.0 | 100.0 | 100.0 | 100.0 | 100.0 | | 100.0 | 100.0 |
| Gross Profit | | 62.5 | 51.1 | 47.9 | 53.7 | 58.3 | | 48.5 | 53.0 |
| Operating Expenses | | 59.7 | 43.5 | 42.9 | 48.4 | 44.4 | | 42.3 | 49.4 |
| Operating Profit | | 2.7 | 7.6 | 5.0 | 5.3 | 13.9 | | 6.2 | 3.6 |
| All Other Expenses (net) | | -.5 | .9 | .3 | 2.1 | 1.3 | | 1.6 | 2.0 |
| Profit Before Taxes | | 3.2 | 6.7 | 4.7 | 3.2 | 12.5 | | 4.6 | 1.6 |
| **RATIOS** | | | | | | | | | |
| Current | | 3.7 | 4.0 | 2.6 | 2.2 | 2.8 | | 2.9 | 3.5 |
| | | 1.5 | 2.3 | 2.0 | 1.3 | 2.4 | | 2.0 | 2.2 |
| | | 1.2 | 1.7 | 1.1 | 1.0 | 1.5 | | 1.3 | 1.4 |
| Quick | | 1.2 | 1.9 | 1.5 | 1.4 | 1.6 | | 1.6 | 1.6 |
| | | .8 | 1.1 | 1.0 | .9 | 1.3 | | 1.0 | .9 |
| | | .6 | .7 | .5 | .5 | 1.0 | | .6 | .5 |
| Sales/Receivables | 13 | 29.0 | 30 · 12.0 | 22 · 16.9 | 31 · 11.9 | 64 · 5.7 | | 36 · 10.0 | 31 · 11.6 |
| | 34 | 10.8 | 53 · 6.9 | 51 · 7.2 | 48 · 7.6 | 78 · 4.7 | | 57 · 6.4 | 51 · 7.1 |
| | 76 | 4.8 | 85 · 4.3 | 63 · 5.8 | 78 · 4.7 | 130 · 2.8 | | 91 · 4.0 | 71 · 5.2 |
| Cost of Sales/Inventory | 25 | 14.4 | 79 · 4.6 | 62 · 5.9 | 42 · 8.6 | 87 · 4.2 | | 62 · 5.9 | 50 · 7.3 |
| | 281 | 1.3 | 182 · 2.0 | 99 · 3.7 | 130 · 2.8 | 94 · 3.9 | | 151 · 2.4 | 174 · 2.1 |
| | 456 | .8 | 243 · 1.5 | 159 · 2.3 | 174 · 2.1 | 166 · 2.2 | | 276 · 1.3 | 247 · 1.5 |
| Cost of Sales/Payables | 34 | 10.8 | 9 · 38.7 | 27 · 13.3 | 41 · 8.9 | 45 · 8.2 | | 24 · 15.1 | 24 · 15.1 |
| | 62 | 5.9 | 40 · 9.1 | 48 · 7.6 | 50 · 7.3 | 114 · 3.2 | | 48 · 7.7 | 51 · 7.2 |
| | 83 | 4.4 | 79 · 4.6 | 69 · 5.3 | 81 · 4.5 | 215 · 1.7 | | 98 · 3.7 | 75 · 4.8 |
| Sales/Working Capital | | 1.8 | 2.7 | 2.4 | 2.8 | 2.5 | | 2.6 | 2.7 |
| | | 10.1 | 4.7 | 6.1 | 9.8 | 3.0 | | 4.0 | 5.2 |
| | | 31.0 | 7.9 | 123.2 | NM | 7.6 | | 13.4 | 10.2 |
| EBIT/Interest | | 8.7 | 35.0 | 31.7 | 36.6 | 99.4 | | 10.2 | 6.3 |
| | (11) | 2.8 | (27) 8.2 | (21) 2.1 | (12) 7.9 | (10) 4.9 | | (84) 3.6 | (78) 2.3 |
| | | 1.0 | 2.2 | -2.3 | .1 | 1.8 | | .7 | .4 |
| Net Profit + Depr., Dep., Amort./Cur. Mat. L/T/D | | | | | | | | 8.9 | 6.7 |
| | | | | | | | | (20) 2.5 | (21) 1.7 |
| | | | | | | | | 1.2 | .7 |
| Fixed/Worth | | .0 | .0 | .1 | .2 | .0 | | .1 | .1 |
| | | .3 | .1 | .4 | .4 | .1 | | .2 | .3 |
| | | -.1 | .4 | 1.4 | -.3 | -.9 | | 1.1 | 1.0 |
| Debt/Worth | | .8 | .4 | .6 | .7 | .6 | | .6 | .5 |
| | | 2.7 | .9 | 1.2 | 2.2 | 5.7 | | 1.4 | 1.5 |
| | | -3.5 | 5.7 | 3.2 | -2.3 | -12.7 | | 7.7 | 6.7 |
| % Profit Before Taxes/Tangible Net Worth | | | 59.0 | 36.0 | 40.9 | | | 35.8 | 19.3 |
| | | | (25) 11.0 | (22) 9.5 | (10) 15.0 | | | (87) 12.3 | (75) 5.1 |
| | | | -.2 | -8.8 | 6.1 | | | 1.9 | -2.6 |
| % Profit Before Taxes/Total Assets | | 18.7 | 21.1 | 12.8 | 10.5 | 10.3 | | 12.7 | 7.7 |
| | | 4.1 | 8.3 | 4.7 | 4.9 | 7.4 | | 4.9 | 2.3 |
| | | -.2 | .2 | -4.1 | -3.8 | 2.9 | | -.9 | -2.2 |
| Sales/Net Fixed Assets | | 94.8 | 154.1 | 52.2 | 28.1 | 137.0 | | 79.1 | 37.9 |
| | | 43.6 | 44.8 | 15.4 | 13.7 | 32.3 | | 22.3 | 22.7 |
| | | 20.6 | 19.3 | 4.9 | 7.9 | 10.4 | | 7.9 | 7.4 |
| Sales/Total Assets | | 3.7 | 2.6 | 1.9 | 1.2 | 1.0 | | 2.0 | 2.2 |
| | | 1.6 | 1.8 | 1.2 | 1.0 | .9 | | 1.4 | 1.5 |
| | | 1.3 | 1.4 | .8 | .8 | .5 | | 1.0 | 1.0 |
| % Depr., Dep., Amort./Sales | | | .4 | .9 | | | | .7 | 1.0 |
| | | | (21) .9 | (16) 2.4 | | | | (69) 1.7 | (67) 1.7 |
| | | | 1.6 | 5.2 | | | | 2.7 | 3.0 |
| % Officers', Directors' Owners' Comp/Sales | | | | | | | | 2.0 | 3.2 |
| | | | | | | | | (21) 3.6 | (18) 6.3 |
| | | | | | | | | 9.1 | 10.9 |
| Net Sales ($) | 836M | 42032M | 294087M | 734215M | 970127M | 1416577M | | 3283561M | 2874421M |
| Total Assets ($) | 418M | 17023M | 145146M | 559794M | 965236M | 1666909M | | 3081407M | 2702938M |

© RMA 2012

**M = $ thousand　　MM = $ million**
See Pages 9 through 22 for Explanation of Ratios and Data

## Comparative Historical Data | Current Data Sorted by Sales

| Type of Statement | 4/1/09-3/31/10 ALL | 4/1/10-3/31/11 ALL | 4/1/11-3/31/12 ALL | 0-1MM | 1-3MM | 3-5MM | 5-10MM | 10-25MM | 25MM & OVER |
|---|---|---|---|---|---|---|---|---|---|
| Unqualified | 22 | 20 | 16 | | | | 1 | 2 | 13 |
| Reviewed | 22 | 17 | 17 | | 3 | 1 | 6 | 4 | 3 |
| Compiled | 2 | 7 | 8 | 1 | | 1 | 1 | 4 | 1 |
| Tax Returns | 12 | 9 | 10 | | 1 | 3 | 3 | 3 | |
| Other | 41 | 40 | 44 | 3 | 5 | 2 | 3 | 10 | 21 |
| | | | | 20 (4/1-9/30/11) | | | 75 (10/1/11-3/31/12) | | |
| NUMBER OF STATEMENTS | 99 | 93 | 95 | 4 | 9 | 7 | 14 | 23 | 38 |

| | 4/1/09-3/31/10 ALL % | 4/1/10-3/31/11 ALL % | 4/1/11-3/31/12 ALL % | 0-1MM % | 1-3MM % | 3-5MM % | 5-10MM % | 10-25MM % | 25MM & OVER % |
|---|---|---|---|---|---|---|---|---|---|
| **ASSETS** | | | | | | | | | |
| Cash & Equivalents | 12.5 | 14.1 | 12.9 | | | | 7.4 | 10.5 | 14.7 |
| Trade Receivables (net) | 22.2 | 21.8 | 22.6 | | | | 29.5 | 26.0 | 18.9 |
| Inventory | 26.3 | 26.9 | 25.5 | | | | 38.9 | 27.6 | 15.5 |
| All Other Current | 6.5 | 6.6 | 5.6 | | | | 2.8 | 7.6 | 6.5 |
| Total Current | 67.6 | 69.4 | 66.6 | | | | 78.7 | 71.7 | 55.6 |
| Fixed Assets (net) | 11.6 | 10.9 | 10.1 | | | | 7.7 | 14.4 | 7.7 |
| Intangibles (net) | 13.6 | 11.2 | 14.5 | | | | 7.5 | 8.9 | 25.1 |
| All Other Non-Current | 7.2 | 8.5 | 8.9 | | | | 6.1 | 5.0 | 11.6 |
| Total | 100.0 | 100.0 | 100.0 | | | | 100.0 | 100.0 | 100.0 |
| **LIABILITIES** | | | | | | | | | |
| Notes Payable-Short Term | 8.2 | 6.1 | 10.0 | | | | 11.2 | 5.9 | 6.1 |
| Cur. Mat.-L.T.D. | 2.6 | 4.1 | 2.3 | | | | 1.7 | 2.8 | 1.4 |
| Trade Payables | 10.6 | 13.0 | 12.2 | | | | 13.8 | 12.8 | 10.3 |
| Income Taxes Payable | .4 | .4 | .3 | | | | .0 | .1 | .6 |
| All Other Current | 13.4 | 14.8 | 14.0 | | | | 25.4 | 11.9 | 13.7 |
| Total Current | 35.1 | 38.3 | 38.7 | | | | 52.2 | 33.6 | 32.1 |
| Long-Term Debt | 16.0 | 9.9 | 10.3 | | | | 3.2 | 13.9 | 10.2 |
| Deferred Taxes | .4 | .6 | .7 | | | | .6 | .1 | 1.5 |
| All Other Non-Current | 12.6 | 17.8 | 11.8 | | | | 5.9 | 17.2 | 5.3 |
| Net Worth | 35.9 | 33.4 | 38.4 | | | | 38.0 | 35.2 | 50.9 |
| Total Liabilities & Net Worth | 100.0 | 100.0 | 100.0 | | | | 100.0 | 100.0 | 100.0 |
| **INCOME DATA** | | | | | | | | | |
| Net Sales | 100.0 | 100.0 | 100.0 | | | | 100.0 | 100.0 | 100.0 |
| Gross Profit | 53.0 | 53.2 | 53.5 | | | | 50.7 | 50.7 | 53.6 |
| Operating Expenses | 50.2 | 49.6 | 47.0 | | | | 49.2 | 41.6 | 45.8 |
| Operating Profit | 2.8 | 3.7 | 6.5 | | | | 1.5 | 9.1 | 7.9 |
| All Other Expenses (net) | 2.1 | 1.9 | .7 | | | | .6 | .5 | 1.2 |
| Profit Before Taxes | .7 | 1.7 | 5.8 | | | | .9 | 8.6 | 6.7 |
| **RATIOS** | | | | | | | | | |
| Current | 3.2 | 3.4 | 2.8 | | | | 3.7 | 3.9 | 2.6 |
| | 2.1 | 2.2 | 2.0 | | | | 2.3 | 2.2 | 1.8 |
| | 1.3 | 1.3 | 1.3 | | | | 1.4 | 1.6 | 1.2 |
| Quick | 1.8 | 1.7 | 1.5 | | | | 1.6 | 2.1 | 1.5 |
| | .9 | 1.1 | 1.0 | | | | 1.1 | 1.0 | 1.1 |
| | .5 | .5 | .6 | | | | .7 | .5 | |
| Sales/Receivables | 28  13.2 | 23  15.7 | 26  14.1 | | | | 34  10.7 | 36  10.1 | 31  11.9 |
| | 49  7.4 | 50  7.3 | 52  7.0 | | | | 58  6.3 | 51  7.2 | 63  5.8 |
| | 83  4.4 | 88  4.2 | 79  4.6 | | | | 79  4.6 | 81  4.5 | 87  4.2 |
| Cost of Sales/Inventory | 63  5.8 | 58  6.3 | 62  5.9 | | | | 114  3.2 | 62  5.9 | 63  5.8 |
| | 140  2.6 | 116  3.1 | 135  2.7 | | | | 192  1.9 | 118  3.1 | 104  3.5 |
| | 246  1.5 | 237  1.5 | 215  1.7 | | | | 243  1.5 | 203  1.8 | 159  2.3 |
| Cost of Sales/Payables | 23  15.6 | 26  14.0 | 30  12.2 | | | | 9  42.2 | 8  45.8 | 37  9.8 |
| | 47  7.7 | 47  7.8 | 49  7.5 | | | | 40  9.1 | 46  7.9 | 49  7.5 |
| | 87  4.2 | 81  4.5 | 83  4.4 | | | | 69  5.3 | 78  4.7 | 91  4.0 |
| Sales/Working Capital | 2.6 | 2.3 | 2.7 | | | | 2.4 | 2.8 | 2.7 |
| | 4.3 | 4.0 | 5.9 | | | | 4.3 | 5.9 | 5.5 |
| | 11.6 | 10.1 | 13.8 | | | | NM | 9.1 | 25.8 |
| EBIT/Interest | 8.1 | 11.6 | 31.8 | | | | 12.9 | 66.0 | 75.5 |
| | (86)  2.8 | (72)  4.0 | (82)  5.7 | | | | (12)  7.8 | 9.2 | (32)  5.9 |
| | -1.0 | .4 | .7 | | | | -.8 | -.7 | .4 |
| Net Profit + Depr., Dep., Amort./Cur. Mat. L/T/D | 15.3 | 13.5 | 19.6 | | | | | | |
| | (20)  1.8 | (14)  1.5 | (11)  4.4 | | | | | | |
| | .6 | -.3 | 2.1 | | | | | | |
| Fixed/Worth | .1 | .1 | .0 | | | | .0 | .1 | .1 |
| | .3 | .3 | .2 | | | | .1 | .2 | .3 |
| | 1.6 | 1.3 | 1.5 | | | | .4 | 1.0 | -2.1 |
| Debt/Worth | .5 | .6 | .6 | | | | .3 | .7 | .6 |
| | 1.7 | 1.4 | 1.4 | | | | .9 | 1.3 | 1.4 |
| | 34.6 | 24.6 | 60.8 | | | | NM | 3.3 | -67.9 |
| % Profit Before Taxes/Tangible Net Worth | 24.5 | 35.5 | 35.3 | | | | 28.2 | 59.2 | 33.0 |
| | (76)  6.2 | (73)  9.4 | (72)  14.2 | | | | (11)  7.1 | (19)  11.0 | (28)  14.7 |
| | -3.7 | .0 | 2.8 | | | | 3.6 | -11.0 | 8.4 |
| % Profit Before Taxes/Total Assets | 9.4 | 9.1 | 13.5 | | | | 8.3 | 22.6 | 10.8 |
| | 2.4 | 3.5 | 5.7 | | | | 4.0 | 13.4 | 6.4 |
| | -3.4 | -2.5 | -.2 | | | | -9.1 | -4.0 | 2.0 |
| Sales/Net Fixed Assets | 55.2 | 75.9 | 84.3 | | | | 426.0 | 126.6 | 46.0 |
| | 24.6 | 24.1 | 29.5 | | | | 38.7 | 39.6 | 22.8 |
| | 8.2 | 10.0 | 11.0 | | | | 19.1 | 9.0 | 10.4 |
| Sales/Total Assets | 1.8 | 2.1 | 2.0 | | | | 2.6 | 2.7 | 1.5 |
| | 1.4 | 1.5 | 1.4 | | | | 1.6 | 1.6 | 1.1 |
| | 1.0 | .9 | 1.0 | | | | 1.2 | 1.1 | .8 |
| % Depr., Dep., Amort./Sales | .6 | .6 | .5 | | | | .4 | .5 | .7 |
| | (71)  1.8 | (63)  1.5 | (59)  1.1 | | | | (11)  .7 | (16)  1.0 | (23)  1.4 |
| | 2.9 | 2.5 | 2.2 | | | | 1.2 | 5.2 | 2.4 |
| % Officers', Directors' Owners' Comp/Sales | 3.8 | 1.4 | 2.3 | | | | | | |
| | (19)  5.0 | (17)  2.9 | (16)  7.1 | | | | | | |
| | 11.8 | 14.7 | 15.5 | | | | | | |
| Net Sales ($) | 3031102M | 2913090M | 3457874M | 2960M | 17323M | 28118M | 104396M | 359468M | 2945609M |
| Total Assets ($) | 2670146M | 2580931M | 3354526M | 2244M | 14466M | 12763M | 70446M | 245068M | 3009539M |

© RMA 2012

M = $ thousand    MM = $ million
See Pages 9 through 22 for Explanation of Ratios and Data

## Current Data Sorted by Assets

## Comparative Historical Data

| 0-500M | 500M-2MM | 2-10MM | 10-50MM | 50-100MM | 100-250MM | Type of Statement | ALL 4/1/07-3/31/08 | ALL 4/1/08-3/31/09 |
|---|---|---|---|---|---|---|---|---|
|  |  | 2 | 6 | 7 | 1 | Unqualified | 10 | 13 |
|  | 6 | 10 | 4 |  |  | Reviewed | 14 | 8 |
| 1 |  |  |  |  |  | Compiled | 4 | 5 |
| 1 | 5 | 4 |  |  |  | Tax Returns | 5 | 8 |
| 1 | 4 | 6 | 6 |  | 4 | Other | 30 | 28 |
|  | 13 (4/1-9/30/11) |  | 55 (10/1/11-3/31/12) |  |  |  |  |  |
| 3 | 15 | 22 | 16 | 7 | 5 | NUMBER OF STATEMENTS | 63 | 62 |
| % | % | % | % | % | % | ASSETS | % | % |
|  | 14.7 | 12.2 | 16.5 |  |  | Cash & Equivalents | 12.0 | 13.0 |
|  | 32.8 | 20.6 | 24.6 |  |  | Trade Receivables (net) | 26.9 | 26.5 |
|  | 17.7 | 18.6 | 10.7 |  |  | Inventory | 15.3 | 14.6 |
|  | 5.9 | 5.8 | 5.4 |  |  | All Other Current | 4.9 | 4.8 |
|  | 71.1 | 57.2 | 57.2 |  |  | Total Current | 59.1 | 59.0 |
|  | 14.1 | 20.9 | 16.9 |  |  | Fixed Assets (net) | 16.3 | 16.8 |
|  | 8.6 | 8.9 | 20.0 |  |  | Intangibles (net) | 11.5 | 13.7 |
|  | 6.2 | 13.0 | 5.9 |  |  | All Other Non-Current | 13.1 | 10.6 |
|  | 100.0 | 100.0 | 100.0 |  |  | Total | 100.0 | 100.0 |
|  |  |  |  |  |  | LIABILITIES |  |  |
|  | 11.8 | 4.9 | 2.5 |  |  | Notes Payable-Short Term | 10.3 | 9.7 |
|  | .9 | 7.6 | 5.0 |  |  | Cur. Mat.-L.T.D. | 2.7 | 3.9 |
|  | 17.3 | 10.8 | 16.4 |  |  | Trade Payables | 11.2 | 14.5 |
|  | .0 | .1 | .0 |  |  | Income Taxes Payable | .6 | .9 |
|  | 6.8 | 20.2 | 19.3 |  |  | All Other Current | 17.6 | 15.7 |
|  | 36.8 | 43.6 | 43.2 |  |  | Total Current | 42.4 | 44.7 |
|  | 14.9 | 18.5 | 13.1 |  |  | Long-Term Debt | 17.0 | 16.8 |
|  | .0 | .6 | .3 |  |  | Deferred Taxes | .5 | .9 |
|  | 31.8 | 12.6 | 12.1 |  |  | All Other Non-Current | 13.4 | 11.2 |
|  | 16.4 | 24.6 | 31.4 |  |  | Net Worth | 26.7 | 26.4 |
|  | 100.0 | 100.0 | 100.0 |  |  | Total Liabilities & Net Worth | 100.0 | 100.0 |
|  |  |  |  |  |  | INCOME DATA |  |  |
|  | 100.0 | 100.0 | 100.0 |  |  | Net Sales | 100.0 | 100.0 |
|  | 59.0 | 54.3 | 53.4 |  |  | Gross Profit | 49.2 | 50.9 |
|  | 53.6 | 49.3 | 45.4 |  |  | Operating Expenses | 42.1 | 46.2 |
|  | 5.3 | 4.9 | 8.0 |  |  | Operating Profit | 7.1 | 4.6 |
|  | .9 | 1.5 | 2.7 |  |  | All Other Expenses (net) | 1.1 | 1.8 |
|  | 4.4 | 3.4 | 5.3 |  |  | Profit Before Taxes | 6.1 | 2.8 |
|  |  |  |  |  |  | RATIOS |  |  |
|  | 3.0 | 4.0 | 1.7 |  |  | Current | 2.5 | 2.4 |
|  | 2.4 | 1.4 | 1.4 |  |  |  | 1.3 | 1.4 |
|  | 1.6 | .9 | .9 |  |  |  | 1.1 | .9 |
|  | 2.2 | 2.2 | 1.4 |  |  | Quick | 1.5 | 1.4 |
|  | 1.1 | .9 | 1.1 |  |  |  | 1.0 | .9 |
|  | .7 | .5 | .6 |  |  |  | .6 | .5 |
| 6 | 66.3 | 21 | 17.4 | 36 | 10.0 | Sales/Receivables | 29 12.5 | 26 13.9 |
| 35 | 10.4 | 43 | 8.5 | 54 | 6.8 |  | 46 8.0 | 48 7.5 |
| 62 | 5.9 | 61 | 6.0 | 78 | 4.7 |  | 62 5.8 | 65 5.6 |
| 0 | UND | 0 | UND | 4 | 85.5 | Cost of Sales/Inventory | 2 169.1 | 0 UND |
| 26 | 14.2 | 13 | 27.7 | 30 | 12.0 |  | 32 11.2 | 31 11.8 |
| 39 | 9.4 | 215 | 1.7 | 83 | 4.4 |  | 105 3.5 | 128 2.9 |
| 13 | 27.7 | 18 | 20.5 | 42 | 8.7 | Cost of Sales/Payables | 17 21.6 | 18 20.5 |
| 33 | 11.2 | 42 | 8.6 | 85 | 4.3 |  | 37 9.9 | 30 12.1 |
| 83 | 4.4 | 96 | 3.8 | 111 | 3.3 |  | 53 6.9 | 89 4.1 |
|  | 4.0 | 2.7 | 6.3 |  |  | Sales/Working Capital | 5.9 | 4.9 |
|  | 10.8 | 11.5 | 9.7 |  |  |  | 18.1 | 15.1 |
|  | 17.8 | -62.0 | NM |  |  |  | 110.4 | -36.0 |
|  | 17.2 | 15.7 | 38.3 |  |  | EBIT/Interest | 12.5 | 6.1 |
|  | (13) 6.9 | (18) 5.3 | (14) 7.5 |  |  |  | (51) 4.7 | (48) 3.2 |
|  | 5.1 | 1.3 | 2.1 |  |  |  | 1.2 | .3 |
|  |  |  |  |  |  | Net Profit + Depr., Dep., Amort./Cur. Mat. L/T/D | 4.0 | 5.8 |
|  |  |  |  |  |  |  | (14) 2.3 | (16) 1.0 |
|  |  |  |  |  |  |  | .6 | .1 |
|  | .1 | .2 | .4 |  |  | Fixed/Worth | .1 | .2 |
|  | .2 | .6 | 2.7 |  |  |  | .6 | 1.1 |
|  | -.4 | 2.1 | -.2 |  |  |  | -3.1 | -1.0 |
|  | 1.3 | 1.0 | 1.3 |  |  | Debt/Worth | .7 | 1.0 |
|  | 9.2 | 2.0 | 5.0 |  |  |  | 2.3 | 5.0 |
|  | -2.9 | 11.9 | -3.4 |  |  |  | -69.0 | -8.2 |
|  | 147.3 | 45.5 | 65.6 |  |  | % Profit Before Taxes/Tangible Net Worth | 73.6 | 111.8 |
|  | (10) 40.5 | (18) 15.8 | (10) 29.5 |  |  |  | (47) 35.2 | (42) 23.9 |
|  | 2.5 | 2.3 | 11.2 |  |  |  | 7.9 | 1.3 |
|  | 20.0 | 11.8 | 16.8 |  |  | % Profit Before Taxes/Total Assets | 27.1 | 15.9 |
|  | 10.8 | 5.1 | 7.9 |  |  |  | 8.4 | 5.7 |
|  | .7 | .3 | 4.2 |  |  |  | 1.9 | -2.3 |
|  | 193.0 | 90.9 | 43.1 |  |  | Sales/Net Fixed Assets | 49.9 | 72.0 |
|  | 70.4 | 21.5 | 18.9 |  |  |  | 21.0 | 16.2 |
|  | 19.9 | 5.7 | 3.4 |  |  |  | 6.9 | 6.9 |
|  | 6.0 | 2.8 | 2.3 |  |  | Sales/Total Assets | 3.1 | 3.1 |
|  | 3.2 | 1.9 | 1.5 |  |  |  | 2.1 | 1.8 |
|  | 2.2 | 1.3 | 1.2 |  |  |  | 1.3 | 1.3 |
|  | .4 | .7 | 1.3 |  |  | % Depr., Dep., Amort./Sales | .7 | .8 |
|  | (12) .8 | (16) 1.5 | (11) 3.0 |  |  |  | (52) 1.7 | (44) 2.3 |
|  | 2.2 | 2.4 | 5.3 |  |  |  | 3.4 | 3.5 |
|  | 2.6 |  |  |  |  | % Officers', Directors' Owners' Comp/Sales | 2.0 | 2.6 |
|  | (11) 5.0 |  |  |  |  |  | (15) 5.2 | (16) 3.8 |
|  | 7.2 |  |  |  |  |  | 8.4 | 9.7 |
| 2694M | 52275M | 187621M | 571682M | 672934M | 594966M | Net Sales ($) | 2019283M | 2466502M |
| 919M | 15132M | 94146M | 353287M | 448330M | 801940M | Total Assets ($) | 1452575M | 1420493M |

M = $ thousand    MM = $ million
See Pages 9 through 22 for Explanation of Ratios and Data

## Comparative Historical Data                                    ## Current Data Sorted by Sales

| | | | Type of Statement | 0-1MM | 1-3MM | 3-5MM | 5-10MM | 10-25MM | 25MM & OVER |
|---|---|---|---|---|---|---|---|---|---|
| 17 | 17 | 16 | Unqualified | | 1 | | | 2 | 13 |
| 9 | 11 | 20 | Reviewed | 1 | 2 | 2 | 7 | 6 | 2 |
| 2 | 3 | 1 | Compiled | 1 | | | | | |
| 3 | 6 | 10 | Tax Returns | 1 | 3 | 3 | 2 | 1 | |
| 29 | 23 | 21 | Other | | 3 | 3 | 5 | 1 | 9 |
| 4/1/09-3/31/10 ALL | 4/1/10-3/31/11 ALL | 4/1/11-3/31/12 ALL | | 13 (4/1-9/30/11) | | | 55 (10/1/11-3/31/12) | | |
| 60 | 60 | 68 | **NUMBER OF STATEMENTS** | 3 | 9 | 8 | 14 | 10 | 24 |
| % | % | % | **ASSETS** | % | % | % | % | % | % |
| 13.7 | 17.8 | 15.2 | Cash & Equivalents | | | | 15.1 | 20.4 | 14.0 |
| 25.2 | 25.5 | 23.1 | Trade Receivables (net) | | | | 23.1 | 17.4 | 22.5 |
| 12.1 | 13.4 | 14.6 | Inventory | | | | 16.8 | 16.1 | 11.5 |
| 5.2 | 5.7 | 6.6 | All Other Current | | | | 3.3 | 3.5 | 5.2 |
| 56.2 | 62.3 | 59.5 | Total Current | | | | 58.3 | 57.4 | 53.1 |
| 16.4 | 13.3 | 16.3 | Fixed Assets (net) | | | | 20.6 | 20.7 | 14.4 |
| 19.7 | 17.2 | 15.6 | Intangibles (net) | | | | 9.7 | 12.2 | 25.0 |
| 7.7 | 7.2 | 8.6 | All Other Non-Current | | | | 11.4 | 9.8 | 7.5 |
| 100.0 | 100.0 | 100.0 | Total | | | | 100.0 | 100.0 | 100.0 |
| | | | **LIABILITIES** | | | | | | |
| 7.2 | 9.0 | 6.5 | Notes Payable-Short Term | | | | 11.4 | 2.2 | 4.3 |
| 2.7 | 2.2 | 5.4 | Cur. Mat.-L.T.D. | | | | 6.0 | 1.7 | 7.5 |
| 15.0 | 14.7 | 12.9 | Trade Payables | | | | 10.8 | 10.2 | 13.0 |
| .2 | .8 | .1 | Income Taxes Payable | | | | .0 | .1 | .2 |
| 15.9 | 16.0 | 16.7 | All Other Current | | | | 22.9 | 18.9 | 21.1 |
| 40.9 | 42.8 | 41.6 | Total Current | | | | 51.1 | 33.2 | 46.1 |
| 13.7 | 11.2 | 15.4 | Long-Term Debt | | | | 20.1 | 5.3 | 12.4 |
| .8 | .4 | .3 | Deferred Taxes | | | | .3 | 1.1 | .2 |
| 17.2 | 13.6 | 18.2 | All Other Non-Current | | | | 23.3 | 2.8 | 17.0 |
| 27.5 | 32.0 | 24.5 | Net Worth | | | | 5.3 | 57.6 | 24.3 |
| 100.0 | 100.0 | 100.0 | Total Liabilities & Net Worth | | | | 100.0 | 100.0 | 100.0 |
| | | | **INCOME DATA** | | | | | | |
| 100.0 | 100.0 | 100.0 | Net Sales | | | | 100.0 | 100.0 | 100.0 |
| 52.0 | 55.5 | 54.7 | Gross Profit | | | | 54.9 | 62.8 | 48.9 |
| 47.0 | 47.9 | 48.5 | Operating Expenses | | | | 50.4 | 56.4 | 41.8 |
| 5.0 | 7.6 | 6.2 | Operating Profit | | | | 4.5 | 6.4 | 7.1 |
| 3.0 | 2.5 | 2.6 | All Other Expenses (net) | | | | 2.8 | .4 | 4.7 |
| 2.0 | 5.1 | 3.6 | Profit Before Taxes | | | | 1.7 | 6.0 | 2.4 |
| | | | **RATIOS** | | | | | | |
| 2.1 | 2.5 | 2.9 | | | | | 4.0 | 4.7 | 1.7 |
| 1.4 | 1.4 | 1.5 | Current | | | | 1.9 | 1.4 | 1.2 |
| 1.0 | 1.0 | .9 | | | | | .6 | 1.0 | .8 |
| 1.5 | 1.6 | 1.9 | | | | | 2.1 | 2.4 | 1.3 |
| 1.0 | 1.0 | .9 | Quick | | | | 1.1 | 1.0 | .8 |
| .6 | .6 | .6 | | | | | .6 | .6 | .4 |
| 32   11.3 | 26   14.0 | 20   18.0 | | | | | 20   18.3 | 12   30.7 | 31   11.7 |
| 44   8.2 | 41   8.8 | 43   8.5 | Sales/Receivables | | | | 42   8.6 | 26   13.8 | 59   6.2 |
| 64   5.7 | 65   5.6 | 66   5.5 | | | | | 57   6.4 | 46   7.9 | 78   4.7 |
| 0   UND | 0   UND | 0   UND | | | | | 0   UND | 0   UND | 0   UND |
| 15   25.1 | 20   18.2 | 23   15.6 | Cost of Sales/Inventory | | | | 6   58.6 | 33   10.9 | 42   8.6 |
| 77   4.7 | 88   4.1 | 94   3.9 | | | | | 49   7.4 | 228   1.6 | 94   3.9 |
| 17   22.1 | 16   22.8 | 26   14.2 | | | | | 11   31.8 | 30   12.2 | 27   13.4 |
| 42   8.6 | 45   8.1 | 47   7.7 | Cost of Sales/Payables | | | | 29   12.4 | 61   6.0 | 54   6.7 |
| 82   4.5 | 91   4.0 | 89   4.1 | | | | | 50   7.3 | 99   3.7 | 91   4.0 |
| 5.6 | 4.3 | 4.0 | | | | | 2.7 | 3.9 | 7.5 |
| 16.6 | 15.8 | 12.5 | Sales/Working Capital | | | | 11.8 | 10.3 | 81.3 |
| -78.4 | 201.2 | -69.8 | | | | | -12.1 | NM | -9.4 |
| 8.9 | 22.1 | 15.1 | | | | | 6.6 | | 22.4 |
| (53) 3.2 | (49) 5.1 | (57) 5.2 | EBIT/Interest | | | | (12) 4.5 | | (21) 2.9 |
| .2 | .9 | 1.2 | | | | | 1.5 | | -.3 |
| 6.8 | 5.4 | 4.5 | Net Profit + Depr., Dep., | | | | | | |
| (12) 4.1 | (14) 2.0 | (10) 2.7 | Amort./Cur. Mat. L/T/D | | | | | | |
| 1.1 | .5 | 1.1 | | | | | | | |
| .2 | .1 | .2 | | | | | .3 | .1 | .7 |
| 1.6 | .6 | 1.1 | Fixed/Worth | | | | .8 | .6 | -1.5 |
| -.7 | NM | -.4 | | | | | -135.2 | 1.4 | -.2 |
| 1.3 | 1.0 | 1.2 | | | | | 1.1 | .7 | 1.9 |
| 6.5 | 6.3 | 5.4 | Debt/Worth | | | | 3.8 | 1.1 | -8.7 |
| -4.0 | -9.3 | -4.5 | | | | | -172.2 | 2.1 | -3.4 |
| 80.8 | 110.5 | 63.5 | % Profit Before Taxes/Tangible | | | | 58.7 | | 126.0 |
| (37) 18.0 | (41) 24.7 | (44) 18.8 | Net Worth | | | | (10) 13.4 | | (11) 46.3 |
| -6.5 | 3.4 | 6.4 | | | | | -1.2 | | 12.7 |
| 15.2 | 19.6 | 13.8 | % Profit Before Taxes/Total | | | | 10.5 | 17.2 | 13.4 |
| 5.2 | 6.8 | 6.9 | Assets | | | | 3.4 | 9.3 | 7.9 |
| -6.4 | .3 | .4 | | | | | -.4 | 3.4 | -9.1 |
| 61.3 | 107.3 | 101.5 | | | | | 50.6 | 62.2 | 43.1 |
| 19.9 | 27.7 | 21.3 | Sales/Net Fixed Assets | | | | 19.5 | 12.6 | 16.7 |
| 6.4 | 6.4 | 6.6 | | | | | 5.4 | 3.8 | 6.9 |
| 2.7 | 2.9 | 2.9 | | | | | 3.4 | 3.0 | 2.0 |
| 1.9 | 1.8 | 1.9 | Sales/Total Assets | | | | 1.9 | 2.1 | 1.5 |
| 1.1 | 1.0 | 1.2 | | | | | 1.2 | 1.2 | 1.0 |
| .7 | .7 | .7 | | | | | .7 | | 1.3 |
| (41) 1.9 | (37) 1.5 | (47) 1.5 | % Depr., Dep., Amort./Sales | | | | (13) 1.1 | (14) 3.3 | 3.3 |
| 3.5 | 3.3 | 3.0 | | | | | 2.3 | | 4.8 |
| | 2.6 | 2.7 | % Officers', Directors' | | | | | | |
| | (16) 3.6 | (22) 5.2 | Owners' Comp/Sales | | | | | | |
| | 10.1 | 8.6 | | | | | | | |
| 1988380M | 2331661M | 2082172M | Net Sales ($) | 2167M | 19892M | 32584M | 101902M | 137782M | 1787845M |
| 1673610M | 1986798M | 1713754M | Total Assets ($) | 1250M | 10893M | 14163M | 62509M | 108627M | 1516312M |

M = $ thousand     MM = $ million
See Pages 9 through 22 for Explanation of Ratios and Data

INFORMATION—Software Publishers  NAICS 511210

| Current Data Sorted by Assets | | | | | | | Comparative Historical Data | |

## Type of Statement

| 0-500M | 500M-2MM | 2-10MM | 10-50MM | 50-100MM | 100-250MM | Type of Statement | | |
|---|---|---|---|---|---|---|---|---|
|  |  | 7 | 16 | 12 | 20 | Unqualified | 71 | 76 |
|  | 6 | 11 | 4 |  |  | Reviewed | 17 | 14 |
| 2 | 2 | 4 |  |  |  | Compiled | 17 | 8 |
| 7 | 10 | 8 | 1 |  |  | Tax Returns | 15 | 17 |
| 5 | 11 | 58 | 41 | 32 | 38 | Other | 97 | 122 |
|  | 43 (4/1-9/30/11) | | | 252 (10/1/11-3/31/12) | | | 4/1/07-3/31/08 ALL | 4/1/08-3/31/09 ALL |
| 14 | 29 | 88 | 62 | 44 | 58 | NUMBER OF STATEMENTS | 217 | 237 |

| 0-500M | 500M-2MM | 2-10MM | 10-50MM | 50-100MM | 100-250MM | | ALL | ALL |
|---|---|---|---|---|---|---|---|---|
| % | % | % | % | % | % | **ASSETS** | % | % |
| 45.3 | 23.8 | 25.7 | 27.0 | 25.0 | 20.5 | Cash & Equivalents | 24.9 | 25.9 |
| 43.7 | 36.1 | 33.1 | 24.8 | 18.9 | 11.6 | Trade Receivables (net) | 28.7 | 25.7 |
| .1 | 3.4 | 1.4 | 2.5 | 1.7 | .6 | Inventory | 1.8 | 1.6 |
| 7.0 | 4.4 | 4.9 | 6.9 | 6.7 | 4.6 | All Other Current | 4.3 | 5.2 |
| 96.0 | 67.6 | 65.1 | 61.3 | 52.2 | 37.3 | Total Current | 59.7 | 58.4 |
| 2.3 | 17.7 | 12.3 | 8.3 | 8.0 | 5.2 | Fixed Assets (net) | 10.2 | 10.0 |
| .1 | 7.9 | 12.1 | 20.6 | 33.7 | 52.2 | Intangibles (net) | 22.5 | 23.8 |
| 1.6 | 6.8 | 10.5 | 9.9 | 6.1 | 5.3 | All Other Non-Current | 7.6 | 7.8 |
| 100.0 | 100.0 | 100.0 | 100.0 | 100.0 | 100.0 | Total | 100.0 | 100.0 |
|  |  |  |  |  |  | **LIABILITIES** | | |
| 11.1 | 6.6 | 6.5 | 2.1 | .8 | .7 | Notes Payable-Short Term | 5.4 | 7.3 |
| 1.2 | 4.8 | 3.1 | 4.8 | 2.9 | 1.7 | Cur. Mat.-L.T.D. | 2.8 | 2.6 |
| 16.9 | 12.9 | 9.5 | 7.0 | 8.5 | 2.9 | Trade Payables | 9.2 | 7.2 |
| .0 | .2 | .6 | .4 | .9 | .9 | Income Taxes Payable | .7 | .6 |
| 23.8 | 19.3 | 28.0 | 42.7 | 25.3 | 22.3 | All Other Current | 25.0 | 27.2 |
| 53.1 | 43.8 | 47.7 | 56.9 | 38.3 | 28.5 | Total Current | 43.0 | 44.8 |
| 21.5 | 22.8 | 7.3 | 15.2 | 19.5 | 18.5 | Long-Term Debt | 16.8 | 15.8 |
| .2 | .0 | .1 | .6 | 2.6 | 3.0 | Deferred Taxes | .6 | 1.1 |
| 7.9 | 15.7 | 13.5 | 12.6 | 10.8 | 12.7 | All Other Non-Current | 13.5 | 10.6 |
| 17.4 | 17.6 | 31.4 | 14.7 | 28.8 | 37.3 | Net Worth | 26.1 | 27.7 |
| 100.0 | 100.0 | 100.0 | 100.0 | 100.0 | 100.0 | Total Liabilities & Net Worth | 100.0 | 100.0 |
|  |  |  |  |  |  | **INCOME DATA** | | |
| 100.0 | 100.0 | 100.0 | 100.0 | 100.0 | 100.0 | Net Sales | 100.0 | 100.0 |
|  |  |  |  |  |  | Gross Profit | | |
| 82.4 | 94.8 | 88.5 | 93.6 | 92.0 | 91.5 | Operating Expenses | 94.1 | 94.8 |
| 17.6 | 5.2 | 11.5 | 6.4 | 8.0 | 8.5 | Operating Profit | 5.9 | 5.2 |
| .2 | 2.5 | 1.1 | 2.4 | 4.3 | 5.6 | All Other Expenses (net) | 2.1 | 2.7 |
| 17.4 | 2.7 | 10.4 | 4.0 | 3.7 | 3.0 | Profit Before Taxes | 3.8 | 2.5 |
|  |  |  |  |  |  | **RATIOS** | | |
| 6.1 | 12.4 | 4.0 | 1.9 | 2.3 | 1.9 |  | 2.2 | 2.6 |
| 2.2 | 2.1 | 1.6 | 1.2 | 1.3 | 1.1 | Current | 1.4 | 1.3 |
| 1.6 | .8 | .9 | .7 | .9 | .8 |  | .9 | .9 |
| 6.1 | 12.3 | 3.7 | 1.8 | 2.1 | 1.7 |  | 2.1 | 2.1 |
| 2.2 | 1.4 | 1.4 | 1.0 | 1.2 | 1.0 | Quick | 1.2 | 1.2 |
| 1.4 | .8 | .7 | .5 | .6 | .5 |  | .7 | .7 |
| 5 72.4 | 7 54.0 | 34 10.8 | 34 10.6 | 46 8.0 | 46 7.9 |  | 41 9.0 | 40 9.0 |
| 33 11.1 | 35 10.4 | 59 6.2 | 59 6.2 | 66 5.5 | 68 5.4 | Sales/Receivables | 68 5.4 | 61 6.0 |
| 48 7.6 | 60 6.1 | 87 4.2 | 83 4.4 | 87 4.2 | 85 4.3 |  | 90 4.1 | 81 4.5 |
|  |  |  |  |  |  | Cost of Sales/Inventory | | |
|  |  |  |  |  |  | Cost of Sales/Payables | | |
| 7.1 | 4.7 | 3.1 | 5.2 | 3.5 | 4.0 |  | 3.4 | 4.0 |
| 11.5 | 13.4 | 13.0 | 14.5 | 10.2 | 15.7 | Sales/Working Capital | 9.3 | 12.5 |
| 23.8 | -34.9 | -37.7 | -6.5 | -14.4 | -8.7 |  | -19.7 | -15.5 |
|  | 19.6 | 98.2 | 79.7 | 9.9 | 4.8 |  | 13.5 | 15.6 |
|  | (20) 2.7 | (57) 12.3 | (41) 5.6 | (36) 3.0 | (48) 2.0 | EBIT/Interest | (153) 3.2 | (165) 2.3 |
|  | -4.5 | 1.1 | -2.0 | -1.8 | -1.0 |  | -.9 | -1.7 |
|  |  | 53.8 | 45.7 | 74.1 |  |  | 10.1 | 44.4 |
|  |  | (10) 7.0 | (16) 2.6 | (12) 6.9 |  | Net Profit + Depr., Dep., Amort./Cur. Mat. L/T/D | (37) 4.3 | (30) 3.1 |
|  |  | 1.2 | .1 | .8 |  |  | 1.0 | 1.6 |
| .0 | .1 | .1 | .1 | .2 | .5 |  | .1 | .2 |
| .0 | .9 | .4 | 2.1 | 9.3 | -.2 | Fixed/Worth | .6 | .9 |
| .0 | -.4 | 32.9 | -.1 | -.1 | -.1 |  | -.4 | -.1 |
| .4 | .4 | .6 | 1.2 | 1.1 | 2.3 |  | .9 | .9 |
| .9 | 3.3 | 2.9 | 27.2 | 19.6 | -2.7 | Debt/Worth | 4.6 | 5.7 |
| NM | -3.8 | 770.9 | -2.6 | -2.1 | -1.5 |  | -3.9 | -2.6 |
| 190.3 | 136.1 | 93.1 | 84.6 | 37.3 | 65.0 |  | 56.7 | 56.9 |
| (11) 60.4 | (20) 10.8 | (67) 52.7 | (32) 34.0 | (23) 9.1 | (18) 23.1 | % Profit Before Taxes/Tangible Net Worth | (135) 26.5 | (138) 22.1 |
| 11.2 | -27.4 | 21.4 | 1.9 | -4.1 | 3.6 |  | -1.1 | -.2 |
| 104.1 | 30.3 | 35.0 | 18.4 | 11.2 | 5.3 |  | 19.2 | 18.6 |
| 44.1 | 7.5 | 12.5 | 6.2 | 4.3 | 2.6 | % Profit Before Taxes/Total Assets | 6.2 | 4.1 |
| 8.9 | -8.1 | 1.8 | -9.1 | -2.1 | -3.9 |  | -3.8 | -3.2 |
| UND | 152.5 | 82.6 | 55.5 | 48.0 | 39.0 |  | 47.5 | 42.2 |
| UND | 50.0 | 38.6 | 30.1 | 19.3 | 18.2 | Sales/Net Fixed Assets | 21.2 | 22.1 |
| 301.5 | 15.4 | 14.4 | 13.2 | 11.3 | 10.8 |  | 12.3 | 12.4 |
| 7.5 | 5.2 | 3.0 | 1.9 | 1.4 | .8 |  | 2.3 | 2.4 |
| 5.4 | 3.0 | 1.7 | 1.3 | .9 | .6 | Sales/Total Assets | 1.4 | 1.3 |
| 3.6 | 2.4 | 1.1 | .9 | .7 | .4 |  | .8 | .8 |
|  | .2 | .6 | 1.0 | 1.7 | 2.2 |  | .8 | .9 |
|  | (18) 1.2 | (52) 1.2 | (37) 2.0 | (22) 3.3 | (15) 4.1 | % Depr., Dep., Amort./Sales | (124) 2.1 | (124) 2.2 |
|  | 2.7 | 2.4 | 3.4 | 4.7 | 7.9 |  | 4.4 | 4.1 |
|  | 1.8 | 2.8 |  |  |  |  | 5.5 | 3.8 |
|  | (12) 4.8 | (22) 4.1 |  |  |  | % Officers', Directors' Owners' Comp/Sales | (30) 9.7 | (29) 8.7 |
|  | 10.3 | 6.1 |  |  |  |  | 18.9 | 18.9 |
| 27437M | 121339M | 901216M | 2045929M | 3486438M | 6133121M | Net Sales ($) | 9940731M | 11215388M |
| 3869M | 30063M | 439921M | 1388264M | 3228911M | 9328106M | Total Assets ($) | 10928344M | 12148508M |

M = $ thousand    MM = $ million
See Pages 9 through 22 for Explanation of Ratios and Data

## Comparative Historical Data                    Current Data Sorted by Sales

Right-side columns are grouped: **43 (4/1-9/30/11)** covers 0-1MM, 1-3MM, 3-5MM; **252 (10/1/11-3/31/12)** covers 5-10MM, 10-25MM, 25MM & OVER.

| 4/1/09-3/31/10 ALL | 4/1/10-3/31/11 ALL | 4/1/11-3/31/12 ALL | | 0-1MM | 1-3MM | 3-5MM | 5-10MM | 10-25MM | 25MM & OVER |
|---|---|---|---|---|---|---|---|---|---|
| | | | **Type of Statement** | | | | | | |
| 86 | 89 | 55 | Unqualified | 1 | | 1 | 4 | 8 | 41 |
| 17 | 14 | 21 | Reviewed | | 7 | | 4 | 7 | 3 |
| 6 | 11 | 8 | Compiled | 1 | 1 | 2 | 2 | 1 | 1 |
| 15 | 21 | 26 | Tax Returns | 2 | 10 | 2 | 8 | 4 | |
| 135 | 137 | 185 | Other | 4 | 15 | 7 | 29 | 42 | 88 |
| 259 | 272 | 295 | **NUMBER OF STATEMENTS** | 8 | 33 | 12 | 47 | 62 | 133 |
| % | % | % | **ASSETS** | % | % | % | % | % | % |
| 26.2 | 24.1 | 25.6 | Cash & Equivalents | 21.3 | 28.6 | 30.4 | | 28.2 | 23.1 |
| 24.2 | 24.9 | 25.8 | Trade Receivables (net) | 37.6 | 24.6 | 32.4 | | 29.0 | 19.5 |
| 1.7 | 1.9 | 1.6 | Inventory | 1.5 | .5 | 1.8 | | 2.2 | 1.6 |
| 5.8 | 6.9 | 5.6 | All Other Current | 7.4 | 2.4 | 4.3 | | 5.6 | 6.1 |
| 57.8 | 57.8 | 58.7 | Total Current | 67.8 | 56.1 | 69.0 | | 65.2 | 50.3 |
| 10.7 | 9.3 | 9.5 | Fixed Assets (net) | 12.2 | 7.9 | 9.6 | | 8.9 | 6.9 |
| 22.1 | 24.4 | 24.0 | Intangibles (net) | 12.0 | 21.4 | 9.2 | | 17.8 | 36.8 |
| 9.4 | 8.4 | 7.9 | All Other Non-Current | 8.0 | 14.6 | 12.2 | | 8.1 | 6.1 |
| 100.0 | 100.0 | 100.0 | Total | 100.0 | 100.0 | 100.0 | | 100.0 | 100.0 |
| | | | **LIABILITIES** | | | | | | |
| 6.5 | 5.1 | 3.8 | Notes Payable-Short Term | 8.8 | 6.9 | 5.6 | | 5.0 | 1.2 |
| 4.0 | 4.6 | 3.2 | Cur. Mat.-L.T.D. | 3.0 | 1.9 | 3.7 | | 4.1 | 3.0 |
| 5.9 | 9.4 | 8.2 | Trade Payables | 10.5 | 4.8 | 8.5 | | 11.2 | 6.6 |
| .7 | 1.0 | .6 | Income Taxes Payable | .2 | .0 | .2 | | .6 | .9 |
| 31.8 | 30.6 | 28.5 | All Other Current | 19.9 | 13.4 | 19.3 | | 42.4 | 28.6 |
| 49.0 | 50.7 | 44.3 | Total Current | 42.4 | 27.0 | 37.4 | | 63.3 | 40.2 |
| 16.8 | 16.8 | 15.2 | Long-Term Debt | 10.7 | 11.8 | 5.9 | | 10.0 | 18.6 |
| 1.1 | 1.2 | 1.1 | Deferred Taxes | .1 | .0 | .2 | | .4 | 2.2 |
| 9.5 | 11.3 | 12.7 | All Other Non-Current | 20.4 | 16.6 | 8.6 | | 13.0 | 11.9 |
| 23.7 | 19.9 | 26.6 | Net Worth | 26.4 | 44.5 | 47.9 | | 13.4 | 27.1 |
| 100.0 | 100.0 | 100.0 | Total Liabilties & Net Worth | 100.0 | 100.0 | 100.0 | | 100.0 | 100.0 |
| | | | **INCOME DATA** | | | | | | |
| 100.0 | 100.0 | 100.0 | Net Sales | 100.0 | 100.0 | 100.0 | | 100.0 | 100.0 |
| | | | Gross Profit | | | | | | |
| 92.9 | 92.9 | 91.0 | Operating Expenses | 95.3 | 84.8 | 88.3 | | 94.7 | 91.4 |
| 7.1 | 7.1 | 9.0 | Operating Profit | 4.7 | 15.2 | 11.7 | | 5.3 | 8.6 |
| 3.8 | 3.7 | 2.8 | All Other Expenses (net) | .9 | .8 | .3 | | 1.4 | 4.5 |
| 3.4 | 3.4 | 6.1 | Profit Before Taxes | 3.8 | 14.4 | 11.4 | | 3.9 | 4.1 |
| | | | **RATIOS** | | | | | | |
| 2.4 | 2.0 | 2.7 | | 4.0 | 26.6 | 4.6 | | 2.3 | 1.9 |
| 1.3 | 1.2 | 1.4 | Current | 1.7 | 2.6 | 2.0 | | 1.2 | 1.2 |
| .8 | .8 | .8 | | .8 | .6 | 1.1 | | .7 | .8 |
| 2.1 | 1.6 | 2.4 | | 3.6 | 26.4 | 4.6 | | 1.8 | 1.7 |
| 1.0 | 1.0 | 1.2 | Quick | 1.5 | 2.2 | 1.8 | | 1.1 | 1.0 |
| .6 | .8 | .6 | | .6 | .5 | .9 | | .5 | .6 |
| 39  9.5 | 36  10.1 | 34  10.6 | | 23  16.0 | 20  18.2 | 35  10.3 | | 44  11.9 | 44  8.3 |
| 59  6.2 | 56  6.5 | 58  6.3 | Sales/Receivables | 61  6.0 | 27  13.5 | 61  6.0 | | 51  7.2 | 65  5.6 |
| 80  4.6 | 77  4.7 | 81  4.5 | | 114  3.2 | 41  9.0 | 87  4.2 | | 78  4.7 | 83  4.4 |
| | | | Cost of Sales/Inventory | | | | | | |
| | | | Cost of Sales/Payables | | | | | | |
| 4.5 | 5.5 | 3.9 | | 3.2 | 4.4 | 3.0 | | 4.8 | 4.6 |
| 15.1 | 18.5 | 13.2 | Sales/Working Capital | 11.2 | 10.2 | 7.8 | | 14.1 | 14.8 |
| -12.4 | -17.3 | -14.1 | | -19.9 | -5.6 | 29.9 | | -9.7 | -11.7 |
| 12.3 | 11.4 | 22.7 | | | 11.6 | | 113.8 | 38.7 | 9.9 |
| (190) 3.1 | (201) 2.3 | (209) 3.9 | EBIT/Interest | | (24) 3.9 | | (26) 18.9 | (45) 6.0 | (106) 2.1 |
| -1.6 | -1.3 | -.6 | | | -1.6 | | -.2 | -.1 | -.9 |
| 8.0 | 4.1 | 32.8 | Net Profit + Depr., Dep., | | | | | 62.4 | 20.3 |
| (35) 2.8 | (51) 1.3 | (47) 2.6 | Amort./Cur. Mat. L/T/D | | | | | (10) 22.4 | (30) 2.9 |
| -.3 | .0 | .7 | | | | | | 1.3 | -.1 |
| .2 | .1 | .1 | | .0 | .1 | .0 | | .1 | .3 |
| .7 | 1.0 | 1.0 | Fixed/Worth | .9 | .5 | .1 | | 1.0 | -.7 |
| -.2 | -.1 | -.2 | | -.4 | -.3 | .8 | | -.2 | -.1 |
| .9 | 1.3 | .9 | | .4 | .6 | .5 | | .8 | 1.4 |
| 5.2 | 8.7 | 6.3 | Debt/Worth | 10.1 | 1.3 | 1.1 | | 4.7 | -8.0 |
| -2.7 | -2.2 | -2.7 | | -4.2 | -7.8 | 5.2 | | -3.6 | -1.7 |
| 74.3 | 97.5 | 90.1 | % Profit Before Taxes/Tangible | | 58.2 | | 93.1 | 96.4 | 48.5 |
| (162) 21.2 | (154) 25.9 | (171) 34.9 | Net Worth | | (20) 14.3 | | (43) 46.2 | (37) 53.1 | (57) 20.2 |
| .9 | 2.5 | 5.4 | | | -.1 | | 9.0 | 25.1 | -1.6 |
| 16.3 | 16.0 | 18.3 | % Profit Before Taxes/Total | 18.1 | 69.5 | 43.0 | | 26.4 | 11.0 |
| 4.7 | 4.9 | 5.6 | Assets | 7.3 | 12.8 | 14.6 | | 9.4 | 3.0 |
| -6.2 | -4.8 | -2.0 | | -.2 | 7.3 | 2.9 | | -1.4 | -3.5 |
| 48.2 | 53.7 | 62.7 | | 191.0 | 424.9 | 97.9 | | 64.6 | 47.9 |
| 19.7 | 27.5 | 30.6 | Sales/Net Fixed Assets | 35.9 | 45.8 | 44.0 | | 35.6 | 23.9 |
| 11.3 | 14.0 | 13.2 | | 7.8 | 19.4 | 18.1 | | 13.3 | 12.3 |
| 2.2 | 2.4 | 2.5 | | 3.4 | 5.2 | 3.2 | | 2.6 | 1.5 |
| 1.2 | 1.4 | 1.3 | Sales/Total Assets | 2.4 | 1.8 | 1.7 | | 1.7 | .9 |
| .8 | .7 | .7 | | .8 | 1.0 | 1.1 | | 1.2 | .6 |
| 1.2 | 1.1 | .9 | | | 1.1 | | .5 | .8 | 1.2 |
| (142) 2.5 | (139) 2.5 | (147) 1.8 | % Depr., Dep., Amort./Sales | | (18) 2.2 | | (27) 1.5 | (43) 1.3 | (54) 2.9 |
| 4.7 | 4.6 | 3.7 | | | 4.3 | | 2.9 | 3.1 | 4.9 |
| 4.2 | 3.2 | 2.7 | % Officers', Directors' | | 3.2 | | 1.9 | | |
| (28) 9.5 | (37) 7.6 | (45) 4.3 | Owners' Comp/Sales | | (16) 6.3 | | (11) 4.3 | | |
| 15.1 | 12.6 | 10.2 | | | 14.8 | | 6.0 | | |
| 12382776M | 13201487M | 12715480M | Net Sales ($) | 3414M | 66538M | 45517M | 357408M | 1040349M | 11202254M |
| 14052707M | 14279089M | 14419134M | Total Assets ($) | 7165M | 56940M | 28028M | 241484M | 802488M | 13283029M |

M = $ thousand    MM = $ million
See Pages 9 through 22 for Explanation of Ratios and Data

## Current Data Sorted by Assets

## Comparative Historical Data

| | 0-500M | 500M-2MM | 2-10MM | 10-50MM | 50-100MM | 100-250MM | Type of Statement | 4/1/07-3/31/08 ALL | 4/1/08-3/31/09 ALL |
|---|---|---|---|---|---|---|---|---|---|
| | | | 3 | 9 | 1 | 6 | Unqualified | 17 | 15 |
| | | 4 | 14 | 2 | 1 | | Reviewed | 19 | 21 |
| | 4 | 9 | 7 | 6 | | | Compiled | 13 | 15 |
| | 18 | 12 | 12 | 3 | | | Tax Returns | 26 | 23 |
| | 17 | 18 | 19 | 7 | 4 | 8 | Other | 52 | 52 |
| | | 18 (4/1-9/30/11) | | 166 (10/1/11-3/31/12) | | | | | |
| | 39 | 43 | 55 | 27 | 6 | 14 | **NUMBER OF STATEMENTS** | 127 | 126 |
| | % | % | % | % | % | % | **ASSETS** | % | % |
| | 23.9 | 19.1 | 19.2 | 17.1 | | 6.6 | Cash & Equivalents | 14.6 | 16.9 |
| | 18.0 | 20.6 | 27.5 | 12.2 | | 10.9 | Trade Receivables (net) | 26.3 | 21.5 |
| | 2.5 | .3 | 3.4 | 7.5 | | 2.2 | Inventory | 3.6 | 4.1 |
| | 1.1 | 3.6 | 3.3 | 6.5 | | 7.6 | All Other Current | 5.2 | 6.0 |
| | 45.5 | 43.6 | 53.3 | 43.3 | | 27.2 | Total Current | 49.7 | 48.4 |
| | 36.5 | 33.8 | 28.6 | 43.7 | | 12.5 | Fixed Assets (net) | 34.7 | 36.0 |
| | 5.1 | 3.6 | 5.6 | 5.7 | | 45.0 | Intangibles (net) | 5.4 | 4.7 |
| | 12.9 | 19.0 | 12.4 | 7.4 | | 15.4 | All Other Non-Current | 10.2 | 10.9 |
| | 100.0 | 100.0 | 100.0 | 100.0 | | 100.0 | Total | 100.0 | 100.0 |
| | | | | | | | **LIABILITIES** | | |
| | 27.5 | 10.0 | 6.4 | 4.1 | | 19.7 | Notes Payable-Short Term | 9.9 | 9.9 |
| | 7.0 | 5.8 | 3.7 | 5.0 | | 8.2 | Cur. Mat.-L.T.D. | 5.1 | 5.5 |
| | 12.1 | 10.8 | 14.7 | 4.7 | | 8.8 | Trade Payables | 18.3 | 10.9 |
| | .2 | .3 | .3 | .3 | | .0 | Income Taxes Payable | .3 | .2 |
| | 35.1 | 24.6 | 19.2 | 10.9 | | 18.9 | All Other Current | 17.6 | 13.1 |
| | 81.9 | 51.5 | 44.3 | 25.0 | | 55.7 | Total Current | 51.1 | 39.7 |
| | 15.0 | 46.6 | 11.5 | 22.6 | | 30.4 | Long-Term Debt | 23.8 | 24.8 |
| | .0 | 1.1 | .2 | 1.5 | | .5 | Deferred Taxes | .7 | .7 |
| | 5.5 | 21.7 | 5.4 | 17.3 | | 16.1 | All Other Non-Current | 13.8 | 8.9 |
| | -2.4 | -20.9 | 38.5 | 33.7 | | -2.7 | Net Worth | 10.7 | 25.9 |
| | 100.0 | 100.0 | 100.0 | 100.0 | | 100.0 | Total Liabilties & Net Worth | 100.0 | 100.0 |
| | | | | | | | **INCOME DATA** | | |
| | 100.0 | 100.0 | 100.0 | 100.0 | | 100.0 | Net Sales | 100.0 | 100.0 |
| | | | | | | | Gross Profit | | |
| | 91.4 | 89.8 | 92.6 | 88.6 | | 95.8 | Operating Expenses | 91.4 | 91.1 |
| | 8.6 | 10.2 | 7.4 | 11.4 | | 4.2 | Operating Profit | 8.6 | 8.9 |
| | .0 | 4.3 | 1.7 | 2.0 | | 19.8 | All Other Expenses (net) | 1.5 | 3.5 |
| | 8.6 | 5.9 | 5.8 | 9.4 | | -15.6 | Profit Before Taxes | 7.2 | 5.4 |
| | | | | | | | **RATIOS** | | |
| | 2.1 | 2.5 | 4.0 | 3.9 | | 1.3 | | 2.4 | 2.3 |
| | .8 | 1.0 | 2.0 | 1.8 | | .6 | Current | 1.3 | 1.3 |
| | .3 | .4 | .9 | .9 | | .2 | | .8 | .7 |
| | 2.1 | 2.5 | 3.3 | 3.2 | | 1.0 | | 2.1 | 1.8 |
| | .8 | .9 | 1.8 | 1.1 | | .5 | Quick | 1.1 | 1.0 |
| | .2 | .3 | .6 | .4 | | .1 | | .6 | .4 |
| | 0 UND | 0 UND | 13 27.4 | 8 45.9 | | 7 53.1 | | 17 21.9 | 8 44.8 |
| | 1 696.0 | 16 22.2 | 39 9.4 | 35 10.5 | | 17 20.9 | Sales/Receivables | 47 7.7 | 36 10.2 |
| | 27 13.5 | 34 10.8 | 74 4.9 | 55 6.6 | | 38 9.5 | | 68 5.4 | 62 5.9 |
| | | | | | | | Cost of Sales/Inventory | | |
| | | | | | | | Cost of Sales/Payables | | |
| | 17.5 | 13.4 | 4.9 | 3.7 | | 13.2 | | 7.5 | 5.9 |
| | -62.6 | -425.6 | 9.9 | 7.8 | | -9.5 | Sales/Working Capital | 22.6 | 22.1 |
| | -8.7 | -11.7 | -66.3 | -18.0 | | -1.4 | | -30.5 | -19.7 |
| | 31.4 | 8.1 | 41.8 | 11.2 | | .1 | | 13.7 | 12.8 |
| | (22) 11.5 | (31) 4.0 | (43) 7.1 | (22) 4.9 | | (13) -2.7 | EBIT/Interest | (107) 5.1 | (107) 4.2 |
| | 3.7 | .7 | .9 | 1.8 | | -4.2 | | 1.4 | .9 |
| | | | | | | | Net Profit + Depr., Dep., Amort./Cur. Mat. L/T/D | 3.9 | 4.9 |
| | | | | | | | | (18) 2.3 | (20) 2.9 |
| | | | | | | | | 1.4 | 1.4 |
| | .5 | .3 | .2 | .3 | | .0 | | .4 | .3 |
| | 1.5 | 16.9 | .5 | 1.8 | | .0 | Fixed/Worth | 1.6 | 1.3 |
| | -4.5 | -1.0 | 1.5 | 4.4 | | NM | | 8.3 | 17.2 |
| | .8 | 1.2 | .5 | .5 | | 15.6 | | .9 | .8 |
| | 2.4 | 20.6 | 1.0 | 1.8 | | -1.6 | Debt/Worth | 3.0 | 2.7 |
| | -10.4 | -3.8 | 3.7 | 4.9 | | -1.4 | | -115.2 | NM |
| | 241.0 | 44.8 | 53.1 | 55.7 | | | % Profit Before Taxes/Tangible Net Worth | 94.1 | 99.9 |
| | (24) 109.1 | (23) 15.7 | (50) 26.0 | (23) 22.2 | | | | (94) 43.3 | (95) 26.8 |
| | 44.3 | 7.5 | 8.1 | 7.0 | | | | 12.4 | 7.6 |
| | 75.9 | 13.4 | 17.6 | 15.3 | | -5.0 | % Profit Before Taxes/Total Assets | 31.1 | 17.9 |
| | 34.5 | 5.3 | 11.1 | 5.0 | | -6.9 | | 10.9 | 6.3 |
| | 9.2 | -.3 | .3 | .2 | | -30.6 | | .7 | -2.7 |
| | 42.0 | 47.0 | 45.5 | 23.6 | | UND | Sales/Net Fixed Assets | 19.5 | 25.2 |
| | 18.4 | 12.7 | 12.4 | 2.3 | | 371.0 | | 9.0 | 7.9 |
| | 11.0 | 4.9 | 3.7 | 1.3 | | 22.0 | | 3.4 | 2.8 |
| | 8.0 | 4.8 | 2.8 | 1.4 | | 1.6 | Sales/Total Assets | 3.2 | 3.1 |
| | 4.8 | 2.9 | 2.1 | 1.1 | | .6 | | 2.1 | 1.9 |
| | 2.3 | 1.2 | 1.4 | .7 | | .3 | | 1.2 | 1.0 |
| | .8 | 1.1 | 1.3 | 3.6 | | | % Depr., Dep., Amort./Sales | 1.8 | 1.7 |
| | (19) 1.8 | (29) 2.2 | (42) 3.8 | (19) 11.5 | | | | (89) 3.7 | (85) 3.7 |
| | 2.8 | 7.2 | 6.9 | 21.8 | | | | 7.5 | 8.5 |
| | 4.8 | 2.3 | 2.5 | | | | % Officers', Directors' Owners' Comp/Sales | 4.4 | 5.1 |
| | (18) 8.1 | (18) 5.3 | (31) 4.0 | | | | | (44) 7.0 | (48) 6.5 |
| | 16.6 | 7.0 | 6.4 | | | | | 12.0 | 10.3 |
| | 52364M | 184886M | 520986M | 1433161M | 259258M | 2080007M | Net Sales ($) | 2614474M | 2641816M |
| | 9504M | 50028M | 239817M | 772714M | 436112M | 2237571M | Total Assets ($) | 2079897M | 2289836M |

M = $ thousand   MM = $ million
See Pages 9 through 22 for Explanation of Ratios and Data

## Comparative Historical Data | Current Data Sorted by Sales

| Type of Statement | 4/1/09-3/31/10 ALL | 4/1/10-3/31/11 ALL | 4/1/11-3/31/12 ALL | 0-1MM | 1-3MM | 3-5MM | 5-10MM | 10-25MM | 25MM & OVER |
|---|---|---|---|---|---|---|---|---|---|
| Unqualified | 16 | 17 | 19 | | 1 | | 6 | 12 | |
| Reviewed | 19 | 30 | 21 | | 2 | 5 | 4 | 8 | 2 |
| Compiled | 12 | 18 | 26 | 4 | 5 | 1 | 8 | 6 | 2 |
| Tax Returns | 32 | 34 | 45 | 15 | 11 | 8 | 9 | 1 | 1 |
| Other | 62 | 59 | 73 | 14 | | 6 | 17 | 9 | 18 |
| | | | | 18 (4/1-9/30/11) | | 166 (10/1/11-3/31/12) | | | |
| NUMBER OF STATEMENTS | 141 | 158 | 184 | 33 | 28 | 20 | 38 | 30 | 35 |
| **ASSETS** | % | % | % | % | % | % | % | % | % |
| Cash & Equivalents | 16.9 | 19.1 | 18.4 | 16.3 | 21.2 | 22.5 | 18.7 | 20.1 | 13.9 |
| Trade Receivables (net) | 23.0 | 21.9 | 19.8 | 13.9 | 17.9 | 15.2 | 27.5 | 26.9 | 14.7 |
| Inventory | 3.7 | 2.8 | 3.0 | 2.4 | 1.0 | 2.2 | 1.3 | 4.3 | 6.3 |
| All Other Current | 6.7 | 4.8 | 4.0 | .8 | 1.2 | 2.2 | 4.3 | 4.8 | 9.0 |
| Total Current | 50.3 | 48.7 | 45.1 | 33.5 | 41.2 | 42.1 | 51.8 | 56.1 | 43.9 |
| Fixed Assets (net) | 36.0 | 33.6 | 32.6 | 45.1 | 38.3 | 39.6 | 24.5 | 30.1 | 23.1 |
| Intangibles (net) | 4.8 | 8.4 | 8.6 | 5.2 | 6.5 | 2.8 | 6.0 | 5.5 | 22.2 |
| All Other Non-Current | 8.9 | 9.3 | 13.7 | 16.1 | 13.9 | 15.6 | 17.6 | 8.2 | 10.8 |
| Total | 100.0 | 100.0 | 100.0 | 100.0 | 100.0 | 100.0 | 100.0 | 100.0 | 100.0 |
| **LIABILITIES** | | | | | | | | | |
| Notes Payable-Short Term | 10.3 | 12.4 | 12.5 | 23.0 | 16.0 | 8.3 | 9.2 | 6.3 | 11.1 |
| Cur. Mat.-L.T.D. | 4.9 | 5.2 | 5.4 | 4.3 | 10.6 | 4.4 | 4.6 | 4.3 | 4.9 |
| Trade Payables | 9.3 | 8.8 | 11.0 | 6.8 | 13.1 | 8.6 | 11.5 | 17.1 | 8.9 |
| Income Taxes Payable | .4 | .3 | .2 | .2 | .1 | .5 | .2 | .4 | .1 |
| All Other Current | 17.0 | 19.3 | 22.2 | 31.1 | 14.7 | 38.1 | 22.7 | 13.0 | 17.8 |
| Total Current | 41.9 | 45.9 | 51.3 | 65.4 | 54.5 | 59.9 | 48.1 | 41.1 | 42.8 |
| Long-Term Debt | 21.6 | 25.8 | 24.3 | 22.2 | 36.0 | 18.6 | 30.1 | 14.0 | 22.6 |
| Deferred Taxes | .4 | .4 | .6 | .0 | .6 | 1.5 | .2 | 1.4 | .7 |
| All Other Non-Current | 8.0 | 9.6 | 11.9 | 6.5 | 9.0 | 30.3 | 6.3 | 7.1 | 18.9 |
| Net Worth | 28.1 | 18.3 | 11.9 | 6.0 | -.1 | -10.3 | 15.3 | 36.4 | 15.1 |
| Total Liabilities & Net Worth | 100.0 | 100.0 | 100.0 | 100.0 | 100.0 | 100.0 | 100.0 | 100.0 | 100.0 |
| **INCOME DATA** | | | | | | | | | |
| Net Sales | 100.0 | 100.0 | 100.0 | 100.0 | 100.0 | 100.0 | 100.0 | 100.0 | 100.0 |
| Gross Profit | | | | | | | | | |
| Operating Expenses | 91.1 | 90.5 | 91.0 | 82.7 | 94.7 | 92.9 | 92.2 | 92.3 | 92.3 |
| Operating Profit | 8.9 | 9.5 | 9.0 | 17.3 | 5.3 | 7.1 | 7.8 | 7.7 | 7.7 |
| All Other Expenses (net) | 2.2 | 3.3 | 3.4 | 4.8 | 2.0 | 2.0 | .7 | 1.2 | 8.9 |
| Profit Before Taxes | 6.7 | 6.3 | 5.6 | 12.5 | 3.2 | 5.1 | 7.1 | 6.5 | -1.2 |
| **RATIOS** | | | | | | | | | |
| Current | 2.9 | 2.7 | 2.9 | 2.1 | 2.1 | 2.5 | 4.6 | 2.9 | 2.9 |
| | 1.3 | 1.2 | 1.3 | .7 | 1.1 | .9 | 2.0 | 1.9 | 1.1 |
| | .8 | .7 | .5 | .2 | .4 | .4 | 1.0 | .5 | .7 |
| Quick | 2.4 | 2.4 | 2.5 | 2.1 | 2.0 | 2.4 | 4.6 | 2.8 | 1.2 |
| | .9 | 1.0 | 1.0 | .5 | .9 | .5 | 1.9 | 1.4 | .9 |
| | .5 | .5 | .4 | .1 | .2 | .3 | .7 | .4 | .5 |
| Sales/Receivables | 7   50.4 | 5   69.1 | 1   676.6 | 0   UND | 0   UND | 0   UND | 13   28.0 | 19   19.1 | 11   33.3 |
| | 37   9.8 | 33   11.1 | 24   15.5 | 0   UND | 15   24.1 | 11   32.6 | 32   11.3 | 41   8.9 | 26   14.2 |
| | 64   5.7 | 58   6.3 | 54   6.8 | 27   13.3 | 40   9.2 | 44   8.3 | 59   6.2 | 62   5.9 | 54   6.8 |
| Cost of Sales/Inventory | | | | | | | | | |
| Cost of Sales/Payables | | | | | | | | | |
| Sales/Working Capital | 5.9 | 5.4 | 6.5 | 16.8 | 9.1 | 9.0 | 5.5 | 5.0 | 5.3 |
| | 25.1 | 28.0 | 30.0 | -52.9 | 158.7 | NM | 11.6 | 15.0 | 29.9 |
| | -16.7 | -16.5 | -11.5 | -3.2 | -18.5 | -5.8 | NM | -6.7 | -11.8 |
| EBIT/Interest | 14.0 | 15.6 | 17.5 | 37.5 | 12.2 | 8.6 | 20.7 | 27.4 | 14.0 |
| | (110) 4.3 | (120) 4.5 | (137) 4.9 | (16) 9.1 | (21) 3.0 | (14) 3.7 | (32) 7.1 | (22) 5.7 | (32) 2.7 |
| | -.1 | 1.0 | .6 | 1.9 | -.9 | 1.8 | .9 | 2.0 | -2.5 |
| Net Profit + Depr., Dep., Amort./Cur. Mat. L/T/D | 4.5 | 5.3 | 6.1 | | | | | | |
| | (21) 2.0 | (21) 3.0 | (23) 3.7 | | | | | | |
| | .9 | 1.5 | 1.6 | | | | | | |
| Fixed/Worth | .3 | .2 | .2 | .5 | .5 | .1 | .2 | .2 | .0 |
| | .9 | 1.2 | 1.0 | 2.2 | 2.4 | 1.2 | .5 | .8 | .7 |
| | 5.7 | 47.2 | -31.3 | -13.7 | -.7 | NM | NM | 4.4 | 2.9 |
| Debt/Worth | .6 | .7 | .7 | .7 | 1.0 | .7 | .3 | .5 | 1.5 |
| | 2.0 | 2.9 | 2.5 | 2.6 | 4.9 | 2.6 | 1.0 | 2.1 | 3.6 |
| | 19.9 | -61.8 | -11.5 | -7.2 | -3.0 | NM | NM | 6.5 | -1.7 |
| % Profit Before Taxes/Tangible Net Worth | 67.9 | 70.3 | 70.1 | 131.9 | 204.8 | 72.5 | 55.7 | 38.7 | 68.5 |
| | (113) 21.1 | (116) 26.3 | (128) 26.5 | (21) 44.8 | (17) 18.0 | (15) 24.9 | (29) 27.0 | (25) 22.5 | (21) 24.0 |
| | 2.2 | 4.4 | 8.7 | 8.4 | 5.2 | 9.4 | 5.2 | 16.6 | -4.4 |
| % Profit Before Taxes/Total Assets | 21.3 | 22.9 | 23.9 | 46.2 | 34.1 | 15.5 | 35.9 | 16.7 | 15.3 |
| | 6.7 | 9.1 | 8.5 | 17.6 | 6.5 | 7.7 | 12.3 | 11.3 | 1.3 |
| | -1.5 | .0 | -.3 | 2.1 | -8.2 | 3.8 | -.6 | 2.8 | -7.5 |
| Sales/Net Fixed Assets | 23.8 | 38.7 | 53.8 | 31.9 | 23.2 | 98.3 | 40.7 | 49.0 | 423.8 |
| | 7.2 | 10.5 | 13.4 | 13.6 | 12.5 | 13.4 | 14.7 | 12.3 | 52.8 |
| | 2.6 | 3.3 | 3.4 | 1.3 | 4.0 | 3.7 | 6.6 | 3.5 | 2.2 |
| Sales/Total Assets | 3.3 | 3.7 | 4.3 | 4.8 | 4.7 | 6.0 | 4.7 | 2.8 | 1.6 |
| | 1.9 | 2.1 | 2.1 | 1.9 | 2.8 | 2.4 | 2.6 | 2.2 | 1.2 |
| | 1.1 | 1.2 | 1.1 | .8 | 1.2 | 1.4 | 1.5 | 1.1 | .6 |
| % Depr., Dep., Amort./Sales | 2.1 | 1.1 | 1.2 | 2.3 | 1.2 | .8 | 1.7 | 1.2 | .3 |
| | (90) 4.7 | (108) 3.9 | (114) 3.3 | (18) 6.3 | (20) 2.3 | (14) 2.0 | (25) 3.6 | (23) 4.0 | (14) 2.4 |
| | 10.1 | 7.6 | 7.6 | 13.7 | 6.9 | 6.1 | 6.7 | 8.1 | 10.7 |
| % Officers', Directors' Owners' Comp/Sales | 5.0 | 4.0 | 3.1 | 6.1 | 3.3 | 4.1 | 2.8 | 2.0 | |
| | (50) 8.3 | (64) 7.1 | (70) 5.5 | (11) 7.8 | (17) 6.0 | (10) 7.7 | (21) 4.0 | (10) 3.0 | |
| | 12.7 | 13.8 | 8.3 | 23.0 | 9.0 | 13.7 | 7.6 | 4.5 | |
| Net Sales ($) | 2440448M | 2849522M | 4530662M | 16006M | 55736M | 76031M | 264289M | 477746M | 3640854M |
| Total Assets ($) | 1998862M | 2535649M | 3745746M | 17053M | 43862M | 61263M | 151469M | 426257M | 3045842M |

© RMA 2012

M = $ thousand    MM = $ million
See Pages 9 through 22 for Explanation of Ratios and Data

## Current Data Sorted by Assets      Comparative Historical Data

| 0-500M | 500M-2MM | 2-10MM | 10-50MM | 50-100MM | 100-250MM | Type of Statement | 4/1/07-3/31/08 ALL | 4/1/08-3/31/09 ALL |
|---|---|---|---|---|---|---|---|---|
| | | 2 | 14 | 5 | 4 | Unqualified | 14 | 18 |
| | | 5 | 4 | 1 | | Reviewed | 11 | 12 |
| 1 | 8 | 11 | 3 | | | Compiled | 10 | 16 |
| 3 | 9 | 4 | 1 | | | Tax Returns | 15 | 13 |
| 5 | 8 | 22 | 13 | 5 | 1 | Other | 37 | 50 |
| | 4 (4/1-9/30/11) | | 125 (10/1/11-3/31/12) | | | | | |
| 9 | 25 | 44 | 35 | 11 | 5 | **NUMBER OF STATEMENTS** | 87 | 109 |
| % | % | % | % | % | % | **ASSETS** | % | % |
| | 8.6 | 8.6 | 7.4 | 8.9 | | Cash & Equivalents | 11.2 | 7.4 |
| | 2.5 | 1.0 | 1.7 | 1.9 | | Trade Receivables (net) | .4 | .9 |
| | 1.5 | .6 | 1.0 | .4 | | Inventory | .9 | 1.3 |
| | 2.3 | 4.7 | 1.4 | 1.2 | | All Other Current | 1.7 | 2.4 |
| | 14.9 | 14.9 | 11.5 | 12.4 | | Total Current | 14.3 | 12.0 |
| | 73.3 | 74.5 | 77.5 | 67.7 | | Fixed Assets (net) | 75.2 | 77.7 |
| | 1.0 | 3.7 | 4.8 | 16.3 | | Intangibles (net) | 3.0 | 5.1 |
| | 10.9 | 6.9 | 6.2 | 3.7 | | All Other Non-Current | 7.5 | 5.1 |
| | 100.0 | 100.0 | 100.0 | 100.0 | | Total | 100.0 | 100.0 |
| | | | | | | **LIABILITIES** | | |
| | 3.3 | 3.9 | 2.1 | 2.0 | | Notes Payable-Short Term | 1.8 | 2.5 |
| | 6.0 | 3.7 | 5.9 | 2.9 | | Cur. Mat.-L.T.D. | 3.7 | 6.3 |
| | 6.6 | 2.6 | 5.1 | 3.8 | | Trade Payables | 7.0 | 5.5 |
| | .0 | .1 | .1 | .1 | | Income Taxes Payable | .1 | .0 |
| | 9.8 | 5.3 | 7.2 | 9.8 | | All Other Current | 8.9 | 8.8 |
| | 25.7 | 15.5 | 20.4 | 18.6 | | Total Current | 21.4 | 23.1 |
| | 40.8 | 51.5 | 47.4 | 45.6 | | Long-Term Debt | 44.8 | 46.3 |
| | .0 | .0 | .1 | .0 | | Deferred Taxes | .1 | .2 |
| | 19.4 | 6.9 | 12.4 | 13.7 | | All Other Non-Current | 17.4 | 11.6 |
| | 14.1 | 26.1 | 19.7 | 22.1 | | Net Worth | 16.3 | 18.9 |
| | 100.0 | 100.0 | 100.0 | 100.0 | | Total Liabilities & Net Worth | 100.0 | 100.0 |
| | | | | | | **INCOME DATA** | | |
| | 100.0 | 100.0 | 100.0 | 100.0 | | Net Sales | 100.0 | 100.0 |
| | | | | | | Gross Profit | | |
| | 87.9 | 91.3 | 86.6 | 93.5 | | Operating Expenses | 93.0 | 89.7 |
| | 12.1 | 8.7 | 13.4 | 6.5 | | Operating Profit | 7.0 | 10.3 |
| | 5.8 | 6.9 | 8.2 | 3.3 | | All Other Expenses (net) | 6.8 | 7.5 |
| | 6.3 | 1.7 | 5.3 | 3.2 | | Profit Before Taxes | .2 | 2.8 |
| | | | | | | **RATIOS** | | |
| | 1.5 | 2.3 | .7 | 1.8 | | | 1.3 | 1.0 |
| | .6 | .8 | .5 | .8 | | Current | .5 | .3 |
| | .2 | .4 | .3 | .5 | | | .3 | .1 |
| | 1.3 | 1.5 | .7 | 1.6 | | | .7 | .8 |
| | .3 | .6 | .4 | .5 | | Quick | .4 (108) | .2 |
| | .1 | .2 | .3 | .4 | | | .2 | .1 |
| | 0 UND | 0 UND | 0 999.8 | 0 UND | | | 0 UND | 0 UND |
| | 0 UND | 0 UND | 3 133.6 | 4 98.7 | | Sales/Receivables | 0 UND | 0 UND |
| | 1 602.5 | 1 298.8 | 8 45.3 | 6 65.9 | | | 2 182.4 | 1 380.8 |
| | | | | | | Cost of Sales/Inventory | | |
| | | | | | | Cost of Sales/Payables | | |
| | 49.9 | 11.0 | -33.2 | 10.4 | | | 123.0 | -207.4 |
| | -47.0 | -70.9 | -12.7 | -28.8 | | Sales/Working Capital | -14.2 | -13.7 |
| | -9.2 | -10.6 | -5.0 | -14.2 | | | -6.4 | -4.8 |
| | 9.7 | 3.0 | 3.1 | 3.2 | | | 2.4 | 3.3 |
| | (21) 4.3 | (41) 1.9 | (28) 1.7 | 2.1 | | EBIT/Interest | (69) 1.3 | (83) 1.5 |
| | 2.4 | .5 | .4 | 1.2 | | | .3 | .4 |
| | | | | | | | 4.7 | 5.6 |
| | | | | | | Net Profit + Depr., Dep., Amort./Cur. Mat. L/T/D | (14) 1.7 | (12) 2.0 |
| | | | | | | | .7 | .9 |
| | 1.3 | 1.3 | 2.5 | 2.4 | | | 2.1 | 2.3 |
| | 2.7 | 4.1 | 4.8 | 37.5 | | Fixed/Worth | 5.0 | 5.1 |
| | -2.7 | UND | 42.5 | -2.4 | | | 155.3 | -13.3 |
| | .9 | .8 | 1.9 | 1.6 | | | 1.5 | 1.8 |
| | 3.6 | 3.4 | 4.2 | 42.5 | | Debt/Worth | 4.4 | 5.0 |
| | -4.9 | UND | 42.6 | -4.7 | | | 159.6 | -17.9 |
| | 71.7 | 23.8 | 53.0 | | | | 32.9 | 33.8 |
| | (15) 27.5 | (34) 9.3 | (27) 12.7 | | | % Profit Before Taxes/Tangible Net Worth | (67) 5.2 | (74) 10.8 |
| | 14.9 | -3.3 | -5.6 | | | | -19.6 | -2.5 |
| | 19.8 | 7.0 | 7.3 | 8.1 | | | 7.8 | 7.7 |
| | 9.0 | 3.1 | 2.2 | 5.6 | | % Profit Before Taxes/Total Assets | 1.4 | 1.5 |
| | -.5 | -2.0 | -1.7 | .6 | | | -4.0 | -3.5 |
| | 5.7 | 2.0 | 2.0 | 3.3 | | | 2.8 | 2.8 |
| | 2.4 | .8 | 1.2 | 1.2 | | Sales/Net Fixed Assets | .9 | 1.0 |
| | 1.0 | .5 | .6 | .9 | | | .5 | .6 |
| | 3.1 | 1.1 | 1.5 | 1.4 | | | 1.6 | 1.8 |
| | 1.5 | .6 | .9 | .9 | | Sales/Total Assets | .8 | .9 |
| | .8 | .4 | .4 | .8 | | | .5 | .5 |
| | 2.3 | 4.9 | 5.6 | 6.8 | | | 4.2 | 4.4 |
| | (22) 4.1 | (40) 7.7 | (33) 8.4 | 7.9 | | % Depr., Dep., Amort./Sales | (83) 6.7 | (94) 7.0 |
| | 7.2 | 11.0 | 11.2 | 9.2 | | | 10.5 | 11.2 |
| | 1.4 | | | | | | 1.8 | 1.9 |
| | (10) 2.7 | | | | | % Officers', Directors' Owners' Comp/Sales | (22) 3.7 | (21) 4.9 |
| | 5.6 | | | | | | 7.7 | 9.9 |
| 8936M | 53399M | 262541M | 949923M | 757104M | 759061M | Net Sales ($) | 1959478M | 2143388M |
| 1509M | 27584M | 244941M | 862848M | 743992M | 839949M | Total Assets ($) | 2124375M | 2263197M |

M = $ thousand     MM = $ million
See Pages 9 through 22 for Explanation of Ratios and Data

## Comparative Historical Data | Current Data Sorted by Sales

| Hist | Hist | Hist | Type of Statement | 0-1MM | 1-3MM | 3-5MM | 5-10MM | 10-25MM | 25MM & OVER |
|---|---|---|---|---|---|---|---|---|---|
| 14 | 17 | 25 | Unqualified | | 1 | 1 | 3 | 5 | 15 |
| 14 | 5 | 10 | Reviewed | | 4 | 1 | 1 | 3 | 1 |
| 18 | 22 | 23 | Compiled | 2 | 8 | 5 | 5 | 3 | |
| 21 | 32 | 17 | Tax Returns | 4 | 13 | | | | |
| 54 | 43 | 54 | Other | 7 | 17 | 6 | 5 | 7 | 12 |
| 4/1/09-3/31/10 ALL | 4/1/10-3/31/11 ALL | 4/1/11-3/31/12 ALL | | 4 (4/1-9/30/11) | | | 125 (10/1/11-3/31/12) | | |
| 121 | 119 | 129 | **NUMBER OF STATEMENTS** | 13 | 43 | 13 | 14 | 18 | 28 |
| % | % | % | **ASSETS** | % | % | % | % | % | % |
| 9.8 | 13.0 | 9.7 | Cash & Equivalents | 14.7 | 8.7 | 10.6 | 7.2 | 8.1 | 10.8 |
| .8 | 2.5 | 1.9 | Trade Receivables (net) | 1.6 | 2.4 | .1 | 2.8 | 1.8 | 1.7 |
| 1.2 | 1.4 | 1.3 | Inventory | 3.7 | .9 | .4 | 1.5 | 1.3 | 1.1 |
| 1.8 | 1.2 | 2.6 | All Other Current | 1.1 | 3.0 | 6.7 | .4 | 2.3 | 1.8 |
| 13.6 | 18.0 | 15.4 | Total Current | 21.1 | 15.0 | 17.9 | 11.9 | 13.5 | 15.3 |
| 75.9 | 73.0 | 71.9 | Fixed Assets (net) | 60.1 | 75.1 | 74.0 | 73.7 | 75.9 | 67.8 |
| 4.9 | 3.5 | 5.6 | Intangibles (net) | 10.0 | 1.9 | 1.5 | 6.6 | 4.3 | 11.3 |
| 5.5 | 5.5 | 7.2 | All Other Non-Current | 9.0 | 8.0 | 6.6 | 7.8 | 6.3 | 5.5 |
| 100.0 | 100.0 | 100.0 | Total | 100.0 | 100.0 | 100.0 | 100.0 | 100.0 | 100.0 |
| | | | **LIABILITIES** | | | | | | |
| 2.7 | 7.7 | 4.8 | Notes Payable-Short Term | 18.1 | 5.0 | 3.3 | 3.1 | 1.2 | 2.0 |
| 6.6 | 5.0 | 4.7 | Cur. Mat.-L.T.D. | 2.2 | 4.9 | 6.4 | 2.2 | 8.8 | 3.4 |
| 8.0 | 7.5 | 5.3 | Trade Payables | 4.0 | 4.3 | 2.5 | 3.1 | 9.0 | 7.5 |
| .2 | .0 | .1 | Income Taxes Payable | .7 | .0 | .0 | .0 | .1 | .0 |
| 9.9 | 8.8 | 9.0 | All Other Current | 8.8 | 9.9 | 3.2 | 5.4 | 8.9 | 12.4 |
| 27.3 | 29.0 | 23.9 | Total Current | 33.7 | 24.1 | 15.5 | 13.8 | 28.1 | 25.4 |
| 42.0 | 49.3 | 47.9 | Long-Term Debt | 42.4 | 56.5 | 46.0 | 37.5 | 47.8 | 43.3 |
| .1 | .0 | .0 | Deferred Taxes | .0 | .0 | .0 | .0 | .0 | .2 |
| 12.6 | 8.1 | 13.1 | All Other Non-Current | 28.8 | 12.0 | 2.2 | 10.8 | 2.6 | 20.5 |
| 17.9 | 13.7 | 15.1 | Net Worth | -4.9 | 7.4 | 36.4 | 37.9 | 21.5 | 10.7 |
| 100.0 | 100.0 | 100.0 | Total Liabilities & Net Worth | 100.0 | 100.0 | 100.0 | 100.0 | 100.0 | 100.0 |
| | | | **INCOME DATA** | | | | | | |
| 100.0 | 100.0 | 100.0 | Net Sales | 100.0 | 100.0 | 100.0 | 100.0 | 100.0 | 100.0 |
| | | | Gross Profit | | | | | | |
| 86.6 | 88.6 | 90.2 | Operating Expenses | 85.1 | 89.9 | 85.6 | 96.9 | 88.4 | 93.2 |
| 13.4 | 11.4 | 9.8 | Operating Profit | 14.9 | 10.1 | 14.4 | 3.1 | 11.6 | 6.8 |
| 7.2 | 6.2 | 6.2 | All Other Expenses (net) | 10.1 | 8.6 | 6.5 | 3.5 | 4.9 | 2.8 |
| 6.3 | 5.2 | 3.5 | Profit Before Taxes | 4.7 | 1.5 | 7.9 | -.5 | 6.7 | 4.0 |
| | | | **RATIOS** | | | | | | |
| 1.0 | 1.3 | 1.4 | | 4.1 | 1.4 | 2.0 | 2.3 | 1.4 | .8 |
| .5 | .7 | .6 | Current | .4 | .5 | .9 | 1.1 | .5 | .6 |
| .2 | .3 | .3 | | .1 | .2 | .4 | .4 | .3 | .4 |
| .8 | 1.1 | 1.1 | | 3.4 | 1.0 | 1.5 | 2.2 | 1.0 | .6 |
| .4 | .5 | .4 | Quick | .4 | .4 | .7 | .6 | .4 | .5 |
| .1 | .2 | .2 | | .1 | .1 | .3 | .3 | .2 | .3 |
| 0 UND | 0 UND | 0 UND | | 0 UND | 0 UND | 0 UND | 0 UND | 0 UND | 1 576.4 |
| 0 UND | 0 UND | 0 999.8 | Sales/Receivables | 0 UND | 0 UND | 0 UND | 0 UND | 2 202.6 | 4 98.7 |
| 3 129.9 | 3 123.3 | 4 95.6 | | 0 UND | 1 368.2 | 1 658.0 | 16 23.2 | 9 40.3 | 6 59.2 |
| | | | Cost of Sales/Inventory | | | | | | |
| | | | Cost of Sales/Payables | | | | | | |
| UND | 52.1 | 25.8 | | 8.2 | 56.3 | 13.3 | 11.0 | 45.2 | -41.6 |
| -17.3 | -25.9 | -17.8 | Sales/Working Capital | -17.8 | -13.6 | -80.6 | NM | -12.1 | -20.2 |
| -5.6 | -7.3 | -8.0 | | -7.1 | -6.2 | -15.1 | -8.0 | -7.2 | -7.0 |
| 4.0 | 4.7 | 4.3 | | | 4.4 | 12.8 | 6.4 | 3.9 | 3.3 |
| (93) 2.1 | (97) 2.1 | (112) 2.2 | EBIT/Interest | (38) 1.5 | (11) 3.0 | (13) 2.4 | (17) 2.0 | (26) 2.1 | |
| 1.4 | .8 | .7 | | .3 | 1.9 | .0 | 1.1 | .7 | |
| 15.5 | 9.6 | 4.0 | Net Profit + Depr., Dep., | | | | | | 7.5 |
| (17) 3.1 | (12) 2.3 | (23) 1.7 | Amort./Cur. Mat. L/T/D | | | | | (11) 3.9 | |
| 1.4 | 1.0 | 1.0 | | | | | | | 1.7 |
| 2.0 | 1.7 | 1.8 | | 1.4 | 1.6 | 1.2 | 1.3 | 2.5 | 2.6 |
| 4.0 | 3.7 | 4.7 | Fixed/Worth | 4.7 | 5.2 | 3.2 | 2.9 | 5.5 | 4.8 |
| -28.3 | 68.4 | -10.0 | | -1.3 | -5.3 | UND | NM | NM | -3.1 |
| 1.5 | 1.5 | 1.5 | | 1.3 | 1.1 | .7 | .9 | 1.9 | 2.0 |
| 3.5 | 3.5 | 4.3 | Debt/Worth | -17.8 | 5.8 | 2.9 | 2.4 | 5.8 | 4.5 |
| -30.0 | 133.0 | -10.9 | | -2.1 | -8.3 | UND | NM | NM | -4.8 |
| 46.7 | 51.4 | 38.2 | % Profit Before Taxes/Tangible | | 27.5 | 77.7 | 23.8 | 84.9 | 40.6 |
| (89) 18.5 | (93) 15.3 | (86) 11.4 | Net Worth | (27) 9.7 | (11) 18.7 | (11) 8.4 | (14) 15.0 | (17) 16.8 | |
| 6.8 | -1.3 | -.1 | | | -5.6 | 2.7 | .1 | 4.3 | -3.8 |
| 10.5 | 8.2 | 9.2 | % Profit Before Taxes/Total | 10.5 | 7.8 | 13.2 | 6.1 | 12.5 | 9.2 |
| 3.6 | 2.9 | 3.6 | Assets | 3.1 | 1.3 | 6.5 | 2.6 | 3.5 | 5.5 |
| 1.2 | -.7 | -1.3 | | -4.5 | -3.2 | 1.8 | -2.0 | .6 | -.9 |
| 2.8 | 3.4 | 3.3 | | 58.0 | 3.9 | 2.7 | 2.4 | 2.1 | 3.8 |
| 1.1 | 1.1 | 1.2 | Sales/Net Fixed Assets | 1.2 | .9 | 1.0 | .8 | 1.3 | 1.9 |
| .6 | .6 | .6 | | .4 | .5 | .6 | .5 | .8 | 1.2 |
| 2.1 | 2.1 | 1.9 | | 5.7 | 2.2 | 1.1 | 1.5 | 1.5 | 2.0 |
| 1.0 | .9 | .9 | Sales/Total Assets | .8 | .7 | .7 | .7 | .9 | 1.3 |
| .5 | .5 | .5 | | .2 | .4 | .5 | .4 | .7 | 1.0 |
| 4.3 | 4.4 | 4.3 | | | 3.7 | 5.2 | 4.9 | 3.5 | 4.6 |
| (115) 6.5 | (108) 7.3 | (113) 6.8 | % Depr., Dep., Amort./Sales | (39) 6.7 | (11) 8.3 | (13) 9.1 | 7.5 | (24) 6.7 | |
| 10.1 | 10.9 | 10.2 | | | 14.1 | 13.0 | 11.6 | 9.2 | 8.1 |
| 1.4 | 1.6 | 1.9 | % Officers', Directors' | | 2.3 | | | | |
| (20) 2.9 | (27) 3.6 | (29) 3.4 | Owners' Comp/Sales | | (13) 3.6 | | | | |
| 5.4 | 6.7 | 7.8 | | | 9.7 | | | | |
| 2637099M | 1884436M | 2790964M | Net Sales ($) | 6563M | 81248M | 52119M | 100416M | 305128M | 2245490M |
| 2579884M | 2061277M | 2720823M | Total Assets ($) | 15869M | 183921M | 80767M | 191512M | 351469M | 1897285M |

M = $ thousand    MM = $ million
See Pages 9 through 22 for Explanation of Ratios and Data

## Current Data Sorted by Assets

## Comparative Historical Data

| | 0-500M | 500M-2MM | 2-10MM | 10-50MM | 50-100MM | 100-250MM | Type of Statement | 4/1/07-3/31/08 ALL | 4/1/08-3/31/09 ALL |
|---|---|---|---|---|---|---|---|---|---|
| | | | 1 | | 1 | | Unqualified | 2 | 4 |
| | | | 3 | 1 | | | Reviewed | 3 | 7 |
| | | | 3 | | | | Compiled | 1 | 6 |
| 5 | 1 | 3 | | | | | Tax Returns | | 3 |
| 3 | 3 | 5 | 1 | | | | Other | 8 | 15 |
| | 5 (4/1-9/30/11) | | | 25 (10/1/11-3/31/12) | | | | | |
| 8 | 4 | 15 | 2 | 1 | | NUMBER OF STATEMENTS | 14 | 35 |
| % | % | % | % | % | % | ASSETS | % | % |
| | | 12.0 | | | | Cash & Equivalents | 9.7 | 13.8 |
| | | 21.6 | | | | Trade Receivables (net) | 26.8 | 27.4 |
| | | 5.8 | | | | Inventory | 5.5 | 1.1 |
| | | 1.2 | | | | All Other Current | 2.1 | 4.2 |
| | | 40.7 | | | | Total Current | 44.1 | 46.5 |
| | | 43.1 | | | | Fixed Assets (net) | 36.6 | 37.2 |
| | | 6.2 | | | | Intangibles (net) | 10.9 | 6.8 |
| | | 10.1 | | | | All Other Non-Current | 8.5 | 9.5 |
| | | 100.0 | | | | Total | 100.0 | 100.0 |
| | | | | | | LIABILITIES | | |
| | | 2.9 | | | | Notes Payable-Short Term | 4.9 | 15.3 |
| | | 5.0 | | | | Cur. Mat.-L.T.D. | 19.8 | 5.0 |
| | | 12.5 | | | | Trade Payables | 11.0 | 10.6 |
| | | .2 | | | | Income Taxes Payable | .4 | .4 |
| | | 7.3 | | | | All Other Current | 9.5 | 11.9 |
| | | 27.8 | | | | Total Current | 45.5 | 43.1 |
| | | 31.5 | | | | Long-Term Debt | 18.3 | 22.3 |
| | | 1.5 | | | | Deferred Taxes | .4 | .5 |
| | | 11.5 | | | | All Other Non-Current | 21.4 | 3.3 |
| | | 27.7 | | | | Net Worth | 14.4 | 30.8 |
| | | 100.0 | | | | Total Liabilties & Net Worth | 100.0 | 100.0 |
| | | | | | | INCOME DATA | | |
| | | 100.0 | | | | Net Sales | 100.0 | 100.0 |
| | | | | | | Gross Profit | | |
| | | 94.0 | | | | Operating Expenses | 98.4 | 93.5 |
| | | 6.0 | | | | Operating Profit | 1.6 | 6.5 |
| | | 1.6 | | | | All Other Expenses (net) | 2.2 | 1.1 |
| | | 4.4 | | | | Profit Before Taxes | -.6 | 5.4 |
| | | | | | | RATIOS | | |
| | | 2.3 / 1.1 / .8 | | | | Current | 1.7 / 1.3 / .8 | 2.6 / 1.5 / .8 |
| | | 2.1 / 1.0 / .7 | | | | Quick | 1.4 / 1.2 / .6 | 2.3 / 1.4 / .7 |
| | | 23  15.6 / 37  9.9 / 49  7.5 | | | | Sales/Receivables | 26  13.8 / 56  6.5 / 71  5.1 | 28  13.0 / 43  8.4 / 62  5.8 |
| | | | | | | Cost of Sales/Inventory | | |
| | | | | | | Cost of Sales/Payables | | |
| | | 8.2 / 53.6 / -33.1 | | | | Sales/Working Capital | 9.9 / 24.6 / -11.3 | 6.7 / 16.7 / -23.1 |
| | | 9.8 / (13) 4.3 / -1.3 | | | | EBIT/Interest | 9.9 / (11) 2.3 / .4 | 8.7 / (31) 2.2 / -1.2 |
| | | | | | | Net Profit + Depr., Dep., Amort./Cur. Mat. L/T/D | | |
| | | .7 / 1.7 / 6.5 | | | | Fixed/Worth | .6 / 1.5 / NM | .5 / 1.3 / 5.1 |
| | | 1.2 / 1.5 / 5.7 | | | | Debt/Worth | .8 / 2.8 / NM | .6 / 2.2 / 12.8 |
| | | 48.0 / (13) 32.8 / -3.1 | | | | % Profit Before Taxes/Tangible Net Worth | 29.0 / (11) 16.9 / 7.3 | 68.7 / (30) 19.5 / -9.3 |
| | | 18.0 / 8.6 / -1.9 | | | | % Profit Before Taxes/Total Assets | 7.5 / 4.7 / -3.4 | 14.8 / 8.4 / -2.9 |
| | | 13.1 / 4.6 / 2.3 | | | | Sales/Net Fixed Assets | 29.7 / 7.7 / 1.9 | 18.5 / 5.8 / 3.5 |
| | | 2.5 / 2.1 / 1.3 | | | | Sales/Total Assets | 3.3 / 1.4 / 1.0 | 3.2 / 2.0 / 1.5 |
| | | 3.3 / (12) 5.3 / 8.3 | | | | % Depr., Dep., Amort./Sales | .7 / (12) 6.2 / 13.4 | 4.2 / (25) 5.3 / 9.3 |
| | | | | | | % Officers', Directors' Owners' Comp/Sales | | 1.7 / (12) 10.7 / 24.8 |
| 11194M | 16831M | 202944M | 39113M | 92528M | | Net Sales ($) | 292599M | 1523206M |
| 1730M | 4351M | 69724M | 20601M | 89481M | | Total Assets ($) | 230210M | 438427M |

*Note: For the current-data columns 0-500M, 500M-2MM, 10-50MM, 50-100MM, and 100-250MM, the ASSETS through RATIOS detail is marked "DATA NOT AVAILABLE."*

## Comparative Historical Data | Current Data Sorted by Sales

### Type of Statement

| Type of Statement | 4/1/09-3/31/10 ALL | 4/1/10-3/31/11 ALL | 4/1/11-3/31/12 ALL | | 0-1MM | 1-3MM | 3-5MM | 5-10MM | 10-25MM | 25MM & OVER |
|---|---|---|---|---|---|---|---|---|---|---|
| | | | | | | 5 (4/1-9/30/11) | | | 25 (10/1/11-3/31/12) | |
| Unqualified | | | 2 | | | | | | 1 | 1 |
| Reviewed | 3 | 2 | 3 | | | | | 2 | 1 | |
| Compiled | 2 | 2 | 4 | | | | | 2 | 2 | |
| Tax Returns | | 9 | 9 | | 3 | 2 | 3 | 1 | | |
| Other | 13 | 13 | 12 | | 1 | 4 | 1 | 1 | 1 | 2 |
| **NUMBER OF STATEMENTS** | 18 | 26 | 30 | | 4 | 6 | 4 | 8 | 5 | 3 |
| | % | % | % | | % | % | % | % | % | % |

### ASSETS

| | 4/1/09-3/31/10 | 4/1/10-3/31/11 | 4/1/11-3/31/12 | | 0-1MM | 1-3MM | 3-5MM | 5-10MM | 10-25MM | 25MM & OVER |
|---|---|---|---|---|---|---|---|---|---|---|
| Cash & Equivalents | 13.5 | 23.4 | 18.8 | | | | | | | |
| Trade Receivables (net) | 24.1 | 20.7 | 19.2 | | | | | | | |
| Inventory | .6 | 2.4 | 3.0 | | | | | | | |
| All Other Current | 3.4 | 1.5 | .9 | | | | | | | |
| Total Current | 41.6 | 48.0 | 41.9 | | | | | | | |
| Fixed Assets (net) | 38.1 | 30.4 | 38.2 | | | | | | | |
| Intangibles (net) | 6.2 | 9.7 | 7.9 | | | | | | | |
| All Other Non-Current | 14.1 | 12.0 | 12.0 | | | | | | | |
| Total | 100.0 | 100.0 | 100.0 | | | | | | | |

### LIABILITIES

| | | | | | | | | | | |
|---|---|---|---|---|---|---|---|---|---|---|
| Notes Payable-Short Term | 16.0 | 10.6 | 13.3 | | | | | | | |
| Cur. Mat.-L.T.D. | 5.9 | 3.0 | 9.1 | | | | | | | |
| Trade Payables | 12.8 | 6.1 | 11.1 | | | | | | | |
| Income Taxes Payable | .2 | .2 | 5.2 | | | | | | | |
| All Other Current | 12.6 | 13.4 | 9.9 | | | | | | | |
| Total Current | 47.5 | 33.4 | 48.5 | | | | | | | |
| Long-Term Debt | 23.8 | 24.1 | 35.0 | | | | | | | |
| Deferred Taxes | .7 | .0 | .7 | | | | | | | |
| All Other Non-Current | 20.9 | 14.3 | 25.7 | | | | | | | |
| Net Worth | 7.1 | 28.3 | -9.9 | | | | | | | |
| Total Liabilities & Net Worth | 100.0 | 100.0 | 100.0 | | | | | | | |

### INCOME DATA

| | | | | | | | | | | |
|---|---|---|---|---|---|---|---|---|---|---|
| Net Sales | 100.0 | 100.0 | 100.0 | | | | | | | |
| Gross Profit | | | | | | | | | | |
| Operating Expenses | 99.0 | 90.0 | 90.7 | | | | | | | |
| Operating Profit | 1.0 | 10.0 | 9.3 | | | | | | | |
| All Other Expenses (net) | 2.6 | 3.0 | 2.9 | | | | | | | |
| Profit Before Taxes | -1.6 | 7.0 | 6.4 | | | | | | | |

### RATIOS

| | | | | | | | | | | |
|---|---|---|---|---|---|---|---|---|---|---|
| Current | 1.6 / 1.2 / .7 | 4.4 / 1.2 / .7 | 1.7 / 1.0 / .5 | | | | | | | |
| Quick | 1.5 / .9 / .6 | 4.2 / 1.1 / .7 | 1.7 / .8 / .4 | | | | | | | |
| Sales/Receivables | 27 13.6 / 41 8.9 / 74 4.9 | 0 UND / 44 8.4 / 72 5.1 | 0 UND / 30 12.1 / 51 7.2 | | | | | | | |
| Cost of Sales/Inventory | | | | | | | | | | |
| Cost of Sales/Payables | | | | | | | | | | |
| Sales/Working Capital | 6.7 / 32.3 / -17.9 | 4.0 / 25.1 / -44.7 | 10.1 / NM / -20.6 | | | | | | | |
| EBIT/Interest | 5.0 / (16) 1.1 / -13.5 | 41.8 / (22) 11.6 / 1.6 | 11.0 / (26) 4.2 / .1 | | | | | | | |
| Net Profit + Depr., Dep., Amort./Cur. Mat. L/T/D | | | | | | | | | | |
| Fixed/Worth | .8 / 1.5 / NM | .2 / 1.2 / 3.1 | .5 / 1.7 / -1.0 | | | | | | | |
| Debt/Worth | 1.0 / 2.1 / NM | .5 / 1.9 / 15.9 | 1.3 / 3.5 / -2.3 | | | | | | | |
| % Profit Before Taxes/Tangible Net Worth | 47.0 / (14) -17.2 / -47.5 | 178.2 / (22) 45.6 / 7.9 | 84.2 / (20) 36.0 / -3.8 | | | | | | | |
| % Profit Before Taxes/Total Assets | 13.2 / .8 / -24.7 | 29.1 / 9.3 / 1.1 | 49.1 / 14.9 / -2.7 | | | | | | | |
| Sales/Net Fixed Assets | 27.5 / 4.9 / 3.4 | 72.8 / 10.0 / 2.8 | 56.9 / 12.3 / 2.9 | | | | | | | |
| Sales/Total Assets | 3.2 / 1.9 / 1.3 | 3.0 / 2.0 / 1.2 | 3.8 / 2.5 / 1.5 | | | | | | | |
| % Depr., Dep., Amort./Sales | 2.5 / (13) 4.4 / 12.7 | 3.5 / (15) 6.1 / 8.7 | 1.9 / (22) 4.3 / 7.7 | | | | | | | |
| % Officers', Directors' Owners' Comp/Sales | | (17) | 4.4 / 7.5 / 9.3 | | | | | | | |

| | | | | | | | | | | |
|---|---|---|---|---|---|---|---|---|---|---|
| Net Sales ($) | 437719M | 202496M | 362610M | | 2544M | 8914M | 16475M | 59378M | 81547M | 193752M |
| Total Assets ($) | 315694M | 129629M | 185887M | | 370M | 6492M | 6494M | 28290M | 41715M | 102526M |

© RMA 2012

M = $ thousand     MM = $ million

See Pages 9 through 22 for Explanation of Ratios and Data

## Current Data Sorted by Assets      Comparative Historical Data

| 0-500M | 500M-2MM | 2-10MM | 10-50MM | 50-100MM | 100-250MM | Type of Statement | 4/1/07-3/31/08 ALL | 4/1/08-3/31/09 ALL |
|---|---|---|---|---|---|---|---|---|
| | | | | 2 | 1 | Unqualified | 3 | 2 |
| | | 3 | 1 | | | Reviewed | 4 | 1 |
| 1 | 1 | 1 | | | | Compiled | 2 | 5 |
| 3 | 2 | 2 | | | | Tax Returns | 7 | 1 |
| 1 | 4 | 9 | | | | Other | 17 | 16 |
| | 5 (4/1-9/30/11) | | 29 (10/1/11-3/31/12) | | | | | |
| 5 | 7 | 15 | 3 | 3 | 1 | **NUMBER OF STATEMENTS** | 33 | 25 |
| % | % | % | % | % | % | | % | % |
| | | | | | | **ASSETS** | | |
| | | 10.3 | | | | Cash & Equivalents | 15.5 | 11.4 |
| | | 27.8 | | | | Trade Receivables (net) | 26.1 | 21.4 |
| | | 1.8 | | | | Inventory | 2.6 | 3.4 |
| | | 1.2 | | | | All Other Current | 1.9 | 2.4 |
| | | 41.0 | | | | Total Current | 46.0 | 38.7 |
| | | 45.2 | | | | Fixed Assets (net) | 34.3 | 42.5 |
| | | 4.8 | | | | Intangibles (net) | 7.8 | 6.7 |
| | | 9.0 | | | | All Other Non-Current | 11.9 | 12.1 |
| | | 100.0 | | | | Total | 100.0 | 100.0 |
| | | | | | | **LIABILITIES** | | |
| | | 9.6 | | | | Notes Payable-Short Term | 8.7 | 4.9 |
| | | 5.9 | | | | Cur. Mat.-L.T.D. | 3.8 | 9.9 |
| | | 15.2 | | | | Trade Payables | 8.3 | 10.0 |
| | | .3 | | | | Income Taxes Payable | .8 | .1 |
| | | 8.5 | | | | All Other Current | 18.6 | 10.1 |
| | | 39.4 | | | | Total Current | 40.1 | 35.1 |
| | | 19.8 | | | | Long-Term Debt | 15.7 | 32.9 |
| | | 2.2 | | | | Deferred Taxes | .1 | .3 |
| | | 5.1 | | | | All Other Non-Current | 6.1 | 6.0 |
| | | 33.4 | | | | Net Worth | 37.9 | 25.9 |
| | | 100.0 | | | | Total Liabilties & Net Worth | 100.0 | 100.0 |
| | | | | | | **INCOME DATA** | | |
| | | 100.0 | | | | Net Sales | 100.0 | 100.0 |
| | | | | | | Gross Profit | | |
| | | 93.7 | | | | Operating Expenses | 95.1 | 98.7 |
| | | 6.3 | | | | Operating Profit | 4.9 | 1.3 |
| | | 1.5 | | | | All Other Expenses (net) | 1.0 | 1.2 |
| | | 4.8 | | | | Profit Before Taxes | 3.9 | .1 |
| | | | | | | **RATIOS** | | |
| | | 1.7 | | | | | 2.6 | 2.9 |
| | | 1.1 | | | | Current | 1.6 | 1.5 |
| | | .7 | | | | | .5 | .6 |
| | | 1.6 | | | | | 2.5 | 2.3 |
| | | 1.0 | | | | Quick | 1.4 | 1.2 |
| | | .7 | | | | | .5 | .5 |
| | 31 | 11.7 | | | | | 22 16.9 | 24 15.1 |
| | 49 | 7.5 | | | | Sales/Receivables | 44 8.3 | 51 7.2 |
| | 83 | 4.4 | | | | | 63 5.8 | 66 5.5 |
| | | | | | | Cost of Sales/Inventory | | |
| | | | | | | Cost of Sales/Payables | | |
| | | 13.5 | | | | | 6.0 | 5.4 |
| | | 129.4 | | | | Sales/Working Capital | 13.0 | 16.2 |
| | | -9.3 | | | | | -13.5 | -28.0 |
| | | 13.0 | | | | | (30) 38.3 | (21) 18.6 |
| | (14) | 3.6 | | | | EBIT/Interest | 2.3 | 2.2 |
| | | 1.5 | | | | | .4 | -.9 |
| | | | | | | Net Profit + Depr., Dep., Amort./Cur. Mat. L/T/D | | |
| | | .5 | | | | | .2 | .5 |
| | | 1.8 | | | | Fixed/Worth | .8 | 2.0 |
| | | -9.3 | | | | | 5.5 | -179.0 |
| | | .8 | | | | | .4 | .4 |
| | | 2.8 | | | | Debt/Worth | 1.6 | 3.3 |
| | | -16.9 | | | | | NM | -262.8 |
| | | 69.4 | | | | % Profit Before Taxes/Tangible Net Worth | 51.4 | 35.1 |
| | (10) | 26.5 | | | | | (25) 14.6 | (18) 13.9 |
| | | -.5 | | | | | -1.2 | -26.2 |
| | | 11.6 | | | | % Profit Before Taxes/Total Assets | 16.4 | 12.0 |
| | | 5.5 | | | | | 2.9 | 4.4 |
| | | -2.9 | | | | | -2.5 | -10.7 |
| | | 6.4 | | | | | 21.9 | 11.5 |
| | | 4.5 | | | | Sales/Net Fixed Assets | 6.3 | 5.3 |
| | | 2.5 | | | | | 3.2 | 2.2 |
| | | 2.9 | | | | | 4.1 | 2.8 |
| | | 1.9 | | | | Sales/Total Assets | 1.8 | 1.3 |
| | | 1.3 | | | | | 1.0 | 1.0 |
| | | 3.7 | | | | % Depr., Dep., Amort./Sales | 2.2 | 3.8 |
| | (13) | 4.4 | | | | | (27) 5.6 | (20) 8.4 |
| | | 8.4 | | | | | 9.4 | 10.5 |
| | | | | | | % Officers', Directors' Owners' Comp/Sales | 2.6 | 3.7 |
| | | | | | | | (13) 7.7 | (12) 10.0 |
| | | | | | | | 14.9 | 16.8 |
| 7298M | 20161M | 132355M | 133865M | 177535M | 184433M | Net Sales ($) | 586661M | 402404M |
| 1623M | 7279M | 64943M | 45885M | 198514M | 113456M | Total Assets ($) | 492300M | 346614M |

© RMA 2012

M = $ thousand    MM = $ million
See Pages 9 through 22 for Explanation of Ratios and Data

## Comparative Historical Data          Current Data Sorted by Sales

| Type of Statement | 4/1/09-3/31/10 ALL | 4/1/10-3/31/11 ALL | 4/1/11-3/31/12 ALL | 0-1MM | 1-3MM | 3-5MM | 5-10MM | 10-25MM | 25MM & OVER |
|---|---|---|---|---|---|---|---|---|---|
| Unqualified | 1 | 2 | 3 |  |  |  |  | 1 | 2 |
| Reviewed | 4 | 7 | 4 |  |  |  | 3 | 1 |  |
| Compiled | 6 | 2 | 3 |  |  |  |  | 1 |  |
| Tax Returns | 5 | 6 | 7 | 1 | 1 | 1 | 1 | 1 |  |
| Other | 12 | 13 | 17 | 5 | 6 | 2 | 4 | 2 | 2 |
|  | | | | 5 (4/1-9/30/11) | | | 29 (10/1/11-3/31/12) | | |
| **NUMBER OF STATEMENTS** | 28 | 30 | 34 | 6 | 7 | 3 | 8 | 6 | 4 |
|  | % | % | % | % | % | % | % | % | % |
| **ASSETS** | | | | | | | | | |
| Cash & Equivalents | 15.7 | 17.1 | 12.2 | | | | | | |
| Trade Receivables (net) | 25.5 | 29.3 | 23.8 | | | | | | |
| Inventory | 5.8 | 3.2 | 2.9 | | | | | | |
| All Other Current | 4.3 | 4.2 | 2.7 | | | | | | |
| Total Current | 51.3 | 53.9 | 41.7 | | | | | | |
| Fixed Assets (net) | 35.2 | 32.4 | 40.0 | | | | | | |
| Intangibles (net) | 2.5 | 6.8 | 3.9 | | | | | | |
| All Other Non-Current | 10.9 | 6.9 | 14.3 | | | | | | |
| Total | 100.0 | 100.0 | 100.0 | | | | | | |
| **LIABILITIES** | | | | | | | | | |
| Notes Payable-Short Term | 13.7 | 9.7 | 8.7 | | | | | | |
| Cur. Mat.-L.T.D. | 6.3 | 8.3 | 3.8 | | | | | | |
| Trade Payables | 10.3 | 13.5 | 17.8 | | | | | | |
| Income Taxes Payable | .4 | .6 | .2 | | | | | | |
| All Other Current | 9.2 | 12.0 | 8.9 | | | | | | |
| Total Current | 40.0 | 44.1 | 39.4 | | | | | | |
| Long-Term Debt | 18.4 | 16.2 | 26.4 | | | | | | |
| Deferred Taxes | .7 | .2 | 1.3 | | | | | | |
| All Other Non-Current | 11.3 | 5.4 | 6.3 | | | | | | |
| Net Worth | 29.6 | 34.1 | 26.5 | | | | | | |
| Total Liabilties & Net Worth | 100.0 | 100.0 | 100.0 | | | | | | |
| **INCOME DATA** | | | | | | | | | |
| Net Sales | 100.0 | 100.0 | 100.0 | | | | | | |
| Gross Profit | | | | | | | | | |
| Operating Expenses | 94.8 | 95.7 | 89.3 | | | | | | |
| Operating Profit | 5.2 | 4.3 | 10.7 | | | | | | |
| All Other Expenses (net) | 1.2 | .7 | 3.8 | | | | | | |
| Profit Before Taxes | 4.0 | 3.6 | 6.9 | | | | | | |
| **RATIOS** | | | | | | | | | |
| Current | 3.2 | 2.0 | 4.9 | | | | | | |
| | 1.3 | 1.2 | 1.3 | | | | | | |
| | .8 | .7 | .6 | | | | | | |
| Quick | 2.5 | 1.6 | 2.8 | | | | | | |
| | 1.2 | 1.0 | 1.0 | | | | | | |
| | .6 | .6 | .5 | | | | | | |
| Sales/Receivables | 28  13.1 | 36  10.2 | 20  18.1 | | | | | | |
| | 39  9.3 | 54  6.7 | 41  8.8 | | | | | | |
| | 60  6.1 | 71  5.1 | 63  5.8 | | | | | | |
| Cost of Sales/Inventory | | | | | | | | | |
| Cost of Sales/Payables | | | | | | | | | |
| Sales/Working Capital | 7.1 | 5.9 | 7.6 | | | | | | |
| | 14.1 | 32.1 | 45.0 | | | | | | |
| | -18.0 | -9.1 | -9.2 | | | | | | |
| EBIT/Interest | 8.3 | 19.7 | 26.1 | | | | | | |
| | (27) 2.8 | (26) 4.0 | (29) 5.6 | | | | | | |
| | .8 | -.7 | 1.7 | | | | | | |
| Net Profit + Depr., Dep., Amort./Cur. Mat. L/T/D | | | | | | | | | |
| Fixed/Worth | .5 | .4 | .4 | | | | | | |
| | 1.3 | .9 | 1.5 | | | | | | |
| | 3.7 | 11.1 | -18.6 | | | | | | |
| Debt/Worth | .5 | .6 | .6 | | | | | | |
| | 2.2 | 3.9 | 2.6 | | | | | | |
| | 17.3 | 61.5 | -25.3 | | | | | | |
| % Profit Before Taxes/Tangible Net Worth | 56.5 | 73.3 | 56.3 | | | | | | |
| | (24) 8.1 | (24) 24.3 | (25) 23.9 | | | | | | |
| | -.7 | 1.3 | 6.6 | | | | | | |
| % Profit Before Taxes/Total Assets | 7.5 | 22.9 | 29.2 | | | | | | |
| | 4.1 | 6.3 | 6.7 | | | | | | |
| | -.4 | -2.0 | .4 | | | | | | |
| Sales/Net Fixed Assets | 30.8 | 24.5 | 13.3 | | | | | | |
| | 5.6 | 6.0 | 5.8 | | | | | | |
| | 2.7 | 3.1 | 2.2 | | | | | | |
| Sales/Total Assets | 3.0 | 2.6 | 3.0 | | | | | | |
| | 2.2 | 1.9 | 1.6 | | | | | | |
| | 1.2 | 1.4 | 1.0 | | | | | | |
| % Depr., Dep., Amort./Sales | 1.9 | 2.1 | 2.4 | | | | | | |
| | (21) 4.3 | (23) 5.8 | (24) 4.4 | | | | | | |
| | 10.9 | 10.1 | 9.4 | | | | | | |
| % Officers', Directors' Owners' Comp/Sales | 2.2 | 6.0 | 2.5 | | | | | | |
| | (13) 4.7 | (11) 6.7 | (12) 6.9 | | | | | | |
| | 12.5 | 15.9 | 11.3 | | | | | | |
| Net Sales ($) | 717648M | 583586M | 655647M | 3911M | 12583M | 11271M | 64219M | 92538M | 471125M |
| Total Assets ($) | 520012M | 391512M | 431700M | 15031M | 10537M | 4361M | 33697M | 95328M | 272746M |

© RMA 2012  
M = $ thousand    MM = $ million  
See Pages 9 through 22 for Explanation of Ratios and Data

## Current Data Sorted by Assets | Comparative Historical Data

| Type of Statement | 0-500M | 500M-2MM | 2-10MM | 10-50MM | 50-100MM | 100-250MM | | 4/1/07-3/31/08 ALL | 4/1/08-3/31/09 ALL |
|---|---|---|---|---|---|---|---|---|---|
| Unqualified | | | 2 | 1 | 2 | 3 | | 4 | 2 |
| Reviewed | | 1 | 2 | | | | | 1 | |
| Compiled | | | 3 | | | | | | 3 |
| Tax Returns | | 3 | 2 | | | | | 3 | 2 |
| Other | | 3 | 7 | | 1 | | | 10 | 7 |
| | | 6 (4/1-9/30/11) | | 24 (10/1/11-3/31/12) | | | | | |
| NUMBER OF STATEMENTS | | 7 | 16 | 1 | 3 | 3 | | 18 | 14 |
| | % | % | % | % | % | % | **ASSETS** | % | % |
| Cash & Equivalents | | | 14.9 | | | | | 7.1 | 11.5 |
| Trade Receivables (net) | | | 15.0 | | | | | 14.4 | 5.7 |
| Inventory | | | .1 | | | | | .0 | .0 |
| All Other Current | | | 1.5 | | | | | 2.2 | 1.5 |
| Total Current | | | 31.5 | | | | | 23.7 | 18.8 |
| Fixed Assets (net) | | | 28.6 | | | | | 29.7 | 30.7 |
| Intangibles (net) | | | 29.2 | | | | | 37.7 | 39.1 |
| All Other Non-Current | | | 10.6 | | | | | 8.9 | 11.5 |
| Total | | | 100.0 | | | | | 100.0 | 100.0 |
| | | | | | | | **LIABILITIES** | | |
| Notes Payable-Short Term | | | 1.4 | | | | | 1.8 | 3.7 |
| Cur. Mat.-L.T.D. | | | 14.9 | | | | | 4.5 | 2.1 |
| Trade Payables | | | 6.7 | | | | | 5.9 | 1.7 |
| Income Taxes Payable | | | .0 | | | | | 1.2 | .0 |
| All Other Current | | | 16.4 | | | | | 3.3 | 2.3 |
| Total Current | | | 39.5 | | | | | 16.7 | 9.7 |
| Long-Term Debt | | | 22.6 | | | | | 64.0 | 57.0 |
| Deferred Taxes | | | .3 | | | | | .9 | .0 |
| All Other Non-Current | | | 11.8 | | | | | 21.3 | 19.5 |
| Net Worth | | | 25.7 | | | | | -2.8 | 13.7 |
| Total Liabilities & Net Worth | | | 100.0 | | | | | 100.0 | 100.0 |
| | | | | | | | **INCOME DATA** | | |
| Net Sales | | | 100.0 | | | | | 100.0 | 100.0 |
| Gross Profit | | | | | | | | | |
| Operating Expenses | | | 84.4 | | | | | 82.2 | 87.1 |
| Operating Profit | | | 15.6 | | | | | 17.8 | 12.9 |
| All Other Expenses (net) | | | 1.9 | | | | | 8.3 | 8.4 |
| Profit Before Taxes | | | 13.7 | | | | | 9.5 | 4.5 |
| | | | | | | | **RATIOS** | | |
| Current | | | 5.5 | | | | | 2.2 | 6.5 |
| | | | 1.8 | | | | | 1.6 | 3.3 |
| | | | .6 | | | | | 1.2 | 1.1 |
| Quick | | | 3.0 | | | | | 2.1 | 5.5 |
| | | | 1.2 | | | | | 1.4 | 2.1 |
| | | | .3 | | | | | .8 | .8 |
| Sales/Receivables | | | 0 UND | | | | | 0 UND | 0 UND |
| | | | 48 7.6 | | | | | 49 7.4 | 34 10.8 |
| | | | 74 4.9 | | | | | 70 5.2 | 56 6.6 |
| Cost of Sales/Inventory | | | | | | | | | |
| Cost of Sales/Payables | | | | | | | | | |
| Sales/Working Capital | | | 4.0 | | | | | 5.4 | 3.2 |
| | | | 7.7 | | | | | 10.9 | 4.5 |
| | | | -7.6 | | | | | 46.0 | 145.7 |
| EBIT/Interest | | | 20.4 | | | | | 3.8 | 2.2 |
| | | (12) | 5.1 | | | | | (17) 1.4 | (10) 2.0 |
| | | | .7 | | | | | .9 | .2 |
| Net Profit + Depr., Dep., Amort./Cur. Mat. L/T/D | | | | | | | | | |
| Fixed/Worth | | | .5 | | | | | 31.3 | .9 |
| | | | 6.8 | | | | | -.6 | -2.1 |
| | | | -.6 | | | | | -.2 | -.4 |
| Debt/Worth | | | .8 | | | | | 33.8 | .9 |
| | | | 16.4 | | | | | -2.2 | -3.7 |
| | | | -2.4 | | | | | -1.6 | -1.5 |
| % Profit Before Taxes/Tangible Net Worth | | | | | | | | | |
| % Profit Before Taxes/Total Assets | | | 25.6 | | | | | 11.7 | 9.5 |
| | | | 12.3 | | | | | 3.7 | 3.5 |
| | | | -.8 | | | | | -.2 | -4.4 |
| Sales/Net Fixed Assets | | | 14.9 | | | | | 8.0 | 4.9 |
| | | | 3.3 | | | | | 3.5 | 2.9 |
| | | | 2.1 | | | | | 2.1 | 1.5 |
| Sales/Total Assets | | | 1.3 | | | | | 1.1 | 1.1 |
| | | | .9 | | | | | .6 | .8 |
| | | | .5 | | | | | .4 | .4 |
| % Depr., Dep., Amort./Sales | | | 2.4 | | | | | 4.6 | 2.1 |
| | | (10) | 5.7 | | | | | (14) 6.5 | (13) 5.2 |
| | | | 9.4 | | | | | 10.4 | 12.0 |
| % Officers', Directors' Owners' Comp/Sales | | | | | | | | | |
| Net Sales ($) | | 16056M | 122141M | 6559M | 159197M | 182495M | | 322714M | 155916M |
| Total Assets ($) | | 8148M | 91291M | 18715M | 226028M | 528581M | | 774840M | 374841M |

*(Left-hand columns 0-500M through 100-250MM marked "DATA NOT AVAILABLE")*

M = $ thousand   MM = $ million
See Pages 9 through 22 for Explanation of Ratios and Data

## Comparative Historical Data

## Current Data Sorted by Sales

| | | | Type of Statement | | | | | | |
|---|---|---|---|---|---|---|---|---|---|
| 3 | 9 | 8 | Unqualified | | 1 | | 1 | 1 | 5 |
| | 3 | 3 | Reviewed | | 1 | | 1 | | |
| 4 | 3 | 3 | Compiled | | | 2 | 1 | | |
| 3 | 2 | 5 | Tax Returns | 1 | 2 | 1 | 1 | | |
| 15 | 10 | 11 | Other | 2 | 2 | 3 | 1 | 2 | 1 |
| 4/1/09- 3/31/10 ALL | 4/1/10- 3/31/11 ALL | 4/1/11- 3/31/12 ALL | | 0-1MM | 6 (4/1-9/30/11) 1-3MM | 3-5MM | 5-10MM | 24 (10/1/11-3/31/12) 10-25MM | 25MM & OVER |
| 25 | 27 | 30 | **NUMBER OF STATEMENTS** | 3 | 6 | 7 | 5 | 3 | 6 |
| % | % | % | **ASSETS** | % | % | % | % | % | % |
| 16.2 | 14.9 | 11.1 | Cash & Equivalents | | | | | | |
| 12.0 | 10.0 | 16.1 | Trade Receivables (net) | | | | | | |
| 2.8 | .9 | .4 | Inventory | | | | | | |
| 1.9 | 3.5 | 2.3 | All Other Current | | | | | | |
| 32.9 | 29.3 | 29.8 | Total Current | | | | | | |
| 26.7 | 29.0 | 27.2 | Fixed Assets (net) | | | | | | |
| 22.8 | 25.9 | 32.8 | Intangibles (net) | | | | | | |
| 17.7 | 15.8 | 10.3 | All Other Non-Current | | | | | | |
| 100.0 | 100.0 | 100.0 | Total | | | | | | |
| | | | **LIABILITIES** | | | | | | |
| 1.2 | .6 | 4.4 | Notes Payable-Short Term | | | | | | |
| 4.2 | 3.1 | 11.5 | Cur. Mat.-L.T.D. | | | | | | |
| 3.9 | 5.5 | 6.2 | Trade Payables | | | | | | |
| .0 | .0 | .0 | Income Taxes Payable | | | | | | |
| 16.5 | 10.8 | 11.2 | All Other Current | | | | | | |
| 25.7 | 20.0 | 33.3 | Total Current | | | | | | |
| 42.2 | 37.9 | 26.4 | Long-Term Debt | | | | | | |
| 1.5 | .8 | 1.1 | Deferred Taxes | | | | | | |
| 9.5 | 13.0 | 10.7 | All Other Non-Current | | | | | | |
| 21.0 | 28.4 | 28.5 | Net Worth | | | | | | |
| 100.0 | 100.0 | 100.0 | Total Liabilities & Net Worth | | | | | | |
| | | | **INCOME DATA** | | | | | | |
| 100.0 | 100.0 | 100.0 | Net Sales | | | | | | |
| | | | Gross Profit | | | | | | |
| 89.0 | 87.1 | 86.3 | Operating Expenses | | | | | | |
| 11.0 | 12.9 | 13.7 | Operating Profit | | | | | | |
| 4.1 | 4.3 | 3.1 | All Other Expenses (net) | | | | | | |
| 6.8 | 8.6 | 10.7 | Profit Before Taxes | | | | | | |
| | | | **RATIOS** | | | | | | |
| 4.3 | 2.7 | 2.3 | | | | | | | |
| 1.6 | 1.4 | 1.3 | Current | | | | | | |
| .9 | .9 | .6 | | | | | | | |
| 3.8 | 2.7 | 2.3 | | | | | | | |
| 1.3 | 1.2 | .9 | Quick | | | | | | |
| .7 | .6 | .5 | | | | | | | |
| 14  25.2 | 7  53.7 | 26  14.0 | | | | | | | |
| 45  8.1 | 36  10.2 | 52  7.0 | Sales/Receivables | | | | | | |
| 57  6.4 | 58  6.3 | 65  5.6 | | | | | | | |
| | | | Cost of Sales/Inventory | | | | | | |
| | | | Cost of Sales/Payables | | | | | | |
| 4.1 | 4.3 | 6.0 | | | | | | | |
| 11.5 | 14.6 | 15.1 | Sales/Working Capital | | | | | | |
| NM | -51.3 | -6.5 | | | | | | | |
| 6.9 | 13.3 | 7.2 | | | | | | | |
| (17)  1.7 | (19)  3.6 | (23)  2.6 | EBIT/Interest | | | | | | |
| .3 | .7 | 1.0 | | | | | | | |
| | | | Net Profit + Depr., Dep., Amort./Cur. Mat. L/T/D | | | | | | |
| .5 | .2 | .5 | | | | | | | |
| 1.4 | 1.3 | 6.8 | Fixed/Worth | | | | | | |
| -.4 | -.4 | -.4 | | | | | | | |
| .5 | .6 | .8 | | | | | | | |
| 3.5 | 1.7 | 17.3 | Debt/Worth | | | | | | |
| -1.7 | -2.0 | -1.8 | | | | | | | |
| 93.5 | 35.9 | 62.0 | | | | | | | |
| (16)  15.3 | (17)  14.8 | (17)  27.1 | % Profit Before Taxes/Tangible Net Worth | | | | | | |
| .7 | -6.3 | 2.7 | | | | | | | |
| 9.8 | 16.1 | 15.3 | | | | | | | |
| 2.9 | 6.3 | 7.6 | % Profit Before Taxes/Total Assets | | | | | | |
| -1.3 | -.6 | -.1 | | | | | | | |
| 26.6 | 15.9 | 16.1 | | | | | | | |
| 3.1 | 4.0 | 4.6 | Sales/Net Fixed Assets | | | | | | |
| 1.9 | 2.1 | 2.0 | | | | | | | |
| 1.3 | 1.4 | 1.4 | | | | | | | |
| .8 | .9 | .9 | Sales/Total Assets | | | | | | |
| .5 | .4 | .5 | | | | | | | |
| 2.2 | 2.3 | 2.3 | | | | | | | |
| (20)  4.6 | (22)  5.6 | (21)  3.7 | % Depr., Dep., Amort./Sales | | | | | | |
| 9.0 | 8.8 | 7.0 | | | | | | | |
| | | | % Officers', Directors' Owners' Comp/Sales | | | | | | |
| 531408M | 423374M | 486448M | Net Sales ($) | 2295M | 11221M | 27905M | 34639M | 45211M | 365177M |
| 911732M | 840094M | 872763M | Total Assets ($) | 3028M | 16358M | 39250M | 39055M | 183094M | 591978M |

M = $ thousand    MM = $ million
See Pages 9 through 22 for Explanation of Ratios and Data

## Current Data Sorted by Assets　　　　　　Comparative Historical Data

| | 0-500M | 500M-2MM | 2-10MM | 10-50MM | 50-100MM | 100-250MM | | 4/1/07-3/31/08 ALL | 4/1/08-3/31/09 ALL |
|---|---|---|---|---|---|---|---|---|---|
| Type of Statement | | | | | | | | | |
| Unqualified | | 2 | 3 | 14 | 3 | 2 | | 39 | 26 |
| Reviewed | | | 5 | 4 | | | | 5 | 9 |
| Compiled | 1 | 1 | 2 | 1 | | | | 8 | 10 |
| Tax Returns | 6 | 4 | 5 | 1 | | | | 12 | 18 |
| Other | 4 | 10 | 13 | 11 | 4 | 3 | | 46 | 53 |
| | | | 21 (4/1-9/30/11) | | 77 (10/1/11-3/31/12) | | | | |
| NUMBER OF STATEMENTS | 11 | 17 | 28 | 30 | 7 | 5 | | 110 | 116 |
| | % | % | % | % | % | % | ASSETS | % | % |
| | 28.6 | 10.8 | 7.0 | 7.9 | | | Cash & Equivalents | 10.9 | 10.3 |
| | 7.0 | 13.7 | 9.3 | 7.8 | | | Trade Receivables (net) | 10.5 | 10.2 |
| | .0 | .5 | .2 | .1 | | | Inventory | .4 | .2 |
| | 5.1 | 1.9 | 3.3 | 3.1 | | | All Other Current | 2.8 | 2.6 |
| | 40.6 | 26.9 | 19.8 | 18.8 | | | Total Current | 24.6 | 23.4 |
| | 27.6 | 27.3 | 29.1 | 23.1 | | | Fixed Assets (net) | 25.3 | 27.0 |
| | 18.4 | 37.3 | 41.9 | 46.8 | | | Intangibles (net) | 38.3 | 37.4 |
| | 13.4 | 8.6 | 9.1 | 11.2 | | | All Other Non-Current | 11.8 | 12.3 |
| | 100.0 | 100.0 | 100.0 | 100.0 | | | Total | 100.0 | 100.0 |
| | | | | | | | LIABILITIES | | |
| | 24.4 | 10.6 | 6.7 | 1.2 | | | Notes Payable-Short Term | 4.1 | 4.5 |
| | 4.7 | 14.4 | 5.6 | 2.4 | | | Cur. Mat.-L.T.D. | 4.2 | 5.0 |
| | 6.3 | 5.3 | 2.5 | 1.8 | | | Trade Payables | 2.2 | 3.3 |
| | .0 | .0 | .0 | .0 | | | Income Taxes Payable | .0 | .2 |
| | 19.8 | 14.1 | 9.5 | 3.3 | | | All Other Current | 5.8 | 6.7 |
| | 55.2 | 44.4 | 24.3 | 8.7 | | | Total Current | 16.3 | 19.6 |
| | 55.3 | 51.5 | 46.8 | 27.3 | | | Long-Term Debt | 40.5 | 44.9 |
| | .0 | .0 | .0 | .1 | | | Deferred Taxes | .7 | .8 |
| | 23.2 | 14.2 | 16.5 | 24.9 | | | All Other Non-Current | 7.8 | 10.9 |
| | -33.8 | -10.1 | 12.4 | 39.0 | | | Net Worth | 34.7 | 23.9 |
| | 100.0 | 100.0 | 100.0 | 100.0 | | | Total Liabilities & Net Worth | 100.0 | 100.0 |
| | | | | | | | INCOME DATA | | |
| | 100.0 | 100.0 | 100.0 | 100.0 | | | Net Sales | 100.0 | 100.0 |
| | | | | | | | Gross Profit | | |
| | 94.5 | 92.2 | 90.1 | 86.4 | | | Operating Expenses | 88.8 | 90.4 |
| | 5.5 | 7.8 | 9.9 | 13.6 | | | Operating Profit | 11.2 | 9.6 |
| | 5.0 | 4.9 | 6.2 | 9.3 | | | All Other Expenses (net) | 7.9 | 9.4 |
| | .5 | 2.9 | 3.7 | 4.2 | | | Profit Before Taxes | 3.3 | .2 |
| | | | | | | | RATIOS | | |
| | 3.7 | 3.9 | 3.9 | 3.3 | | | | 4.1 | 3.0 |
| | 1.1 | 1.0 | 1.9 | 2.3 | | | Current | 1.9 | 1.5 |
| | .2 | .4 | .5 | 1.3 | | | | .9 | .6 |
| | 2.2 | 3.7 | 2.8 | 2.8 | | | | 3.8 | 2.6 |
| | 1.0 | 1.0 | 1.7 | 1.9 | | | Quick | 1.6 | 1.2 |
| | .1 | .4 | .5 | 1.0 | | | | .7 | .5 |
| | 0 UND | 22 16.4 | 29 12.8 | 45 8.1 | | | | 34 10.8 | 29 12.7 |
| | 0 UND | 40 9.2 | 47 7.7 | 49 7.4 | | | Sales/Receivables | 51 7.2 | 48 7.6 |
| | 42 8.7 | 64 5.7 | 63 5.8 | 62 5.9 | | | | 61 6.0 | 57 6.4 |
| | | | | | | | Cost of Sales/Inventory | | |
| | | | | | | | Cost of Sales/Payables | | |
| | 3.7 | 5.4 | 4.8 | 4.4 | | | | 4.3 | 4.5 |
| | 134.0 | 128.3 | 9.2 | 7.5 | | | Sales/Working Capital | 8.7 | 13.0 |
| | -5.8 | -8.0 | -6.4 | 24.7 | | | | -55.4 | -12.4 |
| | 7.8 | 4.4 | 5.9 | 8.5 | | | | 8.1 | 3.9 |
| | (10) 2.8 | (14) 2.0 | (25) 2.1 | (25) 2.8 | | | EBIT/Interest | (85) 2.1 | (85) 1.3 |
| | -.2 | .5 | .5 | .1 | | | | .4 | -.4 |
| | | | | | | | | 8.7 | 3.3 |
| | | | | | | | Net Profit + Depr., Dep., Amort./Cur. Mat. L/T/D | (18) 1.7 | (22) .8 |
| | | | | | | | | 1.0 | -.9 |
| | .9 | 1.4 | 3.9 | .7 | | | | .7 | .8 |
| | -2.3 | -.3 | -1.4 | 9.0 | | | Fixed/Worth | NM | -3.1 |
| | -.3 | -.2 | -.2 | -.2 | | | | -.3 | -.3 |
| | 1.9 | 2.0 | 5.2 | .6 | | | | 1.0 | 1.4 |
| | -4.6 | -2.4 | -6.5 | 15.9 | | | Debt/Worth | NM | -5.5 |
| | -1.5 | -1.3 | -1.7 | -1.4 | | | | -1.8 | -1.7 |
| | | | 130.5 | 122.9 | | | | 80.8 | 43.2 |
| | | (11) 22.1 | (17) 17.0 | | | | % Profit Before Taxes/Tangible Net Worth | (55) 28.4 | (51) 14.9 |
| | | | .2 | 3.5 | | | | 8.7 | -1.2 |
| | 28.4 | 11.3 | 8.4 | 9.4 | | | | 11.5 | 6.8 |
| | 8.3 | 3.4 | 1.3 | 3.5 | | | % Profit Before Taxes/Total Assets | 2.3 | .7 |
| | -11.5 | -2.6 | -1.9 | -3.5 | | | | -3.8 | -4.7 |
| | 28.2 | 13.4 | 8.0 | 6.0 | | | | 8.8 | 7.4 |
| | 6.7 | 3.9 | 3.0 | 2.7 | | | Sales/Net Fixed Assets | 3.7 | 3.4 |
| | 4.0 | 1.8 | 1.5 | 1.7 | | | | 2.1 | 1.8 |
| | 2.8 | 1.6 | 1.1 | .8 | | | | 1.2 | 1.2 |
| | 2.1 | .7 | .6 | .5 | | | Sales/Total Assets | .7 | .6 |
| | 1.3 | .6 | .5 | .4 | | | | .4 | .4 |
| | | 1.6 | 2.8 | 3.3 | | | | 3.0 | 3.1 |
| | (14) 7.6 | (23) 5.2 | 4.4 | | | | % Depr., Dep., Amort./Sales | (92) 5.8 | (107) 5.6 |
| | | 13.8 | 8.6 | 7.9 | | | | 8.5 | 10.3 |
| | | | | | | | | 2.9 | 4.3 |
| | | | | | | | % Officers', Directors' Owners' Comp/Sales | (21) 5.1 | (19) 6.5 |
| | | | | | | | | 7.7 | 10.7 |
| | 7168M | 24855M | 104081M | 436731M | 408617M | 314670M | Net Sales ($) | 1740783M | 2057681M |
| | 2638M | 22136M | 139742M | 750154M | 482519M | 808531M | Total Assets ($) | 3381785M | 3651609M |

© RMA 2012

M = $ thousand　　MM = $ million
See Pages 9 through 22 for Explanation of Ratios and Data

## Comparative Historical Data | Current Data Sorted by Sales

| 4/1/09-3/31/10 ALL | 4/1/10-3/31/11 ALL | 4/1/11-3/31/12 ALL | Type of Statement | 0-1MM | 1-3MM | 3-5MM | 5-10MM | 10-25MM | 25MM & OVER |
|---|---|---|---|---|---|---|---|---|---|
| | | | | | | | 5 | 2 | 10 | 7 |
| 25 | 31 | 24 | Unqualified | | | 5 | 2 | 10 | 7 |
| 5 | 9 | 9 | Reviewed | | 1 | 1 | 5 | 1 | 1 |
| 8 | 5 | 5 | Compiled | 2 | 2 | 1 | | | |
| 12 | 15 | 15 | Tax Returns | 9 | 6 | | | | |
| 63 | 64 | 45 | Other | 9 | 12 | 5 | | 8 | 6 |
| | | | | 21 (4/1-9/30/11) | | | 77 (10/1/11-3/31/12) | | |
| 113 | 124 | 98 | NUMBER OF STATEMENTS | 20 | 21 | 12 | 12 | 19 | 14 |
| % | % | % | **ASSETS** | % | % | % | % | % | % |
| 7.8 | 10.5 | 10.0 | Cash & Equivalents | 14.8 | 9.4 | 14.6 | 3.7 | 11.2 | 3.5 |
| 12.4 | 9.4 | 9.2 | Trade Receivables (net) | 7.3 | 10.9 | 12.1 | 7.0 | 8.0 | 10.1 |
| .2 | .0 | .2 | Inventory | .0 | .6 | .0 | .0 | .0 | .1 |
| 2.8 | 3.4 | 3.5 | All Other Current | 2.9 | 3.7 | 3.5 | 1.4 | 6.2 | 2.4 |
| 23.1 | 23.3 | 22.8 | Total Current | 25.1 | 24.6 | 30.2 | 12.2 | 25.5 | 16.1 |
| 23.1 | 25.1 | 24.5 | Fixed Assets (net) | 30.1 | 28.2 | 27.2 | 18.3 | 22.2 | 17.3 |
| 42.4 | 40.8 | 43.0 | Intangibles (net) | 30.2 | 45.0 | 26.7 | 59.4 | 42.4 | 59.2 |
| 11.3 | 10.8 | 9.7 | All Other Non-Current | 14.7 | 2.3 | 15.9 | 10.2 | 10.0 | 7.5 |
| 100.0 | 100.0 | 100.0 | Total | 100.0 | 100.0 | 100.0 | 100.0 | 100.0 | 100.0 |
| | | | **LIABILITIES** | | | | | | |
| 7.9 | 2.7 | 7.0 | Notes Payable-Short Term | 20.3 | 10.4 | 1.0 | .6 | 2.0 | .0 |
| 6.9 | 9.9 | 7.8 | Cur. Mat.-L.T.D. | 12.0 | 6.4 | 5.9 | 1.9 | 2.5 | 17.8 |
| 4.1 | 2.8 | 3.3 | Trade Payables | 5.2 | 4.1 | 2.6 | 1.5 | 1.7 | 3.9 |
| .0 | .3 | .1 | Income Taxes Payable | .0 | .0 | .0 | .0 | .0 | .5 |
| 17.1 | 11.0 | 8.8 | All Other Current | 18.2 | 6.3 | 18.5 | 2.3 | 3.3 | 3.7 |
| 36.0 | 26.7 | 27.0 | Total Current | 55.8 | 27.3 | 28.1 | 6.3 | 9.6 | 25.9 |
| 40.0 | 44.2 | 40.7 | Long-Term Debt | 57.8 | 61.0 | 23.3 | 31.8 | 26.4 | 28.1 |
| .6 | .3 | .6 | Deferred Taxes | .0 | .0 | .1 | .0 | .0 | 4.0 |
| 15.9 | 15.9 | 18.0 | All Other Non-Current | 25.1 | 9.1 | 15.1 | 25.8 | 26.0 | 6.3 |
| 7.4 | 12.9 | 13.7 | Net Worth | -38.6 | 2.5 | 33.5 | 36.1 | 38.1 | 35.6 |
| 100.0 | 100.0 | 100.0 | Total Liabilities & Net Worth | 100.0 | 100.0 | 100.0 | 100.0 | 100.0 | 100.0 |
| | | | **INCOME DATA** | | | | | | |
| 100.0 | 100.0 | 100.0 | Net Sales | 100.0 | 100.0 | 100.0 | 100.0 | 100.0 | 100.0 |
| | | | Gross Profit | | | | | | |
| 91.5 | 88.5 | 88.6 | Operating Expenses | 93.0 | 88.3 | 93.7 | 87.7 | 85.3 | 83.7 |
| 8.5 | 11.5 | 11.4 | Operating Profit | 7.0 | 11.7 | 6.3 | 12.3 | 14.7 | 16.3 |
| 10.9 | 7.4 | 6.7 | All Other Expenses (net) | 8.1 | 5.0 | 5.4 | 7.7 | 8.9 | 4.3 |
| -2.4 | 4.1 | 4.7 | Profit Before Taxes | -1.1 | 6.7 | .9 | 4.6 | 5.7 | 12.0 |
| | | | **RATIOS** | | | | | | |
| 2.4 | 2.7 | 3.2 | | 3.1 | 6.1 | 3.0 | 2.8 | 9.8 | 2.4 |
| 1.3 | 1.2 | 1.8 | Current | .9 | 1.3 | 1.3 | 2.3 | 2.8 | 1.5 |
| .5 | .5 | .7 | | .2 | .4 | .7 | 1.2 | 1.9 | .6 |
| 2.2 | 2.3 | 2.6 | | 1.8 | 3.3 | 2.8 | 2.4 | 6.9 | 2.1 |
| 1.1 | 1.0 | 1.3 | Quick | .9 | 1.2 | 1.3 | 1.9 | 2.4 | 1.2 |
| .5 | .4 | .6 | | .1 | .4 | .6 | 1.2 | 1.2 | .5 |
| 39  9.4 | 23  15.7 | 27  13.5 | | 0  UND | 30  12.3 | 21  17.3 | 46  8.0 | 13  28.4 | 49  7.5 |
| 55  6.6 | 45  8.1 | 47  7.7 | Sales/Receivables | 29  12.5 | 50  7.3 | 40  9.2 | 48  7.6 | 48  7.6 | 54  6.8 |
| 67  5.5 | 59  6.2 | 59  6.2 | | 54  6.8 | 64  5.7 | 60  6.1 | 54  6.7 | 63  5.8 | 58  6.3 |
| | | | Cost of Sales/Inventory | | | | | | |
| | | | Cost of Sales/Payables | | | | | | |
| 5.6 | 6.3 | 4.7 | | 5.0 | 4.2 | 6.3 | 5.9 | 1.7 | 7.1 |
| 15.9 | 23.9 | 11.6 | Sales/Working Capital | UND | 33.3 | 22.6 | 8.1 | 6.5 | 12.9 |
| -5.3 | -4.8 | -17.5 | | -6.1 | -4.9 | -34.1 | 31.4 | 12.3 | -17.9 |
| 3.0 | 3.6 | 6.0 | | 3.0 | 6.2 | | 9.1 | 7.9 | 8.0 |
| (88)  1.0 | (94)  1.5 | (86)  2.1 | EBIT/Interest | (18)  1.1 | (19)  2.3 | | 1.9 | (15)  3.5 | 4.1 |
| -.6 | .4 | .5 | | -.2 | .9 | | -.2 | .1 | 1.8 |
| 2.8 | 3.5 | | Net Profit + Depr., Dep., | | | | | | |
| (20)  1.0 | (16)  1.1 | | Amort./Cur. Mat. L/T/D | | | | | | |
| .1 | .6 | | | | | | | | |
| 1.5 | 1.1 | 1.6 | | NM | 8.3 | .7 | 3.6 | .4 | 1.7 |
| -.8 | -1.2 | -1.4 | Fixed/Worth | -.4 | -.9 | NM | -.5 | 1.3 | -.3 |
| -.2 | -.2 | -.2 | | -.1 | -.2 | -.5 | -.1 | -1.3 | -.1 |
| 5.5 | 1.6 | 2.0 | | NM | 10.7 | .9 | 5.9 | .4 | 3.8 |
| -2.9 | -3.3 | -4.6 | Debt/Worth | -3.0 | -3.1 | NM | -3.2 | 1.5 | -2.8 |
| -1.5 | -1.5 | -1.5 | | -1.3 | -1.4 | -2.1 | -1.3 | -3.2 | -1.3 |
| 45.5 | 72.0 | 123.9 | % Profit Before Taxes/Tangible | | | | | 67.0 | |
| (37)  5.9 | (48)  14.3 | (40)  23.5 | Net Worth | | | | | (13)  17.0 | |
| -1.0 | .2 | 5.1 | | | | | | 6.2 | |
| 3.9 | 8.9 | 9.6 | % Profit Before Taxes/Total | 7.8 | 11.3 | 17.6 | 8.9 | 9.5 | 11.2 |
| -.3 | 1.7 | 3.4 | Assets | .5 | 3.9 | -.4 | 3.0 | 6.9 | 4.7 |
| -7.2 | -1.7 | -1.9 | | -6.4 | -.9 | -6.6 | -3.7 | -2.4 | 2.6 |
| 8.4 | 8.6 | 7.2 | | 12.3 | 10.5 | 10.2 | 12.0 | 5.1 | 6.8 |
| 3.2 | 3.7 | 3.9 | Sales/Net Fixed Assets | 4.5 | 3.4 | 3.5 | 4.0 | 3.4 | 5.2 |
| 1.8 | 1.8 | 1.9 | | 1.7 | 1.5 | 2.0 | 1.6 | 2.1 | 2.5 |
| 1.0 | 1.0 | 1.0 | | 2.0 | 1.2 | 1.6 | .7 | .8 | .9 |
| .5 | .6 | .6 | Sales/Total Assets | .8 | .6 | 1.0 | .5 | .5 | .5 |
| .4 | .4 | .4 | | .5 | .5 | .6 | .4 | .4 | .3 |
| 3.4 | 3.3 | 2.9 | | 3.8 | 2.5 | 2.6 | 2.9 | 3.2 | 2.9 |
| (97)  6.3 | (98)  6.1 | (84)  5.0 | % Depr., Dep., Amort./Sales | (16)  7.3 | (17)  6.8 | (11)  3.5 | (11)  5.9 | (18)  3.9 | (11)  5.0 |
| 10.0 | 10.1 | 8.6 | | 14.6 | 11.0 | 5.7 | 8.6 | 6.3 | 8.0 |
| 3.3 | 5.2 | 5.2 | % Officers', Directors' | | | | | | |
| (20)  5.9 | (25)  6.4 | (16)  7.2 | Owners' Comp/Sales | | | | | | |
| 8.4 | 9.6 | 11.7 | | | | | | | |
| 1852322M | 1717165M | 1296122M | Net Sales ($) | 10226M | 41809M | 48179M | 83855M | 299032M | 813021M |
| 3626548M | 2991759M | 2205720M | Total Assets ($) | 19907M | 63644M | 62211M | 177508M | 561083M | 1321367M |

M = $ thousand     MM = $ million
See Pages 9 through 22 for Explanation of Ratios and Data

## Current Data Sorted by Assets      Comparative Historical Data

| | 0-500M | 500M-2MM | 2-10MM | 10-50MM | 50-100MM | 100-250MM | Type of Statement | 4/1/07-3/31/08 ALL | 4/1/08-3/31/09 ALL |
|---|---|---|---|---|---|---|---|---|---|
| | 1 | | 9 | 17 | 3 | 5 | Unqualified | 42 | 40 |
| | | | 1 | 2 | 1 | | Reviewed | 3 | 5 |
| | | | 2 | | 1 | 1 | Compiled | 3 | 8 |
| | 1 | 3 | 1 | | | | Tax Returns | 3 | 1 |
| | 1 | 4 | 7 | 11 | 6 | 5 | Other | 34 | 42 |
| | | 38 (4/1-9/30/11) | | 44 (10/1/11-3/31/12) | | | | | |
| | 3 | 7 | 20 | 30 | 11 | 11 | NUMBER OF STATEMENTS | 85 | 96 |
| | % | % | % | % | % | % | | % | % |
| | | | | | | | **ASSETS** | | |
| Cash & Equivalents | | | 13.1 | 12.9 | 8.5 | 9.4 | | 9.7 | 10.3 |
| Trade Receivables (net) | | | 11.5 | 6.9 | 7.8 | 10.8 | | 12.4 | 12.0 |
| Inventory | | | .0 | .4 | .3 | .0 | | .3 | .8 |
| All Other Current | | | 2.0 | 6.4 | 3.7 | 3.6 | | 5.6 | 5.9 |
| Total Current | | | 26.6 | 26.5 | 20.4 | 23.9 | | 27.9 | 29.0 |
| Fixed Assets (net) | | | 51.0 | 42.1 | 36.8 | 16.7 | | 40.7 | 38.5 |
| Intangibles (net) | | | 13.3 | 13.5 | 30.0 | 39.6 | | 17.3 | 19.2 |
| All Other Non-Current | | | 9.1 | 17.9 | 12.8 | 19.8 | | 14.1 | 13.3 |
| Total | | | 100.0 | 100.0 | 100.0 | 100.0 | | 100.0 | 100.0 |
| | | | | | | | **LIABILITIES** | | |
| Notes Payable-Short Term | | | 4.5 | 2.9 | .0 | .4 | | 4.0 | 6.3 |
| Cur. Mat.-L.T.D. | | | 11.5 | 4.8 | 3.2 | 2.2 | | 4.7 | 7.4 |
| Trade Payables | | | 5.5 | 4.8 | 2.5 | 3.3 | | 5.1 | 4.7 |
| Income Taxes Payable | | | .0 | .1 | .1 | .0 | | .4 | .2 |
| All Other Current | | | 4.8 | 4.4 | 6.6 | 3.0 | | 12.7 | 7.6 |
| Total Current | | | 26.2 | 16.9 | 12.4 | 8.8 | | 26.8 | 26.1 |
| Long-Term Debt | | | 20.6 | 24.0 | 35.6 | 54.0 | | 28.5 | 28.2 |
| Deferred Taxes | | | .5 | .7 | .0 | 1.7 | | .8 | .8 |
| All Other Non-Current | | | 2.8 | 10.7 | 7.7 | 15.3 | | 13.3 | 14.9 |
| Net Worth | | | 49.8 | 47.7 | 44.3 | 20.2 | | 30.6 | 30.1 |
| Total Liabilities & Net Worth | | | 100.0 | 100.0 | 100.0 | 100.0 | | 100.0 | 100.0 |
| | | | | | | | **INCOME DATA** | | |
| Net Sales | | | 100.0 | 100.0 | 100.0 | 100.0 | | 100.0 | 100.0 |
| Gross Profit | | | | | | | | | |
| Operating Expenses | | | 94.5 | 90.5 | 87.7 | 81.0 | | 92.7 | 94.6 |
| Operating Profit | | | 5.5 | 9.5 | 12.3 | 19.0 | | 7.3 | 5.4 |
| All Other Expenses (net) | | | 2.4 | 2.1 | 5.3 | 6.3 | | 4.3 | 6.3 |
| Profit Before Taxes | | | 3.1 | 7.4 | 6.9 | 12.7 | | 3.0 | -.9 |
| | | | | | | | **RATIOS** | | |
| Current | | | 4.9 | 3.9 | 2.7 | 3.4 | | 2.6 | 3.0 |
| | | | 1.7 | 1.3 | 1.4 | 2.4 | | 1.7 | 1.4 |
| | | | .6 | .8 | 1.0 | 1.4 | | .9 | .7 |
| Quick | | | 4.5 | 2.6 | 2.0 | 3.0 | | 2.0 | 2.0 |
| | | | 1.6 | 1.0 | 1.0 | 1.9 | | 1.4 | .9 |
| | | | .6 | .4 | .8 | 1.0 | | .7 | .4 |
| Sales/Receivables | | | 8   46.9 | 6   62.4 | 29   12.8 | 49   7.5 | | 17   21.7 | 19   19.6 |
| | | | 29   12.6 | 33   11.0 | 44   8.3 | 62   5.9 | | 46   7.9 | 41   9.0 |
| | | | 54   6.7 | 59   6.2 | 64   5.7 | 70   5.2 | | 72   5.1 | 56   6.6 |
| Cost of Sales/Inventory | | | | | | | | | |
| Cost of Sales/Payables | | | | | | | | | |
| Sales/Working Capital | | | 5.1 | 3.6 | 4.3 | 2.9 | | 4.9 | 4.6 |
| | | | 7.7 | 15.7 | 18.5 | 5.8 | | 8.7 | 15.2 |
| | | | -11.8 | -15.3 | -91.5 | 9.2 | | -43.5 | -12.3 |
| EBIT/Interest | | | 8.3 | 27.4 | | | | 8.9 | 5.4 |
| | | | (18) -.3 | (25) 3.7 | | | | (68) 2.2 | (79) .6 |
| | | | -13.4 | 1.0 | | | | .1 | -3.0 |
| Net Profit + Depr., Dep., Amort./Cur. Mat. L/T/D | | | | | | | | 8.2 | |
| | | | | | | | | (10) 3.9 | |
| | | | | | | | | -1.0 | |
| Fixed/Worth | | | .6 | .6 | 2.2 | .3 | | .7 | .6 |
| | | | 1.0 | .9 | -22.6 | -2.5 | | 1.8 | 1.1 |
| | | | NM | 6.1 | -1.1 | -.3 | | -1.8 | -1.6 |
| Debt/Worth | | | .2 | .3 | 1.7 | .3 | | .3 | .3 |
| | | | .5 | .8 | -37.1 | -5.6 | | 2.9 | 1.3 |
| | | | NM | 7.5 | -4.4 | -1.5 | | -4.0 | -3.5 |
| % Profit Before Taxes/Tangible Net Worth | | | 5.7 | 21.7 | | | | 26.5 | 32.0 |
| | | | (15) -6.1 | (24) 6.6 | | | | (56) 8.0 | (63) 2.5 |
| | | | -12.8 | -4.9 | | | | -1.9 | -11.1 |
| % Profit Before Taxes/Total Assets | | | 9.5 | 10.6 | 6.7 | 7.6 | | 10.2 | 7.2 |
| | | | -1.7 | 3.8 | 2.8 | 5.1 | | 2.5 | -1.6 |
| | | | -8.9 | -2.0 | .6 | 3.2 | | -2.3 | -9.0 |
| Sales/Net Fixed Assets | | | 4.9 | 4.5 | 3.0 | 4.1 | | 4.1 | 4.4 |
| | | | 1.4 | 1.6 | 2.4 | 2.5 | | 2.0 | 2.1 |
| | | | .8 | .8 | .8 | 2.1 | | 1.1 | 1.2 |
| Sales/Total Assets | | | 1.0 | .9 | .8 | .6 | | 1.0 | 1.1 |
| | | | .8 | .6 | .6 | .5 | | .7 | .7 |
| | | | .6 | .4 | .3 | .4 | | .5 | .5 |
| % Depr., Dep., Amort./Sales | | | 9.2 | 6.3 | | | | 4.3 | 4.9 |
| | | | (17) 14.5 | (29) 11.0 | | | | (75) 6.6 | (83) 9.3 |
| | | | 19.3 | 15.6 | | | | 11.4 | 15.1 |
| % Officers', Directors' Owners' Comp/Sales | | | | | | | | | 9.3 |
| | | | | | | | | | (10) 14.4 |
| | | | | | | | | | 32.8 |
| Net Sales ($) | 1195M | 11928M | 88421M | 537413M | 460467M | 1012766M | | 2301767M | 2477685M |
| Total Assets ($) | 620M | 7956M | 111530M | 767488M | 740797M | 1778140M | | 3370153M | 3547446M |

© RMA 2012

M = $ thousand    MM = $ million
See Pages 9 through 22 for Explanation of Ratios and Data

## Comparative Historical Data | Current Data Sorted by Sales

| 4/1/09-3/31/10 ALL | 4/1/10-3/31/11 ALL | 4/1/11-3/31/12 ALL | Type of Statement | 0-1MM | 1-3MM | 3-5MM | 5-10MM | 10-25MM | 25MM & OVER |
|---|---|---|---|---|---|---|---|---|---|
| 40 | 47 | 35 | Unqualified | 1 | 3 | 3 | 9 | 8 | 11 |
| 2 | 4 | 4 | Reviewed | | 1 | | 1 | 2 | |
| 5 | 3 | 4 | Compiled | | 1 | 1 | | 1 | 1 |
| 2 | 2 | 5 | Tax Returns | 2 | 3 | | | | |
| 32 | 31 | 34 | Other | 3 | 3 | 3 | 5 | 7 | 11 |
| | | | | 38 (4/1-9/30/11) | 38 (4/1-9/30/11) | 38 (4/1-9/30/11) | 44 (10/1/11-3/31/12) | 44 (10/1/11-3/31/12) | 44 (10/1/11-3/31/12) |
| 81 | 87 | 82 | NUMBER OF STATEMENTS | 6 | 12 | 8 | 15 | 18 | 23 |
| % | % | % | **ASSETS** | % | % | % | % | % | % |
| 8.4 | 11.3 | 12.6 | Cash & Equivalents | | 10.5 | | 10.5 | 13.5 | 11.4 |
| 8.8 | 10.9 | 8.9 | Trade Receivables (net) | | 3.3 | | 11.8 | 6.5 | 11.5 |
| .2 | .5 | .9 | Inventory | | .3 | | .2 | .2 | .4 |
| 5.1 | 4.9 | 4.7 | All Other Current | | 3.0 | | 3.7 | 6.9 | 4.7 |
| 22.6 | 27.5 | 27.0 | Total Current | | 17.2 | | 26.2 | 27.0 | 27.9 |
| 41.2 | 41.0 | 39.6 | Fixed Assets (net) | | 50.3 | | 42.5 | 42.6 | 26.2 |
| 20.7 | 17.4 | 18.6 | Intangibles (net) | | 17.6 | | 13.6 | 13.0 | 30.1 |
| 15.5 | 14.2 | 14.7 | All Other Non-Current | | 15.0 | | 17.8 | 17.4 | 15.7 |
| 100.0 | 100.0 | 100.0 | Total | | 100.0 | | 100.0 | 100.0 | 100.0 |
| | | | **LIABILITIES** | | | | | | |
| 3.9 | 2.2 | 3.6 | Notes Payable-Short Term | | 6.0 | | 1.2 | 4.3 | .2 |
| 5.2 | 3.5 | 5.5 | Cur. Mat.-L.T.D. | | 2.3 | | 5.8 | 3.1 | 3.5 |
| 4.3 | 4.8 | 5.5 | Trade Payables | | 7.7 | | 5.0 | 5.2 | 4.5 |
| .1 | .1 | .1 | Income Taxes Payable | | .0 | | .0 | .2 | .0 |
| 7.1 | 6.7 | 5.7 | All Other Current | | 2.0 | | 3.7 | 5.1 | 5.3 |
| 20.5 | 17.3 | 20.2 | Total Current | | 18.1 | | 15.6 | 17.9 | 13.5 |
| 35.1 | 31.2 | 31.7 | Long-Term Debt | | 32.3 | | 16.9 | 20.8 | 42.7 |
| .6 | .8 | .6 | Deferred Taxes | | .8 | | .7 | .6 | .8 |
| 11.5 | 5.6 | 8.0 | All Other Non-Current | | 3.0 | | 8.5 | 10.9 | 10.8 |
| 32.3 | 45.2 | 39.4 | Net Worth | | 45.8 | | 58.3 | 49.9 | 32.2 |
| 100.0 | 100.0 | 100.0 | Total Liabilties & Net Worth | | 100.0 | | 100.0 | 100.0 | 100.0 |
| | | | **INCOME DATA** | | | | | | |
| 100.0 | 100.0 | 100.0 | Net Sales | | 100.0 | | 100.0 | 100.0 | 100.0 |
| | | | Gross Profit | | | | | | |
| 98.0 | 92.6 | 91.5 | Operating Expenses | | 101.3 | | 88.0 | 92.3 | 87.0 |
| 2.0 | 7.4 | 8.5 | Operating Profit | | -1.3 | | 12.0 | 7.7 | 13.0 |
| 4.6 | 3.3 | 3.1 | All Other Expenses (net) | | 4.4 | | 1.5 | 1.3 | 4.2 |
| -2.6 | 4.1 | 5.4 | Profit Before Taxes | | -5.7 | | 10.5 | 6.4 | 8.8 |
| | | | **RATIOS** | | | | | | |
| 2.7 | 2.6 | 3.5 | | | 2.9 | | 4.4 | 5.1 | 3.4 |
| 1.3 | 1.4 | 1.5 | Current | | 1.3 | | 1.7 | 1.2 | 2.1 |
| .5 | .9 | .9 | | | .4 | | .7 | .8 | 1.3 |
| 2.2 | 2.2 | 2.6 | | | 2.5 | | 3.6 | 3.1 | 2.5 |
| 1.0 | 1.2 | 1.2 | Quick | | .7 | | 1.6 | 1.1 | 1.5 |
| .4 | .7 | .6 | | | .1 | | .6 | .7 | .9 |
| 16  23.5 | 21  17.0 | 10  38.3 | | 0  UND | | 7  54.7 | 25  14.4 | 42  8.7 |
| 42  8.7 | 46  8.0 | 42  8.7 | Sales/Receivables | 7  51.7 | | 43  8.5 | 42  8.6 | 57  6.4 |
| 61  6.0 | 67  5.5 | 61  6.0 | | 25  14.6 | | 54  6.8 | 59  6.2 | 70  5.2 |
| | | | Cost of Sales/Inventory | | | | | | |
| | | | Cost of Sales/Payables | | | | | | |
| 4.7 | 4.4 | 4.2 | | | 4.7 | | 3.8 | 1.8 | 4.3 |
| 16.1 | 14.1 | 9.7 | Sales/Working Capital | | 28.3 | | 6.1 | 24.6 | 8.9 |
| -8.1 | -45.3 | -24.9 | | | -4.9 | | -16.2 | -12.4 | 28.4 |
| 3.9 | 7.1 | 10.0 | | | 5.0 | | 27.1 | 19.5 | 11.0 |
| (63) 1.3 | (71) 3.1 | (69) 3.1 | EBIT/Interest | | (10) -.2 | (11) 1.2 | (17) 4.3 | (19) 4.4 | |
| -4.1 | -.7 | -.3 | | | -6.9 | | -16.9 | 1.6 | 2.8 |
| | 3.0 | 12.8 | Net Profit + Depr., Dep., | | | | | | |
| | (12) 2.7 | (10) 1.8 | Amort./Cur. Mat. L/T/D | | | | | | |
| | 1.0 | 1.2 | | | | | | | |
| .7 | .5 | .6 | | | 1.0 | | .5 | .7 | .3 |
| 1.3 | 1.0 | 1.1 | Fixed/Worth | | 1.6 | | .7 | .9 | 6.0 |
| -1.1 | -2.6 | -1.7 | | | NM | | 3.4 | 10.2 | -.7 |
| .3 | .2 | .3 | | | .5 | | .1 | .4 | .3 |
| 1.3 | .9 | 1.1 | Debt/Worth | | 1.0 | | .3 | .9 | 17.6 |
| -2.6 | -5.5 | -4.3 | | | NM | | 3.1 | 11.6 | -2.2 |
| 10.7 | 17.8 | 16.1 | % Profit Before Taxes/Tangible | | | | 36.6 | 23.7 | 38.0 |
| (52) .8 | (60) 3.6 | (54) 3.9 | Net Worth | | | (12) 2.1 | (15) 8.3 | (12) 7.3 | |
| -16.1 | -8.3 | -10.2 | | | | | -6.4 | -.3 | 3.3 |
| 3.8 | 9.0 | 7.4 | | | 2.3 | | 13.7 | 5.3 | 8.7 |
| .1 | 3.0 | 2.7 | % Profit Before Taxes/Total Assets | | -3.7 | | 1.2 | 4.6 | 5.1 |
| -8.3 | -4.2 | -4.4 | | | -10.6 | | -5.6 | -.2 | 2.7 |
| 3.4 | 3.8 | 5.2 | | | 5.1 | | 7.1 | 3.4 | 4.3 |
| 1.7 | 2.1 | 2.1 | Sales/Net Fixed Assets | | 1.4 | | 1.6 | 1.9 | 2.6 |
| 1.2 | 1.1 | 1.0 | | | .5 | | .8 | .8 | 2.1 |
| 1.0 | .9 | 1.0 | | | 1.0 | | 1.1 | .9 | .8 |
| .6 | .7 | .6 | Sales/Total Assets | | .7 | | .7 | .6 | .6 |
| .4 | .5 | .4 | | | .3 | | .4 | .4 | .4 |
| 5.8 | 5.5 | 5.8 | | | 8.3 | | 7.3 | 5.8 | 4.0 |
| (71) 10.0 | (73) 8.7 | (69) 10.1 | % Depr., Dep., Amort./Sales | | (10) 14.7 | (12) 14.1 | (17) 11.0 | (18) 7.4 | |
| 16.2 | 15.7 | 15.6 | | | 33.3 | | 15.7 | 16.5 | 9.2 |
| | | 3.2 | % Officers', Directors' | | | | | | |
| | (11) 8.6 | | Owners' Comp/Sales | | | | | | |
| | | 12.6 | | | | | | | |
| 1834048M | 2479403M | 2112190M | Net Sales ($) | 3449M | 25037M | 32879M | 104823M | 303260M | 1642742M |
| 3218520M | 3789133M | 3406531M | Total Assets ($) | 9991M | 106997M | 51781M | 192024M | 596883M | 2448855M |

© RMA 2012

M = $ thousand     MM = $ million
See Pages 9 through 22 for Explanation of Ratios and Data

## Current Data Sorted by Assets     Comparative Historical Data

| | | | | | | Type of Statement | | |
|---|---|---|---|---|---|---|---|---|
| 1 | | 4 | 3 | 2 | 8 | Unqualified | 25 | 21 |
| | | 1 | 2 | | | Reviewed | 11 | 9 |
| 1 | 1 | 2 | 1 | | | Compiled | 4 | 4 |
| 2 | 4 | 2 | | | | Tax Returns | 5 | 7 |
| 3 | 4 | 6 | 7 | 3 | 2 | Other | 19 | 19 |
| | 7 (4/1-9/30/11) | | 52 (10/1/11-3/31/12) | | | | 4/1/07- 3/31/08 | 4/1/08- 3/31/09 |
| 0-500M | 500M-2MM | 2-10MM | 10-50MM | 50-100MM | 100-250MM | | ALL | ALL |
| 7 | 9 | 15 | 13 | 5 | 10 | NUMBER OF STATEMENTS | 64 | 60 |
| % | % | % | % | % | % | ASSETS | % | % |
| | | 10.0 | 16.7 | | 8.7 | Cash & Equivalents | 14.0 | 11.7 |
| | | 16.1 | 25.2 | | 9.5 | Trade Receivables (net) | 13.5 | 17.9 |
| | | 6.9 | .5 | | .0 | Inventory | 2.7 | 2.7 |
| | | .9 | 4.3 | | 3.5 | All Other Current | 4.0 | 2.3 |
| | | 34.0 | 46.7 | | 21.7 | Total Current | 34.1 | 34.6 |
| | | 38.5 | 30.1 | | 29.2 | Fixed Assets (net) | 41.5 | 36.1 |
| | | 16.6 | 15.8 | | 34.1 | Intangibles (net) | 19.3 | 23.2 |
| | | 11.0 | 7.4 | | 15.0 | All Other Non-Current | 5.1 | 6.0 |
| | | 100.0 | 100.0 | | 100.0 | Total | 100.0 | 100.0 |
| | | | | | | LIABILITIES | | |
| | | 3.3 | 3.4 | | .0 | Notes Payable-Short Term | 4.6 | 4.4 |
| | | 2.3 | 3.5 | | 2.6 | Cur. Mat.-L.T.D. | 5.2 | 4.4 |
| | | 9.3 | 9.0 | | 4.4 | Trade Payables | 11.6 | 10.0 |
| | | .0 | .1 | | 1.5 | Income Taxes Payable | .3 | .1 |
| | | 11.6 | 9.6 | | 6.5 | All Other Current | 10.7 | 11.6 |
| | | 26.5 | 25.7 | | 15.0 | Total Current | 32.4 | 30.5 |
| | | 39.9 | 20.5 | | 62.9 | Long-Term Debt | 38.8 | 29.7 |
| | | .7 | 1.1 | | 3.3 | Deferred Taxes | .9 | .6 |
| | | 4.2 | 7.0 | | 54.6 | All Other Non-Current | 7.2 | 3.8 |
| | | 28.7 | 45.8 | | -35.8 | Net Worth | 20.6 | 35.4 |
| | | 100.0 | 100.0 | | 100.0 | Total Liabilities & Net Worth | 100.0 | 100.0 |
| | | | | | | INCOME DATA | | |
| | | 100.0 | 100.0 | | 100.0 | Net Sales | 100.0 | 100.0 |
| | | | | | | Gross Profit | | |
| | | 89.3 | 95.8 | | 81.2 | Operating Expenses | 92.9 | 90.9 |
| | | 10.7 | 4.2 | | 18.8 | Operating Profit | 7.1 | 9.1 |
| | | 5.5 | 1.9 | | 8.3 | All Other Expenses (net) | 4.7 | 5.8 |
| | | 5.2 | 2.3 | | 10.5 | Profit Before Taxes | 2.4 | 3.3 |
| | | | | | | RATIOS | | |
| | | 2.7 | 2.1 | | 2.2 | | 1.8 | 1.8 |
| | | 1.4 | 1.8 | | .9 | Current | .9 | 1.0 |
| | | .7 | .9 | | .6 | | .5 | .6 |
| | | 2.7 | 2.1 | | 1.9 | | 1.4 | 1.7 |
| | | .7 | 1.1 | | .7 | Quick | .7 | .8 |
| | | .6 | .4 | | .6 | | .4 | .4 |
| | | 4   89.1 | 7   49.2 | 16   22.9 | | | 6   58.6 | 9   40.7 |
| | | 19   19.2 | 32   11.4 | 30   12.3 | | Sales/Receivables | 20   18.3 | 27   13.7 |
| | | 41   8.8 | 73   5.0 | 66   5.5 | | | 46   7.9 | 47   7.7 |
| | | | | | | Cost of Sales/Inventory | | |
| | | | | | | Cost of Sales/Payables | | |
| | | 10.9 | 4.8 | | 6.2 | | 12.2 | 12.2 |
| | | 24.8 | 10.9 | | -37.7 | Sales/Working Capital | -51.2 | -203.1 |
| | | -14.0 | NM | | -13.5 | | -9.8 | -11.9 |
| | | 20.7 | 265.2 | | | | 6.6 | 7.5 |
| | | (11)   4.9 | (10)   9.2 | | | EBIT/Interest | (55)   2.5 | (47)   2.3 |
| | | 2.2 | 2.9 | | | | .9 | .2 |
| | | | | | | | | 30.9 |
| | | | | | | Net Profit + Depr., Dep., Amort./Cur. Mat. L/T/D | (10)   8.3 | |
| | | | | | | | | 2.1 |
| | | .5 | .0 | | 8.5 | | .6 | .4 |
| | | 1.4 | 1.0 | | -1.2 | Fixed/Worth | 2.7 | 2.8 |
| | | -1.6 | NM | | -.5 | | -2.4 | -1.6 |
| | | .7 | .5 | | 32.4 | | 1.0 | 1.0 |
| | | 2.7 | 1.1 | | -2.9 | Debt/Worth | 3.6 | 6.1 |
| | | -3.5 | NM | | -1.6 | | -5.1 | -3.7 |
| | | 97.4 | 65.1 | | | | 35.8 | 60.1 |
| | | (11)   31.5 | (10)   24.8 | | | % Profit Before Taxes/Tangible Net Worth | (40)   23.1 | (35)   20.6 |
| | | 5.1 | -15.6 | | | | 7.8 | 6.6 |
| | | 24.3 | 28.7 | | 11.3 | | 13.5 | 15.1 |
| | | 10.5 | 5.1 | | 5.9 | % Profit Before Taxes/Total Assets | 4.1 | 3.8 |
| | | 1.4 | -1.1 | | -.1 | | -2.0 | -2.2 |
| | | 40.7 | 103.9 | | 5.4 | | 16.0 | 23.4 |
| | | 3.4 | 4.5 | | 2.0 | Sales/Net Fixed Assets | 2.5 | 3.0 |
| | | 1.5 | 1.3 | | 1.6 | | 1.2 | 1.4 |
| | | 4.9 | 2.4 | | 1.1 | | 3.3 | 2.4 |
| | | 1.8 | 1.0 | | .7 | Sales/Total Assets | 1.1 | 1.2 |
| | | .9 | .5 | | .4 | | .6 | .4 |
| | | 1.2 | | | | | 2.0 | 1.7 |
| | | (12)   8.8 | | | | % Depr., Dep., Amort./Sales | (48)   7.0 | (46)   6.7 |
| | | 19.3 | | | | | 16.1 | 15.0 |
| | | | | | | | 1.8 | 1.5 |
| | | | | | | % Officers', Directors' Owners' Comp/Sales | (15)   2.8 | (16)   2.5 |
| | | | | | | | 9.3 | 7.4 |
| 20056M | 26977M | 152304M | 440431M | 337991M | 1334161M | Net Sales ($) | 2212336M | 1811565M |
| 1361M | 10567M | 74646M | 312965M | 311224M | 1774304M | Total Assets ($) | 2471393M | 2339127M |

M = $ thousand    MM = $ million
See Pages 9 through 22 for Explanation of Ratios and Data

## Comparative Historical Data

## Current Data Sorted by Sales

| 4/1/09-3/31/10 ALL | 4/1/10-3/31/11 ALL | 4/1/11-3/31/12 ALL | | 7 (4/1-9/30/11) | | | 52 (10/1/11-3/31/12) | | |
|---|---|---|---|---|---|---|---|---|---|
| | | | | 0-1MM | 1-3MM | 3-5MM | 5-10MM | 10-25MM | 25MM & OVER |
| | | | **Type of Statement** | | | | | | |
| 25 | 23 | 18 | Unqualified | 1 | 1 | 2 | 1 | 2 | 11 |
| 6 | 5 | 3 | Reviewed | | 1 | | | | 2 |
| 5 | 7 | 5 | Compiled | 1 | 1 | | | 2 | 1 |
| 10 | 3 | 8 | Tax Returns | 2 | | | 2 | 2 | |
| 21 | 25 | 25 | Other | 3 | 2 | 2 | 5 | 6 | 8 |
| 67 | 63 | 59 | **NUMBER OF STATEMENTS** | 7 | 5 | 5 | 8 | 12 | 22 |
| % | % | % | **ASSETS** | % | % | % | % | % | % |
| 15.3 | 14.0 | 13.0 | Cash & Equivalents | | | | | 11.3 | 14.6 |
| 16.2 | 18.6 | 16.6 | Trade Receivables (net) | | | | | 20.8 | 18.1 |
| 2.6 | 2.6 | 3.5 | Inventory | | | | | 7.4 | 1.6 |
| 3.7 | 2.8 | 2.3 | All Other Current | | | | | 2.8 | 4.2 |
| 37.8 | 38.0 | 35.4 | Total Current | | | | | 42.3 | 38.5 |
| 35.6 | 39.3 | 34.2 | Fixed Assets (net) | | | | | 31.8 | 27.4 |
| 18.2 | 15.4 | 19.9 | Intangibles (net) | | | | | 17.7 | 22.9 |
| 8.4 | 7.3 | 10.5 | All Other Non-Current | | | | | 8.2 | 11.2 |
| 100.0 | 100.0 | 100.0 | Total | | | | | 100.0 | 100.0 |
| | | | **LIABILITIES** | | | | | | |
| 5.8 | 5.4 | 7.9 | Notes Payable-Short Term | | | | | 3.7 | 3.7 |
| 6.5 | 4.7 | 3.4 | Cur. Mat.-L.T.D. | | | | | 2.0 | 3.7 |
| 9.1 | 12.5 | 12.0 | Trade Payables | | | | | 14.3 | 6.7 |
| .3 | .1 | .3 | Income Taxes Payable | | | | | .0 | .8 |
| 15.3 | 15.4 | 21.2 | All Other Current | | | | | 10.0 | 10.8 |
| 36.9 | 38.1 | 44.8 | Total Current | | | | | 29.9 | 25.7 |
| 35.2 | 32.4 | 35.8 | Long-Term Debt | | | | | 17.5 | 36.8 |
| .9 | 1.1 | 1.1 | Deferred Taxes | | | | | .4 | 2.1 |
| 8.5 | 9.3 | 12.6 | All Other Non-Current | | | | | 8.5 | 27.7 |
| 18.5 | 19.1 | 5.7 | Net Worth | | | | | 43.7 | 7.7 |
| 100.0 | 100.0 | 100.0 | Total Liabilities & Net Worth | | | | | 100.0 | 100.0 |
| | | | **INCOME DATA** | | | | | | |
| 100.0 | 100.0 | 100.0 | Net Sales | | | | | 100.0 | 100.0 |
| | | | Gross Profit | | | | | | |
| 91.7 | 91.5 | 89.1 | Operating Expenses | | | | | 95.2 | 88.1 |
| 8.3 | 8.5 | 10.9 | Operating Profit | | | | | 4.8 | 11.9 |
| 4.1 | 4.2 | 3.9 | All Other Expenses (net) | | | | | 2.2 | 3.7 |
| 4.2 | 4.3 | 7.0 | Profit Before Taxes | | | | | 2.6 | 8.2 |
| | | | **RATIOS** | | | | | | |
| 1.4 | 2.1 | 2.0 | | | | | | 2.0 | 2.3 |
| .8 | 1.1 | 1.1 | Current | | | | | 1.7 | 1.4 |
| .4 | .5 | .6 | | | | | | .8 | .7 |
| 1.3 | 2.0 | 2.0 | | | | | | 1.8 | 2.2 |
| .6 | .8 | .8 | Quick | | | | | .9 | 1.1 |
| .3 | .4 | .4 | | | | | | .4 | .6 |
| 8 46.9 | 10 36.6 | 6 57.8 | | | | | | 6 65.2 | 23 16.1 |
| 21 17.4 | 26 13.8 | 29 12.6 | Sales/Receivables | | | | | 19 18.9 | 35 10.5 |
| 38 9.5 | 48 7.6 | 59 6.2 | | | | | | 59 6.2 | 63 5.8 |
| | | | Cost of Sales/Inventory | | | | | | |
| | | | Cost of Sales/Payables | | | | | | |
| 14.5 | 6.6 | 7.0 | | | | | | 6.0 | 6.8 |
| -24.7 | 127.5 | 55.4 | Sales/Working Capital | | | | | 21.2 | 13.6 |
| -7.8 | -7.5 | -11.8 | | | | | | NM | -14.9 |
| 11.5 | 11.5 | 21.5 | | | | | | 34.2 | 7.9 |
| (60) 3.4 | (50) 3.1 | (42) 4.5 | EBIT/Interest | | | | | (10) 6.6 | (18) 4.2 |
| .9 | 1.1 | 1.6 | | | | | | 3.0 | 1.5 |
| | | | Net Profit + Depr., Dep., Amort./Cur. Mat. L/T/D | | | | | | |
| .3 | .4 | .5 | | | | | | .2 | .5 |
| 2.3 | 1.9 | 2.6 | Fixed/Worth | | | | | 1.1 | 40.5 |
| -1.3 | -3.6 | -1.0 | | | | | | 3.3 | -1.0 |
| 1.2 | 1.0 | .7 | | | | | | .7 | .9 |
| 4.9 | 3.1 | 4.8 | Debt/Worth | | | | | 2.2 | 212.3 |
| -5.6 | -6.0 | -2.9 | | | | | | 6.2 | -2.9 |
| 51.5 | 79.4 | 79.3 | | | | | | 71.5 | 73.0 |
| (39) 21.5 | (44) 30.8 | (38) 26.9 | % Profit Before Taxes/Tangible Net Worth | | | | | (10) 28.9 | (12) 33.6 |
| 7.6 | 9.4 | 4.2 | | | | | | 4.9 | -13.4 |
| 16.0 | 16.0 | 21.4 | | | | | | 29.1 | 22.7 |
| 5.4 | 6.6 | 5.7 | % Profit Before Taxes/Total Assets | | | | | 8.6 | 6.8 |
| .5 | 1.2 | -.1 | | | | | | 1.7 | -.1 |
| 36.2 | 20.6 | 27.8 | | | | | | 108.5 | 10.7 |
| 3.4 | 3.5 | 3.7 | Sales/Net Fixed Assets | | | | | 16.7 | 4.8 |
| 1.3 | 1.3 | 1.5 | | | | | | 1.3 | 1.9 |
| 2.8 | 2.7 | 2.4 | | | | | | 4.3 | 1.8 |
| 1.3 | 1.0 | 1.3 | Sales/Total Assets | | | | | 2.1 | 1.1 |
| .6 | .6 | .5 | | | | | | .6 | .6 |
| 1.4 | 1.5 | 2.1 | | | | | | | 1.8 |
| (52) 8.3 | (40) 6.9 | (37) 8.5 | % Depr., Dep., Amort./Sales | | | | | | (12) 4.0 |
| 17.7 | 17.6 | 20.1 | | | | | | | 9.4 |
| .6 | | | | | | | | | |
| (12) 3.1 | | | % Officers', Directors' Owners' Comp/Sales | | | | | | |
| 9.3 | | | | | | | | | |
| 2494963M | 2596689M | 2311920M | Net Sales ($) | 2032M | 8951M | 18986M | 57698M | 194133M | 2030120M |
| 2648726M | 2874178M | 2485067M | Total Assets ($) | 3616M | 15237M | 26779M | 24685M | 180089M | 2234661M |

M = $ thousand    MM = $ million
See Pages 9 through 22 for Explanation of Ratios and Data

## Current Data Sorted by Assets      Comparative Historical Data

| Type of Statement | 0-500M | 500M-2MM | 2-10MM | 10-50MM | 50-100MM | 100-250MM | 4/1/07-3/31/08 ALL | 4/1/08-3/31/09 ALL |
|---|---|---|---|---|---|---|---|---|
| Unqualified | 1 | 1 | 26 | 63 | 33 | 30 | 139 | 109 |
| Reviewed | | 4 | 11 | 2 | | | 18 | 35 |
| Compiled | 2 | 5 | 7 | 3 | | 1 | 11 | 19 |
| Tax Returns | 9 | 9 | 7 | | | | 31 | 35 |
| Other | 8 | 16 | 40 | 32 | 13 | 14 | 121 | 142 |
| | | 29 (4/1-9/30/11) | | | 308 (10/1/11-3/31/12) | | | |
| NUMBER OF STATEMENTS | 20 | 35 | 91 | 100 | 46 | 45 | 320 | 340 |
| | % | % | % | % | % | % | % | % |
| **ASSETS** | | | | | | | | |
| Cash & Equivalents | 26.9 | 19.2 | 12.6 | 11.1 | 8.7 | 8.4 | 14.5 | 12.6 |
| Trade Receivables (net) | 16.4 | 22.0 | 22.0 | 11.7 | 8.6 | 11.1 | 17.5 | 20.9 |
| Inventory | .2 | 9.8 | 4.0 | 3.5 | 1.5 | 2.0 | 4.0 | 3.9 |
| All Other Current | 5.3 | 6.4 | 5.5 | 2.4 | 2.7 | 3.6 | 3.0 | 3.7 |
| Total Current | 48.8 | 57.4 | 44.1 | 28.7 | 21.5 | 25.1 | 39.1 | 41.1 |
| Fixed Assets (net) | 24.6 | 28.8 | 37.9 | 50.7 | 54.7 | 43.3 | 39.7 | 38.1 |
| Intangibles (net) | 8.3 | 4.6 | 8.5 | 10.1 | 14.2 | 25.7 | 11.3 | 10.4 |
| All Other Non-Current | 18.3 | 9.3 | 9.5 | 10.4 | 9.5 | 5.9 | 9.9 | 10.3 |
| Total | 100.0 | 100.0 | 100.0 | 100.0 | 100.0 | 100.0 | 100.0 | 100.0 |
| **LIABILITIES** | | | | | | | | |
| Notes Payable-Short Term | 14.6 | 14.9 | 5.2 | 3.8 | 2.3 | 1.8 | 7.8 | 7.6 |
| Cur. Mat.-L.T.D. | 6.1 | 5.1 | 4.9 | 4.1 | 2.9 | 3.0 | 4.5 | 4.5 |
| Trade Payables | 6.2 | 18.2 | 16.1 | 7.4 | 6.3 | 4.9 | 11.6 | 12.0 |
| Income Taxes Payable | .0 | .0 | .2 | .8 | .3 | .2 | .3 | .3 |
| All Other Current | 26.2 | 22.2 | 13.4 | 10.0 | 6.5 | 9.3 | 13.1 | 13.3 |
| Total Current | 53.1 | 60.4 | 39.8 | 26.2 | 18.5 | 19.2 | 37.4 | 37.6 |
| Long-Term Debt | 46.0 | 26.5 | 19.4 | 26.1 | 26.0 | 29.8 | 25.2 | 26.1 |
| Deferred Taxes | .0 | .0 | 1.1 | 1.6 | 1.6 | 1.2 | .8 | .8 |
| All Other Non-Current | 3.3 | 17.9 | 6.7 | 7.7 | 8.1 | 7.0 | 9.3 | 8.3 |
| Net Worth | -2.4 | -4.9 | 33.0 | 38.5 | 45.8 | 42.8 | 27.3 | 27.1 |
| Total Liabilities & Net Worth | 100.0 | 100.0 | 100.0 | 100.0 | 100.0 | 100.0 | 100.0 | 100.0 |
| **INCOME DATA** | | | | | | | | |
| Net Sales | 100.0 | 100.0 | 100.0 | 100.0 | 100.0 | 100.0 | 100.0 | 100.0 |
| Gross Profit | | | | | | | | |
| Operating Expenses | 93.4 | 88.3 | 95.5 | 90.6 | 90.2 | 85.6 | 91.7 | 92.0 |
| Operating Profit | 6.6 | 11.7 | 4.5 | 9.4 | 9.8 | 14.4 | 8.3 | 8.0 |
| All Other Expenses (net) | 1.8 | 4.8 | .7 | 2.7 | 3.3 | 4.6 | 2.2 | 2.7 |
| Profit Before Taxes | 4.8 | 6.9 | 3.8 | 6.8 | 6.5 | 9.8 | 6.1 | 5.3 |
| **RATIOS** | | | | | | | | |
| Current | 5.1 | 2.1 | 2.2 | 2.1 | 1.6 | 1.7 | 2.1 | 2.1 |
| | 1.2 | 1.0 | 1.2 | 1.3 | 1.1 | 1.2 | 1.2 | 1.2 |
| | .4 | .6 | .6 | .7 | .8 | .8 | .8 | .8 |
| Quick | 5.1 | 1.9 | 1.7 | 1.7 | 1.1 | 1.5 | 1.6 | 1.6 |
| | .8 | (34) .8 | .9 | .9 | .8 | 1.0 | 1.0 | 1.0 |
| | .2 | .3 | .5 | .5 | .6 | .6 | .6 | .6 |
| Sales/Receivables | 0 UND | 0 UND | 17 21.4 | 18 19.8 | 24 14.9 | 25 14.8 | 17 20.9 | 19 19.4 |
| | 0 UND | 18 19.8 | 34 10.7 | 31 11.9 | 35 10.3 | 42 8.6 | 34 10.9 | 35 10.5 |
| | 16 23.3 | 36 10.2 | 57 6.4 | 42 8.7 | 43 8.4 | 68 5.4 | 57 6.4 | 52 7.0 |
| Cost of Sales/Inventory | | | | | | | | |
| Cost of Sales/Payables | | | | | | | | |
| Sales/Working Capital | 17.5 | 9.7 | 6.1 | 4.2 | 9.6 | 7.8 | 5.8 | 6.1 |
| | NM | 316.9 | 24.9 | 25.7 | 63.2 | 16.2 | 21.3 | 23.6 |
| | -16.7 | -12.1 | -11.9 | -11.6 | -17.1 | -21.8 | -20.1 | -21.3 |
| EBIT/Interest | 21.2 | 30.2 | 34.7 | 9.3 | 7.9 | 10.0 | 10.0 | 9.9 |
| | (13) 3.6 | (28) 8.5 | (82) 6.8 | (96) 3.2 | (43) 3.8 | (40) 4.1 | (266) 3.2 | (287) 3.3 |
| | -.8 | 1.9 | 1.5 | .7 | 1.1 | 1.2 | 1.0 | .9 |
| Net Profit + Depr., Dep., Amort./Cur. Mat. L/T/D | | | 10.3 | 7.8 | 5.2 | | 10.8 | 8.7 |
| | | (26) 3.3 | (52) 2.8 | (23) 2.5 | | | (111) 3.2 | (106) 3.4 |
| | | 1.9 | 1.6 | 1.9 | | | 1.8 | 1.9 |
| Fixed/Worth | .0 | .4 | .5 | .8 | 1.1 | 1.1 | .6 | .5 |
| | .2 | 1.1 | 1.0 | 1.4 | 1.7 | 3.1 | 1.6 | 1.5 |
| | 5.7 | -3.7 | 18.0 | 4.3 | 3.5 | -1.7 | -6.9 | NM |
| Debt/Worth | .4 | .7 | .6 | .7 | .7 | .9 | .8 | .7 |
| | 1.2 | 2.7 | 1.5 | 1.6 | 1.5 | 3.2 | 2.4 | 2.6 |
| | NM | -4.7 | 136.7 | 4.8 | 3.9 | -4.1 | -13.9 | -48.4 |
| % Profit Before Taxes/Tangible Net Worth | 165.3 | 157.3 | 55.5 | 31.9 | 23.7 | 53.8 | 55.2 | 53.7 |
| | (15) 32.2 | (25) 46.8 | (69) 17.0 | (81) 10.2 | (39) 14.0 | (29) 19.0 | (233) 14.7 | (253) 16.8 |
| | 6.8 | 10.6 | 3.1 | 1.6 | 2.1 | 6.7 | 4.1 | 1.8 |
| % Profit Before Taxes/Total Assets | 73.3 | 24.2 | 17.4 | 10.2 | 9.9 | 10.7 | 13.9 | 14.7 |
| | 11.0 | 10.9 | 8.3 | 4.6 | 4.8 | 5.3 | 5.2 | 5.4 |
| | -17.8 | 1.7 | .7 | -.4 | 1.0 | .1 | -.2 | -.8 |
| Sales/Net Fixed Assets | UND | 57.7 | 26.7 | 4.6 | 2.8 | 10.3 | 17.6 | 22.9 |
| | 61.9 | 18.8 | 7.8 | 1.1 | .9 | 1.1 | 3.6 | 5.0 |
| | 15.0 | 5.8 | 1.1 | .6 | .6 | .6 | .8 | .9 |
| Sales/Total Assets | 8.7 | 5.5 | 3.0 | 1.2 | .9 | .9 | 2.8 | 3.0 |
| | 6.1 | 4.3 | 2.0 | .6 | .6 | .6 | 1.1 | 1.5 |
| | 2.7 | 1.9 | .7 | .4 | .4 | .4 | .5 | .5 |
| % Depr., Dep., Amort./Sales | | 1.2 | 1.2 | 7.7 | 10.3 | 3.2 | 2.3 | 2.1 |
| | | (21) 1.5 | (76) 7.4 | (95) 16.5 | (37) 19.1 | (17) 9.4 | (250) 9.8 | (261) 7.0 |
| | | 5.1 | 16.3 | 23.0 | 24.4 | 27.0 | 19.4 | 18.5 |
| % Officers', Directors', Owners' Comp/Sales | | 4.1 | 2.1 | | | | 3.0 | 1.9 |
| | | (13) 7.7 | (24) 3.8 | | | | (43) 5.6 | (49) 4.5 |
| | | 11.1 | 7.2 | | | | 10.5 | 8.0 |
| Net Sales ($) | 24946M | 153333M | 1118940M | 2234842M | 2527785M | 6300510M | 11556539M | 11859267M |
| Total Assets ($) | 4901M | 38430M | 492240M | 2407974M | 3446607M | 7466230M | 12523005M | 11964160M |

© RMA 2012

M = $ thousand    MM = $ million
See Pages 9 through 22 for Explanation of Ratios and Data

## Comparative Historical Data

## Current Data Sorted by Sales

| Hist 1 | Hist 2 | Hist 3 | Type of Statement | 0-1MM | 1-3MM | 3-5MM | 5-10MM | 10-25MM | 25MM & OVER |
|---|---|---|---|---|---|---|---|---|---|
| 169 | 143 | 154 | Unqualified | 2 | 9 | 15 | 25 | 30 | 73 |
| 39 | 14 | 17 | Reviewed | | 3 | 2 | 5 | 6 | 1 |
| 16 | 18 | 18 | Compiled | 4 | 2 | 2 | 4 | 5 | 1 |
| 36 | 23 | 25 | Tax Returns | 3 | 9 | 4 | 4 | 5 | |
| 133 | 139 | 123 | Other | 8 | 10 | 10 | 20 | 23 | 52 |
| 4/1/09-3/31/10 ALL | 4/1/10-3/31/11 ALL | 4/1/11-3/31/12 ALL | | 29 (4/1-9/30/11) | | 308 (10/1/11-3/31/12) | | | |
| 393 | 337 | 337 | NUMBER OF STATEMENTS | 17 | 33 | 33 | 58 | 69 | 127 |
| % | % | % | ASSETS | % | % | % | % | % | % |
| 14.0 | 12.7 | 12.6 | Cash & Equivalents | 9.1 | 20.4 | 13.3 | 10.9 | 11.6 | 12.2 |
| 17.0 | 16.8 | 15.3 | Trade Receivables (net) | 13.3 | 10.7 | 19.2 | 14.4 | 16.2 | 15.8 |
| 3.8 | 3.2 | 3.6 | Inventory | .1 | 5.3 | 4.7 | 3.7 | 3.2 | 3.5 |
| 4.1 | 3.8 | 4.0 | All Other Current | 7.8 | 4.2 | 1.0 | 4.5 | 5.7 | 3.1 |
| 39.0 | 36.6 | 35.6 | Total Current | 30.2 | 40.6 | 38.2 | 33.5 | 36.6 | 34.6 |
| 41.1 | 43.6 | 43.0 | Fixed Assets (net) | 41.4 | 36.8 | 47.1 | 46.6 | 42.1 | 42.6 |
| 10.4 | 9.8 | 11.7 | Intangibles (net) | 13.7 | 9.0 | 2.6 | 8.9 | 13.9 | 14.5 |
| 9.5 | 10.1 | 9.8 | All Other Non-Current | 14.7 | 13.6 | 12.0 | 11.0 | 7.4 | 8.3 |
| 100.0 | 100.0 | 100.0 | Total | 100.0 | 100.0 | 100.0 | 100.0 | 100.0 | 100.0 |
| | | | LIABILITIES | | | | | | |
| 5.2 | 5.7 | 5.5 | Notes Payable-Short Term | 5.7 | 9.3 | 5.8 | 8.7 | 5.3 | 3.1 |
| 4.6 | 3.8 | 4.2 | Cur. Mat.-L.T.D. | 5.7 | 4.5 | 3.2 | 5.2 | 5.2 | 3.3 |
| 10.4 | 10.9 | 10.3 | Trade Payables | 5.5 | 6.1 | 10.5 | 9.5 | 13.1 | 10.9 |
| .3 | .4 | .4 | Income Taxes Payable | .0 | .1 | .4 | .2 | .1 | .7 |
| 11.5 | 11.4 | 12.6 | All Other Current | 27.8 | 18.5 | 9.2 | 15.5 | 9.2 | 10.4 |
| 32.0 | 32.2 | 33.0 | Total Current | 44.8 | 38.5 | 29.2 | 39.1 | 32.9 | 28.4 |
| 22.9 | 25.1 | 26.0 | Long-Term Debt | 31.5 | 36.3 | 16.9 | 34.4 | 18.8 | 25.0 |
| 1.2 | 1.1 | 1.1 | Deferred Taxes | .0 | .3 | 1.0 | 1.2 | 1.4 | 1.4 |
| 7.6 | 8.4 | 8.2 | All Other Non-Current | 8.4 | 7.4 | 6.4 | 11.3 | 7.2 | 7.9 |
| 36.3 | 33.2 | 31.7 | Net Worth | 15.4 | 17.5 | 46.4 | 13.9 | 39.7 | 37.4 |
| 100.0 | 100.0 | 100.0 | Total Liabilities & Net Worth | 100.0 | 100.0 | 100.0 | 100.0 | 100.0 | 100.0 |
| | | | INCOME DATA | | | | | | |
| 100.0 | 100.0 | 100.0 | Net Sales | 100.0 | 100.0 | 100.0 | 100.0 | 100.0 | 100.0 |
| | | | Gross Profit | | | | | | |
| 91.6 | 91.3 | 91.1 | Operating Expenses | 82.2 | 93.9 | 90.2 | 93.4 | 92.8 | 89.9 |
| 8.4 | 8.7 | 8.9 | Operating Profit | 17.8 | 6.1 | 9.8 | 6.6 | 7.2 | 10.1 |
| 1.8 | 2.2 | 2.7 | All Other Expenses (net) | 9.9 | .7 | 1.5 | 2.6 | 2.6 | 2.5 |
| 6.6 | 6.5 | 6.2 | Profit Before Taxes | 7.9 | 5.3 | 8.3 | 3.9 | 4.6 | 7.6 |
| | | | RATIOS | | | | | | |
| 2.1 | 2.1 | 2.0 | | .9 | 3.7 | 4.1 | 2.2 | 2.0 | 1.8 |
| 1.3 | 1.2 | 1.1 | Current | .5 | 1.4 | 1.4 | 1.2 | 1.1 | 1.2 |
| .8 | .7 | .7 | | .2 | .6 | .6 | .6 | .7 | .8 |
| 1.8 | 1.7 | 1.7 | | .7 | 2.6 | 3.3 | 1.7 | 1.7 | 1.5 |
| .9 | .9 (336) | .9 | Quick | .3 | .7 | 1.1 (57) | .9 | .8 | .9 |
| .6 | .5 | .5 | | .1 | .4 | .5 | .4 | .4 | .6 |
| 17   21.9 | 19   19.7 | 16   23.5 | | 0 UND | 1   584.9 | 21   17.4 | 15   24.4 | 15   24.1 | 22   16.6 |
| 32   11.3 | 31   11.7 | 31   11.8 | Sales/Receivables | 4   94.0 | 19   19.3 | 34   10.7 | 32   11.4 | 27   13.4 | 34   10.6 |
| 49   7.4 | 48   7.6 | 49   7.5 | | 46   7.9 | 45   8.1 | 50   7.3 | 52   7.0 | 47   7.7 | 52   7.0 |
| | | | Cost of Sales/Inventory | | | | | | |
| | | | Cost of Sales/Payables | | | | | | |
| 6.2 | 6.3 | 7.0 | | -176.6 | 7.5 | 4.3 | 5.2 | 7.1 | 8.8 |
| 21.0 | 24.4 | 36.9 | Sales/Working Capital | -8.5 | 34.0 | 12.0 | 30.3 | 50.5 | 26.4 |
| -23.4 | -17.4 | -14.1 | | -5.0 | -15.6 | -11.9 | -10.3 | -16.9 | -21.5 |
| 12.1 | 14.3 | 14.2 | | | 14.3 | 17.5 | 8.1 | 20.5 | 17.7 |
| (349)   4.1 | (306)   4.6 | (302)   4.3 | EBIT/Interest | (27)   3.8 | (31)   8.1 | (57)   2.8 | (63)   4.6 | (116)   4.9 | |
| 1.5 | 1.1 | 1.2 | | | .1 | 1.6 | .7 | 1.4 | 1.1 |
| 6.6 | 6.3 | 7.6 | | | 12.6 | 5.6 | 5.8 | 9.2 | |
| (131)   3.4 | (112)   3.4 | (110)   3.0 | Net Profit + Depr., Dep., Amort./Cur. Mat. L/T/D | (15)   3.4 | (20)   2.7 | (27)   2.8 | (40)   4.2 | | |
| 1.9 | 2.0 | 1.7 | | | 1.7 | 1.7 | 1.7 | 1.5 | |
| .6 | .7 | .7 | | .1 | .2 | .5 | .7 | .8 | .7 |
| 1.3 | 1.4 | 1.4 | Fixed/Worth | 1.7 | .9 | 1.0 | 1.4 | 1.4 | 1.6 |
| 5.8 | 5.7 | 15.5 | | NM | 5.1 | 2.2 | -5.3 | -6.5 | 22.9 |
| .7 | .7 | .7 | | .7 | .4 | .5 | .8 | .6 | .9 |
| 1.8 | 1.9 | 1.8 | Debt/Worth | 5.4 | 1.5 | .8 | 1.5 | 2.0 | 1.9 |
| 10.9 | 14.1 | 48.2 | | -8.2 | NM | 3.9 | -14.2 | -100.0 | 48.0 |
| 44.5 | 49.3 | 44.3 | | 97.1 | 43.0 | 59.0 | 25.1 | 50.3 | 38.4 |
| (310)   15.4 | (268)   13.2 | (258)   14.7 | % Profit Before Taxes/Tangible Net Worth | (12)   5.1 | (25)   12.8 | (30)   20.6 | (43)   9.7 | (51)   15.4 | (97)   20.9 |
| 4.0 | 1.6 | 3.0 | | -8.5 | 1.6 | 4.4 | 1.5 | 4.5 | 5.7 |
| 15.0 | 14.1 | 13.1 | | 12.4 | 20.0 | 17.8 | 10.6 | 14.1 | 12.4 |
| 5.7 | 5.9 | 5.5 | % Profit Before Taxes/Total Assets | 2.2 | 5.5 | 6.5 | 2.8 | 5.2 | 6.7 |
| 1.2 | .5 | .5 | | -.9 | -.3 | 1.9 | -.8 | .7 | .4 |
| 18.1 | 18.3 | 18.1 | | UND | 47.2 | 21.4 | 11.7 | 21.3 | 16.5 |
| 3.2 | 2.5 | 2.0 | Sales/Net Fixed Assets | 1.0 | 10.9 | 1.5 | 1.4 | 1.7 | 2.1 |
| .8 | .8 | .7 | | .3 | .9 | .6 | .6 | .7 | .9 |
| 2.6 | 2.6 | 2.4 | | 2.9 | 6.1 | 2.3 | 2.5 | 2.9 | 2.1 |
| 1.1 | 1.0 | .9 | Sales/Total Assets | .3 | 2.1 | .7 | .8 | 1.1 | .8 |
| .5 | .5 | .5 | | .2 | .6 | .4 | .4 | .5 | .5 |
| 2.3 | 2.7 | 3.1 | | | 1.1 | 9.5 | 3.4 | 3.3 | 2.6 |
| (311)   9.3 | (262)   10.7 | (252)   12.2 | % Depr., Dep., Amort./Sales | (24)   10.2 | (25)   15.4 | (52)   15.1 | (60)   13.0 | (83)   9.1 | |
| 20.3 | 20.8 | 20.8 | | | 20.1 | 20.5 | 24.6 | 21.9 | 18.3 |
| 2.3 | 2.3 | 3.1 | | | 3.9 | | | 2.3 | |
| (64)   6.1 | (48)   5.0 | (50)   5.0 | % Officers', Directors' Owners' Comp/Sales | (12)   7.5 | | | | (12)   4.5 | |
| 11.3 | 8.5 | 9.8 | | | 18.0 | | | 9.5 | |
| 14737964M | 13141903M | 12360356M | Net Sales ($) | 7899M | 65846M | 129804M | 424836M | 1077164M | 10654807M |
| 14971540M | 13392894M | 13856382M | Total Assets ($) | 18893M | 77193M | 197832M | 716393M | 1664436M | 11181635M |

M = $ thousand       MM = $ million
See Pages 9 through 22 for Explanation of Ratios and Data

## Current Data Sorted by Assets | Comparative Historical Data

**Type of Statement**

| Type of Statement | 0-500M | 500M-2MM | 2-10MM | 10-50MM | 50-100MM | 100-250MM | 4/1/07-3/31/08 ALL | 4/1/08-3/31/09 ALL |
|---|---|---|---|---|---|---|---|---|
| Unqualified | 1 | 1 | 4 | 12 | 4 | 8 | 26 | 32 |
| Reviewed | | 2 | 1 | 4 | 1 | | 15 | 11 |
| Compiled | 3 | 4 | 2 | 1 | | | 10 | 13 |
| Tax Returns | 4 | 9 | 7 | | | | 15 | 15 |
| Other | 1 | 5 | 17 | 14 | 3 | 3 | 31 | 40 |
| | | 16 (4/1-9/30/11) | | 95 (10/1/11-3/31/12) | | | 31 | 40 |
| NUMBER OF STATEMENTS | 9 | 21 | 31 | 31 | 8 | 11 | 97 | 111 |

| | 0-500M | 500M-2MM | 2-10MM | 10-50MM | 50-100MM | 100-250MM | 4/1/07-3/31/08 ALL | 4/1/08-3/31/09 ALL |
|---|---|---|---|---|---|---|---|---|
| | % | % | % | % | % | % | % | % |
| **ASSETS** | | | | | | | | |
| Cash & Equivalents | | 13.0 | 14.1 | 18.6 | | 8.8 | 11.7 | 12.0 |
| Trade Receivables (net) | | 30.6 | 26.5 | 18.7 | | 14.9 | 21.3 | 19.4 |
| Inventory | | 10.1 | 13.1 | 9.1 | | 6.7 | 10.6 | 10.4 |
| All Other Current | | 5.9 | 3.3 | 4.8 | | 1.6 | 5.0 | 4.8 |
| Total Current | | 59.7 | 57.0 | 51.2 | | 32.1 | 48.5 | 46.5 |
| Fixed Assets (net) | | 25.6 | 24.5 | 31.2 | | 48.7 | 38.6 | 34.2 |
| Intangibles (net) | | 8.0 | 9.2 | 9.1 | | 12.3 | 7.3 | 9.4 |
| All Other Non-Current | | 6.8 | 9.3 | 8.5 | | 6.9 | 5.6 | 9.9 |
| Total | | 100.0 | 100.0 | 100.0 | | 100.0 | 100.0 | 100.0 |
| **LIABILITIES** | | | | | | | | |
| Notes Payable-Short Term | | 17.9 | 5.4 | 3.8 | | 1.2 | 6.0 | 8.7 |
| Cur. Mat.-L.T.D. | | 3.5 | 5.1 | 4.8 | | 2.3 | 4.1 | 3.5 |
| Trade Payables | | 18.5 | 26.5 | 18.3 | | 16.9 | 15.1 | 15.0 |
| Income Taxes Payable | | .0 | .1 | .1 | | .0 | .3 | .1 |
| All Other Current | | 11.5 | 12.9 | 10.0 | | 7.0 | 11.3 | 12.3 |
| Total Current | | 51.4 | 50.0 | 36.9 | | 27.4 | 36.8 | 39.7 |
| Long-Term Debt | | 19.9 | 21.2 | 18.6 | | 25.5 | 24.7 | 19.1 |
| Deferred Taxes | | .0 | .5 | .6 | | 1.0 | .3 | .5 |
| All Other Non-Current | | 6.9 | 7.7 | 2.7 | | 11.8 | 5.9 | 5.3 |
| Net Worth | | 21.8 | 20.7 | 41.1 | | 34.2 | 32.2 | 35.5 |
| Total Liabilities & Net Worth | | 100.0 | 100.0 | 100.0 | | 100.0 | 100.0 | 100.0 |
| **INCOME DATA** | | | | | | | | |
| Net Sales | | 100.0 | 100.0 | 100.0 | | 100.0 | 100.0 | 100.0 |
| Gross Profit | | | | | | | | |
| Operating Expenses | | 97.1 | 96.5 | 92.6 | | 91.3 | 93.1 | 91.0 |
| Operating Profit | | 2.9 | 3.5 | 7.4 | | 8.7 | 6.9 | 9.0 |
| All Other Expenses (net) | | 1.8 | 3.5 | 2.1 | | 2.8 | 1.7 | 2.3 |
| Profit Before Taxes | | 1.1 | .1 | 5.3 | | 5.9 | 5.2 | 6.8 |
| **RATIOS** | | | | | | | | |
| Current | | 2.0 | 1.6 | 2.4 | | 3.0 | 2.3 | 2.0 |
| | | 1.2 | 1.2 | 1.3 | | 1.4 | 1.5 | 1.4 |
| | | .7 | .9 | 1.0 | | .8 | 1.0 | .9 |
| Quick | | 1.7 | 1.2 | 1.4 | | 1.3 | 1.6 | 1.5 |
| | | .8 | .8 | 1.0 | | .9 | 1.0 | 1.0 |
| | | .4 | .5 | .7 | | .5 | .6 | .5 |
| Sales/Receivables | | 10  35.4 | 19  18.8 | 17  21.4 | | 28  12.9 | 22  16.7 | 12  31.2 |
| | | 20  18.4 | 31  11.9 | 31  11.8 | | 38  9.6 | 35  10.5 | 28  13.0 |
| | | 47  7.8 | 55  6.6 | 43  8.4 | | 43  8.5 | 57  6.4 | 50  7.2 |
| Cost of Sales/Inventory | | | | | | | | |
| Cost of Sales/Payables | | | | | | | | |
| Sales/Working Capital | | 10.8 | 8.0 | 4.7 | | 3.9 | 6.7 | 7.1 |
| | | 34.0 | 23.1 | 25.2 | | 17.4 | 15.0 | 19.1 |
| | | -11.1 | -46.4 | -553.2 | | -34.1 | -131.4 | -71.9 |
| EBIT/Interest | | 33.7 | 20.3 | 27.0 | | 10.3 | 13.1 | 13.9 |
| | (16) 4.5 | (21) 2.8 | (26) 3.6 | | 4.0 | (83) 3.9 | (91) 5.4 |
| | | 2.8 | -6.9 | .6 | | -.6 | 1.5 | 1.7 |
| Net Profit + Depr., Dep., Amort./Cur. Mat. L/T/D | | | | | | | 9.8 | 17.1 |
| | | | | | | (12) 3.1 | (13) 3.6 |
| | | | | | | | 1.8 | 1.6 |
| Fixed/Worth | | .2 | .3 | .2 | | 1.3 | .5 | .3 |
| | | 1.8 | .7 | .9 | | 3.7 | 1.4 | 1.1 |
| | | -1.0 | -1.5 | 13.4 | | 5.8 | 2.8 | 10.0 |
| Debt/Worth | | .7 | 1.3 | .3 | | .8 | .8 | .5 |
| | | 1.8 | 3.2 | 2.9 | | 4.4 | 2.0 | 2.0 |
| | | -11.9 | -6.9 | 27.6 | | 12.8 | 8.6 | 119.1 |
| % Profit Before Taxes/Tangible Net Worth | | 34.0 | 35.5 | 65.9 | | | 60.8 | 80.9 |
| | (15) 19.9 | (22) 14.3 | (24) 24.2 | | | (80) 24.6 | (84) 25.6 |
| | | 7.8 | -11.4 | 5.4 | | | 6.8 | 6.8 |
| % Profit Before Taxes/Total Assets | | 16.3 | 13.9 | 18.3 | | 13.9 | 17.1 | 23.1 |
| | | 7.4 | 5.5 | 5.2 | | 5.4 | 7.0 | 9.3 |
| | | 1.8 | -3.5 | -1.2 | | -1.9 | 1.0 | 1.2 |
| Sales/Net Fixed Assets | | 118.2 | 47.9 | 54.1 | | 9.2 | 21.1 | 42.6 |
| | | 21.3 | 15.7 | 9.2 | | 2.2 | 6.7 | 8.8 |
| | | 3.4 | 4.7 | 1.3 | | 1.0 | 1.5 | 1.8 |
| Sales/Total Assets | | 6.4 | 4.5 | 2.8 | | 3.8 | 3.7 | 4.0 |
| | | 2.8 | 2.6 | 1.2 | | .7 | 1.8 | 1.9 |
| | | 1.6 | 1.4 | .7 | | .5 | .7 | .9 |
| % Depr., Dep., Amort./Sales | | .8 | 1.1 | .7 | | | 1.1 | 1.0 |
| | (14) 2.0 | (26) 2.6 | (28) 4.9 | | | (83) 2.4 | (81) 3.0 |
| | | 11.0 | 6.9 | 14.2 | | | 12.1 | 11.0 |
| % Officers', Directors', Owners' Comp/Sales | | | | | | | 2.4 | 2.5 |
| | | | | | | | (24) 6.3 | (32) 5.0 |
| | | | | | | | 10.3 | 7.8 |
| Net Sales ($) | 13570M | 116521M | 526813M | 1436356M | 658650M | 2680767M | 3158379M | 5120257M |
| Total Assets ($) | 2237M | 26365M | 158766M | 712479M | 563814M | 1668495M | 2671600M | 3796638M |

## Comparative Historical Data / Current Data Sorted by Sales

| | | | Type of Statement | | | | | | |
|---|---|---|---|---|---|---|---|---|---|
| 36 | 38 | 29 | Unqualified | 2 | 1 | 1 | 2 | 8 | 15 |
| 13 | 14 | 8 | Reviewed | 1 | | 1 | 1 | 2 | 3 |
| 9 | 8 | 11 | Compiled | 3 | 3 | 1 | 1 | 1 | 2 |
| 25 | 23 | 20 | Tax Returns | 4 | 3 | 1 | 4 | 5 | 3 |
| 39 | 45 | 43 | Other | 2 | 3 | 3 | 7 | 11 | 17 |
| 4/1/09- | 4/1/10- | 4/1/11- | | 16 (4/1-9/30/11) | | | 95 (10/1/11-3/31/12) | | |
| 3/31/10 | 3/31/11 | 3/31/12 | | | | | | | |
| ALL | ALL | ALL | | 0-1MM | 1-3MM | 3-5MM | 5-10MM | 10-25MM | 25MM & OVER |
| 122 | 128 | 111 | **NUMBER OF STATEMENTS** | 12 | 10 | 7 | 15 | 27 | 40 |
| % | % | % | **ASSETS** | % | % | % | % | % | % |
| 14.5 | 14.4 | 15.0 | Cash & Equivalents | 7.6 | 9.4 | | 15.4 | 19.3 | 17.0 |
| 17.3 | 22.4 | 23.5 | Trade Receivables (net) | 13.2 | 25.8 | | 18.9 | 26.9 | 25.3 |
| 12.3 | 12.1 | 10.8 | Inventory | 9.5 | 9.6 | | 18.1 | 6.2 | 10.9 |
| 4.6 | 4.1 | 4.4 | All Other Current | 5.4 | 6.7 | | 4.8 | 4.0 | 4.2 |
| 48.7 | 53.0 | 53.7 | Total Current | 35.7 | 51.5 | | 57.1 | 56.4 | 57.4 |
| 33.2 | 29.8 | 28.9 | Fixed Assets (net) | 43.4 | 30.4 | | 22.3 | 27.7 | 25.4 |
| 11.0 | 9.2 | 9.7 | Intangibles (net) | 11.3 | 10.8 | | 6.6 | 6.5 | 12.6 |
| 7.1 | 8.0 | 7.7 | All Other Non-Current | 9.6 | 7.3 | | 13.9 | 9.3 | 4.7 |
| 100.0 | 100.0 | 100.0 | Total | 100.0 | 100.0 | | 100.0 | 100.0 | 100.0 |
| | | | **LIABILITIES** | | | | | | |
| 10.1 | 6.7 | 7.6 | Notes Payable-Short Term | 13.7 | 19.0 | | 9.7 | 3.6 | 4.4 |
| 4.8 | 3.9 | 4.2 | Cur. Mat.-L.T.D. | 4.8 | 5.8 | | 2.6 | 4.4 | 3.8 |
| 15.9 | 19.6 | 21.0 | Trade Payables | 5.7 | 24.7 | | 18.8 | 20.0 | 26.3 |
| .1 | .1 | .0 | Income Taxes Payable | .0 | .0 | | .0 | .2 | .0 |
| 11.8 | 10.1 | 11.4 | All Other Current | 18.6 | 7.4 | | 7.9 | 16.2 | 9.7 |
| 42.7 | 40.3 | 44.3 | Total Current | 42.8 | 57.0 | | 39.0 | 44.3 | 44.2 |
| 19.5 | 22.2 | 22.0 | Long-Term Debt | 52.3 | 41.3 | | 11.1 | 14.8 | 15.9 |
| .4 | .6 | .6 | Deferred Taxes | .5 | .0 | | 1.9 | .0 | .9 |
| 8.2 | 9.3 | 6.1 | All Other Non-Current | 7.3 | 8.6 | | 1.9 | 3.6 | 5.3 |
| 29.3 | 27.6 | 27.0 | Net Worth | -2.8 | -7.0 | | 46.1 | 37.3 | 33.8 |
| 100.0 | 100.0 | 100.0 | Total Liabilities & Net Worth | 100.0 | 100.0 | | 100.0 | 100.0 | 100.0 |
| | | | **INCOME DATA** | | | | | | |
| 100.0 | 100.0 | 100.0 | Net Sales | 100.0 | 100.0 | | 100.0 | 100.0 | 100.0 |
| | | | Gross Profit | | | | | | |
| 91.0 | 91.6 | 94.9 | Operating Expenses | 86.7 | 99.2 | | 96.0 | 97.3 | 93.7 |
| 9.0 | 8.4 | 5.1 | Operating Profit | 13.3 | .8 | | 4.0 | 2.7 | 6.3 |
| 1.3 | 2.2 | 2.5 | All Other Expenses (net) | 8.5 | 3.1 | | .8 | .7 | 2.3 |
| 7.8 | 6.2 | 2.6 | Profit Before Taxes | 4.9 | -2.3 | | 3.2 | 2.0 | 4.0 |
| | | | **RATIOS** | | | | | | |
| 2.1 | 2.4 | 2.0 | | 1.5 | 1.9 | | 2.7 | 2.2 | 2.0 |
| 1.2 | 1.3 | 1.3 | Current | .8 | .9 | | 1.6 | 1.4 | 1.4 |
| .8 | .9 | .9 | | .5 | .5 | | 1.2 | .9 | 1.0 |
| 1.4 | 1.8 | 1.5 | | .9 | 1.7 | | 1.8 | 1.7 | 1.5 |
| .8 | .9 | .9 | Quick | .4 | .6 | | 1.0 | 1.0 | .9 |
| .4 | .5 | .5 | | .3 | .2 | | .5 | .8 | .6 |
| 8 | 47.5 | 14 | 26.8 | 15 | 24.2 | Sales/Receivables | 4 | 100.5 | 15 | 24.2 | | 0 | 914.9 | 21 | 17.5 | 24 | 14.9 |

| Sales/Receivables (detail) | | | | | | | | | | | |
|---|---|---|---|---|---|---|---|---|---|---|---|
| 8 | 47.5 | 14 | 26.8 | 15 | 24.2 | 4 | 100.5 | 15 | 24.2 | 0 | 914.9 | 21 | 17.5 | 24 | 14.9 |
| 25 | 14.7 | 33 | 10.9 | 31 | 11.9 | 16 | 22.3 | 21 | 17.6 | 21 | 17.6 | 36 | 10.0 | 32 | 11.4 |
| 46 | 8.0 | 55 | 6.6 | 47 | 7.7 | 37 | 9.9 | 46 | 7.9 | 47 | 7.7 | 55 | 6.6 | 49 | 7.4 |

| | | | | | | | | | |
|---|---|---|---|---|---|---|---|---|---|
| | | | Cost of Sales/Inventory | | | | | | |
| | | | Cost of Sales/Payables | | | | | | |
| 8.1 | 7.3 | 7.3 | Sales/Working Capital | 9.5 | 13.2 | | 8.0 | 5.5 | 6.0 |
| 32.7 | 20.0 | 23.1 | | -28.4 | NM | | 12.9 | 14.6 | 23.3 |
| -30.2 | -41.2 | -42.3 | | -4.3 | -7.1 | | 27.7 | -81.6 | NM |
| | 28.7 | | 19.9 | | 19.9 | EBIT/Interest | | | | | | | 55.0 | | 32.3 | | 11.9 |
| (104) | 6.4 | (108) | 5.0 | (88) | 3.6 | | | | | | (11) | 12.0 | (20) | 11.6 | (35) | 3.4 |
| | 1.6 | | 1.8 | | .8 | | | | | | | 1.0 | | .3 | | .8 |
| | | 28.0 | | 19.4 | Net Profit + Depr., Dep., Amort./Cur. Mat. L/T/D | | | | | | |
| | (15) | 2.6 | (16) | 3.3 | | | | | | | |
| | | 1.0 | | -.1 | | | | | | | |
| .4 | .3 | .3 | Fixed/Worth | 1.0 | .8 | | .1 | .3 | .2 |
| .9 | 1.0 | 1.1 | | 2.8 | -2.5 | | .5 | .7 | 1.4 |
| 37.5 | 5.4 | -10.6 | | -.4 | -.3 | | 1.4 | 2.6 | 11.1 |
| .7 | .8 | .7 | Debt/Worth | 1.2 | .5 | | .3 | .3 | .9 |
| 2.4 | 2.0 | 2.4 | | 4.3 | -20.0 | | 1.6 | 1.7 | 4.3 |
| NM | 16.1 | -27.1 | | -2.6 | -1.8 | | 4.9 | 12.1 | 23.9 |
| | 99.4 | | 78.6 | | 40.5 | % Profit Before Taxes/Tangible Net Worth | | | | | | | 29.6 | | 30.3 | | 83.8 |
| (92) | 35.8 | (103) | 24.5 | (83) | 16.0 | | | | | | (13) | 8.3 | (22) | 16.1 | (31) | 25.6 |
| | 7.8 | | 6.6 | | 5.0 | | | | | | | 3.4 | | -3.2 | | 7.6 |
| 26.8 | 18.5 | 16.0 | % Profit Before Taxes/Total Assets | 5.4 | 19.2 | | 16.0 | 19.9 | 18.0 |
| 10.5 | 8.1 | 5.2 | | 1.6 | 4.7 | | 7.4 | 7.2 | 6.1 |
| 1.9 | 1.3 | -.5 | | -2.7 | -23.4 | | 2.8 | -2.3 | -.3 |
| 41.9 | 51.4 | 45.3 | Sales/Net Fixed Assets | 36.7 | 35.3 | | 129.6 | 44.4 | 87.4 |
| 9.0 | 11.7 | 13.7 | | 3.9 | 13.3 | | 13.4 | 14.4 | 15.6 |
| 2.0 | 1.9 | 2.2 | | .4 | 3.0 | | 3.5 | 1.7 | 2.3 |
| 4.0 | 4.0 | 4.0 | Sales/Total Assets | 3.4 | 5.2 | | 4.0 | 4.1 | 4.4 |
| 2.1 | 2.1 | 2.2 | | .4 | 2.2 | | 3.1 | 2.1 | 2.1 |
| .9 | .8 | .9 | | .2 | 1.5 | | 1.0 | .9 | .9 |
| | .7 | | .7 | | .9 | % Depr., Dep., Amort./Sales | 1.8 | | | | | 1.7 | | 1.3 | | .5 |
| (90) | 2.9 | (91) | 2.9 | (82) | 2.7 | | (10) | 15.1 | | | (10) | 3.6 | (23) | 5.0 | (24) | 1.4 |
| | 11.0 | | 11.4 | | 10.9 | | | 31.2 | | | | 7.1 | | 11.6 | | 3.0 |
| | 1.8 | | 1.2 | | 1.2 | % Officers', Directors' Owners' Comp/Sales | | | | | | |
| (36) | 3.1 | (33) | 3.3 | (26) | 4.7 | | | | | | | |
| | 7.6 | | 6.2 | | 7.9 | | | | | | | |
| 5795849M | 5016317M | 5432677M | Net Sales ($) | 7507M | 19129M | 29300M | 105475M | 442314M | 4828952M |
| 4028142M | 4197576M | 3132156M | Total Assets ($) | 18082M | 19516M | 27780M | 80750M | 323625M | 2662403M |

M = $ thousand    MM = $ million
See Pages 9 through 22 for Explanation of Ratios and Data

## Current Data Sorted by Assets      Comparative Historical Data

| 0-500M | 500M-2MM | 2-10MM | 10-50MM | 50-100MM | 100-250MM | Type of Statement | 4/1/07-3/31/08 ALL | 4/1/08-3/31/09 ALL |
|---|---|---|---|---|---|---|---|---|
| | | 3 | 10 | 1 | 2 | Unqualified | 7 | 9 |
| | | 3 | 1 | | | Reviewed | 2 | 3 |
| | 1 | 2 | | | | Compiled | 3 | 2 |
| 2 | 5 | 3 | 1 | | | Tax Returns | 1 | 5 |
| 2 | 2 | 13 | 5 | 4 | 4 | Other | 12 | 12 |
| | | 6 (4/1-9/30/11) | 58 (10/1/11-3/31/12) | | | | 12 | 12 |
| 4 | 8 | 24 | 17 | 5 | 6 | NUMBER OF STATEMENTS | 25 | 31 |
| % | % | % | % | % | % | ASSETS | % | % |
| | | 16.9 | 24.9 | | | Cash & Equivalents | 16.5 | 10.6 |
| | | 22.2 | 24.0 | | | Trade Receivables (net) | 28.5 | 27.2 |
| | | 13.5 | 7.1 | | | Inventory | 14.6 | 11.9 |
| | | 4.5 | 3.6 | | | All Other Current | 2.9 | 4.2 |
| | | 57.1 | 59.7 | | | Total Current | 62.4 | 53.9 |
| | | 25.3 | 23.3 | | | Fixed Assets (net) | 21.8 | 17.8 |
| | | 6.6 | 9.6 | | | Intangibles (net) | 9.1 | 14.3 |
| | | 11.0 | 7.5 | | | All Other Non-Current | 6.7 | 14.0 |
| | | 100.0 | 100.0 | | | Total | 100.0 | 100.0 |
| | | | | | | **LIABILITIES** | | |
| | | 3.5 | 4.1 | | | Notes Payable-Short Term | 15.7 | 11.5 |
| | | 2.0 | 5.6 | | | Cur. Mat.-L.T.D. | 3.4 | 2.6 |
| | | 24.2 | 18.6 | | | Trade Payables | 18.9 | 36.1 |
| | | .7 | .7 | | | Income Taxes Payable | .3 | .5 |
| | | 21.9 | 15.5 | | | All Other Current | 12.6 | 12.2 |
| | | 52.2 | 44.7 | | | Total Current | 50.9 | 62.9 |
| | | 9.2 | 15.4 | | | Long-Term Debt | 8.5 | 18.5 |
| | | .0 | .4 | | | Deferred Taxes | .9 | .7 |
| | | 2.2 | 4.5 | | | All Other Non-Current | 4.2 | 13.4 |
| | | 36.4 | 35.1 | | | Net Worth | 35.5 | 4.5 |
| | | 100.0 | 100.0 | | | Total Liabilities & Net Worth | 100.0 | 100.0 |
| | | | | | | **INCOME DATA** | | |
| | | 100.0 | 100.0 | | | Net Sales | 100.0 | 100.0 |
| | | | | | | Gross Profit | | |
| | | 94.4 | 93.2 | | | Operating Expenses | 92.2 | 92.8 |
| | | 5.6 | 6.8 | | | Operating Profit | 7.8 | 7.2 |
| | | 2.3 | 1.6 | | | All Other Expenses (net) | .5 | 3.0 |
| | | 3.3 | 5.2 | | | Profit Before Taxes | 7.3 | 4.2 |
| | | | | | | **RATIOS** | | |
| | | 1.7 | 1.7 | | | Current | 1.8 | 1.6 |
| | | 1.1 | 1.3 | | | | 1.3 | 1.2 |
| | | .6 | 1.1 | | | | .9 | .8 |
| | | 1.1 | 1.5 | | | Quick | 1.4 | 1.2 |
| | | .8 | 1.0 | | | | 1.0 | .8 |
| | | .4 | .6 | | | | .6 | .6 |
| | | 4   91.6 | 24   14.9 | | | Sales/Receivables | 23   15.9 | 18   20.0 |
| | | 16   22.5 | 39   9.3 | | | | 38   9.7 | 31   11.7 |
| | | 48   7.6 | 60   6.1 | | | | 51   7.2 | 55   6.7 |
| | | | | | | Cost of Sales/Inventory | | |
| | | | | | | Cost of Sales/Payables | | |
| | | 9.9 | 9.8 | | | Sales/Working Capital | 8.2 | 9.0 |
| | | 119.5 | 16.4 | | | | 18.1 | 50.5 |
| | | -36.0 | 101.1 | | | | -65.3 | -33.6 |
| | | 137.1 | 20.2 | | | EBIT/Interest | 12.6 | 5.0 |
| | | (17)   11.1 | (15)   7.1 | | | | (23)   4.4 | (26)   1.9 |
| | | 1.8 | 1.6 | | | | 1.3 | -1.0 |
| | | | | | | Net Profit + Depr., Dep., Amort./Cur. Mat. L/T/D | | |
| | | .2 | .1 | | | Fixed/Worth | .4 | .5 |
| | | .9 | 1.3 | | | | .6 | 2.7 |
| | | 3.1 | 4.1 | | | | NM | -.4 |
| | | .8 | 1.1 | | | Debt/Worth | 1.0 | 1.9 |
| | | 3.2 | 1.8 | | | | 1.8 | 11.5 |
| | | 27.4 | 22.1 | | | | NM | -4.9 |
| | | 84.9 | 106.1 | | | % Profit Before Taxes/Tangible Net Worth | 64.2 | 98.2 |
| | | (20)   29.7 | (14)   30.9 | | | | (19)   31.4 | (19)   28.5 |
| | | 7.4 | 5.3 | | | | 16.2 | 11.7 |
| | | 26.2 | 27.6 | | | % Profit Before Taxes/Total Assets | 19.1 | 10.8 |
| | | 11.4 | 11.4 | | | | 9.9 | 4.2 |
| | | .6 | 2.3 | | | | 2.8 | -10.2 |
| | | 171.3 | 74.8 | | | Sales/Net Fixed Assets | 58.1 | 213.4 |
| | | 32.2 | 34.2 | | | | 23.7 | 41.1 |
| | | 3.5 | 8.9 | | | | 7.1 | 11.2 |
| | | 6.8 | 3.3 | | | Sales/Total Assets | 3.7 | 4.3 |
| | | 3.4 | 2.4 | | | | 2.9 | 1.8 |
| | | .9 | .8 | | | | 1.6 | 1.1 |
| | | .3 | .7 | | | % Depr., Dep., Amort./Sales | .4 | .4 |
| | | (21)   .7 | (14)   1.9 | | | | (21)   1.3 | (21)   .9 |
| | | 13.7 | 21.2 | | | | 6.7 | 3.4 |
| | | | | | | % Officers', Directors' Owners' Comp/Sales | | |
| 10340M | 37830M | 831836M | 1009485M | 938050M | 1967170M | Net Sales ($) | 1389514M | 1605716M |
| 717M | 8297M | 124352M | 447843M | 340872M | 944951M | Total Assets ($) | 917596M | 1056762M |

M = $ thousand     MM = $ million
See Pages 9 through 22 for Explanation of Ratios and Data

## Comparative Historical Data  |  Current Data Sorted by Sales

| | | | Type of Statement | 0-1MM | 1-3MM | 3-5MM | 5-10MM | 10-25MM | 25MM & OVER |
|---|---|---|---|---|---|---|---|---|---|
| 6 | 12 | 16 | Unqualified | | 1 | 1 | 2 | 3 | 9 |
| 7 | 10 | 4 | Reviewed | | | | | 3 | 1 |
| 3 | 2 | 3 | Compiled | | 1 | | 1 | | 1 |
| 6 | 5 | 11 | Tax Returns | 4 | 3 | | 1 | 3 | |
| 15 | 19 | 30 | Other | 2 | 1 | 3 | 2 | 3 | 19 |
| 4/1/09-3/31/10 ALL | 4/1/10-3/31/11 ALL | 4/1/11-3/31/12 ALL | | \_\_\_\_ | 6 (4/1-9/30/11) | \_\_\_\_ | \_\_\_\_ | 58 (10/1/11-3/31/12) | \_\_\_\_ |
| 37 | 48 | 64 | NUMBER OF STATEMENTS | 6 | 6 | 4 | 6 | 12 | 30 |
| % | % | % | ASSETS | % | % | % | % | % | % |
| 10.8 | 12.7 | 21.0 | Cash & Equivalents | | | | | 22.5 | 29.7 |
| 28.2 | 28.0 | 23.1 | Trade Receivables (net) | | | | | 23.0 | 25.3 |
| 14.5 | 12.6 | 11.9 | Inventory | | | | | 11.8 | 9.8 |
| 5.4 | 9.4 | 6.3 | All Other Current | | | | | 1.6 | 7.1 |
| 58.9 | 62.8 | 62.3 | Total Current | | | | | 58.8 | 71.9 |
| 16.9 | 19.2 | 21.3 | Fixed Assets (net) | | | | | 23.9 | 11.6 |
| 12.1 | 11.9 | 7.6 | Intangibles (net) | | | | | 7.8 | 9.8 |
| 12.0 | 6.1 | 8.9 | All Other Non-Current | | | | | 9.5 | 6.7 |
| 100.0 | 100.0 | 100.0 | Total | | | | | 100.0 | 100.0 |
| | | | LIABILITIES | | | | | | |
| 17.2 | 8.0 | 6.7 | Notes Payable-Short Term | | | | | 2.7 | 3.2 |
| 3.8 | 3.0 | 3.7 | Cur. Mat.-L.T.D. | | | | | 1.6 | 3.6 |
| 28.0 | 29.6 | 24.2 | Trade Payables | | | | | 13.6 | 25.9 |
| .4 | .6 | .6 | Income Taxes Payable | | | | | .6 | 1.1 |
| 16.3 | 12.4 | 20.2 | All Other Current | | | | | 17.2 | 24.6 |
| 65.6 | 53.5 | 55.4 | Total Current | | | | | 35.6 | 58.3 |
| 18.9 | 12.6 | 16.3 | Long-Term Debt | | | | | 11.8 | 7.2 |
| .4 | 1.1 | .6 | Deferred Taxes | | | | | .0 | 1.2 |
| 7.0 | 5.9 | 4.1 | All Other Non-Current | | | | | 1.3 | 4.8 |
| 8.1 | 27.0 | 23.6 | Net Worth | | | | | 51.2 | 28.6 |
| 100.0 | 100.0 | 100.0 | Total Liabilties & Net Worth | | | | | 100.0 | 100.0 |
| | | | INCOME DATA | | | | | | |
| 100.0 | 100.0 | 100.0 | Net Sales | | | | | 100.0 | 100.0 |
| | | | Gross Profit | | | | | | |
| 93.6 | 97.2 | 93.1 | Operating Expenses | | | | | 94.8 | 92.1 |
| 6.4 | 2.8 | 6.9 | Operating Profit | | | | | 5.2 | 7.9 |
| 2.8 | 1.4 | 2.5 | All Other Expenses (net) | | | | | 1.0 | .9 |
| 3.6 | 1.5 | 4.4 | Profit Before Taxes | | | | | 4.2 | 7.0 |
| | | | RATIOS | | | | | | |
| 1.7 | 1.7 | 1.8 | Current | | | | | 7.0 | 1.8 |
| 1.0 | 1.2 | 1.2 | | | | | | 1.5 | 1.3 |
| .6 | .9 | .8 | | | | | | .7 | 1.0 |
| .9 | 1.2 | 1.5 | Quick | | | | | 5.5 | 1.6 |
| .6 (47) | .7 | .8 | | | | | | 1.1 | .9 |
| .4 | .5 | .5 | | | | | | .6 | .6 |
| 13 27.7 | 19 18.7 | 6 57.1 | Sales/Receivables | | | | | 2 200.6 | 16 22.2 |
| 31 11.9 | 34 10.9 | 26 13.8 | | | | | | 52 7.0 | 25 14.4 |
| 51 7.1 | 46 7.9 | 53 6.9 | | | | | | 65 5.6 | 41 8.8 |
| | | | Cost of Sales/Inventory | | | | | | |
| | | | Cost of Sales/Payables | | | | | | |
| 10.7 | 6.3 | 9.0 | Sales/Working Capital | | | | | 4.9 | 8.9 |
| -152.5 | 34.2 | 45.9 | | | | | | 18.3 | 18.1 |
| -9.8 | -79.3 | -56.1 | | | | | | NM | 180.0 |
| 16.7 | 36.3 | 37.1 | EBIT/Interest | | | | | 436.8 | 90.3 |
| (33) 5.3 | (42) 6.3 | (48) 7.1 | | | | | | 15.1 | (21) 17.4 |
| .6 | 2.5 | 1.7 | | | | | | -.2 | 5.8 |
| | | 6.0 | Net Profit + Depr., Dep., Amort./Cur. Mat. L/T/D | | | | | | |
| | (11) | 2.6 | | | | | | | |
| | | .3 | | | | | | | |
| .3 | .2 | .1 | Fixed/Worth | | | | | .1 | .2 |
| 2.1 | 1.2 | .5 | | | | | | .3 | .5 |
| -.4 | -26.2 | 3.1 | | | | | | 2.4 | 3.8 |
| 1.7 | 1.7 | 1.0 | Debt/Worth | | | | | .2 | 1.0 |
| -17.0 | 4.8 | 2.5 | | | | | | 1.2 | 4.2 |
| -2.9 | -28.0 | 32.5 | | | | | | 2.1 | 32.7 |
| 84.5 | 84.8 | 100.0 | % Profit Before Taxes/Tangible Net Worth | | | | | 37.6 | 283.8 |
| (18) 24.1 | (34) 30.5 | (51) 29.7 | | | | | | (10) 28.0 | (24) 87.8 |
| 11.2 | -1.9 | 5.4 | | | | | | 1.4 | 31.9 |
| 18.2 | 17.9 | 28.1 | % Profit Before Taxes/Total Assets | | | | | 26.8 | 37.8 |
| 6.5 | 6.6 | 10.9 | | | | | | 8.3 | 16.3 |
| -.8 | .0 | .8 | | | | | | -2.1 | 7.1 |
| 120.5 | 120.3 | 154.0 | Sales/Net Fixed Assets | | | | | 171.3 | 153.7 |
| 36.7 | 44.0 | 32.3 | | | | | | 38.2 | 43.7 |
| 12.3 | 10.0 | 9.1 | | | | | | 5.9 | 16.7 |
| 5.9 | 5.2 | 4.7 | Sales/Total Assets | | | | | 6.0 | 4.5 |
| 3.2 | 3.0 | 2.7 | | | | | | 2.1 | 3.3 |
| 1.7 | 1.1 | 1.1 | | | | | | .7 | 2.3 |
| .5 | .4 | .3 | % Depr., Dep., Amort./Sales | | | | | .1 | .3 |
| (27) .9 | (33) .8 | (51) 1.0 | | | | | | (10) .9 | (23) .7 |
| 2.8 | 3.5 | 3.8 | | | | | | 21.2 | 1.9 |
| | .7 | .7 | % Officers', Directors' Owners' Comp/Sales | | | | | | |
| | (11) 3.0 | (11) 3.3 | | | | | | | |
| | 9.7 | 7.1 | | | | | | | |
| 2351557M | 2520018M | 4794711M | Net Sales ($) | 3975M | 12501M | 14281M | 49199M | 199327M | 4515428M |
| 1316658M | 1791794M | 1867032M | Total Assets ($) | 9641M | 8440M | 16521M | 40662M | 130137M | 1661631M |

© RMA 2012

M = $ thousand    MM = $ million

See Pages 9 through 22 for Explanation of Ratios and Data

## Current Data Sorted by Assets      Comparative Historical Data

| Type of Statement | 0-500M | 500M-2MM | 2-10MM | 10-50MM | 50-100MM | 100-250MM | | 4/1/07-3/31/08 ALL | 4/1/08-3/31/09 ALL |
|---|---|---|---|---|---|---|---|---|---|
| Unqualified | | | 3 | 9 | 6 | 5 | | 36 | 34 |
| Reviewed | | 7 | 15 | 3 | | | | 9 | 16 |
| Compiled | 2 | 10 | 8 | | | | | 15 | 14 |
| Tax Returns | 3 | 5 | 1 | | | | | 12 | 14 |
| Other | 8 | 11 | 26 | 12 | 9 | 7 | | 58 | 71 |
| | 17 (4/1-9/30/11) | | | 133 (10/1/11-3/31/12) | | | | | |
| **NUMBER OF STATEMENTS** | 13 | 33 | 53 | 24 | 15 | 12 | | 130 | 149 |
| **ASSETS** | % | % | % | % | % | % | | % | % |
| Cash & Equivalents | 32.2 | 10.3 | 10.7 | 12.9 | 7.9 | 11.3 | | 14.5 | 15.1 |
| Trade Receivables (net) | 18.0 | 36.5 | 32.1 | 28.0 | 13.0 | 18.1 | | 31.5 | 31.9 |
| Inventory | 4.5 | 8.9 | 8.0 | 11.0 | 2.8 | 6.9 | | 7.3 | 6.6 |
| All Other Current | 2.5 | 2.9 | 6.8 | 4.9 | 4.1 | 4.7 | | 4.8 | 4.8 |
| Total Current | 57.2 | 58.5 | 57.6 | 56.8 | 27.8 | 41.0 | | 58.1 | 58.4 |
| Fixed Assets (net) | 29.6 | 30.2 | 21.3 | 24.3 | 45.4 | 24.7 | | 24.4 | 26.7 |
| Intangibles (net) | 1.8 | 4.4 | 7.1 | 12.1 | 16.2 | 20.5 | | 7.9 | 6.6 |
| All Other Non-Current | 11.5 | 6.9 | 14.0 | 6.7 | 10.6 | 13.7 | | 9.7 | 8.4 |
| Total | 100.0 | 100.0 | 100.0 | 100.0 | 100.0 | 100.0 | | 100.0 | 100.0 |
| **LIABILITIES** | | | | | | | | | |
| Notes Payable-Short Term | 8.2 | 10.3 | 9.1 | 6.2 | 2.5 | 1.6 | | 10.7 | 9.3 |
| Cur. Mat.-L.T.D. | 4.3 | 5.9 | 3.1 | 3.9 | 5.1 | 1.8 | | 4.2 | 4.6 |
| Trade Payables | 29.9 | 18.4 | 20.2 | 23.0 | 14.6 | 14.8 | | 17.5 | 18.4 |
| Income Taxes Payable | .0 | .1 | .0 | .1 | .1 | .3 | | .4 | .3 |
| All Other Current | 17.7 | 12.3 | 15.3 | 11.3 | 7.1 | 12.6 | | 16.6 | 15.1 |
| Total Current | 60.1 | 46.9 | 47.8 | 44.5 | 29.3 | 31.1 | | 49.4 | 47.6 |
| Long-Term Debt | 15.7 | 26.1 | 11.1 | 16.8 | 18.7 | 20.0 | | 19.5 | 18.3 |
| Deferred Taxes | .0 | .1 | .2 | .8 | .9 | 1.7 | | .4 | .2 |
| All Other Non-Current | 1.9 | 7.2 | 9.0 | 5.2 | 12.3 | 4.0 | | 6.6 | 4.7 |
| Net Worth | 22.2 | 19.6 | 31.9 | 32.7 | 38.8 | 43.3 | | 24.2 | 29.2 |
| Total Liabilties & Net Worth | 100.0 | 100.0 | 100.0 | 100.0 | 100.0 | 100.0 | | 100.0 | 100.0 |
| **INCOME DATA** | | | | | | | | | |
| Net Sales | 100.0 | 100.0 | 100.0 | 100.0 | 100.0 | 100.0 | | 100.0 | 100.0 |
| Gross Profit | | | | | | | | | |
| Operating Expenses | 83.8 | 89.2 | 93.8 | 94.0 | 95.6 | 87.0 | | 91.4 | 92.8 |
| Operating Profit | 16.2 | 10.8 | 6.2 | 6.0 | 4.4 | 13.0 | | 8.6 | 7.2 |
| All Other Expenses (net) | .7 | 1.7 | .9 | 2.4 | 5.0 | 2.2 | | 2.4 | 2.7 |
| Profit Before Taxes | 15.5 | 9.1 | 5.2 | 3.6 | -.7 | 10.7 | | 6.2 | 4.6 |
| **RATIOS** | | | | | | | | | |
| Current | 2.9 | 2.4 | 2.3 | 1.7 | 1.6 | 2.2 | | 1.9 | 2.0 |
| | 1.7 | 1.1 | 1.3 | 1.2 | .8 | 1.4 | | 1.3 | 1.2 |
| | .3 | .8 | .7 | .7 | .5 | .9 | | .8 | .8 |
| Quick | 2.9 | 2.4 | 1.9 | 1.4 | 1.2 | 1.7 | | 1.5 | 1.6 |
| | 1.2 | 1.0 | .9 | .6 | .7 | 1.3 | | 1.0 | 1.0 |
| | .3 | .5 | .5 | .4 | .3 | .6 | | .5 | .6 |
| Sales/Receivables | 0 UND | 17   22.1 | 26   13.8 | 19   19.7 | 10   35.1 | 38   9.5 | | 24   15.5 | 22   16.4 |
| | 0 999.8 | 39   9.3 | 41   8.8 | 34   10.7 | 36   10.2 | 49   7.5 | | 44   8.3 | 41   8.9 |
| | 37   9.8 | 52   7.0 | 68   5.4 | 65   5.6 | 52   7.0 | 56   6.5 | | 71   5.1 | 64   5.7 |
| Cost of Sales/Inventory | | | | | | | | | |
| Cost of Sales/Payables | | | | | | | | | |
| Sales/Working Capital | 4.7 | 10.0 | 6.7 | 10.6 | 6.2 | 4.2 | | 8.2 | 7.2 |
| | 46.1 | 62.9 | 16.8 | 24.2 | -37.2 | 13.8 | | 19.8 | 24.6 |
| | -38.9 | -55.9 | -16.7 | -30.0 | -8.1 | NM | | -26.1 | -43.4 |
| EBIT/Interest | | 10.7 | 20.3 | 20.0 | 6.6 | 25.0 | | 9.7 | 18.5 |
| | | (27) 3.0 | (44) 6.5 | (21) 5.2 | (13) 1.6 | (10) 6.5 | | (100) 3.8 | (114) 4.2 |
| | | .3 | 1.2 | 2.1 | -4.8 | 2.2 | | 1.2 | .8 |
| Net Profit + Depr., Dep., Amort./Cur. Mat. L/T/D | | | | | | | | 4.9 | 9.4 |
| | | | | | | | | (21) 2.4 | (23) 1.9 |
| | | | | | | | | 1.3 | .7 |
| Fixed/Worth | .1 | .3 | .2 | .1 | .8 | .2 | | .2 | .3 |
| | .5 | 1.0 | .4 | 1.2 | 3.0 | 1.0 | | 1.0 | .8 |
| | NM | -2.0 | 2.3 | 4.1 | 3.4 | NM | | 17.1 | 7.4 |
| Debt/Worth | .3 | .9 | 1.0 | 1.4 | 1.1 | .8 | | 1.2 | .8 |
| | 1.5 | 3.7 | 2.2 | 4.2 | 2.3 | 6.7 | | 3.1 | 3.0 |
| | NM | -24.1 | 29.1 | 6.9 | 6.3 | NM | | 69.6 | 53.2 |
| % Profit Before Taxes/Tangible Net Worth | 316.4 | 116.0 | 50.4 | 37.4 | 28.2 | | | 86.8 | 69.3 |
| | (10) 66.5 | (22) 26.1 | (41) 30.1 | (20) 21.5 | (13) 3.2 | | | (100) 33.1 | (116) 35.2 |
| | 19.7 | 5.6 | 7.6 | 7.4 | -26.9 | | | 10.1 | 3.8 |
| % Profit Before Taxes/Total Assets | 99.7 | 38.6 | 19.1 | 12.7 | 8.0 | 9.4 | | 23.0 | 21.3 |
| | 29.6 | 4.9 | 7.7 | 5.7 | 1.5 | 6.9 | | 7.0 | 6.7 |
| | 8.6 | -3.4 | .8 | 2.4 | -4.3 | 3.2 | | .8 | -.7 |
| Sales/Net Fixed Assets | 172.6 | 81.5 | 53.1 | 87.0 | 14.1 | 68.2 | | 49.1 | 47.4 |
| | 53.8 | 40.6 | 19.6 | 23.4 | 2.1 | 11.4 | | 17.6 | 19.2 |
| | 8.3 | 6.3 | 6.3 | 2.8 | 1.1 | .7 | | 6.2 | 5.6 |
| Sales/Total Assets | 14.2 | 5.7 | 3.2 | 3.9 | 1.5 | 2.5 | | 3.8 | 3.7 |
| | 3.6 | 3.6 | 2.4 | 1.7 | 1.1 | .7 | | 2.6 | 2.7 |
| | 1.6 | 2.1 | 1.6 | .9 | .6 | .3 | | 1.3 | 1.3 |
| % Depr., Dep., Amort./Sales | | .4 | 1.1 | .6 | 3.1 | | | .8 | .7 |
| | | (27) 1.2 | (37) 2.2 | (20) 1.4 | (12) 6.7 | | | (99) 1.9 | (113) 1.8 |
| | | 7.5 | 3.5 | 21.5 | 20.6 | | | 5.3 | 6.8 |
| % Officers', Directors' Owners' Comp/Sales | | | 1.2 | | | | | 2.2 | 1.4 |
| | | | (12) 2.0 | | | | | (33) 5.0 | (36) 3.4 |
| | | | 4.7 | | | | | 11.7 | 9.7 |
| Net Sales ($) | 23677M | 187772M | 643764M | 1141589M | 1362494M | 2661709M | | 5010857M | 5524499M |
| Total Assets ($) | 2628M | 42503M | 259873M | 548972M | 1081867M | 2228272M | | 3283391M | 3102250M |

M = $ thousand     MM = $ million
See Pages 9 through 22 for Explanation of Ratios and Data

## Comparative Historical Data | Current Data Sorted by Sales

| CHD | CHD | CHD | Type of Statement | 0-1MM | 1-3MM | 3-5MM | 5-10MM | 10-25MM | 25MM & OVER |
|---|---|---|---|---|---|---|---|---|---|
| 40 | 33 | 23 | Unqualified | | | | 2 | 7 | 14 |
| 15 | 13 | 25 | Reviewed | 1 | | 6 | 4 | 11 | 3 |
| 11 | 20 | 20 | Compiled | 2 | 1 | 5 | 6 | 6 | |
| 17 | 24 | 9 | Tax Returns | 1 | 3 | | 3 | 2 | |
| 89 | 71 | 73 | Other | 9 | 6 | 9 | 11 | 10 | 28 |
| 4/1/09-3/31/10 ALL | 4/1/10-3/31/11 ALL | 4/1/11-3/31/12 ALL | | 17 (4/1-9/30/11) | | | 133 (10/1/11-3/31/12) | | |
| 172 | 161 | 150 | NUMBER OF STATEMENTS | 13 | 10 | 20 | 26 | 36 | 45 |
| % | % | % | **ASSETS** | % | % | % | % | % | % |
| 14.0 | 11.9 | 12.6 | Cash & Equivalents | 14.6 | 26.9 | 14.4 | 11.8 | 10.8 | 9.9 |
| 24.9 | 28.6 | 28.2 | Trade Receivables (net) | 17.2 | 17.3 | 25.3 | 35.9 | 33.4 | 26.4 |
| 6.6 | 6.4 | 7.7 | Inventory | .5 | 8.6 | 7.7 | 7.4 | 9.0 | 8.9 |
| 5.5 | 4.4 | 4.8 | All Other Current | 2.4 | 10.2 | 3.2 | 2.9 | 5.1 | 5.9 |
| 50.9 | 51.4 | 53.4 | Total Current | 34.7 | 63.0 | 50.6 | 57.9 | 58.4 | 51.1 |
| 29.0 | 29.7 | 27.1 | Fixed Assets (net) | 51.2 | 23.0 | 24.9 | 23.6 | 23.6 | 27.0 |
| 11.6 | 9.5 | 8.8 | Intangibles (net) | 2.1 | 3.0 | 11.3 | 7.3 | 9.4 | 11.3 |
| 8.5 | 9.4 | 10.7 | All Other Non-Current | 12.1 | 11.0 | 13.1 | 11.2 | 8.5 | 10.5 |
| 100.0 | 100.0 | 100.0 | Total | 100.0 | 100.0 | 100.0 | 100.0 | 100.0 | 100.0 |
| | | | **LIABILITIES** | | | | | | |
| 9.4 | 11.2 | 7.6 | Notes Payable-Short Term | 6.5 | 8.1 | 10.4 | 8.8 | 6.4 | 6.6 |
| 3.9 | 3.9 | 4.0 | Cur. Mat.-L.T.D. | 6.3 | 3.7 | 5.6 | 2.9 | 3.6 | 3.9 |
| 15.2 | 14.1 | 20.1 | Trade Payables | 27.8 | 7.8 | 15.8 | 20.5 | 18.8 | 23.3 |
| .1 | .4 | .1 | Income Taxes Payable | .0 | .0 | .0 | .1 | .0 | .1 |
| 18.3 | 13.2 | 13.2 | All Other Current | 14.0 | 21.4 | 6.3 | 21.3 | 10.7 | 11.4 |
| 46.8 | 42.7 | 44.9 | Total Current | 54.6 | 41.0 | 38.1 | 53.6 | 39.6 | 45.4 |
| 22.5 | 23.3 | 17.2 | Long-Term Debt | 39.6 | 12.1 | 9.3 | 18.0 | 19.3 | 13.1 |
| .7 | .5 | .5 | Deferred Taxes | .0 | .1 | .0 | .5 | .5 | .8 |
| 7.0 | 8.5 | 7.3 | All Other Non-Current | 2.0 | 6.8 | 5.7 | 12.0 | 6.3 | 7.8 |
| 23.0 | 24.9 | 30.1 | Net Worth | 3.7 | 40.0 | 46.9 | 16.0 | 34.3 | 32.9 |
| 100.0 | 100.0 | 100.0 | Total Liabilities & Net Worth | 100.0 | 100.0 | 100.0 | 100.0 | 100.0 | 100.0 |
| | | | **INCOME DATA** | | | | | | |
| 100.0 | 100.0 | 100.0 | Net Sales | 100.0 | 100.0 | 100.0 | 100.0 | 100.0 | 100.0 |
| | | | Gross Profit | | | | | | |
| 93.7 | 90.5 | 91.6 | Operating Expenses | 74.1 | 91.5 | 92.6 | 93.2 | 93.3 | 94.0 |
| 6.3 | 9.5 | 8.4 | Operating Profit | 25.9 | 8.5 | 7.4 | 6.8 | 6.7 | 6.0 |
| 1.9 | 3.7 | 1.8 | All Other Expenses (net) | 3.9 | 2.1 | .8 | .6 | 2.8 | 1.6 |
| 4.4 | 5.8 | 6.6 | Profit Before Taxes | 22.0 | 6.4 | 6.5 | 6.2 | 3.9 | 4.5 |
| | | | **RATIOS** | | | | | | |
| 1.7 | 2.2 | 2.2 | Current | 2.5 | 11.0 | 3.5 | 1.7 | 2.5 | 1.7 |
| 1.1 | 1.3 | 1.2 | | 1.0 | 1.4 | 1.8 | 1.0 | 1.4 | 1.1 |
| .6 | .7 | .7 | | .3 | .4 | .8 | .7 | 1.0 | .7 |
| 1.4 | 1.8 | 1.8 | Quick | 2.5 | 10.5 | 3.0 | 1.6 | 1.8 | 1.4 |
| .8 | 1.0 | .9 | | 1.0 | .7 | 1.8 | .9 | 1.0 | .7 |
| .5 | .5 | .5 | | .3 | .2 | .5 | .5 | .6 | .5 |
| 17  21.4 | 18  20.1 | 21  17.0 | Sales/Receivables | 0  UND | 0  UND | 22  16.5 | 28  13.1 | 23  16.2 | 22  16.7 |
| 38  9.6 | 39  9.3 | 39  9.4 | | 29  12.7 | 34  10.6 | 41  9.0 | 38  9.7 | 38  9.7 | 41  8.8 |
| 60  6.1 | 63  5.8 | 59  6.2 | | 45  8.2 | 55  6.6 | 60  6.1 | 57  6.4 | 64  5.7 | 58  6.3 |
| | | | Cost of Sales/Inventory | | | | | | |
| | | | Cost of Sales/Payables | | | | | | |
| 10.7 | 6.2 | 6.7 | Sales/Working Capital | 4.7 | 3.8 | 9.1 | 10.4 | 4.9 | 8.4 |
| 46.5 | 19.4 | 24.0 | | 228.7 | 15.6 | 20.4 | NM | 17.0 | 44.8 |
| -13.4 | -27.9 | -17.6 | | -2.8 | -6.6 | -23.2 | -15.0 | NM | -30.5 |
| 13.9 | 19.7 | 14.5 | EBIT/Interest | | | 9.8 | 19.4 | 24.4 | 15.6 |
| (141) 3.7 | (139) 4.5 | (120) 5.2 | | | (16) .9 | (20) 6.0 | (32) 5.9 | (40) 5.4 |  |
| 1.0 | 1.2 | 1.4 | | | | -.8 | 2.2 | 1.6 | 1.5 |
| 8.1 | 7.1 | 8.2 | Net Profit + Depr., Dep., Amort./Cur. Mat. L/T/D | | | | | | 9.9 |
| (30) 3.3 | (26) 2.5 | (26) 2.2 | | | | | | (11) 2.8 |  |
| 1.1 | 1.4 | 1.4 | | | | | | | 1.1 |
| .3 | .3 | .2 | Fixed/Worth | .3 | .0 | .2 | .2 | .2 | .2 |
| 1.4 | 1.2 | 1.1 | | 3.4 | .2 | .4 | 1.7 | .7 | 1.4 |
| -2.5 | 42.0 | 5.0 | | -23.1 | NM | 1.1 | -1.1 | 4.1 | 3.3 |
| 1.3 | 1.0 | 1.0 | Debt/Worth | .4 | .2 | .4 | 1.9 | .8 | 1.3 |
| 4.1 | 2.7 | 2.7 | | 2.5 | 4.3 | 1.0 | 3.1 | 2.1 | 4.3 |
| -5.4 | 134.1 | 22.4 | | -31.0 | NM | NM | -10.3 | 10.9 | 9.0 |
| 66.0 | 66.5 | 63.7 | % Profit Before Taxes/Tangible Net Worth | | | 104.1 | 100.0 | 50.3 | 64.3 |
| (119) 26.0 | (122) 25.7 | (115) 25.9 | | | (15) 16.3 | (16) 36.8 | (30) 24.3 | (38) 22.6 |  |
| 8.3 | 4.3 | 6.7 | | | | -4.0 | 10.2 | 6.3 | 4.6 |
| 14.4 | 18.9 | 16.2 | % Profit Before Taxes/Total Assets | 34.3 | 51.1 | 20.3 | 24.2 | 17.8 | 11.0 |
| 6.4 | 7.6 | 6.7 | | 12.8 | 3.8 | 2.0 | 9.7 | 5.4 | 6.8 |
| .9 | .3 | 1.0 | | 3.6 | 1.0 | -3.9 | 3.8 | 1.1 | 1.2 |
| 48.5 | 46.2 | 62.9 | Sales/Net Fixed Assets | 35.9 | 118.3 | 68.8 | 64.2 | 54.7 | 67.9 |
| 14.8 | 14.6 | 19.2 | | 4.3 | 45.9 | 19.6 | 24.4 | 23.8 | 18.3 |
| 3.7 | 3.1 | 4.4 | | .2 | 4.7 | 6.4 | 5.1 | 5.1 | 2.8 |
| 3.3 | 3.5 | 3.7 | Sales/Total Assets | 2.7 | 5.6 | 3.9 | 4.5 | 4.1 | 3.7 |
| 2.0 | 1.9 | 2.4 | | 1.2 | 1.6 | 2.5 | 2.5 | 2.8 | 1.6 |
| 1.0 | .9 | 1.1 | | .2 | .9 | 1.5 | 2.0 | 1.4 | 1.0 |
| 1.1 | 1.1 | .7 | % Depr., Dep., Amort./Sales | | | .7 | .7 | .7 | .7 |
| (123) 2.3 | (124) 2.5 | (107) 2.2 | | | (15) 2.7 | (20) 1.8 | (29) 2.2 | (31) 1.3 |  |
| 8.1 | 8.3 | 6.9 | | | | 7.5 | 4.3 | 14.6 | 4.8 |
| 1.1 | 1.9 | 1.4 | % Officers', Directors' Owners' Comp/Sales | | | | | 1.1 | |
| (32) 4.6 | (35) 4.5 | (29) 4.0 | | | | | | (10) 2.0 |  |
| 13.1 | 9.8 | 9.9 | | | | | | 6.1 | |
| 6157303M | 6632604M | 6021005M | Net Sales ($) | 5230M | 17253M | 85657M | 177578M | 575068M | 5160219M |
| 4221608M | 4884092M | 4164115M | Total Assets ($) | 8668M | 13327M | 45995M | 91655M | 578985M | 3425485M |

© RMA 2012

M = $ thousand    MM = $ million

See Pages 9 through 22 for Explanation of Ratios and Data

## Current Data Sorted by Assets | Comparative Historical Data

| Type of Statement | 0-500M | 500M-2MM | 2-10MM | 10-50MM | 50-100MM | 100-250MM | 4/1/07-3/31/08 ALL | 4/1/08-3/31/09 ALL |
|---|---|---|---|---|---|---|---|---|
| Unqualified | | 2 | 12 | 19 | 17 | 14 | 61 | 80 |
| Reviewed | 1 | 4 | 14 | 9 | 1 | | 17 | 27 |
| Compiled | 2 | 5 | 11 | | 2 | 2 | 15 | 24 |
| Tax Returns | 16 | 15 | 11 | 2 | | | 29 | 22 |
| Other | 5 | 35 | 48 | 49 | 13 | 8 | 127 | 127 |
| | | 39 (4/1-9/30/11) | | 278 (10/1/11-3/31/12) | | | | |
| **NUMBER OF STATEMENTS** | 24 | 61 | 96 | 79 | 33 | 24 | 249 | 280 |
| **ASSETS** | % | % | % | % | % | % | % | % |
| Cash & Equivalents | 28.9 | 18.8 | 19.4 | 16.6 | 13.9 | 17.4 | 20.3 | 17.6 |
| Trade Receivables (net) | 24.3 | 37.5 | 34.0 | 24.0 | 17.5 | 13.8 | 32.7 | 30.2 |
| Inventory | 2.2 | 4.1 | 3.5 | 1.1 | .9 | .3 | 2.7 | 2.3 |
| All Other Current | 7.5 | 2.3 | 4.0 | 7.4 | 7.5 | 5.3 | 4.5 | 5.5 |
| Total Current | 62.8 | 62.6 | 60.9 | 49.2 | 39.8 | 36.7 | 60.2 | 55.6 |
| Fixed Assets (net) | 20.3 | 22.4 | 23.2 | 25.8 | 26.0 | 22.1 | 19.7 | 20.7 |
| Intangibles (net) | 4.7 | 5.9 | 6.4 | 15.9 | 25.8 | 30.8 | 11.1 | 15.6 |
| All Other Non-Current | 12.2 | 9.1 | 9.4 | 9.1 | 8.4 | 10.3 | 9.0 | 8.1 |
| Total | 100.0 | 100.0 | 100.0 | 100.0 | 100.0 | 100.0 | 100.0 | 100.0 |
| **LIABILITIES** | | | | | | | | |
| Notes Payable-Short Term | 20.4 | 12.5 | 5.3 | 4.6 | .6 | 3.9 | 12.2 | 10.3 |
| Cur. Mat.-L.T.D. | 3.5 | 2.8 | 2.8 | 3.6 | 3.2 | 2.4 | 3.4 | 6.3 |
| Trade Payables | 7.8 | 11.2 | 16.3 | 12.5 | 8.2 | 3.6 | 11.8 | 12.6 |
| Income Taxes Payable | .0 | .4 | .8 | .3 | .7 | .6 | .6 | .3 |
| All Other Current | 26.6 | 17.4 | 15.0 | 20.6 | 18.1 | 18.2 | 20.8 | 21.1 |
| Total Current | 58.3 | 44.3 | 40.3 | 41.4 | 30.7 | 28.7 | 48.8 | 50.6 |
| Long-Term Debt | 27.7 | 15.8 | 14.4 | 15.9 | 22.7 | 26.6 | 16.3 | 19.3 |
| Deferred Taxes | .2 | .2 | .7 | 1.0 | .9 | 1.1 | .4 | .6 |
| All Other Non-Current | 17.6 | 12.3 | 10.9 | 9.2 | 7.2 | 6.9 | 10.7 | 8.1 |
| Net Worth | -3.7 | 27.5 | 33.6 | 32.6 | 38.6 | 36.7 | 23.8 | 21.4 |
| Total Liabilties & Net Worth | 100.0 | 100.0 | 100.0 | 100.0 | 100.0 | 100.0 | 100.0 | 100.0 |
| **INCOME DATA** | | | | | | | | |
| Net Sales | 100.0 | 100.0 | 100.0 | 100.0 | 100.0 | 100.0 | 100.0 | 100.0 |
| Gross Profit | | | | | | | | |
| Operating Expenses | 92.9 | 93.8 | 92.8 | 89.6 | 94.9 | 91.4 | 91.8 | 94.0 |
| Operating Profit | 7.1 | 6.2 | 7.2 | 10.4 | 5.1 | 8.6 | 8.2 | 6.0 |
| All Other Expenses (net) | .4 | 1.1 | 1.5 | 2.1 | 4.0 | 5.7 | 1.5 | 2.2 |
| Profit Before Taxes | 6.7 | 5.1 | 5.7 | 8.3 | 1.1 | 2.9 | 6.7 | 3.9 |
| **RATIOS** | | | | | | | | |
| Current | 3.9 | 2.9 | 2.6 | 2.1 | 2.4 | 2.1 | 2.3 | 2.3 |
| | 1.4 | 1.4 | 1.5 | 1.2 | 1.3 | 1.2 | 1.4 | 1.3 |
| | .5 | 1.0 | .9 | .8 | .8 | 1.0 | .9 | .8 |
| Quick | 2.9 | 2.7 | 2.4 | 2.0 | 1.9 | 1.7 | 2.1 | 2.1 |
| | 1.1 | 1.2 | 1.2 | 1.0 | 1.0 | 1.0 | 1.3 | 1.1 |
| | .3 | .8 | .7 | .6 | .6 | .7 | .7 | .6 |
| Sales/Receivables | 0 UND | 12 30.6 | 26 13.9 | 19 19.4 | 29 12.6 | 25 14.5 | 28 12.8 | 23 15.8 |
| | 14 26.2 | 36 10.1 | 43 8.5 | 37 9.9 | 40 9.1 | 44 8.3 | 49 7.5 | 44 8.2 |
| | 34 10.8 | 50 7.3 | 62 5.9 | 68 5.4 | 65 5.6 | 70 5.2 | 70 5.2 | 62 5.9 |
| Cost of Sales/Inventory | | | | | | | | |
| Cost of Sales/Payables | | | | | | | | |
| Sales/Working Capital | 11.8 | 8.6 | 6.1 | 6.1 | 3.9 | 7.9 | 6.5 | 6.9 |
| | 32.2 | 18.9 | 15.6 | 15.8 | 22.4 | 29.8 | 21.1 | 20.5 |
| | -16.6 | NM | -100.4 | -13.9 | -17.8 | NM | -66.0 | -34.9 |
| EBIT/Interest | 46.3 | 29.9 | 22.5 | 31.1 | 16.8 | 22.1 | 16.4 | 14.8 |
| | (17) 7.0 | (53) 12.6 | (74) 7.6 | (68) 4.5 | (27) 2.5 | (18) 1.5 | (190) 5.1 | (223) 3.7 |
| | -2.4 | 2.2 | 1.6 | .6 | .8 | -.8 | 1.0 | .4 |
| Net Profit + Depr., Dep., Amort./Cur. Mat. L/T/D | | | 3.6 | 20.2 | | | 13.4 | 5.0 |
| | | (22) | 1.9 | (25) 2.3 | | | (36) 1.8 | (46) 2.8 |
| | | | .6 | .9 | | | .8 | 1.4 |
| Fixed/Worth | .0 | .1 | .2 | .2 | .4 | .3 | .2 | .2 |
| | .5 | .7 | .7 | .8 | 1.8 | 1.7 | .7 | 1.2 |
| | -1.7 | 2.9 | 5.8 | -140.6 | -.6 | NM | -8.3 | -1.0 |
| Debt/Worth | .7 | .5 | .8 | 1.0 | .9 | 1.2 | .9 | 1.0 |
| | 4.3 | 2.6 | 1.8 | 3.3 | 4.8 | 6.9 | 2.6 | 4.4 |
| | -2.9 | 20.9 | 19.7 | -65.7 | -3.0 | NM | -20.3 | -5.1 |
| % Profit Before Taxes/Tangible Net Worth | 173.1 | 123.8 | 55.7 | 63.0 | 48.9 | 69.8 | 90.6 | 74.4 |
| | (15) 91.9 | (49) 71.3 | (77) 25.3 | (58) 32.8 | (19) 15.0 | (18) 10.3 | (181) 42.0 | (186) 30.9 |
| | 41.7 | 20.0 | 7.1 | 9.4 | -3.4 | -48.0 | 13.4 | 9.7 |
| % Profit Before Taxes/Total Assets | 74.1 | 33.4 | 18.4 | 14.9 | 10.0 | 6.7 | 27.9 | 19.3 |
| | 25.2 | 20.4 | 8.1 | 6.5 | 5.0 | .9 | 11.0 | 6.9 |
| | -.8 | 2.6 | 1.0 | .5 | -2.9 | -2.0 | .8 | -.8 |
| Sales/Net Fixed Assets | 881.4 | 169.1 | 88.4 | 31.6 | 16.2 | 18.8 | 66.4 | 58.0 |
| | 58.8 | 32.0 | 21.8 | 12.6 | 8.8 | 8.4 | 19.2 | 17.0 |
| | 13.8 | 7.5 | 5.1 | 4.0 | 2.1 | 2.3 | 8.2 | 6.4 |
| Sales/Total Assets | 8.2 | 5.3 | 3.8 | 2.7 | 1.9 | 1.1 | 3.9 | 3.7 |
| | 4.7 | 3.7 | 2.5 | 1.6 | .9 | .8 | 2.3 | 2.3 |
| | 3.0 | 2.2 | 1.5 | .7 | .5 | .4 | 1.5 | 1.2 |
| % Depr., Dep., Amort./Sales | .5 | .8 | 1.1 | 1.0 | 3.3 | | .7 | .7 |
| | (11) 1.9 | (35) 1.6 | (69) 2.6 | (67) 2.9 | (23) 4.9 | | (175) 2.2 | (177) 2.2 |
| | 4.9 | 4.1 | 7.3 | 7.7 | 13.0 | | 4.8 | 5.3 |
| % Officers', Directors' Owners' Comp/Sales | 7.3 | 3.5 | 2.7 | | | | 2.7 | 2.3 |
| | (17) 12.5 | (22) 7.9 | (27) 5.2 | | | | (66) 6.8 | (65) 5.9 |
| | 18.7 | 11.9 | 12.5 | | | | 10.5 | 11.7 |
| Net Sales ($) | 33575M | 289428M | 1478658M | 3081490M | 2937700M | 3513725M | 7081062M | 12580482M |
| Total Assets ($) | 5178M | 67021M | 498422M | 1835245M | 2422400M | 3728725M | 5058850M | 8226720M |

© RMA 2012

M = $ thousand    MM = $ million
See Pages 9 through 22 for Explanation of Ratios and Data

## Comparative Historical Data | Current Data Sorted by Sales

| 4/1/09-3/31/10 ALL | 4/1/10-3/31/11 ALL | 4/1/11-3/31/12 ALL | Type of Statement | 0-1MM | 1-3MM | 3-5MM | 5-10MM | 10-25MM | 25MM & OVER |
|---|---|---|---|---|---|---|---|---|---|
| 93 | 77 | 64 | Unqualified | 1 |  | 1 | 3 | 16 | 43 |
| 21 | 42 | 29 | Reviewed | 2 |  |  | 9 | 11 | 7 |
| 20 | 22 | 22 | Compiled | 1 | 2 | 6 | 3 | 6 | 4 |
| 34 | 31 | 44 | Tax Returns | 9 | 17 | 6 | 4 | 7 | 1 |
| 149 | 152 | 158 | Other | 4 | 17 | 16 | 25 | 41 | 55 |
|  |  |  |  | 39 (4/1-9/30/11) | | | 278 (10/1/11-3/31/12) | | |
| 317 | 324 | 317 | NUMBER OF STATEMENTS | 17 | 36 | 29 | 44 | 81 | 110 |
| % | % | % | ASSETS | % | % | % | % | % | % |
| 19.6 | 22.2 | 18.6 | Cash & Equivalents | 22.6 | 18.3 | 22.3 | 20.5 | 18.4 | 16.4 |
| 26.7 | 27.1 | 28.2 | Trade Receivables (net) | 16.6 | 24.0 | 35.5 | 34.9 | 29.8 | 25.6 |
| 1.8 | 1.4 | 2.4 | Inventory | 2.8 | 4.0 | 2.0 | 3.1 | 2.2 | 1.8 |
| 5.1 | 5.6 | 5.2 | All Other Current | 6.0 | 3.2 | 3.5 | 4.5 | 5.5 | 6.4 |
| 53.2 | 56.3 | 54.4 | Total Current | 48.1 | 49.5 | 63.3 | 63.0 | 55.9 | 50.2 |
| 21.7 | 22.2 | 23.7 | Fixed Assets (net) | 31.1 | 33.3 | 20.1 | 22.8 | 23.6 | 20.8 |
| 14.3 | 12.5 | 12.4 | Intangibles (net) | 10.2 | 7.4 | 7.0 | 4.7 | 10.8 | 20.1 |
| 10.7 | 9.0 | 9.5 | All Other Non-Current | 10.7 | 9.8 | 9.7 | 9.6 | 9.8 | 8.8 |
| 100.0 | 100.0 | 100.0 | Total | 100.0 | 100.0 | 100.0 | 100.0 | 100.0 | 100.0 |
|  |  |  | LIABILITIES |  |  |  |  |  |  |
| 13.1 | 7.1 | 7.0 | Notes Payable-Short Term | 8.3 | 14.4 | 14.7 | 3.9 | 6.9 | 3.8 |
| 3.9 | 4.8 | 3.1 | Cur. Mat.-L.T.D. | 2.2 | 3.3 | 3.5 | 2.4 | 3.5 | 2.9 |
| 10.8 | 12.3 | 11.9 | Trade Payables | 9.4 | 7.6 | 10.2 | 13.8 | 11.4 | 13.8 |
| .4 | .4 | .5 | Income Taxes Payable | .0 | .0 | .3 | 1.8 | .2 | .5 |
| 19.4 | 18.5 | 18.3 | All Other Current | 29.7 | 15.3 | 16.0 | 10.3 | 22.2 | 18.4 |
| 47.6 | 43.1 | 40.8 | Total Current | 49.6 | 40.5 | 44.6 | 32.2 | 44.3 | 39.5 |
| 18.3 | 17.4 | 17.8 | Long-Term Debt | 16.5 | 40.5 | 9.5 | 9.6 | 14.9 | 18.2 |
| .7 | .6 | .7 | Deferred Taxes | .5 | .2 | .0 | .3 | 1.3 | .8 |
| 10.7 | 10.0 | 10.6 | All Other Non-Current | 10.4 | 18.3 | 14.2 | 17.2 | 6.6 | 7.4 |
| 22.8 | 28.9 | 30.1 | Net Worth | 23.0 | .5 | 31.6 | 40.6 | 33.0 | 34.2 |
| 100.0 | 100.0 | 100.0 | Total Liabilities & Net Worth | 100.0 | 100.0 | 100.0 | 100.0 | 100.0 | 100.0 |
|  |  |  | INCOME DATA |  |  |  |  |  |  |
| 100.0 | 100.0 | 100.0 | Net Sales | 100.0 | 100.0 | 100.0 | 100.0 | 100.0 | 100.0 |
|  |  |  | Gross Profit |  |  |  |  |  |  |
| 92.9 | 92.5 | 92.3 | Operating Expenses | 87.2 | 89.2 | 90.7 | 95.2 | 92.6 | 93.2 |
| 7.1 | 7.5 | 7.7 | Operating Profit | 12.8 | 10.8 | 9.3 | 4.8 | 7.4 | 6.8 |
| 2.4 | 1.8 | 2.1 | All Other Expenses (net) | 3.8 | 2.5 | .1 | 1.5 | 1.7 | 2.7 |
| 4.6 | 5.7 | 5.6 | Profit Before Taxes | 9.0 | 8.3 | 9.2 | 3.3 | 5.6 | 4.1 |
|  |  |  | RATIOS |  |  |  |  |  |  |
| 2.1 | 3.2 | 2.5 | Current | 5.3 | 2.6 | 3.4 | 3.7 | 2.1 | 2.1 |
| 1.2 | 1.4 | 1.3 |  | 1.1 | 1.3 | 1.5 | 2.0 | 1.3 | 1.2 |
| .8 | .8 | .9 |  | .4 | .7 | 1.0 | 1.2 | .8 | .8 |
| 1.9 | 2.9 | 2.0 | Quick | 2.8 | 2.3 | 2.9 | 3.3 | 2.0 | 1.8 |
| (316) 1.0 | 1.2 | 1.1 |  | .5 | 1.1 | 1.2 | 1.7 | 1.1 | 1.1 |
| .7 | .7 | .7 |  | .3 | .4 | .8 | 1.0 | .6 | .7 |
| 20 18.1 | 16 22.4 | 20 18.4 | Sales/Receivables | 0 UND | 2 236.5 | 16 23.2 | 27 13.4 | 18 20.8 | 27 13.6 |
| 42 8.6 | 42 8.8 | 38 9.7 |  | 27 13.3 | 23 16.2 | 41 8.9 | 43 8.4 | 42 8.6 | 40 9.2 |
| 60 6.0 | 63 5.8 | 62 5.9 |  | 47 7.7 | 45 8.1 | 56 6.5 | 69 5.3 | 57 6.4 | 68 5.4 |
|  |  |  | Cost of Sales/Inventory |  |  |  |  |  |  |
|  |  |  | Cost of Sales/Payables |  |  |  |  |  |  |
| 7.4 | 5.1 | 7.0 | Sales/Working Capital | 7.4 | 9.4 | 6.3 | 4.7 | 7.0 | 8.0 |
| 27.1 | 16.3 | 18.9 |  | 34.9 | 84.7 | 20.3 | 9.2 | 18.1 | 19.4 |
| -37.3 | -31.1 | -31.9 |  | -3.3 | -18.7 | 533.0 | 39.1 | -25.4 | -31.8 |
| 17.6 | 32.5 | 29.9 | EBIT/Interest |  | 17.7 | 58.9 | 31.4 | 32.3 | 40.6 |
| (251) 3.7 | (251) 5.6 | (257) 5.7 |  |  | (34) 4.4 | (24) 11.2 | (31) 7.7 | (70) 6.5 | (90) 3.7 |
| .4 | .6 | 1.2 |  |  | 1.4 | 5.5 | .7 | 1.6 | .7 |
| 12.7 | 8.2 | 7.4 | Net Profit + Depr., Dep., Amort./Cur. Mat. L/T/D |  |  |  |  | 4.3 | 24.2 |
| (50) 2.8 | (54) 2.2 | (61) 2.3 |  |  |  |  |  | (20) 2.1 | (30) 3.1 |
| 1.1 | .9 | 1.1 |  |  |  |  |  | .5 | 1.1 |
| .2 | .1 | .2 | Fixed/Worth | .0 | .3 | .1 | .1 | .2 | .3 |
| 1.0 | .8 | .8 |  | 1.1 | 2.3 | .6 | .5 | .9 | .9 |
| -3.3 | -4.7 | 108.7 |  | -.8 | -3.0 | 1.5 | 1.4 | 5.7 | -2.2 |
| .9 | .6 | .8 | Debt/Worth | .3 | 1.9 | .5 | .5 | .8 | 1.0 |
| 3.1 | 2.7 | 2.7 |  | 5.0 | 18.4 | 1.8 | 1.7 | 2.6 | 3.5 |
| -10.2 | -16.7 | -64.9 |  | -2.6 | -6.6 | 3.6 | 5.0 | 17.8 | -6.9 |
| 67.1 | 75.8 | 86.1 | % Profit Before Taxes/Tangible Net Worth | 112.2 | 425.0 | 106.1 | 63.5 | 57.9 | 59.3 |
| (215) 26.0 | (230) 32.3 | (236) 32.8 |  | (10) 54.2 | (23) 114.9 | (25) 66.0 | (39) 28.0 | (63) 24.6 | (76) 32.1 |
| 8.4 | 5.6 | 8.6 |  | 10.3 | 20.4 | 22.1 | -3.0 | 7.4 | 3.7 |
| 18.1 | 27.0 | 22.8 | % Profit Before Taxes/Total Assets | 38.5 | 32.6 | 41.3 | 22.7 | 18.8 | 15.1 |
| 7.0 | 8.7 | 8.0 |  | 5.4 | 15.4 | 22.8 | 8.3 | 8.5 | 5.5 |
| -1.8 | .3 | .4 |  | -1.4 | .6 | 7.4 | -1.4 | 1.3 | -1.0 |
| 48.6 | 53.7 | 66.7 | Sales/Net Fixed Assets | 367.0 | 64.3 | 131.3 | 78.6 | 82.5 | 44.4 |
| 14.4 | 15.7 | 14.6 |  | 26.7 | 12.8 | 23.6 | 26.8 | 14.6 | 12.8 |
| 6.6 | 5.5 | 5.0 |  | 1.7 | 3.9 | 6.2 | 4.9 | 5.6 | 4.9 |
| 3.8 | 3.6 | 3.7 | Sales/Total Assets | 3.5 | 5.0 | 4.5 | 3.8 | 3.8 | 2.9 |
| 1.9 | 2.0 | 2.2 |  | 2.3 | 2.8 | 3.5 | 2.4 | 2.2 | 1.8 |
| 1.1 | 1.1 | 1.1 |  | .5 | 1.6 | 1.6 | 1.2 | 1.3 | .9 |
| .9 | 1.0 | 1.1 | % Depr., Dep., Amort./Sales |  | 1.5 | 1.0 | .9 | 1.1 | .8 |
| (204) 2.8 | (221) 2.8 | (213) 2.8 |  |  | (22) 3.4 | (21) 2.7 | (30) 2.3 | (59) 3.4 | (74) 2.4 |
| 6.3 | 5.8 | 7.0 |  |  | 7.9 | 8.1 | 8.1 | 8.3 | 5.9 |
| 2.4 | 2.5 | 2.9 | % Officers', Directors' Owners' Comp/Sales |  | 4.3 |  |  | 4.7 | 2.2 |
| (67) 4.8 | (82) 6.1 | (76) 6.6 |  |  | (20) 10.9 |  | (10) 7.6 | (23) 3.7 |  |
| 12.6 | 13.0 | 12.5 |  |  | 13.2 |  | 12.1 | 7.9 |  |
| 11368362M | 12886710M | 11334576M | Net Sales ($) | 7951M | 68854M | 116060M | 327963M | 1270214M | 9543534M |
| 8915552M | 8863154M | 8556991M | Total Assets ($) | 28868M | 51961M | 66991M | 345520M | 888657M | 7174994M |

© RMA 2012

M = $ thousand    MM = $ million
See Pages 9 through 22 for Explanation of Ratios and Data

## Current Data Sorted by Assets | Comparative Historical Data

| Type of Statement | 0-500M | 500M-2MM | 2-10MM | 10-50MM | 50-100MM | 100-250MM | | 4/1/07-3/31/08 ALL | 4/1/08-3/31/09 ALL |
|---|---|---|---|---|---|---|---|---|---|
| Unqualified | | 2 | 2 | 4 | | 2 | | 2 | 4 |
| Reviewed | | | | 1 | | | | 1 | 2 |
| Compiled | 1 | 2 | 1 | 1 | | | | 1 | 2 |
| Tax Returns | 1 | 4 | | | | | | 1 | 4 |
| Other | | 6 | 8 | 2 | 3 | 7 | | 12 | 18 |
| | | 9 (4/1-9/30/11) | | 38 (10/1/11-3/31/12) | | | | | |
| **NUMBER OF STATEMENTS** | 2 | 14 | 11 | 8 | 3 | 9 | | 17 | 30 |
| **ASSETS** | % | % | % | % | % | % | | % | % |
| Cash & Equivalents | | 16.7 | 21.6 | | | | | 13.9 | 17.6 |
| Trade Receivables (net) | | 25.7 | 36.2 | | | | | 25.2 | 33.8 |
| Inventory | | 3.6 | .2 | | | | | 3.8 | 1.5 |
| All Other Current | | 4.4 | 5.5 | | | | | 3.7 | 6.9 |
| Total Current | | 50.4 | 63.5 | | | | | 46.5 | 59.7 |
| Fixed Assets (net) | | 40.6 | 10.6 | | | | | 14.0 | 19.3 |
| Intangibles (net) | | 2.3 | 10.9 | | | | | 28.1 | 12.9 |
| All Other Non-Current | | 6.7 | 15.0 | | | | | 11.4 | 8.1 |
| Total | | 100.0 | 100.0 | | | | | 100.0 | 100.0 |
| **LIABILITIES** | | | | | | | | | |
| Notes Payable-Short Term | | 14.1 | 9.9 | | | | | 7.6 | 13.5 |
| Cur. Mat.-L.T.D. | | 1.5 | .4 | | | | | 2.7 | 4.4 |
| Trade Payables | | 10.5 | 6.8 | | | | | 8.1 | 18.7 |
| Income Taxes Payable | | .0 | .7 | | | | | .0 | 2.8 |
| All Other Current | | 8.2 | 29.9 | | | | | 22.2 | 18.7 |
| Total Current | | 34.2 | 47.6 | | | | | 40.6 | 58.0 |
| Long-Term Debt | | 22.7 | 8.5 | | | | | 6.8 | 23.8 |
| Deferred Taxes | | .5 | .0 | | | | | .1 | .1 |
| All Other Non-Current | | 8.0 | 1.0 | | | | | 7.9 | 11.6 |
| Net Worth | | 34.7 | 42.9 | | | | | 44.5 | 6.5 |
| Total Liabilities & Net Worth | | 100.0 | 100.0 | | | | | 100.0 | 100.0 |
| **INCOME DATA** | | | | | | | | | |
| Net Sales | | 100.0 | 100.0 | | | | | 100.0 | 100.0 |
| Gross Profit | | | | | | | | | |
| Operating Expenses | | 83.5 | 90.4 | | | | | 92.3 | 92.7 |
| Operating Profit | | 16.5 | 9.6 | | | | | 7.7 | 7.3 |
| All Other Expenses (net) | | 7.7 | -.7 | | | | | 1.9 | 2.9 |
| Profit Before Taxes | | 8.8 | 10.3 | | | | | 5.8 | 4.5 |
| **RATIOS** | | | | | | | | | |
| Current | | 2.3 | 5.2 | | | | | 2.5 | 2.1 |
| | | 1.3 | 1.0 | | | | | 1.6 | 1.3 |
| | | .7 | .7 | | | | | .7 | .6 |
| Quick | | 2.3 | 5.1 | | | | | 2.4 | 1.8 |
| | | .9 | .9 | | | | | 1.1 | 1.1 |
| | | .4 | .5 | | | | | .5 | .4 |
| Sales/Receivables | 0 UND | | 12 31.7 | | | | | 15 24.0 | 9 38.8 |
| | 11 32.4 | | 43 8.5 | | | | | 43 8.4 | 35 10.5 |
| | 50 7.3 | | 99 3.7 | | | | | 54 6.7 | 59 6.2 |
| Cost of Sales/Inventory | | | | | | | | | |
| Cost of Sales/Payables | | | | | | | | | |
| Sales/Working Capital | | 8.1 | 6.4 | | | | | 10.8 | 9.1 |
| | | 97.9 | 814.0 | | | | | 28.1 | 23.4 |
| | | -17.7 | -7.0 | | | | | -9.3 | -8.2 |
| EBIT/Interest | | | | | | | | 147.6 | 12.8 |
| | | | | | | | | (11) 5.8 | (22) .9 |
| | | | | | | | | .7 | -2.5 |
| Net Profit + Depr., Dep., Amort./Cur. Mat. L/T/D | | | | | | | | | |
| Fixed/Worth | | .2 | .1 | | | | | .2 | .2 |
| | | 2.2 | .3 | | | | | .7 | 1.8 |
| | | NM | -.2 | | | | | -.2 | -.4 |
| Debt/Worth | | .4 | .2 | | | | | .6 | 1.4 |
| | | 2.3 | .9 | | | | | 1.5 | 4.9 |
| | | NM | -4.2 | | | | | -3.3 | -2.9 |
| % Profit Before Taxes/Tangible Net Worth | | 105.4 | | | | | | 62.5 | 102.9 |
| | (11) | 63.6 | | | | | | (11) 47.0 | (18) 42.4 |
| | | 15.7 | | | | | | 13.8 | -26.4 |
| % Profit Before Taxes/Total Assets | | 58.0 | 55.8 | | | | | 29.3 | 22.5 |
| | | 15.4 | 18.3 | | | | | 6.8 | 2.8 |
| | | 2.4 | .0 | | | | | 1.9 | -11.3 |
| Sales/Net Fixed Assets | | 77.4 | 75.8 | | | | | 101.9 | 89.8 |
| | | 17.0 | 38.0 | | | | | 33.8 | 30.3 |
| | | 3.7 | 22.7 | | | | | 11.9 | 13.3 |
| Sales/Total Assets | | 6.1 | 3.9 | | | | | 6.1 | 5.1 |
| | | 3.5 | 2.3 | | | | | 1.5 | 2.9 |
| | | 1.7 | 1.5 | | | | | .9 | 1.3 |
| % Depr., Dep., Amort./Sales | | | | | | | | | .6 |
| | | | | | | | | (16) | 1.7 |
| | | | | | | | | | 4.4 |
| % Officers', Directors' Owners' Comp/Sales | | | | | | | | | |
| Net Sales ($) | 4706M | 67301M | 119030M | 285574M | 301600M | 1383952M | | 819731M | 977983M |
| Total Assets ($) | 572M | 14452M | 50017M | 211950M | 258547M | 1720990M | | 525773M | 500831M |

© RMA 2012

M = $ thousand   MM = $ million
See Pages 9 through 22 for Explanation of Ratios and Data

## Comparative Historical Data | Current Data Sorted by Sales

| 7 | 3 | 10 | Type of Statement | | | | | | |
|---|---|---|---|---|---|---|---|---|---|
|  | 1 | 1 | Unqualified | | | 1 | 1 | 3 | 5 |
| 3 |  | 1 | Reviewed | | | | | 1 | |
| 5 | 5 | 5 | Compiled | | 2 | 1 | | 1 | 1 |
| 15 | 21 | 5 | Tax Returns | | | 3 | | 1 | |
|  |  | 26 | Other | 1 | 3 | 1 | 5 | 4 | 12 |
| 4/1/09-3/31/10 ALL | 4/1/10-3/31/11 ALL | 4/1/11-3/31/12 ALL | | \<1MM | 9 (4/1-9/30/11) | | 38 (10/1/11-3/31/12) | | |
| | | | | 0-1MM | 1-3MM | 3-5MM | 5-10MM | 10-25MM | 25MM & OVER |
| 30 | 30 | 47 | NUMBER OF STATEMENTS | 2 | 5 | 6 | 6 | 10 | 18 |
| % | % | % | ASSETS | % | % | % | % | % | % |
| 28.5 | 26.1 | 19.6 | Cash & Equivalents | | | | | 17.0 | 22.3 |
| 19.2 | 24.1 | 22.8 | Trade Receivables (net) | | | | | 28.5 | 12.9 |
| 3.3 | 1.2 | 1.2 | Inventory | | | | | 5.0 | .1 |
| 7.6 | 5.1 | 4.1 | All Other Current | | | | | 6.2 | 3.7 |
| 58.5 | 56.5 | 47.6 | Total Current | | | | | 56.6 | 39.1 |
| 11.7 | 13.9 | 18.8 | Fixed Assets (net) | | | | | 11.9 | 7.6 |
| 22.2 | 21.1 | 23.4 | Intangibles (net) | | | | | 27.4 | 43.7 |
| 7.6 | 8.5 | 10.3 | All Other Non-Current | | | | | 4.1 | 9.6 |
| 100.0 | 100.0 | 100.0 | Total | | | | | 100.0 | 100.0 |
| | | | LIABILITIES | | | | | | |
| 26.0 | 1.7 | 7.1 | Notes Payable-Short Term | | | | | 14.1 | .6 |
| 2.6 | 1.8 | 1.3 | Cur. Mat.-L.T.D. | | | | | .8 | 1.8 |
| 11.8 | 11.2 | 9.8 | Trade Payables | | | | | 4.9 | 11.5 |
| .2 | .3 | .2 | Income Taxes Payable | | | | | .7 | .2 |
| 22.5 | 32.4 | 20.4 | All Other Current | | | | | 19.4 | 27.0 |
| 63.1 | 47.3 | 38.8 | Total Current | | | | | 39.9 | 41.1 |
| 24.0 | 10.7 | 17.1 | Long-Term Debt | | | | | 20.7 | 10.7 |
| .2 | .6 | 1.2 | Deferred Taxes | | | | | .0 | 2.7 |
| 8.7 | 4.6 | 6.5 | All Other Non-Current | | | | | 2.3 | 9.2 |
| 4.1 | 36.8 | 36.5 | Net Worth | | | | | 37.1 | 36.3 |
| 100.0 | 100.0 | 100.0 | Total Liabilities & Net Worth | | | | | 100.0 | 100.0 |
| | | | INCOME DATA | | | | | | |
| 100.0 | 100.0 | 100.0 | Net Sales | | | | | 100.0 | 100.0 |
| | | | Gross Profit | | | | | | |
| 95.1 | 92.0 | 88.3 | Operating Expenses | | | | | 88.2 | 90.7 |
| 4.9 | 8.0 | 11.7 | Operating Profit | | | | | 11.8 | 9.3 |
| 1.0 | 1.3 | 3.4 | All Other Expenses (net) | | | | | 1.2 | 3.0 |
| 3.9 | 6.7 | 8.3 | Profit Before Taxes | | | | | 10.6 | 6.3 |
| | | | RATIOS | | | | | | |
| 2.4 | 2.6 | 2.2 | | | | | | 6.3 | 1.8 |
| 1.4 | 1.3 | 1.1 | Current | | | | | 1.4 | 1.0 |
| .9 | .8 | .7 | | | | | | .9 | .5 |
| 2.4 | 2.3 | 2.2 | | | | | | 5.8 | 1.6 |
| 1.1 | 1.1 | 1.0 | Quick | | | | | .8 | 1.0 |
| .7 | .7 | .5 | | | | | | .5 | .5 |
| 3  139.8 | 6  64.3 | 4  81.9 | | | | | | 0  UND | 17  21.1 |
| 23  16.2 | 40  9.1 | 29  12.5 | Sales/Receivables | | | | | 27  13.5 | 31  11.9 |
| 62  5.9 | 66  5.6 | 53  6.9 | | | | | | 51  7.2 | 50  7.3 |
| | | | Cost of Sales/Inventory | | | | | | |
| | | | Cost of Sales/Payables | | | | | | |
| 8.1 | 5.8 | 6.9 | | | | | | 6.8 | 7.0 |
| 15.9 | 39.7 | 149.8 | Sales/Working Capital | | | | | 273.7 | NM |
| -25.6 | -15.4 | -16.7 | | | | | | -269.5 | -3.0 |
| 12.4 | 51.3 | 14.0 | | | | | | | 7.0 |
| (22) 3.5 | (19) 5.4 | (30) 4.9 | EBIT/Interest | | | | | | (13) 4.6 |
| -4.3 | 1.1 | .3 | | | | | | | .5 |
| | | | Net Profit + Depr., Dep., Amort./Cur. Mat. L/T/D | | | | | | |
| .1 | .2 | .2 | | | | | | .1 | .4 |
| 1.5 | .5 | 2.4 | Fixed/Worth | | | | | .8 | -.2 |
| -.4 | -1.4 | -.1 | | | | | | -.2 | -.1 |
| 1.8 | .7 | .5 | | | | | | .3 | 1.0 |
| 13.3 | 2.9 | 11.1 | Debt/Worth | | | | | 6.3 | -4.3 |
| -1.9 | -10.0 | -3.0 | | | | | | -2.4 | -1.6 |
| 90.4 | 124.4 | 86.4 | % Profit Before Taxes/Tangible Net Worth | | | | | | |
| (16) 45.1 | (21) 61.9 | (27) 55.1 | | | | | | | |
| 17.1 | 9.2 | .1 | | | | | | | |
| 32.3 | 24.6 | 27.8 | % Profit Before Taxes/Total Assets | | | | | 65.3 | 12.4 |
| 9.0 | 8.7 | 6.6 | | | | | | 15.6 | 2.8 |
| -2.9 | -1.0 | -.2 | | | | | | 2.1 | -1.1 |
| 116.7 | 60.7 | 71.8 | | | | | | 98.6 | 40.5 |
| 32.9 | 36.6 | 30.4 | Sales/Net Fixed Assets | | | | | 36.8 | 21.6 |
| 19.3 | 16.6 | 8.8 | | | | | | 22.9 | 8.2 |
| 6.0 | 3.3 | 3.8 | | | | | | 6.7 | 1.4 |
| 2.3 | 2.0 | 1.7 | Sales/Total Assets | | | | | 3.6 | 1.1 |
| 1.3 | 1.3 | 1.1 | | | | | | 1.6 | .6 |
| .5 | .4 | .6 | | | | | | | |
| (17) 1.4 | (19) 1.7 | (24) 2.0 | % Depr., Dep., Amort./Sales | | | | | | |
| 2.7 | 5.2 | 5.6 | | | | | | | |
| | | | % Officers', Directors' Owners' Comp/Sales | | | | | | |
| 1632322M | 1651943M | 2162163M | Net Sales ($) | 373M | 8923M | 22353M | 38850M | 153904M | 1937760M |
| 1130920M | 1170826M | 2256528M | Total Assets ($) | 2390M | 3435M | 12794M | 13605M | 54688M | 2169616M |

M = $ thousand     MM = $ million
See Pages 9 through 22 for Explanation of Ratios and Data

## Current Data Sorted by Assets        Comparative Historical Data

| 0-500M | 500M-2MM | 2-10MM | 10-50MM | 50-100MM | 100-250MM | | 4/1/07-3/31/08 ALL | 4/1/08-3/31/09 ALL |
|---|---|---|---|---|---|---|---|---|
| | | 7 (4/1-9/30/11) | 67 (10/1/11-3/31/12) | | | **Type of Statement** | | |
| | 3 | 5 | 3 | 4 | 1 | Unqualified | 5 | 41 |
| | | 2 | 1 | | | Reviewed | 3 | 11 |
| | | 2 | | | | Compiled | | 16 |
| 13 | 3 | | | | | Tax Returns | 3 | 18 |
| 4 | 10 | 11 | 8 | 4 | | Other | 8 | 67 |
| 17 | 16 | 20 | 12 | 8 | 1 | **NUMBER OF STATEMENTS** | 19 | 153 |
| % | % | % | % | % | % | **ASSETS** | % | % |
| 35.3 | 15.9 | 23.1 | 11.5 | | | Cash & Equivalents | 13.3 | 18.3 |
| 21.0 | 34.2 | 36.6 | 31.3 | | | Trade Receivables (net) | 31.6 | 24.3 |
| 3.1 | 9.0 | 3.4 | .8 | | | Inventory | 4.1 | 7.9 |
| 5.9 | 3.2 | 6.9 | 7.8 | | | All Other Current | 4.5 | 4.3 |
| 65.3 | 62.4 | 70.0 | 51.4 | | | Total Current | 53.6 | 54.8 |
| 21.1 | 25.0 | 16.3 | 13.2 | | | Fixed Assets (net) | 15.1 | 25.6 |
| .1 | 6.3 | 7.6 | 29.8 | | | Intangibles (net) | 19.2 | 7.8 |
| 13.5 | 6.4 | 6.0 | 5.6 | | | All Other Non-Current | 12.1 | 11.8 |
| 100.0 | 100.0 | 100.0 | 100.0 | | | Total | 100.0 | 100.0 |
| | | | | | | **LIABILITIES** | | |
| 5.0 | 6.4 | 5.6 | 9.7 | | | Notes Payable-Short Term | 38.7 | 9.0 |
| 1.5 | 1.1 | 2.0 | 1.6 | | | Cur. Mat.-L.T.D. | 8.5 | 2.8 |
| 26.9 | 12.5 | 21.8 | 13.3 | | | Trade Payables | 6.6 | 10.7 |
| .0 | .0 | 1.8 | .2 | | | Income Taxes Payable | .4 | .4 |
| 49.8 | 13.8 | 10.4 | 28.8 | | | All Other Current | 18.4 | 16.1 |
| 83.2 | 33.8 | 41.6 | 53.6 | | | Total Current | 72.6 | 38.9 |
| 25.7 | 20.6 | 11.6 | 30.1 | | | Long-Term Debt | 24.6 | 18.9 |
| .0 | .0 | .6 | .4 | | | Deferred Taxes | .7 | .5 |
| 18.3 | 5.0 | 10.2 | 8.1 | | | All Other Non-Current | 7.6 | 7.9 |
| -27.2 | 40.6 | 36.0 | 7.7 | | | Net Worth | -5.5 | 33.8 |
| 100.0 | 100.0 | 100.0 | 100.0 | | | Total Liabilities & Net Worth | 100.0 | 100.0 |
| | | | | | | **INCOME DATA** | | |
| 100.0 | 100.0 | 100.0 | 100.0 | | | Net Sales | 100.0 | 100.0 |
| | | | | | | Gross Profit | | |
| 78.6 | 95.1 | 89.2 | 89.3 | | | Operating Expenses | 89.6 | 92.9 |
| 21.4 | 4.9 | 10.8 | 10.7 | | | Operating Profit | 10.4 | 7.1 |
| .8 | .4 | 2.9 | 2.1 | | | All Other Expenses (net) | 5.6 | 2.2 |
| 20.7 | 4.5 | 7.9 | 8.6 | | | Profit Before Taxes | 4.7 | 4.9 |
| | | | | | | **RATIOS** | | |
| 7.3 | 5.0 | 4.8 | 1.3 | | | | 2.4 | 3.2 |
| .9 | 2.7 | 1.6 | .9 | | | Current | .9 | 1.5 |
| .3 | 1.2 | 1.1 | .7 | | | | .6 | 1.0 |
| 5.3 | 4.1 | 4.6 | 1.2 | | | | 2.3 | 2.5 |
| .7 | 2.4 | 1.3 | .8 | | | Quick | .8 | 1.2 |
| .3 | .8 | .8 | .5 | | | | .3 | .6 |
| 0 UND | 2 194.2 | 32 11.4 | 36 10.1 | | | | 15 24.4 | 11 32.2 |
| 2 217.3 | 33 11.1 | 57 6.4 | 65 5.6 | | | Sales/Receivables | 45 8.0 | 39 9.4 |
| 30 12.2 | 65 5.6 | 74 4.9 | 104 3.5 | | | | 83 4.4 | 61 6.0 |
| | | | | | | Cost of Sales/Inventory | | |
| | | | | | | Cost of Sales/Payables | | |
| 7.4 | 6.2 | 4.1 | 15.1 | | | | 6.5 | 5.4 |
| -138.3 | 9.9 | 12.6 | -51.9 | | | Sales/Working Capital | -60.7 | 13.9 |
| -9.9 | 33.0 | 80.8 | -10.8 | | | | -9.1 | 335.4 |
| 60.5 | 35.1 | 34.5 | 41.2 | | | | 10.9 | 15.0 |
| (11) 19.6 | (12) 11.3 | (16) 5.2 | (10) 2.8 | | | EBIT/Interest | (18) 2.0 | (120) 3.1 |
| 1.3 | 8.0 | -1.6 | -1.9 | | | | .1 | .5 |
| | | | | | | Net Profit + Depr., Dep., | | 31.2 |
| | | | | | | Amort./Cur. Mat. L/T/D | (18) 5.5 | |
| | | | | | | | | 1.5 |
| .0 | .0 | .1 | .4 | | | | .1 | .2 |
| .2 | .2 | .4 | NM | | | Fixed/Worth | 1.6 | .7 |
| -111.6 | 5.3 | 73.5 | -.1 | | | | -.3 | 5.0 |
| .6 | .3 | .7 | 3.7 | | | | 1.2 | .8 |
| 4.3 | 1.4 | 2.0 | -7.9 | | | Debt/Worth | 10.2 | 2.0 |
| -2.4 | NM | 81.1 | -1.6 | | | | -2.0 | 16.8 |
| | | 68.7 | 95.8 | | | % Profit Before Taxes/Tangible | 51.9 | 51.9 |
| | (12) 25.8 | (16) 28.3 | | | | Net Worth | (10) 29.8 | (120) 17.6 |
| | | 13.5 | -9.2 | | | | 8.4 | 3.7 |
| 143.5 | 47.9 | 48.9 | 21.1 | | | % Profit Before Taxes/Total | 15.6 | 16.8 |
| 19.1 | 16.3 | 8.1 | 7.4 | | | Assets | 6.5 | 5.3 |
| 7.0 | 4.2 | -1.7 | -2.8 | | | | -1.2 | -.5 |
| UND | 149.2 | 89.7 | 80.7 | | | | 64.2 | 52.5 |
| 128.0 | 82.0 | 33.6 | 17.0 | | | Sales/Net Fixed Assets | 22.1 | 18.9 |
| 17.2 | 4.8 | 12.5 | 10.5 | | | | 13.3 | 4.7 |
| 8.8 | 4.2 | 2.8 | 2.5 | | | | 5.1 | 4.0 |
| 5.7 | 3.6 | 2.4 | 1.8 | | | Sales/Total Assets | 2.6 | 1.8 |
| 2.3 | 2.4 | 1.9 | .7 | | | | .9 | .9 |
| | | .6 | | | | | .3 | .8 |
| | (18) 1.0 | | | | | % Depr., Dep., Amort./Sales | (10) 1.0 | (111) 1.8 |
| | | 2.4 | | | | | 3.7 | 4.5 |
| 2.8 | | | | | | | | 2.2 |
| (10) 6.6 | | | | | | % Officers', Directors' | | (38) 6.1 |
| 17.2 | | | | | | Owners' Comp/Sales | | 9.1 |
| 13754M | 67425M | 252125M | 395883M | 697281M | 139518M | Net Sales ($) | 902002M | 4616574M |
| 3156M | 18636M | 99368M | 269074M | 651394M | 163815M | Total Assets ($) | 864962M | 3786595M |

M = $ thousand     MM = $ million
See Pages 9 through 22 for Explanation of Ratios and Data

## Comparative Historical Data                              Current Data Sorted by Sales

| 4/1/09-3/31/10 ALL | 4/1/10-3/31/11 ALL | 4/1/11-3/31/12 ALL | Type of Statement | 0-1MM | 1-3MM | 3-5MM | 5-10MM | 10-25MM | 25MM & OVER |
|---|---|---|---|---|---|---|---|---|---|
| 12 | 9 | 13 | Unqualified | | 1 | | | 6 | 6 |
| 9 | 4 | 6 | Reviewed | | 1 | | 1 | 1 | 1 |
| 1 | 1 | 2 | Compiled | | | | 2 | | 1 |
| 16 | 12 | 16 | Tax Returns | 7 | 7 | 2 | | | |
| 21 | 35 | 37 | Other | 5 | 5 | 3 | 9 | 6 | 9 |
| | | | | 7 (4/1-9/30/11) | | | 67 (10/1/11-3/31/12) | | |
| 59 | 61 | 74 | **NUMBER OF STATEMENTS** | 12 | 14 | 6 | 12 | 13 | 17 |
| % | % | % | **ASSETS** | % | % | % | % | % | % |
| 18.8 | 28.5 | 22.2 | Cash & Equivalents | 39.6 | 14.0 | | 23.7 | 22.7 | 16.8 |
| 34.4 | 27.4 | 29.3 | Trade Receivables (net) | 14.5 | 26.8 | | 34.6 | 39.1 | 31.4 |
| 7.1 | 3.3 | 3.9 | Inventory | 1.7 | 9.1 | | 2.3 | .7 | 1.5 |
| 3.0 | 6.0 | 5.6 | All Other Current | .1 | 8.7 | | 3.3 | 5.4 | 7.2 |
| 63.3 | 65.2 | 61.1 | Total Current | 55.8 | 58.6 | | 63.9 | 67.9 | 56.9 |
| 17.3 | 14.8 | 17.6 | Fixed Assets (net) | 28.8 | 24.6 | | 12.6 | 10.6 | 10.0 |
| 9.5 | 11.5 | 13.0 | Intangibles (net) | .1 | 10.7 | | 14.6 | 14.8 | 25.2 |
| 9.9 | 8.5 | 8.3 | All Other Non-Current | 15.4 | 6.0 | | 8.8 | 6.7 | 7.8 |
| 100.0 | 100.0 | 100.0 | Total | 100.0 | 100.0 | | 100.0 | 100.0 | 100.0 |
| | | | **LIABILITIES** | | | | | | |
| 13.9 | 10.6 | 5.7 | Notes Payable-Short Term | 5.4 | 4.2 | | 7.8 | 3.4 | 8.8 |
| 3.0 | 1.5 | 1.7 | Cur. Mat.-L.T.D. | .4 | 1.6 | | 1.4 | 1.5 | 1.9 |
| 14.6 | 17.3 | 17.8 | Trade Payables | 39.3 | 5.2 | | 14.4 | 17.4 | 15.5 |
| .2 | .4 | .6 | Income Taxes Payable | .0 | .3 | | .5 | 1.9 | .4 |
| 20.1 | 19.3 | 23.4 | All Other Current | 37.6 | 31.3 | | 13.6 | 12.9 | 20.9 |
| 51.9 | 49.1 | 49.1 | Total Current | 82.7 | 42.6 | | 37.7 | 37.1 | 47.5 |
| 13.8 | 14.2 | 20.4 | Long-Term Debt | 26.2 | 26.6 | | 7.8 | 9.4 | 22.5 |
| .5 | .7 | .5 | Deferred Taxes | .0 | .4 | | .1 | .4 | 1.3 |
| 8.6 | 6.8 | 9.8 | All Other Non-Current | 18.5 | 12.2 | | 1.9 | 18.4 | 4.0 |
| 25.2 | 29.2 | 20.2 | Net Worth | -27.4 | 18.1 | | 52.5 | 34.7 | 24.6 |
| 100.0 | 100.0 | 100.0 | Total Liabilities & Net Worth | 100.0 | 100.0 | | 100.0 | 100.0 | 100.0 |
| | | | **INCOME DATA** | | | | | | |
| 100.0 | 100.0 | 100.0 | Net Sales | 100.0 | 100.0 | | 100.0 | 100.0 | 100.0 |
| | | | Gross Profit | | | | | | |
| 93.1 | 93.2 | 87.8 | Operating Expenses | 81.7 | 88.8 | | 86.3 | 90.2 | 88.8 |
| 6.9 | 6.8 | 12.2 | Operating Profit | 18.3 | 11.2 | | 13.7 | 9.8 | 11.2 |
| 1.4 | 1.2 | 1.7 | All Other Expenses (net) | 1.1 | 1.1 | | .2 | 2.1 | 1.9 |
| 5.5 | 5.6 | 10.5 | Profit Before Taxes | 17.2 | 10.1 | | 13.5 | 7.7 | 9.3 |
| | | | **RATIOS** | | | | | | |
| 2.4 | 3.7 | 3.4 | | 7.5 | 6.4 | | 4.1 | 5.2 | 2.1 |
| 1.4 | 1.6 | 1.4 | Current | .8 | 1.9 | | 2.0 | 1.8 | 1.2 |
| 1.0 | .8 | .8 | | .3 | .8 | | .7 | 1.1 | 1.0 |
| 2.0 | 3.5 | 2.8 | | 7.5 | 3.1 | | 3.7 | 4.9 | 1.8 |
| 1.2 | 1.5 | 1.2 | Quick | .7 | 1.2 | | 2.0 | 1.7 | 1.1 |
| .5 | .6 | .7 | | .3 | .5 | | .5 | .9 | .8 |
| 18 20.5 | 4 93.4 | 19 18.8 | | 0 UND | 0 UND | | 19 18.9 | 51 7.2 | 45 8.2 |
| 39 9.4 | 31 11.7 | 47 7.7 | Sales/Receivables | 0 UND | 41 8.9 | | 51 7.2 | 66 5.5 | 57 6.4 |
| 63 5.8 | 58 6.3 | 70 5.2 | | 25 14.8 | 66 5.5 | | 76 4.8 | 94 3.9 | 79 4.6 |
| | | | | | | | | | |
| | | | Cost of Sales/Inventory | | | | | | |
| | | | | | | | | | |
| | | | Cost of Sales/Payables | | | | | | |
| 5.5 | 5.2 | 5.3 | | 7.2 | 6.7 | | 5.2 | 4.2 | 4.3 |
| 19.7 | 16.4 | 16.9 | Sales/Working Capital | -106.8 | 22.1 | | 13.4 | 7.1 | 18.2 |
| 117.3 | -40.0 | -28.2 | | -6.8 | -27.9 | | -17.8 | 34.4 | -86.7 |
| 12.4 | 25.2 | 35.8 | | | 59.4 | | | 35.0 | 38.8 |
| (45) 3.6 | (36) 7.1 | (55) 7.5 | EBIT/Interest | | (12) 23.4 | | | (10) 7.6 | (13) 2.5 |
| .4 | 1.8 | .3 | | | 1.7 | | | -1.9 | .3 |
| | | 5.3 | | | | | | | |
| | | (10) 3.4 | Net Profit + Depr., Dep., Amort./Cur. Mat. L/T/D | | | | | | |
| | | .9 | | | | | | | |
| .1 | .1 | .1 | | .0 | .0 | | .0 | .1 | .2 |
| .5 | .4 | .5 | Fixed/Worth | .4 | .4 | | .2 | .4 | 1.0 |
| 1.7 | -5.7 | -2.1 | | NM | NM | | 1.2 | NM | -.2 |
| .9 | .8 | .7 | | .6 | .7 | | .4 | .8 | 1.4 |
| 2.3 | 2.7 | 3.5 | Debt/Worth | 7.5 | 3.6 | | .8 | 3.4 | 6.0 |
| 19.5 | -17.0 | -4.6 | | -3.4 | -3.7 | | NM | NM | -3.4 |
| 54.4 | 106.4 | 95.5 | | | | | | 97.1 | |
| (46) 22.7 | (44) 56.9 | (47) 28.6 | % Profit Before Taxes/Tangible Net Worth | | | | | (10) 39.1 | |
| .3 | 3.3 | 14.4 | | | | | | -5.7 | |
| 12.3 | 50.6 | 49.1 | | 259.7 | 68.1 | | 54.8 | 37.8 | 17.2 |
| 6.7 | 12.2 | 11.1 | % Profit Before Taxes/Total Assets | 16.1 | 15.8 | | 14.7 | 10.0 | 4.8 |
| -.8 | 1.3 | -.1 | | 1.5 | 2.1 | | 7.7 | .8 | -1.1 |
| 168.9 | 197.2 | 115.5 | | UND | UND | | 326.4 | 87.0 | 65.9 |
| 30.4 | 46.2 | 38.6 | Sales/Net Fixed Assets | 82.0 | 75.8 | | 68.7 | 39.3 | 17.8 |
| 10.6 | 14.4 | 10.8 | | 1.5 | 9.2 | | 12.6 | 13.4 | 10.2 |
| 5.0 | 6.1 | 4.1 | | 8.3 | 5.9 | | 4.5 | 2.8 | 2.5 |
| 2.5 | 3.0 | 2.4 | Sales/Total Assets | 4.4 | 3.5 | | 2.7 | 2.3 | 1.4 |
| 1.3 | 1.4 | 1.3 | | .6 | 2.0 | | 2.1 | 1.4 | 1.0 |
| .4 | .9 | .7 | | | | | | .5 | .8 |
| (37) 1.6 | (32) 2.1 | (44) 1.4 | % Depr., Dep., Amort./Sales | | | | | (10) 1.1 | (12) 1.9 |
| 3.1 | 3.9 | 3.6 | | | | | | 2.4 | 4.2 |
| 2.8 | 2.3 | 3.7 | | | | | | | |
| (19) 6.3 | (15) 6.8 | (21) 6.5 | % Officers', Directors' Owners' Comp/Sales | | | | | | |
| 22.6 | 9.6 | 12.1 | | | | | | | |
| 1737488M | 1698987M | 1565986M | Net Sales ($) | 4983M | 27986M | 24257M | 88530M | 216440M | 1203790M |
| 1541380M | 1262831M | 1205443M | Total Assets ($) | 2263M | 17576M | 10484M | 56538M | 141511M | 977071M |

M = $ thousand     MM = $ million
See Pages 9 through 22 for Explanation of Ratios and Data

# FINANCE AND INSURANCE

## Current Data Sorted by Assets      Comparative Historical Data

| 0-500M | 500M-2MM | 2-10MM | 10-50MM | 50-100MM | 100-250MM | Type of Statement | 4/1/07-3/31/08 ALL | 4/1/08-3/31/09 ALL |
|---|---|---|---|---|---|---|---|---|
| | | 5 | 6 | 3 | 2 | Unqualified | 8 | 16 |
| | | 1 | | | | Reviewed | 2 | |
| | | | | | | Compiled | 1 | |
| 2 | 2 | 4 | 1 | 1 | 2 | Tax Returns | 2 | |
| 1 | 2 | 2 | | | 2 | Other | 17 | 15 |
| | 1 (4/1-9/30/11) | | 34 (10/1/11-3/31/12) | | | | | |
| 3 | 4 | 12 | 8 | 4 | 4 | NUMBER OF STATEMENTS | 30 | 34 |
| % | % | % | % | % | % | | % | % |
| | | | | | | **ASSETS** | | |
| | | 7.1 | | | | Cash & Equivalents | 13.4 | 22.7 |
| | | 60.6 | | | | Trade Receivables (net) | 53.4 | 44.9 |
| | | .3 | | | | Inventory | 1.0 | 3.4 |
| | | .3 | | | | All Other Current | 5.9 | 5.5 |
| | | 68.3 | | | | Total Current | 73.7 | 76.5 |
| | | 5.9 | | | | Fixed Assets (net) | 10.6 | 5.6 |
| | | .5 | | | | Intangibles (net) | 5.5 | 4.2 |
| | | 25.3 | | | | All Other Non-Current | 10.2 | 13.8 |
| | | 100.0 | | | | Total | 100.0 | 100.0 |
| | | | | | | **LIABILITIES** | | |
| | | 18.6 | | | | Notes Payable-Short Term | 23.4 | 21.7 |
| | | .2 | | | | Cur. Mat.-L.T.D. | 2.0 | 2.9 |
| | | 8.9 | | | | Trade Payables | 2.1 | 5.4 |
| | | .0 | | | | Income Taxes Payable | .1 | .1 |
| | | 27.6 | | | | All Other Current | 22.3 | 22.5 |
| | | 55.2 | | | | Total Current | 49.8 | 52.6 |
| | | 7.8 | | | | Long-Term Debt | 15.2 | 13.6 |
| | | .0 | | | | Deferred Taxes | .0 | .6 |
| | | 8.4 | | | | All Other Non-Current | 8.9 | 11.4 |
| | | 28.6 | | | | Net Worth | 26.1 | 21.8 |
| | | 100.0 | | | | Total Liabilities & Net Worth | 100.0 | 100.0 |
| | | | | | | **INCOME DATA** | | |
| | | 100.0 | | | | Net Sales | 100.0 | 100.0 |
| | | | | | | Gross Profit | | |
| | | 65.0 | | | | Operating Expenses | 62.1 | 74.4 |
| | | 35.0 | | | | Operating Profit | 37.9 | 25.6 |
| | | 14.7 | | | | All Other Expenses (net) | 19.5 | 14.0 |
| | | 20.3 | | | | Profit Before Taxes | 18.5 | 11.7 |
| | | | | | | **RATIOS** | | |
| | | 1.4 | | | | | 3.0 | 2.4 |
| | | 1.3 | | | | Current | 1.3 | 1.4 |
| | | .6 | | | | | 1.1 | 1.1 |
| | | 1.4 | | | | | 2.3 | 2.4 |
| | | 1.3 | | | | Quick | 1.3 | 1.2 |
| | | .5 | | | | | 1.0 | .7 |
| | 37 | 9.8 | | | | | 4   102.0 | 1   383.6 |
| | 406 | .9 | | | | Sales/Receivables | 213   1.7 | 64   5.7 |
| | 1217 | .3 | | | | | 1518   .2 | 1376   .3 |
| | | | | | | Cost of Sales/Inventory | | |
| | | | | | | Cost of Sales/Payables | | |
| | | .7 | | | | | .7 | .8 |
| | | 4.6 | | | | Sales/Working Capital | 1.7 | 3.6 |
| | | NM | | | | | 19.6 | 17.0 |
| | | 4.2 | | | | | 8.2 | 13.2 |
| | (10) | 2.9 | | | | EBIT/Interest | (20) 4.4 | (17) 3.8 |
| | | 2.1 | | | | | 2.0 | 1.2 |
| | | | | | | Net Profit + Depr., Dep., Amort./Cur. Mat. L/T/D | | |
| | | .0 | | | | | .0 | .0 |
| | | .1 | | | | Fixed/Worth | .0 | .1 |
| | | .5 | | | | | 2.4 | .3 |
| | | 1.0 | | | | | 1.7 | 1.6 |
| | | 2.6 | | | | Debt/Worth | 3.9 | 3.6 |
| | | 9.9 | | | | | NM | 12.4 |
| | | 74.9 | | | | | 42.9 | 56.7 |
| | (11) | 39.5 | | | | % Profit Before Taxes/Tangible Net Worth | (23) 25.3 | (30) 22.6 |
| | | 10.6 | | | | | 6.1 | 5.5 |
| | | 11.0 | | | | | 15.6 | 13.8 |
| | | 5.6 | | | | % Profit Before Taxes/Total Assets | 9.0 | 4.2 |
| | | 3.9 | | | | | 2.0 | .6 |
| | | 904.1 | | | | | 748.1 | 196.2 |
| | | 29.7 | | | | Sales/Net Fixed Assets | 35.4 | 38.7 |
| | | 3.7 | | | | | 9.2 | 21.9 |
| | | 1.0 | | | | | 1.7 | 2.2 |
| | | .3 | | | | Sales/Total Assets | .4 | .6 |
| | | .2 | | | | | .1 | .1 |
| | | | | | | | .4 | .4 |
| | | | | | | % Depr., Dep., Amort./Sales | (19) 1.1 | (19) 1.0 |
| | | | | | | | 3.6 | 2.2 |
| | | | | | | % Officers', Directors' Owners' Comp/Sales | | |
| 3850M | 10599M | 80815M | 62326M | 127047M | 435756M | Net Sales ($) | 709441M | 1451828M |
| 609M | 3052M | 55869M | 176016M | 310408M | 699918M | Total Assets ($) | 1342908M | 1903519M |

M = $ thousand     MM = $ million
See Pages 9 through 22 for Explanation of Ratios and Data

## Comparative Historical Data / Current Data Sorted by Sales

| 7 | 9 | 16 | Type of Statement | 2 | 3 | 3 | 2 | 2 | 4 |
|---|---|---|---|---|---|---|---|---|---|
|  |  |  | Unqualified |  |  |  |  |  |  |
| 1 | 1 | 1 | Reviewed |  |  |  |  |  | 1 |
| 1 | 1 | 2 | Compiled |  |  |  |  |  |  |
| 5 | 1 | 9 | Tax Returns | 4 | 5 |  | 1 | 3 | 1 |
| 12 | 3 | 9 | Other | 1 | 3 |  |  |  |  |
| 4/1/09- | 4/1/10- | 4/1/11- |  | 1 (4/1-9/30/11) |  |  | 34 (10/1/11-3/31/12) |  |  |
| 3/31/10 | 3/31/11 | 3/31/12 |  | 0-1MM | 1-3MM | 3-5MM | 5-10MM | 10-25MM | 25MM & OVER |
| ALL | ALL | ALL |  |  |  |  |  |  |  |
| 26 | 16 | 35 | **NUMBER OF STATEMENTS** | 7 | 11 | 3 | 3 | 5 | 6 |
| % | % | % | **ASSETS** | % | % | % | % | % | % |
| 17.6 | 7.3 | 7.3 | Cash & Equivalents |  | 8.0 |  |  |  |  |
| 45.2 | 50.8 | 56.0 | Trade Receivables (net) |  | 51.9 |  |  |  |  |
| .4 | .7 | 1.8 | Inventory |  | 5.6 |  |  |  |  |
| 3.5 | 4.3 | 2.4 | All Other Current |  | 4.5 |  |  |  |  |
| 66.8 | 63.0 | 67.5 | Total Current |  | 70.1 |  |  |  |  |
| 8.1 | 3.7 | 8.1 | Fixed Assets (net) |  | 4.3 |  |  |  |  |
| 4.8 | 8.6 | 1.1 | Intangibles (net) |  | .0 |  |  |  |  |
| 20.4 | 24.6 | 23.3 | All Other Non-Current |  | 25.6 |  |  |  |  |
| 100.0 | 100.0 | 100.0 | Total |  | 100.0 |  |  |  |  |
|  |  |  | **LIABILITIES** |  |  |  |  |  |  |
| 24.3 | 19.3 | 20.0 | Notes Payable-Short Term |  | 23.1 |  |  |  |  |
| 2.6 | 3.6 | 1.1 | Cur. Mat.-L.T.D. |  | .5 |  |  |  |  |
| 5.2 | 8.4 | 5.3 | Trade Payables |  | 8.3 |  |  |  |  |
| .2 | .0 | .0 | Income Taxes Payable |  | .0 |  |  |  |  |
| 18.3 | 16.4 | 22.4 | All Other Current |  | 24.5 |  |  |  |  |
| 50.6 | 47.6 | 48.7 | Total Current |  | 56.5 |  |  |  |  |
| 15.3 | 11.3 | 15.9 | Long-Term Debt |  | 19.5 |  |  |  |  |
| .4 | .2 | .8 | Deferred Taxes |  | .0 |  |  |  |  |
| 7.1 | 18.8 | 9.4 | All Other Non-Current |  | 22.3 |  |  |  |  |
| 26.7 | 22.1 | 25.1 | Net Worth |  | 1.8 |  |  |  |  |
| 100.0 | 100.0 | 100.0 | Total Liabilities & Net Worth |  | 100.0 |  |  |  |  |
|  |  |  | **INCOME DATA** |  |  |  |  |  |  |
| 100.0 | 100.0 | 100.0 | Net Sales |  | 100.0 |  |  |  |  |
|  |  |  | Gross Profit |  |  |  |  |  |  |
| 85.0 | 66.0 | 63.6 | Operating Expenses |  | 68.8 |  |  |  |  |
| 15.0 | 34.0 | 36.4 | Operating Profit |  | 31.2 |  |  |  |  |
| 5.3 | 9.3 | 11.4 | All Other Expenses (net) |  | 10.2 |  |  |  |  |
| 9.7 | 24.7 | 24.9 | Profit Before Taxes |  | 21.0 |  |  |  |  |
|  |  |  | **RATIOS** |  |  |  |  |  |  |
| 2.9 | 2.7 | 2.6 |  |  | 1.6 |  |  |  |  |
| 1.2 | 1.7 | 1.3 | Current |  | 1.3 |  |  |  |  |
| .8 | 1.1 | 1.0 |  |  | .5 |  |  |  |  |
| 2.8 | 2.2 | 2.5 |  |  | 1.4 |  |  |  |  |
| 1.2 | 1.3 | 1.3 | Quick |  | 1.2 |  |  |  |  |
| .8 | .7 | .4 |  |  | .3 |  |  |  |  |
| 0 UND | 33 11.0 | 20 18.6 |  | 0 UND |  |  |  |  |  |
| 431 .8 | 195 1.9 | 406 .9 | Sales/Receivables | 261 1.4 |  |  |  |  |  |
| 1522 .2 | 1036 .4 | 1217 .3 |  | 1217 .3 |  |  |  |  |  |
|  |  |  | Cost of Sales/Inventory |  |  |  |  |  |  |
|  |  |  | Cost of Sales/Payables |  |  |  |  |  |  |
| .9 | .8 | .8 |  |  | 1.1 |  |  |  |  |
| 5.3 | 1.7 | 3.0 | Sales/Working Capital |  | 5.9 |  |  |  |  |
| -28.4 | 216.9 | 86.1 |  |  | -34.1 |  |  |  |  |
| 5.0 | 8.7 | 6.3 |  |  |  |  |  |  |  |
| (15) 3.4 | (14) 4.7 | (27) 3.3 | EBIT/Interest |  |  |  |  |  |  |
| 2.3 | 3.0 | 2.0 |  |  |  |  |  |  |  |
|  |  |  | Net Profit + Depr., Dep., Amort./Cur. Mat. L/T/D |  |  |  |  |  |  |
| .0 | .0 | .0 |  |  | .0 |  |  |  |  |
| .1 | .0 | .1 | Fixed/Worth |  | .1 |  |  |  |  |
| 7.4 | NM | .5 |  |  | -.8 |  |  |  |  |
| 1.5 | 1.5 | 1.0 |  |  | 2.4 |  |  |  |  |
| 3.7 | 4.9 | 3.1 | Debt/Worth |  | 6.1 |  |  |  |  |
| 18.7 | NM | 7.8 |  |  | -6.0 |  |  |  |  |
| 103.9 | 63.1 | 66.5 |  |  |  |  |  |  |  |
| (21) 13.6 | (12) 37.5 | (32) 41.5 | % Profit Before Taxes/Tangible Net Worth |  |  |  |  |  |  |
| 8.2 | 12.9 | 11.2 |  |  |  |  |  |  |  |
| 17.8 | 22.4 | 14.5 |  |  | 16.2 |  |  |  |  |
| 4.8 | 9.5 | 5.9 | % Profit Before Taxes/Total Assets |  | 5.9 |  |  |  |  |
| 1.1 | 5.2 | 3.7 |  |  | 1.7 |  |  |  |  |
| 171.1 | 796.6 | 365.3 |  |  | 999.8 |  |  |  |  |
| 95.0 | 187.1 | 37.7 | Sales/Net Fixed Assets |  | 215.8 |  |  |  |  |
| 21.2 | 27.4 | 13.1 |  |  | 11.9 |  |  |  |  |
| 3.2 | 1.0 | 1.1 |  |  | 4.0 |  |  |  |  |
| .3 | .4 | .4 | Sales/Total Assets |  | .4 |  |  |  |  |
| .2 | .2 | .2 |  |  | .2 |  |  |  |  |
| .7 |  | .3 |  |  |  |  |  |  |  |
| (11) .9 |  | (21) .9 | % Depr., Dep., Amort./Sales |  |  |  |  |  |  |
| 2.0 |  | 2.3 |  |  |  |  |  |  |  |
|  |  |  | % Officers', Directors' Owners' Comp/Sales |  |  |  |  |  |  |
| 344718M | 816110M | 720393M | Net Sales ($) | 3127M | 21117M | 11232M | 22006M | 81661M | 581250M |
| 806053M | 1114913M | 1245872M | Total Assets ($) | 24104M | 45153M | 68719M | 128603M | 291903M | 687390M |

© RMA 2012

M = $ thousand     MM = $ million
See Pages 9 through 22 for Explanation of Ratios and Data

# FINANCE—Sales Financing  NAICS 522220

| Current Data Sorted by Assets | | | | | | | Comparative Historical Data | |
|---|---|---|---|---|---|---|---|---|
| | 2 | 12 | 43 | 21 | 22 | **Type of Statement** | | |
| | 1 | 22 | 18 | | 2 | Unqualified | 58 | 84 |
| 2 | 6 | 7 | 1 | | | Reviewed | 33 | 36 |
| 9 | 11 | 7 | 3 | | | Compiled | 20 | 17 |
| 4 | 16 | 37 | 44 | 20 | 12 | Tax Returns | 14 | 29 |
| | 27 (4/1-9/30/11) | | 295 (10/1/11-3/31/12) | | | Other | 100 | 99 |
| | | | | | | | 4/1/07- | 4/1/08- |
| | | | | | | | 3/31/08 | 3/31/09 |
| 0-500M | 500M-2MM | 2-10MM | 10-50MM | 50-100MM | 100-250MM | | ALL | ALL |
| 15 | 36 | 85 | 109 | 41 | 36 | NUMBER OF STATEMENTS | 225 | 265 |
| % | % | % | % | % | % | **ASSETS** | % | % |
| 35.2 | 15.6 | 6.4 | 3.5 | 7.1 | 3.0 | Cash & Equivalents | 5.8 | 5.2 |
| 31.5 | 27.7 | 54.5 | 49.7 | 54.3 | 48.6 | Trade Receivables (net) | 46.1 | 46.8 |
| .0 | 11.1 | 5.1 | 4.7 | 8.2 | 6.7 | Inventory | 5.1 | 4.0 |
| .5 | 8.9 | 6.0 | 8.3 | 11.8 | 8.6 | All Other Current | 11.9 | 8.0 |
| 67.1 | 63.2 | 72.0 | 66.2 | 81.3 | 66.8 | Total Current | 68.9 | 64.0 |
| 21.1 | 10.0 | 8.3 | 12.1 | 4.4 | 4.4 | Fixed Assets (net) | 10.2 | 13.3 |
| .1 | 6.9 | 1.5 | .9 | .3 | 3.6 | Intangibles (net) | 1.2 | .9 |
| 11.6 | 19.9 | 18.2 | 20.8 | 14.1 | 25.2 | All Other Non-Current | 19.7 | 21.8 |
| 100.0 | 100.0 | 100.0 | 100.0 | 100.0 | 100.0 | Total | 100.0 | 100.0 |
| | | | | | | **LIABILITIES** | | |
| 59.8 | 17.1 | 24.7 | 29.7 | 35.8 | 19.3 | Notes Payable-Short Term | 27.8 | 29.3 |
| 10.5 | 1.4 | 4.7 | 5.7 | 3.5 | 7.9 | Cur. Mat.-L.T.D. | 5.1 | 5.3 |
| 7.0 | 4.5 | 3.3 | 2.6 | 4.0 | 4.3 | Trade Payables | 4.1 | 3.2 |
| .2 | .0 | .0 | .1 | .5 | 1.0 | Income Taxes Payable | .1 | .1 |
| 16.7 | 22.3 | 14.3 | 6.4 | 5.2 | 6.9 | All Other Current | 8.1 | 8.5 |
| 94.2 | 45.3 | 47.0 | 44.5 | 48.9 | 39.3 | Total Current | 45.2 | 46.3 |
| 5.4 | 9.3 | 13.3 | 18.2 | 18.0 | 29.0 | Long-Term Debt | 21.0 | 19.8 |
| .7 | .4 | .3 | .5 | .9 | 1.7 | Deferred Taxes | .6 | .4 |
| 3.2 | 6.9 | 10.7 | 8.5 | 5.8 | 5.6 | All Other Non-Current | 9.3 | 7.8 |
| -3.4 | 38.1 | 28.7 | 28.4 | 26.4 | 24.4 | Net Worth | 23.9 | 25.7 |
| 100.0 | 100.0 | 100.0 | 100.0 | 100.0 | 100.0 | Total Liabilties & Net Worth | 100.0 | 100.0 |
| | | | | | | **INCOME DATA** | | |
| 100.0 | 100.0 | 100.0 | 100.0 | 100.0 | 100.0 | Net Sales | 100.0 | 100.0 |
| | | | | | | Gross Profit | | |
| 59.4 | 59.5 | 72.4 | 69.7 | 66.5 | 69.6 | Operating Expenses | 66.8 | 69.1 |
| 40.6 | 40.5 | 27.6 | 30.3 | 33.5 | 30.4 | Operating Profit | 33.2 | 30.9 |
| 12.0 | 14.9 | 8.9 | 12.7 | 10.1 | 10.3 | All Other Expenses (net) | 17.3 | 15.7 |
| 28.7 | 25.6 | 18.7 | 17.6 | 23.4 | 20.1 | Profit Before Taxes | 15.9 | 15.2 |
| | | | | | | **RATIOS** | | |
| 9.0 | 7.8 | 2.6 | 2.9 | 2.5 | 2.5 | | 2.9 | 2.4 |
| 1.3 | 2.0 | 1.6 | 1.4 | 1.4 | 1.3 | Current | 1.4 | 1.3 |
| .3 | .7 | 1.2 | 1.0 | 1.2 | 1.2 | | 1.1 | .9 |
| 9.0 | 5.8 | 2.3 | 1.7 | 1.8 | 1.9 | | 2.2 | 1.9 |
| 1.3 | 1.2 | 1.3 | 1.2 | 1.3 | 1.2 | Quick | 1.2 | 1.2 |
| .3 | .1 | .5 | .4 | .3 | .3 | | .4 | .3 |
| 0 UND | 0 UND | 27 13.5 | 38 9.7 | 14 25.2 | 21 17.1 | | 6 63.2 | 14 25.2 |
| 0 UND | 5 72.1 | 365 1.0 | 521 .7 | 456 .8 | 456 .8 | Sales/Receivables | 281 1.3 | 340 1.1 |
| 1825 .2 | 912 .4 | 1217 .3 | 1217 .3 | 1217 .3 | 1217 .3 | | 1117 .3 | 1295 .3 |
| | | | | | | Cost of Sales/Inventory | | |
| | | | | | | Cost of Sales/Payables | | |
| .4 | .3 | .6 | .7 | .6 | .5 | | .6 | .7 |
| 116.0 | 7.3 | 1.3 | 1.8 | 1.0 | 1.2 | Sales/Working Capital | 2.0 | 2.2 |
| -2.0 | -24.5 | 10.0 | NM | 3.1 | 17.3 | | 20.5 | -55.9 |
| | 15.2 | 6.7 | 4.9 | 5.8 | 8.4 | | 6.5 | 4.8 |
| (21) | 7.3 | (64) 4.0 | (79) 2.8 | (32) 3.6 | (29) 2.8 | EBIT/Interest | (118) 2.5 | (145) 2.4 |
| | 2.7 | 2.0 | 1.7 | 2.6 | 2.0 | | 1.4 | 1.4 |
| | | | 43.2 | | | | 22.9 | 39.6 |
| | | (11) | .4 | | | Net Profit + Depr., Dep., | (15) 1.5 | (13) 2.8 |
| | | | .0 | | | Amort./Cur. Mat. L/T/D | .1 | .2 |
| .0 | .0 | .0 | .0 | .0 | .0 | | .0 | .0 |
| .0 | .0 | .0 | .1 | .0 | .0 | Fixed/Worth | .0 | .0 |
| 8.6 | .3 | .2 | .6 | .2 | .2 | | .3 | .5 |
| .6 | .3 | 1.4 | 1.7 | 2.3 | 2.8 | | 1.9 | 1.6 |
| 3.4 | 2.4 | 3.3 | 3.1 | 3.5 | 4.3 | Debt/Worth | 4.7 | 3.9 |
| -22.0 | 19.4 | 7.8 | 7.2 | 5.1 | 7.1 | | 10.9 | 10.7 |
| 147.8 | 61.5 | 50.5 | 43.6 | 54.5 | 50.6 | % Profit Before Taxes/Tangible | 43.2 | 25.2 |
| (11) 21.6 | (29) 16.3 | (75) 27.7 | (107) 20.4 | 26.8 | 24.8 | Net Worth | (213) 20.5 | (242) 14.0 |
| 12.5 | 5.5 | 8.6 | 5.3 | 16.7 | 10.9 | | 8.6 | 4.2 |
| 31.2 | 15.2 | 12.5 | 9.3 | 10.1 | 8.1 | % Profit Before Taxes/Total | 7.7 | 6.9 |
| 10.8 | 5.6 | 6.3 | 4.6 | 5.7 | 5.1 | Assets | 3.5 | 3.1 |
| 7.0 | 2.3 | 1.7 | 1.3 | 3.8 | 1.6 | | 1.1 | .5 |
| UND | UND | UND | 135.3 | 188.3 | 181.9 | | 348.0 | 201.4 |
| UND | UND | 83.2 | 34.3 | 43.3 | 50.9 | Sales/Net Fixed Assets | 47.4 | 44.2 |
| 1.9 | 44.2 | 17.9 | 5.2 | 13.5 | 8.1 | | 12.4 | 5.8 |
| 11.4 | 2.1 | .9 | .5 | .5 | .5 | | .5 | .4 |
| 1.0 | .3 | .4 | .3 | .3 | .2 | Sales/Total Assets | .3 | .3 |
| .1 | .1 | .2 | .2 | .2 | .1 | | .2 | .2 |
| | .2 | .3 | .4 | .5 | .3 | | .4 | .6 |
| (11) | .4 | (45) .5 | (79) 1.1 | (26) 1.0 | (24) .7 | % Depr., Dep., Amort./Sales | (142) 1.0 | (159) 1.1 |
| | 45.6 | 4.3 | 3.5 | 2.0 | 2.1 | | 2.6 | 5.2 |
| | | 4.1 | | | | | 2.2 | 2.4 |
| | (21) | 8.5 | | | | % Officers', Directors' | (45) 5.7 | (43) 7.6 |
| | | 16.3 | | | | Owners' Comp/Sales | 11.0 | 16.3 |
| 16968M | 75305M | 311640M | 1291431M | 1723033M | 3723625M | Net Sales ($) | 4310857M | 4093600M |
| 3815M | 42614M | 452648M | 2599755M | 3051296M | 5870103M | Total Assets ($) | 7877668M | 9119247M |

M = $ thousand    MM = $ million
See Pages 9 through 22 for Explanation of Ratios and Data

## Comparative Historical Data / Current Data Sorted by Sales

| | | | Type of Statement | 0-1MM | 1-3MM | 3-5MM | 5-10MM | 10-25MM | 25MM & OVER |
|---|---|---|---|---|---|---|---|---|---|
| 88 | 81 | 100 | Unqualified | 2 | 11 | 7 | 16 | 31 | 33 |
| 37 | 33 | 43 | Reviewed | 9 | 12 | 6 | 10 | 2 | 4 |
| 25 | 24 | 16 | Compiled | 6 | 6 | 2 | | 2 | |
| 24 | 24 | 30 | Tax Returns | 19 | 6 | 3 | 2 | | |
| 88 | 98 | 133 | Other | 29 | 24 | 8 | 29 | 21 | 22 |
| 4/1/09-3/31/10 ALL | 4/1/10-3/31/11 ALL | 4/1/11-3/31/12 ALL | | 27 (4/1-9/30/11) | 295 (10/1/11-3/31/12) | | | | |
| 262 | 260 | 322 | **NUMBER OF STATEMENTS** | 65 | 59 | 26 | 57 | 56 | 59 |
| % | % | % | **ASSETS** | % | % | % | % | % | % |
| 6.1 | 8.6 | 7.5 | Cash & Equivalents | 13.4 | 5.3 | 9.6 | 4.4 | 8.4 | 4.2 |
| 46.0 | 43.0 | 48.1 | Trade Receivables (net) | 43.3 | 51.5 | 43.5 | 49.8 | 50.2 | 48.5 |
| 4.8 | 4.1 | 6.0 | Inventory | 2.9 | 1.7 | 5.9 | 6.0 | 4.1 | 15.4 |
| 7.5 | 8.7 | 7.9 | All Other Current | 7.0 | 8.0 | 8.5 | 10.3 | 8.8 | 5.1 |
| 64.4 | 64.4 | 69.4 | Total Current | 66.6 | 66.6 | 67.5 | 70.6 | 71.5 | 73.1 |
| 13.9 | 13.4 | 9.4 | Fixed Assets (net) | 9.8 | 9.4 | 11.5 | 6.3 | 11.2 | 9.5 |
| 1.6 | 1.3 | 1.9 | Intangibles (net) | .9 | .5 | 3.5 | 2.5 | 1.9 | 3.2 |
| 20.1 | 20.9 | 19.2 | All Other Non-Current | 22.7 | 23.5 | 17.5 | 20.7 | 15.3 | 14.3 |
| 100.0 | 100.0 | 100.0 | Total | 100.0 | 100.0 | 100.0 | 100.0 | 100.0 | 100.0 |
| | | | **LIABILITIES** | | | | | | |
| 26.2 | 23.1 | 28.0 | Notes Payable-Short Term | 26.1 | 24.1 | 30.6 | 27.9 | 32.3 | 28.9 |
| 6.2 | 7.3 | 5.1 | Cur. Mat.-L.T.D. | 6.9 | 5.7 | 2.7 | 4.7 | 5.3 | 4.0 |
| 3.8 | 3.2 | 3.5 | Trade Payables | 2.2 | 1.0 | 2.3 | 4.9 | 5.1 | 5.4 |
| .2 | .2 | .2 | Income Taxes Payable | .0 | .0 | .2 | .2 | .3 | .6 |
| 9.7 | 10.1 | 10.6 | All Other Current | 21.7 | 10.9 | 5.3 | 7.7 | 7.1 | 6.6 |
| 46.1 | 43.9 | 47.5 | Total Current | 57.0 | 41.7 | 41.0 | 45.3 | 50.1 | 45.5 |
| 22.7 | 19.0 | 16.5 | Long-Term Debt | 9.5 | 18.5 | 14.2 | 14.0 | 21.2 | 21.2 |
| .7 | .7 | .6 | Deferred Taxes | .4 | .4 | 1.1 | .3 | .5 | 1.5 |
| 7.9 | 7.6 | 8.0 | All Other Non-Current | 8.3 | 12.1 | 10.9 | 8.4 | 5.2 | 4.5 |
| 22.5 | 28.7 | 27.4 | Net Worth | 24.8 | 27.4 | 32.8 | 32.1 | 23.0 | 27.4 |
| 100.0 | 100.0 | 100.0 | Total Liabilities & Net Worth | 100.0 | 100.0 | 100.0 | 100.0 | 100.0 | 100.0 |
| | | | **INCOME DATA** | | | | | | |
| 100.0 | 100.0 | 100.0 | Net Sales | 100.0 | 100.0 | 100.0 | 100.0 | 100.0 | 100.0 |
| | | | Gross Profit | | | | | | |
| 74.1 | 71.1 | 68.4 | Operating Expenses | 52.2 | 65.6 | 74.2 | 75.3 | 71.1 | 77.2 |
| 25.9 | 28.9 | 31.6 | Operating Profit | 47.8 | 34.4 | 25.8 | 24.7 | 28.9 | 22.8 |
| 12.7 | 11.7 | 11.3 | All Other Expenses (net) | 18.9 | 11.0 | 9.3 | 9.5 | 11.1 | 5.9 |
| 13.2 | 17.2 | 20.3 | Profit Before Taxes | 28.9 | 23.3 | 16.5 | 15.2 | 17.9 | 16.9 |
| | | | **RATIOS** | | | | | | |
| 2.4 | 2.9 | 3.0 | | 5.4 | 3.2 | 3.6 | 2.8 | 1.9 | 2.6 |
| 1.4 | 1.5 | 1.5 | Current | 1.5 | 1.4 | 1.7 | 1.5 | 1.3 | 1.4 |
| 1.0 | 1.1 | 1.1 | | .8 | 1.0 | 1.3 | 1.2 | 1.1 | 1.2 |
| 2.0 | 2.4 | 2.3 | | 4.6 | 3.2 | 2.7 | 1.6 | 1.7 | 2.0 |
| 1.3 | 1.3 | 1.3 | Quick | 1.3 | 1.3 | 1.4 | 1.2 | 1.2 | 1.2 |
| .2 | .3 | .3 | | .1 | .2 | .2 | .4 | .4 | .4 |
| 5  76.4 | 6  65.4 | 14  25.2 | | 0 UND | 31  11.6 | 10  37.6 | 24  14.9 | 11  32.2 | 20  18.6 |
| 252  1.4 | 178  2.0 | 365  1.0 | Sales/Receivables | 730  .5 | 912  .4 | 365  1.0 | 304  1.2 | 332  1.1 | 281  1.3 |
| 1193  .3 | 1025  .4 | 1217  .3 | | 1825  .2 | 1217  .3 | 1217  .3 | 730  .5 | 912  .4 | 912  .4 |
| | | | Cost of Sales/Inventory | | | | | | |
| | | | Cost of Sales/Payables | | | | | | |
| .7 | .7 | .6 | | .3 | .5 | .7 | .7 | .7 | .8 |
| 2.0 | 2.0 | 1.5 | Sales/Working Capital | .8 | 1.2 | 1.4 | 2.1 | 2.1 | 2.4 |
| 188.3 | 60.0 | 21.8 | | -4.4 | -64.1 | 16.7 | 7.9 | 36.9 | 24.4 |
| 5.8 | 7.2 | 6.5 | | 10.9 | 6.2 | 4.1 | 6.3 | 5.0 | 8.6 |
| (177)  2.4 | (171)  3.1 | (232)  3.5 | EBIT/Interest | (33)  4.2 | (34)  3.8 | (22)  2.4 | (42)  3.7 | (45)  2.7 | (56)  4.2 |
| 1.4 | 1.6 | 1.9 | | 2.0 | 2.0 | 1.5 | 1.6 | 1.9 | 2.6 |
| 2.0 | 5.3 | 2.3 | | | | | | | 9.6 |
| (15)  .5 | (18)  .3 | (29)  .4 | Net Profit + Depr., Dep., Amort./Cur. Mat. L/T/D | | | | | (10)  1.6 | |
| .1 | .1 | .1 | | | | | | | .6 |
| .0 | .0 | .0 | | .0 | .0 | .0 | .0 | .0 | .0 |
| .1 | .0 | .0 | Fixed/Worth | .0 | .0 | .1 | .0 | .1 | .1 |
| .7 | .5 | .3 | | .0 | .1 | .3 | .2 | .5 | .8 |
| 1.6 | 1.2 | 1.6 | | .6 | 1.6 | .8 | 1.1 | 2.4 | 2.2 |
| 3.5 | 3.4 | 3.4 | Debt/Worth | 3.4 | 3.3 | 2.7 | 2.6 | 4.3 | 3.5 |
| 7.7 | 7.0 | 7.3 | | 14.8 | 6.8 | 8.1 | 8.6 | 7.0 | 5.3 |
| 30.8 | 38.9 | 48.8 | | 49.9 | 34.6 | 55.3 | 41.4 | 39.7 | 65.1 |
| (237)  13.2 | (237)  17.0 | (299)  23.7 | % Profit Before Taxes/Tangible Net Worth | (57)  15.1 | (53)  17.4 | (24)  18.2 | (53)  22.6 | (53)  23.8 | 41.1 |
| 4.0 | 5.7 | 8.5 | | 5.0 | 7.2 | 4.3 | 6.8 | 10.2 | 23.9 |
| 7.1 | 9.0 | 10.8 | | 10.8 | 10.2 | 11.6 | 9.9 | 9.5 | 14.0 |
| 3.0 | 4.2 | 5.2 | % Profit Before Taxes/Total Assets | 4.2 | 3.6 | 4.7 | 5.8 | 5.1 | 7.9 |
| .6 | 1.3 | 1.8 | | .8 | 1.7 | 1.3 | 1.5 | 1.9 | 5.0 |
| 235.9 | 264.0 | 916.3 | | UND | 999.8 | 138.5 | 294.5 | 73.7 | 120.1 |
| 38.7 | 49.4 | 60.1 | Sales/Net Fixed Assets | UND | 113.1 | 43.1 | 44.6 | 23.9 | 40.8 |
| 7.0 | 6.5 | 9.6 | | 33.7 | 13.6 | 6.7 | 19.8 | 4.8 | 8.8 |
| .6 | .7 | .7 | | .3 | .4 | .9 | 1.0 | .6 | 1.2 |
| .3 | .3 | .3 | Sales/Total Assets | .2 | .2 | .3 | .4 | .4 | .6 |
| .2 | .2 | .2 | | .1 | .1 | .2 | .2 | .2 | .3 |
| .4 | .4 | .3 | | .3 | .2 | .4 | .4 | .4 | .3 |
| (157)  1.1 | (156)  .9 | (191)  .8 | % Depr., Dep., Amort./Sales | (18)  5.4 | (34)  .5 | (16)  .6 | (39)  .6 | (42)  1.1 | (42)  .7 |
| 4.0 | 4.9 | 2.6 | | 46.5 | 5.0 | 1.3 | 1.8 | 3.7 | 2.0 |
| 3.8 | 2.3 | 3.7 | | 7.5 | 5.2 | | | | |
| (43)  7.4 | (37)  7.1 | (45)  10.8 | % Officers', Directors' Owners' Comp/Sales | (13)  14.4 | (13)  12.0 | | | | |
| 19.3 | 15.7 | 19.1 | | 21.8 | 14.8 | | | | |
| 5453004M | 4167742M | 7142002M | Net Sales ($) | 26747M | 114867M | 103718M | 408392M | 874049M | 5614229M |
| 9259504M | 8469361M | 12020231M | Total Assets ($) | 163302M | 705721M | 372342M | 1467420M | 3030503M | 6280943M |

M = $ thousand    MM = $ million
See Pages 9 through 22 for Explanation of Ratios and Data

## Current Data Sorted by Assets     Comparative Historical Data

| 0-500M | 500M-2MM | 2-10MM | 10-50MM | 50-100MM | 100-250MM | Type of Statement | 4/1/07-3/31/08 ALL | 4/1/08-3/31/09 ALL |
|---|---|---|---|---|---|---|---|---|
| | 1 | 11 | 29 | 11 | 19 | Unqualified | 75 | 82 |
| | 3 | 20 | 12 | | | Reviewed | 28 | 28 |
| 3 | 18 | 16 | 9 | | | Compiled | 28 | 33 |
| 3 | 8 | 4 | 3 | | | Tax Returns | 25 | 19 |
| 10 | 13 | 32 | 34 | 10 | 19 | Other | 102 | 134 |
| | 45 (4/1-9/30/11) | | 243 (10/1/11-3/31/12) | | | | | |
| 16 | 43 | 83 | 87 | 21 | 38 | **NUMBER OF STATEMENTS** | 258 | 296 |
| % | % | % | % | % | % | **ASSETS** | % | % |
| 27.9 | 7.9 | 6.2 | 6.5 | 5.7 | 5.8 | Cash & Equivalents | 6.5 | 7.3 |
| 47.4 | 65.7 | 61.9 | 73.5 | 76.4 | 65.7 | Trade Receivables (net) | 70.8 | 68.1 |
| 5.0 | 1.0 | 3.4 | 1.3 | 1.6 | 1.6 | Inventory | 1.5 | 1.4 |
| 9.4 | 2.2 | 4.1 | 4.3 | .6 | 6.7 | All Other Current | 5.4 | 6.3 |
| 89.7 | 76.7 | 75.6 | 85.6 | 84.3 | 79.9 | Total Current | 84.2 | 83.1 |
| 2.6 | 11.2 | 5.3 | 3.8 | 3.6 | 4.3 | Fixed Assets (net) | 5.8 | 4.9 |
| .4 | 1.8 | 1.0 | 2.3 | .5 | 5.8 | Intangibles (net) | 1.9 | 1.4 |
| 7.3 | 10.3 | 18.1 | 8.3 | 11.6 | 10.0 | All Other Non-Current | 8.1 | 10.6 |
| 100.0 | 100.0 | 100.0 | 100.0 | 100.0 | 100.0 | Total | 100.0 | 100.0 |
| | | | | | | **LIABILITIES** | | |
| 30.7 | 28.0 | 33.5 | 40.4 | 29.2 | 31.7 | Notes Payable-Short Term | 41.1 | 38.2 |
| .0 | 2.9 | .9 | 3.1 | 4.6 | 2.3 | Cur. Mat.-L.T.D. | 2.8 | 3.4 |
| 3.4 | 1.3 | 2.3 | 1.5 | 1.2 | 2.2 | Trade Payables | 2.1 | 2.7 |
| .0 | .0 | .1 | .2 | .1 | .3 | Income Taxes Payable | .1 | .1 |
| 7.3 | 9.3 | 8.2 | 4.4 | 4.4 | 9.3 | All Other Current | 9.0 | 7.4 |
| 41.5 | 41.5 | 45.1 | 49.6 | 39.4 | 45.9 | Total Current | 55.1 | 51.7 |
| 4.7 | 16.2 | 7.4 | 5.8 | 15.1 | 17.2 | Long-Term Debt | 9.6 | 11.2 |
| .0 | .3 | .0 | .0 | .0 | .6 | Deferred Taxes | .0 | .0 |
| 11.5 | 18.3 | 15.6 | 12.3 | 12.9 | 7.9 | All Other Non-Current | 11.5 | 9.9 |
| 42.3 | 23.8 | 31.9 | 32.3 | 32.6 | 28.5 | Net Worth | 23.7 | 27.2 |
| 100.0 | 100.0 | 100.0 | 100.0 | 100.0 | 100.0 | Total Liabilities & Net Worth | 100.0 | 100.0 |
| | | | | | | **INCOME DATA** | | |
| 100.0 | 100.0 | 100.0 | 100.0 | 100.0 | 100.0 | Net Sales | 100.0 | 100.0 |
| | | | | | | Gross Profit | | |
| 68.8 | 76.2 | 73.7 | 68.7 | 63.6 | 72.3 | Operating Expenses | 71.4 | 77.1 |
| 31.2 | 23.8 | 26.3 | 31.3 | 36.4 | 27.7 | Operating Profit | 28.6 | 22.9 |
| 5.3 | 11.4 | 9.2 | 12.1 | 12.0 | 7.9 | All Other Expenses (net) | 15.9 | 13.0 |
| 25.9 | 12.4 | 17.1 | 19.2 | 24.4 | 19.9 | Profit Before Taxes | 12.7 | 9.9 |
| | | | | | | **RATIOS** | | |
| 3.1 | 4.4 | 2.4 | 2.5 | 6.8 | 2.2 | Current | 2.3 | 2.8 |
| 2.4 | 1.9 | 1.7 | 1.7 | 1.7 | 1.5 | | 1.4 | 1.5 |
| 1.9 | 1.3 | 1.3 | 1.4 | 1.4 | 1.3 | | 1.2 | 1.2 |
| 2.5 | 3.9 | 2.4 | 2.5 | 6.8 | 1.7 | Quick | 2.1 | 2.5 |
| 1.9 | 1.9 | 1.5 | 1.5 | 1.5 | 1.4 | | 1.3 | 1.4 |
| 1.4 | 1.3 | 1.2 | 1.3 | 1.4 | 1.1 | | 1.1 | 1.1 |
| 0 UND | 79 4.6 | 51 7.2 | 332 1.1 | 406 .9 | 140 2.6 | Sales/Receivables | 176 2.1 | 125 2.9 |
| 107 3.4 | 521 .7 | 608 .6 | 912 .4 | 912 .4 | 730 .5 | | 871 .4 | 697 .5 |
| 608 .6 | 912 .4 | 912 .4 | 1217 .3 | 1825 .2 | 1217 .3 | | 1370 .3 | 1147 .3 |
| | | | | | | Cost of Sales/Inventory | | |
| | | | | | | Cost of Sales/Payables | | |
| .7 | .8 | .7 | .6 | .4 | .6 | Sales/Working Capital | .7 | .7 |
| 1.0 | 1.3 | 1.5 | 1.1 | .6 | 1.5 | | 1.4 | 1.7 |
| 6.4 | 3.6 | 7.0 | 1.9 | 2.2 | 3.9 | | 5.7 | 3.9 |
| 8.1 | 5.1 | 7.1 | 5.1 | 6.0 | 6.8 | EBIT/Interest | 3.5 | 4.2 |
| (12) 3.5 | (33) 2.3 | (66) 3.4 | (66) 3.6 | (13) 4.0 | (28) 4.3 | | (138) 2.0 | (193) 2.2 |
| 1.8 | 1.3 | 1.8 | 2.1 | 3.3 | 2.7 | | 1.3 | 1.3 |
| | | 17.1 | 129.2 | | | Net Profit + Depr., Dep., Amort./Cur. Mat. L/T/D | 4.7 | 12.3 |
| | | (10) 2.9 | (10) 10.0 | | | | (12) .9 | (24) 4.5 |
| | | .8 | 2.2 | | | | .2 | .1 |
| .0 | .0 | .0 | .0 | .0 | .0 | Fixed/Worth | .0 | .0 |
| .0 | .1 | .0 | .0 | .0 | .1 | | .1 | .1 |
| .1 | 3.7 | .3 | .2 | .1 | .3 | | .4 | .4 |
| .7 | .9 | 1.2 | 1.3 | 1.3 | 1.8 | Debt/Worth | 2.0 | 1.5 |
| 1.1 | 3.3 | 2.4 | 2.6 | 2.8 | 2.9 | | 4.2 | 4.0 |
| 7.4 | 28.7 | 4.9 | 5.0 | 6.4 | 8.6 | | 10.5 | 11.4 |
| 138.9 | 38.8 | 41.0 | 42.0 | 52.4 | 48.3 | % Profit Before Taxes/Tangible Net Worth | 38.4 | 44.3 |
| 37.5 | (33) 21.2 | (77) 22.1 | (80) 19.3 | 24.7 | (35) 27.8 | | (231) 16.7 | (262) 17.2 |
| 18.9 | 8.6 | 5.4 | 9.8 | 8.6 | 15.4 | | 5.3 | 4.6 |
| 21.2 | 11.0 | 11.1 | 9.9 | 12.3 | 12.1 | % Profit Before Taxes/Total Assets | 6.8 | 7.5 |
| 14.7 | 4.2 | 5.2 | 5.7 | 4.5 | 6.5 | | 3.2 | 3.7 |
| 5.3 | .8 | 1.1 | 2.1 | 2.2 | 2.0 | | .9 | .5 |
| UND | 361.0 | 250.5 | 241.2 | 124.7 | 56.3 | Sales/Net Fixed Assets | 120.4 | 121.4 |
| 200.5 | 51.9 | 38.1 | 41.0 | 41.4 | 32.3 | | 30.6 | 33.2 |
| 37.7 | 10.0 | 14.2 | 18.4 | 26.5 | 8.5 | | 15.2 | 12.3 |
| 2.5 | .8 | .8 | .6 | .5 | .9 | Sales/Total Assets | .6 | .8 |
| .5 | .4 | .3 | .3 | .3 | .3 | | .3 | .3 |
| .4 | .3 | .2 | .2 | .1 | .2 | | .2 | .2 |
| | .3 | .4 | .4 | .3 | .6 | % Depr., Dep., Amort./Sales | .6 | .5 |
| | (29) .8 | (59) .8 | (57) .8 | (17) .7 | (27) 1.1 | | (169) 1.1 | (188) 1.2 |
| | 3.4 | 1.9 | 1.6 | 1.3 | 3.1 | | 2.3 | 2.4 |
| | | 1.3 | 3.6 | | | % Officers', Directors' Owners' Comp/Sales | 4.1 | 3.2 |
| | | (14) 4.9 | (17) 9.6 | | | | (51) 11.7 | (50) 7.7 |
| | | 14.3 | 17.4 | | | | 23.1 | 18.8 |
| 6795M | 28902M | 307932M | 1204340M | 525977M | 3378172M | Net Sales ($) | 4326682M | 5785172M |
| 3991M | 48333M | 460943M | 1960076M | 1441826M | 6039379M | Total Assets ($) | 7687990M | 10274047M |

## Comparative Historical Data / Current Data Sorted by Sales

| Type of Statement | 4/1/09-3/31/10 ALL | 4/1/10-3/31/11 ALL | 4/1/11-3/31/12 ALL | 0-1MM | 1-3MM | 3-5MM | 5-10MM | 10-25MM | 25MM & OVER |
|---|---|---|---|---|---|---|---|---|---|
| Unqualified | 76 | 79 | 71 | 3 | 9 | 11 | 17 | 11 | 20 |
| Reviewed | 23 | 25 | 35 | 9 | 10 | 10 | 1 | 5 | |
| Compiled | 55 | 49 | 46 | 18 | 14 | 4 | 4 | 2 | 4 |
| Tax Returns | 21 | 15 | 18 | 10 | 5 | 1 | | | 2 |
| Other | 122 | 89 | 118 | 28 | 22 | 12 | 17 | 10 | 29 |
| | | | | 45 (4/1-9/30/11) | | | 243 (10/1/11-3/31/12) | | |
| **NUMBER OF STATEMENTS** | 297 | 257 | 288 | 68 | 60 | 38 | 39 | 28 | 55 |
| **ASSETS** | % | % | % | % | % | % | % | % | % |
| Cash & Equivalents | 7.5 | 7.4 | 7.6 | 7.7 | 7.6 | 4.3 | 9.4 | 11.5 | 6.8 |
| Trade Receivables (net) | 70.5 | 68.3 | 66.7 | 59.4 | 68.4 | 81.3 | 61.6 | 68.6 | 66.6 |
| Inventory | 1.4 | .8 | 2.1 | .3 | 2.8 | 1.5 | 2.3 | 3.4 | 3.3 |
| All Other Current | 4.9 | 6.0 | 4.3 | 3.8 | 5.6 | .9 | 7.2 | 3.2 | 4.1 |
| Total Current | 84.3 | 82.5 | 80.8 | 71.2 | 84.3 | 88.0 | 80.5 | 86.7 | 80.9 |
| Fixed Assets (net) | 4.4 | 4.7 | 5.3 | 6.5 | 5.2 | 3.6 | 4.1 | 2.7 | 7.4 |
| Intangibles (net) | 2.4 | 2.1 | 2.1 | .9 | 1.2 | 1.1 | 1.6 | 1.8 | 5.5 |
| All Other Non-Current | 8.9 | 10.6 | 11.8 | 21.4 | 9.3 | 7.3 | 13.7 | 8.8 | 6.2 |
| Total | 100.0 | 100.0 | 100.0 | 100.0 | 100.0 | 100.0 | 100.0 | 100.0 | 100.0 |
| **LIABILITIES** | | | | | | | | | |
| Notes Payable-Short Term | 35.4 | 32.9 | 34.1 | 31.1 | 41.6 | 39.0 | 32.6 | 26.9 | 30.8 |
| Cur. Mat.-L.T.D. | 1.9 | 2.5 | 2.3 | 1.8 | .1 | 3.2 | 4.9 | 4.5 | 1.5 |
| Trade Payables | 2.0 | 2.0 | 1.9 | 1.2 | .9 | 2.3 | 2.0 | 3.7 | 2.5 |
| Income Taxes Payable | .1 | .1 | .1 | .0 | .1 | .1 | .1 | .4 | .3 |
| All Other Current | 10.2 | 9.8 | 7.0 | 6.3 | 4.6 | 10.7 | 9.9 | 9.8 | 4.6 |
| Total Current | 49.6 | 47.3 | 45.4 | 40.3 | 47.4 | 55.2 | 49.6 | 45.3 | 39.7 |
| Long-Term Debt | 11.4 | 10.8 | 9.9 | 10.5 | 7.4 | 3.2 | 11.8 | 13.8 | 13.2 |
| Deferred Taxes | .0 | .0 | .1 | .0 | .2 | .0 | .0 | .0 | .4 |
| All Other Non-Current | 13.7 | 14.3 | 13.6 | 19.5 | 13.2 | 11.7 | 8.0 | 13.4 | 12.0 |
| Net Worth | 25.3 | 27.5 | 31.0 | 29.7 | 31.7 | 29.9 | 30.6 | 27.4 | 34.7 |
| Total Liabilities & Net Worth | 100.0 | 100.0 | 100.0 | 100.0 | 100.0 | 100.0 | 100.0 | 100.0 | 100.0 |
| **INCOME DATA** | | | | | | | | | |
| Net Sales | 100.0 | 100.0 | 100.0 | 100.0 | 100.0 | 100.0 | 100.0 | 100.0 | 100.0 |
| Gross Profit | | | | | | | | | |
| Operating Expenses | 74.7 | 72.9 | 71.4 | 68.1 | 69.5 | 70.3 | 72.2 | 76.1 | 75.1 |
| Operating Profit | 25.3 | 27.1 | 28.6 | 31.9 | 30.5 | 29.7 | 27.8 | 23.9 | 24.9 |
| All Other Expenses (net) | 12.3 | 11.2 | 10.2 | 12.8 | 12.3 | 11.1 | 8.0 | 7.2 | 7.2 |
| Profit Before Taxes | 13.0 | 15.9 | 18.4 | 19.1 | 18.2 | 18.6 | 19.7 | 16.7 | 17.6 |

### RATIOS

| | 4/1/09-3/31/10 ALL | 4/1/10-3/31/11 ALL | 4/1/11-3/31/12 ALL | 0-1MM | 1-3MM | 3-5MM | 5-10MM | 10-25MM | 25MM & OVER |
|---|---|---|---|---|---|---|---|---|---|
| Current | 2.7 | 3.2 | 2.8 | 2.9 | 5.2 | 2.5 | 1.8 | 2.8 | 4.5 |
| | 1.6 | 1.7 | 1.7 | 1.9 | 1.7 | 1.6 | 1.6 | 1.7 | 1.8 |
| | 1.3 | 1.3 | 1.3 | 1.2 | 1.3 | 1.3 | 1.4 | 1.5 | 1.4 |
| Quick | 2.6 | 2.9 | 2.6 | 2.7 | 3.5 | 2.5 | 1.8 | 2.7 | 3.3 |
| | 1.4 | 1.5 | 1.5 | 1.8 | 1.6 | 1.5 | 1.5 | 1.5 | 1.5 |
| | 1.2 | 1.3 | 1.3 | 1.0 | 1.2 | 1.2 | 1.1 | 1.3 | 1.3 |
| Sales/Receivables | 276  1.3 | 165  2.2 | 135  2.7 | 0  UND | 159  2.3 | 608  .6 | 66  5.5 | 61  6.0 | 130  2.8 |
| | 716  .5 | 680  .5 | 730  .5 | 608  .6 | 912  .4 | 912  .4 | 456  .8 | 456  .8 | 332  1.1 |
| | 1207  .3 | 1176  .3 | 1217  .3 | 1217  .3 | 1217  .3 | 1217  .3 | 1217  .3 | 1217  .3 | 912  .4 |
| Cost of Sales/Inventory | | | | | | | | | |
| Cost of Sales/Payables | | | | | | | | | |
| Sales/Working Capital | .7 | .6 | .7 | .5 | .6 | .5 | .9 | .6 | 1.0 |
| | 1.3 | 1.3 | 1.3 | .9 | 1.2 | 1.1 | 1.7 | 1.3 | 1.8 |
| | 3.0 | 3.1 | 3.1 | 9.1 | 2.2 | 1.7 | 3.1 | 4.1 | 4.1 |
| EBIT/Interest | 4.9 | 5.3 | 6.2 | 4.1 | 5.8 | 4.3 | 6.3 | 9.0 | 7.0 |
| | (234)  2.7 | (193)  2.8 | (218)  3.5 | (49)  2.5 | (41)  4.1 | (32)  3.2 | (30)  4.0 | (21)  4.7 | (45)  4.3 |
| | 1.5 | 1.6 | 1.8 | 1.5 | 1.7 | 1.5 | 2.2 | 2.2 | 2.7 |
| Net Profit + Depr., Dep., Amort./Cur. Mat. L/T/D | 36.0 | 8.8 | 24.8 | | | | | | 33.2 |
| | (21)  5.2 | (19)  1.6 | (27)  4.7 | | | | | (10)  4.0 | |
| | 1.5 | .2 | .8 | | | | | | .8 |
| Fixed/Worth | .0 | .0 | .0 | .0 | .0 | .0 | .0 | .0 | .0 |
| | .1 | .1 | .0 | .0 | .0 | .1 | .1 | .1 | .1 |
| | .3 | .3 | .3 | .3 | .2 | .3 | .2 | .1 | .5 |
| Debt/Worth | 1.5 | 1.5 | 1.2 | .9 | 1.2 | 1.1 | 1.4 | 1.1 | 1.5 |
| | 3.9 | 3.5 | 2.7 | 3.6 | 2.7 | 2.1 | 2.9 | 2.8 | 2.4 |
| | 10.0 | 9.6 | 6.8 | 8.6 | 4.6 | 6.3 | 5.7 | 15.6 | 3.8 |
| % Profit Before Taxes/Tangible Net Worth | 47.2 | 49.7 | 43.8 | 38.6 | 39.0 | 36.7 | 63.4 | 60.9 | 48.4 |
| | (265)  20.6 | (231)  21.5 | (262)  24.5 | (58)  14.0 | (55)  19.8 | (35)  14.1 | 31.7 | (26)  34.8 | (49)  28.6 |
| | 6.4 | 6.9 | 9.6 | 5.0 | 9.9 | 8.9 | 10.8 | 10.9 | 14.8 |
| % Profit Before Taxes/Total Assets | 9.6 | 10.5 | 11.7 | 9.5 | 11.2 | 8.8 | 13.8 | 14.9 | 12.5 |
| | 4.3 | 4.6 | 5.7 | 4.0 | 5.0 | 5.5 | 6.8 | 7.8 | 8.7 |
| | 1.4 | 1.5 | 1.7 | 1.3 | 2.1 | 1.6 | 3.0 | 1.2 | 3.0 |
| Sales/Net Fixed Assets | 138.5 | 186.0 | 205.8 | UND | 397.3 | 179.8 | 92.5 | 142.3 | 70.5 |
| | 36.3 | 36.7 | 41.1 | 123.6 | 40.9 | 37.0 | 28.3 | 39.8 | 34.5 |
| | 13.4 | 13.2 | 14.8 | 14.3 | 14.8 | 12.9 | 11.4 | 22.4 | 16.1 |
| Sales/Total Assets | .7 | .7 | .7 | .4 | .9 | .4 | .7 | 1.0 | 1.1 |
| | .4 | .4 | .4 | .3 | .3 | .3 | .4 | .4 | .7 |
| | .2 | .2 | .2 | .2 | .2 | .3 | .2 | .3 | .3 |
| % Depr., Dep., Amort./Sales | .5 | .5 | .4 | .3 | .3 | .3 | .4 | .6 | .6 |
| | (190)  1.1 | (169)  1.0 | (192)  .8 | (34)  .6 | (43)  .8 | (28)  .7 | (30)  .8 | (19)  .9 | (38)  1.0 |
| | 2.1 | 2.2 | 1.9 | 2.5 | 1.8 | 1.9 | 2.5 | 1.8 | 1.8 |
| % Officers', Directors' Owners' Comp/Sales | 3.3 | 3.4 | 2.9 | | 2.0 | | | | |
| | (68)  7.6 | (52)  6.3 | (41)  6.6 | | (15)  4.0 | | | | |
| | 15.8 | 15.1 | 16.1 | | 9.6 | | | | |
| Net Sales ($) | 5943353M | 4348672M | 5452118M | 28871M | 110844M | 148137M | 283392M | 453959M | 4426915M |
| Total Assets ($) | 9528417M | 8159287M | 9954548M | 172799M | 415305M | 492314M | 1210170M | 1287586M | 6376374M |

© RMA 2012

M = $ thousand    MM = $ million
See Pages 9 through 22 for Explanation of Ratios and Data

## Current Data Sorted by Assets      Comparative Historical Data

| Type of Statement | 0-500M | 500M-2MM | 2-10MM | 10-50MM | 50-100MM | 100-250MM | 4/1/07-3/31/08 ALL | 4/1/08-3/31/09 ALL |
|---|---|---|---|---|---|---|---|---|
| Unqualified | | 6 | 39 | 83 | 30 | 26 | 247 | 182 |
| Reviewed | | | 3 | 4 | | | 13 | 15 |
| Compiled | 2 | 2 | 5 | 2 | | | 12 | 12 |
| Tax Returns | 6 | 4 | 5 | 4 | | | 28 | 40 |
| Other | 2 | 10 | 24 | 22 | 7 | 4 | 109 | 99 |
| | | 32 (4/1-9/30/11) | | 258 (10/1/11-3/31/12) | | | | |
| **NUMBER OF STATEMENTS** | 10 | 22 | 76 | 115 | 37 | 30 | 409 | 348 |
| **ASSETS** | % | % | % | % | % | % | % | % |
| Cash & Equivalents | 27.4 | 26.0 | 14.5 | 9.4 | 6.3 | 8.9 | 15.8 | 13.2 |
| Trade Receivables (net) | 8.3 | 8.7 | 22.9 | 27.0 | 24.2 | 15.2 | 25.2 | 27.3 |
| Inventory | .0 | 4.5 | 13.5 | 27.0 | 47.0 | 42.7 | 5.5 | 6.2 |
| All Other Current | 1.1 | 19.8 | 9.1 | 11.1 | 8.7 | 14.1 | 25.6 | 21.1 |
| Total Current | 36.9 | 58.9 | 59.9 | 74.5 | 86.2 | 80.8 | 72.2 | 67.7 |
| Fixed Assets (net) | 32.4 | 21.5 | 8.3 | 3.0 | 1.6 | 1.9 | 7.3 | 8.4 |
| Intangibles (net) | 4.0 | .4 | .7 | 1.5 | .5 | 2.0 | 2.0 | 2.7 |
| All Other Non-Current | 26.7 | 19.1 | 31.1 | 21.0 | 11.7 | 15.3 | 18.5 | 21.3 |
| Total | 100.0 | 100.0 | 100.0 | 100.0 | 100.0 | 100.0 | 100.0 | 100.0 |
| **LIABILITIES** | | | | | | | | |
| Notes Payable-Short Term | 32.6 | 15.4 | 39.2 | 57.5 | 68.0 | 60.1 | 43.0 | 38.8 |
| Cur. Mat.-L.T.D. | .3 | .5 | 2.0 | .7 | .1 | 1.2 | 1.8 | 2.0 |
| Trade Payables | 1.1 | 2.7 | 1.6 | 1.4 | 2.3 | 1.5 | 6.0 | 8.4 |
| Income Taxes Payable | .0 | .0 | .2 | .2 | .1 | .1 | .2 | .1 |
| All Other Current | 8.9 | 13.7 | 6.4 | 6.3 | 7.1 | 3.7 | 7.2 | 8.1 |
| Total Current | 42.9 | 32.4 | 49.3 | 66.1 | 77.7 | 66.6 | 58.1 | 57.5 |
| Long-Term Debt | 8.2 | 14.8 | 14.5 | 8.4 | 5.8 | 7.9 | 8.4 | 9.2 |
| Deferred Taxes | .0 | .0 | .2 | .3 | .0 | .4 | .3 | .3 |
| All Other Non-Current | .4 | 3.0 | 5.9 | 2.0 | .7 | 1.4 | 3.8 | 3.6 |
| Net Worth | 48.6 | 49.8 | 30.2 | 23.3 | 15.8 | 23.7 | 29.4 | 29.3 |
| Total Liabilties & Net Worth | 100.0 | 100.0 | 100.0 | 100.0 | 100.0 | 100.0 | 100.0 | 100.0 |
| **INCOME DATA** | | | | | | | | |
| Net Sales | 100.0 | 100.0 | 100.0 | 100.0 | 100.0 | 100.0 | 100.0 | 100.0 |
| Gross Profit | | | | | | | | |
| Operating Expenses | 76.4 | 76.0 | 73.3 | 76.6 | 79.4 | 79.8 | 77.6 | 78.4 |
| Operating Profit | 23.6 | 24.0 | 26.7 | 23.4 | 20.6 | 20.2 | 22.4 | 21.6 |
| All Other Expenses (net) | 8.4 | 13.2 | 16.1 | 8.7 | 10.6 | 4.7 | 13.2 | 12.7 |
| Profit Before Taxes | 15.2 | 10.8 | 10.6 | 14.7 | 10.0 | 15.6 | 9.2 | 8.9 |
| **RATIOS** | | | | | | | | |
| Current | 8.3 | 6.2 | 1.9 | 1.2 | 1.1 | 1.3 | 1.8 | 1.8 |
| | 2.5 | 2.1 | 1.2 | 1.1 | 1.1 | 1.1 | 1.2 | 1.1 |
| | .5 | .8 | 1.0 | 1.0 | 1.0 | 1.1 | 1.0 | 1.0 |
| Quick | 8.3 | 3.4 | 1.6 | 1.1 | 1.1 | .5 | 1.4 | 1.3 |
| | 1.9 | 1.2 | .8 | .4 | .1 | .1 | (408) .9 | (347) .8 |
| | .0 | .3 | .1 | .1 | .1 | .1 | .1 | .1 |
| Sales/Receivables | 0 UND | 0 UND | 0 UND | 0 999.8 | 2 147.1 | 3 109.6 | 0 UND | 0 UND |
| | 0 UND | 0 UND | 13 27.7 | 25 14.7 | 7 50.2 | 8 47.9 | 9 41.6 | 19 18.8 |
| | 5 67.9 | 21 17.7 | 521 .7 | 608 .6 | 912 .4 | 39 9.4 | 430 .8 | 662 .6 |
| Cost of Sales/Inventory | | | | | | | | |
| Cost of Sales/Payables | | | | | | | | |
| Sales/Working Capital | 6.2 | 2.0 | 1.4 | 2.1 | 2.9 | 2.6 | 1.3 | 1.4 |
| | 38.6 | 7.6 | 2.8 | 4.7 | 4.8 | 5.6 | 4.9 | 5.0 |
| | -6.7 | -24.5 | NM | 11.7 | 8.5 | 7.1 | 44.0 | 82.5 |
| EBIT/Interest | | 16.8 | 6.4 | 5.0 | 2.7 | 7.5 | 3.7 | 3.4 |
| | (12) 1.5 | (43) 3.3 | (89) 2.7 | (30) 1.7 | (28) 3.5 | | (240) 1.3 | (219) 1.9 |
| | | 1.0 | 1.0 | 1.4 | 1.1 | 1.4 | .5 | 1.1 |
| Net Profit + Depr., Dep., Amort./Cur. Mat. L/T/D | | | | | | | 5.3 | 5.2 |
| | | | | | | | (26) .1 | (19) .5 |
| | | | | | | | -12.9 | .0 |
| Fixed/Worth | .0 | .0 | .0 | .0 | .0 | .0 | .0 | .0 |
| | .2 | .1 | .0 | .1 | .1 | .1 | .1 | .1 |
| | 1.9 | 1.2 | .3 | .2 | .1 | .1 | .3 | .3 |
| Debt/Worth | .0 | .2 | 1.4 | 2.4 | 6.1 | 2.6 | 1.4 | 1.4 |
| | .2 | 1.0 | 2.9 | 5.7 | 9.4 | 6.9 | 3.7 | 3.6 |
| | 1.6 | 3.6 | 5.7 | 10.1 | 14.6 | 9.4 | 9.1 | 8.6 |
| % Profit Before Taxes/Tangible Net Worth | | 17.4 | 23.1 | 32.9 | 40.6 | 45.6 | 25.9 | 24.4 |
| | (21) 6.1 | (73) 9.0 | (113) 14.6 | 18.4 | 23.5 | | (386) 6.9 | (331) 8.9 |
| | | -1.2 | .2 | 4.8 | 5.8 | 6.4 | -4.7 | .6 |
| % Profit Before Taxes/Total Assets | 52.7 | 8.3 | 5.7 | 5.3 | 4.6 | 8.8 | 5.9 | 5.1 |
| | .8 | 1.5 | 1.6 | 2.6 | 1.8 | 4.9 | 1.6 | 1.7 |
| | -19.1 | -.2 | .0 | .9 | .3 | .7 | -1.3 | .0 |
| Sales/Net Fixed Assets | UND | UND | 207.2 | 161.4 | 96.6 | 112.3 | 132.3 | 172.4 |
| | 8.8 | 30.9 | 46.6 | 53.6 | 42.5 | 50.3 | 31.6 | 36.2 |
| | 2.5 | 1.5 | 5.9 | 17.4 | 19.8 | 25.2 | 11.5 | 10.9 |
| Sales/Total Assets | 5.6 | 1.8 | .5 | .4 | .4 | .5 | .8 | .7 |
| | 2.5 | .6 | .3 | .3 | .3 | .4 | .4 | .3 |
| | .2 | .2 | .1 | .2 | .2 | .2 | .1 | .1 |
| % Depr., Dep., Amort./Sales | | .2 | .4 | .3 | .4 | .5 | .6 | .7 |
| | (13) .4 | (48) .8 | (85) .7 | (27) .7 | (25) 1.0 | | (261) 1.2 | (207) 1.3 |
| | | 2.4 | 1.9 | 1.2 | 1.3 | 1.6 | 2.1 | 2.1 |
| % Officers', Directors' Owners' Comp/Sales | | | 8.4 | 1.0 | | | 3.0 | 3.3 |
| | | | (13) 12.8 | (11) 6.0 | | | (86) 5.8 | (78) 7.3 |
| | | | 19.9 | 11.2 | | | 12.3 | 14.2 |
| Net Sales ($) | 3256M | 24389M | 148770M | 999352M | 786548M | 7925881M | 6505606M | 3770623M |
| Total Assets ($) | 2220M | 25756M | 406431M | 2873976M | 2608380M | 4769301M | 12346643M | 9464493M |

| Comparative Historical Data | | | Type of Statement | Current Data Sorted by Sales | | | | | |
|---|---|---|---|---|---|---|---|---|---|
| 177 | 166 | 184 | Unqualified | 8 | 39 | 23 | 31 | 50 | 33 |
| 6 | 7 | 7 | Reviewed | 1 | 3 | 1 | 1 | 1 | |
| 12 | 15 | 11 | Compiled | 5 | 4 | 1 | 1 | 1 | |
| 27 | 20 | 19 | Tax Returns | 13 | 4 | 1 | 1 | | |
| 94 | 87 | 69 | Other | 26 | 17 | 6 | 5 | 8 | 7 |
| 4/1/09-3/31/10 ALL | 4/1/10-3/31/11 ALL | 4/1/11-3/31/12 ALL | | 32 (4/1-9/30/11) | | 258 (10/1/11-3/31/12) | | | |
| | | | | 0-1MM | 1-3MM | 3-5MM | 5-10MM | 10-25MM | 25MM & OVER |
| 316 | 295 | 290 | NUMBER OF STATEMENTS | 53 | 67 | 31 | 39 | 60 | 40 |
| % | % | % | ASSETS | % | % | % | % | % | % |
| 14.1 | 13.0 | 12.2 | Cash & Equivalents | 10.3 | 19.1 | 13.9 | 12.6 | 6.9 | 9.0 |
| 25.2 | 26.3 | 22.3 | Trade Receivables (net) | 16.9 | 23.3 | 32.5 | 26.1 | 19.5 | 20.6 |
| 13.5 | 14.5 | 25.0 | Inventory | 5.4 | 11.7 | 16.4 | 29.4 | 45.4 | 44.9 |
| 17.4 | 13.5 | 10.9 | All Other Current | 7.0 | 14.0 | 7.9 | 12.0 | 10.5 | 12.6 |
| 70.2 | 67.3 | 70.3 | Total Current | 39.6 | 68.1 | 70.7 | 80.3 | 82.2 | 87.1 |
| 7.5 | 8.2 | 6.5 | Fixed Assets (net) | 18.6 | 5.9 | 4.5 | 3.8 | 2.0 | 2.4 |
| 2.9 | 2.1 | 1.2 | Intangibles (net) | 1.0 | .9 | 2.4 | .1 | 1.8 | 1.3 |
| 19.5 | 22.4 | 21.9 | All Other Non-Current | 40.7 | 25.1 | 22.4 | 15.8 | 14.0 | 9.2 |
| 100.0 | 100.0 | 100.0 | Total | 100.0 | 100.0 | 100.0 | 100.0 | 100.0 | 100.0 |
| | | | LIABILITIES | | | | | | |
| 41.6 | 42.0 | 50.3 | Notes Payable-Short Term | 23.5 | 41.7 | 55.3 | 56.0 | 67.1 | 65.4 |
| 2.0 | 1.8 | 1.0 | Cur. Mat.-L.T.D. | .6 | 2.6 | 1.0 | .2 | .3 | .7 |
| 4.4 | 4.1 | 1.7 | Trade Payables | 1.2 | 1.0 | 2.0 | 2.0 | 1.5 | 3.0 |
| .2 | .1 | .2 | Income Taxes Payable | .0 | .0 | .7 | .1 | .2 | .1 |
| 7.6 | 7.0 | 6.8 | All Other Current | 8.4 | 7.7 | 4.6 | 6.3 | 7.1 | 5.0 |
| 55.8 | 55.0 | 59.9 | Total Current | 33.7 | 53.0 | 63.5 | 64.6 | 76.2 | 74.1 |
| 10.5 | 11.8 | 10.1 | Long-Term Debt | 23.7 | 11.6 | 6.7 | 8.8 | 3.4 | 3.3 |
| .2 | .3 | .2 | Deferred Taxes | .0 | .0 | 1.2 | .2 | .0 | .3 |
| 4.3 | 4.0 | 2.8 | All Other Non-Current | 4.8 | 3.4 | 1.9 | 4.7 | .7 | 1.2 |
| 29.3 | 28.9 | 27.1 | Net Worth | 37.8 | 32.1 | 26.7 | 21.6 | 19.7 | 21.1 |
| 100.0 | 100.0 | 100.0 | Total Liabilities & Net Worth | 100.0 | 100.0 | 100.0 | 100.0 | 100.0 | 100.0 |
| | | | INCOME DATA | | | | | | |
| 100.0 | 100.0 | 100.0 | Net Sales | 100.0 | 100.0 | 100.0 | 100.0 | 100.0 | 100.0 |
| | | | Gross Profit | | | | | | |
| 74.2 | 74.9 | 76.4 | Operating Expenses | 60.5 | 70.3 | 82.9 | 82.8 | 85.0 | 83.2 |
| 25.8 | 25.1 | 23.6 | Operating Profit | 39.5 | 29.7 | 17.1 | 17.2 | 15.0 | 16.8 |
| 10.5 | 11.1 | 10.8 | All Other Expenses (net) | 26.5 | 11.0 | 9.5 | 6.6 | 4.6 | 4.0 |
| 15.3 | 14.0 | 12.9 | Profit Before Taxes | 13.0 | 18.7 | 7.7 | 10.5 | 10.4 | 12.9 |
| | | | RATIOS | | | | | | |
| 1.8 | 1.8 | 1.6 | | 6.6 | 2.0 | 1.4 | 2.0 | 1.1 | 1.1 |
| 1.2 | 1.1 | 1.1 | Current | 1.6 | 1.3 | 1.1 | 1.1 | 1.1 | 1.1 |
| 1.0 | 1.0 | 1.0 | | .2 | 1.1 | 1.0 | 1.0 | 1.0 | 1.1 |
| 1.4 | 1.3 | 1.1 | | 4.8 | 1.6 | 1.1 | 1.9 | 1.0 | .9 |
| .8 | (294) .9 | .5 | Quick | .7 | 1.1 | .9 | .6 | .1 | .1 |
| .1 | .1 | .1 | | .1 | .2 | .1 | .1 | .1 | .1 |
| 0 UND | 0 UND | 0 UND | | 0 UND | 0 UND | 3 134.6 | 0 UND | 0 999.8 | 3 116.2 |
| 15 23.7 | 18 20.7 | 13 28.4 | Sales/Receivables | 0 UND | 7 52.5 | 57 6.4 | 19 18.8 | 13 28.4 | 13 28.3 |
| 452 .8 | 473 .8 | 456 .8 | | 81 4.5 | 521 .7 | 730 .5 | 608 .6 | 49 7.5 | 60 6.1 |
| | | | Cost of Sales/Inventory | | | | | | |
| | | | Cost of Sales/Payables | | | | | | |
| 1.6 | 1.7 | 1.9 | | .3 | 1.3 | 1.6 | 2.7 | 3.5 | 3.7 |
| 4.6 | 4.9 | 4.7 | Sales/Working Capital | 7.9 | 2.3 | 3.0 | 3.9 | 5.2 | 5.9 |
| 15.3 | 19.0 | 13.3 | | -2.0 | 5.7 | 13.7 | 9.2 | 15.0 | 9.5 |
| 6.5 | 7.1 | 5.2 | | 2.3 | 11.7 | 4.2 | 6.6 | 2.9 | 7.7 |
| (207) 3.2 | (200) 3.0 | (204) 2.6 | EBIT/Interest | (15) 1.1 | (43) 4.2 | (25) 1.5 | (32) 2.8 | (51) 2.0 | (38) 3.4 |
| 1.7 | 1.7 | 1.3 | | .9 | 1.6 | .3 | 1.3 | 1.3 | 1.7 |
| 13.1 | 13.7 | 14.0 | Net Profit + Depr., Dep., Amort./Cur. Mat. L/T/D | | | | | | |
| (20) 1.9 | (24) 3.3 | (20) 4.3 | | | | | | | |
| 1.0 | .6 | .7 | | | | | | | |
| .0 | .0 | .0 | | .0 | .0 | .0 | .0 | .0 | .0 |
| .1 | .1 | .1 | Fixed/Worth | .0 | .0 | .1 | .0 | .1 | .1 |
| .2 | .3 | .2 | | .5 | .2 | .3 | .2 | .1 | .2 |
| 1.4 | 1.4 | 1.6 | | .3 | 1.4 | 1.6 | 3.1 | 4.0 | 3.4 |
| 4.0 | 3.9 | 4.8 | Debt/Worth | 1.6 | 2.9 | 3.4 | 6.0 | 7.6 | 7.4 |
| 7.8 | 7.9 | 9.7 | | 12.7 | 5.8 | 7.3 | 11.9 | 12.3 | 11.0 |
| 53.7 | 43.8 | 30.8 | | 12.4 | 25.2 | 21.1 | 35.5 | 33.6 | 49.4 |
| (299) 21.1 | (285) 16.0 | (283) 13.4 | % Profit Before Taxes/Tangible Net Worth | (50) 1.6 | (65) 12.6 | (30) 9.8 | (38) 17.3 | 15.5 | 33.8 |
| 4.3 | 5.5 | 2.0 | | -1.7 | 2.1 | -.9 | 6.1 | 7.2 | 15.5 |
| 9.2 | 7.3 | 5.9 | | 3.9 | 9.0 | 5.1 | 5.5 | 4.7 | 7.1 |
| 4.4 | 3.7 | 2.3 | % Profit Before Taxes/Total Assets | .5 | 3.1 | 2.1 | 2.5 | 2.2 | 5.8 |
| .8 | .9 | .3 | | -.4 | .5 | .1 | .6 | .7 | 1.9 |
| 152.5 | 162.3 | 139.9 | | UND | 257.4 | 76.9 | 138.5 | 100.7 | 67.1 |
| 49.8 | 49.0 | 47.5 | Sales/Net Fixed Assets | 53.0 | 53.0 | 28.0 | 54.2 | 47.5 | 45.7 |
| 12.9 | 10.1 | 11.7 | | 1.3 | 8.1 | 6.2 | 15.0 | 23.1 | 24.6 |
| .7 | .6 | .5 | | .2 | .5 | .5 | .5 | .5 | .5 |
| .4 | .4 | .3 | Sales/Total Assets | .1 | .3 | .3 | .4 | .4 | .4 |
| .1 | .1 | .2 | | .1 | .1 | .2 | .2 | .3 | .3 |
| .4 | .4 | .4 | | .4 | .4 | .5 | .2 | .4 | .4 |
| (191) .8 | (184) .8 | (203) .7 | % Depr., Dep., Amort./Sales | (19) 1.1 | (46) .7 | (23) 1.1 | (32) .4 | (48) .6 | (35) .9 |
| 1.5 | 1.5 | 1.3 | | 7.1 | 1.8 | 1.5 | .8 | 1.0 | 1.2 |
| 3.2 | 2.5 | 4.5 | | | | | | | |
| (60) 6.5 | (49) 6.1 | (33) 9.2 | % Officers', Directors' Owners' Comp/Sales | | | | | | |
| 14.0 | 18.4 | 15.1 | | | | | | | |
| 3996577M | 3925121M | 9888196M | Net Sales ($) | 19997M | 131891M | 122877M | 288892M | 971409M | 8353130M |
| 10197336M | 10349510M | 10686064M | Total Assets ($) | 176749M | 741951M | 585928M | 1032555M | 2968378M | 5180503M |

M = $ thousand    MM = $ million
See Pages 9 through 22 for Explanation of Ratios and Data

**Current Data Sorted by Assets**           **Comparative Historical Data**

| 0-500M | 500M-2MM 11 (4/1-9/30/11) | 2-10MM | 10-50MM 19 (10/1/11-3/31/12) | 50-100MM | 100-250MM | Type of Statement | 4/1/07- 3/31/08 ALL | 4/1/08- 3/31/09 ALL |
|---|---|---|---|---|---|---|---|---|
| 1 | 1 | | 5 | 2 | 1 | Unqualified | 18 | 11 |
| | | 1 | 1 | | | Reviewed | 3 | 3 |
| | 1 | | 1 | | | Compiled | 1 | |
| 1 | 2 | | 1 | | | Tax Returns | 5 | 5 |
| 1 | | 9 | | 1 | 1 | Other | 8 | 9 |
| 3 | 4 | 10 | 8 | 3 | 2 | **NUMBER OF STATEMENTS** | 35 | 28 |
| % | % | % | % | % | % | **ASSETS** | % | % |
| | | 8.4 | | | | Cash & Equivalents | 16.5 | 12.3 |
| | | 36.8 | | | | Trade Receivables (net) | 34.6 | 36.9 |
| | | 2.8 | | | | Inventory | .3 | 1.4 |
| | | 12.2 | | | | All Other Current | 10.6 | 12.5 |
| | | 60.3 | | | | Total Current | 62.0 | 63.2 |
| | | 1.1 | | | | Fixed Assets (net) | 20.0 | 11.7 |
| | | 6.7 | | | | Intangibles (net) | .6 | 1.0 |
| | | 31.9 | | | | All Other Non-Current | 17.3 | 24.1 |
| | | 100.0 | | | | Total | 100.0 | 100.0 |
| | | | | | | **LIABILITIES** | | |
| | | 16.1 | | | | Notes Payable-Short Term | 19.7 | 23.0 |
| | | 2.1 | | | | Cur. Mat.-L.T.D. | 5.8 | 4.7 |
| | | 4.3 | | | | Trade Payables | 3.1 | 1.7 |
| | | .0 | | | | Income Taxes Payable | .0 | .0 |
| | | 11.9 | | | | All Other Current | 4.8 | 7.0 |
| | | 34.5 | | | | Total Current | 33.3 | 36.5 |
| | | 18.1 | | | | Long-Term Debt | 22.0 | 24.3 |
| | | .0 | | | | Deferred Taxes | .0 | .1 |
| | | 7.8 | | | | All Other Non-Current | 8.2 | 6.6 |
| | | 39.6 | | | | Net Worth | 36.5 | 32.6 |
| | | 100.0 | | | | Total Liabilties & Net Worth | 100.0 | 100.0 |
| | | | | | | **INCOME DATA** | | |
| | | 100.0 | | | | Net Sales | 100.0 | 100.0 |
| | | | | | | Gross Profit | | |
| | | 62.1 | | | | Operating Expenses | 65.1 | 61.6 |
| | | 37.9 | | | | Operating Profit | 34.9 | 38.4 |
| | | 4.0 | | | | All Other Expenses (net) | 17.2 | 19.9 |
| | | 34.0 | | | | Profit Before Taxes | 17.8 | 18.5 |
| | | | | | | **RATIOS** | | |
| | | 5.7 | | | | | 4.7 | 5.5 |
| | | 1.7 | | | | Current | 2.0 | 2.0 |
| | | 1.1 | | | | | 1.2 | .9 |
| | | 5.7 | | | | | 3.3 | 4.0 |
| | | 1.2 | | | | Quick | 1.8 | 1.5 |
| | | .6 | | | | | 1.2 | .7 |
| | 1 | 302.1 | | | | | 2   209.0 | 3   107.5 |
| | 50 | 7.3 | | | | Sales/Receivables | 63   5.8 | 528   .7 |
| | 456 | .8 | | | | | 1325   .3 | 1497   .2 |
| | | | | | | Cost of Sales/Inventory | | |
| | | | | | | Cost of Sales/Payables | | |
| | | 1.1 | | | | | .7 | .4 |
| | | 2.9 | | | | Sales/Working Capital | 1.6 | .8 |
| | | NM | | | | | 4.7 | NM |
| | | | | | | | 8.2 | 4.0 |
| | | | | | | EBIT/Interest | (14)   3.2 | (13)   2.1 |
| | | | | | | | 1.3 | 1.1 |
| | | | | | | Net Profit + Depr., Dep., Amort./Cur. Mat. L/T/D | | |
| | | .0 | | | | | .0 | .0 |
| | | .0 | | | | Fixed/Worth | .1 | .0 |
| | | .1 | | | | | .8 | .9 |
| | | .8 | | | | | .4 | .8 |
| | | 1.7 | | | | Debt/Worth | 3.1 | 2.9 |
| | | 4.7 | | | | | 12.2 | 10.1 |
| | | | | | | | 44.5 | 16.7 |
| | | | | | | % Profit Before Taxes/Tangible Net Worth | (32)   14.8 | (26)   9.7 |
| | | | | | | | 8.8 | 4.6 |
| | | 17.7 | | | | | 11.7 | 7.6 |
| | | 10.7 | | | | % Profit Before Taxes/Total Assets | 5.0 | 3.1 |
| | | 2.2 | | | | | .8 | .4 |
| | | UND | | | | | UND | UND |
| | | 917.2 | | | | Sales/Net Fixed Assets | 35.1 | 86.7 |
| | | 19.5 | | | | | 2.8 | 7.9 |
| | | 1.0 | | | | | .8 | .3 |
| | | .4 | | | | Sales/Total Assets | .3 | .2 |
| | | .1 | | | | | .1 | .1 |
| | | | | | | | .9 | .6 |
| | | | | | | % Depr., Dep., Amort./Sales | (16)   3.2 | (14)   2.0 |
| | | | | | | | 5.5 | 4.9 |
| | | | | | | % Officers', Directors' Owners' Comp/Sales | | |
| 256M | 2426M | 39459M | 28673M | 87583M | 204699M | Net Sales ($) | 517597M | 211105M |
| 821M | 5756M | 53759M | 209261M | 182021M | 337796M | Total Assets ($) | 1133106M | 1029680M |

M = $ thousand    MM = $ million
See Pages 9 through 22 for Explanation of Ratios and Data

## Comparative Historical Data | Current Data Sorted by Sales

| | 4/1/09-3/31/10 ALL | 4/1/10-3/31/11 ALL | 4/1/11-3/31/12 ALL | 0-1MM | 1-3MM | 3-5MM | 5-10MM | 10-25MM | 25MM & OVER |
|---|---|---|---|---|---|---|---|---|---|
| **Type of Statement** | | | | | | | | | |
| Unqualified | 11 | 14 | 10 | 1 | 4 | | 2 | 1 | 2 |
| Reviewed | 2 | 3 | 2 | 1 | | | | 1 | |
| Compiled | 2 | | | | | | | | |
| Tax Returns | 8 | 2 | 4 | 3 | | 1 | | | |
| Other | 12 | 7 | 14 | 5 | 4 | 1 | 3 | | 1 |
| | | | | | 11 (4/1-9/30/11) | | 19 (10/1/11-3/31/12) | | |
| **NUMBER OF STATEMENTS** | 35 | 26 | 30 | 10 | 8 | 1 | 6 | 2 | 3 |
| | % | % | % | % | % | % | % | % | % |
| **ASSETS** | | | | | | | | | |
| Cash & Equivalents | 15.3 | 14.4 | 14.6 | 8.2 | | | | | |
| Trade Receivables (net) | 38.6 | 39.1 | 31.0 | 24.6 | | | | | |
| Inventory | 2.1 | 1.7 | 1.0 | .0 | | | | | |
| All Other Current | 7.4 | 7.7 | 5.4 | 3.1 | | | | | |
| Total Current | 63.4 | 63.0 | 52.0 | 35.9 | | | | | |
| Fixed Assets (net) | 9.9 | 7.2 | 11.5 | 10.1 | | | | | |
| Intangibles (net) | 2.7 | 1.0 | 2.6 | 6.0 | | | | | |
| All Other Non-Current | 23.9 | 28.8 | 33.9 | 48.1 | | | | | |
| Total | 100.0 | 100.0 | 100.0 | 100.0 | | | | | |
| **LIABILITIES** | | | | | | | | | |
| Notes Payable-Short Term | 24.0 | 23.8 | 20.5 | 19.0 | | | | | |
| Cur. Mat.-L.T.D. | 8.4 | 1.1 | 2.5 | .0 | | | | | |
| Trade Payables | 4.3 | 2.3 | 4.4 | .1 | | | | | |
| Income Taxes Payable | .0 | .2 | .0 | .0 | | | | | |
| All Other Current | 11.5 | 8.8 | 9.1 | 16.3 | | | | | |
| Total Current | 48.2 | 36.1 | 36.5 | 35.5 | | | | | |
| Long-Term Debt | 17.5 | 17.4 | 18.9 | 15.2 | | | | | |
| Deferred Taxes | .0 | .0 | .0 | .0 | | | | | |
| All Other Non-Current | 11.1 | 6.6 | 7.2 | 9.5 | | | | | |
| Net Worth | 23.1 | 39.9 | 37.5 | 39.8 | | | | | |
| Total Liabilities & Net Worth | 100.0 | 100.0 | 100.0 | 100.0 | | | | | |
| **INCOME DATA** | | | | | | | | | |
| Net Sales | 100.0 | 100.0 | 100.0 | 100.0 | | | | | |
| Gross Profit | | | | | | | | | |
| Operating Expenses | 72.8 | 71.4 | 70.6 | 61.8 | | | | | |
| Operating Profit | 27.2 | 28.6 | 29.4 | 38.2 | | | | | |
| All Other Expenses (net) | 17.5 | 10.4 | 9.7 | 14.5 | | | | | |
| Profit Before Taxes | 9.7 | 18.3 | 19.7 | 23.7 | | | | | |
| **RATIOS** | | | | | | | | | |
| Current | 4.5 | 14.3 | 4.5 | 9.1 | | | | | |
| | 1.4 | 2.1 | 1.5 | .6 | | | | | |
| | 1.1 | 1.3 | .3 | .1 | | | | | |
| Quick | 2.9 | 7.7 | 4.5 | 9.1 | | | | | |
| | 1.4 | 1.9 | 1.1 | .4 | | | | | |
| | .9 | 1.0 | .2 | .1 | | | | | |
| Sales/Receivables | 9  40.8 | 0  UND | 1  310.5 | 0  UND | | | | | |
| | 173  2.1 | 63  5.8 | 40  9.1 | 9  39.3 | | | | | |
| | 1579  .2 | 2000  .2 | 608  .6 | 608  .6 | | | | | |
| Cost of Sales/Inventory | | | | | | | | | |
| Cost of Sales/Payables | | | | | | | | | |
| Sales/Working Capital | .7 | .2 | .8 | 1.4 | | | | | |
| | 2.1 | 1.6 | 2.9 | -1.8 | | | | | |
| | 14.8 | 49.4 | -1.4 | -.5 | | | | | |
| EBIT/Interest | 6.4 | 7.4 | 25.1 | | | | | | |
| | (19)  2.8 | (11)  5.2 | (14)  6.4 | | | | | | |
| | 1.5 | .3 | 3.7 | | | | | | |
| Net Profit + Depr., Dep., Amort./Cur. Mat. L/T/D | | | | | | | | | |
| Fixed/Worth | .0 | .0 | .0 | .0 | | | | | |
| | .0 | .0 | .0 | .0 | | | | | |
| | .6 | .2 | .3 | 3.3 | | | | | |
| Debt/Worth | .7 | .6 | .8 | .8 | | | | | |
| | 5.4 | 1.1 | 2.2 | 1.9 | | | | | |
| | 43.6 | 8.3 | 7.6 | 42.9 | | | | | |
| % Profit Before Taxes/Tangible Net Worth | 31.1 | 13.0 | 41.1 | | | | | | |
| | (27)  8.5 | (25)  6.6 | (28)  13.2 | | | | | | |
| | -1.1 | -4.7 | -1.3 | | | | | | |
| % Profit Before Taxes/Total Assets | 3.8 | 5.6 | 12.2 | 7.7 | | | | | |
| | 1.6 | 1.6 | 2.9 | 1.8 | | | | | |
| | -.6 | -2.4 | -.1 | -3.6 | | | | | |
| Sales/Net Fixed Assets | UND | UND | UND | UND | | | | | |
| | 106.2 | 999.8 | 548.5 | UND | | | | | |
| | 10.3 | 5.2 | 11.2 | 88.4 | | | | | |
| Sales/Total Assets | .7 | .8 | .8 | .4 | | | | | |
| | .3 | .2 | .2 | .2 | | | | | |
| | .1 | .1 | .1 | .1 | | | | | |
| % Depr., Dep., Amort./Sales | 1.0 | .1 | .5 | | | | | | |
| | (17)  1.5 | (12)  .6 | (13)  2.3 | | | | | | |
| | 7.5 | 4.8 | 9.5 | | | | | | |
| % Officers', Directors' Owners' Comp/Sales | | | | | | | | | |
| Net Sales ($) | 344971M | 177180M | 363096M | 2954M | 16861M | 4370M | 36996M | 27221M | 274694M |
| Total Assets ($) | 1057572M | 741470M | 789414M | 21063M | 133322M | 5295M | 208900M | 79321M | 341513M |

M = $ thousand    MM = $ million
See Pages 9 through 22 for Explanation of Ratios and Data

## Current Data Sorted by Assets      Comparative Historical Data

| Type of Statement | 0-500M | 500M-2MM | 2-10MM | 10-50MM | 50-100MM | 100-250MM | | 4/1/07-3/31/08 ALL | 4/1/08-3/31/09 ALL |
|---|---|---|---|---|---|---|---|---|---|
| Unqualified | 2 | 4 | 19 | 61 | 22 | 19 | | 144 | 100 |
| Reviewed | 1 | 2 | 15 | 14 | 1 | 1 | | 28 | 18 |
| Compiled | 1 | 1 | 8 | 3 | 3 | | | 15 | 19 |
| Tax Returns | 5 | 7 | 7 | 3 | | | | 27 | 20 |
| Other | 4 | 14 | 29 | 28 | 12 | 11 | | 107 | 84 |
| | | 35 (4/1-9/30/11) | | 259 (10/1/11-3/31/12) | | | | | |
| NUMBER OF STATEMENTS | 13 | 28 | 78 | 109 | 35 | 31 | | 321 | 241 |

| ASSETS | % | % | % | % | % | % | | % | % |
|---|---|---|---|---|---|---|---|---|---|
| Cash & Equivalents | 26.9 | 17.2 | 11.6 | 9.5 | 5.5 | 6.3 | | 8.8 | 8.6 |
| Trade Receivables (net) | 24.5 | 32.6 | 46.8 | 54.1 | 62.9 | 57.4 | | 53.7 | 50.6 |
| Inventory | 16.0 | 8.3 | 3.9 | 1.9 | .3 | 4.4 | | 2.1 | 3.1 |
| All Other Current | 5.6 | 8.6 | 8.3 | 11.8 | 7.7 | 7.4 | | 10.1 | 9.0 |
| Total Current | 73.0 | 66.7 | 70.7 | 77.3 | 76.4 | 75.5 | | 74.7 | 71.3 |
| Fixed Assets (net) | 12.7 | 20.8 | 10.5 | 4.7 | 1.5 | 4.8 | | 6.8 | 7.7 |
| Intangibles (net) | 5.1 | 3.4 | 2.0 | 1.9 | 1.7 | 7.4 | | 1.7 | 2.9 |
| All Other Non-Current | 9.2 | 9.1 | 16.8 | 16.1 | 20.4 | 12.3 | | 16.8 | 18.0 |
| Total | 100.0 | 100.0 | 100.0 | 100.0 | 100.0 | 100.0 | | 100.0 | 100.0 |

| LIABILITIES | | | | | | | | | |
|---|---|---|---|---|---|---|---|---|---|
| Notes Payable-Short Term | 27.4 | 13.2 | 21.6 | 33.9 | 39.1 | 32.5 | | 32.5 | 30.7 |
| Cur. Mat.-L.T.D. | 3.2 | 2.9 | 3.0 | 3.9 | 2.1 | 2.4 | | 3.6 | 2.4 |
| Trade Payables | 1.4 | 5.9 | 3.8 | 3.3 | 6.6 | 2.4 | | 5.1 | 4.2 |
| Income Taxes Payable | .1 | .0 | .1 | .0 | .0 | .2 | | .1 | .1 |
| All Other Current | 20.1 | 11.3 | 8.9 | 7.6 | 3.2 | 9.5 | | 7.5 | 8.5 |
| Total Current | 52.3 | 33.2 | 37.5 | 48.8 | 51.0 | 47.0 | | 48.7 | 46.8 |
| Long-Term Debt | 12.7 | 22.0 | 17.7 | 14.9 | 17.7 | 24.4 | | 16.5 | 16.8 |
| Deferred Taxes | .0 | .0 | .0 | .1 | .0 | 2.3 | | .2 | .1 |
| All Other Non-Current | 6.4 | 8.7 | 9.8 | 11.4 | 7.3 | 2.8 | | 9.0 | 7.3 |
| Net Worth | 28.6 | 36.0 | 34.9 | 24.8 | 24.0 | 23.5 | | 25.6 | 29.1 |
| Total Liabilities & Net Worth | 100.0 | 100.0 | 100.0 | 100.0 | 100.0 | 100.0 | | 100.0 | 100.0 |

| INCOME DATA | | | | | | | | | |
|---|---|---|---|---|---|---|---|---|---|
| Net Sales | 100.0 | 100.0 | 100.0 | 100.0 | 100.0 | 100.0 | | 100.0 | 100.0 |
| Gross Profit | | | | | | | | | |
| Operating Expenses | 83.4 | 77.1 | 72.0 | 68.3 | 59.9 | 65.9 | | 65.8 | 72.4 |
| Operating Profit | 16.6 | 22.9 | 28.0 | 31.7 | 40.1 | 34.1 | | 34.2 | 27.6 |
| All Other Expenses (net) | 9.1 | 10.2 | 12.4 | 11.6 | 17.1 | 12.1 | | 16.4 | 14.8 |
| Profit Before Taxes | 7.5 | 12.7 | 15.6 | 20.2 | 23.0 | 22.0 | | 17.8 | 12.9 |

| RATIOS | | | | | | | | | |
|---|---|---|---|---|---|---|---|---|---|
| Current | 4.8 | 5.6 | 4.1 | 2.5 | 1.9 | 3.4 | | 2.5 | 3.1 |
| | 1.5 | 1.9 | 1.9 | 1.5 | 1.4 | 1.4 | | 1.5 | 1.5 |
| | 1.1 | .8 | 1.2 | 1.3 | 1.2 | 1.1 | | 1.2 | 1.1 |
| Quick | 3.8 | 5.0 | 3.6 | 2.2 | 1.6 | 3.3 | | 2.2 | 2.7 |
| | 1.1 | 1.5 | 1.6 | 1.4 | 1.4 | 1.3 | | 1.3 | 1.3 |
| | .3 | .5 | .8 | 1.0 | 1.2 | .7 | | .8 | .7 |
| Sales/Receivables | 0 UND | 0 UND | 8 43.7 | 26 13.8 | 332 1.1 | 42 8.6 | | 18 19.8 | 25 14.9 |
| | 4 92.5 | 16 23.1 | 126 2.9 | 730 .5 | 1825 .2 | 730 .5 | | 771 .5 | 502 .7 |
| | 66 5.5 | 130 2.8 | 912 .4 | 1825 .2 | 2000 .1 | 1825 .2 | | 1725 .2 | 1526 .2 |
| Cost of Sales/Inventory | | | | | | | | | |
| | | | | | | | | | |
| | | | | | | | | | |
| Cost of Sales/Payables | | | | | | | | | |
| | | | | | | | | | |
| | | | | | | | | | |
| Sales/Working Capital | 2.8 | 1.4 | .5 | .4 | .3 | .4 | | .5 | .6 |
| | 9.3 | 5.3 | 1.6 | .9 | .6 | 1.4 | | 1.2 | 1.5 |
| | 31.5 | -84.9 | 9.1 | 2.3 | 2.0 | 24.0 | | 7.0 | 16.6 |
| EBIT/Interest | | 21.9 | 6.1 | 5.0 | 4.9 | 10.2 | | 6.2 | 6.0 |
| | | (18) 5.1 | (49) 3.2 | (64) 3.2 | (16) 3.2 | (16) 6.5 | | (133) 2.7 | (110) 2.2 |
| | | | 2.3 | 1.8 | 1.9 | 2.7 | 2.7 | 1.5 | 1.3 |
| Net Profit + Depr., Dep., Amort./Cur. Mat. L/T/D | | | | | | | | 8.0 | 2.4 |
| | | | | | | | | (24) .9 | (18) .3 |
| | | | | | | | | .4 | .0 |
| Fixed/Worth | .0 | .0 | .0 | .0 | .0 | .0 | | .0 | .0 |
| | .1 | .1 | .0 | .0 | .0 | .0 | | .0 | .0 |
| | .8 | 1.8 | .3 | .2 | .0 | .5 | | .2 | .4 |
| Debt/Worth | .9 | .6 | .8 | 1.8 | 2.4 | 2.4 | | 1.8 | 1.4 |
| | 2.1 | 2.1 | 1.8 | 3.4 | 3.0 | 4.5 | | 3.8 | 3.8 |
| | 6.8 | 13.2 | 9.2 | 7.4 | 6.8 | 15.7 | | 10.1 | 11.8 |
| % Profit Before Taxes/Tangible Net Worth | 120.4 | 73.3 | 46.4 | 40.0 | 37.6 | 58.6 | | 34.4 | 27.7 |
| | (11) 11.4 | (25) 17.4 | (70) 20.9 | (103) 16.7 | 16.6 | (26) 14.3 | | (294) 18.2 | (213) 12.3 |
| | .0 | 3.5 | 4.8 | 5.4 | 7.2 | 8.8 | | 6.5 | 2.8 |
| % Profit Before Taxes/Total Assets | 49.6 | 18.0 | 13.5 | 6.9 | 5.3 | 11.3 | | 6.9 | 6.9 |
| | 7.8 | 4.5 | 4.4 | 3.5 | 2.7 | 5.6 | | 3.3 | 2.3 |
| | -.9 | 1.4 | 1.3 | 1.7 | 1.3 | 1.7 | | 1.2 | .6 |
| Sales/Net Fixed Assets | UND | UND | 999.8 | 369.1 | 483.4 | 579.8 | | 555.9 | 270.5 |
| | 162.8 | 92.2 | 69.9 | 50.4 | 90.6 | 76.5 | | 54.1 | 43.1 |
| | 13.9 | 4.6 | 9.5 | 12.8 | 36.9 | 10.1 | | 13.9 | 14.4 |
| Sales/Total Assets | 4.1 | 4.2 | 1.1 | .4 | .2 | .9 | | .4 | .7 |
| | 2.6 | 1.1 | .4 | .2 | .1 | .3 | | .2 | .3 |
| | .8 | .2 | .2 | .1 | .1 | .1 | | .1 | .1 |
| % Depr., Dep., Amort./Sales | | .6 | .5 | .6 | .3 | .4 | | .4 | .5 |
| | | (11) 1.0 | (42) 1.3 | (64) 1.2 | (17) .5 | (14) .7 | | (180) 1.2 | (139) 1.2 |
| | | 27.8 | 3.7 | 2.9 | 3.2 | 2.2 | | 2.6 | 2.7 |
| % Officers', Directors' Owners' Comp/Sales | | 2.0 | 5.3 | 6.2 | | | | 5.2 | 4.2 |
| | | (13) 6.4 | (20) 10.2 | (16) 8.8 | | | | (63) 10.1 | (41) 11.7 |
| | | 18.2 | 24.4 | 15.0 | | | | 19.9 | 17.9 |
| Net Sales ($) | 11393M | 115083M | 382226M | 1072113M | 477079M | 2306383M | | 4687210M | 4227075M |
| Total Assets ($) | 3612M | 38039M | 412329M | 2869980M | 2612027M | 4794070M | | 12510136M | 9168676M |

M = $ thousand   MM = $ million
See Pages 9 through 22 for Explanation of Ratios and Data

## Comparative Historical Data / Current Data Sorted by Sales

| | 4/1/09-3/31/10 ALL | 4/1/10-3/31/11 ALL | 4/1/11-3/31/12 ALL | 0-1MM | 1-3MM | 3-5MM | 5-10MM | 10-25MM | 25MM & OVER |
|---|---|---|---|---|---|---|---|---|---|
| **Type of Statement** | | | | | | | | | |
| Unqualified | 134 | 118 | 127 | 9 | 22 | 12 | 38 | 23 | 23 |
| Reviewed | 28 | 26 | 34 | 3 | 10 | 9 | 5 | 4 | 3 |
| Compiled | 14 | 19 | 13 | 2 | 5 | 2 | 2 | 1 | 1 |
| Tax Returns | 31 | 26 | 22 | 7 | 5 | 2 | 6 | 1 | 1 |
| Other | 122 | 109 | 98 | 26 | 14 | 15 | 17 | 13 | 13 |
| | | | | 35 (4/1-9/30/11) | | | 259 (10/1/11-3/31/12) | | |
| **NUMBER OF STATEMENTS** | 329 | 298 | 294 | 47 | 56 | 40 | 68 | 42 | 41 |
| **ASSETS** | % | % | % | % | % | % | % | % | % |
| Cash & Equivalents | 10.7 | 11.4 | 10.8 | 14.5 | 11.0 | 7.6 | 8.5 | 10.9 | 12.8 |
| Trade Receivables (net) | 49.7 | 49.4 | 50.2 | 39.6 | 46.7 | 47.9 | 61.1 | 52.2 | 49.3 |
| Inventory | 3.3 | 2.8 | 3.7 | 2.0 | 5.0 | 1.0 | 3.7 | 5.0 | 5.5 |
| All Other Current | 7.5 | 9.6 | 9.3 | 7.3 | 9.8 | 14.3 | 6.8 | 8.3 | 11.4 |
| Total Current | 71.1 | 73.1 | 74.0 | 63.4 | 72.5 | 70.9 | 80.1 | 76.4 | 79.0 |
| Fixed Assets (net) | 8.4 | 8.3 | 7.8 | 11.6 | 8.6 | 5.1 | 5.0 | 9.3 | 7.8 |
| Intangibles (net) | 2.9 | 2.6 | 2.8 | 1.5 | 1.0 | 2.7 | 2.5 | 1.8 | 8.2 |
| All Other Non-Current | 17.5 | 16.0 | 15.4 | 23.5 | 17.9 | 21.3 | 12.5 | 12.4 | 5.0 |
| Total | 100.0 | 100.0 | 100.0 | 100.0 | 100.0 | 100.0 | 100.0 | 100.0 | 100.0 |
| **LIABILITIES** | | | | | | | | | |
| Notes Payable-Short Term | 27.3 | 28.6 | 28.9 | 25.6 | 24.1 | 29.5 | 34.4 | 28.9 | 29.3 |
| Cur. Mat.-L.T.D. | 4.3 | 3.1 | 3.1 | 2.1 | 4.7 | 4.4 | 2.7 | 1.8 | 3.1 |
| Trade Payables | 4.6 | 4.0 | 3.9 | 2.0 | 2.5 | 3.9 | 3.6 | 6.6 | 5.7 |
| Income Taxes Payable | .2 | .1 | .1 | .0 | .1 | .0 | .1 | .1 | .2 |
| All Other Current | 9.0 | 9.3 | 8.5 | 9.1 | 6.5 | 6.8 | 8.1 | 7.6 | 13.9 |
| Total Current | 45.3 | 45.2 | 44.5 | 38.8 | 37.9 | 44.6 | 48.9 | 45.0 | 52.3 |
| Long-Term Debt | 16.1 | 16.5 | 17.6 | 16.4 | 23.0 | 21.5 | 14.1 | 17.9 | 13.1 |
| Deferred Taxes | .3 | .2 | .3 | .0 | .1 | .2 | .0 | .0 | 1.8 |
| All Other Non-Current | 7.7 | 8.1 | 9.1 | 7.0 | 10.3 | 12.4 | 8.1 | 6.7 | 10.8 |
| Net Worth | 30.6 | 30.0 | 28.5 | 37.7 | 28.7 | 21.4 | 28.9 | 30.3 | 22.0 |
| Total Liabilities & Net Worth | 100.0 | 100.0 | 100.0 | 100.0 | 100.0 | 100.0 | 100.0 | 100.0 | 100.0 |
| **INCOME DATA** | | | | | | | | | |
| Net Sales | 100.0 | 100.0 | 100.0 | 100.0 | 100.0 | 100.0 | 100.0 | 100.0 | 100.0 |
| Gross Profit | | | | | | | | | |
| Operating Expenses | 73.7 | 71.5 | 69.5 | 63.8 | 72.0 | 63.4 | 67.2 | 72.1 | 79.7 |
| Operating Profit | 26.3 | 28.5 | 30.5 | 36.2 | 28.0 | 36.6 | 32.8 | 27.9 | 20.3 |
| All Other Expenses (net) | 9.8 | 11.7 | 12.3 | 19.7 | 12.2 | 13.4 | 11.5 | 11.4 | 4.7 |
| Profit Before Taxes | 16.5 | 16.7 | 18.2 | 16.5 | 15.8 | 23.1 | 21.2 | 16.5 | 15.6 |
| **RATIOS** | | | | | | | | | |
| Current | 3.1 | 3.0 | 3.2 | 5.6 | 3.8 | 2.7 | 3.1 | 3.4 | 2.1 |
| | 1.5 | 1.5 | 1.6 | 1.6 | 1.8 | 1.7 | 1.5 | 1.5 | 1.4 |
| | 1.1 | 1.2 | 1.2 | 1.0 | 1.3 | 1.2 | 1.3 | 1.2 | 1.2 |
| Quick | 2.4 | 2.5 | 2.7 | 4.3 | 3.3 | 2.3 | 2.6 | 2.6 | 2.0 |
| | 1.4 | 1.4 | 1.4 | 1.5 | 1.7 | 1.4 | 1.4 | 1.4 | 1.2 |
| | .8 | .9 | .9 | .4 | .8 | .4 | 1.2 | 1.1 | .7 |
| Sales/Receivables | 17  21.6 | 21  17.1 | 12  29.5 | 0  UND | 13  27.6 | 5  78.9 | 68  5.4 | 15  23.9 | 14  26.3 |
| | 526  .7 | 609  .6 | 456  .8 | 89  4.1 | 243  1.5 | 456  .8 | 1217  .3 | 332  1.1 | 74  4.9 |
| | 1439  .3 | 1552  .2 | 1217  .3 | 1825  .2 | 1825  .2 | 1217  .3 | 1825  .2 | 1825  .2 | 730  .5 |
| Cost of Sales/Inventory | | | | | | | | | |
| Cost of Sales/Payables | | | | | | | | | |
| Sales/Working Capital | .6 | .5 | .5 | .3 | .4 | .4 | .5 | .7 | 1.4 |
| | 1.4 | 1.2 | 1.2 | 1.2 | 1.0 | .9 | .9 | 2.1 | 7.0 |
| | 10.8 | 7.0 | 7.3 | 10.4 | 3.0 | 6.8 | 2.6 | 6.8 | 20.5 |
| EBIT/Interest | 5.7 | 5.1 | 7.2 | 10.8 | 4.7 | 5.8 | 5.3 | 7.2 | 15.7 |
| | (196) 2.5 | (168) 3.0 | (172) 3.4 | (22) 4.8 | (29) 2.5 | (24) 3.4 | (39) 3.2 | (25) 3.6 | (33) 5.1 |
| | 1.5 | 1.4 | 2.0 | 2.1 | 1.5 | 2.0 | 1.8 | 1.9 | 2.1 |
| Net Profit + Depr., Dep., Amort./Cur. Mat. L/T/D | 5.5 | 7.9 | 3.8 | | | | | | |
| | (26) 2.1 | (10) 2.1 | (16) 1.5 | | | | | | |
| | .1 | .3 | .1 | | | | | | |
| Fixed/Worth | .0 | .0 | .0 | .0 | .0 | .0 | .0 | .0 | .0 |
| | .0 | .0 | .0 | .0 | .0 | .0 | .0 | .0 | .1 |
| | .4 | .3 | .2 | .1 | .3 | .1 | .2 | .3 | .8 |
| Debt/Worth | 1.4 | 1.3 | 1.4 | .4 | 1.2 | 1.9 | 1.6 | 1.6 | 1.8 |
| | 3.2 | 3.1 | 3.0 | 2.2 | 2.4 | 3.4 | 2.9 | 4.7 | 4.0 |
| | 9.5 | 7.7 | 8.1 | 8.7 | 8.1 | 30.0 | 6.6 | 7.1 | 12.5 |
| % Profit Before Taxes/Tangible Net Worth | 33.0 | 38.9 | 43.8 | 28.8 | 29.0 | 76.6 | 41.7 | 76.3 | 81.0 |
| | (297) 15.1 | (276) 15.8 | (270) 16.9 | (42) 8.9 | (53) 11.5 | (34) 23.4 | (66) 18.3 | (40) 16.2 | (35) 34.2 |
| | 4.8 | 4.6 | 5.7 | 1.5 | 2.4 | 9.2 | 8.7 | 4.3 | 13.5 |
| % Profit Before Taxes/Total Assets | 7.7 | 8.0 | 10.0 | 8.6 | 8.0 | 8.2 | 8.6 | 9.6 | 17.8 |
| | 3.2 | 3.5 | 3.9 | 2.6 | 2.3 | 3.7 | 4.7 | 4.4 | 8.3 |
| | 1.1 | 1.0 | 1.5 | .6 | .4 | 1.9 | 2.3 | 1.7 | 2.7 |
| Sales/Net Fixed Assets | 258.2 | 603.2 | 526.5 | UND | 355.1 | 999.8 | 185.7 | 394.7 | 175.7 |
| | 45.0 | 47.7 | 69.1 | 494.0 | 59.1 | 84.7 | 56.8 | 62.0 | 57.2 |
| | 11.3 | 10.1 | 13.0 | 10.3 | 13.5 | 15.9 | 10.5 | 13.7 | 10.8 |
| Sales/Total Assets | .6 | .5 | .9 | .3 | .5 | .5 | .4 | 1.0 | 2.0 |
| | .3 | .2 | .3 | .2 | .3 | .2 | .2 | .3 | .9 |
| | .2 | .1 | .1 | .1 | .1 | .1 | .1 | .1 | .4 |
| % Depr., Dep., Amort./Sales | .5 | .6 | .5 | .5 | .4 | .3 | .6 | .5 | .4 |
| | (185) 1.3 | (148) 1.5 | (152) 1.1 | (12) 2.3 | (35) 1.0 | (21) .9 | (40) 1.2 | (23) 1.3 | (21) .7 |
| | 3.0 | 3.4 | 3.3 | 22.1 | 4.0 | 1.7 | 3.1 | 3.4 | 2.4 |
| % Officers', Directors' Owners' Comp/Sales | 4.3 | 3.5 | 3.5 | 6.3 | 6.4 | | 1.6 | | |
| | (64) 11.5 | (60) 10.1 | (64) 6.6 | (11) 17.6 | (21) 10.5 | | (12) 3.2 | | |
| | 20.0 | 15.9 | 17.2 | 34.6 | 17.0 | | 6.1 | | |
| Net Sales ($) | 5251124M | 4150995M | 4364277M | 22515M | 100652M | 159852M | 489239M | 633913M | 2958106M |
| Total Assets ($) | 11549976M | 11932117M | 10730057M | 160600M | 555276M | 848088M | 2691449M | 2561168M | 3913476M |

M = $ thousand    MM = $ million
See Pages 9 through 22 for Explanation of Ratios and Data

## Current Data Sorted by Assets

| | | | | | | | Comparative Historical Data |
|---|---|---|---|---|---|---|---|

| | | | | | | Type of Statement | | |
|---|---|---|---|---|---|---|---|---|
| 6 | 4 | 32 | 71 | 26 | 8 | Unqualified | 108 | 106 |
| | | 2 | 2 | | | Reviewed | 8 | 5 |
| 1 | 1 | 3 | 2 | | | Compiled | 17 | 11 |
| 5 | 4 | 2 | 1 | 1 | | Tax Returns | 22 | 21 |
| 4 | 4 | 8 | 11 | 6 | 5 | Other | 53 | 68 |
| | 26 (4/1-9/30/11) | | 183 (10/1/11-3/31/12) | | | | 4/1/07-3/31/08 | 4/1/08-3/31/09 |
| 0-500M | 500M-2MM | 2-10MM | 10-50MM | 50-100MM | 100-250MM | | ALL | ALL |
| 16 | 13 | 47 | 87 | 33 | 13 | NUMBER OF STATEMENTS | 208 | 211 |
| % | % | % | % | % | % | ASSETS | % | % |
| 36.5 | 18.4 | 18.8 | 10.7 | 10.3 | 6.1 | Cash & Equivalents | 15.5 | 15.7 |
| 16.2 | 17.2 | 18.4 | 7.2 | 3.4 | 15.3 | Trade Receivables (net) | 22.7 | 20.1 |
| .0 | 10.2 | 21.1 | 49.3 | 47.2 | 26.9 | Inventory | 6.5 | 8.9 |
| 3.8 | 13.7 | 16.9 | 9.1 | 16.7 | 17.1 | All Other Current | 22.7 | 18.1 |
| 56.5 | 59.5 | 75.1 | 76.4 | 77.5 | 65.4 | Total Current | 67.5 | 62.8 |
| 13.6 | 12.9 | 6.4 | 5.0 | 2.0 | 6.1 | Fixed Assets (net) | 13.2 | 12.3 |
| 3.2 | 1.3 | 2.8 | 1.8 | .1 | 5.5 | Intangibles (net) | 2.0 | -2.5 |
| 26.7 | 26.3 | 15.7 | 16.8 | 20.3 | 23.0 | All Other Non-Current | 17.4 | 22.3 |
| 100.0 | 100.0 | 100.0 | 100.0 | 100.0 | 100.0 | Total | 100.0 | 100.0 |
| | | | | | | LIABILITIES | | |
| 21.0 | 23.5 | 40.3 | 59.0 | 54.2 | 39.0 | Notes Payable-Short Term | 37.6 | 41.4 |
| .7 | 1.6 | .6 | 1.0 | 2.4 | .9 | Cur. Mat.-L.T.D. | 2.7 | 2.9 |
| 9.6 | 2.4 | 4.3 | 3.0 | 3.7 | 2.1 | Trade Payables | 3.3 | 3.3 |
| .3 | .2 | .3 | .2 | .0 | .0 | Income Taxes Payable | .1 | .1 |
| 26.2 | 6.7 | 10.2 | 7.8 | 9.2 | 3.5 | All Other Current | 10.4 | 8.8 |
| 57.7 | 34.4 | 55.8 | 71.1 | 69.5 | 45.5 | Total Current | 54.1 | 56.5 |
| 14.4 | 8.1 | 6.1 | 5.8 | 6.4 | 26.7 | Long-Term Debt | 12.7 | 14.4 |
| .0 | .6 | .1 | .1 | .0 | .2 | Deferred Taxes | .1 | .1 |
| 4.7 | 4.4 | 1.9 | .7 | 1.2 | 3.0 | All Other Non-Current | 3.8 | 3.0 |
| 23.2 | 52.6 | 36.2 | 22.3 | 22.9 | 24.5 | Net Worth | 29.2 | 26.0 |
| 100.0 | 100.0 | 100.0 | 100.0 | 100.0 | 100.0 | Total Liabilities & Net Worth | 100.0 | 100.0 |
| | | | | | | INCOME DATA | | |
| 100.0 | 100.0 | 100.0 | 100.0 | 100.0 | 100.0 | Net Sales | 100.0 | 100.0 |
| | | | | | | Gross Profit | | |
| 91.3 | 77.8 | 85.8 | 82.8 | 79.0 | 74.4 | Operating Expenses | 83.8 | 83.4 |
| 8.7 | 22.2 | 14.2 | 17.2 | 21.0 | 25.6 | Operating Profit | 16.2 | 16.6 |
| 1.1 | 7.8 | 4.7 | 5.1 | 4.7 | 16.5 | All Other Expenses (net) | 8.0 | 7.9 |
| 7.6 | 14.4 | 9.5 | 12.1 | 16.3 | 9.1 | Profit Before Taxes | 8.2 | 8.7 |
| | | | | | | RATIOS | | |
| 3.3 | 4.0 | 1.9 | 1.2 | 1.2 | 5.6 | | 1.7 | 2.0 |
| 1.0 | 1.9 | 1.3 | 1.1 | 1.1 | 1.1 | Current | 1.2 | 1.1 |
| .3 | .9 | 1.1 | 1.0 | 1.1 | 1.0 | | 1.0 | .9 |
| 2.9 | 2.0 | 1.3 | .3 | .4 | 2.9 | | 1.3 | 1.5 |
| 1.0 | 1.2 | .5 | .1 | .1 | .5 | Quick | .8 | .5 |
| .2 | .2 | .2 | .1 | .1 | .1 | | .1 | .1 |
| 0 UND | 0 UND | 0 UND | 0 UND | 1 335.6 | 7 55.1 | | 0 UND | 0 UND |
| 0 UND | 0 UND | 4 92.9 | 3 128.6 | 4 97.0 | 28 13.2 | Sales/Receivables | 9 41.0 | 6 59.0 |
| 11 32.7 | 57 6.4 | 78 4.7 | 30 12.0 | 37 9.9 | 104 3.5 | | 206 1.8 | 132 2.8 |
| | | | | | | Cost of Sales/Inventory | | |
| | | | | | | Cost of Sales/Payables | | |
| 9.1 | 2.6 | 1.3 | 2.4 | 2.1 | .9 | | 1.8 | 1.9 |
| NM | 3.4 | 2.6 | 5.4 | 6.0 | 6.7 | Sales/Working Capital | 6.5 | 9.4 |
| -6.7 | NM | 25.3 | 18.0 | 8.7 | 11.3 | | 69.0 | -15.2 |
| | | 9.8 | 7.6 | 5.6 | | | 6.2 | 5.0 |
| | (34) 2.2 | (76) 2.6 | (27) 2.7 | | EBIT/Interest | (133) 1.8 | (135) 2.0 |
| | | 1.1 | 1.5 | 1.6 | | | .5 | .8 |
| | | | | | | | 14.2 | |
| | | | | | | Net Profit + Depr., Dep., | (13) 1.0 | |
| | | | | | | Amort./Cur. Mat. L/T/D | -1.1 | |
| .0 | .0 | .0 | .0 | .0 | .0 | | .0 | .0 |
| .1 | .0 | .0 | .1 | .1 | .0 | Fixed/Worth | .1 | .1 |
| .4 | 1.1 | .1 | .1 | .2 | .2 | | .5 | .6 |
| .3 | .3 | .8 | 3.3 | 2.5 | 1.6 | | 1.4 | 1.2 |
| 1.1 | .9 | 2.3 | 5.8 | 7.1 | 6.4 | Debt/Worth | 3.8 | 4.4 |
| 11.7 | 3.2 | 4.6 | 8.5 | 11.2 | 11.7 | | 8.5 | 10.2 |
| 240.7 | 44.0 | 37.6 | 35.7 | 47.4 | 41.2 | % Profit Before Taxes/Tangible | 38.0 | 37.5 |
| (13) 81.7 | (12) 7.6 | (44) 12.9 | (86) 17.0 | 25.1 | 30.8 | Net Worth | (199) 9.7 | (192) 11.9 |
| 19.0 | -8.0 | .0 | 6.3 | 10.8 | .3 | | -4.6 | .1 |
| 62.3 | 30.7 | 12.1 | 5.8 | 8.3 | 8.9 | % Profit Before Taxes/Total | 7.4 | 6.9 |
| 28.8 | 1.9 | 2.5 | 3.5 | 3.5 | 2.9 | Assets | 1.9 | 2.4 |
| -5.0 | -2.8 | .0 | .9 | 1.2 | .0 | | -.8 | -.2 |
| 298.0 | UND | 115.6 | 77.2 | 63.9 | 128.4 | | 98.1 | 163.6 |
| 82.9 | 169.6 | 63.5 | 46.7 | 41.2 | 70.4 | Sales/Net Fixed Assets | 28.0 | 43.3 |
| 23.4 | 13.7 | 18.6 | 15.8 | 20.8 | 30.2 | | 8.3 | 10.6 |
| 7.0 | 2.3 | 1.0 | .4 | .5 | .5 | | 1.4 | 1.5 |
| 4.9 | 1.7 | .4 | .3 | .3 | .3 | Sales/Total Assets | .5 | .5 |
| 2.7 | .3 | .3 | .2 | .2 | .1 | | .2 | .2 |
| | | .4 | .4 | .5 | .4 | | .6 | .5 |
| | (37) .9 | (73) .8 | (28) .9 | (12) .8 | % Depr., Dep., Amort./Sales | (145) 1.3 | (136) 1.1 |
| | | 1.6 | 1.2 | 1.3 | 1.8 | | 2.1 | 2.2 |
| | | 10.0 | | | | | 4.1 | 5.8 |
| | (10) 20.1 | | | | % Officers', Directors' | (45) 10.4 | (46) 9.0 |
| | | 37.3 | | | | Owners' Comp/Sales | 28.8 | 17.4 |
| 18843M | 27024M | 146796M | 801874M | 874829M | 5999693M | Net Sales ($) | 2167591M | 1552604M |
| 3822M | 17312M | 240469M | 2212933M | 2297802M | 1877713M | Total Assets ($) | 4444657M | 4196594M |

M = $ thousand    MM = $ million
See Pages 9 through 22 for Explanation of Ratios and Data

## Comparative Historical Data | | | | Current Data Sorted by Sales

| Hist 4/1/09-3/31/10 ALL | Hist 4/1/10-3/31/11 ALL | Hist 4/1/11-3/31/12 ALL | Type of Statement | 0-1MM | 1-3MM | 3-5MM | 5-10MM | 10-25MM | 25MM & OVER |
|---|---|---|---|---|---|---|---|---|---|
| 105 | 87 | 147 | Unqualified | 5 | 32 | 22 | 32 | 37 | 19 |
| 5 | 1 | 4 | Reviewed | | 2 | 1 | | 1 | |
| 6 | 5 | 7 | Compiled | 1 | 2 | 1 | 2 | 1 | |
| 21 | 13 | 13 | Tax Returns | 5 | 3 | 2 | 2 | 1 | |
| 74 | 41 | 38 | Other | 6 | 10 | 6 | 4 | 5 | 7 |
| | | | | | 26 (4/1-9/30/11) | | 183 (10/1/11-3/31/12) | | |
| 211 | 147 | 209 | NUMBER OF STATEMENTS | 17 | 49 | 32 | 40 | 45 | 26 |
| % | % | % | ASSETS | % | % | % | % | % | % |
| 18.1 | 19.9 | 14.6 | Cash & Equivalents | 11.0 | 28.2 | 16.3 | 6.8 | 9.6 | 10.3 |
| 26.3 | 13.3 | 10.9 | Trade Receivables (net) | 16.7 | 15.0 | 10.3 | 10.1 | 7.2 | 7.7 |
| 9.8 | 13.0 | 35.0 | Inventory | 4.5 | 19.7 | 29.4 | 54.2 | 50.5 | 34.6 |
| 15.6 | 23.6 | 12.4 | All Other Current | 6.3 | 14.7 | 8.4 | 10.4 | 9.9 | 24.7 |
| 69.8 | 69.8 | 73.0 | Total Current | 38.6 | 77.6 | 64.4 | 81.5 | 77.2 | 77.4 |
| 8.6 | 8.7 | 6.1 | Fixed Assets (net) | 18.3 | 3.7 | 8.2 | 5.9 | .3 | 5.2 |
| 1.8 | 2.5 | 2.1 | Intangibles (net) | 2.8 | 1.6 | 3.0 | .6 | 2.6 | 2.8 |
| 19.8 | 19.0 | 18.8 | All Other Non-Current | 40.4 | 17.1 | 24.4 | 11.9 | 17.2 | 14.6 |
| 100.0 | 100.0 | 100.0 | Total | 100.0 | 100.0 | 100.0 | 100.0 | 100.0 | 100.0 |
| | | | LIABILITIES | | | | | | |
| 42.5 | 38.1 | 47.7 | Notes Payable-Short Term | 24.9 | 35.9 | 45.2 | 59.7 | 57.8 | 51.9 |
| 2.2 | 1.6 | 1.2 | Cur. Mat.-L.T.D. | 2.7 | 1.5 | .4 | 2.2 | .3 | .5 |
| 3.9 | 3.7 | 3.8 | Trade Payables | 7.5 | 4.4 | 3.2 | 3.7 | 2.9 | 2.9 |
| .1 | .3 | .2 | Income Taxes Payable | .0 | .4 | .1 | .0 | .3 | .1 |
| 9.7 | 9.1 | 9.6 | All Other Current | 4.3 | 18.7 | 7.8 | 4.9 | 6.8 | 10.5 |
| 58.4 | 52.9 | 62.5 | Total Current | 39.3 | 60.8 | 56.6 | 70.5 | 68.1 | 65.8 |
| 10.2 | 11.6 | 8.1 | Long-Term Debt | 29.2 | 4.7 | 3.3 | 7.7 | 9.2 | 4.9 |
| .1 | .2 | .1 | Deferred Taxes | .0 | .0 | .3 | .1 | .2 | .1 |
| 3.6 | 1.8 | 1.7 | All Other Non-Current | 4.4 | .2 | 5.1 | .8 | 1.1 | 1.2 |
| 27.8 | 33.5 | 27.6 | Net Worth | 27.1 | 34.2 | 34.7 | 20.8 | 21.3 | 28.0 |
| 100.0 | 100.0 | 100.0 | Total Liabilities & Net Worth | 100.0 | 100.0 | 100.0 | 100.0 | 100.0 | 100.0 |
| | | | INCOME DATA | | | | | | |
| 100.0 | 100.0 | 100.0 | Net Sales | 100.0 | 100.0 | 100.0 | 100.0 | 100.0 | 100.0 |
| | | | Gross Profit | | | | | | |
| 79.6 | 80.2 | 82.7 | Operating Expenses | 69.6 | 85.7 | 82.2 | 86.1 | 81.8 | 82.5 |
| 20.4 | 19.8 | 17.3 | Operating Profit | 30.4 | 14.3 | 17.8 | 13.9 | 18.2 | 17.5 |
| 8.3 | 6.4 | 5.6 | All Other Expenses (net) | 11.5 | 3.5 | 8.2 | 4.9 | 6.1 | 2.4 |
| 12.1 | 13.4 | 11.8 | Profit Before Taxes | 18.9 | 10.8 | 9.6 | 9.0 | 12.1 | 15.1 |
| | | | RATIOS | | | | | | |
| 2.0 / 1.2 / 1.0 | 1.9 / 1.2 / 1.1 | 1.5 / 1.1 / 1.0 | Current | 1.6 / .5 / .2 | 2.0 / 1.3 / 1.0 | 1.9 / 1.2 / .9 | 1.2 / 1.1 / 1.0 | 1.3 / 1.1 / 1.1 | 1.4 / 1.1 / 1.1 |
| 1.5 / .9 / .1 | 1.5 / .3 / .1 | 1.0 / .2 / .1 | Quick | 1.3 / .2 / .1 | 1.6 / .5 / .2 | 1.4 / .2 / .1 | .3 / .1 / .1 | .4 / .1 / .1 | .7 / .1 / .1 |
| 0 UND / 13 28.2 / 403 .9 | 0 UND / 4 84.3 / 33 11.2 | 0 UND / 4 90.9 / 37 9.9 | Sales/Receivables | 0 UND / 0 UND / 192 1.9 | 0 UND / 0 UND / 39 9.4 | 0 UND / 3 132.8 / 41 9.0 | 0 UND / 4 91.3 / 31 11.9 | 2 217.2 / 17 22.0 / 41 9.0 | 1 324.4 / 5 68.7 / 32 11.4 |
| | | | Cost of Sales/Inventory | | | | | | |
| | | | Cost of Sales/Payables | | | | | | |
| 1.8 / 6.1 / 269.0 | 2.6 / 6.4 / 18.6 | 2.2 / 5.5 / 19.9 | Sales/Working Capital | 1.1 / -12.7 / -3.0 | 1.6 / 3.4 / NM | 2.1 / 4.1 / NM | 2.3 / 5.4 / 16.4 | 2.3 / 5.7 / 9.3 | 4.6 / 6.8 / 10.4 |
| 8.8 / (132) 3.3 / 2.0 | 9.1 / (99) 3.6 / 2.2 | 7.9 / (163) 2.6 / 1.5 | EBIT/Interest | 12.0 / (10) 3.2 / 1.7 | 11.7 / (35) 2.3 / 1.0 | 23.3 / (23) 2.9 / 1.6 | 4.1 / (34) 1.9 / 1.1 | 5.5 / (37) 2.6 / 1.6 | 11.1 / (24) 4.1 / 2.6 |
| | 24.7 / (10) 2.4 / 1.1 | 13.3 / (11) 2.3 / .9 | Net Profit + Depr., Dep., Amort./Cur. Mat. L/T/D | | | | | | |
| .0 / .1 / .4 | .0 / .1 / .2 | .0 / .0 / .1 | Fixed/Worth | .0 / .1 / 1.2 | .0 / .0 / .1 | .0 / .0 / .1 | .0 / .1 / .2 | .0 / .1 / .1 | .0 / .1 / .2 |
| 1.3 / 3.3 / 7.6 | 1.0 / 3.4 / 6.6 | 1.4 / 4.6 / 8.5 | Debt/Worth | .7 / 1.6 / 9.6 | .7 / 2.1 / 6.7 | .8 / 3.3 / 5.3 | 3.6 / 6.5 / 9.5 | 2.8 / 6.3 / 11.0 | 1.4 / 6.5 / 9.8 |
| 57.7 / (193) 21.1 / 6.8 | 51.3 / (142) 24.6 / 8.4 | 42.5 / (201) 18.0 / 3.6 | % Profit Before Taxes/Tangible Net Worth | 96.3 / (14) 8.7 / -.3 | 38.5 / (46) 14.5 / .0 | 41.2 / (31) 14.1 / -1.6 | 33.8 / 14.5 / 1.0 | 40.0 / (44) 26.8 / 7.3 | 59.2 / 37.8 / 20.1 |
| 11.6 / 4.9 / 1.1 | 12.6 / 5.0 / 1.5 | 7.9 / 3.0 / .5 | % Profit Before Taxes/Total Assets | 13.1 / 2.2 / -.9 | 11.9 / 2.5 / .0 | 6.7 / 2.9 / -.3 | 7.0 / 1.6 / .2 | 6.5 / 3.9 / 1.4 | 12.2 / 6.7 / 3.3 |
| 257.2 / 48.3 / 14.9 | 223.5 / 51.6 / 15.0 | 107.4 / 48.3 / 19.5 | Sales/Net Fixed Assets | UND / 22.5 / 6.8 | 188.5 / 80.6 / 38.8 | 135.2 / 55.4 / 20.2 | 80.5 / 45.3 / 8.9 | 71.6 / 48.2 / 24.8 | 62.0 / 42.2 / 23.6 |
| 1.5 / .5 / .2 | 1.0 / .5 / .2 | .6 / .4 / .2 | Sales/Total Assets | 2.1 / .3 / .1 | 1.5 / .4 / .2 | 1.2 / .4 / .2 | .4 / .3 / .2 | .4 / .3 / .2 | .6 / .5 / .4 |
| .5 / (138) .9 / 1.7 | .4 / (98) .9 / 1.5 | .4 / (164) .8 / 1.3 | % Depr., Dep., Amort./Sales | | .4 / (35) .7 / 1.3 | .3 / (22) .6 / 1.0 | .5 / (37) .8 / 1.1 | .5 / (38) .7 / 1.3 | .4 / (24) 1.0 / 1.7 |
| 6.6 / (33) 14.9 / 26.0 | 4.2 / (32) 10.5 / 26.3 | 6.4 / (29) 11.7 / 27.6 | % Officers', Directors' Owners' Comp/Sales | 8.0 / (14) 15.7 / 32.2 | | | | | |
| 3465399M | 6818169M | 7869059M | Net Sales ($) | 7369M | 98435M | 125555M | 288506M | 699473M | 6649721M |
| 7080365M | 4578036M | 6650051M | Total Assets ($) | 45063M | 292395M | 483164M | 954171M | 2488661M | 2386597M |

M = $ thousand    MM = $ million
See Pages 9 through 22 for Explanation of Ratios and Data

## Current Data Sorted by Assets　　　　Comparative Historical Data

| 0-500M | 500M-2MM | 2-10MM | 10-50MM | 50-100MM | 100-250MM | | 4/1/07-3/31/08 ALL | 4/1/08-3/31/09 ALL |
|---|---|---|---|---|---|---|---|---|
| | | 11 (4/1-9/30/11) | | | 99 (10/1/11-3/31/12) | Type of Statement | | |
| 1 | 4 | 11 | 20 | 2 | 10 | Unqualified | 28 | 46 |
| 1 | 2 | | | | 1 | Reviewed | 2 | 3 |
| 2 | 1 | 1 | | | | Compiled | 4 | 8 |
| 3 | 2 | | | | | Tax Returns | 1 | 11 |
| 3 | 5 | 12 | 13 | 6 | 11 | Other | 36 | 49 |
| 9 | 13 | 25 | 33 | 8 | 22 | NUMBER OF STATEMENTS | 71 | 117 |
| % | % | % | % | % | % | ASSETS | % | % |
| | 29.5 | 37.3 | 36.2 | | 21.9 | Cash & Equivalents | 29.2 | 32.3 |
| | 17.8 | 14.7 | 22.2 | | 16.4 | Trade Receivables (net) | 19.5 | 24.0 |
| | 4.7 | 2.4 | 2.7 | | .1 | Inventory | 2.4 | 1.7 |
| | 7.7 | 7.3 | 8.7 | | 6.3 | All Other Current | 7.4 | 8.8 |
| | 59.6 | 61.7 | 69.8 | | 44.7 | Total Current | 58.5 | 66.8 |
| | 27.1 | 18.3 | 8.7 | | 8.0 | Fixed Assets (net) | 18.1 | 13.7 |
| | 10.0 | 5.8 | 16.0 | | 30.1 | Intangibles (net) | 10.7 | 9.8 |
| | 3.4 | 14.1 | 5.4 | | 17.2 | All Other Non-Current | 12.7 | 9.7 |
| | 100.0 | 100.0 | 100.0 | | 100.0 | Total | 100.0 | 100.0 |
| | | | | | | LIABILITIES | | |
| | 9.8 | 3.9 | 10.2 | | 3.6 | Notes Payable-Short Term | 10.0 | 13.6 |
| | 4.7 | 2.2 | 3.1 | | 1.3 | Cur. Mat.-L.T.D. | 3.6 | 5.0 |
| | 9.2 | 8.1 | 17.3 | | 9.2 | Trade Payables | 12.4 | 11.4 |
| | 1.0 | .2 | .2 | | .9 | Income Taxes Payable | .3 | .5 |
| | 11.5 | 15.8 | 23.5 | | 30.6 | All Other Current | 18.2 | 22.9 |
| | 36.2 | 30.2 | 54.2 | | 45.5 | Total Current | 44.5 | 53.3 |
| | 51.6 | 18.0 | 17.1 | | 25.4 | Long-Term Debt | 24.0 | 16.7 |
| | .1 | .3 | .4 | | 1.2 | Deferred Taxes | .3 | .1 |
| | 8.2 | 12.4 | 7.9 | | 1.8 | All Other Non-Current | 7.3 | 7.3 |
| | 3.9 | 39.1 | 20.4 | | 26.1 | Net Worth | 23.8 | 22.6 |
| | 100.0 | 100.0 | 100.0 | | 100.0 | Total Liabilities & Net Worth | 100.0 | 100.0 |
| | | | | | | INCOME DATA | | |
| | 100.0 | 100.0 | 100.0 | | 100.0 | Net Sales | 100.0 | 100.0 |
| | | | | | | Gross Profit | | |
| | 88.4 | 88.5 | 87.2 | | 90.2 | Operating Expenses | 91.7 | 87.1 |
| | 11.6 | 11.6 | 12.8 | | 9.8 | Operating Profit | 8.3 | 12.9 |
| | 4.0 | .6 | 2.2 | | 2.7 | All Other Expenses (net) | 2.6 | 2.1 |
| | 7.7 | 11.0 | 10.6 | | 7.1 | Profit Before Taxes | 5.7 | 10.9 |
| | | | | | | RATIOS | | |
| | 3.9 | 3.7 | 1.7 | | 1.6 | Current | 2.2 | 2.1 |
| | 2.3 | 2.4 | 1.3 | | 1.0 | | 1.2 | 1.3 |
| | 1.5 | 1.3 | 1.0 | | .8 | | .9 | 1.0 |
| | 3.8 | 3.5 | 1.5 | | 1.5 | Quick | 1.9 | 1.9 |
| | 1.4 | 1.7 | 1.1 | | .9 | | 1.1 | 1.1 |
| | .8 | 1.0 | .9 | | .5 | | .7 | .7 |
| 1　586.8 | 2　218.4 | 16　22.6 | | | 11　33.6 | Sales/Receivables | 3　109.7 | 4　91.0 |
| 10　35.1 | 22　16.6 | 38　9.5 | | | 35　10.4 | | 28　12.9 | 28　12.9 |
| 46　7.9 | 35　10.3 | 107　3.4 | | | 114　3.2 | | 57　6.4 | 92　3.9 |
| | | | | | | Cost of Sales/Inventory | | |
| | | | | | | Cost of Sales/Payables | | |
| | 3.7 | 5.1 | 3.6 | | 4.9 | Sales/Working Capital | 4.7 | 2.7 |
| | 7.3 | 9.3 | 9.5 | | 23.6 | | 13.8 | 8.8 |
| | 44.2 | 20.9 | 40.9 | | -14.4 | | -104.7 | -75.9 |
| | 12.3 | 81.4 | 10.8 | | 9.3 | EBIT/Interest | 14.0 | 27.7 |
| | (11)　2.0 | (16)　13.9 | (16)　5.9 | | (19)　6.4 | | (50)　2.7 | (78)　4.9 |
| | 1.1 | 3.4 | 3.6 | | 2.6 | | .0 | .9 |
| | | | | | | Net Profit + Depr., Dep., Amort./Cur. Mat. L/T/D | 15.3 | 80.5 |
| | | | | | | | (16)　6.7 | (16)　13.9 |
| | | | | | | | 1.6 | 2.0 |
| | .1 | .1 | .1 | | .4 | Fixed/Worth | .2 | .1 |
| | .8 | .5 | .3 | | 1.0 | | .6 | .3 |
| | -34.8 | 1.9 | 2.2 | | -.2 | | 23.5 | NM |
| | .5 | .6 | 1.9 | | 1.6 | Debt/Worth | .9 | .9 |
| | 2.3 | 1.4 | 5.4 | | 26.9 | | 3.5 | 4.3 |
| | -39.3 | 12.0 | 41.2 | | -5.4 | | -7.4 | -12.1 |
| | | 126.3 | 83.2 | | 50.7 | % Profit Before Taxes/Tangible Net Worth | 64.9 | 82.1 |
| | (20)　47.6 | (26)　33.6 | | | (13)　11.6 | | (53)　22.0 | (86)　25.4 |
| | 29.6 | 8.5 | | | -.5 | | -6.4 | 8.1 |
| | 24.7 | 41.1 | 15.9 | | 14.2 | % Profit Before Taxes/Total Assets | 20.4 | 20.9 |
| | 6.2 | 20.4 | 6.7 | | 4.8 | | 8.1 | 5.8 |
| | 1.7 | 6.9 | 1.5 | | .7 | | -2.4 | 1.1 |
| | 105.9 | 51.8 | 80.2 | | 36.8 | Sales/Net Fixed Assets | 45.9 | 82.0 |
| | 22.0 | 24.6 | 36.3 | | 15.1 | | 15.4 | 25.9 |
| | 10.0 | 7.4 | 7.1 | | 9.8 | | 6.4 | 6.5 |
| | 4.3 | 3.7 | 1.8 | | 1.5 | Sales/Total Assets | 2.7 | 2.5 |
| | 2.4 | 2.3 | .8 | | .9 | | 1.7 | 1.4 |
| | 1.1 | 1.3 | .4 | | .4 | | .7 | .5 |
| | | .6 | .6 | | 2.3 | % Depr., Dep., Amort./Sales | 1.4 | .8 |
| | (20)　1.4 | (23)　1.5 | | | (12)　3.4 | | (44)　2.1 | (70)　2.4 |
| | 3.3 | 2.9 | | | 5.6 | | 5.5 | 4.3 |
| | | | | | | % Officers', Directors', Owners' Comp/Sales | 1.8 | 2.0 |
| | | | | | | | (17)　5.3 | (24)　5.0 |
| | | | | | | | 13.6 | 10.0 |
| 18056M | 92717M | 365478M | 867195M | 1581774M | 4125624M | Net Sales ($) | 2924124M | 4244305M |
| 1762M | 16261M | 110813M | 715761M | 656512M | 3879875M | Total Assets ($) | 2468796M | 3939846M |

M = $ thousand　　MM = $ million
See Pages 9 through 22 for Explanation of Ratios and Data

## Comparative Historical Data

## Current Data Sorted by Sales

| | | | | Type of Statement | | | | | | |
|---|---|---|---|---|---|---|---|---|---|---|
| 42 | | 54 | 48 | Unqualified | 1 | 2 | 5 | 9 | 10 | 21 |
| 3 | | 2 | 4 | Reviewed | | 1 | 2 | | 1 | |
| 2 | | | 3 | Compiled | 2 | 1 | | | | |
| 5 | | 9 | 5 | Tax Returns | 3 | 1 | | | 1 | |
| 46 | | 36 | 50 | Other | 3 | 4 | 5 | 8 | 7 | 23 |
| 4/1/09-3/31/10 | | 4/1/10-3/31/11 | 4/1/11-3/31/12 | | | 11 (4/1-9/30/11) | | 99 (10/1/11-3/31/12) | | |
| ALL | | ALL | ALL | | 0-1MM | 1-3MM | 3-5MM | 5-10MM | 10-25MM | 25MM & OVER |
| 98 | | 101 | 110 | NUMBER OF STATEMENTS | 9 | 9 | 12 | 17 | 19 | 44 |
| % | | % | % | ASSETS | % | % | % | % | % | % |
| 27.6 | | 29.1 | 32.6 | Cash & Equivalents | | | 30.5 | 34.5 | 35.5 | 29.3 |
| 15.9 | | 19.9 | 17.7 | Trade Receivables (net) | | | 17.6 | 12.9 | 19.7 | 18.3 |
| 2.2 | | 1.1 | 2.0 | Inventory | | | 4.4 | 7.8 | .1 | .7 |
| 12.4 | | 12.1 | 6.8 | All Other Current | | | 4.7 | 8.5 | 7.2 | 7.3 |
| 58.0 | | 62.2 | 59.0 | Total Current | | | 57.2 | 63.7 | 62.5 | 55.5 |
| 15.6 | | 14.0 | 14.3 | Fixed Assets (net) | | | 16.9 | 14.0 | 9.8 | 11.1 |
| 17.6 | | 14.9 | 16.2 | Intangibles (net) | | | 9.7 | 13.9 | 13.0 | 24.5 |
| 8.8 | | 8.9 | 10.5 | All Other Non-Current | | | 16.2 | 8.4 | 14.7 | 8.8 |
| 100.0 | | 100.0 | 100.0 | Total | | | 100.0 | 100.0 | 100.0 | 100.0 |
| | | | | LIABILITIES | | | | | | |
| 8.4 | | 12.2 | 8.4 | Notes Payable-Short Term | | | 14.4 | 11.4 | .4 | 3.7 |
| 5.8 | | 3.4 | 3.0 | Cur. Mat.-L.T.D. | | | 2.1 | 2.6 | 1.9 | 2.5 |
| 15.3 | | 13.8 | 10.5 | Trade Payables | | | 16.2 | 14.2 | 16.7 | 8.5 |
| .5 | | .2 | .4 | Income Taxes Payable | | | .1 | .3 | .1 | .6 |
| 18.9 | | 16.4 | 20.1 | All Other Current | | | 19.3 | 14.9 | 17.3 | 27.6 |
| 48.9 | | 46.1 | 42.4 | Total Current | | | 52.1 | 43.4 | 36.4 | 42.8 |
| 19.6 | | 23.3 | 27.5 | Long-Term Debt | | | 42.4 | 13.6 | 11.7 | 24.9 |
| .5 | | .3 | .4 | Deferred Taxes | | | .0 | .7 | .0 | .8 |
| 6.6 | | 7.4 | 6.8 | All Other Non-Current | | | 12.3 | 15.0 | 2.0 | 5.5 |
| 24.3 | | 23.0 | 22.9 | Net Worth | | | -6.9 | 27.3 | 49.9 | 26.0 |
| 100.0 | | 100.0 | 100.0 | Total Liabilities & Net Worth | | | 100.0 | 100.0 | 100.0 | 100.0 |
| | | | | INCOME DATA | | | | | | |
| 100.0 | | 100.0 | 100.0 | Net Sales | | | 100.0 | 100.0 | 100.0 | 100.0 |
| | | | | Gross Profit | | | | | | |
| 90.2 | | 88.2 | 86.9 | Operating Expenses | | | 85.5 | 83.1 | 86.9 | 91.5 |
| 9.8 | | 11.8 | 13.1 | Operating Profit | | | 14.5 | 16.9 | 13.1 | 8.5 |
| 2.8 | | 2.1 | 2.4 | All Other Expenses (net) | | | 4.3 | 4.1 | .2 | 1.8 |
| 7.0 | | 9.7 | 10.7 | Profit Before Taxes | | | 10.2 | 12.8 | 12.9 | 6.7 |
| | | | | RATIOS | | | | | | |
| 1.8 | | 2.7 | 2.6 | | | | 4.2 | 2.6 | 3.3 | 2.1 |
| 1.2 | | 1.5 | 1.5 | Current | | | 1.1 | 1.4 | 1.8 | 1.2 |
| .8 | | 1.1 | 1.0 | | | | .9 | 1.1 | 1.3 | .9 |
| 1.5 | | 2.3 | 2.2 | | | | 3.8 | 1.9 | 3.0 | 1.6 |
| 1.0 | | 1.2 | 1.3 | Quick | | | 1.0 | 1.3 | 1.7 | 1.1 |
| .5 | | .6 | .8 | | | | .6 | .7 | 1.2 | .8 |
| 4  81.1 | 7 | 53.1 | 6  66.2 | | 6  58.9 | 0  999.8 | | 3  124.7 | 9  39.2 | |
| 21  17.4 | 31 | 11.8 | 24  14.9 | Sales/Receivables | 26  13.8 | 29  12.8 | | 38  9.6 | 22  16.6 | |
| 50  7.2 | 66 | 5.5 | 60  6.1 | | 111  3.3 | 50  7.3 | | 47  7.8 | 81  4.5 | |
| | | | | Cost of Sales/Inventory | | | | | | |
| | | | | Cost of Sales/Payables | | | | | | |
| 5.3 | | 3.6 | 4.3 | | | | 2.1 | 2.4 | 5.0 | 6.7 |
| 17.0 | | 7.5 | 11.1 | Sales/Working Capital | | | 6.8 | 7.3 | 9.9 | 21.1 |
| -29.0 | | 64.1 | 76.8 | | | | -18.3 | 30.6 | 17.8 | -105.2 |
| 19.5 | | 24.8 | 16.0 | | | | 13.7 | 150.7 | 14.8 | |
| (66)  3.3 | (77) | 5.5 | (70)  6.7 | EBIT/Interest | | (10)  7.0 | (10)  25.2 | (32)  5.6 | | |
| -.7 | | 1.6 | 2.5 | | | | 3.4 | 9.4 | 2.6 | |
| 25.5 | | 10.3 | 12.2 | | | | | | | 10.6 |
| (18)  4.7 | (10) | 4.0 | (20)  6.0 | Net Profit + Depr., Dep., Amort./Cur. Mat. L/T/D | | | | | (10)  7.6 | |
| 1.7 | | 2.9 | 2.5 | | | | | | | 2.3 |
| .1 | | .1 | .1 | | | | .1 | .2 | .1 | .3 |
| .6 | | .5 | .4 | Fixed/Worth | | | 2.1 | .8 | .2 | .5 |
| -1.0 | | -1.1 | -52.6 | | | | NM | -1.4 | .4 | -.2 |
| 1.1 | | .8 | .8 | | | | 1.7 | 1.7 | .5 | 1.1 |
| 4.6 | | 3.1 | 3.9 | Debt/Worth | | | 28.1 | 3.6 | 1.1 | 4.8 |
| -4.3 | | -5.4 | -18.5 | | | | NM | -11.2 | 5.4 | -6.1 |
| 87.2 | | 83.6 | 121.6 | | | | 74.6 | 120.0 | 86.4 | |
| (67)  34.0 | (71) | 43.4 | (81)  37.9 | % Profit Before Taxes/Tangible Net Worth | | (12)  31.9 | (17)  38.6 | (29)  31.3 | | |
| 1.9 | | 6.2 | 8.8 | | | | 2.5 | 20.4 | 4.2 | |
| 20.3 | | 23.5 | 25.5 | | | | 11.2 | 27.6 | 58.7 | 20.1 |
| 5.4 | | 10.7 | 8.9 | % Profit Before Taxes/Total Assets | | | 4.6 | 5.4 | 18.2 | 9.3 |
| -3.3 | | 1.1 | 1.7 | | | | .9 | .9 | 2.8 | 1.8 |
| 57.7 | | 54.4 | 62.1 | | | | 136.7 | 43.2 | 61.8 | 59.1 |
| 15.9 | | 23.0 | 25.3 | Sales/Net Fixed Assets | | | 39.0 | 14.6 | 32.5 | 26.7 |
| 6.2 | | 8.7 | 8.7 | | | | 6.4 | 6.6 | 11.2 | 10.5 |
| 2.5 | | 2.9 | 2.7 | | | | 2.2 | 2.4 | 3.3 | 3.2 |
| 1.3 | | 1.4 | 1.5 | Sales/Total Assets | | | 1.2 | .9 | 1.6 | 1.5 |
| .6 | | .8 | .7 | | | | .1 | .3 | .7 | .9 |
| 1.6 | | 1.0 | .7 | | | | | | .6 | .7 |
| (61)  3.1 | (64) | 2.9 | (73)  1.8 | % Depr., Dep., Amort./Sales | | | | (16)  1.0 | (29)  2.2 | |
| 5.1 | | 5.1 | 3.9 | | | | | | 2.9 | 3.4 |
| 2.1 | | 2.2 | 2.7 | | | | | | | |
| (22)  4.9 | (15) | 5.5 | (15)  4.9 | % Officers', Directors' Owners' Comp/Sales | | | | | | |
| 10.1 | | 10.2 | 17.9 | | | | | | | |
| 4537676M | | 5309381M | 7050844M | Net Sales ($) | 3889M | 19565M | 48883M | 109771M | 303685M | 6565051M |
| 4138907M | | 3948505M | 5380984M | Total Assets ($) | 3916M | 15474M | 298811M | 282902M | 315027M | 4464854M |

M = $ thousand     MM = $ million
See Pages 9 through 22 for Explanation of Ratios and Data

## Current Data Sorted by Assets     Comparative Historical Data

| 0-500M | 500M-2MM | 2-10MM | 10-50MM | 50-100MM | 100-250MM | Type of Statement | 4/1/07-3/31/08 ALL | 4/1/08-3/31/09 ALL |
|---|---|---|---|---|---|---|---|---|
| 19 | 37 | 21 | 26 | 9 | 7 | Unqualified | 87 | 98 |
| 1 | 1 | 4 | 2 |  |  | Reviewed | 4 | 6 |
| 3 |  | 4 | 1 |  |  | Compiled | 18 | 19 |
| 6 | 7 | 2 |  | 6 |  | Tax Returns | 13 | 11 |
|  | 6 | 5 | 13 |  | 11 | Other | 30 | 42 |
|  | 10 (4/1-9/30/11) |  | 181 (10/1/11-3/31/12) |  |  | | | |
| 29 | 51 | 36 | 42 | 15 | 18 | NUMBER OF STATEMENTS | 152 | 176 |
| % | % | % | % | % | % | ASSETS | % | % |
| 72.6 | 61.4 | 39.8 | 22.6 | 11.2 | 24.9 | Cash & Equivalents | 45.1 | 43.9 |
| 1.1 | 5.6 | 16.7 | 20.2 | 25.4 | 18.7 | Trade Receivables (net) | 17.7 | 14.4 |
| .0 | .1 | .4 | 5.9 | 11.7 | 10.0 | Inventory | 1.1 | 1.5 |
| .9 | 4.6 | 3.9 | 17.8 | 33.9 | 13.9 | All Other Current | 5.7 | 5.8 |
| 74.6 | 71.7 | 60.7 | 66.5 | 82.2 | 67.5 | Total Current | 69.6 | 65.6 |
| 13.2 | 16.8 | 15.5 | 11.0 | 4.3 | 5.8 | Fixed Assets (net) | 15.5 | 15.6 |
| 6.0 | 5.2 | 13.3 | 8.6 | 3.0 | 21.6 | Intangibles (net) | 4.9 | 7.4 |
| 6.2 | 6.3 | 10.5 | 13.9 | 10.4 | 5.0 | All Other Non-Current | 10.0 | 11.4 |
| 100.0 | 100.0 | 100.0 | 100.0 | 100.0 | 100.0 | Total | 100.0 | 100.0 |
|  |  |  |  |  |  | LIABILITIES | | |
| 6.2 | 13.5 | 13.6 | 24.4 | 41.5 | 33.8 | Notes Payable-Short Term | 19.0 | 16.1 |
| .7 | .6 | 1.9 | 2.6 | 5.6 | 2.9 | Cur. Mat.-L.T.D. | 3.8 | 4.6 |
| 15.0 | 16.9 | 14.2 | 7.5 | 2.1 | 12.7 | Trade Payables | 11.6 | 8.6 |
| .0 | .0 | .2 | .4 | .0 | .4 | Income Taxes Payable | .2 | .2 |
| 12.2 | 12.4 | 7.5 | 17.0 | 19.1 | 8.8 | All Other Current | 14.7 | 14.6 |
| 34.1 | 43.4 | 37.4 | 52.0 | 68.4 | 58.6 | Total Current | 49.3 | 44.1 |
| 1.2 | 10.3 | 8.5 | 10.5 | 1.5 | 4.1 | Long-Term Debt | 10.9 | 11.8 |
| .0 | .0 | .1 | .5 | .1 | .3 | Deferred Taxes | .1 | .1 |
| 7.1 | 8.4 | 6.7 | 13.1 | 8.6 | 11.6 | All Other Non-Current | 9.9 | 12.4 |
| 57.6 | 37.9 | 47.3 | 23.9 | 21.4 | 25.4 | Net Worth | 29.8 | 31.7 |
| 100.0 | 100.0 | 100.0 | 100.0 | 100.0 | 100.0 | Total Liabilities & Net Worth | 100.0 | 100.0 |
|  |  |  |  |  |  | INCOME DATA | | |
| 100.0 | 100.0 | 100.0 | 100.0 | 100.0 | 100.0 | Net Sales | 100.0 | 100.0 |
|  |  |  |  |  |  | Gross Profit | | |
| 90.7 | 85.7 | 86.0 | 86.8 | 79.1 | 92.2 | Operating Expenses | 82.6 | 83.8 |
| 9.3 | 14.3 | 14.0 | 13.2 | 20.9 | 7.8 | Operating Profit | 17.4 | 16.2 |
| .9 | 2.9 | 3.5 | 5.5 | 5.4 | 2.2 | All Other Expenses (net) | 6.7 | 5.5 |
| 8.4 | 11.4 | 10.5 | 7.7 | 15.6 | 5.6 | Profit Before Taxes | 10.7 | 10.7 |
|  |  |  |  |  |  | RATIOS | | |
| 7.1 | 4.1 | 3.6 | 2.1 | 1.4 | 1.6 | Current | 3.1 | 3.2 |
| 2.4 | 1.4 | 1.3 | 1.4 | 1.1 | 1.1 | | 1.6 | 1.5 |
| 1.3 | 1.1 | 1.1 | 1.1 | 1.1 | 1.0 | | 1.1 | 1.0 |
| 7.1 | 4.1 | 2.5 | 1.6 | 1.1 | 1.2 | Quick | 2.8 | 3.0 |
| 2.3 | 1.3 | 1.2 | 1.0 | .2 | .8 | | 1.4 | 1.3 |
| 1.3 | 1.1 | 1.1 | .2 | .1 | .1 | | 1.0 | .9 |
| 0 UND | 0 UND | 3 131.7 | 5 76.8 | 0 UND | 10 37.5 | Sales/Receivables | 0 UND | 0 UND |
| 0 888.0 | 3 116.7 | 10 36.5 | 23 16.2 | 40 9.1 | 35 10.3 | | 2 150.2 | 2 172.5 |
| 4 98.3 | 11 33.2 | 39 9.3 | 72 5.1 | 730 .5 | 87 4.2 | | 56 6.6 | 31 11.9 |
|  |  |  |  |  |  | Cost of Sales/Inventory | | |
|  |  |  |  |  |  | Cost of Sales/Payables | | |
| 1.6 | 1.9 | 1.7 | 2.1 | 1.1 | 3.6 | Sales/Working Capital | 2.1 | 2.3 |
| 3.0 | 5.0 | 9.8 | 4.8 | 3.3 | 5.5 | | 4.6 | 5.4 |
| 12.9 | 17.8 | 22.7 | 16.9 | 4.4 | -381.9 | | 20.0 | 36.3 |
| 13.3 | 20.6 | 15.6 | 7.3 | 9.2 | 3.7 | EBIT/Interest | 13.4 | 15.9 |
| (15) 4.5 | (38) 4.6 | (31) 5.5 | (34) 2.1 | (13) 2.7 | (15) 2.4 | | (113) 5.0 | (124) 3.7 |
| -.2 | .8 | 2.0 | 1.1 | 2.0 | 1.9 | | 1.3 | 1.7 |
|  |  |  | 6.2 |  |  | Net Profit + Depr., Dep., Amort./Cur. Mat. L/T/D | 16.1 | 9.3 |
|  |  |  | (11) 2.8 |  |  | | (18) 2.1 | (29) 2.6 |
|  |  |  | 1.1 |  |  | | .7 | .5 |
| .1 | .1 | .1 | .0 | .0 | .1 | Fixed/Worth | .1 | .1 |
| .2 | .3 | .4 | .2 | .0 | .2 | | .3 | .3 |
| .5 | .9 | 1.2 | .7 | .2 | NM | | 1.2 | 1.7 |
| .3 | .8 | .8 | 1.5 | 2.7 | 2.4 | Debt/Worth | 1.1 | 1.0 |
| .7 | 1.7 | 1.8 | 4.7 | 7.3 | 7.5 | | 2.7 | 3.0 |
| 2.1 | 5.4 | 5.2 | 10.5 | 12.5 | -4.9 | | 7.9 | 12.8 |
| 39.4 | 56.8 | 45.0 | 52.0 | 38.8 | 24.8 | % Profit Before Taxes/Tangible Net Worth | 47.9 | 49.1 |
| (28) 9.0 | (46) 16.6 | (33) 14.4 | (35) 21.1 | (13) 21.8 | (13) 19.1 | | (132) 19.8 | (146) 25.6 |
| 1.8 | 1.1 | 2.5 | 4.4 | 12.2 | 9.0 | | 6.5 | 9.0 |
| 23.1 | 18.5 | 13.0 | 10.0 | 7.0 | 4.1 | % Profit Before Taxes/Total Assets | 16.5 | 15.9 |
| 5.4 | 6.5 | 3.9 | 3.1 | 3.8 | 2.5 | | 5.9 | 6.5 |
| .4 | .1 | .8 | .5 | 1.8 | 1.6 | | .8 | 2.1 |
| 81.8 | 27.9 | 43.4 | 76.0 | 119.0 | 52.7 | Sales/Net Fixed Assets | 52.7 | 54.1 |
| 17.9 | 7.9 | 9.2 | 27.4 | 63.2 | 14.3 | | 17.9 | 15.4 |
| 4.7 | 4.4 | 3.7 | 7.6 | 34.2 | 7.3 | | 6.5 | 6.2 |
| 1.6 | 1.3 | 1.4 | 1.4 | .5 | .9 | Sales/Total Assets | 1.7 | 1.6 |
| 1.2 | .8 | .9 | .7 | .3 | .6 | | 1.1 | 1.0 |
| .8 | .6 | .7 | .3 | .2 | .4 | | .5 | .5 |
| .8 | .7 | 1.1 | .6 | .4 | .9 | % Depr., Dep., Amort./Sales | .7 | .9 |
| (22) 1.1 | (43) 1.7 | (25) 1.8 | (35) 2.0 | (12) .7 | (15) 2.5 | | (123) 1.7 | (136) 1.5 |
| 2.1 | 2.5 | 3.6 | 3.9 | 2.3 | 3.7 | | 3.2 | 3.0 |
| 9.8 | 6.4 | 6.4 |  |  |  | % Officers', Directors' Owners' Comp/Sales | 6.1 | 6.8 |
| (17) 14.9 | (25) 11.5 | (17) 9.0 |  |  |  | | (73) 11.1 | (66) 12.6 |
| 23.1 | 21.7 | 13.5 |  |  |  | | 19.6 | 26.4 |
| 26700M | 59261M | 194112M | 1027293M | 370521M | 2014283M | Net Sales ($) | 2467847M | 4024922M |
| 8985M | 56158M | 163758M | 1083119M | 1082404M | 2965956M | Total Assets ($) | 3150060M | 3307047M |

M = $ thousand    MM = $ million
See Pages 9 through 22 for Explanation of Ratios and Data

## Comparative Historical Data

## Current Data Sorted by Sales

| | | | Type of Statement | 0-1MM | 1-3MM | 3-5MM | 5-10MM | 10-25MM | 25MM & OVER |
|---|---|---|---|---|---|---|---|---|---|
| 124 | 94 | 119 | Unqualified | 41 | 27 | 6 | 8 | 18 | 19 |
| 9 | 5 | 8 | Reviewed | 2 | | 2 | 2 | 2 | |
| 11 | 11 | 8 | Compiled | 5 | 2 | 1 | | | |
| 19 | 10 | 15 | Tax Returns | 8 | 5 | 2 | 2 | | |
| 49 | 31 | 41 | Other | 3 | 6 | 2 | | 12 | 18 |
| 4/1/09-3/31/10 ALL | 4/1/10-3/31/11 ALL | 4/1/11-3/31/12 ALL | | 10 (4/1-9/30/11) | | | 181 (10/1/11-3/31/12) | | |
| 212 | 151 | 191 | **NUMBER OF STATEMENTS** | 59 | 40 | 13 | 10 | 32 | 37 |
| % | % | % | **ASSETS** | % | % | % | % | % | % |
| 47.5 | 45.2 | 43.1 | Cash & Equivalents | 66.9 | 47.2 | 26.1 | 44.7 | 25.7 | 21.4 |
| 15.4 | 14.3 | 13.0 | Trade Receivables (net) | 1.6 | 16.4 | 17.1 | 23.6 | 9.9 | 25.8 |
| 1.2 | .8 | 3.3 | Inventory | .1 | .2 | .5 | .0 | 8.4 | 9.1 |
| 4.8 | 7.3 | 10.0 | All Other Current | 3.0 | 2.8 | 22.3 | 10.9 | 28.7 | 8.2 |
| 69.0 | 67.5 | 69.4 | Total Current | 71.5 | 66.6 | 66.1 | 79.2 | 72.7 | 64.6 |
| 13.5 | 15.1 | 12.7 | Fixed Assets (net) | 14.7 | 15.0 | 14.6 | 13.0 | 4.7 | 13.2 |
| 8.4 | 9.1 | 9.0 | Intangibles (net) | 5.7 | 9.7 | 11.2 | 2.0 | 10.9 | 12.8 |
| 9.1 | 8.3 | 8.9 | All Other Non-Current | 8.1 | 8.6 | 8.1 | 5.8 | 11.7 | 9.3 |
| 100.0 | 100.0 | 100.0 | Total | 100.0 | 100.0 | 100.0 | 100.0 | 100.0 | 100.0 |
| | | | **LIABILITIES** | | | | | | |
| 17.3 | 15.4 | 18.9 | Notes Payable-Short Term | 11.2 | 17.3 | 19.9 | 10.4 | 32.9 | 22.8 |
| 3.6 | 2.8 | 1.9 | Cur. Mat.-L.T.D. | .5 | 1.0 | 2.9 | 1.2 | 4.3 | 3.0 |
| 10.3 | 12.3 | 12.5 | Trade Payables | 15.5 | 16.6 | 7.4 | 10.0 | 6.3 | 11.1 |
| .2 | .2 | .2 | Income Taxes Payable | .0 | .1 | .2 | .3 | .4 | .3 |
| 11.0 | 12.7 | 12.6 | All Other Current | 9.5 | 11.8 | 15.7 | 24.6 | 14.6 | 12.4 |
| 42.4 | 43.4 | 46.2 | Total Current | 36.8 | 46.9 | 46.1 | 46.5 | 58.5 | 49.6 |
| 11.4 | 8.0 | 7.3 | Long-Term Debt | 8.1 | 6.2 | 8.8 | 8.0 | 7.0 | 6.9 |
| .1 | .2 | .2 | Deferred Taxes | .0 | .0 | .7 | .3 | .0 | .5 |
| 7.7 | 10.7 | 9.2 | All Other Non-Current | 8.9 | 7.7 | .3 | 6.0 | 16.3 | 9.5 |
| 38.3 | 37.6 | 37.1 | Net Worth | 46.3 | 39.2 | 44.1 | 39.2 | 18.2 | 33.5 |
| 100.0 | 100.0 | 100.0 | Total Liabilties & Net Worth | 100.0 | 100.0 | 100.0 | 100.0 | 100.0 | 100.0 |
| | | | **INCOME DATA** | | | | | | |
| 100.0 | 100.0 | 100.0 | Net Sales | 100.0 | 100.0 | 100.0 | 100.0 | 100.0 | 100.0 |
| | | | Gross Profit | | | | | | |
| 83.1 | 87.0 | 86.8 | Operating Expenses | 85.4 | 84.3 | 83.1 | 96.7 | 88.5 | 89.1 |
| 16.9 | 13.0 | 13.2 | Operating Profit | 14.6 | 15.7 | 16.9 | 3.3 | 11.5 | 10.9 |
| 5.2 | 3.6 | 3.4 | All Other Expenses (net) | 2.0 | 5.1 | 6.6 | .3 | 4.8 | 2.2 |
| 11.7 | 9.4 | 9.8 | Profit Before Taxes | 12.6 | 10.6 | 10.3 | 3.0 | 6.7 | 8.7 |
| | | | **RATIOS** | | | | | | |
| 3.4 | 3.1 | 3.1 | | 6.6 | 3.6 | 3.3 | 5.4 | 2.0 | 1.8 |
| 1.6 | 1.5 | 1.4 | Current | 2.0 | 1.2 | 1.5 | 1.2 | 1.2 | 1.2 |
| 1.1 | 1.1 | 1.1 | | 1.2 | 1.1 | .8 | 1.1 | 1.1 | 1.1 |
| 3.3 | 2.9 | 2.7 | | 5.0 | 2.6 | 2.8 | 4.7 | 1.3 | 1.6 |
| 1.5 | 1.4 | 1.2 | Quick | 2.0 | 1.2 | .7 | 1.2 | .4 | 1.1 |
| 1.1 | .9 | .8 | | 1.2 | 1.1 | .6 | 1.0 | .1 | .6 |
| 0  UND | 1  719.0 | 0  UND | | 0  UND | 0  UND | 0  UND | 3  144.1 | 1  457.1 | 13  27.3 |
| 3  114.1 | 7  51.2 | 8  44.3 | Sales/Receivables | 0  UND | 4  81.8 | 12  30.2 | 19  19.2 | 16  22.7 | 58  6.3 |
| 53  6.9 | 47  7.8 | 40  9.2 | | 6  61.5 | 28  12.9 | 69  5.3 | 107  3.4 | 36  10.0 | 114  3.2 |
| | | | Cost of Sales/Inventory | | | | | | |
| | | | Cost of Sales/Payables | | | | | | |
| 1.6 | 2.0 | 1.7 | | 1.4 | 2.0 | 1.3 | .7 | 2.5 | 3.7 |
| 4.1 | 4.7 | 4.8 | Sales/Working Capital | 3.0 | 6.5 | 8.1 | 7.2 | 4.4 | 6.0 |
| 18.5 | 24.9 | 17.2 | | 10.3 | 20.9 | -15.6 | 46.3 | 17.2 | 40.5 |
| 16.6 | 9.0 | 12.5 | | 24.9 | 5.6 | | | 6.8 | 10.3 |
| (154)  5.2 | (110)  3.2 | (146)  3.3 | EBIT/Interest | (38)  6.1 | (33)  2.3 | | (27)  2.1 | (34)  3.4 | |
| 1.7 | 1.1 | 1.3 | | 1.1 | .1 | | | 1.2 | 2.0 |
| 9.9 | 5.7 | 6.1 | Net Profit + Depr., Dep., Amort./Cur. Mat. L/T/D | | | | | | 3.2 |
| (33)  2.8 | (21)  3.0 | (35)  1.8 | | | | | | (12)  1.9 | |
| 1.0 | 1.3 | .8 | | | | | | | .9 |
| .1 | .1 | .0 | | .0 | .1 | .1 | .1 | .0 | .1 |
| .3 | .3 | .2 | Fixed/Worth | .2 | .5 | .3 | .3 | .1 | .4 |
| 1.1 | 1.4 | .8 | | .6 | 1.1 | .7 | .9 | .1 | 2.4 |
| .6 | .7 | .8 | | .5 | 1.1 | .5 | 1.0 | 2.7 | 1.0 |
| 1.8 | 2.2 | 2.4 | Debt/Worth | 1.2 | 3.8 | 1.6 | 2.4 | 4.7 | 6.2 |
| 7.3 | 6.0 | 7.1 | | 2.8 | 6.6 | 38.6 | 4.7 | 9.9 | 12.1 |
| 44.8 | 40.1 | 43.4 | % Profit Before Taxes/Tangible Net Worth | 39.5 | 45.1 | 54.8 | 69.2 | 35.3 | 47.2 |
| (182)  20.6 | (125)  11.1 | (168)  17.7 | | (55)  16.2 | (36)  9.7 | (11)  15.7 | (26)  4.0 | (30)  19.2 | 24.0 |
| 6.3 | 2.7 | 3.2 | | 2.0 | -4.0 | 2.3 | -1.3 | 4.4 | 11.3 |
| 16.9 | 13.3 | 12.5 | % Profit Before Taxes/Total Assets | 19.1 | 7.4 | 8.8 | 11.9 | 10.4 | 11.6 |
| 6.8 | 3.9 | 3.6 | | 7.5 | 3.4 | 2.6 | 1.3 | 2.8 | 4.7 |
| 1.7 | .5 | .6 | | .5 | -1.5 | -.8 | .5 | 2.0 | |
| 54.3 | 42.0 | 55.3 | Sales/Net Fixed Assets | 34.4 | 30.4 | 62.8 | 37.1 | 118.0 | 39.1 |
| 12.1 | 12.7 | 14.3 | | 12.9 | 7.5 | 13.6 | 15.5 | 60.1 | 14.2 |
| 5.8 | 5.4 | 5.1 | | 4.0 | 4.3 | 5.0 | 3.8 | 27.4 | 6.6 |
| 1.3 | 1.4 | 1.2 | Sales/Total Assets | 1.2 | 1.1 | 2.1 | 1.6 | 1.4 | 1.5 |
| .9 | .9 | .8 | | .8 | .9 | .7 | .9 | .6 | .9 |
| .5 | .6 | .5 | | .6 | .6 | .1 | .6 | .3 | .5 |
| .6 | .8 | .7 | % Depr., Dep., Amort./Sales | .7 | 1.5 | | | .4 | .9 |
| (160)  1.8 | (120)  1.7 | (152)  1.7 | | (47)  1.2 | (28)  2.2 | | (25)  .9 | (34)  2.6 | |
| 3.1 | 3.1 | 3.1 | | 2.2 | 3.3 | | | 2.0 | 3.9 |
| 7.0 | 8.8 | 6.9 | % Officers', Directors' Owners' Comp/Sales | 7.6 | 6.9 | | | | |
| (88)  12.2 | (59)  13.9 | (65)  11.3 | | (33)  13.8 | (19)  9.8 | | | | |
| 22.5 | 23.5 | 21.4 | | 24.2 | 15.5 | | | | |
| 4424124M | 2175828M | 3692170M | Net Sales ($) | 31191M | 75108M | 51888M | 67779M | 524525M | 2941679M |
| 4543056M | 2950025M | 5360380M | Total Assets ($) | 43771M | 166910M | 211271M | 161323M | 1204660M | 3572445M |

M = $ thousand    MM = $ million
See Pages 9 through 22 for Explanation of Ratios and Data

## Current Data Sorted by Assets | Comparative Historical Data

| | | | | | | Type of Statement | | |
|---|---|---|---|---|---|---|---|---|
| | 5 | 3 | 12 | 6 | 6 | Unqualified | 45 | 32 |
| | | 2 | | | | Reviewed | 1 | 3 |
| | | 2 | 1 | | | Compiled | 3 | 2 |
| 5 | 4 | 4 | | | | Tax Returns | 2 | 5 |
| 2 | 8 | 8 | 3 | 2 | 2 | Other | 27 | 21 |
| | 9 (4/1-9/30/11) | | 58 (10/1/11-3/31/12) | | | | 4/1/07-3/31/08 | 4/1/08-3/31/09 |
| 0-500M | 500M-2MM | 2-10MM | 10-50MM | 50-100MM | 100-250MM | | ALL | ALL |
| 7 | 9 | 19 | 16 | 8 | 8 | NUMBER OF STATEMENTS | 78 | 63 |
| % | % | % | % | % | % | ASSETS | % | % |
| | | 34.1 | 22.7 | | | Cash & Equivalents | 28.8 | 32.6 |
| | | 13.2 | 25.6 | | | Trade Receivables (net) | 17.5 | 17.2 |
| | | 4.1 | 15.2 | | | Inventory | 6.3 | 4.3 |
| | | 6.8 | 8.0 | | | All Other Current | 9.1 | 6.9 |
| | | 58.2 | 71.5 | | | Total Current | 61.6 | 61.0 |
| | | 23.1 | 4.1 | | | Fixed Assets (net) | 9.8 | 17.4 |
| | | 11.5 | 4.9 | | | Intangibles (net) | 6.9 | 4.6 |
| | | 7.2 | 19.6 | | | All Other Non-Current | 21.7 | 17.0 |
| | | 100.0 | 100.0 | | | Total | 100.0 | 100.0 |
| | | | | | | LIABILITIES | | |
| | | 10.4 | 10.5 | | | Notes Payable-Short Term | 12.1 | 6.5 |
| | | 12.1 | 1.9 | | | Cur. Mat.-L.T.D. | 1.2 | 4.4 |
| | | 7.9 | 18.5 | | | Trade Payables | 13.7 | 13.0 |
| | | .0 | .0 | | | Income Taxes Payable | .3 | .4 |
| | | 27.4 | 16.4 | | | All Other Current | 20.7 | 19.5 |
| | | 57.9 | 47.3 | | | Total Current | 48.0 | 43.8 |
| | | 19.1 | 14.1 | | | Long-Term Debt | 10.4 | 13.4 |
| | | .0 | .4 | | | Deferred Taxes | .3 | .0 |
| | | 3.0 | 5.8 | | | All Other Non-Current | 2.4 | 3.9 |
| | | 20.0 | 32.4 | | | Net Worth | 38.8 | 38.9 |
| | | 100.0 | 100.0 | | | Total Liabilties & Net Worth | 100.0 | 100.0 |
| | | | | | | INCOME DATA | | |
| | | 100.0 | 100.0 | | | Net Sales | 100.0 | 100.0 |
| | | | | | | Gross Profit | | |
| | | 80.6 | 78.4 | | | Operating Expenses | 74.6 | 77.1 |
| | | 19.4 | 21.6 | | | Operating Profit | 25.4 | 22.9 |
| | | 3.3 | 1.4 | | | All Other Expenses (net) | 4.0 | 8.7 |
| | | 16.0 | 20.2 | | | Profit Before Taxes | 21.4 | 14.2 |
| | | | | | | RATIOS | | |
| | | 2.5 | 1.8 | | | | 4.3 | 3.1 |
| | | 1.5 | 1.4 | | | Current | 1.4 | 1.6 |
| | | 1.0 | 1.2 | | | | 1.0 | 1.0 |
| | | 2.3 | 1.6 | | | | 3.1 | 2.4 |
| | | 1.5 | 1.2 | | | Quick | 1.1 | 1.2 |
| | | .4 | .4 | | | | .5 | .5 |
| | 0 | UND | 9 | 41.9 | | | 0 | UND | 0 | UND |
| | 9 | 39.7 | 51 | 7.2 | | Sales/Receivables | 14 | 25.8 | 12 | 31.2 |
| | 31 | 11.8 | 122 | 3.0 | | | 83 | 4.4 | 61 | 6.0 |
| | | | | | | Cost of Sales/Inventory | | |
| | | | | | | Cost of Sales/Payables | | |
| | | 5.0 | 3.7 | | | | 2.4 | 2.3 |
| | | 18.5 | 5.8 | | | Sales/Working Capital | 5.2 | 5.0 |
| | | -57.0 | 12.0 | | | | -137.1 | 93.3 |
| | | 223.9 | 9.5 | | | | 21.7 | 59.5 |
| | (15) | 10.8 | (10) | 5.3 | | EBIT/Interest | (38) | 3.2 | (35) | 13.0 |
| | | 2.9 | 1.5 | | | | .8 | 1.2 |
| | | | | | | Net Profit + Depr., Dep., Amort./Cur. Mat. L/T/D | | |
| | | .0 | .0 | | | | .0 | .0 |
| | | .3 | .0 | | | Fixed/Worth | .1 | .1 |
| | | 3.4 | .1 | | | | .5 | .7 |
| | | .6 | .6 | | | | .5 | .7 |
| | | 2.2 | 2.3 | | | Debt/Worth | 1.6 | 1.8 |
| | | 4.7 | 7.2 | | | | 6.1 | 6.0 |
| | | 93.2 | 76.5 | | | | 49.0 | 48.1 |
| | (16) | 47.7 | (15) | 19.6 | | % Profit Before Taxes/Tangible Net Worth | (67) | 19.9 | (57) | 20.8 |
| | | -.7 | 11.2 | | | | 5.5 | 2.4 |
| | | 45.1 | 20.6 | | | | 25.5 | 18.6 |
| | | 14.2 | 9.3 | | | % Profit Before Taxes/Total Assets | 6.2 | 5.7 |
| | | 1.5 | 1.1 | | | | 1.2 | .4 |
| | | 131.6 | UND | | | | 324.3 | 83.7 |
| | | 44.3 | 50.3 | | | Sales/Net Fixed Assets | 74.2 | 32.8 |
| | | 3.8 | 34.9 | | | | 26.7 | 6.2 |
| | | 3.6 | 2.1 | | | | 2.4 | 2.0 |
| | | 1.7 | 1.0 | | | Sales/Total Assets | .9 | .7 |
| | | .8 | .4 | | | | .3 | .3 |
| | | .4 | .5 | | | | .3 | .7 |
| | (16) | .8 | (10) | 1.0 | | % Depr., Dep., Amort./Sales | (48) | .7 | (42) | 1.3 |
| | | 3.6 | 1.7 | | | | 1.3 | 3.1 |
| | | | | | | % Officers', Directors' Owners' Comp/Sales | 3.3 | 3.4 |
| | | | | | | | (12) | 18.4 | (17) | 13.2 |
| | | | | | | | 35.0 | 20.5 |
| 9832M | 25888M | 193872M | 423921M | 574829M | 660157M | Net Sales ($) | 2351609M | 2637569M |
| 937M | 10185M | 85660M | 351523M | 542686M | 1099984M | Total Assets ($) | 2710295M | 3112435M |

M = $ thousand    MM = $ million
See Pages 9 through 22 for Explanation of Ratios and Data

## Comparative Historical Data     Current Data Sorted by Sales

| | | | Type of Statement | | | | | | |
|---|---|---|---|---|---|---|---|---|---|
| 31 | 25 | 32 | Unqualified | | 3 | 5 | 4 | 5 | 15 |
| 1 | 2 | 2 | Reviewed | | | | | 2 | |
| 3 | 1 | 3 | Compiled | | 1 | 2 | | | |
| 6 | 8 | 13 | Tax Returns | 5 | 1 | 5 | 1 | | 1 |
| 22 | 15 | 17 | Other | | 3 | 1 | 5 | 3 | 5 |
| 4/1/09-3/31/10 ALL | 4/1/10-3/31/11 ALL | 4/1/11-3/31/12 ALL | | 0-1MM | 9 (4/1-9/30/11)<br>1-3MM | 3-5MM | 58 (10/1/11-3/31/12)<br>5-10MM | 10-25MM | 25MM & OVER |
| 63 | 51 | 67 | **NUMBER OF STATEMENTS** | 5 | 8 | 13 | 10 | 10 | 21 |
| % | % | % | **ASSETS** | % | % | % | % | % | % |
| 30.7 | 33.5 | 30.6 | Cash & Equivalents | | | 33.4 | 20.0 | 28.6 | 34.2 |
| 16.5 | 14.2 | 20.5 | Trade Receivables (net) | | | 23.1 | 20.8 | 27.4 | 26.0 |
| 2.9 | 4.2 | 5.4 | Inventory | | | 1.0 | 13.7 | 10.8 | 4.9 |
| 11.1 | 7.4 | 9.2 | All Other Current | | | 7.0 | .0 | 7.4 | 17.1 |
| 61.2 | 59.3 | 65.6 | Total Current | | | 64.5 | 54.5 | 74.2 | 82.1 |
| 13.6 | 12.1 | 13.1 | Fixed Assets (net) | | | 6.0 | 16.2 | 5.1 | 4.3 |
| 6.6 | 6.7 | 8.5 | Intangibles (net) | | | 8.1 | 6.1 | 15.1 | 5.2 |
| 18.6 | 21.9 | 12.8 | All Other Non-Current | | | 21.4 | 23.2 | 5.6 | 8.4 |
| 100.0 | 100.0 | 100.0 | Total | | | 100.0 | 100.0 | 100.0 | 100.0 |
| | | | **LIABILITIES** | | | | | | |
| 8.8 | 16.4 | 13.4 | Notes Payable-Short Term | | | 10.6 | 14.4 | 10.3 | 6.4 |
| 1.3 | 2.7 | 4.6 | Cur. Mat.-L.T.D. | | | 1.6 | 1.9 | 20.2 | 2.4 |
| 11.3 | 11.9 | 10.7 | Trade Payables | | | 15.5 | 3.1 | 8.9 | 17.1 |
| .1 | .0 | .1 | Income Taxes Payable | | | .1 | .0 | .0 | .2 |
| 15.4 | 14.3 | 20.6 | All Other Current | | | 12.8 | 22.9 | 46.1 | 21.9 |
| 36.8 | 45.3 | 49.4 | Total Current | | | 40.6 | 42.3 | 85.5 | 48.0 |
| 8.1 | 12.2 | 11.8 | Long-Term Debt | | | 8.8 | 16.1 | 11.7 | 9.0 |
| .6 | .4 | .2 | Deferred Taxes | | | .0 | .6 | .3 | .0 |
| 4.1 | 7.8 | 8.0 | All Other Non-Current | | | 4.3 | .1 | 7.6 | 7.1 |
| 50.4 | 34.3 | 30.7 | Net Worth | | | 46.2 | 41.0 | -5.1 | 35.9 |
| 100.0 | 100.0 | 100.0 | Total Liabilities & Net Worth | | | 100.0 | 100.0 | 100.0 | 100.0 |
| | | | **INCOME DATA** | | | | | | |
| 100.0 | 100.0 | 100.0 | Net Sales | | | 100.0 | 100.0 | 100.0 | 100.0 |
| | | | Gross Profit | | | | | | |
| 81.8 | 87.2 | 83.5 | Operating Expenses | | | 88.7 | 83.2 | 89.8 | 82.2 |
| 18.2 | 12.8 | 16.5 | Operating Profit | | | 11.3 | 16.8 | 10.2 | 17.8 |
| 3.3 | 1.9 | 2.6 | All Other Expenses (net) | | | -2.1 | -.5 | 1.1 | 2.7 |
| 14.9 | 10.9 | 13.9 | Profit Before Taxes | | | 13.4 | 17.3 | 9.1 | 15.1 |
| | | | **RATIOS** | | | | | | |
| 2.9 | 3.2 | 2.5 | Current | | | 3.2 | 14.9 | 2.3 | 1.8 |
| 1.9 | 1.5 | 1.5 | | | | 1.5 | 1.0 | 1.4 | 1.6 |
| 1.1 | 1.1 | 1.1 | | | | 1.1 | .6 | 1.3 | 1.3 |
| 2.1 | 2.1 | 2.2 | Quick | | | 3.2 | 11.2 | 2.0 | 1.6 |
| 1.4 | 1.3 | 1.2 | | | | 1.5 | .9 | 1.3 | 1.2 |
| .5 | .6 | .6 | | | | 1.0 | .2 | .7 | .8 |
| 0 UND | 0 UND | 0 999.8 | Sales/Receivables | 0 UND | 0 UND | 6 63.0 | 13 28.8 | | |
| 8 44.5 | 16 22.5 | 14 27.0 | | 8 43.7 | 58 6.3 | 11 32.3 | 36 10.2 | | |
| 81 4.5 | 42 8.7 | 64 5.7 | | 64 5.7 | 99 3.7 | 78 4.7 | 81 4.5 | | |
| | | | Cost of Sales/Inventory | | | | | | |
| | | | Cost of Sales/Payables | | | | | | |
| 2.4 | 3.2 | 3.6 | Sales/Working Capital | | | 3.4 | 2.0 | 3.3 | 3.7 |
| 4.5 | 7.1 | 6.3 | | | | 5.7 | 11.1 | 6.8 | 5.2 |
| 241.0 | 75.2 | 26.4 | | | | 516.7 | -16.4 | 20.5 | 11.0 |
| 57.6 | 39.0 | 28.3 | EBIT/Interest | | | | | | 223.9 |
| (33) 15.6 | (32) 6.6 | (42) 6.6 | | | | | | (15) | 10.8 |
| 2.7 | 1.0 | 2.9 | | | | | | | 3.1 |
| | | | Net Profit + Depr., Dep.,<br>Amort./Cur. Mat. L/T/D | | | | | | |
| .0 | .0 | .0 | Fixed/Worth | | | .0 | .0 | .0 | .0 |
| .1 | .1 | .1 | | | | .1 | .2 | .1 | .1 |
| .5 | 1.0 | 1.3 | | | | .7 | 2.7 | -5.0 | .3 |
| .5 | .6 | .5 | Debt/Worth | | | .4 | .4 | 1.4 | 1.0 |
| 1.2 | 1.7 | 1.8 | | | | .9 | 5.4 | 2.6 | 1.3 |
| 3.1 | 3.9 | 6.5 | | | | 5.5 | 9.7 | -14.6 | 3.1 |
| 80.9 | 74.0 | 78.4 | % Profit Before Taxes/Tangible<br>Net Worth | | | 304.7 | | | 94.3 |
| (59) 19.3 | (44) 24.6 | (58) 23.6 | | | | (12) 16.7 | | (20) | 42.9 |
| 2.0 | .7 | 5.1 | | | | 4.6 | | | 15.2 |
| 31.9 | 36.7 | 31.3 | % Profit Before Taxes/Total<br>Assets | | | 31.4 | 30.2 | 54.6 | 37.1 |
| 6.5 | 6.5 | 10.1 | | | | 9.0 | 8.0 | 5.9 | 14.2 |
| .5 | .1 | 1.5 | | | | 1.7 | .2 | -6.6 | 5.8 |
| 356.2 | 136.9 | 159.9 | Sales/Net Fixed Assets | | | 237.8 | UND | 744.2 | 113.9 |
| 39.3 | 38.0 | 45.3 | | | | 131.6 | 9.9 | 53.8 | 44.2 |
| 17.5 | 14.0 | 14.4 | | | | 73.6 | 2.6 | 26.4 | 22.1 |
| 2.0 | 3.2 | 2.7 | Sales/Total Assets | | | 7.5 | 1.6 | 3.3 | 2.3 |
| 1.0 | 1.7 | 1.4 | | | | 1.7 | .4 | 1.6 | 1.4 |
| .3 | .7 | .7 | | | | .6 | .1 | .9 | .9 |
| .6 | .5 | .5 | % Depr., Dep., Amort./Sales | | | | | | .4 |
| (35) .9 | (36) .9 | (47) 1.0 | | | | | | (16) | 1.1 |
| 1.9 | 2.2 | 2.2 | | | | | | | 2.1 |
| 3.3 | 3.4 | 2.6 | % Officers', Directors'<br>Owners' Comp/Sales | | | | | | |
| (14) 7.3 | (12) 10.3 | (12) 7.9 | | | | | | | |
| 29.7 | 27.1 | 17.2 | | | | | | | |
| 3077773M | 1341641M | 1888499M | Net Sales ($) | 1347M | 15041M | 51113M | 71870M | 170319M | 1578809M |
| 2654327M | 1383849M | 2090975M | Total Assets ($) | 4171M | 15498M | 67311M | 512024M | 166404M | 1325567M |

M = $ thousand    MM = $ million
See Pages 9 through 22 for Explanation of Ratios and Data

## Current Data Sorted by Assets

## Comparative Historical Data

| | | | | | | Type of Statement | | |
|---|---|---|---|---|---|---|---|---|
| 1 | 8 | 10 | 14 | 9 | 3 | Unqualified | 59 | 66 |
| 1 | | 1 | 2 | | 1 | Reviewed | 3 | 1 |
| | 2 | | | | | Compiled | 7 | 2 |
| 8 | 6 | 5 | 1 | | | Tax Returns | 12 | 15 |
| 7 | 7 | 9 | 7 | 6 | 6 | Other | 36 | 19 |
| | 17 (4/1-9/30/11) | | 97 (10/1/11-3/31/12) | | | | 4/1/07-3/31/08 | 4/1/08-3/31/09 |
| 0-500M | 500M-2MM | 2-10MM | 10-50MM | 50-100MM | 100-250MM | | ALL | ALL |
| 17 | 23 | 25 | 24 | 15 | 10 | NUMBER OF STATEMENTS | 117 | 103 |
| % | % | % | % | % | % | ASSETS | % | % |
| 40.0 | 28.3 | 34.3 | 39.2 | 38.2 | 20.4 | Cash & Equivalents | 35.5 | 37.4 |
| 4.1 | 19.6 | 18.5 | 14.9 | 18.4 | 10.6 | Trade Receivables (net) | 13.2 | 15.6 |
| .0 | 2.7 | 1.7 | 6.3 | .0 | 15.5 | Inventory | 3.9 | 1.7 |
| 16.1 | 2.1 | 5.8 | 7.1 | 11.5 | 27.4 | All Other Current | 9.9 | 11.3 |
| 60.2 | 52.8 | 60.3 | 67.5 | 68.1 | 73.8 | Total Current | 62.4 | 66.1 |
| 11.7 | 23.7 | 14.5 | 5.9 | 2.8 | 18.2 | Fixed Assets (net) | 11.0 | 9.5 |
| 11.3 | 6.5 | 4.1 | 2.0 | 3.0 | 3.1 | Intangibles (net) | 6.1 | 5.7 |
| 16.7 | 17.1 | 21.0 | 24.5 | 26.1 | 4.9 | All Other Non-Current | 20.4 | 18.8 |
| 100.0 | 100.0 | 100.0 | 100.0 | 100.0 | 100.0 | Total | 100.0 | 100.0 |
| | | | | | | LIABILITIES | | |
| 22.9 | 7.1 | 2.2 | 10.5 | 5.6 | 19.3 | Notes Payable-Short Term | 6.1 | 7.6 |
| .9 | 2.6 | 1.1 | 2.3 | .0 | .4 | Cur. Mat.-L.T.D. | 2.8 | 2.0 |
| 2.7 | 12.2 | 17.2 | 16.0 | 13.7 | 3.6 | Trade Payables | 8.9 | 9.9 |
| 1.8 | .2 | .0 | .4 | 1.3 | .3 | Income Taxes Payable | .5 | .4 |
| 29.0 | 6.8 | 17.5 | 10.8 | 22.9 | 33.2 | All Other Current | 24.9 | 19.9 |
| 57.3 | 29.0 | 38.0 | 40.0 | 43.5 | 56.8 | Total Current | 43.2 | 39.7 |
| 6.2 | 16.2 | 9.4 | 8.2 | 1.0 | 5.7 | Long-Term Debt | 9.1 | 9.5 |
| .0 | .0 | .0 | .0 | .0 | .2 | Deferred Taxes | .0 | .0 |
| 9.9 | 17.3 | 5.5 | 3.8 | 1.2 | 2.2 | All Other Non-Current | 4.0 | 2.2 |
| 26.6 | 37.5 | 47.1 | 48.0 | 54.3 | 35.1 | Net Worth | 43.7 | 48.6 |
| 100.0 | 100.0 | 100.0 | 100.0 | 100.0 | 100.0 | Total Liabilities & Net Worth | 100.0 | 100.0 |
| | | | | | | INCOME DATA | | |
| 100.0 | 100.0 | 100.0 | 100.0 | 100.0 | 100.0 | Net Sales | 100.0 | 100.0 |
| | | | | | | Gross Profit | | |
| 82.2 | 88.2 | 84.3 | 86.7 | 79.5 | 82.1 | Operating Expenses | 82.0 | 87.5 |
| 17.8 | 11.8 | 15.7 | 13.3 | 20.5 | 17.9 | Operating Profit | 18.0 | 12.5 |
| .2 | 3.4 | 4.5 | 3.5 | 2.7 | -.1 | All Other Expenses (net) | 4.2 | 2.5 |
| 17.6 | 8.3 | 11.2 | 9.8 | 17.8 | 17.9 | Profit Before Taxes | 13.9 | 10.0 |
| | | | | | | RATIOS | | |
| 3.1 | 3.5 | 3.1 | 2.1 | 2.8 | 1.3 | | 2.5 | 3.1 |
| 1.1 | 1.7 | 2.0 | 1.6 | 1.6 | 1.2 | Current | 1.5 | 1.8 |
| .6 | .5 | 1.0 | 1.2 | 1.3 | 1.0 | | 1.0 | 1.3 |
| 2.4 | 3.5 | 3.1 | 2.0 | 2.7 | 1.1 | | 2.2 | 2.7 |
| .8 | 1.6 | 1.5 | 1.3 | 1.5 | .7 | Quick | 1.3 | 1.6 |
| .4 | .5 | 1.0 | .8 | .6 | .0 | | .5 | .7 |
| 0 UND | 0 UND | 1 587.4 | 0 817.4 | 3 110.1 | 0 UND | | 0 UND | 0 UND |
| 0 UND | 9 41.6 | 10 36.2 | 11 33.8 | 37 9.8 | 19 18.9 | Sales/Receivables | 7 51.7 | 8 44.9 |
| 0 UND | 31 11.8 | 32 11.4 | 38 9.5 | 64 5.7 | 89 4.1 | | 41 8.8 | 34 10.7 |
| | | | | | | Cost of Sales/Inventory | | |
| | | | | | | Cost of Sales/Payables | | |
| 14.2 | 5.8 | 4.7 | 1.6 | 2.4 | 1.6 | | 3.4 | 3.6 |
| 129.6 | 18.6 | 11.8 | 4.5 | 4.7 | 12.6 | Sales/Working Capital | 12.1 | 9.9 |
| -73.8 | -67.4 | NM | 17.3 | 19.0 | NM | | NM | 29.7 |
| | | 127.0 | 13.9 | 144.6 | | | 28.0 | 32.5 |
| | (11) 14.0 | (14) .5 | (10) 28.6 | | | EBIT/Interest | (62) 12.0 | (52) 7.2 |
| | 3.9 | -3.4 | 5.9 | | | | 2.0 | 1.1 |
| | | | | | | Net Profit + Depr., Dep., Amort./Cur. Mat. L/T/D | | |
| .0 | .0 | .0 | .0 | .0 | .1 | | .0 | .0 |
| .1 | .0 | .1 | .0 | .1 | .4 | Fixed/Worth | .1 | .1 |
| .6 | 5.7 | 1.0 | .1 | .1 | 1.7 | | .3 | .2 |
| .3 | .5 | .4 | .4 | .6 | 1.0 | | .4 | .4 |
| 3.4 | 1.5 | .6 | 1.2 | 1.1 | 3.0 | Debt/Worth | 1.2 | 1.0 |
| -4.8 | -34.9 | 5.5 | 4.4 | 1.8 | 4.3 | | 3.6 | 2.3 |
| 999.8 | 74.8 | 93.3 | 27.0 | 50.8 | | % Profit Before Taxes/Tangible Net Worth | 65.5 | 71.2 |
| (11) 250.0 | (17) 32.5 | (22) 42.1 | (22) 11.4 | 21.3 | | | (105) 21.7 | (92) 29.0 |
| 63.1 | 3.9 | 7.2 | -3.9 | 3.0 | | | 5.0 | 2.6 |
| 300.4 | 54.7 | 64.0 | 10.4 | 21.7 | 30.7 | % Profit Before Taxes/Total Assets | 28.5 | 31.8 |
| 55.3 | 8.0 | 12.1 | 3.1 | 11.7 | 6.3 | | 9.3 | 13.6 |
| 15.5 | .4 | 4.5 | -3.5 | .9 | 2.3 | | 1.7 | .6 |
| UND | UND | UND | UND | 531.8 | 37.2 | | 328.2 | 382.8 |
| 786.3 | 169.1 | 170.5 | 108.0 | 46.3 | 15.9 | Sales/Net Fixed Assets | 53.0 | 70.3 |
| 37.2 | 11.2 | 20.1 | 34.4 | 21.9 | 5.0 | | 20.5 | 26.4 |
| 17.3 | 6.5 | 4.8 | 1.9 | 1.8 | 2.2 | | 4.2 | 4.6 |
| 7.0 | 3.2 | 2.9 | .7 | 1.2 | 1.0 | Sales/Total Assets | 1.8 | 2.1 |
| 4.5 | .5 | 1.2 | .2 | .7 | .4 | | .8 | .9 |
| | .1 | .5 | .4 | .7 | | | .4 | .3 |
| | (11) .5 | (13) 1.1 | (15) .9 | (10) 1.2 | | % Depr., Dep., Amort./Sales | (75) .9 | (70) .7 |
| | 22.3 | 2.0 | 2.2 | 1.4 | | | 1.5 | 1.7 |
| | | | | | | % Officers', Directors' Owners' Comp/Sales | 4.7 | 6.7 |
| | | | | | | | (19) 12.8 | (15) 18.5 |
| | | | | | | | 27.9 | 29.0 |
| 21740M | 163132M | 476784M | 671172M | 1476295M | 1647568M | Net Sales ($) | 6140279M | 6189125M |
| 3031M | 27492M | 125463M | 501609M | 1059466M | 1471262M | Total Assets ($) | 4423202M | 3241434M |

M = $ thousand     MM = $ million
See Pages 9 through 22 for Explanation of Ratios and Data

## Comparative Historical Data  |  Current Data Sorted by Sales

| | | | | Type of Statement | 0-1MM | 1-3MM | 3-5MM | 5-10MM | 10-25MM | 25MM & OVER |
|---|---|---|---|---|---|---|---|---|---|---|
| | 62 | 55 | 45 | Unqualified | 2 | 3 | 3 | 5 | 10 | 22 |
| | 3 | 5 | 5 | Reviewed | | 1 | 2 | 1 | 1 | |
| | 4 | 2 | 2 | Compiled | | | 1 | | | 1 |
| | 15 | 26 | 20 | Tax Returns | 5 | 6 | 3 | 3 | 2 | 1 |
| | 32 | 51 | 42 | Other | 8 | 6 | 4 | 5 | 4 | 15 |
| | 4/1/09-3/31/10 ALL | 4/1/10-3/31/11 ALL | 4/1/11-3/31/12 ALL | | 17 (4/1-9/30/11) | | | 97 (10/1/11-3/31/12) | | |
| | 116 | 139 | 114 | NUMBER OF STATEMENTS | 15 | 16 | 13 | 14 | 17 | 39 |
| | % | % | % | **ASSETS** | % | % | % | % | % | % |
| | 33.2 | 38.0 | 34.3 | Cash & Equivalents | 30.2 | 35.7 | 22.9 | 23.0 | 41.3 | 40.0 |
| | 17.2 | 13.2 | 15.1 | Trade Receivables (net) | 5.5 | 4.4 | 20.1 | 24.8 | 17.0 | 17.3 |
| | 2.3 | 2.1 | 3.6 | Inventory | .0 | .0 | 4.3 | 10.4 | 3.2 | 4.0 |
| | 9.0 | 13.0 | 9.5 | All Other Current | 1.5 | 12.4 | 5.6 | 7.9 | 13.7 | 11.5 |
| | 61.7 | 66.3 | 62.5 | Total Current | 37.1 | 52.6 | 52.9 | 65.9 | 75.3 | 72.7 |
| | 10.8 | 12.5 | 12.9 | Fixed Assets (net) | 32.9 | 15.9 | 14.2 | 13.3 | 2.5 | 8.0 |
| | 6.7 | 5.0 | 5.0 | Intangibles (net) | 6.6 | 8.0 | 2.6 | 6.5 | 5.0 | 3.4 |
| | 20.7 | 16.3 | 19.6 | All Other Non-Current | 23.3 | 23.5 | 30.3 | 14.3 | 17.1 | 15.9 |
| | 100.0 | 100.0 | 100.0 | Total | 100.0 | 100.0 | 100.0 | 100.0 | 100.0 | 100.0 |
| | | | | **LIABILITIES** | | | | | | |
| | 9.8 | 6.7 | 10.0 | Notes Payable-Short Term | 3.7 | 22.9 | 13.0 | 12.4 | 5.5 | 7.2 |
| | 2.9 | 1.9 | 1.4 | Cur. Mat.-L.T.D. | 1.0 | 1.7 | 3.2 | 3.8 | .2 | .6 |
| | 12.8 | 13.5 | 12.1 | Trade Payables | 8.5 | 2.7 | 5.4 | 14.5 | 15.8 | 17.2 |
| | .4 | .4 | .6 | Income Taxes Payable | .0 | 1.9 | .0 | .4 | .5 | .6 |
| | 17.4 | 20.8 | 17.7 | All Other Current | 19.4 | 9.8 | 19.3 | 8.6 | 12.4 | 25.5 |
| | 43.3 | 43.3 | 41.9 | Total Current | 32.7 | 39.0 | 40.9 | 39.6 | 34.4 | 50.9 |
| | 11.5 | 11.3 | 8.6 | Long-Term Debt | 27.8 | 7.8 | 9.3 | 12.2 | 4.4 | 1.8 |
| | .3 | .0 | .0 | Deferred Taxes | .0 | .0 | .0 | .1 | .0 | .0 |
| | 5.2 | 6.5 | 7.3 | All Other Non-Current | 6.4 | 21.7 | 20.1 | 1.4 | 2.3 | 1.9 |
| | 39.6 | 38.8 | 42.2 | Net Worth | 33.1 | 31.5 | 29.8 | 46.7 | 58.9 | 45.3 |
| | 100.0 | 100.0 | 100.0 | Total Liabilities & Net Worth | 100.0 | 100.0 | 100.0 | 100.0 | 100.0 | 100.0 |
| | | | | **INCOME DATA** | | | | | | |
| | 100.0 | 100.0 | 100.0 | Net Sales | 100.0 | 100.0 | 100.0 | 100.0 | 100.0 | 100.0 |
| | | | | Gross Profit | | | | | | |
| | 83.4 | 87.2 | 84.5 | Operating Expenses | 74.0 | 83.4 | 82.5 | 80.7 | 93.7 | 86.9 |
| | 16.6 | 12.8 | 15.5 | Operating Profit | 26.0 | 16.6 | 17.5 | 19.3 | 6.3 | 13.1 |
| | 2.9 | 1.4 | 2.8 | All Other Expenses (net) | 8.1 | 1.9 | 8.4 | 1.4 | -.1 | 1.0 |
| | 13.7 | 11.4 | 12.7 | Profit Before Taxes | 17.9 | 14.7 | 9.1 | 17.8 | 6.5 | 12.0 |
| | | | | **RATIOS** | | | | | | |
| | 3.3 | 2.8 | 2.8 | | 2.1 | 3.4 | 3.2 | 4.3 | 4.7 | 2.0 |
| | 1.7 | 1.7 | 1.6 | Current | 1.0 | 1.5 | 1.4 | 1.5 | 2.7 | 1.6 |
| | 1.0 | 1.1 | 1.0 | | .4 | .6 | .6 | 1.1 | 1.4 | 1.2 |
| | 2.9 | 2.4 | 2.5 | | 2.1 | 2.6 | 2.6 | 2.4 | 3.8 | 2.0 |
| | 1.4 | 1.5 | 1.4 | Quick | 1.0 | 1.1 | 1.2 | 1.4 | 1.7 | 1.3 |
| | .6 | .6 | .6 | | .4 | .4 | .4 | .7 | .8 | .8 |
| | 0 UND | 0 UND | 0 UND | | 0 UND | 0 UND | 0 UND | 0 UND | 6 66.0 | 1 376.4 |
| | 15 23.7 | 10 37.4 | 9 40.9 | Sales/Receivables | 0 UND | 0 UND | 3 136.3 | 13 28.7 | 13 28.1 | 16 23.0 |
| | 40 9.1 | 34 10.8 | 37 9.9 | | 21 17.4 | 8 47.9 | 72 5.1 | 43 8.4 | 59 6.2 | 36 10.1 |
| | | | | Cost of Sales/Inventory | | | | | | |
| | | | | Cost of Sales/Payables | | | | | | |
| | 3.1 | 2.5 | 4.3 | | 5.5 | 5.8 | 2.8 | 3.7 | 1.8 | 4.0 |
| | 7.9 | 9.5 | 12.1 | Sales/Working Capital | 43.1 | 62.4 | 33.5 | 8.8 | 4.6 | 14.3 |
| | NM | 60.8 | 348.2 | | -8.0 | -222.1 | -10.5 | NM | 11.4 | 27.6 |
| | 32.9 | 53.7 | 40.9 | | | | | | | 90.3 |
| | (68) 10.6 | (76) 6.7 | (56) 8.2 | EBIT/Interest | | | | | (20) 26.2 | |
| | 1.2 | 1.9 | 1.6 | | | | | | | 2.8 |
| | | | 4.6 | | | | | | | |
| | | (12) | 1.7 | Net Profit + Depr., Dep., Amort./Cur. Mat. L/T/D | | | | | | |
| | | | .3 | | | | | | | |
| | .0 | .0 | .0 | | .0 | .0 | .0 | .0 | .0 | .0 |
| | .1 | .1 | .1 | Fixed/Worth | .0 | .1 | .0 | .1 | .0 | .1 |
| | .6 | .4 | .4 | | 3.7 | 6.3 | NM | NM | .1 | .2 |
| | .4 | .4 | .4 | | .4 | .3 | .3 | .1 | .4 | .7 |
| | 1.2 | 1.3 | 1.2 | Debt/Worth | 2.8 | 3.6 | 2.4 | 1.7 | .6 | 1.2 |
| | 10.2 | 7.4 | 4.5 | | 17.6 | -55.7 | -29.1 | NM | 1.3 | 2.2 |
| | 61.4 | 44.7 | 71.4 | | 70.5 | 999.8 | | 61.0 | 82.6 | 73.1 |
| | (93) 23.2 | (118) 18.1 | (96) 27.6 | % Profit Before Taxes/Tangible Net Worth | (12) 52.6 | (11) 78.1 | | (11) 32.9 | (16) 14.3 | (37) 25.9 |
| | 4.0 | 1.0 | 5.9 | | 8.5 | 3.3 | | 16.9 | -9.8 | 7.2 |
| | 28.2 | 24.7 | 48.2 | | 46.6 | 110.8 | 15.6 | 58.9 | 64.0 | 37.0 |
| | 8.6 | 5.9 | 9.9 | % Profit Before Taxes/Total Assets | 8.0 | 22.4 | 3.7 | 18.3 | 4.1 | 11.7 |
| | .2 | .5 | 1.8 | | .6 | 4.8 | -5.3 | 5.3 | -5.4 | 1.9 |
| | 391.5 | 737.1 | UND | | UND | UND | UND | 999.9 | UND | 518.3 |
| | 67.9 | 83.8 | 85.7 | Sales/Net Fixed Assets | UND | 107.2 | 124.4 | 43.3 | 239.8 | 60.2 |
| | 22.9 | 25.3 | 20.4 | | .3 | 20.9 | 17.2 | 9.9 | 63.8 | 24.5 |
| | 3.9 | 5.6 | 5.1 | | 5.3 | 10.0 | 3.7 | 4.4 | 4.3 | 5.1 |
| | 1.5 | 1.9 | 1.9 | Sales/Total Assets | .5 | 4.5 | .8 | 2.8 | 2.3 | 1.8 |
| | .6 | .6 | .7 | | .1 | .9 | .2 | 1.3 | .7 | 1.0 |
| | .3 | .4 | .5 | | | | | | | .6 |
| | (73) .8 | (84) .8 | (63) .9 | % Depr., Dep., Amort./Sales | | | | | (27) .8 | |
| | 2.3 | 1.9 | 2.2 | | | | | | | 1.3 |
| | 4.1 | 3.7 | 2.9 | | | | | | | |
| | (22) 8.2 | (33) 16.0 | (22) 9.1 | % Officers', Directors' Owners' Comp/Sales | | | | | | |
| | 27.3 | 23.3 | 21.8 | | | | | | | |
| | 5139257M | 6257429M | 4456691M | Net Sales ($) | 6385M | 29889M | 49446M | 96540M | 268588M | 4005843M |
| | 3688502M | 4036662M | 3188323M | Total Assets ($) | 21810M | 35372M | 132907M | 165291M | 345559M | 2487384M |

© RMA 2012  
M = $ thousand    MM = $ million  
See Pages 9 through 22 for Explanation of Ratios and Data

## Current Data Sorted by Assets      Comparative Historical Data

| 0-500M | 500M-2MM | 2-10MM | 10-50MM | 50-100MM | 100-250MM | Type of Statement | 4/1/07-3/31/08 ALL | 4/1/08-3/31/09 ALL |
|---|---|---|---|---|---|---|---|---|
|  |  | 5 | 9 |  | 3 | Unqualified | 7 | 10 |
|  |  |  | 1 |  |  | Reviewed | 3 | 5 |
|  | 1 | 3 | 2 |  |  | Compiled | 5 | 4 |
| 1 | 3 |  | 1 |  |  | Tax Returns | 6 | 3 |
| 1 | 4 | 4 | 6 | 2 |  | Other | 15 | 14 |
|  |  | 6 (4/1-9/30/11) |  | 40 (10/1/11-3/31/12) |  |  |  |  |
| 2 | 8 | 12 | 19 | 2 | 3 | **NUMBER OF STATEMENTS** | 36 | 36 |
| % | % | % | % | % | % | **ASSETS** | % | % |
|  |  | 33.5 | 37.7 |  |  | Cash & Equivalents | 23.9 | 19.0 |
|  |  | 22.1 | 17.1 |  |  | Trade Receivables (net) | 26.2 | 26.3 |
|  |  | .0 | 9.1 |  |  | Inventory | 9.8 | 13.4 |
|  |  | 9.2 | 5.4 |  |  | All Other Current | 5.3 | 9.2 |
|  |  | 64.8 | 69.3 |  |  | Total Current | 65.2 | 68.0 |
|  |  | 23.6 | 12.8 |  |  | Fixed Assets (net) | 19.8 | 20.3 |
|  |  | 3.9 | 5.7 |  |  | Intangibles (net) | 1.2 | 1.2 |
|  |  | 7.6 | 12.2 |  |  | All Other Non-Current | 13.8 | 10.6 |
|  |  | 100.0 | 100.0 |  |  | Total | 100.0 | 100.0 |
|  |  |  |  |  |  | **LIABILITIES** |  |  |
|  |  | 18.5 | 8.7 |  |  | Notes Payable-Short Term | 14.7 | 13.0 |
|  |  | 2.9 | 4.9 |  |  | Cur. Mat.-L.T.D. | 1.5 | 1.8 |
|  |  | 16.0 | 15.0 |  |  | Trade Payables | 24.6 | 9.6 |
|  |  | 1.3 | .0 |  |  | Income Taxes Payable | .2 | .2 |
|  |  | 11.6 | 10.7 |  |  | All Other Current | 3.6 | 14.1 |
|  |  | 50.3 | 39.4 |  |  | Total Current | 44.6 | 38.7 |
|  |  | 13.8 | 20.4 |  |  | Long-Term Debt | 23.1 | 25.5 |
|  |  | 4.0 | .5 |  |  | Deferred Taxes | .0 | .0 |
|  |  | 1.5 | 5.1 |  |  | All Other Non-Current | 7.1 | 4.3 |
|  |  | 30.4 | 34.6 |  |  | Net Worth | 25.2 | 31.5 |
|  |  | 100.0 | 100.0 |  |  | Total Liabilities & Net Worth | 100.0 | 100.0 |
|  |  |  |  |  |  | **INCOME DATA** |  |  |
|  |  | 100.0 | 100.0 |  |  | Net Sales | 100.0 | 100.0 |
|  |  |  |  |  |  | Gross Profit |  |  |
|  |  | 78.8 | 79.9 |  |  | Operating Expenses | 67.8 | 74.7 |
|  |  | 21.2 | 20.1 |  |  | Operating Profit | 32.2 | 25.3 |
|  |  | 3.6 | 6.8 |  |  | All Other Expenses (net) | 7.4 | 8.3 |
|  |  | 17.5 | 13.3 |  |  | Profit Before Taxes | 24.8 | 17.0 |
|  |  |  |  |  |  | **RATIOS** |  |  |
|  |  | 2.3 | 3.7 |  |  | Current | 7.3 | 5.8 |
|  |  | 1.3 | 2.2 |  |  |  | 2.6 | 2.5 |
|  |  | .7 | 1.1 |  |  |  | 1.2 | 1.1 |
|  |  | 2.3 | 2.8 |  |  | Quick | 5.0 | 4.2 |
|  |  | 1.3 | 1.5 |  |  |  | 2.2 | 1.5 |
|  |  | .3 | .8 |  |  |  | .9 | .6 |
|  |  | 0   UND | 36   10.0 |  |  | Sales/Receivables | 1   581.2 | 0   UND |
|  |  | 28   12.9 | 49   7.5 |  |  |  | 16   22.5 | 12   30.6 |
|  |  | 55   6.6 | 174   2.1 |  |  |  | 57   6.4 | 69   5.3 |
|  |  |  |  |  |  | Cost of Sales/Inventory |  |  |
|  |  |  |  |  |  | Cost of Sales/Payables |  |  |
|  |  | 3.0 | 1.0 |  |  | Sales/Working Capital | 1.5 | 1.0 |
|  |  | 84.9 | 1.6 |  |  |  | 6.0 | 3.9 |
|  |  | -4.9 | 5.1 |  |  |  | 27.9 | 42.2 |
|  |  |  | 42.0 |  |  | EBIT/Interest | 30.6 | 9.9 |
|  |  |  | (16)   3.4 |  |  |  | (21)   15.6 | (25)   4.8 |
|  |  |  | 1.1 |  |  |  | 2.5 | 1.7 |
|  |  |  |  |  |  | Net Profit + Depr., Dep., Amort./Cur. Mat. L/T/D |  |  |
|  |  | .0 | .0 |  |  | Fixed/Worth | .0 | .0 |
|  |  | .2 | .2 |  |  |  | .2 | .2 |
|  |  | 2.5 | 1.1 |  |  |  | 1.3 | 1.1 |
|  |  | .7 | 1.2 |  |  | Debt/Worth | .6 | .8 |
|  |  | 2.0 | 3.5 |  |  |  | 1.4 | 2.6 |
|  |  | 29.5 | 7.1 |  |  |  | 6.8 | 9.0 |
|  |  | 207.4 | 49.4 |  |  | % Profit Before Taxes/Tangible Net Worth | 79.8 | 47.6 |
|  |  | (11)   51.1 | (17)   21.2 |  |  |  | (31)   37.0 | (32)   28.2 |
|  |  | 12.5 | 2.2 |  |  |  | 14.9 | 12.1 |
|  |  | 26.1 | 9.0 |  |  | % Profit Before Taxes/Total Assets | 32.5 | 17.0 |
|  |  | 12.8 | 3.1 |  |  |  | 10.2 | 6.7 |
|  |  | .5 | .6 |  |  |  | 2.7 | 2.4 |
|  |  | UND | 62.1 |  |  | Sales/Net Fixed Assets | 999.8 | 855.0 |
|  |  | 22.0 | 20.7 |  |  |  | 26.4 | 31.3 |
|  |  | 6.0 | 2.4 |  |  |  | 2.6 | 1.7 |
|  |  | 3.5 | .9 |  |  | Sales/Total Assets | 4.2 | 4.1 |
|  |  | 1.7 | .4 |  |  |  | .7 | .7 |
|  |  | .5 | .2 |  |  |  | .2 | .2 |
|  |  |  | .9 |  |  | % Depr., Dep., Amort./Sales | .1 | .1 |
|  |  |  | (13)   1.7 |  |  |  | (24)   1.4 | (23)   1.1 |
|  |  |  | 5.3 |  |  |  | 4.6 | 5.5 |
|  |  |  |  |  |  | % Officers', Directors' Owners' Comp/Sales |  |  |
| 32160M | 33963M | 135243M | 311042M | 109112M | 3626762M | Net Sales ($) | 2621812M | 3820859M |
| 435M | 9630M | 59438M | 470778M | 147976M | 543708M | Total Assets ($) | 988991M | 1389676M |

## Comparative Historical Data | Current Data Sorted by Sales

| | | | Type of Statement | | | | | | |
|---|---|---|---|---|---|---|---|---|---|
| 14 | 16 | 17 | Unqualified | | 1 | 1 | 3 | 6 | 6 |
| 2 | 4 | 1 | Reviewed | | | 1 | | | |
| 2 | 5 | 6 | Compiled | | 1 | 3 | | 1 | |
| 6 | 7 | 5 | Tax Returns | 1 | | | 2 | 1 | |
| 19 | 15 | 17 | Other | 2 | 1 | | 2 | 1 | |
| 4/1/09- | 4/1/10- | 4/1/11- | | 3 | 1 | 1 | 5 | 2 | 5 |
| 3/31/10 | 3/31/11 | 3/31/12 | | | 6 (4/1-9/30/11) | | | 40 (10/1/11-3/31/12) | |
| ALL | ALL | ALL | | 0-1MM | 1-3MM | 3-5MM | 5-10MM | 10-25MM | 25MM & OVER |
| 43 | 47 | 46 | NUMBER OF STATEMENTS | 6 | 3 | 6 | 10 | 10 | 11 |
| % | % | % | ASSETS | % | % | % | % | % | % |
| 28.6 | 23.6 | 32.6 | Cash & Equivalents | | | | 24.8 | 37.0 | 38.5 |
| 21.9 | 24.3 | 21.4 | Trade Receivables (net) | | | | 28.0 | 20.5 | 30.5 |
| 8.9 | 9.5 | 7.0 | Inventory | | | | 14.7 | .0 | 9.1 |
| 9.1 | 10.3 | 6.9 | All Other Current | | | | 7.8 | 5.1 | 6.9 |
| 68.5 | 67.8 | 68.0 | Total Current | | | | 75.2 | 62.6 | 85.0 |
| 22.5 | 15.3 | 17.5 | Fixed Assets (net) | | | | 18.2 | 22.4 | 8.5 |
| 1.7 | 2.9 | 3.5 | Intangibles (net) | | | | 3.3 | 11.6 | .3 |
| 7.2 | 14.0 | 10.9 | All Other Non-Current | | | | 3.4 | 3.2 | 6.2 |
| 100.0 | 100.0 | 100.0 | Total | | | | 100.0 | 100.0 | 100.0 |
| | | | LIABILITIES | | | | | | |
| 13.2 | 17.8 | 12.9 | Notes Payable-Short Term | | | | 11.0 | 10.0 | 10.6 |
| 1.6 | 1.3 | 3.0 | Cur. Mat.-L.T.D. | | | | 6.7 | 3.8 | 1.0 |
| 8.5 | 9.8 | 15.8 | Trade Payables | | | | 8.4 | 22.4 | 31.1 |
| .1 | .2 | .3 | Income Taxes Payable | | | | .1 | 1.5 | .0 |
| 16.7 | 12.5 | 10.4 | All Other Current | | | | -11.8 | 11.7 | 8.6 |
| 40.1 | 41.6 | 42.4 | Total Current | | | | 38.0 | 49.4 | 51.3 |
| 17.2 | 12.8 | 16.4 | Long-Term Debt | | | | 27.7 | 9.5 | 9.0 |
| .0 | .2 | 1.2 | Deferred Taxes | | | | .0 | 5.5 | .2 |
| 4.1 | 4.7 | 3.3 | All Other Non-Current | | | | 5.2 | 1.6 | .9 |
| 38.6 | 40.7 | 36.7 | Net Worth | | | | 29.1 | 34.0 | 38.7 |
| 100.0 | 100.0 | 100.0 | Total Liabilties & Net Worth | | | | 100.0 | 100.0 | 100.0 |
| | | | INCOME DATA | | | | | | |
| 100.0 | 100.0 | 100.0 | Net Sales | | | | 100.0 | 100.0 | 100.0 |
| | | | Gross Profit | | | | | | |
| 70.3 | 73.9 | 82.0 | Operating Expenses | | | | 94.4 | 88.4 | 80.6 |
| 29.7 | 26.1 | 18.0 | Operating Profit | | | | 5.6 | 11.6 | 19.4 |
| 8.6 | 4.7 | 4.5 | All Other Expenses (net) | | | | 3.0 | .3 | 8.7 |
| 21.0 | 21.4 | 13.5 | Profit Before Taxes | | | | 2.6 | 11.2 | 10.7 |
| | | | RATIOS | | | | | | |
| 5.1 | 3.6 | 3.2 | | | | | 2.7 | 2.7 | 4.0 |
| 1.4 | 1.3 | 1.9 | Current | | | | 2.3 | 1.3 | 1.9 |
| 1.0 | 1.1 | 1.0 | | | | | 1.9 | .9 | 1.1 |
| 3.4 | 3.4 | 2.5 | | | | | 2.4 | 2.5 | 3.8 |
| 1.0 | 1.1 | 1.5 | Quick | | | | 1.9 | 1.2 | 1.9 |
| .5 | .6 | .6 | | | | | .8 | .8 | .8 |
| 0 UND | 7 56.0 | 0 UND | | | 6 60.2 | 0 UND | | 21 17.1 | |
| 22 16.9 | 35 10.5 | 38 9.5 | Sales/Receivables | | 43 8.5 | 36 10.2 | | 61 6.0 | |
| 66 5.5 | 94 3.9 | 87 4.2 | | | 281 1.3 | 44 8.3 | | 99 3.7 | |
| | | | Cost of Sales/Inventory | | | | | | |
| | | | Cost of Sales/Payables | | | | | | |
| 1.4 | 1.7 | 1.6 | | | | | 1.2 | 10.0 | 1.2 |
| 7.1 | 6.4 | 5.7 | Sales/Working Capital | | | | 1.6 | 39.6 | 5.1 |
| 999.8 | 65.9 | 143.1 | | | | | 7.6 | -209.2 | 141.4 |
| 16.5 | 32.0 | 43.7 | | | | | | | |
| (24) 7.8 | (33) 7.0 | (33) 4.0 | EBIT/Interest | | | | | | |
| 3.7 | 2.2 | 1.6 | | | | | | | |
| | | | Net Profit + Depr., Dep., Amort./Cur. Mat. L/T/D | | | | | | |
| .0 | .0 | .0 | | | | | .1 | .0 | .0 |
| .2 | .1 | .2 | Fixed/Worth | | | | .5 | 1.1 | .2 |
| 1.0 | .6 | 1.4 | | | | | 8.4 | NM | .5 |
| .5 | .5 | .6 | | | | | .8 | .7 | .4 |
| 2.4 | 1.7 | 2.6 | Debt/Worth | | | | 4.8 | 3.5 | 1.7 |
| 6.2 | 7.0 | 7.9 | | | | | 11.7 | NM | 7.7 |
| 50.2 | 61.7 | 54.6 | | | | | | | 53.0 |
| (40) 24.1 | (43) 29.4 | (42) 33.0 | % Profit Before Taxes/Tangible Net Worth | | | | | | 33.5 |
| 8.6 | 8.3 | 8.5 | | | | | | | 2.8 |
| 17.4 | 23.9 | 19.8 | | | | | 9.1 | 48.8 | 18.5 |
| 9.5 | 8.6 | 7.0 | % Profit Before Taxes/Total Assets | | | | 2.7 | 18.9 | 6.1 |
| 2.2 | 1.7 | 1.3 | | | | | -1.8 | 4.8 | .3 |
| 590.4 | 626.3 | 448.5 | | | | | 178.8 | 167.8 | 414.2 |
| 38.8 | 42.5 | 24.9 | Sales/Net Fixed Assets | | | | 16.4 | 36.4 | 29.6 |
| .9 | 6.0 | 6.5 | | | | | 1.0 | 6.5 | 10.0 |
| 2.9 | 2.8 | 3.4 | | | | | 4.6 | 17.7 | 3.9 |
| .5 | .8 | .9 | Sales/Total Assets | | | | .3 | 3.1 | 1.3 |
| .1 | .2 | .3 | | | | | .2 | 1.0 | .8 |
| .6 | .4 | .5 | | | | | | | |
| (29) 1.6 | (30) 1.2 | (29) 1.4 | % Depr., Dep., Amort./Sales | | | | | | |
| 8.8 | 3.2 | 3.0 | | | | | | | |
| | .4 | .5 | % Officers', Directors' Owners' Comp/Sales | | | | | | |
| | (10) 1.6 | (11) 2.0 | | | | | | | |
| | | 12.9 | | | | | | | |
| 2411412M | 1919101M | 4248282M | Net Sales ($) | 3209M | 5567M | 22156M | 75993M | 160743M | 3980614M |
| 1137772M | 1314870M | 1231965M | Total Assets ($) | 23172M | 7969M | 79665M | 222287M | 77171M | 821701M |

M = $ thousand    MM = $ million
See Pages 9 through 22 for Explanation of Ratios and Data

## Current Data Sorted by Assets

## Comparative Historical Data

| | | | | | | Type of Statement | | |
|---|---|---|---|---|---|---|---|---|
| | | 2 | 6 | | 2 | Unqualified | 7 | 5 |
| | | 3 | 1 | | | Reviewed | 4 | 3 |
| | | | 1 | | | Compiled | 1 | 2 |
| 2 | 1 | 2 | | 2 | | Tax Returns | 2 | 2 |
| 6 | | 2 | | | | Other | 10 | 6 |
| 6 (4/1-9/30/11) | | | 24 (10/1/11-3/31/12) | | | | 4/1/07-3/31/08 | 4/1/08-3/31/09 |
| 0-500M | 500M-2MM | 2-10MM | 10-50MM | 50-100MM | 100-250MM | | ALL | ALL |
| 2 | 7 | 9 | 8 | 2 | 2 | NUMBER OF STATEMENTS | 24 | 18 |
| % | % | % | % | % | % | ASSETS | % | % |
| | | | | | | Cash & Equivalents | 16.7 | 15.1 |
| | | | | | | Trade Receivables (net) | 36.1 | 42.5 |
| | | | | | | Inventory | 17.3 | 15.3 |
| | | | | | | All Other Current | 12.3 | 2.6 |
| | | | | | | Total Current | 82.4 | 75.4 |
| | | | | | | Fixed Assets (net) | 8.3 | 11.2 |
| | | | | | | Intangibles (net) | .0 | .4 |
| | | | | | | All Other Non-Current | 9.3 | 12.9 |
| | | | | | | Total | 100.0 | 100.0 |
| | | | | | | **LIABILITIES** | | |
| | | | | | | Notes Payable-Short Term | 16.0 | 16.3 |
| | | | | | | Cur. Mat.-L.T.D. | .3 | 2.2 |
| | | | | | | Trade Payables | 24.3 | 26.4 |
| | | | | | | Income Taxes Payable | .0 | .1 |
| | | | | | | All Other Current | 15.9 | 11.2 |
| | | | | | | Total Current | 56.6 | 56.3 |
| | | | | | | Long-Term Debt | 6.3 | 6.5 |
| | | | | | | Deferred Taxes | .0 | .0 |
| | | | | | | All Other Non-Current | 4.5 | 2.9 |
| | | | | | | Net Worth | 32.6 | 34.3 |
| | | | | | | Total Liabilities & Net Worth | 100.0 | 100.0 |
| | | | | | | **INCOME DATA** | | |
| | | | | | | Net Sales | 100.0 | 100.0 |
| | | | | | | Gross Profit | | |
| | | | | | | Operating Expenses | 89.8 | 90.9 |
| | | | | | | Operating Profit | 10.2 | 9.1 |
| | | | | | | All Other Expenses (net) | -.5 | -1.8 |
| | | | | | | Profit Before Taxes | 10.7 | 10.9 |
| | | | | | | **RATIOS** | | |
| | | | | | | Current | 2.1 | 1.8 |
| | | | | | | | 1.3 | 1.4 |
| | | | | | | | 1.1 | 1.1 |
| | | | | | | Quick | 1.7 | 1.4 |
| | | | | | | | 1.0 | 1.0 |
| | | | | | | | .4 | .4 |
| | | | | | | Sales/Receivables | 17   21.4 | 11   34.4 |
| | | | | | | | 33   11.0 | 22   16.4 |
| | | | | | | | 60   6.0 | 49   7.5 |
| | | | | | | Cost of Sales/Inventory | | |
| | | | | | | Cost of Sales/Payables | | |
| | | | | | | Sales/Working Capital | 4.2 | 14.5 |
| | | | | | | | 11.1 | 31.2 |
| | | | | | | | 28.3 | 160.6 |
| | | | | | | EBIT/Interest | 6.6 | 10.5 |
| | | | | | | | (19)   4.3 | (13)   2.7 |
| | | | | | | | 2.3 | 1.6 |
| | | | | | | Net Profit + Depr., Dep., Amort./Cur. Mat. L/T/D | | |
| | | | | | | Fixed/Worth | .0 | .0 |
| | | | | | | | .0 | .2 |
| | | | | | | | .7 | .7 |
| | | | | | | Debt/Worth | .8 | 1.4 |
| | | | | | | | 3.5 | 2.6 |
| | | | | | | | 8.6 | 8.9 |
| | | | | | | % Profit Before Taxes/Tangible Net Worth | 81.3 | 96.2 |
| | | | | | | | 35.2 | (17)   48.8 |
| | | | | | | | 15.7 | 9.5 |
| | | | | | | % Profit Before Taxes/Total Assets | 14.4 | 28.1 |
| | | | | | | | 6.5 | 7.1 |
| | | | | | | | 2.9 | 1.1 |
| | | | | | | Sales/Net Fixed Assets | 999.8 | 999.8 |
| | | | | | | | 598.6 | 219.1 |
| | | | | | | | 17.2 | 7.0 |
| | | | | | | Sales/Total Assets | 4.9 | 8.0 |
| | | | | | | | 3.2 | 4.6 |
| | | | | | | | .9 | 1.1 |
| | | | | | | % Depr., Dep., Amort./Sales | .0 | .0 |
| | | | | | | | (15)   .7 | (11)   1.4 |
| | | | | | | | 2.6 | 3.6 |
| | | | | | | % Officers', Directors' Owners' Comp/Sales | | |
| 992M | 29123M | 261675M | 1527590M | 1726113M | 186786M | Net Sales ($) | 1530871M | 1853983M |
| 231M | 8548M | 42817M | 177698M | 148730M | 355143M | Total Assets ($) | 879205M | 323047M |

© RMA 2012

M = $ thousand    MM = $ million
See Pages 9 through 22 for Explanation of Ratios and Data

## Comparative Historical Data | Current Data Sorted by Sales

| | | | | | | Type of Statement | | | | | | |
|---|---|---|---|---|---|---|---|---|---|---|---|---|
| | 7 | | 3 | | 10 | Unqualified | | | 1 | | 5 | 4 |
| | 2 | | 5 | | 4 | Reviewed | | | | | | 4 |
| | 1 | | 1 | | 1 | Compiled | | | | | | 1 |
| | 5 | | 4 | | 5 | Tax Returns | | | 1 | | | 2 |
| | 14 | | 10 | | 10 | Other | 2 | | 2 | | 1 | 2 |
| | 4/1/09- | | 4/1/10- | | 4/1/11- | | 1 | | 1 | | 2 | |
| | 3/31/10 | | 3/31/11 | | 3/31/12 | | | 6 (4/1-9/30/11) | | | 24 (10/1/11-3/31/12) | |
| | ALL | | ALL | | ALL | | 0-1MM | 1-3MM | 3-5MM | 5-10MM | 10-25MM | 25MM & OVER |
| | 29 | | 23 | | 30 | NUMBER OF STATEMENTS | 3 | 1 | 3 | 4 | 6 | 13 |
| | % | | % | | % | ASSETS | % | % | % | % | % | % |
| | 19.7 | | 23.5 | | 24.0 | Cash & Equivalents | | | | | | 22.4 |
| | 43.4 | | 42.7 | | 40.5 | Trade Receivables (net) | | | | | | 48.1 |
| | 7.5 | | 6.7 | | 11.3 | Inventory | | | | | | 18.7 |
| | 3.9 | | 6.1 | | 5.0 | All Other Current | | | | | | 3.8 |
| | 74.4 | | 79.0 | | 80.7 | Total Current | | | | | | 93.0 |
| | 9.6 | | 8.9 | | 11.8 | Fixed Assets (net) | | | | | | 5.4 |
| | 1.6 | | 1.6 | | 1.1 | Intangibles (net) | | | | | | .5 |
| | 14.4 | | 10.6 | | 6.4 | All Other Non-Current | | | | | | 1.1 |
| | 100.0 | | 100.0 | | 100.0 | Total | | | | | | 100.0 |
| | | | | | | LIABILITIES | | | | | | |
| | 16.2 | | 7.3 | | 10.6 | Notes Payable-Short Term | | | | | | 8.1 |
| | 1.5 | | 1.0 | | 1.6 | Cur. Mat.-L.T.D. | | | | | | .6 |
| | 24.3 | | 32.2 | | 28.0 | Trade Payables | | | | | | 44.2 |
| | .6 | | .3 | | .5 | Income Taxes Payable | | | | | | .1 |
| | 15.4 | | 5.5 | | 15.8 | All Other Current | | | | | | 6.8 |
| | 57.9 | | 46.2 | | 56.6 | Total Current | | | | | | 59.8 |
| | 7.0 | | 34.7 | | 2.9 | Long-Term Debt | | | | | | 1.5 |
| | .3 | | .8 | | 1.3 | Deferred Taxes | | | | | | .0 |
| | .5 | | 4.5 | | 6.9 | All Other Non-Current | | | | | | 5.2 |
| | 34.2 | | 13.9 | | 32.3 | Net Worth | | | | | | 33.6 |
| | 100.0 | | 100.0 | | 100.0 | Total Liabilties & Net Worth | | | | | | 100.0 |
| | | | | | | INCOME DATA | | | | | | |
| | 100.0 | | 100.0 | | 100.0 | Net Sales | | | | | | 100.0 |
| | | | | | | Gross Profit | | | | | | |
| | 88.4 | | 91.7 | | 91.3 | Operating Expenses | | | | | | 98.3 |
| | 11.6 | | 8.3 | | 8.7 | Operating Profit | | | | | | 1.7 |
| | .2 | | 1.6 | | 1.0 | All Other Expenses (net) | | | | | | .1 |
| | 11.4 | | 6.7 | | 7.7 | Profit Before Taxes | | | | | | 1.6 |
| | | | | | | RATIOS | | | | | | |
| | 2.4 | | 3.7 | | 1.9 | | | | | | | 1.6 |
| | 1.4 | | 1.6 | | 1.4 | Current | | | | | | 1.4 |
| | 1.1 | | 1.2 | | 1.2 | | | | | | | 1.3 |
| | 2.4 | | 2.9 | | 1.7 | | | | | | | 1.3 |
| | 1.2 | | 1.5 | | 1.2 | Quick | | | | | | 1.1 |
| | .6 | | .6 | | .7 | | | | | | | .8 |
| 8 | 46.9 | 8 | 48.4 | 11 | 34.1 | | | | | | 11 | 34.3 |
| 28 | 13.0 | 28 | 13.1 | 26 | 14.3 | Sales/Receivables | | | | | 24 | 15.2 |
| 50 | 7.2 | 49 | 7.4 | 43 | 8.4 | | | | | | 35 | 10.5 |
| | | | | | | Cost of Sales/Inventory | | | | | | |
| | | | | | | Cost of Sales/Payables | | | | | | |
| | 9.5 | | 8.2 | | 7.2 | | | | | | | 21.7 |
| | 26.0 | | 22.4 | | 19.5 | Sales/Working Capital | | | | | | 31.5 |
| | 105.7 | | 57.7 | | 42.0 | | | | | | | 53.3 |
| | 64.3 | | 97.6 | | 45.6 | | | | | | | 33.4 |
| (23) | 12.4 | (16) | 18.2 | (25) | 8.3 | EBIT/Interest | | | | | (12) | 13.2 |
| | 2.2 | | 2.9 | | 2.9 | | | | | | | 4.9 |
| | | | | | | Net Profit + Depr., Dep., Amort./Cur. Mat. L/T/D | | | | | | |
| | .0 | | .0 | | .0 | | | | | | | .0 |
| | .1 | | .0 | | .1 | Fixed/Worth | | | | | | .1 |
| | .7 | | .5 | | .5 | | | | | | | .5 |
| | .9 | | .8 | | 1.4 | | | | | | | 1.5 |
| | 2.8 | | 3.7 | | 2.1 | Debt/Worth | | | | | | 2.5 |
| | 7.1 | | 5.8 | | 3.9 | | | | | | | 3.1 |
| | 73.0 | | 69.3 | | 42.4 | | | | | | | 38.9 |
| (26) | 36.7 | (21) | 25.1 | (28) | 20.7 | % Profit Before Taxes/Tangible Net Worth | | | | | | 18.4 |
| | 8.8 | | 2.3 | | 14.5 | | | | | | | 13.7 |
| | 26.0 | | 15.5 | | 13.4 | | | | | | | 12.6 |
| | 7.8 | | 8.6 | | 8.0 | % Profit Before Taxes/Total Assets | | | | | | 7.5 |
| | 2.2 | | 2.5 | | 4.0 | | | | | | | 3.9 |
| | 999.8 | | UND | | 999.8 | | | | | | | 999.8 |
| | 614.5 | | 999.8 | | 129.3 | Sales/Net Fixed Assets | | | | | | 999.8 |
| | 40.6 | | 89.7 | | 15.8 | | | | | | | 113.2 |
| | 11.1 | | 9.8 | | 8.7 | | | | | | | 11.0 |
| | 6.3 | | 4.2 | | 4.8 | Sales/Total Assets | | | | | | 8.5 |
| | 2.5 | | 2.2 | | 2.4 | | | | | | | 5.3 |
| | .0 | | .0 | | .0 | | | | | | | .0 |
| (17) | .2 | (12) | .1 | (22) | .5 | % Depr., Dep., Amort./Sales | | | | | (11) | .0 |
| | 2.0 | | 1.9 | | 1.8 | | | | | | | .6 |
| | 1.6 | | | | | | | | | | | |
| (11) | 2.6 | | | | | % Officers', Directors' Owners' Comp/Sales | | | | | | |
| | 7.7 | | | | | | | | | | | |
| | 2806273M | | 3479431M | | 3732279M | Net Sales ($) | 1258M | 1981M | 13362M | 31180M | 96858M | 3587640M |
| | 473719M | | 564112M | | 733167M | Total Assets ($) | 1649M | 1227M | 2535M | 42861M | 173070M | 511825M |

M = $ thousand    MM = $ million
See Pages 9 through 22 for Explanation of Ratios and Data

### Current Data Sorted by Assets     Comparative Historical Data

| | 0-500M | 500M-2MM | 2-10MM | 10-50MM | 50-100MM | 100-250MM | | 4/1/07-3/31/08 ALL | 4/1/08-3/31/09 ALL |
|---|---|---|---|---|---|---|---|---|---|
| | | 11 (4/1-9/30/11) | | 171 (10/1/11-3/31/12) | | | **Type of Statement** | | |
| Unqualified | 2 | | 4 | 14 | 6 | 4 | | 25 | 53 |
| Reviewed | 1 | 1 | 5 | 7 | | | | 11 | 11 |
| Compiled | | 5 | 3 | 2 | | | | 14 | 11 |
| Tax Returns | 15 | 16 | 14 | 1 | | | | 26 | 25 |
| Other | 12 | 18 | 25 | 15 | 3 | 9 | | 68 | 92 |
| **NUMBER OF STATEMENTS** | 30 | 40 | 51 | 39 | 9 | 13 | | 144 | 192 |
| **ASSETS** | % | % | % | % | % | % | | % | % |
| Cash & Equivalents | 47.0 | 8.7 | 18.6 | 13.4 | | 28.4 | | 13.7 | 13.1 |
| Trade Receivables (net) | 6.0 | 12.1 | 17.0 | 18.3 | | 27.0 | | 12.4 | 21.2 |
| Inventory | 5.9 | 3.7 | 2.1 | 2.6 | | 5.8 | | 4.6 | 1.8 |
| All Other Current | 6.9 | 7.5 | 5.5 | 14.6 | | 2.9 | | 7.8 | 13.7 |
| Total Current | 65.9 | 32.0 | 43.2 | 49.0 | | 64.1 | | 38.5 | 49.8 |
| Fixed Assets (net) | 11.8 | 38.0 | 32.9 | 13.3 | | 8.7 | | 32.9 | 23.1 |
| Intangibles (net) | 4.4 | 6.4 | 5.0 | 6.3 | | .8 | | 4.0 | 3.4 |
| All Other Non-Current | 17.9 | 23.7 | 18.9 | 31.4 | | 26.5 | | 24.5 | 23.7 |
| Total | 100.0 | 100.0 | 100.0 | 100.0 | | 100.0 | | 100.0 | 100.0 |
| **LIABILITIES** | | | | | | | | | |
| Notes Payable-Short Term | 5.2 | 11.1 | 14.5 | 13.0 | | 7.8 | | 12.1 | 19.5 |
| Cur. Mat.-L.T.D. | 6.2 | 3.8 | 1.8 | 3.5 | | 1.9 | | 4.9 | 2.3 |
| Trade Payables | 1.4 | 5.1 | 3.5 | 4.4 | | .7 | | 4.2 | 5.7 |
| Income Taxes Payable | .3 | .2 | .0 | .4 | | .0 | | .1 | .1 |
| All Other Current | 25.9 | 16.9 | 12.3 | 12.8 | | 9.4 | | 10.0 | 12.7 |
| Total Current | 39.0 | 37.1 | 32.1 | 34.0 | | 19.8 | | 31.3 | 40.3 |
| Long-Term Debt | 3.8 | 23.0 | 26.8 | 11.9 | | 23.6 | | 28.2 | 26.2 |
| Deferred Taxes | .0 | .1 | .2 | .2 | | .2 | | .1 | .1 |
| All Other Non-Current | 12.7 | 7.1 | 5.1 | 7.7 | | .1 | | 3.7 | 6.2 |
| Net Worth | 44.7 | 32.8 | 35.8 | 46.1 | | 56.3 | | 36.7 | 27.2 |
| Total Liabilties & Net Worth | 100.0 | 100.0 | 100.0 | 100.0 | | 100.0 | | 100.0 | 100.0 |
| **INCOME DATA** | | | | | | | | | |
| Net Sales | 100.0 | 100.0 | 100.0 | 100.0 | | 100.0 | | 100.0 | 100.0 |
| Gross Profit | | | | | | | | | |
| Operating Expenses | 74.6 | 68.4 | 65.9 | 71.9 | | 47.2 | | 59.3 | 67.1 |
| Operating Profit | 25.4 | 31.6 | 34.1 | 28.1 | | 52.8 | | 40.7 | 32.9 |
| All Other Expenses (net) | .8 | 15.5 | 15.3 | 6.3 | | 19.1 | | 15.0 | 14.6 |
| Profit Before Taxes | 24.6 | 16.1 | 18.8 | 21.8 | | 33.7 | | 25.8 | 18.3 |
| **RATIOS** | | | | | | | | | |
| | 19.3 | 2.3 | 4.8 | 2.7 | | 47.8 | | 3.2 | 2.6 |
| Current | 4.3 | 1.1 | 1.7 | 1.5 | | 2.4 | | 1.3 | 1.3 |
| | .5 | .2 | .5 | .7 | | 1.2 | | .4 | .5 |
| | 16.4 | 1.9 | 4.8 | 2.7 | | 46.7 | | 2.0 | 1.9 |
| Quick | 2.3 | .3 | 1.2 | .7 | | 2.2 | | (143) .6 | .9 |
| | .5 | .1 | .1 | .1 | | .7 | | .1 | .2 |
| | 0 UND | 0 UND | 0 UND | 0 UND | | 0 UND | | 0 UND | 0 UND |
| Sales/Receivables | 0 UND | 0 UND | 2 198.5 | 9 41.9 | | 36 10.2 | | 0 999.8 | 5 77.2 |
| | 0 UND | 22 16.6 | 64 5.7 | 91 4.0 | | 182 2.0 | | 34 10.6 | 69 5.3 |
| Cost of Sales/Inventory | | | | | | | | | |
| Cost of Sales/Payables | | | | | | | | | |
| | 10.8 | 4.2 | 1.3 | .6 | | .3 | | 2.1 | 1.3 |
| Sales/Working Capital | 63.8 | 137.1 | 9.7 | 4.4 | | 1.1 | | 25.0 | 11.6 |
| | -77.0 | -2.1 | -5.1 | -13.9 | | NM | | -4.6 | -12.1 |
| | 172.5 | 21.0 | 20.4 | 16.4 | | | | 10.4 | 7.3 |
| EBIT/Interest | (10) 58.8 | (22) 3.2 | (22) 4.9 | (24) 3.8 | | | | (71) 5.5 | (101) 3.0 |
| | 10.1 | -1.0 | 1.2 | 2.3 | | | | 2.5 | 1.4 |
| | | | | | | | | | 17.8 |
| Net Profit + Depr., Dep., Amort./Cur. Mat. L/T/D | | | | | | | | (12) 10.3 | |
| | | | | | | | | | 2.0 |
| | .0 | .0 | .0 | .0 | | .0 | | .0 | .0 |
| Fixed/Worth | .1 | .7 | .2 | .1 | | .0 | | .5 | .1 |
| | .5 | 7.1 | 4.3 | .8 | | .3 | | 6.6 | 3.1 |
| | .2 | .6 | .7 | .3 | | .1 | | .5 | .8 |
| Debt/Worth | 1.7 | 2.0 | 2.6 | 1.8 | | .6 | | 2.0 | 2.8 |
| | 10.7 | 17.2 | 10.4 | 6.9 | | 3.3 | | 18.1 | 14.3 |
| | 625.0 | 58.6 | 62.8 | 43.3 | | 15.2 | | 68.2 | 49.5 |
| % Profit Before Taxes/Tangible Net Worth | (27) 70.6 | (34) 21.6 | (44) 11.5 | (34) 15.5 | | (12) 8.0 | | (116) 18.2 | (156) 16.1 |
| | 37.0 | 1.2 | -.7 | 2.0 | | -.7 | | 4.9 | 5.0 |
| | 206.6 | 18.5 | 9.6 | 11.2 | | 6.7 | | 21.7 | 15.4 |
| % Profit Before Taxes/Total Assets | 66.3 | 2.4 | 3.0 | 4.9 | | 4.5 | | 6.1 | 4.9 |
| | 17.7 | -.7 | .0 | 1.1 | | -.4 | | 1.6 | 1.1 |
| | UND | UND | UND | 265.4 | | UND | | 337.6 | 549.2 |
| Sales/Net Fixed Assets | 543.2 | 9.0 | 17.8 | 22.2 | | 22.9 | | 13.4 | 27.4 |
| | 63.8 | .2 | .3 | 3.3 | | 3.8 | | .6 | 1.8 |
| | 24.0 | 1.9 | 1.2 | 1.0 | | .8 | | 1.7 | 1.7 |
| Sales/Total Assets | 7.8 | .4 | .2 | .4 | | .1 | | .4 | .4 |
| | 4.3 | .1 | .1 | .1 | | .1 | | .1 | .1 |
| | .2 | 2.4 | .5 | .9 | | | | 1.2 | .6 |
| % Depr., Dep., Amort./Sales | (11) .4 | (21) 11.2 | (29) 2.2 | (23) 1.3 | | | | (86) 3.4 | (112) 1.6 |
| | .9 | 25.4 | 20.5 | 3.2 | | | | 13.6 | 5.2 |
| | | | | | | | | 2.5 | 4.9 |
| % Officers', Directors' Owners' Comp/Sales | | | | | | | | (23) 6.7 | (28) 12.8 |
| | | | | | | | | 15.3 | 20.6 |
| Net Sales ($) | 63651M | 83302M | 219068M | 993767M | 117405M | 843707M | | 2383313M | 3586580M |
| Total Assets ($) | 5076M | 45894M | 232324M | 907832M | 557718M | 2031156M | | 4009584M | 5064696M |

M = $ thousand     MM = $ million
See Pages 9 through 22 for Explanation of Ratios and Data

## Comparative Historical Data | Current Data Sorted by Sales

| | 4/1/09-3/31/10 ALL | 4/1/10-3/31/11 ALL | 4/1/11-3/31/12 ALL | 0-1MM | 1-3MM | 3-5MM | 5-10MM | 10-25MM | 25MM & OVER |
|---|---|---|---|---|---|---|---|---|---|
| **Type of Statement** | | | | | 11 (4/1-9/30/11) | | 171 (10/1/11-3/31/12) | | |
| Unqualified | 43 | 36 | 30 | 6 | 4 | 1 | 5 | 7 | 7 |
| Reviewed | 13 | 7 | 14 | 3 | 2 | 3 | 2 | 2 | 2 |
| Compiled | 9 | 9 | 10 | 5 | 3 | 1 | | 1 | |
| Tax Returns | 26 | 39 | 46 | 31 | 10 | 4 | 1 | | |
| Other | 74 | 81 | 82 | 25 | 10 | 9 | 12 | 13 | 10 |
| **NUMBER OF STATEMENTS** | 165 | 172 | 182 | 70 | 32 | 18 | 20 | 23 | 19 |
| **ASSETS** | % | % | % | % | % | % | % | % | % |
| Cash & Equivalents | 14.6 | 15.4 | 20.2 | 16.5 | 23.1 | 26.5 | 28.8 | 20.5 | 13.6 |
| Trade Receivables (net) | 13.3 | 12.2 | 14.9 | 8.3 | 15.6 | 19.5 | 12.9 | 26.5 | 21.6 |
| Inventory | 3.3 | 3.7 | 3.7 | 1.7 | 2.8 | 10.0 | 3.7 | 1.8 | 9.4 |
| All Other Current | 9.4 | 10.4 | 8.3 | 5.4 | 9.1 | 14.7 | 5.2 | 9.1 | 13.7 |
| Total Current | 40.6 | 41.7 | 47.1 | 31.8 | 50.5 | 70.8 | 50.6 | 57.8 | 58.3 |
| Fixed Assets (net) | 26.7 | 30.0 | 23.6 | 37.7 | 22.7 | 5.7 | 15.1 | 9.0 | 17.0 |
| Intangibles (net) | 2.5 | 5.9 | 4.9 | 3.8 | 8.7 | .3 | 6.1 | 5.8 | 5.0 |
| All Other Non-Current | 30.1 | 22.4 | 24.4 | 26.7 | 18.1 | 23.2 | 28.2 | 27.4 | 19.7 |
| Total | 100.0 | 100.0 | 100.0 | 100.0 | 100.0 | 100.0 | 100.0 | 100.0 | 100.0 |
| **LIABILITIES** | | | | | | | | | |
| Notes Payable-Short Term | 14.8 | 12.0 | 11.4 | 10.6 | 16.6 | 14.6 | 9.5 | 11.2 | 5.0 |
| Cur. Mat.-L.T.D. | 1.9 | 2.7 | 3.3 | 2.0 | 3.8 | 4.6 | 6.6 | .9 | 5.0 |
| Trade Payables | 5.3 | 5.2 | 3.3 | .4 | 1.7 | 4.5 | 5.7 | 8.7 | 6.8 |
| Income Taxes Payable | .1 | .1 | .2 | .0 | .1 | .3 | .0 | .4 | .8 |
| All Other Current | 8.6 | 11.7 | 15.0 | 10.4 | 23.6 | 8.8 | 11.0 | 22.8 | 17.9 |
| Total Current | 30.7 | 31.8 | 33.2 | 23.4 | 45.8 | 32.8 | 32.9 | 44.0 | 35.5 |
| Long-Term Debt | 22.6 | 25.7 | 18.2 | 27.7 | 17.5 | 1.5 | 6.1 | 9.0 | 23.7 |
| Deferred Taxes | .0 | .1 | .1 | .0 | .1 | .0 | .3 | .5 | .2 |
| All Other Non-Current | 4.9 | 3.8 | 7.0 | 7.7 | 8.9 | 10.0 | 1.6 | 3.9 | 7.7 |
| Net Worth | 41.8 | 38.6 | 41.6 | 41.3 | 27.7 | 55.8 | 59.1 | 42.7 | 32.9 |
| Total Liabilities & Net Worth | 100.0 | 100.0 | 100.0 | 100.0 | 100.0 | 100.0 | 100.0 | 100.0 | 100.0 |
| **INCOME DATA** | | | | | | | | | |
| Net Sales | 100.0 | 100.0 | 100.0 | 100.0 | 100.0 | 100.0 | 100.0 | 100.0 | 100.0 |
| Gross Profit | | | | | | | | | |
| Operating Expenses | 65.9 | 65.6 | 66.7 | 58.3 | 63.6 | 78.9 | 64.4 | 75.7 | 82.9 |
| Operating Profit | 34.1 | 34.4 | 33.3 | 41.7 | 36.4 | 21.1 | 35.6 | 24.3 | 17.1 |
| All Other Expenses (net) | 13.6 | 12.5 | 11.8 | 17.9 | 10.3 | 3.3 | 10.1 | 8.5 | 5.8 |
| Profit Before Taxes | 20.5 | 21.9 | 21.5 | 23.9 | 26.2 | 17.8 | 25.5 | 15.7 | 11.3 |
| **RATIOS** | | | | | | | | | |
| Current | 3.8 | 2.8 | 9.2 | 11.2 | 9.7 | 12.9 | 10.7 | 2.4 | 2.5 |
| | 1.4 | 1.3 | 1.6 | 1.4 | 1.4 | 2.7 | 2.3 | 1.4 | 1.4 |
| | .5 | .5 | .5 | .2 | .5 | 1.1 | 1.0 | .8 | .7 |
| Quick | 2.9 | 2.1 | 5.7 | 7.4 | 9.7 | 6.2 | 10.4 | 1.9 | 2.1 |
| | 1.0 | .8 | 1.1 | 1.1 | .9 | 2.5 | 1.9 | 1.2 | .7 |
| | .2 | .2 | .1 | .1 | .1 | .8 | .6 | .6 | .3 |
| Sales/Receivables | 0 UND | 0 UND | 0 UND | 0 UND | 0 UND | 0 UND | 0 UND | 7 55.8 | 6 61.0 |
| | 2 203.3 | 1 276.2 | 0 860.7 | 0 UND | 0 UND | 0 UND | 2 210.5 | 29 12.8 | 15 24.2 |
| | 41 9.0 | 34 10.6 | 36 10.2 | 20 18.2 | 28 12.9 | 33 11.2 | 76 4.8 | 58 6.3 | 114 3.2 |
| Cost of Sales/Inventory | | | | | | | | | |
| Cost of Sales/Payables | | | | | | | | | |
| Sales/Working Capital | 2.0 | 2.0 | 1.5 | 1.2 | .8 | 1.6 | .7 | 5.2 | 1.8 |
| | 9.5 | 14.8 | 18.0 | 11.2 | 31.5 | 4.1 | 9.7 | 17.6 | 19.9 |
| | -7.8 | -10.5 | -14.5 | -2.9 | -5.9 | 75.0 | NM | -66.7 | -21.6 |
| EBIT/Interest | 25.3 | 17.2 | 21.5 | 20.8 | 26.5 | | 40.5 | 166.2 | 10.8 |
| | (84) 3.7 | (100) 4.2 | (93) 4.8 | (29) 4.7 | (16) 3.7 | (13) 11.0 | (14) 11.3 | | (12) 3.2 |
| | 1.2 | 2.1 | 1.6 | .6 | 1.3 | | 2.9 | -.8 | 2.4 |
| Net Profit + Depr., Dep., Amort./Cur. Mat. L/T/D | | | | | | | | | |
| Fixed/Worth | .0 | .0 | .0 | .0 | .0 | .0 | .0 | .0 | .0 |
| | .1 | .5 | .1 | .4 | .0 | .0 | .0 | .1 | .2 |
| | 2.1 | 3.5 | 1.9 | 2.8 | 1.6 | .2 | .8 | 2.0 | 8.0 |
| Debt/Worth | .3 | .5 | .5 | .5 | .7 | .1 | .1 | .5 | .7 |
| | 1.7 | 1.7 | 1.7 | 1.8 | 3.1 | 1.2 | .5 | 1.3 | 2.5 |
| | 8.1 | 11.1 | 8.4 | 8.4 | 39.0 | 2.0 | 8.7 | 26.8 | 10.8 |
| % Profit Before Taxes/Tangible Net Worth | 37.9 | 49.5 | 63.4 | 46.8 | 100.9 | 48.7 | 95.0 | 67.3 | 80.8 |
| | (143) 9.5 | (144) 15.6 | (160) 19.7 | (64) 11.5 | (26) 32.7 | (18) 28.0 | (18) 10.4 | (18) 15.5 | (16) 35.0 |
| | 1.3 | 3.0 | 2.4 | 1.9 | 4.0 | 1.7 | 2.7 | -2.4 | 17.5 |
| % Profit Before Taxes/Total Assets | 11.1 | 19.8 | 21.7 | 13.6 | 52.0 | 26.3 | 33.6 | 21.4 | 27.2 |
| | 3.6 | 4.9 | 5.3 | 2.6 | 6.0 | 8.8 | 5.1 | 7.9 | 8.1 |
| | .6 | 1.4 | .9 | .7 | .9 | .9 | 1.7 | -1.1 | 4.5 |
| Sales/Net Fixed Assets | UND | 724.1 | UND | UND | UND | UND | UND | 343.7 | 115.3 |
| | 30.7 | 21.5 | 32.4 | 4.2 | 114.3 | 266.7 | 49.2 | 28.7 | 22.9 |
| | 1.0 | .6 | 2.8 | .2 | 3.5 | 40.8 | 5.8 | 9.2 | 14.4 |
| Sales/Total Assets | 1.5 | 1.7 | 2.5 | .7 | 3.7 | 8.0 | 4.0 | 3.2 | 2.7 |
| | .2 | .4 | .5 | .1 | .5 | 1.2 | .6 | 1.6 | 1.0 |
| | .1 | .1 | .1 | .1 | .2 | .2 | .1 | .3 | .8 |
| % Depr., Dep., Amort./Sales | .7 | .9 | .5 | 1.4 | .2 | | | .7 | .2 |
| | (89) 2.4 | (101) 3.5 | (93) 1.6 | (35) 12.6 | (17) .5 | | (12) 1.9 | (14) 1.1 | |
| | 17.6 | 16.3 | 12.8 | 25.0 | 2.6 | | | 3.0 | 2.5 |
| % Officers', Directors' Owners' Comp/Sales | 3.9 | 4.8 | 3.4 | | | | | | |
| | (18) 9.6 | (16) 10.4 | (25) 10.1 | | | | | | |
| | 22.9 | 25.3 | 27.3 | | | | | | |
| Net Sales ($) | 2739279M | 4274657M | 2320900M | 29378M | 59782M | 74155M | 144473M | 347965M | 1665147M |
| Total Assets ($) | 4794079M | 4217115M | 3780000M | 213476M | 288437M | 186455M | 772423M | 875307M | 1443902M |

© RMA 2012

M = $ thousand    MM = $ million
See Pages 9 through 22 for Explanation of Ratios and Data

## Current Data Sorted by Assets

## Comparative Historical Data

| | | | | | | Type of Statement | | |
|---|---|---|---|---|---|---|---|---|
| | | 11 | 19 | 6 | 7 | Unqualified | 36 | 42 |
| | 1 | | 2 | | | Reviewed | 4 | 10 |
| 2 | 2 | 1 | | | | Compiled | 10 | 4 |
| 10 | 10 | 4 | 1 | 5 | 9 | Tax Returns | 19 | 18 |
| 12 | 11 | 23 | 13 | | | Other | 58 | 62 |
| | 14 (4/1-9/30/11) | | 135 (10/1/11-3/31/12) | | | | 4/1/07-3/31/08 | 4/1/08-3/31/09 |
| 0-500M | 500M-2MM | 2-10MM | 10-50MM | 50-100MM | 100-250MM | | ALL | ALL |
| 24 | 24 | 39 | 35 | 11 | 16 | NUMBER OF STATEMENTS | 127 | 136 |
| % | % | % | % | % | % | ASSETS | % | % |
| 27.1 | 22.9 | 24.6 | 27.8 | 26.0 | 18.8 | Cash & Equivalents | 26.2 | 24.2 |
| 4.6 | 21.5 | 20.3 | 11.6 | 16.9 | 2.8 | Trade Receivables (net) | 14.7 | 15.8 |
| .1 | .0 | 1.8 | .0 | .0 | 3.7 | Inventory | 1.2 | .3 |
| 12.6 | 2.5 | 2.4 | 11.8 | 10.9 | 7.2 | All Other Current | 9.5 | 8.5 |
| 44.4 | 46.9 | 49.1 | 51.3 | 53.8 | 32.4 | Total Current | 51.6 | 48.8 |
| 25.9 | 32.1 | 30.2 | 18.5 | 5.1 | 7.5 | Fixed Assets (net) | 16.6 | 23.9 |
| 16.2 | 9.3 | 4.8 | 13.4 | 8.6 | 19.2 | Intangibles (net) | 5.7 | 6.5 |
| 13.4 | 11.8 | 15.9 | 16.8 | 32.5 | 40.8 | All Other Non-Current | 26.1 | 20.7 |
| 100.0 | 100.0 | 100.0 | 100.0 | 100.0 | 100.0 | Total | 100.0 | 100.0 |
| | | | | | | LIABILITIES | | |
| 70.2 | 16.2 | 9.1 | 11.4 | 3.2 | 10.1 | Notes Payable-Short Term | 15.1 | 12.0 |
| 5.7 | 3.8 | 5.5 | 1.5 | 3.4 | .7 | Cur. Mat.-L.T.D. | 2.4 | 3.8 |
| 2.0 | 4.2 | 4.0 | 5.7 | 7.0 | 2.2 | Trade Payables | 5.2 | 4.9 |
| .0 | .0 | .0 | .0 | .0 | .0 | Income Taxes Payable | .3 | .3 |
| 47.9 | 21.6 | 10.5 | 7.6 | 20.6 | 5.2 | All Other Current | 18.4 | 15.9 |
| 125.8 | 45.8 | 29.0 | 26.2 | 34.3 | 18.2 | Total Current | 41.4 | 36.9 |
| 37.1 | 24.4 | 22.3 | 12.8 | 14.2 | 24.3 | Long-Term Debt | 16.9 | 25.3 |
| .0 | .0 | .0 | .5 | .1 | 1.0 | Deferred Taxes | .3 | .3 |
| 2.0 | 6.2 | 13.8 | 4.9 | 9.2 | 2.8 | All Other Non-Current | 8.2 | 6.3 |
| -64.9 | 23.6 | 34.9 | 55.5 | 42.2 | 53.8 | Net Worth | 33.2 | 31.1 |
| 100.0 | 100.0 | 100.0 | 100.0 | 100.0 | 100.0 | Total Liabilities & Net Worth | 100.0 | 100.0 |
| | | | | | | INCOME DATA | | |
| 100.0 | 100.0 | 100.0 | 100.0 | 100.0 | 100.0 | Net Sales | 100.0 | 100.0 |
| | | | | | | Gross Profit | | |
| 71.8 | 71.3 | 69.1 | 68.7 | 63.5 | 70.5 | Operating Expenses | 69.4 | 70.7 |
| 28.2 | 28.7 | 30.9 | 31.3 | 36.5 | 29.5 | Operating Profit | 30.6 | 29.3 |
| 2.8 | 9.7 | 9.0 | 6.3 | 7.0 | 17.7 | All Other Expenses (net) | 5.8 | 8.1 |
| 25.4 | 19.0 | 21.8 | 25.0 | 29.5 | 11.9 | Profit Before Taxes | 24.8 | 21.2 |
| | | | | | | RATIOS | | |
| 1.9 | 6.1 | 4.8 | 5.2 | 2.9 | 17.9 | | 5.0 | 5.5 |
| .6 | 2.0 | 2.2 | 2.7 | 2.0 | 1.9 | Current | 1.9 | 1.9 |
| .1 | .2 | .5 | .7 | 1.1 | .9 | | .9 | .6 |
| 1.8 | 5.5 | 4.5 | 4.4 | 2.7 | 17.1 | | 3.8 | 4.2 |
| .4 | 1.3 | 2.2 | 2.1 | 1.6 | 1.4 | Quick | 1.3 | 1.4 |
| .1 | .2 | .3 | .4 | .6 | .4 | | .4 | .4 |
| 0 UND | 0 UND | 0 UND | 0 UND | 0 UND | 0 UND | | 0 UND | 0 UND |
| 0 UND | 0 UND | 17 21.3 | 22 16.9 | 15 24.4 | 5 69.3 | Sales/Receivables | 2 214.3 | 1 414.9 |
| 0 UND | 62 5.9 | 65 5.6 | 45 8.2 | 60 6.1 | 36 10.2 | | 41 9.0 | 41 8.9 |
| | | | | | | Cost of Sales/Inventory | | |
| | | | | | | Cost of Sales/Payables | | |
| 52.2 | 4.2 | 3.5 | 1.5 | 3.4 | .7 | | 2.6 | 3.3 |
| -110.1 | 29.2 | 5.4 | 4.4 | 9.8 | 3.4 | Sales/Working Capital | 9.7 | 16.5 |
| -8.9 | -3.1 | -5.4 | -18.2 | 41.7 | NM | | -28.4 | -11.7 |
| 209.0 | 12.3 | 20.4 | 125.4 | | | | 41.5 | 36.2 |
| (15) 53.4 | (11) 8.4 | (18) 5.8 | (16) 45.0 | | | EBIT/Interest | (64) 10.5 | (77) 7.2 |
| 3.1 | -2.9 | 2.2 | 8.4 | | | | 2.2 | 1.9 |
| | | | | | | Net Profit + Depr., Dep., Amort./Cur. Mat. L/T/D | | 8.8 |
| | | | | | | | (11) 2.3 | |
| | | | | | | | | .7 |
| .2 | .0 | .0 | .0 | .0 | .0 | | .0 | .0 |
| NM | .8 | .3 | .1 | .3 | .1 | Fixed/Worth | .1 | .3 |
| -.2 | 29.1 | 2.0 | .5 | 5.2 | 9.2 | | 2.9 | 3.8 |
| .8 | .5 | .4 | .2 | .2 | .2 | | .4 | .4 |
| -3.3 | 3.5 | 1.1 | 1.0 | 3.2 | 1.2 | Debt/Worth | 1.6 | 1.9 |
| -1.4 | 30.7 | 4.1 | 3.1 | 69.5 | 23.1 | | 20.8 | 21.7 |
| 999.8 | 173.1 | 108.6 | 84.6 | 551.9 | 14.8 | | 109.5 | 118.6 |
| (10) 359.0 | (20) 58.0 | (34) 19.4 | (30) 38.8 | (10) 100.7 | (13) .5 | % Profit Before Taxes/Tangible Net Worth | (105) 33.7 | (111) 41.7 |
| 36.7 | 4.0 | 8.7 | 8.6 | 7.5 | -3.0 | | 6.6 | 3.5 |
| 721.6 | 32.3 | 24.4 | 42.9 | 91.5 | 5.3 | | 36.7 | 40.8 |
| 89.3 | 14.7 | 7.0 | 19.0 | 10.4 | .8 | % Profit Before Taxes/Total Assets | 10.2 | 13.1 |
| 6.6 | 1.0 | 2.0 | 2.9 | 5.0 | -.9 | | 2.1 | 1.0 |
| 293.0 | 343.1 | 92.5 | 120.9 | 105.7 | UND | | 999.8 | 410.0 |
| 60.7 | 40.9 | 23.0 | 34.4 | 43.9 | 28.3 | Sales/Net Fixed Assets | 51.0 | 32.8 |
| 18.8 | 3.8 | .9 | 10.5 | 19.7 | 11.3 | | 12.1 | 7.3 |
| 22.0 | 3.7 | 2.8 | 1.3 | 2.3 | .5 | | 3.2 | 3.9 |
| 7.7 | 1.9 | 1.2 | .8 | 1.6 | .2 | Sales/Total Assets | 1.5 | 1.6 |
| 3.6 | .2 | .2 | .5 | .1 | .1 | | .3 | .3 |
| .2 | .6 | .7 | .7 | | | | .5 | .5 |
| (11) .7 | (12) 1.9 | (26) 1.2 | (26) 1.4 | | | % Depr., Dep., Amort./Sales | (76) 1.2 | (78) 1.8 |
| 6.2 | 13.8 | 10.8 | 5.5 | | | | 3.2 | 4.3 |
| 6.5 | | | | | | | 7.6 | 10.3 |
| (10) 12.1 | | | | | | % Officers', Directors' Owners' Comp/Sales | (29) 22.5 | (23) 20.2 |
| 24.3 | | | | | | | 35.5 | 38.2 |
| 61993M | 50384M | 276736M | 1023863M | 1260868M | 1919914M | Net Sales ($) | 2301211M | 4913207M |
| 5630M | 23101M | 191802M | 948431M | 825503M | 2719004M | Total Assets ($) | 2824370M | 3000777M |

M = $ thousand    MM = $ million
See Pages 9 through 22 for Explanation of Ratios and Data

## Comparative Historical Data | | | | ## Current Data Sorted by Sales

| | | | Type of Statement | | | | | | |
|---|---|---|---|---|---|---|---|---|---|
| 36 | 33 | 43 | Unqualified | 1 | 1 | 1 | 8 | 12 | 20 |
| 7 | 6 | 3 | Reviewed | | 2 | 1 | | | |
| 5 | 5 | 5 | Compiled | | 1 | 1 | | | |
| 29 | 21 | 25 | Tax Returns | 3 | 1 | 1 | | | |
| 64 | 72 | 73 | Other | 12 | 8 | 1 | 4 | | |
| 4/1/09-3/31/10 ALL | 4/1/10-3/31/11 ALL | 4/1/11-3/31/12 ALL | | 14 | 13 (4/1-9/30/11) | 10 | 13 (10/1/11-3/31/12) | 13 | 13 |
| | | | | 0-1MM | 1-3MM | 3-5MM | 5-10MM | 10-25MM | 25MM & OVER |
| 141 | 137 | 149 | NUMBER OF STATEMENTS | 30 | 25 | 14 | 22 | 25 | 33 |
| % | % | % | ASSETS | % | % | % | % | % | % |
| 25.8 | 24.0 | 25.0 | Cash & Equivalents | 14.1 | 26.4 | 19.4 | 27.5 | 35.0 | 26.9 |
| 15.1 | 17.9 | 13.8 | Trade Receivables (net) | 5.2 | 12.0 | 16.2 | 14.6 | 21.3 | 15.7 |
| .6 | 1.5 | .9 | Inventory | .1 | .1 | 4.7 | .0 | .0 | 1.8 |
| 9.8 | 10.5 | 7.4 | All Other Current | 5.4 | 5.4 | 3.6 | 6.6 | 7.4 | 13.0 |
| 51.2 | 53.9 | 47.1 | Total Current | 24.8 | 43.9 | 43.9 | 48.7 | 63.7 | 57.4 |
| 19.4 | 18.0 | 22.8 | Fixed Assets (net) | 44.9 | 24.7 | 31.9 | 20.0 | 10.8 | 8.2 |
| 7.4 | 10.9 | 11.2 | Intangibles (net) | 6.6 | 17.5 | 4.4 | 13.4 | 5.6 | 16.2 |
| 21.9 | 17.2 | 19.0 | All Other Non-Current | 23.7 | 13.9 | 19.7 | 17.9 | 19.9 | 18.2 |
| 100.0 | 100.0 | 100.0 | Total | 100.0 | 100.0 | 100.0 | 100.0 | 100.0 | 100.0 |
| | | | LIABILITIES | | | | | | |
| 15.6 | 17.4 | 20.3 | Notes Payable-Short Term | 41.8 | 26.3 | 22.6 | 14.5 | 5.3 | 10.4 |
| 4.4 | 3.5 | 3.6 | Cur. Mat.-L.T.D. | 5.7 | 2.1 | 2.6 | 8.2 | 1.8 | 1.7 |
| 4.5 | 6.2 | 4.1 | Trade Payables | .7 | 2.0 | 4.6 | 2.5 | 7.3 | 7.3 |
| .2 | .3 | .0 | Income Taxes Payable | .0 | .0 | .0 | .0 | .0 | .1 |
| 19.8 | 16.2 | 17.8 | All Other Current | 27.5 | 11.2 | 25.7 | 16.2 | 14.5 | 14.2 |
| 44.4 | 43.7 | 45.9 | Total Current | 75.8 | 41.6 | 55.4 | 41.4 | 29.0 | 33.7 |
| 25.7 | 20.1 | 22.4 | Long-Term Debt | 36.5 | 35.8 | 30.9 | 8.7 | 11.7 | 13.0 |
| .3 | .3 | .2 | Deferred Taxes | .0 | .0 | .5 | .5 | .2 | .5 |
| 8.3 | 3.6 | 7.1 | All Other Non-Current | 3.4 | 5.7 | 4.9 | 17.0 | 5.8 | 6.7 |
| 21.2 | 32.2 | 24.4 | Net Worth | -15.7 | 16.8 | 8.7 | 32.3 | 53.3 | 46.1 |
| 100.0 | 100.0 | 100.0 | Total Liabilities & Net Worth | 100.0 | 100.0 | 100.0 | 100.0 | 100.0 | 100.0 |
| | | | INCOME DATA | | | | | | |
| 100.0 | 100.0 | 100.0 | Net Sales | 100.0 | 100.0 | 100.0 | 100.0 | 100.0 | 100.0 |
| | | | Gross Profit | | | | | | |
| 75.6 | 70.2 | 69.5 | Operating Expenses | 43.4 | 77.8 | 69.8 | 81.3 | 74.4 | 75.4 |
| 24.4 | 29.8 | 30.5 | Operating Profit | 56.6 | 22.2 | 30.2 | 18.7 | 25.6 | 24.6 |
| 6.2 | 6.0 | 8.3 | All Other Expenses (net) | 21.6 | 4.5 | 14.9 | 2.7 | 5.8 | 1.9 |
| 18.2 | 23.8 | 22.2 | Profit Before Taxes | 35.1 | 17.7 | 15.3 | 16.0 | 19.9 | 22.6 |
| | | | RATIOS | | | | | | |
| 4.2 | 4.7 | 5.0 | | 5.4 | 2.7 | 5.7 | 6.3 | 6.7 | 3.4 |
| 1.9 | 1.9 | 1.9 | Current | .3 | 1.0 | 1.8 | 2.3 | 2.7 | 1.9 |
| .9 | .9 | .5 | | .0 | .4 | .4 | .5 | 2.0 | 1.1 |
| 3.6 | 3.6 | 4.2 | | 4.0 | 2.1 | 4.9 | 5.9 | 6.6 | 2.5 |
| 1.3 | 1.5 | 1.5 | Quick | .3 | .6 | 1.7 | 2.2 | 2.7 | 1.3 |
| .5 | .4 | .4 | | .0 | .2 | .2 | .4 | 1.9 | .5 |
| 0 UND | 0 UND | 0 UND | | 0 UND | 0 UND | 0 UND | 0 UND | 0 UND | 6 56.3 |
| 2 177.8 | 7 48.7 | 6 63.1 | Sales/Receivables | 0 UND | 0 UND | 27 13.3 | 23 15.8 | 14 26.7 | 28 13.0 |
| 38 9.6 | 41 9.0 | 41 8.9 | | 0 UND | 12 29.2 | 73 5.0 | 41 8.9 | 68 5.4 | 56 6.5 |
| | | | Cost of Sales/Inventory | | | | | | |
| | | | Cost of Sales/Payables | | | | | | |
| 3.3 | 3.2 | 3.3 | | 4.0 | 4.5 | 2.5 | 2.6 | 2.8 | 3.4 |
| 11.6 | 9.5 | 10.4 | Sales/Working Capital | -11.9 | UND | 8.8 | 7.5 | 4.8 | 6.1 |
| -16.9 | -59.1 | -9.5 | | -.6 | -5.3 | -14.5 | -10.8 | 11.0 | NM |
| (78) 47.4 | (69) 52.4 | (75) 63.3 | | 24.8 | 12.3 | | 789.3 | | 89.3 |
| 7.4 | 9.4 | 10.0 | EBIT/Interest | (10) 7.9 | (15) 3.1 | | (12) 43.5 | | (20) 10.9 |
| 1.2 | 1.9 | 3.0 | | 2.8 | 1.9 | | 7.7 | | 1.4 |
| 19.3 | 9.3 | 6.1 | | | | | | | |
| (10) 2.3 | (11) 1.8 | (15) 2.1 | Net Profit + Depr., Dep., Amort./Cur. Mat. L/T/D | | | | | | |
| .4 | .2 | 1.0 | | | | | | | |
| .0 | .0 | .0 | | .0 | .0 | .1 | .0 | .0 | .0 |
| .4 | .2 | .2 | Fixed/Worth | 1.9 | 1.0 | .5 | .1 | .1 | .2 |
| 14.7 | 3.4 | 5.4 | | NM | -3.9 | NM | 5.4 | .4 | 7.3 |
| .3 | .3 | .4 | | 1.0 | .5 | .6 | .1 | .3 | .4 |
| 1.5 | 1.4 | 1.4 | Debt/Worth | 3.5 | 4.5 | 2.4 | .3 | .9 | 1.7 |
| -154.2 | 15.8 | 51.8 | | -2.9 | -2.9 | NM | 11.6 | 1.5 | 198.1 |
| 84.7 | 124.4 | 120.7 | | 65.1 | 151.0 | 86.7 | 197.1 | 106.5 | 181.0 |
| (105) 22.2 | (112) 41.2 | (117) 29.3 | % Profit Before Taxes/Tangible Net Worth | (21) 16.7 | (17) 15.9 | (11) 18.8 | (19) 37.7 | (23) 20.6 | (26) 74.3 |
| 2.1 | 10.6 | 4.9 | | 3.6 | 2.2 | .0 | 3.1 | 12.4 | 17.5 |
| 42.1 | 53.2 | 47.5 | | 15.3 | 57.8 | 40.3 | 142.8 | 59.8 | 56.1 |
| 9.8 | 10.5 | 9.6 | % Profit Before Taxes/Total Assets | 4.4 | 9.6 | 8.3 | 6.7 | 14.4 | 28.0 |
| .2 | 2.8 | 1.9 | | .8 | .7 | .2 | 2.1 | 2.8 | 4.7 |
| 208.1 | 250.2 | 206.2 | | UND | 554.9 | 72.8 | 112.1 | 250.3 | 70.6 |
| 35.0 | 44.6 | 40.0 | Sales/Net Fixed Assets | 14.5 | 62.7 | 17.2 | 56.8 | 53.8 | 27.7 |
| 8.6 | 15.3 | 10.3 | | .2 | 6.1 | 2.6 | 25.2 | 18.7 | 16.3 |
| 3.4 | 3.7 | 3.0 | | 1.7 | 5.1 | 2.7 | 7.1 | 3.3 | 2.2 |
| 1.6 | 1.5 | 1.3 | Sales/Total Assets | .2 | 2.0 | 1.5 | 1.1 | 1.9 | 1.3 |
| .3 | .3 | .2 | | .1 | .2 | .2 | .4 | .8 | .7 |
| .6 | .6 | .7 | | 6.5 | .6 | 1.1 | .3 | .7 | .5 |
| (92) 1.5 | (71) 1.8 | (88) 1.3 | % Depr., Dep., Amort./Sales | (13) 12.0 | (11) 1.2 | (10) 1.9 | (15) .7 | (17) 1.0 | (22) 1.2 |
| 5.0 | 6.1 | 6.9 | | 19.3 | 10.3 | 8.7 | 1.5 | 2.1 | 2.1 |
| 9.4 | 7.2 | 5.0 | | | | | | | |
| (24) 18.7 | (29) 11.8 | (27) 12.9 | % Officers', Directors' Owners' Comp/Sales | | | | | | |
| 27.2 | 20.3 | 24.7 | | | | | | | |
| 3482531M | 5087890M | 4593758M | Net Sales ($) | 10414M | 42748M | 55627M | 166495M | 383670M | 3934804M |
| 3519422M | 4313200M | 4713471M | Total Assets ($) | 68193M | 213038M | 313979M | 549027M | 702322M | 2866912M |

M = $ thousand    MM = $ million
See Pages 9 through 22 for Explanation of Ratios and Data

## Current Data Sorted by Assets

## Comparative Historical Data

| | | | | | | Type of Statement | | |
|---|---|---|---|---|---|---|---|---|
| 2 | 1 | 10 | 14 | 4 | 8 | Unqualified | 41 | 29 |
| | 2 | 4 | 1 | | | Reviewed | 6 | 6 |
| 3 | 5 | 3 | 1 | | 1 | Compiled | 10 | 13 |
| 18 | 10 | 4 | 2 | | | Tax Returns | 29 | 30 |
| 17 | 27 | 16 | 18 | .1 | 2 | Other | 65 | 72 |
| | 11 (4/1-9/30/11) | | 163 (10/1/11-3/31/12) | | | | 4/1/07-3/31/08 ALL | 4/1/08-3/31/09 ALL |
| 0-500M | 500M-2MM | 2-10MM | 10-50MM | 50-100MM | 100-250MM | | | |
| 40 | 45 | 37 | 36 | 5 | 11 | NUMBER OF STATEMENTS | 151 | 150 |
| % | % | % | % | % | % | ASSETS | % | % |
| 36.9 | 30.7 | 17.8 | 24.0 | | 21.9 | Cash & Equivalents | 28.8 | 28.2 |
| 3.3 | 20.5 | 20.1 | 21.9 | | 22.5 | Trade Receivables (net) | 18.6 | 17.8 |
| .0 | 1.4 | 2.5 | .2 | | .0 | Inventory | 1.4 | 1.0 |
| 6.4 | 5.7 | 7.2 | 8.7 | | 1.7 | All Other Current | 4.9 | 6.5 |
| 46.6 | 58.3 | 47.5 | 54.8 | | 46.1 | Total Current | 53.7 | 53.5 |
| 28.1 | 20.4 | 23.4 | 13.8 | | 5.2 | Fixed Assets (net) | 16.6 | 20.7 |
| 8.4 | 5.9 | 11.3 | 14.2 | | 30.2 | Intangibles (net) | 12.3 | 9.3 |
| 17.0 | 15.4 | 17.8 | 17.2 | | 18.5 | All Other Non-Current | 17.5 | 16.5 |
| 100.0 | 100.0 | 100.0 | 100.0 | | 100.0 | Total | 100.0 | 100.0 |
| | | | | | | LIABILITIES | | |
| 29.5 | 9.9 | 4.4 | 13.7 | | 5.7 | Notes Payable-Short Term | 10.7 | 15.2 |
| 3.0 | 1.5 | 2.6 | 2.7 | | 5.3 | Cur. Mat.-L.T.D. | 2.8 | 3.0 |
| 2.1 | 3.4 | 5.1 | 4.6 | | 1.1 | Trade Payables | 3.6 | 5.1 |
| .0 | .2 | .5 | .6 | | 2.1 | Income Taxes Payable | .1 | .4 |
| 17.6 | 21.4 | 12.6 | 33.7 | | 26.7 | All Other Current | 18.5 | 15.8 |
| 52.2 | 36.3 | 25.2 | 55.3 | | 41.0 | Total Current | 35.8 | 39.4 |
| 22.2 | 16.5 | 29.7 | 11.7 | | 14.3 | Long-Term Debt | 18.6 | 24.3 |
| .0 | .0 | 1.1 | .0 | | .1 | Deferred Taxes | .3 | .4 |
| 14.0 | 5.6 | 7.5 | 11.2 | | 27.6 | All Other Non-Current | 4.7 | 7.5 |
| 11.6 | 41.5 | 36.4 | 21.8 | | 17.1 | Net Worth | 40.6 | 28.4 |
| 100.0 | 100.0 | 100.0 | 100.0 | | 100.0 | Total Liabilties & Net Worth | 100.0 | 100.0 |
| | | | | | | INCOME DATA | | |
| 100.0 | 100.0 | 100.0 | 100.0 | | 100.0 | Net Sales | 100.0 | 100.0 |
| | | | | | | Gross Profit | | |
| 76.8 | 82.2 | 77.5 | 76.2 | | 73.1 | Operating Expenses | 75.9 | 80.1 |
| 23.2 | 17.8 | 22.5 | 23.8 | | 26.9 | Operating Profit | 24.1 | 19.9 |
| 2.0 | 2.7 | 6.4 | 2.5 | | 4.9 | All Other Expenses (net) | 3.2 | 4.4 |
| 21.2 | 15.1 | 16.1 | 21.3 | | 22.0 | Profit Before Taxes | 20.9 | 15.5 |
| | | | | | | RATIOS | | |
| 4.5 | 7.3 | 3.2 | 2.3 | | 3.6 | | 5.4 | 3.5 |
| 1.1 | 2.9 | 1.6 | 1.6 | | 1.5 | Current | 1.8 | 1.5 |
| .2 | .8 | .8 | 1.2 | | .7 | | .8 | .9 |
| 4.1 | 6.1 | 2.4 | 2.2 | | 3.6 | | 4.3 | 2.9 |
| 1.1 | 2.6 | 1.4 | 1.4 | | 1.5 | Quick | 1.5 | 1.3 |
| .1 | .6 | .5 | 1.0 | | .7 | | .6 | .6 |
| 0 UND | 0 UND | 0 UND | 8 44.5 | | 25 14.7 | | 0 UND | 0 UND |
| 0 UND | 6 59.5 | 17 21.7 | 36 10.2 | | 66 5.5 | Sales/Receivables | 8 47.6 | 5 67.5 |
| 0 UND | 39 9.3 | 47 7.8 | 74 4.9 | | 99 3.7 | | 51 7.2 | 52 7.0 |
| | | | | | | Cost of Sales/Inventory | | |
| | | | | | | Cost of Sales/Payables | | |
| 12.5 | 4.7 | 4.1 | 4.8 | | 1.9 | | 4.5 | 5.2 |
| 333.7 | 12.4 | 10.2 | 7.9 | | 4.8 | Sales/Working Capital | 17.1 | 21.4 |
| -28.9 | -33.1 | -112.7 | 20.1 | | -5.9 | | -54.8 | -66.1 |
| 57.2 | 50.5 | 190.8 | 62.8 | | | | 91.7 | 64.7 |
| (19) 25.3 | (29) 7.1 | (24) 37.3 | (25) 28.7 | | | EBIT/Interest | (93) 12.8 | (97) 7.6 |
| 4.6 | .4 | 5.1 | 8.1 | | | | 1.5 | 1.8 |
| | | | | | | Net Profit + Depr., Dep., Amort./Cur. Mat. L/T/D | | 6.6 |
| | | | | | | | | (13) 1.7 |
| | | | | | | | | .6 |
| .1 | .0 | .1 | .1 | | .1 | | .1 | .1 |
| .6 | .2 | .5 | .3 | | .2 | Fixed/Worth | .3 | .5 |
| -1.1 | 2.0 | 12.4 | .7 | | -.2 | | 1.8 | 8.3 |
| .2 | .2 | .7 | .8 | | .8 | | .4 | .4 |
| 1.3 | .9 | 1.3 | 1.5 | | 4.8 | Debt/Worth | 1.2 | 1.6 |
| -3.9 | 29.7 | 17.0 | 4.8 | | -2.4 | | 7.3 | NM |
| 664.5 | 130.4 | 152.4 | 142.2 | | | | 225.5 | 138.6 |
| (25) 118.5 | (35) 46.1 | (31) 59.3 | (31) 58.6 | | | % Profit Before Taxes/Tangible Net Worth | (126) 64.4 | (113) 50.8 |
| 65.0 | 13.5 | 19.2 | 8.1 | | | | 13.9 | 13.6 |
| 301.5 | 56.1 | 49.2 | 52.3 | | 33.6 | | 83.6 | 66.3 |
| 69.3 | 21.1 | 26.6 | 20.3 | | 6.8 | % Profit Before Taxes/Total Assets | 26.2 | 16.4 |
| 28.6 | 1.1 | 3.1 | 4.4 | | 2.7 | | 4.0 | 2.8 |
| 188.9 | 586.4 | 89.9 | 70.6 | | 73.9 | | 119.3 | 86.5 |
| 53.2 | 42.7 | 30.8 | 29.6 | | 19.3 | Sales/Net Fixed Assets | 39.1 | 31.6 |
| 24.8 | 17.5 | 8.0 | 8.2 | | 11.9 | | 14.6 | 12.2 |
| 15.5 | 5.0 | 3.0 | 2.2 | | 1.2 | | 5.1 | 5.2 |
| 6.5 | 2.7 | 2.1 | 1.5 | | .7 | Sales/Total Assets | 2.6 | 2.5 |
| 3.8 | 1.4 | .8 | .9 | | .5 | | 1.2 | 1.4 |
| .3 | .6 | .5 | .7 | | | | .5 | .5 |
| (20) .7 | (26) 1.2 | (28) 1.0 | (28) 1.3 | | | % Depr., Dep., Amort./Sales | (97) 1.1 | (104) 1.1 |
| 2.4 | 3.2 | 2.8 | 3.1 | | | | 2.3 | 2.5 |
| 12.2 | 10.9 | | | | | | 8.4 | 7.0 |
| (26) 18.8 | (12) 25.7 | | | | | % Officers', Directors' Owners' Comp/Sales | (51) 20.7 | (43) 15.0 |
| 26.0 | 38.3 | | | | | | 30.5 | 24.2 |
| 59799M | 189474M | 316294M | 3232326M | 225732M | 2000160M | Net Sales ($) | 3958636M | 3995016M |
| 7649M | 52434M | 176619M | 879945M | 373888M | 2020636M | Total Assets ($) | 1961048M | 2177934M |

M = $ thousand    MM = $ million
See Pages 9 through 22 for Explanation of Ratios and Data

## Comparative Historical Data   |   Current Data Sorted by Sales

| 4/1/09-3/31/10 ALL | 4/1/10-3/31/11 ALL | 4/1/11-3/31/12 ALL | Type of Statement | 0-1MM | 1-3MM | 3-5MM | 5-10MM | 10-25MM | 25MM & OVER |
|---|---|---|---|---|---|---|---|---|---|
| 29 | 31 | 39 | Unqualified | 3 | 1 | 4 | 3 | 10 | 18 |
| 4 | 8 | 7 | Reviewed | | | 2 | 1 | 4 | |
| 13 | 10 | 13 | Compiled | 2 | 3 | 2 | 3 | 1 | 2 |
| 36 | 31 | 34 | Tax Returns | 11 | 11 | 6 | 4 | 1 | 1 |
| 68 | 58 | 81 | Other | 14 | 18 | 12 | 11 | 12 | 14 |
| 4/1/09-3/31/10 ALL | 4/1/10-3/31/11 ALL | 4/1/11-3/31/12 ALL | | 11 (4/1-9/30/11) | | 163 (10/1/11-3/31/12) | | | |
| 150 | 138 | 174 | NUMBER OF STATEMENTS | 30 | 33 | 26 | 22 | 28 | 35 |
| % | % | % | ASSETS | % | % | % | % | % | % |
| 25.1 | 25.7 | 27.0 | Cash & Equivalents | 19.6 | 34.2 | 25.8 | 37.1 | 23.7 | 23.9 |
| 15.4 | 17.3 | 16.8 | Trade Receivables (net) | 8.7 | 8.0 | 17.9 | 16.1 | 28.0 | 22.8 |
| 1.0 | 1.2 | .9 | Inventory | .0 | .0 | .0 | 2.8 | 3.3 | .2 |
| 7.1 | 6.6 | 6.4 | All Other Current | 8.5 | 4.1 | 5.3 | 10.5 | 6.2 | 5.2 |
| 48.7 | 50.7 | 51.2 | Total Current | 36.8 | 46.3 | 48.9 | 66.6 | 61.3 | 52.1 |
| 22.5 | 20.8 | 20.1 | Fixed Assets (net) | 42.7 | 25.8 | 15.3 | 9.7 | 11.4 | 12.6 |
| 15.0 | 10.3 | 11.6 | Intangibles (net) | 8.0 | 5.7 | 14.9 | 7.2 | 14.1 | 18.7 |
| 13.8 | 18.1 | 17.0 | All Other Non-Current | 12.5 | 22.2 | 20.9 | 16.5 | 13.2 | 16.5 |
| 100.0 | 100.0 | 100.0 | Total | 100.0 | 100.0 | 100.0 | 100.0 | 100.0 | 100.0 |
| | | | LIABILITIES | | | | | | |
| 22.6 | 16.8 | 13.5 | Notes Payable-Short Term | 9.2 | 17.2 | 12.8 | 27.1 | 4.2 | 13.1 |
| 4.8 | 5.4 | 2.7 | Cur. Mat.-L.T.D. | 3.4 | 1.8 | 1.7 | 1.3 | 3.4 | 4.1 |
| 4.7 | 4.1 | 3.5 | Trade Payables | 1.5 | 2.3 | 2.5 | 2.5 | 7.1 | 4.8 |
| .4 | .3 | .4 | Income Taxes Payable | .0 | .0 | .5 | .1 | .3 | 1.3 |
| 18.5 | 18.9 | 21.6 | All Other Current | 5.9 | 18.8 | 19.2 | 14.8 | 20.3 | 44.7 |
| 51.1 | 45.5 | 41.7 | Total Current | 20.0 | 40.2 | 36.6 | 45.7 | 35.2 | 68.0 |
| 23.3 | 24.8 | 19.3 | Long-Term Debt | 38.7 | 22.0 | 9.4 | 5.8 | 21.3 | 14.3 |
| .4 | .3 | .3 | Deferred Taxes | .0 | .1 | .0 | 1.3 | .5 | .0 |
| 14.2 | 7.6 | 11.9 | All Other Non-Current | 1.9 | 1.5 | 30.0 | 6.5 | 5.8 | 24.9 |
| 11.1 | 21.8 | 26.9 | Net Worth | 39.4 | 36.2 | 24.0 | 40.7 | 37.2 | -7.3 |
| 100.0 | 100.0 | 100.0 | Total Liabilties & Net Worth | 100.0 | 100.0 | 100.0 | 100.0 | 100.0 | 100.0 |
| | | | INCOME DATA | | | | | | |
| 100.0 | 100.0 | 100.0 | Net Sales | 100.0 | 100.0 | 100.0 | 100.0 | 100.0 | 100.0 |
| | | | Gross Profit | | | | | | |
| 79.1 | 77.8 | 77.7 | Operating Expenses | 64.3 | 76.3 | 83.2 | 92.5 | 79.5 | 75.7 |
| 20.9 | 22.2 | 22.3 | Operating Profit | 35.7 | 23.7 | 16.8 | 7.5 | 20.5 | 24.3 |
| 5.3 | 4.2 | 3.5 | All Other Expenses (net) | 10.6 | 3.0 | 1.2 | -.2 | .7 | 4.2 |
| 15.7 | 18.0 | 18.8 | Profit Before Taxes | 25.2 | 20.6 | 15.6 | 7.7 | 19.8 | 20.0 |
| | | | RATIOS | | | | | | |
| 3.4 | 2.9 | 4.6 | | 10.9 | 5.0 | 5.3 | 6.0 | 3.3 | 2.9 |
| 1.4 | 1.4 | 1.6 | Current | 1.7 | 1.3 | 1.8 | 2.1 | 1.7 | 1.5 |
| .5 | .6 | .8 | | .2 | .4 | .6 | 1.4 | 1.2 | .9 |
| 2.9 | 2.7 | 3.5 | | 6.3 | 4.7 | 3.3 | 6.0 | 2.5 | 2.6 |
| 1.1 | .9 | 1.5 | Quick | 1.4 | 1.3 | 1.2 | 2.0 | 1.6 | 1.5 |
| .4 | .4 | .6 | | .2 | .2 | .5 | .5 | 1.2 | .9 |
| 0 UND | 0 UND | 0 UND | | 0 UND | 0 UND | 0 UND | 0 UND | 15 24.3 | 22 16.4 |
| 4 88.6 | 3 114.6 | 10 35.6 | Sales/Receivables | 0 UND | 0 UND | 7 50.8 | 4 88.0 | 33 11.2 | 52 7.0 |
| 50 7.3 | 65 5.6 | 49 7.5 | | 24 15.1 | 0 UND | 43 8.4 | 29 12.5 | 78 4.7 | 81 4.5 |
| | | | Cost of Sales/Inventory | | | | | | |
| | | | Cost of Sales/Payables | | | | | | |
| 5.3 | 6.7 | 5.2 | | 5.5 | 7.7 | 3.7 | 5.2 | 4.1 | 4.7 |
| 39.2 | 60.6 | 14.5 | Sales/Working Capital | 68.9 | 120.5 | 19.5 | 9.4 | 9.0 | 8.1 |
| -15.3 | -19.1 | -83.5 | | -7.1 | -33.5 | -26.1 | 30.3 | 22.4 | -133.5 |
| 37.8 | 74.2 | 60.2 | | 33.5 | 62.3 | 56.8 | 102.5 | 113.0 | 54.9 |
| (89) 5.2 | (84) 15.1 | (109) 20.9 | EBIT/Interest | (14) 6.2 | (17) 35.3 | (19) 5.6 | (12) 42.4 | (21) 49.2 | (26) 19.3 |
| 2.0 | 3.2 | 3.2 | | 1.5 | 3.3 | -.7 | -1.1 | 15.2 | 10.0 |
| 13.2 | | | | | | | | | |
| (12) 1.2 | | | Net Profit + Depr., Dep., Amort./Cur. Mat. L/T/D | | | | | | |
| -.2 | | | | | | | | | |
| .1 | .0 | .1 | | .1 | .1 | .1 | .0 | .1 | .1 |
| .5 | .4 | .4 | Fixed/Worth | 1.4 | .3 | .5 | .1 | .2 | .4 |
| -2.0 | 23.7 | 3.3 | | -30.6 | 10.0 | -.4 | .5 | .6 | -.2 |
| .4 | .6 | .5 | | .1 | .2 | .3 | .6 | .7 | 1.0 |
| 2.3 | 2.4 | 1.4 | Debt/Worth | 2.8 | .9 | 1.4 | .8 | 1.5 | 2.3 |
| -3.0 | -14.7 | NM | | -34.0 | 11.7 | -4.7 | 2.3 | 4.0 | -2.1 |
| 112.8 | 148.2 | 142.2 | | 222.2 | 135.8 | 165.7 | 107.5 | 162.7 | 142.2 |
| (98) 44.2 | (100) 62.3 | (131) 59.3 | % Profit Before Taxes/Tangible Net Worth | (19) 65.9 | (27) 77.8 | (18) 56.0 | (20) 34.4 | (24) 81.9 | (23) 56.1 |
| 6.4 | 10.9 | 15.7 | | 13.5 | 37.3 | 8.2 | -3.9 | 32.8 | 8.5 |
| 52.1 | 71.9 | 63.6 | | 74.1 | 125.6 | 51.2 | 74.4 | 54.0 | 55.1 |
| 12.2 | 23.6 | 26.9 | % Profit Before Taxes/Total Assets | 17.4 | 44.6 | 12.8 | 13.1 | 33.1 | 21.6 |
| 1.5 | 3.6 | 6.0 | | 2.7 | 16.7 | -.3 | -1.2 | 22.5 | 6.8 |
| 118.5 | 177.9 | 117.0 | | 107.9 | 187.2 | 284.1 | 999.8 | 90.1 | 70.5 |
| 36.0 | 38.4 | 34.4 | Sales/Net Fixed Assets | 17.3 | 45.7 | 50.5 | 54.3 | 35.8 | 25.4 |
| 12.8 | 14.7 | 12.7 | | .5 | 18.6 | 20.1 | 29.2 | 14.2 | 11.9 |
| 5.7 | 5.8 | 4.8 | | 4.0 | 9.8 | 3.7 | 6.7 | 3.0 | 2.3 |
| 2.1 | 2.6 | 2.2 | Sales/Total Assets | 1.6 | 5.5 | 2.3 | 4.3 | 2.2 | 1.7 |
| .7 | .9 | 1.1 | | .3 | 1.5 | 1.1 | 1.3 | 1.3 | .9 |
| .7 | .5 | .6 | | .7 | .3 | .6 | .5 | .8 | .7 |
| (92) 1.3 | (78) 1.3 | (113) 1.1 | % Depr., Dep., Amort./Sales | (18) 2.3 | (17) .6 | (17) 1.3 | (12) .7 | (20) 1.1 | (29) 1.7 |
| 3.3 | 3.2 | 3.0 | | 19.0 | 3.0 | 2.5 | .9 | 3.2 | 3.1 |
| 9.9 | 7.6 | 12.3 | | 15.8 | 10.4 | | | | |
| (32) 16.0 | (41) 17.0 | (49) 19.3 | % Officers', Directors' Owners' Comp/Sales | (15) 19.1 | (17) 16.3 | | | | |
| 28.4 | 25.9 | 30.7 | | 29.2 | 23.8 | | | | |
| 4278754M | 4343406M | 6023785M | Net Sales ($) | 15014M | 62568M | 95578M | 151108M | 421557M | 5277960M |
| 3625264M | 2538518M | 3511171M | Total Assets ($) | 33227M | 104434M | 108004M | 102295M | 346722M | 2816489M |

© RMA 2012

M = $ thousand    MM = $ million

See Pages 9 through 22 for Explanation of Ratios and Data

## Current Data Sorted by Assets      Comparative Historical Data

| 0-500M | 500M-2MM | 2-10MM | 10-50MM | 50-100MM | 100-250MM | Type of Statement | 4/1/07-3/31/08 ALL | 4/1/08-3/31/09 ALL |
|---|---|---|---|---|---|---|---|---|
| 1 | 1 | 3 | 8 | | 1 | Unqualified | 12 | 13 |
| | | 1 | | | | Reviewed | 1 | 1 |
| 1 | | | | | | Compiled | 6 | 7 |
| 2 | 1 | 4 | 6 | | | Tax Returns | 2 | 1 |
| 2 | 2 | 6 | 6 | 5 | | Other | 12 | 19 |
| | | 7 (4/1-9/30/11) | | 37 (10/1/11-3/31/12) | | | | |
| 6 | 4 | 14 | 14 | 5 | 1 | NUMBER OF STATEMENTS | 33 | 41 |
| % | % | % | % | % | % | ASSETS | % | % |
| | | 23.0 | 38.1 | | | Cash & Equivalents | 33.7 | 23.2 |
| | | 15.8 | 9.1 | | | Trade Receivables (net) | 10.0 | 14.6 |
| | | .0 | 4.9 | | | Inventory | 3.4 | 3.7 |
| | | 8.2 | 4.2 | | | All Other Current | 4.0 | 7.3 |
| | | 47.0 | 56.3 | | | Total Current | 51.1 | 48.8 |
| | | 24.8 | 15.2 | | | Fixed Assets (net) | 17.5 | 21.7 |
| | | 9.6 | 9.0 | | | Intangibles (net) | 3.4 | 5.6 |
| | | 18.6 | 19.4 | | | All Other Non-Current | 27.9 | 23.9 |
| | | 100.0 | 100.0 | | | Total | 100.0 | 100.0 |
| | | | | | | LIABILITIES | | |
| | | 3.1 | .5 | | | Notes Payable-Short Term | 1.2 | 3.1 |
| | | 7.5 | 1.2 | | | Cur. Mat.-L.T.D. | 1.4 | 3.3 |
| | | 7.0 | 4.7 | | | Trade Payables | 6.9 | 4.5 |
| | | .0 | .4 | | | Income Taxes Payable | .1 | .2 |
| | | 9.5 | 8.3 | | | All Other Current | 11.8 | 21.4 |
| | | 27.1 | 15.1 | | | Total Current | 21.4 | 32.5 |
| | | 25.7 | 19.6 | | | Long-Term Debt | 12.7 | 16.4 |
| | | .2 | .0 | | | Deferred Taxes | .7 | .3 |
| | | 2.1 | 5.1 | | | All Other Non-Current | 3.7 | 7.2 |
| | | 44.9 | 60.2 | | | Net Worth | 61.6 | 43.7 |
| | | 100.0 | 100.0 | | | Total Liabilities & Net Worth | 100.0 | 100.0 |
| | | | | | | INCOME DATA | | |
| | | 100.0 | 100.0 | | | Net Sales | 100.0 | 100.0 |
| | | | | | | Gross Profit | | |
| | | 74.5 | 78.8 | | | Operating Expenses | 68.1 | 73.8 |
| | | 25.5 | 21.2 | | | Operating Profit | 31.9 | 26.2 |
| | | 8.6 | 8.1 | | | All Other Expenses (net) | 6.0 | 7.1 |
| | | 16.9 | 13.1 | | | Profit Before Taxes | 26.0 | 19.1 |
| | | | | | | RATIOS | | |
| | | 3.1 | 15.2 | | | | 8.1 | 2.4 |
| | | 2.3 | 7.2 | | | Current | 2.7 | 1.6 |
| | | .7 | 2.2 | | | | 1.6 | .9 |
| | | 3.1 | 15.0 | | | | 6.8 | 2.2 |
| | | 1.9 | 7.0 | | | Quick | 2.0 | 1.1 |
| | | .6 | 1.4 | | | | 1.3 | .5 |
| | 0   UND | 0   UND | | | | | 0   UND | 0   UND |
| | 20   18.0 | 28   13.0 | | | | Sales/Receivables | 10   36.0 | 23   15.8 |
| | 47   7.7 | 52   7.0 | | | | | 34   10.7 | 46   7.9 |
| | | | | | | Cost of Sales/Inventory | | |
| | | | | | | Cost of Sales/Payables | | |
| | | 2.6 | .4 | | | | .7 | 1.6 |
| | | 8.0 | .8 | | | Sales/Working Capital | 3.0 | 9.7 |
| | | -25.0 | 6.1 | | | | 36.6 | UND |
| | | | | | | | 31.2 | 25.0 |
| | | | | | | EBIT/Interest | (12) 5.7 | (21) 5.5 |
| | | | | | | | .7 | 1.8 |
| | | | | | | Net Profit + Depr., Dep., Amort./Cur. Mat. L/T/D | | |
| | | .0 | .0 | | | | .0 | .0 |
| | | .2 | .1 | | | Fixed/Worth | .1 | .2 |
| | | 2.9 | .5 | | | | .6 | 2.7 |
| | | .3 | .1 | | | | .2 | .3 |
| | | .6 | .6 | | | Debt/Worth | .5 | 1.3 |
| | | 2.5 | 1.1 | | | | 1.5 | 24.8 |
| | | 35.5 | 25.5 | | | % Profit Before Taxes/Tangible Net Worth | 24.5 | 41.8 |
| | (12) 12.0 | (13) 14.9 | | | | (30) 11.1 | (35) 14.4 |
| | | 3.0 | -1.6 | | | | 2.7 | 3.8 |
| | | 14.6 | 13.5 | | | % Profit Before Taxes/Total Assets | 14.1 | 13.3 |
| | | 8.3 | 8.5 | | | | 6.6 | 6.5 |
| | | 1.2 | -2.2 | | | | 1.6 | .9 |
| | | 92.0 | 57.4 | | | Sales/Net Fixed Assets | UND | 999.8 |
| | | 26.8 | 18.5 | | | | 37.2 | 23.8 |
| | | .3 | 2.2 | | | | 4.9 | .6 |
| | | 1.8 | 2.0 | | | Sales/Total Assets | 2.6 | 1.7 |
| | | .9 | .5 | | | | .6 | .5 |
| | | .2 | .2 | | | | .1 | .1 |
| | | .8 | | | | % Depr., Dep., Amort./Sales | .8 | .8 |
| | (10) 1.5 | | | | | | (18) 1.8 | (21) 2.4 |
| | | 9.4 | | | | | 4.6 | 11.5 |
| | | | | | | % Officers', Directors' Owners' Comp/Sales | | |
| 6657M | 4506M | 93803M | 388934M | 160921M | 100012M | Net Sales ($) | 912367M | 988463M |
| 1417M | 6112M | 68179M | 322852M | 410357M | 102906M | Total Assets ($) | 1172343M | 1124565M |

M = $ thousand    MM = $ million
See Pages 9 through 22 for Explanation of Ratios and Data

## Comparative Historical Data | Current Data Sorted by Sales

| | | | Type of Statement | | | | | | |
|---|---|---|---|---|---|---|---|---|---|
| 12 | 19 | 14 | Unqualified | 1 | 2 | 2 | 3 | 3 | 3 |
| 1 | 1 | 1 | Reviewed | 1 | | | | | |
| 6 | 6 | 1 | Compiled | | 1 | | | | |
| 3 | 7 | 7 | Tax Returns | 4 | 1 | 1 | 1 | 1 | |
| 20 | 15 | 21 | Other | 7 | 2 | 1 | 4 | 3 | 4 |
| 4/1/09-3/31/10 ALL | 4/1/10-3/31/11 ALL | 4/1/11-3/31/12 ALL | | 7 (4/1-9/30/11) | | | 37 (10/1/11-3/31/12) | | |
| | | | | 0-1MM | 1-3MM | 3-5MM | 5-10MM | 10-25MM | 25MM & OVER |
| 42 | 44 | 44 | **NUMBER OF STATEMENTS** | 13 | 6 | 3 | 8 | 7 | 7 |
| % | % | % | **ASSETS** | % | % | % | % | % | % |
| 31.9 | 33.2 | 35.0 | Cash & Equivalents | 23.1 | | | | | |
| 13.3 | 11.3 | 11.1 | Trade Receivables (net) | 8.4 | | | | | |
| 4.1 | 1.7 | 1.6 | Inventory | .0 | | | | | |
| 5.7 | 3.9 | 6.4 | All Other Current | 6.7 | | | | | |
| 55.0 | 50.1 | 54.2 | Total Current | 38.3 | | | | | |
| 23.4 | 17.4 | 18.9 | Fixed Assets (net) | 44.2 | | | | | |
| 4.7 | 13.0 | 7.8 | Intangibles (net) | 6.7 | | | | | |
| 17.0 | 19.4 | 19.1 | All Other Non-Current | 10.8 | | | | | |
| 100.0 | 100.0 | 100.0 | Total | 100.0 | | | | | |
| | | | **LIABILITIES** | | | | | | |
| 2.8 | 4.0 | 2.9 | Notes Payable-Short Term | 4.6 | | | | | |
| 2.0 | 3.6 | 2.9 | Cur. Mat.-L.T.D. | .5 | | | | | |
| 5.7 | 4.2 | 6.1 | Trade Payables | .6 | | | | | |
| 1.0 | 1.0 | .1 | Income Taxes Payable | .0 | | | | | |
| 21.1 | 18.1 | 13.7 | All Other Current | 12.8 | | | | | |
| 32.7 | 30.9 | 25.7 | Total Current | 18.6 | | | | | |
| 26.4 | 25.3 | 21.3 | Long-Term Debt | 35.7 | | | | | |
| .2 | 1.0 | .0 | Deferred Taxes | .0 | | | | | |
| 5.6 | 6.1 | 6.8 | All Other Non-Current | .9 | | | | | |
| 35.1 | 36.7 | 46.2 | Net Worth | 44.8 | | | | | |
| 100.0 | 100.0 | 100.0 | Total Liabilties & Net Worth | 100.0 | | | | | |
| | | | **INCOME DATA** | | | | | | |
| 100.0 | 100.0 | 100.0 | Net Sales | 100.0 | | | | | |
| | | | Gross Profit | | | | | | |
| 76.0 | 79.2 | 76.2 | Operating Expenses | 59.0 | | | | | |
| 24.0 | 20.8 | 23.8 | Operating Profit | 41.0 | | | | | |
| 7.7 | 4.9 | 8.8 | All Other Expenses (net) | 15.6 | | | | | |
| 16.3 | 16.0 | 15.0 | Profit Before Taxes | 25.4 | | | | | |
| | | | **RATIOS** | | | | | | |
| 4.2 | 4.5 | 6.4 | | 3.4 | | | | | |
| 1.8 | 1.7 | 2.5 | Current | 2.6 | | | | | |
| 1.0 | 1.0 | 1.0 | | .7 | | | | | |
| 4.2 | 4.5 | 5.7 | | 2.9 | | | | | |
| 1.3 | 1.7 | 2.2 | Quick | 1.4 | | | | | |
| .8 | .7 | .7 | | .3 | | | | | |
| 0 UND | 0 UND | 0 UND | | 0 UND | | | | | |
| 30 12.1 | 23 15.9 | 15 23.8 | Sales/Receivables | 0 UND | | | | | |
| 52 7.0 | 48 7.7 | 45 8.2 | | 22 16.6 | | | | | |
| | | | Cost of Sales/Inventory | | | | | | |
| | | | Cost of Sales/Payables | | | | | | |
| 2.0 | 2.2 | .8 | | 1.3 | | | | | |
| 7.6 | 6.2 | 5.4 | Sales/Working Capital | 11.9 | | | | | |
| -830.0 | -138.5 | UND | | -32.4 | | | | | |
| 12.4 | 117.5 | 37.3 | | | | | | | |
| (18) 7.0 | (23) 7.9 | (17) 6.0 | EBIT/Interest | | | | | | |
| 1.3 | 1.4 | -.9 | | | | | | | |
| | | | Net Profit + Depr., Dep., Amort./Cur. Mat. L/T/D | | | | | | |
| .0 | .0 | .0 | | .2 | | | | | |
| .5 | .2 | .1 | Fixed/Worth | 1.2 | | | | | |
| 1.7 | 10.2 | 1.2 | | UND | | | | | |
| .5 | .5 | .3 | | .3 | | | | | |
| 1.6 | 1.5 | .7 | Debt/Worth | .6 | | | | | |
| 9.2 | UND | 5.8 | | UND | | | | | |
| 31.2 | 64.1 | 29.1 | | 17.3 | | | | | |
| (35) 8.9 | (34) 17.3 | (38) 15.5 | % Profit Before Taxes/Tangible Net Worth | (11) 9.7 | | | | | |
| 1.0 | .6 | 1.8 | | .1 | | | | | |
| 13.2 | 17.8 | 14.3 | | 10.1 | | | | | |
| 3.6 | 8.5 | 7.4 | % Profit Before Taxes/Total Assets | 3.2 | | | | | |
| .2 | .2 | .1 | | .6 | | | | | |
| 857.8 | 104.3 | 127.8 | | 81.1 | | | | | |
| 23.0 | 28.1 | 24.1 | Sales/Net Fixed Assets | .6 | | | | | |
| 1.6 | 6.1 | 4.7 | | .2 | | | | | |
| 2.4 | 2.1 | 2.1 | | 2.2 | | | | | |
| .7 | .7 | .6 | Sales/Total Assets | .2 | | | | | |
| .2 | .2 | .2 | | .1 | | | | | |
| 1.3 | .8 | 1.0 | | | | | | | |
| (24) 2.3 | (26) 1.3 | (24) 1.9 | % Depr., Dep., Amort./Sales | | | | | | |
| 9.3 | 5.3 | 6.7 | | | | | | | |
| | | | % Officers', Directors' Owners' Comp/Sales | | | | | | |
| 1011906M | 1161967M | 754833M | Net Sales ($) | 5755M | 13324M | 11863M | 51552M | 124057M | 548282M |
| 973511M | 1262930M | 911823M | Total Assets ($) | 42887M | 123143M | 50825M | 164666M | 165492M | 364810M |

© RMA 2012

M = $ thousand    MM = $ million
See Pages 9 through 22 for Explanation of Ratios and Data

## Current Data Sorted by Assets        Comparative Historical Data

| | 0-500M | 500M-2MM | 2-10MM | 10-50MM | 50-100MM | 100-250MM | Type of Statement | 4/1/07-3/31/08 ALL | 4/1/08-3/31/09 ALL |
|---|---|---|---|---|---|---|---|---|---|
| | 1 | 1 | 5 | 12 | 4 | 7 | Unqualified | 14 | 30 |
| | | | 1 | 1 | | | Reviewed | | |
| | 1 | 1 | | | | | Compiled | 13 | 12 |
| | 11 | 3 | 6 | 2 | | | Tax Returns | 6 | 12 |
| | 14 | 8 | 11 | 13 | 6 | 2 | Other | 31 | 46 |
| | | 11 (4/1-9/30/11) | | 99 (10/1/11-3/31/12) | | | | | |
| | 27 | 13 | 23 | 28 | 10 | 9 | NUMBER OF STATEMENTS | 64 | 100 |
| | % | % | % | % | % | % | ASSETS | % | % |
| | 29.6 | 17.9 | 14.1 | 15.3 | 14.2 | | Cash & Equivalents | 18.7 | 20.8 |
| | 12.0 | 9.9 | 21.6 | 9.7 | 3.6 | | Trade Receivables (net) | 18.9 | 19.0 |
| | .0 | .9 | 3.3 | 1.5 | .1 | | Inventory | 2.1 | 2.7 |
| | 6.7 | 13.9 | 8.5 | 7.5 | 2.6 | | All Other Current | 12.9 | 8.8 |
| | 48.2 | 42.7 | 47.6 | 34.0 | 20.4 | | Total Current | 52.6 | 51.3 |
| | 19.2 | 43.3 | 20.0 | 8.8 | 15.5 | | Fixed Assets (net) | 17.8 | 14.6 |
| | 14.9 | 6.6 | 9.2 | 1.1 | .8 | | Intangibles (net) | 5.2 | 3.0 |
| | 17.6 | 7.5 | 23.1 | 56.2 | 63.2 | | All Other Non-Current | 24.4 | 31.1 |
| | 100.0 | 100.0 | 100.0 | 100.0 | 100.0 | | Total | 100.0 | 100.0 |
| | | | | | | | LIABILITIES | | |
| | 33.2 | .0 | 12.0 | 13.2 | 10.3 | | Notes Payable-Short Term | 27.4 | 28.2 |
| | 1.8 | 1.0 | 10.6 | 6.7 | 1.1 | | Cur. Mat.-L.T.D. | 2.3 | 2.0 |
| | 5.0 | 1.9 | 3.7 | 3.8 | .9 | | Trade Payables | 2.6 | 3.3 |
| | .2 | .3 | .6 | .0 | .0 | | Income Taxes Payable | .0 | .1 |
| | 28.8 | 10.7 | 12.0 | 7.5 | 7.3 | | All Other Current | 7.9 | 8.7 |
| | 69.0 | 13.9 | 38.9 | 31.3 | 19.6 | | Total Current | 40.2 | 42.3 |
| | 26.0 | 35.1 | 26.4 | 26.2 | 25.9 | | Long-Term Debt | 20.5 | 26.1 |
| | .0 | .0 | 1.3 | .1 | .0 | | Deferred Taxes | .0 | .1 |
| | 8.3 | 3.0 | 9.5 | 7.4 | 2.3 | | All Other Non-Current | 4.4 | 11.7 |
| | -3.3 | 48.0 | 23.9 | 35.1 | 52.2 | | Net Worth | 34.8 | 19.8 |
| | 100.0 | 100.0 | 100.0 | 100.0 | 100.0 | | Total Liabilities & Net Worth | 100.0 | 100.0 |
| | | | | | | | INCOME DATA | | |
| | 100.0 | 100.0 | 100.0 | 100.0 | 100.0 | | Net Sales | 100.0 | 100.0 |
| | | | | | | | Gross Profit | | |
| | 76.8 | 64.0 | 71.3 | 47.6 | 63.4 | | Operating Expenses | 51.7 | 58.8 |
| | 23.2 | 36.0 | 28.7 | 52.4 | 36.6 | | Operating Profit | 48.3 | 41.2 |
| | 5.0 | 7.0 | 13.0 | 13.8 | 28.1 | | All Other Expenses (net) | 23.4 | 18.9 |
| | 18.1 | 28.9 | 15.7 | 38.7 | 8.5 | | Profit Before Taxes | 24.9 | 22.3 |
| | | | | | | | RATIOS | | |
| | 2.9 | 14.4 | 3.8 | 4.0 | 4.7 | | Current | 4.4 | 4.3 |
| | .7 | 3.0 | 1.9 | 1.6 | 2.1 | | | 1.7 | 1.5 |
| | .2 | 1.5 | .8 | 1.2 | .6 | | | .9 | .6 |
| | 2.9 | 10.4 | 3.8 | 3.0 | 4.0 | | Quick | 3.3 | 2.5 |
| | .6 | 2.4 | 1.5 | 1.4 | 1.6 | | | 1.0  (99) | 1.1 |
| | .1 | .4 | .3 | .7 | .4 | | | .1 | .3 |
| | 0  UND | 0  UND | 0  UND | 0  UND | 0  UND | | Sales/Receivables | 0  UND | 0  UND |
| | 0  UND | 0  999.8 | 3  106.0 | 4  91.2 | 0  UND | | | 2  197.9 | 0  904.7 |
| | 4  82.0 | 16  23.4 | 49  7.5 | 40  9.2 | 6  65.5 | | | 86  4.3 | 71  5.1 |
| | | | | | | | Cost of Sales/Inventory | | |
| | | | | | | | Cost of Sales/Payables | | |
| | 11.3 | 3.3 | 1.4 | 1.8 | .7 | | Sales/Working Capital | .8 | 1.3 |
| | -94.6 | 7.3 | 4.5 | 4.9 | 2.1 | | | 4.9 | 6.2 |
| | -12.4 | 144.3 | -13.4 | 51.5 | -1.9 | | | -36.5 | -13.3 |
| | 63.1 | | 4.9 | 105.9 | | | EBIT/Interest | 162.9 | 18.9 |
| | (16) 19.6 | | (11) 3.9 | (14) 14.3 | | | | (13) 16.1 | (44) 5.4 |
| | 2.3 | | 1.4 | 3.5 | | | | 2.0 | 1.8 |
| | | | | | | | Net Profit + Depr., Dep., Amort./Cur. Mat. L/T/D | | |
| | .0 | .2 | .0 | .0 | .0 | | Fixed/Worth | .0 | .0 |
| | .1 | .8 | .2 | .0 | .1 | | | .0 | .0 |
| | 11.2 | NM | 1.3 | .4 | .5 | | | 1.1 | 1.0 |
| | .5 | .2 | .3 | .1 | .1 | | Debt/Worth | .4 | .6 |
| | 6.5 | 1.7 | 1.1 | .8 | .8 | | | 3.8 | 2.3 |
| | -1.7 | NM | -188.6 | 16.9 | 14.1 | | | 79.6 | 27.6 |
| | 202.5 | 95.0 | 25.2 | 55.6 | 9.9 | | % Profit Before Taxes/Tangible Net Worth | 43.7 | 60.2 |
| | (16) 88.6 | (10) 32.1 | (17) 14.8 | (23) 11.1 | 1.8 | | | (51) 21.6 | (83) 18.0 |
| | 11.6 | 18.1 | 2.5 | 2.4 | -1.9 | | | 4.7 | 2.6 |
| | 102.3 | 58.9 | 10.7 | 16.9 | 3.7 | | % Profit Before Taxes/Total Assets | 7.5 | 12.4 |
| | 40.4 | 24.2 | 4.6 | 5.0 | .2 | | | 2.8 | 3.3 |
| | -.6 | 5.3 | .5 | 1.7 | -1.1 | | | 1.0 | .3 |
| | UND | 43.9 | 202.6 | UND | UND | | Sales/Net Fixed Assets | UND | UND |
| | 999.8 | 10.4 | 20.3 | UND | UND | | | 281.2 | 173.6 |
| | 27.8 | .3 | 2.8 | 12.5 | .3 | | | 10.0 | 9.1 |
| | 9.7 | 3.4 | 1.9 | 1.1 | .1 | | Sales/Total Assets | .4 | 1.7 |
| | 4.5 | 2.0 | .4 | .2 | .1 | | | .2 | .2 |
| | 1.7 | .3 | .1 | .1 | .0 | | | .1 | .1 |
| | | 1.4 | 1.1 | .3 | | | % Depr., Dep., Amort./Sales | 1.0 | .7 |
| | | (10) 6.2 | (14) 2.0 | (11) .6 | | | | (22) 2.9 | (38) 2.4 |
| | | 19.7 | 6.9 | 3.5 | | | | 14.2 | 9.9 |
| | | | | | | | % Officers', Directors' Owners' Comp/Sales | | |
| | 34068M | 31056M | 124312M | 555422M | 79677M | 248828M | Net Sales ($) | 670215M | 1001419M |
| | 6149M | 12898M | 105402M | 773766M | 602790M | 1489742M | Total Assets ($) | 2291084M | 3374631M |

© RMA 2012

M = $ thousand    MM = $ million
See Pages 9 through 22 for Explanation of Ratios and Data

## Comparative Historical Data | Current Data Sorted by Sales

| | | | Type of Statement | | | | | | |
|---|---|---|---|---|---|---|---|---|---|
| 18 | 21 | 30 | Unqualified | 1 | 6 | 2 | 5 | 7 | 9 |
| 2 | 3 | 2 | Reviewed | 1 | | | | 1 | |
| 4 | 4 | 2 | Compiled | 2 | | | | | |
| 20 | 19 | 22 | Tax Returns | 10 | 5 | 5 | 2 | | |
| 66 | 36 | 54 | Other | 20 | 14 | 6 | 8 | 5 | 1 |
| 4/1/09-3/31/10 | 4/1/10-3/31/11 | 4/1/11-3/31/12 | | | 11 (4/1-9/30/11) | | | 99 (10/1/11-3/31/12) | |
| ALL | ALL | ALL | | 0-1MM | 1-3MM | 3-5MM | 5-10MM | 10-25MM | 25MM & OVER |
| 110 | 83 | 110 | **NUMBER OF STATEMENTS** | 34 | 25 | 13 | 15 | 13 | 10 |
| % | % | % | **ASSETS** | % | % | % | % | % | % |
| 16.6 | 22.6 | 19.5 | Cash & Equivalents | 15.4 | 22.3 | 20.7 | 22.5 | 20.1 | 20.1 |
| 18.1 | 11.4 | 12.9 | Trade Receivables (net) | 12.5 | 11.4 | 1.7 | 9.7 | 31.0 | 14.1 |
| .8 | .7 | 1.2 | Inventory | .0 | .0 | 6.8 | .0 | 3.3 | .3 |
| 8.8 | 10.7 | 7.7 | All Other Current | 9.1 | 6.4 | 3.3 | 12.7 | 3.6 | 9.6 |
| 44.4 | 45.5 | 41.4 | Total Current | 36.9 | 40.2 | 32.6 | 44.8 | 58.0 | 44.1 |
| 27.5 | 20.0 | 18.7 | Fixed Assets (net) | 31.1 | 15.6 | 14.1 | 9.2 | 5.1 | 21.7 |
| 3.8 | 4.7 | 7.6 | Intangibles (net) | 10.0 | 10.0 | 4.6 | 1.2 | 7.4 | 6.7 |
| 24.4 | 29.8 | 32.4 | All Other Non-Current | 21.9 | 34.1 | 48.6 | 44.7 | 29.5 | 27.5 |
| 100.0 | 100.0 | 100.0 | Total | 100.0 | 100.0 | 100.0 | 100.0 | 100.0 | 100.0 |
| | | | **LIABILITIES** | | | | | | |
| 20.3 | 19.7 | 17.0 | Notes Payable-Short Term | 20.0 | 15.9 | 25.2 | 8.8 | 24.2 | 2.3 |
| 4.6 | 1.4 | 4.7 | Cur. Mat.-L.T.D. | 2.9 | 1.2 | 2.9 | 11.7 | 8.0 | 7.4 |
| 3.0 | 3.1 | 3.6 | Trade Payables | 1.8 | 4.2 | 3.1 | 3.6 | 6.4 | 5.4 |
| .1 | .1 | .2 | Income Taxes Payable | .2 | .0 | .0 | .3 | 1.1 | .0 |
| 10.7 | 10.2 | 13.5 | All Other Current | 15.7 | 12.7 | 8.1 | 14.3 | 4.3 | 25.7 |
| 38.7 | 34.6 | 39.1 | Total Current | 40.6 | 34.1 | 39.4 | 38.7 | 44.0 | 40.8 |
| 32.4 | 21.1 | 25.5 | Long-Term Debt | 31.7 | 24.4 | 23.0 | 7.4 | 18.4 | 47.0 |
| .2 | .0 | .3 | Deferred Taxes | .0 | .5 | .0 | .0 | 1.5 | .2 |
| 5.3 | 7.4 | 7.3 | All Other Non-Current | 9.6 | 3.8 | .3 | 7.2 | 15.9 | 6.5 |
| 23.4 | 36.9 | 27.8 | Net Worth | 18.2 | 37.2 | 37.3 | 46.7 | 20.2 | 5.5 |
| 100.0 | 100.0 | 100.0 | Total Liabilities & Net Worth | 100.0 | 100.0 | 100.0 | 100.0 | 100.0 | 100.0 |
| | | | **INCOME DATA** | | | | | | |
| 100.0 | 100.0 | 100.0 | Net Sales | 100.0 | 100.0 | 100.0 | 100.0 | 100.0 | 100.0 |
| | | | Gross Profit | | | | | | |
| 64.0 | 57.4 | 65.0 | Operating Expenses | 52.9 | 73.3 | 63.6 | 73.6 | 67.6 | 71.1 |
| 36.0 | 42.6 | 35.0 | Operating Profit | 47.1 | 26.7 | 36.4 | 26.4 | 32.4 | 28.9 |
| 13.8 | 15.1 | 12.2 | All Other Expenses (net) | 17.2 | 7.1 | 20.1 | 11.5 | 11.0 | .1 |
| 22.2 | 27.5 | 22.8 | Profit Before Taxes | 29.9 | 19.5 | 16.3 | 14.9 | 21.4 | 28.8 |
| | | | **RATIOS** | | | | | | |
| 3.6 | 4.7 | 4.6 | | 6.2 | 8.5 | 2.0 | 2.7 | 7.5 | 2.8 |
| 1.5 | 1.7 | 1.8 | Current | 2.3 | 1.3 | 1.3 | 1.6 | 2.1 | 1.8 |
| .5 | .6 | .6 | | .4 | .4 | .3 | 1.1 | .9 | 1.3 |
| 2.9 | 3.8 | 3.9 | | 6.2 | 3.8 | 1.1 | 2.7 | 7.4 | 2.3 |
| 1.2 (82) | 1.3 | 1.4 | Quick | 1.9 | 1.3 | .6 | 1.4 | 2.0 | 1.4 |
| .4 | .2 | .3 | | .2 | .2 | .2 | .3 | .7 | .5 |
| 0 UND | 0 UND | 0 UND | | 0 UND | 0 UND | 0 UND | 0 UND | 1 533.0 | 0 UND |
| 0 UND | 0 UND | 0 999.8 | Sales/Receivables | 0 UND | 2 147.5 | 0 UND | 0 UND | 33 10.9 | 19 19.3 |
| 52 7.0 | 25 14.7 | 41 8.9 | | 8 48.5 | 21 17.8 | 3 129.4 | 40 9.2 | 87 4.2 | 58 6.3 |
| | | | Cost of Sales/Inventory | | | | | | |
| | | | Cost of Sales/Payables | | | | | | |
| .9 | 1.0 | 2.1 | | 1.1 | 3.3 | 4.5 | 2.6 | 1.5 | 2.2 |
| 10.3 | 6.4 | 8.0 | Sales/Working Capital | 3.8 | 11.1 | 11.3 | 10.0 | 8.2 | 5.4 |
| -6.9 | -7.2 | -26.1 | | -23.7 | -14.3 | -4.7 | 38.6 | NM | NM |
| 18.2 | 22.7 | 56.8 | | 201.8 | 27.8 | | | | |
| (47) 4.2 | (32) 6.1 | (56) 9.9 | EBIT/Interest | (14) 9.8 | (17) 10.2 | | | | |
| 1.2 | 2.0 | 3.2 | | 2.8 | 1.4 | | | | |
| 25.0 | | | | | | | | | |
| (10) 1.7 | | | Net Profit + Depr., Dep., Amort./Cur. Mat. L/T/D | | | | | | |
| .8 | | | | | | | | | |
| .0 | .0 | .0 | | .0 | .0 | .0 | .0 | .0 | .1 |
| .1 | .1 | .1 | Fixed/Worth | .1 | .0 | .0 | .2 | .0 | .9 |
| 2.4 | 1.4 | 1.1 | | 4.0 | 1.1 | .6 | .5 | .3 | -.1 |
| .5 | .3 | .3 | | .3 | .2 | .5 | .3 | .2 | .3 |
| 2.1 | 1.3 | 1.1 | Debt/Worth | 1.7 | 1.5 | 1.0 | .6 | 1.8 | 1.1 |
| 8.2 | 9.7 | 157.5 | | -11.8 | NM | 50.1 | 4.0 | -3.9 | -1.7 |
| 58.2 | 48.4 | 65.0 | % Profit Before Taxes/Tangible Net Worth | 70.2 | 91.8 | 66.8 | 39.8 | | |
| (93) 12.5 | (71) 16.4 | (84) 15.1 | | (24) 15.8 | (19) 8.3 | (11) 11.1 | (14) 13.3 | | |
| 3.0 | 4.7 | 1.7 | | .7 | 1.7 | 3.0 | 1.8 | | |
| 19.3 | 16.6 | 29.9 | % Profit Before Taxes/Total Assets | 28.7 | 48.5 | 29.8 | 17.0 | 29.9 | 45.7 |
| 3.8 | 5.5 | 5.5 | | 4.1 | 4.0 | 10.4 | 4.5 | 5.7 | 12.2 |
| .5 | 1.8 | .4 | | .0 | .8 | -.5 | 1.3 | -1.0 | 9.0 |
| UND | UND | UND | | UND | UND | UND | UND | UND | UND |
| 40.3 | 39.1 | 67.2 | Sales/Net Fixed Assets | 231.9 | 104.3 | 88.9 | 72.9 | 74.4 | 28.6 |
| .5 | 3.6 | 6.4 | | .4 | 10.5 | 5.7 | 12.6 | 25.8 | 1.0 |
| 1.3 | 1.5 | 2.8 | | 1.8 | 6.1 | 2.7 | 4.0 | 2.2 | 2.8 |
| .3 | .2 | .5 | Sales/Total Assets | .3 | 1.1 | .2 | .3 | .6 | 1.3 |
| .1 | .1 | .1 | | .1 | .1 | .1 | .2 | .2 | .4 |
| 1.0 | .7 | .8 | | 4.1 | .7 | | | | |
| (55) 5.8 | (37) 2.5 | (47) 2.5 | % Depr., Dep., Amort./Sales | (12) 12.3 | (11) 1.6 | | | | |
| 22.9 | 19.8 | 10.8 | | 35.0 | 4.7 | | | | |
| 3.7 | 4.4 | 1.6 | % Officers', Directors' Owners' Comp/Sales | | | | | | |
| (13) 17.2 | (12) 12.7 | (22) 8.2 | | | | | | | |
| 22.6 | 17.9 | 33.0 | | | | | | | |
| 973144M | 917200M | 1073363M | Net Sales ($) | 15108M | 49081M | 49635M | 98930M | 216577M | 644032M |
| 3043527M | 2560168M | 2990747M | Total Assets ($) | 141954M | 551044M | 276977M | 396698M | 727840M | 896234M |

© RMA 2012

M = $ thousand    MM = $ million
See Pages 9 through 22 for Explanation of Ratios and Data

## Current Data Sorted by Assets       Comparative Historical Data

| 0-500M | 500M-2MM | 2-10MM | 10-50MM | 50-100MM | 100-250MM | Type of Statement | 4/1/07-3/31/08 ALL | 4/1/08-3/31/09 ALL |
|---|---|---|---|---|---|---|---|---|
|  | 1 | 1 | 2 | 4 | 6 | Unqualified | 12 | 12 |
|  | 2 | 2 | 1 |  |  | Reviewed |  | 2 |
|  | 1 | 2 |  |  |  | Compiled | 1 | 2 |
| 1 | 2 | 1 | 2 |  |  | Tax Returns | 2 | 6 |
| 2 | 1 | 5 | 4 | 2 | 2 | Other | 9 | 11 |
|  | 1 (4/1-9/30/11) |  | 41 (10/1/11-3/31/12) |  |  |  |  |  |
| 3 | 5 | 11 | 9 | 6 | 8 | NUMBER OF STATEMENTS | 24 | 33 |
| % | % | % | % | % | % | ASSETS | % | % |
|  |  | 30.8 |  |  |  | Cash & Equivalents | 31.0 | 40.3 |
|  |  | 15.4 |  |  |  | Trade Receivables (net) | 19.2 | 11.6 |
|  |  | .0 |  |  |  | Inventory | 1.9 | .0 |
|  |  | 7.5 |  |  |  | All Other Current | 15.2 | 5.8 |
|  |  | 53.7 |  |  |  | Total Current | 67.3 | 57.7 |
|  |  | 11.6 |  |  |  | Fixed Assets (net) | 11.8 | 13.5 |
|  |  | 16.3 |  |  |  | Intangibles (net) | 1.5 | 6.0 |
|  |  | 18.4 |  |  |  | All Other Non-Current | 19.4 | 22.8 |
|  |  | 100.0 |  |  |  | Total | 100.0 | 100.0 |
|  |  |  |  |  |  | LIABILITIES |  |  |
|  |  | .3 |  |  |  | Notes Payable-Short Term | 10.9 | 12.1 |
|  |  | 1.3 |  |  |  | Cur. Mat.-L.T.D. | .8 | .8 |
|  |  | 16.0 |  |  |  | Trade Payables | 21.7 | 15.6 |
|  |  | .1 |  |  |  | Income Taxes Payable | 1.1 | .1 |
|  |  | 25.2 |  |  |  | All Other Current | 24.1 | 27.0 |
|  |  | 42.9 |  |  |  | Total Current | 58.6 | 55.6 |
|  |  | 29.6 |  |  |  | Long-Term Debt | 14.2 | 14.8 |
|  |  | .0 |  |  |  | Deferred Taxes | .4 | .1 |
|  |  | 7.9 |  |  |  | All Other Non-Current | 14.3 | 3.7 |
|  |  | 19.6 |  |  |  | Net Worth | 12.6 | 25.9 |
|  |  | 100.0 |  |  |  | Total Liabilties & Net Worth | 100.0 | 100.0 |
|  |  |  |  |  |  | INCOME DATA |  |  |
|  |  | 100.0 |  |  |  | Net Sales | 100.0 | 100.0 |
|  |  |  |  |  |  | Gross Profit |  |  |
|  |  | 90.2 |  |  |  | Operating Expenses | 85.4 | 84.6 |
|  |  | 9.8 |  |  |  | Operating Profit | 14.6 | 15.4 |
|  |  | 7.0 |  |  |  | All Other Expenses (net) | 6.3 | 6.3 |
|  |  | 2.8 |  |  |  | Profit Before Taxes | 8.3 | 9.1 |
|  |  |  |  |  |  | RATIOS |  |  |
|  |  | 2.9 |  |  |  |  | 1.6 | 1.7 |
|  |  | 1.0 |  |  |  | Current | 1.2 | 1.1 |
|  |  | .4 |  |  |  |  | .9 | .8 |
|  |  | 2.8 |  |  |  |  | 1.5 | 1.7 |
|  |  | 1.0 |  |  |  | Quick | 1.0 | .9 |
|  |  | .4 |  |  |  |  | .5 | .7 |
|  | 17 | 20.9 |  |  |  |  | 0   UND | 0   UND |
|  | 30 | 12.2 |  |  |  | Sales/Receivables | 30   12.3 | 13   27.6 |
|  | 114 | 3.2 |  |  |  |  | 132   2.8 | 91   4.0 |
|  |  |  |  |  |  | Cost of Sales/Inventory |  |  |
|  |  |  |  |  |  | Cost of Sales/Payables |  |  |
|  |  | 3.1 |  |  |  |  | 1.0 | 3.4 |
|  |  | 108.2 |  |  |  | Sales/Working Capital | 11.0 | 29.9 |
|  |  | -4.2 |  |  |  |  | -22.9 | -5.1 |
|  |  |  |  |  |  |  | 17.8 | 29.4 |
|  |  |  |  |  |  | EBIT/Interest | (15) 8.2 | (20) 7.3 |
|  |  |  |  |  |  |  | 3.2 | 1.8 |
|  |  |  |  |  |  | Net Profit + Depr., Dep., Amort./Cur. Mat. L/T/D |  |  |
|  |  | .0 |  |  |  |  | .0 | .0 |
|  |  | .4 |  |  |  | Fixed/Worth | .1 | .1 |
|  |  | -.1 |  |  |  |  | 2.1 | 1.7 |
|  |  | 1.3 |  |  |  |  | 2.2 | 1.5 |
|  |  | 19.8 |  |  |  | Debt/Worth | 6.7 | 5.2 |
|  |  | -2.2 |  |  |  |  | 43.1 | 16.2 |
|  |  |  |  |  |  |  | 46.3 | 33.9 |
|  |  |  |  |  |  | % Profit Before Taxes/Tangible Net Worth | (20) 20.5 | (28) 9.8 |
|  |  |  |  |  |  |  | 8.6 | 1.1 |
|  |  | 6.3 |  |  |  |  | 14.7 | 8.5 |
|  |  | 1.8 |  |  |  | % Profit Before Taxes/Total Assets | 1.9 | 2.2 |
|  |  | -.4 |  |  |  |  | .9 | .3 |
|  |  | UND |  |  |  |  | UND | UND |
|  |  | 158.0 |  |  |  | Sales/Net Fixed Assets | 63.6 | 51.2 |
|  |  | 22.4 |  |  |  |  | 14.6 | 16.9 |
|  |  | 1.8 |  |  |  |  | 2.5 | 1.6 |
|  |  | .9 |  |  |  | Sales/Total Assets | .7 | .4 |
|  |  | .3 |  |  |  |  | .1 | .2 |
|  |  |  |  |  |  |  |  | .8 |
|  |  |  |  |  |  | % Depr., Dep., Amort./Sales | (12) 2.0 | 2.0 |
|  |  |  |  |  |  |  |  | 3.9 |
|  |  |  |  |  |  | % Officers', Directors' Owners' Comp/Sales |  |  |
| 4338M | 7498M | 73210M | 110946M | 284268M | 557199M | Net Sales ($) | 887816M | 1824893M |
| 814M | 4835M | 61968M | 179663M | 422886M | 987163M | Total Assets ($) | 1543109M | 1654699M |

M = $ thousand    MM = $ million
See Pages 9 through 22 for Explanation of Ratios and Data

## Comparative Historical Data | Current Data Sorted by Sales

| | | | | Type of Statement | | | | | | |
|---|---|---|---|---|---|---|---|---|---|---|
| | 15 | 10 | 14 | Unqualified | 2 | | 2 | | 2 | 8 |
| | 3 | 2 | 3 | Reviewed | | | | 1 | 1 | 1 |
| | 2 | 5 | 3 | Compiled | | 1 | | 2 | | |
| | 4 | 2 | 6 | Tax Returns | 1 | 1 | 3 | | 1 | |
| | 16 | 16 | 16 | Other | 3 | 3 | 2 | 3 | 3 | 2 |
| | 4/1/09-3/31/10 | 4/1/10-3/31/11 | 4/1/11-3/31/12 | | | 1 (4/1-9/30/11) | | 41 (10/1/11-3/31/12) | | |
| | ALL | ALL | ALL | | 0-1MM | 1-3MM | 3-5MM | 5-10MM | 10-25MM | 25MM & OVER |
| | 40 | 35 | 42 | NUMBER OF STATEMENTS | 6 | 5 | 7 | 6 | 7 | 11 |
| | % | % | % | ASSETS | % | % | % | % | % | % |
| | 49.5 | 43.6 | 40.6 | Cash & Equivalents | | | | | | 41.6 |
| | 12.8 | 14.4 | 9.2 | Trade Receivables (net) | | | | | | 10.2 |
| | 2.2 | .2 | .0 | Inventory | | | | | | .2 |
| | 5.3 | 7.5 | 7.2 | All Other Current | | | | | | 3.7 |
| | 69.9 | 65.7 | 57.1 | Total Current | | | | | | 55.7 |
| | 5.6 | 7.6 | 9.1 | Fixed Assets (net) | | | | | | 4.3 |
| | 5.7 | 6.7 | 10.8 | Intangibles (net) | | | | | | 11.6 |
| | 18.8 | 20.0 | 23.0 | All Other Non-Current | | | | | | 28.3 |
| | 100.0 | 100.0 | 100.0 | Total | | | | | | 100.0 |
| | | | | LIABILITIES | | | | | | |
| | 6.7 | 3.8 | 8.6 | Notes Payable-Short Term | | | | | | 1.1 |
| | 3.9 | 1.7 | 2.0 | Cur. Mat.-L.T.D. | | | | | | 1.8 |
| | 10.6 | 6.0 | 13.5 | Trade Payables | | | | | | 2.0 |
| | .1 | .2 | .2 | Income Taxes Payable | | | | | | .1 |
| | 45.4 | 29.5 | 35.8 | All Other Current | | | | | | 32.7 |
| | 66.8 | 41.3 | 60.1 | Total Current | | | | | | 37.7 |
| | 11.6 | 12.4 | 12.3 | Long-Term Debt | | | | | | 12.2 |
| | .1 | .0 | .2 | Deferred Taxes | | | | | | .3 |
| | 6.9 | 8.3 | 6.4 | All Other Non-Current | | | | | | 9.7 |
| | 14.6 | 38.0 | 21.0 | Net Worth | | | | | | 40.1 |
| | 100.0 | 100.0 | 100.0 | Total Liabilities & Net Worth | | | | | | 100.0 |
| | | | | INCOME DATA | | | | | | |
| | 100.0 | 100.0 | 100.0 | Net Sales | | | | | | 100.0 |
| | | | | Gross Profit | | | | | | |
| | 90.0 | 86.1 | 88.1 | Operating Expenses | | | | | | 97.7 |
| | 10.0 | 13.9 | 11.9 | Operating Profit | | | | | | 2.3 |
| | 3.2 | 3.6 | 3.3 | All Other Expenses (net) | | | | | | -.3 |
| | 6.8 | 10.3 | 8.6 | Profit Before Taxes | | | | | | 2.6 |
| | | | | RATIOS | | | | | | |
| | 2.2 | 4.3 | 2.1 | | | | | | | 2.1 |
| | 1.2 | 1.5 | 1.1 | Current | | | | | | 1.8 |
| | .9 | 1.0 | .7 | | | | | | | 1.0 |
| | 2.1 | 4.3 | 2.1 | | | | | | | 2.1 |
| | 1.1 | 1.5 | 1.0 | Quick | | | | | | 1.3 |
| | .7 | .9 | .5 | | | | | | | 1.0 |
| 0 | 857.8 | 0 | 999.8 | 0 762.1 | Sales/Receivables | | | | | 7 53.9 |
| 18 | 20.0 | 22 | 16.4 | 25 14.8 | | | | | | 33 11.2 |
| 66 | 5.5 | 133 | 2.7 | 53 6.9 | | | | | | 49 7.4 |
| | | | | Cost of Sales/Inventory | | | | | | |
| | | | | Cost of Sales/Payables | | | | | | |
| | 1.6 | 1.0 | 2.1 | | | | | | | 2.6 |
| | 7.8 | 5.5 | 12.1 | Sales/Working Capital | | | | | | 7.0 |
| | -5.5 | -119.1 | -3.3 | | | | | | | 353.8 |
| | 29.1 | 60.0 | 28.7 | | | | | | | |
| (24) | 6.7 | (16) 18.6 | (21) 7.2 | EBIT/Interest | | | | | | |
| | 2.6 | 3.6 | 2.0 | | | | | | | |
| | | | | Net Profit + Depr., Dep., Amort./Cur. Mat. L/T/D | | | | | | |
| | .0 | .0 | .0 | | | | | | | .0 |
| | .0 | .0 | .0 | Fixed/Worth | | | | | | .1 |
| | .8 | .3 | 1.6 | | | | | | | .4 |
| | 1.3 | .5 | 1.0 | | | | | | | .9 |
| | 4.8 | 2.2 | 4.7 | Debt/Worth | | | | | | 3.3 |
| | 16.2 | 11.5 | NM | | | | | | | 7.6 |
| | 42.6 | 55.8 | 35.0 | % Profit Before Taxes/Tangible Net Worth | | | | | | |
| (33) | 14.4 | (31) 15.2 | (32) 10.7 | | | | | | | |
| | 4.5 | 3.7 | .6 | | | | | | | |
| | 11.7 | 18.2 | 8.6 | % Profit Before Taxes/Total Assets | | | | | | 16.8 |
| | 3.4 | 5.1 | 2.4 | | | | | | | 2.0 |
| | .6 | .6 | .0 | | | | | | | -2.0 |
| | UND | UND | UND | | | | | | | 677.6 |
| | 114.6 | 81.5 | 175.8 | Sales/Net Fixed Assets | | | | | | 30.2 |
| | 31.9 | 19.7 | 19.2 | | | | | | | 16.2 |
| | 2.2 | 2.0 | 1.8 | | | | | | | 2.0 |
| | .8 | .9 | .5 | Sales/Total Assets | | | | | | .7 |
| | .2 | .3 | .3 | | | | | | | .5 |
| | .5 | .5 | .4 | | | | | | | |
| (16) | 1.6 | (15) 1.6 | (16) 2.0 | % Depr., Dep., Amort./Sales | | | | | | |
| | 3.7 | 2.8 | 4.0 | | | | | | | |
| | | | | % Officers', Directors' Owners' Comp/Sales | | | | | | |
| | 1842034M | 1986552M | 1037459M | Net Sales ($) | 2760M | 10368M | 29039M | 46929M | 115087M | 833276M |
| | 2182467M | 2208299M | 1657329M | Total Assets ($) | 14054M | 12753M | 116984M | 85865M | 500524M | 927149M |

© RMA 2012

M = $ thousand    MM = $ million
See Pages 9 through 22 for Explanation of Ratios and Data

**Current Data Sorted by Assets** | **Comparative Historical Data**

| 0-500M | 500M-2MM | 2-10MM | 10-50MM | 50-100MM | 100-250MM | Type of Statement | 4/1/07-3/31/08 ALL | 4/1/08-3/31/09 ALL |
|---|---|---|---|---|---|---|---|---|
|  | 1 | 6 | 19 | 9 | 9 | Unqualified | 40 | 46 |
|  |  | 1 | 1 |  |  | Reviewed | 2 |  |
| 1 | 1 | 1 |  |  |  | Compiled | 3 | 5 |
| 1 | 2 | 1 |  |  |  | Tax Returns | 3 | 2 |
| 2 | 2 | 7 | 10 | 6 | 8 | Other | 27 | 26 |
| 17 (4/1-9/30/11) |  | 70 (10/1/11-3/31/12) |  |  |  |  |  |  |
| 4 | 6 | 15 | 30 | 15 | 17 | **NUMBER OF STATEMENTS** | 75 | 79 |
| % | % | % | % | % | % | **ASSETS** | % | % |
|  |  | 32.1 | 55.4 | 56.3 | 34.6 | Cash & Equivalents | 35.1 | 43.5 |
|  |  | 18.0 | 12.8 | 9.4 | 15.0 | Trade Receivables (net) | 15.5 | 15.0 |
|  |  | .2 | .2 | .2 | .2 | Inventory | .7 | .5 |
|  |  | 5.5 | 4.0 | 10.7 | 5.9 | All Other Current | 4.6 | 4.7 |
|  |  | 55.8 | 72.4 | 76.6 | 55.7 | Total Current | 55.8 | 63.6 |
|  |  | 32.2 | 10.4 | 6.3 | 6.3 | Fixed Assets (net) | 18.1 | 12.8 |
|  |  | 6.1 | 2.4 | 3.7 | 20.2 | Intangibles (net) | 8.8 | 8.1 |
|  |  | 6.0 | 14.8 | 13.4 | 17.8 | All Other Non-Current | 17.3 | 15.5 |
|  |  | 100.0 | 100.0 | 100.0 | 100.0 | Total | 100.0 | 100.0 |
|  |  |  |  |  |  | **LIABILITIES** |  |  |
|  |  | 3.2 | .4 | .7 | .3 | Notes Payable-Short Term | 3.5 | 9.5 |
|  |  | 2.9 | 1.2 | .5 | .9 | Cur. Mat.-L.T.D. | 2.1 | 1.2 |
|  |  | 12.6 | 15.0 | 14.8 | 22.4 | Trade Payables | 12.4 | 13.4 |
|  |  | .2 | .4 | .2 | .3 | Income Taxes Payable | .2 | .4 |
|  |  | 11.2 | 31.6 | 29.9 | 22.4 | All Other Current | 23.5 | 28.4 |
|  |  | 30.1 | 48.6 | 46.2 | 46.3 | Total Current | 41.6 | 52.8 |
|  |  | 33.1 | 10.4 | 1.8 | 15.6 | Long-Term Debt | 17.5 | 8.8 |
|  |  | .5 | .4 | .5 | 2.1 | Deferred Taxes | .4 | .3 |
|  |  | .8 | 2.0 | 4.0 | 4.0 | All Other Non-Current | 8.6 | 5.1 |
|  |  | 35.5 | 38.5 | 47.5 | 32.0 | Net Worth | 31.9 | 33.0 |
|  |  | 100.0 | 100.0 | 100.0 | 100.0 | Total Liabilities & Net Worth | 100.0 | 100.0 |
|  |  |  |  |  |  | **INCOME DATA** |  |  |
|  |  | 100.0 | 100.0 | 100.0 | 100.0 | Net Sales | 100.0 | 100.0 |
|  |  |  |  |  |  | Gross Profit |  |  |
|  |  | 85.4 | 93.0 | 97.0 | 94.5 | Operating Expenses | 95.9 | 93.4 |
|  |  | 14.6 | 7.0 | 3.0 | 5.5 | Operating Profit | 4.1 | 6.6 |
|  |  | 6.1 | 2.6 | -.7 | 2.1 | All Other Expenses (net) | -.7 | .6 |
|  |  | 8.4 | 4.4 | 3.7 | 3.3 | Profit Before Taxes | 4.9 | 6.0 |
|  |  |  |  |  |  | **RATIOS** |  |  |
|  |  | 7.0 | 2.2 | 3.3 | 1.6 | Current | 2.3 | 2.3 |
|  |  | 1.9 | 1.4 | 1.7 | 1.3 |  | 1.5 | 1.5 |
|  |  | 1.0 | 1.1 | 1.2 | 1.0 |  | 1.0 | 1.0 |
|  |  | 6.9 | 2.1 | 3.2 | 1.4 | Quick | 2.1 | 2.0 |
|  |  | 1.6 | 1.4 | 1.4 | 1.1 |  | 1.4 | 1.4 |
|  |  | .9 | 1.0 | .8 | .8 |  | .8 | .9 |
|  |  | 0 UND | 3 109.4 | 2 147.8 | 8 44.7 | Sales/Receivables | 4 99.6 | 3 134.6 |
|  |  | 27 13.3 | 12 30.0 | 9 42.4 | 22 16.8 |  | 18 19.8 | 18 20.3 |
|  |  | 60 6.1 | 30 12.2 | 23 16.2 | 39 9.3 |  | 39 9.4 | 36 10.0 |
|  |  |  |  |  |  | Cost of Sales/Inventory |  |  |
|  |  |  |  |  |  | Cost of Sales/Payables |  |  |
|  |  | 2.8 | 4.6 | 3.3 | 9.3 | Sales/Working Capital | 6.1 | 7.3 |
|  |  | 7.6 | 16.9 | 10.5 | 26.5 |  | 15.1 | 15.9 |
|  |  | -97.7 | NM | 37.7 | -115.8 |  | 163.1 | -55.4 |
|  |  | 71.2 | 164.7 |  | 32.9 | EBIT/Interest | 22.5 | 25.6 |
|  |  | (11) 36.7 | (14) 65.2 |  | (11) 11.4 |  | (46) 6.0 | (37) 9.7 |
|  |  | 1.2 | 12.0 |  | 1.9 |  | 1.9 | 1.6 |
|  |  |  |  |  |  | Net Profit + Depr., Dep., Amort./Cur. Mat. L/T/D |  | 17.1 |
|  |  |  |  |  |  |  |  | (11) 12.0 |
|  |  |  |  |  |  |  |  | .4 |
|  |  | .0 | .0 | .0 | .1 | Fixed/Worth | .1 | .0 |
|  |  | .4 | .1 | .1 | .2 |  | .3 | .2 |
|  |  | 2.1 | .5 | .2 | -.3 |  | 1.1 | .8 |
|  |  | .7 | .7 | .4 | 1.3 | Debt/Worth | .7 | .6 |
|  |  | 2.0 | 1.9 | .9 | 2.4 |  | 1.3 | 1.3 |
|  |  | 14.2 | 4.4 | 3.4 | -7.2 |  | 9.7 | 11.4 |
|  |  | 97.3 | 40.2 | 41.3 | 35.1 | % Profit Before Taxes/Tangible Net Worth | 44.3 | 41.8 |
|  |  | (12) 28.5 | (27) 11.3 | (12) 12.9 | 13.4 |  | (65) 18.7 | (65) 16.6 |
|  |  | 1.1 | 6.6 | 9.3 | 2.7 |  | 5.7 | 2.5 |
|  |  | 35.1 | 16.3 | 8.9 | 7.5 | % Profit Before Taxes/Total Assets | 14.9 | 11.6 |
|  |  | 10.2 | 7.0 | 6.2 | 5.1 |  | 8.2 | 5.0 |
|  |  | .5 | 2.2 | 3.2 | .4 |  | 2.4 | 1.1 |
|  |  | 999.8 | 999.8 | 999.8 | 90.9 | Sales/Net Fixed Assets | 154.6 | 295.7 |
|  |  | 17.5 | 167.9 | 76.3 | 38.5 |  | 20.1 | 60.9 |
|  |  | 1.6 | 16.5 | 18.4 | 23.3 |  | 8.4 | 13.0 |
|  |  | 3.0 | 4.3 | 5.4 | 3.7 | Sales/Total Assets | 3.9 | 4.0 |
|  |  | 1.9 | 2.2 | 3.1 | 2.2 |  | 2.2 | 2.8 |
|  |  | 1.0 | 1.1 | 1.6 | .9 |  | 1.2 | 1.2 |
|  |  | 1.9 | .1 |  | .2 | % Depr., Dep., Amort./Sales | .3 | .2 |
|  |  | (10) 3.5 | (20) 1.3 |  | (10) .5 |  | (58) 1.5 | (55) .7 |
|  |  | 13.5 | 4.2 |  | 1.4 |  | 2.9 | 2.4 |
|  |  |  |  |  |  | % Officers', Directors' Owners' Comp/Sales |  |  |
| 8066M | 15761M | 177087M | 2726270M | 3337459M | 6551736M | Net Sales ($) | 9971497M | 12004306M |
| 1063M | 7534M | 82533M | 913946M | 984624M | 2691831M | Total Assets ($) | 4103183M | 4268118M |

M = $ thousand    MM = $ million
See Pages 9 through 22 for Explanation of Ratios and Data

## Comparative Historical Data    Current Data Sorted by Sales

| 4/1/09-3/31/10 ALL | 4/1/10-3/31/11 ALL | 4/1/11-3/31/12 ALL | Type of Statement | 0-1MM | 1-3MM | 3-5MM | 5-10MM | 10-25MM | 25MM & OVER |
|---|---|---|---|---|---|---|---|---|---|
| 51 | 43 | 44 | Unqualified | 3 | | 1 | 3 | 5 | 32 |
| 1 | | 2 | Reviewed | | | | | 1 | 1 |
| 11 | 2 | 2 | Compiled | 1 | | 1 | | | |
| 1 | 4 | 4 | Tax Returns | | 1 | 2 | | | |
| 33 | 37 | 35 | Other | 2 | 4 | | 3 | 2 | 24 |
| | | | | 17 (4/1-9/30/11) | | | 70 (10/1/11-3/31/12) | | |
| 97 | 86 | 87 | NUMBER OF STATEMENTS | 6 | 5 | 4 | 7 | 8 | 57 |
| % | % | % | ASSETS | % | % | % | % | % | % |
| 43.0 | 47.1 | 44.7 | Cash & Equivalents | | | | | | 47.2 |
| 16.3 | 12.8 | 14.3 | Trade Receivables (net) | | | | | | 13.8 |
| .4 | .3 | .2 | Inventory | | | | | | .2 |
| 5.4 | 7.5 | 5.4 | All Other Current | | | | | | 6.8 |
| 65.1 | 67.6 | 64.6 | Total Current | | | | | | 68.1 |
| 15.6 | 12.5 | 12.6 | Fixed Assets (net) | | | | | | 8.6 |
| 7.3 | 5.6 | 7.9 | Intangibles (net) | | | | | | 8.2 |
| 12.0 | 14.2 | 15.0 | All Other Non-Current | | | | | | 15.1 |
| 100.0 | 100.0 | 100.0 | Total | | | | | | 100.0 |
| | | | LIABILITIES | | | | | | |
| 3.7 | .5 | 3.1 | Notes Payable-Short Term | | | | | | .5 |
| 1.2 | 1.3 | 1.3 | Cur. Mat.-L.T.D. | | | | | | 1.2 |
| 12.9 | 17.5 | 18.1 | Trade Payables | | | | | | 14.1 |
| .2 | .3 | .3 | Income Taxes Payable | | | | | | .4 |
| 26.2 | 24.7 | 23.9 | All Other Current | | | | | | 29.2 |
| 44.2 | 44.3 | 46.7 | Total Current | | | | | | 45.3 |
| 10.3 | 12.7 | 13.6 | Long-Term Debt | | | | | | 10.0 |
| .5 | .7 | .7 | Deferred Taxes | | | | | | 1.0 |
| 6.1 | 6.6 | 4.0 | All Other Non-Current | | | | | | 3.3 |
| 39.0 | 35.7 | 35.0 | Net Worth | | | | | | 40.5 |
| 100.0 | 100.0 | 100.0 | Total Liabilties & Net Worth | | | | | | 100.0 |
| | | | INCOME DATA | | | | | | |
| 100.0 | 100.0 | 100.0 | Net Sales | | | | | | 100.0 |
| | | | Gross Profit | | | | | | |
| 93.8 | 92.1 | 92.2 | Operating Expenses | | | | | | 94.9 |
| 6.2 | 7.9 | 7.8 | Operating Profit | | | | | | 5.1 |
| .4 | 2.1 | 2.3 | All Other Expenses (net) | | | | | | .6 |
| 5.7 | 5.9 | 5.5 | Profit Before Taxes | | | | | | 4.6 |
| | | | RATIOS | | | | | | |
| 3.3 | 2.4 | 2.4 | Current | | | | | | 2.1 |
| 1.6 | 1.4 | 1.4 | | | | | | | 1.4 |
| 1.0 | 1.1 | 1.0 | | | | | | | 1.1 |
| 3.0 | 2.3 | 2.2 | Quick | | | | | | 2.0 |
| 1.5 | 1.3 | 1.3 | | | | | | | 1.3 |
| .8 | .9 | .9 | | | | | | | .9 |
| 5   77.4 | 2   149.1 | 3   111.4 | Sales/Receivables | | | | | | 4   96.3 |
| 18   20.4 | 15   24.6 | 13   28.9 | | | | | | | 12   30.4 |
| 33   10.9 | 25   14.9 | 33   10.9 | | | | | | | 29   12.4 |
| | | | Cost of Sales/Inventory | | | | | | |
| | | | Cost of Sales/Payables | | | | | | |
| 5.2 | 5.8 | 5.3 | Sales/Working Capital | | | | | | 6.8 |
| 12.3 | 17.1 | 16.5 | | | | | | | 18.4 |
| UND | 77.5 | -336.1 | | | | | | | 46.8 |
| 58.4 | 51.5 | 67.4 | EBIT/Interest | | | | | | 107.0 |
| (53) 6.6 | (40) 6.6 | (48) 17.8 | | | | | | | (29) 32.9 |
| 1.9 | 1.4 | 3.6 | | | | | | | 5.2 |
| 18.6 | 9.6 | 30.6 | Net Profit + Depr., Dep., Amort./Cur. Mat. L/T/D | | | | | | 30.6 |
| (17) 4.0 | (14) 5.8 | (14) 9.1 | | | | | | | (10) 13.0 |
| 1.1 | 1.5 | 1.6 | | | | | | | 1.7 |
| .0 | .0 | .0 | Fixed/Worth | | | | | | .0 |
| .3 | .2 | .2 | | | | | | | .2 |
| 1.4 | 1.6 | 1.2 | | | | | | | .5 |
| .6 | .7 | .9 | Debt/Worth | | | | | | .7 |
| 1.5 | 1.3 | 1.9 | | | | | | | 1.6 |
| 11.5 | 14.6 | 11.1 | | | | | | | 3.1 |
| 38.3 | 42.6 | 53.2 | % Profit Before Taxes/Tangible Net Worth | | | | | | 55.7 |
| (81) 15.9 | (73) 13.0 | (72) 15.7 | | | | | | | (49) 17.9 |
| 1.1 | 3.0 | 6.7 | | | | | | | 7.4 |
| 13.8 | 15.8 | 14.8 | % Profit Before Taxes/Total Assets | | | | | | 15.4 |
| 6.1 | 5.1 | 7.0 | | | | | | | 7.3 |
| .4 | .6 | 2.0 | | | | | | | 3.4 |
| 362.1 | 625.0 | 730.0 | Sales/Net Fixed Assets | | | | | | 668.9 |
| 43.6 | 71.3 | 48.8 | | | | | | | 51.0 |
| 10.9 | 19.2 | 16.5 | | | | | | | 17.8 |
| 4.2 | 4.6 | 4.1 | Sales/Total Assets | | | | | | 4.5 |
| 2.4 | 2.8 | 2.2 | | | | | | | 2.6 |
| 1.0 | 1.4 | 1.1 | | | | | | | 1.7 |
| .2 | .2 | .2 | % Depr., Dep., Amort./Sales | | | | | | .1 |
| (65) .8 | (58) .5 | (53) 1.4 | | | | | | | (37) .4 |
| 2.8 | 1.8 | 3.8 | | | | | | | 2.2 |
| 4.7 | 4.1 | | % Officers', Directors' Owners' Comp/Sales | | | | | | |
| (11) 7.5 | (10) 7.5 | | | | | | | | |
| 14.2 | 10.2 | | | | | | | | |
| 12983816M | 16200942M | 12816379M | Net Sales ($) | 4179M | 8186M | 14004M | 51344M | 140785M | 12597881M |
| 4754326M | 5300395M | 4681531M | Total Assets ($) | 27598M | 20408M | 4900M | 45501M | 262207M | 4320917M |

M = $ thousand    MM = $ million
See Pages 9 through 22 for Explanation of Ratios and Data

## Current Data Sorted by Assets       Comparative Historical Data

| 0-500M | 500M-2MM | 2-10MM | 10-50MM | 50-100MM | 100-250MM | Type of Statement | 4/1/07-3/31/08 ALL | 4/1/08-3/31/09 ALL |
|---|---|---|---|---|---|---|---|---|
| 1 | | 1 | 8 | 6 | 13 | Unqualified | 23 | 28 |
| | | 3 | | | | Reviewed | | 2 |
| | 1 | 1 | 1 | | 1 | Compiled | 1 | |
| 6 | 3 | 1 | 1 | | | Tax Returns | 3 | 5 |
| 1 | 3 | 5 | 15 | 4 | 9 | Other | 46 | 44 |
| | 8 (4/1-9/30/11) | | 76 (10/1/11-3/31/12) | | | | | |
| 8 | 7 | 11 | 25 | 10 | 23 | **NUMBER OF STATEMENTS** | 73 | 79 |
| % | % | % | % | % | % | **ASSETS** | % | % |
| | | 19.0 | 61.0 | 54.3 | 50.9 | Cash & Equivalents | 41.6 | 47.7 |
| | | 15.4 | 11.4 | 6.8 | 11.6 | Trade Receivables (net) | 10.8 | 12.9 |
| | | .0 | .0 | .0 | .0 | Inventory | .6 | .0 |
| | | 17.2 | 2.8 | 7.5 | 9.5 | All Other Current | 9.8 | 9.4 |
| | | 51.6 | 75.2 | 68.6 | 72.0 | Total Current | 62.8 | 70.0 |
| | | 20.4 | 2.0 | 3.4 | 2.5 | Fixed Assets (net) | 5.2 | 6.9 |
| | | 9.4 | 6.4 | .1 | 1.2 | Intangibles (net) | 4.1 | 5.8 |
| | | 18.6 | 16.4 | 27.9 | 24.3 | All Other Non-Current | 27.9 | 17.3 |
| | | 100.0 | 100.0 | 100.0 | 100.0 | Total | 100.0 | 100.0 |
| | | | | | | **LIABILITIES** | | |
| | | 5.1 | .9 | 5.7 | 1.3 | Notes Payable-Short Term | 6.2 | 1.3 |
| | | 1.1 | .1 | .3 | .6 | Cur. Mat.-L.T.D. | .5 | 1.4 |
| | | 20.8 | 18.1 | 5.2 | 4.8 | Trade Payables | 8.2 | 12.5 |
| | | .1 | 2.4 | .2 | 2.8 | Income Taxes Payable | .5 | .6 |
| | | 18.9 | 36.1 | 32.0 | 42.4 | All Other Current | 32.5 | 34.2 |
| | | 46.1 | 57.5 | 43.4 | 51.9 | Total Current | 48.0 | 50.0 |
| | | 22.0 | 3.0 | 2.7 | 1.2 | Long-Term Debt | 11.8 | 8.9 |
| | | .0 | .0 | .1 | .1 | Deferred Taxes | .1 | .2 |
| | | 2.5 | 9.4 | 7.0 | 14.6 | All Other Non-Current | 9.1 | 13.1 |
| | | 29.5 | 30.1 | 46.8 | 32.2 | Net Worth | 31.1 | 27.9 |
| | | 100.0 | 100.0 | 100.0 | 100.0 | Total Liabilities & Net Worth | 100.0 | 100.0 |
| | | | | | | **INCOME DATA** | | |
| | | 100.0 | 100.0 | 100.0 | 100.0 | Net Sales | 100.0 | 100.0 |
| | | | | | | Gross Profit | | |
| | | 93.7 | 97.3 | 97.6 | 98.4 | Operating Expenses | 83.6 | 90.4 |
| | | 6.3 | 2.7 | 2.4 | 1.6 | Operating Profit | 16.4 | 9.6 |
| | | 4.3 | -1.8 | -3.0 | -2.6 | All Other Expenses (net) | -.7 | -1.2 |
| | | 2.0 | 4.4 | 5.4 | 4.2 | Profit Before Taxes | 17.1 | 10.8 |
| | | | | | | **RATIOS** | | |
| | | 1.9 | 1.6 | 2.8 | 3.4 | | 1.9 | 2.6 |
| | | 1.1 | 1.3 | 1.8 | 1.3 | Current | 1.4 | 1.7 |
| | | .8 | .9 | 1.2 | 1.1 | | 1.0 | 1.1 |
| | | 1.8 | 1.6 | 2.8 | 2.5 | | 1.7 | 2.5 |
| | | .8 | 1.3 | 1.6 | 1.2 | Quick | 1.2 | 1.3 |
| | | .2 | .9 | 1.0 | 1.0 | | .6 | .8 |
| | | 0   999.8 | 0   UND | 23   16.1 | 32   11.5 | | 0   UND | 0   UND |
| | | 20   18.6 | 46   8.0 | 49   7.4 | 70   5.2 | Sales/Receivables | 33   11.2 | 45   8.2 |
| | | 52   7.0 | 79   4.6 | 94   3.9 | 126   2.9 | | 81   4.5 | 97   3.8 |
| | | | | | | Cost of Sales/Inventory | | |
| | | | | | | Cost of Sales/Payables | | |
| | | 7.2 | 1.2 | .9 | .9 | | 1.3 | 1.0 |
| | | 18.4 | 3.9 | 1.9 | 3.6 | Sales/Working Capital | 4.0 | 3.6 |
| | | -12.6 | NM | 6.6 | 21.4 | | 112.3 | 156.1 |
| | | | | | | | 25.1 | 15.6 |
| | | | | | | EBIT/Interest | (32) 7.1 | (33) 4.9 |
| | | | | | | | 3.4 | -1.0 |
| | | | | | | Net Profit + Depr., Dep., Amort./Cur. Mat. L/T/D | | |
| | | .2 | .0 | .0 | .0 | | .0 | .0 |
| | | .3 | .0 | .0 | .1 | Fixed/Worth | .0 | .0 |
| | | 2.0 | .1 | .2 | .2 | | .1 | .3 |
| | | 1.1 | 1.2 | .7 | 1.5 | | 1.0 | 1.3 |
| | | 2.0 | 2.3 | 1.4 | 2.1 | Debt/Worth | 1.9 | 2.4 |
| | | 7.4 | 5.2 | 2.3 | 4.9 | | 3.8 | 13.8 |
| | | | 22.5 | 8.2 | 25.8 | | 34.5 | 45.3 |
| | | | (21) 12.1 | 2.1 | 7.2 | % Profit Before Taxes/Tangible Net Worth | (67) 19.9 | (66) 12.6 |
| | | | -2.2 | -7.8 | -4.4 | | 10.8 | 1.0 |
| | | 13.8 | 7.8 | 3.5 | 5.9 | | 12.5 | 12.2 |
| | | 2.7 | 3.5 | .9 | 3.1 | % Profit Before Taxes/Total Assets | 7.9 | 4.8 |
| | | -1.4 | -4.0 | -3.8 | -.9 | | 2.8 | -.1 |
| | | 54.9 | UND | UND | 562.5 | | UND | UND |
| | | 20.3 | 132.8 | 43.2 | 41.5 | Sales/Net Fixed Assets | 41.3 | 67.7 |
| | | 6.3 | 38.0 | 13.7 | 11.4 | | 18.7 | 20.4 |
| | | 3.7 | 1.0 | .7 | .7 | | 1.0 | 1.0 |
| | | 1.5 | .6 | .4 | .5 | Sales/Total Assets | .5 | .5 |
| | | .4 | .3 | .2 | .3 | | .3 | .3 |
| | | | | | .1 | | .6 | .2 |
| | | | | (15) | .7 | % Depr., Dep., Amort./Sales | (32) 1.1 | (31) 1.2 |
| | | | | | 1.5 | | 1.8 | 2.4 |
| | | | | | | % Officers', Directors' Owners' Comp/Sales | | |
| 6647M | 5560M | 104542M | 639831M | 374596M | 2585648M | Net Sales ($) | 2119747M | 3013461M |
| 1369M | 5818M | 49728M | 696289M | 732784M | 3997572M | Total Assets ($) | 4220942M | 5325827M |

© RMA 2012

**M = $ thousand    MM = $ million**
See Pages 9 through 22 for Explanation of Ratios and Data

## Comparative Historical Data | Current Data Sorted by Sales

| Type of Statement | | | | 0-1MM | 1-3MM | 3-5MM | 5-10MM | 10-25MM | 25MM & OVER |
|---|---|---|---|---|---|---|---|---|---|
| 32 | 20 | 29 | Unqualified | 1 | 1 | 1 | 1 | 5 | 20 |
| 3 | 2 | 3 | Reviewed | | | | 2 | 1 | |
| 5 | 5 | 4 | Compiled | 1 | 1 | 1 | | | 1 |
| 3 | 7 | 11 | Tax Returns | 6 | 4 | 1 | | | |
| 39 | 39 | 37 | Other | 5 | 1 | 1 | 3 | 11 | 16 |
| 4/1/09- 3/31/10 ALL | 4/1/10- 3/31/11 ALL | 4/1/11- 3/31/12 ALL | | | 8 (4/1-9/30/11) | | | 76 (10/1/11-3/31/12) | |
| 82 | 73 | 84 | **NUMBER OF STATEMENTS** | 13 | 7 | 4 | 6 | 17 | 37 |
| % | % | % | **ASSETS** | % | % | % | % | % | % |
| 44.8 | 49.5 | 47.2 | Cash & Equivalents | 24.4 | | | | 56.3 | 55.1 |
| 13.8 | 15.7 | 10.9 | Trade Receivables (net) | 6.8 | | | | 9.0 | 12.6 |
| .3 | .0 | .0 | Inventory | .1 | | | | .0 | .0 |
| 8.3 | 4.2 | 7.0 | All Other Current | 2.7 | | | | 7.6 | 6.3 |
| 67.2 | 69.4 | 65.1 | Total Current | 34.0 | | | | 72.9 | 74.0 |
| 3.3 | 4.0 | 8.8 | Fixed Assets (net) | 35.6 | | | | 5.6 | 3.0 |
| 2.5 | 5.3 | 3.8 | Intangibles (net) | 1.1 | | | | 5.0 | 2.4 |
| 27.0 | 21.3 | 22.3 | All Other Non-Current | 29.3 | | | | 16.5 | 20.5 |
| 100.0 | 100.0 | 100.0 | Total | 100.0 | | | | 100.0 | 100.0 |
| | | | **LIABILITIES** | | | | | | |
| 4.2 | 3.8 | 6.1 | Notes Payable-Short Term | 8.1 | | | | 2.7 | 2.5 |
| 1.1 | .7 | .8 | Cur. Mat.-L.T.D. | 1.8 | | | | .2 | .4 |
| 13.6 | 10.6 | 11.3 | Trade Payables | 6.5 | | | | 11.8 | 9.9 |
| .2 | .3 | 1.5 | Income Taxes Payable | .0 | | | | 1.0 | 2.7 |
| 33.6 | 35.6 | 31.5 | All Other Current | 16.4 | | | | 36.5 | 38.2 |
| 52.7 | 51.0 | 51.2 | Total Current | 32.9 | | | | 52.4 | 53.7 |
| 4.0 | 5.0 | 8.6 | Long-Term Debt | 30.3 | | | | 3.6 | 1.7 |
| .0 | .1 | .0 | Deferred Taxes | .0 | | | | .1 | .0 |
| 9.0 | 6.7 | 8.7 | All Other Non-Current | 3.0 | | | | 9.5 | 12.8 |
| 34.2 | 37.2 | 31.4 | Net Worth | 33.8 | | | | 34.6 | 31.7 |
| 100.0 | 100.0 | 100.0 | Total Liabilties & Net Worth | 100.0 | | | | 100.0 | 100.0 |
| | | | **INCOME DATA** | | | | | | |
| 100.0 | 100.0 | 100.0 | Net Sales | 100.0 | | | | 100.0 | 100.0 |
| | | | Gross Profit | | | | | | |
| 90.6 | 92.6 | 95.2 | Operating Expenses | 79.9 | | | | 93.0 | 101.9 |
| 9.4 | 7.4 | 4.8 | Operating Profit | 20.1 | | | | 7.0 | -1.9 |
| -1.1 | -2.9 | -.3 | All Other Expenses (net) | 8.5 | | | | -1.9 | -2.8 |
| 10.6 | 10.2 | 5.1 | Profit Before Taxes | 11.6 | | | | 8.8 | .9 |
| | | | **RATIOS** | | | | | | |
| 1.9 | 2.1 | 2.3 | | 4.3 | | | | 2.3 | 2.2 |
| 1.5 | 1.6 | 1.3 | Current | 1.9 | | | | 1.3 | 1.4 |
| 1.0 | .9 | 1.0 | | .5 | | | | 1.0 | 1.1 |
| 1.7 | 2.1 | 2.0 | | 3.5 | | | | 2.2 | 2.2 |
| 1.3 | 1.5 | 1.3 | Quick | 1.5 | | | | 1.3 | 1.3 |
| .7 | .7 | .8 | | .5 | | | | .9 | 1.0 |
| 2   188.6 | 7   51.7 | 1   623.2 | | 0   UND | | | | 5   67.0 | 18   19.8 |
| 39   9.3 | 65   5.6 | 39   9.3 | Sales/Receivables | 0   UND | | | | 39   9.4 | 55   6.6 |
| 109   3.3 | 127   2.9 | 76   4.8 | | 6   61.6 | | | | 89   4.1 | 89   4.1 |
| | | | Cost of Sales/Inventory | | | | | | |
| | | | Cost of Sales/Payables | | | | | | |
| 1.0 | .8 | 1.7 | | 6.1 | | | | 1.0 | 1.6 |
| 3.9 | 4.3 | 5.9 | Sales/Working Capital | 11.7 | | | | 2.1 | 4.6 |
| NM | -19.5 | NM | | -7.3 | | | | NM | 25.6 |
| 17.6 | 26.8 | 17.5 | | | | | | | 17.2 |
| (30)   3.6 | (24)   11.9 | (33)   3.8 | EBIT/Interest | | | | | (14)   6.5 | |
| 2.2 | 3.0 | -1.5 | | | | | | | -65.5 |
| | | | Net Profit + Depr., Dep., Amort./Cur. Mat. L/T/D | | | | | | |
| .0 | .0 | .0 | | .0 | | | | .0 | .0 |
| .0 | .0 | .0 | Fixed/Worth | .5 | | | | .0 | .1 |
| .2 | .1 | .4 | | 3.4 | | | | .4 | .2 |
| .8 | .9 | 1.0 | | .5 | | | | 1.4 | 1.0 |
| 2.0 | 1.6 | 2.1 | Debt/Worth | 2.0 | | | | 3.3 | 2.0 |
| 4.6 | 3.6 | 5.0 | | 7.5 | | | | 4.8 | 4.6 |
| 20.7 | 16.4 | 25.1 | | 55.3 | | | | 16.7 | 25.9 |
| (75)   9.8 | (65)   7.9 | (75)   10.9 | % Profit Before Taxes/Tangible Net Worth | (11)   14.3 | | | | (16)   12.5 | (34)   6.4 |
| 2.5 | 4.0 | -1.7 | | 2.1 | | | | 3.8 | -11.4 |
| 7.0 | 7.9 | 7.3 | | 16.5 | | | | 6.9 | 6.9 |
| 3.3 | 3.3 | 2.8 | % Profit Before Taxes/Total Assets | 3.2 | | | | 3.1 | 2.3 |
| .4 | 1.2 | -1.1 | | .9 | | | | .3 | -4.7 |
| UND | UND | UND | | UND | | | | UND | 781.1 |
| 116.5 | 88.6 | 47.3 | Sales/Net Fixed Assets | 5.8 | | | | 127.6 | 42.6 |
| 21.7 | 27.6 | 14.2 | | .7 | | | | 10.4 | 20.3 |
| 1.2 | 1.0 | 1.4 | | 1.9 | | | | .9 | 1.1 |
| .5 | .5 | .6 | Sales/Total Assets | 1.0 | | | | .5 | .6 |
| .3 | .3 | .3 | | .3 | | | | .3 | .4 |
| .5 | .4 | .4 | | | | | | | .3 |
| (28)   1.0 | (21)   .9 | (44)   1.1 | % Depr., Dep., Amort./Sales | | | | | | (20)   .6 |
| 1.7 | 1.8 | 1.5 | | | | | | | 1.4 |
| 5.7 | 1.9 | 8.6 | | | | | | | |
| (10)   9.9 | (15)   9.3 | (14)   10.4 | % Officers', Directors' Owners' Comp/Sales | | | | | | |
| 22.1 | 22.8 | 23.7 | | | | | | | |
| 2439278M | 2273684M | 3716824M | Net Sales ($) | 7299M | 11202M | 15231M | 44602M | 281964M | 3356526M |
| 5236832M | 4794458M | 5483560M | Total Assets ($) | 15353M | 17887M | 50907M | 121324M | 819578M | 4458511M |

© RMA 2012

M = $ thousand    MM = $ million
See Pages 9 through 22 for Explanation of Ratios and Data

## Current Data Sorted by Assets      Comparative Historical Data

| Type of Statement | 0-500M | 500M-2MM | 2-10MM | 10-50MM | 50-100MM | 100-250MM | 4/1/07-3/31/08 ALL | 4/1/08-3/31/09 ALL |
|---|---|---|---|---|---|---|---|---|
| Unqualified | 1 | 2 | 4 | 3 | 2 | 1 | 20 | 17 |
| Reviewed | | | 1 | 1 | | | 2 | 2 |
| Compiled | 1 | | | | | | 2 | 3 |
| Tax Returns | 5 | 3 | 1 | | | | 11 | 8 |
| Other | 1 | 3 | 7 | 5 | 2 | | 37 | 21 |
| | | 3 (4/1-9/30/11) | | 40 (10/1/11-3/31/12) | | | | |
| **NUMBER OF STATEMENTS** | 8 | 8 | 13 | 9 | 4 | 1 | 72 | 51 |
| | % | % | % | % | % | % | % | % |
| **ASSETS** | | | | | | | | |
| Cash & Equivalents | | | 31.6 | | | | 32.8 | 33.3 |
| Trade Receivables (net) | | | 7.9 | | | | 6.7 | 7.0 |
| Inventory | | | .1 | | | | 1.7 | 1.4 |
| All Other Current | | | 3.2 | | | | 10.7 | 11.3 |
| Total Current | | | 42.8 | | | | 51.8 | 53.1 |
| Fixed Assets (net) | | | 32.1 | | | | 19.1 | 18.7 |
| Intangibles (net) | | | 5.9 | | | | 9.8 | 6.6 |
| All Other Non-Current | | | 19.2 | | | | 19.3 | 21.7 |
| Total | | | 100.0 | | | | 100.0 | 100.0 |
| **LIABILITIES** | | | | | | | | |
| Notes Payable-Short Term | | | 1.7 | | | | 11.3 | 17.1 |
| Cur. Mat.-L.T.D. | | | 1.6 | | | | 1.6 | 1.7 |
| Trade Payables | | | 4.8 | | | | 9.8 | 7.2 |
| Income Taxes Payable | | | .0 | | | | .8 | 1.0 |
| All Other Current | | | 12.0 | | | | 20.1 | 18.8 |
| Total Current | | | 20.1 | | | | 43.6 | 45.9 |
| Long-Term Debt | | | 28.3 | | | | 13.3 | 13.6 |
| Deferred Taxes | | | .0 | | | | .5 | .3 |
| All Other Non-Current | | | 2.6 | | | | 13.0 | 10.7 |
| Net Worth | | | 49.1 | | | | 29.6 | 29.6 |
| Total Liabilities & Net Worth | | | 100.0 | | | | 100.0 | 100.0 |
| **INCOME DATA** | | | | | | | | |
| Net Sales | | | 100.0 | | | | 100.0 | 100.0 |
| Gross Profit | | | | | | | | |
| Operating Expenses | | | 85.0 | | | | 101.7 | 102.2 |
| Operating Profit | | | 15.0 | | | | -1.7 | -2.2 |
| All Other Expenses (net) | | | 4.2 | | | | -2.6 | 1.4 |
| Profit Before Taxes | | | 10.8 | | | | .9 | -3.6 |
| **RATIOS** | | | | | | | | |
| Current | | | 2.9 | | | | 3.0 | 2.9 |
| Current | | | 1.8 | | | | 1.2 | 1.6 |
| Current | | | 1.4 | | | | .7 | .9 |
| Quick | | | 2.6 | | | | 2.3 | 2.4 |
| Quick | | | 1.7 | | | | (71) 1.0 | 1.1 |
| Quick | | | 1.2 | | | | .5 | .5 |
| Sales/Receivables | 0 | UND | | | | | 0 UND | 0 UND |
| Sales/Receivables | 7 | 52.2 | | | | | 5 69.5 | 8 45.4 |
| Sales/Receivables | 19 | 19.4 | | | | | 15 24.5 | 21 17.7 |
| Cost of Sales/Inventory | | | | | | | | |
| Cost of Sales/Payables | | | | | | | | |
| Sales/Working Capital | | | 4.4 | | | | 7.4 | 5.5 |
| Sales/Working Capital | | | 12.0 | | | | 24.7 | 13.4 |
| Sales/Working Capital | | | 19.2 | | | | -21.9 | -55.5 |
| EBIT/Interest | | | 44.0 | | | | 7.1 | 6.0 |
| EBIT/Interest | | (11) | 3.9 | | | | (39) 1.6 | (28) -.5 |
| EBIT/Interest | | | 1.9 | | | | -6.1 | -17.6 |
| Net Profit + Depr., Dep., Amort./Cur. Mat. L/T/D | | | | | | | 5.2 | |
| Net Profit + Depr., Dep., Amort./Cur. Mat. L/T/D | | | | | | | (11) 1.2 | |
| Net Profit + Depr., Dep., Amort./Cur. Mat. L/T/D | | | | | | | -2.3 | |
| Fixed/Worth | | | .0 | | | | .1 | .1 |
| Fixed/Worth | | | .3 | | | | .4 | .3 |
| Fixed/Worth | | | 1.0 | | | | NM | 1.9 |
| Debt/Worth | | | .6 | | | | .6 | .4 |
| Debt/Worth | | | .9 | | | | 1.3 | 1.8 |
| Debt/Worth | | | 3.9 | | | | -84.7 | 16.0 |
| % Profit Before Taxes/Tangible Net Worth | | | 65.2 | | | | 48.9 | 33.3 |
| % Profit Before Taxes/Tangible Net Worth | | (12) | 29.5 | | | | (53) 3.2 | (40) -4.4 |
| % Profit Before Taxes/Tangible Net Worth | | | 9.0 | | | | -29.1 | -47.6 |
| % Profit Before Taxes/Total Assets | | | 20.7 | | | | 16.4 | 11.5 |
| % Profit Before Taxes/Total Assets | | | 11.0 | | | | 1.0 | -4.6 |
| % Profit Before Taxes/Total Assets | | | 4.1 | | | | -19.0 | -21.7 |
| Sales/Net Fixed Assets | | | 94.6 | | | | 60.1 | 49.1 |
| Sales/Net Fixed Assets | | | 17.7 | | | | 17.2 | 19.8 |
| Sales/Net Fixed Assets | | | 1.1 | | | | 8.9 | 11.4 |
| Sales/Total Assets | | | 3.2 | | | | 4.2 | 3.7 |
| Sales/Total Assets | | | 1.1 | | | | 2.3 | 1.9 |
| Sales/Total Assets | | | .6 | | | | 1.3 | 1.0 |
| % Depr., Dep., Amort./Sales | | | .8 | | | | 1.2 | 1.0 |
| % Depr., Dep., Amort./Sales | | (11) | 1.8 | | | | (51) 2.1 | (36) 2.6 |
| % Depr., Dep., Amort./Sales | | | 2.6 | | | | 3.3 | 3.5 |
| % Officers', Directors' Owners' Comp/Sales | | | | | | | 6.6 | |
| % Officers', Directors' Owners' Comp/Sales | | | | | | | (17) 14.2 | |
| % Officers', Directors' Owners' Comp/Sales | | | | | | | 22.9 | |
| Net Sales ($) | 8912M | 28036M | 137240M | 482639M | 387927M | 93259M | 3359721M | 1919185M |
| Total Assets ($) | 1396M | 6819M | 73593M | 201160M | 259344M | 163660M | 1672663M | 1162627M |

M = $ thousand    MM = $ million
See Pages 9 through 22 for Explanation of Ratios and Data

## Comparative Historical Data | Current Data Sorted by Sales

| | 4/1/09-3/31/10 ALL | 4/1/10-3/31/11 ALL | 4/1/11-3/31/12 ALL | Type of Statement | 0-1MM | 1-3MM | 3-5MM | 5-10MM | 10-25MM | 25MM & OVER |
|---|---|---|---|---|---|---|---|---|---|---|
| | 9 | 16 | 13 | Unqualified | 2 | | 2 | 1 | 3 | 5 |
| | 2 | 1 | 2 | Reviewed | | | | | | 2 |
| | 3 | 2 | 1 | Compiled | | 1 | | | | |
| | 8 | 5 | 9 | Tax Returns | 5 | 3 | | 1 | | |
| | 17 | 18 | 18 | Other | 2 | 4 | 3 | 1 | 3 | 5 |
| | | | | | 3 (4/1-9/30/11) | | | 40 (10/1/11-3/31/12) | | |
| **NUMBER OF STATEMENTS** | 39 | 42 | 43 | | 9 | 8 | 5 | 3 | 6 | 12 |
| | % | % | % | **ASSETS** | % | % | % | % | % | % |
| Cash & Equivalents | 31.6 | 36.0 | 34.2 | | | | | | | 34.3 |
| Trade Receivables (net) | 5.3 | 7.4 | 6.9 | | | | | | | 12.0 |
| Inventory | .3 | .0 | .0 | | | | | | | .0 |
| All Other Current | 5.5 | 10.7 | 12.3 | | | | | | | 20.3 |
| Total Current | 42.8 | 54.2 | 53.5 | | | | | | | 66.7 |
| Fixed Assets (net) | 24.1 | 15.2 | 20.2 | | | | | | | 12.5 |
| Intangibles (net) | 13.9 | 12.3 | 8.2 | | | | | | | 12.8 |
| All Other Non-Current | 19.3 | 18.4 | 18.1 | | | | | | | 8.1 |
| Total | 100.0 | 100.0 | 100.0 | | | | | | | 100.0 |
| | | | | **LIABILITIES** | | | | | | |
| Notes Payable-Short Term | 9.9 | 6.8 | 8.0 | | | | | | | 9.0 |
| Cur. Mat.-L.T.D. | 2.1 | 2.9 | 1.7 | | | | | | | .4 |
| Trade Payables | 5.6 | 9.7 | 9.1 | | | | | | | 13.8 |
| Income Taxes Payable | .6 | .4 | .7 | | | | | | | .1 |
| All Other Current | 13.3 | 21.1 | 22.9 | | | | | | | 19.5 |
| Total Current | 31.5 | 40.9 | 42.4 | | | | | | | 42.8 |
| Long-Term Debt | 24.1 | 12.5 | 17.8 | | | | | | | .8 |
| Deferred Taxes | .7 | .8 | .2 | | | | | | | .6 |
| All Other Non-Current | 13.3 | 12.1 | 7.2 | | | | | | | 11.9 |
| Net Worth | 30.5 | 33.7 | 32.4 | | | | | | | 43.9 |
| Total Liabilties & Net Worth | 100.0 | 100.0 | 100.0 | | | | | | | 100.0 |
| | | | | **INCOME DATA** | | | | | | |
| Net Sales | 100.0 | 100.0 | 100.0 | | | | | | | 100.0 |
| Gross Profit | | | | | | | | | | |
| Operating Expenses | 92.6 | 92.2 | 91.4 | | | | | | | 93.1 |
| Operating Profit | 7.4 | 7.8 | 8.6 | | | | | | | 6.9 |
| All Other Expenses (net) | 2.9 | .9 | 1.2 | | | | | | | -.6 |
| Profit Before Taxes | 4.5 | 7.0 | 7.5 | | | | | | | 7.5 |
| | | | | **RATIOS** | | | | | | |
| Current | 4.3 | 3.5 | 2.7 | | | | | | | 2.5 |
| | 1.5 | 1.6 | 1.5 | | | | | | | 1.7 |
| | 1.0 | 1.0 | 1.0 | | | | | | | 1.2 |
| Quick | 2.6 | 2.9 | 2.4 | | | | | | | 1.8 |
| | 1.4 | 1.4 | 1.3 | | | | | | | 1.2 |
| | .9 | .6 | .8 | | | | | | | .9 |
| Sales/Receivables | 0 UND | 0 UND | 0 UND | | | | | | 4 | 97.4 |
| | 3 110.5 | 5 66.4 | 3 113.7 | | | | | | 16 | 22.7 |
| | 14 27.0 | 16 23.3 | 22 16.8 | | | | | | 30 | 12.1 |
| Cost of Sales/Inventory | | | | | | | | | | |
| Cost of Sales/Payables | | | | | | | | | | |
| Sales/Working Capital | 6.7 | 5.1 | 4.6 | | | | | | | 4.6 |
| | 18.4 | 12.7 | 13.0 | | | | | | | 9.9 |
| | 368.1 | NM | -999.8 | | | | | | | 18.4 |
| EBIT/Interest | 37.1 | 33.3 | 44.0 | | | | | | | |
| | (28) 5.3 | (31) 6.6 | (27) 6.3 | | | | | | | |
| | .4 | 1.4 | 1.9 | | | | | | | |
| Net Profit + Depr., Dep., Amort./Cur. Mat. L/T/D | | | | | | | | | | |
| Fixed/Worth | .2 | .2 | .1 | | | | | | | .1 |
| | .9 | .5 | .3 | | | | | | | .2 |
| | -.6 | 18.2 | 1.2 | | | | | | | .5 |
| Debt/Worth | .6 | .7 | .6 | | | | | | | .5 |
| | 1.8 | 2.4 | 2.0 | | | | | | | 1.3 |
| | -7.3 | 77.8 | 19.9 | | | | | | | 4.8 |
| % Profit Before Taxes/Tangible Net Worth | 90.0 | 66.3 | 95.5 | | | | | | | 100.6 |
| | (28) 22.7 | (33) 27.9 | (35) 20.3 | | | | | | (11) | 36.1 |
| | -1.5 | -.9 | 5.5 | | | | | | | 14.4 |
| % Profit Before Taxes/Total Assets | 32.9 | 24.4 | 17.2 | | | | | | | 31.2 |
| | 6.3 | 6.7 | 8.2 | | | | | | | 13.1 |
| | -1.5 | .1 | -.3 | | | | | | | 5.1 |
| Sales/Net Fixed Assets | 56.0 | 108.6 | 166.0 | | | | | | | 167.8 |
| | 21.8 | 30.6 | 31.3 | | | | | | | 24.3 |
| | 7.0 | 10.5 | 10.9 | | | | | | | 8.7 |
| Sales/Total Assets | 3.5 | 3.6 | 4.2 | | | | | | | 4.2 |
| | 2.3 | 1.9 | 1.9 | | | | | | | 2.5 |
| | .8 | 1.0 | .6 | | | | | | | .6 |
| % Depr., Dep., Amort./Sales | .7 | .4 | .6 | | | | | | | |
| | (27) 1.3 | (34) 1.2 | (30) 1.0 | | | | | | | |
| | 3.5 | 2.1 | 2.4 | | | | | | | |
| % Officers', Directors' Owners' Comp/Sales | | | | | | | | | | |
| Net Sales ($) | 1172388M | 2469121M | 1138013M | | 4857M | 14452M | 18567M | 22888M | 94574M | 982675M |
| Total Assets ($) | 880119M | 862802M | 705972M | | 5952M | 11163M | 42291M | 11091M | 44671M | 590804M |

M = $ thousand   MM = $ million
See Pages 9 through 22 for Explanation of Ratios and Data

## Current Data Sorted by Assets      Comparative Historical Data

| Type of Statement | 0-500M | 500M-2MM | 2-10MM | 10-50MM | 50-100MM | 100-250MM | 4/1/07-3/31/08 ALL | 4/1/08-3/31/09 ALL |
|---|---|---|---|---|---|---|---|---|
| Unqualified | | | 7 | 9 | 3 | 7 | 29 | 33 |
| Reviewed | | | 1 | | | 1 | 3 | 3 |
| Compiled | | | | 1 | | | 2 | 5 |
| Tax Returns | 1 | 2 | | 1 | | | 6 | 4 |
| Other | 2 | 3 | 7 | 10 | 3 | 4 | 25 | 29 |
| | 6 (4/1-9/30/11) | | 56 (10/1/11-3/31/12) | | | | | |
| **NUMBER OF STATEMENTS** | 3 | 5 | 15 | 21 | 6 | 12 | 65 | 74 |
| | % | % | % | % | % | % | % | % |
| **ASSETS** | | | | | | | | |
| Cash & Equivalents | | | 47.2 | 52.8 | | 51.6 | 49.0 | 52.1 |
| Trade Receivables (net) | | | 8.2 | 16.3 | | 5.0 | 11.0 | 9.7 |
| Inventory | | | .0 | .0 | | .1 | .0 | .2 |
| All Other Current | | | 9.1 | 6.2 | | 1.2 | 7.1 | 5.0 |
| Total Current | | | 64.5 | 75.2 | | 57.9 | 67.1 | 67.0 |
| Fixed Assets (net) | | | 5.3 | 2.3 | | 3.2 | 7.6 | 5.4 |
| Intangibles (net) | | | 1.5 | 6.8 | | 6.7 | 5.6 | 4.6 |
| All Other Non-Current | | | 28.7 | 15.7 | | 32.2 | 19.7 | 23.0 |
| Total | | | 100.0 | 100.0 | | 100.0 | 100.0 | 100.0 |
| **LIABILITIES** | | | | | | | | |
| Notes Payable-Short Term | | | 4.9 | 1.8 | | 3.6 | 8.2 | 4.7 |
| Cur. Mat.-L.T.D. | | | 1.5 | 1.0 | | .2 | 2.5 | .6 |
| Trade Payables | | | 8.1 | 6.1 | | 19.2 | 11.7 | 10.6 |
| Income Taxes Payable | | | .0 | 1.2 | | .5 | .8 | .6 |
| All Other Current | | | 27.4 | 35.4 | | 21.8 | 26.0 | 31.1 |
| Total Current | | | 41.9 | 45.4 | | 45.2 | 49.3 | 47.6 |
| Long-Term Debt | | | 12.8 | 3.2 | | 8.1 | 5.1 | 6.5 |
| Deferred Taxes | | | .1 | 1.1 | | .5 | .3 | .4 |
| All Other Non-Current | | | 17.6 | 8.8 | | 10.5 | 13.5 | 15.0 |
| Net Worth | | | 27.6 | 41.5 | | 35.8 | 31.9 | 30.5 |
| Total Liabilities & Net Worth | | | 100.0 | 100.0 | | 100.0 | 100.0 | 100.0 |
| **INCOME DATA** | | | | | | | | |
| Net Sales | | | 100.0 | 100.0 | | 100.0 | 100.0 | 100.0 |
| Gross Profit | | | | | | | | |
| Operating Expenses | | | 91.1 | 94.5 | | 94.6 | 88.8 | 88.9 |
| Operating Profit | | | 8.9 | 5.5 | | 5.4 | 11.2 | 11.1 |
| All Other Expenses (net) | | | .5 | -1.6 | | -1.7 | -.2 | .4 |
| Profit Before Taxes | | | 8.5 | 7.1 | | 7.1 | 11.4 | 10.7 |
| **RATIOS** | | | | | | | | |
| Current | | | 2.5 | 3.6 | | 2.6 | 2.7 | 2.7 |
| | | | 1.3 | 1.4 | | 1.3 | 1.6 | 1.6 |
| | | | 1.0 | 1.1 | | .6 | 1.0 | 1.0 |
| Quick | | | 1.6 | 3.5 | | 2.5 | 2.6 | 2.7 |
| | | | 1.0 | 1.4 | | 1.3 | 1.4 | 1.4 |
| | | | .8 | .9 | | .6 | .8 | .8 |
| Sales/Receivables | | | 0   UND | 0   UND | | 10   36.0 | 0   UND | 0   UND |
| | | | 11   34.5 | 27   13.3 | | 34   10.7 | 8   46.2 | 7   48.9 |
| | | | 73   5.0 | 94   3.9 | | 76   4.8 | 43   8.4 | 44   8.3 |
| Cost of Sales/Inventory | | | | | | | | |
| Cost of Sales/Payables | | | | | | | | |
| Sales/Working Capital | | | 1.5 | 1.0 | | .6 | 1.8 | 1.4 |
| | | | 8.1 | 2.8 | | 1.8 | 4.9 | 4.4 |
| | | | -74.1 | 23.3 | | NM | UND | 133.4 |
| EBIT/Interest | | | | | | | 21.7 | 23.3 |
| | | | | | | | (28) 9.1 | (31) 9.5 |
| | | | | | | | 1.4 | 1.7 |
| Net Profit + Depr., Dep., Amort./Cur. Mat. L/T/D | | | | | | | | |
| Fixed/Worth | | | .0 | .0 | | .0 | .0 | .0 |
| | | | .1 | .0 | | .0 | .0 | .0 |
| | | | 1.3 | .1 | | .2 | 1.4 | .4 |
| Debt/Worth | | | 1.7 | .8 | | .9 | 1.3 | .9 |
| | | | 2.7 | 1.9 | | 3.4 | 3.0 | 2.2 |
| | | | 12.0 | 4.3 | | 4.8 | 8.0 | 14.4 |
| % Profit Before Taxes/Tangible Net Worth | | | 40.8 | 33.6 | | 16.3 | 61.5 | 57.9 |
| | | | (12) 10.7 | (19) 12.4 | | (11) 7.8 | (57) 31.1 | (62) 16.9 |
| | | | -22.1 | -4.4 | | -14.0 | 9.9 | 2.6 |
| % Profit Before Taxes/Total Assets | | | 10.9 | 13.0 | | 4.9 | 14.9 | 15.2 |
| | | | 2.7 | 3.6 | | 1.7 | 5.6 | 4.8 |
| | | | -5.4 | -2.9 | | -3.5 | 1.7 | .5 |
| Sales/Net Fixed Assets | | | UND | UND | | 195.7 | UND | UND |
| | | | 423.0 | 318.0 | | 31.0 | 127.9 | 283.3 |
| | | | 15.2 | 43.3 | | 10.8 | 23.6 | 40.4 |
| Sales/Total Assets | | | 1.4 | 1.6 | | .7 | 2.4 | 2.4 |
| | | | .8 | .6 | | .3 | .7 | .7 |
| | | | .4 | .3 | | .1 | .4 | .3 |
| % Depr., Dep., Amort./Sales | | | | | | | .5 | .3 |
| | | | | | | | (27) 1.1 | (25) .7 |
| | | | | | | | 2.2 | 1.3 |
| % Officers', Directors' Owners' Comp/Sales | | | | | | | 3.3 | 2.7 |
| | | | | | | | (10) 9.0 | (10) 15.6 |
| | | | | | | | 15.2 | 25.9 |
| Net Sales ($) | 2114M | 8014M | 92417M | 508459M | 135537M | 749630M | 2824851M | 2695775M |
| Total Assets ($) | 662M | 6016M | 81081M | 558939M | 499533M | 1699603M | 2968794M | 4184720M |

M = $ thousand    MM = $ million
See Pages 9 through 22 for Explanation of Ratios and Data

## Comparative Historical Data | Current Data Sorted by Sales

| 4/1/09-3/31/10 ALL | 4/1/10-3/31/11 ALL | 4/1/11-3/31/12 ALL | Type of Statement | 0-1MM | 1-3MM | 3-5MM | 5-10MM | 10-25MM | 25MM & OVER |
|---|---|---|---|---|---|---|---|---|---|
| 25 | 25 | 26 | Unqualified | | 4 | 3 | 3 | 6 | 10 |
| | 1 | 2 | Reviewed | | | | | 1 | 1 |
| 3 | 4 | 1 | Compiled | | | | | 1 | |
| 10 | 7 | 4 | Tax Returns | 1 | 2 | | | | 1 |
| 19 | 23 | 29 | Other | 5 | 4 | 3 | 5 | 7 | 5 |
| | | | | | 6 (4/1-9/30/11) | | 56 (10/1/11-3/31/12) | | |
| 57 | 60 | 62 | **NUMBER OF STATEMENTS** | 6 | 10 | 6 | 8 | 15 | 17 |
| % | % | % | **ASSETS** | % | % | % | % | % | % |
| 48.5 | 51.1 | 50.1 | Cash & Equivalents | | 47.6 | | | 58.7 | 46.7 |
| 8.7 | 11.6 | 13.7 | Trade Receivables (net) | | 17.0 | | | 10.0 | 17.4 |
| .8 | .6 | .0 | Inventory | | .0 | | | .0 | .1 |
| 5.0 | 5.8 | 4.9 | All Other Current | | 1.0 | | | 7.5 | 1.3 |
| 63.0 | 69.1 | 68.7 | Total Current | | 65.6 | | | 76.2 | 65.6 |
| 3.8 | 5.7 | 2.9 | Fixed Assets (net) | | 6.0 | | | 1.3 | 4.3 |
| 10.5 | 5.6 | 5.8 | Intangibles (net) | | 7.4 | | | 3.4 | 8.6 |
| 22.7 | 19.7 | 22.5 | All Other Non-Current | | 20.9 | | | 19.2 | 21.6 |
| 100.0 | 100.0 | 100.0 | Total | | 100.0 | | | 100.0 | 100.0 |
| | | | **LIABILITIES** | | | | | | |
| 10.6 | 4.9 | 3.2 | Notes Payable-Short Term | | .0 | | | 5.0 | 2.3 |
| 2.0 | .4 | .7 | Cur. Mat.-L.T.D. | | 2.2 | | | .2 | 1.0 |
| 10.2 | 12.3 | 12.3 | Trade Payables | | 23.2 | | | 11.5 | 17.0 |
| .6 | .1 | .5 | Income Taxes Payable | | .0 | | | .9 | .9 |
| 28.2 | 31.0 | 29.4 | All Other Current | | 28.7 | | | 30.0 | 22.7 |
| 51.5 | 48.7 | 46.1 | Total Current | | 54.2 | | | 47.6 | 43.9 |
| 5.4 | 7.0 | 5.9 | Long-Term Debt | | 5.5 | | | .5 | 4.8 |
| .7 | .6 | .6 | Deferred Taxes | | .1 | | | 1.6 | .7 |
| 13.0 | 6.4 | 11.3 | All Other Non-Current | | 14.8 | | | 16.5 | 9.7 |
| 29.4 | 37.4 | 36.1 | Net Worth | | 25.4 | | | 33.8 | 40.9 |
| 100.0 | 100.0 | 100.0 | Total Liabilities & Net Worth | | 100.0 | | | 100.0 | 100.0 |
| | | | **INCOME DATA** | | | | | | |
| 100.0 | 100.0 | 100.0 | Net Sales | | 100.0 | | | 100.0 | 100.0 |
| | | | Gross Profit | | | | | | |
| 89.3 | 86.8 | 90.5 | Operating Expenses | | 96.8 | | | 85.8 | 97.9 |
| 10.7 | 13.2 | 9.5 | Operating Profit | | 3.2 | | | 14.2 | 2.1 |
| .1 | -.2 | -1.0 | All Other Expenses (net) | | -2.2 | | | -2.9 | -1.4 |
| 10.7 | 13.3 | 10.5 | Profit Before Taxes | | 5.4 | | | 17.0 | 3.5 |
| | | | **RATIOS** | | | | | | |
| 2.8 / 1.5 / .9 | 2.4 / 1.5 / 1.0 | 2.7 / 1.4 / 1.0 | Current | | 1.9 / 1.1 / .7 | | | 2.6 / 1.6 / 1.1 | 2.8 / 1.4 / 1.1 |
| 2.7 / 1.4 / .7 | 2.1 / 1.4 / .9 | 2.5 / 1.3 / .8 | Quick | | 1.9 / 1.1 / .7 | | | 2.4 / 1.6 / .7 | 2.7 / 1.3 / 1.0 |
| 0 UND / 7 50.6 / 43 8.5 | 0 867.6 / 15 24.7 / 48 7.6 | 0 835.8 / 28 13.1 / 81 4.5 | Sales/Receivables | | 9 40.8 / 53 6.9 / 107 3.4 | | | 0 UND / 29 12.8 / 57 6.4 | 14 26.9 / 58 6.3 / 107 3.4 |
| | | | Cost of Sales/Inventory | | | | | | |
| | | | Cost of Sales/Payables | | | | | | |
| 1.7 / 6.6 / -20.7 | 1.7 / 7.7 / 97.1 | 1.1 / 5.5 / -61.4 | Sales/Working Capital | | 3.3 / 8.1 / -7.3 | | | .6 / 3.9 / 27.4 | 1.6 / 4.1 / 20.3 |
| 31.2 / (26) 7.8 / .4 | 40.5 / (30) 9.7 / 2.0 | 20.1 / (24) 4.4 / -1.9 | EBIT/Interest | | | | | (10) | 20.5 / 10.1 / -1.9 |
| | | | Net Profit + Depr., Dep., Amort./Cur. Mat. L/T/D | | | | | | |
| .0 / .0 / .2 | .0 / .0 / .3 | .0 / .0 / .2 | Fixed/Worth | | .0 / .1 / NM | | | .0 / .0 / .1 | .0 / .1 / .2 |
| .8 / 2.7 / 9.8 | .9 / 2.1 / 10.5 | 1.3 / 2.6 / 6.4 | Debt/Worth | | 1.4 / 3.8 / -46.3 | | | .6 / 3.8 / 4.7 | 1.0 / 2.4 / 4.1 |
| 53.1 / (48) 13.8 / 1.4 | 41.9 / (53) 13.8 / 3.8 | 45.7 / (54) 14.4 / -5.0 | % Profit Before Taxes/Tangible Net Worth | | | | | 122.5 / (13) 16.7 / 2.4 | 17.9 / (15) 10.8 / -14.0 |
| 18.5 / 4.3 / .1 | 11.5 / 5.6 / .6 | 11.2 / 3.4 / -2.7 | % Profit Before Taxes/Total Assets | | 10.6 / 3.0 / -3.1 | | | 20.8 / 6.6 / .5 | 8.6 / 2.7 / -3.5 |
| UND / 164.0 / 26.6 | UND / 254.3 / 25.6 | UND / 144.5 / 33.5 | Sales/Net Fixed Assets | | UND / 389.0 / 21.8 | | | UND / 231.6 / 41.0 | 99.6 / 51.4 / 16.1 |
| 2.3 / .7 / .4 | 2.6 / .7 / .3 | 1.4 / .6 / .3 | Sales/Total Assets | | 1.3 / .6 / .3 | | | 1.7 / .5 / .2 | 1.6 / .8 / .3 |
| .3 / (21) .9 / 1.8 | .3 / (24) .6 / 1.9 | .3 / (24) .9 / 1.9 | % Depr., Dep., Amort./Sales | | | | | | |
| | 2.5 / (10) 8.6 / 18.6 | | % Officers', Directors' Owners' Comp/Sales | | | | | | |
| 2398420M | 3035917M | 1496171M | Net Sales ($) | 3376M | 22571M | 26371M | 58671M | 289026M | 1096156M |
| 3127302M | 3831212M | 2845834M | Total Assets ($) | 6026M | 53951M | 82635M | 309504M | 835452M | 1558266M |

M = $ thousand     MM = $ million
See Pages 9 through 22 for Explanation of Ratios and Data

## Current Data Sorted by Assets | Comparative Historical Data

| | | | | | | Type of Statement | | |
|---|---|---|---|---|---|---|---|---|
| | 2 | 30 | 38 | 13 | 19 | Unqualified | 100 | 101 |
| 2 | 18 | 33 | 26 | 2 | | Reviewed | 111 | 98 |
| 18 | 43 | 28 | 6 | 2 | | Compiled | 100 | 98 |
| 151 | 97 | 49 | 2 | 1 | 1 | Tax Returns | 242 | 250 |
| 81 | 72 | 87 | 46 | 12 | 20 | Other | 297 | 309 |
| | 97 (4/1-9/30/11) | | | 800 (10/1/11-3/31/12) | | | 4/1/07- 3/31/08 | 4/1/08- 3/31/09 |
| 0-500M | 500M-2MM | 2-10MM | 10-50MM | 50-100MM | 100-250MM | | ALL | ALL |
| 252 | 232 | 227 | 118 | 28 | 40 | NUMBER OF STATEMENTS | 850 | 856 |
| % | % | % | % | % | % | ASSETS | % | % |
| 34.8 | 23.6 | 28.5 | 30.7 | 34.6 | 34.1 | Cash & Equivalents | 30.6 | 29.6 |
| 8.2 | 16.1 | 23.2 | 18.2 | 21.8 | 10.9 | Trade Receivables (net) | 17.9 | 18.3 |
| .0 | .0 | .4 | .2 | .0 | .2 | Inventory | .2 | .1 |
| 4.4 | 4.9 | 4.3 | 6.9 | 7.5 | 6.7 | All Other Current | 5.7 | 6.2 |
| 47.4 | 44.5 | 56.4 | 55.9 | 63.9 | 51.9 | Total Current | 54.5 | 54.2 |
| 21.7 | 15.8 | 11.7 | 8.8 | 5.9 | 5.0 | Fixed Assets (net) | 13.6 | 14.1 |
| 17.5 | 24.2 | 18.7 | 16.6 | 14.9 | 17.0 | Intangibles (net) | 17.5 | 17.8 |
| 13.4 | 15.4 | 13.2 | 18.7 | 15.3 | 26.1 | All Other Non-Current | 14.4 | 13.9 |
| 100.0 | 100.0 | 100.0 | 100.0 | 100.0 | 100.0 | Total | 100.0 | 100.0 |
| | | | | | | LIABILITIES | | |
| 24.8 | 9.2 | 5.6 | 3.4 | .9 | 6.1 | Notes Payable-Short Term | 9.6 | 10.5 |
| 4.1 | 4.2 | 2.7 | 2.2 | 1.6 | .9 | Cur. Mat.-L.T.D. | 4.1 | 3.3 |
| 16.2 | 17.5 | 23.7 | 19.2 | 19.7 | 11.5 | Trade Payables | 20.6 | 20.0 |
| .3 | .1 | .1 | .4 | .4 | .3 | Income Taxes Payable | .7 | .3 |
| 14.9 | 13.9 | 15.5 | 28.3 | 35.8 | 26.9 | All Other Current | 18.5 | 20.5 |
| 60.3 | 44.9 | 47.7 | 53.6 | 58.4 | 45.8 | Total Current | 53.5 | 54.6 |
| 25.6 | 28.1 | 16.9 | 9.9 | 11.5 | 12.7 | Long-Term Debt | 21.1 | 20.5 |
| .0 | .1 | .1 | .4 | .2 | .7 | Deferred Taxes | .2 | .2 |
| 11.6 | 8.0 | 5.9 | 6.6 | 10.9 | 6.2 | All Other Non-Current | 6.0 | 6.9 |
| 2.5 | 18.9 | 29.4 | 29.5 | 18.9 | 34.5 | Net Worth | 19.2 | 17.8 |
| 100.0 | 100.0 | 100.0 | 100.0 | 100.0 | 100.0 | Total Liabilties & Net Worth | 100.0 | 100.0 |
| | | | | | | INCOME DATA | | |
| 100.0 | 100.0 | 100.0 | 100.0 | 100.0 | 100.0 | Net Sales | 100.0 | 100.0 |
| | | | | | | Gross Profit | | |
| 87.3 | 89.8 | 88.0 | 89.0 | 85.9 | 84.3 | Operating Expenses | 87.3 | 89.3 |
| 12.7 | 10.2 | 12.0 | 11.0 | 14.1 | 15.7 | Operating Profit | 12.7 | 10.7 |
| 1.3 | 3.0 | 2.8 | .4 | 2.8 | 2.9 | All Other Expenses (net) | 1.6 | 2.1 |
| 11.4 | 7.2 | 9.2 | 10.7 | 11.2 | 12.8 | Profit Before Taxes | 11.0 | 8.6 |
| | | | | | | RATIOS | | |
| 2.6 | 1.8 | 1.6 | 1.3 | 1.6 | 1.8 | | 1.7 | 1.7 |
| .9 | 1.0 | 1.1 | 1.1 | 1.1 | 1.1 | Current | 1.1 | 1.1 |
| .4 | .5 | .8 | .8 | .9 | .9 | | .7 | .6 |
| 2.4 | 1.5 | 1.5 | 1.2 | 1.5 | 1.7 | | 1.5 | 1.5 |
| .9 | .9 | 1.0 | 1.0 | 1.0 | 1.1 | Quick | (849) 1.0 | 1.0 |
| .3 | .4 | .7 | .6 | .6 | .6 | | .5 | .5 |
| 0 UND | 0 UND | 4 83.2 | 10 37.8 | 23 15.7 | 0 UND | | 0 UND | 0 UND |
| 0 UND | 7 52.6 | 34 10.6 | 43 8.4 | 51 7.2 | 23 15.6 | Sales/Receivables | 17 21.1 | 18 20.6 |
| 5 67.4 | 36 10.0 | 89 4.1 | 87 4.2 | 174 2.1 | 91 4.0 | | 64 5.7 | 66 5.5 |
| | | | | | | Cost of Sales/Inventory | | |
| | | | | | | Cost of Sales/Payables | | |
| 19.5 | 11.0 | 5.5 | 6.9 | 4.4 | 1.4 | | 7.7 | 8.0 |
| -317.1 | -314.5 | 29.1 | 20.1 | 38.3 | 21.6 | Sales/Working Capital | 66.6 | 97.7 |
| -13.3 | -9.8 | -14.5 | -12.1 | -11.3 | -14.5 | | -14.0 | -10.8 |
| 19.5 | 16.6 | 24.7 | 54.6 | 90.2 | 25.6 | | 23.1 | 18.3 |
| (154) 7.4 | (179) 5.2 | (161) 5.5 | (80) 10.9 | (23) 14.0 | (26) 8.1 | EBIT/Interest | (600) 5.9 | (591) 5.0 |
| 2.1 | 1.4 | 1.9 | 3.4 | 5.7 | 3.6 | | 1.6 | 1.3 |
| | 7.7 | 3.8 | 17.2 | | | Net Profit + Depr., Dep., | 9.3 | 6.9 |
| | (15) 3.4 | (23) 1.4 | (26) 4.7 | | | Amort./Cur. Mat. L/T/D | (104) 3.2 | (80) 2.1 |
| | .9 | .4 | 1.4 | | | | 1.3 | .9 |
| .1 | .1 | .1 | .1 | .0 | .0 | | .1 | .1 |
| 1.2 | 1.3 | .6 | .5 | .4 | .1 | Fixed/Worth | .7 | .6 |
| -.4 | -.4 | -.6 | 4.0 | NM | -3.8 | | -1.0 | -.8 |
| .6 | 1.8 | 1.4 | 2.2 | 2.5 | 1.3 | | 1.7 | 1.4 |
| 83.0 | 18.5 | 6.3 | 4.8 | 6.7 | 7.0 | Debt/Worth | 6.8 | 6.7 |
| -2.2 | -3.0 | -5.8 | 97.3 | NM | -15.4 | | -5.5 | -4.4 |
| 543.8 | 108.9 | 85.2 | 74.4 | 212.6 | 28.9 | % Profit Before Taxes/Tangible | 146.5 | 112.6 |
| (129) 120.0 | (125) 42.8 | (146) 26.0 | (92) 32.6 | (21) 56.1 | (29) 10.0 | Net Worth | (559) 44.7 | (552) 36.3 |
| 20.3 | 8.9 | 5.9 | 8.4 | 28.7 | 4.0 | | 10.3 | 5.9 |
| 87.9 | 26.2 | 17.1 | 14.7 | 10.7 | 7.2 | % Profit Before Taxes/Total | 26.6 | 23.3 |
| 28.1 | 7.0 | 6.2 | 7.2 | 7.6 | 3.7 | Assets | 9.6 | 6.7 |
| 3.3 | 1.0 | 1.3 | 1.8 | 2.4 | 1.3 | | 1.4 | .4 |
| 577.7 | 153.4 | 88.7 | 55.0 | 553.7 | 180.3 | | 101.6 | 115.7 |
| 58.7 | 40.7 | 36.6 | 23.3 | 36.7 | 42.3 | Sales/Net Fixed Assets | 29.8 | 32.7 |
| 16.9 | 13.8 | 15.9 | 10.7 | 13.8 | 17.7 | | 11.7 | 13.5 |
| 9.4 | 3.2 | 2.0 | 1.5 | 1.3 | .9 | | 3.2 | 3.5 |
| 4.6 | 1.9 | 1.2 | .9 | .9 | .5 | Sales/Total Assets | 1.6 | 1.7 |
| 2.6 | 1.0 | .8 | .5 | .6 | .3 | | .8 | .8 |
| .5 | .7 | .7 | 1.2 | 1.1 | .4 | | .8 | .8 |
| (116) .9 | (123) 1.6 | (143) 1.2 | (81) 1.8 | (17) 2.0 | (20) 1.3 | % Depr., Dep., Amort./Sales | (519) 1.6 | (487) 1.4 |
| 2.2 | 3.9 | 2.1 | 2.7 | 2.9 | 1.5 | | 2.9 | 2.7 |
| 9.9 | 7.4 | 5.5 | 4.4 | | | % Officers', Directors' | 8.2 | 6.6 |
| (165) 16.8 | (135) 11.7 | (77) 13.4 | (19) 6.8 | | | Owners' Comp/Sales | (365) 14.1 | (371) 13.7 |
| 27.1 | 19.6 | 21.6 | 21.0 | | | | 22.2 | 22.7 |
| 317036M | 613413M | 1819275M | 2851006M | 3218100M | 7142699M | Net Sales ($) | 12287714M | 11552528M |
| 54827M | 245101M | 1095406M | 2775751M | 2013040M | 6598031M | Total Assets ($) | 12645205M | 11639528M |

© RMA 2012

## Comparative Historical Data | Current Data Sorted by Sales

| Type of Statement | | | | | 0-1MM | 1-3MM | 3-5MM | 5-10MM | 10-25MM | 25MM & OVER |
|---|---|---|---|---|---|---|---|---|---|---|
| Unqualified | 107 | 119 | 102 | | 3 | 6 | 11 | 10 | 23 | 49 |
| Reviewed | 92 | 93 | 81 | | 7 | 10 | 15 | 16 | 22 | 11 |
| Compiled | 106 | 98 | 95 | | 17 | 29 | 19 | 19 | 6 | 5 |
| Tax Returns | 262 | 255 | 301 | | 132 | 99 | 31 | 30 | 5 | 4 |
| Other | 312 | 313 | 318 | | 68 | 85 | 33 | 46 | 32 | 54 |
| | 4/1/09-3/31/10 ALL | 4/1/10-3/31/11 ALL | 4/1/11-3/31/12 ALL | | 97 (4/1-9/30/11) | | | 800 (10/1/11-3/31/12) | | |
| NUMBER OF STATEMENTS | 879 | 878 | 897 | | 227 | 229 | 109 | 121 | 88 | 123 |
| **ASSETS** | % | % | % | | % | % | % | % | % | % |
| Cash & Equivalents | 29.7 | 28.3 | 29.7 | | 25.1 | 28.0 | 32.0 | 33.5 | 33.7 | 33.0 |
| Trade Receivables (net) | 16.9 | 15.4 | 15.9 | | 9.3 | 16.1 | 15.9 | 23.4 | 18.1 | 18.6 |
| Inventory | .2 | .3 | .1 | | .1 | .3 | .0 | .0 | .0 | .2 |
| All Other Current | 6.4 | 6.0 | 5.0 | | 3.4 | 4.9 | 4.2 | 3.8 | 7.0 | 9.0 |
| Total Current | 53.1 | 50.1 | 50.8 | | 37.8 | 49.3 | 52.1 | 60.7 | 58.7 | 60.8 |
| Fixed Assets (net) | 13.1 | 15.4 | 14.7 | | 25.0 | 14.0 | 10.6 | 8.0 | 11.8 | 9.4 |
| Intangibles (net) | 17.6 | 19.9 | 19.3 | | 21.3 | 21.8 | 22.2 | 16.4 | 13.2 | 15.8 |
| All Other Non-Current | 16.1 | 14.7 | 15.2 | | 15.9 | 15.0 | 15.1 | 14.9 | 16.2 | 14.0 |
| Total | 100.0 | 100.0 | 100.0 | | 100.0 | 100.0 | 100.0 | 100.0 | 100.0 | 100.0 |
| **LIABILITIES** | | | | | | | | | | |
| Notes Payable-Short Term | 10.4 | 11.9 | 11.5 | | 17.2 | 15.4 | 11.3 | 7.0 | 5.2 | 2.9 |
| Cur. Mat.-L.T.D. | 4.8 | 4.0 | 3.3 | | 3.7 | 4.6 | 3.0 | 2.4 | 3.0 | 1.8 |
| Trade Payables | 19.1 | 18.6 | 18.7 | | 10.4 | 22.1 | 22.4 | 23.2 | 22.7 | 17.4 |
| Income Taxes Payable | .3 | .1 | .2 | | .0 | .4 | .2 | .1 | .3 | .4 |
| All Other Current | 20.0 | 18.7 | 17.7 | | 12.2 | 14.8 | 15.0 | 19.9 | 25.1 | 28.6 |
| Total Current | 54.5 | 53.2 | 51.5 | | 43.5 | 57.3 | 51.8 | 52.6 | 56.3 | 51.0 |
| Long-Term Debt | 19.5 | 22.0 | 21.0 | | 36.7 | 23.1 | 13.3 | 12.3 | 10.8 | 10.6 |
| Deferred Taxes | .1 | .3 | .1 | | .0 | .0 | .1 | .2 | .4 | .4 |
| All Other Non-Current | 7.6 | 7.3 | 8.3 | | 9.9 | 9.8 | 8.7 | 5.5 | 4.4 | 7.8 |
| Net Worth | 18.2 | 17.2 | 19.0 | | 9.8 | 9.8 | 26.1 | 29.5 | 28.1 | 30.1 |
| Total Liabilities & Net Worth | 100.0 | 100.0 | 100.0 | | 100.0 | 100.0 | 100.0 | 100.0 | 100.0 | 100.0 |
| **INCOME DATA** | | | | | | | | | | |
| Net Sales | 100.0 | 100.0 | 100.0 | | 100.0 | 100.0 | 100.0 | 100.0 | 100.0 | 100.0 |
| Gross Profit | | | | | | | | | | |
| Operating Expenses | 88.1 | 89.1 | 88.2 | | 82.7 | 89.5 | 91.6 | 88.9 | 89.9 | 90.7 |
| Operating Profit | 11.9 | 10.9 | 11.8 | | 17.3 | 10.5 | 8.4 | 11.1 | 10.1 | 9.3 |
| All Other Expenses (net) | 2.3 | 2.0 | 2.1 | | 5.7 | .9 | 1.6 | 1.4 | -.1 | .6 |
| Profit Before Taxes | 9.5 | 8.9 | 9.7 | | 11.6 | 9.7 | 6.8 | 9.7 | 10.2 | 8.8 |
| **RATIOS** | | | | | | | | | | |
| Current | 1.7 | 1.7 | 1.7 | | 2.4 | 1.9 | 1.4 | 1.7 | 1.5 | 1.5 |
| | 1.0 | 1.0 | 1.0 | | 1.0 | 1.0 | 1.0 | 1.1 | 1.1 | 1.2 |
| | .6 | .6 | .6 | | .3 | .4 | .7 | .8 | .8 | .9 |
| Quick | 1.6 | 1.5 | 1.6 | | 2.2 | 1.6 | 1.4 | 1.6 | 1.4 | 1.3 |
| | .9 | .9 | 1.0 | | .9 | .9 | 1.0 | 1.0 | 1.0 | 1.0 |
| | .4 | .4 | .5 | | .3 | .3 | .5 | .7 | .7 | .7 |
| Sales/Receivables | 0 UND | 0 UND | 0 UND | | 0 UND | 0 UND | 0 UND | 2 171.3 | 2 196.9 | 10 35.3 |
| | 17 21.6 | 13 27.9 | 13 28.8 | | 0 UND | 7 49.5 | 18 20.0 | 35 10.3 | 23 16.0 | 36 10.0 |
| | 59 6.2 | 53 6.9 | 51 7.1 | | 11 33.6 | 43 8.5 | 45 8.1 | 81 4.5 | 54 6.7 | 78 4.7 |
| Cost of Sales/Inventory | | | | | | | | | | |
| Cost of Sales/Payables | | | | | | | | | | |
| Sales/Working Capital | 7.3 | 9.4 | 9.8 | | 11.6 | 12.2 | 12.0 | 5.2 | 7.3 | 7.9 |
| | 83.8 | 118.3 | 116.4 | | -177.0 | -296.8 | 185.1 | 41.0 | 26.1 | 24.4 |
| | -10.2 | -11.1 | -12.3 | | -9.2 | -9.5 | -14.8 | -18.5 | -19.1 | -25.2 |
| EBIT/Interest | 25.5 | 21.7 | 24.3 | | 14.4 | 18.2 | 20.1 | 27.8 | 57.8 | 62.8 |
| | (624) 6.0 | (624) 5.7 | (623) 7.0 | | (137) 4.0 | (165) 5.4 | (79) 5.5 | (87) 8.9 | (64) 10.5 | (91) 10.7 |
| | 1.8 | 1.7 | 2.0 | | 1.4 | 1.5 | 2.8 | 2.1 | 3.1 | 3.7 |
| Net Profit + Depr., Dep., Amort./Cur. Mat. L/T/D | 8.0 | 9.6 | 13.6 | | | 9.8 | | 1.8 | 9.0 | 20.2 |
| | (98) 1.9 | (96) 2.6 | (84) 2.6 | | | (10) 2.4 | | (11) .9 | (16) 2.3 | (34) 13.5 |
| | .8 | .7 | 1.0 | | | .8 | | -2.1 | 1.0 | 2.1 |
| Fixed/Worth | .1 | .1 | .1 | | .0 | .1 | .1 | .1 | .1 | .1 |
| | .6 | .9 | .8 | | 1.7 | 1.0 | 2.3 | .4 | .8 | .5 |
| | -.8 | -.5 | -.6 | | -.8 | -.3 | -.3 | -.9 | -3.5 | 44.2 |
| Debt/Worth | 1.3 | 1.5 | 1.4 | | .9 | 1.5 | 1.7 | 1.1 | 2.0 | 1.5 |
| | 6.2 | 8.4 | 8.8 | | 34.3 | 27.6 | 19.8 | 5.9 | 4.7 | 4.5 |
| | -4.4 | -3.3 | -3.6 | | -2.3 | -2.3 | -3.7 | -9.0 | -25.4 | 132.2 |
| % Profit Before Taxes/Tangible Net Worth | 119.7 | 114.1 | 133.6 | | 213.0 | 173.2 | 142.5 | 80.1 | 125.0 | 101.5 |
| | (567) 31.3 | (527) 33.8 | (542) 40.5 | | (122) 47.2 | (120) 59.4 | (61) 40.4 | (83) 30.6 | (63) 43.5 | (93) 32.7 |
| | 6.3 | 7.1 | 8.4 | | 4.8 | 11.5 | 7.2 | 6.7 | 8.6 | 10.0 |
| % Profit Before Taxes/Total Assets | 21.7 | 24.6 | 28.6 | | 50.8 | 33.6 | 29.3 | 21.3 | 20.2 | 18.0 |
| | 7.1 | 7.7 | 8.3 | | 9.1 | 7.9 | 8.4 | 8.3 | 7.3 | 7.6 |
| | 1.1 | 1.6 | 1.8 | | .4 | 2.2 | .9 | 1.6 | 2.4 | 2.4 |
| Sales/Net Fixed Assets | 131.6 | 99.6 | 152.5 | | 574.0 | 213.7 | 158.0 | 128.4 | 66.5 | 78.5 |
| | 33.5 | 32.1 | 38.6 | | 35.4 | 37.2 | 51.5 | 49.6 | 33.2 | 26.0 |
| | 13.7 | 12.0 | 14.7 | | 6.5 | 14.7 | 26.8 | 22.2 | 19.2 | 11.4 |
| Sales/Total Assets | 3.2 | 3.5 | 3.6 | | 4.3 | 4.2 | 4.2 | 2.7 | 2.3 | 2.3 |
| | 1.6 | 1.6 | 1.7 | | 1.9 | 2.2 | 1.9 | 1.5 | 1.5 | 1.1 |
| | .8 | .8 | .8 | | .5 | 1.2 | 1.1 | .9 | .9 | .7 |
| % Depr., Dep., Amort./Sales | .7 | .7 | .7 | | .7 | .6 | .6 | .6 | .6 | .8 |
| | (495) 1.4 | (525) 1.6 | (500) 1.4 | | (109) 1.9 | (111) 1.4 | (62) 1.1 | (72) 1.1 | (61) 1.5 | (85) 1.5 |
| | 2.6 | 2.7 | 2.5 | | 7.0 | 2.5 | 2.0 | 1.6 | 2.0 | 2.7 |
| % Officers', Directors' Owners' Comp/Sales | 6.8 | 7.1 | 7.7 | | 10.1 | 8.0 | 7.2 | 5.6 | 2.9 | 1.5 |
| | (389) 13.4 | (391) 13.7 | (407) 14.3 | | (123) 17.5 | (137) 14.2 | (54) 13.1 | (48) 10.2 | (23) | (22) 6.0 |
| | 22.5 | 21.6 | 22.2 | | 22.5 | 22.0 | 22.1 | 17.4 | 26.6 | 15.5 |
| Net Sales ($) | 10809436M | 14802575M | 15961529M | | 115698M | 413204M | 422716M | 826504M | 1389831M | 12793576M |
| Total Assets ($) | 12505704M | 13704714M | 12782156M | | 151399M | 377989M | 302663M | 1184753M | 1775759M | 8989593M |

© RMA 2012

M = $ thousand    MM = $ million
See Pages 9 through 22 for Explanation of Ratios and Data

# FINANCE—Claims Adjusting NAICS 524291

## Current Data Sorted by Assets / Comparative Historical Data

| 0-500M | 500M-2MM | 2-10MM | 10-50MM | 50-100MM | 100-250MM | Type of Statement | 4/1/07-3/31/08 ALL | 4/1/08-3/31/09 ALL |
|---|---|---|---|---|---|---|---|---|
| | | 1 | 3 | 1 | 1 | Unqualified | 3 | 5 |
| | | 1 | | | | Reviewed | 3 | 1 |
| | 2 | | | | | Compiled | 1 | |
| 5 | 3 | 1 | | | | Tax Returns | 4 | 4 |
| 2 | 4 | 7 | | | 1 | Other | 4 | 3 |
| | | 5 (4/1-9/30/11) | 30 (10/1/11-3/31/12) | | | | | |
| 8 | 9 | 10 | 5 | 1 | 2 | NUMBER OF STATEMENTS | 15 | 13 |
| % | % | % | % | % | % | | % | % |
| | | | | | | **ASSETS** | | |
| | | 15.7 | | | | Cash & Equivalents | 27.7 | 19.8 |
| | | 52.6 | | | | Trade Receivables (net) | 20.0 | 31.4 |
| | | .0 | | | | Inventory | .0 | 1.1 |
| | | 2.8 | | | | All Other Current | 15.0 | 6.6 |
| | | 71.0 | | | | Total Current | 62.7 | 58.9 |
| | | 9.2 | | | | Fixed Assets (net) | 16.4 | 18.8 |
| | | 14.1 | | | | Intangibles (net) | 8.9 | 9.7 |
| | | 5.7 | | | | All Other Non-Current | 12.0 | 12.6 |
| | | 100.0 | | | | Total | 100.0 | 100.0 |
| | | | | | | **LIABILITIES** | | |
| | | 3.2 | | | | Notes Payable-Short Term | 13.1 | 8.8 |
| | | .8 | | | | Cur. Mat.-L.T.D. | 7.1 | 1.3 |
| | | 9.7 | | | | Trade Payables | 5.8 | 9.6 |
| | | 2.4 | | | | Income Taxes Payable | .2 | .3 |
| | | 26.3 | | | | All Other Current | 24.2 | 13.8 |
| | | 42.4 | | | | Total Current | 50.4 | 33.9 |
| | | 12.1 | | | | Long-Term Debt | 20.3 | 13.6 |
| | | .0 | | | | Deferred Taxes | .1 | .0 |
| | | 37.1 | | | | All Other Non-Current | 5.6 | 13.7 |
| | | 8.5 | | | | Net Worth | 23.6 | 38.9 |
| | | 100.0 | | | | Total Liabilities & Net Worth | 100.0 | 100.0 |
| | | | | | | **INCOME DATA** | | |
| | | 100.0 | | | | Net Sales | 100.0 | 100.0 |
| | | | | | | Gross Profit | | |
| | | 89.7 | | | | Operating Expenses | 92.7 | 90.7 |
| | | 10.3 | | | | Operating Profit | 7.3 | 9.3 |
| | | 2.0 | | | | All Other Expenses (net) | .6 | 1.3 |
| | | 8.3 | | | | Profit Before Taxes | 6.7 | 7.9 |
| | | | | | | **RATIOS** | | |
| | | 2.4 | | | | Current | 1.9 | 4.3 |
| | | 1.7 | | | | | 1.1 | 2.1 |
| | | 1.0 | | | | | 1.0 | 1.0 |
| | | 2.2 | | | | Quick | 1.9 | 4.0 |
| | | 1.6 | | | | | 1.0 | 1.6 |
| | | 1.0 | | | | | .4 | .8 |
| | | 24  15.4 | | | | Sales/Receivables | 0  UND | 19  18.9 |
| | | 40  9.2 | | | | | 27  13.5 | 31  11.6 |
| | | 79  4.6 | | | | | 33  10.9 | 43  8.5 |
| | | | | | | Cost of Sales/Inventory | | |
| | | | | | | Cost of Sales/Payables | | |
| | | 4.7 | | | | Sales/Working Capital | 8.3 | 6.5 |
| | | 16.7 | | | | | 269.4 | 11.1 |
| | | -801.7 | | | | | -209.6 | -539.2 |
| | | | | | | EBIT/Interest | 277.9 | 86.8 |
| | | | | | | | (11) 12.4 | (11) 10.7 |
| | | | | | | | 1.8 | 6.8 |
| | | | | | | Net Profit + Depr., Dep., Amort./Cur. Mat. L/T/D | | |
| | | .1 | | | | Fixed/Worth | .3 | .2 |
| | | .3 | | | | | .6 | 1.2 |
| | | .0 | | | | | -12.2 | NM |
| | | .6 | | | | Debt/Worth | .9 | .5 |
| | | 1.5 | | | | | 8.9 | 4.7 |
| | | -2.0 | | | | | -77.3 | NM |
| | | | | | | % Profit Before Taxes/Tangible Net Worth | 235.7 | 334.3 |
| | | | | | | | (11) 97.5 | (10) 48.5 |
| | | | | | | | 37.5 | 16.5 |
| | | 67.2 | | | | % Profit Before Taxes/Total Assets | 46.4 | 43.8 |
| | | 15.6 | | | | | 16.1 | 11.2 |
| | | 2.0 | | | | | 2.9 | 7.9 |
| | | 407.5 | | | | Sales/Net Fixed Assets | 78.2 | 185.7 |
| | | 68.4 | | | | | 24.0 | 21.5 |
| | | 19.5 | | | | | 15.3 | 14.8 |
| | | 7.3 | | | | Sales/Total Assets | 5.9 | 8.9 |
| | | 2.1 | | | | | 3.5 | 3.0 |
| | | 1.1 | | | | | 1.8 | 1.6 |
| | | | | | | % Depr., Dep., Amort./Sales | .5 | |
| | | | | | | | (10) 1.1 | |
| | | | | | | | 1.9 | |
| | | | | | | % Officers', Directors' Owners' Comp/Sales | | |
| 7473M | 47292M | 156549M | 138110M | 25342M | 106679M | Net Sales ($) | 146449M | 302398M |
| 2016M | 9269M | 47771M | 111859M | 50488M | 336600M | Total Assets ($) | 50411M | 135842M |

M = $ thousand     MM = $ million
See Pages 9 through 22 for Explanation of Ratios and Data

## Comparative Historical Data      Current Data Sorted by Sales

| | | | Type of Statement | | | | | | |
|---|---|---|---|---|---|---|---|---|---|
| 8 | 6 | 6 | Unqualified | | | | 2 | 2 | 2 |
| 4 | | 2 | Reviewed | | 1 | | 1 | | |
| 1 | 1 | 2 | Compiled | 1 | 1 | | | | |
| 4 | 7 | 9 | Tax Returns | 5 | | 1 | 2 | | |
| 6 | 10 | 16 | Other | 1 | 4 | 1 | 3 | 1 | 6 |
| 4/1/09-3/31/10 ALL | 4/1/10-3/31/11 ALL | 4/1/11-3/31/12 ALL | | 0-1MM | 1-3MM | 3-5MM | 5-10MM | 10-25MM | 25MM & OVER |
| | | | | | 5 (4/1-9/30/11) | | 30 (10/1/11-3/31/12) | | |
| 23 | 24 | 35 | **NUMBER OF STATEMENTS** | 7 | 6 | 2 | 8 | 4 | 8 |
| % | % | % | **ASSETS** | % | % | % | % | % | % |
| 29.2 | 29.4 | 17.8 | Cash & Equivalents | | | | | | |
| 16.6 | 23.2 | 31.0 | Trade Receivables (net) | | | | | | |
| 1.0 | .0 | .3 | Inventory | | | | | | |
| 4.1 | 13.3 | 6.8 | All Other Current | | | | | | |
| 50.9 | 66.0 | 55.9 | Total Current | | | | | | |
| 18.7 | 10.7 | 13.5 | Fixed Assets (net) | | | | | | |
| 13.5 | 11.3 | 16.8 | Intangibles (net) | | | | | | |
| 16.9 | 12.1 | 13.7 | All Other Non-Current | | | | | | |
| 100.0 | 100.0 | 100.0 | Total | | | | | | |
| | | | **LIABILITIES** | | | | | | |
| 7.0 | 5.7 | 7.1 | Notes Payable-Short Term | | | | | | |
| 1.5 | 3.2 | 1.8 | Cur. Mat.-L.T.D. | | | | | | |
| 4.9 | 5.8 | 10.7 | Trade Payables | | | | | | |
| .0 | .0 | .8 | Income Taxes Payable | | | | | | |
| 32.4 | 25.2 | 28.5 | All Other Current | | | | | | |
| 45.8 | 39.9 | 49.0 | Total Current | | | | | | |
| 12.8 | 15.0 | 13.7 | Long-Term Debt | | | | | | |
| .5 | .6 | .6 | Deferred Taxes | | | | | | |
| 19.4 | 5.3 | 12.8 | All Other Non-Current | | | | | | |
| 21.5 | 39.2 | 23.9 | Net Worth | | | | | | |
| 100.0 | 100.0 | 100.0 | Total Liabilities & Net Worth | | | | | | |
| | | | **INCOME DATA** | | | | | | |
| 100.0 | 100.0 | 100.0 | Net Sales | | | | | | |
| | | | Gross Profit | | | | | | |
| 89.3 | 90.4 | 85.4 | Operating Expenses | | | | | | |
| 10.7 | 9.6 | 14.6 | Operating Profit | | | | | | |
| 6.8 | 1.7 | 1.8 | All Other Expenses (net) | | | | | | |
| 3.9 | 7.9 | 12.8 | Profit Before Taxes | | | | | | |
| | | | **RATIOS** | | | | | | |
| 2.2 | 3.8 | 2.5 | Current | | | | | | |
| 1.2 | 1.7 | 1.3 | | | | | | | |
| .6 | 1.1 | .6 | | | | | | | |
| 1.8 | 3.2 | 1.7 | Quick | | | | | | |
| 1.0 | 1.4 | 1.0 | | | | | | | |
| .6 | .7 | .3 | | | | | | | |
| 0 UND | 0 UND | 0 UND | Sales/Receivables | | | | | | |
| 19 19.0 | 27 13.7 | 25 14.8 | | | | | | | |
| 33 11.1 | 53 6.9 | 47 7.7 | | | | | | | |
| | | | Cost of Sales/Inventory | | | | | | |
| | | | Cost of Sales/Payables | | | | | | |
| 9.9 | 5.9 | 5.5 | Sales/Working Capital | | | | | | |
| 30.8 | 14.1 | 22.2 | | | | | | | |
| -6.1 | 83.6 | -19.8 | | | | | | | |
| 66.5 | 51.4 | 31.2 | EBIT/Interest | | | | | | |
| (16) 4.9 | (16) 14.4 | (26) 7.9 | | | | | | | |
| 1.9 | 1.9 | 2.5 | | | | | | | |
| | 15.8 | | Net Profit + Depr., Dep., Amort./Cur. Mat. L/T/D | | | | | | |
| | (10) 5.5 | | | | | | | | |
| | .6 | | | | | | | | |
| .3 | .1 | .1 | Fixed/Worth | | | | | | |
| .6 | .3 | .6 | | | | | | | |
| -.2 | .8 | -.4 | | | | | | | |
| 1.0 | .5 | .9 | Debt/Worth | | | | | | |
| 3.1 | 2.0 | 4.5 | | | | | | | |
| -15.8 | 43.4 | -5.8 | | | | | | | |
| 141.0 | 80.6 | 119.3 | % Profit Before Taxes/Tangible Net Worth | | | | | | |
| (15) 19.9 | (20) 28.3 | (23) 38.1 | | | | | | | |
| 3.2 | 17.8 | 6.9 | | | | | | | |
| 26.8 | 34.1 | 34.3 | % Profit Before Taxes/Total Assets | | | | | | |
| 8.0 | 11.7 | 8.8 | | | | | | | |
| 2.8 | 3.8 | 2.3 | | | | | | | |
| 111.4 | 122.1 | 598.5 | Sales/Net Fixed Assets | | | | | | |
| 23.8 | 41.6 | 63.7 | | | | | | | |
| 13.7 | 12.0 | 14.8 | | | | | | | |
| 3.7 | 4.0 | 4.8 | Sales/Total Assets | | | | | | |
| 2.0 | 2.4 | 1.8 | | | | | | | |
| 1.1 | 1.4 | .8 | | | | | | | |
| 1.2 | .6 | .7 | % Depr., Dep., Amort./Sales | | | | | | |
| (15) 2.2 | (16) 1.1 | (13) 2.7 | | | | | | | |
| 3.3 | 1.7 | 5.2 | | | | | | | |
| | 4.0 | 2.0 | % Officers', Directors' Owners' Comp/Sales | | | | | | |
| | (10) 7.2 | (15) 9.8 | | | | | | | |
| | 15.7 | 21.0 | | | | | | | |
| 512492M | 503401M | 481445M | Net Sales ($) | 1514M | 11030M | 7784M | 63903M | 75788M | 321426M |
| 379420M | 267919M | 558003M | Total Assets ($) | 2432M | 6841M | 1101M | 43450M | 144594M | 359585M |

© RMA 2012

M = $ thousand     MM = $ million

See Pages 9 through 22 for Explanation of Ratios and Data

## Current Data Sorted by Assets        Comparative Historical Data

| 0-500M | 500M-2MM | 2-10MM | 10-50MM | 50-100MM | 100-250MM | Type of Statement | 4/1/07-3/31/08 ALL | 4/1/08-3/31/09 ALL |
|---|---|---|---|---|---|---|---|---|
| 1 | 6 | 13 | 10 | 8 | 5 | Unqualified | 20 | 33 |
|  | 2 | 1 | 1 |  |  | Reviewed | 3 | 6 |
| 7 | 1 | 3 |  |  |  | Compiled | 1 | 4 |
|  | 5 | 2 | 1 |  |  | Tax Returns | 4 | 8 |
| 2 | 8 | 15 | 10 | 4 | 2 | Other | 30 | 25 |
|  | 21 (4/1-9/30/11) | | 85 (10/1/11-3/31/12) | | | | | |
| 10 | 22 | 34 | 21 | 12 | 7 | NUMBER OF STATEMENTS | 58 | 76 |
| % | % | % | % | % | % | ASSETS | % | % |
| 37.2 | 32.2 | 24.6 | 30.7 | 23.5 |  | Cash & Equivalents | 26.6 | 32.1 |
| 6.3 | 23.4 | 17.0 | 17.4 | 28.5 |  | Trade Receivables (net) | 21.8 | 22.0 |
| .0 | .0 | 1.9 | 4.5 | .0 |  | Inventory | .2 | .2 |
| 12.0 | 5.9 | 15.6 | 9.3 | 3.3 |  | All Other Current | 7.8 | 7.0 |
| 55.5 | 61.4 | 59.1 | 61.9 | 55.2 |  | Total Current | 56.5 | 61.3 |
| 24.5 | 18.3 | 20.5 | 7.5 | 9.1 |  | Fixed Assets (net) | 13.3 | 11.6 |
| 2.9 | 11.6 | 11.0 | 15.2 | 14.7 |  | Intangibles (net) | 11.7 | 12.1 |
| 17.1 | 8.6 | 9.4 | 15.4 | 20.9 |  | All Other Non-Current | 18.5 | 15.0 |
| 100.0 | 100.0 | 100.0 | 100.0 | 100.0 |  | Total | 100.0 | 100.0 |
|  |  |  |  |  |  | LIABILITIES | | |
| 11.9 | 3.1 | 15.4 | 20.0 | 1.8 |  | Notes Payable-Short Term | 8.4 | 7.1 |
| .2 | 2.9 | 2.4 | 2.2 | .8 |  | Cur. Mat.-L.T.D. | 3.9 | 2.3 |
| 26.1 | 20.8 | 9.3 | 9.7 | 15.2 |  | Trade Payables | 18.1 | 19.1 |
| .1 | .1 | .3 | 1.3 | .0 |  | Income Taxes Payable | .3 | .3 |
| 54.0 | 29.8 | 42.1 | 18.3 | 18.1 |  | All Other Current | 25.9 | 22.9 |
| 92.3 | 56.8 | 69.4 | 51.5 | 35.9 |  | Total Current | 56.6 | 51.7 |
| 7.1 | 29.7 | 10.2 | 8.9 | 9.7 |  | Long-Term Debt | 15.0 | 12.0 |
| .0 | .6 | .5 | 1.4 | 2.0 |  | Deferred Taxes | .8 | .4 |
| 2.1 | 24.1 | 8.8 | 9.1 | 5.7 |  | All Other Non-Current | 19.4 | 9.0 |
| -1.5 | -11.1 | 11.1 | 29.0 | 46.7 |  | Net Worth | 8.1 | 27.0 |
| 100.0 | 100.0 | 100.0 | 100.0 | 100.0 |  | Total Liabilities & Net Worth | 100.0 | 100.0 |
|  |  |  |  |  |  | INCOME DATA | | |
| 100.0 | 100.0 | 100.0 | 100.0 | 100.0 |  | Net Sales | 100.0 | 100.0 |
|  |  |  |  |  |  | Gross Profit | | |
| 84.0 | 87.9 | 92.2 | 91.8 | 90.7 |  | Operating Expenses | 91.9 | 93.6 |
| 16.0 | 12.1 | 7.8 | 8.2 | 9.3 |  | Operating Profit | 8.1 | 6.4 |
| 2.9 | 1.2 | 2.5 | -.5 | 1.4 |  | All Other Expenses (net) | 1.2 | .6 |
| 13.1 | 10.9 | 5.4 | 8.7 | 7.9 |  | Profit Before Taxes | 6.9 | 5.8 |
|  |  |  |  |  |  | RATIOS | | |
| 6.7 | 1.6 | 1.7 | 2.5 | 2.2 |  | | 2.1 | 2.1 |
| 1.4 | 1.2 | 1.1 | 1.2 | 1.5 |  | Current | .9 | 1.3 |
| .3 | .9 | .7 | .9 | 1.2 |  | | .6 | 1.0 |
| 4.9 | 1.6 | 1.3 | 1.9 | 2.0 |  | | 1.9 | 1.9 |
| 1.1 | 1.2 | .9 | 1.0 | 1.3 |  | Quick | .9 | 1.2 |
| .2 | .8 | .2 | .6 | 1.1 |  | | .4 | .7 |
| 0 UND | 0 UND | 1 402.2 | 9 42.8 | 4 101.7 |  | | 6 66.2 | 7 55.9 |
| 0 UND | 16 22.8 | 14 26.6 | 24 15.1 | 27 13.6 |  | Sales/Receivables | 25 14.6 | 30 12.0 |
| 1 599.3 | 36 10.0 | 30 12.1 | 61 6.0 | 104 3.5 |  | | 45 8.2 | 47 7.7 |
|  |  |  |  |  |  | Cost of Sales/Inventory | | |
|  |  |  |  |  |  | Cost of Sales/Payables | | |
| 11.5 | 17.6 | 12.4 | 3.5 | 3.5 |  | | 8.1 | 6.0 |
| NM | 99.3 | 36.2 | 12.7 | 5.6 |  | Sales/Working Capital | -42.6 | 25.1 |
| -19.6 | -37.1 | -16.0 | -75.4 | 48.6 |  | | -8.8 | -63.5 |
|  | 89.5 | 52.0 | 12.7 |  |  | | 26.0 | 37.8 |
|  | (14) 8.7 | (27) 7.6 | (16) 8.6 |  |  | EBIT/Interest | (42) 4.7 | (52) 4.7 |
|  | 5.2 | 1.4 | 4.4 |  |  | | 1.7 | .8 |
|  |  |  |  |  |  | | 22.0 | 5.0 |
|  |  |  |  |  |  | Net Profit + Depr., Dep., Amort./Cur. Mat. L/T/D | (12) 5.6 | (11) 3.2 |
|  |  |  |  |  |  | | 1.8 | 1.4 |
| .0 | .0 | .3 | .0 | .1 |  | | .1 | .1 |
| .6 | -2.4 | .8 | .3 | .3 |  | Fixed/Worth | .5 | .5 |
| UND | -.4 | NM | NM | 1.6 |  | | -1.1 | -6.5 |
| .4 | 2.0 | 1.5 | 1.8 | .8 |  | | 1.3 | 1.1 |
| 2.0 | -31.4 | 3.9 | 4.0 | 1.3 |  | Debt/Worth | 10.6 | 5.1 |
| -1.8 | -3.9 | -25.5 | -20.4 | 19.7 |  | | -3.9 | -17.4 |
|  |  | 107.9 | 50.5 | 84.2 |  | % Profit Before Taxes/Tangible Net Worth | 83.9 | 98.5 |
|  | (25) 36.0 | (15) 23.3 | (10) 24.5 |  |  | | (34) 43.7 | (53) 38.2 |
|  |  | 3.0 | 7.3 | 9.2 |  | | 14.9 | 9.7 |
| 118.0 | 31.3 | 38.4 | 10.9 | 13.3 |  | % Profit Before Taxes/Total Assets | 27.3 | 22.0 |
| 21.0 | 13.9 | 6.8 | 7.5 | 6.0 |  | | 13.1 | 6.7 |
| -4.1 | 6.0 | .5 | 3.0 | 2.5 |  | | 1.6 | -.6 |
| UND | 415.1 | 100.6 | 706.1 | 28.4 |  | | 138.6 | 170.8 |
| 91.2 | 40.8 | 22.1 | 31.3 | 11.4 |  | Sales/Net Fixed Assets | 25.2 | 31.0 |
| 12.0 | 16.0 | 9.2 | 14.1 | 6.1 |  | | 13.3 | 13.3 |
| 23.9 | 5.6 | 4.5 | 2.0 | 1.8 |  | | 4.4 | 4.0 |
| 7.3 | 3.6 | 2.1 | 1.7 | 1.2 |  | Sales/Total Assets | 2.4 | 2.2 |
| 4.5 | 1.5 | 1.1 | .8 | .7 |  | | 1.2 | .9 |
|  | .2 | .6 | 1.0 | 1.3 |  | | .6 | .6 |
|  | (15) 1.4 | (30) 1.8 | (14) 2.2 | (10) 2.1 |  | % Depr., Dep., Amort./Sales | (41) 1.8 | (48) 1.3 |
|  | 2.6 | 2.7 | 3.2 | 6.5 |  | | 3.4 | 2.6 |
|  |  |  |  |  |  | | | 3.8 |
|  |  |  |  |  |  | % Officers', Directors' Owners' Comp/Sales | | (16) 6.5 |
|  |  |  |  |  |  | | | 11.6 |
| 29368M | 189009M | 454914M | 978213M | 1209295M | 1181895M | Net Sales ($) | 3009437M | 2976965M |
| 2304M | 25979M | 150383M | 476398M | 779829M | 1014629M | Total Assets ($) | 1564872M | 1710346M |

M = $ thousand    MM = $ million
See Pages 9 through 22 for Explanation of Ratios and Data

## Comparative Historical Data — Current Data Sorted by Sales

| Hist 4/1/09-3/31/10 ALL | Hist 4/1/10-3/31/11 ALL | Hist 4/1/11-3/31/12 ALL | Type of Statement | 0-1MM | 1-3MM | 3-5MM | 5-10MM | 10-25MM | 25MM & OVER |
|---|---|---|---|---|---|---|---|---|---|
| 40 | 41 | 43 | Unqualified | 1 | 4 | 4 | 3 | 10 | 21 |
| 2 | 4 | 3 | Reviewed | 1 | 2 | | | 1 | |
| 4 | 5 | 4 | Compiled | | | | 3 | 1 | |
| 13 | 10 | 15 | Tax Returns | 6 | 4 | 4 | 1 | | |
| 40 | 48 | 41 | Other | 3 | 4 | 1 | 9 | 9 | 15 |
| | | | | 21 (4/1-9/30/11) | | | 85 (10/1/11-3/31/12) | | |
| 99 | 108 | 106 | NUMBER OF STATEMENTS | 11 | 12 | 11 | 16 | 20 | 36 |
| % | % | % | **ASSETS** | % | % | % | % | % | % |
| 27.5 | 28.9 | 29.1 | Cash & Equivalents | 31.4 | 46.8 | 32.7 | 22.7 | 26.2 | 25.7 |
| 17.3 | 14.9 | 18.6 | Trade Receivables (net) | 11.3 | 6.4 | 12.7 | 17.5 | 20.7 | 26.0 |
| 1.3 | .1 | 1.5 | Inventory | .0 | 5.5 | 7.9 | .0 | .3 | .0 |
| 8.2 | 7.1 | 9.8 | All Other Current | 7.1 | 5.3 | 15.0 | 18.8 | 9.6 | 6.5 |
| 54.2 | 51.0 | 58.9 | Total Current | 49.7 | 64.0 | 68.3 | 59.0 | 56.8 | 58.3 |
| 19.1 | 17.7 | 15.5 | Fixed Assets (net) | 35.3 | 16.2 | 11.5 | 22.5 | 11.9 | 9.3 |
| 14.6 | 16.6 | 12.0 | Intangibles (net) | 2.1 | 10.1 | 11.4 | 5.4 | 13.6 | 17.8 |
| 12.0 | 14.7 | 13.6 | All Other Non-Current | 12.8 | 9.7 | 8.8 | 13.2 | 17.8 | 14.6 |
| 100.0 | 100.0 | 100.0 | Total | 100.0 | 100.0 | 100.0 | 100.0 | 100.0 | 100.0 |
| | | | **LIABILITIES** | | | | | | |
| 6.2 | 10.7 | 11.2 | Notes Payable-Short Term | 16.9 | 14.5 | 8.2 | 6.7 | 7.4 | 13.4 |
| 3.9 | 2.8 | 2.0 | Cur. Mat.-L.T.D. | .4 | .0 | 5.0 | 1.8 | 3.1 | 1.6 |
| 11.9 | 14.1 | 14.4 | Trade Payables | 26.5 | 1.3 | 9.4 | 19.2 | 9.8 | 17.2 |
| .4 | .5 | .4 | Income Taxes Payable | .0 | .1 | .2 | .0 | .5 | .8 |
| 26.5 | 23.3 | 31.8 | All Other Current | 28.5 | 24.3 | 44.5 | 51.1 | 27.9 | 24.9 |
| 48.9 | 51.4 | 59.8 | Total Current | 72.3 | 40.2 | 67.3 | 78.8 | 48.7 | 57.9 |
| 16.3 | 13.9 | 13.5 | Long-Term Debt | 26.0 | 10.1 | 2.8 | 28.5 | 9.3 | 9.8 |
| .4 | .8 | .9 | Deferred Taxes | .0 | .0 | 1.3 | .0 | 1.1 | 1.6 |
| 10.7 | 10.0 | 11.5 | All Other Non-Current | .0 | 17.2 | 3.4 | 29.3 | 11.4 | 7.7 |
| 23.7 | 23.9 | 14.4 | Net Worth | 1.7 | 32.6 | 25.2 | -36.6 | 29.4 | 23.1 |
| 100.0 | 100.0 | 100.0 | Total Liabilities & Net Worth | 100.0 | 100.0 | 100.0 | 100.0 | 100.0 | 100.0 |
| | | | **INCOME DATA** | | | | | | |
| 100.0 | 100.0 | 100.0 | Net Sales | 100.0 | 100.0 | 100.0 | 100.0 | 100.0 | 100.0 |
| | | | Gross Profit | | | | | | |
| 88.2 | 89.6 | 90.6 | Operating Expenses | 73.1 | 94.9 | 84.9 | 92.2 | 92.3 | 94.7 |
| 11.8 | 10.4 | 9.4 | Operating Profit | 26.9 | 5.1 | 15.1 | 7.8 | 7.7 | 5.3 |
| 1.6 | 1.0 | 1.3 | All Other Expenses (net) | 5.9 | 1.7 | -.6 | .3 | 1.4 | .8 |
| 10.2 | 9.4 | 8.1 | Profit Before Taxes | 20.9 | 3.5 | 15.7 | 7.5 | 6.4 | 4.6 |
| | | | **RATIOS** | | | | | | |
| 2.2 | 2.0 | 1.9 | Current | 1.9 | 5.4 | 1.2 | 1.3 | 1.9 | 2.1 |
| 1.2 | 1.1 | 1.2 | | 1.2 | 1.5 | 1.0 | 1.0 | 1.4 | 1.3 |
| .7 | .7 | .9 | | .5 | 1.2 | .9 | .4 | 1.1 | 1.0 |
| 1.8 | 1.7 | 1.7 | Quick | 1.9 | 5.4 | 1.0 | 1.3 | 1.6 | 1.9 |
| 1.0 | 1.0 | 1.1 | | 1.2 | 1.5 | .8 | .4 | 1.2 | 1.1 |
| .6 | .6 | .5 | | .1 | 1.0 | .4 | .2 | .7 | .8 |
| 1  583.8 | 1  552.0 | 1  340.6 | Sales/Receivables | 0  UND | 0  UND | 0  UND | 0  UND | 3  116.6 | 14  25.6 |
| 17  21.3 | 17  21.4 | 15  23.7 | | 0  UND | 0  UND | 3  116.5 | 14  26.3 | 15  24.1 | 30  12.2 |
| 39  9.4 | 35  10.5 | 35  10.3 | | 28  12.9 | 33  11.2 | 29  12.7 | 21  17.3 | 40  9.1 | 59  6.2 |
| | | | Cost of Sales/Inventory | | | | | | |
| | | | Cost of Sales/Payables | | | | | | |
| 5.9 | 7.4 | 6.1 | Sales/Working Capital | 8.4 | 2.0 | 18.4 | 24.2 | 7.9 | 4.8 |
| 29.0 | 39.1 | 25.0 | | 30.4 | 9.1 | -209.0 | NM | 17.3 | 15.5 |
| -15.9 | -17.5 | -37.1 | | -35.3 | 22.4 | -27.2 | -10.5 | 175.6 | NM |
| 38.6 | 52.7 | 42.2 | EBIT/Interest | | | | 40.6 | 14.4 | 34.9 |
| (77) 10.6 | (75) 8.3 | (71) 6.7 | | | | | (12) 6.9 | (15) 8.1 | (25) 6.6 |
| 2.0 | 1.8 | 3.0 | | | | | 4.8 | -2.2 | 3.4 |
| 12.7 | 24.1 | 22.3 | Net Profit + Depr., Dep., Amort./Cur. Mat. L/T/D | | | | | | |
| (17) 2.5 | (18) 3.7 | (15) 3.3 | | | | | | | |
| 1.6 | .9 | 1.1 | | | | | | | |
| .2 | .1 | .1 | Fixed/Worth | .0 | .0 | .0 | .5 | .1 | .1 |
| 1.0 | .7 | .6 | | 2.8 | .5 | 1.6 | 2.8 | .4 | .4 |
| -2.0 | -1.3 | -3.1 | | -1.1 | NM | -1.6 | -.7 | 1.5 | 3.0 |
| 1.2 | 1.0 | 1.1 | Debt/Worth | 1.1 | .9 | 2.2 | 3.5 | .9 | 1.0 |
| 4.4 | 2.9 | 4.1 | | 5.6 | 2.8 | 12.5 | NM | 2.5 | 3.5 |
| -9.8 | -4.8 | -7.9 | | -4.2 | NM | -23.3 | -2.5 | 10.7 | -12.9 |
| 115.3 | 87.4 | 73.3 | % Profit Before Taxes/Tangible Net Worth | | | | | 111.2 | 63.9 |
| (68) 35.5 | (73) 26.5 | (72) 25.5 | | | | | | (16) 30.4 | (26) 22.2 |
| 7.9 | 6.3 | 7.1 | | | | | | 8.1 | 8.1 |
| 27.9 | 19.2 | 19.6 | % Profit Before Taxes/Total Assets | 37.8 | 12.1 | 12.5 | 44.0 | 39.8 | 12.1 |
| 8.4 | 5.4 | 7.7 | | 12.9 | 3.5 | 3.4 | 23.0 | 8.8 | 6.8 |
| 2.2 | 1.3 | 1.8 | | 1.8 | .2 | -.9 | 7.8 | -3.8 | 2.2 |
| 50.5 | 84.7 | 125.0 | Sales/Net Fixed Assets | UND | UND | UND | 56.9 | 108.3 | 83.8 |
| 19.3 | 27.6 | 28.2 | | 67.7 | 59.8 | 54.2 | 15.3 | 33.2 | 26.6 |
| 9.4 | 7.8 | 10.6 | | .3 | 8.4 | 15.6 | 9.3 | 19.4 | 8.3 |
| 3.8 | 3.6 | 4.7 | Sales/Total Assets | 8.0 | 2.0 | 5.3 | 6.5 | 4.7 | 2.8 |
| 1.8 | 1.7 | 1.9 | | 1.5 | .7 | 2.3 | 3.1 | 2.6 | 1.8 |
| .8 | .9 | 1.1 | | .2 | .3 | 1.1 | 2.0 | 1.6 | 1.2 |
| .8 | .6 | .7 | % Depr., Dep., Amort./Sales | | | | 1.0 | .4 | .8 |
| (72) 1.9 | (74) 1.5 | (80) 1.6 | | | | | (13) 1.9 | (17) 1.0 | (30) 1.8 |
| 2.9 | 3.1 | 2.9 | | | | | 3.3 | 2.3 | 3.2 |
| 3.7 | 3.7 | 2.7 | % Officers', Directors' Owners' Comp/Sales | | | | | | |
| (20) 7.0 | (11) 5.7 | (16) 6.7 | | | | | | | |
| 10.2 | 7.1 | 14.1 | | | | | | | |
| 3667818M | 4949379M | 4042694M | Net Sales ($) | 5036M | 21358M | 44458M | 115092M | 349400M | 3507350M |
| 2285801M | 3822606M | 2449522M | Total Assets ($) | 6627M | 48943M | 51526M | 40438M | 238041M | 2063947M |

M = $ thousand    MM = $ million
See Pages 9 through 22 for Explanation of Ratios and Data

## Current Data Sorted by Assets — Comparative Historical Data

| | 0-500M | 500M-2MM | 2-10MM | 10-50MM | 50-100MM | 100-250MM | | 4/1/07-3/31/08 ALL | 4/1/08-3/31/09 ALL |
|---|---|---|---|---|---|---|---|---|---|
| **Type of Statement** | | | | | | | | | |
| Unqualified | | 1 | 9 | 7 | 3 | 3 | | 6 | 15 |
| Reviewed | | 1 | 1 | 1 | | | | | |
| Compiled | 4 | 2 | 2 | | | 1 | | 2 | 2 |
| Tax Returns | 4 | 3 | 2 | | | | | 4 | 4 |
| Other | 4 | 3 | 8 | 7 | 1 | 4 | | 15 | 12 |
| | 9 (4/1-9/30/11) | | | 63 (10/1/11-3/31/12) | | | | | |
| NUMBER OF STATEMENTS | 12 | 10 | 22 | 15 | 5 | 8 | | 27 | 33 |
| | % | % | % | % | % | % | | % | % |
| **ASSETS** | | | | | | | | | |
| Cash & Equivalents | 25.4 | 20.6 | 34.3 | 23.4 | | | | 26.6 | 29.9 |
| Trade Receivables (net) | 36.7 | 30.1 | 18.6 | 25.8 | | | | 28.6 | 26.2 |
| Inventory | .0 | .1 | .0 | .3 | | | | .0 | .3 |
| All Other Current | 16.9 | 4.5 | 3.4 | 5.1 | | | | 11.1 | 7.3 |
| Total Current | 78.9 | 55.3 | 56.4 | 54.6 | | | | 66.4 | 63.8 |
| Fixed Assets (net) | 10.4 | 24.5 | 15.0 | 8.1 | | | | 9.8 | 13.7 |
| Intangibles (net) | .7 | 7.7 | 10.6 | 17.3 | | | | 5.7 | 10.3 |
| All Other Non-Current | 10.1 | 12.4 | 18.0 | 20.0 | | | | 18.1 | 12.3 |
| Total | 100.0 | 100.0 | 100.0 | 100.0 | | | | 100.0 | 100.0 |
| **LIABILITIES** | | | | | | | | | |
| Notes Payable-Short Term | 14.2 | 15.6 | 2.4 | 1.2 | | | | 25.6 | 18.9 |
| Cur. Mat.-L.T.D. | 7.2 | 4.1 | .7 | 3.8 | | | | 1.0 | 2.4 |
| Trade Payables | 33.3 | 5.0 | 14.9 | 16.4 | | | | 13.3 | 13.5 |
| Income Taxes Payable | .0 | .3 | .3 | .0 | | | | .3 | .5 |
| All Other Current | 47.2 | 35.7 | 27.8 | 30.5 | | | | 23.7 | 24.4 |
| Total Current | 101.9 | 60.7 | 46.1 | 52.0 | | | | 63.9 | 59.8 |
| Long-Term Debt | 26.8 | 20.3 | 10.9 | 3.9 | | | | 11.0 | 11.6 |
| Deferred Taxes | .0 | .0 | .0 | .1 | | | | .4 | .5 |
| All Other Non-Current | 41.0 | .0 | 9.3 | 9.3 | | | | 9.8 | 11.8 |
| Net Worth | -69.8 | 19.0 | 33.8 | 34.8 | | | | 14.9 | 16.5 |
| Total Liabilities & Net Worth | 100.0 | 100.0 | 100.0 | 100.0 | | | | 100.0 | 100.0 |
| **INCOME DATA** | | | | | | | | | |
| Net Sales | 100.0 | 100.0 | 100.0 | 100.0 | | | | 100.0 | 100.0 |
| Gross Profit | | | | | | | | | |
| Operating Expenses | 98.3 | 87.6 | 95.1 | 92.4 | | | | 79.8 | 87.4 |
| Operating Profit | 1.7 | 12.4 | 4.9 | 7.6 | | | | 20.2 | 12.6 |
| All Other Expenses (net) | -1.3 | 2.8 | 1.8 | .0 | | | | 1.2 | 1.8 |
| Profit Before Taxes | 3.0 | 9.6 | 3.2 | 7.6 | | | | 19.0 | 10.9 |
| **RATIOS** | | | | | | | | | |
| Current | 1.6 | 3.8 | 3.0 | 1.7 | | | | 1.8 | 2.4 |
| | 1.1 | 1.1 | 1.1 | 1.1 | | | | 1.4 | 1.4 |
| | .6 | .7 | .7 | .7 | | | | .9 | 1.1 |
| Quick | 1.6 | | 3.0 | 1.5 | | | | 1.6 | 2.3 |
| | .9 | | 1.1 | 1.0 | | | | 1.3 | 1.2 |
| | .2 | | .5 | .5 | | | | .8 | .9 |
| Sales/Receivables | 0 UND | 0 UND | 0 UND | 35 10.3 | | | | 11 33.3 | 4 81.7 |
| | 14 26.3 | 40 9.1 | 13 27.2 | 60 6.1 | | | | 36 10.0 | 29 12.7 |
| | 46 8.0 | 73 5.0 | 48 7.6 | 130 2.8 | | | | 91 4.0 | 48 7.6 |
| Cost of Sales/Inventory | | | | | | | | | |
| Cost of Sales/Payables | | | | | | | | | |
| Sales/Working Capital | 11.5 | 4.9 | 3.4 | 6.3 | | | | 3.5 | 5.2 |
| | 73.8 | 293.4 | 514.7 | 32.6 | | | | 11.6 | 16.1 |
| | -20.2 | -42.8 | -16.7 | -6.9 | | | | -93.2 | 127.2 |
| EBIT/Interest | | | 34.4 | 80.5 | | | | 31.9 | 71.9 |
| | | (10) 16.0 | | (10) 23.9 | | | | (17) 10.7 | (22) 14.7 |
| | | | 5.4 | 8.5 | | | | 7.9 | 3.0 |
| Net Profit + Depr., Dep., Amort./Cur. Mat. L/T/D | | | | | | | | | |
| Fixed/Worth | .0 | .1 | .0 | .1 | | | | .1 | .0 |
| | .7 | .4 | 1.2 | .2 | | | | .4 | .3 |
| | -.1 | 3.4 | -4.1 | 3.8 | | | | 2.1 | NM |
| Debt/Worth | 2.1 | .4 | .7 | 2.1 | | | | 1.3 | .9 |
| | -4.3 | 2.4 | 13.4 | 5.0 | | | | 1.7 | 1.9 |
| | -1.8 | NM | -23.5 | 10.5 | | | | 26.6 | NM |
| % Profit Before Taxes/Tangible Net Worth | | | 235.7 | 127.8 | | | | 221.0 | 72.8 |
| | | (16) 32.4 | | (12) 37.9 | | | | (22) 75.7 | (25) 54.3 |
| | | | -6.6 | .7 | | | | 27.3 | 15.1 |
| % Profit Before Taxes/Total Assets | 45.4 | 35.7 | 24.4 | 20.3 | | | | 32.6 | 31.3 |
| | 9.7 | 11.2 | 6.6 | 7.0 | | | | 15.5 | 11.2 |
| | -1.2 | 2.4 | -1.2 | .6 | | | | 10.2 | 3.3 |
| Sales/Net Fixed Assets | UND | 66.8 | UND | 118.9 | | | | 147.1 | 162.2 |
| | 191.7 | 30.5 | 55.6 | 44.5 | | | | 36.1 | 41.8 |
| | 42.4 | 5.2 | 7.1 | 19.0 | | | | 19.1 | 16.2 |
| Sales/Total Assets | 9.3 | 4.1 | 2.8 | 2.5 | | | | 4.0 | 4.7 |
| | 6.2 | 3.0 | 1.2 | .9 | | | | 2.3 | 2.8 |
| | 3.1 | .9 | .8 | .5 | | | | .9 | .9 |
| % Depr., Dep., Amort./Sales | | | .2 | .7 | | | | .5 | .4 |
| | | (10) 1.1 | | (10) 1.3 | | | | (17) 1.4 | (24) 1.2 |
| | | | 2.4 | 3.3 | | | | 2.1 | 2.1 |
| % Officers', Directors' Owners' Comp/Sales | | | | | | | | | |
| Net Sales ($) | 17499M | 28863M | 263170M | 567151M | 917717M | 2099351M | | 877594M | 2184549M |
| Total Assets ($) | 2976M | 10152M | 125928M | 396715M | 405398M | 1380319M | | 696595M | 1020893M |

M = $ thousand    MM = $ million
See Pages 9 through 22 for Explanation of Ratios and Data

## Comparative Historical Data | Current Data Sorted by Sales

| 4/1/09-3/31/10 ALL | 4/1/10-3/31/11 ALL | 4/1/11-3/31/12 ALL | Type of Statement | 0-1MM | 1-3MM | 3-5MM | 5-10MM | 10-25MM | 25MM & OVER |
|---|---|---|---|---|---|---|---|---|---|
| 10 | 21 | 23 | Unqualified | | 2 | 5 | 3 | 4 | 9 |
| 1 | 1 | 2 | Reviewed | | | 1 | 1 | | |
| 7 | 3 | 11 | Compiled | 2 | 5 | | | 2 | 2 |
| 5 | 8 | 9 | Tax Returns | 5 | 1 | 2 | 3 | 3 | 1 |
| 23 | 23 | 27 | Other | 2 | 4 | 2 | | | 13 |
| | | | | | 9 (4/1-9/30/11) | | 63 (10/1/11-3/31/12) | | |
| 46 | 56 | 72 | **NUMBER OF STATEMENTS** | 9 | 12 | 10 | 7 | 9 | 25 |
| % | % | % | **ASSETS** | % | % | % | % | % | % |
| 27.7 | 24.5 | 25.4 | Cash & Equivalents | | 17.6 | 43.0 | | | 21.3 |
| 23.1 | 22.3 | 25.4 | Trade Receivables (net) | | 43.4 | 10.1 | | | 26.0 |
| .1 | .3 | .1 | Inventory | | .1 | .0 | | | .2 |
| 8.6 | 9.5 | 8.1 | All Other Current | | 2.8 | 2.1 | | | 9.4 |
| 59.5 | 56.7 | 59.0 | Total Current | | 63.8 | 55.2 | | | 56.9 |
| 11.5 | 12.5 | 13.2 | Fixed Assets (net) | | 14.9 | 13.2 | | | 11.6 |
| 16.5 | 14.1 | 13.0 | Intangibles (net) | | 7.1 | 16.9 | | | 22.5 |
| 12.5 | 16.7 | 14.8 | All Other Non-Current | | 14.3 | 14.6 | | | 8.9 |
| 100.0 | 100.0 | 100.0 | Total | | 100.0 | 100.0 | | | 100.0 |
| | | | **LIABILITIES** | | | | | | |
| 10.4 | 11.9 | 5.5 | Notes Payable-Short Term | | 6.9 | 15.7 | | | .1 |
| 1.9 | 2.9 | 3.0 | Cur. Mat.-L.T.D. | | 6.3 | 2.2 | | | 2.9 |
| 12.8 | 9.6 | 17.0 | Trade Payables | | 33.5 | 5.2 | | | 18.6 |
| .6 | .3 | .2 | Income Taxes Payable | | .2 | .0 | | | .1 |
| 20.9 | 20.8 | 31.8 | All Other Current | | 20.4 | 34.2 | | | 23.7 |
| 46.7 | 45.5 | 57.4 | Total Current | | 67.3 | 57.3 | | | 45.4 |
| 12.2 | 18.1 | 15.2 | Long-Term Debt | | 25.1 | 8.2 | | | 14.4 |
| .4 | .8 | .4 | Deferred Taxes | | .0 | .0 | | | 1.2 |
| 10.4 | 15.2 | 12.6 | All Other Non-Current | | 17.0 | .8 | | | 7.9 |
| 30.3 | 20.4 | 14.3 | Net Worth | | -9.5 | 33.6 | | | 31.1 |
| 100.0 | 100.0 | 100.0 | Total Liabilities & Net Worth | | 100.0 | 100.0 | | | 100.0 |
| | | | **INCOME DATA** | | | | | | |
| 100.0 | 100.0 | 100.0 | Net Sales | | 100.0 | 100.0 | | | 100.0 |
| | | | Gross Profit | | | | | | |
| 85.0 | 90.3 | 94.1 | Operating Expenses | | 97.4 | 96.8 | | | 93.4 |
| 15.0 | 9.7 | 5.9 | Operating Profit | | 2.6 | 3.2 | | | 6.6 |
| 1.8 | .5 | .8 | All Other Expenses (net) | | .3 | -.4 | | | .6 |
| 13.1 | 9.2 | 5.1 | Profit Before Taxes | | 2.3 | 3.6 | | | 6.0 |
| | | | **RATIOS** | | | | | | |
| 1.8 | 2.1 | 1.9 | | | 6.7 | 1.1 | | | 2.0 |
| 1.3 | 1.5 | 1.2 | Current | | 1.4 | .9 | | | 1.3 |
| .7 | .8 | .8 | | | .7 | .4 | | | .8 |
| 1.7 | 1.7 | 1.7 | | | 7.9 | 1.1 | | | 1.8 |
| 1.2 | 1.1 | (71) 1.0 | Quick | (11) 1.6 | .9 | | | | 1.2 |
| .5 | .6 | .6 | | | .6 | .3 | | | .7 |
| 8 43.7 | 4 94.6 | 0 UND | | 0 UND | 0 UND | | | | 30 12.0 |
| 35 10.3 | 24 15.3 | 35 10.3 | Sales/Receivables | 23 16.0 | 0 UND | | | | 37 9.8 |
| 49 7.5 | 46 7.9 | 60 6.1 | | 89 4.1 | 40 9.1 | | | | 51 7.1 |
| | | | Cost of Sales/Inventory | | | | | | |
| | | | Cost of Sales/Payables | | | | | | |
| 5.7 | 4.8 | 6.1 | | | 5.2 | 80.7 | | | 6.2 |
| 16.9 | 14.1 | 31.0 | Sales/Working Capital | | 17.1 | -58.0 | | | 20.0 |
| -24.1 | -40.7 | -22.1 | | | -40.6 | -9.7 | | | -29.3 |
| 54.4 | 41.0 | 37.4 | | | 33.0 | | | | 66.7 |
| (29) 3.8 | (34) 10.0 | (45) 13.8 | EBIT/Interest | (10) 17.7 | | | | (21) 18.8 |
| -5.1 | 1.2 | 2.3 | | | 5.0 | | | | 3.5 |
| | | 111.8 | Net Profit + Depr., Dep., | | | | | | |
| | | (12) 14.3 | Amort./Cur. Mat. L/T/D | | | | | | |
| | | 2.0 | | | | | | | |
| .0 | .1 | .0 | | | .0 | .1 | | | .2 |
| .3 | .5 | .5 | Fixed/Worth | | .4 | 1.8 | | | 1.9 |
| NM | -.2 | -1.1 | | | -.1 | UND | | | -.1 |
| 1.1 | .8 | 1.5 | | | .4 | 2.7 | | | 1.6 |
| 2.7 | 2.3 | 4.7 | Debt/Worth | | 1.2 | 4.7 | | | 5.1 |
| -7.4 | -4.9 | -8.6 | | | -3.1 | UND | | | -4.8 |
| 81.1 | 80.8 | 113.0 | % Profit Before Taxes/Tangible | | | | | | 122.0 |
| (34) 35.6 | (37) 37.5 | (49) 30.4 | Net Worth | | | | | (15) 64.4 |
| 6.8 | 9.1 | 2.9 | | | | | | | 21.6 |
| 20.4 | 29.9 | 23.2 | % Profit Before Taxes/Total | | 32.3 | 30.4 | | | 23.8 |
| 7.5 | 11.1 | 6.9 | Assets | | 10.5 | 6.5 | | | 14.0 |
| -.7 | 1.4 | .8 | | | 3.4 | -2.9 | | | 3.1 |
| 359.1 | 171.7 | 568.1 | | | 382.9 | UND | | | 163.5 |
| 33.9 | 36.8 | 46.8 | Sales/Net Fixed Assets | | 47.6 | 32.0 | | | 45.5 |
| 17.8 | 12.1 | 14.0 | | | 19.1 | 7.3 | | | 14.1 |
| 3.8 | 4.0 | 4.0 | | | 6.5 | -3.3 | | | 3.4 |
| 1.7 | 1.5 | 2.0 | Sales/Total Assets | | 3.0 | 1.3 | | | 2.3 |
| .4 | .6 | .8 | | | .9 | .5 | | | .9 |
| .6 | .8 | .4 | | | | | | | .5 |
| (24) 1.4 | (32) 1.7 | (37) 1.2 | % Depr., Dep., Amort./Sales | | | | | (14) 1.0 |
| 2.4 | 3.1 | 3.6 | | | | | | | 2.5 |
| 5.3 | 4.3 | 4.0 | % Officers', Directors' | | | | | | |
| (13) 7.6 | (14) 6.1 | (17) 9.2 | Owners' Comp/Sales | | | | | | |
| 27.0 | 13.0 | 19.9 | | | | | | | |
| 1873209M | 2292998M | 3893751M | Net Sales ($) | 4327M | 22218M | 39555M | 55361M | 129430M | 3642860M |
| 1403162M | 1841038M | 2321488M | Total Assets ($) | 6674M | 17907M | 42929M | 43187M | 146500M | 2064291M |

M = $ thousand    MM = $ million
See Pages 9 through 22 for Explanation of Ratios and Data

## Current Data Sorted by Assets | Comparative Historical Data

| 0-500M | 500M-2MM | 2-10MM | 10-50MM | 50-100MM | 100-250MM | Type of Statement | 4/1/07-3/31/08 ALL | 4/1/08-3/31/09 ALL |
|---|---|---|---|---|---|---|---|---|
| | 1 | 1 | 9 | 2 | 7 | Unqualified | 15 | 26 |
| | | | 1 | | | Reviewed | 2 | 3 |
| 1 | 1 | 1 | | | | Compiled | 3 | 5 |
| | 1 | 2 | | | | Tax Returns | 5 | 8 |
| 1 | 2 | 8 | 3 | 3 | 2 | Other | 31 | 24 |
| | | 9 (4/1-9/30/11) | 37 (10/1/11-3/31/12) | | | | | |
| 2 | 5 | 12 | 13 | 5 | 9 | **NUMBER OF STATEMENTS** | 56 | 66 |
| % | % | % | % | % | % | **ASSETS** | % | % |
| | | 11.6 | 34.3 | | | Cash & Equivalents | 23.8 | 22.8 |
| | | 10.1 | 21.6 | | | Trade Receivables (net) | 15.2 | 11.1 |
| | | .0 | 6.0 | | | Inventory | 2.0 | 2.0 |
| | | 3.8 | 5.3 | | | All Other Current | 7.6 | 6.8 |
| | | 25.4 | 67.2 | | | Total Current | 48.6 | 42.7 |
| | | 46.3 | 5.1 | | | Fixed Assets (net) | 18.8 | 17.5 |
| | | 7.0 | .2 | | | Intangibles (net) | 4.9 | 7.2 |
| | | 21.3 | 27.6 | | | All Other Non-Current | 27.7 | 32.6 |
| | | 100.0 | 100.0 | | | Total | 100.0 | 100.0 |
| | | | | | | **LIABILITIES** | | |
| | | .8 | 27.8 | | | Notes Payable-Short Term | 11.6 | 9.0 |
| | | 3.8 | .0 | | | Cur. Mat.-L.T.D. | 4.5 | 4.2 |
| | | 3.3 | 5.5 | | | Trade Payables | 6.3 | 4.8 |
| | | .0 | .0 | | | Income Taxes Payable | .2 | .0 |
| | | 1.3 | 13.3 | | | All Other Current | 12.3 | 13.2 |
| | | 9.1 | 46.6 | | | Total Current | 34.9 | 31.1 |
| | | 25.2 | 1.1 | | | Long-Term Debt | 21.5 | 27.1 |
| | | .2 | .0 | | | Deferred Taxes | .7 | .4 |
| | | 1.8 | 2.5 | | | All Other Non-Current | 7.8 | 7.4 |
| | | 63.8 | 49.8 | | | Net Worth | 35.2 | 34.0 |
| | | 100.0 | 100.0 | | | Total Liabilities & Net Worth | 100.0 | 100.0 |
| | | | | | | **INCOME DATA** | | |
| | | 100.0 | 100.0 | | | Net Sales | 100.0 | 100.0 |
| | | | | | | Gross Profit | | |
| | | 53.1 | 69.7 | | | Operating Expenses | 63.1 | 64.8 |
| | | 46.9 | 30.3 | | | Operating Profit | 36.9 | 35.2 |
| | | 13.9 | 7.7 | | | All Other Expenses (net) | 7.6 | 10.6 |
| | | 33.0 | 22.6 | | | Profit Before Taxes | 29.3 | 24.5 |
| | | | | | | **RATIOS** | | |
| | | 11.9 | 5.7 | | | | 9.2 | 5.0 |
| | | 1.4 | 1.4 | | | Current | 1.6 | 1.7 |
| | | .1 | .9 | | | | .7 | .5 |
| | | 9.3 | 5.4 | | | | 7.6 | 4.3 |
| | | 1.3 | 1.1 | | | Quick | 1.0 | 1.1 |
| | | .1 | .6 | | | | .4 | .4 |
| | | 0 UND | 0 UND | | | | 0 UND | 0 UND |
| | | 0 UND | 33 11.2 | | | Sales/Receivables | 1 680.0 | 0 730.3 |
| | | 31 11.8 | 76 4.8 | | | | 54 6.8 | 47 7.8 |
| | | | | | | Cost of Sales/Inventory | | |
| | | | | | | Cost of Sales/Payables | | |
| | | 4.6 | 1.2 | | | | 2.8 | 3.5 |
| | | 127.4 | 3.0 | | | Sales/Working Capital | 8.7 | 14.0 |
| | | -2.6 | -179.7 | | | | -19.1 | -8.5 |
| | | | | | | | 55.9 | 176.7 |
| | | | | | | EBIT/Interest | (27) 4.6 | (35) 5.7 |
| | | | | | | | 2.0 | 3.0 |
| | | | | | | Net Profit + Depr., Dep., Amort./Cur. Mat. L/T/D | | |
| | | .2 | .0 | | | | .0 | .0 |
| | | .5 | .1 | | | Fixed/Worth | .1 | .1 |
| | | 2.3 | .2 | | | | 4.2 | 8.6 |
| | | .1 | .1 | | | | .2 | .1 |
| | | .5 | 2.2 | | | Debt/Worth | 1.0 | 1.4 |
| | | 1.5 | 4.1 | | | | 29.9 | -72.4 |
| | | 65.3 | 102.2 | | | % Profit Before Taxes/Tangible Net Worth | 115.6 | 66.1 |
| | | 20.0 (12) | 8.9 | | | | (46) 38.7 | (49) 20.2 |
| | | 5.5 | -1.2 | | | | 5.8 | 3.8 |
| | | 44.9 | 8.3 | | | % Profit Before Taxes/Total Assets | 80.0 | 54.3 |
| | | 11.7 | 4.0 | | | | 9.5 | 5.5 |
| | | 1.6 | .4 | | | | 2.9 | 1.4 |
| | | 23.3 | UND | | | | 222.6 | UND |
| | | 1.2 | 90.1 | | | Sales/Net Fixed Assets | 32.9 | 50.7 |
| | | .2 | 15.9 | | | | 7.4 | 10.8 |
| | | 1.4 | 1.2 | | | | 3.0 | 2.4 |
| | | .4 | .6 | | | Sales/Total Assets | .9 | .8 |
| | | .1 | .1 | | | | .2 | .1 |
| | | | | | | | .6 | .6 |
| | | | | | | % Depr., Dep., Amort./Sales | (29) 2.0 | (39) 1.2 |
| | | | | | | | 7.3 | 7.6 |
| | | | | | | % Officers', Directors' Owners' Comp/Sales | | |
| 2438M | 25648M | 60063M | 277694M | 641016M | 1225520M | Net Sales ($) | 1354813M | 1586311M |
| 906M | 4875M | 47873M | 389942M | 373155M | 1570496M | Total Assets ($) | 1494673M | 2028657M |

© RMA 2012

M = $ thousand    MM = $ million
See Pages 9 through 22 for Explanation of Ratios and Data

## Comparative Historical Data

## Current Data Sorted by Sales

| | | | Type of Statement | | | | | | |
|---|---|---|---|---|---|---|---|---|---|
| | | | Unqualified | | 2 | 1 | 3 | 4 | 10 |
| | | | Reviewed | | 1 | | | | |
| | | | Compiled | 1 | 1 | 1 | | | |
| | | | Tax Returns | 3 | | | | | |
| | | | Other | 6 | 1 | 2 | | 4 | 6 |
| 21 | 16 | 20 | | | | | | | |
| 3 | 2 | 1 | | | | | | | |
| 2 | 2 | 3 | | | | | | | |
| 6 | 5 | 3 | | | | | | | |
| 26 | 31 | 19 | | | | | | | |
| 4/1/09-3/31/10 ALL | 4/1/10-3/31/11 ALL | 4/1/11-3/31/12 ALL | | 0-1MM | 9 (4/1-9/30/11) 1-3MM | 3-5MM | 37 (10/1/11-3/31/12) 5-10MM | 10-25MM | 25MM & OVER |
| 58 | 56 | 46 | **NUMBER OF STATEMENTS** | 10 | 5 | 4 | 3 | 8 | 16 |
| % | % | % | **ASSETS** | % | % | % | % | % | % |
| 20.1 | 32.2 | 24.4 | Cash & Equivalents | 3.8 | | | | | 28.6 |
| 13.3 | 11.1 | 17.5 | Trade Receivables (net) | 4.2 | | | | | 26.9 |
| 1.8 | 1.1 | 5.1 | Inventory | 9.3 | | | | | 8.8 |
| 6.1 | 6.8 | 4.4 | All Other Current | 3.7 | | | | | 2.0 |
| 41.3 | 51.1 | 51.4 | Total Current | 21.0 | | | | | 66.2 |
| 14.0 | 18.3 | 19.2 | Fixed Assets (net) | 58.5 | | | | | 9.5 |
| 3.0 | 4.3 | 6.0 | Intangibles (net) | 5.7 | | | | | 7.3 |
| 41.7 | 26.4 | 23.3 | All Other Non-Current | 14.9 | | | | | 17.0 |
| 100.0 | 100.0 | 100.0 | Total | 100.0 | | | | | 100.0 |
| | | | **LIABILITIES** | | | | | | |
| 7.6 | 12.8 | 12.2 | Notes Payable-Short Term | 2.1 | | | | | 8.4 |
| 2.7 | 1.8 | 1.3 | Cur. Mat.-L.T.D. | 4.4 | | | | | .0 |
| 3.4 | 4.0 | 8.5 | Trade Payables | 5.3 | | | | | 7.4 |
| .1 | .0 | .0 | Income Taxes Payable | .0 | | | | | .0 |
| 11.7 | 8.7 | 7.1 | All Other Current | 1.1 | | | | | 7.4 |
| 25.5 | 27.3 | 29.0 | Total Current | 12.8 | | | | | 23.2 |
| 13.5 | 20.5 | 13.7 | Long-Term Debt | 36.7 | | | | | 8.3 |
| .9 | .6 | .4 | Deferred Taxes | .0 | | | | | .0 |
| 3.2 | 5.2 | 6.8 | All Other Non-Current | 3.9 | | | | | 14.1 |
| 57.0 | 46.5 | 50.1 | Net Worth | 46.6 | | | | | 54.3 |
| 100.0 | 100.0 | 100.0 | Total Liabilities & Net Worth | 100.0 | | | | | 100.0 |
| | | | **INCOME DATA** | | | | | | |
| 100.0 | 100.0 | 100.0 | Net Sales | 100.0 | | | | | 100.0 |
| | | | Gross Profit | | | | | | |
| 66.8 | 68.9 | 63.9 | Operating Expenses | 60.2 | | | | | 73.2 |
| 33.2 | 31.1 | 36.1 | Operating Profit | 39.8 | | | | | 26.8 |
| 8.4 | 8.1 | 9.9 | All Other Expenses (net) | 19.3 | | | | | 3.9 |
| 24.8 | 23.0 | 26.3 | Profit Before Taxes | 20.5 | | | | | 22.9 |
| | | | **RATIOS** | | | | | | |
| 6.8 | 16.1 | 10.8 | | 3.6 | | | | | 16.8 |
| 1.7 | 2.2 | 1.4 | Current | .6 | | | | | 5.2 |
| .6 | 1.0 | .7 | | .1 | | | | | 1.3 |
| 4.9 | 13.7 | 9.7 | | 2.5 | | | | | 16.4 |
| 1.5 | 1.7 | 1.2 | Quick | .3 | | | | | 5.0 |
| .4 | .6 | .5 | | .1 | | | | | .9 |
| 0 UND | 0 UND | 0 UND | | 0 UND | | | | 17 | 21.0 |
| 5 73.3 | 25 14.4 | 5 79.9 | Sales/Receivables | 0 UND | | | | 34 | 10.7 |
| 44 8.3 | 48 7.7 | 55 6.6 | | 57 6.4 | | | | 62 | 5.9 |
| | | | Cost of Sales/Inventory | | | | | | |
| | | | Cost of Sales/Payables | | | | | | |
| 1.7 | 1.8 | 2.3 | | 3.7 | | | | | 2.5 |
| 8.6 | 4.0 | 6.1 | Sales/Working Capital | -83.3 | | | | | 4.0 |
| -6.1 | NM | -38.8 | | -2.2 | | | | | 15.1 |
| 127.3 | 161.3 | 139.8 | | | | | | | 568.6 |
| (29) 9.5 | (29) 12.2 | (24) 10.3 | EBIT/Interest | | | | | (10) | 6.4 |
| 2.4 | 1.6 | 2.0 | | | | | | | 2.1 |
| | | | Net Profit + Depr., Dep., Amort./Cur. Mat. L/T/D | | | | | | |
| .0 | .0 | .0 | | .2 | | | | | .0 |
| .1 | .1 | .1 | Fixed/Worth | 1.3 | | | | | .1 |
| .7 | 1.2 | 1.2 | | 2.8 | | | | | .8 |
| .1 | .1 | .1 | | .4 | | | | | .1 |
| .6 | .7 | 1.5 | Debt/Worth | 1.6 | | | | | .6 |
| 2.6 | 7.3 | 2.8 | | 2.6 | | | | | 3.3 |
| 41.5 | 102.7 | 58.5 | % Profit Before Taxes/Tangible Net Worth | 18.4 | | | | | 78.3 |
| (49) 13.5 | (49) 11.7 | (41) 8.2 | | 4.4 | | | | (13) | 7.3 |
| 1.7 | 1.3 | 4.1 | | 1.1 | | | | | 6.2 |
| 30.2 | 40.7 | 20.8 | % Profit Before Taxes/Total Assets | 8.7 | | | | | 89.6 |
| 7.4 | 6.1 | 5.7 | | 1.4 | | | | | 7.5 |
| 1.2 | .5 | 1.8 | | .4 | | | | | 2.6 |
| UND | UND | UND | | 10.8 | | | | | 79.3 |
| 40.6 | 35.2 | 38.7 | Sales/Net Fixed Assets | .2 | | | | | 35.9 |
| 7.4 | 6.0 | 7.1 | | .1 | | | | | 10.6 |
| 2.1 | 1.8 | 2.2 | | .6 | | | | | 2.6 |
| .4 | .7 | .6 | Sales/Total Assets | .1 | | | | | 1.3 |
| .1 | .2 | .1 | | .1 | | | | | .6 |
| .7 | .5 | .6 | | | | | | | .4 |
| (33) 1.2 | (29) 1.3 | (28) 1.3 | % Depr., Dep., Amort./Sales | | | | | (12) | 1.1 |
| 6.6 | 4.5 | 8.4 | | | | | | | 2.7 |
| | | | % Officers', Directors' Owners' Comp/Sales | | | | | | |
| 1282887M | 2182649M | 2232379M | Net Sales ($) | 4722M | 7501M | 17017M | 19591M | 110029M | 2073519M |
| 2631580M | 1686805M | 2387247M | Total Assets ($) | 25374M | 79154M | 55699M | 150214M | 582267M | 1494539M |

© RMA 2012

M = $ thousand    MM = $ million

See Pages 9 through 22 for Explanation of Ratios and Data

# FINANCE—Other Financial Vehicles  NAICS 525990

**Current Data Sorted by Assets**                    **Comparative Historical Data**

| Type of Statement | 0-500M | 500M-2MM | 2-10MM | 10-50MM | 50-100MM | 100-250MM | 4/1/07-3/31/08 ALL | 4/1/08-3/31/09 ALL |
|---|---|---|---|---|---|---|---|---|
| Unqualified | 1 | 2 | 2 | 5 | 7 | 9 | 36 | 30 |
| Reviewed | 1 | 1 | 4 | 6 | | | 9 | 10 |
| Compiled | | 4 | 2 | 2 | | | 13 | 13 |
| Tax Returns | 11 | 17 | 17 | 4 | | | 50 | 50 |
| Other | 4 | 13 | 22 | 23 | 8 | 8 | 60 | 77 |
| | 20 (4/1-9/30/11) | | | 153 (10/1/11-3/31/12) | | | | |
| **NUMBER OF STATEMENTS** | 17 | 37 | 47 | 40 | 15 | 17 | 168 | 180 |
| | % | % | % | % | % | % | % | % |
| **ASSETS** | | | | | | | | |
| Cash & Equivalents | 39.6 | 23.8 | 11.1 | 13.7 | 9.4 | 11.4 | 14.3 | 15.7 |
| Trade Receivables (net) | 2.0 | 7.2 | 16.7 | 15.1 | 24.7 | 18.1 | 10.7 | 10.2 |
| Inventory | 2.5 | 1.3 | 1.5 | .0 | 8.6 | .3 | 1.8 | 1.4 |
| All Other Current | 6.3 | 2.6 | 4.7 | 4.7 | 2.2 | 10.0 | 5.7 | 5.1 |
| Total Current | 50.4 | 35.0 | 34.0 | 33.5 | 44.9 | 39.7 | 32.4 | 32.4 |
| Fixed Assets (net) | 26.6 | 44.9 | 36.8 | 28.6 | 16.6 | 20.5 | 44.2 | 42.8 |
| Intangibles (net) | 15.8 | 3.9 | 6.1 | 5.5 | 7.7 | 12.0 | 4.3 | 4.8 |
| All Other Non-Current | 7.4 | 16.3 | 23.0 | 32.4 | 30.8 | 27.8 | 19.1 | 20.0 |
| Total | 100.0 | 100.0 | 100.0 | 100.0 | 100.0 | 100.0 | 100.0 | 100.0 |
| **LIABILITIES** | | | | | | | | |
| Notes Payable-Short Term | 12.1 | 6.1 | 8.1 | 13.4 | 16.5 | 20.1 | 11.3 | 10.9 |
| Cur. Mat.-L.T.D. | 7.2 | 4.0 | 2.1 | 4.8 | 1.5 | .4 | 3.1 | 3.6 |
| Trade Payables | 9.2 | 7.1 | 4.2 | 1.0 | 2.0 | 4.5 | 3.4 | 2.6 |
| Income Taxes Payable | .0 | .3 | .1 | .0 | .9 | 1.0 | .0 | .2 |
| All Other Current | 17.3 | 14.6 | 13.9 | 3.6 | 5.3 | 6.9 | 9.1 | 9.1 |
| Total Current | 45.9 | 32.1 | 28.4 | 22.9 | 26.3 | 32.9 | 27.0 | 26.3 |
| Long-Term Debt | 14.6 | 37.3 | 28.8 | 28.0 | 29.7 | 7.5 | 34.8 | 36.4 |
| Deferred Taxes | .0 | .2 | .0 | .1 | .2 | .3 | .3 | .2 |
| All Other Non-Current | 8.6 | 4.6 | 5.9 | 3.3 | 6.5 | 6.7 | 7.4 | 6.6 |
| Net Worth | 31.0 | 25.8 | 37.0 | 45.7 | 37.4 | 52.7 | 30.5 | 30.5 |
| Total Liabilties & Net Worth | 100.0 | 100.0 | 100.0 | 100.0 | 100.0 | 100.0 | 100.0 | 100.0 |
| **INCOME DATA** | | | | | | | | |
| Net Sales | 100.0 | 100.0 | 100.0 | 100.0 | 100.0 | 100.0 | 100.0 | 100.0 |
| Gross Profit | | | | | | | | |
| Operating Expenses | 85.0 | 59.2 | 60.5 | 55.4 | 53.8 | 70.6 | 60.5 | 59.0 |
| Operating Profit | 15.0 | 40.8 | 39.5 | 44.6 | 46.2 | 29.4 | 39.5 | 41.0 |
| All Other Expenses (net) | 7.9 | 15.4 | 14.5 | 12.2 | 27.8 | 10.1 | 20.2 | 19.8 |
| Profit Before Taxes | 7.1 | 25.4 | 25.1 | 32.4 | 18.4 | 19.3 | 19.3 | 21.2 |
| **RATIOS** | | | | | | | | |
| Current | 8.7 | 2.2 | 2.7 | 7.0 | 10.0 | 3.2 | 3.5 | 4.1 |
| | 1.1 | 1.0 | 1.0 | 1.5 | 1.6 | 1.2 | 1.1 | 1.2 |
| | .4 | .5 | .5 | .6 | 1.1 | .3 | .3 | .3 |
| Quick | 7.4 | 2.0 | 1.9 | 7.4 | 8.6 | 2.5 | 2.9 | 3.0 |
| | .9 | .7 | .9 | (39) 1.2 | 1.4 | .7 | .8 | 1.0 |
| | .1 | .4 | .2 | .2 | .1 | .1 | .1 | .2 |
| Sales/Receivables | 0 UND | 0 UND | 0 UND | 0 UND | 4 82.9 | 0 UND | 0 UND | 0 UND |
| | 0 UND | 0 UND | 0 UND | 1 446.9 | 45 8.1 | 29 12.6 | 0 UND | 0 UND |
| | 0 UND | 13 27.2 | 60 6.1 | 49 7.5 | 521 .7 | 304 1.2 | 35 10.5 | 35 10.3 |
| Cost of Sales/Inventory | | | | | | | | |
| Cost of Sales/Payables | | | | | | | | |
| Sales/Working Capital | 3.8 | 6.2 | 2.5 | 1.1 | .2 | .6 | 2.4 | 1.8 |
| | 34.6 | UND | 203.8 | 5.3 | 1.6 | 3.1 | 32.3 | 14.3 |
| | -5.5 | -5.5 | -4.2 | -6.4 | 17.4 | -25.5 | -2.3 | -3.5 |
| EBIT/Interest | 9.6 | | 17.2 | 11.2 | | 9.7 | 12.5 | 8.7 |
| | (17) 4.8 | | (28) 6.2 | (20) 4.3 | | (10) 6.8 | (77) 4.1 | (75) 4.0 |
| | 2.1 | | 2.3 | 2.2 | | .8 | 1.3 | 1.5 |
| Net Profit + Depr., Dep., Amort./Cur. Mat. L/T/D | | | | | | | | |
| Fixed/Worth | .0 | .3 | .0 | .0 | .0 | .0 | .0 | .0 |
| | .7 | 3.4 | .4 | .1 | .0 | .3 | 1.6 | 1.2 |
| | 4.3 | -2.8 | 3.1 | 2.3 | .8 | .7 | 6.3 | 6.2 |
| Debt/Worth | .7 | .6 | .4 | .4 | .5 | .5 | .7 | .7 |
| | 4.3 | 5.4 | 1.8 | 1.8 | 2.5 | .8 | 3.1 | 2.9 |
| | -6.2 | -7.1 | 13.2 | 4.3 | 14.6 | 3.7 | 11.4 | 13.1 |
| % Profit Before Taxes/Tangible Net Worth | 66.7 | 109.5 | 65.8 | 23.8 | 38.1 | 21.4 | 33.0 | 32.8 |
| | (11) 20.1 | (26) 22.3 | (39) 10.4 | (37) 13.0 | (13) 5.7 | (16) 10.7 | (135) 10.5 | (150) 9.2 |
| | -14.3 | 11.9 | 3.7 | 2.3 | .0 | 4.2 | 1.5 | .7 |
| % Profit Before Taxes/Total Assets | 89.7 | 20.8 | 15.6 | 8.6 | 7.0 | 6.4 | 10.9 | 8.1 |
| | 6.0 | 7.0 | 4.4 | 4.5 | 1.4 | 3.9 | 4.0 | 2.9 |
| | -3.8 | .5 | 1.8 | .8 | .0 | 1.1 | .0 | .0 |
| Sales/Net Fixed Assets | UND | 45.8 | 307.3 | 193.8 | 979.5 | UND | 100.9 | 173.5 |
| | 10.6 | 4.7 | 10.2 | 14.8 | 50.6 | 6.0 | 2.6 | 2.5 |
| | .8 | .2 | .2 | .2 | 1.3 | .5 | .2 | .2 |
| Sales/Total Assets | 6.1 | 2.1 | 1.1 | .3 | .3 | .4 | .7 | .6 |
| | 1.4 | .5 | .3 | .2 | .1 | .1 | .2 | .1 |
| | .2 | .1 | .1 | .1 | .1 | .1 | .1 | .1 |
| % Depr., Dep., Amort./Sales | .7 | 1.1 | 1.7 | .3 | | 1.0 | 2.0 | 2.9 |
| | (10) 9.0 | (25) 12.6 | (30) 8.5 | (26) 5.2 | | (11) 7.2 | (105) 8.0 | (106) 14.1 |
| | 24.4 | 21.6 | 19.5 | 19.9 | | 31.4 | 20.0 | 25.4 |
| % Officers', Directors' Owners' Comp/Sales | | | | | | | 4.5 | 4.1 |
| | | | | | | | (19) 9.0 | (18) 11.6 |
| | | | | | | | 16.2 | 15.4 |
| Net Sales ($) | 13829M | 189633M | 174098M | 267191M | 375655M | 956803M | 6088659M | 2826103M |
| Total Assets ($) | 3597M | 46493M | 199743M | 1009757M | 1102025M | 2986745M | 4535727M | 4787222M |

M = $ thousand   MM = $ million
See Pages 9 through 22 for Explanation of Ratios and Data

## Comparative Historical Data

## Current Data Sorted by Sales

| 4/1/09-3/31/10 ALL | 4/1/10-3/31/11 ALL | 4/1/11-3/31/12 ALL | Type of Statement | 0-1MM | 1-3MM | 3-5MM | 5-10MM | 10-25MM | 25MM & OVER |
|---|---|---|---|---|---|---|---|---|---|
| 23 | 26 | 26 | Unqualified | 5 | 4 | 2 | 3 | 5 | 7 |
| 5 | 8 | 11 | Reviewed | 1 | 2 | 3 | 3 | 2 | |
| 14 | 14 | 9 | Compiled | 5 | 3 | | 1 | | |
| 49 | 47 | 49 | Tax Returns | 27 | 14 | 2 | 3 | 2 | 1 |
| 86 | 66 | 78 | Other | 21 | 17 | 10 | 10 | 13 | 7 |
| | | | | 20 (4/1-9/30/11) | | 153 (10/1/11-3/31/12) | | | |
| 177 | 161 | 173 | **NUMBER OF STATEMENTS** | 59 | 40 | 17 | 20 | 22 | 15 |
| % | % | % | **ASSETS** | % | % | % | % | % | % |
| 16.1 | 17.0 | 17.1 | Cash & Equivalents | 17.9 | 15.5 | 6.3 | 16.9 | 24.6 | 19.8 |
| 13.2 | 11.1 | 13.7 | Trade Receivables (net) | 3.7 | 9.0 | 22.4 | 30.9 | 24.6 | 16.9 |
| 1.6 | 1.5 | 1.7 | Inventory | .6 | .2 | .5 | 3.7 | 5.9 | 2.9 |
| 7.6 | 8.0 | 4.7 | All Other Current | 5.4 | 4.7 | 1.5 | 3.9 | 3.6 | 8.0 |
| 38.6 | 37.7 | 37.2 | Total Current | 27.6 | 29.3 | 30.8 | 55.4 | 58.7 | 47.7 |
| 39.9 | 36.0 | 32.3 | Fixed Assets (net) | 50.7 | 34.8 | 25.8 | 10.0 | 19.1 | 9.7 |
| 3.3 | 6.3 | 7.2 | Intangibles (net) | 5.7 | 5.5 | 11.2 | 9.7 | 6.4 | 10.5 |
| 18.2 | 19.9 | 23.4 | All Other Non-Current | 16.1 | 30.4 | 32.1 | 25.0 | 15.8 | 32.1 |
| 100.0 | 100.0 | 100.0 | Total | 100.0 | 100.0 | 100.0 | 100.0 | 100.0 | 100.0 |
| | | | **LIABILITIES** | | | | | | |
| 13.6 | 10.3 | 11.2 | Notes Payable-Short Term | 5.0 | 11.6 | 18.5 | 21.3 | 13.2 | 10.0 |
| 3.1 | 4.2 | 3.4 | Cur. Mat.-L.T.D. | 5.1 | 2.5 | .5 | 7.7 | .8 | .6 |
| 2.7 | 4.6 | 4.4 | Trade Payables | .3 | 2.4 | 5.1 | 11.2 | 7.2 | 12.1 |
| .2 | .1 | .3 | Income Taxes Payable | .0 | .0 | .0 | .3 | .5 | 2.1 |
| 7.8 | 9.4 | 10.6 | All Other Current | 9.2 | 11.0 | 3.0 | 14.6 | 18.1 | 7.2 |
| 27.4 | 28.7 | 29.9 | Total Current | 19.6 | 27.4 | 27.1 | 55.2 | 39.8 | 32.0 |
| 37.4 | 30.4 | 27.0 | Long-Term Debt | 37.5 | 30.1 | 33.0 | 11.4 | 12.3 | 13.6 |
| .3 | .1 | .1 | Deferred Taxes | .0 | .0 | .1 | .3 | .1 | .3 |
| 7.6 | 3.8 | 5.4 | All Other Non-Current | 4.0 | 8.8 | 3.8 | 4.7 | 2.0 | 9.7 |
| 27.4 | 37.1 | 37.6 | Net Worth | 38.9 | 33.8 | 36.1 | 28.5 | 45.8 | 44.4 |
| 100.0 | 100.0 | 100.0 | Total Liabilities & Net Worth | 100.0 | 100.0 | 100.0 | 100.0 | 100.0 | 100.0 |
| | | | **INCOME DATA** | | | | | | |
| 100.0 | 100.0 | 100.0 | Net Sales | 100.0 | 100.0 | 100.0 | 100.0 | 100.0 | 100.0 |
| | | | Gross Profit | | | | | | |
| 64.6 | 65.7 | 61.8 | Operating Expenses | 52.0 | 68.8 | 49.2 | 68.9 | 70.9 | 73.5 |
| 35.4 | 34.3 | 38.2 | Operating Profit | 48.0 | 31.2 | 50.8 | 31.1 | 29.1 | 26.5 |
| 18.0 | 14.5 | 14.2 | All Other Expenses (net) | 20.3 | 12.1 | 17.6 | 13.4 | 5.9 | 5.4 |
| 17.4 | 19.8 | 23.9 | Profit Before Taxes | 27.7 | 19.1 | 33.2 | 17.7 | 23.2 | 21.0 |
| | | | **RATIOS** | | | | | | |
| 3.5 | 3.5 | 3.7 | Current | 3.6 | 8.7 | 3.4 | 2.9 | 4.8 | 2.3 |
| 1.4 | 1.4 | 1.2 | | 1.1 | 1.0 | 1.2 | 1.0 | 1.4 | 1.3 |
| .4 | .5 | .6 | | .4 | .2 | .7 | .5 | .8 | 1.0 |
| 2.8 | 2.9 | 2.8 | Quick | 2.4 | 5.8 | 2.0 | 2.9 | 4.1 | 2.3 |
| 1.1 | 1.0 (172) | .9 | | .8 | (39) 1.0 | .9 | .8 | 1.1 | 1.0 |
| .2 | .2 | .2 | | .2 | .1 | .6 | .6 | .6 | .5 |
| 0 UND | 0 UND | 0 UND | Sales/Receivables | 0 UND | 0 UND | 0 UND | 0 UND | 0 UND | 0 UND |
| 0 UND | 0 999.8 | 0 UND | | 0 UND | 0 UND | 12 29.7 | 45 8.1 | 38 9.5 | 16 23.1 |
| 41 8.8 | 38 9.5 | 42 8.6 | | 0 UND | 15 24.0 | 135 2.7 | 912 .4 | 64 5.7 | 72 5.1 |
| | | | Cost of Sales/Inventory | | | | | | |
| | | | Cost of Sales/Payables | | | | | | |
| 1.9 | 2.1 | 1.6 | Sales/Working Capital | .7 | 2.1 | 1.2 | 1.6 | 1.6 | 2.6 |
| 9.8 | 18.7 | 33.1 | | 39.4 | 45.8 | 12.8 | NM | 7.1 | 8.7 |
| -5.7 | -7.2 | -5.8 | | -4.4 | -3.7 | -8.7 | -2.2 | -37.2 | -128.2 |
| 15.7 | 26.7 | 12.3 | EBIT/Interest | 10.3 | 5.8 | | 27.2 | 40.0 | 20.3 |
| (88) 5.1 | (85) 5.0 | (87) 5.6 | | (23) 6.2 | (20) 2.8 | | (11) 4.5 | (12) 6.0 | (12) 9.9 |
| 1.3 | 1.6 | 2.0 | | 4.0 | -1.2 | | -.2 | .3 | 6.7 |
| | | | Net Profit + Depr., Dep., Amort./Cur. Mat. L/T/D | | | | | | |
| .0 | .0 | .0 | Fixed/Worth | .1 | .0 | .0 | .0 | .0 | .0 |
| 1.0 | 1.1 | .6 | | 1.3 | .2 | .1 | .2 | .1 | .3 |
| 8.0 | 6.4 | 3.7 | | 6.0 | 4.7 | 1.7 | NM | 2.1 | .7 |
| .7 | .5 | .5 | Debt/Worth | .5 | .3 | 1.0 | 1.0 | .4 | .6 |
| 3.2 | 2.3 | 2.1 | | 2.0 | 2.0 | 2.5 | 3.5 | 1.9 | .8 |
| 19.4 | 13.9 | 12.9 | | 8.4 | 93.6 | 10.5 | NM | 11.7 | 8.0 |
| 35.4 | 45.5 | 34.6 | % Profit Before Taxes/Tangible Net Worth | 20.0 | 30.2 | 29.3 | 124.2 | 367.2 | 71.4 |
| (144) 13.4 | (132) 16.4 | (142) 13.6 | | (48) 7.8 | (31) 11.3 | (15) 20.8 | (15) 24.4 | (19) 31.8 | (14) 23.4 |
| .9 | 3.2 | 2.9 | | 1.8 | .2 | 6.4 | 4.2 | 6.0 | 11.9 |
| 9.0 | 14.9 | 11.8 | % Profit Before Taxes/Total Assets | 7.2 | 13.2 | 13.5 | 21.4 | 69.3 | 11.2 |
| 2.6 | 4.4 | 4.3 | | 3.0 | 3.3 | 6.6 | 4.1 | 13.0 | 6.8 |
| .0 | .1 | 1.0 | | .7 | .1 | 1.5 | .2 | 2.3 | 3.9 |
| 72.4 | 86.2 | 170.3 | Sales/Net Fixed Assets | 31.0 | 123.9 | 650.8 | 122.8 | 110.4 | 324.2 |
| 4.3 | 7.1 | 10.4 | | .4 | 5.0 | 31.1 | 67.6 | 47.8 | 83.4 |
| .2 | .2 | .2 | | .1 | .2 | .3 | 10.5 | 12.1 | 5.4 |
| .9 | 1.2 | 1.0 | Sales/Total Assets | .4 | .9 | .6 | 2.8 | 5.2 | 1.1 |
| .2 | .2 | .2 | | .1 | .2 | .2 | .4 | 1.1 | .6 |
| .1 | .1 | .1 | | .1 | .1 | .1 | .1 | .1 | .4 |
| 2.7 | 1.8 | 1.1 | % Depr., Dep., Amort./Sales | 12.2 | 3.2 | | .3 | .4 | |
| (105) 9.1 | (97) 9.3 | (110) 8.1 | | (38) 18.2 | (26) 9.8 | | (11) 1.0 | (17) 1.0 | |
| 22.2 | 18.8 | 19.9 | | 24.0 | 17.2 | | 3.3 | 5.2 | |
| 2.1 | 2.9 | 3.0 | % Officers', Directors' Owners' Comp/Sales | | | | | | |
| (23) 10.9 | (25) 7.8 | (17) 11.6 | | | | | | | |
| 15.6 | 16.4 | 25.2 | | | | | | | |
| 1562705M | 2853546M | 1977209M | Net Sales ($) | 19464M | 71116M | 66863M | 142440M | 348127M | 1329199M |
| 4347235M | 4221452M | 5348360M | Total Assets ($) | 261510M | 609234M | 519425M | 733931M | 1262021M | 1962239M |

© RMA 2012

M = $ thousand    MM = $ million
See Pages 9 through 22 for Explanation of Ratios and Data

# REAL ESTATE AND RENTAL
# AND LEASING

## Current Data Sorted by Assets

## Comparative Historical Data

| | | | | | | Type of Statement | | |
|---|---|---|---|---|---|---|---|---|
| 6 | 86 | 174 | 65 | 19 | 17 | Unqualified | 251 | 264 |
| 3 | 11 | 39 | 15 | 4 | 4 | Reviewed | 57 | 68 |
| 29 | 66 | 78 | 29 | 2 | 1 | Compiled | 199 | 182 |
| 265 | 706 | 595 | 81 | 3 | 2 | Tax Returns | 961 | 1219 |
| 88 | 264 | 379 | 135 | 16 | 15 | Other | 467 | 690 |
| | 191 (4/1-9/30/11) | | 3,006 (10/1/11-3/31/12) | | | | 4/1/07-3/31/08 | 4/1/08-3/31/09 |
| 0-500M | 500M-2MM | 2-10MM | 10-50MM | 50-100MM | 100-250MM | | ALL | ALL |
| 391 | 1133 | 1265 | 325 | 44 | 39 | NUMBER OF STATEMENTS | 1935 | 2423 |
| % | % | % | % | % | % | ASSETS | % | % |
| 13.4 | 6.1 | 4.9 | 6.0 | 7.9 | 9.7 | Cash & Equivalents | 6.8 | 6.8 |
| 2.3 | .9 | 1.4 | 3.1 | 8.3 | 2.6 | Trade Receivables (net) | 2.3 | 2.4 |
| .7 | .9 | .9 | 3.1 | 1.1 | 2.6 | Inventory | 3.2 | 2.1 |
| 3.0 | .9 | 1.2 | 2.5 | 5.6 | 2.6 | All Other Current | 2.4 | 2.1 |
| 19.3 | 8.9 | 8.3 | 14.6 | 22.9 | 17.5 | Total Current | 14.7 | 13.3 |
| 71.9 | 82.5 | 82.9 | 71.2 | 57.6 | 65.9 | Fixed Assets (net) | 76.2 | 76.3 |
| 2.3 | 1.8 | 1.6 | 1.8 | 4.4 | 1.8 | Intangibles (net) | 1.7 | 1.6 |
| 6.5 | 6.9 | 7.3 | 12.4 | 15.1 | 14.9 | All Other Non-Current | 7.4 | 8.8 |
| 100.0 | 100.0 | 100.0 | 100.0 | 100.0 | 100.0 | Total | 100.0 | 100.0 |
| | | | | | | LIABILITIES | | |
| 6.1 | 3.0 | 2.5 | 4.7 | 4.6 | 2.4 | Notes Payable-Short Term | 6.1 | 5.1 |
| 5.6 | 4.0 | 2.9 | 2.0 | 3.0 | 1.8 | Cur. Mat.-L.T.D. | 4.0 | 4.7 |
| 3.8 | 1.0 | 1.0 | 2.1 | 4.2 | 2.5 | Trade Payables | 2.1 | 1.6 |
| .0 | .0 | .1 | .2 | .1 | .0 | Income Taxes Payable | .0 | .1 |
| 17.3 | 5.6 | 5.8 | 5.4 | 8.7 | 4.2 | All Other Current | 6.9 | 7.8 |
| 32.9 | 13.6 | 12.3 | 14.4 | 20.5 | 10.8 | Total Current | 19.2 | 19.2 |
| 71.6 | 76.3 | 68.5 | 60.8 | 48.7 | 61.5 | Long-Term Debt | 68.9 | 69.8 |
| .0 | .0 | .0 | .0 | .1 | .0 | Deferred Taxes | | |
| 5.6 | 3.8 | 3.1 | 3.3 | 9.4 | 4.7 | All Other Non-Current | 3.1 | 3.4 |
| -10.1 | 6.2 | 16.0 | 21.3 | 21.3 | 22.9 | Net Worth | 8.9 | 7.5 |
| 100.0 | 100.0 | 100.0 | 100.0 | 100.0 | 100.0 | Total Liabilities & Net Worth | 100.0 | 100.0 |
| | | | | | | INCOME DATA | | |
| 100.0 | 100.0 | 100.0 | 100.0 | 100.0 | 100.0 | Net Sales | 100.0 | 100.0 |
| | | | | | | Gross Profit | | |
| 67.7 | 64.2 | 67.4 | 72.3 | 82.3 | 78.4 | Operating Expenses | 70.2 | 69.0 |
| 32.3 | 35.8 | 32.6 | 27.7 | 17.7 | 21.6 | Operating Profit | 29.8 | 31.0 |
| 19.3 | 22.8 | 24.1 | 21.0 | 10.6 | 22.1 | All Other Expenses (net) | 23.0 | 23.9 |
| 12.9 | 13.0 | 8.5 | 6.7 | 7.2 | -.5 | Profit Before Taxes | 6.7 | 7.1 |
| | | | | | | RATIOS | | |
| 1.7 | 1.7 | 1.8 | 2.6 | 1.6 | 3.5 | | 1.9 | 1.8 |
| .7 | .5 | .6 | .9 | 1.0 | 1.3 | Current | .7 | .6 |
| .2 | .1 | .2 | .2 | .5 | .8 | | .2 | .2 |
| 1.5 | 1.4 | 1.5 | 1.7 | 1.3 | 2.1 | | 1.3 | 1.3 |
| .5 | .4 (1264) | .5 (324) | .6 | .7 | 1.0 | Quick | .4 (2421) | .4 |
| .1 | .1 | .1 | .1 | .3 | .5 | | .1 | .1 |
| 0 UND | 0 UND | 0 UND | 0 UND | 0 UND | 0 UND | | 0 UND | 0 UND |
| 0 UND | 0 UND | 0 UND | 1 579.9 | 15 24.1 | 5 78.9 | Sales/Receivables | 0 UND | 0 UND |
| 0 UND | 0 UND | 2 215.5 | 10 36.1 | 43 8.4 | 17 21.3 | | 3 133.4 | 2 147.0 |
| | | | | | | Cost of Sales/Inventory | | |
| | | | | | | Cost of Sales/Payables | | |
| 18.0 | 11.6 | 7.6 | 3.8 | 8.7 | 2.3 | | 9.1 | 9.3 |
| -21.0 | -11.3 | -12.9 | -36.9 | NM | 7.2 | Sales/Working Capital | -15.8 | -11.9 |
| -3.3 | -2.7 | -2.7 | -2.7 | -5.4 | -16.6 | | -3.0 | -2.6 |
| 4.7 | 5.6 | 4.5 | 5.7 | 6.2 | 7.4 | | 4.9 | 4.6 |
| (144) 2.9 | (428) 3.0 | (459) 2.1 | (126) 2.3 | (26) 1.6 | (14) 1.2 | EBIT/Interest | (712) 2.4 | (899) 2.2 |
| 1.2 | 1.4 | .7 | .6 | -.9 | .1 | | 1.1 | .9 |
| | 6.1 | 4.2 | 2.2 | | | | 2.3 | 3.0 |
| (11) | 1.1 (34) | 1.3 (20) | 1.5 | | | Net Profit + Depr., Dep., Amort./Cur. Mat. L/T/D | (41) 1.1 (52) | 1.2 |
| | .6 | .6 | .9 | | | | .7 | .4 |
| 1.4 | 2.3 | 2.1 | 1.4 | .8 | 1.4 | | 1.9 | 2.0 |
| 8.3 | 6.8 | 5.1 | 4.8 | 2.7 | 3.4 | Fixed/Worth | 5.7 | 7.2 |
| -3.1 | -8.5 | -34.8 | 87.5 | NM | 16.5 | | -19.7 | -13.1 |
| 1.4 | 1.7 | 1.6 | 1.4 | .9 | 1.4 | | 1.8 | 1.8 |
| 12.6 | 6.7 | 5.0 | 6.1 | 3.8 | 3.2 | Debt/Worth | 6.4 | 8.4 |
| -4.5 | -10.3 | -39.5 | 90.9 | NM | 25.2 | | -21.4 | -15.2 |
| 53.6 | 28.9 | 20.6 | 21.6 | 18.6 | 20.9 | | 29.8 | 28.0 |
| (231) 17.6 | (732) 9.9 | (911) 5.8 | (249) 5.8 | (33) 7.2 | (31) .7 | % Profit Before Taxes/Tangible Net Worth | (1329) 7.6 | (1606) 7.4 |
| .0 | -.4 | -3.0 | -1.9 | -.3 | -8.5 | | -4.2 | -4.2 |
| 18.2 | 7.5 | 4.4 | 4.2 | 5.4 | 1.9 | | 6.4 | 6.1 |
| 3.7 | 2.4 | 1.2 | 1.1 | .8 | .3 | % Profit Before Taxes/Total Assets | 1.4 | 1.3 |
| -.9 | -.5 | -1.1 | -1.2 | -.8 | -1.4 | | -1.5 | -1.6 |
| 2.6 | .4 | .3 | .5 | 3.4 | .5 | | .6 | .6 |
| .4 | .2 | .2 | .2 | .4 | .2 | Sales/Net Fixed Assets | .3 | .2 |
| .2 | .1 | .1 | .1 | .2 | .1 | | .2 | .1 |
| 1.1 | .3 | .3 | .3 | .7 | .2 | | .4 | .4 |
| .3 | .2 | .2 | .2 | .2 | .2 | Sales/Total Assets | .2 | .2 |
| .2 | .1 | .1 | .1 | .2 | .1 | | .1 | .1 |
| 8.2 | 12.0 | 13.7 | 9.8 | 6.0 | 8.8 | | 9.1 | 9.8 |
| (302) 17.2 | (989) 18.9 | (1072) 21.2 | (257) 19.7 | (35) 13.5 | (28) 16.2 | % Depr., Dep., Amort./Sales | (1696) 16.6 | (2049) 17.7 |
| 25.0 | 27.1 | 31.2 | 28.8 | 19.3 | 29.1 | | 25.0 | 26.7 |
| 5.0 | 2.5 | 3.0 | 2.9 | | | | 3.3 | 3.5 |
| (34) 7.0 | (90) 6.0 | (105) 6.4 | (40) 5.8 | | | % Officers', Directors' Owners' Comp/Sales | (220) 6.0 | (236) 6.5 |
| 12.3 | 10.9 | 14.3 | 10.3 | | | | 13.2 | 11.3 |
| 111210M | 538171M | 1546438M | 2151721M | 2262017M | 2138503M | Net Sales ($) | 8004279M | 8263148M |
| 110784M | 1314383M | 5431558M | 6280173M | 3047477M | 6049387M | Total Assets ($) | 13712681M | 18088802M |

M = $ thousand    MM = $ million
See Pages 9 through 22 for Explanation of Ratios and Data

## Comparative Historical Data

## Current Data Sorted by Sales

| Comparative Historical Data | | | Type of Statement | Current Data Sorted by Sales | | | | | |
|---|---|---|---|---|---|---|---|---|---|
| | | | | | | | | | |
| 308 | 334 | 367 | Unqualified | 204 | 73 | 20 | 23 | 24 | 23 |
| 70 | 53 | 76 | Reviewed | 29 | 17 | 6 | 5 | 11 | 8 |
| 229 | 221 | 205 | Compiled | 139 | 41 | 11 | 6 | 4 | 4 |
| 1527 | 1436 | 1652 | Tax Returns | 1370 | 219 | 28 | 23 | 8 | 4 |
| 788 | 893 | 897 | Other | 589 | 178 | 49 | 37 | 27 | 17 |
| 4/1/09-3/31/10 ALL | 4/1/10-3/31/11 ALL | 4/1/11-3/31/12 ALL | | 191 (4/1-9/30/11) | | | 3,006 (10/1/11-3/31/12) | | |
| | | | | 0-1MM | 1-3MM | 3-5MM | 5-10MM | 10-25MM | 25MM & OVER |
| 2922 | 2937 | 3197 | NUMBER OF STATEMENTS | 2331 | 528 | 114 | 94 | 74 | 56 |
| % | % | % | ASSETS | % | % | % | % | % | % |
| 6.5 | 6.5 | 6.5 | Cash & Equivalents | 5.1 | 8.3 | 14.7 | 12.5 | 14.3 | 11.5 |
| 2.0 | 1.8 | 1.6 | Trade Receivables (net) | .6 | 2.2 | 2.2 | 5.5 | 10.5 | 17.3 |
| 1.6 | 1.3 | 1.1 | Inventory | .4 | 1.1 | 3.8 | 5.4 | 8.5 | 7.2 |
| 1.5 | 2.1 | 1.5 | All Other Current | 1.0 | 1.6 | 4.2 | 3.2 | 6.0 | 7.6 |
| 11.6 | 11.7 | 10.8 | Total Current | 7.2 | 13.3 | 24.8 | 26.7 | 39.3 | 43.6 |
| 78.6 | 79.2 | 79.6 | Fixed Assets (net) | 84.9 | 74.0 | 61.3 | 55.1 | 42.5 | 41.8 |
| 1.6 | 1.7 | 1.8 | Intangibles (net) | 1.6 | 2.4 | 1.9 | 1.8 | 2.7 | 3.4 |
| 8.2 | 7.4 | 7.8 | All Other Non-Current | 6.3 | 10.4 | 12.0 | 16.5 | 15.6 | 11.1 |
| 100.0 | 100.0 | 100.0 | Total | 100.0 | 100.0 | 100.0 | 100.0 | 100.0 | 100.0 |
| | | | LIABILITIES | | | | | | |
| 3.6 | 4.1 | 3.4 | Notes Payable-Short Term | 3.2 | 3.1 | 2.6 | 5.1 | 5.8 | 8.0 |
| 4.2 | 3.9 | 3.5 | Cur. Mat.-L.T.D. | 3.7 | 3.2 | 2.5 | 3.5 | 3.1 | 3.0 |
| 1.3 | 1.6 | 1.5 | Trade Payables | .9 | 1.7 | 2.2 | 4.1 | 8.9 | 10.5 |
| .0 | .0 | .1 | Income Taxes Payable | .0 | .4 | .0 | .1 | .1 | .0 |
| 7.5 | 6.6 | 7.1 | All Other Current | 6.6 | 8.0 | 8.3 | 9.8 | 8.5 | 11.4 |
| 16.5 | 16.1 | 15.6 | Total Current | 14.4 | 16.3 | 15.6 | 22.6 | 26.5 | 32.9 |
| 73.1 | 70.9 | 70.5 | Long-Term Debt | 71.8 | 80.1 | 60.0 | 46.7 | 34.4 | 35.4 |
| .1 | .0 | .0 | Deferred Taxes | .0 | .1 | .4 | .4 | .1 | .2 |
| 3.1 | 3.8 | 3.8 | All Other Non-Current | 3.7 | 3.5 | 3.6 | 3.8 | 6.4 | 8.0 |
| 7.3 | 9.1 | 10.0 | Net Worth | 10.0 | .0 | 20.7 | 26.6 | 32.6 | 23.4 |
| 100.0 | 100.0 | 100.0 | Total Liabilities & Net Worth | 100.0 | 100.0 | 100.0 | 100.0 | 100.0 | 100.0 |
| | | | INCOME DATA | | | | | | |
| 100.0 | 100.0 | 100.0 | Net Sales | 100.0 | 100.0 | 100.0 | 100.0 | 100.0 | 100.0 |
| | | | Gross Profit | | | | | | |
| 67.5 | 67.8 | 67.1 | Operating Expenses | 64.5 | 69.5 | 75.6 | 81.4 | 83.9 | 91.7 |
| 32.5 | 32.2 | 32.9 | Operating Profit | 35.5 | 30.5 | 24.4 | 18.6 | 16.1 | 8.3 |
| 24.2 | 23.5 | 22.5 | All Other Expenses (net) | 25.1 | 19.2 | 13.1 | 10.1 | 8.2 | 4.7 |
| 8.3 | 8.7 | 10.3 | Profit Before Taxes | 10.4 | 11.4 | 11.4 | 8.5 | 7.8 | 3.6 |
| | | | RATIOS | | | | | | |
| 1.8 | 1.8 | 1.8 | | 1.5 | 2.3 | 4.4 | 3.5 | 4.2 | 2.0 |
| .6 | .6 | .6 | Current | .5 | .8 | 1.3 | 1.2 | 1.4 | 1.2 |
| .1 | .2 | .2 | | .1 | .2 | .4 | .4 | .9 | .8 |
| 1.4 | 1.4 | 1.5 | | 1.3 | 1.9 | 2.6 | 2.6 | 2.6 | 1.3 |
| (2921) .4 | (2935) .5 | (3195) .5 | Quick | .4 (526) .6 | | 1.0 | .8 | 1.1 | .8 |
| .1 | .1 | .1 | | .1 | .2 | .3 | .3 | .4 | .4 |
| 0 UND | 0 UND | 0 UND | | 0 UND | 0 UND | 0 UND | 0 UND | 1 470.8 | 5 77.8 |
| 0 UND | 0 UND | 0 UND | Sales/Receivables | 0 UND | 0 UND | 0 UND | 1 268.9 | 9 40.2 | 30 12.3 |
| 2 171.4 | 2 174.4 | 2 236.0 | | 0 UND | 4 103.8 | 6 56.5 | 18 20.4 | 38 9.7 | 51 7.2 |
| | | | Cost of Sales/Inventory | | | | | | |
| | | | Cost of Sales/Payables | | | | | | |
| 10.5 | 9.1 | 9.3 | | 13.5 | 6.5 | 3.2 | 4.4 | 3.0 | 6.5 |
| -11.1 | -12.8 | -14.3 | Sales/Working Capital | -9.4 | -51.7 | 18.8 | 26.9 | 11.8 | 26.3 |
| -2.6 | -2.7 | -2.8 | | -2.3 | -4.0 | -7.7 | -6.8 | -68.0 | -22.0 |
| 5.5 | 5.5 | 5.2 | | 4.6 | 5.1 | 7.0 | 7.1 | 19.2 | 7.4 |
| (1054) 2.6 | (1063) 2.5 | (1197) 2.5 | EBIT/Interest | (729) 2.5 | (268) 2.5 | (52) 2.4 | (59) 2.9 | (45) 2.7 | (44) 2.0 |
| 1.1 | 1.1 | 1.0 | | 1.0 | 1.2 | .9 | 1.1 | 1.3 | -.1 |
| 4.4 | 4.4 | 3.2 | | 2.3 | 6.0 | | | | |
| (41) 2.1 | (59) 1.6 | (72) 1.4 | Net Profit + Depr., Dep., Amort./Cur. Mat. L/T/D | (27) .9 | (16) 2.5 | | | | |
| .5 | .5 | .6 | | .5 | 1.0 | | | | |
| 2.1 | 2.0 | 2.0 | | 2.2 | 2.3 | .8 | .6 | .2 | .4 |
| 6.8 | 6.0 | 5.8 | Fixed/Worth | 6.1 | 7.6 | 4.3 | 2.4 | 1.5 | 1.6 |
| -11.2 | -14.6 | -15.0 | | -19.8 | -4.8 | -8.4 | 13.7 | 5.3 | 14.5 |
| 1.9 | 1.6 | 1.6 | | 1.7 | 2.1 | .9 | .8 | 1.1 | 1.1 |
| 7.3 | 6.5 | 6.2 | Debt/Worth | 6.2 | 8.7 | 6.1 | 3.6 | 2.7 | 3.6 |
| -13.4 | -16.1 | -17.5 | | -21.4 | -6.7 | -10.5 | 26.6 | 8.3 | 16.5 |
| 27.8 | 26.7 | 26.7 | | 24.6 | 33.2 | 40.5 | 29.2 | 28.3 | 45.6 |
| (1939) 7.0 | (2002) 7.6 | (2187) 7.7 | % Profit Before Taxes/Tangible Net Worth | (1603) 6.5 | (320) 12.2 | (79) 11.3 | (78) 8.9 | (63) 11.0 | (44) 13.5 |
| -3.2 | -2.7 | -2.0 | | -2.4 | -.1 | .2 | -1.2 | .0 | -1.3 |
| 6.0 | 5.8 | 6.0 | | 5.3 | 8.2 | 7.0 | 8.9 | 11.5 | 9.7 |
| 1.3 | 1.5 | 1.8 | % Profit Before Taxes/Total Assets | 1.5 | 2.8 | 2.2 | 3.4 | 3.5 | 2.4 |
| -1.5 | -1.3 | -1.0 | | -1.1 | -.8 | -.3 | -.2 | -.4 | -1.0 |
| .5 | .5 | .4 | | .3 | .8 | 3.2 | 15.9 | 42.5 | 23.8 |
| .2 | .2 | .2 | Sales/Net Fixed Assets | .2 | .3 | .5 | .7 | 2.7 | 4.9 |
| .1 | .1 | .1 | | .1 | .2 | .2 | .2 | .3 | .5 |
| .3 | .3 | .3 | | .3 | .5 | .6 | 1.3 | 2.2 | 2.9 |
| .2 | .2 | .2 | Sales/Total Assets | .2 | .2 | .3 | .3 | .5 | 1.2 |
| .1 | .1 | .1 | | .1 | .2 | .2 | .2 | .2 | .4 |
| 11.0 | 11.6 | 12.0 | | 14.2 | 8.6 | 1.9 | 1.9 | .8 | 1.1 |
| (2512) 18.8 | (2457) 19.2 | (2683) 19.7 | % Depr., Dep., Amort./Sales | (1990) 21.4 | (435) 16.3 | (81) 12.5 | (76) 8.7 | (59) 3.7 | (42) 2.7 |
| 27.1 | 28.4 | 28.6 | | 30.4 | 24.6 | 19.7 | 17.0 | 16.3 | 10.0 |
| 2.7 | 3.0 | 3.0 | | 4.0 | 2.5 | 2.4 | 2.3 | 1.4 | 1.3 |
| (270) 5.3 | (255) 5.6 | (277) 6.4 | % Officers', Directors' Owners' Comp/Sales | (143) 7.0 | (67) 5.0 | (23) 5.0 | (18) 5.5 | (12) 2.0 | (14) 3.4 |
| 11.0 | 10.7 | 12.1 | | 12.5 | 12.8 | 13.5 | 10.2 | 4.4 | 12.2 |
| 9240220M | 7496952M | 8748060M | Net Sales ($) | 789242M | 874044M | 447493M | 659054M | 1130253M | 4847974M |
| 22183155M | 20663249M | 22233762M | Total Assets ($) | 5065168M | 3997251M | 1750458M | 2793997M | 3626267M | 5000621M |

M = $ thousand    MM = $ million
See Pages 9 through 22 for Explanation of Ratios and Data

## Current Data Sorted by Assets      Comparative Historical Data

| | | | | | | Type of Statement | | |
|---|---|---|---|---|---|---|---|---|
| 6 | 20 | 66 | 69 | 22 | 22 | Unqualified | 206 | 238 |
| 11 | 66 | 160 | 78 | 14 | 12 | Reviewed | 248 | 291 |
| 64 | 358 | 454 | 123 | 9 | 3 | Compiled | 720 | 851 |
| 796 | 3378 | 2771 | 266 | 12 | 11 | Tax Returns | 3887 | 5067 |
| 246 | 1166 | 1567 | 455 | 65 | 46 | Other | 1668 | 2144 |
| | 343 (4/1-9/30/11) | | 11,993 (10/1/11-3/31/12) | | | | 4/1/07-3/31/08 | 4/1/08-3/31/09 |
| 0-500M | 500M-2MM | 2-10MM | 10-50MM | 50-100MM | 100-250MM | | ALL | ALL |
| 1123 | 4988 | 5018 | 991 | 122 | 94 | NUMBER OF STATEMENTS | 6729 | 8591 |
| % | % | % | % | % | % | **ASSETS** | % | % |
| 11.2 | 4.4 | 3.9 | 4.4 | 6.1 | 6.1 | Cash & Equivalents | 5.0 | 5.0 |
| 2.2 | 1.1 | 1.2 | 2.0 | 3.1 | 2.7 | Trade Receivables (net) | 1.6 | 1.5 |
| 1.5 | .5 | .6 | 2.1 | 1.1 | 2.4 | Inventory | 1.1 | 1.0 |
| 2.1 | 1.0 | 1.3 | 2.4 | 2.7 | 2.2 | All Other Current | 1.8 | 1.5 |
| 16.9 | 7.0 | 7.0 | 11.0 | 13.0 | 13.5 | Total Current | 9.5 | 9.0 |
| 76.3 | 87.0 | 85.9 | 76.4 | 72.2 | 70.9 | Fixed Assets (net) | 83.2 | 83.2 |
| 1.8 | 1.5 | 1.7 | 2.7 | 2.6 | 3.9 | Intangibles (net) | 1.4 | 1.5 |
| 5.0 | 4.5 | 5.4 | 9.9 | 12.2 | 11.8 | All Other Non-Current | 5.9 | 6.3 |
| 100.0 | 100.0 | 100.0 | 100.0 | 100.0 | 100.0 | Total | 100.0 | 100.0 |
| | | | | | | **LIABILITIES** | | |
| 5.5 | 2.5 | 2.5 | 3.0 | 4.6 | 2.1 | Notes Payable-Short Term | 3.4 | 3.6 |
| 5.4 | 4.1 | 3.5 | 3.4 | 2.9 | 4.6 | Cur. Mat.-L.T.D. | 4.5 | 4.3 |
| 2.8 | .7 | .6 | 1.3 | 2.4 | 2.4 | Trade Payables | 1.2 | 1.1 |
| .0 | .0 | .0 | .0 | .0 | .2 | Income Taxes Payable | .0 | .0 |
| 11.1 | 3.3 | 3.3 | 3.8 | 3.2 | 3.3 | All Other Current | 4.3 | 4.1 |
| 24.8 | 10.7 | 9.9 | 11.5 | 13.2 | 12.6 | Total Current | 13.4 | 13.2 |
| 63.8 | 70.1 | 68.4 | 57.9 | 52.2 | 52.2 | Long-Term Debt | 67.3 | 68.1 |
| .0 | .0 | .0 | .2 | .4 | .5 | Deferred Taxes | .1 | .0 |
| 6.2 | 2.7 | 3.0 | 3.2 | 4.6 | 4.8 | All Other Non-Current | 3.1 | 2.9 |
| 5.2 | 16.5 | 18.8 | 27.2 | 29.7 | 29.9 | Net Worth | 16.2 | 15.7 |
| 100.0 | 100.0 | 100.0 | 100.0 | 100.0 | 100.0 | Total Liabilties & Net Worth | 100.0 | 100.0 |
| | | | | | | **INCOME DATA** | | |
| 100.0 | 100.0 | 100.0 | 100.0 | 100.0 | 100.0 | Net Sales | 100.0 | 100.0 |
| | | | | | | Gross Profit | | |
| 52.1 | 45.9 | 48.4 | 57.7 | 65.5 | 67.4 | Operating Expenses | 48.8 | 49.2 |
| 47.9 | 54.1 | 51.6 | 42.3 | 34.5 | 32.6 | Operating Profit | 51.2 | 50.8 |
| 21.1 | 30.1 | 30.1 | 24.4 | 19.4 | 21.2 | All Other Expenses (net) | 30.2 | 30.3 |
| 26.7 | 24.0 | 21.5 | 17.9 | 15.1 | 11.4 | Profit Before Taxes | 21.1 | 20.5 |
| | | | | | | **RATIOS** | | |
| 1.6 | 1.7 | 1.8 | 2.2 | 2.0 | 2.1 | | 1.8 | 1.8 |
| .5 | .5 | .6 | .8 | 1.0 | 1.0 | Current | .5 | .6 |
| .2 | .1 | .2 | .2 | .3 | .3 | | .2 | .2 |
| 1.4 | 1.4 | 1.4 | 1.7 | 1.5 | 1.5 | | 1.3 | 1.3 |
| .4 (4984) | .4 (5017) | .4 (990) | .5 | .6 | .6 | Quick (6723) | .4 (8587) | .4 |
| .1 | .1 | .1 | .1 | .2 | .2 | | .1 | .1 |
| 0 UND | 0 UND | 0 UND | 0 UND | 0 UND | 0 UND | | 0 UND | 0 UND |
| 0 UND | 0 UND | 0 UND | 0 UND | 6 58.1 | 6 58.5 | Sales/Receivables | 0 UND | 0 UND |
| 0 UND | 0 UND | 0 UND | 11 34.1 | 31 11.8 | 33 11.2 | | 0 UND | 0 UND |
| | | | | | | Cost of Sales/Inventory | | |
| | | | | | | Cost of Sales/Payables | | |
| 15.9 | 9.9 | 8.2 | 4.6 | 3.0 | 4.5 | | 9.7 | 9.6 |
| -12.0 | -8.7 | -9.0 | -26.3 | 163.6 | -114.4 | Sales/Working Capital | -10.0 | -9.9 |
| -2.8 | -2.8 | -2.7 | -2.5 | -2.9 | -3.0 | | -2.6 | -2.7 |
| 9.7 | 7.2 | 7.0 | 6.4 | 7.3 | 8.4 | | 6.8 | 6.7 |
| (443) 5.1 (1349) | 4.5 (1383) | 4.0 (358) | 3.5 (56) | 2.6 (40) | 2.4 | EBIT/Interest (1764) | 4.0 (2320) | 3.9 |
| 2.7 | 2.7 | 2.4 | 1.7 | 1.2 | 1.4 | | 2.2 | 2.1 |
| | 3.0 | 4.1 | 3.4 | 5.5 | 3.5 | | 4.3 | 3.7 |
| (51) | 1.7 (137) | 2.2 (92) | 1.6 (13) | 2.3 (18) | 1.5 | Net Profit + Depr., Dep., Amort./Cur. Mat. L/T/D (257) | 1.9 (278) | 1.9 |
| | .9 | 1.2 | .9 | .8 | .2 | | .9 | .8 |
| 1.5 | 2.5 | 2.4 | 1.5 | 1.4 | 1.4 | | 2.3 | 2.3 |
| 4.1 | 5.3 | 5.3 | 3.6 | 2.9 | 3.3 | Fixed/Worth | 5.2 | 5.3 |
| -20.6 | 67.2 | 68.0 | 14.1 | 11.0 | 11.3 | | 66.5 | 128.5 |
| 1.1 | 1.8 | 1.8 | 1.2 | 1.0 | 1.2 | | 1.8 | 1.8 |
| 4.1 | 4.8 | 4.8 | 3.4 | 2.8 | 3.5 | Debt/Worth | 5.0 | 5.2 |
| -14.0 | 82.3 | 77.6 | 16.3 | 11.7 | 11.5 | | 81.4 | 180.5 |
| 55.0 | 33.8 | 28.7 | 22.5 | 13.0 | 19.5 | | 35.2 | 33.9 |
| (797) 22.2 (3823) | 15.7 (3879) | 13.3 (816) | 9.1 (99) | 6.0 (78) | 6.3 | % Profit Before Taxes/Tangible Net Worth (5208) | 15.9 (6552) | 14.9 |
| 6.7 | 4.5 | 3.3 | 1.8 | .2 | -1.0 | | 4.5 | 3.5 |
| 18.5 | 7.9 | 6.1 | 5.3 | 4.1 | 4.1 | | 7.8 | 7.3 |
| 6.5 | 3.6 | 2.8 | 2.2 | 1.4 | 1.4 | % Profit Before Taxes/Total Assets | 3.4 | 3.1 |
| 1.0 | .8 | .5 | .2 | -.2 | -.5 | | .6 | .4 |
| 1.0 | .3 | .2 | .3 | .3 | .4 | | .3 | .3 |
| .3 | .2 | .2 | .2 | .2 | .2 | Sales/Net Fixed Assets | .2 | .2 |
| .2 | .1 | .1 | .1 | .1 | .1 | | .1 | .1 |
| .6 | .2 | .2 | .2 | .2 | .2 | | .3 | .2 |
| .3 | .2 | .1 | .1 | .1 | .1 | Sales/Total Assets | .2 | .2 |
| .1 | .1 | .1 | .1 | .1 | .1 | | .1 | .1 |
| 7.9 | 12.9 | 14.3 | 13.3 | 12.8 | 9.1 | | 11.1 | 11.7 |
| (913) 14.7 (4508) | 18.5 (4448) | 19.7 (875) | 20.3 (103) | 20.1 (73) | 19.2 | % Depr., Dep., Amort./Sales (6113) | 16.6 (7807) | 17.4 |
| 21.4 | 25.0 | 26.7 | 28.4 | 27.2 | 25.3 | | 23.3 | 24.3 |
| 4.5 | 2.5 | 2.6 | 1.7 | .9 | | | 2.7 | 2.1 |
| (82) 11.7 (239) | 5.7 (283) | 5.2 (87) | 4.8 (18) | 3.6 | | % Officers', Directors' Owners' Comp/Sales (429) | 5.9 (540) | 5.2 |
| 19.3 | 12.7 | 11.7 | 11.9 | 8.1 | | | 13.0 | 11.6 |
| 341238M | 1667174M | 4633206M | 6681189M | 3731913M | 4894957M | Net Sales ($) | 20406044M | 20685589M |
| 347584M | 5974736M | 20988688M | 19711400M | 8491760M | 15749926M | Total Assets ($) | 39567965M | 52875159M |

© RMA 2012

## Comparative Historical Data | | | Type of Statement | Current Data Sorted by Sales

| | | | Type of Statement | | | | | | |
|---|---|---|---|---|---|---|---|---|---|
| 222 | 203 | 205 | Unqualified | 54 | 43 | 18 | 34 | 19 | 37 |
| 263 | 314 | 341 | Reviewed | 151 | 74 | 29 | 26 | 36 | 25 |
| 918 | 868 | 1011 | Compiled | 763 | 175 | 34 | 19 | 13 | 7 |
| 5789 | 6072 | 7234 | Tax Returns | 6512 | 583 | 68 | 39 | 20 | 12 |
| 2498 | 3100 | 3545 | Other | 2610 | 554 | 131 | 106 | 90 | 54 |
| 4/1/09-3/31/10 ALL | 4/1/10-3/31/11 ALL | 4/1/11-3/31/12 ALL | | 343 (4/1-9/30/11) | | 11,993 (10/1/11-3/31/12) | | | |
| | | | | 0-1MM | 1-3MM | 3-5MM | 5-10MM | 10-25MM | 25MM & OVER |
| 9690 | 10557 | 12336 | NUMBER OF STATEMENTS | 10090 | 1429 | 280 | 224 | 178 | 135 |
| % | % | % | **ASSETS** | % | % | % | % | % | % |
| 4.7 | 4.8 | 4.8 | Cash & Equivalents | 4.3 | 6.0 | 6.6 | 11.2 | 8.6 | 9.2 |
| 1.3 | 1.5 | 1.3 | Trade Receivables (net) | .7 | 1.8 | 4.6 | 7.5 | 9.8 | 14.3 |
| .9 | .8 | .8 | Inventory | .2 | 1.6 | 3.1 | 5.8 | 8.4 | 11.3 |
| 1.3 | 1.6 | 1.4 | All Other Current | 1.1 | 2.1 | 2.5 | 2.9 | 5.0 | 4.2 |
| 8.2 | 8.6 | 8.3 | Total Current | 6.4 | 11.5 | 16.8 | 27.3 | 31.8 | 39.0 |
| 84.5 | 84.1 | 84.5 | Fixed Assets (net) | 87.5 | 78.1 | 70.1 | 57.0 | 51.3 | 46.9 |
| 1.7 | 1.7 | 1.7 | Intangibles (net) | 1.5 | 2.5 | 2.5 | 2.9 | 5.3 | 3.4 |
| 5.7 | 5.6 | 5.5 | All Other Non-Current | 4.6 | 8.0 | 10.6 | 12.8 | 11.6 | 10.7 |
| 100.0 | 100.0 | 100.0 | Total | 100.0 | 100.0 | 100.0 | 100.0 | 100.0 | 100.0 |
| | | | **LIABILITIES** | | | | | | |
| 3.3 | 3.4 | 2.8 | Notes Payable-Short Term | 2.6 | 2.9 | 3.3 | 4.9 | 5.5 | 7.8 |
| 4.5 | 4.2 | 3.9 | Cur. Mat.-L.T.D. | 3.9 | 3.9 | 4.3 | 3.8 | 4.3 | 2.4 |
| 1.0 | .9 | .9 | Trade Payables | .5 | 1.1 | 3.4 | 6.3 | 6.9 | 10.2 |
| .0 | .0 | .0 | Income Taxes Payable | .0 | .0 | .1 | .1 | .1 | .2 |
| 4.1 | 4.1 | 4.1 | All Other Current | 3.7 | 4.8 | 7.1 | 9.3 | 6.5 | 6.8 |
| 12.9 | 12.6 | 11.7 | Total Current | 10.7 | 12.8 | 18.2 | 24.4 | 23.5 | 27.4 |
| 68.1 | 67.5 | 67.5 | Long-Term Debt | 69.1 | 68.4 | 55.2 | 45.9 | 44.4 | 33.5 |
| .0 | .0 | .0 | Deferred Taxes | .0 | .0 | .1 | .4 | .3 | .4 |
| 2.6 | 2.9 | 3.2 | All Other Non-Current | 2.9 | 3.9 | 3.6 | 6.4 | 8.0 | 4.3 |
| 16.3 | 17.0 | 17.5 | Net Worth | 17.3 | 14.8 | 22.9 | 23.0 | 23.8 | 34.4 |
| 100.0 | 100.0 | 100.0 | Total Liabilities & Net Worth | 100.0 | 100.0 | 100.0 | 100.0 | 100.0 | 100.0 |
| | | | **INCOME DATA** | | | | | | |
| 100.0 | 100.0 | 100.0 | Net Sales | 100.0 | 100.0 | 100.0 | 100.0 | 100.0 | 100.0 |
| | | | Gross Profit | | | | | | |
| 49.2 | 48.9 | 48.8 | Operating Expenses | 45.7 | 56.0 | 66.8 | 74.7 | 79.8 | 85.1 |
| 50.8 | 51.1 | 51.2 | Operating Profit | 54.3 | 44.0 | 33.2 | 25.3 | 20.2 | 14.9 |
| 29.7 | 29.0 | 28.7 | All Other Expenses (net) | 31.0 | 21.4 | 17.2 | 12.9 | 10.8 | 6.4 |
| 21.1 | 22.0 | 22.5 | Profit Before Taxes | 23.3 | 22.6 | 16.0 | 12.4 | 9.4 | 8.5 |
| | | | **RATIOS** | | | | | | |
| 1.7 | 1.8 | 1.8 | | 1.6 | 2.5 | 2.3 | 2.3 | 2.3 | 2.1 |
| .5 | .6 | .6 | Current | .5 | .8 | .8 | 1.1 | 1.2 | 1.2 |
| .1 | .2 | .2 | | .1 | .2 | .3 | .4 | .6 | .7 |
| 1.4 | 1.4 | 1.4 | | 1.4 | 1.9 | 1.8 | 1.9 | 1.6 | 1.4 |
| (9684) .4 | (10552) .4 | (12330) .4 | Quick | (10087) .4 | (1426) .6 | .5 | .7 | .7 | .7 |
| .1 | .1 | .1 | | .1 | .2 | .1 | .2 | .3 | .3 |
| 0 UND | 0 UND | 0 UND | | 0 UND | 0 UND | 0 UND | 0 UND | 1 693.8 | 2 179.4 |
| 0 UND | 0 UND | 0 UND | Sales/Receivables | 0 UND | 0 UND | 2 162.5 | 6 65.1 | 8 45.6 | 14 27.0 |
| 0 UND | 0 UND | 0 UND | | 0 UND | 4 88.0 | 18 20.2 | 25 14.4 | 41 8.8 | 43 8.5 |
| | | | Cost of Sales/Inventory | | | | | | |
| | | | Cost of Sales/Payables | | | | | | |
| 9.1 | 8.5 | 8.7 | | 10.0 | 5.5 | 6.9 | 6.8 | 6.3 | 6.1 |
| -9.5 | -9.8 | -9.8 | Sales/Working Capital | -7.9 | -31.0 | -31.3 | 39.3 | 22.5 | 25.8 |
| -2.6 | -2.7 | -2.7 | | -2.6 | -3.6 | -3.2 | -4.2 | -10.0 | -23.8 |
| 7.0 | 7.0 | 7.4 | | 7.2 | 7.2 | 6.3 | 9.5 | 12.9 | 14.2 |
| (2779) 4.0 | (3123) 4.1 | (3629) 4.3 | EBIT/Interest | (2535) 4.4 | (625) 3.8 | (126) 3.5 | (123) 3.0 | (115) 2.9 | (105) 3.9 |
| 2.2 | 2.4 | 2.4 | | 2.7 | 1.9 | 1.6 | 1.3 | 1.3 | 1.5 |
| 3.3 | 3.5 | 3.6 | | 3.0 | 3.7 | 2.9 | 3.4 | 4.7 | 9.9 |
| (267) 1.6 | (310) 1.8 | (314) 1.9 | Net Profit + Depr., Dep., Amort./Cur. Mat. L/T/D | (142) 1.9 | (65) 2.1 | (29) 1.0 | (20) 1.7 | (26) 1.5 | (32) 3.0 |
| .8 | 1.0 | 1.0 | | 1.1 | 1.3 | .6 | .6 | .7 | 1.2 |
| 2.3 | 2.2 | 2.2 | | 2.4 | 1.9 | 1.4 | .8 | .7 | .3 |
| 5.6 | 5.1 | 4.9 | Fixed/Worth | 5.2 | 4.8 | 4.1 | 2.3 | 2.8 | 1.1 |
| 118.2 | 94.9 | 64.3 | | 61.6 | -107.9 | 57.7 | 12.3 | 25.9 | 4.4 |
| 1.8 | 1.7 | 1.7 | | 1.8 | 1.5 | 1.2 | 1.1 | 1.1 | .9 |
| 5.3 | 4.8 | 4.6 | Debt/Worth | 4.7 | 5.0 | 4.0 | 3.2 | 3.8 | 2.5 |
| 164.1 | 125.6 | 79.2 | | 70.4 | -74.5 | UND | 25.7 | 64.5 | 6.2 |
| 33.3 | 33.2 | 31.7 | % Profit Before Taxes/Tangible Net Worth | 30.9 | 40.2 | 34.8 | 37.8 | 32.9 | 28.8 |
| (7378) 14.2 | (8065) 14.6 | (9492) 14.2 | | (7805) 13.9 | (1047) 16.1 | (211) 15.3 | (176) 11.3 | (135) 12.1 | (118) 15.2 |
| 3.1 | 3.6 | 3.6 | | 3.6 | 4.3 | 3.5 | 1.1 | 2.4 | 4.7 |
| 7.0 | 7.2 | 7.3 | % Profit Before Taxes/Total Assets | 7.0 | 8.7 | 7.6 | 9.5 | 10.4 | 8.8 |
| 3.0 | 3.2 | 3.2 | | 3.1 | 3.9 | 3.4 | 3.5 | 3.3 | 4.1 |
| .3 | .5 | .6 | | .5 | .9 | .5 | -.2 | .1 | .7 |
| .3 | .3 | .3 | | .2 | .4 | .7 | 11.6 | 17.4 | 26.8 |
| .2 | .2 | .2 | Sales/Net Fixed Assets | .2 | .2 | .3 | .4 | 1.5 | 4.6 |
| .1 | .1 | .1 | | .1 | .1 | .2 | .2 | .2 | .4 |
| .2 | .2 | .2 | | .2 | .3 | .4 | 2.7 | 2.4 | 3.4 |
| .1 | .1 | .1 | Sales/Total Assets | .1 | .2 | .2 | .3 | .5 | 1.3 |
| .1 | .1 | .1 | | .1 | .1 | .1 | .1 | .2 | .3 |
| 12.6 | 12.5 | 13.0 | | 13.8 | 10.7 | 10.1 | 2.1 | 1.9 | .9 |
| (8784) 18.5 | (9377) 18.5 | 18.8 | % Depr., Dep., Amort./Sales | (8982) 19.3 | (1261) 16.8 | (236) 16.6 | (188) 14.1 | (148) 8.7 | (105) 2.8 |
| 25.4 | 25.5 | 25.7 | | 26.1 | 24.6 | 23.6 | 23.0 | 20.0 | 10.5 |
| 2.4 | 2.4 | 2.6 | | 3.2 | 2.8 | 1.7 | 1.2 | 1.0 | .5 |
| (584) 5.3 | (640) 5.6 | (714) 5.6 | % Officers', Directors' Owners' Comp/Sales | (405) 6.3 | (167) 5.7 | (48) 4.3 | (38) 3.2 | (32) 2.9 | (24) 1.3 |
| 11.8 | 12.4 | 12.8 | | 12.8 | 11.9 | 6.0 | 6.0 | | |
| 19871403M | 22771902M | 21949677M | Net Sales ($) | 3181251M | 2319169M | 1058105M | 1566850M | 2712591M | 11111711M |
| 56315124M | 60456042M | 71264094M | Total Assets ($) | 22850122M | 14054613M | 5589842M | 6880927M | 9571672M | 12316918M |

## Current Data Sorted by Assets      Comparative Historical Data

| 0-500M | 500M-2MM | 2-10MM | 10-50MM | 50-100MM | 100-250MM | Type of Statement | | |
|---|---|---|---|---|---|---|---|---|
| | 2 | 3 | 3 | 1 | 3 | Unqualified | 7 | 13 |
| | 2 | 1 | 4 | 1 | | Reviewed | 11 | 8 |
| 3 | 21 | 19 | 4 | | | Compiled | 23 | 28 |
| 42 | 152 | 100 | 10 | | 1 | Tax Returns | 185 | 193 |
| 25 | 96 | 97 | 19 | | | Other | 93 | 164 |
| | 13 (4/1-9/30/11) | | 596 (10/1/11-3/31/12) | | | | 4/1/07-3/31/08 ALL | 4/1/08-3/31/09 ALL |
| 70 | 273 | 220 | 40 | 3 | 3 | **NUMBER OF STATEMENTS** | 319 | 406 |
| % | % | % | % | % | % | **ASSETS** | % | % |
| 25.1 | 3.9 | 3.8 | 3.2 | | | Cash & Equivalents | 7.0 | 6.6 |
| 3.2 | 1.6 | 1.4 | .5 | | | Trade Receivables (net) | 2.0 | 2.1 |
| 1.6 | .8 | .6 | 2.4 | | | Inventory | 1.7 | 1.1 |
| 2.6 | 1.2 | .8 | .8 | | | All Other Current | 2.2 | 1.4 |
| 32.6 | 7.5 | 6.6 | 7.0 | | | Total Current | 12.9 | 11.3 |
| 53.8 | 86.2 | 85.2 | 78.9 | | | Fixed Assets (net) | 80.3 | 81.1 |
| 3.1 | 2.0 | 2.0 | 2.9 | | | Intangibles (net) | 2.1 | 1.9 |
| 10.6 | 4.2 | 6.2 | 11.3 | | | All Other Non-Current | 4.7 | 5.8 |
| 100.0 | 100.0 | 100.0 | 100.0 | | | Total | 100.0 | 100.0 |
| | | | | | | **LIABILITIES** | | |
| 6.1 | 4.3 | 3.4 | 3.9 | | | Notes Payable-Short Term | 3.6 | 4.7 |
| 4.1 | 3.6 | 2.8 | 2.9 | | | Cur. Mat.-L.T.D. | 4.3 | 4.2 |
| 2.9 | .9 | .7 | .9 | | | Trade Payables | 1.3 | 1.5 |
| .0 | .0 | .0 | .0 | | | Income Taxes Payable | .1 | .1 |
| 25.5 | 4.9 | 5.6 | 3.7 | | | All Other Current | 10.0 | 6.0 |
| 38.7 | 13.7 | 12.5 | 11.5 | | | Total Current | 19.3 | 16.5 |
| 57.3 | 79.0 | 69.9 | 63.1 | | | Long-Term Debt | 68.1 | 66.5 |
| .0 | .0 | .0 | .4 | | | Deferred Taxes | .1 | .0 |
| 10.4 | 3.4 | 3.3 | 2.0 | | | All Other Non-Current | 4.0 | 5.5 |
| -6.3 | 3.9 | 14.3 | 23.0 | | | Net Worth | 8.5 | 11.5 |
| 100.0 | 100.0 | 100.0 | 100.0 | | | Total Liabilities & Net Worth | 100.0 | 100.0 |
| | | | | | | **INCOME DATA** | | |
| 100.0 | 100.0 | 100.0 | 100.0 | | | Net Sales | 100.0 | 100.0 |
| | | | | | | Gross Profit | | |
| 75.5 | 61.0 | 59.5 | 68.5 | | | Operating Expenses | 62.2 | 64.5 |
| 24.5 | 39.0 | 40.5 | 31.5 | | | Operating Profit | 37.8 | 35.5 |
| 9.5 | 21.9 | 25.3 | 20.4 | | | All Other Expenses (net) | 23.9 | 23.4 |
| 15.0 | 17.1 | 15.2 | 11.0 | | | Profit Before Taxes | 13.9 | 12.0 |
| | | | | | | **RATIOS** | | |
| 3.8 | 1.4 | 1.7 | 1.7 | | | | 2.2 | 2.0 |
| 1.0 | .5 | .7 | .3 | | | Current | .8 | .7 |
| .3 | .1 | .2 | .2 | | | | .3 | .2 |
| 3.5 | 1.2 | 1.5 | .8 | | | | 1.8 | 1.6 |
| 1.0 | .4 | .6 | .3 | | | Quick | .6 | .6 |
| .3 | .1 | .1 | .1 | | | | .2 | .1 |
| 0 UND | 0 UND | 0 UND | 0 UND | | | | 0 UND | 0 UND |
| 0 UND | 0 UND | 0 UND | 3 133.9 | | | Sales/Receivables | 0 UND | 0 UND |
| 0 UND | 0 UND | 3 125.3 | 14 25.9 | | | | 3 128.0 | 4 98.4 |
| | | | | | | Cost of Sales/Inventory | | |
| | | | | | | Cost of Sales/Payables | | |
| 13.2 | 28.3 | 12.2 | 5.6 | | | | 12.4 | 15.7 |
| UND | -10.9 | -17.6 | -6.3 | | | Sales/Working Capital | -34.3 | -25.7 |
| -8.1 | -2.8 | -3.0 | -1.9 | | | | -4.5 | -3.2 |
| 6.1 | 5.5 | 6.4 | 5.3 | | | | 8.8 | 4.7 |
| (29) 2.6 | (117) 3.2 | (83) 3.3 | (13) 2.9 | | | EBIT/Interest | (117) 3.7 | (142) 2.7 |
| 1.5 | 1.6 | 2.0 | 1.8 | | | | 2.0 | 1.6 |
| | | | | | | | 5.8 | 7.8 |
| | | | | | | Net Profit + Depr., Dep., Amort./Cur. Mat. L/T/D | (13) 2.6 | (14) 1.6 |
| | | | | | | | 1.3 | .6 |
| .8 | 2.7 | 2.6 | 1.7 | | | | 2.6 | 2.7 |
| 5.1 | 15.1 | 7.3 | 3.8 | | | Fixed/Worth | 9.2 | 7.4 |
| -1.3 | -4.8 | -13.9 | 18.8 | | | | -8.8 | -17.6 |
| .5 | 2.2 | 2.0 | 1.3 | | | | 2.0 | 2.2 |
| 13.9 | 15.1 | 7.6 | 3.4 | | | Debt/Worth | 10.3 | 8.1 |
| -3.9 | -6.1 | -16.3 | 31.4 | | | | -10.8 | -19.3 |
| 100.0 | 47.4 | 32.4 | 19.9 | | | % Profit Before Taxes/Tangible Net Worth | 51.9 | 40.9 |
| (42) 22.7 | (165) 18.7 | (145) 13.1 | (33) 7.8 | | | | (199) 21.9 | (282) 14.8 |
| -.8 | 4.3 | 2.8 | -1.8 | | | | 3.8 | 1.0 |
| 23.2 | 9.4 | 6.9 | 4.0 | | | % Profit Before Taxes/Total Assets | 9.3 | 6.9 |
| 7.9 | 3.6 | 2.5 | 1.8 | | | | 3.2 | 2.7 |
| 1.3 | .4 | -.2 | -.5 | | | | -.3 | .0 |
| 46.1 | .4 | .3 | .3 | | | | .6 | .5 |
| 3.5 | .3 | .2 | .2 | | | Sales/Net Fixed Assets | .3 | .3 |
| .4 | .2 | .1 | .1 | | | | .2 | .2 |
| 6.0 | .3 | .2 | .2 | | | | .5 | .4 |
| 1.5 | .2 | .2 | .1 | | | Sales/Total Assets | .2 | .2 |
| .4 | .2 | .1 | .1 | | | | .2 | .1 |
| 2.0 | 11.8 | 12.1 | 14.8 | | | % Depr., Dep., Amort./Sales | 7.6 | 9.1 |
| (43) 8.8 | (213) 16.4 | (182) 18.1 | (32) 20.7 | | | | (271) 12.7 | (310) 14.2 |
| 17.1 | 23.6 | 25.9 | 25.1 | | | | 18.5 | 20.5 |
| 1.9 | 5.3 | 2.1 | | | | % Officers', Directors' Owners' Comp/Sales | 4.9 | 3.5 |
| (12) 4.2 | (38) 8.2 | (30) 4.8 | | | | | (40) 10.5 | (44) 7.0 |
| 6.6 | 12.5 | 7.0 | | | | | 13.8 | 12.3 |
| 30768M | 113596M | 237086M | 464076M | 465967M | 84218M | Net Sales ($) | 1424935M | 938197M |
| 15321M | 336121M | 866099M | 885630M | 245924M | 528425M | Total Assets ($) | 1880863M | 2388156M |

## Comparative Historical Data

## Current Data Sorted by Sales

| | | | Type of Statement | | | | | | |
|---|---|---|---|---|---|---|---|---|---|
| 6 | 9 | 12 | Unqualified | 4 | 1 | | 4 | 1 | 2 |
| 19 | 19 | 8 | Reviewed | 2 | 1 | 3 | 1 | | 1 |
| 37 | 56 | 47 | Compiled | 38 | 4 | 4 | 1 | | |
| 216 | 296 | 305 | Tax Returns | 276 | 21 | 2 | 1 | 3 | 2 |
| 159 | 186 | 237 | Other | 192 | 33 | 8 | 1 | 2 | 1 |
| 4/1/09-3/31/10 ALL | 4/1/10-3/31/11 ALL | 4/1/11-3/31/12 ALL | | 13 (4/1-9/30/11) 0-1MM | 1-3MM | 3-5MM | 596 (10/1/11-3/31/12) 5-10MM | 10-25MM | 25MM & OVER |
| 437 | 566 | 609 | **NUMBER OF STATEMENTS** | 512 | 60 | 17 | 8 | 6 | 6 |
| % | % | % | **ASSETS** | % | % | % | % | % | % |
| 7.0 | 6.6 | 6.3 | Cash & Equivalents | 6.1 | 7.2 | 6.6 | | | |
| 1.8 | 1.1 | 1.6 | Trade Receivables (net) | 1.0 | 3.3 | 3.7 | | | |
| 1.5 | .9 | .9 | Inventory | .4 | 4.0 | .1 | | | |
| 1.4 | 1.4 | 1.3 | All Other Current | 1.3 | .4 | .7 | | | |
| 11.7 | 10.1 | 10.2 | Total Current | 8.8 | 14.9 | 11.1 | | | |
| 81.2 | 82.4 | 81.4 | Fixed Assets (net) | 83.3 | 77.6 | 73.1 | | | |
| 2.0 | 2.9 | 2.2 | Intangibles (net) | 2.2 | 1.4 | .9 | | | |
| 5.2 | 4.6 | 6.2 | All Other Non-Current | 5.8 | 6.1 | 15.0 | | | |
| 100.0 | 100.0 | 100.0 | Total | 100.0 | 100.0 | 100.0 | | | |
| | | | **LIABILITIES** | | | | | | |
| 3.5 | 3.8 | 4.1 | Notes Payable-Short Term | 4.2 | 2.6 | 4.7 | | | |
| 3.5 | 3.9 | 3.3 | Cur. Mat.-L.T.D. | 3.3 | 3.3 | 3.8 | | | |
| 1.3 | 1.0 | 1.1 | Trade Payables | .5 | 1.9 | 1.9 | | | |
| .0 | .0 | .0 | Income Taxes Payable | .0 | .1 | .0 | | | |
| 6.3 | 8.9 | 7.4 | All Other Current | 8.0 | 4.6 | 4.8 | | | |
| 14.6 | 17.7 | 16.0 | Total Current | 16.1 | 12.4 | 15.2 | | | |
| 68.7 | 73.1 | 71.7 | Long-Term Debt | 74.1 | 65.3 | 54.1 | | | |
| .0 | .1 | .0 | Deferred Taxes | .0 | .0 | .7 | | | |
| 2.8 | 4.7 | 4.1 | All Other Non-Current | 4.1 | 4.2 | 5.4 | | | |
| 13.9 | 4.5 | 8.2 | Net Worth | 5.8 | 18.1 | 24.5 | | | |
| 100.0 | 100.0 | 100.0 | Total Liabilities & Net Worth | 100.0 | 100.0 | 100.0 | | | |
| | | | **INCOME DATA** | | | | | | |
| 100.0 | 100.0 | 100.0 | Net Sales | 100.0 | 100.0 | 100.0 | | | |
| | | | Gross Profit | | | | | | |
| 64.0 | 64.5 | 62.8 | Operating Expenses | 61.4 | 65.9 | 71.1 | | | |
| 36.0 | 35.5 | 37.2 | Operating Profit | 38.6 | 34.1 | 28.9 | | | |
| 23.5 | 23.7 | 21.4 | All Other Expenses (net) | 22.8 | 16.1 | 15.1 | | | |
| 12.6 | 11.8 | 15.7 | Profit Before Taxes | 15.8 | 18.1 | 13.7 | | | |
| | | | **RATIOS** | | | | | | |
| 2.2 | 1.2 | 1.7 | | 1.5 | 2.6 | 1.8 | | | |
| .6 | .5 | .6 | Current | .6 | 1.1 | .5 | | | |
| .2 | .2 | .2 | | .2 | .2 | .2 | | | |
| 1.7 | 1.0 | 1.4 | | 1.3 | 2.0 | 1.5 | | | |
| .5 | (565) .4 | .5 | Quick | .5 | .8 | .5 | | | |
| .1 | .1 | .1 | | .1 | .2 | .2 | | | |
| 0 UND | 0 UND | 0 UND | | 0 UND | 0 UND | 2 203.8 | | | |
| 0 UND | 0 UND | 0 UND | Sales/Receivables | 0 UND | 0 999.8 | 13 27.2 | | | |
| 3 120.0 | 0 UND | 1 394.8 | | 0 UND | 8 44.9 | 20 17.9 | | | |
| | | | Cost of Sales/Inventory | | | | | | |
| | | | Cost of Sales/Payables | | | | | | |
| 11.8 | 44.3 | 15.7 | | 20.5 | 7.6 | 5.1 | | | |
| -19.7 | -8.6 | -15.8 | Sales/Working Capital | -11.9 | 52.0 | -17.4 | | | |
| -3.0 | -3.1 | -3.0 | | -2.8 | -4.9 | -1.4 | | | |
| 5.0 | 4.5 | 5.8 | | 5.5 | 5.9 | | | | |
| (166) 2.8 | (204) 2.9 | (246) 3.2 | EBIT/Interest | (193) 3.2 | (34) 3.7 | | | | |
| 1.7 | 1.6 | 1.8 | | 1.8 | 2.4 | | | | |
| 2.3 | 3.8 | 3.7 | Net Profit + Depr., Dep., Amort./Cur. Mat. L/T/D | | | | | | |
| (13) 1.4 | (16) 2.4 | (12) 1.8 | | | | | | | |
| .7 | 1.2 | .8 | | | | | | | |
| 2.4 | 2.8 | 2.3 | | 2.6 | 1.7 | 1.5 | | | |
| 6.6 | 10.7 | 7.4 | Fixed/Worth | 10.0 | 4.2 | 4.5 | | | |
| -24.0 | -7.7 | -9.2 | | -6.4 | -35.1 | 21.1 | | | |
| 1.7 | 2.4 | 1.7 | | 1.9 | 1.2 | .8 | | | |
| 6.6 | 12.0 | 8.6 | Debt/Worth | 10.8 | 4.1 | 5.2 | | | |
| -26.4 | -9.1 | -11.5 | | -8.8 | -39.1 | 30.7 | | | |
| 40.4 | 39.2 | 37.1 | % Profit Before Taxes/Tangible Net Worth | 35.5 | 44.0 | 43.5 | | | |
| (294) 15.6 | (342) 15.0 | (391) 15.5 | | (316) 15.4 | (44) 20.1 | (15) 27.7 | | | |
| 1.2 | .4 | 3.0 | | 2.7 | 6.0 | 6.4 | | | |
| 7.9 | 7.1 | 8.8 | % Profit Before Taxes/Total Assets | 8.4 | 12.0 | 18.1 | | | |
| 2.7 | 2.4 | 3.2 | | 2.9 | 4.3 | 3.7 | | | |
| -.2 | -.5 | .2 | | .1 | 1.3 | 1.2 | | | |
| .4 | .4 | .4 | | .4 | .8 | 1.1 | | | |
| .2 | .2 | .2 | Sales/Net Fixed Assets | .2 | .3 | .3 | | | |
| .2 | .2 | .2 | | .2 | .2 | .2 | | | |
| .4 | .3 | .3 | | .3 | .6 | .8 | | | |
| .2 | .2 | .2 | Sales/Total Assets | .2 | .2 | .2 | | | |
| .1 | .1 | .1 | | .1 | .2 | .1 | | | |
| 10.5 | 11.1 | 11.3 | % Depr., Dep., Amort./Sales | 11.7 | 9.5 | 13.8 | | | |
| (346) 15.4 | (454) 16.8 | (476) 17.1 | | (399) 17.4 | (45) 13.1 | (16) 17.8 | | | |
| 22.9 | 22.9 | 23.8 | | 23.7 | 24.9 | 26.0 | | | |
| 3.7 | 2.9 | 3.5 | % Officers', Directors' Owners' Comp/Sales | 3.0 | 3.9 | | | | |
| (60) 7.1 | (63) 6.5 | (83) 5.3 | | (69) 5.5 | (11) 4.9 | | | | |
| 14.0 | 13.2 | 10.0 | | 9.8 | 8.7 | | | | |
| 1121534M | 1357345M | 1395711M | Net Sales ($) | 203536M | 102393M | 66415M | 54662M | 102050M | 866655M |
| 2662511M | 3163383M | 2877520M | Total Assets ($) | 1024721M | 447819M | 331020M | 372142M | 230006M | 471812M |

M = $ thousand    MM = $ million
See Pages 9 through 22 for Explanation of Ratios and Data

## Current Data Sorted by Assets | Comparative Historical Data

| | 0-500M | 500M-2MM | 2-10MM | 10-50MM | 50-100MM | 100-250MM | Type of Statement | 4/1/07-3/31/08 ALL | 4/1/08-3/31/09 ALL |
|---|---|---|---|---|---|---|---|---|---|
| | | 10 | 23 | 28 | 6 | 11 | Unqualified | 82 | 99 |
| | 5 | 12 | 38 | 25 | 2 | 4 | Reviewed | 89 | 102 |
| | 14 | 72 | 109 | 31 | 3 | | Compiled | 241 | 262 |
| | 143 | 491 | 375 | 30 | | | Tax Returns | 902 | 1071 |
| | 45 | 212 | 263 | 92 | 10 | 8 | Other | 533 | 584 |
| | | 111 (4/1-9/30/11) | | 1,951 (10/1/11-3/31/12) | | | | | |
| | 207 | 797 | 808 | 206 | 21 | 23 | **NUMBER OF STATEMENTS** | 1847 | 2118 |
| | % | % | % | % | % | % | **ASSETS** | % | % |
| | 12.8 | 5.7 | 4.7 | 6.1 | 3.0 | 6.8 | Cash & Equivalents | 6.2 | 6.0 |
| | 3.3 | 1.2 | 1.4 | 3.3 | 5.9 | 2.4 | Trade Receivables (net) | 2.2 | 2.2 |
| | 2.5 | .9 | 1.1 | 2.2 | 7.8 | 2.5 | Inventory | 2.6 | 1.7 |
| | 1.5 | 1.4 | 1.6 | 3.4 | 1.7 | 1.5 | All Other Current | 2.5 | 2.2 |
| | 20.2 | 9.1 | 8.8 | 15.0 | 18.5 | 13.3 | Total Current | 13.4 | 12.0 |
| | 69.7 | 83.3 | 81.4 | 70.1 | 68.0 | 78.3 | Fixed Assets (net) | 78.2 | 79.5 |
| | 2.6 | 2.3 | 2.0 | 3.7 | 2.5 | 1.8 | Intangibles (net) | 1.6 | 1.9 |
| | 7.6 | 5.2 | 7.7 | 11.2 | 11.0 | 6.7 | All Other Non-Current | 6.7 | 6.5 |
| | 100.0 | 100.0 | 100.0 | 100.0 | 100.0 | 100.0 | Total | 100.0 | 100.0 |
| | | | | | | | **LIABILITIES** | | |
| | 7.2 | 3.7 | 2.7 | 5.3 | 1.5 | 5.1 | Notes Payable-Short Term | 3.9 | 4.4 |
| | 5.5 | 4.8 | 4.0 | 4.8 | 4.4 | 6.8 | Cur. Mat.-L.T.D. | 4.5 | 4.8 |
| | 1.9 | .8 | .7 | 2.0 | 5.9 | 1.7 | Trade Payables | 1.5 | 1.4 |
| | .0 | .0 | .1 | .0 | .0 | .1 | Income Taxes Payable | .1 | .1 |
| | 15.0 | 4.1 | 3.9 | 3.9 | 5.5 | 5.8 | All Other Current | 5.3 | 5.0 |
| | 29.7 | 13.4 | 11.4 | 16.1 | 17.3 | 19.6 | Total Current | 15.2 | 15.8 |
| | 69.3 | 64.1 | 62.6 | 54.6 | 45.9 | 50.9 | Long-Term Debt | 59.5 | 64.2 |
| | .0 | .0 | .1 | .2 | 1.7 | .3 | Deferred Taxes | .1 | .0 |
| | 7.8 | 4.1 | 4.4 | 5.6 | 7.1 | 8.7 | All Other Non-Current | 3.8 | 3.8 |
| | -6.8 | 18.4 | 21.5 | 23.6 | 28.1 | 20.6 | Net Worth | 21.5 | 16.2 |
| | 100.0 | 100.0 | 100.0 | 100.0 | 100.0 | 100.0 | Total Liabilities & Net Worth | 100.0 | 100.0 |
| | | | | | | | **INCOME DATA** | | |
| | 100.0 | 100.0 | 100.0 | 100.0 | 100.0 | 100.0 | Net Sales | 100.0 | 100.0 |
| | | | | | | | Gross Profit | | |
| | 57.6 | 49.6 | 50.9 | 61.2 | 72.7 | 80.1 | Operating Expenses | 52.8 | 53.4 |
| | 42.4 | 50.4 | 49.1 | 38.8 | 27.3 | 19.9 | Operating Profit | 47.2 | 46.6 |
| | 16.0 | 26.4 | 27.3 | 20.7 | 20.9 | 13.3 | All Other Expenses (net) | 25.9 | 27.1 |
| | 26.4 | 24.0 | 21.8 | 18.1 | 6.3 | 6.6 | Profit Before Taxes | 21.3 | 19.5 |
| | | | | | | | **RATIOS** | | |
| | 2.0 | 1.9 | 1.9 | 3.1 | 2.5 | 1.7 | | 2.1 | 2.0 |
| | .6 | .5 | .7 | .9 | 1.0 | .8 | Current | .7 | .7 |
| | .2 | .2 | .2 | .2 | .5 | .5 | | .2 | .2 |
| | 1.6 | 1.4 | 1.5 | 1.8 | 1.6 | 1.4 | | 1.4 | 1.5 |
| | .6 | .4 | (805) .5 | .7 | .4 | .6 | Quick | (1845) .5 | .4 |
| | .2 | .1 | .1 | .1 | .1 | .1 | | .1 | .1 |
| | 0 UND | 0 UND | 0 UND | 0 UND | 0 UND | 4 90.3 | | 0 UND | 0 UND |
| | 0 UND | 0 UND | 0 UND | 1 648.7 | 10 36.5 | 17 20.9 | Sales/Receivables | 0 UND | 0 UND |
| | 0 UND | 0 UND | 0 UND | 18 20.8 | 43 8.4 | 37 9.9 | | 1 331.0 | 1 446.6 |
| | | | | | | | Cost of Sales/Inventory | | |
| | | | | | | | Cost of Sales/Payables | | |
| | 13.0 | 9.4 | 6.3 | 3.8 | 8.2 | 2.5 | | 6.4 | 7.4 |
| | -19.3 | -9.0 | -14.4 | -138.3 | 568.7 | -12.5 | Sales/Working Capital | -15.5 | -13.4 |
| | -3.5 | -2.7 | -2.4 | -2.2 | -2.5 | -1.6 | | -2.9 | -2.7 |
| | 8.9 | 8.3 | 7.4 | 5.7 | 5.6 | 3.0 | | 6.9 | 7.0 |
| | (87) 5.0 | (266) 4.4 | (278) 3.9 | (93) 3.0 | (15) 1.3 | (14) 1.6 | EBIT/Interest | (624) 3.7 | (668) 4.0 |
| | 1.8 | 2.3 | 2.0 | 1.3 | -.1 | 1.1 | | 1.8 | 1.9 |
| | | 4.3 | 2.8 | 2.1 | | | | 3.7 | 3.0 |
| | | (19) 1.6 | (36) 2.1 | (18) 1.0 | | | Net Profit + Depr., Dep., Amort./Cur. Mat. L/T/D | (82) 2.0 | (91) 1.7 |
| | | 1.0 | 1.4 | .4 | | | | 1.0 | .9 |
| | 1.1 | 2.0 | 1.8 | 1.4 | 1.1 | 2.1 | | 1.8 | 1.9 |
| | 3.6 | 4.7 | 4.4 | 3.1 | 3.2 | 7.1 | Fixed/Worth | 4.1 | 4.5 |
| | -7.0 | 47.3 | 33.5 | 13.3 | 5.0 | 31.9 | | 22.6 | 85.2 |
| | .9 | 1.4 | 1.4 | 1.4 | 1.2 | 1.7 | | 1.4 | 1.5 |
| | 3.4 | 4.4 | 4.2 | 3.3 | 3.5 | 6.9 | Debt/Worth | 4.0 | 4.5 |
| | -5.7 | 55.2 | 33.6 | 24.3 | 5.3 | 32.6 | | 27.1 | 155.1 |
| | 61.7 | 35.7 | 29.6 | 23.8 | 15.4 | 25.1 | | 37.5 | 33.5 |
| | (145) 18.5 | (619) 15.0 | (638) 13.6 | (159) 11.3 | (18) 2.0 | (19) 12.4 | % Profit Before Taxes/Tangible Net Worth | (1476) 16.6 | (1610) 13.8 |
| | 6.6 | 4.5 | 3.4 | 1.4 | -6.4 | 3.4 | | 4.7 | 2.5 |
| | 25.8 | 9.2 | 6.8 | 6.0 | 3.2 | 4.4 | | 8.7 | 8.2 |
| | 7.8 | 3.8 | 3.0 | 2.8 | .5 | 1.0 | % Profit Before Taxes/Total Assets | 3.8 | 3.2 |
| | 1.6 | .7 | .3 | .1 | -2.4 | -1.5 | | .6 | .1 |
| | 3.2 | .3 | .3 | .4 | 1.1 | .3 | | .4 | .4 |
| | .4 | .2 | .2 | .2 | .3 | .2 | Sales/Net Fixed Assets | .2 | .2 |
| | .2 | .1 | .1 | .1 | .1 | .1 | | .1 | .1 |
| | 1.2 | .3 | .2 | .3 | .7 | .2 | | .3 | .3 |
| | .3 | .2 | .1 | .1 | .2 | .2 | Sales/Total Assets | .2 | .2 |
| | .2 | .1 | .1 | .1 | .1 | .1 | | .1 | .1 |
| | 5.2 | 10.7 | 12.4 | 8.7 | 5.5 | 10.7 | | 9.0 | 9.9 |
| | (155) 12.9 | (694) 17.8 | (728) 19.7 | (187) 17.0 | (19) 19.2 | (22) 18.1 | % Depr., Dep., Amort./Sales | (1621) 15.7 | (1874) 17.1 |
| | 20.4 | 24.9 | 27.9 | 28.2 | 26.8 | 24.7 | | 22.7 | 25.0 |
| | 3.5 | 3.7 | 3.4 | 1.5 | | | | 2.2 | 3.1 |
| | (27) 7.6 | (43) 5.9 | (48) 5.8 | (21) 3.9 | | | % Officers', Directors', Owners' Comp/Sales | (160) 5.4 | (165) 6.3 |
| | 15.7 | 11.7 | 10.8 | 8.3 | | | | 13.1 | 12.5 |
| | 65520M | 334722M | 894726M | 1520633M | 716875M | 1160257M | Net Sales ($) | 8903227M | 5639253M |
| | 61044M | 959926M | 3419544M | 4111741M | 1393079M | 4152390M | Total Assets ($) | 12889684M | 14673104M |

M = $ thousand　　MM = $ million
See Pages 9 through 22 for Explanation of Ratios and Data

## Comparative Historical Data | Current Data Sorted by Sales

| | 4/1/09-3/31/10 ALL | 4/1/10-3/31/11 ALL | 4/1/11-3/31/12 ALL | Type of Statement | 0-1MM | 1-3MM | 3-5MM | 5-10MM | 10-25MM | 25MM & OVER |
|---|---|---|---|---|---|---|---|---|---|---|
| | 99 | 73 | 78 | Unqualified | 22 | 14 | 10 | 5 | 14 | 13 |
| | 100 | 83 | 86 | Reviewed | 40 | 17 | 7 | 10 | 7 | 5 |
| | 256 | 221 | 229 | Compiled | 149 | 61 | 10 | 4 | 4 | 1 |
| | 1008 | 997 | 1039 | Tax Returns | 921 | 99 | 8 | 10 | 1 | |
| | 607 | 609 | 630 | Other | 434 | 114 | 24 | 16 | 25 | 17 |
| | | | | | | 111 (4/1-9/30/11) | | 1,951 (10/1/11-3/31/12) | | |
| | 2070 | 1983 | 2062 | NUMBER OF STATEMENTS | 1566 | 305 | 59 | 45 | 51 | 36 |
| | % | % | % | ASSETS | % | % | % | % | % | % |
| | 5.7 | 6.4 | 6.1 | Cash & Equivalents | 5.0 | 8.2 | 13.0 | 10.3 | 10.5 | 10.1 |
| | 2.1 | 1.6 | 1.8 | Trade Receivables (net) | .8 | 1.9 | 8.1 | 8.8 | 7.8 | 13.6 |
| | 1.5 | 1.4 | 1.3 | Inventory | .4 | 2.5 | 7.2 | 4.0 | 8.0 | 9.7 |
| | 2.0 | 1.9 | 1.7 | All Other Current | 1.4 | 1.9 | 4.1 | 3.3 | 5.4 | 2.4 |
| | 11.2 | 11.4 | 10.8 | Total Current | 7.6 | 14.5 | 32.3 | 26.4 | 31.7 | 35.7 |
| | 79.7 | 79.6 | 79.7 | Fixed Assets (net) | 84.4 | 73.1 | 51.0 | 57.3 | 50.4 | 47.4 |
| | 2.0 | 2.0 | 2.4 | Intangibles (net) | 1.8 | 3.6 | 4.6 | 4.5 | 4.2 | 9.2 |
| | 7.1 | 7.1 | 7.1 | All Other Non-Current | 6.3 | 8.7 | 12.0 | 11.8 | 13.7 | 7.7 |
| | 100.0 | 100.0 | 100.0 | Total | 100.0 | 100.0 | 100.0 | 100.0 | 100.0 | 100.0 |
| | | | | LIABILITIES | | | | | | |
| | 3.9 | 4.4 | 3.8 | Notes Payable-Short Term | 3.5 | 4.5 | 6.4 | 4.6 | 5.1 | 6.6 |
| | 5.3 | 4.4 | 4.6 | Cur. Mat.-L.T.D. | 4.5 | 5.3 | 3.0 | 2.7 | 5.3 | 5.8 |
| | 1.3 | 1.2 | 1.1 | Trade Payables | .3 | 1.7 | 3.0 | 6.6 | 6.2 | 9.8 |
| | .0 | .0 | .0 | Income Taxes Payable | .0 | .1 | .1 | .2 | .2 | .1 |
| | 5.2 | 5.3 | 5.2 | All Other Current | 4.7 | 5.3 | 7.6 | 6.2 | 9.8 | 10.2 |
| | 15.8 | 15.3 | 14.6 | Total Current | 13.0 | 16.9 | 20.2 | 20.4 | 26.5 | 32.4 |
| | 64.7 | 61.2 | 62.8 | Long-Term Debt | 64.0 | 71.2 | 42.3 | 38.6 | 43.6 | 26.2 |
| | .1 | .0 | .1 | Deferred Taxes | .0 | .0 | .0 | .5 | .6 | .8 |
| | 3.7 | 4.9 | 4.8 | All Other Non-Current | 4.0 | 6.8 | 13.5 | 7.4 | 5.8 | 6.4 |
| | 15.8 | 18.5 | 17.7 | Net Worth | 18.9 | 5.1 | 24.0 | 33.0 | 23.5 | 34.1 |
| | 100.0 | 100.0 | 100.0 | Total Liabilties & Net Worth | 100.0 | 100.0 | 100.0 | 100.0 | 100.0 | 100.0 |
| | | | | INCOME DATA | | | | | | |
| | 100.0 | 100.0 | 100.0 | Net Sales | 100.0 | 100.0 | 100.0 | 100.0 | 100.0 | 100.0 |
| | | | | Gross Profit | | | | | | |
| | 53.6 | 53.2 | 52.7 | Operating Expenses | 48.0 | 59.6 | 74.2 | 77.9 | 82.5 | 85.5 |
| | 46.4 | 46.8 | 47.3 | Operating Profit | 52.0 | 40.4 | 25.8 | 22.1 | 17.5 | 14.5 |
| | 25.2 | 25.5 | 24.9 | All Other Expenses (net) | 28.1 | 18.2 | 12.1 | 9.0 | 9.8 | 6.9 |
| | 21.3 | 21.2 | 22.4 | Profit Before Taxes | 23.9 | 22.2 | 13.7 | 13.1 | 7.7 | 7.6 |
| | | | | RATIOS | | | | | | |
| | 2.2 | 2.1 | 2.1 | | 1.7 | 2.9 | 4.4 | 3.0 | 3.2 | 2.3 |
| | .6 | .6 | .6 | Current | .5 | 1.0 | 1.8 | 1.1 | 1.1 | 1.3 |
| | .2 | .2 | .2 | | .1 | .2 | .6 | .7 | .6 | .7 |
| | 1.6 | 1.5 | 1.5 | | 1.4 | 2.0 | 2.8 | 2.4 | 1.9 | 1.8 |
| | (2068) .4 | .4 | (2059) .5 | Quick | (1563) .4 | .7 | 1.1 | .9 | .7 | .9 |
| | .1 | .1 | .1 | | .1 | .2 | .3 | .4 | .2 | .4 |
| | 0 UND | 0 UND | 0 UND | | 0 UND | 0 UND | 0 UND | 0 UND | 1 497.1 | 7 56.1 |
| | 0 UND | 0 UND | 0 UND | Sales/Receivables | 0 UND | 0 UND | 1 305.1 | 4 98.4 | 11 34.3 | 27 13.3 |
| | 2 214.3 | 0 UND | 0 UND | | 0 UND | 4 91.7 | 33 10.9 | 34 10.8 | 36 10.2 | 48 7.6 |
| | | | | Cost of Sales/Inventory | | | | | | |
| | | | | Cost of Sales/Payables | | | | | | |
| | 6.5 | 6.5 | 7.1 | | 9.8 | 5.0 | 2.9 | 6.3 | 6.5 | 6.6 |
| | -12.6 | -11.0 | -13.1 | Sales/Working Capital | -8.7 | -176.3 | 9.5 | 45.0 | 88.8 | 20.1 |
| | -2.4 | -2.6 | -2.6 | | -2.4 | -3.6 | -6.7 | -29.8 | -6.0 | -12.4 |
| | 7.6 | 7.9 | 7.8 | | 7.9 | 6.0 | 8.6 | 28.6 | 6.3 | 11.5 |
| | (756) 4.2 | (695) 4.2 | (753) 4.0 | EBIT/Interest | (459) 4.4 | (156) 3.4 | (36) 2.1 | (34) 4.2 | (37) 2.3 | (31) 2.8 |
| | 2.0 | 2.0 | 1.9 | | 2.3 | 1.4 | 1.0 | 2.1 | 1.1 | .9 |
| | 2.8 | 2.9 | 3.1 | | 3.3 | 5.4 | | | 2.5 | |
| | (77) 1.8 | (66) 1.7 | (88) 1.9 | Net Profit + Depr., Dep., Amort./Cur. Mat. L/T/D | (41) 2.1 | (18) 2.2 | | | (11) 1.5 | |
| | 1.0 | .9 | 1.0 | | .9 | 1.6 | | | .3 | |
| | 1.8 | 1.7 | 1.8 | | 2.0 | 1.9 | .4 | .7 | .3 | .7 |
| | 4.6 | 4.2 | 4.3 | Fixed/Worth | 4.5 | 5.0 | 1.7 | 1.9 | 2.1 | 2.0 |
| | 116.0 | 31.7 | 44.4 | | 33.2 | -7.5 | 7.7 | 7.9 | 4.7 | 12.1 |
| | 1.5 | 1.4 | 1.4 | | 1.4 | 1.8 | 1.0 | .7 | 1.4 | 1.2 |
| | 4.6 | 3.9 | 4.1 | Debt/Worth | 4.1 | 5.9 | 2.6 | 2.2 | 2.5 | 2.3 |
| | 198.6 | 46.5 | 56.7 | | 34.9 | -9.7 | 23.0 | 8.5 | 6.9 | 23.5 |
| | 33.3 | 30.8 | 32.4 | | 30.4 | 42.8 | 44.8 | 46.0 | 40.5 | 34.0 |
| | (1567) 14.6 | (1543) 13.6 | (1598) 14.2 | % Profit Before Taxes/Tangible Net Worth | (1243) 13.6 | (199) 17.6 | (45) 12.6 | (37) 16.9 | (43) 18.2 | (31) 12.7 |
| | 3.0 | 2.4 | 3.4 | | 3.4 | 4.9 | .0 | 4.8 | 1.9 | -.8 |
| | 8.2 | 8.1 | 8.1 | | 7.6 | 10.5 | 13.6 | 12.5 | 14.6 | 6.9 |
| | 3.4 | 3.2 | 3.5 | % Profit Before Taxes/Total Assets | 3.3 | 4.3 | 3.3 | 5.1 | 2.8 | 2.5 |
| | .2 | .2 | .5 | | .5 | .7 | .0 | 1.0 | .4 | -.7 |
| | .4 | .4 | .4 | | .3 | .8 | 16.4 | 12.5 | 29.7 | 16.5 |
| | .2 | .2 | .2 | Sales/Net Fixed Assets | .2 | .3 | .8 | .8 | 1.5 | 3.1 |
| | .1 | .1 | .1 | | .1 | .2 | .2 | .3 | .3 | .3 |
| | .3 | .3 | .3 | | .2 | .5 | 1.1 | 2.1 | 2.3 | 2.2 |
| | .2 | .2 | .2 | Sales/Total Assets | .1 | .2 | .3 | .5 | .5 | .9 |
| | .1 | .1 | .1 | | .1 | .1 | .2 | .2 | .3 | .3 |
| | 10.6 | 11.0 | 10.8 | | 12.7 | 7.5 | 2.3 | 2.4 | 1.1 | .9 |
| | (1839) 17.3 | (1719) 17.9 | (1805) 17.9 | % Depr., Dep., Amort./Sales | (1367) 19.3 | (268) 16.5 | (52) 10.6 | (38) 10.2 | (46) 7.0 | (34) 2.6 |
| | 25.0 | 26.4 | 25.9 | | 26.7 | 24.6 | 22.2 | 14.9 | 17.9 | 11.2 |
| | 4.0 | 2.4 | 3.3 | | 3.6 | 3.5 | 3.6 | 2.9 | | |
| | (173) 7.1 | (143) 6.0 | (141) 5.9 | % Officers', Directors' Owners' Comp/Sales | (58) 8.5 | (48) 5.6 | (10) 4.9 | (13) 7.1 | | |
| | 13.2 | 13.5 | 11.2 | | 16.1 | 8.2 | 6.8 | 14.7 | | |
| | 5826073M | 3923703M | 4692733M | Net Sales ($) | 503943M | 499297M | 230133M | 309506M | 833196M | 2316658M |
| | 16954725M | 11508371M | 14097724M | Total Assets ($) | 3468885M | 2707524M | 1019801M | 981701M | 2374961M | 3544852M |

M = $ thousand   MM = $ million
See Pages 9 through 22 for Explanation of Ratios and Data

## Current Data Sorted by Assets      Comparative Historical Data

| | 0-500M | 500M-2MM | 2-10MM | 10-50MM | 50-100MM | 100-250MM | Type of Statement | 4/1/07-3/31/08 ALL | 4/1/08-3/31/09 ALL |
|---|---|---|---|---|---|---|---|---|---|
| | 4 | 3 | 10 | 10 | 4 | 7 | Unqualified | 63 | 44 |
| | 2 | 9 | 16 | 9 | 4 | 1 | Reviewed | 53 | 47 |
| | 12 | 35 | 22 | 7 | 1 | | Compiled | 97 | 94 |
| | 159 | 102 | 63 | 8 | | | Tax Returns | 404 | 366 |
| | 99 | 93 | 88 | 39 | 8 | 12 | Other | 296 | 314 |
| | 61 (4/1-9/30/11) | | | 766 (10/1/11-3/31/12) | | | | | |
| NUMBER OF STATEMENTS | 276 | 242 | 199 | 73 | 17 | 20 | | 913 | 865 |
| | % | % | % | % | % | % | ASSETS | % | % |
| | 35.5 | 19.0 | 13.4 | 15.2 | 19.7 | 16.5 | Cash & Equivalents | 16.8 | 18.0 |
| | 7.3 | 5.7 | 6.1 | 9.0 | 7.8 | 13.6 | Trade Receivables (net) | 6.8 | 6.8 |
| | .6 | 2.4 | 1.8 | 6.5 | 6.7 | 7.0 | Inventory | 4.9 | 3.5 |
| | 6.0 | 3.7 | 5.9 | 5.1 | 6.4 | 6.9 | All Other Current | 7.5 | 6.3 |
| | 49.4 | 30.7 | 27.1 | 35.8 | 40.6 | 44.0 | Total Current | 36.0 | 34.6 |
| | 31.5 | 47.8 | 51.7 | 41.3 | 38.8 | 26.5 | Fixed Assets (net) | 44.3 | 46.1 |
| | 5.5 | 5.5 | 7.6 | 7.2 | 9.3 | 14.2 | Intangibles (net) | 6.4 | 6.3 |
| | 13.6 | 15.9 | 13.6 | 15.6 | 11.3 | 15.3 | All Other Non-Current | 13.3 | 12.9 |
| | 100.0 | 100.0 | 100.0 | 100.0 | 100.0 | 100.0 | Total | 100.0 | 100.0 |
| | | | | | | | LIABILITIES | | |
| | 24.9 | 12.5 | 6.3 | 8.6 | 7.9 | 4.3 | Notes Payable-Short Term | 13.3 | 14.6 |
| | 3.9 | 2.9 | 3.9 | 2.9 | 8.1 | 1.8 | Cur. Mat.-L.T.D. | 4.5 | 5.0 |
| | 6.5 | 4.8 | 4.3 | 4.8 | 5.8 | 4.8 | Trade Payables | 4.8 | 5.0 |
| | .1 | .0 | .0 | .1 | .0 | .1 | Income Taxes Payable | .1 | .2 |
| | 31.5 | 14.0 | 11.2 | 10.8 | 10.2 | 12.4 | All Other Current | 18.5 | 16.5 |
| | 66.9 | 34.2 | 25.6 | 27.2 | 31.9 | 23.5 | Total Current | 41.2 | 41.3 |
| | 18.8 | 43.9 | 47.1 | 29.5 | 32.3 | 35.0 | Long-Term Debt | 34.6 | 35.0 |
| | .0 | .0 | .0 | .7 | .2 | 1.9 | Deferred Taxes | .1 | .1 |
| | 25.2 | 5.4 | 8.6 | 9.0 | 4.8 | 3.4 | All Other Non-Current | 5.7 | 8.8 |
| | -11.0 | 16.5 | 18.7 | 33.6 | 30.7 | 36.2 | Net Worth | 18.4 | 14.9 |
| | 100.0 | 100.0 | 100.0 | 100.0 | 100.0 | 100.0 | Total Liabilities & Net Worth | 100.0 | 100.0 |
| | | | | | | | INCOME DATA | | |
| | 100.0 | 100.0 | 100.0 | 100.0 | 100.0 | 100.0 | Net Sales | 100.0 | 100.0 |
| | | | | | | | Gross Profit | | |
| | 89.3 | 76.8 | 74.5 | 79.6 | 88.1 | 89.2 | Operating Expenses | 80.7 | 82.4 |
| | 10.7 | 23.2 | 25.5 | 20.4 | 11.9 | 10.8 | Operating Profit | 19.3 | 17.6 |
| | 2.9 | 11.1 | 12.3 | 9.8 | 9.1 | 9.1 | All Other Expenses (net) | 9.8 | 10.8 |
| | 7.7 | 12.0 | 13.2 | 10.6 | 2.8 | 1.7 | Profit Before Taxes | 9.5 | 6.8 |
| | | | | | | | RATIOS | | |
| | 3.5 | 2.6 | 2.4 | 2.2 | 2.6 | 4.3 | | 2.2 | 2.1 |
| | 1.1 | 1.2 | 1.1 | 1.4 | 1.8 | 1.8 | Current | 1.0 | 1.0 |
| | .3 | .3 | .3 | .5 | .6 | 1.0 | | .3 | .3 |
| | 3.2 | 2.3 | 2.1 | 2.0 | 2.3 | 2.9 | | 1.6 | 1.6 |
| | .9 | 1.0 | .6 | .8 | .8 | .9 | Quick | .6 (863) | .6 |
| | .2 | .2 | .2 | .2 | .3 | .5 | | .1 | .2 |
| | 0 UND | 0 UND | 0 UND | 0 UND | 0 UND | 8 44.0 | | 0 UND | 0 UND |
| | 0 UND | 0 UND | 0 UND | 2 211.6 | 9 39.3 | 38 9.7 | Sales/Receivables | 0 UND | 0 UND |
| | 1 263.7 | 6 58.3 | 8 44.1 | 34 10.7 | 35 10.4 | 59 6.2 | | 8 46.7 | 9 42.8 |
| | | | | | | | Cost of Sales/Inventory | | |
| | | | | | | | Cost of Sales/Payables | | |
| | 15.7 | 8.1 | 6.3 | 4.2 | 3.0 | 1.3 | | 9.9 | 12.6 |
| | 341.5 | 110.9 | 129.5 | 24.5 | 14.7 | 10.2 | Sales/Working Capital | 779.8 | -999.8 |
| | -14.5 | -4.5 | -6.0 | -10.3 | -3.5 | NM | | -7.8 | -6.8 |
| | 13.3 | 16.2 | 12.4 | 11.1 | 5.9 | 5.8 | | 10.2 | 7.6 |
| | (132) 4.8 | (138) 5.2 | (114) 4.2 | (37) 3.7 | (11) -.2 | (15) 2.7 | EBIT/Interest | (512) 2.9 | (482) 1.2 |
| | .1 | 1.3 | 1.8 | .2 | -17.2 | 1.5 | | .1 | -2.9 |
| | | | | | | | Net Profit + Depr., Dep., Amort./Cur. Mat. L/T/D | 4.5 | 2.6 |
| | | | | | | | | (36) 1.6 | (38) 1.7 |
| | | | | | | | | .4 | -1.6 |
| | .0 | .3 | .6 | .2 | .4 | .2 | | .3 | .4 |
| | .8 | 2.1 | 3.3 | 1.1 | 1.4 | .9 | Fixed/Worth | 1.9 | 2.4 |
| | -2.7 | -44.5 | -10.9 | 7.0 | -311.6 | NM | | UND | -30.9 |
| | .5 | .9 | 1.4 | .7 | .8 | 1.2 | | 1.0 | .9 |
| | 3.5 | 3.0 | 4.0 | 1.9 | 3.6 | 2.5 | Debt/Worth | 3.5 | 4.3 |
| | -3.3 | -46.9 | -16.2 | 7.1 | -331.5 | NM | | -40.0 | -22.2 |
| | 134.6 | 67.0 | 50.1 | 25.7 | 40.7 | 26.9 | % Profit Before Taxes/Tangible Net Worth | 77.9 | 40.1 |
| | (177) 42.3 | (175) 21.0 | (141) 21.9 | (61) 4.3 | (12) 1.0 | (15) 8.5 | | (663) 22.0 | (615) 10.9 |
| | 3.5 | .3 | 2.9 | -1.6 | -3.5 | -.2 | | 2.2 | -6.4 |
| | 50.0 | 16.9 | 12.5 | 6.7 | 4.8 | 8.6 | % Profit Before Taxes/Total Assets | 17.7 | 9.8 |
| | 12.3 | 5.3 | 4.4 | 3.2 | .0 | 2.2 | | 4.4 | 1.5 |
| | -5.2 | -.3 | .8 | -.1 | -4.1 | .0 | | -1.8 | -5.7 |
| | 547.5 | 56.4 | 18.0 | 37.7 | 33.7 | 27.2 | Sales/Net Fixed Assets | 55.5 | 48.8 |
| | 49.8 | 6.0 | 1.2 | 4.2 | 5.5 | 11.9 | | 11.4 | 8.2 |
| | 9.9 | .3 | .2 | .2 | .3 | 1.0 | | .4 | .3 |
| | 11.7 | 3.9 | 2.5 | 2.2 | 1.9 | 1.6 | Sales/Total Assets | 5.4 | 5.2 |
| | 5.5 | 1.0 | .5 | .5 | .8 | .8 | | 1.5 | 1.4 |
| | 2.0 | .2 | .2 | .1 | .2 | .2 | | .3 | .2 |
| | .4 | .7 | 1.6 | 1.0 | 3.2 | 1.1 | % Depr., Dep., Amort./Sales | .8 | 1.0 |
| | (143) 1.1 | (174) 5.5 | (152) 7.8 | (54) 2.9 | (10) 9.6 | (14) 3.2 | | (671) 2.8 | (641) 3.3 |
| | 3.4 | 18.2 | 18.8 | 16.4 | 17.4 | 13.2 | | 12.6 | 14.9 |
| | 3.3 | 1.9 | 2.2 | .6 | | | % Officers', Directors' Owners' Comp/Sales | 2.7 | 1.7 |
| | (105) 6.1 | (62) 3.7 | (50) 3.6 | (15) 3.3 | | | | (239) 5.4 | (221) 4.9 |
| | 16.1 | 8.7 | 7.2 | 6.3 | | | | 15.7 | 11.8 |
| | 496341M | 685275M | 1527068M | 2301876M | 2073117M | 3105798M | Net Sales ($) | 11119705M | 8892674M |
| | 58911M | 267831M | 841393M | 1566500M | 1251785M | 3306406M | Total Assets ($) | 6749598M | 5829371M |

## Comparative Historical Data     Current Data Sorted by Sales

| | | | Type of Statement | | | | | | |
|---|---|---|---|---|---|---|---|---|---|
| 46 | 38 | 38 | Unqualified | 5 | 4 | 3 | 5 | 8 | 13 |
| 40 | 33 | 41 | Reviewed | 9 | 8 | 4 | 2 | 7 | 11 |
| 96 | 86 | 77 | Compiled | 28 | 16 | 10 | 9 | 12 | 2 |
| 363 | 304 | 332 | Tax Returns | 192 | 81 | 16 | 27 | 14 | 2 |
| 289 | 306 | 339 | Other | 117 | 86 | 22 | 39 | 32 | 43 |
| 4/1/09-3/31/10 | 4/1/10-3/31/11 | 4/1/11-3/31/12 | | 61 (4/1-9/30/11) | | | 766 (10/1/11-3/31/12) | | |
| ALL | ALL | ALL | | 0-1MM | 1-3MM | 3-5MM | 5-10MM | 10-25MM | 25MM & OVER |
| 834 | 767 | 827 | **NUMBER OF STATEMENTS** | 351 | 195 | 55 | 82 | 73 | 71 |
| % | % | % | **ASSETS** | % | % | % | % | % | % |
| 20.0 | 21.1 | 22.8 | Cash & Equivalents | 17.2 | 29.7 | 26.0 | 25.3 | 24.1 | 24.6 |
| 6.0 | 6.0 | 6.8 | Trade Receivables (net) | 3.5 | 6.4 | 8.0 | 10.4 | 8.4 | 18.1 |
| 2.7 | 2.0 | 2.2 | Inventory | 1.0 | 1.9 | 3.2 | 2.7 | 2.7 | 7.0 |
| 5.3 | 6.0 | 5.2 | All Other Current | 3.4 | 6.1 | 7.3 | 4.4 | 10.1 | 6.2 |
| 34.0 | 35.1 | 37.0 | Total Current | 25.1 | 44.2 | 44.4 | 42.8 | 45.3 | 55.9 |
| 45.7 | 45.0 | 42.0 | Fixed Assets (net) | 60.4 | 34.4 | 32.2 | 24.7 | 24.7 | 17.8 |
| 6.2 | 6.6 | 6.5 | Intangibles (net) | 2.8 | 7.5 | 8.4 | 6.5 | 12.0 | 14.1 |
| 14.1 | 13.4 | 14.5 | All Other Non-Current | 11.8 | 13.9 | 15.0 | 26.0 | 17.9 | 12.2 |
| 100.0 | 100.0 | 100.0 | Total | 100.0 | 100.0 | 100.0 | 100.0 | 100.0 | 100.0 |
| | | | **LIABILITIES** | | | | | | |
| 15.9 | 13.7 | 14.5 | Notes Payable-Short Term | 13.5 | 17.1 | 25.7 | 14.6 | 9.5 | 8.7 |
| 4.5 | 4.0 | 3.5 | Cur. Mat.-L.T.D. | 3.5 | 3.7 | 6.4 | 2.1 | 2.9 | 3.5 |
| 4.3 | 4.0 | 5.3 | Trade Payables | 2.8 | 4.8 | 7.9 | 8.4 | 7.5 | 10.6 |
| .1 | .1 | .1 | Income Taxes Payable | .0 | .1 | .0 | .1 | .0 | .1 |
| 15.5 | 17.1 | 18.8 | All Other Current | 15.8 | 25.2 | 16.0 | 20.1 | 16.5 | 18.4 |
| 40.3 | 38.8 | 42.1 | Total Current | 35.7 | 50.9 | 56.1 | 45.2 | 36.5 | 41.4 |
| 36.7 | 38.1 | 34.6 | Long-Term Debt | 49.5 | 23.1 | 20.8 | 23.9 | 23.0 | 27.3 |
| .0 | .0 | .1 | Deferred Taxes | .0 | .1 | .0 | .0 | .1 | .8 |
| 8.2 | 11.9 | 13.1 | All Other Non-Current | 11.0 | 15.9 | 17.9 | 9.3 | 17.3 | 11.8 |
| 14.7 | 11.2 | 10.1 | Net Worth | 3.8 | 10.0 | 5.2 | 21.6 | 23.1 | 18.7 |
| 100.0 | 100.0 | 100.0 | Total Liabilties & Net Worth | 100.0 | 100.0 | 100.0 | 100.0 | 100.0 | 100.0 |
| | | | **INCOME DATA** | | | | | | |
| 100.0 | 100.0 | 100.0 | Net Sales | 100.0 | 100.0 | 100.0 | 100.0 | 100.0 | 100.0 |
| | | | Gross Profit | | | | | | |
| 79.9 | 80.0 | 81.2 | Operating Expenses | 66.8 | 87.3 | 95.2 | 95.9 | 94.8 | 94.1 |
| 20.1 | 20.0 | 18.8 | Operating Profit | 33.2 | 12.7 | 4.8 | 4.1 | 5.2 | 5.9 |
| 10.5 | 9.6 | 8.5 | All Other Expenses (net) | 17.3 | 3.1 | .9 | 1.1 | 2.3 | .2 |
| 9.7 | 10.4 | 10.3 | Profit Before Taxes | 15.9 | 9.6 | 3.9 | 3.0 | 2.9 | 5.7 |
| | | | **RATIOS** | | | | | | |
| 2.8 | 2.9 | 2.9 | | 2.7 | 3.5 | 3.0 | 2.8 | 3.3 | 2.4 |
| 1.1 | 1.2 | 1.2 | Current | .8 | 1.3 | 1.0 | 1.2 | 1.5 | 1.5 |
| .3 | .4 | .3 | | .2 | .4 | .5 | .5 | .6 | .9 |
| 2.1 | 2.3 | 2.3 | | 2.3 | 2.8 | 2.3 | 2.6 | 2.4 | 2.0 |
| (832) .7 | .8 | .8 | Quick | .5 | 1.0 | .8 | 1.1 | 1.0 | 1.3 |
| .2 | .2 | .2 | | .1 | .3 | .3 | .3 | .3 | .5 |
| 0 UND | 0 UND | 0 UND | | 0 UND | 0 UND | 0 UND | 0 UND | 0 UND | 1 254.8 |
| 0 UND | 0 UND | 0 UND | Sales/Receivables | 0 UND | 0 UND | 1 421.2 | 0 949.0 | 2 178.5 | 9 39.3 |
| 9 41.6 | 7 52.3 | 7 55.6 | | 1 446.0 | 8 44.0 | 8 43.1 | 7 51.7 | 13 28.7 | 49 7.4 |
| | | | Cost of Sales/Inventory | | | | | | |
| | | | Cost of Sales/Payables | | | | | | |
| 7.9 | 8.0 | 8.9 | | 6.9 | 9.6 | 15.1 | 17.4 | 8.5 | 6.7 |
| 177.3 | 105.6 | 109.0 | Sales/Working Capital | -57.0 | 46.2 | -376.0 | 110.9 | 55.0 | 18.0 |
| -6.1 | -8.5 | -8.0 | | -3.1 | -15.8 | -10.7 | -48.2 | -32.4 | -51.5 |
| 9.0 | 9.7 | 12.0 | | 8.6 | 11.2 | 15.0 | 22.5 | 18.3 | 28.5 |
| (471) 2.6 | (428) 3.3 | (447) 4.3 | EBIT/Interest | (124) 4.1 | (122) 4.4 | (36) 5.8 | (52) 6.7 | (58) 5.2 | (55) 3.7 |
| -.6 | .4 | 1.0 | | 1.2 | .7 | 1.3 | .4 | .2 | 1.5 |
| 2.6 | 2.9 | 4.9 | | | | | | | 22.8 |
| (42) 1.3 | (29) 1.7 | (30) 1.0 | Net Profit + Depr., Dep., Amort./Cur. Mat. L/T/D | | | | | (12) 1.0 | |
| .2 | .5 | .3 | | | | | | | .7 |
| .3 | .3 | .2 | | .7 | .1 | .2 | .1 | .2 | .2 |
| 2.0 | 2.2 | 1.7 | Fixed/Worth | 3.6 | 1.1 | 1.1 | .6 | .8 | .4 |
| -21.4 | -12.0 | -16.4 | | -46.4 | -12.5 | -4.4 | -18.6 | -4.3 | -8.8 |
| .8 | .8 | .8 | | 1.3 | .5 | .5 | .5 | .7 | .8 |
| 3.4 | 3.5 | 3.3 | Debt/Worth | 5.0 | 2.1 | 3.1 | 2.2 | 1.6 | 2.7 |
| -12.4 | -12.4 | -13.8 | | -19.5 | -11.2 | -13.7 | -14.1 | -10.9 | -12.2 |
| 50.5 | 70.5 | 66.8 | % Profit Before Taxes/Tangible Net Worth | 54.8 | 75.5 | 63.3 | 75.6 | 103.3 | 41.6 |
| (589) 14.8 | (531) 20.6 | (581) 21.6 | | (248) 19.7 | (136) 31.9 | (39) 27.9 | (57) 23.2 | (51) 20.8 | (50) 12.3 |
| .9 | 2.0 | 1.3 | | 1.5 | 3.0 | 2.4 | 2.3 | -3.6 | -.1 |
| 12.6 | 18.6 | 19.6 | % Profit Before Taxes/Total Assets | 13.3 | 30.8 | 18.3 | 29.9 | 20.2 | 15.9 |
| 3.4 | 4.6 | 5.1 | | 3.7 | 7.4 | 6.1 | 9.1 | 7.9 | 4.6 |
| -2.0 | -.8 | -.3 | | -.1 | -.8 | .1 | -1.2 | -1.2 | .8 |
| 51.6 | 52.1 | 77.6 | Sales/Net Fixed Assets | 17.1 | 96.4 | 92.5 | 171.6 | 104.7 | 81.2 |
| 6.9 | 8.1 | 12.1 | | .4 | 27.9 | 19.7 | 34.3 | 40.3 | 29.4 |
| .3 | .3 | .4 | | .2 | 2.0 | 4.6 | 9.3 | 7.8 | 15.3 |
| 4.8 | 5.3 | 5.2 | Sales/Total Assets | 1.8 | 7.3 | 8.2 | 9.6 | 8.5 | 5.1 |
| 1.1 | 1.4 | 1.7 | | .2 | 3.0 | 3.9 | 5.0 | 3.3 | 2.5 |
| .2 | .2 | .2 | | .1 | .7 | 1.2 | 2.1 | 1.6 | 1.5 |
| 1.0 | .8 | .8 | % Depr., Dep., Amort./Sales | 4.7 | .4 | .4 | .3 | .5 | .8 |
| (621) 4.3 | (526) 3.0 | (547) 2.9 | | (245) 14.6 | (126) 1.1 | (32) 1.1 | (49) .7 | (50) 1.4 | (45) 1.3 |
| 16.4 | 14.8 | 15.5 | | 22.2 | 4.2 | 2.3 | 2.4 | 3.0 | 2.4 |
| 2.3 | 2.2 | 2.3 | % Officers', Directors' Owners' Comp/Sales | 5.6 | 2.9 | 1.3 | 1.5 | 1.9 | .8 |
| (221) 6.1 | (226) 5.2 | (236) 4.8 | | (63) 11.9 | (71) 4.6 | (25) 2.6 | (34) 3.1 | (27) 3.5 | (16) 2.7 |
| 12.9 | 13.3 | 10.5 | | 18.6 | 8.6 | 7.4 | 7.1 | 5.4 | 4.3 |
| 10899980M | 10089862M | 10189475M | Net Sales ($) | 133886M | 342888M | 213566M | 580942M | 1140967M | 7777226M |
| 8329032M | 6026779M | 7292826M | Total Assets ($) | 534689M | 484460M | 245129M | 530667M | 1405058M | 4092823M |

© RMA 2012

**M = $ thousand    MM = $ million**

See Pages 9 through 22 for Explanation of Ratios and Data

## Current Data Sorted by Assets

## Comparative Historical Data

| 0-500M | 500M-2MM | 2-10MM | 10-50MM | 50-100MM | 100-250MM | Type of Statement | | 4/1/07-3/31/08 ALL | 4/1/08-3/31/09 ALL |
|---|---|---|---|---|---|---|---|---|---|
| 4 | 16 | 30 | 14 | 5 | 5 | Unqualified | | 38 | 48 |
| | 4 | 10 | 10 | 1 | | Reviewed | | 10 | 12 |
| 11 | 16 | 18 | 4 | | | Compiled | | 17 | 21 |
| 83 | 105 | 80 | 8 | | | Tax Returns | | 77 | 145 |
| 56 | 70 | 88 | 35 | 4 | 4 | Other | | 83 | 170 |
| 0-500M | 49 (4/1-9/30/11) 500M-2MM | 2-10MM | 632 (10/1/11-3/31/12) 10-50MM | 50-100MM | 100-250MM | | | | |
| 154 | 211 | 226 | 71 | 10 | 9 | NUMBER OF STATEMENTS | | 225 | 396 |
| % | % | % | % | % | % | ASSETS | | % | % |
| 32.8 | 17.8 | 9.5 | 13.2 | 8.2 | | Cash & Equivalents | | 20.0 | 19.1 |
| 8.1 | 5.7 | 5.4 | 9.6 | 7.6 | | Trade Receivables (net) | | 7.0 | 7.2 |
| 2.3 | 1.8 | 2.4 | 6.4 | 8.5 | | Inventory | | 6.9 | 4.3 |
| 3.5 | 2.5 | 2.8 | 4.9 | 1.1 | | All Other Current | | 5.4 | 4.2 |
| 46.8 | 27.8 | 20.1 | 34.0 | 25.4 | | Total Current | | 39.3 | 34.8 |
| 32.5 | 55.7 | 65.4 | 47.1 | 47.0 | | Fixed Assets (net) | | 42.4 | 46.5 |
| 4.5 | 2.9 | 3.5 | 1.9 | 1.5 | | Intangibles (net) | | 2.8 | 3.8 |
| 16.2 | 13.6 | 10.9 | 17.1 | 26.1 | | All Other Non-Current | | 15.4 | 14.9 |
| 100.0 | 100.0 | 100.0 | 100.0 | 100.0 | | Total | | 100.0 | 100.0 |
| | | | | | | LIABILITIES | | | |
| 9.5 | 5.1 | 3.6 | 3.9 | 1.2 | | Notes Payable-Short Term | | 9.2 | 8.0 |
| 3.9 | 3.8 | 2.7 | 2.2 | 1.5 | | Cur. Mat.-L.T.D. | | 7.9 | 4.3 |
| 5.8 | 3.4 | 2.4 | 3.7 | 6.8 | | Trade Payables | | 5.8 | 4.2 |
| .0 | .0 | .1 | .0 | .0 | | Income Taxes Payable | | .0 | .0 |
| 46.9 | 14.1 | 13.0 | 11.1 | 24.1 | | All Other Current | | 14.8 | 20.4 |
| 66.1 | 26.4 | 21.9 | 21.1 | 33.6 | | Total Current | | 37.7 | 36.8 |
| 34.7 | 47.1 | 52.7 | 41.6 | 26.4 | | Long-Term Debt | | 41.0 | 44.6 |
| .0 | .0 | .1 | .3 | .0 | | Deferred Taxes | | .0 | .0 |
| 6.6 | 3.8 | 4.0 | 3.6 | .4 | | All Other Non-Current | | 2.9 | 3.5 |
| -7.4 | 22.7 | 21.3 | 33.5 | 39.5 | | Net Worth | | 18.4 | 15.1 |
| 100.0 | 100.0 | 100.0 | 100.0 | 100.0 | | Total Liabilities & Net Worth | | 100.0 | 100.0 |
| | | | | | | INCOME DATA | | | |
| 100.0 | 100.0 | 100.0 | 100.0 | 100.0 | | Net Sales | | 100.0 | 100.0 |
| | | | | | | Gross Profit | | | |
| 84.7 | 71.5 | 71.3 | 76.7 | 81.0 | | Operating Expenses | | 82.9 | 79.9 |
| 15.3 | 28.5 | 28.7 | 23.3 | 19.0 | | Operating Profit | | 17.1 | 20.1 |
| 3.9 | 16.7 | 18.7 | 14.0 | 6.1 | | All Other Expenses (net) | | 9.6 | 12.5 |
| 11.3 | 11.8 | 10.0 | 9.3 | 12.9 | | Profit Before Taxes | | 7.5 | 7.6 |
| | | | | | | RATIOS | | | |
| 3.2 | 3.0 | 2.1 | 2.6 | 1.9 | | Current | | 3.4 | 2.6 |
| 1.0 | 1.1 | .8 | 1.5 | .8 | | | | 1.1 | 1.0 |
| .3 | .2 | .1 | .6 | .4 | | | | .4 | .3 |
| 2.9 | 2.4 | 1.6 | 2.0 | 1.7 | | Quick | | 2.1 | 2.2 |
| (153) 1.0 | .9 | .6 | .9 | .5 | | | | (224) .7 | .5 |
| .2 | .1 | .1 | .4 | .1 | | | | .1 | .1 |
| 0 UND | 0 UND | 0 UND | 0 UND | 3 120.7 | | Sales/Receivables | | 0 UND | 0 UND |
| 0 UND | 0 UND | 0 UND | 6 60.2 | 19 19.2 | | | | 1 326.2 | 0 999.8 |
| 4 89.0 | 5 73.6 | 15 23.7 | 35 10.5 | 30 12.3 | | | | 18 20.5 | 14 26.1 |
| | | | | | | Cost of Sales/Inventory | | | |
| | | | | | | Cost of Sales/Payables | | | |
| 12.4 | 4.5 | 6.3 | 2.7 | 3.4 | | Sales/Working Capital | | 4.2 | 4.9 |
| UND | 47.9 | -37.4 | 12.2 | NM | | | | 61.3 | -94.4 |
| -11.4 | -2.7 | -2.9 | -8.3 | -2.4 | | | | -4.2 | -3.7 |
| 18.2 | 8.2 | 13.0 | 14.3 | | | EBIT/Interest | | 8.9 | 9.5 |
| (70) 3.5 | (83) 3.1 | (107) 2.7 | (31) 4.6 | | | | | (108) 3.3 | (185) 2.6 |
| .2 | 1.1 | .9 | .9 | | | | | .7 | .1 |
| | | 3.2 | | | | Net Profit + Depr., Dep., Amort./Cur. Mat. L/T/D | | | 4.2 |
| | | (11) 2.0 | | | | | | (19) | 1.3 |
| | | .3 | | | | | | | .0 |
| .0 | .2 | 1.2 | .2 | .3 | | Fixed/Worth | | .1 | .1 |
| .8 | 2.5 | 3.8 | 1.2 | .9 | | | | 1.6 | 1.9 |
| -9.8 | -104.5 | -66.0 | 7.3 | 3.4 | | | | 124.0 | 21.1 |
| .4 | .8 | 1.1 | .6 | .4 | | Debt/Worth | | .7 | .9 |
| 3.8 | 3.7 | 4.4 | 2.5 | 2.5 | | | | 3.2 | 3.9 |
| -5.0 | -29.9 | -76.1 | 71.9 | 8.1 | | | | -120.4 | -34.6 |
| 204.9 | 42.2 | 39.7 | 25.0 | 34.4 | | % Profit Before Taxes/Tangible Net Worth | | 47.2 | 55.9 |
| (101) 40.7 | (151) 11.0 | (165) 11.2 | (56) 7.2 | 9.0 | | | | (166) 14.6 | (292) 10.8 |
| 1.9 | 1.6 | -.4 | -.9 | -6.4 | | | | -.4 | -3.8 |
| 51.4 | 9.3 | 8.5 | 8.3 | 6.7 | | % Profit Before Taxes/Total Assets | | 12.5 | 12.7 |
| 9.7 | 3.2 | 2.0 | 2.3 | 2.9 | | | | 2.5 | 2.0 |
| -2.7 | -.3 | -1.6 | -.7 | -4.4 | | | | -1.4 | -2.0 |
| UND | 29.0 | 4.7 | 26.3 | 62.7 | | Sales/Net Fixed Assets | | 97.5 | 65.8 |
| 48.1 | .6 | .3 | 1.1 | .6 | | | | 6.9 | 2.1 |
| 4.1 | .2 | .1 | .1 | .3 | | | | .3 | .2 |
| 8.9 | 1.3 | .8 | 1.0 | .6 | | Sales/Total Assets | | 2.1 | 2.2 |
| 2.7 | .3 | .2 | .3 | .2 | | | | .8 | .5 |
| .7 | .1 | .1 | .1 | .2 | | | | .2 | .2 |
| .8 | 3.9 | 3.4 | 1.3 | | | % Depr., Dep., Amort./Sales | | 1.1 | 2.0 |
| (67) 3.1 | (146) 14.5 | (178) 16.0 | (58) 7.2 | | | | | (152) 5.9 | (261) 8.9 |
| 11.4 | 23.2 | 25.2 | 23.4 | | | | | 14.5 | 18.8 |
| 8.0 | 4.6 | 1.9 | | | | % Officers', Directors' Owners' Comp/Sales | | 4.3 | 4.3 |
| (45) 13.2 | (28) 7.5 | (32) 7.4 | | | | | | (46) 8.3 | (68) 9.0 |
| 19.1 | 17.8 | 11.8 | | | | | | 14.5 | 19.4 |
| 158606M | 251306M | 880302M | 1293199M | 653939M | 1169247M | Net Sales ($) | | 2209381M | 3943306M |
| 32306M | 239969M | 1030610M | 1313896M | 711425M | 1541123M | Total Assets ($) | | 1707626M | 3121525M |

## Comparative Historical Data

## Current Data Sorted by Sales

| | | | Type of Statement | | | | | | |
|---|---|---|---|---|---|---|---|---|---|
| 63 | 43 | 74 | Unqualified | 27 | 17 | 4 | 6 | 14 | 6 |
| 20 | 13 | 25 | Reviewed | 2 | 6 | 2 | 2 | 7 | 6 |
| 42 | 32 | 49 | Compiled | 29 | 10 | 6 | 3 | 1 | |
| 234 | 218 | 276 | Tax Returns | 211 | 44 | 5 | 12 | 2 | 2 |
| 189 | 207 | 257 | Other | 115 | 68 | 21 | 23 | 18 | 12 |
| 4/1/09-3/31/10 ALL | 4/1/10-3/31/11 ALL | 4/1/11-3/31/12 ALL | | 49 (4/1-9/30/11) | 632 (10/1/11-3/31/12) | | | | |
| | | | | 0-1MM | 1-3MM | 3-5MM | 5-10MM | 10-25MM | 25MM & OVER |
| 548 | 513 | 681 | NUMBER OF STATEMENTS | 384 | 145 | 38 | 46 | 42 | 26 |
| % | % | % | ASSETS | % | % | % | % | % | % |
| 17.9 | 18.3 | 17.7 | Cash & Equivalents | 15.9 | 19.0 | 21.3 | 19.5 | 24.1 | 18.4 |
| 7.0 | 7.0 | 6.6 | Trade Receivables (net) | 2.8 | 6.6 | 15.0 | 12.7 | 17.0 | 21.9 |
| 2.8 | 3.4 | 2.8 | Inventory | 2.0 | 2.8 | 6.6 | 1.6 | 2.2 | 11.4 |
| 3.0 | 3.0 | 3.0 | All Other Current | 1.4 | 4.5 | 3.3 | 6.2 | 7.3 | 5.6 |
| 30.7 | 31.7 | 30.1 | Total Current | 22.2 | 32.9 | 46.2 | 40.0 | 50.7 | 57.3 |
| 50.6 | 51.1 | 52.7 | Fixed Assets (net) | 63.2 | 45.4 | 35.9 | 33.3 | 36.9 | 22.4 |
| 4.1 | 3.1 | 3.4 | Intangibles (net) | 2.6 | 5.5 | 1.5 | 5.2 | 2.0 | 5.9 |
| 14.5 | 14.0 | 13.8 | All Other Non-Current | 12.0 | 16.3 | 16.4 | 21.4 | 10.5 | 14.5 |
| 100.0 | 100.0 | 100.0 | Total | 100.0 | 100.0 | 100.0 | 100.0 | 100.0 | 100.0 |
| | | | LIABILITIES | | | | | | |
| 8.9 | 9.0 | 5.4 | Notes Payable-Short Term | 4.5 | 5.7 | 7.5 | 9.4 | 6.6 | 5.7 |
| 3.2 | 3.2 | 3.2 | Cur. Mat.-L.T.D. | 3.3 | 4.0 | 1.7 | 3.0 | 2.2 | 5.5 |
| 4.5 | 3.5 | 3.7 | Trade Payables | 1.8 | 5.1 | 5.8 | 3.9 | 8.3 | 12.6 |
| .1 | .1 | .1 | Income Taxes Payable | .0 | .0 | .7 | .0 | .5 | .0 |
| 20.3 | 17.7 | 20.9 | All Other Current | 20.1 | 20.6 | 24.2 | 23.7 | 20.6 | 23.8 |
| 37.0 | 33.5 | 33.3 | Total Current | 29.8 | 35.4 | 39.9 | 40.0 | 38.1 | 44.6 |
| 41.5 | 43.8 | 45.2 | Long-Term Debt | 54.2 | 43.0 | 33.0 | 28.5 | 19.0 | 15.4 |
| .1 | .0 | .1 | Deferred Taxes | .0 | .1 | .0 | .1 | .4 | .2 |
| 3.1 | 4.3 | 4.4 | All Other Non-Current | 4.7 | 4.5 | 3.8 | 5.8 | 1.1 | 4.0 |
| 18.3 | 18.3 | 17.0 | Net Worth | 11.4 | 17.0 | 23.2 | 25.6 | 41.4 | 35.8 |
| 100.0 | 100.0 | 100.0 | Total Liabilities & Net Worth | 100.0 | 100.0 | 100.0 | 100.0 | 100.0 | 100.0 |
| | | | INCOME DATA | | | | | | |
| 100.0 | 100.0 | 100.0 | Net Sales | 100.0 | 100.0 | 100.0 | 100.0 | 100.0 | 100.0 |
| | | | Gross Profit | | | | | | |
| 76.7 | 75.1 | 75.3 | Operating Expenses | 67.7 | 80.3 | 89.6 | 90.0 | 87.7 | 93.9 |
| 23.3 | 24.9 | 24.7 | Operating Profit | 32.3 | 19.7 | 10.4 | 10.0 | 12.3 | 6.1 |
| 14.0 | 13.1 | 13.9 | All Other Expenses (net) | 20.1 | 9.8 | 2.6 | 2.2 | 2.6 | .6 |
| 9.3 | 11.8 | 10.8 | Profit Before Taxes | 12.2 | 9.9 | 7.7 | 7.8 | 9.7 | 5.5 |
| | | | RATIOS | | | | | | |
| 2.0 | 2.9 | 2.5 | | 2.7 | 2.8 | 2.4 | 3.0 | 2.0 | 1.8 |
| .8 | .9 | 1.0 | Current | .9 | .9 | 1.4 | 1.3 | 1.2 | 1.3 |
| .2 | .2 | .2 | | .1 | .2 | .6 | .7 | .7 | .8 |
| 1.7 | 2.1 | 2.0 | | 2.2 | 2.1 | 2.2 | 2.3 | 1.5 | 1.4 |
| .6 (512) | .7 (680) | .7 | Quick | .7 (383) | .6 | 1.0 | 1.1 | .9 | .8 |
| .1 | .2 | .2 | | .1 | .1 | .3 | .4 | .5 | .5 |
| 0 UND | 0 UND | 0 UND | | 0 UND | 0 UND | 0 UND | 0 UND | 2 182.1 | 5 69.0 |
| 0 UND | 0 UND | 0 UND | Sales/Receivables | 0 UND | 1 363.8 | 7 54.4 | 6 63.3 | 16 22.6 | 18 20.2 |
| 14 25.6 | 14 26.2 | 12 30.5 | | 1 293.5 | 12 31.1 | 42 8.7 | 37 9.8 | 53 6.9 | 36 10.0 |
| | | | Cost of Sales/Inventory | | | | | | |
| | | | Cost of Sales/Payables | | | | | | |
| 8.5 | 6.4 | 5.3 | | 4.8 | 5.7 | 4.7 | 6.8 | 3.9 | 9.5 |
| -29.4 | -50.3 | UND | Sales/Working Capital | -106.1 | -154.3 | 28.7 | 30.4 | 75.5 | 25.2 |
| -3.3 | -4.2 | -4.0 | | -2.2 | -5.6 | -19.6 | -38.5 | -14.3 | -69.4 |
| 10.7 | 13.7 | 11.6 | | 5.9 | 12.8 | 14.0 | 22.2 | 29.7 | 86.5 |
| (256) 3.3 | (232) 3.2 | (301) 3.1 | EBIT/Interest | (109) 3.1 | (88) 2.3 | (24) 1.9 | (38) 7.9 | (21) 6.0 | (21) 6.2 |
| .9 | 1.2 | .8 | | .9 | .7 | -.1 | 1.4 | 1.1 | 2.1 |
| 13.2 | 14.6 | 5.2 | | | | | | | |
| (23) 3.1 | (16) 4.2 | (27) 1.9 | Net Profit + Depr., Dep., Amort./Cur. Mat. L/T/D | | | | | | |
| 1.3 | 2.7 | .1 | | | | | | | |
| .2 | .2 | .3 | | .6 | .1 | .1 | .3 | .2 | .2 |
| 2.3 | 2.3 | 2.5 | Fixed/Worth | 3.3 | 1.8 | .8 | 1.1 | 1.0 | .4 |
| 275.7 | 36.6 | -159.7 | | -64.4 | -13.1 | -8.1 | 8.0 | 3.4 | 4.4 |
| 1.0 | .9 | .8 | | 1.0 | .8 | .8 | .6 | .5 | .8 |
| 4.3 | 4.0 | 3.7 | Debt/Worth | 4.3 | 4.3 | 2.0 | 3.1 | 1.3 | 2.0 |
| -39.7 | -194.1 | -24.2 | | -15.6 | -12.1 | -16.3 | 30.8 | 8.4 | 15.1 |
| 47.0 | 59.9 | 50.7 | | 35.7 | 101.2 | 64.6 | 117.8 | 57.6 | 96.1 |
| (394) 15.1 | (383) 17.4 | (490) 12.6 | % Profit Before Taxes/Tangible Net Worth | (270) 10.7 | (99) 11.8 | (27) 7.8 | (37) 28.1 | (35) 20.5 | (22) 18.4 |
| .2 | 2.1 | .4 | | .5 | -1.1 | -9.1 | 4.0 | .4 | 12.3 |
| 12.2 | 13.9 | 12.2 | | 7.8 | 15.2 | 26.4 | 41.5 | 32.1 | 25.3 |
| 3.2 | 3.9 | 3.0 | % Profit Before Taxes/Total Assets | 2.2 | 3.4 | 1.4 | 10.3 | 7.0 | 6.7 |
| -.8 | .0 | -.8 | | -1.0 | -1.1 | -2.3 | 2.4 | .6 | 2.2 |
| 54.5 | 39.1 | 42.6 | | 17.4 | 83.4 | 45.7 | 71.6 | 44.8 | 95.3 |
| 1.2 | 1.8 | 1.1 | Sales/Net Fixed Assets | .3 | 5.5 | 11.7 | 15.7 | 8.1 | 32.1 |
| .2 | .2 | .2 | | .1 | .3 | 1.3 | 2.1 | 1.0 | 11.8 |
| 2.1 | 2.2 | 1.8 | | .7 | 2.2 | 4.2 | 5.0 | 2.5 | 5.2 |
| .5 | .6 | .4 | Sales/Total Assets | .2 | .7 | 1.2 | 1.8 | 1.2 | 3.5 |
| .1 | .1 | .1 | | .1 | .2 | .5 | .8 | .5 | 1.4 |
| 1.8 | 1.7 | 1.9 | | 10.1 | 1.1 | 1.1 | .8 | .6 | .3 |
| (391) 9.6 | (330) 9.7 | (462) 12.3 | % Depr., Dep., Amort./Sales | (260) 18.8 | (88) 7.5 | (27) 2.9 | (32) 1.8 | (34) 1.8 | (21) .7 |
| 19.4 | 19.9 | 23.2 | | 28.3 | 19.9 | 11.3 | 4.3 | 7.6 | 1.7 |
| 3.1 | 3.2 | 3.5 | | 6.3 | 5.3 | | 2.8 | | |
| (102) 7.0 | (99) 6.3 | (113) 8.8 | % Officers', Directors' Owners' Comp/Sales | (45) 11.9 | (36) 9.6 | | (13) 4.5 | | |
| 14.2 | 12.3 | 15.5 | | 21.4 | 14.8 | | 8.8 | | |
| 5422831M | 4027960M | 4406599M | Net Sales ($) | 139798M | 258516M | 146065M | 317789M | 677284M | 2867147M |
| 4254321M | 3714879M | 4869329M | Total Assets ($) | 696615M | 808011M | 186899M | 425181M | 1384191M | 1368432M |

M = $ thousand    MM = $ million
See Pages 9 through 22 for Explanation of Ratios and Data

## Current Data Sorted by Assets | | | | | | Comparative Historical Data

| 0-500M | 500M-2MM | 2-10MM | 10-50MM | 50-100MM | 100-250MM | Type of Statement | 4/1/07-3/31/08 ALL | 4/1/08-3/31/09 ALL |
|---|---|---|---|---|---|---|---|---|
|  | 1 | 4 | 6 | 3 | 1 | Unqualified | 12 | 18 |
|  |  | 8 | 6 | 2 |  | Reviewed | 11 | 14 |
| 3 | 9 | 15 | 5 |  |  | Compiled | 32 | 35 |
| 27 | 60 | 45 | 9 |  | 1 | Tax Returns | 71 | 123 |
| 29 | 50 | 50 | 20 | 6 | 6 | Other | 106 | 144 |
| | 24 (4/1-9/30/11) | | 342 (10/1/11-3/31/12) | | | | | |
| 59 | 120 | 122 | 46 | 11 | 8 | NUMBER OF STATEMENTS | 232 | 334 |
| % | % | % | % | % | % | ASSETS | % | % |
| 23.0 | 7.8 | 11.3 | 7.8 | 3.2 |  | Cash & Equivalents | 11.9 | 9.6 |
| 8.3 | 5.0 | 7.2 | 6.0 | .5 |  | Trade Receivables (net) | 4.8 | 5.1 |
| 1.1 | .9 | 1.8 | 1.9 | 2.4 |  | Inventory | 1.3 | 1.3 |
| 4.8 | 3.0 | 4.0 | 4.2 | 1.9 |  | All Other Current | 3.6 | 3.1 |
| 37.2 | 16.6 | 24.2 | 19.9 | 8.0 |  | Total Current | 21.5 | 19.1 |
| 47.2 | 71.3 | 61.9 | 60.1 | 68.2 |  | Fixed Assets (net) | 64.7 | 66.5 |
| 6.3 | 3.0 | 3.4 | 4.5 | 1.0 |  | Intangibles (net) | 1.8 | 2.1 |
| 9.3 | 9.1 | 10.5 | 15.5 | 22.7 |  | All Other Non-Current | 12.0 | 12.3 |
| 100.0 | 100.0 | 100.0 | 100.0 | 100.0 |  | Total | 100.0 | 100.0 |
|  |  |  |  |  |  | LIABILITIES |  |  |
| 19.2 | 7.8 | 5.5 | 1.4 | 6.4 |  | Notes Payable-Short Term | 6.5 | 5.6 |
| 5.1 | 5.3 | 3.7 | 2.6 | 3.2 |  | Cur. Mat.-L.T.D. | 2.8 | 3.4 |
| 9.1 | 4.2 | 4.0 | 4.3 | 1.2 |  | Trade Payables | 2.9 | 3.0 |
| .1 | .0 | .1 | .5 | .1 |  | Income Taxes Payable | .1 | .1 |
| 17.1 | 6.7 | 7.7 | 6.3 | 4.4 |  | All Other Current | 9.4 | 6.0 |
| 50.5 | 24.0 | 20.9 | 15.2 | 15.3 |  | Total Current | 21.7 | 18.0 |
| 47.3 | 53.9 | 42.7 | 43.1 | 36.4 |  | Long-Term Debt | 51.0 | 53.9 |
| .0 | .0 | .0 | .9 | 1.0 |  | Deferred Taxes | .0 | .0 |
| 9.8 | 4.3 | 6.9 | 4.1 | 1.1 |  | All Other Non-Current | 4.0 | 4.7 |
| -7.7 | 17.8 | 29.5 | 36.8 | 46.3 |  | Net Worth | 23.3 | 23.4 |
| 100.0 | 100.0 | 100.0 | 100.0 | 100.0 |  | Total Liabilities & Net Worth | 100.0 | 100.0 |
|  |  |  |  |  |  | INCOME DATA |  |  |
| 100.0 | 100.0 | 100.0 | 100.0 | 100.0 |  | Net Sales | 100.0 | 100.0 |
|  |  |  |  |  |  | Gross Profit |  |  |
| 71.9 | 62.1 | 62.8 | 69.4 | 51.2 |  | Operating Expenses | 61.4 | 61.4 |
| 28.1 | 37.9 | 37.2 | 30.6 | 48.8 |  | Operating Profit | 38.6 | 38.6 |
| 10.1 | 20.7 | 19.7 | 13.8 | 21.8 |  | All Other Expenses (net) | 19.7 | 20.7 |
| 17.9 | 17.3 | 17.6 | 16.8 | 27.0 |  | Profit Before Taxes | 18.9 | 18.0 |
|  |  |  |  |  |  | RATIOS |  |  |
| 2.9 | 1.7 | 2.7 | 3.1 | 2.8 |  | Current | 2.3 | 2.8 |
| 1.1 | .6 | 1.1 | 1.1 | .8 |  |  | .8 | .9 |
| .2 | .1 | .4 | .5 | .1 |  |  | .2 | .3 |
| 2.8 | 1.4 | 2.2 | 1.6 | 1.6 |  | Quick | 1.9 | 2.3 |
| 1.0 | .5 | .9 | .7 | .2 |  |  | .6 | .7 |
| .1 | .1 | .3 | .2 | .0 |  |  | .2 | .2 |
| 0 UND | 0 UND | 0 UND | 0 UND | 1 693.0 |  | Sales/Receivables | 0 UND | 0 UND |
| 0 UND | 0 UND | 0 UND | 0 881.8 | 6 63.3 |  |  | 0 UND | 0 UND |
| 5 76.6 | 3 121.3 | 16 22.2 | 18 20.1 | 27 13.5 |  |  | 13 27.2 | 12 30.7 |
|  |  |  |  |  |  | Cost of Sales/Inventory |  |  |
|  |  |  |  |  |  | Cost of Sales/Payables |  |  |
| 12.4 | 7.4 | 4.8 | 5.4 | 2.7 |  | Sales/Working Capital | 6.3 | 7.9 |
| 519.5 | -14.3 | 42.0 | 71.7 | -13.3 |  |  | -35.3 | -115.4 |
| -5.3 | -3.1 | -5.8 | -6.1 | -.7 |  |  | -3.2 | -4.9 |
| 24.2 | 11.3 | 16.5 | 17.2 |  |  | EBIT/Interest | 8.4 | 8.6 |
| (23) 7.5 | (53) 4.7 | (57) 5.1 | (25) 5.4 |  |  |  | (93) 4.3 | (142) 4.2 |
| 1.6 | 1.8 | 1.9 | 2.2 |  |  |  | 1.6 | 1.5 |
|  |  |  |  |  |  | Net Profit + Depr., Dep., Amort./Cur. Mat. L/T/D | 4.9 | 5.4 |
|  |  |  |  |  |  |  | (10) 2.1 | (17) 3.1 |
|  |  |  |  |  |  |  | 1.4 | 1.7 |
| .1 | 1.8 | .7 | .6 | 1.1 |  | Fixed/Worth | .8 | 1.1 |
| 1.4 | 4.3 | 2.4 | 1.7 | 1.9 |  |  | 3.3 | 3.6 |
| -6.6 | -64.7 | 32.9 | 8.6 | 3.0 |  |  | 64.5 | 15.3 |
| .5 | 1.4 | .9 | .8 | .6 |  | Debt/Worth | .9 | 1.1 |
| 2.9 | 4.4 | 3.1 | 2.3 | 1.3 |  |  | 3.4 | 3.7 |
| -3.5 | -88.1 | 40.2 | 7.9 | 2.6 |  |  | 114.1 | 19.3 |
| 105.6 | 39.1 | 34.0 | 27.5 | 30.9 |  | % Profit Before Taxes/Tangible Net Worth | 47.1 | 46.6 |
| (39) 27.4 | (89) 15.6 | (94) 15.3 | (41) 8.9 | 6.3 |  |  | (178) 16.7 | (272) 14.3 |
| 10.6 | 6.3 | 1.1 | .4 | -2.9 |  |  | 2.7 | 3.3 |
| 57.9 | 11.2 | 9.8 | 7.7 | 6.4 |  | % Profit Before Taxes/Total Assets | 12.1 | 9.8 |
| 14.4 | 3.1 | 3.9 | 2.9 | 2.3 |  |  | 4.1 | 3.5 |
| 1.8 | .9 | .2 | .5 | -.9 |  |  | .3 | .4 |
| 173.9 | 3.7 | 10.3 | 3.3 | .3 |  | Sales/Net Fixed Assets | 10.9 | 4.9 |
| 9.0 | .2 | .3 | .3 | .2 |  |  | .3 | .3 |
| .4 | .1 | .1 | .2 | .1 |  |  | .2 | .2 |
| 7.0 | 1.0 | 1.0 | .9 | .3 |  | Sales/Total Assets | 1.1 | .8 |
| 2.9 | .2 | .2 | .2 | .1 |  |  | .2 | .2 |
| .3 | .1 | .1 | .1 | .1 |  |  | .1 | .1 |
| 1.1 | 5.2 | 5.0 | 4.6 |  |  | % Depr., Dep., Amort./Sales | 3.6 | 5.6 |
| (35) 8.6 | (95) 13.7 | (93) 14.9 | (39) 18.9 |  |  |  | (175) 12.2 | (266) 14.5 |
| 14.7 | 22.4 | 23.2 | 24.6 |  |  |  | 19.6 | 22.1 |
| 4.8 | 1.2 | 1.6 |  |  |  | % Officers', Directors' Owners' Comp/Sales | 3.0 | 4.8 |
| (12) 5.8 | (12) 9.2 | (12) 2.8 |  |  |  |  | (23) 5.7 | (35) 8.8 |
| 22.5 | 25.5 | 10.9 |  |  |  |  | 14.4 | 12.4 |
| 48237M | 202292M | 531676M | 551310M | 140106M | 765492M | Net Sales ($) | 1781986M | 3039662M |
| 14185M | 134010M | 533481M | 901261M | 770239M | 1155744M | Total Assets ($) | 2403171M | 3243923M |

M = $ thousand   MM = $ million
See Pages 9 through 22 for Explanation of Ratios and Data

## Comparative Historical Data      Current Data Sorted by Sales

| | | | Type of Statement | | | | | | |
|---|---|---|---|---|---|---|---|---|---|
| 20 | 22 | 15 | Unqualified | 2 | 2 | | 3 | 5 | 3 |
| 17 | 20 | 16 | Reviewed | 4 | 4 | 1 | 1 | 5 | 1 |
| 37 | 36 | 32 | Compiled | 16 | 11 | 2 | 2 | 1 | |
| 108 | 119 | 142 | Tax Returns | 107 | 21 | 4 | 5 | 3 | 2 |
| 123 | 136 | 161 | Other | 68 | 41 | 15 | 10 | 15 | 12 |
| 4/1/09-<br>3/31/10<br>ALL | 4/1/10-<br>3/31/11<br>ALL | 4/1/11-<br>3/31/12<br>ALL | | | 24 (4/1-9/30/11) | | 342 (10/1/11-3/31/12) | | |
| | | | | 0-1MM | 1-3MM | 3-5MM | 5-10MM | 10-25MM | 25MM & OVER |
| 305 | 333 | 366 | NUMBER OF STATEMENTS | 197 | 79 | 22 | 21 | 29 | 18 |
| % | % | % | ASSETS | % | % | % | % | % | % |
| 12.2 | 11.3 | 11.4 | Cash & Equivalents | 6.9 | 13.3 | 21.0 | 16.2 | 21.8 | 17.4 |
| 4.3 | 5.7 | 6.6 | Trade Receivables (net) | 2.2 | 6.6 | 12.5 | 7.6 | 18.1 | 29.4 |
| 1.6 | 1.3 | 1.4 | Inventory | .4 | 1.9 | 2.3 | 5.0 | 2.5 | 3.6 |
| 3.7 | 4.8 | 3.7 | All Other Current | 1.7 | 4.7 | 9.0 | 5.8 | 9.6 | 2.8 |
| 21.7 | 23.1 | 23.2 | Total Current | 11.2 | 26.6 | 44.8 | 34.6 | 52.0 | 53.1 |
| 65.0 | 62.3 | 62.3 | Fixed Assets (net) | 78.1 | 57.1 | 34.5 | 43.2 | 29.9 | 21.0 |
| 3.2 | 3.1 | 3.8 | Intangibles (net) | 2.8 | 4.0 | 5.4 | 11.1 | 1.7 | 6.0 |
| 10.0 | 11.5 | 10.7 | All Other Non-Current | 7.8 | 12.4 | 15.3 | 11.0 | 16.4 | 19.9 |
| 100.0 | 100.0 | 100.0 | Total | 100.0 | 100.0 | 100.0 | 100.0 | 100.0 | 100.0 |
| | | | LIABILITIES | | | | | | |
| 7.3 | 9.7 | 8.0 | Notes Payable-Short Term | 8.6 | 7.2 | 8.0 | 10.3 | 4.4 | 6.8 |
| 4.7 | 3.9 | 4.2 | Cur. Mat.-L.T.D. | 5.6 | 3.5 | 1.4 | 2.1 | 2.2 | 1.4 |
| 2.3 | 5.4 | 5.0 | Trade Payables | .8 | 5.8 | 7.9 | 17.8 | 10.2 | 20.2 |
| .0 | .0 | .1 | Income Taxes Payable | .0 | .0 | .0 | .0 | .9 | .1 |
| 10.0 | 8.9 | 8.6 | All Other Current | 4.2 | 11.8 | 5.4 | 24.6 | 15.7 | 16.4 |
| 24.4 | 27.8 | 25.9 | Total Current | 19.3 | 28.3 | 22.8 | 54.8 | 33.3 | 44.9 |
| 48.3 | 50.2 | 46.7 | Long-Term Debt | 60.3 | 43.2 | 22.6 | 28.3 | 13.8 | 17.4 |
| .1 | .1 | .2 | Deferred Taxes | .0 | .0 | .5 | .0 | 1.4 | .0 |
| 5.1 | 7.8 | 5.9 | All Other Non-Current | 5.9 | 7.9 | 4.4 | 3.4 | 5.3 | 2.7 |
| 22.2 | 14.1 | 21.4 | Net Worth | 14.5 | 20.5 | 49.8 | 13.5 | 46.2 | 34.9 |
| 100.0 | 100.0 | 100.0 | Total Liabilities & Net Worth | 100.0 | 100.0 | 100.0 | 100.0 | 100.0 | 100.0 |
| | | | INCOME DATA | | | | | | |
| 100.0 | 100.0 | 100.0 | Net Sales | 100.0 | 100.0 | 100.0 | 100.0 | 100.0 | 100.0 |
| | | | Gross Profit | | | | | | |
| 65.7 | 63.8 | 64.8 | Operating Expenses | 52.3 | 75.2 | 80.3 | 76.7 | 86.6 | 87.3 |
| 34.3 | 36.2 | 35.2 | Operating Profit | 47.7 | 24.8 | 19.7 | 23.3 | 13.4 | 12.7 |
| 18.9 | 19.5 | 17.5 | All Other Expenses (net) | 26.2 | 11.6 | 3.7 | 4.5 | 3.7 | 3.4 |
| 15.4 | 16.6 | 17.7 | Profit Before Taxes | 21.5 | 13.3 | 16.0 | 18.8 | 9.7 | 9.3 |
| | | | RATIOS | | | | | | |
| 2.7 | 2.4 | 2.5 | | 1.6 | 3.5 | 4.3 | 3.3 | 3.1 | 2.7 |
| .9 | .9 | .9 | Current | .6 | 1.3 | 2.3 | 1.3 | 1.5 | 1.2 |
| .2 | .3 | .3 | | .1 | .4 | .8 | .6 | 1.0 | .5 |
| 2.2 | 1.8 | 1.7 | | 1.5 | 2.5 | 4.3 | 1.6 | 2.3 | 2.5 |
| (304) .7 | .6 | .7 | Quick | .5 | .9 | 1.1 | .8 | 1.4 | 1.2 |
| .2 | .1 | .2 | | .1 | .2 | .4 | .1 | .6 | .3 |
| 0 UND | 0 UND | 0 UND | | 0 UND | 0 UND | 0 UND | 0 UND | 3 107.4 | 6 61.7 |
| 0 UND | 0 UND | 0 UND | Sales/Receivables | 0 UND | 0 999.8 | 0 UND | 3 110.2 | 12 31.3 | 34 10.6 |
| 8 44.6 | 11 32.2 | 11 33.9 | | 0 UND | 7 50.7 | 47 7.8 | 21 17.2 | 38 9.6 | 61 6.0 |
| | | | Cost of Sales/Inventory | | | | | | |
| | | | Cost of Sales/Payables | | | | | | |
| 5.5 | 7.0 | 5.8 | | 7.5 | 5.0 | 2.1 | 5.8 | 3.9 | 7.1 |
| -79.7 | -59.8 | -68.0 | Sales/Working Capital | -9.7 | 23.2 | 19.5 | 27.0 | 26.3 | 25.4 |
| -3.4 | -3.9 | -4.6 | | -2.9 | -7.2 | -32.9 | -13.2 | NM | -9.9 |
| 9.3 | 14.0 | 15.3 | | 8.5 | 16.9 | 38.5 | 12.2 | 26.8 | 15.2 |
| (135) 4.2 | (137) 4.2 | (167) 5.0 | EBIT/Interest | (69) 4.6 | (36) 3.9 | (15) 14.1 | (15) 4.8 | (18) 15.2 | (14) 8.0 |
| 1.7 | 1.5 | 1.9 | | 1.9 | 1.4 | 4.6 | 2.2 | 2.9 | 1.7 |
| 3.5 | 4.2 | 5.7 | Net Profit + Depr., Dep., | | | | | | |
| (15) 2.4 | (15) 2.4 | (20) 2.1 | Amort./Cur. Mat. L/T/D | | | | | | |
| .6 | .7 | .6 | | | | | | | |
| 1.0 | .9 | .9 | | 1.9 | .8 | .1 | .2 | .1 | .1 |
| 3.6 | 3.4 | 2.6 | Fixed/Worth | 4.2 | 2.3 | .7 | 1.4 | .5 | .3 |
| 15.6 | 70.3 | 30.9 | | NM | 40.3 | 2.6 | -6.7 | 1.3 | NM |
| 1.0 | 1.2 | .9 | | 1.4 | .8 | .4 | .7 | .4 | .9 |
| 3.6 | 4.1 | 3.0 | Debt/Worth | 4.3 | 3.7 | .8 | 1.6 | 1.2 | 2.6 |
| 19.2 | UND | 41.4 | | -144.3 | UND | 3.2 | -8.0 | 3.2 | NM |
| 43.7 | 37.2 | 41.0 | | 28.8 | 60.1 | 44.7 | 48.5 | 41.5 | 66.4 |
| (247) 14.7 | (250) 13.9 | (280) 15.1 | % Profit Before Taxes/Tangible<br>Net Worth | (146) 12.4 | (60) 23.6 | (19) 12.2 | (14) 21.8 | (27) 15.2 | (14) 26.1 |
| 1.9 | 1.8 | 2.4 | | 2.0 | 1.4 | 1.1 | 4.4 | -.1 | 5.9 |
| 10.9 | 8.9 | 13.4 | | 7.8 | 15.9 | 37.2 | 37.4 | 15.5 | 22.6 |
| 3.4 | 3.5 | 3.9 | % Profit Before Taxes/Total<br>Assets | 2.7 | 4.7 | 8.1 | 9.4 | 7.0 | 6.1 |
| .0 | .2 | .6 | | .4 | .5 | .8 | 3.0 | -.4 | 2.3 |
| 10.3 | 15.0 | 9.9 | | .4 | 14.5 | 29.3 | 56.9 | 51.5 | 132.9 |
| .2 | .3 | .3 | Sales/Net Fixed Assets | .2 | .9 | 9.3 | 7.4 | 17.9 | 51.8 |
| .1 | .1 | .1 | | .1 | .2 | 1.0 | .3 | 1.8 | 1.2 |
| 1.0 | .9 | 1.5 | | .3 | 4.2 | 4.3 | 5.1 | 4.3 | 4.5 |
| .2 | .2 | .2 | Sales/Total Assets | .1 | .4 | 1.4 | 1.5 | 1.9 | 2.8 |
| .1 | .1 | .1 | | .1 | .2 | .2 | .2 | .8 | .6 |
| 4.2 | 4.4 | 4.3 | | 11.5 | 1.6 | .4 | 1.2 | .4 | .4 |
| (245) 15.6 | (259) 14.2 | (277) 14.1 | % Depr., Dep., Amort./Sales | (155) 17.2 | (59) 9.2 | (17) 2.6 | (14) 11.0 | (20) 1.1 | (12) .5 |
| 24.5 | 22.4 | 22.8 | | 24.9 | 19.0 | 17.8 | 20.6 | 16.2 | 4.8 |
| 4.1 | 3.2 | 2.4 | | 2.9 | 3.7 | | | | |
| (49) 9.8 | (52) 8.6 | (41) 5.5 | % Officers', Directors'<br>Owners' Comp/Sales | (12) 13.3 | (13) 6.1 | | | | |
| 19.6 | 18.1 | 14.8 | | 40.3 | 26.2 | | | | |
| 1654231M | 1624055M | 2239113M | Net Sales ($) | 64281M | 143933M | 80995M | 147592M | 451386M | 1350926M |
| 2863515M | 3248009M | 3508920M | Total Assets ($) | 386470M | 538691M | 258190M | 487596M | 683436M | 1154537M |

© RMA 2012     M = $ thousand    MM = $ million
See Pages 9 through 22 for Explanation of Ratios and Data

## Current Data Sorted by Assets

## Comparative Historical Data

| | | 2 | | 2 | | | Type of Statement | | |
|---|---|---|---|---|---|---|---|---|---|
| | | 1 | | | | | Unqualified | | 2 |
| 1 | | 1 | | | | | Reviewed | 1 | |
| 6 | 3 | 1 | | | | | Compiled | 1 | 4 |
| 3 | 5 | 3 | | | | | Tax Returns | 18 | 8 |
| | 2 (4/1-9/30/11) | | 2 | 27 (10/1/11-3/31/12) | | | Other | 4 | 2 |
| | | | | | | | | 4/1/07- | 4/1/08- |
| | | | | | | | | 3/31/08 | 3/31/09 |
| 0-500M | 500M-2MM | 2-10MM | 10-50MM | 50-100MM | 100-250MM | | | ALL | ALL |
| 10 | 8 | 7 | 2 | 2 | | NUMBER OF STATEMENTS | | 24 | 16 |
| % | % | % | % | % | % | ASSETS | | % | % |
| 30.9 | | | | | | Cash & Equivalents | | 23.4 | 27.8 |
| 12.6 | | | | | | Trade Receivables (net) | | 12.5 | 10.9 |
| .0 | | | | | | Inventory | | 11.9 | 6.2 |
| 14.8 | | | | | | All Other Current | | 4.6 | 1.6 |
| 58.2 | | | | | | Total Current | | 52.5 | 46.5 |
| 23.4 | | | | | | Fixed Assets (net) | | 30.9 | 38.2 |
| 9.1 | | | | | | Intangibles (net) | | 4.5 | 9.0 |
| 9.6 | | | | | | All Other Non-Current | | 12.1 | 6.4 |
| 100.0 | | | | | | Total | | 100.0 | 100.0 |
| | | | | | | LIABILITIES | | | |
| 49.7 | | | | | | Notes Payable-Short Term | | 31.1 | 22.3 |
| 10.0 | | | | | | Cur. Mat.-L.T.D. | | 3.8 | 3.2 |
| 2.8 | | | | | | Trade Payables | | 1.3 | 4.8 |
| .0 | | | | | | Income Taxes Payable | | .0 | .4 |
| 65.5 | | | | | | All Other Current | | 30.6 | 16.9 |
| 128.1 | | | | | | Total Current | | 66.7 | 47.6 |
| 30.3 | | | | | | Long-Term Debt | | 20.2 | 20.0 |
| .0 | | | | | | Deferred Taxes | | .0 | .0 |
| 3.9 | | | | | | All Other Non-Current | | 1.8 | 3.9 |
| -62.3 | | | | | | Net Worth | | 11.3 | 28.6 |
| 100.0 | | | | | | Total Liabilities & Net Worth | | 100.0 | 100.0 |
| | | | | | | INCOME DATA | | | |
| 100.0 | | | | | | Net Sales | | 100.0 | 100.0 |
| | | | | | | Gross Profit | | | |
| 82.6 | | | | | | Operating Expenses | | 83.0 | 87.5 |
| 17.4 | | | | | | Operating Profit | | 17.0 | 12.5 |
| .5 | | | | | | All Other Expenses (net) | | 3.3 | 3.8 |
| 16.9 | | | | | | Profit Before Taxes | | 13.7 | 8.7 |
| | | | | | | RATIOS | | | |
| 3.2 | | | | | | | | 17.3 | 2.4 |
| .8 | | | | | | Current | | 1.1 | .8 |
| .3 | | | | | | | | .4 | .5 |
| 2.3 | | | | | | | | 6.2 | 2.1 |
| .8 | | | | | | Quick | | .6 | .7 |
| .0 | | | | | | | | .3 | .2 |
| 0 UND | | | | | | | | 0 UND | 0 UND |
| 0 UND | | | | | | Sales/Receivables | | 0 UND | 0 UND |
| 0 UND | | | | | | | | 17 21.1 | 22 16.2 |
| | | | | | | Cost of Sales/Inventory | | | |
| | | | | | | Cost of Sales/Payables | | | |
| 32.9 | | | | | | | | 4.8 | 15.2 |
| NM | | | | | | Sales/Working Capital | | 15.2 | -542.6 |
| -16.4 | | | | | | | | -24.9 | -17.8 |
| | | | | | | | | 69.4 | 5.7 |
| | | | | | | EBIT/Interest | | (17) 5.3 | (10) 1.6 |
| | | | | | | | | 1.3 | -9.7 |
| | | | | | | Net Profit + Depr., Dep., Amort./Cur. Mat. L/T/D | | | |
| .3 | | | | | | | | .0 | .2 |
| 14.1 | | | | | | Fixed/Worth | | .8 | 1.3 |
| -.2 | | | | | | | | 2.6 | 7.7 |
| 1.9 | | | | | | | | .5 | .5 |
| 44.4 | | | | | | Debt/Worth | | 1.4 | 1.5 |
| -1.6 | | | | | | | | NM | 6.9 |
| | | | | | | % Profit Before Taxes/Tangible Net Worth | | 109.7 | 116.3 |
| | | | | | | | | (18) 24.6 | (13) 5.1 |
| | | | | | | | | 2.6 | -47.0 |
| 401.2 | | | | | | % Profit Before Taxes/Total Assets | | 75.9 | 80.5 |
| 123.7 | | | | | | | | 11.9 | 4.9 |
| -3.5 | | | | | | | | .7 | -22.8 |
| 234.7 | | | | | | | | 900.4 | 200.4 |
| 109.2 | | | | | | Sales/Net Fixed Assets | | 34.4 | 24.8 |
| 38.4 | | | | | | | | 4.9 | 2.5 |
| 30.4 | | | | | | | | 6.9 | 7.7 |
| 10.9 | | | | | | Sales/Total Assets | | 3.7 | 3.8 |
| 5.8 | | | | | | | | .7 | 1.5 |
| | | | | | | | | .3 | .4 |
| | | | | | | % Depr., Dep., Amort./Sales | | (16) .9 | (12) 1.8 |
| | | | | | | | | 2.6 | 3.4 |
| | | | | | | % Officers', Directors' Owners' Comp/Sales | | 6.0 | |
| | | | | | | | | (16) 10.6 | |
| | | | | | | | | 17.5 | |
| 27957M | 54263M | 167475M | 56100M | 353652M | | Net Sales ($) | | 98930M | 258977M |
| 1835M | 8568M | 34639M | 65132M | 161842M | | Total Assets ($) | | 58909M | 126565M |

Note: In columns 10-50MM, 50-100MM, and 100-250MM of the Current Data the ratios area is marked **DATA NOT AVAILABLE**.

M = $ thousand    MM = $ million
See Pages 9 through 22 for Explanation of Ratios and Data

## Comparative Historical Data | Current Data Sorted by Sales

| | | | | | Type of Statement | | | | | | |
|---|---|---|---|---|---|---|---|---|---|---|---|
| | 4 | | 6 | | 4 | Unqualified | | | | 1 | 3 |
| | 2 | | 1 | | 1 | Reviewed | | | | 1 | |
| | 1 | | 1 | | 1 | Compiled | | | | | |
| | 7 | | 10 | | 10 | Tax Returns | 1 | 3 | 1 | | 1 | |
| | 3 | | 12 | | 13 | Other | 5 | 3 | 2 | 2 | | 3 |
| | 4/1/09- | | 4/1/10- | | 4/1/11- | | 3 | 3 | | | | |
| | 3/31/10 | | 3/31/11 | | 3/31/12 | | | 2 (4/1-9/30/11) | | 27 (10/1/11-3/31/12) | | |
| | ALL | | ALL | | ALL | | 0-1MM | 1-3MM | 3-5MM | 5-10MM | 10-25MM | 25MM & OVER |
| | 17 | | 30 | | 29 | NUMBER OF STATEMENTS | 9 | 6 | 3 | 2 | 3 | 6 |
| | % | | % | | % | ASSETS | % | % | % | % | % | % |
| | 15.9 | | 16.8 | | 18.8 | Cash & Equivalents | | | | | | |
| | 21.9 | | 21.3 | | 20.3 | Trade Receivables (net) | | | | | | |
| | .0 | | .2 | | .0 | Inventory | | | | | | |
| | 4.4 | | 6.2 | | 7.4 | All Other Current | | | | | | |
| | 42.2 | | 44.4 | | 46.5 | Total Current | | | | | | |
| | 26.4 | | 36.1 | | 32.7 | Fixed Assets (net) | | | | | | |
| | 8.3 | | 7.7 | | 9.7 | Intangibles (net) | | | | | | |
| | 23.1 | | 11.8 | | 11.2 | All Other Non-Current | | | | | | |
| | 100.0 | | 100.0 | | 100.0 | Total | | | | | | |
| | | | | | | LIABILITIES | | | | | | |
| | 25.8 | | 15.9 | | 19.2 | Notes Payable-Short Term | | | | | | |
| | 2.7 | | 2.1 | | 7.1 | Cur. Mat.-L.T.D. | | | | | | |
| | 5.8 | | 5.7 | | 4.9 | Trade Payables | | | | | | |
| | .1 | | .3 | | .1 | Income Taxes Payable | | | | | | |
| | 19.2 | | 24.6 | | 29.4 | All Other Current | | | | | | |
| | 53.7 | | 48.7 | | 60.8 | Total Current | | | | | | |
| | 24.8 | | 14.9 | | 33.9 | Long-Term Debt | | | | | | |
| | .1 | | .8 | | .1 | Deferred Taxes | | | | | | |
| | .4 | | 6.2 | | 2.4 | All Other Non-Current | | | | | | |
| | 20.9 | | 29.5 | | 2.9 | Net Worth | | | | | | |
| | 100.0 | | 100.0 | | 100.0 | Total Liabilities & Net Worth | | | | | | |
| | | | | | | INCOME DATA | | | | | | |
| | 100.0 | | 100.0 | | 100.0 | Net Sales | | | | | | |
| | | | | | | Gross Profit | | | | | | |
| | 86.5 | | 88.7 | | 83.2 | Operating Expenses | | | | | | |
| | 13.5 | | 11.3 | | 16.8 | Operating Profit | | | | | | |
| | 6.1 | | 2.6 | | 4.6 | All Other Expenses (net) | | | | | | |
| | 7.3 | | 8.7 | | 12.2 | Profit Before Taxes | | | | | | |
| | | | | | | RATIOS | | | | | | |
| | 5.4 | | 2.2 | | 2.4 | | | | | | | |
| | .8 | | 1.4 | | 1.3 | Current | | | | | | |
| | .3 | | .7 | | .4 | | | | | | | |
| | 5.4 | | 1.7 | | 2.4 | | | | | | | |
| | .7 | | 1.2 | | 1.2 | Quick | | | | | | |
| | .2 | | .7 | | .3 | | | | | | | |
| 0 | UND | 0 | UND | 0 | UND | | | | | | | |
| 12 | 30.9 | 6 | 56.6 | 2 | 189.8 | Sales/Receivables | | | | | | |
| 34 | 10.9 | 57 | 6.4 | 46 | 8.0 | | | | | | | |
| | | | | | | Cost of Sales/Inventory | | | | | | |
| | | | | | | Cost of Sales/Payables | | | | | | |
| | 10.2 | | 8.7 | | 7.1 | | | | | | | |
| | -27.5 | | 33.4 | | 61.2 | Sales/Working Capital | | | | | | |
| | -4.5 | | -27.5 | | -17.1 | | | | | | | |
| | 9.9 | | 27.0 | | 41.7 | | | | | | | |
| (14) | 2.2 | (23) | 8.0 | (21) | 7.6 | EBIT/Interest | | | | | | |
| | .8 | | .2 | | -3.2 | | | | | | | |
| | | | | | | Net Profit + Depr., Dep., Amort./Cur. Mat. L/T/D | | | | | | |
| | .1 | | .2 | | .1 | | | | | | | |
| | 1.2 | | 1.0 | | 1.6 | Fixed/Worth | | | | | | |
| | 60.8 | | 3.9 | | NM | | | | | | | |
| | .6 | | .6 | | .8 | | | | | | | |
| | 2.0 | | 2.2 | | 2.5 | Debt/Worth | | | | | | |
| | 69.1 | | 5.1 | | NM | | | | | | | |
| | 125.9 | | 69.4 | | 68.4 | % Profit Before Taxes/Tangible Net Worth | | | | | | |
| (14) | 13.2 | (25) | 15.4 | (22) | 31.1 | | | | | | | |
| | -2.6 | | -15.5 | | 5.9 | | | | | | | |
| | 31.5 | | 20.1 | | 51.1 | % Profit Before Taxes/Total Assets | | | | | | |
| | 4.2 | | 8.1 | | 7.5 | | | | | | | |
| | -1.6 | | -6.0 | | .4 | | | | | | | |
| | 173.8 | | 54.3 | | 170.8 | Sales/Net Fixed Assets | | | | | | |
| | 35.9 | | 18.0 | | 43.4 | | | | | | | |
| | 8.6 | | 6.2 | | 3.6 | | | | | | | |
| | 4.1 | | 5.3 | | 9.7 | Sales/Total Assets | | | | | | |
| | 2.4 | | 3.3 | | 3.5 | | | | | | | |
| | 1.7 | | 1.5 | | 1.2 | | | | | | | |
| | | | .8 | | .3 | % Depr., Dep., Amort./Sales | | | | | | |
| | | (24) | 1.6 | (20) | .7 | | | | | | | |
| | | | 3.2 | | 2.2 | | | | | | | |
| | | | | | | % Officers', Directors' Owners' Comp/Sales | | | | | | |
| | 559217M | | 487834M | | 659447M | Net Sales ($) | 3399M | 11779M | 10739M | 12303M | 48116M | 573111M |
| | 234261M | | 250784M | | 272016M | Total Assets ($) | 7709M | 4366M | 21368M | 1733M | 9970M | 226870M |

© RMA 2012

M = $ thousand    MM = $ million
See Pages 9 through 22 for Explanation of Ratios and Data

## Current Data Sorted by Assets     Comparative Historical Data

| | 0-500M | 500M-2MM | 2-10MM | 10-50MM | 50-100MM | 100-250MM | Type of Statement | 4/1/07-3/31/08 ALL | 4/1/08-3/31/09 ALL |
|---|---|---|---|---|---|---|---|---|---|
| | 3 | 9 | 22 | 27 | 15 | 13 | Unqualified | 88 | 101 |
| | 3 | 6 | 22 | 16 | 5 | 1 | Reviewed | 37 | 46 |
| | 14 | 33 | 53 | 8 | 1 | | Compiled | 106 | 95 |
| | 147 | 373 | 343 | 46 | 3 | | Tax Returns | 625 | 743 |
| | 76 | 170 | 257 | 95 | 17 | 13 | Other | 471 | 571 |
| | 76 (4/1-9/30/11) | | | 1,715 (10/1/11-3/31/12) | | | | | |
| NUMBER OF STATEMENTS | 243 | 591 | 697 | 192 | 41 | 27 | | 1327 | 1556 |
| | % | % | % | % | % | % | **ASSETS** | % | % |
| | 26.0 | 7.7 | 6.1 | 8.8 | 8.5 | 10.4 | Cash & Equivalents | 8.9 | 9.7 |
| | 5.1 | 2.6 | 3.4 | 6.9 | 11.8 | 10.5 | Trade Receivables (net) | 5.0 | 4.6 |
| | 4.8 | 8.6 | 7.4 | 9.8 | 9.2 | 15.9 | Inventory | 18.6 | 13.8 |
| | 6.2 | 2.4 | 2.4 | 3.9 | 7.0 | 3.2 | All Other Current | 4.8 | 3.4 |
| | 42.0 | 21.2 | 19.4 | 29.5 | 36.5 | 40.1 | Total Current | 37.3 | 31.5 |
| | 42.0 | 66.8 | 66.2 | 48.3 | 30.3 | 34.0 | Fixed Assets (net) | 45.7 | 53.3 |
| | 2.2 | 2.5 | 2.4 | 2.9 | 8.5 | 6.1 | Intangibles (net) | 2.0 | 1.5 |
| | 13.8 | 9.5 | 12.0 | 19.4 | 24.7 | 19.8 | All Other Non-Current | 15.0 | 13.7 |
| | 100.0 | 100.0 | 100.0 | 100.0 | 100.0 | 100.0 | Total | 100.0 | 100.0 |
| | | | | | | | **LIABILITIES** | | |
| | 18.5 | 7.0 | 5.4 | 7.0 | 18.0 | 8.7 | Notes Payable-Short Term | 13.8 | 11.1 |
| | 3.1 | 4.2 | 3.2 | 2.8 | 3.7 | 2.3 | Cur. Mat.-L.T.D. | 4.2 | 4.2 |
| | 2.6 | 1.7 | 1.8 | 1.7 | 4.3 | 3.3 | Trade Payables | 3.3 | 2.7 |
| | .1 | .0 | .0 | .1 | .0 | .4 | Income Taxes Payable | .1 | .0 |
| | 22.1 | 7.1 | 7.3 | 8.5 | 4.3 | 9.1 | All Other Current | 10.2 | 10.4 |
| | 46.4 | 20.0 | 17.6 | 20.1 | 30.3 | 23.8 | Total Current | 31.5 | 28.4 |
| | 28.9 | 55.0 | 55.9 | 39.4 | 34.9 | 29.4 | Long-Term Debt | 42.5 | 48.3 |
| | .0 | .0 | .0 | .1 | .4 | .6 | Deferred Taxes | .1 | .2 |
| | 9.9 | 4.0 | 5.3 | 4.9 | 3.4 | 6.6 | All Other Non-Current | 5.0 | 5.1 |
| | 14.8 | 21.0 | 21.2 | 35.5 | 31.0 | 39.6 | Net Worth | 20.9 | 17.9 |
| | 100.0 | 100.0 | 100.0 | 100.0 | 100.0 | 100.0 | Total Liabilities & Net Worth | 100.0 | 100.0 |
| | | | | | | | **INCOME DATA** | | |
| | 100.0 | 100.0 | 100.0 | 100.0 | 100.0 | 100.0 | Net Sales | 100.0 | 100.0 |
| | | | | | | | Gross Profit | | |
| | 76.7 | 60.2 | 61.7 | 71.4 | 89.4 | 82.5 | Operating Expenses | 70.9 | 70.8 |
| | 23.3 | 39.8 | 38.3 | 28.6 | 10.6 | 17.5 | Operating Profit | 29.1 | 29.2 |
| | 10.1 | 23.7 | 24.3 | 17.2 | 7.8 | 9.3 | All Other Expenses (net) | 16.6 | 19.0 |
| | 13.2 | 16.1 | 13.9 | 11.4 | 2.8 | 8.2 | Profit Before Taxes | 12.5 | 10.2 |
| | | | | | | | **RATIOS** | | |
| | 3.6 | 2.3 | 2.5 | 3.4 | 2.5 | 4.6 | | 2.6 | 2.7 |
| | 1.0 | .7 | .8 | 1.4 | 1.2 | 1.3 | Current | 1.1 | 1.0 |
| | .3 | .2 | .2 | .3 | .9 | .7 | | .3 | .2 |
| | 2.3 | 1.4 | 1.4 | 1.9 | 1.5 | 3.2 | | 1.3 | 1.5 |
| | .6 | .4 | (696) .4 | .6 | .8 | 1.0 | Quick | (1326) .3 | (1555) .4 |
| | .1 | .1 | .1 | .1 | .4 | .3 | | .1 | .1 |
| | 0 UND | 0 UND | 0 UND | 0 UND | 0 UND | 6 60.7 | | 0 UND | 0 UND |
| | 0 UND | 0 UND | 0 UND | 2 237.3 | 25 14.7 | 22 16.3 | Sales/Receivables | 0 UND | 0 UND |
| | 0 UND | 0 UND | 2 217.9 | 19 18.8 | 57 6.4 | 72 5.1 | | 8 45.1 | 7 50.9 |
| | | | | | | | Cost of Sales/Inventory | | |
| | | | | | | | Cost of Sales/Payables | | |
| | 8.1 | 6.5 | 4.5 | 1.5 | 1.7 | 1.3 | | 2.7 | 3.0 |
| | -583.0 | -19.5 | -27.6 | 13.7 | 10.8 | 5.6 | Sales/Working Capital | 45.7 | UND |
| | -5.0 | -2.5 | -2.6 | -3.3 | -145.3 | -9.2 | | -4.5 | -3.0 |
| | 19.1 | 11.6 | 7.8 | 10.8 | 9.0 | 23.9 | | 8.8 | 8.0 |
| | (108) 4.4 | (220) 4.0 | (243) 2.9 | (93) 3.0 | (28) 2.4 | (15) 2.4 | EBIT/Interest | (598) 2.8 | (632) 2.4 |
| | .9 | 1.2 | 1.1 | 1.1 | -.1 | 1.4 | | .8 | .3 |
| | | | 4.0 | | | | | 6.7 | 5.8 |
| | | | (16) 2.6 | | | | Net Profit + Depr., Dep., Amort./Cur. Mat. L/T/D | (35) 2.2 | (42) 2.5 |
| | | | 1.5 | | | | | .9 | .5 |
| | .1 | 1.1 | 1.1 | .1 | .0 | .0 | | .0 | .2 |
| | 1.1 | 3.6 | 3.8 | 1.5 | .5 | 1.1 | Fixed/Worth | 1.8 | 2.8 |
| | 53.4 | 24.2 | 21.3 | 8.9 | 4.9 | 4.1 | | 17.2 | 45.7 |
| | .5 | 1.4 | 1.6 | .6 | .9 | .7 | | 1.3 | 1.4 |
| | 2.1 | 4.2 | 4.5 | 2.7 | 4.3 | 2.3 | Debt/Worth | 4.4 | 5.0 |
| | -24.8 | 63.1 | 41.3 | 10.7 | 6.9 | 8.0 | | 90.5 | UND |
| | 101.4 | 36.0 | 29.8 | 24.7 | 25.7 | 26.0 | % Profit Before Taxes/Tangible Net Worth | 48.8 | 37.5 |
| | (177) 17.5 | (459) 13.2 | (544) 10.5 | (160) 6.5 | (38) 7.9 | (23) 12.9 | | (1030) 15.4 | (1169) 10.9 |
| | .9 | .8 | 1.0 | -.6 | -7.3 | -.8 | | .8 | -.9 |
| | 34.2 | 8.1 | 5.9 | 5.2 | 6.5 | 8.5 | % Profit Before Taxes/Total Assets | 10.3 | 6.8 |
| | 8.6 | 2.7 | 2.2 | 2.0 | 1.7 | 3.6 | | 2.6 | 1.6 |
| | -.4 | -.2 | -.1 | -.6 | -2.2 | -.5 | | -.4 | -1.1 |
| | 318.0 | 2.5 | 1.5 | 14.2 | 47.3 | 61.9 | | 98.8 | 25.0 |
| | 15.0 | .2 | .2 | .4 | 7.3 | 2.5 | Sales/Net Fixed Assets | 1.9 | .6 |
| | .4 | .1 | .1 | .1 | .5 | .3 | | .2 | .1 |
| | 5.7 | .4 | .3 | .4 | 1.0 | .6 | | 1.1 | .7 |
| | 1.6 | .2 | .1 | .2 | .3 | .3 | Sales/Total Assets | .3 | .2 |
| | .2 | .1 | .1 | .1 | .1 | .1 | | .1 | .1 |
| | 1.7 | 9.9 | 6.2 | 1.9 | .9 | 1.3 | | 1.6 | 2.1 |
| | (128) 8.4 | (420) 18.2 | (515) 17.2 | (136) 12.5 | (27) 2.8 | (18) 10.2 | % Depr., Dep., Amort./Sales | (810) 8.9 | (1023) 12.3 |
| | 22.0 | 25.5 | 26.3 | 22.9 | 12.2 | 25.7 | | 18.4 | 21.4 |
| | 5.9 | 2.3 | 1.5 | .8 | | | | 2.2 | 1.9 |
| | (57) 12.1 | (57) 6.9 | (57) 4.5 | (19) 1.4 | | | % Officers', Directors' Owners' Comp/Sales | (195) 5.1 | (212) 5.0 |
| | 21.9 | 14.3 | 9.8 | 4.7 | | | | 14.3 | 12.1 |
| | 160188M | 387680M | 1614598M | 2158710M | 2399909M | 2318699M | Net Sales ($) | 10404961M | 8493209M |
| | 57246M | 700576M | 3048755M | 3877299M | 2936786M | 4357413M | Total Assets ($) | 15187587M | 14557198M |

© RMA 2012

M = $ thousand    MM = $ million
See Pages 9 through 22 for Explanation of Ratios and Data

## Comparative Historical Data / Current Data Sorted by Sales

| | Comparative Historical Data | | | Current Data Sorted by Sales | | | | | |
|---|---|---|---|---|---|---|---|---|---|
| **Type of Statement** | | | | | | | | | |
| Unqualified | 97 | 101 | 89 | 11 | 16 | 9 | 9 | 17 | 27 |
| Reviewed | 48 | 53 | 53 | 12 | 14 | 5 | 4 | 10 | 8 |
| Compiled | 95 | 95 | 109 | 66 | 26 | 7 | 5 | 5 | |
| Tax Returns | 817 | 784 | 912 | 722 | 127 | 29 | 22 | 5 | 7 |
| Other | 581 | 654 | 628 | 371 | 118 | 47 | 33 | 26 | 33 |
| | 4/1/09-3/31/10 ALL | 4/1/10-3/31/11 ALL | 4/1/11-3/31/12 ALL | 76 (4/1-9/30/11) | | | 1,715 (10/1/11-3/31/12) | | |
| | | | | 0-1MM | 1-3MM | 3-5MM | 5-10MM | 10-25MM | 25MM & OVER |
| **NUMBER OF STATEMENTS** | 1638 | 1687 | 1791 | 1182 | 301 | 97 | 73 | 63 | 75 |
| **ASSETS** | % | % | % | % | % | % | % | % | % |
| Cash & Equivalents | 9.3 | 11.4 | 9.7 | 7.5 | 11.6 | 19.2 | 15.3 | 15.8 | 15.4 |
| Trade Receivables (net) | 4.7 | 4.7 | 4.0 | 1.4 | 4.9 | 9.1 | 9.1 | 15.2 | 20.9 |
| Inventory | 12.5 | 8.5 | 7.9 | 5.4 | 11.9 | 9.9 | 15.8 | 14.1 | 15.1 |
| All Other Current | 2.8 | 3.6 | 3.2 | 2.4 | 3.9 | 6.4 | 4.5 | 5.2 | 6.0 |
| Total Current | 29.3 | 28.1 | 24.9 | 16.7 | 32.3 | 44.6 | 44.8 | 50.3 | 57.5 |
| Fixed Assets (net) | 55.0 | 57.2 | 59.9 | 71.5 | 47.7 | 33.0 | 27.4 | 27.5 | 18.9 |
| Intangibles (net) | 2.3 | 2.3 | 2.6 | 1.8 | 3.8 | 2.5 | 4.7 | 2.1 | 8.8 |
| All Other Non-Current | 13.4 | 12.4 | 12.6 | 10.0 | 16.2 | 19.9 | 23.2 | 20.1 | 14.8 |
| Total | 100.0 | 100.0 | 100.0 | 100.0 | 100.0 | 100.0 | 100.0 | 100.0 | 100.0 |
| **LIABILITIES** | | | | | | | | | |
| Notes Payable-Short Term | 11.4 | 9.3 | 8.2 | 6.9 | 8.7 | 12.8 | 16.6 | 8.4 | 12.6 |
| Cur. Mat.-L.T.D. | 4.0 | 3.3 | 3.4 | 3.6 | 3.6 | 1.9 | 2.3 | 2.6 | 4.0 |
| Trade Payables | 2.8 | 2.2 | 1.9 | .8 | 1.9 | 6.7 | 4.0 | 4.5 | 9.7 |
| Income Taxes Payable | .1 | .0 | .0 | .0 | .0 | .0 | .0 | .1 | .3 |
| All Other Current | 11.2 | 9.8 | 9.3 | 7.6 | 12.7 | 13.1 | 14.5 | 12.6 | 10.0 |
| Total Current | 29.4 | 24.7 | 23.0 | 19.0 | 27.0 | 34.5 | 37.4 | 28.2 | 36.7 |
| Long-Term Debt | 48.2 | 49.2 | 49.3 | 56.6 | 46.1 | 29.6 | 25.7 | 19.3 | 20.4 |
| Deferred Taxes | .1 | .1 | .0 | .0 | .0 | .2 | .1 | .2 | .3 |
| All Other Non-Current | 5.1 | 5.2 | 5.4 | 4.7 | 6.7 | 9.3 | 6.3 | 7.4 | 5.0 |
| Net Worth | 17.1 | 20.8 | 22.3 | 19.8 | 20.2 | 26.3 | 30.5 | 44.9 | 37.7 |
| Total Liabilities & Net Worth | 100.0 | 100.0 | 100.0 | 100.0 | 100.0 | 100.0 | 100.0 | 100.0 | 100.0 |
| **INCOME DATA** | | | | | | | | | |
| Net Sales | 100.0 | 100.0 | 100.0 | 100.0 | 100.0 | 100.0 | 100.0 | 100.0 | 100.0 |
| Gross Profit | | | | | | | | | |
| Operating Expenses | 69.4 | 67.1 | 65.2 | 57.1 | 74.4 | 84.5 | 90.0 | 88.4 | 88.9 |
| Operating Profit | 30.6 | 32.9 | 34.8 | 42.9 | 25.6 | 15.5 | 10.0 | 11.6 | 11.1 |
| All Other Expenses (net) | 20.1 | 19.6 | 20.8 | 27.2 | 11.7 | 7.4 | 3.9 | 5.3 | 2.5 |
| Profit Before Taxes | 10.5 | 13.3 | 14.0 | 15.7 | 13.9 | 8.1 | 6.1 | 6.3 | 8.6 |
| **RATIOS** | | | | | | | | | |
| Current | 2.5 | 3.1 | 2.7 | 2.1 | 4.2 | 3.5 | 3.5 | 5.7 | 3.3 |
| | .9 | 1.0 | .9 | .6 | 1.2 | 1.4 | 1.3 | 1.9 | 1.4 |
| | .2 | .2 | .2 | .1 | .3 | .4 | .7 | 1.0 | 1.0 |
| Quick | 1.3 | 1.7 | 1.6 | 1.3 | 2.1 | 2.8 | 1.9 | 2.1 | 2.2 |
| | (1635) .3 | (1685) .4 | (1790) .5 | .3 | (300) .5 | .7 | .8 | 1.1 | .9 |
| | .1 | .1 | .1 | .1 | .1 | .1 | .2 | .5 | .4 |
| Sales/Receivables | 0 UND | 0 UND | 0 UND | 0 UND | 0 UND | 0 UND | 0 UND | 0 999.8 | 6 58.4 |
| | 0 UND | 0 UND | 0 UND | 0 UND | 0 UND | 2 155.9 | 0 999.8 | 11 32.7 | 25 14.7 |
| | 5 69.6 | 4 84.0 | 3 128.3 | 0 UND | 5 73.3 | 20 18.5 | 12 30.5 | 45 8.1 | 56 6.5 |
| Cost of Sales/Inventory | | | | | | | | | |
| Cost of Sales/Payables | | | | | | | | | |
| Sales/Working Capital | 3.8 | 3.5 | 4.6 | 6.4 | 3.2 | 4.0 | 3.5 | 2.1 | 3.1 |
| | -50.6 | -166.7 | -57.1 | -11.7 | 29.8 | 16.6 | 21.8 | 8.6 | 14.4 |
| | -2.8 | -3.3 | -3.0 | -2.2 | -5.2 | -6.6 | -21.1 | 363.8 | 384.8 |
| EBIT/Interest | 7.2 | 9.4 | 10.0 | 8.6 | 8.3 | 9.4 | 9.9 | 34.7 | 21.0 |
| | (671) 2.6 | (683) 3.5 | (707) 3.4 | (325) 3.6 | (172) 2.7 | (55) 2.6 | (48) 3.9 | (45) 7.3 | (62) 5.3 |
| | .6 | 1.2 | 1.1 | 1.3 | .8 | 1.1 | -1.9 | .6 | 1.5 |
| Net Profit + Depr., Dep., Amort./Cur. Mat. L/T/D | 6.6 | 5.2 | 5.3 | 4.0 | | | | | 11.2 |
| | (45) 2.4 | (39) 2.1 | (46) 2.6 | (12) 1.7 | | | | (13) 3.3 | |
| | .8 | .5 | .9 | .6 | | | | | .9 |
| Fixed/Worth | .3 | .4 | .6 | 1.4 | .1 | .0 | .0 | .0 | .1 |
| | 2.8 | 2.7 | 3.0 | 3.9 | 2.0 | .9 | .5 | .4 | .4 |
| | 27.1 | 24.6 | 18.1 | 22.8 | 38.4 | 8.0 | 5.4 | 1.6 | 1.9 |
| Debt/Worth | 1.3 | 1.0 | 1.2 | 1.5 | .9 | .7 | .6 | .5 | .7 |
| | 4.9 | 3.9 | 3.9 | 4.3 | 4.7 | 2.3 | 3.0 | 1.5 | 2.1 |
| | 942.6 | 63.4 | 45.0 | 54.5 | -158.0 | 26.0 | 19.7 | 5.7 | 7.3 |
| % Profit Before Taxes/Tangible Net Worth | 36.4 | 39.1 | 33.6 | 25.9 | 50.1 | 66.4 | 61.5 | 58.7 | 60.2 |
| | (1244) 9.6 | (1316) 12.0 | (1401) 11.5 | (920) 10.1 | (222) 14.6 | (77) 15.7 | (59) 20.9 | (58) 15.1 | (65) 21.1 |
| | -.7 | .7 | .5 | .3 | .8 | 1.9 | -2.5 | -.7 | 8.2 |
| % Profit Before Taxes/Total Assets | 7.0 | 9.2 | 7.6 | 6.0 | 10.6 | 15.8 | 19.6 | 22.3 | 19.9 |
| | 1.7 | 2.7 | 2.5 | 2.1 | 3.1 | 3.3 | 4.1 | 5.5 | 6.2 |
| | -.9 | -.2 | -.2 | -.2 | -.1 | .0 | -1.5 | -.7 | 2.5 |
| Sales/Net Fixed Assets | 25.2 | 22.5 | 13.8 | .5 | 34.6 | 219.0 | 173.8 | 127.7 | 74.5 |
| | .4 | .3 | .3 | .2 | 1.5 | 18.3 | 21.4 | 15.2 | 30.9 |
| | .1 | .1 | .1 | .1 | .2 | .5 | 1.2 | 1.6 | 7.3 |
| Sales/Total Assets | .7 | .8 | .6 | .2 | 1.1 | 2.8 | 2.9 | 3.0 | 2.8 |
| | .2 | .2 | .2 | .1 | .4 | .8 | 1.0 | 1.2 | 1.2 |
| | .1 | .1 | .1 | .1 | .2 | .2 | .4 | .3 | .5 |
| % Depr., Dep., Amort./Sales | 2.8 | 3.6 | 5.0 | 12.3 | 1.4 | .7 | .5 | .5 | .4 |
| | (1094) 13.9 | (1130) 14.6 | (1244) 16.0 | (860) 19.5 | (190) 7.1 | (52) 4.1 | (46) 1.9 | (45) 2.2 | (51) 1.2 |
| | 23.4 | 24.0 | 25.1 | 27.5 | 18.0 | 14.6 | 7.5 | 6.8 | 2.8 |
| % Officers', Directors', Owners' Comp/Sales | 2.1 | 2.2 | 1.9 | 4.3 | 2.4 | 1.3 | 2.0 | .9 | .4 |
| | (218) 5.1 | (236) 5.5 | (195) 6.3 | (76) 10.1 | (59) 7.5 | (21) 4.5 | (15) 2.6 | (14) 1.5 | (10) .9 |
| | 12.6 | 13.8 | 14.2 | 18.6 | 14.3 | 8.2 | 8.8 | 5.0 | 2.3 |
| Net Sales ($) | 9677855M | 11293104M | 9039784M | 374208M | 540356M | 373084M | 518854M | 982781M | 6250501M |
| Total Assets ($) | 15751710M | 14869047M | 14978075M | 2763188M | 2156035M | 1041290M | 1299435M | 2077371M | 5640756M |

M = $ thousand    MM = $ million
See Pages 9 through 22 for Explanation of Ratios and Data

## REAL ESTATE—Passenger Car Rental NAICS 532111

### Current Data Sorted by Assets | Comparative Historical Data

| | 0-500M | 500M-2MM | 2-10MM | 10-50MM | 50-100MM | 100-250MM | Type of Statement | 4/1/07-3/31/08 ALL | 4/1/08-3/31/09 ALL |
|---|---|---|---|---|---|---|---|---|---|
| | | 2 | 6 | 19 | 7 | 4 | Unqualified | 23 | 24 |
| | 1 | 2 | 10 | 8 | | | Reviewed | 14 | 14 |
| | 3 | 6 | 12 | 3 | | | Compiled | 19 | 14 |
| | 13 | 17 | 10 | 1 | | | Tax Returns | 11 | 10 |
| | 6 | 20 | 26 | 15 | 2 | 2 | Other | 30 | 34 |
| | | 28 (4/1-9/30/11) | | 167 (10/1/11-3/31/12) | | | | | |
| NUMBER OF STATEMENTS | 23 | 47 | 64 | 46 | 9 | 6 | | 97 | 96 |

| | 0-500M | 500M-2MM | 2-10MM | 10-50MM | 50-100MM | 100-250MM | | 4/1/07-3/31/08 ALL | 4/1/08-3/31/09 ALL |
|---|---|---|---|---|---|---|---|---|---|
| | % | % | % | % | % | % | **ASSETS** | % | % |
| | 27.9 | 15.8 | 9.3 | 5.7 | | | Cash & Equivalents | 6.8 | 8.3 |
| | 5.3 | 3.7 | 5.5 | 5.9 | | | Trade Receivables (net) | 4.6 | 6.7 |
| | .9 | 7.0 | 7.4 | 8.5 | | | Inventory | 17.8 | 16.0 |
| | 5.3 | 1.7 | .9 | 4.8 | | | All Other Current | 8.1 | 3.8 |
| | 39.4 | 28.2 | 23.1 | 24.9 | | | Total Current | 37.3 | 34.9 |
| | 47.2 | 59.6 | 61.8 | 65.7 | | | Fixed Assets (net) | 53.5 | 52.4 |
| | 6.3 | 6.5 | 6.7 | 1.7 | | | Intangibles (net) | 3.2 | 2.8 |
| | 7.2 | 5.7 | 8.5 | 7.8 | | | All Other Non-Current | 5.9 | 9.9 |
| | 100.0 | 100.0 | 100.0 | 100.0 | | | Total | 100.0 | 100.0 |
| | | | | | | | **LIABILITIES** | | |
| | 12.1 | 15.8 | 18.4 | 19.2 | | | Notes Payable-Short Term | 34.9 | 27.6 |
| | 8.8 | 5.7 | 3.9 | 5.3 | | | Cur. Mat.-L.T.D. | 6.1 | 7.6 |
| | .4 | 3.9 | 3.0 | 3.6 | | | Trade Payables | 3.9 | 4.5 |
| | .8 | .0 | .4 | .5 | | | Income Taxes Payable | .2 | .1 |
| | 42.0 | 7.4 | 8.4 | 3.1 | | | All Other Current | 5.9 | 6.6 |
| | 64.1 | 33.0 | 34.1 | 31.7 | | | Total Current | 51.1 | 46.4 |
| | 30.6 | 34.1 | 39.2 | 39.2 | | | Long-Term Debt | 26.2 | 32.8 |
| | .0 | .0 | .3 | 1.2 | | | Deferred Taxes | .7 | .7 |
| | .1 | 14.2 | 4.8 | 5.9 | | | All Other Non-Current | 4.5 | 4.5 |
| | 5.1 | 18.8 | 21.6 | 21.9 | | | Net Worth | 17.5 | 15.6 |
| | 100.0 | 100.0 | 100.0 | 100.0 | | | Total Liabilities & Net Worth | 100.0 | 100.0 |
| | | | | | | | **INCOME DATA** | | |
| | 100.0 | 100.0 | 100.0 | 100.0 | | | Net Sales | 100.0 | 100.0 |
| | | | | | | | Gross Profit | | |
| | 86.0 | 92.5 | 90.0 | 89.4 | | | Operating Expenses | 91.9 | 94.6 |
| | 14.0 | 7.5 | 10.0 | 10.6 | | | Operating Profit | 8.1 | 5.4 |
| | 1.6 | 2.8 | 4.0 | 2.9 | | | All Other Expenses (net) | 6.8 | 3.0 |
| | 12.4 | 4.7 | 6.1 | 7.7 | | | Profit Before Taxes | 1.3 | 2.4 |
| | | | | | | | **RATIOS** | | |
| | 2.4 | 2.9 | 2.5 | 2.7 | | | Current | 1.2 | 1.5 |
| | .8 | 1.1 | 1.1 | 1.3 | | | | .7 | .9 |
| | .2 | .3 | .4 | .3 | | | | .2 | .3 |
| | 2.2 | 2.8 | 2.5 | 2.2 | | | Quick | .5 | .9 |
| | .8 | .8 | .8 | .6 | | | | .2 | .3 |
| | .2 | .2 | .2 | .1 | | | | .1 | .1 |
| | 0 UND | 0 UND | 0 UND | 8 46.4 | | | Sales/Receivables | 4 90.4 | 3 131.9 |
| | 0 UND | 1 282.3 | 9 40.4 | 15 23.8 | | | | 13 28.9 | 12 31.1 |
| | 12 31.5 | 10 37.7 | 22 16.3 | 33 11.1 | | | | 25 14.7 | 30 12.3 |
| | | | | | | | Cost of Sales/Inventory | | |
| | | | | | | | Cost of Sales/Payables | | |
| | 29.8 | 5.0 | 9.5 | 5.4 | | | Sales/Working Capital | 10.3 | 11.0 |
| | -42.0 | 48.2 | 86.7 | 30.4 | | | | -24.3 | -79.8 |
| | -1.7 | -7.5 | -3.4 | -3.1 | | | | -2.4 | -3.1 |
| | 6.5 | 4.6 | 4.5 | 4.0 | | | EBIT/Interest | 1.8 | 2.6 |
| | (14) 2.1 | (40) 2.4 | (54) 1.8 | (43) 2.1 | | | | (84) 1.1 | (89) 1.4 |
| | 1.1 | 1.0 | 1.1 | 1.5 | | | | .7 | .5 |
| | | | | | | | Net Profit + Depr., Dep., Amort./Cur. Mat. L/T/D | 19.3 | 12.0 |
| | | | | | | | | (10) 3.6 (10) 2.7 | |
| | | | | | | | | 1.6 | 1.4 |
| | .2 | 1.1 | 1.2 | 1.9 | | | Fixed/Worth | .3 | .4 |
| | 1.9 | 3.0 | 4.3 | 5.0 | | | | 3.2 | 3.4 |
| | -18.3 | 10.7 | 10.1 | 8.1 | | | | 11.1 | 16.2 |
| | .8 | 1.2 | 2.7 | 2.7 | | | Debt/Worth | 2.4 | 2.3 |
| | 2.0 | 4.4 | 5.2 | 5.6 | | | | 6.1 | 7.3 |
| | -25.4 | 74.5 | 26.1 | 9.5 | | | | 17.3 | 33.8 |
| | 134.7 | 72.4 | 35.4 | 41.1 | | | % Profit Before Taxes/Tangible Net Worth | 22.6 | 32.1 |
| | (17) 31.2 | (37) 21.2 | (52) 18.0 | (44) 25.8 | | | | (85) 11.0 (76) 14.3 | |
| | 10.5 | 4.7 | 2.2 | 10.0 | | | | -4.1 | .2 |
| | 63.3 | 10.0 | 7.5 | 7.9 | | | % Profit Before Taxes/Total Assets | 3.7 | 5.5 |
| | 8.2 | 5.4 | 3.1 | 3.8 | | | | 1.1 | 2.0 |
| | 1.4 | .0 | .2 | 1.0 | | | | -1.2 | -2.3 |
| | 351.4 | 8.0 | 2.3 | 2.4 | | | Sales/Net Fixed Assets | 12.5 | 19.1 |
| | 3.0 | 2.1 | 1.0 | .8 | | | | 1.4 | 1.4 |
| | 1.2 | 1.0 | .7 | .5 | | | | .8 | .8 |
| | 5.0 | 2.1 | 1.2 | .8 | | | Sales/Total Assets | 1.1 | 1.2 |
| | 1.1 | 1.2 | .7 | .6 | | | | .7 | .7 |
| | .5 | .6 | .4 | .5 | | | | .5 | .6 |
| | 11.3 | 8.4 | 11.7 | 14.5 | | | % Depr., Dep., Amort./Sales | 11.4 | 14.7 |
| | (14) 34.2 | (37) 21.1 | (52) 28.4 | (37) 33.0 | | | | (66) 21.5 (59) 31.6 | |
| | 42.9 | 29.1 | 36.9 | 40.8 | | | | 37.1 | 43.9 |
| | | 2.5 | 1.6 | 1.4 | | | % Officers', Directors' Owners' Comp/Sales | 2.1 | 1.0 |
| | | (17) 5.5 | (21) 3.3 | (11) 2.5 | | | | (31) 4.0 (33) 2.8 | |
| | | 8.5 | 5.1 | 3.5 | | | | 7.3 | 4.4 |
| | 19185M | 101800M | 344532M | 969663M | 382332M | 622195M | Net Sales ($) | 1373745M | 1820826M |
| | 5432M | 51833M | 300114M | 1071076M | 691700M | 1043636M | Total Assets ($) | 1865883M | 2034269M |

M = $ thousand   MM = $ million
See Pages 9 through 22 for Explanation of Ratios and Data

## Comparative Historical Data      Current Data Sorted by Sales

| 4/1/09-3/31/10 ALL | 4/1/10-3/31/11 ALL | 4/1/11-3/31/12 ALL | Type of Statement | 28 (4/1-9/30/11) 0-1MM | 1-3MM | 3-5MM | 167 (10/1/11-3/31/12) 5-10MM | 10-25MM | 25MM & OVER |
|---|---|---|---|---|---|---|---|---|---|
| 26 | 24 | 38 | Unqualified | 2 | 2 | 2 | 9 | 12 | 11 |
| 17 | 22 | 21 | Reviewed | 1 | 3 | 5 | 4 | 6 | 2 |
| 21 | 15 | 24 | Compiled | 7 | 9 | 2 | 1 | 4 | 1 |
| 31 | 19 | 41 | Tax Returns | 18 | 14 | 8 | | 1 | |
| 42 | 45 | 71 | Other | 16 | 17 | 10 | 9 | 11 | 8 |
| 137 | 125 | 195 | **NUMBER OF STATEMENTS** | 44 | 45 | 27 | 23 | 34 | 22 |
| % | % | % | **ASSETS** | % | % | % | % | % | % |
| 10.9 | 9.2 | 12.3 | Cash & Equivalents | 13.9 | 16.9 | 10.0 | 10.4 | 11.1 | 6.1 |
| 7.9 | 7.0 | 5.4 | Trade Receivables (net) | 3.3 | 3.3 | 4.9 | 3.8 | 4.9 | 16.8 |
| 12.5 | 12.5 | 7.3 | Inventory | 5.9 | 8.0 | 1.2 | .7 | 14.3 | 11.9 |
| 4.7 | 4.8 | 2.6 | All Other Current | 2.9 | .5 | 3.0 | 1.8 | 3.3 | 5.3 |
| 36.0 | 33.4 | 27.5 | Total Current | 26.0 | 28.8 | 19.0 | 16.7 | 33.7 | 40.0 |
| 53.2 | 55.3 | 59.6 | Fixed Assets (net) | 60.9 | 59.7 | 65.2 | 74.0 | 50.9 | 48.3 |
| 2.2 | 1.9 | 5.3 | Intangibles (net) | 4.5 | 4.7 | 6.6 | 1.9 | 9.3 | 4.1 |
| 8.6 | 9.3 | 7.6 | All Other Non-Current | 8.7 | 6.8 | 9.3 | 7.4 | 6.2 | 7.5 |
| 100.0 | 100.0 | 100.0 | Total | 100.0 | 100.0 | 100.0 | 100.0 | 100.0 | 100.0 |
| | | | **LIABILITIES** | | | | | | |
| 27.4 | 22.8 | 16.7 | Notes Payable-Short Term | 9.9 | 14.0 | 20.2 | 25.2 | 25.4 | 9.0 |
| 7.2 | 8.5 | 5.6 | Cur. Mat.-L.T.D. | 7.1 | 5.2 | 6.4 | 1.2 | 5.0 | 7.4 |
| 5.2 | 3.1 | 3.0 | Trade Payables | 1.3 | 1.8 | 4.3 | 2.9 | 2.9 | 7.7 |
| .2 | .3 | .5 | Income Taxes Payable | .1 | .4 | .0 | .0 | 1.8 | .5 |
| 9.8 | 7.8 | 10.6 | All Other Current | 22.9 | 5.6 | 6.8 | 4.7 | 11.8 | 5.1 |
| 49.7 | 42.4 | 36.3 | Total Current | 41.2 | 27.0 | 37.8 | 34.1 | 46.9 | 29.6 |
| 28.9 | 26.9 | 37.7 | Long-Term Debt | 40.7 | 39.4 | 35.1 | 48.5 | 21.9 | 44.4 |
| .5 | .6 | .6 | Deferred Taxes | .0 | .2 | .2 | 1.1 | .9 | 2.2 |
| 2.7 | 4.0 | 6.7 | All Other Non-Current | 9.4 | 6.8 | 8.3 | 6.7 | 4.5 | 2.7 |
| 18.1 | 26.1 | 18.7 | Net Worth | 8.6 | 26.6 | 18.7 | 9.6 | 25.8 | 21.1 |
| 100.0 | 100.0 | 100.0 | Total Liabilities & Net Worth | 100.0 | 100.0 | 100.0 | 100.0 | 100.0 | 100.0 |
| | | | **INCOME DATA** | | | | | | |
| 100.0 | 100.0 | 100.0 | Net Sales | 100.0 | 100.0 | 100.0 | 100.0 | 100.0 | 100.0 |
| | | | Gross Profit | | | | | | |
| 89.0 | 85.6 | 89.7 | Operating Expenses | 77.4 | 95.3 | 94.1 | 94.1 | 91.7 | 90.1 |
| 11.0 | 14.4 | 10.3 | Operating Profit | 22.6 | 4.7 | 5.9 | 5.9 | 8.3 | 9.9 |
| 3.3 | 3.7 | 3.0 | All Other Expenses (net) | 6.7 | 2.7 | 1.7 | .9 | 1.8 | 2.0 |
| 7.7 | 10.8 | 7.3 | Profit Before Taxes | 15.9 | 2.0 | 4.3 | 5.1 | 6.5 | 7.9 |
| | | | **RATIOS** | | | | | | |
| 1.5 | 1.9 | 2.6 | | 2.6 | 2.8 | 2.5 | 2.8 | 1.7 | 2.8 |
| .8 | 1.1 | 1.2 | Current | .9 | 1.5 | .8 | 1.7 | .7 | 1.6 |
| .2 | .3 | .3 | | .2 | .4 | .2 | .7 | .3 | 1.0 |
| .9 | 1.4 | 2.4 | | 2.4 | 2.7 | 2.1 | 2.4 | .9 | 2.5 |
| .3 | .4 | .8 | Quick | .8 | 1.0 | .7 | 1.4 | .3 | 1.1 |
| .1 | .1 | .2 | | .2 | .3 | .1 | .6 | .2 | .2 |
| 3   107.1 | 2   167.6 | 0   UND | | 0   UND | 0   UND | 0   UND | 4   97.0 | 3   115.6 | 9   42.7 |
| 13   28.3 | 11   33.3 | 8   46.4 | Sales/Receivables | 0   UND | 5   72.1 | 9   40.7 | 9   39.7 | 16   23.0 | 19   19.1 |
| 29   12.4 | 32   11.3 | 23   15.8 | | 9   41.6 | 24   14.9 | 16   22.5 | 18   20.8 | 33   11.1 | 35   10.5 |
| | | | Cost of Sales/Inventory | | | | | | |
| | | | Cost of Sales/Payables | | | | | | |
| 10.7 | 7.2 | 6.8 | | 3.8 | 9.0 | 14.5 | 8.3 | 5.9 | 5.1 |
| -19.7 | 40.8 | 48.6 | Sales/Working Capital | -60.8 | 29.8 | -351.4 | 30.2 | -26.1 | 23.2 |
| -2.2 | -2.0 | -4.1 | | -2.3 | -7.4 | -2.2 | -10.1 | -3.1 | NM |
| 5.8 | 4.8 | 4.5 | | 5.9 | 4.3 | 4.3 | 3.5 | 4.2 | 6.6 |
| (120) 1.7 | (108) 2.3 | (165) 2.2 | EBIT/Interest | (32) 2.2 | (40) 1.9 | (24) 1.7 | (22) 2.2 | (26) 2.4 | (21) 2.4 |
| 1.1 | 1.4 | 1.3 | | .8 | 1.2 | .9 | 1.2 | 1.5 | 1.7 |
| 6.5 | 10.7 | 8.3 | | | | | | | |
| (14) 2.8 | (10) 1.6 | (11) 4.3 | Net Profit + Depr., Dep., Amort./Cur. Mat. L/T/D | | | | | | |
| .8 | .1 | 1.1 | | | | | | | |
| .7 | .6 | 1.1 | | .8 | 1.0 | 1.9 | 3.3 | .4 | .4 |
| 2.6 | 2.0 | 4.0 | Fixed/Worth | 2.9 | 3.4 | 4.9 | 6.9 | 3.2 | 4.5 |
| 8.6 | 7.7 | 10.3 | | 11.9 | 7.8 | 42.4 | 13.9 | 5.4 | 8.5 |
| 1.9 | 1.6 | 2.2 | | 1.2 | 1.1 | 2.3 | 2.9 | 2.4 | 4.6 |
| 4.3 | 3.8 | 5.5 | Debt/Worth | 4.4 | 4.7 | 4.7 | 6.7 | 4.2 | 7.2 |
| 15.6 | 12.5 | 14.0 | | 29.6 | 17.5 | 47.6 | 15.7 | 14.4 | 10.1 |
| 39.6 | 47.4 | 44.3 | | 47.0 | 49.2 | 39.6 | 61.5 | 32.8 | 78.0 |
| (117) 15.4 | (111) 19.7 | (164) 22.4 | % Profit Before Taxes/Tangible Net Worth | (34) 21.1 | (38) 21.3 | (22) 13.5 | (20) 32.9 | (29) 18.6 | (21) 38.2 |
| 2.1 | 7.8 | 9.5 | | 4.4 | 5.7 | -5.1 | 8.9 | 10.8 | 22.1 |
| 7.6 | 8.3 | 9.7 | | 10.3 | 9.9 | 9.4 | 6.6 | 8.1 | 9.8 |
| 2.7 | 4.1 | 4.1 | % Profit Before Taxes/Total Assets | 4.6 | 4.8 | 3.2 | 4.1 | 3.7 | 5.6 |
| .2 | .9 | .8 | | .5 | .5 | -.4 | .7 | 1.0 | 2.6 |
| 6.5 | 7.4 | 5.5 | | 4.0 | 5.1 | 4.2 | 2.0 | 21.0 | 15.1 |
| 1.5 | 1.3 | 1.2 | Sales/Net Fixed Assets | 1.1 | 1.3 | 1.4 | .9 | 1.1 | 1.8 |
| .8 | .6 | .6 | | .3 | .8 | .7 | .6 | .6 | .9 |
| 1.2 | 1.0 | 1.3 | | 1.1 | 1.8 | 1.6 | 1.1 | 2.6 | 1.6 |
| .7 | .7 | .7 | Sales/Total Assets | .5 | .9 | .9 | .7 | .7 | .8 |
| .5 | .5 | .5 | | .2 | .5 | .5 | .5 | .5 | .6 |
| 7.9 | 10.0 | 12.2 | | 20.6 | 9.2 | 14.1 | 23.9 | 7.9 | |
| (94) 22.7 | (86) 25.3 | (142) 27.2 | % Depr., Dep., Amort./Sales | (31) 28.9 | (37) 21.5 | (25) 28.1 | (20) 34.5 | (21) 27.6 | |
| 38.4 | 37.4 | 38.0 | | 41.3 | 34.7 | 39.1 | 40.7 | 37.2 | |
| 1.5 | 1.3 | 1.6 | | | 2.8 | 1.6 | | 1.0 | |
| (40) 2.9 | (34) 3.2 | (60) 3.5 | % Officers', Directors' Owners' Comp/Sales | | (19) 5.5 | (10) 3.5 | | (12) 2.5 | |
| 7.2 | 5.8 | 5.9 | | | 8.0 | 5.1 | | 3.3 | |
| 2135919M | 2359232M | 2439707M | Net Sales ($) | 17655M | 87242M | 101555M | 163742M | 496440M | 1573073M |
| 2693886M | 2627599M | 3163791M | Total Assets ($) | 51758M | 113103M | 165676M | 244692M | 736613M | 1851949M |

M = $ thousand    MM = $ million
See Pages 9 through 22 for Explanation of Ratios and Data

## Current Data Sorted by Assets      Comparative Historical Data

| | 0-500M | 500M-2MM | 2-10MM | 10-50MM | 50-100MM | 100-250MM | Type of Statement | 4/1/07-3/31/08 ALL | 4/1/08-3/31/09 ALL |
|---|---|---|---|---|---|---|---|---|---|
| | | 28 (4/1-9/30/11) | | 97 (10/1/11-3/31/12) | | | | | |
| Unqualified | | | 3 | 11 | 4 | 6 | | 22 | 23 |
| Reviewed | | | 6 | 19 | 1 | 3 | | 23 | 27 |
| Compiled | 2 | | 8 | 2 | 2 | 1 | | 30 | 18 |
| Tax Returns | 4 | 7 | 4 | 2 | | | | 13 | 21 |
| Other | 1 | 4 | 13 | 15 | 6 | 3 | | 59 | 60 |
| **NUMBER OF STATEMENTS** | 7 | 11 | 34 | 49 | 11 | 13 | | 147 | 149 |

### ASSETS (%)

| | 0-500M | 500M-2MM | 2-10MM | 10-50MM | 50-100MM | 100-250MM | | 4/1/07-3/31/08 ALL | 4/1/08-3/31/09 ALL |
|---|---|---|---|---|---|---|---|---|---|
| Cash & Equivalents | | 13.3 | 5.3 | 4.5 | 4.8 | 6.9 | | 5.8 | 5.5 |
| Trade Receivables (net) | | 4.7 | 10.0 | 4.4 | 22.3 | 2.8 | | 9.8 | 13.2 |
| Inventory | | 10.7 | 3.8 | 10.0 | 1.2 | .6 | | 6.9 | 6.6 |
| All Other Current | | 2.9 | 7.9 | 10.2 | 1.0 | 17.1 | | 7.7 | 8.4 |
| Total Current | | 31.7 | 27.0 | 29.1 | 29.4 | 27.4 | | 30.2 | 33.7 |
| Fixed Assets (net) | | 65.9 | 50.9 | 49.9 | 51.5 | 52.0 | | 45.8 | 46.4 |
| Intangibles (net) | | .2 | 3.5 | 1.6 | .7 | .6 | | 1.4 | 1.2 |
| All Other Non-Current | | 2.2 | 18.6 | 19.4 | 18.5 | 20.0 | | 22.6 | 18.7 |
| Total | | 100.0 | 100.0 | 100.0 | 100.0 | 100.0 | | 100.0 | 100.0 |

### LIABILITIES

| | 0-500M | 500M-2MM | 2-10MM | 10-50MM | 50-100MM | 100-250MM | | 4/1/07-3/31/08 ALL | 4/1/08-3/31/09 ALL |
|---|---|---|---|---|---|---|---|---|---|
| Notes Payable-Short Term | | 8.8 | 11.4 | 12.9 | 7.9 | 25.5 | | 18.5 | 16.9 |
| Cur. Mat.-L.T.D. | | 15.1 | 6.3 | 9.2 | 7.4 | .3 | | 7.0 | 8.1 |
| Trade Payables | | 4.2 | 4.7 | 1.0 | 9.0 | 1.7 | | 3.4 | 3.2 |
| Income Taxes Payable | | .1 | .5 | .0 | .0 | .3 | | .2 | .2 |
| All Other Current | | 3.4 | 7.3 | 1.9 | 6.4 | 3.4 | | 3.9 | 6.2 |
| Total Current | | 31.5 | 30.2 | 25.1 | 30.7 | 31.2 | | 33.1 | 34.6 |
| Long-Term Debt | | 41.8 | 50.7 | 53.3 | 47.1 | 40.5 | | 44.9 | 45.7 |
| Deferred Taxes | | .0 | .2 | 2.0 | 1.1 | 2.1 | | .8 | .8 |
| All Other Non-Current | | .9 | 8.4 | 3.6 | 1.4 | 1.9 | | 4.9 | 3.9 |
| Net Worth | | 25.8 | 10.4 | 16.0 | 19.6 | 24.3 | | 16.3 | 15.1 |
| Total Liabilities & Net Worth | | 100.0 | 100.0 | 100.0 | 100.0 | 100.0 | | 100.0 | 100.0 |

### INCOME DATA

| | 0-500M | 500M-2MM | 2-10MM | 10-50MM | 50-100MM | 100-250MM | | 4/1/07-3/31/08 ALL | 4/1/08-3/31/09 ALL |
|---|---|---|---|---|---|---|---|---|---|
| Net Sales | | 100.0 | 100.0 | 100.0 | 100.0 | 100.0 | | 100.0 | 100.0 |
| Gross Profit | | | | | | | | | |
| Operating Expenses | | 81.6 | 80.4 | 83.0 | 85.8 | 79.6 | | 82.9 | 82.4 |
| Operating Profit | | 18.4 | 19.6 | 17.0 | 14.2 | 20.4 | | 17.1 | 17.6 |
| All Other Expenses (net) | | 5.8 | 10.6 | 9.3 | 5.0 | 9.3 | | 11.1 | 12.3 |
| Profit Before Taxes | | 12.6 | 9.0 | 7.7 | 9.3 | 11.1 | | 6.0 | 5.3 |

### RATIOS

| Ratio | 0-500M | 500M-2MM | 2-10MM | 10-50MM | 50-100MM | 100-250MM | | 4/1/07-3/31/08 ALL | 4/1/08-3/31/09 ALL |
|---|---|---|---|---|---|---|---|---|---|
| Current | | 6.0 | 3.2 | 4.1 | 4.6 | 1.6 | | 2.9 | 2.1 |
| | | 1.2 | 1.4 | 1.2 | 1.3 | 1.2 | | 1.1 | 1.1 |
| | | .4 | .5 | .4 | 1.0 | .5 | | .3 | .3 |
| Quick | | 6.0 | 2.6 | 1.8 | 3.2 | 1.0 | | 1.7 | 1.6 |
| | | .6 | .7 | .5 | 1.2 | .6 | | (146) .5 | .5 |
| | | .2 | .2 | .2 | 1.0 | .1 | | .1 | .1 |
| Sales/Receivables | | 0 UND | 5 72.5 | 4 97.0 | 9 38.5 | 5 67.7 | | 3 114.5 | 2 161.7 |
| | | 0 UND | 28 13.2 | 10 37.8 | 30 12.2 | 23 15.6 | | 17 21.0 | 14 25.7 |
| | | 8 43.8 | 49 7.4 | 29 12.5 | 365 1.0 | 26 14.3 | | 51 7.1 | 54 6.7 |
| Cost of Sales/Inventory | | | | | | | | | |
| Cost of Sales/Payables | | | | | | | | | |
| Sales/Working Capital | | 8.5 | 4.3 | 2.0 | 4.1 | 3.0 | | 3.7 | 3.1 |
| | | 91.5 | 14.2 | 16.6 | 14.6 | 19.6 | | 27.8 | 68.4 |
| | | -1.5 | -3.5 | -2.1 | -38.5 | -18.1 | | -3.5 | -2.2 |
| EBIT/Interest | | | 3.5 | 2.9 | 3.8 | 4.2 | | 2.4 | 2.6 |
| | | | (27) 1.7 | (42) 1.7 | 2.7 | (11) 2.0 | | (106) 1.4 | (106) 1.3 |
| | | | 1.0 | 1.3 | 1.7 | 1.7 | | 1.1 | 1.0 |
| Net Profit + Depr., Dep., Amort./Cur. Mat. L/T/D | | | | | | | | | |
| Fixed/Worth | | .2 | .8 | .1 | 1.0 | .0 | | .2 | .2 |
| | | 2.2 | 3.8 | 3.3 | 2.1 | 3.4 | | 3.1 | 3.1 |
| | | -50.1 | 27.1 | 6.7 | 6.2 | 3.8 | | 11.0 | 8.1 |
| Debt/Worth | | .5 | 3.6 | 4.5 | 2.9 | 2.8 | | 3.8 | 3.7 |
| | | 4.3 | 11.6 | 6.3 | 5.4 | 3.5 | | 8.1 | 7.5 |
| | | -60.0 | -13.5 | 12.8 | 11.7 | 11.9 | | 20.5 | 21.8 |
| % Profit Before Taxes/Tangible Net Worth | | | 60.2 | 35.5 | 33.5 | 18.7 | | 32.6 | 26.4 |
| | | | (25) 26.3 | (47) 17.0 | 18.3 | (12) 12.0 | | (126) 13.6 | (129) 12.3 |
| | | | 2.3 | 7.9 | 13.9 | 8.0 | | 4.2 | 1.9 |
| % Profit Before Taxes/Total Assets | | 10.7 | 5.8 | 3.5 | 6.3 | 5.1 | | 4.3 | 3.3 |
| | | 7.6 | 2.2 | 1.9 | 4.6 | 2.4 | | 1.7 | 1.0 |
| | | 5.0 | .4 | 1.0 | 2.1 | 1.4 | | .3 | .0 |
| Sales/Net Fixed Assets | | 42.9 | 23.3 | 14.0 | 6.2 | 35.8 | | 36.7 | 29.8 |
| | | .6 | .9 | .8 | .7 | 1.0 | | 1.3 | 1.1 |
| | | .4 | .5 | .4 | .5 | .5 | | .5 | .5 |
| Sales/Total Assets | | 4.7 | .7 | .6 | .5 | .7 | | .7 | .6 |
| | | .5 | .4 | .4 | .4 | .4 | | .5 | .4 |
| | | .3 | .2 | .3 | .3 | .2 | | .3 | .2 |
| % Depr., Dep., Amort./Sales | | | 8.7 | 10.2 | | | | 3.5 | 3.8 |
| | | | (24) 35.0 | (32) 43.0 | | | | (106) 25.1 | (97) 27.5 |
| | | | 59.6 | 63.8 | | | | 58.9 | 60.7 |
| % Officers', Directors' Owners' Comp/Sales | | | 1.4 | 1.6 | | | | 2.6 | 1.8 |
| | | | (17) 4.6 | (13) 3.5 | | | | (36) 5.2 | (36) 3.7 |
| | | | 11.3 | 6.8 | | | | 7.7 | 7.4 |
| **Net Sales ($)** | 3617M | 25029M | 194668M | 554895M | 555402M | 1115065M | | 1777787M | 2343406M |
| **Total Assets ($)** | 1742M | 10026M | 195680M | 1325107M | 767409M | 2279213M | | 4074451M | 4930160M |

© RMA 2012

M = $ thousand    MM = $ million
See Pages 9 through 22 for Explanation of Ratios and Data

## Comparative Historical Data        Current Data Sorted by Sales

| | | | Type of Statement | 0-1MM | 1-3MM | 3-5MM | 5-10MM | 10-25MM | 25MM & OVER |
|---|---|---|---|---|---|---|---|---|---|
| 27 | 22 | 24 | Unqualified | | 3 | | 2 | 9 | 10 |
| 24 | 23 | 29 | Reviewed | 1 | 2 | 10 | 2 | 12 | 2 |
| 27 | 13 | 13 | Compiled | 3 | 4 | 4 | | 2 | |
| 18 | 14 | 17 | Tax Returns | 9 | 1 | 4 | 3 | | |
| 38 | 31 | 42 | Other | 7 | 7 | 4 | 9 | 7 | 8 |
| 4/1/09-3/31/10 ALL | 4/1/10-3/31/11 ALL | 4/1/11-3/31/12 ALL | | | 28 (4/1-9/30/11) | | 97 (10/1/11-3/31/12) | | |
| 134 | 103 | 125 | NUMBER OF STATEMENTS | 20 | 17 | 22 | 16 | 30 | 20 |
| % | % | % | ASSETS | % | % | % | % | % | % |
| 6.0 | 5.4 | 6.3 | Cash & Equivalents | 8.7 | 5.1 | 7.6 | 4.2 | 6.3 | 5.4 |
| 9.0 | 9.6 | 7.5 | Trade Receivables (net) | 7.0 | 4.0 | 4.2 | 8.7 | 7.1 | 14.2 |
| 4.6 | 5.0 | 7.4 | Inventory | 8.6 | 1.2 | 1.6 | 25.3 | 8.7 | 1.7 |
| 4.7 | 6.4 | 8.5 | All Other Current | 5.1 | 7.8 | 7.6 | 8.8 | 12.3 | 7.3 |
| 24.4 | 26.4 | 29.7 | Total Current | 29.3 | 18.2 | 21.0 | 46.9 | 34.4 | 28.5 |
| 53.3 | 52.8 | 51.3 | Fixed Assets (net) | 57.8 | 43.2 | 65.7 | 25.9 | 49.7 | 58.3 |
| 1.0 | 1.4 | 2.2 | Intangibles (net) | 4.3 | 6.8 | 1.0 | .7 | .9 | .7 |
| 21.3 | 19.3 | 16.9 | All Other Non-Current | 8.6 | 31.8 | 12.3 | 26.6 | 15.0 | 12.5 |
| 100.0 | 100.0 | 100.0 | Total | 100.0 | 100.0 | 100.0 | 100.0 | 100.0 | 100.0 |
| | | | **LIABILITIES** | | | | | | |
| 10.8 | 12.1 | 13.1 | Notes Payable-Short Term | 6.8 | 15.7 | 3.9 | 15.0 | 14.9 | 23.0 |
| 9.8 | 10.1 | 8.5 | Cur. Mat.-L.T.D. | 19.0 | 4.7 | 13.5 | 3.8 | 7.6 | 1.1 |
| 2.8 | 2.4 | 3.1 | Trade Payables | .9 | 1.2 | 1.2 | 2.3 | 3.8 | 8.4 |
| .2 | .1 | .2 | Income Taxes Payable | .0 | .6 | .4 | .0 | .1 | .1 |
| 7.1 | 6.4 | 4.0 | All Other Current | .6 | 4.7 | 3.2 | 2.7 | 4.8 | 7.5 |
| 30.8 | 31.1 | 28.9 | Total Current | 27.2 | 26.9 | 22.2 | 23.9 | 31.2 | 40.2 |
| 54.9 | 49.6 | 49.9 | Long-Term Debt | 54.6 | 53.4 | 56.7 | 58.1 | 46.1 | 33.9 |
| .9 | 1.2 | 1.1 | Deferred Taxes | .0 | .8 | .7 | .9 | 2.7 | .8 |
| 5.3 | 5.5 | 4.8 | All Other Non-Current | 7.6 | 8.1 | 4.8 | .9 | 4.2 | 2.9 |
| 8.2 | 12.7 | 15.3 | Net Worth | 10.6 | 10.8 | 15.6 | 16.1 | 15.7 | 22.2 |
| 100.0 | 100.0 | 100.0 | Total Liabilities & Net Worth | 100.0 | 100.0 | 100.0 | 100.0 | 100.0 | 100.0 |
| | | | **INCOME DATA** | | | | | | |
| 100.0 | 100.0 | 100.0 | Net Sales | 100.0 | 100.0 | 100.0 | 100.0 | 100.0 | 100.0 |
| | | | Gross Profit | | | | | | |
| 86.9 | 84.7 | 82.2 | Operating Expenses | 73.0 | 80.3 | 82.4 | 84.9 | 86.1 | 84.7 |
| 13.1 | 15.3 | 17.8 | Operating Profit | 27.0 | 19.7 | 17.6 | 15.1 | 13.9 | 15.3 |
| 10.6 | 9.4 | 8.5 | All Other Expenses (net) | 9.9 | 11.1 | 13.0 | 6.7 | 6.4 | 4.3 |
| 2.5 | 5.9 | 9.4 | Profit Before Taxes | 17.0 | 8.6 | 4.6 | 8.4 | 7.6 | 11.0 |
| | | | **RATIOS** | | | | | | |
| 2.6 | 3.0 | 3.9 | | 5.8 | 3.7 | 3.5 | 13.9 | 4.2 | 1.4 |
| 1.0 | 1.0 | 1.2 | Current | 1.0 | 1.0 | 1.5 | 2.0 | 1.3 | 1.0 |
| .3 | .2 | .4 | | .4 | .2 | .3 | 1.2 | 1.0 | .2 |
| 1.5 | 2.0 | 2.1 | | 5.3 | 2.7 | 2.5 | 2.7 | 2.6 | .9 |
| .5 | .4 | .6 | Quick | .4 | .5 | .5 | 1.2 | .9 | .6 |
| .2 | .1 | .2 | | .2 | .1 | .1 | .2 | .3 | .1 |
| 4 88.2 | 3 109.0 | 3 107.2 | | 0 UND | 5 80.4 | 3 130.7 | 1 266.6 | 5 72.8 | 5 80.9 |
| 15 24.8 | 20 17.8 | 12 31.6 | Sales/Receivables | 0 UND | 26 14.0 | 13 27.2 | 9 41.7 | 13 27.3 | 24 15.1 |
| 38 9.7 | 51 7.2 | 33 11.0 | | 63 5.8 | 47 7.8 | 63 5.8 | 14 25.2 | 32 11.5 | 29 12.5 |
| | | | Cost of Sales/Inventory | | | | | | |
| | | | Cost of Sales/Payables | | | | | | |
| 4.2 | 3.5 | 3.9 | | 1.2 | 6.9 | 2.0 | .8 | 3.9 | 17.4 |
| NM | -84.1 | 16.7 | Sales/Working Capital | 183.5 | 13.0 | 9.2 | 13.7 | 9.0 | NM |
| -2.4 | -1.8 | -3.3 | | -1.9 | -2.1 | -2.0 | 79.1 | -86.6 | -2.7 |
| 2.5 | 2.9 | 3.5 | | 6.7 | 3.3 | 2.3 | 6.5 | 2.8 | 11.3 |
| (99) 1.4 | (79) 1.7 | (107) 1.9 | EBIT/Interest | (14) 2.6 | (14) 1.9 | (16) 1.3 | (15) 1.7 | (29) 1.7 | (19) 3.4 |
| 1.0 | 1.0 | 1.4 | | 1.2 | 1.2 | 1.0 | 1.3 | 1.5 | 1.9 |
| 1.0 | | 12.6 | | | | | | | |
| (10) .8 | | (10) 1.2 | Net Profit + Depr., Dep., Amort./Cur. Mat. L/T/D | | | | | | |
| -.1 | | .1 | | | | | | | |
| 1.4 | .7 | .3 | | .9 | .1 | 1.7 | .0 | .1 | 1.4 |
| 5.8 | 3.8 | 3.3 | Fixed/Worth | 2.4 | 8.3 | 4.2 | .7 | 3.0 | 3.3 |
| 86.3 | 20.0 | 9.9 | | NM | -6.1 | 11.6 | 7.1 | 6.2 | 15.6 |
| 3.9 | 3.6 | 3.4 | | 2.1 | 6.2 | 3.4 | 4.1 | 3.8 | 1.7 |
| 10.2 | 7.6 | 6.3 | Debt/Worth | 15.6 | 13.2 | 6.0 | 9.9 | 5.5 | 3.8 |
| 600.3 | 46.4 | 20.0 | | -21.6 | -9.6 | 21.8 | 17.3 | 7.2 | 18.7 |
| 22.5 | 35.0 | 39.7 | | 142.9 | 31.9 | 41.3 | 55.8 | 23.9 | 56.1 |
| (102) 11.9 | (83) 13.7 | (108) 16.3 | % Profit Before Taxes/Tangible Net Worth | (14) 28.2 | (12) 7.5 | (19) 13.9 | (29) 34.6 | (29) 13.9 | (18) 25.2 |
| 1.9 | 4.2 | 8.0 | | 3.0 | -5.1 | 5.1 | 8.2 | 9.4 | 13.2 |
| 3.4 | 4.4 | 5.9 | | 7.9 | 4.5 | 3.8 | 6.7 | 4.6 | 8.2 |
| 1.2 | 1.9 | 2.5 | % Profit Before Taxes/Total Assets | 4.9 | 2.3 | 1.3 | 2.3 | 2.4 | 4.1 |
| .1 | .1 | 1.2 | | .8 | .4 | .3 | 1.1 | 1.3 | 2.4 |
| 12.2 | 11.4 | 18.3 | | 1.8 | 39.7 | 1.5 | 591.9 | 16.6 | 16.3 |
| .8 | .9 | .8 | Sales/Net Fixed Assets | .6 | 1.6 | .5 | 7.4 | 1.0 | 1.0 |
| .5 | .5 | .5 | | .3 | .4 | .4 | .6 | .5 | .7 |
| .6 | .6 | .6 | | .6 | .5 | .6 | .6 | .6 | .8 |
| .4 | .4 | .4 | Sales/Total Assets | .3 | .3 | .4 | .5 | .4 | .7 |
| .3 | .2 | .2 | | .1 | .2 | .2 | .3 | .3 | .5 |
| 6.3 | 6.0 | 7.0 | | 46.5 | | 16.2 | 5.8 | 5.8 | |
| (86) 36.9 | (63) 30.3 | (79) 36.2 | % Depr., Dep., Amort./Sales | (16) 61.4 | | (21) 59.7 | (10) 22.4 | (14) 19.6 | |
| 70.6 | 57.2 | 64.2 | | 72.0 | | 72.3 | 60.2 | 45.6 | |
| 2.3 | 2.6 | 1.3 | | | | | | | |
| (39) 3.4 | (30) 4.5 | (35) 3.5 | % Officers', Directors' Owners' Comp/Sales | | | | | | |
| 5.7 | 7.8 | 8.5 | | | | | | | |
| 1732376M | 1759416M | 2448676M | Net Sales ($) | 7936M | 32514M | 86351M | 116518M | 522728M | 1682629M |
| 3529629M | 3581762M | 4579177M | Total Assets ($) | 40548M | 117735M | 346896M | 296147M | 1441165M | 2336686M |

**Current Data Sorted by Assets**　　　　　　　　　　　**Comparative Historical Data**

| Type of Statement | 0-500M | 500M-2MM | 2-10MM | 10-50MM | 50-100MM | 100-250MM | | 4/1/07-3/31/08 ALL | 4/1/08-3/31/09 ALL |
|---|---|---|---|---|---|---|---|---|---|
| Unqualified |  |  | 6 | 21 | 9 | 15 | | 50 | 58 |
| Reviewed | 1 | 3 | 20 | 49 | 2 | 2 | | 53 | 67 |
| Compiled | 2 | 7 | 18 | 4 |  |  | | 37 | 45 |
| Tax Returns | 12 | 11 | 6 |  |  |  | | 34 | 39 |
| Other | 17 | 21 | 33 | 36 | 11 | 13 | | 102 | 117 |
| | | 47 (4/1-9/30/11) | | 272 (10/1/11-3/31/12) | | | | | |
| **NUMBER OF STATEMENTS** | 32 | 42 | 83 | 110 | 22 | 30 | | 276 | 326 |
| **ASSETS** | % | % | % | % | % | % | | % | % |
| Cash & Equivalents | 15.2 | 16.1 | 12.1 | 7.7 | 6.0 | 3.9 | | 7.5 | 6.5 |
| Trade Receivables (net) | 9.4 | 11.2 | 11.3 | 10.0 | 15.7 | 9.0 | | 10.5 | 11.7 |
| Inventory | 4.1 | 5.3 | 10.7 | 8.5 | 8.4 | 7.5 | | 7.8 | 6.4 |
| All Other Current | 2.5 | 3.8 | 2.4 | 5.9 | 2.7 | 5.5 | | 4.1 | 4.6 |
| Total Current | 31.3 | 36.4 | 36.6 | 32.2 | 32.9 | 25.9 | | 30.0 | 29.3 |
| Fixed Assets (net) | 56.5 | 48.3 | 55.1 | 56.4 | 53.9 | 49.7 | | 61.8 | 60.5 |
| Intangibles (net) | 1.6 | 1.7 | 1.8 | 2.3 | 2.3 | 1.8 | | 1.7 | 1.5 |
| All Other Non-Current | 10.6 | 13.6 | 6.5 | 9.1 | 11.0 | 22.5 | | 6.5 | 8.7 |
| Total | 100.0 | 100.0 | 100.0 | 100.0 | 100.0 | 100.0 | | 100.0 | 100.0 |
| **LIABILITIES** | | | | | | | | | |
| Notes Payable-Short Term | 14.4 | 6.6 | 9.4 | 7.7 | 9.9 | 9.5 | | 11.4 | 9.3 |
| Cur. Mat.-L.T.D. | 13.5 | 13.2 | 11.2 | 11.9 | 9.9 | 9.0 | | 11.7 | 12.8 |
| Trade Payables | 6.9 | 7.1 | 4.6 | 4.4 | 3.8 | 3.1 | | 4.5 | 4.4 |
| Income Taxes Payable | .0 | .2 | .4 | .2 | .2 | .1 | | .3 | .2 |
| All Other Current | 8.0 | 8.0 | 8.4 | 4.4 | 3.2 | 6.0 | | 6.0 | 7.2 |
| Total Current | 42.8 | 35.0 | 34.1 | 28.6 | 27.0 | 27.6 | | 33.9 | 33.9 |
| Long-Term Debt | 69.7 | 37.5 | 38.0 | 35.9 | 38.5 | 42.2 | | 38.0 | 40.5 |
| Deferred Taxes | .0 | .0 | 1.0 | 2.3 | 4.1 | 5.2 | | 2.0 | 1.8 |
| All Other Non-Current | 15.1 | 3.9 | 4.2 | 2.7 | 1.2 | 3.2 | | 3.9 | 4.9 |
| Net Worth | -27.6 | 23.5 | 22.7 | 30.5 | 29.2 | 21.9 | | 22.2 | 18.9 |
| Total Liabilities & Net Worth | 100.0 | 100.0 | 100.0 | 100.0 | 100.0 | 100.0 | | 100.0 | 100.0 |
| **INCOME DATA** | | | | | | | | | |
| Net Sales | 100.0 | 100.0 | 100.0 | 100.0 | 100.0 | 100.0 | | 100.0 | 100.0 |
| Gross Profit | | | | | | | | | |
| Operating Expenses | 83.3 | 78.9 | 84.3 | 88.6 | 85.2 | 89.0 | | 86.6 | 88.5 |
| Operating Profit | 16.7 | 21.1 | 15.7 | 11.4 | 14.8 | 11.0 | | 13.4 | 11.5 |
| All Other Expenses (net) | 4.9 | 2.4 | 5.3 | 2.4 | 5.6 | 6.6 | | 5.8 | 5.9 |
| Profit Before Taxes | 11.8 | 18.7 | 10.4 | 9.0 | 9.1 | 4.4 | | 7.6 | 5.5 |
| **RATIOS** | | | | | | | | | |
| Current | 2.6 | 2.1 | 1.9 | 1.7 | 2.6 | 1.2 | | 1.6 | 1.8 |
| | .5 | 1.3 | 1.1 | 1.1 | 1.1 | .9 | | .9 | .9 |
| | .2 | .3 | .4 | .6 | .6 | .3 | | .4 | .3 |
| Quick | 2.1 | 1.9 | 1.5 | 1.3 | 2.4 | .6 | | 1.1 | 1.1 |
| | .4 | .5 | .6 | .6 | .8 | .3 | | .5 | .5 |
| | .1 | .2 | .3 | .2 | .3 | .2 | | .2 | .2 |
| Sales/Receivables | 0 UND | 0 UND | 0 UND | 12 30.3 | 19 19.1 | 21 17.3 | | 2 183.2 | 1 324.7 |
| | 0 UND | 17 21.5 | 24 15.2 | 28 12.9 | 34 10.7 | 34 10.7 | | 28 12.9 | 26 14.2 |
| | 48 7.6 | 35 10.4 | 42 8.6 | 42 8.6 | 62 5.9 | 45 8.2 | | 44 8.2 | 46 7.9 |
| Cost of Sales/Inventory | | | | | | | | | |
| Cost of Sales/Payables | | | | | | | | | |
| Sales/Working Capital | 8.6 | 4.7 | 5.1 | 4.9 | 6.3 | 9.6 | | 10.2 | 9.4 |
| | -40.5 | 16.6 | 51.2 | 85.4 | 46.5 | -13.2 | | -98.7 | -36.4 |
| | -2.3 | -3.9 | -5.3 | -8.9 | -6.7 | -4.3 | | -4.2 | -4.0 |
| EBIT/Interest | 8.7 | 9.2 | 5.8 | 5.9 | 4.0 | 4.0 | | 3.7 | 2.8 |
| | (24) 2.5 | (36) 4.3 | (76) 2.5 | (99) 2.5 | (21) 3.3 | (26) 1.8 | | (243) 1.8 | (266) 1.5 |
| | -.8 | 1.1 | 1.1 | 1.4 | 2.6 | 1.4 | | 1.2 | .9 |
| Net Profit + Depr., Dep., Amort./Cur. Mat. L/T/D | | | 3.5 | 2.8 | | | | 2.5 | 2.6 |
| | | | (12) 1.4 | (33) 1.4 | | | | (56) 1.2 | (60) 1.2 |
| | | | .9 | 1.1 | | | | .9 | .9 |
| Fixed/Worth | 1.5 | .4 | 1.0 | 1.2 | .9 | .8 | | 1.3 | 1.3 |
| | 6.2 | 1.6 | 2.2 | 1.9 | 2.3 | 2.4 | | 2.7 | 2.6 |
| | -1.4 | -7.3 | 18.3 | 4.0 | 4.0 | 3.9 | | 7.3 | 10.7 |
| Debt/Worth | 2.1 | .8 | 1.5 | 1.3 | 1.8 | 2.7 | | 1.8 | 1.5 |
| | 13.4 | 3.1 | 3.1 | 3.0 | 3.1 | 5.3 | | 3.6 | 3.7 |
| | -2.7 | -11.1 | 28.6 | 5.7 | 6.6 | 7.4 | | 10.2 | 20.6 |
| % Profit Before Taxes/Tangible Net Worth | 170.6 | 53.0 | 48.3 | 33.1 | 33.1 | 22.7 | | 30.2 | 25.4 |
| | (19) 41.7 | (30) 23.4 | (65) 21.7 | (103) 19.2 | (21) 21.0 | (28) 15.4 | | (237) 14.2 | (270) 9.5 |
| | -1.1 | 8.4 | 7.8 | 7.2 | 13.8 | 9.0 | | 5.6 | 1.5 |
| % Profit Before Taxes/Total Assets | 23.8 | 25.0 | 13.5 | 9.1 | 8.2 | 4.3 | | 8.0 | 5.7 |
| | 4.8 | 12.1 | 4.5 | 4.3 | 4.6 | 2.5 | | 3.3 | 2.1 |
| | -2.0 | 1.6 | .5 | 1.3 | 3.7 | 1.1 | | .9 | -.8 |
| Sales/Net Fixed Assets | 7.0 | 12.0 | 6.7 | 5.4 | 6.2 | 11.1 | | 3.8 | 4.5 |
| | 1.9 | 2.5 | 1.1 | 1.3 | 1.3 | 1.2 | | 1.2 | 1.1 |
| | 1.1 | 1.0 | .5 | .7 | .6 | .6 | | .6 | .6 |
| Sales/Total Assets | 2.6 | 1.7 | 1.7 | 1.7 | 1.3 | .9 | | 1.6 | 1.7 |
| | 1.3 | 1.0 | .6 | .8 | .7 | .6 | | .8 | .7 |
| | .6 | .6 | .3 | .4 | .4 | .3 | | .4 | .4 |
| % Depr., Dep., Amort./Sales | 11.9 | 9.7 | 6.5 | 4.5 | 2.2 | | | 6.0 | 6.8 |
| | (15) 33.1 | (24) 17.6 | (68) 26.2 | (98) 16.9 | (19) 9.7 | | | (210) 19.5 | (247) 22.3 |
| | 52.2 | 29.1 | 48.3 | 29.3 | 31.3 | | | 42.5 | 42.5 |
| % Officers', Directors' Owners' Comp/Sales | | | 1.3 | 2.2 | | | | 1.0 | .8 |
| | | (17) 2.9 | (16) 8.0 | | | | | (48) 3.2 | (52) 2.8 |
| | | 6.6 | 23.4 | | | | | 6.3 | 7.1 |
| Net Sales ($) | 11039M | 76250M | 620355M | 3193636M | 1320411M | 3182186M | | 8551283M | 7209273M |
| Total Assets ($) | 7947M | 49109M | 471450M | 2729105M | 1524231M | 4290387M | | 8665091M | 8964143M |

M = $ thousand　　MM = $ million
See Pages 9 through 22 for Explanation of Ratios and Data

## Comparative Historical Data / Current Data Sorted by Sales

| | | | Type of Statement | | | | | | |
|---|---|---|---|---|---|---|---|---|---|
| 45 | 56 | 51 | Unqualified | | 6 | 1 | 6 | 9 | 29 |
| 62 | 75 | 77 | Reviewed | 4 | 7 | 14 | 13 | 20 | 19 |
| 47 | 41 | 31 | Compiled | 7 | 10 | 4 | 6 | 3 | 1 |
| 33 | 30 | 29 | Tax Returns | 17 | 7 | 2 | 2 | | 1 |
| 117 | 133 | 131 | Other | 33 | 16 | 8 | 14 | 18 | 42 |
| 4/1/09-3/31/10 ALL | 4/1/10-3/31/11 ALL | 4/1/11-3/31/12 ALL | | \<--- 47 (4/1-9/30/11) ---\> | | \<--- 272 (10/1/11-3/31/12) ---\> | | | |
| | | | | 0-1MM | 1-3MM | 3-5MM | 5-10MM | 10-25MM | 25MM & OVER |
| 304 | 335 | 319 | NUMBER OF STATEMENTS | 61 | 46 | 29 | 41 | 50 | 92 |
| % | % | % | ASSETS | % | % | % | % | % | % |
| 7.7 | 8.7 | 10.2 | Cash & Equivalents | 13.2 | 14.9 | 13.0 | 8.0 | 10.8 | 5.6 |
| 10.5 | 10.5 | 10.7 | Trade Receivables (net) | 5.3 | 12.2 | 9.2 | 9.5 | 14.1 | 12.8 |
| 9.1 | 7.1 | 8.1 | Inventory | 3.2 | 2.7 | 4.0 | 15.8 | 7.9 | 12.2 |
| 4.5 | 4.5 | 4.1 | All Other Current | 4.1 | 1.7 | 8.5 | 4.0 | 5.9 | 3.1 |
| 31.7 | 30.9 | 33.2 | Total Current | 25.9 | 31.6 | 34.8 | 37.3 | 38.6 | 33.7 |
| 57.6 | 55.8 | 54.2 | Fixed Assets (net) | 60.3 | 52.6 | 54.6 | 55.4 | 51.1 | 52.0 |
| 1.7 | 2.3 | 2.0 | Intangibles (net) | 1.3 | 2.0 | 1.5 | 2.6 | 1.7 | 2.4 |
| 9.0 | 11.0 | 10.6 | All Other Non-Current | 12.5 | 13.8 | 9.1 | 4.7 | 8.6 | 11.9 |
| 100.0 | 100.0 | 100.0 | Total | 100.0 | 100.0 | 100.0 | 100.0 | 100.0 | 100.0 |
| | | | LIABILITIES | | | | | | |
| 12.4 | 11.2 | 9.0 | Notes Payable-Short Term | 10.7 | 7.4 | 3.5 | 10.6 | 4.7 | 12.0 |
| 12.0 | 11.0 | 11.6 | Cur. Mat.-L.T.D. | 13.1 | 11.2 | 15.1 | 12.8 | 12.0 | 9.1 |
| 5.0 | 4.4 | 4.9 | Trade Payables | 3.8 | 4.6 | 3.8 | 4.7 | 4.9 | 6.2 |
| .2 | .1 | .2 | Income Taxes Payable | .1 | .1 | 1.0 | .0 | .1 | .3 |
| 9.0 | 7.6 | 6.3 | All Other Current | 9.6 | 8.0 | 2.6 | 4.4 | 5.0 | 6.1 |
| 38.5 | 34.5 | 32.1 | Total Current | 37.3 | 31.3 | 26.0 | 32.5 | 26.6 | 33.7 |
| 35.6 | 34.7 | 40.8 | Long-Term Debt | 58.2 | 38.4 | 45.2 | 32.1 | 37.1 | 35.0 |
| 1.9 | 1.8 | 1.8 | Deferred Taxes | .0 | .6 | .9 | 1.4 | 2.1 | 4.0 |
| 4.9 | 3.2 | 4.4 | All Other Non-Current | 9.2 | 4.5 | 5.4 | 3.6 | 3.1 | 2.1 |
| 19.0 | 25.9 | 20.8 | Net Worth | -4.7 | 25.2 | 22.4 | 30.3 | 31.1 | 25.2 |
| 100.0 | 100.0 | 100.0 | Total Liabilities & Net Worth | 100.0 | 100.0 | 100.0 | 100.0 | 100.0 | 100.0 |
| | | | INCOME DATA | | | | | | |
| 100.0 | 100.0 | 100.0 | Net Sales | 100.0 | 100.0 | 100.0 | 100.0 | 100.0 | 100.0 |
| | | | Gross Profit | | | | | | |
| 90.7 | 86.3 | 85.5 | Operating Expenses | 72.9 | 81.0 | 85.3 | 87.3 | 87.4 | 94.2 |
| 9.3 | 13.7 | 14.5 | Operating Profit | 27.1 | 19.0 | 14.7 | 12.7 | 12.6 | 5.8 |
| 5.1 | 4.4 | 4.1 | All Other Expenses (net) | 7.2 | 4.9 | 5.0 | 3.7 | 2.0 | 2.6 |
| 4.2 | 9.4 | 10.5 | Profit Before Taxes | 19.9 | 14.1 | 9.7 | 9.0 | 10.6 | 3.3 |
| | | | RATIOS | | | | | | |
| 1.6 | 1.7 | 1.8 | | 1.7 | 2.7 | 2.0 | 1.9 | 2.7 | 1.4 |
| .9 | 1.0 | 1.0 | Current | .7 | 1.2 | 1.4 | 1.1 | 1.2 | 1.0 |
| .4 | .4 | .4 | | .2 | .3 | .4 | .4 | .7 | .7 |
| 1.1 | 1.3 | 1.4 | | 1.3 | 2.6 | 1.6 | 1.0 | 1.7 | .9 |
| .5 | .5 | .5 | Quick | .4 | .9 | 1.1 | .4 | .7 | .5 |
| .2 | .2 | .2 | | .1 | .3 | .1 | .2 | .3 | .2 |
| 4  99.3 | 1  271.3 | 6  62.0 | | 0  UND | 0  UND | 0  755.4 | 16  22.8 | 17  21.0 | 16  23.2 |
| 27  13.7 | 26  13.8 | 24  14.9 | Sales/Receivables | 0  UND | 20  18.3 | 16  23.4 | 29  12.7 | 29  12.5 | 27  13.4 |
| 42  8.6 | 45  8.1 | 44  8.3 | | 33  11.0 | 55  6.6 | 49  7.4 | 46  8.0 | 46  8.0 | 44  8.3 |
| | | | Cost of Sales/Inventory | | | | | | |
| | | | Cost of Sales/Payables | | | | | | |
| 8.3 | 7.2 | 6.2 | | 4.2 | 3.4 | 2.6 | 4.8 | 4.1 | 15.7 |
| -59.5 | -117.0 | 97.4 | Sales/Working Capital | -12.2 | 30.6 | 6.4 | 35.5 | 17.0 | -222.3 |
| -3.9 | -4.6 | -5.2 | | -2.3 | -3.1 | -3.0 | -3.2 | -15.2 | -10.3 |
| 3.1 | 5.3 | 5.9 | | 10.2 | 6.4 | 3.4 | 5.1 | 9.2 | 4.0 |
| (265)  1.5 | (290)  2.2 | (282)  2.7 | EBIT/Interest | (48)  3.7 | (40)  2.7 | (24)  2.1 | (39)  2.5 | (44)  3.7 | (87)  2.6 |
| .3 | 1.2 | 1.3 | | .7 | 1.1 | 1.1 | 1.3 | 1.6 | 1.5 |
| 2.9 | 2.4 | 3.0 | Net Profit + Depr., Dep., | | | | | 3.1 | 3.2 |
| (59)  1.3 | (55)  1.2 | (58)  1.3 | Amort./Cur. Mat. L/T/D | | | | (11)  1.4 | (31)  1.2 | |
| .9 | 1.0 | 1.0 | | | | | | 1.3 | 1.0 |
| 1.2 | 1.0 | 1.0 | | 1.5 | .7 | 1.2 | 1.0 | .5 | 1.3 |
| 2.3 | 2.0 | 2.1 | Fixed/Worth | 3.6 | 1.9 | 2.4 | 1.8 | 1.5 | 2.3 |
| 11.7 | 6.3 | 5.8 | | -4.1 | 5.9 | 17.1 | 4.2 | 3.4 | 4.7 |
| 1.4 | 1.2 | 1.5 | | 1.7 | 1.3 | 1.4 | 1.4 | .9 | 1.9 |
| 3.6 | 2.9 | 3.2 | Debt/Worth | 7.8 | 3.7 | 3.2 | 2.6 | 2.0 | 3.4 |
| 26.5 | 13.4 | 11.5 | | -6.5 | 11.7 | 17.7 | 6.1 | 5.2 | 6.7 |
| 25.4 | 30.7 | 37.5 | % Profit Before Taxes/Tangible | 76.4 | 32.1 | 36.4 | 37.6 | 39.9 | 35.0 |
| (244)  9.6 | (274)  14.4 | (266)  19.0 | Net Worth | (39)  23.4 | (37)  17.7 | (24)  16.7 | (39)  12.7 | (42)  21.7 | (85)  18.3 |
| .1 | 5.1 | 8.2 | | 3.6 | 2.8 | 8.2 | 3.3 | 10.2 | 9.4 |
| 5.9 | 8.9 | 10.8 | % Profit Before Taxes/Total | 23.2 | 14.7 | 7.5 | 7.9 | 15.4 | 6.5 |
| 1.7 | 3.4 | 4.6 | Assets | 6.8 | 6.0 | 3.0 | 4.7 | 7.1 | 3.8 |
| -2.0 | .6 | .8 | | .0 | .1 | .5 | .8 | 1.8 | 1.7 |
| 4.9 | 5.5 | 6.5 | | 4.5 | 6.9 | 4.0 | 10.7 | 6.5 | 8.6 |
| 1.4 | 1.6 | 1.4 | Sales/Net Fixed Assets | 1.4 | 1.2 | .6 | 1.1 | 1.4 | 2.7 |
| .7 | .7 | .6 | | .5 | .6 | .5 | .5 | .9 | 1.2 |
| 1.5 | 1.5 | 1.7 | | 1.3 | 1.3 | .9 | 1.2 | 2.0 | 2.3 |
| .8 | .9 | .8 | Sales/Total Assets | .6 | .6 | .4 | .6 | .9 | 1.2 |
| .4 | .4 | .4 | | .3 | .3 | .3 | .3 | .5 | .8 |
| 5.6 | 6.1 | 4.7 | | 16.7 | 15.1 | 19.6 | 10.4 | 5.1 | 2.3 |
| (232)  20.6 | (241)  16.9 | (233)  17.0 | % Depr., Dep., Amort./Sales | (34)  28.4 | (34)  41.1 | (26)  35.4 | (33)  22.3 | (41)  12.3 | (65)  6.0 |
| 38.8 | 35.5 | 35.9 | | 51.3 | 56.5 | 63.7 | 37.1 | 25.9 | 10.8 |
| 1.4 | 1.6 | 2.0 | % Officers', Directors' | | | | 1.9 | | |
| (56)  2.6 | (49)  3.4 | (45)  4.6 | Owners' Comp/Sales | | | | (15)  4.1 | | |
| 8.0 | 7.3 | 15.7 | | | | | 10.0 | | |
| 6466322M | 8225728M | 8403877M | Net Sales ($) | 28601M | 80693M | 117395M | 293367M | 855150M | 7028671M |
| 8297885M | 9892467M | 9072229M | Total Assets ($) | 72633M | 199769M | 336368M | 622746M | 1612983M | 6227730M |

M = $ thousand    MM = $ million
See Pages 9 through 22 for Explanation of Ratios and Data

## Current Data Sorted by Assets | Comparative Historical Data

| | 0-500M | 500M-2MM | 2-10MM | 10-50MM | 50-100MM | 100-250MM | | 4/1/07-3/31/08 ALL | 4/1/08-3/31/09 ALL |
|---|---|---|---|---|---|---|---|---|---|
| | | 6 (4/1-9/30/11) | | 84 (10/1/11-3/31/12) | | | Type of Statement | | |
| Unqualified | | 1 | 2 | 4 | 1 | 1 | | 11 | 10 |
| Reviewed | | 1 | 9 | 2 | | | | 10 | 14 |
| Compiled | 4 | 4 | 5 | 4 | | | | 22 | 28 |
| Tax Returns | 8 | 14 | 4 | 1 | | | | 12 | 23 |
| Other | 4 | 7 | 6 | 8 | 3 | 1 | | 24 | 25 |
| | 16 | 27 | 26 | 15 | 4 | 2 | NUMBER OF STATEMENTS | 79 | 100 |
| | % | % | % | % | % | % | ASSETS | % | % |
| | 18.4 | 15.9 | 3.5 | 5.4 | | | Cash & Equivalents | 7.7 | 9.2 |
| | 6.1 | 9.5 | 7.9 | 13.0 | | | Trade Receivables (net) | 12.5 | 12.6 |
| | 15.6 | 9.6 | 26.1 | 12.8 | | | Inventory | 15.9 | 15.9 |
| | .2 | 1.6 | 5.0 | 6.7 | | | All Other Current | 4.3 | 4.1 |
| | 40.3 | 36.6 | 42.4 | 37.9 | | | Total Current | 40.4 | 41.9 |
| | 33.0 | 50.6 | 41.9 | 34.0 | | | Fixed Assets (net) | 46.1 | 44.8 |
| | 5.6 | 8.2 | 5.4 | 11.0 | | | Intangibles (net) | 4.9 | 3.2 |
| | 21.1 | 4.7 | 10.3 | 17.1 | | | All Other Non-Current | 8.6 | 10.1 |
| | 100.0 | 100.0 | 100.0 | 100.0 | | | Total | 100.0 | 100.0 |
| | | | | | | | LIABILITIES | | |
| | 8.2 | 16.4 | 40.2 | 15.0 | | | Notes Payable-Short Term | 17.1 | 21.9 |
| | 2.4 | 7.9 | 5.1 | 5.4 | | | Cur. Mat.-L.T.D. | 8.2 | 8.6 |
| | 6.3 | 4.1 | 5.5 | 5.2 | | | Trade Payables | 9.0 | 7.2 |
| | .0 | .8 | .7 | .0 | | | Income Taxes Payable | .1 | .2 |
| | 20.0 | 12.1 | 9.3 | 9.6 | | | All Other Current | 7.0 | 8.7 |
| | 36.8 | 41.3 | 60.8 | 35.1 | | | Total Current | 41.6 | 46.6 |
| | 15.1 | 25.6 | 13.7 | 27.6 | | | Long-Term Debt | 30.5 | 28.9 |
| | .0 | .3 | .3 | 1.0 | | | Deferred Taxes | .5 | .3 |
| | 25.7 | 12.4 | 6.0 | 10.4 | | | All Other Non-Current | 9.5 | 9.8 |
| | 22.4 | 20.4 | 19.2 | 25.9 | | | Net Worth | 18.0 | 14.4 |
| | 100.0 | 100.0 | 100.0 | 100.0 | | | Total Liabilities & Net Worth | 100.0 | 100.0 |
| | | | | | | | INCOME DATA | | |
| | 100.0 | 100.0 | 100.0 | 100.0 | | | Net Sales | 100.0 | 100.0 |
| | | | | | | | Gross Profit | | |
| | 85.2 | 87.3 | 94.5 | 89.7 | | | Operating Expenses | 89.3 | 89.8 |
| | 14.8 | 12.7 | 5.5 | 10.3 | | | Operating Profit | 10.7 | 10.2 |
| | -.2 | 3.2 | 1.8 | 3.2 | | | All Other Expenses (net) | 6.4 | 4.8 |
| | 15.0 | 9.5 | 3.7 | 7.1 | | | Profit Before Taxes | 4.2 | 5.5 |
| | | | | | | | RATIOS | | |
| | 7.4 | 2.2 | 1.3 | 2.1 | | | | 2.1 | 2.0 |
| | 2.1 | 1.0 | .8 | 1.2 | | | Current | 1.0 | 1.1 |
| | .2 | .3 | .1 | .3 | | | | .3 | .4 |
| | 2.9 | 1.7 | .7 | 1.5 | | | | 1.4 | 1.4 |
| | 1.1 | .7 | .1 | .8 | | | Quick | .4 | .5 |
| | .1 | .1 | .0 | .1 | | | | .1 | .1 |
| | 0 UND | 0 UND | 0 UND | 2 231.2 | | | | 0 UND | 0 UND |
| | 0 UND | 0 999.8 | 0 783.5 | 21 17.8 | | | Sales/Receivables | 6 57.6 | 10 36.6 |
| | 4 82.9 | 24 15.0 | 21 17.4 | 101 3.6 | | | | 29 12.6 | 37 9.9 |
| | | | | | | | Cost of Sales/Inventory | | |
| | | | | | | | Cost of Sales/Payables | | |
| | 6.0 | 6.7 | 47.9 | 3.5 | | | | 6.7 | 5.2 |
| | 26.0 | 411.0 | -14.6 | 9.8 | | | Sales/Working Capital | 103.6 | 47.7 |
| | -6.3 | -4.2 | -3.3 | -13.1 | | | | -5.1 | -5.6 |
| | | 14.6 | 5.2 | 4.6 | | | | 3.5 | 6.4 |
| | (23) | 3.2 | 2.3 | (13) 2.7 | | | EBIT/Interest | (65) 1.9 | (85) 1.9 |
| | | 1.2 | .9 | 1.3 | | | | 1.0 | .8 |
| | | | | | | | Net Profit + Depr., Dep., | 4.5 | 9.8 |
| | | | | | | | Amort./Cur. Mat. L/T/D | (15) 2.9 | (11) 2.5 |
| | | | | | | | | 1.8 | 1.2 |
| | .0 | .6 | 1.0 | .1 | | | | .5 | .6 |
| | 1.4 | 5.3 | 4.2 | 1.8 | | | Fixed/Worth | 4.1 | 1.8 |
| | -2.6 | -2.1 | -1.7 | 18.7 | | | | -16.0 | -5.9 |
| | .2 | .6 | 2.1 | 2.7 | | | | 1.5 | .9 |
| | 3.8 | 8.4 | 5.1 | 3.8 | | | Debt/Worth | 6.2 | 3.1 |
| | -7.1 | -4.1 | -9.2 | 26.2 | | | | -23.3 | -10.2 |
| | 335.3 | 54.9 | 36.8 | 99.0 | | | % Profit Before Taxes/Tangible | 58.2 | 52.7 |
| | (10) 48.7 | (15) 35.3 | (17) 12.0 | (12) 14.5 | | | Net Worth | (55) 22.1 | (72) 17.7 |
| | 16.5 | 11.1 | .3 | 2.5 | | | | 4.6 | 4.5 |
| | 71.6 | 29.5 | 8.3 | 14.2 | | | % Profit Before Taxes/Total | 9.0 | 13.9 |
| | 19.8 | 6.9 | 3.9 | 4.8 | | | Assets | 4.2 | 3.1 |
| | 3.4 | 1.3 | .0 | .8 | | | | .0 | -.6 |
| | UND | 14.7 | 25.3 | 19.5 | | | | 15.7 | 12.2 |
| | 15.3 | 3.4 | 5.7 | 9.4 | | | Sales/Net Fixed Assets | 3.0 | 5.1 |
| | 2.6 | 1.8 | 2.1 | 2.4 | | | | 1.4 | 1.6 |
| | 3.9 | 3.5 | 2.2 | 1.8 | | | | 2.3 | 2.5 |
| | 2.3 | 1.9 | 1.8 | 1.4 | | | Sales/Total Assets | 1.5 | 1.6 |
| | 1.1 | 1.0 | 1.2 | .4 | | | | .7 | .8 |
| | | 4.8 | 6.5 | 2.4 | | | | 3.5 | 3.6 |
| | (19) | 21.6 | (16) 29.0 | (11) 6.8 | | | % Depr., Dep., Amort./Sales | (61) 15.1 | (70) 9.3 |
| | | 32.3 | 32.6 | 25.5 | | | | 31.2 | 30.1 |
| | | 1.2 | | | | | % Officers', Directors' | 2.6 | 3.6 |
| | (12) | 2.7 | | | | | Owners' Comp/Sales | (22) 4.5 | (31) 7.1 |
| | | 6.3 | | | | | | 10.8 | 10.8 |
| | 9421M | 68207M | 211326M | 463295M | 364617M | 388123M | Net Sales ($) | 860370M | 1338007M |
| | 3575M | 32463M | 131032M | 455603M | 306997M | 290016M | Total Assets ($) | 792676M | 1330760M |

M = $ thousand   MM = $ million
See Pages 9 through 22 for Explanation of Ratios and Data

## Comparative Historical Data — Current Data Sorted by Sales

| | | | Type of Statement | | | 6 (4/1-9/30/11) | 84 (10/1/11-3/31/12) | | |
|---|---|---|---|---|---|---|---|---|---|
| 14 | 8 | 9 | Unqualified | | 1 | 1 | 2 | 1 | 4 |
| 14 | 13 | 12 | Reviewed | 1 | 2 | | 3 | 4 | 2 |
| 10 | 13 | 13 | Compiled | 5 | 3 | 1 | 3 | 1 | |
| 25 | 20 | 27 | Tax Returns | 9 | 9 | 4 | 4 | 1 | |
| 27 | 22 | 29 | Other | 6 | 2 | 4 | 4 | 1 | 10 |
| 4/1/09-3/31/10 ALL | 4/1/10-3/31/11 ALL | 4/1/11-3/31/12 ALL | | 0-1MM | 1-3MM | 3-5MM | 5-10MM | 10-25MM | 25MM & OVER |
| 90 | 76 | 90 | **NUMBER OF STATEMENTS** | 21 | 17 | 10 | 18 | 8 | 16 |
| % | % | % | **ASSETS** | % | % | % | % | % | % |
| 9.1 | 7.2 | 10.4 | Cash & Equivalents | 14.7 | 13.1 | 18.5 | 6.2 | | 4.4 |
| 10.6 | 10.7 | 9.8 | Trade Receivables (net) | 3.2 | 5.5 | 22.1 | 4.0 | | 17.2 |
| 15.6 | 15.7 | 16.7 | Inventory | 11.4 | 10.9 | 16.8 | 22.9 | | 19.1 |
| 3.4 | 2.3 | 3.3 | All Other Current | .3 | 6.5 | 1.6 | 7.1 | | 1.5 |
| 38.7 | 35.9 | 40.1 | Total Current | 29.6 | 36.1 | 59.0 | 40.3 | | 42.2 |
| 44.6 | 46.6 | 41.0 | Fixed Assets (net) | 47.6 | 48.5 | 29.5 | 38.2 | | 43.4 |
| 4.8 | 6.8 | 7.7 | Intangibles (net) | 6.6 | 6.8 | 3.2 | 7.1 | | 9.3 |
| 12.0 | 10.7 | 11.2 | All Other Non-Current | 16.2 | 8.6 | 8.3 | 14.5 | | 5.2 |
| 100.0 | 100.0 | 100.0 | Total | 100.0 | 100.0 | 100.0 | 100.0 | | 100.0 |
| | | | **LIABILITIES** | | | | | | |
| 14.9 | 19.6 | 21.9 | Notes Payable-Short Term | 8.4 | 23.7 | 11.1 | 45.3 | | 19.0 |
| 7.5 | 8.2 | 5.5 | Cur. Mat.-L.T.D. | 4.5 | 5.8 | 8.4 | 5.8 | | 4.7 |
| 7.3 | 9.1 | 5.3 | Trade Payables | 2.5 | 3.5 | 9.8 | 4.9 | | 7.7 |
| .3 | .3 | .4 | Income Taxes Payable | .0 | 1.3 | .0 | .2 | | .0 |
| 10.2 | 11.5 | 11.9 | All Other Current | 21.2 | 7.7 | 7.8 | 8.4 | | 10.7 |
| 40.2 | 48.7 | 45.0 | Total Current | 36.6 | 42.1 | 37.0 | 64.7 | | 42.0 |
| 37.9 | 33.8 | 20.7 | Long-Term Debt | 20.4 | 28.6 | 13.9 | 16.6 | | 25.3 |
| .6 | .4 | .4 | Deferred Taxes | .0 | .5 | .0 | .0 | | 1.3 |
| 13.9 | 9.8 | 13.2 | All Other Non-Current | 25.6 | 9.8 | 12.2 | 4.5 | | 12.9 |
| 7.5 | 7.3 | 20.6 | Net Worth | 17.4 | 19.0 | 36.9 | 14.2 | | 18.4 |
| 100.0 | 100.0 | 100.0 | Total Liabilities & Net Worth | 100.0 | 100.0 | 100.0 | 100.0 | | 100.0 |
| | | | **INCOME DATA** | | | | | | |
| 100.0 | 100.0 | 100.0 | Net Sales | 100.0 | 100.0 | 100.0 | 100.0 | | 100.0 |
| | | | Gross Profit | | | | | | |
| 88.8 | 90.2 | 89.7 | Operating Expenses | 81.6 | 91.5 | 87.2 | 91.6 | | 93.0 |
| 11.2 | 9.8 | 10.3 | Operating Profit | 18.4 | 8.5 | 12.8 | 8.4 | | 7.0 |
| 6.5 | 4.6 | 2.4 | All Other Expenses (net) | 3.3 | 2.4 | 2.6 | 3.2 | | 1.6 |
| 4.6 | 5.1 | 8.0 | Profit Before Taxes | 15.1 | 6.1 | 10.2 | 5.2 | | 5.4 |
| | | | **RATIOS** | | | | | | |
| 2.1 | 1.4 | 2.1 | Current | 2.9 | 2.6 | 3.8 | 1.1 | | 1.5 |
| 1.1 | .8 | 1.0 | | 1.0 | 1.0 | 1.7 | .6 | | .9 |
| .4 | .2 | .3 | | .2 | .3 | 1.1 | .1 | | .4 |
| 1.2 | .9 | 1.3 | Quick | 2.0 | 1.7 | 2.4 | .3 | | 1.1 |
| .5 | .3 | .6 | | .7 | .6 | 1.4 | .1 | | .8 |
| .2 | .1 | .1 | | .1 | .0 | .8 | .0 | | .1 |
| 0 UND | 0 UND | 0 UND | Sales/Receivables | 0 UND | 0 UND | 0 UND | 0 UND | | 1 414.0 |
| 11 33.0 | 4 87.4 | 1 285.3 | | 0 UND | 2 175.8 | 2 224.8 | 0 999.8 | | 23 16.2 |
| 33 11.2 | 35 10.3 | 27 13.4 | | 4 83.0 | 22 16.9 | 45 8.2 | 14 25.2 | | 45 8.1 |
| | | | Cost of Sales/Inventory | | | | | | |
| | | | Cost of Sales/Payables | | | | | | |
| 7.1 | 9.6 | 7.5 | Sales/Working Capital | 6.9 | 4.9 | 4.6 | 764.7 | | 8.3 |
| 118.9 | -22.7 | -549.7 | | -199.3 | 100.8 | 13.5 | -7.8 | | -462.5 |
| -7.4 | -4.4 | -4.5 | | -2.9 | -5.3 | NM | -3.1 | | -10.7 |
| 4.9 | 5.8 | 5.8 | EBIT/Interest | 4.6 | 6.1 | | 6.0 | | 4.8 |
| (73) 2.6 | (66) 3.3 | (75) 2.5 | | (12) 1.8 | (15) 5.1 | | 2.5 | | (15) 3.1 |
| 1.1 | 1.0 | 1.2 | | 1.1 | 1.2 | | 1.3 | | 1.0 |
| 2.6 | | | Net Profit + Depr., Dep., Amort./Cur. Mat. L/T/D | | | | | | |
| (10) 1.8 | | | | | | | | | |
| .6 | | | | | | | | | |
| .6 | .9 | .5 | Fixed/Worth | .2 | .5 | .1 | .8 | | 1.4 |
| 3.0 | 4.0 | 2.9 | | 4.1 | 2.1 | .5 | 5.1 | | 3.4 |
| -4.7 | -3.6 | -2.4 | | -2.8 | -2.2 | NM | -.9 | | NM |
| 1.1 | 1.5 | 1.2 | Debt/Worth | .3 | 1.7 | .3 | 2.5 | | 2.7 |
| 4.7 | 5.4 | 4.9 | | 8.0 | 6.9 | 1.7 | 9.3 | | 9.6 |
| -11.8 | -10.1 | -8.6 | | -7.7 | -4.0 | NM | -6.2 | | NM |
| 49.9 | 57.8 | 55.7 | % Profit Before Taxes/Tangible Net Worth | 59.0 | 39.5 | | 53.2 | | 376.8 |
| (64) 16.9 | (46) 26.8 | (58) 22.6 | | (13) 35.3 | (10) 14.0 | | (10) 27.6 | | (12) 39.0 |
| 2.3 | 5.6 | 7.4 | | 12.2 | 1.7 | | 3.3 | | 9.3 |
| 10.6 | 12.8 | 18.0 | % Profit Before Taxes/Total Assets | 28.5 | 18.2 | 49.9 | 16.1 | | 13.8 |
| 4.1 | 5.4 | 5.7 | | 4.4 | 7.4 | 15.4 | 6.6 | | 6.1 |
| .3 | .4 | .8 | | .4 | .6 | -.5 | .8 | | .7 |
| 13.8 | 11.5 | 19.4 | Sales/Net Fixed Assets | 47.0 | 9.7 | 116.7 | 25.3 | | 15.2 |
| 4.9 | 3.9 | 5.4 | | 2.8 | 4.3 | 11.6 | 14.7 | | 4.4 |
| 1.9 | 2.0 | 2.2 | | .6 | 2.7 | 2.5 | 2.2 | | 2.3 |
| 2.8 | 2.3 | 2.4 | Sales/Total Assets | 2.4 | 3.0 | 4.1 | 2.3 | | 1.9 |
| 1.8 | 1.6 | 1.7 | | 1.0 | 1.9 | 2.4 | 1.9 | | 1.5 |
| .8 | .8 | .9 | | .4 | 1.2 | 1.1 | 1.3 | | 1.1 |
| 2.2 | 4.4 | 3.9 | % Depr., Dep., Amort./Sales | 6.3 | 4.8 | | 3.1 | | 2.5 |
| (72) 8.1 | (52) 10.3 | (56) 11.0 | | (13) 21.6 | (11) 10.2 | | (11) 30.3 | | (10) 6.7 |
| 22.3 | 22.9 | 29.6 | | 62.8 | 21.7 | | 32.7 | | 21.9 |
| 3.1 | 2.6 | 1.7 | % Officers', Directors' Owners' Comp/Sales | | | | | | |
| (38) 5.5 | (23) 5.1 | (33) 3.3 | | | | | | | |
| 10.1 | 9.9 | 10.7 | | | | | | | |
| 1209335M | 1151641M | 1504989M | Net Sales ($) | 8023M | 34397M | 37971M | 134268M | 116484M | 1173846M |
| 1289414M | 1036857M | 1219686M | Total Assets ($) | 11531M | 29996M | 48818M | 137099M | 114553M | 877689M |

M = $ thousand    MM = $ million
See Pages 9 through 22 for Explanation of Ratios and Data

# REAL ESTATE—Home Health Equipment Rental  NAICS 532291

**Current Data Sorted by Assets** | **Comparative Historical Data**

### Statement type composition (number of statements by asset size)

| Type of Statement | 0-500M | 500M-2MM | 2-10MM | 10-50MM | 50-100MM | 100-250MM |
|---|---|---|---|---|---|---|
| Unqualified | | | 1 | 5 | | 1 |
| Reviewed | 1 | 2 | 3 | 2 | | |
| Compiled | | 5 | 3 | | | |
| Tax Returns | 4 | 9 | 6 | | | |
| Other | 1 | | 12 | 3 | | 2 |

6 (4/1-9/30/11)  54 (10/1/11-3/31/12)

### Main data

| | 0-500M | 500M-2MM | 2-10MM | 10-50MM | 50-100MM | 100-250MM | | 4/1/07-3/31/08 ALL | 4/1/08-3/31/09 ALL |
|---|---|---|---|---|---|---|---|---|---|
| Type of Statement | | | | | | | | | |
| Unqualified | | | | | | | | 6 | 5 |
| Reviewed | | | | | | | | 12 | 8 |
| Compiled | | | | | | | | 7 | 5 |
| Tax Returns | | | | | | | | 12 | 18 |
| Other | | | | | | | | 34 | 30 |
| **NUMBER OF STATEMENTS** | 6 | 16 | 25 | 10 | | 3 | | 71 | 66 |
| | % | % | % | % | % | % | | % | % |
| **ASSETS** | | | | | | | | | |
| Cash & Equivalents | | 8.1 | 5.0 | 6.9 | | | | 13.0 | 10.1 |
| Trade Receivables (net) | | 19.0 | 29.4 | 23.9 | | | | 22.2 | 27.5 |
| Inventory | | 2.1 | 8.3 | 8.6 | | | | 5.5 | 9.4 |
| All Other Current | | 6.2 | 3.7 | 5.9 | | | | 2.9 | 3.6 |
| Total Current | | 35.3 | 46.4 | 45.3 | | | | 43.5 | 50.7 |
| Fixed Assets (net) | | 49.9 | 45.3 | 43.6 | | | | 40.9 | 36.7 |
| Intangibles (net) | | 7.3 | 2.7 | 5.4 | | | | 7.6 | 6.0 |
| All Other Non-Current | | 7.4 | 5.6 | 5.7 | | | | 8.0 | 6.6 |
| Total | | 100.0 | 100.0 | 100.0 | | | | 100.0 | 100.0 |
| **LIABILITIES** | | | | | | | | | |
| Notes Payable-Short Term | | 5.0 | 9.4 | 8.8 | | | | 9.8 | 11.3 |
| Cur. Mat.-L.T.D. | | 6.6 | 8.8 | 11.4 | | | | 9.6 | 8.7 |
| Trade Payables | | 8.1 | 10.6 | 6.9 | | | | 8.5 | 12.0 |
| Income Taxes Payable | | 1.2 | .1 | .9 | | | | .1 | .2 |
| All Other Current | | 7.0 | 4.2 | 5.9 | | | | 10.4 | 8.6 |
| Total Current | | 27.8 | 33.1 | 34.0 | | | | 38.4 | 40.8 |
| Long-Term Debt | | 37.8 | 17.2 | 21.7 | | | | 29.4 | 21.4 |
| Deferred Taxes | | .0 | .8 | 2.2 | | | | .6 | .5 |
| All Other Non-Current | | .9 | 1.3 | 5.8 | | | | 3.7 | 4.7 |
| Net Worth | | 33.4 | 47.6 | 36.3 | | | | 27.9 | 32.6 |
| Total Liabilities & Net Worth | | 100.0 | 100.0 | 100.0 | | | | 100.0 | 100.0 |
| **INCOME DATA** | | | | | | | | | |
| Net Sales | | 100.0 | 100.0 | 100.0 | | | | 100.0 | 100.0 |
| Gross Profit | | | | | | | | | |
| Operating Expenses | | 79.4 | 90.7 | 92.4 | | | | 84.8 | 89.7 |
| Operating Profit | | 20.6 | 9.3 | 7.6 | | | | 15.2 | 10.3 |
| All Other Expenses (net) | | 2.7 | 2.7 | 3.8 | | | | 3.5 | 2.6 |
| Profit Before Taxes | | 17.9 | 6.7 | 3.9 | | | | 11.6 | 7.7 |
| **RATIOS** | | | | | | | | | |
| Current | | 4.2 | 3.1 | 2.3 | | | | 1.9 | 2.1 |
| | | 1.6 | 1.3 | 1.3 | | | | 1.1 | 1.3 |
| | | 1.0 | .9 | .9 | | | | .6 | .8 |
| Quick | | 3.1 | 2.3 | 1.4 | | | | 1.4 | 1.5 |
| | | 1.1 | 1.1 | .8 | | | | .9 | .9 |
| | | .3 | .8 | .7 | | | | .5 | .6 |
| Sales/Receivables | 0 UND | | 41 8.8 | 34 10.7 | | | 2 | 238.9 | 17 21.4 |
| | 17 21.0 | | 62 5.9 | 61 6.0 | | | 51 | 7.1 | 51 7.2 |
| | 52 7.0 | | 81 4.5 | 122 3.0 | | | 75 | 4.9 | 80 4.6 |
| Cost of Sales/Inventory | | | | | | | | | |
| Cost of Sales/Payables | | | | | | | | | |
| Sales/Working Capital | | 5.2 | 4.9 | 6.0 | | | | 6.4 | 6.8 |
| | | 10.7 | 26.5 | 15.5 | | | | 49.7 | 43.2 |
| | | UND | -87.5 | -102.1 | | | | -8.9 | -19.9 |
| EBIT/Interest | | 52.6 | 28.9 | 14.5 | | | | 8.7 | 9.7 |
| | | (15) 14.2 | (20) 6.0 | 3.2 | | | (60) | 4.3 | (61) 3.7 |
| | | .8 | 2.2 | .9 | | | | 2.2 | 1.5 |
| Net Profit + Depr., Dep., Amort./Cur. Mat. L/T/D | | | | | | | | 4.4 | 10.8 |
| | | | | | | | (12) | 1.8 | (10) 1.7 |
| | | | | | | | | .9 | .6 |
| Fixed/Worth | | .8 | .5 | .6 | | | | .7 | .4 |
| | | 1.2 | 1.0 | 1.7 | | | | 2.2 | 1.5 |
| | | 33.9 | 2.9 | 3.3 | | | | -21.8 | -65.1 |
| Debt/Worth | | .4 | .5 | 1.6 | | | | .9 | .8 |
| | | 2.0 | 1.0 | 2.4 | | | | 2.8 | 1.8 |
| | | 33.3 | 4.1 | 3.7 | | | | -63.1 | -73.4 |
| % Profit Before Taxes/Tangible Net Worth | | 140.2 | 53.0 | | | | | 88.7 | 76.1 |
| | | (13) 47.7 | 21.6 | | | | (52) | 30.7 | (49) 21.9 |
| | | 2.1 | 1.9 | | | | | 14.4 | 11.3 |
| % Profit Before Taxes/Total Assets | | 38.4 | 15.7 | 11.3 | | | | 25.2 | 22.6 |
| | | 24.5 | 6.4 | 4.9 | | | | 11.4 | 7.0 |
| | | -.9 | 1.2 | -1.0 | | | | 1.7 | 1.9 |
| Sales/Net Fixed Assets | | 8.8 | 7.6 | 5.8 | | | | 11.0 | 22.5 |
| | | 4.7 | 4.8 | 2.8 | | | | 4.7 | 6.9 |
| | | 1.1 | 2.1 | 2.5 | | | | 1.9 | 3.0 |
| Sales/Total Assets | | 2.8 | 2.6 | 1.6 | | | | 2.4 | 3.2 |
| | | 2.0 | 1.9 | 1.4 | | | | 1.6 | 1.9 |
| | | .6 | 1.1 | .9 | | | | 1.0 | 1.2 |
| % Depr., Dep., Amort./Sales | | 3.2 | 3.9 | | | | | 2.8 | 1.8 |
| | | (10) 6.3 | (21) 6.9 | | | | (56) | 6.4 | (48) 6.4 |
| | | 15.9 | 13.2 | | | | | 17.9 | 12.9 |
| % Officers', Directors' Owners' Comp/Sales | | | .8 | | | | | 1.5 | 3.0 |
| | | | (12) 1.6 | | | | (14) | 9.8 | (20) 4.5 |
| | | | 4.6 | | | | | 21.4 | 8.9 |
| Net Sales ($) | 3817M | 33871M | 260144M | 184944M | | 399981M | | 1162678M | 1367061M |
| Total Assets ($) | 1200M | 19190M | 136937M | 171434M | | 407291M | | 1119888M | 1266479M |

DATA NOT AVAILABLE (50-100MM column)

© RMA 2012

M = $ thousand     MM = $ million
See Pages 9 through 22 for Explanation of Ratios and Data

## Comparative Historical Data

## Current Data Sorted by Sales

| | | | Type of Statement | | | | | | |
|---|---|---|---|---|---|---|---|---|---|
| 8 | 7 | 7 | Unqualified | | | | 1 | 4 | 2 |
| 12 | 11 | 6 | Reviewed | 1 | | | 1 | 3 | |
| 6 | 6 | 5 | Compiled | | 1 | 2 | | 2 | |
| 20 | 15 | 15 | Tax Returns | 8 | 2 | 1 | | 4 | |
| 29 | 35 | 27 | Other | 3 | 4 | 4 | 6 | 7 | 3 |
| 4/1/09-3/31/10 ALL | 4/1/10-3/31/11 ALL | 4/1/11-3/31/12 ALL | | | 6 (4/1-9/30/11) | | | 54 (10/1/11-3/31/12) | |
| | | | | 0-1MM | 1-3MM | 3-5MM | 5-10MM | 10-25MM | 25MM & OVER |
| 75 | 74 | 60 | NUMBER OF STATEMENTS | 12 | 7 | 8 | 8 | 20 | 5 |
| % | % | % | ASSETS | % | % | % | % | % | % |
| 8.2 | 10.6 | 10.2 | Cash & Equivalents | 21.6 | | | | 4.8 | |
| 20.8 | 19.0 | 22.7 | Trade Receivables (net) | .9 | | | | 27.0 | |
| 9.8 | 9.7 | 7.4 | Inventory | 3.2 | | | | 11.9 | |
| 2.2 | 3.6 | 4.5 | All Other Current | 6.6 | | | | 4.8 | |
| 41.0 | 43.0 | 44.8 | Total Current | 32.4 | | | | 48.6 | |
| 44.9 | 39.8 | 41.9 | Fixed Assets (net) | 52.0 | | | | 41.6 | |
| 5.8 | 5.8 | 4.8 | Intangibles (net) | 8.3 | | | | 2.4 | |
| 8.3 | 11.4 | 8.5 | All Other Non-Current | 7.3 | | | | 7.4 | |
| 100.0 | 100.0 | 100.0 | Total | 100.0 | | | | 100.0 | |
| | | | LIABILITIES | | | | | | |
| 7.9 | 9.3 | 8.7 | Notes Payable-Short Term | 1.6 | | | | 9.7 | |
| 8.7 | 8.4 | 7.7 | Cur. Mat.-L.T.D. | 3.6 | | | | 11.2 | |
| 8.9 | 7.6 | 8.2 | Trade Payables | 1.4 | | | | 10.1 | |
| .3 | .4 | .5 | Income Taxes Payable | .0 | | | | .5 | |
| 7.7 | 8.1 | 15.2 | All Other Current | 52.7 | | | | 4.8 | |
| 33.6 | 33.9 | 40.3 | Total Current | 59.3 | | | | 36.3 | |
| 32.8 | 26.7 | 24.5 | Long-Term Debt | 50.5 | | | | 17.5 | |
| .7 | .8 | .8 | Deferred Taxes | .0 | | | | 1.0 | |
| 6.5 | 8.2 | 2.3 | All Other Non-Current | .4 | | | | 2.7 | |
| 26.4 | 30.5 | 32.1 | Net Worth | -10.2 | | | | 42.6 | |
| 100.0 | 100.0 | 100.0 | Total Liabilities & Net Worth | 100.0 | | | | 100.0 | |
| | | | INCOME DATA | | | | | | |
| 100.0 | 100.0 | 100.0 | Net Sales | 100.0 | | | | 100.0 | |
| | | | Gross Profit | | | | | | |
| 88.4 | 90.6 | 87.6 | Operating Expenses | 70.9 | | | | 92.3 | |
| 11.6 | 9.4 | 12.4 | Operating Profit | 29.1 | | | | 7.7 | |
| 4.0 | 3.5 | 2.9 | All Other Expenses (net) | 8.4 | | | | 2.7 | |
| 7.6 | 5.9 | 9.5 | Profit Before Taxes | 20.7 | | | | 4.9 | |
| | | | RATIOS | | | | | | |
| 1.9 | 2.2 | 2.7 | | 7.6 | | | | 2.7 | |
| 1.2 | 1.2 | 1.4 | Current | 1.8 | | | | 1.2 | |
| .9 | .7 | 1.0 | | .6 | | | | .9 | |
| 1.6 | 1.6 | 2.3 | | 7.1 | | | | 1.4 | |
| .9 | .9 | 1.0 | Quick | 1.6 | | | | .8 | |
| .5 | .4 | .7 | | .1 | | | | .5 | |
| 7   52.7 | 0   UND | 0   UND | | 0   UND | | | | 24   15.4 | |
| 46   8.0 | 37   9.9 | 49   7.5 | Sales/Receivables | 0   UND | | | | 54   6.8 | |
| 64   5.7 | 64   5.7 | 73   5.0 | | 0   UND | | | | 73   5.0 | |
| | | | Cost of Sales/Inventory | | | | | | |
| | | | Cost of Sales/Payables | | | | | | |
| 8.6 | 8.4 | 5.0 | | 4.5 | | | | 6.6 | |
| 37.7 | 57.1 | 12.3 | Sales/Working Capital | 6.3 | | | | 22.7 | |
| -27.4 | -17.3 | UND | | NM | | | | -46.4 | |
| 8.0 | 13.8 | 20.8 | | | | | | 31.2 | |
| (66)   4.1 | (66)   3.9 | (51)   6.8 | EBIT/Interest | | | | (16)   4.9 | | |
| 1.1 | .8 | 1.9 | | | | | | .4 | |
| 3.7 | 7.7 | 2.7 | Net Profit + Depr., Dep., | | | | | | |
| (11)   1.9 | (15)   1.2 | (10)   1.5 | Amort./Cur. Mat. L/T/D | | | | | | |
| 1.2 | .6 | 1.0 | | | | | | | |
| .6 | .5 | .6 | | .6 | | | | .6 | |
| 1.7 | 1.3 | 1.2 | Fixed/Worth | 6.6 | | | | 1.4 | |
| -99.1 | 14.0 | 3.7 | | NM | | | | 2.1 | |
| .9 | .8 | .5 | | .7 | | | | .5 | |
| 2.6 | 2.3 | 1.7 | Debt/Worth | 6.0 | | | | 1.9 | |
| -159.5 | 25.8 | 6.0 | | NM | | | | 4.2 | |
| 69.3 | 57.4 | 63.3 | | | | | | 42.8 | |
| (56)   24.2 | (60)   21.3 | (54)   27.9 | % Profit Before Taxes/Tangible Net Worth | | | | (19)   21.6 | | |
| 6.7 | .4 | 6.4 | | | | | | 9.7 | |
| 18.8 | 20.1 | 23.7 | | 26.5 | | | | 17.4 | |
| 6.8 | 6.4 | 7.9 | % Profit Before Taxes/Total Assets | 5.3 | | | | 6.3 | |
| .3 | -.3 | .8 | | -.9 | | | | 1.3 | |
| 12.3 | 14.2 | 9.2 | | 16.0 | | | | 8.8 | |
| 4.9 | 6.3 | 4.6 | Sales/Net Fixed Assets | 1.6 | | | | 3.8 | |
| 2.2 | 2.3 | 2.5 | | .2 | | | | 2.5 | |
| 2.6 | 2.7 | 2.8 | | 2.4 | | | | 2.5 | |
| 1.8 | 1.6 | 1.7 | Sales/Total Assets | .6 | | | | 1.7 | |
| .9 | .9 | 1.0 | | .2 | | | | 1.3 | |
| 2.3 | 3.1 | 3.2 | | | | | | 3.8 | |
| (55)   6.2 | (50)   7.4 | (46)   6.9 | % Depr., Dep., Amort./Sales | | | | (18)   7.8 | | |
| 17.6 | 15.1 | 15.1 | | | | | | 15.2 | |
| 3.0 | 2.5 | 1.4 | % Officers', Directors' | | | | | | |
| (21)   5.7 | (26)   5.6 | (20)   2.9 | Owners' Comp/Sales | | | | | | |
| 17.0 | 13.9 | 9.5 | | | | | | | |
| 1234311M | 1267885M | 882757M | Net Sales ($) | 6022M | 12458M | 29497M | 53183M | 311482M | 470115M |
| 1231979M | 1228176M | 736052M | Total Assets ($) | 14315M | 5861M | 18823M | 68382M | 323242M | 305429M |

M = $ thousand    MM = $ million
See Pages 9 through 22 for Explanation of Ratios and Data

## Current Data Sorted by Assets

## Comparative Historical Data

| | | | | | | Type of Statement | | |
|---|---|---|---|---|---|---|---|---|
| | | 1 | 5 | | 2 | Unqualified | 3 | 5 |
| | | 2 | 1 | | | Reviewed | 5 | 7 |
| 5 | 4 | 8 | | 1 | | Compiled | 9 | 12 |
| 13 | 16 | 5 | | | | Tax Returns | 13 | 12 |
| 3 | 9 | 15 | 4 | 2 | 2 | Other | 13 | 22 |
| | 18 (4/1-9/30/11) | | 80 (10/1/11-3/31/12) | | | | 4/1/07-3/31/08 | 4/1/08-3/31/09 |
| | | | | | | | ALL | ALL |
| 0-500M | 500M-2MM | 2-10MM | 10-50MM | 50-100MM | 100-250MM | | | |
| 21 | 29 | 31 | 10 | 3 | 4 | NUMBER OF STATEMENTS | 43 | 58 |
| % | % | % | % | % | % | ASSETS | % | % |
| 15.6 | 21.2 | 8.5 | 2.7 | | | Cash & Equivalents | 6.9 | 11.4 |
| 10.4 | 11.6 | 15.1 | 9.5 | | | Trade Receivables (net) | 10.6 | 17.1 |
| 2.8 | 8.9 | 11.3 | 16.9 | | | Inventory | 13.9 | 10.1 |
| 1.4 | .9 | 5.5 | 10.4 | | | All Other Current | 3.7 | 3.1 |
| 30.2 | 42.7 | 40.3 | 39.4 | | | Total Current | 35.2 | 41.6 |
| 48.5 | 41.8 | 48.2 | 45.2 | | | Fixed Assets (net) | 53.0 | 42.4 |
| 14.8 | 4.0 | 5.2 | 5.9 | | | Intangibles (net) | 2.8 | 6.0 |
| 6.6 | 11.5 | 6.3 | 9.5 | | | All Other Non-Current | 9.1 | 10.0 |
| 100.0 | 100.0 | 100.0 | 100.0 | | | Total | 100.0 | 100.0 |
| | | | | | | LIABILITIES | | |
| 2.5 | 11.4 | 10.5 | 26.2 | | | Notes Payable-Short Term | 16.0 | 16.1 |
| 6.9 | 6.5 | 6.5 | 10.6 | | | Cur. Mat.-L.T.D. | 13.8 | 6.1 |
| 6.1 | 9.7 | 12.1 | 6.7 | | | Trade Payables | 5.9 | 6.5 |
| .1 | .0 | .1 | .0 | | | Income Taxes Payable | .2 | .2 |
| 3.2 | 4.8 | 7.6 | 7.2 | | | All Other Current | 11.8 | 13.0 |
| 18.8 | 32.4 | 36.7 | 50.7 | | | Total Current | 47.8 | 41.9 |
| 26.7 | 23.4 | 26.5 | 27.6 | | | Long-Term Debt | 32.8 | 32.6 |
| .0 | .0 | .2 | 1.7 | | | Deferred Taxes | .5 | .5 |
| 11.4 | 12.9 | 13.6 | 3.9 | | | All Other Non-Current | 10.2 | 11.2 |
| 43.1 | 31.3 | 23.0 | 16.1 | | | Net Worth | 8.7 | 13.9 |
| 100.0 | 100.0 | 100.0 | 100.0 | | | Total Liabilities & Net Worth | 100.0 | 100.0 |
| | | | | | | INCOME DATA | | |
| 100.0 | 100.0 | 100.0 | 100.0 | | | Net Sales | 100.0 | 100.0 |
| | | | | | | Gross Profit | | |
| 90.5 | 90.7 | 91.6 | 90.8 | | | Operating Expenses | 91.3 | 91.3 |
| 9.5 | 9.3 | 8.4 | 9.2 | | | Operating Profit | 8.7 | 8.7 |
| 3.2 | 1.1 | 3.8 | 5.8 | | | All Other Expenses (net) | 5.5 | 5.0 |
| 6.3 | 8.2 | 4.6 | 3.5 | | | Profit Before Taxes | 3.2 | 3.7 |
| | | | | | | RATIOS | | |
| 6.2 | 3.4 | 2.5 | 1.3 | | | | 2.1 | 2.6 |
| 3.1 | 1.7 | .9 | .9 | | | Current | .8 | .9 |
| .6 | .6 | .6 | .3 | | | | .4 | .4 |
| 6.2 | 3.4 | 1.5 | 1.0 | | | | .9 | 1.4 |
| 1.6 | 1.2 | .7 | .2 | | | Quick | .4 | .5 |
| .3 | .4 | .3 | .1 | | | | .2 | .2 |
| 0 UND | 0 UND | 1 UND | 1 425.5 | 1 310.5 | | | 0 UND | 0 UND |
| 0 UND | 10 37.1 | 24 15.2 | 18 20.5 | | | Sales/Receivables | 17 22.1 | 22 16.4 |
| 12 30.3 | 26 14.3 | 40 9.2 | 53 6.9 | | | | 30 12.0 | 62 5.9 |
| | | | | | | Cost of Sales/Inventory | | |
| | | | | | | Cost of Sales/Payables | | |
| 8.9 | 6.0 | 8.8 | 7.8 | | | | 9.9 | 5.2 |
| 23.0 | 16.6 | -72.3 | NM | | | Sales/Working Capital | -36.1 | -86.7 |
| -75.3 | -11.8 | -8.0 | -3.7 | | | | -3.9 | -6.2 |
| 8.3 | 19.2 | 6.3 | | | | | 3.8 | 4.9 |
| (14) 4.8 | (26) 8.6 | (27) 2.7 | | | | EBIT/Interest | (36) .9 | (48) 1.5 |
| -.6 | 2.6 | 1.5 | | | | | -.1 | -.5 |
| | | | | | | Net Profit + Depr., Dep., Amort./Cur. Mat. L/T/D | | |
| .4 | .6 | .5 | .4 | | | | .9 | .5 |
| 1.1 | 1.2 | 6.1 | 2.2 | | | Fixed/Worth | 2.1 | 1.9 |
| 2.8 | 8.3 | -3.4 | -2.7 | | | | -5.1 | -151.6 |
| .2 | .6 | .8 | 2.1 | | | | 1.3 | 1.4 |
| .7 | 1.5 | 7.5 | 2.9 | | | Debt/Worth | 4.0 | 2.7 |
| NM | NM | -14.1 | -4.4 | | | | -8.4 | -203.6 |
| 106.4 | 53.2 | 35.1 | | | | % Profit Before Taxes/Tangible Net Worth | 68.0 | 28.3 |
| (16) 17.6 | (22) 27.8 | (22) 15.8 | | | | | (27) 13.7 | (42) 8.3 |
| -6.6 | 10.7 | 4.2 | | | | | -3.7 | -2.7 |
| 41.1 | 21.8 | 12.9 | 4.1 | | | % Profit Before Taxes/Total Assets | 11.5 | 11.3 |
| 9.6 | 9.6 | 3.6 | 1.2 | | | | 1.1 | 1.8 |
| -3.7 | 2.4 | 1.6 | -1.0 | | | | -4.3 | -3.4 |
| 14.0 | 17.1 | 9.1 | 24.7 | | | | 5.9 | 17.7 |
| 6.6 | 5.9 | 3.5 | 2.5 | | | Sales/Net Fixed Assets | 3.1 | 5.0 |
| 2.0 | 2.7 | 1.9 | 1.0 | | | | 1.9 | 2.0 |
| 4.1 | 3.4 | 2.2 | 1.7 | | | | 2.4 | 2.5 |
| 1.9 | 2.2 | 1.7 | 1.3 | | | Sales/Total Assets | 1.7 | 1.4 |
| 1.3 | 1.7 | 1.1 | .7 | | | | 1.0 | .8 |
| 5.6 | 3.5 | 3.5 | | | | | 5.5 | 2.9 |
| (13) 13.9 | (16) 8.6 | (27) 7.6 | | | | % Depr., Dep., Amort./Sales | (32) 10.7 | (49) 9.7 |
| 21.1 | 17.1 | 13.4 | | | | | 16.4 | 14.4 |
| | 4.8 | 2.2 | | | | | 2.5 | 3.4 |
| | (18) 6.1 | (14) 3.6 | | | | % Officers', Directors' Owners' Comp/Sales | (20) 4.8 | (21) 5.5 |
| | 11.1 | 4.9 | | | | | 7.7 | 7.4 |
| 17155M | 75616M | 205568M | 250128M | 127356M | 876167M | Net Sales ($) | 776385M | 1590813M |
| 6165M | 30731M | 123660M | 219420M | 168733M | 708953M | Total Assets ($) | 718472M | 825935M |

M = $ thousand    MM = $ million
See Pages 9 through 22 for Explanation of Ratios and Data

## Comparative Historical Data | Current Data Sorted by Sales

| | | | | Type of Statement | | | | | | |
|---|---|---|---|---|---|---|---|---|---|---|
| 4 | 4 | 8 | | Unqualified | | | 1 | 2 | 3 | 4 |
| 13 | 14 | 4 | | Reviewed | | | | | 2 | |
| 16 | 14 | 17 | | Compiled | 3 | 5 | 5 | 4 | | |
| 19 | 24 | 34 | | Tax Returns | 14 | 11 | 4 | 5 | | |
| 30 | 25 | 35 | | Other | 5 | 8 | 3 | 5 | 7 | 7 |
| 4/1/09-<br>3/31/10 | 4/1/10-<br>3/31/11 | 4/1/11-<br>3/31/12 | | | | 18 (4/1-9/30/11) | | 80 (10/1/11-3/31/12) | | |
| ALL | ALL | ALL | | | 0-1MM | 1-3MM | 3-5MM | 5-10MM | 10-25MM | 25MM & OVER |
| 82 | 81 | 98 | | **NUMBER OF STATEMENTS** | 22 | 24 | 13 | 16 | 12 | 11 |
| % | % | % | | **ASSETS** | % | % | % | % | % | % |
| 9.9 | 11.0 | 12.8 | | Cash & Equivalents | 13.0 | 22.9 | 10.6 | 7.9 | 9.8 | 3.3 |
| 12.4 | 12.7 | 12.0 | | Trade Receivables (net) | 9.7 | 8.9 | 16.1 | 17.0 | 14.7 | 8.4 |
| 14.2 | 7.4 | 8.6 | | Inventory | .7 | 8.3 | 5.2 | 8.2 | 27.6 | 8.6 |
| 2.4 | 2.7 | 4.1 | | All Other Current | 1.4 | 1.1 | 7.1 | 3.9 | 2.8 | 14.0 |
| 38.8 | 33.8 | 37.4 | | Total Current | 24.7 | 41.2 | 38.9 | 37.0 | 54.9 | 34.3 |
| 47.9 | 53.6 | 45.0 | | Fixed Assets (net) | 56.7 | 43.2 | 42.3 | 51.4 | 31.7 | 33.5 |
| 6.5 | 5.2 | 8.8 | | Intangibles (net) | 13.7 | 3.4 | 5.7 | 5.5 | 4.3 | 23.5 |
| 6.8 | 7.4 | 8.9 | | All Other Non-Current | 4.9 | 12.2 | 13.0 | 6.1 | 9.1 | 8.6 |
| 100.0 | 100.0 | 100.0 | | Total | 100.0 | 100.0 | 100.0 | 100.0 | 100.0 | 100.0 |
| | | | | **LIABILITIES** | | | | | | |
| 15.2 | 15.8 | 10.6 | | Notes Payable-Short Term | 1.4 | 8.2 | 14.3 | 10.0 | 25.9 | 13.9 |
| 6.2 | 9.5 | 7.2 | | Cur. Mat.-L.T.D. | 4.7 | 8.5 | 8.8 | 10.8 | 4.2 | 5.4 |
| 6.5 | 7.0 | 9.2 | | Trade Payables | 6.3 | 5.7 | 6.0 | 14.3 | 18.8 | 8.3 |
| .1 | .1 | .0 | | Income Taxes Payable | .1 | .0 | .1 | .1 | .0 | .0 |
| 5.8 | 6.5 | 6.2 | | All Other Current | 1.2 | 4.7 | 8.1 | 6.9 | 7.7 | 15.0 |
| 34.0 | 38.9 | 33.2 | | Total Current | 13.5 | 27.1 | 37.4 | 42.1 | 56.6 | 42.6 |
| 34.3 | 31.4 | 27.8 | | Long-Term Debt | 27.9 | 34.4 | 25.0 | 21.1 | 8.5 | 47.2 |
| .5 | .6 | .2 | | Deferred Taxes | .0 | .0 | .3 | .7 | .5 | .2 |
| 11.5 | 12.2 | 11.6 | | All Other Non-Current | 6.2 | 16.8 | 16.0 | 17.3 | 4.3 | 5.0 |
| 19.8 | 16.9 | 27.2 | | Net Worth | 52.4 | 21.7 | 21.3 | 18.8 | 30.0 | 5.0 |
| 100.0 | 100.0 | 100.0 | | Total Liabilties & Net Worth | 100.0 | 100.0 | 100.0 | 100.0 | 100.0 | 100.0 |
| | | | | **INCOME DATA** | | | | | | |
| 100.0 | 100.0 | 100.0 | | Net Sales | 100.0 | 100.0 | 100.0 | 100.0 | 100.0 | 100.0 |
| | | | | Gross Profit | | | | | | |
| 89.7 | 96.0 | 92.0 | | Operating Expenses | 81.0 | 93.5 | 91.5 | 97.0 | 95.6 | 99.8 |
| 10.3 | 4.0 | 8.0 | | Operating Profit | 19.0 | 6.5 | 8.5 | 3.0 | 4.4 | .2 |
| 5.9 | 3.0 | 3.4 | | All Other Expenses (net) | 7.3 | .9 | 4.4 | .8 | 1.7 | 5.7 |
| 4.4 | 1.0 | 4.6 | | Profit Before Taxes | 11.6 | 5.6 | 4.1 | 2.2 | 2.6 | -5.5 |
| | | | | **RATIOS** | | | | | | |
| 2.4 | 2.5 | 3.1 | | | 5.2 | 9.0 | 1.7 | 1.8 | 3.1 | 1.3 |
| 1.0 | 1.1 | 1.2 | | Current | 2.4 | 2.3 | 1.1 | .8 | .8 | .6 |
| .6 | .4 | .5 | | | .6 | .5 | .6 | .4 | .6 | .3 |
| 1.5 | 1.9 | 2.3 | | | 5.2 | 4.5 | 1.3 | 1.6 | 1.4 | .5 |
| .6 | .6 | .7 | | Quick | 1.6 | 1.6 | .7 | .6 | .7 | .3 |
| .2 | .2 | .2 | | | .4 | .2 | .3 | .4 | .1 | .2 |
| 0 UND | 0 UND | 0 UND | | | 0 UND | 0 UND | 6 62.7 | 5 77.4 | 0 UND | 5 80.8 |
| 17 21.1 | 16 22.8 | 15 24.9 | | Sales/Receivables | 0 UND | 3 109.6 | 24 14.9 | 24 15.3 | 11 32.7 | 24 14.9 |
| 40 9.1 | 41 8.9 | 33 10.9 | | | 35 10.3 | 20 18.1 | 37 9.9 | 39 9.4 | 47 7.8 | 46 8.0 |
| | | | | Cost of Sales/Inventory | | | | | | |
| | | | | Cost of Sales/Payables | | | | | | |
| 4.9 | 7.3 | 8.4 | | | 7.8 | 5.7 | 7.0 | 10.9 | 8.9 | 8.6 |
| 268.5 | 85.0 | 59.0 | | Sales/Working Capital | 22.5 | 11.4 | 116.2 | -132.7 | -16.3 | -12.0 |
| -8.9 | -6.4 | -8.8 | | | -11.5 | -11.5 | -12.6 | -6.0 | -4.3 | -5.7 |
| 4.3 | 5.4 | 9.1 | | | 14.4 | 16.3 | 4.8 | 14.4 | 6.6 | 2.7 |
| (65) 1.7 | (72) 2.2 | (83) 3.3 | | EBIT/Interest | (13) 4.0 | (21) 6.8 | (12) 1.7 | (15) 2.7 | (11) 2.4 | .8 |
| -.7 | -.1 | .9 | | | -.2 | 3.0 | .7 | 1.1 | 1.4 | -.3 |
| 2.6 | 5.5 | 6.5 | | Net Profit + Depr., Dep., | | | | | | |
| (11) 1.9 | (11) 2.4 | (10) 1.6 | | Amort./Cur. Mat. L/T/D | | | | | | |
| 1.2 | 1.1 | .8 | | | | | | | | |
| .7 | .8 | .7 | | | .6 | .6 | .4 | .7 | .3 | 1.3 |
| 2.3 | 2.3 | 1.8 | | Fixed/Worth | 1.1 | 1.1 | 1.2 | 15.9 | 3.0 | 2.2 |
| UND | -7.8 | -24.0 | | | 2.7 | NM | -2.8 | -3.1 | NM | -.2 |
| 1.4 | 1.4 | .7 | | | .2 | .6 | .9 | 1.0 | .5 | 2.1 |
| 4.6 | 4.0 | 2.4 | | Debt/Worth | .9 | 1.9 | 1.8 | 22.1 | 4.1 | 9.3 |
| -42.1 | -8.7 | -13.6 | | | 6.6 | -12.4 | -6.4 | -5.8 | NM | -1.4 |
| 39.4 | 40.1 | 48.8 | | | 75.7 | 57.6 | | 141.4 | | |
| (61) 12.3 | (55) 14.5 | (71) 17.4 | | % Profit Before Taxes/Tangible<br>Net Worth | (20) 21.1 | (17) 17.4 | | (10) 24.3 | | |
| -6.8 | 2.7 | 3.6 | | | -4.6 | 7.3 | | 3.3 | | |
| 15.1 | 12.0 | 17.7 | | | 39.5 | 23.1 | 3.6 | 14.0 | 11.8 | 6.1 |
| 3.0 | 3.2 | 3.7 | | % Profit Before Taxes/Total<br>Assets | 5.6 | 10.7 | 2.8 | 3.6 | 3.7 | -.9 |
| -3.7 | -3.1 | -.8 | | | -1.7 | 4.3 | -1.9 | .5 | 1.1 | -24.9 |
| 13.7 | 8.8 | 14.8 | | | 12.1 | 13.0 | 25.5 | 15.3 | 58.0 | 8.9 |
| 3.9 | 3.1 | 5.0 | | Sales/Net Fixed Assets | 2.0 | 5.8 | 4.9 | 5.0 | 10.6 | 5.3 |
| 1.7 | 1.4 | 2.2 | | | .5 | 3.1 | 2.8 | 2.0 | 2.0 | 2.5 |
| 2.3 | 2.6 | 2.6 | | | 2.0 | 3.3 | 2.3 | 3.5 | 3.7 | 1.7 |
| 1.4 | 1.6 | 1.7 | | Sales/Total Assets | 1.3 | 2.3 | 1.8 | 2.0 | 1.9 | 1.3 |
| .7 | 1.0 | 1.1 | | | .3 | 1.7 | 1.2 | 1.4 | 1.1 | .9 |
| 5.0 | 6.0 | 4.3 | | | 12.9 | 3.0 | 3.1 | 2.1 | | |
| (61) 11.7 | (63) 11.9 | (64) 9.4 | | % Depr., Dep., Amort./Sales | (14) 21.1 | (15) 7.9 | (10) 8.4 | (13) 6.8 | | |
| 17.9 | 18.9 | 19.3 | | | 30.5 | 13.4 | 13.3 | 16.6 | | |
| 3.1 | 4.1 | 2.7 | | | | | 4.3 | 2.4 | | |
| (29) 5.1 | (33) 5.5 | (41) 5.0 | | % Officers', Directors'<br>Owners' Comp/Sales | | (12) 6.1 | | (10) 4.4 | | |
| 9.9 | 6.7 | 6.9 | | | | 11.3 | | 5.6 | | |
| 872902M | 708460M | 1551990M | | Net Sales ($) | 11386M | 44810M | 49843M | 107283M | 165373M | 1173295M |
| 1126218M | 554125M | 1257662M | | Total Assets ($) | 17604M | 26584M | 58655M | 59944M | 145952M | 948923M |

M = $ thousand    MM = $ million
See Pages 9 through 22 for Explanation of Ratios and Data

## Current Data Sorted by Assets      Comparative Historical Data

| | | | | | | Type of Statement | | |
|---|---|---|---|---|---|---|---|---|
| | | 4 | 4 | 1 | 5 | Unqualified | 10 | 11 |
| 1 | 1 | 5 | 2 | 2 | 1 | Reviewed | 10 | 12 |
| 9 | 13 | 4 | 1 | | | Compiled | 23 | 13 |
| 15 | 23 | 13 | | | 3 | Tax Returns | 34 | 39 |
| 10 | 13 | 28 | 4 | 2 | 1 | Other | 61 | 46 |
| | 20 (4/1-9/30/11) | | 145 (10/1/11-3/31/12) | | | | 4/1/07-3/31/08 | 4/1/08-3/31/09 |
| 0-500M | 500M-2MM | 2-10MM | 10-50MM | 50-100MM | 100-250MM | | ALL | ALL |
| 35 | 50 | 54 | 11 | 5 | 10 | NUMBER OF STATEMENTS | 138 | 121 |
| % | % | % | % | % | % | ASSETS | % | % |
| 12.7 | 9.8 | 6.6 | 11.7 | | 2.6 | Cash & Equivalents | 6.4 | 9.7 |
| 4.7 | 8.7 | 10.9 | 5.7 | | 17.0 | Trade Receivables (net) | 9.7 | 8.5 |
| 11.6 | 11.7 | 12.3 | 22.1 | | .3 | Inventory | 9.7 | 9.6 |
| 1.0 | 2.3 | 1.8 | .6 | | 1.1 | All Other Current | 4.1 | 3.5 |
| 30.0 | 32.5 | 31.6 | 40.1 | | 21.0 | Total Current | 29.9 | 31.3 |
| 49.9 | 57.6 | 58.2 | 34.4 | | 59.8 | Fixed Assets (net) | 60.0 | 60.6 |
| 7.4 | 3.4 | 2.4 | 5.6 | | 6.8 | Intangibles (net) | 3.7 | 2.8 |
| 12.7 | 6.5 | 7.7 | 19.9 | | 12.5 | All Other Non-Current | 6.4 | 5.2 |
| 100.0 | 100.0 | 100.0 | 100.0 | | 100.0 | Total | 100.0 | 100.0 |
| | | | | | | LIABILITIES | | |
| 18.2 | 8.4 | 8.6 | 19.9 | | 4.2 | Notes Payable-Short Term | 10.1 | 12.5 |
| 6.0 | 7.9 | 3.4 | 4.4 | | 14.6 | Cur. Mat.-L.T.D. | 8.5 | 7.8 |
| 8.0 | 5.5 | 6.4 | 6.5 | | 17.5 | Trade Payables | 5.4 | 5.3 |
| .0 | .1 | .1 | .0 | | .4 | Income Taxes Payable | .1 | .2 |
| 17.9 | 4.5 | 11.2 | 6.3 | | 3.6 | All Other Current | 5.5 | 6.2 |
| 50.2 | 26.4 | 29.7 | 37.2 | | 40.4 | Total Current | 29.6 | 32.0 |
| 49.2 | 42.4 | 31.2 | 19.5 | | 65.4 | Long-Term Debt | 38.3 | 39.1 |
| .0 | .0 | .3 | .2 | | .6 | Deferred Taxes | .6 | .6 |
| 20.0 | 9.6 | 11.1 | 4.2 | | 7.2 | All Other Non-Current | 6.6 | 7.0 |
| -19.4 | 21.5 | 27.6 | 38.9 | | -13.5 | Net Worth | 25.0 | 21.3 |
| 100.0 | 100.0 | 100.0 | 100.0 | | 100.0 | Total Liabilties & Net Worth | 100.0 | 100.0 |
| | | | | | | INCOME DATA | | |
| 100.0 | 100.0 | 100.0 | 100.0 | | 100.0 | Net Sales | 100.0 | 100.0 |
| | | | | | | Gross Profit | | |
| 91.1 | 87.2 | 74.0 | 88.1 | | 86.9 | Operating Expenses | 85.4 | 85.6 |
| 8.9 | 12.8 | 26.0 | 11.9 | | 13.1 | Operating Profit | 14.6 | 14.4 |
| 5.5 | 6.5 | 10.5 | 7.1 | | 11.2 | All Other Expenses (net) | 5.9 | 5.5 |
| 3.4 | 6.3 | 15.4 | 4.7 | | 1.9 | Profit Before Taxes | 8.7 | 8.9 |
| | | | | | | RATIOS | | |
| 1.5 | 2.6 | 4.2 | 1.6 | | 1.9 | | 1.8 | 2.3 |
| .8 | 1.2 | 1.4 | 1.3 | | .6 | Current | 1.0 | 1.0 |
| .3 | .4 | .7 | .8 | | .1 | | .4 | .4 |
| 1.0 | 2.2 | 2.4 | 1.2 | | 1.8 | | 1.1 | 1.8 |
| .3 | .6 | .9 | .8 | | .4 | Quick | (136) .5 | .6 |
| .2 | .2 | .3 | .0 | | .1 | | .1 | .1 |
| 0 UND | 0 UND | 0 UND | 0 UND | | 0 UND | | 0 UND | 0 UND |
| 0 UND | 12 29.8 | 17 20.9 | 0 999.8 | | 3 104.8 | Sales/Receivables | 14 26.2 | 11 31.9 |
| 14 26.2 | 29 12.4 | 37 9.8 | 5 73.2 | | 96 3.8 | | 39 9.5 | 35 10.4 |
| | | | | | | Cost of Sales/Inventory | | |
| | | | | | | Cost of Sales/Payables | | |
| 27.5 | 6.6 | 6.5 | 5.1 | | 12.2 | | 10.3 | 7.5 |
| -44.0 | 38.3 | 17.7 | 18.3 | | -8.6 | Sales/Working Capital | UND | UND |
| -6.5 | -8.3 | -17.1 | -9.2 | | -4.2 | | -5.3 | -7.2 |
| 8.1 | 4.7 | 14.9 | | | | | 5.2 | 4.6 |
| (26) 1.6 | (37) 1.6 | (39) 4.9 | | | | EBIT/Interest | (120) 2.4 | (101) 2.6 |
| -1.3 | 1.0 | 2.3 | | | | | .8 | .3 |
| | | | | | | Net Profit + Depr., Dep., | 4.9 | 4.5 |
| | | | | | | Amort./Cur. Mat. L/T/D | (12) 2.2 | (12) 2.5 |
| | | | | | | | 1.6 | 1.1 |
| 1.4 | 1.0 | .6 | .2 | | 1.3 | | 1.0 | .9 |
| -5.0 | 2.7 | 1.7 | .5 | | 11.1 | Fixed/Worth | 2.3 | 2.3 |
| -.5 | -10.9 | 9.2 | 2.1 | | -.8 | | 10.1 | 103.4 |
| 1.4 | .9 | .7 | .7 | | 2.8 | | 1.1 | 1.0 |
| -7.8 | 3.0 | 2.0 | 1.4 | | 25.0 | Debt/Worth | 3.8 | 3.0 |
| -1.8 | -15.1 | 12.3 | 4.1 | | -1.9 | | 20.3 | 133.4 |
| 100.0 | 29.1 | 25.1 | 45.9 | | | % Profit Before Taxes/Tangible | 51.5 | 44.1 |
| (15) 30.8 | (37) 10.1 | (43) 16.8 | (10) 20.5 | | | Net Worth | (114) 23.8 | (93) 19.5 |
| 5.7 | .7 | 6.9 | 1.1 | | | | 7.8 | 2.2 |
| 29.6 | 9.3 | 10.6 | 20.5 | | 3.1 | % Profit Before Taxes/Total | 13.6 | 11.6 |
| 4.5 | 2.0 | 5.8 | 4.8 | | .1 | Assets | 5.5 | 5.1 |
| -10.3 | -.1 | 2.7 | 1.2 | | -26.6 | | -.8 | -.6 |
| 27.6 | 5.5 | 9.9 | 37.9 | | 5.1 | | 5.2 | 7.8 |
| 8.4 | 2.7 | 1.9 | 8.5 | | 2.1 | Sales/Net Fixed Assets | 2.5 | 2.6 |
| 3.2 | 1.1 | .2 | .4 | | .6 | | 1.1 | .8 |
| 5.3 | 2.2 | 1.9 | 2.6 | | 2.7 | | 2.1 | 2.1 |
| 2.8 | 1.5 | 1.0 | 1.3 | | .9 | Sales/Total Assets | 1.4 | 1.4 |
| 1.6 | .7 | .2 | .1 | | .2 | | .5 | .5 |
| 4.4 | 7.5 | 3.4 | | | | | 7.5 | 6.6 |
| (20) 13.5 | (34) 11.5 | (38) 11.6 | | | | % Depr., Dep., Amort./Sales | (110) 13.3 | (92) 13.3 |
| 18.8 | 18.9 | 23.3 | | | | | 21.2 | 28.2 |
| 5.3 | 3.3 | 1.1 | | | | % Officers', Directors' | 2.3 | 3.2 |
| (15) 7.1 | (23) 6.9 | (11) 2.2 | | | | Owners' Comp/Sales | (47) 5.2 | (35) 4.6 |
| 12.6 | 12.1 | 3.7 | | | | | 9.4 | 6.7 |
| 31060M | 82682M | 287893M | 353253M | 177110M | 2345526M | Net Sales ($) | 2202984M | 1451582M |
| 9599M | 56829M | 244928M | 281084M | 305144M | 1712422M | Total Assets ($) | 1758507M | 1526148M |

M = $ thousand     MM = $ million
See Pages 9 through 22 for Explanation of Ratios and Data

## Comparative Historical Data / Current Data Sorted by Sales

| | 4/1/09-3/31/10 ALL | 4/1/10-3/31/11 ALL | 4/1/11-3/31/12 ALL | 20 (4/1-9/30/11) 0-1MM | 20 (4/1-9/30/11) 1-3MM | 145 (10/1/11-3/31/12) 3-5MM | 145 (10/1/11-3/31/12) 5-10MM | 145 (10/1/11-3/31/12) 10-25MM | 145 (10/1/11-3/31/12) 25MM & OVER |
|---|---|---|---|---|---|---|---|---|---|
| **Type of Statement** | | | | | | | | | |
| Unqualified | 11 | 13 | 14 | | 1 | | 3 | 3 | 7 |
| Reviewed | 12 | 11 | 12 | 2 | | 2 | 2 | 2 | 4 |
| Compiled | 22 | 19 | 27 | 11 | 9 | 4 | 1 | 2 | |
| Tax Returns | 44 | 46 | 54 | 28 | 13 | 4 | 5 | 1 | 3 |
| Other | 41 | 51 | 58 | 19 | 20 | 5 | 7 | 4 | 3 |
| **NUMBER OF STATEMENTS** | 130 | 140 | 165 | 60 | 43 | 15 | 18 | 12 | 17 |
| **ASSETS** | % | % | % | % | % | % | % | % | % |
| Cash & Equivalents | 8.8 | 8.7 | 9.1 | 6.7 | 9.2 | 14.7 | 11.9 | 10.4 | 8.1 |
| Trade Receivables (net) | 6.6 | 9.7 | 8.9 | 3.0 | 7.5 | 18.5 | 16.9 | 15.7 | 11.4 |
| Inventory | 10.0 | 10.1 | 12.1 | 9.1 | 8.1 | 13.1 | 15.3 | 35.1 | 12.0 |
| All Other Current | 3.0 | 2.6 | 1.7 | 1.0 | 2.6 | .9 | .5 | 5.5 | .8 |
| Total Current | 28.5 | 31.1 | 31.7 | 19.8 | 27.5 | 47.1 | 44.6 | 66.7 | 32.3 |
| Fixed Assets (net) | 60.4 | 59.4 | 54.0 | 70.9 | 55.2 | 39.9 | 31.7 | 17.5 | 53.0 |
| Intangibles (net) | 3.3 | 4.1 | 4.4 | 4.0 | 4.2 | 3.0 | 2.8 | 5.0 | 8.4 |
| All Other Non-Current | 7.8 | 5.4 | 10.0 | 5.4 | 13.1 | 9.9 | 20.8 | 10.8 | 6.3 |
| Total | 100.0 | 100.0 | 100.0 | 100.0 | 100.0 | 100.0 | 100.0 | 100.0 | 100.0 |
| **LIABILITIES** | | | | | | | | | |
| Notes Payable-Short Term | 12.4 | 12.3 | 11.0 | 11.3 | 13.2 | 3.6 | 9.3 | 12.4 | 12.2 |
| Cur. Mat.-L.T.D. | 8.1 | 8.8 | 6.0 | 5.4 | 5.4 | 7.3 | 6.1 | 5.4 | 8.8 |
| Trade Payables | 4.5 | 6.0 | 7.0 | 4.5 | 4.4 | 5.7 | 16.0 | 6.4 | 14.3 |
| Income Taxes Payable | .1 | .2 | .1 | .0 | .0 | .3 | .1 | .1 | .3 |
| All Other Current | 6.0 | 7.8 | 9.6 | 10.6 | 5.6 | 9.1 | 9.1 | 26.2 | 5.4 |
| Total Current | 31.1 | 35.1 | 33.7 | 31.7 | 28.7 | 26.0 | 40.7 | 50.5 | 40.9 |
| Long-Term Debt | 44.3 | 44.6 | 39.0 | 59.6 | 31.9 | 22.3 | 25.9 | 15.7 | 29.7 |
| Deferred Taxes | .5 | .6 | .6 | .2 | .0 | .0 | .2 | 4.8 | 1.3 |
| All Other Non-Current | 11.3 | 11.0 | 11.5 | 12.9 | 12.3 | 12.5 | 14.9 | 4.1 | 5.4 |
| Net Worth | 12.8 | 8.7 | 15.2 | -4.4 | 27.1 | 39.2 | 18.3 | 24.9 | 22.6 |
| Total Liabilities & Net Worth | 100.0 | 100.0 | 100.0 | 100.0 | 100.0 | 100.0 | 100.0 | 100.0 | 100.0 |
| **INCOME DATA** | | | | | | | | | |
| Net Sales | 100.0 | 100.0 | 100.0 | 100.0 | 100.0 | 100.0 | 100.0 | 100.0 | 100.0 |
| Gross Profit | | | | | | | | | |
| Operating Expenses | 88.5 | 86.4 | 83.6 | 70.3 | 93.6 | 85.9 | 93.6 | 83.4 | 92.9 |
| Operating Profit | 11.5 | 13.6 | 16.4 | 29.7 | 6.4 | 14.1 | 6.4 | 16.6 | 7.1 |
| All Other Expenses (net) | 6.9 | 6.4 | 7.8 | 17.2 | 2.0 | -.2 | 3.2 | 4.8 | 3.8 |
| Profit Before Taxes | 4.6 | 7.2 | 8.6 | 12.5 | 4.4 | 14.3 | 3.2 | 11.8 | 3.3 |
| **RATIOS** | | | | | | | | | |
| Current | 2.1 | 2.1 | 2.4 | 1.6 | 3.1 | 4.3 | 2.0 | 5.3 | 2.4 |
| | .8 | .9 | 1.1 | .6 | 1.1 | 2.0 | 1.3 | 2.4 | 1.1 |
| | .3 | .4 | .4 | .2 | .5 | 1.4 | .9 | 1.1 | .1 |
| Quick | 1.1 | 1.3 | 1.6 | 1.2 | 2.4 | 2.3 | 1.7 | 3.5 | 1.1 |
| | .5 | .6 | .6 | .3 | .7 | 1.3 | 1.0 | .4 | .8 |
| | .2 | .2 | .2 | .1 | .2 | .6 | .4 | .2 | .1 |
| Sales/Receivables | 0 UND | 0 UND | 0 UND | 0 UND | 0 UND | 15 23.7 | 3 120.7 | 0 UND | 0 UND |
| | 12 29.3 | 12 29.3 | 8 46.4 | 0 UND | 12 30.5 | 28 12.9 | 27 13.5 | 0 UND | 5 73.2 |
| | 36 10.1 | 38 9.6 | 30 12.3 | 13 29.0 | 33 10.9 | 41 9.0 | 40 9.1 | 32 11.5 | 57 6.4 |
| Cost of Sales/Inventory | | | | | | | | | |
| Cost of Sales/Payables | | | | | | | | | |
| Sales/Working Capital | 9.5 | 6.6 | 7.4 | 12.7 | 7.7 | 3.6 | 7.0 | 3.0 | 11.6 |
| | -32.5 | -78.7 | 66.7 | -24.4 | 269.5 | 10.8 | 18.7 | 7.3 | 56.3 |
| | -4.7 | -7.0 | -8.7 | -3.2 | -9.7 | 20.2 | -594.8 | 23.3 | -4.7 |
| EBIT/Interest | 3.5 | 4.5 | 8.5 | 7.2 | 6.0 | 12.8 | 7.7 | | 30.5 |
| | (106) 1.0 | (118) 2.8 | (122) 2.8 | (33) 1.7 | (36) 1.7 | (14) 4.5 | (16) 3.5 | | (15) 4.2 |
| | -.9 | .6 | .9 | -1.2 | .9 | 2.4 | 1.3 | | -.2 |
| Net Profit + Depr., Dep., Amort./Cur. Mat. L/T/D | 4.6 | | | | | | | | |
| | (15) 1.6 | | | | | | | | |
| | 1.0 | | | | | | | | |
| Fixed/Worth | 1.2 | 1.2 | .7 | 2.1 | 1.1 | .5 | .4 | .1 | .4 |
| | 2.9 | 3.3 | 2.3 | 7.7 | 1.7 | 1.0 | 1.3 | .3 | 1.2 |
| | -7.5 | -4.0 | -4.9 | -2.2 | -12.9 | 4.6 | -2.7 | 6.8 | -57.0 |
| Debt/Worth | 1.2 | 1.3 | .9 | 1.4 | .7 | .8 | .8 | .2 | .6 |
| | 2.9 | 4.2 | 3.1 | 11.5 | 1.9 | 1.7 | 5.0 | 1.7 | 1.2 |
| | -12.7 | -6.1 | -9.9 | -3.6 | -16.1 | 5.2 | -11.9 | 30.8 | -68.6 |
| % Profit Before Taxes/Tangible Net Worth | 30.2 | 41.7 | 31.4 | 28.2 | 21.6 | 34.9 | 60.7 | 48.6 | 38.7 |
| | (91) 7.1 | (91) 13.7 | (116) 14.7 | (37) 10.5 | (32) 9.9 | (13) 25.1 | (12) 13.9 | (10) 25.8 | (12) 20.8 |
| | -4.8 | 2.6 | 3.1 | 1.1 | .0 | 12.1 | 1.4 | 14.7 | 2.2 |
| % Profit Before Taxes/Total Assets | 7.9 | 10.6 | 11.1 | 5.9 | 10.2 | 16.0 | 9.8 | 21.8 | 12.2 |
| | .4 | 4.5 | 3.8 | 3.3 | 2.5 | 7.6 | 6.7 | 9.6 | 2.9 |
| | -5.0 | -1.5 | .0 | -1.1 | -1.4 | 4.5 | 2.3 | 1.3 | -6.8 |
| Sales/Net Fixed Assets | 5.4 | 5.9 | 11.6 | 4.3 | 12.0 | 8.0 | 62.3 | 37.7 | 16.5 |
| | 2.3 | 3.1 | 3.5 | .4 | 3.4 | 4.4 | 9.3 | 15.5 | 4.8 |
| | .6 | 1.0 | .5 | .1 | 1.6 | 3.5 | 4.2 | 7.8 | 1.1 |
| Sales/Total Assets | 2.2 | 2.5 | 2.3 | 1.6 | 2.8 | 2.3 | 2.5 | 2.5 | 3.9 |
| | 1.3 | 1.5 | 1.4 | .3 | 1.5 | 1.9 | 1.8 | 1.9 | 1.3 |
| | .4 | .6 | .3 | .1 | .9 | 1.2 | 1.2 | .6 | .8 |
| % Depr., Dep., Amort./Sales | 8.9 | 5.8 | 4.9 | 11.8 | 7.0 | | 1.2 | | |
| | (104) 16.2 | (100) 11.2 | (102) 12.2 | (38) 17.5 | (31) 12.3 | | (12) 4.4 | | |
| | 28.7 | 21.9 | 21.6 | 23.5 | 22.5 | | 11.6 | | |
| % Officers', Directors' Owners' Comp/Sales | 2.9 | 2.6 | 2.2 | 6.9 | 3.0 | | | | |
| | (51) 5.8 | (41) 7.5 | (50) 5.7 | (15) 10.3 | (17) 8.7 | | | | |
| | 11.5 | 12.5 | 10.5 | 12.6 | 12.6 | | | | |
| Net Sales ($) | 1148233M | 3702456M | 3277524M | 29976M | 72295M | 57053M | 121569M | 203843M | 2792788M |
| Total Assets ($) | 1309845M | 2707227M | 2610006M | 103006M | 121169M | 65950M | 155118M | 527569M | 1637194M |

© RMA 2012

M = $ thousand    MM = $ million
See Pages 9 through 22 for Explanation of Ratios and Data

## Current Data Sorted by Assets | Comparative Historical Data

### Type of Statement / Number of Statements

| 0-500M | 500M-2MM | 2-10MM | 10-50MM | 50-100MM | 100-250MM | Type of Statement | 4/1/07-3/31/08 ALL | 4/1/08-3/31/09 ALL |
|---|---|---|---|---|---|---|---|---|
| | 1 | | 8 | 7 | 8 | Unqualified | 8 | 12 |
| 1 | 2 | 8 | 11 | | | Reviewed | 8 | 16 |
| 1 | 3 | 8 | 1 | 1 | | Compiled | 15 | 11 |
| 25 | 26 | 16 | 1 | | 1 | Tax Returns | 22 | 25 |
| 13 | 21 | 28 | 20 | 1 | 10 | Other | 21 | 44 |
| 40 | 53 | 60 | 40 | 10 | 18 | NUMBER OF STATEMENTS | 74 | 108 |

Asset size ranges: 20 (4/1-9/30/11) covers 0-500M, 500M-2MM, 2-10MM; 201 (10/1/11-3/31/12) covers 10-50MM, 50-100MM, 100-250MM.

### Main Data (all figures %, except ratios and dollar totals)

| 0-500M | 500M-2MM | 2-10MM | 10-50MM | 50-100MM | 100-250MM | Account | 4/1/07-3/31/08 ALL | 4/1/08-3/31/09 ALL |
|---|---|---|---|---|---|---|---|---|
| % | % | % | % | % | % | **ASSETS** | % | % |
| 18.9 | 9.0 | 9.3 | 8.3 | 10.2 | 3.5 | Cash & Equivalents | 10.0 | 8.0 |
| 3.2 | 8.2 | 13.9 | 11.9 | 3.1 | 6.0 | Trade Receivables (net) | 5.3 | 14.1 |
| 2.0 | 2.4 | 3.7 | 4.8 | .8 | 1.9 | Inventory | 3.6 | 4.5 |
| 1.7 | 1.6 | 1.3 | 5.8 | 1.2 | 1.5 | All Other Current | 2.8 | 3.0 |
| 25.8 | 21.2 | 28.2 | 30.9 | 15.2 | 12.9 | Total Current | 21.7 | 29.6 |
| 58.7 | 64.9 | 57.7 | 59.6 | 52.5 | 77.8 | Fixed Assets (net) | 67.8 | 60.6 |
| 3.0 | 6.1 | 3.5 | 1.3 | 1.0 | 3.9 | Intangibles (net) | 1.1 | 2.0 |
| 12.6 | 7.8 | 10.6 | 8.2 | 31.2 | 5.4 | All Other Non-Current | 9.5 | 7.8 |
| 100.0 | 100.0 | 100.0 | 100.0 | 100.0 | 100.0 | Total | 100.0 | 100.0 |
| | | | | | | **LIABILITIES** | | |
| 25.5 | 2.6 | 2.2 | 5.5 | .5 | 4.8 | Notes Payable-Short Term | 8.4 | 8.2 |
| 12.3 | 10.1 | 6.8 | 9.1 | 6.6 | 6.7 | Cur. Mat.-L.T.D. | 12.6 | 10.2 |
| 3.4 | 2.0 | 4.4 | 4.0 | 1.6 | 3.6 | Trade Payables | 2.7 | 6.6 |
| .0 | .0 | .0 | .2 | .1 | .1 | Income Taxes Payable | .0 | .0 |
| 30.4 | 7.0 | 8.0 | 7.8 | .7 | 6.5 | All Other Current | 5.0 | 8.1 |
| 71.6 | 21.6 | 21.4 | 26.6 | 9.4 | 21.6 | Total Current | 28.7 | 33.2 |
| 33.1 | 73.2 | 41.7 | 28.3 | 44.6 | 36.7 | Long-Term Debt | 48.1 | 47.8 |
| .0 | .1 | .4 | 1.5 | .8 | 1.3 | Deferred Taxes | .4 | .8 |
| 14.5 | 4.4 | 4.4 | 1.7 | 7.6 | 2.0 | All Other Non-Current | 5.5 | 4.6 |
| -19.5 | .7 | 32.1 | 41.8 | 37.6 | 38.4 | Net Worth | 17.4 | 13.6 |
| 100.0 | 100.0 | 100.0 | 100.0 | 100.0 | 100.0 | Total Liabilties & Net Worth | 100.0 | 100.0 |
| | | | | | | **INCOME DATA** | | |
| 100.0 | 100.0 | 100.0 | 100.0 | 100.0 | 100.0 | Net Sales | 100.0 | 100.0 |
| | | | | | | Gross Profit | | |
| 76.5 | 66.6 | 78.2 | 85.0 | 74.9 | 73.3 | Operating Expenses | 77.1 | 77.7 |
| 23.5 | 33.4 | 21.8 | 15.0 | 25.1 | 26.7 | Operating Profit | 22.9 | 22.3 |
| 8.7 | 13.5 | 5.4 | 3.3 | 8.1 | 8.9 | All Other Expenses (net) | 9.2 | 7.2 |
| 14.8 | 19.9 | 16.4 | 11.7 | 17.0 | 17.8 | Profit Before Taxes | 13.7 | 15.2 |
| | | | | | | **RATIOS** | | |
| 1.6 | 2.2 | 2.4 | 2.5 | 2.3 | 1.5 | Current | 2.0 | 2.0 |
| .5 | 1.1 | 1.1 | 1.2 | 1.2 | .9 | | .8 | .8 |
| .1 | .3 | .5 | .7 | .9 | .2 | | .4 | .3 |
| 1.5 | 2.2 | 2.3 | 1.3 | 2.3 | 1.1 | Quick | 1.8 | 1.4 |
| .4 | .7 | .8 | .8 | 1.1 | .6 | | .6 | .6 |
| .1 | .2 | .4 | .4 | .6 | .1 | | .2 | .1 |
| 0 UND | 0 UND | 0 UND | 8 46.9 | 0 UND | 21 17.6 | Sales/Receivables | 0 UND | 0 UND |
| 0 UND | 0 UND | 24 14.9 | 33 10.9 | 13 27.2 | 33 11.2 | | 12 29.7 | 24 15.1 |
| 0 UND | 33 11.2 | 51 7.2 | 59 6.2 | 64 5.7 | 69 5.3 | | 35 10.5 | 55 6.6 |
| | | | | | | Cost of Sales/Inventory | | |
| | | | | | | Cost of Sales/Payables | | |
| 15.1 | 6.3 | 4.8 | 5.8 | 3.5 | 8.2 | Sales/Working Capital | 8.5 | 7.1 |
| -6.6 | 100.0 | 287.3 | 21.9 | 51.1 | NM | | -17.4 | -23.3 |
| -1.9 | -2.8 | -5.2 | -8.2 | -78.5 | -2.2 | | -3.4 | -3.2 |
| 7.6 | 19.7 | 14.7 | 12.3 | | 13.9 | EBIT/Interest | 7.6 | 10.0 |
| (25) 2.3 | (35) 3.3 | (48) 5.4 | (36) 4.5 | | (15) 5.6 | | (54) 2.4 | (86) 3.5 |
| 1.1 | 1.1 | 1.0 | 2.5 | | 2.5 | | 1.3 | 1.6 |
| | | | 21.0 | | | Net Profit + Depr., Dep., Amort./Cur. Mat. L/T/D | | 3.3 |
| | | | (12) 4.6 | | | | | (17) 1.6 |
| | | | 2.4 | | | | | .7 |
| .9 | 1.2 | .7 | .9 | .8 | 1.7 | Fixed/Worth | 1.2 | 1.0 |
| 2.9 | 3.4 | 2.2 | 1.3 | 1.8 | 2.6 | | 2.6 | 1.9 |
| -2.8 | -17.1 | 7.8 | 2.3 | 3.8 | 3.1 | | -41.5 | 12.1 |
| .6 | .9 | .9 | .7 | .9 | 1.5 | Debt/Worth | .9 | .9 |
| 4.6 | 3.9 | 2.0 | 1.4 | 2.7 | 2.0 | | 2.8 | 3.3 |
| -2.3 | -25.7 | 7.4 | 2.4 | 4.3 | 2.6 | | -44.4 | 27.1 |
| 72.7 | 53.7 | 44.5 | 39.0 | 35.9 | 32.1 | % Profit Before Taxes/Tangible Net Worth | 61.2 | 52.3 |
| (26) 15.6 | (37) 20.0 | (50) 23.0 | (38) 20.3 | 15.2 | 12.0 | | (55) 17.1 | (84) 19.7 |
| .8 | 3.4 | 3.0 | 11.3 | 3.1 | 5.0 | | 4.6 | 6.7 |
| 23.5 | 16.1 | 20.0 | 13.8 | 7.0 | 11.0 | % Profit Before Taxes/Total Assets | 15.0 | 14.8 |
| 7.9 | 3.5 | 6.2 | 7.2 | 5.2 | 5.7 | | 4.6 | 5.9 |
| .1 | .1 | .0 | 2.1 | 1.5 | 1.6 | | .2 | 1.1 |
| 12.7 | 3.0 | 5.4 | 2.6 | UND | .8 | Sales/Net Fixed Assets | 2.3 | 5.0 |
| 1.6 | .7 | 1.5 | 1.3 | .6 | .3 | | .7 | 1.0 |
| .6 | .2 | .4 | .4 | .5 | .2 | | .4 | .5 |
| 2.7 | 1.5 | 1.3 | 1.1 | .4 | .5 | Sales/Total Assets | 1.1 | 1.6 |
| .9 | .4 | .7 | .7 | .3 | .3 | | .5 | .8 |
| .4 | .2 | .3 | .3 | .1 | .1 | | .3 | .2 |
| 17.7 | 9.8 | 8.7 | 7.8 | | 12.3 | % Depr., Dep., Amort./Sales | 10.9 | 3.8 |
| (25) 37.8 | (38) 22.3 | (48) 21.5 | (35) 15.8 | | (10) 28.9 | | (59) 24.9 | (92) 21.6 |
| 59.6 | 54.8 | 33.7 | 25.0 | | 38.3 | | 51.9 | 48.4 |
| | | | 1.8 | | | % Officers', Directors' Owners' Comp/Sales | 1.3 | .9 |
| | | (13) 3.6 | | | | | (13) 3.0 | (18) 3.0 |
| | | | 6.7 | | | | 7.0 | 7.3 |
| 14851M | 57479M | 290353M | 876319M | 249703M | 1054857M | Net Sales ($) | 974667M | 2324748M |
| 9568M | 59721M | 260267M | 1008963M | 712926M | 2832611M | Total Assets ($) | 2059477M | 2721026M |

M = $ thousand   MM = $ million
See Pages 9 through 22 for Explanation of Ratios and Data

## Comparative Historical Data / Current Data Sorted by Sales

| Hist 4/1/09-3/31/10 ALL | Hist 4/1/10-3/31/11 ALL | Hist 4/1/11-3/31/12 ALL | Type of Statement | 0-1MM | 1-3MM | 3-5MM | 5-10MM | 10-25MM | 25MM & OVER |
|---|---|---|---|---|---|---|---|---|---|
| | | | | | 20 (4/1-9/30/11) | | 201 (10/1/11-3/31/12) | | |
| 15 | 22 | 24 | Unqualified | 1 | | 2 | 2 | 7 | 12 |
| 19 | 18 | 22 | Reviewed | 4 | 3 | 1 | 2 | 7 | 5 |
| 16 | 14 | 14 | Compiled | 3 | 3 | 2 | 3 | 1 | 2 |
| 49 | 49 | 68 | Tax Returns | 49 | 10 | 5 | 3 | 1 | |
| 63 | 55 | 93 | Other | 32 | 15 | 10 | 14 | 12 | 10 |
| 162 | 158 | 221 | NUMBER OF STATEMENTS | 89 | 31 | 20 | 24 | 28 | 29 |
| % | % | % | ASSETS | % | % | % | % | % | % |
| 9.9 | 10.8 | 10.3 | Cash & Equivalents | 10.7 | 11.0 | 10.7 | 11.7 | 8.9 | 8.5 |
| 10.1 | 11.4 | 9.1 | Trade Receivables (net) | 3.6 | 13.1 | 11.9 | 13.0 | 7.1 | 18.5 |
| 2.4 | 3.9 | 3.0 | Inventory | 1.3 | 5.0 | 6.5 | 3.4 | 3.5 | 3.2 |
| 3.5 | 3.3 | 2.3 | All Other Current | 1.9 | 1.4 | .6 | 3.9 | 2.5 | 3.9 |
| 25.9 | 29.4 | 24.8 | Total Current | 17.6 | 30.5 | 29.6 | 32.0 | 21.8 | 34.1 |
| 60.8 | 58.2 | 61.3 | Fixed Assets (net) | 67.8 | 56.5 | 53.7 | 47.2 | 67.0 | 58.1 |
| 2.1 | 1.0 | 3.5 | Intangibles (net) | 4.7 | 4.9 | 1.1 | 2.7 | 3.1 | 1.5 |
| 11.2 | 11.4 | 10.4 | All Other Non-Current | 10.0 | 8.1 | 15.6 | 18.0 | 8.1 | 6.2 |
| 100.0 | 100.0 | 100.0 | Total | 100.0 | 100.0 | 100.0 | 100.0 | 100.0 | 100.0 |
| | | | LIABILITIES | | | | | | |
| 7.4 | 5.7 | 7.2 | Notes Payable-Short Term | 12.4 | 2.7 | 7.5 | 2.6 | 4.0 | 3.3 |
| 10.2 | 8.8 | 9.0 | Cur. Mat.-L.T.D. | 10.2 | 10.1 | 3.4 | 12.9 | 6.5 | 7.1 |
| 5.7 | 5.2 | 3.4 | Trade Payables | 1.9 | 2.7 | 1.7 | 5.4 | 4.5 | 6.9 |
| .0 | .1 | .1 | Income Taxes Payable | .0 | .0 | .0 | .3 | .0 | .1 |
| 8.6 | 9.4 | 11.3 | All Other Current | 14.9 | 11.3 | 5.0 | 10.9 | 5.0 | 11.2 |
| 32.0 | 29.3 | 31.0 | Total Current | 39.4 | 26.8 | 17.5 | 32.1 | 20.0 | 28.6 |
| 51.8 | 47.5 | 45.0 | Long-Term Debt | 49.4 | 65.5 | 53.1 | 34.9 | 30.1 | 26.8 |
| .8 | .4 | .5 | Deferred Taxes | .0 | .0 | .0 | 1.1 | 2.1 | 1.1 |
| 5.2 | 5.0 | 5.7 | All Other Non-Current | 8.6 | 5.5 | 3.0 | 5.0 | 3.4 | 1.7 |
| 10.2 | 17.9 | 17.8 | Net Worth | 2.5 | 2.2 | 26.3 | 27.0 | 44.4 | 41.8 |
| 100.0 | 100.0 | 100.0 | Total Liabilities & Net Worth | 100.0 | 100.0 | 100.0 | 100.0 | 100.0 | 100.0 |
| | | | INCOME DATA | | | | | | |
| 100.0 | 100.0 | 100.0 | Net Sales | 100.0 | 100.0 | 100.0 | 100.0 | 100.0 | 100.0 |
| | | | Gross Profit | | | | | | |
| 74.2 | 75.1 | 75.8 | Operating Expenses | 64.7 | 84.8 | 76.8 | 83.4 | 85.0 | 84.3 |
| 25.8 | 24.9 | 24.2 | Operating Profit | 35.3 | 15.2 | 23.2 | 16.6 | 15.0 | 15.7 |
| 10.1 | 9.1 | 8.0 | All Other Expenses (net) | 13.6 | 4.3 | 7.5 | 4.3 | 3.6 | 2.0 |
| 15.7 | 15.8 | 16.3 | Profit Before Taxes | 21.7 | 10.9 | 15.7 | 12.3 | 11.4 | 13.7 |
| | | | RATIOS | | | | | | |
| 1.7 | 2.5 | 2.0 | | 1.8 | 3.0 | 6.3 | 2.2 | 1.8 | 1.7 |
| .8 | 1.1 | 1.0 | Current | .5 | 1.5 | 1.9 | 1.1 | 1.0 | 1.2 |
| .3 | .4 | .4 | | .1 | .7 | .8 | .5 | .6 | .9 |
| 1.5 | 2.0 | 1.7 | | 1.2 | 3.0 | 6.3 | 2.0 | 1.2 | 1.4 |
| .5 | .8 | .8 | Quick | .4 | 1.3 | 1.3 | .8 | .8 | 1.0 |
| .2 | .2 | .2 | | .1 | .5 | .7 | .3 | .3 | .5 |
| 0 UND | 0 UND | 0 UND | | 0 UND | 0 UND | 0 UND | 0 UND | 15 25.1 | 30 12.2 |
| 10 35.7 | 22 16.7 | 13 28.4 | Sales/Receivables | 0 UND | 18 20.2 | 17 21.8 | 21 17.6 | 26 13.9 | 47 7.7 |
| 52 7.0 | 51 7.1 | 45 8.2 | | 4 98.2 | 51 7.2 | 54 6.8 | 66 5.5 | 46 8.0 | 72 5.1 |
| | | | Cost of Sales/Inventory | | | | | | |
| | | | Cost of Sales/Payables | | | | | | |
| 8.0 | 5.1 | 6.5 | | 8.1 | 5.9 | 3.0 | 4.0 | 6.4 | 9.0 |
| -16.5 | 36.2 | 462.1 | Sales/Working Capital | -6.1 | 17.3 | 19.4 | 89.0 | 321.1 | 21.8 |
| -3.2 | -5.3 | -3.8 | | -1.7 | -6.4 | -30.8 | -8.9 | -6.7 | -18.0 |
| 6.8 | 10.3 | 12.5 | | 8.3 | 19.7 | 11.1 | 16.6 | 12.9 | 12.7 |
| (126) 2.9 | (124) 3.9 | (167) 4.3 | EBIT/Interest | (51) 3.1 | (27) 6.9 | (16) 3.8 | (21) 2.7 | (24) 5.2 | (28) 5.1 |
| 1.1 | 1.0 | 1.5 | | 1.2 | 1.9 | 1.0 | .5 | 1.6 | 3.2 |
| 10.6 | 5.8 | 15.1 | | | | | | | |
| (16) 3.1 | (15) 1.9 | (21) 4.1 | Net Profit + Depr., Dep., Amort./Cur. Mat. L/T/D | | | | | | |
| 1.0 | .7 | 1.8 | | | | | | | |
| 1.0 | .8 | 1.0 | | 1.1 | 1.2 | .3 | .6 | 1.1 | 1.0 |
| 2.4 | 1.8 | 2.2 | Fixed/Worth | 2.9 | 2.2 | 3.0 | 1.7 | 1.7 | 1.7 |
| UND | 10.7 | 8.6 | | -544.3 | -2.4 | 39.9 | 4.3 | 3.0 | 2.5 |
| 1.0 | .8 | .9 | | .9 | .9 | .7 | 1.3 | .8 | .8 |
| 3.4 | 2.2 | 2.1 | Debt/Worth | 2.8 | 2.1 | 3.1 | 2.8 | 1.3 | 1.6 |
| -51.0 | 22.5 | 11.8 | | -97.8 | -5.0 | 43.1 | 9.2 | 2.2 | 2.4 |
| 47.5 | 51.9 | 40.6 | | 35.1 | 41.5 | 40.8 | 39.7 | 40.9 | 44.2 |
| (120) 12.4 | (122) 16.4 | (179) 18.4 | % Profit Before Taxes/Tangible Net Worth | (65) 15.4 | (22) 23.0 | (16) 27.0 | (20) 19.8 | (27) 13.8 | 24.0 |
| 1.9 | 5.5 | 3.9 | | 2.7 | 8.8 | .1 | .2 | 2.7 | 10.9 |
| 15.6 | 17.9 | 15.6 | | 14.5 | 18.1 | 27.5 | 12.1 | 15.2 | 12.7 |
| 5.4 | 5.9 | 6.2 | % Profit Before Taxes/Total Assets | 4.0 | 11.5 | 5.7 | 5.6 | 7.0 | 8.5 |
| .4 | -.1 | .6 | | .3 | -.9 | .0 | -1.1 | .5 | 4.6 |
| 3.2 | 3.8 | 2.8 | | 1.7 | 6.9 | 20.6 | 11.0 | 2.3 | 2.9 |
| 1.1 | 1.3 | 1.1 | Sales/Net Fixed Assets | .5 | 1.7 | 1.6 | 2.4 | 1.0 | 1.7 |
| .5 | .4 | .4 | | .2 | .6 | .3 | .8 | .2 | .5 |
| 1.5 | 1.4 | 1.3 | | .8 | 2.1 | 1.3 | 2.5 | 1.2 | 1.6 |
| .6 | .7 | .5 | Sales/Total Assets | .3 | .7 | .7 | 1.0 | .7 | .8 |
| .3 | .3 | .2 | | .1 | .5 | .3 | .4 | .2 | .5 |
| 8.2 | 8.4 | 9.4 | | 19.4 | 7.2 | 13.8 | 6.3 | 10.2 | 2.1 |
| (125) 21.7 | (124) 20.2 | (163) 21.3 | % Depr., Dep., Amort./Sales | (67) 31.7 | (21) 23.3 | (13) 33.3 | (19) 9.6 | (24) 18.1 | (19) 8.3 |
| 39.5 | 43.9 | 38.7 | | 59.4 | 43.3 | 36.9 | 25.6 | 28.1 | 16.8 |
| 2.6 | 1.2 | 2.3 | | | | | | | |
| (33) 4.0 | (24) 3.3 | (35) 3.6 | % Officers', Directors' Owners' Comp/Sales | | | | | | |
| 9.5 | 4.7 | 6.6 | | | | | | | |
| 1581112M | 1759274M | 2543562M | Net Sales ($) | 28340M | 59331M | 77398M | 183660M | 478084M | 1716749M |
| 2747322M | 2955014M | 4884056M | Total Assets ($) | 103242M | 92143M | 221213M | 485721M | 1444113M | 2537624M |

© RMA 2012

M = $ thousand    MM = $ million
See Pages 9 through 22 for Explanation of Ratios and Data

## Current Data Sorted by Assets       Comparative Historical Data

| | | | | | | Type of Statement | | |
|---|---|---|---|---|---|---|---|---|
| | 2 | 9 | 22 | 15 | 16 | Unqualified | 68 | 66 |
| 5 | 5 | 38 | 30 | 6 | 3 | Reviewed | 113 | 98 |
| 3 | 16 | 31 | 6 | 2 | | Compiled | 78 | 57 |
| 16 | 18 | 15 | 1 | | | Tax Returns | 47 | 46 |
| 8 | 25 | 57 | 46 | 14 | 11 | Other | 156 | 161 |
| | 68 (4/1-9/30/11) | | 352 (10/1/11-3/31/12) | | | | 4/1/07-3/31/08 | 4/1/08-3/31/09 |
| 0-500M | 500M-2MM | 2-10MM | 10-50MM | 50-100MM | 100-250MM | | ALL | ALL |
| 32 | 66 | 150 | 105 | 37 | 30 | NUMBER OF STATEMENTS | 462 | 428 |
| % | % | % | % | % | % | ASSETS | % | % |
| 24.7 | 13.2 | 9.9 | 6.5 | 7.1 | 3.1 | Cash & Equivalents | 7.1 | 7.7 |
| 16.9 | 12.0 | 18.0 | 15.9 | 12.7 | 11.2 | Trade Receivables (net) | 13.4 | 12.8 |
| 5.1 | 11.2 | 11.6 | 14.1 | 9.8 | 11.1 | Inventory | 10.1 | 12.8 |
| .4 | 3.6 | 2.8 | 2.1 | 2.6 | 2.3 | All Other Current | 3.2 | 2.5 |
| 47.2 | 40.0 | 42.2 | 38.6 | 32.2 | 27.7 | Total Current | 33.9 | 35.8 |
| 33.6 | 50.5 | 50.5 | 50.8 | 56.8 | 59.3 | Fixed Assets (net) | 59.7 | 56.8 |
| .9 | 3.9 | 1.6 | 1.4 | 2.6 | 9.6 | Intangibles (net) | 1.7 | 2.1 |
| 18.3 | 5.6 | 5.7 | 9.2 | 8.4 | 3.4 | All Other Non-Current | 4.7 | 5.3 |
| 100.0 | 100.0 | 100.0 | 100.0 | 100.0 | 100.0 | Total | 100.0 | 100.0 |
| | | | | | | LIABILITIES | | |
| 12.9 | 5.6 | 11.1 | 10.7 | 8.2 | 10.3 | Notes Payable-Short Term | 9.7 | 10.1 |
| 10.0 | 10.7 | 9.1 | 9.6 | 8.0 | 6.0 | Cur. Mat.-L.T.D. | 10.3 | 9.6 |
| 11.0 | 5.2 | 6.4 | 5.4 | 6.6 | 4.0 | Trade Payables | 6.0 | 5.1 |
| .0 | .0 | .4 | .6 | .3 | .2 | Income Taxes Payable | .4 | .2 |
| 16.2 | 6.2 | 7.6 | 4.5 | 4.7 | 3.5 | All Other Current | 4.5 | 5.5 |
| 50.1 | 27.7 | 34.6 | 30.7 | 27.7 | 24.0 | Total Current | 30.8 | 30.5 |
| 38.6 | 26.9 | 25.0 | 25.2 | 30.3 | 32.0 | Long-Term Debt | 37.0 | 34.0 |
| .0 | .7 | 1.7 | 1.6 | 2.4 | 2.8 | Deferred Taxes | .8 | .8 |
| 4.2 | 5.7 | 4.4 | 2.9 | 3.0 | 4.6 | All Other Non-Current | 3.5 | 3.3 |
| 6.8 | 39.0 | 34.3 | 39.6 | 36.6 | 36.6 | Net Worth | 27.9 | 31.4 |
| 100.0 | 100.0 | 100.0 | 100.0 | 100.0 | 100.0 | Total Liabilties & Net Worth | 100.0 | 100.0 |
| | | | | | | INCOME DATA | | |
| 100.0 | 100.0 | 100.0 | 100.0 | 100.0 | 100.0 | Net Sales | 100.0 | 100.0 |
| | | | | | | Gross Profit | | |
| 77.0 | 82.9 | 91.0 | 90.2 | 89.0 | 89.7 | Operating Expenses | 84.6 | 85.9 |
| 23.0 | 17.1 | 9.0 | 9.8 | 11.0 | 10.3 | Operating Profit | 15.4 | 14.1 |
| .8 | 2.6 | 1.8 | 1.8 | 3.3 | 6.6 | All Other Expenses (net) | 4.0 | 4.4 |
| 22.2 | 14.6 | 7.2 | 8.1 | 7.7 | 3.7 | Profit Before Taxes | 11.3 | 9.7 |
| | | | | | | RATIOS | | |
| 2.8 | 3.4 | 2.2 | 2.0 | 2.2 | 2.3 | | 2.0 | 2.2 |
| 1.1 | 1.5 | 1.3 | 1.2 | 1.1 | 1.3 | Current | 1.1 | 1.2 |
| .3 | .4 | .7 | .7 | .8 | .6 | | .5 | .6 |
| 2.7 | 2.3 | 1.7 | 1.4 | 1.5 | 1.3 | | 1.4 | 1.5 |
| 1.0 | .9 | .9 | .7 | .8 | .7 | Quick | .6 | .7 |
| .3 | .3 | .4 | .4 | .4 | .3 | | .3 | .3 |
| 0 UND | 0 UND | 25 14.6 | 36 10.0 | 41 8.9 | 24 15.1 | | 13 27.6 | 17 20.9 |
| 8 48.2 | 19 19.0 | 49 7.4 | 57 6.4 | 53 6.9 | 46 7.9 | Sales/Receivables | 40 9.2 | 40 9.2 |
| 49 7.4 | 49 7.4 | 72 5.1 | 85 4.3 | 65 5.6 | 66 5.5 | | 64 5.7 | 63 5.8 |
| | | | | | | | | |
| | | | | | | Cost of Sales/Inventory | | |
| | | | | | | | | |
| | | | | | | Cost of Sales/Payables | | |
| | | | | | | | | |
| 7.3 | 3.5 | 4.3 | 4.7 | 5.7 | 4.3 | | 7.1 | 5.5 |
| 342.3 | 11.2 | 13.8 | 15.2 | 31.7 | 15.5 | Sales/Working Capital | 30.2 | 18.7 |
| -5.3 | -6.8 | -8.6 | -9.8 | -12.8 | -6.0 | | -5.6 | -8.6 |
| 31.4 | 12.6 | 9.3 | 5.7 | 6.3 | 6.2 | | 6.2 | 6.1 |
| (23) 4.9 | (57) 3.9 | (139) 2.9 | (96) 3.1 | (36) 3.1 | (28) 2.7 | EBIT/Interest | (420) 3.0 | (395) 2.8 |
| .7 | 1.1 | 1.3 | 1.7 | 1.4 | .4 | | 1.5 | 1.1 |
| | | 3.9 | 2.7 | 6.3 | | | 3.0 | 3.7 |
| | (46) 1.9 | (33) 1.8 | (10) 2.7 | | | Net Profit + Depr., Dep., Amort./Cur. Mat. L/T/D | (95) 1.6 | (91) 1.8 |
| | | 1.2 | .9 | .8 | | | 1.2 | 1.1 |
| .1 | .5 | .6 | .5 | 1.1 | .9 | | 1.0 | .9 |
| .8 | 1.2 | 1.4 | 1.2 | 1.8 | 2.1 | Fixed/Worth | 2.3 | 1.9 |
| 4.3 | 2.9 | 2.9 | 2.5 | 3.2 | 11.6 | | 5.8 | 4.5 |
| .4 | .7 | .8 | .6 | 1.1 | 1.2 | | 1.3 | 1.1 |
| 2.9 | 1.5 | 1.8 | 1.7 | 1.5 | 2.2 | Debt/Worth | 2.9 | 2.5 |
| 167.3 | 4.0 | 3.6 | 3.2 | 5.0 | 12.3 | | 7.0 | 6.5 |
| 271.0 | 49.2 | 36.3 | 27.8 | 23.3 | 19.9 | | 51.1 | 41.1 |
| (25) 82.4 | (58) 19.8 | (135) 15.0 | (101) 11.8 | (34) 15.6 | (24) 10.2 | % Profit Before Taxes/Tangible Net Worth | (410) 27.5 | (380) 21.6 |
| 12.6 | 4.1 | 3.0 | 5.4 | 3.4 | 4.2 | | 12.0 | 4.7 |
| 73.3 | 18.6 | 13.4 | 9.2 | 8.1 | 7.3 | | 13.8 | 13.1 |
| 27.8 | 8.3 | 4.9 | 4.5 | 4.1 | 3.6 | % Profit Before Taxes/Total Assets | 6.7 | 6.2 |
| 1.6 | .4 | .8 | 1.6 | 1.0 | -3.1 | | 1.9 | .4 |
| 108.3 | 8.9 | 5.8 | 6.2 | 2.5 | 2.0 | | 4.1 | 4.6 |
| 10.4 | 2.0 | 2.2 | 1.8 | 1.0 | .9 | Sales/Net Fixed Assets | 1.5 | 1.6 |
| 1.9 | .6 | 1.0 | .8 | .7 | .5 | | .7 | .8 |
| 3.5 | 2.1 | 1.6 | 1.3 | 1.0 | 1.0 | | 1.5 | 1.5 |
| 1.8 | 1.0 | 1.0 | .9 | .7 | .5 | Sales/Total Assets | .9 | .9 |
| .9 | .4 | .6 | .5 | .6 | .3 | | .5 | .5 |
| 4.5 | 6.0 | 4.6 | 5.1 | 8.8 | | | 6.2 | 6.3 |
| (15) 12.8 | (53) 17.6 | (130) 11.5 | (87) 12.1 | (30) 12.9 | | % Depr., Dep., Amort./Sales | (401) 14.4 | (352) 13.8 |
| 30.1 | 51.4 | 22.3 | 24.5 | 16.3 | | | 29.7 | 27.3 |
| 2.8 | 1.8 | 2.0 | 1.9 | | | | 1.6 | 1.2 |
| (10) 12.2 | (20) 5.1 | (47) 3.7 | (18) 2.9 | | | % Officers', Directors' Owners' Comp/Sales | (101) 3.2 | (102) 3.7 |
| 16.2 | 16.4 | 5.4 | 6.5 | | | | 7.1 | 7.5 |
| 33184M | 112147M | 923248M | 2480528M | 2053514M | 3559546M | Net Sales ($) | 9920573M | 10394268M |
| 9068M | 79007M | 771677M | 2563209M | 2481540M | 5281614M | Total Assets ($) | 10279818M | 11236597M |

M = $ thousand     MM = $ million
See Pages 9 through 22 for Explanation of Ratios and Data

## Comparative Historical Data | Current Data Sorted by Sales

| | | | Type of Statement | | | | | | |
|---|---|---|---|---|---|---|---|---|---|
| 57 | 73 | 64 | Unqualified | 3 | 2 | 2 | 6 | 13 | 38 |
| 98 | 90 | 87 | Reviewed | 6 | 7 | 13 | 21 | 23 | 17 |
| 59 | 47 | 58 | Compiled | 14 | 9 | 12 | 13 | 7 | 3 |
| 42 | 67 | 50 | Tax Returns | 23 | 9 | 8 | 10 | | |
| 141 | 149 | 161 | Other | 24 | 29 | 17 | 19 | 28 | 44 |
| 4/1/09-3/31/10 ALL | 4/1/10-3/31/11 ALL | 4/1/11-3/31/12 ALL | | 68 (4/1-9/30/11) | | | 352 (10/1/11-3/31/12) | | |
| | | | | 0-1MM | 1-3MM | 3-5MM | 5-10MM | 10-25MM | 25MM & OVER |
| 397 | 426 | 420 | **NUMBER OF STATEMENTS** | 70 | 56 | 52 | 69 | 71 | 102 |
| % | % | % | **ASSETS** | % | % | % | % | % | % |
| 8.6 | 9.1 | 10.0 | Cash & Equivalents | 13.5 | 16.7 | 12.7 | 9.2 | 7.0 | 5.1 |
| 13.3 | 14.1 | 15.5 | Trade Receivables (net) | 10.3 | 15.5 | 14.9 | 18.9 | 17.3 | 15.8 |
| 11.2 | 10.8 | 11.5 | Inventory | 4.7 | 5.5 | 10.2 | 14.5 | 16.0 | 14.8 |
| 3.0 | 3.1 | 2.5 | All Other Current | 1.6 | 4.9 | 2.4 | 2.3 | 2.3 | 2.1 |
| 36.0 | 37.0 | 39.4 | Total Current | 30.1 | 42.5 | 40.1 | 44.8 | 42.5 | 37.9 |
| 54.7 | 52.8 | 50.5 | Fixed Assets (net) | 57.1 | 47.2 | 50.9 | 49.1 | 47.0 | 50.9 |
| 3.0 | 2.7 | 2.5 | Intangibles (net) | 3.2 | 1.4 | 2.5 | 1.1 | 1.5 | 4.3 |
| 6.3 | 7.5 | 7.6 | All Other Non-Current | 9.7 | 8.9 | 6.4 | 4.9 | 8.9 | 6.9 |
| 100.0 | 100.0 | 100.0 | Total | 100.0 | 100.0 | 100.0 | 100.0 | 100.0 | 100.0 |
| | | | **LIABILITIES** | | | | | | |
| 9.7 | 9.1 | 9.9 | Notes Payable-Short Term | 7.6 | 6.5 | 8.0 | 12.6 | 9.1 | 13.3 |
| 9.8 | 8.5 | 9.2 | Cur. Mat.-L.T.D. | 12.3 | 9.3 | 8.9 | 8.4 | 10.8 | 6.7 |
| 4.8 | 5.7 | 6.2 | Trade Payables | 4.3 | 6.8 | 6.1 | 5.7 | 7.0 | 6.8 |
| .3 | .3 | .3 | Income Taxes Payable | .0 | .1 | .7 | .4 | .3 | .4 |
| 5.5 | 6.0 | 6.7 | All Other Current | 5.0 | 11.3 | 11.1 | 5.0 | 4.9 | 5.4 |
| 30.0 | 29.6 | 32.4 | Total Current | 29.3 | 34.0 | 34.8 | 32.1 | 32.1 | 32.7 |
| 30.6 | 28.8 | 27.4 | Long-Term Debt | 34.4 | 32.8 | 23.5 | 23.1 | 22.3 | 27.9 |
| 1.1 | 1.3 | 1.5 | Deferred Taxes | .8 | 1.0 | 1.3 | 1.3 | 2.5 | 1.9 |
| 4.6 | 4.7 | 4.1 | All Other Non-Current | 4.4 | 4.0 | 6.1 | 3.3 | 4.2 | 3.5 |
| 33.7 | 35.6 | 34.6 | Net Worth | 31.0 | 28.3 | 34.4 | 40.1 | 38.9 | 34.1 |
| 100.0 | 100.0 | 100.0 | Total Liabilities & Net Worth | 100.0 | 100.0 | 100.0 | 100.0 | 100.0 | 100.0 |
| | | | **INCOME DATA** | | | | | | |
| 100.0 | 100.0 | 100.0 | Net Sales | 100.0 | 100.0 | 100.0 | 100.0 | 100.0 | 100.0 |
| | | | Gross Profit | | | | | | |
| 91.4 | 89.4 | 88.2 | Operating Expenses | 73.0 | 88.3 | 92.0 | 92.6 | 92.5 | 90.5 |
| 8.6 | 10.6 | 11.8 | Operating Profit | 27.0 | 11.7 | 8.0 | 7.4 | 7.5 | 9.5 |
| 4.6 | 3.2 | 2.3 | All Other Expenses (net) | 4.5 | 2.8 | -.6 | 1.5 | 1.4 | 3.2 |
| 4.0 | 7.4 | 9.5 | Profit Before Taxes | 22.4 | 8.9 | 8.7 | 6.0 | 6.1 | 6.3 |
| | | | **RATIOS** | | | | | | |
| 2.2 | 2.4 | 2.3 | | 2.6 | 3.7 | 2.1 | 2.2 | 2.2 | 2.1 |
| 1.2 | 1.3 | 1.3 | Current | 1.0 | 1.5 | 1.2 | 1.4 | 1.2 | 1.2 |
| .6 | .6 | .6 | | .3 | .6 | .5 | .9 | .8 | .8 |
| 1.5 | 1.7 | 1.6 | | 1.8 | 2.7 | 1.7 | 1.6 | 1.4 | 1.3 |
| (396) .7 | (425) .7 | .8 | Quick | .6 | 1.0 | .8 | 1.0 | .8 | .7 |
| .3 | .4 | .4 | | .2 | .4 | .4 | .4 | .4 | .3 |
| 21 17.5 | 22 17.0 | 19 19.1 | | 0 UND | 11 32.3 | 14 26.6 | 33 11.0 | 41 8.9 | 32 11.4 |
| 41 8.8 | 45 8.0 | 46 7.9 | Sales/Receivables | 3 118.5 | 43 8.5 | 37 9.8 | 51 7.2 | 56 6.5 | 51 7.1 |
| 64 5.7 | 69 5.3 | 72 5.1 | | 63 5.8 | 74 4.9 | 65 5.6 | 76 4.8 | 76 4.8 | 63 5.8 |
| | | | Cost of Sales/Inventory | | | | | | |
| | | | Cost of Sales/Payables | | | | | | |
| 5.0 | 4.6 | 4.5 | | 2.5 | 3.4 | 5.2 | 5.1 | 4.8 | 5.0 |
| 24.4 | 16.6 | 17.0 | Sales/Working Capital | 62.7 | 7.5 | 40.2 | 15.2 | 13.1 | 16.1 |
| -6.6 | -7.7 | -8.6 | | -2.6 | -5.3 | -7.5 | -50.7 | -11.3 | -14.0 |
| 4.5 | 5.7 | 8.3 | | 12.7 | 14.0 | 13.3 | 5.9 | 6.2 | 6.0 |
| (353) 1.6 | (389) 2.2 | (379) 3.1 | EBIT/Interest | (56) 3.7 | (49) 3.0 | (44) 4.6 | (68) 2.3 | (64) 3.4 | (98) 3.0 |
| -.4 | .7 | 1.4 | | 1.3 | .8 | 1.6 | 1.3 | 1.8 | 1.4 |
| 2.8 | 3.0 | 3.7 | Net Profit + Depr., Dep., | | | 4.7 | 2.7 | 2.6 | 9.5 |
| (100) 1.2 | (84) 1.6 | (102) 1.9 | Amort./Cur. Mat. L/T/D | | | (10) 2.0 | (24) 1.6 | (29) 1.7 | (24) 2.9 |
| .5 | .9 | 1.0 | | | | 1.2 | .9 | .9 | 1.0 |
| .8 | .7 | .6 | | .7 | .4 | .5 | .4 | .5 | .7 |
| 1.8 | 1.5 | 1.4 | Fixed/Worth | 1.5 | 1.1 | 1.5 | 1.3 | 1.3 | 1.5 |
| 4.5 | 3.3 | 2.9 | | 4.5 | 3.5 | 3.0 | 2.4 | 2.4 | 3.2 |
| .9 | .9 | .9 | | .7 | .5 | .6 | .8 | 1.0 | 1.1 |
| 2.1 | 1.7 | 1.7 | Debt/Worth | 2.0 | 1.2 | 1.8 | 1.6 | 1.8 | 2.0 |
| 5.7 | 4.8 | 3.9 | | 5.3 | 4.9 | 5.2 | 3.2 | 3.3 | 4.4 |
| 24.6 | 26.4 | 36.5 | % Profit Before Taxes/Tangible | 73.5 | 36.7 | 56.1 | 28.3 | 32.2 | 29.5 |
| (348) 6.7 | (381) 9.2 | (377) 15.0 | Net Worth | (62) 21.8 | (46) 9.4 | (43) 30.6 | (66) 10.3 | (70) 14.8 | (90) 14.8 |
| -11.2 | -.3 | 4.5 | | 5.9 | 1.9 | 8.1 | 2.1 | 5.1 | 6.0 |
| 8.5 | 9.1 | 12.6 | % Profit Before Taxes/Total | 20.2 | 13.2 | 19.6 | 11.2 | 10.6 | 8.6 |
| 1.4 | 2.7 | 5.2 | Assets | 8.0 | 5.7 | 8.1 | 4.6 | 5.3 | 3.9 |
| -4.7 | -1.3 | .8 | | .5 | .0 | 2.5 | .9 | 1.2 | 1.4 |
| 4.9 | 5.9 | 7.2 | | 2.9 | 9.3 | 6.4 | 10.4 | 7.4 | 6.7 |
| 1.4 | 1.6 | 1.9 | Sales/Net Fixed Assets | 1.0 | 1.7 | 2.5 | 2.6 | 2.7 | 1.9 |
| .7 | .8 | .8 | | .4 | .7 | 1.2 | 1.0 | .9 | .8 |
| 1.4 | 1.4 | 1.5 | | .9 | 1.5 | 1.9 | 1.8 | 1.6 | 1.3 |
| .8 | .8 | .9 | Sales/Total Assets | .5 | .9 | 1.2 | 1.0 | 1.0 | 1.0 |
| .5 | .5 | .5 | | .3 | .5 | .7 | .7 | .6 | .6 |
| 6.8 | 7.1 | 5.2 | | 18.0 | 8.0 | 5.1 | 4.4 | 3.8 | 3.9 |
| (317) 14.4 | (337) 14.8 | (324) 12.3 | % Depr., Dep., Amort./Sales | (52) 35.0 | (43) 19.8 | (45) 11.3 | (56) 11.3 | (60) 9.9 | (68) 8.0 |
| 30.3 | 28.1 | 24.1 | | 61.1 | 50.6 | 19.5 | 20.6 | 18.2 | 14.8 |
| 2.2 | 1.8 | 1.8 | % Officers', Directors' | 7.6 | 4.0 | 2.2 | 1.6 | 1.6 | |
| (86) 4.2 | (89) 4.1 | (100) 3.6 | Owners' Comp/Sales | (12) 13.7 | (17) 6.6 | (23) 3.7 | (18) 3.2 | (22) 2.6 | |
| 7.4 | 7.2 | 6.7 | | 15.1 | 9.9 | 5.0 | 4.8 | 3.9 | |
| 8742446M | 9404533M | 9162167M | Net Sales ($) | 33898M | 107872M | 201607M | 499837M | 1143048M | 7175905M |
| 10872783M | 10785786M | 11186115M | Total Assets ($) | 83778M | 198043M | 201110M | 575886M | 1366828M | 8760470M |

© RMA 2012     M = $ thousand    MM = $ million
See Pages 9 through 22 for Explanation of Ratios and Data

## Current Data Sorted by Assets / Comparative Historical Data

| 0-500M | 500M-2MM | 2-10MM | 10-50MM | 50-100MM | 100-250MM | | 4/1/07-3/31/08 ALL | 4/1/08-3/31/09 ALL |
|---|---|---|---|---|---|---|---|---|
| | | | | | | **Type of Statement** | | |
| 1 | 2 | 2 | 6 | 2 | 3 | Unqualified | 24 | 21 |
| 2 | 6 | 6 | 6 | | | Reviewed | 17 | 18 |
| 3 | 7 | 14 | 1 | 2 | | Compiled | 17 | 12 |
| 14 | 14 | 9 | | | 1 | Tax Returns | 21 | 34 |
| 4 | 5 | 14 | 12 | | 2 | Other | 44 | 56 |
| 14 (4/1-9/30/11) | | | 118 (10/1/11-3/31/12) | | | | | |
| 24 | 28 | 45 | 25 | 4 | 6 | **NUMBER OF STATEMENTS** | 123 | 141 |
| % | % | % | % | % | % | **ASSETS** | % | % |
| 17.0 | 13.8 | 5.0 | 6.9 | | | Cash & Equivalents | 7.6 | 7.5 |
| 6.7 | 14.4 | 14.1 | 20.7 | | | Trade Receivables (net) | 13.5 | 15.5 |
| 3.0 | 9.4 | 8.3 | 4.8 | | | Inventory | 7.3 | 7.0 |
| 1.5 | 4.3 | 6.8 | 8.2 | | | All Other Current | 6.7 | 7.3 |
| 28.2 | 41.9 | 34.2 | 40.6 | | | Total Current | 35.1 | 37.3 |
| 60.0 | 48.6 | 53.1 | 39.3 | | | Fixed Assets (net) | 42.4 | 41.3 |
| 2.9 | 2.9 | 2.2 | 4.2 | | | Intangibles (net) | 1.9 | 2.2 |
| 8.9 | 6.6 | 10.5 | 15.9 | | | All Other Non-Current | 20.5 | 19.2 |
| 100.0 | 100.0 | 100.0 | 100.0 | | | Total | 100.0 | 100.0 |
| | | | | | | **LIABILITIES** | | |
| 18.3 | 12.0 | 7.3 | 9.1 | | | Notes Payable-Short Term | 16.2 | 15.8 |
| 11.9 | 9.2 | 7.3 | 11.5 | | | Cur. Mat.-L.T.D. | 10.4 | 10.0 |
| 2.3 | 9.8 | 6.3 | 6.5 | | | Trade Payables | 5.7 | 6.8 |
| .4 | .0 | .7 | .1 | | | Income Taxes Payable | .3 | .1 |
| 5.3 | 7.9 | 5.8 | 12.2 | | | All Other Current | 7.2 | 7.1 |
| 38.2 | 38.8 | 27.3 | 39.5 | | | Total Current | 39.8 | 39.8 |
| 26.6 | 46.0 | 27.0 | 24.0 | | | Long-Term Debt | 31.6 | 34.4 |
| .0 | .0 | .0 | .7 | | | Deferred Taxes | .6 | .4 |
| 7.4 | 6.3 | 8.1 | 3.2 | | | All Other Non-Current | 6.4 | 5.6 |
| 27.8 | 8.8 | 37.6 | 32.6 | | | Net Worth | 21.6 | 19.8 |
| 100.0 | 100.0 | 100.0 | 100.0 | | | Total Liabilities & Net Worth | 100.0 | 100.0 |
| | | | | | | **INCOME DATA** | | |
| 100.0 | 100.0 | 100.0 | 100.0 | | | Net Sales | 100.0 | 100.0 |
| | | | | | | Gross Profit | | |
| 70.8 | 84.0 | 77.8 | 83.4 | | | Operating Expenses | 74.0 | 78.5 |
| 29.2 | 16.0 | 22.2 | 16.6 | | | Operating Profit | 26.0 | 21.5 |
| 3.6 | 3.4 | 4.7 | 6.8 | | | All Other Expenses (net) | 12.3 | 9.2 |
| 25.6 | 12.6 | 17.4 | 9.8 | | | Profit Before Taxes | 13.8 | 12.3 |
| | | | | | | **RATIOS** | | |
| 2.1 | 2.0 | 2.3 | 1.9 | | | | 1.4 | 1.9 |
| .6 | 1.1 | 1.4 | 1.1 | | | Current | .9 | .9 |
| .1 | .4 | .4 | .6 | | | | .4 | .3 |
| 1.7 | 1.4 | 1.6 | 1.2 | | | | 1.1 | 1.4 |
| .6 | .7 | .6 | .7 | | | Quick | .4 | .5 |
| .1 | .3 | .2 | .2 | | | | .1 | .1 |
| 0 UND | 0 UND | 3 133.3 | 5 73.9 | | | | 0 UND | 0 UND |
| 0 UND | 11 33.9 | 31 11.6 | 47 7.7 | | | Sales/Receivables | 23 16.1 | 17 21.6 |
| 19 19.7 | 35 10.3 | 48 7.6 | 64 5.7 | | | | 45 8.1 | 51 7.1 |
| | | | | | | Cost of Sales/Inventory | | |
| | | | | | | Cost of Sales/Payables | | |
| 8.2 | 8.9 | 5.9 | 6.2 | | | | 6.6 | 4.5 |
| -25.8 | 47.9 | 19.8 | 34.2 | | | Sales/Working Capital | -22.3 | -66.2 |
| -2.2 | -4.6 | -4.1 | -4.3 | | | | -2.2 | -3.2 |
| 19.4 | 8.6 | 8.4 | 11.3 | | | | 5.7 | 7.9 |
| (17) 4.0 | (21) 2.6 | (38) 3.3 | (19) 2.2 | | | EBIT/Interest | (88) 2.2 | (98) 2.6 |
| 1.9 | 1.1 | 1.7 | 1.4 | | | | 1.3 | 1.3 |
| | | | | | | | 2.7 | 3.2 |
| | | | | | | Net Profit + Depr., Dep., Amort./Cur. Mat. L/T/D | (19) 1.3 | (14) 1.3 |
| | | | | | | | .9 | .4 |
| 1.0 | .7 | .5 | .1 | | | | .1 | .1 |
| 2.3 | 2.6 | 1.5 | .9 | | | Fixed/Worth | 1.5 | 1.2 |
| NM | -4.8 | 6.4 | 3.7 | | | | 9.7 | 5.5 |
| .8 | .9 | .6 | 1.2 | | | | 1.8 | 1.5 |
| 2.2 | 11.7 | 1.8 | 3.2 | | | Debt/Worth | 5.7 | 4.3 |
| NM | -8.7 | 8.5 | 7.5 | | | | 30.1 | 18.3 |
| 188.2 | 113.0 | 37.0 | 43.4 | | | | 43.7 | 51.7 |
| (18) 39.3 | (19) 36.7 | (40) 18.1 | (23) 12.2 | | | % Profit Before Taxes/Tangible Net Worth | (99) 23.2 | (115) 20.0 |
| 8.7 | 22.9 | 5.1 | 2.5 | | | | 9.1 | 7.5 |
| 23.0 | 14.5 | 13.0 | 9.8 | | | | 11.8 | 14.9 |
| 12.9 | 4.6 | 6.4 | 4.5 | | | % Profit Before Taxes/Total Assets | 4.4 | 4.8 |
| 2.9 | -.5 | 2.5 | .5 | | | | 1.3 | .8 |
| 8.8 | 29.3 | 10.4 | 60.6 | | | | 36.5 | 30.7 |
| 2.0 | 1.9 | 1.6 | 2.0 | | | Sales/Net Fixed Assets | 3.9 | 4.3 |
| .6 | .8 | .5 | 1.1 | | | | .7 | .9 |
| 2.0 | 2.5 | 2.0 | 1.4 | | | | 1.4 | 1.8 |
| .9 | 1.4 | .7 | .7 | | | Sales/Total Assets | .5 | .7 |
| .5 | .4 | .3 | .4 | | | | .3 | .3 |
| 8.2 | 1.2 | 5.2 | .9 | | | | 2.8 | 2.2 |
| (13) 21.4 | (20) 15.5 | (37) 20.7 | (20) 8.9 | | | % Depr., Dep., Amort./Sales | (89) 15.4 | (93) 11.3 |
| 47.5 | 48.4 | 50.3 | 15.6 | | | | 49.9 | 44.0 |
| | 2.2 | 2.1 | | | | | 4.7 | 2.9 |
| | (11) 3.5 | (14) 3.4 | | | | % Officers', Directors' Owners' Comp/Sales | (25) 8.6 | (35) 6.2 |
| | 9.7 | 12.0 | | | | | 13.8 | 12.0 |
| 9532M | 56135M | 265501M | 569463M | 194321M | 1003775M | Net Sales ($) | 1506604M | 1288523M |
| 5934M | 32348M | 208502M | 536098M | 312362M | 1064992M | Total Assets ($) | 2685582M | 2251517M |

M = $ thousand    MM = $ million
See Pages 9 through 22 for Explanation of Ratios and Data

| Comparative Historical Data | | | Type of Statement | Current Data Sorted by Sales | | | | | |
|---|---|---|---|---|---|---|---|---|---|
| 18 | 14 | 14 | Unqualified | 1 | 1 | | 4 | 1 | 7 |
| 9 | 19 | 16 | Reviewed | 3 | 4 | 3 | 2 | 2 | 2 |
| 17 | 21 | 27 | Compiled | 11 | 4 | 2 | 4 | 3 | 3 |
| 22 | 31 | 38 | Tax Returns | 21 | 11 | 1 | 1 | 3 | 1 |
| 44 | 40 | 37 | Other | 8 | 8 | 2 | 7 | 6 | 6 |
| 4/1/09-3/31/10 ALL | 4/1/10-3/31/11 ALL | 4/1/11-3/31/12 ALL | | 14 (4/1-9/30/11) | | | 118 (10/1/11-3/31/12) | | |
| | | | | 0-1MM | 1-3MM | 3-5MM | 5-10MM | 10-25MM | 25MM & OVER |
| 110 | 125 | 132 | NUMBER OF STATEMENTS | 44 | 28 | 8 | 18 | 15 | 19 |
| % | % | % | ASSETS | % | % | % | % | % | % |
| 11.1 | 11.9 | 9.5 | Cash & Equivalents | 13.2 | 13.1 | | 4.4 | 4.9 | 5.2 |
| 14.5 | 14.2 | 15.0 | Trade Receivables (net) | 5.4 | 11.9 | | 16.8 | 28.4 | 28.2 |
| 7.4 | 7.0 | 6.5 | Inventory | .4 | 8.1 | | 10.9 | 14.6 | 6.1 |
| 8.4 | 6.9 | 5.5 | All Other Current | 5.7 | 6.7 | | 7.5 | 4.9 | 3.9 |
| 41.4 | 40.0 | 36.6 | Total Current | 24.7 | 39.8 | | 39.7 | 52.8 | 43.4 |
| 41.5 | 43.4 | 48.8 | Fixed Assets (net) | 60.8 | 47.5 | | 47.1 | 33.8 | 34.4 |
| 2.0 | 2.9 | 3.3 | Intangibles (net) | .7 | 2.8 | | 1.9 | 8.4 | 6.3 |
| 15.1 | 13.7 | 11.3 | All Other Non-Current | 13.8 | 9.9 | | 11.3 | 5.0 | 15.8 |
| 100.0 | 100.0 | 100.0 | Total | 100.0 | 100.0 | | 100.0 | 100.0 | 100.0 |
| | | | LIABILITIES | | | | | | |
| 10.4 | 15.8 | 11.0 | Notes Payable-Short Term | 12.0 | 12.4 | | 9.0 | 11.0 | 11.1 |
| 9.3 | 8.4 | 9.6 | Cur. Mat.-L.T.D. | 10.5 | 10.0 | | 13.1 | 4.4 | 8.9 |
| 6.9 | 7.4 | 6.1 | Trade Payables | .6 | 7.3 | | 8.7 | 9.0 | 10.1 |
| .2 | .1 | .4 | Income Taxes Payable | .4 | .1 | | .1 | 1.4 | .7 |
| 12.9 | 9.8 | 8.4 | All Other Current | 3.6 | 8.1 | | 8.4 | 13.5 | 17.1 |
| 39.6 | 41.5 | 35.5 | Total Current | 27.2 | 37.9 | | 39.4 | 39.4 | 47.9 |
| 30.3 | 30.0 | 29.3 | Long-Term Debt | 42.8 | 32.1 | | 21.2 | 12.0 | 13.7 |
| .5 | .4 | .2 | Deferred Taxes | .0 | .3 | | .5 | .1 | .2 |
| 6.4 | 5.7 | 7.2 | All Other Non-Current | 6.3 | 4.6 | | 11.9 | 6.1 | 10.0 |
| 23.3 | 22.4 | 27.8 | Net Worth | 23.8 | 25.1 | | 27.1 | 42.4 | 28.3 |
| 100.0 | 100.0 | 100.0 | Total Liabilities & Net Worth | 100.0 | 100.0 | | 100.0 | 100.0 | 100.0 |
| | | | INCOME DATA | | | | | | |
| 100.0 | 100.0 | 100.0 | Net Sales | 100.0 | 100.0 | | 100.0 | 100.0 | 100.0 |
| | | | Gross Profit | | | | | | |
| 84.8 | 80.4 | 79.2 | Operating Expenses | 63.3 | 84.7 | | 87.4 | 88.1 | 88.6 |
| 15.2 | 19.6 | 20.8 | Operating Profit | 36.7 | 15.3 | | 12.6 | 11.9 | 11.4 |
| 6.6 | 5.6 | 4.6 | All Other Expenses (net) | 6.5 | 4.4 | | 3.3 | 3.9 | 2.9 |
| 8.6 | 14.0 | 16.2 | Profit Before Taxes | 30.2 | 10.8 | | 9.4 | 8.0 | 8.5 |
| | | | RATIOS | | | | | | |
| 2.4 | 2.4 | 2.0 | | 1.8 | 4.4 | | 1.8 | 2.4 | 1.5 |
| 1.2 | 1.0 | 1.0 | Current | .7 | 1.3 | | 1.0 | 1.5 | .8 |
| .5 | .4 | .4 | | .2 | .3 | | .5 | .7 | .5 |
| 1.8 | 1.5 | 1.4 | | 1.7 | 1.7 | | .8 | 1.3 | 1.2 |
| .7 | .5 | .6 | Quick | .4 | .6 | | .5 | .8 | .6 |
| .2 | .2 | .2 | | .2 | .2 | | .1 | .5 | .3 |
| 0  UND | 0  UND | 0  UND | | 0  UND | 0  UND | 10  36.5 | 30  12.1 | 32  11.4 | |
| 19  19.2 | 21  17.5 | 21  17.3 | Sales/Receivables | 0  UND | 6  65.9 | 35  10.3 | 35  10.4 | 51  7.1 | |
| 52  7.1 | 51  7.1 | 47  7.8 | | 19  19.7 | 36  10.0 | 49  7.5 | 54  6.7 | 73  5.0 | |
| | | | Cost of Sales/Inventory | | | | | | |
| | | | Cost of Sales/Payables | | | | | | |
| 2.7 | 5.2 | 7.1 | | 4.7 | 3.4 | | 8.5 | 6.3 | 13.6 |
| 17.4 | -281.0 | NM | Sales/Working Capital | -30.2 | 16.8 | | -93.4 | 10.1 | -13.7 |
| -5.6 | -4.5 | -4.0 | | -2.7 | -2.9 | | -7.6 | -5.9 | -4.2 |
| 7.1 | 9.5 | 9.8 | | 19.3 | 9.5 | | 9.4 | 17.7 | 11.0 |
| (91)  2.3 | (92)  2.8 | (105)  3.2 | EBIT/Interest | (29)  4.0 | (20)  3.3 | (17)  2.2 | (14)  3.4 | (18)  3.4 | |
| 1.0 | 1.2 | 1.7 | | 2.0 | 1.5 | | 1.0 | 1.6 | .1 |
| | | 8.6 | Net Profit + Depr., Dep., | | | | | | |
| | (17)  4.0 | Amort./Cur. Mat. L/T/D | | | | | | | |
| | | 1.5 | | | | | | | |
| .2 | .3 | .5 | | .8 | .5 | | .9 | .2 | .4 |
| 1.8 | 1.7 | 1.7 | Fixed/Worth | 2.3 | 1.7 | | 1.8 | 1.0 | 1.0 |
| 7.4 | 7.4 | 8.5 | | 34.7 | NM | | 20.8 | 3.1 | 8.6 |
| 1.5 | 1.0 | .9 | | .7 | 1.1 | | 1.7 | .6 | .8 |
| 3.8 | 3.3 | 2.9 | Debt/Worth | 2.3 | 2.8 | | 3.1 | 1.8 | 4.7 |
| 26.3 | 26.2 | 12.4 | | 54.1 | NM | | 27.3 | 5.4 | 8.7 |
| 42.8 | 51.3 | 57.4 | % Profit Before Taxes/Tangible Net Worth | 121.9 | 59.7 | | 68.2 | 56.0 | 48.7 |
| (87)  16.9 | (100)  19.7 | (108)  23.8 | | (36)  28.3 | (21)  23.9 | (16)  20.2 | (14)  24.8 | (15)  15.7 | |
| 2.6 | 9.5 | 7.5 | | 9.0 | 9.4 | | 1.0 | 6.5 | 5.6 |
| 12.1 | 15.5 | 14.7 | % Profit Before Taxes/Total Assets | 19.8 | 15.3 | | 12.5 | 14.0 | 12.7 |
| 4.5 | 5.1 | 6.1 | | 7.1 | 4.4 | | 5.5 | 7.6 | 5.4 |
| .0 | .2 | 1.5 | | 2.4 | -.6 | | .1 | 1.4 | -.9 |
| 37.6 | 20.6 | 12.1 | | 2.6 | 29.2 | | 12.0 | 29.1 | 12.3 |
| 2.6 | 2.3 | 2.0 | Sales/Net Fixed Assets | .9 | 2.0 | | 2.4 | 10.2 | 3.5 |
| .8 | .7 | .7 | | .4 | .6 | | 1.1 | 2.2 | 1.7 |
| 1.7 | 2.0 | 1.9 | | .9 | 1.9 | | 2.1 | 3.1 | 1.9 |
| .7 | .8 | .8 | Sales/Total Assets | .5 | .6 | | .9 | 2.1 | 1.2 |
| .4 | .4 | .4 | | .2 | .3 | | .5 | .8 | .6 |
| 2.4 | 2.9 | 2.6 | | 14.3 | 3.0 | | 1.2 | .9 | .7 |
| (70)  14.6 | (83)  16.5 | (96)  13.3 | % Depr., Dep., Amort./Sales | (29)  36.4 | (20)  16.0 | (16)  12.6 | (12)  2.6 | (12)  6.8 | |
| 62.3 | 54.5 | 37.3 | | 67.5 | 43.9 | | 19.4 | 6.9 | 9.5 |
| 4.2 | 1.8 | 2.2 | % Officers', Directors' Owners' Comp/Sales | | 3.2 | | | | |
| (19)  5.3 | (24)  7.0 | (34)  5.8 | | | (10)  8.3 | | | | |
| 11.8 | 11.4 | 11.3 | | | 10.0 | | | | |
| 1612105M | 1231676M | 2098727M | Net Sales ($) | 16405M | 51462M | 32985M | 126604M | 214357M | 1656914M |
| 2952130M | 1430599M | 2160236M | Total Assets ($) | 51585M | 139069M | 27518M | 157111M | 211174M | 1573779M |

© RMA 2012          M = $ thousand    MM = $ million
See Pages 9 through 22 for Explanation of Ratios and Data

| Current Data Sorted by Assets | | | | | | | Comparative Historical Data | |
|---|---|---|---|---|---|---|---|---|
| | | | | | | Type of Statement | | |
| 2 | 3 | 8 | 35 | 9 | 18 | Unqualified | 87 | 69 |
| 4 | 7 | 45 | 27 | 2 | | Reviewed | 93 | 77 |
| 10 | 31 | 43 | 8 | | | Compiled | 101 | 75 |
| 44 | 55 | 43 | 3 | | | Tax Returns | 109 | 129 |
| 23 | 68 | 98 | 52 | 14 | 16 | Other | 226 | 225 |
| | 79 (4/1-9/30/11) | | 589 (10/1/11-3/31/12) | | | | 4/1/07-3/31/08 ALL | 4/1/08-3/31/09 ALL |
| 0-500M | 500M-2MM | 2-10MM | 10-50MM | 50-100MM | 100-250MM | | | |
| 83 | 164 | 237 | 125 | 25 | 34 | NUMBER OF STATEMENTS | 616 | 575 |
| % | % | % | % | % | % | ASSETS | % | % |
| 23.3 | 10.9 | 9.2 | 7.5 | 11.0 | 4.1 | Cash & Equivalents | 8.5 | 9.5 |
| 9.1 | 11.3 | 14.0 | 16.6 | 11.4 | 16.8 | Trade Receivables (net) | 15.1 | 13.7 |
| 3.2 | 6.2 | 4.8 | 8.1 | 6.8 | 2.0 | Inventory | 7.6 | 6.7 |
| 2.1 | 2.9 | 4.8 | 4.1 | 5.7 | 4.1 | All Other Current | 4.2 | 4.7 |
| 37.7 | 31.3 | 32.7 | 36.3 | 34.9 | 27.0 | Total Current | 35.4 | 34.6 |
| 47.7 | 57.6 | 57.4 | 51.4 | 44.8 | 46.7 | Fixed Assets (net) | 53.9 | 53.3 |
| 4.0 | 3.4 | 2.9 | 3.1 | 4.5 | 9.1 | Intangibles (net) | 2.2 | 2.4 |
| 10.5 | 7.7 | 7.0 | 9.2 | 15.9 | 17.2 | All Other Non-Current | 8.6 | 9.7 |
| 100.0 | 100.0 | 100.0 | 100.0 | 100.0 | 100.0 | Total | 100.0 | 100.0 |
| | | | | | | LIABILITIES | | |
| 15.4 | 8.1 | 7.2 | 10.4 | 15.1 | 6.8 | Notes Payable-Short Term | 11.0 | 9.7 |
| 10.7 | 7.8 | 7.2 | 6.9 | 4.7 | 5.7 | Cur. Mat.-L.T.D. | 9.9 | 10.1 |
| 5.3 | 4.9 | 4.7 | 5.4 | 4.4 | 5.0 | Trade Payables | 6.1 | 5.2 |
| .0 | .0 | .3 | .1 | .1 | .3 | Income Taxes Payable | .2 | .2 |
| 7.5 | 8.3 | 6.6 | 6.1 | 3.0 | 5.7 | All Other Current | 8.0 | 6.9 |
| 38.8 | 29.2 | 26.1 | 28.9 | 27.3 | 23.4 | Total Current | 35.2 | 32.1 |
| 41.5 | 44.7 | 35.4 | 28.2 | 36.4 | 35.3 | Long-Term Debt | 35.4 | 36.6 |
| .1 | .4 | .6 | 1.5 | 2.0 | 2.0 | Deferred Taxes | .7 | .6 |
| 9.6 | 5.8 | 5.0 | 5.6 | 9.4 | 5.3 | All Other Non-Current | 4.4 | 5.1 |
| 10.1 | 20.0 | 32.8 | 35.7 | 25.0 | 34.0 | Net Worth | 24.3 | 25.6 |
| 100.0 | 100.0 | 100.0 | 100.0 | 100.0 | 100.0 | Total Liabilties & Net Worth | 100.0 | 100.0 |
| | | | | | | INCOME DATA | | |
| 100.0 | 100.0 | 100.0 | 100.0 | 100.0 | 100.0 | Net Sales | 100.0 | 100.0 |
| | | | | | | Gross Profit | | |
| 72.2 | 74.6 | 74.8 | 83.3 | 71.3 | 78.8 | Operating Expenses | 81.0 | 80.1 |
| 27.8 | 25.4 | 25.2 | 16.7 | 28.7 | 21.2 | Operating Profit | 19.0 | 19.9 |
| 4.3 | 8.1 | 10.2 | 4.8 | 15.5 | 7.7 | All Other Expenses (net) | 6.4 | 7.1 |
| 23.5 | 17.3 | 15.0 | 11.9 | 13.2 | 13.4 | Profit Before Taxes | 12.6 | 12.8 |
| | | | | | | RATIOS | | |
| 3.3 | 2.9 | 2.4 | 2.8 | 3.5 | 2.3 | | 1.9 | 1.9 |
| 1.1 | 1.2 | 1.1 | 1.3 | 1.4 | 1.3 | Current | 1.0 | 1.0 |
| .3 | .5 | .5 | .7 | .9 | .5 | | .5 | .5 |
| 3.0 | 1.9 | 1.8 | 1.7 | 3.3 | 1.8 | | 1.3 | 1.4 |
| .8 | .7 | (236) .7 | .8 | 1.0 | .8 | Quick | .7 | .7 |
| .2 | .3 | .3 | .4 | .3 | .3 | | .3 | .3 |
| 0 UND | 0 UND | 0 UND | 22 16.9 | 6 64.7 | 21 17.2 | | 0 UND | 0 UND |
| 0 UND | 10 37.9 | 28 13.2 | 43 8.5 | 33 10.9 | 58 6.3 | Sales/Receivables | 28 13.1 | 23 15.8 |
| 26 14.0 | 40 9.2 | 51 7.2 | 70 5.2 | 69 5.3 | 101 3.6 | | 57 6.4 | 48 7.6 |
| | | | | | | Cost of Sales/Inventory | | |
| | | | | | | Cost of Sales/Payables | | |
| 4.8 | 6.9 | 4.2 | 3.8 | 1.6 | 5.7 | | 6.2 | 6.6 |
| 41.8 | 27.8 | 46.6 | 16.8 | 3.9 | 12.1 | Sales/Working Capital | 129.1 | 154.6 |
| -5.3 | -5.8 | -4.9 | -13.1 | -20.0 | -6.1 | | -6.4 | -6.6 |
| 19.2 | 14.0 | 10.4 | 9.7 | 6.4 | 11.7 | | 6.5 | 6.7 |
| (63) 5.8 | (123) 4.2 | (177) 4.3 | (111) 3.9 | (17) 3.6 | (26) 6.3 | EBIT/Interest | (490) 2.9 | (457) 2.6 |
| 1.3 | 1.4 | 1.8 | 1.8 | 1.4 | 2.0 | | 1.3 | 1.0 |
| | | 4.1 | 7.0 | | | | 4.3 | 4.1 |
| | | (50) 2.5 | (26) 2.1 | | | Net Profit + Depr., Dep., Amort./Cur. Mat. L/T/D | (98) 1.9 | (79) 1.7 |
| | | 1.5 | 1.6 | | | | 1.3 | 1.1 |
| .4 | .8 | .8 | .5 | .7 | .7 | | .7 | .8 |
| 1.8 | 1.8 | 1.7 | 1.6 | 2.0 | 1.7 | Fixed/Worth | 1.9 | 2.1 |
| -5.4 | 39.1 | 5.6 | 3.1 | 10.0 | 3.2 | | 7.5 | 8.2 |
| .6 | .8 | .8 | .8 | 1.2 | 1.5 | | 1.3 | 1.1 |
| 3.4 | 2.5 | 2.1 | 1.9 | 3.7 | 2.3 | Debt/Worth | 3.3 | 3.1 |
| -4.8 | 39.4 | 7.6 | 4.5 | 17.1 | 11.0 | | 12.8 | 13.6 |
| 122.7 | 53.2 | 43.7 | 30.6 | 29.0 | 47.9 | | 54.8 | 54.6 |
| (50) 40.9 | (124) 20.7 | (209) 19.9 | (117) 13.3 | (20) 16.2 | (29) 23.4 | % Profit Before Taxes/Tangible Net Worth | (521) 26.2 | (479) 21.2 |
| 1.6 | 5.0 | 5.7 | 7.3 | 7.2 | 9.5 | | 9.0 | 3.4 |
| 45.4 | 20.7 | 12.4 | 10.1 | 9.1 | 13.7 | | 15.6 | 15.5 |
| 18.9 | 6.1 | 5.6 | 5.3 | 4.0 | 4.1 | % Profit Before Taxes/Total Assets | 6.2 | 4.9 |
| .9 | .8 | 1.6 | 1.6 | 1.2 | 1.5 | | 1.1 | .0 |
| 11.0 | 7.3 | 6.2 | 7.1 | 11.7 | 7.0 | | 7.3 | 7.0 |
| 2.8 | 1.7 | 1.6 | 1.7 | .7 | 1.1 | Sales/Net Fixed Assets | 2.1 | 2.0 |
| 1.2 | .4 | .3 | .7 | .5 | .6 | | .7 | .7 |
| 2.7 | 2.2 | 1.9 | 1.4 | .8 | 1.2 | | 1.9 | 1.8 |
| 1.2 | .8 | .6 | .8 | .3 | .5 | Sales/Total Assets | .9 | .9 |
| .5 | .3 | .2 | .3 | .1 | .2 | | .4 | .4 |
| 11.5 | 6.5 | 5.8 | 6.2 | 4.5 | 3.8 | | 4.6 | 5.5 |
| (44) 31.4 | (122) 16.1 | (201) 15.2 | (110) 14.8 | (19) 10.7 | (11) 8.3 | % Depr., Dep., Amort./Sales | (500) 13.2 | (459) 15.2 |
| 51.8 | 31.4 | 27.8 | 26.9 | 21.1 | 21.8 | | 33.0 | 33.0 |
| 3.0 | 2.5 | 2.3 | 1.4 | | | | 2.2 | 2.2 |
| (17) 7.2 | (41) 4.0 | (52) 5.1 | (25) 4.4 | | | % Officers', Directors' Owners' Comp/Sales | (152) 4.5 | (125) 5.5 |
| 11.9 | 10.2 | 11.8 | 7.5 | | | | 8.5 | 10.3 |
| 46117M | 251166M | 1229166M | 2863294M | 1084582M | 3577743M | Net Sales ($) | 8465540M | 7865076M |
| 22798M | 187140M | 1111819M | 2803989M | 1734544M | 5578623M | Total Assets ($) | 10056888M | 9468348M |

M = $ thousand    MM = $ million
See Pages 9 through 22 for Explanation of Ratios and Data

## Comparative Historical Data

## Current Data Sorted by Sales

| Type of Statement | 4/1/09-3/31/10 ALL | 4/1/10-3/31/11 ALL | 4/1/11-3/31/12 ALL | 0-1MM | 1-3MM | 3-5MM | 5-10MM | 10-25MM | 25MM & OVER |
|---|---|---|---|---|---|---|---|---|---|
| Unqualified | 74 | 69 | 75 | 6 | 3 | 4 | 10 | 21 | 31 |
| Reviewed | 85 | 95 | 85 | 13 | 16 | 9 | 15 | 19 | 13 |
| Compiled | 69 | 81 | 92 | 34 | 26 | 16 | 11 | 4 | 1 |
| Tax Returns | 114 | 108 | 145 | 89 | 35 | 7 | 6 | 7 | 1 |
| Other | 220 | 207 | 271 | 85 | 47 | 30 | 31 | 41 | 37 |
| | | | | 79 (4/1-9/30/11) | | | 589 (10/1/11-3/31/12) | | |
| NUMBER OF STATEMENTS | 562 | 560 | 668 | 227 | 127 | 66 | 73 | 92 | 83 |
| **ASSETS** | % | % | % | % | % | % | % | % | % |
| Cash & Equivalents | 9.2 | 9.2 | 10.9 | 11.5 | 10.4 | 13.7 | 13.5 | 9.6 | 6.6 |
| Trade Receivables (net) | 14.1 | 15.0 | 13.3 | 6.0 | 12.4 | 16.6 | 17.9 | 21.5 | 18.6 |
| Inventory | 6.9 | 6.0 | 5.5 | .3 | 6.2 | 7.7 | 8.6 | 6.8 | 12.2 |
| All Other Current | 4.5 | 4.6 | 3.8 | 3.5 | 3.7 | 5.3 | 2.6 | 4.3 | 4.5 |
| Total Current | 34.7 | 34.8 | 33.4 | 21.3 | 32.8 | 43.3 | 42.6 | 42.3 | 42.0 |
| Fixed Assets (net) | 53.2 | 52.7 | 54.1 | 66.1 | 55.8 | 43.3 | 46.9 | 44.7 | 44.1 |
| Intangibles (net) | 2.3 | 3.3 | 3.6 | 2.8 | 4.7 | 3.6 | 2.1 | 3.2 | 5.0 |
| All Other Non-Current | 9.8 | 9.2 | 8.9 | 9.8 | 6.8 | 9.9 | 8.3 | 9.8 | 8.0 |
| Total | 100.0 | 100.0 | 100.0 | 100.0 | 100.0 | 100.0 | 100.0 | 100.0 | 100.0 |
| **LIABILITIES** | | | | | | | | | |
| Notes Payable-Short Term | 10.8 | 9.8 | 9.3 | 8.0 | 7.7 | 12.1 | 11.4 | 9.6 | 11.3 |
| Cur. Mat.-L.T.D. | 10.3 | 10.1 | 7.6 | 8.1 | 9.0 | 7.9 | 7.6 | 6.2 | 5.0 |
| Trade Payables | 5.3 | 5.9 | 5.0 | 1.9 | 4.3 | 7.0 | 6.6 | 7.5 | 8.4 |
| Income Taxes Payable | .1 | .3 | .2 | .0 | .0 | .3 | .3 | .5 | .2 |
| All Other Current | 7.7 | 7.8 | 6.8 | 5.2 | 6.4 | 9.0 | 7.1 | 8.4 | 8.5 |
| Total Current | 34.2 | 34.0 | 28.9 | 23.2 | 27.4 | 36.4 | 32.9 | 32.2 | 33.4 |
| Long-Term Debt | 32.3 | 32.6 | 37.1 | 50.4 | 42.3 | 24.4 | 24.8 | 23.8 | 28.4 |
| Deferred Taxes | .6 | .8 | .8 | .0 | .8 | .4 | 1.6 | 1.2 | 1.8 |
| All Other Non-Current | 5.8 | 7.4 | 6.1 | 4.9 | 9.4 | 3.5 | 6.8 | 4.1 | 7.6 |
| Net Worth | 27.2 | 25.2 | 27.2 | 21.4 | 20.1 | 35.3 | 33.9 | 38.7 | 28.7 |
| Total Liabilities & Net Worth | 100.0 | 100.0 | 100.0 | 100.0 | 100.0 | 100.0 | 100.0 | 100.0 | 100.0 |
| **INCOME DATA** | | | | | | | | | |
| Net Sales | 100.0 | 100.0 | 100.0 | 100.0 | 100.0 | 100.0 | 100.0 | 100.0 | 100.0 |
| Gross Profit | | | | | | | | | |
| Operating Expenses | 82.6 | 83.2 | 76.1 | 59.1 | 79.2 | 85.1 | 88.2 | 85.9 | 89.3 |
| Operating Profit | 17.4 | 16.8 | 23.9 | 40.9 | 20.8 | 14.9 | 11.8 | 14.1 | 10.7 |
| All Other Expenses (net) | 6.8 | 5.3 | 8.0 | 15.3 | 6.2 | 4.2 | 3.3 | 3.0 | 3.6 |
| Profit Before Taxes | 10.6 | 11.5 | 15.9 | 25.7 | 14.7 | 10.7 | 8.5 | 11.1 | 7.1 |
| **RATIOS** | | | | | | | | | |
| Current | 2.2 | 2.3 | 2.6 | 2.3 | 3.3 | 2.9 | 2.7 | 2.5 | 2.3 |
| | 1.1 | 1.1 | 1.2 | .8 | 1.2 | 1.5 | 1.4 | 1.2 | 1.3 |
| | .5 | .5 | .5 | .2 | .4 | .9 | .8 | .7 | .8 |
| Quick | 1.5 | 1.7 | 1.9 | 2.0 | 2.4 | 2.1 | 2.0 | 1.9 | 1.4 |
| | .7 | .7 (667) | .8 | (226) .6 | .7 | 1.2 | 1.0 | .9 | .7 |
| | .3 | .3 | .3 | .1 | .3 | .5 | .5 | .4 | .4 |
| Sales/Receivables | 0 UND | 1 490.2 | 0 UND | 0 UND | 0 UND | 4 88.8 | 17 21.8 | 26 14.0 | 25 14.6 |
| | 27 13.3 | 31 11.8 | 26 14.2 | 0 UND | 18 20.2 | 28 13.1 | 35 10.3 | 46 7.9 | 43 8.5 |
| | 55 6.7 | 59 6.2 | 54 6.8 | 29 12.4 | 46 8.0 | 54 6.8 | 57 6.4 | 73 5.0 | 61 6.0 |
| Cost of Sales/Inventory | | | | | | | | | |
| Cost of Sales/Payables | | | | | | | | | |
| Sales/Working Capital | 5.5 | 5.2 | 4.5 | 2.5 | 5.2 | 4.3 | 4.7 | 4.4 | 6.3 |
| | 40.9 | 49.4 | 22.4 | -18.8 | 30.2 | 12.2 | 12.2 | 24.7 | 16.8 |
| | -6.3 | -6.6 | -6.3 | -2.5 | -6.6 | -37.1 | -31.6 | -15.3 | -18.8 |
| EBIT/Interest | 6.0 | 8.4 | 11.2 | 13.1 | 7.8 | 12.4 | 10.0 | 13.6 | 13.9 |
| | (454) 2.2 | (483) 3.2 | (517) 4.2 | (133) 4.0 | (102) 2.9 | (60) 4.5 | (67) 4.4 | (81) 4.6 | (74) 4.8 |
| | .5 | 1.1 | 1.6 | 1.5 | 1.4 | 1.5 | 1.8 | 2.0 | 2.0 |
| Net Profit + Depr., Dep., Amort./Cur. Mat. L/T/D | 4.0 | 5.0 | 4.1 | 2.7 | 3.3 | | 4.5 | 6.3 | 11.4 |
| | (76) 1.6 | (87) 2.1 | (92) 2.2 | (14) 1.5 | (15) 2.6 | | (15) 3.3 | (23) 2.3 | (16) 2.4 |
| | 1.0 | 1.0 | 1.4 | 1.1 | 1.5 | | 1.7 | 1.5 | 1.6 |
| Fixed/Worth | .7 | .8 | .7 | 1.0 | .8 | .3 | .6 | .4 | .6 |
| | 1.8 | 1.8 | 1.8 | 2.2 | 2.2 | 1.1 | 1.3 | 1.4 | 1.8 |
| | 9.5 | 9.6 | 6.0 | 23.9 | 10.3 | 2.8 | 2.5 | 2.6 | 4.0 |
| Debt/Worth | .9 | .9 | .9 | .9 | 1.0 | .7 | .8 | .8 | 1.2 |
| | 2.6 | 2.3 | 2.3 | 2.8 | 3.0 | 1.4 | 1.7 | 2.0 | 2.3 |
| | 15.9 | 14.8 | 9.8 | -224.0 | 40.8 | 5.7 | 3.8 | 5.5 | 7.9 |
| % Profit Before Taxes/Tangible Net Worth | 40.0 | 40.8 | 45.1 | 43.2 | 45.5 | 44.8 | 44.2 | 50.5 | 39.4 |
| | (456) 16.4 | (450) 18.2 | (549) 19.0 | (170) 14.8 | (97) 21.5 | (59) 14.5 | (67) 20.5 | (85) 24.8 | (71) 21.5 |
| | 1.8 | 2.6 | 6.3 | 4.5 | 3.1 | 3.7 | 8.1 | 9.4 | 10.0 |
| % Profit Before Taxes/Total Assets | 13.6 | 14.1 | 15.1 | 14.3 | 15.9 | 16.3 | 17.9 | 12.3 | 13.7 |
| | 3.4 | 4.9 | 5.9 | 4.9 | 6.0 | 4.7 | 7.3 | 6.6 | 6.0 |
| | -1.0 | .1 | 1.3 | .9 | .3 | 1.1 | 2.3 | 2.5 | 2.3 |
| Sales/Net Fixed Assets | 6.3 | 6.0 | 7.0 | 1.8 | 7.4 | 13.8 | 10.7 | 12.8 | 10.8 |
| | 1.8 | 2.2 | 1.7 | .5 | 2.0 | 3.6 | 3.8 | 2.8 | 3.1 |
| | .7 | .8 | .5 | .2 | .4 | .9 | 1.3 | 1.0 | 1.1 |
| Sales/Total Assets | 1.5 | 1.8 | 1.8 | .7 | 2.3 | 2.6 | 2.5 | 2.1 | 2.0 |
| | .8 | .9 | .8 | .3 | .9 | 1.2 | 1.7 | 1.3 | 1.3 |
| | .4 | .4 | .3 | .1 | .3 | .4 | .8 | .6 | .7 |
| % Depr., Dep., Amort./Sales | 5.3 | 6.5 | 6.4 | 16.6 | 7.9 | 4.1 | 3.6 | 3.3 | 2.4 |
| | (446) 16.6 | (449) 15.1 | (507) 15.4 | (171) 26.1 | (97) 18.8 | (49) 11.0 | (61) 9.9 | (75) 11.4 | (54) 6.2 |
| | 35.5 | 35.2 | 28.9 | 49.2 | 34.5 | 25.6 | 19.6 | 17.5 | 10.6 |
| % Officers', Directors' Owners' Comp/Sales | 2.2 | 1.9 | 2.1 | 5.4 | 2.6 | 3.1 | 1.9 | 1.3 | |
| | (114) 4.5 | (122) 4.9 | (140) 4.7 | (27) 10.9 | (32) 13.2 | (27) 5.2 | (20) 4.2 | (25) 2.2 | |
| | 10.2 | 9.6 | 9.8 | 23.1 | 13.2 | 9.3 | 7.7 | 4.8 | |
| Net Sales ($) | 10671039M | 7744054M | 9052068M | 94648M | 223994M | 272062M | 532944M | 1478718M | 6449702M |
| Total Assets ($) | 10084459M | 8810970M | 11438913M | 427253M | 493128M | 564608M | 821428M | 2389514M | 6742982M |

© RMA 2012

M = $ thousand    MM = $ million

See Pages 9 through 22 for Explanation of Ratios and Data

## Current Data Sorted by Assets

## Comparative Historical Data

| | 0-500M | 500M-2MM | 2-10MM | 10-50MM | 50-100MM | 100-250MM | Type of Statement | | 4/1/07-3/31/08 ALL | 4/1/08-3/31/09 ALL |
|---|---|---|---|---|---|---|---|---|---|---|
| | 1 | 4 | 3 | 13 | 3 | 7 | Unqualified | | 12 | 21 |
| | | | 3 | | | | Reviewed | | 2 | 4 |
| | 2 | 2 | 1 | | | | Compiled | | 6 | 3 |
| | 6 | 9 | 9 | | | | Tax Returns | | 15 | 10 |
| | | 3 | 12 | 8 | 4 | 1 | Other | | 26 | 26 |
| | | 7 (4/1-9/30/11) | | 84 (10/1/11-3/31/12) | | | | | | |
| | 9 | 18 | 28 | 21 | 7 | 8 | NUMBER OF STATEMENTS | | 61 | 64 |
| | % | % | % | % | % | % | ASSETS | | % | % |
| | | 10.9 | 7.7 | 20.6 | | | Cash & Equivalents | | 10.9 | 9.2 |
| | | 5.6 | 2.9 | 9.0 | | | Trade Receivables (net) | | 11.7 | 14.3 |
| | | 6.0 | 2.5 | 13.0 | | | Inventory | | 8.3 | 3.3 |
| | | 6.8 | 8.5 | 8.4 | | | All Other Current | | 5.0 | 4.0 |
| | | 29.3 | 21.5 | 50.9 | | | Total Current | | 35.8 | 30.8 |
| | | 52.0 | 57.4 | 22.3 | | | Fixed Assets (net) | | 46.6 | 43.6 |
| | | 12.6 | 5.3 | 11.6 | | | Intangibles (net) | | 6.0 | 12.4 |
| | | 6.1 | 15.9 | 15.2 | | | All Other Non-Current | | 11.6 | 13.2 |
| | | 100.0 | 100.0 | 100.0 | | | Total | | 100.0 | 100.0 |
| | | | | | | | LIABILITIES | | | |
| | | 12.8 | 2.5 | 6.7 | | | Notes Payable-Short Term | | 7.0 | 14.1 |
| | | 4.6 | 5.2 | 3.6 | | | Cur. Mat.-L.T.D. | | 3.7 | 2.8 |
| | | 4.8 | 1.6 | 3.1 | | | Trade Payables | | 8.8 | 7.2 |
| | | .0 | .0 | .2 | | | Income Taxes Payable | | .0 | .0 |
| | | 6.2 | 8.6 | 15.3 | | | All Other Current | | 13.6 | 11.8 |
| | | 28.4 | 17.9 | 29.0 | | | Total Current | | 33.1 | 35.9 |
| | | 46.0 | 54.3 | 18.8 | | | Long-Term Debt | | 44.0 | 38.3 |
| | | .0 | .0 | .3 | | | Deferred Taxes | | .4 | .5 |
| | | 15.3 | 2.0 | 1.4 | | | All Other Non-Current | | 4.7 | 7.4 |
| | | 10.3 | 25.9 | 50.5 | | | Net Worth | | 17.9 | 17.8 |
| | | 100.0 | 100.0 | 100.0 | | | Total Liabilties & Net Worth | | 100.0 | 100.0 |
| | | | | | | | INCOME DATA | | | |
| | | 100.0 | 100.0 | 100.0 | | | Net Sales | | 100.0 | 100.0 |
| | | | | | | | Gross Profit | | | |
| | | 68.2 | 55.9 | 74.0 | | | Operating Expenses | | 72.7 | 70.2 |
| | | 31.8 | 44.1 | 26.0 | | | Operating Profit | | 27.3 | 29.8 |
| | | 7.9 | 20.9 | 10.6 | | | All Other Expenses (net) | | 11.6 | 11.4 |
| | | 23.9 | 23.2 | 15.4 | | | Profit Before Taxes | | 15.7 | 18.4 |
| | | | | | | | RATIOS | | | |
| | | 2.9 | 3.5 | 4.1 | | | | | 1.5 | 2.3 |
| | | 1.1 | .6 | 1.4 | | | Current | | .9 | 1.0 |
| | | .5 | .2 | .9 | | | | | .5 | .4 |
| | | 1.4 | 1.0 | 3.5 | | | | | 1.3 | 1.4 |
| | | .6 | .5 | .9 | | | Quick | | .6 | .7 |
| | | .2 | .1 | .2 | | | | | .1 | .3 |
| | 0 UND | 0 UND | 3 140.0 | | | | | 0 UND | 0 UND | |
| | 4 94.6 | 0 UND | 26 13.9 | | | Sales/Receivables | | 3 126.8 | 14 25.6 |
| | 26 13.8 | 18 20.5 | 49 7.5 | | | | | 30 12.1 | 44 8.3 |
| | | | | | | | Cost of Sales/Inventory | | | |
| | | | | | | | Cost of Sales/Payables | | | |
| | | 3.5 | 2.8 | 2.3 | | | | | 11.4 | 8.6 |
| | | UND | -7.7 | 4.7 | | | Sales/Working Capital | | -31.0 | -816.0 |
| | | -11.7 | -2.9 | -218.7 | | | | | -5.9 | -5.7 |
| | | 38.6 | | 38.6 | | | | | 11.4 | 13.0 |
| | (14) | 5.4 | (12) 2.7 | | | | EBIT/Interest | (37) 4.5 | (40) 4.8 |
| | | 2.0 | | 1.6 | | | | | 1.5 | 1.9 |
| | | | | | | | Net Profit + Depr., Dep., Amort./Cur. Mat. L/T/D | | | 8.8 |
| | | | | | | | | | (10) 4.1 | |
| | | | | | | | | | | 2.0 |
| | | .9 | .4 | .1 | | | | | .5 | .5 |
| | | 7.0 | 3.4 | .3 | | | Fixed/Worth | | 3.5 | 3.1 |
| | | -5.4 | NM | 1.4 | | | | | -5.0 | 111.2 |
| | | 3.4 | 1.3 | .3 | | | | | 1.3 | 1.4 |
| | | 56.3 | 6.6 | 2.3 | | | Debt/Worth | | 4.3 | 5.2 |
| | | -3.5 | -51.4 | 4.8 | | | | | -14.0 | 213.2 |
| | | 418.7 | 101.8 | 27.5 | | | | | 113.8 | 163.2 |
| | (11) | 53.3 | (20) 15.3 | (20) 14.0 | | | % Profit Before Taxes/Tangible Net Worth | (41) 34.2 | (49) 44.1 |
| | | 11.1 | 4.5 | 7.8 | | | | | 6.6 | 20.3 |
| | | 30.2 | 12.3 | 18.3 | | | | | 19.9 | 24.2 |
| | | 13.6 | 4.8 | 4.5 | | | % Profit Before Taxes/Total Assets | | 8.0 | 7.7 |
| | | 4.0 | 1.0 | .9 | | | | | .9 | 1.3 |
| | | 26.3 | 12.9 | 43.6 | | | | | 30.7 | 23.5 |
| | | 2.9 | .2 | 8.2 | | | Sales/Net Fixed Assets | | 3.6 | 4.7 |
| | | .3 | .1 | 2.0 | | | | | .3 | .3 |
| | | 2.3 | .5 | 1.3 | | | | | 2.2 | 1.9 |
| | | .7 | .2 | .7 | | | Sales/Total Assets | | .9 | .9 |
| | | .2 | .1 | .2 | | | | | .2 | .2 |
| | | 1.3 | 1.4 | .6 | | | | | 1.7 | 1.2 |
| | (13) | 4.1 | (25) 15.2 | (15) 2.1 | | | % Depr., Dep., Amort./Sales | (46) 5.3 | (48) 3.8 |
| | | 15.0 | 25.7 | 9.1 | | | | | 16.3 | 18.4 |
| | | | | | | | | | | 2.7 |
| | | | | | | | % Officers', Directors' Owners' Comp/Sales | (11) 8.3 | |
| | | | | | | | | | 31.4 | |
| | 3587M | 23365M | 52588M | 353101M | 313248M | 1809473M | Net Sales ($) | | 859047M | 1026808M |
| | 2019M | 19140M | 123154M | 475992M | 478492M | 1325473M | Total Assets ($) | | 719907M | 997162M |

M = $ thousand   MM = $ million
See Pages 9 through 22 for Explanation of Ratios and Data

## Comparative Historical Data | | Type of Statement | ## Current Data Sorted by Sales

| | | | Type of Statement | | | | | | |
|---|---|---|---|---|---|---|---|---|---|
| 22 | 22 | 31 | Unqualified | 3 | 3 | 1 | 4 | 9 | 11 |
| 1 | 7 | 3 | Reviewed | 1 | 2 | | | | |
| 4 | 4 | 5 | Compiled | 4 | | 1 | | | |
| 17 | 17 | 24 | Tax Returns | 18 | 5 | 1 | 2 | | |
| 24 | 24 | 28 | Other | 9 | 8 | | 2 | 4 | 3 |
| 4/1/09-3/31/10 ALL | 4/1/10-3/31/11 ALL | 4/1/11-3/31/12 ALL | | 7 (4/1-9/30/11) | | | 84 (10/1/11-3/31/12) | | |
| | | | | 0-1MM | 1-3MM | 3-5MM | 5-10MM | 10-25MM | 25MM & OVER |
| 68 | 74 | 91 | NUMBER OF STATEMENTS | 35 | 18 | 4 | 7 | 13 | 14 |
| % | % | % | ASSETS | % | % | % | % | % | % |
| 14.4 | 21.2 | 14.4 | Cash & Equivalents | 8.8 | 12.8 | | | 22.0 | 25.1 |
| 8.2 | 8.1 | 5.7 | Trade Receivables (net) | 1.9 | 8.1 | | | 9.7 | 9.1 |
| 2.1 | 3.6 | 6.2 | Inventory | 1.5 | 10.9 | | | 7.5 | 11.4 |
| 8.4 | 7.8 | 7.7 | All Other Current | 3.8 | 14.3 | | | 11.9 | 8.4 |
| 33.1 | 40.7 | 33.9 | Total Current | 15.9 | 46.1 | | | 51.2 | 54.0 |
| 39.6 | 39.0 | 40.7 | Fixed Assets (net) | 71.0 | 22.8 | | | 16.8 | 18.7 |
| 11.9 | 9.7 | 10.5 | Intangibles (net) | 4.6 | 13.6 | | | 20.0 | 16.9 |
| 15.3 | 10.6 | 14.9 | All Other Non-Current | 8.5 | 17.5 | | | 12.0 | 10.4 |
| 100.0 | 100.0 | 100.0 | Total | 100.0 | 100.0 | | | 100.0 | 100.0 |
| | | | LIABILITIES | | | | | | |
| 7.5 | 5.9 | 6.7 | Notes Payable-Short Term | 5.6 | 6.8 | | | 9.3 | 3.9 |
| 11.6 | 5.2 | 6.6 | Cur. Mat.-L.T.D. | 10.5 | 1.7 | | | 5.1 | 2.4 |
| 4.9 | 5.9 | 4.1 | Trade Payables | .8 | 7.3 | | | 4.2 | 8.0 |
| .1 | .3 | .1 | Income Taxes Payable | .0 | .0 | | | .3 | .1 |
| 11.9 | 13.2 | 9.5 | All Other Current | 5.5 | 4.8 | | | 17.8 | 17.9 |
| 36.0 | 30.5 | 26.9 | Total Current | 22.5 | 20.6 | | | 36.7 | 32.3 |
| 35.9 | 29.1 | 39.2 | Long-Term Debt | 70.1 | 26.7 | | | 12.0 | 16.9 |
| .3 | .4 | .7 | Deferred Taxes | .0 | .1 | | | .4 | 2.9 |
| 6.5 | 4.2 | 5.3 | All Other Non-Current | 4.7 | 10.2 | | | 1.4 | 3.2 |
| 21.3 | 35.7 | 27.9 | Net Worth | 2.7 | 42.4 | | | 49.5 | 44.6 |
| 100.0 | 100.0 | 100.0 | Total Liabilties & Net Worth | 100.0 | 100.0 | | | 100.0 | 100.0 |
| | | | INCOME DATA | | | | | | |
| 100.0 | 100.0 | 100.0 | Net Sales | 100.0 | 100.0 | | | 100.0 | 100.0 |
| | | | Gross Profit | | | | | | |
| 74.6 | 70.2 | 65.3 | Operating Expenses | 50.4 | 76.6 | | | 78.6 | 78.9 |
| 25.4 | 29.8 | 34.7 | Operating Profit | 49.6 | 23.4 | | | 21.4 | 21.1 |
| 14.1 | 9.7 | 12.5 | All Other Expenses (net) | 21.1 | 6.1 | | | 11.1 | 2.1 |
| 11.3 | 20.1 | 22.2 | Profit Before Taxes | 28.4 | 17.4 | | | 10.3 | 19.0 |
| | | | RATIOS | | | | | | |
| 2.9 | 4.0 | 3.7 | | 2.5 | 53.8 | | | 2.4 | 4.8 |
| 1.0 | 1.2 | 1.1 | Current | .7 | 4.7 | | | 1.1 | 1.7 |
| .5 | .5 | .5 | | .3 | .7 | | | .8 | 1.0 |
| 1.4 | 2.4 | 2.5 | | 1.7 | 11.0 | | | 2.2 | 4.7 |
| .6 | .7 | .7 | Quick | .5 | .8 | | | .6 | 1.5 |
| .2 | .1 | .2 | | .1 | .3 | | | .3 | .5 |
| 0 UND | 0 UND | 0 UND | | 0 UND | 1 332.3 | | 4 83.5 | 6 65.3 | |
| 5 68.1 | 5 76.0 | 3 109.8 | Sales/Receivables | 0 UND | 21 17.6 | | 17 22.1 | 28 12.9 | |
| 29 12.7 | 33 11.2 | 31 11.7 | | 0 UND | 51 7.1 | | 29 12.6 | 50 7.3 | |
| | | | Cost of Sales/Inventory | | | | | | |
| | | | Cost of Sales/Payables | | | | | | |
| 6.4 | 3.5 | 2.6 | | 5.3 | 1.0 | | | 2.4 | 2.2 |
| 208.0 | 30.1 | 22.9 | Sales/Working Capital | -9.1 | 6.4 | | | 14.6 | 8.6 |
| -4.8 | -4.9 | -4.6 | | -3.1 | -29.8 | | | -204.6 | -699.2 |
| 16.3 | 23.9 | 21.8 | | 16.0 | 10.4 | | | | |
| (44) 4.1 | (40) 7.2 | (48) 4.6 | EBIT/Interest | (14) 5.0 | (11) 2.7 | | | | |
| 1.0 | 3.0 | 1.8 | | 2.4 | .2 | | | | |
| 8.9 | | | Net Profit + Depr., Dep., | | | | | | |
| (10) 1.1 | | | Amort./Cur. Mat. L/T/D | | | | | | |
| .5 | | | | | | | | | |
| .5 | .1 | .1 | | 2.2 | .0 | | | .1 | .0 |
| 2.7 | 1.4 | 1.4 | Fixed/Worth | 12.6 | .1 | | | .7 | .2 |
| -1.6 | 9.3 | 67.9 | | -5.7 | NM | | | 1.9 | 1.9 |
| 1.2 | .5 | 1.0 | | 2.0 | .2 | | | .4 | .4 |
| 5.9 | 2.5 | 5.3 | Debt/Worth | 72.2 | 1.9 | | | 4.0 | 3.5 |
| -8.7 | -87.2 | -32.9 | | -6.4 | -80.9 | | | 9.7 | 17.6 |
| 57.2 | 71.8 | 85.9 | % Profit Before Taxes/Tangible | 140.4 | 23.6 | | | 28.6 | 183.9 |
| (43) 18.1 | (55) 25.2 | (66) 22.6 | Net Worth | (19) 12.9 | (13) 13.9 | | (11) 16.0 | (12) 57.6 | |
| .2 | 12.6 | 7.5 | | 1.1 | 8.0 | | | 9.5 | 22.3 |
| 14.9 | 25.0 | 17.6 | % Profit Before Taxes/Total | 20.6 | 14.1 | | | 18.3 | 26.2 |
| 3.7 | 8.5 | 6.1 | Assets | 5.0 | 5.5 | | | 3.9 | 11.0 |
| -2.1 | 3.4 | 1.7 | | .6 | 1.7 | | | .7 | 4.3 |
| 33.8 | 114.5 | 50.8 | | .9 | 151.6 | | | 235.6 | 288.5 |
| 4.9 | 5.3 | 3.1 | Sales/Net Fixed Assets | .3 | 22.5 | | | 11.7 | 30.6 |
| .3 | .4 | .3 | | .1 | 1.7 | | | 4.4 | 2.8 |
| 1.8 | 1.5 | 1.2 | | .6 | 3.1 | | | 1.2 | 1.7 |
| .7 | .7 | .5 | Sales/Total Assets | .2 | .5 | | | .7 | 1.2 |
| .2 | .3 | .2 | | .1 | .2 | | | .3 | .4 |
| 1.5 | 1.0 | 1.3 | | 9.4 | .6 | | | | .2 |
| (52) 3.9 | (51) 3.8 | (67) 4.6 | % Depr., Dep., Amort./Sales | (28) 16.7 | (13) 3.3 | | | (11) 3.2 | |
| 16.3 | 12.7 | 17.5 | | 31.6 | 9.2 | | | | 3.9 |
| 2.1 | | | % Officers', Directors' | | | | | | |
| (11) 8.8 | | | Owners' Comp/Sales | | | | | | |
| 16.8 | | | | | | | | | |
| 2484571M | 2229393M | 2555362M | Net Sales ($) | 14776M | 37722M | 14536M | 50252M | 218182M | 2219894M |
| 1551292M | 1097087M | 2424270M | Total Assets ($) | 69442M | 120941M | 67209M | 264064M | 497365M | 1405249M |

© RMA 2012

M = $ thousand   MM = $ million
See Pages 9 through 22 for Explanation of Ratios and Data

# PROFESSIONAL, SCIENTIFIC, AND TECHNICAL SERVICES

## Current Data Sorted by Assets      Comparative Historical Data

| Type of Statement | 0-500M | 500M-2MM | 2-10MM | 10-50MM | 50-100MM | 100-250MM | | 4/1/07-3/31/08 ALL | 4/1/08-3/31/09 ALL |
|---|---|---|---|---|---|---|---|---|---|
| Unqualified | 5 | 12 | 29 | 38 | 13 | 12 | | 100 | 117 |
| Reviewed | 7 | 32 | 107 | 78 | 8 | 5 | | 176 | 202 |
| Compiled | 88 | 112 | 89 | 22 | 1 | 1 | | 244 | 259 |
| Tax Returns | 412 | 209 | 111 | 15 | 1 | 4 | | 469 | 566 |
| Other | 304 | 306 | 297 | 149 | 29 | 17 | | 769 | 905 |
| | 129 (4/1-9/30/11) | | | 2,383 (10/1/11-3/31/12) | | | | | |
| **NUMBER OF STATEMENTS** | 816 | 671 | 633 | 302 | 51 | 39 | | 1758 | 2049 |
| | % | % | % | % | % | % | | % | % |
| **ASSETS** | | | | | | | | | |
| Cash & Equivalents | 40.0 | 34.1 | 28.5 | 29.1 | 33.1 | 46.4 | | 31.9 | 30.7 |
| Trade Receivables (net) | 6.7 | 11.9 | 22.2 | 23.9 | 17.1 | 8.0 | | 16.0 | 16.9 |
| Inventory | .6 | 1.0 | 1.4 | 3.6 | .0 | .1 | | 1.1 | 1.5 |
| All Other Current | 12.6 | 15.0 | 16.3 | 14.8 | 11.7 | 9.3 | | 13.2 | 13.7 |
| Total Current | 59.9 | 61.9 | 68.4 | 71.4 | 61.9 | 63.7 | | 62.3 | 62.8 |
| Fixed Assets (net) | 21.8 | 20.0 | 16.8 | 15.7 | 22.6 | 26.8 | | 21.8 | 21.1 |
| Intangibles (net) | 3.6 | 3.2 | 2.2 | 1.7 | 5.2 | 1.8 | | 2.4 | 3.1 |
| All Other Non-Current | 14.6 | 14.9 | 12.5 | 11.2 | 10.3 | 7.7 | | 13.4 | 13.0 |
| Total | 100.0 | 100.0 | 100.0 | 100.0 | 100.0 | 100.0 | | 100.0 | 100.0 |
| **LIABILITIES** | | | | | | | | | |
| Notes Payable-Short Term | 48.2 | 18.9 | 13.5 | 5.3 | 4.1 | 3.5 | | 26.6 | 27.6 |
| Cur. Mat.-L.T.D. | 5.0 | 3.1 | 2.7 | 2.1 | 2.2 | 1.9 | | 4.6 | 4.4 |
| Trade Payables | 2.7 | 2.7 | 3.5 | 4.7 | 2.4 | 2.3 | | 2.8 | 3.2 |
| Income Taxes Payable | .2 | .2 | .7 | 1.0 | .3 | .5 | | .4 | .5 |
| All Other Current | 41.3 | 31.5 | 26.2 | 23.2 | 20.8 | 22.2 | | 31.9 | 29.6 |
| Total Current | 97.3 | 56.4 | 46.6 | 36.3 | 29.8 | 30.5 | | 66.2 | 65.2 |
| Long-Term Debt | 18.4 | 14.0 | 11.6 | 7.8 | 6.2 | 6.7 | | 13.3 | 13.6 |
| Deferred Taxes | .0 | .0 | .5 | .6 | .0 | .0 | | .2 | .2 |
| All Other Non-Current | 8.7 | 5.6 | 5.6 | 6.7 | 3.3 | 1.7 | | 5.8 | 5.1 |
| Net Worth | -24.4 | 24.0 | 35.7 | 48.5 | 60.6 | 61.1 | | 14.5 | 15.9 |
| Total Liabilties & Net Worth | 100.0 | 100.0 | 100.0 | 100.0 | 100.0 | 100.0 | | 100.0 | 100.0 |
| **INCOME DATA** | | | | | | | | | |
| Net Sales | 100.0 | 100.0 | 100.0 | 100.0 | 100.0 | 100.0 | | 100.0 | 100.0 |
| Gross Profit | | | | | | | | | |
| Operating Expenses | 85.0 | 82.2 | 79.2 | 75.8 | 69.4 | 61.4 | | 79.5 | 79.4 |
| Operating Profit | 15.0 | 17.8 | 20.8 | 24.2 | 30.6 | 38.6 | | 20.5 | 20.6 |
| All Other Expenses (net) | .8 | 2.1 | 1.9 | 1.7 | 2.5 | 1.6 | | 1.5 | 1.4 |
| Profit Before Taxes | 14.2 | 15.7 | 18.9 | 22.5 | 28.1 | 37.1 | | 19.1 | 19.2 |
| **RATIOS** | | | | | | | | | |
| | 2.1 | 2.7 | 3.7 | 5.0 | 6.5 | 10.1 | | 2.9 | 2.9 |
| Current | .9 | 1.1 | 1.5 | 2.3 | 2.4 | 3.3 | | 1.2 | 1.2 |
| | .3 | .7 | .9 | 1.2 | 1.2 | 1.3 | | .6 | .6 |
| | 1.6 | 2.1 | 2.8 | 4.1 | 5.6 | 8.4 | | 2.2 | 2.2 |
| Quick | (815) .6 | (670) .9 | (632) 1.1 | 1.6 | 1.9 | 3.0 | | (1753) 1.0 | (2046) 1.0 |
| | .2 | .3 | .5 | .9 | .9 | 1.0 | | .3 | .3 |
| | 0 UND | 0 UND | 0 UND | 0 UND | 0 UND | 0 UND | | 0 UND | 0 UND |
| Sales/Receivables | 0 UND | 0 UND | 4 83.2 | 17 21.4 | 7 54.3 | 3 137.9 | | 0 UND | 0 UND |
| | 0 UND | 5 69.6 | 58 6.3 | 74 4.9 | 52 7.0 | 7 53.6 | | 21 17.3 | 31 11.9 |
| Cost of Sales/Inventory | | | | | | | | | |
| Cost of Sales/Payables | | | | | | | | | |
| | 34.7 | 10.4 | 4.8 | 3.9 | 4.9 | 4.9 | | 8.7 | 8.6 |
| Sales/Working Capital | -175.2 | 86.7 | 15.3 | 8.0 | 11.1 | 8.8 | | 65.2 | 57.1 |
| | -15.3 | -21.7 | -98.5 | 30.4 | 29.5 | 80.8 | | -29.1 | -25.2 |
| | 55.6 | 95.6 | 176.3 | 268.0 | 490.1 | 325.0 | | 91.2 | 108.6 |
| EBIT/Interest | (562) 11.3 | (495) 12.2 | (508) 25.5 | (240) 62.2 | (41) 109.4 | (31) 122.8 | | (1464) 17.8 | (1647) 19.3 |
| | .8 | 1.2 | 2.9 | 7.2 | 18.5 | 73.5 | | 2.4 | 2.1 |
| | 1.7 | 6.4 | 6.5 | 10.6 | | | | 7.1 | 6.3 |
| Net Profit + Depr., Dep., Amort./Cur. Mat. L/T/D | (13) 1.1 | (20) 2.9 | (60) 1.9 | (39) 1.8 | | | | (120) 2.5 | (139) 1.9 |
| | .1 | 1.6 | .6 | .8 | | | | .8 | .9 |
| | .0 | .1 | .1 | .1 | .2 | .2 | | .2 | .1 |
| Fixed/Worth | 1.0 | .5 | .3 | .3 | .4 | .4 | | .7 | .6 |
| | -.5 | 8.9 | 2.6 | .7 | .6 | .8 | | UND | -38.0 |
| | .9 | .6 | .6 | .3 | .2 | .1 | | .6 | .6 |
| Debt/Worth | 42.0 | 2.5 | 1.8 | 1.0 | .7 | .3 | | 2.9 | 2.5 |
| | -2.6 | 219.5 | 14.0 | 3.7 | 2.2 | 1.9 | | -26.5 | -20.8 |
| | 794.7 | 334.2 | 238.5 | 214.5 | 316.3 | 338.3 | | 388.0 | 355.1 |
| % Profit Before Taxes/Tangible Net Worth | (433) 182.8 | (508) 85.2 | (519) 87.0 | (288) 90.7 | (48) 161.5 | (37) 185.3 | | (1273) 147.8 | (1465) 119.2 |
| | 31.1 | 12.3 | 11.4 | 15.7 | 53.5 | 159.6 | | 24.4 | 20.7 |
| | 189.3 | 101.9 | 98.9 | 126.0 | 171.6 | 161.4 | | 163.2 | 154.2 |
| % Profit Before Taxes/Total Assets | 39.4 | 17.7 | 20.3 | 38.2 | 112.7 | 131.5 | | 43.6 | 41.2 |
| | .0 | 1.2 | 2.4 | 3.8 | 8.8 | 91.5 | | 3.2 | 3.0 |
| | 916.6 | 195.5 | 141.3 | 55.2 | 27.6 | 19.5 | | 107.4 | 130.7 |
| Sales/Net Fixed Assets | 113.6 | 58.2 | 43.8 | 28.3 | 19.5 | 15.0 | | 39.3 | 40.8 |
| | 34.3 | 22.2 | 19.0 | 16.8 | 12.4 | 10.5 | | 17.8 | 17.8 |
| | 20.4 | 7.7 | 5.0 | 4.3 | 5.1 | 4.2 | | 9.7 | 9.1 |
| Sales/Total Assets | 9.8 | 4.0 | 2.9 | 2.5 | 3.5 | 3.3 | | 4.6 | 4.5 |
| | 4.8 | 2.1 | 1.7 | 1.6 | 1.9 | 2.9 | | 2.5 | 2.3 |
| | .2 | .3 | .5 | .7 | .9 | .7 | | .5 | .4 |
| % Depr., Dep., Amort./Sales | (347) .5 | (364) .7 | (422) .9 | (244) 1.1 | (43) 1.5 | (24) 1.1 | | (1174) .9 | (1292) .9 |
| | 1.2 | 1.3 | 1.5 | 1.7 | 2.3 | 1.8 | | 1.5 | 1.6 |
| | 12.4 | 9.9 | 5.9 | 6.4 | 2.7 | 15.8 | | 11.7 | 11.1 |
| % Officers', Directors' Owners' Comp/Sales | (481) 22.0 | (321) 20.5 | (250) 15.1 | (108) 18.3 | (11) 16.5 | (15) 24.4 | | (777) 23.1 | (877) 21.0 |
| | 34.2 | 34.8 | 31.9 | 36.0 | 41.5 | 34.1 | | 33.7 | 34.2 |
| Net Sales ($) | 2156605M | 3959216M | 11738721M | 21674702M | 11621299M | 22724384M | | 68261416M | 87407896M |
| Total Assets ($) | 175995M | 717863M | 3068219M | 6901510M | 3388013M | 6204181M | | 16701460M | 22186517M |

M = $ thousand     MM = $ million
See Pages 9 through 22 for Explanation of Ratios and Data

## Comparative Historical Data | Current Data Sorted by Sales

| 4/1/09-3/31/10 ALL | 4/1/10-3/31/11 ALL | 4/1/11-3/31/12 ALL | Type of Statement | 0-1MM | 1-3MM | 3-5MM | 5-10MM | 10-25MM | 25MM & OVER |
|---|---|---|---|---|---|---|---|---|---|
| 115 | 109 | 109 | Unqualified | 2 | 4 | 7 | 10 | 20 | 66 |
| 209 | 222 | 237 | Reviewed | | 9 | 8 | 33 | 64 | 123 |
| 275 | 263 | 313 | Compiled | 32 | 72 | 46 | 68 | 61 | 34 |
| 654 | 643 | 751 | Tax Returns | 203 | 233 | 93 | 119 | 72 | 31 |
| 938 | 962 | 1102 | Other | 123 | 227 | 134 | 188 | 209 | 221 |
| 4/1/09-3/31/10 ALL | 4/1/10-3/31/11 ALL | 4/1/11-3/31/12 ALL | | 129 (4/1-9/30/11) | | | 2,383 (10/1/11-3/31/12) | | |
| 2191 | 2199 | 2512 | **NUMBER OF STATEMENTS** | 360 | 545 | 288 | 418 | 426 | 475 |
| % | % | % | **ASSETS** | % | % | % | % | % | % |
| 33.4 | 34.2 | 34.2 | Cash & Equivalents | 32.5 | 37.7 | 35.9 | 31.4 | 33.1 | 33.6 |
| 16.1 | 15.4 | 14.3 | Trade Receivables (net) | 7.3 | 10.3 | 12.4 | 16.2 | 19.1 | 19.3 |
| 1.3 | 1.0 | 1.3 | Inventory | .9 | .6 | 1.2 | 1.1 | 2.1 | 1.7 |
| 12.0 | 13.7 | 14.4 | All Other Current | 9.9 | 14.8 | 16.3 | 16.2 | 16.8 | 12.3 |
| 62.7 | 64.3 | 64.1 | Total Current | 50.5 | 63.4 | 65.9 | 65.0 | 71.0 | 67.0 |
| 21.0 | 19.1 | 19.4 | Fixed Assets (net) | 31.1 | 18.8 | 15.5 | 15.3 | 15.7 | 20.8 |
| 2.8 | 2.5 | 2.9 | Intangibles (net) | 3.1 | 3.7 | 2.8 | 3.8 | 1.9 | 2.2 |
| 13.5 | 14.2 | 13.6 | All Other Non-Current | 15.2 | 14.1 | 15.8 | 15.9 | 11.5 | 10.1 |
| 100.0 | 100.0 | 100.0 | Total | 100.0 | 100.0 | 100.0 | 100.0 | 100.0 | 100.0 |
| | | | **LIABILITIES** | | | | | | |
| 26.0 | 26.0 | 24.9 | Notes Payable-Short Term | 35.1 | 37.5 | 35.2 | 22.6 | 15.6 | 6.6 |
| 4.4 | 4.1 | 3.5 | Cur. Mat.-L.T.D. | 3.4 | 4.2 | 3.3 | 4.1 | 2.0 | 3.5 |
| 2.9 | 3.1 | 3.1 | Trade Payables | 2.8 | 2.3 | 3.0 | 3.6 | 3.2 | 3.9 |
| .6 | .5 | .4 | Income Taxes Payable | .1 | .1 | .5 | .4 | .6 | .9 |
| 30.6 | 32.5 | 32.0 | All Other Current | 28.9 | 35.5 | 32.4 | 37.0 | 33.4 | 24.3 |
| 64.4 | 66.3 | 63.8 | Total Current | 70.4 | 79.6 | 74.3 | 67.7 | 54.8 | 39.3 |
| 14.6 | 12.3 | 13.8 | Long-Term Debt | 29.7 | 15.9 | 12.0 | 10.3 | 8.5 | 8.4 |
| .2 | .2 | .2 | Deferred Taxes | .0 | .1 | .1 | .3 | .2 | .5 |
| 6.9 | 6.4 | 6.6 | All Other Non-Current | 9.2 | 7.8 | 4.7 | 6.9 | 6.0 | 4.8 |
| 13.9 | 14.7 | 15.5 | Net Worth | -9.2 | -3.3 | 8.9 | 14.8 | 30.6 | 47.0 |
| 100.0 | 100.0 | 100.0 | Total Liabilities & Net Worth | 100.0 | 100.0 | 100.0 | 100.0 | 100.0 | 100.0 |
| | | | **INCOME DATA** | | | | | | |
| 100.0 | 100.0 | 100.0 | Net Sales | 100.0 | 100.0 | 100.0 | 100.0 | 100.0 | 100.0 |
| | | | Gross Profit | | | | | | |
| 80.7 | 81.1 | 81.0 | Operating Expenses | 79.2 | 83.9 | 84.1 | 82.9 | 81.2 | 75.3 |
| 19.3 | 18.9 | 19.0 | Operating Profit | 20.8 | 16.1 | 15.9 | 17.1 | 18.8 | 24.7 |
| 1.5 | 1.6 | 1.6 | All Other Expenses (net) | 5.8 | .8 | .3 | .7 | .6 | 1.7 |
| 17.7 | 17.4 | 17.4 | Profit Before Taxes | 15.0 | 15.4 | 15.6 | 16.4 | 18.2 | 23.0 |
| | | | **RATIOS** | | | | | | |
| 2.9 | 3.0 | 3.3 | Current | 2.7 | 2.2 | 2.7 | 3.3 | 3.5 | 4.7 |
| 1.2 | 1.2 | 1.3 | | .9 | 1.0 | 1.2 | 1.2 | 1.5 | 2.1 |
| .6 | .6 | .7 | | .3 | .5 | .5 | .6 | .9 | 1.1 |
| 2.3 | 2.3 | 2.5 | Quick | 1.7 | 1.7 | 2.0 | 2.4 | 2.7 | 3.9 |
| (2187) 1.0 | (2192) 1.0 | (2509) 1.0 | | (544) .7 | (287) .7 | .8 | (425) .9 | 1.1 | 1.5 |
| .4 | .3 | .3 | | .2 | .2 | .2 | .2 | .5 | .8 |
| 0 UND | 0 UND | 0 UND | Sales/Receivables | 0 UND | 0 UND | 0 UND | 0 UND | 0 UND | 0 UND |
| 0 UND | 0 UND | 0 UND | | 0 UND | 0 UND | 0 UND | 0 UND | 2 164.4 | 5 72.9 |
| 24 15.1 | 18 20.2 | 17 21.8 | | 0 UND | 1 713.1 | 8 46.8 | 22 16.5 | 45 8.1 | 46 7.9 |
| | | | Cost of Sales/Inventory | | | | | | |
| | | | Cost of Sales/Payables | | | | | | |
| 8.0 | 8.0 | 7.8 | Sales/Working Capital | 10.9 | 13.8 | 8.9 | 8.0 | 5.9 | 5.7 |
| 51.2 | 54.0 | 49.4 | | -92.4 | 575.0 | 81.9 | 54.4 | 29.8 | 15.2 |
| -29.2 | -28.8 | -30.4 | | -6.2 | -14.5 | -25.6 | -37.2 | -142.8 | 163.6 |
| 118.6 | 124.0 | 131.6 | EBIT/Interest | 18.9 | 68.8 | 92.7 | 133.7 | 200.6 | 284.8 |
| (1715) 17.9 | (1730) 17.9 | (1877) 18.5 | | (216) 7.0 | (403) 15.0 | (222) 9.9 | (323) 20.2 | (326) 31.3 | (387) 74.8 |
| 1.8 | 2.2 | 2.1 | | .2 | 1.0 | 1.7 | 1.4 | 2.9 | 6.4 |
| 7.5 | 7.2 | 7.0 | Net Profit + Depr., Dep., Amort./Cur. Mat. L/T/D | | 3.0 | | 8.4 | 10.5 | 10.0 |
| (136) 1.8 | (144) 2.0 | (143) 2.0 | | | (13) 1.1 | | (18) 2.0 | (40) 2.2 | (64) 2.0 |
| .6 | .8 | .7 | | | .1 | | .5 | .7 | .8 |
| .1 | .1 | .1 | Fixed/Worth | .0 | .0 | .0 | .1 | .1 | .1 |
| .6 | .4 | .4 | | 2.0 | .5 | .3 | .3 | .4 | .4 |
| -24.3 | 16.1 | 10.2 | | -1.8 | -1.2 | -3.2 | 41.7 | 1.8 | 1.1 |
| .6 | .6 | .6 | Debt/Worth | 1.2 | .9 | .6 | .6 | .5 | .3 |
| 3.0 | 2.5 | 2.5 | | 8.2 | 6.1 | 2.4 | 2.6 | 1.8 | 1.1 |
| -17.0 | -36.2 | -29.5 | | -4.3 | -4.4 | -11.5 | -21.8 | 17.3 | 3.8 |
| 340.1 | 335.1 | 328.2 | % Profit Before Taxes/Tangible Net Worth | 207.9 | 439.3 | 347.7 | 342.5 | 309.6 | 310.1 |
| (1541) 118.2 | (1605) 111.0 | (1833) 106.7 | | (217) 44.8 | (336) 119.5 | (198) 105.3 | (305) 114.0 | (346) 106.1 | (431) 144.9 |
| 17.7 | 19.1 | 18.5 | | 13.5 | 21.1 | 22.1 | 20.0 | 13.1 | 34.4 |
| 129.0 | 131.9 | 128.8 | % Profit Before Taxes/Total Assets | 53.5 | 126.8 | 116.5 | 142.3 | 118.0 | 165.9 |
| 31.0 | 31.1 | 28.5 | | 12.3 | 28.6 | 25.4 | 25.4 | 30.7 | 73.3 |
| 1.8 | 1.8 | 2.2 | | .0 | .8 | 2.6 | 2.0 | 3.1 | 5.8 |
| 158.6 | 170.9 | 211.2 | Sales/Net Fixed Assets | 565.3 | 392.8 | 361.3 | 298.6 | 163.1 | 59.9 |
| 43.3 | 49.0 | 53.5 | | 37.1 | 76.9 | 81.9 | 89.2 | 52.9 | 28.4 |
| 17.8 | 19.4 | 20.5 | | 4.2 | 22.4 | 34.3 | 33.0 | 23.5 | 16.5 |
| 8.9 | 8.8 | 9.0 | Sales/Total Assets | 5.9 | 10.4 | 12.6 | 11.4 | 8.9 | 6.7 |
| 4.2 | 4.3 | 4.3 | | 2.5 | 4.8 | 5.0 | 5.2 | 3.9 | 4.2 |
| 2.2 | 2.4 | 2.2 | | .8 | 2.3 | 2.5 | 2.5 | 2.3 | 2.6 |
| .4 | .4 | .4 | % Depr., Dep., Amort./Sales | .8 | .3 | .2 | .2 | .4 | .7 |
| (1354) .9 | (1313) .9 | (1444) .8 | | (160) 1.9 | (262) .6 | (145) .5 | (229) .6 | (272) .9 | (376) 1.1 |
| 1.6 | 1.6 | 1.5 | | 14.9 | 1.1 | 1.1 | 1.2 | 1.4 | 1.6 |
| 9.6 | 9.7 | 9.5 | % Officers', Directors' Owners' Comp/Sales | 12.1 | 11.3 | 9.3 | 7.7 | 7.6 | 7.3 |
| (1038) 22.0 | (1032) 22.2 | (1186) 20.4 | | (173) 20.3 | (304) 20.5 | (141) 18.3 | (210) 20.4 | (186) 21.7 | (172) 20.8 |
| 34.1 | 34.5 | 34.1 | | 31.0 | 35.0 | 30.9 | 33.3 | 36.5 | 36.1 |
| 82554282M | 71199502M | 73874927M | Net Sales ($) | 183909M | 1041355M | 1115834M | 3034972M | 6761507M | 61737350M |
| 19999008M | 18856727M | 20455781M | Total Assets ($) | 187253M | 447203M | 379401M | 1048949M | 2297864M | 16095111M |

**Current Data Sorted by Assets**  |  **Comparative Historical Data**

| 0-500M | 500M-2MM | 2-10MM | 10-50MM | 50-100MM | 100-250MM | Type of Statement | 4/1/07-3/31/08 ALL | 4/1/08-3/31/09 ALL |
|---|---|---|---|---|---|---|---|---|
|  |  | 3 | 3 |  | 1 | Unqualified | 3 | 5 |
|  |  | 3 |  |  |  | Reviewed | 2 | 4 |
| 2 | 5 | 7 |  |  |  | Compiled | 3 | 14 |
| 21 | 15 | 5 | 1 |  |  | Tax Returns | 20 | 23 |
| 12 | 19 | 8 | 5 | 1 |  | Other | 41 | 44 |
| | 11 (4/1-9/30/11) | | | 100 (10/1/11-3/31/12) | | | | |
| 35 | 39 | 26 | 9 | 1 | 1 | **NUMBER OF STATEMENTS** | 69 | 90 |
| % | % | % | % | % | % | **ASSETS** | % | % |
| 50.2 | 27.8 | 31.7 |  |  |  | Cash & Equivalents | 27.6 | 32.6 |
| 7.0 | 17.5 | 17.2 |  |  |  | Trade Receivables (net) | 12.0 | 9.0 |
| .0 | .6 | .1 |  |  |  | Inventory | .4 | 1.4 |
| 3.8 | 4.0 | 13.8 |  |  |  | All Other Current | 8.4 | 6.0 |
| 61.1 | 49.9 | 62.7 |  |  |  | Total Current | 48.4 | 49.1 |
| 18.6 | 22.3 | 18.7 |  |  |  | Fixed Assets (net) | 23.5 | 21.5 |
| 13.6 | 11.7 | 4.6 |  |  |  | Intangibles (net) | 11.5 | 14.5 |
| 6.7 | 16.1 | 14.1 |  |  |  | All Other Non-Current | 16.6 | 14.9 |
| 100.0 | 100.0 | 100.0 |  |  |  | Total | 100.0 | 100.0 |
|  |  |  |  |  |  | **LIABILITIES** |  |  |
| 14.6 | 10.8 | 3.6 |  |  |  | Notes Payable-Short Term | 15.9 | 22.9 |
| 1.5 | 1.4 | 2.2 |  |  |  | Cur. Mat.-L.T.D. | 1.9 | 4.2 |
| 16.4 | 6.9 | 11.9 |  |  |  | Trade Payables | 8.4 | 7.9 |
| .0 | .0 | .0 |  |  |  | Income Taxes Payable | .6 | .2 |
| 26.0 | 20.5 | 29.1 |  |  |  | All Other Current | 27.6 | 20.1 |
| 58.5 | 39.6 | 46.8 |  |  |  | Total Current | 54.3 | 55.2 |
| 12.9 | 27.1 | 12.1 |  |  |  | Long-Term Debt | 16.8 | 14.0 |
| .0 | .4 | .0 |  |  |  | Deferred Taxes | .1 | .3 |
| 10.3 | 9.5 | 12.7 |  |  |  | All Other Non-Current | 4.7 | 3.9 |
| 18.3 | 23.4 | 28.4 |  |  |  | Net Worth | 24.1 | 26.7 |
| 100.0 | 100.0 | 100.0 |  |  |  | Total Liabilities & Net Worth | 100.0 | 100.0 |
|  |  |  |  |  |  | **INCOME DATA** |  |  |
| 100.0 | 100.0 | 100.0 |  |  |  | Net Sales | 100.0 | 100.0 |
|  |  |  |  |  |  | Gross Profit |  |  |
| 91.7 | 86.9 | 93.3 |  |  |  | Operating Expenses | 96.1 | .93.7 |
| 8.3 | 13.1 | 6.7 |  |  |  | Operating Profit | 3.9 | 6.3 |
| 2.8 | 2.7 | 1.8 |  |  |  | All Other Expenses (net) | -.8 | 1.2 |
| 5.6 | 10.4 | 4.9 |  |  |  | Profit Before Taxes | 4.7 | 5.1 |
|  |  |  |  |  |  | **RATIOS** |  |  |
| 3.9 | 3.8 | 3.2 |  |  |  |  | 2.8 | 2.6 |
| 1.5 | 1.5 | 1.3 |  |  |  | Current | 1.1 | 1.1 |
| .6 | .7 | .8 |  |  |  |  | .6 | .5 |
| 3.3 | 3.7 | 2.0 |  |  |  |  | 2.3 | 2.1 |
| 1.3 | 1.4 | 1.1 |  |  |  | Quick | 1.0 | 1.0 |
| .6 | .6 | .6 |  |  |  |  | .4 | .3 |
| 0 UND | 0 UND | 0 UND |  |  |  |  | 0 UND | 0 UND |
| 0 UND | 5 67.7 | 7 50.2 |  |  |  | Sales/Receivables | 3 130.9 | 3 130.4 |
| 1 334.0 | 59 6.2 | 48 7.6 |  |  |  |  | 20 18.6 | 25 14.5 |
|  |  |  |  |  |  | Cost of Sales/Inventory |  |  |
|  |  |  |  |  |  | Cost of Sales/Payables |  |  |
| 9.6 | 6.9 | 5.0 |  |  |  |  | 10.3 | 8.7 |
| 90.3 | 18.6 | 17.3 |  |  |  | Sales/Working Capital | 75.9 | 107.6 |
| -24.6 | -18.5 | -20.6 |  |  |  |  | -14.9 | -8.8 |
| 10.9 | 30.0 | 149.5 |  |  |  |  | 28.0 | 19.0 |
| (19) .8 | (22) 8.2 | (21) 17.2 |  |  |  | EBIT/Interest | (51) 3.3 | (58) 1.8 |
| -5.3 | 2.7 | -4.9 |  |  |  |  | -3.0 | -6.1 |
|  |  |  |  |  |  | Net Profit + Depr., Dep., Amort./Cur. Mat. L/T/D |  |  |
| .0 | .1 | .1 |  |  |  |  | .3 | .2 |
| .5 | .3 | .5 |  |  |  | Fixed/Worth | .9 | .9 |
| -.4 | 12.4 | NM |  |  |  |  | -2.5 | -.8 |
| .2 | .5 | .6 |  |  |  |  | .5 | .5 |
| 1.8 | 3.0 | 2.7 |  |  |  | Debt/Worth | 2.3 | 3.9 |
| -3.1 | -40.4 | NM |  |  |  |  | -8.4 | -4.4 |
| 170.6 | 144.9 | 69.3 |  |  |  |  | 148.2 | 84.2 |
| (22) 52.1 | (29) 54.4 | (20) 18.7 |  |  |  | % Profit Before Taxes/Tangible Net Worth | (51) 31.1 | (62) 27.4 |
| 4.6 | 6.9 | -.2 |  |  |  |  | -5.7 | 4.9 |
| 55.4 | 31.1 | 21.0 |  |  |  |  | 32.7 | 31.6 |
| 10.3 | 12.7 | 7.1 |  |  |  | % Profit Before Taxes/Total Assets | 5.0 | 4.7 |
| -19.5 | 3.1 | -1.6 |  |  |  |  | -12.1 | -3.5 |
| UND | 85.7 | 111.8 |  |  |  |  | 38.9 | 75.9 |
| 54.3 | 22.3 | 33.0 |  |  |  | Sales/Net Fixed Assets | 18.9 | 19.9 |
| 19.4 | 8.6 | 7.3 |  |  |  |  | 8.9 | 8.3 |
| 9.9 | 4.2 | 2.8 |  |  |  |  | 5.3 | 4.2 |
| 5.1 | 2.9 | 1.8 |  |  |  | Sales/Total Assets | 2.9 | 2.3 |
| 2.3 | .9 | 1.4 |  |  |  |  | 1.3 | 1.2 |
| .4 | .8 | .3 |  |  |  |  | .8 | 1.2 |
| (18) .8 | (23) 1.7 | (20) 1.3 |  |  |  | % Depr., Dep., Amort./Sales | (51) 1.9 | (53) 2.3 |
| 1.5 | 3.7 | 3.0 |  |  |  |  | 4.0 | 3.9 |
| 7.0 | 3.7 |  |  |  |  |  | 4.7 | 5.7 |
| (19) 9.5 | (17) 7.9 |  |  |  |  | % Officers', Directors' Owners' Comp/Sales | (18) 9.5 | (28) 11.4 |
| 14.1 | 14.3 |  |  |  |  |  | 27.6 | 27.6 |
| 38954M | 147489M | 247054M | 532115M | 130980M | 57028M | Net Sales ($) | 692954M | 1185962M |
| 7104M | 42852M | 114324M | 227650M | 85745M | 197634M | Total Assets ($) | 420367M | 877575M |

M = $ thousand    MM = $ million
See Pages 9 through 22 for Explanation of Ratios and Data

## Comparative Historical Data | | | | ## Current Data Sorted by Sales

| 10 / 4 / 11 / 33 / 43 | 8 / 5 / 9 / 24 / 47 | 7 / 3 / 14 / 42 / 45 | Type of Statement | 0-1MM | 1-3MM | 3-5MM | 5-10MM | 10-25MM | 25MM & OVER |
|---|---|---|---|---|---|---|---|---|---|
| | | | Unqualified | | | | 1 | 1 | 4 |
| | | | Reviewed | | | | 1 | 1 | 1 |
| | | | Compiled | 1 | 3 | 6 | 3 | 1 | |
| | | | Tax Returns | 21 | 12 | 5 | 2 | 1 | 1 |
| | | | Other | 13 | 8 | 8 | 7 | 4 | 5 |
| 4/1/09-3/31/10 ALL | 4/1/10-3/31/11 ALL | 4/1/11-3/31/12 ALL | | **11 (4/1-9/30/11)** | | | **100 (10/1/11-3/31/12)** | | |
| 101 | 93 | 111 | **NUMBER OF STATEMENTS** | 35 | 23 | 20 | 14 | 8 | 11 |
| % | % | % | **ASSETS** | % | % | % | % | % | % |
| 34.0 | 33.9 | 34.8 | Cash & Equivalents | 37.5 | 32.2 | 44.0 | 30.0 | | 27.2 |
| 10.1 | 9.3 | 14.1 | Trade Receivables (net) | 3.8 | 21.8 | 14.2 | 18.4 | | 19.7 |
| .7 | .9 | .2 | Inventory | .0 | .0 | .0 | 1.8 | | .0 |
| 7.6 | 9.7 | 7.0 | All Other Current | 3.9 | 5.0 | 3.6 | 7.0 | | 13.7 |
| 52.4 | 53.8 | 56.1 | Total Current | 45.2 | 58.9 | 61.9 | 57.3 | | 60.5 |
| 23.4 | 18.6 | 19.7 | Fixed Assets (net) | 26.9 | 15.7 | 18.8 | 21.7 | | 11.9 |
| 10.5 | 11.2 | 12.5 | Intangibles (net) | 14.4 | 11.7 | 6.4 | 8.8 | | 25.3 |
| 13.7 | 16.4 | 11.7 | All Other Non-Current | 13.5 | 13.6 | 12.9 | 12.3 | | 2.3 |
| 100.0 | 100.0 | 100.0 | Total | 100.0 | 100.0 | 100.0 | 100.0 | | 100.0 |
| | | | **LIABILITIES** | | | | | | |
| 12.6 | 16.1 | 9.5 | Notes Payable-Short Term | 6.4 | 20.9 | 10.9 | 6.3 | | 2.1 |
| 1.6 | 2.8 | 1.7 | Cur. Mat.-L.T.D. | 1.1 | 1.6 | 2.0 | 3.2 | | 2.4 |
| 14.6 | 8.2 | 11.2 | Trade Payables | 7.5 | 17.9 | 7.2 | 13.3 | | 9.3 |
| .2 | .1 | .0 | Income Taxes Payable | .0 | .1 | .0 | .0 | | .0 |
| 23.7 | 23.4 | 23.8 | All Other Current | 27.4 | 16.9 | 27.9 | 23.5 | | 15.8 |
| 52.7 | 50.7 | 46.3 | Total Current | 42.4 | 57.4 | 48.0 | 46.2 | | 29.7 |
| 14.3 | 13.1 | 17.6 | Long-Term Debt | 22.9 | 24.9 | 9.3 | 18.1 | | 10.9 |
| .2 | .2 | .3 | Deferred Taxes | .0 | .6 | .0 | .0 | | .6 |
| 7.7 | 10.2 | 9.9 | All Other Non-Current | 16.2 | 5.7 | 4.8 | 16.7 | | 3.8 |
| 25.1 | 25.7 | 25.9 | Net Worth | 18.5 | 11.4 | 38.0 | 18.9 | | 54.9 |
| 100.0 | 100.0 | 100.0 | Total Liabilities & Net Worth | 100.0 | 100.0 | 100.0 | 100.0 | | 100.0 |
| | | | **INCOME DATA** | | | | | | |
| 100.0 | 100.0 | 100.0 | Net Sales | 100.0 | 100.0 | 100.0 | 100.0 | | 100.0 |
| | | | Gross Profit | | | | | | |
| 92.1 | 89.1 | 90.0 | Operating Expenses | 82.5 | 91.5 | 99.6 | 91.9 | | 88.5 |
| 7.9 | 10.9 | 10.0 | Operating Profit | 17.5 | 8.5 | .4 | 8.1 | | 11.5 |
| .9 | 1.6 | 2.4 | All Other Expenses (net) | 7.5 | -.7 | -1.3 | 1.7 | | 1.4 |
| 7.0 | 9.3 | 7.7 | Profit Before Taxes | 9.9 | 9.2 | 1.7 | 6.5 | | 10.1 |
| | | | **RATIOS** | | | | | | |
| 2.3 | 2.1 | 3.3 | | 3.2 | 5.4 | 2.6 | 3.1 | | 3.0 |
| 1.1 | 1.2 | 1.6 | Current | 1.3 | 2.0 | 1.3 | 1.4 | | 2.1 |
| .6 | .7 | .8 | | .6 | .8 | .7 | .8 | | 1.6 |
| 2.0 | 2.0 | 3.1 | | 3.1 | 5.4 | 2.6 | 2.7 | | 2.1 |
| 1.0 | 1.0 | 1.3 | Quick | 1.0 | 2.0 | 1.1 | 1.2 | | 1.7 |
| .4 | .4 | .6 | | .5 | .8 | .7 | .6 | | .8 |
| 0 UND | 0 UND | 0 UND | | 0 UND | 0 UND | 0 UND | 0 UND | | 8 43.8 |
| 1 279.8 | 2 211.6 | 1 334.0 | Sales/Receivables | 0 UND | 5 66.8 | 0 UND | 7 50.2 | | 24 15.4 |
| 24 15.0 | 17 22.1 | 26 14.3 | | 0 UND | 62 5.9 | 29 12.6 | 51 7.1 | | 47 7.8 |
| | | | Cost of Sales/Inventory | | | | | | |
| | | | Cost of Sales/Payables | | | | | | |
| 9.7 | 10.4 | 6.8 | | 9.2 | 6.8 | 8.8 | 6.7 | | 5.4 |
| 114.5 | 48.8 | 20.7 | Sales/Working Capital | 90.3 | 24.5 | 21.9 | 19.6 | | 11.5 |
| -20.8 | -18.0 | -24.6 | | -11.6 | -33.6 | -20.5 | -20.6 | | 27.8 |
| 26.5 | 32.4 | 27.7 | | 7.6 | 19.6 | 39.1 | 164.3 | | |
| (71) 10.5 | (68) 6.9 | (70) 7.4 | EBIT/Interest | (17) 2.9 | (14) 11.2 | (13) 2.3 | (11) 17.7 | | |
| .4 | .3 | -.8 | | -3.5 | 2.7 | -8.2 | -.6 | | |
| | 11.6 | 5.2 | | | | | | | |
| | (10) 6.4 | (10) 3.0 | Net Profit + Depr., Dep., Amort./Cur. Mat. L/T/D | | | | | | |
| | 2.1 | -5.9 | | | | | | | |
| .2 | .1 | .1 | | .1 | .0 | .2 | .1 | | .2 |
| .9 | .6 | .4 | Fixed/Worth | .9 | .4 | .4 | .5 | | .4 |
| -4.9 | -6.9 | 70.2 | | -4.4 | -3.1 | 20.2 | NM | | -.2 |
| .6 | .7 | .5 | | .6 | .4 | .5 | .4 | | .5 |
| 2.0 | 2.4 | 2.3 | Debt/Worth | 8.1 | 1.8 | 2.9 | 9.1 | | 1.1 |
| -22.7 | -12.1 | -7.4 | | -3.1 | -3.1 | 55.7 | -30.2 | | -5.9 |
| 168.3 | 147.9 | 116.0 | | 151.7 | 95.7 | 235.9 | 95.4 | | |
| (73) 71.0 | (65) 51.3 | (78) 40.0 | % Profit Before Taxes/Tangible Net Worth | (22) 31.7 | (15) 59.0 | (17) 40.4 | (10) 33.6 | | |
| 12.4 | 9.0 | 4.8 | | -1.3 | 12.2 | -6.9 | -50.8 | | |
| 50.8 | 39.1 | 31.1 | | 18.2 | 44.3 | 26.0 | 45.5 | | 49.2 |
| 16.2 | 11.5 | 11.0 | % Profit Before Taxes/Total Assets | 5.4 | 24.5 | 7.6 | 18.3 | | 27.4 |
| .4 | -.3 | -.1 | | -2.3 | 3.5 | -10.6 | -1.9 | | 7.9 |
| 53.5 | 76.4 | 137.4 | | 317.7 | 999.8 | 82.4 | 117.0 | | 205.3 |
| 24.0 | 30.2 | 29.1 | Sales/Net Fixed Assets | 18.8 | 54.3 | 24.9 | 15.1 | | 23.9 |
| 10.6 | 11.7 | 10.6 | | 4.6 | 23.8 | 9.8 | 7.4 | | 14.9 |
| 5.9 | 4.6 | 4.6 | | 3.9 | 5.7 | 4.2 | 5.0 | | 4.6 |
| 2.7 | 2.7 | 2.5 | Sales/Total Assets | 2.1 | 3.6 | 2.7 | 3.4 | | 2.5 |
| 1.5 | 1.4 | 1.5 | | .5 | 2.5 | 1.8 | 2.3 | | 1.5 |
| .9 | .6 | .4 | | .7 | .4 | .2 | .7 | | |
| (68) 1.6 | (62) 1.7 | (71) 1.2 | % Depr., Dep., Amort./Sales | (21) 1.2 | (11) .8 | (12) 1.5 | (11) 1.5 | | |
| 3.2 | 2.5 | 2.6 | | 6.6 | 1.3 | 3.4 | 3.9 | | |
| 4.7 | 3.7 | 4.7 | | 9.2 | 4.8 | | | | |
| (41) 9.3 | (31) 6.8 | (44) 7.3 | % Officers', Directors' Owners' Comp/Sales | (15) 13.1 | (14) 6.8 | | | | |
| 26.7 | 27.5 | 13.7 | | 18.4 | 10.1 | | | | |
| 897930M | 977044M | 1153620M | Net Sales ($) | 17024M | 44140M | 81993M | 100586M | 127444M | 782433M |
| 464161M | 533688M | 675309M | Total Assets ($) | 21245M | 21556M | 34676M | 35020M | 88532M | 474280M |

M = $ thousand    MM = $ million
See Pages 9 through 22 for Explanation of Ratios and Data

## Current Data Sorted by Assets      Comparative Historical Data

| | 0-500M | 500M-2MM | 2-10MM | 10-50MM | 50-100MM | 100-250MM | | 4/1/07-3/31/08 ALL | 4/1/08-3/31/09 ALL |
|---|---|---|---|---|---|---|---|---|---|
| | | | | | | | **Type of Statement** | | |
| | | 1 | 2 | 1 | | | Unqualified | 4 | 6 |
| | | | 3 | 1 | | | Reviewed | 1 | 2 |
| | 1 | 3 | 2 | | | | Compiled | 1 | |
| | 4 | 1 | 1 | | | | Tax Returns | 1 | 4 |
| | 4 | 5 | 11 | 5 | 1 | | Other | 7 | 12 |
| | | 5 (4/1-9/30/11) | | 41 (10/1/11-3/31/12) | | | | | |
| | 9 | 10 | 19 | 7 | 1 | | **NUMBER OF STATEMENTS** | 14 | 24 |
| | % | % | % | % | % | % | | % | % |
| | | | | | | | **ASSETS** | | |
| Cash & Equivalents | | 25.7 | 20.2 | | | | | 34.5 | 30.1 |
| Trade Receivables (net) | | 10.4 | 46.6 | | | | | 25.8 | 23.9 |
| Inventory | | .5 | 2.6 | | | | | .2 | .3 |
| All Other Current | | 13.5 | 8.8 | | | | | 6.4 | 12.9 |
| Total Current | | 50.1 | 78.2 | | | | | 66.8 | 67.3 |
| Fixed Assets (net) | | 41.3 | 11.3 | | | | | 17.3 | 20.0 |
| Intangibles (net) | | .0 | 6.4 | DATA | | | | 10.3 | 3.4 |
| All Other Non-Current | | 8.6 | 4.2 | NOT | | | | 5.5 | 9.3 |
| Total | | 100.0 | 100.0 | AVAILABLE | | | | 100.0 | 100.0 |
| | | | | | | | **LIABILITIES** | | |
| Notes Payable-Short Term | | 3.5 | 9.7 | | | | | 11.4 | 13.0 |
| Cur. Mat.-L.T.D. | | 1.3 | 3.4 | | | | | 1.7 | 3.3 |
| Trade Payables | | 2.1 | 4.2 | | | | | 4.1 | 4.8 |
| Income Taxes Payable | | .0 | .7 | | | | | .9 | .1 |
| All Other Current | | 8.4 | 13.1 | | | | | 36.5 | 28.1 |
| Total Current | | 15.3 | 31.1 | | | | | 54.6 | 49.3 |
| Long-Term Debt | | 25.0 | 5.4 | | | | | 4.6 | 12.7 |
| Deferred Taxes | | .0 | .9 | | | | | .2 | .5 |
| All Other Non-Current | | 1.3 | 9.9 | | | | | 12.8 | 11.8 |
| Net Worth | | 58.4 | 52.7 | | | | | 27.8 | 25.7 |
| Total Liabilities & Net Worth | | 100.0 | 100.0 | | | | | 100.0 | 100.0 |
| | | | | | | | **INCOME DATA** | | |
| Net Sales | | 100.0 | 100.0 | | | | | 100.0 | 100.0 |
| Gross Profit | | | | | | | | | |
| Operating Expenses | | 74.0 | 87.1 | | | | | 86.3 | 84.5 |
| Operating Profit | | 26.0 | 12.9 | | | | | 13.7 | 15.5 |
| All Other Expenses (net) | | 4.6 | .8 | | | | | .8 | 1.8 |
| Profit Before Taxes | | 21.4 | 12.2 | | | | | 12.9 | 13.7 |
| | | | | | | | **RATIOS** | | |
| | | 5.3 | 7.3 | | | | | 2.6 | 3.5 |
| Current | | 2.5 | 2.6 | | | | | 1.3 | 1.6 |
| | | .9 | 1.7 | | | | | .9 | 1.1 |
| | | 5.3 | 7.1 | | | | | 2.5 | 2.0 |
| Quick | | 1.8 | 2.1 | | | | | 1.3 | 1.4 |
| | | .3 | 1.6 | | | | | .9 | .9 |
| | 0 UND | 0 UND | 41 8.9 | | | | | 0 UND | 0 UND |
| Sales/Receivables | 0 UND | 0 UND | 69 5.3 | | | | | 14 26.8 | 4 84.8 |
| | 19 18.8 | 19 18.8 | 87 4.2 | | | | | 72 5.1 | 61 6.0 |
| | | | | | | | Cost of Sales/Inventory | | |
| | | | | | | | Cost of Sales/Payables | | |
| | | 2.2 | 3.3 | | | | | 5.3 | 7.1 |
| Sales/Working Capital | | 7.4 | 6.1 | | | | | 17.8 | 14.8 |
| | | UND | 10.9 | | | | | NM | 135.6 |
| | | | 305.5 | | | | | 9.7 | 84.6 |
| EBIT/Interest | | (15) | 33.6 | | | | | (10) 3.9 | (18) 23.4 |
| | | | 3.4 | | | | | 2.2 | 3.8 |
| | | | | | | | Net Profit + Depr., Dep., Amort./Cur. Mat. L/T/D | | |
| | | .0 | .0 | | | | | .2 | .1 |
| Fixed/Worth | | .5 | .2 | | | | | .6 | .6 |
| | | 2.3 | .4 | | | | | NM | 1.4 |
| | | .2 | .5 | | | | | .6 | .6 |
| Debt/Worth | | .6 | 1.1 | | | | | 2.2 | 1.3 |
| | | 2.4 | 1.5 | | | | | NM | 5.9 |
| | | 124.7 | 183.5 | | | | | 360.7 | 188.1 |
| % Profit Before Taxes/Tangible Net Worth | | 24.9 | (18) 47.9 | | | | | (11) 38.8 | (20) 65.5 |
| | | 2.8 | 15.8 | | | | | 14.8 | 5.6 |
| | | 51.1 | 50.5 | | | | | 42.0 | 108.5 |
| % Profit Before Taxes/Total Assets | | 9.8 | 21.3 | | | | | 17.8 | 18.4 |
| | | 1.5 | 4.6 | | | | | 5.7 | 1.7 |
| | | UND | 164.0 | | | | | 48.6 | 74.7 |
| Sales/Net Fixed Assets | | 12.9 | 34.5 | | | | | 25.0 | 19.5 |
| | | .4 | 13.8 | | | | | 16.0 | 10.5 |
| | | 2.3 | 3.0 | | | | | 5.9 | 5.4 |
| Sales/Total Assets | | 1.2 | 2.7 | | | | | 3.5 | 3.0 |
| | | .4 | 2.2 | | | | | 2.2 | 2.3 |
| | | | .6 | | | | | .8 | .6 |
| % Depr., Dep., Amort./Sales | | (14) | 1.6 | | | | | (13) 1.7 | (19) 1.7 |
| | | | 2.6 | | | | | 2.4 | 3.1 |
| | | | | | | | % Officers', Directors' Owners' Comp/Sales | | |
| Net Sales ($) | 17253M | 19669M | 315253M | 383814M | 78311M | | | 374466M | 1012573M |
| Total Assets ($) | 1835M | 13432M | 118189M | 180897M | 69099M | | | 400346M | 448253M |

M = $ thousand    MM = $ million
See Pages 9 through 22 for Explanation of Ratios and Data

## Comparative Historical Data    Current Data Sorted by Sales

| Type of Statement | 0-1MM | 1-3MM | 3-5MM | 5-10MM | 10-25MM | 25MM & OVER |
|---|---|---|---|---|---|---|
| Unqualified | | | | 2 | 1 | 1 |
| Reviewed | | | | 1 | 2 | 1 |
| Compiled | 2 | 1 | 1 | 1 | 1 | |
| Tax Returns | 3 | 2 | | | 1 | |
| Other | 3 | 4 | 1 | 4 | 9 | 5 |

Historical columns — Type of Statement totals:

| | | |
|---|---|---|
| 5 | 5 | 4 |
| 1 | 1 | 4 |
| 2 | 3 | 6 |
| 7 | 6 | 6 |
| 13 | 25 | 26 |
| 4/1/09- 3/31/10 ALL | 4/1/10- 3/31/11 ALL | 4/1/11- 3/31/12 ALL |

Current data date spans: **5 (4/1-9/30/11)** and **41 (10/1/11-3/31/12)**

| 4/1/09-3/31/10 ALL | 4/1/10-3/31/11 ALL | 4/1/11-3/31/12 ALL | | 0-1MM | 1-3MM | 3-5MM | 5-10MM | 10-25MM | 25MM & OVER |
|---|---|---|---|---|---|---|---|---|---|
| 28 | 40 | 46 | **NUMBER OF STATEMENTS** | 8 | 7 | 2 | 8 | 14 | 7 |
| % | % | % | **ASSETS** | % | % | % | % | % | % |
| 33.1 | 26.8 | 26.4 | Cash & Equivalents | | | | | 10.4 | |
| 19.5 | 24.1 | 31.8 | Trade Receivables (net) | | | | | 48.4 | |
| .1 | 2.8 | 1.2 | Inventory | | | | | 1.8 | |
| 13.6 | 6.3 | 8.1 | All Other Current | | | | | 10.4 | |
| 66.3 | 60.0 | 67.5 | Total Current | | | | | 71.0 | |
| 14.3 | 20.7 | 17.5 | Fixed Assets (net) | | | | | 7.7 | |
| 10.2 | 11.1 | 6.4 | Intangibles (net) | | | | | 13.3 | |
| 9.2 | 8.2 | 8.6 | All Other Non-Current | | | | | 8.1 | |
| 100.0 | 100.0 | 100.0 | Total | | | | | 100.0 | |
| | | | **LIABILITIES** | | | | | | |
| 17.5 | 14.0 | 13.2 | Notes Payable-Short Term | | | | | 12.2 | |
| 3.1 | 2.9 | 2.3 | Cur. Mat.-L.T.D. | | | | | 3.3 | |
| 4.8 | 2.7 | 3.3 | Trade Payables | | | | | 5.4 | |
| .0 | .3 | .4 | Income Taxes Payable | | | | | 1.2 | |
| 15.3 | 15.6 | 18.3 | All Other Current | | | | | 11.5 | |
| 40.7 | 35.5 | 37.3 | Total Current | | | | | 33.5 | |
| 12.3 | 12.9 | 9.6 | Long-Term Debt | | | | | 4.5 | |
| .3 | .6 | .5 | Deferred Taxes | | | | | 1.2 | |
| 7.6 | 8.3 | 8.1 | All Other Non-Current | | | | | 12.7 | |
| 39.1 | 42.7 | 44.5 | Net Worth | | | | | 48.1 | |
| 100.0 | 100.0 | 100.0 | Total Liabilities & Net Worth | | | | | 100.0 | |
| | | | **INCOME DATA** | | | | | | |
| 100.0 | 100.0 | 100.0 | Net Sales | | | | | 100.0 | |
| | | | Gross Profit | | | | | | |
| 80.4 | 85.5 | 84.8 | Operating Expenses | | | | | 86.2 | |
| 19.6 | 14.5 | 15.2 | Operating Profit | | | | | 13.8 | |
| 1.3 | .8 | 1.7 | All Other Expenses (net) | | | | | .5 | |
| 18.3 | 13.7 | 13.5 | Profit Before Taxes | | | | | 13.3 | |
| | | | **RATIOS** | | | | | | |
| 2.8 | 5.4 | 3.7 | | | | | | 3.6 | |
| 1.6 | 2.3 | 2.2 | Current | | | | | 2.0 | |
| .8 | 1.2 | 1.6 | | | | | | 1.7 | |
| 2.5 | 4.6 | 2.9 | | | | | | 2.4 | |
| 1.0 | 2.1 | 1.8 | Quick | | | | | 1.8 | |
| .5 | .6 | 1.1 | | | | | | 1.6 | |
| 0  UND | 0  UND | 0  UND | | | | | | 46  7.9 | |
| 0  UND | 34  10.8 | 36  10.1 | Sales/Receivables | | | | | 76  4.8 | |
| 49  7.5 | 59  6.2 | 85  4.3 | | | | | | 87  4.2 | |
| | | | Cost of Sales/Inventory | | | | | | |
| | | | Cost of Sales/Payables | | | | | | |
| 6.5 | 5.5 | 4.0 | | | | | | 3.3 | |
| 12.7 | 9.4 | 7.5 | Sales/Working Capital | | | | | 6.3 | |
| -20.1 | 121.9 | 25.1 | | | | | | 9.3 | |
| 170.6 | 42.1 | 170.3 | | | | | | 114.6 | |
| (21)  38.4 | (31)  8.3 | (33)  12.5 | EBIT/Interest | | | | | (10)  9.5 | |
| 3.4 | 1.5 | 3.3 | | | | | | 3.4 | |
| | | | Net Profit + Depr., Dep., Amort./Cur. Mat. L/T/D | | | | | | |
| .0 | .1 | .0 | | | | | | .1 | |
| .2 | .4 | .2 | Fixed/Worth | | | | | .2 | |
| 3.9 | NM | .8 | | | | | | .4 | |
| .5 | .5 | .5 | | | | | | .9 | |
| 1.2 | 1.0 | 1.2 | Debt/Worth | | | | | 1.5 | |
| 30.4 | NM | 4.1 | | | | | | 2.9 | |
| 245.1 | 125.0 | 143.3 | | | | | | 142.3 | |
| (22)  80.9 | (30)  69.5 | (40)  49.4 | % Profit Before Taxes/Tangible Net Worth | | | | | (13)  61.1 | |
| 38.9 | 15.7 | 7.3 | | | | | | 17.8 | |
| 68.9 | 47.7 | 47.4 | | | | | | 34.2 | |
| 37.1 | 16.7 | 14.7 | % Profit Before Taxes/Total Assets | | | | | 20.8 | |
| 6.3 | 1.9 | 3.3 | | | | | | 8.0 | |
| 284.7 | 97.8 | 204.7 | | | | | | 99.8 | |
| 59.2 | 27.9 | 30.6 | Sales/Net Fixed Assets | | | | | 41.1 | |
| 13.2 | 10.8 | 12.5 | | | | | | 13.8 | |
| 4.7 | 4.9 | 4.2 | | | | | | 2.9 | |
| 3.0 | 2.5 | 2.7 | Sales/Total Assets | | | | | 2.3 | |
| 1.6 | 1.1 | 1.6 | | | | | | 2.1 | |
| .4 | .4 | .6 | | | | | | .9 | |
| (16)  1.7 | (27)  1.2 | (31)  1.4 | % Depr., Dep., Amort./Sales | | | | | (11)  1.7 | |
| 2.8 | 2.9 | 2.7 | | | | | | 2.9 | |
| | 11.0 | 6.1 | % Officers', Directors' Owners' Comp/Sales | | | | | | |
| | (10)  19.8 | (11)  21.7 | | | | | | | |
| | | 23.7 | | | | | | | 26.8 | |
| 937527M | 1037540M | 814300M | Net Sales ($) | 3861M | 14753M | 6170M | 55674M | 255133M | 478709M |
| 376407M | 703529M | 383452M | Total Assets ($) | 6590M | 4454M | 2247M | 32282M | 163513M | 174366M |

M = $ thousand    MM = $ million
See Pages 9 through 22 for Explanation of Ratios and Data

## Current Data Sorted by Assets / Comparative Historical Data

| | 0-500M | 500M-2MM | 2-10MM | 10-50MM | 50-100MM | 100-250MM | Type of Statement | 4/1/07-3/31/08 ALL | 4/1/08-3/31/09 ALL |
|---|---|---|---|---|---|---|---|---|---|
| | | | 9 | 3 | 1 | 5 | Unqualified | 19 | 36 |
| | | 3 | 2 | 3 | | | Reviewed | 7 | 15 |
| | 18 | 38 | 30 | 7 | 1 | 3 | Compiled | 100 | 82 |
| | 151 | 68 | 18 | 4 | 1 | | Tax Returns | 165 | 167 |
| | 144 | 140 | 179 | 45 | 13 | 14 | Other | 454 | 490 |
| | 178 (4/1-9/30/11) | | | 722 (10/1/11-3/31/12) | | | | | |
| NUMBER OF STATEMENTS | 313 | 249 | 238 | 62 | 16 | 22 | | 745 | 790 |
| | % | % | % | % | % | % | ASSETS | % | % |
| | 28.4 | 13.2 | 13.1 | 19.1 | 16.9 | 10.7 | Cash & Equivalents | 17.1 | 15.4 |
| | 17.7 | 32.6 | 37.7 | 36.2 | 31.7 | 41.2 | Trade Receivables (net) | 31.3 | 33.0 |
| | .7 | 3.9 | 5.2 | 4.4 | 4.7 | 2.2 | Inventory | 3.8 | 4.1 |
| | 4.6 | 5.8 | 7.3 | 6.2 | 14.8 | 8.7 | All Other Current | 7.6 | 6.8 |
| | 51.4 | 55.6 | 63.3 | 65.8 | 68.1 | 62.8 | Total Current | 59.8 | 59.3 |
| | 22.9 | 19.8 | 16.1 | 13.4 | 13.4 | 10.7 | Fixed Assets (net) | 18.0 | 19.0 |
| | 14.5 | 14.5 | 10.9 | 8.2 | 10.6 | 16.0 | Intangibles (net) | 11.9 | 9.9 |
| | 11.2 | 10.1 | 9.7 | 12.6 | 7.9 | 10.5 | All Other Non-Current | 10.3 | 11.8 |
| | 100.0 | 100.0 | 100.0 | 100.0 | 100.0 | 100.0 | Total | 100.0 | 100.0 |
| | | | | | | | LIABILITIES | | |
| | 34.2 | 13.7 | 9.1 | 7.3 | 9.5 | 5.4 | Notes Payable-Short Term | 17.2 | 17.6 |
| | 3.8 | 4.1 | 3.0 | 3.7 | 1.8 | 2.9 | Cur. Mat.-L.T.D. | 5.6 | 4.5 |
| | 2.6 | 1.7 | 3.7 | 6.6 | 2.2 | 9.4 | Trade Payables | 3.8 | 4.8 |
| | .1 | .4 | .2 | .6 | .0 | .3 | Income Taxes Payable | .3 | .4 |
| | 24.2 | 12.5 | 13.9 | 16.0 | 15.1 | 22.4 | All Other Current | 19.8 | 18.8 |
| | 64.9 | 32.4 | 29.9 | 34.1 | 28.7 | 40.4 | Total Current | 46.6 | 46.0 |
| | 22.4 | 21.6 | 13.6 | 12.9 | 10.1 | 11.0 | Long-Term Debt | 17.8 | 16.6 |
| | .0 | .2 | .3 | .0 | .0 | .4 | Deferred Taxes | .1 | .2 |
| | 9.4 | 7.0 | 8.7 | 7.4 | 8.3 | 4.0 | All Other Non-Current | 8.1 | 7.0 |
| | 3.3 | 38.8 | 47.4 | 45.6 | 52.9 | 44.2 | Net Worth | 27.3 | 30.3 |
| | 100.0 | 100.0 | 100.0 | 100.0 | 100.0 | 100.0 | Total Liabilities & Net Worth | 100.0 | 100.0 |
| | | | | | | | INCOME DATA | | |
| | 100.0 | 100.0 | 100.0 | 100.0 | 100.0 | 100.0 | Net Sales | 100.0 | 100.0 |
| | | | | | | | Gross Profit | | |
| | 85.4 | 82.2 | 84.8 | 80.8 | 74.8 | 77.7 | Operating Expenses | 83.7 | 84.0 |
| | 14.6 | 17.8 | 15.2 | 19.2 | 25.2 | 22.3 | Operating Profit | 16.3 | 16.0 |
| | 1.3 | 3.8 | 3.0 | 3.7 | 5.2 | .3 | All Other Expenses (net) | 2.0 | 2.8 |
| | 13.4 | 14.0 | 12.2 | 15.5 | 19.9 | 22.0 | Profit Before Taxes | 14.3 | 13.2 |
| | | | | | | | RATIOS | | |
| | 2.8 | 5.5 | 4.6 | 5.8 | 4.4 | 2.2 | Current | 3.6 | 3.5 |
| | 1.0 | 1.8 | 2.2 | 2.1 | 2.1 | 1.7 | | 1.7 | 1.7 |
| | .3 | .9 | 1.4 | 1.2 | 1.6 | 1.1 | | .8 | .8 |
| | 2.5 | 4.9 | 3.8 | 4.6 | 3.8 | 2.1 | Quick | 3.0 | 2.9 |
| | (312) .9 | 1.4 | 1.7 | 1.9 | 1.8 | 1.3 | | (744) 1.3 | 1.4 |
| | .3 | .7 | 1.0 | 1.0 | 1.4 | 1.0 | | .6 | .6 |
| | 0 UND | 0 UND | 31 11.6 | 35 10.5 | 31 11.8 | 54 6.7 | Sales/Receivables | 0 UND | 0 UND |
| | 0 UND | 45 8.1 | 52 7.0 | 56 6.5 | 60 6.1 | 81 4.5 | | 42 8.7 | 45 8.2 |
| | 31 11.8 | 72 5.1 | 73 5.0 | 83 4.4 | 83 4.4 | 111 3.3 | | 70 5.2 | 74 4.9 |
| | | | | | | | Cost of Sales/Inventory | | |
| | | | | | | | Cost of Sales/Payables | | |
| | 15.7 | 4.8 | 4.9 | 3.7 | 4.1 | 5.1 | Sales/Working Capital | 5.4 | 5.4 |
| | UND | 11.3 | 7.8 | 8.1 | 7.1 | 8.2 | | 12.0 | 12.3 |
| | -16.8 | -77.0 | 17.0 | 27.5 | 8.5 | 28.8 | | -65.2 | -78.3 |
| | 38.5 | 29.3 | 47.3 | 125.4 | 137.8 | 145.0 | EBIT/Interest | 31.4 | 33.8 |
| | (234) 12.4 | (198) 7.7 | (207) 12.6 | (46) 22.1 | (15) 50.1 | (20) 31.8 | | (608) 8.9 | (642) 8.5 |
| | 2.6 | 2.7 | 2.5 | 6.0 | 12.3 | 16.7 | | 2.4 | 2.2 |
| | | | 2.6 | | | | Net Profit + Depr., Dep., Amort./Cur. Mat. L/T/D | 5.6 | 6.9 |
| | | (13) 1.4 | | | | | | (46) 2.1 | (50) 1.9 |
| | | .5 | | | | | | 1.0 | 1.0 |
| | .0 | .1 | .1 | .1 | .2 | .2 | Fixed/Worth | .1 | .1 |
| | .8 | .3 | .3 | .2 | .3 | .3 | | .4 | .4 |
| | -1.4 | 24.1 | 1.4 | .8 | .5 | .9 | | 22.1 | 5.3 |
| | .8 | .4 | .4 | .2 | .3 | .9 | Debt/Worth | .5 | .6 |
| | 8.8 | 2.3 | 1.3 | 1.5 | 1.4 | 2.2 | | 1.8 | 1.9 |
| | -2.5 | -15.0 | 5.8 | 4.4 | 3.0 | 8.1 | | -27.9 | 63.1 |
| | 528.6 | 108.0 | 114.3 | 128.3 | 198.2 | 167.4 | % Profit Before Taxes/Tangible Net Worth | 153.5 | 143.1 |
| | (183) 137.1 | (182) 38.5 | (202) 37.4 | (56) 61.0 | (14) 116.8 | (19) 137.2 | | (540) 72.3 | (605) 58.8 |
| | 43.8 | 10.5 | 10.3 | 17.8 | 58.2 | 76.8 | | 16.4 | 13.9 |
| | 107.1 | 40.1 | 44.7 | 60.0 | 84.4 | 63.6 | % Profit Before Taxes/Total Assets | 70.8 | 66.6 |
| | 39.1 | 11.1 | 15.0 | 16.7 | 55.0 | 52.2 | | 22.0 | 18.2 |
| | 5.9 | 2.9 | 2.7 | 4.3 | 9.0 | 13.9 | | 4.1 | 3.2 |
| | 778.6 | 92.0 | 60.1 | 62.0 | 27.1 | 25.5 | Sales/Net Fixed Assets | 83.6 | 80.1 |
| | 54.1 | 33.0 | 31.0 | 29.4 | 18.9 | 17.0 | | 29.3 | 29.9 |
| | 17.5 | 14.2 | 15.7 | 16.1 | 12.2 | 11.3 | | 15.5 | 15.4 |
| | 11.3 | 3.8 | 3.3 | 3.1 | 2.9 | 2.4 | Sales/Total Assets | 4.7 | 4.5 |
| | 5.7 | 2.6 | 2.4 | 2.4 | 2.4 | 1.9 | | 2.8 | 2.9 |
| | 3.0 | 1.5 | 1.8 | 1.6 | 1.6 | 1.2 | | 2.0 | 2.0 |
| | .7 | .9 | .9 | .8 | 1.4 | 1.1 | % Depr., Dep., Amort./Sales | .9 | .9 |
| | (146) 1.3 | (161) 1.5 | (177) 1.4 | (52) 1.1 | (13) 2.3 | (17) 1.6 | | (477) 1.5 | (538) 1.5 |
| | 2.2 | 3.3 | 2.5 | 2.2 | 2.7 | 2.1 | | 2.5 | 2.5 |
| | 14.5 | 11.1 | 15.5 | 4.9 | | | % Officers', Directors' Owners' Comp/Sales | 14.2 | 11.8 |
| | (201) 22.6 | (129) 19.9 | (102) 23.9 | (25) 16.5 | | | | (366) 22.8 | (375) 21.4 |
| | 30.4 | 30.9 | 30.0 | 27.8 | | | | 30.9 | 30.3 |
| | 427839M | 843131M | 2807042M | 3562721M | 3136168M | 6468372M | Net Sales ($) | 16594587M | 15157413M |
| | 63466M | 273884M | 1087762M | 1144933M | 1218878M | 3611919M | Total Assets ($) | 5944918M | 5826677M |

© RMA 2012

M = $ thousand    MM = $ million
See Pages 9 through 22 for Explanation of Ratios and Data

## Comparative Historical Data / Current Data Sorted by Sales

| | 4/1/09-3/31/10 ALL | 4/1/10-3/31/11 ALL | 4/1/11-3/31/12 ALL | 0-1MM | 1-3MM | 3-5MM | 5-10MM | 10-25MM | 25MM & OVER |
|---|---|---|---|---|---|---|---|---|---|
| **Type of Statement** | | | | | | | | | |
| Unqualified | 37 | 23 | 18 | | | 1 | 2 | 6 | 9 |
| Reviewed | 9 | 7 | 8 | | 2 | | 3 | 1 | 2 |
| Compiled | 81 | 88 | 97 | 20 | 22 | 16 | 14 | 15 | 10 |
| Tax Returns | 225 | 222 | 242 | 105 | 72 | 23 | 26 | 10 | 6 |
| Other | 480 | 499 | 535 | 105 | 118 | 56 | 74 | 112 | 70 |
| | | | | 178 (4/1-9/30/11) | | 722 (10/1/11-3/31/12) | | | |
| **NUMBER OF STATEMENTS** | 832 | 839 | 900 | 230 | 214 | 96 | 119 | 144 | 97 |
| | % | % | % | % | % | % | % | % | % |
| **ASSETS** | | | | | | | | | |
| Cash & Equivalents | 17.4 | 17.7 | 18.9 | 21.5 | 20.1 | 18.4 | 16.1 | 17.0 | 16.9 |
| Trade Receivables (net) | 31.7 | 30.2 | 29.2 | 16.7 | 29.4 | 29.8 | 36.0 | 35.9 | 39.4 |
| Inventory | 3.3 | 3.5 | 3.1 | .7 | 3.3 | 4.3 | 3.3 | 5.0 | 4.3 |
| All Other Current | 5.3 | 7.2 | 6.1 | 5.0 | 5.2 | 5.1 | 5.6 | 8.3 | 8.8 |
| Total Current | 57.7 | 58.5 | 57.3 | 43.9 | 58.0 | 57.6 | 61.0 | 66.1 | 69.5 |
| Fixed Assets (net) | 18.4 | 18.2 | 19.1 | 31.2 | 16.4 | 15.4 | 15.9 | 14.3 | 11.6 |
| Intangibles (net) | 12.1 | 12.2 | 13.1 | 15.5 | 14.9 | 15.0 | 10.4 | 10.0 | 9.1 |
| All Other Non-Current | 11.8 | 11.1 | 10.5 | 9.4 | 10.8 | 12.0 | 12.6 | 9.6 | 9.9 |
| Total | 100.0 | 100.0 | 100.0 | 100.0 | 100.0 | 100.0 | 100.0 | 100.0 | 100.0 |
| **LIABILITIES** | | | | | | | | | |
| Notes Payable-Short Term | 18.2 | 19.1 | 18.9 | 24.2 | 23.8 | 21.4 | 16.7 | 10.6 | 7.8 |
| Cur. Mat.-L.T.D. | 5.1 | 3.6 | 3.6 | 3.1 | 4.0 | 5.8 | 3.7 | 2.8 | 2.9 |
| Trade Payables | 3.8 | 3.4 | 3.1 | 2.3 | 2.0 | 2.1 | 3.0 | 4.1 | 6.7 |
| Income Taxes Payable | .2 | .3 | .3 | .1 | .2 | .3 | .3 | .3 | .5 |
| All Other Current | 19.2 | 18.8 | 17.5 | 15.0 | 16.9 | 26.0 | 17.2 | 16.6 | 17.9 |
| Total Current | 46.5 | 45.3 | 43.3 | 44.8 | 46.9 | 55.6 | 40.9 | 34.4 | 35.8 |
| Long-Term Debt | 17.0 | 18.6 | 18.7 | 29.8 | 21.3 | 12.2 | 13.9 | 12.1 | 8.6 |
| Deferred Taxes | .3 | .2 | .2 | .0 | .1 | .0 | .3 | .4 | .2 |
| All Other Non-Current | 6.2 | 7.2 | 8.3 | 7.4 | 9.1 | 10.2 | 10.6 | 6.4 | 6.7 |
| Net Worth | 29.9 | 28.8 | 29.6 | 18.0 | 22.6 | 21.9 | 34.3 | 46.8 | 48.7 |
| Total Liabilities & Net Worth | 100.0 | 100.0 | 100.0 | 100.0 | 100.0 | 100.0 | 100.0 | 100.0 | 100.0 |
| **INCOME DATA** | | | | | | | | | |
| Net Sales | 100.0 | 100.0 | 100.0 | 100.0 | 100.0 | 100.0 | 100.0 | 100.0 | 100.0 |
| Gross Profit | | | | | | | | | |
| Operating Expenses | 84.1 | 83.4 | 83.7 | 76.1 | 85.1 | 91.4 | 89.3 | 85.5 | 81.1 |
| Operating Profit | 15.9 | 16.6 | 16.3 | 23.9 | 14.9 | 8.6 | 10.7 | 14.5 | 18.9 |
| All Other Expenses (net) | 2.7 | 2.6 | 2.6 | 5.8 | 1.5 | .7 | .9 | 2.0 | 2.7 |
| Profit Before Taxes | 13.3 | 13.9 | 13.7 | 18.1 | 13.4 | 7.9 | 9.8 | 12.5 | 16.2 |
| **RATIOS** | | | | | | | | | |
| Current | 3.8 | 4.0 | 4.0 | 3.3 | 4.8 | 4.1 | 5.1 | 3.9 | 3.7 |
| | 1.6 | 1.7 | 1.7 | 1.0 | 1.5 | 1.7 | 2.2 | 2.0 | 2.0 |
| | .8 | .9 | .9 | .4 | .6 | .9 | 1.1 | 1.3 | 1.3 |
| Quick | 3.2 | 3.1 | 3.5 | 2.8 | 3.9 | 3.3 | 4.5 | 3.2 | 3.0 |
| | 1.3 | (838) 1.4 | (899) 1.4 | (229) 1.0 | 1.2 | 1.4 | 1.7 | 1.6 | 1.7 |
| | .6 | .7 | .7 | .3 | .5 | .5 | 1.0 | 1.0 | 1.0 |
| Sales/Receivables | 0 UND | 0 UND | 0 UND | 0 UND | 0 UND | 0 UND | 12 29.7 | 29 12.6 | 34 10.8 |
| | 41 8.9 | 41 8.9 | 38 9.7 | 0 UND | 27 13.5 | 43 8.5 | 49 7.5 | 48 7.6 | 56 6.5 |
| | 68 5.3 | 69 5.3 | 65 5.6 | 41 8.8 | 69 5.3 | 72 5.1 | 69 5.3 | 64 5.7 | 83 4.4 |
| Cost of Sales/Inventory | | | | | | | | | |
| Cost of Sales/Payables | | | | | | | | | |
| Sales/Working Capital | 5.6 | 5.2 | 5.8 | 8.9 | 5.7 | 5.4 | 5.1 | 5.5 | 4.8 |
| | 15.5 | 12.5 | 14.4 | 397.5 | 25.9 | 13.3 | 9.8 | 9.2 | 7.9 |
| | -45.7 | -102.7 | -63.5 | -11.3 | -34.2 | -50.8 | 53.0 | 21.2 | 19.7 |
| EBIT/Interest | 33.7 | 46.0 | 44.9 | 34.3 | 34.1 | 24.6 | 38.6 | 54.1 | 137.8 |
| | (657) 9.6 | (662) 10.5 | (720) 12.6 | (149) 9.3 | (177) 11.9 | (83) 6.2 | (102) 6.6 | (126) 17.3 | (83) 33.2 |
| | 2.0 | 2.3 | 2.9 | 3.7 | 3.3 | 1.0 | 1.3 | 2.4 | 6.8 |
| Net Profit + Depr., Dep., Amort./Cur. Mat. L/T/D | 8.1 | 6.8 | 3.9 | | | | | | 11.8 |
| | (34) 3.2 | (40) 3.2 | (39) 2.1 | | | | | | (14) 3.3 |
| | .7 | 1.3 | .5 | | | | | | .9 |
| Fixed/Worth | .1 | .1 | .1 | .1 | .0 | .1 | .1 | .1 | .1 |
| | .3 | .3 | .3 | 1.3 | .2 | .3 | .3 | 1.3 | .3 |
| | 4.3 | 4.3 | 12.1 | -5.6 | -4.0 | -1.5 | 3.8 | 1.0 | .5 |
| Debt/Worth | .5 | .5 | .5 | .9 | .5 | .6 | .5 | .5 | .4 |
| | 1.9 | 1.9 | 2.2 | 8.6 | 3.9 | 2.1 | 1.8 | 1.3 | 1.2 |
| | UND | -90.0 | -15.8 | -4.5 | -4.0 | -6.1 | 277.8 | 4.0 | 3.2 |
| % Profit Before Taxes/Tangible Net Worth | 151.6 | 152.9 | 154.4 | 322.3 | 221.2 | 74.7 | 133.0 | 118.5 | 149.0 |
| | (629) 57.5 | (622) 63.7 | (656) 65.2 | (145) 84.7 | (142) 90.0 | (65) 25.2 | (90) 36.9 | (126) 59.5 | (88) 80.5 |
| | 8.8 | 10.0 | 16.2 | 25.0 | 16.5 | 5.6 | 5.3 | 12.4 | 27.1 |
| % Profit Before Taxes/Total Assets | 68.0 | 64.2 | 61.1 | 76.7 | 70.0 | 32.1 | 46.2 | 58.2 | 63.9 |
| | 18.7 | 20.3 | 20.3 | 23.6 | 28.1 | 9.9 | 9.5 | 21.0 | 35.5 |
| | 2.0 | 2.6 | 3.8 | 5.2 | 5.7 | .0 | 1.0 | 3.3 | 7.5 |
| Sales/Net Fixed Assets | 120.5 | 110.8 | 105.6 | 224.8 | 278.9 | 110.6 | 75.2 | 63.1 | 44.9 |
| | 31.4 | 33.3 | 34.0 | 27.2 | 51.2 | 36.4 | 34.9 | 32.2 | 25.8 |
| | 15.1 | 16.1 | 16.1 | 4.7 | 19.8 | 23.7 | 19.1 | 16.2 | 16.9 |
| Sales/Total Assets | 5.0 | 4.7 | 5.1 | 6.2 | 6.6 | 5.5 | 4.7 | 4.3 | 3.4 |
| | 3.0 | 2.9 | 3.0 | 2.4 | 3.7 | 3.0 | 3.2 | 2.7 | 2.6 |
| | 1.9 | 1.9 | 1.9 | .8 | 2.1 | 1.9 | 2.3 | 2.1 | 2.0 |
| % Depr., Dep., Amort./Sales | .9 | .9 | .9 | 1.0 | .7 | 1.1 | .9 | .8 | .8 |
| | (511) 1.6 | (524) 1.5 | (566) 1.4 | (123) 2.3 | (110) 1.3 | (62) 1.4 | (84) 1.4 | (110) 1.3 | (77) 1.3 |
| | 2.8 | 2.5 | 2.5 | 11.2 | 2.1 | 2.2 | 2.3 | 2.2 | 1.9 |
| % Officers', Directors' Owners' Comp/Sales | 10.9 | 13.1 | 12.1 | 11.2 | 13.1 | 16.1 | 11.3 | 16.3 | 5.8 |
| | (406) 21.9 | (438) 21.8 | (463) 22.3 | (130) 20.1 | (115) 21.5 | (58) 25.1 | (60) 20.4 | (65) 24.6 | (35) 20.4 |
| | 31.7 | 31.1 | 30.9 | 28.4 | 32.7 | 34.5 | 34.2 | 31.9 | 32.6 |
| Net Sales ($) | 18739443M | 18540903M | 17245273M | 112645M | 387120M | 376543M | 843245M | 2113440M | 13412280M |
| Total Assets ($) | 6881308M | 6524767M | 7400842M | 107579M | 166441M | 169786M | 337470M | 903048M | 5716518M |

© RMA 2012

M = $ thousand    MM = $ million
See Pages 9 through 22 for Explanation of Ratios and Data

## Current Data Sorted by Assets        Comparative Historical Data

| 0-500M | 500M-2MM | 2-10MM | 10-50MM | 50-100MM | 100-250MM | Type of Statement | 4/1/07-3/31/08 ALL | 4/1/08-3/31/09 ALL |
|---|---|---|---|---|---|---|---|---|
| | | | | | | Unqualified | 8 | 7 |
| 2 | | 4 | 7 | 1 | 2 | Reviewed | 2 | 2 |
| 4 | | 2 | 3 | | 1 | Compiled | 4 | 3 |
| 2 | | 1 | 1 | .1 | | Tax Returns | 2 | 5 |
| 4 | 2 | 3 | 1 | | | Other | | |
| 12 | 11 | 7 | 6 | 2 | 1 | | 10 | 19 |
| | 14 (4/1-9/30/11) | | 59 (10/1/11-3/31/12) | | | | | |
| 18 | 13 | 17 | 17 | 4 | 4 | NUMBER OF STATEMENTS | 26 | 36 |
| % | % | % | % | % | % | ASSETS | % | % |
| 36.5 | 61.2 | 43.4 | 24.6 | | | Cash & Equivalents | 32.9 | 27.8 |
| 9.7 | .7 | 24.5 | 14.3 | | | Trade Receivables (net) | 16.5 | 17.5 |
| .0 | .0 | 1.2 | .1 | | | Inventory | .1 | .3 |
| 9.9 | 9.7 | 8.6 | 25.9 | | | All Other Current | 23.3 | 21.1 |
| 56.2 | 71.6 | 77.7 | 64.9 | | | Total Current | 72.8 | 66.6 |
| 20.6 | 8.6 | 6.3 | 6.3 | | | Fixed Assets (net) | 11.7 | 10.1 |
| 12.1 | 13.9 | 10.4 | 16.7 | | | Intangibles (net) | 8.9 | 10.1 |
| 11.2 | 5.9 | 5.6 | 12.1 | | | All Other Non-Current | 6.6 | 13.2 |
| 100.0 | 100.0 | 100.0 | 100.0 | | | Total | 100.0 | 100.0 |
| | | | | | | LIABILITIES | | |
| 28.8 | 1.8 | 4.9 | 4.1 | | | Notes Payable-Short Term | 9.5 | 11.6 |
| 7.6 | .4 | .7 | 2.1 | | | Cur. Mat.-L.T.D. | .4 | 5.5 |
| 9.4 | 9.8 | 12.4 | 9.8 | | | Trade Payables | 3.4 | 5.0 |
| .0 | .0 | .0 | .1 | | | Income Taxes Payable | .0 | .1 |
| 29.9 | 53.9 | 40.2 | 58.0 | | | All Other Current | 45.5 | 47.6 |
| 75.7 | 66.0 | 58.3 | 74.1 | | | Total Current | 58.8 | 69.9 |
| 10.5 | 9.8 | 13.7 | 12.0 | | | Long-Term Debt | 20.6 | 13.8 |
| .0 | .0 | .2 | .0 | | | Deferred Taxes | .1 | .1 |
| .9 | .6 | 2.6 | 11.7 | | | All Other Non-Current | 4.2 | 12.3 |
| 12.9 | 23.7 | 25.4 | 2.2 | | | Net Worth | 16.3 | 3.9 |
| 100.0 | 100.0 | 100.0 | 100.0 | | | Total Liabilties & Net Worth | 100.0 | 100.0 |
| | | | | | | INCOME DATA | | |
| 100.0 | 100.0 | 100.0 | 100.0 | | | Net Sales | 100.0 | 100.0 |
| | | | | | | Gross Profit | | |
| 88.8 | 94.6 | 91.5 | 91.3 | | | Operating Expenses | 93.9 | 96.6 |
| 11.2 | 5.4 | 8.5 | 8.7 | | | Operating Profit | 6.1 | 3.4 |
| .1 | 2.7 | .4 | 1.0 | | | All Other Expenses (net) | 2.7 | .9 |
| 11.0 | 2.8 | 8.0 | 7.8 | | | Profit Before Taxes | 3.4 | 2.5 |
| | | | | | | RATIOS | | |
| 1.7 | 1.3 | 2.1 | 1.0 | | | | 1.7 | 1.8 |
| 1.1 | 1.0 | 1.4 | 1.0 | | | Current | 1.1 | 1.3 |
| .5 | .9 | 1.0 | .8 | | | | 1.0 | 1.0 |
| 1.4 | 1.0 | 1.6 | 1.0 | | | | 1.5 | 1.5 |
| .9 | .9 | 1.0 | .7 | | | Quick | 1.0 | 1.0 |
| .3 | .8 | .9 | .4 | | | | .1 | .3 |
| 0 UND | 0 UND | 0 919.8 | 1 323.7 | | | | 1 503.3 | 3 130.5 |
| 0 UND | 0 999.8 | 6 57.8 | 7 50.3 | | | Sales/Receivables | 9 38.5 | 9 42.4 |
| 1 371.1 | 3 107.3 | 34 10.7 | 61 6.0 | | | | 29 12.6 | 26 14.1 |
| | | | | | | Cost of Sales/Inventory | | |
| | | | | | | Cost of Sales/Payables | | |
| 38.2 | 38.4 | 12.3 | 16.1 | | | | 3.2 | 9.5 |
| 436.8 | -420.0 | 53.7 | -25.3 | | | Sales/Working Capital | 20.5 | 77.9 |
| -49.3 | -4.3 | -87.6 | -4.8 | | | | -37.1 | -26.4 |
| | | | 50.3 | | | | 20.6 | 19.5 |
| | | | (15) 6.1 | | | EBIT/Interest | (17) 3.2 | (27) 1.3 |
| | | | 1.7 | | | | -3.8 | -3.9 |
| | | | | | | Net Profit + Depr., Dep., Amort./Cur. Mat. L/T/D | | |
| .0 | .0 | .1 | .5 | | | | .1 | .1 |
| .1 | .0 | .3 | -1.4 | | | Fixed/Worth | .7 | 2.0 |
| 2.4 | NM | -24.9 | -.1 | | | | -.9 | -.3 |
| .6 | 3.3 | 1.2 | 18.9 | | | | 1.3 | 3.2 |
| 5.3 | 34.0 | 4.7 | -26.5 | | | Debt/Worth | 13.7 | 57.0 |
| UND | -13.0 | -589.8 | -3.1 | | | | -7.9 | -5.6 |
| 862.5 | | 61.2 | | | | % Profit Before Taxes/Tangible Net Worth | 107.5 | 117.1 |
| (14) 142.9 | | (12) 35.1 | | | | | (17) 20.2 | (24) 51.9 |
| 44.0 | | 14.7 | | | | | 5.3 | -9.6 |
| 87.2 | 30.3 | 10.6 | 4.8 | | | % Profit Before Taxes/Total Assets | 9.4 | 18.7 |
| 28.9 | 9.7 | 5.7 | 3.5 | | | | 2.9 | 2.9 |
| 5.9 | .3 | 2.1 | .8 | | | | -4.0 | -2.1 |
| UND | UND | 999.8 | 81.9 | | | | 87.1 | 598.5 |
| UND | 999.8 | 46.0 | 32.5 | | | Sales/Net Fixed Assets | 12.8 | 26.0 |
| 16.1 | 20.6 | 18.4 | 12.5 | | | | 7.6 | 9.9 |
| 28.9 | 6.0 | 9.9 | 1.3 | | | | 3.0 | 14.9 |
| 10.8 | 2.8 | 2.4 | .4 | | | Sales/Total Assets | .6 | 1.6 |
| 3.5 | .2 | .4 | .3 | | | | .3 | .3 |
| | | .0 | 1.3 | | | | .9 | .2 |
| | (14) | .3 | (12) 2.1 | | | % Depr., Dep., Amort./Sales | (14) 1.9 | (24) 1.1 |
| | | 2.6 | 3.4 | | | | 3.8 | 3.9 |
| | | | | | | % Officers', Directors' Owners' Comp/Sales | | |
| 70611M | 187401M | 823635M | 453584M | 601494M | 4338618M | Net Sales ($) | 2899234M | 4249877M |
| 3664M | 16975M | 75322M | 390820M | 248081M | 709196M | Total Assets ($) | 1240071M | 1621390M |

M = $ thousand     MM = $ million
See Pages 9 through 22 for Explanation of Ratios and Data

## Comparative Historical Data / Current Data Sorted by Sales

| Hist 1 | Hist 2 | Hist 3 | Type of Statement | 0-1MM | 1-3MM | 3-5MM | 5-10MM | 10-25MM | 25MM & OVER |
|---|---|---|---|---|---|---|---|---|---|
| 8 | 10 | 14 | Unqualified | | 1 | 3 | 1 | 3 | 6 |
| 7 | 4 | 6 | Reviewed | | | 1 | 1 | 2 | 2 |
| 2 | 4 | 4 | Compiled | 1 | 2 | | | 1 | 1 |
| 13 | 10 | 10 | Tax Returns | 6 | 2 | 1 | | 1 | 1 |
| 17 | 28 | 39 | Other | 10 | 4 | 5 | 5 | 7 | 8 |
| 4/1/09-3/31/10 ALL | 4/1/10-3/31/11 ALL | 4/1/11-3/31/12 ALL | | | 14 (4/1-9/30/11) | | | 59 (10/1/11-3/31/12) | |
| 47 | 56 | 73 | **NUMBER OF STATEMENTS** | 17 | 9 | 10 | 7 | 14 | 16 |
| % | % | % | **ASSETS** | % | % | % | % | % | % |
| 33.9 | 34.3 | 37.4 | Cash & Equivalents | 58.0 | | 45.0 | | 34.9 | 17.4 |
| 7.8 | 15.3 | 12.8 | Trade Receivables (net) | 3.2 | | 5.7 | | 25.5 | 24.8 |
| .4 | .4 | .3 | Inventory | .0 | | .0 | | .4 | .0 |
| 23.8 | 20.8 | 15.0 | All Other Current | .6 | | 22.6 | | 15.2 | 20.5 |
| 65.9 | 70.8 | 65.5 | Total Current | 61.8 | | 73.4 | | 75.9 | 62.7 |
| 13.4 | 8.3 | 9.9 | Fixed Assets (net) | 19.0 | | 3.5 | | 6.8 | 7.5 |
| 5.7 | 8.1 | 13.8 | Intangibles (net) | 14.2 | | 4.4 | | 10.2 | 17.5 |
| 14.9 | 12.9 | 10.8 | All Other Non-Current | 4.9 | | 18.7 | | 7.1 | 12.2 |
| 100.0 | 100.0 | 100.0 | Total | 100.0 | | 100.0 | | 100.0 | 100.0 |
| | | | **LIABILITIES** | | | | | | |
| 14.7 | 10.4 | 9.5 | Notes Payable-Short Term | 2.1 | | 2.1 | | 4.8 | 4.3 |
| 1.8 | .7 | 2.8 | Cur. Mat.-L.T.D. | 2.9 | | .0 | | 7.7 | 2.9 |
| 3.7 | 2.2 | 9.6 | Trade Payables | 15.7 | | 2.0 | | 10.9 | 11.9 |
| 2.6 | .6 | 1.4 | Income Taxes Payable | .0 | | .0 | | .1 | .1 |
| 45.8 | 57.0 | 45.8 | All Other Current | 40.7 | | 64.6 | | 41.5 | 44.6 |
| 68.6 | 70.9 | 69.1 | Total Current | 61.4 | | 68.7 | | 65.0 | 63.8 |
| 8.6 | 7.6 | 11.7 | Long-Term Debt | 15.6 | | 6.6 | | 12.0 | 17.2 |
| .1 | .1 | .0 | Deferred Taxes | .0 | | .0 | | .2 | .0 |
| 15.8 | 6.1 | 4.0 | All Other Non-Current | .5 | | 9.5 | | 1.4 | 8.1 |
| 6.9 | 15.3 | 15.1 | Net Worth | 22.5 | | 15.2 | | 21.4 | 10.9 |
| 100.0 | 100.0 | 100.0 | Total Liabilties & Net Worth | 100.0 | | 100.0 | | 100.0 | 100.0 |
| | | | **INCOME DATA** | | | | | | |
| 100.0 | 100.0 | 100.0 | Net Sales | 100.0 | | 100.0 | | 100.0 | 100.0 |
| | | | Gross Profit | | | | | | |
| 93.5 | 94.8 | 91.5 | Operating Expenses | 85.0 | | 89.4 | | 96.7 | 94.1 |
| 6.5 | 5.2 | 8.5 | Operating Profit | 15.0 | | 10.6 | | 3.3 | 5.9 |
| 1.4 | .5 | 1.0 | All Other Expenses (net) | 2.1 | | -.1 | | .5 | 1.3 |
| 5.1 | 4.7 | 7.5 | Profit Before Taxes | 13.0 | | 10.7 | | 2.8 | 4.6 |
| | | | **RATIOS** | | | | | | |
| 1.8 | 1.5 | 1.5 | | 1.1 | | 2.3 | | 1.6 | 1.4 |
| 1.0 | 1.0 | 1.0 | Current | 1.0 | | 1.0 | | 1.1 | 1.0 |
| 1.0 | .9 | .8 | | .4 | | .9 | | .9 | .6 |
| 1.7 | 1.3 | 1.2 | | 1.0 | | 2.0 | | 1.6 | .9 |
| 1.0 | .9 | .9 | Quick | 1.0 | | 1.0 | | 1.0 | .7 |
| .1 | .2 | .3 | | .4 | | .3 | | .6 | .3 |
| 0 UND | 0 UND | 0 UND | | 0 UND | 0 UND | | | 1 403.8 | 1 349.7 |
| 1 325.4 | 7 50.7 | 2 178.1 | Sales/Receivables | 0 UND | 1 708.6 | | | 11 34.2 | 11 33.0 |
| 11 32.9 | 34 10.7 | 29 12.6 | | 3 124.5 | 13 27.8 | | | 34 10.8 | 44 8.3 |
| | | | | | | | | | |
| | | | Cost of Sales/Inventory | | | | | | |
| | | | | | | | | | |
| | | | Cost of Sales/Payables | | | | | | |
| 8.8 | 10.8 | 17.1 | | 75.8 | | 11.6 | | 15.0 | 72.5 |
| 47.4 | 131.5 | 578.6 | Sales/Working Capital | -49.5 | | 16.9 | | 769.1 | 789.2 |
| -16.5 | -16.5 | -15.3 | | -3.6 | | -33.1 | | -16.8 | -102.9 |
| 15.0 | 28.7 | 49.3 | | | | | | | 7.2 |
| (32) 5.8 | (33) 3.1 | (40) 8.7 | EBIT/Interest | | | | | (13) 2.1 | 2.1 |
| -1.7 | -.1 | 2.1 | | | | | | | 1.5 |
| | | | Net Profit + Depr., Dep., Amort./Cur. Mat. L/T/D | | | | | | |
| .0 | .0 | .0 | | .0 | | .0 | | .0 | .2 |
| .8 | .5 | .5 | Fixed/Worth | .9 | | .3 | | .2 | 1.6 |
| -.8 | -2.1 | -.6 | | -1.1 | | -1.0 | | NM | -.1 |
| 2.3 | 1.8 | 2.3 | | 2.3 | | 5.6 | | 1.3 | 7.7 |
| 23.1 | 12.1 | 33.9 | Debt/Worth | 82.0 | | 21.5 | | 12.1 | NM |
| -30.4 | -21.0 | -9.1 | | -11.8 | | -39.7 | | -10.3 | -3.8 |
| 205.5 | 90.1 | 170.3 | | 862.5 | | | | 53.5 | |
| (32) 42.7 | (37) 27.3 | (46) 70.3 | % Profit Before Taxes/Tangible Net Worth | (10) 346.5 | | | | (10) 38.5 | |
| 12.8 | 7.2 | 32.1 | | 87.3 | | | | 7.5 | |
| 16.6 | 10.0 | 21.5 | | 62.2 | | 25.7 | | 22.2 | 8.3 |
| 5.3 | 4.7 | 4.3 | % Profit Before Taxes/Total Assets | 4.9 | | 8.3 | | 6.5 | 4.2 |
| .2 | .1 | 1.7 | | -.6 | | 3.0 | | 1.9 | 3.0 |
| 303.0 | 885.2 | UND | | UND | | UND | | UND | 999.8 |
| 30.9 | 45.5 | 65.4 | Sales/Net Fixed Assets | 19.5 | | 61.7 | | 95.0 | 208.8 |
| 8.5 | 13.4 | 16.4 | | 7.8 | | 28.4 | | 14.7 | 39.6 |
| 9.5 | 5.9 | 9.9 | | 4.3 | | 4.5 | | 32.8 | 30.2 |
| 1.4 | .9 | 2.2 | Sales/Total Assets | .6 | | .7 | | 4.7 | 5.8 |
| .3 | .3 | .3 | | .2 | | .3 | | 1.2 | 1.1 |
| .5 | .3 | .3 | | | | | | .1 | .0 |
| (24) 1.4 | (36) 1.4 | (43) 1.5 | % Depr., Dep., Amort./Sales | | | | | (10) 1.2 | (12) .3 |
| 2.8 | 2.9 | 2.9 | | | | | | 2.7 | 1.3 |
| 2.1 | 3.5 | 4.5 | | | | | | | |
| (13) 8.2 | (12) 7.7 | (15) 13.7 | % Officers', Directors' Owners' Comp/Sales | | | | | | |
| 12.7 | 14.5 | 22.3 | | | | | | | |
| 4541762M | 5719627M | 6475343M | Net Sales ($) | 6470M | 16982M | 40970M | 52949M | 211538M | 6146434M |
| 1920120M | 1793793M | 1444058M | Total Assets ($) | 18411M | 112205M | 95337M | 133502M | 120263M | 964340M |

© RMA 2012

M = $ thousand    MM = $ million
See Pages 9 through 22 for Explanation of Ratios and Data

## Current Data Sorted by Assets     Comparative Historical Data

| | 0-500M | 500M-2MM | 2-10MM | 10-50MM | 50-100MM | 100-250MM | Type of Statement | 4/1/07-3/31/08 ALL | 4/1/08-3/31/09 ALL |
|---|---|---|---|---|---|---|---|---|---|
| | | | | | | | Unqualified | 9 | 20 |
| | | 2 | 5 | 7 | | 2 | Reviewed | 9 | 8 |
| | 6 | 1 | 3 | 1 | | | Compiled | 18 | 16 |
| | 34 | 13 | 4 | 2 | | | Tax Returns | 30 | 40 |
| | 31 | 25 | 31 | 6 | 3 | 3 | Other | 66 | 81 |
| | | 16 (4/1-9/30/11) | | 163 (10/1/11-3/31/12) | | | | | |
| **NUMBER OF STATEMENTS** | 71 | 41 | 43 | 16 | 3 | 5 | | 132 | 165 |
| | % | % | % | % | % | % | **ASSETS** | % | % |
| | 34.2 | 27.3 | 21.8 | 18.6 | | | Cash & Equivalents | 22.2 | 22.1 |
| | 13.1 | 26.0 | 33.1 | 24.9 | | | Trade Receivables (net) | 22.6 | 24.8 |
| | .2 | 1.6 | 1.8 | .2 | | | Inventory | 2.9 | 2.9 |
| | 6.3 | 2.4 | 5.8 | 17.2 | | | All Other Current | 8.1 | 7.0 |
| | 53.9 | 57.3 | 62.5 | 60.8 | | | Total Current | 55.8 | 56.8 |
| | 20.6 | 18.0 | 11.3 | 7.9 | | | Fixed Assets (net) | 20.4 | 18.5 |
| | 8.2 | 13.0 | 18.8 | 13.0 | | | Intangibles (net) | 9.6 | 12.3 |
| | 17.4 | 11.6 | 7.5 | 18.4 | | | All Other Non-Current | 14.2 | 12.4 |
| | 100.0 | 100.0 | 100.0 | 100.0 | | | Total | 100.0 | 100.0 |
| | | | | | | | **LIABILITIES** | | |
| | 26.9 | 7.2 | 9.2 | 9.8 | | | Notes Payable-Short Term | 15.3 | 15.5 |
| | 2.9 | 3.3 | 1.1 | 1.7 | | | Cur. Mat.-L.T.D. | 5.2 | 3.0 |
| | 5.6 | 6.2 | 8.3 | 12.5 | | | Trade Payables | 5.8 | 7.2 |
| | 1.3 | .1 | .0 | .7 | | | Income Taxes Payable | .8 | .3 |
| | 20.7 | 14.3 | 28.0 | 26.7 | | | All Other Current | 22.3 | 22.8 |
| | 57.4 | 31.2 | 46.7 | 51.5 | | | Total Current | 49.4 | 49.0 |
| | 20.2 | 15.4 | 15.7 | 7.0 | | | Long-Term Debt | 17.8 | 14.8 |
| | .0 | .0 | .1 | .8 | | | Deferred Taxes | .2 | .2 |
| | 19.5 | 9.0 | 5.2 | 26.6 | | | All Other Non-Current | 11.7 | 8.9 |
| | 2.8 | 44.4 | 32.3 | 14.2 | | | Net Worth | 21.0 | 27.1 |
| | 100.0 | 100.0 | 100.0 | 100.0 | | | Total Liabilities & Net Worth | 100.0 | 100.0 |
| | | | | | | | **INCOME DATA** | | |
| | 100.0 | 100.0 | 100.0 | 100.0 | | | Net Sales | 100.0 | 100.0 |
| | | | | | | | Gross Profit | | |
| | 82.9 | 80.5 | 87.3 | 90.2 | | | Operating Expenses | 88.8 | 90.0 |
| | 17.1 | 19.5 | 12.7 | 9.8 | | | Operating Profit | 11.2 | 10.0 |
| | .8 | 1.8 | 2.2 | -.2 | | | All Other Expenses (net) | .3 | 1.7 |
| | 16.3 | 17.6 | 10.5 | 10.0 | | | Profit Before Taxes | 10.8 | 8.4 |
| | | | | | | | **RATIOS** | | |
| | 6.0 | 6.6 | 2.6 | 3.2 | | | | 2.6 | 2.4 |
| | 1.4 | 2.1 | 1.3 | 1.3 | | | Current | 1.3 | 1.3 |
| | .4 | 1.0 | 1.0 | .7 | | | | .6 | .7 |
| | 6.0 | 6.6 | 2.5 | 2.1 | | | | 2.3 | 2.1 |
| (70) | 1.2 | 1.8 | 1.2 | .8 | | | Quick | 1.1 | 1.1 |
| | .2 | 1.0 | .8 | .5 | | | | .4 | .5 |
| 0 | UND | 0 UND | 4 93.8 | 7 52.9 | | | | 0 UND | 0 UND |
| 0 | UND | 17 21.7 | 36 10.0 | 39 9.3 | | | Sales/Receivables | 25 14.8 | 21 17.0 |
| 11 | 32.9 | 56 6.5 | 76 4.8 | 50 7.3 | | | | 50 7.3 | 49 7.5 |
| | | | | | | | Cost of Sales/Inventory | | |
| | | | | | | | Cost of Sales/Payables | | |
| | 12.0 | 6.2 | 6.2 | 5.1 | | | | 7.6 | 8.3 |
| | 53.1 | 10.4 | 23.1 | 38.1 | | | Sales/Working Capital | 20.1 | 29.5 |
| | -20.8 | 143.9 | -72.4 | -7.3 | | | | -25.6 | -24.6 |
| | 50.2 | 78.1 | 42.3 | 26.4 | | | | 17.5 | 18.9 |
| (42) | 19.4 | (28) 17.7 | (33) 9.7 | (11) 8.8 | | | EBIT/Interest | (104) 4.5 | (118) 4.9 |
| | 4.5 | 5.6 | 3.4 | 1.0 | | | | 1.3 | 1.3 |
| | | | | | | | | | 6.5 |
| | | | | | | | Net Profit + Depr., Dep., Amort./Cur. Mat. L/T/D | (14) 1.8 | |
| | | | | | | | | | .9 |
| | .0 | .0 | .0 | .1 | | | | .2 | .1 |
| | .5 | .1 | .6 | .8 | | | Fixed/Worth | .6 | .5 |
| | -1.5 | 10.0 | -.3 | -.6 | | | | 19.2 | 37.7 |
| | .4 | .3 | 1.0 | 3.0 | | | | 1.0 | 1.0 |
| | 2.3 | 1.3 | 7.4 | 9.5 | | | Debt/Worth | 3.0 | 5.0 |
| | -2.3 | NM | -5.1 | -8.7 | | | | -21.0 | -21.6 |
| | 271.9 | 131.7 | 110.2 | 141.2 | | | | 143.8 | 102.6 |
| (43) | 100.0 | (31) 70.3 | (28) 52.6 | (10) 82.5 | | | % Profit Before Taxes/Tangible Net Worth | (97) 61.0 | (117) 48.7 |
| | 36.5 | 19.9 | 23.5 | 18.3 | | | | 10.6 | 5.4 |
| | 121.6 | 58.9 | 32.3 | 32.1 | | | | 48.0 | 42.4 |
| | 61.5 | 22.5 | 11.0 | 12.4 | | | % Profit Before Taxes/Total Assets | 14.9 | 7.5 |
| | 23.1 | 8.0 | 1.9 | 1.1 | | | | 1.1 | .5 |
| | UND | 381.2 | 340.2 | 65.3 | | | | 90.7 | 84.2 |
| | 71.8 | 74.0 | 46.9 | 30.5 | | | Sales/Net Fixed Assets | 21.0 | 24.6 |
| | 21.5 | 24.6 | 19.2 | 14.9 | | | | 11.4 | 10.8 |
| | 11.3 | 4.2 | 4.1 | 3.3 | | | | 5.2 | 5.7 |
| | 6.4 | 3.1 | 2.1 | 1.6 | | | Sales/Total Assets | 2.9 | 2.6 |
| | 3.6 | 1.0 | .9 | .6 | | | | 1.5 | 1.3 |
| | .6 | .5 | .8 | .5 | | | | 1.0 | 1.0 |
| (25) | 1.2 | (19) 1.0 | (26) 1.4 | (14) 1.3 | | | % Depr., Dep., Amort./Sales | (85) 1.6 | (103) 1.7 |
| | 2.5 | 4.3 | 2.4 | 3.4 | | | | 2.7 | 2.6 |
| | 8.8 | 4.9 | 1.0 | | | | | 4.5 | 3.6 |
| (41) | 14.6 | (14) 7.4 | (14) 4.4 | | | | % Officers', Directors' Owners' Comp/Sales | (46) 13.0 | (49) 11.2 |
| | 20.8 | 17.3 | 19.3 | | | | | 20.3 | 22.3 |
| | 81343M | 136795M | 619535M | 1160655M | 279879M | 5155857M | Net Sales ($) | 1844282M | 6529696M |
| | 11464M | 43756M | 192017M | 361412M | 208451M | 893055M | Total Assets ($) | 1215294M | 2418742M |

© RMA 2012

M = $ thousand    MM = $ million
See Pages 9 through 22 for Explanation of Ratios and Data

## Comparative Historical Data | Current Data Sorted by Sales

| 4/1/09-3/31/10 ALL | 4/1/10-3/31/11 ALL | 4/1/11-3/31/12 ALL | Type of Statement | 0-1MM | 1-3MM | 3-5MM | 5-10MM | 10-25MM | 25MM & OVER |
|---|---|---|---|---|---|---|---|---|---|
| 18 | 23 | 16 | Unqualified |  |  |  | 1 | 6 | 9 |
| 11 | 6 | 4 | Reviewed |  | 1 |  | 2 |  | 1 |
| 7 | 9 | 7 | Compiled | 3 | 3 |  | 1 |  |  |
| 63 | 48 | 53 | Tax Returns | 26 | 14 | 10 | 1 |  | 2 |
| 82 | 89 | 99 | Other | 27 | 24 | 7 | 21 | 6 | 14 |
|  |  |  |  | 16 (4/1-9/30/11) | | | 163 (10/1/11-3/31/12) | | |
| 181 | 175 | 179 | NUMBER OF STATEMENTS | 56 | 42 | 17 | 26 | 12 | 26 |
| % | % | % | **ASSETS** | % | % | % | % | % | % |
| 23.9 | 23.1 | 27.2 | Cash & Equivalents | 31.7 | 35.5 | 18.8 | 21.1 | 15.8 | 20.6 |
| 21.8 | 22.1 | 22.6 | Trade Receivables (net) | 10.4 | 14.4 | 31.6 | 34.2 | 39.5 | 36.5 |
| 1.4 | 1.7 | 1.0 | Inventory | .2 | .0 | 6.1 | 1.3 | .0 | 1.3 |
| 6.2 | 8.6 | 6.5 | All Other Current | 6.3 | 5.8 | 5.8 | 6.5 | 5.4 | 9.2 |
| 53.2 | 55.5 | 57.3 | Total Current | 48.6 | 55.8 | 62.4 | 63.2 | 60.8 | 67.6 |
| 19.1 | 17.0 | 16.2 | Fixed Assets (net) | 27.5 | 14.5 | 12.2 | 7.7 | 8.6 | 8.9 |
| 12.3 | 13.2 | 13.3 | Intangibles (net) | 9.4 | 13.7 | 19.4 | 15.8 | 7.3 | 17.1 |
| 15.4 | 14.2 | 13.3 | All Other Non-Current | 14.6 | 16.0 | 6.0 | 13.3 | 23.3 | 6.4 |
| 100.0 | 100.0 | 100.0 | Total | 100.0 | 100.0 | 100.0 | 100.0 | 100.0 | 100.0 |
|  |  |  | **LIABILITIES** |  |  |  |  |  |  |
| 12.9 | 19.1 | 15.6 | Notes Payable-Short Term | 25.2 | 16.7 | 5.5 | 13.2 | 8.5 | 5.6 |
| 4.9 | 2.5 | 2.4 | Cur. Mat.-L.T.D. | 1.8 | 3.1 | 3.3 | 2.9 | 2.6 | 1.4 |
| 6.2 | 5.8 | 7.1 | Trade Payables | 3.7 | 6.7 | 6.5 | 10.6 | 7.4 | 11.4 |
| .3 | .4 | .6 | Income Taxes Payable | .0 | 2.2 | .0 | .2 | .0 | .4 |
| 25.0 | 28.1 | 21.4 | All Other Current | 14.1 | 32.9 | 12.1 | 14.4 | 29.5 | 28.0 |
| 49.3 | 55.9 | 47.1 | Total Current | 44.9 | 61.6 | 27.3 | 41.3 | 47.9 | 46.8 |
| 21.2 | 16.9 | 16.6 | Long-Term Debt | 16.3 | 23.9 | 19.0 | 13.2 | 13.5 | 8.8 |
| .2 | .4 | .2 | Deferred Taxes | .0 | .0 | .0 | .0 | .0 | 1.0 |
| 16.4 | 7.8 | 13.6 | All Other Non-Current | 15.2 | 16.7 | 12.2 | 9.6 | 15.5 | 9.0 |
| 12.9 | 19.0 | 22.5 | Net Worth | 23.4 | -2.3 | 41.5 | 35.9 | 23.1 | 34.3 |
| 100.0 | 100.0 | 100.0 | Total Liabilities & Net Worth | 100.0 | 100.0 | 100.0 | 100.0 | 100.0 | 100.0 |
|  |  |  | **INCOME DATA** |  |  |  |  |  |  |
| 100.0 | 100.0 | 100.0 | Net Sales | 100.0 | 100.0 | 100.0 | 100.0 | 100.0 | 100.0 |
|  |  |  | Gross Profit |  |  |  |  |  |  |
| 87.9 | 87.2 | 84.1 | Operating Expenses | 77.2 | 88.8 | 83.4 | 85.8 | 88.9 | 88.0 |
| 12.1 | 12.8 | 15.9 | Operating Profit | 22.8 | 11.2 | 16.6 | 14.2 | 11.1 | 12.0 |
| 1.3 | 1.2 | 1.3 | All Other Expenses (net) | 2.1 | .6 | 1.0 | 1.1 | 3.5 | .3 |
| 10.8 | 11.7 | 14.6 | Profit Before Taxes | 20.7 | 10.6 | 15.6 | 13.1 | 7.6 | 11.8 |
|  |  |  | **RATIOS** |  |  |  |  |  |  |
| 3.2 | 2.5 | 3.6 |  | 3.6 | 6.1 | 19.1 | 3.1 | 1.7 | 2.7 |
| 1.2 | 1.2 | 1.4 | Current | 1.3 | 1.3 | 2.1 | 1.7 | 1.2 | 1.4 |
| .6 | .6 | .7 |  | .4 | .5 | 1.2 | .7 | 1.1 | 1.0 |
| 2.8 | 2.1 | 3.4 |  | 3.6 | 6.1 | 9.2 | 2.5 | 1.5 | 2.0 |
| 1.0 | 1.0 | (178) 1.2 | Quick | (55) 1.0 | 1.2 | 1.8 | 1.3 | 1.2 | 1.4 |
| .4 | .4 | .5 |  | .3 | .2 | .7 | .5 | 1.0 | .6 |
| 0 UND | 0 UND | 0 UND |  | 0 UND | 0 UND | 1 538.4 | 0 UND | 31 11.6 | 20 18.0 |
| 13 27.1 | 8 47.1 | 6 56.8 | Sales/Receivables | 0 UND | 0 UND | 20 18.1 | 36 10.2 | 42 8.6 | 48 7.6 |
| 54 6.7 | 51 7.1 | 51 7.2 |  | 9 38.9 | 36 10.2 | 69 5.3 | 66 5.5 | 83 4.4 | 68 5.4 |
|  |  |  | Cost of Sales/Inventory |  |  |  |  |  |  |
|  |  |  | Cost of Sales/Payables |  |  |  |  |  |  |
| 6.2 | 7.6 | 7.1 |  | 8.7 | 6.3 | 4.9 | 6.2 | 13.9 | 5.7 |
| 38.5 | 34.8 | 28.6 | Sales/Working Capital | 50.3 | 36.1 | 12.6 | 12.1 | 23.1 | 15.6 |
| -16.1 | -20.2 | -34.1 |  | -9.3 | -26.4 | NM | -42.9 | 42.1 | NM |
| 22.6 | 28.6 | 51.7 |  | 41.0 | 59.8 | 69.0 | 80.7 | 25.6 | 127.7 |
| (122) 5.6 | (124) 7.3 | (122) 12.4 | EBIT/Interest | (31) 11.9 | (29) 17.0 | (11) 9.3 | (19) 24.1 | 17.5 | (20) 9.7 |
| 1.2 | 1.8 | 4.0 |  | 3.3 | 5.4 | 6.8 | 2.9 | -1.8 | 4.4 |
| 4.2 | 14.8 | 6.5 | Net Profit + Depr., Dep., Amort./Cur. Mat. L/T/D |  |  |  |  |  |  |
| (12) 3.1 | (15) 6.6 | (12) 4.7 |  |  |  |  |  |  |  |
| 1.1 | 2.3 | 1.6 |  |  |  |  |  |  |  |
| .1 | .1 | .0 |  | .0 | .0 | .0 | .0 | .1 | .1 |
| .7 | .5 | .5 | Fixed/Worth | .4 | .7 | 1.2 | .3 | .4 | .5 |
| UND | -2.5 | -1.4 |  | 4.4 | -.3 | -.2 | -.6 | NM | -.5 |
| .7 | .8 | .5 |  | .4 | .8 | .1 | .6 | 1.3 | .5 |
| 4.6 | 4.8 | 3.3 | Debt/Worth | 2.4 | 22.1 | 12.8 | 2.2 | 5.4 | 4.0 |
| -9.4 | -4.3 | -5.1 |  | -17.5 | -2.1 | -7.5 | -7.7 | NM | -6.4 |
| 122.5 | 125.3 | 168.2 |  | 201.0 | 120.2 | 656.8 | 193.5 |  | 122.4 |
| (129) 49.2 | (111) 55.1 | (117) 77.1 | % Profit Before Taxes/Tangible Net Worth | (39) 98.3 | (24) 48.4 | (11) 124.7 | (17) 75.8 |  | (17) 76.8 |
| 13.6 | 21.4 | 31.8 |  | 31.4 | 17.6 | 66.6 | 27.5 |  | 38.6 |
| 38.8 | 47.6 | 73.7 |  | 94.9 | 80.9 | 109.3 | 70.2 | 16.7 | 41.5 |
| 11.7 | 13.3 | 27.1 | % Profit Before Taxes/Total Assets | 46.4 | 26.1 | 32.3 | 29.5 | 5.1 | 19.6 |
| .6 | 3.2 | 6.5 |  | 8.5 | 7.6 | 10.8 | 5.7 | -7.8 | 7.7 |
| 86.6 | 177.0 | 473.1 |  | UND | 426.0 | 702.8 | 233.1 | 91.6 | 119.5 |
| 23.5 | 37.7 | 51.7 | Sales/Net Fixed Assets | 43.0 | 66.4 | 74.0 | 58.9 | 40.0 | 45.6 |
| 9.8 | 11.7 | 19.2 |  | 7.2 | 29.6 | 11.3 | 28.7 | 15.4 | 22.8 |
| 5.0 | 5.3 | 6.1 |  | 7.6 | 8.2 | 4.7 | 4.4 | 4.8 | 4.7 |
| 2.5 | 3.0 | 3.5 | Sales/Total Assets | 3.5 | 4.0 | 3.4 | 4.0 | 2.0 | 2.9 |
| 1.1 | 1.5 | 1.5 |  | .9 | 1.2 | 1.8 | 2.2 | 1.0 | 1.6 |
| .9 | .7 | .6 |  | 1.1 | .3 |  | .3 |  | .9 |
| (102) 1.4 | (101) 1.4 | (92) 1.2 | % Depr., Dep., Amort./Sales | (21) 2.5 | (18) .7 |  | (15) .9 |  | (21) 1.6 |
| 2.8 | 3.1 | 2.8 |  | 6.7 | 2.5 |  | 1.5 |  | 2.8 |
| 8.9 | 4.7 | 5.6 |  | 11.7 | 5.2 | 4.8 |  |  |  |
| (66) 17.8 | (71) 9.8 | (73) 12.5 | % Officers', Directors' Owners' Comp/Sales | (31) 14.4 | (15) 10.3 | (10) 7.4 |  |  |  |
| 30.5 | 25.2 | 20.5 |  | 20.1 | 24.2 | 16.5 |  |  |  |
| 6112608M | 7431157M | 7434064M | Net Sales ($) | 24561M | 70492M | 67807M | 179111M | 172983M | 6919110M |
| 2678154M | 2411204M | 1710155M | Total Assets ($) | 23382M | 42221M | 47011M | 68560M | 112918M | 1416063M |

M = $ thousand    MM = $ million
See Pages 9 through 22 for Explanation of Ratios and Data

## Current Data Sorted by Assets      Comparative Historical Data

**Type of Statement**

| Type of Statement | 0-500M | 500M-2MM | 2-10MM | 10-50MM | 50-100MM | 100-250MM | 4/1/07-3/31/08 ALL | 4/1/08-3/31/09 ALL |
|---|---|---|---|---|---|---|---|---|
| Unqualified | | | 7 | 23 | 4 | 2 | 28 | 39 |
| Reviewed | 2 | 8 | 68 | 32 | 3 | 1 | 104 | 127 |
| Compiled | 12 | 43 | 36 | 4 | | | 74 | 96 |
| Tax Returns | 86 | 43 | 15 | | 1 | 1 | 90 | 112 |
| Other | 39 | 67 | 73 | 20 | 5 | 1 | 190 | 221 |
| | 0-500M | 52 (4/1-9/30/11) 500M-2MM | 2-10MM | 544 (10/1/11-3/31/12) 10-50MM | 50-100MM | 100-250MM | | |

| | 0-500M | 500M-2MM | 2-10MM | 10-50MM | 50-100MM | 100-250MM | | 4/1/07-3/31/08 ALL | 4/1/08-3/31/09 ALL |
|---|---|---|---|---|---|---|---|---|---|
| **NUMBER OF STATEMENTS** | 139 | 161 | 199 | 79 | 13 | 5 | | 486 | 595 |
| | % | % | % | % | % | % | **ASSETS** | % | % |
| | 29.5 | 17.0 | 11.0 | 12.6 | 19.6 | | Cash & Equivalents | 14.3 | 15.2 |
| | 18.7 | 38.8 | 52.9 | 52.6 | 28.6 | | Trade Receivables (net) | 45.2 | 45.2 |
| | .3 | 3.3 | 1.8 | 2.2 | .5 | | Inventory | 2.1 | 2.5 |
| | 4.4 | 3.8 | 6.5 | 9.6 | 19.8 | | All Other Current | 5.9 | 6.1 |
| | 52.9 | 63.0 | 72.2 | 77.0 | 68.6 | | Total Current | 67.5 | 69.1 |
| | 29.5 | 24.1 | 15.8 | 12.6 | 12.3 | | Fixed Assets (net) | 19.4 | 19.0 |
| | 4.3 | 2.6 | 2.7 | 3.5 | 5.9 | | Intangibles (net) | 2.9 | 2.2 |
| | 13.2 | 10.3 | 9.3 | 7.0 | 13.3 | | All Other Non-Current | 10.1 | 9.7 |
| | 100.0 | 100.0 | 100.0 | 100.0 | 100.0 | | Total | 100.0 | 100.0 |
| | | | | | | | **LIABILITIES** | | |
| | 34.8 | 14.3 | 8.6 | 5.1 | 15.0 | | Notes Payable-Short Term | 16.0 | 15.0 |
| | 4.5 | 2.9 | 1.9 | 1.6 | 2.8 | | Cur. Mat.-L.T.D. | 3.8 | 3.2 |
| | 8.4 | 13.9 | 17.8 | 18.8 | 12.8 | | Trade Payables | 15.2 | 15.8 |
| | .1 | 1.1 | 2.3 | 1.6 | .6 | | Income Taxes Payable | 1.7 | 1.6 |
| | 21.8 | 9.2 | 13.9 | 22.5 | 27.2 | | All Other Current | 19.3 | 19.6 |
| | 69.7 | 41.5 | 44.6 | 49.6 | 58.4 | | Total Current | 56.0 | 55.3 |
| | 26.6 | 12.3 | 7.3 | 6.6 | 6.1 | | Long-Term Debt | 10.6 | 10.1 |
| | .0 | .3 | 1.4 | .8 | .5 | | Deferred Taxes | 1.1 | 1.2 |
| | 26.1 | 5.3 | 3.9 | 5.4 | 1.8 | | All Other Non-Current | 7.2 | 4.8 |
| | -22.4 | 40.6 | 42.8 | 37.7 | 33.2 | | Net Worth | 25.1 | 28.6 |
| | 100.0 | 100.0 | 100.0 | 100.0 | 100.0 | | Total Liabilties & Net Worth | 100.0 | 100.0 |
| | | | | | | | **INCOME DATA** | | |
| | 100.0 | 100.0 | 100.0 | 100.0 | 100.0 | | Net Sales | 100.0 | 100.0 |
| | | | | | | | Gross Profit | | |
| | 92.8 | 90.3 | 94.0 | 94.5 | 96.7 | | Operating Expenses | 91.7 | 93.8 |
| | 7.2 | 9.7 | 6.0 | 5.5 | 3.3 | | Operating Profit | 8.3 | 6.2 |
| | .6 | 2.3 | 1.1 | .7 | .4 | | All Other Expenses (net) | 1.1 | 1.4 |
| | 6.6 | 7.4 | 4.9 | 4.9 | 2.9 | | Profit Before Taxes | 7.2 | 4.8 |
| | | | | | | | **RATIOS** | | |
| | 4.9 | 3.4 | 2.5 | 2.1 | 1.9 | | | 2.3 | 2.4 |
| | 1.1 | 1.8 | 1.7 | 1.5 | 1.3 | | Current | 1.5 | 1.5 |
| | .3 | .8 | 1.2 | 1.2 | 1.1 | | | 1.0 | .9 |
| | 4.3 | 3.1 | 2.3 | 1.8 | 1.3 | | | 2.2 | 2.1 |
| | .9 | 1.6 | 1.5 | 1.3 | 1.0 | | Quick | 1.3 | 1.3 |
| | .2 | .7 | 1.1 | .9 | .7 | | | .8 | .7 |
| | 0 UND | 0 UND | 57 6.4 | 65 5.6 | 38 9.6 | | | 7 52.5 | 14 26.5 |
| | 0 UND | 55 6.6 | 85 4.3 | 83 4.4 | 54 6.7 | | Sales/Receivables | 71 5.1 | 69 5.3 |
| | 23 15.8 | 87 4.2 | 114 3.2 | 114 3.2 | 61 6.0 | | | 103 3.6 | 104 3.5 |
| | | | | | | | Cost of Sales/Inventory | | |
| | | | | | | | Cost of Sales/Payables | | |
| | 13.2 | 5.3 | 4.9 | 5.3 | 5.4 | | | 5.9 | 5.8 |
| | 999.8 | 13.0 | 7.7 | 9.0 | 11.2 | | Sales/Working Capital | 13.2 | 13.2 |
| | -14.8 | -98.3 | 17.0 | 17.4 | 45.2 | | | -207.7 | -130.3 |
| | 19.4 | 34.0 | 24.8 | 61.2 | 38.6 | | | 30.5 | 30.7 |
| | (93) 7.1 | (125) 6.3 | (161) 7.1 | (73) 13.1 | (11) 7.1 | | EBIT/Interest | (388) 9.0 | (475) 7.2 |
| | .1 | .8 | 1.1 | 3.1 | 1.1 | | | 2.5 | 1.1 |
| | | | 13.9 | 20.6 | | | | 7.5 | 9.8 |
| | | (43) 2.4 | (23) 5.0 | | | | Net Profit + Depr., Dep., Amort./Cur. Mat. L/T/D | (92) 3.5 | (123) 3.3 |
| | | .3 | 1.4 | | | | | 1.2 | 1.3 |
| | .1 | .1 | .1 | .1 | .2 | | | .1 | .2 |
| | 1.7 | .4 | .2 | .3 | .4 | | Fixed/Worth | .4 | .4 |
| | -.5 | 2.1 | .5 | .6 | .8 | | | 1.3 | 1.4 |
| | .5 | .4 | .7 | .9 | 1.0 | | | .7 | .7 |
| | 21.7 | 1.1 | 1.3 | 2.0 | 1.5 | | Debt/Worth | 1.9 | 2.0 |
| | -2.9 | 6.6 | 3.0 | 4.1 | 5.7 | | | 7.8 | 6.6 |
| | 158.7 | 70.4 | 40.6 | 33.6 | 28.3 | | | 77.7 | 71.0 |
| | (73) 69.7 | (133) 20.4 | (189) 15.8 | (77) 18.9 | (12) 18.6 | | % Profit Before Taxes/Tangible Net Worth | (411) 35.3 | (504) 26.5 |
| | 11.5 | 2.6 | .9 | 5.8 | -10.4 | | | 12.6 | 3.8 |
| | 64.2 | 25.7 | 16.0 | 13.4 | 11.2 | | | 35.2 | 24.8 |
| | 21.7 | 10.0 | 5.5 | 5.9 | 7.0 | | % Profit Before Taxes/Total Assets | 12.5 | 7.9 |
| | -2.2 | -.1 | .2 | 2.0 | -1.4 | | | 3.1 | .5 |
| | 318.0 | 49.4 | 48.9 | 51.1 | 39.2 | | | 65.7 | 61.1 |
| | 37.2 | 23.3 | 24.5 | 22.9 | 16.0 | | Sales/Net Fixed Assets | 27.6 | 25.9 |
| | 12.4 | 10.1 | 13.1 | 15.5 | 9.0 | | | 13.5 | 14.1 |
| | 12.6 | 4.0 | 2.9 | 2.7 | 2.5 | | | 4.3 | 4.3 |
| | 7.2 | 2.7 | 2.2 | 2.2 | 1.7 | | Sales/Total Assets | 2.7 | 2.7 |
| | 4.0 | 1.8 | 1.6 | 1.7 | 1.5 | | | 2.1 | 2.0 |
| | .4 | .7 | .9 | .8 | 1.0 | | | .7 | .8 |
| | (73) 1.2 | (120) 1.2 | (163) 1.4 | (73) 1.5 | (11) 2.3 | | % Depr., Dep., Amort./Sales | (372) 1.2 | (427) 1.4 |
| | 2.2 | 1.9 | 2.2 | 2.2 | 2.7 | | | 1.9 | 2.2 |
| | 8.3 | 7.6 | 4.6 | 2.5 | | | | 6.2 | 4.9 |
| | (97) 14.7 | (69) 11.0 | (48) 7.8 | (19) 8.6 | | | % Officers', Directors' Owners' Comp/Sales | (208) 11.6 | (244) 10.7 |
| | 20.5 | 16.4 | 13.0 | 14.3 | | | | 19.2 | 18.2 |
| | 246009M | 557192M | 2128957M | 3721136M | 2059280M | 2165838M | Net Sales ($) | 7474408M | 14120626M |
| | 30427M | 176941M | 935887M | 1638254M | 896021M | 816752M | Total Assets ($) | 3373499M | 5633092M |

M = $ thousand    MM = $ million
See Pages 9 through 22 for Explanation of Ratios and Data

## Comparative Historical Data / Current Data Sorted by Sales

| 42 | 41 | 36 | Type of Statement | | | | | | |
|---|---|---|---|---|---|---|---|---|---|
| 112 | 129 | 114 | Unqualified | | | | 3 | 5 | 28 |
| 99 | 91 | 95 | Reviewed | | 3 | 7 | 31 | 48 | 25 |
| 127 | 129 | 146 | Compiled | 6 | 22 | 17 | 31 | 18 | 1 |
| 222 | 212 | 205 | Tax Returns | 43 | 53 | 22 | 18 | 8 | 2 |
| 4/1/09-3/31/10 ALL | 4/1/10-3/31/11 ALL | 4/1/11-3/31/12 ALL | Other | 34 | 54 | 27 | 30 | 37 | 23 |
| | | | | 52 (4/1-9/30/11) | | | 544 (10/1/11-3/31/12) | | |
| | | | | 0-1MM | 1-3MM | 3-5MM | 5-10MM | 10-25MM | 25MM & OVER |
| 602 | 602 | 596 | NUMBER OF STATEMENTS | 83 | 132 | 73 | 113 | 116 | 79 |
| % | % | % | **ASSETS** | % | % | % | % | % | % |
| 16.4 | 17.2 | 17.4 | Cash & Equivalents | 20.1 | 18.2 | 24.6 | 16.7 | 12.0 | 15.3 |
| 40.5 | 39.3 | 40.3 | Trade Receivables (net) | 17.0 | 35.6 | 34.2 | 47.2 | 55.5 | 46.5 |
| 1.5 | 1.7 | 1.9 | Inventory | .4 | 2.3 | 3.0 | 2.2 | 1.8 | 1.4 |
| 6.7 | 7.9 | 6.0 | All Other Current | 4.9 | 3.8 | 1.5 | 7.0 | 7.0 | 12.1 |
| 65.2 | 66.1 | 65.6 | Total Current | 42.5 | 59.9 | 63.4 | 73.1 | 76.3 | 75.3 |
| 21.5 | 20.8 | 20.8 | Fixed Assets (net) | 44.6 | 23.4 | 19.6 | 15.5 | 12.1 | 13.2 |
| 3.1 | 3.3 | 3.2 | Intangibles (net) | 2.7 | 4.5 | 5.3 | 1.9 | 2.6 | 2.8 |
| 10.2 | 9.8 | 10.3 | All Other Non-Current | 10.4 | 12.2 | 11.7 | 9.5 | 9.0 | 8.8 |
| 100.0 | 100.0 | 100.0 | Total | 100.0 | 100.0 | 100.0 | 100.0 | 100.0 | 100.0 |
| | | | **LIABILITIES** | | | | | | |
| 18.8 | 16.0 | 16.0 | Notes Payable-Short Term | 23.0 | 25.4 | 24.7 | 8.4 | 7.9 | 7.8 |
| 3.4 | 2.9 | 2.8 | Cur. Mat.-L.T.D. | 3.0 | 4.7 | 1.1 | 3.4 | 1.5 | 2.0 |
| 14.5 | 14.9 | 14.5 | Trade Payables | 6.5 | 13.8 | 12.3 | 13.7 | 22.2 | 16.1 |
| 1.9 | 1.8 | 1.4 | Income Taxes Payable | .0 | .4 | .7 | 1.9 | 3.2 | 1.5 |
| 19.5 | 20.4 | 16.1 | All Other Current | 15.3 | 14.9 | 11.8 | 15.3 | 14.0 | 26.8 |
| 58.2 | 55.9 | 50.8 | Total Current | 47.9 | 59.3 | 50.7 | 42.7 | 48.8 | 54.2 |
| 11.1 | 10.8 | 13.2 | Long-Term Debt | 36.5 | 17.8 | 7.0 | 8.0 | 4.2 | 7.3 |
| 1.0 | .8 | .7 | Deferred Taxes | .0 | .1 | .2 | .8 | 1.9 | .7 |
| 5.9 | 8.3 | 9.6 | All Other Non-Current | 15.7 | 19.1 | 5.1 | 6.3 | 4.2 | 4.6 |
| 23.7 | 24.2 | 25.7 | Net Worth | .0 | 3.7 | 37.0 | 42.3 | 40.9 | 33.2 |
| 100.0 | 100.0 | 100.0 | Total Liabilities & Net Worth | 100.0 | 100.0 | 100.0 | 100.0 | 100.0 | 100.0 |
| | | | **INCOME DATA** | | | | | | |
| 100.0 | 100.0 | 100.0 | Net Sales | 100.0 | 100.0 | 100.0 | 100.0 | 100.0 | 100.0 |
| | | | Gross Profit | | | | | | |
| 97.2 | 94.7 | 92.9 | Operating Expenses | 80.7 | 92.7 | 93.4 | 95.7 | 97.1 | 95.4 |
| 2.8 | 5.3 | 7.1 | Operating Profit | 19.3 | 7.3 | 6.6 | 4.3 | 2.9 | 4.6 |
| 1.7 | 1.5 | 1.2 | All Other Expenses (net) | 6.3 | .4 | .0 | .4 | .5 | .6 |
| 1.1 | 3.8 | 5.9 | Profit Before Taxes | 13.0 | 6.9 | 6.5 | 4.0 | 2.3 | 4.0 |
| | | | **RATIOS** | | | | | | |
| 2.4 | 2.6 | 2.7 | Current | 4.7 | 3.3 | 4.2 | 3.1 | 2.3 | 2.0 |
| 1.4 | 1.4 | 1.5 | | 1.0 | 1.4 | 1.8 | 2.0 | 1.5 | 1.4 |
| .9 | 1.0 | 1.0 | | .2 | .7 | .8 | 1.3 | 1.2 | 1.1 |
| 2.2 | 2.2 | 2.5 | Quick | 4.0 | 3.0 | 4.1 | 3.0 | 2.1 | 1.6 |
| (601) 1.2 | 1.2 | 1.3 | | .9 | 1.2 | 1.6 | 1.7 | 1.3 | 1.1 |
| .7 | .8 | .8 | | .1 | .5 | .7 | 1.1 | 1.1 | .9 |
| 0 UND | 0 UND | 0 UND | Sales/Receivables | 0 UND | 0 UND | 0 UND | 35 10.3 | 59 6.2 | 55 6.6 |
| 63 5.8 | 60 6.0 | 61 6.0 | | 0 UND | 40 9.1 | 46 7.9 | 74 4.9 | 89 4.1 | 73 5.0 |
| 102 3.6 | 91 4.0 | 96 3.8 | | 37 9.8 | 85 4.3 | 87 4.2 | 99 3.7 | 114 3.2 | 89 4.1 |
| | | | Cost of Sales/Inventory | | | | | | |
| | | | Cost of Sales/Payables | | | | | | |
| 5.6 | 5.7 | 5.6 | Sales/Working Capital | 6.2 | 6.0 | 5.4 | 5.0 | 5.5 | 5.7 |
| 13.7 | 12.8 | 12.3 | | 348.0 | 25.3 | 14.4 | 7.3 | 10.3 | 11.2 |
| -54.0 | -234.2 | 802.3 | | -6.9 | -22.4 | -139.4 | 17.0 | 20.5 | 21.7 |
| 19.4 | 21.3 | 29.3 | EBIT/Interest | 8.3 | 28.2 | 45.8 | 41.1 | 28.6 | 48.4 |
| (473) 2.3 | (463) 5.3 | (468) 7.6 | | (47) 2.7 | (103) 7.6 | (56) 10.1 | (95) 6.9 | (98) 10.5 | (69) 9.6 |
| -8.6 | -1.9 | 1.1 | | -2.1 | 1.2 | .8 | .9 | 1.1 | 3.5 |
| 5.9 | 5.5 | 10.3 | Net Profit + Depr., Dep., Amort./Cur. Mat. L/T/D | | | | 13.9 | 13.5 | 9.4 |
| (123) 1.6 | (105) 2.5 | (88) 2.8 | | | | | (23) 1.7 | (30) 2.1 | (28) 4.0 |
| -1.1 | .5 | .7 | | | | | .7 | .2 | 1.2 |
| .1 | .2 | .1 | Fixed/Worth | .3 | .1 | .1 | .1 | .2 | .2 |
| .4 | .4 | .4 | | 2.2 | .7 | .3 | .3 | .3 | .4 |
| 2.4 | 1.4 | 1.4 | | -4.5 | -2.1 | 1.0 | .7 | .5 | .6 |
| .7 | .7 | .6 | Debt/Worth | .5 | .6 | .4 | .4 | .7 | 1.0 |
| 1.9 | 1.9 | 1.7 | | 5.6 | 2.3 | 1.1 | 1.1 | 1.6 | 2.0 |
| 7.3 | 7.0 | 7.2 | | -5.0 | -5.3 | 4.8 | 3.2 | 3.0 | 4.4 |
| 47.6 | 52.0 | 58.6 | % Profit Before Taxes/Tangible Net Worth | 87.3 | 108.1 | 73.5 | 49.4 | 34.0 | 31.7 |
| (496) 11.2 | (494) 16.7 | (488) 19.6 | | (53) 28.8 | (89) 32.6 | (61) 25.9 | (98) 16.4 | (112) 12.7 | (75) 19.1 |
| -20.6 | -4.9 | 2.9 | | 1.4 | 3.9 | 8.6 | 2.0 | .3 | 6.0 |
| 17.6 | 21.7 | 22.9 | % Profit Before Taxes/Total Assets | 36.8 | 45.2 | 35.0 | 21.6 | 12.2 | 13.1 |
| 2.4 | 5.2 | 8.0 | | 6.2 | 12.4 | 13.7 | 7.7 | 3.9 | 5.6 |
| -11.8 | -3.4 | .5 | | -4.8 | .6 | -.2 | .6 | -.3 | 2.0 |
| 54.6 | 54.7 | 55.0 | Sales/Net Fixed Assets | 37.2 | 83.2 | 120.6 | 54.1 | 49.1 | 48.1 |
| 23.4 | 23.4 | 25.8 | | 10.3 | 30.3 | 30.6 | 31.8 | 26.5 | 22.5 |
| 10.9 | 11.3 | 12.1 | | .6 | 13.4 | 15.1 | 13.1 | 17.6 | 13.0 |
| 4.3 | 3.9 | 4.3 | Sales/Total Assets | 4.5 | 7.7 | 6.1 | 3.9 | 3.3 | 2.9 |
| 2.6 | 2.6 | 2.6 | | 2.0 | 3.3 | 3.1 | 2.4 | 2.5 | 2.3 |
| 1.7 | 1.8 | 1.7 | | .5 | 2.2 | 1.8 | 1.7 | 1.8 | 1.7 |
| .7 | .8 | .7 | % Depr., Dep., Amort./Sales | 1.1 | .6 | .5 | .6 | .8 | .9 |
| (453) 1.5 | (442) 1.5 | (444) 1.4 | | (49) 3.3 | (84) 1.4 | (45) .9 | (97) 1.3 | (99) 1.4 | (70) 1.4 |
| 2.5 | 2.4 | 2.2 | | 12.3 | 1.9 | 1.8 | 2.1 | 2.0 | 2.3 |
| 6.4 | 4.5 | 6.5 | % Officers', Directors' Owners' Comp/Sales | 11.3 | 8.2 | 7.1 | 5.0 | 3.0 | 2.7 |
| (249) 12.4 | (249) 9.6 | (235) 11.4 | | (42) 18.8 | (75) 12.5 | (38) 12.2 | (39) 6.5 | (28) 8.3 | (13) 9.8 |
| 19.5 | 17.9 | 17.9 | | 23.3 | 17.7 | 16.9 | 9.9 | 13.1 | 26.3 |
| 9757855M | 10780629M | 10878412M | Net Sales ($) | 42398M | 246861M | 278795M | 809697M | 1867660M | 7633001M |
| 4513410M | 5240868M | 4494282M | Total Assets ($) | 58614M | 90671M | 113268M | 341200M | 824041M | 3066488M |

M = $ thousand    MM = $ million
See Pages 9 through 22 for Explanation of Ratios and Data

## Current Data Sorted by Assets     Comparative Historical Data

| Type of Statement | 0-500M | 500M-2MM | 2-10MM | 10-50MM | 50-100MM | 100-250MM | | 4/1/07-3/31/08 ALL | 4/1/08-3/31/09 ALL |
|---|---|---|---|---|---|---|---|---|---|
| Unqualified | 1 | 1 | 5 | 3 | 1 | | | 7 | 6 |
| Reviewed | | 6 | 11 | 2 | 1 | 1 | | 26 | 35 |
| Compiled | 2 | 14 | 3 | | | | | 25 | 25 |
| Tax Returns | 32 | 16 | 4 | | | 1 | | 33 | 57 |
| Other | 18 | 22 | 14 | 2 | 1 | 1 | | 57 | 61 |
| | | 22 (4/1-9/30/11) | | 139 (10/1/11-3/31/12) | | | | | |
| **NUMBER OF STATEMENTS** | 53 | 59 | 37 | 7 | 3 | 2 | | 148 | 184 |
| | % | % | % | % | % | % | **ASSETS** | % | % |
| | 20.1 | 12.8 | 10.4 | | | | Cash & Equivalents | 11.9 | 11.7 |
| | 19.6 | 30.6 | 32.4 | | | | Trade Receivables (net) | 30.9 | 31.0 |
| | 5.7 | 6.8 | 7.0 | | | | Inventory | 6.7 | 6.6 |
| | 2.0 | 4.8 | 7.0 | | | | All Other Current | 4.0 | 3.9 |
| | 47.4 | 55.0 | 56.8 | | | | Total Current | 53.6 | 53.2 |
| | 35.7 | 34.2 | 32.1 | | | | Fixed Assets (net) | 33.9 | 36.2 |
| | 2.7 | 3.3 | 2.4 | | | | Intangibles (net) | 4.2 | 2.2 |
| | 14.2 | 7.5 | 8.7 | | | | All Other Non-Current | 8.4 | 8.3 |
| | 100.0 | 100.0 | 100.0 | | | | Total | 100.0 | 100.0 |
| | | | | | | | **LIABILITIES** | | |
| | 29.4 | 9.3 | 9.0 | | | | Notes Payable-Short Term | 11.4 | 14.0 |
| | 8.2 | 3.4 | 5.3 | | | | Cur. Mat.-L.T.D. | 7.2 | 4.7 |
| | 14.5 | 11.5 | 9.9 | | | | Trade Payables | 13.4 | 9.3 |
| | .0 | .2 | .1 | | | | Income Taxes Payable | .5 | .6 |
| | 17.3 | 8.6 | 11.7 | | | | All Other Current | 14.1 | 10.5 |
| | 69.3 | 33.0 | 36.1 | | | | Total Current | 46.5 | 39.1 |
| | 41.9 | 26.0 | 15.1 | | | | Long-Term Debt | 22.6 | 26.9 |
| | .0 | .5 | .3 | | | | Deferred Taxes | .5 | .7 |
| | 9.0 | 3.7 | 4.3 | | | | All Other Non-Current | 3.0 | 4.9 |
| | -20.2 | 36.8 | 44.2 | | | | Net Worth | 27.5 | 28.5 |
| | 100.0 | 100.0 | 100.0 | | | | Total Liabilties & Net Worth | 100.0 | 100.0 |
| | | | | | | | **INCOME DATA** | | |
| | 100.0 | 100.0 | 100.0 | | | | Net Sales | 100.0 | 100.0 |
| | | | | | | | Gross Profit | | |
| | 94.2 | 91.5 | 93.4 | | | | Operating Expenses | 94.3 | 93.0 |
| | 5.8 | 8.5 | 6.6 | | | | Operating Profit | 5.7 | 7.0 |
| | .9 | 2.9 | 2.8 | | | | All Other Expenses (net) | 1.0 | 2.1 |
| | 4.9 | 5.6 | 3.8 | | | | Profit Before Taxes | 4.7 | 4.9 |
| | | | | | | | **RATIOS** | | |
| | 2.2 | 4.0 | 2.4 | | | | | 2.5 | 2.7 |
| | 1.1 | 1.9 | 1.6 | | | | Current | 1.4 | 1.6 |
| | .2 | 1.0 | 1.0 | | | | | .8 | .9 |
| | 1.9 | 3.1 | 1.9 | | | | | 2.1 | 2.2 |
| | .8 | 1.3 | 1.2 | | | | Quick | 1.1 | 1.1 |
| | .2 | .7 | .7 | | | | | .6 | .6 |
| | 0 UND | 14 25.7 | 25 14.4 | | | | | 15 25.0 | 12 29.4 |
| | 5 75.8 | 36 10.0 | 43 8.5 | | | | Sales/Receivables | 39 9.3 | 37 9.8 |
| | 27 13.7 | 50 7.3 | 66 5.5 | | | | | 61 6.0 | 64 5.7 |
| | | | | | | | Cost of Sales/Inventory | | |
| | | | | | | | Cost of Sales/Payables | | |
| | 16.6 | 4.6 | 6.2 | | | | | 7.0 | 5.7 |
| | 169.5 | 12.8 | 12.1 | | | | Sales/Working Capital | 20.8 | 17.1 |
| | -12.6 | -164.0 | 231.5 | | | | | -38.6 | -74.1 |
| | 18.0 | 18.8 | 9.4 | | | | | 12.4 | 10.9 |
| | (37) 4.1 | (52) 6.8 | (32) 4.4 | | | | EBIT/Interest | (134) 3.5 | (155) 3.8 |
| | .5 | 1.9 | 1.2 | | | | | 1.0 | 1.4 |
| | | | | | | | | 3.4 | 2.5 |
| | | | | | | | Net Profit + Depr., Dep., Amort./Cur. Mat. L/T/D | (23) 2.4 | (27) 1.5 |
| | | | | | | | | 1.5 | .7 |
| | .6 | .3 | .3 | | | | | .4 | .3 |
| | 4.5 | 1.2 | .8 | | | | Fixed/Worth | .9 | .9 |
| | -.6 | 3.4 | 1.5 | | | | | 4.1 | 3.5 |
| | 1.4 | .8 | .6 | | | | | .8 | .8 |
| | 15.6 | 2.2 | 1.1 | | | | Debt/Worth | 2.1 | 2.1 |
| | -2.6 | 7.3 | 2.6 | | | | | 10.5 | 5.8 |
| | 257.5 | 97.3 | 33.5 | | | | | 61.2 | 57.7 |
| | (33) 77.1 | (52) 28.1 | (35) 9.2 | | | | % Profit Before Taxes/Tangible Net Worth | (119) 27.4 | (156) 20.0 |
| | 33.8 | 8.1 | .8 | | | | | 8.5 | 3.9 |
| | 42.4 | 20.1 | 13.4 | | | | | 21.0 | 20.6 |
| | 15.5 | 7.7 | 3.9 | | | | % Profit Before Taxes/Total Assets | 8.0 | 6.1 |
| | .9 | 1.9 | .4 | | | | | .8 | .6 |
| | 41.9 | 28.8 | 21.7 | | | | | 24.9 | 23.6 |
| | 20.2 | 10.1 | 8.9 | | | | Sales/Net Fixed Assets | 11.2 | 10.4 |
| | 9.2 | 3.9 | 4.0 | | | | | 5.9 | 4.7 |
| | 10.5 | 4.0 | 3.0 | | | | | 4.1 | 4.0 |
| | 4.4 | 2.7 | 2.3 | | | | Sales/Total Assets | 2.9 | 2.8 |
| | 3.6 | 1.4 | 1.6 | | | | | 2.0 | 1.7 |
| | .8 | 1.6 | 1.5 | | | | | 1.9 | 1.6 |
| | (31) 2.0 | (41) 2.7 | (32) 2.8 | | | | % Depr., Dep., Amort./Sales | (120) 3.1 | (140) 3.3 |
| | 4.7 | 4.3 | 5.5 | | | | | 4.7 | 5.3 |
| | 3.4 | 3.1 | 1.9 | | | | | 3.3 | 2.9 |
| | (32) 7.0 | (39) 5.8 | (17) 3.0 | | | | % Officers', Directors' Owners' Comp/Sales | (70) 5.5 | (93) 6.4 |
| | 11.4 | 7.5 | 5.9 | | | | | 8.7 | 12.1 |
| | 79081M | 194044M | 366811M | 201741M | 234564M | 604060M | Net Sales ($) | 2752603M | 1841212M |
| | 13482M | 66132M | 156410M | 138618M | 172582M | 294750M | Total Assets ($) | 1006258M | 807845M |

M = $ thousand    MM = $ million
See Pages 9 through 22 for Explanation of Ratios and Data

## Comparative Historical Data | Current Data Sorted by Sales

| | | | | Type of Statement | | | | | | |
|---|---|---|---|---|---|---|---|---|---|---|
| 6 | 11 | 10 | | Unqualified | | 1 | 1 | 3 | 1 | 4 |
| 33 | 33 | 21 | | Reviewed | | 2 | 5 | 4 | 8 | 2 |
| 19 | 16 | 19 | | Compiled | 2 | 8 | 5 | 3 | 1 | |
| 61 | 52 | 53 | | Tax Returns | 22 | 16 | 9 | 4 | 1 | 1 |
| 72 | 64 | 58 | | Other | 10 | 21 | 7 | 12 | 7 | 1 |
| 4/1/09-3/31/10 | 4/1/10-3/31/11 | 4/1/11-3/31/12 | | | | 22 (4/1-9/30/11) | | 139 (10/1/11-3/31/12) | | |
| ALL | ALL | ALL | | | 0-1MM | 1-3MM | 3-5MM | 5-10MM | 10-25MM | 25MM & OVER |
| 191 | 176 | 161 | | NUMBER OF STATEMENTS | 34 | 48 | 27 | 26 | 18 | 8 |
| % | % | % | | ASSETS | % | % | % | % | % | % |
| 14.1 | 15.6 | 14.8 | | Cash & Equivalents | 16.8 | 15.6 | 14.7 | 11.8 | 12.9 | |
| 30.0 | 29.5 | 26.5 | | Trade Receivables (net) | 13.4 | 26.8 | 29.0 | 30.9 | 38.0 | |
| 6.1 | 7.0 | 6.3 | | Inventory | 5.0 | 9.3 | 3.6 | 7.6 | 5.1 | |
| 4.0 | 4.3 | 4.5 | | All Other Current | 5.9 | 1.4 | 5.7 | 4.5 | 7.7 | |
| 54.3 | 56.4 | 52.0 | | Total Current | 41.1 | 53.1 | 53.0 | 54.8 | 63.7 | |
| 33.2 | 30.6 | 35.0 | | Fixed Assets (net) | 42.7 | 36.1 | 30.7 | 33.3 | 25.5 | |
| 3.2 | 3.0 | 2.8 | | Intangibles (net) | 2.0 | 2.3 | 3.9 | 5.2 | 1.5 | |
| 9.3 | 10.0 | 10.2 | | All Other Non-Current | 14.2 | 8.5 | 12.4 | 6.7 | 9.2 | |
| 100.0 | 100.0 | 100.0 | | Total | 100.0 | 100.0 | 100.0 | 100.0 | 100.0 | |
| | | | | LIABILITIES | | | | | | |
| 16.1 | 16.1 | 15.4 | | Notes Payable-Short Term | 14.1 | 24.0 | 9.8 | 14.7 | 6.8 | |
| 6.5 | 4.8 | 5.7 | | Cur. Mat.-L.T.D. | 8.0 | 5.3 | 4.5 | 5.2 | 4.6 | |
| 13.1 | 12.1 | 11.9 | | Trade Payables | 8.0 | 13.1 | 13.7 | 12.7 | 12.9 | |
| .8 | .6 | .1 | | Income Taxes Payable | .2 | .0 | .2 | .0 | .3 | |
| 16.4 | 11.0 | 12.7 | | All Other Current | 14.1 | 12.2 | 9.8 | 10.8 | 17.6 | |
| 52.8 | 44.6 | 45.8 | | Total Current | 44.4 | 54.6 | 37.9 | 43.5 | 42.1 | |
| 20.5 | 20.9 | 28.2 | | Long-Term Debt | 48.9 | 32.7 | 18.9 | 16.4 | 12.9 | |
| .3 | .1 | .2 | | Deferred Taxes | .0 | .6 | .1 | .3 | .1 | |
| 7.0 | 6.8 | 5.6 | | All Other Non-Current | 7.9 | 4.8 | 6.4 | 5.2 | 3.9 | |
| 19.4 | 27.7 | 20.2 | | Net Worth | -1.1 | 7.4 | 36.7 | 34.6 | 41.0 | |
| 100.0 | 100.0 | 100.0 | | Total Liabilities & Net Worth | 100.0 | 100.0 | 100.0 | 100.0 | 100.0 | |
| | | | | INCOME DATA | | | | | | |
| 100.0 | 100.0 | 100.0 | | Net Sales | 100.0 | 100.0 | 100.0 | 100.0 | 100.0 | |
| | | | | Gross Profit | | | | | | |
| 96.3 | 93.0 | 93.1 | | Operating Expenses | 82.0 | 96.2 | 96.2 | 95.2 | 97.2 | |
| 3.7 | 7.0 | 6.9 | | Operating Profit | 18.0 | 3.8 | 3.8 | 4.8 | 2.8 | |
| 1.8 | 2.2 | 2.0 | | All Other Expenses (net) | 7.3 | .6 | -.2 | 1.8 | .4 | |
| 1.9 | 4.8 | 4.8 | | Profit Before Taxes | 10.6 | 3.2 | 4.0 | 2.9 | 2.4 | |
| | | | | RATIOS | | | | | | |
| 2.4 | 3.3 | 2.6 | | | 4.1 | 3.8 | 3.1 | 2.1 | 2.5 | |
| 1.5 | 1.6 | 1.4 | | Current | 1.4 | 1.4 | 1.5 | 1.4 | 1.8 | |
| .7 | .8 | .8 | | | .2 | .8 | .7 | .9 | .9 | |
| 1.9 | 2.4 | 2.2 | | | 3.0 | 3.3 | 2.6 | 1.7 | 2.3 | |
| 1.1 | 1.1 | 1.1 | | Quick | 1.2 | 1.1 | 1.2 | 1.2 | 1.0 | |
| .5 | .5 | .4 | | | .2 | .4 | .6 | .8 | .6 | |
| 8 45.7 | 9 42.3 | 4 88.3 | | | 0 UND | 5 71.5 | 4 84.5 | 19 19.2 | 30 12.0 | |
| 39 9.4 | 32 11.4 | 29 12.7 | | Sales/Receivables | 0 UND | 25 14.4 | 27 13.4 | 36 10.1 | 46 8.0 | |
| 69 5.3 | 59 6.2 | 54 6.8 | | | 33 10.9 | 46 8.0 | 51 7.1 | 54 6.7 | 72 5.1 | |
| | | | | Cost of Sales/Inventory | | | | | | |
| | | | | Cost of Sales/Payables | | | | | | |
| 6.5 | 6.4 | 6.9 | | | 3.9 | 6.1 | 7.5 | 11.0 | 6.3 | |
| 18.1 | 18.9 | 24.7 | | Sales/Working Capital | 27.7 | 37.5 | 19.0 | 28.9 | 12.6 | |
| -25.7 | -43.8 | -32.7 | | | -9.7 | -20.8 | -22.3 | -135.8 | -59.8 | |
| 8.4 | 12.9 | 12.5 | | | 6.0 | 22.9 | 43.0 | 11.2 | 11.1 | |
| (154) 2.1 | (144) 4.2 | (132) 4.7 | | EBIT/Interest | (19) 3.2 | (41) 4.1 | (24) 6.4 | (25) 8.0 | (15) 2.8 | |
| -1.1 | -.8 | 1.4 | | | .7 | .9 | 1.2 | 4.2 | -.3 | |
| 3.4 | 6.6 | 6.0 | | | | | | | | |
| (28) 1.4 | (16) 1.0 | (17) 3.8 | | Net Profit + Depr., Dep., Amort./Cur. Mat. L/T/D | | | | | | |
| -.3 | .2 | 2.0 | | | | | | | | |
| .3 | .3 | .4 | | | .5 | .5 | .2 | .5 | .2 | |
| .8 | .9 | 1.0 | | Fixed/Worth | 3.6 | 1.4 | .8 | 1.1 | .6 | |
| 86.7 | 33.5 | 5.1 | | | -8.4 | NM | 2.2 | 3.4 | 1.4 | |
| .8 | .6 | .8 | | | 1.5 | .8 | .4 | .8 | .7 | |
| 2.1 | 1.9 | 2.1 | | Debt/Worth | 4.7 | 2.3 | 1.7 | 1.7 | 2.0 | |
| UND | 80.8 | 15.8 | | | -11.9 | NM | 6.0 | 8.9 | 2.5 | |
| 52.0 | 71.8 | 89.0 | | | 135.7 | 103.4 | 102.6 | 74.1 | 29.2 | |
| (144) 15.0 | (135) 18.4 | (131) 24.0 | | % Profit Before Taxes/Tangible Net Worth | (23) 39.4 | (36) 39.8 | (24) 34.9 | (23) 24.0 | 8.7 | |
| -4.0 | -1.6 | 4.8 | | | 6.6 | 8.5 | 2.9 | 4.6 | 1.8 | |
| 16.6 | 22.2 | 21.6 | | | 27.0 | 23.8 | 32.1 | 18.9 | 11.0 | |
| 4.1 | 4.8 | 8.5 | | % Profit Before Taxes/Total Assets | 9.3 | 9.4 | 11.6 | 10.9 | 3.8 | |
| -4.7 | -3.5 | 1.1 | | | 1.2 | -2.3 | .4 | 1.9 | .6 | |
| 28.9 | 36.0 | 30.4 | | | 35.6 | 28.3 | 36.6 | 25.6 | 36.1 | |
| 11.5 | 14.7 | 12.3 | | Sales/Net Fixed Assets | 6.1 | 16.2 | 20.0 | 10.3 | 12.4 | |
| 5.2 | 6.4 | 5.1 | | | 1.5 | 4.9 | 6.5 | 6.9 | 6.7 | |
| 4.1 | 4.1 | 4.4 | | | 4.3 | 5.0 | 6.1 | 4.6 | 3.9 | |
| 2.6 | 2.9 | 2.9 | | Sales/Total Assets | 2.0 | 3.5 | 3.8 | 3.0 | 2.8 | |
| 1.6 | 1.8 | 1.7 | | | .7 | 1.8 | 1.9 | 2.2 | 1.7 | |
| 1.5 | 1.2 | 1.2 | | | 2.8 | 1.2 | 1.0 | 1.5 | .9 | |
| (140) 2.9 | (124) 2.7 | (113) 2.8 | | % Depr., Dep., Amort./Sales | (19) 6.9 | (33) 2.0 | (20) 2.3 | (20) 3.2 | (16) 2.4 | |
| 4.8 | 5.1 | 4.7 | | | 10.9 | 4.2 | 4.2 | 5.1 | 3.1 | |
| 3.9 | 2.5 | 3.0 | | | 5.4 | 3.8 | 2.5 | 1.9 | | |
| (88) 6.8 | (85) 5.5 | (90) 5.6 | | % Officers', Directors' Owners' Comp/Sales | (20) 9.6 | (28) 6.6 | (20) 4.1 | (14) 3.1 | | |
| 11.5 | 9.3 | 9.0 | | | 14.1 | 9.6 | 6.5 | 5.5 | | |
| 1427877M | 2616312M | 1680301M | | Net Sales ($) | 18933M | 88033M | 101893M | 183603M | 280923M | 1006916M |
| 716433M | 1193809M | 841974M | | Total Assets ($) | 21409M | 35246M | 53129M | 69186M | 259431M | 403573M |

## Current Data Sorted by Assets

## Comparative Historical Data

| | | | | | | Type of Statement | | |
|---|---|---|---|---|---|---|---|---|
| 1 | 5 | 68 | 105 | 25 | 23 | Unqualified | 224 | 249 |
| 7 | 56 | 204 | 71 | 5 | 2 | Reviewed | 313 | 324 |
| 23 | 92 | 121 | 16 | 1 | | Compiled | 199 | 218 |
| 174 | 128 | 60 | 6 | | | Tax Returns | 244 | 289 |
| 97 | 181 | 262 | 147 | 25 | 25 | Other | 589 | 657 |
| | 202 (4/1-9/30/11) | | 1,728 (10/1/11-3/31/12) | | | | 4/1/07-3/31/08 | 4/1/08-3/31/09 |
| 0-500M | 500M-2MM | 2-10MM | 10-50MM | 50-100MM | 100-250MM | | ALL | ALL |
| 302 | 462 | 715 | 345 | 56 | 50 | **NUMBER OF STATEMENTS** | 1569 | 1737 |
| % | % | % | % | % | % | **ASSETS** | % | % |
| 32.7 | 16.5 | 13.1 | 13.0 | 14.2 | 13.8 | Cash & Equivalents | 14.2 | 14.2 |
| 17.3 | 42.6 | 49.4 | 45.7 | 41.6 | 34.4 | Trade Receivables (net) | 46.4 | 44.4 |
| 2.7 | 4.3 | 4.5 | 4.2 | 1.7 | 3.2 | Inventory | 3.9 | 3.9 |
| 4.6 | 4.1 | 6.3 | 11.1 | 10.7 | 13.3 | All Other Current | 7.0 | 6.7 |
| 57.4 | 67.5 | 73.3 | 74.0 | 68.1 | 64.6 | Total Current | 71.6 | 69.2 |
| 27.2 | 22.5 | 15.4 | 13.5 | 11.6 | 11.7 | Fixed Assets (net) | 18.1 | 18.6 |
| 4.0 | 2.6 | 3.2 | 5.5 | 14.7 | 16.2 | Intangibles (net) | 2.9 | 3.6 |
| 11.3 | 7.4 | 8.0 | 7.0 | 5.6 | 7.5 | All Other Non-Current | 7.4 | 8.5 |
| 100.0 | 100.0 | 100.0 | 100.0 | 100.0 | 100.0 | Total | 100.0 | 100.0 |
| | | | | | | **LIABILITIES** | | |
| 41.9 | 12.7 | 9.4 | 6.2 | 2.5 | 2.0 | Notes Payable-Short Term | 12.0 | 14.0 |
| 4.6 | 2.8 | 2.2 | 2.3 | 1.8 | 4.3 | Cur. Mat.-L.T.D. | 3.2 | 3.5 |
| 6.2 | 10.3 | 11.0 | 11.5 | 14.5 | 11.1 | Trade Payables | 11.0 | 10.8 |
| .0 | .6 | 1.8 | 3.4 | 3.0 | 2.1 | Income Taxes Payable | 1.7 | 1.7 |
| 18.9 | 11.8 | 14.7 | 17.8 | 22.3 | 21.3 | All Other Current | 17.0 | 16.5 |
| 71.7 | 38.3 | 39.1 | 41.2 | 44.1 | 40.7 | Total Current | 44.9 | 46.5 |
| 26.4 | 15.8 | 9.3 | 7.6 | 9.3 | 7.6 | Long-Term Debt | 11.9 | 12.8 |
| .0 | .5 | 1.1 | 1.6 | 1.3 | 1.2 | Deferred Taxes | 1.0 | .9 |
| 11.3 | 5.7 | 4.3 | 5.7 | 5.7 | 5.4 | All Other Non-Current | 4.5 | 6.3 |
| -9.3 | 39.7 | 46.2 | 44.0 | 39.6 | 45.1 | Net Worth | 37.6 | 33.5 |
| 100.0 | 100.0 | 100.0 | 100.0 | 100.0 | 100.0 | Total Liabilities & Net.Worth | 100.0 | 100.0 |
| | | | | | | **INCOME DATA** | | |
| 100.0 | 100.0 | 100.0 | 100.0 | 100.0 | 100.0 | Net Sales | 100.0 | 100.0 |
| | | | | | | Gross Profit | | |
| 93.4 | 91.2 | 92.7 | 94.0 | 93.2 | 91.6 | Operating Expenses | 92.3 | 93.4 |
| 6.6 | 8.8 | 7.3 | 6.0 | 6.8 | 8.4 | Operating Profit | 7.7 | 6.6 |
| 1.1 | 2.4 | 1.4 | .6 | 1.4 | 1.1 | All Other Expenses (net) | 1.5 | 1.5 |
| 5.5 | 6.3 | 5.9 | 5.4 | 5.4 | 7.2 | Profit Before Taxes | 6.2 | 5.1 |
| | | | | | | **RATIOS** | | |
| 3.4 | 4.2 | 3.2 | 2.8 | 2.0 | 2.3 | | 2.9 | 2.9 |
| 1.1 | 2.0 | 1.9 | 1.8 | 1.5 | 1.7 | Current | 1.7 | 1.7 |
| .4 | 1.2 | 1.3 | 1.3 | 1.2 | 1.3 | | 1.2 | 1.1 |
| 3.0 | 3.8 | 2.6 | 2.3 | 1.7 | 1.8 | | 2.5 | 2.5 |
| 1.0 | 1.7 | 1.6 | 1.4 | 1.2 | 1.3 | Quick | (1567) 1.5 | 1.4 |
| .2 | 1.0 | 1.1 | 1.0 | .9 | .9 | | .9 | .9 |

| | | | | | | | | | | | | | Sales/Receivables | | | | |
|---|---|---|---|---|---|---|---|---|---|---|---|---|---|---|---|---|---|
| 0 | UND | 22 | 16.9 | 49 | 7.5 | 54 | 6.7 | 70 | 5.2 | 58 | 6.3 | | | 42 | 8.7 | 37 | 9.8 |
| 0 | UND | 54 | 6.7 | 73 | 5.0 | 74 | 4.9 | 85 | 4.3 | 76 | 4.8 | | | 69 | 5.3 | 64 | 5.7 |
| 30 | 12.3 | 87 | 4.2 | 101 | 3.6 | 99 | 3.7 | 99 | 3.7 | 85 | 4.3 | | | 96 | 3.8 | 94 | 3.9 |

Cost of Sales/Inventory

Cost of Sales/Payables

| | | | | | | | | Sales/Working Capital | | |
|---|---|---|---|---|---|---|---|---|---|---|
| 13.1 | 4.9 | 4.4 | 4.2 | 5.1 | 3.7 | | | 5.1 | 5.2 |
| 189.4 | 9.2 | 7.3 | 6.6 | 7.6 | 7.5 | | | 9.0 | 9.7 |
| -17.9 | 32.4 | 17.4 | 13.4 | 14.7 | 14.0 | | | 28.0 | 42.4 |

| | | | | | | | | | | | | | EBIT/Interest | | | | |
|---|---|---|---|---|---|---|---|---|---|---|---|---|---|---|---|---|---|
| | 27.7 | | 27.1 | | 44.9 | | 50.2 | | 46.2 | | 27.3 | | | | 25.5 | | 26.2 |
| (215) | 6.6 | (370) | 6.9 | (586) | 11.5 | (300) | 12.0 | (47) | 14.2 | (40) | 13.4 | | | (1283) | 7.5 | (1444) | 6.8 |
| | .0 | | 1.1 | | 2.4 | | 3.0 | | 4.9 | | 3.2 | | | | 2.0 | | 1.2 |

| | | | | | | | | | | | | | Net Profit + Depr., Dep., Amort./Cur. Mat. L/T/D | | | | |
|---|---|---|---|---|---|---|---|---|---|---|---|---|---|---|---|---|---|
| | | | 5.2 | | 14.3 | | 10.6 | | 5.1 | | 9.7 | | | | 8.4 | | 9.2 |
| | | (38) | 2.7 | (134) | 3.2 | (130) | 3.4 | (20) | 4.2 | (17) | 3.5 | | | (339) | 2.8 | (393) | 3.3 |
| | | | .4 | | 1.3 | | 1.3 | | 2.3 | | 1.5 | | | | 1.2 | | 1.2 |

| | | | | | | | | Fixed/Worth | | |
|---|---|---|---|---|---|---|---|---|---|---|
| .1 | .1 | .1 | .1 | .2 | .2 | | | .1 | .1 |
| 1.0 | .3 | .2 | .3 | .4 | .4 | | | .3 | .4 |
| -.7 | 1.6 | .6 | .7 | .9 | .8 | | | .9 | 1.2 |

| | | | | | | | | Debt/Worth | | |
|---|---|---|---|---|---|---|---|---|---|---|
| .5 | .4 | .6 | .7 | .9 | .9 | | | .6 | .6 |
| 4.2 | 1.3 | 1.2 | 1.3 | 2.2 | 1.7 | | | 1.4 | 1.5 |
| -3.1 | 4.8 | 2.6 | 3.3 | 8.2 | 5.6 | | | 4.3 | 4.7 |

| | | | | | | | | | | | | | % Profit Before Taxes/Tangible Net Worth | | | | |
|---|---|---|---|---|---|---|---|---|---|---|---|---|---|---|---|---|---|
| | 162.2 | | 70.5 | | 48.8 | | 45.8 | | 44.3 | | 61.0 | | | | 66.0 | | 59.7 |
| (183) | 56.2 | (391) | 27.0 | (672) | 22.5 | (327) | 22.4 | (45) | 27.7 | (44) | 29.2 | | | (1408) | 30.6 | (1505) | 26.1 |
| | 11.2 | | 4.4 | | 6.7 | | 7.0 | | 14.0 | | 16.6 | | | | 9.0 | | 5.0 |

| | | | | | | | | % Profit Before Taxes/Total Assets | | |
|---|---|---|---|---|---|---|---|---|---|---|
| 76.8 | 27.2 | 20.8 | 16.7 | 13.2 | 12.1 | | | 25.0 | 23.2 |
| 19.3 | 10.9 | 9.0 | 8.2 | 8.0 | 7.6 | | | 10.8 | 8.6 |
| -1.3 | .4 | 2.4 | 2.0 | 4.1 | 3.9 | | | 2.5 | .6 |

| | | | | | | | | Sales/Net Fixed Assets | | |
|---|---|---|---|---|---|---|---|---|---|---|
| 318.6 | 74.2 | 76.2 | 52.6 | 45.7 | 41.7 | | | 60.7 | 61.7 |
| 47.4 | 26.5 | 28.4 | 22.7 | 21.2 | 18.5 | | | 24.8 | 25.4 |
| 17.6 | 10.2 | 12.6 | 10.4 | 12.0 | 9.3 | | | 11.5 | 12.3 |

| | | | | | | | | Sales/Total Assets | | |
|---|---|---|---|---|---|---|---|---|---|---|
| 13.4 | 4.0 | 3.2 | 2.6 | 2.2 | 2.2 | | | 3.7 | 3.8 |
| 7.1 | 2.8 | 2.4 | 2.1 | 1.8 | 1.6 | | | 2.6 | 2.6 |
| 3.8 | 1.9 | 1.7 | 1.6 | 1.4 | 1.2 | | | 1.9 | 1.9 |

| | | | | | | | | | | | | | % Depr., Dep., Amort./Sales | | | | |
|---|---|---|---|---|---|---|---|---|---|---|---|---|---|---|---|---|---|
| | .5 | | .6 | | .6 | | .7 | | 1.0 | | 1.1 | | | | .7 | | .7 |
| (151) | 1.1 | (320) | 1.3 | (569) | 1.3 | (298) | 1.4 | (45) | 1.4 | (38) | 1.9 | | | (1250) | 1.4 | (1349) | 1.5 |
| | 2.3 | | 2.7 | | 2.3 | | 2.2 | | 2.2 | | 2.6 | | | | 2.3 | | 2.5 |

| | | | | | | | | | | | | | % Officers', Directors' Owners' Comp/Sales | | | | |
|---|---|---|---|---|---|---|---|---|---|---|---|---|---|---|---|---|---|
| | 5.9 | | 4.3 | | 2.4 | | 1.0 | | | | | | | | 3.7 | | 3.4 |
| (186) | 12.2 | (192) | 8.2 | (182) | 5.0 | (47) | 3.1 | | | | | | | (511) | 7.6 | (537) | 7.5 |
| | 20.1 | | 13.1 | | 8.6 | | 9.8 | | | | | | | | 14.7 | | 13.7 |

| | | | | | | | | | |
|---|---|---|---|---|---|---|---|---|---|
| 631166M | 1798927M | 8697052M | 15972246M | 7128452M | 12958894M | Net Sales ($) | 48440781M | 53653005M |
| 71572M | 553468M | 3403545M | 7229837M | 3812291M | 7710090M | Total Assets ($) | 19812964M | 21904315M |

M = $ thousand    MM = $ million
See Pages 9 through 22 for Explanation of Ratios and Data

## Comparative Historical Data | Current Data Sorted by Sales

| Hist 1 | Hist 2 | Hist 3 | Type of Statement | 0-1MM | 1-3MM | 3-5MM | 5-10MM | 10-25MM | 25MM & OVER |
|---|---|---|---|---|---|---|---|---|---|
| 222 | 243 | 227 | Unqualified | 2 | 4 | 1 | 16 | 57 | 147 |
| 353 | 337 | 345 | Reviewed | 5 | 20 | 34 | 90 | 129 | 67 |
| 219 | 248 | 253 | Compiled | 15 | 54 | 47 | 63 | 62 | 12 |
| 286 | 315 | 368 | Tax Returns | 83 | 131 | 55 | 61 | 35 | 3 |
| 634 | 709 | 737 | Other | 65 | 131 | 89 | 122 | 141 | 189 |
| 4/1/09-3/31/10 ALL | 4/1/10-3/31/11 ALL | 4/1/11-3/31/12 ALL | | 202 (4/1-9/30/11) | | | 1,728 (10/1/11-3/31/12) | | |
| 1714 | 1852 | 1930 | **NUMBER OF STATEMENTS** | 170 | 340 | 226 | 352 | 424 | 418 |
| % | % | % | **ASSETS** | % | % | % | % | % | % |
| 15.8 | 16.6 | 17.0 | Cash & Equivalents | 20.3 | 24.3 | 18.7 | 14.8 | 14.3 | 13.4 |
| 41.8 | 41.9 | 41.5 | Trade Receivables (net) | 16.9 | 31.8 | 41.5 | 47.0 | 49.2 | 46.8 |
| 4.0 | 3.8 | 4.0 | Inventory | 4.0 | 3.4 | 5.2 | 4.4 | 4.3 | 3.3 |
| 7.2 | 6.8 | 6.7 | All Other Current | 3.0 | 4.8 | 5.3 | 5.6 | 7.5 | 10.4 |
| 68.7 | 69.2 | 69.2 | Total Current | 44.2 | 64.4 | 70.8 | 71.8 | 75.3 | 74.0 |
| 18.6 | 18.3 | 18.4 | Fixed Assets (net) | 41.9 | 22.6 | 17.7 | 16.6 | 14.1 | 11.7 |
| 4.6 | 4.1 | 4.3 | Intangibles (net) | 2.6 | 4.1 | 3.4 | 3.6 | 2.9 | 7.5 |
| 8.1 | 8.4 | 8.1 | All Other Non-Current | 11.4 | 9.0 | 8.1 | 8.0 | 7.7 | 6.7 |
| 100.0 | 100.0 | 100.0 | Total | 100.0 | 100.0 | 100.0 | 100.0 | 100.0 | 100.0 |
| | | | **LIABILITIES** | | | | | | |
| 15.2 | 13.1 | 14.3 | Notes Payable-Short Term | 24.3 | 23.0 | 18.1 | 13.7 | 10.5 | 5.8 |
| 3.8 | 3.2 | 2.8 | Cur. Mat.-L.T.D. | 3.1 | 3.5 | 2.3 | 3.0 | 2.6 | 2.3 |
| 10.0 | 10.8 | 10.3 | Trade Payables | 5.5 | 6.6 | 9.9 | 10.9 | 11.3 | 13.7 |
| 1.7 | 1.7 | 1.6 | Income Taxes Payable | .1 | .2 | 1.3 | 1.5 | 2.2 | 3.0 |
| 16.2 | 16.0 | 15.6 | All Other Current | 10.9 | 13.5 | 14.4 | 16.2 | 15.8 | 19.3 |
| 47.0 | 45.0 | 44.6 | Total Current | 43.7 | 46.8 | 46.1 | 45.3 | 42.3 | 44.0 |
| 12.6 | 11.4 | 13.2 | Long-Term Debt | 32.6 | 21.6 | 10.9 | 10.6 | 8.4 | 6.7 |
| .9 | 1.0 | .9 | Deferred Taxes | .1 | .2 | .8 | .9 | 1.4 | 1.2 |
| 6.2 | 5.2 | 6.0 | All Other Non-Current | 10.9 | 7.8 | 5.5 | 5.4 | 4.3 | 5.2 |
| 33.4 | 37.5 | 35.3 | Net Worth | 12.7 | 23.6 | 36.8 | 37.7 | 43.6 | 42.9 |
| 100.0 | 100.0 | 100.0 | Total Liabilties & Net Worth | 100.0 | 100.0 | 100.0 | 100.0 | 100.0 | 100.0 |
| | | | **INCOME DATA** | | | | | | |
| 100.0 | 100.0 | 100.0 | Net Sales | 100.0 | 100.0 | 100.0 | 100.0 | 100.0 | 100.0 |
| | | | Gross Profit | | | | | | |
| 95.0 | 93.7 | 92.7 | Operating Expenses | 79.2 | 93.2 | 94.8 | 94.7 | 93.8 | 93.8 |
| 5.0 | 6.3 | 7.3 | Operating Profit | 20.8 | 6.8 | 5.2 | 5.3 | 6.2 | 6.2 |
| 1.3 | 1.4 | 1.4 | All Other Expenses (net) | 10.0 | 1.1 | .2 | .4 | .6 | .7 |
| 3.7 | 4.8 | 5.9 | Profit Before Taxes | 10.8 | 5.7 | 5.0 | 4.9 | 5.6 | 5.5 |
| | | | **RATIOS** | | | | | | |
| 3.0 | 3.1 | 3.1 | | 4.2 | 4.8 | 3.6 | 3.3 | 3.1 | 2.4 |
| 1.8 | 1.8 | 1.8 | Current | 1.0 | 1.9 | 1.8 | 1.9 | 1.9 | 1.7 |
| 1.1 | 1.2 | 1.2 | | .4 | 1.0 | 1.2 | 1.3 | 1.3 | 1.3 |
| 2.6 | 2.7 | 2.7 | | 3.6 | 4.2 | 3.3 | 2.7 | 2.6 | 2.0 |
| (1711) 1.4 | 1.5 | 1.5 | Quick | .9 | 1.7 | 1.6 | 1.6 | 1.6 | 1.3 |
| .9 | .9 | .9 | | .3 | .7 | 1.0 | 1.1 | 1.0 | 1.0 |
| 33  11.0 | 35  10.6 | 32  11.4 | | 0  UND | 0  UND | 34  10.6 | 40  9.1 | 46  8.0 | 52  7.0 |
| 62  5.9 | 66  5.6 | 63  5.8 | Sales/Receivables | 0  UND | 39  9.3 | 63  5.8 | 69  5.3 | 70  5.2 | 70  5.2 |
| 93  3.9 | 94  3.9 | 91  4.0 | | 65  5.6 | 87  4.2 | 94  3.9 | 94  3.9 | 96  3.8 | 94  3.9 |
| | | | Cost of Sales/Inventory | | | | | | |
| | | | Cost of Sales/Payables | | | | | | |
| 5.0 | 4.6 | 4.8 | | 5.9 | 4.6 | 4.8 | 4.9 | 4.4 | 5.0 |
| 9.2 | 8.8 | 8.8 | Sales/Working Capital | 162.3 | 11.4 | 8.2 | 8.2 | 7.9 | 7.8 |
| 43.2 | 40.0 | 31.7 | | -6.0 | UND | 26.2 | 22.2 | 18.6 | 17.1 |
| 24.8 | 30.7 | 37.5 | | 14.7 | 28.1 | 26.5 | 36.2 | 50.3 | 51.5 |
| (1403) 5.5 | (1483) 7.4 | (1558) 10.0 | EBIT/Interest | (88) 3.8 | (276) 5.7 | (189) 7.7 | (284) 9.3 | (366) 12.7 | (355) 15.3 |
| .2 | 1.3 | 2.0 | | -.4 | .0 | 1.5 | 1.8 | 2.9 | 4.1 |
| 6.4 | 9.3 | 10.6 | Net Profit + Depr., Dep., | | 6.7 | 18.2 | 9.1 | 12.0 | 10.8 |
| (342) 2.5 | (380) 2.5 | (341) 3.3 | Amort./Cur. Mat. L/T/D | (15) 2.1 | (26) 3.8 | (53) 2.9 | (99) 2.8 | (144) 4.3 | |
| .8 | .8 | 1.4 | | -.4 | -.2 | 1.0 | 1.1 | 2.0 | |
| .1 | .1 | .1 | | .1 | .1 | .1 | .1 | .1 | .1 |
| .3 | .3 | .3 | Fixed/Worth | 2.1 | .4 | .3 | .3 | .2 | .3 |
| 1.2 | 1.0 | 1.0 | | UND | 6.9 | 1.2 | .8 | .7 | .6 |
| .6 | .6 | .6 | | .7 | .4 | .4 | .5 | .6 | .8 |
| 1.5 | 1.4 | 1.4 | Debt/Worth | 3.4 | 1.4 | 1.2 | 1.2 | 1.3 | 1.5 |
| 5.6 | 4.2 | 4.4 | | -11.3 | 17.9 | 3.7 | 3.7 | 2.6 | 3.5 |
| 50.4 | 53.1 | 58.6 | % Profit Before Taxes/Tangible | 73.4 | 82.8 | 56.8 | 55.6 | 52.3 | 57.2 |
| (1442) 20.0 | (1635) 21.7 | (1662) 25.2 | Net Worth | (120) 25.1 | (259) 29.2 | (191) 22.2 | (311) 22.5 | (396) 24.7 | (385) 26.8 |
| .9 | 3.3 | 7.1 | | 7.0 | 1.6 | 4.5 | 4.3 | 9.0 | 11.3 |
| 21.3 | 21.5 | 23.8 | % Profit Before Taxes/Total | 24.7 | 39.0 | 21.8 | 24.9 | 22.6 | 18.1 |
| 7.0 | 7.9 | 9.9 | Assets | 7.5 | 11.9 | 11.3 | 8.8 | 10.5 | 9.1 |
| -1.0 | .8 | 1.8 | | .0 | -1.2 | 1.0 | 1.3 | 3.0 | 3.4 |
| 67.0 | 65.8 | 78.8 | | 68.7 | 89.7 | 73.0 | 80.0 | 85.8 | 71.1 |
| 25.7 | 26.4 | 28.4 | Sales/Net Fixed Assets | 9.6 | 28.8 | 25.5 | 30.9 | 29.3 | 28.3 |
| 11.0 | 11.3 | 12.1 | | .3 | 11.8 | 12.9 | 14.7 | 13.3 | 14.2 |
| 3.7 | 3.7 | 3.9 | | 4.2 | 6.5 | 4.1 | 4.0 | 3.5 | 3.1 |
| 2.6 | 2.4 | 2.5 | Sales/Total Assets | 1.7 | 3.3 | 2.6 | 2.7 | 2.5 | 2.2 |
| 1.8 | 1.8 | 1.8 | | .2 | 1.9 | 1.9 | 2.0 | 1.9 | 1.8 |
| .7 | .7 | .7 | | .9 | .7 | .6 | .6 | .7 | .6 |
| (1327) 1.5 | (1406) 1.4 | (1421) 1.3 | % Depr., Dep., Amort./Sales | (104) 4.8 | (206) 1.5 | (156) 1.4 | (270) 1.3 | (348) 1.2 | (337) 1.3 |
| 2.6 | 2.6 | 2.4 | | 17.6 | 2.7 | 2.4 | 2.1 | 2.0 | 2.1 |
| 4.2 | 3.4 | 3.5 | % Officers', Directors' | 4.1 | 5.8 | 4.1 | 2.7 | 2.1 | 1.2 |
| (551) 8.9 | (567) 7.2 | (611) 7.4 | Owners' Comp/Sales | (60) 19.1 | (173) 9.8 | (104) 7.1 | (130) 5.7 | (99) 3.7 | (45) 3.0 |
| 15.4 | 13.3 | 13.7 | | 25.4 | 15.2 | 12.3 | 9.9 | 8.4 | 8.8 |
| 45127541M | 46965845M | 47186737M | Net Sales ($) | 80182M | 678555M | 896515M | 2574685M | 6838414M | 36118386M |
| 19972985M | 20998610M | 22780803M | Total Assets ($) | 121062M | 284079M | 385829M | 1102752M | 2977112M | 17909969M |

© RMA 2012

**M = $ thousand    MM = $ million**
See Pages 9 through 22 for Explanation of Ratios and Data

## Current Data Sorted by Assets / Comparative Historical Data

| 0-500M | 500M-2MM | 2-10MM | 10-50MM | 50-100MM | 100-250MM | Type of Statement | 3 / 4/1/07-3/31/08 ALL | 6 / 4/1/08-3/31/09 ALL |
|---|---|---|---|---|---|---|---|---|
| | 1 | 2 | 1 | 1 | | Unqualified | 3 | 6 |
| 1 | 3 | 6 | | | | Reviewed | 10 | 9 |
| 1 | 5 | 4 | | | | Compiled | 11 | 8 |
| 13 | 4 | 2 | | | | Tax Returns | 24 | 20 |
| 5 | 13 | 6 | 5 | | 2 | Other | 36 | 32 |
| | 9 (4/1-9/30/11) | | 66 (10/1/11-3/31/12) | | | | | |
| 20 | 26 | 20 | 6 | 1 | 2 | NUMBER OF STATEMENTS | 84 | 75 |
| % | % | % | % | % | % | **ASSETS** | % | % |
| 19.4 | 12.5 | 9.5 | | | | Cash & Equivalents | 14.9 | 14.3 |
| 30.2 | 44.3 | 41.7 | | | | Trade Receivables (net) | 35.6 | 34.9 |
| 2.9 | 5.1 | 6.4 | | | | Inventory | 2.9 | 1.8 |
| 4.9 | 1.3 | 8.0 | | | | All Other Current | 4.9 | 4.6 |
| 57.4 | 63.3 | 65.6 | | | | Total Current | 58.4 | 55.6 |
| 17.2 | 20.0 | 15.6 | | | | Fixed Assets (net) | 27.6 | 25.9 |
| 5.4 | 7.4 | 5.9 | | | | Intangibles (net) | 6.6 | 7.8 |
| 19.4 | 9.4 | 12.9 | | | | All Other Non-Current | 7.5 | 10.8 |
| 100.0 | 100.0 | 100.0 | | | | Total | 100.0 | 100.0 |
| | | | | | | **LIABILITIES** | | |
| 43.0 | 11.9 | 8.8 | | | | Notes Payable-Short Term | 12.2 | 17.8 |
| 7.2 | 3.6 | 4.6 | | | | Cur. Mat.-L.T.D. | 6.2 | 3.5 |
| 4.3 | 4.7 | 10.0 | | | | Trade Payables | 6.0 | 6.3 |
| .3 | 1.2 | 2.0 | | | | Income Taxes Payable | 2.0 | 1.7 |
| 17.2 | 11.3 | 19.6 | | | | All Other Current | 10.3 | 10.7 |
| 72.0 | 32.6 | 45.1 | | | | Total Current | 36.7 | 40.0 |
| 39.6 | 16.3 | 10.3 | | | | Long-Term Debt | 19.8 | 19.2 |
| .3 | 3.8 | .9 | | | | Deferred Taxes | 1.4 | .9 |
| .4 | 10.5 | 1.9 | | | | All Other Non-Current | 6.1 | 6.7 |
| -12.3 | 36.8 | 41.9 | | | | Net Worth | 35.9 | 33.3 |
| 100.0 | 100.0 | 100.0 | | | | Total Liabilties & Net Worth | 100.0 | 100.0 |
| | | | | | | **INCOME DATA** | | |
| 100.0 | 100.0 | 100.0 | | | | Net Sales | 100.0 | 100.0 |
| | | | | | | Gross Profit | | |
| 93.8 | 97.5 | 94.8 | | | | Operating Expenses | 94.1 | 97.6 |
| 6.2 | 2.5 | 5.2 | | | | Operating Profit | 5.9 | 2.4 |
| 2.1 | -.1 | 1.2 | | | | All Other Expenses (net) | 1.2 | 1.3 |
| 4.1 | 2.6 | 4.0 | | | | Profit Before Taxes | 4.8 | 1.0 |
| | | | | | | **RATIOS** | | |
| 9.3 | 6.2 | 2.9 | | | | | 4.4 | 4.2 |
| 1.5 | 1.9 | 1.4 | | | | Current | 1.6 | 1.6 |
| .3 | 1.0 | 1.0 | | | | | 1.1 | 1.0 |
| 4.9 | 6.0 | 2.4 | | | | | 3.4 | 4.1 |
| .6 | 1.7 | 1.2 | | | | Quick | 1.4 | 1.4 |
| .2 | .6 | .7 | | | | | .9 | .8 |
| 0 UND | 43 8.5 | 36 10.2 | | | | | 9 39.7 | 2 157.7 |
| 14 26.2 | 70 5.2 | 70 5.2 | | | | Sales/Receivables | 64 5.7 | 53 6.8 |
| 76 4.8 | 99 3.7 | 118 3.1 | | | | | 87 4.2 | 84 4.4 |
| | | | | | | Cost of Sales/Inventory | | |
| | | | | | | Cost of Sales/Payables | | |
| 6.2 | 3.9 | 4.6 | | | | | 4.5 | 5.9 |
| 126.0 | 9.3 | 13.4 | | | | Sales/Working Capital | 9.3 | 20.7 |
| -7.9 | NM | -55.1 | | | | | 193.2 | -293.0 |
| 16.7 | 6.3 | 17.1 | | | | | 23.2 | 8.3 |
| (17) 2.9 | (20) 1.2 | 7.8 | | | | EBIT/Interest | (73) 3.4 | (66) 3.1 |
| -3.5 | -1.9 | .3 | | | | | .6 | -3.8 |
| | | | | | | | 5.6 | |
| | | | | | | Net Profit + Depr., Dep., Amort./Cur. Mat. L/T/D | (18) 1.6 | |
| | | | | | | | .8 | |
| .1 | .1 | .1 | | | | | .3 | .3 |
| .8 | .4 | .3 | | | | Fixed/Worth | .5 | .9 |
| -.2 | NM | 3.4 | | | | | 1.8 | 10.6 |
| .6 | .2 | .5 | | | | | .5 | .5 |
| 3.1 | 1.7 | 1.7 | | | | Debt/Worth | 1.3 | 2.1 |
| -2.7 | NM | 7.0 | | | | | 4.3 | 72.7 |
| 110.9 | 49.0 | 65.0 | | | | | 71.4 | 62.1 |
| (11) 50.4 | (20) 22.7 | (17) 27.0 | | | | % Profit Before Taxes/Tangible Net Worth | (70) 17.2 | (57) 13.5 |
| 19.4 | -9.4 | -.5 | | | | | 1.9 | -21.4 |
| 44.0 | 23.9 | 21.8 | | | | | 29.1 | 23.0 |
| 7.8 | 4.1 | 8.3 | | | | % Profit Before Taxes/Total Assets | 7.1 | 4.6 |
| -9.1 | -4.7 | -1.5 | | | | | -1.1 | -12.9 |
| 115.8 | 50.1 | 37.2 | | | | | 25.0 | 31.5 |
| 32.9 | 20.7 | 19.8 | | | | Sales/Net Fixed Assets | 12.9 | 12.0 |
| 18.4 | 7.7 | 9.1 | | | | | 6.8 | 8.8 |
| 8.4 | 3.4 | 2.8 | | | | | 4.0 | 3.9 |
| 3.7 | 2.5 | 2.1 | | | | Sales/Total Assets | 2.5 | 2.4 |
| 1.8 | 1.9 | 1.5 | | | | | 1.8 | 1.8 |
| .9 | 1.4 | 1.2 | | | | | 1.5 | 2.0 |
| (10) 1.6 | (15) 2.8 | (17) 1.9 | | | | % Depr., Dep., Amort./Sales | (66) 2.7 | (56) 2.8 |
| 2.5 | 4.1 | 3.0 | | | | | 5.2 | 5.2 |
| 8.3 | 4.6 | 2.8 | | | | | 3.7 | 5.2 |
| (14) 13.9 | (11) 7.7 | (10) 7.2 | | | | % Officers', Directors' Owners' Comp/Sales | (44) 8.0 | (30) 8.9 |
| 31.0 | 20.3 | 15.7 | | | | | 14.7 | 15.1 |
| 23110M | 78600M | 219443M | 157539M | 76131M | 1330326M | Net Sales ($) | 790824M | 923992M |
| 4862M | 27299M | 95627M | 142682M | 64794M | 328358M | Total Assets ($) | 514482M | 564291M |

M = $ thousand   MM = $ million
See Pages 9 through 22 for Explanation of Ratios and Data

## Comparative Historical Data

## Current Data Sorted by Sales

| | | | Type of Statement | | | | | | | |
|---|---|---|---|---|---|---|---|---|---|---|
| 9 | 7 | 5 | Unqualified | | | 1 | | | 3 | 1 |
| 7 | 5 | 10 | Reviewed | 1 | 2 | | 5 | | 2 | |
| 7 | 7 | 10 | Compiled | 2 | 2 | 1 | 4 | | | 1 |
| 26 | 27 | 19 | Tax Returns | 9 | 5 | | 5 | | | |
| 23 | 30 | 31 | Other | 5 | 9 | 6 | 1 | | 5 | 5 |
| 4/1/09- 3/31/10 ALL | 4/1/10- 3/31/11 ALL | 4/1/11- 3/31/12 ALL | | 9 (4/1-9/30/11) | | | 66 (10/1/11-3/31/12) | | | |
| | | | | 0-1MM | 1-3MM | 3-5MM | 5-10MM | 10-25MM | 25MM & OVER | |
| 72 | 76 | 75 | NUMBER OF STATEMENTS | 17 | 18 | 8 | 15 | 10 | 7 | |
| % | % | % | ASSETS | % | % | % | % | % | % | |
| 14.9 | 13.8 | 13.3 | Cash & Equivalents | 8.8 | 19.6 | | 19.6 | 8.5 | | |
| 28.8 | 32.8 | 38.3 | Trade Receivables (net) | 35.0 | 38.6 | | 32.9 | 39.8 | | |
| 1.7 | 2.2 | 4.6 | Inventory | 6.0 | 4.6 | | 3.1 | 8.1 | | |
| 5.4 | 6.2 | 4.7 | All Other Current | 2.2 | 3.8 | | 6.3 | 4.1 | | |
| 50.8 | 55.1 | 60.8 | Total Current | 52.1 | 66.6 | | 61.8 | 60.4 | | |
| 24.2 | 25.4 | 17.7 | Fixed Assets (net) | 17.0 | 18.6 | | 15.8 | 12.4 | | |
| 8.6 | 4.8 | 8.9 | Intangibles (net) | 8.7 | 2.0 | | 10.3 | 19.2 | | |
| 16.4 | 14.8 | 12.4 | All Other Non-Current | 21.5 | 12.7 | | 12.0 | 8.1 | | |
| 100.0 | 100.0 | 100.0 | Total | 100.0 | 100.0 | | 100.0 | 100.0 | | |
| | | | LIABILITIES | | | | | | | |
| 25.8 | 14.4 | 18.1 | Notes Payable-Short Term | 40.4 | 20.0 | | 11.4 | 9.0 | | |
| 7.8 | 6.3 | 4.6 | Cur. Mat.-L.T.D. | 7.0 | 2.9 | | 4.9 | 2.3 | | |
| 8.0 | 6.0 | 6.3 | Trade Payables | 2.8 | 5.1 | | 5.5 | 12.8 | | |
| .3 | 1.2 | 1.1 | Income Taxes Payable | .0 | 1.6 | | 2.7 | .5 | | |
| 11.4 | 19.2 | 15.2 | All Other Current | 18.5 | 5.5 | | 20.6 | 25.3 | | |
| 53.2 | 47.0 | 45.4 | Total Current | 68.7 | 35.1 | | 45.1 | 49.9 | | |
| 26.8 | 32.4 | 20.8 | Long-Term Debt | 42.9 | 19.9 | | 8.7 | 6.4 | | |
| 1.0 | 1.1 | 2.2 | Deferred Taxes | .0 | 2.5 | | .0 | 5.8 | | |
| 15.5 | 11.8 | 5.6 | All Other Non-Current | 6.5 | 4.3 | | 2.7 | 4.8 | | |
| 3.5 | 7.6 | 26.0 | Net Worth | -18.2 | 38.3 | | 43.5 | 33.1 | | |
| 100.0 | 100.0 | 100.0 | Total Liabilities & Net Worth | 100.0 | 100.0 | | 100.0 | 100.0 | | |
| | | | INCOME DATA | | | | | | | |
| 100.0 | 100.0 | 100.0 | Net Sales | 100.0 | 100.0 | | 100.0 | 100.0 | | |
| | | | Gross Profit | | | | | | | |
| 96.2 | 96.7 | 94.5 | Operating Expenses | 92.6 | 97.6 | | 96.9 | 93.5 | | |
| 3.8 | 3.3 | 5.5 | Operating Profit | 7.4 | 2.4 | | 3.1 | 6.5 | | |
| 2.4 | 1.2 | 1.0 | All Other Expenses (net) | 2.2 | 1.1 | | .4 | 1.0 | | |
| 1.4 | 2.1 | 4.5 | Profit Before Taxes | 5.2 | 1.3 | | 2.8 | 5.4 | | |
| | | | RATIOS | | | | | | | |
| 4.1 | 2.4 | 4.4 | | 6.4 | 7.7 | | 4.4 | 1.7 | | |
| 1.3 | 1.4 | 1.6 | Current | 1.0 | 3.0 | | 1.3 | 1.5 | | |
| .7 | .6 | .9 | | .3 | .8 | | .9 | 1.1 | | |
| 3.3 | 2.3 | 3.4 | | 2.3 | 7.0 | | 3.4 | 1.6 | | |
| 1.1 | 1.0 | 1.3 | Quick | .5 | 3.0 | | 1.2 | 1.2 | | |
| .5 | .5 | .6 | | .2 | .6 | | .5 | .9 | | |
| 0  UND | 0  UND | 31  11.6 | | 0  UND | 0  UND | | 0  UND | 35  10.5 | | |
| 49  7.4 | 48  7.6 | 68  5.4 | Sales/Receivables | 47  7.7 | 59  6.2 | | 60  6.1 | 72  5.1 | | |
| 93  3.9 | 89  4.1 | 99  3.7 | | 91  4.0 | 89  4.1 | | 114  3.2 | 87  4.2 | | |
| | | | Cost of Sales/Inventory | | | | | | | |
| | | | Cost of Sales/Payables | | | | | | | |
| 5.0 | 5.6 | 4.5 | | 5.5 | 3.4 | | 5.0 | 8.4 | | |
| 30.1 | 34.7 | 10.2 | Sales/Working Capital | 199.0 | 5.9 | | 16.0 | 13.8 | | |
| -16.9 | -15.9 | -43.7 | | -5.1 | -14.4 | | -43.7 | NM | | |
| 10.1 | 7.2 | 15.4 | | 9.8 | 6.5 | | 19.3 | | | |
| (60) 3.3 | (66) 1.9 | (63) 3.1 | EBIT/Interest | (15) 1.8 | (15) 1.9 | | (13) 1.3 | | | |
| -4.8 | -2.0 | -1.3 | | -.7 | -9.2 | | -5.2 | | | |
| | 18.4 | 10.1 | Net Profit + Depr., Dep., | | | | | | | |
| | (10) 2.7 | (15) 2.8 | Amort./Cur. Mat. L/T/D | | | | | | | |
| | 1.8 | 1.1 | | | | | | | | |
| .1 | .2 | .1 | | .1 | .1 | | .1 | .1 | | |
| .8 | 1.0 | .4 | Fixed/Worth | .4 | .4 | | .4 | .4 | | |
| -.6 | -1.7 | -1.6 | | -.3 | NM | | 1.7 | -.6 | | |
| .5 | .6 | .5 | | .7 | .2 | | .5 | .8 | | |
| 3.0 | 3.1 | 2.2 | Debt/Worth | 3.2 | .9 | | 1.0 | 2.7 | | |
| -2.8 | -4.5 | -7.7 | | -2.0 | NM | | 6.4 | -2.8 | | |
| 48.5 | 80.8 | 59.8 | % Profit Before Taxes/Tangible | | 32.9 | | 93.0 | | | |
| (44) 9.1 | (50) 11.5 | (54) 28.3 | Net Worth | | (14) 18.4 | | (13) 59.4 | | | |
| -17.7 | -7.6 | .6 | | | -7.2 | | -2.0 | | | |
| 18.3 | 18.1 | 24.4 | % Profit Before Taxes/Total | 29.5 | 20.5 | | 25.1 | 16.4 | | |
| 2.6 | 3.4 | 7.5 | Assets | 5.0 | 5.3 | | 12.0 | 8.5 | | |
| -22.9 | -8.5 | -2.4 | | -8.5 | -7.5 | | -3.6 | 5.3 | | |
| 47.3 | 41.3 | 50.2 | | 84.1 | 65.9 | | 100.5 | 122.0 | | |
| 17.7 | 13.7 | 23.9 | Sales/Net Fixed Assets | 33.7 | 22.4 | | 32.1 | 40.0 | | |
| 8.6 | 7.4 | 10.2 | | 11.5 | 7.7 | | 11.2 | 10.8 | | |
| 4.2 | 4.2 | 3.5 | | 4.7 | 3.5 | | 9.2 | 3.0 | | |
| 2.5 | 2.5 | 2.3 | Sales/Total Assets | 2.1 | 2.5 | | 2.6 | 2.3 | | |
| 1.3 | 1.5 | 1.5 | | 1.1 | 1.8 | | 2.0 | 1.3 | | |
| 1.0 | 1.3 | 1.4 | | | 1.4 | | 1.3 | | | |
| (54) 2.7 | (47) 2.1 | (48) 2.4 | % Depr., Dep., Amort./Sales | | (11) 2.0 | | (10) 2.1 | | | |
| 4.0 | 4.8 | 4.0 | | | 4.5 | | 2.9 | | | |
| 5.9 | 6.7 | 5.3 | % Officers', Directors' | 8.0 | | | | | | |
| (35) 12.6 | (35) 14.9 | (35) 11.7 | Owners' Comp/Sales | (12) 16.5 | | | | | | |
| 19.6 | 24.4 | 21.3 | | 33.1 | | | | | | |
| 1052927M | 933394M | 1885149M | Net Sales ($) | 9099M | 35866M | 28799M | 106628M | 165389M | 1539368M | |
| 938693M | 738636M | 663622M | Total Assets ($) | 5233M | 20636M | 12052M | 40876M | 88238M | 496587M | |

M = $ thousand    MM = $ million
See Pages 9 through 22 for Explanation of Ratios and Data

## Current Data Sorted by Assets      Comparative Historical Data

| Type of Statement | 0-500M | 500M-2MM | 2-10MM | 10-50MM | 50-100MM | 100-250MM | 4/1/07-3/31/08 ALL | 4/1/08-3/31/09 ALL |
|---|---|---|---|---|---|---|---|---|
| Unqualified | | 1 | 3 | 11 | 3 | 6 | 27 | 38 |
| Reviewed | | 4 | 19 | 6 | 1 | | 32 | 29 |
| Compiled | 4 | 13 | 12 | 1 | | | 35 | 31 |
| Tax Returns | 23 | 26 | 14 | | | | 32 | 44 |
| Other | 10 | 28 | 28 | 22 | 4 | 1 | 72 | 93 |
| | | 38 (4/1-9/30/11) | | 202 (10/1/11-3/31/12) | | | | |
| **NUMBER OF STATEMENTS** | 37 | 72 | 76 | 40 | 8 | 7 | 198 | 235 |

| | % | % | % | % | % | % | % | % |
|---|---|---|---|---|---|---|---|---|
| **ASSETS** | | | | | | | | |
| Cash & Equivalents | 25.4 | 15.8 | 12.3 | 11.6 | | | 10.7 | 11.8 |
| Trade Receivables (net) | 9.5 | 29.6 | 34.1 | 29.8 | | | 32.5 | 32.4 |
| Inventory | 1.8 | 2.9 | 2.4 | 4.2 | | | 4.1 | 3.5 |
| All Other Current | 3.5 | 1.7 | 4.4 | 7.4 | | | 3.7 | 4.4 |
| Total Current | 40.2 | 50.0 | 53.3 | 53.0 | | | 50.9 | 52.2 |
| Fixed Assets (net) | 44.7 | 33.4 | 36.8 | 33.6 | | | 37.9 | 35.5 |
| Intangibles (net) | 4.7 | 5.7 | 3.0 | 7.9 | | | 4.4 | 5.4 |
| All Other Non-Current | 10.4 | 10.9 | 6.9 | 5.6 | | | 6.7 | 7.0 |
| Total | 100.0 | 100.0 | 100.0 | 100.0 | | | 100.0 | 100.0 |
| **LIABILITIES** | | | | | | | | |
| Notes Payable-Short Term | 16.8 | 6.4 | 6.1 | 5.8 | | | 9.6 | 9.5 |
| Cur. Mat.-L.T.D. | 13.2 | 6.7 | 3.6 | 2.7 | | | 5.0 | 4.4 |
| Trade Payables | 6.2 | 6.1 | 6.3 | 7.1 | | | 10.0 | 8.3 |
| Income Taxes Payable | .0 | .2 | .7 | .4 | | | .6 | .6 |
| All Other Current | 14.4 | 6.1 | 9.6 | 16.2 | | | 10.7 | 12.3 |
| Total Current | 50.6 | 25.6 | 26.2 | 32.2 | | | 35.9 | 35.1 |
| Long-Term Debt | 34.8 | 22.1 | 17.6 | 16.3 | | | 21.6 | 19.8 |
| Deferred Taxes | .0 | .6 | .9 | .6 | | | .8 | .8 |
| All Other Non-Current | 8.3 | 9.1 | 7.1 | 4.4 | | | 5.4 | 5.8 |
| Net Worth | 6.2 | 42.6 | 48.2 | 46.5 | | | 36.3 | 38.5 |
| Total Liabilties & Net Worth | 100.0 | 100.0 | 100.0 | 100.0 | | | 100.0 | 100.0 |
| **INCOME DATA** | | | | | | | | |
| Net Sales | 100.0 | 100.0 | 100.0 | 100.0 | | | 100.0 | 100.0 |
| Gross Profit | | | | | | | | |
| Operating Expenses | 87.2 | 89.8 | 87.7 | 89.8 | | | 90.0 | 91.5 |
| Operating Profit | 12.8 | 10.2 | 12.3 | 10.2 | | | 10.0 | 8.5 |
| All Other Expenses (net) | 2.5 | 2.7 | .9 | 1.0 | | | 2.5 | 1.8 |
| Profit Before Taxes | 10.3 | 7.5 | 11.4 | 9.2 | | | 7.4 | 6.7 |

| **RATIOS** | 0-500M | 500M-2MM | 2-10MM | 10-50MM | | | 4/1/07-3/31/08 | 4/1/08-3/31/09 |
|---|---|---|---|---|---|---|---|---|
| Current | 4.7 | 5.1 | 3.5 | 3.0 | | | 2.9 | 3.0 |
| | 1.0 | 2.2 | 2.2 | 1.9 | | | 1.6 | 1.6 |
| | .2 | 1.0 | 1.3 | 1.1 | | | 1.0 | 1.0 |
| Quick | 3.8 | 5.1 | 3.3 | 2.4 | | | 2.2 | 2.4 |
| | .8 | 1.7 | 2.0 | 1.3 | | | (197) 1.3 | 1.3 |
| | .2 | .9 | 1.2 | .9 | | | .8 | .8 |
| Sales/Receivables | 0 UND | 32 11.3 | 42 8.7 | 54 6.7 | | | 33 11.0 | 36 10.1 |
| | 0 UND | 49 7.5 | 58 6.3 | 69 5.3 | | | 55 6.6 | 56 6.5 |
| | 30 12.0 | 63 5.8 | 79 4.6 | 94 3.9 | | | 75 4.9 | 73 5.0 |
| Cost of Sales/Inventory | | | | | | | | |
| Cost of Sales/Payables | | | | | | | | |
| Sales/Working Capital | 9.0 | 5.3 | 4.4 | 3.6 | | | 5.4 | 5.0 |
| | -405.5 | 12.4 | 7.0 | 7.5 | | | 11.5 | 12.2 |
| | -9.7 | NM | 22.5 | 57.2 | | | -999.8 | -107.4 |
| EBIT/Interest | 31.7 | 16.4 | 37.4 | 43.8 | | | 14.5 | 13.4 |
| | (29) 8.3 | (55) 5.1 | (65) 15.1 | (34) 8.8 | | | (170) 5.2 | (202) 4.6 |
| | .2 | 2.5 | 3.8 | 3.6 | | | 1.7 | 1.7 |
| Net Profit + Depr., Dep., Amort./Cur. Mat. L/T/D | | 4.3 | 19.6 | 14.4 | | | 9.2 | 11.0 |
| | | (12) 1.7 | (17) 6.1 | (13) 2.6 | | | (49) 4.1 | (61) 4.7 |
| | | .5 | 1.6 | 1.0 | | | 2.1 | 2.2 |
| Fixed/Worth | .5 | .3 | .3 | .5 | | | .4 | .4 |
| | 1.8 | .8 | .7 | .9 | | | 1.0 | .9 |
| | -2.6 | 7.1 | 1.4 | 2.0 | | | 2.8 | 2.5 |
| Debt/Worth | .8 | .3 | .5 | .5 | | | .6 | .6 |
| | 2.7 | 1.0 | .9 | 1.3 | | | 1.6 | 1.4 |
| | -4.6 | 10.6 | 2.5 | 4.0 | | | 6.4 | 4.8 |
| % Profit Before Taxes/Tangible Net Worth | 159.9 | 59.4 | 49.2 | 54.3 | | | 59.2 | 60.0 |
| | (25) 93.6 | (57) 27.4 | (70) 24.6 | (35) 26.2 | | | (170) 32.8 | (200) 27.4 |
| | 38.3 | 9.4 | 11.5 | 15.8 | | | 11.8 | 7.8 |
| % Profit Before Taxes/Total Assets | 67.9 | 25.8 | 21.6 | 20.7 | | | 21.3 | 22.8 |
| | 38.1 | 12.1 | 12.6 | 10.5 | | | 12.8 | 8.5 |
| | 9.4 | 2.8 | 6.0 | 4.3 | | | 2.4 | 1.9 |
| Sales/Net Fixed Assets | 29.6 | 21.5 | 19.0 | 7.7 | | | 13.1 | 12.9 |
| | 10.6 | 9.9 | 6.8 | 4.7 | | | 6.5 | 6.3 |
| | 5.5 | 3.7 | 3.1 | 2.7 | | | 3.7 | 3.9 |
| Sales/Total Assets | 8.0 | 3.3 | 2.7 | 2.2 | | | 3.0 | 2.8 |
| | 3.6 | 2.4 | 2.0 | 1.3 | | | 2.2 | 2.0 |
| | 2.4 | 1.5 | 1.2 | 1.0 | | | 1.4 | 1.4 |
| % Depr., Dep., Amort./Sales | 1.2 | 2.1 | 1.5 | 3.3 | | | 1.9 | 2.0 |
| | (29) 3.3 | (57) 3.5 | (64) 3.6 | (34) 4.8 | | | (162) 3.5 | (193) 3.9 |
| | 10.6 | 7.1 | 5.4 | 5.8 | | | 5.3 | 6.1 |
| % Officers', Directors' Owners' Comp/Sales | 4.7 | 4.1 | 2.5 | | | | 2.6 | 2.6 |
| | (21) 7.3 | (39) 6.9 | (29) 4.5 | | | | (60) 5.6 | (75) 4.9 |
| | 13.9 | 9.2 | 8.2 | | | | 9.4 | 8.1 |
| Net Sales ($) | 47104M | 204928M | 808192M | 1297668M | 973256M | 1274654M | 2998309M | 4890000M |
| Total Assets ($) | 9738M | 77986M | 343808M | 802079M | 565292M | 1172418M | 1891566M | 3485207M |

© RMA 2012

M = $ thousand     MM = $ million
See Pages 9 through 22 for Explanation of Ratios and Data

## Comparative Historical Data                 ## Current Data Sorted by Sales

| | | | Type of Statement | | | | | | |
|---|---|---|---|---|---|---|---|---|---|
| 35 | 27 | 24 | Unqualified | | 1 | | 2 | 6 | 15 |
| 33 | 36 | 30 | Reviewed | | 5 | 2 | 8 | 10 | 5 |
| 22 | 28 | 30 | Compiled | 4 | 7 | 8 | 9 | 1 | 1 |
| 43 | 53 | 63 | Tax Returns | 19 | 20 | 10 | 9 | 4 | 1 |
| 97 | 97 | 93 | Other | 16 | 20 | 6 | 17 | 16 | 18 |
| 4/1/09- | 4/1/10- | 4/1/11- | | | 38 (4/1-9/30/11) | | 202 (10/1/11-3/31/12) | | |
| 3/31/10 | 3/31/11 | 3/31/12 | | | | | | | |
| ALL | ALL | ALL | | 0-1MM | 1-3MM | 3-5MM | 5-10MM | 10-25MM | 25MM & OVER |
| 230 | 241 | 240 | NUMBER OF STATEMENTS | 39 | 53 | 26 | 45 | 37 | 40 |
| % | % | % | ASSETS | % | % | % | % | % | % |
| 13.6 | 12.4 | 15.0 | Cash & Equivalents | 18.5 | 15.5 | 17.5 | 14.5 | 15.4 | 9.8 |
| 29.6 | 30.1 | 27.8 | Trade Receivables (net) | 7.0 | 30.1 | 26.3 | 36.0 | 31.8 | 32.9 |
| 3.2 | 3.9 | 2.7 | Inventory | .1 | 2.2 | 5.8 | 2.4 | 4.4 | 2.7 |
| 4.6 | 3.5 | 4.1 | All Other Current | 3.4 | 2.5 | 1.2 | 2.0 | 8.4 | 7.0 |
| 51.0 | 49.8 | 49.6 | Total Current | 29.0 | 50.3 | 50.8 | 55.0 | 60.0 | 52.4 |
| 34.2 | 34.2 | 36.0 | Fixed Assets (net) | 51.0 | 33.4 | 36.1 | 36.7 | 27.5 | 31.9 |
| 7.3 | 6.6 | 6.0 | Intangibles (net) | 9.2 | 3.7 | 5.2 | 1.4 | 7.1 | 10.5 |
| 7.5 | 9.4 | 8.4 | All Other Non-Current | 10.8 | 12.6 | 7.8 | 6.9 | 5.4 | 5.2 |
| 100.0 | 100.0 | 100.0 | Total | 100.0 | 100.0 | 100.0 | 100.0 | 100.0 | 100.0 |
| | | | LIABILITIES | | | | | | |
| 9.5 | 10.0 | 7.5 | Notes Payable-Short Term | 9.7 | 9.9 | 9.6 | 4.4 | 5.1 | 6.8 |
| 5.2 | 5.5 | 6.2 | Cur. Mat.-L.T.D. | 12.7 | 4.5 | 3.1 | 7.4 | 3.3 | 5.5 |
| 6.9 | 8.0 | 6.3 | Trade Payables | 3.1 | 7.4 | 8.8 | 5.2 | 7.8 | 6.0 |
| .3 | .4 | .4 | Income Taxes Payable | .0 | .0 | .3 | .7 | .9 | .4 |
| 11.4 | 11.1 | 10.9 | All Other Current | 12.0 | 6.0 | 7.3 | 8.9 | 12.5 | 19.8 |
| 33.4 | 35.1 | 31.3 | Total Current | 37.4 | 27.7 | 29.2 | 26.7 | 29.6 | 38.6 |
| 18.4 | 18.6 | 21.4 | Long-Term Debt | 33.0 | 25.5 | 24.8 | 17.9 | 12.5 | 14.9 |
| .7 | .9 | .7 | Deferred Taxes | .0 | .8 | .5 | 1.5 | .2 | 1.0 |
| 5.1 | 7.8 | 8.8 | All Other Non-Current | 5.2 | 12.4 | 8.3 | 7.2 | 4.9 | 13.5 |
| 42.4 | 37.7 | 37.7 | Net Worth | 24.4 | 33.7 | 37.3 | 46.8 | 52.9 | 32.1 |
| 100.0 | 100.0 | 100.0 | Total Liabilties & Net Worth | 100.0 | 100.0 | 100.0 | 100.0 | 100.0 | 100.0 |
| | | | INCOME DATA | | | | | | |
| 100.0 | 100.0 | 100.0 | Net Sales | 100.0 | 100.0 | 100.0 | 100.0 | 100.0 | 100.0 |
| | | | Gross Profit | | | | | | |
| 90.9 | 91.2 | 88.9 | Operating Expenses | 78.7 | 91.2 | 93.7 | 90.8 | 89.5 | 89.9 |
| 9.1 | 8.8 | 11.1 | Operating Profit | 21.3 | 8.8 | 6.3 | 9.2 | 10.5 | 10.1 |
| 2.1 | 2.0 | 1.9 | All Other Expenses (net) | 7.5 | .8 | .2 | .5 | .6 | 1.9 |
| 7.0 | 6.8 | 9.2 | Profit Before Taxes | 13.8 | 8.1 | 6.1 | 8.7 | 9.9 | 8.2 |
| | | | RATIOS | | | | | | |
| 3.2 | 3.0 | 3.5 | | 3.9 | 5.3 | 3.6 | 5.2 | 3.0 | 2.4 |
| 1.8 | 1.8 | 1.9 | Current | 1.0 | 2.3 | 1.8 | 2.3 | 2.1 | 1.6 |
| 1.0 | 1.0 | 1.0 | | .1 | .9 | 1.0 | 1.6 | 1.3 | 1.0 |
| 2.8 | 2.7 | 3.4 | | 3.9 | 4.9 | 3.4 | 4.7 | 2.5 | 1.9 |
| 1.5 | 1.6 | 1.5 | Quick | .8 | 1.7 | 1.3 | 2.0 | 1.6 | 1.3 |
| .8 | .8 | .9 | | .1 | .9 | .9 | 1.3 | .9 | .8 |
| 38  9.7 | 34  10.6 | 32  11.3 | Sales/Receivables | 0 UND | 33  11.1 | 30  12.3 | 46  7.9 | 41  8.8 | 49  7.5 |
| 55  6.6 | 55  6.6 | 53  6.9 | | 0 UND | 50  7.3 | 47  7.8 | 63  5.8 | 54  6.7 | 68  5.4 |
| 73  5.0 | 73  5.0 | 72  5.1 | | 37  9.9 | 68  5.4 | 65  5.6 | 83  4.4 | 76  4.8 | 81  4.5 |
| | | | Cost of Sales/Inventory | | | | | | |
| | | | Cost of Sales/Payables | | | | | | |
| 5.2 | 5.5 | 4.9 | | 6.0 | 4.7 | 4.9 | 4.5 | 4.2 | 5.3 |
| 11.4 | 11.4 | 9.4 | Sales/Working Capital | -405.5 | 10.3 | 16.3 | 7.4 | 6.9 | 12.2 |
| -194.0 | NM | 336.1 | | -3.9 | -59.0 | NM | 15.3 | 14.8 | -123.8 |
| 17.9 | 18.9 | 29.2 | | 12.0 | 35.6 | 30.5 | 22.3 | 64.1 | 51.5 |
| (191)  5.2 | (205)  6.5 | (198)  8.2 | EBIT/Interest | (26)  7.7 | (44)  7.1 | (21)  5.7 | (40)  10.9 | (32)  17.3 | (35)  8.2 |
| 1.0 | 1.8 | 2.7 | | 2.4 | .9 | 2.2 | 3.3 | 5.5 | 2.6 |
| 7.1 | 7.4 | 12.3 | Net Profit + Depr., Dep., | | | | 6.1 | | 13.7 |
| (52)  2.8 | (66)  2.6 | (50)  2.6 | Amort./Cur. Mat. L/T/D | | | (15)  2.2 | | (14)  2.5 | |
| 1.3 | 1.1 | 1.1 | | | | | .8 | | 1.6 |
| .4 | .4 | .4 | | .9 | .3 | .4 | .5 | .3 | .5 |
| .9 | 1.0 | .9 | Fixed/Worth | 2.6 | .7 | .9 | .7 | .6 | 1.1 |
| 2.8 | 4.5 | 3.3 | | -2.7 | NM | 2.3 | 1.3 | 1.0 | 5.3 |
| .5 | .5 | .5 | | .8 | .3 | .6 | .4 | .5 | .8 |
| 1.2 | 1.3 | 1.3 | Debt/Worth | 3.0 | .9 | 1.5 | .9 | .8 | 2.3 |
| 6.7 | 9.1 | 7.0 | | -9.6 | NM | 5.8 | 2.1 | 2.1 | 8.5 |
| 66.1 | 58.7 | 70.8 | % Profit Before Taxes/Tangible | 99.2 | 53.1 | 116.9 | 46.8 | 77.3 | 58.6 |
| (193)  22.8 | (200)  27.0 | (198)  27.9 | Net Worth | (28)  45.2 | (40)  28.4 | (23)  24.3 | (40)  26.3 | (34)  22.8 | (33)  32.1 |
| 6.5 | 7.4 | 13.2 | | 8.9 | 11.2 | 17.3 | 12.1 | 10.2 | 19.0 |
| 21.1 | 24.4 | 26.6 | % Profit Before Taxes/Total | 38.9 | 27.8 | 28.5 | 28.2 | 23.2 | 22.0 |
| 7.5 | 9.5 | 12.4 | Assets | 12.3 | 15.9 | 10.6 | 15.5 | 10.9 | 8.3 |
| .3 | 2.3 | 3.4 | | 4.1 | 1.4 | 2.6 | 3.4 | 4.3 | 2.5 |
| 13.5 | 16.8 | 17.8 | | 13.9 | 24.7 | 26.5 | 14.2 | 21.6 | 12.2 |
| 5.9 | 6.6 | 7.0 | Sales/Net Fixed Assets | 5.6 | 9.2 | 10.1 | 6.9 | 8.0 | 6.0 |
| 3.4 | 3.5 | 3.6 | | 1.3 | 3.8 | 3.4 | 3.5 | 3.2 | 4.3 |
| 2.8 | 2.9 | 3.1 | | 3.1 | 3.2 | 3.9 | 3.2 | 2.8 | 2.6 |
| 1.9 | 2.0 | 2.1 | Sales/Total Assets | 1.6 | 2.3 | 2.4 | 2.1 | 1.7 | 1.9 |
| 1.1 | 1.2 | 1.2 | | .4 | 1.4 | 1.6 | 1.4 | 1.1 | 1.2 |
| 2.1 | 2.0 | 1.8 | | 3.2 | 1.7 | 1.4 | 1.6 | 1.5 | 2.8 |
| (179)  3.8 | (190)  3.8 | (195)  3.8 | % Depr., Dep., Amort./Sales | (30)  10.6 | (42)  3.2 | (20)  3.6 | (40)  3.7 | (32)  3.5 | (31)  4.7 |
| 6.0 | 6.2 | 5.9 | | 14.9 | 5.2 | 5.6 | 6.0 | 5.3 | 5.6 |
| 2.9 | 2.9 | 3.4 | % Officers', Directors' | 5.9 | 3.7 | 4.3 | 3.8 | | |
| (63)  6.2 | (90)  6.1 | (94)  6.0 | Owners' Comp/Sales | (16)  10.6 | (28)  6.5 | (11)  5.9 | (26)  6.0 | | |
| 11.0 | 9.9 | 9.1 | | 15.5 | 9.9 | 8.2 | 9.1 | | |
| 4398189M | 4863611M | 4605802M | Net Sales ($) | 19771M | 110085M | 100019M | 330143M | 567812M | 3477972M |
| 3275100M | 3518265M | 2971321M | Total Assets ($) | 27117M | 69869M | 49404M | 190029M | 359065M | 2275837M |

M = $ thousand    MM = $ million
See Pages 9 through 22 for Explanation of Ratios and Data

## Current Data Sorted by Assets   |   Comparative Historical Data

**Type of Statement**

| Type of Statement | 0-500M | 500M-2MM | 2-10MM | 10-50MM | 50-100MM | 100-250MM | | 2 4/1/07-3/31/08 ALL | 3 4/1/08-3/31/09 ALL |
|---|---|---|---|---|---|---|---|---|---|
| Unqualified | 1 | | 4 | 5 | | | | 2 | 3 |
| Reviewed | 1 | 4 | 8 | 2 | | | | 4 | 7 |
| Compiled | 1 | 5 | 4 | | | | | 8 | 16 |
| Tax Returns | 22 | 22 | 4 | | | 2 | | 20 | 33 |
| Other | 16 | 26 | 11 | 2 | | | | 27 | 29 |

Current date groupings: 9 (4/1-9/30/11) · 131 (10/1/11-3/31/12)

| | 0-500M | 500M-2MM | 2-10MM | 10-50MM | 50-100MM | 100-250MM | | 2 4/1/07-3/31/08 ALL | 3 4/1/08-3/31/09 ALL |
|---|---|---|---|---|---|---|---|---|---|
| **NUMBER OF STATEMENTS** | 41 | 57 | 31 | 9 | | 2 | | 61 | 88 |
| | % | % | % | % | % | % | | % | % |
| **ASSETS** | | | | | | | | | |
| Cash & Equivalents | 21.4 | 13.6 | 11.2 | | | | | 13.8 | 17.0 |
| Trade Receivables (net) | 24.2 | 31.8 | 44.4 | | | | | 29.4 | 27.1 |
| Inventory | 14.6 | 21.7 | 15.3 | | | | | 21.0 | 19.3 |
| All Other Current | 2.3 | 1.5 | 7.0 | | | | | 5.5 | 6.4 |
| Total Current | 62.5 | 68.5 | 77.9 | | | | | 69.8 | 69.9 |
| Fixed Assets (net) | 24.9 | 16.2 | 13.3 | | | | | 17.3 | 19.8 |
| Intangibles (net) | 2.5 | 1.6 | 4.9 | | | | | 2.7 | 1.6 |
| All Other Non-Current | 10.0 | 13.7 | 4.0 | | | | | 10.3 | 8.7 |
| Total | 100.0 | 100.0 | 100.0 | | | | | 100.0 | 100.0 |
| **LIABILITIES** | | | | | | | | | |
| Notes Payable-Short Term | 27.6 | 18.7 | 7.4 | | | | | 17.3 | 13.5 |
| Cur. Mat.-L.T.D. | 3.1 | .9 | 2.0 | | | | | 5.7 | 4.0 |
| Trade Payables | 11.8 | 16.8 | 17.6 | | | | | 18.0 | 13.6 |
| Income Taxes Payable | .0 | .1 | 1.1 | | | | | .1 | .2 |
| All Other Current | 38.2 | 21.8 | 18.0 | | | | | 24.5 | 24.6 |
| Total Current | 80.6 | 58.2 | 46.1 | | | | | 65.6 | 56.0 |
| Long-Term Debt | 8.1 | 15.1 | 11.6 | | | | | 15.8 | 15.8 |
| Deferred Taxes | .0 | .0 | .0 | | | | | .0 | .1 |
| All Other Non-Current | 27.4 | 11.7 | 6.3 | | | | | 5.9 | 7.9 |
| Net Worth | -16.1 | 15.0 | 36.0 | | | | | 12.7 | 20.2 |
| Total Liabilities & Net Worth | 100.0 | 100.0 | 100.0 | | | | | 100.0 | 100.0 |
| **INCOME DATA** | | | | | | | | | |
| Net Sales | 100.0 | 100.0 | 100.0 | | | | | 100.0 | 100.0 |
| Gross Profit | | | | | | | | | |
| Operating Expenses | 100.0 | 94.4 | 90.9 | | | | | 93.7 | 94.8 |
| Operating Profit | .0 | 5.6 | 9.1 | | | | | 6.3 | 5.2 |
| All Other Expenses (net) | .1 | 2.1 | 1.6 | | | | | 1.1 | .4 |
| Profit Before Taxes | -.2 | 3.6 | 7.5 | | | | | 5.2 | 4.9 |
| **RATIOS** | | | | | | | | | |
| Current | 2.1 | 2.2 | 2.6 | | | | | 2.0 | 2.1 |
| | .8 | 1.4 | 1.9 | | | | | 1.3 | 1.3 |
| | .4 | .7 | 1.2 | | | | | .9 | 1.0 |
| Quick | 1.3 | 1.6 | 2.2 | | | | | 1.6 | 1.4 |
| | .7 | .8 | 1.3 | | | | | .7 | .8 |
| | .2 | .3 | .9 | | | | | .3 | .3 |
| Sales/Receivables | 0 UND | 7 48.7 | 16 22.2 | | | | | 8 43.7 | 3 111.0 |
| | 4 89.9 | 26 13.8 | 47 7.7 | | | | | 27 13.6 | 25 14.9 |
| | 34 10.7 | 55 6.6 | 76 4.8 | | | | | 49 7.4 | 54 6.7 |
| Cost of Sales/Inventory | | | | | | | | | |
| Cost of Sales/Payables | | | | | | | | | |
| Sales/Working Capital | 11.8 | 6.6 | 4.5 | | | | | 6.7 | 8.1 |
| | -103.5 | 17.7 | 9.7 | | | | | 22.6 | 20.0 |
| | -18.6 | -20.6 | 29.1 | | | | | -43.2 | UND |
| EBIT/Interest | 19.3 | 23.5 | 26.6 | | | | | 20.8 | 17.3 |
| | (24) 3.5 | (46) 3.4 | (26) 6.5 | | | | | (53) 6.0 | (73) 5.3 |
| | -5.2 | .2 | 2.2 | | | | | 1.9 | 1.1 |
| Net Profit + Depr., Dep., Amort./Cur. Mat. L/T/D | | | | | | | | | |
| Fixed/Worth | .1 | .1 | .1 | | | | | .2 | .1 |
| | 1.3 | .4 | .2 | | | | | .6 | .5 |
| | -.5 | 3.0 | 1.4 | | | | | 6.7 | -47.0 |
| Debt/Worth | 1.0 | 1.1 | 1.0 | | | | | 1.1 | .9 |
| | 13.4 | 3.2 | 1.8 | | | | | 3.5 | 2.9 |
| | -3.8 | 12.2 | 9.8 | | | | | 44.5 | -38.4 |
| % Profit Before Taxes/Tangible Net Worth | 297.5 | 145.0 | 63.0 | | | | | 86.5 | 75.3 |
| | (24) 51.5 | (46) 24.0 | (29) 36.6 | | | | | (48) 45.9 | (63) 30.0 |
| | .4 | 2.2 | 5.2 | | | | | 17.8 | 9.1 |
| % Profit Before Taxes/Total Assets | 29.7 | 28.4 | 18.5 | | | | | 24.6 | 25.9 |
| | 3.8 | 4.7 | 7.3 | | | | | 9.1 | 9.5 |
| | -19.0 | -.6 | 1.9 | | | | | 1.5 | -.2 |
| Sales/Net Fixed Assets | 275.7 | 96.1 | 142.4 | | | | | 78.5 | 86.8 |
| | 43.0 | 31.1 | 52.0 | | | | | 37.9 | 29.7 |
| | 19.8 | 13.6 | 18.4 | | | | | 14.1 | 11.8 |
| Sales/Total Assets | 11.6 | 4.8 | 3.9 | | | | | 4.8 | 4.9 |
| | 5.7 | 3.0 | 3.0 | | | | | 3.4 | 3.2 |
| | 3.5 | 1.9 | 1.9 | | | | | 1.8 | 2.1 |
| % Depr., Dep., Amort./Sales | .2 | .3 | .3 | | | | | .5 | .4 |
| | (20) .7 | (36) .6 | (26) .7 | | | | | (47) .9 | (63) .9 |
| | 1.4 | 1.7 | 1.6 | | | | | 1.8 | 1.8 |
| % Officers', Directors' Owners' Comp/Sales | 8.1 | 3.9 | | | | | | 2.4 | 2.4 |
| | (28) 11.0 | (27) 6.2 | | | | | | (30) 4.6 | (46) 5.2 |
| | 14.0 | 12.1 | | | | | | 7.2 | 8.8 |
| Net Sales ($) | 51885M | 223025M | 466191M | 475093M | | 6757875M | | 1059035M | 1284723M |
| Total Assets ($) | 8636M | 61092M | 149503M | 208921M | 239314M | | | 272260M | 473650M |

(Columns 10-50MM, 50-100MM, and 100-250MM display "DATA NOT AVAILABLE" across the ASSETS through RATIOS sections.)

M = $ thousand   MM = $ million
See Pages 9 through 22 for Explanation of Ratios and Data

## Comparative Historical Data | | | Current Data Sorted by Sales

| | | | Type of Statement | | | | | | |
|---|---|---|---|---|---|---|---|---|---|
| 1 | 3 | 10 | Unqualified | 1 | | 3 | 3 | 3 | 6 |
| 8 | 6 | 15 | Reviewed | | 2 | | | 3 | 4 |
| 10 | 8 | 10 | Compiled | 1 | 2 | 1 | 4 | 1 | 1 |
| 28 | 27 | 50 | Tax Returns | 11 | 22 | 6 | 7 | 2 | 2 |
| 38 | 44 | 55 | Other | 13 | 16 | 7 | 11 | 5 | 3 |
| 4/1/09-3/31/10 ALL | 4/1/10-3/31/11 ALL | 4/1/11-3/31/12 ALL | | 0-1MM | 9 (4/1-9/30/11) 1-3MM | 3-5MM | 5-10MM | 131 (10/1/11-3/31/12) 10-25MM | 25MM & OVER |
| 85 | 88 | 140 | NUMBER OF STATEMENTS | 26 | 42 | 17 | 25 | 14 | 16 |
| % | % | % | ASSETS | % | % | % | % | % | % |
| 22.1 | 14.6 | 15.2 | Cash & Equivalents | 13.9 | 21.6 | 11.4 | 9.7 | 20.5 | 8.4 |
| 25.4 | 29.6 | 32.4 | Trade Receivables (net) | 20.9 | 28.0 | 30.6 | 46.6 | 38.1 | 37.9 |
| 14.1 | 18.1 | 17.6 | Inventory | 17.2 | 21.0 | 16.2 | 16.1 | 9.5 | 19.9 |
| 6.3 | 4.4 | 3.7 | All Other Current | 3.1 | 1.5 | 3.2 | 1.4 | 6.3 | 12.4 |
| 67.9 | 66.7 | 68.9 | Total Current | 55.0 | 72.0 | 61.4 | 73.8 | 74.4 | 78.5 |
| 22.1 | 19.9 | 17.6 | Fixed Assets (net) | 31.0 | 20.1 | 13.7 | 13.4 | 8.1 | 8.2 |
| 3.1 | 2.7 | 3.3 | Intangibles (net) | 1.9 | 1.2 | 6.8 | 1.8 | 3.1 | 10.0 |
| 6.9 | 10.8 | 10.2 | All Other Non-Current | 12.1 | 6.7 | 18.2 | 10.9 | 14.5 | 3.3 |
| 100.0 | 100.0 | 100.0 | Total | 100.0 | 100.0 | 100.0 | 100.0 | 100.0 | 100.0 |
| | | | LIABILITIES | | | | | | |
| 19.4 | 26.8 | 18.1 | Notes Payable-Short Term | 25.3 | 24.1 | 16.7 | 10.9 | 12.6 | 8.2 |
| 2.0 | 1.9 | 1.8 | Cur. Mat.-L.T.D. | 2.1 | 1.9 | .8 | 1.9 | 2.1 | 1.8 |
| 22.7 | 13.9 | 15.3 | Trade Payables | 10.2 | 14.2 | 10.7 | 25.4 | 12.4 | 17.7 |
| 1.5 | .2 | .3 | Income Taxes Payable | .0 | .0 | .0 | .4 | 2.0 | .0 |
| 24.6 | 23.6 | 25.4 | All Other Current | 39.0 | 20.1 | 26.3 | 26.2 | 22.6 | 17.8 |
| 70.3 | 66.4 | 60.8 | Total Current | 76.5 | 60.2 | 54.5 | 64.7 | 51.9 | 45.5 |
| 14.4 | 14.4 | 12.1 | Long-Term Debt | 15.1 | 7.7 | 11.2 | 20.4 | 5.7 | 12.6 |
| .3 | .1 | .1 | Deferred Taxes | .0 | .0 | .0 | .0 | .5 | .5 |
| 4.0 | 7.7 | 16.1 | All Other Non-Current | 39.2 | 13.1 | 11.6 | 5.6 | 8.2 | 14.6 |
| 11.2 | 11.5 | 10.8 | Net Worth | -30.8 | 19.0 | 22.7 | 9.2 | 33.6 | 26.7 |
| 100.0 | 100.0 | 100.0 | Total Liabilities & Net Worth | 100.0 | 100.0 | 100.0 | 100.0 | 100.0 | 100.0 |
| | | | INCOME DATA | | | | | | |
| 100.0 | 100.0 | 100.0 | Net Sales | 100.0 | 100.0 | 100.0 | 100.0 | 100.0 | 100.0 |
| | | | Gross Profit | | | | | | |
| 98.4 | 92.8 | 95.5 | Operating Expenses | 96.1 | 95.5 | 94.4 | 95.3 | 93.4 | 97.5 |
| 1.6 | 7.2 | 4.5 | Operating Profit | 3.9 | 4.5 | 5.6 | 4.7 | 6.6 | 2.5 |
| 1.6 | 1.5 | 1.3 | All Other Expenses (net) | 4.5 | 1.0 | .0 | .6 | -.1 | .6 |
| .0 | 5.7 | 3.3 | Profit Before Taxes | -.6 | 3.5 | 5.7 | 4.1 | 6.6 | 1.9 |
| | | | RATIOS | | | | | | |
| 2.4 | 2.4 | 2.3 | | 3.1 | 2.8 | 2.1 | 2.3 | 2.5 | 2.1 |
| 1.2 | 1.4 | 1.3 | Current | .7 | 1.5 | 1.3 | 1.2 | 1.3 | 1.8 |
| .7 | .9 | .8 | | .4 | .8 | .8 | .9 | 1.0 | 1.4 |
| 1.6 | 1.5 | 1.6 | | 1.1 | 2.1 | 1.6 | 1.8 | 2.2 | 1.6 |
| .8 | 1.0 | 1.0 | Quick | .5 | 1.1 | .8 | 1.1 | 1.0 | 1.1 |
| .4 | .3 | .4 | | .2 | .3 | .5 | .4 | .9 | .7 |
| 0 UND | 4 92.6 | 6 61.1 | | 0 UND | 0 UND | 4 81.6 | 12 29.9 | 9 40.2 | 30 12.2 |
| 24 15.1 | 31 11.7 | 27 13.7 | Sales/Receivables | 11 33.4 | 26 14.0 | 23 15.6 | 31 11.6 | 51 7.1 | 44 8.3 |
| 47 7.8 | 66 5.5 | 61 6.0 | | 28 13.2 | 54 6.7 | 57 6.4 | 74 4.9 | 89 4.1 | 64 5.7 |
| | | | Cost of Sales/Inventory | | | | | | |
| | | | Cost of Sales/Payables | | | | | | |
| 8.2 | 8.1 | 7.0 | | 6.9 | 5.0 | 6.1 | 8.6 | 9.9 | 8.6 |
| 46.7 | 18.4 | 20.8 | Sales/Working Capital | -44.2 | 11.5 | 18.8 | 38.2 | 23.4 | 10.3 |
| -15.6 | -35.1 | -34.0 | | -10.2 | -25.3 | -64.4 | -65.1 | NM | 23.0 |
| 21.5 | 19.6 | 21.4 | | 19.3 | 17.4 | 18.1 | 26.5 | 127.3 | 19.0 |
| (64) 1.7 | (66) 5.2 | (105) 4.6 | EBIT/Interest | (16) 4.0 | (29) 1.7 | (12) 4.3 | (21) 3.0 | (12) 20.2 | (15) 5.8 |
| -1.5 | 1.3 | 1.3 | | -5.8 | -.9 | 2.0 | 1.7 | 7.2 | 1.4 |
| 8.5 | | 7.1 | | | | | | | |
| (10) 1.7 | | (10) 1.8 | Net Profit + Depr., Dep., Amort./Cur. Mat. L/T/D | | | | | | |
| .1 | | -.6 | | | | | | | |
| .1 | .1 | .1 | | .1 | .1 | .1 | .1 | .1 | .1 |
| .6 | .5 | .4 | Fixed/Worth | 3.6 | .7 | .2 | .4 | .2 | .2 |
| NM | 10.0 | 3.8 | | -.6 | 2.6 | 1.9 | 1.5 | NM | 1.4 |
| .7 | .8 | 1.0 | | .8 | .8 | 1.1 | 1.3 | 1.1 | 1.0 |
| 2.8 | 3.2 | 3.3 | Debt/Worth | -24.0 | 2.0 | 3.3 | 3.4 | 2.9 | 2.1 |
| -13.2 | 92.1 | 114.1 | | -3.7 | 11.6 | 40.6 | 12.0 | NM | 12.5 |
| 93.0 | 114.4 | 139.5 | | 342.8 | 101.0 | 195.2 | 150.1 | 190.2 | 67.0 |
| (61) 33.8 | (67) 30.5 | (108) 34.0 | % Profit Before Taxes/Tangible Net Worth | (12) 15.7 | (35) 14.0 | (15) 92.0 | (20) 36.7 | (11) 61.3 | (15) 44.1 |
| -6.2 | 5.7 | 4.3 | | 2.6 | -13.9 | 4.2 | 8.6 | 20.9 | 7.5 |
| 26.3 | 22.3 | 27.7 | | 27.5 | 25.2 | 43.0 | 34.9 | 37.9 | 15.9 |
| 2.4 | 9.8 | 6.2 | % Profit Before Taxes/Total Assets | .6 | 4.0 | 9.6 | 14.1 | 15.7 | 10.2 |
| -11.2 | 1.3 | .0 | | -28.1 | -5.8 | 1.3 | 1.9 | 4.8 | 2.0 |
| 217.2 | 88.9 | 139.9 | | 150.3 | 113.4 | 113.1 | 167.0 | 168.4 | 146.5 |
| 26.7 | 27.7 | 39.6 | Sales/Net Fixed Assets | 26.2 | 30.8 | 34.3 | 40.9 | 67.4 | 55.5 |
| 9.6 | 10.7 | 16.1 | | 9.7 | 12.5 | 16.5 | 18.8 | 35.0 | 24.7 |
| 5.4 | 4.2 | 5.6 | | 6.1 | 4.2 | 7.4 | 6.0 | 4.2 | 4.5 |
| 3.3 | 3.0 | 3.5 | Sales/Total Assets | 3.4 | 3.3 | 3.1 | 4.2 | 3.6 | 3.7 |
| 2.0 | 1.8 | 2.2 | | 1.3 | 1.7 | 2.3 | 2.9 | 2.1 | 2.7 |
| .4 | .4 | .3 | | .6 | .4 | .3 | .3 | .3 | .3 |
| (53) .9 | (56) .9 | (92) .7 | % Depr., Dep., Amort./Sales | (14) 1.2 | (23) .7 | (10) .4 | (18) .6 | (13) .9 | (14) .6 |
| 3.0 | 2.3 | 1.6 | | 8.8 | 1.4 | 1.1 | 1.6 | 1.6 | 1.7 |
| 3.5 | 4.1 | 4.0 | | 8.3 | 5.3 | | 2.1 | | |
| (44) 7.1 | (37) 6.3 | (65) 8.0 | % Officers', Directors' Owners' Comp/Sales | (12) 10.6 | (28) 9.4 | | (13) 3.1 | | |
| 13.7 | 8.5 | 12.5 | | 13.6 | 14.8 | | 8.3 | | |
| 2882128M | 652176M | 7974069M | Net Sales ($) | 13117M | 77851M | 64112M | 175200M | 210398M | 7433391M |
| 566116M | 233752M | 667466M | Total Assets ($) | 9871M | 31088M | 22132M | 48343M | 76784M | 479248M |

M = $ thousand     MM = $ million
See Pages 9 through 22 for Explanation of Ratios and Data

## Current Data Sorted by Assets

## Comparative Historical Data

| | | | | | | Type of Statement | | |
|---|---|---|---|---|---|---|---|---|
| | | 3 | 8 | | | Unqualified | 18 | 13 |
| | 5 | 14 | 5 | | | Reviewed | 21 | 22 |
| 9 | 6 | 8 | | | | Compiled | 30 | 26 |
| 13 | 15 | 8 | | | | Tax Returns | 25 | 35 |
| 11 | 16 | 17 | 9 | 2 | 1 | Other | 62 | 72 |
| | 22 (4/1-9/30/11) | | 128 (10/1/11-3/31/12) | | | | 4/1/07-3/31/08 | 4/1/08-3/31/09 |
| 0-500M | 500M-2MM | 2-10MM | 10-50MM | 50-100MM | 100-250MM | | ALL | ALL |
| 33 | 42 | 50 | 22 | 2 | 1 | NUMBER OF STATEMENTS | 156 | 168 |
| % | % | % | % | % | % | ASSETS | % | % |
| 35.6 | 16.8 | 10.1 | 6.2 | | | Cash & Equivalents | 14.3 | 14.2 |
| 20.7 | 34.7 | 38.1 | 22.4 | | | Trade Receivables (net) | 30.4 | 30.5 |
| 3.0 | 9.0 | 12.5 | 8.3 | | | Inventory | 5.7 | 7.7 |
| 5.4 | 5.0 | 3.7 | 8.0 | | | All Other Current | 3.7 | 4.8 |
| 64.7 | 65.6 | 64.5 | 44.9 | | | Total Current | 54.0 | 57.3 |
| 21.4 | 24.9 | 25.4 | 31.2 | | | Fixed Assets (net) | 32.7 | 29.1 |
| 1.7 | 3.5 | 2.8 | 12.4 | | | Intangibles (net) | 4.3 | 5.4 |
| 12.2 | 5.9 | 7.3 | 11.5 | | | All Other Non-Current | 9.0 | 8.2 |
| 100.0 | 100.0 | 100.0 | 100.0 | | | Total | 100.0 | 100.0 |
| | | | | | | LIABILITIES | | |
| 26.9 | 11.1 | 7.8 | 4.6 | | | Notes Payable-Short Term | 18.1 | 14.9 |
| 12.6 | 3.0 | 3.1 | 2.7 | | | Cur. Mat.-L.T.D. | 4.0 | 6.5 |
| 14.0 | 12.3 | 12.5 | 7.8 | | | Trade Payables | 11.7 | 11.6 |
| .1 | .4 | .4 | .0 | | | Income Taxes Payable | .5 | .2 |
| 13.8 | 9.1 | 15.7 | 9.4 | | | All Other Current | 14.0 | 13.5 |
| 67.4 | 35.9 | 39.5 | 24.6 | | | Total Current | 48.3 | 46.7 |
| 10.4 | 15.8 | 14.2 | 19.5 | | | Long-Term Debt | 19.3 | 19.1 |
| .1 | .6 | .5 | .5 | | | Deferred Taxes | .4 | .2 |
| 23.8 | 6.9 | 8.0 | 5.5 | | | All Other Non-Current | 5.5 | 6.0 |
| -1.7 | 40.8 | 37.8 | 49.8 | | | Net Worth | 26.5 | 28.0 |
| 100.0 | 100.0 | 100.0 | 100.0 | | | Total Liabilities & Net Worth | 100.0 | 100.0 |
| | | | | | | INCOME DATA | | |
| 100.0 | 100.0 | 100.0 | 100.0 | | | Net Sales | 100.0 | 100.0 |
| | | | | | | Gross Profit | | |
| 87.6 | 92.9 | 92.3 | 89.9 | | | Operating Expenses | 95.3 | 95.7 |
| 12.4 | 7.1 | 7.7 | 10.1 | | | Operating Profit | 4.7 | 4.3 |
| 1.1 | .6 | 1.1 | 4.0 | | | All Other Expenses (net) | 1.3 | 1.1 |
| 11.3 | 6.5 | 6.7 | 6.1 | | | Profit Before Taxes | 3.4 | 3.2 |
| | | | | | | RATIOS | | |
| 6.3 | 5.3 | 2.7 | 2.4 | | | | 2.4 | 2.9 |
| 1.4 | 2.1 | 1.6 | 1.6 | | | Current | 1.5 | 1.4 |
| .6 | .9 | 1.1 | 1.2 | | | | .9 | 1.0 |
| 4.4 | 5.2 | 2.2 | 1.9 | | | | 2.1 | 2.3 |
| 1.3 | 1.5 | 1.3 | 1.2 | | | Quick | 1.1 | 1.1 |
| .4 | .7 | .9 | .7 | | | | .7 | .6 |
| 0 UND | 13 28.7 | 31 11.8 | 29 12.7 | | | | 17 21.0 | 22 16.4 |
| 0 UND | 44 8.3 | 54 6.8 | 39 9.4 | | | Sales/Receivables | 43 8.5 | 40 9.2 |
| 44 8.3 | 63 5.8 | 63 5.8 | 54 6.8 | | | | 63 5.8 | 59 6.2 |
| | | | | | | Cost of Sales/Inventory | | |
| | | | | | | Cost of Sales/Payables | | |
| 8.8 | 5.5 | 6.1 | 6.5 | | | | 6.7 | 7.7 |
| 68.3 | 11.3 | 11.6 | 11.8 | | | Sales/Working Capital | 16.0 | 18.9 |
| -22.7 | -109.1 | 58.1 | 32.3 | | | | -62.9 | 183.8 |
| 15.9 | 18.0 | 21.0 | 31.5 | | | | 9.9 | 13.5 |
| (14) 2.8 | (35) 6.4 | (46) 8.7 | (18) 6.7 | | | EBIT/Interest | (133) 3.3 | (150) 3.5 |
| .6 | 2.5 | 2.3 | 2.1 | | | | .8 | -.1 |
| | | 6.9 | 7.2 | | | | 3.3 | 3.4 |
| | | (10) 5.6 | (11) 2.1 | | | Net Profit + Depr., Dep., Amort./Cur. Mat. L/T/D | (23) 1.7 | (24) 1.3 |
| | | 2.7 | 1.1 | | | | .8 | -.2 |
| .1 | .1 | .3 | .2 | | | | .4 | .4 |
| .6 | .7 | .6 | .7 | | | Fixed/Worth | .8 | .9 |
| UND | 3.3 | 1.7 | 1.9 | | | | 3.4 | 4.2 |
| .2 | .3 | .8 | .6 | | | | .6 | .7 |
| 1.1 | 1.8 | 1.3 | 1.5 | | | Debt/Worth | 1.8 | 2.2 |
| -5.0 | 13.6 | 4.3 | 3.9 | | | | 10.2 | 11.6 |
| 142.9 | 98.2 | 56.9 | 67.1 | | | | 68.8 | 61.2 |
| (24) 68.1 | (33) 36.8 | (43) 26.0 | (20) 17.6 | | | % Profit Before Taxes/Tangible Net Worth | (129) 24.0 | (134) 19.1 |
| 16.2 | 5.6 | 7.7 | 2.8 | | | | 3.8 | 1.6 |
| 64.6 | 40.4 | 25.3 | 14.3 | | | | 20.7 | 19.4 |
| 14.5 | 7.5 | 9.3 | 5.0 | | | % Profit Before Taxes/Total Assets | 6.6 | 5.7 |
| 4.9 | 1.3 | 1.7 | 1.3 | | | | -.5 | -3.7 |
| 209.1 | 54.2 | 29.4 | 29.5 | | | | 31.3 | 41.4 |
| 37.3 | 20.7 | 15.4 | 9.1 | | | Sales/Net Fixed Assets | 10.1 | 13.4 |
| 15.4 | 5.9 | 6.3 | 2.3 | | | | 4.0 | 4.8 |
| 7.9 | 4.7 | 3.4 | 2.3 | | | | 3.9 | 4.5 |
| 4.9 | 3.0 | 2.5 | 1.4 | | | Sales/Total Assets | 2.4 | 2.7 |
| 2.7 | 2.2 | 1.7 | 1.1 | | | | 1.6 | 1.7 |
| .7 | .7 | 1.1 | 1.6 | | | | 1.3 | 1.1 |
| (14) 1.4 | (31) 1.2 | (43) 2.3 | (21) 2.1 | | | % Depr., Dep., Amort./Sales | (119) 2.5 | (125) 2.5 |
| 1.8 | 2.4 | 4.1 | 4.8 | | | | 4.6 | 5.3 |
| 6.9 | 4.6 | 3.6 | | | | | 3.4 | 4.4 |
| (15) 13.5 | (24) 6.3 | (19) 6.0 | | | | % Officers', Directors' Owners' Comp/Sales | (65) 6.9 | (77) 7.5 |
| 22.8 | 10.5 | 8.9 | | | | | 13.6 | 14.0 |
| 45532M | 170413M | 552006M | 844345M | 152727M | 530078M | Net Sales ($) | 3828919M | 2879799M |
| 7922M | 47746M | 209454M | 497524M | 143290M | 170418M | Total Assets ($) | 1993521M | 1317493M |

M = $ thousand    MM = $ million
See Pages 9 through 22 for Explanation of Ratios and Data

## Comparative Historical Data | | | | Current Data Sorted by Sales

| Type of Statement | | | | 22 (4/1-9/30/11) | | | 128 (10/1/11-3/31/12) | | |
|---|---|---|---|---|---|---|---|---|---|
| 13 | 15 | 11 | Unqualified |  | 2 |  | 1 | 4 | 4 |
| 21 | 21 | 24 | Reviewed |  | 3 | 3 | 9 | 5 | 4 |
| 19 | 13 | 23 | Compiled | 5 | 7 | 4 | 4 | 3 |  |
| 36 | 26 | 36 | Tax Returns | 9 | 8 | 8 | 9 | 2 |  |
| 54 | 54 | 56 | Other | 7 | 9 | 13 | 5 | 10 | 12 |
| 4/1/09-3/31/10 ALL | 4/1/10-3/31/11 ALL | 4/1/11-3/31/12 ALL |  | 0-1MM | 1-3MM | 3-5MM | 5-10MM | 10-25MM | 25MM & OVER |
| 143 | 129 | 150 | **NUMBER OF STATEMENTS** | 21 | 29 | 28 | 28 | 24 | 20 |
| % | % | % | **ASSETS** | % | % | % | % | % | % |
| 18.8 | 15.8 | 17.0 | Cash & Equivalents | 31.5 | 20.9 | 21.4 | 12.1 | 11.2 | 4.0 |
| 28.9 | 29.1 | 30.8 | Trade Receivables (net) | 26.5 | 18.6 | 33.9 | 35.3 | 39.3 | 32.1 |
| 6.6 | 8.5 | 8.7 | Inventory | .3 | 7.9 | 10.8 | 10.5 | 10.8 | 10.4 |
| 3.5 | 3.2 | 5.0 | All Other Current | 1.2 | 8.1 | 1.9 | 6.9 | 6.2 | 4.7 |
| 57.8 | 56.6 | 61.5 | Total Current | 59.6 | 55.3 | 68.1 | 64.8 | 67.5 | 51.2 |
| 30.3 | 29.8 | 25.0 | Fixed Assets (net) | 32.0 | 24.2 | 26.3 | 23.3 | 23.5 | 21.2 |
| 4.2 | 6.8 | 4.4 | Intangibles (net) | 2.7 | 3.6 | 1.6 | 4.1 | .7 | 16.0 |
| 7.7 | 6.8 | 9.1 | All Other Non-Current | 5.7 | 16.8 | 4.0 | 7.8 | 8.3 | 11.5 |
| 100.0 | 100.0 | 100.0 | Total | 100.0 | 100.0 | 100.0 | 100.0 | 100.0 | 100.0 |
|  |  |  | **LIABILITIES** |  |  |  |  |  |  |
| 23.7 | 17.2 | 12.4 | Notes Payable-Short Term | 27.2 | 18.3 | 8.9 | 9.9 | 5.1 | 5.8 |
| 4.4 | 4.1 | 5.1 | Cur. Mat.-L.T.D. | 16.2 | 2.8 | 4.1 | 4.2 | 2.4 | 2.5 |
| 12.2 | 11.4 | 12.0 | Trade Payables | 9.4 | 12.3 | 9.7 | 13.2 | 14.6 | 12.9 |
| .3 | .3 | .3 | Income Taxes Payable | .0 | .2 | .3 | .6 | .3 | .0 |
| 13.0 | 11.2 | 12.3 | All Other Current | 13.2 | 8.1 | 13.2 | 12.1 | 15.5 | 12.6 |
| 53.5 | 44.2 | 42.1 | Total Current | 66.0 | 41.8 | 36.2 | 40.0 | 37.8 | 33.8 |
| 15.0 | 16.7 | 14.5 | Long-Term Debt | 13.9 | 19.4 | 14.8 | 13.8 | 9.9 | 13.6 |
| .2 | .2 | .4 | Deferred Taxes | .2 | .1 | 1.1 | .5 | .0 | .7 |
| 8.7 | 12.7 | 10.7 | All Other Non-Current | 25.5 | 14.5 | 7.9 | 9.3 | 5.8 | 1.0 |
| 22.6 | 26.2 | 32.4 | Net Worth | -5.7 | 24.2 | 40.0 | 36.4 | 46.4 | 50.9 |
| 100.0 | 100.0 | 100.0 | Total Liabilities & Net Worth | 100.0 | 100.0 | 100.0 | 100.0 | 100.0 | 100.0 |
|  |  |  | **INCOME DATA** |  |  |  |  |  |  |
| 100.0 | 100.0 | 100.0 | Net Sales | 100.0 | 100.0 | 100.0 | 100.0 | 100.0 | 100.0 |
|  |  |  | Gross Profit |  |  |  |  |  |  |
| 96.1 | 92.7 | 91.1 | Operating Expenses | 83.8 | 89.9 | 88.6 | 94.2 | 95.0 | 95.2 |
| 3.9 | 7.3 | 8.9 | Operating Profit | 16.2 | 10.1 | 11.4 | 5.8 | 5.0 | 4.8 |
| 1.1 | 2.3 | 1.3 | All Other Expenses (net) | 4.7 | 2.3 | .4 | .0 | .7 | .3 |
| 2.8 | 5.1 | 7.5 | Profit Before Taxes | 11.5 | 7.8 | 11.0 | 5.8 | 4.2 | 4.5 |
|  |  |  | **RATIOS** |  |  |  |  |  |  |
| 2.8 | 3.3 | 3.4 | Current | 12.1 | 3.1 | 6.6 | 3.0 | 2.6 | 2.4 |
| 1.4 | 1.4 | 1.6 |  | 1.4 | 1.4 | 1.9 | 1.8 | 1.9 | 1.6 |
| .9 | .9 | 1.0 |  | .3 | .8 | 1.3 | 1.0 | 1.2 | 1.2 |
| 2.2 | 2.9 | 3.1 | Quick | 11.4 | 2.6 | 5.9 | 2.2 | 1.8 | 1.9 |
| 1.2 | 1.1 | 1.3 |  | 1.3 | .9 | 1.6 | 1.3 | 1.3 | 1.2 |
| .6 | .6 | .7 |  | .3 | .5 | 1.1 | .8 | .9 | .8 |
| 18  20.2 | 22  16.5 | 11  32.5 | Sales/Receivables | 0  UND | 0  UND | 0  UND | 17  21.1 | 27  13.4 | 33  11.0 |
| 38  9.5 | 43  8.4 | 42  8.7 |  | 35  10.4 | 10  36.8 | 53  6.9 | 44  8.3 | 46  7.9 | 42  8.7 |
| 60  6.0 | 66  5.5 | 61  6.0 |  | 55  6.6 | 49  7.4 | 78  4.7 | 62  5.9 | 62  5.9 | 56  6.5 |
|  |  |  | Cost of Sales/Inventory |  |  |  |  |  |  |
|  |  |  | Cost of Sales/Payables |  |  |  |  |  |  |
| 6.0 | 6.0 | 6.5 | Sales/Working Capital | 8.4 | 4.7 | 4.3 | 6.8 | 5.3 | 8.3 |
| 15.3 | 14.3 | 13.0 |  | 33.3 | 22.3 | 11.1 | 14.5 | 9.9 | 13.0 |
| -58.2 | -66.6 | UND |  | -2.3 | -27.9 | 31.9 | NM | 22.6 | 39.7 |
| 11.0 | 17.8 | 19.3 | EBIT/Interest |  | 9.5 | 194.3 | 16.1 | 34.1 | 34.9 |
| (120) 2.8 | (110) 3.7 | (115) 6.4 |  | (19) 5.6 | (23) 10.8 | (23) 4.7 | (22) 9.5 | (19) 10.0 | |
| -1.1 | 1.0 | 2.0 |  | 1.0 | 3.3 | 2.0 | 1.6 | 3.6 | |
| 4.7 | 5.1 | 6.2 | Net Profit + Depr., Dep., Amort./Cur. Mat. L/T/D |  |  |  |  |  |  |
| (24) 2.0 | (15) 1.8 | (29) 2.8 |  |  |  |  |  |  |  |
| .3 | .3 | 1.2 |  |  |  |  |  |  |  |
| .3 | .3 | .2 | Fixed/Worth | .2 | .1 | .1 | .3 | .2 | .2 |
| .7 | .8 | .6 |  | 1.0 | .7 | .7 | .6 | .4 | .6 |
| 4.7 | 7.0 | 2.1 |  | -4.0 | UND | 2.7 | 1.5 | 1.1 | 1.8 |
| .6 | .5 | .4 | Debt/Worth | .1 | .3 | .3 | .7 | .7 | .6 |
| 2.0 | 1.7 | 1.3 |  | 3.9 | 1.6 | 1.0 | 1.6 | 1.1 | 1.1 |
| 19.8 | 162.1 | 7.5 |  | -5.0 | UND | 10.8 | 2.8 | 2.2 | 5.6 |
| 45.2 | 70.6 | 79.0 | % Profit Before Taxes/Tangible Net Worth | 68.7 | 104.7 | 159.9 | 100.2 | 36.6 | 81.0 |
| (114) 12.1 | (98) 19.6 | (123) 27.7 |  | (14) 19.6 | (23) 36.0 | (22) 46.6 | (23) 27.3 | (23) 17.2 | (18) 31.7 |
| -.3 | 2.6 | 6.6 |  | 5.9 | 3.5 | 15.4 | 9.2 | 5.9 | 5.1 |
| 15.3 | 21.1 | 26.0 | % Profit Before Taxes/Total Assets | 30.2 | 22.6 | 64.1 | 33.2 | 20.7 | 14.4 |
| 4.5 | 6.1 | 9.3 |  | 8.0 | 9.4 | 19.6 | 8.2 | 5.5 | 9.7 |
| -4.5 | -.4 | 1.9 |  | 2.0 | -.1 | 5.8 | 1.8 | 1.1 | 2.4 |
| 38.4 | 38.7 | 49.0 | Sales/Net Fixed Assets | 191.1 | 94.9 | 106.3 | 35.4 | 30.6 | 49.7 |
| 12.7 | 14.0 | 18.6 |  | 17.7 | 18.7 | 18.3 | 21.4 | 19.1 | 15.4 |
| 5.5 | 4.0 | 6.1 |  | 2.1 | 6.9 | 5.4 | 9.6 | 5.0 | 5.5 |
| 4.2 | 3.7 | 4.5 | Sales/Total Assets | 5.1 | 4.3 | 4.3 | 4.8 | 4.3 | 3.1 |
| 2.6 | 2.4 | 2.7 |  | 2.6 | 2.8 | 2.5 | 3.4 | 2.7 | 2.4 |
| 1.9 | 1.4 | 1.8 |  | 1.1 | 1.5 | 1.9 | 2.2 | 1.8 | 1.4 |
| .9 | 1.0 | 1.0 | % Depr., Dep., Amort./Sales |  | 1.1 | .7 | .7 | 1.2 | 1.2 |
| (113) 2.2 | (95) 2.5 | (110) 1.7 |  | (21) 1.5 | (19) 2.9 | (23) 1.3 | (20) 2.0 | (18) 2.1 | |
| 4.5 | 4.5 | 3.6 |  | 2.7 | 3.9 | 3.8 | 2.7 | 4.2 | |
| 5.3 | 3.1 | 4.2 | % Officers', Directors' Owners' Comp/Sales |  | 6.3 | 3.5 | 4.4 |  |  |
| (65) 10.1 | (54) 6.9 | (62) 7.1 |  | (16) 10.7 | (15) 6.5 | (14) 5.9 |  |  | |
| 19.0 | 11.7 | 12.2 |  | 17.6 | 11.9 | 9.4 |  |  | |
| 1373045M | 2066632M | 2295101M | Net Sales ($) | 9525M | 54901M | 118056M | 200947M | 395556M | 1516116M |
| 732035M | 1353247M | 1076354M | Total Assets ($) | 7554M | 60634M | 50402M | 79478M | 181491M | 696795M |

M = $ thousand   MM = $ million
See Pages 9 through 22 for Explanation of Ratios and Data

## Current Data Sorted by Assets     Comparative Historical Data

| | 0-500M | 500M-2MM | 2-10MM | 10-50MM | 50-100MM | 100-250MM | Type of Statement | 4/1/07-3/31/08 ALL | 4/1/08-3/31/09 ALL |
|---|---|---|---|---|---|---|---|---|---|
| | | 2 | | 1 | | | Unqualified | 3 | 2 |
| | | 2 | 3 | 2 | | | Reviewed | 1 | 3 |
| | 3 | 4 | 3 | | | 1 | Compiled | 2 | 1 |
| | 5 | 3 | 1 | 6 | | | Tax Returns | 3 | 1 |
| | | 5 (4/1-9/30/11) | | 31 (10/1/11-3/31/12) | | | Other | 9 | 8 |
| | 0-500M | 500M-2MM | 2-10MM | 10-50MM | 50-100MM | 100-250MM | NUMBER OF STATEMENTS | 18 | 15 |
| | 8 | 11 | 7 | 9 | 1 | | | | |
| | % | % | % | % | % | % | **ASSETS** | % | % |
| | | 22.7 | | | | | Cash & Equivalents | 10.0 | 10.5 |
| | | 28.9 | | | | | Trade Receivables (net) | 31.1 | 27.2 |
| | | 4.7 | | | | | Inventory | 12.7 | 22.0 |
| | | 5.0 | | | | | All Other Current | 4.1 | 6.9 |
| | | 61.4 | | | | | Total Current | 57.9 | 66.6 |
| | | 21.9 | | | | | Fixed Assets (net) | 23.2 | 25.5 |
| | | 6.3 | | | | | Intangibles (net) | 10.3 | 1.9 |
| | | 10.4 | | | | | All Other Non-Current | 8.6 | 6.1 |
| | | 100.0 | | | | | Total | 100.0 | 100.0 |
| | | | | | | | **LIABILITIES** | | |
| | | 10.1 | | | | | Notes Payable-Short Term | 18.5 | 12.6 |
| | | 4.4 | | | | | Cur. Mat.-L.T.D. | 1.6 | 2.7 |
| | | 11.6 | | | | | Trade Payables | 20.1 | 12.3 |
| | | .0 | | | | | Income Taxes Payable | .0 | .4 |
| | | 17.4 | | | | | All Other Current | 10.9 | 21.1 |
| | | 43.5 | | | | | Total Current | 51.0 | 49.1 |
| | | 16.4 | | | | | Long-Term Debt | 12.0 | 10.6 |
| | | .0 | | | | | Deferred Taxes | .1 | .0 |
| | | .1 | | | | | All Other Non-Current | 7.0 | 9.2 |
| | | 40.0 | | | | | Net Worth | 30.0 | 31.0 |
| | | 100.0 | | | | | Total Liabilities & Net Worth | 100.0 | 100.0 |
| | | | | | | | **INCOME DATA** | | |
| | | 100.0 | | | | | Net Sales | 100.0 | 100.0 |
| | | | | | | | Gross Profit | | |
| | | 93.0 | | | | | Operating Expenses | 97.0 | 95.2 |
| | | 7.0 | | | | | Operating Profit | 3.0 | 4.8 |
| | | 3.5 | | | | | All Other Expenses (net) | 3.6 | 1.5 |
| | | 3.5 | | | | | Profit Before Taxes | -.6 | 3.3 |
| | | | | | | | **RATIOS** | | |
| | | 2.5 | | | | | Current | 1.8 | 2.0 |
| | | 1.2 | | | | | | 1.1 | 1.4 |
| | | .9 | | | | | | .7 | 1.1 |
| | | 2.1 | | | | | Quick | 1.1 | 1.2 |
| | | 1.1 | | | | | | .9 | .8 |
| | | .8 | | | | | | .5 | .4 |
| | 0 UND | | | | | | Sales/Receivables | 0 UND   23 15.7 | |
| | 39 9.4 | | | | | | | 42 8.7   33 11.1 | |
| | 63 5.8 | | | | | | | 57 6.4   51 7.2 | |
| | | | | | | | Cost of Sales/Inventory | | |
| | | | | | | | Cost of Sales/Payables | | |
| | | 9.4 | | | | | Sales/Working Capital | 9.7 | 7.3 |
| | | 28.4 | | | | | | NM | 17.1 |
| | | -64.2 | | | | | | -18.8 | 215.6 |
| | | | | | | | EBIT/Interest | 52.4 | 33.3 |
| | | | | | | | | (13) 1.8   (14) 5.4 | |
| | | | | | | | | -23.0 | 1.4 |
| | | | | | | | Net Profit + Depr., Dep., Amort./Cur. Mat. L/T/D | | |
| | | .1 | | | | | Fixed/Worth | .4 | .2 |
| | | .6 | | | | | | .9 | .6 |
| | | 2.1 | | | | | | -4.9 | 1.7 |
| | | .8 | | | | | Debt/Worth | .7 | .7 |
| | | 2.9 | | | | | | 4.2 | 2.2 |
| | | 10.3 | | | | | | -8.5 | 11.6 |
| | | 69.6 | | | | | % Profit Before Taxes/Tangible Net Worth | 93.6 | 101.0 |
| | (10) | 32.6 | | | | | | (11) 50.2   (14) 14.7 | |
| | | 3.3 | | | | | | -1.7 | 3.4 |
| | | 19.3 | | | | | % Profit Before Taxes/Total Assets | 27.8 | 14.2 |
| | | 13.1 | | | | | | 4.5 | 6.3 |
| | | -2.5 | | | | | | -20.8 | .8 |
| | | 83.7 | | | | | Sales/Net Fixed Assets | 48.7 | 62.5 |
| | | 33.6 | | | | | | 20.6 | 12.2 |
| | | 9.2 | | | | | | 7.1 | 6.3 |
| | | 3.6 | | | | | Sales/Total Assets | 4.9 | 3.7 |
| | | 2.8 | | | | | | 2.7 | 2.8 |
| | | 1.8 | | | | | | 1.7 | 2.2 |
| | | | | | | | % Depr., Dep., Amort./Sales | .7 | .3 |
| | | | | | | | | (14) 1.6   (14) 1.8 | |
| | | | | | | | | 4.3 | 3.9 |
| | | | | | | | % Officers', Directors' Owners' Comp/Sales | | |
| | 9314M | 34547M | 51701M | 353841M | 76834M | | Net Sales ($) | 647891M | 504492M |
| | 1997M | 12949M | 29462M | 182891M | 70694M | | Total Assets ($) | 247613M | 235183M |

Note: The central "DATA NOT AVAILABLE" band covers columns 2-10MM, 10-50MM, 50-100MM and 100-250MM for the ASSETS and LIABILITIES sections.

M = $ thousand    MM = $ million
See Pages 9 through 22 for Explanation of Ratios and Data

## Comparative Historical Data      Current Data Sorted by Sales

| | | | | Type of Statement | | | | | | |
|---|---|---|---|---|---|---|---|---|---|---|
| | | | | Unqualified | | | | | | |
| 1 | | 2 | 1 | Reviewed | | | | 1 | 1 | 1 |
| 5 | | 7 | 7 | Compiled | | | 3 | 2 | 1 | 2 |
| | | 1 | 6 | Tax Returns | | | 2 | 2 | | 1 |
| 3 | | | 7 | Other | 3 | 2 | 2 | | | |
| 4 | | 7 | 15 | | 4 | 5 | | | 2 | 4 |
| 4/1/09- | | 4/1/10- | 4/1/11- | | | 5 (4/1-9/30/11) | | 31 (10/1/11-3/31/12) | | |
| 3/31/10 | | 3/31/11 | 3/31/12 | | | | | | | |
| ALL | | ALL | ALL | | 0-1MM | 1-3MM | 3-5MM | 5-10MM | 10-25MM | 25MM & OVER |
| 13 | | 17 | 36 | **NUMBER OF STATEMENTS** | 7 | 7 | 7 | 3 | 4 | 8 |
| % | | % | % | **ASSETS** | % | % | % | % | % | % |
| 8.6 | | 8.9 | 18.1 | Cash & Equivalents | | | | | | |
| 33.1 | | 34.9 | 23.6 | Trade Receivables (net) | | | | | | |
| 16.6 | | 19.5 | 15.8 | Inventory | | | | | | |
| 8.7 | | 6.0 | 4.2 | All Other Current | | | | | | |
| 67.0 | | 69.2 | 61.6 | Total Current | | | | | | |
| 21.5 | | 14.8 | 24.0 | Fixed Assets (net) | | | | | | |
| 7.0 | | 9.0 | 7.2 | Intangibles (net) | | | | | | |
| 4.5 | | 7.1 | 7.3 | All Other Non-Current | | | | | | |
| 100.0 | | 100.0 | 100.0 | Total | | | | | | |
| | | | | **LIABILITIES** | | | | | | |
| 21.4 | | 12.9 | 9.1 | Notes Payable-Short Term | | | | | | |
| 2.2 | | 4.2 | 5.0 | Cur. Mat.-L.T.D. | | | | | | |
| 17.8 | | 14.8 | 11.0 | Trade Payables | | | | | | |
| .2 | | .9 | .0 | Income Taxes Payable | | | | | | |
| 9.8 | | 10.9 | 22.1 | All Other Current | | | | | | |
| 51.4 | | 43.7 | 47.1 | Total Current | | | | | | |
| 13.7 | | 10.1 | 15.9 | Long-Term Debt | | | | | | |
| 1.0 | | .0 | .4 | Deferred Taxes | | | | | | |
| 10.9 | | 5.3 | 19.3 | All Other Non-Current | | | | | | |
| 23.0 | | 40.8 | 17.5 | Net Worth | | | | | | |
| 100.0 | | 100.0 | 100.0 | Total Liabilties & Net Worth | | | | | | |
| | | | | **INCOME DATA** | | | | | | |
| 100.0 | | 100.0 | 100.0 | Net Sales | | | | | | |
| | | | | Gross Profit | | | | | | |
| 99.8 | | 93.2 | 91.4 | Operating Expenses | | | | | | |
| .2 | | 6.8 | 8.6 | Operating Profit | | | | | | |
| 1.0 | | 2.3 | 2.2 | All Other Expenses (net) | | | | | | |
| -.8 | | 4.5 | 6.3 | Profit Before Taxes | | | | | | |
| | | | | **RATIOS** | | | | | | |
| 1.7 | | 2.6 | 3.0 | | | | | | | |
| 1.2 | | 1.4 | 1.6 | Current | | | | | | |
| .9 | | 1.1 | 1.0 | | | | | | | |
| 1.1 | | 2.0 | 2.3 | | | | | | | |
| .8 | | 1.0 (35) | 1.0 | Quick | | | | | | |
| .4 | | .6 | .6 | | | | | | | |
| 19   19.7 | 21   17.0 | | 0   UND | | | | | | | |
| 46   8.0 | 48   7.6 | | 30   12.1 | Sales/Receivables | | | | | | |
| 57   6.4 | 62   5.9 | | 57   6.4 | | | | | | | |
| | | | | Cost of Sales/Inventory | | | | | | |
| | | | | Cost of Sales/Payables | | | | | | |
| 7.9 | | 7.6 | 4.0 | | | | | | | |
| 27.0 | | 12.9 | 12.1 | Sales/Working Capital | | | | | | |
| -62.4 | | 33.0 | -141.4 | | | | | | | |
| 8.9 | | 32.1 | 8.3 | | | | | | | |
| 4.2 (14) | | 5.1 (27) | 3.4 | EBIT/Interest | | | | | | |
| -1.0 | | 1.6 | .3 | | | | | | | |
| | | | | Net Profit + Depr., Dep., Amort./Cur. Mat. L/T/D | | | | | | |
| .3 | | .1 | .2 | | | | | | | |
| 1.1 | | .4 | .7 | Fixed/Worth | | | | | | |
| NM | | 1.2 | 3.9 | | | | | | | |
| 1.5 | | 1.0 | .9 | | | | | | | |
| 4.7 | | 1.7 | 3.4 | Debt/Worth | | | | | | |
| NM | | 4.2 | NM | | | | | | | |
| 79.0 | | 53.9 | 68.3 | | | | | | | |
| (10)   25.6 | (16)   20.9 | | (27)   23.8 | % Profit Before Taxes/Tangible Net Worth | | | | | | |
| -110.6 | | 9.6 | 13.3 | | | | | | | |
| 17.2 | | 14.3 | 19.3 | | | | | | | |
| 4.5 | | 8.0 | 8.9 | % Profit Before Taxes/Total Assets | | | | | | |
| -13.1 | | 1.8 | 1.7 | | | | | | | |
| 72.1 | | 85.7 | 68.6 | | | | | | | |
| 27.0 | | 25.7 | 25.5 | Sales/Net Fixed Assets | | | | | | |
| 11.0 | | 14.4 | 5.2 | | | | | | | |
| 4.4 | | 3.4 | 3.5 | | | | | | | |
| 3.7 | | 2.9 | 2.3 | Sales/Total Assets | | | | | | |
| 2.5 | | 1.8 | 1.3 | | | | | | | |
| .9 | | .6 | 1.1 | | | | | | | |
| (10)   1.2 | (11)   1.4 | | (25)   2.0 | % Depr., Dep., Amort./Sales | | | | | | |
| 3.1 | | 3.7 | 4.4 | | | | | | | |
| | | | 1.8 | | | | | | | |
| | | | (15)   7.6 | % Officers', Directors' Owners' Comp/Sales | | | | | | |
| | | | 23.7 | | | | | | | |
| 378779M | | 277733M | 526237M | Net Sales ($) | 2596M | 14948M | 28577M | 20754M | 76687M | 382675M |
| 129582M | | 159880M | 297993M | Total Assets ($) | 2621M | 10252M | 10470M | 13040M | 49247M | 212363M |

M = $ thousand    MM = $ million
See Pages 9 through 22 for Explanation of Ratios and Data

**Current Data Sorted by Assets**      **Comparative Historical Data**

| 0-500M | 500M-2MM | 2-10MM | 10-50MM | 50-100MM | 100-250MM | Type of Statement | 4/1/07-3/31/08 ALL | 4/1/08-3/31/09 ALL |
|---|---|---|---|---|---|---|---|---|
| 3 | 4 | 38 | 43 | 8 | 18 | Unqualified | 86 | 112 |
| 2 | 15 | 41 | 19 | 2 | | Reviewed | 57 | 68 |
| 4 | 24 | 31 | 2 | | | Compiled | 38 | 57 |
| 51 | 60 | 28 | 2 | | 1 | Tax Returns | 75 | 105 |
| 38 | 98 | 131 | 66 | 17 | 19 | Other | 260 | 280 |
| | 78 (4/1-9/30/11) | | 687 (10/1/11-3/31/12) | | | | | |
| 98 | 201 | 269 | 132 | 27 | 38 | NUMBER OF STATEMENTS | 516 | 622 |
| % | % | % | % | % | % | **ASSETS** | % | % |
| 38.6 | 21.4 | 20.9 | 22.0 | 21.6 | 28.8 | Cash & Equivalents | 19.6 | 21.7 |
| 25.5 | 41.2 | 45.6 | 33.6 | 28.0 | 20.9 | Trade Receivables (net) | 41.0 | 40.8 |
| 2.0 | 2.5 | 2.2 | 1.8 | 1.5 | 1.8 | Inventory | 2.4 | 2.1 |
| 4.2 | 2.6 | 4.1 | 5.8 | 6.9 | 6.0 | All Other Current | 5.3 | 5.1 |
| 70.3 | 67.7 | 72.8 | 63.2 | 58.1 | 57.4 | Total Current | 68.2 | 69.7 |
| 16.4 | 14.7 | 12.8 | 9.5 | 10.4 | 9.1 | Fixed Assets (net) | 12.4 | 13.1 |
| 2.8 | 5.8 | 5.9 | 19.0 | 25.2 | 25.6 | Intangibles (net) | 10.1 | 8.8 |
| 10.4 | 11.8 | 8.6 | 8.3 | 6.4 | 7.9 | All Other Non-Current | 9.3 | 8.5 |
| 100.0 | 100.0 | 100.0 | 100.0 | 100.0 | 100.0 | Total | 100.0 | 100.0 |
| | | | | | | **LIABILITIES** | | |
| 32.2 | 13.0 | 7.5 | 5.6 | 2.7 | 1.9 | Notes Payable-Short Term | 13.2 | 13.3 |
| 3.7 | 2.9 | 1.9 | 2.4 | 6.0 | 1.3 | Cur. Mat.-L.T.D. | 2.8 | 3.2 |
| 11.9 | 11.0 | 12.2 | 9.0 | 9.0 | 4.5 | Trade Payables | 10.8 | 12.8 |
| .1 | .1 | .4 | 1.0 | .4 | .5 | Income Taxes Payable | .8 | .6 |
| 21.4 | 18.5 | 21.8 | 25.1 | 28.4 | 25.0 | All Other Current | 21.0 | 22.0 |
| 69.3 | 45.5 | 43.8 | 43.2 | 46.4 | 33.2 | Total Current | 48.6 | 51.9 |
| 22.0 | 11.8 | 7.8 | 8.4 | 9.3 | 12.5 | Long-Term Debt | 10.0 | 12.3 |
| .0 | .3 | .3 | .6 | .9 | 1.4 | Deferred Taxes | .5 | .4 |
| 13.9 | 13.8 | 9.9 | 12.8 | 10.3 | 4.3 | All Other Non-Current | 7.9 | 9.6 |
| -5.2 | 28.6 | 38.2 | 35.0 | 33.1 | 48.5 | Net Worth | 33.1 | 25.8 |
| 100.0 | 100.0 | 100.0 | 100.0 | 100.0 | 100.0 | Total Liabilities & Net Worth | 100.0 | 100.0 |
| | | | | | | **INCOME DATA** | | |
| 100.0 | 100.0 | 100.0 | 100.0 | 100.0 | 100.0 | Net Sales | 100.0 | 100.0 |
| | | | | | | Gross Profit | | |
| 93.2 | 90.7 | 90.8 | 91.2 | 94.0 | 90.2 | Operating Expenses | 94.5 | 94.0 |
| 6.8 | 9.3 | 9.2 | 8.8 | 6.0 | 9.8 | Operating Profit | 5.5 | 6.0 |
| .7 | 1.7 | 1.0 | .8 | 1.5 | 1.7 | All Other Expenses (net) | 1.3 | 1.4 |
| 6.2 | 7.6 | 8.3 | 8.0 | 4.5 | 8.0 | Profit Before Taxes | 4.2 | 4.5 |
| | | | | | | **RATIOS** | | |
| 3.9 | 4.1 | 3.5 | 2.6 | 2.5 | 3.2 | | 2.8 | 2.8 |
| 1.9 | 1.6 | 1.8 | 1.5 | 1.3 | 1.8 | Current | 1.6 | 1.5 |
| .7 | 1.0 | 1.2 | 1.0 | 1.0 | 1.0 | | 1.0 | 1.0 |
| 3.7 | 3.8 | 3.0 | 2.2 | 2.5 | 2.6 | | 2.6 | 2.6 |
| 1.6 | 1.5 | 1.6 | 1.3 | 1.0 | 1.4 | Quick | 1.4 (621) | 1.3 |
| .5 | .9 | 1.1 | .8 | .7 | .9 | | .9 | .8 |
| 0 UND | 12 31.7 | 36 10.0 | 43 8.5 | 39 9.4 | 52 7.0 | | 35 10.6 | 31 11.6 |
| 8 47.8 | 38 9.6 | 54 6.7 | 61 6.0 | 68 5.4 | 64 5.7 | Sales/Receivables | 58 6.3 | 52 7.0 |
| 39 9.3 | 58 6.3 | 76 4.8 | 85 4.3 | 99 3.7 | 85 4.3 | | 78 4.7 | 74 4.9 |
| | | | | | | Cost of Sales/Inventory | | |
| | | | | | | Cost of Sales/Payables | | |
| 11.6 | 6.8 | 5.0 | 4.0 | 2.5 | 2.5 | | 5.8 | 5.8 |
| 52.7 | 17.8 | 10.1 | 8.9 | 12.7 | 7.3 | Sales/Working Capital | 12.9 | 13.4 |
| -33.2 | UND | 30.8 | NM | -117.8 | 283.3 | | 362.3 | -130.4 |
| 42.3 | 39.9 | 63.2 | 46.7 | 23.3 | 149.1 | | 19.9 | 29.7 |
| (62) 8.8 | (134) 11.6 | (192) 15.1 | (102) 7.3 | (18) 7.8 | (24) 4.0 | EBIT/Interest | (373) 5.2 | (469) 7.1 |
| .8 | 2.4 | 4.3 | 2.5 | 1.1 | 1.3 | | .9 | .9 |
| | 5.8 | 25.7 | 14.9 | | | Net Profit + Depr., Dep., | 30.0 | 10.8 |
| | (10) 2.9 | (27) 6.3 | (27) 3.3 | | | Amort./Cur. Mat. L/T/D | (61) 3.8 | (74) 4.0 |
| | .7 | 1.4 | .8 | | | | .5 | .8 |
| .0 | .0 | .0 | .1 | .1 | .1 | | .1 | .1 |
| .3 | .2 | .2 | .5 | .5 | .5 | Fixed/Worth | .3 | .3 |
| -1.2 | 1.9 | .9 | -5.4 | -.2 | -.8 | | 1.9 | 5.1 |
| .4 | .5 | .6 | 1.1 | 1.1 | .6 | | .6 | .7 |
| 2.6 | 1.8 | 1.4 | 3.6 | 3.5 | 2.2 | Debt/Worth | 1.8 | 2.1 |
| -3.6 | 12.8 | 4.8 | -72.4 | -8.1 | -9.2 | | 13.3 | 69.1 |
| 176.9 | 89.0 | 77.4 | 78.7 | 68.5 | 34.4 | % Profit Before Taxes/Tangible | 70.5 | 82.3 |
| (64) 75.3 | (164) 41.8 | (226) 40.8 | (96) 38.1 | (18) 23.2 | (25) 20.2 | Net Worth | (407) 34.6 | (473) 34.0 |
| 9.4 | 14.6 | 14.2 | 15.0 | 9.5 | 4.6 | | 9.3 | 6.9 |
| 100.0 | 40.2 | 33.4 | 17.6 | 14.2 | 14.1 | % Profit Before Taxes/Total | 24.1 | 26.2 |
| 35.1 | 16.2 | 13.4 | 9.5 | 4.9 | 7.3 | Assets | 9.3 | -10.1 |
| .0 | 3.6 | 5.5 | 3.0 | 1.0 | .7 | | .2 | .2 |
| 999.8 | 315.2 | 173.1 | 61.7 | 67.5 | 38.7 | | 109.3 | 130.4 |
| 131.8 | 68.2 | 45.7 | 31.6 | 18.3 | 18.8 | Sales/Net Fixed Assets | 36.2 | 39.2 |
| 24.7 | 30.0 | 16.4 | 13.3 | 10.0 | 9.2 | | 15.8 | 15.2 |
| 13.5 | 5.7 | 4.2 | 2.4 | 2.2 | 1.4 | | 4.2 | 4.6 |
| 6.0 | 3.7 | 2.9 | 1.6 | 1.1 | 1.0 | Sales/Total Assets | 2.7 | 2.9 |
| 3.7 | 2.5 | 1.8 | 1.0 | .7 | .6 | | 1.5 | 1.6 |
| .2 | .3 | .3 | .5 | 1.1 | 1.7 | | .4 | .4 |
| (41) .7 | (107) .8 | (183) .9 | (85) 1.4 | (14) 3.9 | (19) 2.5 | % Depr., Dep., Amort./Sales | (331) 1.1 | (376) 1.0 |
| 1.5 | 1.8 | 1.9 | 2.8 | 5.2 | 5.9 | | 2.7 | 2.6 |
| 5.3 | 2.9 | 1.7 | .9 | | | | 3.1 | 3.0 |
| (52) 10.0 | (73) 6.2 | (74) 3.7 | (17) 1.8 | | | % Officers', Directors' Owners' Comp/Sales | (149) 6.6 | (158) 5.9 |
| 15.2 | 12.1 | 7.4 | 18.2 | | | | 13.5 | 13.1 |
| 229379M | 963778M | 3497995M | 5730612M | 2782993M | 6864736M | Net Sales ($) | 12854996M | 19137886M |
| 23458M | 228758M | 1158165M | 2897613M | 1990967M | 6024324M | Total Assets ($) | 9278578M | 10387008M |

© RMA 2012

M = $ thousand     MM = $ million
See Pages 9 through 22 for Explanation of Ratios and Data

## Comparative Historical Data | Current Data Sorted by Sales

| Type of Statement | 4/1/09-3/31/10 ALL | 4/1/10-3/31/11 ALL | 4/1/11-3/31/12 ALL | 0-1MM | 1-3MM | 3-5MM | 5-10MM | 10-25MM | 25MM & OVER |
|---|---|---|---|---|---|---|---|---|---|
| Unqualified | 126 | 118 | 114 | 3 | 2 | 4 | 9 | 41 | 55 |
| Reviewed | 73 | 76 | 79 | 1 | 4 | 8 | 18 | 30 | 18 |
| Compiled | 64 | 55 | 61 | 2 | 13 | 9 | 19 | 15 | 3 |
| Tax Returns | 101 | 102 | 142 | 19 | 39 | 25 | 38 | 16 | 5 |
| Other | 338 | 341 | 369 | 30 | 41 | 48 | 81 | 83 | 86 |

78 (4/1-9/30/11)    687 (10/1/11-3/31/12)

| | 4/1/09-3/31/10 ALL | 4/1/10-3/31/11 ALL | 4/1/11-3/31/12 ALL | 0-1MM | 1-3MM | 3-5MM | 5-10MM | 10-25MM | 25MM & OVER |
|---|---|---|---|---|---|---|---|---|---|
| **NUMBER OF STATEMENTS** | 702 | 692 | 765 | 55 | 99 | 94 | 165 | 185 | 167 |
| | % | % | % | % | % | % | % | % | % |
| **ASSETS** | | | | | | | | | |
| Cash & Equivalents | 23.4 | 22.0 | 23.9 | 22.2 | 27.4 | 31.1 | 22.6 | 20.1 | 23.8 |
| Trade Receivables (net) | 38.4 | 39.9 | 37.9 | 19.9 | 33.8 | 30.6 | 43.4 | 45.7 | 36.5 |
| Inventory | 1.8 | 2.3 | 2.1 | 1.0 | 2.9 | 1.7 | 2.3 | 2.0 | 2.2 |
| All Other Current | 6.0 | 4.5 | 4.2 | 3.3 | 3.1 | 2.9 | 3.4 | 5.3 | 5.5 |
| Total Current | 69.6 | 68.8 | 68.2 | 46.3 | 67.1 | 66.4 | 71.8 | 73.2 | 68.0 |
| Fixed Assets (net) | 11.9 | 12.5 | 12.9 | 35.3 | 14.3 | 11.7 | 14.0 | 8.9 | 8.8 |
| Intangibles (net) | 9.8 | 9.2 | 9.4 | 7.4 | 5.1 | 8.8 | 5.5 | 9.6 | 16.5 |
| All Other Non-Current | 8.7 | 9.5 | 9.5 | 11.0 | 13.5 | 13.0 | 8.8 | 8.3 | 6.8 |
| Total | 100.0 | 100.0 | 100.0 | 100.0 | 100.0 | 100.0 | 100.0 | 100.0 | 100.0 |
| **LIABILITIES** | | | | | | | | | |
| Notes Payable-Short Term | 14.1 | 11.8 | 11.3 | 20.1 | 23.2 | 11.2 | 10.9 | 7.7 | 5.9 |
| Cur. Mat.-L.T.D. | 3.2 | 2.1 | 2.6 | 3.3 | 3.0 | 2.9 | 2.4 | 2.5 | 2.3 |
| Trade Payables | 11.9 | 11.0 | 10.8 | 10.5 | 7.9 | 8.7 | 10.7 | 13.6 | 11.0 |
| Income Taxes Payable | .6 | .4 | .4 | .0 | .0 | .2 | .2 | .8 | .5 |
| All Other Current | 24.3 | 23.0 | 21.8 | 27.2 | 12.0 | 18.9 | 23.3 | 21.5 | 26.5 |
| Total Current | 54.1 | 48.3 | 47.0 | 61.1 | 46.2 | 41.8 | 47.5 | 46.0 | 46.3 |
| Long-Term Debt | 9.5 | 9.0 | 11.0 | 25.3 | 14.6 | 16.2 | 8.2 | 6.1 | 9.5 |
| Deferred Taxes | .4 | .4 | .4 | .0 | .0 | .6 | .4 | .4 | .7 |
| All Other Non-Current | 10.9 | 10.9 | 11.7 | 15.4 | 12.7 | 20.9 | 8.9 | 11.3 | 7.9 |
| Net Worth | 25.1 | 31.4 | 29.9 | -1.8 | 26.5 | 20.5 | 35.0 | 36.1 | 35.6 |
| Total Liabilities & Net Worth | 100.0 | 100.0 | 100.0 | 100.0 | 100.0 | 100.0 | 100.0 | 100.0 | 100.0 |
| **INCOME DATA** | | | | | | | | | |
| Net Sales | 100.0 | 100.0 | 100.0 | 100.0 | 100.0 | 100.0 | 100.0 | 100.0 | 100.0 |
| Gross Profit | | | | | | | | | |
| Operating Expenses | 93.5 | 91.4 | 91.2 | 82.7 | 90.3 | 92.8 | 92.0 | 92.2 | 91.8 |
| Operating Profit | 6.5 | 8.6 | 8.8 | 17.3 | 9.7 | 7.2 | 8.0 | 7.8 | 8.2 |
| All Other Expenses (net) | 1.2 | 1.3 | 1.1 | 5.2 | .6 | .8 | 1.0 | .7 | .9 |
| Profit Before Taxes | 5.3 | 7.4 | 7.6 | 12.1 | 9.1 | 6.5 | 7.0 | 7.0 | 7.3 |
| **RATIOS** | | | | | | | | | |
| Current | 2.8 | 3.0 | 3.4 | 5.0 | 5.2 | 5.8 | 3.8 | 2.6 | 2.4 |
| | 1.6 | 1.6 | 1.6 | 1.3 | 2.2 | 1.9 | 1.6 | 1.6 | 1.5 |
| | 1.0 | 1.0 | 1.0 | .3 | .9 | .9 | 1.1 | 1.1 | 1.1 |
| Quick | 2.5 | 2.7 | 3.0 | 4.8 | 5.0 | 5.7 | 3.4 | 2.5 | 2.2 |
| | (701) 1.4 | 1.4 | 1.5 | 1.2 | 2.0 | 1.8 | 1.5 | 1.5 | 1.4 |
| | .8 | .9 | .9 | .2 | .7 | .8 | 1.0 | .9 | .9 |
| Sales/Receivables | 29  12.7 | 33  10.9 | 25  14.7 | 0  UND | 0  UND | 15  24.3 | 27  13.6 | 35  10.4 | 43  8.5 |
| | 52  7.0 | 55  6.7 | 49  7.5 | 9  39.6 | 36  10.0 | 34  10.8 | 50  7.3 | 54  6.7 | 60  6.1 |
| | 75  4.9 | 76  4.8 | 73  5.0 | 43  8.4 | 65  5.6 | 59  6.2 | 70  5.2 | 74  4.9 | 79  4.6 |
| Cost of Sales/Inventory | | | | | | | | | |
| Cost of Sales/Payables | | | | | | | | | |
| Sales/Working Capital | 5.4 | 5.1 | 5.5 | 5.0 | 4.7 | 4.9 | 5.9 | 6.7 | 4.9 |
| | 13.8 | 11.4 | 12.7 | 51.8 | 12.2 | 16.9 | 15.0 | 11.8 | 10.9 |
| | -174.0 | 395.3 | 201.6 | -3.9 | -370.7 | -100.7 | 109.2 | 49.2 | 51.5 |
| EBIT/Interest | 27.2 | 53.2 | 49.9 | 15.9 | 40.1 | 21.7 | 62.3 | 89.7 | 55.1 |
| | (495) 7.4 | (496) 14.1 | (532) 11.3 | (28) 1.8 | (66) 8.3 | (59) 7.9 | (120) 16.0 | (142) 15.6 | (117) 8.2 |
| | .7 | 3.0 | 2.8 | -.6 | 2.2 | 2.8 | 3.9 | 4.4 | 1.9 |
| Net Profit + Depr., Dep., Amort./Cur. Mat. L/T/D | 14.1 | 19.1 | 19.1 | | | | | 25.5 | 32.1 |
| | (72) 3.4 | (65) 3.6 | (79) 3.9 | | | | | (24) 11.7 | (34) 4.1 |
| | .5 | 1.9 | 1.4 | | | | | 1.2 | 1.8 |
| Fixed/Worth | .1 | .1 | .1 | .0 | .0 | .0 | .1 | .1 | .1 |
| | .3 | .2 | .3 | .9 | .2 | .2 | .3 | .2 | .3 |
| | 6.0 | 1.9 | 3.4 | -1.2 | 3.2 | -197.5 | 1.2 | 1.2 | 4.7 |
| Debt/Worth | .7 | .7 | .6 | .8 | .3 | .3 | .6 | .7 | .9 |
| | 2.0 | 1.9 | 1.7 | 4.0 | 1.6 | 1.1 | 1.6 | 1.7 | 2.8 |
| | 182.1 | 14.9 | 23.7 | -3.8 | -26.8 | -12.8 | 14.5 | 10.5 | 27.7 |
| % Profit Before Taxes/Tangible Net Worth | 78.5 | 83.9 | 85.9 | 75.0 | 107.1 | 65.8 | 96.0 | 87.0 | 78.8 |
| | (530) 30.5 | (550) 40.1 | (593) 41.0 | (38) 22.5 | (74) 50.3 | (68) 37.2 | (136) 52.2 | (150) 43.4 | (127) 33.4 |
| | 9.8 | 14.1 | 13.1 | .0 | 13.7 | 14.0 | 10.7 | 18.8 | 12.8 |
| % Profit Before Taxes/Total Assets | 24.4 | 29.9 | 34.1 | 29.0 | 58.3 | 30.5 | 40.8 | 34.1 | 21.5 |
| | 10.0 | 13.6 | 13.1 | 4.8 | 17.7 | 14.0 | 16.8 | 14.0 | 9.4 |
| | .9 | 3.0 | 3.4 | -.9 | 4.2 | 4.2 | 4.8 | 5.6 | 2.0 |
| Sales/Net Fixed Assets | 145.4 | 152.6 | 185.9 | 310.0 | 284.4 | 195.5 | 143.6 | 217.6 | 94.3 |
| | 44.1 | 44.4 | 46.2 | 22.4 | 60.3 | 49.6 | 49.7 | 51.9 | 34.9 |
| | 16.6 | 16.7 | 16.7 | .9 | 21.3 | 25.9 | 16.0 | 20.5 | 13.7 |
| Sales/Total Assets | 4.3 | 4.2 | 4.7 | 4.6 | 5.6 | 5.8 | 5.0 | 4.7 | 3.1 |
| | 2.8 | 2.6 | 2.8 | 1.8 | 3.2 | 3.1 | 3.2 | 3.3 | 1.9 |
| | 1.6 | 1.5 | 1.5 | .3 | 2.1 | 1.9 | 2.2 | 1.7 | 1.1 |
| % Depr., Dep., Amort./Sales | .4 | .3 | .3 | 1.0 | .3 | .4 | .4 | .2 | .4 |
| | (409) 1.0 | (410) .9 | (449) 1.0 | (25) 2.7 | (50) .8 | (53) .9 | (102) .9 | (113) .9 | (106) 1.3 |
| | 2.2 | 2.2 | 2.2 | 10.2 | 1.6 | 1.7 | 1.9 | 1.9 | 3.3 |
| % Officers', Directors' Owners' Comp/Sales | 2.7 | 2.6 | 2.3 | 7.5 | 5.1 | 4.3 | 2.3 | 1.2 | .8 |
| | (191) 6.0 | (168) 6.9 | (219) 5.2 | (15) 15.3 | (45) 10.2 | (36) 7.6 | (56) 4.1 | (46) 2.6 | (21) 1.6 |
| | 11.9 | 13.8 | 11.9 | 22.4 | 15.0 | 13.2 | 7.4 | 4.5 | 4.2 |
| Net Sales ($) | 17538981M | 18634430M | 20069493M | 24979M | 198011M | 372897M | 1187807M | 2965721M | 15320078M |
| Total Assets ($) | 11756229M | 11618559M | 12323285M | 31283M | 102071M | 147296M | 480921M | 1440913M | 10120801M |

M = $ thousand    MM = $ million
See Pages 9 through 22 for Explanation of Ratios and Data

## Current Data Sorted by Assets | Comparative Historical Data

| Type of Statement | 0-500M | 500M-2MM | 2-10MM | 10-50MM | 50-100MM | 100-250MM | | 4/1/07-3/31/08 ALL | 4/1/08-3/31/09 ALL |
|---|---|---|---|---|---|---|---|---|---|
| Unqualified | 1 | 8 | 50 | 59 | 18 | 15 | | 102 | 126 |
| Reviewed | 6 | 21 | 73 | 18 | | | | 75 | 102 |
| Compiled | 57 | 22 | 29 | 2 | | 1 | | 43 | 53 |
| Tax Returns | 35 | 45 | 26 | 1 | | 1 | | 63 | 82 |
| Other | | 96 | 167 | 98 | 18 | 18 | | 262 | 283 |
| | 93 (4/1-9/30/11) | | | 792 (10/1/11-3/31/12) | | | | | |
| **NUMBER OF STATEMENTS** | 99 | 192 | 345 | 178 | 36 | 35 | | 545 | 646 |
| **ASSETS** | % | % | % | % | % | % | | % | % |
| Cash & Equivalents | 31.6 | 20.4 | 18.4 | 17.9 | 15.3 | 12.8 | | 14.4 | 16.1 |
| Trade Receivables (net) | 27.6 | 44.4 | 49.3 | 44.6 | 32.2 | 28.2 | | 45.4 | 45.5 |
| Inventory | 3.1 | 4.0 | 4.1 | 5.3 | 5.7 | 5.7 | | 5.4 | 4.7 |
| All Other Current | 3.1 | 3.2 | 4.6 | 6.8 | 7.1 | 7.0 | | 4.7 | 5.1 |
| Total Current | 65.3 | 72.0 | 76.4 | 74.5 | 60.2 | 53.6 | | 70.0 | 71.4 |
| Fixed Assets (net) | 15.9 | 13.5 | 10.8 | 8.3 | 9.1 | 9.1 | | 13.4 | 11.5 |
| Intangibles (net) | 4.5 | 5.5 | 6.7 | 11.1 | 25.3 | 30.1 | | 9.4 | 8.8 |
| All Other Non-Current | 14.3 | 9.0 | 6.0 | 6.0 | 5.4 | 7.2 | | 7.3 | 8.3 |
| Total | 100.0 | 100.0 | 100.0 | 100.0 | 100.0 | 100.0 | | 100.0 | 100.0 |
| **LIABILITIES** | | | | | | | | | |
| Notes Payable-Short Term | 32.3 | 13.7 | 6.9 | 7.0 | 5.5 | 2.1 | | 13.1 | 15.5 |
| Cur. Mat.-L.T.D. | 4.3 | 1.9 | 2.0 | 1.7 | 2.0 | 1.7 | | 2.8 | 2.4 |
| Trade Payables | 14.2 | 17.9 | 19.5 | 19.5 | 17.6 | 16.1 | | 17.5 | 18.0 |
| Income Taxes Payable | .0 | .4 | .5 | .7 | .8 | .8 | | .7 | .6 |
| All Other Current | 29.1 | 17.2 | 19.8 | 21.5 | 21.2 | 15.9 | | 17.4 | 17.9 |
| Total Current | 80.0 | 51.2 | 48.6 | 50.3 | 47.1 | 36.6 | | 51.6 | 54.4 |
| Long-Term Debt | 14.5 | 13.0 | 6.5 | 6.7 | 10.5 | 15.9 | | 10.5 | 11.2 |
| Deferred Taxes | .0 | .1 | .4 | .5 | .8 | 1.4 | | .5 | .3 |
| All Other Non-Current | 6.0 | 7.3 | 5.6 | 5.0 | 2.6 | 8.3 | | 7.7 | 7.5 |
| Net Worth | -.6 | 28.4 | 38.9 | 37.5 | 39.0 | 37.9 | | 29.7 | 26.5 |
| Total Liabilties & Net Worth | 100.0 | 100.0 | 100.0 | 100.0 | 100.0 | 100.0 | | 100.0 | 100.0 |
| **INCOME DATA** | | | | | | | | | |
| Net Sales | 100.0 | 100.0 | 100.0 | 100.0 | 100.0 | 100.0 | | 100.0 | 100.0 |
| Gross Profit | | | | | | | | | |
| Operating Expenses | 93.6 | 91.9 | 93.7 | 93.3 | 93.6 | 91.3 | | 94.4 | 94.5 |
| Operating Profit | 6.4 | 8.1 | 6.3 | 6.7 | 6.4 | 8.7 | | 5.6 | 5.5 |
| All Other Expenses (net) | 1.0 | 1.0 | .7 | .8 | 1.5 | 1.7 | | .9 | 1.4 |
| Profit Before Taxes | 5.4 | 7.1 | 5.6 | 5.9 | 4.9 | 7.0 | | 4.7 | 4.2 |
| **RATIOS** | | | | | | | | | |
| Current | 2.8 | 2.9 | 2.9 | 2.2 | 1.9 | 2.1 | | 2.3 | 2.3 |
| | 1.0 | 1.6 | 1.6 | 1.5 | 1.3 | 1.4 | | 1.4 | 1.5 |
| | .6 | 1.0 | 1.1 | 1.1 | 1.1 | 1.1 | | 1.0 | 1.0 |
| Quick | 2.5 | 2.8 | 2.5 | 1.8 | 1.5 | 1.5 | | 2.0 | 2.1 |
| | 1.0 | 1.4 | 1.5 | 1.2 | 1.1 | 1.1 | | 1.2 | 1.3 |
| | .4 | .9 | .9 | .9 | .7 | .7 | | .8 | .8 |
| Sales/Receivables | 0 UND | 26 14.3 | 41 9.0 | 45 8.2 | 36 10.1 | 42 8.6 | | 38 9.6 | 33 11.1 |
| | 10 37.3 | 45 8.2 | 54 6.7 | 63 5.8 | 64 5.7 | 54 6.7 | | 56 6.5 | 53 6.9 |
| | 41 8.8 | 65 5.6 | 72 5.1 | 79 4.6 | 76 4.8 | 78 4.7 | | 77 4.7 | 72 5.1 |
| Cost of Sales/Inventory | | | | | | | | | |
| Cost of Sales/Payables | | | | | | | | | |
| Sales/Working Capital | 12.6 | 7.4 | 5.8 | 5.2 | 6.8 | 4.0 | | 6.9 | 6.6 |
| | 155.1 | 14.7 | 11.2 | 11.4 | 11.9 | 12.5 | | 14.6 | 14.0 |
| | -32.5 | 843.6 | 45.1 | 39.2 | 97.7 | 73.4 | | -999.8 | 299.8 |
| EBIT/Interest | 22.5 | 37.4 | 72.8 | 66.8 | 86.5 | 26.8 | | 25.3 | 26.5 |
| | (53) 7.3 | (135) 8.7 | (257) 13.6 | (134) 14.8 | (31) 15.5 | (29) 5.6 | | (445) 5.7 | (510) 7.0 |
| | .1 | 2.1 | 3.8 | 3.8 | 1.8 | 2.1 | | 1.7 | 1.1 |
| Net Profit + Depr., Dep., Amort./Cur. Mat. L/T/D | | | 25.3 | 33.0 | | | | 11.5 | 11.4 |
| | | (39) 8.0 | (33) 8.5 | | | | | (74) 3.3 | (83) 3.5 |
| | | | 2.2 | 2.6 | | | | 1.3 | .7 |
| Fixed/Worth | .0 | .0 | .0 | .1 | .1 | .2 | | .1 | .1 |
| | .4 | .2 | .2 | .2 | .3 | 2.5 | | .3 | .3 |
| | -1.3 | 1.8 | .9 | 1.1 | -.3 | -.1 | | 2.6 | 2.2 |
| Debt/Worth | .6 | .7 | .7 | 1.0 | 1.0 | 1.0 | | .9 | .9 |
| | 2.8 | 1.8 | 1.6 | 2.1 | 3.8 | 8.8 | | 2.4 | 2.4 |
| | -4.1 | 11.1 | 6.1 | 10.0 | -6.3 | -3.7 | | 23.0 | 35.7 |
| % Profit Before Taxes/Tangible Net Worth | 196.3 | 93.7 | 78.0 | 75.7 | 63.3 | 50.7 | | 76.7 | 66.7 |
| | (63) 70.4 | (150) 49.3 | (300) 39.6 | (147) 38.4 | (25) 41.0 | (18) 18.6 | | (425) 38.8 | (502) 35.7 |
| | 17.9 | 12.4 | 15.0 | 16.7 | 15.0 | 3.4 | | 12.9 | 10.6 |
| % Profit Before Taxes/Total Assets | 67.3 | 35.9 | 26.4 | 22.7 | 16.8 | 11.4 | | 24.1 | 22.4 |
| | 19.9 | 14.3 | 12.6 | 11.3 | 8.4 | 5.0 | | 10.4 | 9.6 |
| | -1.7 | 2.7 | 3.9 | 3.8 | 2.4 | 2.0 | | 1.9 | .8 |
| Sales/Net Fixed Assets | UND | 322.0 | 186.3 | 201.0 | 92.3 | 96.5 | | 122.9 | 144.5 |
| | 120.0 | 76.0 | 65.2 | 71.2 | 37.1 | 38.2 | | 43.3 | 50.9 |
| | 36.1 | 24.1 | 19.8 | 24.2 | 14.6 | 12.3 | | 17.4 | 22.1 |
| Sales/Total Assets | 14.8 | 5.1 | 4.3 | 3.7 | 2.5 | 2.2 | | 4.3 | 4.4 |
| | 7.3 | 3.8 | 3.1 | 2.4 | 1.6 | 1.3 | | 2.9 | 3.3 |
| | 4.2 | 2.7 | 2.0 | 1.4 | 1.0 | .7 | | 1.8 | 2.0 |
| % Depr., Dep., Amort./Sales | .2 | .3 | .3 | .3 | .2 | .4 | | .4 | .3 |
| | (39) .7 | (99) .8 | (237) .7 | (123) .5 | (22) .9 | (22) 1.1 | | (368) .9 | (431) .7 |
| | 2.1 | 2.1 | 1.6 | 1.4 | 3.9 | 3.2 | | 2.2 | 1.7 |
| % Officers', Directors' Owners' Comp/Sales | 6.5 | 3.7 | 1.8 | 1.5 | | | | 2.5 | 2.2 |
| | (54) 10.7 | (77) 6.9 | (77) 4.0 | (13) 5.9 | | | | (136) 5.1 | (142) 4.7 |
| | 14.2 | 11.6 | 7.3 | 19.3 | | | | 9.3 | 8.7 |
| Net Sales ($) | 207113M | 930103M | 5663642M | 9386255M | 4814165M | 9860406M | | 18391158M | 23302122M |
| Total Assets ($) | 23777M | 225073M | 1771961M | 3741837M | 2582789M | 5608056M | | 10003424M | 11331466M |

M = $ thousand  MM = $ million
See Pages 9 through 22 for Explanation of Ratios and Data

## Comparative Historical Data / Current Data Sorted by Sales

| | | | Type of Statement | 0-1MM | 1-3MM | 3-5MM | 5-10MM | 10-25MM | 25MM & OVER |
|---|---|---|---|---|---|---|---|---|---|
| 161 | 166 | 150 | Unqualified | | 2 | 2 | 17 | 41 | 88 |
| 102 | 123 | 113 | Reviewed | 1 | 5 | 4 | 32 | 45 | 26 |
| 53 | 61 | 60 | Compiled | 2 | 9 | 13 | 15 | 16 | 5 |
| 91 | 88 | 130 | Tax Returns | 21 | 34 | 23 | 29 | 19 | 4 |
| 368 | 381 | 432 | Other | 18 | 54 | 39 | 65 | 122 | 134 |
| 4/1/09-3/31/10 ALL | 4/1/10-3/31/11 ALL | 4/1/11-3/31/12 ALL | | 93 (4/1-9/30/11) | | | 792 (10/1/11-3/31/12) | | |
| 775 | 819 | 885 | NUMBER OF STATEMENTS | 42 | 104 | 81 | 158 | 243 | 257 |
| % | % | % | ASSETS | % | % | % | % | % | % |
| 17.8 | 17.6 | 19.9 | Cash & Equivalents | 20.8 | 27.7 | 22.6 | 22.2 | 19.4 | 14.7 |
| 44.8 | 45.3 | 43.3 | Trade Receivables (net) | 26.5 | 32.3 | 39.3 | 42.3 | 48.4 | 47.7 |
| 4.8 | 4.6 | 4.3 | Inventory | 5.0 | 2.3 | 4.9 | 3.0 | 4.6 | 5.4 |
| 5.2 | 5.5 | 4.7 | All Other Current | 1.8 | 3.5 | 2.8 | 5.2 | 4.6 | 6.2 |
| 72.7 | 73.0 | 72.3 | Total Current | 54.2 | 65.8 | 69.6 | 72.6 | 77.1 | 74.0 |
| 11.1 | 10.4 | 11.3 | Fixed Assets (net) | 24.1 | 15.7 | 12.6 | 13.3 | 9.5 | 7.6 |
| 8.9 | 8.9 | 8.8 | Intangibles (net) | 7.9 | 6.4 | 7.9 | 5.8 | 7.8 | 12.8 |
| 7.4 | 7.8 | 7.6 | All Other Non-Current | 13.9 | 12.2 | 9.8 | 8.3 | 5.6 | 5.6 |
| 100.0 | 100.0 | 100.0 | Total | 100.0 | 100.0 | 100.0 | 100.0 | 100.0 | 100.0 |
| | | | LIABILITIES | | | | | | |
| 14.4 | 12.5 | 11.0 | Notes Payable-Short Term | 19.2 | 22.1 | 16.4 | 11.1 | 7.3 | 6.8 |
| 3.0 | 2.3 | 2.2 | Cur. Mat.-L.T.D. | 3.3 | 3.9 | 1.5 | 2.8 | 1.7 | 1.5 |
| 17.5 | 16.9 | 18.3 | Trade Payables | 18.0 | 11.0 | 18.1 | 15.6 | 18.7 | 22.7 |
| .5 | .6 | .5 | Income Taxes Payable | .0 | .3 | .5 | .4 | .6 | .6 |
| 19.1 | 21.1 | 20.5 | All Other Current | 39.4 | 16.7 | 14.3 | 22.2 | 19.9 | 20.5 |
| 54.5 | 53.4 | 52.5 | Total Current | 79.8 | 54.1 | 50.8 | 52.1 | 48.2 | 52.2 |
| 10.8 | 9.3 | 9.4 | Long-Term Debt | 25.2 | 14.2 | 9.6 | 10.7 | 5.6 | 7.6 |
| .4 | .3 | .4 | Deferred Taxes | .0 | .1 | .1 | .3 | .5 | .6 |
| 6.2 | 7.5 | 5.9 | All Other Non-Current | 7.8 | 6.3 | 9.9 | 6.1 | 5.9 | 4.1 |
| 28.1 | 29.5 | 31.9 | Net Worth | -12.8 | 25.4 | 29.6 | 30.9 | 39.8 | 35.6 |
| 100.0 | 100.0 | 100.0 | Total Liabilities & Net Worth | 100.0 | 100.0 | 100.0 | 100.0 | 100.0 | 100.0 |
| | | | INCOME DATA | | | | | | |
| 100.0 | 100.0 | 100.0 | Net Sales | 100.0 | 100.0 | 100.0 | 100.0 | 100.0 | 100.0 |
| | | | Gross Profit | | | | | | |
| 94.3 | 94.2 | 93.1 | Operating Expenses | 82.5 | 92.4 | 94.6 | 93.7 | 93.1 | 94.3 |
| 5.7 | 5.8 | 6.9 | Operating Profit | 17.5 | 7.6 | 5.4 | 6.3 | 6.9 | 5.7 |
| 1.3 | .7 | .9 | All Other Expenses (net) | 3.9 | 1.0 | .5 | .8 | .8 | .7 |
| 4.4 | 5.1 | 6.0 | Profit Before Taxes | 13.6 | 6.7 | 4.9 | 5.5 | 6.1 | 5.0 |
| | | | RATIOS | | | | | | |
| 2.2 | 2.4 | 2.6 | | 1.9 | 4.7 | 2.8 | 3.1 | 2.8 | 1.9 |
| 1.4 | 1.5 | 1.5 | Current | .9 | 1.9 | 1.5 | 1.8 | 1.6 | 1.4 |
| 1.0 | 1.1 | 1.0 | | .5 | .8 | .9 | 1.0 | 1.1 | 1.1 |
| 1.9 | 2.2 | 2.3 | | 1.7 | 4.2 | 2.6 | 2.7 | 2.4 | 1.7 |
| 1.3 | 1.3 | 1.3 | Quick | .8 | 1.5 | 1.4 | 1.5 | 1.5 | 1.2 |
| .8 | .8 | .8 | | .4 | .7 | .8 | .9 | .9 | .8 |
| 35  10.4 | 37  9.9 | 33  11.0 | | 0  UND | 0  UND | 19  19.7 | 27  13.5 | 40  9.1 | 43  8.4 |
| 55  6.7 | 57  6.4 | 51  7.1 | Sales/Receivables | 16  22.2 | 41  9.0 | 42  8.6 | 49  7.5 | 54  6.7 | 58  6.3 |
| 73  5.0 | 74  4.9 | 70  5.2 | | 58  6.3 | 64  5.7 | 69  5.3 | 66  5.5 | 74  4.9 | 73  5.0 |
| | | | Cost of Sales/Inventory | | | | | | |
| | | | Cost of Sales/Payables | | | | | | |
| 6.7 | 6.6 | 6.5 | | 9.0 | 6.5 | 6.6 | 5.6 | 5.9 | 7.3 |
| 14.4 | 14.1 | 13.2 | Sales/Working Capital | -148.6 | 15.3 | 15.4 | 11.7 | 11.2 | 15.4 |
| 793.9 | 95.7 | 155.2 | | -13.3 | -107.4 | -138.2 | 337.5 | 51.2 | 57.9 |
| 32.6 | 37.4 | 48.2 | | 21.7 | 14.0 | 20.1 | 56.5 | 97.3 | 54.8 |
| (604)  7.6 | (643)  11.3 | (639)  11.1 | EBIT/Interest | (28)  7.6 | (62)  5.5 | (53)  5.8 | (108)  10.6 | (184)  15.5 | (204)  15.9 |
| 1.1 | 2.4 | 3.1 | | 3.2 | -.3 | 1.3 | 2.2 | 3.9 | 4.0 |
| 15.6 | 21.6 | 15.9 | | | | | 11.4 | 17.8 | 26.6 |
| (103)  3.4 | (112)  5.0 | (92)  5.1 | Net Profit + Depr., Dep., Amort./Cur. Mat. L/T/D | | | (12)  8.4 | (31)  3.7 | (42)  4.9 | |
| .6 | 1.8 | 1.7 | | | | | 3.5 | 1.5 | 2.2 |
| .1 | .1 | .0 | | .0 | .0 | .0 | .0 | .0 | .1 |
| .3 | .2 | .2 | Fixed/Worth | 1.6 | .3 | .2 | .2 | .2 | .2 |
| 2.8 | 1.4 | 1.7 | | -.8 | 6.5 | 2.0 | 1.2 | 1.0 | 1.9 |
| .9 | .8 | .7 | | 2.1 | .3 | .7 | .6 | .7 | 1.1 |
| 2.4 | 2.3 | 2.0 | Debt/Worth | 5.8 | 1.4 | 1.8 | 1.4 | 1.7 | 2.7 |
| 38.4 | 12.4 | 12.9 | | -3.2 | NM | 21.9 | 7.0 | 7.2 | 26.0 |
| 64.5 | 73.8 | 83.0 | | 174.2 | 104.4 | 117.4 | 73.2 | 82.0 | 74.9 |
| (602)  30.1 | (654)  38.9 | (703)  42.2 | % Profit Before Taxes/Tangible Net Worth | (24)  67.6 | (78)  47.7 | (64)  56.7 | (126)  37.6 | (207)  42.4 | (204)  39.6 |
| 8.0 | 13.3 | 14.9 | | 18.2 | 1.5 | 18.2 | 8.5 | 21.0 | 16.6 |
| 21.8 | 24.3 | 28.2 | | 51.1 | 40.3 | 30.8 | 32.7 | 29.6 | 21.5 |
| 8.0 | 10.9 | 12.3 | % Profit Before Taxes/Total Assets | 14.7 | 13.4 | 13.0 | 12.5 | 13.8 | 10.2 |
| .3 | 2.6 | 3.2 | | .4 | -1.9 | 3.5 | 2.7 | 4.5 | 4.3 |
| 157.9 | 187.1 | 220.3 | | UND | 522.2 | 632.2 | 170.4 | 177.3 | 218.2 |
| 58.0 | 66.2 | 68.7 | Sales/Net Fixed Assets | 72.0 | 44.1 | 86.8 | 59.4 | 69.5 | 79.6 |
| 20.9 | 22.9 | 22.0 | | 3.8 | 20.2 | 26.6 | 18.0 | 25.6 | 24.0 |
| 4.3 | 4.4 | 4.6 | | 7.6 | 6.3 | 5.6 | 4.8 | 4.5 | 4.1 |
| 3.0 | 3.1 | 3.2 | Sales/Total Assets | 3.7 | 3.6 | 3.7 | 3.3 | 3.0 | 3.0 |
| 1.9 | 1.8 | 1.9 | | .6 | 2.1 | 2.6 | 2.0 | 1.9 | 1.7 |
| .3 | .3 | .3 | | .8 | .5 | .4 | .2 | .2 | .2 |
| (490)  .7 | (544)  .7 | (542)  .7 | % Depr., Dep., Amort./Sales | (19)  7.2 | (48)  1.5 | (40)  .9 | (100)  .9 | (161)  .6 | (174)  .5 |
| 1.6 | 1.7 | 1.7 | | 14.2 | 3.2 | 1.7 | 2.0 | 1.4 | 1.3 |
| 2.4 | 2.9 | 2.8 | | 5.8 | 6.3 | 4.1 | 2.7 | 1.9 | .9 |
| (186)  5.2 | (173)  5.4 | (223)  6.3 | % Officers', Directors' Owners' Comp/Sales | (16)  12.4 | (47)  10.6 | (34)  6.9 | (54)  4.6 | (55)  4.0 | (17)  1.7 |
| 10.9 | 10.8 | 11.7 | | 17.0 | 14.3 | 11.7 | 9.6 | 7.5 | 15.9 |
| 27717292M | 32220806M | 30861684M | Net Sales ($) | 22373M | 211394M | 313618M | 1116597M | 3953694M | 25244008M |
| 14067052M | 15261793M | 13953493M | Total Assets ($) | 16947M | 82821M | 107667M | 468568M | 1645278M | 11632212M |

M = $ thousand    MM = $ million
See Pages 9 through 22 for Explanation of Ratios and Data

## Current Data Sorted by Assets

## Comparative Historical Data

| 0-500M | 500M-2MM | 2-10MM | 10-50MM | 50-100MM | 100-250MM | Type of Statement | 4/1/07-3/31/08 ALL | 4/1/08-3/31/09 ALL |
|---|---|---|---|---|---|---|---|---|
| | | 3 | 3 | 2 | 1 | Unqualified | 5 | 3 |
| 1 | | 3 | | | | Reviewed | | 1 |
| 1 | | | | | | Compiled | 1 | 2 |
| 5 | 4 | 2 | | | | Tax Returns | 2 | 1 |
| | 2 | 4 | 3 | 1 | 1 | Other | 14 | 8 |
| 1 (4/1-9/30/11) | | | 35 (10/1/11-3/31/12) | | | | | |
| 7 | 6 | 12 | 6 | 3 | 2 | NUMBER OF STATEMENTS | 22 | 15 |
| % | % | % | % | % | % | ASSETS | % | % |
| | | 15.7 | | | | Cash & Equivalents | 11.0 | 10.0 |
| | | 59.6 | | | | Trade Receivables (net) | 46.4 | 50.4 |
| | | 2.3 | | | | Inventory | 3.3 | 9.7 |
| | | 5.2 | | | | All Other Current | 8.5 | 7.3 |
| | | 82.7 | | | | Total Current | 69.1 | 77.4 |
| | | 10.6 | | | | Fixed Assets (net) | 12.5 | 17.2 |
| | | 2.2 | | | | Intangibles (net) | 8.2 | 4.3 |
| | | 4.5 | | | | All Other Non-Current | 10.2 | 1.1 |
| | | 100.0 | | | | Total | 100.0 | 100.0 |
| | | | | | | LIABILITIES | | |
| | | 6.6 | | | | Notes Payable-Short Term | 17.1 | 18.4 |
| | | 3.3 | | | | Cur. Mat.-L.T.D. | 3.7 | 3.9 |
| | | 15.8 | | | | Trade Payables | 16.7 | 28.3 |
| | | .0 | | | | Income Taxes Payable | 1.7 | 2.4 |
| | | 22.2 | | | | All Other Current | 22.2 | 24.6 |
| | | 47.8 | | | | Total Current | 61.4 | 77.6 |
| | | 6.0 | | | | Long-Term Debt | 15.4 | 6.2 |
| | | .0 | | | | Deferred Taxes | .5 | .6 |
| | | 8.0 | | | | All Other Non-Current | 2.2 | .6 |
| | | 38.1 | | | | Net Worth | 20.4 | 14.9 |
| | | 100.0 | | | | Total Liabilities & Net Worth | 100.0 | 100.0 |
| | | | | | | INCOME DATA | | |
| | | 100.0 | | | | Net Sales | 100.0 | 100.0 |
| | | 40.9 | | | | Gross Profit | 42.0 | 47.1 |
| | | 34.6 | | | | Operating Expenses | 36.6 | 39.9 |
| | | 6.3 | | | | Operating Profit | 5.4 | 7.1 |
| | | -.3 | | | | All Other Expenses (net) | 1.9 | 2.4 |
| | | 6.6 | | | | Profit Before Taxes | 3.6 | 4.8 |
| | | | | | | RATIOS | | |
| | | 2.6 | | | | | 1.7 | 1.5 |
| | | 1.8 | | | | Current | 1.2 | 1.0 |
| | | 1.1 | | | | | .9 | .7 |
| | | 2.1 | | | | | 1.6 | 1.5 |
| | | 1.5 | | | | Quick | 1.0 | .7 |
| | | 1.1 | | | | | .5 | .3 |
| | 42 | 8.6 | | | | | 22   16.7 | 29   12.6 |
| | 56 | 6.5 | | | | Sales/Receivables | 53   6.9 | 52   7.0 |
| | 72 | 5.1 | | | | | 86   4.3 | 72   5.1 |
| | 0 | UND | | | | | 0   UND | 0   UND |
| | 0 | UND | | | | Cost of Sales/Inventory | 0   UND | 3   112.3 |
| | 5 | 78.9 | | | | | 3   113.6 | 5   71.5 |
| | 13 | 28.0 | | | | | 9   41.5 | 22   16.7 |
| | 20 | 18.3 | | | | Cost of Sales/Payables | 35   10.3 | 32   11.5 |
| | 74 | 4.9 | | | | | 56   6.5 | 149   2.5 |
| | | 6.7 | | | | | 8.6 | 10.5 |
| | | 12.4 | | | | Sales/Working Capital | 20.5 | -393.1 |
| | | 32.7 | | | | | -33.4 | -10.0 |
| | | | | | | | 42.4 | 22.7 |
| | | | | | | EBIT/Interest | (18)   5.9 | 5.2 |
| | | | | | | | -.2 | -.2 |
| | | | | | | Net Profit + Depr., Dep., Amort./Cur. Mat. L/T/D | | |
| | | .1 | | | | | .1 | .1 |
| | | .2 | | | | Fixed/Worth | .3 | 1.1 |
| | | .7 | | | | | -1.2 | -.6 |
| | | .9 | | | | | 1.2 | 1.8 |
| | | 2.0 | | | | Debt/Worth | 3.0 | 6.6 |
| | | 10.3 | | | | | -5.0 | -8.2 |
| | | 112.3 | | | | | 55.2 | |
| | (11) | 54.5 | | | | % Profit Before Taxes/Tangible Net Worth | (15)   43.5 | |
| | | 32.2 | | | | | 12.4 | |
| | | 27.4 | | | | | 28.4 | 16.7 |
| | | 24.3 | | | | % Profit Before Taxes/Total Assets | 11.0 | 4.4 |
| | | 11.5 | | | | | -3.4 | -6.8 |
| | | 152.4 | | | | | 116.3 | 113.0 |
| | | 70.0 | | | | Sales/Net Fixed Assets | 61.1 | 44.3 |
| | | 29.2 | | | | | 24.8 | 17.6 |
| | | 5.4 | | | | | 4.2 | 4.6 |
| | | 3.4 | | | | Sales/Total Assets | 3.2 | 3.6 |
| | | 2.8 | | | | | 2.3 | 2.2 |
| | | .3 | | | | | .4 | .4 |
| | (10) | .7 | | | | % Depr., Dep., Amort./Sales | (14)   .7 | (11)   .9 |
| | | 1.7 | | | | | 1.2 | 1.2 |
| | | | | | | % Officers', Directors' Owners' Comp/Sales | | |
| 13176M | 29000M | 211745M | 373342M | 279572M | 614655M | Net Sales ($) | 1765383M | 782225M |
| 1752M | 7084M | 56443M | 112295M | 175849M | 223227M | Total Assets ($) | 700695M | 314950M |

M = $ thousand    MM = $ million
See Pages 9 through 22 for Explanation of Ratios and Data

## Comparative Historical Data — Current Data Sorted by Sales

| Type of Statement | 4/1/09-3/31/10 ALL | 4/1/10-3/31/11 ALL | 4/1/11-3/31/12 ALL | 0-1MM | 1-3MM | 3-5MM | 5-10MM | 10-25MM | 25MM & OVER |
|---|---|---|---|---|---|---|---|---|---|
| Unqualified | 4 | 12 | 9 | | | | | 2 | 7 |
| Reviewed | 1 | 3 | 4 | | 1 | | | 2 | 1 |
| Compiled | 3 | | 1 | | | 1 | | | |
| Tax Returns | 3 | 3 | 11 | 2 | 4 | 2 | 1 | 1 | 1 |
| Other | 10 | 13 | 11 | | | | 1 | 3 | 4 |
|  |  |  |  | 1 (4/1-9/30/11) | | | 35 (10/1/11-3/31/12) | | |
| NUMBER OF STATEMENTS | 21 | 31 | 36 | 2 | 6 | 4 | 3 | 8 | 13 |
| ASSETS | % | % | % | % | % | % | % | % | % |
| Cash & Equivalents | 17.1 | 15.5 | 18.1 | | | | | | 12.6 |
| Trade Receivables (net) | 36.0 | 36.3 | 47.0 | | | | | | 49.0 |
| Inventory | 3.0 | 4.3 | 4.1 | | | | | | 3.0 |
| All Other Current | 3.5 | 10.5 | 6.1 | | | | | | 7.7 |
| Total Current | 59.6 | 66.7 | 75.4 | | | | | | 72.3 |
| Fixed Assets (net) | 26.6 | 12.2 | 11.5 | | | | | | 12.2 |
| Intangibles (net) | 6.0 | 10.8 | 6.2 | | | | | | 11.3 |
| All Other Non-Current | 7.9 | 10.3 | 7.0 | | | | | | 4.2 |
| Total | 100.0 | 100.0 | 100.0 | | | | | | 100.0 |
| LIABILITIES | | | | | | | | | |
| Notes Payable-Short Term | 8.4 | 8.1 | 6.7 | | | | | | 6.8 |
| Cur. Mat.-L.T.D. | 7.5 | 2.8 | 3.2 | | | | | | 3.8 |
| Trade Payables | 19.3 | 15.3 | 19.4 | | | | | | 11.4 |
| Income Taxes Payable | .2 | .3 | .1 | | | | | | .2 |
| All Other Current | 15.5 | 21.4 | 26.7 | | | | | | 22.9 |
| Total Current | 50.9 | 47.9 | 56.0 | | | | | | 45.1 |
| Long-Term Debt | 16.6 | 8.6 | 10.7 | | | | | | 9.3 |
| Deferred Taxes | .7 | .4 | .2 | | | | | | .6 |
| All Other Non-Current | 3.8 | 12.1 | 6.6 | | | | | | 7.1 |
| Net Worth | 28.0 | 31.1 | 26.5 | | | | | | 37.9 |
| Total Liabilities & Net Worth | 100.0 | 100.0 | 100.0 | | | | | | 100.0 |
| INCOME DATA | | | | | | | | | |
| Net Sales | 100.0 | 100.0 | 100.0 | | | | | | 100.0 |
| Gross Profit | 45.4 | 47.4 | 46.9 | | | | | | 35.7 |
| Operating Expenses | 35.7 | 39.6 | 40.4 | | | | | | 27.0 |
| Operating Profit | 9.7 | 7.8 | 6.5 | | | | | | 8.7 |
| All Other Expenses (net) | 2.5 | 3.4 | .6 | | | | | | 1.5 |
| Profit Before Taxes | 7.2 | 4.5 | 5.9 | | | | | | 7.2 |
| RATIOS | | | | | | | | | |
| Current | 2.1 / 1.3 / .7 | 1.9 / 1.3 / .8 | 2.6 / 1.5 / 1.1 | | | | | | 2.4 / 1.4 / 1.1 |
| Quick | 1.8 / 1.0 / .6 | 1.6 / 1.1 / .5 | 2.0 / 1.4 / .9 | | | | | | 2.0 / 1.2 / 1.0 |
| Sales/Receivables | 16 22.5 / 41 9.0 / 74 4.9 | 23 15.8 / 52 7.0 / 81 4.5 | 38 9.6 / 52 7.0 / 65 5.6 | | | | | | 44 8.3 / 51 7.1 / 69 5.3 |
| Cost of Sales/Inventory | 0 UND / 0 UND / 8 43.9 | 0 UND / 0 999.8 / 9 40.8 | 0 UND / 0 UND / 4 93.7 | | | | | | 0 UND / 0 UND / 2 169.9 |
| Cost of Sales/Payables | 14 25.3 / 42 8.7 / 115 3.2 | 19 19.6 / 41 8.9 / 128 2.8 | 9 40.3 / 23 15.8 / 46 8.0 | | | | | | 7 49.4 / 13 29.1 / 39 9.4 |
| Sales/Working Capital | 8.8 / 21.7 / -18.2 | 6.7 / 20.3 / -14.7 | 7.9 / 14.4 / 130.3 | | | | | | 6.9 / 10.6 / 51.5 |
| EBIT/Interest | 22.8 / (18) 4.1 / 1.0 | 100.6 / (24) 7.5 / 1.7 | 42.8 / (29) 17.3 / 2.4 | | | | | (10) | 80.1 / 23.7 / 2.6 |
| Net Profit + Depr., Dep., Amort./Cur. Mat. L/T/D | | | | | | | | | |
| Fixed/Worth | .2 / 1.2 / UND | .1 / .3 / 45.8 | .1 / .2 / 4.2 | | | | | | .1 / .2 / 2.9 |
| Debt/Worth | 1.0 / 6.0 / UND | 1.0 / 2.5 / 52.6 | .9 / 1.7 / 12.7 | | | | | | .9 / 1.9 / 8.9 |
| % Profit Before Taxes/Tangible Net Worth | 181.0 / (17) 76.9 / 33.2 | 70.2 / (24) 31.8 / 7.2 | 105.3 / (29) 52.0 / 32.1 | | | | | (11) | 98.3 / 52.0 / 34.9 |
| % Profit Before Taxes/Total Assets | 48.9 / 12.0 / 2.4 | 20.4 / 6.8 / .8 | 30.3 / 21.6 / 6.4 | | | | | | 35.6 / 15.0 / 8.0 |
| Sales/Net Fixed Assets | 100.6 / 22.5 / 8.2 | 147.2 / 63.0 / 20.7 | 127.2 / 62.7 / 37.5 | | | | | | 113.3 / 69.3 / 41.8 |
| Sales/Total Assets | 4.2 / 2.9 / 1.9 | 3.6 / 2.3 / .9 | 5.5 / 3.7 / 2.5 | | | | | | 4.6 / 3.8 / 1.4 |
| % Depr., Dep., Amort./Sales | .7 / (14) 2.7 / 5.4 | .3 / (19) .6 / 1.9 | .4 / (28) .7 / 1.6 | | | | | (12) | .3 / .6 / 1.8 |
| % Officers', Directors', Owners' Comp/Sales | | | 5.1 / (13) 7.3 / 17.1 | | | | | | |
| Net Sales ($) | 675775M | 1582728M | 1521490M | 1557M | 13105M | 16326M | 24458M | 97959M | 1368085M |
| Total Assets ($) | 490627M | 1224585M | 576650M | 427M | 3166M | 3661M | 21145M | 30029M | 518222M |

© RMA 2012

M = $ thousand    MM = $ million
See Pages 9 through 22 for Explanation of Ratios and Data

## Current Data Sorted by Assets | Comparative Historical Data

| Type of Statement | 0-500M | 500M-2MM | 2-10MM | 10-50MM | 50-100MM | 100-250MM | 4/1/07-3/31/08 ALL | 4/1/08-3/31/09 ALL |
|---|---|---|---|---|---|---|---|---|
| Unqualified | | 3 | 26 | 27 | 8 | 3 | 59 | 81 |
| Reviewed | | 17 | 49 | 11 | | | 61 | 72 |
| Compiled | 5 | 23 | 26 | 4 | | 1 | 40 | 53 |
| Tax Returns | 80 | 65 | 33 | 2 | | 2 | 93 | 125 |
| Other | 54 | 104 | 125 | 40 | 10 | 11 | 216 | 205 |
| | | 45 (4/1-9/30/11) | | 684 (10/1/11-3/31/12) | | | | |
| **NUMBER OF STATEMENTS** | 139 | 212 | 259 | 84 | 18 | 17 | 469 | 536 |

| | 0-500M % | 500M-2MM % | 2-10MM % | 10-50MM % | 50-100MM % | 100-250MM % | ALL % | ALL % |
|---|---|---|---|---|---|---|---|---|
| **ASSETS** | | | | | | | | |
| Cash & Equivalents | 33.7 | 18.0 | 17.9 | 16.4 | 14.5 | 10.7 | 16.7 | 16.6 |
| Trade Receivables (net) | 25.8 | 46.8 | 47.2 | 41.5 | 41.0 | 21.9 | 42.3 | 40.5 |
| Inventory | 2.3 | 4.0 | 3.5 | 4.4 | 2.0 | 5.1 | 5.8 | 5.3 |
| All Other Current | 3.6 | 1.6 | 3.9 | 9.6 | 6.2 | 3.9 | 4.1 | 4.4 |
| Total Current | 65.4 | 70.4 | 72.5 | 71.9 | 63.7 | 41.6 | 69.0 | 66.9 |
| Fixed Assets (net) | 19.4 | 13.9 | 14.3 | 9.3 | 12.7 | 12.5 | 15.1 | 15.9 |
| Intangibles (net) | 5.2 | 5.7 | 5.2 | 10.1 | 16.5 | 30.6 | 7.6 | 8.9 |
| All Other Non-Current | 9.9 | 10.0 | 8.0 | 8.7 | 7.2 | 15.4 | 8.3 | 8.4 |
| Total | 100.0 | 100.0 | 100.0 | 100.0 | 100.0 | 100.0 | 100.0 | 100.0 |
| **LIABILITIES** | | | | | | | | |
| Notes Payable-Short Term | 22.8 | 12.7 | 7.8 | 6.4 | 6.0 | 12.8 | 16.8 | 14.6 |
| Cur. Mat.-L.T.D. | 4.4 | 2.7 | 1.9 | 1.8 | 2.6 | 5.2 | 3.2 | 3.9 |
| Trade Payables | 10.7 | 16.0 | 15.7 | 17.7 | 19.5 | 12.0 | 16.1 | 14.7 |
| Income Taxes Payable | .0 | .3 | .5 | .3 | .5 | .1 | .4 | .4 |
| All Other Current | 20.7 | 13.2 | 16.2 | 20.2 | 15.7 | 12.8 | 18.7 | 17.1 |
| Total Current | 58.7 | 45.0 | 42.0 | 46.4 | 44.2 | 43.0 | 55.2 | 50.7 |
| Long-Term Debt | 19.3 | 11.3 | 11.1 | 7.5 | 26.2 | 21.4 | 13.0 | 15.9 |
| Deferred Taxes | .0 | .2 | .1 | .9 | .5 | 3.5 | .2 | .2 |
| All Other Non-Current | 15.3 | 11.0 | 8.4 | 6.9 | 4.8 | 6.3 | 10.6 | 10.3 |
| Net Worth | 6.7 | 32.6 | 38.3 | 38.3 | 24.3 | 25.8 | 21.1 | 22.8 |
| Total Liabilities & Net Worth | 100.0 | 100.0 | 100.0 | 100.0 | 100.0 | 100.0 | 100.0 | 100.0 |
| **INCOME DATA** | | | | | | | | |
| Net Sales | 100.0 | 100.0 | 100.0 | 100.0 | 100.0 | 100.0 | 100.0 | 100.0 |
| Gross Profit | | | | | | | | |
| Operating Expenses | 89.6 | 91.5 | 91.8 | 92.5 | 94.0 | 91.3 | 94.9 | 95.0 |
| Operating Profit | 10.4 | 8.5 | 8.2 | 7.5 | 6.0 | 8.7 | 5.1 | 5.0 |
| All Other Expenses (net) | 1.3 | 1.0 | 1.1 | .6 | 1.8 | 2.9 | .8 | 1.1 |
| Profit Before Taxes | 9.1 | 7.5 | 7.1 | 7.0 | 4.2 | 5.9 | 4.3 | 3.9 |

### RATIOS

| | 0-500M | 500M-2MM | 2-10MM | 10-50MM | 50-100MM | 100-250MM | ALL | ALL |
|---|---|---|---|---|---|---|---|---|
| Current | 3.9 / 1.6 / .7 | 3.8 / 1.7 / 1.0 | 3.1 / 1.8 / 1.1 | 2.4 / 1.5 / 1.1 | 2.8 / 1.2 / .9 | 2.4 / 1.6 / .8 | 2.5 / 1.4 / .9 | 2.6 / 1.5 / 1.0 |
| Quick | 3.7 / 1.4 / .6 | 3.6 / 1.5 / .9 | 2.9 / 1.6 / 1.0 | 2.0 / 1.2 / .8 | 2.5 / 1.1 / .8 | 1.9 / 1.3 / .6 | 2.2 / 1.2 / .7 | 2.3 / 1.3 / .8 |
| Sales/Receivables | 0 UND / 2 200.5 / 38 9.5 | 26 14.2 / 45 8.1 / 66 5.5 | 39 9.4 / 55 6.6 / 74 4.9 | 45 8.1 / 59 6.2 / 87 4.2 | 43 8.4 / 65 5.6 / 104 3.5 | 31 11.7 / 60 6.1 / 79 4.6 | 30 12.0 / 48 7.5 / 69 5.3 | 26 14.1 / 47 7.7 / 69 5.3 |
| Cost of Sales/Inventory | | | | | | | | |
| Cost of Sales/Payables | | | | | | | | |
| Sales/Working Capital | 11.2 / 41.6 / -35.4 | 6.3 / 13.9 / -555.5 | 5.5 / 10.2 / 44.1 | 5.8 / 11.2 / 35.3 | 3.3 / 18.8 / -116.8 | 6.1 / 9.6 / -18.1 | 7.6 / 18.6 / -74.3 | 6.9 / 14.9 / -381.2 |
| EBIT/Interest | (87) 34.6 / 9.4 / 2.5 | (152) 40.6 / 12.4 / 2.6 | (203) 42.0 / 11.9 / 2.5 | (60) 45.2 / 6.6 / 2.0 | (15) 19.2 / 2.8 / .7 | (16) 44.8 / 2.5 / -.2 | (369) 17.0 / 5.5 / 1.2 | (428) 21.4 / 5.1 / 1.2 |
| Net Profit + Depr., Dep., Amort./Cur. Mat. L/T/D | | | (30) 13.5 / 5.4 / 1.8 | (15) 10.7 / 4.2 / 2.7 | | | (47) 10.1 / 2.6 / .9 | (53) 9.8 / 3.4 / 1.1 |
| Fixed/Worth | .0 / .3 / 41.0 | .0 / .2 / 2.7 | .0 / .2 / 1.4 | .1 / .2 / 1.2 | .1 / 1.0 / -.7 | .1 / -.6 / -.1 | .1 / .4 / 10.3 | .1 / .4 / 8.0 |
| Debt/Worth | .5 / 2.4 / -3.4 | .5 / 1.9 / 14.0 | .5 / 1.6 / 6.0 | 1.0 / 1.9 / 7.0 | .6 / 8.8 / -5.6 | 61.3 / -6.2 / -2.8 | .8 / 2.9 / -54.1 | .8 / 2.7 / -72.3 |
| % Profit Before Taxes/Tangible Net Worth | (95) 221.1 / 70.0 / 31.9 | (169) 103.6 / 60.6 / 26.7 | (219) 82.7 / 47.5 / 16.4 | (73) 69.4 / 40.1 / 12.1 | (11) 33.1 / 14.4 / .1 | | (347) 96.4 / 42.0 / 12.0 | (399) 75.2 / 36.8 / 11.6 |
| % Profit Before Taxes/Total Assets | 70.5 / 30.2 / 2.8 | 45.7 / 19.4 / 5.9 | 33.7 / 14.2 / 3.8 | 20.9 / 10.8 / 3.4 | 16.4 / 6.9 / -.4 | 10.7 / 5.2 / -1.7 | 27.8 / 11.2 / 1.5 | 29.3 / 10.7 / .6 |
| Sales/Net Fixed Assets | UND / 106.3 / 26.1 | 495.6 / 85.7 / 20.8 | 214.0 / 55.9 / 16.9 | 163.9 / 54.4 / 18.7 | 71.7 / 28.5 / 6.7 | 146.8 / 16.8 / 6.2 | 167.4 / 43.5 / 15.8 | 165.9 / 43.9 / 14.8 |
| Sales/Total Assets | 10.5 / 6.4 / 3.9 | 5.3 / 3.7 / 2.7 | 4.1 / 2.9 / 2.1 | 3.1 / 2.3 / 1.4 | 2.4 / 1.6 / 1.2 | 2.7 / 1.2 / .8 | 5.0 / 3.3 / 2.1 | 4.7 / 3.4 / 2.0 |
| % Depr., Dep., Amort./Sales | (53) .7 / 1.3 / 3.1 | (105) .3 / .8 / 2.2 | (179) .2 / .7 / 2.0 | (62) .4 / .8 / 2.0 | (16) .6 / 1.2 / 5.2 | (10) .6 / 3.4 / 6.7 | (308) .4 / 1.0 / 2.8 | (346) .4 / 1.0 / 2.4 |
| % Officers', Directors' Owners' Comp/Sales | (72) 3.7 / 8.7 / 15.0 | (82) 2.4 / 5.6 / 8.8 | (74) 1.7 / 3.4 / 6.1 | (10) 1.4 / 5.4 / 13.0 | | | (157) 2.9 / 6.4 / 11.7 | (177) 2.9 / 6.2 / 10.8 |
| Net Sales ($) | 265936M | 1003828M | 3582677M | 4300985M | 2737612M | 5516110M | 12201138M | 13931296M |
| Total Assets ($) | 33134M | 243497M | 1180676M | 1865465M | 1296685M | 2734401M | 5597101M | 6459643M |

M = $ thousand MM = $ million
See Pages 9 through 22 for Explanation of Ratios and Data

## Comparative Historical Data  /  Current Data Sorted by Sales

| | | | Type of Statement | 0-1MM | 1-3MM | 3-5MM | 5-10MM | 10-25MM | 25MM & OVER |
|---|---|---|---|---|---|---|---|---|---|
| 81 | 71 | 67 | Unqualified | | | 2 | 9 | 21 | 35 |
| 68 | 78 | 77 | Reviewed | | 4 | 8 | 18 | 32 | 15 |
| 47 | 45 | 59 | Compiled | 2 | 7 | 7 | 24 | 14 | 5 |
| 128 | 170 | 182 | Tax Returns | 39 | 52 | 29 | 34 | 24 | 4 |
| 294 | 301 | 344 | Other | 26 | 62 | 48 | 74 | 67 | 67 |
| 4/1/09- 3/31/10 ALL | 4/1/10- 3/31/11 ALL | 4/1/11- 3/31/12 ALL | | 45 (4/1-9/30/11) | | | 684 (10/1/11-3/31/12) | | |
| 618 | 665 | 729 | **NUMBER OF STATEMENTS** | 67 | 125 | 94 | 159 | 158 | 126 |
| % | % | % | **ASSETS** | % | % | % | % | % | % |
| 16.9 | 19.6 | 20.5 | Cash & Equivalents | 29.2 | 26.7 | 19.4 | 19.1 | 17.3 | 16.3 |
| 42.1 | 41.3 | 41.6 | Trade Receivables (net) | 16.2 | 37.1 | 41.1 | 44.3 | 50.7 | 45.2 |
| 4.2 | 3.2 | 3.5 | Inventory | 2.2 | 2.6 | 4.7 | 3.9 | 3.1 | 4.4 |
| 4.3 | 4.6 | 3.9 | All Other Current | 1.9 | 3.1 | 1.8 | 3.3 | 4.1 | 7.6 |
| 67.5 | 68.7 | 69.5 | Total Current | 49.5 | 69.6 | 67.1 | 70.6 | 75.1 | 73.5 |
| 15.0 | 14.9 | 14.5 | Fixed Assets (net) | 35.2 | 14.6 | 15.7 | 12.8 | 11.6 | 8.4 |
| 8.8 | 7.9 | 6.8 | Intangibles (net) | 7.2 | 6.1 | 4.7 | 7.2 | 5.0 | 10.7 |
| 8.7 | 8.5 | 9.2 | All Other Non-Current | 8.1 | 9.8 | 12.5 | 9.5 | 8.3 | 7.4 |
| 100.0 | 100.0 | 100.0 | Total | 100.0 | 100.0 | 100.0 | 100.0 | 100.0 | 100.0 |
| | | | **LIABILITIES** | | | | | | |
| 14.8 | 13.8 | 12.0 | Notes Payable-Short Term | 19.0 | 19.3 | 13.8 | 9.4 | 7.6 | 8.5 |
| 4.1 | 2.8 | 2.7 | Cur. Mat.-L.T.D. | 3.8 | 3.1 | 2.0 | 3.0 | 2.7 | 2.0 |
| 15.7 | 15.2 | 15.1 | Trade Payables | 9.6 | 12.2 | 13.8 | 15.4 | 16.2 | 19.8 |
| .2 | .4 | .3 | Income Taxes Payable | .0 | .0 | .3 | .4 | .4 | .5 |
| 18.4 | 19.1 | 16.6 | All Other Current | 25.7 | 14.2 | 12.5 | 15.7 | 16.5 | 18.3 |
| 53.3 | 51.1 | 46.6 | Total Current | 58.0 | 48.9 | 42.4 | 43.8 | 43.4 | 49.1 |
| 16.1 | 13.0 | 12.9 | Long-Term Debt | 25.2 | 18.1 | 8.7 | 11.0 | 10.7 | 9.7 |
| .2 | .3 | .3 | Deferred Taxes | .0 | .0 | .2 | .3 | .3 | .7 |
| 11.1 | 9.5 | 10.1 | All Other Non-Current | 19.4 | 10.9 | 16.3 | 9.7 | 6.8 | 4.7 |
| 19.3 | 26.1 | 30.0 | Net Worth | -2.8 | 22.1 | 32.5 | 35.1 | 38.8 | 35.8 |
| 100.0 | 100.0 | 100.0 | Total Liabilities & Net Worth | 100.0 | 100.0 | 100.0 | 100.0 | 100.0 | 100.0 |
| | | | **INCOME DATA** | | | | | | |
| 100.0 | 100.0 | 100.0 | Net Sales | 100.0 | 100.0 | 100.0 | 100.0 | 100.0 | 100.0 |
| | | | Gross Profit | | | | | | |
| 94.4 | 91.7 | 91.4 | Operating Expenses | 81.9 | 89.8 | 94.2 | 91.6 | 93.0 | 93.7 |
| 5.6 | 8.3 | 8.6 | Operating Profit | 18.1 | 10.2 | 5.8 | 8.4 | 7.0 | 6.3 |
| 1.4 | 1.4 | 1.1 | All Other Expenses (net) | 6.1 | .6 | .5 | .6 | .5 | 1.0 |
| 4.2 | 6.9 | 7.5 | Profit Before Taxes | 12.0 | 9.6 | 5.3 | 7.8 | 6.5 | 5.3 |
| | | | **RATIOS** | | | | | | |
| 2.7 | 2.8 | 3.2 | | 2.3 | 4.2 | 3.3 | 3.4 | 3.2 | 2.3 |
| 1.5 | 1.4 | 1.7 | Current | 1.2 | 2.1 | 1.5 | 1.8 | 1.9 | 1.5 |
| .9 | 1.0 | 1.0 | | .2 | .9 | 1.0 | 1.0 | 1.2 | 1.1 |
| 2.3 | 2.4 | 3.1 | | 2.3 | 4.1 | 3.0 | 3.1 | 3.1 | 2.0 |
| 1.2 (664) | 1.3 | 1.4 | Quick | 1.2 | 1.8 | 1.4 | 1.5 | 1.6 | 1.3 |
| .7 | .8 | .9 | | .2 | .8 | .9 | 1.0 | 1.0 | .9 |
| 26  14.1 | 17  21.7 | 23  16.1 | | 0  UND | 4  93.6 | 21  17.2 | 27  13.6 | 39  9.3 | 41  8.9 |
| 49  7.5 | 47  7.8 | 47  7.7 | Sales/Receivables | 0  UND | 41  8.8 | 41  8.9 | 51  7.2 | 54  6.7 | 55  6.6 |
| 70  5.2 | 68  5.3 | 69  5.3 | | 30  12.2 | 68  5.4 | 60  6.1 | 69  5.3 | 76  4.8 | 74  4.9 |
| | | | Cost of Sales/Inventory | | | | | | |
| | | | Cost of Sales/Payables | | | | | | |
| 7.1 | 7.1 | 6.2 | | 10.1 | 5.6 | 7.7 | 5.9 | 6.2 | 6.6 |
| 16.2 | 16.9 | 14.4 | Sales/Working Capital | 100.4 | 11.7 | 19.0 | 11.5 | 11.2 | 14.1 |
| -98.8 | -256.5 | 239.5 | | -6.2 | -107.5 | UND | 113.7 | 40.8 | 41.8 |
| 24.4 | 42.0 | 40.3 | | 25.3 | 29.5 | 25.6 | 69.2 | 37.9 | 55.0 |
| (487) 5.3 | (507) 7.5 | (533) 10.0 | EBIT/Interest | (33) 9.4 | (86) 8.6 | (69) 5.3 | (125) 10.4 | (121) 16.6 | (99) 9.4 |
| 1.0 | 1.8 | 2.3 | | 4.2 | 1.5 | 1.6 | 2.6 | 2.5 | 2.2 |
| 14.4 | 10.7 | 10.0 | | | | | 63.0 | 11.2 | 8.6 |
| (42) 3.8 | (63) 2.8 | (57) 4.2 | Net Profit + Depr., Dep., Amort./Cur. Mat. L/T/D | | | | (11) 8.2 | (15) 4.4 | (23) 4.2 |
| 1.4 | .9 | 1.9 | | | | | 3.2 | 2.7 | 2.8 |
| .1 | .1 | .0 | | .0 | .0 | .0 | .0 | .0 | .1 |
| .3 | .3 | .2 | Fixed/Worth | 1.4 | .3 | .3 | .1 | .2 | .2 |
| 37.3 | 5.3 | 2.7 | | -26.1 | UND | 1.2 | 2.5 | 1.2 | 2.6 |
| .7 | .6 | .6 | | 1.3 | .5 | .5 | .6 | .5 | .9 |
| 2.7 | 2.3 | 1.9 | Debt/Worth | 8.9 | 2.3 | 1.6 | 1.7 | 1.5 | 2.2 |
| -70.9 | 45.6 | 22.7 | | -2.7 | -9.1 | 8.2 | 8.1 | 4.6 | 105.4 |
| 77.7 | 91.4 | 95.7 | | 291.7 | 108.6 | 95.8 | 97.4 | 90.3 | 68.4 |
| (461) 33.4 | (506) 51.0 | (572) 50.4 | % Profit Before Taxes/Tangible Net Worth | (41) 57.9 | (89) 54.3 | (78) 49.2 | (129) 55.8 | (137) 51.2 | (98) 42.0 |
| 7.4 | 19.8 | 17.7 | | 5.8 | 25.0 | 13.6 | 28.5 | 18.9 | 15.0 |
| 24.3 | 34.3 | 39.1 | | 77.6 | 52.2 | 37.8 | 39.1 | 38.3 | 21.2 |
| 8.4 | 13.2 | 16.6 | % Profit Before Taxes/Total Assets | 23.9 | 19.8 | 13.2 | 19.0 | 17.7 | 10.7 |
| .5 | 3.2 | 3.7 | | 1.0 | 3.9 | 2.7 | 6.1 | 4.6 | 3.4 |
| 172.4 | 183.0 | 317.7 | | UND | 912.3 | 503.0 | 292.8 | 328.8 | 190.4 |
| 52.2 | 58.3 | 65.3 | Sales/Net Fixed Assets | 30.4 | 62.5 | 72.5 | 67.8 | 84.3 | 64.1 |
| 15.9 | 18.6 | 19.1 | | 4.8 | 17.9 | 17.4 | 19.8 | 24.6 | 26.8 |
| 4.9 | 5.3 | 5.0 | | 8.0 | 5.9 | 5.7 | 4.7 | 5.0 | 4.1 |
| 3.2 | 3.3 | 3.3 | Sales/Total Assets | 3.4 | 3.6 | 3.8 | 3.2 | 3.2 | 3.0 |
| 1.9 | 2.2 | 2.2 | | 1.6 | 2.2 | 2.7 | 2.3 | 2.2 | 1.7 |
| .3 | .3 | .3 | | 1.7 | .7 | .3 | .3 | .2 | .3 |
| (387) .8 | (402) .9 | (425) .9 | % Depr., Dep., Amort./Sales | (34) 3.5 | (50) 1.3 | (47) 1.0 | (96) .8 | (102) .6 | (96) .7 |
| 2.5 | 2.3 | 2.2 | | 18.6 | 4.3 | 2.2 | 1.9 | 2.0 | 1.5 |
| 2.2 | 2.8 | 2.4 | | 9.3 | 5.5 | 2.6 | 2.2 | 1.5 | .7 |
| (201) 5.6 | (246) 6.0 | (240) 5.3 | % Officers', Directors' Owners' Comp/Sales | (28) 14.4 | (51) 9.0 | (35) 4.9 | (59) 3.9 | (47) 2.6 | (20) 2.7 |
| 10.2 | 10.7 | 9.9 | | 18.1 | 12.9 | 7.6 | 6.2 | 6.1 | 5.5 |
| 14904573M | 17327406M | 17407148M | Net Sales ($) | 36715M | 238553M | 372091M | 1119370M | 2444615M | 13195804M |
| 7623524M | 7531513M | 7353858M | Total Assets ($) | 26233M | 86301M | 132868M | 443624M | 933015M | 5731817M |

M = $ thousand     MM = $ million
See Pages 9 through 22 for Explanation of Ratios and Data

## Current Data Sorted by Assets

## Comparative Historical Data

| | | | | | | Type of Statement | | |
|---|---|---|---|---|---|---|---|---|
| 1 | 9 | 49 | 42 | 13 | 17 | Unqualified | 88 | 108 |
| 1 | 18 | 42 | 12 | | | Reviewed | 52 | 73 |
| 16 | 25 | 36 | 4 | | 1 | Compiled | 49 | 46 |
| 103 | 45 | 30 | 5 | 1 | 1 | Tax Returns | 71 | 129 |
| 64 | 106 | 139 | 55 | 13 | 20 | Other | 210 | 248 |
| | 89 (4/1-9/30/11) | | 779 (10/1/11-3/31/12) | | | | 4/1/07-3/31/08 | 4/1/08-3/31/09 |
| 0-500M | 500M-2MM | 2-10MM | 10-50MM | 50-100MM | 100-250MM | | ALL | ALL |
| 185 | 203 | 296 | 118 | 27 | 39 | **NUMBER OF STATEMENTS** | 470 | 604 |
| % | % | % | % | % | % | **ASSETS** | % | % |
| 36.5 | 20.8 | 17.0 | 17.0 | 12.9 | 18.4 | Cash & Equivalents | 19.6 | 19.6 |
| 15.7 | 34.9 | 42.5 | 42.7 | 29.7 | 26.7 | Trade Receivables (net) | 37.3 | 36.2 |
| 1.6 | 1.7 | 1.6 | 2.1 | 2.3 | 1.2 | Inventory | 2.0 | 2.1 |
| 4.9 | 5.4 | 6.9 | 6.4 | 14.7 | 8.4 | All Other Current | 5.8 | 6.6 |
| 58.7 | 62.9 | 67.9 | 68.2 | 59.7 | 54.7 | Total Current | 64.8 | 64.4 |
| 17.8 | 14.6 | 12.2 | 12.3 | 9.4 | 13.5 | Fixed Assets (net) | 15.2 | 17.0 |
| 4.5 | 6.3 | 6.1 | 8.3 | 21.9 | 17.7 | Intangibles (net) | 7.4 | 6.6 |
| 19.1 | 16.3 | 13.8 | 11.1 | 9.0 | 14.1 | All Other Non-Current | 12.6 | 12.0 |
| 100.0 | 100.0 | 100.0 | 100.0 | 100.0 | 100.0 | Total | 100.0 | 100.0 |
| | | | | | | **LIABILITIES** | | |
| 30.0 | 12.4 | 7.9 | 9.1 | 9.8 | 4.4 | Notes Payable-Short Term | 14.2 | 15.6 |
| 6.4 | 2.1 | 2.3 | 2.4 | 3.0 | 3.2 | Cur. Mat.-L.T.D. | 4.1 | 2.9 |
| 7.8 | 10.4 | 11.6 | 13.2 | 7.1 | 7.4 | Trade Payables | 10.1 | 9.5 |
| .3 | .2 | .8 | .9 | .4 | 1.1 | Income Taxes Payable | .8 | .7 |
| 23.4 | 18.7 | 20.0 | 19.3 | 21.2 | 21.5 | All Other Current | 20.6 | 22.4 |
| 67.8 | 43.8 | 42.5 | 44.9 | 41.5 | 37.7 | Total Current | 49.8 | 51.1 |
| 16.3 | 13.3 | 8.3 | 8.6 | 16.5 | 21.6 | Long-Term Debt | 11.7 | 11.7 |
| .0 | .2 | .4 | .2 | .5 | 1.2 | Deferred Taxes | .5 | .4 |
| 12.1 | 5.8 | 6.0 | 5.4 | 10.4 | 3.1 | All Other Non-Current | 8.2 | 5.8 |
| 3.8 | 36.9 | 42.7 | 40.9 | 31.0 | 36.4 | Net Worth | 29.8 | 31.0 |
| 100.0 | 100.0 | 100.0 | 100.0 | 100.0 | 100.0 | Total Liabilities & Net Worth | 100.0 | 100.0 |
| | | | | | | **INCOME DATA** | | |
| 100.0 | 100.0 | 100.0 | 100.0 | 100.0 | 100.0 | Net Sales | 100.0 | 100.0 |
| | | | | | | Gross Profit | | |
| 83.0 | 88.1 | 88.4 | 90.3 | 91.5 | 91.3 | Operating Expenses | 90.1 | 89.6 |
| 17.0 | 11.9 | 11.6 | 9.7 | 8.5 | 8.7 | Operating Profit | 9.9 | 10.4 |
| 1.8 | .9 | 1.5 | 1.9 | 1.4 | 3.2 | All Other Expenses (net) | 1.6 | 2.0 |
| 15.2 | 11.1 | 10.1 | 7.8 | 7.2 | 5.4 | Profit Before Taxes | 8.3 | 8.4 |
| | | | | | | **RATIOS** | | |
| 3.9 | 4.5 | 3.0 | 2.3 | 2.0 | 2.4 | | 3.0 | 2.6 |
| 1.2 | 1.7 | 1.7 | 1.6 | 1.4 | 1.5 | Current | 1.5 | 1.5 |
| .4 | .8 | 1.0 | 1.1 | 1.2 | 1.2 | | 1.0 | 1.0 |
| 3.8 | 3.7 | 3.0 | 2.2 | 1.6 | 2.1 | | 2.7 | 2.3 |
| 1.0 | 1.5 | 1.5 | 1.3 | (26) 1.3 | 1.1 | Quick | 1.3 | 1.3 |
| .3 | .7 | .8 | .9 | .7 | .8 | | .8 | .8 |
| 0 UND | 0 UND | 18 20.7 | 38 9.7 | 31 11.8 | 36 10.0 | | 7 50.5 | 6 57.9 |
| 0 UND | 36 10.0 | 47 7.8 | 63 5.8 | 65 5.6 | 59 6.2 | Sales/Receivables | 48 7.5 | 45 8.1 |
| 26 14.1 | 61 6.0 | 72 5.1 | 78 4.7 | 81 4.5 | 83 4.4 | | 76 4.8 | 70 5.2 |
| | | | | | | Cost of Sales/Inventory | | |
| | | | | | | Cost of Sales/Payables | | |
| 10.8 | 5.7 | 5.3 | 5.4 | 5.7 | 3.2 | | 5.7 | 7.2 |
| 131.0 | 15.3 | 10.7 | 12.5 | 11.2 | 7.0 | Sales/Working Capital | 15.7 | 15.9 |
| -15.0 | -71.3 | 999.8 | 98.0 | 19.0 | 21.6 | | -388.9 | -304.4 |
| 43.0 | 62.8 | 68.8 | 52.8 | 35.5 | 98.9 | | 25.6 | 29.9 |
| (96) 9.2 | (145) 12.6 | (215) 16.7 | (85) 24.7 | (24) 7.1 | (32) 11.0 | EBIT/Interest | (357) 6.7 | (451) 8.0 |
| .9 | 1.8 | 2.6 | 3.6 | 1.4 | 1.9 | | 2.0 | 2.1 |
| | 5.9 | 9.9 | 6.8 | | | | 18.2 | 16.8 |
| | (11) 2.3 | (37) 3.0 | (26) 2.5 | | | Net Profit + Depr., Dep., Amort./Cur. Mat. L/T/D | (52) 4.2 | (74) 4.5 |
| | -.7 | .9 | .8 | | | | 1.5 | 1.1 |
| .0 | .0 | .0 | .1 | .1 | .2 | | .1 | .1 |
| .3 | .2 | .2 | .2 | .4 | .7 | Fixed/Worth | .3 | .3 |
| UND | 1.1 | .8 | 1.0 | -1.3 | -1.2 | | 2.0 | 2.3 |
| .3 | .4 | .4 | .7 | 1.3 | .6 | | .7 | .7 |
| 2.8 | 1.3 | 1.4 | 1.7 | 5.7 | 2.3 | Debt/Worth | 2.3 | 2.0 |
| -4.8 | 9.2 | 4.8 | 7.2 | -9.9 | -5.2 | | 12.7 | 12.4 |
| 251.5 | 108.9 | 81.2 | 79.2 | 94.2 | 70.5 | | 81.8 | 90.4 |
| (122) 100.0 | (167) 51.9 | (252) 44.9 | (106) 45.2 | (19) 30.7 | (28) 23.4 | % Profit Before Taxes/Tangible Net Worth | (375) 37.9 | (495) 38.7 |
| 22.4 | 12.2 | 15.2 | 14.4 | 13.9 | 6.2 | | 11.0 | 10.8 |
| 118.5 | 47.3 | 37.0 | 27.4 | 14.5 | 13.9 | | 30.5 | 35.1 |
| 45.8 | 17.2 | 15.4 | 13.8 | 8.2 | 5.6 | % Profit Before Taxes/Total Assets | 12.1 | 11.5 |
| 1.8 | 2.9 | 3.9 | 4.2 | 1.8 | .9 | | 3.0 | 1.4 |
| UND | 339.4 | 214.4 | 129.1 | 111.6 | 61.6 | | 135.3 | 128.8 |
| 165.4 | 79.1 | 60.7 | 49.4 | 33.3 | 17.9 | Sales/Net Fixed Assets | 44.1 | 46.0 |
| 24.9 | 23.2 | 22.6 | 19.9 | 16.6 | 4.3 | | 14.6 | 14.0 |
| 13.7 | 4.7 | 4.4 | 3.4 | 2.3 | 1.7 | | 4.3 | 4.6 |
| 5.4 | 3.1 | 3.0 | 2.4 | 1.9 | 1.2 | Sales/Total Assets | 2.8 | 2.9 |
| 2.6 | 1.7 | 1.9 | 1.6 | 1.1 | .5 | | 1.6 | 1.8 |
| .3 | .3 | .3 | .4 | .6 | .7 | | .4 | .4 |
| (64) .9 | (115) .8 | (206) .7 | (92) .8 | (16) 1.3 | (22) 1.8 | % Depr., Dep., Amort./Sales | (315) 1.0 | (407) 1.0 |
| 1.8 | 2.5 | 1.9 | 2.3 | 3.3 | 3.1 | | 2.1 | 2.1 |
| 6.7 | 3.5 | 2.2 | .5 | | | | 3.4 | 3.4 |
| (76) 12.2 | (69) 8.1 | (65) 5.8 | (11) 1.8 | | | % Officers', Directors' Owners' Comp/Sales | (119) 8.6 | (166) 6.9 |
| 24.3 | 16.3 | 14.4 | 14.4 | | | | 16.7 | 12.8 |
| 283896M | 869215M | 5080344M | 8349345M | 4290964M | 8117025M | Net Sales ($) | 16782558M | 22653996M |
| 36341M | 229690M | 1389165M | 2552508M | 2020394M | 6509081M | Total Assets ($) | 8546200M | 9406455M |

M = $ thousand    MM = $ million
See Pages 9 through 22 for Explanation of Ratios and Data

## Comparative Historical Data | Current Data Sorted by Sales

| | 4/1/09-3/31/10 ALL | 4/1/10-3/31/11 ALL | 4/1/11-3/31/12 ALL | Type of Statement | 0-1MM | 1-3MM | 3-5MM | 5-10MM | 10-25MM | 25MM & OVER |
|---|---|---|---|---|---|---|---|---|---|---|
| | 130 | 129 | 131 | Unqualified | 4 | 2 | 7 | 12 | 36 | 70 |
| | 78 | 73 | 73 | Reviewed | 2 | 2 | 10 | 15 | 26 | 18 |
| | 61 | 66 | 82 | Compiled | 12 | 16 | 7 | 18 | 23 | 6 |
| | 137 | 139 | 185 | Tax Returns | 68 | 46 | 27 | 21 | 17 | 6 |
| | 310 | 351 | 397 | Other | 63 | 63 | 38 | 59 | 78 | 96 |
| | | | | | 89 (4/1-9/30/11) | | | 779 (10/1/11-3/31/12) | | |
| NUMBER OF STATEMENTS | 716 | 758 | 868 | | 149 | 129 | 89 | 125 | 180 | 196 |
| | % | % | % | ASSETS | % | % | % | % | % | % |
| Cash & Equivalents | 20.4 | 20.0 | 22.0 | | 30.1 | 25.5 | 22.2 | 21.8 | 18.1 | 17.2 |
| Trade Receivables (net) | 34.8 | 35.3 | 33.9 | | 11.6 | 24.1 | 32.6 | 40.0 | 48.6 | 40.6 |
| Inventory | 2.2 | 1.9 | 1.7 | | 1.8 | 1.6 | 1.2 | 1.7 | 2.0 | 1.6 |
| All Other Current | 7.0 | 6.8 | 6.4 | | 4.2 | 6.0 | 4.6 | 5.9 | 6.1 | 9.6 |
| Total Current | 64.4 | 64.0 | 64.0 | | 47.6 | 57.2 | 60.6 | 69.5 | 74.8 | 69.0 |
| Fixed Assets (net) | 16.5 | 15.7 | 13.9 | | 22.1 | 17.1 | 14.2 | 12.4 | 9.8 | 10.3 |
| Intangibles (net) | 6.5 | 7.1 | 7.1 | | 6.6 | 5.9 | 6.2 | 5.0 | 5.9 | 11.2 |
| All Other Non-Current | 12.6 | 13.1 | 15.0 | | 23.7 | 19.9 | 19.1 | 13.1 | 9.6 | 9.5 |
| Total | 100.0 | 100.0 | 100.0 | | 100.0 | 100.0 | 100.0 | 100.0 | 100.0 | 100.0 |
| | | | | LIABILITIES | | | | | | |
| Notes Payable-Short Term | 14.1 | 14.3 | 13.7 | | 20.3 | 19.1 | 19.6 | 13.2 | 8.7 | 7.6 |
| Cur. Mat.-L.T.D. | 3.4 | 2.8 | 3.2 | | 3.5 | 6.5 | 1.9 | 1.9 | 2.9 | 2.4 |
| Trade Payables | 10.5 | 11.4 | 10.4 | | 6.3 | 8.6 | 11.8 | 8.7 | 11.2 | 14.3 |
| Income Taxes Payable | .4 | .6 | .6 | | .3 | .0 | .8 | .5 | .6 | 1.0 |
| All Other Current | 20.0 | 21.4 | 20.4 | | 20.6 | 16.7 | 17.9 | 18.0 | 22.7 | 23.4 |
| Total Current | 48.4 | 50.5 | 48.3 | | 51.1 | 50.9 | 51.9 | 42.3 | 46.1 | 48.7 |
| Long-Term Debt | 12.0 | 11.8 | 12.1 | | 17.0 | 19.1 | 16.5 | 10.2 | 5.1 | 9.2 |
| Deferred Taxes | .5 | .4 | .3 | | .1 | .0 | .3 | .2 | .5 | .5 |
| All Other Non-Current | 8.1 | 8.1 | 7.2 | | 12.1 | 7.1 | 4.8 | 5.6 | 7.2 | 5.5 |
| Net Worth | 31.0 | 29.2 | 32.2 | | 19.8 | 22.9 | 26.4 | 41.6 | 41.0 | 36.0 |
| Total Liabilities & Net Worth | 100.0 | 100.0 | 100.0 | | 100.0 | 100.0 | 100.0 | 100.0 | 100.0 | 100.0 |
| | | | | INCOME DATA | | | | | | |
| Net Sales | 100.0 | 100.0 | 100.0 | | 100.0 | 100.0 | 100.0 | 100.0 | 100.0 | 100.0 |
| Gross Profit | | | | | | | | | | |
| Operating Expenses | 90.2 | 90.0 | 87.7 | | 74.6 | 88.8 | 87.8 | 88.1 | 92.0 | 92.5 |
| Operating Profit | 9.8 | 10.0 | 12.3 | | 25.4 | 11.2 | 12.2 | 11.9 | 8.0 | 7.5 |
| All Other Expenses (net) | 1.8 | 1.6 | 1.6 | | 5.1 | 1.0 | .1 | 1.1 | .4 | 1.2 |
| Profit Before Taxes | 8.0 | 8.5 | 10.8 | | 20.3 | 10.1 | 12.1 | 10.8 | 7.6 | 6.3 |
| | | | | RATIOS | | | | | | |
| Current | 2.8 | 2.9 | 3.1 | | 3.7 | 4.6 | 3.6 | 3.8 | 3.2 | 2.2 |
| | 1.5 | 1.6 | 1.6 | | 1.0 | 1.4 | 1.7 | 1.7 | 1.8 | 1.5 |
| | .9 | .9 | .9 | | .3 | .7 | .8 | 1.1 | 1.2 | 1.1 |
| Quick | 2.4 | 2.5 | 2.8 | | 3.7 | 3.9 | 3.6 | 3.4 | 3.1 | 2.0 |
| | 1.3 (757) | 1.3 (867) | 1.3 | | .9 | 1.2 | 1.6 | 1.6 | 1.6 (195) | 1.2 |
| | .7 | .7 | .7 | | .2 | .6 | .6 | .8 | 1.0 | .8 |
| Sales/Receivables | 8 47.1 | 8 44.6 | 0 UND | | 0 UND | 0 UND | 0 UND | 9 38.8 | 29 12.6 | 31 11.7 |
| | 42 8.6 | 45 8.2 | 39 9.3 | | 0 UND | 14 25.8 | 36 10.2 | 48 7.6 | 55 6.6 | 56 6.5 |
| | 67 5.5 | 72 5.1 | 68 5.4 | | 30 12.3 | 58 6.3 | 58 6.3 | 70 5.2 | 74 4.9 | 73 5.0 |
| Cost of Sales/Inventory | | | | | | | | | | |
| Cost of Sales/Payables | | | | | | | | | | |
| Sales/Working Capital | 5.8 | 5.8 | 5.8 | | 6.3 | 5.0 | 6.8 | 4.8 | 5.6 | 6.9 |
| | 14.5 | 14.9 | 14.8 | | UND | 31.3 | 16.5 | 11.0 | 10.7 | 13.0 |
| | -125.4 | -94.5 | -112.1 | | -6.3 | -14.8 | -71.8 | 130.2 | 52.3 | 157.4 |
| EBIT/Interest | 31.0 | 43.5 | 59.2 | | 20.0 | 44.8 | 71.2 | 70.5 | 91.1 | 71.9 |
| | (515) 8.4 | (533) 10.0 | (597) 15.0 | | (71) 4.7 | (79) 10.6 | (68) 17.0 | (82) 6.6 | (143) 17.1 | (154) 23.1 |
| | 1.4 | 2.1 | 2.2 | | .7 | 1.3 | 2.2 | 1.0 | 2.8 | 5.1 |
| Net Profit + Depr., Dep., Amort./Cur. Mat. L/T/D | 8.3 | 9.9 | 9.9 | | | | | | 9.9 | 15.6 |
| | (73) 2.5 | (74) 2.8 | (89) 2.7 | | | | | | (33) 2.7 | (36) 3.1 |
| | .4 | 1.3 | .6 | | | | | | .6 | .9 |
| Fixed/Worth | .1 | .1 | .0 | | .0 | .0 | .0 | .0 | .0 | .1 |
| | .3 | .3 | .2 | | .1 | .3 | .2 | .1 | .2 | .2 |
| | 2.8 | 2.9 | 1.5 | | 8.3 | 4.7 | 1.3 | .6 | .6 | 1.5 |
| Debt/Worth | .6 | .6 | .4 | | .3 | .4 | .4 | .4 | .4 | .8 |
| | 1.9 | 2.0 | 1.6 | | 1.7 | 2.1 | 1.0 | 1.4 | 1.2 | 2.2 |
| | 16.0 | 21.1 | 16.4 | | -19.9 | -14.0 | UND | 3.7 | 5.4 | 16.5 |
| % Profit Before Taxes/Tangible Net Worth | 80.8 | 94.1 | 108.9 | | 130.8 | 129.7 | 126.4 | 95.0 | 91.1 | 116.1 |
| | (568) 33.7 | (597) 38.3 | (694) 50.3 | | (110) 33.7 | (95) 46.4 | (67) 61.5 | (107) 41.3 | (154) 48.8 | (161) 56.6 |
| | 9.1 | 10.7 | 14.4 | | 4.3 | 13.5 | 14.6 | 13.8 | 15.8 | 20.4 |
| % Profit Before Taxes/Total Assets | 31.9 | 32.0 | 44.4 | | 69.6 | 52.0 | 56.5 | 47.7 | 39.7 | 28.9 |
| | 10.4 | 12.4 | 15.6 | | 14.7 | 15.7 | 17.6 | 19.1 | 17.9 | 13.9 |
| | 1.2 | 1.9 | 3.1 | | .1 | 2.0 | 3.1 | 2.7 | 5.5 | 4.2 |
| Sales/Net Fixed Assets | 137.0 | 148.0 | 287.6 | | UND | 627.9 | 223.1 | 209.2 | 250.0 | 129.3 |
| | 43.0 | 49.3 | 64.4 | | 121.3 | 56.7 | 73.4 | 65.7 | 67.2 | 56.3 |
| | 15.0 | 15.5 | 20.2 | | 7.5 | 15.1 | 22.6 | 25.8 | 27.6 | 20.2 |
| Sales/Total Assets | 4.7 | 4.6 | 4.9 | | 4.7 | 5.2 | 6.3 | 4.5 | 5.0 | 4.7 |
| | 2.8 | 2.9 | 3.0 | | 1.9 | 2.9 | 3.4 | 3.2 | 3.3 | 2.7 |
| | 1.5 | 1.6 | 1.7 | | .5 | 1.5 | 1.8 | 2.1 | 2.5 | 1.6 |
| % Depr., Dep., Amort./Sales | .5 | .4 | .4 | | .9 | .4 | .3 | .3 | .3 | .4 |
| | (467) 1.0 | (476) 1.0 | (515) .8 | | (52) 2.2 | (62) 1.1 | (48) .9 | (78) .7 | (133) .7 | (142) .7 |
| | 2.4 | 2.3 | 2.1 | | 10.7 | 2.7 | 2.4 | 1.6 | 1.4 | 1.7 |
| % Officers', Directors' Owners' Comp/Sales | 3.7 | 3.1 | 3.2 | | 9.0 | 7.3 | 5.6 | 3.7 | 1.2 | .5 |
| | (191) 10.2 | (189) 6.8 | (227) 8.2 | | (44) 17.2 | (48) 12.2 | (36) 8.3 | (34) 7.4 | (44) 2.8 | (21) 3.1 |
| | 17.3 | 16.3 | 17.5 | | 27.7 | 25.4 | 14.5 | 15.7 | 6.3 | 6.1 |
| Net Sales ($) | 20531091M | 20173293M | 26990789M | | 65837M | 239396M | 350622M | 890218M | 2833047M | 22611669M |
| Total Assets ($) | 10385864M | 10065959M | 12737179M | | 104826M | 247057M | 151676M | 651439M | 1406653M | 10175528M |

© RMA 2012   M = $ thousand   MM = $ million
See Pages 9 through 22 for Explanation of Ratios and Data

## Current Data Sorted by Assets      Comparative Historical Data

| 0-500M | 500M-2MM | 2-10MM | 10-50MM | 50-100MM | 100-250MM | Type of Statement | 4/1/07-3/31/08 ALL | 4/1/08-3/31/09 ALL |
|---|---|---|---|---|---|---|---|---|
| 2 | 3 | 12 | 7 | 1 | 1 | Unqualified | 20 | 27 |
|  | 3 | 12 | 4 |  |  | Reviewed | 23 | 15 |
| 5 | 7 | 9 |  |  |  | Compiled | 15 | 19 |
| 13 | 6 | 4 | 1 |  |  | Tax Returns | 10 | 18 |
| 5 | 13 | 26 | 11 |  | 5 | Other | 51 | 75 |
|  | 23 (4/1-9/30/11) |  | 127 (10/1/11-3/31/12) |  |  |  |  |  |
| 25 | 32 | 63 | 23 | 1 | 6 | **NUMBER OF STATEMENTS** | 119 | 154 |
| % | % | % | % | % | % | **ASSETS** | % | % |
| 39.8 | 20.2 | 15.2 | 21.4 |  |  | Cash & Equivalents | 16.3 | 20.7 |
| 15.2 | 44.8 | 48.7 | 35.4 |  |  | Trade Receivables (net) | 44.7 | 41.7 |
| .0 | .1 | .1 | 1.8 |  |  | Inventory | .8 | .8 |
| 9.3 | 4.0 | 7.7 | 13.6 |  |  | All Other Current | 4.8 | 6.6 |
| 64.3 | 69.0 | 71.7 | 72.2 |  |  | Total Current | 66.6 | 69.7 |
| 17.5 | 13.3 | 10.8 | 5.1 |  |  | Fixed Assets (net) | 13.5 | 13.6 |
| 10.2 | 10.0 | 7.4 | 13.7 |  |  | Intangibles (net) | 6.2 | 7.4 |
| 8.1 | 7.7 | 10.2 | 9.0 |  |  | All Other Non-Current | 13.6 | 9.3 |
| 100.0 | 100.0 | 100.0 | 100.0 |  |  | Total | 100.0 | 100.0 |
|  |  |  |  |  |  | **LIABILITIES** |  |  |
| 54.1 | 14.0 | 10.1 | 8.6 |  |  | Notes Payable-Short Term | 21.3 | 15.8 |
| 3.8 | 1.0 | 2.3 | 1.7 |  |  | Cur. Mat.-L.T.D. | 3.2 | 2.0 |
| 16.8 | 7.9 | 12.0 | 11.6 |  |  | Trade Payables | 10.4 | 8.7 |
| .0 | .1 | 1.6 | .4 |  |  | Income Taxes Payable | .7 | .5 |
| 21.6 | 25.4 | 26.6 | 38.3 |  |  | All Other Current | 27.5 | 23.2 |
| 96.3 | 48.4 | 52.6 | 60.7 |  |  | Total Current | 63.2 | 50.2 |
| 11.8 | 10.6 | 6.9 | 5.8 |  |  | Long-Term Debt | 7.4 | 14.7 |
| .0 | .0 | .1 | .9 |  |  | Deferred Taxes | .6 | .4 |
| 3.5 | 15.0 | 9.9 | 5.7 |  |  | All Other Non-Current | 6.3 | 6.2 |
| -11.5 | 26.0 | 30.5 | 26.9 |  |  | Net Worth | 22.7 | 28.5 |
| 100.0 | 100.0 | 100.0 | 100.0 |  |  | Total Liabilties & Net Worth | 100.0 | 100.0 |
|  |  |  |  |  |  | **INCOME DATA** |  |  |
| 100.0 | 100.0 | 100.0 | 100.0 |  |  | Net Sales | 100.0 | 100.0 |
|  |  |  |  |  |  | Gross Profit |  |  |
| 96.1 | 96.2 | 97.8 | 93.3 |  |  | Operating Expenses | 95.7 | 95.4 |
| 3.9 | 3.8 | 2.2 | 6.7 |  |  | Operating Profit | 4.3 | 4.6 |
| -.4 | 1.3 | .4 | 2.5 |  |  | All Other Expenses (net) | .8 | 1.0 |
| 4.3 | 2.6 | 1.8 | 4.3 |  |  | Profit Before Taxes | 3.5 | 3.6 |
|  |  |  |  |  |  | **RATIOS** |  |  |
| 1.5 | 3.7 | 2.4 | 1.6 |  |  |  | 2.4 | 2.6 |
| .6 | 1.9 | 1.4 | 1.2 |  |  | Current | 1.3 | 1.4 |
| .4 | 1.0 | .9 | .9 |  |  |  | .8 | 1.0 |
| 1.5 | 3.7 | 2.2 | 1.3 |  |  |  | 2.2 | 2.5 |
| .5 | 1.6 | 1.2 | 1.0 |  |  | Quick | 1.2 | 1.2 |
| .3 | 1.0 | .8 | .6 |  |  |  | .7 | .8 |
| 0 UND | 7 52.4 | 26 14.2 | 17 21.8 |  |  |  | 12 30.5 | 9 42.1 |
| 0 UND | 34 10.8 | 45 8.2 | 36 10.0 |  |  | Sales/Receivables | 44 8.3 | 36 10.1 |
| 25 14.4 | 60 6.1 | 63 5.8 | 63 5.8 |  |  |  | 62 5.9 | 59 6.2 |
|  |  |  |  |  |  | Cost of Sales/Inventory |  |  |
|  |  |  |  |  |  | Cost of Sales/Payables |  |  |
| 15.7 | 6.1 | 9.4 | 9.8 |  |  |  | 9.0 | 8.4 |
| -72.1 | 13.1 | 26.7 | 28.2 |  |  | Sales/Working Capital | 25.2 | 22.0 |
| -20.3 | UND | -309.5 | -102.3 |  |  |  | -85.1 | -977.9 |
| 18.2 | 42.3 | 32.4 | 43.2 |  |  |  | 19.3 | 21.7 |
| (19) 3.5 | (20) 7.9 | (50) 7.8 | (19) 16.0 |  |  | EBIT/Interest | (97) 4.8 | (123) 6.3 |
| -1.8 | 1.4 | .3 | 4.6 |  |  |  | 1.0 | 1.3 |
|  |  |  |  |  |  |  | 34.8 | 31.0 |
|  |  |  |  |  |  | Net Profit + Depr., Dep., Amort./Cur. Mat. L/T/D | (10) 16.9 | (12) 12.2 |
|  |  |  |  |  |  |  | 3.6 | 1.2 |
| .0 | .0 | .1 | .1 |  |  |  | .1 | .1 |
| .4 | .1 | .2 | .3 |  |  | Fixed/Worth | .3 | .3 |
| -1.9 | -2.4 | 3.6 | 109.9 |  |  |  | 25.0 | 2.1 |
| 1.7 | .4 | .7 | 1.8 |  |  |  | .7 | .8 |
| -11.7 | 1.5 | 2.1 | 4.5 |  |  | Debt/Worth | 2.7 | 1.8 |
| -1.9 | -8.9 | 84.3 | 784.9 |  |  |  | -94.0 | 19.4 |
| 123.2 | 41.1 | 74.1 | 213.3 |  |  |  | 68.0 | 79.6 |
| (11) 64.4 | (23) 20.8 | (48) 20.7 | (18) 49.6 |  |  | % Profit Before Taxes/Tangible Net Worth | (89) 32.8 | (125) 33.8 |
| 28.2 | 1.7 | 2.7 | 22.1 |  |  |  | 4.6 | 5.3 |
| 41.9 | 20.9 | 17.6 | 15.6 |  |  |  | 22.8 | 28.5 |
| 15.9 | 11.9 | 6.3 | 7.3 |  |  | % Profit Before Taxes/Total Assets | 8.9 | 10.1 |
| -2.5 | -2.4 | .1 | 4.1 |  |  |  | 2.6 | .7 |
| UND | 445.2 | 395.4 | 351.5 |  |  |  | 290.0 | 383.8 |
| 90.6 | 133.3 | 107.2 | 112.0 |  |  | Sales/Net Fixed Assets | 71.8 | 76.0 |
| 36.7 | 28.1 | 26.3 | 29.3 |  |  |  | 28.9 | 21.6 |
| 18.2 | 6.9 | 6.7 | 4.3 |  |  |  | 6.7 | 6.9 |
| 5.7 | 4.6 | 4.6 | 2.6 |  |  | Sales/Total Assets | 4.2 | 4.2 |
| 2.9 | 2.7 | 2.6 | 1.2 |  |  |  | 2.5 | 2.1 |
| .5 | .1 | .1 | .1 |  |  |  | .2 | .2 |
| (13) 1.2 | (18) .5 | (44) .3 | (15) .4 |  |  | % Depr., Dep., Amort./Sales | (82) .5 | (106) .6 |
| 2.4 | 1.6 | 1.0 | 1.0 |  |  |  | 1.0 | 1.7 |
| 5.5 |  | .8 |  |  |  |  | 1.4 | 1.9 |
| (15) 17.3 |  | (15) 3.4 |  |  |  | % Officers', Directors' Owners' Comp/Sales | (22) 3.5 | (45) 3.8 |
| 21.7 |  | 13.5 |  |  |  |  | 7.9 | 10.0 |
| 59404M | 200817M | 1778824M | 2023991M | 168922M | 3232385M | Net Sales ($) | 3957832M | 9053837M |
| 6917M | 38187M | 291785M | 539184M | 81906M | 1242557M | Total Assets ($) | 1188674M | 2066991M |

© RMA 2012

**M = $ thousand    MM = $ million**
See Pages 9 through 22 for Explanation of Ratios and Data

## Comparative Historical Data / Current Data Sorted by Sales

| Hist. 4/1/09-3/31/10 ALL | Hist. 4/1/10-3/31/11 ALL | Hist. 4/1/11-3/31/12 ALL | Type of Statement | 0-1MM | 1-3MM | 3-5MM | 5-10MM | 10-25MM | 25MM & OVER |
|---|---|---|---|---|---|---|---|---|---|
| 30 | 24 | 26 | Unqualified | | 2 | 2 | 6 | 7 | 9 |
| 23 | 24 | 19 | Reviewed | | 2 | | 3 | 5 | 9 |
| 14 | 14 | 21 | Compiled | 2 | 2 | 4 | 6 | 4 | 3 |
| 15 | 19 | 24 | Tax Returns | 4 | 8 | 3 | 6 | 2 | 1 |
| 65 | 70 | 60 | Other | 4 | 5 | 5 | 8 | 10 | 28 |
| | | | | | 23 (4/1-9/30/11) | | 127 (10/1/11-3/31/12) | | |
| 147 | 151 | 150 | **NUMBER OF STATEMENTS** | 10 | 19 | 14 | 29 | 28 | 50 |
| % | % | % | **ASSETS** | % | % | % | % | % | % |
| 22.3 | 20.1 | 21.5 | Cash & Equivalents | 23.3 | 36.7 | 23.4 | 17.9 | 18.6 | 18.6 |
| 33.9 | 41.4 | 39.6 | Trade Receivables (net) | 6.6 | 32.0 | 33.3 | 39.6 | 48.8 | 45.7 |
| .5 | 1.3 | .5 | Inventory | .0 | .0 | .2 | .1 | .2 | 1.4 |
| 5.3 | 7.4 | 8.0 | All Other Current | 8.7 | 7.9 | 7.4 | 7.6 | 4.6 | 10.2 |
| 62.1 | 70.2 | 69.6 | Total Current | 38.6 | 76.6 | 64.4 | 65.2 | 72.2 | 75.8 |
| 15.3 | 11.2 | 11.6 | Fixed Assets (net) | 44.7 | 10.7 | 7.0 | 13.3 | 10.5 | 6.2 |
| 10.0 | 9.7 | 9.8 | Intangibles (net) | 11.3 | 6.9 | 21.1 | 8.9 | 6.7 | 9.7 |
| 12.6 | 8.9 | 9.0 | All Other Non-Current | 5.4 | 5.9 | 7.5 | 12.6 | 10.6 | 8.4 |
| 100.0 | 100.0 | 100.0 | Total | 100.0 | 100.0 | 100.0 | 100.0 | 100.0 | 100.0 |
| | | | **LIABILITIES** | | | | | | |
| 16.9 | 19.7 | 17.7 | Notes Payable-Short Term | 22.5 | 36.4 | 28.2 | 12.6 | 16.1 | 10.5 |
| 3.5 | 1.4 | 2.1 | Cur. Mat.-L.T.D. | 1.3 | 3.6 | 5.5 | 1.4 | 1.3 | 1.5 |
| 10.2 | 8.0 | 11.5 | Trade Payables | 29.1 | 7.2 | 6.3 | 13.2 | 7.9 | 11.9 |
| .6 | .4 | .8 | Income Taxes Payable | .0 | .0 | .2 | 1.6 | 1.1 | .9 |
| 25.3 | 25.7 | 27.4 | All Other Current | 19.7 | 29.3 | 16.5 | 30.7 | 25.6 | 30.4 |
| 56.6 | 55.3 | 59.5 | Total Current | 72.6 | 76.5 | 56.8 | 59.5 | 52.1 | 55.2 |
| 13.5 | 8.4 | 8.6 | Long-Term Debt | 34.5 | 3.3 | 19.6 | 3.7 | 8.0 | 5.6 |
| .5 | .4 | .2 | Deferred Taxes | .0 | .0 | .0 | .0 | .2 | .6 |
| 5.4 | 8.1 | 9.3 | All Other Non-Current | .0 | 9.5 | 5.9 | 14.8 | 9.7 | 8.7 |
| 24.0 | 27.7 | 22.3 | Net Worth | -6.7 | 10.7 | 17.6 | 22.1 | 30.0 | 29.8 |
| 100.0 | 100.0 | 100.0 | Total Liabilities & Net Worth | 100.0 | 100.0 | 100.0 | 100.0 | 100.0 | 100.0 |
| | | | **INCOME DATA** | | | | | | |
| 100.0 | 100.0 | 100.0 | Net Sales | 100.0 | 100.0 | 100.0 | 100.0 | 100.0 | 100.0 |
| | | | Gross Profit | | | | | | |
| 94.8 | 94.8 | 96.2 | Operating Expenses | 86.5 | 99.0 | 97.6 | 98.1 | 97.4 | 94.9 |
| 5.2 | 5.2 | 3.8 | Operating Profit | 13.5 | 1.0 | 2.4 | 1.9 | 2.6 | 5.1 |
| 1.5 | .8 | .9 | All Other Expenses (net) | 4.7 | -.5 | 1.0 | -.2 | .4 | 1.5 |
| 3.7 | 4.5 | 2.9 | Profit Before Taxes | 8.8 | 1.5 | 1.3 | 2.1 | 2.1 | 3.6 |
| | | | **RATIOS** | | | | | | |
| 2.5 | 4.0 | 2.4 | Current | 1.0 | 5.0 | 2.2 | 2.6 | 3.5 | 2.2 |
| 1.3 | 1.4 | 1.3 | | .4 | 2.3 | 1.5 | 1.1 | 1.8 | 1.3 |
| .9 | 1.0 | .9 | | .3 | .5 | .7 | .6 | .9 | 1.0 |
| 2.4 | 3.4 | 2.2 | Quick | 1.0 | 5.0 | 2.2 | 2.5 | 3.2 | 1.9 |
| 1.2 | (150) 1.3 | 1.2 | | .4 | 1.9 | 1.4 | 1.1 | 1.6 | 1.2 |
| .8 | .9 | .7 | | .1 | .5 | .3 | .4 | .8 | .9 |
| 9 39.0 | 8 45.5 | 8 48.4 | Sales/Receivables | 0 UND | 4 96.5 | 0 UND | 5 67.0 | 28 12.9 | 16 22.4 |
| 35 10.6 | 40 9.1 | 35 10.3 | | 0 UND | 46 7.9 | 33 11.1 | 33 10.9 | 45 8.1 | 37 9.9 |
| 53 6.9 | 60 6.1 | 57 6.4 | | 23 15.6 | 73 5.0 | 64 5.7 | 72 5.1 | 54 6.8 | 56 6.5 |
| | | | Cost of Sales/Inventory | | | | | | |
| | | | Cost of Sales/Payables | | | | | | |
| 8.7 | 7.9 | 9.3 | Sales/Working Capital | UND | 3.4 | 10.5 | 7.8 | 8.3 | 10.7 |
| 22.5 | 16.7 | 27.0 | | -49.1 | 8.1 | 20.9 | 30.7 | 12.0 | 30.2 |
| -141.8 | -211.3 | -81.0 | | -8.6 | -27.4 | -66.4 | -30.1 | -84.1 | NM |
| 14.9 | 33.0 | 36.9 | EBIT/Interest | | 44.8 | 12.4 | 36.9 | 35.7 | 45.6 |
| (106) 4.1 | (110) 10.5 | (115) 9.2 | | | (12) 6.5 | (12) 3.8 | (19) 13.6 | (25) 6.9 | (41) 13.1 |
| -.1 | 2.2 | 2.1 | | | -15.0 | 1.2 | 2.2 | -.8 | 4.4 |
| 8.5 | 19.7 | | Net Profit + Depr., Dep., Amort./Cur. Mat. L/T/D | | | | | | |
| (12) 2.1 | (13) 2.8 | | | | | | | | |
| -.4 | 1.5 | | | | | | | | |
| .0 | .0 | .0 | Fixed/Worth | .0 | .0 | .1 | .0 | .0 | .1 |
| .3 | .1 | .3 | | 3.8 | .1 | .3 | .1 | .2 | .3 |
| 7.1 | 2.0 | -3.7 | | -6.7 | -3.0 | -.1 | -1.1 | 3.1 | 28.6 |
| .6 | .6 | .8 | Debt/Worth | 2.9 | .2 | 1.1 | .5 | .6 | 1.3 |
| 1.7 | 2.2 | 3.0 | | -19.9 | 2.4 | NM | 1.8 | 2.5 | 3.5 |
| -808.2 | -20.0 | -10.3 | | -1.9 | -3.7 | -2.2 | -4.5 | 38.5 | 259.5 |
| 74.0 | 83.0 | 78.4 | % Profit Before Taxes/Tangible Net Worth | | 75.3 | | 36.6 | 159.6 | 109.8 |
| (110) 28.9 | (112) 26.5 | (105) 28.2 | | | (13) 39.5 | | (20) 15.9 | (22) 36.8 | (39) 45.5 |
| 4.5 | 8.5 | 10.9 | | | -7.1 | | 2.1 | 9.2 | 13.2 |
| 26.0 | 23.6 | 20.6 | % Profit Before Taxes/Total Assets | 43.0 | 31.6 | 16.4 | 17.3 | 26.0 | 18.1 |
| 7.0 | 9.4 | 8.7 | | 7.2 | 19.0 | 10.0 | 7.2 | 7.8 | 8.9 |
| -1.2 | 2.2 | 1.1 | | 3.5 | -8.1 | -1.7 | .5 | -3.5 | 4.1 |
| 364.0 | 999.8 | 405.5 | Sales/Net Fixed Assets | UND | 188.5 | 319.7 | 392.3 | 872.9 | 413.3 |
| 62.5 | 133.4 | 110.9 | | 27.4 | 72.1 | 102.9 | 76.1 | 169.7 | 191.7 |
| 15.3 | 33.1 | 29.8 | | 1.3 | 21.4 | 45.4 | 20.4 | 33.1 | 43.6 |
| 6.5 | 6.2 | 6.9 | Sales/Total Assets | 8.3 | 5.5 | 10.5 | 5.8 | 6.4 | 8.0 |
| 3.7 | 4.2 | 4.2 | | 2.1 | 3.4 | 5.4 | 3.4 | 4.6 | 4.8 |
| 1.8 | 2.2 | 2.2 | | 1.1 | 2.0 | 2.0 | 1.8 | 2.9 | 2.8 |
| .3 | .1 | .1 | % Depr., Dep., Amort./Sales | | .2 | | .1 | .2 | .1 |
| (89) .7 | (85) .7 | (95) .4 | | | (11) 1.0 | | (19) .4 | (17) .4 | (35) .3 |
| 1.9 | 1.5 | 1.6 | | | 2.0 | | 2.2 | .7 | .8 |
| 2.9 | 1.7 | 1.9 | % Officers', Directors' Owners' Comp/Sales | | | | | | |
| (40) 5.4 | (40) 4.8 | (40) 5.3 | | | | | | | |
| 14.9 | 10.3 | 17.1 | | | | | | | |
| 6068615M | 5576264M | 7464343M | Net Sales ($) | 5227M | 36324M | 59733M | 200183M | 453666M | 6709210M |
| 2234487M | 1679920M | 2200536M | Total Assets ($) | 3968M | 15468M | 20191M | 116093M | 153618M | 1891198M |

## Current Data Sorted by Assets      Comparative Historical Data

### Type of Statement

| | 0-500M | 500M-2MM | 2-10MM | 10-50MM | 50-100MM | 100-250MM | | 4/1/07-3/31/08 ALL | 4/1/08-3/31/09 ALL |
|---|---|---|---|---|---|---|---|---|---|
| Unqualified | | | 9 | 12 | 7 | 5 | | 19 | 22 |
| Reviewed | 1 | 4 | 22 | 5 | | | | 12 | 13 |
| Compiled | 3 | 7 | 15 | 4 | | | | 15 | 21 |
| Tax Returns | 10 | 17 | 6 | | | | | 24 | 28 |
| Other | 20 | 26 | 39 | 21 | 1 | 3 | | 67 | 74 |
| | 19 (4/1-9/30/11) | | | 218 (10/1/11-3/31/12) | | | | | |
| **NUMBER OF STATEMENTS** | 34 | 54 | 91 | 42 | 8 | 8 | | 137 | 158 |
| **ASSETS** | % | % | % | % | % | % | | % | % |
| Cash & Equivalents | 33.3 | 21.1 | 17.2 | 15.8 | | | | 18.8 | 17.6 |
| Trade Receivables (net) | 16.6 | 29.8 | 40.4 | 39.3 | | | | 30.7 | 31.5 |
| Inventory | 3.1 | 2.7 | 3.4 | 3.1 | | | | 4.0 | 4.1 |
| All Other Current | 4.4 | 8.1 | 8.5 | 10.2 | | | | 7.8 | 7.3 |
| Total Current | 57.4 | 61.8 | 69.5 | 68.5 | | | | 61.3 | 60.5 |
| Fixed Assets (net) | 18.6 | 20.3 | 16.4 | 10.4 | | | | 15.2 | 14.8 |
| Intangibles (net) | 4.0 | 6.6 | 7.5 | 16.6 | | | | 10.1 | 11.8 |
| All Other Non-Current | 20.1 | 11.3 | 6.7 | 4.4 | | | | 13.4 | 13.0 |
| Total | 100.0 | 100.0 | 100.0 | 100.0 | | | | 100.0 | 100.0 |
| **LIABILITIES** | | | | | | | | | |
| Notes Payable-Short Term | 21.6 | 9.2 | 9.4 | 7.8 | | | | 16.8 | 22.4 |
| Cur. Mat.-L.T.D. | 2.0 | 2.1 | 1.9 | 4.1 | | | | 2.4 | 3.3 |
| Trade Payables | 8.2 | 11.6 | 13.0 | 18.3 | | | | 13.5 | 13.9 |
| Income Taxes Payable | .0 | .4 | 1.3 | .3 | | | | .6 | .1 |
| All Other Current | 21.4 | 22.5 | 22.9 | 24.1 | | | | 22.9 | 18.3 |
| Total Current | 53.1 | 45.7 | 48.3 | 54.6 | | | | 56.2 | 58.0 |
| Long-Term Debt | 21.7 | 12.9 | 10.4 | 15.0 | | | | 10.8 | 11.0 |
| Deferred Taxes | .0 | .0 | .5 | .4 | | | | .2 | .2 |
| All Other Non-Current | 6.7 | 16.1 | 4.5 | 9.0 | | | | 10.4 | 13.8 |
| Net Worth | 18.3 | 25.3 | 36.3 | 21.1 | | | | 22.5 | 17.0 |
| Total Liabilities & Net Worth | 100.0 | 100.0 | 100.0 | 100.0 | | | | 100.0 | 100.0 |
| **INCOME DATA** | | | | | | | | | |
| Net Sales | 100.0 | 100.0 | 100.0 | 100.0 | | | | 100.0 | 100.0 |
| Gross Profit | | | | | | | | | |
| Operating Expenses | 87.8 | 86.2 | 92.0 | 92.8 | | | | 92.0 | 94.8 |
| Operating Profit | 12.2 | 13.8 | 8.0 | 7.2 | | | | 8.0 | 5.2 |
| All Other Expenses (net) | .4 | 3.7 | .9 | 1.4 | | | | 1.3 | 1.5 |
| Profit Before Taxes | 11.9 | 10.1 | 7.1 | 5.8 | | | | 6.7 | 3.7 |
| **RATIOS** | | | | | | | | | |
| Current | 5.0 | 2.9 | 2.7 | 1.8 | | | | 2.2 | 2.2 |
| | 1.3 | 1.4 | 1.6 | 1.3 | | | | 1.3 | 1.3 |
| | .5 | .7 | 1.0 | 1.0 | | | | 1.0 | .8 |
| Quick | 3.6 | 2.1 | 2.4 | 1.7 | | | | 2.0 | 1.9 |
| | 1.1 | 1.0 | 1.2 | 1.0 | | | | 1.0 | 1.0 |
| | .4 | .5 | .7 | .8 | | | | .6 | .5 |
| Sales/Receivables | 0   UND | 0   UND | 23   16.0 | 42   8.6 | | | | 13   28.8 | 17   22.0 |
| | 0   UND | 25   14.7 | 47   7.7 | 62   5.9 | | | | 47   7.8 | 41   8.9 |
| | 20   18.3 | 58   6.3 | 76   4.8 | 78   4.7 | | | | 68   5.4 | 60   6.0 |
| Cost of Sales/Inventory | | | | | | | | | |
| Cost of Sales/Payables | | | | | | | | | |
| Sales/Working Capital | 9.2 | 7.7 | 6.6 | 6.7 | | | | 8.0 | 7.4 |
| | 96.0 | 19.0 | 14.3 | 15.8 | | | | 24.2 | 25.8 |
| | -17.8 | -38.6 | -168.9 | 426.6 | | | | -188.2 | -29.2 |
| EBIT/Interest | 29.0 | 57.0 | 40.2 | 26.1 | | | | 29.1 | 22.5 |
| | (22) 9.2 | (33) 15.6 | (65) 11.5 | (35) 7.6 | | | | (102) 4.5 | (123) 3.3 |
| | 2.8 | .2 | 3.2 | 1.8 | | | | 1.3 | -1.2 |
| Net Profit + Depr., Dep., Amort./Cur. Mat. L/T/D | | | 12.8 | 8.0 | | | | 16.4 | 6.9 |
| | | (10) | 7.1 | (10) 5.4 | | | | (17) 4.6 | (21) 1.9 |
| | | | 2.0 | 1.7 | | | | -2.0 | -.4 |
| Fixed/Worth | .0 | .0 | .1 | .1 | | | | .1 | .1 |
| | .6 | .5 | .4 | .6 | | | | .4 | .6 |
| | UND | 21.6 | 5.2 | -.3 | | | | 4.9 | -1.2 |
| Debt/Worth | .4 | .5 | .6 | 1.8 | | | | .9 | 1.0 |
| | 1.1 | 3.6 | 1.7 | 6.1 | | | | 3.7 | 3.8 |
| | UND | UND | 30.7 | -5.0 | | | | 176.3 | -7.1 |
| % Profit Before Taxes/Tangible Net Worth | 237.6 | 113.6 | 106.8 | 113.4 | | | | 104.6 | 109.1 |
| | (26) 74.2 | (42) 63.7 | (74) 34.2 | (28) 51.0 | | | | (105) 44.1 | (107) 33.0 |
| | 20.2 | 7.4 | 12.0 | 19.1 | | | | 3.1 | 7.2 |
| % Profit Before Taxes/Total Assets | 103.0 | 40.8 | 26.7 | 19.7 | | | | 29.2 | 22.2 |
| | 29.6 | 10.8 | 12.8 | 10.0 | | | | 10.6 | 8.0 |
| | 12.4 | 1.3 | 2.9 | 3.7 | | | | .4 | -1.4 |
| Sales/Net Fixed Assets | 718.0 | 337.4 | 102.2 | 109.3 | | | | 135.9 | 134.3 |
| | 86.3 | 52.8 | 39.2 | 41.6 | | | | 36.5 | 31.4 |
| | 21.1 | 14.5 | 12.5 | 18.1 | | | | 11.1 | 13.8 |
| Sales/Total Assets | 10.9 | 5.8 | 4.0 | 3.0 | | | | 4.2 | 4.3 |
| | 5.9 | 3.0 | 2.7 | 1.9 | | | | 2.7 | 3.0 |
| | 3.2 | 2.0 | 2.1 | 1.6 | | | | 1.6 | 1.8 |
| % Depr., Dep., Amort./Sales | .4 | .4 | .3 | .7 | | | | .5 | .6 |
| | (14) 1.0 | (32) .8 | (71) .9 | (28) 1.2 | | | | (98) 1.3 | (96) 1.3 |
| | 2.7 | 1.7 | 2.0 | 2.1 | | | | 2.5 | 3.0 |
| % Officers', Directors' Owners' Comp/Sales | 5.3 | 2.7 | 2.8 | | | | | 4.2 | 2.9 |
| | (17) 10.5 | (23) 4.9 | (22) 4.3 | | | | | (38) 6.7 | (47) 4.4 |
| | 24.6 | 7.2 | 6.3 | | | | | 12.4 | 13.4 |
| Net Sales ($) | 60580M | 340983M | 1468509M | 2164560M | 605105M | 1469368M | | 4202060M | 8142211M |
| Total Assets ($) | 7290M | 68248M | 441484M | 940178M | 676922M | 1263812M | | 2907232M | 3642460M |

## Comparative Historical Data      Current Data Sorted by Sales

| | | | Type of Statement | 0-1MM | 1-3MM | 3-5MM | 5-10MM | 10-25MM | 25MM & OVER |
|---|---|---|---|---|---|---|---|---|---|
| 24 | 23 | 33 | Unqualified | | | | 3 | 11 | 19 |
| 21 | 22 | 32 | Reviewed | 2 | 1 | 2 | 6 | 10 | 11 |
| 23 | 25 | 29 | Compiled | | 5 | 8 | 7 | 4 | 5 |
| 29 | 21 | 33 | Tax Returns | 6 | 9 | 7 | 3 | 5 | 3 |
| 76 | 108 | 110 | Other | 12 | 17 | 9 | 14 | 34 | 24 |
| 4/1/09-3/31/10 ALL | 4/1/10-3/31/11 ALL | 4/1/11-3/31/12 ALL | | | 19 (4/1-9/30/11) | | 218 (10/1/11-3/31/12) | | |
| 173 | 199 | 237 | NUMBER OF STATEMENTS | 20 | 32 | 26 | 33 | 64 | 62 |
| % | % | % | ASSETS | % | % | % | % | % | % |
| 20.0 | 20.4 | 20.4 | Cash & Equivalents | 21.4 | 25.1 | 23.1 | 17.9 | 20.6 | 17.6 |
| 32.2 | 33.0 | 33.0 | Trade Receivables (net) | 8.4 | 24.4 | 27.7 | 47.4 | 38.7 | 34.2 |
| 5.5 | 4.2 | 3.3 | Inventory | 2.9 | 2.7 | 1.8 | 5.3 | 2.3 | 4.2 |
| 5.3 | 7.1 | 8.1 | All Other Current | 4.3 | 10.3 | 10.8 | 3.3 | 4.6 | 13.1 |
| 63.0 | 64.7 | 64.7 | Total Current | 37.0 | 62.4 | 63.3 | 73.9 | 66.2 | 69.0 |
| 14.7 | 14.8 | 16.3 | Fixed Assets (net) | 44.0 | 16.3 | 16.3 | 13.1 | 15.4 | 10.0 |
| 10.5 | 10.6 | 9.9 | Intangibles (net) | 6.2 | 4.5 | 3.5 | 7.2 | 12.6 | 15.2 |
| 11.8 | 9.9 | 9.1 | All Other Non-Current | 12.9 | 16.8 | 16.8 | 5.7 | 5.8 | 5.8 |
| 100.0 | 100.0 | 100.0 | Total | 100.0 | 100.0 | 100.0 | 100.0 | 100.0 | 100.0 |
| | | | LIABILITIES | | | | | | |
| 11.6 | 14.6 | 10.5 | Notes Payable-Short Term | 20.7 | 13.7 | 7.0 | 10.2 | 9.2 | 8.7 |
| 2.9 | 4.1 | 2.6 | Cur. Mat.-L.T.D. | .7 | 2.3 | 3.0 | 1.7 | 2.5 | 3.8 |
| 14.8 | 13.1 | 12.7 | Trade Payables | 2.8 | 11.5 | 14.7 | 9.8 | 12.9 | 16.9 |
| .4 | .3 | .6 | Income Taxes Payable | .0 | .0 | .0 | .0 | 2.1 | .3 |
| 19.7 | 21.3 | 22.2 | All Other Current | 14.2 | 16.5 | 21.8 | 25.7 | 24.1 | 24.3 |
| 49.4 | 53.5 | 48.7 | Total Current | 38.4 | 43.9 | 46.5 | 47.4 | 50.7 | 53.9 |
| 11.0 | 13.4 | 13.8 | Long-Term Debt | 46.8 | 9.1 | 17.1 | 4.8 | 10.3 | 12.8 |
| .3 | .2 | .3 | Deferred Taxes | .0 | .0 | .1 | .1 | .7 | .4 |
| 8.6 | 8.5 | 8.7 | All Other Non-Current | 12.7 | 5.9 | 20.0 | 9.2 | 5.3 | 7.2 |
| 30.7 | 24.4 | 28.5 | Net Worth | 1.9 | 41.2 | 16.4 | 38.4 | 33.1 | 25.7 |
| 100.0 | 100.0 | 100.0 | Total Liabilities & Net Worth | 100.0 | 100.0 | 100.0 | 100.0 | 100.0 | 100.0 |
| | | | INCOME DATA | | | | | | |
| 100.0 | 100.0 | 100.0 | Net Sales | 100.0 | 100.0 | 100.0 | 100.0 | 100.0 | 100.0 |
| | | | Gross Profit | | | | | | |
| 92.6 | 90.1 | 89.8 | Operating Expenses | 65.0 | 88.6 | 90.7 | 95.9 | 92.2 | 92.4 |
| 7.4 | 9.9 | 10.2 | Operating Profit | 35.0 | 11.4 | 9.3 | 4.1 | 7.8 | 7.6 |
| 1.3 | 1.4 | 1.8 | All Other Expenses (net) | 9.7 | .1 | 2.3 | .6 | 1.4 | .8 |
| 6.1 | 8.5 | 8.4 | Profit Before Taxes | 25.3 | 11.3 | 7.0 | 3.4 | 6.4 | 6.7 |
| | | | RATIOS | | | | | | |
| 2.5 | 2.8 | 2.5 | Current | 4.7 | 3.2 | 3.5 | 3.4 | 2.3 | 1.9 |
| 1.3 | 1.4 | 1.4 | | .7 | 1.6 | 1.6 | 1.4 | 1.4 | 1.3 |
| .9 | 1.0 | .9 | | .4 | .8 | .7 | 1.1 | 1.0 | 1.0 |
| 1.9 | 2.2 | 2.1 | Quick | 4.1 | 2.5 | 2.4 | 2.9 | 2.3 | 1.6 |
| 1.2 | 1.2 | 1.1 | | .6 | 1.4 | 1.3 | 1.3 | 1.2 | 1.0 |
| .7 | .7 | .7 | | .2 | .4 | .5 | .9 | .7 | .7 |
| 18   20.1 | 16   23.5 | 12   29.5 | Sales/Receivables | 0   UND | 0   UND | 0   UND | 26   13.8 | 23   15.8 | 25   14.5 |
| 43   8.5 | 42   8.6 | 46   8.0 | | 0   UND | 15   24.4 | 39   9.4 | 55   6.6 | 53   6.9 | 50   7.3 |
| 68   5.3 | 65   5.6 | 69   5.3 | | 3   114.0 | 55   6.6 | 54   6.7 | 83   4.4 | 76   4.8 | 73   5.0 |
| | | | Cost of Sales/Inventory | | | | | | |
| | | | Cost of Sales/Payables | | | | | | |
| 7.7 | 6.9 | 7.1 | Sales/Working Capital | 7.8 | 6.6 | 6.8 | 5.8 | 6.6 | 8.3 |
| 19.6 | 16.6 | 17.4 | | -19.5 | 15.2 | 13.1 | 14.1 | 12.6 | 29.1 |
| -57.7 | -367.9 | -69.3 | | -5.6 | -72.4 | -23.4 | 93.0 | -123.5 | -319.5 |
| 24.7 | 30.5 | 36.7 | EBIT/Interest | 42.8 | 18.2 | 39.2 | 28.0 | 46.9 | 76.7 |
| (134) 3.7 | (147) 7.5 | (168) 8.6 | | (12) 17.2 | (18) 5.9 | (15) 9.4 | (25) 5.6 | (46) 12.3 | (52) 9.1 |
| .7 | 2.0 | 2.2 | | 3.2 | 1.3 | .0 | -.3 | 2.4 | 2.5 |
| 4.3 | 21.8 | 8.0 | Net Profit + Depr., Dep., Amort./Cur. Mat. L/T/D | | | | | | 8.7 |
| (15) 1.5 | (18) 8.2 | (26) 3.7 | | | | | | | (15) 4.3 |
| .7 | 2.8 | 1.2 | | | | | | | 2.0 |
| .1 | .1 | .1 | Fixed/Worth | .1 | .0 | .0 | .1 | .2 | .1 |
| .5 | .4 | .5 | | 4.7 | .3 | .4 | .3 | .7 | .7 |
| -2.5 | -9.1 | UND | | -42.3 | 5.6 | 16.7 | 5.2 | 7.8 | -.3 |
| .8 | .9 | .7 | Debt/Worth | .4 | .3 | .4 | .5 | .9 | 1.4 |
| 3.4 | 2.4 | 3.3 | | 5.5 | 1.3 | 1.5 | 2.8 | 3.3 | 7.6 |
| -12.2 | -12.6 | -258.5 | | -44.1 | UND | NM | 13.6 | 58.5 | -5.8 |
| 108.2 | 135.6 | 116.3 | % Profit Before Taxes/Tangible Net Worth | 240.8 | 138.9 | 88.7 | 85.7 | 120.7 | 122.4 |
| (122) 39.1 | (144) 51.4 | (177) 51.3 | | (13) 69.2 | (26) 77.3 | (20) 36.2 | (29) 23.1 | (50) 49.8 | (39) 64.4 |
| 4.7 | 11.6 | 15.1 | | 20.1 | 7.4 | 6.1 | 5.2 | 8.9 | 25.6 |
| 25.9 | 41.5 | 31.6 | % Profit Before Taxes/Total Assets | 55.4 | 61.1 | 42.6 | 21.1 | 32.2 | 29.2 |
| 7.5 | 11.0 | 12.8 | | 20.2 | 27.8 | 8.7 | 8.3 | 14.6 | 11.4 |
| .2 | 2.5 | 2.7 | | 2.9 | 2.8 | 1.6 | -1.8 | 2.7 | 3.3 |
| 111.6 | 104.1 | 160.8 | Sales/Net Fixed Assets | 175.8 | 999.8 | 217.2 | 205.9 | 67.0 | 205.4 |
| 35.2 | 37.3 | 38.3 | | 15.6 | 58.9 | 44.9 | 54.1 | 35.1 | 48.9 |
| 12.8 | 15.3 | 14.7 | | .2 | 12.8 | 14.1 | 13.3 | 18.5 | 18.2 |
| 4.6 | 4.5 | 4.5 | Sales/Total Assets | 3.1 | 7.2 | 5.0 | 4.1 | 4.0 | 4.9 |
| 2.7 | 2.8 | 2.7 | | 1.6 | 4.1 | 2.8 | 2.7 | 2.7 | 2.6 |
| 1.7 | 1.7 | 1.8 | | .2 | 2.1 | 2.0 | 2.2 | 1.9 | 1.4 |
| .6 | .5 | .5 | % Depr., Dep., Amort./Sales | 2.7 | .4 | .4 | .6 | .5 | .2 |
| (109) 1.4 | (121) 1.0 | (154) 1.1 | | (10) 5.3 | (17) .7 | (17) .7 | (21) 1.1 | (46) 1.0 | (43) 1.1 |
| 2.2 | 2.3 | 2.1 | | 18.2 | 1.7 | 1.3 | 2.0 | 2.1 | 2.2 |
| 2.9 | 2.5 | 3.3 | % Officers', Directors', Owners' Comp/Sales | | 5.0 | 2.8 | 2.3 | 3.0 | |
| (60) 6.5 | (57) 6.3 | (68) 5.3 | | | (16) 9.0 | (15) 6.6 | (10) 4.0 | (12) 5.0 | |
| 15.3 | 11.7 | 10.6 | | | 14.1 | 13.4 | 8.9 | 10.0 | |
| 6096471M | 5756488M | 6109105M | Net Sales ($) | 8920M | 58563M | 106026M | 237731M | 1060148M | 4637717M |
| 3131834M | 3088800M | 3397934M | Total Assets ($) | 20242M | 18712M | 43884M | 97957M | 528696M | 2688443M |

© RMA 2012    M = $ thousand    MM = $ million
See Pages 9 through 22 for Explanation of Ratios and Data

**Current Data Sorted by Assets** | | | | | | | **Comparative Historical Data**

| 0-500M | 500M-2MM | 2-10MM | 10-50MM | 50-100MM | 100-250MM | Type of Statement | 4/1/07-3/31/08 ALL | 4/1/08-3/31/09 ALL |
|---|---|---|---|---|---|---|---|---|
| | 2 | 10 | 12 | 5 | 3 | Unqualified | 14 | 27 |
| 1 | 1 | 8 | 9 | | | Reviewed | 7 | 13 |
| 1 | 5 | 4 | 1 | 1 | | Compiled | 14 | 8 |
| 3 | 4 | 1 | | | | Tax Returns | 8 | 9 |
| 5 | 10 | 22 | 20 | 4 | 7 | Other | 42 | 51 |
| | 20 (4/1-9/30/11) | | 119 (10/1/11-3/31/12) | | | | | |
| 10 | 22 | 45 | 42 | 10 | 10 | NUMBER OF STATEMENTS | 85 | 108 |
| % | % | % | % | % | % | ASSETS | % | % |
| 39.1 | 11.4 | 14.2 | 8.9 | 12.3 | 4.4 | Cash & Equivalents | 13.3 | 12.7 |
| 35.9 | 42.0 | 51.3 | 36.3 | 20.4 | 38.1 | Trade Receivables (net) | 39.2 | 43.7 |
| 1.5 | 1.2 | 2.5 | 2.0 | 5.6 | 4.6 | Inventory | 4.4 | 5.0 |
| 9.3 | 2.5 | 6.5 | 11.5 | 4.9 | 5.2 | All Other Current | 7.2 | 5.0 |
| 85.6 | 57.0 | 74.5 | 58.8 | 43.2 | 52.3 | Total Current | 64.2 | 66.3 |
| 6.3 | 23.1 | 12.4 | 27.5 | 32.4 | 10.2 | Fixed Assets (net) | 15.6 | 15.6 |
| 3.0 | 1.3 | 2.8 | 7.5 | 20.8 | 25.4 | Intangibles (net) | 10.9 | 8.0 |
| 5.1 | 18.6 | 10.2 | 6.3 | 3.6 | 12.0 | All Other Non-Current | 9.3 | 10.1 |
| 100.0 | 100.0 | 100.0 | 100.0 | 100.0 | 100.0 | Total | 100.0 | 100.0 |
| | | | | | | LIABILITIES | | |
| 45.5 | 8.8 | 11.8 | 9.3 | 5.5 | 10.7 | Notes Payable-Short Term | 14.9 | 16.3 |
| .0 | 3.2 | 1.8 | 3.3 | 5.3 | 3.3 | Cur. Mat.-L.T.D. | 2.8 | 3.0 |
| 9.1 | 9.8 | 21.5 | 16.3 | 6.8 | 17.3 | Trade Payables | 16.0 | 22.5 |
| .0 | .1 | 1.4 | .4 | .9 | .2 | Income Taxes Payable | .5 | .2 |
| 33.3 | 10.2 | 19.5 | 16.3 | 9.5 | 15.7 | All Other Current | 19.1 | 17.1 |
| 87.9 | 32.1 | 55.9 | 45.5 | 28.0 | 47.1 | Total Current | 53.3 | 59.1 |
| 11.4 | 10.8 | 8.0 | 18.4 | 25.7 | 24.7 | Long-Term Debt | 12.1 | 14.3 |
| .0 | .2 | .3 | 1.0 | 3.4 | .5 | Deferred Taxes | .2 | .3 |
| 2.2 | 18.9 | 6.6 | 4.4 | 2.6 | 7.7 | All Other Non-Current | 7.1 | 4.5 |
| -1.5 | 38.0 | 29.2 | 30.7 | 40.3 | 20.0 | Net Worth | 27.2 | 21.7 |
| 100.0 | 100.0 | 100.0 | 100.0 | 100.0 | 100.0 | Total Liabilities & Net Worth | 100.0 | 100.0 |
| | | | | | | INCOME DATA | | |
| 100.0 | 100.0 | 100.0 | 100.0 | 100.0 | 100.0 | Net Sales | 100.0 | 100.0 |
| | | | | | | Gross Profit | | |
| 87.8 | 88.1 | 94.5 | 93.4 | 95.0 | 90.1 | Operating Expenses | 94.4 | 95.2 |
| 12.2 | 11.9 | 5.5 | 6.6 | 5.0 | 9.9 | Operating Profit | 5.6 | 4.8 |
| .3 | 1.3 | .5 | .6 | 2.3 | 2.6 | All Other Expenses (net) | 1.9 | .5 |
| 11.9 | 10.6 | 5.0 | 6.0 | 2.7 | 7.3 | Profit Before Taxes | 3.8 | 4.3 |
| | | | | | | RATIOS | | |
| 7.2 | 7.0 | 2.8 | 1.9 | 2.5 | 1.4 | | 2.3 | 1.8 |
| 1.2 | 2.6 | 1.7 | 1.2 | 1.5 | 1.1 | Current | 1.3 | 1.2 |
| .7 | .8 | 1.0 | 1.0 | 1.1 | .8 | | .9 | .9 |
| 7.2 | 7.0 | 2.6 | 1.5 | 2.3 | 1.3 | | 1.8 | 1.6 |
| 1.0 | 2.1 | 1.5 | 1.0 | 1.3 | .9 | Quick | 1.0 | 1.0 |
| .4 | .7 | .9 | .7 | .6 | .6 | | .7 | .7 |
| 0 UND | 22 16.5 | 31 11.9 | 33 11.1 | 43 8.5 | 31 11.9 | | 25 14.6 | 26 14.1 |
| 0 UND | 43 8.4 | 46 8.0 | 45 8.1 | 53 6.9 | 55 6.6 | Sales/Receivables | 38 9.6 | 39 9.3 |
| 35 10.3 | 69 5.3 | 78 4.7 | 73 5.0 | 66 5.5 | 94 3.9 | | 61 6.0 | 59 6.2 |
| | | | | | | Cost of Sales/Inventory | | |
| | | | | | | Cost of Sales/Payables | | |
| 9.5 | 5.1 | 6.6 | 10.4 | 4.2 | 9.2 | | 9.4 | 11.8 |
| UND | 13.4 | 14.2 | 29.4 | 16.8 | 45.4 | Sales/Working Capital | 24.9 | 38.6 |
| -49.6 | -175.7 | 448.0 | 411.7 | NM | -33.1 | | -159.9 | -82.4 |
| | 44.4 | 69.6 | 30.1 | | 12.8 | | 17.3 | 13.3 |
| | (12) 19.2 | (37) 15.6 | (35) 6.7 | | 6.1 | EBIT/Interest | (72) 5.3 | (91) 4.8 |
| | 2.3 | 4.0 | 2.6 | | 3.4 | | 1.7 | 1.3 |
| | | | 6.9 | | | | 32.5 | 8.4 |
| | | | (12) 2.7 | | | Net Profit + Depr., Dep., Amort./Cur. Mat. L/T/D | (11) 6.4 | (18) 3.2 |
| | | | 1.2 | | | | 1.4 | 1.2 |
| .0 | .1 | .0 | .4 | .9 | .4 | | .1 | .1 |
| .0 | .3 | .3 | 1.2 | 2.6 | NM | Fixed/Worth | .5 | .4 |
| UND | 1.5 | 1.2 | NM | NM | -.2 | | 4.0 | 2.4 |
| 1.0 | .4 | .5 | .9 | 1.1 | 4.4 | | .8 | 1.0 |
| UND | .8 | 2.9 | 3.1 | 4.6 | NM | Debt/Worth | 2.8 | 3.2 |
| -3.7 | 8.8 | 6.4 | -170.7 | NM | -3.1 | | -50.1 | 86.5 |
| | 69.2 | 72.7 | 50.0 | | | | 79.0 | 85.4 |
| | (19) 46.0 | (39) 31.9 | (31) 31.4 | | | % Profit Before Taxes/Tangible Net Worth | (63) 44.0 | (85) 35.0 |
| | 19.6 | 12.8 | 6.3 | | | | 10.9 | 12.6 |
| 189.2 | 67.3 | 27.8 | 19.7 | 12.8 | 11.0 | | 27.3 | 19.4 |
| 108.0 | 18.6 | 10.7 | 9.5 | 6.5 | 6.7 | % Profit Before Taxes/Total Assets | 9.0 | 7.0 |
| 31.2 | 5.8 | 2.9 | 1.6 | .5 | 2.4 | | 2.0 | 1.0 |
| UND | 141.7 | 243.7 | 51.5 | 20.9 | 177.4 | | 210.9 | 251.1 |
| UND | 25.0 | 64.2 | 18.0 | 6.7 | 25.9 | Sales/Net Fixed Assets | 38.7 | 50.9 |
| 86.9 | 10.7 | 15.9 | 3.3 | 3.0 | 12.6 | | 13.0 | 18.1 |
| 19.3 | 6.0 | 4.8 | 3.2 | 2.0 | 4.3 | | 6.5 | 7.0 |
| 9.3 | 3.6 | 3.4 | 2.4 | 1.5 | 1.6 | Sales/Total Assets | 3.5 | 3.9 |
| 5.2 | 2.1 | 2.5 | 1.5 | .9 | .6 | | 2.0 | 2.2 |
| | .3 | .3 | .6 | | | | .4 | .4 |
| | (15) 1.3 | (33) .7 | (36) 1.6 | | | % Depr., Dep., Amort./Sales | (48) .9 | (67) .9 |
| | 2.5 | 2.0 | 3.7 | | | | 2.2 | 2.5 |
| | | | | | | | 1.4 | 1.6 |
| | | | | | | % Officers', Directors' Owners' Comp/Sales | (17) 5.5 | (17) 3.5 |
| | | | | | | | 7.7 | 11.0 |
| 18620M | 197041M | 854783M | 2425289M | 1078012M | 4917417M | Net Sales ($) | 5730996M | 13110248M |
| 2441M | 27807M | 233232M | 900056M | 749420M | 1674070M | Total Assets ($) | 2000834M | 2817040M |

## Comparative Historical Data / Current Data Sorted by Sales

| | | | Type of Statement | | | | | | |
|---|---|---|---|---|---|---|---|---|---|
| 32 | 30 | 32 | Unqualified | | | | 5 | 5 | 22 |
| 18 | 19 | 19 | Reviewed | | 3 | | 2 | 6 | 8 |
| 14 | 17 | 12 | Compiled | 1 | 2 | 2 | 4 | 1 | 2 |
| 12 | 14 | 8 | Tax Returns | 2 | 1 | 1 | 2 | | 2 |
| 59 | 67 | 68 | Other | 3 | 7 | 4 | 5 | 13 | 36 |
| 4/1/09-3/31/10 | 4/1/10-3/31/11 | 4/1/11-3/31/12 | | | 20 (4/1-9/30/11) | | | 119 (10/1/11-3/31/12) | |
| ALL | ALL | ALL | | 0-1MM | 1-3MM | 3-5MM | 5-10MM | 10-25MM | 25MM & OVER |
| 135 | 147 | 139 | NUMBER OF STATEMENTS | 6 | 13 | 7 | 18 | 25 | 70 |
| % | % | % | ASSETS | % | % | % | % | % | % |
| 11.8 | 12.5 | 13.1 | Cash & Equivalents | | 22.9 | | 13.0 | 10.0 | 11.6 |
| 41.4 | 43.3 | 41.0 | Trade Receivables (net) | | 39.4 | | 52.3 | 47.6 | 38.9 |
| 4.7 | 3.4 | 2.5 | Inventory | | .1 | | 2.3 | 1.0 | 3.5 |
| 5.8 | 8.0 | 7.4 | All Other Current | | 15.2 | | 2.8 | 7.8 | 7.9 |
| 63.6 | 67.2 | 63.9 | Total Current | | 77.6 | | 70.5 | 66.4 | 61.9 |
| 17.7 | 17.1 | 19.5 | Fixed Assets (net) | | 5.4 | | 11.6 | 25.4 | 18.8 |
| 7.2 | 8.2 | 6.9 | Intangibles (net) | | 1.3 | | 3.3 | 1.7 | 11.3 |
| 11.5 | 7.5 | 9.6 | All Other Non-Current | | 15.6 | | 14.7 | 6.6 | 7.9 |
| 100.0 | 100.0 | 100.0 | Total | | 100.0 | | 100.0 | 100.0 | 100.0 |
| | | | LIABILITIES | | | | | | |
| 16.1 | 15.5 | 12.4 | Notes Payable-Short Term | | 29.9 | | 9.2 | 18.4 | 7.8 |
| 4.1 | 2.7 | 2.7 | Cur. Mat.-L.T.D. | | .1 | | 1.8 | 4.2 | 3.0 |
| 18.4 | 18.0 | 15.8 | Trade Payables | | 12.3 | | 14.6 | 17.3 | 18.2 |
| .4 | .3 | .7 | Income Taxes Payable | | .0 | | .1 | 1.0 | .9 |
| 12.3 | 15.4 | 17.1 | All Other Current | | 29.4 | | 12.7 | 6.7 | 21.0 |
| 51.3 | 51.9 | 48.7 | Total Current | | 71.8 | | 38.3 | 47.6 | 50.8 |
| 7.4 | 9.9 | 14.3 | Long-Term Debt | | .5 | | 2.9 | 18.5 | 16.0 |
| .4 | .5 | .7 | Deferred Taxes | | .0 | | .5 | .1 | 1.1 |
| 5.0 | 7.1 | 7.4 | All Other Non-Current | | 18.9 | | 5.5 | 14.5 | 3.5 |
| 36.0 | 30.6 | 29.0 | Net Worth | | 8.8 | | 52.7 | 19.3 | 28.5 |
| 100.0 | 100.0 | 100.0 | Total Liabilities & Net Worth | | 100.0 | | 100.0 | 100.0 | 100.0 |
| | | | INCOME DATA | | | | | | |
| 100.0 | 100.0 | 100.0 | Net Sales | | 100.0 | | 100.0 | 100.0 | 100.0 |
| | | | Gross Profit | | | | | | |
| 95.9 | 92.7 | 92.4 | Operating Expenses | | 92.2 | | 95.2 | 92.2 | 93.4 |
| 4.1 | 7.3 | 7.6 | Operating Profit | | 7.8 | | 4.8 | 7.8 | 6.6 |
| .8 | 1.0 | .9 | All Other Expenses (net) | | -.1 | | .4 | .6 | .9 |
| 3.3 | 6.4 | 6.7 | Profit Before Taxes | | 7.9 | | 4.4 | 7.2 | 5.6 |
| | | | RATIOS | | | | | | |
| 2.1 | 2.2 | 2.6 | | | 5.7 | | 4.1 | 2.3 | 2.0 |
| 1.2 | 1.4 | 1.4 | Current | | 1.2 | | 2.2 | 1.5 | 1.3 |
| .9 | 1.0 | 1.0 | | | .8 | | 1.2 | 1.1 | 1.0 |
| 1.8 | 2.0 | 2.4 | | | 5.7 | | 4.0 | 2.1 | 1.6 |
| 1.0 | 1.1 | 1.1 | Quick | | .8 | | 1.9 | 1.4 | 1.1 |
| .7 | .7 | .7 | | | .4 | | 1.2 | .9 | .7 |
| 29  12.8 | 32  11.4 | 30  12.1 | | 0  UND | | 33  11.2 | 41  9.0 | 33  11.1 | |
| 45  8.1 | 47  7.8 | 45  8.2 | Sales/Receivables | 45  8.2 | | 43  8.4 | 47  7.8 | 46  7.9 | |
| 63  5.8 | 66  5.5 | 70  5.2 | | 69  5.3 | | 76  4.8 | 78  4.7 | 70  5.2 | |
| | | | Cost of Sales/Inventory | | | | | | |
| | | | Cost of Sales/Payables | | | | | | |
| 9.1 | 6.9 | 7.4 | | | 6.5 | | 4.6 | 7.7 | 9.6 |
| 33.9 | 16.5 | 19.1 | Sales/Working Capital | | 13.9 | | 9.8 | 14.2 | 22.3 |
| -42.3 | -144.0 | -215.6 | | | -16.1 | | NM | 177.0 | NM |
| 16.0 | 30.6 | 30.1 | | | 39.9 | | 42.9 | 30.1 | |
| (112)  4.5 | (117)  6.9 | (107)  8.5 | EBIT/Interest | | (13)  15.3 | (22)  8.5 | (59)  7.1 | |
| .5 | 2.6 | 3.0 | | | -10.7 | | 3.5 | 2.8 | |
| 6.0 | 20.8 | 7.9 | | | | | | | 14.8 |
| (26)  2.3 | (26)  4.2 | (27)  3.0 | Net Profit + Depr., Dep., Amort./Cur. Mat. L/T/D | | | | | (17)  3.3 | |
| .7 | 1.6 | 1.4 | | | | | | | 1.2 |
| .1 | .1 | .1 | | | .0 | | .0 | .1 | .2 |
| .3 | .5 | .5 | Fixed/Worth | | .1 | | .2 | 1.1 | 1.0 |
| 1.8 | 6.0 | 5.6 | | | .3 | | .5 | 2.0 | -34.7 |
| .7 | .8 | .7 | | | .2 | | .4 | 1.3 | .9 |
| 2.3 | 2.4 | 3.1 | Debt/Worth | | 3.9 | | .7 | 3.3 | 4.6 |
| 7.3 | 30.8 | 33.0 | | | -5.6 | | 2.6 | 9.7 | -170.7 |
| 55.9 | 69.7 | 69.2 | | | 57.5 | | 81.5 | 73.6 | |
| (113)  20.2 | (114)  29.6 | (107)  32.3 | % Profit Before Taxes/Tangible Net Worth | | (17)  31.8 | (21)  36.6 | (51)  32.3 | |
| 2.7 | 11.6 | 12.3 | | | -8.2 | | 11.3 | 12.8 | |
| 16.8 | 28.6 | 29.4 | | | 88.8 | | 30.4 | 29.1 | 15.9 |
| 5.9 | 10.2 | 10.7 | % Profit Before Taxes/Total Assets | | 36.6 | | 10.4 | 8.5 | 10.5 |
| .0 | 2.2 | 2.8 | | | -5.5 | | -.9 | 3.1 | 3.0 |
| 124.4 | 143.0 | 139.1 | | | UND | | 229.9 | 145.8 | 110.5 |
| 39.4 | 32.8 | 28.1 | Sales/Net Fixed Assets | | 91.7 | | 56.2 | 18.1 | 28.6 |
| 13.8 | 13.9 | 9.2 | | | 20.0 | | 15.0 | 5.1 | 10.5 |
| 5.0 | 4.9 | 4.6 | | | 5.9 | | 4.0 | 5.2 | 4.4 |
| 3.3 | 3.2 | 2.8 | Sales/Total Assets | | 3.4 | | 3.4 | 3.0 | 2.7 |
| 2.0 | 1.7 | 1.7 | | | 2.0 | | 2.8 | 1.4 | 1.7 |
| .4 | .4 | .3 | | | | | .3 | .5 | .3 |
| (88)  1.0 | (109)  .8 | (99)  1.1 | % Depr., Dep., Amort./Sales | | | (11)  .9 | (22)  2.0 | (53)  .8 | |
| 2.5 | 2.6 | 3.2 | | | | | 1.7 | 3.2 | 3.3 |
| 2.3 | 1.5 | 1.7 | | | | | | | |
| (27)  3.4 | (39)  2.5 | (26)  4.1 | % Officers', Directors' Owners' Comp/Sales | | | | | | |
| 6.9 | 7.3 | 15.1 | | | | | | | |
| 8503553M | 11037564M | 9491162M | Net Sales ($) | 4033M | 27899M | 26134M | 133612M | 425144M | 8874340M |
| 3036446M | 3989416M | 3587026M | Total Assets ($) | 9164M | 16520M | 15948M | 44417M | 183950M | 3317027M |

M = $ thousand    MM = $ million
See Pages 9 through 22 for Explanation of Ratios and Data

## Current Data Sorted by Assets            Comparative Historical Data

| | | 3 | | 17 | | 25 | | 6 | | 5 | Type of Statement | | | | |
|---|---|---|---|---|---|---|---|---|---|---|---|---|---|---|---|
| | 2 | 13 | | 30 | | 9 | | 1 | | | Unqualified | | | 80 | 78 |
| | 9 | 6 | | 17 | | 6 | | | | | Reviewed | | | 42 | 53 |
| | 25 | 30 | | 8 | | 6 | | | | | Compiled | | | 41 | 43 |
| | 40 | 51 | | 64 | | 2 | | 8 | | 6 | Tax Returns | | | 48 | 76 |
| | | | | | | 30 | | | | | Other | | | 154 | 165 |
| | | 50 (4/1-9/30/11) | | | | 363 (10/1/11-3/31/12) | | | | | | | | 4/1/07- | 4/1/08- |
| | | | | | | | | | | | | | | 3/31/08 | 3/31/09 |
| | 0-500M | 500M-2MM | | 2-10MM | | 10-50MM | | 50-100MM | | 100-250MM | | | | ALL | ALL |
| | 76 | 103 | | 136 | | 72 | | 15 | | 11 | NUMBER OF STATEMENTS | | | 365 | 415 |
| | % | % | | % | | % | | % | | % | ASSETS | | | % | % |
| | 32.6 | 21.6 | | 17.9 | | 14.7 | | 9.4 | | 12.7 | Cash & Equivalents | | | 15.7 | 17.6 |
| | 23.0 | 37.3 | | 47.3 | | 41.8 | | 33.1 | | 35.8 | Trade Receivables (net) | | | 42.8 | 41.6 |
| | .5 | 1.6 | | 1.9 | | .4 | | 1.7 | | .0 | Inventory | | | 2.5 | 3.0 |
| | 5.5 | 3.0 | | 6.7 | | 12.6 | | 9.8 | | 8.5 | All Other Current | | | 6.7 | 6.1 |
| | 61.7 | 63.6 | | 73.9 | | 69.5 | | 54.0 | | 56.9 | Total Current | | | 67.6 | 68.3 |
| | 16.0 | 22.7 | | 11.9 | | 11.1 | | 12.1 | | 6.6 | Fixed Assets (net) | | | 16.1 | 14.9 |
| | 6.0 | 5.5 | | 6.4 | | 9.0 | | 25.9 | | 33.8 | Intangibles (net) | | | 7.0 | 6.5 |
| | 16.3 | 8.3 | | 7.8 | | 10.5 | | 7.9 | | 2.7 | All Other Non-Current | | | 9.2 | 10.3 |
| | 100.0 | 100.0 | | 100.0 | | 100.0 | | 100.0 | | 100.0 | Total | | | 100.0 | 100.0 |
| | | | | | | | | | | | LIABILITIES | | | | |
| | 37.3 | 12.2 | | 7.9 | | 7.9 | | 7.4 | | 2.0 | Notes Payable-Short Term | | | 12.7 | 17.7 |
| | 4.2 | 1.6 | | 2.8 | | 3.2 | | 3.2 | | 2.6 | Cur. Mat.-L.T.D. | | | 3.1 | 4.3 |
| | 9.6 | 10.1 | | 14.0 | | 10.6 | | 14.0 | | 6.3 | Trade Payables | | | 14.5 | 12.0 |
| | .4 | .1 | | 1.0 | | 2.0 | | 1.5 | | 2.4 | Income Taxes Payable | | | .8 | .8 |
| | 33.6 | 12.1 | | 19.1 | | 19.2 | | 17.6 | | 11.6 | All Other Current | | | 19.6 | 20.3 |
| | 85.2 | 36.1 | | 44.7 | | 42.9 | | 43.6 | | 24.9 | Total Current | | | 50.7 | 54.9 |
| | 8.7 | 16.8 | | 6.9 | | 7.1 | | 20.4 | | 17.9 | Long-Term Debt | | | 14.1 | 15.2 |
| | .1 | .0 | | .3 | | .8 | | 1.4 | | 1.4 | Deferred Taxes | | | .3 | .6 |
| | 4.7 | 4.3 | | 7.1 | | 8.6 | | 9.0 | | 7.2 | All Other Non-Current | | | 8.4 | 6.0 |
| | 1.3 | 42.8 | | 40.8 | | 40.6 | | 25.6 | | 48.5 | Net Worth | | | 26.5 | 23.3 |
| | 100.0 | 100.0 | | 100.0 | | 100.0 | | 100.0 | | 100.0 | Total Liabilties & Net Worth | | | 100.0 | 100.0 |
| | | | | | | | | | | | INCOME DATA | | | | |
| | 100.0 | 100.0 | | 100.0 | | 100.0 | | 100.0 | | 100.0 | Net Sales | | | 100.0 | 100.0 |
| | | | | | | | | | | | Gross Profit | | | | |
| | 87.2 | 87.1 | | 87.6 | | 90.4 | | 84.4 | | 90.5 | Operating Expenses | | | 90.2 | 90.8 |
| | 12.8 | 12.9 | | 12.4 | | 9.6 | | 15.6 | | 9.5 | Operating Profit | | | 9.8 | 9.2 |
| | 1.1 | 2.8 | | 1.5 | | 1.7 | | 4.8 | | 2.8 | All Other Expenses (net) | | | 2.0 | 2.6 |
| | 11.7 | 10.1 | | 10.9 | | 7.9 | | 10.8 | | 6.7 | Profit Before Taxes | | | 7.9 | 6.6 |
| | | | | | | | | | | | RATIOS | | | | |
| | 3.9 | 6.8 | | 3.2 | | 2.5 | | 1.9 | | 4.2 | | | | 2.6 | 2.4 |
| | 1.0 | 1.6 | | 1.6 | | 1.6 | | 1.0 | | 2.1 | Current | | | 1.5 | 1.5 |
| | .4 | 1.1 | | 1.1 | | 1.1 | | .9 | | 1.3 | | | | 1.0 | 1.0 |
| | 2.4 | 5.8 | | 3.1 | | 2.1 | | 1.4 | | 3.2 | | | | 2.3 | 2.1 |
| | .7 | 1.5 | | 1.5 | | 1.4 | | .9 | | 2.0 | Quick | (364) | 1.3 | (414) | 1.3 |
| | .2 | .9 | | 1.0 | | .8 | | .7 | | 1.1 | | | | .8 | .8 |

| | | | | | | | | | | | | | | | | | | | | |
|---|---|---|---|---|---|---|---|---|---|---|---|---|---|---|---|---|---|---|---|---|
| 0 | UND | | 3 | 118.6 | 42 | 8.7 | 43 | 8.5 | 29 | 12.4 | 60 | 6.1 | | | 21 | 17.0 | 23 | 15.6 | | |
| 0 | UND | | 38 | 9.7 | 60 | 6.1 | 63 | 5.8 | 60 | 6.1 | 87 | 4.2 | Sales/Receivables | | 55 | 6.6 | 50 | 7.3 | | |
| 29 | 12.8 | | 66 | 5.5 | 83 | 4.4 | 83 | 4.4 | 81 | 4.5 | 91 | 4.0 | | | 86 | 4.2 | 80 | 4.6 | | |

| | | | | | | | | | | | |
|---|---|---|---|---|---|---|---|---|---|---|---|
| | | | | | | | | | Cost of Sales/Inventory | | |
| | | | | | | | | | Cost of Sales/Payables | | |

| | | | | | | | | | |
|---|---|---|---|---|---|---|---|---|---|
| 14.8 | 6.3 | | 4.6 | 3.4 | 8.4 | 3.0 | | 5.6 | 6.0 |
| UND | 11.9 | | 9.6 | 10.0 | 155.8 | 6.9 | Sales/Working Capital | 13.6 | 14.6 |
| -19.3 | 76.6 | | 34.5 | 46.7 | -41.0 | 14.3 | | UND | -131.3 |

| | | | | | | | | | | | | | |
|---|---|---|---|---|---|---|---|---|---|---|---|---|---|
| | 24.4 | | 34.3 | | 71.7 | | 84.9 | 59.7 | | | 20.1 | | 27.0 |
| (46) | 8.2 | (63) | 6.7 | (103) | 20.3 | (61) | 16.8 | (13) 11.3 | EBIT/Interest | (271) | 6.7 | (322) | 8.0 |
| | 2.2 | | 2.8 | | 4.6 | | 4.0 | .8 | | | 1.8 | | 2.0 |

| | | | | | | | | | | | |
|---|---|---|---|---|---|---|---|---|---|---|---|
| | | | | 9.4 | | 26.8 | | | | 5.0 | 14.9 |
| | | (11) | 1.6 | (15) | 4.0 | | | Net Profit + Depr., Dep., | (43) 2.4 (61) | 3.0 |
| | | | 1.0 | | 1.2 | | | Amort./Cur. Mat. L/T/D | 1.3 | 1.0 |

| | | | | | | | | | |
|---|---|---|---|---|---|---|---|---|---|
| .0 | .0 | | .0 | .1 | .4 | .1 | | .1 | .1 |
| .3 | .2 | | .2 | .2 | 2.0 | .4 | Fixed/Worth | .3 | .3 |
| -2.2 | 1.8 | | .9 | .4 | -.2 | -.1 | | 7.1 | 3.4 |

| | | | | | | | | | |
|---|---|---|---|---|---|---|---|---|---|
| .4 | .5 | | .6 | .7 | .8 | .5 | | .7 | .7 |
| 5.6 | 1.6 | | 1.7 | 1.8 | 6.3 | 2.6 | Debt/Worth | 2.2 | 2.1 |
| -4.5 | 6.1 | | 4.3 | 6.1 | -3.1 | -1.8 | | 50.4 | 47.4 |

| | | | | | | | | | | | | |
|---|---|---|---|---|---|---|---|---|---|---|---|---|
| | 344.1 | | 84.2 | | 77.4 | 72.0 | | | % Profit Before Taxes/Tangible | 80.3 | | 83.4 |
| (49) | 87.1 | (89) | 38.4 | (113) | 45.9 | (60) 26.9 | | | Net Worth | (281) 34.0 | (320) | 36.0 |
| | 11.7 | | 7.0 | | 13.8 | 13.1 | | | | 11.3 | | 8.4 |

| | | | | | | | | |
|---|---|---|---|---|---|---|---|---|
| 82.1 | 34.4 | 33.1 | 20.2 | 20.8 | 14.6 | % Profit Before Taxes/Total | 27.2 | 28.6 |
| 31.3 | 14.9 | 17.7 | 11.2 | 9.5 | 13.2 | Assets | 11.0 | 11.5 |
| 2.7 | 3.0 | 4.4 | 3.6 | 2.5 | -1.1 | | 2.4 | 1.7 |

| | | | | | | | | |
|---|---|---|---|---|---|---|---|---|
| UND | 311.3 | 224.4 | 113.8 | 49.5 | 46.8 | | 115.2 | 151.9 |
| 103.2 | 51.9 | 62.8 | 45.1 | 24.4 | 33.0 | Sales/Net Fixed Assets | 41.0 | 43.8 |
| 27.2 | 7.4 | 21.7 | 19.7 | 11.6 | 13.3 | | 15.3 | 15.7 |

| | | | | | | | | |
|---|---|---|---|---|---|---|---|---|
| 12.3 | 4.8 | 4.0 | 3.4 | 2.4 | 1.9 | | 4.0 | 4.6 |
| 6.2 | 3.1 | 2.8 | 1.9 | 1.8 | 1.3 | Sales/Total Assets | 2.7 | 2.8 |
| 3.4 | 1.9 | 1.7 | 1.2 | 1.2 | .7 | | 1.7 | 1.8 |

| | | | | | | | | | | | | |
|---|---|---|---|---|---|---|---|---|---|---|---|---|
| | .3 | | .4 | | .2 | .4 | | | | .4 | | .5 |
| (31) | 1.0 | (54) | 1.0 | (96) | .6 | (54) 1.4 | | % Depr., Dep., Amort./Sales | (259) 1.0 | (264) | 1.2 |
| | 1.7 | | 3.9 | | 1.8 | 2.8 | | | | 2.2 | | 2.4 |

| | | | | | | | | | | | |
|---|---|---|---|---|---|---|---|---|---|---|---|
| | 6.1 | | 3.9 | | 1.7 | | | % Officers', Directors' | | 3.2 | 3.1 |
| (33) | 8.8 | (33) | 6.6 | (29) | 3.3 | | | Owners' Comp/Sales | (90) 6.3 | (107) | 8.2 |
| | 16.1 | | 11.0 | | 10.5 | | | | | 15.6 | 17.0 |

| | | | | | | | | |
|---|---|---|---|---|---|---|---|---|
| 101305M | 379344M | 1914414M | 4328089M | 2230222M | 3609660M | Net Sales ($) | 10382991M | 15472197M |
| 17087M | 117877M | 639517M | 1537244M | 1146249M | 1679595M | Total Assets ($) | 5551582M | 7298284M |

© RMA 2012

M = $ thousand    MM = $ million
See Pages 9 through 22 for Explanation of Ratios and Data

## Comparative Historical Data | | Current Data Sorted by Sales

| | | | Type of Statement | | | | | | |
|---|---|---|---|---|---|---|---|---|---|
| 90 | 87 | 56 | Unqualified | 3 | 3 | 1 | 3 | 12 | 34 |
| 50 | 65 | 55 | Reviewed | 2 | 4 | 7 | 14 | 16 | 12 |
| 42 | 40 | 38 | Compiled | 5 | 11 | 7 | 4 | 10 | 1 |
| 74 | 73 | 65 | Tax Returns | 22 | 16 | 11 | 12 | 2 | 2 |
| 187 | 208 | 199 | Other | 24 | 40 | 24 | 31 | 35 | 45 |
| 4/1/09-3/31/10 ALL | 4/1/10-3/31/11 ALL | 4/1/11-3/31/12 ALL | | 0-1MM | 50 (4/1-9/30/11) 1-3MM | 3-5MM | 363 (10/1/11-3/31/12) 5-10MM | 10-25MM | 25MM & OVER |
| 443 | 473 | 413 | **NUMBER OF STATEMENTS** | 56 | 74 | 50 | 64 | 75 | 94 |
| % | % | % | **ASSETS** | % | % | % | % | % | % |
| 18.6 | 18.8 | 20.5 | Cash & Equivalents | 21.7 | 25.2 | 21.2 | 25.7 | 17.7 | 14.6 |
| 39.5 | 42.7 | 38.6 | Trade Receivables (net) | 15.9 | 26.8 | 40.1 | 47.9 | 47.8 | 46.8 |
| 2.7 | 2.5 | 1.3 | Inventory | .0 | 1.4 | 4.0 | 1.5 | .8 | .6 |
| 7.3 | 6.5 | 6.8 | All Other Current | 5.9 | 5.4 | 5.6 | 3.8 | 8.6 | 9.5 |
| 68.1 | 70.4 | 67.1 | Total Current | 43.6 | 58.7 | 71.0 | 78.9 | 74.9 | 71.5 |
| 15.3 | 13.6 | 15.1 | Fixed Assets (net) | 33.2 | 20.3 | 16.9 | 7.8 | 9.2 | 8.7 |
| 6.9 | 6.5 | 8.0 | Intangibles (net) | 5.0 | 8.1 | 5.0 | 7.3 | 6.6 | 12.8 |
| 9.7 | 9.4 | 9.8 | All Other Non-Current | 18.2 | 12.8 | 7.2 | 5.9 | 9.3 | 7.0 |
| 100.0 | 100.0 | 100.0 | Total | 100.0 | 100.0 | 100.0 | 100.0 | 100.0 | 100.0 |
| | | | **LIABILITIES** | | | | | | |
| 16.2 | 14.7 | 14.2 | Notes Payable-Short Term | 23.6 | 19.1 | 22.3 | 10.4 | 8.0 | 7.9 |
| 3.3 | 2.5 | 2.8 | Cur. Mat.-L.T.D. | 1.9 | 3.5 | 5.4 | 1.3 | 1.5 | 3.6 |
| 12.8 | 14.1 | 11.4 | Trade Payables | 4.2 | 9.8 | 15.0 | 10.9 | 14.3 | 13.3 |
| .9 | .6 | .9 | Income Taxes Payable | .2 | .3 | .2 | .4 | 1.5 | 2.0 |
| 22.7 | 19.1 | 19.8 | All Other Current | 23.0 | 18.2 | 15.8 | 19.2 | 21.3 | 20.5 |
| 55.9 | 51.0 | 49.1 | Total Current | 52.9 | 50.9 | 58.6 | 42.3 | 46.6 | 47.3 |
| 10.2 | 9.6 | 10.5 | Long-Term Debt | 22.8 | 12.4 | 10.7 | 5.3 | 5.6 | 9.1 |
| .3 | .4 | .4 | Deferred Taxes | .5 | .0 | .0 | .2 | .3 | .9 |
| 7.4 | 5.8 | 6.3 | All Other Non-Current | 7.8 | 5.9 | 4.2 | 5.7 | 7.5 | 6.2 |
| 26.3 | 33.1 | 33.7 | Net Worth | 16.0 | 30.8 | 26.5 | 46.5 | 40.0 | 36.5 |
| 100.0 | 100.0 | 100.0 | Total Liabilties & Net Worth | 100.0 | 100.0 | 100.0 | 100.0 | 100.0 | 100.0 |
| | | | **INCOME DATA** | | | | | | |
| 100.0 | 100.0 | 100.0 | Net Sales | 100.0 | 100.0 | 100.0 | 100.0 | 100.0 | 100.0 |
| | | | Gross Profit | | | | | | |
| 92.1 | 90.9 | 87.8 | Operating Expenses | 73.3 | 87.2 | 91.9 | 90.4 | 90.3 | 91.1 |
| 7.9 | 9.1 | 12.2 | Operating Profit | 26.7 | 12.8 | 8.1 | 9.6 | 9.7 | 8.9 |
| 2.0 | 1.4 | 2.0 | All Other Expenses (net) | 7.6 | 1.5 | .1 | .5 | 1.2 | 1.5 |
| 5.9 | 7.7 | 10.2 | Profit Before Taxes | 19.1 | 11.3 | 8.0 | 9.1 | 8.5 | 7.4 |
| | | | **RATIOS** | | | | | | |
| 2.5 | 3.1 | 3.3 | | 2.2 | 6.6 | 3.6 | 5.5 | 2.7 | 2.2 |
| 1.4 | 1.6 | 1.5 | Current | .8 | 1.7 | 1.6 | 2.0 | 1.5 | 1.6 |
| 1.0 | 1.0 | 1.0 | | .3 | .8 | 1.0 | 1.3 | 1.1 | 1.1 |
| 2.1 | 2.8 | 2.9 | | 1.4 | 5.8 | 3.4 | 5.4 | 2.6 | 2.0 |
| 1.2 | 1.4 | 1.4 | Quick | .7 | 1.5 | 1.5 | 1.9 | 1.4 | 1.3 |
| .7 | .8 | .7 | | .2 | .6 | .7 | 1.2 | .9 | .8 |
| 21 17.7 | 25 14.7 | 14 26.0 | | 0 UND | 0 UND | 19 18.9 | 42 8.7 | 35 10.3 | 45 8.1 |
| 51 7.1 | 52 7.0 | 50 7.3 | Sales/Receivables | 0 UND | 23 16.1 | 51 7.2 | 60 6.1 | 60 6.1 | 64 5.7 |
| 78 4.7 | 79 4.6 | 74 4.9 | | 21 17.0 | 57 6.4 | 79 4.6 | 83 4.4 | 76 4.8 | 81 4.5 |
| | | | Cost of Sales/Inventory | | | | | | |
| | | | Cost of Sales/Payables | | | | | | |
| 6.2 | 5.6 | 5.7 | | 10.1 | 5.4 | 4.5 | 4.6 | 5.7 | 6.2 |
| 14.7 | 12.1 | 13.1 | Sales/Working Capital | -136.4 | 17.7 | 10.6 | 8.3 | 10.2 | 13.5 |
| -140.7 | 99.0 | -547.7 | | -10.2 | -49.7 | -774.8 | 18.6 | 65.8 | 55.1 |
| 42.4 | 46.4 | 45.1 | | 10.4 | 34.9 | 44.4 | 49.3 | 87.5 | 73.1 |
| (335) 8.0 | (333) 13.7 | (295) 14.4 | EBIT/Interest | (33) 4.1 | (50) 8.3 | (35) 10.1 | (42) 11.2 | (54) 23.3 | (81) 16.8 |
| 1.6 | 2.8 | 3.1 | | 2.0 | 1.2 | 3.3 | 2.9 | 13.2 | 4.2 |
| 17.6 | 17.0 | 7.2 | Net Profit + Depr., Dep., Amort./Cur. Mat. L/T/D | | | | | | 23.8 |
| (60) 2.6 | (59) 3.8 | (40) 2.9 | | | | | | (20) 4.0 |
| .9 | .9 | .8 | | | | | | | 1.1 |
| .1 | .0 | .0 | | .0 | .0 | .0 | .0 | .0 | .1 |
| .3 | .2 | .2 | Fixed/Worth | 1.5 | .3 | .2 | .1 | .1 | .2 |
| 2.0 | 1.3 | 1.9 | | -9.4 | 1.7 | 3.6 | .5 | .8 | 2.1 |
| .7 | .5 | .6 | | .9 | .4 | .3 | .4 | .6 | .8 |
| 2.1 | 1.6 | 1.8 | Debt/Worth | 4.5 | 1.6 | 1.7 | 1.3 | 1.8 | 2.2 |
| 22.5 | 12.1 | 12.0 | | -11.1 | 70.8 | 13.9 | 3.6 | 5.1 | 14.7 |
| 71.3 | 88.9 | 87.1 | % Profit Before Taxes/Tangible Net Worth | 165.0 | 95.4 | 70.0 | 96.4 | 72.2 | 86.5 |
| (345) 32.7 | (384) 39.4 | (326) 43.3 | | (40) 32.1 | (57) 51.1 | (39) 30.6 | (54) 47.7 | (64) 36.7 | (72) 48.5 |
| 8.3 | 13.7 | 12.5 | | 2.8 | 11.6 | 8.8 | 13.9 | 13.7 | 23.7 |
| 25.7 | 29.9 | 34.7 | % Profit Before Taxes/Total Assets | 49.2 | 46.8 | 32.8 | 42.6 | 28.7 | 25.9 |
| 9.8 | 12.4 | 14.8 | | 8.0 | 19.2 | 11.2 | 18.9 | 16.8 | 14.0 |
| .8 | 3.1 | 3.3 | | 1.4 | 2.5 | 3.4 | 4.0 | 4.6 | 7.2 |
| 143.9 | 179.4 | 243.9 | | UND | 999.8 | 280.4 | 271.1 | 233.6 | 116.9 |
| 43.8 | 54.2 | 54.1 | Sales/Net Fixed Assets | 25.2 | 52.9 | 52.1 | 87.0 | 63.0 | 47.9 |
| 16.6 | 17.6 | 19.7 | | .6 | 10.5 | 15.9 | 29.5 | 26.4 | 24.7 |
| 4.4 | 4.4 | 4.4 | | 6.7 | 6.2 | 5.2 | 4.5 | 4.3 | 4.1 |
| 3.0 | 2.9 | 2.8 | Sales/Total Assets | 1.2 | 3.4 | 2.9 | 3.2 | 2.8 | 2.7 |
| 1.7 | 1.8 | 1.6 | | .3 | 1.6 | 1.9 | 2.0 | 2.0 | 1.6 |
| .4 | .3 | .3 | | .7 | .7 | .1 | .2 | .3 | .3 |
| (287) .9 | (310) .8 | (249) 1.1 | % Depr., Dep., Amort./Sales | (32) 2.3 | (36) 1.7 | (27) .9 | (46) .5 | (46) .8 | (62) 1.3 |
| 2.1 | 2.0 | 2.3 | | 12.4 | 2.8 | 2.0 | 1.4 | 2.2 | 2.1 |
| 2.3 | 3.5 | 3.3 | | 6.6 | 3.6 | 2.8 | 2.9 | 3.0 | .7 |
| (119) 5.0 | (122) 6.9 | (106) 6.9 | % Officers', Directors' Owners' Comp/Sales | (12) 10.9 | (30) 7.9 | (20) 5.9 | (18) 5.7 | (16) 10.1 | (10) 5.2 |
| 9.8 | 14.4 | 12.0 | | 17.0 | 15.7 | 9.9 | 11.7 | 12.0 | 17.0 |
| 13614314M | 14657336M | 12563034M | Net Sales ($) | 24127M | 143486M | 187722M | 461422M | 1168920M | 10577357M |
| 6757700M | 7033760M | 5137569M | Total Assets ($) | 36812M | 134533M | 88715M | 208581M | 585095M | 4083833M |

© RMA 2012    **M = $ thousand    MM = $ million**
See Pages 9 through 22 for Explanation of Ratios and Data

## Current Data Sorted by Assets    Comparative Historical Data

| 0-500M | 500M-2MM | 2-10MM | 10-50MM | 50-100MM | 100-250MM | Type of Statement | 4/1/07-3/31/08 ALL | 4/1/08-3/31/09 ALL |
|---|---|---|---|---|---|---|---|---|
| 1 | 1 | 8 | 12 | 4 | | Unqualified | 14 | 14 |
| | 3 | 29 | 7 | | | Reviewed | 13 | 20 |
| 1 | 16 | 9 | | | | Compiled | 6 | 15 |
| 17 | 7 | 4 | | | | Tax Returns | 13 | 20 |
| 6 | 29 | 38 | 7 | | 2 | Other | 36 | 57 |
| **19 (4/1-9/30/11)** | | | **182 (10/1/11-3/31/12)** | | | | | |
| 25 | 56 | 88 | 26 | 4 | 2 | **NUMBER OF STATEMENTS** | 82 | 126 |
| % | % | % | % | % | % | **ASSETS** | % | % |
| 35.3 | 13.1 | 11.5 | 13.3 | | | Cash & Equivalents | 10.8 | 15.4 |
| 9.8 | 46.9 | 51.2 | 44.3 | | | Trade Receivables (net) | 43.8 | 38.7 |
| 3.4 | 2.7 | 2.8 | 5.3 | | | Inventory | 2.2 | 2.2 |
| 1.5 | 5.1 | 6.8 | 8.3 | | | All Other Current | 5.7 | 6.3 |
| 50.0 | 67.8 | 72.4 | 71.2 | | | Total Current | 62.5 | 62.6 |
| 29.6 | 21.4 | 14.9 | 15.0 | | | Fixed Assets (net) | 25.5 | 22.3 |
| 6.0 | 3.3 | 5.0 | 7.0 | | | Intangibles (net) | 3.1 | 5.0 |
| 14.4 | 7.4 | 7.8 | 6.8 | | | All Other Non-Current | 8.9 | 10.1 |
| 100.0 | 100.0 | 100.0 | 100.0 | | | Total | 100.0 | 100.0 |
| | | | | | | **LIABILITIES** | | |
| 23.7 | 11.6 | 7.5 | 6.3 | | | Notes Payable-Short Term | 14.7 | 13.1 |
| 5.3 | 4.3 | 3.3 | 3.2 | | | Cur. Mat.-L.T.D. | 4.5 | 4.8 |
| 6.3 | 12.7 | 13.9 | 17.4 | | | Trade Payables | 14.1 | 13.0 |
| .4 | .2 | 1.2 | .9 | | | Income Taxes Payable | 1.3 | .9 |
| 21.5 | 9.1 | 11.6 | 12.4 | | | All Other Current | 11.9 | 12.7 |
| 57.2 | 37.8 | 37.5 | 40.2 | | | Total Current | 46.5 | 44.5 |
| 24.3 | 19.0 | 8.0 | 7.9 | | | Long-Term Debt | 20.8 | 15.9 |
| .0 | .5 | 1.1 | 1.8 | | | Deferred Taxes | .5 | .4 |
| 2.4 | 6.9 | 3.7 | 3.0 | | | All Other Non-Current | 3.8 | 4.6 |
| 16.1 | 35.8 | 49.7 | 47.0 | | | Net Worth | 28.4 | 34.7 |
| 100.0 | 100.0 | 100.0 | 100.0 | | | Total Liabilities & Net Worth | 100.0 | 100.0 |
| | | | | | | **INCOME DATA** | | |
| 100.0 | 100.0 | 100.0 | 100.0 | | | Net Sales | 100.0 | 100.0 |
| | | | | | | Gross Profit | | |
| 90.6 | 92.9 | 92.0 | 93.5 | | | Operating Expenses | 93.1 | 94.3 |
| 9.4 | 7.1 | 8.0 | 6.5 | | | Operating Profit | 6.9 | 5.7 |
| 1.9 | 1.5 | .7 | .7 | | | All Other Expenses (net) | 1.8 | 1.4 |
| 7.5 | 5.6 | 7.3 | 5.7 | | | Profit Before Taxes | 5.1 | 4.3 |
| | | | | | | **RATIOS** | | |
| 8.4 | 3.7 | 3.3 | 2.6 | | | | 2.1 | 2.4 |
| 1.6 | 2.0 | 1.9 | 1.7 | | | Current | 1.4 | 1.6 |
| .3 | 1.2 | 1.4 | 1.3 | | | | 1.1 | 1.0 |
| 8.2 | 3.6 | 3.0 | 2.3 | | | | 1.9 | 2.3 |
| 1.5 | 1.7 | 1.6 | 1.5 | | | Quick | 1.2 | 1.3 |
| .2 | 1.0 | 1.1 | 1.1 | | | | .8 | .9 |
| 0 UND | 31 11.8 | 59 6.2 | 53 6.9 | | | | 53 7.0 | 33 11.0 |
| 0 UND | 58 6.3 | 79 4.6 | 76 4.8 | | | Sales/Receivables | 75 4.9 | 59 6.2 |
| 21 17.1 | 94 3.9 | 104 3.5 | 118 3.1 | | | | 98 3.7 | 83 4.4 |
| | | | | | | | | |
| | | | | | | Cost of Sales/Inventory | | |
| | | | | | | | | |
| | | | | | | Cost of Sales/Payables | | |
| 9.4 | 5.8 | 4.2 | 3.7 | | | | 5.9 | 6.3 |
| 18.8 | 10.6 | 6.6 | 7.2 | | | Sales/Working Capital | 12.6 | 13.3 |
| -21.8 | 30.0 | 12.6 | 12.9 | | | | 92.0 | 178.9 |
| 31.3 | 24.0 | 52.3 | 24.5 | | | | 21.3 | 23.8 |
| (16) 8.1 | (50) 6.0 | (75) 11.7 | (20) 13.1 | | | EBIT/Interest | (67) 5.5 | (105) 7.4 |
| 2.6 | 1.6 | 2.7 | 4.4 | | | | 1.7 | 1.5 |
| | | 8.0 | 20.3 | | | | 8.1 | 16.5 |
| | (24) 3.4 | (10) 6.2 | | | | Net Profit + Depr., Dep., Amort./Cur. Mat. L/T/D | (13) 1.6 | (15) 7.0 |
| | 1.2 | 2.9 | | | | | 1.3 | 1.4 |
| .4 | .1 | .1 | .1 | | | | .2 | .2 |
| 1.5 | .4 | .2 | .3 | | | Fixed/Worth | .6 | .5 |
| -.3 | 1.7 | .6 | .7 | | | | 3.1 | 2.5 |
| .2 | .5 | .5 | .8 | | | | .9 | .7 |
| 3.0 | 1.2 | 1.1 | 1.5 | | | Debt/Worth | 1.9 | 1.6 |
| -4.8 | 4.2 | 2.3 | 4.2 | | | | 6.1 | 6.6 |
| 145.8 | 59.1 | 49.3 | 33.8 | | | | 52.2 | 56.0 |
| (16) 54.3 | (48) 28.9 | (85) 27.7 | (24) 22.5 | | | % Profit Before Taxes/Tangible Net Worth | (69) 28.6 | (106) 24.3 |
| 14.1 | 1.7 | 13.1 | 13.7 | | | | 14.4 | 8.1 |
| 92.7 | 31.4 | 22.7 | 14.1 | | | | 23.5 | 21.0 |
| 32.7 | 9.4 | 11.3 | 9.6 | | | % Profit Before Taxes/Total Assets | 9.4 | 8.9 |
| 15.2 | .9 | 5.3 | 3.9 | | | | 2.7 | .5 |
| 448.0 | 62.5 | 49.3 | 61.9 | | | | 40.0 | 49.1 |
| 46.9 | 25.0 | 23.5 | 18.4 | | | Sales/Net Fixed Assets | 17.3 | 21.2 |
| 8.3 | 10.2 | 10.1 | 7.6 | | | | 6.0 | 9.1 |
| 10.0 | 4.1 | 2.9 | 2.3 | | | | 3.3 | 3.6 |
| 4.6 | 3.0 | 2.2 | 1.7 | | | Sales/Total Assets | 2.2 | 2.6 |
| 2.6 | 1.9 | 1.7 | 1.4 | | | | 1.6 | 1.8 |
| 1.0 | .7 | .8 | .6 | | | | 1.0 | 1.0 |
| (10) 3.1 | (40) 1.0 | (77) 1.4 | (25) 1.2 | | | % Depr., Dep., Amort./Sales | (69) 2.1 | (93) 1.9 |
| 3.7 | 3.1 | 2.3 | 2.2 | | | | 3.9 | 3.5 |
| 4.0 | 4.1 | 1.6 | | | | | 2.4 | 2.8 |
| (17) 9.6 | (20) 6.2 | (27) 4.4 | | | | % Officers', Directors' Owners' Comp/Sales | (25) 5.6 | (40) 8.9 |
| 12.8 | 11.1 | 9.8 | | | | | 13.2 | 14.9 |
| 42863M | 187740M | 988779M | 1073587M | 699225M | 321607M | Net Sales ($) | 1509591M | 2326648M |
| 5920M | 59995M | 433100M | 574994M | 337809M | 369486M | Total Assets ($) | 755692M | 1058086M |

## Comparative Historical Data

## Current Data Sorted by Sales

| | | | Type of Statement | | | | | | |
|---|---|---|---|---|---|---|---|---|---|
| 20 | 28 | 26 | Unqualified | | 1 | | 3 | 9 | 13 |
| 28 | 42 | 39 | Reviewed | | 2 | 2 | 12 | 17 | 6 |
| 15 | 23 | 26 | Compiled | | 9 | 8 | 6 | 3 | |
| 24 | 33 | 28 | Tax Returns | 7 | 12 | 2 | 6 | 1 | |
| 57 | 55 | 82 | Other | 10 | 14 | 12 | 17 | 22 | 7 |
| 4/1/09-3/31/10 ALL | 4/1/10-3/31/11 ALL | 4/1/11-3/31/12 ALL | | 0-1MM | 19 (4/1-9/30/11) 1-3MM | 3-5MM | 182 (10/1/11-3/31/12) 5-10MM | 10-25MM | 25MM & OVER |
| 144 | 181 | 201 | **NUMBER OF STATEMENTS** | 17 | 38 | 24 | 44 | 52 | 26 |
| % | % | % | **ASSETS** | % | % | % | % | % | % |
| 15.0 | 14.4 | 14.9 | Cash & Equivalents | 22.5 | 18.6 | 17.8 | 14.5 | 11.2 | 10.1 |
| 44.2 | 43.0 | 43.3 | Trade Receivables (net) | 12.4 | 31.7 | 53.4 | 48.2 | 52.4 | 44.2 |
| 2.0 | 2.1 | 3.2 | Inventory | 5.3 | 4.7 | 2.9 | 2.3 | 3.1 | 2.0 |
| 5.6 | 5.8 | 6.1 | All Other Current | .3 | 5.5 | 5.3 | 3.6 | 8.3 | 11.3 |
| 66.8 | 65.4 | 67.5 | Total Current | 40.5 | 60.5 | 79.4 | 68.6 | 75.0 | 67.6 |
| 19.2 | 20.8 | 18.6 | Fixed Assets (net) | 40.3 | 22.2 | 16.2 | 16.8 | 12.3 | 17.0 |
| 4.8 | 5.1 | 5.6 | Intangibles (net) | 8.7 | 4.5 | 1.4 | 5.6 | 4.8 | 10.7 |
| 9.2 | 8.7 | 8.3 | All Other Non-Current | 10.3 | 12.9 | 3.0 | 9.0 | 7.8 | 4.7 |
| 100.0 | 100.0 | 100.0 | Total | 100.0 | 100.0 | 100.0 | 100.0 | 100.0 | 100.0 |
| | | | **LIABILITIES** | | | | | | |
| 11.0 | 14.4 | 10.3 | Notes Payable-Short Term | 3.5 | 23.2 | 9.0 | 8.1 | 9.0 | 3.6 |
| 3.8 | 6.9 | 3.8 | Cur. Mat.-L.T.D. | 2.7 | 6.1 | 3.4 | 4.2 | 2.2 | 3.7 |
| 11.5 | 14.4 | 13.1 | Trade Payables | 7.4 | 8.3 | 12.2 | 12.8 | 16.2 | 18.9 |
| .9 | .5 | .8 | Income Taxes Payable | .0 | .2 | 1.0 | .5 | 1.4 | 1.0 |
| 12.5 | 13.6 | 12.2 | All Other Current | 17.4 | 11.5 | 8.0 | 12.2 | 11.9 | 14.2 |
| 39.7 | 49.8 | 40.2 | Total Current | 31.1 | 49.4 | 33.6 | 37.9 | 40.9 | 41.3 |
| 13.4 | 12.9 | 13.1 | Long-Term Debt | 30.8 | 26.5 | 9.5 | 7.9 | 6.7 | 7.0 |
| .7 | 1.0 | .9 | Deferred Taxes | .0 | .0 | .8 | 1.2 | 1.2 | 2.0 |
| 3.5 | 4.3 | 4.5 | All Other Non-Current | 10.8 | 5.1 | 5.8 | 1.6 | 4.2 | 3.5 |
| 42.6 | 32.0 | 41.3 | Net Worth | 27.3 | 19.0 | 50.2 | 51.5 | 47.0 | 46.2 |
| 100.0 | 100.0 | 100.0 | Total Liabilties & Net Worth | 100.0 | 100.0 | 100.0 | 100.0 | 100.0 | 100.0 |
| | | | **INCOME DATA** | | | | | | |
| 100.0 | 100.0 | 100.0 | Net Sales | 100.0 | 100.0 | 100.0 | 100.0 | 100.0 | 100.0 |
| | | | Gross Profit | | | | | | |
| 94.5 | 92.4 | 92.4 | Operating Expenses | 79.4 | 94.3 | 91.6 | 93.7 | 93.7 | 94.0 |
| 5.5 | 7.6 | 7.6 | Operating Profit | 20.6 | 5.7 | 8.4 | 6.3 | 6.3 | 6.0 |
| .7 | 1.0 | 1.1 | All Other Expenses (net) | 6.3 | 1.0 | .4 | .7 | .3 | .7 |
| 4.8 | 6.6 | 6.5 | Profit Before Taxes | 14.3 | 4.7 | 8.1 | 5.7 | 6.0 | 5.3 |
| | | | **RATIOS** | | | | | | |
| 2.8 | 2.5 | 3.4 | | 6.2 | 4.0 | 3.6 | 3.7 | 2.7 | 2.0 |
| 1.8 | 1.6 | 1.9 | Current | 3.4 | 1.4 | 2.2 | 1.9 | 1.9 | 1.7 |
| 1.1 | 1.1 | 1.3 | | .7 | .7 | 1.7 | 1.4 | 1.3 | 1.3 |
| 2.6 | 2.2 | 3.2 | | 6.2 | 3.6 | 3.2 | 3.7 | 2.4 | 1.7 |
| 1.5 | 1.4 | 1.6 | Quick | 3.4 | 1.1 | 2.2 | 1.7 | 1.6 | 1.2 |
| 1.0 | .9 | 1.0 | | .6 | .4 | 1.6 | 1.1 | 1.0 | 1.0 |
| 35   10.5 | 36   10.2 | 39   9.3 | | 0   UND | 0   UND | 48   7.6 | 45   8.2 | 60   6.1 | 51   7.1 |
| 63   5.8 | 66   5.5 | 68   5.4 | Sales/Receivables | 16   22.4 | 44   8.3 | 70   5.2 | 69   5.3 | 78   4.7 | 69   5.3 |
| 91   4.0 | 93   3.9 | 96   3.8 | | 74   4.9 | 89   4.1 | 107   3.4 | 99   3.7 | 96   3.8 | 104   3.5 |
| | | | Cost of Sales/Inventory | | | | | | |
| | | | Cost of Sales/Payables | | | | | | |
| 5.0 | 5.4 | 4.7 | | 4.7 | 4.9 | 3.9 | 4.2 | 4.6 | 6.2 |
| 8.8 | 10.2 | 8.5 | Sales/Working Capital | 10.3 | 19.9 | 7.4 | 8.0 | 7.5 | 8.2 |
| 51.0 | 103.5 | 20.4 | | -26.6 | -28.1 | 10.9 | 15.4 | 17.0 | 22.1 |
| 34.5 | 30.0 | 32.3 | | | 23.8 | 29.5 | 36.3 | 55.4 | 35.2 |
| (115)   8.3 | (150)   7.9 | (167)   8.8 | EBIT/Interest | (33)   4.0 | 7.1 | (34)   8.2 | (45)   15.9 | (22)   16.2 |
| 1.2 | 1.7 | 2.4 | | | 1.6 | 4.3 | 1.6 | 3.4 | 6.5 |
| 10.1 | 6.2 | 11.3 | | | | | | 9.5 | |
| (20)   3.1 | (35)   2.9 | (39)   3.8 | Net Profit + Depr., Dep., Amort./Cur. Mat. L/T/D | | | | (18)   3.8 | |
| .8 | 1.3 | 1.1 | | | | | | .9 | |
| .1 | .1 | .1 | | .3 | .1 | .1 | .1 | .1 | .2 |
| .4 | .3 | .4 | Fixed/Worth | 1.0 | .8 | .3 | .3 | .2 | .3 |
| 1.3 | 1.3 | 1.0 | | -4.9 | -.9 | .9 | .9 | .6 | .8 |
| .5 | .7 | .5 | | .1 | .7 | .5 | .4 | .7 | .8 |
| 1.1 | 1.5 | 1.2 | Debt/Worth | 3.0 | 2.1 | .9 | .8 | 1.4 | 1.2 |
| 4.0 | 4.1 | 3.3 | | -7.0 | -9.9 | 1.6 | 2.6 | 2.5 | 2.7 |
| 47.3 | 62.3 | 53.8 | % Profit Before Taxes/Tangible Net Worth | 91.4 | 62.4 | 57.1 | 42.5 | 56.8 | 43.9 |
| (126)   20.1 | (154)   29.7 | (177)   27.4 | | (12)   28.0 | (27)   19.0 | (23)   36.5 | (42)   25.2 | (50)   31.1 | (23)   26.2 |
| 3.5 | 7.9 | 11.5 | | 3.4 | 1.3 | 8.2 | 7.4 | 16.0 | 19.3 |
| 23.8 | 27.5 | 24.3 | % Profit Before Taxes/Total Assets | 37.2 | 32.7 | 32.3 | 25.1 | 22.9 | 15.6 |
| 9.2 | 11.4 | 11.4 | | 6.7 | 19.8 | 13.3 | 13.0 | 10.8 | 10.3 |
| .2 | 3.0 | 3.9 | | .9 | 1.1 | 2.6 | 3.2 | 5.4 | 5.8 |
| 56.5 | 52.2 | 62.4 | Sales/Net Fixed Assets | 40.0 | 62.3 | 87.3 | 48.5 | 68.8 | 65.0 |
| 20.8 | 26.1 | 23.9 | | 5.8 | 27.5 | 23.2 | 22.8 | 29.4 | 23.2 |
| 8.8 | 9.5 | 9.5 | | .4 | 10.0 | 7.4 | 13.3 | 15.5 | 7.7 |
| 3.7 | 3.6 | 3.4 | Sales/Total Assets | 3.0 | 4.6 | 4.4 | 3.3 | 3.0 | 2.8 |
| 2.6 | 2.5 | 2.3 | | 1.1 | 3.1 | 2.8 | 2.4 | 2.3 | 2.2 |
| 1.7 | 1.8 | 1.7 | | .2 | 1.9 | 1.7 | 1.6 | 1.8 | 1.6 |
| .7 | .9 | .7 | | 1.1 | .7 | .6 | .8 | .6 | .7 |
| (119)   1.4 | (135)   1.6 | (155)   1.2 | % Depr., Dep., Amort./Sales | (10)   5.3 | (22)   1.0 | (20)   1.6 | (34)   1.4 | (46)   1.2 | (23)   1.2 |
| 3.4 | 3.2 | 2.6 | | 18.5 | 3.3 | 2.5 | 3.2 | 2.1 | 1.8 |
| 4.3 | 2.7 | 2.4 | % Officers', Directors' Owners' Comp/Sales | | 3.8 | | 4.2 | 1.5 | |
| (54)   7.9 | (69)   5.2 | (71)   5.6 | | (18)   7.6 | | (18)   8.6 | (12)   2.9 | |
| 13.7 | 12.2 | 11.5 | | | 11.7 | | | 6.5 | |
| 2081202M | 3721799M | 3313801M | Net Sales ($) | 7003M | 74360M | 96847M | 316549M | 787089M | 2031953M |
| 939104M | 1845876M | 1781304M | Total Assets ($) | 23937M | 26655M | 42321M | 144858M | 380291M | 1163242M |

© RMA 2012

M = $ thousand     MM = $ million
See Pages 9 through 22 for Explanation of Ratios and Data

## Current Data Sorted by Assets      Comparative Historical Data

| | | | | | | | Type of Statement | | |
|---|---|---|---|---|---|---|---|---|---|
| | | 4 | 16 | 16 | 4 | 5 | Unqualified | 24 | 35 |
| | 6 | 17 | 4 | | | | Reviewed | 12 | 20 |
| 3 | 6 | 5 | | | | | Compiled | 15 | 25 |
| 14 | 6 | 9 | | | | | Tax Returns | 14 | 20 |
| 20 | 41 | 59 | 22 | 5 | 4 | | Other | 72 | 84 |
| | 26 (4/1-9/30/11) | | 240 (10/1/11-3/31/12) | | | | | 4/1/07-3/31/08 | 4/1/08-3/31/09 |
| 0-500M | 500M-2MM | 2-10MM | 10-50MM | 50-100MM | 100-250MM | | | ALL | ALL |
| 37 | 63 | 106 | 42 | 9 | 9 | **NUMBER OF STATEMENTS** | 137 | 184 |
| % | % | % | % | % | % | **ASSETS** | % | % |
| 26.8 | 14.0 | 19.1 | 17.6 | | | Cash & Equivalents | 13.9 | 19.9 |
| 29.6 | 45.2 | 46.8 | 41.8 | | | Trade Receivables (net) | 46.0 | 38.0 |
| 4.1 | 2.5 | 3.5 | 2.0 | | | Inventory | 3.3 | 2.6 |
| .8 | 6.4 | 4.9 | 5.6 | | | All Other Current | 7.1 | 5.9 |
| 61.3 | 68.1 | 74.3 | 67.0 | | | Total Current | 70.3 | 66.4 |
| 21.5 | 20.6 | 13.3 | 10.1 | | | Fixed Assets (net) | 16.0 | 19.3 |
| 3.7 | 1.4 | 4.5 | 13.4 | | | Intangibles (net) | 6.7 | 7.4 |
| 13.5 | 9.9 | 8.0 | 9.5 | | | All Other Non-Current | 6.9 | 6.9 |
| 100.0 | 100.0 | 100.0 | 100.0 | | | Total | 100.0 | 100.0 |
| | | | | | | **LIABILITIES** | | |
| 26.9 | 12.7 | 10.6 | 7.7 | | | Notes Payable-Short Term | 13.3 | 12.6 |
| 4.7 | 4.4 | 1.5 | 1.2 | | | Cur. Mat.-L.T.D. | 2.5 | 3.0 |
| 7.9 | 15.6 | 11.1 | 13.3 | | | Trade Payables | 15.9 | 12.8 |
| .2 | .1 | .3 | 1.6 | | | Income Taxes Payable | .7 | .5 |
| 15.4 | 19.6 | 20.2 | 15.0 | | | All Other Current | 19.2 | 19.1 |
| 55.2 | 52.5 | 43.8 | 38.8 | | | Total Current | 51.6 | 48.0 |
| 15.0 | 15.7 | 9.3 | 8.3 | | | Long-Term Debt | 10.0 | 13.2 |
| .0 | .2 | .7 | .2 | | | Deferred Taxes | .6 | .7 |
| 15.5 | 6.7 | 5.3 | 5.9 | | | All Other Non-Current | 5.2 | 11.7 |
| 14.4 | 24.9 | 40.9 | 46.8 | | | Net Worth | 32.5 | 26.5 |
| 100.0 | 100.0 | 100.0 | 100.0 | | | Total Liabilities & Net Worth | 100.0 | 100.0 |
| | | | | | | **INCOME DATA** | | |
| 100.0 | 100.0 | 100.0 | 100.0 | | | Net Sales | 100.0 | 100.0 |
| | | | | | | Gross Profit | | |
| 92.8 | 91.7 | 92.3 | 90.6 | | | Operating Expenses | 92.0 | 90.1 |
| 7.2 | 8.3 | 7.7 | 9.4 | | | Operating Profit | 8.0 | 9.9 |
| .4 | 3.4 | 1.4 | 1.5 | | | All Other Expenses (net) | .7 | 2.2 |
| 6.7 | 4.9 | 6.4 | 7.9 | | | Profit Before Taxes | 7.3 | 7.6 |
| | | | | | | **RATIOS** | | |
| 3.5 | 2.7 | 3.6 | 2.7 | | | | 2.2 | 2.5 |
| 1.3 | 1.5 | 1.8 | 1.7 | | | Current | 1.5 | 1.5 |
| .7 | 1.0 | 1.2 | 1.2 | | | | 1.0 | 1.1 |
| 3.2 | 2.5 | 3.5 | 2.7 | | | | 2.0 | 2.3 |
| 1.3 | 1.3 | 1.6 | 1.6 | | | Quick | 1.2 | 1.3 |
| .6 | .7 | 1.0 | 1.0 | | | | .8 | .8 |
| 0   UND | 12   30.9 | 34   10.8 | 42   8.7 | | | | 34   10.7 | 25   14.7 |
| 13   27.5 | 46   7.9 | 57   6.4 | 63   5.8 | | | Sales/Receivables | 58   6.3 | 49   7.5 |
| 48   7.6 | 63   5.8 | 87   4.2 | 76   4.8 | | | | 82   4.5 | 77   4.7 |
| | | | | | | Cost of Sales/Inventory | | |
| | | | | | | Cost of Sales/Payables | | |
| 8.1 | 7.0 | 4.3 | 4.4 | | | | 6.9 | 5.7 |
| 54.0 | 18.7 | 8.3 | 9.9 | | | Sales/Working Capital | 14.7 | 15.4 |
| -61.6 | -452.9 | 28.6 | 30.2 | | | | 982.7 | 89.7 |
| | 75.0 | | 124.2 | 48.4 | | | | 27.1 | 28.4 |
| (25)   15.0 | (44)   9.4 | (79)   9.6 | (29)   10.0 | | | EBIT/Interest | (106)   5.8 | (141)   8.4 |
| 1.6 | 4.0 | 1.6 | .7 | | | | 1.8 | 1.8 |
| | | 27.0 | | | | | | 9.5 | 13.2 |
| | | (12)   4.6 | | | | Net Profit + Depr., Dep., Amort./Cur. Mat. L/T/D | (17)   2.6 | (28)   3.4 |
| | | 1.0 | | | | | .4 | 1.3 |
| .0 | .1 | .0 | .1 | | | | .1 | .1 |
| .2 | .3 | .2 | .2 | | | Fixed/Worth | .4 | .5 |
| 1.3 | 5.9 | .9 | 1.1 | | | | 2.6 | 7.6 |
| .3 | .6 | .5 | .5 | | | | .8 | .7 |
| 2.0 | 2.5 | 1.4 | 1.6 | | | Debt/Worth | 2.3 | 2.2 |
| -4.9 | -78.1 | 3.3 | 18.0 | | | | 16.2 | 57.4 |
| 146.6 | 80.7 | 77.8 | 69.5 | | | % Profit Before Taxes/Tangible Net Worth | 99.0 | 83.2 |
| (26)   73.7 | (47)   31.9 | (92)   35.1 | (35)   40.0 | | | | (112)   50.3 | (142)   38.6 |
| 27.1 | 10.5 | 9.1 | 5.7 | | | | 15.5 | 10.3 |
| 54.7 | 38.0 | 32.8 | 25.6 | | | % Profit Before Taxes/Total Assets | 36.6 | 28.9 |
| 30.0 | 9.9 | 14.4 | 11.7 | | | | 13.4 | 14.8 |
| -3.1 | 2.6 | 2.6 | .4 | | | | 2.0 | 2.1 |
| UND | 228.2 | 144.5 | 256.1 | | | | 111.6 | 117.5 |
| 88.7 | 44.2 | 59.4 | 57.8 | | | Sales/Net Fixed Assets | 37.3 | 30.8 |
| 22.5 | 13.1 | 16.5 | 14.2 | | | | 13.9 | 9.3 |
| 9.7 | 5.5 | 3.9 | 3.4 | | | | 4.6 | 4.7 |
| 5.0 | 3.7 | 2.7 | 2.2 | | | Sales/Total Assets | 3.1 | 3.1 |
| 3.1 | 2.3 | 1.8 | 1.3 | | | | 1.9 | 1.5 |
| .2 | .4 | .2 | .4 | | | | .6 | .4 |
| (14)   .8 | (34)   .9 | (74)   .5 | (28)   .9 | | | % Depr., Dep., Amort./Sales | (83)   1.0 | (127)   1.2 |
| 2.2 | 2.2 | 1.6 | 2.7 | | | | 1.8 | 2.7 |
| 5.6 | 1.9 | 2.3 | | | | | 2.8 | 2.7 |
| (15)   11.7 | (19)   5.4 | (22)   3.4 | | | | % Officers', Directors' Owners' Comp/Sales | (28)   5.0 | (41)   7.5 |
| 21.3 | 10.6 | 5.0 | | | | | 13.5 | 14.8 |
| 52071M | 393575M | 1401507M | 2294109M | 1130617M | 2316598M | Net Sales ($) | 4850063M | 5880581M |
| 9089M | 76465M | 449825M | 902002M | 644671M | 1413638M | Total Assets ($) | 2465929M | 2641159M |

M = $ thousand    MM = $ million
See Pages 9 through 22 for Explanation of Ratios and Data

## Comparative Historical Data | Current Data Sorted by Sales

| Hist 1 | Hist 2 | Hist 3 | Type of Statement | 0-1MM | 1-3MM | 3-5MM | 5-10MM | 10-25MM | 25MM & OVER |
|---|---|---|---|---|---|---|---|---|---|
| 52 | 60 | 45 | Unqualified | | 4 | 3 | 4 | 12 | 22 |
| 32 | 33 | 27 | Reviewed | | 1 | 2 | 8 | 12 | 4 |
| 14 | 15 | 14 | Compiled | 3 | 2 | 3 | 3 | 2 | 1 |
| 28 | 27 | 29 | Tax Returns | 3 | 12 | 5 | 8 | 1 | |
| 112 | 148 | 151 | Other | 24 | 14 | 17 | 28 | 32 | 36 |
| 4/1/09-3/31/10 ALL | 4/1/10-3/31/11 ALL | 4/1/11-3/31/12 ALL | | 26 (4/1-9/30/11) | | | 240 (10/1/11-3/31/12) | | |
| 238 | 283 | 266 | **NUMBER OF STATEMENTS** | 30 | 33 | 30 | 51 | 59 | 63 |
| % | % | % | **ASSETS** | % | % | % | % | % | % |
| 17.7 | 17.7 | 18.3 | Cash & Equivalents | 16.2 | 20.4 | 26.0 | 19.1 | 16.3 | 15.9 |
| 42.1 | 39.6 | 42.6 | Trade Receivables (net) | 22.3 | 27.8 | 37.9 | 50.0 | 53.0 | 46.6 |
| 2.9 | 2.3 | 3.2 | Inventory | .4 | 7.0 | 2.1 | 5.7 | 1.3 | 2.7 |
| 5.6 | 6.9 | 4.8 | All Other Current | 3.1 | 7.1 | 3.2 | 2.2 | 6.3 | 5.7 |
| 68.2 | 66.5 | 68.9 | Total Current | 42.0 | 62.3 | 69.1 | 77.0 | 76.9 | 71.0 |
| 16.4 | 16.9 | 15.7 | Fixed Assets (net) | 36.3 | 22.9 | 16.3 | 11.4 | 10.5 | 10.1 |
| 7.2 | 8.7 | 6.3 | Intangibles (net) | 3.4 | 1.6 | 1.0 | 6.4 | 6.8 | 11.9 |
| 8.1 | 8.0 | 9.1 | All Other Non-Current | 18.3 | 13.2 | 12.6 | 5.1 | 5.8 | 7.1 |
| 100.0 | 100.0 | 100.0 | Total | 100.0 | 100.0 | 100.0 | 100.0 | 100.0 | 100.0 |
| | | | **LIABILITIES** | | | | | | |
| 10.7 | 10.6 | 12.5 | Notes Payable-Short Term | 19.0 | 15.2 | 13.3 | 8.8 | 14.1 | 9.0 |
| 3.1 | 2.6 | 2.6 | Cur. Mat.-L.T.D. | 1.0 | 4.7 | 6.0 | 3.4 | 1.6 | 1.1 |
| 12.6 | 10.9 | 12.1 | Trade Payables | 8.8 | 6.7 | 10.0 | 13.9 | 12.4 | 15.8 |
| .6 | .7 | .5 | Income Taxes Payable | .3 | .1 | .1 | .2 | .5 | 1.3 |
| 19.0 | 18.4 | 18.6 | All Other Current | 17.4 | 16.8 | 16.0 | 17.9 | 20.8 | 19.9 |
| 46.0 | 43.2 | 46.3 | Total Current | 46.4 | 43.4 | 45.3 | 44.3 | 49.3 | 47.2 |
| 14.4 | 10.8 | 12.0 | Long-Term Debt | 22.9 | 19.1 | 10.4 | 10.3 | 8.6 | 8.6 |
| .6 | .7 | .4 | Deferred Taxes | .0 | .0 | .6 | .8 | .4 | .5 |
| 7.0 | 4.6 | 7.6 | All Other Non-Current | 23.8 | 3.5 | 3.7 | 7.3 | 6.3 | 5.5 |
| 32.0 | 40.7 | 33.6 | Net Worth | 7.0 | 34.0 | 40.0 | 37.3 | 35.4 | 38.2 |
| 100.0 | 100.0 | 100.0 | Total Liabilities & Net Worth | 100.0 | 100.0 | 100.0 | 100.0 | 100.0 | 100.0 |
| | | | **INCOME DATA** | | | | | | |
| 100.0 | 100.0 | 100.0 | Net Sales | 100.0 | 100.0 | 100.0 | 100.0 | 100.0 | 100.0 |
| | | | Gross Profit | | | | | | |
| 92.8 | 91.1 | 91.8 | Operating Expenses | 84.0 | 94.2 | 93.0 | 92.0 | 93.7 | 91.7 |
| 7.2 | 8.9 | 8.2 | Operating Profit | 16.0 | 5.8 | 7.0 | 8.0 | 6.3 | 8.3 |
| 1.6 | 1.7 | 1.9 | All Other Expenses (net) | 8.9 | .8 | .2 | .9 | .9 | 1.6 |
| 5.6 | 7.3 | 6.3 | Profit Before Taxes | 7.1 | 5.0 | 6.9 | 7.2 | 5.4 | 6.6 |
| | | | **RATIOS** | | | | | | |
| 3.1 | 3.1 | 3.1 | | 3.0 | 5.0 | 5.2 | 4.6 | 2.7 | 2.2 |
| 1.6 | 1.6 | 1.7 | Current | 1.2 | 2.0 | 1.8 | 2.3 | 1.7 | 1.5 |
| 1.1 | 1.1 | 1.1 | | .4 | 1.1 | 1.1 | 1.2 | 1.1 | 1.1 |
| 2.7 | 2.8 | 3.0 | | 3.0 | 4.0 | 5.0 | 3.9 | 2.4 | 1.9 |
| 1.4 | 1.4 | 1.5 | Quick | 1.2 | 1.8 | 1.7 | 2.2 | 1.5 | 1.3 |
| .9 | .8 | .9 | | .2 | .6 | 1.0 | 1.2 | .9 | .9 |
| 30  12.1 | 27  13.4 | 24  15.1 | | 0 UND | 3 133.2 | 20 17.9 | 40 9.2 | 35 10.3 | 34 10.7 |
| 54  6.7 | 55  6.6 | 53  6.9 | Sales/Receivables | 0 UND | 30 12.1 | 52 7.0 | 59 6.2 | 61 6.0 | 58 6.3 |
| 75  4.9 | 78  4.7 | 74  4.9 | | 42 8.6 | 55 6.6 | 76 4.8 | 74 4.9 | 87 4.2 | 74 4.9 |
| | | | Cost of Sales/Inventory | | | | | | |
| | | | Cost of Sales/Payables | | | | | | |
| 5.3 | 5.0 | 5.1 | | 5.8 | 4.4 | 4.3 | 4.6 | 6.6 | 5.1 |
| 13.0 | 9.5 | 12.8 | Sales/Working Capital | 27.1 | 13.1 | 12.4 | 8.8 | 12.7 | 15.6 |
| 79.3 | 87.0 | 163.0 | | -9.5 | 217.6 | 50.7 | 33.3 | 77.6 | 66.2 |
| 38.3 | 42.7 | 58.1 | | 15.9 | 15.7 | 85.5 | 75.7 | 81.1 | 70.6 |
| (175) 8.0 | (208) 12.8 | (193) 10.3 | EBIT/Interest | (13) 6.2 | (24) 9.6 | (25) 12.5 | (41) 10.3 | (45) 8.1 | (45) 15.2 |
| 1.5 | 2.2 | 1.6 | | -.8 | .9 | 2.5 | 3.6 | 1.6 | 2.0 |
| 19.6 | 17.5 | 18.9 | | | | | | | |
| (34) 2.3 | (39) 3.3 | (22) 2.4 | Net Profit + Depr., Dep., Amort./Cur. Mat. L/T/D | | | | | | |
| 1.2 | 1.4 | 1.3 | | | | | | | |
| .1 | .1 | .1 | | .0 | .1 | .0 | .0 | .1 | .1 |
| .4 | .3 | .2 | Fixed/Worth | .9 | .3 | .2 | .2 | .2 | .2 |
| 2.2 | 1.6 | 1.5 | | NM | 1.4 | 1.0 | 2.6 | .9 | 1.6 |
| .7 | .5 | .6 | | .9 | .5 | .3 | .5 | .8 | .9 |
| 2.3 | 1.9 | 1.7 | Debt/Worth | 7.1 | 1.1 | 1.1 | .9 | 1.8 | 2.5 |
| 12.5 | 7.3 | 9.8 | | -4.9 | 3.7 | 4.0 | -42.3 | 5.2 | 10.4 |
| 77.9 | 77.3 | 81.1 | | 31.5 | 77.1 | 110.7 | 83.5 | 78.4 | 100.9 |
| (195) 36.6 | (239) 38.0 | (213) 38.3 | % Profit Before Taxes/Tangible Net Worth | (17) 24.5 | (29) 25.5 | (26) 58.3 | (38) 42.6 | (50) 37.3 | (53) 50.2 |
| 8.5 | 8.6 | 10.7 | | 3.1 | 2.6 | 10.4 | 23.8 | 10.9 | 17.4 |
| 26.6 | 29.3 | 33.8 | | 23.2 | 37.5 | 58.3 | 44.9 | 25.4 | 26.8 |
| 10.0 | 10.1 | 12.8 | % Profit Before Taxes/Total Assets | 2.7 | 10.1 | 10.2 | 17.6 | 15.7 | 13.5 |
| 1.6 | 1.8 | 2.4 | | -7.3 | .5 | 4.8 | 5.8 | 1.5 | 3.2 |
| 125.9 | 114.0 | 179.1 | | UND | 90.1 | 389.6 | 311.3 | 161.7 | 214.6 |
| 38.7 | 40.5 | 53.0 | Sales/Net Fixed Assets | 19.0 | 29.7 | 37.4 | 70.0 | 61.3 | 60.6 |
| 11.6 | 12.8 | 15.9 | | .7 | 10.4 | 9.7 | 25.0 | 20.7 | 22.1 |
| 4.5 | 3.9 | 4.7 | | 4.7 | 5.5 | 6.5 | 4.3 | 5.2 | 4.5 |
| 2.9 | 2.6 | 3.0 | Sales/Total Assets | 1.3 | 3.1 | 3.0 | 3.0 | 3.1 | 2.8 |
| 1.6 | 1.5 | 1.6 | | .2 | 1.2 | 1.5 | 2.1 | 2.3 | 1.5 |
| .4 | .4 | .3 | | 1.2 | .2 | .6 | .3 | .2 | .3 |
| (164) 1.0 | (183) 1.3 | (163) .7 | % Depr., Dep., Amort./Sales | (11) 4.1 | (20) 1.0 | (10) 3.1 | (33) .7 | (48) .5 | (41) .7 |
| 2.2 | 2.4 | 2.1 | | 23.0 | 2.2 | 4.7 | 2.0 | 1.1 | 2.6 |
| 2.3 | 2.4 | 2.3 | | | 2.8 | 2.4 | 2.4 | 2.0 | |
| (54) 4.8 | (56) 4.2 | (62) 4.6 | % Officers', Directors' Owners' Comp/Sales | | (12) 7.6 | (11) 3.9 | (15) 5.1 | (12) 2.9 | |
| 11.2 | 12.1 | 9.8 | | | 18.5 | 11.4 | 8.4 | 4.4 | |
| 8004503M | 10416688M | 7588477M | Net Sales ($) | 14574M | 62998M | 118043M | 345340M | 917207M | 6130315M |
| 3769377M | 5233833M | 3495690M | Total Assets ($) | 19694M | 44233M | 46299M | 147483M | 336380M | 2901601M |

M = $ thousand     MM = $ million
See Pages 9 through 22 for Explanation of Ratios and Data

## Current Data Sorted by Assets | Comparative Historical Data

| 0-500M | 500M-2MM | 2-10MM | 10-50MM | 50-100MM | 100-250MM | Type of Statement | 4/1/07-3/31/08 ALL | 4/1/08-3/31/09 ALL |
|---|---|---|---|---|---|---|---|---|
|  |  | 2 | 4 |  |  | Unqualified | 4 | 6 |
|  |  | 1 | 2 | 1 |  | Reviewed |  |  |
| 1 |  | 2 | 1 |  |  | Compiled | 1 | 1 |
| 3 |  | 2 | 1 |  |  | Tax Returns | 2 | 4 |
| 4 |  | 8 | 8 | 4 | 3 | Other | 3 | 5 |
|  | 8 (4/1-9/30/11) |  | 37 (10/1/11-3/31/12) |  |  |  |  |  |
| 8 | 4 | 15 | 10 | 5 | 3 | **NUMBER OF STATEMENTS** | 10 | 16 |
| % | % | % | % | % | % | **ASSETS** | % | % |
|  |  | 19.6 | 18.7 |  |  | Cash & Equivalents | 24.0 | 14.8 |
|  |  | 30.2 | 18.1 |  |  | Trade Receivables (net) | 12.4 | 16.2 |
|  |  | 2.4 | 9.7 |  |  | Inventory | 3.0 | 8.0 |
|  |  | 10.8 | 4.3 |  |  | All Other Current | 4.7 | 5.7 |
|  |  | 63.0 | 50.8 |  |  | Total Current | 44.0 | 44.6 |
|  |  | 21.0 | 33.3 |  |  | Fixed Assets (net) | 29.9 | 35.5 |
|  |  | 8.2 | .1 |  |  | Intangibles (net) | 13.9 | 13.9 |
|  |  | 7.9 | 15.7 |  |  | All Other Non-Current | 12.2 | 6.0 |
|  |  | 100.0 | 100.0 |  |  | Total | 100.0 | 100.0 |
|  |  |  |  |  |  | **LIABILITIES** |  |  |
|  |  | 8.4 | 6.1 |  |  | Notes Payable-Short Term | 3.3 | 5.8 |
|  |  | 1.8 | 2.5 |  |  | Cur. Mat.-L.T.D. | 5.2 | 3.5 |
|  |  | 13.9 | 10.0 |  |  | Trade Payables | 6.2 | 13.4 |
|  |  | .2 | .9 |  |  | Income Taxes Payable | .0 | .1 |
|  |  | 14.8 | 14.2 |  |  | All Other Current | 23.1 | 14.6 |
|  |  | 39.1 | 33.7 |  |  | Total Current | 37.9 | 37.4 |
|  |  | 6.0 | 19.3 |  |  | Long-Term Debt | 16.4 | 20.6 |
|  |  | .5 | 2.3 |  |  | Deferred Taxes | .3 | .4 |
|  |  | 11.1 | 5.5 |  |  | All Other Non-Current | .5 | 3.2 |
|  |  | 43.3 | 39.1 |  |  | Net Worth | 44.9 | 38.4 |
|  |  | 100.0 | 100.0 |  |  | Total Liabilities & Net Worth | 100.0 | 100.0 |
|  |  |  |  |  |  | **INCOME DATA** |  |  |
|  |  | 100.0 | 100.0 |  |  | Net Sales | 100.0 | 100.0 |
|  |  |  |  |  |  | Gross Profit |  |  |
|  |  | 93.4 | 89.4 |  |  | Operating Expenses | 87.1 | 89.5 |
|  |  | 6.6 | 10.6 |  |  | Operating Profit | 12.9 | 10.5 |
|  |  | .4 | 2.6 |  |  | All Other Expenses (net) | 2.0 | 2.3 |
|  |  | 6.1 | 8.0 |  |  | Profit Before Taxes | 10.9 | 8.1 |
|  |  |  |  |  |  | **RATIOS** |  |  |
|  |  | 2.9 | 4.3 |  |  | Current | 1.9 | 1.7 |
|  |  | 2.2 | 1.5 |  |  |  | 1.3 | 1.2 |
|  |  | 1.1 | .8 |  |  |  | .7 | .8 |
|  |  | 2.5 | 4.1 |  |  | Quick | 1.7 | 1.3 |
|  |  | 1.6 | 1.2 |  |  |  | 1.1 | .7 |
|  |  | .9 | .3 |  |  |  | .3 | .5 |
|  |  | 34   10.6 | 30   12.3 |  |  | Sales/Receivables | 0   UND | 12   31.6 |
|  |  | 74   4.9 | 37   9.8 |  |  |  | 17   21.5 | 38   9.5 |
|  |  | 91   4.0 | 47   7.7 |  |  |  | 48   7.7 | 47   7.7 |
|  |  |  |  |  |  | Cost of Sales/Inventory |  |  |
|  |  |  |  |  |  | Cost of Sales/Payables |  |  |
|  |  | 2.9 | 2.5 |  |  | Sales/Working Capital | 7.9 | 6.7 |
|  |  | 6.7 | 15.1 |  |  |  | 27.0 | 20.7 |
|  |  | 27.4 | -9.1 |  |  |  | -14.7 | -30.0 |
|  |  | 141.0 |  |  |  | EBIT/Interest |  | 25.7 |
|  |  | (12) 23.9 |  |  |  |  | (15) 4.2 |
|  |  | 2.2 |  |  |  |  |  | 2.8 |
|  |  |  |  |  |  | Net Profit + Depr., Dep., Amort./Cur. Mat. L/T/D |  |  |
|  |  | .2 | .2 |  |  | Fixed/Worth | .1 | .3 |
|  |  | .5 | 1.0 |  |  |  | .5 | 1.1 |
|  |  | 1.6 | NM |  |  |  | NM | 3.1 |
|  |  | .4 | .7 |  |  | Debt/Worth | .4 | .8 |
|  |  | 1.0 | 1.3 |  |  |  | 1.5 | 2.1 |
|  |  | 2.4 | NM |  |  |  | -3.4 | 8.5 |
|  |  | 92.3 |  |  |  | % Profit Before Taxes/Tangible Net Worth |  | 74.0 |
|  |  | (13) 30.1 |  |  |  |  | (13) 31.1 |
|  |  | 5.3 |  |  |  |  |  | 10.8 |
|  |  | 34.0 | 30.6 |  |  | % Profit Before Taxes/Total Assets | 27.7 | 25.3 |
|  |  | 9.0 | 9.0 |  |  |  | 15.5 | 13.7 |
|  |  | -1.0 | .5 |  |  |  | 2.5 | 3.8 |
|  |  | 40.6 | 14.9 |  |  | Sales/Net Fixed Assets | 143.2 | 36.3 |
|  |  | 7.9 | 5.1 |  |  |  | 6.4 | 3.3 |
|  |  | 2.6 | 1.7 |  |  |  | 2.6 | 2.0 |
|  |  | 2.2 | 1.8 |  |  | Sales/Total Assets | 3.0 | 2.0 |
|  |  | 1.5 | 1.1 |  |  |  | 1.5 | 1.5 |
|  |  | 1.1 | .6 |  |  |  | 1.0 | 1.0 |
|  |  | 1.8 | .4 |  |  | % Depr., Dep., Amort./Sales |  | 1.2 |
|  |  | (11) 3.7 | 2.6 |  |  |  | (12) 6.0 |
|  |  | 5.3 | 4.9 |  |  |  |  | 10.5 |
|  |  |  |  |  |  | % Officers', Directors' Owners' Comp/Sales |  |  |
| 18576M | 10944M | 150585M | 516020M | 490904M | 562090M | Net Sales ($) | 239484M | 481906M |
| 2634M | 4076M | 76124M | 281174M | 438096M | 506864M | Total Assets ($) | 376961M | 520465M |

M = $ thousand    MM = $ million
See Pages 9 through 22 for Explanation of Ratios and Data

## Comparative Historical Data | Current Data Sorted by Sales

| | Hist 1 | Hist 2 | Hist 3 | | Type of Statement | 0-1MM | 1-3MM | 3-5MM | 5-10MM | 10-25MM | 25MM & OVER |
|---|---|---|---|---|---|---|---|---|---|---|---|
| | 11 | 6 | 6 | | Unqualified | | | | 3 | 3 | |
| | 1 | 2 | 4 | | Reviewed | | | | 1 | | 3 |
| | 3 | 1 | 3 | | Compiled | 1 | | 1 | 1 | | |
| | 1 | 2 | 6 | | Tax Returns | | 1 | | 2 | 1 | 1 |
| | 10 | 15 | 26 | | Other | 4 | 3 | 4 | 3 | 1 | 11 |
| | 4/1/09-3/31/10 ALL | 4/1/10-3/31/11 ALL | 4/1/11-3/31/12 ALL | | | | 8 (4/1-9/30/11) | | 37 (10/1/11-3/31/12) | | |
| | 26 | 26 | 45 | | NUMBER OF STATEMENTS | 5 | 4 | 6 | 9 | 6 | 15 |
| | % | % | % | | **ASSETS** | % | % | % | % | % | % |
| | 16.7 | 18.5 | 24.0 | | Cash & Equivalents | | | | | | 25.0 |
| | 19.8 | 18.0 | 20.9 | | Trade Receivables (net) | | | | | | 25.7 |
| | 1.9 | 4.2 | 4.9 | | Inventory | | | | | | 7.7 |
| | 6.8 | 7.1 | 6.3 | | All Other Current | | | | | | 7.3 |
| | 45.2 | 47.8 | 56.1 | | Total Current | | | | | | 65.7 |
| | 25.1 | 33.1 | 25.1 | | Fixed Assets (net) | | | | | | 19.6 |
| | 16.1 | 9.9 | 7.9 | | Intangibles (net) | | | | | | 7.0 |
| | 13.5 | 9.2 | 10.9 | | All Other Non-Current | | | | | | 7.7 |
| | 100.0 | 100.0 | 100.0 | | Total | | | | | | 100.0 |
| | | | | | **LIABILITIES** | | | | | | |
| | 15.9 | 7.8 | 9.7 | | Notes Payable-Short Term | | | | | | 3.0 |
| | .7 | 1.6 | 1.3 | | Cur. Mat.-L.T.D. | | | | | | .8 |
| | 8.4 | 8.6 | 9.8 | | Trade Payables | | | | | | 12.2 |
| | .3 | .1 | .3 | | Income Taxes Payable | | | | | | .9 |
| | 13.0 | 14.5 | 13.3 | | All Other Current | | | | | | 16.1 |
| | 38.2 | 32.5 | 34.4 | | Total Current | | | | | | 33.0 |
| | 11.7 | 21.0 | 17.1 | | Long-Term Debt | | | | | | 18.0 |
| | .8 | .9 | .8 | | Deferred Taxes | | | | | | 1.9 |
| | 4.0 | 6.3 | 7.1 | | All Other Non-Current | | | | | | 8.4 |
| | 45.2 | 39.3 | 40.6 | | Net Worth | | | | | | 38.7 |
| | 100.0 | 100.0 | 100.0 | | Total Liabilities & Net Worth | | | | | | 100.0 |
| | | | | | **INCOME DATA** | | | | | | |
| | 100.0 | 100.0 | 100.0 | | Net Sales | | | | | | 100.0 |
| | | | | | Gross Profit | | | | | | |
| | 90.2 | 96.7 | 90.0 | | Operating Expenses | | | | | | 91.1 |
| | 9.8 | 3.3 | 10.0 | | Operating Profit | | | | | | 8.9 |
| | 2.5 | 2.2 | .9 | | All Other Expenses (net) | | | | | | 1.5 |
| | 7.3 | 1.1 | 9.0 | | Profit Before Taxes | | | | | | 7.5 |
| | | | | | **RATIOS** | | | | | | |
| | 2.5 | 2.9 | 4.6 | | Current | | | | | | 4.7 |
| | 1.6 | 1.4 | 1.6 | | | | | | | | 1.6 |
| | 1.0 | .9 | .9 | | | | | | | | 1.2 |
| | 2.3 | 2.4 | 3.7 | | Quick | | | | | | 4.4 |
| | 1.3 | 1.3 | 1.4 | | | | | | | | 1.3 |
| | .7 | .7 | .6 | | | | | | | | 1.0 |
| 16 | 23.1 | 23  16.2 | 20  18.0 | | Sales/Receivables | | | | | 31 | 11.9 |
| 54 | 6.7 | 49  7.5 | 41  9.0 | | | | | | | 46 | 8.0 |
| 71 | 5.1 | 63  5.8 | 69  5.3 | | | | | | | 65 | 5.6 |
| | | | | | Cost of Sales/Inventory | | | | | | |
| | | | | | Cost of Sales/Payables | | | | | | |
| | 4.9 | 5.0 | 4.4 | | Sales/Working Capital | | | | | | 2.1 |
| | 13.4 | 12.7 | 11.2 | | | | | | | | 11.2 |
| | NM | -37.2 | -79.7 | | | | | | | | 18.0 |
| | 39.3 | 30.5 | 66.4 | | EBIT/Interest | | | | | | 47.6 |
| (20) | 7.6 | (18)  2.1 | (30)  13.1 | | | | | | | (10) | 17.6 |
| | 1.6 | -2.9 | 1.4 | | | | | | | | 3.1 |
| | | | | | Net Profit + Depr., Dep., Amort./Cur. Mat. L/T/D | | | | | | |
| | .2 | .2 | .2 | | Fixed/Worth | | | | | | .1 |
| | .5 | 1.2 | .6 | | | | | | | | .5 |
| | 1.4 | 41.9 | 5.4 | | | | | | | | UND |
| | .6 | .5 | .5 | | Debt/Worth | | | | | | .5 |
| | 1.0 | 3.0 | 1.2 | | | | | | | | 1.2 |
| | 3.6 | 124.6 | UND | | | | | | | | UND |
| | 68.2 | 35.2 | 86.4 | | % Profit Before Taxes/Tangible Net Worth | | | | | | 105.9 |
| (23) | 23.5 | (21)  12.9 | (34)  19.1 | | | | | | | (12) | 19.1 |
| | -.3 | -21.4 | 3.4 | | | | | | | | 4.7 |
| | 20.8 | 15.6 | 35.3 | | % Profit Before Taxes/Total Assets | | | | | | 52.4 |
| | 5.2 | 2.3 | 10.9 | | | | | | | | 9.6 |
| | -.2 | -4.9 | .8 | | | | | | | | 4.9 |
| | 29.9 | 24.8 | 38.4 | | Sales/Net Fixed Assets | | | | | | 39.7 |
| | 13.3 | 6.2 | 7.9 | | | | | | | | 7.9 |
| | 2.5 | 1.9 | 4.4 | | | | | | | | 4.6 |
| | 1.7 | 2.2 | 2.8 | | Sales/Total Assets | | | | | | 2.3 |
| | 1.3 | 1.3 | 1.5 | | | | | | | | 1.4 |
| | .7 | .7 | .9 | | | | | | | | 1.1 |
| | 1.3 | 2.0 | 1.7 | | % Depr., Dep., Amort./Sales | | | | | | |
| (20) | 2.7 | (17)  5.1 | (29)  3.1 | | | | | | | | |
| | 3.9 | 10.4 | 4.7 | | | | | | | | |
| | | | 1.4 | | % Officers', Directors' Owners' Comp/Sales | | | | | | |
| | | (12) | 6.1 | | | | | | | | |
| | | | 9.0 | | | | | | | | |
| | 1106825M | 529984M | 1749119M | | Net Sales ($) | 3314M | 5686M | 24989M | 62622M | 98946M | 1553562M |
| | 1393361M | 738630M | 1308968M | | Total Assets ($) | 5290M | 5700M | 9831M | 52127M | 121082M | 1114938M |

M = $ thousand     MM = $ million
See Pages 9 through 22 for Explanation of Ratios and Data

## Current Data Sorted by Assets     Comparative Historical Data

Type of Statement counts:

| Type of Statement | 0-500M | 500M-2MM | 2-10MM | 10-50MM | 50-100MM | 100-250MM | | 4/1/07-3/31/08 ALL | 4/1/08-3/31/09 ALL |
|---|---|---|---|---|---|---|---|---|---|
| Unqualified | 1 | 3 | 14 | 27 | 11 | 16 | | 77 | 81 |
| Reviewed | 2 | 2 | 7 | 5 | 1 | | | 17 | 24 |
| Compiled | | 3 | 5 | | | | | 15 | 9 |
| Tax Returns | 8 | 8 | 8 | 1 | | | | 19 | 22 |
| Other | 6 | 19 | 28 | 26 | 14 | 16 | | 89 | 101 |
| | 51 (4/1-9/30/11) | | | 180 (10/1/11-3/31/12) | | | | | |

| | 0-500M | 500M-2MM | 2-10MM | 10-50MM | 50-100MM | 100-250MM | | 4/1/07-3/31/08 ALL | 4/1/08-3/31/09 ALL |
|---|---|---|---|---|---|---|---|---|---|
| **NUMBER OF STATEMENTS** | 17 | 35 | 62 | 59 | 26 | 32 | | 217 | 237 |
| | % | % | % | % | % | % | **ASSETS** | % | % |
| | 46.8 | 19.3 | 19.5 | 21.3 | 23.1 | 14.4 | Cash & Equivalents | 19.2 | 20.0 |
| | 16.1 | 33.2 | 32.4 | 26.0 | 21.5 | 13.0 | Trade Receivables (net) | 28.4 | 30.4 |
| | .0 | 6.4 | 6.6 | 4.6 | 2.7 | 3.3 | Inventory | 5.1 | 4.5 |
| | .7 | 9.1 | 5.7 | 6.1 | 5.9 | 7.7 | All Other Current | 5.7 | 5.6 |
| | 63.5 | 68.0 | 64.2 | 58.0 | 53.2 | 38.5 | Total Current | 58.3 | 60.5 |
| | 20.3 | 16.1 | 23.4 | 22.4 | 30.1 | 26.4 | Fixed Assets (net) | 23.5 | 23.9 |
| | .2 | 3.2 | 4.0 | 8.2 | 10.3 | 17.4 | Intangibles (net) | 6.4 | 5.2 |
| | 16.1 | 12.7 | 8.3 | 11.4 | 6.4 | 17.7 | All Other Non-Current | 11.8 | 10.4 |
| | 100.0 | 100.0 | 100.0 | 100.0 | 100.0 | 100.0 | Total | 100.0 | 100.0 |
| | | | | | | | **LIABILITIES** | | |
| | 39.6 | 6.6 | 7.7 | 4.1 | 1.4 | 2.4 | Notes Payable-Short Term | 7.8 | 6.7 |
| | .0 | .5 | 2.0 | 1.8 | 1.7 | 3.3 | Cur. Mat.-L.T.D. | 2.3 | 2.0 |
| | 15.7 | 13.7 | 8.8 | 10.8 | 11.0 | 7.7 | Trade Payables | 9.2 | 10.3 |
| | .0 | .3 | .6 | .5 | .0 | .5 | Income Taxes Payable | .4 | .3 |
| | 77.3 | 14.2 | 18.1 | 17.9 | 20.9 | 12.4 | All Other Current | 20.3 | 17.2 |
| | 132.7 | 35.2 | 37.2 | 35.2 | 35.1 | 26.3 | Total Current | 39.9 | 36.5 |
| | 26.1 | 7.0 | 10.3 | 11.9 | 16.1 | 20.3 | Long-Term Debt | 12.9 | 14.6 |
| | .0 | .0 | .3 | .5 | .5 | 1.0 | Deferred Taxes | .3 | .4 |
| | 2.3 | 7.0 | 6.8 | 7.0 | 6.6 | 16.1 | All Other Non-Current | 7.6 | 4.7 |
| | -61.1 | 50.8 | 45.4 | 45.5 | 41.7 | 36.3 | Net Worth | 39.3 | 43.8 |
| | 100.0 | 100.0 | 100.0 | 100.0 | 100.0 | 100.0 | Total Liabilities & Net Worth | 100.0 | 100.0 |
| | | | | | | | **INCOME DATA** | | |
| | 100.0 | 100.0 | 100.0 | 100.0 | 100.0 | 100.0 | Net Sales | 100.0 | 100.0 |
| | | | | | | | Gross Profit | | |
| | 102.2 | 94.1 | 95.3 | 91.3 | 97.2 | 93.3 | Operating Expenses | 93.2 | 93.7 |
| | -2.2 | 5.9 | 4.7 | 8.7 | 2.8 | 6.7 | Operating Profit | 6.8 | 6.3 |
| | .3 | -.4 | .4 | 1.5 | .2 | 6.0 | All Other Expenses (net) | .7 | 2.1 |
| | -2.5 | 6.3 | 4.3 | 7.2 | 2.6 | .7 | Profit Before Taxes | 6.2 | 4.3 |
| | | | | | | | **RATIOS** | | |
| | 1.3 | 6.4 | 3.1 | 3.0 | 3.3 | 2.1 | | 3.7 | 3.3 |
| | .5 | 2.9 | 1.6 | 1.9 | 1.4 | 1.6 | Current | 1.7 | 1.8 |
| | .2 | 1.4 | 1.1 | 1.1 | .9 | 1.1 | | 1.1 | 1.2 |
| | 1.3 | 4.2 | 2.6 | 2.3 | 2.7 | 1.5 | | 2.9 | 2.9 |
| | .5 | 2.4 | 1.3 | 1.5 | 1.3 | 1.1 | Quick | 1.4 | 1.5 |
| | .2 | 1.0 | .9 | .9 | .7 | .7 | | .8 | .9 |
| | 0 UND | 17 21.4 | 24 15.0 | 31 11.9 | 31 11.8 | 30 12.2 | | 27 13.5 | 32 11.4 |
| | 0 UND | 36 10.2 | 47 7.8 | 52 7.0 | 44 8.3 | 51 7.1 | Sales/Receivables | 51 7.2 | 52 7.0 |
| | 2 149.1 | 53 6.9 | 69 5.3 | 74 4.9 | 72 5.1 | 70 5.2 | | 80 4.6 | 76 4.8 |
| | | | | | | | Cost of Sales/Inventory | | |
| | | | | | | | Cost of Sales/Payables | | |
| | 74.8 | 4.0 | 3.6 | 3.4 | 1.9 | 3.9 | | 3.4 | 3.9 |
| | -23.9 | 6.3 | 9.1 | 7.0 | 7.0 | 8.4 | Sales/Working Capital | 9.2 | 7.8 |
| | -3.0 | 22.0 | 31.0 | 33.2 | -72.1 | 64.9 | | 89.2 | 37.7 |
| | | 41.7 | 31.1 | 46.4 | 9.9 | 26.8 | | 15.6 | 23.0 |
| | | (20) 10.3 | (49) 11.2 | (43) 5.9 | (18) 2.5 | (27) 5.4 | EBIT/Interest | (151) 5.7 | (163) 3.6 |
| | | -.3 | 2.0 | 1.6 | .4 | -.1 | | 1.6 | -.5 |
| | | | 20.1 | | | 8.4 | Net Profit + Depr., Dep., | 8.9 | 15.3 |
| | | | (11) 4.4 | | | (11) 2.6 | Amort./Cur. Mat. L/T/D | (41) 4.4 | (37) 4.3 |
| | | | 2.4 | | | .4 | | 1.5 | 1.6 |
| | .0 | .1 | .1 | .1 | .2 | .4 | | .2 | .1 |
| | -32.0 | .2 | .3 | .3 | 1.1 | .7 | Fixed/Worth | .5 | .4 |
| | -.3 | .6 | 1.3 | 1.9 | 3.0 | NM | | 1.8 | 1.1 |
| | 3.0 | .3 | .5 | .6 | 1.0 | .5 | | .4 | .4 |
| | -2.5 | .7 | 1.1 | 1.0 | 2.0 | 1.2 | Debt/Worth | 1.4 | 1.1 |
| | -1.9 | 2.6 | 3.0 | 2.5 | 4.5 | NM | | 5.8 | 3.4 |
| | | 76.2 | 49.7 | 43.6 | 17.3 | 29.9 | % Profit Before Taxes/Tangible | 54.4 | 44.9 |
| | (31) 25.0 | (55) 25.0 | (52) 12.1 | (22) 5.5 | (24) 8.1 | | Net Worth | (189) 20.7 | (214) 18.6 |
| | 3.6 | 4.0 | 2.0 | -1.6 | -.3 | | | 1.9 | -1.0 |
| | 46.2 | 37.6 | 18.8 | 16.0 | 8.8 | 7.6 | % Profit Before Taxes/Total | 19.0 | 18.3 |
| | -10.0 | 6.5 | 9.5 | 5.2 | 2.8 | 3.1 | Assets | 8.3 | 5.4 |
| | -63.9 | .9 | .2 | .8 | -.8 | -3.3 | | .5 | -1.1 |
| | UND | 50.2 | 53.2 | 61.9 | 54.1 | 20.0 | | 44.8 | 67.4 |
| | 54.3 | 20.1 | 14.4 | 15.4 | 5.6 | 4.2 | Sales/Net Fixed Assets | 14.5 | 16.5 |
| | 16.0 | 12.6 | 3.5 | 4.6 | 1.2 | 1.4 | | 4.3 | 3.5 |
| | 18.9 | 4.3 | 2.8 | 2.3 | 2.3 | 1.5 | | 3.1 | 3.1 |
| | 6.4 | 2.5 | 1.8 | 1.6 | 1.1 | .7 | Sales/Total Assets | 1.8 | 1.9 |
| | 3.4 | 1.6 | 1.1 | .9 | .6 | .5 | | .9 | 1.0 |
| | | .6 | 1.2 | .6 | 2.1 | 2.2 | | 1.0 | .7 |
| | | (23) 1.1 | (50) 2.6 | (49) 2.4 | (21) 3.9 | (26) 5.6 | % Depr., Dep., Amort./Sales | (174) 2.3 | (176) 2.3 |
| | | 2.5 | 4.9 | 5.7 | 7.6 | 8.3 | | 4.3 | 5.5 |
| | | | 4.2 | | | | % Officers', Directors' | 3.2 | 3.0 |
| | | (14) 7.4 | | | | | Owners' Comp/Sales | (31) 7.5 | (34) 9.2 |
| | | | 8.9 | | | | | 16.6 | 13.9 |
| | 17803M | 117094M | 637977M | 2385332M | 2818713M | 4813944M | Net Sales ($) | 9239155M | 11651357M |
| | 2215M | 40261M | 310972M | 1334904M | 1873547M | 4903198M | Total Assets ($) | 6850277M | 8568654M |

© RMA 2012

M = $ thousand    MM = $ million
See Pages 9 through 22 for Explanation of Ratios and Data

## Comparative Historical Data | Current Data Sorted by Sales

| Type of Statement | | | | | | | | | |
|---|---|---|---|---|---|---|---|---|---|
| Unqualified | 92 | 74 | 72 | 1 | 6 | 3 | 5 | 17 | 40 |
| Reviewed | 21 | 25 | 15 | | 4 | 1 | 7 | | 3 |
| Compiled | 8 | 12 | 10 | 1 | 2 | 2 | 2 | 3 | |
| Tax Returns | 20 | 23 | 25 | 7 | 13 | 3 | 2 | | |
| Other | 101 | 115 | 109 | 8 | 6 | 12 | 17 | 18 | 48 |
| | 4/1/09-3/31/10 ALL | 4/1/10-3/31/11 ALL | 4/1/11-3/31/12 ALL | 51 (4/1-9/30/11) | | | 180 (10/1/11-3/31/12) | | |
| | | | | 0-1MM | 1-3MM | 3-5MM | 5-10MM | 10-25MM | 25MM & OVER |

| | | | | | | | | | |
|---|---|---|---|---|---|---|---|---|---|
| **NUMBER OF STATEMENTS** | 242 | 249 | 231 | 17 | 27 | 24 | 27 | 45 | 91 |
| **ASSETS** | % | % | % | % | % | % | % | % | % |
| Cash & Equivalents | 21.5 | 20.4 | 21.7 | 41.1 | 20.9 | 21.4 | 17.3 | 20.0 | 20.4 |
| Trade Receivables (net) | 27.6 | 29.5 | 25.8 | 19.3 | 19.8 | 27.4 | 31.4 | 30.7 | 24.2 |
| Inventory | 5.3 | 4.9 | 4.7 | .2 | 7.5 | 4.6 | 6.3 | 5.1 | 4.0 |
| All Other Current | 6.5 | 6.7 | 6.2 | .0 | 6.5 | 5.5 | 6.6 | 6.1 | 7.5 |
| Total Current | 60.8 | 61.5 | 58.3 | 60.6 | 54.7 | 58.9 | 61.6 | 61.9 | 56.1 |
| Fixed Assets (net) | 22.8 | 21.8 | 23.0 | 14.7 | 30.0 | 24.3 | 26.0 | 23.0 | 21.2 |
| Intangibles (net) | 5.1 | 6.2 | 7.3 | 6.8 | 6.5 | 1.1 | 3.5 | 5.6 | 11.1 |
| All Other Non-Current | 11.3 | 10.6 | 11.4 | 17.9 | 8.8 | 15.7 | 8.9 | 9.6 | 11.5 |
| Total | 100.0 | 100.0 | 100.0 | 100.0 | 100.0 | 100.0 | 100.0 | 100.0 | 100.0 |
| **LIABILITIES** | | | | | | | | | |
| Notes Payable-Short Term | 5.7 | 7.1 | 7.5 | 27.3 | 4.6 | 19.2 | 7.0 | 3.1 | 3.9 |
| Cur. Mat.-L.T.D. | 1.8 | 1.6 | 1.7 | .2 | .9 | 1.3 | 2.0 | 1.2 | 2.6 |
| Trade Payables | 10.6 | 9.4 | 10.6 | 15.2 | 5.0 | 7.6 | 15.1 | 9.7 | 11.4 |
| Income Taxes Payable | .5 | .4 | .4 | .0 | .0 | .4 | .6 | .5 | .5 |
| All Other Current | 16.8 | 16.8 | 21.3 | 78.3 | 8.5 | 9.9 | 20.4 | 19.5 | 18.7 |
| Total Current | 35.4 | 35.3 | 41.7 | 121.1 | 19.0 | 38.4 | 45.2 | 33.9 | 37.1 |
| Long-Term Debt | 10.3 | 11.1 | 13.4 | 24.6 | 17.2 | 8.9 | 10.9 | 9.0 | 14.3 |
| Deferred Taxes | .4 | .7 | .4 | .0 | .0 | .1 | .0 | .4 | .8 |
| All Other Non-Current | 6.3 | 6.0 | 7.8 | 5.5 | 11.7 | 5.7 | 4.3 | 6.6 | 9.3 |
| Net Worth | 47.6 | 46.9 | 36.7 | -51.2 | 52.1 | 46.9 | 39.6 | 50.0 | 38.4 |
| Total Liabilties & Net Worth | 100.0 | 100.0 | 100.0 | 100.0 | 100.0 | 100.0 | 100.0 | 100.0 | 100.0 |
| **INCOME DATA** | | | | | | | | | |
| Net Sales | 100.0 | 100.0 | 100.0 | 100.0 | 100.0 | 100.0 | 100.0 | 100.0 | 100.0 |
| Gross Profit | | | | | | | | | |
| Operating Expenses | 93.0 | 91.5 | 94.5 | 105.8 | 95.8 | 90.4 | 94.7 | 91.9 | 94.4 |
| Operating Profit | 7.0 | 8.5 | 5.5 | -5.8 | 4.2 | 9.6 | 5.3 | 8.1 | 5.6 |
| All Other Expenses (net) | 1.2 | .7 | 1.3 | 1.2 | 1.6 | -.4 | 1.2 | -.3 | 2.5 |
| Profit Before Taxes | 5.8 | 7.8 | 4.1 | -6.9 | 2.6 | 10.0 | 4.1 | 8.4 | 3.0 |
| **RATIOS** | | | | | | | | | |
| Current | 3.5 | 3.3 | 3.0 | 1.6 | 7.4 | 3.7 | 3.2 | 3.2 | 2.7 |
| | 1.9 | 1.8 | 1.7 | .5 | 2.9 | 1.8 | 1.6 | 2.0 | 1.6 |
| | 1.2 | 1.2 | 1.1 | .3 | 1.3 | 1.1 | 1.0 | 1.2 | 1.1 |
| Quick | 2.9 | 2.8 | 2.5 | 1.6 | 7.3 | 3.2 | 2.1 | 2.8 | 2.0 |
| | 1.5 | 1.5 | 1.3 | .5 | 1.7 | 1.5 | 1.3 | 1.4 | 1.2 |
| | .9 | .8 | .7 | .3 | .4 | 1.0 | .7 | .9 | .8 |
| Sales/Receivables | 28  13.2 | 26  14.1 | 21  17.1 | 0  UND | 5  75.2 | 10  36.5 | 24  15.1 | 33  11.2 | 35  10.5 |
| | 48  7.7 | 51  7.2 | 46  8.0 | 0  UND | 23  15.7 | 38  9.5 | 46  7.9 | 51  7.2 | 51  7.2 |
| | 68  5.3 | 75  4.8 | 70  5.2 | 91  4.0 | 53  6.9 | 66  5.5 | 74  4.9 | 72  5.1 | 72  5.1 |
| Cost of Sales/Inventory | | | | | | | | | |
| Cost of Sales/Payables | | | | | | | | | |
| Sales/Working Capital | 3.2 | 3.3 | 3.8 | 11.4 | 3.4 | 4.3 | 3.5 | 3.5 | 3.8 |
| | 7.6 | 7.3 | 8.6 | -23.9 | 5.7 | 10.5 | 8.1 | 7.3 | 8.2 |
| | 24.7 | 26.6 | 68.0 | -2.3 | 33.0 | 27.4 | -310.7 | 23.4 | 71.1 |
| EBIT/Interest | 38.4 | 51.7 | 27.6 | | 12.8 | 38.7 | 33.3 | 21.6 | 34.6 |
| | (168)  8.8 | (176)  8.3 | (162)  6.3 | | (18)  1.5 | (14)  8.9 | (20)  4.9 | (32)  12.1 | (72)  7.1 |
| | 1.4 | 1.3 | .7 | | -4.1 | 5.3 | 1.3 | 2.1 | .3 |
| Net Profit + Depr., Dep., Amort./Cur. Mat. L/T/D | 9.4 | 34.5 | 12.1 | | | | | | 11.9 |
| | (34)  3.5 | (43)  7.8 | (38)  3.5 | | | | | (27)  | 3.2 |
| | 1.4 | 2.9 | 1.5 | | | | | | .8 |
| Fixed/Worth | .1 | .1 | .1 | .0 | .2 | .1 | .1 | .1 | .2 |
| | .4 | .3 | .4 | -1.2 | .4 | .2 | .9 | .3 | .5 |
| | 1.1 | 1.3 | 1.9 | -.2 | 1.0 | 1.5 | 2.0 | 1.1 | 2.5 |
| Debt/Worth | .4 | .5 | .5 | 3.0 | .3 | .4 | .5 | .4 | .7 |
| | 1.0 | 1.1 | 1.2 | -3.2 | .6 | 1.1 | .9 | 1.1 | 1.4 |
| | 2.8 | 3.9 | 4.7 | -1.6 | 3.6 | 2.3 | 4.4 | 2.2 | 4.5 |
| % Profit Before Taxes/Tangible Net Worth | 51.0 | 53.7 | 47.2 | | 49.4 | 90.0 | 44.4 | 44.8 | 45.1 |
| | (216)  14.7 | (221)  20.9 | (189)  14.3 | | (23)  9.5 | (21)  16.6 | (24)  18.1 | (42)  18.5 | (74)  12.7 |
| | .7 | 3.8 | 1.8 | | -.9 | 3.1 | .3 | 4.0 | -1.3 |
| % Profit Before Taxes/Total Assets | 19.7 | 26.1 | 16.4 | 4.6 | 19.8 | 42.5 | 20.1 | 17.5 | 12.7 |
| | 7.0 | 8.6 | 4.9 | -10.0 | 3.4 | 9.6 | 10.1 | 5.9 | 4.7 |
| | .2 | .6 | -.7 | -63.9 | -.8 | 1.2 | .0 | 2.2 | -.9 |
| Sales/Net Fixed Assets | 44.6 | 57.4 | 50.2 | UND | 30.8 | 38.0 | 62.0 | 65.6 | 49.5 |
| | 14.6 | 19.0 | 15.0 | 34.0 | 8.1 | 16.2 | 13.6 | 15.0 | 12.1 |
| | 3.5 | 4.0 | 3.3 | 13.4 | 1.9 | 7.1 | 2.5 | 5.1 | 2.5 |
| Sales/Total Assets | 2.8 | 3.2 | 2.8 | 6.9 | 3.4 | 3.2 | 2.8 | 2.9 | 2.4 |
| | 1.7 | 1.8 | 1.6 | 4.4 | 1.5 | 2.0 | 1.8 | 1.7 | 1.5 |
| | 1.0 | .9 | .9 | 1.5 | .8 | 1.4 | .9 | .8 | .8 |
| % Depr., Dep., Amort./Sales | 1.0 | .9 | 1.1 | | .8 | .9 | 1.4 | .6 | 1.0 |
| | (187)  2.6 | (178)  2.1 | (176)  2.5 | | (22)  3.3 | (18)  1.7 | (22)  2.9 | (34)  2.0 | (73)  2.6 |
| | 5.9 | 4.6 | 5.7 | | 6.3 | 3.9 | 5.3 | 5.9 | 6.4 |
| % Officers', Directors', Owners' Comp/Sales | 3.9 | 1.8 | 3.7 | | 4.3 | | | | |
| | (33)  8.6 | (34)  6.6 | (35)  6.0 | | (12)  6.5 | | | | |
| | 12.9 | 14.8 | 10.1 | | 9.2 | | | | |
| Net Sales ($) | 9982321M | 10609510M | 10790863M | 9532M | 56263M | 91605M | 191677M | 709651M | 9732135M |
| Total Assets ($) | 7387910M | 7575469M | 8465097M | 36090M | 85912M | 55292M | 220748M | 730150M | 7336905M |

## Current Data Sorted by Assets                                   Comparative Historical Data

| | | | | | | Type of Statement | | |
|---|---|---|---|---|---|---|---|---|
| | 1 | 10 | 8 | 2 | 12 | Unqualified | 20 | 31 |
| | 1 | 1 | 3 | | | Reviewed | 5 | 8 |
| | 4 | | | | | Compiled | 7 | 3 |
| 1 | 1 | 2 | | | | Tax Returns | 2 | 7 |
| 1 | 7 | 4 | 7 | 2 | 4 | Other | 26 | 21 |
| | 30 (4/1-9/30/11) | | 41 (10/1/11-3/31/12) | | | | 4/1/07-3/31/08 | 4/1/08-3/31/09 |
| 0-500M | 500M-2MM | 2-10MM | 10-50MM | 50-100MM | 100-250MM | | ALL | ALL |
| 2 | 14 | 17 | 18 | 4 | 16 | **NUMBER OF STATEMENTS** | 60 | 70 |
| % | % | % | % | % | % | **ASSETS** | % | % |
| | 24.6 | 36.0 | 24.1 | | 21.2 | Cash & Equivalents | 24.4 | 26.6 |
| | 39.7 | 26.8 | 27.9 | | 23.0 | Trade Receivables (net) | 27.5 | 31.0 |
| | 4.7 | 1.2 | .0 | | .0 | Inventory | 1.3 | .8 |
| | 4.0 | 6.7 | 5.7 | | 1.5 | All Other Current | 6.4 | 4.3 |
| | 73.0 | 70.7 | 57.6 | | 45.8 | Total Current | 59.6 | 62.7 |
| | 14.6 | 16.2 | 14.9 | | 22.5 | Fixed Assets (net) | 21.8 | 16.1 |
| | 8.5 | 2.8 | 2.4 | | 6.2 | Intangibles (net) | 12.8 | 7.2 |
| | 4.0 | 10.3 | 25.0 | | 25.5 | All Other Non-Current | 5.9 | 14.1 |
| | 100.0 | 100.0 | 100.0 | | 100.0 | Total | 100.0 | 100.0 |
| | | | | | | **LIABILITIES** | | |
| | 12.3 | 2.8 | 4.5 | | .5 | Notes Payable-Short Term | 8.6 | 9.4 |
| | .2 | .9 | .2 | | .8 | Cur. Mat.-L.T.D. | 3.2 | 4.0 |
| | 7.3 | 8.5 | 9.2 | | 5.3 | Trade Payables | 8.0 | 8.5 |
| | .2 | .0 | .3 | | .0 | Income Taxes Payable | 1.5 | .2 |
| | 21.8 | 16.8 | 19.6 | | 16.6 | All Other Current | 18.4 | 22.1 |
| | 41.9 | 28.9 | 33.7 | | 23.2 | Total Current | 39.7 | 44.1 |
| | 4.3 | 5.7 | 2.2 | | 12.0 | Long-Term Debt | 14.2 | 11.7 |
| | .0 | .0 | .4 | | .5 | Deferred Taxes | .2 | .4 |
| | 9.7 | 2.3 | 6.4 | | 12.4 | All Other Non-Current | 8.3 | 6.3 |
| | 44.0 | 63.1 | 57.2 | | 52.0 | Net Worth | 37.7 | 37.5 |
| | 100.0 | 100.0 | 100.0 | | 100.0 | Total Liabilties & Net Worth | 100.0 | 100.0 |
| | | | | | | **INCOME DATA** | | |
| | 100.0 | 100.0 | 100.0 | | 100.0 | Net Sales | 100.0 | 100.0 |
| | | | | | | Gross Profit | | |
| | 96.0 | 84.8 | 94.0 | | 83.0 | Operating Expenses | 91.8 | 94.0 |
| | 4.0 | 15.2 | 6.0 | | 17.0 | Operating Profit | 8.2 | 6.0 |
| | 1.6 | 1.2 | -.1 | | 1.6 | All Other Expenses (net) | 1.5 | 2.6 |
| | 2.4 | 14.0 | 6.1 | | 15.4 | Profit Before Taxes | 6.7 | 3.4 |
| | | | | | | **RATIOS** | | |
| | 4.5 | 5.0 | 2.6 | | 4.7 | | 2.8 | 2.9 |
| | 2.5 | 2.8 | 1.7 | | 2.0 | Current | 1.7 | 2.0 |
| | 1.1 | 1.4 | 1.3 | | 1.0 | | 1.1 | 1.1 |
| | 3.7 | 4.9 | 2.3 | | 4.6 | | 2.4 | 2.7 |
| | 1.8 | 2.8 | 1.5 | | 1.9 | Quick | 1.4 | 1.5 |
| | .8 | 1.4 | 1.1 | | .8 | | .9 | .9 |

| | | | | | | | | | | | | |
|---|---|---|---|---|---|---|---|---|---|---|---|---|
| 0 | UND | 1 | 552.9 | 3 | 112.7 | 43 | 8.5 | Sales/Receivables | 32 | 11.3 | 17 | 21.9 |
| 49 | 7.4 | 47 | 7.7 | 40 | 9.2 | 59 | 6.2 | | 61 | 6.0 | 57 | 6.4 |
| 74 | 4.9 | 62 | 5.9 | 85 | 4.3 | 94 | 3.9 | | 76 | 4.8 | 86 | 4.3 |
| | | | | | | | | Cost of Sales/Inventory | | | | |
| | | | | | | | | Cost of Sales/Payables | | | | |
| | 3.5 | | 2.7 | | 6.0 | | 1.8 | Sales/Working Capital | | 3.8 | | 3.9 |
| | 29.1 | | 5.7 | | 13.7 | | 3.1 | | | 6.1 | | 7.5 |
| | NM | | 14.1 | | 78.2 | | NM | | | 62.4 | | 45.2 |
| | 95.3 | | | | | | | EBIT/Interest | | 32.6 | | 11.8 |
| (10) | 36.6 | | | | | | | | (46) | 9.4 | (50) | 1.8 |
| | .7 | | | | | | | | | 1.3 | | -5.9 |
| | | | | | | | | Net Profit + Depr., Dep., Amort./Cur. Mat. L/T/D | | 17.9 | | 17.1 |
| | | | | | | | | | (13) | 4.5 | (12) | 4.3 |
| | | | | | | | | | | 2.5 | | 1.9 |
| | .0 | | .0 | | .0 | | .0 | Fixed/Worth | | .1 | | .1 |
| | .1 | | .1 | | .2 | | .5 | | | .7 | | .3 |
| | .8 | | .3 | | .6 | | .9 | | | NM | | 1.6 |
| | .4 | | .2 | | .2 | | .2 | Debt/Worth | | .5 | | .5 |
| | .9 | | .5 | | .7 | | .6 | | | 2.1 | | 1.1 |
| | NM | | 1.4 | | 2.1 | | 23.0 | | | -19.6 | | 8.8 |
| | 136.6 | | 69.1 | | 36.4 | | 47.7 | % Profit Before Taxes/Tangible Net Worth | | 68.2 | | 46.9 |
| (11) | 24.8 | | 32.8 | | 19.2 | (13) | 11.5 | | (44) | 18.6 | (59) | 8.0 |
| | 7.2 | | 16.3 | | 2.9 | | -3.9 | | | 6.2 | | -6.9 |
| | 37.2 | | 38.8 | | 19.0 | | 17.5 | % Profit Before Taxes/Total Assets | | 25.4 | | 12.8 |
| | 18.7 | | 23.6 | | 9.3 | | 4.1 | | | 8.1 | | 1.5 |
| | 3.4 | | 11.5 | | 1.8 | | -3.7 | | | .3 | | -5.1 |
| | 988.6 | | 65.2 | | 657.3 | | 31.3 | Sales/Net Fixed Assets | | 49.8 | | 89.0 |
| | 109.3 | | 54.4 | | 39.7 | | 5.8 | | | 13.8 | | 23.4 |
| | 21.1 | | 5.8 | | 3.8 | | 1.3 | | | 5.1 | | 5.2 |
| | 4.9 | | 2.8 | | 5.2 | | 1.5 | Sales/Total Assets | | 2.4 | | 2.9 |
| | 3.9 | | 1.8 | | 2.1 | | .7 | | | 1.6 | | 1.6 |
| | 2.5 | | 1.3 | | 1.0 | | .5 | | | .8 | | .8 |
| | | | .5 | | .6 | | .7 | % Depr., Dep., Amort./Sales | | .8 | | .7 |
| | | (16) | .8 | (13) | .9 | (12) | 1.1 | | (44) | 2.6 | (54) | 1.7 |
| | | | 1.8 | | 3.1 | | 4.5 | | | 4.8 | | 3.2 |
| | | | | | | | | % Officers', Directors' Owners' Comp/Sales | | | | 5.4 |
| | | | | | | | | | | | (15) | 9.3 |
| | | | | | | | | | | | | 14.2 |

| 4651M | 64808M | 173512M | 4113397M | 568772M | 2776524M | Net Sales ($) | 2352509M | 2515838M |
|---|---|---|---|---|---|---|---|---|
| 738M | 14462M | 84772M | 454320M | 309606M | 2719650M | Total Assets ($) | 2079081M | 2087681M |

© RMA 2012

M = $ thousand     MM = $ million
See Pages 9 through 22 for Explanation of Ratios and Data

| Comparative Historical Data | | | Type of Statement | Current Data Sorted by Sales | | | | | |
|---|---|---|---|---|---|---|---|---|---|
| 35 | 29 | 33 | Unqualified | | | 4 | 4 | 6 | 19 |
| 5 | 3 | 5 | Reviewed | | | 1 | | 2 | 2 |
| 6 | 6 | 4 | Compiled | 1 | 1 | 1 | 1 | | |
| 4 | 3 | 4 | Tax Returns | | | 1 | 2 | 1 | |
| 18 | 27 | 25 | Other | 2 | 3 | 3 | 3 | 3 | 11 |
| 4/1/09-3/31/10 | 4/1/10-3/31/11 | 4/1/11-3/31/12 | | | 30 (4/1-9/30/11) | | 41 (10/1/11-3/31/12) | | |
| ALL | ALL | ALL | | 0-1MM | 1-3MM | 3-5MM | 5-10MM | 10-25MM | 25MM & OVER |
| 68 | 68 | 71 | **NUMBER OF STATEMENTS** | 3 | 4 | 10 | 10 | 12 | 32 |
| % | % | % | **ASSETS** | % | % | % | % | % | % |
| 23.0 | 26.9 | 27.5 | Cash & Equivalents | | | 28.0 | 31.9 | 39.3 | 22.6 |
| 30.0 | 25.6 | 28.1 | Trade Receivables (net) | | | 32.7 | 37.0 | 21.2 | 28.7 |
| 1.0 | .9 | 1.2 | Inventory | | | .0 | .0 | 1.7 | .0 |
| 6.6 | 6.6 | 4.6 | All Other Current | | | 8.2 | 1.8 | 2.4 | 4.7 |
| 60.6 | 60.1 | 61.4 | Total Current | | | 68.9 | 70.7 | 64.6 | 56.0 |
| 18.8 | 19.8 | 16.4 | Fixed Assets (net) | | | 12.8 | 11.9 | 12.7 | 18.7 |
| 6.8 | 3.8 | 4.5 | Intangibles (net) | | | .4 | 3.6 | 1.4 | 4.4 |
| 13.7 | 16.3 | 17.7 | All Other Non-Current | | | 17.9 | 13.8 | 21.4 | 20.8 |
| 100.0 | 100.0 | 100.0 | Total | | | 100.0 | 100.0 | 100.0 | 100.0 |
| | | | **LIABILITIES** | | | | | | |
| 10.6 | 6.4 | 4.4 | Notes Payable-Short Term | | | 10.0 | 4.4 | 3.3 | 2.2 |
| 1.9 | 1.6 | .6 | Cur. Mat.-L.T.D. | | | .0 | 1.2 | .0 | .7 |
| 10.1 | 6.7 | 7.5 | Trade Payables | | | 5.1 | 8.9 | 6.6 | 8.6 |
| .1 | .2 | .1 | Income Taxes Payable | | | .0 | .3 | .3 | .1 |
| 16.8 | 19.5 | 18.6 | All Other Current | | | 14.9 | 8.7 | 27.2 | 20.2 |
| 39.5 | 34.5 | 31.2 | Total Current | | | 30.1 | 23.6 | 37.5 | 31.8 |
| 10.2 | 13.7 | 6.8 | Long-Term Debt | | | 10.2 | 5.4 | .4 | 7.8 |
| .1 | .2 | .2 | Deferred Taxes | | | .0 | .0 | .0 | .5 |
| 5.9 | 6.8 | 7.1 | All Other Non-Current | | | 2.3 | 4.0 | 2.1 | 9.3 |
| 44.4 | 44.8 | 54.6 | Net Worth | | | 57.4 | 67.0 | 60.0 | 50.6 |
| 100.0 | 100.0 | 100.0 | Total Liabilties & Net Worth | | | 100.0 | 100.0 | 100.0 | 100.0 |
| | | | **INCOME DATA** | | | | | | |
| 100.0 | 100.0 | 100.0 | Net Sales | | | 100.0 | 100.0 | 100.0 | 100.0 |
| | | | Gross Profit | | | | | | |
| 99.2 | 95.5 | 89.7 | Operating Expenses | | | 89.2 | 93.3 | 82.6 | 91.7 |
| .8 | 4.5 | 10.3 | Operating Profit | | | 10.8 | 6.7 | 17.4 | 8.3 |
| .9 | 1.6 | 1.1 | All Other Expenses (net) | | | -.5 | -1.4 | .2 | 1.2 |
| -.1 | 2.9 | 9.1 | Profit Before Taxes | | | 11.3 | 8.0 | 17.2 | 7.1 |
| | | | **RATIOS** | | | | | | |
| 2.9 | 3.5 | 3.5 | | | | 7.2 | 5.1 | 4.9 | 2.7 |
| 1.7 | 2.1 | 2.1 | Current | | | 2.0 | 2.8 | 2.2 | 1.5 |
| 1.1 | 1.3 | 1.3 | | | | 1.0 | 1.6 | 1.0 | 1.2 |
| 2.6 | 3.0 | 3.4 | | | | 5.2 | 5.0 | 4.8 | 2.4 |
| 1.5 | 1.7 | 1.6 | Quick | | | 2.0 | 2.7 | 2.1 | 1.5 |
| .7 | 1.0 | 1.0 | | | | .8 | 1.6 | .9 | 1.0 |
| 6  63.5 | 14  26.5 | 5  78.9 | | 0  UND | 31  11.8 | 2  187.1 | 29  12.7 | | |
| 53  6.8 | 52  7.0 | 47  7.7 | Sales/Receivables | 41  9.0 | 49  7.5 | 42  8.7 | 50  7.3 | | |
| 84  4.3 | 74  5.0 | 74  4.9 | | 78  4.7 | 69  5.3 | 73  5.0 | 81  4.5 | | |
| | | | Cost of Sales/Inventory | | | | | | |
| | | | Cost of Sales/Payables | | | | | | |
| 3.4 | 2.9 | 2.9 | | | | 2.2 | 5.3 | 2.5 | 2.9 |
| 10.1 | 7.1 | 8.4 | Sales/Working Capital | | | 17.6 | 7.2 | 6.6 | 12.2 |
| 73.3 | 29.4 | 39.3 | | | | NM | 15.8 | 216.8 | 53.3 |
| 25.1 | 61.9 | 75.5 | | | | | | | 104.0 |
| (45)  6.0 | (44)  8.6 | (36)  29.2 | EBIT/Interest | | | | | (17)  8.0 | |
| -3.8 | -.1 | .2 | | | | | | | -.8 |
| | | | Net Profit + Depr., Dep., Amort./Cur. Mat. L/T/D | | | | | | |
| .1 | .1 | .0 | | | | .0 | .0 | .0 | .0 |
| .3 | .3 | .1 | Fixed/Worth | | | .0 | .0 | .2 | .2 |
| 1.6 | 1.0 | .6 | | | | .5 | .3 | .5 | .6 |
| .5 | .3 | .3 | | | | .2 | .2 | .2 | .4 |
| 1.3 | 1.1 | .6 | Debt/Worth | | | .4 | .5 | .5 | .9 |
| 4.7 | 3.7 | 2.3 | | | | 3.7 | .9 | 3.5 | 2.1 |
| 34.6 | 36.4 | 47.7 | % Profit Before Taxes/Tangible Net Worth | | | 52.0 | 221.0 | | 46.0 |
| (59)  7.6 | (60)  15.1 | (65)  19.8 | | | | 36.0 | 21.1 | (29)  18.7 | |
| -5.0 | 2.1 | 6.1 | | | | 1.1 | 14.3 | | .9 |
| 12.9 | 16.6 | 25.9 | % Profit Before Taxes/Total Assets | | | 48.8 | 35.8 | 38.6 | 20.8 |
| 2.4 | 5.9 | 9.8 | | | | 16.9 | 24.0 | 16.2 | 7.3 |
| -4.5 | -.6 | 2.3 | | | | 5.0 | 2.2 | 9.2 | -1.8 |
| 75.7 | 69.6 | 105.3 | Sales/Net Fixed Assets | | | 337.7 | 272.9 | 75.9 | 68.9 |
| 24.7 | 19.0 | 36.0 | | | | 59.7 | 59.1 | 32.5 | 27.1 |
| 4.5 | 4.4 | 5.1 | | | | 11.2 | 14.2 | 4.6 | 2.8 |
| 3.4 | 2.9 | 3.6 | | | | 4.1 | 4.9 | 2.6 | 3.4 |
| 2.1 | 1.7 | 1.8 | Sales/Total Assets | | | 2.5 | 2.7 | 1.4 | 1.6 |
| .9 | .7 | 1.0 | | | | 1.3 | 1.7 | 1.1 | .7 |
| .9 | .7 | .6 | | | | | | .3 | .7 |
| (48)  1.8 | (54)  1.5 | (54)  1.0 | % Depr., Dep., Amort./Sales | | | | | .9 | (24)  1.0 |
| 3.6 | 3.4 | 3.1 | | | | | | 2.4 | 4.1 |
| 6.6 | 3.7 | | % Officers', Directors' Owners' Comp/Sales | | | | | | |
| (16)  15.3 | (14)  17.5 | | | | | | | | |
| 20.9 | 31.1 | | | | | | | | |
| 6259637M | 7717288M | 7701664M | Net Sales ($) | 1160M | 8030M | 36961M | 80893M | 192320M | 7382300M |
| 2423251M | 3529552M | 3583548M | Total Assets ($) | 9847M | 2554M | 18983M | 47724M | 243373M | 3261067M |

M = $ thousand     MM = $ million
See Pages 9 through 22 for Explanation of Ratios and Data

## Current Data Sorted by Assets

## Comparative Historical Data

| | | | 7 | 14 | 4 | 8 | Type of Statement | | | |
|---|---|---|---|---|---|---|---|---|---|---|
| | | 6 | 39 | 16 | 1 | 1 | Unqualified | | 26 | 28 |
| | 6 | 22 | 32 | 3 | | | Reviewed | | 52 | 55 |
| | 58 | 39 | 30 | 1 | 2 | | Compiled | | 63 | 59 |
| | 30 | 57 | 61 | 27 | 2 | 6 | Tax Returns | | 68 | 94 |
| | | | | | | | Other | | 161 | 170 |
| | | 42 (4/1-9/30/11) | | 430 (10/1/11-3/31/12) | | | | | 4/1/07-3/31/08 | 4/1/08-3/31/09 |
| | 0-500M | 500M-2MM | 2-10MM | 10-50MM | 50-100MM | 100-250MM | | | ALL | ALL |
| | 94 | 124 | 169 | 61 | 9 | 15 | NUMBER OF STATEMENTS | | 370 | 406 |
| | % | % | % | % | % | % | ASSETS | | % | % |
| | 29.4 | 17.0 | 20.1 | 17.6 | | 12.8 | Cash & Equivalents | | 16.2 | 16.9 |
| | 25.0 | 40.7 | 44.1 | 42.6 | | 20.7 | Trade Receivables (net) | | 46.7 | 44.6 |
| | 2.2 | .9 | 3.1 | 2.0 | | .2 | Inventory | | 3.1 | 2.9 |
| | 4.5 | 3.1 | 4.6 | 7.4 | | 2.4 | All Other Current | | 5.9 | 4.9 |
| | 61.2 | 61.7 | 71.9 | 69.5 | | 36.1 | Total Current | | 71.9 | 69.4 |
| | 21.4 | 18.4 | 14.2 | 11.7 | | 5.4 | Fixed Assets (net) | | 13.4 | 15.1 |
| | 5.2 | 4.3 | 4.7 | 8.5 | | 54.0 | Intangibles (net) | | 6.0 | 6.2 |
| | 12.2 | 15.6 | 9.2 | 10.3 | | 4.5 | All Other Non-Current | | 8.7 | 9.4 |
| | 100.0 | 100.0 | 100.0 | 100.0 | | 100.0 | Total | | 100.0 | 100.0 |
| | | | | | | | LIABILITIES | | | |
| | 47.4 | 11.9 | 5.8 | 5.3 | | .1 | Notes Payable-Short Term | | 12.6 | 15.9 |
| | 3.3 | 1.5 | 1.7 | 2.0 | | 4.4 | Cur. Mat.-L.T.D. | | 4.0 | 3.5 |
| | 15.3 | 22.9 | 29.4 | 28.6 | | 15.5 | Trade Payables | | 28.2 | 29.9 |
| | .1 | .4 | .1 | .2 | | 2.2 | Income Taxes Payable | | .3 | .2 |
| | 24.6 | 16.7 | 21.2 | 20.9 | | 13.3 | All Other Current | | 20.0 | 19.1 |
| | 90.7 | 53.5 | 58.2 | 57.0 | | 35.4 | Total Current | | 65.1 | 68.7 |
| | 24.2 | 10.9 | 8.8 | 7.3 | | 19.2 | Long-Term Debt | | 11.5 | 10.1 |
| | .0 | .5 | .2 | .2 | | 1.2 | Deferred Taxes | | .2 | .2 |
| | 9.7 | 6.8 | 4.9 | 6.5 | | 3.1 | All Other Non-Current | | 9.5 | 8.5 |
| | -24.7 | 28.3 | 28.0 | 29.0 | | 41.1 | Net Worth | | 13.7 | 12.5 |
| | 100.0 | 100.0 | 100.0 | 100.0 | | 100.0 | Total Liabilties & Net Worth | | 100.0 | 100.0 |
| | | | | | | | INCOME DATA | | | |
| | 100.0 | 100.0 | 100.0 | 100.0 | | 100.0 | Net Sales | | 100.0 | 100.0 |
| | | | | | | | Gross Profit | | | |
| | 95.1 | 92.7 | 93.7 | 93.5 | | 89.5 | Operating Expenses | | 94.5 | 95.0 |
| | 4.9 | 7.3 | 6.3 | 6.5 | | 10.5 | Operating Profit | | 5.5 | 5.0 |
| | 1.2 | 1.9 | .6 | .9 | | 4.1 | All Other Expenses (net) | | 1.3 | 1.3 |
| | 3.7 | 5.4 | 5.6 | 5.6 | | 6.3 | Profit Before Taxes | | 4.2 | 3.7 |
| | | | | | | | RATIOS | | | |
| | 1.5 | 2.1 | 1.7 | 1.7 | | 1.2 | | | 1.8 | 1.8 |
| | .8 | 1.1 | 1.3 | 1.1 | | 1.0 | Current | | 1.1 | 1.1 |
| | .4 | .7 | .9 | 1.0 | | .9 | | | .8 | .8 |
| | 1.4 | 2.0 | 1.5 | 1.4 | | 1.1 | | | 1.5 | 1.6 |
| | .7 | 1.1 | 1.1 | 1.0 | | .9 | Quick | (368) | 1.0 | 1.0 |
| | .3 | .7 | .8 | .8 | | .7 | | | .7 | .7 |

| | | | | | | | | | | | | | | | |
|---|---|---|---|---|---|---|---|---|---|---|---|---|---|---|---|
| 0 | UND | 22 | 16.5 | 29 | 12.4 | 48 | 7.6 | | | 57 | 6.4 | | 26 | 14.0 | 28 | 13.3 |
| 1 | 340.2 | 40 | 9.1 | 49 | 7.4 | 69 | 5.3 | | | 74 | 4.9 | Sales/Receivables | 49 | 7.5 | 45 | 8.1 |
| 37 | 9.8 | 68 | 5.4 | 74 | 4.9 | 101 | 3.6 | | | 96 | 3.8 | | 71 | 5.1 | 72 | 5.0 |

(Cost of Sales/Inventory — no data)

(Cost of Sales/Payables — no data)

| | | | | | | | | | | | |
|---|---|---|---|---|---|---|---|---|---|---|---|
| | 38.2 | | 10.1 | | 10.1 | | 6.1 | | 19.2 | | 12.0 | 12.0 |
| | -91.2 | | 70.6 | | 28.4 | | 26.2 | | 45.2 | Sales/Working Capital | 46.1 | 51.9 |
| | -13.5 | | -25.6 | | -71.9 | | -999.8 | | -15.9 | | -37.3 | -27.0 |
| | 18.3 | | 26.8 | | 86.9 | | 54.7 | | 7.1 | | 24.9 | 24.5 |
| (60) | 4.5 | (84) | 5.3 | (124) | 17.2 | (46) | 11.0 | (14) | 3.2 | EBIT/Interest | (277) 6.0 | (312) 5.9 |
| | -1.6 | | -3.1 | | 4.0 | | 2.5 | | .9 | | 1.3 | .7 |
| | | | | | 69.1 | | 7.8 | | | | 7.5 | 7.0 |
| | | | (15) | 4.5 | | 4.5 | (14) | 4.7 | | | Net Profit + Depr., Dep., Amort./Cur. Mat. L/T/D | (35) 2.4 | (47) 2.1 |
| | | | | 1.8 | | 1.8 | | | | | | 1.3 | .6 |
| | .1 | | .1 | | .1 | | .2 | | -10.8 | | .2 | .2 |
| | 1.5 | | .4 | | .4 | | .4 | | -.4 | Fixed/Worth | .5 | .6 |
| | -.5 | | 11.9 | | 2.2 | | 5.6 | | -.1 | | -3.7 | -3.4 |
| | 1.5 | | .7 | | 1.3 | | 1.3 | | -524.2 | | 1.4 | 1.2 |
| | 8.9 | | 3.1 | | 3.6 | | 4.5 | | -2.9 | Debt/Worth | 5.4 | 5.4 |
| | -2.6 | | UND | | 21.2 | | 34.2 | | -1.8 | | -15.3 | -20.9 |
| | 167.5 | | 80.9 | | 109.3 | | 79.7 | | | | 95.0 | 100.0 |
| (57) | 78.2 | (93) | 21.8 | (141) | 50.3 | (48) | 38.5 | | | % Profit Before Taxes/Tangible Net Worth | (259) 43.0 | (285) 36.3 |
| | 9.8 | | 3.2 | | 15.7 | | 11.9 | | | | 14.9 | 7.0 |
| | 53.3 | | 22.5 | | 23.0 | | 16.2 | | 10.2 | | 24.4 | 23.4 |
| | 16.6 | | 6.7 | | 10.5 | | 7.0 | | 3.2 | % Profit Before Taxes/Total Assets | 7.2 | 7.4 |
| | -8.4 | | -1.4 | | 3.5 | | 2.7 | | -.3 | | .9 | -.1 |
| | 432.9 | | 208.8 | | 121.2 | | 66.2 | | 38.0 | | 116.7 | 111.6 |
| | 80.0 | | 51.7 | | 41.7 | | 36.7 | | 26.5 | Sales/Net Fixed Assets | 46.0 | 40.3 |
| | 24.2 | | 16.0 | | 17.8 | | 13.1 | | 12.2 | | 19.2 | 18.8 |
| | 12.3 | | 5.0 | | 4.4 | | 3.1 | | 1.1 | | 5.3 | 5.5 |
| | 6.4 | | 3.3 | | 3.2 | | 2.1 | | .8 | Sales/Total Assets | 3.7 | 3.7 |
| | 3.9 | | 1.8 | | 2.2 | | 1.2 | | .6 | | 2.3 | 2.3 |
| | .5 | | .6 | | .4 | | .4 | | | | .4 | .5 |
| (50) | .7 | (77) | 1.0 | (132) | .9 | (51) | 1.2 | | | % Depr., Dep., Amort./Sales | (267) .8 | (280) .9 |
| | 1.9 | | 2.2 | | 1.5 | | 1.9 | | | | 1.8 | 2.0 |
| | 5.4 | | 4.9 | | 2.1 | | 1.2 | | | | 2.7 | 2.5 |
| (56) | 8.7 | (52) | 7.4 | (61) | 4.2 | (10) | 1.4 | | | % Officers', Directors' Owners' Comp/Sales | (160) 5.7 | (168) 5.8 |
| | 15.7 | | 13.8 | | 9.9 | | 3.2 | | | | 12.0 | 11.3 |

| | | | | | | | | |
|---|---|---|---|---|---|---|---|---|
| 187105M | 512149M | 2738059M | 3007515M | 1480714M | 2312106M | Net Sales ($) | 9144795M | 9121021M |
| 21710M | 139086M | 783642M | 1283338M | 636315M | 2388743M | Total Assets ($) | 3556690M | 4319658M |

M = $ thousand    MM = $ million
See Pages 9 through 22 for Explanation of Ratios and Data

## Comparative Historical Data

## Current Data Sorted by Sales

| | | | | | | Type of Statement | | | | | | |
|---|---|---|---|---|---|---|---|---|---|---|---|---|
| | 29 | | 26 | | 33 | Unqualified | | | | 1 | 6 | 26 |
| | 67 | | 70 | | 63 | Reviewed | | 5 | | 18 | 17 | 23 |
| | 61 | | 60 | | 63 | Compiled | 7 | 10 | 8 | 12 | 22 | 4 |
| | 96 | | 107 | | 130 | Tax Returns | 25 | 41 | 21 | 22 | 14 | 7 |
| | 195 | | 209 | | 183 | Other | 24 | 34 | 24 | 24 | 36 | 39 |
| | 4/1/09-3/31/10 ALL | | 4/1/10-3/31/11 ALL | | 4/1/11-3/31/12 ALL | | 0-1MM | 42 (4/1-9/30/11) 1-3MM | 3-5MM | 430 (10/1/11-3/31/12) 5-10MM | 10-25MM | 25MM & OVER |
| | 448 | | 472 | | 472 | NUMBER OF STATEMENTS | 56 | 90 | 53 | 79 | 95 | 99 |
| | % | | % | | % | ASSETS | % | % | % | % | % | % |
| | 18.9 | | 21.9 | | 20.7 | Cash & Equivalents | 20.1 | 23.5 | 20.9 | 16.8 | 22.2 | 20.1 |
| | 40.7 | | 39.8 | | 38.3 | Trade Receivables (net) | 19.7 | 33.0 | 37.2 | 46.5 | 44.5 | 41.7 |
| | 3.3 | | 2.7 | | 2.1 | Inventory | .9 | 1.7 | 2.5 | 2.7 | 3.3 | 1.3 |
| | 5.0 | | 4.9 | | 4.5 | All Other Current | 4.4 | 4.2 | 2.3 | 6.4 | 4.4 | 4.6 |
| | 67.9 | | 69.2 | | 65.6 | Total Current | 45.1 | 62.4 | 62.9 | 72.4 | 74.5 | 67.6 |
| | 15.7 | | 15.0 | | 16.0 | Fixed Assets (net) | 35.8 | 20.4 | 12.4 | 12.9 | 10.8 | 10.3 |
| | 5.9 | | 6.7 | | 6.9 | Intangibles (net) | 4.2 | 5.3 | 4.7 | 3.7 | 6.5 | 13.7 |
| | 10.6 | | 9.0 | | 11.5 | All Other Non-Current | 14.9 | 11.9 | 20.0 | 11.0 | 8.1 | 8.3 |
| | 100.0 | | 100.0 | | 100.0 | Total | 100.0 | 100.0 | 100.0 | 100.0 | 100.0 | 100.0 |
| | | | | | | LIABILITIES | | | | | | |
| | 17.2 | | 13.9 | | 15.4 | Notes Payable-Short Term | 28.9 | 31.2 | 18.7 | 12.3 | 6.2 | 3.0 |
| | 3.1 | | 2.9 | | 2.1 | Cur. Mat.-L.T.D. | 4.1 | 2.1 | 1.4 | 2.1 | 1.2 | 2.2 |
| | 27.5 | | 26.6 | | 24.4 | Trade Payables | 12.5 | 17.0 | 23.1 | 23.5 | 31.9 | 32.3 |
| | .2 | | .2 | | .3 | Income Taxes Payable | .1 | .3 | .5 | .1 | .2 | .5 |
| | 22.9 | | 22.3 | | 20.4 | All Other Current | 25.1 | 15.0 | 22.2 | 24.8 | 20.0 | 18.5 |
| | 70.9 | | 65.8 | | 62.6 | Total Current | 70.6 | 65.5 | 65.8 | 62.7 | 59.4 | 56.5 |
| | 10.8 | | 11.7 | | 12.5 | Long-Term Debt | 29.8 | 18.3 | 11.5 | 6.4 | 5.6 | 9.7 |
| | .2 | | .2 | | .3 | Deferred Taxes | .0 | .6 | .1 | .2 | .3 | .3 |
| | 7.9 | | 8.6 | | 6.6 | All Other Non-Current | 14.0 | 7.3 | 2.7 | 4.9 | 5.2 | 6.5 |
| | 10.2 | | 13.6 | | 18.0 | Net Worth | -14.5 | 8.4 | 19.9 | 25.7 | 29.4 | 27.0 |
| | 100.0 | | 100.0 | | 100.0 | Total Liabilities & Net Worth | 100.0 | 100.0 | 100.0 | 100.0 | 100.0 | 100.0 |
| | | | | | | INCOME DATA | | | | | | |
| | 100.0 | | 100.0 | | 100.0 | Net Sales | 100.0 | 100.0 | 100.0 | 100.0 | 100.0 | 100.0 |
| | | | | | | Gross Profit | | | | | | |
| | 96.3 | | 93.4 | | 93.5 | Operating Expenses | 84.9 | 95.3 | 95.5 | 95.1 | 94.1 | 94.1 |
| | 3.7 | | 6.6 | | 6.5 | Operating Profit | 15.1 | 4.7 | 4.5 | 4.9 | 5.9 | 5.9 |
| | 1.1 | | 1.3 | | 1.2 | All Other Expenses (net) | 6.8 | .1 | .7 | .3 | .3 | 1.0 |
| | 2.6 | | 5.3 | | 5.2 | Profit Before Taxes | 8.3 | 4.6 | 3.8 | 4.6 | 5.6 | 5.0 |
| | | | | | | RATIOS | | | | | | |
| | 1.7 | | 2.1 | | 1.7 | | 1.5 | 2.8 | 1.6 | 1.6 | 1.7 | 1.5 |
| | 1.1 | | 1.1 | | 1.1 | Current | .7 | 1.2 | 1.0 | 1.1 | 1.2 | 1.1 |
| | .7 | | .8 | | .8 | | .2 | .7 | .6 | .9 | 1.0 | 1.0 |
| | 1.5 | | 1.8 | | 1.5 | | 1.5 | 2.5 | 1.5 | 1.5 | 1.6 | 1.3 |
| (447) | .9 | | 1.0 | | 1.0 | Quick | .6 | 1.1 | 1.0 | 1.0 | 1.1 | 1.0 |
| | .6 | | .7 | | .7 | | .2 | .6 | .5 | .7 | .8 | .8 |
| 24 | 15.4 | 21 | 17.7 | 21 | 17.6 | | 0 UND | 0 UND | 9 40.0 | 32 11.4 | 29 12.8 | 33 11.2 |
| 46 | 7.9 | 45 | 8.0 | 46 | 8.0 | Sales/Receivables | 2 150.9 | 38 9.7 | 34 10.8 | 53 6.9 | 49 7.4 | 51 7.2 |
| 76 | 4.8 | 68 | 5.4 | 72 | 5.1 | | 51 7.2 | 65 5.6 | 62 5.9 | 78 4.7 | 76 4.8 | 72 5.1 |
| | | | | | | Cost of Sales/Inventory | | | | | | |
| | | | | | | Cost of Sales/Payables | | | | | | |
| | 10.1 | | 8.9 | | 10.9 | | 13.3 | 8.0 | 11.6 | 13.0 | 9.7 | 13.5 |
| | 65.2 | | 39.1 | | 46.6 | Sales/Working Capital | -33.3 | 47.4 | 944.2 | 38.9 | 29.1 | 34.4 |
| | -18.6 | | -27.1 | | -33.5 | | -4.5 | -19.6 | -20.9 | -43.8 | -204.2 | -164.3 |
| | 20.9 | | 38.7 | | 41.3 | | 18.0 | 26.0 | 27.3 | 27.3 | 91.1 | 59.6 |
| (336) | 3.7 | (328) | 8.0 | (335) | 9.7 | EBIT/Interest | (25) 3.0 | (67) 5.6 | (40) 4.3 | (53) 9.5 | (72) 22.3 | (78) 11.0 |
| | -2.4 | | 1.2 | | 1.6 | | .1 | -4.2 | -1.6 | 1.8 | 7.2 | 1.8 |
| | 9.1 | | 14.1 | | 9.1 | Net Profit + Depr., Dep., | | | | | 7.4 | 13.1 |
| (37) | 2.1 | (50) | 4.3 | (41) | 3.7 | Amort./Cur. Mat. L/T/D | | | | (10) 2.0 | (16) 4.7 |
| | .5 | | 2.1 | | 1.4 | | | | | | 1.4 | 2.1 |
| | .2 | | .1 | | .1 | | .0 | .1 | .1 | .2 | .1 | .2 |
| | .7 | | .6 | | .5 | Fixed/Worth | 3.0 | .6 | .3 | .3 | .4 | .8 |
| | -1.1 | | -1.8 | | 12.9 | | -1.9 | NM | UND | 1.8 | 6.6 | -4.9 |
| | 1.3 | | 1.1 | | 1.1 | | 1.6 | .6 | .8 | 1.1 | 1.1 | 2.2 |
| | 5.6 | | 5.9 | | 4.3 | Debt/Worth | 6.3 | 3.0 | 4.0 | 3.8 | 3.8 | 7.9 |
| | -6.5 | | -8.4 | | -41.8 | | -3.0 | -13.2 | -17.5 | 11.5 | 47.5 | -25.7 |
| | 99.7 | | 112.1 | | 95.3 | % Profit Before Taxes/Tangible | 89.9 | 92.7 | 87.4 | 85.8 | 109.4 | 135.1 |
| (296) | 31.1 | (323) | 43.3 | (348) | 44.2 | Net Worth | (36) 35.3 | (65) 41.9 | (38) 21.7 | (64) 35.9 | (75) 55.9 | (70) 48.2 |
| | .7 | | 7.2 | | 11.4 | | 7.9 | -2.4 | -3.7 | 9.1 | 22.7 | 15.5 |
| | 22.1 | | 26.6 | | 24.6 | % Profit Before Taxes/Total | 35.7 | 36.6 | 20.7 | 24.0 | 26.1 | 16.1 |
| | 5.1 | | 8.8 | | 8.8 | Assets | 6.9 | 13.0 | 8.4 | 6.0 | 13.6 | 7.4 |
| | -4.3 | | .6 | | 1.1 | | -3.4 | -7.8 | -2.1 | 1.2 | 4.9 | 1.5 |
| | 99.6 | | 120.3 | | 139.4 | | 136.7 | 161.8 | 262.0 | 112.6 | 154.3 | 95.1 |
| | 37.5 | | 40.6 | | 42.4 | Sales/Net Fixed Assets | 22.3 | 41.5 | 60.2 | 40.1 | 46.1 | 41.7 |
| | 16.1 | | 18.4 | | 17.2 | | 1.0 | 18.2 | 22.5 | 14.0 | 23.5 | 18.3 |
| | 5.1 | | 5.3 | | 5.2 | | 5.7 | 5.7 | 6.7 | 4.3 | 4.9 | 5.1 |
| | 3.4 | | 3.3 | | 3.3 | Sales/Total Assets | 1.6 | 3.7 | 4.4 | 3.2 | 3.5 | 2.8 |
| | 1.8 | | 1.9 | | 1.9 | | .4 | 1.9 | 2.6 | 2.2 | 2.4 | 1.5 |
| | .5 | | .4 | | .5 | | .7 | .6 | .6 | .6 | .3 | .3 |
| (306) | 1.1 | (318) | 1.0 | (321) | .9 | % Depr., Dep., Amort./Sales | (37) 3.6 | (51) 1.1 | (33) .7 | (56) 1.0 | (74) .7 | (70) .9 |
| | 2.1 | | 2.1 | | 2.0 | | 16.6 | 2.1 | 1.2 | 2.3 | 1.3 | 1.6 |
| | 3.2 | | 3.8 | | 3.0 | % Officers', Directors' | 5.9 | 6.4 | 3.7 | 3.4 | 1.4 | .9 |
| (182) | 5.8 | (193) | 6.7 | (181) | 6.3 | Owners' Comp/Sales | (17) 9.5 | (52) 10.2 | (29) 6.1 | (34) 5.7 | (29) 2.6 | (20) 2.0 |
| | 11.1 | | 12.3 | | 12.4 | | 19.7 | 15.9 | 11.7 | 10.9 | 5.3 | 5.0 |
| | 8527079M | | 8093203M | | 10237648M | Net Sales ($) | 25715M | 180286M | 215425M | 584880M | 1481605M | 7749737M |
| | 4271237M | | 4028991M | | 5252834M | Total Assets ($) | 27970M | 78007M | 72256M | 248725M | 554901M | 4270975M |

© RMA 2012

M = $ thousand    MM = $ million
See Pages 9 through 22 for Explanation of Ratios and Data

| Current Data Sorted by Assets | | | | | | | Comparative Historical Data | |
|---|---|---|---|---|---|---|---|---|
| 2 | | 6 | 5 | | 2 | Type of Statement<br>Unqualified | 15 | 15 |
| | 3 | 8 | | | | Reviewed | 13 | 14 |
| 2 | 5 | 1 | | | | Compiled | 11 | 10 |
| 7 | 5 | 2 | | | | Tax Returns | 10 | 13 |
| 9 | 12 | 9 | 6 | 1 | 1 | Other | 16 | 21 |
| | 15 (4/1-9/30/11) | | 71 (10/1/11-3/31/12) | | | | 4/1/07-<br>3/31/08 | 4/1/08-<br>3/31/09 |
| 0-500M | 500M-2MM | 2-10MM | 10-50MM | 50-100MM | 100-250MM | | ALL | ALL |
| 20 | 25 | 26 | 11 | 1 | 3 | NUMBER OF STATEMENTS | 65 | 73 |
| % | % | % | % | % | % | ASSETS | % | % |
| 38.8 | 20.5 | 27.2 | 24.1 | | | Cash & Equivalents | 23.6 | 22.7 |
| 21.7 | 40.3 | 36.4 | 28.9 | | | Trade Receivables (net) | 41.3 | 38.2 |
| .1 | .0 | 5.2 | .3 | | | Inventory | 3.5 | 3.8 |
| 5.4 | 2.8 | 4.0 | 7.8 | | | All Other Current | 4.0 | 4.5 |
| 65.9 | 63.5 | 72.9 | 61.1 | | | Total Current | 72.3 | 69.3 |
| 17.2 | 14.0 | 11.5 | 19.7 | | | Fixed Assets (net) | 16.7 | 17.2 |
| 4.7 | 10.2 | 8.8 | 13.2 | | | Intangibles (net) | 4.9 | 4.3 |
| 12.3 | 12.2 | 6.8 | 6.0 | | | All Other Non-Current | 6.1 | 9.2 |
| 100.0 | 100.0 | 100.0 | 100.0 | | | Total | 100.0 | 100.0 |
| | | | | | | LIABILITIES | | |
| 40.5 | 8.7 | 5.1 | 3.3 | | | Notes Payable-Short Term | 13.9 | 14.1 |
| .1 | 3.3 | 2.6 | 1.9 | | | Cur. Mat.-L.T.D. | 6.3 | 10.5 |
| 13.9 | 15.8 | 13.6 | 8.4 | | | Trade Payables | 10.5 | 11.3 |
| .2 | .5 | .4 | .7 | | | Income Taxes Payable | .7 | .9 |
| 22.7 | 14.3 | 26.5 | 22.1 | | | All Other Current | 14.2 | 16.7 |
| 77.3 | 42.7 | 48.2 | 36.3 | | | Total Current | 45.5 | 53.5 |
| 5.4 | 14.3 | 10.8 | 17.3 | | | Long-Term Debt | 6.7 | 8.2 |
| .0 | .4 | .1 | .0 | | | Deferred Taxes | .5 | .7 |
| 8.4 | 10.7 | 2.8 | 22.0 | | | All Other Non-Current | 10.6 | 7.3 |
| 8.9 | 32.0 | 38.1 | 24.4 | | | Net Worth | 36.8 | 30.3 |
| 100.0 | 100.0 | 100.0 | 100.0 | | | Total Liabilties & Net Worth | 100.0 | 100.0 |
| | | | | | | INCOME DATA | | |
| 100.0 | 100.0 | 100.0 | 100.0 | | | Net Sales | 100.0 | 100.0 |
| | | | | | | Gross Profit | | |
| 94.7 | 91.0 | 94.6 | 89.3 | | | Operating Expenses | 92.0 | 93.4 |
| 5.3 | 9.0 | 5.4 | 10.7 | | | Operating Profit | 8.0 | 6.6 |
| .0 | .9 | .9 | 7.2 | | | All Other Expenses (net) | 3.3 | 2.4 |
| 5.3 | 8.1 | 4.5 | 3.5 | | | Profit Before Taxes | 4.6 | 4.2 |
| | | | | | | RATIOS | | |
| 5.1 | 3.7 | 3.4 | 2.1 | | | Current | 3.4 | 3.2 |
| 1.3 | 2.0 | 2.1 | 1.6 | | | | 1.6 | 1.6 |
| .3 | 1.0 | 1.0 | .8 | | | | 1.1 | 1.0 |
| 5.1 | 3.6 | 3.4 | 2.1 | | | Quick | 3.2 | 2.7 |
| 1.1 | 1.8 | 1.9 | 1.4 | | | | 1.5 | 1.5 |
| .3 | 1.0 | .8 | .6 | | | | .9 | .9 |
| 0 UND | 0 UND | 26 13.8 | 23 15.6 | | | Sales/Receivables | 23 15.9 | 13 27.2 |
| 0 UND | 41 8.8 | 46 8.0 | 54 6.8 | | | | 51 7.1 | 44 8.2 |
| 33 11.0 | 72 5.1 | 69 5.3 | 70 5.2 | | | | 75 4.9 | 68 5.4 |
| | | | | | | Cost of Sales/Inventory | | |
| | | | | | | Cost of Sales/Payables | | |
| 15.0 | 6.2 | 3.4 | 6.1 | | | Sales/Working Capital | 7.0 | 6.9 |
| 176.1 | 13.6 | 9.9 | 14.6 | | | | 11.3 | 14.1 |
| -13.9 | NM | 303.6 | -24.1 | | | | 131.0 | -575.4 |
| 108.2 | 22.3 | 20.2 | | | | EBIT/Interest | 18.7 | 20.4 |
| (13) 16.0 | (22) 9.4 | (18) 4.9 | | | | | (50) 4.3 | (51) 5.4 |
| 5.8 | 1.2 | 1.4 | | | | | .9 | -1.8 |
| | | | | | | Net Profit + Depr., Dep.,<br>Amort./Cur. Mat. L/T/D | | |
| .0 | .1 | .1 | .1 | | | Fixed/Worth | .1 | .1 |
| .4 | .4 | .2 | .3 | | | | .3 | .3 |
| -.5 | -.9 | .6 | -.2 | | | | 1.7 | 1.4 |
| .5 | .6 | .4 | .7 | | | Debt/Worth | .5 | .7 |
| 9.6 | 1.6 | 1.2 | 2.2 | | | | 1.5 | 1.4 |
| -6.4 | -8.6 | 9.1 | -1.9 | | | | 9.3 | 4.2 |
| 297.6 | 80.5 | 46.0 | | | | % Profit Before Taxes/Tangible<br>Net Worth | 94.8 | 91.9 |
| (12) 144.4 | (17) 26.3 | (21) 10.9 | | | | | (53) 20.8 | (61) 30.7 |
| 22.2 | -8.8 | .7 | | | | | -3.7 | 1.5 |
| 93.6 | 37.5 | 14.3 | 24.5 | | | % Profit Before Taxes/Total<br>Assets | 18.5 | 31.4 |
| 34.2 | 18.0 | 6.8 | 12.1 | | | | 7.4 | 10.4 |
| 3.8 | -.5 | -.1 | -.6 | | | | -1.5 | -2.3 |
| UND | 105.7 | 70.2 | 59.3 | | | Sales/Net Fixed Assets | 115.8 | 82.6 |
| 279.7 | 34.7 | 36.1 | 29.5 | | | | 29.4 | 43.0 |
| 35.9 | 17.7 | 20.9 | 13.9 | | | | 15.1 | 18.7 |
| 15.8 | 5.7 | 3.3 | 2.8 | | | Sales/Total Assets | 5.1 | 5.4 |
| 7.7 | 3.3 | 2.5 | 1.8 | | | | 3.4 | 3.2 |
| 5.3 | 2.3 | 1.9 | 1.4 | | | | 2.0 | 2.4 |
| | .6 | .5 | | | | % Depr., Dep., Amort./Sales | .5 | .5 |
| | (15) .8 | (22) 1.1 | | | | | (47) 1.1 | (53) 1.0 |
| | 1.6 | 2.0 | | | | | 2.1 | 2.0 |
| 6.6 | 6.3 | | | | | % Officers', Directors'<br>Owners' Comp/Sales | 4.8 | 4.8 |
| (14) 14.3 | (14) 11.6 | | | | | | (20) 8.0 | (22) 7.2 |
| 25.6 | 24.1 | | | | | | 17.6 | 11.6 |
| 39467M | 127274M | 291493M | 595084M | 297895M | 320654M | Net Sales ($) | 3098599M | 1424649M |
| 4398M | 29632M | 113605M | 273938M | 99648M | 375405M | Total Assets ($) | 901622M | 705769M |

M = $ thousand    MM = $ million
See Pages 9 through 22 for Explanation of Ratios and Data

## Comparative Historical Data | | Current Data Sorted by Sales

| | | | Type of Statement | 0-1MM | 1-3MM | 3-5MM | 5-10MM | 10-25MM | 25MM & OVER |
|---|---|---|---|---|---|---|---|---|---|
| 19 | 11 | 15 | Unqualified | 2 | 2 | 1 | 1 | 3 | 6 |
| 9 | 10 | 11 | Reviewed | | 1 | 2 | 2 | 5 | 1 |
| 14 | 12 | 8 | Compiled | 1 | 3 | 1 | 3 | | |
| 13 | 8 | 14 | Tax Returns | | 5 | 4 | 3 | 2 | |
| 22 | 36 | 38 | Other | 4 | 11 | 4 | 4 | 8 | 6 |
| 4/1/09-3/31/10 ALL | 4/1/10-3/31/11 ALL | 4/1/11-3/31/12 ALL | | | 15 (4/1-9/30/11) | | 71 (10/1/11-3/31/12) | | |
| 77 | 77 | 86 | **NUMBER OF STATEMENTS** | 7 | 22 | 12 | 17 | 15 | 13 |
| % | % | % | **ASSETS** | % | % | % | % | % | % |
| 23.9 | 19.9 | 27.5 | Cash & Equivalents | | 23.4 | 26.5 | 28.7 | 29.6 | 20.0 |
| 39.0 | 37.6 | 32.3 | Trade Receivables (net) | | 32.3 | 36.3 | 35.1 | 35.8 | 31.9 |
| 2.9 | 1.6 | 2.1 | Inventory | | .1 | .0 | .3 | 5.4 | 6.7 |
| 3.5 | 3.4 | 5.0 | All Other Current | | 2.5 | 3.5 | 4.2 | 3.3 | 9.0 |
| 69.2 | 62.5 | 66.9 | Total Current | | 58.3 | 66.3 | 68.3 | 74.1 | 67.7 |
| 14.6 | 17.0 | 14.6 | Fixed Assets (net) | | 19.6 | 18.0 | 13.3 | 9.4 | 10.5 |
| 5.4 | 9.0 | 8.9 | Intangibles (net) | | 10.3 | 7.9 | 6.0 | 10.6 | 14.3 |
| 10.7 | 11.4 | 9.6 | All Other Non-Current | | 11.8 | 7.9 | 12.4 | 5.9 | 7.5 |
| 100.0 | 100.0 | 100.0 | Total | | 100.0 | 100.0 | 100.0 | 100.0 | 100.0 |
| | | | **LIABILITIES** | | | | | | |
| 12.7 | 12.3 | 14.0 | Notes Payable-Short Term | | 26.3 | 6.8 | 6.2 | 3.9 | 5.1 |
| 3.0 | 2.8 | 2.1 | Cur. Mat.-L.T.D. | | 1.1 | 3.4 | 3.5 | 2.0 | 1.8 |
| 12.3 | 10.7 | 13.3 | Trade Payables | | 8.1 | 8.8 | 14.0 | 20.7 | 10.1 |
| .7 | .8 | .4 | Income Taxes Payable | | .7 | .0 | .1 | .5 | .9 |
| 22.0 | 16.3 | 21.6 | All Other Current | | 21.3 | 10.9 | 24.9 | 29.7 | 22.2 |
| 50.8 | 43.0 | 51.4 | Total Current | | 57.5 | 29.9 | 48.7 | 56.8 | 40.0 |
| 11.5 | 13.4 | 11.4 | Long-Term Debt | | 10.7 | 13.3 | 17.4 | 7.0 | 11.0 |
| .7 | .6 | .1 | Deferred Taxes | | .4 | .0 | .0 | .2 | .0 |
| 9.3 | 9.1 | 8.8 | All Other Non-Current | | 8.4 | 12.4 | 5.6 | 4.3 | 17.7 |
| 27.7 | 33.9 | 28.2 | Net Worth | | 22.9 | 44.5 | 28.4 | 31.7 | 31.3 |
| 100.0 | 100.0 | 100.0 | Total Liabilities & Net Worth | | 100.0 | 100.0 | 100.0 | 100.0 | 100.0 |
| | | | **INCOME DATA** | | | | | | |
| 100.0 | 100.0 | 100.0 | Net Sales | | 100.0 | 100.0 | 100.0 | 100.0 | 100.0 |
| | | | Gross Profit | | | | | | |
| 93.0 | 92.5 | 92.9 | Operating Expenses | | 93.6 | 92.6 | 93.1 | 93.8 | 93.4 |
| 7.0 | 7.5 | 7.1 | Operating Profit | | 6.4 | 7.4 | 6.9 | 6.2 | 6.6 |
| 1.7 | .6 | 1.5 | All Other Expenses (net) | | 2.6 | 1.5 | .1 | 1.0 | 2.8 |
| 5.4 | 6.9 | 5.6 | Profit Before Taxes | | 3.8 | 5.9 | 6.8 | 5.2 | 3.8 |
| | | | **RATIOS** | | | | | | |
| 2.7 | 2.7 | 3.4 | | | 3.3 | 4.2 | 3.5 | 3.4 | 2.2 |
| 1.4 | 1.5 | 1.7 | Current | | 1.4 | 2.6 | 1.8 | 1.9 | 1.6 |
| .8 | .9 | .9 | | | .6 | 1.4 | .9 | 1.0 | 1.3 |
| 2.3 | 2.6 | 3.4 | | | 3.3 | 4.2 | 3.5 | 3.4 | 2.0 |
| 1.3 | 1.5 | 1.5 | Quick | | 1.4 | 2.5 | 1.8 | 1.9 | 1.4 |
| .8 | .7 | .7 | | | .6 | 1.2 | .8 | .7 | .8 |
| 25  14.5 | 13  27.7 | 1  347.5 | | | 0  UND | 0  UND | 16  23.2 | 26  14.2 | 24  15.0 |
| 45  8.1 | 52  7.0 | 39  9.4 | Sales/Receivables | | 41  8.8 | 26  14.0 | 41  8.9 | 46  8.0 | 44  8.3 |
| 68  5.4 | 70  5.2 | 65  5.6 | | | 70  5.2 | 91  4.0 | 57  6.4 | 74  4.9 | 65  5.6 |
| | | | Cost of Sales/Inventory | | | | | | |
| | | | Cost of Sales/Payables | | | | | | |
| 6.1 | 5.5 | 6.2 | | | 9.7 | 5.9 | 6.2 | 4.5 | 6.4 |
| 21.6 | 14.3 | 15.0 | Sales/Working Capital | | 38.6 | 7.3 | 18.8 | 13.6 | 11.7 |
| -47.1 | -94.3 | -79.8 | | | -11.8 | 26.1 | -53.4 | 999.8 | 15.2 |
| 23.9 | 29.8 | 27.6 | | | 19.7 | | 61.3 | 37.3 | 42.8 |
| (58) 7.2 | (58) 7.0 | (62) 10.1 | EBIT/Interest | | (17) 8.0 | | (12) 11.4 | (10) 7.5 | (11) 12.3 |
| 1.1 | 1.9 | 2.8 | | | -.1 | | 3.3 | -2.4 | 3.0 |
| 14.8 | | | Net Profit + Depr., Dep., | | | | | | |
| (13) 2.7 | | | Amort./Cur. Mat. L/T/D | | | | | | |
| .9 | | | | | | | | | |
| .1 | .1 | .1 | | | .1 | .0 | .1 | .1 | .1 |
| .4 | .5 | .3 | Fixed/Worth | | 3.6 | .3 | .3 | .2 | .3 |
| -8.0 | 13.7 | NM | | | -.4 | 1.1 | 2.4 | -.5 | NM |
| .9 | .6 | .6 | | | .5 | .4 | .6 | .5 | 1.1 |
| 2.3 | 1.7 | 2.1 | Debt/Worth | | 5.9 | .7 | 1.6 | 1.4 | 2.2 |
| -30.9 | NM | -9.2 | | | -6.4 | 21.0 | NM | -3.2 | NM |
| 87.2 | 94.7 | 96.9 | % Profit Before Taxes/Tangible | | 93.8 | 144.3 | 110.4 | 55.1 | 99.2 |
| (56) 25.7 | (58) 30.4 | (62) 19.6 | Net Worth | | (13) 5.9 | (10) 9.4 | (13) 36.8 | (11) 19.6 | (10) 29.3 |
| 3.5 | 4.0 | 1.0 | | | -10.6 | -8.1 | 3.6 | 1.3 | .0 |
| 32.2 | 29.8 | 30.8 | % Profit Before Taxes/Total | | 32.8 | 49.4 | 57.7 | 24.5 | 22.9 |
| 7.7 | 9.6 | 10.6 | Assets | | 13.4 | 14.2 | 15.9 | 10.2 | 8.0 |
| -.1 | .7 | -.4 | | | -1.2 | -1.6 | -.2 | .0 | -.4 |
| 112.6 | 204.5 | 175.9 | | | 470.7 | 384.1 | 84.9 | 110.5 | 61.3 |
| 36.0 | 41.7 | 39.3 | Sales/Net Fixed Assets | | 43.5 | 34.6 | 34.1 | 42.6 | 33.8 |
| 19.3 | 17.2 | 19.4 | | | 17.8 | 11.0 | 22.2 | 20.1 | 16.9 |
| 4.9 | 4.7 | 5.6 | | | 7.4 | 8.2 | 5.8 | 3.5 | 4.1 |
| 3.3 | 2.7 | 3.1 | Sales/Total Assets | | 3.4 | 3.2 | 3.4 | 2.5 | 2.3 |
| 2.2 | 1.6 | 2.1 | | | 2.1 | 2.1 | 2.4 | 2.0 | 1.4 |
| .4 | .7 | .6 | | | .5 | .6 | .4 | | .5 |
| (60) 1.0 | (46) 1.2 | (56) .8 | % Depr., Dep., Amort./Sales | | (13) .8 | (11) .8 | (12) 1.1 | | (10) .9 |
| 1.6 | 1.8 | 1.5 | | | 1.4 | 1.9 | 1.4 | | 1.3 |
| 6.0 | 6.5 | 6.2 | % Officers', Directors' | | 8.6 | | | | |
| (28) 10.5 | (31) 12.0 | (37) 11.6 | Owners' Comp/Sales | | (13) 14.2 | | | | |
| 16.1 | 16.5 | 22.6 | | | 27.3 | | | | |
| 1891481M | 2918938M | 1671867M | Net Sales ($) | 3540M | 44753M | 48188M | 124245M | 221045M | 1230096M |
| 1041493M | 1028158M | 896626M | Total Assets ($) | 3729M | 38171M | 20750M | 38116M | 84395M | 711465M |

© RMA 2012

M = $ thousand     MM = $ million
See Pages 9 through 22 for Explanation of Ratios and Data

## Current Data Sorted by Assets | Comparative Historical Data

| 0-500M | 500M-2MM | 2-10MM | 10-50MM | 50-100MM | 100-250MM | Type of Statement | 4/1/07-3/31/08 ALL | 4/1/08-3/31/09 ALL |
|---|---|---|---|---|---|---|---|---|
| | | 1 | 1 | 1 | 1 | Unqualified | 4 | 6 |
| | 2 | 1 | | | | Reviewed | 3 | 4 |
| | 1 | 2 | | | | Compiled | 4 | 4 |
| 1 | 2 | 3 | 2 | | 1 | Tax Returns | 3 | 2 |
| 1 | 7 | 2 | 3 | 2 | | Other | 8 | 16 |
| | 4 (4/1-9/30/11) | | 28 (10/1/11-3/31/12) | | | | | |
| 2 | 12 | 9 | 4 | 3 | 2 | NUMBER OF STATEMENTS | 22 | 32 |
| % | % | % | % | % | % | ASSETS | % | % |
| | 19.9 | | | | | Cash & Equivalents | 14.0 | 13.8 |
| | 36.2 | | | | | Trade Receivables (net) | 41.4 | 35.3 |
| | .0 | | | | | Inventory | 1.0 | 3.1 |
| | 4.7 | | | | | All Other Current | 2.8 | 4.5 |
| | 60.8 | | | | | Total Current | 59.2 | 56.7 |
| | 14.5 | | | | | Fixed Assets (net) | 21.9 | 20.6 |
| | 7.1 | | | | | Intangibles (net) | 11.8 | 15.4 |
| | 17.6 | | | | | All Other Non-Current | 7.1 | 7.2 |
| | 100.0 | | | | | Total | 100.0 | 100.0 |
| | | | | | | LIABILITIES | | |
| | 8.4 | | | | | Notes Payable-Short Term | 7.4 | 12.4 |
| | 1.4 | | | | | Cur. Mat.-L.T.D. | 3.0 | 3.5 |
| | 15.7 | | | | | Trade Payables | 27.5 | 25.3 |
| | .2 | | | | | Income Taxes Payable | .2 | .0 |
| | 26.0 | | | | | All Other Current | 13.3 | 11.3 |
| | 51.7 | | | | | Total Current | 51.4 | 52.6 |
| | 13.2 | | | | | Long-Term Debt | 32.5 | 20.3 |
| | .0 | | | | | Deferred Taxes | .4 | .8 |
| | 14.2 | | | | | All Other Non-Current | 3.8 | 5.3 |
| | 20.9 | | | | | Net Worth | 11.9 | 21.1 |
| | 100.0 | | | | | Total Liabilities & Net Worth | 100.0 | 100.0 |
| | | | | | | INCOME DATA | | |
| | 100.0 | | | | | Net Sales | 100.0 | 100.0 |
| | | | | | | Gross Profit | | |
| | 91.1 | | | | | Operating Expenses | 92.1 | 96.1 |
| | 8.9 | | | | | Operating Profit | 7.9 | 3.9 |
| | 1.2 | | | | | All Other Expenses (net) | 4.3 | 4.2 |
| | 7.7 | | | | | Profit Before Taxes | 3.5 | -.2 |
| | | | | | | RATIOS | | |
| | 5.5 | | | | | | 2.6 | 1.6 |
| | 1.8 | | | | | Current | 1.2 | 1.1 |
| | 1.0 | | | | | | .7 | .8 |
| | 3.6 | | | | | | 2.5 | 1.4 |
| | 1.5 | | | | | Quick | 1.0 | .9 |
| | .9 | | | | | | .7 | .6 |
| 0 UND | | | | | | | 25  14.3 | 29  12.6 |
| 32 11.4 | | | | | | Sales/Receivables | 47  7.7 | 51  7.2 |
| 91 4.0 | | | | | | | 85  4.3 | 79  4.6 |
| | | | | | | Cost of Sales/Inventory | | |
| | | | | | | Cost of Sales/Payables | | |
| | 9.6 | | | | | | 8.0 | 9.1 |
| | 23.7 | | | | | Sales/Working Capital | 39.8 | 57.3 |
| | NM | | | | | | -16.2 | -25.0 |
| | 64.2 | | | | | | 7.6 | 8.3 |
| (10) | 31.0 | | | | | EBIT/Interest | (16)  1.8 | (25)  1.4 |
| | 5.4 | | | | | | -.3 | -.1 |
| | | | | | | Net Profit + Depr., Dep., Amort./Cur. Mat. L/T/D | | |
| | .0 | | | | | | .3 | .3 |
| | .1 | | | | | Fixed/Worth | 2.8 | 1.1 |
| | .9 | | | | | | -2.0 | -21.1 |
| | .4 | | | | | | 1.5 | 2.2 |
| | 1.7 | | | | | Debt/Worth | 12.7 | 13.8 |
| | NM | | | | | | -6.8 | -13.9 |
| | | | | | | % Profit Before Taxes/Tangible Net Worth | (13)  104.9 / 41.0 / 11.7 | (21)  93.9 / 32.8 / -6.5 |
| | 59.4 | | | | | | 18.8 | 11.5 |
| | 32.6 | | | | | % Profit Before Taxes/Total Assets | 4.1 | 1.9 |
| | 21.4 | | | | | | -1.6 | -3.7 |
| | 504.2 | | | | | | 80.9 | 71.3 |
| | 133.4 | | | | | Sales/Net Fixed Assets | 31.6 | 17.4 |
| | 45.8 | | | | | | 8.4 | 5.8 |
| | 9.4 | | | | | | 4.4 | 4.4 |
| | 4.9 | | | | | Sales/Total Assets | 2.8 | 2.0 |
| | 2.3 | | | | | | 1.4 | .5 |
| | | | | | | % Depr., Dep., Amort./Sales | (20)  .6 / 1.3 / 4.3 | (24)  .5 / 2.2 / 4.6 |
| | | | | | | % Officers', Directors' Owners' Comp/Sales | | |
| 5784M | 82556M | 85203M | 290028M | 441977M | 630078M | Net Sales ($) | 786942M | 970467M |
| 695M | 12277M | 39158M | 150025M | 216060M | 386329M | Total Assets ($) | 337030M | 804828M |

M = $ thousand   MM = $ million
See Pages 9 through 22 for Explanation of Ratios and Data

| Comparative Historical Data | | | | Current Data Sorted by Sales | | | | | |
|---|---|---|---|---|---|---|---|---|---|
| | | | **Type of Statement** | | | | | | |
| 6 | 7 | 4 | Unqualified | 1 | | | | | 3 |
| 2 | 2 | 3 | Reviewed | | | | 1 | 2 | |
| 2 | 1 | 3 | Compiled | | | | 2 | 1 | |
| 8 | 3 | 6 | Tax Returns | 2 | | | 1 | 3 | |
| 16 | 16 | 16 | Other | 4 | 2 | | 4 | | 6 |
| 4/1/09-3/31/10 ALL | 4/1/10-3/31/11 ALL | 4/1/11-3/31/12 ALL | | 0-1MM | 4 (4/1-9/30/11) 1-3MM | 3-5MM | 28 (10/1/11-3/31/12) 5-10MM | 10-25MM | 25MM & OVER |
| 34 | 29 | 32 | **NUMBER OF STATEMENTS** | | 7 | 2 | 8 | 6 | 9 |
| % | % | % | **ASSETS** | % | % | % | % | % | % |
| 12.9 | 20.8 | 21.7 | Cash & Equivalents | D | | | | | |
| 32.2 | 32.3 | 29.5 | Trade Receivables (net) | A | | | | | |
| 2.4 | 2.5 | 2.4 | Inventory | T | | | | | |
| 1.8 | 2.9 | 2.9 | All Other Current | A | | | | | |
| 49.4 | 58.5 | 56.6 | Total Current | | | | | | |
| 21.4 | 15.4 | 16.0 | Fixed Assets (net) | N | | | | | |
| 17.4 | 18.4 | 13.8 | Intangibles (net) | O | | | | | |
| 11.8 | 7.7 | 13.6 | All Other Non-Current | T | | | | | |
| 100.0 | 100.0 | 100.0 | Total | | | | | | |
| | | | **LIABILITIES** | A | | | | | |
| 17.2 | 15.4 | 10.1 | Notes Payable-Short Term | V | | | | | |
| 2.2 | 1.6 | 1.1 | Cur. Mat.-L.T.D. | A | | | | | |
| 16.3 | 20.3 | 16.9 | Trade Payables | I | | | | | |
| 2.7 | .1 | .1 | Income Taxes Payable | L | | | | | |
| 14.9 | 26.5 | 24.7 | All Other Current | A | | | | | |
| 53.2 | 63.9 | 52.9 | Total Current | B | | | | | |
| 18.5 | 10.8 | 9.1 | Long-Term Debt | L | | | | | |
| .8 | .2 | .8 | Deferred Taxes | E | | | | | |
| 7.0 | 3.4 | 9.3 | All Other Non-Current | | | | | | |
| 20.5 | 21.7 | 27.9 | Net Worth | | | | | | |
| 100.0 | 100.0 | 100.0 | Total Liabilties & Net Worth | | | | | | |
| | | | **INCOME DATA** | | | | | | |
| 100.0 | 100.0 | 100.0 | Net Sales | | | | | | |
| | | | Gross Profit | | | | | | |
| 99.3 | 94.0 | 93.3 | Operating Expenses | | | | | | |
| .7 | 6.0 | 6.7 | Operating Profit | | | | | | |
| 1.9 | 1.2 | 1.1 | All Other Expenses (net) | | | | | | |
| -1.1 | 4.8 | 5.7 | Profit Before Taxes | | | | | | |
| | | | **RATIOS** | | | | | | |
| 1.5 | 1.9 | 1.9 | | | | | | | |
| 1.1 | 1.1 | 1.3 | Current | | | | | | |
| .7 | .6 | .8 | | | | | | | |
| 1.4 | 1.5 | 1.7 | | | | | | | |
| .9 | 1.0 | 1.0 | Quick | | | | | | |
| .6 | .6 | .7 | | | | | | | |
| 12  31.0 | 12  30.2 | 15  24.3 | | | | | | | |
| 52  7.0 | 46  8.0 | 33  11.0 | Sales/Receivables | | | | | | |
| 77  4.8 | 85  4.3 | 87  4.2 | | | | | | | |
| | | | Cost of Sales/Inventory | | | | | | |
| | | | Cost of Sales/Payables | | | | | | |
| 9.2 | 7.2 | 10.6 | | | | | | | |
| 323.3 | 50.6 | 29.4 | Sales/Working Capital | | | | | | |
| -14.2 | -15.8 | -25.8 | | | | | | | |
| 4.6 | 21.8 | 74.0 | | | | | | | |
| (26)  -.5 | (21)  2.6 | (24)  8.2 | EBIT/Interest | | | | | | |
| -7.7 | -4.8 | .7 | | | | | | | |
| | | | Net Profit + Depr., Dep., Amort./Cur. Mat. L/T/D | | | | | | |
| .4 | .2 | .1 | | | | | | | |
| 2.3 | .5 | .6 | Fixed/Worth | | | | | | |
| -1.0 | -12.6 | 26.5 | | | | | | | |
| 1.2 | 1.7 | 1.2 | | | | | | | |
| 15.4 | 4.4 | 2.4 | Debt/Worth | | | | | | |
| -4.2 | -11.5 | NM | | | | | | | |
| 66.1 | 188.0 | 107.9 | | | | | | | |
| (20)  1.2 | (19)  36.9 | (24)  59.0 | % Profit Before Taxes/Tangible Net Worth | | | | | | |
| -102.5 | -12.2 | 12.9 | | | | | | | |
| 9.5 | 33.7 | 42.0 | | | | | | | |
| -.9 | 7.7 | 13.9 | % Profit Before Taxes/Total Assets | | | | | | |
| -13.7 | -.5 | -.2 | | | | | | | |
| 87.5 | 121.9 | 164.3 | | | | | | | |
| 21.6 | 29.3 | 56.2 | Sales/Net Fixed Assets | | | | | | |
| 7.6 | 9.2 | 11.0 | | | | | | | |
| 4.7 | 4.1 | 5.2 | | | | | | | |
| 2.3 | 2.3 | 2.5 | Sales/Total Assets | | | | | | |
| 1.3 | 1.5 | 1.5 | | | | | | | |
| 1.7 | .6 | .3 | | | | | | | |
| (18)  2.4 | (18)  2.0 | (16)  .6 | % Depr., Dep., Amort./Sales | | | | | | |
| 4.3 | 5.3 | 3.0 | | | | | | | |
| 4.0 | | 2.7 | | | | | | | |
| (13)  7.4 | | (10)  7.0 | % Officers', Directors' Owners' Comp/Sales | | | | | | |
| 9.3 | | 12.4 | | | | | | | |
| 994235M | 1365000M | 1535626M | Net Sales ($) | | 16381M | 7423M | 52074M | 97665M | 1362083M |
| 736528M | 697137M | 804544M | Total Assets ($) | | 7278M | 2483M | 23313M | 19056M | 752414M |

© RMA 2012

**M = $ thousand    MM = $ million**
See Pages 9 through 22 for Explanation of Ratios and Data

## Current Data Sorted by Assets     Comparative Historical Data

| Type of Statement | 0-500M | 500M-2MM | 2-10MM | 10-50MM | 50-100MM | 100-250MM | 4/1/07-3/31/08 ALL | 4/1/08-3/31/09 ALL |
|---|---|---|---|---|---|---|---|---|
| Unqualified | | | 3 | 3 | | 2 | 12 | 9 |
| Reviewed | | 2 | 10 | 2 | | | 7 | 10 |
| Compiled | 1 | 4 | 5 | | | | 12 | 7 |
| Tax Returns | 5 | 5 | 5 | | | | 8 | 13 |
| Other | 5 | 16 | 10 | 10 | 1 | 2 | 45 | 39 |
| | 8 (4/1-9/30/11) | | | 81 (10/1/11-3/31/12) | | | | |
| NUMBER OF STATEMENTS | 11 | 27 | 31 | 15 | 1 | 4 | 84 | 78 |
| **ASSETS** | % | % | % | % | % | % | % | % |
| Cash & Equivalents | 31.3 | 16.6 | 15.4 | 8.6 | | | 11.0 | 10.4 |
| Trade Receivables (net) | 11.2 | 30.7 | 24.6 | 15.6 | | | 22.5 | 22.9 |
| Inventory | 5.6 | 8.3 | 7.6 | 6.0 | | | 6.2 | 7.2 |
| All Other Current | 7.6 | 2.6 | 3.3 | 4.4 | | | 3.2 | 2.1 |
| Total Current | 55.6 | 58.1 | 50.8 | 34.5 | | | 42.9 | 42.7 |
| Fixed Assets (net) | 29.8 | 29.6 | 36.3 | 41.0 | | | 43.1 | 40.3 |
| Intangibles (net) | 5.8 | 5.2 | 3.4 | 12.4 | | | 5.2 | 8.3 |
| All Other Non-Current | 8.8 | 7.2 | 9.5 | 12.0 | | | 8.8 | 8.7 |
| Total | 100.0 | 100.0 | 100.0 | 100.0 | | | 100.0 | 100.0 |
| **LIABILITIES** | | | | | | | | |
| Notes Payable-Short Term | 11.3 | 8.9 | 10.8 | 3.9 | | | 12.9 | 11.7 |
| Cur. Mat.-L.T.D. | 5.7 | 8.6 | 3.9 | 3.0 | | | 5.0 | 4.4 |
| Trade Payables | 11.6 | 15.9 | 12.3 | 8.8 | | | 11.9 | 9.8 |
| Income Taxes Payable | .0 | .2 | .0 | .4 | | | .0 | .0 |
| All Other Current | 9.2 | 18.0 | 10.3 | 8.2 | | | 11.1 | 11.0 |
| Total Current | 37.9 | 51.7 | 37.3 | 24.3 | | | 40.9 | 37.0 |
| Long-Term Debt | 96.8 | 26.1 | 22.3 | 22.9 | | | 30.2 | 28.1 |
| Deferred Taxes | .0 | .0 | .7 | .0 | | | .1 | .2 |
| All Other Non-Current | 7.4 | 25.1 | 22.2 | 1.7 | | | 12.9 | 4.4 |
| Net Worth | -42.6 | -2.9 | 17.4 | 51.1 | | | 15.9 | 30.4 |
| Total Liabilities & Net Worth | 100.0 | 100.0 | 100.0 | 100.0 | | | 100.0 | 100.0 |
| **INCOME DATA** | | | | | | | | |
| Net Sales | 100.0 | 100.0 | 100.0 | 100.0 | | | 100.0 | 100.0 |
| Gross Profit | | | | | | | | |
| Operating Expenses | 85.6 | 86.2 | 90.1 | 91.4 | | | 86.2 | 86.6 |
| Operating Profit | 14.4 | 13.8 | 9.9 | 8.6 | | | 13.8 | 13.4 |
| All Other Expenses (net) | 2.1 | 5.2 | 3.4 | 2.1 | | | 4.0 | 2.9 |
| Profit Before Taxes | 12.2 | 8.6 | 6.5 | 6.6 | | | 9.9 | 10.6 |
| **RATIOS** | | | | | | | | |
| | 5.1 | 2.9 | 2.7 | 2.1 | | | 2.5 | 2.4 |
| Current | 1.6 | 1.4 | 1.3 | 1.6 | | | 1.2 | 1.3 |
| | .7 | .5 | .8 | .9 | | | .7 | .8 |
| | 2.8 | 2.2 | 2.3 | 1.7 | | | 1.8 | 1.9 |
| Quick | .7 | 1.0 | 1.0 | .9 | | | .9 (77) | 1.0 |
| | .6 | .4 | .5 | .6 | | | .4 | .6 |
| | 0 UND | 16   22.4 | 22   16.3 | 28   12.9 | | | 12   29.4 | 16   22.3 |
| Sales/Receivables | 3   126.0 | 38   9.7 | 41   8.8 | 34   10.8 | | | 38   9.7 | 35   10.5 |
| | 22   16.5 | 51   7.1 | 55   6.6 | 58   6.3 | | | 58   6.3 | 48   7.6 |
| Cost of Sales/Inventory | | | | | | | | |
| Cost of Sales/Payables | | | | | | | | |
| | 3.4 | 5.1 | 6.1 | 6.8 | | | 6.5 | 8.4 |
| Sales/Working Capital | 39.1 | 18.0 | 21.4 | 13.3 | | | 25.1 | 23.6 |
| | -15.2 | -10.6 | -16.6 | -24.2 | | | -16.2 | -29.2 |
| | | 14.7 | 31.8 | 33.3 | | | 9.7 | 12.0 |
| EBIT/Interest | | (16) 4.9 | (28) 2.6 | (13) 6.6 | | | (72) 3.1 | (70) 3.6 |
| | | -1.0 | 1.4 | .9 | | | 1.0 | 1.2 |
| Net Profit + Depr., Dep., Amort./Cur. Mat. L/T/D | | | | | | | | 10.3 |
| | | | | | | | (10) 3.2 | |
| | | | | | | | | .9 |
| | .0 | .3 | .2 | .2 | | | .6 | .3 |
| Fixed/Worth | -.6 | 3.8 | 1.5 | 1.0 | | | 1.4 | 1.1 |
| | -.3 | -.4 | 4.7 | 1.9 | | | 20.8 | 3.4 |
| | .6 | .5 | .6 | .5 | | | .9 | .9 |
| Debt/Worth | -3.6 | 5.6 | 2.9 | .9 | | | 2.3 | 2.2 |
| | -1.7 | -5.0 | 11.5 | 3.0 | | | 47.4 | 5.8 |
| | | 117.0 | 71.1 | 23.9 | | | 64.1 | 81.6 |
| % Profit Before Taxes/Tangible Net Worth | | (17) 40.3 | (27) 26.9 | (14) 17.2 | | | (66) 32.4 | (67) 31.4 |
| | | 18.2 | 10.9 | -1.3 | | | 6.2 | 7.1 |
| | 109.1 | 30.6 | 21.6 | 13.2 | | | 22.1 | 25.2 |
| % Profit Before Taxes/Total Assets | 25.4 | 16.5 | 5.5 | 9.1 | | | 9.3 | 8.8 |
| | -4.5 | 1.3 | 1.8 | -.7 | | | -.9 | .5 |
| | 391.4 | 50.6 | 47.1 | 13.9 | | | 24.5 | 28.4 |
| Sales/Net Fixed Assets | 47.7 | 16.8 | 10.4 | 2.4 | | | 5.6 | 6.3 |
| | 1.6 | 2.2 | 1.2 | 1.1 | | | 1.2 | 1.2 |
| | 10.1 | 3.9 | 3.7 | 1.5 | | | 2.8 | 3.4 |
| Sales/Total Assets | 4.4 | 2.2 | 1.6 | 1.1 | | | 1.7 | 1.9 |
| | 1.4 | 1.1 | .8 | .5 | | | .8 | .7 |
| | | .7 | .5 | 3.0 | | | 1.3 | 1.0 |
| % Depr., Dep., Amort./Sales | | (18) 1.7 | (25) 2.6 | (13) 11.0 | | | (66) 4.6 | (64) 3.9 |
| | | 11.6 | 10.3 | 16.0 | | | 12.4 | 11.9 |
| | | 2.0 | 3.2 | | | | 3.0 | 3.4 |
| % Officers', Directors' Owners' Comp/Sales | | (15) 5.6 | (16) 5.1 | | | | (34) 4.7 | (28) 5.1 |
| | | 8.1 | 10.2 | | | | 8.2 | 13.5 |
| Net Sales ($) | 12864M | 79589M | 340397M | 397372M | 175766M | 712616M | 1029640M | 2158521M |
| Total Assets ($) | 3024M | 31276M | 167746M | 343523M | 79981M | 579960M | 784367M | 1344595M |

© RMA 2012

**M = $ thousand    MM = $ million**
See Pages 9 through 22 for Explanation of Ratios and Data

## Comparative Historical Data | | Current Data Sorted by Sales

| | | | Type of Statement | 0-1MM | 1-3MM | 3-5MM | 5-10MM | 10-25MM | 25MM & OVER |
|---|---|---|---|---|---|---|---|---|---|
| 9 | 13 | 8 | Unqualified | | | | 4 | 2 | 2 |
| 13 | 9 | 14 | Reviewed | | 2 | 3 | 5 | 4 | |
| 12 | 8 | 10 | Compiled | 1 | 3 | 2 | 1 | 3 | |
| 14 | 8 | 13 | Tax Returns | 7 | 7 | 1 | 3 | 2 | |
| 24 | 31 | 44 | Other | 7 | 7 | 8 | 5 | 7 | 10 |
| 4/1/09-3/31/10 ALL | 4/1/10-3/31/11 ALL | 4/1/11-3/31/12 ALL | | 8 (4/1-9/30/11) | | | 81 (10/1/11-3/31/12) | | |
| 72 | 69 | 89 | NUMBER OF STATEMENTS | 15 | 12 | 14 | 18 | 18 | 12 |
| % | % | % | **ASSETS** | % | % | % | % | % | % |
| 12.3 | 12.3 | 16.0 | Cash & Equivalents | 23.2 | 14.1 | 17.5 | 15.3 | 10.3 | 16.8 |
| 21.9 | 21.4 | 23.7 | Trade Receivables (net) | 6.8 | 27.8 | 32.7 | 18.3 | 31.9 | 25.8 |
| 7.3 | 6.6 | 7.5 | Inventory | .6 | 16.2 | 2.6 | 5.9 | 10.0 | 11.8 |
| 5.5 | 5.8 | 3.8 | All Other Current | 6.0 | 1.6 | 3.7 | 1.3 | 4.9 | 5.6 |
| 47.0 | 46.0 | 51.0 | Total Current | 36.6 | 59.7 | 56.5 | 40.8 | 57.1 | 60.0 |
| 39.0 | 34.1 | 33.6 | Fixed Assets (net) | 52.7 | 19.8 | 34.7 | 41.6 | 26.5 | 20.7 |
| 6.4 | 10.4 | 6.2 | Intangibles (net) | 4.2 | 11.3 | .3 | 5.0 | 7.7 | 9.8 |
| 7.6 | 9.6 | 9.3 | All Other Non-Current | 6.5 | 9.2 | 8.5 | 12.6 | 8.7 | 9.5 |
| 100.0 | 100.0 | 100.0 | Total | 100.0 | 100.0 | 100.0 | 100.0 | 100.0 | 100.0 |
| | | | **LIABILITIES** | | | | | | |
| 10.2 | 7.5 | 8.9 | Notes Payable-Short Term | 9.3 | 12.8 | 6.6 | 9.8 | 6.1 | 10.1 |
| 4.9 | 4.5 | 5.3 | Cur. Mat.-L.T.D. | 13.0 | 5.1 | 4.9 | 4.8 | 2.1 | 1.6 |
| 12.6 | 11.9 | 12.3 | Trade Payables | 4.8 | 18.9 | 10.7 | 15.4 | 13.1 | 11.0 |
| .0 | .1 | .1 | Income Taxes Payable | .0 | .0 | .2 | .2 | .2 | .2 |
| 14.0 | 12.2 | 12.7 | All Other Current | 5.7 | 10.0 | 21.5 | 14.3 | 10.5 | 15.1 |
| 41.7 | 36.2 | 39.4 | Total Current | 32.9 | 46.8 | 44.0 | 44.5 | 32.1 | 38.1 |
| 41.3 | 34.4 | 37.1 | Long-Term Debt | 74.4 | 52.3 | 21.1 | 23.3 | 15.2 | 47.8 |
| .3 | .3 | .3 | Deferred Taxes | .0 | .0 | .7 | .7 | .0 | .0 |
| 4.3 | 9.1 | 16.9 | All Other Non-Current | 5.4 | 4.7 | 42.1 | 6.0 | 3.9 | 50.1 |
| 12.5 | 20.0 | 6.2 | Net Worth | -13.0 | -3.8 | -7.8 | 25.5 | 48.8 | -36.1 |
| 100.0 | 100.0 | 100.0 | Total Liabilties & Net Worth | 100.0 | 100.0 | 100.0 | 100.0 | 100.0 | 100.0 |
| | | | **INCOME DATA** | | | | | | |
| 100.0 | 100.0 | 100.0 | Net Sales | 100.0 | 100.0 | 100.0 | 100.0 | 100.0 | 100.0 |
| | | | Gross Profit | | | | | | |
| 91.5 | 90.7 | 88.6 | Operating Expenses | 74.5 | 88.5 | 92.3 | 92.2 | 89.8 | 94.6 |
| 8.5 | 9.3 | 11.4 | Operating Profit | 25.5 | 11.5 | 7.7 | 7.8 | 10.2 | 5.4 |
| 4.3 | 3.6 | 3.8 | All Other Expenses (net) | 10.4 | 4.3 | 2.7 | 2.5 | .7 | 3.2 |
| 4.1 | 5.7 | 7.6 | Profit Before Taxes | 15.0 | 7.1 | 5.0 | 5.3 | 9.4 | 2.2 |
| | | | **RATIOS** | | | | | | |
| 2.0 | 2.2 | 2.6 | | 3.7 | 2.3 | 2.8 | 1.8 | 2.5 | 2.6 |
| 1.1 | 1.3 | 1.4 | Current | .8 | 1.3 | 1.7 | .8 | 1.8 | 1.8 |
| .9 | .8 | .8 | | .2 | .7 | .8 | .5 | 1.3 | 1.2 |
| 1.6 | 1.5 | 2.1 | | 2.2 | 1.5 | 2.4 | 1.7 | 2.1 | 2.2 |
| (71) .9 | 1.0 | 1.0 | Quick | .7 | .7 | 1.3 | .7 | 1.2 | 1.1 |
| .4 | .5 | .5 | | .4 | .4 | .6 | .4 | .9 | .7 |
| 17 20.9 | 20 18.3 | 18 19.8 | | 0 UND | 17 20.9 | 31 11.8 | 14 25.2 | 33 10.9 | 28 13.2 |
| 39 9.3 | 42 8.6 | 38 9.7 | Sales/Receivables | 0 UND | 42 8.7 | 40 9.1 | 30 12.2 | 52 7.0 | 51 7.2 |
| 57 6.4 | 61 6.0 | 54 6.7 | | 23 16.1 | 49 7.4 | 72 5.1 | 43 8.5 | 62 5.9 | 81 4.5 |
| | | | Cost of Sales/Inventory | | | | | | |
| | | | Cost of Sales/Payables | | | | | | |
| 6.9 | 4.8 | 5.9 | | 5.0 | 4.3 | 5.3 | 15.6 | 5.5 | 4.6 |
| 32.2 | 22.7 | 18.0 | Sales/Working Capital | -34.7 | 64.4 | 9.0 | -40.0 | 11.4 | 10.6 |
| -45.7 | -17.3 | -19.8 | | -3.6 | -17.7 | NM | -10.6 | 20.9 | 27.8 |
| 4.8 | 7.7 | 29.2 | | | | 12.4 | 34.2 | 54.7 | |
| (62) 1.8 | (58) 2.0 | (67) 4.0 | EBIT/Interest | | (10) 3.6 | | (17) 4.4 | (17) 13.1 | |
| .2 | .4 | 1.1 | | | .2 | | 1.5 | 1.3 | |
| | | 10.4 | Net Profit + Depr., Dep., | | | | | | |
| | | (13) 3.1 | Amort./Cur. Mat. L/T/D | | | | | | |
| | | 1.3 | | | | | | | |
| .6 | .3 | .2 | | .0 | .3 | .2 | .8 | .2 | .2 |
| 1.7 | 2.6 | 1.5 | Fixed/Worth | 9.6 | NM | 1.6 | 3.3 | .9 | 1.2 |
| -14.6 | -1.3 | -3.7 | | -1.4 | -.2 | 4.5 | NM | 1.5 | -.3 |
| 1.5 | 1.0 | .6 | | .6 | .9 | .5 | 1.5 | .5 | .6 |
| 5.0 | 3.5 | 3.0 | Debt/Worth | -5.6 | NM | 2.1 | 5.3 | 1.0 | 6.2 |
| -16.4 | -4.2 | -7.2 | | -2.4 | -2.5 | 32.6 | NM | 3.9 | -2.0 |
| 46.6 | 39.7 | 63.6 | % Profit Before Taxes/Tangible | | | 61.3 | 84.1 | 64.4 | |
| (51) 10.8 | (47) 18.4 | (63) 26.2 | Net Worth | | | (12) 30.5 | (14) 16.8 | (17) 27.2 | |
| -11.8 | .7 | 9.3 | | | | 14.0 | 6.6 | 19.4 | |
| 10.1 | 16.0 | 25.9 | % Profit Before Taxes/Total | 51.3 | 25.7 | 33.5 | 15.8 | 27.5 | 9.3 |
| 1.4 | 3.6 | 9.1 | Assets | 7.1 | 13.2 | 13.6 | 4.8 | 12.2 | 4.9 |
| -2.7 | -1.0 | .5 | | -.7 | -4.0 | 1.1 | 1.8 | 1.0 | -6.2 |
| 28.3 | 26.2 | 44.0 | | 62.0 | 103.8 | 34.2 | 38.3 | 49.4 | 17.3 |
| 9.7 | 6.3 | 10.3 | Sales/Net Fixed Assets | 1.6 | 30.5 | 10.9 | 6.9 | 18.8 | 14.0 |
| 1.0 | 1.1 | 1.5 | | .6 | 7.1 | 1.1 | 1.2 | 2.0 | 6.4 |
| 2.7 | 2.4 | 3.3 | | 1.8 | 2.6 | 3.9 | 4.2 | 3.1 | 2.8 |
| 1.6 | 1.5 | 1.7 | Sales/Total Assets | .9 | 1.8 | 2.4 | 1.8 | 1.8 | 1.7 |
| .7 | .6 | .9 | | .5 | 1.5 | .8 | .8 | 1.0 | 1.2 |
| 1.1 | 1.1 | .8 | | 4.5 | | 1.3 | 1.6 | .4 | |
| (59) 3.9 | (58) 3.6 | (64) 4.0 | % Depr., Dep., Amort./Sales | (10) 12.0 | | (11) 2.5 | (13) 5.3 | (15) 3.7 | |
| 14.4 | 13.0 | 13.0 | | 24.8 | | 8.9 | 17.0 | 11.0 | |
| 3.2 | 4.3 | 3.2 | % Officers', Directors' | | | | | | |
| (28) 5.2 | (19) 7.4 | (36) 5.6 | Owners' Comp/Sales | | | | | | |
| 8.5 | 10.9 | 10.6 | | | | | | | |
| 1846735M | 1733658M | 1718604M | Net Sales ($) | 6875M | 25806M | 56297M | 133994M | 294373M | 1201259M |
| 1220077M | 1882220M | 1205510M | Total Assets ($) | 12062M | 13207M | 42998M | 113896M | 217362M | 805985M |

© RMA 2012          M = $ thousand     MM = $ million
See Pages 9 through 22 for Explanation of Ratios and Data

## Current Data Sorted by Assets | Comparative Historical Data

| Type of Statement | 0-500M | 500M-2MM | 2-10MM | 10-50MM | 50-100MM | 100-250MM | | 4/1/07-3/31/08 ALL | 4/1/08-3/31/09 ALL |
|---|---|---|---|---|---|---|---|---|---|
| Unqualified | | | | 10 | 2 | 1 | | 14 | 15 |
| Reviewed | | 4 | 11 | 6 | | | | 15 | 17 |
| Compiled | 2 | 4 | 7 | 3 | | | | 18 | 23 |
| Tax Returns | 12 | 14 | 4 | | | | | 13 | 19 |
| Other | 6 | 13 | 19 | 15 | | 1 | | 43 | 45 |
| | 19 (4/1-9/30/11) | | | 115 (10/1/11-3/31/12) | | | | | |
| NUMBER OF STATEMENTS | 20 | 35 | 41 | 34 | 2 | 2 | | 103 | 119 |
| **ASSETS** | % | % | % | % | % | % | | % | % |
| Cash & Equivalents | 18.0 | 21.6 | 14.4 | 13.2 | | | | 14.1 | 14.2 |
| Trade Receivables (net) | 22.3 | 21.6 | 35.0 | 30.4 | | | | 36.0 | 33.9 |
| Inventory | .2 | 1.7 | 3.9 | 2.6 | | | | 4.6 | 3.4 |
| All Other Current | .4 | 2.8 | 1.8 | 6.7 | | | | 3.6 | 4.7 |
| Total Current | 40.9 | 47.7 | 55.1 | 52.9 | | | | 58.2 | 56.2 |
| Fixed Assets (net) | 23.6 | 27.4 | 30.2 | 17.9 | | | | 24.8 | 25.7 |
| Intangibles (net) | 21.8 | 12.1 | 3.5 | 21.1 | | | | 11.6 | 11.3 |
| All Other Non-Current | 13.7 | 12.9 | 11.2 | 8.0 | | | | 5.4 | 6.8 |
| Total | 100.0 | 100.0 | 100.0 | 100.0 | | | | 100.0 | 100.0 |
| **LIABILITIES** | | | | | | | | | |
| Notes Payable-Short Term | 27.4 | 8.8 | 9.0 | 5.5 | | | | 7.9 | 12.0 |
| Cur. Mat.-L.T.D. | 20.1 | 6.0 | 2.9 | 6.7 | | | | 5.4 | 5.7 |
| Trade Payables | 14.6 | 15.2 | 17.4 | 18.7 | | | | 18.9 | 16.7 |
| Income Taxes Payable | .0 | .0 | .2 | .2 | | | | .1 | .2 |
| All Other Current | 14.4 | 19.4 | 22.8 | 18.6 | | | | 17.5 | 18.0 |
| Total Current | 76.4 | 49.4 | 52.2 | 49.7 | | | | 49.7 | 52.8 |
| Long-Term Debt | 22.3 | 27.6 | 21.2 | 17.0 | | | | 22.9 | 29.0 |
| Deferred Taxes | .0 | .1 | .2 | .6 | | | | .4 | 1.0 |
| All Other Non-Current | 31.4 | 16.9 | 6.8 | 13.9 | | | | 6.6 | 8.0 |
| Net Worth | -30.1 | 6.1 | 19.6 | 18.7 | | | | 20.4 | 9.2 |
| Total Liabilties & Net Worth | 100.0 | 100.0 | 100.0 | 100.0 | | | | 100.0 | 100.0 |
| **INCOME DATA** | | | | | | | | | |
| Net Sales | 100.0 | 100.0 | 100.0 | 100.0 | | | | 100.0 | 100.0 |
| Gross Profit | | | | | | | | | |
| Operating Expenses | 91.1 | 92.3 | 92.8 | 95.8 | | | | 94.9 | 95.6 |
| Operating Profit | 8.9 | 7.7 | 7.2 | 4.2 | | | | 5.1 | 4.4 |
| All Other Expenses (net) | 1.2 | 1.5 | 1.8 | 1.6 | | | | 1.4 | 2.1 |
| Profit Before Taxes | 7.8 | 6.1 | 5.4 | 2.6 | | | | 3.7 | 2.3 |
| **RATIOS** | | | | | | | | | |
| Current | 5.4 | 3.5 | 1.9 | 1.8 | | | | 1.9 | 1.8 |
| | 1.0 | 1.2 | 1.4 | 1.0 | | | | 1.1 | 1.1 |
| | .1 | .4 | .8 | .7 | | | | .8 | .7 |
| Quick | 5.4 | 3.5 | 1.6 | 1.4 | | | | 1.6 | 1.6 |
| | 1.0 | .8 | 1.2 | .9 | | | | 1.1 | .9 |
| | .1 | .3 | .6 | .6 | | | | .7 | .6 |
| Sales/Receivables | 0 UND | 0 UND | 27 13.4 | 35 10.5 | | | | 31 11.9 | 22 16.3 |
| | 16 22.4 | 14 27.0 | 42 8.7 | 49 7.4 | | | | 50 7.3 | 41 8.9 |
| | 49 7.5 | 33 11.1 | 64 5.7 | 72 5.1 | | | | 60 6.1 | 63 5.8 |
| Cost of Sales/Inventory | | | | | | | | | |
| Cost of Sales/Payables | | | | | | | | | |
| Sales/Working Capital | 12.7 | 11.1 | 6.7 | 7.1 | | | | 10.6 | 12.4 |
| | NM | 153.8 | 57.5 | 278.6 | | | | 74.7 | 43.5 |
| | -4.1 | -8.7 | -21.5 | -10.4 | | | | -32.4 | -23.3 |
| EBIT/Interest | 11.0 | 30.0 | 42.5 | 11.0 | | | | 24.8 | 9.2 |
| | (15) 6.0 | (27) 5.3 | (34) 6.2 | (30) 4.1 | | | | (97) 3.9 | (104) 1.9 |
| | 1.3 | .3 | 2.0 | 1.4 | | | | 1.2 | .8 |
| Net Profit + Depr., Dep., Amort./Cur. Mat. L/T/D | | | 5.3 | 6.9 | | | | 7.3 | 2.5 |
| | | (11) 1.6 | | (11) 2.2 | | | | (26) 3.3 | (22) 1.4 |
| | | | .5 | 1.5 | | | | 1.3 | .6 |
| Fixed/Worth | .0 | .0 | .5 | .6 | | | | .5 | .5 |
| | 3.1 | 1.0 | 1.6 | 1.7 | | | | 1.7 | 2.0 |
| | -.3 | -1.4 | -9.7 | -1.0 | | | | -.9 | -.7 |
| Debt/Worth | 4.1 | .5 | 1.4 | 1.1 | | | | 1.4 | 1.7 |
| | -3.6 | 2.6 | 3.9 | 11.5 | | | | 4.1 | 6.1 |
| | -1.6 | -4.1 | -18.8 | -3.7 | | | | -6.2 | -5.8 |
| % Profit Before Taxes/Tangible Net Worth | 86.1 | | 62.8 | 138.0 | | | | 93.2 | 57.0 |
| | | (21) 21.4 | (28) 30.5 | (22) 39.0 | | | | (69) 38.3 | (76) 18.7 |
| | | 1.7 | 8.3 | 6.7 | | | | 10.2 | .1 |
| % Profit Before Taxes/Total Assets | 57.0 | 19.2 | 20.0 | 12.5 | | | | 21.4 | 14.8 |
| | 21.8 | 7.6 | 9.2 | 4.3 | | | | 7.6 | 3.6 |
| | -2.7 | -3.4 | 1.8 | -.2 | | | | .6 | -1.0 |
| Sales/Net Fixed Assets | 870.4 | 312.9 | 35.2 | 37.1 | | | | 27.5 | 36.3 |
| | 35.3 | 47.9 | 9.9 | 11.0 | | | | 13.7 | 14.8 |
| | 15.0 | 14.2 | 5.6 | 5.5 | | | | 8.1 | 7.3 |
| Sales/Total Assets | 6.7 | 8.1 | 3.9 | 2.4 | | | | 4.0 | 4.2 |
| | 5.5 | 3.7 | 2.6 | 1.8 | | | | 2.6 | 2.9 |
| | 2.9 | 2.3 | 2.0 | 1.3 | | | | 1.9 | 1.8 |
| % Depr., Dep., Amort./Sales | .9 | .6 | 1.0 | 1.5 | | | | 1.0 | .8 |
| | (13) 1.5 | (23) 1.8 | (33) 2.1 | (29) 2.3 | | | | (88) 2.3 | (92) 2.6 |
| | 2.9 | 5.1 | 3.5 | 6.1 | | | | 4.0 | 4.8 |
| % Officers', Directors' Owners' Comp/Sales | 5.7 | 2.2 | 1.9 | | | | | 2.0 | 2.4 |
| | (11) 8.6 | (19) 5.0 | (19) 3.6 | | | | | (35) 3.7 | (43) 5.0 |
| | 13.0 | 8.7 | 8.1 | | | | | 6.4 | 11.2 |
| Net Sales ($) | 19733M | 196964M | 572898M | 1346774M | 122332M | 404353M | | 2956738M | 3097872M |
| Total Assets ($) | 3545M | 39647M | 195442M | 792071M | 115504M | 319748M | | 1654461M | 1690755M |

M = $ thousand    MM = $ million
See Pages 9 through 22 for Explanation of Ratios and Data

## Comparative Historical Data                                    Current Data Sorted by Sales

| 4/1/09-3/31/10 ALL | 4/1/10-3/31/11 ALL | 4/1/11-3/31/12 ALL | Type of Statement | 0-1MM | 1-3MM | 3-5MM | 5-10MM | 10-25MM | 25MM & OVER |
|---|---|---|---|---|---|---|---|---|---|
| 12 | 14 | 13 | Unqualified | | 1 | 2 | 7 | 6 | 13 |
| 28 | 25 | 21 | Reviewed | | 1 | | | | 5 |
| 14 | 11 | 16 | Compiled | 3 | 1 | | 6 | 5 | 1 |
| 19 | 14 | 30 | Tax Returns | 11 | 5 | 4 | 8 | 2 | |
| 51 | 44 | 54 | Other | 5 | 8 | 3 | 10 | 10 | 18 |
| | | | | 19 (4/1-9/30/11) | | | 115 (10/1/11-3/31/12) | | |
| 124 | 108 | 134 | NUMBER OF STATEMENTS | 19 | 15 | 9 | 31 | 23 | 37 |
| % | % | % | ASSETS | % | % | % | % | % | % |
| 16.3 | 14.2 | 16.5 | Cash & Equivalents | 14.3 | 22.6 | | 16.5 | 16.7 | 13.8 |
| 31.6 | 30.9 | 27.9 | Trade Receivables (net) | 19.4 | 25.3 | | 32.3 | 33.3 | 29.8 |
| 3.6 | 3.3 | 2.4 | Inventory | .4 | 1.4 | | 3.9 | 1.4 | 3.1 |
| 4.7 | 3.8 | 3.2 | All Other Current | .1 | 1.5 | | 2.0 | 3.1 | 6.0 |
| 56.2 | 52.2 | 50.0 | Total Current | 34.1 | 50.8 | | 54.7 | 54.5 | 52.8 |
| 24.8 | 26.0 | 24.7 | Fixed Assets (net) | 36.6 | 20.0 | | 26.1 | 28.0 | 17.9 |
| 12.4 | 14.0 | 14.0 | Intangibles (net) | 16.8 | 18.8 | | 5.1 | 5.8 | 21.5 |
| 6.5 | 7.7 | 11.2 | All Other Non-Current | 12.4 | 10.3 | | 14.1 | 11.7 | 7.8 |
| 100.0 | 100.0 | 100.0 | Total | 100.0 | 100.0 | | 100.0 | 100.0 | 100.0 |
| | | | LIABILITIES | | | | | | |
| 7.0 | 6.9 | 10.6 | Notes Payable-Short Term | 23.5 | 17.2 | | 9.4 | 7.9 | 5.9 |
| 7.8 | 4.2 | 7.2 | Cur. Mat.-L.T.D. | 22.5 | 2.3 | | 3.6 | 3.6 | 6.5 |
| 15.3 | 17.8 | 16.5 | Trade Payables | 13.2 | 13.5 | | 15.1 | 24.7 | 17.1 |
| .3 | .1 | .1 | Income Taxes Payable | .0 | .0 | | .0 | .1 | .4 |
| 17.7 | 18.7 | 19.2 | All Other Current | 12.0 | 14.4 | | 17.4 | 20.0 | 21.7 |
| 48.1 | 47.8 | 53.6 | Total Current | 71.1 | 47.4 | | 45.4 | 56.3 | 51.6 |
| 22.0 | 24.0 | 21.6 | Long-Term Debt | 33.2 | 14.8 | | 25.8 | 16.1 | 16.3 |
| .3 | .5 | .3 | Deferred Taxes | .0 | .0 | | .2 | .0 | .8 |
| 9.3 | 9.7 | 15.0 | All Other Non-Current | 38.3 | 3.3 | | 16.8 | 4.5 | 14.0 |
| 20.4 | 18.0 | 9.6 | Net Worth | -42.6 | 34.4 | | 11.7 | 23.0 | 17.3 |
| 100.0 | 100.0 | 100.0 | Total Liabilities & Net Worth | 100.0 | 100.0 | | 100.0 | 100.0 | 100.0 |
| | | | INCOME DATA | | | | | | |
| 100.0 | 100.0 | 100.0 | Net Sales | 100.0 | 100.0 | | 100.0 | 100.0 | 100.0 |
| | | | Gross Profit | | | | | | |
| 95.0 | 93.5 | 93.2 | Operating Expenses | 78.6 | 95.3 | | 96.6 | 95.4 | 94.9 |
| 5.0 | 6.5 | 6.8 | Operating Profit | 21.4 | 4.7 | | 3.4 | 4.6 | 5.1 |
| 1.8 | 2.4 | 1.6 | All Other Expenses (net) | 6.3 | 1.8 | | -.2 | .8 | 1.6 |
| 3.2 | 4.1 | 5.2 | Profit Before Taxes | 15.1 | 2.9 | | 3.6 | 3.8 | 3.5 |
| | | | RATIOS | | | | | | |
| 1.9 | 1.7 | 2.0 | | 2.0 | 2.7 | | 3.5 | 1.7 | 1.8 |
| 1.3 | 1.1 | 1.1 | Current | .6 | 1.2 | | 1.5 | 1.1 | 1.0 |
| .9 | .7 | .6 | | .1 | .4 | | .7 | .8 | .7 |
| 1.6 | 1.5 | 1.7 | | 2.0 | 2.7 | | 3.4 | 1.6 | 1.3 |
| 1.0 | .9 | .9 | Quick | .6 | 1.2 | | 1.3 | 1.1 | .9 |
| .7 | .6 | .5 | | .1 | .2 | | .5 | .6 | .6 |
| 28  13.2 | 22  17.0 | 13  28.0 | | 0  UND | 4  100.8 | | 5  75.5 | 14  25.6 | 33  11.1 |
| 45  8.1 | 46  8.0 | 36  10.1 | Sales/Receivables | 16  22.9 | 22  16.4 | | 44  8.3 | 28  13.1 | 44  8.3 |
| 69  5.3 | 65  5.6 | 62  5.9 | | 83  4.4 | 54  6.8 | | 73  5.0 | 42  8.7 | 69  5.3 |
| | | | Cost of Sales/Inventory | | | | | | |
| | | | Cost of Sales/Payables | | | | | | |
| 7.4 | 10.0 | 8.4 | | 11.5 | 6.9 | | 6.7 | 10.9 | 9.8 |
| 34.5 | 65.2 | 144.4 | Sales/Working Capital | -10.7 | 25.8 | | 19.5 | 292.5 | 304.3 |
| -43.6 | -15.6 | -10.6 | | -3.7 | -20.2 | | -38.7 | -22.4 | -11.5 |
| 12.2 | 10.0 | 18.9 | | 10.5 | | | 43.7 | 12.9 | 11.4 |
| (108) 3.2 | (89) 2.2 | (109) 5.3 | EBIT/Interest | (11) 4.6 | | | (27) 6.2 | (21) 6.0 | (33) 4.6 |
| .9 | .1 | 1.4 | | 1.3 | | | .3 | 1.1 | 1.6 |
| 3.5 | 5.2 | 5.3 | Net Profit + Depr., Dep., | | | | | | 6.1 |
| (23) 1.4 | (17) 2.3 | (25) 1.8 | Amort./Cur. Mat. L/T/D | | | | | (13) | 1.9 |
| .3 | 1.3 | 1.2 | | | | | | | 1.5 |
| .3 | .4 | .3 | | .5 | .0 | | .4 | .6 | .5 |
| 1.4 | 2.3 | 1.5 | Fixed/Worth | 13.7 | .2 | | 1.6 | 1.5 | 2.1 |
| -1.9 | -1.1 | -1.3 | | -.3 | 1.1 | | -1.3 | -5.1 | -.8 |
| 1.2 | 1.5 | 1.2 | | 5.0 | .5 | | .8 | 1.3 | 1.4 |
| 3.6 | 4.8 | 8.6 | Debt/Worth | -4.1 | 2.0 | | 5.1 | 3.2 | 13.6 |
| -6.7 | -4.8 | -4.0 | | -1.5 | -4.2 | | -4.5 | -10.4 | -3.1 |
| 70.8 | 63.7 | 67.7 | % Profit Before Taxes/Tangible | | 12.7 | | 61.2 | 72.0 | 115.6 |
| (84) 24.9 | (71) 21.0 | (80) 27.7 | Net Worth | (10) .8 | | | (19) 25.8 | (17) 18.0 | (21) 45.7 |
| 1.6 | .6 | 6.3 | | | -12.1 | | 7.8 | 2.0 | 13.0 |
| 15.9 | 11.8 | 19.3 | % Profit Before Taxes/Total | 50.0 | 19.4 | | 20.5 | 21.5 | 14.3 |
| 5.2 | 5.4 | 7.0 | Assets | 7.4 | 1.1 | | 11.1 | 6.9 | 5.4 |
| -2.0 | -.2 | .2 | | -16.1 | -3.9 | | -1.5 | .2 | 1.0 |
| 33.4 | 28.5 | 88.6 | | 482.0 | 783.7 | | 92.2 | 74.0 | 43.0 |
| 12.6 | 14.3 | 18.2 | Sales/Net Fixed Assets | 16.4 | 28.1 | | 17.8 | 20.6 | 14.6 |
| 6.1 | 6.4 | 6.9 | | 1.5 | 14.1 | | 7.5 | 4.7 | 6.6 |
| 3.3 | 3.5 | 4.5 | | 5.6 | 5.9 | | 5.4 | 6.8 | 2.8 |
| 2.4 | 2.3 | 2.6 | Sales/Total Assets | 2.9 | 3.2 | | 2.9 | 3.0 | 2.0 |
| 1.5 | 1.4 | 1.7 | | .8 | 2.1 | | 2.0 | 1.8 | 1.4 |
| 1.2 | 1.2 | .9 | | 1.2 | | | 1.0 | .6 | 1.0 |
| (94) 2.8 | (85) 2.3 | (101) 2.2 | % Depr., Dep., Amort./Sales | (14) 2.5 | | | (24) 2.3 | (18) 1.6 | (32) 2.2 |
| 5.2 | 4.6 | 4.1 | | 20.0 | | | 3.5 | 3.0 | 5.7 |
| 1.9 | 2.2 | 2.3 | % Officers', Directors' | | | | 3.1 | | |
| (44) 4.9 | (32) 5.4 | (55) 5.6 | Owners' Comp/Sales | | | | (21) 5.9 | | |
| 9.3 | 9.1 | 9.0 | | | | | 8.8 | | |
| 3411150M | 3175894M | 2663054M | Net Sales ($) | 8739M | 30118M | 36654M | 242291M | 362532M | 1982720M |
| 2114650M | 1997676M | 1465957M | Total Assets ($) | 9516M | 19632M | 10757M | 104830M | 137622M | 1183600M |

## Current Data Sorted by Assets     Comparative Historical Data

**Type of Statement**

| Type of Statement | 0-500M | 500M-2MM | 2-10MM | 10-50MM | 50-100MM | 100-250MM | 4/1/07-3/31/08 ALL | 4/1/08-3/31/09 ALL |
|---|---|---|---|---|---|---|---|---|
| Unqualified | | 1 | 2 | 7 | 1 | 1 | 10 | 4 |
| Reviewed | | 4 | 2 | | 1 | | 7 | 15 |
| Compiled | | 1 | 2 | | | | 5 | 2 |
| Tax Returns | 4 | 7 | 2 | | | | 7 | 6 |
| Other | 2 | 5 | 8 | 3 | 2 | 3 | 26 | 12 |

Periods: 11 (4/1-9/30/11); 47 (10/1/11-3/31/12)

| | 0-500M | 500M-2MM | 2-10MM | 10-50MM | 50-100MM | 100-250MM | 4/1/07-3/31/08 ALL | 4/1/08-3/31/09 ALL |
|---|---|---|---|---|---|---|---|---|
| **NUMBER OF STATEMENTS** | 6 | 14 | 18 | 12 | 4 | 4 | 55 | 39 |
| | % | % | % | % | % | % | % | % |
| **ASSETS** | | | | | | | | |
| Cash & Equivalents | | 14.7 | 13.3 | 6.5 | | | 8.9 | 11.7 |
| Trade Receivables (net) | | 40.3 | 36.1 | 30.3 | | | 41.7 | 39.2 |
| Inventory | | 6.9 | 4.4 | 10.9 | | | 6.8 | 10.0 |
| All Other Current | | .7 | 12.3 | 4.7 | | | 5.6 | 5.0 |
| Total Current | | 62.7 | 66.1 | 52.4 | | | 63.0 | 66.0 |
| Fixed Assets (net) | | 23.9 | 18.9 | 25.3 | | | 17.9 | 22.2 |
| Intangibles (net) | | 1.7 | 8.4 | 14.9 | | | 11.6 | 4.5 |
| All Other Non-Current | | 11.7 | 6.6 | 7.4 | | | 7.4 | 7.3 |
| Total | | 100.0 | 100.0 | 100.0 | | | 100.0 | 100.0 |
| **LIABILITIES** | | | | | | | | |
| Notes Payable-Short Term | | 11.8 | 10.6 | 9.3 | | | 10.1 | 13.2 |
| Cur. Mat.-L.T.D. | | 2.2 | 3.3 | 4.1 | | | 5.9 | 3.6 |
| Trade Payables | | 23.5 | 11.3 | 10.1 | | | 18.9 | 18.4 |
| Income Taxes Payable | | .1 | .0 | .5 | | | .1 | .0 |
| All Other Current | | 9.5 | 20.2 | 16.7 | | | 13.5 | 12.2 |
| Total Current | | 47.1 | 45.3 | 40.8 | | | 48.5 | 47.4 |
| Long-Term Debt | | 21.2 | 13.7 | 16.4 | | | 12.2 | 14.1 |
| Deferred Taxes | | .0 | .1 | 1.5 | | | .1 | .0 |
| All Other Non-Current | | 5.1 | 9.4 | 1.7 | | | 13.5 | 6.5 |
| Net Worth | | 26.6 | 31.5 | 39.6 | | | 25.6 | 32.0 |
| Total Liabilities & Net Worth | | 100.0 | 100.0 | 100.0 | | | 100.0 | 100.0 |
| **INCOME DATA** | | | | | | | | |
| Net Sales | | 100.0 | 100.0 | 100.0 | | | 100.0 | 100.0 |
| Gross Profit | | | | | | | | |
| Operating Expenses | | 89.4 | 87.7 | 94.2 | | | 93.5 | 91.4 |
| Operating Profit | | 10.6 | 12.3 | 5.8 | | | 6.5 | 8.6 |
| All Other Expenses (net) | | 6.6 | .8 | .7 | | | 1.8 | 1.7 |
| Profit Before Taxes | | 4.1 | 11.4 | 5.0 | | | 4.7 | 6.9 |
| **RATIOS** | | | | | | | | |
| Current | | 2.3 | 2.2 | 3.0 | | | 2.4 | 2.7 |
| Current | | 1.5 | 1.4 | 1.1 | | | 1.3 | 1.4 |
| Current | | .9 | 1.0 | .8 | | | .9 | .9 |
| Quick | | 2.3 | 1.7 | 2.3 | | | 1.6 | 1.8 |
| Quick | | 1.2 | 1.0 | .8 | | | 1.1 | 1.2 |
| Quick | | .8 | .6 | .5 | | | .6 | .7 |
| Sales/Receivables | | 31  11.8 | 35  10.4 | 31  11.7 | | | 33  11.1 | 27  13.3 |
| Sales/Receivables | | 41  9.0 | 68  5.4 | 59  6.2 | | | 47  7.7 | 50  7.3 |
| Sales/Receivables | | 61  6.0 | 182  2.0 | 66  5.5 | | | 71  5.2 | 74  4.9 |
| Cost of Sales/Inventory | | | | | | | | |
| Cost of Sales/Payables | | | | | | | | |
| Sales/Working Capital | | 8.5 | 3.1 | 5.2 | | | 8.6 | 7.1 |
| Sales/Working Capital | | 24.8 | 8.5 | 89.0 | | | 24.0 | 12.6 |
| Sales/Working Capital | | -121.0 | -709.3 | -25.1 | | | -58.1 | -49.6 |
| EBIT/Interest | | | 6.7 | 17.2 | | | 12.1 | 11.9 |
| EBIT/Interest | | | (16) 4.6 | (11) 3.7 | | | (45) 5.6 | (30) 4.2 |
| EBIT/Interest | | | 2.5 | 2.1 | | | 1.4 | 1.2 |
| Net Profit + Depr., Dep., Amort./Cur. Mat. L/T/D | | | | | | | 5.7 | |
| Net Profit + Depr., Dep., Amort./Cur. Mat. L/T/D | | | | | | | (13) 2.0 | |
| Net Profit + Depr., Dep., Amort./Cur. Mat. L/T/D | | | | | | | 1.1 | |
| Fixed/Worth | | .1 | .2 | .4 | | | .2 | .1 |
| Fixed/Worth | | .7 | .5 | 1.3 | | | .6 | .6 |
| Fixed/Worth | | 7.5 | 2.6 | NM | | | 5.9 | 1.7 |
| Debt/Worth | | .7 | .7 | .6 | | | 1.0 | .8 |
| Debt/Worth | | 3.6 | 2.6 | 1.3 | | | 3.3 | 2.2 |
| Debt/Worth | | 28.0 | 6.2 | NM | | | 31.2 | 6.7 |
| % Profit Before Taxes/Tangible Net Worth | | 63.3 | 37.7 | | | | 88.4 | 60.7 |
| % Profit Before Taxes/Tangible Net Worth | | (12) 15.3 | (15) 20.6 | | | | (42) 43.5 | (32) 27.5 |
| % Profit Before Taxes/Tangible Net Worth | | 10.0 | 5.3 | | | | 4.0 | 11.7 |
| % Profit Before Taxes/Total Assets | | 7.6 | 9.8 | 20.6 | | | 28.2 | 21.0 |
| % Profit Before Taxes/Total Assets | | 2.9 | 7.2 | 6.2 | | | 10.4 | 6.7 |
| % Profit Before Taxes/Total Assets | | 1.7 | 2.9 | 3.4 | | | -1.4 | 2.0 |
| Sales/Net Fixed Assets | | 184.0 | 22.4 | 37.5 | | | 80.5 | 54.0 |
| Sales/Net Fixed Assets | | 35.5 | 12.9 | 23.7 | | | 25.3 | 22.7 |
| Sales/Net Fixed Assets | | 6.5 | 5.1 | 3.1 | | | 11.7 | 5.5 |
| Sales/Total Assets | | 4.6 | 2.2 | 2.7 | | | 3.8 | 4.0 |
| Sales/Total Assets | | 3.1 | 1.6 | 2.4 | | | 2.8 | 2.2 |
| Sales/Total Assets | | 1.9 | .9 | 1.6 | | | 1.8 | 1.6 |
| % Depr., Dep., Amort./Sales | | | 1.0 | .9 | | | .8 | .6 |
| % Depr., Dep., Amort./Sales | | | (17) 2.4 | 1.6 | | | (39) 1.7 | (30) 1.5 |
| % Depr., Dep., Amort./Sales | | | 4.9 | 4.9 | | | 3.5 | 3.3 |
| % Officers', Directors' Owners' Comp/Sales | | | | | | | 2.6 | 2.5 |
| % Officers', Directors' Owners' Comp/Sales | | | | | | | (15) 6.0 | (10) 5.6 |
| % Officers', Directors' Owners' Comp/Sales | | | | | | | 10.7 | 14.0 |
| Net Sales ($) | 9956M | 58520M | 145860M | 573887M | 346686M | 790460M | 1550293M | 1447504M |
| Total Assets ($) | 1340M | 17696M | 95438M | 250163M | 318832M | 560917M | 695112M | 565455M |

M = $ thousand    MM = $ million
See Pages 9 through 22 for Explanation of Ratios and Data

## Comparative Historical Data / Current Data Sorted by Sales

### Type of Statement

| 4/1/09-3/31/10 ALL | 4/1/10-3/31/11 ALL | 4/1/11-3/31/12 ALL | Type of Statement | 0-1MM | 1-3MM | 3-5MM | 5-10MM | 10-25MM | 25MM & OVER |
|---|---|---|---|---|---|---|---|---|---|
| 14 | 8 | 12 | Unqualified | | 1 | | | 3 | 8 |
| 15 | 13 | 7 | Reviewed | | | 1 | 1 | 3 | 2 |
| 2 | 3 | 3 | Compiled | | | 2 | 1 | | |
| 7 | 8 | 13 | Tax Returns | 3 | 2 | 2 | 5 | 1 | |
| 32 | 22 | 23 | Other | 4 | 2 | 2 | 4 | | 8 |
| | | | | | 11 (4/1-9/30/11) | | | 47 (10/1/11-3/31/12) | |
| 70 | 54 | 58 | NUMBER OF STATEMENTS | 7 | 7 | 7 | 11 | 8 | 18 |

### Assets / Liabilities / Income / Ratios

| H 4/1/09-3/31/10 | H 4/1/10-3/31/11 | H 4/1/11-3/31/12 | | 0-1MM | 1-3MM | 3-5MM | 5-10MM | 10-25MM | 25MM & OVER |
|---|---|---|---|---|---|---|---|---|---|
| % | % | % | **ASSETS** | % | % | % | % | % | % |
| 13.5 | 14.4 | 12.8 | Cash & Equivalents | | | | 8.2 | | 9.7 |
| 35.0 | 32.8 | 32.7 | Trade Receivables (net) | | | | 51.2 | | 25.1 |
| 8.4 | 8.2 | 6.0 | Inventory | | | | 10.3 | | 8.1 |
| 5.0 | 6.7 | 5.5 | All Other Current | | | | 1.2 | | 4.8 |
| 61.8 | 62.0 | 57.0 | Total Current | | | | 71.0 | | 47.7 |
| 21.6 | 17.8 | 19.3 | Fixed Assets (net) | | | | 16.6 | | 15.4 |
| 12.7 | 12.8 | 14.7 | Intangibles (net) | | | | 3.8 | | 31.5 |
| 3.8 | 7.4 | 9.0 | All Other Non-Current | | | | 8.6 | | 5.4 |
| 100.0 | 100.0 | 100.0 | Total | | | | 100.0 | | 100.0 |
| | | | **LIABILITIES** | | | | | | |
| 12.4 | 14.3 | 12.2 | Notes Payable-Short Term | | | | 9.5 | | 7.0 |
| 6.9 | 9.5 | 2.7 | Cur. Mat.-L.T.D. | | | | 2.9 | | 3.0 |
| 20.2 | 18.4 | 17.9 | Trade Payables | | | | 26.3 | | 10.4 |
| .3 | .1 | .2 | Income Taxes Payable | | | | .1 | | .4 |
| 19.9 | 19.8 | 14.4 | All Other Current | | | | 20.1 | | 18.4 |
| 59.7 | 62.1 | 47.4 | Total Current | | | | 58.9 | | 39.3 |
| 16.1 | 15.9 | 16.0 | Long-Term Debt | | | | 18.0 | | 15.5 |
| .7 | .6 | .7 | Deferred Taxes | | | | .0 | | 1.2 |
| 5.5 | 6.8 | 5.0 | All Other Non-Current | | | | 6.8 | | 1.4 |
| 18.0 | 14.7 | 30.9 | Net Worth | | | | 16.3 | | 42.5 |
| 100.0 | 100.0 | 100.0 | Total Liabilities & Net Worth | | | | 100.0 | | 100.0 |
| | | | **INCOME DATA** | | | | | | |
| 100.0 | 100.0 | 100.0 | Net Sales | | | | 100.0 | | 100.0 |
| | | | Gross Profit | | | | | | |
| 94.8 | 93.7 | 89.2 | Operating Expenses | | | | 96.3 | | 94.3 |
| 5.2 | 6.3 | 10.8 | Operating Profit | | | | 3.7 | | 5.7 |
| 1.9 | 2.1 | 2.3 | All Other Expenses (net) | | | | .7 | | 1.0 |
| 3.4 | 4.2 | 8.5 | Profit Before Taxes | | | | 3.1 | | 4.6 |
| | | | **RATIOS** | | | | | | |
| 2.3<br>1.2<br>.8 | 1.9<br>1.3<br>.9 | 2.1<br>1.2<br>.8 | Current | | | | 1.4<br>1.2<br>1.0 | | 2.0<br>1.0<br>.8 |
| 1.7<br>.9<br>.5 | 1.6<br>1.0<br>.5 | 1.7<br>1.0<br>.6 | Quick | | | | 1.1<br>.9<br>.9 | | 1.5<br>.7<br>.6 |
| 24 15.3<br>42 8.6<br>63 5.8 | 22 16.8<br>40 9.2<br>56 6.5 | 31 11.6<br>49 7.5<br>68 5.4 | Sales/Receivables | | | | 40 9.1<br>45 8.1<br>79 4.6 | | 37 9.9<br>52 7.0<br>64 5.7 |
| | | | Cost of Sales/Inventory | | | | | | |
| | | | Cost of Sales/Payables | | | | | | |
| 7.0<br>31.8<br>-27.1 | 7.4<br>26.5<br>-22.5 | 6.8<br>28.5<br>-30.1 | Sales/Working Capital | | | | 8.5<br>38.5<br>-904.2 | | 7.0<br>NM<br>-17.2 |
| 13.5<br>(62) 2.6<br>.6 | 12.9<br>(48) 4.9<br>2.0 | 14.8<br>(44) 3.9<br>2.2 | EBIT/Interest | | | | | | 16.0<br>(14) 3.3<br>1.1 |
| 2.2<br>(11) .3<br>-.4 | | | Net Profit + Depr., Dep., Amort./Cur. Mat. L/T/D | | | | | | |
| .2<br>1.2<br>-1.0 | .1<br>.6<br>-3.7 | .2<br>.8<br>NM | Fixed/Worth | | | | .2<br>.6<br>1.0 | | .2<br>1.4<br>-.2 |
| 1.1<br>3.4<br>-4.6 | .7<br>2.6<br>-44.5 | .9<br>3.8<br>-17.7 | Debt/Worth | | | | 2.7<br>4.5<br>8.2 | | 1.0<br>12.9<br>-2.4 |
| 64.9<br>(48) 17.4<br>2.9 | 77.0<br>(39) 26.2<br>11.8 | 38.0<br>(42) 20.5<br>7.7 | % Profit Before Taxes/Tangible Net Worth | | | | 47.8<br>(10) 26.5<br>12.7 | | 28.8<br>(11) 20.5<br>.3 |
| 12.9<br>3.6<br>-.7 | 17.0<br>8.2<br>2.4 | 13.4<br>6.2<br>2.4 | % Profit Before Taxes/Total Assets | | | | 8.3<br>5.5<br>2.7 | | 14.3<br>6.5<br>.1 |
| 82.9<br>23.2<br>7.3 | 99.1<br>29.9<br>10.1 | 75.9<br>19.9<br>6.5 | Sales/Net Fixed Assets | | | | 398.3<br>30.9<br>9.3 | | 51.5<br>29.2<br>12.2 |
| 4.2<br>2.6<br>1.7 | 4.6<br>2.6<br>1.6 | 3.0<br>2.1<br>1.1 | Sales/Total Assets | | | | 4.7<br>3.6<br>2.0 | | 2.6<br>2.2<br>1.5 |
| .6<br>(56) 1.4<br>3.9 | .3<br>(41) 1.2<br>3.2 | .7<br>(45) 1.4<br>3.1 | % Depr., Dep., Amort./Sales | | | | | | .7<br>(15) 1.3<br>2.2 |
| 1.0<br>(19) 4.8<br>10.2 | 2.7<br>(12) 5.9<br>13.4 | 3.9<br>(14) 6.8<br>15.6 | % Officers', Directors' Owners' Comp/Sales | | | | | | |
| 2470391M | 1313010M | 1925369M | Net Sales ($) | 3381M | 16340M | 28197M | 77892M | 114412M | 1685147M |
| 1216555M | 811422M | 1244386M | Total Assets ($) | 15976M | 7807M | 19844M | 32497M | 73623M | 1094639M |

© RMA 2012

M = $ thousand    MM = $ million
See Pages 9 through 22 for Explanation of Ratios and Data

| Current Data Sorted by Assets | | | | | | | Comparative Historical Data | |
|---|---|---|---|---|---|---|---|---|

**Type of Statement**

| 0-500M | 500M-2MM | 2-10MM | 10-50MM | 50-100MM | 100-250MM | | 4/1/07-3/31/08 ALL | 4/1/08-3/31/09 ALL |
|---|---|---|---|---|---|---|---|---|
| | 2 | 1 | 7 | 8 | 1 | Unqualified | 14 | 18 |
| 3 | 10 | 12 | 4 | | | Reviewed | 8 | 17 |
| 12 | 14 | 6 | 1 | 4 | | Compiled | 14 | 22 |
| 13 | 27 | 4 | 1 | | 6 | Tax Returns | 13 | 27 |
| | | 21 | 11 | | | Other | 45 | 61 |
| 13 (4/1-9/30/11) | | 155 (10/1/11-3/31/12) | | | | | | |
| 28 | 53 | 44 | 24 | 12 | 7 | **NUMBER OF STATEMENTS** | 94 | 145 |

| 0-500M % | 500M-2MM % | 2-10MM % | 10-50MM % | 50-100MM % | 100-250MM % | | % | % |
|---|---|---|---|---|---|---|---|---|
| | | | | | | **ASSETS** | | |
| 29.6 | 14.7 | 15.6 | 18.5 | 9.0 | | Cash & Equivalents | 16.6 | 15.2 |
| 28.0 | 31.6 | 38.0 | 31.7 | 24.9 | | Trade Receivables (net) | 41.2 | 36.2 |
| 2.8 | 11.1 | 10.2 | 11.0 | 2.1 | | Inventory | 11.0 | 9.3 |
| 5.7 | 3.6 | 4.6 | 3.9 | 2.5 | | All Other Current | 3.6 | 4.7 |
| 66.1 | 61.0 | 68.5 | 65.2 | 38.5 | | Total Current | 72.4 | 65.4 |
| 23.9 | 17.6 | 16.4 | 14.4 | 16.8 | | Fixed Assets (net) | 14.4 | 17.6 |
| 6.2 | 12.3 | 7.9 | 10.6 | 39.5 | | Intangibles (net) | 5.4 | 9.0 |
| 3.8 | 9.1 | 7.2 | 9.7 | 5.2 | | All Other Non-Current | 7.8 | 8.1 |
| 100.0 | 100.0 | 100.0 | 100.0 | 100.0 | | Total | 100.0 | 100.0 |
| | | | | | | **LIABILITIES** | | |
| 31.8 | 13.8 | 10.2 | 7.2 | 4.7 | | Notes Payable-Short Term | 13.3 | 14.2 |
| 5.0 | 1.3 | 3.4 | 2.1 | 4.1 | | Cur. Mat.-L.T.D. | 4.6 | 5.8 |
| 14.6 | 16.3 | 26.8 | 18.3 | 13.2 | | Trade Payables | 18.9 | 17.5 |
| .0 | .1 | .1 | .5 | .2 | | Income Taxes Payable | .3 | .7 |
| 21.4 | 12.1 | 20.3 | 11.9 | 10.7 | | All Other Current | 18.5 | 18.1 |
| 72.9 | 43.7 | 60.8 | 40.0 | 32.8 | | Total Current | 55.6 | 56.4 |
| 16.7 | 19.1 | 9.5 | 16.1 | 25.2 | | Long-Term Debt | 19.8 | 17.8 |
| .0 | .0 | .6 | .5 | .3 | | Deferred Taxes | .1 | .3 |
| 8.2 | 6.7 | 7.9 | 12.2 | 7.5 | | All Other Non-Current | 5.2 | 6.5 |
| 2.2 | 30.4 | 21.1 | 31.2 | 34.1 | | Net Worth | 19.2 | 19.1 |
| 100.0 | 100.0 | 100.0 | 100.0 | 100.0 | | Total Liabilities & Net Worth | 100.0 | 100.0 |
| | | | | | | **INCOME DATA** | | |
| 100.0 | 100.0 | 100.0 | 100.0 | 100.0 | | Net Sales | 100.0 | 100.0 |
| | | | | | | Gross Profit | | |
| 89.5 | 91.2 | 93.2 | 88.2 | 89.5 | | Operating Expenses | 93.9 | 96.1 |
| 10.5 | 8.8 | 6.8 | 11.8 | 10.5 | | Operating Profit | 6.1 | 3.9 |
| .9 | 2.6 | 1.5 | .5 | 2.3 | | All Other Expenses (net) | 1.2 | 1.4 |
| 9.5 | 6.3 | 5.3 | 11.3 | 8.2 | | Profit Before Taxes | 4.9 | 2.5 |
| | | | | | | **RATIOS** | | |
| 2.0 | 2.8 | 1.7 | 2.7 | 1.6 | | Current | 2.2 | 2.1 |
| 1.3 | 1.4 | 1.3 | 1.4 | 1.0 | | | 1.4 | 1.3 |
| .5 | .7 | .9 | 1.2 | .8 | | | 1.0 | .9 |
| 2.0 | 2.2 | 1.5 | 2.1 | 1.5 | | Quick | 1.7 | 1.5 |
| 1.2 | .9 | .9 | 1.3 | .8 | | | 1.1 | 1.0 |
| .4 | .5 | .6 | .9 | .7 | | | .7 | .6 |
| 0 UND | 8 45.0 | 24 15.0 | 36 10.2 | 36 10.0 | | Sales/Receivables | 29 12.6 | 21 17.1 |
| 17 21.7 | 34 10.8 | 35 10.3 | 47 7.7 | 47 7.7 | | | 49 7.5 | 38 9.5 |
| 41 9.0 | 52 7.0 | 69 5.3 | 70 5.2 | 65 5.6 | | | 64 5.7 | 58 6.3 |
| | | | | | | Cost of Sales/Inventory | | |
| | | | | | | Cost of Sales/Payables | | |
| 8.4 | 8.5 | 8.3 | 4.0 | 12.3 | | Sales/Working Capital | 6.9 | 7.3 |
| 381.1 | 19.1 | 17.3 | 9.2 | NM | | | 16.1 | 25.9 |
| -17.4 | -34.7 | -33.8 | 19.1 | -16.9 | | | 390.6 | -43.0 |
| 4.9 | 13.2 | 31.3 | 74.1 | 14.4 | | EBIT/Interest | 14.2 | 12.3 |
| (15) 1.7 | (37) 3.4 | (38) 9.4 | (17) 6.1 | (10) 2.7 | | | (79) 4.1 | (124) 4.1 |
| -.6 | 1.1 | 2.5 | 3.4 | 1.5 | | | .9 | .7 |
| | | | | | | Net Profit + Depr., Dep., Amort./Cur. Mat. L/T/D | 13.1 | 8.3 |
| | | | | | | | (21) 4.7 | (31) 2.1 |
| | | | | | | | .5 | 1.1 |
| .1 | .0 | .3 | .1 | 2.7 | | Fixed/Worth | .1 | .2 |
| .8 | .5 | .5 | .2 | -1.5 | | | .4 | 1.0 |
| -2.4 | -4.7 | NM | 2.0 | -.2 | | | 1.8 | -2.4 |
| .9 | .9 | 1.2 | .7 | 4.8 | | Debt/Worth | 1.0 | 1.2 |
| 2.3 | 3.9 | 3.5 | 1.5 | -6.1 | | | 2.8 | 3.6 |
| -4.1 | -8.1 | -32.8 | 18.1 | -3.3 | | | 26.5 | -10.1 |
| 201.5 | 51.2 | 61.6 | 36.0 | | | % Profit Before Taxes/Tangible Net Worth | 68.0 | 73.7 |
| (19) 46.8 | (35) 19.4 | (32) 29.5 | (19) 18.5 | | | | (72) 21.5 | (104) 23.6 |
| 7.3 | -3.5 | 10.7 | 7.8 | | | | 5.0 | .9 |
| 81.6 | 19.8 | 18.4 | 21.3 | 10.0 | | % Profit Before Taxes/Total Assets | 19.0 | 20.0 |
| 16.5 | 4.5 | 9.6 | 6.9 | 6.0 | | | 7.7 | 5.3 |
| -.6 | .1 | 4.6 | 4.1 | 2.6 | | | | -.7 |
| 248.6 | 350.2 | 95.5 | 286.6 | 46.9 | | Sales/Net Fixed Assets | 133.7 | 73.7 |
| 45.5 | 57.8 | 41.1 | 32.3 | 16.9 | | | 41.0 | 27.9 |
| 21.0 | 16.5 | 15.2 | 10.6 | 5.1 | | | 13.0 | 11.2 |
| 12.2 | 4.4 | 3.6 | 2.8 | 2.9 | | Sales/Total Assets | 5.0 | 4.9 |
| 5.6 | 3.2 | 3.0 | 1.9 | 1.5 | | | 2.9 | 3.0 |
| 3.1 | 1.8 | 2.0 | .9 | .9 | | | 2.1 | 2.0 |
| .5 | .4 | .3 | .6 | | | % Depr., Dep., Amort./Sales | .4 | .6 |
| (13) 1.3 | (27) 1.2 | (35) .5 | (17) 1.7 | | | | (71) 1.0 | (117) 1.5 |
| 2.4 | 2.0 | 1.9 | 5.2 | | | | 2.2 | 2.9 |
| 6.3 | 4.3 | 1.1 | | | | % Officers', Directors', Owners' Comp/Sales | 2.8 | 2.4 |
| (17) 8.4 | (23) 6.1 | (20) 2.3 | | | | | (38) 4.8 | (58) 4.9 |
| 16.3 | 9.5 | 4.3 | | | | | 9.1 | 9.1 |
| 51512M | 272598M | 592918M | 980407M | 1664549M | 1299589M | Net Sales ($) | 4477065M | 6228423M |
| 6898M | 64547M | 206024M | 459505M | 895662M | 1090895M | Total Assets ($) | 1868305M | 2622109M |

© RMA 2012

M = $ thousand     MM = $ million
See Pages 9 through 22 for Explanation of Ratios and Data

## Comparative Historical Data / Current Data Sorted by Sales

| | | | Type of Statement | | | | | | |
|---|---|---|---|---|---|---|---|---|---|
| 21 | 25 | 17 | Unqualified | | 1 | | | 2 | 14 |
| 17 | 19 | 18 | Reviewed | 1 | | | 4 | 9 | 4 |
| 13 | 17 | 20 | Compiled | 6 | 2 | | 5 | 4 | 3 |
| 33 | 29 | 31 | Tax Returns | 8 | 5 | | 7 | 3 | |
| 71 | 89 | 82 | Other | 8 | 8 | | 10 | 17 | 17 |
| | | | | 9 | 19 | 10 | | | |
| 4/1/09-3/31/10 ALL | 4/1/10-3/31/11 ALL | 4/1/11-3/31/12 ALL | | 13 (4/1-9/30/11) | | | 155 (10/1/11-3/31/12) | | |
| | | | | 0-1MM | 1-3MM | 3-5MM | 5-10MM | 10-25MM | 25MM & OVER |
| 155 | 179 | 168 | NUMBER OF STATEMENTS | 17 | 34 | 18 | 26 | 35 | 38 |
| % | % | % | ASSETS | % | % | % | % | % | % |
| 19.8 | 17.3 | 17.0 | Cash & Equivalents | 21.4 | 19.0 | 19.1 | 15.8 | 16.3 | 13.8 |
| 33.6 | 30.6 | 31.8 | Trade Receivables (net) | 19.1 | 29.0 | 27.5 | 38.6 | 39.6 | 30.1 |
| 7.1 | 12.8 | 8.6 | Inventory | 2.3 | 6.0 | 12.5 | 8.2 | 11.2 | 9.6 |
| 5.6 | 3.9 | 4.2 | All Other Current | 2.3 | 4.0 | 8.5 | 4.5 | 4.0 | 3.2 |
| 66.1 | 64.6 | 61.6 | Total Current | 45.1 | 58.0 | 67.7 | 67.1 | 71.0 | 56.8 |
| 15.7 | 14.8 | 17.4 | Fixed Assets (net) | 47.7 | 16.2 | 15.9 | 17.6 | 11.4 | 11.1 |
| 10.2 | 10.9 | 13.9 | Intangibles (net) | .6 | 18.0 | 9.1 | 7.0 | 9.3 | 27.3 |
| 8.0 | 9.6 | 7.2 | All Other Non-Current | 6.6 | 7.9 | 7.4 | 8.3 | 8.3 | 4.8 |
| 100.0 | 100.0 | 100.0 | Total | 100.0 | 100.0 | 100.0 | 100.0 | 100.0 | 100.0 |
| | | | LIABILITIES | | | | | | |
| 14.2 | 15.1 | 13.9 | Notes Payable-Short Term | 18.6 | 24.1 | 19.0 | 8.8 | 11.2 | 6.3 |
| 4.4 | 2.3 | 2.8 | Cur. Mat.-L.T.D. | 9.8 | 1.1 | .1 | 2.2 | 2.8 | 3.0 |
| 20.6 | 17.6 | 18.5 | Trade Payables | 5.1 | 12.8 | 16.8 | 15.9 | 35.2 | 16.8 |
| .4 | .8 | .2 | Income Taxes Payable | .0 | .0 | .0 | .1 | .1 | .6 |
| 19.1 | 16.2 | 15.6 | All Other Current | 13.0 | 17.8 | 11.2 | 26.0 | 12.0 | 12.9 |
| 58.7 | 52.1 | 51.0 | Total Current | 46.5 | 55.8 | 47.1 | 53.1 | 61.4 | 39.5 |
| 14.9 | 12.1 | 16.7 | Long-Term Debt | 31.2 | 19.0 | 15.6 | 17.2 | 3.6 | 20.4 |
| .4 | .3 | .4 | Deferred Taxes | .0 | .0 | .1 | .9 | .4 | .6 |
| 6.7 | 5.2 | 8.0 | All Other Non-Current | 7.6 | 10.4 | 5.4 | 3.5 | 7.7 | 10.6 |
| 19.3 | 30.3 | 24.0 | Net Worth | 14.7 | 14.8 | 31.9 | 25.4 | 26.8 | 29.0 |
| 100.0 | 100.0 | 100.0 | Total Liabilities & Net Worth | 100.0 | 100.0 | 100.0 | 100.0 | 100.0 | 100.0 |
| | | | INCOME DATA | | | | | | |
| 100.0 | 100.0 | 100.0 | Net Sales | 100.0 | 100.0 | 100.0 | 100.0 | 100.0 | 100.0 |
| | | | Gross Profit | | | | | | |
| 95.8 | 91.8 | 90.8 | Operating Expenses | 71.7 | 90.9 | 92.9 | 95.1 | 94.0 | 92.6 |
| 4.2 | 8.2 | 9.2 | Operating Profit | 28.3 | 9.1 | 7.1 | 4.9 | 6.0 | 7.4 |
| 2.0 | 1.6 | 1.7 | All Other Expenses (net) | 10.5 | .9 | .5 | -.1 | .5 | 1.5 |
| 2.2 | 6.6 | 7.4 | Profit Before Taxes | 17.8 | 8.1 | 6.5 | 5.0 | 5.5 | 6.0 |
| | | | RATIOS | | | | | | |
| 2.1 | 2.5 | 2.1 | | 2.8 | 2.5 | 4.3 | 2.1 | 1.7 | 2.1 |
| 1.2 | 1.3 | 1.4 | Current | 1.6 | 1.4 | 1.5 | 1.5 | 1.2 | 1.3 |
| .8 | .9 | .7 | | .4 | .5 | .8 | .9 | .8 | 1.0 |
| 1.8 | 1.8 | 1.8 | | 2.3 | 2.3 | 2.7 | 1.9 | 1.5 | 1.4 |
| 1.0 | 1.0 | 1.0 | Quick | 1.5 | .8 | 1.0 | 1.0 | .9 | 1.1 |
| .5 | .5 | .6 | | .2 | .4 | .4 | .4 | .5 | .7 |

| | | | | | | | Sales/Receivables | | | | | |
|---|---|---|---|---|---|---|---|---|---|---|---|---|
| 23 | 15.6 | 22 | 16.7 | 14 | 25.5 | 0 UND | 3 140.8 | 0 UND | 14 25.6 | 25 14.6 | 34 10.6 |
| 41 | 8.8 | 40 | 9.1 | 38 | 9.5 | 14 25.5 | 33 11.2 | 21 17.1 | 42 8.6 | 38 9.5 | 51 7.2 |
| 62 | 5.9 | 61 | 6.0 | 61 | 6.0 | 43 8.5 | 47 7.8 | 49 7.4 | 64 5.7 | 69 5.3 | 65 5.6 |

Cost of Sales/Inventory

Cost of Sales/Payables

| | | | | | Sales/Working Capital | | | | | | |
|---|---|---|---|---|---|---|---|---|---|---|---|
| 6.5 | | 7.3 | | 8.2 | | 5.0 | 8.3 | 7.7 | 8.4 | 9.3 | 8.2 |
| 24.8 | | 19.2 | | 18.2 | | 18.3 | 23.1 | 16.0 | 15.2 | 23.7 | 21.4 |
| -27.6 | | -61.7 | | -37.9 | | -6.4 | -20.5 | -83.3 | -92.8 | -32.3 | NM |

| | | | | | | EBIT/Interest | | | | | | |
|---|---|---|---|---|---|---|---|---|---|---|---|---|
| | 12.1 | | 13.5 | | 18.6 | | 5.8 | 66.4 | 29.9 | 29.8 | 26.4 |
| (132) | 2.6 | (132) | 4.8 | (124) | 4.6 | (21) 1.6 | (12) 3.5 | (22) 11.8 | (29) 5.2 | (31) 5.0 |
| | .6 | | 1.4 | | 1.5 | | -.1 | .3 | 2.6 | 1.6 | 1.6 |

| | | | | | | Net Profit + Depr., Dep., Amort./Cur. Mat. L/T/D | | | | | | |
|---|---|---|---|---|---|---|---|---|---|---|---|---|
| | 6.5 | | 7.6 | | 16.3 | | | | | | |
| (21) | 1.7 | (21) | 1.9 | (13) | 4.4 | | | | | | |
| | .8 | | 1.3 | | 1.8 | | | | | | |

| | | | | | Fixed/Worth | | | | | | |
|---|---|---|---|---|---|---|---|---|---|---|---|
| .1 | | .1 | | .1 | | .1 | .1 | .1 | .1 | .1 | .2 |
| .8 | | .3 | | .6 | | 1.7 | .5 | .6 | .9 | .3 | 2.9 |
| -1.3 | | 30.1 | | -1.0 | | -5.9 | -1.0 | NM | -2.0 | 2.3 | -.3 |

| | | | | | Debt/Worth | | | | | | |
|---|---|---|---|---|---|---|---|---|---|---|---|
| 1.1 | | .8 | | 1.0 | | .6 | 1.0 | .4 | 1.0 | 1.3 | 1.4 |
| 4.2 | | 2.8 | | 4.0 | | 1.5 | 3.9 | 3.0 | 2.3 | 3.7 | 6.7 |
| -6.6 | | 296.0 | | -5.1 | | -7.4 | -3.5 | -22.3 | -10.7 | -104.7 | -3.0 |

| | | | | | | % Profit Before Taxes/Tangible Net Worth | | | | | | |
|---|---|---|---|---|---|---|---|---|---|---|---|---|
| | 52.7 | | 73.9 | | 62.4 | | 74.6 | 56.7 | 139.2 | 121.4 | 44.4 | 59.0 |
| (102) | 12.4 | (135) | 28.7 | (110) | 26.5 | (12) 16.1 | (20) 16.9 | (13) 38.5 | (19) 34.5 | (26) 23.0 | (20) 26.7 |
| | -4.3 | | 9.5 | | 5.9 | | 8.0 | -14.3 | -2.5 | 12.0 | 4.9 | 10.0 |

| | | | | | % Profit Before Taxes/Total Assets | | | | | | |
|---|---|---|---|---|---|---|---|---|---|---|---|
| 16.8 | | 20.3 | | 20.6 | | 32.8 | 38.3 | 66.3 | 21.7 | 15.1 | 11.2 |
| 3.2 | | 7.9 | | 7.6 | | 8.7 | 4.2 | 13.9 | 12.2 | 7.5 | 7.1 |
| -3.3 | | 1.9 | | 1.9 | | 1.8 | -2.0 | .5 | 4.2 | 1.7 | 2.5 |

| | | | | | Sales/Net Fixed Assets | | | | | | |
|---|---|---|---|---|---|---|---|---|---|---|---|
| 120.4 | | 169.6 | | 149.4 | | 78.7 | 268.5 | 346.0 | 189.9 | 150.8 | 95.2 |
| 30.7 | | 48.4 | | 39.0 | | 4.7 | 45.5 | 89.7 | 35.1 | 47.0 | 32.3 |
| 12.2 | | 13.5 | | 11.8 | | .2 | 17.6 | 30.0 | 10.9 | 33.0 | 10.5 |

| | | | | | Sales/Total Assets | | | | | | |
|---|---|---|---|---|---|---|---|---|---|---|---|
| 4.6 | | 4.4 | | 4.1 | | 3.9 | 5.1 | 5.7 | 4.4 | 5.3 | 3.3 |
| 2.5 | | 2.6 | | 2.9 | | 1.8 | 3.1 | 3.9 | 2.9 | 3.4 | 2.3 |
| 1.6 | | 1.5 | | 1.8 | | .2 | 1.8 | 2.9 | 2.1 | 1.9 | 1.4 |

| | | | | | | % Depr., Dep., Amort./Sales | | | | | | |
|---|---|---|---|---|---|---|---|---|---|---|---|---|
| | .6 | | .4 | | .5 | | 1.8 | .4 | | .4 | .3 | .7 |
| (112) | 1.4 | (122) | 1.1 | (105) | 1.2 | (11) 12.5 | (19) 1.2 | (16) | .6 | (26) .5 | (25) 2.0 |
| | 3.3 | | 3.2 | | 2.8 | | 13.7 | 2.2 | 2.0 | 1.7 | 3.0 |

| | | | | | | % Officers', Directors' Owners' Comp/Sales | | | | | | |
|---|---|---|---|---|---|---|---|---|---|---|---|---|
| | 2.6 | | 2.6 | | 2.2 | | | 5.4 | 2.1 | 1.0 | |
| (63) | 5.5 | (59) | 5.1 | (64) | 5.2 | | (19) 7.8 | (14) 4.5 | (13) 2.2 | |
| | 11.6 | | 9.8 | | 9.2 | | | 13.7 | 8.5 | 2.8 | |

| | | | Net Sales ($) | | | | | | |
|---|---|---|---|---|---|---|---|---|---|
| 4213893M | 5303910M | 4861573M | | 7097M | 62017M | 67739M | 186537M | 573392M | 3964791M |
| 2271723M | 2989774M | 2723531M | Total Assets ($) | 13215M | 53891M | 31854M | 69798M | 259351M | 2295422M |

© RMA 2012

M = $ thousand     MM = $ million
See Pages 9 through 22 for Explanation of Ratios and Data

## Current Data Sorted by Assets

## Comparative Historical Data

| | | | | | | Type of Statement | | |
|---|---|---|---|---|---|---|---|---|
| 1 | 1 | 9 | 5 | 5 | 6 | Unqualified | 16 | 22 |
| | 2 | 11 | 3 | | | Reviewed | 9 | 14 |
| | 4 | 11 | 1 | | | Compiled | 11 | 13 |
| 8 | 15 | 8 | | | | Tax Returns | 19 | 20 |
| 11 | 25 | 14 | 14 | 4 | 2 | Other | 34 | 43 |
| | 28 (4/1-9/30/11) | | 132 (10/1/11-3/31/12) | | | | 4/1/07-3/31/08 | 4/1/08-3/31/09 |
| 0-500M | 500M-2MM | 2-10MM | 10-50MM | 50-100MM | 100-250MM | | ALL | ALL |
| 20 | 47 | 53 | 23 | 9 | 8 | NUMBER OF STATEMENTS | 89 | 112 |
| % | % | % | % | % | % | ASSETS | % | % |
| 45.5 | 15.8 | 15.1 | 17.0 | | | Cash & Equivalents | 16.6 | 19.2 |
| 29.0 | 43.0 | 40.0 | 38.6 | | | Trade Receivables (net) | 38.3 | 35.4 |
| .0 | 2.9 | 2.3 | 3.3 | | | Inventory | 1.2 | 2.4 |
| 1.1 | 3.7 | 7.9 | 5.7 | | | All Other Current | 6.5 | 5.4 |
| 75.5 | 65.4 | 65.3 | 64.7 | | | Total Current | 62.8 | 62.4 |
| 10.5 | 18.9 | 17.7 | 10.8 | | | Fixed Assets (net) | 20.2 | 20.6 |
| 9.1 | 6.4 | 6.8 | 11.7 | | | Intangibles (net) | 7.8 | 8.0 |
| 4.9 | 9.3 | 10.3 | 12.9 | | | All Other Non-Current | 9.3 | 9.0 |
| 100.0 | 100.0 | 100.0 | 100.0 | | | Total | 100.0 | 100.0 |
| | | | | | | LIABILITIES | | |
| 24.1 | 14.8 | 9.1 | 6.0 | | | Notes Payable-Short Term | 15.6 | 14.6 |
| 1.5 | 2.6 | 3.7 | 2.1 | | | Cur. Mat.-L.T.D. | 5.9 | 3.7 |
| 13.1 | 13.2 | 11.7 | 15.3 | | | Trade Payables | 13.9 | 13.2 |
| .0 | .2 | 1.0 | 2.9 | | | Income Taxes Payable | .4 | .4 |
| 24.0 | 22.5 | 23.2 | 19.4 | | | All Other Current | 21.6 | 19.6 |
| 62.6 | 53.3 | 48.7 | 45.7 | | | Total Current | 57.5 | 51.4 |
| 3.3 | 17.4 | 10.6 | 8.7 | | | Long-Term Debt | 15.8 | 12.5 |
| .0 | .1 | .4 | 1.3 | | | Deferred Taxes | .2 | .3 |
| 8.2 | 9.5 | 3.5 | 13.9 | | | All Other Non-Current | 6.4 | 8.3 |
| 25.8 | 19.8 | 36.8 | 30.4 | | | Net Worth | 20.1 | 27.4 |
| 100.0 | 100.0 | 100.0 | 100.0 | | | Total Liabilties & Net Worth | 100.0 | 100.0 |
| | | | | | | INCOME DATA | | |
| 100.0 | 100.0 | 100.0 | 100.0 | | | Net Sales | 100.0 | 100.0 |
| | | | | | | Gross Profit | | |
| 93.3 | 95.7 | 92.9 | 95.8 | | | Operating Expenses | 94.6 | 95.7 |
| 6.7 | 4.3 | 7.1 | 4.2 | | | Operating Profit | 5.4 | 4.3 |
| 1.1 | .8 | 1.8 | 2.2 | | | All Other Expenses (net) | 1.7 | 1.7 |
| 5.6 | 3.5 | 5.3 | 2.1 | | | Profit Before Taxes | 3.7 | 2.7 |
| | | | | | | RATIOS | | |
| 3.4 | 4.0 | 2.5 | 1.9 | | | | 2.4 | 2.5 |
| 1.5 | 1.4 | 1.4 | 1.3 | | | Current | 1.3 | 1.3 |
| .8 | .8 | 1.0 | .9 | | | | .9 | .9 |
| 3.4 | 3.5 | 2.2 | 1.7 | | | | 2.1 | 2.2 |
| 1.4 | 1.4 | 1.0 | 1.1 | | | Quick | 1.1 (111) | 1.2 |
| .8 | .6 | .7 | .8 | | | | .7 | .8 |
| 0 UND | 25 14.4 | 39 9.4 | 44 8.3 | | | | 28 13.2 | 23 15.6 |
| 5 77.5 | 41 8.9 | 61 6.0 | 58 6.3 | | | Sales/Receivables | 51 7.2 | 47 7.7 |
| 35 10.3 | 79 4.6 | 79 4.6 | 74 4.9 | | | | 68 5.3 | 64 5.7 |
| | | | | | | Cost of Sales/Inventory | | |
| | | | | | | Cost of Sales/Payables | | |
| 9.4 | 6.0 | 6.5 | 5.7 | | | | 8.6 | 7.2 |
| 33.0 | 22.5 | 20.4 | 18.1 | | | Sales/Working Capital | 22.8 | 28.5 |
| -45.0 | -33.4 | NM | -103.8 | | | | -37.3 | -49.9 |
| 32.7 | 22.8 | 48.9 | 185.5 | | | | 17.3 | 23.5 |
| (15) 11.8 | (36) 2.5 | (42) 14.4 | (17) 5.6 | | | EBIT/Interest | (69) 2.9 | (93) 4.1 |
| 2.2 | -1.0 | 1.5 | 1.5 | | | | 1.1 | .9 |
| | | 16.4 | | | | | 7.6 | 20.7 |
| | | (11) 3.0 | | | | Net Profit + Depr., Dep., Amort./Cur. Mat. L/T/D | (13) 3.7 | (19) 2.7 |
| | | 1.6 | | | | | 2.0 | 1.3 |
| .0 | .1 | .1 | .1 | | | | .2 | .2 |
| .2 | .4 | .3 | .2 | | | Fixed/Worth | .6 | .6 |
| NM | 6.0 | 2.2 | .9 | | | | -1.8 | UND |
| .5 | .5 | .9 | .9 | | | | .8 | .9 |
| 1.8 | 1.8 | 2.4 | 3.3 | | | Debt/Worth | 3.3 | 2.7 |
| -10.1 | 17.4 | 5.2 | 12.7 | | | | -10.2 | UND |
| 510.9 | 106.5 | 63.1 | 52.2 | | | | 91.4 | 82.6 |
| (14) 115.6 | (36) 38.0 | (45) 32.3 | (19) 25.3 | | | % Profit Before Taxes/Tangible Net Worth | (61) 26.5 | (85) 20.2 |
| 9.8 | 6.0 | 4.6 | 6.6 | | | | 8.4 | 2.7 |
| 94.7 | 27.3 | 21.0 | 15.6 | | | | 23.0 | 23.2 |
| 21.8 | 9.0 | 9.0 | 8.1 | | | % Profit Before Taxes/Total Assets | 6.2 | 5.8 |
| 2.0 | .1 | 1.2 | .4 | | | | .6 | -.1 |
| 960.8 | 172.1 | 104.0 | 194.9 | | | | 54.7 | 56.8 |
| 123.3 | 49.5 | 31.5 | 66.0 | | | Sales/Net Fixed Assets | 28.4 | 24.4 |
| 37.1 | 13.7 | 12.0 | 15.9 | | | | 11.3 | 11.4 |
| 19.4 | 5.0 | 3.2 | 3.8 | | | | 4.5 | 4.9 |
| 7.3 | 3.5 | 2.4 | 2.2 | | | Sales/Total Assets | 3.0 | 3.0 |
| 4.5 | 2.3 | 1.8 | 1.7 | | | | 2.1 | 2.1 |
| | .5 | .6 | .3 | | | | .7 | .9 |
| | (28) 1.2 | (43) 1.3 | (18) .6 | | | % Depr., Dep., Amort./Sales | (68) 1.3 | (79) 1.5 |
| | 2.3 | 2.9 | 1.3 | | | | 2.1 | 2.5 |
| 5.3 | 4.2 | 2.1 | | | | | 2.8 | 4.3 |
| (13) 13.3 | (22) 7.6 | (17) 4.0 | | | | % Officers', Directors' Owners' Comp/Sales | (27) 8.0 | (42) 9.8 |
| 19.4 | 14.1 | 10.2 | | | | | 16.8 | 21.4 |
| 49578M | 211537M | 639919M | 1118738M | 982907M | 1656478M | Net Sales ($) | 4874062M | 3465487M |
| 5018M | 53001M | 255843M | 436152M | 659840M | 1411611M | Total Assets ($) | 1558431M | 1921247M |

© RMA 2012

M = $ thousand    MM = $ million
See Pages 9 through 22 for Explanation of Ratios and Data

## Comparative Historical Data | Current Data Sorted by Sales

| 4/1/09-3/31/10 ALL | 4/1/10-3/31/11 ALL | 4/1/11-3/31/12 ALL | Type of Statement | 0-1MM | 1-3MM | 3-5MM | 5-10MM | 10-25MM | 25MM & OVER |
|---|---|---|---|---|---|---|---|---|---|
| | | | Unqualified | | | 1 | 3 | 4 | 18 |
| 25 | 22 | 26 | Reviewed | 1 | 3 | 6 | 3 | | 4 |
| 14 | 17 | 17 | Compiled | | 4 | 4 | 4 | 4 | |
| 16 | 18 | 16 | Tax Returns | 3 | 10 | 5 | 6 | 7 | |
| 17 | 16 | 31 | Other | 5 | 15 | 9 | | | 18 |
| 66 | 62 | 70 | | | 28 (4/1-9/30/11) | | 132 (10/1/11-3/31/12) | | |
| 138 | 135 | 160 | **NUMBER OF STATEMENTS** | 9 | 32 | 19 | 32 | 28 | 40 |
| % | % | % | **ASSETS** | % | % | % | % | % | % |
| 16.7 | 17.4 | 19.6 | Cash & Equivalents | | 22.6 | 24.1 | 20.0 | 15.8 | 17.3 |
| 37.6 | 40.5 | 37.4 | Trade Receivables (net) | | 37.2 | 31.3 | 45.0 | 37.7 | 35.4 |
| 2.3 | 2.3 | 2.1 | Inventory | | 2.4 | 2.3 | .9 | 5.3 | 1.1 |
| 5.9 | 5.2 | 5.4 | All Other Current | | 2.2 | 2.9 | 5.7 | 13.2 | 4.7 |
| 62.5 | 65.5 | 64.5 | Total Current | | 64.3 | 60.7 | 71.6 | 72.0 | 58.6 |
| 19.2 | 16.0 | 15.4 | Fixed Assets (net) | | 15.7 | 27.0 | 15.2 | 8.8 | 11.1 |
| 8.7 | 8.6 | 10.9 | Intangibles (net) | | 7.7 | 6.1 | 4.7 | 8.4 | 21.8 |
| 9.6 | 9.9 | 9.2 | All Other Non-Current | | 12.2 | 6.2 | 8.4 | 10.8 | 8.5 |
| 100.0 | 100.0 | 100.0 | Total | | 100.0 | 100.0 | 100.0 | 100.0 | 100.0 |
| | | | **LIABILITIES** | | | | | | |
| 12.4 | 16.2 | 11.2 | Notes Payable-Short Term | | 17.6 | 16.9 | 9.0 | 11.3 | 5.5 |
| 6.5 | 2.5 | 2.8 | Cur. Mat.-L.T.D. | | 2.2 | 5.3 | 3.3 | 2.1 | 2.4 |
| 14.6 | 15.0 | 12.6 | Trade Payables | | 11.8 | 13.2 | 12.3 | 13.9 | 13.9 |
| .2 | .4 | .9 | Income Taxes Payable | | .2 | .6 | .8 | .8 | 1.8 |
| 19.3 | 22.0 | 22.2 | All Other Current | | 16.9 | 15.4 | 22.0 | 34.7 | 18.6 |
| 53.0 | 56.1 | 49.6 | Total Current | | 48.6 | 51.5 | 47.3 | 62.8 | 42.3 |
| 16.3 | 11.5 | 12.0 | Long-Term Debt | | 11.6 | 16.2 | 7.6 | 14.5 | 12.0 |
| .5 | .6 | .6 | Deferred Taxes | | .1 | .0 | .0 | 1.8 | 1.0 |
| 7.9 | 10.8 | 8.0 | All Other Non-Current | | 6.8 | 9.1 | 4.5 | 19.7 | 5.1 |
| 22.3 | 21.0 | 29.8 | Net Worth | | 32.9 | 23.2 | 40.6 | 1.2 | 39.7 |
| 100.0 | 100.0 | 100.0 | Total Liabilties & Net Worth | | 100.0 | 100.0 | 100.0 | 100.0 | 100.0 |
| | | | **INCOME DATA** | | | | | | |
| 100.0 | 100.0 | 100.0 | Net Sales | | 100.0 | 100.0 | 100.0 | 100.0 | 100.0 |
| | | | Gross Profit | | | | | | |
| 93.7 | 92.0 | 94.1 | Operating Expenses | | 93.7 | 96.8 | 94.1 | 97.3 | 93.8 |
| 6.3 | 8.0 | 5.9 | Operating Profit | | 6.3 | 3.2 | 5.9 | 2.7 | 6.2 |
| 2.6 | 2.3 | 1.6 | All Other Expenses (net) | | .9 | 1.6 | .7 | 1.0 | 1.7 |
| 3.7 | 5.7 | 4.3 | Profit Before Taxes | | 5.4 | 1.6 | 5.2 | 1.7 | 4.4 |
| | | | **RATIOS** | | | | | | |
| 2.3 | 2.7 | 2.6 | | | 3.0 | 6.0 | 3.5 | 1.9 | 1.7 |
| 1.4 | 1.3 | 1.3 | Current | | 1.4 | 1.4 | 1.9 | 1.2 | 1.2 |
| 1.0 | .9 | 1.0 | | | .9 | .7 | 1.0 | 1.0 | 1.0 |
| 2.1 | 2.4 | 2.5 | | | 3.0 | 6.0 | 3.5 | 1.4 | 1.7 |
| 1.2 | 1.1 | 1.1 | Quick | | 1.3 | 1.1 | 1.7 | 1.0 | 1.0 |
| .8 | .7 | .7 | | | .7 | .7 | .7 | .6 | .8 |
| 30   12.0 | 25   14.8 | 25   14.6 | | | 5   75.8 | 12   30.9 | 34   10.8 | 9   39.6 | 38   9.6 |
| 50   7.3 | 54   6.7 | 51   7.2 | Sales/Receivables | | 40   9.2 | 32   11.4 | 51   7.1 | 58   6.3 | 58   6.3 |
| 77   4.7 | 76   4.8 | 76   4.8 | | | 78   4.7 | 53   6.9 | 76   4.8 | 78   4.7 | 76   4.8 |
| | | | Cost of Sales/Inventory | | | | | | |
| | | | Cost of Sales/Payables | | | | | | |
| 6.0 | 6.3 | 6.5 | | | 8.7 | 7.0 | 5.1 | 10.6 | 7.1 |
| 18.3 | 24.9 | 20.4 | Sales/Working Capital | | 27.5 | 14.7 | 11.7 | 41.6 | 18.0 |
| -195.5 | -35.1 | -114.5 | | | -165.2 | -20.6 | NM | 682.1 | NM |
| 19.5 | 29.8 | 35.8 | | | 30.0 | 43.0 | 54.1 | 51.8 | 18.5 |
| (103)   5.4 | (105)   7.0 | (124)   7.5 | EBIT/Interest | (24)   6.0 | (16)   6.2 | (25)   21.4 | (22)   9.8 | (32)   6.4 | |
| .9 | 1.3 | 1.3 | | | -.4 | .3 | 1.0 | -7.2 | 1.6 |
| 8.6 | 13.3 | 16.6 | Net Profit + Depr., Dep., | | | | | | |
| (21)   4.4 | (13)   7.4 | (22)   3.1 | Amort./Cur. Mat. L/T/D | | | | | | |
| 2.1 | 3.6 | 1.6 | | | | | | | |
| .1 | .1 | .1 | | | .1 | .1 | .1 | .1 | .1 |
| .5 | .5 | .4 | Fixed/Worth | | .2 | .6 | .3 | .3 | .4 |
| 4.1 | 4.3 | 4.4 | | | 4.1 | -3.1 | 1.0 | 42.2 | -.8 |
| .8 | .8 | .6 | | | .5 | 1.3 | .4 | 2.5 | 1.0 |
| 2.7 | 2.9 | 2.4 | Debt/Worth | | 1.6 | 3.2 | 1.0 | 4.1 | 2.6 |
| 36.7 | 107.7 | 41.7 | | | 13.9 | -14.9 | 5.7 | -7.7 | -9.2 |
| 64.3 | 86.7 | 94.0 | % Profit Before Taxes/Tangible | | 147.3 | 151.3 | 57.2 | 100.2 | 51.4 |
| (106)   21.6 | (103)   39.8 | (122)   31.8 | Net Worth | (26)   39.2 | (14)   51.2 | (26)   26.8 | (20)   39.1 | (28)   28.4 | |
| 2.1 | 10.0 | 6.3 | | | 10.3 | 14.3 | 1.2 | 16.4 | 6.3 |
| 19.5 | 19.4 | 22.4 | % Profit Before Taxes/Total | | 37.2 | 27.3 | 27.3 | 20.4 | 17.2 |
| 6.7 | 7.8 | 8.9 | Assets | | 15.0 | 9.0 | 8.7 | 7.9 | 6.9 |
| -1.1 | .7 | 1.1 | | | 2.0 | -18.5 | .2 | -7.6 | .7 |
| 70.8 | 97.3 | 131.9 | | | 159.2 | 85.7 | 122.1 | 213.8 | 72.5 |
| 27.0 | 38.6 | 43.4 | Sales/Net Fixed Assets | | 44.4 | 32.8 | 43.6 | 74.2 | 33.5 |
| 9.8 | 13.5 | 14.0 | | | 16.4 | 3.5 | 13.5 | 29.6 | 11.7 |
| 4.0 | 4.6 | 4.3 | | | 6.8 | 5.0 | 4.8 | 5.1 | 3.4 |
| 2.5 | 2.7 | 2.6 | Sales/Total Assets | | 2.8 | 2.6 | 3.0 | 2.9 | 2.1 |
| 1.6 | 1.8 | 1.8 | | | 2.0 | 1.7 | 2.3 | 2.0 | 1.2 |
| .7 | .6 | .5 | | | .6 | .9 | .4 | .5 | .4 |
| (100)   1.5 | (90)   1.0 | (103)   1.2 | % Depr., Dep., Amort./Sales | (16)   1.4 | (11)   1.4 | (26)   1.2 | (20)   .9 | (26)   .9 | |
| 2.6 | 1.8 | 2.4 | | | 2.8 | 5.0 | 2.2 | 1.3 | 2.4 |
| 3.3 | 2.3 | 3.9 | % Officers', Directors' | | 5.3 | 7.3 | 4.2 | 1.0 | |
| (33)   8.2 | (38)   4.4 | (55)   7.3 | Owners' Comp/Sales | (17)   10.1 | (11)   16.5 | (10)   6.2 | (14)   2.4 | | |
| 16.3 | 8.9 | 15.5 | | | 15.6 | 20.9 | 9.4 | 6.7 | | |
| 3765111M | 4142290M | 4659157M | Net Sales ($) | 4969M | 68853M | 73454M | 245053M | 467445M | 3799383M |
| 2314504M | 2349560M | 2821465M | Total Assets ($) | 9803M | 25416M | 35147M | 95949M | 176083M | 2479067M |

M = $ thousand    MM = $ million
See Pages 9 through 22 for Explanation of Ratios and Data

## Current Data Sorted by Assets

## Comparative Historical Data

| | | | | | | Type of Statement | | |
|---|---|---|---|---|---|---|---|---|
| | 2 | | | 2 | | Unqualified | 1 | 4 |
| 2 | 1 | 3 | 1 | | | Reviewed | 7 | 7 |
| 18 | 6 | 3 | | | 1 | Compiled | 4 | 6 |
| 9 | 3 | 2 | | | 1 | Tax Returns | 6 | 17 |
| | 9 (4/1-9/30/11) | | 48 (10/1/11-3/31/12) | | | Other | 15 | 19 |
| | | | | | | | 4/1/07-3/31/08 | 4/1/08-3/31/09 |
| 0-500M | 500M-2MM | 2-10MM | 10-50MM | 50-100MM | 100-250MM | | ALL | ALL |
| 29 | 12 | 8 | 4 | 2 | 2 | NUMBER OF STATEMENTS | 33 | 53 |
| % | % | % | % | % | % | ASSETS | % | % |
| 21.2 | 19.3 | | | | | Cash & Equivalents | 18.5 | 15.5 |
| 12.8 | 19.5 | | | | | Trade Receivables (net) | 10.9 | 10.2 |
| 6.0 | 7.1 | | | | | Inventory | 4.9 | 5.9 |
| .8 | 2.3 | | | | | All Other Current | 4.2 | 2.5 |
| 40.7 | 48.2 | | | | | Total Current | 38.4 | 34.1 |
| 37.2 | 29.9 | | | | | Fixed Assets (net) | 47.1 | 40.8 |
| 14.3 | 1.9 | | | | | Intangibles (net) | 10.5 | 14.0 |
| 7.7 | 20.0 | | | | | All Other Non-Current | 3.9 | 11.1 |
| 100.0 | 100.0 | | | | | Total | 100.0 | 100.0 |
| | | | | | | LIABILITIES | | |
| 22.2 | 4.7 | | | | | Notes Payable-Short Term | 7.3 | 13.5 |
| 4.3 | 4.9 | | | | | Cur. Mat.-L.T.D. | 3.9 | 5.2 |
| 7.0 | 15.8 | | | | | Trade Payables | 10.8 | 6.7 |
| .0 | .0 | | | | | Income Taxes Payable | .7 | .6 |
| 29.3 | 10.6 | | | | | All Other Current | 13.0 | 18.4 |
| 62.8 | 36.1 | | | | | Total Current | 35.7 | 44.4 |
| 24.2 | 17.8 | | | | | Long-Term Debt | 28.7 | 27.8 |
| .0 | .0 | | | | | Deferred Taxes | .7 | .5 |
| 18.1 | 6.4 | | | | | All Other Non-Current | 8.9 | 16.8 |
| -5.1 | 39.8 | | | | | Net Worth | 26.0 | 10.4 |
| 100.0 | 100.0 | | | | | Total Liabilties & Net Worth | 100.0 | 100.0 |
| | | | | | | INCOME DATA | | |
| 100.0 | 100.0 | | | | | Net Sales | 100.0 | 100.0 |
| | | | | | | Gross Profit | | |
| 99.9 | 85.8 | | | | | Operating Expenses | 95.4 | 95.8 |
| .1 | 14.2 | | | | | Operating Profit | 4.6 | 4.2 |
| .8 | 3.0 | | | | | All Other Expenses (net) | 1.8 | 1.5 |
| -.6 | 11.2 | | | | | Profit Before Taxes | 2.9 | 2.7 |
| | | | | | | RATIOS | | |
| 1.9 | 2.4 | | | | | | 1.7 | 1.9 |
| .9 | 1.8 | | | | | Current | 1.2 | .7 |
| .2 | .9 | | | | | | .6 | .3 |
| 1.5 | 2.3 | | | | | | 1.4 | 1.4 |
| .6 | 1.3 | | | | | Quick | (32) .9 | .5 |
| .2 | .7 | | | | | | .3 | .2 |
| 0 UND | 0 UND | | | | | | 1 384.9 | 0 UND |
| 1 449.0 | 14 25.9 | | | | | Sales/Receivables | 5 72.2 | 4 96.5 |
| 26 14.2 | 33 11.2 | | | | | | 20 18.1 | 15 24.2 |
| | | | | | | Cost of Sales/Inventory | | |
| | | | | | | Cost of Sales/Payables | | |
| 22.1 | 8.4 | | | | | | 7.5 | 12.1 |
| -113.8 | 14.3 | | | | | Sales/Working Capital | 75.1 | -31.7 |
| -5.5 | NM | | | | | | -22.7 | -9.2 |
| 5.6 | | | | | | | 7.9 | 6.1 |
| (20) .7 | | | | | | EBIT/Interest | (32) 2.7 | (44) 1.6 |
| -4.8 | | | | | | | .2 | -.9 |
| | | | | | | Net Profit + Depr., Dep., Amort./Cur. Mat. L/T/D | | |
| 1.6 | .4 | | | | | | .8 | .8 |
| 5.5 | .8 | | | | | Fixed/Worth | 2.0 | 4.3 |
| -.3 | 3.2 | | | | | | -3.7 | -.8 |
| 2.8 | .4 | | | | | | 1.0 | 1.3 |
| 13.8 | 1.2 | | | | | Debt/Worth | 2.4 | 8.2 |
| -1.9 | 14.4 | | | | | | -6.9 | -2.8 |
| 48.3 | 92.6 | | | | | | 58.8 | 42.0 |
| (15) 29.4 | (10) 19.0 | | | | | % Profit Before Taxes/Tangible Net Worth | (22) 30.0 | (30) 15.6 |
| -135.5 | 7.7 | | | | | | 4.9 | -10.2 |
| 19.5 | 15.6 | | | | | | 16.3 | 14.3 |
| -1.0 | 12.3 | | | | | % Profit Before Taxes/Total Assets | 5.3 | 2.2 |
| -25.8 | 4.4 | | | | | | -5.4 | -8.6 |
| 24.0 | 19.5 | | | | | | 8.7 | 18.1 |
| 17.3 | 11.7 | | | | | Sales/Net Fixed Assets | 6.2 | 8.2 |
| 6.9 | 5.3 | | | | | | 3.0 | 4.4 |
| 8.7 | 4.2 | | | | | | 3.0 | 3.9 |
| 3.7 | 3.7 | | | | | Sales/Total Assets | 2.4 | 2.6 |
| 2.2 | 1.6 | | | | | | 1.8 | 1.8 |
| 1.6 | .4 | | | | | | 2.4 | 1.8 |
| (19) 2.2 | (10) 4.3 | | | | | % Depr., Dep., Amort./Sales | (29) 3.2 | (40) 3.5 |
| 8.2 | 6.3 | | | | | | 6.2 | 5.7 |
| 7.0 | | | | | | | 2.5 | 4.0 |
| (17) 8.8 | | | | | | % Officers', Directors' Owners' Comp/Sales | (19) 8.8 | (21) 9.8 |
| 19.8 | | | | | | | 12.2 | 15.9 |
| 26858M | 38840M | 74813M | 229826M | 405036M | 798010M | Net Sales ($) | 1060655M | 2160688M |
| 5733M | 13826M | 36893M | 95771M | 159202M | 300282M | Total Assets ($) | 573752M | 1059621M |

M = $ thousand    MM = $ million
See Pages 9 through 22 for Explanation of Ratios and Data

## Comparative Historical Data  /  Current Data Sorted by Sales

| Type of Statement | 4/1/09-3/31/10 ALL | 4/1/10-3/31/11 ALL | 4/1/11-3/31/12 ALL | | 0-1MM | 1-3MM | 3-5MM | 5-10MM | 10-25MM | 25MM & OVER |
|---|---|---|---|---|---|---|---|---|---|---|
| Unqualified | | | | | | | 4 | | 1 | 2 |
| Reviewed | | | | | | | | | | 1 |
| Compiled | | | | | 2 | 1 | | 3 | | 1 |
| Tax Returns | | | | | 13 | 8 | 2 | 1 | 2 | 1 |
| Other | | | | | 6 | 5 | 1 | | | 4 |
| | 4 | 4 | 2 | | | | | | | |
| | 3 | 1 | 6 | | | | | | | |
| | 8 | 6 | 6 | | | | | | | |
| | 21 | 17 | 27 | | | 9 (4/1-9/30/11) | | | 48 (10/1/11-3/31/12) | |
| | 14 | 21 | 16 | | | | | | | |

| | 4/1/09-3/31/10 ALL | 4/1/10-3/31/11 ALL | 4/1/11-3/31/12 ALL | | 0-1MM | 1-3MM | 3-5MM | 5-10MM | 10-25MM | 25MM & OVER |
|---|---|---|---|---|---|---|---|---|---|---|
| **NUMBER OF STATEMENTS** | 50 | 49 | 57 | | 21 | 14 | 7 | 4 | 3 | 8 |
| **ASSETS** | % | % | % | | % | % | % | % | % | % |
| Cash & Equivalents | 17.9 | 19.3 | 20.9 | | 17.2 | 20.9 | | | | |
| Trade Receivables (net) | 5.3 | 11.6 | 13.2 | | 14.2 | 11.4 | | | | |
| Inventory | 7.3 | 4.7 | 7.3 | | 6.5 | 2.7 | | | | |
| All Other Current | 3.1 | 3.4 | 1.4 | | 1.1 | 1.7 | | | | |
| Total Current | 33.5 | 38.9 | 42.7 | | 39.0 | 36.7 | | | | |
| Fixed Assets (net) | 38.9 | 39.1 | 30.1 | | 34.3 | 36.5 | | | | |
| Intangibles (net) | 16.6 | 13.2 | 13.8 | | 11.2 | 13.1 | | | | |
| All Other Non-Current | 11.1 | 8.7 | 13.4 | | 15.5 | 13.8 | | | | |
| Total | 100.0 | 100.0 | 100.0 | | 100.0 | 100.0 | | | | |
| **LIABILITIES** | | | | | | | | | | |
| Notes Payable-Short Term | 24.0 | 14.9 | 13.2 | | 23.9 | 14.6 | | | | |
| Cur. Mat.-L.T.D. | 4.6 | 3.3 | 3.7 | | 5.9 | 2.7 | | | | |
| Trade Payables | 11.0 | 10.5 | 9.7 | | 6.7 | 9.8 | | | | |
| Income Taxes Payable | .1 | .1 | .1 | | .0 | .0 | | | | |
| All Other Current | 15.9 | 13.5 | 21.8 | | 32.1 | 13.7 | | | | |
| Total Current | 55.7 | 42.3 | 48.5 | | 68.5 | 40.7 | | | | |
| Long-Term Debt | 33.2 | 29.2 | 22.7 | | 24.5 | 22.5 | | | | |
| Deferred Taxes | .2 | .3 | .4 | | .0 | .0 | | | | |
| All Other Non-Current | 9.2 | 7.5 | 16.8 | | 18.9 | 12.3 | | | | |
| Net Worth | 1.8 | 20.8 | 11.7 | | -12.0 | 24.5 | | | | |
| Total Liabilties & Net Worth | 100.0 | 100.0 | 100.0 | | 100.0 | 100.0 | | | | |
| **INCOME DATA** | | | | | | | | | | |
| Net Sales | 100.0 | 100.0 | 100.0 | | 100.0 | 100.0 | | | | |
| Gross Profit | | | | | | | | | | |
| Operating Expenses | 96.9 | 92.5 | 96.8 | | 95.6 | 95.1 | | | | |
| Operating Profit | 3.1 | 7.5 | 3.2 | | 4.4 | 4.9 | | | | |
| All Other Expenses (net) | 3.0 | 1.9 | 1.7 | | 2.3 | 2.4 | | | | |
| Profit Before Taxes | .1 | 5.6 | 1.5 | | 2.2 | 2.4 | | | | |
| **RATIOS** | | | | | | | | | | |
| Current | 2.1 | 2.3 | 2.4 | | 1.8 | 2.1 | | | | |
| | .6 | 1.2 | 1.2 | | .8 | 1.4 | | | | |
| | .3 | .4 | .5 | | .2 | .4 | | | | |
| Quick | 1.3 | 2.1 | 1.9 | | 1.4 | 1.9 | | | | |
| | .4 | .7 | 1.0 | | .6 | 1.2 | | | | |
| | .2 | .2 | .4 | | .2 | .3 | | | | |
| Sales/Receivables | 0 UND | 0 UND | 0 UND | | 0 UND | 0 UND | | | | |
| | 1 364.3 | 4 90.5 | 5 72.3 | | 10 36.3 | 4 86.8 | | | | |
| | 8 44.9 | 21 17.5 | 26 14.1 | | 27 13.5 | 18 19.8 | | | | |
| Cost of Sales/Inventory | | | | | | | | | | |
| Cost of Sales/Payables | | | | | | | | | | |
| Sales/Working Capital | 13.1 | 10.2 | 10.9 | | 60.3 | 12.7 | | | | |
| | -32.9 | 56.6 | 123.7 | | -21.1 | 41.6 | | | | |
| | -7.3 | -10.7 | -10.1 | | -3.7 | -74.8 | | | | |
| EBIT/Interest | 4.4 | 8.6 | 8.2 | | 5.1 | 28.7 | | | | |
| | (38) .0 | (41) 3.5 | (43) 2.1 | | (13) .0 | (10) 7.1 | | | | |
| | -4.0 | 1.3 | -3.0 | | -8.5 | -.2 | | | | |
| Net Profit + Depr., Dep., Amort./Cur. Mat. L/T/D | | | | | | | | | | |
| Fixed/Worth | .7 | .8 | .7 | | .7 | .8 | | | | |
| | NM | 2.3 | 3.2 | | -2.5 | 2.3 | | | | |
| | -.6 | -1.0 | -.4 | | -.3 | NM | | | | |
| Debt/Worth | .9 | .8 | .8 | | 1.6 | 1.6 | | | | |
| | NM | 3.3 | 5.7 | | -5.1 | 4.2 | | | | |
| | -2.1 | -3.8 | -2.0 | | -1.9 | NM | | | | |
| % Profit Before Taxes/Tangible Net Worth | 121.0 | 75.4 | 40.8 | | | 112.7 | | | | |
| | (25) 8.9 | (32) 26.1 | (33) 14.9 | | | (11) 41.9 | | | | |
| | -9.4 | 6.3 | -.2 | | | -6.5 | | | | |
| % Profit Before Taxes/Total Assets | 12.8 | 14.9 | 15.5 | | 19.5 | 19.5 | | | | |
| | -1.1 | 7.9 | 4.8 | | -3.2 | 10.3 | | | | |
| | -15.5 | 1.9 | -17.4 | | -26.0 | -16.3 | | | | |
| Sales/Net Fixed Assets | 20.2 | 19.4 | 23.4 | | 23.0 | 23.1 | | | | |
| | 12.4 | 7.6 | 13.8 | | 11.6 | 15.1 | | | | |
| | 5.9 | 4.4 | 6.7 | | 4.7 | 7.3 | | | | |
| Sales/Total Assets | 6.2 | 3.7 | 4.3 | | 6.3 | 7.4 | | | | |
| | 3.1 | 2.3 | 3.2 | | 2.4 | 4.0 | | | | |
| | 1.7 | 1.4 | 1.6 | | 1.5 | 3.0 | | | | |
| % Depr., Dep., Amort./Sales | 1.6 | 3.1 | .9 | | 1.9 | | | | | |
| | (37) 3.0 | (31) 4.1 | (39) 2.8 | | (15) 5.4 | | | | | |
| | 5.8 | 6.6 | 6.9 | | 10.9 | | | | | |
| % Officers', Directors' Owners' Comp/Sales | 3.5 | 2.2 | 2.4 | | 7.8 | 2.0 | | | | |
| | (25) 8.7 | (20) 6.6 | (30) 5.3 | | (10) 14.4 | (11) 4.0 | | | | |
| | 18.4 | 15.7 | 9.4 | | 22.5 | 8.4 | | | | |
| Net Sales ($) | 1105905M | 1621031M | 1573383M | | 8094M | 27492M | 28918M | 31969M | 44038M | 1432872M |
| Total Assets ($) | 550991M | 699591M | 611707M | | 5352M | 8798M | 12064M | 12285M | 17953M | 555255M |

M = $ thousand     MM = $ million
See Pages 9 through 22 for Explanation of Ratios and Data

## Current Data Sorted by Assets

## Comparative Historical Data

| | | | | | | | Type of Statement | | |
|---|---|---|---|---|---|---|---|---|---|
| 1 | | | | | | | Unqualified | | |
| 1 | 3 | 4 | | | | | Reviewed | 2 | 1 |
| 1 | 1 | | 1 | | | | Compiled | 2 | 4 |
| 4 | 3 | 1 | | | | | Tax Returns | 4 | 3 |
| 2 | 5 | 9 | 9 | | | | Other | 5 | 6 |
| | 5 (4/1-9/30/11) | | | 32 (10/1/11-3/31/12) | | | | 14<br>4/1/07-<br>3/31/08 | 11<br>4/1/08-<br>3/31/09 |
| 0-500M | 500M-2MM | 2-10MM | 10-50MM | 50-100MM | 100-250MM | | | ALL | ALL |
| 8 | 12 | 14 | 2 | 1 | | | NUMBER OF STATEMENTS | 27 | 25 |
| % | % | % | % | % | % | | ASSETS | % | % |
| | 16.8 | 8.3 | | | | D | Cash & Equivalents | 13.0 | 12.1 |
| | 28.8 | 20.1 | | | | A | Trade Receivables (net) | 20.2 | 24.7 |
| | 3.2 | 9.2 | | | | T | Inventory | 7.8 | 8.1 |
| | 6.9 | 4.7 | | | | A | All Other Current | 4.2 | 5.5 |
| | 55.8 | 42.2 | | | | | Total Current | 45.2 | 50.3 |
| | 36.7 | 34.9 | | | | N | Fixed Assets (net) | 40.5 | 38.8 |
| | .4 | .9 | | | | O | Intangibles (net) | 4.7 | 2.6 |
| | 7.1 | 21.9 | | | | T | All Other Non-Current | 9.6 | 8.4 |
| | 100.0 | 100.0 | | | | | Total | 100.0 | 100.0 |
| | | | | | | A | LIABILITIES | | |
| | 9.6 | 9.0 | | | | V | Notes Payable-Short Term | 16.7 | 15.0 |
| | 4.6 | 3.8 | | | | A | Cur. Mat.-L.T.D. | 13.7 | 11.4 |
| | 9.9 | 14.6 | | | | I | Trade Payables | 16.7 | 20.1 |
| | .0 | .6 | | | | L | Income Taxes Payable | .3 | .9 |
| | 8.1 | 15.8 | | | | A | All Other Current | 11.2 | 11.7 |
| | 32.1 | 43.8 | | | | B | Total Current | 58.6 | 59.2 |
| | 33.3 | 21.5 | | | | L | Long-Term Debt | 26.1 | 39.0 |
| | 1.5 | 1.9 | | | | E | Deferred Taxes | .4 | .9 |
| | 3.3 | 4.0 | | | | | All Other Non-Current | 4.0 | 4.8 |
| | 29.7 | 28.7 | | | | | Net Worth | 10.8 | -3.9 |
| | 100.0 | 100.0 | | | | | Total Liabilties & Net Worth | 100.0 | 100.0 |
| | | | | | | | INCOME DATA | | |
| | 100.0 | 100.0 | | | | | Net Sales | 100.0 | 100.0 |
| | | | | | | | Gross Profit | | |
| | 99.5 | 96.3 | | | | | Operating Expenses | 90.1 | 88.2 |
| | .5 | 3.7 | | | | | Operating Profit | 9.9 | 11.8 |
| | .6 | .3 | | | | | All Other Expenses (net) | 3.1 | 4.2 |
| | -.1 | 3.4 | | | | | Profit Before Taxes | 6.8 | 7.6 |
| | | | | | | | RATIOS | | |
| | 12.8 | 1.4 | | | | | | 3.2 | 2.7 |
| | 2.3 | 1.0 | | | | | Current | 1.0 | 1.1 |
| | .7 | .5 | | | | | | .6 | .4 |
| | 10.4 | 1.3 | | | | | | 2.4 | 2.0 |
| | 1.4 | .5 | | | | | Quick | .7 | .7 |
| | .7 | .2 | | | | | | .3 | .3 |
| 9 | 41.7 | 5 | 75.4 | | | | | 4 | 100.8 | 19 | 19.6 |
| 44 | 8.3 | 29 | 12.6 | | | | Sales/Receivables | 32 | 11.6 | 48 | 7.6 |
| 59 | 6.2 | 69 | 5.3 | | | | | 63 | 5.8 | 68 | 5.4 |
| | | | | | | | Cost of Sales/Inventory | | |
| | | | | | | | Cost of Sales/Payables | | |
| | 5.0 | 9.8 | | | | | | 7.1 | 6.2 |
| | 8.0 | NM | | | | | Sales/Working Capital | -162.0 | 18.8 |
| | -26.6 | -19.9 | | | | | | -10.0 | -6.9 |
| | 30.7 | 13.9 | | | | | | 8.6 | 9.2 |
| (11) | 4.6 | (13) | 2.2 | | | | EBIT/Interest | (20) | 2.2 | (21) | 1.8 |
| | 1.1 | 1.1 | | | | | | .1 | .1 |
| | | | | | | | Net Profit + Depr., Dep.,<br>Amort./Cur. Mat. L/T/D | | |
| | .3 | .7 | | | | | | .5 | .7 |
| | 1.6 | 1.1 | | | | | Fixed/Worth | 1.3 | 1.4 |
| | NM | 13.5 | | | | | | -2.7 | -31.5 |
| | .2 | 1.0 | | | | | | .7 | 1.1 |
| | 1.7 | 3.0 | | | | | Debt/Worth | 2.0 | 3.5 |
| | NM | 26.0 | | | | | | -7.2 | -44.3 |
| | | 54.9 | | | | | | 82.3 | 51.9 |
| | (12) | 13.1 | | | | | % Profit Before Taxes/Tangible<br>Net Worth | (20) | 44.9 | (18) | 19.7 |
| | | 1.4 | | | | | | 5.3 | 1.2 |
| | 21.3 | 17.9 | | | | | | 33.0 | 21.3 |
| | 12.2 | 1.7 | | | | | % Profit Before Taxes/Total<br>Assets | 8.8 | 9.7 |
| | .8 | -1.7 | | | | | | .6 | -.5 |
| | 23.0 | 19.8 | | | | | | 22.2 | 17.8 |
| | 14.4 | 10.4 | | | | | Sales/Net Fixed Assets | 8.9 | 5.9 |
| | 4.5 | 3.1 | | | | | | 3.3 | 3.0 |
| | 3.8 | 4.8 | | | | | | 4.5 | 3.9 |
| | 2.8 | 3.1 | | | | | Sales/Total Assets | 2.5 | 2.4 |
| | 1.9 | 1.3 | | | | | | 1.4 | .9 |
| | | 1.2 | | | | | | .9 | 2.1 |
| | (12) | 2.0 | | | | | % Depr., Dep., Amort./Sales | (18) | 3.1 | (19) | 3.8 |
| | | 2.5 | | | | | | 3.8 | 7.7 |
| | | | | | | | % Officers', Directors'<br>Owners' Comp/Sales | 5.9 | |
| | | | | | | | | (11) | 8.6 | |
| | | | | | | | | 15.8 | |
| 6787M | 53110M | 191465M | 37646M | 44221M | | | Net Sales ($) | 439095M | 304448M |
| 1664M | 13163M | 71674M | 56799M | 63443M | | | Total Assets ($) | 236851M | 140088M |

M = $ thousand    MM = $ million
See Pages 9 through 22 for Explanation of Ratios and Data

## Comparative Historical Data

## Current Data Sorted by Sales

| | | | | Type of Statement | | | | | | |
|---|---|---|---|---|---|---|---|---|---|---|
| | 1 | 2 | 1 | Unqualified | 1 | | | 2 | 2 | 2 |
| | 6 | 7 | 7 | Reviewed | | | | | | |
| | 2 | 2 | 3 | Compiled | 1 | | 1 | 1 | 1 | |
| | 8 | 3 | 8 | Tax Returns | 4 | 2 | 1 | 1 | | |
| | 10 | 17 | 18 | Other | 4 | 1 | 1 | 3 | 5 | 4 |
| | 4/1/09-3/31/10 | 4/1/10-3/31/11 | 4/1/11-3/31/12 | | | 5 (4/1-9/30/11) | | | 32 (10/1/11-3/31/12) | |
| | ALL | ALL | ALL | | 0-1MM | 1-3MM | 3-5MM | 5-10MM | 10-25MM | 25MM & OVER |
| | 27 | 31 | 37 | NUMBER OF STATEMENTS | 10 | 3 | 5 | 6 | 8 | 5 |
| | % | % | % | ASSETS | % | % | % | % | % | % |
| | 12.1 | 7.2 | 13.1 | Cash & Equivalents | 15.6 | | | | | |
| | 18.4 | 24.1 | 21.0 | Trade Receivables (net) | 11.2 | | | | | |
| | 5.6 | 3.9 | 5.4 | Inventory | 3.3 | | | | | |
| | 7.0 | 7.2 | 8.5 | All Other Current | 11.7 | | | | | |
| | 43.1 | 42.4 | 48.0 | Total Current | 41.7 | | | | | |
| | 41.3 | 43.2 | 37.1 | Fixed Assets (net) | 43.9 | | | | | |
| | 7.3 | 5.5 | 3.0 | Intangibles (net) | .3 | | | | | |
| | 8.3 | 8.9 | 11.9 | All Other Non-Current | 14.0 | | | | | |
| | 100.0 | 100.0 | 100.0 | Total | 100.0 | | | | | |
| | | | | LIABILITIES | | | | | | |
| | 13.3 | 22.6 | 10.4 | Notes Payable-Short Term | 6.6 | | | | | |
| | 7.0 | 8.5 | 5.1 | Cur. Mat.-L.T.D. | 7.3 | | | | | |
| | 12.1 | 16.5 | 11.2 | Trade Payables | 4.7 | | | | | |
| | .1 | .3 | .3 | Income Taxes Payable | .2 | | | | | |
| | 26.5 | 18.4 | 12.0 | All Other Current | 5.3 | | | | | |
| | 58.9 | 66.2 | 39.0 | Total Current | 24.1 | | | | | |
| | 29.9 | 19.3 | 28.7 | Long-Term Debt | 30.0 | | | | | |
| | .9 | .7 | 1.5 | Deferred Taxes | 1.5 | | | | | |
| | 7.3 | 4.6 | 11.4 | All Other Non-Current | 30.6 | | | | | |
| | 3.0 | 9.3 | 19.5 | Net Worth | 13.8 | | | | | |
| | 100.0 | 100.0 | 100.0 | Total Liabilties & Net Worth | 100.0 | | | | | |
| | | | | INCOME DATA | | | | | | |
| | 100.0 | 100.0 | 100.0 | Net Sales | 100.0 | | | | | |
| | | | | Gross Profit | | | | | | |
| | 95.3 | 90.0 | 96.3 | Operating Expenses | 94.7 | | | | | |
| | 4.7 | 10.0 | 3.7 | Operating Profit | 5.3 | | | | | |
| | 3.2 | 2.0 | .8 | All Other Expenses (net) | 2.7 | | | | | |
| | 1.5 | 8.1 | 2.9 | Profit Before Taxes | 2.6 | | | | | |
| | | | | RATIOS | | | | | | |
| | 1.5 | 2.5 | 2.4 | | 5.5 | | | | | |
| | .9 | 1.1 | 1.2 | Current | 1.9 | | | | | |
| | .4 | .6 | .6 | | .6 | | | | | |
| | 1.0 | 2.1 | 2.2 | | 3.4 | | | | | |
| | .7 | .8 | .7 | Quick | .8 | | | | | |
| | .2 | .3 | .3 | | .2 | | | | | |
| | 2  222.7 | 2  196.0 | 6  64.8 | | 14  26.2 | | | | | |
| | 23  15.9 | 41  9.0 | 29  12.4 | Sales/Receivables | 28  13.2 | | | | | |
| | 61  6.0 | 62  5.9 | 59  6.2 | | 42  8.7 | | | | | |
| | | | | Cost of Sales/Inventory | | | | | | |
| | | | | Cost of Sales/Payables | | | | | | |
| | 9.7 | 7.6 | 5.5 | | 4.8 | | | | | |
| | -75.0 | 23.3 | 17.1 | Sales/Working Capital | 9.2 | | | | | |
| | -11.7 | -15.0 | -20.8 | | -18.4 | | | | | |
| | 3.5 | 12.1 | 12.1 | | | | | | | |
| | (22) 1.0 | (25) 4.6 | (33) 3.4 | EBIT/Interest | | | | | | |
| | -.5 | .3 | 1.3 | | | | | | | |
| | | | | Net Profit + Depr., Dep., Amort./Cur. Mat. L/T/D | | | | | | |
| | .9 | .6 | .5 | | .4 | | | | | |
| | 5.4 | 1.6 | 1.5 | Fixed/Worth | .6 | | | | | |
| | -2.1 | UND | NM | | NM | | | | | |
| | 1.3 | 1.0 | .7 | | .1 | | | | | |
| | 7.9 | 4.3 | 3.0 | Debt/Worth | .8 | | | | | |
| | -6.5 | UND | NM | | NM | | | | | |
| | 36.0 | 57.2 | 53.4 | % Profit Before Taxes/Tangible Net Worth | | | | | | |
| | (18) 7.7 | (24) 39.7 | (28) 29.9 | | | | | | | |
| | -25.5 | -36.0 | 4.9 | | | | | | | |
| | 8.0 | 26.6 | 23.5 | % Profit Before Taxes/Total Assets | 25.5 | | | | | |
| | .0 | 10.7 | 9.3 | | 13.3 | | | | | |
| | -7.4 | -.8 | .5 | | -9.4 | | | | | |
| | 19.3 | 17.7 | 18.4 | | 8.7 | | | | | |
| | 12.0 | 8.9 | 10.2 | Sales/Net Fixed Assets | 3.2 | | | | | |
| | 3.1 | 2.1 | 2.9 | | 1.3 | | | | | |
| | 5.8 | 3.8 | 3.6 | | 2.5 | | | | | |
| | 1.9 | 2.5 | 2.6 | Sales/Total Assets | 1.5 | | | | | |
| | 1.2 | .9 | 1.3 | | .9 | | | | | |
| | 3.3 | 2.2 | 1.5 | | | | | | | |
| | (19) 4.6 | (25) 2.9 | (27) 2.2 | % Depr., Dep., Amort./Sales | | | | | | |
| | 6.1 | 7.0 | 5.9 | | | | | | | |
| | 4.5 | 2.4 | 3.6 | % Officers', Directors' Owners' Comp/Sales | | | | | | |
| | (12) 6.4 | (12) 4.7 | (18) 8.6 | | | | | | | |
| | 18.7 | 9.9 | 16.4 | | | | | | | |
| | 196316M | 261483M | 333229M | Net Sales ($) | 5239M | 5264M | 17948M | 38534M | 111126M | 155118M |
| | 127408M | 181007M | 206743M | Total Assets ($) | 12592M | 2164M | 8983M | 19641M | 63016M | 100347M |

© RMA 2012

M = $ thousand    MM = $ million

See Pages 9 through 22 for Explanation of Ratios and Data

## Current Data Sorted by Assets

## Comparative Historical Data

| Type of Statement | 0-500M | 500M-2MM | 2-10MM | 10-50MM | 50-100MM | 100-250MM | 4/1/07-3/31/08 ALL | 4/1/08-3/31/09 ALL |
|---|---|---|---|---|---|---|---|---|
| Unqualified | 2 | 2 | 2 | 1 | 5 | | 6 | 6 |
| Reviewed | 46 | 33 | 9 | 2 | 1 | | 12 | 11 |
| Compiled | 212 | 88 | 8 | 1 | | | 72 | 78 |
| Tax Returns | 118 | 62 | 16 | | | 1 | 158 | 194 |
| Other | | | 32 | 4 | | 1 | 103 | 107 |
| | 29 (4/1-9/30/11) | | | 617 (10/1/11-3/31/12) | | | | |
| **NUMBER OF STATEMENTS** | 378 | 185 | 67 | 8 | 6 | 2 | 351 | 396 |
| **ASSETS** | % | % | % | % | % | % | % | % |
| Cash & Equivalents | 27.3 | 14.0 | 12.1 | | | | 19.3 | 19.0 |
| Trade Receivables (net) | 5.3 | 3.0 | 6.3 | | | | 6.7 | 4.6 |
| Inventory | 12.4 | 4.7 | 4.9 | | | | 10.1 | 11.0 |
| All Other Current | 2.5 | .5 | 1.0 | | | | 2.8 | 2.7 |
| Total Current | 47.4 | 22.3 | 24.2 | | | | 38.9 | 37.3 |
| Fixed Assets (net) | 31.6 | 46.1 | 57.6 | | | | 37.8 | 36.7 |
| Intangibles (net) | 11.2 | 20.4 | 11.1 | | | | 12.7 | 15.7 |
| All Other Non-Current | 9.8 | 11.2 | 7.1 | | | | 10.6 | 10.4 |
| Total | 100.0 | 100.0 | 100.0 | | | | 100.0 | 100.0 |
| **LIABILITIES** | | | | | | | | |
| Notes Payable-Short Term | 13.8 | 5.3 | 4.2 | | | | 10.0 | 10.2 |
| Cur. Mat.-L.T.D. | 6.1 | 4.9 | 4.9 | | | | 5.2 | 5.4 |
| Trade Payables | 11.1 | 4.8 | 5.4 | | | | 8.3 | 9.2 |
| Income Taxes Payable | .1 | .1 | .0 | | | | .1 | .1 |
| All Other Current | 17.0 | 6.8 | 6.6 | | | | 13.1 | 15.6 |
| Total Current | 48.0 | 21.9 | 21.1 | | | | 36.6 | 40.4 |
| Long-Term Debt | 38.7 | 55.1 | 49.6 | | | | 36.5 | 38.9 |
| Deferred Taxes | .0 | .1 | .1 | | | | .1 | .1 |
| All Other Non-Current | 8.9 | 3.6 | 1.6 | | | | 7.8 | 5.7 |
| Net Worth | 4.4 | 19.3 | 27.6 | | | | 19.0 | 14.9 |
| Total Liabilities & Net Worth | 100.0 | 100.0 | 100.0 | | | | 100.0 | 100.0 |
| **INCOME DATA** | | | | | | | | |
| Net Sales | 100.0 | 100.0 | 100.0 | | | | 100.0 | 100.0 |
| Gross Profit | | | | | | | | |
| Operating Expenses | 91.5 | 85.7 | 79.6 | | | | 89.8 | 90.0 |
| Operating Profit | 8.5 | 14.3 | 20.4 | | | | 10.2 | 10.0 |
| All Other Expenses (net) | 1.4 | 5.7 | 11.3 | | | | 2.0 | 3.1 |
| Profit Before Taxes | 7.2 | 8.6 | 9.0 | | | | 8.2 | 6.9 |
| **RATIOS** | | | | | | | | |
| Current | 3.5 | 2.8 | 2.7 | | | | 3.0 | 2.9 |
| | 1.2 | 1.0 | 1.2 | | | | 1.2 | 1.1 |
| | .5 | .3 | .5 | | | | .5 | .4 |
| Quick | 2.4 | 2.2 | 2.3 | | | | 2.1 | 1.8 |
| | (376) .8 | .7 | .8 | | | | (350) .7 | .6 |
| | .2 | .2 | .3 | | | | .2 | .2 |
| Sales/Receivables | 0 UND | 0 UND | 0 UND | | | | 0 UND | 0 UND |
| | 0 UND | 0 UND | 0 999.8 | | | | 0 UND | 0 UND |
| | 3 143.3 | 3 105.0 | 6 62.8 | | | | 4 81.8 | 3 132.2 |
| Cost of Sales/Inventory | | | | | | | | |
| Cost of Sales/Payables | | | | | | | | |
| Sales/Working Capital | 17.9 | 18.9 | 11.6 | | | | 17.3 | 19.2 |
| | 116.4 | 200.8 | 64.9 | | | | 85.4 | 400.0 |
| | -28.8 | -15.1 | -7.8 | | | | -30.1 | -16.2 |
| EBIT/Interest | 26.4 | 10.6 | 13.0 | | | | 16.4 | 12.7 |
| | (285) 6.3 | (147) 4.5 | (49) 3.6 | | | | (279) 4.9 | (301) 3.4 |
| | 2.0 | 1.4 | 1.5 | | | | 1.5 | 1.0 |
| Net Profit + Depr., Dep., Amort./Cur. Mat. L/T/D | | | | | | | 7.1 | 5.2 |
| | | | | | | | (14) 3.5 | (16) 4.1 |
| | | | | | | | 2.1 | .7 |
| Fixed/Worth | .2 | 1.6 | 1.2 | | | | .5 | .5 |
| | 1.8 | 8.4 | 3.3 | | | | 2.2 | 4.4 |
| | -1.2 | -1.5 | 30.4 | | | | -2.0 | -1.1 |
| Debt/Worth | .7 | 1.7 | 1.5 | | | | .8 | 1.1 |
| | 6.3 | 9.6 | 3.6 | | | | 3.8 | 15.0 |
| | -3.1 | -4.2 | 47.0 | | | | -5.2 | -3.2 |
| % Profit Before Taxes/Tangible Net Worth | 213.8 | 113.5 | 76.5 | | | | 227.0 | 180.8 |
| | (228) 78.6 | (111) 52.5 | (52) 33.1 | | | | (232) 83.6 | (220) 62.8 |
| | 30.1 | 14.3 | 9.8 | | | | 31.2 | 20.7 |
| % Profit Before Taxes/Total Assets | 67.2 | 29.7 | 16.1 | | | | 58.3 | 46.8 |
| | 29.0 | 9.1 | 5.7 | | | | 21.1 | 14.9 |
| | 6.3 | 1.9 | 1.8 | | | | 3.9 | .7 |
| Sales/Net Fixed Assets | 131.5 | 32.2 | 9.6 | | | | 63.9 | 62.9 |
| | 28.8 | 7.7 | 2.8 | | | | 15.5 | 20.5 |
| | 10.9 | 2.0 | .4 | | | | 5.6 | 6.7 |
| Sales/Total Assets | 10.8 | 3.6 | 2.9 | | | | 8.1 | 9.3 |
| | 6.6 | 2.0 | 1.6 | | | | 3.8 | 4.4 |
| | 3.6 | 1.1 | .3 | | | | 2.1 | 2.0 |
| % Depr., Dep., Amort./Sales | .8 | 1.8 | 2.3 | | | | .9 | 1.0 |
| | (199) 1.8 | (120) 3.1 | (55) 4.0 | | | | (242) 2.0 | (246) 2.0 |
| | 3.6 | 7.0 | 9.9 | | | | 3.8 | 4.2 |
| % Officers', Directors' Owners' Comp/Sales | 6.4 | 4.3 | 5.3 | | | | 5.5 | 5.3 |
| | (261) 9.6 | (100) 8.8 | (22) 6.7 | | | | (218) 9.4 | (243) 9.0 |
| | 14.2 | 13.8 | 15.0 | | | | 15.3 | 15.1 |
| Net Sales ($) | 539286M | 498367M | 543008M | 356104M | 451573M | 2772012M | 6697572M | 3343372M |
| Total Assets ($) | 85299M | 193934M | 268173M | 132397M | 430625M | 348424M | 1671296M | 1013487M |

M = $ thousand    MM = $ million
See Pages 9 through 22 for Explanation of Ratios and Data

## Comparative Historical Data | Current Data Sorted by Sales

| Type of Statement | Hist 1 | Hist 2 | Hist 3 | 0-1MM | 1-3MM | 3-5MM | 5-10MM | 10-25MM | 25MM & OVER |
|---|---|---|---|---|---|---|---|---|---|
| Unqualified | 8 | 7 | 8 | | | | 2 | | 6 |
| Reviewed | 13 | 12 | 16 | 1 | 2 | 2 | 1 | 6 | 4 |
| Compiled | 74 | 84 | 88 | 25 | 40 | 11 | 8 | 2 | 2 |
| Tax Returns | 280 | 251 | 317 | 110 | 162 | 26 | 14 | 2 | 3 |
| Other | 132 | 164 | 217 | 70 | 103 | 16 | 12 | 11 | 5 |
| | 4/1/09-3/31/10 ALL | 4/1/10-3/31/11 ALL | 4/1/11-3/31/12 ALL | 29 (4/1-9/30/11) | | | 617 (10/1/11-3/31/12) | | |
| **NUMBER OF STATEMENTS** | 507 | 518 | 646 | 206 | 307 | 55 | 37 | 21 | 20 |
| | % | % | % | % | % | % | % | % | % |
| **ASSETS** | | | | | | | | | |
| Cash & Equivalents | 18.4 | 20.7 | 21.6 | 19.1 | 23.6 | 23.0 | 22.5 | 18.1 | 16.2 |
| Trade Receivables (net) | 4.6 | 4.4 | 4.8 | 3.4 | 4.3 | 5.1 | 8.9 | 11.8 | 10.6 |
| Inventory | 8.4 | 8.6 | 9.4 | 8.8 | 9.4 | 10.2 | 9.0 | 8.6 | 13.7 |
| All Other Current | 1.6 | 2.3 | 1.7 | 2.4 | 1.4 | 1.5 | 1.4 | 2.3 | 1.5 |
| Total Current | 33.1 | 36.1 | 37.5 | 33.7 | 38.7 | 39.7 | 41.8 | 40.9 | 42.0 |
| Fixed Assets (net) | 40.5 | 39.7 | 38.5 | 43.3 | 36.6 | 36.3 | 35.3 | 40.1 | 30.1 |
| Intangibles (net) | 16.4 | 14.3 | 13.9 | 15.0 | 13.6 | 14.9 | 12.7 | 7.3 | 13.3 |
| All Other Non-Current | 10.0 | 9.9 | 10.0 | 8.0 | 11.1 | 9.1 | 10.3 | 11.8 | 14.6 |
| Total | 100.0 | 100.0 | 100.0 | 100.0 | 100.0 | 100.0 | 100.0 | 100.0 | 100.0 |
| **LIABILITIES** | | | | | | | | | |
| Notes Payable-Short Term | 12.2 | 11.2 | 10.2 | 11.4 | 10.5 | 10.5 | 3.7 | 4.3 | 9.1 |
| Cur. Mat.-L.T.D. | 5.8 | 6.0 | 5.6 | 5.0 | 5.6 | 7.2 | 5.3 | 6.7 | 5.6 |
| Trade Payables | 8.2 | 10.6 | 8.6 | 5.6 | 9.3 | 10.4 | 15.2 | 7.7 | 13.5 |
| Income Taxes Payable | .0 | .1 | .1 | .0 | .1 | .2 | .0 | .0 | .0 |
| All Other Current | 16.0 | 13.8 | 12.7 | 14.3 | 12.1 | 13.1 | 12.3 | 11.1 | 7.9 |
| Total Current | 42.1 | 41.7 | 37.1 | 36.4 | 37.5 | 41.3 | 36.4 | 29.8 | 36.2 |
| Long-Term Debt | 45.4 | 44.3 | 44.1 | 51.8 | 41.8 | 37.2 | 40.2 | 55.9 | 13.9 |
| Deferred Taxes | .1 | .1 | .0 | .1 | .0 | .0 | .1 | .0 | .0 |
| All Other Non-Current | 4.5 | 11.9 | 6.5 | 10.6 | 5.0 | 2.9 | 2.5 | 7.4 | 3.2 |
| Net Worth | 7.9 | 2.0 | 12.3 | 1.2 | 15.7 | 18.5 | 20.8 | 6.9 | 46.8 |
| Total Liabilities & Net Worth | 100.0 | 100.0 | 100.0 | 100.0 | 100.0 | 100.0 | 100.0 | 100.0 | 100.0 |
| **INCOME DATA** | | | | | | | | | |
| Net Sales | 100.0 | 100.0 | 100.0 | 100.0 | 100.0 | 100.0 | 100.0 | 100.0 | 100.0 |
| Gross Profit | | | | | | | | | |
| Operating Expenses | 90.4 | 89.7 | 88.7 | 81.3 | 91.6 | 90.8 | 96.3 | 93.5 | 95.4 |
| Operating Profit | 9.6 | 10.3 | 11.3 | 18.7 | 8.4 | 9.2 | 3.7 | 6.5 | 4.6 |
| All Other Expenses (net) | 3.4 | 2.9 | 3.7 | 8.9 | 1.4 | .9 | .8 | .5 | 1.7 |
| Profit Before Taxes | 6.2 | 7.4 | 7.6 | 9.8 | 7.0 | 8.3 | 2.9 | 6.0 | 2.9 |
| **RATIOS** | | | | | | | | | |
| Current | 2.5 | 3.1 | 3.2 | 3.5 | 3.2 | 3.5 | 2.9 | 2.9 | 2.3 |
| | .9 | 1.0 | 1.2 | .9 | 1.2 | 1.3 | 1.3 | 1.6 | 1.4 |
| | .4 | .4 | .5 | .3 | .5 | .6 | .6 | 1.2 | .6 |
| Quick | 1.8 | 2.2 | 2.3 | 2.6 | 2.3 | 2.2 | 2.5 | 2.4 | 1.7 |
| | (506) .5 | (517) .6 | (644) .8 | (205) .5 | (306) .8 | 1.0 | .8 | 1.2 | .8 |
| | .2 | .2 | .3 | .1 | .3 | .3 | .5 | .6 | .4 |
| Sales/Receivables | 0 UND | 0 UND | 0 UND | 0 UND | 0 UND | 0 UND | 0 UND | 0 999.8 | 1 527.6 |
| | 0 UND | 0 UND | 0 UND | 0 UND | 0 UND | 0 UND | 2 162.5 | 3 114.1 | 5 79.7 |
| | 3 108.7 | 3 106.4 | 3 105.1 | 1 260.6 | 3 122.8 | 3 107.2 | 9 42.8 | 20 18.1 | 24 15.2 |
| Cost of Sales/Inventory | | | | | | | | | |
| Cost of Sales/Payables | | | | | | | | | |
| Sales/Working Capital | 20.4 | 17.6 | 17.0 | 13.8 | 19.0 | 18.9 | 15.4 | 12.0 | 8.9 |
| | -202.0 | 999.8 | 116.4 | -193.9 | 109.9 | 118.3 | 36.7 | 25.3 | 55.2 |
| | -15.1 | -15.8 | -21.6 | -7.6 | -29.2 | -38.3 | -62.0 | 119.5 | -183.4 |
| EBIT/Interest | 12.2 | 16.8 | 18.0 | 9.0 | 20.4 | 30.1 | 16.3 | 17.4 | 25.6 |
| | (391) 3.6 | (404) 4.1 | (495) 5.3 | (126) 3.7 | (252) 5.9 | (48) 11.4 | (33) 5.0 | (18) 9.4 | (18) 8.2 |
| | .9 | 1.3 | 1.7 | .9 | 1.8 | 4.2 | 1.4 | 2.8 | .4 |
| Net Profit + Depr., Dep., Amort./Cur. Mat. L/T/D | 7.0 | 5.4 | 9.7 | | | | | | |
| | (19) 4.8 | (14) 1.5 | (19) 1.6 | | | | | | |
| | 1.1 | .8 | .7 | | | | | | |
| Fixed/Worth | .7 | .7 | .5 | .5 | .5 | .7 | 1.0 | .8 | .3 |
| | 15.1 | 4.2 | 3.3 | 6.0 | 2.9 | 2.6 | 2.7 | 2.4 | .7 |
| | -.8 | -.8 | -1.8 | -1.0 | -1.7 | -1.5 | -1.7 | -4.4 | 2.8 |
| Debt/Worth | 1.2 | 1.0 | .9 | 1.2 | .9 | .9 | 1.4 | 1.1 | .5 |
| | 69.0 | 12.5 | 6.9 | 12.3 | 6.0 | 5.2 | 7.0 | 4.6 | 1.2 |
| | -2.7 | -3.0 | -3.9 | -2.2 | -4.5 | -3.1 | -6.2 | -8.6 | 9.3 |
| % Profit Before Taxes/Tangible Net Worth | 201.1 | 180.8 | 162.4 | 95.2 | 192.6 | 217.5 | 200.1 | 117.0 | 126.9 |
| | (265) 61.4 | (292) 61.4 | (404) 62.4 | (123) 40.7 | (193) 76.8 | (34) 89.1 | (21) 55.3 | (15) 51.6 | (18) 38.4 |
| | 13.1 | 13.8 | 20.3 | 10.7 | 24.0 | 48.6 | 12.0 | 33.8 | 4.3 |
| % Profit Before Taxes/Total Assets | 46.5 | 41.6 | 48.3 | 37.2 | 50.2 | 68.2 | 49.6 | 29.8 | 23.4 |
| | 13.6 | 14.2 | 17.6 | 8.7 | 20.4 | 33.0 | 13.2 | 20.0 | 13.8 |
| | .0 | 1.9 | 3.3 | .4 | 4.6 | 7.8 | 2.5 | 13.8 | .1 |
| Sales/Net Fixed Assets | 45.3 | 52.6 | 67.7 | 49.7 | 85.0 | 62.8 | 56.7 | 31.9 | 59.4 |
| | 15.6 | 15.7 | 17.4 | 10.4 | 21.5 | 21.4 | 18.1 | 9.6 | 10.6 |
| | 4.6 | 4.4 | 4.9 | 1.7 | 6.9 | 8.6 | 5.1 | 5.3 | 3.5 |
| Sales/Total Assets | 7.6 | 7.8 | 7.8 | 5.6 | 9.0 | 10.2 | 7.6 | 4.7 | 5.2 |
| | 3.8 | 3.8 | 3.9 | 2.6 | 4.6 | 6.2 | 5.2 | 3.4 | 3.1 |
| | 1.8 | 1.8 | 1.9 | .7 | 2.6 | 2.4 | 2.2 | 2.6 | 1.9 |
| % Depr., Dep., Amort./Sales | 1.1 | 1.1 | 1.3 | 1.6 | 1.0 | 1.3 | 1.8 | 1.8 | .8 |
| | (347) 2.5 | (323) 2.4 | (385) 2.5 | (118) 5.0 | (168) 2.2 | (38) 1.6 | (27) 2.4 | (19) 2.6 | (15) 2.5 |
| | 4.9 | 4.6 | 5.2 | 14.4 | 4.5 | 2.9 | 3.5 | 4.0 | 3.5 |
| % Officers', Directors' Owners' Comp/Sales | 5.8 | 5.4 | 5.7 | 7.7 | 5.6 | 4.9 | 2.7 | | |
| | (321) 9.6 | (336) 8.4 | (387) 9.1 | (101) 10.5 | (213) 8.7 | (39) 8.6 | (20) 8.7 | | |
| | 14.0 | 14.0 | 14.1 | 14.9 | 13.3 | 16.7 | 15.7 | | |
| Net Sales ($) | 7263151M | 3612776M | 5160350M | 118063M | 530393M | 204948M | 265607M | 285807M | 3755532M |
| Total Assets ($) | 1510029M | 1116320M | 1458852M | 115666M | 184740M | 54372M | 103463M | 88056M | 912555M |

© RMA 2012

M = $ thousand    MM = $ million
See Pages 9 through 22 for Explanation of Ratios and Data

## Current Data Sorted by Assets | Comparative Historical Data

| Type of Statement | 0-500M | 500M-2MM | 2-10MM | 10-50MM | 50-100MM | 100-250MM | 4/1/07-3/31/08 ALL | 4/1/08-3/31/09 ALL |
|---|---|---|---|---|---|---|---|---|
| Unqualified | 4 | 9 | 46 | 49 | 8 | 11 | 99 | 83 |
| Reviewed | 8 | 25 | 66 | 18 | 1 | | 76 | 71 |
| Compiled | 30 | 52 | 50 | 5 | | | 105 | 90 |
| Tax Returns | 207 | 155 | 56 | 3 | | 1 | 242 | 314 |
| Other | 113 | 186 | 166 | 53 | 17 | 5 | 331 | 283 |
| | | 121 (4/1-9/30/11) | | 1,223 (10/1/11-3/31/12) | | | | |
| NUMBER OF STATEMENTS | 362 | 427 | 384 | 128 | 26 | 17 | 853 | 841 |
| **ASSETS** | % | % | % | % | % | % | % | % |
| Cash & Equivalents | 34.7 | 18.2 | 15.7 | 13.4 | 10.9 | 18.6 | 19.3 | 20.6 |
| Trade Receivables (net) | 19.0 | 28.7 | 36.9 | 30.2 | 26.4 | 24.5 | 28.3 | 28.1 |
| Inventory | 3.4 | 5.7 | 6.0 | 6.7 | 5.2 | 5.8 | 6.8 | 5.5 |
| All Other Current | 3.5 | 3.3 | 4.5 | 5.1 | 4.4 | 4.9 | 4.9 | 4.1 |
| Total Current | 60.6 | 55.9 | 63.2 | 55.5 | 46.9 | 53.8 | 59.3 | 58.3 |
| Fixed Assets (net) | 22.2 | 26.6 | 20.6 | 20.3 | 23.4 | 14.8 | 25.2 | 24.1 |
| Intangibles (net) | 3.0 | 6.0 | 5.9 | 15.0 | 23.1 | 28.1 | 4.9 | 5.6 |
| All Other Non-Current | 14.3 | 11.5 | 10.3 | 9.2 | 6.6 | 3.4 | 10.5 | 11.9 |
| Total | 100.0 | 100.0 | 100.0 | 100.0 | 100.0 | 100.0 | 100.0 | 100.0 |
| **LIABILITIES** | | | | | | | | |
| Notes Payable-Short Term | 30.8 | 12.0 | 8.8 | 6.5 | 4.7 | 9.6 | 14.5 | 15.5 |
| Cur. Mat.-L.T.D. | 4.8 | 2.7 | 2.8 | 3.4 | 3.2 | 1.0 | 3.5 | 4.4 |
| Trade Payables | 9.4 | 11.6 | 11.8 | 13.7 | 8.8 | 10.7 | 13.1 | 11.4 |
| Income Taxes Payable | .2 | .1 | .5 | .4 | .2 | .2 | .4 | .2 |
| All Other Current | 22.8 | 14.7 | 16.4 | 14.3 | 19.3 | 15.8 | 17.6 | 17.5 |
| Total Current | 68.0 | 41.1 | 40.3 | 38.3 | 36.3 | 37.3 | 49.1 | 49.1 |
| Long-Term Debt | 21.5 | 19.4 | 14.1 | 15.3 | 19.1 | 16.1 | 18.2 | 17.3 |
| Deferred Taxes | .3 | .3 | .3 | .4 | 1.2 | 2.8 | .2 | .2 |
| All Other Non-Current | 18.5 | 8.8 | 6.4 | 9.2 | 11.6 | 7.2 | 6.3 | 7.4 |
| Net Worth | -8.2 | 30.4 | 38.9 | 36.8 | 31.8 | 36.7 | 26.1 | 26.0 |
| Total Liabilties & Net Worth | 100.0 | 100.0 | 100.0 | 100.0 | 100.0 | 100.0 | 100.0 | 100.0 |
| **INCOME DATA** | | | | | | | | |
| Net Sales | 100.0 | 100.0 | 100.0 | 100.0 | 100.0 | 100.0 | 100.0 | 100.0 |
| Gross Profit | | | | | | | | |
| Operating Expenses | 90.0 | 89.6 | 90.9 | 89.4 | 87.2 | 88.1 | 89.8 | 90.6 |
| Operating Profit | 10.0 | 10.4 | 9.1 | 10.6 | 12.8 | 11.9 | 10.2 | 9.4 |
| All Other Expenses (net) | 1.0 | 2.3 | 1.7 | 2.8 | 7.0 | 2.9 | 2.1 | 2.0 |
| Profit Before Taxes | 9.0 | 8.0 | 7.3 | 7.8 | 5.8 | 9.0 | 8.2 | 7.4 |
| **RATIOS** | | | | | | | | |
| Current | 3.8 | 3.3 | 3.3 | 2.4 | 1.9 | 2.7 | 2.9 | 3.0 |
| | 1.2 | 1.6 | 1.6 | 1.4 | 1.3 | 1.6 | 1.4 | 1.4 |
| | .5 | .8 | 1.0 | 1.0 | 1.0 | 1.3 | .8 | .8 |
| Quick | 3.2 | 2.5 | 2.7 | 1.9 | 1.7 | 1.9 | 2.4 | 2.5 |
| | 1.0 | (426) 1.2 | 1.4 | 1.0 | 1.0 | 1.5 | 1.1 | 1.2 |
| | .4 | .6 | .7 | .6 | .7 | 1.0 | .5 | .5 |
| Sales/Receivables | 0 UND | 0 UND | 27 13.7 | 31 11.6 | 30 12.2 | 36 10.2 | 0 UND | 0 UND |
| | 0 UND | 29 12.6 | 47 7.7 | 49 7.4 | 49 7.5 | 65 5.6 | 29 12.8 | 29 12.8 |
| | 26 14.3 | 51 7.2 | 72 5.1 | 76 4.8 | 101 3.6 | 89 4.1 | 62 5.9 | 57 6.4 |
| Cost of Sales/Inventory | | | | | | | | |
| Cost of Sales/Payables | | | | | | | | |
| Sales/Working Capital | 12.5 | 7.6 | 5.2 | 5.0 | 2.6 | 2.4 | 6.6 | 7.1 |
| | 114.4 | 20.6 | 11.2 | 14.9 | 25.1 | 6.8 | 20.8 | 23.8 |
| | -25.4 | -48.9 | 161.3 | UND | -58.6 | 16.3 | -54.3 | -42.1 |
| EBIT/Interest | 26.9 | 25.9 | 39.4 | 27.8 | 10.8 | 15.8 | 16.9 | 26.6 |
| | (233) 6.9 | (291) 6.8 | (298) 9.1 | (98) 6.3 | (17) 3.2 | (15) 5.9 | (644) 5.1 | (621) 6.5 |
| | 1.2 | 1.4 | 1.8 | 1.5 | .8 | 1.3 | 1.5 | 1.4 |
| Net Profit + Depr., Dep., Amort./Cur. Mat. L/T/D | | 6.4 | 7.3 | 6.4 | | | 7.2 | 7.1 |
| | | (17) 3.2 | (40) 3.0 | (25) 2.5 | | | (71) 3.1 | (58) 3.5 |
| | | 1.1 | 1.3 | .9 | | | .9 | 1.5 |
| Fixed/Worth | .0 | .1 | .1 | .1 | .3 | .2 | .1 | .1 |
| | .6 | .6 | .4 | .6 | 2.4 | .8 | .6 | .7 |
| | -4.0 | 7.2 | 2.0 | 4.4 | -.3 | -.3 | 4.7 | 6.8 |
| Debt/Worth | .5 | .6 | .6 | .8 | 1.6 | .9 | .6 | .6 |
| | 4.1 | 1.8 | 1.6 | 2.4 | 3.5 | 2.6 | 2.3 | 2.7 |
| | -4.6 | 16.2 | 5.9 | 14.6 | -3.2 | -3.7 | 66.2 | 342.5 |
| % Profit Before Taxes/Tangible Net Worth | 337.3 | 86.5 | 71.6 | 58.8 | 56.5 | 24.0 | 93.6 | 101.3 |
| | (234) 92.8 | (339) 41.8 | (324) 34.8 | (102) 31.0 | (14) 12.5 | (10) 21.7 | (657) 40.6 | (643) 43.8 |
| | 32.0 | 9.3 | 7.0 | 8.2 | 5.2 | 18.0 | 11.3 | 9.3 |
| % Profit Before Taxes/Total Assets | 78.2 | 35.1 | 25.9 | 16.2 | 12.5 | 9.4 | 34.0 | 36.8 |
| | 28.1 | 12.3 | 11.0 | 7.8 | 4.2 | 5.4 | 12.0 | 13.2 |
| | 2.0 | 1.8 | 1.7 | 1.3 | -.6 | 1.1 | 1.4 | .9 |
| Sales/Net Fixed Assets | 999.8 | 105.9 | 86.3 | 66.7 | 37.5 | 40.2 | 86.4 | 124.7 |
| | 59.7 | 21.3 | 23.2 | 20.9 | 17.6 | 18.7 | 24.5 | 31.9 |
| | 18.9 | 6.8 | 7.5 | 5.6 | 3.1 | 2.8 | 7.1 | 7.5 |
| Sales/Total Assets | 13.1 | 4.8 | 3.4 | 2.6 | 1.5 | 1.4 | 4.8 | 5.8 |
| | 6.2 | 3.2 | 2.5 | 1.8 | 1.0 | .7 | 2.8 | 3.0 |
| | 3.5 | 1.8 | 1.6 | .9 | .3 | .5 | 1.6 | 1.6 |
| % Depr., Dep., Amort./Sales | .5 | .5 | .4 | .6 | 1.0 | .7 | .6 | .5 |
| | (155) 1.0 | (256) 1.3 | (278) 1.4 | (97) 1.9 | (18) 2.7 | (10) 2.4 | (584) 1.5 | (525) 1.5 |
| | 2.6 | 4.1 | 3.7 | 3.5 | 8.8 | 4.3 | 3.9 | 4.1 |
| % Officers', Directors' Owners' Comp/Sales | 5.1 | 5.0 | 2.1 | | | | 3.3 | 2.8 |
| | (192) 9.3 | (195) 5.6 | (119) 3.2 | | | | (327) 6.2 | (341) 6.1 |
| | 18.1 | 9.2 | 7.2 | | | | 13.0 | 12.0 |
| Net Sales ($) | 693472M | 1701704M | 4423936M | 5076343M | 2100903M | 6073854M | 12909839M | 16366600M |
| Total Assets ($) | 81534M | 479102M | 1683559M | 2761728M | 1876463M | 2786378M | 7953824M | 6377385M |

© RMA 2012

M = $ thousand    MM = $ million
See Pages 9 through 22 for Explanation of Ratios and Data

## Comparative Historical Data | Current Data Sorted by Sales

| | | | Type of Statement | 0-1MM | 1-3MM | 3-5MM | 5-10MM | 10-25MM | 25MM & OVER |
|---|---|---|---|---|---|---|---|---|---|
| 119 | 109 | 127 | Unqualified | 8 | 6 | 8 | 10 | 41 | 54 |
| 103 | 104 | 118 | Reviewed | 5 | 11 | 13 | 31 | 35 | 23 |
| 128 | 96 | 137 | Compiled | 18 | 33 | 23 | 37 | 20 | 6 |
| 334 | 346 | 422 | Tax Returns | 126 | 135 | 57 | 74 | 27 | 3 |
| 373 | 517 | 540 | Other | 85 | 125 | 68 | 111 | 93 | 58 |
| 4/1/09-3/31/10 ALL | 4/1/10-3/31/11 ALL | 4/1/11-3/31/12 ALL | | 121 (4/1-9/30/11) | | | 1,223 (10/1/11-3/31/12) | | |
| 1057 | 1172 | 1344 | NUMBER OF STATEMENTS | 242 | 310 | 169 | 263 | 216 | 144 |
| % | % | % | ASSETS | % | % | % | % | % | % |
| 20.6 | 20.3 | 21.4 | Cash & Equivalents | 28.6 | 22.6 | 20.8 | 21.7 | 16.4 | 13.7 |
| 27.3 | 29.6 | 28.5 | Trade Receivables (net) | 12.8 | 25.7 | 31.3 | 30.8 | 38.0 | 39.0 |
| 5.5 | 5.0 | 5.2 | Inventory | 2.4 | 4.1 | 6.9 | 7.0 | 6.4 | 5.6 |
| 4.4 | 4.0 | 3.9 | All Other Current | 3.4 | 2.9 | 3.6 | 3.9 | 5.0 | 5.7 |
| 57.8 | 59.0 | 59.0 | Total Current | 47.3 | 55.3 | 62.5 | 63.4 | 65.9 | 64.0 |
| 24.4 | 23.6 | 22.9 | Fixed Assets (net) | 34.0 | 26.2 | 21.0 | 19.2 | 17.7 | 13.7 |
| 6.1 | 6.2 | 6.6 | Intangibles (net) | 4.7 | 6.3 | 3.9 | 5.3 | 6.6 | 16.0 |
| 11.7 | 11.2 | 11.5 | All Other Non-Current | 14.0 | 12.2 | 12.5 | 12.2 | 9.8 | 6.3 |
| 100.0 | 100.0 | 100.0 | Total | 100.0 | 100.0 | 100.0 | 100.0 | 100.0 | 100.0 |
| | | | LIABILITIES | | | | | | |
| 16.1 | 13.7 | 15.5 | Notes Payable-Short Term | 19.5 | 19.6 | 14.5 | 14.5 | 11.5 | 8.7 |
| 3.8 | 3.2 | 3.3 | Cur. Mat.-L.T.D. | 2.7 | 4.7 | 4.0 | 2.9 | 2.1 | 3.3 |
| 10.6 | 11.0 | 11.2 | Trade Payables | 6.2 | 10.9 | 11.6 | 12.0 | 12.7 | 16.0 |
| .2 | .3 | .3 | Income Taxes Payable | .1 | .1 | .3 | .4 | .3 | .5 |
| 16.1 | 15.5 | 17.4 | All Other Current | 19.3 | 16.2 | 16.7 | 16.8 | 18.7 | 17.1 |
| 46.7 | 43.6 | 47.7 | Total Current | 47.8 | 51.5 | 47.1 | 46.7 | 45.3 | 45.5 |
| 17.1 | 16.9 | 18.0 | Long-Term Debt | 25.7 | 24.0 | 15.1 | 13.6 | 12.2 | 12.5 |
| .2 | .2 | .3 | Deferred Taxes | .0 | .4 | .0 | .5 | .4 | .9 |
| 7.2 | 9.8 | 10.8 | All Other Non-Current | 19.4 | 12.1 | 7.0 | 8.7 | 6.7 | 7.9 |
| 28.8 | 29.5 | 23.2 | Net Worth | 7.1 | 12.0 | 30.8 | 30.6 | 35.5 | 33.2 |
| 100.0 | 100.0 | 100.0 | Total Liabilities & Net Worth | 100.0 | 100.0 | 100.0 | 100.0 | 100.0 | 100.0 |
| | | | INCOME DATA | | | | | | |
| 100.0 | 100.0 | 100.0 | Net Sales | 100.0 | 100.0 | 100.0 | 100.0 | 100.0 | 100.0 |
| | | | Gross Profit | | | | | | |
| 91.8 | 91.1 | 90.0 | Operating Expenses | 80.5 | 91.8 | 93.1 | 91.9 | 91.6 | 92.6 |
| 8.2 | 8.9 | 10.0 | Operating Profit | 19.5 | 8.2 | 6.9 | 8.1 | 8.4 | 7.4 |
| 1.8 | 2.0 | 2.0 | All Other Expenses (net) | 6.3 | 1.0 | 1.4 | .4 | 1.0 | 1.5 |
| 6.4 | 6.9 | 8.0 | Profit Before Taxes | 13.2 | 7.2 | 5.5 | 7.6 | 7.4 | 5.8 |
| | | | RATIOS | | | | | | |
| 3.3 | 3.5 | 3.2 | Current | 4.8 | 3.4 | 3.7 | 2.9 | 2.8 | 2.2 |
| 1.5 | 1.6 | 1.5 | | 1.3 | 1.2 | 1.7 | 1.5 | 1.6 | 1.4 |
| .8 | .9 | .8 | | .4 | .7 | .9 | 1.0 | 1.0 | 1.0 |
| 2.7 | 3.1 | 2.7 | Quick | 4.3 | 2.8 | 2.7 | 2.5 | 2.5 | 1.8 |
| 1.2 | 1.3 (1343) | 1.2 | | (241) 1.1 | 1.1 | 1.4 | 1.2 | 1.3 | 1.2 |
| .6 | .6 | .6 | | .3 | .5 | .7 | .7 | .8 | .7 |
| 0  UND | 0  UND | 0  UND | Sales/Receivables | 0  UND | 0  UND | 10  35.9 | 5  67.0 | 23  16.0 | 36  10.2 |
| 31  11.9 | 34  10.8 | 32  11.3 | | 0  UND | 21  17.4 | 36  10.1 | 33  11.2 | 45  8.1 | 50  7.3 |
| 58  6.3 | 60  6.0 | 58  6.3 | | 33  11.2 | 49  7.4 | 60  6.1 | 57  6.4 | 69  5.3 | 73  5.0 |
| | | | Cost of Sales/Inventory | | | | | | |
| | | | Cost of Sales/Payables | | | | | | |
| 6.8 | 6.1 | 6.7 | Sales/Working Capital | 6.0 | 8.5 | 5.5 | 7.3 | 6.1 | 6.8 |
| 22.8 | 18.3 | 20.5 | | 43.2 | 47.1 | 13.8 | 19.5 | 13.7 | 17.5 |
| -40.2 | -63.9 | -55.8 | | -9.2 | -22.4 | -134.8 | -654.8 | 223.1 | 151.7 |
| 25.0 | 27.7 | 29.5 | EBIT/Interest | 19.4 | 20.5 | 23.3 | 48.4 | 49.1 | 27.0 |
| (800) 5.3 | (850) 6.1 | (952) 7.3 | | (123) 4.0 | (227) 4.8 | (127) 6.8 | (200) 11.1 | (159) 12.2 | (116) 7.1 |
| .7 | 1.2 | 1.5 | | .1 | 1.1 | 1.7 | 2.5 | 2.6 | 1.4 |
| 6.8 | 8.6 | 6.0 | Net Profit + Depr., Dep., Amort./Cur. Mat. L/T/D | | | | 5.0 | 7.7 | 6.4 |
| (77) 2.7 | (86) 3.0 | (92) 2.5 | | | | | (23) 2.0 | (23) 4.4 | (29) 2.3 |
| .8 | 1.2 | 1.3 | | | | | .2 | 2.7 | 1.1 |
| .1 | .1 | .1 | Fixed/Worth | .0 | .1 | .1 | .1 | .1 | .1 |
| .6 | .5 | .5 | | 1.1 | 1.0 | .4 | .4 | .3 | .5 |
| 6.3 | 4.8 | 6.5 | | 17.6 | -5.8 | 2.3 | 2.1 | 1.9 | -3.1 |
| .6 | .5 | .6 | Debt/Worth | .6 | .5 | .4 | .6 | .6 | 1.0 |
| 1.9 | 2.0 | 2.1 | | 3.3 | 2.6 | 1.8 | 1.4 | 1.9 | 2.5 |
| 64.7 | 26.2 | 269.5 | | -23.6 | -7.6 | 17.4 | 7.6 | 7.6 | -24.8 |
| 81.5 | 91.0 | 97.2 | % Profit Before Taxes/Tangible Net Worth | 116.0 | 125.2 | 78.0 | 108.8 | 78.2 | 67.3 |
| (817) 32.6 | (908) 36.6 | (1023) 43.6 | | (174) 36.7 | (212) 53.0 | (133) 42.9 | (218) 49.3 | (180) 40.4 | (106) 33.4 |
| 4.8 | 6.3 | 10.4 | | 2.9 | 10.0 | 5.6 | 14.3 | 13.5 | 13.0 |
| 31.0 | 33.6 | 36.5 | % Profit Before Taxes/Total Assets | 48.9 | 40.8 | 35.6 | 40.8 | 29.8 | 20.5 |
| 9.5 | 12.2 | 12.7 | | 8.6 | 14.8 | 12.7 | 15.8 | 12.2 | 8.9 |
| -.1 | .8 | 1.6 | | -.5 | 1.9 | .9 | 3.4 | 3.8 | 1.5 |
| 120.7 | 143.6 | 128.9 | Sales/Net Fixed Assets | 319.0 | 101.1 | 134.9 | 180.8 | 117.9 | 81.9 |
| 28.1 | 28.5 | 31.1 | | 17.6 | 24.4 | 28.2 | 41.9 | 37.0 | 35.3 |
| 7.8 | 7.3 | 8.5 | | 1.6 | 8.2 | 10.1 | 11.1 | 12.4 | 13.0 |
| 5.1 | 5.0 | 5.1 | Sales/Total Assets | 4.9 | 5.9 | 4.9 | 6.1 | 4.6 | 3.8 |
| 2.9 | 2.9 | 3.0 | | 1.9 | 3.5 | 3.2 | 3.6 | 2.9 | 2.4 |
| 1.5 | 1.6 | 1.7 | | .5 | 1.9 | 1.9 | 2.2 | 2.1 | 1.4 |
| .5 | .5 | .5 | % Depr., Dep., Amort./Sales | 1.1 | .6 | .6 | .2 | .3 | .5 |
| (716) 1.5 | (763) 1.5 | (814) 1.4 | | (127) 4.0 | (164) 1.4 | (102) 1.5 | (162) 1.0 | (156) 1.0 | (103) 1.0 |
| 3.9 | 3.8 | 3.7 | | 14.8 | 3.8 | 3.7 | 3.2 | 2.1 | 2.6 |
| 3.4 | 3.1 | 2.9 | % Officers', Directors' Owners' Comp/Sales | 7.2 | 3.7 | 4.6 | 2.6 | 1.2 | .9 |
| (455) 7.2 | (457) 7.0 | (518) 6.1 | | (96) 12.3 | (156) 11.6 | (77) 6.9 | (107) 4.1 | (67) 2.4 | (15) 13.7 |
| 14.7 | 13.2 | 11.6 | | 19.0 | 11.6 | 12.4 | 7.5 | 3.4 | 7.6 |
| 14078423M | 19614452M | 20070212M | Net Sales ($) | 116725M | 602447M | 672577M | 1879690M | 3397915M | 13400858M |
| 8524632M | 9922402M | 9668764M | Total Assets ($) | 190606M | 344569M | 372096M | 853948M | 1834581M | 6072964M |

M = $ thousand    MM = $ million
See Pages 9 through 22 for Explanation of Ratios and Data

# MANAGEMENT OF
# COMPANIES AND
# ENTERPRISES

## Current Data Sorted by Assets      Comparative Historical Data

| Type of Statement | 0-500M | 500M-2MM | 2-10MM | 10-50MM | 50-100MM | 100-250MM | | 4/1/07-3/31/08 ALL | 4/1/08-3/31/09 ALL |
|---|---|---|---|---|---|---|---|---|---|
| Unqualified | | | 1 | 1 | | 2 | | 9 | 3 |
| Reviewed | | 2 | | | | | | | 1 |
| Compiled | | 2 | 2 | | | | | 6 | 5 |
| Tax Returns | | 1 | 1 | | | | | 2 | 3 |
| Other | 1 | | 6 | 9 | | 1 | | 9 | 13 |
| | 0-500M | 0 (4/1-9/30/11) 500M-2MM | 2-10MM | 29 (10/1/11-3/31/12) 10-50MM | 50-100MM | 100-250MM | | 4/1/07-3/31/08 | 4/1/08-3/31/09 |
| NUMBER OF STATEMENTS | 1 | 5 | 10 | 10 | | 3 | | 26 | 25 |

| | % | % | % | % | % | % | | % | % |
|---|---|---|---|---|---|---|---|---|---|
| **ASSETS** | | | | | | | | | |
| Cash & Equivalents | | | 8.5 | 8.3 | | | | 7.5 | 8.7 |
| Trade Receivables (net) | | | 26.4 | 9.9 | | | | 14.4 | 19.6 |
| Inventory | | | .4 | 14.6 | | | | 3.2 | 6.1 |
| All Other Current | | | 4.6 | .7 | | | | 11.4 | 4.3 |
| Total Current | | | 39.9 | 33.5 | | | | 36.5 | 38.8 |
| Fixed Assets (net) | | | 35.3 | 26.4 | | | | 17.0 | 30.6 |
| Intangibles (net) | | | .1 | 6.7 | | | | 3.3 | 7.9 |
| All Other Non-Current | | | 24.7 | 33.4 | | | | 43.2 | 22.8 |
| Total | | | 100.0 | 100.0 | | | | 100.0 | 100.0 |
| **LIABILITIES** | | | | | | | | | |
| Notes Payable-Short Term | | | 8.3 | 10.3 | | | | 10.0 | 10.2 |
| Cur. Mat.-L.T.D. | | | 2.4 | 2.9 | | | | 1.4 | 1.3 |
| Trade Payables | | | 7.2 | 6.3 | | | | 9.0 | 7.9 |
| Income Taxes Payable | | | .1 | .0 | | | | .1 | .3 |
| All Other Current | | | 14.7 | 12.7 | | | | 10.6 | 11.6 |
| Total Current | | | 32.6 | 32.2 | | | | 31.0 | 31.3 |
| Long-Term Debt | | | 19.2 | 19.8 | | | | 28.4 | 25.5 |
| Deferred Taxes | | | .1 | 1.3 | | | | .5 | .4 |
| All Other Non-Current | | | 5.6 | .6 | | | | 3.4 | 2.3 |
| Net Worth | | | 42.4 | 46.0 | | | | 36.7 | 40.5 |
| Total Liabilties & Net Worth | | | 100.0 | 100.0 | | | | 100.0 | 100.0 |
| **INCOME DATA** | | | | | | | | | |
| Net Sales | | | 100.0 | 100.0 | | | | 100.0 | 100.0 |
| Gross Profit | | | | | | | | | |
| Operating Expenses | | | 80.5 | 74.2 | | | | 55.9 | 61.4 |
| Operating Profit | | | 19.5 | 25.8 | | | | 44.1 | 38.6 |
| All Other Expenses (net) | | | 8.1 | 3.7 | | | | 9.6 | 16.6 |
| Profit Before Taxes | | | 11.4 | 22.1 | | | | 34.5 | 22.0 |

(Columns for 0-500M, 500M-2MM, 50-100MM and 100-250MM: **DATA NOT AVAILABLE**)

| RATIOS | 2-10MM | 10-50MM | | 4/1/07-3/31/08 | 4/1/08-3/31/09 |
|---|---|---|---|---|---|
| Current | 2.3 | 1.8 | | 1.8 | 1.9 |
| | .8 | 1.1 | | 1.1 | 1.1 |
| | .3 | .4 | | .2 | .7 |
| Quick | 1.9 | 1.4 | | 1.3 | 1.5 |
| | .7 | .7 | | .6 | .8 |
| | .1 | .1 | | .1 | .4 |
| Sales/Receivables | 0 UND | 0 UND | | 0 UND | 0 UND |
| | 37 9.8 | 16 22.2 | | 0 UND | 26 13.8 |
| | 74 4.9 | 51 7.2 | | 50 7.3 | 69 5.3 |
| Cost of Sales/Inventory | | | | | |
| Cost of Sales/Payables | | | | | |
| Sales/Working Capital | 8.8 | 4.2 | | 1.8 | 1.9 |
| | NM | 21.8 | | 10.8 | 18.0 |
| | -6.0 | -3.2 | | -2.8 | -5.7 |
| EBIT/Interest | | 16.6 | | 14.3 | 24.4 |
| | | 5.3 | | (18) 5.3 | (17) 4.9 |
| | | 1.9 | | 2.5 | 1.9 |
| Net Profit + Depr., Dep., Amort./Cur. Mat. L/T/D | | | | | |
| Fixed/Worth | .0 | .0 | | .0 | .0 |
| | 1.1 | .6 | | .3 | .8 |
| | 5.1 | 1.5 | | .7 | 3.1 |
| Debt/Worth | .2 | .4 | | .2 | .5 |
| | 1.7 | 1.0 | | 2.5 | 2.1 |
| | 6.4 | 4.6 | | 11.9 | 8.5 |
| % Profit Before Taxes/Tangible Net Worth | | | | 20.0 | 27.3 |
| | | | | (23) 11.5 | (21) 14.2 |
| | | | | 4.8 | 1.3 |
| % Profit Before Taxes/Total Assets | 17.5 | 8.6 | | 9.8 | 12.6 |
| | 5.0 | 6.9 | | 5.7 | 4.8 |
| | .4 | 2.0 | | 1.0 | .9 |
| Sales/Net Fixed Assets | 314.7 | UND | | UND | 114.3 |
| | 20.4 | 21.4 | | 35.0 | 8.2 |
| | .3 | 1.7 | | 1.4 | .4 |
| Sales/Total Assets | 3.1 | 1.6 | | .6 | 1.0 |
| | 1.6 | .9 | | .2 | .3 |
| | .2 | .1 | | .1 | .1 |
| % Depr., Dep., Amort./Sales | | | | 3.1 | 1.4 |
| | | | | (14) 4.9 | (18) 4.5 |
| | | | | 10.2 | 13.4 |
| % Officers', Directors' Owners' Comp/Sales | | | | | |

| | 0-500M | 500M-2MM | 2-10MM | 10-50MM | 50-100MM | 100-250MM | | 4/1/07-3/31/08 | 4/1/08-3/31/09 |
|---|---|---|---|---|---|---|---|---|---|
| Net Sales ($) | 62M | 13752M | 90822M | 275481M | | 64820M | | 395807M | 273688M |
| Total Assets ($) | 391M | 5075M | 46163M | 274022M | | 569748M | | 1580016M | 880307M |

M = $ thousand    MM = $ million
See Pages 9 through 22 for Explanation of Ratios and Data

## Comparative Historical Data | Current Data Sorted by Sales

| 5 3 5 5 16 4/1/09-3/31/10 ALL | 5 2 3 2 15 4/1/10-3/31/11 ALL | 5 2 2 4 16 4/1/11-3/31/12 ALL | Type of Statement | 0-1MM | 1-3MM | 3-5MM | 5-10MM | 10-25MM | 25MM & OVER |
|---|---|---|---|---|---|---|---|---|---|
|  |  |  | Unqualified |  |  |  | 1 |  | 3 |
|  |  |  | Reviewed |  |  |  | 1 | 1 |  |
|  |  |  | Compiled | 1 |  | 1 | 1 |  |  |
|  |  |  | Tax Returns | 4 |  |  |  |  |  |
|  |  |  | Other | 3 | 1 | 3 |  | 6 | 3 |
|  |  |  |  |  | 0 (4/1-9/30/11) |  | 29 (10/1/11-3/31/12) |  |  |
| 34 | 27 | 29 | **NUMBER OF STATEMENTS** | 8 | 1 | 4 | 3 | 7 | 6 |
| % | % | % | **ASSETS** | % | % | % | % | % | % |
| 7.8 | 11.8 | 10.5 | Cash & Equivalents |  |  |  |  |  |  |
| 18.1 | 11.4 | 16.3 | Trade Receivables (net) |  |  |  |  |  |  |
| 6.6 | 5.2 | 9.2 | Inventory |  |  |  |  |  |  |
| 6.0 | 1.3 | 1.8 | All Other Current |  |  |  |  |  |  |
| 38.4 | 29.7 | 37.9 | Total Current |  |  |  |  |  |  |
| 23.8 | 38.4 | 33.8 | Fixed Assets (net) |  |  |  |  |  |  |
| 7.2 | 8.9 | 3.0 | Intangibles (net) |  |  |  |  |  |  |
| 30.6 | 23.0 | 25.3 | All Other Non-Current |  |  |  |  |  |  |
| 100.0 | 100.0 | 100.0 | Total |  |  |  |  |  |  |
|  |  |  | **LIABILITIES** |  |  |  |  |  |  |
| 14.0 | 10.4 | 8.9 | Notes Payable-Short Term |  |  |  |  |  |  |
| 1.5 | 3.5 | 2.8 | Cur. Mat.-L.T.D. |  |  |  |  |  |  |
| 12.5 | 5.2 | 5.9 | Trade Payables |  |  |  |  |  |  |
| .2 | .0 | .0 | Income Taxes Payable |  |  |  |  |  |  |
| 5.8 | 4.5 | 20.1 | All Other Current |  |  |  |  |  |  |
| 34.0 | 23.7 | 37.7 | Total Current |  |  |  |  |  |  |
| 17.5 | 30.7 | 22.0 | Long-Term Debt |  |  |  |  |  |  |
| .4 | .2 | .5 | Deferred Taxes |  |  |  |  |  |  |
| 2.6 | 5.8 | 2.2 | All Other Non-Current |  |  |  |  |  |  |
| 45.5 | 39.5 | 37.7 | Net Worth |  |  |  |  |  |  |
| 100.0 | 100.0 | 100.0 | Total Liabilities & Net Worth |  |  |  |  |  |  |
|  |  |  | **INCOME DATA** |  |  |  |  |  |  |
| 100.0 | 100.0 | 100.0 | Net Sales |  |  |  |  |  |  |
|  |  |  | Gross Profit |  |  |  |  |  |  |
| 67.2 | 63.9 | 75.2 | Operating Expenses |  |  |  |  |  |  |
| 32.8 | 36.1 | 24.8 | Operating Profit |  |  |  |  |  |  |
| 12.2 | 7.3 | 6.9 | All Other Expenses (net) |  |  |  |  |  |  |
| 20.6 | 28.8 | 17.9 | Profit Before Taxes |  |  |  |  |  |  |
|  |  |  | **RATIOS** |  |  |  |  |  |  |
| 1.9 | 1.9 | 1.6 | Current |  |  |  |  |  |  |
| 1.2 | 1.1 | 1.1 |  |  |  |  |  |  |  |
| .3 | .5 | .4 |  |  |  |  |  |  |  |
| 1.3 | 1.7 | 1.5 | Quick |  |  |  |  |  |  |
| .7 | .9 | .6 |  |  |  |  |  |  |  |
| .1 | .2 | .1 |  |  |  |  |  |  |  |
| 0 UND | 0 UND | 0 UND | Sales/Receivables |  |  |  |  |  |  |
| 1 667.7 | 0 UND | 12 30.5 |  |  |  |  |  |  |  |
| 42 8.6 | 32 11.3 | 49 7.4 |  |  |  |  |  |  |  |
|  |  |  | Cost of Sales/Inventory |  |  |  |  |  |  |
|  |  |  | Cost of Sales/Payables |  |  |  |  |  |  |
| 4.6 | 8.0 | 10.2 | Sales/Working Capital |  |  |  |  |  |  |
| 21.7 | 37.5 | 76.2 |  |  |  |  |  |  |  |
| -4.2 | -8.6 | -2.4 |  |  |  |  |  |  |  |
| 6.3 | 12.6 | 12.1 | EBIT/Interest |  |  |  |  |  |  |
| (17) 3.5 | (19) 4.8 | (19) 5.1 |  |  |  |  |  |  |  |
| .9 | 2.0 | 1.1 |  |  |  |  |  |  |  |
|  |  |  | Net Profit + Depr., Dep., Amort./Cur. Mat. L/T/D |  |  |  |  |  |  |
| .0 | .1 | .0 | Fixed/Worth |  |  |  |  |  |  |
| .3 | 1.1 | .7 |  |  |  |  |  |  |  |
| 2.1 | 8.4 | 3.6 |  |  |  |  |  |  |  |
| .3 | .4 | .4 | Debt/Worth |  |  |  |  |  |  |
| 1.3 | 2.7 | 2.0 |  |  |  |  |  |  |  |
| 7.7 | 12.5 | 9.2 |  |  |  |  |  |  |  |
| 28.1 | 43.8 | 21.5 | % Profit Before Taxes/Tangible Net Worth |  |  |  |  |  |  |
| (30) 7.0 | (23) 14.2 | (26) 11.3 |  |  |  |  |  |  |  |
| 2.8 | 5.5 | 5.5 |  |  |  |  |  |  |  |
| 7.5 | 11.4 | 9.2 | % Profit Before Taxes/Total Assets |  |  |  |  |  |  |
| 3.6 | 6.5 | 6.1 |  |  |  |  |  |  |  |
| .4 | 2.9 | .6 |  |  |  |  |  |  |  |
| UND | 105.1 | 43.1 | Sales/Net Fixed Assets |  |  |  |  |  |  |
| 44.6 | 4.6 | 16.7 |  |  |  |  |  |  |  |
| 2.6 | .4 | .7 |  |  |  |  |  |  |  |
| 1.9 | 1.5 | 2.9 | Sales/Total Assets |  |  |  |  |  |  |
| .4 | .3 | .7 |  |  |  |  |  |  |  |
| .1 | .1 | .1 |  |  |  |  |  |  |  |
| 1.3 | 1.2 | .8 | % Depr., Dep., Amort./Sales |  |  |  |  |  |  |
| (17) 5.2 | (17) 4.1 | (20) 1.8 |  |  |  |  |  |  |  |
| 11.7 | 16.4 | 15.0 |  |  |  |  |  |  |  |
|  |  |  | % Officers', Directors' Owners' Comp/Sales |  |  |  |  |  |  |
| 488754M | 372769M | 444937M | Net Sales ($) | 3536M | 1612M | 16333M | 22591M | 97617M | 303248M |
| 974903M | 482613M | 895399M | Total Assets ($) | 16291M | 15471M | 103270M | 133439M | 290444M | 336484M |

## Current Data Sorted by Assets      Comparative Historical Data

| | | | | | | Type of Statement | | |
|---|---|---|---|---|---|---|---|---|
| 2 | 4 | 11 | 30 | 20 | 27 | Unqualified | 86 | 82 |
| | 7 | 23 | 12 | 2 | 2 | Reviewed | 59 | 52 |
| 10 | 18 | 29 | 15 | 1 | | Compiled | 121 | 112 |
| 50 | 115 | 89 | 10 | 1 | 1 | Tax Returns | 244 | 227 |
| 21 | 59 | 99 | 52 | 16 | 18 | Other | 252 | 261 |
| | 72 (4/1-9/30/11) | | 672 (10/1/11-3/31/12) | | | | 4/1/07-3/31/08 | 4/1/08-3/31/09 |
| 0-500M | 500M-2MM | 2-10MM | 10-50MM | 50-100MM | 100-250MM | | ALL | ALL |
| 83 | 203 | 251 | 119 | 40 | 48 | NUMBER OF STATEMENTS | 762 | 734 |
| % | % | % | % | % | % | ASSETS | % | % |
| 20.7 | 7.9 | 7.9 | 9.5 | 12.4 | 10.1 | Cash & Equivalents | 9.2 | 8.3 |
| 7.8 | 4.8 | 7.6 | 10.4 | 15.7 | 10.9 | Trade Receivables (net) | 8.0 | 8.2 |
| 3.0 | 2.5 | 5.4 | 8.0 | 10.3 | 7.8 | Inventory | 4.9 | 5.5 |
| 6.7 | 2.1 | 2.1 | 6.0 | 5.4 | 2.5 | All Other Current | 3.3 | 3.6 |
| 38.1 | 17.3 | 23.0 | 33.9 | 43.8 | 31.3 | Total Current | 25.5 | 25.6 |
| 43.2 | 69.3 | 55.7 | 46.7 | 32.0 | 32.8 | Fixed Assets (net) | 59.3 | 57.1 |
| 3.5 | 2.0 | 6.6 | 5.4 | 11.5 | 21.5 | Intangibles (net) | 3.3 | 5.0 |
| 15.2 | 11.3 | 14.6 | 14.0 | 12.7 | 14.4 | All Other Non-Current | 12.0 | 12.3 |
| 100.0 | 100.0 | 100.0 | 100.0 | 100.0 | 100.0 | Total | 100.0 | 100.0 |
| | | | | | | LIABILITIES | | |
| 3.4 | 5.2 | 4.1 | 6.6 | 5.9 | 7.9 | Notes Payable-Short Term | 5.3 | 5.9 |
| 4.0 | 5.3 | 4.5 | 5.4 | 2.5 | 3.3 | Cur. Mat.-L.T.D. | 4.1 | 5.4 |
| 4.0 | 2.6 | 4.6 | 7.6 | 11.2 | 4.5 | Trade Payables | 4.7 | 5.1 |
| .0 | .0 | .2 | .3 | .1 | .3 | Income Taxes Payable | .1 | .1 |
| 14.8 | 5.5 | 7.6 | 9.6 | 11.2 | 9.1 | All Other Current | 8.1 | 8.0 |
| 26.3 | 18.5 | 21.0 | 29.6 | 31.0 | 25.1 | Total Current | 22.3 | 24.6 |
| 40.2 | 52.7 | 43.4 | 28.6 | 24.0 | 30.8 | Long-Term Debt | 44.0 | 42.1 |
| .0 | .0 | .1 | .7 | 1.3 | 1.6 | Deferred Taxes | .4 | .2 |
| 7.5 | 7.5 | 5.7 | 7.9 | 9.2 | 12.5 | All Other Non-Current | 4.3 | 5.2 |
| 26.0 | 21.3 | 29.8 | 33.2 | 34.4 | 30.0 | Net Worth | 29.0 | 27.9 |
| 100.0 | 100.0 | 100.0 | 100.0 | 100.0 | 100.0 | Total Liabilties & Net Worth | 100.0 | 100.0 |
| | | | | | | INCOME DATA | | |
| 100.0 | 100.0 | 100.0 | 100.0 | 100.0 | 100.0 | Net Sales | 100.0 | 100.0 |
| | | | | | | Gross Profit | | |
| 75.5 | 56.3 | 65.9 | 72.7 | 88.1 | 82.8 | Operating Expenses | 62.8 | 66.8 |
| 24.5 | 43.7 | 34.1 | 27.3 | 11.9 | 17.2 | Operating Profit | 37.2 | 33.2 |
| 7.4 | 20.3 | 14.8 | 8.7 | 3.9 | 7.4 | All Other Expenses (net) | 16.9 | 16.1 |
| 17.1 | 23.5 | 19.2 | 18.6 | 7.9 | 9.8 | Profit Before Taxes | 20.3 | 17.2 |
| | | | | | | RATIOS | | |
| 5.3 | 2.3 | 1.9 | 1.7 | 2.4 | 2.1 | | 2.4 | 2.0 |
| 1.2 | .6 | .9 | 1.0 | 1.5 | 1.4 | Current | 1.1 | 1.0 |
| .5 | .2 | .2 | .4 | .9 | .6 | | .3 | .3 |
| 4.3 | 1.9 | 1.4 | 1.2 | 1.7 | 1.6 | | 1.7 | 1.3 |
| 1.0 | .4 | .6 | .6 | .8 | .9 | Quick | .7 (733) | .6 |
| .3 | .1 | .2 | .2 | .4 | .3 | | .2 | .2 |
| 0 UND | 0 UND | 0 UND | 0 UND | 20 18.2 | 16 22.6 | | 0 UND | 0 UND |
| 0 UND | 0 UND | 0 UND | 19 19.5 | 38 9.6 | 41 8.9 | Sales/Receivables | 0 UND | 0 UND |
| 5 80.7 | 1 339.0 | 30 12.2 | 47 7.7 | 53 6.9 | 64 5.7 | | 32 11.3 | 34 10.7 |
| | | | | | | Cost of Sales/Inventory | | |
| | | | | | | Cost of Sales/Payables | | |
| 6.1 | 7.2 | 7.1 | 6.7 | 3.6 | 4.6 | | 5.6 | 7.5 |
| 61.7 | -13.3 | -53.5 | 217.5 | 11.9 | 13.1 | Sales/Working Capital | 136.5 | -173.9 |
| -11.6 | -3.4 | -3.3 | -4.2 | -95.3 | -9.4 | | -3.7 | -3.5 |
| 10.3 | 10.7 | 13.8 | 14.6 | 11.4 | 7.0 | | 8.9 | 8.9 |
| (32) 3.5 | (100) 4.4 | (157) 4.8 | (92) 4.6 | (31) 4.9 | (43) 2.4 | EBIT/Interest | (388) 4.1 | (398) 3.6 |
| .9 | 1.8 | 1.8 | 1.9 | 1.2 | 1.2 | | 1.6 | 1.3 |
| | | 3.9 | 7.0 | 4.3 | 7.7 | Net Profit + Depr., Dep., | 5.1 | 8.7 |
| | (19) 2.0 | (26) 3.2 | (16) 2.7 | (15) 2.4 | | Amort./Cur. Mat. L/T/D | (84) 2.2 | (97) 2.8 |
| | 1.1 | 1.3 | 1.5 | 1.4 | | | 1.0 | 1.0 |
| .0 | 1.3 | .7 | .5 | .2 | .4 | | .8 | .7 |
| 1.4 | 3.4 | 2.2 | 1.6 | 1.7 | 2.7 | Fixed/Worth | 2.3 | 2.5 |
| 248.0 | -119.9 | 16.3 | 5.1 | -6.4 | -3.3 | | 7.9 | 13.4 |
| .3 | 1.1 | 1.1 | .9 | .9 | 1.3 | | .9 | 1.1 |
| 1.5 | 3.4 | 2.7 | 2.2 | 2.3 | 7.2 | Debt/Worth | 2.6 | 3.2 |
| -15.0 | -62.9 | 27.4 | 10.8 | -16.8 | -5.5 | | 11.3 | 20.6 |
| 56.0 | 51.2 | 45.1 | 37.2 | 31.0 | 24.3 | % Profit Before Taxes/Tangible | 36.5 | 41.2 |
| (60) 18.5 | (147) 19.1 | (197) 16.2 | (103) 20.5 | (28) 14.1 | (28) 11.1 | Net Worth | (631) 17.0 | (594) 16.3 |
| 2.7 | 6.6 | 2.5 | 7.0 | 2.9 | 1.7 | | 5.2 | 3.1 |
| 21.3 | 12.7 | 10.1 | 11.7 | 9.8 | 6.9 | % Profit Before Taxes/Total | 11.5 | 10.5 |
| 6.3 | 5.5 | 4.2 | 5.9 | 4.0 | 3.6 | Assets | 4.9 | 4.3 |
| -.5 | 1.1 | .4 | 1.3 | .6 | .3 | | .9 | .3 |
| UND | 3.2 | 10.5 | 11.1 | 32.5 | 14.9 | | 8.7 | 10.4 |
| 11.8 | .3 | .5 | 3.2 | 7.4 | 4.7 | Sales/Net Fixed Assets | .4 | .5 |
| .3 | .2 | .1 | .2 | 1.6 | 1.3 | | .2 | .2 |
| 4.9 | .8 | 1.3 | 1.8 | 2.0 | 1.1 | | 1.5 | 1.6 |
| 1.5 | .2 | .2 | 1.0 | 1.2 | .5 | Sales/Total Assets | .2 | .3 |
| .3 | .1 | .1 | .2 | .3 | .2 | | .1 | .1 |
| 2.1 | 7.7 | 2.8 | 1.8 | 1.2 | 2.1 | | 2.8 | 2.1 |
| (46) 8.7 | (169) 14.6 | (207) 14.0 | (107) 5.2 | (36) 3.1 | (32) 3.9 | % Depr., Dep., Amort./Sales | (654) 12.0 | (603) 11.2 |
| 17.1 | 22.5 | 23.7 | 17.0 | 8.2 | 10.4 | | 19.7 | 20.0 |
| 6.7 | 3.4 | 2.0 | .8 | | | | 1.5 | 1.4 |
| (22) 24.1 | (22) 5.2 | (44) 4.1 | (12) 3.0 | | | % Officers', Directors' | (97) 3.8 | (90) 3.0 |
| 33.6 | 19.4 | 9.8 | 7.5 | | | Owners' Comp/Sales | 10.3 | 11.9 |
| 59957M | 204666M | 1234343M | 3141456M | 3713327M | 6047778M | Net Sales ($) | 17092827M | 18547998M |
| 23153M | 231509M | 1202486M | 2744618M | 2814191M | 7874002M | Total Assets ($) | 12427990M | 14695221M |

M = $ thousand    MM = $ million
See Pages 9 through 22 for Explanation of Ratios and Data

## Comparative Historical Data                                   ## Current Data Sorted by Sales

| 4/1/09-3/31/10 ALL | 4/1/10-3/31/11 ALL | 4/1/11-3/31/12 ALL | Type of Statement | 0-1MM | 1-3MM | 3-5MM | 5-10MM | 10-25MM | 25MM & OVER |
|---|---|---|---|---|---|---|---|---|---|
| 89 | 88 | 94 | Unqualified | 4 | 8 | 7 | 3 | 13 | 59 |
| 62 | 50 | 46 | Reviewed | 12 | 5 | 1 | 4 | 12 | 12 |
| 92 | 93 | 73 | Compiled | 32 | 21 | 5 | 3 | 10 | 2 |
| 259 | 248 | 266 | Tax Returns | 191 | 29 | 13 | 18 | 11 | 4 |
| 253 | 270 | 265 | Other | 106 | 46 | 16 | 24 | 28 | 45 |
| | | | | 72 (4/1-9/30/11) | | | 672 (10/1/11-3/31/12) | | |
| 755 | 749 | 744 | NUMBER OF STATEMENTS | 345 | 109 | 42 | 52 | 74 | 122 |
| % | % | % | **ASSETS** | % | % | % | % | % | % |
| 9.1 | 8.8 | 10.0 | Cash & Equivalents | 8.1 | 9.8 | 14.1 | 11.5 | 13.0 | 11.6 |
| 7.7 | 8.8 | 8.0 | Trade Receivables (net) | 2.7 | 6.2 | 9.0 | 9.2 | 16.1 | 18.4 |
| 4.5 | 4.8 | 5.2 | Inventory | .5 | 5.7 | 7.0 | 7.7 | 14.1 | 10.9 |
| 3.3 | 3.4 | 3.4 | All Other Current | 2.5 | 4.1 | 2.3 | 5.6 | 4.0 | 4.6 |
| 24.7 | 25.8 | 26.5 | Total Current | 13.8 | 25.9 | 32.3 | 34.0 | 47.2 | 45.5 |
| 56.7 | 56.4 | 53.8 | Fixed Assets (net) | 73.5 | 46.1 | 41.2 | 36.1 | 32.1 | 30.2 |
| 4.7 | 4.7 | 6.0 | Intangibles (net) | 1.9 | 8.2 | 7.7 | 7.9 | 6.5 | 14.4 |
| 13.9 | 13.0 | 13.6 | All Other Non-Current | 10.8 | 19.9 | 18.7 | 22.1 | 14.2 | 9.9 |
| 100.0 | 100.0 | 100.0 | Total | 100.0 | 100.0 | 100.0 | 100.0 | 100.0 | 100.0 |
| | | | **LIABILITIES** | | | | | | |
| 6.8 | 5.9 | 5.1 | Notes Payable-Short Term | 3.2 | 6.7 | 4.8 | 4.5 | 7.5 | 7.8 |
| 4.5 | 4.1 | 4.6 | Cur. Mat.-L.T.D. | 4.3 | 6.5 | 7.0 | 3.8 | 3.7 | 3.9 |
| 4.4 | 4.1 | 4.8 | Trade Payables | 1.0 | 4.1 | 6.5 | 6.9 | 10.9 | 11.1 |
| .3 | .1 | .2 | Income Taxes Payable | .0 | .1 | .1 | .6 | .5 | .2 |
| 10.0 | 8.7 | 8.4 | All Other Current | 5.1 | 10.3 | 14.7 | 10.8 | 11.7 | 11.1 |
| 26.0 | 22.9 | 23.1 | Total Current | 13.6 | 27.7 | 33.2 | 26.6 | 34.3 | 34.1 |
| 42.6 | 41.6 | 41.4 | Long-Term Debt | 57.7 | 34.8 | 28.9 | 27.2 | 24.1 | 21.7 |
| .3 | .3 | .3 | Deferred Taxes | .0 | .1 | .1 | .2 | .4 | 1.5 |
| 6.3 | 6.3 | 7.4 | All Other Non-Current | 5.3 | 11.6 | 8.0 | 8.7 | 7.0 | 8.9 |
| 24.8 | 28.9 | 27.9 | Net Worth | 23.4 | 25.8 | 29.8 | 37.4 | 34.3 | 33.8 |
| 100.0 | 100.0 | 100.0 | Total Liabilities & Net Worth | 100.0 | 100.0 | 100.0 | 100.0 | 100.0 | 100.0 |
| | | | **INCOME DATA** | | | | | | |
| 100.0 | 100.0 | 100.0 | Net Sales | 100.0 | 100.0 | 100.0 | 100.0 | 100.0 | 100.0 |
| | | | Gross Profit | | | | | | |
| 66.6 | 64.9 | 67.7 | Operating Expenses | 50.9 | 70.6 | 79.1 | 79.6 | 88.7 | 90.9 |
| 33.4 | 35.1 | 32.3 | Operating Profit | 49.1 | 29.4 | 20.9 | 20.4 | 11.3 | 9.1 |
| 15.6 | 14.2 | 13.4 | All Other Expenses (net) | 23.3 | 9.1 | 5.8 | 4.2 | 2.8 | 2.3 |
| 17.8 | 20.8 | 18.8 | Profit Before Taxes | 25.7 | 20.4 | 15.1 | 16.2 | 8.5 | 6.8 |
| | | | **RATIOS** | | | | | | |
| 2.0 | 2.1 | 2.1 | | 2.2 | 2.3 | 1.8 | 2.4 | 2.3 | 2.0 |
| .9 | 1.0 | 1.0 | Current | .6 | .8 | 1.0 | 1.2 | 1.4 | 1.4 |
| .3 | .3 | .3 | | .2 | .2 | .2 | .6 | .8 | .9 |
| 1.4 | 1.5 | 1.6 | | 1.9 | 1.4 | 1.6 | 2.0 | 1.4 | 1.5 |
| .6 | .7 | .6 | Quick | .4 | .5 | .7 | .7 | .8 | .8 |
| .2 | .2 | .2 | | .1 | .1 | .1 | .2 | .4 | .4 |
| 0 UND | 0 UND | 0 UND | | 0 UND | 0 UND | 0 UND | 0 UND | 9 40.1 | 17 21.4 |
| 0 999.8 | 0 UND | 0 999.8 | Sales/Receivables | 0 UND | 0 999.8 | 9 39.7 | 3 124.3 | 33 11.1 | 39 9.3 |
| 29 12.5 | 36 10.0 | 34 10.8 | | 0 UND | 25 14.8 | 33 10.9 | 46 7.9 | 47 7.8 | 54 6.8 |
| | | | Cost of Sales/Inventory | | | | | | |
| | | | Cost of Sales/Payables | | | | | | |
| 8.0 | 6.2 | 6.7 | | 5.6 | 8.9 | 7.8 | 6.8 | 5.7 | 6.5 |
| -71.0 | 173.0 | UND | Sales/Working Capital | -13.3 | -32.9 | NM | 26.6 | 12.5 | 15.8 |
| -3.3 | -4.2 | -4.3 | | -2.6 | -2.6 | -3.6 | -25.4 | -39.6 | -51.3 |
| 8.4 | 12.2 | 11.2 | | 8.4 | 8.7 | 5.5 | 31.5 | 20.3 | 12.7 |
| (415) 3.5 | (424) 4.6 | (455) 4.3 | EBIT/Interest | (139) 4.3 | (68) 3.4 | (23) 4.2 | (42) 6.5 | (69) 5.5 | (114) 4.7 |
| 1.3 | 1.9 | 1.6 | | 2.4 | .6 | .7 | 1.9 | 1.7 | 1.6 |
| 4.3 | 4.5 | 5.1 | | 3.5 | | | | 3.1 | 7.3 |
| (88) 1.8 | (90) 2.1 | (82) 2.5 | Net Profit + Depr., Dep., Amort./Cur. Mat. L/T/D | (10) 1.8 | | | (13) 2.0 | | (48) 3.2 |
| .8 | 1.1 | 1.3 | | 1.0 | | | | 1.1 | 1.5 |
| .7 | .6 | .6 | | 1.4 | .4 | .3 | .1 | .3 | .3 |
| 2.6 | 2.2 | 2.2 | Fixed/Worth | 3.3 | 2.6 | 1.8 | .9 | .8 | 1.4 |
| 21.8 | 8.5 | 38.4 | | 36.2 | -4.6 | NM | 5.1 | 3.6 | -12.8 |
| 1.0 | .9 | .9 | | 1.0 | .6 | .8 | .8 | .8 | 1.0 |
| 3.4 | 2.5 | 2.8 | Debt/Worth | 3.1 | 3.5 | 2.9 | 2.3 | 2.5 | 2.4 |
| 40.4 | 12.9 | 176.2 | | 149.6 | -10.0 | NM | 9.2 | 6.9 | -14.8 |
| 38.6 | 39.3 | 44.1 | | 36.1 | 42.8 | 60.8 | 84.1 | 60.0 | 47.0 |
| (593) 14.8 | (617) 16.7 | (563) 17.7 | % Profit Before Taxes/Tangible Net Worth | (263) 15.9 | (74) 17.1 | (32) 22.2 | (45) 24.5 | (63) 19.7 | (86) 20.6 |
| 3.1 | 3.9 | 4.0 | | 3.4 | 3.6 | 3.8 | 8.9 | 6.1 | 5.2 |
| 9.3 | 11.2 | 11.9 | | 9.9 | 11.9 | 15.6 | 23.0 | 14.8 | 14.2 |
| 4.2 | 5.1 | 4.8 | % Profit Before Taxes/Total Assets | 4.0 | 4.6 | 6.3 | 6.6 | 6.5 | 6.5 |
| .3 | 1.0 | .8 | | .6 | .6 | -.2 | 2.2 | 1.6 | 1.6 |
| 10.0 | 10.9 | 12.6 | | .5 | 28.2 | 68.0 | 89.8 | 26.5 | 24.9 |
| .5 | .6 | 1.1 | Sales/Net Fixed Assets | .2 | 2.0 | 4.1 | 9.9 | 9.6 | 6.7 |
| .2 | .2 | .2 | | .1 | .2 | .4 | .9 | 3.1 | 3.1 |
| 1.3 | 1.4 | 1.6 | | .3 | 1.6 | 3.0 | 2.4 | 2.4 | 2.3 |
| .3 | .3 | .4 | Sales/Total Assets | .2 | .5 | .9 | 1.3 | 1.8 | 1.5 |
| .1 | .1 | .2 | | .1 | .2 | .2 | .5 | .9 | .9 |
| 3.4 | 3.2 | 2.7 | | 2.4 | 1.8 | 1.2 | 1.5 | 1.0 | 1.2 |
| (620) 13.3 | (610) 12.9 | (597) 10.1 | % Depr., Dep., Amort./Sales | (283) 19.0 | (79) 6.5 | (31) 3.0 | (39) 3.7 | (66) 2.5 | (99) 3.0 |
| 21.6 | 21.4 | 21.2 | | 26.3 | 21.7 | 17.8 | 10.3 | 5.2 | 5.1 |
| 2.1 | 1.7 | 2.2 | | 9.0 | 4.8 | 1.4 | 2.1 | 1.1 | .8 |
| (95) 5.2 | (99) 4.6 | (104) 5.1 | % Officers', Directors' Owners' Comp/Sales | (27) 21.8 | (17) 9.2 | (10) 4.2 | (21) 4.0 | (16) 1.7 | (13) 2.5 |
| 13.4 | 15.3 | 19.4 | | 27.9 | 27.9 | 7.6 | 6.0 | 3.7 | 20.8 |
| 13073172M | 15284663M | 14401527M | Net Sales ($) | 114798M | 201075M | 167387M | 374747M | 1220247M | 12323273M |
| 12414948M | 13417041M | 14889959M | Total Assets ($) | 704244M | 753400M | 620014M | 915686M | 1698513M | 10198102M |

© RMA 2012

M = $ thousand     MM = $ million
See Pages 9 through 22 for Explanation of Ratios and Data

## Current Data Sorted by Assets

## Comparative Historical Data

| | | | | | | Type of Statement | | |
|---|---|---|---|---|---|---|---|---|
| | | 1 | 3 | 1 | 2 | Unqualified | 4 | 6 |
| | | 1 | 2 | | | Reviewed | 7 | 6 |
| 3 | 3 | 3 | | | | Compiled | 1 | |
| 2 | 1 | | 1 | | | Tax Returns | 2 | 5 |
| 2 | 3 | | 2 | 3 | 3 | Other | 8 | 10 |
| | 5 (4/1-9/30/11) | | 31 (10/1/11-3/31/12) | | | | 4/1/07-3/31/08 | 4/1/08-3/31/09 |
| 0-500M | 500M-2MM | 2-10MM | 10-50MM | 50-100MM | 100-250MM | | ALL | ALL |
| 7 | 8 | 4 | 8 | 4 | 5 | NUMBER OF STATEMENTS | 22 | 27 |
| % | % | % | % | % | % | ASSETS | % | % |
| | | | | | | Cash & Equivalents | 8.8 | 12.0 |
| | | | | | | Trade Receivables (net) | 21.2 | 17.2 |
| | | | | | | Inventory | 2.5 | 5.8 |
| | | | | | | All Other Current | 13.6 | 9.8 |
| | | | | | | Total Current | 46.2 | 44.9 |
| | | | | | | Fixed Assets (net) | 38.7 | 31.7 |
| | | | | | | Intangibles (net) | 6.1 | 6.9 |
| | | | | | | All Other Non-Current | 9.0 | 16.5 |
| | | | | | | Total | 100.0 | 100.0 |
| | | | | | | LIABILITIES | | |
| | | | | | | Notes Payable-Short Term | 4.6 | 9.8 |
| | | | | | | Cur. Mat.-L.T.D. | 2.2 | 1.9 |
| | | | | | | Trade Payables | 11.1 | 9.2 |
| | | | | | | Income Taxes Payable | .4 | .1 |
| | | | | | | All Other Current | 16.1 | 15.6 |
| | | | | | | Total Current | 34.3 | 36.5 |
| | | | | | | Long-Term Debt | 30.5 | 28.0 |
| | | | | | | Deferred Taxes | .2 | .1 |
| | | | | | | All Other Non-Current | 5.2 | 5.5 |
| | | | | | | Net Worth | 29.8 | 29.8 |
| | | | | | | Total Liabilties & Net Worth | 100.0 | 100.0 |
| | | | | | | INCOME DATA | | |
| | | | | | | Net Sales | 100.0 | 100.0 |
| | | | | | | Gross Profit | | |
| | | | | | | Operating Expenses | 83.2 | 76.6 |
| | | | | | | Operating Profit | 16.8 | 23.4 |
| | | | | | | All Other Expenses (net) | 8.1 | 8.5 |
| | | | | | | Profit Before Taxes | 8.7 | 14.9 |
| | | | | | | RATIOS | | |
| | | | | | | Current | 2.3 | 2.1 |
| | | | | | | | 1.4 | 1.2 |
| | | | | | | | .8 | .7 |
| | | | | | | Quick | 1.5 | 1.4 |
| | | | | | | | .8 | .7 |
| | | | | | | | .5 | .4 |
| | | | | | | Sales/Receivables | 0 UND   0 UND | |
| | | | | | | | 40   9.1   28   12.9 | |
| | | | | | | | 72   5.0   51   7.2 | |
| | | | | | | Cost of Sales/Inventory | | |
| | | | | | | Cost of Sales/Payables | | |
| | | | | | | Sales/Working Capital | 5.1 | 5.0 |
| | | | | | | | 7.2 | 23.7 |
| | | | | | | | -38.9 | -20.1 |
| | | | | | | EBIT/Interest | 3.7     12.0 | |
| | | | | | | | (11) 1.3   (16) 3.7 | |
| | | | | | | | -1.0     1.8 | |
| | | | | | | Net Profit + Depr., Dep., Amort./Cur. Mat. L/T/D | | |
| | | | | | | Fixed/Worth | .5 | .5 |
| | | | | | | | 1.4 | 1.3 |
| | | | | | | | 5.9 | -3.9 |
| | | | | | | Debt/Worth | 1.1 | .8 |
| | | | | | | | 1.9 | 2.8 |
| | | | | | | | 13.5 | -36.0 |
| | | | | | | % Profit Before Taxes/Tangible Net Worth | 22.7     40.9 | |
| | | | | | | | (18) 12.4   (20) 16.2 | |
| | | | | | | | -1.1     5.4 | |
| | | | | | | % Profit Before Taxes/Total Assets | 8.2 | 12.5 |
| | | | | | | | 4.6 | 4.6 |
| | | | | | | | -1.8 | 1.4 |
| | | | | | | Sales/Net Fixed Assets | 24.3 | 32.3 |
| | | | | | | | 6.2 | 7.2 |
| | | | | | | | .7 | .5 |
| | | | | | | Sales/Total Assets | 2.6 | 1.8 |
| | | | | | | | 1.1 | 1.1 |
| | | | | | | | .3 | .2 |
| | | | | | | % Depr., Dep., Amort./Sales | 2.0     .9 | |
| | | | | | | | (20) 3.8   (24) 4.9 | |
| | | | | | | | 12.8     12.4 | |
| | | | | | | % Officers', Directors' Owners' Comp/Sales | | |
| 12302M | 26765M | 24213M | 436846M | 386889M | 945495M | Net Sales ($) | 931772M | 940999M |
| 2437M | 7756M | 21868M | 144400M | 308064M | 867594M | Total Assets ($) | 857309M | 702613M |

M = $ thousand     MM = $ million
See Pages 9 through 22 for Explanation of Ratios and Data

## Comparative Historical Data | Current Data Sorted by Sales

| | | | Type of Statement | | | | | | |
|---|---|---|---|---|---|---|---|---|---|
| 4 | 3 | 7 | Unqualified | | | 1 | | 1 | 5 |
| 5 | 5 | 3 | Reviewed | | 1 | | 1 | | |
| 2 | 3 | 9 | Compiled | 2 | 3 | 3 | | 1 | |
| 5 | 2 | 4 | Tax Returns | 2 | | 1 | 1 | 1 | |
| 11 | 15 | 13 | Other | 2 | 4 | | 1 | 1 | 5 |
| **4/1/09-3/31/10 ALL** | **4/1/10-3/31/11 ALL** | **4/1/11-3/31/12 ALL** | | **0-1MM** | **1-3MM** | **3-5MM** | **5-10MM** | **10-25MM** | **25MM & OVER** |
| | | | | | 5 (4/1-9/30/11) | | 31 (10/1/11-3/31/12) | | |
| 27 | 28 | 36 | **NUMBER OF STATEMENTS** | 6 | 8 | 5 | 3 | 4 | 10 |
| % | % | % | **ASSETS** | % | % | % | % | % | % |
| 11.2 | 8.8 | 18.7 | Cash & Equivalents | | | | | | 11.2 |
| 13.6 | 12.1 | 14.9 | Trade Receivables (net) | | | | | | 16.0 |
| 5.9 | 6.1 | 3.4 | Inventory | | | | | | 8.9 |
| 11.6 | 10.3 | 12.4 | All Other Current | | | | | | 11.1 |
| 42.2 | 37.2 | 49.5 | Total Current | | | | | | 47.2 |
| 32.2 | 37.5 | 28.1 | Fixed Assets (net) | | | | | | 31.2 |
| 11.4 | 8.0 | 11.7 | Intangibles (net) | | | | | | 14.9 |
| 14.1 | 17.3 | 10.8 | All Other Non-Current | | | | | | 6.6 |
| 100.0 | 100.0 | 100.0 | Total | | | | | | 100.0 |
| | | | **LIABILITIES** | | | | | | |
| 5.8 | 8.7 | 12.8 | Notes Payable-Short Term | | | | | | 5.4 |
| 4.5 | 4.8 | 5.2 | Cur. Mat.-L.T.D. | | | | | | 6.8 |
| 7.9 | 11.9 | 8.3 | Trade Payables | | | | | | 9.0 |
| .3 | .2 | .4 | Income Taxes Payable | | | | | | .7 |
| 19.1 | 28.1 | 15.6 | All Other Current | | | | | | 17.6 |
| 37.6 | 53.6 | 42.3 | Total Current | | | | | | 39.5 |
| 29.1 | 28.9 | 28.1 | Long-Term Debt | | | | | | 31.6 |
| .0 | .5 | .4 | Deferred Taxes | | | | | | 1.4 |
| 10.4 | 5.3 | 4.5 | All Other Non-Current | | | | | | 7.6 |
| 22.9 | 11.7 | 24.7 | Net Worth | | | | | | 20.0 |
| 100.0 | 100.0 | 100.0 | Total Liabilties & Net Worth | | | | | | 100.0 |
| | | | **INCOME DATA** | | | | | | |
| 100.0 | 100.0 | 100.0 | Net Sales | | | | | | 100.0 |
| | | | Gross Profit | | | | | | |
| 83.2 | 77.0 | 85.9 | Operating Expenses | | | | | | 93.6 |
| 16.8 | 23.0 | 14.1 | Operating Profit | | | | | | 6.4 |
| 8.6 | 9.2 | 7.4 | All Other Expenses (net) | | | | | | 1.6 |
| 8.2 | 13.8 | 6.7 | Profit Before Taxes | | | | | | 4.8 |
| | | | **RATIOS** | | | | | | |
| 2.0 | 1.5 | 1.5 | Current | | | | | | 1.5 |
| 1.3 | .8 | 1.2 | | | | | | | 1.2 |
| .4 | .2 | .7 | | | | | | | .6 |
| 1.4 | 1.0 | 1.1 | Quick | | | | | | 1.0 |
| .5 | .4 | .8 | | | | | | | .7 |
| .2 | .1 | .5 | | | | | | | .4 |
| 0 UND | 0 UND | 0 UND | Sales/Receivables | | | | | | 20 18.3 |
| 21 17.3 | 10 37.6 | 20 17.9 | | | | | | | 40 9.1 |
| 39 9.4 | 52 7.0 | 48 7.6 | | | | | | | 51 7.1 |
| | | | Cost of Sales/Inventory | | | | | | |
| | | | Cost of Sales/Payables | | | | | | |
| 5.5 | 8.6 | 6.5 | Sales/Working Capital | | | | | | 6.6 |
| 50.1 | -10.0 | 57.5 | | | | | | | 35.6 |
| -5.1 | -3.2 | -7.8 | | | | | | | -25.9 |
| 6.7 | 22.4 | 22.2 | EBIT/Interest | | | | | | 10.2 |
| (19) 2.6 | (23) 6.0 | (30) 6.9 | | | | | | | 4.4 |
| .5 | 1.0 | 1.7 | | | | | | | 2.2 |
| | | | Net Profit + Depr., Dep., Amort./Cur. Mat. L/T/D | | | | | | |
| .1 | .5 | .1 | Fixed/Worth | | | | | | .5 |
| 1.6 | 1.8 | 1.3 | | | | | | | 5.4 |
| -341.3 | -1.8 | 24.6 | | | | | | | -1.3 |
| 1.5 | 1.2 | 1.4 | Debt/Worth | | | | | | 1.8 |
| 2.7 | 3.3 | 3.6 | | | | | | | 9.7 |
| -20.5 | -5.4 | NM | | | | | | | -4.0 |
| 26.8 | 52.9 | 106.4 | % Profit Before Taxes/Tangible Net Worth | | | | | | |
| (19) 9.4 | (18) 31.3 | (27) 37.0 | | | | | | | |
| -1.8 | 1.9 | 5.7 | | | | | | | |
| 12.8 | 15.9 | 19.2 | % Profit Before Taxes/Total Assets | | | | | | 11.8 |
| 1.5 | 7.5 | 7.2 | | | | | | | 9.0 |
| -.7 | .2 | 1.0 | | | | | | | 3.3 |
| 88.3 | 17.7 | 27.9 | Sales/Net Fixed Assets | | | | | | 11.8 |
| 7.1 | 6.5 | 11.5 | | | | | | | 6.4 |
| .7 | .6 | 4.0 | | | | | | | 3.6 |
| 1.9 | 1.8 | 3.9 | Sales/Total Assets | | | | | | 2.3 |
| 1.0 | 1.0 | 1.7 | | | | | | | 1.5 |
| .4 | .3 | .8 | | | | | | | 1.2 |
| 1.0 | 1.5 | 1.3 | % Depr., Dep., Amort./Sales | | | | | | |
| (21) 2.8 | (22) 3.0 | (28) 2.5 | | | | | | | |
| 12.0 | 16.9 | 4.1 | | | | | | | |
| | | | % Officers', Directors' Owners' Comp/Sales | | | | | | |
| 835525M | 1161552M | 1832510M | Net Sales ($) | 3761M | 18785M | 18663M | 20292M | 79502M | 1691507M |
| 834727M | 947444M | 1352119M | Total Assets ($) | 10255M | 101847M | 3576M | 23143M | 170644M | 1042654M |

M = $ thousand    MM = $ million
See Pages 9 through 22 for Explanation of Ratios and Data

# ADMINISTRATIVE AND SUPPORT AND WASTE MANAGEMENT AND REMEDIATION SERVICES

## Current Data Sorted by Assets      Comparative Historical Data

| | | | | | | Type of Statement | | |
|---|---|---|---|---|---|---|---|---|
| | 5 | 14 | 17 | 3 | 8 | Unqualified | 48 | 54 |
| 3 | 6 | 20 | 5 | | | Reviewed | 21 | 21 |
| 7 | 10 | 5 | | 1 | | Compiled | 15 | 19 |
| 43 | 27 | 13 | | 1 | | Tax Returns | 48 | 84 |
| 31 | 41 | 37 | 27 | 5 | 7 | Other | 109 | 140 |
| | 46 (4/1-9/30/11) | | 290 (10/1/11-3/31/12) | | | | 4/1/07-3/31/08 | 4/1/08-3/31/09 |
| 0-500M | 500M-2MM | 2-10MM | 10-50MM | 50-100MM | 100-250MM | | ALL | ALL |
| 84 | 89 | 89 | 49 | 10 | 15 | **NUMBER OF STATEMENTS** | 241 | 318 |
| % | % | % | % | % | % | **ASSETS** | % | % |
| 37.1 | 20.8 | 20.3 | 21.2 | 10.3 | 11.5 | Cash & Equivalents | 19.2 | 19.7 |
| 13.2 | 23.3 | 29.7 | 23.2 | 29.7 | 11.1 | Trade Receivables (net) | 25.9 | 20.4 |
| .6 | 1.1 | 1.8 | 2.8 | .2 | 4.8 | Inventory | 3.3 | 2.5 |
| 7.2 | 7.6 | 4.1 | 9.6 | 6.9 | 8.3 | All Other Current | 8.9 | 7.1 |
| 58.2 | 52.8 | 56.0 | 56.8 | 47.0 | 35.7 | Total Current | 57.3 | 49.7 |
| 17.0 | 20.9 | 27.2 | 21.3 | 25.3 | 30.3 | Fixed Assets (net) | 23.9 | 27.3 |
| 4.5 | 6.5 | 7.0 | 10.5 | 17.2 | 17.6 | Intangibles (net) | 5.6 | 7.4 |
| 20.3 | 19.8 | 9.8 | 11.4 | 10.5 | 16.4 | All Other Non-Current | 13.2 | 15.6 |
| 100.0 | 100.0 | 100.0 | 100.0 | 100.0 | 100.0 | Total | 100.0 | 100.0 |
| | | | | | | **LIABILITIES** | | |
| 14.1 | 9.9 | 6.8 | 5.8 | 4.0 | 3.7 | Notes Payable-Short Term | 11.6 | 9.7 |
| 4.1 | 2.6 | 4.3 | 2.8 | 3.3 | 1.3 | Cur. Mat.-L.T.D. | 4.4 | 3.8 |
| 10.9 | 8.2 | 10.7 | 10.1 | 12.0 | 6.5 | Trade Payables | 9.6 | 9.9 |
| .0 | .1 | .4 | 1.5 | 1.1 | .1 | Income Taxes Payable | .3 | .3 |
| 28.0 | 16.7 | 15.7 | 19.0 | 20.1 | 21.5 | All Other Current | 19.8 | 22.0 |
| 57.1 | 37.6 | 38.0 | 39.2 | 40.5 | 33.1 | Total Current | 45.7 | 45.8 |
| 7.6 | 13.8 | 18.9 | 16.3 | 21.8 | 28.5 | Long-Term Debt | 15.7 | 22.1 |
| .0 | .1 | .1 | .4 | .1 | .8 | Deferred Taxes | .1 | .1 |
| 7.5 | 8.2 | 9.6 | 8.0 | 7.7 | 3.8 | All Other Non-Current | 6.5 | 7.1 |
| 27.9 | 40.4 | 33.4 | 35.8 | 30.0 | 33.8 | Net Worth | 32.0 | 24.9 |
| 100.0 | 100.0 | 100.0 | 100.0 | 100.0 | 100.0 | Total Liabilities & Net Worth | 100.0 | 100.0 |
| | | | | | | **INCOME DATA** | | |
| 100.0 | 100.0 | 100.0 | 100.0 | 100.0 | 100.0 | Net Sales | 100.0 | 100.0 |
| | | | | | | Gross Profit | | |
| 88.9 | 85.8 | 88.8 | 88.8 | 94.1 | 94.0 | Operating Expenses | 89.4 | 87.5 |
| 11.1 | 14.2 | 11.2 | 11.2 | 5.9 | 6.0 | Operating Profit | 10.6 | 12.5 |
| 1.2 | 2.1 | 3.4 | 2.9 | 1.0 | 2.8 | All Other Expenses (net) | 1.8 | 3.4 |
| 10.0 | 12.1 | 7.8 | 8.3 | 4.9 | 3.2 | Profit Before Taxes | 8.8 | 9.2 |
| | | | | | | **RATIOS** | | |
| 4.3 | 3.3 | 2.8 | 2.6 | 1.6 | 1.8 | | 2.5 | 2.3 |
| 1.2 | 1.6 | 1.5 | 1.5 | 1.2 | 1.4 | Current | 1.3 | 1.3 |
| .4 | .6 | .9 | 1.0 | .9 | .5 | | .8 | .6 |
| 3.4 | 2.6 | 2.7 | 2.2 | 1.3 | 1.5 | | 1.9 | 2.0 |
| 1.1 | 1.3 | 1.2 | 1.1 | 1.0 | 1.0 | Quick | (240) 1.1 | (317) 1.0 |
| .3 | .5 | .7 | .7 | .4 | .3 | | .6 | .4 |
| 0 UND | 0 UND | 0 999.8 | 18 20.5 | 16 23.1 | 15 24.4 | | 0 UND | 0 UND |
| 0 UND | 15 24.1 | 29 12.7 | 32 11.3 | 60 6.1 | 33 11.0 | Sales/Receivables | 26 14.1 | 18 20.8 |
| 4 81.9 | 60 6.1 | 66 5.5 | 62 5.9 | 85 4.3 | 54 6.7 | | 56 6.5 | 50 7.3 |
| | | | | | | Cost of Sales/Inventory | | |
| | | | | | | Cost of Sales/Payables | | |
| 9.6 | 6.7 | 5.1 | 4.4 | 8.0 | 4.8 | | 5.8 | 7.4 |
| 78.9 | 21.5 | 22.1 | 8.9 | 29.6 | 8.0 | Sales/Working Capital | 27.6 | 38.5 |
| -22.1 | -49.2 | -41.6 | 239.9 | NM | -6.6 | | -62.9 | -17.8 |
| 29.0 | 63.1 | 22.9 | 11.6 | | 8.0 | | 21.9 | 16.6 |
| (39) 10.2 | (53) 15.6 | (67) 7.7 | (35) 4.5 | | (12) 4.8 | EBIT/Interest | (178) 6.5 | (228) 5.5 |
| 2.0 | 4.1 | 1.6 | 1.6 | | -.6 | | 1.4 | 1.4 |
| | | 6.0 | 16.9 | | | Net Profit + Depr., Dep., | 12.3 | 7.3 |
| | (14) 2.4 | (12) 3.7 | | | | Amort./Cur. Mat. L/T/D | (31) 5.5 | (30) 2.7 |
| | | 1.2 | 2.2 | | | | 1.6 | 1.3 |
| .0 | .1 | .0 | .1 | .4 | .5 | | .1 | .1 |
| .1 | .4 | .7 | .5 | 1.5 | .8 | Fixed/Worth | .5 | .9 |
| 2.0 | 6.2 | 4.5 | 1.8 | -8.6 | -1.9 | | 4.8 | 19.5 |
| .5 | .3 | .7 | .9 | 1.9 | .7 | | .8 | .8 |
| 1.8 | 1.1 | 2.3 | 2.1 | 3.0 | 1.6 | Debt/Worth | 2.3 | 2.8 |
| 53.3 | NM | 17.5 | 22.0 | -12.3 | -3.7 | | 15.4 | UND |
| 137.5 | 95.5 | 70.3 | 96.9 | | 69.8 | % Profit Before Taxes/Tangible | 83.5 | 111.6 |
| (66) 32.9 | (67) 37.2 | (72) 16.8 | (41) 19.2 | | (11) 17.1 | Net Worth | (194) 36.4 | (240) 38.7 |
| 7.5 | 15.0 | 3.5 | 5.0 | | 7.6 | | 9.0 | 9.4 |
| 60.7 | 39.6 | 23.3 | 14.9 | 18.9 | 11.0 | % Profit Before Taxes/Total | 26.6 | 32.6 |
| 21.0 | 16.0 | 5.4 | 6.7 | 5.3 | 6.5 | Assets | 10.5 | 8.8 |
| 2.1 | 3.2 | 1.6 | 2.3 | .9 | -.2 | | 1.4 | 1.2 |
| UND | 151.3 | 150.5 | 95.7 | 49.1 | 10.9 | | 216.4 | 123.2 |
| 280.3 | 27.8 | 26.4 | 11.3 | 21.7 | 5.5 | Sales/Net Fixed Assets | 32.6 | 21.4 |
| 25.5 | 9.4 | 3.6 | 3.5 | 4.6 | 2.1 | | 6.5 | 5.0 |
| 11.5 | 4.9 | 4.1 | 2.6 | 3.3 | 1.9 | | 4.9 | 4.7 |
| 4.8 | 2.6 | 2.2 | 1.5 | 2.2 | .9 | Sales/Total Assets | 2.6 | 2.4 |
| 2.7 | 1.2 | .9 | .6 | 1.2 | .3 | | 1.3 | 1.0 |
| .3 | .6 | .6 | .8 | | | | .4 | .6 |
| (29) 1.6 | (55) 1.6 | (65) 2.4 | (38) 2.5 | | | % Depr., Dep., Amort./Sales | (154) 1.3 | (205) 2.0 |
| 2.7 | 4.0 | 5.0 | 3.7 | | | | 4.1 | 5.5 |
| 5.3 | 3.7 | 2.1 | 1.1 | | | % Officers', Directors' | 2.0 | 3.2 |
| (32) 10.0 | (33) 7.1 | (24) 4.7 | (10) 5.0 | | | Owners' Comp/Sales | (55) 7.8 | (73) 9.1 |
| 18.6 | 11.3 | 14.6 | 18.6 | | | | 14.2 | 17.9 |
| 129997M | 332964M | 1239101M | 2178378M | 3607284M | 2679369M | Net Sales ($) | 8221137M | 9473596M |
| 17308M | 98083M | 433017M | 1171983M | 676273M | 2308138M | Total Assets ($) | 3937202M | 5596866M |

© RMA 2012

M = $ thousand    MM = $ million
See Pages 9 through 22 for Explanation of Ratios and Data

| Comparative Historical Data | | | Type of Statement | Current Data Sorted by Sales | | | | | |
|---|---|---|---|---|---|---|---|---|---|
| 47 | 52 | 47 | Unqualified | 2 | 4 | 1 | 6 | 14 | 20 |
| 40 | 29 | 34 | Reviewed | 4 | 2 | 2 | 10 | 10 | 6 |
| 16 | 19 | 23 | Compiled | 8 | 5 | 3 | 2 | 4 | 1 |
| 67 | 84 | 84 | Tax Returns | 32 | 25 | 14 | 8 | 4 | 1 |
| 142 | 157 | 148 | Other | 29 | 29 | 16 | 18 | 21 | 35 |
| 4/1/09-3/31/10 ALL | 4/1/10-3/31/11 ALL | 4/1/11-3/31/12 ALL | | 46 (4/1-9/30/11) | | | 290 (10/1/11-3/31/12) | | |
| | | | | 0-1MM | 1-3MM | 3-5MM | 5-10MM | 10-25MM | 25MM & OVER |
| 312 | 341 | 336 | NUMBER OF STATEMENTS | 75 | 65 | 36 | 44 | 53 | 63 |
| % | % | % | ASSETS | % | % | % | % | % | % |
| 20.1 | 19.9 | 24.1 | Cash & Equivalents | 26.0 | 24.9 | 27.6 | 27.2 | 22.0 | 18.4 |
| 22.8 | 21.5 | 22.1 | Trade Receivables (net) | 13.7 | 15.8 | 26.3 | 21.6 | 32.2 | 28.1 |
| 2.5 | 1.9 | 1.6 | Inventory | .8 | .7 | 1.3 | 1.1 | 1.4 | 4.0 |
| 6.7 | 8.8 | 6.9 | All Other Current | 9.9 | 6.4 | 4.7 | 3.2 | 7.8 | 6.9 |
| 52.2 | 52.1 | 54.6 | Total Current | 50.3 | 47.8 | 59.8 | 53.1 | 63.4 | 57.4 |
| 24.5 | 25.3 | 22.2 | Fixed Assets (net) | 25.2 | 22.0 | 15.0 | 28.7 | 19.0 | 21.3 |
| 9.6 | 5.9 | 7.5 | Intangibles (net) | 5.0 | 7.0 | 9.6 | 2.9 | 9.3 | 11.6 |
| 13.7 | 16.7 | 15.6 | All Other Non-Current | 19.6 | 23.1 | 15.6 | 15.2 | 8.3 | 9.7 |
| 100.0 | 100.0 | 100.0 | Total | 100.0 | 100.0 | 100.0 | 100.0 | 100.0 | 100.0 |
| | | | LIABILITIES | | | | | | |
| 12.2 | 6.7 | 9.1 | Notes Payable-Short Term | 12.8 | 11.2 | 13.3 | 4.6 | 6.2 | 5.6 |
| 3.0 | 3.3 | 3.4 | Cur. Mat.-L.T.D. | 2.7 | 3.3 | 2.9 | 5.3 | 3.8 | 3.2 |
| 10.8 | 9.8 | 9.9 | Trade Payables | 11.3 | 4.8 | 7.7 | 8.3 | 12.7 | 13.2 |
| .5 | .3 | .4 | Income Taxes Payable | .1 | .0 | .4 | .2 | 1.2 | .7 |
| 19.1 | 22.0 | 19.9 | All Other Current | 22.9 | 18.6 | 14.5 | 17.3 | 22.0 | 20.9 |
| 45.5 | 42.0 | 42.7 | Total Current | 49.7 | 37.9 | 38.8 | 35.7 | 46.0 | 43.6 |
| 22.8 | 18.8 | 14.9 | Long-Term Debt | 16.6 | 14.2 | 10.7 | 15.8 | 14.0 | 16.0 |
| .2 | .2 | .1 | Deferred Taxes | .0 | .0 | .0 | .2 | .3 | .4 |
| 9.4 | 9.7 | 8.2 | All Other Non-Current | 8.7 | 9.2 | 3.0 | 8.6 | 11.9 | 6.0 |
| 22.0 | 29.3 | 34.1 | Net Worth | 25.1 | 38.6 | 47.5 | 39.7 | 27.8 | 34.1 |
| 100.0 | 100.0 | 100.0 | Total Liabilities & Net Worth | 100.0 | 100.0 | 100.0 | 100.0 | 100.0 | 100.0 |
| | | | INCOME DATA | | | | | | |
| 100.0 | 100.0 | 100.0 | Net Sales | 100.0 | 100.0 | 100.0 | 100.0 | 100.0 | 100.0 |
| | | | Gross Profit | | | | | | |
| 90.2 | 87.4 | 88.4 | Operating Expenses | 83.8 | 85.4 | 86.1 | 92.2 | 90.3 | 94.2 |
| 9.8 | 12.6 | 11.6 | Operating Profit | 16.2 | 14.6 | 13.9 | 7.8 | 9.7 | 5.8 |
| 2.9 | 2.9 | 2.3 | All Other Expenses (net) | 6.0 | 1.2 | 2.0 | .7 | 1.3 | 1.4 |
| 6.9 | 9.7 | 9.3 | Profit Before Taxes | 10.3 | 13.4 | 11.8 | 7.1 | 8.4 | 4.5 |
| | | | RATIOS | | | | | | |
| 2.7 | 3.0 | 2.8 | | 4.0 | 5.6 | 4.5 | 2.6 | 2.7 | 2.0 |
| 1.4 | 1.5 | 1.4 | Current | 1.2 | 1.2 | 1.7 | 1.9 | 1.5 | 1.3 |
| .7 | .8 | .7 | | .3 | .3 | 1.0 | 1.1 | .9 | 1.0 |
| 2.3 | 2.2 | 2.5 | | 3.0 | 5.5 | 4.0 | 2.4 | 2.3 | 1.7 |
| 1.1 | 1.1 | 1.2 | Quick | 1.0 | .9 | 1.5 | 1.5 | 1.2 | 1.1 |
| .4 | .5 | .4 | | .2 | .2 | .8 | .9 | .7 | .6 |
| 0 UND | 0 UND | 0 UND | | 0 UND | 0 UND | 0 UND | 0 UND | 0 UND | 15 24.4 |
| 19 19.1 | 13 27.1 | 14 26.9 | Sales/Receivables | 0 UND | 0 UND | 27 13.7 | 17 22.1 | 32 11.4 | 35 10.5 |
| 54 6.8 | 50 7.3 | 53 6.9 | | 21 17.4 | 28 12.9 | 54 6.8 | 54 6.8 | 73 5.0 | 61 6.0 |
| | | | Cost of Sales/Inventory | | | | | | |
| | | | Cost of Sales/Payables | | | | | | |
| 6.3 | 6.2 | 6.1 | | 5.4 | 5.3 | 7.7 | 4.2 | 6.4 | 7.4 |
| 22.9 | 19.2 | 21.8 | Sales/Working Capital | 29.4 | 25.1 | 22.5 | 15.4 | 14.4 | 22.2 |
| -49.3 | -35.7 | -41.4 | | -14.1 | -16.3 | NM | 277.0 | -44.7 | -94.2 |
| 26.0 | 27.6 | 23.8 | | 11.4 | 33.6 | 49.5 | 18.7 | 38.1 | 16.7 |
| (228) 6.7 | (223) 7.0 | (215) 8.0 | EBIT/Interest | (27) 3.4 | (41) 9.9 | (26) 21.7 | (35) 8.8 | (38) 8.4 | (48) 7.2 |
| 1.1 | 1.6 | 2.0 | | .1 | 1.2 | 8.4 | 1.4 | 2.4 | 2.6 |
| 7.5 | 15.1 | 7.7 | | | | | | 12.4 | 20.8 |
| (32) 2.5 | (29) 4.6 | (36) 3.4 | Net Profit + Depr., Dep., Amort./Cur. Mat. L/T/D | | | | (10) 2.1 | (12) 4.2 | |
| 1.0 | 2.1 | 1.7 | | | | | | .7 | 3.1 |
| .1 | .1 | .0 | | .0 | .0 | .0 | .1 | .0 | .3 |
| .7 | .5 | .4 | Fixed/Worth | .2 | .4 | .2 | .7 | .4 | .6 |
| 26.7 | 7.5 | 3.3 | | 15.7 | 2.8 | .9 | 1.8 | 9.3 | 2.3 |
| .7 | .6 | .6 | | .6 | .4 | .3 | .5 | .8 | 1.1 |
| 2.8 | 2.0 | 1.8 | Debt/Worth | 2.2 | 1.4 | 1.0 | 1.3 | 3.1 | 2.1 |
| -41.7 | -144.5 | 28.2 | | -17.0 | 20.9 | 4.1 | 5.4 | -36.4 | 8.9 |
| 74.7 | 88.7 | 92.4 | | 65.0 | 136.1 | 107.8 | 72.3 | 136.5 | 62.7 |
| (229) 40.0 | (252) 24.6 | (264) 30.2 | % Profit Before Taxes/Tangible Net Worth | (54) 23.3 | (52) 40.0 | (29) 63.4 | (38) 11.1 | (39) 65.5 | (52) 30.3 |
| 8.7 | 6.0 | 8.0 | | 6.5 | 5.2 | 16.4 | .9 | 14.3 | 9.0 |
| 26.1 | 28.5 | 27.6 | | 22.7 | 59.6 | 45.8 | 27.6 | 27.1 | 15.1 |
| 9.3 | 8.4 | 9.7 | % Profit Before Taxes/Total Assets | 8.1 | 16.8 | 21.2 | 8.9 | 13.0 | 6.5 |
| .1 | .9 | 1.8 | | .7 | 1.8 | 3.6 | .9 | 4.2 | 2.5 |
| 112.8 | 137.8 | 282.0 | | UND | 605.4 | UND | 67.9 | 659.3 | 88.9 |
| 26.0 | 22.7 | 29.2 | Sales/Net Fixed Assets | 30.7 | 31.0 | 53.9 | 19.7 | 36.6 | 21.4 |
| 6.1 | 5.0 | 6.4 | | 2.4 | 7.4 | 14.6 | 3.3 | 10.9 | 5.5 |
| 4.5 | 5.0 | 4.8 | | 4.7 | 4.7 | 5.0 | 5.6 | 5.2 | 4.5 |
| 2.5 | 2.3 | 2.5 | Sales/Total Assets | 1.9 | 2.6 | 2.7 | 2.7 | 2.4 | 2.8 |
| 1.2 | 1.0 | 1.0 | | .3 | 1.2 | 1.3 | 1.0 | 1.5 | 1.5 |
| .5 | .6 | .6 | | .5 | .5 | .5 | .7 | .5 | .4 |
| (210) 1.8 | (232) 2.1 | (202) 1.9 | % Depr., Dep., Amort./Sales | (32) 3.0 | (34) 1.7 | (19) 2.0 | (35) 2.4 | (37) 1.9 | (45) 1.3 |
| 4.1 | 5.4 | 4.0 | | 12.0 | 4.2 | 4.0 | 5.2 | 2.6 | 3.5 |
| 3.9 | 3.4 | 2.5 | | 5.6 | 3.5 | 2.2 | 4.6 | 1.6 | 1.0 |
| (79) 7.9 | (75) 8.9 | (103) 7.4 | % Officers', Directors' Owners' Comp/Sales | (20) 11.3 | (30) 10.0 | (12) 4.9 | (17) 8.0 | (13) 2.4 | (11) 2.3 |
| 20.1 | 18.0 | 15.3 | | 26.0 | 17.1 | 8.5 | 12.0 | 7.2 | 9.1 |
| 10977076M | 8068743M | 10167093M | Net Sales ($) | 34888M | 119308M | 144292M | 298448M | 817825M | 8752332M |
| 5183679M | 5572062M | 4704802M | Total Assets ($) | 59500M | 89307M | 94287M | 362702M | 457064M | 3641942M |

© RMA 2012

M = $ thousand    MM = $ million
See Pages 9 through 22 for Explanation of Ratios and Data

## Current Data Sorted by Assets      Comparative Historical Data

| 0-500M | 500M-2MM | 2-10MM | 10-50MM | 50-100MM | 100-250MM | Type of Statement | 4/1/07-3/31/08 ALL | 4/1/08-3/31/09 ALL |
|---|---|---|---|---|---|---|---|---|
| | 3 | 14 | 14 | 2 | 1 | Unqualified | 30 | 33 |
| 1 | 3 | 12 | 4 | | | Reviewed | 9 | 16 |
| 1 | 2 | 2 | 2 | | | Compiled | 6 | 5 |
| 7 | 5 | 6 | 1 | | | Tax Returns | 9 | 12 |
| 4 | 13 | 25 | 15 | 2 | 2 | Other | 30 | 41 |
| | 20 (4/1-9/30/11) | | 121 (10/1/11-3/31/12) | | | | | |
| 13 | 26 | 59 | 36 | 4 | 3 | **NUMBER OF STATEMENTS** | 84 | 107 |
| % | % | % | % | % | % | **ASSETS** | % | % |
| 32.0 | 19.6 | 13.5 | 10.9 | | | Cash & Equivalents | 14.3 | 15.6 |
| 13.0 | 39.3 | 49.1 | 39.0 | | | Trade Receivables (net) | 43.3 | 39.3 |
| 11.1 | 1.2 | 2.2 | 1.6 | | | Inventory | 2.3 | 2.0 |
| 6.7 | 3.5 | 5.3 | 10.4 | | | All Other Current | 6.5 | 6.1 |
| 62.9 | 63.6 | 70.1 | 62.0 | | | Total Current | 66.5 | 63.0 |
| 22.0 | 27.6 | 21.5 | 21.5 | | | Fixed Assets (net) | 23.3 | 22.8 |
| 4.6 | 5.6 | 1.5 | 5.4 | | | Intangibles (net) | 2.3 | 2.8 |
| 10.6 | 3.2 | 6.9 | 11.1 | | | All Other Non-Current | 7.9 | 11.4 |
| 100.0 | 100.0 | 100.0 | 100.0 | | | Total | 100.0 | 100.0 |
| | | | | | | **LIABILITIES** | | |
| 30.2 | 5.2 | 12.3 | 7.2 | | | Notes Payable-Short Term | 9.9 | 7.9 |
| 16.1 | 2.8 | 2.9 | 3.3 | | | Cur. Mat.-L.T.D. | 4.5 | 3.9 |
| 14.3 | 13.0 | 15.6 | 12.8 | | | Trade Payables | 13.2 | 14.8 |
| .0 | .0 | .1 | .3 | | | Income Taxes Payable | .2 | .6 |
| 11.4 | 13.0 | 14.0 | 17.2 | | | All Other Current | 17.5 | 15.9 |
| 72.0 | 34.0 | 45.0 | 40.8 | | | Total Current | 45.4 | 43.0 |
| 11.1 | 11.0 | 11.4 | 14.1 | | | Long-Term Debt | 13.1 | 14.5 |
| .0 | .0 | .2 | .8 | | | Deferred Taxes | .3 | .3 |
| 9.4 | 2.3 | 3.3 | 1.0 | | | All Other Non-Current | 2.7 | 2.2 |
| 7.5 | 52.8 | 40.1 | 43.3 | | | Net Worth | 38.5 | 40.0 |
| 100.0 | 100.0 | 100.0 | 100.0 | | | Total Liabilities & Net Worth | 100.0 | 100.0 |
| | | | | | | **INCOME DATA** | | |
| 100.0 | 100.0 | 100.0 | 100.0 | | | Net Sales | 100.0 | 100.0 |
| | | | | | | Gross Profit | | |
| 88.3 | 86.6 | 90.4 | 91.5 | | | Operating Expenses | 90.6 | 91.6 |
| 11.7 | 13.4 | 9.6 | 8.5 | | | Operating Profit | 9.4 | 8.4 |
| 1.4 | -.4 | 1.7 | .5 | | | All Other Expenses (net) | 2.0 | .8 |
| 10.2 | 13.9 | 7.9 | 8.0 | | | Profit Before Taxes | 7.4 | 7.6 |
| | | | | | | **RATIOS** | | |
| 4.6 | 3.8 | 2.9 | 2.4 | | | | 2.5 | 2.4 |
| 1.3 | 2.2 | 1.4 | 1.5 | | | Current | 1.6 | 1.5 |
| .6 | 1.2 | 1.2 | 1.0 | | | | 1.1 | 1.0 |
| 3.3 | 3.8 | 2.9 | 1.7 | | | | 2.4 | 1.9 |
| .7 | 2.1 | 1.3 | 1.1 | | | Quick | 1.5 | 1.3 |
| .4 | 1.2 | 1.0 | .9 | | | | .9 | .9 |
| 0 UND | 2 224.1 | 29 12.6 | 34 10.6 | | | | 27 13.3 | 27 13.7 |
| 0 UND | 32 11.3 | 47 7.7 | 51 7.2 | | | Sales/Receivables | 52 7.1 | 48 7.6 |
| 0 UND | 54 6.7 | 64 5.7 | 63 5.8 | | | | 71 5.1 | 66 5.6 |
| | | | | | | Cost of Sales/Inventory | | |
| | | | | | | Cost of Sales/Payables | | |
| 6.8 | 6.3 | 5.9 | 6.6 | | | | 6.5 | 7.0 |
| 56.7 | 12.4 | 19.4 | 14.2 | | | Sales/Working Capital | 14.0 | 16.6 |
| -25.5 | 35.3 | 46.9 | 126.5 | | | | 58.4 | 350.0 |
| | 73.3 | 32.2 | 63.1 | | | | 31.3 | 29.5 |
| | (13) 46.9 | (50) 13.7 | (30) 12.3 | | | EBIT/Interest | (66) 9.1 | (87) 11.4 |
| | 4.5 | 2.8 | 5.2 | | | | 3.2 | 2.6 |
| | | 20.0 | | | | | 24.4 | 22.0 |
| | | (10) 7.9 | | | | Net Profit + Depr., Dep., Amort./Cur. Mat. L/T/D | (23) 5.6 | (19) 8.6 |
| | | 2.1 | | | | | 2.0 | 5.4 |
| .0 | .1 | .1 | .1 | | | | .1 | .1 |
| .5 | .3 | .3 | .3 | | | Fixed/Worth | .4 | .4 |
| NM | 1.0 | 1.1 | 1.1 | | | | 1.5 | 1.1 |
| .5 | .3 | .7 | .7 | | | | .6 | .7 |
| -14.9 | .8 | 2.0 | 1.8 | | | Debt/Worth | 1.5 | 1.5 |
| -2.9 | 2.9 | 3.3 | 4.0 | | | | 7.7 | 4.6 |
| | 106.2 | 59.1 | 62.8 | | | | 72.2 | 74.3 |
| | (23) 58.6 | (57) 29.7 | (34) 31.1 | | | % Profit Before Taxes/Tangible Net Worth | (76) 38.6 | (99) 38.8 |
| | 13.3 | 4.2 | 11.3 | | | | 20.0 | 12.3 |
| 144.2 | 43.9 | 23.0 | 17.2 | | | | 24.4 | 25.5 |
| 20.8 | 21.1 | 10.2 | 11.9 | | | % Profit Before Taxes/Total Assets | 13.2 | 12.1 |
| .3 | 6.5 | 2.5 | 4.6 | | | | 3.4 | 3.3 |
| UND | 206.5 | 153.3 | 114.5 | | | | 126.2 | 157.4 |
| 164.5 | 34.3 | 39.7 | 51.4 | | | Sales/Net Fixed Assets | 20.3 | 29.4 |
| 28.4 | 5.5 | 5.9 | 4.4 | | | | 5.3 | 5.8 |
| 16.1 | 6.0 | 5.2 | 4.0 | | | | 4.3 | 4.1 |
| 5.9 | 3.6 | 3.9 | 2.9 | | | Sales/Total Assets | 3.0 | 3.2 |
| 1.0 | 2.0 | 1.5 | 1.2 | | | | 1.4 | 1.7 |
| | .4 | .3 | .4 | | | | .3 | .4 |
| | (18) 1.4 | (48) .9 | (29) .8 | | | % Depr., Dep., Amort./Sales | (64) 1.0 | (70) 1.5 |
| | 4.4 | 3.5 | 3.4 | | | | 3.4 | 3.8 |
| | | .6 | | | | | .8 | 1.4 |
| | | (11) 2.1 | | | | % Officers', Directors' Owners' Comp/Sales | (19) 1.9 | (22) 2.8 |
| | | 9.8 | | | | | 10.0 | 5.5 |
| 31767M | 157292M | 1049424M | 2110347M | 545298M | 566702M | Net Sales ($) | 3755832M | 4988406M |
| 3619M | 34927M | 287392M | 730307M | 309408M | 511693M | Total Assets ($) | 1899437M | 2530255M |

M = $ thousand    MM = $ million
See Pages 9 through 22 for Explanation of Ratios and Data

## Comparative Historical Data

## Current Data Sorted by Sales

| | | | | | Type of Statement | | | | | | |
|---|---|---|---|---|---|---|---|---|---|---|---|
| | 30 | | 31 | | 34 | Unqualified | | 1 | 4 | 5 | 5 | 19 |
| | 19 | | 15 | | 20 | Reviewed | | | | 5 | 7 | 8 |
| | 7 | | 5 | | 7 | Compiled | 1 | 1 | 1 | 2 | 2 | 2 |
| | 16 | | 17 | | 19 | Tax Returns | 4 | 3 | 1 | 5 | 5 | 1 |
| | 47 | | 45 | | 61 | Other | 8 | 5 | 7 | 11 | 13 | 17 |
| | 4/1/09-3/31/10 ALL | | 4/1/10-3/31/11 ALL | | 4/1/11-3/31/12 ALL | | 0-1MM | 20 (4/1-9/30/11) 1-3MM | 3-5MM | 121 (10/1/11-3/31/12) 5-10MM | 10-25MM | 25MM & OVER |
| | 119 | | 113 | | 141 | NUMBER OF STATEMENTS | 13 | 10 | 13 | 26 | 32 | 47 |
| | % | | % | | % | ASSETS | % | % | % | % | % | % |
| | 17.2 | | 16.1 | | 15.8 | Cash & Equivalents | 13.2 | 34.3 | 18.3 | 16.3 | 14.2 | 12.8 |
| | 36.3 | | 41.7 | | 39.9 | Trade Receivables (net) | 6.6 | 13.0 | 34.4 | 35.8 | 50.6 | 51.5 |
| | 2.6 | | 2.4 | | 2.7 | Inventory | 9.4 | 2.3 | .4 | 4.6 | .8 | 1.6 |
| | 5.5 | | 8.1 | | 6.3 | All Other Current | 6.4 | 1.3 | 4.5 | 4.1 | 6.9 | 8.7 |
| | 61.6 | | 68.4 | | 64.7 | Total Current | 35.6 | 50.8 | 57.7 | 60.7 | 72.5 | 74.6 |
| | 25.8 | | 22.1 | | 23.6 | Fixed Assets (net) | 50.6 | 23.9 | 34.1 | 27.3 | 19.8 | 13.7 |
| | 4.9 | | 3.4 | | 3.8 | Intangibles (net) | 10.7 | 4.4 | 1.7 | .5 | 1.9 | 5.5 |
| | 7.7 | | 6.1 | | 7.9 | All Other Non-Current | 3.1 | 20.9 | 6.4 | 11.5 | 5.8 | 6.2 |
| | 100.0 | | 100.0 | | 100.0 | Total | 100.0 | 100.0 | 100.0 | 100.0 | 100.0 | 100.0 |
| | | | | | | LIABILITIES | | | | | | |
| | 9.9 | | 10.7 | | 10.7 | Notes Payable-Short Term | 13.2 | 23.5 | 8.3 | 5.0 | 10.5 | 11.4 |
| | 3.9 | | 2.8 | | 4.2 | Cur. Mat.-L.T.D. | 1.9 | 4.5 | 2.0 | 10.1 | 1.6 | 3.9 |
| | 10.3 | | 14.1 | | 13.8 | Trade Payables | 9.4 | 7.4 | 8.2 | 15.6 | 12.6 | 17.8 |
| | .3 | | .5 | | .2 | Income Taxes Payable | .0 | .0 | .0 | .1 | .1 | .3 |
| | 16.1 | | 17.3 | | 14.1 | All Other Current | 3.3 | 7.5 | 2.8 | 14.7 | 18.5 | 18.4 |
| | 40.5 | | 45.4 | | 43.0 | Total Current | 27.8 | 42.9 | 21.4 | 45.5 | 43.3 | 51.8 |
| | 18.6 | | 14.0 | | 12.8 | Long-Term Debt | 14.9 | 9.7 | 24.6 | 18.6 | 8.2 | 9.4 |
| | .2 | | .9 | | .4 | Deferred Taxes | .0 | .0 | .0 | .3 | .4 | .6 |
| | 4.7 | | 6.0 | | 3.0 | All Other Non-Current | 8.0 | 2.5 | 2.2 | 3.0 | 3.9 | 1.4 |
| | 36.0 | | 33.7 | | 40.8 | Net Worth | 49.2 | 44.9 | 51.8 | 32.6 | 44.2 | 36.8 |
| | 100.0 | | 100.0 | | 100.0 | Total Liabilities & Net Worth | 100.0 | 100.0 | 100.0 | 100.0 | 100.0 | 100.0 |
| | | | | | | INCOME DATA | | | | | | |
| | 100.0 | | 100.0 | | 100.0 | Net Sales | 100.0 | 100.0 | 100.0 | 100.0 | 100.0 | 100.0 |
| | | | | | | Gross Profit | | | | | | |
| | 90.5 | | 91.8 | | 90.1 | Operating Expenses | 63.5 | 82.4 | 80.6 | 92.5 | 96.0 | 96.4 |
| | 9.5 | | 8.2 | | 9.9 | Operating Profit | 36.5 | 17.6 | 19.4 | 7.5 | 4.0 | 3.6 |
| | 2.6 | | 1.5 | | 1.0 | All Other Expenses (net) | 6.5 | 1.8 | .1 | .8 | .4 | .1 |
| | 6.9 | | 6.7 | | 8.9 | Profit Before Taxes | 30.0 | 15.8 | 19.3 | 6.7 | 3.6 | 3.5 |
| | | | | | | RATIOS | | | | | | |
| | 2.6 | | 2.7 | | 2.8 | | 19.6 | 5.0 | 8.6 | 2.8 | 3.7 | 2.2 |
| | 1.5 | | 1.7 | | 1.7 | Current | 2.4 | 1.7 | 2.7 | 2.1 | 1.4 | 1.4 |
| | 1.0 | | 1.2 | | 1.2 | | .8 | .5 | 1.4 | 1.2 | 1.2 | 1.1 |
| | 2.4 | | 2.4 | | 2.7 | | 9.3 | 4.9 | 8.2 | 2.8 | 3.6 | 1.8 |
| | 1.3 | | 1.3 | | 1.3 | Quick | 2.4 | 1.7 | 2.7 | 1.5 | 1.3 | 1.3 |
| | .9 | | 1.0 | | 1.0 | | .5 | .4 | .9 | .9 | 1.0 | 1.0 |
| 20 | 18.5 | 31 | 12.0 | 25 | 14.8 | | 0 UND | 0 UND | 34 10.6 | 26 14.3 | 26 14.2 | 38 9.5 |
| 43 | 8.5 | 44 | 8.4 | 46 | 8.0 | Sales/Receivables | 0 UND | 0 UND | 54 6.8 | 44 8.3 | 47 7.7 | 50 7.3 |
| 62 | 5.9 | 63 | 5.8 | 62 | 5.9 | | 0 UND | 45 8.2 | 99 3.7 | 59 6.2 | 61 6.0 | 63 5.8 |
| | | | | | | Cost of Sales/Inventory | | | | | | |
| | | | | | | Cost of Sales/Payables | | | | | | |
| | 6.8 | | 5.8 | | 6.1 | | 5.0 | 5.5 | 2.5 | 5.0 | 7.1 | 7.7 |
| | 14.1 | | 10.4 | | 13.4 | Sales/Working Capital | 12.2 | 22.1 | 5.6 | 13.4 | 20.4 | 14.2 |
| | 964.0 | | 42.8 | | 56.5 | | -16.0 | -37.2 | NM | 34.4 | 45.7 | 68.7 |
| | 31.8 | | 22.7 | | 46.9 | | | | | 33.7 | 72.3 | 60.3 |
| (94) | 6.9 | (84) | 8.3 | (107) | 12.3 | EBIT/Interest | | | (21) 17.7 | (28) 23.0 | (40) 10.8 |
| | 1.2 | | 1.6 | | 3.7 | | | | | 1.2 | 7.9 | 1.5 |
| | 6.2 | | 9.2 | | 25.4 | | | | | | | 12.4 |
| (15) | 2.0 | (19) | 2.8 | (21) | 6.1 | Net Profit + Depr., Dep., Amort./Cur. Mat. L/T/D | | | | | (12) 3.1 |
| | .3 | | 1.6 | | 2.2 | | | | | | | 2.1 |
| | .1 | | .1 | | .1 | | .0 | .0 | .1 | .2 | .1 | .1 |
| | .4 | | .3 | | .3 | Fixed/Worth | 1.0 | .5 | .3 | .4 | .3 | .2 |
| | 2.6 | | 1.7 | | 1.0 | | 2.1 | .6 | 1.7 | 1.6 | 1.5 | 1.0 |
| | .7 | | .7 | | .6 | | .0 | .1 | .4 | .6 | .8 | .8 |
| | 1.9 | | 1.7 | | 1.7 | Debt/Worth | 2.4 | 1.1 | 1.0 | 1.9 | 1.9 | 2.3 |
| | 4.8 | | 4.7 | | 4.0 | | -5.3 | 3.5 | 1.7 | 4.9 | 3.1 | 4.3 |
| | 60.1 | | 79.3 | | 68.1 | % Profit Before Taxes/Tangible Net Worth | | 57.9 | 70.0 | 72.6 | 63.5 |
| (102) | 29.4 | (100) | 35.6 | (127) | 31.3 | | (12) 39.2 | (23) 30.3 | (30) 35.3 | (45) 32.7 |
| | 5.8 | | 13.3 | | 8.0 | | | 6.0 | 3.3 | 7.8 | 12.3 |
| | 23.2 | | 26.0 | | 24.9 | % Profit Before Taxes/Total Assets | 26.6 | 50.1 | 32.4 | 35.3 | 28.0 | 17.4 |
| | 10.0 | | 13.6 | | 13.0 | | 11.8 | 21.3 | 12.2 | 16.5 | 9.8 | 11.8 |
| | .5 | | 3.8 | | 3.1 | | 2.7 | 12.2 | 4.7 | 4.0 | 4.0 | 3.2 |
| | 138.2 | | 127.2 | | 151.5 | | UND | UND | 39.2 | 51.9 | 404.8 | 138.1 |
| | 27.4 | | 41.4 | | 40.4 | Sales/Net Fixed Assets | .8 | 17.4 | 18.5 | 28.3 | 101.2 | 64.2 |
| | 4.5 | | 5.6 | | 5.7 | | .2 | 6.6 | .8 | 4.7 | 6.2 | 16.8 |
| | 4.7 | | 5.0 | | 5.1 | | 1.0 | 5.6 | 3.1 | 5.0 | 5.3 | 5.2 |
| | 2.8 | | 3.4 | | 3.2 | Sales/Total Assets | .6 | 2.6 | 1.7 | 3.1 | 4.6 | 4.0 |
| | 1.4 | | 1.6 | | 1.4 | | .2 | .9 | .5 | 1.5 | 2.3 | 2.9 |
| | .4 | | .5 | | .4 | | | | | .7 | .3 | .2 |
| (82) | 1.8 | (82) | 1.3 | (106) | 1.0 | % Depr., Dep., Amort./Sales | | | (21) 1.3 | (27) .7 | (37) .5 |
| | 3.1 | | 3.6 | | 3.8 | | | | | 3.8 | 3.0 | 1.9 |
| | 1.1 | | 1.5 | | .8 | % Officers', Directors' Owners' Comp/Sales | | | | | |
| (24) | 3.2 | (24) | 4.9 | (23) | 2.6 | | | | | | |
| | 5.4 | | 7.3 | | 7.1 | | | | | | | |
| | 4394957M | | 4606991M | | 4460830M | Net Sales ($) | 5696M | 22440M | 51223M | 185367M | 530542M | 3665562M |
| | 2053514M | | 1948687M | | 1877346M | Total Assets ($) | 20320M | 24870M | 77843M | 102657M | 263054M | 1388602M |

© RMA 2012

M = $ thousand    MM = $ million
See Pages 9 through 22 for Explanation of Ratios and Data

## Current Data Sorted by Assets

## Comparative Historical Data

| | | | | | | | Type of Statement | | |
|---|---|---|---|---|---|---|---|---|---|
| | 2 | 15 | 22 | 2 | | | Unqualified | 52 | 52 |
| | 12 | 30 | 4 | | | | Reviewed | 62 | 57 |
| 6 | 27 | 16 | | 2 | | | Compiled | 41 | 59 |
| 43 | 27 | 8 | 1 | | | | Tax Returns | 50 | 63 |
| 30 | 74 | 80 | 25 | 6 | 6 | | Other | 130 | 141 |
| | 29 (4/1-9/30/11) | | 407 (10/1/11-3/31/12) | | | | | 4/1/07-3/31/08 | 4/1/08-3/31/09 |
| 0-500M | 500M-2MM | 2-10MM | 10-50MM | 50-100MM | 100-250MM | | | ALL | ALL |
| 79 | 142 | 149 | 52 | 8 | 6 | NUMBER OF STATEMENTS | | 335 | 372 |
| % | % | % | % | % | % | **ASSETS** | | % | % |
| 33.3 | 17.3 | 12.9 | 9.5 | | | Cash & Equivalents | | 13.8 | 16.4 |
| 27.5 | 59.0 | 65.3 | 60.7 | | | Trade Receivables (net) | | 53.8 | 46.6 |
| .1 | .0 | .5 | 1.2 | | | Inventory | | .1 | .5 |
| 9.5 | 4.6 | 3.4 | 5.2 | | | All Other Current | | 7.1 | 7.5 |
| 70.4 | 80.9 | 82.1 | 76.7 | | | Total Current | | 74.9 | 71.0 |
| 9.7 | 6.7 | 5.5 | 4.4 | | | Fixed Assets (net) | | 9.0 | 10.1 |
| 7.7 | 5.3 | 3.6 | 13.0 | | | Intangibles (net) | | 5.4 | 7.6 |
| 12.3 | 7.1 | 8.8 | 5.9 | | | All Other Non-Current | | 10.7 | 11.3 |
| 100.0 | 100.0 | 100.0 | 100.0 | | | Total | | 100.0 | 100.0 |
| | | | | | | **LIABILITIES** | | | |
| 30.3 | 21.3 | 19.1 | 17.2 | | | Notes Payable-Short Term | | 21.8 | 21.6 |
| 4.7 | 2.1 | .9 | 2.6 | | | Cur. Mat.-L.T.D. | | 3.0 | 3.0 |
| 8.9 | 6.1 | 8.8 | 10.2 | | | Trade Payables | | 7.4 | 6.8 |
| .0 | .5 | .3 | .2 | | | Income Taxes Payable | | .7 | .4 |
| 23.2 | 21.4 | 18.6 | 22.5 | | | All Other Current | | 21.7 | 19.9 |
| 67.1 | 51.4 | 47.8 | 52.6 | | | Total Current | | 54.5 | 51.8 |
| 20.3 | 5.9 | 5.3 | 14.1 | | | Long-Term Debt | | 8.6 | 14.1 |
| .0 | .0 | .3 | .0 | | | Deferred Taxes | | .2 | .1 |
| 25.5 | 4.8 | 3.6 | 7.3 | | | All Other Non-Current | | 6.6 | 7.6 |
| -13.0 | 37.9 | 43.1 | 25.9 | | | Net Worth | | 30.1 | 26.4 |
| 100.0 | 100.0 | 100.0 | 100.0 | | | Total Liabilties & Net Worth | | 100.0 | 100.0 |
| | | | | | | **INCOME DATA** | | | |
| 100.0 | 100.0 | 100.0 | 100.0 | | | Net Sales | | 100.0 | 100.0 |
| | | | | | | Gross Profit | | | |
| 94.0 | 94.9 | 96.4 | 96.4 | | | Operating Expenses | | 95.9 | 95.9 |
| 6.0 | 5.1 | 3.6 | 3.6 | | | Operating Profit | | 4.1 | 4.1 |
| .1 | .7 | .2 | .7 | | | All Other Expenses (net) | | 1.3 | 1.3 |
| 5.9 | 4.4 | 3.3 | 2.9 | | | Profit Before Taxes | | 2.8 | 2.7 |
| | | | | | | **RATIOS** | | | |
| 3.9 | 3.2 | 2.9 | 2.1 | | | | | 2.3 | 2.8 |
| 1.4 | 1.7 | 1.7 | 1.3 | | | Current | | 1.4 | 1.6 |
| .7 | 1.1 | 1.3 | 1.1 | | | | | 1.0 | 1.0 |
| 3.0 | 3.2 | 2.8 | 1.8 | | | | | 2.2 | 2.5 |
| 1.1 | 1.6 | 1.7 | 1.2 | | | Quick | | 1.3 | 1.4 |
| .5 | 1.1 | 1.2 | 1.0 | | | | | .9 | .8 |

| | | | | | | | | | | | | | | | | |
|---|---|---|---|---|---|---|---|---|---|---|---|---|---|---|---|---|
| 0 | UND | 26 | 13.9 | 35 | 10.4 | 41 | 8.9 | | | | | Sales/Receivables | | 23 | 15.9 | 13 | 28.2 |
| 0 | UND | 41 | 8.9 | 51 | 7.2 | 48 | 7.6 | | | | | | | 39 | 9.4 | 35 | 10.5 |
| 36 | 10.0 | 55 | 6.6 | 68 | 5.4 | 63 | 5.8 | | | | | | | 56 | 6.5 | 51 | 7.1 |

| | | | | | | | Cost of Sales/Inventory | | |
| | | | | | | | Cost of Sales/Payables | | |

| 9.8 | 9.0 | 8.7 | 9.8 | | | Sales/Working Capital | | 11.1 | 10.1 |
|---|---|---|---|---|---|---|---|---|---|
| 131.0 | 17.4 | 14.5 | 24.6 | | | | | 25.2 | 22.4 |
| -50.3 | 98.3 | 30.6 | 49.2 | | | | | 433.2 | UND |

| | | | | | | | | | | |
|---|---|---|---|---|---|---|---|---|---|---|
| | 36.3 | | 29.1 | | 36.8 | | 52.2 | | 12.5 | 13.6 |
| (53) | 5.7 | (105) | 9.4 | (121) | 10.7 | (47) | 8.8 | EBIT/Interest | (275) 4.2 (292) 3.5 |
| | -.8 | | 2.5 | | 2.9 | | 1.7 | | 1.1 .3 |

| | | | | | | | | |
|---|---|---|---|---|---|---|---|---|
| | | | | | | 38.2 | Net Profit + Depr., Dep., | 14.1 9.3 |
| | | | | (12) | 6.2 | Amort./Cur. Mat. L/T/D | (34) 2.8 (38) 2.1 |
| | | | | | 3.4 | | -.1 -1.5 |

| .0 | .0 | .0 | .0 | | | | | .0 | .0 |
|---|---|---|---|---|---|---|---|---|---|
| .1 | .1 | .1 | .2 | | | Fixed/Worth | | .2 | .2 |
| -1.1 | .5 | .2 | .5 | | | | | 1.0 | 1.3 |
| .5 | .6 | .6 | 1.1 | | | | | .8 | .7 |
| 15.1 | 1.7 | 1.3 | 2.4 | | | Debt/Worth | | 2.0 | 1.9 |
| -2.0 | 5.6 | 3.6 | 19.5 | | | | | 7.3 | 26.9 |

| | | | | | | | | |
|---|---|---|---|---|---|---|---|---|
| | 177.4 | | 87.1 | | 55.5 | | 60.3 | 73.6 73.4 |
| (45) | 60.6 | (119) | 44.0 | (138) | 30.3 | (43) | 38.7 | % Profit Before Taxes/Tangible Net Worth (277) 31.5 (287) 24.8 |
| | 12.3 | | 8.1 | | 11.2 | | 17.6 | 5.5 2.0 |

| 75.3 | 28.2 | 22.3 | 21.0 | | | % Profit Before Taxes/Total Assets | | 24.5 | 24.3 |
|---|---|---|---|---|---|---|---|---|---|
| 20.8 | 14.1 | 12.5 | 12.0 | | | | | 10.0 | 7.7 |
| .0 | 2.4 | 3.4 | 2.9 | | | | | .8 | -.7 |
| UND | 999.8 | 626.2 | 272.3 | | | Sales/Net Fixed Assets | | 435.5 | 507.8 |
| 432.4 | 248.5 | 202.9 | 146.2 | | | | | 131.8 | 148.5 |
| 63.9 | 81.8 | 92.3 | 77.2 | | | | | 54.8 | 48.7 |
| 15.9 | 8.3 | 6.8 | 5.6 | | | Sales/Total Assets | | 7.8 | 8.3 |
| 6.9 | 5.7 | 4.9 | 4.3 | | | | | 5.6 | 5.5 |
| 3.9 | 3.8 | 3.6 | 3.2 | | | | | 4.1 | 3.5 |

| | | | | | | | | |
|---|---|---|---|---|---|---|---|---|
| | .1 | | .1 | | .1 | | .2 | .1 .1 |
| (25) | .2 | (70) | .2 | (102) | .2 | (41) | .3 | % Depr., Dep., Amort./Sales (216) .3 (250) .3 |
| | .7 | | .4 | | .4 | | .6 | .6 .6 |

| | | | | | | | | |
|---|---|---|---|---|---|---|---|---|
| | 3.6 | | 1.8 | | .9 | | | 1.4 1.7 |
| (38) | 6.5 | (47) | 4.5 | (39) | 2.3 | | | % Officers', Directors' Owners' Comp/Sales (109) 3.2 (132) 3.5 |
| | 13.4 | | 8.0 | | 4.0 | | | 8.7 8.3 |

| 178402M | 1263644M | 4053201M | 4480675M | 1719116M | 4998793M | Net Sales ($) | | 14600806M | 16493689M |
|---|---|---|---|---|---|---|---|---|---|
| 18466M | 169370M | 694633M | 1043944M | 578131M | 1059840M | Total Assets ($) | | 3069114M | 3874510M |

M = $ thousand    MM = $ million
See Pages 9 through 22 for Explanation of Ratios and Data

## Comparative Historical Data / Current Data Sorted by Sales

| | | Comparative Historical Data | | Type of Statement | Current Data Sorted by Sales | | | | | |
|---|---|---|---|---|---|---|---|---|---|---|
| | 45 | 42 | 41 | Unqualified | | 2 | | 2 | 6 | 31 |
| | 61 | 43 | 46 | Reviewed | | 1 | 3 | 6 | 17 | 19 |
| | 43 | 44 | 49 | Compiled | 2 | 6 | 8 | 12 | 20 | 1 |
| | 50 | 75 | 79 | Tax Returns | 12 | 25 | 13 | 16 | 10 | 3 |
| | 155 | 211 | 221 | Other | 16 | 22 | 20 | 36 | 52 | 75 |
| | 4/1/09-3/31/10 ALL | 4/1/10-3/31/11 ALL | 4/1/11-3/31/12 ALL | | 29 (4/1-9/30/11) | | 407 (10/1/11-3/31/12) | | | |
| | | | | | 0-1MM | 1-3MM | 3-5MM | 5-10MM | 10-25MM | 25MM & OVER |
| NUMBER OF STATEMENTS | 354 | 415 | 436 | | 30 | 56 | 44 | 72 | 105 | 129 |
| | % | % | % | **ASSETS** | % | % | % | % | % | % |
| Cash & Equivalents | 14.4 | 15.8 | 17.5 | | 34.4 | 31.6 | 17.6 | 17.3 | 12.2 | 11.8 |
| Trade Receivables (net) | 51.5 | 53.1 | 55.2 | | 16.9 | 38.3 | 55.4 | 59.1 | 66.3 | 60.3 |
| Inventory | .6 | .3 | .4 | | .0 | .1 | .0 | .0 | .2 | 1.0 |
| All Other Current | 6.8 | 7.1 | 5.3 | | 13.3 | 6.3 | 3.1 | 4.6 | 3.6 | 5.5 |
| Total Current | 73.2 | 76.3 | 78.4 | | 64.6 | 76.3 | 76.2 | 81.1 | 82.3 | 78.6 |
| Fixed Assets (net) | 10.0 | 9.4 | 6.5 | | 13.8 | 8.3 | 8.8 | 5.1 | 4.8 | 5.6 |
| Intangibles (net) | 5.5 | 5.0 | 6.6 | | 13.3 | 5.8 | 5.7 | 5.1 | 4.6 | 8.1 |
| All Other Non-Current | 11.3 | 9.3 | 8.5 | | 8.3 | 9.7 | 9.4 | 8.7 | 8.3 | 7.7 |
| Total | 100.0 | 100.0 | 100.0 | | 100.0 | 100.0 | 100.0 | 100.0 | 100.0 | 100.0 |
| | | | | **LIABILITIES** | | | | | | |
| Notes Payable-Short Term | 20.3 | 22.0 | 21.4 | | 25.0 | 23.2 | 27.5 | 22.4 | 21.0 | 17.3 |
| Cur. Mat.-L.T.D. | 3.1 | 2.6 | 2.2 | | 5.8 | 1.8 | 1.3 | 2.3 | 2.5 | 1.5 |
| Trade Payables | 7.4 | 8.5 | 8.1 | | 2.7 | 7.3 | 12.7 | 6.7 | 6.6 | 10.1 |
| Income Taxes Payable | .5 | .6 | .3 | | .0 | .1 | .0 | .2 | .2 | .6 |
| All Other Current | 22.7 | 23.0 | 20.9 | | 15.9 | 28.6 | 10.6 | 23.2 | 17.5 | 23.9 |
| Total Current | 54.0 | 56.8 | 52.9 | | 49.4 | 61.0 | 52.2 | 54.6 | 47.9 | 53.4 |
| Long-Term Debt | 9.1 | 8.3 | 9.5 | | 21.7 | 6.9 | 12.8 | 7.0 | 7.3 | 9.8 |
| Deferred Taxes | .2 | .1 | .1 | | .0 | .0 | .0 | .0 | .3 | .1 |
| All Other Non-Current | 5.8 | 9.8 | 8.5 | | 26.1 | 9.1 | 10.3 | 13.8 | 3.4 | 4.8 |
| Net Worth | 30.9 | 25.0 | 29.0 | | 2.7 | 22.9 | 24.8 | 24.6 | 41.1 | 31.8 |
| Total Liabilties & Net Worth | 100.0 | 100.0 | 100.0 | | 100.0 | 100.0 | 100.0 | 100.0 | 100.0 | 100.0 |
| | | | | **INCOME DATA** | | | | | | |
| Net Sales | 100.0 | 100.0 | 100.0 | | 100.0 | 100.0 | 100.0 | 100.0 | 100.0 | 100.0 |
| Gross Profit | | | | | | | | | | |
| Operating Expenses | 98.5 | 96.1 | 95.5 | | 88.8 | 90.3 | 97.8 | 96.8 | 96.4 | 97.0 |
| Operating Profit | 1.5 | 3.9 | 4.5 | | 11.2 | 9.7 | 2.2 | 3.2 | 3.6 | 3.0 |
| All Other Expenses (net) | .9 | 1.0 | .4 | | 1.8 | .3 | .3 | .2 | .3 | .4 |
| Profit Before Taxes | .7 | 2.9 | 4.1 | | 9.5 | 9.4 | 1.9 | 2.9 | 3.3 | 2.6 |
| | | | | **RATIOS** | | | | | | |
| Current | 2.8 | 2.7 | 3.0 | | 4.2 | 5.2 | 3.2 | 3.0 | 3.2 | 2.3 |
| | 1.5 | 1.6 | 1.6 | | 1.7 | 1.7 | 1.6 | 1.6 | 1.8 | 1.4 |
| | 1.0 | 1.0 | 1.1 | | .8 | .8 | 1.0 | 1.2 | 1.2 | 1.1 |
| Quick | 2.5 | 2.4 | 2.8 | | 3.1 | 4.8 | 3.1 | 2.9 | 3.0 | 2.2 |
| | 1.4 | 1.4 | 1.5 | | 1.5 | 1.6 | 1.6 | 1.5 | 1.7 | 1.3 |
| | .9 | .9 | 1.0 | | .5 | .7 | 1.0 | 1.1 | 1.2 | 1.0 |
| Sales/Receivables | 27  13.7 | 21  17.7 | 26  14.3 | | 0  UND | 0  UND | 24  14.9 | 31  11.8 | 30  12.3 | 32  11.3 |
| | 43  8.4 | 42  8.8 | 43  8.5 | | 7  50.8 | 32  11.3 | 43  8.5 | 43  8.4 | 46  7.9 | 44  8.3 |
| | 63  5.8 | 61  6.0 | 60  6.1 | | 38  9.5 | 60  6.1 | 62  5.9 | 56  6.5 | 65  5.6 | 56  6.5 |
| Cost of Sales/Inventory | | | | | | | | | | |
| Cost of Sales/Payables | | | | | | | | | | |
| Sales/Working Capital | 9.4 | 10.0 | 9.1 | | 2.5 | 6.6 | 9.4 | 8.5 | 9.0 | 10.6 |
| | 18.4 | 18.5 | 18.1 | | 10.2 | 14.3 | 17.1 | 16.9 | 17.3 | 23.2 |
| | NM | 574.0 | 114.8 | | -54.3 | -70.5 | 427.6 | 64.4 | 41.8 | 105.8 |
| EBIT/Interest | 14.4 | 26.7 | 34.6 | | 33.0 | 79.4 | 29.3 | 22.1 | 32.0 | 38.0 |
| | (283) 2.9 | (331) 6.5 | (337) 9.7 | | (19) 8.2 | (34) 12.1 | (31) 3.0 | (61) 6.1 | (82) 10.5 | (110) 11.5 |
| | -2.2 | 1.9 | 2.4 | | .0 | 1.8 | -.7 | 2.5 | 2.2 | 3.4 |
| Net Profit + Depr., Dep., Amort./Cur. Mat. L/T/D | 10.4 | 15.8 | 42.9 | | | | | | | 49.8 |
| | (34) 2.4 | (25) 2.3 | (27) 16.6 | | | | | | (19) | 33.3 |
| | .0 | .7 | 3.0 | | | | | | | 4.7 |
| Fixed/Worth | .0 | .0 | .0 | | .0 | .0 | .0 | .0 | .0 | .0 |
| | .2 | .1 | .1 | | .1 | .1 | .1 | .1 | .1 | .1 |
| | 1.1 | 1.1 | .5 | | NM | .7 | .7 | .7 | .2 | .6 |
| Debt/Worth | .6 | .7 | .6 | | .4 | .3 | .5 | .9 | .6 | .9 |
| | 1.8 | 1.9 | 1.8 | | 12.4 | 1.7 | 2.0 | 2.0 | 1.3 | 2.0 |
| | 11.1 | 14.7 | 14.5 | | -1.9 | UND | NM | 13.7 | 4.1 | 9.9 |
| % Profit Before Taxes/Tangible Net Worth | 57.4 | 78.2 | 70.4 | | 69.8 | 164.8 | 63.6 | 73.3 | 64.6 | 60.7 |
| | (288) 15.1 | (332) 34.0 | (355) 36.4 | | (17) 30.2 | (43) 73.1 | (33) 7.6 | (58) 36.9 | (96) 37.4 | (108) 34.4 |
| | -4.2 | 9.0 | 10.9 | | 5.4 | 30.2 | -6.5 | 7.7 | 17.4 | 21.3 |
| % Profit Before Taxes/Total Assets | 16.3 | 25.6 | 27.4 | | 48.1 | 77.8 | 24.7 | 27.2 | 27.9 | 20.5 |
| | 5.1 | 11.6 | 13.4 | | 18.9 | 27.4 | 3.0 | 14.4 | 15.4 | 11.2 |
| | -5.7 | 1.6 | 2.8 | | -.3 | 5.8 | -1.6 | 2.4 | 4.2 | 4.7 |
| Sales/Net Fixed Assets | 438.7 | 490.5 | 827.7 | | UND | UND | 999.8 | 985.4 | 865.6 | 415.8 |
| | 124.8 | 158.5 | 210.9 | | 90.2 | 259.3 | 263.9 | 311.3 | 211.9 | 201.4 |
| | 37.8 | 55.6 | 83.0 | | 16.9 | 47.8 | 66.5 | 90.5 | 94.2 | 93.7 |
| Sales/Total Assets | 6.7 | 7.6 | 7.7 | | 4.8 | 7.7 | 8.2 | 6.6 | 8.4 | 7.7 |
| | 4.7 | 5.3 | 5.3 | | 2.4 | 4.8 | 5.6 | 5.5 | 5.6 | 5.4 |
| | 3.0 | 3.5 | 3.6 | | .9 | 3.2 | 3.6 | 3.7 | 4.0 | 3.9 |
| % Depr., Dep., Amort./Sales | .1 | .1 | .1 | | .4 | .1 | .1 | .1 | .1 | .1 |
| | (248) .4 | (257) .3 | (248) .2 | | (11) 1.8 | (20) .3 | (18) .2 | (34) .2 | (66) .2 | (99) .2 |
| | .7 | .7 | .5 | | 3.9 | .7 | .6 | .5 | .4 | .4 |
| % Officers', Directors' Owners' Comp/Sales | 1.5 | 1.5 | 1.9 | | 3.6 | 4.2 | 3.6 | 1.6 | 1.1 | 1.0 |
| | (105) 2.8 | (125) 3.7 | (129) 4.1 | | (15) 15.5 | (23) 7.8 | (18) 5.6 | (23) 3.8 | (29) 2.3 | (21) 3.5 |
| | 7.2 | 8.0 | 8.1 | | 19.2 | 13.3 | 8.7 | 5.2 | 4.0 | 5.8 |
| Net Sales ($) | 13266747M | 15099783M | 16693831M | | 17220M | 105513M | 171201M | 530270M | 1727165M | 14142462M |
| Total Assets ($) | 3059295M | 3560467M | 3564384M | | 9665M | 30360M | 44596M | 138659M | 364366M | 2976738M |

© RMA 2012

M = $ thousand    MM = $ million
See Pages 9 through 22 for Explanation of Ratios and Data

## Current Data Sorted by Assets      Comparative Historical Data

| 0-500M | 500M-2MM | 2-10MM | 10-50MM | 50-100MM | 100-250MM | Type of Statement | 4/1/07-3/31/08 ALL | 4/1/08-3/31/09 ALL |
|---|---|---|---|---|---|---|---|---|
| 3 | 3 | 22 | 26 | 3 | 6 | Unqualified | 53 | 60 |
| | 7 | 39 | 9 | | | Reviewed | 42 | 57 |
| 9 | 27 | 27 | 1 | | | Compiled | 45 | 49 |
| 16 | 11 | 4 | | | | Tax Returns | 39 | 36 |
| 16 | 49 | 80 | 35 | 7 | 4 | Other | 136 | 167 |
| | 38 (4/1-9/30/11) | | 366 (10/1/11-3/31/12) | | | | | |
| 44 | 97 | 172 | 71 | 10 | 10 | NUMBER OF STATEMENTS | 315 | 369 |
| % | % | % | % | % | % | **ASSETS** | % | % |
| 27.8 | 11.7 | 9.2 | 11.9 | 12.3 | 3.3 | Cash & Equivalents | 13.3 | 14.6 |
| 37.9 | 59.4 | 65.4 | 56.4 | 37.7 | 61.9 | Trade Receivables (net) | 53.9 | 51.7 |
| 1.0 | .3 | .2 | .4 | .0 | .0 | Inventory | .4 | .4 |
| 6.9 | 5.0 | 4.9 | 5.5 | 3.1 | 4.5 | All Other Current | 5.9 | 6.6 |
| 73.7 | 76.5 | 79.7 | 74.3 | 53.1 | 69.7 | Total Current | 73.4 | 73.2 |
| 13.8 | 10.5 | 6.4 | 5.0 | 10.3 | 5.4 | Fixed Assets (net) | 9.4 | 8.8 |
| 2.6 | 4.2 | 4.8 | 12.8 | 30.6 | 17.2 | Intangibles (net) | 7.3 | 7.8 |
| 10.0 | 8.8 | 9.1 | 7.9 | 6.0 | 7.7 | All Other Non-Current | 10.0 | 10.2 |
| 100.0 | 100.0 | 100.0 | 100.0 | 100.0 | 100.0 | Total | 100.0 | 100.0 |
| | | | | | | **LIABILITIES** | | |
| 26.2 | 22.4 | 19.9 | 15.4 | 4.7 | 7.4 | Notes Payable-Short Term | 22.6 | 21.6 |
| 6.9 | 2.1 | 1.3 | 2.3 | 2.0 | 2.8 | Cur. Mat.-L.T.D. | 1.8 | 2.8 |
| 8.3 | 5.5 | 5.6 | 8.7 | 9.7 | 14.3 | Trade Payables | 7.6 | 7.7 |
| .0 | .3 | .3 | .3 | .1 | .3 | Income Taxes Payable | .5 | .6 |
| 35.8 | 19.1 | 18.1 | 23.9 | 12.7 | 17.8 | All Other Current | 23.6 | 19.8 |
| 77.2 | 49.6 | 45.2 | 50.6 | 29.1 | 42.6 | Total Current | 56.1 | 52.5 |
| 9.1 | 8.5 | 4.4 | 8.1 | 28.5 | 23.8 | Long-Term Debt | 9.4 | 9.1 |
| .0 | .0 | .1 | .5 | .2 | 2.1 | Deferred Taxes | .1 | .3 |
| 10.9 | 5.5 | 4.3 | 4.8 | 9.7 | 11.4 | All Other Non-Current | 7.0 | 6.9 |
| 2.8 | 36.4 | 45.9 | 36.0 | 32.4 | 20.1 | Net Worth | 27.5 | 31.1 |
| 100.0 | 100.0 | 100.0 | 100.0 | 100.0 | 100.0 | Total Liabilties & Net Worth | 100.0 | 100.0 |
| | | | | | | **INCOME DATA** | | |
| 100.0 | 100.0 | 100.0 | 100.0 | 100.0 | 100.0 | Net Sales | 100.0 | 100.0 |
| | | | | | | Gross Profit | | |
| 98.0 | 95.8 | 96.1 | 97.1 | 99.8 | 94.8 | Operating Expenses | 96.1 | 97.1 |
| 2.0 | 4.2 | 3.9 | 2.9 | .2 | 5.2 | Operating Profit | 3.9 | 2.9 |
| .5 | .8 | .5 | .4 | 1.3 | .9 | All Other Expenses (net) | .8 | .7 |
| 1.5 | 3.4 | 3.4 | 2.4 | -1.1 | 4.3 | Profit Before Taxes | 3.0 | 2.1 |
| | | | | | | **RATIOS** | | |
| 3.3 | 3.3 | 2.8 | 2.0 | 2.6 | 2.5 | | 2.3 | 2.5 |
| 1.3 | 1.8 | 1.8 | 1.4 | 2.0 | 1.7 | Current | 1.4 | 1.5 |
| .5 | 1.0 | 1.3 | 1.1 | 1.4 | 1.2 | | 1.0 | 1.1 |
| 3.0 | 3.0 | 2.6 | 1.9 | 2.2 | 2.1 | | 2.2 | 2.2 |
| 1.2 | 1.7 | 1.7 | 1.3 | 1.9 | 1.7 | Quick | 1.3 | 1.3 |
| .4 | 1.0 | 1.2 | 1.0 | 1.4 | 1.1 | | 1.0 | .9 |
| 0 UND | 26   13.9 | 34   10.8 | 34   10.7 | 46   7.9 | 50   7.3 | | 24   15.0 | 21   17.2 |
| 17   21.1 | 33   11.0 | 47   7.8 | 46   8.0 | 51   7.2 | 60   6.1 | Sales/Receivables | 39   9.3 | 35   10.5 |
| 27   13.4 | 50   7.3 | 62   5.9 | 64   5.7 | 58   6.3 | 107   3.4 | | 55   6.6 | 49   7.4 |
| | | | | | | Cost of Sales/Inventory | | |
| | | | | | | Cost of Sales/Payables | | |
| 15.1 | 9.8 | 9.3 | 10.9 | 6.5 | 8.8 | | 10.9 | 11.3 |
| 183.7 | 19.2 | 15.1 | 22.7 | 11.2 | 12.9 | Sales/Working Capital | 25.7 | 23.4 |
| -13.4 | 182.0 | 35.6 | 83.7 | 20.0 | 26.4 | | 275.7 | 233.0 |
| 38.0 | 20.8 | 41.8 | 28.3 | 11.3 | 16.1 | | 13.1 | 15.4 |
| (24) 3.4 | (79) 5.9 | (141) 12.5 | (57) 6.8 | 3.0 | 10.5 | EBIT/Interest | (265) 5.3 | (313) 3.8 |
| -6.1 | 2.0 | 3.6 | 3.0 | -3.5 | 5.0 | | 1.6 | 1.0 |
| | | 44.1 | | | | | 30.8 | 11.8 |
| | (16) | 4.2 | | | | Net Profit + Depr., Dep., Amort./Cur. Mat. L/T/D | (36) 4.2 | (49) 1.9 |
| | | 1.3 | | | | | -.2 | .0 |
| .0 | .0 | .0 | .0 | .5 | .2 | | .1 | .1 |
| .0 | .1 | .1 | .1 | NM | NM | Fixed/Worth | .2 | .2 |
| 6.4 | .8 | .2 | .6 | .0 | -.1 | | .9 | .9 |
| .5 | .6 | .5 | 1.0 | 1.0 | 5.1 | | .9 | .7 |
| 4.6 | 1.5 | 1.2 | 2.1 | NM | NM | Debt/Worth | 2.5 | 2.1 |
| -4.3 | 7.7 | 3.2 | 7.8 | -2.0 | -5.7 | | 8.7 | 9.6 |
| 76.9 | 65.8 | 68.7 | 77.9 | | | | 74.1 | 62.3 |
| (27) 43.7 | (84) 27.2 | (155) 36.4 | (62) 34.0 | | | % Profit Before Taxes/Tangible Net Worth | (260) 38.9 | (303) 22.9 |
| 16.5 | 5.3 | 16.0 | 12.1 | | | | 11.2 | 4.8 |
| 30.0 | 24.0 | 27.5 | 17.8 | 11.7 | 23.4 | | 20.7 | 18.1 |
| 10.6 | 12.5 | 16.2 | 7.5 | .0 | 10.0 | % Profit Before Taxes/Total Assets | 11.5 | 7.6 |
| .1 | 1.8 | 5.0 | 3.2 | -10.2 | 4.2 | | 2.0 | .2 |
| UND | 595.6 | 443.0 | 310.9 | 184.3 | 372.8 | | 347.1 | 341.9 |
| 878.1 | 157.6 | 165.6 | 158.1 | 89.6 | 100.7 | Sales/Net Fixed Assets | 127.9 | 128.9 |
| 57.7 | 49.8 | 83.4 | 69.6 | 20.5 | 46.1 | | 62.5 | 57.7 |
| 14.8 | 7.9 | 6.5 | 6.4 | 3.8 | 4.5 | | 8.2 | 8.0 |
| 8.1 | 6.1 | 5.1 | 4.7 | 2.9 | 2.5 | Sales/Total Assets | 5.6 | 5.6 |
| 4.7 | 4.4 | 4.0 | 3.0 | 1.6 | 2.2 | | 3.7 | 3.7 |
| .1 | .1 | .1 | .1 | | | | .1 | .1 |
| (18) .3 | (62) .3 | (128) .2 | (49) .2 | | | % Depr., Dep., Amort./Sales | (226) .3 | (252) .3 |
| 1.4 | .5 | .4 | .4 | | | | .5 | .5 |
| 1.7 | 1.6 | 1.1 | | | | | 1.3 | 1.1 |
| (21) 3.0 | (30) 2.9 | (56) 1.9 | | | | % Officers', Directors' Owners' Comp/Sales | (101) 2.7 | (115) 2.1 |
| 12.8 | 3.8 | 3.5 | | | | | 6.7 | 5.2 |
| 168987M | 702419M | 4174695M | 7795399M | 1968789M | 5649597M | Net Sales ($) | 22896790M | 21760986M |
| 10505M | 114658M | 786995M | 1441196M | 664595M | 1779754M | Total Assets ($) | 4762416M | 5077454M |

© RMA 2012

M = $ thousand    MM = $ million
See Pages 9 through 22 for Explanation of Ratios and Data

## Comparative Historical Data | Current Data Sorted by Sales

| | | | | Type of Statement | 0-1MM | 1-3MM | 3-5MM | 5-10MM | 10-25MM | 25MM & OVER |
|---|---|---|---|---|---|---|---|---|---|---|
| | 55 | 57 | 63 | Unqualified | | 5 | 1 | 2 | 10 | 45 |
| | 67 | 46 | 55 | Reviewed | | 1 | 2 | 10 | 19 | 23 |
| | 43 | 58 | 64 | Compiled | 3 | 7 | 8 | 18 | 20 | 8 |
| | 36 | 44 | 31 | Tax Returns | 8 | 6 | 3 | 8 | 5 | 1 |
| | 178 | 199 | 191 | Other | 16 | 6 | 10 | 25 | 59 | 75 |
| | 4/1/09-3/31/10 ALL | 4/1/10-3/31/11 ALL | 4/1/11-3/31/12 ALL | | 38 (4/1-9/30/11) | | 366 (10/1/11-3/31/12) | | | |
| | 379 | 404 | 404 | **NUMBER OF STATEMENTS** | 27 | 25 | 24 | 63 | 113 | 152 |
| | % | % | % | **ASSETS** | % | % | % | % | % | % |
| | 14.0 | 12.5 | 12.2 | Cash & Equivalents | 22.9 | 14.5 | 16.0 | 14.4 | 9.7 | 10.4 |
| | 52.5 | 55.1 | 58.6 | Trade Receivables (net) | 26.6 | 50.2 | 49.9 | 59.7 | 66.1 | 61.0 |
| | .1 | .2 | .4 | Inventory | .4 | .2 | 2.1 | .3 | .2 | .2 |
| | 7.6 | 7.7 | 5.2 | All Other Current | 8.4 | 1.3 | 9.3 | 5.1 | 3.7 | 5.9 |
| | 74.2 | 75.5 | 76.4 | Total Current | 58.4 | 66.2 | 77.4 | 79.5 | 79.7 | 77.4 |
| | 8.4 | 8.1 | 8.0 | Fixed Assets (net) | 30.3 | 11.6 | 9.0 | 5.6 | 6.4 | 5.5 |
| | 6.6 | 6.5 | 6.8 | Intangibles (net) | 6.3 | 8.5 | 3.8 | 3.3 | 5.7 | 9.3 |
| | 10.8 | 9.9 | 8.8 | All Other Non-Current | 4.9 | 13.7 | 9.8 | 11.5 | 8.3 | 7.8 |
| | 100.0 | 100.0 | 100.0 | Total | 100.0 | 100.0 | 100.0 | 100.0 | 100.0 | 100.0 |
| | | | | **LIABILITIES** | | | | | | |
| | 19.4 | 21.4 | 19.7 | Notes Payable-Short Term | 20.1 | 37.0 | 22.4 | 23.5 | 19.9 | 14.7 |
| | 2.8 | 3.2 | 2.4 | Cur. Mat.-L.T.D. | 1.8 | 10.7 | 1.7 | 2.6 | 1.3 | 1.8 |
| | 7.6 | 7.1 | 6.7 | Trade Payables | 8.2 | 2.6 | 8.6 | 5.9 | 6.1 | 7.6 |
| | .4 | .5 | .3 | Income Taxes Payable | .0 | .1 | .1 | .6 | .3 | .2 |
| | 22.0 | 23.2 | 21.2 | All Other Current | 23.6 | 9.3 | 37.2 | 18.6 | 18.3 | 23.3 |
| | 52.1 | 55.4 | 50.2 | Total Current | 53.6 | 59.7 | 70.0 | 51.3 | 46.0 | 47.7 |
| | 7.1 | 8.5 | 7.6 | Long-Term Debt | 22.6 | 8.5 | 6.6 | 5.9 | 4.7 | 7.9 |
| | .2 | .2 | .2 | Deferred Taxes | .0 | .0 | .0 | .0 | .2 | .2 |
| | 8.6 | 8.5 | 5.7 | All Other Non-Current | 13.4 | 15.9 | 3.5 | 4.6 | 3.0 | 5.5 |
| | 32.0 | 27.5 | 36.2 | Net Worth | 10.4 | 15.9 | 19.9 | 38.2 | 46.1 | 38.6 |
| | 100.0 | 100.0 | 100.0 | Total Liabilities & Net Worth | 100.0 | 100.0 | 100.0 | 100.0 | 100.0 | 100.0 |
| | | | | **INCOME DATA** | | | | | | |
| | 100.0 | 100.0 | 100.0 | Net Sales | 100.0 | 100.0 | 100.0 | 100.0 | 100.0 | 100.0 |
| | | | | Gross Profit | | | | | | |
| | 98.6 | 96.2 | 96.5 | Operating Expenses | 92.4 | 96.7 | 97.2 | 96.8 | 96.3 | 97.0 |
| | 1.4 | 3.8 | 3.5 | Operating Profit | 7.6 | 3.3 | 2.8 | 3.2 | 3.7 | 3.0 |
| | .6 | .8 | .6 | All Other Expenses (net) | 4.6 | .3 | .7 | .2 | .3 | .3 |
| | .8 | 3.0 | 2.9 | Profit Before Taxes | 3.0 | 3.0 | 2.0 | 3.0 | 3.4 | 2.7 |
| | | | | **RATIOS** | | | | | | |
| | 2.5 | 2.5 | 2.7 | Current | 4.0 | 3.1 | 2.1 | 3.5 | 2.9 | 2.3 |
| | 1.5 | 1.5 | 1.7 | | 1.4 | 1.5 | 1.2 | 1.7 | 1.8 | 1.7 |
| | 1.0 | 1.0 | 1.1 | | .6 | .7 | .9 | 1.1 | 1.1 | 1.2 |
| | 2.3 | 2.3 | 2.5 | Quick | 2.8 | 3.1 | 2.0 | 2.4 | 2.9 | 2.1 |
| | 1.4 | 1.3 | 1.6 | | 1.4 | 1.5 | 1.0 | 1.6 | 1.7 | 1.6 |
| | .9 | .9 | 1.1 | | .7 | .7 | .8 | 1.1 | 1.1 | 1.1 |
| | 26  14.1 | 27  13.4 | 28  12.9 | Sales/Receivables | 0  UND | 23  16.0 | 5  73.8 | 31  11.9 | 32  11.5 | 32  11.4 |
| | 42  8.7 | 40  9.2 | 42  8.6 | | 15  23.7 | 41  9.0 | 31  11.9 | 47  7.7 | 47  7.8 | 42  8.6 |
| | 56  6.5 | 57  6.4 | 57  6.4 | | 36  10.1 | 69  5.3 | 47  7.8 | 63  5.8 | 63  5.8 | 54  6.7 |
| | | | | Cost of Sales/Inventory | | | | | | |
| | | | | Cost of Sales/Payables | | | | | | |
| | 10.2 | 9.9 | 9.7 | Sales/Working Capital | 4.3 | 9.3 | 19.9 | 8.9 | 9.5 | 10.3 |
| | 20.8 | 22.0 | 17.9 | | 15.7 | 14.7 | 215.9 | 15.9 | 17.7 | 18.0 |
| | 209.4 | 291.8 | 74.6 | | -11.8 | -17.6 | -51.5 | 66.3 | 48.2 | 43.5 |
| | 15.6 | 26.2 | 29.8 | EBIT/Interest | 10.0 | 22.1 | 20.7 | 21.5 | 44.1 | 33.5 |
| (321) | 3.3 | (336)  7.0 | (321)  7.8 | | (14)  3.9 | (22)  3.1 | (14)  8.4 | (49)  6.6 | (93)  11.3 | (129)  10.8 |
| | -2.1 | 2.0 | 2.7 | | -3.3 | -1.6 | .3 | 2.4 | 2.9 | 3.4 |
| | 13.0 | 41.8 | 40.9 | Net Profit + Depr., Dep., | | | | | 26.6 | 44.5 |
| (45) | 3.2 | (45)  4.9 | (35)  4.6 | Amort./Cur. Mat. L/T/D | | | | (11)  4.6 | 4.6 | (19)  5.3 |
| | -.3 | 1.5 | 1.3 | | | | | | 2.9 | .8 |
| | .0 | .0 | .0 | Fixed/Worth | .0 | .0 | .0 | .0 | .0 | .0 |
| | .2 | .2 | .1 | | .3 | .0 | .3 | .1 | .1 | .1 |
| | 1.1 | 1.1 | .6 | | 6.6 | NM | 2.9 | .4 | .5 | .6 |
| | .6 | .8 | .7 | Debt/Worth | .8 | .4 | .9 | .7 | .5 | .8 |
| | 1.8 | 2.3 | 1.6 | | 3.2 | 3.0 | 5.4 | 1.5 | 1.1 | 1.7 |
| | 9.3 | 14.3 | 7.6 | | -6.1 | -24.3 | 47.1 | 5.0 | 4.7 | 5.9 |
| | 51.9 | 85.7 | 68.7 | % Profit Before Taxes/Tangible | 53.5 | 62.7 | 80.4 | 63.4 | 66.6 | 77.4 |
| (308) | 15.3 | (324)  39.5 | (338)  34.9 | Net Worth | (20)  28.1 | (16)  17.2 | (19)  16.7 | (53)  34.6 | (101)  33.5 | (129)  38.2 |
| | -2.9 | 14.5 | 11.8 | | 5.9 | -2.1 | -14.7 | 7.7 | 16.9 | 14.5 |
| | 15.2 | 25.7 | 24.3 | % Profit Before Taxes/Total | 14.3 | 22.7 | 33.9 | 20.8 | 24.3 | 25.0 |
| | 3.7 | 11.3 | 12.5 | Assets | 3.5 | 7.3 | 13.6 | 10.0 | 14.3 | 13.2 |
| | -4.6 | 2.5 | 3.5 | | -1.6 | -4.0 | -.4 | 3.0 | 4.9 | 4.8 |
| | 353.1 | 470.2 | 488.7 | Sales/Net Fixed Assets | UND | UND | 999.8 | 546.3 | 458.1 | 336.7 |
| | 135.3 | 146.9 | 166.0 | | 46.4 | 279.2 | 284.2 | 147.7 | 151.7 | 172.8 |
| | 48.8 | 61.1 | 67.3 | | 3.4 | 41.5 | 39.8 | 69.8 | 69.7 | 103.0 |
| | 6.9 | 7.3 | 7.2 | Sales/Total Assets | 6.4 | 7.8 | 9.6 | 7.3 | 6.8 | 7.4 |
| | 4.9 | 5.1 | 5.2 | | 1.6 | 4.7 | 6.4 | 5.0 | 5.3 | 5.4 |
| | 3.6 | 3.6 | 3.8 | | .5 | 2.7 | 4.6 | 3.7 | 4.0 | 4.0 |
| | .1 | .1 | .1 | % Depr., Dep., Amort./Sales | .8 | .1 | .1 | .1 | .1 | .1 |
| (272) | .3 | (274)  .2 | (269)  .2 | | (12)  3.5 | (12)  .3 | (13)  .2 | (41)  .2 | (77)  .2 | (114)  .2 |
| | .6 | .6 | .5 | | 20.6 | 1.3 | .4 | .4 | .5 | .3 |
| | 1.1 | 1.3 | 1.2 | % Officers', Directors' | | 1.6 | | 1.6 | 1.6 | .4 |
| (131) | 2.5 | (124)  2.9 | (118)  2.3 | Owners' Comp/Sales | | (12)  6.2 | | (26)  2.8 | (35)  2.7 | (36)  1.1 |
| | 29333582M | 24368330M | 20459886M | Net Sales ($) | 12549M | 52310M | 98892M | 457346M | 1816565M | 18022224M |
| | 6046474M | 5624884M | 4797703M | Total Assets ($) | 14939M | 24852M | 16587M | 139778M | 421406M | 4180141M |

## Current Data Sorted by Assets      Comparative Historical Data

| Type of Statement | 0-500M | 500M-2MM | 2-10MM | 10-50MM | 50-100MM | 100-250MM | 4/1/07-3/31/08 ALL | 4/1/08-3/31/09 ALL |
|---|---|---|---|---|---|---|---|---|
| Unqualified | 1 | | 2 | 6 | 1 | 1 | 9 | 15 |
| Reviewed | | 2 | 7 | | | | 3 | 8 |
| Compiled | 1 | | 2 | 1 | | | 4 | 2 |
| Tax Returns | 5 | 4 | 2 | 1 | | | 5 | 5 |
| Other | 8 | 14 | 20 | 14 | 2 | 2 | 11 | 25 |
| | | 4 (4/1-9/30/11) | | 92 (10/1/11-3/31/12) | | | | |
| NUMBER OF STATEMENTS | 15 | 20 | 33 | 22 | 3 | 3 | 32 | 55 |
| **ASSETS** | % | % | % | % | % | % | % | % |
| Cash & Equivalents | 48.0 | 25.2 | 20.1 | 19.3 | | | 14.6 | 27.7 |
| Trade Receivables (net) | 33.3 | 38.4 | 45.8 | 30.1 | | | 37.7 | 29.9 |
| Inventory | .3 | .0 | .0 | .0 | | | .0 | .0 |
| All Other Current | 5.7 | 8.4 | 13.4 | 10.0 | | | 14.8 | 12.0 |
| Total Current | 87.3 | 72.0 | 79.3 | 59.3 | | | 67.1 | 69.6 |
| Fixed Assets (net) | 4.8 | 7.8 | 9.8 | 6.9 | | | 6.3 | 9.9 |
| Intangibles (net) | .4 | 1.9 | 6.3 | 23.9 | | | 8.9 | 7.3 |
| All Other Non-Current | 7.5 | 18.3 | 4.7 | 9.9 | | | 17.7 | 13.2 |
| Total | 100.0 | 100.0 | 100.0 | 100.0 | | | 100.0 | 100.0 |
| **LIABILITIES** | | | | | | | | |
| Notes Payable-Short Term | 61.7 | 15.0 | 15.9 | 5.2 | | | 17.1 | 10.3 |
| Cur. Mat.-L.T.D. | .1 | 2.3 | 1.1 | 2.9 | | | 4.6 | 2.0 |
| Trade Payables | 14.2 | 1.8 | 5.7 | 4.2 | | | 6.4 | 7.0 |
| Income Taxes Payable | .0 | .1 | .8 | .2 | | | 1.0 | 1.3 |
| All Other Current | 37.1 | 36.0 | 41.8 | 41.9 | | | 29.0 | 43.5 |
| Total Current | 113.0 | 55.3 | 65.3 | 54.4 | | | 58.1 | 64.1 |
| Long-Term Debt | .3 | 1.7 | 9.0 | 13.1 | | | 9.4 | 15.7 |
| Deferred Taxes | .0 | .0 | .3 | 1.0 | | | .1 | .2 |
| All Other Non-Current | 21.7 | 9.5 | 4.1 | 18.8 | | | 7.2 | 9.2 |
| Net Worth | -35.0 | 33.5 | 21.2 | 12.8 | | | 25.1 | 10.8 |
| Total Liabilities & Net Worth | 100.0 | 100.0 | 100.0 | 100.0 | | | 100.0 | 100.0 |
| **INCOME DATA** | | | | | | | | |
| Net Sales | 100.0 | 100.0 | 100.0 | 100.0 | | | 100.0 | 100.0 |
| Gross Profit | | | | | | | | |
| Operating Expenses | 100.1 | 97.0 | 96.8 | 99.5 | | | 92.9 | 95.2 |
| Operating Profit | -.1 | 3.0 | 3.2 | .5 | | | 7.1 | 4.8 |
| All Other Expenses (net) | .3 | -.4 | .3 | 1.1 | | | 1.6 | .6 |
| Profit Before Taxes | -.4 | 3.4 | 2.9 | -.6 | | | 5.5 | 4.2 |
| **RATIOS** | | | | | | | | |
| Current | 2.3 | 2.9 | 1.9 | 1.6 | | | 1.4 | 1.9 |
| | 1.0 | 2.0 | 1.2 | .9 | | | 1.1 | 1.1 |
| | .5 | 1.0 | .9 | .8 | | | .9 | .9 |
| Quick | 2.1 | 2.9 | 1.8 | 1.5 | | | 1.4 | 1.7 |
| | 1.0 | 1.8 | 1.1 | .9 | | | 1.0 | 1.0 |
| | .5 | .7 | .6 | .6 | | | .4 | .6 |
| Sales/Receivables | 0 UND | 2 189.6 | 6 64.9 | 6 59.9 | | | 1 494.2 | 0 897.1 |
| | 2 154.1 | 6 63.9 | 34 10.7 | 18 20.1 | | | 33 11.0 | 9 42.5 |
| | 40 9.1 | 41 9.0 | 59 6.2 | 37 9.9 | | | 63 5.8 | 44 8.4 |
| Cost of Sales/Inventory | | | | | | | | |
| Cost of Sales/Payables | | | | | | | | |
| Sales/Working Capital | 67.2 | 12.3 | 10.6 | 15.5 | | | 16.2 | 16.6 |
| | UND | 37.5 | 31.4 | -292.9 | | | 147.7 | 119.3 |
| | -28.3 | -999.8 | -425.8 | -43.9 | | | -84.1 | -280.8 |
| EBIT/Interest | | 105.0 | 57.1 | 38.1 | | | 26.7 | 45.6 |
| | (11) 22.5 | (28) 8.8 | (19) 3.2 | | | | (24) 4.5 | (42) -8.6 |
| | | 4.6 | 1.3 | -.1 | | | 1.6 | 2.9 |
| Net Profit + Depr., Dep., Amort./Cur. Mat. L/T/D | | | | | | | | |
| Fixed/Worth | .0 | .0 | .1 | .3 | | | .0 | .0 |
| | .0 | .1 | .3 | -5.6 | | | .2 | .3 |
| | 1.2 | 1.0 | 2.3 | -.1 | | | 2.0 | 14.8 |
| Debt/Worth | .7 | .4 | 1.2 | 7.3 | | | 1.8 | 1.5 |
| | 4.9 | 2.2 | 5.2 | -67.9 | | | 5.4 | 6.8 |
| | -2.2 | 19.9 | -155.2 | -1.9 | | | 24.8 | -107.5 |
| % Profit Before Taxes/Tangible Net Worth | | 95.5 | 99.1 | 134.0 | | | 91.3 | 166.7 |
| | (16) 61.3 | (24) 32.7 | (10) 50.5 | | | | (26) 37.5 | (40) 68.3 |
| | | 5.0 | 7.7 | 10.2 | | | 20.9 | 12.5 |
| % Profit Before Taxes/Total Assets | 122.8 | 41.6 | 20.2 | 10.8 | | | 17.9 | 27.8 |
| | 19.8 | 11.6 | 6.2 | 6.3 | | | 10.4 | 9.7 |
| | .0 | 1.1 | .3 | -9.7 | | | 3.4 | 3.1 |
| Sales/Net Fixed Assets | UND | UND | 777.5 | 356.6 | | | 999.8 | 999.8 |
| | UND | 712.1 | 188.7 | 149.7 | | | 431.1 | 168.8 |
| | 339.1 | 107.2 | 53.0 | 46.1 | | | 47.4 | 44.9 |
| Sales/Total Assets | 69.0 | 30.3 | 17.9 | 12.5 | | | 15.1 | 21.6 |
| | 34.0 | 6.3 | 5.5 | 4.6 | | | 5.7 | 6.9 |
| | 5.5 | 4.9 | 4.2 | 1.9 | | | 2.5 | 3.1 |
| % Depr., Dep., Amort./Sales | | | .1 | .1 | | | | .1 |
| | | (21) .2 | (14) .4 | | | | (16) .4 | (35) .2 |
| | | | .4 | .6 | | | 2.0 | .8 |
| % Officers', Directors' Owners' Comp/Sales | | | .5 | | | | | 1.2 |
| | | (13) 1.9 | | | | | (10) 1.9 | (11) 7.0 |
| | | | 6.5 | | | | 4.6 | 4.8 |
| Net Sales ($) | 137421M | 371498M | 2183417M | 3612350M | 1670345M | 2532849M | 2943922M | 4113094M |
| Total Assets ($) | 3913M | 22686M | 162082M | 498434M | 174391M | 509733M | 696302M | 1025196M |

## Comparative Historical Data

## Current Data Sorted by Sales

| | | | Type of Statement | | | | | | |
|---|---|---|---|---|---|---|---|---|---|
| 19 | 16 | 11 | Unqualified | | | | | 3 | 8 |
| 7 | 11 | 9 | Reviewed | | | | 2 | 2 | 5 |
| 7 | 4 | 4 | Compiled | | | 1 | 1 | | 2 |
| 6 | 11 | 12 | Tax Returns | | | 1 | 3 | 3 | 1 |
| 32 | 36 | 60 | Other | 1 | 3 | 3 | 4 | 12 | 34 |
| 4/1/09- | 4/1/10- | 4/1/11- | | 3 | 4 | | | | |
| 3/31/10 | 3/31/11 | 3/31/12 | | | 4 (4/1-9/30/11) | | 92 (10/1/11-3/31/12) | | |
| ALL | ALL | ALL | | 0-1MM | 1-3MM | 3-5MM | 5-10MM | 10-25MM | 25MM & OVER |
| 71 | 78 | 96 | NUMBER OF STATEMENTS | 4 | 7 | 5 | 10 | 20 | 50 |
| % | % | % | ASSETS | % | % | % | % | % | % |
| 31.8 | 23.2 | 25.5 | Cash & Equivalents | | | | 35.7 | 18.7 | 22.3 |
| 26.4 | 35.2 | 38.4 | Trade Receivables (net) | | | | 32.1 | 48.1 | 37.1 |
| .1 | .1 | .0 | Inventory | | | | .0 | .0 | .0 |
| 14.7 | 11.3 | 10.3 | All Other Current | | | | 4.0 | 6.1 | 13.9 |
| 73.0 | 69.8 | 74.2 | Total Current | | | | 71.7 | 72.9 | 73.2 |
| 9.3 | 9.9 | 7.6 | Fixed Assets (net) | | | | 10.0 | 14.1 | 6.0 |
| 8.9 | 10.4 | 8.8 | Intangibles (net) | | | | 2.5 | 4.1 | 12.3 |
| 8.8 | 9.9 | 9.4 | All Other Non-Current | | | | 15.7 | 8.9 | 8.4 |
| 100.0 | 100.0 | 100.0 | Total | | | | 100.0 | 100.0 | 100.0 |
| | | | LIABILITIES | | | | | | |
| 9.5 | 10.6 | 19.4 | Notes Payable-Short Term | | | | 20.9 | 12.2 | 7.4 |
| 1.2 | 1.5 | 1.6 | Cur. Mat.-L.T.D. | | | | .1 | 1.3 | 1.8 |
| 4.2 | 6.1 | 5.7 | Trade Payables | | | | 3.8 | 3.7 | 4.2 |
| 1.8 | .7 | .4 | Income Taxes Payable | | | | .6 | .4 | .3 |
| 42.8 | 32.9 | 40.1 | All Other Current | | | | 22.4 | 33.4 | 52.0 |
| 59.5 | 51.8 | 67.2 | Total Current | | | | 47.7 | 51.1 | 65.7 |
| 9.0 | 10.7 | 7.1 | Long-Term Debt | | | | .3 | 7.4 | 7.8 |
| .3 | .2 | .4 | Deferred Taxes | | | | .0 | .7 | .5 |
| 3.1 | 5.6 | 12.1 | All Other Non-Current | | | | 2.3 | 8.3 | 9.7 |
| 28.0 | 31.7 | 13.1 | Net Worth | | | | 49.7 | 32.5 | 16.3 |
| 100.0 | 100.0 | 100.0 | Total Liabilities & Net Worth | | | | 100.0 | 100.0 | 100.0 |
| | | | INCOME DATA | | | | | | |
| 100.0 | 100.0 | 100.0 | Net Sales | | | | 100.0 | 100.0 | 100.0 |
| | | | Gross Profit | | | | | | |
| 97.1 | 95.5 | 98.2 | Operating Expenses | | | | 95.2 | 96.7 | 99.0 |
| 2.9 | 4.5 | 1.8 | Operating Profit | | | | 4.8 | 3.3 | 1.0 |
| 1.9 | .8 | .3 | All Other Expenses (net) | | | | -.4 | .4 | .4 |
| 1.0 | 3.7 | 1.5 | Profit Before Taxes | | | | 5.2 | 2.9 | .7 |
| | | | RATIOS | | | | | | |
| 2.1 | 2.5 | 2.1 | | | | | 3.5 | 2.9 | 1.6 |
| 1.2 | 1.4 | 1.2 | Current | | | | 1.7 | 1.8 | 1.1 |
| .9 | 1.0 | .9 | | | | | 1.1 | 1.0 | .9 |
| 1.8 | 2.2 | 1.9 | | | | | 3.5 | 2.9 | 1.5 |
| 1.0 | 1.3 | 1.1 | Quick | | | | 1.5 | 1.5 | .9 |
| .6 | .8 | .6 | | | | | 1.1 | .9 | .6 |
| 0 UND | 1 255.3 | 3 142.8 | | | | | 0 UND | 6 61.3 | 2 234.0 |
| 5 67.8 | 22 16.7 | 24 15.2 | Sales/Receivables | | | | 9 38.8 | 37 9.9 | 10 38.4 |
| 42 8.7 | 53 6.9 | 43 8.4 | | | | | 41 8.8 | 62 5.9 | 35 10.4 |
| | | | Cost of Sales/Inventory | | | | | | |
| | | | Cost of Sales/Payables | | | | | | |
| 11.4 | 11.2 | 12.5 | | | | | 12.0 | 10.9 | 18.8 |
| 115.1 | 31.4 | 120.7 | Sales/Working Capital | | | | 27.2 | 29.2 | 587.1 |
| -497.4 | NM | -163.9 | | | | | NM | NM | -197.2 |
| 27.7 | 30.1 | 62.9 | | | | | | 116.0 | 56.6 |
| (46) 3.7 | (53) 9.8 | (70) 8.8 | EBIT/Interest | | | | (18) | 8.8 (36) | 16.9 |
| .5 | 2.8 | 1.0 | | | | | | 2.6 | .7 |
| 12.7 | 5.6 | | Net Profit + Depr., Dep., | | | | | | |
| (11) 3.5 | (12) 1.8 | | Amort./Cur. Mat. L/T/D | | | | | | |
| .8 | .8 | | | | | | | | |
| .0 | .0 | .0 | | | | | .0 | .0 | .1 |
| .2 | .2 | .4 | Fixed/Worth | | | | .1 | .2 | .8 |
| .9 | 1.4 | -4.8 | | | | | .4 | 2.4 | -.8 |
| 1.2 | .9 | 1.1 | | | | | .3 | .5 | 2.6 |
| 3.3 | 2.9 | 7.6 | Debt/Worth | | | | 1.1 | 2.4 | 15.2 |
| 14.3 | 22.3 | -11.5 | | | | | 1.5 | 38.4 | -12.5 |
| 64.2 | 107.4 | 96.2 | | | | | | 120.5 | 92.0 |
| (59) 20.4 | (64) 41.5 | (63) 36.6 | % Profit Before Taxes/Tangible | | | | (16) | 69.8 (30) | 61.6 |
| .6 | 13.9 | 6.2 | Net Worth | | | | | 17.8 | 18.4 |
| 16.7 | 26.8 | 21.7 | % Profit Before Taxes/Total | | | | 91.1 | 45.3 | 16.5 |
| 2.7 | 10.5 | 8.1 | Assets | | | | 7.6 | 15.8 | 7.3 |
| -.7 | 2.7 | .4 | | | | | -.7 | 2.1 | .4 |
| 999.8 | 977.7 | 999.8 | | | | | 475.0 | 999.8 | 999.8 |
| 419.6 | 239.7 | 236.5 | Sales/Net Fixed Assets | | | | 122.4 | 93.1 | 255.6 |
| 66.6 | 45.8 | 76.0 | | | | | 76.5 | 37.6 | 103.5 |
| 23.6 | 16.1 | 21.5 | | | | | 23.6 | 14.5 | 24.2 |
| 9.8 | 5.4 | 6.1 | Sales/Total Assets | | | | 5.9 | 5.5 | 10.5 |
| 4.1 | 3.3 | 4.3 | | | | | 4.4 | 3.3 | 4.9 |
| .1 | .1 | .1 | | | | | | .1 | .1 |
| (37) .2 | (45) .2 | (48) .1 | % Depr., Dep., Amort./Sales | | | | (10) | .2 (30) | .1 |
| 1.1 | .5 | .4 | | | | | | 1.6 | .4 |
| .8 | 1.3 | .8 | % Officers', Directors' | | | | | | |
| (16) 1.6 | (16) 2.9 | (26) 2.2 | Owners' Comp/Sales | | | | | | |
| 5.8 | 7.3 | 6.0 | | | | | | | |
| 7891491M | 6389591M | 10507880M | Net Sales ($) | 1103M | 14122M | 19901M | 81695M | 320161M | 10070898M |
| 1327616M | 1426389M | 1371239M | Total Assets ($) | 472M | 17260M | 7242M | 11936M | 88530M | 1245799M |

M = $ thousand    MM = $ million
See Pages 9 through 22 for Explanation of Ratios and Data

## Current Data Sorted by Assets      Comparative Historical Data

| 0-500M | 500M-2MM | 2-10MM | 10-50MM | 50-100MM | 100-250MM | | 4/1/07-3/31/08 ALL | 4/1/08-3/31/09 ALL |
|---|---|---|---|---|---|---|---|---|
| | | 3 | | 1 | 1 | Type of Statement | | |
| | 1 | 1 | 2 | | | Unqualified | 4 | 8 |
| 1 | | | 1 | | | Reviewed | 3 | 2 |
| 1 | 1 | | | | | Compiled | 3 | 1 |
| 1 | 3 | 8 | 9 | 2 | 1 | Tax Returns | 5 | 2 |
| | 6 (4/1-9/30/11) | | 31 (10/1/11-3/31/12) | | | Other | 8 | 7 |
| 3 | 5 | 12 | 12 | 3 | 2 | NUMBER OF STATEMENTS | 23 | 20 |
| % | % | % | % | % | % | ASSETS | % | % |
| | | 9.3 | 8.8 | | | Cash & Equivalents | 13.3 | 9.4 |
| | | 49.8 | 32.0 | | | Trade Receivables (net) | 35.2 | 38.6 |
| | | .0 | .3 | | | Inventory | .6 | .2 |
| | | 3.8 | 6.4 | | | All Other Current | 2.7 | 9.0 |
| | | 62.9 | 47.4 | | | Total Current | 51.8 | 57.2 |
| | | 20.4 | 17.5 | | | Fixed Assets (net) | 26.7 | 26.0 |
| | | 11.2 | 24.9 | | | Intangibles (net) | 4.0 | 7.2 |
| | | 5.5 | 10.2 | | | All Other Non-Current | 17.5 | 9.7 |
| | | 100.0 | 100.0 | | | Total | 100.0 | 100.0 |
| | | | | | | LIABILITIES | | |
| | | 4.9 | 5.8 | | | Notes Payable-Short Term | 12.7 | 18.6 |
| | | 4.2 | 1.7 | | | Cur. Mat.-L.T.D. | 8.6 | 4.6 |
| | | 14.4 | 9.2 | | | Trade Payables | 6.6 | 5.6 |
| | | .2 | 1.1 | | | Income Taxes Payable | .4 | .3 |
| | | 39.4 | 9.5 | | | All Other Current | 14.1 | 16.1 |
| | | 63.1 | 27.3 | | | Total Current | 42.5 | 45.1 |
| | | 5.3 | 22.1 | | | Long-Term Debt | 18.4 | 12.0 |
| | | .2 | .5 | | | Deferred Taxes | .3 | .2 |
| | | 14.9 | 10.7 | | | All Other Non-Current | 4.6 | 5.4 |
| | | 16.5 | 39.4 | | | Net Worth | 34.3 | 37.3 |
| | | 100.0 | 100.0 | | | Total Liabilities & Net Worth | 100.0 | 100.0 |
| | | | | | | INCOME DATA | | |
| | | 100.0 | 100.0 | | | Net Sales | 100.0 | 100.0 |
| | | | | | | Gross Profit | | |
| | | 102.7 | 93.8 | | | Operating Expenses | 92.7 | 95.7 |
| | | -2.7 | 6.2 | | | Operating Profit | 7.3 | 4.3 |
| | | .1 | 2.0 | | | All Other Expenses (net) | 1.6 | 1.3 |
| | | -2.8 | 4.2 | | | Profit Before Taxes | 5.7 | 3.0 |
| | | | | | | RATIOS | | |
| | | 2.0 | 3.2 | | | | 2.5 | 2.4 |
| | | 1.3 | 1.5 | | | Current | 1.8 | 1.2 |
| | | .6 | 1.0 | | | | .6 | .9 |
| | | 1.9 | 3.1 | | | | 2.1 | 2.2 |
| | | 1.3 | 1.3 | | | Quick | 1.4 | 1.2 |
| | | .6 | .8 | | | | .4 | .9 |
| | | 24   15.3 | 25   14.5 | | | | 17   21.0 | 37   9.9 |
| | | 47   7.8 | 38   9.5 | | | Sales/Receivables | 49   7.4 | 53   6.9 |
| | | 53   6.9 | 61   6.0 | | | | 66   5.5 | 69   5.3 |
| | | | | | | | | |
| | | | | | | Cost of Sales/Inventory | | |
| | | | | | | | | |
| | | | | | | | | |
| | | | | | | Cost of Sales/Payables | | |
| | | | | | | | | |
| | | 13.6 | 8.0 | | | | 6.0 | 9.0 |
| | | 31.7 | 27.7 | | | Sales/Working Capital | 23.9 | 29.9 |
| | | -17.4 | -259.6 | | | | -196.4 | NM |
| | | 17.9 | 18.2 | | | | 22.0 | 7.2 |
| | | (10)   4.7 | (10)   3.9 | | | EBIT/Interest | 7.6 | (18)   3.4 |
| | | -42.8 | .2 | | | | 1.0 | .1 |
| | | | | | | Net Profit + Depr., Dep., Amort./Cur. Mat. L/T/D | | |
| | | | | | | | | |
| | | .3 | .4 | | | | .2 | .3 |
| | | .8 | .7 | | | Fixed/Worth | .5 | .7 |
| | | -2.1 | NM | | | | 2.3 | 3.0 |
| | | .9 | 1.1 | | | | .7 | .7 |
| | | 1.4 | 2.3 | | | Debt/Worth | 2.2 | 2.6 |
| | | -11.5 | NM | | | | 6.3 | 4.6 |
| | | | | | | % Profit Before Taxes/Tangible Net Worth | 163.8 | 75.1 |
| | | | | | | | (20)   45.5 | (17)   43.7 |
| | | | | | | | 10.1 | 1.8 |
| | | 44.5 | 28.9 | | | | 31.7 | 29.5 |
| | | 10.6 | 6.3 | | | % Profit Before Taxes/Total Assets | 12.8 | 7.9 |
| | | -62.2 | -5.8 | | | | .2 | -2.5 |
| | | 41.0 | 36.1 | | | | 98.2 | 40.6 |
| | | 29.5 | 21.1 | | | Sales/Net Fixed Assets | 20.3 | 19.9 |
| | | 14.3 | 11.0 | | | | 6.1 | 8.0 |
| | | 5.5 | 4.0 | | | | 4.0 | 4.4 |
| | | 4.0 | 2.1 | | | Sales/Total Assets | 3.0 | 2.4 |
| | | 3.1 | 1.3 | | | | 1.6 | 2.0 |
| | | 1.1 | 1.7 | | | | 1.2 | 1.2 |
| | | (11)   2.1 | (10)   2.1 | | | % Depr., Dep., Amort./Sales | (14)   2.2 | (14)   2.2 |
| | | 3.5 | 3.0 | | | | 3.3 | 3.7 |
| | | | | | | % Officers', Directors' Owners' Comp/Sales | | |
| 11535M | 37583M | 208716M | 482131M | 415991M | 314297M | Net Sales ($) | 1192617M | 1375898M |
| 773M | 6710M | 49103M | 204260M | 189298M | 262468M | Total Assets ($) | 592728M | 562256M |

M = $ thousand    MM = $ million
See Pages 9 through 22 for Explanation of Ratios and Data

## Comparative Historical Data                                   Current Data Sorted by Sales

| | | | Type of Statement | | | | | | |
|---|---|---|---|---|---|---|---|---|---|
| 7 | 9 | 5 | Unqualified | | | 1 | | 1 | 3 |
| 2 | | 4 | Reviewed | | | | 1 | 1 | 2 |
| 2 | 1 | 2 | Compiled | 1 | | | | 1 | |
| 2 | 3 | 2 | Tax Returns | | | | 1 | 1 | |
| 15 | 22 | 24 | Other | | | 1 | 4 | 8 | 11 |
| 4/1/09-3/31/10 ALL | 4/1/10-3/31/11 ALL | 4/1/11-3/31/12 ALL | | 0-1MM | 6 (4/1-9/30/11) 1-3MM | 3-5MM | 31 (10/1/11-3/31/12) 5-10MM | 10-25MM | 25MM & OVER |
| 28 | 35 | 37 | NUMBER OF STATEMENTS | 1 | 2 | 2 | 6 | 12 | 16 |
| % | % | % | | % | % | % | % | % | % |
| | | | ASSETS | | | | | | |
| 9.7 | 12.7 | 12.4 | Cash & Equivalents | | | | | 7.6 | 7.5 |
| 41.9 | 36.0 | 36.2 | Trade Receivables (net) | D | | | | 46.3 | 36.8 |
| .4 | 3.1 | .1 | Inventory | A | | | | .0 | .2 |
| 8.4 | 8.9 | 5.3 | All Other Current | T | | | | 5.9 | 4.3 |
| 60.4 | 60.6 | 54.0 | Total Current | A | | | | 59.7 | 48.9 |
| 22.7 | 20.5 | 22.4 | Fixed Assets (net) | | | | | 19.2 | 26.4 |
| 8.9 | 14.5 | 14.8 | Intangibles (net) | N | | | | 17.7 | 14.8 |
| 7.9 | 4.4 | 8.8 | All Other Non-Current | O | | | | 3.4 | 9.9 |
| 100.0 | 100.0 | 100.0 | Total | T | | | | 100.0 | 100.0 |
| | | | LIABILITIES | A | | | | | |
| 24.0 | 9.9 | 8.5 | Notes Payable-Short Term | V | | | | 3.5 | 6.9 |
| 6.3 | 3.8 | 3.2 | Cur. Mat.-L.T.D. | A | | | | 1.4 | 4.9 |
| 11.1 | 9.6 | 10.5 | Trade Payables | I | | | | 13.4 | 12.2 |
| .6 | .5 | .5 | Income Taxes Payable | L | | | | .1 | .9 |
| 26.1 | 20.6 | 21.0 | All Other Current | A | | | | 33.8 | 15.1 |
| 68.1 | 44.3 | 43.8 | Total Current | B | | | | 52.1 | 40.1 |
| 14.4 | 14.4 | 16.5 | Long-Term Debt | L | | | | 21.1 | 17.5 |
| .4 | .3 | .3 | Deferred Taxes | E | | | | .2 | .6 |
| 5.5 | 8.1 | 14.4 | All Other Non-Current | | | | | 13.1 | 10.7 |
| 11.6 | 32.8 | 24.9 | Net Worth | | | | | 13.5 | 31.1 |
| 100.0 | 100.0 | 100.0 | Total Liabilties & Net Worth | | | | | 100.0 | 100.0 |
| | | | INCOME DATA | | | | | | |
| 100.0 | 100.0 | 100.0 | Net Sales | | | | | 100.0 | 100.0 |
| | | | Gross Profit | | | | | | |
| 96.3 | 94.7 | 97.2 | Operating Expenses | | | | | 99.0 | 98.5 |
| 3.7 | 5.3 | 2.8 | Operating Profit | | | | | 1.0 | 1.5 |
| 1.4 | 2.0 | 1.5 | All Other Expenses (net) | | | | | 1.8 | .8 |
| 2.3 | 3.3 | 1.4 | Profit Before Taxes | | | | | -.8 | .7 |
| | | | RATIOS | | | | | | |
| 2.4 | 2.8 | 2.4 | | | | | | 3.8 | 2.3 |
| 1.4 | 1.7 | 1.2 | Current | | | | | 1.4 | 1.2 |
| .4 | 1.2 | .8 | | | | | | .8 | .8 |
| 2.2 | 2.4 | 2.0 | | | | | | 3.6 | 2.0 |
| 1.2 | 1.5 | 1.1 | Quick | | | | | 1.3 | 1.1 |
| .3 | .8 | .6 | | | | | | .5 | .8 |
| 35  10.4 | 26  14.0 | 21  17.4 | | | | | 22  16.4 | 37  9.8 | |
| 45  8.1 | 45  8.1 | 43  8.4 | Sales/Receivables | | | | 39  9.4 | 51  7.1 | |
| 60  6.1 | 64  5.7 | 57  6.4 | | | | | 64  5.7 | 64  5.7 | |
| | | | Cost of Sales/Inventory | | | | | | |
| | | | Cost of Sales/Payables | | | | | | |
| 10.9 | 6.3 | 10.0 | | | | | | 6.4 | 10.4 |
| 19.1 | 12.4 | 43.2 | Sales/Working Capital | | | | | 31.7 | 40.7 |
| -18.4 | 56.4 | -54.1 | | | | | | -50.6 | -64.5 |
| 20.2 | 12.8 | 17.8 | | | | | | 10.3 | 8.5 |
| (25)  1.9 | (31)  6.4 | (31)  5.0 | EBIT/Interest | | | (10) | 1.8 | (14)  .5 | |
| -.8 | -1.9 | -2.6 | | | | | | -23.9 | -10.2 |
| | | | Net Profit + Depr., Dep., Amort./Cur. Mat. L/T/D | | | | | | |
| .3 | .3 | .4 | | | | | | .3 | .4 |
| .9 | .9 | 1.2 | Fixed/Worth | | | | | 1.0 | .9 |
| -1.3 | -6.1 | -2.3 | | | | | | -.5 | NM |
| .5 | .8 | 1.0 | | | | | | .7 | 1.1 |
| 3.7 | 2.8 | 2.9 | Debt/Worth | | | | | 7.8 | 2.3 |
| -2.6 | -20.6 | -13.9 | | | | | | -3.3 | NM |
| 51.4 | 96.1 | 127.1 | | | | | | | 97.5 |
| (17)  40.7 | (25)  43.9 | (25)  50.9 | % Profit Before Taxes/Tangible Net Worth | | | | | (12)  18.3 | |
| 1.2 | 4.1 | -16.1 | | | | | | | -50.5 |
| 20.0 | 30.3 | 35.0 | | | | | | 44.5 | 15.0 |
| 4.4 | 12.0 | 8.5 | % Profit Before Taxes/Total Assets | | | | | 2.9 | 1.3 |
| -10.8 | -4.4 | -7.4 | | | | | | -10.7 | -12.0 |
| 47.6 | 32.7 | 39.7 | | | | | | 38.6 | 21.5 |
| 21.1 | 15.5 | 22.0 | Sales/Net Fixed Assets | | | | | 36.3 | 11.2 |
| 10.9 | 11.1 | 9.0 | | | | | | 20.2 | 6.0 |
| 5.1 | 4.3 | 5.3 | | | | | | 7.0 | 4.3 |
| 3.4 | 2.4 | 3.3 | Sales/Total Assets | | | | | 3.5 | 2.7 |
| 2.1 | 1.7 | 2.1 | | | | | | 1.3 | 2.1 |
| 1.1 | 1.2 | 1.4 | | | | | | | 1.7 |
| (19)  2.0 | (28)  2.2 | (28)  2.1 | % Depr., Dep., Amort./Sales | | | | | (14)  2.2 | |
| 3.0 | 3.1 | 2.8 | | | | | | | 4.4 |
| | | | % Officers', Directors' Owners' Comp/Sales | | | | | | |
| 2441258M | 3035183M | 1470253M | Net Sales ($) | 900M | | 8409M | 40662M | 177952M | 1242330M |
| 909557M | 1329773M | 712612M | Total Assets ($) | 200M | | 4212M | 8655M | 90952M | 608593M |

M = $ thousand     MM = $ million
See Pages 9 through 22 for Explanation of Ratios and Data

## Current Data Sorted by Assets                                              Comparative Historical Data

| | | | | | | Type of Statement | | |
|---|---|---|---|---|---|---|---|---|
| | | 4 | 2 | | 3 | Unqualified | 10 | 7 |
| | 2 | 4 | 2 | | | Reviewed | 10 | 12 |
| 1 | 2 | 2 | 2 | | | Compiled | 15 | 17 |
| 17 | 5 | 6 | 5 | 1 | | Tax Returns | 20 | 27 |
| 9 | 6 | 8 | | | | Other | 36 | 35 |
| | 12 (4/1-9/30/11) | | 67 (10/1/11-3/31/12) | | | | 4/1/07-3/31/08 ALL | 4/1/08-3/31/09 ALL |
| 0-500M | 500M-2MM | 2-10MM | 10-50MM | 50-100MM | 100-250MM | **NUMBER OF STATEMENTS** | | |
| 27 | 15 | 24 | 9 | 1 | 3 | | 91 | 98 |
| % | % | % | % | % | % | **ASSETS** | % | % |
| 16.5 | 11.6 | 16.6 | | | | Cash & Equivalents | 14.4 | 14.9 |
| 23.6 | 39.0 | 21.6 | | | | Trade Receivables (net) | 22.9 | 28.0 |
| 6.2 | 7.4 | 9.9 | | | | Inventory | 8.1 | 9.5 |
| 1.9 | .7 | 1.9 | | | | All Other Current | 2.2 | 2.5 |
| 48.2 | 58.7 | 50.0 | | | | Total Current | 47.6 | 54.9 |
| 28.5 | 28.8 | 36.4 | | | | Fixed Assets (net) | 32.2 | 31.9 |
| 8.7 | .6 | 8.1 | | | | Intangibles (net) | 11.9 | 6.6 |
| 14.5 | 11.9 | 5.5 | | | | All Other Non-Current | 8.3 | 6.6 |
| 100.0 | 100.0 | 100.0 | | | | Total | 100.0 | 100.0 |
| | | | | | | **LIABILITIES** | | |
| 31.3 | 5.3 | 4.2 | | | | Notes Payable-Short Term | 8.4 | 12.9 |
| 4.5 | 4.2 | 7.7 | | | | Cur. Mat.-L.T.D. | 5.9 | 5.9 |
| 10.5 | 16.6 | 9.6 | | | | Trade Payables | 10.9 | 11.8 |
| .1 | .1 | .3 | | | | Income Taxes Payable | .5 | .1 |
| 24.2 | 15.6 | 12.6 | | | | All Other Current | 10.6 | 13.6 |
| 70.6 | 41.8 | 34.4 | | | | Total Current | 36.2 | 44.2 |
| 25.3 | 25.4 | 24.4 | | | | Long-Term Debt | 26.8 | 25.6 |
| .0 | 1.0 | .4 | | | | Deferred Taxes | .4 | .3 |
| 4.4 | 6.6 | 3.5 | | | | All Other Non-Current | 5.7 | 6.4 |
| -.3 | 25.2 | 37.3 | | | | Net Worth | 31.0 | 23.4 |
| 100.0 | 100.0 | 100.0 | | | | Total Liabilities & Net Worth | 100.0 | 100.0 |
| | | | | | | **INCOME DATA** | | |
| 100.0 | 100.0 | 100.0 | | | | Net Sales | 100.0 | 100.0 |
| | | | | | | Gross Profit | | |
| 95.6 | 94.1 | 91.8 | | | | Operating Expenses | 92.3 | 94.2 |
| 4.4 | 5.9 | 8.2 | | | | Operating Profit | 7.7 | 5.8 |
| .3 | .8 | 3.8 | | | | All Other Expenses (net) | 1.6 | 1.3 |
| 4.0 | 5.1 | 4.3 | | | | Profit Before Taxes | 6.1 | 4.5 |
| | | | | | | **RATIOS** | | |
| 1.5 | 5.2 | 3.5 | | | | | 2.4 | 2.5 |
| .9 | 1.1 | 1.4 | | | | Current | 1.5 | 1.3 |
| .5 | .9 | .8 | | | | | .8 | .9 |
| 1.3 | 5.0 | 3.2 | | | | | 2.0 | 2.1 |
| .6 | 1.1 | .9 | | | | Quick | 1.1 | 1.0 |
| .4 | .6 | .6 | | | | | .5 | .6 |
| 0 UND | 33  11.2 | 17  21.1 | | | | | 21  17.0 | 22  16.5 |
| 16  22.7 | 38  9.7 | 29  12.7 | | | | Sales/Receivables | 36  10.3 | 35  10.5 |
| 30  12.1 | 73  5.0 | 54  6.7 | | | | | 54  6.7 | 48  7.6 |
| | | | | | | Cost of Sales/Inventory | | |
| | | | | | | Cost of Sales/Payables | | |
| 43.7 | 5.4 | 5.7 | | | | | 8.2 | 7.8 |
| -85.0 | 53.6 | 17.1 | | | | Sales/Working Capital | 18.9 | 24.4 |
| -8.8 | -34.3 | -43.9 | | | | | -21.8 | -30.9 |
| 15.5 | 7.1 | 22.4 | | | | | 9.8 | 10.7 |
| (22)  6.3 | (12)  4.9 | (23)  2.5 | | | | EBIT/Interest | (78)  3.7 | (88)  2.7 |
| 1.1 | -.1 | 1.1 | | | | | 1.6 | .9 |
| | | | | | | | 3.6 | 2.0 |
| | | | | | | Net Profit + Depr., Dep., Amort./Cur. Mat. L/T/D | (15)  2.1 | (16)  1.7 |
| | | | | | | | 1.4 | .6 |
| .4 | .0 | .6 | | | | | .5 | .4 |
| 2.6 | .8 | 1.7 | | | | Fixed/Worth | 1.4 | 1.5 |
| -.7 | 1.9 | 2.8 | | | | | -2.4 | -2.2 |
| 1.2 | 1.5 | .8 | | | | | 1.1 | .9 |
| 4.6 | 2.6 | 2.2 | | | | Debt/Worth | 2.8 | 2.5 |
| -2.1 | 18.1 | 4.4 | | | | | -8.7 | -6.8 |
| 212.5 | 116.4 | 50.3 | | | | | 70.8 | 77.1 |
| (18)  52.8 | (12)  54.1 | (21)  15.1 | | | | % Profit Before Taxes/Tangible Net Worth | (64)  38.0 | (67)  33.2 |
| 19.7 | 25.7 | .5 | | | | | 8.4 | 7.1 |
| 52.8 | 36.1 | 18.5 | | | | | 19.1 | 30.4 |
| 18.4 | 13.0 | 4.1 | | | | % Profit Before Taxes/Total Assets | 9.0 | 7.7 |
| -1.5 | 1.7 | .3 | | | | | 1.7 | -.9 |
| 71.1 | 197.9 | 25.5 | | | | | 18.9 | 28.9 |
| 25.1 | 15.4 | 7.2 | | | | Sales/Net Fixed Assets | 8.7 | 11.7 |
| 9.5 | 4.6 | 3.2 | | | | | 4.3 | 5.4 |
| 8.9 | 6.1 | 3.2 | | | | | 3.8 | 4.6 |
| 5.4 | 2.9 | 2.4 | | | | Sales/Total Assets | 2.3 | 2.9 |
| 2.6 | 1.5 | 1.6 | | | | | 1.5 | 1.9 |
| .8 | | 2.0 | | | | | 2.5 | 1.4 |
| (14)  1.3 | | (21)  4.2 | | | | % Depr., Dep., Amort./Sales | (75)  3.8 | (75)  3.0 |
| 4.7 | | 8.2 | | | | | 6.3 | 6.6 |
| 5.9 | | 5.1 | | | | | 3.0 | 3.6 |
| (21)  9.0 | | (14)  6.4 | | | | % Officers', Directors' Owners' Comp/Sales | (42)  6.1 | (42)  6.1 |
| 13.3 | | 11.8 | | | | | 9.4 | 9.9 |
| 53088M | 69888M | 364574M | 303455M | 56569M | 389488M | Net Sales ($) | 1070455M | 1545097M |
| 6796M | 18394M | 134512M | 209771M | 58599M | 490351M | Total Assets ($) | 725758M | 891013M |

M = $ thousand    MM = $ million
See Pages 9 through 22 for Explanation of Ratios and Data

## Comparative Historical Data

## Current Data Sorted by Sales

| | | | | Type of Statement | | | | | | |
|---|---|---|---|---|---|---|---|---|---|---|
| 12 | | 8 | 9 | Unqualified | | 2 | 1 | | 2 | 4 |
| 9 | | 8 | 6 | Reviewed | | 2 | | | 3 | 1 |
| 10 | | 8 | 5 | Compiled | 1 | 1 | 2 | | 1 | |
| 15 | | 24 | 30 | Tax Returns | 10 | 4 | 5 | | 2 | 2 |
| 26 | | 39 | 29 | Other | 5 | 2 | | | 8 | 6 |
| 4/1/09- | | 4/1/10- | 4/1/11- | | 8 | | | | | |
| 3/31/10 | | 3/31/11 | 3/31/12 | | 12 (4/1-9/30/11) | | 67 (10/1/11-3/31/12) | | | |
| ALL | | ALL | ALL | | 0-1MM | 1-3MM | 3-5MM | 5-10MM | 10-25MM | 25MM & OVER |
| 72 | | 87 | 79 | **NUMBER OF STATEMENTS** | 15 | 16 | 11 | 8 | 16 | 13 |
| % | | % | % | **ASSETS** | % | % | % | % | % | % |
| 13.3 | | 16.8 | 15.3 | Cash & Equivalents | 12.4 | 15.9 | 10.4 | | 12.8 | 22.3 |
| 31.0 | | 24.2 | 25.4 | Trade Receivables (net) | 15.5 | 29.5 | 30.9 | | 30.1 | 25.1 |
| 8.6 | | 5.8 | 7.3 | Inventory | 5.2 | 2.9 | 8.7 | | 12.0 | 4.7 |
| 1.8 | | 5.4 | 2.2 | All Other Current | 1.0 | 3.3 | 2.8 | | 2.3 | 3.1 |
| 54.7 | | 52.3 | 50.2 | Total Current | 34.1 | 51.6 | 52.7 | | 57.2 | 55.1 |
| 27.1 | | 27.9 | 31.5 | Fixed Assets (net) | 38.0 | 32.2 | 35.7 | | 26.5 | 23.2 |
| 10.9 | | 8.1 | 7.8 | Intangibles (net) | 8.5 | 6.0 | 7.2 | | 8.3 | 13.1 |
| 7.3 | | 11.7 | 10.5 | All Other Non-Current | 19.4 | 10.1 | 4.3 | | 7.9 | 8.6 |
| 100.0 | | 100.0 | 100.0 | Total | 100.0 | 100.0 | 100.0 | | 100.0 | 100.0 |
| | | | | **LIABILITIES** | | | | | | |
| 13.3 | | 14.2 | 15.7 | Notes Payable-Short Term | 30.1 | 29.3 | 2.9 | | 8.5 | 10.8 |
| 5.3 | | 4.6 | 5.2 | Cur. Mat.-L.T.D. | 4.5 | 3.3 | 12.3 | | 5.9 | 2.7 |
| 15.8 | | 14.9 | 10.6 | Trade Payables | 5.4 | 10.8 | 14.1 | | 15.9 | 4.8 |
| 1.2 | | .1 | .2 | Income Taxes Payable | .0 | .0 | .2 | | .5 | .4 |
| 14.5 | | 14.5 | 17.3 | All Other Current | 20.4 | 17.0 | 22.2 | | 11.2 | 16.5 |
| 50.1 | | 48.3 | 49.1 | Total Current | 60.5 | 60.3 | 51.7 | | 42.0 | 35.3 |
| 19.5 | | 22.9 | 23.6 | Long-Term Debt | 29.4 | 19.7 | 39.5 | | 20.5 | 14.0 |
| .7 | | .3 | .4 | Deferred Taxes | .0 | .0 | 1.3 | | .7 | .4 |
| 7.3 | | 12.3 | 4.5 | All Other Non-Current | 3.2 | 8.3 | 3.2 | | 5.0 | 4.2 |
| 22.5 | | 16.2 | 22.4 | Net Worth | 6.9 | 11.7 | 4.3 | | 31.8 | 46.2 |
| 100.0 | | 100.0 | 100.0 | Total Liabilties & Net Worth | 100.0 | 100.0 | 100.0 | | 100.0 | 100.0 |
| | | | | **INCOME DATA** | | | | | | |
| 100.0 | | 100.0 | 100.0 | Net Sales | 100.0 | 100.0 | 100.0 | | 100.0 | 100.0 |
| | | | | Gross Profit | | | | | | |
| 98.3 | | 95.0 | 93.9 | Operating Expenses | 90.7 | 95.6 | 95.0 | | 95.8 | 91.5 |
| 1.7 | | 5.0 | 6.1 | Operating Profit | 9.3 | 4.4 | 5.0 | | 4.2 | 8.5 |
| 1.1 | | 1.5 | 2.6 | All Other Expenses (net) | 6.8 | .1 | 1.7 | | 2.1 | 1.4 |
| .6 | | 3.5 | 3.5 | Profit Before Taxes | 2.6 | 4.3 | 3.3 | | 2.1 | 7.1 |
| | | | | **RATIOS** | | | | | | |
| 2.0 | | 2.5 | 2.3 | | 4.5 | 4.5 | 1.6 | | 3.2 | 3.9 |
| 1.4 | | 1.1 | 1.1 | Current | .8 | 1.2 | 1.1 | | 1.2 | 1.1 |
| .7 | | .7 | .8 | | .4 | .5 | .7 | | .8 | .9 |
| 1.6 | | 1.4 | 2.0 | | 2.0 | 4.4 | 1.4 | | 2.2 | 3.8 |
| .9 | | .8 | .9 | Quick | .6 | 1.1 | .7 | | .8 | 1.0 |
| .5 | | .5 | .5 | | .3 | .1 | .6 | | .6 | .8 |
| 21  17.6 | 8  48.3 | 16  23.1 | | | 0  UND | 0  UND | 33  11.2 | | 20  18.4 | 38  9.7 |
| 40  9.2 | 33  11.0 | 31  11.8 | | Sales/Receivables | 23  15.7 | 16  23.2 | 38  9.7 | | 23  15.6 | 64  5.7 |
| 66  5.5 | 50  7.3 | 51  7.1 | | | 35  10.3 | 46  7.9 | 56  6.5 | | 51  7.1 | 79  4.6 |
| | | | | Cost of Sales/Inventory | | | | | | |
| | | | | Cost of Sales/Payables | | | | | | |
| 9.4 | | 8.7 | 7.0 | | 5.1 | 8.7 | 5.4 | | 6.9 | 5.3 |
| 24.0 | | 64.6 | 61.3 | Sales/Working Capital | -25.0 | NM | 61.3 | | 104.9 | 26.4 |
| -15.7 | | -16.4 | -25.0 | | -5.2 | -10.4 | -26.1 | | -28.7 | -72.9 |
| 8.7 | | 17.7 | 11.8 | | 8.1 | 24.3 | 5.5 | | 11.1 | 127.8 |
| (61)  2.3 | (72)  4.1 | (65)  3.9 | EBIT/Interest | (13)  5.4 | (13)  7.5 | 1.3 | (15)  4.7 | (10)  5.9 | |
| -.6 | 1.0 | 1.2 | | .7 | .8 | 1.0 | | 1.1 | .9 |
| 3.2 | | 5.7 | 4.1 | Net Profit + Depr., Dep., | | | | | | |
| (17)  1.9 | (13)  2.5 | (13)  1.1 | Amort./Cur. Mat. L/T/D | | | | | | |
| .7 | .9 | .9 | | | | | | | |
| .4 | | .5 | .4 | | 1.0 | .5 | .8 | | .3 | .2 |
| 1.6 | | 1.9 | 1.3 | Fixed/Worth | 2.8 | 1.3 | 1.3 | | 1.5 | .8 |
| -2.1 | | -.8 | UND | | -2.1 | NM | -1.1 | | 3.6 | NM |
| 1.1 | | 1.0 | 1.0 | | 2.0 | 1.2 | 1.7 | | 1.0 | .8 |
| 2.8 | | 6.7 | 2.5 | Debt/Worth | 6.8 | 1.7 | 2.6 | | 2.4 | 1.1 |
| -6.5 | | -4.6 | UND | | -4.5 | NM | -3.0 | | 9.1 | NM |
| 42.4 | | 65.3 | 72.5 | % Profit Before Taxes/Tangible | 107.0 | 202.3 | | | 54.8 | 109.0 |
| (45)  15.1 | (53)  36.7 | (60)  33.5 | Net Worth | (10)  45.0 | (12)  49.7 | | (13)  25.7 | (10)  39.5 | |
| -15.0 | 3.3 | 1.6 | | -1.9 | 23.9 | | | -9.0 | 11.4 |
| 15.4 | | 23.4 | 30.7 | % Profit Before Taxes/Total | 33.5 | 44.0 | 11.5 | | 30.5 | 27.4 |
| 2.2 | | 9.8 | 7.6 | Assets | 6.6 | 19.0 | 3.2 | | 10.4 | 10.3 |
| -8.2 | | .3 | .4 | | -.8 | -.3 | .0 | | .7 | 2.7 |
| 30.0 | | 37.5 | 39.4 | | 16.3 | 51.4 | 11.7 | | 42.7 | 29.8 |
| 14.7 | | 15.7 | 11.6 | Sales/Net Fixed Assets | 9.5 | 24.7 | 4.9 | | 18.0 | 9.4 |
| 5.4 | | 6.4 | 4.9 | | 3.9 | 9.4 | 3.9 | | 5.9 | 5.8 |
| 4.3 | | 5.0 | 5.4 | | 3.2 | 7.3 | 2.9 | | 3.6 | 2.8 |
| 2.8 | | 2.8 | 2.7 | Sales/Total Assets | 2.3 | 5.7 | 2.4 | | 3.0 | 1.9 |
| 2.1 | | 1.7 | 1.7 | | .7 | 3.0 | 1.5 | | 2.3 | .9 |
| 1.1 | | 1.0 | 1.3 | | | .8 | | | 1.0 | 2.0 |
| (55)  2.7 | (62)  2.8 | (54)  4.2 | % Depr., Dep., Amort./Sales | | (10)  1.2 | | (13)  2.1 | (11)  5.2 | |
| 5.4 | 5.5 | 6.7 | | | 5.1 | | | 4.6 | 7.2 |
| 3.6 | | 2.8 | 4.3 | | | 6.5 | | | | |
| (25)  8.8 | (36)  7.6 | (40)  6.9 | % Officers', Directors' | | (12)  9.4 | | | | |
| 14.8 | 16.5 | 12.4 | Owners' Comp/Sales | | 12.7 | | | | |
| 1262133M | 1841372M | 1237062M | Net Sales ($) | 9092M | 24739M | 46484M | 55784M | 235468M | 865495M |
| 859549M | 796731M | 918423M | Total Assets ($) | 23312M | 5330M | 31801M | 41140M | 89023M | 727817M |

M = $ thousand    MM = $ million
See Pages 9 through 22 for Explanation of Ratios and Data

**Current Data Sorted by Assets**      **Comparative Historical Data**

| | | | | | | Type of Statement | | 40 | 56 |
|---|---|---|---|---|---|---|---|---|---|
| 2 | 8 | 23 | 31 | 5 | 3 | Unqualified | | 40 | 56 |
| | 7 | 12 | 4 | | | Reviewed | | 16 | 22 |
| 4 | 10 | 10 | 1 | | 1 | Compiled | | 21 | 16 |
| 11 | 9 | 4 | 1 | | | Tax Returns | | 26 | 25 |
| 5 | 21 | 33 | 19 | 9 | 4 | Other | | 45 | 75 |
| | | 23 (4/1-9/30/11) | | 214 (10/1/11-3/31/12) | | | | 4/1/07-3/31/08 | 4/1/08-3/31/09 |
| 0-500M | 500M-2MM | 2-10MM | 10-50MM | 50-100MM | 100-250MM | | | ALL | ALL |
| 22 | 55 | 82 | 56 | 14 | 8 | NUMBER OF STATEMENTS | | 148 | 194 |
| % | % | % | % | % | % | ASSETS | | % | % |
| 37.3 | 30.9 | 24.4 | 19.1 | 12.3 | | Cash & Equivalents | | 26.8 | 24.0 |
| 10.7 | 25.6 | 26.2 | 22.5 | 28.3 | | Trade Receivables (net) | | 24.8 | 25.8 |
| 8.0 | 1.4 | .0 | .0 | .0 | | Inventory | | 1.6 | 1.0 |
| 9.1 | 4.4 | 11.4 | 11.3 | 8.5 | | All Other Current | | 6.4 | 9.4 |
| 65.0 | 62.3 | 62.1 | 52.9 | 49.0 | | Total Current | | 59.6 | 60.2 |
| 24.4 | 16.5 | 17.9 | 16.1 | 7.1 | | Fixed Assets (net) | | 18.5 | 17.8 |
| 1.0 | 7.4 | 8.2 | 15.9 | 41.0 | | Intangibles (net) | | 9.7 | 11.7 |
| 9.2 | 13.7 | 11.8 | 15.1 | 2.9 | | All Other Non-Current | | 12.2 | 10.4 |
| 100.0 | 100.0 | 100.0 | 100.0 | 100.0 | | Total | | 100.0 | 100.0 |
| | | | | | | LIABILITIES | | | |
| 75.4 | 8.1 | 9.3 | 10.2 | 2.9 | | Notes Payable-Short Term | | 10.9 | 12.7 |
| 7.0 | 3.8 | 3.5 | 2.9 | 2.7 | | Cur. Mat.-L.T.D. | | 4.6 | 5.1 |
| 11.8 | 12.5 | 9.1 | 8.5 | 3.2 | | Trade Payables | | 10.3 | 9.4 |
| .3 | .0 | .1 | .1 | .1 | | Income Taxes Payable | | .2 | .4 |
| 29.7 | 17.4 | 19.4 | 14.0 | 8.0 | | All Other Current | | 17.7 | 21.4 |
| 124.1 | 41.8 | 41.3 | 35.6 | 16.9 | | Total Current | | 43.8 | 49.0 |
| 10.1 | 11.0 | 16.5 | 14.6 | 25.8 | | Long-Term Debt | | 16.5 | 16.8 |
| .0 | .1 | .3 | .5 | 1.1 | | Deferred Taxes | | .2 | .3 |
| 5.6 | 7.7 | 4.6 | 15.9 | 4.6 | | All Other Non-Current | | 8.5 | 5.1 |
| -39.9 | 39.4 | 37.4 | 33.3 | 51.6 | | Net Worth | | 31.1 | 28.9 |
| 100.0 | 100.0 | 100.0 | 100.0 | 100.0 | | Total Liabilties & Net Worth | | 100.0 | 100.0 |
| | | | | | | INCOME DATA | | | |
| 100.0 | 100.0 | 100.0 | 100.0 | 100.0 | | Net Sales | | 100.0 | 100.0 |
| | | | | | | Gross Profit | | | |
| 90.8 | 90.7 | 90.4 | 89.1 | 71.0 | | Operating Expenses | | 89.9 | 91.5 |
| 9.2 | 9.3 | 9.6 | 10.9 | 29.0 | | Operating Profit | | 10.1 | 8.5 |
| 2.4 | 1.2 | 1.5 | 2.6 | 6.8 | | All Other Expenses (net) | | 2.8 | 2.6 |
| 6.9 | 8.1 | 8.2 | 8.4 | 22.2 | | Profit Before Taxes | | 7.3 | 5.9 |
| | | | | | | RATIOS | | | |
| 5.4 | 2.2 | 2.8 | 2.6 | 10.2 | | | | 2.8 | 2.3 |
| 1.1 | 1.6 | 1.5 | 1.4 | 2.0 | | Current | | 1.5 | 1.3 |
| .2 | 1.0 | .8 | 1.0 | .9 | | | | .8 | .9 |
| 5.3 | 2.2 | 2.4 | 2.3 | 5.5 | | | | 2.6 | 1.8 |
| .6 | 1.4 | 1.2 | 1.2 | 1.9 | | Quick | | 1.3 | 1.1 |
| .2 | .8 | .7 | .7 | .7 | | | | .7 | .7 |
| 0   UND | 6   65.0 | 15   23.9 | 20   18.4 | 18   20.8 | | | | 9   39.3 | 8   44.6 |
| 0   UND | 22   16.9 | 27   13.6 | 30   12.0 | 42   8.6 | | Sales/Receivables | | 24   15.0 | 27   13.7 |
| 7   52.0 | 36   10.2 | 42   8.7 | 48   7.6 | 159   2.3 | | | | 46   7.9 | 50   7.3 |
| | | | | | | Cost of Sales/Inventory | | | |
| | | | | | | Cost of Sales/Payables | | | |
| 10.4 | 8.0 | 6.8 | 4.0 | .9 | | | | 5.7 | 6.2 |
| 731.7 | 28.4 | 20.0 | 13.5 | 12.0 | | Sales/Working Capital | | 17.4 | 29.2 |
| -5.2 | -701.0 | -37.9 | 250.6 | -41.7 | | | | -45.1 | -39.7 |
| 27.1 | 36.8 | 37.8 | 28.5 | 285.2 | | | | 14.9 | 19.4 |
| (14) 7.6 | (38) 8.8 | (71) 10.4 | (44) 4.3 | (13) 9.1 | | EBIT/Interest | | (114) 5.5 | (150) 5.4 |
| -.8 | 3.0 | 3.3 | 1.2 | 2.7 | | | | 1.8 | 1.2 |
| | | | | | | Net Profit + Depr., Dep., | | 6.7 | 7.9 |
| | | | | | | Amort./Cur. Mat. L/T/D | | (21) 2.3   (29) 2.5 | |
| | | | | | | | | -.9 | .8 |
| .0 | .1 | .1 | .2 | .0 | | | | .2 | .2 |
| .9 | .4 | .4 | .5 | NM | | Fixed/Worth | | .5 | .7 |
| -.5 | 2.3 | 1.9 | 1.5 | -.2 | | | | 2.6 | 7.2 |
| .2 | .7 | .5 | .7 | .5 | | | | .7 | 1.0 |
| 3.9 | 1.1 | 1.6 | 2.4 | NM | | Debt/Worth | | 2.7 | 3.1 |
| -2.2 | 8.9 | 6.3 | 15.7 | -1.8 | | | | 23.7 | NM |
| 222.4 | 157.1 | 92.6 | 73.6 | | | % Profit Before Taxes/Tangible | | 90.6 | 73.1 |
| (13) 88.1 | (46) 50.7 | (71) 33.9 | (43) 43.0 | | | Net Worth | | (118) 41.9 | (146) 38.4 |
| 19.7 | 20.7 | 14.8 | 12.1 | | | | | 10.7 | 8.8 |
| 88.8 | 37.0 | 27.7 | 23.9 | 20.7 | | % Profit Before Taxes/Total | | 29.7 | 24.6 |
| 34.1 | 20.8 | 11.9 | 10.0 | 10.6 | | Assets | | 9.7 | 9.7 |
| -5.5 | 4.7 | 4.2 | 1.7 | 5.9 | | | | 2.1 | 1.0 |
| UND | 118.7 | 52.9 | 41.1 | UND | | | | 50.4 | 54.7 |
| 246.3 | 41.9 | 30.3 | 25.8 | 37.1 | | Sales/Net Fixed Assets | | 21.5 | 20.0 |
| 29.6 | 19.7 | 15.5 | 8.2 | 10.7 | | | | 10.9 | 11.3 |
| 24.1 | 5.8 | 4.0 | 2.6 | 1.2 | | | | 4.6 | 4.2 |
| 7.0 | 3.9 | 3.3 | 1.8 | .8 | | Sales/Total Assets | | 2.8 | 2.7 |
| 3.1 | 2.5 | 2.1 | .9 | .7 | | | | 1.5 | 1.4 |
| | .5 | .7 | 1.2 | | | | | 1.1 | 1.0 |
| | (39) 1.0 | (61) 1.6 | (44) 1.7 | | | % Depr., Dep., Amort./Sales | | (119) 1.9 | (139) 2.0 |
| | 1.9 | 2.6 | 3.5 | | | | | 3.0 | 3.1 |
| 5.5 | 3.3 | 2.5 | | | | % Officers', Directors' | | 4.4 | 2.9 |
| (11) 10.2 | (25) 8.0 | (16) 5.0 | | | | Owners' Comp/Sales | | (35) 5.6   (41) 4.3 | |
| 20.8 | 13.0 | 6.4 | | | | | | 9.8 | 8.5 |
| 42631M | 307940M | 1336068M | 1923709M | 1061549M | 2687819M | Net Sales ($) | | 3585516M | 6585775M |
| 4683M | 67127M | 425743M | 1125429M | 993360M | 1287793M | Total Assets ($) | | 2309209M | 4058734M |

## Comparative Historical Data

| | | | | | | Type of Statement | | | | | | |
|---|---|---|---|---|---|---|---|---|---|---|---|---|

| | | | | | | | Current Data Sorted by Sales | | | | | |
|---|---|---|---|---|---|---|---|---|---|---|---|---|

| | | | | | | **Type of Statement** | | | | | | |
|---|---|---|---|---|---|---|---|---|---|---|---|---|
| | 72 | | 75 | | 72 | Unqualified | 2 | 4 | 2 | 14 | 15 | 35 |
| | 25 | | 21 | | 23 | Reviewed | | 1 | 1 | 7 | 12 | 3 |
| | 26 | | 21 | | 26 | Compiled | 2 | 6 | 5 | 6 | 4 | 3 |
| | 28 | | 28 | | 25 | Tax Returns | 7 | 6 | 4 | 6 | 2 | |
| | 77 | | 91 | | 91 | Other | 4 | 10 | 7 | 12 | 22 | 36 |
| | 4/1/09-3/31/10 ALL | | 4/1/10-3/31/11 ALL | | 4/1/11-3/31/12 ALL | | | 23 (4/1-9/30/11) | | | 214 (10/1/11-3/31/12) | |
| | | | | | | | 0-1MM | 1-3MM | 3-5MM | 5-10MM | 10-25MM | 25MM & OVER |
| | 228 | | 236 | | 237 | **NUMBER OF STATEMENTS** | 15 | 26 | 19 | 45 | 55 | 77 |
| | % | | % | | % | **ASSETS** | % | % | % | % | % | % |
| | 26.0 | | 26.2 | | 24.7 | Cash & Equivalents | 28.1 | 32.7 | 27.7 | 23.4 | 25.4 | 20.7 |
| | 24.6 | | 23.8 | | 23.6 | Trade Receivables (net) | .7 | 23.3 | 19.7 | 27.1 | 25.3 | 25.8 |
| | 1.4 | | 1.3 | | 1.1 | Inventory | 11.7 | 3.0 | .0 | .0 | .0 | .0 |
| | 10.4 | | 8.2 | | 9.6 | All Other Current | 10.6 | 8.9 | 14.4 | 5.4 | 9.4 | 11.0 |
| | 62.4 | | 59.7 | | 58.9 | Total Current | 51.0 | 68.0 | 61.8 | 55.9 | 60.2 | 57.5 |
| | 18.0 | | 18.0 | | 16.8 | Fixed Assets (net) | 27.5 | 19.2 | 17.8 | 17.6 | 15.0 | 14.5 |
| | 11.0 | | 12.4 | | 12.3 | Intangibles (net) | 8.2 | 5.7 | 4.5 | 9.7 | 12.5 | 18.7 |
| | 8.6 | | 10.0 | | 11.9 | All Other Non-Current | 12.7 | 7.1 | 15.9 | 16.8 | 12.3 | 9.3 |
| | 100.0 | | 100.0 | | 100.0 | Total | 100.0 | 100.0 | 100.0 | 100.0 | 100.0 | 100.0 |
| | | | | | | **LIABILITIES** | | | | | | |
| | 9.2 | | 12.3 | | 14.8 | Notes Payable-Short Term | 34.5 | 15.2 | 10.2 | 28.9 | 9.5 | 7.4 |
| | 4.2 | | 4.1 | | 3.8 | Cur. Mat.-L.T.D. | 6.0 | 1.8 | 6.6 | 5.6 | 2.4 | 3.3 |
| | 10.5 | | 9.0 | | 9.6 | Trade Payables | 6.9 | 10.2 | 8.4 | 8.9 | 12.7 | 8.3 |
| | .3 | | .2 | | .1 | Income Taxes Payable | .0 | .0 | .0 | .2 | .1 | .1 |
| | 19.4 | | 17.2 | | 17.7 | All Other Current | 14.2 | 26.9 | 16.4 | 18.0 | 14.3 | 17.8 |
| | 43.4 | | 42.8 | | 45.9 | Total Current | 61.4 | 54.0 | 41.6 | 61.6 | 39.1 | 36.9 |
| | 16.4 | | 16.3 | | 14.8 | Long-Term Debt | 22.0 | 14.3 | 14.8 | 10.9 | 8.7 | 20.1 |
| | .5 | | .3 | | .3 | Deferred Taxes | .0 | .1 | .2 | .3 | .5 | .4 |
| | 6.9 | | 5.8 | | 8.2 | All Other Non-Current | 4.2 | 9.4 | 1.5 | 12.4 | 5.9 | 9.4 |
| | 32.7 | | 34.8 | | 30.7 | Net Worth | 12.4 | 22.2 | 41.9 | 14.7 | 45.8 | 33.1 |
| | 100.0 | | 100.0 | | 100.0 | Total Liabilties & Net Worth | 100.0 | 100.0 | 100.0 | 100.0 | 100.0 | 100.0 |
| | | | | | | **INCOME DATA** | | | | | | |
| | 100.0 | | 100.0 | | 100.0 | Net Sales | 100.0 | 100.0 | 100.0 | 100.0 | 100.0 | 100.0 |
| | | | | | | Gross Profit | | | | | | |
| | 90.4 | | 90.0 | | 88.7 | Operating Expenses | 77.7 | 85.6 | 82.8 | 94.3 | 91.7 | 87.9 |
| | 9.6 | | 10.0 | | 11.3 | Operating Profit | 22.3 | 14.4 | 17.2 | 5.7 | 8.3 | 12.1 |
| | 1.4 | | 2.3 | | 2.1 | All Other Expenses (net) | 7.0 | 2.2 | 1.1 | .9 | 1.1 | 2.8 |
| | 8.2 | | 7.7 | | 9.2 | Profit Before Taxes | 15.3 | 12.2 | 16.1 | 4.8 | 7.2 | 9.3 |
| | | | | | | **RATIOS** | | | | | | |
| | 2.8 | | 2.8 | | 2.7 | | 1.8 | 9.4 | 4.1 | 2.4 | 2.5 | 2.7 |
| | 1.4 | | 1.5 | | 1.5 | Current | .7 | 2.1 | 1.6 | 1.2 | 1.4 | 1.6 |
| | 1.0 | | 1.0 | | .9 | | .3 | 1.0 | 1.0 | .8 | 1.0 | .9 |
| | 2.2 | | 2.3 | | 2.4 | | 1.8 | 6.9 | 1.8 | 2.4 | 1.8 | 2.4 |
| | 1.2 | | 1.3 | | 1.2 | Quick | .4 | 2.1 | 1.1 | 1.1 | 1.3 | 1.3 |
| | .7 | | .8 | | .7 | | .1 | .7 | .6 | .6 | .8 | .7 |
| 8 | 46.7 | 8 | 44.1 | 9 | 40.4 | | 0 UND | 0 UND | 0 999.8 | 13 27.3 | 10 36.7 | 17 21.1 |
| 27 | 13.6 | 26 | 13.8 | 26 | 14.2 | Sales/Receivables | 0 UND | 15 24.0 | 24 15.5 | 25 14.4 | 27 13.5 | 30 12.2 |
| 45 | 8.2 | 43 | 8.5 | 42 | 8.6 | | 0 UND | 51 7.2 | 32 11.4 | 37 9.8 | 42 8.7 | 47 7.7 |
| | | | | | | Cost of Sales/Inventory | | | | | | |
| | | | | | | Cost of Sales/Payables | | | | | | |
| | 7.0 | | 7.2 | | 6.6 | | 2.8 | 2.4 | 7.1 | 8.7 | 7.0 | 5.5 |
| | 19.7 | | 18.1 | | 17.7 | Sales/Working Capital | -158.4 | 7.3 | 10.8 | 49.3 | 20.2 | 14.5 |
| | 653.0 | | -192.5 | | -100.5 | | -3.0 | NM | 272.4 | -20.6 | 294.9 | -58.6 |
| | 36.6 | | 31.3 | | 33.3 | | 7.1 | 17.8 | 32.2 | 32.2 | 52.7 | 48.2 |
| (174) | 7.9 | (183) | 5.6 | (188) | 8.1 | EBIT/Interest | (10) 4.5 | (17) 5.2 | (15) 12.5 | (37) 9.8 | (44) 11.7 | (65) 7.5 |
| | 1.9 | | 1.5 | | 1.8 | | 1.2 | 2.2 | 1.4 | -1.3 | 2.5 | 1.9 |
| | 4.8 | | 6.4 | | 13.8 | | | | | | | 10.4 |
| (30) | 2.7 | (29) | 2.4 | (23) | 4.2 | Net Profit + Depr., Dep., Amort./Cur. Mat. L/T/D | | | | | (11) | 5.9 |
| | .6 | | .7 | | 1.7 | | | | | | | 3.3 |
| | .2 | | .2 | | .1 | | .0 | .0 | .1 | .1 | .2 | .2 |
| | .5 | | .5 | | .5 | Fixed/Worth | 4.8 | .2 | .3 | .8 | .4 | .6 |
| | 2.8 | | 5.6 | | 5.3 | | -1.0 | 11.4 | .9 | NM | 1.0 | -.5 |
| | .7 | | .7 | | .6 | | 1.8 | .2 | .5 | .8 | .6 | .5 |
| | 2.3 | | 2.3 | | 2.1 | Debt/Worth | 4.7 | 1.2 | 1.0 | 2.9 | 1.5 | 2.7 |
| | 13.3 | | 31.5 | | 18.8 | | -3.8 | NM | 4.1 | NM | 5.0 | -2.3 |
| | 89.4 | | 107.0 | | 92.6 | | 131.7 | 117.2 | 174.3 | 88.4 | 87.9 | 75.3 |
| (183) | 49.5 | (182) | 45.2 | (183) | 45.8 | % Profit Before Taxes/Tangible Net Worth | (10) 41.8 | (20) 54.0 | (16) 64.6 | (34) 44.8 | (48) 43.6 | (55) 44.7 |
| | 22.7 | | 13.5 | | 16.6 | | 5.0 | 22.4 | 17.1 | 9.4 | 15.4 | 16.6 |
| | 34.1 | | 35.1 | | 33.2 | | 49.0 | 47.6 | 44.5 | 28.9 | 33.4 | 28.4 |
| | 15.4 | | 12.7 | | 12.2 | % Profit Before Taxes/Total Assets | 7.2 | 18.1 | 26.1 | 14.0 | 11.3 | 11.0 |
| | 3.8 | | 2.3 | | 3.1 | | -3.8 | 1.8 | 3.3 | -8.1 | 4.4 | 3.0 |
| | 62.4 | | 61.9 | | 69.3 | | UND | 710.0 | 160.5 | 79.4 | 55.0 | 44.2 |
| | 25.3 | | 27.2 | | 31.3 | Sales/Net Fixed Assets | 111.3 | 49.3 | 54.5 | 35.0 | 26.6 | 29.3 |
| | 11.6 | | 13.7 | | 14.1 | | .8 | 21.6 | 26.5 | 14.2 | 17.0 | 13.0 |
| | 4.7 | | 4.5 | | 4.4 | | 4.2 | 6.4 | 5.0 | 5.3 | 4.6 | 3.7 |
| | 3.1 | | 3.3 | | 2.9 | Sales/Total Assets | 1.1 | 2.4 | 2.8 | 3.6 | 3.2 | 2.4 |
| | 1.5 | | 1.6 | | 1.5 | | .5 | 1.4 | 1.7 | 2.3 | 1.7 | 1.1 |
| | .8 | | .8 | | .7 | | | .4 | .5 | .6 | .9 | 1.0 |
| (156) | 1.7 | (169) | 1.8 | (163) | 1.5 | % Depr., Dep., Amort./Sales | | (19) 1.1 | (12) .8 | (30) 1.5 | (41) 1.5 | (55) 1.8 |
| | 2.8 | | 2.7 | | 2.8 | | | 2.3 | 1.9 | 2.4 | 2.8 | 2.9 |
| | 2.5 | | 2.9 | | 2.8 | | | 5.5 | 2.6 | 4.2 | | 2.0 |
| (51) | 4.6 | (53) | 4.9 | (59) | 6.0 | % Officers', Directors' Owners' Comp/Sales | | (12) 12.2 | (10) 4.1 | (13) 6.0 | | (11) 3.1 |
| | 9.8 | | 10.1 | | 10.9 | | | 14.5 | 8.7 | 10.1 | | 4.8 |
| 6969291M | | 8278977M | | 7359716M | | Net Sales ($) | 7176M | 49909M | 80997M | 326653M | 904247M | 5990734M |
| 4048188M | | 3928459M | | 3904135M | | Total Assets ($) | 12646M | 53498M | 41384M | 168802M | 468509M | 3159296M |

M = $ thousand    MM = $ million
See Pages 9 through 22 for Explanation of Ratios and Data

## Current Data Sorted by Assets | Comparative Historical Data

| | 0-500M | 500M-2MM | 2-10MM | 10-50MM | 50-100MM | 100-250MM | Type of Statement | | 4/1/07-3/31/08 ALL | 4/1/08-3/31/09 ALL |
|---|---|---|---|---|---|---|---|---|---|---|
| | 2 | 8 | 27 | 31 | 10 | 12 | Unqualified | | 101 | 116 |
| | | 11 | 32 | 12 | | | Reviewed | | 99 | 88 |
| | 15 | 26 | 25 | 2 | | | Compiled | | 78 | 100 |
| | 64 | 60 | 22 | 2 | | | Tax Returns | | 116 | 124 |
| | 49 | 62 | 101 | 45 | 11 | 16 | Other | | 247 | 273 |
| | | 80 (4/1-9/30/11) | | 565 (10/1/11-3/31/12) | | | | | | |
| | 130 | 167 | 207 | 92 | 21 | 28 | **NUMBER OF STATEMENTS** | | 641 | 701 |
| | % | % | % | % | % | % | **ASSETS** | | % | % |
| | 31.5 | 18.6 | 17.4 | 20.1 | 19.1 | 16.8 | Cash & Equivalents | | 16.6 | 15.7 |
| | 17.5 | 24.8 | 32.5 | 27.2 | 24.2 | 20.8 | Trade Receivables (net) | | 29.7 | 29.0 |
| | 6.2 | 7.0 | 7.1 | 6.5 | 5.4 | 1.6 | Inventory | | 6.7 | 7.1 |
| | 6.1 | 3.4 | 6.3 | 6.8 | 6.9 | 11.2 | All Other Current | | 6.1 | 6.4 |
| | 61.3 | 53.8 | 63.3 | 60.6 | 55.6 | 50.4 | Total Current | | 59.2 | 58.2 |
| | 23.0 | 28.7 | 22.6 | 17.0 | 16.6 | 8.8 | Fixed Assets (net) | | 24.9 | 25.2 |
| | 7.4 | 4.2 | 5.7 | 12.2 | 19.8 | 28.7 | Intangibles (net) | | 7.1 | 7.5 |
| | 8.3 | 13.3 | 8.5 | 10.2 | 8.0 | 12.1 | All Other Non-Current | | 8.8 | 9.1 |
| | 100.0 | 100.0 | 100.0 | 100.0 | 100.0 | 100.0 | Total | | 100.0 | 100.0 |
| | | | | | | | **LIABILITIES** | | | |
| | 15.9 | 8.1 | 7.9 | 6.6 | 7.5 | 2.4 | Notes Payable-Short Term | | 11.1 | 12.5 |
| | 3.2 | 3.6 | 3.4 | 2.2 | 3.1 | 2.2 | Cur. Mat.-L.T.D. | | 4.1 | 4.0 |
| | 16.1 | 11.8 | 16.3 | 11.8 | 9.7 | 11.0 | Trade Payables | | 11.2 | 12.5 |
| | .0 | .1 | .2 | .3 | .1 | .5 | Income Taxes Payable | | .3 | .4 |
| | 25.8 | 16.4 | 13.8 | 20.8 | 22.6 | 24.6 | All Other Current | | 19.0 | 16.3 |
| | 61.0 | 40.0 | 41.6 | 41.7 | 43.0 | 40.7 | Total Current | | 45.8 | 45.6 |
| | 26.5 | 19.9 | 15.4 | 10.6 | 20.2 | 12.7 | Long-Term Debt | | 17.3 | 17.3 |
| | .0 | .2 | .4 | .3 | .1 | 1.9 | Deferred Taxes | | .3 | .3 |
| | 13.4 | 7.1 | 8.6 | 10.3 | 6.5 | 3.1 | All Other Non-Current | | 6.4 | 6.7 |
| | -.9 | 32.8 | 34.0 | 37.1 | 30.3 | 41.6 | Net Worth | | 30.2 | 30.1 |
| | 100.0 | 100.0 | 100.0 | 100.0 | 100.0 | 100.0 | Total Liabilities & Net Worth | | 100.0 | 100.0 |
| | | | | | | | **INCOME DATA** | | | |
| | 100.0 | 100.0 | 100.0 | 100.0 | 100.0 | 100.0 | Net Sales | | 100.0 | 100.0 |
| | | | | | | | Gross Profit | | | |
| | 90.7 | 89.0 | 92.0 | 89.0 | 87.8 | 89.3 | Operating Expenses | | 89.9 | 91.9 |
| | 9.3 | 11.0 | 8.0 | 11.0 | 12.2 | 10.7 | Operating Profit | | 10.1 | 8.1 |
| | 1.6 | 3.2 | 2.1 | 2.4 | 1.9 | 1.8 | All Other Expenses (net) | | 2.5 | 2.9 |
| | 7.7 | 7.8 | 5.9 | 8.6 | 10.3 | 8.9 | Profit Before Taxes | | 7.7 | 5.1 |
| | | | | | | | **RATIOS** | | | |
| | 3.1 | 2.8 | 2.9 | 2.5 | 1.9 | 2.5 | Current | | 2.6 | 2.4 |
| | 1.4 | 1.3 | 1.6 | 1.4 | 1.2 | 1.4 | | | 1.4 | 1.3 |
| | .6 | .8 | 1.0 | 1.0 | 1.0 | 1.0 | | | .9 | .9 |
| | 2.5 | 2.3 | 2.4 | 2.1 | 1.8 | 2.0 | Quick | | 2.2 | 1.9 |
| | 1.0 | 1.1 | 1.3 | 1.1 | 1.0 | .9 | | | (640) 1.1 | 1.1 |
| | .3 | .5 | .7 | .7 | .6 | .5 | | | .6 | .5 |
| | 0 UND | 0 UND | 21 17.2 | 20 18.6 | 21 17.7 | 20 18.5 | Sales/Receivables | | 7 49.1 | 9 39.7 |
| | 0 UND | 29 12.7 | 41 8.9 | 40 9.1 | 55 6.6 | 46 8.0 | | | 38 9.5 | 37 9.9 |
| | 25 14.8 | 45 8.1 | 62 5.9 | 63 5.8 | 79 4.6 | 68 5.4 | | | 63 5.8 | 61 6.0 |
| | | | | | | | Cost of Sales/Inventory | | | |
| | | | | | | | Cost of Sales/Payables | | | |
| | 12.6 | 8.5 | 5.5 | 4.7 | 4.1 | 3.0 | Sales/Working Capital | | 6.6 | 6.7 |
| | 69.9 | 32.2 | 10.3 | 9.9 | 18.4 | 9.2 | | | 19.8 | 23.7 |
| | -22.2 | -38.7 | 639.9 | 399.0 | -106.9 | -79.3 | | | -59.6 | -48.1 |
| | 19.9 | 23.1 | 32.5 | 51.4 | 92.6 | 45.6 | EBIT/Interest | | 20.7 | 16.8 |
| | (74) 6.9 | (114) 6.9 | (164) 6.9 | (70) 7.3 | (19) 3.1 | (24) 7.6 | | | (498) 5.4 | (562) 4.6 |
| | 1.6 | 2.1 | 2.1 | 2.6 | 1.0 | .6 | | | 1.3 | 1.0 |
| | | 10.0 | 8.7 | 43.5 | | | Net Profit + Depr., Dep., Amort./Cur. Mat. L/T/D | | 10.6 | 11.9 |
| | | (12) 4.8 | (28) 2.8 | (13) 4.4 | | | | | (92) 3.5 | (89) 3.3 |
| | | 2.4 | .8 | 1.8 | | | | | 1.1 | .8 |
| | .0 | .1 | .1 | .2 | .2 | .0 | Fixed/Worth | | .1 | .2 |
| | .6 | .7 | .6 | .5 | 1.0 | .5 | | | .7 | .8 |
| | -19.2 | 5.0 | 2.2 | 2.1 | -.6 | -.1 | | | 3.3 | 6.0 |
| | .8 | .6 | .6 | .6 | 1.1 | .6 | Debt/Worth | | .8 | .9 |
| | 4.1 | 2.0 | 1.8 | 2.4 | 5.8 | 4.3 | | | 2.4 | 2.5 |
| | -4.8 | 15.9 | 8.3 | 6.2 | -3.8 | -2.9 | | | 14.3 | 32.7 |
| | 190.0 | 77.4 | 66.3 | 66.9 | 85.7 | 25.2 | % Profit Before Taxes/Tangible Net Worth | | 87.0 | 70.3 |
| | (83) 90.1 | (131) 27.7 | (172) 33.0 | (75) 32.0 | (13) 34.7 | (17) 17.8 | | | (515) 38.9 | (539) 27.9 |
| | 18.7 | 5.9 | 8.5 | 10.8 | 20.9 | 4.3 | | | 8.7 | 3.6 |
| | 50.0 | 26.2 | 25.1 | 16.8 | 18.1 | 10.5 | % Profit Before Taxes/Total Assets | | 25.8 | 19.6 |
| | 18.2 | 8.4 | 9.9 | 9.0 | 8.1 | 5.3 | | | 9.5 | 7.0 |
| | .6 | .7 | 1.6 | 4.3 | 1.5 | -.3 | | | 1.0 | -.1 |
| | UND | 91.4 | 68.1 | 74.3 | 38.6 | 121.3 | Sales/Net Fixed Assets | | 72.6 | 66.1 |
| | 89.4 | 22.8 | 26.1 | 22.7 | 10.2 | 57.2 | | | 20.0 | 18.5 |
| | 15.8 | 5.3 | 6.7 | 7.8 | 6.4 | 13.8 | | | 6.4 | 6.0 |
| | 10.8 | 5.0 | 3.5 | 2.8 | 2.7 | 1.8 | Sales/Total Assets | | 4.3 | 4.2 |
| | 5.4 | 2.9 | 2.4 | 1.7 | 1.5 | .7 | | | 2.5 | 2.5 |
| | 3.1 | 1.7 | 1.6 | 1.1 | .7 | .5 | | | 1.4 | 1.4 |
| | .5 | .6 | .5 | .8 | 1.5 | .3 | % Depr., Dep., Amort./Sales | | .6 | .7 |
| | (58) 1.6 | (115) 1.4 | (160) 1.2 | (73) 2.0 | (15) 2.4 | (13) .8 | | | (476) 1.6 | (500) 1.7 |
| | 4.2 | 4.3 | 2.5 | 3.9 | 2.5 | 4.5 | | | 3.8 | 4.5 |
| | 3.3 | 3.5 | 2.2 | | | | % Officers', Directors' Owners' Comp/Sales | | 2.4 | 2.2 |
| | (59) 8.8 | (62) 5.1 | (46) 4.0 | | | | | | (212) 5.5 | (228) 5.0 |
| | 16.5 | 11.3 | 6.4 | | | | | | 10.9 | 10.4 |
| | 211267M | 725631M | 2781032M | 4670720M | 2789853M | 8152729M | Net Sales ($) | | 18954331M | 22642162M |
| | 30831M | 196801M | 986022M | 2025315M | 1480462M | 4534008M | Total Assets ($) | | 9302770M | 11600157M |

M = $ thousand    MM = $ million
See Pages 9 through 22 for Explanation of Ratios and Data

## Comparative Historical Data

## Current Data Sorted by Sales

| | | | Type of Statement | | | | | | |
|---|---|---|---|---|---|---|---|---|---|
| 115 | 100 | 90 | Unqualified | 4 | 4 | 2 | 8 | 22 | 50 |
| 102 | 76 | 55 | Reviewed | 1 | 2 | 8 | 14 | 22 | 8 |
| 93 | 77 | 68 | Compiled | 11 | 14 | 16 | 15 | 10 | 2 |
| 174 | 139 | 148 | Tax Returns | 45 | 48 | 23 | 21 | 8 | 3 |
| 359 | 318 | 284 | Other | 31 | 47 | 32 | 49 | 57 | 68 |
| 4/1/09-3/31/10 ALL | 4/1/10-3/31/11 ALL | 4/1/11-3/31/12 ALL | | 80 (4/1-9/30/11) | | | 565 (10/1/11-3/31/12) | | |
| | | | | 0-1MM | 1-3MM | 3-5MM | 5-10MM | 10-25MM | 25MM & OVER |
| 843 | 710 | 645 | **NUMBER OF STATEMENTS** | 92 | 115 | 81 | 107 | 119 | 131 |
| % | % | % | **ASSETS** | % | % | % | % | % | % |
| 18.2 | 20.3 | 21.0 | Cash & Equivalents | 21.1 | 24.4 | 20.8 | 19.7 | 19.2 | 20.7 |
| 28.2 | 26.7 | 26.0 | Trade Receivables (net) | 7.6 | 20.6 | 27.3 | 31.3 | 36.3 | 29.1 |
| 7.2 | 6.8 | 6.5 | Inventory | 2.2 | 7.2 | 10.8 | 7.8 | 6.2 | 5.7 |
| 6.1 | 5.5 | 5.8 | All Other Current | 2.6 | 7.4 | 5.6 | 4.1 | 6.0 | 7.9 |
| 59.7 | 59.3 | 59.2 | Total Current | 33.4 | 59.5 | 64.5 | 62.8 | 67.7 | 63.3 |
| 24.1 | 23.4 | 22.7 | Fixed Assets (net) | 47.2 | 22.4 | 22.5 | 21.1 | 16.7 | 12.4 |
| 7.7 | 8.5 | 8.0 | Intangibles (net) | 8.7 | 5.9 | 4.1 | 4.5 | 6.4 | 16.1 |
| 8.6 | 8.9 | 10.1 | All Other Non-Current | 10.6 | 12.2 | 8.8 | 11.5 | 9.2 | 8.2 |
| 100.0 | 100.0 | 100.0 | Total | 100.0 | 100.0 | 100.0 | 100.0 | 100.0 | 100.0 |
| | | | **LIABILITIES** | | | | | | |
| 12.1 | 9.6 | 9.1 | Notes Payable-Short Term | 5.6 | 15.9 | 8.8 | 10.2 | 8.3 | 5.6 |
| 4.0 | 3.7 | 3.2 | Cur. Mat.-L.T.D. | 3.7 | 3.8 | 2.5 | 3.4 | 3.1 | 2.5 |
| 11.9 | 13.1 | 14.0 | Trade Payables | 6.5 | 15.1 | 18.6 | 12.9 | 12.7 | 17.5 |
| .5 | .5 | .2 | Income Taxes Payable | .0 | .0 | .1 | .3 | .2 | .3 |
| 19.5 | 19.5 | 18.6 | All Other Current | 15.3 | 22.7 | 17.5 | 12.7 | 19.2 | 22.4 |
| 47.9 | 46.4 | 45.1 | Total Current | 31.1 | 57.6 | 47.5 | 39.6 | 43.5 | 48.4 |
| 17.7 | 17.2 | 18.2 | Long-Term Debt | 36.8 | 28.0 | 13.4 | 13.2 | 9.6 | 11.4 |
| .3 | .4 | .3 | Deferred Taxes | .0 | .2 | .3 | .2 | .6 | .4 |
| 8.3 | 8.4 | 9.1 | All Other Non-Current | 10.5 | 9.8 | 9.6 | 6.5 | 7.8 | 10.5 |
| 25.7 | 27.5 | 27.3 | Net Worth | 21.5 | 4.5 | 29.3 | 40.5 | 38.4 | 29.3 |
| 100.0 | 100.0 | 100.0 | Total Liabilities & Net Worth | 100.0 | 100.0 | 100.0 | 100.0 | 100.0 | 100.0 |
| | | | **INCOME DATA** | | | | | | |
| 100.0 | 100.0 | 100.0 | Net Sales | 100.0 | 100.0 | 100.0 | 100.0 | 100.0 | 100.0 |
| | | | Gross Profit | | | | | | |
| 91.6 | 89.7 | 90.3 | Operating Expenses | 79.0 | 89.5 | 95.2 | 92.8 | 93.0 | 91.4 |
| 8.4 | 10.3 | 9.7 | Operating Profit | 21.0 | 10.5 | 4.8 | 7.2 | 7.0 | 8.6 |
| 2.9 | 2.8 | 2.3 | All Other Expenses (net) | 10.0 | 2.0 | .5 | .5 | .8 | 1.2 |
| 5.4 | 7.5 | 7.4 | Profit Before Taxes | 11.0 | 8.5 | 4.3 | 6.7 | 6.2 | 7.4 |
| | | | **RATIOS** | | | | | | |
| 2.8 | 2.8 | 2.8 | Current | 3.2 | 2.9 | 2.7 | 4.1 | 2.8 | 2.4 |
| 1.4 | 1.5 | 1.5 | | 1.4 | 1.2 | 1.6 | 1.7 | 1.6 | 1.4 |
| .9 | .9 | .9 | | .3 | .7 | 1.0 | 1.0 | 1.1 | 1.0 |
| 2.1 | 2.3 | 2.3 | Quick | 2.7 | 2.3 | 2.1 | 2.8 | 2.3 | 2.0 |
| (842) 1.1 | 1.1 | 1.1 | | 1.0 | .9 | 1.2 | 1.3 | 1.4 | 1.1 |
| .5 | .6 | .6 | | .2 | .3 | .6 | .7 | .8 | .7 |
| 8  46.1 | 6  62.0 | 2  170.8 | Sales/Receivables | 0  UND | 0  UND | 4  82.2 | 15  24.7 | 26  14.3 | 20  18.1 |
| 36  10.2 | 31  11.6 | 32  11.3 | | 0  UND | 10  35.1 | 33  10.9 | 35  10.3 | 41  8.9 | 40  9.1 |
| 60  6.1 | 58  6.3 | 54  6.7 | | 17  21.9 | 46  8.0 | 57  6.4 | 56  6.5 | 66  5.5 | 56  6.5 |
| | | | Cost of Sales/Inventory | | | | | | |
| | | | Cost of Sales/Payables | | | | | | |
| 5.7 | 6.6 | 6.5 | Sales/Working Capital | 5.3 | 8.7 | 6.7 | 6.0 | 5.2 | 6.5 |
| 15.8 | 16.3 | 18.3 | | 75.8 | 77.0 | 18.2 | 13.1 | 10.0 | 18.4 |
| -54.6 | -55.7 | -67.9 | | -4.9 | -18.4 | 622.4 | 943.3 | 133.9 | -999.8 |
| 16.4 | 24.4 | 28.8 | EBIT/Interest | 12.2 | 19.3 | 22.3 | 32.7 | 39.8 | 71.2 |
| (637) 3.9 | (515) 5.3 | (465) 6.9 | | (42) 3.7 | (82) 6.0 | (59) 5.1 | (81) 6.9 | (95) 11.9 | (106) 7.9 |
| .5 | 1.5 | 2.1 | | 1.0 | 1.2 | 2.4 | 2.4 | 2.4 | 2.3 |
| 8.3 | 10.6 | 10.1 | Net Profit + Depr., Dep., Amort./Cur. Mat. L/T/D | | | | 23.0 | 7.8 | 16.3 |
| (79) 2.8 | (71) 3.8 | (63) 3.8 | | | | | (11) 3.1 | (19) 2.7 | (22) 5.5 |
| .9 | 1.2 | 1.4 | | | | | .9 | 1.1 | 2.1 |
| .1 | .1 | .1 | Fixed/Worth | .0 | .1 | .1 | .1 | .1 | .1 |
| .7 | .7 | .6 | | 2.4 | .8 | .6 | .4 | .4 | .5 |
| 11.4 | 16.6 | 5.0 | | UND | -3.5 | 1.9 | 2.2 | 1.6 | -1.2 |
| .8 | .7 | .7 | Debt/Worth | .9 | .5 | .9 | .4 | .6 | .8 |
| 2.5 | 2.5 | 2.2 | | 3.4 | 3.9 | 2.0 | 1.4 | 1.6 | 2.6 |
| 378.0 | -935.8 | 57.6 | | -14.7 | -6.0 | 9.4 | 8.3 | 6.2 | -6.8 |
| 64.1 | 77.5 | 82.4 | % Profit Before Taxes/Tangible Net Worth | 65.9 | 147.0 | 77.9 | 73.5 | 66.9 | 83.2 |
| (640) 22.9 | (532) 35.2 | (491) 33.0 | | (65) 19.1 | (76) 63.7 | (69) 27.5 | (88) 41.8 | (99) 34.3 | (94) 35.8 |
| 2.7 | 8.4 | 8.2 | | -.9 | 3.5 | 3.0 | 15.8 | 12.1 | 16.2 |
| 20.6 | 24.2 | 27.5 | % Profit Before Taxes/Total Assets | 17.5 | 47.6 | 18.9 | 28.9 | 27.6 | 21.8 |
| 6.1 | 9.0 | 10.3 | | 4.9 | 14.8 | 8.7 | 13.9 | 11.8 | 9.9 |
| -.5 | 1.2 | 1.6 | | -.6 | -1.4 | .7 | 3.4 | 3.5 | 2.5 |
| 75.0 | 87.9 | 114.6 | Sales/Net Fixed Assets | 152.5 | 188.3 | 97.3 | 88.7 | 99.2 | 164.8 |
| 23.8 | 22.6 | 28.3 | | 4.4 | 36.8 | 21.0 | 24.4 | 31.4 | 35.9 |
| 6.4 | 7.2 | 7.8 | | .2 | 8.5 | 8.1 | 10.2 | 11.7 | 13.4 |
| 4.1 | 4.2 | 4.9 | Sales/Total Assets | 3.3 | 6.8 | 4.7 | 5.0 | 4.3 | 4.2 |
| 2.5 | 2.4 | 2.6 | | 1.0 | 3.6 | 2.8 | 2.9 | 2.7 | 2.4 |
| 1.2 | 1.3 | 1.5 | | .2 | 1.9 | 1.9 | 2.1 | 1.7 | 1.3 |
| .6 | .7 | .6 | % Depr., Dep., Amort./Sales | 3.6 | .5 | .7 | .6 | .5 | .4 |
| (574) 1.7 | (486) 1.6 | (434) 1.5 | | (51) 11.0 | (67) 1.5 | (56) 1.5 | (78) 1.2 | (89) 1.1 | (93) 1.5 |
| 4.6 | 4.3 | 3.4 | | 20.8 | 3.6 | 3.1 | 2.3 | 2.4 | 2.6 |
| 2.4 | 2.7 | 2.7 | % Officers', Directors' Owners' Comp/Sales | 3.9 | 3.6 | 2.9 | 2.7 | 1.7 | 1.0 |
| (236) 4.9 | (194) 5.2 | (178) 5.0 | | (21) 16.8 | (52) 7.0 | (33) 5.1 | (35) 4.1 | (24) 4.2 | (13) 2.0 |
| 11.1 | 10.5 | 11.6 | | 32.7 | 14.2 | 9.3 | 6.1 | 6.1 | 5.8 |
| 23152596M | 22770488M | 19331232M | Net Sales ($) | 42065M | 217069M | 321246M | 752261M | 1924747M | 16073844M |
| 12929000M | 11841992M | 9253439M | Total Assets ($) | 122570M | 130137M | 129113M | 337529M | 1072275M | 7461815M |

M = $ thousand    MM = $ million
See Pages 9 through 22 for Explanation of Ratios and Data

## Current Data Sorted by Assets      Comparative Historical Data

| 0-500M | 500M-2MM | 2-10MM | 10-50MM | 50-100MM | 100-250MM | Type of Statement | 4/1/07-3/31/08 ALL | 4/1/08-3/31/09 ALL |
|---|---|---|---|---|---|---|---|---|
| | 4 | 4 | 8 | 2 | 4 | Unqualified | 12 | 8 |
| 1 | 2 | 2 | 7 | | | Reviewed | 16 | 15 |
| 3 | 7 | 5 | 1 | | | Compiled | 12 | 14 |
| 17 | 15 | 8 | 1 | | | Tax Returns | 21 | 21 |
| 9 | 16 | 17 | 11 | 3 | | Other | 32 | 38 |
| | 29 (4/1-9/30/11) | | 118 (10/1/11-3/31/12) | | | | | |
| 30 | 44 | 36 | 28 | 5 | 4 | **NUMBER OF STATEMENTS** | 93 | 96 |
| % | % | % | % | % | % | **ASSETS** | % | % |
| 36.1 | 38.5 | 29.6 | 41.1 | | | Cash & Equivalents | 33.0 | 35.1 |
| 8.7 | 17.5 | 19.5 | 19.6 | | | Trade Receivables (net) | 14.8 | 16.2 |
| .6 | .3 | .0 | .2 | | | Inventory | .8 | .1 |
| 6.0 | 5.6 | 20.1 | 5.9 | | | All Other Current | 7.7 | 9.7 |
| 51.4 | 61.9 | 69.2 | 66.8 | | | Total Current | 56.4 | 61.0 |
| 12.8 | 17.1 | 8.9 | 10.2 | | | Fixed Assets (net) | 20.2 | 15.7 |
| 8.2 | 4.9 | 5.5 | 10.8 | | | Intangibles (net) | 10.4 | 6.8 |
| 27.6 | 16.1 | 16.5 | 12.2 | | | All Other Non-Current | 13.0 | 16.5 |
| 100.0 | 100.0 | 100.0 | 100.0 | | | Total | 100.0 | 100.0 |
| | | | | | | **LIABILITIES** | | |
| 10.0 | 8.8 | 3.8 | 3.8 | | | Notes Payable-Short Term | 10.4 | 12.0 |
| 1.7 | 2.2 | .8 | .3 | | | Cur. Mat.-L.T.D. | 2.2 | 1.6 |
| 13.6 | 18.3 | 18.2 | 14.4 | | | Trade Payables | 19.7 | 14.6 |
| .2 | .2 | .1 | .6 | | | Income Taxes Payable | .8 | .2 |
| 19.9 | 30.9 | 53.8 | 26.4 | | | All Other Current | 37.2 | 26.4 |
| 45.3 | 60.4 | 76.7 | 45.4 | | | Total Current | 70.3 | 54.7 |
| 24.6 | 7.6 | 1.8 | 3.8 | | | Long-Term Debt | 11.5 | 8.0 |
| .0 | .2 | .0 | .7 | | | Deferred Taxes | .1 | .1 |
| 35.9 | 16.4 | 6.6 | 7.4 | | | All Other Non-Current | 9.1 | 8.7 |
| -5.8 | 15.4 | 14.9 | 42.8 | | | Net Worth | 9.0 | 28.5 |
| 100.0 | 100.0 | 100.0 | 100.0 | | | Total Liabilities & Net Worth | 100.0 | 100.0 |
| | | | | | | **INCOME DATA** | | |
| 100.0 | 100.0 | 100.0 | 100.0 | | | Net Sales | 100.0 | 100.0 |
| | | | | | | Gross Profit | | |
| 98.8 | 94.4 | 97.6 | 95.2 | | | Operating Expenses | 95.0 | 95.4 |
| 1.2 | 5.6 | 2.4 | 4.8 | | | Operating Profit | 5.0 | 4.6 |
| .3 | 1.6 | .1 | .0 | | | All Other Expenses (net) | 1.1 | .1 |
| .9 | 4.0 | 2.4 | 4.9 | | | Profit Before Taxes | 3.9 | 4.5 |
| | | | | | | **RATIOS** | | |
| 3.8 | 1.4 | 1.5 | 2.4 | | | | 1.6 | 3.2 |
| 1.3 | 1.0 | 1.1 | 1.7 | | | Current | .8 | 1.3 |
| .5 | .6 | .7 | 1.0 | | | | .5 | .8 |
| 3.4 | 1.3 | 1.1 | 2.1 | | | | 1.3 | 2.3 |
| 1.0 | .9 | .7 | 1.6 | | | Quick | .7 | 1.1 |
| .3 | .5 | .4 | .9 | | | | .3 | .5 |
| 0 UND | 0 UND | 1 351.1 | 7 54.7 | | | | 0 UND | 0 742.1 |
| 0 UND | 3 114.1 | 6 63.2 | 21 17.4 | | | Sales/Receivables | 5 79.8 | 7 54.4 |
| 6 65.3 | 21 17.7 | 32 11.4 | 47 7.7 | | | | 29 12.4 | 26 14.0 |
| | | | | | | Cost of Sales/Inventory | | |
| | | | | | | Cost of Sales/Payables | | |
| 44.2 | 17.7 | 18.7 | 3.2 | | | | 20.9 | 9.5 |
| 143.7 | 461.5 | 862.5 | 10.8 | | | Sales/Working Capital | -118.5 | 49.4 |
| -36.2 | -28.2 | -10.9 | -112.8 | | | | -9.1 | -34.0 |
| 18.2 | 23.0 | 35.1 | 539.4 | | | | 20.4 | 36.0 |
| (14) 4.5 | (23) 7.5 | (19) 11.9 | (13) 14.5 | | | EBIT/Interest | (60) 6.1 | (53) 6.5 |
| -4.3 | 2.1 | 4.5 | 2.0 | | | | .8 | 1.8 |
| | | | | | | Net Profit + Depr., Dep., | | 22.0 |
| | | | | | | Amort./Cur. Mat. L/T/D | (12) 3.8 | |
| | | | | | | | | 1.1 |
| .0 | .0 | .1 | .1 | | | | .2 | .1 |
| .2 | .4 | .6 | .3 | | | Fixed/Worth | 1.1 | .4 |
| -.2 | 4.0 | -.5 | 1.1 | | | | -.6 | 2.4 |
| .4 | 1.9 | 1.1 | .7 | | | | 1.1 | .6 |
| 2.4 | 3.4 | 4.0 | 1.3 | | | Debt/Worth | 7.5 | 1.9 |
| -2.4 | -46.7 | -17.7 | 9.4 | | | | -5.1 | 15.3 |
| 103.4 | 81.5 | 127.4 | 89.4 | | | % Profit Before Taxes/Tangible | 60.4 | 51.5 |
| (17) 26.7 | (32) 28.3 | (24) 58.6 | (25) 16.1 | | | Net Worth | (60) 25.4 | (77) 16.4 |
| 5.1 | 9.3 | 22.7 | 10.2 | | | | 12.4 | 4.7 |
| 46.6 | 20.0 | 29.2 | 17.9 | | | % Profit Before Taxes/Total | 14.8 | 18.2 |
| 19.8 | 6.3 | 10.2 | 7.0 | | | Assets | 5.0 | 5.7 |
| -1.9 | 2.3 | 2.4 | 2.7 | | | | -1.2 | .6 |
| UND | 409.5 | 252.3 | 81.1 | | | | 153.6 | 301.5 |
| 396.6 | 104.7 | 109.9 | 30.0 | | | Sales/Net Fixed Assets | 41.9 | 58.3 |
| 102.3 | 20.1 | 45.5 | 12.5 | | | | 10.4 | 18.2 |
| 30.7 | 11.9 | 8.0 | 3.7 | | | | 10.3 | 13.4 |
| 12.9 | 5.4 | 4.2 | 1.7 | | | Sales/Total Assets | 3.0 | 3.3 |
| 6.1 | 2.2 | 2.2 | .9 | | | | 1.5 | 1.7 |
| .1 | .1 | .1 | .6 | | | | .2 | .3 |
| (14) .2 | (31) .4 | (25) .3 | (22) 1.4 | | | % Depr., Dep., Amort./Sales | (70) .6 | (58) .8 |
| .4 | 1.0 | .8 | 2.7 | | | | 2.1 | 2.5 |
| 1.9 | 1.0 | .2 | | | | | .9 | 1.3 |
| (17) 3.0 | (15) 4.5 | (11) 3.4 | | | | % Officers', Directors' Owners' Comp/Sales | (26) 3.0 | (35) 3.0 |
| 6.1 | 9.8 | 5.1 | | | | | 7.0 | 13.1 |
| 101312M | 393605M | 1548066M | 2002286M | 717516M | 2535665M | Net Sales ($) | 3431306M | 1945610M |
| 6390M | 46507M | 174681M | 665262M | 412098M | 613170M | Total Assets ($) | 1403468M | 664155M |

M = $ thousand    MM = $ million
See Pages 9 through 22 for Explanation of Ratios and Data

## Comparative Historical Data | | | | Current Data Sorted by Sales

| 4/1/09-3/31/10 ALL | 4/1/10-3/31/11 ALL | 4/1/11-3/31/12 ALL | Type of Statement | 0-1MM | 1-3MM | 3-5MM | 5-10MM | 10-25MM | 25MM & OVER |
|---|---|---|---|---|---|---|---|---|---|
| 14 | 18 | 22 | Unqualified | | 1 | 3 | 2 | 3 | 13 |
| 10 | 21 | 12 | Reviewed | 1 | | 1 | 3 | 2 | 5 |
| 23 | 15 | 16 | Compiled | | 2 | 3 | 3 | 3 | 5 |
| 23 | 39 | 41 | Tax Returns | 4 | 13 | 9 | 8 | 5 | 2 |
| 59 | 54 | 56 | Other | 3 | 6 | 6 | 9 | 11 | 21 |
| | | | | | 29 (4/1-9/30/11) | | 118 (10/1/11-3/31/12) | | |
| 129 | 147 | 147 | **NUMBER OF STATEMENTS** | 8 | 22 | 22 | 25 | 24 | 46 |
| % | % | % | **ASSETS** | % | % | % | % | % | % |
| 37.1 | 37.8 | 35.6 | Cash & Equivalents | | 38.8 | 45.6 | 32.3 | 37.0 | 33.6 |
| 15.5 | 16.8 | 16.4 | Trade Receivables (net) | | 13.9 | 11.9 | 18.9 | 9.5 | 24.0 |
| .4 | .6 | .3 | Inventory | | .1 | .3 | .7 | .3 | .1 |
| 8.8 | 9.5 | 9.5 | All Other Current | | 2.9 | 11.3 | 14.1 | 16.3 | 7.3 |
| 61.8 | 64.7 | 61.8 | Total Current | | 55.7 | 69.0 | 66.0 | 63.3 | 65.1 |
| 14.1 | 12.6 | 13.4 | Fixed Assets (net) | | 10.9 | 10.3 | 7.0 | 9.2 | 15.8 |
| 10.3 | 9.2 | 7.3 | Intangibles (net) | | 8.3 | 4.0 | 6.7 | 10.9 | 7.1 |
| 13.8 | 13.6 | 17.6 | All Other Non-Current | | 25.0 | 16.7 | 20.3 | 16.6 | 12.0 |
| 100.0 | 100.0 | 100.0 | Total | | 100.0 | 100.0 | 100.0 | 100.0 | 100.0 |
| | | | **LIABILITIES** | | | | | | |
| 8.8 | 8.8 | 6.8 | Notes Payable-Short Term | | 8.1 | 4.9 | 16.0 | 3.8 | 3.9 |
| 1.9 | 2.6 | 1.9 | Cur. Mat.-L.T.D. | | .5 | .5 | 1.7 | .5 | 2.6 |
| 17.3 | 18.3 | 16.6 | Trade Payables | | 12.8 | 15.8 | 14.9 | 16.6 | 20.3 |
| .2 | .3 | .4 | Income Taxes Payable | | .2 | .2 | .2 | .4 | .6 |
| 37.1 | 32.5 | 33.9 | All Other Current | | 25.7 | 33.1 | 32.1 | 55.3 | 31.3 |
| 65.3 | 62.4 | 59.5 | Total Current | | 47.3 | 54.5 | 64.8 | 76.6 | 58.7 |
| 14.8 | 8.3 | 8.9 | Long-Term Debt | | 6.7 | 3.1 | 7.0 | 2.9 | 4.8 |
| .1 | .3 | .2 | Deferred Taxes | | .3 | .0 | .0 | .3 | .3 |
| 8.4 | 12.6 | 15.6 | All Other Non-Current | | 22.7 | 12.2 | 29.9 | 3.4 | 13.3 |
| 11.4 | 16.3 | 15.8 | Net Worth | | 22.9 | 30.2 | -1.8 | 16.7 | 22.9 |
| 100.0 | 100.0 | 100.0 | Total Liabilities & Net Worth | | 100.0 | 100.0 | 100.0 | 100.0 | 100.0 |
| | | | **INCOME DATA** | | | | | | |
| 100.0 | 100.0 | 100.0 | Net Sales | | 100.0 | 100.0 | 100.0 | 100.0 | 100.0 |
| | | | Gross Profit | | | | | | |
| 96.3 | 95.5 | 96.3 | Operating Expenses | | 91.2 | 98.7 | 99.2 | 94.3 | 96.7 |
| 3.7 | 4.5 | 3.7 | Operating Profit | | 8.8 | 1.3 | .8 | 5.7 | 3.3 |
| .9 | -.1 | .6 | All Other Expenses (net) | | .1 | .7 | .0 | -.3 | .1 |
| 2.8 | 4.6 | 3.1 | Profit Before Taxes | | 8.8 | .5 | .8 | 6.0 | 3.2 |
| | | | **RATIOS** | | | | | | |
| 1.6 | 2.0 | 1.9 | | | 2.9 | 3.8 | 1.9 | 2.0 | 1.7 |
| 1.0 | 1.2 | 1.1 | Current | | 1.2 | 1.1 | 1.2 | .9 | 1.2 |
| .6 | .7 | .7 | | | .6 | .7 | .6 | .6 | .8 |
| 1.5 | 1.7 | 1.7 | | | 2.9 | 3.7 | 1.2 | 2.0 | 1.6 |
| .8 | 1.0 | .9 | Quick | | 1.2 | 1.0 | .8 | .7 | 1.1 |
| .4 | .6 | .5 | | | .6 | .6 | .5 | .4 | .7 |
| 0 999.8 | 0 999.8 | 0 999.8 | | 0 UND | 0 UND | 0 UND | 0 UND | 0 UND | 1 284.9 |
| 6 64.8 | 4 81.2 | 5 66.6 | Sales/Receivables | | 4 85.1 | 4 81.2 | 4 94.1 | 4 88.7 | 9 42.7 |
| 25 14.7 | 31 11.7 | 23 16.1 | | | 18 20.7 | 16 22.5 | 26 14.0 | 29 12.4 | 35 10.4 |
| | | | Cost of Sales/Inventory | | | | | | |
| | | | Cost of Sales/Payables | | | | | | |
| 10.4 | 11.6 | 15.9 | | | 9.0 | 27.3 | 15.6 | 10.4 | 13.0 |
| -947.2 | 65.5 | 145.0 | Sales/Working Capital | | 36.6 | 133.0 | 133.3 | -69.1 | 97.3 |
| -12.0 | -22.0 | -34.7 | | | -33.7 | -24.8 | -41.9 | -22.3 | -62.2 |
| 21.6 | 33.4 | 30.0 | | | 53.7 | 22.1 | 47.1 | | 33.3 |
| (75) 3.7 | (76) 8.5 | (76) 7.3 | EBIT/Interest | | (12) 19.5 | (14) 8.3 | (12) 10.1 | | (25) 7.7 |
| -.4 | 1.9 | 2.2 | | | 2.7 | 6.0 | -.9 | | 3.4 |
| | 30.5 | 12.3 | | | | | | | |
| (13) 11.0 | (13) 3.0 | | Net Profit + Depr., Dep., Amort./Cur. Mat. L/T/D | | | | | | |
| 2.4 | 1.1 | | | | | | | | |
| .1 | .1 | .1 | | | .0 | .0 | .1 | .0 | .1 |
| .7 | .4 | .3 | Fixed/Worth | | .2 | .2 | .3 | .3 | .4 |
| -1.6 | -33.3 | -6.5 | | | 9.7 | 6.0 | -.1 | -11.6 | 5.9 |
| 1.1 | 1.1 | .9 | | | .4 | .6 | 2.1 | .7 | .9 |
| 6.5 | 4.3 | 3.3 | Debt/Worth | | 1.4 | 2.6 | 12.9 | 3.7 | 2.8 |
| -7.0 | -47.3 | -21.9 | | | 264.6 | 259.4 | -7.3 | -12.8 | 53.7 |
| 58.6 | 82.5 | 108.5 | | | 151.6 | 83.2 | 138.6 | 86.9 | 113.4 |
| (87) 17.6 | (106) 33.7 | (103) 31.7 | % Profit Before Taxes/Tangible Net Worth | (18) 33.0 | (18) 25.4 | (14) 30.6 | (15) 31.7 | (36) 33.9 | |
| 3.7 | 13.4 | 11.5 | | | 9.4 | 6.9 | 15.1 | 11.5 | 11.7 |
| 12.4 | 21.6 | 23.1 | | | 26.8 | 19.7 | 25.8 | 23.1 | 23.4 |
| 4.6 | 8.9 | 7.8 | % Profit Before Taxes/Total Assets | | 12.6 | 3.4 | 7.8 | 9.3 | 8.5 |
| -.6 | 2.7 | 2.0 | | | 4.0 | 1.1 | 2.4 | 2.3 | 2.7 |
| 240.2 | 277.0 | 388.8 | | | 457.6 | 632.7 | 748.3 | 208.9 | 163.9 |
| 48.6 | 73.7 | 93.7 | Sales/Net Fixed Assets | | 106.3 | 128.9 | 174.5 | 70.9 | 78.2 |
| 14.9 | 22.3 | 26.3 | | | 19.4 | 33.5 | 76.0 | 28.6 | 23.0 |
| 6.7 | 7.4 | 11.5 | | | 8.3 | 12.9 | 19.3 | 9.2 | 13.7 |
| 2.6 | 3.1 | 4.5 | Sales/Total Assets | | 3.3 | 5.7 | 6.3 | 3.2 | 5.4 |
| 1.4 | 1.6 | 2.1 | | | 1.9 | 2.3 | 2.4 | 1.3 | 2.3 |
| .3 | .2 | .1 | | | .3 | .1 | .1 | .3 | .1 |
| (90) .7 | (97) .7 | (97) .5 | % Depr., Dep., Amort./Sales | (13) .5 | (15) .3 | (16) .2 | (15) .7 | (33) .6 | |
| 2.4 | 1.7 | 1.3 | | | 1.3 | .8 | .6 | 2.1 | 1.4 |
| 1.6 | 1.0 | 1.2 | | | 2.9 | 1.9 | | | |
| (43) 3.3 | (52) 2.5 | (48) 3.0 | % Officers', Directors' Owners' Comp/Sales | (11) 6.0 | (12) 4.7 | | | | |
| 6.7 | 6.5 | 6.7 | | | 12.1 | 8.2 | | | |
| 14477811M | 3958779M | 7298450M | Net Sales ($) | 4505M | 43073M | 85652M | 190464M | 381617M | 6593139M |
| 1936846M | 1646473M | 1918108M | Total Assets ($) | 3195M | 14494M | 37003M | 66733M | 180573M | 1616110M |

M = $ thousand     MM = $ million
See Pages 9 through 22 for Explanation of Ratios and Data

## Current Data Sorted by Assets / Comparative Historical Data

| | | | | | | Type of Statement | | |
|---|---|---|---|---|---|---|---|---|
| | | | 2 | 3 | 4 | Unqualified | 12 | 11 |
| | | 1 | 2 | | | Reviewed | 3 | 6 |
| | | 1 | 2 | | | Compiled | 9 | 7 |
| 6 | 6 | 3 | 1 | | | Tax Returns | 11 | 12 |
| 7 | 5 | 4 | 1 | 4 | 1 | Other | 29 | 21 |
| | 7 (4/1-9/30/11) | | 46 (10/1/11-3/31/12) | | | | 4/1/07-3/31/08 | 4/1/08-3/31/09 |
| 0-500M | 500M-2MM | 2-10MM | 10-50MM | 50-100MM | 100-250MM | | ALL | ALL |
| 13 | 11 | 9 | 8 | 7 | 5 | NUMBER OF STATEMENTS | 64 | 57 |
| % | % | % | % | % | % | ASSETS | % | % |
| 40.3 | 34.1 | | | | | Cash & Equivalents | 30.3 | 30.2 |
| 11.5 | 9.1 | | | | | Trade Receivables (net) | 7.3 | 9.2 |
| 2.8 | 1.7 | | | | | Inventory | 2.0 | 1.5 |
| 1.7 | 10.2 | | | | | All Other Current | 8.2 | 10.8 |
| 56.3 | 55.1 | | | | | Total Current | 47.8 | 51.7 |
| 25.4 | 32.8 | | | | | Fixed Assets (net) | 34.6 | 30.1 |
| 6.4 | 1.3 | | | | | Intangibles (net) | 3.4 | 7.2 |
| 11.8 | 10.8 | | | | | All Other Non-Current | 14.1 | 11.0 |
| 100.0 | 100.0 | | | | | Total | 100.0 | 100.0 |
| | | | | | | LIABILITIES | | |
| 35.0 | 3.3 | | | | | Notes Payable-Short Term | 7.2 | 5.3 |
| 6.3 | 5.3 | | | | | Cur. Mat.-L.T.D. | 4.6 | 3.7 |
| 11.3 | 10.8 | | | | | Trade Payables | 14.5 | 13.2 |
| .0 | .0 | | | | | Income Taxes Payable | .1 | .1 |
| 39.0 | 30.6 | | | | | All Other Current | 31.6 | 29.8 |
| 91.7 | 49.9 | | | | | Total Current | 57.9 | 52.1 |
| 23.0 | 36.6 | | | | | Long-Term Debt | 23.4 | 15.1 |
| .0 | .0 | | | | | Deferred Taxes | .4 | .4 |
| 14.2 | 5.6 | | | | | All Other Non-Current | 11.5 | 7.5 |
| -29.0 | 7.8 | | | | | Net Worth | 6.7 | 24.9 |
| 100.0 | 100.0 | | | | | Total Liabilities & Net Worth | 100.0 | 100.0 |
| | | | | | | INCOME DATA | | |
| 100.0 | 100.0 | | | | | Net Sales | 100.0 | 100.0 |
| | | | | | | Gross Profit | | |
| 97.2 | 97.1 | | | | | Operating Expenses | 95.7 | 97.1 |
| 2.8 | 2.9 | | | | | Operating Profit | 4.3 | 2.9 |
| 5.1 | 2.8 | | | | | All Other Expenses (net) | .3 | .7 |
| -2.3 | .0 | | | | | Profit Before Taxes | 4.0 | 2.3 |
| | | | | | | RATIOS | | |
| 1.8 | 2.0 | | | | | | 1.3 | 1.6 |
| .9 | 1.3 | | | | | Current | .8 | 1.0 |
| .3 | .4 | | | | | | .5 | .5 |
| 1.6 | 1.8 | | | | | | 1.1 | 1.4 |
| .7 | 1.3 | | | | | Quick | .6 | .9 |
| .3 | .3 | | | | | | .3 | .4 |
| 0 UND | 0 UND | | | | | | 0 UND | 0 UND |
| 2 177.2 | 1 258.5 | | | | | Sales/Receivables | 3 116.8 | 6 65.5 |
| 20 18.5 | 24 15.1 | | | | | | 12 30.2 | 17 21.8 |
| | | | | | | Cost of Sales/Inventory | | |
| | | | | | | Cost of Sales/Payables | | |
| 24.2 | 4.3 | | | | | | 27.5 | 12.6 |
| -35.4 | 123.1 | | | | | Sales/Working Capital | -50.9 | 170.9 |
| -10.3 | -8.2 | | | | | | -9.0 | -12.4 |
| | | | | | | | 8.5 | 11.5 |
| | | | | | | EBIT/Interest | (43) 2.1 | (36) 2.8 |
| | | | | | | | .9 | .5 |
| | | | | | | Net Profit + Depr., Dep., Amort./Cur. Mat. L/T/D | | |
| .3 | .1 | | | | | | .3 | .2 |
| 1.7 | 2.2 | | | | | Fixed/Worth | 2.7 | 1.3 |
| -.1 | -3.9 | | | | | | -6.0 | -4.5 |
| 1.0 | 2.6 | | | | | | 2.7 | 1.5 |
| -197.0 | 8.5 | | | | | Debt/Worth | 8.2 | 4.6 |
| -2.1 | -5.7 | | | | | | -7.2 | -10.5 |
| | | | | | | % Profit Before Taxes/Tangible Net Worth | 92.7 | 51.1 |
| | | | | | | | (43) 46.0 | (42) 19.7 |
| | | | | | | | 6.1 | .9 |
| 35.7 | 19.9 | | | | | | 16.8 | 12.4 |
| 3.4 | 7.8 | | | | | % Profit Before Taxes/Total Assets | 4.8 | 4.0 |
| -21.7 | -7.2 | | | | | | .1 | -.2 |
| 232.4 | 108.3 | | | | | | 91.3 | 83.2 |
| 60.9 | 33.0 | | | | | Sales/Net Fixed Assets | 13.7 | 15.5 |
| 8.4 | 2.6 | | | | | | 2.7 | 3.4 |
| 13.6 | 14.0 | | | | | | 4.9 | 5.1 |
| 5.0 | 2.0 | | | | | Sales/Total Assets | 2.6 | 2.8 |
| 3.3 | 1.4 | | | | | | 1.2 | 1.5 |
| | .2 | | | | | | .4 | .4 |
| | 2.0 | | | | | % Depr., Dep., Amort./Sales | (47) 1.4 | (42) 2.1 |
| | 11.5 | | | | | | 7.3 | 5.6 |
| | | | | | | % Officers', Directors' Owners' Comp/Sales | 1.1 | 1.1 |
| | | | | | | | (13) 1.8 | (15) 1.8 |
| | | | | | | | 7.8 | 4.8 |
| 31697M | 112523M | 129134M | 333907M | 637484M | 1232806M | Net Sales ($) | 3791407M | 4837804M |
| 3579M | 15079M | 36676M | 127064M | 467747M | 772417M | Total Assets ($) | 1550061M | 1719057M |

© RMA 2012

M = $ thousand   MM = $ million
See Pages 9 through 22 for Explanation of Ratios and Data

## Comparative Historical Data / Current Data Sorted by Sales

| 4/1/09-3/31/10 ALL | 4/1/10-3/31/11 ALL | 4/1/11-3/31/12 ALL | Type of Statement | 0-1MM | 1-3MM | 3-5MM | 5-10MM | 10-25MM | 25MM & OVER |
|---|---|---|---|---|---|---|---|---|---|
| 13 | 12 | 9 | Unqualified | | | | | 1 | 8 |
| 7 | 4 | 3 | Reviewed | | | | | 1 | 2 |
| 10 | 4 | 3 | Compiled | | | | 1 | 1 | 1 |
| 17 | 11 | 16 | Tax Returns | 1 | 6 | 2 | 1 | 2 | 3 |
| 19 | 25 | 22 | Other | 4 | 4 | 5 | 1 | 3 | 6 |
| | | | | | 7 (4/1-9/30/11) | | 46 (10/1/11-3/31/12) | | |
| 66 | 56 | 53 | NUMBER OF STATEMENTS | 5 | 10 | 7 | 3 | 8 | 20 |
| % | % | % | ASSETS | % | % | % | % | % | % |
| 28.0 | 29.9 | 32.0 | Cash & Equivalents | | 34.9 | | | | 37.7 |
| 7.6 | 10.0 | 10.6 | Trade Receivables (net) | | 1.4 | | | | 13.2 |
| .5 | .6 | 1.4 | Inventory | | 4.0 | | | | .7 |
| 6.3 | 10.3 | 9.8 | All Other Current | | 2.2 | | | | 15.9 |
| 42.4 | 50.8 | 53.8 | Total Current | | 42.5 | | | | 67.5 |
| 36.1 | 31.4 | 29.5 | Fixed Assets (net) | | 37.9 | | | | 15.0 |
| 3.5 | 4.8 | 3.4 | Intangibles (net) | | 5.3 | | | | 2.0 |
| 18.0 | 13.0 | 13.3 | All Other Non-Current | | 14.3 | | | | 15.6 |
| 100.0 | 100.0 | 100.0 | Total | | 100.0 | | | | 100.0 |
| | | | LIABILITIES | | | | | | |
| 5.2 | 5.5 | 10.5 | Notes Payable-Short Term | | 3.2 | | | | 3.1 |
| 6.6 | 4.2 | 4.7 | Cur. Mat.-L.T.D. | | 12.9 | | | | 1.5 |
| 8.0 | 11.7 | 10.8 | Trade Payables | | 6.5 | | | | 15.7 |
| .2 | .1 | .1 | Income Taxes Payable | | .0 | | | | .3 |
| 30.8 | 29.9 | 30.9 | All Other Current | | 27.4 | | | | 34.5 |
| 50.8 | 51.5 | 57.0 | Total Current | | 50.0 | | | | 55.1 |
| 24.0 | 21.0 | 23.8 | Long-Term Debt | | 32.1 | | | | 12.0 |
| .2 | .2 | .2 | Deferred Taxes | | .0 | | | | .1 |
| 9.2 | 12.1 | 8.2 | All Other Non-Current | | 10.4 | | | | 1.4 |
| 15.9 | 15.1 | 10.9 | Net Worth | | 7.5 | | | | 31.4 |
| 100.0 | 100.0 | 100.0 | Total Liabilties & Net Worth | | 100.0 | | | | 100.0 |
| | | | INCOME DATA | | | | | | |
| 100.0 | 100.0 | 100.0 | Net Sales | | 100.0 | | | | 100.0 |
| | | | Gross Profit | | | | | | |
| 96.2 | 95.8 | 95.7 | Operating Expenses | | 97.9 | | | | 94.7 |
| 3.8 | 4.2 | 4.3 | Operating Profit | | 2.1 | | | | 5.3 |
| 1.3 | .1 | 2.4 | All Other Expenses (net) | | 1.4 | | | | .3 |
| 2.6 | 4.1 | 1.9 | Profit Before Taxes | | .7 | | | | 5.0 |
| | | | RATIOS | | | | | | |
| 1.4 | 2.1 | 1.9 | | | 1.7 | | | | 2.1 |
| .8 | 1.1 | 1.3 | Current | | 1.1 | | | | 1.4 |
| .4 | .7 | .6 | | | .3 | | | | .8 |
| 1.1 | 1.4 | 1.5 | | | 1.4 | | | | 1.5 |
| .6 | .9 | .9 | Quick | | .7 | | | | 1.1 |
| .6 | .4 | .3 | | | .2 | | | | .5 |
| 0 UND | 0 999.8 | 0 UND | | 0 UND | 0 UND | | | | 1 390.0 |
| 2 156.2 | 5 69.2 | 4 97.5 | Sales/Receivables | | 0 UND | | | | 7 54.4 |
| 10 37.0 | 17 21.6 | 24 15.2 | | | 2 174.4 | | | | 22 16.6 |
| | | | Cost of Sales/Inventory | | | | | | |
| | | | Cost of Sales/Payables | | | | | | |
| 29.5 | 12.6 | 7.7 | | | 20.7 | | | | 5.5 |
| -40.5 | 90.8 | 47.9 | Sales/Working Capital | | NM | | | | 10.6 |
| -6.6 | -12.7 | -11.3 | | | -8.5 | | | | -36.2 |
| | | | | | | | | | 45.6 |
| (34) 9.7 | (35) 24.0 | (38) 12.4 | EBIT/Interest | | | | | (11) 45.6 |  |
| 1.7 | 3.5 | 3.6 | | | | | | | 25.3 |
| .4 | 1.4 | 1.3 | | | | | | | 3.5 |
| | | | Net Profit + Depr., Dep., Amort./Cur. Mat. L/T/D | | | | | | |
| .3 | .2 | .2 | | | .6 | | | | .1 |
| 2.1 | 1.4 | 1.7 | Fixed/Worth | | NM | | | | .3 |
| -6.4 | UND | NM | | | -2.1 | | | | 2.2 |
| 1.2 | 1.2 | 1.2 | | | 1.0 | | | | 1.0 |
| 5.1 | 4.6 | 4.0 | Debt/Worth | | NM | | | | 2.5 |
| -11.5 | UND | -143.7 | | | -5.4 | | | | 7.1 |
| 86.4 | 82.3 | 74.6 | | | | | | | 111.7 |
| (44) 24.4 | (43) 28.6 | (39) 30.2 | % Profit Before Taxes/Tangible Net Worth | | | | | (18) 34.5 |  |
| 9.2 | 9.4 | 5.7 | | | | | | | 6.9 |
| 13.4 | 15.0 | 15.6 | | | 12.9 | | | | 16.6 |
| 5.3 | 6.8 | 4.1 | % Profit Before Taxes/Total Assets | | 5.9 | | | | 8.7 |
| .1 | 1.8 | .3 | | | -7.8 | | | | 3.2 |
| 57.0 | 90.2 | 127.9 | | | 117.5 | | | | 166.4 |
| 17.0 | 24.9 | 33.0 | Sales/Net Fixed Assets | | 22.0 | | | | 36.8 |
| 2.6 | 2.9 | 3.4 | | | 2.4 | | | | 13.7 |
| 4.2 | 4.5 | 4.6 | | | 5.1 | | | | 4.6 |
| 2.0 | 2.3 | 2.6 | Sales/Total Assets | | 2.9 | | | | 2.4 |
| 1.4 | 1.1 | 1.3 | | | 1.5 | | | | 1.2 |
| .6 | .4 | .3 | | | | | | | .2 |
| (53) 2.4 | (46) 1.4 | (44) 1.3 | % Depr., Dep., Amort./Sales | | | | | (17) .7 |  |
| 8.2 | 6.0 | 7.0 | | | | | | | 2.7 |
| .7 | .9 | .9 | | | | | | | |
| (19) 2.4 | (18) 2.5 | (18) 2.5 | % Officers', Directors' Owners' Comp/Sales | | | | | | |
| 4.0 | 6.8 | 4.7 | | | | | | | |
| 3984628M | 2227949M | 2477551M | Net Sales ($) | 1770M | 19211M | 27585M | 22934M | 132212M | 2273839M |
| 2030493M | 1375844M | 1422562M | Total Assets ($) | 1340M | 8839M | 11007M | 24820M | 55644M | 1320912M |

M = $ thousand    MM = $ million
See Pages 9 through 22 for Explanation of Ratios and Data

## Current Data Sorted by Assets

## Comparative Historical Data

| | | | | | | Type of Statement | | |
|---|---|---|---|---|---|---|---|---|
| 1 | | 3 | 7 | 2 | 1 | Unqualified | 13 | 17 |
| | | 3 | 1 | | | Reviewed | 2 | 6 |
| 1 | 1 | 1 | | | | Compiled | 3 | 6 |
| 1 | 1 | 2 | | | | Tax Returns | 3 | 6 |
| 3 | 3 | 10 | 5 | 5 | 4 | Other | 19 | 17 |
| | 11 (4/1-9/30/11) | | 44 (10/1/11-3/31/12) | | | | 4/1/07-3/31/08 | 4/1/08-3/31/09 |
| 0-500M | 500M-2MM | 2-10MM | 10-50MM | 50-100MM | 100-250MM | | ALL | ALL |
| 6 | 5 | 19 | 13 | 7 | 5 | NUMBER OF STATEMENTS | 40 | 52 |
| % | % | % | % | % | % | ASSETS | % | % |
| | | 21.5 | 24.2 | | | Cash & Equivalents | 32.8 | 28.3 |
| | | 21.1 | 12.4 | | | Trade Receivables (net) | 11.8 | 14.2 |
| | | 1.1 | 1.7 | | | Inventory | 1.1 | 2.4 |
| | | 5.9 | 6.7 | | | All Other Current | 13.5 | 7.9 |
| | | 49.6 | 45.0 | | | Total Current | 59.2 | 52.8 |
| | | 26.0 | 24.5 | | | Fixed Assets (net) | 22.8 | 24.8 |
| | | 2.4 | 20.4 | | | Intangibles (net) | 6.9 | 8.0 |
| | | 22.0 | 10.1 | | | All Other Non-Current | 11.1 | 14.4 |
| | | 100.0 | 100.0 | | | Total | 100.0 | 100.0 |
| | | | | | | LIABILITIES | | |
| | | 4.9 | 3.4 | | | Notes Payable-Short Term | 3.8 | 4.7 |
| | | 4.0 | .5 | | | Cur. Mat.-L.T.D. | 5.4 | 1.9 |
| | | 23.2 | 10.6 | | | Trade Payables | 13.5 | 10.4 |
| | | 1.0 | 1.2 | | | Income Taxes Payable | .8 | 2.2 |
| | | 30.0 | 24.9 | | | All Other Current | 21.3 | 19.9 |
| | | 63.2 | 40.6 | | | Total Current | 44.8 | 39.1 |
| | | 14.1 | 6.1 | | | Long-Term Debt | 8.5 | 13.2 |
| | | .0 | .6 | | | Deferred Taxes | .1 | .3 |
| | | 17.9 | 8.0 | | | All Other Non-Current | 5.7 | 9.2 |
| | | 4.8 | 44.7 | | | Net Worth | 40.8 | 38.1 |
| | | 100.0 | 100.0 | | | Total Liabilties & Net Worth | 100.0 | 100.0 |
| | | | | | | INCOME DATA | | |
| | | 100.0 | 100.0 | | | Net Sales | 100.0 | 100.0 |
| | | | | | | Gross Profit | | |
| | | 92.2 | 91.9 | | | Operating Expenses | 88.6 | 93.1 |
| | | 7.8 | 8.1 | | | Operating Profit | 11.4 | 6.9 |
| | | 2.3 | -.3 | | | All Other Expenses (net) | 1.9 | 3.2 |
| | | 5.5 | 8.4 | | | Profit Before Taxes | 9.5 | 3.7 |
| | | | | | | RATIOS | | |
| | | 1.7 | 1.8 | | | | 2.5 | 2.1 |
| | | .9 | 1.0 | | | Current | 1.6 | 1.2 |
| | | .5 | .8 | | | | .9 | 1.0 |
| | | 1.7 | 1.6 | | | | 2.1 | 2.0 |
| | | .8 | .9 | | | Quick | 1.0 | 1.0 |
| | | .5 | .5 | | | | .7 | .6 |
| | 5 | 66.4 | 6 | 61.5 | | | 0 UND | 4 97.2 |
| | 14 | 26.7 | 11 | 32.3 | | Sales/Receivables | 7 54.4 | 11 32.2 |
| | 60 | 6.1 | 59 | 6.2 | | | 46 7.9 | 40 9.2 |
| | | | | | | Cost of Sales/Inventory | | |
| | | | | | | Cost of Sales/Payables | | |
| | | 10.2 | 3.7 | | | | 3.3 | 4.4 |
| | | -91.6 | 190.8 | | | Sales/Working Capital | 9.2 | 18.3 |
| | | -6.4 | -25.1 | | | | -145.4 | -585.8 |
| | | 26.3 | | | | | 22.2 | 11.6 |
| | | (11) 4.2 | | | | EBIT/Interest | (23) 6.1 | (32) 3.2 |
| | | 1.8 | | | | | 1.1 | .8 |
| | | | | | | Net Profit + Depr., Dep., Amort./Cur. Mat. L/T/D | | |
| | | .3 | .5 | | | | .2 | .1 |
| | | 1.6 | 1.0 | | | Fixed/Worth | .6 | .6 |
| | | -.4 | 2.3 | | | | 2.1 | 2.8 |
| | | 1.0 | 1.0 | | | | .5 | .8 |
| | | 5.5 | 1.9 | | | Debt/Worth | 1.7 | 1.8 |
| | | -5.1 | 8.4 | | | | 7.1 | 4.4 |
| | | 90.4 | 69.5 | | | | 67.6 | 45.8 |
| | | (11) 29.8 | (11) 28.8 | | | % Profit Before Taxes/Tangible Net Worth | (36) 19.2 | (43) 10.7 |
| | | 4.3 | 11.4 | | | | 6.2 | .0 |
| | | 53.4 | 10.6 | | | | 19.6 | 16.1 |
| | | 7.0 | 4.5 | | | % Profit Before Taxes/Total Assets | 8.0 | 4.5 |
| | | 1.9 | 2.4 | | | | .8 | -1.1 |
| | | 154.8 | 25.5 | | | | 116.1 | 97.4 |
| | | 17.0 | 16.6 | | | Sales/Net Fixed Assets | 16.2 | 12.2 |
| | | 2.6 | 2.5 | | | | 4.6 | 3.4 |
| | | 5.2 | 2.1 | | | | 3.4 | 2.8 |
| | | 2.3 | .9 | | | Sales/Total Assets | 1.4 | 1.4 |
| | | 1.0 | .6 | | | | .7 | .9 |
| | | .8 | | | | | .4 | .5 |
| | | (13) 1.4 | | | | % Depr., Dep., Amort./Sales | (27) 2.6 | (36) 1.9 |
| | | 9.9 | | | | | 3.9 | 3.5 |
| | | | | | | | | .8 |
| | | | | | | % Officers', Directors' Owners' Comp/Sales | | (11) 6.7 |
| | | | | | | | | 22.3 |
| 17493M | 56838M | 318403M | 373097M | 575562M | 461860M | Net Sales ($) | 1227038M | 3040687M |
| 1357M | 4680M | 91240M | 305232M | 512363M | 662442M | Total Assets ($) | 1013801M | 1994172M |

M = $ thousand    MM = $ million
See Pages 9 through 22 for Explanation of Ratios and Data

## Comparative Historical Data | Current Data Sorted by Sales

| 4/1/09-3/31/10 ALL | 4/1/10-3/31/11 ALL | 4/1/11-3/31/12 ALL | Type of Statement | 0-1MM | 1-3MM | 3-5MM | 5-10MM | 10-25MM | 25MM & OVER |
|---|---|---|---|---|---|---|---|---|---|
| | | | | | 11 (4/1-9/30/11) | | | 44 (10/1/11-3/31/12) | |
| 13 | 10 | 14 | Unqualified | 1 | | 2 | | 5 | 6 |
| 4 | 2 | 4 | Reviewed | 1 | | | 2 | 1 | 1 |
| 2 | 3 | 3 | Compiled | | | | 1 | 1 | 1 |
| 5 | 4 | 4 | Tax Returns | 1 | | | 1 | 1 | 1 |
| 21 | 26 | 30 | Other | 2 | 2 | 2 | | 8 | 12 |
| 45 | 45 | 55 | **NUMBER OF STATEMENTS** | 5 | 2 | 5 | 8 | 14 | 21 |
| % | % | % | **ASSETS** | % | % | % | % | % | % |
| 27.7 | 26.8 | 27.5 | Cash & Equivalents | | | | | 32.6 | 28.8 |
| 16.9 | 17.4 | 15.6 | Trade Receivables (net) | | | | | 15.7 | 15.3 |
| 1.5 | 2.3 | 3.3 | Inventory | | | | | 2.0 | 1.1 |
| 11.6 | 8.7 | 5.7 | All Other Current | | | | | 3.3 | 10.1 |
| 57.7 | 55.1 | 52.1 | Total Current | | | | | 53.5 | 55.3 |
| 22.4 | 20.9 | 22.7 | Fixed Assets (net) | | | | | 25.4 | 17.1 |
| 8.5 | 11.1 | 9.7 | Intangibles (net) | | | | | 7.2 | 16.3 |
| 11.2 | 12.9 | 15.5 | All Other Non-Current | | | | | 13.8 | 11.3 |
| 100.0 | 100.0 | 100.0 | Total | | | | | 100.0 | 100.0 |
| | | | **LIABILITIES** | | | | | | |
| 5.7 | 7.5 | 12.1 | Notes Payable-Short Term | | | | | 1.1 | 2.3 |
| .8 | 1.7 | 3.5 | Cur. Mat.-L.T.D. | | | | | .7 | 3.1 |
| 14.7 | 12.6 | 15.2 | Trade Payables | | | | | 20.3 | 20.8 |
| 1.6 | 1.3 | .9 | Income Taxes Payable | | | | | 1.3 | 1.5 |
| 19.6 | 21.1 | 23.0 | All Other Current | | | | | 36.9 | 25.0 |
| 42.3 | 44.2 | 54.6 | Total Current | | | | | 60.3 | 52.6 |
| 9.4 | 14.3 | 9.9 | Long-Term Debt | | | | | 7.9 | 2.6 |
| .3 | .7 | .4 | Deferred Taxes | | | | | .5 | .8 |
| 14.2 | 6.7 | 13.7 | All Other Non-Current | | | | | 13.6 | 14.1 |
| 34.0 | 34.1 | 21.3 | Net Worth | | | | | 17.7 | 29.9 |
| 100.0 | 100.0 | 100.0 | Total Liabilities & Net Worth | | | | | 100.0 | 100.0 |
| | | | **INCOME DATA** | | | | | | |
| 100.0 | 100.0 | 100.0 | Net Sales | | | | | 100.0 | 100.0 |
| | | | Gross Profit | | | | | | |
| 93.4 | 95.9 | 93.1 | Operating Expenses | | | | | 91.1 | 96.4 |
| 6.6 | 4.1 | 6.9 | Operating Profit | | | | | 8.9 | 3.6 |
| 2.8 | .1 | .6 | All Other Expenses (net) | | | | | -.2 | -.3 |
| 3.8 | 4.0 | 6.4 | Profit Before Taxes | | | | | 9.1 | 3.9 |
| | | | **RATIOS** | | | | | | |
| 2.9 | 2.9 | 2.0 | | | | | | 1.6 | 2.3 |
| 1.4 | 1.3 | 1.0 | Current | | | | | 1.0 | 1.4 |
| .7 | .8 | .6 | | | | | | .7 | .8 |
| 2.8 | 2.1 | 1.6 | | | | | | 1.5 | 1.9 |
| 1.0 | 1.0 | 1.0 | Quick | | | | | .9 | 1.1 |
| .5 | .7 | .5 | | | | | | .6 | .5 |
| 5   72.8 | 5   77.8 | 6   65.2 | | | | | | 5   70.9 | 7   49.2 |
| 21   17.1 | 19   19.1 | 15   24.9 | Sales/Receivables | | | | | 8   46.6 | 15   24.0 |
| 44   8.4 | 40   9.1 | 46   8.0 | | | | | | 39   9.4 | 33   11.0 |
| | | | Cost of Sales/Inventory | | | | | | |
| | | | Cost of Sales/Payables | | | | | | |
| 2.1 | 4.1 | 5.7 | | | | | | 8.7 | 3.1 |
| 12.5 | 35.0 | 999.8 | Sales/Working Capital | | | | | -418.4 | 102.4 |
| -23.5 | -14.5 | -19.0 | | | | | | -20.2 | -26.6 |
| 25.0 | 42.5 | 27.6 | | | | | | | 49.9 |
| (26) 3.8 | (26) 8.3 | (34) 7.1 | EBIT/Interest | | | | | | (14) 8.2 |
| -.3 | .5 | 1.7 | | | | | | | 2.4 |
| | | | Net Profit + Depr., Dep., Amort./Cur. Mat. L/T/D | | | | | | |
| .2 | .2 | .3 | | | | | | .1 | .4 |
| .5 | .9 | 1.0 | Fixed/Worth | | | | | 1.5 | .7 |
| NM | 13.8 | -7.3 | | | | | | -.7 | -1.3 |
| .8 | .7 | 1.0 | | | | | | .9 | 1.1 |
| 1.2 | 1.8 | 2.3 | Debt/Worth | | | | | 4.2 | 2.1 |
| NM | 589.1 | -43.8 | | | | | | -6.7 | -10.9 |
| 32.0 | 95.1 | 90.4 | | | | | | 79.2 | 48.5 |
| (34) 13.2 | (36) 25.4 | (39) 28.8 | % Profit Before Taxes/Tangible Net Worth | | | | | (10) 32.4 | (14) 12.5 |
| -.7 | 12.6 | 6.3 | | | | | | 6.9 | 3.0 |
| 11.1 | 15.2 | 22.3 | | | | | | 30.3 | 14.6 |
| 6.9 | 6.8 | 5.7 | % Profit Before Taxes/Total Assets | | | | | 5.9 | 5.2 |
| -1.6 | 1.6 | 1.0 | | | | | | .4 | 1.0 |
| 64.8 | 62.2 | 63.6 | | | | | | 66.6 | 58.4 |
| 13.1 | 19.4 | 16.6 | Sales/Net Fixed Assets | | | | | 16.7 | 7.6 |
| 4.1 | 3.3 | 3.2 | | | | | | 3.0 | 3.6 |
| 3.3 | 3.5 | 4.5 | | | | | | 4.8 | 2.7 |
| 1.2 | 1.3 | 1.4 | Sales/Total Assets | | | | | 2.1 | 1.2 |
| .7 | .8 | .8 | | | | | | .8 | .8 |
| .3 | 1.1 | 1.3 | | | | | | | .7 |
| (28) 1.9 | (28) 1.9 | (32) 2.1 | % Depr., Dep., Amort./Sales | | | | | | (14) 2.1 |
| 3.5 | 5.1 | 7.9 | | | | | | | 6.1 |
| | | | % Officers', Directors' Owners' Comp/Sales | | | | | | |
| 2016808M | 1535348M | 1803253M | Net Sales ($) | 2123M | 3678M | 21113M | 49300M | 229652M | 1497387M |
| 1765936M | 1438098M | 1577314M | Total Assets ($) | 6796M | 4765M | 16602M | 32650M | 186089M | 1330412M |

© RMA 2012

M = $ thousand   MM = $ million
See Pages 9 through 22 for Explanation of Ratios and Data

## Current Data Sorted by Assets  |  Comparative Historical Data

| | 0-500M | 500M-2MM | 2-10MM | 10-50MM | 50-100MM | 100-250MM | | 4/1/07-3/31/08 ALL | 4/1/08-3/31/09 ALL |
|---|---|---|---|---|---|---|---|---|---|
| **Type of Statement** | | | | | | | | | |
| Unqualified | | | 7 | 4 | | 5 | | 14 | 22 |
| Reviewed | | 5 | 12 | 3 | | | | 16 | 17 |
| Compiled | 2 | 17 | 10 | | | | | 12 | 12 |
| Tax Returns | 8 | 8 | 7 | | | | | 12 | 12 |
| Other | 5 | 11 | 17 | 14 | 2 | 3 | | 28 | 45 |
| | | 16 (4/1-9/30/11) | | 124 (10/1/11-3/31/12) | | | | | |
| **NUMBER OF STATEMENTS** | 15 | 41 | 53 | 21 | 2 | 8 | | 82 | 108 |
| | % | % | % | % | % | % | | % | % |
| **ASSETS** | | | | | | | | | |
| Cash & Equivalents | 16.4 | 17.9 | 11.6 | 9.0 | | | | 13.9 | 7.9 |
| Trade Receivables (net) | 41.5 | 42.1 | 50.4 | 44.9 | | | | 53.9 | 50.8 |
| Inventory | .7 | .5 | 1.1 | 2.5 | | | | 1.1 | 1.3 |
| All Other Current | 4.1 | 1.6 | 5.1 | 5.7 | | | | 5.2 | 6.0 |
| Total Current | 62.7 | 62.0 | 68.1 | 62.1 | | | | 74.1 | 66.0 |
| Fixed Assets (net) | 21.8 | 22.1 | 18.3 | 14.3 | | | | 13.1 | 16.3 |
| Intangibles (net) | .5 | 8.1 | 8.3 | 15.0 | | | | 5.2 | 6.7 |
| All Other Non-Current | 15.1 | 7.8 | 5.3 | 8.6 | | | | 7.6 | 11.0 |
| Total | 100.0 | 100.0 | 100.0 | 100.0 | | | | 100.0 | 100.0 |
| **LIABILITIES** | | | | | | | | | |
| Notes Payable-Short Term | 90.3 | 14.6 | 14.5 | 9.3 | | | | 18.0 | 21.0 |
| Cur. Mat.-L.T.D. | .7 | 1.3 | 4.6 | 7.0 | | | | 2.6 | 2.7 |
| Trade Payables | 3.7 | 9.8 | 5.5 | 9.1 | | | | 7.4 | 7.8 |
| Income Taxes Payable | 1.0 | .4 | .2 | .6 | | | | .8 | .9 |
| All Other Current | 15.4 | 11.2 | 17.0 | 18.7 | | | | 18.6 | 18.5 |
| Total Current | 111.1 | 37.3 | 41.9 | 44.7 | | | | 47.4 | 51.0 |
| Long-Term Debt | 18.4 | 10.8 | 10.7 | 8.3 | | | | 11.1 | 13.9 |
| Deferred Taxes | .0 | .2 | .3 | .2 | | | | .4 | .3 |
| All Other Non-Current | 26.9 | 5.9 | 9.2 | 8.4 | | | | 5.5 | 8.3 |
| Net Worth | -56.4 | 45.8 | 38.0 | 38.4 | | | | 35.7 | 26.6 |
| Total Liabilities & Net Worth | 100.0 | 100.0 | 100.0 | 100.0 | | | | 100.0 | 100.0 |
| **INCOME DATA** | | | | | | | | | |
| Net Sales | 100.0 | 100.0 | 100.0 | 100.0 | | | | 100.0 | 100.0 |
| Gross Profit | | | | | | | | | |
| Operating Expenses | 99.3 | 93.8 | 93.8 | 97.4 | | | | 94.8 | 95.7 |
| Operating Profit | .7 | 6.2 | 6.2 | 2.6 | | | | 5.2 | 4.3 |
| All Other Expenses (net) | .4 | .7 | 1.5 | .7 | | | | .8 | 1.0 |
| Profit Before Taxes | .3 | 5.5 | 4.8 | 1.9 | | | | 4.4 | 3.3 |
| **RATIOS** | | | | | | | | | |
| Current | 2.1 | 3.6 | 2.4 | 1.8 | | | | 2.6 | 1.8 |
| | .8 | 2.1 | 1.6 | 1.2 | | | | 1.4 | 1.3 |
| | .4 | 1.1 | 1.2 | 1.1 | | | | 1.1 | 1.0 |
| Quick | 2.0 | 3.1 | 2.3 | 1.7 | | | | 2.6 | 1.7 |
| | .7 | 1.7 | 1.3 | 1.2 | | | | 1.3 | 1.2 |
| | .3 | 1.1 | 1.0 | .9 | | | | 1.0 | .8 |
| Sales/Receivables | 13  28.8 | 17  21.2 | 35  10.4 | 44  8.3 | | | | 39  9.3 | 34  10.6 |
| | 28  13.0 | 30  12.1 | 43  8.5 | 49  7.4 | | | | 45  8.1 | 43  8.4 |
| | 49  7.5 | 41  9.0 | 52  7.0 | 59  6.2 | | | | 59  6.2 | 59  6.2 |
| Cost of Sales/Inventory | | | | | | | | | |
| Cost of Sales/Payables | | | | | | | | | |
| Sales/Working Capital | 15.3 | 10.7 | 7.5 | 13.7 | | | | 11.1 | 12.6 |
| | -72.9 | 20.3 | 22.7 | 26.8 | | | | 23.6 | 28.1 |
| | -6.3 | 197.3 | 51.7 | 93.6 | | | | 106.8 | -259.2 |
| EBIT/Interest | 15.9 | 32.0 | 28.8 | 3.9 | | | | 13.9 | 13.0 |
| | (10) -1.1 | (35) 13.7 | (46) 7.1 | (16) 2.5 | | | | (69) 4.4 | (98) 3.6 |
| | -20.3 | 2.1 | 2.5 | .3 | | | | 1.9 | 1.2 |
| Net Profit + Depr., Dep., Amort./Cur. Mat. L/T/D | | | | | | | | 9.8 | 7.4 |
| | | | | | | | | (16) 3.1 | (27) 2.1 |
| | | | | | | | | 1.6 | .8 |
| Fixed/Worth | .0 | .2 | .2 | .2 | | | | .1 | .2 |
| | 6.9 | .6 | .4 | .9 | | | | .4 | .5 |
| | -.3 | 1.3 | 2.0 | 2.6 | | | | 2.1 | 2.0 |
| Debt/Worth | 1.4 | .5 | .8 | 1.0 | | | | .6 | 1.2 |
| | 157.0 | 1.3 | 1.8 | 3.9 | | | | 2.5 | 2.2 |
| | -1.9 | 4.0 | 5.2 | 13.3 | | | | 13.1 | 10.9 |
| % Profit Before Taxes/Tangible Net Worth | | 114.6 | 75.1 | 43.3 | | | | 75.3 | 101.6 |
| | (37) 54.7 | (45) 38.8 | (17) 23.7 | | | | | (67) 36.6 | (87) 29.5 |
| | | 11.6 | 14.6 | 3.8 | | | | 15.9 | 6.0 |
| % Profit Before Taxes/Total Assets | 25.5 | 49.0 | 23.6 | 6.4 | | | | 20.2 | 18.3 |
| | 2.8 | 18.8 | 11.6 | 3.0 | | | | 9.0 | 6.9 |
| | -31.2 | 2.3 | 5.2 | .4 | | | | 3.2 | .7 |
| Sales/Net Fixed Assets | 999.8 | 139.2 | 98.8 | 97.2 | | | | 84.0 | 90.8 |
| | 65.8 | 35.4 | 33.3 | 25.0 | | | | 48.4 | 44.8 |
| | 14.0 | 14.3 | 11.9 | 11.7 | | | | 28.0 | 19.9 |
| Sales/Total Assets | 10.5 | 6.5 | 6.3 | 4.3 | | | | 5.6 | 5.9 |
| | 6.1 | 4.6 | 4.2 | 3.8 | | | | 4.5 | 4.5 |
| | 3.3 | 3.6 | 2.9 | 2.4 | | | | 3.2 | 3.1 |
| % Depr., Dep., Amort./Sales | | .3 | .5 | .4 | | | | .4 | .4 |
| | (29) 1.1 | (44) .7 | (14) 1.3 | | | | | (58) .9 | (81) .8 |
| | | 1.5 | 1.6 | 3.2 | | | | 1.2 | 1.3 |
| % Officers', Directors' Owners' Comp/Sales | | 1.6 | 1.3 | | | | | 1.1 | 1.3 |
| | (18) 4.0 | (20) 2.5 | | | | | | (30) 2.0 | (33) 2.2 |
| | | 5.2 | 3.3 | | | | | 4.6 | |
| Net Sales ($) | 24826M | 272061M | 1147398M | 1345915M | 506551M | 3247848M | | 4143862M | 8089752M |
| Total Assets ($) | 3484M | 49125M | 261461M | 390004M | 156237M | 1318218M | | 1189858M | 2226184M |

## Comparative Historical Data | Current Data Sorted by Sales

| | | | Type of Statement | | | | | | |
|---|---|---|---|---|---|---|---|---|---|
| 30 | 17 | 16 | Unqualified | | | | | 4 | 12 |
| 25 | 21 | 20 | Reviewed | | | 1 | 6 | 6 | 7 |
| 17 | 17 | 29 | Compiled | 2 | 3 | 9 | 9 | 5 | 1 |
| 16 | 26 | 23 | Tax Returns | 2 | 6 | 3 | 5 | 5 | 2 |
| 52 | 60 | 52 | Other | 3 | 3 | 4 | 10 | 8 | 24 |
| 4/1/09-3/31/10 ALL | 4/1/10-3/31/11 ALL | 4/1/11-3/31/12 ALL | | 0-1MM | 16 (4/1-9/30/11) 1-3MM | 3-5MM | 124 (10/1/11-3/31/12) 5-10MM | 10-25MM | 25MM & OVER |
| 140 | 141 | 140 | **NUMBER OF STATEMENTS** | 7 | 12 | 17 | 30 | 28 | 46 |
| % | % | % | **ASSETS** | % | % | % | % | % | % |
| 14.0 | 14.6 | 13.1 | Cash & Equivalents | | 9.1 | 17.7 | 14.9 | 16.2 | 8.3 |
| 49.3 | 45.9 | 46.0 | Trade Receivables (net) | | 54.3 | 31.1 | 40.9 | 47.0 | 54.9 |
| 1.3 | 1.4 | 1.1 | Inventory | | .8 | .1 | 2.1 | 1.9 | .6 |
| 6.0 | 5.1 | 4.1 | All Other Current | | 1.5 | 3.2 | 3.8 | 4.6 | 4.9 |
| 70.6 | 67.1 | 64.3 | Total Current | | 65.7 | 52.2 | 61.7 | 69.7 | 68.7 |
| 14.0 | 17.3 | 18.5 | Fixed Assets (net) | | 19.8 | 23.2 | 21.3 | 17.6 | 11.6 |
| 5.5 | 7.3 | 9.4 | Intangibles (net) | | 1.8 | 12.2 | 11.4 | 6.6 | 12.0 |
| 9.9 | 8.3 | 7.9 | All Other Non-Current | | 12.8 | 12.4 | 5.5 | 6.1 | 7.6 |
| 100.0 | 100.0 | 100.0 | Total | | 100.0 | 100.0 | 100.0 | 100.0 | 100.0 |
| | | | **LIABILITIES** | | | | | | |
| 18.8 | 18.7 | 21.2 | Notes Payable-Short Term | | 44.8 | 18.1 | 16.0 | 11.2 | 12.1 |
| 2.9 | 2.7 | 3.7 | Cur. Mat.-L.T.D. | | .0 | 1.5 | 2.1 | 5.1 | 6.0 |
| 7.7 | 7.4 | 7.3 | Trade Payables | | 5.5 | 9.4 | 9.4 | 6.2 | 7.0 |
| .6 | .3 | .4 | Income Taxes Payable | | .0 | .6 | .2 | .3 | .3 |
| 21.2 | 21.3 | 15.7 | All Other Current | | 18.5 | 8.9 | 10.3 | 17.2 | 21.4 |
| 51.2 | 50.3 | 48.2 | Total Current | | 68.8 | 38.5 | 37.9 | 39.9 | 46.8 |
| 12.0 | 12.3 | 11.7 | Long-Term Debt | | 17.4 | 14.3 | 13.1 | 8.7 | 8.4 |
| .1 | .0 | .2 | Deferred Taxes | | .0 | .0 | .3 | .2 | .2 |
| 7.6 | 7.9 | 10.7 | All Other Non-Current | | 16.3 | 5.7 | 2.9 | 15.2 | 7.7 |
| 29.1 | 29.5 | 29.2 | Net Worth | | -2.5 | 41.5 | 45.8 | 35.8 | 36.9 |
| 100.0 | 100.0 | 100.0 | Total Liabilities & Net Worth | | 100.0 | 100.0 | 100.0 | 100.0 | 100.0 |
| | | | **INCOME DATA** | | | | | | |
| 100.0 | 100.0 | 100.0 | Net Sales | | 100.0 | 100.0 | 100.0 | 100.0 | 100.0 |
| | | | Gross Profit | | | | | | |
| 95.8 | 94.8 | 95.0 | Operating Expenses | | 96.8 | 95.9 | 94.0 | 94.1 | 96.7 |
| 4.2 | 5.2 | 5.0 | Operating Profit | | 3.2 | 4.1 | 6.0 | 5.9 | 3.3 |
| .7 | .9 | 1.1 | All Other Expenses (net) | | 2.6 | .1 | .9 | .7 | .9 |
| 3.5 | 4.2 | 3.9 | Profit Before Taxes | | .6 | 4.0 | 5.1 | 5.2 | 2.3 |
| | | | **RATIOS** | | | | | | |
| 2.1 | 2.7 | 2.5 | | | 4.5 | 3.5 | 2.7 | 4.1 | 2.2 |
| 1.5 | 1.4 | 1.5 | Current | | 2.0 | 1.7 | 1.9 | 1.6 | 1.3 |
| 1.0 | 1.0 | 1.1 | | | .8 | .6 | 1.2 | 1.1 | 1.1 |
| 2.1 | 2.5 | 2.3 | | | 4.5 | 2.8 | 2.6 | 4.1 | 2.0 |
| 1.3 | 1.3 | 1.3 | Quick | | 1.9 | 1.6 | 1.6 | 1.3 | 1.3 |
| .8 | .8 | .9 | | | .8 | .5 | .8 | 1.1 | 1.0 |
| 34  10.7 | 31  11.9 | 27  13.4 | | 14  25.8 | 11  33.9 | 24  15.4 | 29  12.4 | 41  9.0 | |
| 41  8.9 | 42  8.7 | 41  8.8 | Sales/Receivables | 35  10.3 | 30  12.0 | 34  10.7 | 41  8.9 | 46  7.9 | |
| 54  6.7 | 54  6.8 | 52  7.0 | | 55  6.6 | 52  7.0 | 48  7.6 | 58  6.3 | 53  6.9 | |
| | | | Cost of Sales/Inventory | | | | | | |
| | | | Cost of Sales/Payables | | | | | | |
| 10.6 | 10.1 | 10.1 | | | 7.9 | 7.5 | 10.5 | 7.6 | 13.4 |
| 23.1 | 22.6 | 22.8 | Sales/Working Capital | | 16.5 | 22.8 | 18.9 | 20.7 | 27.8 |
| UND | NM | 93.8 | | | NM | -15.8 | 50.4 | 90.3 | 53.6 |
| 17.0 | 29.6 | 21.9 | | | 101.4 | 22.8 | 37.6 | 14.4 | |
| (126)  5.5 | (117)  8.9 | (117)  5.9 | EBIT/Interest | | 16.8 | (27)  10.8 | (22)  6.7 | (40)  3.6 | |
| 2.2 | 2.1 | 1.8 | | | -.2 | 1.8 | 2.5 | 1.9 | |
| 6.7 | 11.2 | 19.1 | | | | | | | 16.2 |
| (37)  2.9 | (24)  5.5 | (22)  10.6 | Net Profit + Depr., Dep., Amort./Cur. Mat. L/T/D | | | | | (16)  10.1 | |
| .9 | 2.6 | .4 | | | | | | 1.5 | |
| .1 | .1 | .2 | | | .2 | .2 | .2 | .2 | .2 |
| .3 | .3 | .6 | Fixed/Worth | | 1.3 | .4 | .6 | .5 | .5 |
| 2.0 | 2.2 | 2.4 | | | 25.0 | -2.9 | 1.4 | 4.1 | 2.0 |
| .9 | .8 | .8 | | | 1.8 | .4 | .7 | .3 | 1.1 |
| 1.9 | 1.8 | 2.0 | Debt/Worth | | 20.5 | 1.2 | 1.5 | 2.3 | 2.2 |
| 10.6 | 17.0 | 11.2 | | | NM | -9.3 | 3.2 | 13.2 | 7.9 |
| 79.2 | 81.7 | 85.0 | | | 82.0 | 94.7 | 97.6 | 62.1 | |
| (113)  32.6 | (114)  34.7 | (113)  38.7 | % Profit Before Taxes/Tangible Net Worth | | (12)  34.1 | (27)  56.5 | (22)  41.4 | (39)  23.7 | |
| 11.1 | 18.2 | 11.5 | | | 8.8 | 13.3 | 16.8 | 13.2 | |
| 22.0 | 25.9 | 24.5 | | | 27.0 | 51.6 | 27.4 | 42.0 | 14.7 |
| 10.1 | 12.5 | 8.1 | % Profit Before Taxes/Total Assets | | -.4 | 15.9 | 19.8 | 14.8 | 6.2 |
| 3.2 | 4.1 | 2.4 | | | -26.3 | -2.0 | 2.2 | 4.3 | 3.0 |
| 140.0 | 119.9 | 104.6 | | | 832.7 | 69.5 | 82.3 | 183.5 | 103.2 |
| 59.1 | 50.0 | 33.9 | Sales/Net Fixed Assets | | 91.6 | 35.4 | 25.2 | 33.0 | 59.6 |
| 22.9 | 16.9 | 13.3 | | | 23.5 | 11.2 | 9.0 | 18.8 | 24.9 |
| 5.9 | 6.2 | 6.0 | | | 8.2 | 4.9 | 6.0 | 6.7 | 5.2 |
| 4.4 | 4.1 | 4.2 | Sales/Total Assets | | 5.4 | 4.0 | 4.4 | 4.2 | 4.3 |
| 3.4 | 3.1 | 3.0 | | | 3.6 | 2.9 | 3.0 | 2.7 | 3.5 |
| .3 | .4 | .4 | | | .7 | .4 | .2 | .4 | |
| (102)  .7 | (104)  .7 | (100)  .9 | % Depr., Dep., Amort./Sales | | (13)  1.2 | (22)  1.2 | (23)  .7 | (33)  .8 | |
| 1.4 | 1.7 | 1.7 | | | 2.0 | 2.2 | 1.1 | 1.4 | |
| 1.6 | 1.9 | 1.4 | | | | 2.3 | 1.1 | | |
| (40)  3.8 | (45)  4.3 | (48)  3.0 | % Officers', Directors' Owners' Comp/Sales | | (13)  3.4 | (14)  1.6 | | | |
| 8.2 | 7.9 | 5.0 | | | | 5.3 | 3.1 | | |
| 9659551M | 6630587M | 6544599M | Net Sales ($) | 3019M | 24680M | 66392M | 229611M | 461479M | 5759418M |
| 2195757M | 2234734M | 2178529M | Total Assets ($) | 2837M | 13193M | 18538M | 67521M | 127262M | 1949178M |

© RMA 2012

M = $ thousand     MM = $ million
See Pages 9 through 22 for Explanation of Ratios and Data

## Current Data Sorted by Assets  |  Comparative Historical Data

| Type of Statement | 0-500M | 500M-2MM | 2-10MM | 10-50MM | 50-100MM | 100-250MM | 4/1/07-3/31/08 ALL | 4/1/08-3/31/09 ALL |
|---|---|---|---|---|---|---|---|---|
| Unqualified | | 2 | 10 | 14 | 3 | 10 | 20 | 36 |
| Reviewed | | 13 | 45 | 4 | 1 | | 50 | 58 |
| Compiled | 4 | 10 | 14 | | | | 16 | 27 |
| Tax Returns | 15 | 22 | 10 | | | | 34 | 27 |
| Other | 8 | 31 | 31 | 20 | 3 | 9 | 65 | 83 |
| | | 41 (4/1-9/30/11) | | 238 (10/1/11-3/31/12) | | | | |
| NUMBER OF STATEMENTS | 27 | 78 | 110 | 38 | 7 | 19 | 185 | 231 |
| **ASSETS** | % | % | % | % | % | % | % | % |
| Cash & Equivalents | 18.1 | 14.9 | 12.4 | 6.2 | | 3.3 | 9.1 | 8.9 |
| Trade Receivables (net) | 27.0 | 37.3 | 35.8 | 22.2 | | 17.8 | 35.4 | 33.8 |
| Inventory | 19.3 | 11.2 | 9.4 | 6.2 | | 1.7 | 10.7 | 10.3 |
| All Other Current | 2.1 | 3.1 | 6.4 | 5.2 | | 4.8 | 6.0 | 5.9 |
| Total Current | 66.5 | 66.5 | 64.0 | 39.9 | | 27.6 | 61.2 | 58.9 |
| Fixed Assets (net) | 16.6 | 15.7 | 15.7 | 10.4 | | 4.9 | 18.4 | 16.7 |
| Intangibles (net) | 9.7 | 9.1 | 11.9 | 43.0 | | 51.9 | 12.9 | 14.8 |
| All Other Non-Current | 7.2 | 8.7 | 8.4 | 6.7 | | 15.7 | 7.5 | 9.6 |
| Total | 100.0 | 100.0 | 100.0 | 100.0 | | 100.0 | 100.0 | 100.0 |
| **LIABILITIES** | | | | | | | | |
| Notes Payable-Short Term | 35.1 | 12.8 | 14.6 | 3.0 | | 4.9 | 10.9 | 11.9 |
| Cur. Mat.-L.T.D. | 3.1 | 3.0 | 3.5 | 3.6 | | .8 | 6.0 | 5.4 |
| Trade Payables | 21.8 | 15.7 | 15.5 | 8.7 | | 6.0 | 13.6 | 14.2 |
| Income Taxes Payable | .1 | .2 | .4 | .4 | | .0 | .5 | .7 |
| All Other Current | 12.3 | 15.0 | 17.7 | 16.0 | | 16.1 | 18.0 | 22.8 |
| Total Current | 72.4 | 46.7 | 51.7 | 31.7 | | 27.8 | 49.0 | 54.9 |
| Long-Term Debt | 22.5 | 17.5 | 20.0 | 42.5 | | 51.1 | 24.3 | 26.1 |
| Deferred Taxes | .0 | .1 | .3 | .4 | | .2 | .3 | .4 |
| All Other Non-Current | 6.6 | 8.2 | 5.6 | 10.1 | | 6.3 | 6.1 | 5.6 |
| Net Worth | -1.4 | 27.4 | 22.3 | 15.3 | | 14.6 | 20.3 | 13.0 |
| Total Liabilities & Net Worth | 100.0 | 100.0 | 100.0 | 100.0 | | 100.0 | 100.0 | 100.0 |
| **INCOME DATA** | | | | | | | | |
| Net Sales | 100.0 | 100.0 | 100.0 | 100.0 | | 100.0 | 100.0 | 100.0 |
| Gross Profit | | | | | | | | |
| Operating Expenses | 96.4 | 93.8 | 93.4 | 90.3 | | 97.7 | 93.7 | 94.4 |
| Operating Profit | 3.6 | 6.2 | 6.6 | 9.7 | | 2.3 | 6.3 | 5.6 |
| All Other Expenses (net) | 1.0 | 1.9 | 1.5 | 4.7 | | 9.9 | 1.9 | 2.8 |
| Profit Before Taxes | 2.6 | 4.3 | 5.1 | 5.0 | | -7.7 | 4.5 | 2.8 |
| **RATIOS** | | | | | | | | |
| Current | 2.0 | 3.2 | 2.4 | 1.8 | | 1.1 | 1.9 | 1.8 |
| | 1.0 | 1.5 | 1.5 | 1.1 | | .7 | 1.4 | 1.2 |
| | .4 | 1.0 | .8 | .6 | | .3 | 1.0 | .8 |
| Quick | 1.8 | 2.2 | 1.9 | 1.4 | | .9 | 1.5 | 1.3 |
| | .6 | 1.3 | 1.1 | .9 | | .4 | 1.0 | .9 |
| | .2 | .7 | .6 | .4 | | .2 | .6 | .4 |
| Sales/Receivables | 0 UND | 23 16.0 | 31 11.7 | 31 11.8 | | 10 37.3 | 25 14.5 | 26 14.0 |
| | 18 20.0 | 41 8.9 | 49 7.5 | 43 8.4 | | 28 13.0 | 41 8.8 | 42 8.6 |
| | 35 10.5 | 57 6.4 | 74 4.9 | 59 6.2 | | 74 4.9 | 61 6.0 | 63 5.8 |
| Cost of Sales/Inventory | | | | | | | | |
| Cost of Sales/Payables | | | | | | | | |
| Sales/Working Capital | 17.8 | 6.0 | 5.8 | 8.6 | | 46.0 | 8.9 | 8.7 |
| | -200.3 | 17.0 | 11.5 | 76.6 | | -13.6 | 17.9 | 29.2 |
| | -18.9 | 201.4 | -24.4 | -10.0 | | -8.3 | -170.4 | -22.1 |
| EBIT/Interest | 11.6 | 13.8 | 29.9 | 17.7 | | 6.2 | 10.8 | 13.0 |
| | (24) 5.2 | (65) 5.5 | (95) 6.2 | (35) 3.1 | | (14) 1.1 | (169) 3.7 | (201) 3.4 |
| | -.1 | 1.0 | 1.8 | 1.3 | | -1.1 | 1.3 | .6 |
| Net Profit + Depr., Dep., Amort./Cur. Mat. L/T/D | | | 8.4 | | | | 6.4 | 7.3 |
| | | | (26) 3.9 | | | | (41) 3.7 | (52) 3.0 |
| | | | 1.5 | | | | 1.9 | 1.2 |
| Fixed/Worth | .0 | .2 | .1 | .5 | | .2 | .2 | .2 |
| | 5.0 | .4 | .5 | -.9 | | -.1 | .7 | 1.3 |
| | -.3 | NM | 141.0 | -.2 | | .0 | -1.7 | -.5 |
| Debt/Worth | 1.2 | .8 | .8 | 2.6 | | 4.7 | 1.2 | 1.4 |
| | -17.4 | 2.2 | 2.1 | -5.9 | | -2.0 | 3.3 | 5.4 |
| | -3.0 | -97.2 | NM | -1.3 | | -1.1 | -6.3 | -2.8 |
| % Profit Before Taxes/Tangible Net Worth | 148.2 | 72.0 | 49.4 | 150.7 | | | 79.8 | 65.3 |
| | (13) 72.7 | (58) 24.3 | (83) 31.5 | (17) 53.3 | | | (126) 28.8 | (136) 35.0 |
| | 15.9 | 4.2 | 8.5 | 26.2 | | | 9.3 | 9.4 |
| % Profit Before Taxes/Total Assets | 49.8 | 27.0 | 17.5 | 17.2 | | 4.3 | 20.0 | 20.0 |
| | 14.8 | 10.2 | 7.6 | 6.7 | | .0 | 7.5 | 6.1 |
| | -5.0 | .8 | 1.6 | .5 | | -11.5 | 1.6 | -1.2 |
| Sales/Net Fixed Assets | 699.5 | 82.4 | 69.9 | 41.1 | | 76.4 | 52.1 | 53.2 |
| | 70.6 | 30.0 | 20.4 | 21.2 | | 28.6 | 22.0 | 22.0 |
| | 35.7 | 18.0 | 11.4 | 10.1 | | 15.1 | 11.1 | 11.0 |
| Sales/Total Assets | 8.5 | 4.4 | 3.1 | 2.1 | | 1.7 | 4.1 | 3.8 |
| | 6.1 | 3.5 | 2.2 | 1.5 | | .7 | 2.8 | 2.6 |
| | 3.6 | 2.7 | 1.5 | .8 | | .3 | 1.7 | 1.5 |
| % Depr., Dep., Amort./Sales | .4 | .6 | .7 | 1.0 | | | .9 | .7 |
| | (15) 1.1 | (46) 1.2 | (77) 1.3 | (22) 2.1 | | | (136) 1.8 | (160) 1.5 |
| | 2.0 | 1.7 | 2.5 | 6.5 | | | 3.3 | 2.9 |
| % Officers', Directors', Owners' Comp/Sales | 2.6 | 3.3 | 2.6 | | | | 2.7 | 3.1 |
| | (15) 5.3 | (34) 4.4 | (37) 4.4 | | | | (73) 4.4 | (67) 4.8 |
| | 14.4 | 7.2 | 7.3 | | | | 9.1 | 9.2 |
| Net Sales ($) | 43100M | 317739M | 1231747M | 1568995M | 1008713M | 3515700M | 3689240M | 5849488M |
| Total Assets ($) | 7281M | 87820M | 509197M | 1022044M | 521232M | 3130070M | 1995579M | 3568706M |

M = $ thousand    MM = $ million
See Pages 9 through 22 for Explanation of Ratios and Data

## Comparative Historical Data

## Current Data Sorted by Sales

| H1 | H2 | H3 | Type of Statement | 0-1MM | 1-3MM | 3-5MM | 5-10MM | 10-25MM | 25MM & OVER |
|---|---|---|---|---|---|---|---|---|---|
| 44 | 38 | 39 | Unqualified | | | 4 | 4 | 9 | 22 |
| 43 | 54 | 63 | Reviewed | | 5 | 9 | 17 | 25 | 7 |
| 28 | 27 | 28 | Compiled | 1 | 9 | 6 | 7 | 5 | |
| 42 | 41 | 47 | Tax Returns | 8 | 18 | 10 | 9 | 1 | 1 |
| 93 | 104 | 102 | Other | 4 | 19 | 13 | 20 | 19 | 27 |
| 4/1/09-3/31/10 ALL | 4/1/10-3/31/11 ALL | 4/1/11-3/31/12 ALL | | 41 (4/1-9/30/11) | | | 238 (10/1/11-3/31/12) | | |
| 250 | 264 | 279 | NUMBER OF STATEMENTS | 13 | 51 | 42 | 57 | 59 | 57 |
| % | % | % | **ASSETS** | % | % | % | % | % | % |
| 10.6 | 10.7 | 12.0 | Cash & Equivalents | 17.9 | 16.0 | 16.0 | 11.6 | 10.6 | 5.9 |
| 30.9 | 31.3 | 32.2 | Trade Receivables (net) | 10.7 | 30.1 | 32.6 | 35.6 | 40.2 | 27.1 |
| 10.1 | 10.8 | 9.9 | Inventory | 17.7 | 12.2 | 8.6 | 12.7 | 8.3 | 5.7 |
| 4.6 | 5.8 | 4.7 | All Other Current | .8 | 2.5 | 6.2 | 3.5 | 7.1 | 5.2 |
| 56.2 | 58.7 | 58.8 | Total Current | 47.1 | 60.8 | 63.4 | 63.4 | 66.2 | 44.0 |
| 18.3 | 15.7 | 14.2 | Fixed Assets (net) | 32.3 | 14.7 | 16.4 | 11.8 | 15.0 | 9.7 |
| 15.9 | 15.6 | 18.5 | Intangibles (net) | 7.1 | 15.3 | 12.0 | 15.2 | 14.4 | 36.4 |
| 9.6 | 10.0 | 8.5 | All Other Non-Current | 13.5 | 9.3 | 8.2 | 9.6 | 4.4 | 10.0 |
| 100.0 | 100.0 | 100.0 | Total | 100.0 | 100.0 | 100.0 | 100.0 | 100.0 | 100.0 |
| | | | **LIABILITIES** | | | | | | |
| 12.7 | 13.9 | 13.5 | Notes Payable-Short Term | 48.3 | 16.0 | 13.4 | 18.2 | 7.5 | 5.0 |
| 4.3 | 4.6 | 3.1 | Cur. Mat.-L.T.D. | 1.4 | 3.8 | 4.4 | 2.9 | 2.6 | 2.7 |
| 15.7 | 15.6 | 14.4 | Trade Payables | 10.6 | 15.9 | 13.6 | 17.5 | 15.9 | 10.0 |
| .3 | .7 | .3 | Income Taxes Payable | .0 | .2 | .2 | .7 | .2 | .3 |
| 18.7 | 20.0 | 16.4 | All Other Current | 7.3 | 9.9 | 11.2 | 19.8 | 22.0 | 18.8 |
| 51.7 | 54.8 | 47.8 | Total Current | 67.7 | 45.8 | 42.8 | 59.1 | 48.2 | 36.8 |
| 26.3 | 24.9 | 25.8 | Long-Term Debt | 23.7 | 20.4 | 17.4 | 17.0 | 27.7 | 44.0 |
| .1 | .3 | .3 | Deferred Taxes | .0 | .0 | .1 | .2 | .4 | .5 |
| 9.4 | 9.9 | 7.3 | All Other Non-Current | 12.5 | 6.9 | 6.9 | 5.1 | 8.1 | 8.3 |
| 12.5 | 10.1 | 18.9 | Net Worth | -3.7 | 26.9 | 32.8 | 18.5 | 15.6 | 10.3 |
| 100.0 | 100.0 | 100.0 | Total Liabilities & Net Worth | 100.0 | 100.0 | 100.0 | 100.0 | 100.0 | 100.0 |
| | | | **INCOME DATA** | | | | | | |
| 100.0 | 100.0 | 100.0 | Net Sales | 100.0 | 100.0 | 100.0 | 100.0 | 100.0 | 100.0 |
| | | | Gross Profit | | | | | | |
| 95.6 | 95.2 | 93.8 | Operating Expenses | 84.1 | 93.8 | 93.8 | 94.5 | 94.6 | 94.6 |
| 4.4 | 4.8 | 6.2 | Operating Profit | 15.9 | 6.2 | 6.2 | 5.5 | 5.4 | 5.4 |
| 2.2 | 1.9 | 2.7 | All Other Expenses (net) | 12.1 | 1.0 | .6 | 2.0 | 2.2 | 5.1 |
| 2.2 | 2.9 | 3.4 | Profit Before Taxes | 3.9 | 5.3 | 5.6 | 3.5 | 3.2 | .3 |
| | | | **RATIOS** | | | | | | |
| 2.0 | 1.9 | 2.3 | Current | 4.3 | 2.9 | 3.9 | 2.0 | 2.0 | 1.7 |
| 1.2 | 1.2 | 1.3 | | 1.4 | 1.5 | 1.8 | 1.3 | 1.5 | 1.0 |
| .7 | .8 | .8 | | .2 | .7 | 1.0 | .8 | .9 | .6 |
| 1.4 | 1.4 | 1.6 | Quick | 3.4 | 2.2 | 3.1 | 1.3 | 1.5 | 1.3 |
| .9 | .8 | .9 | | .5 | 1.0 | 1.3 | .9 | 1.1 | .8 |
| .5 | .4 | .5 | | .1 | .4 | .7 | .4 | .6 | .4 |
| 23  16.2 | 23  15.6 | 23  15.9 | Sales/Receivables | 0  UND | 16  23.1 | 25  14.6 | 28  13.0 | 33  10.9 | 19  18.8 |
| 38  9.7 | 41  8.9 | 42  8.7 | | 5  79.8 | 30  12.3 | 38  9.7 | 41  8.8 | 49  7.4 | 45  8.1 |
| 58  6.3 | 60  6.1 | 63  5.8 | | 52  7.0 | 56  6.5 | 54  6.8 | 68  5.4 | 76  4.8 | 66  5.5 |
| | | | Cost of Sales/Inventory | | | | | | |
| | | | | | | | | | |
| | | | | | | | | | |
| | | | Cost of Sales/Payables | | | | | | |
| | | | | | | | | | |
| | | | | | | | | | |
| 8.4 | 7.8 | 7.2 | Sales/Working Capital | 3.1 | 6.7 | 5.1 | 9.0 | 7.9 | 9.8 |
| 29.3 | 26.2 | 20.5 | | 21.0 | 20.8 | 10.9 | 22.4 | 11.0 | 618.9 |
| -20.1 | -20.5 | -20.8 | | -4.1 | -42.4 | NM | -19.0 | -25.1 | -11.9 |
| 12.5 | 16.6 | 16.8 | EBIT/Interest | | 14.3 | 12.1 | 28.6 | 22.8 | 13.7 |
| (225) 3.0 | (224) 3.2 | (239) 4.7 | | (45) 4.7 | (33) 4.7 | (53) 6.7 | (49) 6.3 | (50) 3.7 | |
| .7 | .8 | 1.1 | | | .7 | 2.4 | 1.8 | 1.1 | 1.3 |
| 7.4 | 5.3 | 10.5 | Net Profit + Depr., Dep., Amort./Cur. Mat. L/T/D | | | | | 12.4 | 18.9 |
| (34) 2.5 | (43) 2.7 | (45) 3.8 | | | | | (15) 6.3 | (10) 3.2 | |
| 1.5 | 1.1 | 1.4 | | | | | | 2.2 | 1.5 |
| .2 | .2 | .2 | Fixed/Worth | .1 | .1 | .1 | .2 | .2 | .4 |
| 1.0 | .9 | .7 | | 20.1 | .6 | .4 | .5 | .5 | -1.1 |
| -.6 | -.6 | -.4 | | -.5 | -.6 | -14.5 | NM | -3.0 | -.1 |
| 1.2 | 1.3 | 1.1 | Debt/Worth | 1.9 | .8 | .5 | 1.4 | 1.1 | 2.3 |
| 4.2 | 7.9 | 3.7 | | -46.9 | 2.1 | 1.4 | 3.5 | 2.4 | -7.1 |
| -3.8 | -3.6 | -3.2 | | -4.7 | -4.0 | -16.6 | -4.9 | -8.3 | -1.5 |
| 56.6 | 62.4 | 71.5 | % Profit Before Taxes/Tangible Net Worth | | 103.1 | 69.1 | 58.5 | 65.3 | 129.6 |
| (156) 27.1 | (162) 20.9 | (178) 32.6 | | (34) 31.9 | (30) 22.8 | (42) 37.2 | (41) 35.2 | (25) 39.1 | |
| 4.3 | 4.0 | 8.5 | | | 1.6 | 7.2 | 11.9 | 8.7 | 17.1 |
| 16.7 | 16.0 | 20.0 | % Profit Before Taxes/Total Assets | 17.7 | 30.1 | 30.3 | 16.1 | 20.0 | 17.3 |
| 5.1 | 5.3 | 7.2 | | 1.3 | 10.0 | 10.4 | 8.5 | 6.4 | 5.3 |
| -2.4 | -.5 | .3 | | -3.0 | -.8 | 2.8 | 1.1 | 1.2 | -2.2 |
| 53.5 | 72.0 | 76.4 | Sales/Net Fixed Assets | UND | 155.4 | 54.3 | 76.9 | 69.9 | 48.1 |
| 22.8 | 25.0 | 27.0 | | 28.5 | 39.5 | 22.0 | 27.1 | 20.6 | 28.5 |
| 10.5 | 12.9 | 13.7 | | .4 | 16.9 | 15.3 | 16.5 | 12.4 | 12.1 |
| 3.8 | 3.5 | 3.8 | Sales/Total Assets | 6.2 | 4.7 | 4.1 | 3.8 | 3.5 | 2.9 |
| 2.5 | 2.5 | 2.5 | | 2.4 | 3.5 | 3.0 | 2.4 | 2.6 | 1.6 |
| 1.6 | 1.5 | 1.5 | | .2 | 1.7 | 1.7 | 1.5 | 1.9 | .8 |
| .8 | .7 | .6 | % Depr., Dep., Amort./Sales | | .6 | .5 | .9 | .5 | .7 |
| (173) 1.6 | (183) 1.5 | (169) 1.4 | | (20) 1.8 | (31) 1.3 | (34) 1.3 | (47) 1.1 | (30) 1.7 | |
| 3.1 | 2.6 | 2.4 | | | 2.7 | 2.2 | 2.3 | 2.2 | 3.8 |
| 3.0 | 2.9 | 2.6 | % Officers', Directors' Owners' Comp/Sales | | 3.1 | 3.7 | 3.1 | 2.3 | |
| (98) 4.6 | (83) 4.6 | (91) 4.4 | | (23) 5.2 | (19) 6.4 | (24) 4.3 | (16) 3.1 | | |
| 10.4 | 8.9 | 7.3 | | | 9.6 | 10.3 | 5.7 | 5.5 | |
| 5177143M | 7124041M | 7685994M | Net Sales ($) | 5971M | 101996M | 170260M | 417378M | 893153M | 6097236M |
| 3036239M | 4266530M | 5277644M | Total Assets ($) | 8255M | 53197M | 77114M | 239197M | 558205M | 4341676M |

© RMA 2012

M = $ thousand    MM = $ million
See Pages 9 through 22 for Explanation of Ratios and Data

## Current Data Sorted by Assets | Comparative Historical Data

| 0-500M | 500M-2MM | 2-10MM | 10-50MM | 50-100MM | 100-250MM | Type of Statement | 4/1/07-3/31/08 ALL | 4/1/08-3/31/09 ALL |
|---|---|---|---|---|---|---|---|---|
| | 1 | 3 | 1 | 1 | | Unqualified | 3 | 2 |
| | 1 | 6 | 3 | | | Reviewed | 11 | 18 |
| 4 | 4 | 5 | 1 | 1 | | Compiled | 20 | 10 |
| 10 | 11 | 1 | 1 | | 1 | Tax Returns | 27 | 24 |
| 10 | 18 | 16 | 3 | | | Other | 18 | 24 |
| | 14 (4/1-9/30/11) | | 87 (10/1/11-3/31/12) | | | | | |
| 24 | 35 | 31 | 9 | 1 | 1 | NUMBER OF STATEMENTS | 79 | 78 |
| % | % | % | % | % | % | ASSETS | % | % |
| 28.6 | 15.8 | 15.9 | | | | Cash & Equivalents | 14.6 | 16.4 |
| 12.1 | 21.6 | 20.4 | | | | Trade Receivables (net) | 20.6 | 19.5 |
| 2.5 | 2.5 | 1.7 | | | | Inventory | 3.6 | 4.6 |
| 2.5 | 1.1 | 4.0 | | | | All Other Current | 6.4 | 3.8 |
| 45.8 | 40.9 | 42.0 | | | | Total Current | 45.2 | 44.4 |
| 30.7 | 36.9 | 31.6 | | | | Fixed Assets (net) | 35.3 | 32.1 |
| 18.2 | 10.7 | 17.1 | | | | Intangibles (net) | 10.6 | 12.5 |
| 5.3 | 11.4 | 9.2 | | | | All Other Non-Current | 9.0 | 11.0 |
| 100.0 | 100.0 | 100.0 | | | | Total | 100.0 | 100.0 |
| | | | | | | LIABILITIES | | |
| 22.6 | 7.0 | 6.9 | | | | Notes Payable-Short Term | 8.6 | 14.4 |
| 6.9 | 5.4 | 4.7 | | | | Cur. Mat.-L.T.D. | 7.7 | 10.6 |
| 6.0 | 8.6 | 8.1 | | | | Trade Payables | 8.9 | 8.9 |
| .0 | .2 | .1 | | | | Income Taxes Payable | .2 | .1 |
| 23.1 | 11.0 | 13.7 | | | | All Other Current | 14.1 | 14.8 |
| 58.6 | 32.2 | 33.5 | | | | Total Current | 39.5 | 48.8 |
| 53.2 | 26.0 | 13.7 | | | | Long-Term Debt | 26.5 | 32.3 |
| .0 | .2 | .1 | | | | Deferred Taxes | .2 | .1 |
| 8.8 | 9.2 | 6.6 | | | | All Other Non-Current | 5.0 | 16.6 |
| -20.5 | 32.4 | 46.1 | | | | Net Worth | 28.8 | 2.2 |
| 100.0 | 100.0 | 100.0 | | | | Total Liabilities & Net Worth | 100.0 | 100.0 |
| | | | | | | INCOME DATA | | |
| 100.0 | 100.0 | 100.0 | | | | Net Sales | 100.0 | 100.0 |
| | | | | | | Gross Profit | | |
| 93.7 | 86.3 | 91.0 | | | | Operating Expenses | 94.2 | 94.2 |
| 6.3 | 13.7 | 9.0 | | | | Operating Profit | 5.8 | 5.8 |
| 1.0 | 4.5 | 1.1 | | | | All Other Expenses (net) | 1.7 | 1.3 |
| 5.3 | 9.2 | 7.8 | | | | Profit Before Taxes | 4.1 | 4.5 |
| | | | | | | RATIOS | | |
| 4.3 | 2.5 | 2.5 | | | | | 2.7 | 2.4 |
| .7 | 1.4 | 1.2 | | | | Current | 1.3 | 1.2 |
| .4 | .7 | .8 | | | | | .8 | .6 |
| 4.2 | 2.5 | 2.0 | | | | | 1.9 | 1.9 |
| .6 | 1.1 | 1.1 | | | | Quick | .9 | .9 |
| .3 | .7 | .7 | | | | | .5 | .5 |
| 0 UND | 1 438.7 | 15 24.9 | | | | | 0 UND | 3 138.2 |
| 0 UND | 17 21.6 | 20 17.9 | | | | Sales/Receivables | 21 17.3 | 20 18.3 |
| 21 17.8 | 31 11.9 | 36 10.2 | | | | | 31 11.7 | 30 12.2 |
| | | | | | | Cost of Sales/Inventory | | |
| | | | | | | Cost of Sales/Payables | | |
| 22.4 | 10.7 | 9.4 | | | | | 11.5 | 11.1 |
| -62.9 | 73.7 | 65.9 | | | | Sales/Working Capital | 40.4 | 82.7 |
| -20.0 | -37.3 | -36.9 | | | | | -32.6 | -18.9 |
| 19.5 | 14.6 | 25.1 | | | | | 26.2 | 8.1 |
| (20) 9.4 | (29) 6.6 | (27) 7.7 | | | | EBIT/Interest | (66) 4.1 | (70) 3.5 |
| 2.1 | .7 | 3.7 | | | | | .9 | 1.5 |
| | | | | | | Net Profit + Depr., Dep., | 19.3 | 17.1 |
| | | | | | | Amort./Cur. Mat. L/T/D | (13) 6.7 | (17) 2.5 |
| | | | | | | | 1.1 | .6 |
| .9 | .3 | .5 | | | | | .5 | .7 |
| -1.3 | 1.2 | 1.2 | | | | Fixed/Worth | 1.3 | 3.1 |
| -.3 | 15.0 | 3.9 | | | | | -4.6 | -1.6 |
| 1.8 | .8 | .5 | | | | | .7 | 1.2 |
| -3.6 | 2.7 | 2.9 | | | | Debt/Worth | 2.6 | 6.6 |
| -1.7 | 20.6 | 25.0 | | | | | -8.6 | -4.3 |
| | 91.8 | 89.7 | | | | % Profit Before Taxes/Tangible | 129.2 | 81.8 |
| | (27) 20.4 | (25) 34.7 | | | | Net Worth | (56) 50.3 | (47) 25.5 |
| | 1.7 | 9.5 | | | | | 17.7 | 10.5 |
| 49.5 | 23.1 | 26.2 | | | | % Profit Before Taxes/Total | 24.4 | 18.7 |
| 28.6 | 6.2 | 10.3 | | | | Assets | 8.6 | 9.1 |
| 4.7 | .3 | 2.1 | | | | | -.3 | 2.4 |
| 56.5 | 46.1 | 32.9 | | | | | 29.7 | 34.4 |
| 25.1 | 14.8 | 16.0 | | | | Sales/Net Fixed Assets | 12.6 | 14.1 |
| 10.5 | 5.3 | 4.4 | | | | | 7.5 | 8.8 |
| 6.6 | 5.8 | 4.3 | | | | | 5.6 | 5.0 |
| 5.1 | 3.7 | 2.6 | | | | Sales/Total Assets | 3.5 | 3.2 |
| 3.0 | 1.9 | 1.5 | | | | | 2.2 | 2.2 |
| | .5 | .8 | | | | | 1.5 | 1.6 |
| | (21) 1.6 | (25) 1.9 | | | | % Depr., Dep., Amort./Sales | (71) 2.5 | (57) 2.9 |
| | 4.5 | 4.3 | | | | | 4.0 | 4.4 |
| 6.2 | 4.1 | 2.6 | | | | % Officers', Directors' | 3.2 | 3.6 |
| (14) 7.9 | (17) 5.6 | (11) 3.7 | | | | Owners' Comp/Sales | (52) 5.5 | (47) 5.4 |
| 16.7 | 9.7 | 8.0 | | | | | 12.5 | 8.6 |
| 30486M | 140743M | 378866M | 706567M | 130902M | 1534731M | Net Sales ($) | 1011716M | 1727773M |
| 5905M | 40105M | 136300M | 286863M | 90582M | 212158M | Total Assets ($) | 364440M | 612459M |

© RMA 2012

M = $ thousand    MM = $ million
See Pages 9 through 22 for Explanation of Ratios and Data

## Comparative Historical Data | Current Data Sorted by Sales

| | | | Type of Statement | | | | | | |
|---|---|---|---|---|---|---|---|---|---|
| 4 | 5 | 6 | Unqualified | | 1 | 1 | 1 | 1 | 2 |
| 9 | 10 | 10 | Reviewed | | 1 | | 1 | 3 | 5 |
| 11 | 9 | 14 | Compiled | | 6 | 4 | 1 | 2 | 1 |
| 25 | 27 | 24 | Tax Returns | 6 | 9 | | 5 | 2 | 2 |
| 43 | 33 | 47 | Other | 9 | 9 | 9 | 7 | 10 | 3 |
| 4/1/09-3/31/10 ALL | 4/1/10-3/31/11 ALL | 4/1/11-3/31/12 ALL | | | 14 (4/1-9/30/11) | | 87 (10/1/11-3/31/12) | | |
| | | | | 0-1MM | 1-3MM | 3-5MM | 5-10MM | 10-25MM | 25MM & OVER |
| 92 | 84 | 101 | **NUMBER OF STATEMENTS** | 15 | 26 | 14 | 15 | 18 | 13 |
| % | % | % | **ASSETS** | % | % | % | % | % | % |
| 16.5 | 20.4 | 19.0 | Cash & Equivalents | 16.5 | 24.3 | 13.4 | 19.1 | 19.3 | 16.7 |
| 17.6 | 17.2 | 18.6 | Trade Receivables (net) | 1.7 | 18.0 | 16.4 | 25.2 | 27.5 | 21.9 |
| 3.6 | 3.9 | 2.7 | Inventory | .7 | 2.7 | .6 | 5.2 | 1.9 | 5.3 |
| 6.2 | 4.8 | 2.8 | All Other Current | 2.9 | 1.5 | .1 | 2.1 | 5.7 | 4.8 |
| 43.8 | 46.2 | 43.1 | Total Current | 21.7 | 46.5 | 30.5 | 51.7 | 54.4 | 48.7 |
| 29.8 | 30.6 | 33.3 | Fixed Assets (net) | 63.8 | 27.1 | 45.9 | 14.2 | 24.0 | 32.2 |
| 16.9 | 14.3 | 14.9 | Intangibles (net) | 11.8 | 15.3 | 8.0 | 25.7 | 14.8 | 12.9 |
| 9.5 | 8.9 | 8.7 | All Other Non-Current | 2.6 | 11.1 | 15.7 | 8.4 | 6.8 | 6.2 |
| 100.0 | 100.0 | 100.0 | Total | 100.0 | 100.0 | 100.0 | 100.0 | 100.0 | 100.0 |
| | | | **LIABILITIES** | | | | | | |
| 9.5 | 14.3 | 10.3 | Notes Payable-Short Term | 11.4 | 17.4 | 4.9 | 5.4 | 12.7 | 3.2 |
| 5.6 | 5.7 | 5.2 | Cur. Mat.-L.T.D. | 3.1 | 7.3 | 4.1 | 7.3 | 4.4 | 3.0 |
| 8.0 | 9.5 | 8.1 | Trade Payables | 3.0 | 6.2 | 6.5 | 10.7 | 9.6 | 14.7 |
| .3 | .1 | .1 | Income Taxes Payable | .0 | .2 | .2 | .0 | .0 | .1 |
| 18.7 | 19.9 | 15.7 | All Other Current | 9.3 | 21.9 | 8.4 | 15.7 | 14.8 | 19.6 |
| 42.1 | 49.6 | 39.4 | Total Current | 26.8 | 53.0 | 24.0 | 39.0 | 41.6 | 40.7 |
| 36.8 | 23.3 | 27.7 | Long-Term Debt | 41.3 | 47.1 | 25.5 | 11.9 | 12.6 | 15.0 |
| .0 | .1 | .1 | Deferred Taxes | .0 | .0 | .0 | .0 | .5 | .0 |
| 4.9 | 6.4 | 11.2 | All Other Non-Current | 5.4 | 8.9 | 4.9 | 13.4 | 8.5 | 30.1 |
| 16.2 | 20.7 | 21.7 | Net Worth | 26.5 | -9.0 | 45.7 | 35.6 | 36.9 | 14.2 |
| 100.0 | 100.0 | 100.0 | Total Liabilities & Net Worth | 100.0 | 100.0 | 100.0 | 100.0 | 100.0 | 100.0 |
| | | | **INCOME DATA** | | | | | | |
| 100.0 | 100.0 | 100.0 | Net Sales | 100.0 | 100.0 | 100.0 | 100.0 | 100.0 | 100.0 |
| | | | Gross Profit | | | | | | |
| 89.9 | 92.9 | 90.1 | Operating Expenses | 73.2 | 92.7 | 91.0 | 94.4 | 94.9 | 92.1 |
| 10.1 | 7.1 | 9.9 | Operating Profit | 26.8 | 7.3 | 9.0 | 5.6 | 5.1 | 7.9 |
| 2.1 | 1.8 | 2.1 | All Other Expenses (net) | 12.0 | 1.3 | -.7 | .4 | .2 | .1 |
| 8.1 | 5.2 | 7.7 | Profit Before Taxes | 14.8 | 6.0 | 9.7 | 5.2 | 4.9 | 7.8 |
| | | | **RATIOS** | | | | | | |
| 2.5 | 2.0 | 2.5 | | 2.5 | 5.3 | 4.0 | 2.1 | 2.7 | 2.9 |
| 1.2 | 1.0 | 1.1 | Current | .7 | .8 | 1.3 | 1.2 | 1.4 | 1.1 |
| .6 | .6 | .6 | | .1 | .5 | .5 | .9 | .9 | .5 |
| 2.2 | 1.8 | 2.3 | | 2.5 | 5.3 | 3.4 | 1.8 | 2.6 | 2.0 |
| 1.0 | .7 | .9 | Quick | .6 | .8 | 1.3 | 1.0 | 1.4 | .9 |
| .5 | .1 | .1 | | .1 | .4 | .5 | .8 | .7 | .5 |
| 0 UND | 3 120.0 | 0 UND | | 0 UND | 0 UND | 0 UND | 8 45.8 | 16 22.6 | 14 27.0 |
| 19 19.7 | 19 19.3 | 17 21.3 | Sales/Receivables | 0 UND | 17 21.9 | 12 30.5 | 21 17.1 | 23 16.1 | 20 18.4 |
| 32 11.6 | 31 11.6 | 28 13.0 | | 0 UND | 28 13.2 | 32 11.3 | 31 11.9 | 36 10.2 | 41 8.9 |
| | | | Cost of Sales/Inventory | | | | | | |
| | | | Cost of Sales/Payables | | | | | | |
| 10.0 | 12.7 | 9.6 | | 8.4 | 6.9 | 11.0 | 13.1 | 9.5 | 7.4 |
| 64.9 | -226.7 | 145.5 | Sales/Working Capital | -36.4 | -88.9 | NM | 92.7 | 50.0 | 41.3 |
| -18.0 | -12.0 | -27.4 | | -1.5 | -22.8 | -33.2 | -112.3 | -76.5 | -22.2 |
| 19.0 | 17.8 | 17.0 | | | 15.5 | 43.3 | 29.9 | 17.0 | 48.4 |
| (78) 5.5 | (74) 4.4 | (84) 7.5 | EBIT/Interest | (23) 6.6 | 9.2 | (14) 5.6 | (15) 6.9 | (10) 13.0 | |
| 1.5 | .6 | 2.4 | | 2.1 | .9 | .6 | 3.0 | 6.2 | |
| 17.6 | 6.6 | 9.4 | | | | | | | |
| (15) 7.6 | (15) 2.5 | (10) 5.3 | Net Profit + Depr., Dep., Amort./Cur. Mat. L/T/D | | | | | | |
| .4 | 1.7 | 1.4 | | | | | | | |
| .4 | .5 | .4 | | 1.4 | .5 | .2 | .2 | .4 | .3 |
| 2.5 | 1.8 | 1.7 | Fixed/Worth | 3.8 | NM | 1.0 | 1.8 | 2.0 | .8 |
| -1.5 | -2.6 | -2.3 | | -1.7 | -.3 | 3.6 | -2.8 | -29.9 | NM |
| 1.0 | 1.0 | .8 | | .9 | .8 | .4 | 1.2 | .8 | .6 |
| 7.5 | 3.6 | 3.3 | Debt/Worth | 2.8 | -33.2 | 1.7 | 4.4 | 3.6 | 2.0 |
| -5.2 | -7.1 | -6.1 | | -3.0 | -1.7 | 3.8 | -9.3 | -106.2 | NM |
| 72.3 | 95.0 | 82.8 | % Profit Before Taxes/Tangible Net Worth | 32.8 | 88.8 | 217.3 | 156.2 | 86.6 | 71.9 |
| (52) 31.4 | (54) 23.2 | (69) 23.4 | | (10) 5.6 | (12) 58.6 | (13) 19.1 | (11) 16.0 | (13) 39.8 | (10) 32.4 |
| 13.9 | .3 | 8.5 | | -8.9 | 15.3 | -3.1 | 7.6 | 7.3 | 17.4 |
| 24.1 | 29.8 | 31.5 | % Profit Before Taxes/Total Assets | 26.8 | 45.7 | 65.3 | 30.5 | 26.2 | 30.6 |
| 12.0 | 9.0 | 10.3 | | 5.2 | 13.0 | 13.5 | 4.1 | 10.3 | 16.5 |
| 2.6 | -.4 | 2.6 | | .0 | 4.8 | -.4 | -.2 | 2.1 | 8.9 |
| 37.9 | 29.8 | 38.9 | Sales/Net Fixed Assets | 19.0 | 65.5 | 77.3 | 50.4 | 36.1 | 22.1 |
| 14.6 | 14.8 | 18.8 | | 3.5 | 28.2 | 9.1 | 28.7 | 22.5 | 12.0 |
| 7.7 | 7.0 | 6.0 | | .1 | 7.0 | 2.9 | 19.1 | 10.8 | 5.7 |
| 4.4 | 4.5 | 5.5 | Sales/Total Assets | 2.9 | 6.4 | 5.7 | 6.6 | 5.6 | 4.1 |
| 2.9 | 3.0 | 3.2 | | 1.1 | 3.9 | 4.4 | 4.0 | 3.7 | 2.8 |
| 1.7 | 1.9 | 1.9 | | .1 | 2.3 | 1.9 | 2.2 | 2.9 | 1.7 |
| 1.5 | 1.5 | .8 | % Depr., Dep., Amort./Sales | | .9 | | .4 | .8 | 1.6 |
| (58) 2.9 | (57) 2.6 | (63) 2.2 | | | (10) 3.1 | | (10) .6 | (14) 1.3 | (11) 2.3 |
| 5.1 | 4.0 | 3.9 | | | 4.3 | | 2.9 | 4.0 | 2.9 |
| 3.1 | 2.8 | 3.8 | % Officers', Directors' Owners' Comp/Sales | | 4.5 | | | | |
| (53) 5.1 | (47) 5.2 | (45) 6.4 | | | (14) 6.7 | | | | |
| 8.4 | 9.3 | 9.3 | | | 8.4 | | | | |
| 1246452M | 1509083M | 2922295M | Net Sales ($) | 5415M | 49233M | 54975M | 105038M | 272434M | 2435200M |
| 523619M | 615979M | 771913M | Total Assets ($) | 12398M | 18813M | 21860M | 38764M | 76506M | 603572M |

M = $ thousand    MM = $ million
See Pages 9 through 22 for Explanation of Ratios and Data

## Current Data Sorted by Assets

## Comparative Historical Data

| | | | | | | | Type of Statement | | |
|---|---|---|---|---|---|---|---|---|---|
| | | 7 | 9 | 9 | 6 | 2 | Unqualified | 34 | 39 |
| | | 14 | 37 | 4 | 1 | 1 | Reviewed | 57 | 50 |
| | 7 | 14 | 11 | | | | Compiled | 34 | 32 |
| | 54 | 45 | 4 | | | 1 | Tax Returns | 60 | 63 |
| | 30 | 43 | 45 | 13 | 2 | 4 | Other | 87 | 105 |
| | | 40 (4/1-9/30/11) | | 323 (10/1/11-3/31/12) | | | | 4/1/07-3/31/08 | 4/1/08-3/31/09 |
| | 0-500M | 500M-2MM | 2-10MM | 10-50MM | 50-100MM | 100-250MM | | ALL | ALL |
| | 91 | 123 | 106 | 26 | 9 | 8 | NUMBER OF STATEMENTS | 272 | 289 |
| | % | % | % | % | % | % | ASSETS | % | % |
| | 18.9 | 14.8 | 12.1 | 9.6 | | | Cash & Equivalents | 13.3 | 14.1 |
| | 27.3 | 32.9 | 44.2 | 46.6 | | | Trade Receivables (net) | 38.6 | 38.8 |
| | 1.4 | 3.5 | 1.9 | .4 | | | Inventory | 3.6 | 2.8 |
| | 3.0 | 5.0 | 4.9 | 3.8 | | | All Other Current | 5.9 | 4.3 |
| | 50.5 | 56.2 | 63.1 | 60.4 | | | Total Current | 61.5 | 60.0 |
| | 25.4 | 26.9 | 20.3 | 14.7 | | | Fixed Assets (net) | 20.3 | 20.8 |
| | 13.4 | 7.3 | 8.7 | 14.6 | | | Intangibles (net) | 8.2 | 9.1 |
| | 10.7 | 9.6 | 8.0 | 10.4 | | | All Other Non-Current | 10.0 | 10.1 |
| | 100.0 | 100.0 | 100.0 | 100.0 | | | Total | 100.0 | 100.0 |
| | | | | | | | LIABILITIES | | |
| | 24.6 | 11.1 | 12.6 | 11.7 | | | Notes Payable-Short Term | 14.7 | 12.8 |
| | 3.8 | 3.1 | 2.3 | 2.3 | | | Cur. Mat.-L.T.D. | 4.6 | 5.2 |
| | 11.8 | 9.4 | 14.3 | 10.7 | | | Trade Payables | 12.0 | 13.7 |
| | .2 | .2 | .4 | .2 | | | Income Taxes Payable | .4 | .2 |
| | 15.0 | 14.7 | 13.6 | 19.0 | | | All Other Current | 16.8 | 18.0 |
| | 55.5 | 38.5 | 43.4 | 44.0 | | | Total Current | 48.5 | 49.9 |
| | 34.9 | 20.7 | 10.0 | 12.3 | | | Long-Term Debt | 18.4 | 22.1 |
| | .0 | .1 | .4 | .3 | | | Deferred Taxes | .4 | .2 |
| | 8.6 | 5.8 | 3.8 | 3.8 | | | All Other Non-Current | 6.2 | 8.5 |
| | .9 | 34.9 | 42.5 | 39.6 | | | Net Worth | 26.5 | 19.2 |
| | 100.0 | 100.0 | 100.0 | 100.0 | | | Total Liabilities & Net Worth | 100.0 | 100.0 |
| | | | | | | | INCOME DATA | | |
| | 100.0 | 100.0 | 100.0 | 100.0 | | | Net Sales | 100.0 | 100.0 |
| | | | | | | | Gross Profit | | |
| | 95.2 | 90.0 | 94.7 | 94.3 | | | Operating Expenses | 93.9 | 94.9 |
| | 4.8 | 10.0 | 5.3 | 5.7 | | | Operating Profit | 6.1 | 5.1 |
| | 1.2 | 2.1 | .4 | .3 | | | All Other Expenses (net) | 1.1 | 1.2 |
| | 3.6 | 7.9 | 4.8 | 5.4 | | | Profit Before Taxes | 5.0 | 3.9 |
| | | | | | | | RATIOS | | |
| | 4.0 | 2.6 | 2.2 | 1.9 | | | | 2.2 | 1.8 |
| | 1.2 | 1.5 | 1.5 | 1.2 | | | Current | 1.4 | 1.3 |
| | .5 | 1.0 | 1.0 | 1.0 | | | | 1.0 | .9 |
| | 4.0 | 2.3 | 1.8 | 1.8 | | | | 1.8 | 1.7 |
| | 1.0 | 1.3 | 1.3 | 1.0 | | | Quick | 1.2 | 1.2 |
| | .4 | .8 | .8 | .8 | | | | .7 | .7 |
| 0 UND | 13 28.1 | 28 13.0 | 32 11.4 | | | | | 17 21.1 | 19 19.7 |
| 13 28.1 | 26 13.8 | 38 9.5 | 45 8.1 | | | Sales/Receivables | 35 10.6 | 32 11.5 |
| 31 11.7 | 40 9.1 | 54 6.8 | 57 6.4 | | | | 51 7.1 | 46 7.9 |
| | | | | | | | Cost of Sales/Inventory | | |
| | | | | | | | Cost of Sales/Payables | | |
| | 22.8 | 10.4 | 8.3 | 10.5 | | | | 11.8 | 14.1 |
| | 104.2 | 27.3 | 20.9 | 47.3 | | | Sales/Working Capital | 29.0 | 35.3 |
| | -23.6 | -795.8 | 554.2 | NM | | | | -208.5 | -137.8 |
| | 32.4 | 41.4 | 30.0 | 51.9 | | | | 16.6 | 15.8 |
| (74) | 10.2 (99) | 9.5 (95) | 6.4 (22) | 9.0 | | | EBIT/Interest | (230) 6.8 (251) | 3.9 |
| | 1.6 | 2.0 | 3.2 | 3.8 | | | | 2.1 | 1.3 |
| | | 6.7 | 7.6 | | | | | 13.4 | 14.0 |
| | (10) | 3.5 (21) | 3.8 | | | | Net Profit + Depr., Dep., Amort./Cur. Mat. L/T/D | (55) 3.6 (56) | 4.6 |
| | | 2.4 | 1.7 | | | | | 1.8 | 1.9 |
| | .3 | .1 | .1 | .2 | | | | .2 | .2 |
| | 1.9 | .8 | .4 | .7 | | | Fixed/Worth | .7 | .7 |
| | -.9 | 4.8 | 1.5 | 5.8 | | | | 3.8 | -19.2 |
| | 1.1 | .8 | .9 | 1.1 | | | | .9 | 1.1 |
| | 21.3 | 2.1 | 1.6 | 3.6 | | | Debt/Worth | 2.4 | 2.8 |
| | -2.8 | 16.0 | 3.7 | 28.8 | | | | 13.1 | -32.4 |
| | 327.6 | 108.3 | 79.0 | 172.1 | | | | 93.0 | 91.5 |
| (52) | 77.2 (103) | 32.1 (97) | 35.6 (23) | 67.4 | | | % Profit Before Taxes/Tangible Net Worth | (215) 43.8 (213) | 38.6 |
| | 24.6 | 14.8 | 10.5 | 39.0 | | | | 15.7 | 13.1 |
| | 61.3 | 35.4 | 23.7 | 34.6 | | | | 28.7 | 26.1 |
| | 26.6 | 12.9 | 11.6 | 12.4 | | | % Profit Before Taxes/Total Assets | 12.8 | 10.8 |
| | 1.5 | 3.0 | 3.6 | 8.1 | | | | 3.2 | 1.4 |
| | 164.5 | 114.0 | 89.3 | 94.7 | | | | 75.8 | 104.5 |
| | 41.3 | 28.1 | 34.8 | 43.8 | | | Sales/Net Fixed Assets | 32.8 | 35.2 |
| | 15.2 | 7.8 | 13.3 | 20.4 | | | | 14.9 | 15.8 |
| | 10.4 | 6.2 | 5.5 | 4.8 | | | | 5.8 | 6.3 |
| | 7.1 | 4.1 | 3.6 | 3.8 | | | Sales/Total Assets | 4.2 | 4.5 |
| | 4.1 | 2.5 | 2.4 | 2.7 | | | | 2.9 | 2.9 |
| | .4 | .4 | .5 | .4 | | | | .5 | .4 |
| (55) | 1.2 (96) | 1.1 (89) | 1.0 (22) | .6 | | | % Depr., Dep., Amort./Sales | (207) 1.0 (215) | .9 |
| | 3.1 | 3.0 | 1.7 | 1.0 | | | | 1.8 | 1.9 |
| | 3.3 | 2.2 | 1.5 | | | | | 2.0 | 2.1 |
| (54) | 5.6 (58) | 5.2 (40) | 2.9 | | | | % Officers', Directors' Owners' Comp/Sales | (112) 3.8 (124) | 4.2 |
| | 9.9 | 8.3 | 5.3 | | | | | 6.5 | 7.1 |
| | 145159M | 677221M | 1900409M | 2216625M | 2010698M | 4193510M | Net Sales ($) | 8843258M | 11348126M |
| | 19471M | 137295M | 476989M | 596243M | 630030M | 952820M | Total Assets ($) | 2364077M | 2906522M |

M = $ thousand    MM = $ million
See Pages 9 through 22 for Explanation of Ratios and Data

## Comparative Historical Data | Current Data Sorted by Sales

| | | | Type of Statement | | | | | | |
|---|---|---|---|---|---|---|---|---|---|
| 36 | 34 | 33 | Unqualified | | 1 | 5 | 6 | 3 | 18 |
| 55 | 55 | 57 | Reviewed | | 2 | 4 | 9 | 23 | 19 |
| 29 | 40 | 32 | Compiled | 4 | 6 | 5 | 9 | 7 | 1 |
| 77 | 56 | 104 | Tax Returns | 32 | 34 | 16 | 14 | 7 | 1 |
| 119 | 126 | 137 | Other | 16 | 32 | 6 | 24 | 29 | 30 |
| 4/1/09-3/31/10 | 4/1/10-3/31/11 | 4/1/11-3/31/12 | | | 40 (4/1-9/30/11) | | 323 (10/1/11-3/31/12) | | |
| ALL | ALL | ALL | | 0-1MM | 1-3MM | 3-5MM | 5-10MM | 10-25MM | 25MM & OVER |
| 316 | 311 | 363 | **NUMBER OF STATEMENTS** | 52 | 75 | 36 | 62 | 69 | 69 |
| % | % | % | **ASSETS** | % | % | % | % | % | % |
| 13.3 | 14.0 | 14.4 | Cash & Equivalents | 12.2 | 17.8 | 15.3 | 14.7 | 14.5 | 11.4 |
| 38.0 | 40.0 | 36.0 | Trade Receivables (net) | 21.4 | 28.2 | 35.8 | 33.4 | 46.9 | 47.1 |
| 3.0 | 2.3 | 2.3 | Inventory | 1.5 | 3.0 | 2.7 | 4.2 | 1.4 | 1.1 |
| 5.0 | 4.3 | 4.3 | All Other Current | 1.4 | 3.5 | 9.5 | 5.4 | 4.6 | 3.6 |
| 59.4 | 60.6 | 57.0 | Total Current | 36.5 | 52.4 | 63.3 | 57.7 | 67.4 | 63.3 |
| 20.2 | 19.1 | 23.1 | Fixed Assets (net) | 36.5 | 27.1 | 24.2 | 25.4 | 14.7 | 14.6 |
| 10.9 | 9.9 | 10.7 | Intangibles (net) | 16.1 | 10.4 | 5.5 | 6.5 | 9.3 | 14.6 |
| 9.5 | 10.4 | 9.2 | All Other Non-Current | 11.0 | 10.1 | 7.1 | 10.3 | 8.6 | 7.5 |
| 100.0 | 100.0 | 100.0 | Total | 100.0 | 100.0 | 100.0 | 100.0 | 100.0 | 100.0 |
| | | | **LIABILITIES** | | | | | | |
| 14.6 | 12.9 | 14.6 | Notes Payable-Short Term | 27.1 | 13.8 | 11.4 | 15.6 | 11.8 | 9.7 |
| 5.9 | 4.9 | 3.1 | Cur. Mat.-L.T.D. | 2.5 | 4.6 | 3.9 | 3.4 | 1.8 | 2.6 |
| 12.7 | 12.8 | 11.7 | Trade Payables | 9.6 | 8.6 | 13.0 | 10.3 | 13.9 | 14.9 |
| .5 | .3 | .3 | Income Taxes Payable | .0 | .3 | .1 | .5 | .3 | .3 |
| 16.2 | 16.9 | 14.8 | All Other Current | 9.9 | 13.5 | 11.5 | 15.0 | 18.0 | 18.6 |
| 49.8 | 47.8 | 44.5 | Total Current | 49.1 | 40.7 | 39.8 | 44.9 | 45.7 | 46.1 |
| 17.8 | 18.1 | 20.5 | Long-Term Debt | 51.7 | 23.2 | 17.7 | 16.3 | 8.6 | 11.1 |
| .3 | .2 | .3 | Deferred Taxes | .0 | .0 | .1 | .4 | .3 | .6 |
| 8.4 | 6.9 | 5.9 | All Other Non-Current | 12.9 | 7.1 | 2.3 | 1.6 | 6.5 | 4.4 |
| 23.7 | 27.0 | 28.9 | Net Worth | -13.8 | 29.0 | 40.1 | 36.8 | 38.9 | 37.8 |
| 100.0 | 100.0 | 100.0 | Total Liabilities & Net Worth | 100.0 | 100.0 | 100.0 | 100.0 | 100.0 | 100.0 |
| | | | **INCOME DATA** | | | | | | |
| 100.0 | 100.0 | 100.0 | Net Sales | 100.0 | 100.0 | 100.0 | 100.0 | 100.0 | 100.0 |
| | | | Gross Profit | | | | | | |
| 95.2 | 94.3 | 93.3 | Operating Expenses | 84.0 | 92.6 | 94.5 | 95.4 | 96.0 | 95.8 |
| 4.8 | 5.7 | 6.7 | Operating Profit | 16.0 | 7.4 | 5.5 | 4.6 | 4.0 | 4.2 |
| .7 | .8 | 1.2 | All Other Expenses (net) | 6.6 | .0 | .4 | .3 | .3 | .6 |
| 4.0 | 4.9 | 5.5 | Profit Before Taxes | 9.4 | 7.3 | 5.0 | 4.2 | 3.8 | 3.6 |
| | | | **RATIOS** | | | | | | |
| 2.0 | 2.3 | 2.5 | | 3.1 | 4.2 | 4.3 | 2.5 | 2.1 | 1.8 |
| 1.2 | 1.4 | 1.4 | Current | 1.0 | 1.8 | 1.6 | 1.3 | 1.5 | 1.3 |
| .9 | 1.0 | .9 | | .3 | .8 | 1.0 | 1.0 | 1.1 | 1.0 |
| 1.8 | 2.1 | 2.2 | | 2.1 | 4.1 | 2.5 | 2.1 | 1.8 | 1.7 |
| 1.1 | 1.2 | 1.2 | Quick | .8 | 1.5 | 1.3 | 1.0 | 1.4 | 1.2 |
| .7 | .8 | .8 | | .3 | .6 | .8 | .7 | 1.0 | .9 |
| 18  20.2 | 20  18.3 | 15  24.4 | | 0  UND | 5  73.9 | 19  19.4 | 15  24.5 | 23  16.2 | 27  13.3 |
| 31  11.7 | 33  11.2 | 31  11.9 | Sales/Receivables | 6  59.3 | 28  13.2 | 27  13.4 | 29  12.4 | 37  9.8 | 41  9.0 |
| 49  7.5 | 53  6.9 | 48  7.6 | | 34  10.6 | 40  9.1 | 45  8.1 | 51  7.1 | 51  7.1 | 56  6.5 |
| | | | Cost of Sales/Inventory | | | | | | |
| | | | Cost of Sales/Payables | | | | | | |
| 13.5 | 11.2 | 10.9 | | 11.0 | 8.0 | 7.9 | 10.8 | 14.0 | 12.7 |
| 42.3 | 32.3 | 33.3 | Sales/Working Capital | UND | 28.9 | 23.5 | 37.0 | 24.1 | 34.5 |
| -67.6 | -163.3 | -90.3 | | -8.4 | -48.2 | NM | -638.9 | 194.2 | 331.0 |
| 22.5 | 27.6 | 32.5 | | 13.0 | 41.8 | 18.4 | 26.6 | 56.3 | 44.1 |
| (282)  7.2 | (270)  6.9 | (307)  8.2 | EBIT/Interest | (35)  2.4 | (64)  13.7 | (30)  10.1 | (58)  6.4 | (59)  13.3 | (61)  8.4 |
| 1.9 | 2.5 | 2.4 | | -1.0 | 2.2 | 1.4 | 3.0 | 4.5 | 3.0 |
| 11.8 | 8.1 | 6.8 | | | | | | 6.3 | 11.0 |
| (51)  3.7 | (47)  3.1 | (42)  3.7 | Net Profit + Depr., Dep., Amort./Cur. Mat. L/T/D | | | | | (14)  4.4 | (13)  4.9 |
| 1.2 | 1.7 | 1.6 | | | | | | 1.8 | 1.4 |
| .2 | .2 | .2 | | .3 | .2 | .1 | .2 | .1 | .2 |
| .8 | .6 | .8 | Fixed/Worth | 5.8 | 1.2 | 1.0 | .7 | .4 | .7 |
| 20.8 | 4.4 | 6.1 | | -.6 | -5.8 | 3.8 | 3.0 | 1.1 | 5.4 |
| 1.2 | .9 | .9 | | 1.2 | .5 | .5 | .8 | 1.0 | 1.1 |
| 3.2 | 2.7 | 2.4 | Debt/Worth | 55.9 | 3.8 | 1.5 | 1.8 | 2.0 | 3.2 |
| -72.2 | 22.9 | 31.6 | | -2.0 | -11.4 | 7.3 | 5.5 | 3.9 | 24.9 |
| 103.7 | 100.0 | 104.5 | | 161.5 | 188.0 | 132.2 | 72.7 | 96.9 | 114.2 |
| (234)  46.0 | (247)  46.4 | (284)  44.2 | % Profit Before Taxes/Tangible Net Worth | (27)  32.3 | (53)  61.3 | (33)  28.3 | (53)  31.6 | (62)  48.6 | (56)  49.9 |
| 10.4 | 15.0 | 18.8 | | 14.1 | 21.4 | -1.9 | 9.9 | 21.9 | 25.2 |
| 28.6 | 29.6 | 34.6 | | 29.7 | 48.6 | 39.6 | 24.9 | 29.5 | 24.5 |
| 11.7 | 13.4 | 13.0 | % Profit Before Taxes/Total Assets | 6.4 | 27.6 | 13.3 | 10.3 | 13.4 | 11.6 |
| 3.5 | 3.8 | 3.3 | | -4.2 | 3.7 | -.4 | 3.1 | 6.0 | 4.2 |
| 90.7 | 91.3 | 102.4 | | 83.1 | 64.8 | 187.2 | 74.6 | 122.9 | 99.1 |
| 38.4 | 36.7 | 33.9 | Sales/Net Fixed Assets | 16.4 | 26.5 | 42.2 | 26.7 | 55.3 | 43.4 |
| 15.5 | 15.9 | 12.1 | | 5.0 | 9.0 | 8.7 | 8.7 | 25.5 | 19.5 |
| 6.8 | 6.4 | 6.7 | | 7.3 | 7.7 | 7.2 | 6.1 | 7.3 | 5.7 |
| 4.6 | 4.2 | 4.2 | Sales/Total Assets | 3.0 | 3.8 | 4.6 | 4.3 | 4.9 | 4.5 |
| 2.8 | 2.8 | 2.6 | | 1.0 | 2.5 | 3.1 | 2.4 | 3.0 | 3.1 |
| .5 | .5 | .4 | | 1.4 | .5 | .4 | .5 | .3 | .4 |
| (218)  .9 | (229)  .9 | (273)  1.0 | % Depr., Dep., Amort./Sales | (32)  3.8 | (49)  1.7 | (28)  .9 | (53)  1.0 | (57)  .6 | (54)  .7 |
| 2.0 | 1.8 | 2.1 | | 9.9 | 3.2 | 2.0 | 1.8 | 1.2 | 1.1 |
| 2.6 | 1.9 | 2.2 | | 4.0 | 3.2 | 2.5 | 1.7 | 1.5 | .8 |
| (137)  5.0 | (125)  4.2 | (159)  4.4 | % Officers', Directors' Owners' Comp/Sales | (25)  7.6 | (41)  7.2 | (21)  5.1 | (28)  4.5 | (27)  2.4 | (17)  1.4 |
| 7.4 | 6.8 | 8.1 | | 12.3 | 10.1 | 6.6 | 6.7 | 3.9 | 5.3 |
| 12577136M | 11203189M | 11143622M | Net Sales ($) | 24578M | 138853M | 134784M | 457388M | 1075185M | 9312834M |
| 3010756M | 3145691M | 2812848M | Total Assets ($) | 18216M | 45874M | 34978M | 128334M | 258370M | 2327076M |

© RMA 2012

M = $ thousand    MM = $ million
See Pages 9 through 22 for Explanation of Ratios and Data

## Current Data Sorted by Assets / Comparative Historical Data

| | | | | | | Type of Statement | | |
|---|---|---|---|---|---|---|---|---|
| 1 | 2 | 10 | 8 | 4 | 1 | Unqualified | 26 | 30 |
| 3 | 20 | 55 | 5 | | | Reviewed | 79 | 80 |
| 16 | 45 | 22 | | | | Compiled | 73 | 71 |
| 135 | 67 | 16 | 2 | 1 | 3 | Tax Returns | 182 | 173 |
| 71 | 80 | 58 | 11 | 3 | 3 | Other | 190 | 162 |
| | 43 (4/1-9/30/11) | | 599 (10/1/11-3/31/12) | | | | 4/1/07-3/31/08 ALL | 4/1/08-3/31/09 ALL |
| 0-500M | 500M-2MM | 2-10MM | 10-50MM | 50-100MM | 100-250MM | | | |
| 226 | 214 | 161 | 26 | 8 | 7 | NUMBER OF STATEMENTS | 550 | 516 |
| % | % | % | % | % | % | ASSETS | % | % |
| 17.0 | 10.7 | 9.4 | 10.3 | | | Cash & Equivalents | 10.1 | 11.2 |
| 18.0 | 25.4 | 32.6 | 30.4 | | | Trade Receivables (net) | 26.7 | 26.1 |
| 4.0 | 5.3 | 7.0 | 2.5 | | | Inventory | 6.4 | 6.5 |
| 5.0 | 3.0 | 5.3 | 5.0 | | | All Other Current | 4.1 | 4.2 |
| 44.0 | 44.3 | 54.4 | 48.3 | | | Total Current | 47.4 | 48.1 |
| 40.4 | 36.8 | 32.7 | 33.1 | | | Fixed Assets (net) | 42.3 | 39.2 |
| 5.9 | 7.2 | 3.9 | 8.8 | | | Intangibles (net) | 3.1 | 4.1 |
| 9.8 | 11.7 | 9.1 | 9.9 | | | All Other Non-Current | 7.2 | 8.6 |
| 100.0 | 100.0 | 100.0 | 100.0 | | | Total | 100.0 | 100.0 |
| | | | | | | LIABILITIES | | |
| 19.4 | 10.7 | 8.9 | 10.8 | | | Notes Payable-Short Term | 12.5 | 14.7 |
| 8.7 | 5.7 | 5.5 | 5.0 | | | Cur. Mat.-L.T.D. | 8.2 | 7.2 |
| 12.2 | 13.2 | 14.2 | 11.5 | | | Trade Payables | 11.7 | 10.7 |
| .2 | .1 | .5 | 1.5 | | | Income Taxes Payable | .3 | .3 |
| 16.0 | 8.1 | 8.6 | 11.4 | | | All Other Current | 10.8 | 10.6 |
| 56.4 | 37.8 | 37.6 | 40.2 | | | Total Current | 43.4 | 43.5 |
| 36.3 | 28.4 | 17.9 | 17.3 | | | Long-Term Debt | 31.6 | 30.9 |
| .0 | .5 | 1.0 | .9 | | | Deferred Taxes | .4 | .3 |
| 9.7 | 4.7 | 3.0 | 1.8 | | | All Other Non-Current | 4.8 | 6.4 |
| -2.5 | 28.7 | 40.5 | 39.8 | | | Net Worth | 19.8 | 18.9 |
| 100.0 | 100.0 | 100.0 | 100.0 | | | Total Liabilties & Net Worth | 100.0 | 100.0 |
| | | | | | | INCOME DATA | | |
| 100.0 | 100.0 | 100.0 | 100.0 | | | Net Sales | 100.0 | 100.0 |
| | | | | | | Gross Profit | | |
| 93.7 | 94.7 | 95.6 | 97.0 | | | Operating Expenses | 94.0 | 94.2 |
| 6.3 | 5.3 | 4.4 | 3.0 | | | Operating Profit | 6.0 | 5.8 |
| 1.3 | 1.0 | 1.2 | .1 | | | All Other Expenses (net) | 1.7 | 1.6 |
| 5.0 | 4.3 | 3.1 | 2.9 | | | Profit Before Taxes | 4.4 | 4.2 |
| | | | | | | RATIOS | | |
| 2.4 | 2.2 | 2.2 | 1.9 | | | | 2.0 | 2.2 |
| 1.0 | 1.2 | 1.4 | 1.5 | | | Current | 1.3 | 1.3 |
| .4 | .6 | 1.1 | .7 | | | | .7 | .8 |
| 2.0 | 1.9 | 1.8 | 1.7 | | | | 1.7 | 1.8 |
| .6 | .9 | 1.1 | 1.1 | | | Quick | .9 (514) | 1.0 |
| .2 | .4 | .8 | .6 | | | | .4 | .4 |
| 0 UND | 12 31.2 | 29 12.7 | 28 13.0 | | | | 7 54.8 | 6 57.4 |
| 10 37.2 | 28 13.2 | 43 8.4 | 38 9.5 | | | Sales/Receivables | 32 11.4 | 30 12.4 |
| 25 14.4 | 46 7.9 | 68 5.4 | 76 4.8 | | | | 55 6.6 | 53 6.9 |
| | | | | | | Cost of Sales/Inventory | | |
| | | | | | | Cost of Sales/Payables | | |
| 18.3 | 10.0 | 7.9 | 7.9 | | | | 10.4 | 10.1 |
| UND | 51.2 | 15.7 | 22.5 | | | Sales/Working Capital | 33.7 | 29.0 |
| -13.4 | -17.8 | 81.8 | -14.7 | | | | -27.3 | -36.9 |
| 14.8 | 10.9 | 12.6 | 17.7 | | | | 9.5 | 9.8 |
| (193) 5.3 | (195) 4.3 | (146) 4.7 | (23) 6.6 | | | EBIT/Interest | (510) 3.4 | (456) 3.2 |
| 1.1 | .8 | 1.5 | 2.4 | | | | 1.2 | 1.0 |
| | 3.0 | 6.8 | | | | | 4.2 | 4.7 |
| | (24) 1.5 | (35) 2.6 | | | | Net Profit + Depr., Dep., Amort./Cur. Mat. L/T/D | (76) 2.2 | (71) 2.2 |
| | .4 | 1.6 | | | | | 1.4 | .6 |
| .5 | .5 | .4 | .3 | | | | .6 | .6 |
| 3.8 | 1.4 | .9 | 1.0 | | | Fixed/Worth | 1.7 | 1.5 |
| -1.6 | -229.0 | 2.0 | 3.3 | | | | 11.2 | 33.0 |
| .8 | .9 | .7 | .7 | | | | 1.1 | 1.1 |
| 15.7 | 2.7 | 1.5 | 1.6 | | | Debt/Worth | 2.9 | 2.8 |
| -3.5 | -23.6 | 4.0 | 10.4 | | | | 32.7 | 64.7 |
| 201.4 | 53.3 | 38.0 | 61.0 | | | | 77.0 | 71.5 |
| (130) 53.8 | (156) 17.3 | (146) 16.5 | (23) 22.7 | | | % Profit Before Taxes/Tangible Net Worth | (436) 34.1 | (397) 27.2 |
| 12.3 | 2.4 | 5.0 | 7.1 | | | | 10.0 | 4.5 |
| 42.6 | 17.9 | 13.3 | 11.5 | | | | 23.5 | 21.0 |
| 15.0 | 5.7 | 6.3 | 8.7 | | | % Profit Before Taxes/Total Assets | 9.3 | 7.6 |
| .4 | -.6 | 1.2 | 3.1 | | | | .7 | .0 |
| 45.2 | 18.5 | 16.0 | 16.3 | | | | 17.0 | 19.6 |
| 15.2 | 9.6 | 7.9 | 7.3 | | | Sales/Net Fixed Assets | 8.9 | 10.5 |
| 6.3 | 5.1 | 4.5 | 3.8 | | | | 4.4 | 4.6 |
| 7.6 | 4.4 | 3.0 | 3.0 | | | | 4.6 | 4.7 |
| 4.7 | 3.0 | 2.3 | 2.2 | | | Sales/Total Assets | 3.0 | 3.0 |
| 2.8 | 2.0 | 1.6 | 1.8 | | | | 2.0 | 2.0 |
| 1.4 | 1.8 | 1.9 | 2.1 | | | | 2.0 | 1.8 |
| (134) 2.9 | (155) 3.4 | (138) 3.2 | (24) 3.4 | | | % Depr., Dep., Amort./Sales | (467) 3.7 | (410) 3.6 |
| 5.7 | 5.5 | 5.2 | 5.0 | | | | 6.1 | 5.3 |
| 4.3 | 2.6 | 1.9 | .7 | | | | 2.7 | 2.5 |
| (121) 7.0 | (130) 4.2 | (64) 3.7 | (10) 1.3 | | | % Officers', Directors' Owners' Comp/Sales | (279) 4.3 | (258) 4.5 |
| 10.3 | 6.3 | 4.8 | 3.7 | | | | 7.3 | 8.4 |
| 271257M | 727610M | 1499638M | 1151954M | 1605471M | 6720802M | Net Sales ($) | 12720660M | 8583123M |
| 50649M | 226175M | 638477M | 462967M | 539739M | 1136966M | Total Assets ($) | 3383236M | 2879797M |

M = $ thousand    MM = $ million
See Pages 9 through 22 for Explanation of Ratios and Data

## Comparative Historical Data / Current Data Sorted by Sales

| | | | Type of Statement | | | | | | |
|---|---|---|---|---|---|---|---|---|---|
| 26 | 27 | 26 | Unqualified | 2 | 2 | 1 | 6 | 3 | 12 |
| 72 | 86 | 83 | Reviewed | 3 | 9 | 13 | 32 | 22 | 4 |
| 76 | 82 | 83 | Compiled | 8 | 31 | 16 | 16 | 12 | |
| 193 | 226 | 224 | Tax Returns | 79 | 85 | 32 | 17 | 5 | 6 |
| 184 | 194 | 226 | Other | 52 | 68 | 33 | 35 | 22 | 16 |
| 4/1/09-3/31/10 ALL | 4/1/10-3/31/11 ALL | 4/1/11-3/31/12 ALL | | 43 (4/1-9/30/11) | | | 599 (10/1/11-3/31/12) | | |
| | | | | 0-1MM | 1-3MM | 3-5MM | 5-10MM | 10-25MM | 25MM & OVER |
| 551 | 615 | 642 | **NUMBER OF STATEMENTS** | 144 | 195 | 95 | 106 | 64 | 38 |
| % | % | % | **ASSETS** | % | % | % | % | % | % |
| 12.6 | 11.6 | 12.6 | Cash & Equivalents | 13.7 | 15.3 | 9.2 | 10.3 | 10.4 | 13.2 |
| 22.8 | 24.5 | 24.8 | Trade Receivables (net) | 13.2 | 22.2 | 25.1 | 33.7 | 40.7 | 29.5 |
| 6.5 | 5.6 | 5.1 | Inventory | 4.4 | 4.5 | 6.8 | 6.5 | 4.8 | 3.1 |
| 3.5 | 4.2 | 4.4 | All Other Current | 4.8 | 2.8 | 5.5 | 4.7 | 6.7 | 3.8 |
| 45.4 | 45.9 | 46.9 | Total Current | 36.1 | 44.8 | 46.6 | 55.2 | 62.7 | 49.7 |
| 41.2 | 39.5 | 37.0 | Fixed Assets (net) | 42.0 | 38.6 | 37.4 | 33.7 | 25.7 | 35.9 |
| 4.4 | 6.0 | 6.0 | Intangibles (net) | 9.8 | 5.7 | 3.7 | 3.9 | 4.0 | 8.3 |
| 9.0 | 8.6 | 10.2 | All Other Non-Current | 12.1 | 10.9 | 12.4 | 7.2 | 7.7 | 6.1 |
| 100.0 | 100.0 | 100.0 | Total | 100.0 | 100.0 | 100.0 | 100.0 | 100.0 | 100.0 |
| | | | **LIABILITIES** | | | | | | |
| 15.2 | 15.5 | 13.3 | Notes Payable-Short Term | 15.5 | 15.6 | 12.3 | 10.1 | 9.8 | 11.0 |
| 6.6 | 6.4 | 6.7 | Cur. Mat.-L.T.D. | 6.7 | 7.7 | 7.0 | 5.4 | 5.5 | 6.0 |
| 10.1 | 10.6 | 12.9 | Trade Payables | 12.5 | 10.2 | 15.3 | 15.9 | 15.4 | 10.2 |
| .2 | .2 | .3 | Income Taxes Payable | .0 | .3 | .3 | .2 | .7 | 1.6 |
| 10.9 | 10.4 | 11.2 | All Other Current | 14.1 | 11.2 | 10.4 | 7.7 | 11.5 | 11.8 |
| 43.0 | 43.0 | 44.5 | Total Current | 48.9 | 44.9 | 45.4 | 39.4 | 42.4 | 40.6 |
| 31.7 | 29.9 | 28.0 | Long-Term Debt | 36.8 | 33.4 | 26.0 | 19.0 | 14.1 | 21.2 |
| .3 | .3 | .5 | Deferred Taxes | .0 | .3 | .8 | 1.0 | .5 | .7 |
| 6.1 | 7.7 | 5.9 | All Other Non-Current | 13.3 | 4.6 | 4.4 | 2.9 | 2.6 | 3.1 |
| 18.8 | 19.1 | 21.1 | Net Worth | 1.1 | 16.7 | 23.6 | 37.8 | 40.4 | 34.4 |
| 100.0 | 100.0 | 100.0 | Total Liabilities & Net Worth | 100.0 | 100.0 | 100.0 | 100.0 | 100.0 | 100.0 |
| | | | **INCOME DATA** | | | | | | |
| 100.0 | 100.0 | 100.0 | Net Sales | 100.0 | 100.0 | 100.0 | 100.0 | 100.0 | 100.0 |
| | | | Gross Profit | | | | | | |
| 95.0 | 94.3 | 94.7 | Operating Expenses | 90.4 | 94.4 | 96.6 | 97.6 | 96.8 | 96.2 |
| 5.0 | 5.7 | 5.3 | Operating Profit | 9.6 | 5.6 | 3.4 | 2.4 | 3.2 | 3.8 |
| 2.0 | 1.8 | 1.1 | All Other Expenses (net) | 3.6 | .7 | .3 | .1 | -.2 | .5 |
| 3.0 | 3.9 | 4.2 | Profit Before Taxes | 6.0 | 4.9 | 3.0 | 2.2 | 3.4 | 3.3 |
| | | | **RATIOS** | | | | | | |
| 2.2 | 2.2 | 2.3 | | 2.3 | 2.6 | 2.3 | 2.1 | 2.1 | 2.4 |
| 1.2 | 1.2 | 1.3 | Current | .8 | 1.2 | 1.2 | 1.4 | 1.4 | 1.5 |
| .7 | .7 | .6 | | .3 | .6 | .6 | .9 | 1.2 | .7 |
| 1.8 | 1.9 | 1.9 | | 1.4 | 2.3 | 1.9 | 1.8 | 1.8 | 2.2 |
| .9 (613) | .9 | 1.0 | Quick | .5 | 1.0 | .8 | 1.1 | 1.2 | 1.1 |
| .4 | .5 | .4 | | .2 | .4 | .4 | .7 | .9 | .6 |
| 6   61.2 | 5   69.2 | 8   44.6 | | 0 UND | 2   159.4 | 13   27.1 | 22   16.3 | 31   11.8 | 27   13.6 |
| 27   13.7 | 28   12.9 | 27   13.3 | Sales/Receivables | 10   35.4 | 21   17.7 | 30   12.0 | 34   10.8 | 43   8.5 | 39   9.4 |
| 50   7.4 | 52   7.1 | 47   7.8 | | 28   13.0 | 42   8.6 | 47   7.7 | 62   5.9 | 66   5.5 | 55   6.6 |
| | | | Cost of Sales/Inventory | | | | | | |
| | | | Cost of Sales/Payables | | | | | | |
| 10.2 | 9.9 | 10.7 | | 19.0 | 12.4 | 8.0 | 9.6 | 9.4 | 8.3 |
| 36.8 | 38.4 | 39.3 | Sales/Working Capital | -46.6 | 52.8 | 51.0 | 23.6 | 16.1 | 22.5 |
| -24.6 | -23.3 | -21.6 | | -7.6 | -16.6 | -18.1 | -197.2 | 51.3 | -19.4 |
| 11.3 | 11.2 | 12.9 | | 13.7 | 11.8 | 12.1 | 10.8 | 16.5 | 25.5 |
| (487) 2.9 | (552) 4.1 | (571) 4.8 | EBIT/Interest | (118) 3.9 | (171) 5.3 | (88) 3.9 | (101) 4.6 | (58) 7.0 | (35) 6.6 |
| .3 | 1.0 | 1.3 | | .8 | 1.5 | 1.0 | 1.5 | 1.6 | 2.7 |
| 4.4 | 5.1 | 6.0 | Net Profit + Depr., Dep., | | | 2.2 | 7.4 | 5.1 | |
| (76) 1.8 | (63) 2.0 | (70) 2.3 | Amort./Cur. Mat. L/T/D | | (15) 1.8 | (22) 3.5 | (14) 2.7 | | |
| .7 | .5 | .7 | | | | .4 | 1.3 | 2.0 | |
| .6 | .5 | .5 | | .5 | .5 | .5 | .4 | .4 | .4 |
| 1.5 | 1.5 | 1.2 | Fixed/Worth | 4.5 | 1.9 | 1.4 | .9 | .7 | 1.3 |
| 172.0 | -14.3 | -69.4 | | -1.7 | -4.4 | -64.5 | 2.0 | 1.2 | 3.8 |
| .8 | .8 | .8 | | .9 | .8 | .9 | .7 | .8 | .8 |
| 2.8 | 3.1 | 2.6 | Debt/Worth | 14.2 | 3.9 | 2.0 | 1.5 | 1.4 | 2.1 |
| -639.0 | -18.0 | -34.7 | | -3.1 | -9.7 | -153.1 | 3.6 | 3.4 | 10.4 |
| 65.7 | 63.0 | 61.9 | % Profit Before Taxes/Tangible | 125.6 | 112.3 | 52.0 | 37.5 | 42.5 | 56.5 |
| (413) 20.9 | (439) 25.3 | (467) 23.0 | Net Worth | (82) 50.0 | (129) 26.1 | (71) 13.5 | (94) 15.2 | (59) 23.3 | (32) 23.6 |
| .0 | 3.0 | 5.5 | | 9.9 | 4.7 | 3.3 | 3.0 | 8.4 | 10.3 |
| 22.4 | 20.4 | 20.6 | % Profit Before Taxes/Total | 29.0 | 27.7 | 14.6 | 13.2 | 17.3 | 14.7 |
| 6.1 | 7.9 | 7.9 | Assets | 10.6 | 9.9 | 5.7 | 5.1 | 9.6 | 9.6 |
| -2.4 | .0 | .6 | | -.7 | 1.2 | -.1 | .9 | 3.0 | 4.2 |
| 18.5 | 20.1 | 23.9 | | 29.6 | 25.7 | 20.5 | 18.0 | 27.5 | 20.9 |
| 8.6 | 9.4 | 10.0 | Sales/Net Fixed Assets | 7.6 | 10.6 | 10.2 | 9.2 | 14.1 | 8.4 |
| 4.3 | 4.3 | 5.1 | | 3.2 | 5.5 | 6.6 | 5.3 | 7.5 | 4.4 |
| 4.3 | 4.4 | 5.0 | | 5.4 | 5.4 | 5.1 | 4.0 | 4.7 | 3.5 |
| 2.8 | 2.7 | 3.0 | Sales/Total Assets | 2.6 | 3.4 | 3.3 | 2.9 | 2.9 | 2.5 |
| 1.9 | 1.8 | 2.0 | | 1.4 | 2.0 | 2.2 | 2.2 | 2.2 | 2.0 |
| 2.1 | 2.0 | 1.7 | | 2.0 | 1.5 | 1.6 | 1.9 | 1.7 | 1.6 |
| (427) 3.9 | (472) 3.7 | (459) 3.3 | % Depr., Dep., Amort./Sales | (92) 4.5 | (125) 3.5 | (78) 2.7 | (85) 2.9 | (50) 2.8 | (29) 3.3 |
| 6.1 | 6.1 | 5.3 | | 9.8 | 5.4 | 4.5 | 5.1 | 3.8 | 4.9 |
| 2.6 | 2.8 | 2.7 | % Officers', Directors' | 4.9 | 3.5 | 3.0 | 1.6 | 2.1 | .8 |
| (285) 5.3 | (329) 5.4 | (330) 4.7 | Owners' Comp/Sales | (66) 9.1 | (109) 4.9 | (60) 4.7 | (55) 2.9 | (25) 3.7 | (15) 3.6 |
| 8.8 | 9.3 | 8.2 | | 14.0 | 7.9 | 6.6 | 4.7 | 4.7 | 8.8 |
| 8577746M | 10050545M | 11976732M | Net Sales ($) | 70783M | 365624M | 382617M | 762572M | 932417M | 9462719M |
| 3099988M | 3258990M | 3054973M | Total Assets ($) | 41988M | 158675M | 145882M | 286809M | 334854M | 2086765M |

M = $ thousand    MM = $ million
See Pages 9 through 22 for Explanation of Ratios and Data

## Current Data Sorted by Assets / Comparative Historical Data

For current-data columns 10-50MM, 50-100MM and 100-250MM, the ratio data is marked **DATA NOT AVAILABLE**.

| Type of Statement | 0-500M | 500M-2MM | 2-10MM | 10-50MM | 50-100MM | 100-250MM | | 4/1/07-3/31/08 ALL | 4/1/08-3/31/09 ALL |
|---|---|---|---|---|---|---|---|---|---|
| Unqualified | | | | 2 | 2 | | | 3 | 4 |
| Reviewed | 1 | 1 | 4 | | | | | 4 | 4 |
| Compiled | 3 | 3 | 1 | | | | | 3 | 9 |
| Tax Returns | 13 | 8 | 2 | 1 | 1 | | | 12 | 26 |
| Other | 11 | 11 | 5 | | | | | 19 | 20 |
| | | 5 (4/1-9/30/11) | | 64 (10/1/11-3/31/12) | | | | | |
| **NUMBER OF STATEMENTS** | 28 | 23 | 12 | 3 | 3 | | | 41 | 63 |
| | % | % | % | % | % | % | | % | % |

### ASSETS

| Assets | 0-500M | 500M-2MM | 2-10MM | | | 4/1/07-3/31/08 | 4/1/08-3/31/09 |
|---|---|---|---|---|---|---|---|
| Cash & Equivalents | 24.8 | 11.0 | 12.0 | | | 13.2 | 15.1 |
| Trade Receivables (net) | 17.2 | 25.8 | 26.0 | | | 22.9 | 23.6 |
| Inventory | 4.4 | 3.9 | 5.8 | | | 1.8 | 3.5 |
| All Other Current | 3.7 | 2.2 | 1.9 | | | 1.5 | 3.5 |
| Total Current | 50.1 | 42.9 | 45.7 | | | 39.4 | 45.7 |
| Fixed Assets (net) | 39.8 | 38.8 | 42.4 | | | 37.4 | 34.0 |
| Intangibles (net) | 4.3 | 4.9 | 2.1 | | | 13.0 | 11.2 |
| All Other Non-Current | 5.8 | 13.4 | 9.8 | | | 10.2 | 9.2 |
| Total | 100.0 | 100.0 | 100.0 | | | 100.0 | 100.0 |

### LIABILITIES

| Liabilities | 0-500M | 500M-2MM | 2-10MM | | | 4/1/07-3/31/08 | 4/1/08-3/31/09 |
|---|---|---|---|---|---|---|---|
| Notes Payable-Short Term | 15.8 | 11.0 | 9.9 | | | 20.1 | 18.7 |
| Cur. Mat.-L.T.D. | 5.6 | 4.6 | 15.2 | | | 6.7 | 5.8 |
| Trade Payables | 8.5 | 9.3 | 13.6 | | | 9.2 | 8.5 |
| Income Taxes Payable | .0 | .3 | .1 | | | .1 | .1 |
| All Other Current | 16.9 | 3.9 | 9.2 | | | 6.4 | 10.5 |
| Total Current | 46.7 | 29.1 | 47.9 | | | 42.5 | 43.7 |
| Long-Term Debt | 53.2 | 32.0 | 17.8 | | | 38.5 | 31.5 |
| Deferred Taxes | .0 | .8 | .4 | | | .0 | .0 |
| All Other Non-Current | 17.4 | 2.9 | 10.7 | | | 4.4 | 4.4 |
| Net Worth | -17.4 | 35.2 | 23.1 | | | 14.6 | 20.4 |
| Total Liabilities & Net Worth | 100.0 | 100.0 | 100.0 | | | 100.0 | 100.0 |

### INCOME DATA

| Income Data | 0-500M | 500M-2MM | 2-10MM | | | 4/1/07-3/31/08 | 4/1/08-3/31/09 |
|---|---|---|---|---|---|---|---|
| Net Sales | 100.0 | 100.0 | 100.0 | | | 100.0 | 100.0 |
| Gross Profit | | | | | | | |
| Operating Expenses | 93.2 | 93.0 | 89.2 | | | 93.7 | 90.9 |
| Operating Profit | 6.8 | 7.0 | 10.8 | | | 6.3 | 9.1 |
| All Other Expenses (net) | 1.0 | 2.2 | 1.2 | | | 1.5 | 1.9 |
| Profit Before Taxes | 5.8 | 4.8 | 9.6 | | | 4.8 | 7.2 |

### RATIOS

| Ratio | 0-500M | 500M-2MM | 2-10MM | | | 4/1/07-3/31/08 | 4/1/08-3/31/09 |
|---|---|---|---|---|---|---|---|
| Current | 2.5 | 2.8 | 1.8 | | | 2.6 | 3.0 |
| | 1.1 | 1.6 | 1.0 | | | 1.0 | 1.4 |
| | .7 | .7 | .7 | | | .5 | .6 |
| Quick | 2.3 | 2.5 | 1.8 | | | 1.9 | 2.7 |
| | (27) 1.1 | 1.0 | .9 | | | 1.0 | 1.1 |
| | .7 | .6 | .5 | | | .3 | .5 |
| Sales/Receivables | 0 UND | 5 71.1 | 6 58.8 | | | 1 543.3 | 2 201.4 |
| | 5 70.9 | 32 11.3 | 27 13.5 | | | 15 24.5 | 17 21.4 |
| | 25 14.4 | 51 7.1 | 69 5.3 | | | 51 7.2 | 38 9.5 |
| Cost of Sales/Inventory | | | | | | | |
| Cost of Sales/Payables | | | | | | | |
| Sales/Working Capital | 10.3 | 10.0 | 13.0 | | | 11.6 | 9.6 |
| | 331.1 | 22.1 | 459.0 | | | UND | 36.9 |
| | -63.9 | -16.3 | -16.7 | | | -14.3 | -19.0 |
| EBIT/Interest | 9.6 | 45.5 | 117.6 | | | 8.1 | 17.9 |
| | (24) 5.1 | (20) 2.6 | (11) 6.6 | | | (38) 4.0 | (58) 6.3 |
| | -.1 | 1.4 | 3.5 | | | 1.2 | 2.8 |
| Net Profit + Depr., Dep., Amort./Cur. Mat. L/T/D | | | | | | | |
| Fixed/Worth | .6 | .3 | .4 | | | .6 | .3 |
| | -2.5 | 1.0 | 1.3 | | | 2.2 | 1.0 |
| | -.6 | 9.3 | 4.1 | | | -2.1 | -2.4 |
| Debt/Worth | .9 | .5 | .4 | | | 1.4 | .6 |
| | -6.0 | 1.9 | 2.8 | | | 14.2 | 2.9 |
| | -2.0 | 12.0 | 5.8 | | | -4.8 | -7.6 |
| % Profit Before Taxes/Tangible Net Worth | 103.9 | 70.6 | 50.6 | | | 68.1 | 100.8 |
| | (13) 67.4 | (19) 34.6 | (11) 37.6 | | | (22) 33.6 | (43) 54.2 |
| | 12.7 | 3.0 | 26.4 | | | 6.6 | 21.8 |
| % Profit Before Taxes/Total Assets | 55.8 | 32.4 | 21.9 | | | 24.9 | 46.5 |
| | 18.2 | 4.3 | 10.7 | | | 9.8 | 19.2 |
| | -5.7 | 1.2 | 5.9 | | | .9 | 5.9 |
| Sales/Net Fixed Assets | 34.4 | 25.1 | 11.6 | | | 19.5 | 36.7 |
| | 15.1 | 9.9 | 7.1 | | | 10.3 | 13.6 |
| | 8.9 | 3.3 | 3.9 | | | 6.3 | 7.7 |
| Sales/Total Assets | 7.0 | 3.7 | 3.3 | | | 4.8 | 5.5 |
| | 5.5 | 3.1 | 2.9 | | | 3.3 | 3.7 |
| | 3.6 | 1.3 | 1.6 | | | 2.0 | 2.4 |
| % Depr., Dep., Amort./Sales | 1.0 | 1.8 | 1.6 | | | 1.6 | 1.6 |
| | (15) 2.2 | (16) 2.6 | 2.9 | | | (30) 2.5 | (44) 2.9 |
| | 3.7 | 3.9 | 4.7 | | | 4.2 | 4.6 |
| % Officers', Directors' Owners' Comp/Sales | 3.2 | 2.8 | | | | 2.3 | 3.2 |
| | (17) 6.4 | (10) 7.6 | | | | (17) 7.3 | (32) 6.6 |
| | 11.1 | 12.3 | | | | 10.4 | 9.5 |

| | 0-500M | 500M-2MM | 2-10MM | 10-50MM | 50-100MM | | 4/1/07-3/31/08 | 4/1/08-3/31/09 |
|---|---|---|---|---|---|---|---|---|
| Net Sales ($) | 37364M | 70446M | 120400M | 215801M | 678024M | | 182068M | 452793M |
| Total Assets ($) | 6744M | 23254M | 49674M | 72201M | 221185M | | 70672M | 161748M |

M = $ thousand   MM = $ million
See Pages 9 through 22 for Explanation of Ratios and Data

## Comparative Historical Data      Current Data Sorted by Sales

| | 2<br>7<br>9<br>28<br>24<br>4/1/09-<br>3/31/10<br>ALL | 2<br>2<br>8<br>18<br>30<br>4/1/10-<br>3/31/11<br>ALL | 5<br>5<br>7<br>24<br>28<br>4/1/11-<br>3/31/12<br>ALL | Type of Statement<br>Unqualified<br>Reviewed<br>Compiled<br>Tax Returns<br>Other | 1<br>11<br>6<br>5 (4/1-9/30/11)<br>**0-1MM** | 3<br>7<br>13<br>**1-3MM** | 2<br>1<br>2<br>**3-5MM** | 1<br>3<br>1<br>4<br>4<br>64 (10/1/11-3/31/12)<br>**5-10MM** | 2<br>3<br>**10-25MM** | 4<br>1<br>**25MM & OVER** |
|---|---|---|---|---|---|---|---|---|---|---|
| NUMBER OF STATEMENTS | 70 | 60 | 69 | | 18 | 23 | 6 | 12 | 5 | 5 |
| | % | % | % | **ASSETS** | % | % | % | % | % | % |
| Cash & Equivalents | 16.0 | 14.4 | 16.5 | | 21.4 | 17.4 | | 10.8 | | |
| Trade Receivables (net) | 25.1 | 26.5 | 22.5 | | 12.6 | 23.8 | | 30.8 | | |
| Inventory | 4.6 | 2.6 | 5.2 | | 3.6 | 3.3 | | 3.7 | | |
| All Other Current | 3.8 | 2.2 | 3.5 | | 3.9 | 1.6 | | 2.2 | | |
| Total Current | 49.5 | 45.7 | 47.7 | | 41.4 | 46.2 | | 47.7 | | |
| Fixed Assets (net) | 28.0 | 30.6 | 38.5 | | 41.1 | 40.9 | | 37.9 | | |
| Intangibles (net) | 11.9 | 10.7 | 4.2 | | 2.7 | 7.0 | | 2.3 | | |
| All Other Non-Current | 10.6 | 13.0 | 9.6 | | 14.9 | 5.9 | | 12.2 | | |
| Total | 100.0 | 100.0 | 100.0 | | 100.0 | 100.0 | | 100.0 | | |
| | | | | **LIABILITIES** | | | | | | |
| Notes Payable-Short Term | 22.6 | 9.8 | 12.1 | | 12.1 | 15.4 | | 14.0 | | |
| Cur. Mat.-L.T.D. | 4.6 | 4.0 | 8.0 | | 5.0 | 6.1 | | 5.9 | | |
| Trade Payables | 9.0 | 8.0 | 9.8 | | 4.7 | 10.4 | | 14.8 | | |
| Income Taxes Payable | .0 | .2 | .1 | | .2 | .1 | | .1 | | |
| All Other Current | 10.3 | 8.9 | 11.1 | | 6.6 | 10.2 | | 8.1 | | |
| Total Current | 46.5 | 31.0 | 41.1 | | 28.5 | 42.2 | | 42.9 | | |
| Long-Term Debt | 31.7 | 24.8 | 36.2 | | 58.9 | 43.9 | | 15.6 | | |
| Deferred Taxes | .1 | .0 | .3 | | .3 | .0 | | .4 | | |
| All Other Non-Current | 6.2 | 9.1 | 10.3 | | 13.5 | 12.3 | | 2.3 | | |
| Net Worth | 15.5 | 35.0 | 12.1 | | -1.2 | 1.6 | | 38.7 | | |
| Total Liabilties & Net Worth | 100.0 | 100.0 | 100.0 | | 100.0 | 100.0 | | 100.0 | | |
| | | | | **INCOME DATA** | | | | | | |
| Net Sales | 100.0 | 100.0 | 100.0 | | 100.0 | 100.0 | | 100.0 | | |
| Gross Profit | | | | | | | | | | |
| Operating Expenses | 94.3 | 92.5 | 92.7 | | 83.7 | 94.5 | | 96.4 | | |
| Operating Profit | 5.7 | 7.5 | 7.3 | | 16.3 | 5.5 | | 3.6 | | |
| All Other Expenses (net) | 1.0 | .9 | 1.3 | | 4.7 | .9 | | -1.4 | | |
| Profit Before Taxes | 4.7 | 6.6 | 5.9 | | 11.6 | 4.7 | | 5.0 | | |
| | | | | **RATIOS** | | | | | | |
| Current | 3.2<br>1.5<br>.7 | 4.9<br>1.7<br>.8 | 2.4<br>1.2<br>.8 | | 2.8<br>1.0<br>.7 | 2.5<br>1.3<br>.8 | | 1.8<br>1.1<br>.7 | | |
| Quick | 2.9<br>(69) 1.2<br>.6 | 4.1<br>1.6<br>.7 | 2.3<br>(68) 1.0<br>.6 | | 2.2<br>(17) .9<br>.6 | 2.5<br>1.1<br>.8 | | 1.8<br>.9<br>.6 | | |
| Sales/Receivables | 3 118.2<br>24 15.0<br>48 7.6 | 3 125.1<br>30 12.1<br>57 6.4 | 2 177.0<br>21 17.7<br>46 8.0 | | 0 UND<br>6 59.3<br>28 13.1 | 0 UND<br>29 12.7<br>43 8.4 | | 6 65.1<br>33 11.0<br>69 5.3 | | |
| Cost of Sales/Inventory | | | | | | | | | | |
| Cost of Sales/Payables | | | | | | | | | | |
| Sales/Working Capital | 9.1<br>25.0<br>-21.5 | 8.4<br>19.3<br>-104.3 | 10.0<br>35.3<br>-40.0 | | 10.1<br>NM<br>-35.3 | 10.4<br>32.4<br>-37.0 | | 22.2<br>208.8<br>-18.0 | | |
| EBIT/Interest | 19.6<br>(66) 4.6<br>1.1 | 31.0<br>(54) 8.8<br>1.6 | 21.6<br>(60) 5.1<br>1.4 | | 6.4<br>(14) 5.1<br>1.6 | 23.2<br>(21) 2.2<br>-2.1 | | 42.7<br>4.9<br>3.1 | | |
| Net Profit + Depr., Dep., Amort./Cur. Mat. L/T/D | | | 5.5<br>(10) 2.2<br>1.3 | | | | | | | |
| Fixed/Worth | .3<br>.9<br>-1.6 | .3<br>.8<br>-12.7 | .4<br>1.5<br>-2.5 | | .2<br>2.7<br>-1.5 | .8<br>2.4<br>-.5 | | .4<br>.8<br>4.1 | | |
| Debt/Worth | .8<br>1.6<br>-4.6 | .7<br>1.6<br>-33.9 | .8<br>2.3<br>-6.9 | | 1.1<br>4.9<br>-2.8 | .9<br>2.6<br>-2.9 | | .6<br>2.8<br>5.8 | | |
| % Profit Before Taxes/Tangible Net Worth | 111.4<br>(49) 30.8<br>8.4 | 91.7<br>(44) 36.2<br>3.3 | 75.3<br>(48) 39.9<br>5.3 | | 101.9<br>(12) 47.1<br>23.0 | 90.9<br>(12) 65.9<br>-18.6 | | 102.8<br>44.7<br>23.1 | | |
| % Profit Before Taxes/Total Assets | 27.1<br>9.3<br>-1.2 | 42.3<br>11.4<br>2.3 | 32.7<br>10.9<br>1.1 | | 60.9<br>18.2<br>3.5 | 43.5<br>4.3<br>-8.4 | | 23.0<br>14.5<br>4.7 | | |
| Sales/Net Fixed Assets | 56.6<br>16.7<br>8.2 | 43.3<br>13.3<br>7.1 | 26.6<br>11.9<br>6.1 | | 36.5<br>11.5<br>4.8 | 20.4<br>12.8<br>5.4 | | 23.3<br>7.6<br>4.9 | | |
| Sales/Total Assets | 5.5<br>3.5<br>2.3 | 4.7<br>3.3<br>2.3 | 5.3<br>3.4<br>2.5 | | 6.0<br>4.2<br>1.0 | 5.6<br>3.4<br>2.6 | | 5.1<br>3.3<br>1.9 | | |
| % Depr., Dep., Amort./Sales | .9<br>(38) 2.6<br>5.2 | 1.5<br>(36) 2.9<br>4.5 | 1.5<br>(48) 2.6<br>3.7 | | | (14) 2.6<br>3.9 | | 1.3<br>(10) 2.5<br>4.9 | | |
| % Officers', Directors' Owners' Comp/Sales | 3.1<br>(46) 6.4<br>9.4 | 2.0<br>(30) 5.4<br>10.0 | 3.1<br>(34) 6.3<br>10.3 | | 3.3<br>(10) 5.5<br>8.1 | | | | | |
| Net Sales ($) | 260805M | 554482M | 1122035M | | 11166M | 42783M | 21378M | 85384M | 80035M | 881289M |
| Total Assets ($) | 103130M | 231950M | 373058M | | 7968M | 13713M | 4701M | 32050M | 31765M | 282861M |

© RMA 2012     M = $ thousand    MM = $ million

See Pages 9 through 22 for Explanation of Ratios and Data

## Current Data Sorted by Assets

## Comparative Historical Data

| | | | | | | Type of Statement | | |
|---|---|---|---|---|---|---|---|---|
| 1 | 1 | 1 | 6 | 1 | | Unqualified | 5 | 7 |
| | 5 | 18 | 5 | | | Reviewed | 16 | 19 |
| 1 | 9 | 3 | | | | Compiled | 18 | 20 |
| 22 | 24 | 8 | | | | Tax Returns | 41 | 43 |
| 12 | 26 | 17 | 3 | | 1 | Other | 28 | 49 |
| | 12 (4/1-9/30/11) | | 152 (10/1/11-3/31/12) | | | | 4/1/07-3/31/08 | 4/1/08-3/31/09 |
| 0-500M | 500M-2MM | 2-10MM | 10-50MM | 50-100MM | 100-250MM | | ALL | ALL |
| 36 | 65 | 47 | 14 | 1 | 1 | **NUMBER OF STATEMENTS** | 108 | 138 |
| % | % | % | % | % | % | **ASSETS** | % | % |
| 26.6 | 13.1 | 16.4 | 8.1 | | | Cash & Equivalents | 16.2 | 13.0 |
| 22.3 | 32.3 | 37.2 | 32.7 | | | Trade Receivables (net) | 32.2 | 32.0 |
| 9.4 | 8.8 | 8.1 | 7.6 | | | Inventory | 5.8 | 5.7 |
| 1.1 | 2.5 | 5.9 | 4.8 | | | All Other Current | 5.7 | 4.9 |
| 59.3 | 56.7 | 67.5 | 53.2 | | | Total Current | 60.0 | 55.7 |
| 21.8 | 26.5 | 20.1 | 23.6 | | | Fixed Assets (net) | 29.6 | 31.0 |
| 5.9 | 6.0 | 2.9 | 12.8 | | | Intangibles (net) | 3.3 | 3.8 |
| 13.1 | 10.8 | 9.5 | 10.5 | | | All Other Non-Current | 7.2 | 9.5 |
| 100.0 | 100.0 | 100.0 | 100.0 | | | Total | 100.0 | 100.0 |
| | | | | | | **LIABILITIES** | | |
| 8.6 | 10.9 | 7.0 | 10.2 | | | Notes Payable-Short Term | 17.5 | 13.7 |
| 2.5 | 2.3 | 3.4 | 1.9 | | | Cur. Mat.-L.T.D. | 4.8 | 5.5 |
| 12.1 | 13.4 | 15.7 | 11.5 | | | Trade Payables | 11.6 | 11.9 |
| .0 | .5 | .4 | .0 | | | Income Taxes Payable | .1 | .1 |
| 27.9 | 9.5 | 11.6 | 19.4 | | | All Other Current | 16.4 | 12.6 |
| 51.2 | 36.5 | 37.9 | 42.9 | | | Total Current | 50.4 | 43.8 |
| 39.2 | 27.2 | 15.0 | 13.4 | | | Long-Term Debt | 21.1 | 22.0 |
| .0 | .0 | .3 | 2.2 | | | Deferred Taxes | .2 | .1 |
| 24.7 | 8.6 | 3.4 | 8.4 | | | All Other Non-Current | 6.7 | 4.8 |
| -15.1 | 27.6 | 43.3 | 33.1 | | | Net Worth | 21.6 | 29.3 |
| 100.0 | 100.0 | 100.0 | 100.0 | | | Total Liabilities & Net Worth | 100.0 | 100.0 |
| | | | | | | **INCOME DATA** | | |
| 100.0 | 100.0 | 100.0 | 100.0 | | | Net Sales | 100.0 | 100.0 |
| | | | | | | Gross Profit | | |
| 91.1 | 91.4 | 94.4 | 93.2 | | | Operating Expenses | 92.9 | 91.8 |
| 8.9 | 8.6 | 5.6 | 6.8 | | | Operating Profit | 7.1 | 8.2 |
| 1.6 | .6 | 1.5 | 1.3 | | | All Other Expenses (net) | 2.3 | 2.4 |
| 7.2 | 8.0 | 4.1 | 5.5 | | | Profit Before Taxes | 4.8 | 5.8 |
| | | | | | | **RATIOS** | | |
| 4.1 | 3.3 | 2.9 | 1.9 | | | | 2.4 | 2.3 |
| 1.6 | 1.6 | 1.8 | 1.3 | | | Current | 1.4 | 1.4 |
| .8 | 1.0 | 1.3 | 1.0 | | | | .8 | .8 |
| 3.5 | 2.4 | 2.6 | 1.6 | | | | 1.9 | 2.0 |
| 1.6 | 1.4 | 1.4 | .9 | | | Quick | 1.0 | 1.0 |
| .5 | .7 | .9 | .7 | | | | .5 | .5 |
| 0 UND | 11 34.0 | 26 13.8 | 28 13.1 | | | | 8 47.4 | 9 41.0 |
| 2 185.3 | 30 12.0 | 45 8.1 | 59 6.2 | | | Sales/Receivables | 37 9.9 | 34 10.7 |
| 46 8.0 | 49 7.5 | 73 5.0 | 83 4.4 | | | | 54 6.7 | 61 5.9 |
| | | | | | | Cost of Sales/Inventory | | |
| | | | | | | Cost of Sales/Payables | | |
| 9.8 | 9.3 | 5.5 | 8.2 | | | | 7.7 | 7.7 |
| 26.7 | 16.2 | 9.2 | 15.4 | | | Sales/Working Capital | 27.4 | 23.0 |
| -111.9 | NM | 22.9 | -192.5 | | | | -41.6 | -26.3 |
| 42.5 | 27.7 | 22.8 | 27.3 | | | | 15.9 | 19.8 |
| (27) 11.0 | (56) 6.9 | (42) 7.4 | 8.8 | | | EBIT/Interest | (93) 5.5 | (119) 5.6 |
| 1.3 | 2.9 | 1.3 | 3.4 | | | | 1.7 | 1.6 |
| | | 19.5 | | | | | 6.0 | 13.2 |
| | | (10) 7.7 | | | | Net Profit + Depr., Dep., | (14) 3.1 | (20) 2.5 |
| | | 2.5 | | | | Amort./Cur. Mat. L/T/D | .5 | .8 |
| .1 | .1 | .1 | .4 | | | | .3 | .3 |
| .5 | .9 | .4 | .8 | | | Fixed/Worth | .7 | 1.0 |
| -.6 | NM | .8 | 6.9 | | | | 2.8 | 6.6 |
| .4 | 1.0 | .7 | .7 | | | | .7 | .8 |
| 4.2 | 2.0 | 1.3 | 3.4 | | | Debt/Worth | 1.9 | 2.5 |
| -2.6 | NM | 3.0 | 11.3 | | | | 9.4 | 33.5 |
| 118.0 | 118.5 | 53.7 | 78.8 | | | | 71.2 | 83.3 |
| (21) 62.0 | (49) 54.0 | (44) 18.7 | (12) 44.7 | | | % Profit Before Taxes/Tangible Net Worth | (85) 35.1 | (106) 32.1 |
| 22.4 | 14.0 | 1.5 | 23.9 | | | | 11.2 | 10.6 |
| 61.2 | 34.1 | 21.8 | 17.1 | | | | 30.3 | 25.3 |
| 28.6 | 12.8 | 5.4 | 9.2 | | | % Profit Before Taxes/Total Assets | 13.1 | 12.8 |
| 6.2 | 3.0 | .4 | 6.8 | | | | 2.0 | 1.6 |
| 198.9 | 91.4 | 73.8 | 33.6 | | | | 49.6 | 45.5 |
| 48.9 | 24.6 | 23.3 | 10.7 | | | Sales/Net Fixed Assets | 15.1 | 17.0 |
| 14.7 | 7.3 | 8.1 | 3.5 | | | | 6.7 | 6.1 |
| 9.3 | 4.4 | 3.6 | 3.0 | | | | 5.4 | 5.1 |
| 5.4 | 3.2 | 2.4 | 1.6 | | | Sales/Total Assets | 3.3 | 3.1 |
| 3.6 | 2.3 | 1.7 | 1.1 | | | | 2.1 | 1.9 |
| .8 | .4 | .8 | 1.0 | | | | .9 | 1.0 |
| (18) 2.2 | (39) 1.2 | (37) 1.3 | (13) 2.3 | | | % Depr., Dep., Amort./Sales | (79) 2.2 | (103) 2.3 |
| 3.3 | 3.1 | 2.3 | 3.4 | | | | 5.3 | 5.2 |
| 4.6 | 3.6 | 1.2 | | | | | 2.8 | 2.3 |
| (17) 6.2 | (40) 5.4 | (16) 2.0 | | | | % Officers', Directors' Owners' Comp/Sales | (67) 6.1 | (66) 4.7 |
| 11.2 | 9.2 | 6.0 | | | | | 10.9 | 10.2 |
| 54049M | 271229M | 619203M | 620283M | 349835M | 152846M | Net Sales ($) | 1473264M | 1859301M |
| 9047M | 73798M | 212095M | 278713M | 89071M | 109734M | Total Assets ($) | 467105M | 708136M |

© RMA 2012

M = $ thousand    MM = $ million
See Pages 9 through 22 for Explanation of Ratios and Data

## Comparative Historical Data | Current Data Sorted by Sales

| 9 / 28 / 16 / 38 / 43 | 7 / 29 / 10 / 50 / 39 | 10 / 28 / 13 / 54 / 59 | Type of Statement | 0-1MM | 1-3MM | 3-5MM | 5-10MM | 10-25MM | 25MM & OVER |
|---|---|---|---|---|---|---|---|---|---|
| | | | Unqualified | 1 | | 1 | | 3 | 5 |
| | | | Reviewed | | 2 | 3 | 8 | 11 | 4 |
| | | | Compiled | 1 | 2 | 5 | 2 | 3 | |
| | | | Tax Returns | 13 | 17 | 11 | 9 | 4 | |
| | | | Other | 6 | 20 | 10 | 8 | 8 | 6 |
| 4/1/09-3/31/10 ALL | 4/1/10-3/31/11 ALL | 4/1/11-3/31/12 ALL | | 12 (4/1-9/30/11) | | | 152 (10/1/11-3/31/12) | | |
| 134 | 135 | 164 | **NUMBER OF STATEMENTS** | 21 | 41 | 30 | 28 | 29 | 15 |
| % | % | % | **ASSETS** | % | % | % | % | % | % |
| 14.3 | 18.4 | 16.5 | Cash & Equivalents | 17.7 | 19.9 | 14.2 | 16.1 | 18.1 | 7.4 |
| 33.0 | 29.7 | 31.6 | Trade Receivables (net) | 15.4 | 27.3 | 33.0 | 36.0 | 38.4 | 42.0 |
| 7.2 | 6.8 | 8.5 | Inventory | 7.5 | 9.3 | 4.6 | 12.9 | 6.3 | 11.8 |
| 4.2 | 3.3 | 3.3 | All Other Current | 5.8 | 1.2 | 3.3 | 2.2 | 5.4 | 3.8 |
| 58.7 | 58.1 | 59.9 | Total Current | 46.4 | 57.7 | 55.0 | 67.3 | 68.2 | 65.0 |
| 25.6 | 26.3 | 23.5 | Fixed Assets (net) | 35.9 | 24.5 | 26.0 | 16.5 | 18.8 | 20.5 |
| 6.0 | 4.4 | 5.8 | Intangibles (net) | 6.6 | 7.1 | 7.5 | 2.9 | 5.3 | 3.9 |
| 9.6 | 11.1 | 10.8 | All Other Non-Current | 11.1 | 10.7 | 11.4 | 13.3 | 7.8 | 10.6 |
| 100.0 | 100.0 | 100.0 | Total | 100.0 | 100.0 | 100.0 | 100.0 | 100.0 | 100.0 |
| | | | **LIABILITIES** | | | | | | |
| 13.4 | 14.4 | 9.2 | Notes Payable-Short Term | 5.9 | 12.5 | 9.1 | 8.7 | 7.2 | 10.0 |
| 4.2 | 3.7 | 2.6 | Cur. Mat.-L.T.D. | 3.6 | 1.8 | 1.7 | 3.0 | 3.7 | 2.6 |
| 12.1 | 13.1 | 13.5 | Trade Payables | 2.7 | 12.8 | 14.5 | 14.1 | 19.8 | 15.1 |
| .3 | .3 | .3 | Income Taxes Payable | .0 | .0 | .5 | 1.1 | .3 | .3 |
| 13.1 | 14.9 | 15.1 | All Other Current | 33.1 | 10.3 | 9.0 | 13.0 | 15.2 | 18.5 |
| 43.0 | 46.5 | 40.7 | Total Current | 45.3 | 37.4 | 34.8 | 40.0 | 45.9 | 46.4 |
| 22.1 | 23.3 | 25.0 | Long-Term Debt | 68.8 | 16.9 | 28.9 | 20.4 | 14.2 | 7.4 |
| .3 | .1 | .3 | Deferred Taxes | .0 | .0 | .1 | .4 | .9 | .4 |
| 8.0 | 8.1 | 10.6 | All Other Non-Current | 26.5 | 14.7 | 1.1 | 8.7 | 6.6 | 6.8 |
| 26.6 | 21.9 | 23.5 | Net Worth | -40.6 | 31.0 | 35.1 | 30.5 | 32.4 | 39.0 |
| 100.0 | 100.0 | 100.0 | Total Liabilities & Net Worth | 100.0 | 100.0 | 100.0 | 100.0 | 100.0 | 100.0 |
| | | | **INCOME DATA** | | | | | | |
| 100.0 | 100.0 | 100.0 | Net Sales | 100.0 | 100.0 | 100.0 | 100.0 | 100.0 | 100.0 |
| | | | Gross Profit | | | | | | |
| 92.7 | 92.0 | 92.4 | Operating Expenses | 78.6 | 93.4 | 95.1 | 95.2 | 94.1 | 94.9 |
| 7.3 | 8.0 | 7.6 | Operating Profit | 21.4 | 6.6 | 4.9 | 4.8 | 5.9 | 5.1 |
| 1.1 | 2.0 | 1.1 | All Other Expenses (net) | 7.7 | .1 | -.3 | .5 | .4 | .0 |
| 6.1 | 6.0 | 6.5 | Profit Before Taxes | 13.7 | 6.5 | 5.3 | 4.3 | 5.4 | 5.1 |
| | | | **RATIOS** | | | | | | |
| 2.9 | 2.5 | 3.0 | | 9.2 | 4.0 | 3.9 | 3.2 | 2.2 | 2.0 |
| 1.6 | 1.4 | 1.6 | Current | 1.6 | 2.0 | 1.6 | 1.8 | 1.5 | 1.3 |
| .9 | .8 | 1.0 | | .7 | 1.1 | 1.0 | .9 | 1.2 | 1.1 |
| 2.5 | 2.2 | 2.5 | | 1.9 | 3.9 | 2.5 | 2.8 | 1.8 | 1.5 |
| 1.3 | 1.2 | 1.4 | Quick | .8 | 1.9 | 1.5 | 1.4 | 1.2 | 1.0 |
| .3 | .6 | .7 | | .3 | .5 | .9 | .6 | .9 | .9 |
| 9  41.7 | 5  71.3 | 9  42.2 | | 0  UND | 0  UND | 4  97.2 | 21  17.5 | 19  19.5 | 30  12.3 |
| 37  10.0 | 33  11.0 | 35  10.5 | Sales/Receivables | 1  468.5 | 36  10.0 | 31  11.6 | 34  10.7 | 48  7.6 | 41  9.0 |
| 66  5.5 | 55  6.6 | 59  6.2 | | 31  11.8 | 57  6.4 | 74  4.9 | 55  6.6 | 73  5.0 | 51  7.2 |
| | | | Cost of Sales/Inventory | | | | | | |
| | | | Cost of Sales/Payables | | | | | | |
| 6.9 | 7.9 | 7.5 | | 4.7 | 7.6 | 8.0 | 5.2 | 6.7 | 14.1 |
| 14.8 | 23.4 | 15.4 | Sales/Working Capital | 28.4 | 15.3 | 15.2 | 13.0 | 13.7 | 17.4 |
| -244.0 | -33.5 | 625.9 | | -58.6 | UND | NM | -72.6 | 60.6 | 77.1 |
| 18.7 | 26.7 | 28.5 | | 17.0 | 38.6 | 16.4 | 38.1 | 23.5 | 97.8 |
| (113)  5.6 | (113)  4.7 | (141)  8.2 | EBIT/Interest | (15)  4.4 | (31)  12.5 | (27)  6.7 | (24)  2.6 | 8.4 | 17.6 |
| 1.4 | 1.4 | 2.5 | | 1.2 | 2.6 | 3.8 | 1.0 | 2.4 | 9.7 |
| 7.7 | 6.3 | 11.9 | | | | | | | |
| (21)  2.5 | (11)  2.4 | (17)  6.1 | Net Profit + Depr., Dep., Amort./Cur. Mat. L/T/D | | | | | | |
| .5 | 1.1 | 2.2 | | | | | | | |
| .2 | .1 | .1 | | .5 | .1 | .2 | .1 | .3 | .3 |
| .7 | .7 | .6 | Fixed/Worth | 12.0 | .5 | .6 | .3 | .6 | .5 |
| 5.8 | 5.7 | 5.6 | | -.8 | 5.6 | -6.9 | 1.2 | 1.1 | 1.3 |
| .7 | .9 | .7 | | 1.3 | .4 | .9 | .6 | 1.2 | .7 |
| 2.0 | 2.4 | 1.9 | Debt/Worth | -29.5 | 1.2 | 1.7 | 1.5 | 2.3 | 2.1 |
| 48.2 | 24.8 | 20.3 | | -1.8 | 12.5 | -13.7 | 7.3 | 6.1 | 4.0 |
| 87.7 | 88.2 | 87.0 | | | 105.1 | 91.6 | 86.3 | 87.1 | 110.8 |
| (104)  36.8 | (104)  22.9 | (128)  41.3 | % Profit Before Taxes/Tangible Net Worth | (32)  47.1 | (22)  32.8 | (23)  26.5 | (27)  36.0 | 48.8 | |
| 5.4 | 5.4 | 11.5 | | | 20.7 | 6.2 | 1.0 | 9.0 | 27.3 |
| 27.9 | 25.5 | 34.1 | | 48.3 | 49.6 | 25.9 | 25.3 | 26.1 | 21.8 |
| 11.7 | 8.6 | 12.1 | % Profit Before Taxes/Total Assets | 8.2 | 23.3 | 11.4 | 4.1 | 13.4 | 10.3 |
| .8 | 1.0 | 2.6 | | -1.6 | 4.0 | 3.5 | .1 | 2.3 | 8.0 |
| 72.3 | 79.2 | 80.3 | | 83.1 | 101.5 | 99.8 | 96.9 | 85.1 | 40.5 |
| 22.1 | 26.1 | 24.3 | Sales/Net Fixed Assets | 15.2 | 26.0 | 19.7 | 34.0 | 23.9 | 26.5 |
| 8.7 | 9.3 | 8.4 | | 2.1 | 8.0 | 8.3 | 15.5 | 8.7 | 12.1 |
| 5.2 | 5.2 | 5.0 | | 5.8 | 5.3 | 4.3 | 4.6 | 6.0 | 5.5 |
| 3.1 | 2.9 | 3.2 | Sales/Total Assets | 2.4 | 3.3 | 2.9 | 3.0 | 3.1 | 3.7 |
| 1.9 | 2.1 | 2.0 | | .9 | 2.2 | 2.3 | 2.0 | 1.5 | 2.2 |
| .8 | .7 | .7 | | 1.9 | .4 | .6 | .6 | .9 | .6 |
| (87)  1.6 | (94)  1.5 | (108)  1.3 | % Depr., Dep., Amort./Sales | (14)  3.1 | (19)  1.0 | (21)  2.2 | (19)  1.1 | (22)  1.3 | (13)  1.0 |
| 4.0 | 3.5 | 3.0 | | 4.7 | 3.6 | 3.4 | 2.3 | 2.1 | 1.5 |
| 3.4 | 3.2 | 3.0 | | | 4.7 | 3.2 | 3.1 | 1.2 | |
| (68)  6.8 | (62)  6.7 | (74)  5.3 | % Officers', Directors' Owners' Comp/Sales | (22)  6.4 | (17)  4.7 | (15)  4.8 | (10)  2.0 | | |
| 11.0 | 12.7 | 8.7 | | 9.8 | 7.8 | 10.3 | 4.0 | | |
| 3193842M | 1274605M | 2067445M | Net Sales ($) | 11116M | 82604M | 117293M | 203779M | 456829M | 1195824M |
| 906469M | 524569M | 772458M | Total Assets ($) | 12639M | 28725M | 42181M | 95833M | 193651M | 399429M |

## Current Data Sorted by Assets        Comparative Historical Data

| 0-500M | 500M-2MM | 2-10MM | 10-50MM | 50-100MM | 100-250MM | Type of Statement | 4/1/07-3/31/08 ALL | 4/1/08-3/31/09 ALL |
|---|---|---|---|---|---|---|---|---|
| | 1 | 2 | 8 | | 1 | Unqualified | 5 | 10 |
| 1 | 2 | 12 | 6 | | | Reviewed | 5 | 12 |
| | 3 | 10 | 1 | | | Compiled | 5 | 10 |
| 11 | 11 | 6 | 9 | | | Tax Returns | 9 | 12 |
| 6 | 9 | 9 | 9 | 1 | 2 | Other | 21 | 19 |
| | 17 (4/1-9/30/11) | | 94 (10/1/11-3/31/12) | | | | | |
| 18 | 26 | 39 | 24 | 1 | 3 | **NUMBER OF STATEMENTS** | 45 | 63 |
| % | % | % | % | % | % | **ASSETS** | % | % |
| 27.5 | 12.3 | 7.0 | 3.9 | | | Cash & Equivalents | 7.5 | 8.3 |
| 9.6 | 34.1 | 30.3 | 27.5 | | | Trade Receivables (net) | 25.6 | 29.3 |
| 13.1 | 11.7 | 15.0 | 23.2 | | | Inventory | 14.6 | 16.3 |
| 13.3 | 2.1 | 1.8 | 2.0 | | | All Other Current | 3.0 | 4.7 |
| 63.4 | 60.1 | 54.0 | 56.7 | | | Total Current | 50.7 | 58.7 |
| 15.7 | 26.9 | 34.2 | 24.9 | | | Fixed Assets (net) | 34.1 | 30.9 |
| 13.2 | 3.7 | 5.2 | 15.1 | | | Intangibles (net) | 9.2 | 4.4 |
| 7.7 | 9.3 | 6.6 | 3.3 | | | All Other Non-Current | 6.0 | 6.0 |
| 100.0 | 100.0 | 100.0 | 100.0 | | | Total | 100.0 | 100.0 |
| | | | | | | **LIABILITIES** | | |
| 20.4 | 19.2 | 13.6 | 12.1 | | | Notes Payable-Short Term | 12.7 | 14.9 |
| .5 | 2.4 | 4.4 | 2.9 | | | Cur. Mat.-L.T.D. | 3.7 | 5.7 |
| 7.4 | 18.1 | 15.9 | 18.3 | | | Trade Payables | 15.3 | 21.2 |
| .0 | .0 | .3 | .0 | | | Income Taxes Payable | .0 | .1 |
| 8.5 | 22.8 | 11.7 | 7.9 | | | All Other Current | 13.4 | 15.0 |
| 36.9 | 62.6 | 46.0 | 41.2 | | | Total Current | 45.2 | 56.9 |
| 20.5 | 20.1 | 19.1 | 16.4 | | | Long-Term Debt | 31.8 | 19.7 |
| .0 | .1 | .7 | .0 | | | Deferred Taxes | .1 | .2 |
| 8.3 | 6.9 | 1.2 | 4.3 | | | All Other Non-Current | 10.3 | 4.7 |
| 34.4 | 10.3 | 32.9 | 38.1 | | | Net Worth | 12.7 | 18.6 |
| 100.0 | 100.0 | 100.0 | 100.0 | | | Total Liabilities & Net Worth | 100.0 | 100.0 |
| | | | | | | **INCOME DATA** | | |
| 100.0 | 100.0 | 100.0 | 100.0 | | | Net Sales | 100.0 | 100.0 |
| | | | | | | Gross Profit | | |
| 85.5 | 92.2 | 86.9 | 92.4 | | | Operating Expenses | 86.4 | 95.0 |
| 14.5 | 7.8 | 13.1 | 7.6 | | | Operating Profit | 13.6 | 5.0 |
| .5 | 1.4 | 4.7 | 3.7 | | | All Other Expenses (net) | 6.1 | 2.9 |
| 13.9 | 6.5 | 8.4 | 3.9 | | | Profit Before Taxes | 7.5 | 2.1 |
| | | | | | | **RATIOS** | | |
| 5.3 | 3.8 | 2.3 | 2.1 | | | Current | 1.5 | 1.9 |
| 2.1 | 2.1 | 1.3 | 1.3 | | | | 1.1 | 1.2 |
| .8 | 1.1 | .9 | .9 | | | | .8 | .8 |
| 4.9 | 2.8 | 1.4 | 1.2 | | | Quick | 1.1 | 1.2 |
| .9 | 1.9 | 1.0 | .8 | | | | .7 | .7 |
| .2 | .6 | .4 | .5 | | | | .5 | .4 |
| 0 UND | 19   19.4 | 30   12.2 | 31   11.7 | | | Sales/Receivables | 26   14.0 | 25   14.4 |
| 0 UND | 36   10.2 | 41   8.9 | 42   8.6 | | | | 43   8.5 | 36   10.1 |
| 13   28.4 | 47   7.8 | 66   5.5 | 50   7.3 | | | | 64   5.7 | 59   6.2 |
| | | | | | | Cost of Sales/Inventory | | |
| | | | | | | Cost of Sales/Payables | | |
| 8.4 | 7.7 | 7.4 | 7.5 | | | Sales/Working Capital | 10.8 | 10.9 |
| 58.0 | 15.6 | 16.8 | 23.2 | | | | 28.0 | 36.0 |
| -78.5 | 66.0 | -28.4 | -66.2 | | | | -21.0 | -14.8 |
| 54.5 | 32.6 | 12.2 | 38.5 | | | EBIT/Interest | 10.2 | 10.7 |
| (12) 9.2 | (22) 11.1 | (29) 3.7 | (22) 7.7 | | | | (34) 1.9 | (54) 3.0 |
| -2.6 | .3 | 1.7 | 2.8 | | | | .4 | -.1 |
| | | 5.9 | | | | Net Profit + Depr., Dep., | | |
| | | (10) 2.5 | | | | Amort./Cur. Mat. L/T/D | | |
| | | 1.6 | | | | | | |
| .0 | .3 | .3 | .3 | | | Fixed/Worth | .4 | .4 |
| .3 | .6 | 1.3 | 1.0 | | | | 2.0 | 1.3 |
| -1.4 | NM | 4.6 | 2.0 | | | | -20.6 | -13.2 |
| .3 | .5 | .7 | .9 | | | Debt/Worth | 2.0 | 1.0 |
| 1.4 | 1.8 | 1.9 | 3.0 | | | | 4.1 | 3.3 |
| -5.8 | NM | 8.3 | 6.4 | | | | -7.1 | -36.5 |
| 150.7 | 90.4 | 40.1 | 70.5 | | | % Profit Before Taxes/Tangible | 87.8 | 54.6 |
| (11) 37.7 | (20) 35.5 | (32) 27.2 | (22) 29.6 | | | Net Worth | (32) 32.5 | (45) 27.3 |
| 15.0 | 9.6 | 6.9 | 13.6 | | | | 1.4 | 3.5 |
| 127.8 | 22.5 | 12.9 | 14.5 | | | % Profit Before Taxes/Total | 17.1 | 16.1 |
| 22.4 | 14.4 | 6.3 | 7.5 | | | Assets | 7.0 | 4.9 |
| -1.2 | -.9 | 2.3 | 2.6 | | | | .2 | -3.1 |
| UND | 65.0 | 30.1 | 51.1 | | | Sales/Net Fixed Assets | 36.7 | 26.4 |
| 56.0 | 17.7 | 8.2 | 17.0 | | | | 8.5 | 11.3 |
| 24.9 | 8.3 | 3.9 | 3.1 | | | | 3.2 | 4.7 |
| 11.6 | 4.4 | 2.8 | 3.4 | | | Sales/Total Assets | 2.7 | 3.5 |
| 5.5 | 3.4 | 2.0 | 2.4 | | | | 2.1 | 2.6 |
| 3.5 | 2.6 | 1.5 | 1.3 | | | | 1.4 | 1.9 |
| | 1.4 | 1.1 | .5 | | | % Depr., Dep., Amort./Sales | .8 | 1.3 |
| | (21) 2.1 | (36) 2.1 | (23) 1.4 | | | | (37) 2.0 | (51) 2.7 |
| | 4.4 | 6.5 | 5.8 | | | | 6.3 | 3.7 |
| | | 2.6 | 1.5 | | | % Officers', Directors' | 1.7 | 2.9 |
| | (10) | 4.5 | (12) 4.8 | | | Owners' Comp/Sales | (11) 3.7 | (17) 4.1 |
| | | 9.7 | 6.6 | | | | 8.6 | 8.9 |
| 22687M | 114436M | 460644M | 1072494M | 86751M | 758265M | Net Sales ($) | 1161827M | 1829259M |
| 4336M | 29462M | 199848M | 439387M | 63691M | 420192M | Total Assets ($) | 635369M | 568382M |

© RMA 2012

**M = $ thousand    MM = $ million**
See Pages 9 through 22 for Explanation of Ratios and Data

## Comparative Historical Data / Current Data Sorted by Sales

| | | | Type of Statement | 0-1MM | 1-3MM | 3-5MM | 5-10MM | 10-25MM | 25MM & OVER |
|---|---|---|---|---|---|---|---|---|---|
| 9 | 8 | 12 | Unqualified | | 2 | | 6 | 4 | 6 |
| 9 | 20 | 21 | Reviewed | 1 | | 1 | 7 | 7 | 6 |
| 12 | 14 | 14 | Compiled | 1 | 4 | | 5 | 2 | 2 |
| 16 | 26 | 28 | Tax Returns | 11 | 11 | 2 | 3 | 1 | |
| 42 | 45 | 36 | Other | 3 | 3 | 6 | 7 | 7 | 12 |
| 4/1/09-3/31/10 ALL | 4/1/10-3/31/11 ALL | 4/1/11-3/31/12 ALL | | 17 (4/1-9/30/11) | | | 94 (10/1/11-3/31/12) | | |
| 88 | 113 | 111 | NUMBER OF STATEMENTS | 16 | 20 | 9 | 19 | 21 | 26 |
| % | % | % | **ASSETS** | % | % | % | % | % | % |
| 9.4 | 11.9 | 10.6 | Cash & Equivalents | 21.5 | 16.6 | | 6.6 | 3.9 | 6.3 |
| 25.0 | 29.4 | 27.0 | Trade Receivables (net) | 5.3 | 21.4 | | 31.7 | 32.7 | 33.8 |
| 13.4 | 12.6 | 15.8 | Inventory | 9.9 | 7.0 | | 14.3 | 20.4 | 24.4 |
| 2.5 | 2.6 | 3.8 | All Other Current | 11.0 | 4.4 | | 1.2 | 1.7 | 2.2 |
| 50.4 | 56.5 | 57.2 | Total Current | 47.7 | 49.4 | | 53.7 | 58.8 | 66.8 |
| 34.2 | 27.1 | 26.7 | Fixed Assets (net) | 44.8 | 29.5 | | 34.1 | 21.7 | 17.3 |
| 8.0 | 8.8 | 9.4 | Intangibles (net) | 5.1 | 13.0 | | 4.8 | 12.1 | 12.8 |
| 7.4 | 7.6 | 6.7 | All Other Non-Current | 2.4 | 8.1 | | 7.4 | 7.4 | 3.2 |
| 100.0 | 100.0 | 100.0 | Total | 100.0 | 100.0 | | 100.0 | 100.0 | 100.0 |
| | | | **LIABILITIES** | | | | | | |
| 15.4 | 11.9 | 15.3 | Notes Payable-Short Term | 19.0 | 20.8 | | 15.2 | 10.5 | 12.1 |
| 4.1 | 2.4 | 2.9 | Cur. Mat.-L.T.D. | 1.2 | 1.5 | | 5.4 | 4.0 | 3.1 |
| 16.6 | 18.0 | 15.6 | Trade Payables | 2.3 | 9.8 | | 22.2 | 19.8 | 20.3 |
| .1 | .1 | .1 | Income Taxes Payable | .0 | .0 | | .4 | .2 | .0 |
| 15.6 | 11.1 | 12.9 | All Other Current | 5.8 | 6.2 | | 34.2 | 8.2 | 12.9 |
| 51.8 | 43.6 | 46.7 | Total Current | 28.3 | 38.4 | | 77.3 | 42.8 | 48.5 |
| 27.0 | 19.4 | 19.4 | Long-Term Debt | 26.8 | 36.3 | | 28.6 | 7.9 | 10.9 |
| .1 | .2 | .3 | Deferred Taxes | .0 | .1 | | 1.1 | .4 | .0 |
| 7.5 | 11.5 | 4.8 | All Other Non-Current | .1 | 6.1 | | 1.2 | 2.9 | 5.1 |
| 13.7 | 25.3 | 28.8 | Net Worth | 45.0 | 19.2 | | -8.2 | 46.1 | 35.5 |
| 100.0 | 100.0 | 100.0 | Total Liabilities & Net Worth | 100.0 | 100.0 | | 100.0 | 100.0 | 100.0 |
| | | | **INCOME DATA** | | | | | | |
| 100.0 | 100.0 | 100.0 | Net Sales | 100.0 | 100.0 | | 100.0 | 100.0 | 100.0 |
| | | | Gross Profit | | | | | | |
| 91.8 | 93.2 | 89.3 | Operating Expenses | 57.9 | 90.7 | | 96.1 | 96.2 | 94.3 |
| 8.2 | 6.8 | 10.7 | Operating Profit | 42.1 | 9.3 | | 3.9 | 3.8 | 5.7 |
| 3.5 | 2.1 | 2.9 | All Other Expenses (net) | 12.3 | 4.2 | | 1.8 | -.2 | .8 |
| 4.8 | 4.8 | 7.8 | Profit Before Taxes | 29.8 | 5.1 | | 2.0 | 4.0 | 4.9 |
| | | | **RATIOS** | | | | | | |
| 2.2 | 2.7 | 2.8 | | 9.5 | 4.8 | | 1.5 | 2.8 | 2.1 |
| 1.3 | 1.4 | 1.4 | Current | 2.6 | 2.3 | | 1.1 | 1.5 | 1.3 |
| .8 | .9 | .9 | | .7 | 1.1 | | .6 | .9 | 1.1 |
| 1.5 | 1.8 | 2.1 | | 8.4 | 4.7 | | 1.3 | 1.7 | 1.3 |
| .8 | .9 | .9 | Quick | 1.1 | 1.9 | | .7 | 1.0 | .9 |
| .5 | .5 | .5 | | .3 | .5 | | .4 | .4 | .6 |
| 24  15.0 | 23  16.1 | 14  26.1 | | 0  UND | 0  UND | | 32  11.5 | 32  11.4 | 32  11.5 |
| 36  10.1 | 37  9.9 | 37  9.8 | Sales/Receivables | 0  UND | 35  10.4 | | 41  8.9 | 49  7.4 | 43  8.4 |
| 51  7.1 | 55  6.6 | 53  6.9 | | 0  UND | 46  8.0 | | 62  5.9 | 64  5.7 | 49  7.4 |
| | | | Cost of Sales/Inventory | | | | | | |
| | | | Cost of Sales/Payables | | | | | | |
| 7.7 | 7.1 | 7.4 | | 4.5 | 7.9 | | 10.5 | 5.3 | 9.6 |
| 20.3 | 19.3 | 18.1 | Sales/Working Capital | 19.8 | 13.4 | | 61.2 | 13.8 | 18.5 |
| -19.5 | -52.8 | -86.3 | | -29.6 | 113.2 | | -8.4 | -23.1 | NM |
| 7.9 | 16.1 | 28.6 | | | 13.3 | | 5.2 | 39.6 | 45.1 |
| (69) 2.8 | (96) 5.7 | (88) 5.9 | EBIT/Interest | | (15) 3.4 | | 2.0 | (17) 6.7 | (23) 8.2 |
| .8 | 1.8 | 1.8 | | | .1 | | -2.0 | 2.8 | 2.9 |
| 9.1 | 13.1 | 9.2 | | | | | | | |
| (14) 4.8 | (21) 3.5 | (18) 3.7 | Net Profit + Depr., Dep., Amort./Cur. Mat. L/T/D | | | | | | |
| 1.2 | 1.1 | 2.3 | | | | | | | |
| .5 | .2 | .3 | | .0 | .3 | | .6 | .3 | .3 |
| 1.4 | .9 | 1.1 | Fixed/Worth | .6 | 1.7 | | 1.4 | .5 | .8 |
| NM | 3.1 | 4.0 | | 3.7 | -1.1 | | -.8 | 1.9 | 2.1 |
| .9 | .9 | .7 | | .3 | .9 | | 1.0 | .6 | 1.0 |
| 3.6 | 2.2 | 2.3 | Debt/Worth | 1.8 | 2.3 | | 2.3 | 1.5 | 3.4 |
| -48.4 | 13.3 | 14.5 | | 7.3 | -2.9 | | -3.5 | 4.6 | 12.5 |
| 62.7 | 78.7 | 70.2 | | 105.2 | 30.5 | | 83.0 | 40.0 | 71.2 |
| (65) 23.2 | (87) 26.9 | (87) 28.8 | % Profit Before Taxes/Tangible Net Worth | (14) 41.4 | (13) 16.5 | | (12) 28.6 | (18) 17.0 | (23) 39.0 |
| 3.8 | 8.3 | 12.7 | | 19.4 | -3.4 | | -1.1 | 10.6 | 26.0 |
| 16.3 | 19.0 | 17.8 | | 122.0 | 17.3 | | 18.0 | 12.5 | 14.9 |
| 8.0 | 8.1 | 8.3 | % Profit Before Taxes/Total Assets | 15.4 | 6.4 | | 4.0 | 6.2 | 9.4 |
| .2 | 1.9 | 2.3 | | 2.8 | -3.8 | | -7.8 | 2.6 | 4.8 |
| 21.4 | 44.8 | 55.2 | | 489.6 | 45.0 | | 11.2 | 95.6 | 59.0 |
| 8.8 | 15.4 | 17.1 | Sales/Net Fixed Assets | 14.3 | 17.4 | | 8.0 | 8.7 | 28.4 |
| 4.1 | 5.4 | 5.5 | | .2 | 4.8 | | 4.7 | 4.5 | 7.1 |
| 4.1 | 4.0 | 4.0 | | 5.7 | 4.4 | | 3.3 | 2.8 | 3.9 |
| 2.4 | 2.7 | 2.7 | Sales/Total Assets | .9 | 3.7 | | 2.6 | 1.8 | 2.8 |
| 1.4 | 1.7 | 1.7 | | .2 | 1.7 | | 1.8 | 1.4 | 2.0 |
| 1.3 | .9 | .9 | | | 1.7 | | 1.7 | .7 | .4 |
| (70) 2.8 | (88) 1.7 | (87) 2.1 | % Depr., Dep., Amort./Sales | | (15) 2.7 | | (18) 2.3 | (17) 1.6 | (22) .9 |
| 6.2 | 4.0 | 5.5 | | | 8.2 | | 6.4 | 4.7 | 2.6 |
| 2.3 | 2.1 | 1.7 | | | | | | | |
| (28) 5.4 | (38) 3.8 | (34) 4.2 | % Officers', Directors' Owners' Comp/Sales | | | | | | |
| 11.7 | 6.6 | 6.2 | | | | | | | |
| 1998033M | 2343381M | 2515277M | Net Sales ($) | 7640M | 40642M | 34289M | 134313M | 295236M | 2003157M |
| 825213M | 1058281M | 1156916M | Total Assets ($) | 19707M | 31363M | 8989M | 61924M | 154320M | 880613M |

© RMA 2012

M = $ thousand    MM = $ million
See Pages 9 through 22 for Explanation of Ratios and Data

## Current Data Sorted by Assets      Comparative Historical Data

| 0-500M | 500M-2MM | 2-10MM | 10-50MM | 50-100MM | 100-250MM | Type of Statement | 4/1/07-3/31/08 ALL | 4/1/08-3/31/09 ALL |
|---|---|---|---|---|---|---|---|---|
| | | 1 | 2 | | | Unqualified | 1 | 6 |
| | | 2 | 1 | | | Reviewed | 2 | 3 |
| 2 | 3 | 2 | 1 | | | Compiled | 3 | 3 |
| 1 | 3 | 2 | | | | Tax Returns | 5 | 4 |
| 2 | 3 | 9 | | | | Other | 4 | 8 |
| | 3 (4/1-9/30/11) | | 33 (10/1/11-3/31/12) | | | | | |
| 5 | 9 | 15 | 4 | 3 | | **NUMBER OF STATEMENTS** | 15 | 24 |
| % | % | % | % | % | % | | % | % |
| | | 16.9 | | | | **ASSETS** Cash & Equivalents | 27.5 | 21.9 |
| | | 48.3 | | | | Trade Receivables (net) | 23.6 | 27.2 |
| | | 5.2 | | | | Inventory | 5.1 | 5.7 |
| | | 1.5 | | | | All Other Current | 2.8 | 5.7 |
| | | 71.8 | | | | Total Current | 59.0 | 60.5 |
| | | 15.8 | | | | Fixed Assets (net) | 28.1 | 21.3 |
| | | 2.9 | | | | Intangibles (net) | 2.8 | 10.9 |
| | | 9.5 | | | | All Other Non-Current | 10.1 | 7.4 |
| | | 100.0 | | | | Total | 100.0 | 100.0 |
| | | 16.3 | | | | **LIABILITIES** Notes Payable-Short Term | 16.2 | 9.4 |
| | | .7 | | | | Cur. Mat.-L.T.D. | 2.6 | 2.2 |
| | | 22.7 | | | | Trade Payables | 16.8 | 12.5 |
| | | .6 | | | | Income Taxes Payable | .0 | .1 |
| | | 21.6 | | | | All Other Current | 18.9 | 17.5 |
| | | 61.8 | | | | Total Current | 54.6 | 41.8 |
| | | 3.7 | | | | Long-Term Debt | 14.8 | 20.6 |
| | | .7 | | | | Deferred Taxes | .3 | .3 |
| | | 6.5 | | | | All Other Non-Current | 4.9 | 26.4 |
| | | 27.3 | | | | Net Worth | 25.3 | 10.9 |
| | | 100.0 | | | | Total Liabilities & Net Worth | 100.0 | 100.0 |
| | | 100.0 | | | | **INCOME DATA** Net Sales | 100.0 | 100.0 |
| | | | | | | Gross Profit | | |
| | | 97.6 | | | | Operating Expenses | 95.9 | 93.1 |
| | | 2.4 | | | | Operating Profit | 4.1 | 6.9 |
| | | .4 | | | | All Other Expenses (net) | .6 | 1.6 |
| | | 2.0 | | | | Profit Before Taxes | 3.5 | 5.3 |
| | | 2.7 | | | | **RATIOS** | 2.7 | 3.0 |
| | | 1.2 | | | | Current | 1.5 | 1.5 |
| | | .6 | | | | | 1.0 | .9 |
| | | 2.2 | | | | | 2.5 | 2.8 |
| | | 1.0 | | | | Quick | 1.1 | 1.3 |
| | | .6 | | | | | .8 | .6 |
| | 24 | 15.5 | | | | | 2  171.5 | 13  28.2 |
| | 46 | 7.9 | | | | Sales/Receivables | 12  30.7 | 24  15.1 |
| | 83 | 4.4 | | | | | 36  10.0 | 48  7.5 |
| | | | | | | Cost of Sales/Inventory | | |
| | | | | | | Cost of Sales/Payables | | |
| | | 6.8 | | | | | 6.7 | 7.4 |
| | | 41.3 | | | | Sales/Working Capital | 30.2 | 15.6 |
| | | -14.1 | | | | | -176.7 | -133.1 |
| | | 17.1 | | | | | (11) 30.5 | (21) 17.8 |
| | (12) | 4.1 | | | | EBIT/Interest | 6.2 | 3.7 |
| | | -1.8 | | | | | 1.8 | 2.1 |
| | | | | | | Net Profit + Depr., Dep., Amort./Cur. Mat. L/T/D | | |
| | | .1 | | | | | .1 | .3 |
| | | .5 | | | | Fixed/Worth | .9 | 52.0 |
| | | -.9 | | | | | 2.5 | -.3 |
| | | .6 | | | | | .5 | .9 |
| | | 3.7 | | | | Debt/Worth | 3.2 | 59.5 |
| | | -11.0 | | | | | 9.7 | -3.4 |
| | | 52.3 | | | | | (13) 167.9 | (13) 115.6 |
| | (11) | 29.7 | | | | % Profit Before Taxes/Tangible Net Worth | 60.3 | 37.9 |
| | | .2 | | | | | 26.9 | 10.0 |
| | | 16.0 | | | | | 35.4 | 32.7 |
| | | 4.3 | | | | % Profit Before Taxes/Total Assets | 21.1 | 13.3 |
| | | .1 | | | | | 5.6 | 3.7 |
| | | 91.4 | | | | | 51.6 | 54.0 |
| | | 39.0 | | | | Sales/Net Fixed Assets | 22.0 | 19.1 |
| | | 10.7 | | | | | 7.0 | 10.2 |
| | | 4.6 | | | | | 7.4 | 5.2 |
| | | 3.5 | | | | Sales/Total Assets | 4.4 | 2.8 |
| | | 2.4 | | | | | 2.8 | 1.7 |
| | | .4 | | | | | (13) .6 | (18) .4 |
| | (12) | .8 | | | | % Depr., Dep., Amort./Sales | 1.2 | 1.4 |
| | | 1.7 | | | | | 2.5 | 5.6 |
| | | | | | | % Officers', Directors' Owners' Comp/Sales | | |
| 21365M | 41353M | 254697M | 144478M | 203089M | | Net Sales ($) | 167918M | 677575M |
| 1278M | 11443M | 73110M | 106970M | 226190M | | Total Assets ($) | 40473M | 491416M |

*(Column 100-250MM for the ASSETS and LIABILITIES sections is marked "DATA NOT AVAILABLE".)*

M = $ thousand     MM = $ million
See Pages 9 through 22 for Explanation of Ratios and Data

## Comparative Historical Data | Current Data Sorted by Sales

| 4/1/09-3/31/10 ALL | 4/1/10-3/31/11 ALL | 4/1/11-3/31/12 ALL | Type of Statement | 0-1MM | 1-3MM | 3-5MM | 5-10MM | 10-25MM | 25MM & OVER |
|---|---|---|---|---|---|---|---|---|---|
| 5 | 4 | 3 | Unqualified | | | | | 1 | 2 |
| 4 | 5 | 3 | Reviewed | | | | | | 2 |
| 1 | 2 | 7 | Compiled | | 1 | 2 | 1 | 2 | |
| 2 | 8 | 5 | Tax Returns | 1 | 1 | | 2 | | 1 |
| 15 | 12 | 18 | Other | 1 | 2 | 2 | 3 | 5 | 5 |
| 27 | 31 | 36 | **NUMBER OF STATEMENTS** | 2 | 4 | 4 | 8 | 8 | 10 |
| % | % | % | **ASSETS** | % | % | % | % | % | % |
| 15.3 | 23.5 | 20.9 | Cash & Equivalents | | | | | | 8.7 |
| 29.5 | 23.2 | 32.5 | Trade Receivables (net) | | | | | | 34.3 |
| 5.6 | 8.6 | 5.2 | Inventory | | | | | | 7.4 |
| 8.2 | 5.4 | 2.4 | All Other Current | | | | | | 1.4 |
| 58.5 | 60.7 | 61.0 | Total Current | | | | | | 51.7 |
| 20.8 | 23.8 | 17.7 | Fixed Assets (net) | | | | | | 7.2 |
| 14.1 | 6.4 | 11.0 | Intangibles (net) | | | | | | 30.9 |
| 6.6 | 9.1 | 10.3 | All Other Non-Current | | | | | | 10.2 |
| 100.0 | 100.0 | 100.0 | Total | | | | | | 100.0 |
| | | | **LIABILITIES** | | | | | | |
| 10.9 | 22.1 | 19.3 | Notes Payable-Short Term | | | | | | 7.4 |
| 2.0 | 4.6 | 1.3 | Cur. Mat.-L.T.D. | | | | | | 1.1 |
| 15.0 | 10.5 | 15.1 | Trade Payables | | | | | | 12.0 |
| .0 | .1 | .3 | Income Taxes Payable | | | | | | .3 |
| 25.8 | 39.0 | 21.8 | All Other Current | | | | | | 16.6 |
| 53.7 | 76.2 | 57.8 | Total Current | | | | | | 37.5 |
| 37.8 | 21.8 | 12.3 | Long-Term Debt | | | | | | 10.1 |
| .3 | .1 | .3 | Deferred Taxes | | | | | | .2 |
| 10.8 | 6.1 | 13.4 | All Other Non-Current | | | | | | 24.1 |
| -2.6 | -4.3 | 16.3 | Net Worth | | | | | | 28.2 |
| 100.0 | 100.0 | 100.0 | Total Liabilities & Net Worth | | | | | | 100.0 |
| | | | **INCOME DATA** | | | | | | |
| 100.0 | 100.0 | 100.0 | Net Sales | | | | | | 100.0 |
| | | | Gross Profit | | | | | | |
| 96.2 | 91.1 | 94.2 | Operating Expenses | | | | | | 92.6 |
| 3.8 | 8.9 | 5.8 | Operating Profit | | | | | | 7.4 |
| 2.1 | 1.4 | .6 | All Other Expenses (net) | | | | | | 2.5 |
| 1.7 | 7.5 | 5.2 | Profit Before Taxes | | | | | | 4.9 |
| | | | **RATIOS** | | | | | | |
| 2.8 | 2.1 | 2.8 | Current | | | | | | 9.7 |
| 1.3 | 1.3 | 1.2 | | | | | | | 1.2 |
| .7 | .7 | .8 | | | | | | | .9 |
| 2.0 | 1.5 | 2.6 | Quick | | | | | | 5.2 |
| 1.1 | .9 | 1.0 | | | | | | | 1.0 |
| .4 | .4 | .6 | | | | | | | .8 |
| 15  24.9 | 1  260.3 | 8  47.9 | Sales/Receivables | | | | | | 31  11.9 |
| 24  15.2 | 26  14.1 | 30  12.0 | | | | | | | 53  6.9 |
| 54  6.8 | 67  5.4 | 73  5.0 | | | | | | | 78  4.7 |
| | | | Cost of Sales/Inventory | | | | | | |
| | | | Cost of Sales/Payables | | | | | | |
| 11.5 | 7.9 | 6.4 | Sales/Working Capital | | | | | | 5.6 |
| 25.2 | 33.7 | 36.9 | | | | | | | 36.3 |
| -122.6 | -23.3 | -33.8 | | | | | | | -105.8 |
| 7.6 | 28.7 | 18.5 | EBIT/Interest | | | | | | |
| (23) 2.4 | (28) 4.6 | (27) 4.8 | | | | | | | |
| 1.7 | 1.5 | 1.1 | | | | | | | |
| | | | Net Profit + Depr., Dep., Amort./Cur. Mat. L/T/D | | | | | | |
| .7 | .2 | .1 | Fixed/Worth | | | | | | .3 |
| -504.0 | 1.0 | 1.0 | | | | | | | NM |
| -.5 | 73.6 | -.7 | | | | | | | .0 |
| 1.8 | 1.1 | .9 | Debt/Worth | | | | | | 1.4 |
| -999.8 | 8.0 | 4.2 | | | | | | | NM |
| -3.4 | -22.0 | -5.6 | | | | | | | -1.8 |
| 52.3 | 89.5 | 79.6 | % Profit Before Taxes/Tangible Net Worth | | | | | | |
| (13) 19.5 | (22) 44.9 | (25) 39.3 | | | | | | | |
| 7.0 | 21.9 | 16.9 | | | | | | | |
| 15.1 | 24.3 | 21.1 | % Profit Before Taxes/Total Assets | | | | | | 16.4 |
| 8.5 | 12.8 | 5.8 | | | | | | | 5.6 |
| 2.8 | 3.0 | 1.8 | | | | | | | 3.1 |
| 139.6 | 133.0 | 149.9 | Sales/Net Fixed Assets | | | | | | 104.8 |
| 35.0 | 45.6 | 49.2 | | | | | | | 57.1 |
| 8.5 | 4.6 | 12.1 | | | | | | | 24.9 |
| 4.6 | 5.2 | 5.0 | Sales/Total Assets | | | | | | 4.2 |
| 3.6 | 2.6 | 3.5 | | | | | | | 2.4 |
| 1.4 | 1.4 | 1.5 | | | | | | | .9 |
| .4 | .5 | .4 | % Depr., Dep., Amort./Sales | | | | | | |
| (18) 1.8 | (24) 1.6 | (24) 1.1 | | | | | | | |
| 3.8 | 4.2 | 3.1 | | | | | | | |
| | 2.8 | 1.5 | % Officers', Directors' Owners' Comp/Sales | | | | | | |
| | (14) 5.9 | (14) 3.8 | | | | | | | |
| | 12.7 | 20.8 | | | | | | | |
| 701193M | 564598M | 664982M | Net Sales ($) | 1607M | 8136M | 18170M | 58751M | 133053M | 445265M |
| 545870M | 399607M | 418991M | Total Assets ($) | 857M | 4616M | 6010M | 29424M | 34750M | 343334M |

Column period headings (Current Data): 3 (4/1-9/30/11) · 33 (10/1/11-3/31/12)

M = $ thousand    MM = $ million
See Pages 9 through 22 for Explanation of Ratios and Data

## Current Data Sorted by Assets | Comparative Historical Data

| | | | | | | Type of Statement | | |
|---|---|---|---|---|---|---|---|---|
| | 4 | 13 | 20 | 3 | 3 | Unqualified | 24 | 38 |
| | 5 | 25 | 7 | | | Reviewed | 12 | 26 |
| 9 | 18 | 18 | 2 | | | Compiled | 14 | 23 |
| 26 | 17 | 8 | | | | Tax Returns | 24 | 48 |
| 30 | 44 | 41 | 9 | 7 | 3 | Other | 45 | 61 |
| | 44 (4/1-9/30/11) | | 268 (10/1/11-3/31/12) | | | | 4/1/07-3/31/08 | 4/1/08-3/31/09 |
| 0-500M | 500M-2MM | 2-10MM | 10-50MM | 50-100MM | 100-250MM | | ALL | ALL |
| 65 | 88 | 105 | 38 | 10 | 6 | **NUMBER OF STATEMENTS** | 119 | 196 |
| % | % | % | % | % | % | **ASSETS** | % | % |
| 36.0 | 21.4 | 18.5 | 15.3 | 10.1 | | Cash & Equivalents | 13.8 | 17.3 |
| 13.9 | 28.6 | 32.2 | 26.3 | 23.1 | | Trade Receivables (net) | 29.7 | 26.3 |
| 4.3 | 7.3 | 7.6 | 11.4 | 4.9 | | Inventory | 7.8 | 7.8 |
| 3.1 | 2.6 | 5.1 | 7.3 | 5.3 | | All Other Current | 5.4 | 5.5 |
| 57.3 | 59.9 | 63.3 | 60.4 | 43.5 | | Total Current | 56.7 | 56.9 |
| 25.7 | 29.1 | 24.1 | 23.6 | 19.9 | | Fixed Assets (net) | 27.3 | 25.6 |
| 4.5 | 2.2 | 2.4 | 8.7 | 30.7 | | Intangibles (net) | 7.4 | 8.5 |
| 12.4 | 8.8 | 10.1 | 7.3 | 6.0 | | All Other Non-Current | 8.6 | 9.0 |
| 100.0 | 100.0 | 100.0 | 100.0 | 100.0 | | Total | 100.0 | 100.0 |
| | | | | | | **LIABILITIES** | | |
| 29.3 | 6.0 | 8.2 | 7.5 | 3.6 | | Notes Payable-Short Term | 9.5 | 8.9 |
| 2.2 | 2.4 | 2.5 | 3.1 | .4 | | Cur. Mat.-L.T.D. | 3.5 | 3.9 |
| 8.2 | 10.9 | 12.1 | 14.2 | 10.5 | | Trade Payables | 14.9 | 13.5 |
| .0 | .9 | .2 | .1 | .0 | | Income Taxes Payable | .4 | .4 |
| 21.9 | 15.8 | 12.1 | 15.5 | 13.2 | | All Other Current | 16.4 | 16.0 |
| 61.6 | 36.1 | 35.0 | 40.4 | 27.7 | | Total Current | 44.7 | 42.7 |
| 19.3 | 20.0 | 11.5 | 15.5 | 15.6 | | Long-Term Debt | 22.1 | 19.8 |
| .0 | .1 | .5 | .4 | .2 | | Deferred Taxes | .7 | .6 |
| 19.6 | 7.1 | 6.0 | 8.8 | 5.3 | | All Other Non-Current | 4.2 | 9.5 |
| -.5 | 36.7 | 46.9 | 34.9 | 51.2 | | Net Worth | 28.4 | 27.5 |
| 100.0 | 100.0 | 100.0 | 100.0 | 100.0 | | Total Liabilties & Net Worth | 100.0 | 100.0 |
| | | | | | | **INCOME DATA** | | |
| 100.0 | 100.0 | 100.0 | 100.0 | 100.0 | | Net Sales | 100.0 | 100.0 |
| | | | | | | Gross Profit | | |
| 91.1 | 89.1 | 90.6 | 92.9 | 100.7 | | Operating Expenses | 88.3 | 91.2 |
| 8.9 | 10.9 | 9.4 | 7.1 | -.7 | | Operating Profit | 11.7 | 8.8 |
| .3 | 2.9 | .8 | 1.5 | 3.6 | | All Other Expenses (net) | 2.9 | 1.9 |
| 8.6 | 7.9 | 8.6 | 5.6 | -4.3 | | Profit Before Taxes | 8.9 | 6.9 |
| | | | | | | **RATIOS** | | |
| 4.2 | 4.2 | 3.6 | 2.3 | 3.6 | | | 2.5 | 2.4 |
| 1.3 | 1.8 | 1.9 | 1.5 | 1.6 | | Current | 1.3 | 1.3 |
| .5 | .9 | 1.2 | .9 | 1.2 | | | .8 | .8 |
| 3.3 | 3.8 | 2.8 | 1.6 | 3.4 | | | 2.3 | 1.9 |
| 1.0 | 1.5 | 1.5 | 1.0 | 1.3 | | Quick | 1.0 | 1.1 |
| .3 | .7 | .9 | .6 | .6 | | | .5 | .5 |
| 0　UND | 0　850.9 | 17　21.8 | 21　17.0 | 34　10.7 | | | 12　31.6 | 9　41.4 |
| 0　UND | 25　14.8 | 39　9.3 | 40　9.1 | 47　7.8 | | Sales/Receivables | 45　8.2 | 33　11.1 |
| 24　15.5 | 44　8.3 | 58　6.3 | 63　5.8 | 69　5.3 | | | 70　5.2 | 55　6.7 |
| | | | | | | Cost of Sales/Inventory | | |
| | | | | | | Cost of Sales/Payables | | |
| 13.1 | 5.7 | 5.9 | 5.7 | 4.1 | | | 6.3 | 7.8 |
| 65.4 | 14.3 | 10.7 | 11.7 | 7.4 | | Sales/Working Capital | 18.9 | 25.2 |
| -22.1 | -191.9 | 31.3 | -132.2 | NM | | | -26.4 | -52.1 |
| | 17.5 | 24.1 | 36.6 | 20.9 | | | | 11.4 | 21.9 |
| (35)　5.2 | (68)　8.9 | (81)　11.8 | (32)　5.6 | | | EBIT/Interest | (87)　4.4 | (161)　3.8 |
| .9 | 1.9 | 2.9 | 1.1 | | | | 1.1 | 1.2 |
| | | 8.3 | | | | | 12.7 | 5.6 |
| | (19)　3.5 | | | | Net Profit + Depr., Dep., | (17)　5.5 | (31)　1.6 |
| | | 2.4 | | | | Amort./Cur. Mat. L/T/D | 1.5 | .4 |
| .0 | .1 | .1 | .1 | .5 | | | .2 | .2 |
| 1.0 | .4 | .4 | .9 | 1.2 | | Fixed/Worth | .9 | .8 |
| -1.3 | 2.0 | 1.2 | 2.9 | -.5 | | | 8.3 | 7.1 |
| .5 | .5 | .3 | .9 | .6 | | | 1.0 | .9 |
| 4.2 | 1.3 | 1.4 | 2.0 | 2.4 | | Debt/Worth | 3.6 | 3.1 |
| -4.6 | 4.0 | 3.5 | 12.8 | -2.7 | | | 15.7 | 42.7 |
| 224.4 | 83.2 | 61.0 | 54.5 | | | % Profit Before Taxes/Tangible | 78.9 | 89.1 |
| (42)　74.0 | (76)　28.7 | (99)　27.3 | (31)　40.6 | | | Net Worth | (95)　34.3 | (151)　32.0 |
| 21.4 | 9.7 | 8.6 | 13.8 | | | | 11.0 | 5.3 |
| 82.2 | 28.9 | 25.1 | 22.0 | 5.9 | | % Profit Before Taxes/Total | 24.1 | 21.1 |
| 24.2 | 12.2 | 13.0 | 10.8 | 3.7 | | Assets | 9.1 | 8.2 |
| 1.8 | 2.6 | 3.7 | .6 | -8.7 | | | .9 | .7 |
| 817.6 | 110.3 | 108.9 | 60.5 | 75.2 | | | 41.5 | 99.0 |
| 52.7 | 25.0 | 25.3 | 12.6 | 12.7 | | Sales/Net Fixed Assets | 15.1 | 17.1 |
| 11.5 | 5.7 | 7.1 | 3.1 | 4.2 | | | 4.5 | 5.8 |
| 11.6 | 4.8 | 3.9 | 3.4 | 2.1 | | | 3.8 | 4.3 |
| 5.3 | 3.1 | 2.9 | 1.7 | 1.3 | | Sales/Total Assets | 2.2 | 2.6 |
| 3.0 | 1.6 | 1.7 | .9 | .7 | | | 1.3 | 1.2 |
| .7 | .6 | .3 | .6 | | | | .8 | .6 |
| (26)　1.7 | (49)　1.3 | (80)　.9 | (33)　2.3 | | | % Depr., Dep., Amort./Sales | (84)　2.0 | (143)　2.1 |
| 2.9 | 4.6 | 3.8 | 4.8 | | | | 4.9 | 5.1 |
| 6.0 | 1.6 | 1.8 | | | | % Officers', Directors' | 2.6 | 2.5 |
| (32)　10.9 | (34)　4.7 | (25)　4.3 | | | | Owners' Comp/Sales | (37)　4.0 | (64)　5.1 |
| 20.0 | 8.5 | 8.9 | | | | | 9.3 | 8.2 |
| 105266M | 457352M | 1703345M | 2659471M | 1197808M | 706685M | Net Sales ($) | 4199439M | 7100369M |
| 13339M | 95352M | 464716M | 774597M | 706232M | 901655M | Total Assets ($) | 3189911M | 4090868M |

© RMA 2012

M = $ thousand　　MM = $ million
See Pages 9 through 22 for Explanation of Ratios and Data

## Comparative Historical Data / Current Data Sorted by Sales

| 30 | 37 | 43 | Type of Statement | | | | | | |
|---|---|---|---|---|---|---|---|---|---|
| | | | | | 0-1MM | 1-3MM | 3-5MM | 5-10MM | 10-25MM | 25MM & OVER |
| 30 | 37 | 43 | Unqualified | | 4 | 3 | 6 | 12 | 18 |
| 29 | 41 | 37 | Reviewed | | 4 | 4 | 6 | 13 | 10 |
| 29 | 35 | 47 | Compiled | 7 | 13 | 3 | 10 | 12 | 2 |
| 65 | 48 | 51 | Tax Returns | 19 | 17 | 6 | 4 | 5 | |
| 102 | 111 | 134 | Other | 19 | 30 | 17 | 18 | 28 | 22 |
| 4/1/09-3/31/10 ALL | 4/1/10-3/31/11 ALL | 4/1/11-3/31/12 ALL | | | 44 (4/1-9/30/11) | | | 268 (10/1/11-3/31/12) | | |
| 255 | 272 | 312 | NUMBER OF STATEMENTS | 45 | 68 | 33 | 44 | 70 | 52 |
| % | % | % | ASSETS | % | % | % | % | % | % |
| 16.1 | 16.9 | 22.2 | Cash & Equivalents | 29.8 | 26.7 | 17.8 | 18.8 | 22.1 | 15.2 |
| 23.8 | 29.2 | 26.0 | Trade Receivables (net) | 10.7 | 19.3 | 28.5 | 34.0 | 31.3 | 32.7 |
| 8.1 | 7.2 | 7.1 | Inventory | 3.8 | 6.7 | 5.7 | 8.4 | 8.5 | 8.4 |
| 4.5 | 6.0 | 4.3 | All Other Current | 3.3 | 1.1 | 7.2 | 2.6 | 6.0 | 6.9 |
| 52.5 | 59.3 | 59.6 | Total Current | 47.6 | 53.8 | 59.1 | 63.8 | 68.0 | 63.2 |
| 28.5 | 24.9 | 25.5 | Fixed Assets (net) | 40.5 | 32.6 | 22.1 | 20.5 | 20.2 | 16.5 |
| 9.6 | 7.3 | 4.9 | Intangibles (net) | 4.1 | 3.4 | .9 | 2.8 | 4.7 | 12.3 |
| 9.4 | 8.5 | 10.0 | All Other Non-Current | 7.7 | 10.2 | 17.9 | 12.9 | 7.2 | 8.0 |
| 100.0 | 100.0 | 100.0 | Total | 100.0 | 100.0 | 100.0 | 100.0 | 100.0 | 100.0 |
| | | | LIABILITIES | | | | | | |
| 14.1 | 12.7 | 11.6 | Notes Payable-Short Term | 19.5 | 16.7 | 7.1 | 10.7 | 7.9 | 6.6 |
| 3.6 | 3.9 | 2.4 | Cur. Mat.-L.T.D. | 1.5 | 2.4 | 3.1 | 3.5 | 2.5 | 1.6 |
| 11.1 | 12.8 | 11.1 | Trade Payables | 1.7 | 9.8 | 14.9 | 9.4 | 13.4 | 16.7 |
| .4 | .4 | .3 | Income Taxes Payable | .0 | .1 | .2 | 1.7 | .2 | .1 |
| 15.8 | 22.2 | 15.8 | All Other Current | 20.6 | 11.1 | 18.8 | 13.2 | 14.4 | 19.8 |
| 44.9 | 52.0 | 41.2 | Total Current | 43.3 | 40.0 | 44.2 | 38.5 | 38.3 | 44.8 |
| 20.3 | 18.1 | 16.2 | Long-Term Debt | 16.4 | 30.1 | 15.3 | 11.7 | 11.0 | 8.9 |
| .4 | .4 | .3 | Deferred Taxes | .0 | .1 | .0 | .5 | .7 | .6 |
| 8.1 | 7.5 | 9.6 | All Other Non-Current | 18.3 | 13.8 | 5.2 | 7.2 | 3.7 | 9.0 |
| 26.3 | 22.0 | 32.8 | Net Worth | 21.9 | 15.9 | 35.3 | 42.0 | 46.3 | 36.7 |
| 100.0 | 100.0 | 100.0 | Total Liabilities & Net Worth | 100.0 | 100.0 | 100.0 | 100.0 | 100.0 | 100.0 |
| | | | INCOME DATA | | | | | | |
| 100.0 | 100.0 | 100.0 | Net Sales | 100.0 | 100.0 | 100.0 | 100.0 | 100.0 | 100.0 |
| | | | Gross Profit | | | | | | |
| 92.2 | 91.9 | 90.9 | Operating Expenses | 83.3 | 88.3 | 91.3 | 92.9 | 93.6 | 95.6 |
| 7.8 | 8.1 | 9.1 | Operating Profit | 16.7 | 11.7 | 8.7 | 7.1 | 6.4 | 4.4 |
| 2.1 | 1.9 | 1.5 | All Other Expenses (net) | 5.0 | 1.5 | .6 | .3 | .4 | 1.4 |
| 5.7 | 6.2 | 7.6 | Profit Before Taxes | 11.7 | 10.2 | 8.1 | 6.8 | 6.0 | 3.0 |
| | | | RATIOS | | | | | | |
| 2.6 | 2.7 | 3.4 | Current | 3.6 | 6.4 | 3.2 | 3.1 | 3.6 | 2.2 |
| 1.3 | 1.4 | 1.7 | | 1.3 | 1.8 | 1.5 | 1.9 | 1.8 | 1.4 |
| .8 | .9 | .9 | | .5 | .9 | 1.1 | 1.0 | 1.4 | .9 |
| 2.0 | 2.2 | 2.8 | Quick | 3.1 | 5.7 | 2.0 | 2.7 | 3.0 | 1.4 |
| .9 | 1.1 | 1.3 | | .9 | 1.6 | 1.4 | 1.8 | 1.5 | .9 |
| .4 | .6 | .7 | | .2 | .5 | .9 | .8 | .8 | .7 |
| 3   119.5 | 8   48.1 | 2   157.6 | Sales/Receivables | 0 UND | 0 UND | 13   27.3 | 24   14.9 | 15   24.8 | 15   23.6 |
| 27   13.7 | 35   10.3 | 27   13.5 | | 0 UND | 20   18.4 | 26   14.2 | 40   9.1 | 37   9.9 | 37   9.9 |
| 48   7.5 | 56   6.6 | 52   7.0 | | 33   11.1 | 43   8.4 | 45   8.1 | 69   5.3 | 55   6.6 | 53   6.9 |
| | | | Cost of Sales/Inventory | | | | | | |
| | | | Cost of Sales/Payables | | | | | | |
| 8.8 | 7.4 | 6.2 | Sales/Working Capital | 8.0 | 4.2 | 6.0 | 6.0 | 6.3 | 7.5 |
| 27.9 | 20.7 | 13.7 | | 52.0 | 14.2 | 23.0 | 10.6 | 10.9 | 24.1 |
| -22.1 | -61.9 | -137.8 | | -21.4 | -41.1 | 316.7 | NM | 30.6 | -200.6 |
| 18.1 | 18.8 | 24.5 | EBIT/Interest | 22.2 | 13.1 | 33.0 | 22.5 | 34.1 | 132.0 |
| (198)  3.7 | (203)  5.1 | (227)  6.6 | | (21)  4.3 | (51)  5.7 | (25)  9.5 | (35)  13.7 | (54)  5.8 | (41)  6.7 |
| .4 | 1.0 | 2.1 | | 1.6 | 1.9 | -.4 | 3.0 | 2.2 | 3.0 |
| 11.1 | 8.1 | 8.3 | Net Profit + Depr., Dep., Amort./Cur. Mat. L/T/D | | | | | 59.5 | 13.3 |
| (29)  3.2 | (40)  4.2 | (35)  3.6 | | | | | | (12)  5.6 | (13)  4.2 |
| 1.7 | .9 | 2.1 | | | | | | 2.8 | 2.3 |
| .2 | .2 | .1 | Fixed/Worth | .1 | .2 | .0 | .1 | .1 | .2 |
| .9 | .8 | .6 | | 1.3 | .9 | .2 | .4 | .3 | .9 |
| -6.0 | 5.0 | 2.4 | | UND | 4.0 | 1.7 | 1.4 | 1.3 | 3.6 |
| .8 | .7 | .5 | Debt/Worth | .4 | .4 | .5 | .6 | .4 | .9 |
| 3.2 | 2.0 | 1.7 | | 3.0 | 1.9 | 1.2 | 1.3 | 1.4 | 2.9 |
| -8.8 | 24.6 | 7.8 | | -53.0 | 9.3 | 5.0 | 4.2 | 3.6 | 20.3 |
| 60.0 | 69.7 | 78.2 | % Profit Before Taxes/Tangible Net Worth | 93.6 | 103.4 | 109.3 | 57.3 | 61.6 | 77.3 |
| (181)  23.3 | (211)  31.9 | (258)  29.2 | | (33)  26.7 | (52)  33.0 | (30)  26.0 | (39)  28.5 | (62)  27.4 | (42)  41.5 |
| 2.5 | 9.5 | 11.0 | | 6.2 | 11.7 | 7.7 | 5.9 | 6.9 | 16.4 |
| 20.3 | 29.1 | 29.0 | % Profit Before Taxes/Total Assets | 26.1 | 36.3 | 42.3 | 29.5 | 28.9 | 21.4 |
| 6.4 | 9.2 | 12.4 | | 9.8 | 16.8 | 11.0 | 13.3 | 12.9 | 10.8 |
| -1.7 | .8 | 2.5 | | 2.0 | 3.1 | -2.4 | 2.9 | 2.4 | 2.4 |
| 74.6 | 79.4 | 113.2 | Sales/Net Fixed Assets | 262.6 | 45.7 | 193.8 | 130.2 | 163.3 | 114.4 |
| 15.1 | 20.8 | 25.2 | | 13.8 | 13.1 | 37.1 | 28.3 | 41.0 | 32.9 |
| 5.2 | 6.4 | 6.5 | | 1.2 | 5.1 | 8.1 | 8.3 | 9.1 | 9.1 |
| 4.7 | 4.9 | 5.2 | Sales/Total Assets | 5.2 | 4.9 | 5.9 | 4.0 | 5.5 | 7.3 |
| 2.4 | 3.0 | 3.1 | | 1.9 | 3.0 | 3.1 | 3.0 | 3.3 | 3.3 |
| 1.1 | 1.5 | 1.5 | | .6 | 1.5 | 1.4 | 2.0 | 1.8 | 1.3 |
| .5 | .5 | .6 | % Depr., Dep., Amort./Sales | 1.0 | .9 | .3 | .4 | .4 | .1 |
| (176)  2.3 | (196)  1.5 | (197)  1.3 | | (18)  5.5 | (42)  2.1 | (21)  1.1 | (26)  .8 | (50)  1.2 | (40)  .9 |
| 5.0 | 4.6 | 4.3 | | 15.0 | 4.9 | 4.6 | 3.1 | 3.8 | 2.6 |
| 2.5 | 3.0 | 2.5 | % Officers', Directors' Owners' Comp/Sales | 5.5 | 4.0 | 4.9 | 2.4 | 1.2 | |
| (85)  5.1 | (76)  6.5 | (95)  5.8 | | (16)  10.3 | (30)  9.8 | (10)  6.6 | (13)  5.0 | (20)  2.3 | |
| 9.8 | 13.2 | 12.0 | | 25.4 | 15.2 | 11.5 | 10.0 | 5.3 | |
| 7192441M | 7330894M | 6829927M | Net Sales ($) | 19592M | 127095M | 126328M | 321724M | 1092683M | 5142505M |
| 3655078M | 3446741M | 2955891M | Total Assets ($) | 21959M | 77174M | 88012M | 175139M | 470184M | 2123423M |

M = $ thousand    MM = $ million
See Pages 9 through 22 for Explanation of Ratios and Data

# ADMIN & WASTE MANAGEMENT SERVICES—Solid Waste Collection  NAICS 562111

**Current Data Sorted by Assets**  |  **Comparative Historical Data**

| 0-500M | 500M-2MM | 2-10MM | 10-50MM | 50-100MM | 100-250MM | Type of Statement | 4/1/07-3/31/08 ALL | 4/1/08-3/31/09 ALL |
|---|---|---|---|---|---|---|---|---|
|  |  | 6 | 12 | 3 | 5 | Unqualified | 31 | 28 |
|  | 11 | 18 | 13 | 1 |  | Reviewed | 24 | 32 |
| 5 | 18 | 13 | 2 |  | 1 | Compiled | 26 | 30 |
| 35 | 24 | 20 |  |  |  | Tax Returns | 52 | 72 |
| 6 | 29 | 32 | 24 | 5 | 6 | Other | 59 | 91 |
|  | 33 (4/1-9/30/11) |  | 256 (10/1/11-3/31/12) |  |  |  |  |  |
| 46 | 82 | 89 | 51 | 9 | 12 | **NUMBER OF STATEMENTS** | 192 | 253 |
| % | % | % | % | % | % | **ASSETS** | % | % |
| 18.3 | 11.8 | 10.9 | 8.6 |  | 9.1 | Cash & Equivalents | 9.4 | 10.9 |
| 13.6 | 20.9 | 24.6 | 14.0 |  | 11.4 | Trade Receivables (net) | 16.4 | 18.0 |
| .8 | 2.2 | 2.1 | 1.1 |  | .8 | Inventory | 2.1 | 1.1 |
| 4.4 | 3.9 | 2.1 | 4.2 |  | 3.5 | All Other Current | 2.2 | 3.3 |
| 37.0 | 38.9 | 39.7 | 27.9 |  | 24.7 | Total Current | 30.1 | 33.3 |
| 44.7 | 41.1 | 46.7 | 57.9 |  | 42.6 | Fixed Assets (net) | 53.6 | 51.1 |
| 11.5 | 6.8 | 7.9 | 7.8 |  | 23.3 | Intangibles (net) | 8.4 | 8.3 |
| 6.7 | 13.2 | 5.7 | 6.4 |  | 9.4 | All Other Non-Current | 7.9 | 7.3 |
| 100.0 | 100.0 | 100.0 | 100.0 |  | 100.0 | Total | 100.0 | 100.0 |
|  |  |  |  |  |  | **LIABILITIES** |  |  |
| 18.6 | 8.9 | 4.7 | 3.1 |  | 5.2 | Notes Payable-Short Term | 5.8 | 5.6 |
| 9.6 | 8.3 | 7.7 | 7.9 |  | 3.9 | Cur. Mat.-L.T.D. | 8.1 | 9.1 |
| 12.2 | 12.6 | 13.3 | 7.4 |  | 6.2 | Trade Payables | 9.2 | 9.7 |
| .0 | .3 | .4 | .1 |  | .2 | Income Taxes Payable | .1 | .2 |
| 10.4 | 8.9 | 7.7 | 9.1 |  | 4.9 | All Other Current | 8.7 | 6.9 |
| 50.9 | 39.0 | 33.8 | 27.6 |  | 20.4 | Total Current | 31.8 | 31.4 |
| 64.3 | 34.3 | 26.5 | 30.1 |  | 31.4 | Long-Term Debt | 41.3 | 43.0 |
| .0 | .1 | .8 | .7 |  | 4.2 | Deferred Taxes | .7 | .9 |
| 18.5 | 17.4 | 4.7 | 8.3 |  | 8.0 | All Other Non-Current | 9.0 | 7.5 |
| -33.6 | 9.2 | 34.1 | 33.3 |  | 36.0 | Net Worth | 17.1 | 17.2 |
| 100.0 | 100.0 | 100.0 | 100.0 |  | 100.0 | Total Liabilities & Net Worth | 100.0 | 100.0 |
|  |  |  |  |  |  | **INCOME DATA** |  |  |
| 100.0 | 100.0 | 100.0 | 100.0 |  | 100.0 | Net Sales | 100.0 | 100.0 |
|  |  |  |  |  |  | Gross Profit |  |  |
| 93.6 | 93.4 | 91.9 | 93.4 |  | 89.7 | Operating Expenses | 93.0 | 93.5 |
| 6.4 | 6.6 | 8.1 | 6.6 |  | 10.3 | Operating Profit | 7.0 | 6.5 |
| 1.3 | 2.1 | 1.3 | 1.3 |  | 3.5 | All Other Expenses (net) | 2.4 | 2.9 |
| 5.1 | 4.5 | 6.8 | 5.3 |  | 6.7 | Profit Before Taxes | 4.6 | 3.7 |
|  |  |  |  |  |  | **RATIOS** |  |  |
| 1.7 | 2.0 | 2.0 | 1.4 |  | 1.8 |  | 1.6 | 1.8 |
| .7 | 1.1 | 1.2 | .9 |  | 1.1 | Current | 1.0 | 1.1 |
| .2 | .5 | .7 | .6 |  | .6 |  | .6 | .6 |
| 1.5 | 1.7 | 1.8 | 1.2 |  | 1.4 |  | 1.4 | 1.6 |
| .6 | .9 | 1.0 | .7 |  | .7 | Quick | .8 | .9 |
| .2 | .4 | .6 | .5 |  | .5 |  | .5 | .5 |
| 0 UND | 2 181.3 | 24 15.5 | 23 15.6 |  | 23 16.2 |  | 13 27.1 | 15 24.8 |
| 0 UND | 26 14.1 | 33 11.1 | 34 10.6 |  | 32 11.3 | Sales/Receivables | 33 11.0 | 31 11.7 |
| 17 20.9 | 38 9.7 | 47 7.7 | 46 8.0 |  | 45 8.2 |  | 44 8.3 | 41 8.8 |
|  |  |  |  |  |  | Cost of Sales/Inventory |  |  |
|  |  |  |  |  |  | Cost of Sales/Payables |  |  |
| 27.8 | 14.3 | 10.1 | 17.9 |  | 8.2 |  | 15.4 | 16.2 |
| -46.0 | 118.7 | 47.5 | -122.8 |  | NM | Sales/Working Capital | -158.2 | 196.5 |
| -11.0 | -12.9 | -19.3 | -10.6 |  | -7.9 |  | -12.9 | -14.2 |
| 11.6 | 8.2 | 13.1 | 8.3 |  | 13.5 |  | 5.4 | 5.8 |
| (37) 4.1 | (73) 3.2 | (83) 5.4 | (48) 4.4 |  | 3.6 | EBIT/Interest | (175) 2.6 | (232) 2.9 |
| 1.0 | .1 | 2.1 | 1.8 |  | .9 |  | 1.1 | 1.0 |
|  |  | 10.9 | 2.4 |  |  |  | 2.8 | 2.9 |
|  |  | (16) 2.7 | (11) 1.7 |  |  | Net Profit + Depr., Dep., Amort./Cur. Mat. L/T/D | (44) 1.8 | (54) 1.6 |
|  |  | 1.8 | .8 |  |  |  | 1.3 | 1.0 |
| .9 | .7 | .8 | 1.5 |  | 1.5 |  | 1.3 | 1.0 |
| -1.9 | 2.3 | 1.6 | 2.5 |  | 3.2 | Fixed/Worth | 3.8 | 3.3 |
| -.3 | -2.0 | 9.0 | 6.2 |  | NM |  | -5.0 | -6.0 |
| 1.4 | 1.1 | .9 | 1.5 |  | 1.6 |  | 1.5 | 1.6 |
| -3.6 | 4.9 | 2.3 | 3.1 |  | 4.4 | Debt/Worth | 4.8 | 4.2 |
| -1.7 | -3.8 | 34.4 | 8.6 |  | NM |  | -7.3 | -11.6 |
| 148.8 | 62.3 | 80.7 | 51.1 |  |  |  | 66.6 | 59.2 |
| (18) 78.8 | (54) 32.5 | (70) 34.1 | (48) 29.1 |  |  | % Profit Before Taxes/Tangible Net Worth | (133) 32.3 | (178) 29.3 |
| 19.3 | 8.3 | 17.7 | 14.0 |  |  |  | 10.6 | 7.1 |
| 40.7 | 21.9 | 20.7 | 12.3 |  | 8.5 |  | 14.3 | 15.6 |
| 16.6 | 8.1 | 11.0 | 7.8 |  | 4.7 | % Profit Before Taxes/Total Assets | 6.5 | 5.5 |
| .4 | -3.4 | 3.1 | 1.6 |  | -1.4 |  | .7 | .0 |
| 34.9 | 20.1 | 10.5 | 3.3 |  | 4.5 |  | 6.2 | 8.7 |
| 13.8 | 8.1 | 4.8 | 2.3 |  | 2.3 | Sales/Net Fixed Assets | 3.5 | 3.9 |
| 5.4 | 3.5 | 2.6 | 1.6 |  | 1.2 |  | 1.9 | 2.0 |
| 7.0 | 4.5 | 3.1 | 1.6 |  | 1.3 |  | 2.8 | 3.4 |
| 4.5 | 2.4 | 2.3 | 1.2 |  | 1.0 | Sales/Total Assets | 1.7 | 1.9 |
| 3.1 | 1.5 | 1.6 | .9 |  | .6 |  | 1.2 | 1.2 |
| 3.7 | 1.9 | 3.4 | 5.7 |  |  |  | 4.6 | 5.0 |
| (27) 6.4 | (60) 5.9 | (77) 6.1 | (50) 8.2 |  |  | % Depr., Dep., Amort./Sales | (162) 7.6 | (202) 7.5 |
| 11.9 | 9.1 | 9.4 | 11.3 |  |  |  | 11.2 | 10.6 |
| 3.3 | 2.0 | 1.5 |  |  |  |  | 1.6 | 1.9 |
| (27) 6.2 | (31) 5.0 | (44) 2.9 |  |  |  | % Officers', Directors' Owners' Comp/Sales | (83) 4.1 | (104) 4.0 |
| 8.1 | 10.2 | 4.9 |  |  |  |  | 6.6 | 7.7 |
| 83125M | 319744M | 1012319M | 1553152M | 716287M | 3030476M | Net Sales ($) | 4167555M | 6402782M |
| 11293M | 94357M | 424941M | 1103567M | 646062M | 1846204M | Total Assets ($) | 3680464M | 4526778M |

© RMA 2012

M = $ thousand    MM = $ million
See Pages 9 through 22 for Explanation of Ratios and Data

## Comparative Historical Data | Current Data Sorted by Sales

| Type of Statement | | | | | | | | | |
|---|---|---|---|---|---|---|---|---|---|
| | **Comp. Hist.** | | | | | | | | |
| Unqualified | | | | | 1 | 1 | 2 | 8 | 14 |
| Reviewed | 37 | 29 | 26 | 1 | 2 | 1 | 13 | 19 | 7 |
| Compiled | 43 | 36 | 43 | 6 | 7 | 7 | 12 | 6 | 1 |
| Tax Returns | 50 | 46 | 39 | 20 | 25 | 12 | 12 | 9 | 1 |
| Other | 72 | 49 | 79 | 9 | 16 | 8 | 20 | 21 | 28 |
| | 94 | 98 | 102 | | | | | | |
| | 4/1/09-3/31/10 | 4/1/10-3/31/11 | 4/1/11-3/31/12 | 33 (4/1-9/30/11) | | | 256 (10/1/11-3/31/12) | | |
| | ALL | ALL | ALL | 0-1MM | 1-3MM | 3-5MM | 5-10MM | 10-25MM | 25MM & OVER |
| **NUMBER OF STATEMENTS** | 296 | 258 | 289 | 36 | 51 | 29 | 59 | 63 | 51 |
| | % | % | % | % | % | % | % | % | % |
| **ASSETS** | | | | | | | | | |
| Cash & Equivalents | 11.8 | 11.7 | 11.6 | 9.3 | 14.7 | 12.1 | 12.5 | 12.9 | 7.2 |
| Trade Receivables (net) | 17.0 | 19.3 | 19.0 | 12.6 | 13.5 | 16.1 | 26.7 | 24.4 | 15.0 |
| Inventory | 1.4 | 1.2 | 1.6 | .9 | 2.3 | 1.6 | 1.5 | 1.3 | 2.2 |
| All Other Current | 3.2 | 3.9 | 3.4 | 5.6 | 2.7 | 3.3 | 3.4 | 3.0 | 3.1 |
| Total Current | 33.4 | 36.1 | 35.6 | 28.4 | 33.2 | 33.2 | 44.1 | 41.5 | 27.6 |
| Fixed Assets (net) | 49.4 | 46.3 | 47.2 | 45.2 | 52.0 | 46.9 | 43.4 | 43.3 | 53.1 |
| Intangibles (net) | 8.9 | 9.3 | 8.9 | 16.1 | 5.3 | 10.1 | 5.9 | 6.7 | 13.1 |
| All Other Non-Current | 8.3 | 8.3 | 8.2 | 10.3 | 9.5 | 9.8 | 6.6 | 8.4 | 6.2 |
| Total | 100.0 | 100.0 | 100.0 | 100.0 | 100.0 | 100.0 | 100.0 | 100.0 | 100.0 |
| **LIABILITIES** | | | | | | | | | |
| Notes Payable-Short Term | 5.0 | 8.2 | 7.8 | 17.8 | 7.3 | 8.5 | 5.5 | 7.2 | 4.0 |
| Cur. Mat.-L.T.D. | 7.5 | 6.8 | 8.0 | 7.2 | 7.2 | 15.7 | 7.8 | 6.9 | 6.4 |
| Trade Payables | 9.7 | 10.3 | 11.4 | 5.3 | 12.6 | 11.7 | 16.3 | 11.2 | 8.7 |
| Income Taxes Payable | .3 | .3 | .2 | .0 | .3 | .2 | .1 | .5 | .1 |
| All Other Current | 11.4 | 9.1 | 8.7 | 6.6 | 8.5 | 6.3 | 11.1 | 9.1 | 8.2 |
| Total Current | 33.9 | 34.7 | 36.0 | 36.9 | 36.0 | 42.4 | 40.8 | 35.0 | 27.3 |
| Long-Term Debt | 37.5 | 29.8 | 36.1 | 54.0 | 46.9 | 50.8 | 24.1 | 25.6 | 31.1 |
| Deferred Taxes | .8 | 1.2 | .6 | .0 | .0 | .2 | .3 | 1.1 | 1.7 |
| All Other Non-Current | 8.0 | 8.8 | 11.4 | 20.5 | 24.9 | 10.2 | 4.6 | 5.5 | 7.1 |
| Net Worth | 19.8 | 25.5 | 16.0 | -11.5 | -7.8 | -3.6 | 30.2 | 32.9 | 32.8 |
| Total Liabilities & Net Worth | 100.0 | 100.0 | 100.0 | 100.0 | 100.0 | 100.0 | 100.0 | 100.0 | 100.0 |
| **INCOME DATA** | | | | | | | | | |
| Net Sales | 100.0 | 100.0 | 100.0 | 100.0 | 100.0 | 100.0 | 100.0 | 100.0 | 100.0 |
| Gross Profit | | | | | | | | | |
| Operating Expenses | 93.1 | 91.5 | 92.8 | 88.2 | 92.8 | 93.4 | 93.5 | 93.8 | 93.7 |
| Operating Profit | 6.9 | 8.5 | 7.2 | 11.8 | 7.2 | 6.6 | 6.5 | 6.2 | 6.3 |
| All Other Expenses (net) | 2.3 | 1.8 | 1.6 | 3.8 | 2.2 | 2.0 | .5 | .7 | 1.8 |
| Profit Before Taxes | 4.6 | 6.6 | 5.6 | 8.0 | 5.0 | 4.7 | 6.0 | 5.5 | 4.5 |
| **RATIOS** | | | | | | | | | |
| Current | 2.0 | 1.9 | 1.8 | 2.1 | 2.6 | 1.4 | 1.8 | 2.0 | 1.4 |
| | 1.0 | 1.0 | 1.0 | .8 | .9 | .9 | 1.2 | 1.1 | .9 |
| | .6 | .6 | .6 | .1 | .4 | .5 | .7 | .7 | .6 |
| Quick | 1.7 | 1.7 | 1.5 | 1.5 | 2.3 | 1.4 | 1.7 | 1.7 | 1.0 |
| | (295) .8 | .9 | .8 | .6 | .7 | .7 | 1.0 | 1.0 | .7 |
| | .5 | .5 | .5 | .1 | .3 | .3 | .6 | .6 | .6 |
| Sales/Receivables | 17 21.6 | 19 18.7 | 13 27.3 | 0 UND | 0 UND | 0 UND | 23 15.8 | 25 14.5 | 22 16.6 |
| | 31 11.6 | 32 11.5 | 28 12.9 | 4 88.1 | 20 18.4 | 23 16.2 | 32 11.4 | 36 10.1 | 33 11.0 |
| | 45 8.2 | 45 8.0 | 42 8.6 | 27 13.4 | 36 10.1 | 39 9.3 | 42 8.6 | 48 7.6 | 42 8.7 |
| Cost of Sales/Inventory | | | | | | | | | |
| Cost of Sales/Payables | | | | | | | | | |
| Sales/Working Capital | 11.2 | 10.0 | 14.7 | 15.0 | 10.5 | 31.9 | 13.1 | 9.4 | 26.0 |
| | UND | 174.5 | -999.8 | -79.5 | -163.8 | -66.1 | 37.6 | 76.5 | -128.7 |
| | -14.3 | -17.9 | -13.0 | -6.4 | -11.6 | -12.6 | -21.2 | -17.3 | -12.5 |
| EBIT/Interest | 7.5 | 10.6 | 10.2 | 7.6 | 10.2 | 15.0 | 15.8 | 10.0 | 9.7 |
| | (272) 3.2 | (239) 4.6 | (261) 4.3 | (27) 2.3 | (44) 3.5 | 4.0 | (55) 6.0 | (58) 5.2 | (48) 4.1 |
| | 1.1 | 1.9 | 1.3 | .1 | .5 | .3 | 1.6 | 2.1 | 2.0 |
| Net Profit + Depr., Dep., Amort./Cur. Mat. L/T/D | 3.4 | 2.3 | 6.0 | | | | | 3.6 | 7.6 |
| | (57) 1.9 | (63) 1.8 | (43) 2.4 | | | | (17) 2.4 | (13) 2.4 | |
| | 1.4 | 1.2 | 1.2 | | | | | 1.4 | 1.5 |
| Fixed/Worth | 1.1 | .9 | .9 | 1.2 | .8 | 1.8 | .8 | .6 | 1.6 |
| | 2.8 | 2.1 | 2.5 | -2.1 | 4.5 | 44.7 | 1.4 | 1.6 | 2.7 |
| | -7.2 | -43.0 | -16.3 | -.4 | -2.0 | -.8 | 6.0 | 4.9 | 12.2 |
| Debt/Worth | 1.4 | 1.1 | 1.3 | 1.5 | 1.2 | 2.2 | .9 | .8 | 1.5 |
| | 3.3 | 3.0 | 3.6 | -4.0 | 6.0 | 54.9 | 2.0 | 2.3 | 3.5 |
| | -12.2 | -83.9 | -26.5 | -1.9 | -3.3 | -2.7 | 8.1 | 8.0 | 19.3 |
| % Profit Before Taxes/Tangible Net Worth | 50.2 | 61.4 | 70.8 | 54.4 | 115.8 | 144.0 | 74.8 | 55.5 | 64.6 |
| | (212) 25.7 | (189) 30.0 | (207) 31.9 | (14) 19.9 | (31) 39.5 | (15) 46.8 | (49) 31.9 | (53) 30.9 | (45) 29.1 |
| | 6.4 | 12.3 | 16.9 | 6.7 | 18.0 | 20.9 | 15.8 | 13.3 | 17.5 |
| % Profit Before Taxes/Total Assets | 13.6 | 18.6 | 19.4 | 19.0 | 32.4 | 26.5 | 21.8 | 15.8 | 10.3 |
| | 6.3 | 7.6 | 9.1 | 6.3 | 12.5 | 7.6 | 11.0 | 9.7 | 7.3 |
| | .4 | 1.5 | 1.3 | -4.1 | -.4 | -2.6 | 2.7 | 1.8 | 2.8 |
| Sales/Net Fixed Assets | 8.1 | 10.3 | 12.3 | 15.1 | 18.8 | 10.0 | 19.5 | 12.2 | 4.0 |
| | 3.8 | 4.0 | 4.8 | 5.5 | 6.3 | 5.3 | 7.9 | 4.8 | 2.7 |
| | 1.9 | 2.0 | 2.3 | 2.0 | 2.5 | 3.3 | 2.6 | 2.4 | 1.6 |
| Sales/Total Assets | 2.8 | 3.0 | 3.6 | 4.0 | 4.6 | 3.6 | 4.3 | 3.2 | 2.2 |
| | 1.7 | 1.7 | 2.1 | 1.7 | 2.2 | 2.2 | 3.0 | 2.3 | 1.3 |
| | 1.1 | 1.1 | 1.3 | .8 | 1.5 | 1.7 | 1.6 | 1.2 | 1.0 |
| % Depr., Dep., Amort./Sales | 4.5 | 3.5 | 3.7 | 5.7 | 3.1 | 3.0 | 2.1 | 4.3 | 5.3 |
| | (250) 7.6 | (216) 6.4 | (226) 6.7 | (24) 10.4 | (38) 7.2 | (22) 7.3 | (49) 4.9 | (52) 6.1 | (41) 7.8 |
| | 10.8 | 10.1 | 10.1 | 14.6 | 9.6 | 11.0 | 8.7 | 8.9 | 10.3 |
| % Officers', Directors' Owners' Comp/Sales | 2.3 | 2.6 | 2.2 | 3.3 | 5.0 | 2.9 | 2.1 | 1.2 | |
| | (110) 4.5 | (82) 4.5 | (110) 4.2 | (15) 5.6 | (24) 6.8 | (11) 8.5 | (24) 4.0 | (32) 2.3 | |
| | 6.9 | 7.3 | 6.7 | 7.3 | 11.3 | 8.2 | 5.7 | 4.4 | |
| Net Sales ($) | 5933994M | 4514085M | 6715103M | 22225M | 93273M | 111689M | 439667M | 945621M | 5102628M |
| Total Assets ($) | 4131736M | 3724377M | 4126424M | 18427M | 75552M | 54308M | 200050M | 679733M | 3098354M |

© RMA 2012

M = $ thousand    MM = $ million
See Pages 9 through 22 for Explanation of Ratios and Data

**Current Data Sorted by Assets**     **Comparative Historical Data**

| 0-500M | 500M-2MM | 2-10MM | 10-50MM | 50-100MM | 100-250MM | Type of Statement | 4/1/07-3/31/08 ALL | 4/1/08-3/31/09 ALL |
|---|---|---|---|---|---|---|---|---|
| 2 1 | 3 4 2 | 1 4 3 3 1 5 | 2 3 | 1 | | Unqualified | 4 | 4 |
| | 1 (4/1-9/30/11) | | 31 (10/1/11-3/31/12) | | | Reviewed | 1 | 4 |
| | | | | | | Compiled | 5 | 4 |
| | | | | | | Tax Returns | 6 | 6 |
| | | | | | | Other | 14 | 6 |
| **3** | **9** | **14** | **5** | **1** | | **NUMBER OF STATEMENTS** | **30** | **24** |
| % | % | % | % | % | % | **ASSETS** | % | % |
| | | 4.6 | | | D | Cash & Equivalents | 9.8 | 9.7 |
| | | 26.9 | | | A | Trade Receivables (net) | 17.6 | 19.1 |
| | | 1.6 | | | T | Inventory | 1.5 | 1.8 |
| | | .9 | | | A | All Other Current | 3.0 | 1.7 |
| | | 34.0 | | | | Total Current | 32.0 | 32.3 |
| | | 49.4 | | | N | Fixed Assets (net) | 52.2 | 53.9 |
| | | 6.6 | | | O | Intangibles (net) | 10.6 | 8.7 |
| | | 10.0 | | | T | All Other Non-Current | 5.2 | 5.2 |
| | | 100.0 | | | | Total | 100.0 | 100.0 |
| | | | | | A | **LIABILITIES** | | |
| | | 3.9 | | | V | Notes Payable-Short Term | 15.1 | 5.5 |
| | | 10.4 | | | A | Cur. Mat.-L.T.D. | 7.6 | 10.2 |
| | | 15.3 | | | I | Trade Payables | 8.7 | 7.1 |
| | | .0 | | | L | Income Taxes Payable | .0 | .0 |
| | | 11.3 | | | A | All Other Current | 5.3 | 5.8 |
| | | 41.0 | | | B | Total Current | 36.7 | 28.7 |
| | | 24.4 | | | L | Long-Term Debt | 39.8 | 36.9 |
| | | 1.2 | | | E | Deferred Taxes | .4 | .7 |
| | | 4.5 | | | | All Other Non-Current | 8.3 | 13.5 |
| | | 28.9 | | | | Net Worth | 14.7 | 20.2 |
| | | 100.0 | | | | Total Liabilities & Net Worth | 100.0 | 100.0 |
| | | | | | | **INCOME DATA** | | |
| | | 100.0 | | | | Net Sales | 100.0 | 100.0 |
| | | | | | | Gross Profit | | |
| | | 93.9 | | | | Operating Expenses | 93.4 | 93.9 |
| | | 6.1 | | | | Operating Profit | 6.6 | 6.1 |
| | | 1.1 | | | | All Other Expenses (net) | 3.3 | 2.3 |
| | | 4.9 | | | | Profit Before Taxes | 3.3 | 3.8 |
| | | | | | | **RATIOS** | | |
| | | 1.3 | | | | | 1.9 | 2.6 |
| | | .7 | | | | Current | .9 | .9 |
| | | .5 | | | | | .3 | .6 |
| | | .9 | | | | | 1.6 | 1.5 |
| | | .6 | | | | Quick | .6 | .9 |
| | | .5 | | | | | .3 | .6 |
| | | 3 110.1 | | | | | 17 21.1 | 28 12.9 |
| | | 31 11.6 | | | | Sales/Receivables | 35 10.4 | 40 9.2 |
| | | 43 8.4 | | | | | 46 7.9 | 57 6.4 |
| | | | | | | Cost of Sales/Inventory | | |
| | | | | | | Cost of Sales/Payables | | |
| | | 108.1 | | | | | 13.2 | 11.8 |
| | | -20.1 | | | | Sales/Working Capital | -49.0 | -102.5 |
| | | -12.7 | | | | | -5.9 | -12.5 |
| | | 9.0 | | | | | 6.0 | 6.4 |
| | (12) | 4.4 | | | | EBIT/Interest | (26) 2.2 | 3.6 |
| | | 1.1 | | | | | .7 | 1.1 |
| | | | | | | Net Profit + Depr., Dep., Amort./Cur. Mat. L/T/D | | |
| | | 1.1 | | | | | 1.4 | 1.1 |
| | | 3.2 | | | | Fixed/Worth | 33.2 | 2.6 |
| | | 36.4 | | | | | -4.8 | NM |
| | | .8 | | | | | 1.5 | 1.0 |
| | | 5.2 | | | | Debt/Worth | NM | 3.5 |
| | | 93.7 | | | | | -10.4 | NM |
| | | 72.7 | | | | | 59.0 | 103.2 |
| | (12) | 30.7 | | | | % Profit Before Taxes/Tangible Net Worth | (15) 34.9 | (18) 32.0 |
| | | -17.7 | | | | | 7.9 | 10.0 |
| | | 14.0 | | | | | 18.5 | 15.1 |
| | | 9.3 | | | | % Profit Before Taxes/Total Assets | 7.9 | 7.4 |
| | | -3.1 | | | | | -2.1 | .5 |
| | | 12.0 | | | | | 10.4 | 6.2 |
| | | 5.0 | | | | Sales/Net Fixed Assets | 3.0 | 2.0 |
| | | 3.0 | | | | | 1.3 | 1.7 |
| | | 4.6 | | | | | 3.4 | 1.9 |
| | | 2.6 | | | | Sales/Total Assets | 1.7 | 1.4 |
| | | 1.6 | | | | | .9 | 1.1 |
| | | 1.5 | | | | | 4.9 | 5.8 |
| | (12) | 5.4 | | | | % Depr., Dep., Amort./Sales | (23) 10.7 | (21) 10.1 |
| | | 9.3 | | | | | 13.6 | 12.8 |
| | | | | | | | 2.3 | 1.5 |
| | | | | | | % Officers', Directors' Owners' Comp/Sales | (16) 4.5 | (13) 3.9 |
| | | | | | | | 9.6 | 4.8 |
| 1691M | 21430M | 288629M | 260728M | 45555M | | Net Sales ($) | 594042M | 490659M |
| 681M | 10195M | 63708M | 90738M | 52729M | | Total Assets ($) | 592580M | 473366M |

## Comparative Historical Data                                      Current Data Sorted by Sales

| 3<br>4<br>7<br>10<br>26<br>4/1/09-<br>3/31/10<br>ALL | 2<br>7<br>12<br>10<br>4/1/10-<br>3/31/11<br>ALL | 1<br>4<br>8<br>7<br>12<br>4/1/11-<br>3/31/12<br>ALL | Type of Statement<br>Unqualified<br>Reviewed<br>Compiled<br>Tax Returns<br>Other | 0-1MM | 1 (4/1-9/30/11)<br>1-3MM | 3-5MM | 31 (10/1/11-3/31/12)<br>5-10MM | 10-25MM | 25MM & OVER |
|---|---|---|---|---|---|---|---|---|---|
| 50 | 31 | 32 | **NUMBER OF STATEMENTS** | 2 | 9 | 5 | 3 | 7 | 6 |
| % | % | % | **ASSETS** | % | % | % | % | % | % |
| 7.3 | 11.7 | 5.2 | Cash & Equivalents | | | | | | |
| 16.2 | 20.3 | 22.8 | Trade Receivables (net) | | | | | | |
| 3.3 | 1.1 | 1.7 | Inventory | | | | | | |
| 3.4 | 2.3 | 2.3 | All Other Current | | | | | | |
| 30.2 | 35.4 | 32.1 | Total Current | | | | | | |
| 52.3 | 53.2 | 52.4 | Fixed Assets (net) | | | | | | |
| 6.9 | 3.8 | 7.1 | Intangibles (net) | | | | | | |
| 10.6 | 7.7 | 8.4 | All Other Non-Current | | | | | | |
| 100.0 | 100.0 | 100.0 | Total | | | | | | |
| | | | **LIABILITIES** | | | | | | |
| 6.5 | 5.4 | 5.7 | Notes Payable-Short Term | | | | | | |
| 9.6 | 10.2 | 9.5 | Cur. Mat.-L.T.D. | | | | | | |
| 10.6 | 14.3 | 12.4 | Trade Payables | | | | | | |
| .0 | .0 | .0 | Income Taxes Payable | | | | | | |
| 10.9 | 9.6 | 13.2 | All Other Current | | | | | | |
| 37.7 | 39.5 | 40.8 | Total Current | | | | | | |
| 41.5 | 36.1 | 35.1 | Long-Term Debt | | | | | | |
| .8 | .5 | .5 | Deferred Taxes | | | | | | |
| 2.5 | 9.4 | 3.4 | All Other Non-Current | | | | | | |
| 17.5 | 14.5 | 20.1 | Net Worth | | | | | | |
| 100.0 | 100.0 | 100.0 | Total Liabilities & Net Worth | | | | | | |
| | | | **INCOME DATA** | | | | | | |
| 100.0 | 100.0 | 100.0 | Net Sales | | | | | | |
| | | | Gross Profit | | | | | | |
| 91.3 | 86.8 | 92.3 | Operating Expenses | | | | | | |
| 8.7 | 13.2 | 7.7 | Operating Profit | | | | | | |
| 2.3 | 2.9 | 2.6 | All Other Expenses (net) | | | | | | |
| 6.4 | 10.3 | 5.1 | Profit Before Taxes | | | | | | |
| | | | **RATIOS** | | | | | | |
| 1.5 | 1.7 | 1.6 | Current | | | | | | |
| .8 | .8 | .7 | | | | | | | |
| .4 | .5 | .5 | | | | | | | |
| 1.1 | 1.7 | 1.1 | Quick | | | | | | |
| .6 | .8 | .6 | | | | | | | |
| .3 | .3 | .4 | | | | | | | |
| 7   52.2 | 13   27.2 | 2   217.0 | Sales/Receivables | | | | | | |
| 31   11.8 | 33   11.0 | 29   12.4 | | | | | | | |
| 51   7.1 | 47   7.7 | 42   8.6 | | | | | | | |
| | | | Cost of Sales/Inventory | | | | | | |
| | | | Cost of Sales/Payables | | | | | | |
| 19.8 | 10.9 | 32.7 | Sales/Working Capital | | | | | | |
| -37.4 | -30.2 | -23.1 | | | | | | | |
| -8.3 | -7.1 | -9.5 | | | | | | | |
| 8.0 | 20.0 | 11.7 | EBIT/Interest | | | | | | |
| (46)   2.5 | (28)   5.4 | (29)   3.4 | | | | | | | |
| 1.1 | 2.0 | .4 | | | | | | | |
| | | | Net Profit + Depr., Dep.,<br>Amort./Cur. Mat. L/T/D | | | | | | |
| 1.1 | .7 | 1.3 | Fixed/Worth | | | | | | |
| 2.5 | 2.7 | 4.3 | | | | | | | |
| -16.0 | 19.7 | 95.5 | | | | | | | |
| 1.6 | .8 | 1.7 | Debt/Worth | | | | | | |
| 4.0 | 2.6 | 5.2 | | | | | | | |
| -29.7 | 30.5 | 267.5 | | | | | | | |
| 53.1 | 62.7 | 104.9 | % Profit Before Taxes/Tangible<br>Net Worth | | | | | | |
| (35)   29.2 | (24)   21.0 | (25)   33.2 | | | | | | | |
| 9.7 | 12.8 | -5.4 | | | | | | | |
| 20.6 | 20.8 | 20.5 | % Profit Before Taxes/Total<br>Assets | | | | | | |
| 7.3 | 6.9 | 5.6 | | | | | | | |
| .4 | 2.8 | -2.4 | | | | | | | |
| 9.4 | 10.2 | 9.7 | Sales/Net Fixed Assets | | | | | | |
| 3.8 | 4.4 | 3.9 | | | | | | | |
| 1.6 | 1.4 | 2.2 | | | | | | | |
| 2.9 | 3.3 | 4.0 | Sales/Total Assets | | | | | | |
| 1.7 | 1.8 | 2.2 | | | | | | | |
| 1.0 | .8 | 1.3 | | | | | | | |
| 2.6 | 2.7 | 2.5 | % Depr., Dep., Amort./Sales | | | | | | |
| (40)   7.4 | (26)   8.9 | (28)   8.1 | | | | | | | |
| 12.6 | 13.0 | 12.8 | | | | | | | |
| 2.1 | 3.0 | 2.1 | % Officers', Directors'<br>Owners' Comp/Sales | | | | | | |
| (20)   3.4 | (16)   4.2 | (14)   3.5 | | | | | | | |
| 6.5 | 6.5 | 5.7 | | | | | | | |
| 616788M | 448252M | 618033M | Net Sales ($) | 207M | 17319M | 21570M | 22768M | 134203M | 421966M |
| 461201M | 342906M | 218051M | Total Assets ($) | 494M | 10998M | 9966M | 9275M | 86384M | 100934M |

M = $ thousand        MM = $ million
See Pages 9 through 22 for Explanation of Ratios and Data

### Current Data Sorted by Assets                                   Comparative Historical Data

| 0-500M | 500M-2MM | 2-10MM | 10-50MM | 50-100MM | 100-250MM | Type of Statement | 4/1/07-3/31/08 ALL | 4/1/08-3/31/09 ALL |
|---|---|---|---|---|---|---|---|---|
| | 1 | 1 | 7 | 1 | 3 | Unqualified | 9 | 7 |
| | 2 | 8 | 5 | | | Reviewed | 16 | 9 |
| 3 | 2 | 3 | | | 1 | Compiled | 7 | 11 |
| 1 | 2 | 3 | | | | Tax Returns | 9 | 7 |
| 1 | 2 | 11 | 5 | | 3 | Other | 24 | 31 |
| | 8 (4/1-9/30/11) | | 57 (10/1/11-3/31/12) | | | | | |
| 5 | 9 | 26 | 17 | 1 | 7 | **NUMBER OF STATEMENTS** | 65 | 65 |
| % | % | % | % | % | % | **ASSETS** | % | % |
| | | 10.8 | 12.5 | | | Cash & Equivalents | 8.2 | 8.1 |
| | | 33.5 | 22.1 | | | Trade Receivables (net) | 25.6 | 27.7 |
| | | 2.0 | 1.8 | | | Inventory | 1.6 | 2.0 |
| | | 4.9 | 1.9 | | | All Other Current | 2.7 | 3.5 |
| | | 51.1 | 38.3 | | | Total Current | 38.1 | 41.4 |
| | | 36.9 | 43.4 | | | Fixed Assets (net) | 47.3 | 42.3 |
| | | 5.4 | 10.7 | | | Intangibles (net) | 7.3 | 8.5 |
| | | 6.5 | 7.6 | | | All Other Non-Current | 7.2 | 7.8 |
| | | 100.0 | 100.0 | | | Total | 100.0 | 100.0 |
| | | | | | | **LIABILITIES** | | |
| | | 8.2 | 2.8 | | | Notes Payable-Short Term | 6.7 | 12.8 |
| | | 2.8 | 6.0 | | | Cur. Mat.-L.T.D. | 9.0 | 8.1 |
| | | 11.7 | 11.2 | | | Trade Payables | 13.4 | 13.1 |
| | | .8 | .0 | | | Income Taxes Payable | .3 | .5 |
| | | 8.4 | 7.9 | | | All Other Current | 9.2 | 12.9 |
| | | 32.0 | 28.0 | | | Total Current | 38.7 | 47.4 |
| | | 21.1 | 21.6 | | | Long-Term Debt | 30.8 | 21.7 |
| | | .7 | .7 | | | Deferred Taxes | .3 | .5 |
| | | 3.8 | 3.6 | | | All Other Non-Current | 4.7 | 3.6 |
| | | 42.4 | 46.1 | | | Net Worth | 25.6 | 26.8 |
| | | 100.0 | 100.0 | | | Total Liabilties & Net Worth | 100.0 | 100.0 |
| | | | | | | **INCOME DATA** | | |
| | | 100.0 | 100.0 | | | Net Sales | 100.0 | 100.0 |
| | | | | | | Gross Profit | | |
| | | 94.1 | 91.3 | | | Operating Expenses | 89.7 | 91.1 |
| | | 5.9 | 8.7 | | | Operating Profit | 10.3 | 8.9 |
| | | 1.5 | 2.6 | | | All Other Expenses (net) | 2.2 | 2.1 |
| | | 4.4 | 6.1 | | | Profit Before Taxes | 8.1 | 6.8 |
| | | | | | | **RATIOS** | | |
| | | 2.4 | 2.2 | | | | 1.7 | 1.7 |
| | | 1.6 | 1.0 | | | Current | 1.2 | 1.1 |
| | | .9 | .7 | | | | .8 | .7 |
| | | 1.9 | 1.9 | | | | 1.5 | 1.5 |
| | | 1.4 | .9 | | | Quick | 1.1 (64) | 1.0 |
| | | .9 | .6 | | | | .6 | .6 |
| | | 29 12.7 | 32 11.4 | | | | 25 14.3 | 26 14.1 |
| | | 56 6.5 | 43 8.4 | | | Sales/Receivables | 42 8.7 | 51 7.2 |
| | | 76 4.8 | 62 5.9 | | | | 67 5.4 | 75 4.8 |
| | | | | | | Cost of Sales/Inventory | | |
| | | | | | | Cost of Sales/Payables | | |
| | | 7.5 | 9.0 | | | | 11.0 | 10.5 |
| | | 10.6 | 146.1 | | | Sales/Working Capital | 38.7 | 45.3 |
| | | -129.4 | -14.5 | | | | -24.3 | -12.7 |
| | | 11.5 | 101.0 | | | | 10.6 | 12.2 |
| | | (20) 3.0 | 5.6 | | | EBIT/Interest | (61) 5.2 | (64) 5.2 |
| | | -.3 | 1.8 | | | | 2.2 | .9 |
| | | | | | | Net Profit + Depr., Dep., | 6.2 | 12.1 |
| | | | | | | Amort./Cur. Mat. L/T/D | (13) 3.0 | (16) 3.6 |
| | | | | | | | 1.8 | 2.2 |
| | | .3 | .4 | | | | .8 | .9 |
| | | .7 | 1.4 | | | Fixed/Worth | 1.7 | 1.6 |
| | | 2.6 | 4.5 | | | | NM | 8.9 |
| | | .8 | .6 | | | | .9 | 1.0 |
| | | 1.6 | 2.0 | | | Debt/Worth | 2.4 | 2.2 |
| | | 3.0 | 6.3 | | | | NM | 17.0 |
| | | 40.9 | 31.5 | | | | 69.8 | 59.8 |
| | | (22) 10.8 | (15) 21.9 | | | % Profit Before Taxes/Tangible Net Worth | (49) 35.3 | (50) 27.4 |
| | | .5 | 8.4 | | | | 21.4 | 10.4 |
| | | 17.9 | 18.7 | | | | 22.2 | 18.0 |
| | | 5.5 | 8.1 | | | % Profit Before Taxes/Total Assets | 9.1 | 7.0 |
| | | .1 | 2.5 | | | | 2.5 | -.2 |
| | | 20.8 | 15.7 | | | | 7.9 | 11.6 |
| | | 8.3 | 3.4 | | | Sales/Net Fixed Assets | 4.1 | 3.8 |
| | | 2.6 | 1.9 | | | | 2.3 | 2.0 |
| | | 2.8 | 2.3 | | | | 2.5 | 2.6 |
| | | 2.2 | 1.4 | | | Sales/Total Assets | 1.8 | 1.7 |
| | | 1.5 | 1.1 | | | | 1.2 | 1.1 |
| | | 1.6 | 3.0 | | | | 2.5 | 2.2 |
| | | (23) 2.6 | 4.9 | | | % Depr., Dep., Amort./Sales | (56) 4.7 | (58) 4.6 |
| | | 7.7 | 7.9 | | | | 7.7 | 7.5 |
| | | | | | | % Officers', Directors' Owners' Comp/Sales | 1.2 | 1.9 |
| | | | | | | | (21) 3.0 | (16) 4.0 |
| | | | | | | | 4.8 | 7.7 |
| 26458M | 24253M | 279897M | 486369M | 72970M | 1204183M | Net Sales ($) | 1600044M | 1978251M |
| 1399M | 9660M | 127445M | 333358M | 67615M | 1044983M | Total Assets ($) | 1452324M | 1629671M |

M = $ thousand    MM = $ million
See Pages 9 through 22 for Explanation of Ratios and Data

## Comparative Historical Data         Current Data Sorted by Sales

| 4/1/09-3/31/10 ALL | 4/1/10-3/31/11 ALL | 4/1/11-3/31/12 ALL | | 0-1MM | 1-3MM | 3-5MM | 5-10MM | 10-25MM | 25MM & OVER |
|---|---|---|---|---|---|---|---|---|---|
| | | | **Type of Statement** | | | | | | |
| 8 | 17 | 13 | Unqualified | | 1 | | 1 | 4 | 7 |
| 14 | 16 | 15 | Reviewed | | 1 | | 3 | 8 | 2 |
| 8 | 5 | 9 | Compiled | 1 | 1 | 1 | 3 | 2 | 1 |
| 5 | 5 | 6 | Tax Returns | | 2 | 1 | 3 | | |
| 23 | 28 | 22 | Other | 2 | 1 | 2 | 4 | 5 | 8 |
| | | | | | 8 (4/1-9/30/11) | | 57 (10/1/11-3/31/12) | | |
| 58 | 71 | 65 | **NUMBER OF STATEMENTS** | 3 | 6 | 5 | 14 | 19 | 18 |
| % | % | % | | % | % | % | % | % | % |
| | | | **ASSETS** | | | | | | |
| 8.2 | 9.3 | 10.6 | Cash & Equivalents | | | | 10.2 | 11.3 | 13.7 |
| 25.2 | 28.7 | 28.1 | Trade Receivables (net) | | | | 30.4 | 26.9 | 24.0 |
| 1.7 | 2.6 | 1.7 | Inventory | | | | .4 | 1.2 | 2.9 |
| 5.1 | 3.3 | 4.7 | All Other Current | | | | 5.8 | 5.4 | 3.7 |
| 40.2 | 43.9 | 45.0 | Total Current | | | | 46.8 | 44.9 | 44.2 |
| 39.6 | 40.7 | 38.3 | Fixed Assets (net) | | | | 42.1 | 41.1 | 29.9 |
| 11.1 | 8.9 | 10.0 | Intangibles (net) | | | | 1.1 | 10.1 | 19.0 |
| 9.1 | 6.6 | 6.7 | All Other Non-Current | | | | 10.0 | 4.0 | 6.9 |
| 100.0 | 100.0 | 100.0 | Total | | | | 100.0 | 100.0 | 100.0 |
| | | | **LIABILITIES** | | | | | | |
| 7.5 | 2.8 | 5.4 | Notes Payable-Short Term | | | | 9.2 | 5.6 | 1.3 |
| 8.3 | 6.5 | 3.6 | Cur. Mat.-L.T.D. | | | | 3.0 | 4.0 | 4.6 |
| 13.1 | 14.6 | 11.3 | Trade Payables | | | | 11.0 | 9.4 | 13.8 |
| .2 | .1 | .7 | Income Taxes Payable | | | | 1.8 | .2 | .0 |
| 11.0 | 8.0 | 12.5 | All Other Current | | | | 8.4 | 21.2 | 7.0 |
| 40.1 | 32.0 | 33.4 | Total Current | | | | 33.3 | 40.5 | 26.8 |
| 22.7 | 20.9 | 25.9 | Long-Term Debt | | | | 28.4 | 24.0 | 18.6 |
| .9 | 1.0 | .9 | Deferred Taxes | | | | 1.1 | .2 | 2.3 |
| 4.7 | 3.5 | 3.5 | All Other Non-Current | | | | 3.2 | 2.3 | 3.5 |
| 31.7 | 42.7 | 36.2 | Net Worth | | | | 34.0 | 33.1 | 48.9 |
| 100.0 | 100.0 | 100.0 | Total Liabilities & Net Worth | | | | 100.0 | 100.0 | 100.0 |
| | | | **INCOME DATA** | | | | | | |
| 100.0 | 100.0 | 100.0 | Net Sales | | | | 100.0 | 100.0 | 100.0 |
| | | | Gross Profit | | | | | | |
| 96.5 | 92.6 | 93.1 | Operating Expenses | | | | 97.1 | 92.7 | 91.7 |
| 3.5 | 7.4 | 6.9 | Operating Profit | | | | 2.9 | 7.3 | 8.3 |
| 1.4 | 1.0 | 2.0 | All Other Expenses (net) | | | | .5 | 1.9 | 1.6 |
| 2.1 | 6.5 | 4.8 | Profit Before Taxes | | | | 2.4 | 5.4 | 6.8 |
| | | | **RATIOS** | | | | | | |
| 1.8 | 1.8 | 2.1 | | | | | 2.5 | 2.0 | 2.2 |
| 1.2 | 1.4 | 1.5 | Current | | | | 1.3 | 1.5 | 1.6 |
| .7 | 1.0 | .9 | | | | | .9 | .8 | 1.1 |
| 1.4 | 1.7 | 1.8 | | | | | 2.0 | 2.0 | 1.8 |
| 1.0 | 1.2 | 1.3 | Quick | | | | 1.2 | 1.4 | 1.4 |
| .6 | .8 | .8 | | | | | .8 | .7 | .8 |
| 36  10.1 | 32  11.3 | 32  11.4 | | | | | 30  12.0 | 32  11.4 | 32  11.4 |
| 47  7.7 | 48  7.6 | 49  7.4 | Sales/Receivables | | | | 54  6.8 | 56  6.5 | 43  8.4 |
| 62  5.9 | 68  5.3 | 69  5.3 | | | | | 70  5.2 | 72  5.1 | 72  5.1 |
| | | | Cost of Sales/Inventory | | | | | | |
| | | | Cost of Sales/Payables | | | | | | |
| 8.6 | 8.8 | 7.6 | | | | | 6.9 | 8.4 | 7.3 |
| 31.5 | 20.8 | 12.3 | Sales/Working Capital | | | | 18.5 | 15.7 | 10.7 |
| -25.9 | 128.3 | -74.8 | | | | | -67.2 | -54.0 | NM |
| 11.1 | 18.4 | 19.1 | | | | | 9.3 | 17.6 | 61.4 |
| (55) 3.6 | (65) 6.4 | (56) 3.9 | EBIT/Interest | | | | (11) 3.0 | (17) 3.0 | (17) 13.5 |
| -.3 | 3.4 | 1.8 | | | | | 1.0 | 1.4 | 3.2 |
| 4.4 | 6.9 | 5.3 | Net Profit + Depr., Dep., | | | | | | |
| (17) 1.2 | (18) 1.9 | (13) 1.5 | Amort./Cur. Mat. L/T/D | | | | | | |
| .9 | 1.5 | 1.1 | | | | | | | |
| .7 | .6 | .4 | | | | | .3 | .6 | .3 |
| 1.1 | 1.2 | 1.1 | Fixed/Worth | | | | .7 | 2.2 | 1.1 |
| 3.5 | 2.9 | 4.5 | | | | | 2.0 | 16.3 | 5.6 |
| 1.0 | 1.0 | .8 | | | | | .7 | 1.3 | .7 |
| 1.8 | 1.7 | 1.9 | Debt/Worth | | | | 1.2 | 2.0 | 1.4 |
| 18.7 | 3.4 | 7.8 | | | | | 5.1 | 18.0 | 8.7 |
| 36.2 | 62.2 | 50.0 | % Profit Before Taxes/Tangible | | | | 29.6 | 29.9 | 58.3 |
| (45) 14.8 | (66) 33.1 | (54) 19.3 | Net Worth | | | | (12) 10.0 | (15) 19.3 | (15) 40.5 |
| -7.9 | 14.9 | 8.0 | | | | | .9 | 6.7 | 18.8 |
| 14.3 | 19.8 | 17.9 | % Profit Before Taxes/Total | | | | 9.9 | 18.7 | 20.8 |
| 6.0 | 10.2 | 6.3 | Assets | | | | 5.2 | 7.7 | 8.1 |
| -3.2 | 4.5 | 2.2 | | | | | .1 | 2.1 | 5.1 |
| 14.3 | 10.2 | 21.0 | | | | | 24.3 | 14.2 | 18.7 |
| 5.0 | 5.6 | 6.6 | Sales/Net Fixed Assets | | | | 7.5 | 3.9 | 8.6 |
| 2.5 | 2.3 | 2.7 | | | | | 2.6 | 2.0 | 2.8 |
| 2.5 | 2.7 | 2.9 | | | | | 2.8 | 2.7 | 2.9 |
| 1.6 | 1.9 | 2.1 | Sales/Total Assets | | | | 2.3 | 1.5 | 1.3 |
| 1.2 | 1.2 | 1.2 | | | | | 1.6 | 1.2 | 1.0 |
| 3.9 | 2.1 | 1.9 | | | | | 1.8 | 2.4 | 1.4 |
| (45) 5.3 | (61) 4.1 | (57) 4.2 | % Depr., Dep., Amort./Sales | | | | (13) 4.8 | (17) 4.9 | (16) 2.7 |
| 9.1 | 6.0 | 7.0 | | | | | 7.1 | 8.2 | 5.6 |
| | 1.4 | 2.2 | % Officers', Directors' | | | | | | |
| | (19) 3.2 | (12) 3.5 | Owners' Comp/Sales | | | | | | |
| | 4.3 | 6.6 | | | | | | | |
| 1491693M | 3659995M | 2094130M | Net Sales ($) | 2047M | 12594M | 18619M | 94704M | 307932M | 1658234M |
| 1129551M | 2401453M | 1584460M | Total Assets ($) | 2665M | 5015M | 8764M | 50272M | 228148M | 1289596M |

© RMA 2012

M = $ thousand     MM = $ million
See Pages 9 through 22 for Explanation of Ratios and Data

## Current Data Sorted by Assets | Comparative Historical Data

| 0-500M | 500M-2MM | 2-10MM | 10-50MM | 50-100MM | 100-250MM | Type of Statement | 4/1/07-3/31/08 ALL | 4/1/08-3/31/09 ALL |
|---|---|---|---|---|---|---|---|---|
| | | 1 | 6 | 4 | 4 | Unqualified | 30 | 39 |
| | 2 | 11 | 4 | | | Reviewed | 25 | 24 |
| 1 | 2 | 3 | 1 | | | Compiled | 15 | 14 |
| 1 | 5 | 4 | | | | Tax Returns | 10 | 16 |
| | 2 | 12 | 7 | 3 | 3 | Other | 41 | 41 |
| | 13 (4/1-9/30/11) | | 64 (10/1/11-3/31/12) | | | | | |
| 2 | 12 | 31 | 18 | 7 | 7 | **NUMBER OF STATEMENTS** | 121 | 134 |
| % | % | % | % | % | % | **ASSETS** | % | % |
| | 18.0 | 15.9 | 12.4 | | | Cash & Equivalents | 13.6 | 12.2 |
| | 30.0 | 15.7 | 13.2 | | | Trade Receivables (net) | 18.7 | 14.7 |
| | .3 | 3.0 | 5.3 | | | Inventory | 2.2 | 1.3 |
| | 3.6 | 3.7 | 1.4 | | | All Other Current | 3.0 | 3.7 |
| | 51.7 | 38.2 | 32.3 | | | Total Current | 37.5 | 31.9 |
| | 33.2 | 45.1 | 56.0 | | | Fixed Assets (net) | 46.9 | 51.3 |
| | 7.9 | 8.3 | 1.1 | | | Intangibles (net) | 6.5 | 6.7 |
| | 7.2 | 8.4 | 10.7 | | | All Other Non-Current | 9.1 | 10.1 |
| | 100.0 | 100.0 | 100.0 | | | Total | 100.0 | 100.0 |
| | | | | | | **LIABILITIES** | | |
| | 6.7 | 3.6 | 5.4 | | | Notes Payable-Short Term | 3.8 | 3.3 |
| | 7.2 | 5.4 | 7.0 | | | Cur. Mat.-L.T.D. | 5.8 | 6.0 |
| | 10.8 | 10.2 | 8.3 | | | Trade Payables | 10.3 | 6.8 |
| | .0 | .1 | .0 | | | Income Taxes Payable | .4 | .1 |
| | 5.8 | 7.1 | 6.4 | | | All Other Current | 6.7 | 8.5 |
| | 30.6 | 26.3 | 27.2 | | | Total Current | 27.0 | 24.8 |
| | 18.0 | 21.6 | 19.3 | | | Long-Term Debt | 29.3 | 33.2 |
| | .5 | .4 | .0 | | | Deferred Taxes | .6 | .7 |
| | 5.7 | 5.3 | 12.4 | | | All Other Non-Current | 7.3 | 7.9 |
| | 45.2 | 46.3 | 41.1 | | | Net Worth | 35.8 | 33.5 |
| | 100.0 | 100.0 | 100.0 | | | Total Liabilities & Net Worth | 100.0 | 100.0 |
| | | | | | | **INCOME DATA** | | |
| | 100.0 | 100.0 | 100.0 | | | Net Sales | 100.0 | 100.0 |
| | | | | | | Gross Profit | | |
| | 88.5 | 87.4 | 91.9 | | | Operating Expenses | 86.2 | 90.7 |
| | 11.5 | 12.6 | 8.1 | | | Operating Profit | 13.8 | 9.3 |
| | 4.2 | 1.1 | 1.6 | | | All Other Expenses (net) | 1.8 | 3.4 |
| | 7.3 | 11.6 | 6.5 | | | Profit Before Taxes | 12.1 | 5.9 |
| | | | | | | **RATIOS** | | |
| | 7.4 | 2.3 | 3.2 | | | | 2.1 | 2.2 |
| | 1.3 | 1.5 | 1.3 | | | Current | 1.2 | 1.3 |
| | .9 | .9 | .6 | | | | .9 | .7 |
| | 6.8 | 2.0 | 2.8 | | | | 1.8 | 1.8 |
| | 1.2 | 1.4 | .9 | | | Quick | 1.1 | 1.0 |
| | .9 | .6 | .4 | | | | .7 | .5 |
| | 0 UND | 23 15.7 | 22 16.4 | | | | 21 17.3 | 16 22.9 |
| | 26 14.0 | 30 12.2 | 40 9.1 | | | Sales/Receivables | 37 9.8 | 34 10.9 |
| | 51 7.1 | 43 8.4 | 51 7.2 | | | | 54 6.7 | 49 7.5 |
| | | | | | | | | |
| | | | | | | Cost of Sales/Inventory | | |
| | | | | | | | | |
| | | | | | | Cost of Sales/Payables | | |
| | 4.9 | 8.5 | 3.9 | | | | 6.6 | 6.8 |
| | 29.0 | 20.1 | 95.6 | | | Sales/Working Capital | 26.1 | 29.5 |
| | NM | -14.2 | -10.0 | | | | -50.8 | -17.4 |
| | 53.1 | 25.3 | 23.9 | | | | 10.8 | 7.3 |
| | (10) 5.4 | (27) 7.8 | (16) 4.9 | | | EBIT/Interest | (108) 4.1 | (117) 3.2 |
| | 2.5 | 3.7 | 2.2 | | | | 2.1 | 1.3 |
| | | | | | | Net Profit + Depr., Dep., Amort./Cur. Mat. L/T/D | 3.9 | 4.2 |
| | | | | | | | (41) 2.6 (51) 2.2 | |
| | | | | | | | 1.6 | 1.2 |
| | .1 | .7 | .7 | | | | .9 | 1.0 |
| | .5 | 1.2 | 1.3 | | | Fixed/Worth | 1.7 | 1.9 |
| | 2.0 | 2.3 | 2.4 | | | | 4.3 | 7.4 |
| | .4 | .7 | .7 | | | | .9 | .9 |
| | 1.2 | 1.4 | 1.6 | | | Debt/Worth | 2.1 | 2.4 |
| | 29.4 | 6.4 | 3.2 | | | | 10.8 | 11.5 |
| | 59.5 | 48.9 | 44.2 | | | | 82.3 | 63.3 |
| | (11) 34.1 | (28) 21.4 | (16) 17.8 | | | % Profit Before Taxes/Tangible Net Worth | (105) 39.3 | (116) 21.0 |
| | 9.4 | 7.6 | .6 | | | | 13.0 | 3.9 |
| | 24.7 | 21.6 | 15.9 | | | | 26.4 | 13.8 |
| | 12.4 | 11.9 | 7.2 | | | % Profit Before Taxes/Total Assets | 9.0 | 5.4 |
| | 1.4 | 3.6 | .0 | | | | 4.3 | .6 |
| | 58.3 | 6.8 | 4.5 | | | | 7.0 | 6.2 |
| | 8.7 | 2.8 | 1.6 | | | Sales/Net Fixed Assets | 3.4 | 2.5 |
| | 5.9 | 1.7 | .8 | | | | 1.6 | 1.1 |
| | 4.0 | 2.4 | 1.9 | | | | 2.5 | 2.2 |
| | 3.1 | 1.2 | 1.1 | | | Sales/Total Assets | 1.5 | 1.2 |
| | 2.3 | .7 | .6 | | | | .8 | .7 |
| | | 3.9 | 3.6 | | | | 3.5 | 4.3 |
| | | (26) 6.6 | 8.4 | | | % Depr., Dep., Amort./Sales | (103) 6.7 | (121) 7.4 |
| | | 11.8 | 16.1 | | | | 10.6 | 12.1 |
| | | | | | | | 2.0 | 1.5 |
| | | | | | | % Officers', Directors' Owners' Comp/Sales | (36) 3.4 | (33) 2.8 |
| | | | | | | | 5.8 | 5.0 |
| 4573M | 56575M | 202921M | 532536M | 423412M | 665326M | Net Sales ($) | 3029878M | 3143469M |
| 591M | 14744M | 135147M | 443843M | 461240M | 1114273M | Total Assets ($) | 2692913M | 3260098M |

M = $ thousand    MM = $ million
See Pages 9 through 22 for Explanation of Ratios and Data

## Comparative Historical Data                    Current Data Sorted by Sales

| 4/1/09-3/31/10 ALL | 4/1/10-3/31/11 ALL | 4/1/11-3/31/12 ALL | Type of Statement | 0-1MM | 1-3MM | 3-5MM | 5-10MM | 10-25MM | 25MM & OVER |
|---|---|---|---|---|---|---|---|---|---|
| 31 | 22 | 16 | Unqualified | 1 | | | 4 | 1 | 10 |
| 19 | 17 | 17 | Reviewed | | 2 | | 6 | 7 | 2 |
| 13 | 13 | 7 | Compiled | | 3 | 2 | 2 | 2 | |
| 11 | 5 | 10 | Tax Returns | 4 | 1 | 1 | 3 | 1 | |
| 35 | 37 | 27 | Other | 1 | 5 | 2 | 4 | 4 | 9 |
| | | | | 13 (4/1-9/30/11) | | | 64 (10/1/11-3/31/12) | | |
| 109 | 94 | 77 | NUMBER OF STATEMENTS | 6 | 9 | 7 | 19 | 15 | 21 |
| % | % | % | **ASSETS** | % | % | % | % | % | % |
| 13.1 | 10.3 | 15.4 | Cash & Equivalents | | | | 18.4 | 9.5 | 12.8 |
| 14.5 | 16.1 | 16.4 | Trade Receivables (net) | | | | 18.4 | 26.7 | 13.3 |
| 1.4 | 1.6 | 2.6 | Inventory | | | | 1.1 | 6.0 | 3.4 |
| 4.6 | 2.8 | 3.4 | All Other Current | | | | 1.6 | 1.1 | 1.0 |
| 33.5 | 30.9 | 37.8 | Total Current | | | | 39.4 | 43.3 | 30.5 |
| 50.3 | 53.6 | 45.7 | Fixed Assets (net) | | | | 50.6 | 44.6 | 48.9 |
| 5.2 | 6.0 | 6.5 | Intangibles (net) | | | | 2.8 | 2.8 | 6.9 |
| 10.9 | 9.5 | 10.1 | All Other Non-Current | | | | 7.1 | 9.4 | 13.8 |
| 100.0 | 100.0 | 100.0 | Total | | | | 100.0 | 100.0 | 100.0 |
| | | | **LIABILITIES** | | | | | | |
| 5.5 | 4.2 | 4.9 | Notes Payable-Short Term | | | | 2.3 | 9.6 | 6.4 |
| 4.7 | 7.2 | 5.7 | Cur. Mat.-L.T.D. | | | | 4.4 | 7.8 | 4.6 |
| 9.8 | 7.9 | 9.1 | Trade Payables | | | | 10.5 | 12.9 | 7.7 |
| .1 | .1 | .0 | Income Taxes Payable | | | | .1 | .0 | .0 |
| 12.0 | 9.4 | 7.7 | All Other Current | | | | 6.3 | 6.0 | 12.3 |
| 32.1 | 28.9 | 27.5 | Total Current | | | | 23.6 | 36.4 | 31.0 |
| 29.0 | 24.6 | 21.8 | Long-Term Debt | | | | 16.1 | 17.5 | 26.2 |
| .8 | .5 | .7 | Deferred Taxes | | | | 1.0 | .0 | 1.7 |
| 8.8 | 9.1 | 9.6 | All Other Non-Current | | | | 6.8 | 7.4 | 13.8 |
| 29.3 | 37.0 | 40.4 | Net Worth | | | | 52.4 | 38.7 | 27.3 |
| 100.0 | 100.0 | 100.0 | Total Liabilities & Net Worth | | | | 100.0 | 100.0 | 100.0 |
| | | | **INCOME DATA** | | | | | | |
| 100.0 | 100.0 | 100.0 | Net Sales | | | | 100.0 | 100.0 | 100.0 |
| | | | Gross Profit | | | | | | |
| 91.2 | 89.4 | 88.9 | Operating Expenses | | | | 92.5 | 89.8 | 90.7 |
| 8.8 | 10.6 | 11.1 | Operating Profit | | | | 7.5 | 10.2 | 9.3 |
| 3.1 | 2.6 | 2.5 | All Other Expenses (net) | | | | .6 | 1.3 | 4.0 |
| 5.6 | 7.9 | 8.6 | Profit Before Taxes | | | | 6.8 | 8.9 | 5.3 |
| | | | **RATIOS** | | | | | | |
| 2.8 | 2.2 | 2.7 | | | | | 6.8 | 1.6 | 1.4 |
| 1.3 | 1.1 | 1.3 | Current | | | | 1.7 | 1.4 | 1.0 |
| .6 | .5 | .8 | | | | | 1.0 | .9 | .6 |
| 2.3 | 2.0 | 2.2 | | | | | 6.8 | 1.4 | 1.2 |
| 1.1 | .9 | 1.1 | Quick | | | | 1.4 | 1.0 | .8 |
| .5 | .5 | .6 | | | | | .9 | .5 | .6 |
| 24  15.4 | 25  14.4 | 24  15.4 | | | | | 21  17.3 | 18  20.6 | 34  10.8 |
| 37  10.0 | 39  9.3 | 34  10.8 | Sales/Receivables | | | | 31  11.8 | 30  12.0 | 40  9.1 |
| 50  7.3 | 54  6.8 | 49  7.5 | | | | | 54  6.7 | 47  7.8 | 57  6.4 |
| | | | Cost of Sales/Inventory | | | | | | |
| | | | Cost of Sales/Payables | | | | | | |
| 5.5 | 6.0 | 6.1 | | | | | 4.5 | 13.4 | 7.2 |
| 24.3 | 69.2 | 24.0 | Sales/Working Capital | | | | 20.6 | 23.5 | -793.2 |
| -13.6 | -7.2 | -15.6 | | | | | 999.8 | -33.1 | -10.6 |
| 9.2 | 10.2 | 26.8 | | | | | 27.2 | 23.5 | 26.8 |
| (91) 3.2 | (81) 4.2 | (67) 6.0 | EBIT/Interest | | | | (17) 7.8 | 6.8 | (19) 4.6 |
| .8 | 1.2 | 2.6 | | | | | 3.1 | 4.5 | .7 |
| 3.4 | 3.5 | 14.0 | Net Profit + Depr., Dep., | | | | | | |
| (30) 2.0 | (28) 1.7 | (15) 2.8 | Amort./Cur. Mat. L/T/D | | | | | | |
| 1.4 | 1.3 | 1.5 | | | | | | | |
| .8 | .8 | .7 | | | | | .7 | .7 | 1.0 |
| 1.8 | 1.9 | 1.3 | Fixed/Worth | | | | 1.2 | 1.0 | 3.0 |
| 8.8 | 7.2 | 3.1 | | | | | 1.5 | 2.3 | -9.1 |
| .7 | .8 | .5 | | | | | .5 | 1.2 | 1.5 |
| 2.1 | 1.9 | 1.7 | Debt/Worth | | | | .8 | 1.8 | 3.2 |
| 19.0 | 9.2 | 4.8 | | | | | 2.0 | 4.0 | -42.9 |
| 38.6 | 42.5 | 44.9 | % Profit Before Taxes/Tangible | | | | 40.9 | 54.8 | 41.9 |
| (90) 15.8 | (81) 21.8 | (66) 21.2 | Net Worth | | | | 13.5 | (14) 32.4 | (15) 19.0 |
| -.1 | 5.0 | 6.9 | | | | | 1.9 | 19.0 | 2.2 |
| 13.6 | 14.0 | 18.4 | % Profit Before Taxes/Total | | | | 23.5 | 21.0 | 13.2 |
| 4.6 | 6.3 | 7.2 | Assets | | | | 4.5 | 15.1 | 2.8 |
| -.6 | .4 | 1.0 | | | | | .4 | 4.0 | -.7 |
| 6.7 | 5.2 | 7.6 | | | | | 7.5 | 16.4 | 3.9 |
| 2.2 | 2.0 | 2.7 | Sales/Net Fixed Assets | | | | 2.8 | 5.5 | 1.8 |
| 1.0 | .9 | 1.4 | | | | | .9 | 1.5 | 1.3 |
| 2.4 | 2.1 | 2.4 | | | | | 3.1 | 4.1 | 1.7 |
| 1.2 | 1.1 | 1.1 | Sales/Total Assets | | | | 1.8 | 1.9 | 1.0 |
| .6 | .5 | .7 | | | | | .6 | 1.0 | .6 |
| 4.3 | 4.7 | 3.4 | | | | | 2.8 | 3.8 | 3.3 |
| (92) 7.8 | (88) 8.4 | (62) 7.2 | % Depr., Dep., Amort./Sales | | | | (17) 6.1 | (13) 5.4 | (17) 6.7 |
| 14.0 | 15.1 | 12.9 | | | | | 13.3 | 15.5 | 12.5 |
| 1.9 | 1.7 | 1.8 | % Officers', Directors' | | | | | | |
| (30) 3.3 | (22) 3.4 | (17) 3.2 | Owners' Comp/Sales | | | | | | |
| 5.0 | 4.1 | 4.5 | | | | | | | |
| 2108479M | 1583555M | 1885343M | Net Sales ($) | 3638M | 20131M | 27925M | 128957M | 249410M | 1455282M |
| 2675820M | 1719610M | 2169838M | Total Assets ($) | 13325M | 21085M | 21903M | 139777M | 189022M | 1784726M |

M = $ thousand     MM = $ million
See Pages 9 through 22 for Explanation of Ratios and Data

## Current Data Sorted by Assets

## Comparative Historical Data

| 0-500M | 500M-2MM | 2-10MM | 10-50MM | 50-100MM | 100-250MM | Type of Statement | 4/1/07-3/31/08 ALL | 4/1/08-3/31/09 ALL |
|---|---|---|---|---|---|---|---|---|
| | 1 | 5 | 7 | | | Unqualified | 7 | 8 |
| | 4 | 4 | 2 | 1 | 2 | Reviewed | 5 | 13 |
| 3 | 8 | 6 | | | | Compiled | | 3 |
| 1 | 8 | 10 | 3 | 3 | | Tax Returns | 3 | 5 |
| | | | | | | Other | 8 | 10 |
| | 5 (4/1-9/30/11) | | 63 (10/1/11-3/31/12) | | | | | |
| 4 | 21 | 25 | 12 | 4 | 2 | **NUMBER OF STATEMENTS** | 23 | 39 |

| 0-500M % | 500M-2MM % | 2-10MM % | 10-50MM % | 50-100MM % | 100-250MM % | | % | % |
|---|---|---|---|---|---|---|---|---|
| | | | | | | **ASSETS** | | |
| | 19.7 | 9.2 | 9.4 | | | Cash & Equivalents | 4.2 | 7.6 |
| | 19.5 | 26.0 | 18.6 | | | Trade Receivables (net) | 19.4 | 20.8 |
| | 1.7 | 1.2 | 6.8 | | | Inventory | 1.7 | 2.8 |
| | 4.3 | 5.4 | 1.9 | | | All Other Current | 3.4 | 4.6 |
| | 45.1 | 41.8 | 36.7 | | | Total Current | 28.7 | 35.8 |
| | 36.4 | 46.3 | 50.6 | | | Fixed Assets (net) | 56.9 | 52.7 |
| | 10.0 | 5.2 | 8.6 | | | Intangibles (net) | 8.1 | 6.3 |
| | 8.5 | 6.7 | 4.1 | | | All Other Non-Current | 6.3 | 5.2 |
| | 100.0 | 100.0 | 100.0 | | | Total | 100.0 | 100.0 |
| | | | | | | **LIABILITIES** | | |
| | 11.5 | 3.6 | 3.7 | | | Notes Payable-Short Term | 2.2 | 9.3 |
| | 4.5 | 5.3 | 6.8 | | | Cur. Mat.-L.T.D. | 6.5 | 7.4 |
| | 7.6 | 15.3 | 14.6 | | | Trade Payables | 10.9 | 11.1 |
| | .1 | .0 | .0 | | | Income Taxes Payable | .5 | .0 |
| | 17.5 | 4.4 | 8.9 | | | All Other Current | 5.4 | 6.4 |
| | 41.1 | 28.6 | 34.0 | | | Total Current | 25.6 | 34.2 |
| | 24.0 | 26.9 | 23.3 | | | Long-Term Debt | 38.0 | 29.3 |
| | .5 | .0 | .6 | | | Deferred Taxes | .9 | 1.1 |
| | 12.9 | 10.3 | 7.6 | | | All Other Non-Current | 11.3 | 12.7 |
| | 21.4 | 34.2 | 34.5 | | | Net Worth | 24.2 | 22.7 |
| | 100.0 | 100.0 | 100.0 | | | Total Liabilities & Net Worth | 100.0 | 100.0 |
| | | | | | | **INCOME DATA** | | |
| | 100.0 | 100.0 | 100.0 | | | Net Sales | 100.0 | 100.0 |
| | | | | | | Gross Profit | | |
| | 91.7 | 87.7 | 92.7 | | | Operating Expenses | 88.0 | 93.5 |
| | 8.3 | 12.3 | 7.3 | | | Operating Profit | 12.0 | 6.5 |
| | 1.2 | 1.0 | 2.5 | | | All Other Expenses (net) | 1.8 | 1.3 |
| | 7.1 | 11.3 | 4.8 | | | Profit Before Taxes | 10.2 | 5.2 |

### RATIOS

| 0-500M | 500M-2MM | 2-10MM | 10-50MM | 50-100MM | 100-250MM | Ratio | 4/1/07-3/31/08 ALL | 4/1/08-3/31/09 ALL |
|---|---|---|---|---|---|---|---|---|
| | 3.1 | 3.0 | 2.0 | | | Current | 1.7 | 2.5 |
| | 2.1 | 1.3 | 1.0 | | | | 1.0 | 1.2 |
| | 1.3 | .8 | .6 | | | | .6 | .8 |
| | 3.0 | 2.7 | 1.6 | | | Quick | 1.2 | 1.5 |
| | 1.5 | 1.0 | .8 | | | | .9 | .9 |
| | .9 | .8 | .4 | | | | .5 | .6 |
| 0 UND | | 27 13.5 | 28 12.9 | | | Sales/Receivables | 25 14.4 | 20 17.9 |
| 25 14.4 | | 46 8.0 | 45 8.1 | | | | 37 9.8 | 37 9.8 |
| 49 7.4 | | 62 5.9 | 58 6.3 | | | | 61 5.9 | 46 7.9 |
| | | | | | | Cost of Sales/Inventory | | |
| | | | | | | Cost of Sales/Payables | | |
| | 8.4 | 6.3 | 8.9 | | | Sales/Working Capital | 11.0 | 8.9 |
| | 23.9 | 36.3 | -77.2 | | | | -320.3 | 30.6 |
| | 61.6 | -59.8 | -9.7 | | | | -10.9 | -33.6 |
| | 15.1 | 26.3 | 53.2 | | | EBIT/Interest | 8.3 | 12.7 |
| | (20) 7.5 | (24) 4.9 | 5.4 | | | | (20) 5.9 | (38) 3.3 |
| | 2.1 | 1.9 | -1.8 | | | | 1.4 | .6 |
| | | | | | | Net Profit + Depr., Dep., Amort./Cur. Mat. L/T/D | | |
| | .4 | .5 | .9 | | | Fixed/Worth | 1.2 | .8 |
| | 1.5 | 2.0 | 1.2 | | | | 3.0 | 3.0 |
| | NM | 4.0 | 5.9 | | | | 11.6 | -17.2 |
| | .6 | .8 | .6 | | | Debt/Worth | 1.2 | 1.0 |
| | 2.3 | 1.8 | 2.4 | | | | 2.7 | 3.7 |
| | NM | 5.5 | 15.6 | | | | 12.6 | -27.5 |
| | 84.3 | 76.8 | 57.8 | | | % Profit Before Taxes/Tangible Net Worth | 71.2 | 50.7 |
| | (16) 44.3 | (22) 42.4 | (10) 18.2 | | | | (19) 41.0 | (28) 27.6 |
| | 31.3 | 10.5 | -1.3 | | | | 23.8 | 6.2 |
| | 29.8 | 28.5 | 10.4 | | | % Profit Before Taxes/Total Assets | 23.2 | 16.3 |
| | 11.3 | 9.4 | 4.5 | | | | 10.1 | 5.8 |
| | 5.7 | 2.1 | -7.8 | | | | 2.7 | -2.0 |
| | 13.5 | 9.2 | 4.9 | | | Sales/Net Fixed Assets | 6.1 | 6.6 |
| | 7.5 | 3.8 | 2.8 | | | | 3.3 | 3.7 |
| | 4.2 | 1.7 | 1.4 | | | | 1.8 | 2.1 |
| | 4.1 | 2.4 | 1.8 | | | Sales/Total Assets | 3.0 | 3.3 |
| | 2.8 | 1.7 | 1.6 | | | | 1.6 | 1.9 |
| | 1.6 | 1.1 | .9 | | | | 1.1 | 1.1 |
| | 2.8 | 1.9 | 4.9 | | | % Depr., Dep., Amort./Sales | 3.1 | 2.1 |
| | (13) 7.8 | (23) 4.5 | 7.6 | | | | (19) 5.6 | (34) 4.7 |
| | 12.6 | 10.9 | 8.7 | | | | 9.3 | 8.0 |
| | | 1.0 | | | | % Officers', Directors', Owners' Comp/Sales | | 1.3 |
| | | (10) 2.8 | | | | | | (11) 2.4 |
| | | 3.5 | | | | | | 4.2 |
| 5126M | 70402M | 185663M | 454493M | 313761M | 332126M | Net Sales ($) | 785963M | 1200090M |
| 1337M | 22710M | 108798M | 318100M | 336267M | 296324M | Total Assets ($) | 670117M | 982419M |

M = $ thousand    MM = $ million
See Pages 9 through 22 for Explanation of Ratios and Data

## Comparative Historical Data | Current Data Sorted by Sales

Date ranges for current data: **5 (4/1-9/30/11)** covers 0-1MM and 1-3MM; **63 (10/1/11-3/31/12)** covers 3-5MM, 5-10MM, 10-25MM, 25MM & OVER.

| 4/1/09-3/31/10 ALL | 4/1/10-3/31/11 ALL | 4/1/11-3/31/12 ALL | Type of Statement | 0-1MM | 1-3MM | 3-5MM | 5-10MM | 10-25MM | 25MM & OVER |
|---|---|---|---|---|---|---|---|---|---|
| 10 | 6 | 10 | Unqualified | | | | 1 | | 9 |
| 5 | 2 | 8 | Reviewed | | 2 | | 3 | 3 | |
| 5 | 6 | 8 | Compiled | | 1 | 3 | 1 | 1 | |
| 7 | 12 | 17 | Tax Returns | 2 | 6 | 4 | 4 | 2 | |
| 16 | 18 | 25 | Other | 1 | 6 | 4 | 6 | 2 | 6 |
| 43 | 44 | 68 | NUMBER OF STATEMENTS | 4 | 15 | 11 | 15 | 8 | 15 |
| % | % | % | **ASSETS** | % | % | % | % | % | % |
| 10.0 | 11.2 | 12.7 | Cash & Equivalents | | 11.6 | 6.2 | 22.9 | | 5.7 |
| 16.0 | 16.5 | 21.8 | Trade Receivables (net) | | 23.4 | 28.6 | 15.9 | | 17.2 |
| 2.2 | 2.2 | 2.3 | Inventory | | .0 | .0 | 1.5 | | 6.0 |
| 2.8 | 5.5 | 3.8 | All Other Current | | 7.9 | 3.0 | 3.2 | | 2.0 |
| 31.1 | 35.3 | 40.5 | Total Current | | 42.9 | 37.8 | 43.5 | | 30.9 |
| 54.6 | 49.0 | 44.6 | Fixed Assets (net) | | 43.1 | 49.6 | 38.4 | | 50.5 |
| 6.2 | 4.0 | 8.6 | Intangibles (net) | | 5.5 | 9.9 | 9.0 | | 14.1 |
| 8.1 | 11.7 | 6.3 | All Other Non-Current | | 8.5 | 2.7 | 9.1 | | 4.5 |
| 100.0 | 100.0 | 100.0 | Total | | 100.0 | 100.0 | 100.0 | | 100.0 |
| | | | **LIABILITIES** | | | | | | |
| 4.8 | 5.8 | 5.7 | Notes Payable-Short Term | | 6.4 | 12.9 | 2.8 | | 3.7 |
| 5.0 | 5.9 | 5.3 | Cur. Mat.-L.T.D. | | 4.4 | 5.5 | 3.9 | | 6.8 |
| 10.7 | 9.6 | 11.7 | Trade Payables | | 6.2 | 8.5 | 14.6 | | 12.8 |
| .1 | .1 | .0 | Income Taxes Payable | | .0 | .1 | .0 | | .1 |
| 10.2 | 10.5 | 9.3 | All Other Current | | 20.1 | 8.7 | 4.0 | | 9.2 |
| 30.8 | 31.9 | 32.1 | Total Current | | 37.0 | 35.7 | 25.3 | | 32.7 |
| 27.7 | 27.1 | 29.7 | Long-Term Debt | | 15.4 | 36.0 | 28.0 | | 30.5 |
| 1.3 | .0 | .3 | Deferred Taxes | | .7 | .0 | .0 | | .6 |
| 9.4 | 11.2 | 10.3 | All Other Non-Current | | 18.1 | 2.9 | 14.7 | | 10.5 |
| 30.8 | 29.8 | 27.6 | Net Worth | | 28.7 | 25.4 | 32.1 | | 25.7 |
| 100.0 | 100.0 | 100.0 | Total Liabilities & Net Worth | | 100.0 | 100.0 | 100.0 | | 100.0 |
| | | | **INCOME DATA** | | | | | | |
| 100.0 | 100.0 | 100.0 | Net Sales | | 100.0 | 100.0 | 100.0 | | 100.0 |
| | | | Gross Profit | | | | | | |
| 90.3 | 88.0 | 90.3 | Operating Expenses | | 89.7 | 89.3 | 89.4 | | 93.7 |
| 9.7 | 12.0 | 9.7 | Operating Profit | | 10.3 | 10.7 | 10.6 | | 6.3 |
| 3.7 | 3.5 | 1.5 | All Other Expenses (net) | | 1.4 | 2.3 | .4 | | 2.9 |
| 6.0 | 8.5 | 8.2 | Profit Before Taxes | | 8.9 | 8.3 | 10.2 | | 3.4 |
| | | | **RATIOS** | | | | | | |
| 2.3 | 2.0 | 2.7 | Current | | 3.8 | 2.4 | 3.7 | | 1.5 |
| 1.3 | 1.3 | 1.4 | | | 2.3 | 1.3 | 2.6 | | 1.0 |
| .8 | 1.0 | .9 | | | 1.2 | .9 | .8 | | .6 |
| 1.6 | 1.6 | 2.5 | Quick | | 3.8 | 1.8 | 3.6 | | 1.3 |
| 1.1 | 1.1 | 1.2 | | | 1.5 | 1.0 | 2.4 | | .7 |
| .5 | .7 | .7 | | | .5 | .9 | .8 | | .4 |
| 26  14.2 | 22  16.5 | 21  17.6 | Sales/Receivables | 20  18.0 | 19  19.2 | 10  37.3 | | 27  13.4 |
| 37  10.0 | 32  11.3 | 42  8.7 | | 42  8.6 | 49  7.5 | 28  13.0 | | 42  8.6 |
| 60  6.1 | 42  8.7 | 51  7.1 | | 51  7.2 | 58  6.3 | 46  7.9 | | 51  7.2 |
| | | | Cost of Sales/Inventory | | | | | | |
| | | | Cost of Sales/Payables | | | | | | |
| 11.3 | 8.6 | 8.7 | Sales/Working Capital | | 5.9 | 16.1 | 7.9 | | 13.0 |
| 26.2 | 32.1 | 25.8 | | | 11.9 | 34.4 | 22.4 | | -115.6 |
| -26.7 | -303.9 | -45.1 | | | 67.7 | -137.4 | -80.9 | | -10.1 |
| 12.0 | 17.8 | 16.9 | EBIT/Interest | | 15.7 | 11.4 | 24.1 | | 10.3 |
| (38) 1.4 | (39) 4.8 | (65) 6.9 | | | (14) 7.1 | 3.1 | (14) 9.1 | | 6.0 |
| -.9 | 1.5 | 1.8 | | | 3.4 | 1.8 | 2.6 | | .6 |
| | | | Net Profit + Depr., Dep., Amort./Cur. Mat. L/T/D | | | | | | |
| .8 | .8 | .6 | Fixed/Worth | | .6 | .7 | .5 | | 1.3 |
| 1.5 | 1.6 | 1.7 | | | 1.5 | 2.0 | 1.6 | | 3.6 |
| 10.3 | 11.7 | 9.5 | | | 3.8 | 3.2 | 10.1 | | -171.1 |
| .7 | 1.0 | .7 | Debt/Worth | | .6 | .7 | .5 | | 2.1 |
| 2.5 | 2.1 | 2.2 | | | 2.8 | 1.8 | 1.7 | | 3.7 |
| 13.1 | 14.9 | 13.7 | | | 5.0 | 10.9 | 45.5 | | -348.5 |
| 54.0 | 57.9 | 75.4 | % Profit Before Taxes/Tangible Net Worth | | 50.9 | | 84.3 | | 78.1 |
| (33) 11.8 | (35) 29.9 | (55) 37.0 | | | (13) 30.8 | | (12) 47.9 | | (11) 40.0 |
| -3.9 | 5.0 | 12.4 | | | 11.6 | | 18.3 | | 5.0 |
| 17.4 | 20.3 | 23.6 | % Profit Before Taxes/Total Assets | | 24.0 | 24.7 | 31.5 | | 11.1 |
| 1.9 | 6.4 | 9.4 | | | 11.3 | 6.4 | 11.7 | | 7.1 |
| -4.8 | 1.5 | 2.1 | | | 2.1 | 2.1 | 5.0 | | -2.5 |
| 3.9 | 11.2 | 8.3 | Sales/Net Fixed Assets | | 8.4 | 7.8 | 16.2 | | 5.1 |
| 2.3 | 2.9 | 4.3 | | | 4.3 | 6.6 | 5.6 | | 2.7 |
| 1.2 | 1.3 | 2.0 | | | 1.6 | 1.7 | 3.4 | | 1.5 |
| 1.9 | 2.7 | 2.8 | Sales/Total Assets | | 2.8 | 3.4 | 3.5 | | 1.7 |
| 1.2 | 1.3 | 1.8 | | | 2.2 | 1.8 | 2.2 | | 1.4 |
| .8 | .9 | 1.1 | | | 1.1 | 1.2 | 1.3 | | .9 |
| 4.6 | 3.3 | 2.0 | % Depr., Dep., Amort./Sales | | 1.3 | | .8 | | 2.3 |
| (33) 7.1 | (33) 6.0 | (55) 5.8 | | | (12) 7.7 | | (12) 3.1 | | (13) 6.2 |
| 13.1 | 10.9 | 10.0 | | | 14.9 | | 7.3 | | 8.4 |
| | 2.1 | 2.2 | % Officers', Directors' Owners' Comp/Sales | | | | | | |
| | (13) 3.9 | (21) 3.0 | | | | | | | |
| | 5.6 | | | | | | | | |
| 1176923M | 866797M | 1361571M | Net Sales ($) | 2749M | 27803M | 42813M | 106154M | 126882M | 1055170M |
| 1165373M | 751386M | 1083536M | Total Assets ($) | 5041M | 23136M | 28612M | 81465M | 67651M | 877631M |

© RMA 2012

M = $ thousand     MM = $ million
See Pages 9 through 22 for Explanation of Ratios and Data

## Current Data Sorted by Assets | Comparative Historical Data

| 0-500M | 500M-2MM | 2-10MM | 10-50MM | 50-100MM | 100-250MM | Type of Statement | 4/1/07-3/31/08 ALL | 4/1/08-3/31/09 ALL |
|---|---|---|---|---|---|---|---|---|
|  | 2 | 7 | 13 | 1 | 5 | Unqualified | 9 | 12 |
|  | 8 | 28 | 4 |  |  | Reviewed | 23 | 36 |
| 1 | 5 | 4 |  |  | 1 | Compiled | 11 | 4 |
| 8 | 7 | 3 |  |  |  | Tax Returns | 8 | 8 |
| 6 | 9 | 14 | 11 | 3 | 2 | Other | 21 | 28 |
|  | 24 (4/1-9/30/11) |  | 118 (10/1/11-3/31/12) |  |  |  | 72 | 88 |
| 15 | 31 | 56 | 28 | 4 | 8 | NUMBER OF STATEMENTS | 72 | 88 |
| % | % | % | % | % | % | ASSETS | % | % |
| 21.1 | 12.1 | 10.5 | 10.5 |  |  | Cash & Equivalents | 9.2 | 11.5 |
| 37.7 | 53.0 | 48.2 | 31.9 |  |  | Trade Receivables (net) | 42.7 | 39.7 |
| .1 | .8 | 3.3 | 3.6 |  |  | Inventory | 2.7 | 4.2 |
| 3.4 | 4.0 | 4.3 | 3.9 |  |  | All Other Current | 8.8 | 5.5 |
| 62.2 | 69.9 | 66.2 | 49.9 |  |  | Total Current | 63.5 | 60.9 |
| 26.3 | 25.1 | 24.6 | 34.2 |  |  | Fixed Assets (net) | 26.5 | 25.5 |
| 2.6 | 1.1 | 1.6 | 6.9 |  |  | Intangibles (net) | 3.5 | 5.4 |
| 8.7 | 4.0 | 7.6 | 9.1 |  |  | All Other Non-Current | 6.5 | 8.2 |
| 100.0 | 100.0 | 100.0 | 100.0 |  |  | Total | 100.0 | 100.0 |
|  |  |  |  |  |  | **LIABILITIES** |  |  |
| 14.7 | 8.5 | 10.0 | 7.5 |  |  | Notes Payable-Short Term | 9.3 | 12.1 |
| 6.3 | 3.9 | 4.2 | 3.7 |  |  | Cur. Mat.-L.T.D. | 4.0 | 5.5 |
| 13.2 | 11.1 | 14.7 | 12.4 |  |  | Trade Payables | 12.5 | 13.1 |
| .0 | .1 | .7 | .2 |  |  | Income Taxes Payable | .8 | .4 |
| 12.9 | 12.1 | 11.5 | 9.0 |  |  | All Other Current | 11.4 | 10.7 |
| 47.2 | 35.7 | 41.2 | 32.8 |  |  | Total Current | 38.0 | 41.8 |
| 47.1 | 16.4 | 11.6 | 16.5 |  |  | Long-Term Debt | 19.4 | 20.0 |
| .0 | .0 | .4 | .7 |  |  | Deferred Taxes | .2 | .4 |
| 3.5 | 8.5 | 1.4 | 5.5 |  |  | All Other Non-Current | 1.6 | 4.5 |
| 2.3 | 39.3 | 45.4 | 44.6 |  |  | Net Worth | 40.8 | 33.3 |
| 100.0 | 100.0 | 100.0 | 100.0 |  |  | Total Liabilties & Net Worth | 100.0 | 100.0 |
|  |  |  |  |  |  | **INCOME DATA** |  |  |
| 100.0 | 100.0 | 100.0 | 100.0 |  |  | Net Sales | 100.0 | 100.0 |
|  |  |  |  |  |  | Gross Profit |  |  |
| 85.6 | 96.4 | 94.5 | 92.8 |  |  | Operating Expenses | 90.3 | 93.6 |
| 14.4 | 3.6 | 5.5 | 7.2 |  |  | Operating Profit | 9.7 | 6.4 |
| .7 | .4 | .4 | 1.1 |  |  | All Other Expenses (net) | 2.3 | 1.3 |
| 13.6 | 3.2 | 5.2 | 6.2 |  |  | Profit Before Taxes | 7.4 | 5.1 |
|  |  |  |  |  |  | **RATIOS** |  |  |
| 3.4 | 5.3 | 2.2 | 2.1 |  |  |  | 2.7 | 2.3 |
| 1.5 | 2.1 | 1.5 | 1.5 |  |  | Current | 1.7 | 1.5 |
| .6 | 1.2 | 1.2 | 1.2 |  |  |  | 1.2 | 1.1 |
| 3.4 | 4.8 | 2.1 | 1.8 |  |  |  | 2.4 | 1.9 |
| 1.5 | 1.9 | 1.4 | 1.3 |  |  | Quick | 1.3 | 1.3 |
| .6 | 1.1 | 1.1 | 1.0 |  |  |  | 1.0 | 1.0 |
| 2 167.9 | 52 7.0 | 53 6.9 | 45 8.2 |  |  |  | 33 10.9 | 35 10.3 |
| 31 11.9 | 70 5.2 | 76 4.8 | 59 6.2 |  |  | Sales/Receivables | 68 5.4 | 64 5.7 |
| 49 7.5 | 101 3.6 | 101 3.6 | 85 4.3 |  |  |  | 93 3.9 | 79 4.6 |
|  |  |  |  |  |  | Cost of Sales/Inventory |  |  |
|  |  |  |  |  |  | Cost of Sales/Payables |  |  |
| 7.8 | 4.5 | 6.0 | 5.3 |  |  |  | 5.6 | 6.2 |
| 30.3 | 7.6 | 11.8 | 10.0 |  |  | Sales/Working Capital | 8.7 | 12.8 |
| -48.8 | 32.6 | 28.7 | 53.6 |  |  |  | 29.0 | 45.5 |
| 24.1 | 28.0 | 28.4 | 29.8 |  |  |  | 22.3 | 17.6 |
| (12) 6.9 | (27) 9.3 | (52) 9.5 | (26) 11.1 |  |  | EBIT/Interest | (63) 8.4 | (82) 4.8 |
| 2.7 | 3.0 | 2.2 | 3.2 |  |  |  | 2.5 | 1.0 |
|  |  | 6.1 |  |  |  | Net Profit + Depr., Dep., | 11.7 | 3.9 |
|  | (15) 3.5 |  |  |  |  | Amort./Cur. Mat. L/T/D | (21) 5.1 | (16) 1.2 |
|  |  | .8 |  |  |  |  | 1.5 | .3 |
| .1 | .2 | .2 | .5 |  |  |  | .2 | .2 |
| 2.2 | .4 | .5 | .8 |  |  | Fixed/Worth | .6 | .6 |
| -.8 | 2.2 | 1.0 | 1.7 |  |  |  | 1.2 | 1.5 |
| .7 | .5 | .5 | .8 |  |  |  | .6 | .8 |
| 5.9 | 1.8 | 1.2 | 1.7 |  |  | Debt/Worth | 1.6 | 1.7 |
| -2.8 | 9.9 | 2.4 | 2.8 |  |  |  | 3.3 | 6.2 |
|  | 61.0 | 46.3 | 51.9 |  |  | % Profit Before Taxes/Tangible | 60.9 | 56.8 |
|  | (29) 23.1 | (53) 22.7 | (27) 18.9 |  |  | Net Worth | (65) 33.3 | (74) 26.3 |
|  | 5.3 | 9.2 | 8.4 |  |  |  | 16.5 | 3.2 |
| 73.0 | 26.2 | 24.5 | 18.7 |  |  | % Profit Before Taxes/Total | 23.9 | 25.8 |
| 25.6 | 8.3 | 10.0 | 6.1 |  |  | Assets | 11.3 | 8.9 |
| 14.4 | 1.2 | 2.6 | 2.5 |  |  |  | 4.0 | -.4 |
| 103.2 | 33.9 | 33.2 | 12.8 |  |  |  | 32.9 | 28.6 |
| 42.8 | 14.9 | 11.7 | 5.4 |  |  | Sales/Net Fixed Assets | 15.0 | 13.2 |
| 18.7 | 6.0 | 5.2 | 3.1 |  |  |  | 6.4 | 4.9 |
| 8.9 | 3.2 | 3.6 | 2.1 |  |  |  | 3.3 | 3.1 |
| 5.1 | 2.5 | 2.1 | 1.6 |  |  | Sales/Total Assets | 2.4 | 2.3 |
| 2.1 | 1.9 | 1.6 | 1.2 |  |  |  | 1.8 | 1.8 |
|  | .6 | .9 | 2.3 |  |  |  | .9 | 1.0 |
|  | (23) 2.9 | (49) 1.8 | (24) 3.6 |  |  | % Depr., Dep., Amort./Sales | (59) 2.1 | (70) 2.2 |
|  | 3.4 | 4.0 | 4.3 |  |  |  | 4.2 | 4.9 |
|  | 4.5 | 1.6 |  |  |  |  | 2.1 | 2.5 |
|  | (15) 7.5 | (24) 3.1 |  |  |  | % Officers', Directors', | (30) 4.1 | (36) 4.2 |
|  | 11.4 | 5.4 |  |  |  | Owners' Comp/Sales | 8.8 | 7.5 |
| 18623M | 87012M | 659238M | 1094692M | 463805M | 1370534M | Net Sales ($) | 1475890M | 1517527M |
| 3260M | 34679M | 270287M | 587523M | 377000M | 1275475M | Total Assets ($) | 702751M | 1196402M |

M = $ thousand    MM = $ million
See Pages 9 through 22 for Explanation of Ratios and Data

## Comparative Historical Data | Current Data Sorted by Sales

| | Hist 4/1/09-3/31/10 ALL | Hist 4/1/10-3/31/11 ALL | Hist 4/1/11-3/31/12 ALL | 0-1MM | 1-3MM | 3-5MM | 5-10MM | 10-25MM | 25MM & OVER |
|---|---|---|---|---|---|---|---|---|---|
| **Type of Statement** | | | | | | | | | |
| Unqualified | 21 | 25 | 28 | | 1 | 1 | 1 | 10 | 15 |
| Reviewed | 34 | 35 | 40 | 1 | 4 | 7 | 8 | 17 | 3 |
| Compiled | 11 | 15 | 11 | | 5 | 2 | 1 | 2 | 1 |
| Tax Returns | 18 | 16 | 18 | 4 | 7 | 5 | | 1 | |
| Other | 38 | 39 | 45 | 2 | 9 | 5 | 8 | 10 | 11 |
| | | | | 24 (4/1-9/30/11) | | 118 (10/1/11-3/31/12) | | | |
| **NUMBER OF STATEMENTS** | 122 | 130 | 142 | 7 | 26 | 20 | 19 | 40 | 30 |
| | % | % | % | % | % | % | % | % | % |
| **ASSETS** | | | | | | | | | |
| Cash & Equivalents | 11.5 | 11.6 | 11.7 | | 12.1 | 15.3 | 11.0 | 11.3 | 8.5 |
| Trade Receivables (net) | 37.0 | 37.8 | 42.9 | | 48.4 | 52.6 | 42.9 | 42.1 | 35.7 |
| Inventory | 2.8 | 3.1 | 2.2 | | .6 | 2.2 | .8 | 3.8 | 2.9 |
| All Other Current | 5.3 | 7.7 | 4.2 | | 4.8 | 1.9 | 2.7 | 4.7 | 5.8 |
| Total Current | 56.7 | 60.3 | 61.0 | | 66.0 | 72.1 | 57.3 | 61.8 | 52.9 |
| Fixed Assets (net) | 30.0 | 25.6 | 26.0 | | 27.1 | 21.8 | 31.9 | 26.5 | 20.9 |
| Intangibles (net) | 4.8 | 6.4 | 5.5 | | .5 | 1.0 | 1.7 | 2.8 | 18.4 |
| All Other Non-Current | 8.6 | 7.7 | 7.5 | | 6.4 | 5.2 | 9.2 | 8.9 | 7.7 |
| Total | 100.0 | 100.0 | 100.0 | | 100.0 | 100.0 | 100.0 | 100.0 | 100.0 |
| **LIABILITIES** | | | | | | | | | |
| Notes Payable-Short Term | 11.7 | 9.5 | 9.0 | | 12.5 | 6.2 | 8.6 | 10.3 | 6.2 |
| Cur. Mat.-L.T.D. | 6.2 | 7.4 | 4.1 | | 6.7 | 2.5 | 4.9 | 4.1 | 2.5 |
| Trade Payables | 14.1 | 15.0 | 12.9 | | 12.8 | 8.1 | 13.2 | 14.7 | 14.2 |
| Income Taxes Payable | .6 | .2 | .4 | | .1 | .8 | .6 | .5 | .2 |
| All Other Current | 9.7 | 11.6 | 11.1 | | 14.4 | 10.1 | 4.4 | 11.7 | 11.5 |
| Total Current | 42.2 | 43.7 | 37.6 | | 46.4 | 27.7 | 31.7 | 41.3 | 34.6 |
| Long-Term Debt | 21.7 | 17.8 | 17.9 | | 24.9 | 14.1 | 10.9 | 15.9 | 13.7 |
| Deferred Taxes | .9 | .6 | .7 | | .0 | .3 | .6 | .4 | 2.2 |
| All Other Non-Current | 5.7 | 6.2 | 4.9 | | 6.7 | 7.1 | 4.6 | 2.2 | 6.7 |
| Net Worth | 29.4 | 31.6 | 39.0 | | 22.0 | 50.8 | 52.1 | 40.2 | 42.8 |
| Total Liabilities & Net Worth | 100.0 | 100.0 | 100.0 | | 100.0 | 100.0 | 100.0 | 100.0 | 100.0 |
| **INCOME DATA** | | | | | | | | | |
| Net Sales | 100.0 | 100.0 | 100.0 | | 100.0 | 100.0 | 100.0 | 100.0 | 100.0 |
| Gross Profit | | | | | | | | | |
| Operating Expenses | 95.9 | 94.8 | 93.4 | | 97.1 | 92.7 | 94.5 | 94.0 | 93.0 |
| Operating Profit | 4.1 | 5.2 | 6.6 | | 2.9 | 7.3 | 5.5 | 6.0 | 7.0 |
| All Other Expenses (net) | 1.1 | .9 | .8 | | .3 | .6 | .4 | .7 | 1.5 |
| Profit Before Taxes | 3.0 | 4.2 | 5.8 | | 2.6 | 6.8 | 5.1 | 5.2 | 5.6 |
| **RATIOS** | | | | | | | | | |
| Current | 2.5 | 2.2 | 2.5 | | 3.2 | 5.3 | 2.7 | 2.2 | 2.0 |
| | 1.5 | 1.5 | 1.5 | | 1.6 | 2.9 | 1.6 | 1.4 | 1.5 |
| | 1.1 | 1.1 | 1.2 | | .9 | 1.4 | 1.4 | 1.0 | 1.2 |
| Quick | 2.2 | 2.0 | 2.3 | | 3.0 | 5.0 | 2.3 | 2.0 | 1.7 |
| | 1.3 | 1.2 | 1.4 | | 1.6 | 2.7 | 1.5 | 1.2 | 1.2 |
| | .8 | .8 | 1.0 | | .7 | 1.1 | 1.3 | .9 | 1.1 |
| Sales/Receivables | 35  10.3 | 41  8.9 | 45  8.2 | | 32  11.5 | 55  6.6 | 57  6.4 | 41  8.8 | 53  6.9 |
| | 60  6.1 | 67  5.5 | 69  5.3 | | 54  6.7 | 78  4.7 | 78  4.7 | 58  6.3 | 68  5.4 |
| | 85  4.3 | 83  4.4 | 96  3.8 | | 122  3.0 | 96  3.8 | 114  3.2 | 89  4.1 | 87  4.2 |
| Cost of Sales/Inventory | | | | | | | | | |
| Cost of Sales/Payables | | | | | | | | | |
| Sales/Working Capital | 6.3 | 6.0 | 5.5 | | 5.1 | 4.5 | 4.6 | 6.2 | 5.4 |
| | 13.4 | 11.3 | 10.3 | | 17.7 | 6.5 | 8.2 | 13.3 | 9.7 |
| | 84.8 | 76.2 | 33.4 | | -48.2 | 15.6 | 14.0 | 90.8 | 21.6 |
| EBIT/Interest | 10.5 | 15.6 | 26.7 | | 26.6 | 32.4 | 32.8 | 26.6 | 46.4 |
| | (107) 3.2 | (117) 5.3 | (128) 8.3 | | (24) 7.4 | (18) 15.1 | (17) 6.2 | (38) 7.2 | (28) 7.7 |
| | -.6 | 1.6 | 2.2 | | 1.4 | 4.6 | 2.0 | 1.9 | 1.7 |
| Net Profit + Depr., Dep., Amort./Cur. Mat. L/T/D | 5.1 | 6.3 | 6.1 | | | | | 3.2 | 18.8 |
| | (32) 2.1 | (23) 2.6 | (30) 2.8 | | | | | (10) 1.3 | (10) 2.5 |
| | .5 | 1.2 | .8 | | | | | .8 | .8 |
| Fixed/Worth | .3 | .2 | .3 | | .2 | .1 | .2 | .3 | .4 |
| | .7 | .8 | .6 | | 1.4 | .3 | .6 | .7 | 30 |
| | 3.2 | 3.4 | 1.9 | | 20.5 | .8 | 1.0 | 1.7 | NM |
| Debt/Worth | .7 | .8 | .6 | | .5 | .4 | .2 | .7 | 1.2 |
| | 1.6 | 2.1 | 1.7 | | 5.5 | .8 | 1.3 | 1.5 | 2.0 |
| | 6.5 | 9.2 | 5.6 | | 36.0 | 2.7 | 2.0 | 5.2 | NM |
| % Profit Before Taxes/Tangible Net Worth | 47.6 | 47.6 | 56.1 | | 69.1 | 54.7 | 34.1 | 49.8 | 71.7 |
| | (98) 19.3 | (107) 25.7 | (124) 24.8 | | (21) 26.2 | (19) 31.4 | 15.2 | (38) 24.4 | (23) 27.5 |
| | -4.9 | 10.4 | 8.7 | | 3.9 | 11.1 | 1.8 | 9.4 | 12.3 |
| % Profit Before Taxes/Total Assets | 18.0 | 17.7 | 24.6 | | 20.5 | 29.0 | 18.6 | 24.5 | 15.6 |
| | 5.8 | 7.6 | 9.4 | | 7.8 | 20.4 | 4.7 | 9.5 | 6.5 |
| | -2.6 | 1.8 | 2.5 | | 1.1 | 4.6 | .6 | 2.5 | 2.4 |
| Sales/Net Fixed Assets | 28.1 | 35.0 | 31.8 | | 61.1 | 33.2 | 16.7 | 35.8 | 25.1 |
| | 9.6 | 12.1 | 11.0 | | 22.1 | 16.6 | 5.2 | 10.5 | 7.1 |
| | 3.9 | 5.0 | 4.7 | | 8.9 | 6.3 | 2.8 | 4.0 | 4.8 |
| Sales/Total Assets | 3.2 | 2.9 | 3.3 | | 5.3 | 3.3 | 2.3 | 3.7 | 2.2 |
| | 2.1 | 2.1 | 2.1 | | 2.6 | 2.7 | 1.6 | 2.2 | 1.7 |
| | 1.5 | 1.5 | 1.4 | | 1.7 | 1.9 | 1.1 | 1.6 | 1.2 |
| % Depr., Dep., Amort./Sales | 1.4 | 1.1 | 1.2 | | .8 | .8 | 1.4 | .8 | 1.9 |
| | (103) 2.9 | (104) 2.1 | (109) 2.9 | | (17) 2.9 | (14) 1.5 | (17) 4.0 | (34) 2.2 | (23) 3.1 |
| | 5.8 | 4.1 | 4.2 | | 4.6 | 3.5 | 6.9 | 3.5 | 4.4 |
| % Officers', Directors', Owners' Comp/Sales | 2.8 | 1.5 | 2.1 | | 3.0 | 5.3 | 2.8 | .8 | |
| | (51) 5.8 | (59) 3.0 | (53) 4.3 | | (13) 4.3 | (10) 7.1 | (11) 4.2 | (12) 1.6 | |
| | 10.1 | 6.2 | 7.5 | | 9.5 | 9.3 | 8.3 | 3.5 | |
| Net Sales ($) | 2213531M | 3957630M | 3693904M | 2405M | 52921M | 74969M | 142566M | 621588M | 2799455M |
| Total Assets ($) | 1684133M | 2402559M | 2548224M | 1825M | 26463M | 30682M | 104278M | 296576M | 2088400M |

M = $ thousand    MM = $ million
See Pages 9 through 22 for Explanation of Ratios and Data

| Current Data Sorted by Assets | | | | | | | Comparative Historical Data | |
|---|---|---|---|---|---|---|---|---|
| | | | | | | **Type of Statement** | | |
| 1 | | 1 | 9 | | 1 | Unqualified | 9 | 12 |
| | 5 | 8 | 4 | 1 | | Reviewed | 13 | 18 |
| | 5 | 5 | 4 | | 1 | Compiled | 11 | 15 |
| 2 | 5 | 6 | 1 | | | Tax Returns | 9 | 11 |
| 4 | 11 | 8 | 15 | | 5 | Other | 21 | 31 |
| | 16 (4/1-9/30/11) | | | 86 (10/1/11-3/31/12) | | | 4/1/07-3/31/08 | 4/1/08-3/31/09 |
| 0-500M | 500M-2MM | 2-10MM | 10-50MM | 50-100MM | 100-250MM | | ALL | ALL |
| 7 | 26 | 28 | 33 | 1 | 7 | **NUMBER OF STATEMENTS** | 63 | 87 |
| % | % | % | % | % | % | **ASSETS** | % | % |
| | 24.1 | 13.1 | 12.4 | | | Cash & Equivalents | 9.1 | 11.9 |
| | 22.5 | 18.2 | 19.8 | | | Trade Receivables (net) | 22.2 | 19.6 |
| | 7.3 | 10.7 | 11.3 | | | Inventory | 6.5 | 5.2 |
| | 3.0 | 4.0 | 2.7 | | | All Other Current | 5.1 | 3.5 |
| | 56.9 | 46.0 | 46.2 | | | Total Current | 43.0 | 40.1 |
| | 32.9 | 44.4 | 42.1 | | | Fixed Assets (net) | 44.4 | 44.1 |
| | 3.3 | 1.7 | 5.0 | | | Intangibles (net) | 5.7 | 6.4 |
| | 6.9 | 7.9 | 6.7 | | | All Other Non-Current | 6.9 | 9.4 |
| | 100.0 | 100.0 | 100.0 | | | Total | 100.0 | 100.0 |
| | | | | | | **LIABILITIES** | | |
| | 7.2 | 6.1 | 7.5 | | | Notes Payable-Short Term | 11.7 | 8.1 |
| | 5.3 | 5.4 | 4.4 | | | Cur. Mat.-L.T.D. | 8.2 | 5.6 |
| | 16.5 | 13.5 | 10.6 | | | Trade Payables | 10.2 | 11.7 |
| | .2 | .0 | .4 | | | Income Taxes Payable | .5 | .1 |
| | 11.4 | 6.4 | 6.9 | | | All Other Current | 7.8 | 9.3 |
| | 40.7 | 31.4 | 29.8 | | | Total Current | 38.4 | 34.8 |
| | 28.8 | 22.2 | 23.2 | | | Long-Term Debt | 33.1 | 28.7 |
| | .0 | .5 | .3 | | | Deferred Taxes | .7 | .2 |
| | 8.9 | 4.9 | 7.2 | | | All Other Non-Current | 5.1 | 5.8 |
| | 21.6 | 40.9 | 39.6 | | | Net Worth | 22.8 | 30.5 |
| | 100.0 | 100.0 | 100.0 | | | Total Liabilties & Net Worth | 100.0 | 100.0 |
| | | | | | | **INCOME DATA** | | |
| | 100.0 | 100.0 | 100.0 | | | Net Sales | 100.0 | 100.0 |
| | | | | | | Gross Profit | | |
| | 83.2 | 95.4 | 91.7 | | | Operating Expenses | 93.9 | 91.3 |
| | 16.8 | 4.6 | 8.3 | | | Operating Profit | 6.1 | 8.7 |
| | 6.4 | 1.2 | .5 | | | All Other Expenses (net) | 2.0 | 2.9 |
| | 10.5 | 3.3 | 7.8 | | | Profit Before Taxes | 4.2 | 5.8 |
| | | | | | | **RATIOS** | | |
| | 2.4 | 2.2 | 2.7 | | | | 2.0 | 2.2 |
| | 1.3 | 1.5 | 1.6 | | | Current | 1.2 | 1.3 |
| | .7 | 1.0 | 1.0 | | | | .7 | .7 |
| | 2.1 | 1.5 | 1.7 | | | | 1.5 | 1.7 |
| | .9 | .9 | 1.1 | | | Quick | .9 | 1.0 |
| | .6 | .4 | .8 | | | | .5 | .4 |
| | 1   280.8 | 16   23.3 | 26   14.3 | | | | 17   21.2 | 9   41.2 |
| | 20   18.0 | 27   13.4 | 34   10.8 | | | Sales/Receivables | 32   11.5 | 28   13.2 |
| | 34   10.7 | 36   10.1 | 44   8.3 | | | | 46   8.0 | 49   7.5 |
| | | | | | | Cost of Sales/Inventory | | |
| | | | | | | Cost of Sales/Payables | | |
| | 7.7 | 8.3 | 5.9 | | | | 11.8 | 12.3 |
| | 37.0 | 16.0 | 14.2 | | | Sales/Working Capital | 39.8 | 35.1 |
| | -30.2 | NM | 166.3 | | | | -21.0 | -19.7 |
| | 18.8 | 9.2 | 20.7 | | | | 21.2 | 14.2 |
| | (17) 13.6 | (23) 5.1 | (30) 4.8 | | | EBIT/Interest | (60) 3.9 | (74) 3.6 |
| | 2.3 | .7 | 1.4 | | | | 1.1 | 1.5 |
| | | | | | | Net Profit + Depr., Dep., | 17.2 | 11.9 |
| | | | | | | Amort./Cur. Mat. L/T/D | (17) 3.3 | (13) 2.3 |
| | | | | | | | 1.9 | .6 |
| | .3 | .4 | .7 | | | | .6 | .5 |
| | 2.0 | 1.2 | 1.4 | | | Fixed/Worth | 1.9 | 1.8 |
| | -3.1 | 2.5 | 2.9 | | | | -26.9 | 9.5 |
| | 1.2 | .7 | .7 | | | | 1.2 | .9 |
| | 5.0 | 2.0 | 1.6 | | | Debt/Worth | 2.3 | 2.9 |
| | -8.8 | 3.1 | 5.2 | | | | -33.6 | 18.0 |
| | 79.8 | 61.7 | 46.5 | | | % Profit Before Taxes/Tangible | 79.3 | 72.7 |
| | (18) 41.6 | (26) 23.7 | (29) 28.6 | | | Net Worth | (47) 35.8 | (69) 38.0 |
| | 8.4 | 6.2 | 10.6 | | | | 6.2 | 13.6 |
| | 32.0 | 16.1 | 22.6 | | | % Profit Before Taxes/Total | 21.1 | 27.7 |
| | 16.9 | 8.5 | 10.5 | | | Assets | 8.5 | 7.7 |
| | 3.5 | -.2 | 1.7 | | | | .4 | 2.1 |
| | 30.7 | 16.7 | 8.5 | | | | 17.9 | 14.3 |
| | 17.1 | 6.8 | 4.4 | | | Sales/Net Fixed Assets | 6.2 | 5.6 |
| | 6.5 | 2.2 | 2.3 | | | | 2.1 | 2.2 |
| | 5.2 | 3.8 | 3.0 | | | | 3.9 | 4.0 |
| | 3.5 | 2.2 | 2.0 | | | Sales/Total Assets | 1.9 | 2.1 |
| | 1.7 | 1.3 | 1.0 | | | | 1.1 | 1.3 |
| | .8 | 1.6 | 1.7 | | | | 1.4 | 1.3 |
| | (20) 1.7 | (26) 2.9 | (30) 3.3 | | | % Depr., Dep., Amort./Sales | (58) 3.1 | (72) 2.8 |
| | 3.5 | 7.3 | 5.9 | | | | 7.1 | 7.6 |
| | | | | | | % Officers', Directors' | .9 | .9 |
| | | | | | | Owners' Comp/Sales | (22) 2.8 | (31) 2.5 |
| | | | | | | | 4.7 | 6.3 |
| 8373M | 87852M | 415274M | 1318310M | 268273M | 2463591M | Net Sales ($) | 1934700M | 3479947M |
| 1739M | 30059M | 144246M | 662981M | 62101M | 1077605M | Total Assets ($) | 973837M | 1430503M |

© RMA 2012

M = $ thousand    MM = $ million
See Pages 9 through 22 for Explanation of Ratios and Data

## Comparative Historical Data | Current Data Sorted by Sales

| | 4/1/09-3/31/10 ALL | 4/1/10-3/31/11 ALL | 4/1/11-3/31/12 ALL | 0-1MM | 1-3MM | 3-5MM | 5-10MM | 10-25MM | 25MM & OVER |
|---|---|---|---|---|---|---|---|---|---|
| | | | | 16 (4/1-9/30/11) | | 86 (10/1/11-3/31/12) | | | |
| **Type of Statement** | | | | | | | | | |
| Unqualified | 14 | 19 | 12 | 1 | | 2 | 4 | 2 | 9 |
| Reviewed | 21 | 20 | 18 | | 1 | | | 6 | 5 |
| Compiled | 16 | 21 | 15 | 1 | | 5 | 2 | 3 | 4 |
| Tax Returns | 13 | 7 | 14 | 5 | 3 | 1 | | 3 | 2 |
| Other | 31 | 30 | 43 | 4 | 5 | 8 | 4 | 7 | 15 |
| **NUMBER OF STATEMENTS** | 95 | 97 | 102 | 11 | 9 | 16 | 10 | 21 | 35 |
| | % | % | % | % | % | % | % | % | % |
| **ASSETS** | | | | | | | | | |
| Cash & Equivalents | 10.3 | 12.5 | 16.3 | 15.6 | | 10.7 | 25.6 | 13.4 | 13.9 |
| Trade Receivables (net) | 18.1 | 19.0 | 20.8 | 8.9 | | 20.0 | 27.8 | 18.4 | 22.2 |
| Inventory | 8.4 | 8.2 | 10.1 | 3.0 | | 10.2 | 8.2 | 8.0 | 14.2 |
| All Other Current | 4.0 | 4.1 | 3.3 | 4.6 | | 5.6 | .6 | 2.4 | 2.6 |
| Total Current | 40.8 | 43.8 | 50.6 | 32.1 | | 46.5 | 62.2 | 42.2 | 53.0 |
| Fixed Assets (net) | 47.6 | 41.3 | 37.5 | 61.4 | | 40.9 | 29.3 | 44.6 | 33.3 |
| Intangibles (net) | 3.7 | 7.5 | 5.4 | .1 | | 5.4 | 1.6 | 3.4 | 10.7 |
| All Other Non-Current | 8.0 | 7.4 | 6.5 | 6.4 | | 7.2 | 6.9 | 9.8 | 3.1 |
| Total | 100.0 | 100.0 | 100.0 | 100.0 | | 100.0 | 100.0 | 100.0 | 100.0 |
| **LIABILITIES** | | | | | | | | | |
| Notes Payable-Short Term | 7.6 | 8.2 | 7.1 | 5.3 | | 5.9 | 6.9 | 5.1 | 8.2 |
| Cur. Mat.-L.T.D. | 6.0 | 4.7 | 4.9 | 5.1 | | 8.2 | 3.3 | 5.4 | 3.8 |
| Trade Payables | 11.8 | 9.8 | 12.8 | 3.7 | | 10.0 | 25.1 | 13.3 | 12.1 |
| Income Taxes Payable | .2 | .1 | .2 | .0 | | .4 | .0 | .1 | .5 |
| All Other Current | 9.8 | 7.6 | 7.4 | 8.9 | | 12.3 | 5.2 | 5.4 | 6.0 |
| Total Current | 35.4 | 30.5 | 32.4 | 23.0 | | 36.8 | 40.4 | 29.2 | 30.6 |
| Long-Term Debt | 29.1 | 20.7 | 24.0 | 45.0 | | 40.8 | 14.0 | 28.9 | 13.4 |
| Deferred Taxes | .2 | .5 | .3 | .0 | | .0 | 1.3 | .4 | .2 |
| All Other Non-Current | 7.2 | 6.2 | 6.5 | 1.1 | | 9.4 | 11.4 | 6.0 | 6.3 |
| Net Worth | 28.0 | 42.1 | 36.8 | 30.9 | | 13.1 | 32.9 | 35.6 | 49.6 |
| Total Liabilities & Net Worth | 100.0 | 100.0 | 100.0 | 100.0 | | 100.0 | 100.0 | 100.0 | 100.0 |
| **INCOME DATA** | | | | | | | | | |
| Net Sales | 100.0 | 100.0 | 100.0 | 100.0 | | 100.0 | 100.0 | 100.0 | 100.0 |
| Gross Profit | | | | | | | | | |
| Operating Expenses | 95.3 | 88.6 | 89.3 | 59.8 | | 94.0 | 93.6 | 91.8 | 93.1 |
| Operating Profit | 4.7 | 11.4 | 10.7 | 40.2 | | 6.0 | 6.4 | 8.2 | 6.9 |
| All Other Expenses (net) | 2.1 | 3.7 | 2.3 | 16.9 | | .7 | .3 | .8 | .5 |
| Profit Before Taxes | 2.6 | 7.7 | 8.3 | 23.3 | | 5.3 | 6.1 | 7.3 | 6.4 |
| **RATIOS** | | | | | | | | | |
| Current | 1.8 | 2.6 | 2.3 | 3.5 | | 2.2 | 3.2 | 2.0 | 3.1 |
| | 1.1 | 1.5 | 1.6 | 1.2 | | 1.5 | 1.6 | 1.4 | 1.8 |
| | .7 | .7 | 1.0 | .1 | | .9 | 1.1 | 1.0 | 1.2 |
| Quick | 1.3 | 1.8 | 1.8 | 2.3 | | 2.0 | 2.2 | 1.4 | 1.7 |
| | .8 | .8 | 1.1 | .7 | | .7 | 1.5 | .9 | 1.2 |
| | .4 | .5 | .7 | .1 | | .4 | .8 | .7 | .8 |
| Sales/Receivables | 19  19.0 | 14  26.3 | 15  24.4 | 0  UND | | 19  19.4 | 14  27.0 | 18  20.6 | 22  16.6 |
| | 36  10.1 | 33  10.9 | 29  12.6 | 0  UND | | 28  13.1 | 31  11.8 | 26  13.9 | 34  10.8 |
| | 47  7.8 | 49  7.4 | 41  9.0 | 43  8.4 | | 47  7.8 | 35  10.5 | 48  7.6 | 43  8.4 |
| Cost of Sales/Inventory | | | | | | | | | |
| Cost of Sales/Payables | | | | | | | | | |
| Sales/Working Capital | 11.2 | 8.4 | 7.3 | 5.1 | | 7.5 | 8.2 | 8.4 | 7.1 |
| | 84.9 | 33.3 | 16.0 | 17.4 | | 14.3 | 14.3 | 25.1 | 10.8 |
| | -14.3 | -17.3 | 212.2 | -3.6 | | NM | NM | NM | 43.7 |
| EBIT/Interest | 7.3 | 17.6 | 17.5 | | | 14.5 | | 10.1 | 23.8 |
| | (90) 2.6 | (80) 6.4 | (83) 5.6 | | | (14) 4.1 | (18) 5.5 | (31) 7.8 | |
| | -.2 | 2.4 | 1.5 | | | 1.9 | | .9 | 1.5 |
| Net Profit + Depr., Dep., Amort./Cur. Mat. L/T/D | 7.1 | 10.5 | 8.0 | | | | | | |
| | (18) 2.0 | (27) 1.9 | (17) 3.2 | | | | | | |
| | 1.2 | 1.2 | 1.6 | | | | | | |
| Fixed/Worth | .7 | .5 | .4 | .4 | | .9 | .2 | .5 | .4 |
| | 1.7 | 1.5 | 1.3 | 3.2 | | 5.1 | .9 | 1.6 | 1.0 |
| | 4.1 | 4.4 | 3.2 | -3.4 | | -1.4 | 3.7 | 2.8 | 1.6 |
| Debt/Worth | 1.0 | .6 | .7 | .1 | | 1.7 | 1.0 | 1.5 | .6 |
| | 2.2 | 1.8 | 1.8 | 2.4 | | 9.6 | 1.5 | 2.0 | 1.1 |
| | 5.5 | 6.2 | 6.6 | -4.5 | | -6.4 | 17.0 | 3.2 | 2.7 |
| % Profit Before Taxes/Tangible Net Worth | 33.3 | 80.7 | 63.5 | | | | | 66.5 | 45.5 |
| | (82) 15.2 | (82) 28.7 | (85) 32.5 | | | | | (19) 32.5 | (32) 27.9 |
| | 1.3 | 10.1 | 9.8 | | | | | 10.4 | 10.5 |
| % Profit Before Taxes/Total Assets | 9.7 | 26.7 | 24.3 | 34.2 | | 27.7 | 35.1 | 15.4 | 23.4 |
| | 4.1 | 12.0 | 10.8 | 3.5 | | 10.4 | 18.8 | 9.5 | 12.6 |
| | -1.8 | 3.6 | 2.4 | -1.1 | | 1.1 | 5.1 | .9 | 4.1 |
| Sales/Net Fixed Assets | 10.9 | 19.0 | 24.2 | 6.5 | | 17.3 | 264.7 | 11.0 | 39.2 |
| | 3.6 | 5.8 | 6.8 | .6 | | 6.8 | 14.8 | 4.1 | 7.7 |
| | 2.0 | 2.2 | 2.9 | .1 | | 3.1 | 3.0 | 2.8 | 3.2 |
| Sales/Total Assets | 3.0 | 3.4 | 4.1 | .9 | | 4.0 | 6.5 | 3.4 | 4.0 |
| | 1.6 | 1.9 | 2.3 | .2 | | 2.5 | 3.4 | 2.1 | 2.5 |
| | 1.1 | 1.2 | 1.1 | .1 | | 1.1 | 1.6 | 1.1 | 1.3 |
| % Depr., Dep., Amort./Sales | 2.2 | 1.7 | 1.1 | | | 1.6 | | 2.7 | .9 |
| | (81) 4.8 | (83) 3.3 | (85) 2.7 | | | (14) 2.9 | | (19) 3.3 | (32) 2.1 |
| | 8.5 | 7.4 | 5.2 | | | 7.2 | | 4.8 | 4.1 |
| % Officers', Directors', Owners' Comp/Sales | .7 | 1.0 | .7 | | | | | | |
| | (26) 2.6 | (23) 2.6 | (20) 2.3 | | | | | | |
| | 4.8 | 5.4 | 5.7 | | | | | | |
| Net Sales ($) | 2297197M | 2541930M | 4561673M | 4866M | 20375M | 61249M | 73968M | 352408M | 4048807M |
| Total Assets ($) | 1209899M | 1473549M | 1978731M | 15831M | 6385M | 42339M | 35568M | 192238M | 1686370M |

© RMA 2012

M = $ thousand    MM = $ million

See Pages 9 through 22 for Explanation of Ratios and Data

**Current Data Sorted by Assets**                                                                     **Comparative Historical Data**

| | | | | | | Type of Statement | | |
|---|---|---|---|---|---|---|---|---|
| | | 1 | | 1 | | Unqualified | | |
| 1 | | 5 | | | | Reviewed | 4 | 7 |
| 1 | 4 | 1 | | | | Compiled | 1 | 3 |
| 9 | 3 | 1 | | | | Tax Returns | 3 | 7 |
| 3 | 3 | 3 | | | 2 | Other | 3 | 6 |
| | 2 (4/1-9/30/11) | | 36 (10/1/11-3/31/12) | | | | 4/1/07-3/31/08 | 4/1/08-3/31/09 |
| 0-500M | 500M-2MM | 2-10MM | 10-50MM | 50-100MM | 100-250MM | | ALL | ALL |
| 14 | 10 | 11 | | 1 | 2 | NUMBER OF STATEMENTS | 11 | 23 |
| % | % | % | % | % | % | ASSETS | % | % |
| 19.5 | 9.0 | 12.0 | | | | Cash & Equivalents | 6.1 | 11.8 |
| 19.0 | 15.8 | 31.4 | | | | Trade Receivables (net) | 14.0 | 16.4 |
| .4 | 3.8 | 2.4 | | | | Inventory | 1.4 | 1.7 |
| 1.0 | 1.5 | 3.2 | | | | All Other Current | .3 | 1.5 |
| 39.9 | 30.0 | 49.0 | | | | Total Current | 21.8 | 31.3 |
| 35.4 | 58.5 | 37.3 | | | | Fixed Assets (net) | 63.6 | 50.4 |
| 16.1 | 8.4 | 9.5 | | | | Intangibles (net) | 12.5 | 8.6 |
| 8.6 | *3.1 | 4.2 | | | | All Other Non-Current | 2.0 | 9.5 |
| 100.0 | 100.0 | 100.0 | | | | Total | 100.0 | 100.0 |
| | | | | | | LIABILITIES | | |
| 20.9 | 19.2 | 6.1 | | | | Notes Payable-Short Term | 23.2 | 3.5 |
| 19.8 | 4.8 | 4.5 | | | | Cur. Mat.-L.T.D. | 7.1 | 7.3 |
| 16.0 | 5.9 | 6.1 | | | | Trade Payables | 10.1 | 5.6 |
| .0 | .0 | .0 | | | | Income Taxes Payable | .0 | .0 |
| 11.2 | 7.5 | 5.6 | | | | All Other Current | 2.6 | 5.0 |
| 68.0 | 37.4 | 22.4 | | | | Total Current | 43.0 | 21.4 |
| 59.8 | 56.3 | 12.5 | | | | Long-Term Debt | 46.9 | 36.4 |
| .0 | .8 | 1.3 | | | | Deferred Taxes | .0 | .0 |
| 17.5 | 13.0 | 1.0 | | | | All Other Non-Current | 12.9 | 6.5 |
| -45.3 | -7.5 | 62.8 | | | | Net Worth | -2.9 | 35.8 |
| 100.0 | 100.0 | 100.0 | | | | Total Liabilties & Net Worth | 100.0 | 100.0 |
| | | | | | | INCOME DATA | | |
| 100.0 | 100.0 | 100.0 | | | | Net Sales | 100.0 | 100.0 |
| | | | | | | Gross Profit | | |
| 89.2 | 89.2 | 92.6 | | | | Operating Expenses | 100.0 | 93.8 |
| 10.8 | 10.8 | 7.4 | | | | Operating Profit | .0 | 6.2 |
| 3.0 | 8.1 | 1.0 | | | | All Other Expenses (net) | 2.6 | 1.7 |
| 7.8 | 2.8 | 6.4 | | | | Profit Before Taxes | -2.6 | 4.5 |
| | | | | | | RATIOS | | |
| 3.7 | 2.4 | 4.3 | | | | | 1.9 | 2.7 |
| .6 | 1.0 | 1.8 | | | | Current | .4 | 1.7 |
| .2 | .5 | 1.4 | | | | | .2 | .5 |
| 3.6 | 2.3 | 4.3 | | | | | 1.8 | 2.7 |
| .6 | .8 | 1.6 | | | | Quick | .4 | 1.6 |
| .2 | .4 | 1.1 | | | | | .2 | .5 |
| 0 UND | 0 UND | 33 11.2 | | | | | 10 36.0 | 14 25.3 |
| 9 40.5 | 29 12.7 | 43 8.5 | | | | Sales/Receivables | 17 21.4 | 24 15.3 |
| 38 9.5 | 39 9.4 | 79 4.6 | | | | | 27 13.4 | 34 10.7 |
| | | | | | | Cost of Sales/Inventory | | |
| | | | | | | Cost of Sales/Payables | | |
| 8.2 | 6.6 | 4.4 | | | | | 32.9 | 16.1 |
| -28.0 | NM | 10.2 | | | | Sales/Working Capital | -14.3 | 23.9 |
| -6.8 | -13.0 | 21.4 | | | | | -5.6 | -44.2 |
| 4.5 | | 94.1 | | | | | 5.4 | 13.4 |
| (11) 1.7 | | 18.0 | | | | EBIT/Interest | -.9 | (20) 2.0 |
| 1.0 | | 7.0 | | | | | -1.3 | -.5 |
| | | | | | | Net Profit + Depr., Dep., Amort./Cur. Mat. L/T/D | | |
| .1 | 1.8 | .5 | | | | | 2.7 | .7 |
| -1.6 | 9.1 | .6 | | | | Fixed/Worth | -3.8 | 1.4 |
| -.5 | -2.5 | 1.4 | | | | | -1.4 | -15.7 |
| 2.7 | 1.5 | .3 | | | | | 2.9 | .9 |
| -3.3 | 9.4 | .5 | | | | Debt/Worth | -5.1 | 2.0 |
| -1.9 | -5.7 | 1.9 | | | | | -3.3 | -21.5 |
| | | 47.7 | | | | | | 83.7 |
| | | 18.8 | | | | % Profit Before Taxes/Tangible Net Worth | (17) | 36.8 |
| | | 12.9 | | | | | | 1.4 |
| 59.6 | 14.6 | 25.3 | | | | | 21.4 | 30.7 |
| 10.9 | 3.2 | 11.6 | | | | % Profit Before Taxes/Total Assets | -12.7 | 4.5 |
| 1.2 | -7.1 | 5.6 | | | | | -16.7 | -7.5 |
| 103.4 | 7.7 | 8.6 | | | | | 5.2 | 11.5 |
| 17.9 | 3.2 | 4.4 | | | | Sales/Net Fixed Assets | 2.9 | 4.9 |
| 5.3 | .4 | 3.5 | | | | | 2.2 | 2.1 |
| 4.3 | 3.3 | 2.3 | | | | | 3.2 | 3.5 |
| 3.5 | 1.9 | 1.8 | | | | Sales/Total Assets | 1.9 | 2.0 |
| 2.6 | .3 | 1.7 | | | | | 1.7 | 1.6 |
| | | 1.0 | | | | | 6.5 | 5.1 |
| | | 6.1 | | | | % Depr., Dep., Amort./Sales | (10) 10.4 | (16) 8.2 |
| | | 7.3 | | | | | 14.6 | 13.2 |
| | | | | | | % Officers', Directors' Owners' Comp/Sales | | |
| 12090M | 21983M | 90859M | | 145030M | 312929M | Net Sales ($) | 32034M | 86044M |
| 3217M | 11033M | 48526M | | 57927M | 326052M | Total Assets ($) | 15998M | 46454M |

The letters "D A T A   N O T   A V A I L A B L E" appear vertically in the 10-50MM column area.

M = $ thousand     MM = $ million
See Pages 9 through 22 for Explanation of Ratios and Data

## Comparative Historical Data | Current Data Sorted by Sales

| 3 2 8 6 | 2 5 1 9 7 | 2 6 6 13 11 | Type of Statement | | | | | | |
|---|---|---|---|---|---|---|---|---|---|
| | | | Unqualified | | | | 1 | | 1 |
| | | | Reviewed | 1 | | 1 | 2 | 2 | 1 |
| | | | Compiled | 1 | 2 | 2 | 1 | | |
| | | | Tax Returns | 8 | 4 | 1 | 4 | | 2 |
| | | | Other | 3 | 1 | | | 1 | |
| 3 | 7 | 11 | | | 2 (4/1-9/30/11) | | 36 (10/1/11-3/31/12) | | |
| 4/1/09-3/31/10 ALL | 4/1/10-3/31/11 ALL | 4/1/11-3/31/12 ALL | | 0-1MM | 1-3MM | 3-5MM | 5-10MM | 10-25MM | 25MM & OVER |
| 19 | 24 | 38 | NUMBER OF STATEMENTS | 13 | 7 | 4 | 8 | 3 | 3 |
| % | % | % | ASSETS | % | % | % | % | % | % |
| 18.0 | 14.9 | 13.4 | Cash & Equivalents | 13.9 | | | | | |
| 18.7 | 19.2 | 22.5 | Trade Receivables (net) | 8.9 | | | | | |
| 5.8 | 2.4 | 2.0 | Inventory | 1.6 | | | | | |
| 1.9 | 3.4 | 2.1 | All Other Current | 1.0 | | | | | |
| 44.5 | 40.0 | 39.9 | Total Current | 25.5 | | | | | |
| 43.6 | 43.5 | 41.0 | Fixed Assets (net) | 48.4 | | | | | |
| 6.5 | 11.4 | 13.0 | Intangibles (net) | 17.2 | | | | | |
| 5.5 | 5.0 | 6.1 | All Other Non-Current | 8.9 | | | | | |
| 100.0 | 100.0 | 100.0 | Total | 100.0 | | | | | |
| | | | LIABILITIES | | | | | | |
| 12.3 | 9.8 | 14.9 | Notes Payable-Short Term | 19.3 | | | | | |
| 5.7 | 8.3 | 10.0 | Cur. Mat.-L.T.D. | 9.3 | | | | | |
| 14.4 | 6.8 | 10.1 | Trade Payables | 9.6 | | | | | |
| .0 | .3 | .0 | Income Taxes Payable | .0 | | | | | |
| 8.2 | 9.1 | 8.8 | All Other Current | 5.4 | | | | | |
| 40.6 | 34.3 | 43.9 | Total Current | 43.5 | | | | | |
| 35.1 | 30.4 | 42.0 | Long-Term Debt | 59.1 | | | | | |
| .0 | .0 | .7 | Deferred Taxes | .0 | | | | | |
| 10.4 | 5.9 | 10.1 | All Other Non-Current | 16.9 | | | | | |
| 14.0 | 29.4 | 3.2 | Net Worth | -19.6 | | | | | |
| 100.0 | 100.0 | 100.0 | Total Liabilities & Net Worth | 100.0 | | | | | |
| | | | INCOME DATA | | | | | | |
| 100.0 | 100.0 | 100.0 | Net Sales | 100.0 | | | | | |
| | | | Gross Profit | | | | | | |
| 97.8 | 91.0 | 91.0 | Operating Expenses | 90.2 | | | | | |
| 2.2 | 9.0 | 9.0 | Operating Profit | 9.8 | | | | | |
| 1.4 | 1.1 | 3.6 | All Other Expenses (net) | 6.5 | | | | | |
| .8 | 8.0 | 5.4 | Profit Before Taxes | 3.3 | | | | | |
| | | | RATIOS | | | | | | |
| 3.4 | 2.8 | 2.6 | | 2.8 | | | | | |
| 1.2 | 1.2 | 1.3 | Current | .5 | | | | | |
| .6 | .4 | .5 | | .3 | | | | | |
| 1.8 | 2.0 | 2.5 | | 2.8 | | | | | |
| 1.1 | 1.0 | 1.1 | Quick | .5 | | | | | |
| .5 | .3 | .5 | | .2 | | | | | |
| 3 120.8 | 0 UND | 10 37.9 | | 0 UND | | | | | |
| 19 19.3 | 24 15.3 | 36 10.2 | Sales/Receivables | 8 45.7 | | | | | |
| 43 8.5 | 46 7.9 | 51 7.1 | | 23 15.6 | | | | | |
| | | | Cost of Sales/Inventory | | | | | | |
| | | | Cost of Sales/Payables | | | | | | |
| 10.3 | 8.0 | 6.6 | | 8.2 | | | | | |
| 53.1 | 96.0 | 22.8 | Sales/Working Capital | -25.5 | | | | | |
| -12.0 | -10.3 | -18.1 | | -6.0 | | | | | |
| 3.9 | 17.5 | 18.6 | | | | | | | |
| (18) .7 | (22) 6.1 | (34) 4.4 | EBIT/Interest | | | | | | |
| -4.5 | 1.6 | 1.1 | | | | | | | |
| | | | Net Profit + Depr., Dep., Amort./Cur. Mat. L/T/D | | | | | | |
| .9 | .8 | .5 | | 4.3 | | | | | |
| 2.3 | 3.2 | 2.1 | Fixed/Worth | -2.1 | | | | | |
| -5.4 | -2.0 | -2.0 | | -.7 | | | | | |
| 1.1 | .8 | .8 | | NM | | | | | |
| 3.5 | 3.5 | 4.5 | Debt/Worth | -3.9 | | | | | |
| -13.8 | -4.6 | -3.8 | | -2.3 | | | | | |
| 36.7 | 141.6 | 62.3 | % Profit Before Taxes/Tangible Net Worth | | | | | | |
| (13) 10.7 | (15) 58.0 | (24) 31.7 | | | | | | | |
| -22.5 | 12.9 | 8.9 | | | | | | | |
| 11.9 | 32.8 | 16.3 | % Profit Before Taxes/Total Assets | 15.2 | | | | | |
| -.6 | 16.8 | 7.9 | | 6.5 | | | | | |
| -10.2 | 2.8 | 1.4 | | 1.9 | | | | | |
| 14.5 | 13.2 | 16.9 | | 54.5 | | | | | |
| 5.6 | 5.9 | 6.0 | Sales/Net Fixed Assets | 5.6 | | | | | |
| 2.9 | 2.4 | 3.6 | | 1.4 | | | | | |
| 3.0 | 3.4 | 3.3 | | 3.6 | | | | | |
| 2.4 | 2.2 | 2.4 | Sales/Total Assets | 2.8 | | | | | |
| 1.6 | 1.3 | 1.7 | | 1.0 | | | | | |
| 2.7 | 2.9 | 2.1 | | | | | | | |
| (17) 10.4 | (17) 9.0 | (27) 6.3 | % Depr., Dep., Amort./Sales | | | | | | |
| 16.0 | 17.2 | 9.3 | | | | | | | |
| | 3.6 | 1.9 | % Officers', Directors' Owners' Comp/Sales | | | | | | |
| | (12) 5.5 | (14) 3.8 | | | | | | | |
| | 8.7 | 8.1 | | | | | | | |
| 234291M | 315276M | 582891M | Net Sales ($) | 6247M | 11384M | 15539M | 58183M | 33579M | 457959M |
| 93051M | 226010M | 446755M | Total Assets ($) | 4309M | 4529M | 6221M | 32231M | 15486M | 383979M |

M = $ thousand   MM = $ million
See Pages 9 through 22 for Explanation of Ratios and Data

## Current Data Sorted by Assets

## Comparative Historical Data

| | | | | | | Type of Statement | | |
|---|---|---|---|---|---|---|---|---|
| 2 | 1 | 4 | 9 | 2 | 2 | Unqualified | | |
| 1 | 4 | 13 | 9 | | | Reviewed | 18 | 18 |
| 10 | 5 | 8 | | | | Compiled | 33 | 36 |
| 3 | 8 | 6 | 1 | | | Tax Returns | 18 | 17 |
| | 12 | 17 | 11 | 1 | 1 | Other | 28 | 27 |
| | 21 (4/1-9/30/11) | | 109 (10/1/11-3/31/12) | | | | 48 | 46 |
| | | | | | | | 4/1/07- | 4/1/08- |
| 0-500M | 500M-2MM | 2-10MM | 10-50MM | 50-100MM | 100-250MM | | 3/31/08 | 3/31/09 |
| 16 | 30 | 48 | 30 | 3 | 3 | NUMBER OF STATEMENTS | ALL | ALL |
| | | | | | | | 145 | 144 |
| % | % | % | % | % | % | ASSETS | % | % |
| 13.5 | 22.0 | 10.6 | 8.8 | | | Cash & Equivalents | 9.4 | 12.1 |
| 8.6 | 30.2 | 27.0 | 22.2 | | | Trade Receivables (net) | 25.4 | 25.4 |
| 6.6 | 4.7 | 2.4 | 4.3 | | | Inventory | 2.4 | 2.7 |
| 3.8 | 1.0 | 2.0 | 1.4 | | | All Other Current | 3.7 | 3.4 |
| 32.5 | 57.9 | 41.9 | 36.8 | | | Total Current | 40.9 | 43.5 |
| 43.2 | 32.6 | 42.4 | 49.2 | | | Fixed Assets (net) | 44.9 | 39.6 |
| 6.7 | 3.8 | 7.9 | 7.0 | | | Intangibles (net) | 5.6 | 7.1 |
| 17.7 | 5.7 | 7.7 | 7.1 | | | All Other Non-Current | 8.6 | 9.8 |
| 100.0 | 100.0 | 100.0 | 100.0 | | | Total | 100.0 | 100.0 |
| | | | | | | LIABILITIES | | |
| 14.0 | 7.2 | 2.5 | 4.8 | | | Notes Payable-Short Term | 5.0 | 7.6 |
| 10.0 | 3.5 | 6.0 | 6.6 | | | Cur. Mat.-L.T.D. | 7.2 | 6.8 |
| 9.5 | 10.2 | 10.4 | 9.9 | | | Trade Payables | 12.0 | 9.8 |
| .1 | .0 | .5 | .0 | | | Income Taxes Payable | .7 | .7 |
| 17.6 | 10.2 | 6.5 | 5.4 | | | All Other Current | 6.7 | 6.2 |
| 51.1 | 31.0 | 25.8 | 26.7 | | | Total Current | 31.6 | 31.0 |
| 39.9 | 20.9 | 18.9 | 23.8 | | | Long-Term Debt | 29.8 | 25.9 |
| .0 | .6 | .5 | .4 | | | Deferred Taxes | .6 | .4 |
| 18.0 | 1.2 | 5.4 | 4.2 | | | All Other Non-Current | 9.3 | 5.3 |
| -9.0 | 46.3 | 49.4 | 44.8 | | | Net Worth | 28.7 | 37.3 |
| 100.0 | 100.0 | 100.0 | 100.0 | | | Total Liabilties & Net Worth | 100.0 | 100.0 |
| | | | | | | INCOME DATA | | |
| 100.0 | 100.0 | 100.0 | 100.0 | | | Net Sales | 100.0 | 100.0 |
| | | | | | | Gross Profit | | |
| 99.8 | 95.2 | 93.1 | 94.0 | | | Operating Expenses | 93.8 | 92.0 |
| .2 | 4.8 | 6.9 | 6.0 | | | Operating Profit | 6.2 | 8.0 |
| -.8 | .4 | .4 | 1.1 | | | All Other Expenses (net) | 1.8 | 1.6 |
| .9 | 4.4 | 6.5 | 5.0 | | | Profit Before Taxes | 4.5 | 6.4 |
| | | | | | | RATIOS | | |
| 1.5 | 14.4 | 3.0 | 1.9 | | | | 2.2 | 2.7 |
| .8 | 1.8 | 1.6 | 1.3 | | | Current | 1.3 | 1.4 |
| .3 | 1.0 | 1.1 | 1.0 | | | | .8 | .8 |
| 1.0 | 9.1 | 2.3 | 1.9 | | | | 2.0 | 2.4 |
| .5 | 1.8 | 1.4 | 1.1 | | | Quick | (144) 1.1 | 1.2 |
| .1 | .7 | .9 | .8 | | | | .6 | .6 |
| 0 UND | 20 18.5 | 28 13.2 | 31 11.7 | | | | 20 18.4 | 24 15.5 |
| 0 UND | 34 10.6 | 43 8.5 | 51 7.2 | | | Sales/Receivables | 39 9.4 | 37 9.8 |
| 18 20.3 | 51 7.2 | 73 5.0 | 69 5.3 | | | | 60 6.1 | 65 5.7 |
| | | | | | | Cost of Sales/Inventory | | |
| | | | | | | Cost of Sales/Payables | | |
| 28.0 | 6.9 | 6.5 | 6.8 | | | | 8.6 | 6.5 |
| -58.7 | 13.8 | 14.7 | 23.4 | | | Sales/Working Capital | 36.5 | 25.0 |
| -17.8 | NM | 120.8 | NM | | | | -24.7 | -32.5 |
| 18.8 | 20.5 | 24.5 | 12.6 | | | | 7.5 | 11.3 |
| (13) 2.8 | (22) 3.6 | (45) 8.3 | (29) 5.0 | | | EBIT/Interest | (127) 3.3 | (134) 4.3 |
| .1 | 1.1 | 2.0 | .8 | | | | 1.3 | 1.8 |
| | | | | | | Net Profit + Depr., Dep., | 9.8 | 4.1 |
| | | | | | | Amort./Cur. Mat. L/T/D | (31) 2.3 | (30) 2.0 |
| | | | | | | | 1.0 | 1.1 |
| 1.5 | .3 | .5 | .9 | | | | .5 | .5 |
| NM | .7 | .9 | 1.3 | | | Fixed/Worth | 1.9 | 1.5 |
| -.8 | 2.1 | 2.8 | 1.9 | | | | 7.2 | 5.0 |
| 3.5 | .1 | .4 | .6 | | | | .8 | .7 |
| NM | 1.6 | .8 | 1.5 | | | Debt/Worth | 2.7 | 1.9 |
| -2.8 | 5.6 | 3.8 | 3.9 | | | | 11.5 | 6.3 |
| | 69.5 | 48.7 | 34.5 | | | % Profit Before Taxes/Tangible | 58.1 | 52.9 |
| | (25) 29.9 | (40) 23.9 | (26) 16.6 | | | Net Worth | (119) 27.8 | (120) 25.1 |
| | 4.0 | 2.8 | -1.3 | | | | 10.7 | 12.3 |
| 30.8 | 27.2 | 19.3 | 13.2 | | | % Profit Before Taxes/Total | 16.1 | 22.2 |
| 7.6 | 9.2 | 11.2 | 7.2 | | | Assets | 7.4 | 9.8 |
| .0 | .7 | 2.2 | -2.5 | | | | .7 | 2.7 |
| 24.0 | 67.2 | 9.8 | 6.0 | | | | 11.3 | 14.1 |
| 13.8 | 8.8 | 4.8 | 2.9 | | | Sales/Net Fixed Assets | 5.5 | 6.3 |
| 4.1 | 4.1 | 2.7 | 1.0 | | | | 2.4 | 2.8 |
| 9.3 | 3.5 | 2.5 | 2.3 | | | | 3.0 | 3.0 |
| 5.4 | 2.7 | 2.0 | 1.3 | | | Sales/Total Assets | 2.0 | 2.1 |
| 2.3 | 2.0 | 1.3 | .6 | | | | 1.3 | 1.4 |
| | 2.1 | 2.4 | 3.8 | | | | 2.2 | 2.5 |
| | (21) 4.3 | (45) 5.0 | (29) 7.7 | | | % Depr., Dep., Amort./Sales | (127) 4.9 | (124) 4.9 |
| | 7.4 | 8.3 | 12.1 | | | | 9.3 | 8.9 |
| | 2.5 | 2.7 | | | | | 2.4 | 2.2 |
| | (12) 5.3 | (17) 6.5 | | | | % Officers', Directors' | (62) 5.1 | (60) 4.4 |
| | 6.5 | 10.6 | | | | Owners' Comp/Sales | 7.9 | 9.7 |
| 30258M | 110928M | 469089M | 1098759M | 174369M | 599057M | Net Sales ($) | 2284023M | 1988890M |
| 3974M | 35012M | 230485M | 736824M | 207339M | 441868M | Total Assets ($) | 1539606M | 1363086M |

© RMA 2012

M = $ thousand   MM = $ million
See Pages 9 through 22 for Explanation of Ratios and Data

## Comparative Historical Data / Current Data Sorted by Sales

| Comparative Historical Data | | | Type of Statement | | | | | | |
|---|---|---|---|---|---|---|---|---|---|
| 16 | 20 | 18 | Unqualified | 1 | 5 | 1 | 2 | 3 | 6 |
| 25 | 27 | 28 | Reviewed | 1 | 3 | 5 | 3 | 10 | 6 |
| 22 | 12 | 14 | Compiled | 1 | 3 | 4 | 3 | 3 | |
| 23 | 28 | 25 | Tax Returns | 5 | 8 | 6 | 4 | 2 | |
| 39 | 41 | 45 | Other | 2 | 9 | 5 | 5 | 17 | 7 |
| 4/1/09-3/31/10 ALL | 4/1/10-3/31/11 ALL | 4/1/11-3/31/12 ALL | | 21 (4/1-9/30/11) | | | 109 (10/1/11-3/31/12) | | |
| | | | | 0-1MM | 1-3MM | 3-5MM | 5-10MM | 10-25MM | 25MM & OVER |
| 125 | 128 | 130 | **NUMBER OF STATEMENTS** | 10 | 28 | 21 | 17 | 35 | 19 |
| % | % | % | **ASSETS** | % | % | % | % | % | % |
| 12.0 | 13.5 | 12.9 | Cash & Equivalents | 13.2 | 15.3 | 19.4 | 10.7 | 11.6 | 6.6 |
| 24.2 | 22.6 | 23.8 | Trade Receivables (net) | 6.5 | 20.4 | 18.6 | 26.7 | 28.1 | 33.3 |
| 4.2 | 3.8 | 3.8 | Inventory | .0 | 5.3 | 1.6 | 2.0 | 4.9 | 5.8 |
| 4.1 | 2.6 | 1.9 | All Other Current | .1 | 2.7 | 2.6 | 2.0 | 1.0 | 2.2 |
| 44.5 | 42.5 | 42.4 | Total Current | 19.8 | 43.8 | 42.1 | 41.4 | 45.5 | 48.0 |
| 41.0 | 39.9 | 41.1 | Fixed Assets (net) | 56.2 | 42.5 | 39.9 | 46.4 | 37.3 | 34.6 |
| 6.8 | 8.2 | 7.1 | Intangibles (net) | 6.6 | 3.8 | 6.9 | 4.5 | 9.7 | 10.2 |
| 7.8 | 9.4 | 9.3 | All Other Non-Current | 17.4 | 9.9 | 11.1 | 7.7 | 7.5 | 7.2 |
| 100.0 | 100.0 | 100.0 | Total | 100.0 | 100.0 | 100.0 | 100.0 | 100.0 | 100.0 |
| | | | **LIABILITIES** | | | | | | |
| 9.3 | 8.4 | 5.5 | Notes Payable-Short Term | 18.9 | 7.3 | 1.3 | 2.6 | 3.0 | 7.4 |
| 6.9 | 6.4 | 6.0 | Cur. Mat.-L.T.D. | 5.7 | 5.6 | 4.2 | 5.6 | 6.6 | 7.8 |
| 12.5 | 10.6 | 10.0 | Trade Payables | 12.2 | 9.2 | 5.7 | 8.3 | 10.7 | 14.7 |
| .3 | .4 | .2 | Income Taxes Payable | .0 | .0 | .0 | .8 | .3 | .0 |
| 5.8 | 11.0 | 8.3 | All Other Current | 17.5 | 9.6 | 5.7 | 4.3 | 8.7 | 7.0 |
| 34.7 | 36.7 | 29.8 | Total Current | 54.4 | 31.7 | 16.8 | 21.6 | 29.3 | 37.0 |
| 24.4 | 28.5 | 23.8 | Long-Term Debt | 51.4 | 24.6 | 23.0 | 17.9 | 17.8 | 25.2 |
| .8 | .2 | .4 | Deferred Taxes | .0 | .6 | .0 | .0 | 1.0 | .1 |
| 8.2 | 7.6 | 5.7 | All Other Non-Current | 22.2 | 3.6 | 4.9 | 3.9 | 5.6 | 2.5 |
| 31.9 | 27.0 | 40.3 | Net Worth | -28.1 | 39.5 | 55.3 | 56.7 | 46.4 | 35.2 |
| 100.0 | 100.0 | 100.0 | Total Liabilties & Net Worth | 100.0 | 100.0 | 100.0 | 100.0 | 100.0 | 100.0 |
| | | | **INCOME DATA** | | | | | | |
| 100.0 | 100.0 | 100.0 | Net Sales | 100.0 | 100.0 | 100.0 | 100.0 | 100.0 | 100.0 |
| | | | Gross Profit | | | | | | |
| 94.2 | 92.9 | 94.3 | Operating Expenses | 104.2 | 94.8 | 93.0 | 95.9 | 90.9 | 94.4 |
| 5.8 | 7.1 | 5.7 | Operating Profit | -4.2 | 5.2 | 7.0 | 4.1 | 9.1 | 5.6 |
| 1.8 | 2.0 | .5 | All Other Expenses (net) | -1.2 | .7 | -.9 | .7 | 1.7 | .7 |
| 4.0 | 5.0 | 5.2 | Profit Before Taxes | -3.0 | 4.5 | 7.9 | 3.4 | 7.5 | 4.9 |
| | | | **RATIOS** | | | | | | |
| 2.4 | 2.4 | 2.6 | | 1.6 | 2.0 | 13.4 | 3.1 | 2.7 | 1.6 |
| 1.3 | 1.3 | 1.4 | Current | .5 | 1.4 | 2.8 | 1.8 | 1.3 | 1.3 |
| .8 | .8 | 1.0 | | .1 | .7 | 1.2 | 1.4 | 1.1 | 1.0 |
| 2.0 | 2.1 | 2.1 | | 1.6 | 1.9 | 12.7 | 2.8 | 2.0 | 1.2 |
| 1.0 | 1.1 | 1.2 | Quick | .5 | 1.0 | 2.3 | 1.8 | 1.2 | 1.0 |
| .6 | .6 | .8 | | .1 | .4 | .9 | 1.4 | 1.0 | .8 |
| 25  14.6 | 13  29.1 | 21  17.5 | | 0  UND | 17  21.4 | 16  22.2 | 29  12.6 | 30  12.0 | 32  11.5 |
| 41  9.0 | 39  9.3 | 39  9.3 | Sales/Receivables | 0  UND | 30  12.1 | 42  8.7 | 43  8.5 | 43  8.4 | 61  6.0 |
| 67  5.4 | 52  7.0 | 61  6.0 | | 14  27.0 | 48  7.6 | 60  6.1 | 60  6.1 | 66  5.5 | 73  5.0 |
| | | | Cost of Sales/Inventory | | | | | | |
| | | | Cost of Sales/Payables | | | | | | |
| 7.4 | 7.5 | 7.1 | | 29.0 | 10.2 | 4.9 | 5.4 | 6.7 | 11.6 |
| 24.6 | 31.3 | 18.1 | Sales/Working Capital | -26.1 | 24.9 | 8.9 | 13.0 | 18.7 | 24.3 |
| -24.6 | -28.7 | -463.9 | | -2.9 | -17.4 | 507.4 | 22.9 | 142.8 | 91.5 |
| 8.5 | 9.0 | 15.8 | | | 13.4 | 21.3 | 17.8 | 30.0 | 13.1 |
| (112) 2.9 | (113) 3.7 | (115) 4.6 | EBIT/Interest | (24) | 2.8 (18) | 6.5 (15) | 2.7 (31) | 10.0 | 5.7 |
| 1.0 | 1.1 | 1.2 | | | .7 | 1.2 | -2.6 | 3.2 | 4.1 |
| 4.7 | 3.0 | 5.0 | Net Profit + Depr., Dep., | | | | | | |
| (24) 2.0 | (20) 2.3 | (16) 2.3 | Amort./Cur. Mat. L/T/D | | | | | | |
| 1.4 | 1.2 | 1.5 | | | | | | | |
| .5 | .6 | .6 | | 2.1 | .6 | .3 | .4 | .5 | .7 |
| 1.8 | 1.6 | 1.1 | Fixed/Worth | -2.1 | .8 | 1.1 | .8 | 1.1 | 1.3 |
| 11.1 | 9.8 | 3.6 | | -.7 | 5.0 | 3.0 | 1.3 | 1.8 | 6.5 |
| .8 | .8 | .5 | | 17.7 | .3 | .1 | .4 | .4 | 1.1 |
| 2.7 | 2.5 | 1.5 | Debt/Worth | -3.3 | 1.7 | 1.0 | .7 | 1.1 | 2.8 |
| 20.1 | 226.7 | 9.5 | | -2.1 | 22.3 | 4.5 | 1.0 | 3.1 | 10.9 |
| 49.6 | 66.3 | 54.1 | | | 47.4 | 45.1 | 19.0 | 63.3 | 76.4 |
| (99) 20.8 | (99) 19.3 | (104) 23.9 | % Profit Before Taxes/Tangible Net Worth | (23) | 14.3 (18) | 24.3 (15) | 1.3 (29) | 30.5 (15) | 32.6 |
| 3.9 | 3.2 | 2.2 | | | -2.7 | 4.9 | -5.0 | 11.6 | 19.0 |
| 15.0 | 18.9 | 21.1 | | 7.6 | 20.4 | 23.9 | 11.5 | 24.6 | 19.5 |
| 5.3 | 7.0 | 9.6 | % Profit Before Taxes/Total Assets | 2.0 | 9.2 | 11.7 | 7.8 | 14.7 | 8.7 |
| .0 | .6 | .6 | | -14.6 | -.9 | 2.0 | -2.6 | 4.7 | 4.4 |
| 15.2 | 15.2 | 14.6 | | 15.2 | 19.1 | 55.8 | 9.6 | 15.2 | 10.3 |
| 4.5 | 6.4 | 5.1 | Sales/Net Fixed Assets | 3.6 | 7.1 | 3.6 | 4.9 | 6.9 | 5.1 |
| 2.4 | 3.0 | 2.7 | | 1.9 | 1.9 | 3.0 | 2.7 | 2.1 | 3.6 |
| 2.7 | 3.4 | 3.0 | | 5.9 | 3.4 | 2.5 | 2.6 | 3.1 | 2.7 |
| 1.8 | 2.1 | 2.0 | Sales/Total Assets | 1.9 | 2.5 | 1.9 | 2.0 | 2.2 | 2.1 |
| 1.2 | 1.2 | 1.2 | | 1.0 | 1.0 | 1.3 | 1.4 | 1.0 | 1.3 |
| 2.0 | 2.4 | 2.9 | | | 4.1 | 2.9 | 2.3 | 2.3 | 1.3 |
| (108) 5.4 | (106) 5.9 | (107) 5.1 | % Depr., Dep., Amort./Sales | (19) | 5.1 (17) | 5.1 (16) | 6.4 (31) | 5.2 (16) | 4.3 |
| 10.1 | 10.6 | 9.2 | | | 6.8 | 11.3 | 10.7 | 9.1 | 7.3 |
| 2.1 | 3.1 | 2.3 | | | 3.1 | | | | |
| (40) 4.3 | (46) 5.6 | (39) 5.4 | % Officers', Directors' Owners' Comp/Sales | (12) | 5.3 | | | | |
| 8.3 | 9.0 | 9.2 | | | 10.1 | | | | |
| 1591795M | 1900693M | 2482460M | Net Sales ($) | 5114M | 58221M | 79205M | 119813M | 581497M | 1638610M |
| 1239734M | 1411344M | 1655502M | Total Assets ($) | 6082M | 67891M | 85823M | 98553M | 530688M | 866465M |

M = $ thousand     MM = $ million
See Pages 9 through 22 for Explanation of Ratios and Data

# EDUCATIONAL SERVICES

| Current Data Sorted by Assets | | | | | | | Comparative Historical Data | |
|---|---|---|---|---|---|---|---|---|

| | | | | | | Type of Statement | | |
|---|---|---|---|---|---|---|---|---|
| 33 | 110 | 337 | 613 | 181 | 142 | Unqualified | 1004 | 1234 |
| 2 | 13 | 51 | 20 | 2 | 2 | Reviewed | 68 | 78 |
| 16 | 19 | 26 | 7 | 2 | | Compiled | 47 | 54 |
| 45 | 32 | 35 | | 1 | | Tax Returns | 51 | 65 |
| 50 | 66 | 107 | 97 | 16 | 8 | Other | 277 | 314 |
| | 1,846 (4/1-9/30/11) | | 185 (10/1/11-3/31/12) | | | | 4/1/07-3/31/08 | 4/1/08-3/31/09 |
| 0-500M | 500M-2MM | 2-10MM | 10-50MM | 50-100MM | 100-250MM | | ALL | ALL |
| 146 | 240 | 556 | 737 | 202 | 150 | NUMBER OF STATEMENTS | 1447 | 1745 |
| % | % | % | % | % | % | ASSETS | % | % |
| 38.0 | 30.9 | 21.5 | 19.8 | 17.6 | 18.8 | Cash & Equivalents | 22.6 | 23.2 |
| 9.1 | 12.2 | 6.7 | 4.8 | 5.4 | 5.5 | Trade Receivables (net) | 6.6 | 7.1 |
| .7 | .2 | .4 | .2 | .1 | .2 | Inventory | .3 | .3 |
| 3.8 | 3.2 | 2.2 | 2.4 | 2.3 | 3.7 | All Other Current | 4.0 | 3.6 |
| 51.6 | 46.5 | 30.8 | 27.1 | 25.4 | 28.2 | Total Current | 33.4 | 34.3 |
| 33.5 | 42.4 | 61.0 | 62.2 | 62.2 | 61.9 | Fixed Assets (net) | 54.9 | 52.9 |
| 4.0 | 1.8 | .7 | .6 | .7 | 1.0 | Intangibles (net) | .7 | .9 |
| 11.0 | 9.3 | 7.5 | 10.1 | 11.7 | 8.9 | All Other Non-Current | 10.9 | 11.9 |
| 100.0 | 100.0 | 100.0 | 100.0 | 100.0 | 100.0 | Total | 100.0 | 100.0 |
| | | | | | | LIABILITIES | | |
| 12.0 | 3.1 | 1.9 | 1.3 | 1.1 | .8 | Notes Payable-Short Term | 2.6 | 2.9 |
| 1.9 | 2.0 | 2.5 | 2.1 | 1.8 | 2.2 | Cur. Mat.-L.T.D. | 2.1 | 1.9 |
| 7.1 | 5.3 | 3.0 | 2.1 | 1.9 | 1.5 | Trade Payables | 4.1 | 3.9 |
| .8 | .1 | .0 | .0 | .0 | .2 | Income Taxes Payable | .1 | .1 |
| 34.1 | 16.7 | 9.9 | 8.4 | 6.7 | 5.9 | All Other Current | 10.8 | 10.7 |
| 56.0 | 27.2 | 17.4 | 13.8 | 11.6 | 10.6 | Total Current | 19.7 | 19.6 |
| 24.3 | 20.9 | 31.2 | 32.0 | 37.6 | 38.9 | Long-Term Debt | 28.2 | 28.3 |
| .0 | .1 | .0 | .0 | .0 | .0 | Deferred Taxes | .0 | .0 |
| 22.3 | 10.3 | 5.9 | 4.6 | 4.0 | 5.7 | All Other Non-Current | 5.6 | 5.1 |
| -2.5 | 41.5 | 45.4 | 49.6 | 46.9 | 44.8 | Net Worth | 46.6 | 47.0 |
| 100.0 | 100.0 | 100.0 | 100.0 | 100.0 | 100.0 | Total Liabilities & Net Worth | 100.0 | 100.0 |
| | | | | | | INCOME DATA | | |
| 100.0 | 100.0 | 100.0 | 100.0 | 100.0 | 100.0 | Net Sales | 100.0 | 100.0 |
| | | | | | | Gross Profit | | |
| 93.5 | 93.6 | 93.4 | 93.9 | 92.5 | 95.5 | Operating Expenses | 91.5 | 94.1 |
| 6.5 | 6.4 | 6.6 | 6.1 | 7.5 | 4.5 | Operating Profit | 8.5 | 5.9 |
| 1.8 | 1.7 | 2.5 | 1.0 | 1.3 | 1.1 | All Other Expenses (net) | 1.1 | 2.9 |
| 4.6 | 4.7 | 4.1 | 5.1 | 6.2 | 3.4 | Profit Before Taxes | 7.4 | 3.0 |
| | | | | | | RATIOS | | |
| 4.0 | 4.5 | 4.9 | 4.3 | 4.4 | 4.5 | | 4.4 | 4.4 |
| 1.3 | 1.9 | 2.1 | 2.1 | 2.1 | 2.4 | Current | 1.9 | 2.0 |
| .5 | .9 | 1.0 | 1.0 | 1.2 | 1.5 | | 1.0 | 1.0 |
| 3.7 | 4.2 | 4.5 | 3.8 | 4.2 | 4.1 | | 3.9 | 3.9 |
| 1.3 | 1.8 | 1.9 | 1.8 | 1.8 | 2.1 | Quick | (1445) 1.7 | 1.8 |
| .4 | .8 | .8 | .9 | 1.0 | 1.2 | | .8 | .8 |
| 0 UND | 0 UND | 2 239.7 | 2 181.2 | 3 131.8 | 3 137.6 | | 1 368.2 | 1 370.2 |
| 0 UND | 4 93.1 | 8 46.7 | 9 39.9 | 13 27.6 | 14 25.5 | Sales/Receivables | 7 52.2 | 7 51.8 |
| 9 41.0 | 27 13.5 | 25 14.4 | 33 11.2 | 47 7.8 | 62 5.9 | | 26 14.1 | 28 13.1 |
| | | | | | | Cost of Sales/Inventory | | |
| | | | | | | Cost of Sales/Payables | | |
| 12.4 | 5.3 | 3.3 | 2.4 | 2.0 | 1.8 | | 3.0 | 3.0 |
| 53.5 | 12.2 | 7.9 | 5.7 | 5.1 | 3.9 | Sales/Working Capital | 8.2 | 7.9 |
| -40.4 | -109.1 | -114.1 | 177.4 | 25.4 | 13.4 | | 529.4 | 178.8 |
| 19.3 | 17.4 | 5.2 | 5.9 | 7.2 | 4.0 | | 7.9 | 4.9 |
| (69) 3.7 | (142) 3.4 | (436) 1.7 | (642) 2.5 | (179) 2.4 | (132) 1.9 | EBIT/Interest | (1092) 2.9 | (1321) 1.8 |
| -.9 | .6 | .4 | .9 | 1.4 | .9 | | 1.1 | .3 |
| | | | | | | Net Profit + Depr., Dep., | 7.5 | 7.9 |
| | | | | | | Amort./Cur. Mat. L/T/D | (19) 3.8 | (16) 3.9 |
| | | | | | | | .1 | 1.5 |
| .1 | .3 | .8 | .8 | .8 | .9 | | .6 | .6 |
| 1.0 | .8 | 1.4 | 1.2 | 1.3 | 1.8 | Fixed/Worth | 1.1 | 1.1 |
| -5.4 | 2.8 | 3.0 | 2.0 | 2.8 | 2.9 | | 2.3 | 2.3 |
| .5 | .4 | .4 | .4 | .4 | .6 | | .4 | .4 |
| 2.7 | 1.2 | 1.2 | .9 | 1.1 | 1.6 | Debt/Worth | 1.0 | .9 |
| -4.6 | 5.2 | 3.0 | 2.0 | 3.1 | 3.3 | | 2.6 | 2.7 |
| 118.9 | 40.4 | 17.2 | 11.1 | 11.5 | 9.2 | % Profit Before Taxes/Tangible | 19.3 | 14.9 |
| (100) 40.0 | (207) 15.9 | (521) 6.3 | (715) 4.8 | (193) 5.5 | (146) 4.7 | Net Worth | (1373) 8.6 | (1631) 4.2 |
| .4 | -1.2 | -2.3 | .0 | 1.9 | -.2 | | 1.0 | -2.5 |
| 54.0 | 20.2 | 6.8 | 5.0 | 4.8 | 4.1 | % Profit Before Taxes/Total | 8.8 | 6.2 |
| 15.8 | 7.5 | 2.4 | 2.3 | 2.6 | 1.8 | Assets | 3.9 | 1.8 |
| -3.1 | -.5 | -1.3 | -.2 | .6 | -.1 | | .3 | -1.3 |
| 201.2 | 22.6 | 2.7 | 1.3 | 1.1 | 1.0 | | 3.2 | 3.6 |
| 26.9 | 7.0 | 1.1 | .8 | .8 | .8 | Sales/Net Fixed Assets | 1.1 | 1.1 |
| 10.5 | 1.8 | .7 | .6 | .5 | .6 | | .7 | .7 |
| 9.7 | 3.4 | 1.2 | .7 | .7 | .7 | | 1.4 | 1.4 |
| 5.8 | 1.9 | .7 | .5 | .5 | .5 | Sales/Total Assets | .7 | .7 |
| 3.2 | 1.0 | .5 | .4 | .3 | .3 | | .4 | .4 |
| .7 | 1.0 | 2.7 | 3.8 | 3.5 | 3.5 | | 2.6 | 2.6 |
| (82) 1.8 | (182) 1.9 | (491) 4.7 | (680) 5.8 | (185) 5.8 | (134) 4.9 | % Depr., Dep., Amort./Sales | (1160) 4.5 | (1402) 4.7 |
| 2.9 | 3.3 | 6.5 | 7.9 | 8.0 | 6.9 | | 6.4 | 6.7 |
| 5.0 | 2.5 | 2.9 | 4.2 | 1.5 | 2.2 | | 3.7 | 3.6 |
| (444) 8.6 | (41) 4.2 | (59) 4.8 | (45) 7.1 | (13) 3.5 | (11) 7.7 | % Officers', Directors' | (153) 7.1 | (179) 7.6 |
| 12.4 | 8.7 | 12.9 | 16.8 | 9.7 | 18.4 | Owners' Comp/Sales | 13.3 | 13.8 |
| 223603M | 666521M | 3238834M | 11932171M | 8176020M | 13143765M | Net Sales ($) | 29106068M | 38437550M |
| 34000M | 290608M | 3029055M | 17994107M | 13943222M | 22285775M | Total Assets ($) | 35983798M | 53819064M |

M = $ thousand    MM = $ million
See Pages 9 through 22 for Explanation of Ratios and Data

## Comparative Historical Data  |  Current Data Sorted by Sales

| Hist 1 | Hist 2 | Hist 3 | Type of Statement | 0-1MM | 1-3MM | 3-5MM | 5-10MM | 10-25MM | 25MM & OVER |
|---|---|---|---|---|---|---|---|---|---|
| 1303 | 1412 | 1416 | Unqualified | 20 | 168 | 178 | 295 | 408 | 347 |
| 73 | 88 | 88 | Reviewed | 6 | 28 | 22 | 23 | 6 | 3 |
| 58 | 57 | 70 | Compiled | 20 | 26 | 14 | 3 | 6 | 1 |
| 75 | 85 | 113 | Tax Returns | 38 | 54 | 13 | 4 | 4 | |
| 341 | 356 | 344 | Other | 39 | 103 | 59 | 62 | 47 | 34 |
| 4/1/09-3/31/10 ALL | 4/1/10-3/31/11 ALL | 4/1/11-3/31/12 ALL | | 1,846 (4/1-9/30/11) | | | 185 (10/1/11-3/31/12) | | |
| 1850 | 1998 | 2031 | NUMBER OF STATEMENTS | 123 | 379 | 286 | 387 | 471 | 385 |
| % | % | % | ASSETS | % | % | % | % | % | % |
| 21.5 | 21.6 | 22.6 | Cash & Equivalents | 23.7 | 24.3 | 25.7 | 20.3 | 21.7 | 21.6 |
| 6.3 | 6.4 | 6.6 | Trade Receivables (net) | 4.9 | 7.6 | 6.3 | 6.4 | 5.5 | 8.1 |
| .2 | .2 | .3 | Inventory | .2 | .2 | .3 | .1 | .2 | .6 |
| 2.8 | 3.1 | 2.6 | All Other Current | 1.7 | 2.4 | 1.9 | 2.5 | 2.6 | 3.8 |
| 30.7 | 31.4 | 32.1 | Total Current | 30.6 | 34.5 | 34.1 | 29.3 | 29.9 | 34.1 |
| 59.0 | 56.8 | 57.4 | Fixed Assets (net) | 57.9 | 54.9 | 55.8 | 59.6 | 58.2 | 57.9 |
| .9 | .9 | 1.1 | Intangibles (net) | 4.1 | 2.1 | .8 | .4 | .4 | .7 |
| 9.5 | 10.9 | 9.4 | All Other Non-Current | 7.6 | 8.5 | 9.3 | 10.7 | 11.4 | 7.4 |
| 100.0 | 100.0 | 100.0 | Total | 100.0 | 100.0 | 100.0 | 100.0 | 100.0 | 100.0 |
| | | | LIABILITIES | | | | | | |
| 2.8 | 2.6 | 2.4 | Notes Payable-Short Term | 5.4 | 3.8 | 2.3 | 2.6 | 1.0 | 1.6 |
| 2.3 | 2.0 | 2.2 | Cur. Mat.-L.T.D. | 1.6 | 2.3 | 2.5 | 2.0 | 2.0 | 2.3 |
| 3.3 | 3.3 | 3.0 | Trade Payables | 2.8 | 3.7 | 2.8 | 3.0 | 2.6 | 3.1 |
| .1 | .1 | .1 | Income Taxes Payable | .0 | .4 | .0 | .0 | .0 | .1 |
| 10.7 | 11.5 | 11.3 | All Other Current | 18.2 | 16.3 | 11.2 | 10.5 | 9.0 | 7.8 |
| 19.2 | 19.5 | 19.0 | Total Current | 28.0 | 26.6 | 18.8 | 18.1 | 14.6 | 14.9 |
| 31.4 | 30.7 | 31.0 | Long-Term Debt | 38.6 | 31.5 | 28.2 | 27.2 | 29.7 | 35.5 |
| .0 | .0 | .0 | Deferred Taxes | .0 | .0 | .0 | .0 | .0 | .0 |
| 5.6 | 5.1 | 6.9 | All Other Non-Current | 18.5 | 9.7 | 5.7 | 5.2 | 4.8 | 5.7 |
| 43.8 | 44.6 | 43.1 | Net Worth | 14.9 | 32.2 | 47.3 | 49.5 | 50.9 | 43.9 |
| 100.0 | 100.0 | 100.0 | Total Liabilities & Net Worth | 100.0 | 100.0 | 100.0 | 100.0 | 100.0 | 100.0 |
| | | | INCOME DATA | | | | | | |
| 100.0 | 100.0 | 100.0 | Net Sales | 100.0 | 100.0 | 100.0 | 100.0 | 100.0 | 100.0 |
| | | | Gross Profit | | | | | | |
| 95.9 | 94.6 | 93.7 | Operating Expenses | 89.9 | 92.8 | 94.0 | 94.6 | 93.6 | 94.7 |
| 4.1 | 5.4 | 6.3 | Operating Profit | 10.1 | 7.2 | 6.0 | 5.4 | 6.4 | 5.3 |
| 4.4 | 1.8 | 1.6 | All Other Expenses (net) | 6.7 | 2.6 | 1.1 | 1.2 | .4 | 1.3 |
| -.3 | 3.5 | 4.7 | Profit Before Taxes | 3.5 | 4.6 | 4.9 | 4.2 | 6.0 | 3.9 |
| | | | RATIOS | | | | | | |
| 3.9 | 4.0 | 4.4 | | 4.8 | 4.8 | 4.9 | 4.0 | 4.3 | 4.2 |
| 1.8 | 1.9 | 2.1 | Current | 1.5 | 1.7 | 2.1 | 1.8 | 2.5 | 2.2 |
| .9 | 1.0 | 1.0 | | .5 | .8 | .9 | .9 | 1.2 | 1.3 |
| 3.5 | 3.6 | 4.0 | | 4.0 | 4.5 | 4.7 | 3.5 | 4.0 | 3.8 |
| (1849) 1.6 | 1.6 | 1.8 | Quick | 1.3 | 1.6 | 2.0 | 1.6 | 2.0 | 1.8 |
| .8 | .9 | .9 | | .5 | .7 | .9 | .8 | 1.1 | 1.1 |
| 1 339.4 | 1 277.2 | 1 407.4 | | 0 UND | 0 UND | 1 416.6 | 2 174.7 | 2 150.6 | 1 243.5 |
| 7 54.6 | 8 43.6 | 8 45.7 | Sales/Receivables | 0 UND | 4 86.2 | 8 46.6 | 9 42.6 | 12 31.5 | 12 31.1 |
| 24 15.5 | 28 13.0 | 30 12.3 | | 17 21.0 | 19 19.0 | 28 12.9 | 30 12.0 | 35 10.4 | 43 8.4 |
| | | | Cost of Sales/Inventory | | | | | | |
| | | | Cost of Sales/Payables | | | | | | |
| 3.2 | 3.2 | 3.0 | | 4.5 | 4.2 | 2.7 | 3.3 | 2.4 | 2.6 |
| 9.0 | 8.3 | 7.9 | Sales/Working Capital | 23.1 | 13.3 | 8.1 | 8.2 | 5.5 | 6.1 |
| -163.3 | -318.0 | 621.7 | | -21.4 | -42.8 | -95.0 | -42.7 | 40.8 | 21.1 |
| 3.7 | 5.0 | 6.3 | | 3.1 | 8.1 | 5.9 | 7.5 | 6.7 | 5.2 |
| (1447) 1.2 | (1573) 2.0 | (1600) 2.2 | EBIT/Interest | (64) 1.1 | (281) 2.0 | (205) 1.8 | (319) 2.3 | (402) 2.9 | (329) 2.1 |
| -.7 | .6 | .8 | | -.9 | .5 | .5 | .5 | 1.2 | 1.0 |
| 10.2 | 4.1 | 13.1 | Net Profit + Depr., Dep., | | | | | | |
| (17) 2.7 | (13) 2.1 | (20) 5.6 | Amort./Cur. Mat. L/T/D | | | | | | |
| 1.8 | .9 | .9 | | | | | | | |
| .7 | .7 | .7 | | .9 | .6 | .6 | .8 | .7 | .8 |
| 1.2 | 1.2 | 1.3 | Fixed/Worth | 2.5 | 1.5 | 1.2 | 1.1 | 1.1 | 1.4 |
| 2.5 | 2.4 | 2.6 | | -37.3 | 3.8 | 2.6 | 2.1 | 2.0 | 2.6 |
| .4 | .4 | .4 | | .8 | .5 | .4 | .4 | .4 | .5 |
| 1.1 | 1.0 | 1.1 | Debt/Worth | 3.1 | 1.4 | 1.1 | .9 | .9 | 1.2 |
| 2.6 | 2.7 | 3.0 | | -14.7 | 4.5 | 2.9 | 2.0 | 2.1 | 3.1 |
| 11.8 | 12.3 | 15.5 | % Profit Before Taxes/Tangible | 55.7 | 30.4 | 22.7 | 13.0 | 12.5 | 11.9 |
| (1726) 1.5 | (1865) 4.0 | (1882) 6.1 | Net Worth | (86) 5.4 | (329) 8.9 | (273) 6.9 | (370) 4.9 | (456) 5.6 | (368) 5.5 |
| -6.5 | -1.6 | -.6 | | -6.9 | -1.2 | -2.3 | -1.1 | 1.0 | .3 |
| 5.0 | 5.6 | 6.9 | % Profit Before Taxes/Total | 17.3 | 11.1 | 9.5 | 5.9 | 5.5 | 4.8 |
| .6 | 1.8 | 2.7 | Assets | 1.6 | 3.6 | 2.8 | 2.4 | 2.8 | 2.3 |
| -3.3 | -.8 | -.4 | | -3.6 | -1.0 | -1.0 | -.8 | .4 | .1 |
| 2.6 | 2.7 | 2.9 | | 16.3 | 14.3 | 5.0 | 2.1 | 1.5 | 2.0 |
| 1.0 | 1.0 | 1.0 | Sales/Net Fixed Assets | 1.7 | 1.5 | 1.0 | .9 | .9 | 1.0 |
| .6 | .6 | .6 | | .5 | .7 | .6 | .6 | .6 | .8 |
| 1.3 | 1.3 | 1.3 | | 3.1 | 2.8 | 1.5 | 1.0 | .8 | 1.2 |
| .6 | .6 | .6 | Sales/Total Assets | 1.0 | .9 | .6 | .6 | .5 | .7 |
| .4 | .4 | .4 | | .4 | .5 | .4 | .4 | .4 | .5 |
| 2.6 | 2.9 | 2.7 | | 1.9 | 1.7 | 2.8 | 3.2 | 3.7 | 2.5 |
| (1565) 4.7 | (1689) 5.0 | (1754) 4.8 | % Depr., Dep., Amort./Sales | (82) 4.0 | (304) 3.4 | (247) 5.2 | (354) 5.4 | (436) 5.7 | (331) 4.0 |
| 7.1 | 7.4 | 7.1 | | 9.4 | 6.4 | 7.1 | 7.6 | 7.8 | 5.7 |
| 3.7 | 3.7 | 3.2 | % Officers', Directors' | 5.8 | 2.5 | 3.0 | 3.2 | 3.9 | 2.2 |
| (216) 7.1 | (190) 6.5 | (213) 6.1 | Owners' Comp/Sales | (27) 9.4 | (60) 4.1 | (29) 7.1 | (25) 5.5 | (40) 6.9 | (32) 5.1 |
| 14.4 | 12.4 | 12.4 | | 12.7 | 9.5 | 17.9 | 13.5 | 17.0 | 10.7 |
| 36506660M | 37832362M | 37380914M | Net Sales ($) | 76221M | 746554M | 1130457M | 2833840M | 7346458M | 25247384M |
| 51921585M | 57042299M | 57576767M | Total Assets ($) | 133347M | 1161562M | 1947468M | 5372296M | 14872114M | 34089980M |

M = $ thousand    MM = $ million
See Pages 9 through 22 for Explanation of Ratios and Data

## Current Data Sorted by Assets      Comparative Historical Data

| 0-500M | 500M-2MM | 2-10MM | 10-50MM | 50-100MM | 100-250MM | Type of Statement | 4/1/07-3/31/08 ALL | 4/1/08-3/31/09 ALL |
|---|---|---|---|---|---|---|---|---|
| | 2 | 8 | 13 | 4 | 11 | Unqualified | 41 | 57 |
| | | | | | | Reviewed | | 1 |
| | | 1 | | | | Compiled | 1 | |
| | | | | | | Tax Returns | | 1 |
| | | 2 | 7 | 4 | 1 | Other | 10 | 13 |
| | 46 (4/1-9/30/11) | | 7 (10/1/11-3/31/12) | | | | | |
| 0-500M | 500M-2MM | 2-10MM | 10-50MM | 50-100MM | 100-250MM | | | |
| | 2 | 11 | 20 | 8 | 12 | NUMBER OF STATEMENTS | 52 | 72 |

Note: In the current-data columns marked 0-500M and 500M-2MM the percentage data is shown as **DATA NOT AVAILABLE**.

| 0-500M | 500M-2MM | 2-10MM | 10-50MM | 50-100MM | 100-250MM | | 4/1/07-3/31/08 ALL | 4/1/08-3/31/09 ALL |
|---|---|---|---|---|---|---|---|---|
| % | % | % | % | % | % | **ASSETS** | % | % |
| | | 23.1 | 15.5 | | 17.2 | Cash & Equivalents | 20.7 | 19.7 |
| | | 20.0 | 10.4 | | 8.9 | Trade Receivables (net) | 10.0 | 8.2 |
| | | 1.4 | .5 | | .4 | Inventory | 1.2 | .8 |
| | | 2.9 | 3.3 | | 2.1 | All Other Current | 2.7 | 3.1 |
| | | 47.4 | 29.7 | | 28.7 | Total Current | 34.6 | 31.8 |
| | | 41.9 | 47.3 | | 61.9 | Fixed Assets (net) | 46.9 | 51.8 |
| | | .2 | 5.7 | | .1 | Intangibles (net) | 4.5 | 1.7 |
| | | 10.5 | 17.3 | | 9.3 | All Other Non-Current | 14.0 | 14.7 |
| | | 100.0 | 100.0 | | 100.0 | Total | 100.0 | 100.0 |
| | | | | | | **LIABILITIES** | | |
| | | 3.6 | .2 | | .0 | Notes Payable-Short Term | 1.0 | 1.2 |
| | | 2.3 | 1.5 | | 3.8 | Cur. Mat.-L.T.D. | 1.9 | 3.2 |
| | | 4.1 | 4.3 | | 4.1 | Trade Payables | 4.6 | 3.9 |
| | | .4 | .0 | | .1 | Income Taxes Payable | .3 | .2 |
| | | 17.0 | 9.4 | | 9.7 | All Other Current | 7.0 | 9.3 |
| | | 27.5 | 15.4 | | 17.7 | Total Current | 14.8 | 17.8 |
| | | 22.7 | 20.8 | | 25.9 | Long-Term Debt | 22.8 | 26.1 |
| | | 2.1 | .1 | | .3 | Deferred Taxes | .5 | .2 |
| | | .9 | 4.9 | | 6.5 | All Other Non-Current | 4.3 | 5.0 |
| | | 46.9 | 58.8 | | 49.5 | Net Worth | 57.7 | 50.9 |
| | | 100.0 | 100.0 | | 100.0 | Total Liabilties & Net Worth | 100.0 | 100.0 |
| | | | | | | **INCOME DATA** | | |
| | | 100.0 | 100.0 | | 100.0 | Net Sales | 100.0 | 100.0 |
| | | | | | | Gross Profit | | |
| | | 75.6 | 90.8 | | 95.1 | Operating Expenses | 91.1 | 92.9 |
| | | 24.4 | 9.2 | | 4.9 | Operating Profit | 8.9 | 7.1 |
| | | 5.0 | 1.0 | | .1 | All Other Expenses (net) | -1.0 | 1.3 |
| | | 19.3 | 8.2 | | 4.8 | Profit Before Taxes | 9.9 | 5.8 |
| | | | | | | **RATIOS** | | |
| | | 10.8 | 3.1 | | 3.7 | | 5.2 | 3.2 |
| | | 1.5 | 2.2 | | 1.2 | Current | 2.6 | 1.8 |
| | | .9 | 1.4 | | 1.1 | | 1.4 | 1.1 |
| | | 10.8 | 2.8 | | 3.6 | | 4.9 | 3.1 |
| | | 1.3 | 1.7 | | 1.1 | Quick | 2.2 | 1.7 |
| | | .8 | .8 | | .8 | | 1.0 | .9 |
| | | 8  46.7 | 2  149.6 | | 11  33.6 | | 11  34.6 | 6  57.6 |
| | | 30  12.2 | 22  16.4 | | 20  18.1 | Sales/Receivables | 25  14.7 | 17  22.0 |
| | | 72  5.1 | 60  6.1 | | 66  5.5 | | 46  7.9 | 41  8.8 |
| | | | | | | Cost of Sales/Inventory | | |
| | | | | | | Cost of Sales/Payables | | |
| | | 1.8 | 2.2 | | 2.6 | | 2.4 | 3.2 |
| | | 10.1 | 6.8 | | 24.3 | Sales/Working Capital | 4.5 | 6.9 |
| | | -44.7 | 34.3 | | 75.6 | | 13.8 | 69.4 |
| | | | 18.6 | | 14.4 | | 13.0 | 9.8 |
| | | | (17)  5.3 | | (11)  2.7 | EBIT/Interest | (43)  6.3 | (59)  4.4 |
| | | | 3.4 | | .0 | | 2.8 | 1.8 |
| | | | | | | Net Profit + Depr., Dep., Amort./Cur. Mat. L/T/D | | |
| | | .4 | .6 | | 1.0 | | .6 | .6 |
| | | 1.1 | .8 | | 1.2 | Fixed/Worth | .9 | .9 |
| | | 1.7 | 1.3 | | 2.0 | | 1.2 | 1.5 |
| | | .6 | .3 | | .3 | | .4 | .4 |
| | | 1.0 | .9 | | 1.2 | Debt/Worth | .7 | .8 |
| | | 3.4 | 1.4 | | 4.0 | | 1.5 | 1.6 |
| | | 55.4 | 34.6 | | 8.4 | | 30.9 | 25.1 |
| | | 41.0 | 12.6 | | 1.6 | % Profit Before Taxes/Tangible Net Worth | (50)  10.4 | (68)  5.8 |
| | | 14.0 | 2.4 | | -5.1 | | 5.2 | 1.8 |
| | | 23.5 | 12.1 | | 7.1 | | 12.8 | 8.3 |
| | | 10.2 | 5.4 | | .8 | % Profit Before Taxes/Total Assets | 6.4 | 2.9 |
| | | 3.2 | 1.5 | | -2.5 | | 2.4 | 1.1 |
| | | 11.5 | 6.1 | | 1.7 | | 5.9 | 4.6 |
| | | 2.8 | 1.0 | | .9 | Sales/Net Fixed Assets | 1.4 | 1.2 |
| | | .5 | .7 | | .7 | | .8 | .8 |
| | | 1.6 | 1.4 | | .9 | | 1.2 | 1.5 |
| | | 1.0 | .6 | | .6 | Sales/Total Assets | .8 | .7 |
| | | .2 | .5 | | .4 | | .5 | .5 |
| | | 1.2 | 2.2 | | 4.1 | | 2.4 | 2.5 |
| | | 2.4 | 4.4 | | (10)  4.9 | % Depr., Dep., Amort./Sales | (46)  4.6 | (69)  4.4 |
| | | 6.3 | 7.4 | | 7.1 | | 6.4 | 7.0 |
| | | | | | | % Officers', Directors' Owners' Comp/Sales | | |
| | 3772M | 81019M | 524674M | 555175M | 1753073M | Net Sales ($) | 2399822M | 2885334M |
| | 1469M | 66662M | 525635M | 666224M | 2081509M | Total Assets ($) | 3425107M | 4194995M |

M = $ thousand    MM = $ million
See Pages 9 through 22 for Explanation of Ratios and Data

## Comparative Historical Data | Current Data Sorted by Sales

| | | | | Type of Statement | | | | | | |
|---|---|---|---|---|---|---|---|---|---|---|
| 48 | | 60 | 38 | Unqualified | 1 | 1 | 5 | 8 | 3 | 20 |
| 4 | | | | Reviewed | | | | | | |
| | | 2 | | Compiled | | | | | | |
| 1 | | 2 | 1 | Tax Returns | 1 | | | | | |
| 13 | | 16 | 14 | Other | | 1 | | | 6 | 7 |
| 4/1/09- | | 4/1/10- | 4/1/11- | | | 46 (4/1-9/30/11) | | 7 (10/1/11-3/31/12) | | |
| 3/31/10 | | 3/31/11 | 3/31/12 | | | | | | | |
| ALL | | ALL | ALL | | 0-1MM | 1-3MM | 3-5MM | 5-10MM | 10-25MM | 25MM & OVER |
| 66 | | 80 | 53 | NUMBER OF STATEMENTS | 2 | 2 | 5 | 8 | 9 | 27 |
| % | | % | % | ASSETS | % | % | % | % | % | % |
| 21.4 | | 24.4 | 19.7 | Cash & Equivalents | | | | | | 20.1 |
| 9.1 | | 13.7 | 11.8 | Trade Receivables (net) | | | | | | 11.6 |
| .8 | | .9 | .6 | Inventory | | | | | | .5 |
| 4.4 | | 1.8 | 2.7 | All Other Current | | | | | | 3.3 |
| 35.7 | | 40.8 | 34.9 | Total Current | | | | | | 35.4 |
| 46.4 | | 44.0 | 47.7 | Fixed Assets (net) | | | | | | 48.6 |
| 3.3 | | 2.3 | 3.5 | Intangibles (net) | | | | | | 2.7 |
| 14.6 | | 12.9 | 13.8 | All Other Non-Current | | | | | | 13.2 |
| 100.0 | | 100.0 | 100.0 | Total | | | | | | 100.0 |
| | | | | LIABILITIES | | | | | | |
| 1.2 | | 2.5 | .8 | Notes Payable-Short Term | | | | | | .0 |
| 2.8 | | 1.8 | 2.2 | Cur. Mat.-L.T.D. | | | | | | 2.6 |
| 6.1 | | 4.5 | 4.8 | Trade Payables | | | | | | 5.1 |
| .1 | | .2 | .1 | Income Taxes Payable | | | | | | .1 |
| 12.2 | | 12.1 | 10.6 | All Other Current | | | | | | 11.6 |
| 22.4 | | 21.0 | 18.5 | Total Current | | | | | | 19.5 |
| 20.9 | | 19.6 | 20.3 | Long-Term Debt | | | | | | 18.3 |
| .2 | | .4 | .5 | Deferred Taxes | | | | | | .2 |
| 4.8 | | 5.8 | 3.9 | All Other Non-Current | | | | | | 5.7 |
| 51.7 | | 53.2 | 56.8 | Net Worth | | | | | | 56.3 |
| 100.0 | | 100.0 | 100.0 | Total Liabilities & Net Worth | | | | | | 100.0 |
| | | | | INCOME DATA | | | | | | |
| 100.0 | | 100.0 | 100.0 | Net Sales | | | | | | 100.0 |
| | | | | Gross Profit | | | | | | |
| 94.3 | | 90.4 | 89.2 | Operating Expenses | | | | | | 92.4 |
| 5.7 | | 9.6 | 10.8 | Operating Profit | | | | | | 7.6 |
| 2.6 | | -.5 | 1.2 | All Other Expenses (net) | | | | | | .0 |
| 3.1 | | 10.1 | 9.6 | Profit Before Taxes | | | | | | 7.6 |
| | | | | RATIOS | | | | | | |
| 2.7 | | 4.3 | 3.6 | | | | | | | 2.9 |
| 1.7 | | 2.2 | 2.2 | Current | | | | | | 2.2 |
| 1.2 | | 1.3 | 1.1 | | | | | | | 1.1 |
| 2.4 | | 4.1 | 3.3 | | | | | | | 2.8 |
| 1.5 | | 2.1 | 1.7 | Quick | | | | | | 1.8 |
| .9 | | 1.2 | 1.0 | | | | | | | 1.0 |
| 10  37.2 | 10 | 35.2 | 8  47.4 | | | | | | 9 | 39.4 |
| 23  15.8 | 28 | 12.8 | 24  15.3 | Sales/Receivables | | | | | 21 | 17.7 |
| 45  8.1 | 53 | 6.9 | 63  5.8 | | | | | | 53 | 6.9 |
| | | | | Cost of Sales/Inventory | | | | | | |
| | | | | Cost of Sales/Payables | | | | | | |
| 3.3 | | 2.9 | 2.4 | | | | | | | 4.0 |
| 7.8 | | 6.2 | 6.7 | Sales/Working Capital | | | | | | 7.7 |
| 36.9 | | 14.3 | 39.4 | | | | | | | 37.6 |
| 27.4 | | 34.3 | 31.9 | | | | | | | 82.7 |
| (55)  3.2 | (58) | 8.2 | (43)  6.5 | EBIT/Interest | | | | | (26) | 8.2 |
| .1 | | 3.4 | 3.0 | | | | | | | 2.9 |
| | | | | Net Profit + Depr., Dep., Amort./Cur. Mat. L/T/D | | | | | | |
| .7 | | .5 | .6 | | | | | | | .5 |
| .9 | | .8 | .8 | Fixed/Worth | | | | | | .8 |
| 1.3 | | 1.2 | 1.4 | | | | | | | 1.4 |
| .5 | | .3 | .3 | | | | | | | .4 |
| .8 | | .8 | .7 | Debt/Worth | | | | | | .6 |
| 1.5 | | 2.4 | 1.5 | | | | | | | 1.7 |
| 39.0 | | 39.2 | 38.0 | % Profit Before Taxes/Tangible Net Worth | | | | | | 40.1 |
| (64)  7.1 | (77) | 12.9 | 9.0 | | | | | | | 8.2 |
| -1.0 | | 4.4 | 1.5 | | | | | | | 1.6 |
| 16.0 | | 15.5 | 10.3 | % Profit Before Taxes/Total Assets | | | | | | 10.4 |
| 3.5 | | 6.9 | 4.8 | | | | | | | 5.4 |
| -.9 | | 2.4 | .8 | | | | | | | .9 |
| 6.1 | | 7.9 | 6.7 | | | | | | | 8.3 |
| 1.2 | | 1.6 | 1.2 | Sales/Net Fixed Assets | | | | | | 1.4 |
| .8 | | .9 | .7 | | | | | | | .9 |
| 2.0 | | 1.7 | 1.4 | | | | | | | 2.2 |
| .7 | | .8 | .7 | Sales/Total Assets | | | | | | .8 |
| .5 | | .5 | .5 | | | | | | | .6 |
| 2.3 | | 2.2 | 2.1 | | | | | | | 1.9 |
| (60)  3.7 | (71) | 3.9 | (51)  4.3 | % Depr., Dep., Amort./Sales | | | | | (25) | 3.7 |
| 6.3 | | 6.1 | 6.4 | | | | | | | 5.5 |
| | | | | % Officers', Directors' Owners' Comp/Sales | | | | | | |
| 2874920M | | 2818110M | 2917713M | Net Sales ($) | 1249M | 2343M | 21453M | 59594M | 146875M | 2686199M |
| 3683554M | | 3920339M | 3341499M | Total Assets ($) | 4179M | 13768M | 67946M | 87419M | 224774M | 2943413M |

M = $ thousand   MM = $ million
See Pages 9 through 22 for Explanation of Ratios and Data

## Current Data Sorted by Assets

## Comparative Historical Data

| 0-500M | 500M-2MM | 2-10MM | 10-50MM | 50-100MM | 100-250MM | Type of Statement | | 4/1/07-3/31/08 ALL | | 4/1/08-3/31/09 ALL |
|---|---|---|---|---|---|---|---|---|---|---|
| 4 | 6 | 43 | 161 | 145 | 183 | Unqualified | | 505 | | 613 |
| 1 | 1 | 1 | | | 3 | Reviewed | | 10 | | 3 |
| | | 1 | 1 | | | Compiled | | 3 | | 6 |
| | 1 | 1 | 1 | 1 | | Tax Returns | | 3 | | 6 |
| 2 | 4 | 1 | 5 | 1 | | Other | | 5 | | 6 |
| 7 | 1 | 17 | 36 | 28 | 26 | | | 98 | | 113 |
| | 575 (4/1-9/30/11) | | 104 (10/1/11-3/31/12) | | | | | | | |
| 14 | 13 | 63 | 203 | 174 | 212 | NUMBER OF STATEMENTS | | 621 | | 741 |
| % | % | % | % | % | % | ASSETS | | % | | % |
| 26.6 | 22.2 | 23.4 | 18.0 | 15.2 | 14.3 | Cash & Equivalents | | 16.4 | | 15.5 |
| 14.3 | 15.2 | 10.3 | 7.9 | 3.8 | 3.8 | Trade Receivables (net) | | 5.4 | | 5.1 |
| 1.5 | 1.0 | 1.4 | .5 | .2 | .3 | Inventory | | .5 | | .6 |
| 3.9 | 3.3 | 2.1 | 2.6 | 2.0 | 2.3 | All Other Current | | 3.4 | | 3.3 |
| 46.4 | 41.7 | 37.1 | 29.1 | 21.3 | 20.7 | Total Current | | 25.8 | | 24.6 |
| 43.5 | 39.1 | 43.8 | 51.9 | 54.5 | 49.6 | Fixed Assets (net) | | 47.4 | | 48.0 |
| .0 | 6.3 | 2.7 | 1.6 | 1.5 | 2.1 | Intangibles (net) | | 1.1 | | 1.1 |
| 10.1 | 12.8 | 16.3 | 17.5 | 22.8 | 27.5 | All Other Non-Current | | 25.8 | | 26.3 |
| 100.0 | 100.0 | 100.0 | 100.0 | 100.0 | 100.0 | Total | | 100.0 | | 100.0 |
| | | | | | | LIABILITIES | | | | |
| 1.7 | 6.1 | 2.4 | 2.0 | 1.6 | .7 | Notes Payable-Short Term | | 1.6 | | 1.9 |
| .2 | .8 | 4.2 | 2.1 | 1.4 | 1.4 | Cur. Mat.-L.T.D. | | 1.4 | | 1.5 |
| 5.0 | 4.2 | 5.3 | 3.6 | 2.7 | 2.6 | Trade Payables | | 3.4 | | 2.9 |
| 1.5 | .0 | .0 | .0 | .1 | .1 | Income Taxes Payable | | .2 | | .1 |
| 8.2 | 14.6 | 13.6 | 8.5 | 5.9 | 5.5 | All Other Current | | 5.9 | | 7.0 |
| 16.5 | 25.6 | 25.5 | 16.3 | 11.7 | 10.3 | Total Current | | 12.5 | | 13.3 |
| 13.4 | 36.9 | 25.9 | 30.3 | 31.0 | 25.9 | Long-Term Debt | | 26.7 | | 26.3 |
| .0 | .0 | .1 | .1 | .1 | .1 | Deferred Taxes | | .1 | | .0 |
| 1.1 | 5.1 | 6.1 | 4.4 | 4.3 | 4.8 | All Other Non-Current | | 4.6 | | 4.3 |
| 69.1 | 32.5 | 42.5 | 48.9 | 53.0 | 58.9 | Net Worth | | 56.1 | | 56.1 |
| 100.0 | 100.0 | 100.0 | 100.0 | 100.0 | 100.0 | Total Liabilities & Net Worth | | 100.0 | | 100.0 |
| | | | | | | INCOME DATA | | | | |
| 100.0 | 100.0 | 100.0 | 100.0 | 100.0 | 100.0 | Net Sales | | 100.0 | | 100.0 |
| | | | | | | Gross Profit | | | | |
| 87.3 | 86.9 | 86.6 | 90.4 | 90.5 | 89.9 | Operating Expenses | | 88.7 | | 93.3 |
| 12.7 | 13.1 | 13.4 | 9.6 | 9.5 | 10.1 | Operating Profit | | 11.3 | | 6.7 |
| -.8 | 4.1 | 6.3 | 1.8 | 1.7 | -1.2 | All Other Expenses (net) | | -.1 | | 5.6 |
| 13.4 | 9.0 | 7.1 | 7.8 | 7.8 | 11.3 | Profit Before Taxes | | 11.4 | | 1.1 |
| | | | | | | RATIOS | | | | |
| 6.7 | 3.3 | 3.0 | 3.3 | 3.8 | 3.5 | | | 4.1 | | 3.9 |
| 4.1 | 1.6 | 1.3 | 1.6 | 1.6 | 1.7 | Current | | 1.9 | | 1.8 |
| 2.1 | .8 | .8 | .9 | .9 | 1.1 | | | 1.0 | | 1.0 |
| 4.9 | 3.0 | 3.0 | 2.8 | 3.4 | 2.8 | | | 3.5 | | 3.4 |
| 3.6 | 1.3 | 1.2 | 1.4 | 1.4 | 1.4 | Quick | | 1.5 | | 1.4 |
| 1.9 | .8 | .7 | .8 | .6 | .7 | | | .8 | | .6 |
| 0　UND | 0　UND | 2　209.2 | 6　65.0 | 8　46.0 | 7　51.8 | Sales/Receivables | 7　55.0 | | 7　50.8 | |
| 13　29.0 | 6　57.4 | 10　35.2 | 15　24.2 | 18　20.3 | 18　20.1 | | 15　24.5 | | 16　23.2 | |
| 27　13.7 | 42　8.6 | 27　13.4 | 33　10.9 | 33　11.2 | 28　13.1 | | 34　10.7 | | 36　10.3 | |
| | | | | | | Cost of Sales/Inventory | | | | |
| | | | | | | Cost of Sales/Payables | | | | |
| 3.0 | 3.5 | 3.9 | 2.7 | 2.8 | 3.1 | Sales/Working Capital | | 2.6 | | 2.5 |
| 9.3 | 6.1 | 21.5 | 9.3 | 9.8 | 8.1 | | | 7.3 | | 8.0 |
| 21.5 | -189.4 | -29.0 | -52.4 | -34.4 | 224.4 | | | 206.6 | | -140.4 |
| | | 19.5 | 10.1 | 9.6 | 11.8 | EBIT/Interest | | 9.2 | | 4.7 |
| | (44)　3.7 | | (165)　4.2 | (144)　3.8 | (179)　5.3 | | (474)　5.0 | | (590)　1.5 | |
| | | 1.1 | 1.6 | 1.8 | 2.4 | | | 2.2 | | -1.1 |
| | | | 8.8 | 119.1 | | Net Profit + Depr., Dep., Amort./Cur. Mat. L/T/D | | 8.3 | | 11.0 |
| | | (14)　2.2 | | (11)　16.0 | | | (24)　2.4 | | (30)　3.4 | |
| | | .8 | | 4.6 | | | | .8 | | 1.7 |
| .4 | .2 | .3 | .7 | .7 | .6 | Fixed/Worth | | .6 | | .5 |
| .6 | 1.3 | .8 | 1.0 | 1.0 | .9 | | | .8 | | .8 |
| 1.0 | NM | 2.5 | 1.8 | 1.6 | 1.2 | | | 1.2 | | 1.2 |
| .1 | .5 | .4 | .5 | .5 | .4 | Debt/Worth | | .4 | | .3 |
| .3 | 1.6 | 1.2 | 1.0 | .7 | .6 | | | .7 | | .6 |
| 1.3 | NM | 3.6 | 2.0 | 1.6 | 1.1 | | | 1.2 | | 1.2 |
| 50.1 | 74.8 | 35.8 | 21.2 | 12.9 | 13.9 | % Profit Before Taxes/Tangible Net Worth | | 14.9 | | 7.3 |
| 27.3 | (10)　31.7 | (54)　13.1 | (188)　9.0 | (166)　7.0 | (206)　7.2 | | (595)　8.7 | | (708)　1.3 | |
| 10.4 | 9.8 | 2.2 | 2.3 | 1.3 | 3.2 | | | 3.8 | | -3.3 |
| 43.2 | 32.4 | 10.8 | 8.7 | 7.0 | 7.4 | % Profit Before Taxes/Total Assets | | 8.7 | | 4.2 |
| 11.2 | 6.1 | 5.4 | 4.4 | 3.4 | 4.2 | | | 4.7 | | .7 |
| 8.5 | -4.5 | .4 | .6 | .5 | 1.4 | | | 2.0 | | -2.1 |
| 50.8 | 55.1 | 15.8 | 2.8 | 1.3 | 1.2 | Sales/Net Fixed Assets | | 1.7 | | 1.5 |
| 4.5 | 8.4 | 4.7 | 1.2 | .9 | .8 | | | 1.0 | | .9 |
| 1.0 | .7 | .8 | .8 | .7 | .6 | | | .7 | | .7 |
| 4.7 | 2.8 | 2.4 | 1.0 | .7 | .6 | Sales/Total Assets | | .7 | | .7 |
| 2.0 | 1.3 | .9 | .6 | .5 | .4 | | | .5 | | .5 |
| .6 | .6 | .5 | .4 | .4 | .3 | | | .4 | | .3 |
| 1.1 | | 2.1 | 3.2 | 4.4 | 4.6 | % Depr., Dep., Amort./Sales | | 3.9 | | 4.2 |
| (10)　2.8 | | (58)　3.1 | (193)　4.9 | (168)　5.8 | (190)　6.0 | | (554)　5.3 | | (681)　5.6 | |
| 5.2 | | 7.4 | 6.7 | 8.5 | 7.8 | | | 7.1 | | 7.6 |
| | | | 2.3 | 6.6 | 3.8 | % Officers', Directors' Owners' Comp/Sales | | 3.7 | | 3.7 |
| | | (19)　5.6 | | (13)　12.0 | (20)　9.1 | | (65)　7.7 | | (83)　8.7 | |
| | | | 19.5 | 15.5 | 16.1 | | | 16.3 | | 18.5 |
| 28346M | 26024M | 601771M | 4468287M | 7524104M | 18642993M | Net Sales ($) | | 24067575M | | 29513898M |
| 3198M | 16517M | 358030M | 5762086M | 12946752M | 34106207M | Total Assets ($) | | 47438602M | | 63226488M |

M = $ thousand　　MM = $ million
See Pages 9 through 22 for Explanation of Ratios and Data

## Comparative Historical Data | Current Data Sorted by Sales

| | | | Type of Statement | 0-1MM | 1-3MM | 3-5MM | 5-10MM | 10-25MM | 25MM & OVER |
|---|---|---|---|---|---|---|---|---|---|
| 616 | 646 | 542 | Unqualified | 8 | 16 | 21 | 43 | 122 | 332 |
| 6 | 2 | 6 | Reviewed | 1 | 1 | | 1 | 2 | 1 |
| 3 | 3 | 3 | Compiled | | | 2 | | | 1 |
| 4 | 14 | 13 | Tax Returns | | | | | | 1 |
| 112 | 112 | 115 | Other | 4 | 3 | 1 | 1 | | 4 |
| 4/1/09-3/31/10 ALL | 4/1/10-3/31/11 ALL | 4/1/11-3/31/12 ALL | | 9 | 5 | 8 | 5 | 24 | 64 |
| | | | | | 575 (4/1-9/30/11) | | | 104 (10/1/11-3/31/12) | |
| 741 | 777 | 679 | NUMBER OF STATEMENTS | 22 | 27 | 30 | 50 | 148 | 402 |
| % | % | % | ASSETS | % | % | % | % | % | % |
| 16.0 | 16.8 | 16.9 | Cash & Equivalents | 14.6 | 18.8 | 22.4 | 16.8 | 17.0 | 16.5 |
| 5.7 | 5.3 | 6.1 | Trade Receivables (net) | 4.1 | 8.1 | 8.3 | 6.6 | 6.0 | 5.8 |
| .5 | .6 | .5 | Inventory | .4 | .6 | .7 | .7 | .7 | .4 |
| 3.1 | 3.1 | 2.3 | All Other Current | 1.9 | 3.8 | 1.0 | 4.1 | 1.8 | 2.3 |
| 25.3 | 25.7 | 25.8 | Total Current | 21.1 | 31.3 | 32.4 | 28.1 | 25.5 | 25.0 |
| 51.9 | 51.2 | 50.7 | Fixed Assets (net) | 69.3 | 49.9 | 48.8 | 50.2 | 50.9 | 49.8 |
| 1.7 | 1.3 | 1.9 | Intangibles (net) | .9 | .9 | .9 | 3.6 | 1.1 | 2.2 |
| 21.0 | 21.8 | 21.6 | All Other Non-Current | 8.7 | 17.9 | 17.9 | 18.1 | 22.5 | 23.0 |
| 100.0 | 100.0 | 100.0 | Total | 100.0 | 100.0 | 100.0 | 100.0 | 100.0 | 100.0 |
| | | | LIABILITIES | | | | | | |
| 1.7 | 2.1 | 1.6 | Notes Payable-Short Term | .5 | 2.6 | 2.9 | 3.5 | 1.9 | 1.2 |
| 1.8 | 1.8 | 1.8 | Cur. Mat.-L.T.D. | 5.8 | 1.1 | 1.9 | 1.8 | 1.5 | 1.8 |
| 3.2 | 3.1 | 3.3 | Trade Payables | 2.0 | 3.2 | 2.5 | 2.7 | 2.9 | 3.6 |
| .0 | .1 | .1 | Income Taxes Payable | .0 | .8 | .0 | .0 | .0 | .1 |
| 7.5 | 6.8 | 7.5 | All Other Current | 3.8 | 9.7 | 9.5 | 8.8 | 7.8 | 7.1 |
| 14.2 | 13.9 | 14.3 | Total Current | 12.1 | 17.4 | 16.8 | 16.8 | 14.2 | 13.7 |
| 27.2 | 27.5 | 28.5 | Long-Term Debt | 38.4 | 50.2 | 32.3 | 35.4 | 29.3 | 25.0 |
| .1 | .1 | .1 | Deferred Taxes | .0 | .0 | .0 | .0 | .0 | .1 |
| 4.8 | 5.2 | 4.6 | All Other Non-Current | 4.3 | 3.1 | 5.0 | 6.5 | 4.5 | 4.5 |
| 53.7 | 53.3 | 52.6 | Net Worth | 45.3 | 29.3 | 45.9 | 41.3 | 51.9 | 56.7 |
| 100.0 | 100.0 | 100.0 | Total Liabilities & Net Worth | 100.0 | 100.0 | 100.0 | 100.0 | 100.0 | 100.0 |
| | | | INCOME DATA | | | | | | |
| 100.0 | 100.0 | 100.0 | Net Sales | 100.0 | 100.0 | 100.0 | 100.0 | 100.0 | 100.0 |
| | | | Gross Profit | | | | | | |
| 93.9 | 91.3 | 89.8 | Operating Expenses | 75.1 | 83.0 | 87.4 | 86.5 | 91.6 | 91.0 |
| 6.1 | 8.7 | 10.2 | Operating Profit | 24.9 | 17.0 | 12.6 | 13.5 | 8.4 | 9.0 |
| 9.5 | .8 | 1.2 | All Other Expenses (net) | 8.4 | 14.3 | 6.4 | 5.6 | 2.1 | -1.3 |
| -3.4 | 7.9 | 9.0 | Profit Before Taxes | 16.6 | 2.7 | 6.2 | 8.0 | 6.3 | 10.3 |
| | | | RATIOS | | | | | | |
| 3.5 | 3.8 | 3.5 | | 4.6 | 3.7 | 5.9 | 4.0 | 3.2 | 3.5 |
| 1.7 | 1.7 | 1.6 | Current | 2.1 | 1.6 | 2.5 | 1.3 | 1.6 | 1.7 |
| .9 | .9 | .9 | | 1.2 | .6 | .7 | .7 | .9 | 1.0 |
| 2.9 | 3.1 | 3.3 | | 3.9 | 3.1 | 5.2 | 2.2 | 2.8 | 3.3 |
| 1.4 | 1.4 | 1.4 | Quick | 2.1 | 1.1 | 2.2 | 1.2 | 1.4 | 1.4 |
| .7 | .7 | .7 | | 1.1 | .6 | .6 | .4 | .7 | .8 |
| 6 57.1 | 7 54.5 | 6 57.0 | | 0 UND | 0 UND | 4 89.9 | 3 121.0 | 6 65.0 | 8 45.7 |
| 16 22.8 | 15 23.8 | 16 23.5 | Sales/Receivables | 0 UND | 6 57.4 | 17 22.0 | 15 24.8 | 15 25.0 | 18 20.2 |
| 35 10.4 | 31 11.6 | 31 11.7 | | 14 25.8 | 24 15.5 | 34 10.7 | 30 12.2 | 35 10.4 | 31 11.9 |
| | | | Cost of Sales/Inventory | | | | | | |
| | | | Cost of Sales/Payables | | | | | | |
| 3.2 | 3.0 | 3.0 | | 2.4 | 2.7 | 2.0 | 2.2 | 2.6 | 3.3 |
| 8.8 | 7.4 | 9.9 | Sales/Working Capital | 4.6 | 11.7 | 8.1 | 16.3 | 12.7 | 9.3 |
| -103.7 | -104.6 | -76.6 | | 68.5 | -11.7 | -24.2 | -14.0 | -27.1 | -175.6 |
| 3.7 | 7.6 | 10.8 | | | 15.4 | 4.1 | 12.3 | 8.8 | 12.2 |
| (612) 3.6 | (652) 3.8 | (547) 4.4 | EBIT/Interest | (19) 4.2 | (19) 1.6 | (34) 3.2 | (122) 3.6 | (344) 5.2 | |
| -3.6 | 1.6 | 1.9 | | .8 | .0 | 1.0 | 1.2 | 2.4 | |
| 16.5 | 22.2 | 14.0 | Net Profit + Depr., Dep., | | | | | | 16.7 |
| (37) 6.6 | (29) 12.4 | (38) 6.0 | Amort./Cur. Mat. L/T/D | | | | | (30) 8.6 | |
| 2.8 | 3.3 | 1.6 | | | | | | | 1.8 |
| .7 | .6 | .6 | | .6 | .3 | .4 | .5 | .5 | .6 |
| .9 | .9 | .9 | Fixed/Worth | 1.7 | 1.3 | 1.1 | 1.1 | 1.0 | .9 |
| 1.5 | 1.4 | 1.5 | | 5.8 | -16.6 | 1.8 | NM | 1.5 | 1.3 |
| .4 | .4 | .4 | | .2 | .5 | .3 | .6 | .5 | .4 |
| .8 | .7 | .8 | Debt/Worth | 1.1 | 1.9 | 1.1 | 1.2 | .9 | .7 |
| 1.5 | 1.4 | 1.6 | | 6.0 | -18.7 | 2.3 | NM | 1.7 | 1.3 |
| 7.2 | 12.0 | 17.7 | % Profit Before Taxes/Tangible | 31.7 | 40.1 | 13.0 | 27.3 | 15.7 | 16.7 |
| (715) -1.1 | (749) 6.0 | (638) 7.9 | Net Worth | (20) 13.2 | (18) 6.1 | (27) 3.2 | (38) 12.2 | (145) 7.3 | (390) 8.1 |
| -10.1 | 1.8 | 2.3 | | 7.7 | 1.7 | -1.7 | 3.6 | .5 | 3.2 |
| 4.1 | 6.6 | 8.2 | % Profit Before Taxes/Total | 10.9 | 11.0 | 5.7 | 9.0 | 7.5 | 8.3 |
| -.7 | 3.3 | 4.2 | Assets | 6.0 | 2.1 | 1.3 | 3.0 | 3.5 | 4.7 |
| -5.8 | .7 | .9 | | .9 | -2.8 | -.4 | -.7 | .2 | 1.6 |
| 1.5 | 1.5 | 1.8 | | 1.2 | 17.6 | 4.2 | 5.3 | 1.7 | 1.7 |
| .9 | .9 | 1.0 | Sales/Net Fixed Assets | .7 | 1.1 | 1.0 | .9 | 1.0 | 1.0 |
| .6 | .7 | .7 | | .2 | .3 | .4 | .5 | .6 | .7 |
| .7 | .7 | .8 | | .7 | 1.4 | .9 | .9 | .7 | .8 |
| .5 | .5 | .5 | Sales/Total Assets | .4 | .5 | .4 | .4 | .5 | .5 |
| .3 | .3 | .4 | | .1 | .2 | .2 | .2 | .3 | .4 |
| 4.3 | 4.3 | 3.8 | | 4.4 | 1.6 | 2.2 | 2.4 | 3.8 | 3.9 |
| (679) 6.0 | (714) 5.9 | (627) 5.4 | % Depr., Dep., Amort./Sales | (18) 7.0 | (18) 5.7 | (28) 6.2 | (47) 5.3 | (142) 5.8 | (374) 5.2 |
| 7.8 | 8.2 | 7.5 | | 26.7 | 12.8 | 9.9 | 12.7 | 8.5 | 7.0 |
| 3.6 | 5.4 | 4.0 | % Officers', Directors' | | | | | 2.8 | 6.2 |
| (93) 10.3 | (74) 10.3 | (59) 9.5 | Owners' Comp/Sales | | | | | (12) 5.6 | (35) 11.2 |
| 19.7 | 21.0 | 16.8 | | | | | | 12.4 | 19.5 |
| 31617495M | 32583743M | 31291525M | Net Sales ($) | 10796M | 56080M | 117875M | 367069M | 2581355M | 28158350M |
| 59939574M | 63935007M | 53192790M | Total Assets ($) | 64657M | 201572M | 411856M | 1318601M | 6369595M | 44826509M |

M = $ thousand    MM = $ million
See Pages 9 through 22 for Explanation of Ratios and Data

## Current Data Sorted by Assets

## Comparative Historical Data

| | | | | | | Type of Statement | | |
|---|---|---|---|---|---|---|---|---|
| | 2 | 6 | 10 | | 3 | Unqualified | 23 | 18 |
| | 2 | 6 | | | | Reviewed | 1 | 2 |
| | 2 | | | | | Compiled | 1 | 1 |
| 2 | 1 | | | | | Tax Returns | 7 | 3 |
| 6 | 13 | 12 | 7 | 1 | | Other | 10 | 20 |
| | 24 (4/1-9/30/11) | | 49 (10/1/11-3/31/12) | | | | 4/1/07-3/31/08 | 4/1/08-3/31/09 |
| **0-500M** | **500M-2MM** | **2-10MM** | **10-50MM** | **50-100MM** | **100-250MM** | | **ALL** | **ALL** |
| 8 | 20 | 24 | 17 | 1 | 3 | **NUMBER OF STATEMENTS** | 42 | 44 |
| % | % | % | % | % | % | **ASSETS** | % | % |
| | 24.8 | 19.8 | 21.4 | | | Cash & Equivalents | 21.2 | 24.3 |
| | 20.2 | 22.7 | 17.4 | | | Trade Receivables (net) | 13.1 | 13.7 |
| | 4.7 | .4 | .7 | | | Inventory | 4.3 | 2.4 |
| | 11.8 | 3.9 | 2.3 | | | All Other Current | 4.3 | 5.4 |
| | 61.6 | 46.7 | 41.8 | | | Total Current | 43.0 | 45.7 |
| | 25.7 | 39.5 | 36.6 | | | Fixed Assets (net) | 36.4 | 31.4 |
| | 4.0 | 3.4 | 13.1 | | | Intangibles (net) | 8.2 | 10.3 |
| | 8.8 | 10.4 | 8.6 | | | All Other Non-Current | 12.4 | 12.6 |
| | 100.0 | 100.0 | 100.0 | | | Total | 100.0 | 100.0 |
| | | | | | | **LIABILITIES** | | |
| | 9.8 | 5.8 | 1.0 | | | Notes Payable-Short Term | 7.6 | 2.5 |
| | 1.5 | 1.1 | 2.8 | | | Cur. Mat.-L.T.D. | 4.0 | 2.2 |
| | 5.9 | 7.4 | 5.5 | | | Trade Payables | 5.0 | 6.4 |
| | .3 | .3 | .0 | | | Income Taxes Payable | .1 | .2 |
| | 21.2 | 11.6 | 9.9 | | | All Other Current | 19.1 | 19.5 |
| | 38.8 | 26.2 | 19.2 | | | Total Current | 35.8 | 30.7 |
| | 10.6 | 20.1 | 34.1 | | | Long-Term Debt | 16.3 | 20.1 |
| | .2 | .6 | .3 | | | Deferred Taxes | .2 | .1 |
| | 11.5 | 9.2 | 6.9 | | | All Other Non-Current | 6.8 | 10.2 |
| | 38.9 | 43.9 | 39.6 | | | Net Worth | 40.8 | 38.9 |
| | 100.0 | 100.0 | 100.0 | | | Total Liabilities & Net Worth | 100.0 | 100.0 |
| | | | | | | **INCOME DATA** | | |
| | 100.0 | 100.0 | 100.0 | | | Net Sales | 100.0 | 100.0 |
| | | | | | | Gross Profit | | |
| | 91.8 | 90.2 | 85.4 | | | Operating Expenses | 95.2 | 97.3 |
| | 8.2 | 9.8 | 14.6 | | | Operating Profit | 4.8 | 2.7 |
| | 1.8 | 4.6 | 2.6 | | | All Other Expenses (net) | 1.4 | 1.2 |
| | 6.4 | 5.2 | 12.0 | | | Profit Before Taxes | 3.4 | 1.5 |
| | | | | | | **RATIOS** | | |
| | 13.2 | 4.9 | 6.2 | | | | 2.6 | 3.9 |
| | 2.2 | 1.7 | 2.1 | | | Current | 1.3 | 1.6 |
| | 1.0 | .8 | 1.2 | | | | .8 | .7 |
| | 12.8 | 4.2 | 6.1 | | | | 1.8 | 3.5 |
| | 1.4 | 1.7 | 1.9 | | | Quick | 1.1 | 1.5 |
| | .4 | .7 | 1.0 | | | | .4 | .6 |
| 5 | 73.2 | 4 | 93.5 | 8 | 44.4 | | 1 | 520.8 | 2 | 164.4 |
| 21 | 17.8 | 28 | 12.9 | 31 | 11.9 | Sales/Receivables | 16 | 22.7 | 24 | 15.5 |
| 65 | 5.6 | 54 | 6.7 | 72 | 5.1 | | 46 | 8.0 | 46 | 7.9 |
| | | | | | | Cost of Sales/Inventory | | |
| | | | | | | Cost of Sales/Payables | | |
| | 3.1 | 3.5 | 2.7 | | | | 4.7 | 4.6 |
| | 6.9 | 20.4 | 6.6 | | | Sales/Working Capital | 27.9 | 13.3 |
| | NM | -63.9 | NM | | | | -26.9 | -20.7 |
| | 9.2 | 105.0 | 24.2 | | | | 12.7 | 14.3 |
| (10) | 3.9 | (15) | 9.4 | (12) | 4.0 | EBIT/Interest | (31) | 2.1 | (32) | 3.6 |
| | .8 | 3.0 | 2.4 | | | | -.7 | -.8 |
| | | | | | | Net Profit + Depr., Dep., Amort./Cur. Mat. L/T/D | | |
| | .1 | .1 | .2 | | | | .5 | .3 |
| | .4 | .6 | .9 | | | Fixed/Worth | 1.0 | .8 |
| | 2.4 | 2.3 | 1.8 | | | | 3.8 | 7.6 |
| | .4 | .6 | .6 | | | | .4 | .7 |
| | .9 | 1.5 | 1.5 | | | Debt/Worth | 1.5 | 1.9 |
| | 5.3 | 3.5 | 2.6 | | | | 19.4 | 9.3 |
| | 91.3 | 45.5 | 46.5 | | | % Profit Before Taxes/Tangible Net Worth | 29.8 | 45.3 |
| (18) | 21.9 | (22) | 9.3 | (14) | 14.2 | | (34) | 10.9 | (35) | 11.9 |
| | 1.0 | 2.2 | 8.6 | | | | -3.6 | 3.1 |
| | 26.2 | 17.4 | 22.6 | | | % Profit Before Taxes/Total Assets | 11.3 | 12.1 |
| | 10.8 | 3.8 | 9.5 | | | | 5.0 | 2.7 |
| | .2 | .3 | 2.3 | | | | -3.1 | -3.2 |
| | 67.1 | 36.3 | 25.2 | | | | 31.2 | 37.5 |
| | 31.3 | 6.3 | 4.3 | | | Sales/Net Fixed Assets | 5.9 | 7.6 |
| | 2.9 | 1.8 | 1.8 | | | | 2.3 | 2.5 |
| | 3.6 | 2.6 | 2.1 | | | | 2.9 | 3.3 |
| | 2.3 | 1.5 | 1.1 | | | Sales/Total Assets | 1.5 | 1.5 |
| | 1.0 | .9 | .6 | | | | .9 | .8 |
| | .6 | .4 | 2.1 | | | | 1.0 | 1.4 |
| (11) | 1.5 | (17) | 1.7 | (11) | 3.6 | % Depr., Dep., Amort./Sales | (34) | 2.3 | (31) | 3.1 |
| | 3.7 | 3.5 | 8.8 | | | | 3.9 | 5.7 |
| | | | | | | % Officers', Directors' Owners' Comp/Sales | | 1.8 |
| | | | | | | | (10) | 7.9 |
| | | | | | | | | 18.4 |
| 12821M | 64561M | 209530M | 623096M | 99190M | 567726M | Net Sales ($) | 1285924M | 1386758M |
| 2563M | 21459M | 123812M | 414106M | 67150M | 431562M | Total Assets ($) | 1066058M | 1046362M |

M = $ thousand   MM = $ million
See Pages 9 through 22 for Explanation of Ratios and Data

## Comparative Historical Data
## Current Data Sorted by Sales

| Type of Statement | 4/1/09-3/31/10 ALL | 4/1/10-3/31/11 ALL | 4/1/11-3/31/12 ALL | 0-1MM | 1-3MM | 3-5MM | 5-10MM | 10-25MM | 25MM & OVER |
|---|---|---|---|---|---|---|---|---|---|
| Unqualified | 22 | 32 | 21 | 1 | 1 | 2 | 1 | 10 | 6 |
| Reviewed | 1 | 4 | 8 | | 1 | | 1 | 6 | |
| Compiled | 3 | | 2 | | 1 | 1 | | | |
| Tax Returns | 10 | 11 | 3 | 2 | 1 | | | | |
| Other | 23 | 27 | 39 | 6 | 13 | 5 | 6 | 3 | 6 |
| | | | | | 24 (4/1-9/30/11) | | | 49 (10/1/11-3/31/12) | |
| NUMBER OF STATEMENTS | 59 | 74 | 73 | 9 | 17 | 8 | 8 | 19 | 12 |
| | % | % | % | % | % | % | % | % | % |
| **ASSETS** | | | | | | | | | |
| Cash & Equivalents | 21.3 | 24.2 | 22.3 | | 24.5 | | | 27.0 | 18.9 |
| Trade Receivables (net) | 18.1 | 19.8 | 21.2 | | 24.6 | | | 22.3 | 26.1 |
| Inventory | 1.2 | 1.3 | 2.2 | | 3.2 | | | .4 | 1.0 |
| All Other Current | 7.5 | 3.7 | 6.1 | | 6.8 | | | 2.3 | 3.8 |
| Total Current | 48.1 | 49.1 | 51.8 | | 59.1 | | | 52.1 | 49.7 |
| Fixed Assets (net) | 31.8 | 28.9 | 32.4 | | 30.3 | | | 24.5 | 27.2 |
| Intangibles (net) | 10.0 | 7.7 | 6.7 | | 4.5 | | | 7.2 | 17.3 |
| All Other Non-Current | 10.1 | 14.2 | 9.1 | | 6.1 | | | 16.1 | 5.7 |
| Total | 100.0 | 100.0 | 100.0 | | 100.0 | | | 100.0 | 100.0 |
| **LIABILITIES** | | | | | | | | | |
| Notes Payable-Short Term | 6.5 | 3.4 | 5.2 | | 7.5 | | | 5.2 | 1.4 |
| Cur. Mat.-L.T.D. | 2.9 | 1.5 | 2.9 | | 2.2 | | | 1.4 | 3.4 |
| Trade Payables | 7.1 | 8.2 | 6.2 | | 5.4 | | | 8.7 | 6.4 |
| Income Taxes Payable | .3 | .2 | .2 | | .4 | | | .4 | .1 |
| All Other Current | 20.8 | 15.9 | 19.1 | | 25.8 | | | 11.7 | 16.7 |
| Total Current | 37.5 | 29.2 | 33.5 | | 41.3 | | | 27.3 | 28.0 |
| Long-Term Debt | 18.2 | 13.5 | 18.6 | | 13.9 | | | 15.4 | 29.7 |
| Deferred Taxes | .3 | .2 | .4 | | .3 | | | 1.1 | .5 |
| All Other Non-Current | 9.1 | 17.9 | 8.7 | | 15.7 | | | 9.0 | 7.8 |
| Net Worth | 34.9 | 39.1 | 38.7 | | 28.9 | | | 47.3 | 34.0 |
| Total Liabilities & Net Worth | 100.0 | 100.0 | 100.0 | | 100.0 | | | 100.0 | 100.0 |
| **INCOME DATA** | | | | | | | | | |
| Net Sales | 100.0 | 100.0 | 100.0 | | 100.0 | | | 100.0 | 100.0 |
| Gross Profit | | | | | | | | | |
| Operating Expenses | 93.2 | 93.7 | 89.2 | | 86.9 | | | 94.9 | 88.1 |
| Operating Profit | 6.8 | 6.3 | 10.8 | | 13.1 | | | 5.1 | 11.9 |
| All Other Expenses (net) | 2.0 | 1.3 | 2.7 | | 3.3 | | | -.3 | 1.5 |
| Profit Before Taxes | 4.8 | 5.1 | 8.1 | | 9.7 | | | 5.4 | 10.4 |
| **RATIOS** | | | | | | | | | |
| Current | 3.6 | 4.7 | 6.2 | | 9.5 | | | 4.3 | 3.2 |
| | 1.6 | 1.8 | 1.8 | | 2.1 | | | 2.1 | 1.5 |
| | .6 | .8 | 1.0 | | 1.0 | | | 1.0 | 1.1 |
| Quick | 3.1 | 4.5 | 5.8 | | 9.0 | | | 4.3 | 3.1 |
| | 1.3 | 1.6 | 1.7 | | 2.0 | | | 1.9 | 1.4 |
| | .4 | .7 | .7 | | 1.0 | | | 1.0 | 1.0 |
| Sales/Receivables | 2  174.3 | 1  287.3 | 5  73.8 | 0  UND | | | 6  58.4 | 24  14.9 | |
| | 27  13.4 | 23  15.6 | 30  12.3 | 18  20.4 | | | 30  12.3 | 52  7.0 | |
| | 49  7.5 | 51  7.2 | 57  6.4 | 45  8.1 | | | 58  6.3 | 78  4.7 | |
| Cost of Sales/Inventory | | | | | | | | | |
| Cost of Sales/Payables | | | | | | | | | |
| Sales/Working Capital | 5.0 | 4.7 | 3.3 | | 4.2 | | | 3.2 | 6.9 |
| | 10.7 | 14.8 | 10.3 | | 10.3 | | | 4.4 | 11.6 |
| | -10.2 | -95.9 | -159.2 | | NM | | | -217.5 | NM |
| EBIT/Interest | 13.4 | 48.7 | 35.9 | | 70.0 | | | 158.0 | 55.1 |
| | (40)  3.8 | (44)  7.0 | (48)  7.0 | (11)  12.2 | | | (13)  9.4 | (11)  8.0 | |
| | -.3 | .2 | 2.4 | | 5.2 | | | 3.0 | 2.5 |
| Net Profit + Depr., Dep., Amort./Cur. Mat. L/T/D | | | | | | | | | |
| Fixed/Worth | .4 | .1 | .1 | | .1 | | | .1 | .1 |
| | 1.0 | .6 | .7 | | .3 | | | .4 | .8 |
| | -4.6 | 4.8 | 2.2 | | 2.6 | | | 1.3 | 1.6 |
| Debt/Worth | .4 | .4 | .5 | | .3 | | | .6 | .4 |
| | 1.4 | 1.2 | 1.5 | | 1.0 | | | .9 | 1.6 |
| | -14.2 | 8.7 | 4.6 | | 6.2 | | | 2.1 | 7.7 |
| % Profit Before Taxes/Tangible Net Worth | 44.3 | 73.6 | 66.1 | | 89.8 | | | 41.8 | 100.8 |
| | (43)  10.8 | (61)  21.2 | (64)  20.2 | (15)  24.7 | | | (17)  11.9 | (10)  37.8 | |
| | 1.7 | .3 | 4.3 | | 8.0 | | | 6.7 | 9.6 |
| % Profit Before Taxes/Total Assets | 18.1 | 20.0 | 22.2 | | 50.4 | | | 13.7 | 29.1 |
| | 4.7 | 6.9 | 8.8 | | 12.9 | | | 5.0 | 8.4 |
| | -.9 | -.9 | 2.1 | | 1.4 | | | 2.4 | 1.5 |
| Sales/Net Fixed Assets | 35.3 | 53.7 | 44.0 | | 83.6 | | | 62.4 | 46.2 |
| | 12.3 | 10.9 | 11.6 | | 28.7 | | | 12.6 | 9.2 |
| | 2.3 | 2.8 | 2.7 | | 5.4 | | | 3.5 | 3.9 |
| Sales/Total Assets | 3.6 | 2.8 | 2.9 | | 4.3 | | | 2.7 | 2.4 |
| | 1.9 | 1.8 | 2.0 | | 2.5 | | | 2.1 | 1.9 |
| | .8 | 1.0 | .9 | | 1.7 | | | 1.1 | 1.2 |
| % Depr., Dep., Amort./Sales | 1.1 | .8 | .7 | | | | | .4 | |
| | (39)  2.0 | (52)  2.1 | (44)  2.5 | | | | | (14)  2.0 | |
| | 4.6 | 4.6 | 5.1 | | | | | 2.7 | |
| % Officers', Directors' Owners' Comp/Sales | 4.8 | 3.0 | | | | | | | |
| | (14)  8.6 | (14)  7.3 | | | | | | | |
| | 12.7 | 14.4 | | | | | | | |
| Net Sales ($) | 1458802M | 2205115M | 1576924M | 4539M | 30249M | 31661M | 57301M | 271777M | 1181397M |
| Total Assets ($) | 1122320M | 1333001M | 1060652M | 14729M | 28209M | 34323M | 33671M | 191861M | 757859M |

M = $ thousand   MM = $ million
See Pages 9 through 22 for Explanation of Ratios and Data

## Current Data Sorted by Assets

## Comparative Historical Data

| Type of Statement | 0-500M | 500M-2MM | 2-10MM | 10-50MM | 50-100MM | 100-250MM | | 4/1/07-3/31/08 ALL | 4/1/08-3/31/09 ALL |
|---|---|---|---|---|---|---|---|---|---|
| Unqualified | | 4 | 5 | 6 | | 1 | | 5 | 2 |
| Reviewed | | | 1 | | | | | | 2 |
| Compiled | | 1 | 1 | | | | | 2 | 1 |
| Tax Returns | | | | | | | | 2 | 2 |
| Other | | 2 | 6 | 2 | 1 | | | 6 | 8 |
| | 0-500M | 6 (4/1-9/30/11) 500M-2MM | 2-10MM | 24 (10/1/11-3/31/12) 10-50MM | 50-100MM | 100-250MM | | | |
| NUMBER OF STATEMENTS | | 7 | 13 | 8 | 1 | 1 | | 15 | 15 |
| | % | % | % | % | % | % | | % | % |
| **ASSETS** | | | | | | | | | |
| Cash & Equivalents | | | 26.0 | | | | | 19.5 | 20.0 |
| Trade Receivables (net) | | | 18.3 | | | | | 12.5 | 14.4 |
| Inventory | | | 1.4 | | | | | 9.6 | 5.6 |
| All Other Current | | | 5.2 | | | | | 4.2 | 1.2 |
| Total Current | | | 50.9 | | | | | 45.8 | 41.2 |
| Fixed Assets (net) | | | 30.2 | | | | | 41.1 | 48.1 |
| Intangibles (net) | | | 4.7 | | | | | 3.1 | 7.8 |
| All Other Non-Current | | | 14.2 | | | | | 10.0 | 2.8 |
| Total | | | 100.0 | | | | | 100.0 | 100.0 |
| **LIABILITIES** | | | | | | | | | |
| Notes Payable-Short Term | | | 1.1 | | | | | 9.4 | 5.8 |
| Cur. Mat.-L.T.D. | | | .8 | | | | | 3.9 | 1.3 |
| Trade Payables | | | 2.5 | | | | | 8.1 | 3.3 |
| Income Taxes Payable | | | .0 | | | | | .2 | 2.8 |
| All Other Current | | | 25.1 | | | | | 18.2 | 17.2 |
| Total Current | | | 29.6 | | | | | 39.8 | 30.4 |
| Long-Term Debt | | | 14.5 | | | | | 23.1 | 22.3 |
| Deferred Taxes | | | .0 | | | | | .0 | .3 |
| All Other Non-Current | | | 7.6 | | | | | 10.3 | 22.0 |
| Net Worth | | | 48.3 | | | | | 26.8 | 24.9 |
| Total Liabilities & Net Worth | | | 100.0 | | | | | 100.0 | 100.0 |
| **INCOME DATA** | | | | | | | | | |
| Net Sales | | | 100.0 | | | | | 100.0 | 100.0 |
| Gross Profit | | | | | | | | | |
| Operating Expenses | | | 89.1 | | | | | 95.1 | 90.5 |
| Operating Profit | | | 10.9 | | | | | 4.9 | 9.5 |
| All Other Expenses (net) | | | 1.2 | | | | | 1.2 | 2.0 |
| Profit Before Taxes | | | 9.7 | | | | | 3.7 | 7.5 |
| **RATIOS** | | | | | | | | | |
| Current | | | 3.7 | | | | | 2.1 | 4.7 |
| | | | 1.8 | | | | | 1.1 | 1.3 |
| | | | .8 | | | | | .8 | .6 |
| Quick | | | 3.4 | | | | | 1.8 | 3.6 |
| | | | 1.5 | | | | | .9 | 1.2 |
| | | | .7 | | | | | .4 | .6 |
| Sales/Receivables | | | 2  229.1 | | | | | 0  UND | 0  UND |
| | | | 45  8.2 | | | | | 22  16.6 | 27  13.3 |
| | | | 122  3.0 | | | | | 47  7.8 | 65  5.6 |
| Cost of Sales/Inventory | | | | | | | | | |
| Cost of Sales/Payables | | | | | | | | | |
| Sales/Working Capital | | | 2.1 | | | | | 6.3 | 4.1 |
| | | | 3.0 | | | | | 36.9 | 17.6 |
| | | | -18.7 | | | | | -25.3 | -11.2 |
| EBIT/Interest | | | | | | | | (11) 6.9 | (13) 24.0 |
| | | | | | | | | 3.1 | 11.4 |
| | | | | | | | | .3 | 1.8 |
| Net Profit + Depr., Dep., Amort./Cur. Mat. L/T/D | | | | | | | | | |
| Fixed/Worth | | | .2 | | | | | .6 | 1.3 |
| | | | .5 | | | | | 1.6 | 1.7 |
| | | | 1.4 | | | | | 5.2 | 16.2 |
| Debt/Worth | | | .8 | | | | | .7 | 1.6 |
| | | | 1.1 | | | | | 3.8 | 2.5 |
| | | | 1.8 | | | | | 7.7 | 18.4 |
| % Profit Before Taxes/Tangible Net Worth | | | 50.4 | | | | | (13) 73.1 | (12) 94.7 |
| | | | 22.5 | | | | | 25.0 | 42.2 |
| | | | 1.9 | | | | | 10.0 | 14.0 |
| % Profit Before Taxes/Total Assets | | | 22.4 | | | | | 14.7 | 16.2 |
| | | | 8.4 | | | | | 6.2 | 6.5 |
| | | | 1.2 | | | | | -4.7 | 1.5 |
| Sales/Net Fixed Assets | | | 20.7 | | | | | 8.3 | 8.7 |
| | | | 4.6 | | | | | 3.1 | 3.5 |
| | | | 1.6 | | | | | 2.2 | 1.5 |
| Sales/Total Assets | | | 1.4 | | | | | 2.5 | 2.1 |
| | | | .9 | | | | | 1.3 | 1.3 |
| | | | .4 | | | | | .8 | 1.0 |
| % Depr., Dep., Amort./Sales | | | 1.8 | | | | | (13) 2.0 | 2.2 |
| | | | (12) 4.1 | | | | | 3.5 | 3.6 |
| | | | 5.9 | | | | | 6.9 | 7.3 |
| % Officers', Directors' Owners' Comp/Sales | | | | | | | | | |
| Net Sales ($) | 9607M | 45970M | 312294M | 227985M | 107777M | | | 225584M | 249935M |
| Total Assets ($) | 7267M | 50897M | 186616M | 87511M | 115002M | | | 240878M | 173573M |

M = $ thousand   MM = $ million
See Pages 9 through 22 for Explanation of Ratios and Data

## Comparative Historical Data | Current Data Sorted by Sales

| | | | Type of Statement | | | | | | |
|---|---|---|---|---|---|---|---|---|---|
| 5 | 12 | 16 | Unqualified | 2 | 6 | 1 | | 2 | 5 |
| | | | Reviewed | | | | | | |
| | | | Compiled | | 1 | | | | |
| 1 | 2 | 1 | Tax Returns | 1 | | 1 | | | |
| 2 | 1 | 2 | Other | 1 | 2 | 2 | 3 | 1 | 2 |
| 13 | 11 | 11 | | | | | | | |
| 4/1/09- | 4/1/10- | 4/1/11- | | | 6 (4/1-9/30/11) | | 24 (10/1/11-3/31/12) | | |
| 3/31/10 | 3/31/11 | 3/31/12 | | | | | | | |
| ALL | ALL | ALL | | 0-1MM | 1-3MM | 3-5MM | 5-10MM | 10-25MM | 25MM & OVER |
| 21 | 26 | 30 | **NUMBER OF STATEMENTS** | 4 | 9 | 4 | 3 | 3 | 7 |
| % | % | % | **ASSETS** | % | % | % | % | % | % |
| 21.0 | 16.3 | 26.0 | Cash & Equivalents | | | | | | |
| 16.8 | 17.6 | 19.5 | Trade Receivables (net) | | | | | | |
| 4.2 | 3.3 | 3.3 | Inventory | | | | | | |
| 3.8 | 5.5 | 4.1 | All Other Current | | | | | | |
| 45.8 | 42.7 | 52.9 | Total Current | | | | | | |
| 40.9 | 32.1 | 27.3 | Fixed Assets (net) | | | | | | |
| 2.3 | 8.4 | 5.1 | Intangibles (net) | | | | | | |
| 11.0 | 16.8 | 14.6 | All Other Non-Current | | | | | | |
| 100.0 | 100.0 | 100.0 | Total | | | | | | |
| | | | **LIABILITIES** | | | | | | |
| 5.3 | 6.9 | 2.7 | Notes Payable-Short Term | | | | | | |
| .9 | 1.6 | 2.4 | Cur. Mat.-L.T.D. | | | | | | |
| 3.2 | 3.4 | 3.4 | Trade Payables | | | | | | |
| .1 | .2 | .1 | Income Taxes Payable | | | | | | |
| 25.0 | 21.2 | 22.1 | All Other Current | | | | | | |
| 34.5 | 33.2 | 30.7 | Total Current | | | | | | |
| 13.7 | 16.5 | 14.1 | Long-Term Debt | | | | | | |
| .4 | .4 | .2 | Deferred Taxes | | | | | | |
| 15.7 | 10.7 | 10.0 | All Other Non-Current | | | | | | |
| 35.7 | 39.1 | 45.0 | Net Worth | | | | | | |
| 100.0 | 100.0 | 100.0 | Total Liabilities & Net Worth | | | | | | |
| | | | **INCOME DATA** | | | | | | |
| 100.0 | 100.0 | 100.0 | Net Sales | | | | | | |
| | | | Gross Profit | | | | | | |
| 94.9 | 84.2 | 87.8 | Operating Expenses | | | | | | |
| 5.1 | 15.8 | 12.2 | Operating Profit | | | | | | |
| .9 | .1 | .6 | All Other Expenses (net) | | | | | | |
| 4.2 | 15.7 | 11.6 | Profit Before Taxes | | | | | | |
| | | | **RATIOS** | | | | | | |
| 2.1 | 3.4 | 3.5 | | | | | | | |
| 1.3 | 1.4 | 1.9 | Current | | | | | | |
| .8 | .9 | 1.1 | | | | | | | |
| 2.0 | 1.9 | 3.5 | | | | | | | |
| .9 | 1.2 | 1.4 | Quick | | | | | | |
| .8 | .7 | 1.0 | | | | | | | |
| 5  66.5 | 0  UND | 10  36.7 | Sales/Receivables | | | | | | |
| 25  14.7 | 25  14.5 | 35  10.4 | | | | | | | |
| 152  2.4 | 90  4.1 | 118  3.1 | | | | | | | |
| | | | Cost of Sales/Inventory | | | | | | |
| | | | Cost of Sales/Payables | | | | | | |
| 3.1 | 5.9 | 2.7 | | | | | | | |
| 31.0 | 9.7 | 5.3 | Sales/Working Capital | | | | | | |
| -15.5 | -23.1 | 20.5 | | | | | | | |
| 78.7 | 49.0 | 67.2 | | | | | | | |
| (18) 19.9 | (20) 10.9 | (24) 15.6 | EBIT/Interest | | | | | | |
| 2.4 | 2.8 | 2.9 | | | | | | | |
| | | | Net Profit + Depr., Dep., Amort./Cur. Mat. L/T/D | | | | | | |
| .4 | .4 | .3 | | | | | | | |
| .8 | .6 | .5 | Fixed/Worth | | | | | | |
| 1.9 | 1.7 | 1.3 | | | | | | | |
| .9 | .8 | .9 | | | | | | | |
| 1.3 | 1.6 | 1.1 | Debt/Worth | | | | | | |
| 2.9 | 2.9 | 2.2 | | | | | | | |
| 59.1 | 81.0 | 84.3 | | | | | | | |
| (18) 28.6 | (24) 52.5 | (29) 32.6 | % Profit Before Taxes/Tangible Net Worth | | | | | | |
| 1.3 | 16.6 | 9.7 | | | | | | | |
| 23.3 | 30.8 | 25.6 | | | | | | | |
| 10.6 | 20.5 | 12.7 | % Profit Before Taxes/Total Assets | | | | | | |
| -3.7 | 3.7 | 4.1 | | | | | | | |
| 8.9 | 11.8 | 13.7 | | | | | | | |
| 3.2 | 6.7 | 6.5 | Sales/Net Fixed Assets | | | | | | |
| 1.7 | 2.4 | 3.0 | | | | | | | |
| 1.6 | 1.9 | 1.6 | | | | | | | |
| 1.1 | 1.3 | 1.1 | Sales/Total Assets | | | | | | |
| .6 | .9 | .7 | | | | | | | |
| 1.7 | 1.8 | 2.3 | | | | | | | |
| (18) 3.4 | (22) 3.5 | (25) 3.3 | % Depr., Dep., Amort./Sales | | | | | | |
| 7.6 | 5.4 | 5.5 | | | | | | | |
| | | | % Officers', Directors' Owners' Comp/Sales | | | | | | |
| 893209M | 1162906M | 703633M | Net Sales ($) | 2917M | 16357M | 14471M | 21832M | 51468M | 596588M |
| 777305M | 673976M | 447293M | Total Assets ($) | 4588M | 26510M | 10780M | 16286M | 56422M | 332707M |

M = $ thousand    MM = $ million
See Pages 9 through 22 for Explanation of Ratios and Data

## Current Data Sorted by Assets

## Comparative Historical Data

| | | | | | | Type of Statement | | | |
|---|---|---|---|---|---|---|---|---|---|
| | 7 | 30 | 24 | 7 | 2 | Unqualified | | 52 | 74 |
| | | 1 | 1 | | | Reviewed | | 6 | 2 |
| 3 | 1 | 2 | 1 | | | Compiled | | 8 | 15 |
| 9 | 9 | 3 | | | | Tax Returns | | 12 | 14 |
| 6 | 13 | 23 | 12 | 3 | 3 | Other | | 25 | 33 |
| | 62 (4/1-9/30/11) | | 98 (10/1/11-3/31/12) | | | | | 4/1/07-3/31/08 | 4/1/08-3/31/09 |
| 0-500M | 500M-2MM | 2-10MM | 10-50MM | 50-100MM | 100-250MM | | | ALL | ALL |
| 18 | 30 | 59 | 38 | 10 | 5 | NUMBER OF STATEMENTS | | 103 | 138 |
| % | % | % | % | % | % | ASSETS | | % | % |
| 23.5 | 25.2 | 21.9 | 16.9 | 16.5 | | Cash & Equivalents | | 20.9 | 19.8 |
| 15.6 | 26.8 | 22.3 | 15.7 | 10.2 | | Trade Receivables (net) | | 25.7 | 17.3 |
| 1.9 | 3.9 | 1.9 | 1.0 | .8 | | Inventory | | 1.6 | 1.4 |
| .3 | 2.1 | 5.6 | 3.1 | 2.7 | | All Other Current | | 3.6 | 5.0 |
| 41.4 | 58.0 | 51.7 | 36.7 | 30.2 | | Total Current | | 51.8 | 43.5 |
| 42.5 | 18.7 | 37.7 | 41.6 | 30.5 | | Fixed Assets (net) | | 33.5 | 38.2 |
| 9.3 | 13.5 | 5.0 | 8.8 | 23.9 | | Intangibles (net) | | 7.1 | 9.6 |
| 6.8 | 9.8 | 5.6 | 12.9 | 15.4 | | All Other Non-Current | | 7.6 | 8.7 |
| 100.0 | 100.0 | 100.0 | 100.0 | 100.0 | | Total | | 100.0 | 100.0 |
| | | | | | | LIABILITIES | | | |
| 11.7 | 4.4 | 1.6 | 2.7 | 2.9 | | Notes Payable-Short Term | | 4.6 | 4.8 |
| 3.4 | 1.0 | 2.0 | 2.5 | 1.2 | | Cur. Mat.-L.T.D. | | 3.2 | 2.4 |
| 10.5 | 7.3 | 3.9 | 4.6 | 5.3 | | Trade Payables | | 9.1 | 4.8 |
| .0 | 1.5 | .5 | .1 | .3 | | Income Taxes Payable | | .3 | .4 |
| 44.0 | 23.6 | 22.8 | 22.4 | 17.9 | | All Other Current | | 22.9 | 18.5 |
| 69.6 | 37.9 | 30.8 | 32.4 | 27.6 | | Total Current | | 40.1 | 30.9 |
| 22.1 | 13.1 | 14.7 | 19.0 | 9.9 | | Long-Term Debt | | 13.4 | 18.2 |
| .0 | .0 | .5 | .8 | .7 | | Deferred Taxes | | .1 | .3 |
| 6.9 | 16.4 | 9.6 | 4.8 | 18.4 | | All Other Non-Current | | 5.6 | 7.1 |
| 1.5 | 32.6 | 44.4 | 43.0 | 43.5 | | Net Worth | | 40.8 | 43.5 |
| 100.0 | 100.0 | 100.0 | 100.0 | 100.0 | | Total Liabilties & Net Worth | | 100.0 | 100.0 |
| | | | | | | INCOME DATA | | | |
| 100.0 | 100.0 | 100.0 | 100.0 | 100.0 | | Net Sales | | 100.0 | 100.0 |
| | | | | | | Gross Profit | | | |
| 94.6 | 93.5 | 89.2 | 92.6 | 82.0 | | Operating Expenses | | 92.2 | 92.9 |
| 5.4 | 6.5 | 10.8 | 7.4 | 18.0 | | Operating Profit | | 7.8 | 7.1 |
| .6 | .3 | .7 | 2.4 | 3.1 | | All Other Expenses (net) | | .8 | 1.5 |
| 4.7 | 6.2 | 10.2 | 4.9 | 15.0 | | Profit Before Taxes | | 7.0 | 5.6 |
| | | | | | | RATIOS | | | |
| 2.8 | 3.7 | 3.1 | 2.3 | 1.8 | | | | 2.6 | 2.8 |
| .9 | 1.4 | 2.0 | 1.4 | 1.1 | | Current | | 1.3 | 1.3 |
| .2 | .9 | 1.3 | .8 | .5 | | | | .9 | .9 |
| 1.8 | 2.4 | 2.7 | 2.2 | 1.6 | | | | 2.3 | 2.3 |
| .9 | 1.3 | 1.7 | 1.1 | 1.0 | | Quick | | 1.2 | 1.2 |
| .2 | .7 | 1.1 | .8 | .5 | | | | .9 | .7 |

| | | | | | | | | | | | | | | | | |
|---|---|---|---|---|---|---|---|---|---|---|---|---|---|---|---|---|
| 0 | UND | 2 | 167.1 | 9 | 39.0 | 9 | 40.7 | 7 | 50.4 | | | Sales/Receivables | 14 | 25.3 | 5 | 79.5 |
| 0 | UND | 21 | 17.3 | 36 | 10.0 | 33 | 11.2 | 26 | 13.9 | | | | 36 | 10.0 | 28 | 13.2 |
| 18 | 20.6 | 69 | 5.3 | 89 | 4.1 | 87 | 4.2 | 70 | 5.2 | | | | 98 | 3.7 | 74 | 4.9 |

| | | | | | | | | |
|---|---|---|---|---|---|---|---|---|
| | | | | | | Cost of Sales/Inventory | | |
| | | | | | | Cost of Sales/Payables | | |

| | | | | | | | | | | | | | | | | |
|---|---|---|---|---|---|---|---|---|---|---|---|---|---|---|---|---|
| 13.1 | | 5.2 | | 3.5 | | 3.8 | | 6.9 | | | | Sales/Working Capital | | 5.4 | | 5.0 |
| NM | | 27.8 | | 7.8 | | 12.0 | | 67.7 | | | | | | 12.5 | | 16.0 |
| -5.9 | | -61.6 | | 16.0 | | -17.1 | | -7.8 | | | | | | -136.4 | | -56.3 |
| | 16.5 | | 45.9 | | 60.7 | | 27.3 | | | | | | | 23.8 | | 25.3 |
| (10) | 5.2 | (17) | 13.5 | (42) | 11.9 | (33) | 4.5 | | | | | EBIT/Interest | (77) | 8.8 | (98) | 5.3 |
| | .8 | | 5.0 | | 2.1 | | 2.5 | | | | | | | 1.1 | | 1.5 |
| | | | | | 15.0 | | | | | | | Net Profit + Depr., Dep., | | 12.3 | | 7.9 |
| | | (11) | 5.8 | | | | | | | | | Amort./Cur. Mat. L/T/D | (13) | 3.1 | (26) | 1.9 |
| | | | 1.7 | | | | | | | | | | | 2.1 | | .5 |
| | .4 | | .3 | | .3 | | .7 | | .4 | | | | | .4 | | .4 |
| | 1.4 | | .7 | | .8 | | 1.2 | | 2.5 | | | Fixed/Worth | | .8 | | .9 |
| | -2.4 | | -7.0 | | 1.6 | | 3.4 | | -1.6 | | | | | 1.8 | | 2.3 |
| | .4 | | .7 | | .6 | | .7 | | .6 | | | | | .6 | | .8 |
| | 48.2 | | 4.0 | | 1.3 | | 2.2 | | 2.8 | | | Debt/Worth | | 1.5 | | 1.5 |
| | -3.9 | | -20.1 | | 2.9 | | 4.6 | | -4.4 | | | | | 4.4 | | 3.9 |
| | 231.3 | | 167.0 | | 71.1 | | 35.5 | | | | | % Profit Before Taxes/Tangible | | 54.7 | | 43.8 |
| (11) | 77.4 | (21) | 47.4 | (56) | 18.5 | (34) | 18.1 | | | | | Net Worth | (91) | 25.4 | (115) | 17.4 |
| | 43.6 | | 16.0 | | 3.9 | | 2.0 | | | | | | | 3.4 | | 2.5 |
| | 49.3 | | 32.7 | | 24.1 | | 9.8 | | 54.0 | | | % Profit Before Taxes/Total | | 20.4 | | 17.7 |
| | 13.2 | | 16.4 | | 8.6 | | 4.9 | | 10.3 | | | Assets | | 8.4 | | 7.1 |
| | -2.2 | | 7.2 | | 2.2 | | 1.1 | | -1.0 | | | | | .3 | | 2.6 |
| | 39.6 | | 73.6 | | 14.8 | | 6.8 | | 36.5 | | | | | 16.4 | | 12.6 |
| | 12.2 | | 25.5 | | 5.0 | | 2.7 | | 7.8 | | | Sales/Net Fixed Assets | | 7.8 | | 4.8 |
| | 4.1 | | 11.2 | | 1.8 | | 1.5 | | 1.9 | | | | | 2.5 | | 2.0 |
| | 5.3 | | 3.8 | | 2.2 | | 1.6 | | 2.7 | | | | | 2.4 | | 2.0 |
| | 3.7 | | 2.3 | | 1.4 | | 1.0 | | .8 | | | Sales/Total Assets | | 1.5 | | 1.3 |
| | 1.9 | | 1.3 | | .7 | | .7 | | .4 | | | | | .8 | | .7 |
| | 1.2 | | .9 | | 1.4 | | 2.1 | | | | | | | 1.6 | | 1.8 |
| (12) | 2.2 | (21) | 1.4 | (52) | 2.5 | (37) | 4.0 | | | | % Depr., Dep., Amort./Sales | (82) | 3.0 | (113) | 3.0 |
| | 5.2 | | 3.5 | | 4.9 | | 5.8 | | | | | | | 4.8 | | 5.4 |
| | | | | | | | | | | | | | | 3.2 | | 3.9 |
| | | | | | | | | | | | | % Officers', Directors' | (21) | 6.5 | (24) | 8.9 |
| | | | | | | | | | | | | Owners' Comp/Sales | | 11.9 | | 19.0 |

| | | | | | | | | | |
|---|---|---|---|---|---|---|---|---|---|
| 15209M | 100645M | 471681M | 1002585M | 1028856M | 913908M | Net Sales ($) | | 2092588M | 2394547M |
| 3557M | 33142M | 292197M | 849502M | 663195M | 802717M | Total Assets ($) | | 1726497M | 2247452M |

M = $ thousand　　MM = $ million
See Pages 9 through 22 for Explanation of Ratios and Data

## Comparative Historical Data / Current Data Sorted by Sales

| Type of Statement | | | | | | | | | | |
|---|---|---|---|---|---|---|---|---|---|---|
| | 65 | 63 | 70 | Unqualified | 2 | 11 | 8 | 14 | 17 | 18 |
| | 1 | 2 | 2 | Reviewed | | | 1 | | 1 | |
| | 9 | 6 | 7 | Compiled | 3 | 1 | 1 | | 2 | |
| | 11 | 9 | 21 | Tax Returns | 10 | 4 | 2 | 3 | 2 | |
| | 51 | 59 | 60 | Other | 7 | 12 | 7 | 14 | 11 | 9 |
| | 4/1/09-3/31/10 ALL | 4/1/10-3/31/11 ALL | 4/1/11-3/31/12 ALL | | 0-1MM | 1-3MM (62, 4/1-9/30/11) | 3-5MM | 5-10MM | 10-25MM (98, 10/1/11-3/31/12) | 25MM & OVER |
| **NUMBER OF STATEMENTS** | 137 | 139 | 160 | | 22 | 28 | 19 | 31 | 33 | 27 |
| | % | % | % | **ASSETS** | % | % | % | % | % | % |
| Cash & Equivalents | 20.8 | 22.2 | 21.2 | | 18.9 | 18.9 | 26.8 | 19.2 | 28.5 | 15.1 |
| Trade Receivables (net) | 17.9 | 19.3 | 19.8 | | 16.0 | 24.1 | 16.3 | 22.7 | 19.3 | 18.5 |
| Inventory | 1.7 | 1.7 | 2.0 | | 1.5 | 2.4 | 2.3 | 1.5 | 3.2 | .7 |
| All Other Current | 4.1 | 4.0 | 3.5 | | .3 | 2.8 | 1.6 | 7.6 | 1.4 | 5.8 |
| Total Current | 44.4 | 47.2 | 46.5 | | 36.7 | 48.2 | 46.9 | 51.1 | 52.3 | 40.1 |
| Fixed Assets (net) | 34.8 | 35.4 | 35.0 | | 47.7 | 36.2 | 33.3 | 32.1 | 29.8 | 34.6 |
| Intangibles (net) | 9.2 | 7.8 | 9.5 | | 10.3 | 7.0 | 10.4 | 9.8 | 10.9 | 8.8 |
| All Other Non-Current | 11.5 | 9.7 | 8.9 | | 5.4 | 8.6 | 9.3 | 7.0 | 7.0 | 16.5 |
| Total | 100.0 | 100.0 | 100.0 | | 100.0 | 100.0 | 100.0 | 100.0 | 100.0 | 100.0 |
| | | | | **LIABILITIES** | | | | | | |
| Notes Payable-Short Term | 3.1 | 4.5 | 3.6 | | 9.0 | 3.7 | 3.4 | 2.6 | 1.7 | 2.6 |
| Cur. Mat.-L.T.D. | 3.7 | 2.5 | 2.0 | | 2.9 | 1.6 | 2.4 | .9 | 2.3 | 2.4 |
| Trade Payables | 6.9 | 8.2 | 5.5 | | 8.5 | 2.8 | 4.3 | 7.0 | 4.6 | 6.2 |
| Income Taxes Payable | .5 | .2 | .5 | | .0 | 1.2 | .8 | .3 | .7 | .2 |
| All Other Current | 20.3 | 25.5 | 25.0 | | 32.7 | 23.1 | 15.2 | 24.6 | 24.4 | 28.9 |
| Total Current | 34.6 | 40.9 | 36.7 | | 53.1 | 32.5 | 26.0 | 35.4 | 33.7 | 40.3 |
| Long-Term Debt | 16.1 | 16.7 | 16.1 | | 29.0 | 19.8 | 10.7 | 10.7 | 12.3 | 16.5 |
| Deferred Taxes | .2 | .3 | .4 | | .0 | .0 | .3 | .1 | 1.1 | .9 |
| All Other Non-Current | 7.6 | 6.7 | 9.8 | | 12.5 | 9.5 | 15.2 | 3.2 | 3.7 | 19.2 |
| Net Worth | 41.4 | 35.5 | 36.9 | | 5.5 | 38.2 | 47.7 | 50.6 | 49.2 | 23.1 |
| Total Liabilties & Net Worth | 100.0 | 100.0 | 100.0 | | 100.0 | 100.0 | 100.0 | 100.0 | 100.0 | 100.0 |
| | | | | **INCOME DATA** | | | | | | |
| Net Sales | 100.0 | 100.0 | 100.0 | | 100.0 | 100.0 | 100.0 | 100.0 | 100.0 | 100.0 |
| Gross Profit | | | | | | | | | | |
| Operating Expenses | 88.4 | 89.0 | 90.9 | | 91.9 | 88.9 | 94.4 | 89.8 | 92.3 | 89.3 |
| Operating Profit | 11.6 | 11.0 | 9.1 | | 8.1 | 11.1 | 5.6 | 10.2 | 7.7 | 10.7 |
| All Other Expenses (net) | 2.2 | 1.6 | 1.2 | | 1.9 | 1.5 | .9 | .9 | .9 | 1.3 |
| Profit Before Taxes | 9.4 | 9.4 | 7.9 | | 6.2 | 9.6 | 4.7 | 9.3 | 6.8 | 9.4 |
| | | | | **RATIOS** | | | | | | |
| Current | 2.1 | 2.5 | 2.8 | | 4.6 | 3.2 | 5.9 | 2.7 | 3.1 | 1.6 |
| | 1.3 | 1.3 | 1.5 | | 1.5 | 1.6 | 2.1 | 1.4 | 1.7 | 1.2 |
| | .9 | .9 | .9 | | .2 | 1.0 | .7 | 1.1 | 1.2 | .8 |
| Quick | 1.9 | 2.1 | 2.2 | | 4.6 | 2.1 | 5.9 | 2.1 | 3.0 | 1.3 |
| | (136) 1.2 | 1.1 | 1.4 | | 1.4 | 1.5 | 1.8 | 1.2 | 1.6 | 1.0 |
| | .7 | .7 | .8 | | .2 | 1.0 | .6 | .9 | 1.0 | .7 |
| Sales/Receivables | 8 / 43.2 | 7 / 51.4 | 5 / 78.8 | | 0 UND | 3 / 106.5 | 3 / 105.9 | 5 / 72.2 | 16 / 23.0 | 14 / 25.2 |
| | 28 / 13.2 | 30 / 12.1 | 30 / 12.3 | | 0 UND | 35 / 10.4 | 24 / 15.4 | 33 / 11.1 | 33 / 11.1 | 43 / 8.5 |
| | 68 / 5.3 | 85 / 4.3 | 69 / 5.3 | | 19 / 19.5 | 85 / 4.3 | 89 / 4.1 | 89 / 4.1 | 62 / 5.9 | 70 / 5.2 |
| Cost of Sales/Inventory | | | | | | | | | | |
| Cost of Sales/Payables | | | | | | | | | | |
| Sales/Working Capital | 4.7 | 4.9 | 4.4 | | 6.0 | 3.6 | 3.5 | 5.8 | 4.3 | 8.0 |
| | 11.5 | 18.1 | 11.8 | | 20.5 | 7.0 | 8.2 | 8.9 | 8.3 | 29.5 |
| | -100.2 | -32.1 | -82.3 | | -6.1 | 141.1 | -15.0 | 135.7 | 24.3 | -13.4 |
| EBIT/Interest | 23.9 | 42.0 | 36.3 | | 16.5 | 120.1 | 9.8 | 41.3 | 75.6 | 51.0 |
| | (100) 7.3 | (111) 11.1 | (113) 6.9 | | (14) 5.2 | (17) 4.4 | (10) 7.5 | (24) 9.3 | (26) 25.7 | (22) 6.1 |
| | 3.1 | 3.1 | 2.5 | | -2.0 | 2.0 | 3.9 | 2.6 | 2.7 | 2.6 |
| Net Profit + Depr., Dep., Amort./Cur. Mat. L/T/D | 17.1 | 27.1 | 11.5 | | | | | | 12.2 | |
| | (22) 5.4 | (16) 8.6 | (25) 5.4 | | | | | | (11) 9.8 | |
| | 2.8 | 3.1 | 1.6 | | | | | | 2.0 | |
| Fixed/Worth | .4 | .4 | .4 | | .7 | .3 | .3 | .3 | .3 | .5 |
| | .8 | .9 | .9 | | 2.0 | .7 | .6 | .9 | .9 | 1.1 |
| | 2.1 | 1.9 | 3.7 | | -2.0 | 2.8 | 1.5 | 1.2 | 2.5 | 4.1 |
| Debt/Worth | .7 | .8 | .6 | | .4 | .8 | .5 | .4 | .6 | 1.3 |
| | 1.6 | 1.5 | 1.9 | | 8.1 | 2.0 | 1.0 | 1.0 | 1.8 | 2.5 |
| | 4.1 | 3.8 | 6.2 | | -3.2 | 5.8 | 3.8 | 4.5 | 4.2 | 6.7 |
| % Profit Before Taxes/Tangible Net Worth | 55.7 | 68.5 | 71.1 | | 179.9 | 48.0 | 42.1 | 80.1 | 73.4 | 76.8 |
| | (118) 19.4 | (118) 32.7 | (132) 28.4 | | (14) 72.0 | (23) 15.3 | (17) 12.8 | (27) 18.7 | (29) 26.8 | (22) 36.2 |
| | 5.1 | 8.2 | 6.7 | | 23.4 | 3.9 | -11.1 | 3.6 | 12.5 | 13.1 |
| % Profit Before Taxes/Total Assets | 17.7 | 22.1 | 24.9 | | 42.3 | 25.5 | 24.1 | 22.4 | 24.7 | 33.1 |
| | 7.3 | 11.0 | 7.7 | | 7.0 | 7.5 | 4.5 | 11.3 | 8.6 | 7.9 |
| | 1.8 | 3.9 | 1.9 | | -1.9 | 1.9 | -4.9 | 1.9 | 2.5 | 4.2 |
| Sales/Net Fixed Assets | 15.1 | 14.1 | 18.9 | | 28.6 | 26.0 | 22.5 | 30.1 | 20.9 | 11.2 |
| | 5.4 | 5.2 | 7.1 | | 6.3 | 11.4 | 6.5 | 6.9 | 7.2 | 7.0 |
| | 1.8 | 1.9 | 2.1 | | 2.0 | .8 | 2.1 | 1.8 | 3.0 | 2.6 |
| Sales/Total Assets | 1.9 | 2.2 | 2.5 | | 4.4 | 2.1 | 2.6 | 2.5 | 2.5 | 2.1 |
| | 1.3 | 1.3 | 1.5 | | 2.1 | 1.2 | 1.7 | 1.3 | 1.5 | 1.6 |
| | .7 | .8 | .9 | | .8 | .5 | .9 | .8 | 1.0 | .9 |
| % Depr., Dep., Amort./Sales | 1.5 | 2.0 | 1.5 | | 1.4 | 1.6 | 2.1 | 1.2 | 1.0 | 1.8 |
| | (119) 3.0 | (108) 3.4 | (133) 2.8 | | (17) 2.9 | (21) 4.9 | (15) 2.5 | (24) 2.9 | (31) 2.1 | (25) 3.0 |
| | 5.3 | 5.3 | 4.9 | | 8.2 | 9.6 | 4.8 | 4.3 | 4.6 | 4.6 |
| % Officers', Directors' Owners' Comp/Sales | 4.2 | 4.4 | 3.4 | | | | | | | |
| | (16) 10.4 | (22) 10.9 | (28) 10.3 | | | | | | | |
| | 25.0 | 21.0 | 17.8 | | | | | | | |
| Net Sales ($) | 4543889M | 5677882M | 3532884M | | 11067M | 56192M | 74755M | 232937M | 527158M | 2630775M |
| Total Assets ($) | 3058990M | 3449402M | 2644310M | | 14708M | 73123M | 64968M | 260726M | 476616M | 1754169M |

M = $ thousand   MM = $ million
See Pages 9 through 22 for Explanation of Ratios and Data

## Current Data Sorted by Assets      Comparative Historical Data

| 0-500M | 500M-2MM | 2-10MM | 10-50MM | 50-100MM | 100-250MM | | 4/1/07-3/31/08 ALL | 4/1/08-3/31/09 ALL |
|---|---|---|---|---|---|---|---|---|
| | | | | | | **Type of Statement** | | |
| 2 | 1 | 19 | 15 | 2 | 1 | Unqualified | 27 | 32 |
| | | 3 | | | | Reviewed | 1 | 1 |
| 1 | 1 | 1 | | | | Compiled | 1 | 1 |
| 9 | 7 | 1 | | | | Tax Returns | 7 | 8 |
| 8 | 4 | 5 | 5 | 1 | 1 | Other | 13 | 13 |
| 49 (4/1-9/30/11) | | | 38 (10/1/11-3/31/12) | | | | | |
| 20 | 13 | 29 | 20 | 3 | 2 | **NUMBER OF STATEMENTS** | 49 | 55 |
| % | % | % | % | % | % | **ASSETS** | % | % |
| 37.4 | 13.5 | 12.1 | 19.2 | | | Cash & Equivalents | 20.8 | 20.4 |
| 1.2 | 4.1 | 11.2 | 3.8 | | | Trade Receivables (net) | 6.0 | 4.9 |
| 1.5 | 1.0 | .9 | .7 | | | Inventory | 1.4 | .8 |
| 3.2 | .1 | 4.2 | 1.0 | | | All Other Current | 2.5 | 3.2 |
| 43.4 | 18.7 | 28.3 | 24.6 | | | Total Current | 30.6 | 29.4 |
| 42.2 | 49.7 | 59.5 | 54.2 | | | Fixed Assets (net) | 49.5 | 53.1 |
| 7.3 | 1.2 | 1.0 | .9 | | | Intangibles (net) | 2.8 | 2.7 |
| 6.7 | 30.5 | 11.2 | 20.3 | | | All Other Non-Current | 17.1 | 14.8 |
| 100.0 | 100.0 | 100.0 | 100.0 | | | Total | 100.0 | 100.0 |
| | | | | | | **LIABILITIES** | | |
| 6.6 | 7.2 | 4.1 | .7 | | | Notes Payable-Short Term | 3.6 | 8.1 |
| 3.4 | 2.4 | 2.9 | 1.4 | | | Cur. Mat.-L.T.D. | .9 | 1.8 |
| 7.5 | 2.0 | 3.5 | 2.2 | | | Trade Payables | 6.9 | 2.7 |
| .0 | 4.4 | 1.9 | .0 | | | Income Taxes Payable | .0 | .2 |
| 19.9 | 13.8 | 7.4 | 10.1 | | | All Other Current | 7.4 | 14.5 |
| 37.3 | 29.8 | 19.9 | 14.4 | | | Total Current | 18.9 | 27.3 |
| 22.5 | 30.0 | 19.2 | 27.7 | | | Long-Term Debt | 25.3 | 19.2 |
| .0 | .0 | .0 | .0 | | | Deferred Taxes | .0 | .0 |
| 34.0 | 2.5 | 5.4 | 1.2 | | | All Other Non-Current | 6.5 | 5.4 |
| 6.4 | 37.7 | 55.5 | 56.7 | | | Net Worth | 49.3 | 48.1 |
| 100.0 | 100.0 | 100.0 | 100.0 | | | Total Liabilities & Net Worth | 100.0 | 100.0 |
| | | | | | | **INCOME DATA** | | |
| 100.0 | 100.0 | 100.0 | 100.0 | | | Net Sales | 100.0 | 100.0 |
| | | | | | | Gross Profit | | |
| 92.5 | 81.6 | 93.4 | 98.1 | | | Operating Expenses | 91.2 | 93.8 |
| 7.5 | 18.4 | 6.6 | 1.9 | | | Operating Profit | 8.8 | 6.2 |
| 4.4 | 10.0 | .7 | 1.8 | | | All Other Expenses (net) | 1.9 | 3.1 |
| 3.1 | 8.5 | 5.9 | .1 | | | Profit Before Taxes | 6.9 | 3.1 |
| | | | | | | **RATIOS** | | |
| 3.2 | 1.0 | 3.3 | 5.1 | | | | 5.0 | 4.1 |
| 1.2 | .4 | 1.4 | 1.6 | | | Current | 1.7 | .9 |
| .4 | .2 | .6 | .7 | | | | .6 | .6 |
| 3.1 | 1.0 | 2.3 | 5.1 | | | | 4.3 | 2.7 |
| 1.1 | .3 | 1.1 | 1.6 | | | Quick | 1.6 | .8 |
| .4 | .1 | .5 | .7 | | | | .5 | .5 |
| 0 UND | 0 UND | 1 278.4 | 1 404.5 | | | | 0 UND | 0 UND |
| 0 UND | 0 UND | 7 52.3 | 5 76.9 | | | Sales/Receivables | 5 76.1 | 4 84.9 |
| 2 236.8 | 7 52.2 | 41 8.8 | 38 9.5 | | | | 28 13.3 | 29 12.7 |
| | | | | | | Cost of Sales/Inventory | | |
| | | | | | | Cost of Sales/Payables | | |
| 24.6 | NM | 5.8 | 2.3 | | | | 4.1 | 4.8 |
| 77.0 | -12.2 | 17.3 | 7.1 | | | Sales/Working Capital | 24.6 | -58.2 |
| -12.0 | -5.7 | -13.9 | -32.9 | | | | -18.7 | -11.1 |
| | | 22.2 | 24.5 | | | | 14.6 | 12.1 |
| | (27) 1.8 | | (17) 7.9 | | | EBIT/Interest | (29) 4.4 | (41) 2.6 |
| | | .5 | -.9 | | | | 1.0 | -1.6 |
| | | | | | | Net Profit + Depr., Dep., Amort./Cur. Mat. L/T/D | | |
| .1 | .2 | .7 | .6 | | | | .4 | .4 |
| 1.2 | 1.6 | 1.1 | .8 | | | Fixed/Worth | .8 | 1.1 |
| -4.2 | 3.9 | 1.7 | 1.6 | | | | 2.0 | 2.0 |
| .8 | .7 | .3 | .3 | | | | .2 | .2 |
| 4.5 | 2.6 | .8 | .5 | | | Debt/Worth | .5 | .8 |
| -5.8 | 6.1 | 1.9 | 2.1 | | | | 2.9 | 3.5 |
| 528.9 | 95.6 | 20.3 | 20.9 | | | | 39.8 | 39.5 |
| (13) 39.2 | 26.2 | (27) 4.6 | (18) 5.5 | | | % Profit Before Taxes/Tangible Net Worth | (43) 8.3 | (51) 4.9 |
| -2.9 | -2.1 | -2.6 | -3.1 | | | | .3 | -3.2 |
| 29.6 | 18.6 | 11.1 | 7.3 | | | | 17.8 | 13.8 |
| 8.8 | 7.3 | 1.9 | 2.4 | | | % Profit Before Taxes/Total Assets | 6.5 | 1.4 |
| -2.3 | -.7 | -1.9 | -1.7 | | | | .1 | -2.8 |
| 877.0 | 19.0 | 4.0 | 3.3 | | | | 11.7 | 5.1 |
| 29.1 | 8.1 | 1.1 | 1.1 | | | Sales/Net Fixed Assets | 1.7 | 1.3 |
| 1.7 | .3 | .6 | .5 | | | | .9 | .7 |
| 13.1 | 1.7 | 1.8 | .8 | | | | 2.2 | 1.8 |
| 3.8 | 1.1 | .8 | .5 | | | Sales/Total Assets | 1.0 | .9 |
| 1.1 | .3 | .5 | .4 | | | | .5 | .4 |
| | 1.4 | 3.0 | 3.4 | | | | 2.1 | 2.3 |
| | (11) 2.2 | (27) 4.9 | (19) 5.2 | | | % Depr., Dep., Amort./Sales | (38) 4.0 | (46) 4.6 |
| | 19.8 | 7.0 | 8.0 | | | | 6.2 | 6.7 |
| | | | | | | % Officers', Directors' Owners' Comp/Sales | | 4.7 |
| | | | | | | | (10) | 6.6 |
| | | | | | | | | 12.0 |
| 10999M | 19458M | 168363M | 296668M | 361153M | 115269M | Net Sales ($) | 253299M | 535418M |
| 3271M | 14009M | 149437M | 396701M | 223798M | 396479M | Total Assets ($) | 585768M | 744299M |

M = $ thousand    MM = $ million
See Pages 9 through 22 for Explanation of Ratios and Data

## Comparative Historical Data | Current Data Sorted by Sales

| | | | Type of Statement | | | | | | |
|---|---|---|---|---|---|---|---|---|---|
| 28 | 30 | 40 | Unqualified | 2 | 8 | 8 | 10 | 8 | 4 |
| 1 | 1 | 3 | Reviewed | | 2 | | 1 | | |
| 2 | 2 | 3 | Compiled | 1 | | 2 | | | |
| 10 | 11 | 17 | Tax Returns | 13 | 4 | | | | |
| 15 | 18 | 24 | Other | 10 | 3 | 4 | 2 | 1 | 4 |
| 4/1/09-3/31/10 | 4/1/10-3/31/11 | 4/1/11-3/31/12 | | | 49 (4/1-9/30/11) | | 38 (10/1/11-3/31/12) | | |
| ALL | ALL | ALL | | 0-1MM | 1-3MM | 3-5MM | 5-10MM | 10-25MM | 25MM & OVER |
| 56 | 62 | 87 | NUMBER OF STATEMENTS | 26 | 17 | 14 | 13 | 9 | 8 |
| % | % | % | ASSETS | % | % | % | % | % | % |
| 22.2 | 19.7 | 19.3 | Cash & Equivalents | 27.9 | 15.0 | 13.0 | 16.6 | | |
| 8.4 | 9.4 | 5.6 | Trade Receivables (net) | 2.4 | 1.6 | 10.8 | 7.1 | | |
| 2.8 | .5 | 1.0 | Inventory | 1.1 | .8 | .2 | 1.6 | | |
| 2.5 | .6 | 2.4 | All Other Current | 2.4 | .8 | 1.2 | 1.4 | | |
| 36.0 | 30.1 | 28.2 | Total Current | 33.9 | 18.3 | 25.2 | 26.6 | | |
| 42.6 | 49.8 | 52.3 | Fixed Assets (net) | 51.3 | 54.0 | 56.6 | 56.6 | | |
| 2.1 | 1.8 | 2.4 | Intangibles (net) | 2.3 | 7.2 | .5 | .3 | | |
| 19.2 | 18.2 | 17.0 | All Other Non-Current | 12.2 | 20.5 | 17.8 | 16.5 | | |
| 100.0 | 100.0 | 100.0 | Total | 100.0 | 100.0 | 100.0 | 100.0 | | |
| | | | LIABILITIES | | | | | | |
| 5.4 | 1.7 | 4.2 | Notes Payable-Short Term | 5.3 | 7.4 | .7 | 1.3 | | |
| 1.1 | 1.6 | 2.5 | Cur. Mat.-L.T.D. | 2.2 | 4.0 | 2.5 | 1.8 | | |
| 6.0 | 2.5 | 3.9 | Trade Payables | 3.1 | 6.0 | 2.1 | 4.6 | | |
| .9 | 1.9 | 1.3 | Income Taxes Payable | .4 | 2.8 | 3.2 | .0 | | |
| 12.7 | 12.5 | 11.7 | All Other Current | 14.5 | 9.7 | 9.9 | 6.3 | | |
| 26.0 | 20.2 | 23.6 | Total Current | 25.4 | 29.9 | 18.4 | 14.0 | | |
| 16.9 | 34.8 | 23.7 | Long-Term Debt | 30.7 | 13.7 | 33.4 | 18.9 | | |
| .0 | .0 | .0 | Deferred Taxes | .0 | .0 | .0 | .0 | | |
| 4.9 | 1.9 | 10.5 | All Other Non-Current | 27.4 | 2.2 | 1.8 | 2.4 | | |
| 52.2 | 43.1 | 42.2 | Net Worth | 16.6 | 54.1 | 46.4 | 64.6 | | |
| 100.0 | 100.0 | 100.0 | Total Liabilities & Net Worth | 100.0 | 100.0 | 100.0 | 100.0 | | |
| | | | INCOME DATA | | | | | | |
| 100.0 | 100.0 | 100.0 | Net Sales | 100.0 | 100.0 | 100.0 | 100.0 | | |
| | | | Gross Profit | | | | | | |
| 94.7 | 92.9 | 92.6 | Operating Expenses | 84.1 | 95.3 | 95.1 | 99.4 | | |
| 5.3 | 7.1 | 7.4 | Operating Profit | 15.9 | 4.7 | 4.9 | .6 | | |
| 1.3 | 2.3 | 2.9 | All Other Expenses (net) | 9.0 | -1.7 | 4.6 | -.5 | | |
| 4.0 | 4.8 | 4.5 | Profit Before Taxes | 6.9 | 6.4 | .4 | 1.1 | | |
| | | | RATIOS | | | | | | |
| 6.7 | 4.0 | 3.3 | | 2.7 | 1.9 | 2.3 | 6.9 | | |
| 1.3 | 1.5 | 1.2 | Current | 1.2 | .8 | .8 | 3.8 | | |
| .9 | .5 | .6 | | .4 | .4 | .6 | .7 | | |
| 5.3 | 3.6 | 2.7 | | 2.6 | 1.3 | 2.3 | 5.8 | | |
| 1.1 | 1.4 | 1.1 | Quick | 1.1 | .7 | .7 | 3.3 | | |
| .5 | .4 | .5 | | .3 | .3 | .5 | .7 | | |
| 0 UND | 0 UND | 0 UND | | 0 UND | 0 UND | 2 234.5 | 0 UND | | |
| 4 93.3 | 4 90.1 | 3 110.3 | Sales/Receivables | 0 UND | 2 159.6 | 14 25.2 | 3 109.5 | | |
| 31 11.9 | 37 9.9 | 16 23.5 | | 1 347.5 | 7 51.6 | 62 5.9 | 62 5.9 | | |
| | | | Cost of Sales/Inventory | | | | | | |
| | | | Cost of Sales/Payables | | | | | | |
| 5.0 | 5.4 | 6.1 | | 10.7 | 56.3 | 5.7 | 2.3 | | |
| 28.7 | 37.2 | 49.4 | Sales/Working Capital | 54.1 | -17.1 | -32.6 | 3.3 | | |
| -96.9 | -13.9 | -11.5 | | -9.7 | -7.2 | -10.8 | NM | | |
| 14.0 | 21.6 | 24.3 | | 12.5 | 31.6 | 11.5 | 22.2 | | |
| (35) 3.9 | (42) 5.7 | (62) 5.0 | EBIT/Interest | (11) 4.0 | (14) 2.0 | (11) 1.5 | (11) 7.9 | | |
| -.4 | .6 | .7 | | 1.2 | -.9 | .2 | -1.7 | | |
| | | | Net Profit + Depr., Dep., Amort./Cur. Mat. L/T/D | | | | | | |
| .3 | .3 | .5 | | .1 | .4 | .4 | .7 | | |
| .8 | 1.1 | 1.0 | Fixed/Worth | 1.4 | 1.1 | 1.4 | .8 | | |
| 1.7 | 2.3 | 2.1 | | 6.6 | 2.1 | 2.0 | 1.2 | | |
| .2 | .3 | .4 | | .8 | .3 | .3 | .2 | | |
| .6 | .9 | 1.0 | Debt/Worth | 2.7 | .6 | .9 | .3 | | |
| 2.3 | 2.6 | 3.7 | | 55.1 | 4.8 | NM | 1.3 | | |
| 47.5 | 37.6 | 30.5 | % Profit Before Taxes/Tangible Net Worth | 92.0 | 26.2 | 20.3 | 22.0 | | |
| (52) 10.0 | (57) 12.6 | (76) 6.9 | | (21) 26.3 | (15) 3.6 | (11) -1.6 | 6.0 | | |
| -5.4 | -3.0 | -2.1 | | -2.9 | -2.2 | -2.9 | -5.1 | | |
| 21.9 | 18.4 | 16.6 | % Profit Before Taxes/Total Assets | 26.4 | 20.1 | 16.3 | 7.6 | | |
| 5.6 | 4.8 | 2.7 | | 2.4 | 3.3 | -.8 | 2.8 | | |
| -3.0 | -2.0 | -1.5 | | -1.7 | -1.6 | -1.6 | -4.5 | | |
| 21.7 | 15.5 | 9.0 | Sales/Net Fixed Assets | 79.6 | 29.9 | 9.9 | 4.2 | | |
| 5.8 | 2.2 | 1.5 | | 3.7 | 1.2 | 1.2 | 1.1 | | |
| 1.2 | .9 | .6 | | .2 | .6 | .6 | .6 | | |
| 3.3 | 2.7 | 2.3 | Sales/Total Assets | 4.4 | 1.7 | 1.8 | .9 | | |
| 1.4 | 1.0 | .9 | | 1.1 | .8 | .8 | .7 | | |
| .7 | .5 | .4 | | .2 | .4 | .4 | .5 | | |
| 1.5 | 1.7 | 2.4 | % Depr., Dep., Amort./Sales | 1.4 | 3.4 | 2.5 | 2.5 | | |
| (43) 3.0 | (43) 4.0 | (69) 4.9 | | (17) 7.5 | (12) 5.0 | (13) 5.4 | 4.1 | | |
| 5.1 | 6.4 | 7.9 | | 21.4 | 9.4 | 6.8 | 8.1 | | |
| | 3.7 | 6.0 | % Officers', Directors' Owners' Comp/Sales | | | | | | |
| | (11) 4.3 | (13) 10.8 | | | | | | | |
| | | 16.3 | | 13.1 | | | | | |
| 517202M | 655601M | 971910M | Net Sales ($) | 10404M | 32363M | 58969M | 93656M | 134195M | 642323M |
| 497496M | 670891M | 1183695M | Total Assets ($) | 16991M | 54640M | 107617M | 153547M | 226638M | 624262M |

M = $ thousand    MM = $ million
See Pages 9 through 22 for Explanation of Ratios and Data

## Current Data Sorted by Assets          Comparative Historical Data

| | 1 | 2 | 2 | | | | Type of Statement | 2 | 3 |
|---|---|---|---|---|---|---|---|---|---|
| | | | | | | | Unqualified | | 2 |
| | 3 | 2 | | | | | Reviewed | | |
| | 7 | 7 | 5 | | | | Compiled | 5 | 2 |
| | 7 | 7 | 4 | | | | Tax Returns | 4 | 2 |
| | 7 | 7 | | | | | Other | 9 | 8 |
| | | 8 (4/1-9/30/11) | | 39 (10/1/11-3/31/12) | | | | 4/1/07-3/31/08 ALL | 4/1/08-3/31/09 ALL |
| | 0-500M | 500M-2MM | 2-10MM | 10-50MM | 50-100MM | 100-250MM | | | |
| NUMBER OF STATEMENTS | 18 | 16 | 13 | | | | | 20 | 17 |
| | % | % | % | % | % | % | **ASSETS** | % | % |
| | 32.1 | 13.9 | 19.5 | D | D | D | Cash & Equivalents | 18.7 | 13.9 |
| | 5.2 | 9.1 | 9.4 | A | A | A | Trade Receivables (net) | 4.6 | 7.8 |
| | 1.6 | 4.8 | 1.8 | T | T | T | Inventory | 8.3 | 12.1 |
| | 6.1 | 5.5 | 2.6 | A | A | A | All Other Current | 4.2 | 1.9 |
| | 45.0 | 33.4 | 33.2 | | | | Total Current | 35.7 | 35.8 |
| | 46.3 | 41.0 | 56.6 | N | N | N | Fixed Assets (net) | 52.8 | 40.9 |
| | 1.2 | 1.3 | 5.2 | O | O | O | Intangibles (net) | 1.0 | 9.1 |
| | 7.6 | 24.4 | 5.0 | T | T | T | All Other Non-Current | 10.4 | 14.2 |
| | 100.0 | 100.0 | 100.0 | | | | Total | 100.0 | 100.0 |
| | | | | A | A | A | **LIABILITIES** | | |
| | 17.1 | 2.8 | .8 | V | V | V | Notes Payable-Short Term | 11.6 | 19.4 |
| | 1.0 | 3.7 | 11.1 | A | A | A | Cur. Mat.-L.T.D. | 4.3 | 6.8 |
| | 4.2 | 3.5 | 1.5 | I | I | I | Trade Payables | 6.8 | 9.8 |
| | .0 | .0 | 5.5 | L | L | L | Income Taxes Payable | .0 | .0 |
| | 22.2 | 17.1 | 11.9 | A | A | A | All Other Current | 13.8 | 24.6 |
| | 44.5 | 27.1 | 30.7 | B | B | B | Total Current | 36.4 | 60.6 |
| | 32.2 | 35.9 | 32.5 | L | L | L | Long-Term Debt | 32.1 | 30.9 |
| | .0 | .0 | .0 | E | E | E | Deferred Taxes | .2 | .0 |
| | 17.8 | 2.7 | 11.2 | | | | All Other Non-Current | 11.4 | 24.5 |
| | 5.6 | 34.3 | 25.5 | | | | Net Worth | 19.8 | -16.0 |
| | 100.0 | 100.0 | 100.0 | | | | Total Liabilities & Net Worth | 100.0 | 100.0 |
| | | | | | | | **INCOME DATA** | | |
| | 100.0 | 100.0 | 100.0 | | | | Net Sales | 100.0 | 100.0 |
| | | | | | | | Gross Profit | | |
| | 93.3 | 86.2 | 83.7 | | | | Operating Expenses | 90.4 | 94.7 |
| | 6.7 | 13.8 | 16.3 | | | | Operating Profit | 9.6 | 5.3 |
| | 1.3 | 3.5 | 6.6 | | | | All Other Expenses (net) | 6.3 | 3.2 |
| | 5.4 | 10.3 | 9.7 | | | | Profit Before Taxes | 3.3 | 2.1 |
| | | | | | | | **RATIOS** | | |
| | 3.5 | 4.2 | 4.9 | | | | | 1.6 | 1.8 |
| | 1.3 | 1.3 | 1.1 | | | | Current | .6 | .5 |
| | .3 | .5 | .5 | | | | | .1 | .2 |
| | 3.5 | 2.7 | 4.8 | | | | | 1.3 | 1.3 |
| | 1.1 | .5 | 1.0 | | | | Quick | .4 | .2 |
| | .2 | .2 | .4 | | | | | .1 | .1 |
| | 0 UND | 0 UND | 0 UND | | | | | 0 UND | 0 UND |
| | 0 UND | 2 169.7 | 1 348.6 | | | | Sales/Receivables | 0 UND | 2 192.6 |
| | 0 UND | 18 20.4 | 40 9.1 | | | | | 4 90.4 | 29 12.5 |
| | | | | | | | Cost of Sales/Inventory | | |
| | | | | | | | Cost of Sales/Payables | | |
| | 12.3 | 6.2 | 3.8 | | | | | 17.4 | 26.8 |
| | 185.7 | 129.4 | 47.9 | | | | Sales/Working Capital | -23.7 | -16.7 |
| | -9.1 | -10.2 | -3.4 | | | | | -6.0 | -3.4 |
| | 24.4 | | | | | | | 9.2 | 19.8 |
| | (10) 4.9 | | | | | | EBIT/Interest | (13) 2.1 | (14) 2.0 |
| | -.3 | | | | | | | .1 | .4 |
| | | | | | | | Net Profit + Depr., Dep., Amort./Cur. Mat. L/T/D | | |
| | .2 | .1 | 1.1 | | | | | .3 | .4 |
| | 1.1 | 1.9 | 2.6 | | | | Fixed/Worth | 2.7 | 2.3 |
| | -2.5 | -16.9 | 520.2 | | | | | 18.3 | -.5 |
| | .3 | .2 | 1.0 | | | | | 1.4 | 1.2 |
| | 1.9 | 3.3 | 3.9 | | | | Debt/Worth | 4.2 | 3.9 |
| | -3.9 | -28.1 | 523.6 | | | | | NM | -1.8 |
| | 58.9 | 76.3 | 173.3 | | | | % Profit Before Taxes/Tangible Net Worth | 84.6 | 72.5 |
| | (11) 48.0 | (11) 14.9 | (11) 21.6 | | | | | (15) 42.2 | (10) 17.2 |
| | 17.6 | -1.2 | 3.4 | | | | | -22.0 | -2.5 |
| | 31.2 | 11.4 | 17.8 | | | | % Profit Before Taxes/Total Assets | 21.3 | 13.4 |
| | 16.5 | 4.8 | 4.3 | | | | | 4.8 | 4.0 |
| | 1.9 | -3.0 | 1.5 | | | | | -2.2 | -3.6 |
| | 199.9 | 108.4 | 14.5 | | | | | 45.1 | 67.9 |
| | 8.8 | 10.1 | .6 | | | | Sales/Net Fixed Assets | 5.9 | 7.9 |
| | 3.5 | .9 | .3 | | | | | .8 | 1.1 |
| | 6.2 | 2.9 | 1.6 | | | | | 4.6 | 3.4 |
| | 3.2 | 1.1 | .5 | | | | Sales/Total Assets | 2.1 | 1.5 |
| | 1.8 | .5 | .2 | | | | | .8 | .9 |
| | 1.3 | | 3.9 | | | | | .9 | 2.2 |
| | (11) 1.8 | | (10) 7.9 | | | | % Depr., Dep., Amort./Sales | (13) 3.7 | (12) 4.4 |
| | 8.6 | | 16.0 | | | | | 8.3 | 10.2 |
| | 2.8 | | | | | | | | |
| | (10) 5.9 | | | | | | % Officers', Directors' Owners' Comp/Sales | | |
| | 12.8 | | | | | | | | |
| | 20039M | 45000M | 58676M | | | | Net Sales ($) | 33938M | 89823M |
| | 4052M | 18635M | 62695M | | | | Total Assets ($) | 28031M | 98665M |

M = $ thousand   MM = $ million
See Pages 9 through 22 for Explanation of Ratios and Data

| Comparative Historical Data | | | | Current Data Sorted by Sales | | | | | |
|---|---|---|---|---|---|---|---|---|---|
| 3 | 3 | 3 | Type of Statement | | | | | | |
| | | | Unqualified | 1 | | | 1 | 1 | |
| | 2 | 2 | Reviewed | | 1 | 1 | | | |
| 1 | 4 | 5 | Compiled | 1 | 3 | | 1 | | |
| 6 | 12 | 19 | Tax Returns | 13 | 4 | | 1 | 1 | |
| 9 | 18 | 18 | Other | 10 | 5 | | 2 | 1 | |
| 4/1/09-3/31/10 ALL | 4/1/10-3/31/11 ALL | 4/1/11-3/31/12 ALL | | 8 (4/1-9/30/11) | | 39 (10/1/11-3/31/12) | | | |
| | | | | 0-1MM | 1-3MM | 3-5MM | 5-10MM | 10-25MM | 25MM & OVER |
| 19 | 39 | 47 | NUMBER OF STATEMENTS | 25 | 13 | 1 | 5 | 3 | |
| % | % | % | ASSETS | % | % | % | % | % | % |
| 18.6 | 22.2 | 22.4 | Cash & Equivalents | 21.5 | 18.1 | | | | D |
| 8.5 | 6.6 | 7.7 | Trade Receivables (net) | 1.7 | 8.5 | | | | A |
| 5.6 | 4.5 | 2.7 | Inventory | .5 | 6.2 | | | | T |
| 1.1 | 2.2 | 4.9 | All Other Current | 3.8 | 6.3 | | | | A |
| 33.8 | 35.5 | 37.8 | Total Current | 27.7 | 39.1 | | | | |
| 33.2 | 47.1 | 47.3 | Fixed Assets (net) | 54.3 | 52.8 | | | | N |
| 9.9 | 5.4 | 2.3 | Intangibles (net) | .8 | 1.5 | | | | O |
| 23.1 | 12.1 | 12.6 | All Other Non-Current | 17.3 | 6.5 | | | | T |
| 100.0 | 100.0 | 100.0 | Total | 100.0 | 100.0 | | | | |
| | | | LIABILITIES | | | | | | A |
| 5.4 | 9.3 | 7.7 | Notes Payable-Short Term | 5.3 | 14.9 | | | | V |
| 2.6 | 2.7 | 4.7 | Cur. Mat.-L.T.D. | .9 | 4.6 | | | | A |
| 3.9 | 6.8 | 3.2 | Trade Payables | 2.2 | 4.4 | | | | I |
| .1 | 1.8 | 1.5 | Income Taxes Payable | .0 | .0 | | | | L |
| 15.1 | 16.3 | 17.6 | All Other Current | 16.2 | 20.9 | | | | A |
| 27.1 | 36.8 | 34.8 | Total Current | 24.7 | 44.9 | | | | B |
| 30.7 | 31.4 | 33.5 | Long-Term Debt | 49.2 | 26.0 | | | | L |
| .0 | .0 | .0 | Deferred Taxes | .0 | .0 | | | | E |
| 5.5 | 14.9 | 10.8 | All Other Non-Current | 3.8 | 14.7 | | | | |
| 36.7 | 16.9 | 20.9 | Net Worth | 22.4 | 14.5 | | | | |
| 100.0 | 100.0 | 100.0 | Total Liabilities & Net Worth | 100.0 | 100.0 | | | | |
| | | | INCOME DATA | | | | | | |
| 100.0 | 100.0 | 100.0 | Net Sales | 100.0 | 100.0 | | | | |
| | | | Gross Profit | | | | | | |
| 89.5 | 87.2 | 88.2 | Operating Expenses | 85.4 | 92.2 | | | | |
| 10.5 | 12.8 | 11.8 | Operating Profit | 14.6 | 7.8 | | | | |
| 6.1 | 4.8 | 3.5 | All Other Expenses (net) | 4.8 | 2.0 | | | | |
| 4.4 | 8.0 | 8.3 | Profit Before Taxes | 9.7 | 5.7 | | | | |
| | | | RATIOS | | | | | | |
| 6.8 | 3.8 | 4.0 | | 3.7 | 4.1 | | | | |
| .9 | 1.5 | 1.1 | Current | 1.0 | 1.1 | | | | |
| .2 | .2 | .5 | | .4 | .2 | | | | |
| 4.6 | 3.2 | 3.2 | | 3.0 | 3.5 | | | | |
| .7 | 1.2 | .9 | Quick | .7 | .5 | | | | |
| .1 | .2 | .2 | | .2 | .2 | | | | |
| 0 UND | 0 UND | 0 UND | | 0 UND | 0 UND | | | | |
| 0 999.8 | 1 501.1 | 0 UND | Sales/Receivables | 0 UND | 0 999.8 | | | | |
| 34 10.7 | 18 20.5 | 13 28.1 | | 0 UND | 19 19.0 | | | | |
| | | | Cost of Sales/Inventory | | | | | | |
| | | | Cost of Sales/Payables | | | | | | |
| 4.9 | 5.2 | 6.1 | | 8.3 | 3.6 | | | | |
| -37.3 | 51.1 | 59.5 | Sales/Working Capital | 308.0 | 29.7 | | | | |
| -6.5 | -4.2 | -8.5 | | -9.2 | -5.6 | | | | |
| 6.7 | 4.9 | 15.6 | | 24.4 | | | | | |
| (11) 2.8 | (24) 1.8 | (25) 3.8 | EBIT/Interest | (10) 4.9 | | | | | |
| .0 | -2.3 | .8 | | -.7 | | | | | |
| | | | Net Profit + Depr., Dep., Amort./Cur. Mat. L/T/D | | | | | | |
| .2 | .4 | .3 | | .3 | .4 | | | | |
| .9 | 2.4 | 1.7 | Fixed/Worth | 3.1 | 1.6 | | | | |
| -4.4 | -12.5 | -14.7 | | -11.1 | NM | | | | |
| .2 | .8 | .8 | | .2 | .6 | | | | |
| 2.8 | 3.9 | 2.5 | Debt/Worth | 2.3 | 1.4 | | | | |
| -7.9 | -16.5 | -19.7 | | -13.6 | NM | | | | |
| 48.5 | 93.2 | 62.7 | % Profit Before Taxes/Tangible Net Worth | 89.1 | 26.4 | | | | |
| (14) 15.8 | (28) 13.2 | (33) 27.1 | | (17) 48.0 | (10) 12.2 | | | | |
| -5.3 | -3.0 | 9.3 | | 14.8 | -19.7 | | | | |
| 20.3 | 11.9 | 26.8 | % Profit Before Taxes/Total Assets | 30.1 | 12.8 | | | | |
| 3.8 | 6.3 | 5.0 | | 9.8 | 4.9 | | | | |
| -4.8 | -2.0 | 1.1 | | 1.0 | -9.9 | | | | |
| 32.7 | 22.0 | 44.0 | Sales/Net Fixed Assets | 25.3 | 18.0 | | | | |
| 16.1 | 6.2 | 5.7 | | 5.7 | 3.7 | | | | |
| 2.0 | .6 | .8 | | .5 | .8 | | | | |
| 3.3 | 3.4 | 3.8 | Sales/Total Assets | 3.2 | 3.7 | | | | |
| 1.9 | 2.0 | 1.6 | | 1.4 | 1.3 | | | | |
| .9 | .5 | .5 | | .4 | .5 | | | | |
| 1.4 | 1.9 | 1.5 | % Depr., Dep., Amort./Sales | 1.6 | 1.2 | | | | |
| (16) 2.8 | (28) 4.9 | (30) 3.6 | | (14) 6.0 | (11) 2.5 | | | | |
| 5.7 | 15.8 | 10.0 | | 19.1 | 8.2 | | | | |
| | | 2.5 | % Officers', Directors' Owners' Comp/Sales | 3.2 | | | | | |
| | (21) 6.8 | | | (11) 5.5 | | | | | |
| | | 10.4 | | 13.0 | | | | | |
| 88558M | 149843M | 123715M | Net Sales ($) | 14170M | 24965M | 3836M | 32377M | 48367M | |
| 78410M | 168585M | 85382M | Total Assets ($) | 23209M | 23910M | 9605M | 14880M | 13778M | |

M = $ thousand     MM = $ million
See Pages 9 through 22 for Explanation of Ratios and Data

## Current Data Sorted by Assets      Comparative Historical Data

| | | Type of Statement | | |
|---|---|---|---|---|
| 6 | 24 | 46 | 39 | 6 | 4 | Unqualified | 83 | 204 |

| Type of Statement | 0-500M | 500M-2MM | 2-10MM | 10-50MM | 50-100MM | 100-250MM | 4/1/07-3/31/08 ALL | 4/1/08-3/31/09 ALL |
|---|---|---|---|---|---|---|---|---|
| Unqualified | 6 | 24 | 46 | 39 | 6 | 4 | 83 | 204 |
| Reviewed | 1 | | 6 | 3 | 1 | | 4 | 15 |
| Compiled | 4 | 5 | 5 | 3 | | | 9 | 11 |
| Tax Returns | 30 | 17 | 12 | | | | 24 | 47 |
| Other | 22 | 16 | 18 | 17 | | 1 | 42 | 68 |
|   | | 168 (4/1-9/30/11) | | 118 (10/1/11-3/31/12) | | | | |
| **NUMBER OF STATEMENTS** | 63 | 62 | 87 | 62 | 7 | 5 | 162 | 345 |
| **ASSETS** % | % | % | % | % | % | % | % | % |
| Cash & Equivalents | 43.6 | 29.2 | 21.6 | 20.5 | | | 22.6 | 21.9 |
| Trade Receivables (net) | 8.7 | 12.8 | 11.6 | 9.7 | | | 12.5 | 9.9 |
| Inventory | 4.2 | 2.2 | 1.8 | 1.3 | | | 1.6 | 1.8 |
| All Other Current | 2.1 | 2.3 | 3.7 | 2.6 | | | 5.6 | 4.0 |
| Total Current | 58.6 | 46.6 | 38.7 | 34.0 | | | 42.3 | 37.6 |
| Fixed Assets (net) | 27.2 | 44.4 | 52.1 | 52.4 | | | 46.5 | 44.9 |
| Intangibles (net) | 5.6 | 1.8 | 3.2 | 2.7 | | | 2.2 | 3.5 |
| All Other Non-Current | 8.7 | 7.2 | 6.0 | 10.9 | | | 9.0 | 13.9 |
| Total | 100.0 | 100.0 | 100.0 | 100.0 | | | 100.0 | 100.0 |
| **LIABILITIES** | | | | | | | | |
| Notes Payable-Short Term | 6.4 | 5.9 | 3.1 | 4.5 | | | 6.1 | 4.9 |
| Cur. Mat.-L.T.D. | 1.8 | 4.1 | 2.3 | 5.5 | | | 4.0 | 2.6 |
| Trade Payables | 9.0 | 5.7 | 4.4 | 3.5 | | | 6.2 | 5.0 |
| Income Taxes Payable | .1 | .0 | .0 | .1 | | | .1 | .2 |
| All Other Current | 12.5 | 9.6 | 11.8 | 8.3 | | | 14.6 | 14.8 |
| Total Current | 29.7 | 25.4 | 21.6 | 21.9 | | | 31.0 | 27.5 |
| Long-Term Debt | 10.7 | 19.2 | 25.4 | 24.6 | | | 19.3 | 23.3 |
| Deferred Taxes | .0 | .0 | .0 | .0 | | | .0 | .1 |
| All Other Non-Current | 21.1 | 7.5 | 5.7 | 6.7 | | | 6.4 | 8.6 |
| Net Worth | 38.5 | 48.0 | 47.2 | 46.8 | | | 43.3 | 40.5 |
| Total Liabilities & Net Worth | 100.0 | 100.0 | 100.0 | 100.0 | | | 100.0 | 100.0 |
| **INCOME DATA** | | | | | | | | |
| Net Sales | 100.0 | 100.0 | 100.0 | 100.0 | | | 100.0 | 100.0 |
| Gross Profit | | | | | | | | |
| Operating Expenses | 90.9 | 90.9 | 89.6 | 89.2 | | | 89.8 | 92.4 |
| Operating Profit | 9.1 | 9.1 | 10.4 | 10.8 | | | 10.2 | 7.6 |
| All Other Expenses (net) | 3.0 | 3.6 | 3.7 | 2.6 | | | 1.5 | 3.4 |
| Profit Before Taxes | 6.1 | 5.5 | 6.7 | 8.2 | | | 8.7 | 4.2 |
| **RATIOS** | | | | | | | | |
| Current | 6.7 | 8.5 | 5.0 | 3.9 | | | 3.3 | 4.1 |
| | 2.8 | 2.2 | 2.0 | 2.1 | | | 1.7 | 1.9 |
| | .9 | .8 | 1.0 | .9 | | | .9 | .9 |
| Quick | 6.6 | 8.2 | 4.5 | 3.7 | | | 2.8 | 3.6 |
| | 2.8 | 1.7 | 1.7 | 1.8 | | | 1.4 | 1.5 |
| | .6 | .4 | .7 | .8 | | | .6 | .7 |
| Sales/Receivables | 0 UND | 0 UND | 2 237.9 | 5 73.4 | | | 0 UND | 0 958.0 |
| | 0 UND | 4 85.8 | 15 23.6 | 19 18.9 | | | 10 36.7 | 10 35.7 |
| | 3 111.6 | 26 14.0 | 38 9.7 | 56 6.5 | | | 35 10.6 | 35 10.5 |
| Cost of Sales/Inventory | | | | | | | | |
| Cost of Sales/Payables | | | | | | | | |
| Sales/Working Capital | 11.6 | 4.0 | 3.1 | 2.9 | | | 4.5 | 3.4 |
| | 19.7 | 12.4 | 6.6 | 7.1 | | | 11.7 | 11.1 |
| | -395.5 | -36.8 | -63.8 | -50.9 | | | -68.9 | -115.4 |
| EBIT/Interest | 27.5 | 5.5 | 8.8 | 8.6 | | | 13.2 | 6.6 |
| | (32) 6.5 | (37) 2.5 | (61) 2.4 | (52) 3.9 | | | (122) 3.7 | (246) 2.1 |
| | -.3 | 1.2 | .9 | 1.6 | | | 1.6 | .3 |
| Net Profit + Depr., Dep., Amort./Cur. Mat. L/T/D | | | | | | | | |
| Fixed/Worth | .0 | .3 | .7 | .6 | | | .5 | .4 |
| | .4 | 1.0 | 1.1 | 1.2 | | | 1.0 | 1.0 |
| | 2.2 | 3.1 | 3.2 | 2.3 | | | 2.2 | 2.5 |
| Debt/Worth | .3 | .1 | .3 | .4 | | | .5 | .4 |
| | 1.0 | .9 | 1.0 | 1.0 | | | 1.0 | 1.2 |
| | 6.5 | 4.0 | 3.5 | 2.1 | | | 3.4 | 3.5 |
| % Profit Before Taxes/Tangible Net Worth | 136.0 | 43.7 | 36.2 | 19.9 | | | 44.7 | 24.1 |
| | (51) 80.8 | (53) 14.0 | (79) 8.8 | (58) 10.2 | | | (146) 18.3 | (306) 8.1 |
| | 5.7 | 1.1 | .3 | 1.4 | | | 3.8 | -1.2 |
| % Profit Before Taxes/Total Assets | 64.7 | 22.2 | 11.6 | 9.3 | | | 20.5 | 10.5 |
| | 28.7 | 6.8 | 3.3 | 3.5 | | | 8.1 | 2.2 |
| | .0 | .0 | .1 | .8 | | | 1.6 | -1.4 |
| Sales/Net Fixed Assets | 622.0 | 21.2 | 7.1 | 4.0 | | | 15.9 | 14.1 |
| | 39.2 | 6.8 | 2.0 | 1.3 | | | 4.0 | 2.4 |
| | 11.3 | 1.1 | .8 | .7 | | | 1.1 | .8 |
| Sales/Total Assets | 10.8 | 3.6 | 1.7 | 1.3 | | | 2.9 | 2.4 |
| | 6.0 | 2.3 | 1.0 | .7 | | | 1.6 | 1.0 |
| | 2.7 | .8 | .5 | .4 | | | .7 | .5 |
| % Depr., Dep., Amort./Sales | .5 | .9 | 1.6 | 2.9 | | | 1.2 | 1.5 |
| | (30) 1.1 | (43) 1.7 | (75) 4.1 | (56) 4.6 | | | (123) 2.6 | (274) 3.3 |
| | 3.6 | 3.4 | 7.9 | 5.8 | | | 5.1 | 6.1 |
| % Officers', Directors' Owners' Comp/Sales | 6.0 | 2.7 | 1.3 | | | | 3.0 | 3.4 |
| | (29) 8.7 | (12) 6.7 | (10) 4.5 | | | | (36) 6.4 | (68) 6.5 |
| | 13.5 | 14.3 | 5.8 | | | | 12.4 | 10.4 |
| Net Sales ($) | 79487M | 153160M | 465800M | 1272088M | 475290M | 490027M | 2352552M | 5325230M |
| Total Assets ($) | 12429M | 66747M | 404679M | 1208239M | 459400M | 624729M | 2053192M | 6605063M |

M = $ thousand    MM = $ million
See Pages 9 through 22 for Explanation of Ratios and Data

## Comparative Historical Data | Current Data Sorted by Sales

| | | | Type of Statement | | | | | | |
|---|---|---|---|---|---|---|---|---|---|
| 105 | 120 | 125 | Unqualified | 4 | 25 | 27 | 30 | 26 | 13 |
| 7 | 13 | 11 | Reviewed | 1 | 2 | 2 | 2 | 3 | 1 |
| 7 | 14 | 17 | Compiled | 8 | 3 | 2 | 3 | | 1 |
| 26 | 41 | 59 | Tax Returns | 25 | 20 | 8 | 5 | 1 | |
| 75 | 75 | 74 | Other | 27 | 15 | 9 | 10 | 7 | 6 |
| 4/1/09-3/31/10 ALL | 4/1/10-3/31/11 ALL | 4/1/11-3/31/12 ALL | | 168 (4/1-9/30/11) | | | 118 (10/1/11-3/31/12) | | |
| | | | | 0-1MM | 1-3MM | 3-5MM | 5-10MM | 10-25MM | 25MM & OVER |
| 220 | 263 | 286 | **NUMBER OF STATEMENTS** | 65 | 65 | 48 | 50 | 37 | 21 |
| % | % | % | **ASSETS** | % | % | % | % | % | % |
| 22.9 | 23.2 | 27.8 | Cash & Equivalents | 27.9 | 32.2 | 26.2 | 26.2 | 29.3 | 18.2 |
| 13.0 | 11.7 | 10.6 | Trade Receivables (net) | 4.4 | 7.6 | 16.7 | 13.2 | 10.7 | 19.3 |
| 1.4 | 2.5 | 2.3 | Inventory | 3.0 | 1.7 | 2.2 | 2.4 | 2.1 | 2.0 |
| 4.0 | 3.7 | 2.8 | All Other Current | .6 | 2.3 | 3.2 | 2.6 | 5.8 | 5.7 |
| 41.3 | 41.1 | 43.5 | Total Current | 35.9 | 43.8 | 48.3 | 44.5 | 48.0 | 45.3 |
| 44.2 | 44.1 | 44.2 | Fixed Assets (net) | 52.1 | 47.1 | 39.6 | 41.9 | 40.5 | 33.1 |
| 5.5 | 5.3 | 3.9 | Intangibles (net) | 6.3 | .7 | 3.0 | 3.0 | 3.5 | 11.2 |
| 9.0 | 9.5 | 8.4 | All Other Non-Current | 5.7 | 8.4 | 9.2 | 10.7 | 8.1 | 10.3 |
| 100.0 | 100.0 | 100.0 | Total | 100.0 | 100.0 | 100.0 | 100.0 | 100.0 | 100.0 |
| | | | **LIABILITIES** | | | | | | |
| 6.9 | 5.0 | 4.6 | Notes Payable-Short Term | 4.8 | 4.6 | 3.6 | 5.3 | 3.8 | 6.6 |
| 2.5 | 2.9 | 3.2 | Cur. Mat.-L.T.D. | 3.0 | 2.9 | 1.4 | 3.9 | 1.1 | 10.9 |
| 5.1 | 6.0 | 5.4 | Trade Payables | 3.9 | 4.1 | 8.2 | 4.7 | 7.7 | 5.7 |
| .1 | .1 | .1 | Income Taxes Payable | .1 | .0 | .0 | .1 | .1 | .3 |
| 15.8 | 10.9 | 10.7 | All Other Current | 7.9 | 11.2 | 8.2 | 9.2 | 15.1 | 19.9 |
| 30.3 | 24.9 | 24.1 | Total Current | 19.6 | 22.8 | 21.6 | 23.2 | 27.7 | 43.4 |
| 22.3 | 25.9 | 20.2 | Long-Term Debt | 22.4 | 21.5 | 21.4 | 18.4 | 19.4 | 12.3 |
| .1 | .1 | .1 | Deferred Taxes | .0 | .0 | .0 | .0 | .0 | .8 |
| 10.3 | 12.9 | 9.8 | All Other Non-Current | 15.1 | 10.2 | 7.1 | 9.8 | 3.9 | 9.1 |
| 37.0 | 36.2 | 45.8 | Net Worth | 43.0 | 45.5 | 49.9 | 48.6 | 48.9 | 34.5 |
| 100.0 | 100.0 | 100.0 | Total Liabilities & Net Worth | 100.0 | 100.0 | 100.0 | 100.0 | 100.0 | 100.0 |
| | | | **INCOME DATA** | | | | | | |
| 100.0 | 100.0 | 100.0 | Net Sales | 100.0 | 100.0 | 100.0 | 100.0 | 100.0 | 100.0 |
| | | | Gross Profit | | | | | | |
| 93.0 | 91.0 | 90.3 | Operating Expenses | 83.2 | 92.5 | 93.4 | 91.6 | 92.6 | 90.5 |
| 7.0 | 9.0 | 9.7 | Operating Profit | 16.8 | 7.5 | 6.6 | 8.4 | 7.4 | 9.5 |
| 4.2 | 2.9 | 3.3 | All Other Expenses (net) | 6.6 | 4.5 | 2.4 | 1.2 | .5 | 1.3 |
| 2.8 | 6.1 | 6.4 | Profit Before Taxes | 10.2 | 3.0 | 4.1 | 7.2 | 6.9 | 8.2 |
| | | | **RATIOS** | | | | | | |
| 3.9 | 4.8 | 5.8 | | 6.4 | 5.8 | 7.9 | 6.5 | 4.2 | 3.4 |
| 1.7 | 2.0 | 2.2 | Current | 1.7 | 2.3 | 2.7 | 2.2 | 2.3 | 1.3 |
| .8 | 1.0 | .9 | | .6 | 1.0 | 1.2 | .8 | 1.2 | .9 |
| 3.6 | 3.9 | 5.3 | | 6.3 | 5.8 | 7.9 | 6.0 | 4.0 | 2.8 |
| 1.4 | 1.7 | 2.0 | Quick | 1.6 | 2.3 | 2.6 | 2.2 | 2.2 | 1.0 |
| .8 | .7 | .7 | | .5 | 1.0 | .9 | .6 | 1.1 | .8 |
| 1 636.2 | 0 UND | 0 UND | | 0 UND | 0 UND | 2 163.4 | 4 91.0 | 5 73.5 | 2 154.0 |
| 13 27.9 | 8 43.9 | 6 62.6 | Sales/Receivables | 0 UND | 3 127.0 | 18 19.8 | 23 15.9 | 19 19.4 | 26 14.1 |
| 38 9.6 | 36 10.1 | 32 11.5 | | 4 103.1 | 14 26.5 | 51 7.2 | 53 6.9 | 33 10.9 | 59 6.2 |
| | | | Cost of Sales/Inventory | | | | | | |
| | | | Cost of Sales/Payables | | | | | | |
| 4.5 | 4.0 | 3.9 | | 5.6 | 4.9 | 3.4 | 2.0 | 3.0 | 5.4 |
| 12.7 | 10.0 | 12.1 | Sales/Working Capital | 25.7 | 15.6 | 6.3 | 6.6 | 7.4 | 15.6 |
| -21.1 | -239.9 | -112.8 | | -16.3 | NM | 27.4 | -20.7 | 28.7 | -134.6 |
| 10.1 | 10.5 | 9.5 | | 8.2 | 6.6 | 5.4 | 18.8 | 10.4 | 20.3 |
| (137) 2.5 | (173) 2.9 | (190) 3.3 | EBIT/Interest | (36) 2.7 | (44) 1.8 | (29) 2.4 | (38) 5.1 | (26) 4.2 | (17) 4.5 |
| .4 | .5 | 1.2 | | 1.2 | .3 | 1.2 | 2.0 | 1.6 | 1.4 |
| | 7.7 | | Net Profit + Depr., Dep., | | | | | | |
| | (12) 2.5 | | Amort./Cur. Mat. L/T/D | | | | | | |
| | .8 | | | | | | | | |
| .4 | .4 | .3 | | .2 | .3 | .3 | .3 | .3 | .4 |
| 1.1 | 1.3 | 1.0 | Fixed/Worth | 1.3 | 1.0 | .7 | .9 | 1.0 | .7 |
| 2.9 | 3.5 | 2.6 | | 3.6 | 2.3 | 1.7 | 3.1 | 2.6 | NM |
| .5 | .4 | .3 | | .2 | .4 | .3 | .3 | .3 | .5 |
| 1.3 | 1.3 | 1.0 | Debt/Worth | 1.0 | 1.0 | .9 | .9 | 1.0 | 1.6 |
| 4.8 | 5.9 | 3.1 | | 6.1 | 2.7 | 3.4 | 3.0 | 3.6 | NM |
| 32.5 | 37.5 | 49.2 | % Profit Before Taxes/Tangible | 92.3 | 78.8 | 38.7 | 33.4 | 29.9 | 37.2 |
| (189) 7.3 | (221) 11.9 | (250) 13.2 | Net Worth | (54) 24.4 | (60) 12.0 | (43) 8.8 | (44) 12.1 | (33) 15.1 | (16) 15.4 |
| -3.4 | -.3 | 1.0 | | 1.8 | -2.2 | 2.2 | 1.3 | 2.3 | 2.4 |
| 15.0 | 14.7 | 19.7 | % Profit Before Taxes/Total | 34.5 | 36.8 | 12.5 | 14.6 | 11.2 | 18.8 |
| 3.3 | 5.0 | 5.3 | Assets | 7.2 | 2.9 | 4.8 | 6.1 | 5.0 | 4.2 |
| -1.5 | -.3 | .3 | | .7 | -1.7 | .6 | 1.0 | .9 | 1.7 |
| 21.9 | 24.9 | 24.8 | | 24.6 | 36.1 | 22.1 | 27.8 | 11.4 | 31.3 |
| 4.3 | 4.6 | 3.8 | Sales/Net Fixed Assets | 6.5 | 4.3 | 5.5 | 2.3 | 3.0 | 9.5 |
| .9 | .9 | 1.1 | | .4 | .9 | 1.5 | 1.0 | 1.1 | 2.2 |
| 3.1 | 3.2 | 3.2 | | 4.5 | 6.2 | 3.3 | 2.3 | 2.1 | 3.2 |
| 1.4 | 1.5 | 1.3 | Sales/Total Assets | 1.8 | 1.8 | 1.5 | 1.0 | 1.3 | 1.6 |
| .6 | .6 | .6 | | .4 | .6 | .7 | .5 | .7 | 1.1 |
| 1.5 | 1.4 | 1.4 | | .9 | 1.5 | 1.3 | 1.2 | 1.4 | 1.0 |
| (161) 3.0 | (199) 2.9 | (214) 3.3 | % Depr., Dep., Amort./Sales | (33) 4.1 | (52) 3.8 | (37) 2.1 | (43) 4.6 | (33) 3.0 | (16) 3.1 |
| 6.1 | 5.7 | 5.3 | | 12.5 | 6.6 | 3.6 | 5.8 | 4.6 | 3.5 |
| 3.2 | 3.9 | 4.3 | % Officers', Directors' | 6.3 | 4.3 | | | | |
| (38) 6.3 | (56) 6.5 | (56) 7.5 | Owners' Comp/Sales | (18) 9.9 | (18) 7.9 | | | | |
| 11.2 | 11.1 | 11.8 | | 17.7 | 10.6 | | | | |
| 3624860M | 5221849M | 2935852M | Net Sales ($) | 35645M | 126475M | 185807M | 345696M | 553256M | 1688973M |
| 3651425M | 3359854M | 2776223M | Total Assets ($) | 67776M | 158593M | 262666M | 460306M | 633085M | 1193797M |

M = $ thousand     MM = $ million
See Pages 9 through 22 for Explanation of Ratios and Data

## Current Data Sorted by Assets          Comparative Historical Data

| | | | | | | Type of Statement | | |
|---|---|---|---|---|---|---|---|---|
| 5 | 17 | 59 | 85 | 24 | 32 | Unqualified | 182 | 128 |
| 1 | 3 | 11 | 7 | | | Reviewed | 13 | 10 |
| 1 | | 3 | | | | Compiled | 12 | 3 |
| 16 | 6 | 1 | 1 | | | Tax Returns | 26 | 21 |
| 11 | 15 | 27 | 24 | 7 | 7 | Other | 79 | 46 |
| | 247 (4/1-9/30/11) | | 116 (10/1/11-3/31/12) | | | | 4/1/07-3/31/08 | 4/1/08-3/31/09 |
| 0-500M | 500M-2MM | 2-10MM | 10-50MM | 50-100MM | 100-250MM | | ALL | ALL |
| 34 | 41 | 101 | 117 | 31 | 39 | NUMBER OF STATEMENTS | 312 | 208 |
| % | % | % | % | % | % | ASSETS | % | % |
| 39.9 | 36.1 | 27.8 | 22.4 | 20.7 | 24.5 | Cash & Equivalents | 24.0 | 28.5 |
| 10.7 | 20.8 | 17.8 | 9.0 | 7.7 | 9.2 | Trade Receivables (net) | 16.0 | 15.5 |
| 1.1 | 3.0 | 2.6 | 1.2 | 3.2 | .0 | Inventory | 2.0 | 3.2 |
| 8.3 | 2.2 | 4.2 | 1.9 | 3.3 | 2.8 | All Other Current | 4.2 | 4.4 |
| 60.0 | 62.1 | 52.4 | 34.4 | 34.9 | 36.6 | Total Current | 46.1 | 51.6 |
| 26.9 | 23.6 | 34.9 | 46.7 | 42.7 | 37.4 | Fixed Assets (net) | 38.1 | 30.6 |
| 5.4 | 4.1 | 2.4 | 4.5 | 1.6 | 6.0 | Intangibles (net) | 2.8 | 2.9 |
| 7.6 | 10.2 | 10.3 | 14.3 | 20.9 | 20.0 | All Other Non-Current | 12.9 | 14.8 |
| 100.0 | 100.0 | 100.0 | 100.0 | 100.0 | 100.0 | Total | 100.0 | 100.0 |
| | | | | | | LIABILITIES | | |
| 32.1 | 5.2 | 3.0 | 2.4 | 1.7 | .8 | Notes Payable-Short Term | 3.4 | 5.6 |
| 2.7 | 2.0 | 1.5 | 1.5 | 1.6 | 4.8 | Cur. Mat.-L.T.D. | 2.3 | 1.5 |
| 13.5 | 10.6 | 6.8 | 4.0 | 2.8 | 3.4 | Trade Payables | 5.9 | 7.6 |
| .0 | .0 | .0 | .1 | .0 | .0 | Income Taxes Payable | .1 | .2 |
| 28.7 | 19.6 | 12.6 | 9.9 | 8.9 | 7.2 | All Other Current | 16.9 | 18.1 |
| 76.9 | 37.3 | 23.9 | 17.9 | 15.1 | 16.2 | Total Current | 28.6 | 33.0 |
| 15.7 | 14.2 | 16.1 | 28.4 | 23.8 | 22.9 | Long-Term Debt | 22.6 | 17.9 |
| .0 | .0 | .0 | .1 | .0 | .1 | Deferred Taxes | .1 | .1 |
| 7.5 | 7.4 | 7.8 | 5.8 | 2.1 | 3.1 | All Other Non-Current | 9.5 | 8.1 |
| -.2 | 41.0 | 52.2 | 47.8 | 59.0 | 57.8 | Net Worth | 39.3 | 40.9 |
| 100.0 | 100.0 | 100.0 | 100.0 | 100.0 | 100.0 | Total Liabilities & Net Worth | 100.0 | 100.0 |
| | | | | | | INCOME DATA | | |
| 100.0 | 100.0 | 100.0 | 100.0 | 100.0 | 100.0 | Net Sales | 100.0 | 100.0 |
| | | | | | | Gross Profit | | |
| 95.4 | 92.3 | 93.9 | 91.6 | 92.5 | 87.2 | Operating Expenses | 91.3 | 93.4 |
| 4.6 | 7.7 | 6.1 | 8.4 | 7.5 | 12.8 | Operating Profit | 8.7 | 6.6 |
| .2 | 2.0 | 1.6 | 2.8 | -.2 | 3.5 | All Other Expenses (net) | 1.3 | 4.0 |
| 4.4 | 5.7 | 4.5 | 5.6 | 7.7 | 9.2 | Profit Before Taxes | 7.4 | 2.6 |
| | | | | | | RATIOS | | |
| 2.2 | 7.9 | 5.0 | 4.4 | 6.1 | 7.6 | | 4.4 | 5.0 |
| 1.0 | 3.4 | 2.5 | 2.2 | 2.1 | 2.3 | Current | 1.9 | 2.1 |
| .4 | 1.0 | 1.2 | 1.0 | 1.2 | 1.2 | | 1.0 | 1.0 |
| 2.1 | 6.4 | 4.1 | 4.3 | 4.1 | 7.6 | | 3.5 | 4.3 |
| .6 | 2.8 | 2.0 | 1.9 | 1.7 | 2.2 | Quick | 1.5 | 1.7 |
| .3 | 1.0 | 1.0 | .8 | 1.0 | 1.0 | | .8 | .8 |
| 0 UND | 0 UND | 3 112.1 | 3 105.3 | 8 44.8 | 1 257.1 | | 2 223.2 | 3 116.1 |
| 0 UND | 22 16.6 | 18 20.8 | 16 23.2 | 26 13.8 | 40 9.1 | Sales/Receivables | 21 17.0 | 23 16.1 |
| 2 172.0 | 49 7.4 | 46 8.0 | 44 8.3 | 61 6.0 | 64 5.7 | | 55 6.6 | 49 7.4 |
| | | | | | | Cost of Sales/Inventory | | |
| | | | | | | Cost of Sales/Payables | | |
| 15.9 | 2.3 | 3.0 | 2.3 | 2.0 | 1.3 | | 3.3 | 2.9 |
| UND | 4.9 | 7.1 | 5.4 | 6.3 | 2.7 | Sales/Working Capital | 10.9 | 7.8 |
| -10.5 | -695.3 | 26.0 | NM | 24.7 | 26.4 | | NM | UND |
| 30.6 | 12.7 | 8.6 | 7.6 | 12.2 | 7.3 | | 11.0 | 9.0 |
| (21) 12.3 | (24) 2.5 | (66) 3.1 | (86) 3.0 | (23) 3.5 | (33) 3.5 | EBIT/Interest | (212) 3.1 | (129) 2.5 |
| 1.4 | -1.4 | 1.0 | 1.1 | 1.3 | 1.1 | | 1.2 | .3 |
| | | | | | | Net Profit + Depr., Dep., Amort./Cur. Mat. L/T/D | 15.0 | 13.7 |
| | | | | | | | (11) 3.8 | (12) 5.7 |
| | | | | | | | 1.5 | 1.6 |
| .1 | .0 | .1 | .5 | .2 | .4 | | .2 | .1 |
| 1.0 | .4 | .6 | .9 | .8 | .8 | Fixed/Worth | .8 | .6 |
| -13.5 | 2.9 | 1.5 | 2.7 | 1.5 | 1.5 | | 2.0 | 1.7 |
| .4 | .2 | .3 | .3 | .3 | .4 | | .4 | .3 |
| 3.1 | .9 | .8 | 1.1 | .8 | .6 | Debt/Worth | 1.2 | 1.1 |
| -15.8 | 7.8 | 2.9 | 4.1 | 1.5 | 2.1 | | 3.6 | 3.5 |
| 132.9 | 39.9 | 27.0 | 14.3 | 15.0 | 12.7 | % Profit Before Taxes/Tangible Net Worth | 27.9 | 28.4 |
| (24) 57.4 | (32) 10.1 | (94) 7.0 | (105) 5.9 | 5.4 | (36) 5.1 | | (273) 10.3 | (183) 6.0 |
| -15.4 | -2.0 | 1.2 | .2 | .9 | .0 | | 2.0 | -3.3 |
| 65.4 | 18.6 | 9.8 | 6.3 | 7.9 | 5.1 | % Profit Before Taxes/Total Assets | 12.4 | 13.4 |
| 21.0 | 2.1 | 3.8 | 2.8 | 2.7 | 2.9 | | 4.2 | 1.8 |
| -5.2 | -2.7 | .2 | .1 | .4 | .0 | | .3 | -1.9 |
| 458.1 | 116.0 | 37.0 | 7.6 | 6.5 | 9.6 | Sales/Net Fixed Assets | 28.8 | 40.8 |
| 41.2 | 34.0 | 8.6 | 1.3 | 1.5 | 1.4 | | 5.3 | 9.8 |
| 10.3 | 3.9 | 1.0 | .6 | .8 | .5 | | 1.1 | 1.8 |
| 9.9 | 3.4 | 2.3 | 1.1 | 1.4 | .9 | Sales/Total Assets | 2.5 | 2.9 |
| 6.5 | 1.9 | 1.3 | .6 | .5 | .4 | | 1.2 | 1.4 |
| 4.3 | 1.2 | .7 | .4 | .3 | .2 | | .6 | .7 |
| .6 | .5 | .7 | 1.9 | 1.8 | 1.6 | % Depr., Dep., Amort./Sales | 1.1 | .8 |
| (20) 1.5 | (34) 1.2 | (85) 1.9 | (104) 4.3 | (26) 4.0 | (30) 3.5 | | (235) 3.0 | (168) 2.0 |
| 2.4 | 2.5 | 4.0 | 8.6 | 5.6 | 6.9 | | 5.2 | 4.6 |
| 6.4 | | 3.1 | 2.1 | | | % Officers', Directors' Owners' Comp/Sales | 1.5 | 4.3 |
| (12) 9.9 | (12) | 4.6 | (13) 8.4 | | | | (47) 6.8 | (35) 8.0 |
| 14.1 | | 8.0 | 16.2 | | | | 12.5 | 18.6 |
| 54723M | 134941M | 902640M | 2351014M | 1616720M | 3580915M | Net Sales ($) | 9154602M | 5552332M |
| 6326M | 49582M | 544899M | 2732812M | 2068740M | 5926827M | Total Assets ($) | 7711899M | 6658056M |

M = $ thousand     MM = $ million
See Pages 9 through 22 for Explanation of Ratios and Data

## Comparative Historical Data / Current Data Sorted by Sales

| | | | | | Type of Statement | | 247 (4/1-9/30/11) | | | 116 (10/1/11-3/31/12) | | |
|---|---|---|---|---|---|---|---|---|---|---|---|---|
| | 224 | 232 | 222 | | Unqualified | | 8 | 27 | 19 | 34 | 71 | 63 |
| | 22 | 17 | 22 | | Reviewed | | 2 | 5 | 3 | | 11 | 1 |
| | 14 | 10 | 4 | | Compiled | | | 3 | | 1 | | |
| | 25 | 28 | 24 | | Tax Returns | | 6 | 13 | 4 | | | 1 |
| | 68 | 87 | 91 | | Other | | 9 | 20 | 10 | 8 | 26 | 18 |
| | 4/1/09-3/31/10 ALL | 4/1/10-3/31/11 ALL | 4/1/11-3/31/12 ALL | | | | 0-1MM | 1-3MM | 3-5MM | 5-10MM | 10-25MM | 25MM & OVER |
| | 353 | 374 | 363 | | **NUMBER OF STATEMENTS** | | 25 | 68 | 36 | 43 | 108 | 83 |
| | % | % | % | | **ASSETS** | | % | % | % | % | % | % |
| | 24.5 | 26.2 | 27.2 | | Cash & Equivalents | | 35.6 | 28.6 | 27.1 | 26.9 | 27.6 | 23.1 |
| | 13.0 | 13.4 | 12.8 | | Trade Receivables (net) | | 9.0 | 9.6 | 9.9 | 10.5 | 17.0 | 13.8 |
| | 2.1 | 1.9 | 1.8 | | Inventory | | 1.5 | 1.3 | 2.4 | .5 | 1.7 | 2.9 |
| | 3.7 | 3.7 | 3.4 | | All Other Current | | 7.1 | 3.1 | 1.6 | 1.1 | 4.4 | 3.2 |
| | 43.3 | 45.2 | 45.2 | | Total Current | | 53.2 | 42.6 | 41.1 | 38.9 | 50.6 | 43.0 |
| | 40.3 | 36.4 | 37.6 | | Fixed Assets (net) | | 40.0 | 42.9 | 35.2 | 43.6 | 33.7 | 35.7 |
| | 4.3 | 3.8 | 3.9 | | Intangibles (net) | | 1.9 | 2.7 | 7.2 | .1 | 3.5 | 6.4 |
| | 12.1 | 14.5 | 13.3 | | All Other Non-Current | | 4.9 | 11.8 | 16.5 | 17.3 | 12.2 | 14.8 |
| | 100.0 | 100.0 | 100.0 | | Total | | 100.0 | 100.0 | 100.0 | 100.0 | 100.0 | 100.0 |
| | | | | | **LIABILITIES** | | | | | | | |
| | 8.0 | 5.1 | 5.4 | | Notes Payable-Short Term | | 16.0 | 11.5 | 2.3 | 2.7 | 3.6 | 2.4 |
| | 3.9 | 2.6 | 2.0 | | Cur. Mat.-L.T.D. | | .8 | 1.7 | 2.3 | 1.1 | 2.5 | 2.5 |
| | 6.0 | 7.0 | 6.3 | | Trade Payables | | 6.9 | 6.0 | 4.3 | 5.2 | 7.1 | 6.5 |
| | .2 | .0 | .0 | | Income Taxes Payable | | .0 | .1 | .0 | .0 | .0 | .0 |
| | 14.9 | 15.1 | 13.2 | | All Other Current | | 19.5 | 13.7 | 11.0 | 11.6 | 13.5 | 12.1 |
| | 33.0 | 29.8 | 26.9 | | Total Current | | 43.2 | 33.1 | 19.9 | 20.7 | 26.7 | 23.4 |
| | 22.1 | 20.6 | 21.2 | | Long-Term Debt | | 10.8 | 29.4 | 20.8 | 24.3 | 19.3 | 18.6 |
| | .0 | .1 | .1 | | Deferred Taxes | | .0 | .0 | .0 | .0 | .2 | .1 |
| | 6.7 | 7.1 | 6.1 | | All Other Non-Current | | 8.4 | 3.7 | 10.8 | 3.3 | 7.4 | 4.9 |
| | 38.1 | 42.4 | 45.8 | | Net Worth | | 37.6 | 33.9 | 48.5 | 51.8 | 46.4 | 53.0 |
| | 100.0 | 100.0 | 100.0 | | Total Liabilities & Net Worth | | 100.0 | 100.0 | 100.0 | 100.0 | 100.0 | 100.0 |
| | | | | | **INCOME DATA** | | | | | | | |
| | 100.0 | 100.0 | 100.0 | | Net Sales | | 100.0 | 100.0 | 100.0 | 100.0 | 100.0 | 100.0 |
| | | | | | Gross Profit | | | | | | | |
| | 94.8 | 93.0 | 92.3 | | Operating Expenses | | 93.0 | 91.7 | 87.3 | 93.8 | 94.3 | 91.4 |
| | 5.2 | 7.0 | 7.7 | | Operating Profit | | 7.0 | 8.3 | 12.7 | 6.2 | 5.7 | 8.6 |
| | 4.2 | 1.7 | 1.9 | | All Other Expenses (net) | | 1.3 | 4.5 | 1.5 | 2.0 | .7 | 1.8 |
| | 1.0 | 5.3 | 5.8 | | Profit Before Taxes | | 5.7 | 3.8 | 11.2 | 4.2 | 5.0 | 6.8 |
| | | | | | **RATIOS** | | | | | | | |
| | 4.1 | 4.3 | 5.0 | | | | 7.7 | 5.8 | 5.9 | 4.9 | 5.1 | 3.4 |
| | 1.8 | 1.9 | 2.1 | | Current | | 1.2 | 1.8 | 2.4 | 2.2 | 2.6 | 1.7 |
| | 1.0 | 1.1 | 1.0 | | | | .6 | .6 | 1.0 | 1.0 | 1.2 | 1.1 |
| | 3.5 | 3.9 | 4.4 | | | | 4.6 | 4.7 | 5.1 | 4.7 | 4.5 | 3.1 |
| | 1.5 | (373) 1.7 | 1.8 | | Quick | | 1.2 | 1.5 | 2.2 | 2.1 | 2.6 | 1.4 |
| | .7 | .8 | .9 | | | | .6 | .6 | 1.0 | .9 | 1.0 | .9 |
| | 1  333.9 | 3  107.6 | 1  252.3 | | | | 0  UND | 0  UND | 1  291.1 | 3  124.4 | 6  64.2 | 8  44.8 |
| | 16  22.4 | 19  19.3 | 16  22.4 | | Sales/Receivables | | 1  484.0 | 4  82.2 | 10  35.5 | 15  24.8 | 22  16.6 | 29  12.5 |
| | 44  8.3 | 50  7.2 | 46  8.0 | | | | 26  14.0 | 29  12.5 | 38  9.5 | 40  9.1 | 54  6.8 | 61  6.0 |
| | | | | | Cost of Sales/Inventory | | | | | | | |
| | | | | | Cost of Sales/Payables | | | | | | | |
| | 3.1 | 3.0 | 2.5 | | | | 2.6 | 2.9 | 2.2 | 2.5 | 2.4 | 2.7 |
| | 8.6 | 7.2 | 7.1 | | Sales/Working Capital | | 11.9 | 13.1 | 5.2 | 7.0 | 5.2 | 7.1 |
| | -82.7 | 92.8 | 101.0 | | | | -30.8 | -16.8 | 769.0 | -999.8 | 21.6 | 35.4 |
| | 10.5 | 15.0 | 10.9 | | | | 13.4 | 13.5 | 7.5 | 10.8 | 12.5 | 9.6 |
| | (263) 2.2 | (257) 3.0 | (253) 3.3 | | EBIT/Interest | | (14) 5.7 | (45) 2.4 | (24) 3.3 | (24) 2.4 | (77) 3.8 | (69) 3.5 |
| | -.4 | 1.1 | 1.1 | | | | .4 | .5 | .8 | -1.6 | 1.7 | 1.1 |
| | 7.6 | 7.8 | 9.0 | | Net Profit + Depr., Dep., | | | | | | | |
| | (13) 3.6 | (14) 3.7 | (13) 4.0 | | Amort./Cur. Mat. L/T/D | | | | | | | |
| | 1.6 | 1.2 | 1.3 | | | | | | | | | |
| | .2 | .2 | .2 | | | | .3 | .1 | .2 | .2 | .2 | .3 |
| | 1.0 | .8 | .8 | | Fixed/Worth | | 1.2 | .9 | 1.1 | .8 | .7 | .8 |
| | 2.1 | 1.7 | 2.0 | | | | 3.5 | 3.4 | 2.9 | 3.1 | 1.8 | 1.5 |
| | .4 | .4 | .3 | | | | .3 | .2 | .3 | .2 | .3 | .4 |
| | 1.3 | 1.0 | .9 | | Debt/Worth | | .7 | .8 | .9 | .8 | 1.0 | .9 |
| | 3.5 | 3.5 | 3.4 | | | | 14.7 | 4.3 | 3.2 | 4.1 | 3.1 | 2.4 |
| | 17.5 | 23.0 | 20.6 | | % Profit Before Taxes/Tangible | | 75.7 | 17.2 | 21.8 | 15.6 | 24.2 | 19.4 |
| | (305) 4.0 | (334) 7.9 | (322) 6.5 | | Net Worth | | (21) 8.0 | (55) 4.7 | (30) 8.3 | (42) 5.0 | (97) 8.1 | (77) 6.5 |
| | -5.3 | .3 | .2 | | | | -5.8 | -2.2 | 3.0 | -2.6 | 2.2 | 1.6 |
| | 8.7 | 10.2 | 9.5 | | % Profit Before Taxes/Total | | 30.4 | 14.8 | 12.1 | 5.1 | 8.8 | 8.1 |
| | 1.3 | 3.1 | 3.1 | | Assets | | 3.1 | 2.5 | 3.3 | 1.9 | 3.4 | 3.4 |
| | -2.9 | -.3 | -.1 | | | | -4.8 | -1.2 | 1.0 | -1.3 | .3 | .2 |
| | 30.2 | 25.3 | 31.6 | | | | 413.3 | 43.5 | 36.7 | 13.9 | 26.3 | 20.4 |
| | 3.3 | 4.2 | 4.0 | | Sales/Net Fixed Assets | | 10.9 | 7.0 | 3.4 | 2.6 | 5.2 | 3.8 |
| | .9 | .9 | .8 | | | | 1.1 | .5 | .6 | .7 | .9 | 1.1 |
| | 2.3 | 2.2 | 2.2 | | | | 5.9 | 3.8 | 1.7 | 2.3 | 2.1 | 1.8 |
| | 1.1 | 1.0 | 1.0 | | Sales/Total Assets | | 2.3 | 1.2 | .8 | .7 | .9 | 1.0 |
| | .5 | .5 | .4 | | | | .5 | .3 | .4 | .5 | .4 | .5 |
| | 1.3 | 1.0 | 1.1 | | | | 2.0 | .8 | .8 | 1.3 | 1.1 | 1.0 |
| | (274) 3.4 | (291) 3.0 | (299) 2.7 | | % Depr., Dep., Amort./Sales | | (16) 3.6 | (53) 2.4 | (32) 2.9 | (38) 2.7 | (92) 2.9 | (68) 2.5 |
| | 5.6 | 6.1 | 5.8 | | | | 9.8 | 8.2 | 5.9 | 6.3 | 5.4 | 4.3 |
| | 4.1 | 2.9 | 3.3 | | % Officers', Directors' | | 6.6 | | | | 2.9 | |
| | (51) 8.2 | (45) 6.6 | (49) 8.3 | | Owners' Comp/Sales | | (13) 9.6 | | | (14) 5.8 | | |
| | 12.7 | 12.9 | 13.8 | | | | 11.9 | | | | 20.3 | |
| | 8060336M | 9800108M | 8640953M | | Net Sales ($) | | 12646M | 129741M | 139422M | 317386M | 1680630M | 6361128M |
| | 8871953M | 11780799M | 11329186M | | Total Assets ($) | | 17288M | 271573M | 264913M | 601193M | 2901370M | 7272849M |

M = $ thousand    MM = $ million
See Pages 9 through 22 for Explanation of Ratios and Data

# HEALTH CARE AND SOCIAL ASSISTANCE

## Current Data Sorted by Assets   &   Comparative Historical Data

| Type of Statement | 0-500M | 500M-2MM | 2-10MM | 10-50MM | 50-100MM | 100-250MM | 4/1/07-3/31/08 ALL | 4/1/08-3/31/09 ALL |
|---|---|---|---|---|---|---|---|---|
| Unqualified | 6 | 14 | 69 | 96 | 31 | 28 | 201 | 198 |
| Reviewed | 11 | 34 | 87 | 37 | 1 |  | 132 | 140 |
| Compiled | 378 | 262 | 119 | 15 | 1 | 1 | 579 | 646 |
| Tax Returns | 1213 | 595 | 201 | 18 | 6 | 5 | 1107 | 1324 |
| Other | 638 | 523 | 395 | 164 | 25 | 15 | 1015 | 1263 |
| | 415 (4/1-9/30/11) | | | 4,572 (10/1/11-3/31/12) | | | | |
| NUMBER OF STATEMENTS | 2246 | 1428 | 871 | 330 | 63 | 49 | 3034 | 3571 |
| **ASSETS** | % | % | % | % | % | % | % | % |
| Cash & Equivalents | 42.1 | 27.0 | 16.4 | 14.0 | 15.7 | 18.3 | 27.1 | 27.0 |
| Trade Receivables (net) | 3.1 | 6.7 | 17.1 | 21.7 | 17.9 | 11.5 | 10.2 | 9.7 |
| Inventory | 1.0 | 1.0 | 1.0 | 1.4 | 1.0 | .8 | 1.0 | 1.0 |
| All Other Current | 3.9 | 3.8 | 3.5 | 5.2 | 5.0 | 3.2 | 4.6 | 4.4 |
| Total Current | 50.1 | 38.5 | 38.0 | 42.3 | 39.6 | 33.8 | 42.9 | 42.0 |
| Fixed Assets (net) | 31.6 | 42.8 | 48.1 | 42.4 | 42.7 | 37.7 | 42.1 | 41.6 |
| Intangibles (net) | 4.5 | 5.4 | 4.5 | 3.4 | 8.5 | 10.5 | 3.7 | 4.1 |
| All Other Non-Current | 13.8 | 13.3 | 9.3 | 11.9 | 9.2 | 18.0 | 11.3 | 12.3 |
| Total | 100.0 | 100.0 | 100.0 | 100.0 | 100.0 | 100.0 | 100.0 | 100.0 |
| **LIABILITIES** | | | | | | | | |
| Notes Payable-Short Term | 30.4 | 14.4 | 6.2 | 4.8 | 4.5 | 10.5 | 18.6 | 20.0 |
| Cur. Mat.-L.T.D. | 7.5 | 7.2 | 6.4 | 5.5 | 6.6 | 2.7 | 8.5 | 8.5 |
| Trade Payables | 2.9 | 2.7 | 4.3 | 6.2 | 6.9 | 4.3 | 3.1 | 3.1 |
| Income Taxes Payable | .2 | .1 | .4 | 1.0 | .6 | .4 | .4 | .5 |
| All Other Current | 36.1 | 22.5 | 17.1 | 18.0 | 11.8 | 13.7 | 27.6 | 26.1 |
| Total Current | 77.1 | 46.9 | 34.3 | 35.5 | 30.3 | 31.6 | 58.3 | 58.2 |
| Long-Term Debt | 25.7 | 30.9 | 35.4 | 27.5 | 26.9 | 26.2 | 31.8 | 31.9 |
| Deferred Taxes | .0 | .1 | .2 | .5 | .4 | .7 | .2 | .2 |
| All Other Non-Current | 8.4 | 4.9 | 3.8 | 4.0 | 7.3 | 10.7 | 5.5 | 4.9 |
| Net Worth | -11.1 | 17.1 | 26.3 | 32.5 | 35.1 | 30.5 | 4.3 | 4.9 |
| Total Liabilities & Net Worth | 100.0 | 100.0 | 100.0 | 100.0 | 100.0 | 100.0 | 100.0 | 100.0 |
| **INCOME DATA** | | | | | | | | |
| Net Sales | 100.0 | 100.0 | 100.0 | 100.0 | 100.0 | 100.0 | 100.0 | 100.0 |
| Gross Profit | | | | | | | | |
| Operating Expenses | 89.3 | 84.9 | 82.0 | 86.8 | 90.6 | 91.9 | 89.0 | 87.9 |
| Operating Profit | 10.7 | 15.1 | 18.0 | 13.2 | 9.4 | 8.1 | 11.0 | 12.1 |
| All Other Expenses (net) | .4 | 3.3 | 6.1 | 4.5 | 2.1 | 2.8 | 2.4 | 2.6 |
| Profit Before Taxes | 10.2 | 11.8 | 11.8 | 8.6 | 7.3 | 5.3 | 8.6 | 9.5 |
| **RATIOS** | | | | | | | | |
| Current | 2.2 | 2.1 | 2.3 | 2.1 | 2.0 | 2.2 | 2.0 | 2.0 |
| | .8 | .8 | 1.1 | 1.3 | 1.5 | 1.5 | .9 | .9 |
| | .3 | .3 | .5 | .8 | 1.0 | .9 | .3 | .3 |
| Quick | 2.0 | 1.8 | 2.1 | 1.9 | 1.8 | 1.9 | 1.7 | 1.8 |
| | .7 | .7 | (869) 1.0 | 1.0 | 1.1 | 1.3 | (3027) .7 | (3565) .7 |
| | .2 | .2 | .4 | .6 | .8 | .8 | .2 | .2 |
| Sales/Receivables | 0 UND | 0 UND | 0 UND | 1 341.8 | 11 33.5 | 4 89.8 | 0 UND | 0 UND |
| | 0 UND | 0 UND | 0 UND | 30 12.2 | 33 11.2 | 34 10.8 | 0 UND | 0 UND |
| | 0 UND | 0 UND | 36 10.0 | 47 7.8 | 50 7.3 | 41 8.9 | 9 40.8 | 2 150.0 |
| Cost of Sales/Inventory | | | | | | | | |
| Cost of Sales/Payables | | | | | | | | |
| Sales/Working Capital | 37.3 | 25.6 | 10.7 | 8.5 | 7.6 | 6.8 | 22.4 | 24.5 |
| | -188.1 | -109.5 | 106.6 | 27.3 | 19.6 | 15.5 | -205.2 | -182.9 |
| | -24.6 | -19.3 | -21.0 | -45.4 | -164.7 | -86.6 | -22.5 | -20.1 |
| EBIT/Interest | 32.2 | 31.2 | 31.5 | 25.0 | 15.2 | 14.2 | 16.7 | 22.5 |
| | (1431) 7.8 | (1058) 6.5 | (660) 6.7 | (260) 6.2 | (57) 6.2 | (45) 5.9 | (2309) 3.8 | (2701) 4.2 |
| | 1.0 | 1.2 | 1.5 | 2.0 | 1.5 | 1.6 | .8 | .8 |
| Net Profit + Depr., Dep., Amort./Cur. Mat. L/T/D | 2.6 | 5.1 | 4.2 | 4.8 | 4.1 | | 3.6 | 3.7 |
| | (34) 1.4 | (49) 1.7 | (81) 1.8 | (54) 1.9 | (24) 2.3 | | (184) 1.6 | (204) 1.5 |
| | .4 | .7 | 1.0 | 1.0 | 1.8 | | .9 | .7 |
| Fixed/Worth | .1 | .4 | .6 | .5 | .7 | .7 | .5 | .5 |
| | 2.1 | 2.9 | 2.2 | 1.3 | 1.4 | 1.2 | 2.9 | 2.8 |
| | -1.2 | -3.8 | UND | 3.9 | 3.1 | 15.1 | -3.9 | -3.8 |
| Debt/Worth | .9 | 1.0 | 1.0 | .9 | .8 | .8 | 1.2 | 1.1 |
| | 18.1 | 6.0 | 3.7 | 2.2 | 1.9 | 1.5 | 7.4 | 6.5 |
| | -3.2 | -8.7 | -108.8 | 6.6 | 12.5 | 27.1 | -6.8 | -6.9 |
| % Profit Before Taxes/Tangible Net Worth | 490.7 | 210.6 | 120.2 | 60.0 | 105.7 | 26.2 | 226.1 | 233.4 |
| | (1258) 129.3 | (927) 72.3 | (647) 33.9 | (286) 21.7 | (49) 17.4 | (39) 14.4 | (1916) 59.5 | (2264) 60.2 |
| | 33.3 | 18.5 | 6.2 | 7.2 | 3.9 | 3.9 | 7.1 | 6.5 |
| % Profit Before Taxes/Total Assets | 124.4 | 55.0 | 32.5 | 18.4 | 25.9 | 7.9 | 54.8 | 63.5 |
| | 32.5 | 14.6 | 7.4 | 6.4 | 5.5 | 4.9 | 9.8 | 11.3 |
| | .0 | .8 | .7 | 1.2 | .7 | .9 | -.3 | -.3 |
| Sales/Net Fixed Assets | 401.8 | 73.9 | 27.6 | 22.6 | 12.4 | 21.4 | 69.6 | 75.0 |
| | 63.4 | 22.4 | 10.2 | 6.0 | 5.0 | 4.5 | 21.2 | 21.0 |
| | 21.5 | 7.5 | 2.3 | 2.2 | 2.3 | 2.0 | 7.8 | 7.6 |
| Sales/Total Assets | 23.8 | 12.2 | 6.4 | 3.7 | 3.1 | 2.6 | 14.0 | 13.4 |
| | 11.8 | 5.9 | 3.1 | 2.1 | 1.5 | 1.6 | 6.5 | 6.5 |
| | 5.9 | 2.5 | 1.1 | 1.1 | 1.0 | .8 | 2.7 | 2.7 |
| % Depr., Dep., Amort./Sales | .4 | .8 | 1.2 | 1.5 | 1.6 | 1.2 | .8 | .8 |
| | (1097) 1.0 | (950) 1.7 | (715) 2.5 | (292) 2.8 | (58) 2.9 | (33) 2.8 | (2215) 1.9 | (2468) 1.9 |
| | 2.0 | 4.1 | 7.9 | 5.5 | 5.2 | 3.6 | 3.4 | 4.0 |
| % Officers', Directors' Owners' Comp/Sales | 12.8 | 10.0 | 7.4 | 10.3 | 9.5 | 2.9 | 13.7 | 12.3 |
| | (1494) 22.7 | (771) 21.1 | (299) 17.3 | (79) 24.3 | (18) 19.6 | (12) 27.0 | (1634) 24.9 | (1898) 23.8 |
| | 32.4 | 31.9 | 30.6 | 36.6 | 33.0 | 35.1 | 35.3 | 33.8 |
| Net Sales ($) | 7093197M | 11926484M | 17088650M | 22739298M | 15715207M | 34087566M | 104989116M | 66197860M |
| Total Assets ($) | 486299M | 1441189M | 3920186M | 7035507M | 4330586M | 7926416M | 18078305M | 18538944M |

| Comparative Historical Data | | | Type of Statement | Current Data Sorted by Sales | | | | | |
|---|---|---|---|---|---|---|---|---|---|
| 222 | 247 | 244 | Unqualified | 7 | 9 | 9 | 22 | 58 | 139 |
| 162 | 140 | 170 | Reviewed | 9 | 9 | 12 | 11 | 61 | 68 |
| 698 | 667 | 775 | Compiled | 117 | 219 | 98 | 143 | 146 | 52 |
| 1634 | 1520 | 2038 | Tax Returns | 537 | 585 | 284 | 325 | 215 | 92 |
| 1356 | 1521 | 1760 | Other | 236 | 441 | 210 | 259 | 316 | 298 |
| 4/1/09- 3/31/10 ALL | 4/1/10- 3/31/11 ALL | 4/1/11- 3/31/12 ALL | | 415 (4/1-9/30/11) | | | 4,572 (10/1/11-3/31/12) | | |
| | | | | 0-1MM | 1-3MM | 3-5MM | 5-10MM | 10-25MM | 25MM & OVER |
| 4072 | 4095 | 4987 | NUMBER OF STATEMENTS | 906 | 1263 | 613 | 760 | 796 | 649 |
| % | % | % | ASSETS | % | % | % | % | % | % |
| 27.5 | 28.2 | 30.9 | Cash & Equivalents | 27.2 | 35.8 | 36.2 | 33.2 | 27.6 | 22.8 |
| 9.5 | 9.7 | 8.1 | Trade Receivables (net) | 3.6 | 5.1 | 5.9 | 8.3 | 12.1 | 17.2 |
| 1.0 | 1.1 | 1.0 | Inventory | .6 | 1.0 | 1.2 | 1.3 | 1.1 | 1.4 |
| 4.2 | 3.7 | 3.9 | All Other Current | 2.8 | 4.2 | 3.3 | 3.3 | 4.5 | 5.1 |
| 42.2 | 42.8 | 43.9 | Total Current | 34.2 | 46.0 | 46.6 | 46.0 | 45.2 | 46.5 |
| 41.1 | 40.2 | 38.6 | Fixed Assets (net) | 48.0 | 33.6 | 35.0 | 38.9 | 39.5 | 37.1 |
| 4.5 | 4.7 | 4.8 | Intangibles (net) | 4.2 | 5.8 | 5.1 | 4.3 | 4.2 | 4.7 |
| 12.3 | 12.4 | 12.7 | All Other Non-Current | 13.6 | 14.5 | 13.4 | 10.8 | 11.0 | 11.8 |
| 100.0 | 100.0 | 100.0 | Total | 100.0 | 100.0 | 100.0 | 100.0 | 100.0 | 100.0 |
| | | | LIABILITIES | | | | | | |
| 18.5 | 18.9 | 19.4 | Notes Payable-Short Term | 18.7 | 25.7 | 20.3 | 19.5 | 16.3 | 10.6 |
| 7.9 | 7.0 | 7.0 | Cur. Mat.-L.T.D. | 5.0 | 5.9 | 8.8 | 8.8 | 8.1 | 7.0 |
| 3.2 | 3.4 | 3.4 | Trade Payables | 2.2 | 3.4 | 2.6 | 2.7 | 3.6 | 6.1 |
| .4 | .3 | .3 | Income Taxes Payable | .1 | .2 | .2 | .1 | .2 | .9 |
| 27.3 | 26.5 | 27.2 | All Other Current | 21.2 | 24.7 | 27.1 | 31.6 | 31.9 | 29.5 |
| 57.2 | 56.1 | 57.2 | Total Current | 47.1 | 59.9 | 59.0 | 62.7 | 60.0 | 54.2 |
| 32.6 | 30.1 | 29.0 | Long-Term Debt | 39.4 | 28.3 | 29.4 | 26.6 | 26.2 | 22.0 |
| .1 | .2 | .1 | Deferred Taxes | .0 | .0 | .1 | .1 | .2 | .4 |
| 4.8 | 5.6 | 6.3 | All Other Non-Current | 7.6 | 7.8 | 8.4 | 4.7 | 4.1 | 4.2 |
| 5.2 | 8.0 | 7.4 | Net Worth | 6.0 | 3.9 | 3.1 | 5.9 | 9.5 | 19.2 |
| 100.0 | 100.0 | 100.0 | Total Liabilities & Net Worth | 100.0 | 100.0 | 100.0 | 100.0 | 100.0 | 100.0 |
| | | | INCOME DATA | | | | | | |
| 100.0 | 100.0 | 100.0 | Net Sales | 100.0 | 100.0 | 100.0 | 100.0 | 100.0 | 100.0 |
| | | | Gross Profit | | | | | | |
| 87.8 | 87.1 | 86.7 | Operating Expenses | 71.9 | 86.0 | 88.1 | 92.0 | 92.9 | 93.4 |
| 12.2 | 12.9 | 13.3 | Operating Profit | 28.1 | 14.0 | 11.9 | 8.0 | 7.1 | 6.6 |
| 2.6 | 2.5 | 2.5 | All Other Expenses (net) | 10.7 | 1.6 | .8 | .1 | -.1 | .7 |
| 9.6 | 10.4 | 10.8 | Profit Before Taxes | 17.3 | 12.4 | 11.2 | 7.9 | 7.2 | 6.0 |
| | | | RATIOS | | | | | | |
| 2.1 | 2.3 | 2.2 | | 2.5 | 3.2 | 2.6 | 1.8 | 1.9 | 1.7 |
| .9 | .9 | .9 | Current | .8 | 1.0 | 1.0 | .8 | .9 | 1.1 |
| .3 | .3 | .3 | | .2 | .3 | .4 | .3 | .4 | .6 |
| 1.8 | 2.0 | 1.9 | | 2.2 | 2.7 | 2.3 | 1.6 | 1.6 | 1.4 |
| (4065) .8 | (4089) .8 | (4985) .8 | Quick | .7 | .8 | .9 | .8 | (795) .8 | (648) .9 |
| .2 | .3 | .3 | | .2 | .3 | .3 | .3 | .3 | .4 |
| 0 UND | 0 UND | 0 UND | | 0 UND | 0 UND | 0 UND | 0 UND | 0 UND | 0 UND |
| 0 UND | 0 UND | 0 UND | Sales/Receivables | 0 UND | 0 UND | 0 UND | 0 UND | 0 UND | 6 64.0 |
| 2 174.0 | 5 80.0 | 0 UND | | 0 UND | 0 UND | 0 UND | 0 UND | 26 14.3 | 36 10.1 |
| | | | Cost of Sales/Inventory | | | | | | |
| | | | Cost of Sales/Payables | | | | | | |
| 24.7 | 19.3 | 21.3 | | 14.5 | 17.9 | 21.6 | 34.1 | 23.3 | 19.4 |
| -207.7 | -337.5 | -349.5 | Sales/Working Capital | -81.9 | -745.0 | -774.4 | -212.7 | -285.8 | 295.1 |
| -20.9 | -21.6 | -23.3 | | -6.6 | -19.4 | -26.1 | -29.5 | -32.0 | -38.8 |
| 22.7 | 27.9 | 29.9 | | 23.9 | 32.2 | 51.0 | 28.0 | 26.3 | 28.4 |
| (3073) 5.4 | (3014) 6.3 | (3511) 6.8 | EBIT/Interest | (393) 6.8 | (824) 8.8 | (471) 10.2 | (598) 6.3 | (668) 4.8 | (557) 5.9 |
| 1.0 | 1.1 | 1.2 | | 2.0 | 1.9 | 1.4 | .9 | .8 | 1.3 |
| 4.4 | 4.8 | 4.4 | | | | 5.3 | 4.7 | 4.4 | 4.6 |
| (245) 1.8 | (194) 1.8 | (247) 1.9 | Net Profit + Depr., Dep., Amort./Cur. Mat. L/T/D | | | (21) 1.6 | (35) 1.5 | (67) 1.9 | (108) 2.1 |
| .8 | 1.0 | 1.0 | | | | .9 | .6 | .9 | 1.1 |
| .5 | .4 | .3 | | .2 | .2 | .3 | .5 | .6 | .6 |
| 2.7 | 2.3 | 2.1 | Fixed/Worth | 2.9 | 1.5 | 1.8 | 3.1 | 2.5 | 1.6 |
| -3.4 | -4.3 | -3.8 | | -25.5 | -3.0 | -2.2 | -2.5 | -2.6 | UND |
| 1.1 | .9 | .9 | | .8 | .7 | .8 | 1.1 | 1.1 | 1.1 |
| 6.8 | 5.4 | 5.7 | Debt/Worth | 5.6 | 5.7 | 6.1 | 10.3 | 6.2 | 3.4 |
| -6.6 | -7.4 | -6.6 | | -8.9 | -4.8 | -4.6 | -5.9 | -5.9 | -62.8 |
| 225.1 | 222.2 | 245.6 | % Profit Before Taxes/Tangible Net Worth | 198.1 | 384.0 | 358.2 | 274.6 | 175.7 | 134.5 |
| (2549) 59.3 | (2671) 60.4 | (3206) 71.5 | | (618) 50.3 | (782) 112.8 | (379) 98.4 | (451) 82.9 | (497) 47.1 | (479) 30.0 |
| 9.7 | 10.4 | 13.7 | | 12.0 | 37.1 | 25.3 | 15.2 | 3.8 | 7.6 |
| 58.4 | 64.4 | 70.8 | % Profit Before Taxes/Total Assets | 62.1 | 103.5 | 96.6 | 56.0 | 47.8 | 28.3 |
| 12.0 | 13.9 | 15.4 | | 11.9 | 33.3 | 27.4 | 14.4 | 9.0 | 7.0 |
| .3 | .4 | .7 | | 1.4 | 3.6 | 1.1 | -.1 | -.3 | .4 |
| 82.3 | 86.3 | 124.2 | | 141.3 | 182.2 | 145.4 | 137.9 | 93.2 | 58.1 |
| 22.3 | 22.9 | 27.3 | Sales/Net Fixed Assets | 13.1 | 36.4 | 35.7 | 36.4 | 29.1 | 19.9 |
| 7.8 | 7.6 | 8.4 | | .3 | 10.5 | 13.3 | 14.0 | 11.7 | 7.9 |
| 13.5 | 13.1 | 14.5 | | 7.2 | 13.3 | 16.8 | 19.8 | 19.5 | 12.5 |
| 6.4 | 5.8 | 6.7 | Sales/Total Assets | 2.6 | 6.5 | 8.5 | 11.0 | 9.2 | 5.3 |
| 2.6 | 2.6 | 2.8 | | .2 | 3.1 | 3.9 | 5.2 | 3.6 | 2.7 |
| .8 | .8 | .7 | | 1.4 | .5 | .6 | .6 | .6 | 1.0 |
| (2860) 1.8 | (2739) 1.7 | (3145) 1.7 | % Depr., Dep., Amort./Sales | (543) 9.4 | (657) 1.6 | (360) 1.5 | (487) 1.3 | (592) 1.5 | (506) 1.7 |
| 3.7 | 3.7 | 3.7 | | 20.7 | 4.2 | 2.9 | 2.2 | 2.6 | 2.9 |
| 12.3 | 12.5 | 11.4 | | 13.3 | 10.6 | 9.2 | 14.6 | 10.8 | 10.2 |
| (2193) 23.8 | (2130) 23.0 | (2673) 21.9 | % Officers', Directors' Owners' Comp/Sales | (380) 21.9 | (775) 18.0 | (372) 20.9 | (473) 25.9 | (424) 24.5 | (249) 24.2 |
| 34.0 | 33.0 | 32.2 | | 31.4 | 28.4 | 31.9 | 35.1 | 35.0 | 34.7 |
| 97386418M | 90946410M | 108650402M | Net Sales ($) | 485594M | 2363597M | 2400939M | 5432397M | 12462243M | 85505632M |
| 22074414M | 23196586M | 25140183M | Total Assets ($) | 746501M | 1086665M | 691633M | 1091812M | 3107803M | 18415769M |

M = $ thousand    MM = $ million
See Pages 9 through 22 for Explanation of Ratios and Data

## Current Data Sorted by Assets      Comparative Historical Data

| 0-500M | 500M-2MM | 2-10MM | 10-50MM | 50-100MM | 100-250MM | Type of Statement | 4/1/07-3/31/08 ALL | 4/1/08-3/31/09 ALL |
|---|---|---|---|---|---|---|---|---|
| 1 | 4 | 3 | 6 | 2 | 1 | Unqualified | 9 | 14 |
|  |  | 2 | 1 |  |  | Reviewed |  | 1 |
| 8 | 8 | 5 | 1 |  | 1 | Compiled | 11 | 14 |
| 33 | 13 | 10 | 2 |  |  | Tax Returns | 25 | 27 |
| 19 | 16 | 12 | 5 | 2 | 1 | Other | 13 | 26 |
|  | 18 (4/1-9/30/11) |  | 138 (10/1/11-3/31/12) |  |  |  |  |  |
| 61 | 41 | 32 | 15 | 4 | 3 | NUMBER OF STATEMENTS | 58 | 82 |
| % | % | % | % | % | % | **ASSETS** | % | % |
| 45.7 | 27.2 | 16.2 | 19.9 |  |  | Cash & Equivalents | 34.2 | 25.0 |
| 3.8 | 10.1 | 17.3 | 18.7 |  |  | Trade Receivables (net) | 7.2 | 14.3 |
| 1.0 | .2 | .7 | .9 |  |  | Inventory | .5 | .7 |
| 4.7 | 1.6 | 3.9 | 5.9 |  |  | All Other Current | 6.1 | 5.9 |
| 55.2 | 39.1 | 38.1 | 45.4 |  |  | Total Current | 48.0 | 45.9 |
| 25.2 | 34.0 | 42.1 | 36.7 |  |  | Fixed Assets (net) | 38.7 | 40.8 |
| 8.4 | 12.1 | 6.5 | 10.6 |  |  | Intangibles (net) | 5.1 | 2.9 |
| 11.2 | 14.8 | 13.2 | 7.3 |  |  | All Other Non-Current | 8.1 | 10.3 |
| 100.0 | 100.0 | 100.0 | 100.0 |  |  | Total | 100.0 | 100.0 |
|  |  |  |  |  |  | **LIABILITIES** |  |  |
| 32.8 | 20.8 | 5.8 | 2.6 |  |  | Notes Payable-Short Term | 22.8 | 14.3 |
| 2.3 | 4.7 | 5.3 | 3.7 |  |  | Cur. Mat.-L.T.D. | 9.3 | 4.2 |
| 4.3 | 6.3 | 1.4 | 6.4 |  |  | Trade Payables | 4.3 | 6.0 |
| .1 | .0 | 3.1 | 1.6 |  |  | Income Taxes Payable | .0 | .0 |
| 29.2 | 16.7 | 11.5 | 14.9 |  |  | All Other Current | 30.3 | 24.9 |
| 68.8 | 48.5 | 27.2 | 29.2 |  |  | Total Current | 66.7 | 49.3 |
| 10.7 | 18.7 | 25.0 | 12.7 |  |  | Long-Term Debt | 35.8 | 30.1 |
| .0 | .0 | .0 | .2 |  |  | Deferred Taxes | .4 | .4 |
| 3.9 | 13.7 | 2.2 | 9.9 |  |  | All Other Non-Current | 3.6 | 4.7 |
| 16.8 | 19.0 | 45.5 | 48.0 |  |  | Net Worth | -6.7 | 15.6 |
| 100.0 | 100.0 | 100.0 | 100.0 |  |  | Total Liabilities & Net Worth | 100.0 | 100.0 |
|  |  |  |  |  |  | **INCOME DATA** |  |  |
| 100.0 | 100.0 | 100.0 | 100.0 |  |  | Net Sales | 100.0 | 100.0 |
|  |  |  |  |  |  | Gross Profit |  |  |
| 89.5 | 84.2 | 83.9 | 94.7 |  |  | Operating Expenses | 88.4 | 90.8 |
| 10.5 | 15.8 | 16.1 | 5.3 |  |  | Operating Profit | 11.6 | 9.2 |
| .6 | 4.2 | 4.5 | 2.4 |  |  | All Other Expenses (net) | 1.2 | 3.3 |
| 9.9 | 11.6 | 11.7 | 2.9 |  |  | Profit Before Taxes | 10.4 | 5.9 |
|  |  |  |  |  |  | **RATIOS** |  |  |
| 2.4 | 2.8 | 3.7 | 4.1 |  |  | Current | 3.9 | 3.2 |
| 1.0 | .9 | 1.5 | 1.3 |  |  |  | 1.2 | 1.1 |
| .4 | .4 | .5 | 1.0 |  |  |  | .4 | .4 |
| 2.3 | 2.5 | 3.1 | 3.4 |  |  | Quick | 3.2 | 2.8 |
| .8 | .7 | 1.4 | .9 |  |  |  | .9 | 1.0 |
| .2 | .3 | .5 | .8 |  |  |  | .3 | .3 |
| 0 UND | 0 UND | 0 UND | 11 32.5 |  |  | Sales/Receivables | 0 UND | 0 UND |
| 0 UND | 0 UND | 31 11.9 | 40 9.1 |  |  |  | 0 UND | 0 UND |
| 0 UND | 16 22.9 | 44 8.3 | 48 7.6 |  |  |  | 6 62.4 | 36 10.0 |
|  |  |  |  |  |  | Cost of Sales/Inventory |  |  |
|  |  |  |  |  |  | Cost of Sales/Payables |  |  |
| 43.1 | 10.7 | 6.8 | 3.7 |  |  | Sales/Working Capital | 11.5 | 11.4 |
| UND | -191.1 | 22.0 | 14.9 |  |  |  | 95.0 | 211.3 |
| -31.3 | -12.5 | -9.9 | -457.9 |  |  |  | -36.7 | -20.9 |
| 39.4 | 18.0 | 80.6 | 11.8 |  |  | EBIT/Interest | 25.5 | 27.0 |
| (32) 11.8 | (25) 3.3 | (18) 19.2 | (13) 2.7 |  |  |  | (40) 5.1 | (57) 3.3 |
| 1.6 | -1.2 | 3.0 | -.5 |  |  |  | 1.5 | .5 |
|  |  |  |  |  |  | Net Profit + Depr., Dep., Amort./Cur. Mat. L/T/D |  |  |
| .0 | .3 | .2 | .4 |  |  | Fixed/Worth | .3 | .4 |
| .5 | 2.6 | 1.1 | .9 |  |  |  | 2.8 | 1.8 |
| NM | -2.4 | 5.0 | 4.4 |  |  |  | -.9 | -8.3 |
| .5 | .5 | .3 | .2 |  |  | Debt/Worth | .5 | .6 |
| 2.9 | 3.4 | 1.4 | .8 |  |  |  | 6.3 | 4.5 |
| -5.1 | -6.3 | 11.0 | 7.8 |  |  |  | -3.7 | -13.2 |
| 999.8 | 86.8 | 109.0 | 26.3 |  |  | % Profit Before Taxes/Tangible Net Worth | 147.4 | 137.5 |
| (42) 136.0 | (24) 22.4 | (28) 35.8 | (12) 11.4 |  |  |  | (35) 27.8 | (56) 30.5 |
| 28.7 | -12.5 | 3.4 | -.1 |  |  |  | 8.6 | 5.3 |
| 166.4 | 51.8 | 34.7 | 19.8 |  |  | % Profit Before Taxes/Total Assets | 82.7 | 25.7 |
| 33.9 | 10.2 | 9.2 | 2.7 |  |  |  | 13.5 | 4.1 |
| .0 | -3.0 | .7 | -1.5 |  |  |  | 2.3 | -.7 |
| UND | 46.3 | 37.4 | 25.0 |  |  | Sales/Net Fixed Assets | 103.4 | 89.2 |
| 207.6 | 20.5 | 8.3 | 8.2 |  |  |  | 25.0 | 16.4 |
| 24.3 | 6.2 | 1.8 | 1.5 |  |  |  | 6.1 | 4.0 |
| 22.5 | 7.1 | 4.7 | 3.7 |  |  | Sales/Total Assets | 13.2 | 8.5 |
| 12.5 | 2.7 | 1.6 | 1.4 |  |  |  | 4.5 | 4.0 |
| 7.3 | 1.4 | .8 | .9 |  |  |  | 2.1 | 1.6 |
| .2 | 1.0 | .6 | 1.9 |  |  | % Depr., Dep., Amort./Sales | .5 | .7 |
| (23) 1.2 | (28) 2.1 | (24) 3.3 | (11) 2.8 |  |  |  | (40) 1.9 | (61) 2.0 |
| 3.1 | 4.8 | 8.1 | 4.3 |  |  |  | 3.9 | 4.7 |
| 13.4 | 4.6 |  |  |  |  | % Officers', Directors' Owners' Comp/Sales | 13.3 | 14.6 |
| (38) 21.3 | (15) 8.8 |  |  |  |  |  | (24) 25.6 | (31) 27.1 |
| 35.1 | 30.2 |  |  |  |  |  | 33.6 | 35.2 |
| 107613M | 205387M | 332254M | 1130917M | 784835M | 1696135M | Net Sales ($) | 1928901M | 1229216M |
| 8383M | 42150M | 133004M | 337456M | 329705M | 582181M | Total Assets ($) | 295433M | 547312M |

© RMA 2012

M = $ thousand    MM = $ million
See Pages 9 through 22 for Explanation of Ratios and Data

## Comparative Historical Data | Current Data Sorted by Sales

| | | | | Type of Statement | | | | | | |
|---|---|---|---|---|---|---|---|---|---|---|
| 9 | | 18 | 17 | Unqualified | 1 | 2 | 1 | 2 | 4 | 7 |
| 4 | | 5 | 3 | Reviewed | | | 2 | | | 1 |
| 19 | | 15 | 23 | Compiled | 7 | 1 | 5 | 2 | 5 | 3 |
| 27 | | 24 | 58 | Tax Returns | 24 | 16 | 7 | 4 | 5 | 2 |
| 29 | | 35 | 55 | Other | 11 | 16 | 5 | 8 | 8 | 8 |
| 4/1/09-<br>3/31/10<br>ALL | | 4/1/10-<br>3/31/11<br>ALL | 4/1/11-<br>3/31/12<br>ALL | | 0-1MM | 18 (4/1-9/30/11)<br>1-3MM | 3-5MM | 138 (10/1/11-3/31/12)<br>5-10MM | 10-25MM | 25MM & OVER |
| 88 | | 97 | 156 | NUMBER OF STATEMENTS | 43 | 35 | 20 | 15 | 22 | 21 |
| % | | % | % | ASSETS | % | % | % | % | % | % |
| 19.2 | | 24.2 | 32.0 | Cash & Equivalents | 31.5 | 43.2 | 25.6 | 31.3 | 21.4 | 32.0 |
| 14.8 | | 15.7 | 10.0 | Trade Receivables (net) | 1.4 | 10.2 | 11.6 | 7.7 | 22.0 | 14.7 |
| .4 | | 1.3 | .7 | Inventory | .1 | .6 | 1.9 | 1.1 | .4 | .8 |
| 3.8 | | 4.9 | 3.8 | All Other Current | 5.1 | 2.5 | 2.7 | 3.2 | 3.8 | 4.5 |
| 38.3 | | 46.1 | 46.5 | Total Current | 38.1 | 56.5 | 41.9 | 43.3 | 47.6 | 52.1 |
| 40.0 | | 35.4 | 32.4 | Fixed Assets (net) | 38.8 | 20.7 | 35.7 | 36.0 | 34.2 | 30.9 |
| 6.6 | | 6.0 | 9.2 | Intangibles (net) | 11.7 | 8.6 | 9.0 | 9.0 | 3.7 | 10.4 |
| 15.0 | | 12.5 | 12.0 | All Other Non-Current | 11.5 | 14.1 | 12.4 | 11.6 | 14.5 | 6.6 |
| 100.0 | | 100.0 | 100.0 | Total | 100.0 | 100.0 | 100.0 | 100.0 | 100.0 | 100.0 |
| | | | | LIABILITIES | | | | | | |
| 17.0 | | 17.9 | 19.8 | Notes Payable-Short Term | 17.0 | 37.6 | 8.9 | 15.5 | 18.2 | 11.3 |
| 11.7 | | 4.8 | 3.6 | Cur. Mat.-L.T.D. | 4.3 | 1.0 | 5.4 | 2.9 | 6.1 | 3.0 |
| 6.4 | | 4.9 | 4.6 | Trade Payables | 1.8 | 6.9 | 9.4 | 1.6 | 1.7 | 7.2 |
| .1 | | .7 | .8 | Income Taxes Payable | .0 | .0 | .3 | .0 | 4.5 | 1.1 |
| 24.9 | | 22.4 | 20.3 | All Other Current | 19.8 | 22.7 | 14.0 | 23.4 | 24.5 | 16.7 |
| 60.1 | | 50.6 | 49.2 | Total Current | 42.9 | 68.2 | 38.1 | 43.4 | 55.1 | 39.3 |
| 29.6 | | 25.1 | 16.3 | Long-Term Debt | 26.7 | 6.0 | 23.3 | 10.9 | 13.5 | 12.6 |
| .3 | | .3 | .0 | Deferred Taxes | .0 | .0 | .0 | .0 | .0 | .1 |
| 4.3 | | 5.6 | 6.7 | All Other Non-Current | 4.0 | 3.3 | 10.3 | 17.0 | 5.5 | 8.2 |
| 5.7 | | 18.3 | 27.8 | Net Worth | 26.5 | 22.5 | 28.3 | 28.8 | 25.9 | 39.8 |
| 100.0 | | 100.0 | 100.0 | Total Liabilities & Net Worth | 100.0 | 100.0 | 100.0 | 100.0 | 100.0 | 100.0 |
| | | | | INCOME DATA | | | | | | |
| 100.0 | | 100.0 | 100.0 | Net Sales | 100.0 | 100.0 | 100.0 | 100.0 | 100.0 | 100.0 |
| | | | | Gross Profit | | | | | | |
| 86.8 | | 87.8 | 87.8 | Operating Expenses | 80.5 | 83.9 | 91.7 | 91.6 | 94.1 | 96.4 |
| 13.2 | | 12.2 | 12.2 | Operating Profit | 19.5 | 16.1 | 8.3 | 8.4 | 5.9 | 3.6 |
| 3.7 | | 2.3 | 2.5 | All Other Expenses (net) | 8.3 | .0 | .2 | .3 | -.4 | 1.5 |
| 9.5 | | 9.9 | 9.7 | Profit Before Taxes | 11.2 | 16.2 | 8.1 | 8.2 | 6.3 | 2.2 |
| | | | | RATIOS | | | | | | |
| 2.2 | | 3.4 | 3.1 | | 1.9 | 6.2 | 2.6 | 3.2 | 3.7 | 3.6 |
| .9 | | 1.4 | 1.2 | Current | .6 | 1.7 | 1.3 | 1.6 | 1.1 | 1.6 |
| .4 | | .5 | .5 | | .2 | .5 | .6 | .7 | .5 | 1.0 |
| 1.8 | | 2.9 | 2.9 | | 1.9 | 6.2 | 2.4 | 2.9 | 2.9 | 3.1 |
| .8 | | 1.0 | .9 | Quick | .5 | 1.7 | 1.1 | 1.5 | 1.0 | 1.4 |
| .3 | | .4 | .4 | | .2 | .5 | .4 | .7 | .5 | .8 |
| 0 UND | | 0 UND | 0 UND | | 0 UND | 0 UND | 0 UND | 0 UND | 0 UND | 0 UND |
| 1 428.1 | | 1 276.4 | 0 UND | Sales/Receivables | 0 UND | 0 UND | 0 UND | 1 257.9 | 25 14.7 | 25 14.7 |
| 42 8.6 | | 38 9.5 | 26 13.8 | | 0 UND | 11 31.8 | 33 10.9 | 36 10.0 | 47 7.7 | 42 8.6 |
| | | | | Cost of Sales/Inventory | | | | | | |
| | | | | Cost of Sales/Payables | | | | | | |
| 11.3 | | 6.2 | 10.4 | | 23.2 | 11.2 | 11.8 | 9.7 | 7.0 | 6.0 |
| -302.2 | | 57.3 | 169.2 | Sales/Working Capital | -74.5 | 56.5 | 241.8 | 48.2 | NM | 43.0 |
| -13.1 | | -32.1 | -23.0 | | -8.0 | -17.0 | -24.0 | -76.6 | -34.2 | -133.7 |
| 16.7 | | 44.0 | 31.2 | | 28.9 | 51.0 | 92.6 | 133.7 | 32.7 | 12.5 |
| (68) 3.0 | | (70) 4.7 | (95) 8.0 | EBIT/Interest | (16) 11.0 | (19) 9.3 | (17) 13.0 | (10) 4.0 | (15) 6.5 | (18) 5.8 |
| -.1 | | 1.0 | .7 | | 2.8 | 1.0 | 1.2 | -2.0 | -.4 | .1 |
| | | | | Net Profit + Depr., Dep.,<br>Amort./Cur. Mat. L/T/D | | | | | | |
| .5 | | .3 | .1 | | .0 | .1 | .3 | .2 | .3 | .3 |
| 1.4 | | 1.3 | 1.0 | Fixed/Worth | 1.8 | .5 | 1.6 | 1.2 | 1.0 | .9 |
| -2.7 | | -4.9 | 54.8 | | 24.0 | -10.4 | -17.7 | 5.1 | -2.1 | NM |
| 1.0 | | .4 | .5 | | .9 | .2 | .5 | .6 | .3 | .5 |
| 3.7 | | 2.2 | 2.0 | Debt/Worth | 3.1 | 1.3 | 2.1 | 2.0 | 2.1 | 1.6 |
| -5.7 | | -7.5 | -25.0 | | 69.0 | -5.2 | -11.2 | 24.6 | -4.1 | NM |
| 120.4 | | 177.7 | 138.8 | | 802.8 | 561.5 | 82.4 | 205.4 | 56.8 | 80.1 |
| (60) 26.6 | | (66) 25.8 | (113) 39.3 | % Profit Before Taxes/Tangible<br>Net Worth | (33) 51.9 | (24) 93.5 | (13) 29.3 | (12) 18.1 | (15) 16.9 | (16) 15.5 |
| -.2 | | 3.2 | 1.5 | | 4.3 | 19.6 | -6.3 | -13.2 | 2.0 | 1.4 |
| 50.8 | | 60.5 | 58.9 | | 63.8 | 105.2 | 76.7 | 36.4 | 37.6 | 18.1 |
| 6.8 | | 11.3 | 11.7 | % Profit Before Taxes/Total<br>Assets | 14.3 | 33.4 | 11.0 | 6.3 | 4.9 | 3.5 |
| -1.7 | | .1 | -.1 | | .0 | .3 | .3 | -4.5 | -1.7 | -.2 |
| 47.7 | | 93.2 | 254.0 | | UND | 266.3 | 76.8 | 171.4 | 81.5 | 49.2 |
| 18.9 | | 20.8 | 27.7 | Sales/Net Fixed Assets | 76.6 | 49.0 | 20.6 | 25.9 | 21.0 | 14.9 |
| 3.7 | | 4.0 | 7.4 | | 1.3 | 12.8 | 5.1 | 2.5 | 3.9 | 4.9 |
| 10.2 | | 9.5 | 11.3 | | 12.8 | 13.5 | 7.2 | 15.8 | 7.7 | 6.0 |
| 3.3 | | 3.4 | 4.7 | Sales/Total Assets | 5.1 | 8.1 | 5.0 | 7.2 | 4.6 | 3.4 |
| 1.4 | | 1.5 | 1.5 | | .5 | 2.0 | 2.3 | 1.2 | 1.5 | 1.5 |
| .9 | | .8 | .8 | | 1.9 | .5 | .8 | | .3 | .4 |
| (66) 2.2 | | (64) 2.0 | (91) 2.1 | % Depr., Dep., Amort./Sales | (22) 9.7 | (15) 1.3 | (14) 3.0 | | (17) 2.0 | (16) 1.9 |
| 4.9 | | 3.8 | 4.3 | | 19.8 | 2.8 | 4.5 | | 3.3 | 4.0 |
| 10.4 | | 8.0 | 9.6 | | 14.1 | 6.5 | | | | |
| (32) 16.0 | | (37) 22.5 | (63) 17.3 | % Officers', Directors'<br>Owners' Comp/Sales | (17) 23.2 | (21) 14.4 | | | | |
| 31.2 | | 32.7 | 33.9 | | 36.3 | 35.9 | | | | |
| 1436445M<br>737601M | | 2602003M<br>1152021M | 4257141M<br>1432879M | Net Sales ($)<br>Total Assets ($) | 22954M<br>23191M | 60854M<br>21707M | 79550M<br>26185M | 106024M<br>46643M | 315463M<br>122282M | 3672296M<br>1192871M |

M = $ thousand     MM = $ million
See Pages 9 through 22 for Explanation of Ratios and Data

## Current Data Sorted by Assets      Comparative Historical Data

| | 0-500M | 500M-2MM | 2-10MM | 10-50MM | 50-100MM | 100-250MM | Type of Statement | | 4/1/07-3/31/08 ALL | 4/1/08-3/31/09 ALL |
|---|---|---|---|---|---|---|---|---|---|---|
| | 1 | 3 | 5 | 5 | 2 | 6 | Unqualified | | 19 | 18 |
| | 3 | 1 | 4 | 3 | | | Reviewed | | 19 | 6 |
| | 182 | 90 | 18 | 1 | | 3 | Compiled | | 158 | 187 |
| | 945 | 372 | 16 | 1 | 1 | | Tax Returns | | 520 | 657 |
| | 378 | 213 | 38 | 15 | 2 | 8 | Other | | 243 | 297 |
| | | 95 (4/1-9/30/11) | | | 2,221 (10/1/11-3/31/12) | | | | | |
| | 1509 | 679 | 81 | 25 | 5 | 17 | NUMBER OF STATEMENTS | | 959 | 1165 |
| | % | % | % | % | % | % | ASSETS | | % | % |
| | 29.2 | 16.2 | 11.6 | 12.9 | | 14.6 | Cash & Equivalents | | 21.1 | 20.4 |
| | 2.6 | 3.7 | 13.5 | 12.7 | | 8.6 | Trade Receivables (net) | | 4.5 | 3.3 |
| | .4 | .3 | .9 | .6 | | 2.2 | Inventory | | .4 | .5 |
| | 2.5 | 2.7 | 2.1 | 5.5 | | 2.6 | All Other Current | | 3.1 | 3.6 |
| | 34.6 | 22.7 | 28.1 | 31.8 | | 28.0 | Total Current | | 29.0 | 27.7 |
| | 39.9 | 41.2 | 47.7 | 34.3 | | 32.1 | Fixed Assets (net) | | 45.4 | 46.0 |
| | 14.7 | 24.4 | 12.8 | 24.0 | | 31.4 | Intangibles (net) | | 14.8 | 16.7 |
| | 10.7 | 11.6 | 11.4 | 9.9 | | 8.5 | All Other Non-Current | | 10.8 | 9.5 |
| | 100.0 | 100.0 | 100.0 | 100.0 | | 100.0 | Total | | 100.0 | 100.0 |
| | | | | | | | LIABILITIES | | | |
| | 18.3 | 7.7 | 3.7 | .9 | | 1.7 | Notes Payable-Short Term | | 15.1 | 13.3 |
| | 8.9 | 5.6 | 4.8 | 3.7 | | 6.6 | Cur. Mat.-L.T.D. | | 8.4 | 9.5 |
| | 2.1 | 1.0 | 2.9 | 4.2 | | 3.5 | Trade Payables | | 2.2 | 1.6 |
| | .1 | .0 | .5 | .1 | | .0 | Income Taxes Payable | | .2 | .1 |
| | 19.2 | 7.9 | 6.7 | 19.0 | | 13.6 | All Other Current | | 19.4 | 16.6 |
| | 48.6 | 22.2 | 18.6 | 27.9 | | 25.5 | Total Current | | 45.1 | 41.1 |
| | 51.5 | 55.3 | 41.5 | 25.8 | | 67.5 | Long-Term Debt | | 46.9 | 51.8 |
| | .0 | .0 | .1 | .9 | | 2.7 | Deferred Taxes | | .0 | .1 |
| | 12.4 | 5.3 | 4.8 | 17.5 | | 11.2 | All Other Non-Current | | 6.9 | 5.5 |
| | -12.6 | 17.3 | 35.0 | 28.0 | | -7.0 | Net Worth | | 1.0 | 1.6 |
| | 100.0 | 100.0 | 100.0 | 100.0 | | 100.0 | Total Liabilties & Net Worth | | 100.0 | 100.0 |
| | | | | | | | INCOME DATA | | | |
| | 100.0 | 100.0 | 100.0 | 100.0 | | 100.0 | Net Sales | | 100.0 | 100.0 |
| | | | | | | | Gross Profit | | | |
| | 87.9 | 82.5 | 82.2 | 90.5 | | 94.9 | Operating Expenses | | 87.4 | 87.0 |
| | 12.1 | 17.5 | 17.8 | 9.5 | | 5.1 | Operating Profit | | 12.6 | 13.0 |
| | 1.7 | 4.8 | 5.6 | 1.5 | | 3.8 | All Other Expenses (net) | | 2.6 | 3.2 |
| | 10.5 | 12.7 | 12.3 | 8.0 | | 1.2 | Profit Before Taxes | | 10.0 | 9.9 |
| | | | | | | | RATIOS | | | |
| | 3.2 | 3.4 | 3.0 | 1.6 | | 1.7 | Current | | 1.8 | 2.0 |
| | 1.0 | 1.0 | 1.4 | .9 | | 1.0 | | | .7 | .7 |
| | .3 | .3 | .4 | .6 | | .7 | | | .2 | .2 |
| | 2.9 | 2.9 | 2.9 | 1.4 | | 1.4 | Quick | | 1.6 | 1.8 |
| | .9 | (678) .9 | 1.2 | .8 | | .7 | | (957) .5 | (1161) .6 |
| | .2 | .2 | .2 | .5 | | .4 | | | .2 | .2 |
| | 0 UND | 0 UND | 0 UND | 4 86.8 | | 0 UND | Sales/Receivables | | 0 UND | 0 UND |
| | 0 UND | 0 UND | 0 UND | 18 19.9 | | 25 14.6 | | | 0 UND | 0 UND |
| | 0 UND | 0 UND | 28 13.1 | 28 13.1 | | 33 11.2 | | | 0 UND | 0 UND |
| | | | | | | | Cost of Sales/Inventory | | | |
| | | | | | | | Cost of Sales/Payables | | | |
| | 22.9 | 11.4 | 10.7 | 26.4 | | 16.3 | Sales/Working Capital | | 36.8 | 34.1 |
| | -790.5 | 734.0 | 45.2 | -183.9 | | -999.8 | | | -64.0 | -75.2 |
| | -19.9 | -14.4 | -22.6 | -30.3 | | -17.9 | | | -15.9 | -14.1 |
| | 21.2 | 13.9 | 25.3 | 26.1 | | 4.9 | EBIT/Interest | | 12.4 | 14.2 |
| | (1135) 5.6 | (571) 4.8 | (67) 7.0 | (23) 13.0 | | 1.5 | | (752) 4.0 | (939) 4.1 |
| | 1.5 | 1.8 | 2.0 | 3.9 | | -.2 | | | 1.1 | 1.2 |
| | 5.1 | 3.1 | | | | | Net Profit + Depr., Dep., Amort./Cur. Mat. L/T/D | | 4.8 | 4.8 |
| | (19) 1.6 | (10) 1.7 | | | | | | (26) 1.6 | (34) 1.2 |
| | .6 | .6 | | | | | | | .6 | .5 |
| | .7 | 1.2 | .7 | .6 | | 3.8 | Fixed/Worth | | 1.1 | 1.2 |
| | UND | 139.9 | 2.4 | 4.0 | | -2.7 | | | 188.0 | -54.1 |
| | -.6 | -.8 | 19.1 | -1.7 | | -.2 | | | -1.0 | -.9 |
| | 1.5 | 2.1 | .7 | 1.1 | | 7.2 | Debt/Worth | | 2.0 | 1.9 |
| | -13.0 | -52.0 | 2.9 | 5.1 | | -6.4 | | | -58.8 | -30.2 |
| | -2.0 | -2.2 | 163.3 | -4.1 | | -1.6 | | | -2.5 | -2.4 |
| | 490.3 | 189.7 | 90.8 | 155.5 | | | % Profit Before Taxes/Tangible Net Worth | | 356.4 | 339.4 |
| | (689) 139.3 | (325) 81.6 | (62) 46.6 | (16) 52.4 | | | | (465) 123.3 | (547) 117.8 |
| | 39.9 | 29.1 | 7.5 | 19.7 | | | | | 33.7 | 29.4 |
| | 93.0 | 40.3 | 27.2 | 30.7 | | 8.9 | % Profit Before Taxes/Total Assets | | 66.5 | 63.0 |
| | 31.9 | 16.4 | 10.8 | 12.6 | | 3.5 | | | 19.2 | 19.0 |
| | 4.0 | 3.8 | 1.4 | 7.9 | | -2.5 | | | .8 | 1.4 |
| | 67.8 | 21.9 | 18.2 | 13.8 | | 9.6 | Sales/Net Fixed Assets | | 38.2 | 35.3 |
| | 18.7 | 8.7 | 7.9 | 8.5 | | 5.6 | | | 12.4 | 12.1 |
| | 7.9 | 2.9 | .9 | 4.1 | | 4.0 | | | 5.2 | 4.5 |
| | 10.7 | 3.4 | 3.5 | 3.4 | | 3.5 | Sales/Total Assets | | 8.7 | 8.5 |
| | 5.4 | 2.0 | 2.0 | 2.2 | | 1.7 | | | 4.2 | 3.8 |
| | 2.9 | 1.3 | .5 | 1.6 | | .8 | | | 2.2 | 2.0 |
| | 1.1 | 1.9 | 1.9 | 1.9 | | | % Depr., Dep., Amort./Sales | | 1.2 | 1.4 |
| | (852) 2.6 | (426) 4.1 | (58) 3.1 | (23) 2.8 | | | | (649) 2.7 | (781) 3.4 |
| | 5.4 | 8.1 | 10.0 | 5.2 | | | | | 5.5 | 6.5 |
| | 10.9 | 9.2 | 3.1 | | | | % Officers', Directors' Owners' Comp/Sales | | 11.9 | 10.4 |
| | (1050) 17.7 | (442) 15.2 | (30) 11.3 | | | | | (664) 19.1 | (802) 18.1 |
| | 25.2 | 22.9 | 16.6 | | | | | | 28.8 | 25.8 |
| | 1958337M | 1520244M | 749973M | 1939687M | 1228556M | 6220714M | Net Sales ($) | | 14421648M | 11970487M |
| | 337322M | 596342M | 306128M | 558211M | 352938M | 2838585M | Total Assets ($) | | 3250423M | 2956731M |

© RMA 2012

M = $ thousand    MM = $ million
See Pages 9 through 22 for Explanation of Ratios and Data

## Comparative Historical Data | | Type of Statement | ## Current Data Sorted by Sales

| | | | Type of Statement | | | | | | |
|---|---|---|---|---|---|---|---|---|---|
| 27 | 24 | 22 | Unqualified | 1 | 3 | 1 | 2 | 2 | 13 |
| 7 | 14 | 11 | Reviewed | 2 | 1 | | 4 | 4 | 4 |
| 226 | 235 | 291 | Compiled | 93 | 149 | 22 | 14 | 12 | 1 |
| 792 | 832 | 1338 | Tax Returns | 557 | 630 | 103 | 36 | 7 | 5 |
| 330 | 481 | 654 | Other | 282 | 253 | 58 | 18 | 18 | 25 |
| 4/1/09-3/31/10 ALL | 4/1/10-3/31/11 ALL | 4/1/11-3/31/12 ALL | | 95 (4/1-9/30/11) 0-1MM | 1-3MM | 3-5MM | 2,221 (10/1/11-3/31/12) 5-10MM | 10-25MM | 25MM & OVER |
| 1382 | 1586 | 2316 | NUMBER OF STATEMENTS | 935 | 1035 | 185 | 70 | 43 | 48 |
| % | % | % | ASSETS | % | % | % | % | % | % |
| 22.0 | 23.0 | 24.4 | Cash & Equivalents | 22.8 | 26.2 | 26.3 | 25.8 | 18.1 | 14.7 |
| 4.0 | 4.4 | 3.4 | Trade Receivables (net) | 2.2 | 3.2 | 4.9 | 4.6 | 18.8 | 12.2 |
| .4 | .5 | .4 | Inventory | .4 | .3 | .5 | .7 | .5 | 2.1 |
| 2.9 | 3.1 | 2.6 | All Other Current | 2.7 | 2.2 | 3.1 | 2.1 | 4.0 | 5.0 |
| 29.3 | 30.9 | 30.8 | Total Current | 28.1 | 31.9 | 34.9 | 33.2 | 41.3 | 33.9 |
| 42.8 | 41.8 | 40.4 | Fixed Assets (net) | 43.3 | 38.7 | 36.3 | 44.9 | 39.0 | 32.8 |
| 17.0 | 16.6 | 17.8 | Intangibles (net) | 17.8 | 18.4 | 15.8 | 11.9 | 11.5 | 25.8 |
| 10.8 | 10.7 | 11.0 | All Other Non-Current | 10.8 | 11.0 | 13.0 | 10.0 | 8.2 | 7.5 |
| 100.0 | 100.0 | 100.0 | Total | 100.0 | 100.0 | 100.0 | 100.0 | 100.0 | 100.0 |
| | | | LIABILITIES | | | | | | |
| 13.8 | 13.5 | 14.3 | Notes Payable-Short Term | 13.4 | 16.0 | 14.1 | 13.7 | 9.9 | 1.3 |
| 8.2 | 7.5 | 7.7 | Cur. Mat.-L.T.D. | 6.6 | 8.5 | 9.7 | 7.3 | 7.1 | 5.1 |
| 1.8 | 2.1 | 1.8 | Trade Payables | 1.5 | 1.6 | 2.1 | 6.0 | 3.4 | 4.5 |
| .1 | .1 | .1 | Income Taxes Payable | .1 | .0 | | .3 | .6 | .1 |
| 19.0 | 15.2 | 15.4 | All Other Current | 12.3 | 17.3 | 17.3 | 19.4 | 22.2 | 16.5 |
| 43.0 | 38.4 | 39.3 | Total Current | 33.9 | 43.4 | 43.3 | 46.6 | 43.2 | 27.3 |
| 49.1 | 49.0 | 52.1 | Long-Term Debt | 56.9 | 50.5 | 44.7 | 50.2 | 31.6 | 40.5 |
| .1 | .1 | .0 | Deferred Taxes | .0 | .0 | .0 | .0 | .2 | 1.5 |
| 6.2 | 8.9 | 10.1 | All Other Non-Current | 13.7 | 7.5 | 8.7 | 4.6 | 4.8 | 14.0 |
| 1.5 | 3.6 | -1.5 | Net Worth | -4.5 | -1.5 | 3.4 | -1.4 | 20.2 | 16.7 |
| 100.0 | 100.0 | 100.0 | Total Liabilities & Net Worth | 100.0 | 100.0 | 100.0 | 100.0 | 100.0 | 100.0 |
| | | | INCOME DATA | | | | | | |
| 100.0 | 100.0 | 100.0 | Net Sales | 100.0 | 100.0 | 100.0 | 100.0 | 100.0 | 100.0 |
| | | | Gross Profit | | | | | | |
| 87.1 | 85.4 | 86.2 | Operating Expenses | 83.2 | 87.6 | 89.1 | 90.9 | 90.3 | 93.1 |
| 12.9 | 14.6 | 13.8 | Operating Profit | 16.8 | 12.4 | 10.9 | 9.1 | 9.7 | 6.9 |
| 2.7 | 2.9 | 2.8 | All Other Expenses (net) | 4.7 | 1.5 | .9 | 1.0 | 2.2 | 2.4 |
| 10.2 | 11.6 | 11.1 | Profit Before Taxes | 12.1 | 10.9 | 10.0 | 8.1 | 7.4 | 4.6 |
| | | | RATIOS | | | | | | |
| 2.3 | 2.9 | 3.2 | Current | 4.4 | 2.9 | 2.1 | 1.9 | 2.8 | 2.0 |
| .8 | 1.0 | 1.0 | | 1.1 | .9 | .8 | .6 | 1.3 | 1.0 |
| .2 | .3 | .3 | | .3 | .3 | .3 | .2 | .8 | .7 |
| 2.0 | 2.5 | 2.9 | Quick | 3.8 | 2.7 | 1.9 | 1.8 | 2.6 | 1.6 |
| (1381) .6 | (1583) .8 | (2315) .9 | | 1.0 | .8 | (184) .8 | .6 | 1.0 | .8 |
| .2 | .2 | .2 | | .2 | .2 | .2 | .2 | .5 | .4 |
| 0 UND | 0 UND | 0 UND | Sales/Receivables | 0 UND | 0 UND | 0 UND | 0 UND | 0 UND | 2 151.5 |
| 0 UND | 0 UND | 0 UND | | 0 UND | 0 UND | 0 UND | 0 UND | 8 46.8 | 19 19.6 |
| 0 UND | 0 UND | 0 UND | | 0 UND | 0 UND | 0 UND | 0 UND | 33 11.2 | 29 12.5 |
| | | | Cost of Sales/Inventory | | | | | | |
| | | | Cost of Sales/Payables | | | | | | |
| 25.8 | 19.3 | 18.2 | Sales/Working Capital | 12.7 | 20.9 | 35.3 | 27.8 | 10.7 | 13.8 |
| -111.7 | -855.8 | UND | | 191.0 | -298.4 | -264.8 | -83.9 | 72.4 | -999.8 |
| -14.9 | -17.0 | -17.9 | | -12.5 | -18.6 | -30.3 | -23.9 | -45.3 | -23.8 |
| 15.6 | 18.6 | 19.0 | EBIT/Interest | 12.1 | 23.0 | 27.9 | 33.7 | 23.9 | 26.7 |
| (1107) 4.4 | (1240) 5.7 | (1817) 5.2 | | (665) 3.8 | (852) 6.1 | (151) 11.3 | (66) 5.8 | (37) 6.0 | (46) 7.3 |
| 1.3 | 1.5 | 1.6 | | 1.4 | 1.9 | 2.1 | 1.0 | 1.5 | 1.5 |
| 7.9 | 7.4 | 5.2 | Net Profit + Depr., Dep., Amort./Cur. Mat. L/T/D | | 4.7 | | | | 12.5 |
| (30) 2.5 | (42) 1.6 | (42) 1.8 | | | (13) 1.6 | | | | (10) 2.6 |
| 1.0 | .6 | .7 | | | .5 | | | | 1.1 |
| .9 | .9 | .8 | Fixed/Worth | .9 | .8 | .7 | 1.0 | .8 | .6 |
| UND | 42.5 | 54.8 | | 223.6 | UND | 7.9 | NM | 1.6 | 6.1 |
| -.9 | -.8 | -.7 | | -.6 | -.6 | -.8 | -1.4 | -5.3 | -1.8 |
| 1.6 | 1.5 | 1.6 | Debt/Worth | 1.8 | 1.5 | 1.9 | 1.7 | .7 | 1.1 |
| -24.0 | -137.8 | -25.8 | | -17.4 | -11.4 | 357.0 | -106.4 | 2.5 | 9.9 |
| -2.4 | -2.5 | -2.1 | | -1.9 | -2.0 | -2.5 | -3.1 | -18.9 | -3.5 |
| 283.5 | 296.9 | 302.0 | % Profit Before Taxes/Tangible Net Worth | 267.9 | 352.5 | 562.7 | 199.9 | 169.2 | 103.1 |
| (660) 96.3 | (783) 108.6 | (1103) 105.1 | | (438) 92.8 | (479) 125.0 | (94) 173.0 | (34) 85.0 | (30) 63.7 | (28) 51.9 |
| 24.2 | 30.9 | 31.7 | | 23.0 | 44.9 | 51.2 | 35.7 | 18.9 | 19.7 |
| 61.0 | 71.5 | 68.0 | % Profit Before Taxes/Total Assets | 53.7 | 79.4 | 81.2 | 61.2 | 43.3 | 26.8 |
| 19.7 | 24.6 | 23.5 | | 17.9 | 29.2 | 32.8 | 20.6 | 15.3 | 11.8 |
| 1.4 | 2.6 | 3.7 | | 2.5 | 5.4 | 5.2 | .0 | .8 | 3.4 |
| 36.5 | 38.9 | 44.9 | Sales/Net Fixed Assets | 33.1 | 56.3 | 81.1 | 52.7 | 22.8 | 16.6 |
| 13.1 | 13.2 | 14.0 | | 9.2 | 16.4 | 23.0 | 19.4 | 14.5 | 8.5 |
| 5.5 | 5.3 | 5.5 | | 3.2 | 8.1 | 11.4 | 9.5 | 7.9 | 4.5 |
| 7.8 | 7.8 | 7.8 | Sales/Total Assets | 5.1 | 9.3 | 11.8 | 12.1 | 7.4 | 4.5 |
| 4.0 | 3.7 | 3.7 | | 2.5 | 4.5 | 6.5 | 6.7 | 4.4 | 2.5 |
| 2.1 | 1.9 | 2.0 | | 1.4 | 2.5 | 4.2 | 3.9 | 2.3 | 1.4 |
| 1.3 | 1.3 | 1.4 | % Depr., Dep., Amort./Sales | 2.1 | 1.2 | .8 | 1.0 | 1.3 | 1.9 |
| (910) 2.9 | (1000) 2.8 | (1370) 3.1 | | (545) 5.2 | (610) 2.6 | (100) 1.8 | (49) 1.9 | (31) 2.3 | (35) 2.8 |
| 5.8 | 6.1 | 6.3 | | 9.8 | 4.9 | 2.7 | 2.8 | 4.9 | 4.7 |
| 10.6 | 10.1 | 10.3 | % Officers', Directors' Owners' Comp/Sales | 9.8 | 10.8 | 8.6 | 9.8 | 1.8 | 10.8 |
| (965) 17.7 | (1067) 16.6 | (1533) 16.7 | | (571) 16.0 | (746) 16.6 | (131) 18.5 | (52) 24.2 | (22) 13.5 | (11) 21.2 |
| 26.4 | 25.5 | 24.6 | | 24.2 | 23.8 | 31.0 | 38.3 | 31.1 | 34.5 |
| 19358930M | 23196089M | 13617511M | Net Sales ($) | 582190M | 1732160M | 695719M | 480134M | 623312M | 9503996M |
| 5245972M | 5441375M | 4989526M | Total Assets ($) | 354549M | 489461M | 135356M | 93555M | 190558M | 3726047M |

M = $ thousand    MM = $ million
See Pages 9 through 22 for Explanation of Ratios and Data

## Current Data Sorted by Assets      Comparative Historical Data

| 0-500M | 500M-2MM | 2-10MM | 10-50MM | 50-100MM | 100-250MM | Type of Statement | 4/1/07-3/31/08 ALL | 4/1/08-3/31/09 ALL |
|---|---|---|---|---|---|---|---|---|
| | | 1 | 1 | | | Unqualified | | 1 |
| | | | 1 | | | Reviewed | | 1 |
| 13 | 4 | 1 | 1 | | | Compiled | 19 | 12 |
| 85 | 11 | 1 | 1 | | | Tax Returns | 77 | 64 |
| 49 | 11 | 2 | 3 | | | Other | 34 | 26 |
| | 6 (4/1-9/30/11) | | 175 (10/1/11-3/31/12) | | | | | |
| 147 | 26 | 5 | 3 | | | NUMBER OF STATEMENTS | 130 | 104 |
| % | % | % | % | % | % | **ASSETS** | % | % |
| 30.9 | 15.6 | | | D | D | Cash & Equivalents | 23.4 | 27.8 |
| 6.1 | 3.6 | | | A | A | Trade Receivables (net) | 8.6 | 9.3 |
| 1.2 | .8 | | | T | T | Inventory | .5 | .5 |
| 2.2 | .5 | | | A | A | All Other Current | 4.8 | 3.3 |
| 40.5 | 20.4 | | | | | Total Current | 37.1 | 40.8 |
| 32.1 | 55.3 | | | N | N | Fixed Assets (net) | 35.7 | 38.3 |
| 12.4 | 7.9 | | | O | O | Intangibles (net) | 13.4 | 6.0 |
| 15.1 | 16.4 | | | T | T | All Other Non-Current | 13.8 | 14.8 |
| 100.0 | 100.0 | | | | | Total | 100.0 | 100.0 |
| | | | | A | A | **LIABILITIES** | | |
| 20.5 | 7.5 | | | V | V | Notes Payable-Short Term | 22.6 | 26.9 |
| 6.0 | 4.6 | | | A | A | Cur. Mat.-L.T.D. | 7.0 | 4.3 |
| 3.1 | .7 | | | I | I | Trade Payables | 5.5 | 1.8 |
| .0 | .0 | | | L | L | Income Taxes Payable | .5 | .3 |
| 11.1 | 4.1 | | | A | A | All Other Current | 12.4 | 10.1 |
| 40.8 | 16.9 | | | B | B | Total Current | 47.9 | 43.4 |
| 38.4 | 57.1 | | | L | L | Long-Term Debt | 34.7 | 31.1 |
| .2 | .0 | | | E | E | Deferred Taxes | .0 | .0 |
| 11.1 | 5.4 | | | | | All Other Non-Current | 10.0 | 8.6 |
| 9.5 | 20.6 | | | | | Net Worth | 7.4 | 16.8 |
| 100.0 | 100.0 | | | | | Total Liabilities & Net Worth | 100.0 | 100.0 |
| | | | | | | **INCOME DATA** | | |
| 100.0 | 100.0 | | | | | Net Sales | 100.0 | 100.0 |
| | | | | | | Gross Profit | | |
| 83.8 | 70.4 | | | | | Operating Expenses | 83.7 | 80.5 |
| 16.2 | 29.6 | | | | | Operating Profit | 16.3 | 19.5 |
| 1.7 | 17.7 | | | | | All Other Expenses (net) | 3.1 | 2.7 |
| 14.5 | 11.9 | | | | | Profit Before Taxes | 13.2 | 16.7 |
| | | | | | | **RATIOS** | | |
| 3.8 | 4.1 | | | | | | 2.7 | 3.3 |
| 1.3 | 1.0 | | | | | Current | 1.0 | 1.4 |
| .4 | .1 | | | | | | .3 | .4 |
| 3.4 | 3.9 | | | | | | 2.4 | 3.2 |
| 1.2 | .9 | | | | | Quick | (129) .8 | 1.2 |
| .3 | .1 | | | | | | .2 | .3 |
| 0 UND | 0 UND | | | | | | 0 UND | 0 UND |
| 0 UND | 0 UND | | | | | Sales/Receivables | 0 UND | 0 UND |
| 0 UND | 0 UND | | | | | | 0 UND | 0 UND |
| | | | | | | Cost of Sales/Inventory | | |
| | | | | | | Cost of Sales/Payables | | |
| 14.2 | 10.4 | | | | | | 20.8 | 15.1 |
| 143.2 | NM | | | | | Sales/Working Capital | -270.8 | 75.9 |
| -22.3 | -8.6 | | | | | | -12.5 | -25.1 |
| 30.0 | 12.5 | | | | | | 12.9 | 38.9 |
| (94) 7.6 | (17) 9.0 | | | | | EBIT/Interest | (93) 5.8 | (70) 12.4 |
| 2.1 | 2.8 | | | | | | 2.0 | 1.8 |
| | | | | | | Net Profit + Depr., Dep., Amort./Cur. Mat. L/T/D | | |
| .2 | .7 | | | | | | .3 | .3 |
| 1.3 | 3.1 | | | | | Fixed/Worth | 3.5 | 1.1 |
| -1.6 | -21.8 | | | | | | -.9 | UND |
| .4 | 1.5 | | | | | | .5 | .4 |
| 5.0 | 9.6 | | | | | Debt/Worth | 34.2 | 2.0 |
| -3.0 | -12.6 | | | | | | -2.9 | -85.7 |
| 464.8 | 332.0 | | | | | | 412.5 | 496.7 |
| (91) 136.1 | (18) 50.5 | | | | | % Profit Before Taxes/Tangible Net Worth | (71) 155.3 | (77) 145.8 |
| 44.6 | -.1 | | | | | | 45.8 | 70.0 |
| 112.8 | 33.5 | | | | | | 109.5 | 135.1 |
| 42.3 | 17.1 | | | | | % Profit Before Taxes/Total Assets | 31.1 | 53.2 |
| 9.8 | 2.0 | | | | | | 4.6 | 15.9 |
| 101.0 | 29.4 | | | | | | 52.5 | 51.2 |
| 24.5 | 4.8 | | | | | Sales/Net Fixed Assets | 20.3 | 15.2 |
| 10.1 | .1 | | | | | | 7.4 | 6.0 |
| 8.6 | 2.9 | | | | | | 11.0 | 8.6 |
| 5.0 | 1.4 | | | | | Sales/Total Assets | 4.5 | 4.5 |
| 2.8 | .1 | | | | | | 1.9 | 2.2 |
| 1.1 | 2.5 | | | | | | .9 | .6 |
| (69) 2.5 | (12) 6.6 | | | | | % Depr., Dep., Amort./Sales | (77) 2.3 | (68) 2.0 |
| 4.8 | 24.0 | | | | | | 4.5 | 4.2 |
| 10.7 | | | | | | | 12.7 | 10.9 |
| (102) 16.5 | | | | | | % Officers', Directors' Owners' Comp/Sales | (81) 19.9 | (68) 15.7 |
| 23.0 | | | | | | | 27.4 | 21.7 |
| 88090M | 36433M | 63162M | 55169M | | | Net Sales ($) | 901972M | 1205613M |
| 20903M | 22853M | 20699M | 47750M | | | Total Assets ($) | 328176M | 337105M |

M = $ thousand    MM = $ million
See Pages 9 through 22 for Explanation of Ratios and Data

## Comparative Historical Data     Current Data Sorted by Sales

Type of Statement counts:

| | 3 | 5 | 1 | Type of Statement | | | | | | |
|---|---|---|---|---|---|---|---|---|---|---|
| | 20 | 22 | 18 | Unqualified | 13 | 4 | 1 | | 1 | |
| | | | | Reviewed | | | | | | |
| | 3 | 5 | 1 | Compiled | | | | 1 | | |
| | 79 | 92 | 97 | Tax Returns | 80 | 15 | 2 | | | |
| | 51 | 71 | 65 | Other | 43 | 16 | | 3 | 1 | 2 |

| 4/1/09- 3/31/10 ALL | 4/1/10- 3/31/11 ALL | 4/1/11- 3/31/12 ALL | | 6 (4/1-9/30/11) 0-1MM | 1-3MM | 175 (10/1/11-3/31/12) 3-5MM | 5-10MM | 10-25MM | 25MM & OVER |
|---|---|---|---|---|---|---|---|---|---|
| 153 | 190 | 181 | **NUMBER OF STATEMENTS** | 136 | 35 | 3 | 4 | 1 | 2 |
| % | % | % | **ASSETS** | % | % | % | % | % | % |
| 27.7 | 24.9 | 27.9 | Cash & Equivalents | 28.8 | 27.9 | | | | |
| 11.0 | 7.1 | 7.2 | Trade Receivables (net) | 6.2 | 6.7 | | | | |
| .2 | 1.1 | 1.1 | Inventory | 1.2 | .7 | | | | |
| 2.6 | 1.9 | 2.0 | All Other Current | 1.7 | 3.0 | | | | |
| 41.6 | 35.1 | 38.2 | Total Current | 37.9 | 38.4 | | | | |
| 37.9 | 39.0 | 34.7 | Fixed Assets (net) | 34.9 | 38.2 | | | | |
| 8.1 | 10.3 | 11.8 | Intangibles (net) | 13.0 | 7.8 | | | | |
| 12.3 | 15.7 | 15.4 | All Other Non-Current | 14.3 | 15.6 | | | | |
| 100.0 | 100.0 | 100.0 | Total | 100.0 | 100.0 | | | | |
| | | | **LIABILITIES** | | | | | | |
| 18.6 | 18.1 | 17.7 | Notes Payable-Short Term | 18.6 | 18.0 | | | | |
| 3.8 | 5.0 | 5.6 | Cur. Mat.-L.T.D. | 5.1 | 8.1 | | | | |
| 1.9 | 1.4 | 2.8 | Trade Payables | 3.4 | .8 | | | | |
| .1 | .3 | .0 | Income Taxes Payable | .0 | .0 | | | | |
| 12.9 | 13.8 | 9.8 | All Other Current | 10.4 | 8.8 | | | | |
| 37.3 | 38.7 | 36.0 | Total Current | 37.4 | 35.7 | | | | |
| 33.2 | 28.8 | 40.4 | Long-Term Debt | 42.0 | 34.8 | | | | |
| .3 | .0 | .1 | Deferred Taxes | .0 | .7 | | | | |
| 2.7 | 13.9 | 9.9 | All Other Non-Current | 9.8 | 12.6 | | | | |
| 26.5 | 18.6 | 13.6 | Net Worth | 10.8 | 16.2 | | | | |
| 100.0 | 100.0 | 100.0 | Total Liabilities & Net Worth | 100.0 | 100.0 | | | | |
| | | | **INCOME DATA** | | | | | | |
| 100.0 | 100.0 | 100.0 | Net Sales | 100.0 | 100.0 | | | | |
| | | | Gross Profit | | | | | | |
| 81.1 | 84.1 | 82.0 | Operating Expenses | 80.6 | 86.2 | | | | |
| 18.9 | 15.9 | 18.0 | Operating Profit | 19.4 | 13.8 | | | | |
| 2.2 | 1.9 | 3.9 | All Other Expenses (net) | 4.7 | 2.0 | | | | |
| 16.7 | 14.1 | 14.1 | Profit Before Taxes | 14.8 | 11.7 | | | | |
| | | | **RATIOS** | | | | | | |
| 4.0 | 3.2 | 4.1 | | 4.2 | 3.9 | | | | |
| 1.3 | .8 | 1.3 | Current | 1.2 | 1.7 | | | | |
| .4 | .3 | .4 | | .3 | .4 | | | | |
| 4.0 | 3.2 | 3.9 | | 3.8 | 3.9 | | | | |
| 1.2 | .8 | 1.2 | Quick | 1.1 | 1.1 | | | | |
| .3 | .2 | .3 | | .3 | .3 | | | | |
| 0 UND | 0 UND | 0 UND | | 0 UND | 0 UND | | | | |
| 0 UND | 0 UND | 0 UND | Sales/Receivables | 0 UND | 0 UND | | | | |
| 0 UND | 0 UND | 0 UND | | 0 UND | 0 UND | | | | |
| | | | Cost of Sales/Inventory | | | | | | |
| | | | Cost of Sales/Payables | | | | | | |
| 12.1 | 19.4 | 12.3 | | 12.1 | 14.7 | | | | |
| 68.2 | -126.0 | 103.1 | Sales/Working Capital | 114.2 | 168.0 | | | | |
| -23.9 | -15.5 | -22.1 | | -21.4 | -38.4 | | | | |
| 38.6 | 34.0 | 26.0 | | 28.3 | 22.8 | | | | |
| (101) 12.0 | (123) 9.0 | (116) 7.6 | EBIT/Interest | (81) 7.8 | (28) 6.8 | | | | |
| 3.5 | 4.0 | 2.1 | | 2.3 | 1.9 | | | | |
| | | | Net Profit + Depr., Dep., Amort./Cur. Mat. L/T/D | | | | | | |
| .3 | .4 | .2 | | .3 | .4 | | | | |
| 1.1 | 1.5 | 1.5 | Fixed/Worth | 1.5 | 2.3 | | | | |
| UND | -5.1 | -3.3 | | -1.6 | -6.1 | | | | |
| .3 | .4 | .6 | | .6 | .4 | | | | |
| 2.5 | 2.8 | 4.8 | Debt/Worth | 4.3 | 9.6 | | | | |
| -165.1 | -4.3 | -4.0 | | -3.0 | -10.1 | | | | |
| 415.3 | 289.8 | 381.4 | | 313.0 | 959.4 | | | | |
| (114) 99.8 | (129) 91.9 | (117) 102.5 | % Profit Before Taxes/Tangible Net Worth | (84) 102.2 | (25) 177.5 | | | | |
| 40.5 | 27.6 | 29.0 | | 30.8 | 70.7 | | | | |
| 99.3 | 80.9 | 92.9 | | 106.9 | 82.6 | | | | |
| 43.3 | 36.8 | 33.3 | % Profit Before Taxes/Total Assets | 35.0 | 30.4 | | | | |
| 12.1 | 6.0 | 7.5 | | 6.9 | 10.7 | | | | |
| 59.9 | 51.2 | 95.4 | | 97.1 | 95.1 | | | | |
| 15.2 | 15.9 | 19.3 | Sales/Net Fixed Assets | 19.9 | 16.3 | | | | |
| 6.2 | 6.0 | 8.7 | | 8.7 | 7.7 | | | | |
| 7.4 | 7.2 | 7.4 | | 7.9 | 8.1 | | | | |
| 3.9 | 3.8 | 4.5 | Sales/Total Assets | 4.4 | 4.6 | | | | |
| 2.0 | 1.8 | 1.9 | | 1.8 | 2.9 | | | | |
| .8 | .8 | 1.1 | | 1.2 | .7 | | | | |
| (89) 2.0 | (106) 1.8 | (85) 2.7 | % Depr., Dep., Amort./Sales | (62) 2.8 | (19) 1.9 | | | | |
| 3.9 | 3.5 | 5.1 | | 6.0 | 3.2 | | | | |
| 8.6 | 9.3 | 10.6 | | 11.0 | 8.7 | | | | |
| (93) 15.6 | (123) 13.7 | (112) 16.4 | % Officers', Directors' Owners' Comp/Sales | (89) 16.6 | (21) 14.8 | | | | |
| 25.7 | 20.4 | 22.9 | | 23.4 | 21.8 | | | | |
| 1760090M | 2056374M | 242854M | Net Sales ($) | 60518M | 53544M | 10068M | 26975M | 17871M | 73878M |
| 421249M | 686287M | 112205M | Total Assets ($) | 28163M | 15591M | 4087M | 26935M | 19344M | 18085M |

## Current Data Sorted by Assets | Comparative Historical Data

| | | | | | | Type of Statement | | |
|---|---|---|---|---|---|---|---|---|
| 1 | 2 | | 2 | | | Unqualified | | |
| | 4 | 5 | 2 | 1 | | Reviewed | 7 | 5 |
| 30 | 15 | 12 | | | | Compiled | 5 | 3 |
| 148 | 64 | 11 | | | 1 | Tax Returns | 43 | 47 |
| 43 | 30 | 15 | | | | Other | 87 | 118 |
| | 21 (4/1-9/30/11) | | 370 (10/1/11-3/31/12) | | | | 44 | 80 |
| | | | | | | | 4/1/07- | 4/1/08- |
| | | | | | | | 3/31/08 | 3/31/09 |
| 0-500M | 500M-2MM | 2-10MM | 10-50MM | 50-100MM | 100-250MM | | ALL | ALL |
| 222 | 115 | 43 | 8 | 2 | 1 | NUMBER OF STATEMENTS | 186 | 253 |
| % | % | % | % | % | % | ASSETS | % | % |
| 23.5 | 16.2 | 11.5 | | | | Cash & Equivalents | 18.7 | 16.6 |
| 7.7 | 6.8 | 15.3 | | | | Trade Receivables (net) | 9.8 | 8.5 |
| 16.4 | 7.9 | 7.1 | | | | Inventory | 11.6 | 10.8 |
| 2.0 | 3.1 | 2.0 | | | | All Other Current | 2.8 | 4.0 |
| 49.5 | 34.0 | 36.0 | | | | Total Current | 42.8 | 40.0 |
| 33.1 | 38.7 | 41.9 | | | | Fixed Assets (net) | 39.1 | 38.3 |
| 9.3 | 15.9 | 10.4 | | | | Intangibles (net) | 8.2 | 10.2 |
| 8.1 | 11.4 | 11.7 | | | | All Other Non-Current | 9.9 | 11.5 |
| 100.0 | 100.0 | 100.0 | | | | Total | 100.0 | 100.0 |
| | | | | | | LIABILITIES | | |
| 13.9 | 6.6 | 5.1 | | | | Notes Payable-Short Term | 12.2 | 11.0 |
| 6.7 | 6.8 | 5.9 | | | | Cur. Mat.-L.T.D. | 7.1 | 7.9 |
| 4.3 | 4.0 | 5.2 | | | | Trade Payables | 8.6 | 5.3 |
| .1 | .0 | .2 | | | | Income Taxes Payable | .3 | .4 |
| 23.0 | 16.6 | 16.6 | | | | All Other Current | 16.0 | 16.6 |
| 48.1 | 34.1 | 32.9 | | | | Total Current | 44.2 | 41.2 |
| 35.1 | 33.3 | 31.1 | | | | Long-Term Debt | 39.3 | 40.9 |
| .0 | .0 | .0 | | | | Deferred Taxes | .1 | .0 |
| 8.8 | 3.5 | 2.6 | | | | All Other Non-Current | 7.7 | 7.1 |
| 8.0 | 29.1 | 33.4 | | | | Net Worth | 8.6 | 10.8 |
| 100.0 | 100.0 | 100.0 | | | | Total Liabilties & Net Worth | 100.0 | 100.0 |
| | | | | | | INCOME DATA | | |
| 100.0 | 100.0 | 100.0 | | | | Net Sales | 100.0 | 100.0 |
| | | | | | | Gross Profit | | |
| 92.5 | 86.6 | 83.4 | | | | Operating Expenses | 91.4 | 90.1 |
| 7.5 | 13.4 | 16.6 | | | | Operating Profit | 8.6 | 9.9 |
| .9 | 2.6 | 3.8 | | | | All Other Expenses (net) | 1.4 | 1.7 |
| 6.7 | 10.8 | 12.8 | | | | Profit Before Taxes | 7.3 | 8.2 |
| | | | | | | RATIOS | | |
| 3.3 | 2.6 | 2.0 | | | | | 2.8 | 2.6 |
| 1.4 | 1.1 | 1.2 | | | | Current | 1.1 | 1.2 |
| .7 | .5 | .5 | | | | | .5 | .6 |
| 2.0 | 1.8 | 1.4 | | | | | 1.9 | 1.8 |
| .9 | .8 | 1.0 | | | | Quick | .6 (251) | .7 |
| .3 | .2 | .4 | | | | | .2 | .2 |
| 0 UND | 0 UND | 0 UND | | | | | 0 UND | 0 UND |
| 0 UND | 0 UND | 16 22.2 | | | | Sales/Receivables | 0 UND | 0 UND |
| 8 43.8 | 8 46.6 | 29 12.5 | | | | | 17 21.5 | 19 19.5 |
| | | | | | | Cost of Sales/Inventory | | |
| | | | | | | Cost of Sales/Payables | | |
| 13.6 | 18.5 | 11.8 | | | | | 15.5 | 15.8 |
| 55.6 | 230.4 | 36.0 | | | | Sales/Working Capital | 307.1 | 110.9 |
| -34.1 | -20.8 | -21.4 | | | | | -27.8 | -31.0 |
| 19.4 | 31.1 | 35.0 | | | | | 11.9 | 15.0 |
| (158) 5.4 | (90) 7.7 | (37) 6.4 | | | | EBIT/Interest | (148) 3.7 | (209) 4.2 |
| 1.0 | 1.6 | 1.4 | | | | | 1.0 | .7 |
| | | | | | | Net Profit + Depr., Dep., | | 6.1 |
| | | | | | | Amort./Cur. Mat. L/T/D | (12) 1.1 | |
| | | | | | | | | .5 |
| .3 | .6 | .6 | | | | | .6 | .6 |
| 1.4 | 2.2 | 1.8 | | | | Fixed/Worth | 2.5 | 3.9 |
| -1.4 | -3.0 | -62.8 | | | | | -3.5 | -1.6 |
| .6 | .9 | .8 | | | | | 1.0 | 1.0 |
| 5.0 | 4.8 | 2.8 | | | | Debt/Worth | 5.5 | 8.5 |
| -3.3 | -5.3 | -204.6 | | | | | -6.7 | -4.7 |
| 130.6 | 162.0 | 88.1 | | | | | 150.0 | 211.2 |
| (132) 63.4 | (73) 59.3 | (32) 43.6 | | | | % Profit Before Taxes/Tangible Net Worth | (119) 43.1 | (158) 78.6 |
| 19.0 | 15.2 | 11.9 | | | | | 9.9 | 18.5 |
| 47.2 | 40.2 | 36.4 | | | | | 47.8 | 50.1 |
| 15.9 | 13.7 | 8.6 | | | | % Profit Before Taxes/Total Assets | 12.3 | 15.5 |
| .0 | 1.8 | 1.0 | | | | | .6 | .0 |
| 64.0 | 32.6 | 18.5 | | | | | 43.8 | 37.5 |
| 23.8 | 11.5 | 10.1 | | | | Sales/Net Fixed Assets | 16.3 | 13.7 |
| 10.4 | 7.1 | 4.9 | | | | | 7.6 | 6.6 |
| 9.0 | 6.0 | 4.4 | | | | | 9.3 | 8.0 |
| 5.3 | 3.5 | 2.8 | | | | Sales/Total Assets | 5.5 | 4.4 |
| 3.5 | 2.1 | 1.1 | | | | | 2.6 | 2.3 |
| 1.1 | 1.6 | 1.6 | | | | | 1.1 | 1.7 |
| (128) 2.4 | (76) 2.8 | (36) 3.3 | | | | % Depr., Dep., Amort./Sales | (134) 2.1 | (168) 2.9 |
| 3.7 | 5.2 | 5.0 | | | | | 3.8 | 5.1 |
| 9.1 | 4.9 | 4.8 | | | | | 8.3 | 7.9 |
| (153) 13.6 | (65) 16.7 | (22) 14.9 | | | | % Officers', Directors' Owners' Comp/Sales | (123) 14.2 | (165) 14.2 |
| 21.7 | 25.7 | 24.5 | | | | | 24.5 | 22.1 |
| 359031M | 498653M | 612983M | 300290M | 158298M | 2596620M | Net Sales ($) | 4216963M | 2528226M |
| 53968M | 104981M | 214353M | 128622M | 137452M | 215938M | Total Assets ($) | 1160827M | 1007665M |

M = $ thousand　　MM = $ million
See Pages 9 through 22 for Explanation of Ratios and Data

## Comparative Historical Data

## Current Data Sorted by Sales

| Type of Statement | | | | | | | | | |
|---|---|---|---|---|---|---|---|---|---|
| | | | | | | 2 | | | 2 |
| Unqualified | 4 | 2 | 4 | 3 | 1 | 1 | 1 | 3 | 4 |
| Reviewed | 18 | 15 | 13 | 10 | 16 | 9 | 10 | 10 | 2 |
| Compiled | 45 | 65 | 57 | 87 | 87 | 22 | 20 | 5 | 3 |
| Tax Returns | 148 | 127 | 224 | 22 | 34 | 9 | 10 | 14 | 4 |
| Other | 85 | 89 | 93 | | | | | | |
| | 4/1/09-3/31/10 ALL | 4/1/10-3/31/11 ALL | 4/1/11-3/31/12 ALL | 0-1MM | 21 (4/1-9/30/11) 1-3MM | 3-5MM | 370 (10/1/11-3/31/12) 5-10MM | 10-25MM | 25MM & OVER |
| NUMBER OF STATEMENTS | 300 | 298 | 391 | 122 | 138 | 43 | 41 | 32 | 15 |
| **ASSETS** | % | % | % | % | % | % | % | % | % |
| Cash & Equivalents | 21.5 | 21.6 | 19.9 | 18.6 | 20.1 | 23.9 | 23.5 | 15.4 | 17.3 |
| Trade Receivables (net) | 9.2 | 9.6 | 8.5 | 5.7 | 8.8 | 9.2 | 7.1 | 17.4 | 10.1 |
| Inventory | 12.5 | 11.0 | 12.5 | 13.8 | 15.7 | 7.3 | 9.5 | 7.2 | 7.5 |
| All Other Current | 1.6 | 2.2 | 2.5 | 2.1 | 2.1 | 4.1 | 1.7 | 2.7 | 6.8 |
| Total Current | 44.8 | 44.4 | 43.4 | 40.2 | 46.7 | 44.5 | 41.8 | 42.7 | 41.7 |
| Fixed Assets (net) | 36.7 | 36.9 | 36.0 | 40.1 | 30.7 | 35.3 | 37.5 | 40.9 | 38.1 |
| Intangibles (net) | 10.5 | 9.3 | 11.2 | 11.9 | 10.7 | 9.5 | 13.6 | 8.4 | 14.9 |
| All Other Non-Current | 8.0 | 9.5 | 9.4 | 7.8 | 11.9 | 10.7 | 7.1 | 8.0 | 5.4 |
| Total | 100.0 | 100.0 | 100.0 | 100.0 | 100.0 | 100.0 | 100.0 | 100.0 | 100.0 |
| **LIABILITIES** | | | | | | | | | |
| Notes Payable-Short Term | 10.5 | 9.5 | 10.5 | 10.3 | 11.9 | 11.9 | 8.0 | 8.3 | 6.8 |
| Cur. Mat.-L.T.D. | 9.1 | 7.5 | 6.8 | 5.2 | 6.5 | 7.1 | 9.0 | 8.6 | 10.3 |
| Trade Payables | 5.8 | 5.1 | 4.5 | 3.7 | 4.6 | 3.7 | 6.1 | 4.5 | 8.7 |
| Income Taxes Payable | .1 | .1 | .1 | .0 | .1 | .0 | .1 | .1 | .8 |
| All Other Current | 16.3 | 14.3 | 20.0 | 15.1 | 24.8 | 17.4 | 21.8 | 17.9 | 23.4 |
| Total Current | 41.8 | 36.6 | 41.9 | 34.4 | 48.0 | 40.1 | 45.1 | 39.3 | 50.0 |
| Long-Term Debt | 38.6 | 37.9 | 33.7 | 41.7 | 33.9 | 24.8 | 31.3 | 21.5 | 26.1 |
| Deferred Taxes | .1 | .1 | .0 | .0 | .1 | .0 | .0 | .0 | .0 |
| All Other Non-Current | 6.2 | 5.1 | 6.6 | 10.7 | 4.1 | 4.2 | 5.9 | 5.0 | 8.8 |
| Net Worth | 13.4 | 20.3 | 17.7 | 13.2 | 13.9 | 30.9 | 17.7 | 34.2 | 15.2 |
| Total Liabilities & Net Worth | 100.0 | 100.0 | 100.0 | 100.0 | 100.0 | 100.0 | 100.0 | 100.0 | 100.0 |
| **INCOME DATA** | | | | | | | | | |
| Net Sales | 100.0 | 100.0 | 100.0 | 100.0 | 100.0 | 100.0 | 100.0 | 100.0 | 100.0 |
| Gross Profit | | | | | | | | | |
| Operating Expenses | 87.8 | 88.7 | 89.9 | 84.2 | 91.9 | 91.7 | 93.2 | 93.0 | 95.4 |
| Operating Profit | 12.2 | 11.3 | 10.1 | 15.8 | 8.1 | 8.3 | 6.8 | 7.0 | 4.6 |
| All Other Expenses (net) | 2.7 | 1.8 | 1.6 | 4.4 | .6 | 1.0 | -.8 | .7 | -.6 |
| Profit Before Taxes | 9.5 | 9.5 | 8.5 | 11.4 | 7.4 | 7.3 | 7.6 | 6.3 | 5.2 |
| **RATIOS** | | | | | | | | | |
| Current | 3.2 | 3.6 | 2.8 | 4.6 | 3.0 | 2.5 | 1.8 | 2.7 | 1.9 |
| | 1.3 | 1.4 | 1.3 | 1.6 | 1.3 | 1.2 | 1.1 | 1.3 | .9 |
| | .6 | .7 | .6 | .6 | .6 | .8 | .5 | .7 | .5 |
| Quick | 2.1 | 2.6 | 1.8 | 2.2 | 1.8 | 1.9 | 1.4 | 1.9 | 1.4 |
| | (299) .8 | (296) .9 | .8 | .9 | .8 | .9 | .6 | 1.2 | .6 |
| | .3 | .4 | .3 | .2 | .2 | .4 | .3 | .3 | .1 |
| Sales/Receivables | 0 UND | 0 UND | 0 UND | 0 UND | 0 UND | 0 UND | 0 UND | 0 UND | 0 UND |
| | 0 UND | 0 UND | 0 UND | 0 UND | 0 UND | 0 UND | 0 UND | 17 20.9 | 9 40.9 |
| | 15 24.8 | 14 25.6 | 13 28.9 | 8 48.5 | 9 39.7 | 20 18.4 | 8 48.0 | 30 12.3 | 27 13.7 |
| Cost of Sales/Inventory | | | | | | | | | |
| Cost of Sales/Payables | | | | | | | | | |
| Sales/Working Capital | 15.3 | 12.9 | 14.1 | 9.1 | 14.3 | 14.2 | 26.4 | 17.3 | 24.3 |
| | 75.6 | 58.6 | 60.8 | 27.7 | 77.2 | 85.6 | 550.1 | 47.4 | -42.7 |
| | -30.6 | -35.7 | -30.2 | -17.9 | -30.1 | -32.0 | -52.8 | -30.3 | -21.8 |
| EBIT/Interest | 21.1 | 24.4 | 24.8 | 17.2 | 24.0 | 26.6 | 30.8 | 43.1 | 31.8 |
| | (233) 5.5 | (243) 7.2 | (294) 6.3 | (82) 5.3 | (103) 7.5 | (32) 6.1 | (34) 3.1 | (30) 16.9 | (13) 4.8 |
| | 1.5 | 1.4 | 1.2 | 1.9 | 1.1 | 1.5 | .9 | 1.6 | 2.3 |
| Net Profit + Depr., Dep., Amort./Cur. Mat. L/T/D | 2.5 | 5.9 | 4.0 | | | | | | |
| | (13) 1.6 | (11) 3.8 | (15) 2.5 | | | | | | |
| | .8 | 1.4 | .9 | | | | | | |
| Fixed/Worth | .5 | .4 | .4 | .3 | .4 | .3 | .3 | .6 | .4 |
| | 2.5 | 2.0 | 1.8 | 2.4 | 1.5 | .8 | 2.5 | 1.1 | 1.7 |
| | -1.4 | -3.4 | -2.2 | -2.6 | -1.5 | -11.3 | -1.7 | NM | 6.3 |
| Debt/Worth | 1.1 | .8 | .7 | .7 | .6 | .5 | 1.5 | .6 | 1.3 |
| | 4.9 | 3.6 | 3.8 | 8.2 | 3.6 | 2.6 | 3.8 | 1.2 | 2.5 |
| | -3.8 | -6.3 | -4.5 | -3.7 | -3.8 | -13.6 | -3.0 | NM | -2.7 |
| % Profit Before Taxes/Tangible Net Worth | 172.5 | 190.7 | 131.5 | 122.4 | 136.5 | 201.3 | 268.4 | 90.4 | 143.1 |
| | (187) 70.1 | (199) 62.8 | (247) 57.1 | (70) 62.1 | (85) 67.4 | (31) 48.4 | (26) 56.7 | (24) 46.3 | (11) 23.9 |
| | 14.0 | 15.8 | 14.6 | 20.0 | 18.4 | 6.1 | 11.0 | 11.0 | 8.9 |
| % Profit Before Taxes/Total Assets | 55.3 | 50.2 | 44.0 | 44.3 | 45.8 | 40.2 | 59.6 | 41.2 | 23.7 |
| | 18.5 | 16.7 | 14.0 | 14.0 | 17.3 | 10.7 | 11.9 | 15.3 | 4.9 |
| | 1.9 | 1.1 | .9 | 1.6 | .5 | .8 | -.4 | .6 | 1.0 |
| Sales/Net Fixed Assets | 51.1 | 50.5 | 40.1 | 40.5 | 44.6 | 38.6 | 68.6 | 23.1 | 23.2 |
| | 17.8 | 18.2 | 17.5 | 11.6 | 20.8 | 24.7 | 26.6 | 11.0 | 10.5 |
| | 6.5 | 6.9 | 7.6 | 4.2 | 9.1 | 15.4 | 11.5 | 6.2 | 7.6 |
| Sales/Total Assets | 8.3 | 8.3 | 7.4 | 5.1 | 7.5 | 10.5 | 14.4 | 6.6 | 7.4 |
| | 4.5 | 4.4 | 4.3 | 3.3 | 4.7 | 4.6 | 9.3 | 4.4 | 3.7 |
| | 2.7 | 2.3 | 2.7 | 1.6 | 3.1 | 2.9 | 4.2 | 2.8 | 1.9 |
| % Depr., Dep., Amort./Sales | 1.3 | 1.2 | 1.3 | 1.3 | .9 | 1.9 | 1.5 | 1.7 | 1.3 |
| | (196) 2.5 | (184) 2.2 | (250) 2.6 | (78) 3.8 | (81) 2.6 | (26) 2.5 | (26) 2.2 | (28) 2.3 | (11) 2.4 |
| | 4.3 | 4.3 | 4.5 | 8.1 | 3.8 | 3.7 | 3.1 | 4.1 | 3.5 |
| % Officers', Directors' Owners' Comp/Sales | 8.1 | 8.1 | 8.6 | 9.0 | 7.2 | 8.1 | 9.8 | 11.9 | |
| | (183) 13.6 | (174) 14.6 | (241) 13.7 | (71) 12.6 | (83) 13.2 | (32) 15.3 | (32) 25.1 | (17) 23.7 | |
| | 23.0 | 24.9 | 23.9 | 17.7 | 18.7 | 28.3 | 33.1 | 28.4 | |
| Net Sales ($) | 3185274M | 3178082M | 4525875M | 76285M | 238666M | 165363M | 289089M | 525774M | 3230698M |
| Total Assets ($) | 1150549M | 960793M | 855314M | 56477M | 61796M | 53294M | 55080M | 145587M | 483080M |

© RMA 2012

M = $ thousand    MM = $ million

See Pages 9 through 22 for Explanation of Ratios and Data

## Current Data Sorted by Assets      Comparative Historical Data

| Type of Statement | 0-500M | 500M-2MM | 2-10MM | 10-50MM | 50-100MM | 100-250MM | | 4/1/07-3/31/08 ALL | 4/1/08-3/31/09 ALL |
|---|---|---|---|---|---|---|---|---|---|
| Unqualified | 2 | 8 | 10 | 14 | 3 | | | 15 | 18 |
| Reviewed | | | 1 | | | | | 2 | 1 |
| Compiled | 2 | 4 | 1 | 1 | | | | 5 | 9 |
| Tax Returns | 22 | 9 | 1 | 1 | | | | 14 | 23 |
| Other | 11 | 3 | 6 | 5 | | | | 19 | 19 |
| | 45 (4/1-9/30/11) | | 59 (10/1/11-3/31/12) | | | | | | |
| NUMBER OF STATEMENTS | 37 | 24 | 19 | 21 | 3 | | | 55 | 70 |

Columns 50-100MM (partial) and 100-250MM: DATA NOT AVAILABLE

| | % | % | % | % | % | % | | % | % |
|---|---|---|---|---|---|---|---|---|---|
| **ASSETS** | | | | | | | | | |
| Cash & Equivalents | 42.6 | 25.7 | 18.0 | 21.1 | | | | 26.7 | 22.4 |
| Trade Receivables (net) | 13.1 | 25.3 | 26.1 | 19.8 | | | | 18.2 | 19.3 |
| Inventory | .0 | .1 | .0 | .1 | | | | .4 | .2 |
| All Other Current | 5.9 | 2.8 | 5.6 | 6.1 | | | | 5.2 | 5.7 |
| Total Current | 61.5 | 53.9 | 49.6 | 47.2 | | | | 50.5 | 47.5 |
| Fixed Assets (net) | 21.7 | 32.0 | 40.1 | 45.4 | | | | 32.7 | 35.5 |
| Intangibles (net) | 10.0 | 5.6 | 1.4 | 2.1 | | | | 7.3 | 6.8 |
| All Other Non-Current | 6.9 | 8.4 | 8.9 | 5.4 | | | | 9.5 | 10.2 |
| Total | 100.0 | 100.0 | 100.0 | 100.0 | | | | 100.0 | 100.0 |
| **LIABILITIES** | | | | | | | | | |
| Notes Payable-Short Term | 12.5 | 6.6 | 6.9 | 2.0 | | | | 20.8 | 19.8 |
| Cur. Mat.-L.T.D. | 14.1 | 2.0 | 1.0 | 2.7 | | | | 3.9 | 2.6 |
| Trade Payables | .9 | 5.4 | 4.8 | 6.1 | | | | 4.2 | 5.5 |
| Income Taxes Payable | .7 | .1 | 1.1 | .1 | | | | .2 | .0 |
| All Other Current | 47.3 | 20.7 | 14.6 | 13.5 | | | | 22.0 | 20.1 |
| Total Current | 75.5 | 34.8 | 28.5 | 24.4 | | | | 51.1 | 47.9 |
| Long-Term Debt | 31.1 | 12.7 | 16.5 | 25.5 | | | | 15.9 | 27.0 |
| Deferred Taxes | .0 | 1.1 | .4 | .0 | | | | .0 | .0 |
| All Other Non-Current | 17.6 | 9.1 | .8 | 1.9 | | | | 8.0 | 7.2 |
| Net Worth | -24.2 | 42.4 | 53.7 | 48.2 | | | | 24.9 | 18.0 |
| Total Liabilities & Net Worth | 100.0 | 100.0 | 100.0 | 100.0 | | | | 100.0 | 100.0 |
| **INCOME DATA** | | | | | | | | | |
| Net Sales | 100.0 | 100.0 | 100.0 | 100.0 | | | | 100.0 | 100.0 |
| Gross Profit | | | | | | | | | |
| Operating Expenses | 94.1 | 90.9 | 99.6 | 97.3 | | | | 91.9 | 93.9 |
| Operating Profit | 5.9 | 9.1 | .4 | 2.7 | | | | 8.1 | 6.1 |
| All Other Expenses (net) | 2.3 | 3.8 | .0 | 1.4 | | | | .1 | 1.8 |
| Profit Before Taxes | 3.6 | 5.3 | .4 | 1.4 | | | | 8.0 | 4.3 |
| **RATIOS** | | | | | | | | | |
| Current | 6.5 | 4.7 | 2.9 | 3.6 | | | | 3.0 | 2.3 |
| | 1.5 | 1.9 | 1.7 | 1.8 | | | | 1.5 | 1.3 |
| | .4 | .8 | 1.3 | 1.2 | | | | .8 | .7 |
| Quick | 6.5 | 4.7 | 2.7 | 2.9 | | | | 2.9 | 2.0 |
| | 1.5 | 1.8 | 1.6 | 1.7 | | | | 1.3 | 1.1 |
| | .3 | .7 | 1.1 | .9 | | | | .6 | .6 |
| Sales/Receivables | 0 UND | 0 UND | 20 18.2 | 14 25.8 | | | | 0 UND | 0 UND |
| | 0 UND | 22 16.6 | 37 9.8 | 28 13.0 | | | | 15 24.3 | 17 21.1 |
| | 0 UND | 41 8.8 | 69 5.3 | 42 8.6 | | | | 39 9.3 | 43 8.5 |
| Cost of Sales/Inventory | | | | | | | | | |
| Cost of Sales/Payables | | | | | | | | | |
| Sales/Working Capital | 14.9 | 7.0 | 4.9 | 4.2 | | | | 6.2 | 8.5 |
| | 108.9 | 20.4 | 13.3 | 14.0 | | | | 18.3 | 28.9 |
| | -27.0 | NM | 20.5 | 32.1 | | | | -28.0 | -86.4 |
| EBIT/Interest | 30.5 | 66.2 | 24.1 | 8.3 | | | | 11.0 | 14.3 |
| | (21) 9.0 | (13) 4.3 | (16) 5.6 | (20) 3.2 | | | | (42) 3.9 | (55) 2.5 |
| | 1.6 | -.7 | .4 | 1.3 | | | | 1.2 | .4 |
| Net Profit + Depr., Dep., Amort./Cur. Mat. L/T/D | | | | | | | | | |
| Fixed/Worth | .0 | .1 | .4 | .6 | | | | .3 | .3 |
| | .3 | .5 | .8 | 1.1 | | | | .7 | 1.2 |
| | -.6 | 4.4 | 1.3 | 1.4 | | | | 2.8 | 8.0 |
| Debt/Worth | .5 | .5 | .4 | .5 | | | | .5 | .7 |
| | 5.3 | 2.4 | .8 | 1.1 | | | | 1.5 | 2.4 |
| | -1.5 | 6.9 | 1.5 | 2.0 | | | | 27.0 | 82.6 |
| % Profit Before Taxes/Tangible Net Worth | 194.0 | 64.0 | 17.4 | 15.8 | | | | 98.7 | 92.9 |
| | (20) 110.3 | (22) 12.8 | 9.7 | 7.0 | | | | (44) 16.2 | (56) 14.2 |
| | 48.9 | -8.4 | -.7 | 2.4 | | | | 1.9 | 2.8 |
| % Profit Before Taxes/Total Assets | 80.4 | 32.0 | 9.5 | 5.9 | | | | 38.5 | 20.3 |
| | 28.4 | 4.6 | 5.2 | 3.5 | | | | 7.3 | 3.4 |
| | .0 | -2.5 | -.5 | 1.0 | | | | .8 | -1.2 |
| Sales/Net Fixed Assets | 798.7 | 100.2 | 15.9 | 13.2 | | | | 45.2 | 108.5 |
| | 172.3 | 28.7 | 4.9 | 3.2 | | | | 12.6 | 19.5 |
| | 48.1 | 5.8 | 3.2 | 2.1 | | | | 3.8 | 2.8 |
| Sales/Total Assets | 17.5 | 5.3 | 3.8 | 2.8 | | | | 5.1 | 7.7 |
| | 11.2 | 3.8 | 1.9 | 1.5 | | | | 2.9 | 3.4 |
| | 5.3 | 2.2 | 1.5 | 1.2 | | | | 1.7 | 1.7 |
| % Depr., Dep., Amort./Sales | .3 | .5 | 1.6 | 1.6 | | | | .6 | .5 |
| | (17) .6 | (19) .8 | (17) 2.1 | (20) 2.0 | | | | (40) 1.7 | (51) 1.5 |
| | 1.5 | 3.2 | 3.3 | 3.4 | | | | 3.2 | 3.2 |
| % Officers', Directors' Owners' Comp/Sales | 4.7 | | | | | | | 3.2 | 6.2 |
| | (22) 16.3 | | | | | | | (15) 10.4 | (26) 11.6 |
| | 27.5 | | | | | | | 22.0 | 31.0 |
| Net Sales ($) | 63297M | 89921M | 247550M | 851760M | 192214M | | | 688500M | 698186M |
| Total Assets ($) | 6213M | 26782M | 100447M | 459948M | 210803M | | | 330852M | 380080M |

M = $ thousand    MM = $ million
See Pages 9 through 22 for Explanation of Ratios and Data

## Comparative Historical Data / Current Data Sorted by Sales

| | | | Type of Statement | | | | | | |
|---|---|---|---|---|---|---|---|---|---|
| 17 | 23 | 37 | Unqualified | 2 | 4 | 3 | 7 | 11 | 10 |
| 10 | 2 | 1 | Reviewed | | | | | | 1 |
| 6 | 13 | 8 | Compiled | 2 | 2 | 1 | 1 | 1 | 1 |
| 22 | 25 | 33 | Tax Returns | 11 | 10 | 7 | 3 | 1 | 1 |
| 20 | 21 | 25 | Other | 5 | 6 | 2 | 3 | 4 | 5 |
| 4/1/09-3/31/10 ALL | 4/1/10-3/31/11 ALL | 4/1/11-3/31/12 ALL | | 45 (4/1-9/30/11) 0-1MM | 1-3MM | 3-5MM | 59 (10/1/11-3/31/12) 5-10MM | 10-25MM | 25MM & OVER |
| 75 | 84 | 104 | **NUMBER OF STATEMENTS** | 20 | 22 | 13 | 14 | 17 | 18 |
| % | % | % | **ASSETS** | % | % | % | % | % | % |
| 25.1 | 29.5 | 29.2 | Cash & Equivalents | 38.8 | 40.6 | 23.0 | 25.8 | 20.2 | 20.3 |
| 20.7 | 21.0 | 19.5 | Trade Receivables (net) | 12.7 | 16.8 | 22.8 | 22.1 | 18.3 | 27.2 |
| .2 | .1 | .1 | Inventory | .0 | .1 | .1 | .0 | .0 | .2 |
| 5.0 | 3.7 | 5.0 | All Other Current | 2.9 | 4.3 | 9.6 | 5.5 | 5.2 | 4.3 |
| 51.0 | 54.2 | 53.8 | Total Current | 54.5 | 61.8 | 55.5 | 53.5 | 43.7 | 52.0 |
| 34.6 | 30.3 | 32.1 | Fixed Assets (net) | 33.5 | 25.0 | 20.5 | 32.5 | 46.7 | 33.2 |
| 5.0 | 2.3 | 5.6 | Intangibles (net) | 5.7 | 10.3 | 10.4 | 3.7 | 1.4 | 1.4 |
| 9.4 | 13.2 | 8.6 | All Other Non-Current | 6.4 | 2.9 | 13.6 | 10.3 | 8.2 | 13.4 |
| 100.0 | 100.0 | 100.0 | Total | 100.0 | 100.0 | 100.0 | 100.0 | 100.0 | 100.0 |
| | | | **LIABILITIES** | | | | | | |
| 7.4 | 14.8 | 7.7 | Notes Payable-Short Term | 7.8 | 12.0 | 10.2 | 6.3 | 3.6 | 5.7 |
| 2.0 | 1.6 | 6.2 | Cur. Mat.-L.T.D. | 7.3 | 17.6 | 2.8 | 1.2 | 1.2 | 2.4 |
| 6.8 | 3.8 | 3.7 | Trade Payables | 1.3 | 4.5 | 4.0 | 2.7 | 3.3 | 6.4 |
| .9 | .9 | .5 | Income Taxes Payable | 1.2 | .0 | .0 | .1 | 1.3 | .2 |
| 17.3 | 18.5 | 27.3 | All Other Current | 37.4 | 26.6 | 37.2 | 37.2 | 15.3 | 13.6 |
| 34.4 | 39.7 | 45.5 | Total Current | 55.1 | 60.6 | 54.1 | 47.6 | 24.6 | 28.3 |
| 24.5 | 16.8 | 22.4 | Long-Term Debt | 34.8 | 21.8 | 25.2 | 11.6 | 21.0 | 17.0 |
| .0 | .0 | .3 | Deferred Taxes | .0 | .0 | .0 | 1.9 | .5 | .0 |
| 6.5 | 7.2 | 8.9 | All Other Non-Current | 20.8 | 13.8 | 10.4 | 1.8 | .4 | 2.0 |
| 34.6 | 36.2 | 22.9 | Net Worth | -10.5 | 3.7 | 10.3 | 37.2 | 53.5 | 52.7 |
| 100.0 | 100.0 | 100.0 | Total Liabilties & Net Worth | 100.0 | 100.0 | 100.0 | 100.0 | 100.0 | 100.0 |
| | | | **INCOME DATA** | | | | | | |
| 100.0 | 100.0 | 100.0 | Net Sales | 100.0 | 100.0 | 100.0 | 100.0 | 100.0 | 100.0 |
| | | | Gross Profit | | | | | | |
| 91.5 | 92.3 | 95.2 | Operating Expenses | 85.8 | 96.5 | 97.3 | 98.2 | 97.8 | 97.4 |
| 8.5 | 7.7 | 4.8 | Operating Profit | 14.2 | 3.5 | 2.7 | 1.8 | 2.2 | 2.6 |
| 2.4 | .4 | 2.0 | All Other Expenses (net) | 7.9 | .7 | .3 | .2 | 1.1 | .6 |
| 6.1 | 7.3 | 2.8 | Profit Before Taxes | 6.2 | 2.8 | 2.4 | 1.6 | 1.0 | 2.0 |
| | | | **RATIOS** | | | | | | |
| 3.9 | 4.7 | 3.4 | | 4.7 | 7.1 | 2.9 | 2.4 | 3.3 | 3.2 |
| 1.9 | 2.2 | 1.8 | Current | 2.4 | 2.0 | 1.7 | 1.7 | 1.6 | 1.7 |
| .9 | 1.2 | .9 | | .4 | .6 | .6 | 1.3 | 1.1 | 1.2 |
| 3.8 | 3.9 | 3.3 | | 4.7 | 7.1 | 2.9 | 2.3 | 3.0 | 3.1 |
| 1.8 | 2.1 | 1.6 | Quick | 2.1 | 1.5 | 1.2 | 1.7 | 1.6 | 1.6 |
| .8 | 1.1 | .7 | | .4 | .4 | .3 | 1.0 | 1.0 | .9 |
| 0 UND | 0 UND | 0 UND | | 0 UND | 0 UND | 0 UND | 0 UND | 17 21.3 | 14 25.7 |
| 20 18.7 | 18 20.0 | 15 24.0 | Sales/Receivables | 0 UND | 0 UND | 7 51.0 | 17 21.5 | 29 12.4 | 36 10.1 |
| 48 7.6 | 46 8.0 | 40 9.1 | | 0 UND | 25 14.5 | 57 6.4 | 34 10.6 | 42 8.6 | 54 6.7 |
| | | | Cost of Sales/Inventory | | | | | | |
| | | | Cost of Sales/Payables | | | | | | |
| 9.7 | 6.6 | 6.1 | | 5.0 | 7.0 | 9.6 | 11.6 | 5.1 | 4.2 |
| 22.6 | 13.1 | 20.1 | Sales/Working Capital | 37.0 | 72.2 | 23.8 | 19.6 | 13.3 | 14.7 |
| -87.6 | 82.6 | -202.6 | | -56.0 | -36.8 | -19.8 | 86.1 | 50.9 | 30.9 |
| 16.0 | 39.0 | 21.1 | | | | 31.3 | 26.4 | 11.2 | 8.6 |
| (49) 2.9 | (55) 8.8 | (72) 4.3 | EBIT/Interest | | (15) 6.7 | | (10) 2.7 | (15) 6.3 | (16) 3.5 |
| -.5 | 2.8 | 1.1 | | | 1.3 | | -.7 | 1.7 | 1.9 |
| | | | Net Profit + Depr., Dep., Amort./Cur. Mat. L/T/D | | | | | | |
| .3 | .1 | .1 | | .0 | .0 | .3 | .4 | .5 | .2 |
| .7 | .4 | .7 | Fixed/Worth | .3 | 1.2 | .9 | .5 | 1.0 | .7 |
| 6.8 | 1.3 | 2.9 | | 10.3 | -4.3 | -1.3 | 1.5 | 1.4 | 1.2 |
| .3 | .3 | .5 | | .3 | .4 | 1.2 | .6 | .4 | .4 |
| 1.2 | .8 | 1.4 | Debt/Worth | 1.2 | 6.5 | 3.5 | 1.1 | .9 | 1.0 |
| 7.9 | 3.2 | 6.7 | | NM | -4.6 | -3.3 | 2.8 | 1.5 | 1.7 |
| 97.5 | 80.3 | 51.2 | | 202.8 | 81.8 | | 86.3 | 16.9 | 17.0 |
| (60) 23.2 | (71) 26.7 | (85) 15.1 | % Profit Before Taxes/Tangible Net Worth | (15) 50.0 | (13) 44.7 | (13) 3.3 | | 9.2 | 10.1 |
| .5 | 4.8 | .7 | | -4.0 | -1.9 | | -4.2 | 2.5 | 2.9 |
| 46.2 | 54.6 | 28.1 | | 97.7 | 60.8 | 54.8 | 26.2 | 9.3 | 6.6 |
| 5.1 | 11.4 | 6.1 | % Profit Before Taxes/Total Assets | 19.1 | 12.5 | 16.4 | 1.1 | 5.2 | 4.3 |
| -.2 | 2.6 | -.5 | | -2.4 | -1.1 | -21.6 | -2.6 | 1.2 | 1.4 |
| 71.9 | 153.2 | 173.1 | | UND | 698.1 | 124.4 | 160.1 | 13.4 | 22.6 |
| 20.4 | 24.4 | 23.2 | Sales/Net Fixed Assets | 81.5 | 124.8 | 42.5 | 18.7 | 3.5 | 5.1 |
| 4.4 | 4.0 | 4.0 | | 7.5 | 23.7 | 8.5 | 4.6 | 2.0 | 2.9 |
| 6.6 | 8.1 | 7.0 | | 10.4 | 14.2 | 7.4 | 9.9 | 3.6 | 3.3 |
| 3.5 | 3.7 | 3.6 | Sales/Total Assets | 5.0 | 7.2 | 5.4 | 4.0 | 1.5 | 2.3 |
| 1.8 | 1.5 | 1.6 | | 1.0 | 3.3 | 2.2 | 1.8 | 1.2 | 1.5 |
| .7 | .7 | .6 | | .4 | .3 | .3 | .7 | 1.8 | .7 |
| (64) 1.3 | (56) 2.0 | (76) 1.8 | % Depr., Dep., Amort./Sales | (13) 1.4 | (10) .8 | (10) 2.0 | (11) 1.7 | (15) 2.3 | (17) 1.7 |
| 3.0 | 3.4 | 3.2 | | 11.0 | 1.9 | 3.2 | 3.3 | 3.4 | 2.8 |
| 4.6 | 4.0 | 4.0 | | | 8.7 | | | | |
| (27) 10.2 | (35) 7.7 | (36) 10.7 | % Officers', Directors' Owners' Comp/Sales | | (11) 16.1 | | | | |
| 15.0 | 16.6 | 23.9 | | | 27.4 | | | | |
| 970002M | 964673M | 1444742M | Net Sales ($) | 9310M | 42397M | 51585M | 103402M | 290099M | 947949M |
| 500884M | 716131M | 804193M | Total Assets ($) | 6966M | 8830M | 16303M | 35842M | 194157M | 542095M |

M = $ thousand    MM = $ million
See Pages 9 through 22 for Explanation of Ratios and Data

## Current Data Sorted by Assets / Comparative Historical Data

| 0-500M | 500M-2MM | 2-10MM | 10-50MM | 50-100MM | 100-250MM | Type of Statement | 4/1/07-3/31/08 ALL | 4/1/08-3/31/09 ALL |
|---|---|---|---|---|---|---|---|---|
| 1 | 4 | 7 | 13 | | 2 | Unqualified | 17 | 11 |
| 1 | 3 | 3 | 3 | | | Reviewed | 21 | 10 |
| 20 | 11 | 2 | | | 1 | Compiled | 18 | 10 |
| 89 | 23 | 5 | | 1 | 1 | Tax Returns | 81 | 69 |
| 37 | 32 | 15 | 7 | 2 | 1 | Other | 59 | 63 |
| | 26 (4/1-9/30/11) | | 258 (10/1/11-3/31/12) | | | | | |
| 148 | 73 | 32 | 23 | 3 | 5 | NUMBER OF STATEMENTS | 196 | 163 |
| % | % | % | % | % | % | ASSETS | % | % |
| 33.8 | 11.4 | 18.6 | 12.9 | | | Cash & Equivalents | 26.1 | 25.8 |
| 11.7 | 25.5 | 27.8 | 32.5 | | | Trade Receivables (net) | 16.3 | 18.5 |
| .4 | 1.2 | 1.4 | 2.0 | | | Inventory | .9 | .6 |
| 4.1 | 1.7 | 6.9 | 4.5 | | | All Other Current | 6.2 | 5.9 |
| 50.1 | 39.8 | 54.8 | 52.0 | | | Total Current | 49.5 | 50.7 |
| 31.1 | 37.1 | 31.8 | 30.8 | | | Fixed Assets (net) | 33.1 | 29.8 |
| 5.6 | 12.0 | 5.6 | 10.5 | | | Intangibles (net) | 5.4 | 10.1 |
| 13.3 | 11.0 | 7.8 | 6.7 | | | All Other Non-Current | 12.0 | 9.4 |
| 100.0 | 100.0 | 100.0 | 100.0 | | | Total | 100.0 | 100.0 |
| | | | | | | LIABILITIES | | |
| 25.2 | 17.4 | 4.5 | 6.0 | | | Notes Payable-Short Term | 22.7 | 18.6 |
| 5.2 | 4.5 | 4.0 | 2.2 | | | Cur. Mat.-L.T.D. | 6.0 | 3.9 |
| 4.0 | 3.5 | 4.0 | 3.8 | | | Trade Payables | 5.2 | 3.1 |
| .7 | .0 | .0 | .1 | | | Income Taxes Payable | .1 | .2 |
| 20.8 | 9.0 | 7.8 | 14.9 | | | All Other Current | 19.6 | 16.0 |
| 55.9 | 34.5 | 20.4 | 27.1 | | | Total Current | 53.5 | 41.8 |
| 23.4 | 25.5 | 25.2 | 16.0 | | | Long-Term Debt | 27.2 | 23.9 |
| .0 | .0 | .2 | .9 | | | Deferred Taxes | .3 | .1 |
| 10.0 | 8.9 | 1.5 | 1.0 | | | All Other Non-Current | 4.4 | 6.4 |
| 10.7 | 31.1 | 52.7 | 55.1 | | | Net Worth | 14.6 | 27.8 |
| 100.0 | 100.0 | 100.0 | 100.0 | | | Total Liabilities & Net Worth | 100.0 | 100.0 |
| | | | | | | INCOME DATA | | |
| 100.0 | 100.0 | 100.0 | 100.0 | | | Net Sales | 100.0 | 100.0 |
| | | | | | | Gross Profit | | |
| 89.3 | 84.1 | 87.8 | 95.2 | | | Operating Expenses | 91.1 | 90.4 |
| 10.7 | 15.9 | 12.2 | 4.8 | | | Operating Profit | 8.9 | 9.6 |
| 1.8 | 3.6 | 3.6 | 1.4 | | | All Other Expenses (net) | 1.6 | 1.5 |
| 9.0 | 12.2 | 8.7 | 3.3 | | | Profit Before Taxes | 7.2 | 8.1 |
| | | | | | | RATIOS | | |
| 4.4 | 3.1 | 3.9 | 2.8 | | | | 3.0 | 5.2 |
| 1.1 | 1.6 | 2.6 | 2.0 | | | Current | 1.2 | 1.6 |
| .3 | .5 | 1.1 | 1.2 | | | | .5 | .6 |
| 3.9 | 3.1 | 3.7 | 2.7 | | | | 2.9 | 4.1 |
| .9 | 1.5 | 2.0 | 1.5 | | | Quick | 1.1 | 1.3 |
| .2 | .5 | 1.0 | .8 | | | | .4 | .4 |
| 0 UND | 0 UND | 0 UND | 34 10.6 | | | | 0 UND | 0 UND |
| 0 UND | 11 32.5 | 33 11.0 | 54 6.7 | | | Sales/Receivables | 0 UND | 0 UND |
| 0 840.6 | 54 6.7 | 59 6.2 | 68 5.4 | | | | 38 9.5 | 49 7.5 |
| | | | | | | Cost of Sales/Inventory | | |
| | | | | | | Cost of Sales/Payables | | |
| 13.9 | 10.8 | 3.5 | 4.7 | | | | 10.5 | 7.5 |
| 257.0 | 27.3 | 7.8 | 7.8 | | | Sales/Working Capital | 55.2 | 30.1 |
| -14.9 | -18.1 | 57.2 | 26.7 | | | | -24.4 | -24.3 |
| 28.3 | 21.5 | 54.9 | 31.0 | | | | 18.6 | 24.8 |
| (90) 7.8 | (55) 6.3 | (20) 7.7 | (21) 5.4 | | | EBIT/Interest | (144) 4.9 | (113) 6.7 |
| 1.9 | 2.5 | 3.9 | .9 | | | | 1.0 | 1.4 |
| | | | | | | Net Profit + Depr., Dep., | 2.5 | |
| | | | | | | Amort./Cur. Mat. L/T/D | (15) 1.8 | |
| | | | | | | | 1.2 | |
| .1 | .3 | .0 | .2 | | | | .2 | .1 |
| .8 | 1.1 | .4 | .7 | | | Fixed/Worth | .9 | .8 |
| -7.5 | 32.4 | 5.1 | 1.1 | | | | UND | 65.5 |
| .3 | .7 | .4 | .5 | | | | .5 | .4 |
| 3.4 | 2.3 | .7 | .9 | | | Debt/Worth | 2.4 | 2.4 |
| -5.0 | 64.8 | 5.3 | 2.6 | | | | -27.5 | -26.3 |
| 287.9 | 100.3 | 55.4 | 52.6 | | | | 135.3 | 163.1 |
| (101) 95.8 | (57) 43.0 | (29) 14.9 | (22) 10.7 | | | % Profit Before Taxes/Tangible Net Worth | (143) 44.0 | (118) 68.3 |
| 29.5 | 16.0 | 6.9 | 2.0 | | | | 5.7 | 10.4 |
| 95.8 | 32.6 | 24.3 | 19.1 | | | | 50.6 | 66.7 |
| 33.9 | 13.1 | 8.3 | 4.3 | | | % Profit Before Taxes/Total Assets | 12.8 | 18.5 |
| 2.3 | 3.9 | 2.2 | .4 | | | | .0 | 2.7 |
| 239.2 | 55.8 | 41.3 | 64.5 | | | | 84.1 | 143.0 |
| 39.9 | 17.0 | 17.2 | 15.2 | | | Sales/Net Fixed Assets | 22.8 | 31.0 |
| 10.5 | 3.0 | 4.7 | 1.9 | | | | 6.8 | 9.8 |
| 11.6 | 4.8 | 3.9 | 3.2 | | | | 9.1 | 8.0 |
| 6.1 | 2.7 | 2.1 | 2.0 | | | Sales/Total Assets | 3.9 | 4.1 |
| 3.4 | 1.3 | 1.1 | 1.1 | | | | 2.0 | 2.1 |
| .7 | .6 | .9 | .6 | | | | .5 | .5 |
| (87) 1.4 | (57) 1.7 | (22) 2.3 | (21) 2.2 | | | % Depr., Dep., Amort./Sales | (150) 1.2 | (108) 1.5 |
| 3.0 | 3.4 | 5.5 | 3.4 | | | | 2.7 | 3.2 |
| 9.1 | 4.6 | | | | | | 6.1 | 6.4 |
| (89) 12.7 | (30) 8.2 | | | | | % Officers', Directors' Owners' Comp/Sales | (99) 12.5 | (79) 10.7 |
| 21.3 | 11.8 | | | | | | 21.7 | 18.4 |
| 205423M | 249456M | 366170M | 1008276M | 1604999M | 2568503M | Net Sales ($) | 4883279M | 4488495M |
| 30003M | 77653M | 157885M | 497705M | 213531M | 883976M | Total Assets ($) | 1058195M | 929657M |

M = $ thousand   MM = $ million
See Pages 9 through 22 for Explanation of Ratios and Data

## Comparative Historical Data | | | | Current Data Sorted by Sales

| Hist 1 | Hist 2 | Hist 3 | Type of Statement | 0-1MM | 1-3MM | 3-5MM | 5-10MM | 10-25MM | 25MM & OVER |
|---|---|---|---|---|---|---|---|---|---|
| 18 | 19 | 27 | Unqualified | | 3 | 5 | 3 | 9 | 7 |
| 22 | 14 | 10 | Reviewed | 1 | 1 | 1 | 2 | 2 | 3 |
| 36 | 33 | 34 | Compiled | 9 | 14 | 4 | 3 | 3 | 1 |
| 96 | 90 | 119 | Tax Returns | 64 | 39 | 5 | 6 | 3 | 2 |
| 81 | 94 | 94 | Other | 26 | 23 | 14 | 12 | 9 | 10 |
| 4/1/09-3/31/10 ALL | 4/1/10-3/31/11 ALL | 4/1/11-3/31/12 ALL | | 26 (4/1-9/30/11) | | 258 (10/1/11-3/31/12) | | | |
| 253 | 250 | 284 | **NUMBER OF STATEMENTS** | 100 | 80 | 29 | 26 | 26 | 23 |
| % | % | % | **ASSETS** | % | % | % | % | % | % |
| 24.8 | 26.8 | 24.4 | Cash & Equivalents | 27.0 | 30.0 | 19.0 | 17.4 | 17.2 | 16.6 |
| 18.6 | 18.3 | 18.7 | Trade Receivables (net) | 9.5 | 13.8 | 22.9 | 36.3 | 35.0 | 32.4 |
| .4 | .3 | .9 | Inventory | .2 | 1.6 | .3 | 1.6 | .3 | 2.2 |
| 3.8 | 4.7 | 3.8 | All Other Current | 3.3 | 4.1 | 1.1 | 4.4 | 6.2 | 4.1 |
| 47.6 | 50.2 | 47.8 | Total Current | 40.0 | 49.5 | 43.2 | 59.8 | 58.8 | 55.3 |
| 32.4 | 30.2 | 32.5 | Fixed Assets (net) | 43.2 | 28.4 | 32.7 | 26.9 | 21.1 | 19.9 |
| 7.1 | 7.5 | 8.3 | Intangibles (net) | 5.2 | 9.6 | 10.7 | 4.1 | 7.9 | 19.3 |
| 12.8 | 12.2 | 11.4 | All Other Non-Current | 11.7 | 12.6 | 13.4 | 9.2 | 12.3 | 5.5 |
| 100.0 | 100.0 | 100.0 | Total | 100.0 | 100.0 | 100.0 | 100.0 | 100.0 | 100.0 |
| | | | **LIABILITIES** | | | | | | |
| 18.3 | 17.2 | 18.7 | Notes Payable-Short Term | 24.4 | 19.5 | 18.7 | 16.4 | 7.0 | 6.5 |
| 6.8 | 4.7 | 4.5 | Cur. Mat.-L.T.D. | 3.2 | 4.7 | 10.1 | 6.6 | 3.4 | 1.9 |
| 4.0 | 4.1 | 3.8 | Trade Payables | 3.6 | 4.1 | 1.8 | 3.7 | 5.9 | 4.1 |
| .1 | .1 | .4 | Income Taxes Payable | .0 | 1.3 | .0 | .1 | .1 | .1 |
| 16.8 | 16.9 | 15.6 | All Other Current | 14.6 | 15.2 | 21.9 | 12.8 | 15.2 | 17.8 |
| 46.0 | 42.9 | 43.1 | Total Current | 45.8 | 44.8 | 52.5 | 39.7 | 31.4 | 30.2 |
| 28.3 | 20.3 | 23.5 | Long-Term Debt | 23.9 | 30.7 | 22.2 | 19.7 | 10.7 | 16.5 |
| .1 | .4 | .1 | Deferred Taxes | .0 | .0 | .0 | .0 | .4 | .9 |
| 6.1 | 7.0 | 7.8 | All Other Non-Current | 10.5 | 6.6 | 11.0 | 6.8 | 4.5 | 1.0 |
| 19.5 | 29.4 | 25.6 | Net Worth | 19.9 | 17.9 | 14.2 | 33.8 | 53.0 | 51.4 |
| 100.0 | 100.0 | 100.0 | Total Liabilities & Net Worth | 100.0 | 100.0 | 100.0 | 100.0 | 100.0 | 100.0 |
| | | | **INCOME DATA** | | | | | | |
| 100.0 | 100.0 | 100.0 | Net Sales | 100.0 | 100.0 | 100.0 | 100.0 | 100.0 | 100.0 |
| | | | Gross Profit | | | | | | |
| 87.0 | 89.8 | 88.3 | Operating Expenses | 81.9 | 90.3 | 91.6 | 95.8 | 90.7 | 94.0 |
| 13.0 | 10.2 | 11.7 | Operating Profit | 18.1 | 9.7 | 8.4 | 4.2 | 9.3 | 6.0 |
| 2.1 | 1.0 | 2.4 | All Other Expenses (net) | 5.8 | .7 | 1.4 | -.4 | .0 | .4 |
| 10.9 | 9.2 | 9.3 | Profit Before Taxes | 12.3 | 9.0 | 7.0 | 4.6 | 9.3 | 5.6 |
| | | | **RATIOS** | | | | | | |
| 4.1 | 3.9 | 3.7 | | 4.3 | 4.7 | 3.2 | 3.7 | 3.7 | 2.8 |
| 1.3 | 1.5 | 1.6 | Current | 1.1 | 1.8 | 1.0 | 1.9 | 2.4 | 1.7 |
| .5 | .7 | .5 | | .3 | .5 | .3 | .9 | 1.7 | 1.1 |
| 3.8 | 3.6 | 3.6 | | 3.7 | 4.3 | 3.1 | 3.6 | 3.6 | 2.7 |
| 1.2 | (249) 1.4 | 1.3 | Quick | 1.0 | 1.5 | .8 | 1.6 | 2.0 | 1.5 |
| .4 | .6 | .4 | | .2 | .4 | .2 | .8 | 1.2 | .8 |
| 0 UND | 0 UND | 0 UND | | 0 UND | 0 UND | 0 UND | 0 UND | 20 18.0 | 23 16.2 |
| 0 UND | 0 UND | 0 UND | Sales/Receivables | 0 UND | 0 UND | 2 215.3 | 36 10.1 | 40 9.2 | 47 7.8 |
| 44 8.3 | 40 9.1 | 40 9.2 | | 0 UND | 28 13.0 | 45 8.2 | 55 6.6 | 65 5.6 | 59 6.2 |
| | | | Cost of Sales/Inventory | | | | | | |
| | | | Cost of Sales/Payables | | | | | | |
| 9.3 | 9.8 | 8.3 | | 15.4 | 8.9 | 10.0 | 11.0 | 4.0 | 7.2 |
| 38.9 | 27.4 | 36.3 | Sales/Working Capital | 187.0 | 37.8 | -194.6 | 16.6 | 7.5 | 13.4 |
| -26.1 | -52.0 | -27.9 | | -6.3 | -32.4 | -15.5 | -188.2 | 28.3 | 81.8 |
| 21.7 | 26.2 | 28.7 | | 17.0 | 29.4 | 36.1 | 19.8 | 45.5 | 61.0 |
| (189) 7.1 | (186) 7.7 | (193) 7.6 | EBIT/Interest | (48) 5.2 | (58) 8.1 | (23) 10.4 | (22) 5.9 | (20) 11.8 | (22) 15.2 |
| 1.8 | 1.9 | 2.0 | | 1.6 | 2.2 | .3 | 1.1 | 4.2 | 2.3 |
| 10.6 | 19.1 | 24.5 | Net Profit + Depr., Dep., | | | | | | |
| (16) 3.7 | (24) 3.6 | (13) 2.6 | Amort./Cur. Mat. L/T/D | | | | | | |
| 1.7 | 1.6 | 1.7 | | | | | | | |
| .1 | .2 | .1 | | .2 | .1 | .3 | .2 | .1 | .3 |
| .8 | .7 | .8 | Fixed/Worth | 1.5 | .8 | 2.2 | .6 | .4 | .7 |
| 17.0 | 4.3 | 12.8 | | 11.6 | 57.5 | -.9 | 3.9 | 1.1 | 1.5 |
| .6 | .4 | .4 | | .4 | .3 | .7 | .6 | .4 | .7 |
| 2.2 | 1.6 | 2.2 | Debt/Worth | 4.0 | 1.8 | 3.6 | 2.5 | .5 | 1.7 |
| -14.9 | 85.3 | 439.0 | | -9.9 | -5.7 | -4.2 | 8.8 | 1.9 | 4.6 |
| 210.2 | 200.1 | 128.9 | % Profit Before Taxes/Tangible | 179.5 | 198.0 | 317.7 | 108.9 | 50.4 | 87.9 |
| (185) 66.7 | (190) 62.3 | (215) 49.3 | Net Worth | (73) 40.2 | (58) 78.1 | (20) 99.1 | (23) 43.0 | (21) 19.6 | (20) 28.2 |
| 16.0 | 10.4 | 11.1 | | 11.5 | 27.8 | 3.9 | 5.4 | 9.6 | 10.1 |
| 72.8 | 56.9 | 53.4 | % Profit Before Taxes/Total | 53.4 | 81.9 | 72.6 | 36.6 | 38.4 | 32.7 |
| 22.5 | 21.1 | 16.5 | Assets | 12.7 | 25.1 | 21.9 | 15.7 | 9.6 | 11.8 |
| 3.2 | 3.1 | 2.4 | | .9 | 7.7 | 2.1 | -.3 | 5.4 | 1.4 |
| 88.9 | 94.2 | 91.5 | | 113.1 | 73.5 | 168.4 | 98.8 | 162.4 | 64.5 |
| 22.5 | 27.5 | 23.7 | Sales/Net Fixed Assets | 12.9 | 33.5 | 33.8 | 34.0 | 36.9 | 18.0 |
| 8.0 | 10.2 | 6.5 | | 1.5 | 9.7 | 10.1 | 6.4 | 16.0 | 9.5 |
| 7.9 | 8.5 | 7.2 | | 6.5 | 9.6 | 10.3 | 6.8 | 4.8 | 4.0 |
| 4.0 | 4.2 | 3.9 | Sales/Total Assets | 3.3 | 4.9 | 4.5 | 4.8 | 2.7 | 2.5 |
| 2.2 | 2.1 | 1.9 | | 1.1 | 2.3 | 2.6 | 2.1 | 1.7 | 1.8 |
| .6 | .6 | .7 | | 1.0 | .7 | .3 | .5 | .7 | .4 |
| (173) 1.5 | (173) 1.4 | (193) 1.7 | % Depr., Dep., Amort./Sales | (65) 2.5 | (51) 1.5 | (22) .8 | (17) 1.2 | (18) 2.0 | (20) 1.6 |
| 2.9 | 2.7 | 3.2 | | 11.9 | 2.5 | 2.6 | 2.2 | 2.6 | 2.4 |
| 6.8 | 5.8 | 7.1 | % Officers', Directors' | 10.0 | 5.8 | 6.5 | 2.8 | | |
| (108) 11.9 | (109) 13.6 | (132) 11.2 | Owners' Comp/Sales | (48) 15.7 | (48) 10.5 | (12) 11.0 | (13) 7.7 | | |
| 20.1 | 20.1 | 19.7 | | 24.4 | 18.2 | 29.4 | 10.8 | | |
| 6328356M | 5314787M | 6002827M | Net Sales ($) | 48199M | 140780M | 113872M | 179849M | 416290M | 5103837M |
| 1180297M | 1893239M | 1860753M | Total Assets ($) | 37641M | 56361M | 80676M | 59692M | 185260M | 1441123M |

## Current Data Sorted by Assets       Comparative Historical Data

Note: In the "Current Data" columns, the **50-100MM** and **100-250MM** columns are marked "DATA NOT AVAILABLE" for all line items below.

| Type of Statement | 0-500M | 500M-2MM | 2-10MM | 10-50MM | 50-100MM | 100-250MM | | 4/1/07-3/31/08 ALL | 4/1/08-3/31/09 ALL |
|---|---|---|---|---|---|---|---|---|---|
| Unqualified | | | | | | | | 4 | 5 |
| Reviewed | | | | | | | | 21 | 22 |
| Compiled | 4 | | 1 | 2 | | | | 6 | 5 |
| Tax Returns | 36 | 2 | 3 | 1 | | | | | |
| Other | 15 | 7 | 1 | | | | | | |
| | 2 (4/1-9/30/11) | | 69 (10/1/11-3/31/12) | | | | | | |
| **NUMBER OF STATEMENTS** | 55 | 9 | 4 | 3 | | | | 31 | 32 |

| ASSETS | 0-500M % | 500M-2MM % | 2-10MM % | 10-50MM % | 50-100MM % | 100-250MM % | | 07-08 ALL % | 08-09 ALL % |
|---|---|---|---|---|---|---|---|---|---|
| Cash & Equivalents | 30.6 | | | | | | | 30.3 | 31.7 |
| Trade Receivables (net) | 5.4 | | | | | | | .7 | 5.8 |
| Inventory | 2.5 | | | | | | | .2 | .0 |
| All Other Current | 2.4 | | | | | | | 5.2 | 2.2 |
| Total Current | 41.0 | | | | | | | 36.4 | 39.8 |
| Fixed Assets (net) | 33.2 | | | | | | | 40.4 | 31.9 |
| Intangibles (net) | 10.5 | | | | | | | 6.8 | 6.9 |
| All Other Non-Current | 15.5 | | | | | | | 16.4 | 21.4 |
| Total | 100.0 | | | | | | | 100.0 | 100.0 |

| LIABILITIES | 0-500M | | | | | | | 07-08 ALL | 08-09 ALL |
|---|---|---|---|---|---|---|---|---|---|
| Notes Payable-Short Term | 26.5 | | | | | | | 15.8 | 20.4 |
| Cur. Mat.-L.T.D. | 9.7 | | | | | | | 17.5 | 11.5 |
| Trade Payables | 1.0 | | | | | | | .4 | 2.4 |
| Income Taxes Payable | .0 | | | | | | | .0 | .0 |
| All Other Current | 23.3 | | | | | | | 20.6 | 20.5 |
| Total Current | 60.5 | | | | | | | 54.4 | 54.8 |
| Long-Term Debt | 40.5 | | | | | | | 41.0 | 40.9 |
| Deferred Taxes | .0 | | | | | | | .0 | .4 |
| All Other Non-Current | 10.1 | | | | | | | 4.8 | 2.3 |
| Net Worth | -11.0 | | | | | | | -.1 | 1.6 |
| Total Liabilities & Net Worth | 100.0 | | | | | | | 100.0 | 100.0 |

| INCOME DATA | 0-500M | | | | | | | 07-08 ALL | 08-09 ALL |
|---|---|---|---|---|---|---|---|---|---|
| Net Sales | 100.0 | | | | | | | 100.0 | 100.0 |
| Gross Profit | | | | | | | | | |
| Operating Expenses | 91.0 | | | | | | | 89.0 | 86.6 |
| Operating Profit | 9.0 | | | | | | | 11.0 | 13.4 |
| All Other Expenses (net) | .6 | | | | | | | 2.3 | 2.5 |
| Profit Before Taxes | 8.4 | | | | | | | 8.6 | 10.9 |

| RATIOS | 0-500M | | | | | | | 07-08 ALL | 08-09 ALL |
|---|---|---|---|---|---|---|---|---|---|
| | 2.0 | | | | | | | 1.7 | 4.1 |
| Current | .6 | | | | | | | .8 | 1.2 |
| | .3 | | | | | | | .3 | .1 |
| | 1.5 | | | | | | | 1.7 | 3.2 |
| Quick | (54) .6 | | | | | | | .8 | 1.2 |
| | .2 | | | | | | | .1 | .1 |
| | 0   UND | | | | | | | 0   UND | 0   UND |
| Sales/Receivables | 0   UND | | | | | | | 0   UND | 0   UND |
| | 0   UND | | | | | | | 0   UND | 0   UND |
| | | | | | | | | | |
| Cost of Sales/Inventory | | | | | | | | | |
| | | | | | | | | | |
| | | | | | | | | | |
| Cost of Sales/Payables | | | | | | | | | |
| | | | | | | | | | |
| | 42.9 | | | | | | | 46.1 | 23.5 |
| Sales/Working Capital | -129.7 | | | | | | | -56.6 | 134.1 |
| | -25.3 | | | | | | | -13.4 | -8.8 |
| | 27.3 | | | | | | | 19.7 | 43.8 |
| EBIT/Interest | (43) 5.6 | | | | | | | (25) 4.8 | (26) 12.7 |
| | .7 | | | | | | | 1.4 | .4 |
| | | | | | | | | | |
| Net Profit + Depr., Dep., Amort./Cur. Mat. L/T/D | | | | | | | | | |
| | | | | | | | | | |
| | .6 | | | | | | | .6 | .3 |
| Fixed/Worth | 18.6 | | | | | | | 5.0 | 1.5 |
| | -.8 | | | | | | | -1.0 | -1.4 |
| | 3.7 | | | | | | | .6 | .8 |
| Debt/Worth | 247.0 | | | | | | | -11.2 | 4.2 |
| | -2.6 | | | | | | | -2.7 | -4.4 |
| | 523.6 | | | | | | | 128.0 | 498.8 |
| % Profit Before Taxes/Tangible Net Worth | (29) 159.4 | | | | | | | (14) 65.2 | (21) 138.5 |
| | 82.1 | | | | | | | 24.7 | 68.2 |
| | 74.4 | | | | | | | 55.5 | 131.2 |
| % Profit Before Taxes/Total Assets | 22.2 | | | | | | | 17.5 | 39.6 |
| | -1.0 | | | | | | | 1.1 | -2.7 |
| | 131.2 | | | | | | | 145.0 | 194.7 |
| Sales/Net Fixed Assets | 32.5 | | | | | | | 23.5 | 38.5 |
| | 14.3 | | | | | | | 9.8 | 12.0 |
| | 15.3 | | | | | | | 13.2 | 10.4 |
| Sales/Total Assets | 7.0 | | | | | | | 6.0 | 5.6 |
| | 4.1 | | | | | | | 2.9 | 2.9 |
| | .6 | | | | | | | .8 | .3 |
| % Depr., Dep., Amort./Sales | (35) 1.4 | | | | | | | (16) 2.0 | (21) 1.0 |
| | 2.9 | | | | | | | 6.3 | 3.4 |
| | 9.6 | | | | | | | 15.3 | 14.2 |
| % Officers', Directors' Owners' Comp/Sales | (42) 17.8 | | | | | | | (23) 20.9 | (22) 20.9 |
| | 29.3 | | | | | | | 32.2 | 35.0 |
| Net Sales ($) | 100963M | 29734M | 16175M | 1513277M | | | | 57533M | 49750M |
| Total Assets ($) | 12377M | 9859M | 10993M | 107258M | | | | 10071M | 10263M |

© RMA 2012

M = $ thousand    MM = $ million

See Pages 9 through 22 for Explanation of Ratios and Data

## Comparative Historical Data     Current Data Sorted by Sales

| Type of Statement | | | | | | | | |
|---|---|---|---|---|---|---|---|---|
| | | | Unqualified | 1 | 3 | | | |
| | | | Reviewed | | | | | |
| 13 | 5 | 4 | Compiled | | | | | |
| 39 | 28 | 41 | Tax Returns | 19 | 12 | 3 | 3 | 2 | 2 |
| 9 | 15 | 26 | Other | 12 | 9 | 2 | | 1 | |
| 4/1/09-3/31/10 | 4/1/10-3/31/11 | 4/1/11-3/31/12 | | 2 (4/1-9/30/11) | | 69 (10/1/11-3/31/12) | | | |
| ALL | ALL | ALL | | 0-1MM | 1-3MM | 3-5MM | 5-10MM | 10-25MM | 25MM & OVER |

| 4/1/09-3/31/10 ALL | 4/1/10-3/31/11 ALL | 4/1/11-3/31/12 ALL | | 0-1MM | 1-3MM | 3-5MM | 5-10MM | 10-25MM | 25MM & OVER |
|---|---|---|---|---|---|---|---|---|---|
| 61 | 48 | 71 | **NUMBER OF STATEMENTS** | 32 | 24 | 5 | 5 | 2 | 3 |
| % | % | % | **ASSETS** | % | % | % | % | % | % |
| 25.9 | 26.6 | 26.8 | Cash & Equivalents | 21.7 | 37.9 | | | | |
| 4.0 | 7.7 | 4.9 | Trade Receivables (net) | 5.2 | 5.5 | | | | |
| 1.4 | .8 | 2.0 | Inventory | 3.9 | .6 | | | | |
| 4.6 | 2.9 | 2.4 | All Other Current | 2.9 | 2.9 | | | | |
| 36.0 | 38.1 | 36.0 | Total Current | 33.7 | 46.9 | | | | |
| 32.3 | 30.4 | 36.6 | Fixed Assets (net) | 36.9 | 29.6 | | | | |
| 13.7 | 16.8 | 10.3 | Intangibles (net) | 10.1 | 13.8 | | | | |
| 18.0 | 14.7 | 17.1 | All Other Non-Current | 19.4 | 9.8 | | | | |
| 100.0 | 100.0 | 100.0 | Total | 100.0 | 100.0 | | | | |
| | | | **LIABILITIES** | | | | | | |
| 25.5 | 26.1 | 22.6 | Notes Payable-Short Term | 21.4 | 31.1 | | | | |
| 6.2 | 5.6 | 8.1 | Cur. Mat.-L.T.D. | 2.9 | 16.4 | | | | |
| 4.0 | 3.3 | .9 | Trade Payables | .7 | .5 | | | | |
| .0 | .7 | .0 | Income Taxes Payable | .0 | .0 | | | | |
| 23.2 | 22.1 | 20.6 | All Other Current | 18.7 | 22.1 | | | | |
| 58.9 | 57.7 | 52.2 | Total Current | 43.7 | 70.1 | | | | |
| 45.7 | 34.3 | 40.8 | Long-Term Debt | 52.3 | 25.5 | | | | |
| .0 | .0 | .0 | Deferred Taxes | .0 | .0 | | | | |
| 4.0 | 5.4 | 8.2 | All Other Non-Current | 9.9 | 6.2 | | | | |
| -8.5 | 2.6 | -1.1 | Net Worth | -5.8 | -1.7 | | | | |
| 100.0 | 100.0 | 100.0 | Total Liabilities & Net Worth | 100.0 | 100.0 | | | | |
| | | | **INCOME DATA** | | | | | | |
| 100.0 | 100.0 | 100.0 | Net Sales | 100.0 | 100.0 | | | | |
| | | | Gross Profit | | | | | | |
| 88.9 | 88.8 | 86.0 | Operating Expenses | 78.7 | 91.4 | | | | |
| 11.1 | 11.2 | 14.0 | Operating Profit | 21.3 | 8.6 | | | | |
| 2.9 | 1.0 | 2.1 | All Other Expenses (net) | 4.3 | .2 | | | | |
| 8.1 | 10.2 | 11.9 | Profit Before Taxes | 17.1 | 8.4 | | | | |
| | | | **RATIOS** | | | | | | |
| 5.7 | 1.8 | 2.3 | Current | 2.3 | 2.5 | | | | |
| .6 | .7 | .9 | | .8 | .8 | | | | |
| .1 | .2 | .3 | | .3 | .3 | | | | |
| 5.1 | 1.6 | 2.1 | Quick | 1.3 | 2.4 | | | | |
| .6 | .6 | (70) .7 | | (31) .6 | .8 | | | | |
| .1 | .1 | .2 | | .2 | .3 | | | | |
| 0 UND | 0 UND | 0 UND | Sales/Receivables | 0 UND | 0 UND | | | | |
| 0 UND | 0 UND | 0 UND | | 0 UND | 0 UND | | | | |
| 0 UND | 0 UND | 0 UND | | 0 UND | 0 UND | | | | |
| | | | Cost of Sales/Inventory | | | | | | |
| | | | Cost of Sales/Payables | | | | | | |
| 37.3 | 23.3 | 32.1 | Sales/Working Capital | 14.8 | 27.0 | | | | |
| -46.3 | -92.2 | -174.2 | | -131.8 | -162.9 | | | | |
| -13.5 | -16.7 | -24.9 | | -22.6 | -16.5 | | | | |
| 14.4 | 16.9 | 28.9 | EBIT/Interest | 19.0 | 28.5 | | | | |
| (44) 3.4 | (29) 4.3 | (54) 8.6 | | (22) 7.4 | (19) 5.3 | | | | |
| -.5 | 1.0 | 1.1 | | 3.4 | -2.8 | | | | |
| | | | Net Profit + Depr., Dep., Amort./Cur. Mat. L/T/D | | | | | | |
| .4 | .4 | .6 | Fixed/Worth | .4 | .5 | | | | |
| -40.5 | 2.6 | 13.5 | | 5.4 | UND | | | | |
| -.4 | -.7 | -1.0 | | -1.0 | -.6 | | | | |
| .8 | .6 | 1.0 | Debt/Worth | 1.5 | 1.9 | | | | |
| -7.8 | 17.8 | 22.1 | | 16.2 | UND | | | | |
| -2.1 | -2.0 | -3.4 | | -3.0 | -2.9 | | | | |
| 169.2 | 342.6 | 340.0 | % Profit Before Taxes/Tangible Net Worth | 460.0 | 555.8 | | | | |
| (27) 83.9 | (27) 127.3 | (39) 122.2 | | (19) 146.2 | (13) 159.4 | | | | |
| 18.6 | 54.6 | 58.3 | | 77.1 | 40.4 | | | | |
| 76.7 | 77.3 | 68.8 | % Profit Before Taxes/Total Assets | 78.6 | 68.6 | | | | |
| 31.4 | 32.3 | 22.2 | | 28.1 | 12.5 | | | | |
| -.9 | 3.9 | .5 | | 8.1 | -1.5 | | | | |
| 70.9 | 89.4 | 91.1 | Sales/Net Fixed Assets | 163.3 | 111.2 | | | | |
| 25.8 | 20.5 | 28.1 | | 17.0 | 38.9 | | | | |
| 13.5 | 11.8 | 11.9 | | 4.3 | 19.5 | | | | |
| 10.5 | 10.0 | 12.8 | Sales/Total Assets | 8.8 | 12.6 | | | | |
| 5.3 | 5.2 | 6.1 | | 4.1 | 6.4 | | | | |
| 2.9 | 3.3 | 2.9 | | 1.6 | 4.7 | | | | |
| .9 | .8 | .6 | % Depr., Dep., Amort./Sales | .6 | .7 | | | | |
| (39) 1.9 | (27) 1.5 | (41) 1.4 | | (20) 2.2 | (13) 1.4 | | | | |
| 3.8 | 3.3 | 2.9 | | 3.5 | 2.9 | | | | |
| 11.6 | 10.8 | 11.0 | % Officers', Directors' Owners' Comp/Sales | 9.1 | 11.0 | | | | |
| (49) 19.3 | (36) 17.7 | (50) 17.8 | | (24) 14.8 | (14) 25.1 | | | | |
| 30.8 | 27.3 | 28.1 | | 20.9 | 33.1 | | | | |
| 110355M | 113758M | 1660149M | Net Sales ($) | 21072M | 43696M | 20881M | 39660M | 21563M | 1513277M |
| 24946M | 27125M | 140487M | Total Assets ($) | 15127M | 7373M | 5178M | 5088M | 463M | 107258M |

M = $ thousand    MM = $ million
See Pages 9 through 22 for Explanation of Ratios and Data

## Current Data Sorted by Assets

## Comparative Historical Data

| | | | | | | Type of Statement | | |
|---|---|---|---|---|---|---|---|---|
| | 2 | 10 | 10 | 6 | 1 | Unqualified | 38 | 45 |
| | 5 | 4 | 2 | | | Reviewed | 9 | 31 |
| 12 | 9 | 7 | 1 | | | Compiled | 29 | 34 |
| 85 | 32 | 8 | 2 | | 1 | Tax Returns | 79 | 87 |
| 45 | 45 | 34 | 11 | | 4 | Other | 68 | 99 |
| | 41 (4/1-9/30/11) | | 295 (10/1/11-3/31/12) | | | | 4/1/07-3/31/08 | 4/1/08-3/31/09 |
| 0-500M | 500M-2MM | 2-10MM | 10-50MM | 50-100MM | 100-250MM | | ALL | ALL |
| 142 | 93 | 63 | 26 | 6 | 6 | NUMBER OF STATEMENTS | 223 | 296 |
| % | % | % | % | % | % | ASSETS | % | % |
| 37.3 | 19.8 | 14.4 | 11.5 | | | Cash & Equivalents | 22.1 | 21.6 |
| 7.5 | 15.3 | 27.5 | 20.8 | | | Trade Receivables (net) | 15.8 | 18.6 |
| 4.3 | 2.0 | 1.3 | 1.4 | | | Inventory | 3.0 | 2.9 |
| 2.9 | 3.9 | 6.1 | 2.3 | | | All Other Current | 4.9 | 3.3 |
| 52.0 | 41.1 | 49.2 | 35.9 | | | Total Current | 45.7 | 46.4 |
| 28.9 | 34.3 | 29.1 | 46.8 | | | Fixed Assets (net) | 40.0 | 36.7 |
| 4.4 | 6.1 | 6.8 | 5.5 | | | Intangibles (net) | 3.0 | 4.4 |
| 14.7 | 18.6 | 15.0 | 11.8 | | | All Other Non-Current | 11.3 | 12.5 |
| 100.0 | 100.0 | 100.0 | 100.0 | | | Total | 100.0 | 100.0 |
| | | | | | | LIABILITIES | | |
| 33.1 | 11.6 | 8.1 | 2.8 | | | Notes Payable-Short Term | 17.6 | 16.1 |
| 7.2 | 2.5 | 3.5 | 3.3 | | | Cur. Mat.-L.T.D. | 6.7 | 5.8 |
| 2.1 | 5.7 | 8.2 | 6.6 | | | Trade Payables | 7.0 | 7.8 |
| .0 | .1 | .2 | .0 | | | Income Taxes Payable | .4 | .1 |
| 29.0 | 18.4 | 13.3 | 13.5 | | | All Other Current | 16.6 | 16.0 |
| 71.4 | 38.4 | 33.3 | 26.3 | | | Total Current | 48.3 | 45.7 |
| 25.2 | 23.4 | 17.0 | 28.3 | | | Long-Term Debt | 28.2 | 26.9 |
| .0 | .1 | .0 | .0 | | | Deferred Taxes | .2 | .2 |
| 9.8 | 9.6 | 7.5 | 11.0 | | | All Other Non-Current | 6.9 | 4.2 |
| -6.4 | 28.5 | 42.3 | 34.4 | | | Net Worth | 16.4 | 22.9 |
| 100.0 | 100.0 | 100.0 | 100.0 | | | Total Liabilities & Net Worth | 100.0 | 100.0 |
| | | | | | | INCOME DATA | | |
| 100.0 | 100.0 | 100.0 | 100.0 | | | Net Sales | 100.0 | 100.0 |
| | | | | | | Gross Profit | | |
| 88.5 | 86.4 | 85.3 | 88.8 | | | Operating Expenses | 88.2 | 87.5 |
| 11.5 | 13.6 | 14.7 | 11.2 | | | Operating Profit | 11.8 | 12.5 |
| .9 | 3.0 | 3.4 | 3.5 | | | All Other Expenses (net) | 1.9 | 3.6 |
| 10.6 | 10.6 | 11.3 | 7.7 | | | Profit Before Taxes | 9.8 | 8.9 |
| | | | | | | RATIOS | | |
| 3.1 | 2.8 | 3.4 | 2.9 | | | | 2.5 | 2.8 |
| 1.3 | 1.2 | 1.6 | 1.7 | | | Current | 1.3 | 1.4 |
| .4 | .4 | .8 | .7 | | | | .6 | .6 |
| 2.6 | 2.5 | 2.9 | 2.7 | | | | 2.4 | 2.5 |
| 1.0 | 1.0 | 1.4 | 1.6 | | | Quick | (222) 1.1 | (295) 1.2 |
| .3 | .3 | .6 | .6 | | | | .4 | .4 |
| 0 UND | 0 UND | 8 47.9 | 20 18.2 | | | | 0 UND | 0 UND |
| 0 UND | 0 UND | 30 12.2 | 33 11.2 | | | Sales/Receivables | 2 213.0 | 12 30.7 |
| 0 UND | 40 9.1 | 57 6.4 | 51 7.1 | | | | 40 9.2 | 43 8.4 |
| | | | | | | Cost of Sales/Inventory | | |
| | | | | | | Cost of Sales/Payables | | |
| 21.5 | 8.1 | 5.6 | 6.9 | | | | 8.8 | 9.4 |
| 108.2 | 210.1 | 13.9 | 17.7 | | | Sales/Working Capital | 51.3 | 43.3 |
| -25.9 | -17.1 | -33.1 | -19.7 | | | | -22.8 | -25.4 |
| 24.6 | 59.4 | 23.6 | 15.1 | | | | 24.0 | 25.8 |
| (88) 5.5 | (65) 8.3 | (47) 9.3 | (24) 4.8 | | | EBIT/Interest | (171) 4.3 | (230) 5.8 |
| 1.1 | 2.3 | 2.3 | 2.1 | | | | 1.1 | 1.0 |
| | | | | | | Net Profit + Depr., Dep., Amort./Cur. Mat. L/T/D | | 8.8 |
| | | | | | | | | (24) 3.5 |
| | | | | | | | | .5 |
| .2 | .1 | .1 | .9 | | | | .4 | .4 |
| 1.1 | .7 | .5 | 1.3 | | | Fixed/Worth | 1.3 | 1.2 |
| -2.0 | 11.0 | 2.5 | 2.7 | | | | -69.3 | -40.7 |
| .5 | .5 | .4 | .9 | | | | .7 | .6 |
| 4.9 | 1.7 | 1.0 | 1.3 | | | Debt/Worth | 2.4 | 2.1 |
| -4.7 | NM | 10.7 | 8.7 | | | | -24.8 | -30.5 |
| 716.8 | 102.3 | 68.8 | 61.6 | | | % Profit Before Taxes/Tangible Net Worth | 158.8 | 120.9 |
| (93) 93.9 | (70) 43.2 | (51) 31.8 | (22) 21.2 | | | | (163) 25.3 | (210) 32.3 |
| 24.9 | 11.1 | 7.7 | 9.8 | | | | 3.0 | 6.5 |
| 116.9 | 39.4 | 28.2 | 18.9 | | | % Profit Before Taxes/Total Assets | 60.9 | 47.5 |
| 32.5 | 13.2 | 12.9 | 6.9 | | | | 8.4 | 11.5 |
| 1.9 | 3.1 | 2.5 | 2.0 | | | | -.1 | -.1 |
| 348.5 | 58.3 | 51.7 | 13.4 | | | | 46.1 | 42.1 |
| 47.9 | 17.5 | 15.9 | 3.6 | | | Sales/Net Fixed Assets | 11.8 | 13.1 |
| 15.2 | 4.4 | 2.9 | 1.7 | | | | 3.8 | 3.7 |
| 14.8 | 4.8 | 3.4 | 2.6 | | | | 6.4 | 6.4 |
| 8.0 | 3.0 | 2.1 | 1.9 | | | Sales/Total Assets | 3.3 | 3.2 |
| 3.9 | 1.4 | 1.2 | 1.2 | | | | 1.7 | 1.5 |
| .5 | .7 | .8 | 1.7 | | | | .9 | .8 |
| (75) 1.1 | (59) 1.6 | (49) 2.8 | (23) 2.8 | | | % Depr., Dep., Amort./Sales | (155) 2.2 | (227) 2.2 |
| 3.1 | 4.2 | 4.7 | 3.4 | | | | 5.6 | 4.2 |
| 8.6 | 6.2 | 2.0 | | | | | 6.1 | 5.3 |
| (86) 18.4 | (38) 10.3 | (18) 4.4 | | | | % Officers', Directors' Owners' Comp/Sales | (96) 14.6 | (106) 11.6 |
| 30.3 | 20.1 | 11.5 | | | | | 23.5 | 23.6 |
| 264260M | 363425M | 626307M | 1288512M | 553587M | 2086860M | Net Sales ($) | 2573984M | 4993551M |
| 29957M | 98874M | 269617M | 537513M | 404505M | 1007584M | Total Assets ($) | 1678940M | 2375716M |

© RMA 2012

M = $ thousand    MM = $ million
See Pages 9 through 22 for Explanation of Ratios and Data

## Comparative Historical Data

## Current Data Sorted by Sales

| | | | Type of Statement | | | | | | |
|---|---|---|---|---|---|---|---|---|---|
| 53 | 44 | 29 | Unqualified | 1 | 2 | 1 | 4 | 11 | 10 |
| 23 | 15 | 11 | Reviewed | 2 | 1 | 2 | 4 | 1 | 1 |
| 38 | 30 | 29 | Compiled | 4 | 8 | 4 | 5 | 8 | |
| 124 | 117 | 128 | Tax Returns | 45 | 54 | 12 | 11 | 2 | 4 |
| 92 | 117 | 139 | Other | 24 | 43 | 15 | 22 | 22 | 13 |
| 4/1/09-3/31/10 | 4/1/10-3/31/11 | 4/1/11-3/31/12 | | 41 (4/1-9/30/11) | | | 295 (10/1/11-3/31/12) | | |
| ALL | ALL | ALL | | 0-1MM | 1-3MM | 3-5MM | 5-10MM | 10-25MM | 25MM & OVER |
| 330 | 323 | 336 | **NUMBER OF STATEMENTS** | 76 | 108 | 34 | 46 | 44 | 28 |
| % | % | % | **ASSETS** | % | % | % | % | % | % |
| 21.4 | 23.8 | 25.2 | Cash & Equivalents | 36.3 | 23.1 | 26.2 | 22.3 | 21.6 | 13.0 |
| 16.5 | 14.9 | 14.8 | Trade Receivables (net) | 6.0 | 11.5 | 16.6 | 21.1 | 23.4 | 25.1 |
| 3.2 | 3.2 | 2.8 | Inventory | 3.1 | 4.6 | 2.6 | .8 | .9 | 1.7 |
| 4.3 | 4.1 | 3.7 | All Other Current | .9 | 4.0 | 3.1 | 5.7 | 7.2 | 2.4 |
| 45.3 | 45.9 | 46.6 | Total Current | 46.2 | 43.3 | 48.4 | 49.9 | 53.0 | 42.1 |
| 36.7 | 33.3 | 31.7 | Fixed Assets (net) | 33.2 | 34.4 | 27.5 | 26.6 | 31.5 | 30.6 |
| 5.8 | 7.4 | 6.3 | Intangibles (net) | 4.7 | 5.6 | 9.7 | 4.9 | 2.9 | 16.3 |
| 12.2 | 13.4 | 15.5 | All Other Non-Current | 15.8 | 16.7 | 14.3 | 18.6 | 12.5 | 11.0 |
| 100.0 | 100.0 | 100.0 | Total | 100.0 | 100.0 | 100.0 | 100.0 | 100.0 | 100.0 |
| | | | **LIABILITIES** | | | | | | |
| 14.9 | 16.0 | 19.1 | Notes Payable-Short Term | 24.7 | 19.0 | 22.8 | 20.4 | 13.5 | 6.4 |
| 6.1 | 6.0 | 4.8 | Cur. Mat.-L.T.D. | 8.6 | 3.5 | 5.2 | 4.1 | 2.3 | 3.8 |
| 5.7 | 5.0 | 4.8 | Trade Payables | 2.3 | 3.9 | 4.2 | 5.8 | 8.2 | 8.8 |
| .1 | .3 | .1 | Income Taxes Payable | .1 | .1 | .0 | .0 | .4 | .3 |
| 19.9 | 22.0 | 21.1 | All Other Current | 17.7 | 23.4 | 15.7 | 24.6 | 27.8 | 12.0 |
| 46.8 | 49.3 | 49.9 | Total Current | 53.4 | 49.9 | 47.8 | 54.8 | 52.2 | 31.2 |
| 30.8 | 27.4 | 23.8 | Long-Term Debt | 28.9 | 22.6 | 23.6 | 22.3 | 17.7 | 27.2 |
| .1 | .1 | .1 | Deferred Taxes | .0 | .0 | .4 | .0 | .0 | .2 |
| 8.4 | 7.8 | 9.2 | All Other Non-Current | 9.3 | 7.8 | 7.9 | 18.7 | 4.1 | 8.8 |
| 13.8 | 15.4 | 17.0 | Net Worth | 8.6 | 19.8 | 20.4 | 4.2 | 26.0 | 32.5 |
| 100.0 | 100.0 | 100.0 | Total Liabilities & Net Worth | 100.0 | 100.0 | 100.0 | 100.0 | 100.0 | 100.0 |
| | | | **INCOME DATA** | | | | | | |
| 100.0 | 100.0 | 100.0 | Net Sales | 100.0 | 100.0 | 100.0 | 100.0 | 100.0 | 100.0 |
| | | | Gross Profit | | | | | | |
| 89.9 | 87.7 | 87.4 | Operating Expenses | 79.5 | 88.2 | 86.4 | 90.2 | 95.9 | 89.3 |
| 10.1 | 12.3 | 12.6 | Operating Profit | 20.5 | 11.8 | 13.6 | 9.8 | 4.1 | 10.7 |
| 2.1 | 1.3 | 2.2 | All Other Expenses (net) | 6.9 | 1.0 | .1 | .4 | .3 | 2.8 |
| 8.1 | 11.0 | 10.4 | Profit Before Taxes | 13.6 | 10.8 | 13.5 | 9.5 | 3.8 | 8.0 |
| | | | **RATIOS** | | | | | | |
| 2.5 | 3.4 | 3.0 | | 4.6 | 2.2 | 6.0 | 3.1 | 2.8 | 2.5 |
| 1.3 | 1.3 | 1.4 | Current | 1.5 | 1.0 | 1.8 | 1.4 | 1.4 | 1.6 |
| .5 | .5 | .6 | | .3 | .5 | .6 | .4 | .8 | .9 |
| 2.2 | 2.7 | 2.6 | | 4.5 | 2.0 | 4.6 | 2.6 | 2.6 | 2.2 |
| 1.0 | (322) 1.1 | 1.1 | Quick | 1.3 | .9 | 1.6 | 1.1 | 1.3 | 1.3 |
| .3 | .3 | .4 | | .3 | .3 | .5 | .2 | .7 | .8 |
| 0 UND | 0 UND | 0 UND | | 0 UND | 0 UND | 0 UND | 0 UND | 2 156.6 | 12 30.1 |
| 2 228.3 | 0 UND | 0 UND | Sales/Receivables | 0 UND | 0 UND | 0 UND | 4 93.5 | 21 17.7 | 37 9.9 |
| 36 10.1 | 39 9.4 | 31 11.7 | | 0 UND | 22 16.9 | 51 7.2 | 47 7.7 | 39 9.3 | 56 6.5 |
| | | | Cost of Sales/Inventory | | | | | | |
| | | | Cost of Sales/Payables | | | | | | |
| 9.8 | 8.7 | 9.2 | | 8.1 | 18.0 | 6.0 | 8.4 | 7.8 | 8.9 |
| 50.3 | 54.4 | 59.9 | Sales/Working Capital | 34.5 | 333.3 | 19.0 | 35.7 | 26.9 | 21.2 |
| -23.7 | -24.6 | -23.1 | | -18.5 | -16.5 | -42.2 | -18.5 | -45.1 | -55.8 |
| 22.4 | 20.9 | 27.3 | | 13.0 | 33.3 | 41.0 | 32.5 | 13.7 | 33.1 |
| (249) 6.0 | (222) 5.9 | (236) 6.9 | EBIT/Interest | (38) 6.7 | (79) 8.7 | (25) 5.1 | (37) 8.0 | (31) 3.5 | (26) 11.4 |
| 1.2 | 1.4 | 1.7 | | 1.5 | 1.7 | 1.1 | 2.4 | 1.0 | 1.6 |
| 23.6 | | 3.9 | Net Profit + Depr., Dep., | | | | | | |
| (12) 3.5 | (11) 1.4 | | Amort./Cur. Mat. L/T/D | | | | | | |
| .7 | | -.2 | | | | | | | |
| .3 | .3 | .2 | | .0 | .2 | .2 | .1 | .1 | .5 |
| 1.3 | 1.0 | .9 | Fixed/Worth | .7 | .8 | .8 | .9 | .8 | 1.6 |
| -45.0 | -23.0 | -24.7 | | 18.1 | UND | -7.4 | -6.8 | 5.0 | -.4 |
| .7 | .5 | .5 | | .5 | .5 | .4 | .6 | .5 | .9 |
| 2.7 | 1.9 | 2.0 | Debt/Worth | 2.3 | 1.7 | 1.7 | 1.9 | 1.8 | 2.2 |
| -19.7 | -11.6 | -15.6 | | -13.6 | -9.4 | -30.5 | -8.6 | 56.7 | -5.4 |
| 124.2 | 131.0 | 131.0 | % Profit Before Taxes/Tangible | 144.2 | 179.9 | 158.2 | 205.4 | 117.5 | 102.7 |
| (237) 40.3 | (231) 42.2 | (240) 48.5 | Net Worth | (54) 60.4 | (79) 52.1 | (24) 65.9 | (31) 48.5 | (35) 24.3 | (17) 44.0 |
| 6.8 | 8.0 | 11.1 | | 9.7 | 8.3 | 20.9 | 15.5 | 1.5 | 19.3 |
| 44.9 | 60.3 | 53.6 | % Profit Before Taxes/Total | 77.5 | 62.3 | 55.9 | 42.6 | 22.0 | 42.7 |
| 12.7 | 14.7 | 14.8 | Assets | 23.6 | 19.4 | 15.7 | 19.1 | 7.7 | 11.1 |
| .8 | 1.5 | 2.4 | | 1.9 | 2.8 | 2.5 | 5.4 | .4 | 2.3 |
| 65.4 | 78.2 | 102.3 | | UND | 66.7 | 103.2 | 136.9 | 928.9 | 65.7 |
| 15.3 | 17.2 | 21.9 | Sales/Net Fixed Assets | 28.5 | 17.8 | 18.1 | 34.9 | 22.1 | 14.5 |
| 4.2 | 4.9 | 5.9 | | 4.3 | 6.0 | 7.4 | 11.6 | 2.8 | 3.7 |
| 7.7 | 7.1 | 8.0 | | 11.0 | 8.0 | 7.7 | 8.5 | 7.4 | 4.0 |
| 3.8 | 3.4 | 3.6 | Sales/Total Assets | 3.0 | 3.9 | 4.7 | 3.9 | 3.3 | 2.5 |
| 1.8 | 1.6 | 1.8 | | 1.0 | 2.4 | 1.7 | 2.4 | 1.6 | 1.6 |
| .8 | .8 | .7 | | .6 | .7 | .4 | .6 | 1.1 | 1.6 |
| (244) 2.1 | (211) 2.1 | (212) 1.8 | % Depr., Dep., Amort./Sales | (41) 1.8 | (69) 1.8 | (23) 1.8 | (32) 1.1 | (29) 2.5 | (18) 2.5 |
| 4.3 | 4.4 | 4.0 | | 8.9 | 4.2 | 4.3 | 3.1 | 3.4 | 3.4 |
| 5.9 | 5.5 | 6.6 | % Officers', Directors' | 11.4 | 7.4 | 5.6 | 2.9 | 2.2 | |
| (147) 11.9 | (128) 11.3 | (147) 13.0 | Owners' Comp/Sales | (35) 22.8 | (59) 12.3 | (16) 6.7 | (18) 8.8 | (14) 26.1 | |
| 22.9 | 25.0 | 27.8 | | 30.5 | 23.1 | 27.3 | 19.2 | 43.5 | |
| 8996080M | 6265935M | 5182951M | Net Sales ($) | 37859M | 194155M | 135325M | 309924M | 726819M | 3778869M |
| 2716232M | 2558353M | 2348050M | Total Assets ($) | 33722M | 92265M | 54178M | 108787M | 401647M | 1657451M |

M = $ thousand    MM = $ million
See Pages 9 through 22 for Explanation of Ratios and Data

## Current Data Sorted by Assets      Comparative Historical Data

### Type of Statement

| 0-500M | 500M-2MM | 2-10MM | 10-50MM | 50-100MM | 100-250MM | Type of Statement | 4/1/07-3/31/08 ALL | 4/1/08-3/31/09 ALL |
|---|---|---|---|---|---|---|---|---|
| 2 | 4 | 6 | 12 | 3 | 1 | Unqualified | 18 | 34 |
|  | 1 | 1 | 1 |  |  | Reviewed | 1 |  |
| 2 |  |  |  |  |  | Compiled |  | 1 |
|  | 1 |  |  |  |  | Tax Returns | 2 | 2 |
| 4 | 4 | 4 | 2 | 1 |  | Other | 13 | 14 |

Current period groupings: 19 (4/1-9/30/11) — 29 (10/1/11-3/31/12)

| 0-500M | 500M-2MM | 2-10MM | 10-50MM | 50-100MM | 100-250MM | | 4/1/07-3/31/08 ALL | 4/1/08-3/31/09 ALL |
|---|---|---|---|---|---|---|---|---|
| 8 | 10 | 11 | 14 | 4 | 1 | NUMBER OF STATEMENTS | 34 | 51 |
| % | % | % | % | % | % | **ASSETS** | % | % |
|  | 24.5 | 16.9 | 27.6 |  |  | Cash & Equivalents | 15.3 | 23.8 |
|  | 15.4 | 13.3 | 11.0 |  |  | Trade Receivables (net) | 18.9 | 13.6 |
|  | .2 | 1.7 | 2.6 |  |  | Inventory | 1.1 | 2.0 |
|  | 1.3 | 1.5 | 2.5 |  |  | All Other Current | 5.8 | 6.2 |
|  | 41.5 | 33.4 | 43.6 |  |  | Total Current | 41.2 | 45.6 |
|  | 46.7 | 51.4 | 37.2 |  |  | Fixed Assets (net) | 44.8 | 37.1 |
|  | 4.6 | 3.9 | .2 |  |  | Intangibles (net) | 2.6 | 2.7 |
|  | 7.2 | 11.2 | 19.0 |  |  | All Other Non-Current | 11.4 | 14.6 |
|  | 100.0 | 100.0 | 100.0 |  |  | Total | 100.0 | 100.0 |
|  |  |  |  |  |  | **LIABILITIES** |  |  |
|  | 7.8 | .9 | .2 |  |  | Notes Payable-Short Term | 3.4 | 4.3 |
|  | 5.0 | 1.4 | .5 |  |  | Cur. Mat.-L.T.D. | 3.2 | 2.3 |
|  | 5.8 | 4.3 | 3.2 |  |  | Trade Payables | 7.6 | 7.7 |
|  | .0 | .0 | .0 |  |  | Income Taxes Payable | .3 | .0 |
|  | 9.4 | 5.2 | 5.5 |  |  | All Other Current | 9.6 | 8.7 |
|  | 28.0 | 11.8 | 9.5 |  |  | Total Current | 24.2 | 23.0 |
|  | 23.7 | 21.2 | 12.8 |  |  | Long-Term Debt | 23.3 | 13.0 |
|  | .0 | .0 | .0 |  |  | Deferred Taxes | .0 | .0 |
|  | .5 | 1.1 | .4 |  |  | All Other Non-Current | 1.8 | 1.4 |
|  | 47.8 | 65.9 | 77.4 |  |  | Net Worth | 50.7 | 62.6 |
|  | 100.0 | 100.0 | 100.0 |  |  | Total Liabilities & Net Worth | 100.0 | 100.0 |
|  |  |  |  |  |  | **INCOME DATA** |  |  |
|  | 100.0 | 100.0 | 100.0 |  |  | Net Sales | 100.0 | 100.0 |
|  |  |  |  |  |  | Gross Profit |  |  |
|  | 88.6 | 88.7 | 94.4 |  |  | Operating Expenses | 91.9 | 91.4 |
|  | 11.4 | 11.3 | 5.6 |  |  | Operating Profit | 8.1 | 8.6 |
|  | 1.4 | 3.9 | -1.0 |  |  | All Other Expenses (net) | -.6 | 1.1 |
|  | 9.9 | 7.4 | 6.6 |  |  | Profit Before Taxes | 8.7 | 7.5 |
|  |  |  |  |  |  | **RATIOS** |  |  |
|  | 13.9 | 6.0 | 7.1 |  |  | Current | 3.5 | 4.2 |
|  | 2.3 | 3.8 | 4.0 |  |  |  | 2.0 | 2.3 |
|  | .6 | .9 | 2.6 |  |  |  | 1.1 | 1.2 |
|  | 13.6 | 4.5 | 6.1 |  |  | Quick | 3.2 | 3.8 |
|  | 2.2 | 2.6 | 3.6 |  |  |  | 1.7 | 1.9 |
|  | .6 | .8 | 2.1 |  |  |  | 1.0 | .9 |
|  | 0 UND | 2 193.4 | 29 12.8 |  |  | Sales/Receivables | 5 73.0 | 10 35.7 |
|  | 5 80.9 | 11 33.0 | 41 9.0 |  |  |  | 31 11.6 | 27 13.7 |
|  | 31 11.6 | 27 13.3 | 62 5.9 |  |  |  | 58 6.3 | 44 8.3 |
|  |  |  |  |  |  | Cost of Sales/Inventory |  |  |
|  |  |  |  |  |  | Cost of Sales/Payables |  |  |
|  | 1.9 | 3.5 | 1.9 |  |  | Sales/Working Capital | 4.8 | 2.8 |
|  | 15.2 | 8.9 | 4.3 |  |  |  | 10.5 | 5.9 |
|  | -19.1 | -74.1 | 6.1 |  |  |  | 64.2 | 60.5 |
|  | 13.9 |  | 36.4 |  |  | EBIT/Interest | (28) 24.9 | (34) 35.7 |
|  | 7.9 |  | (11) 11.9 |  |  |  | 6.0 | 3.1 |
|  | 3.1 |  | -2.0 |  |  |  | 2.3 | -1.3 |
|  |  |  |  |  |  | Net Profit + Depr., Dep., Amort./Cur. Mat. L/T/D |  |  |
|  | .7 | .4 | .3 |  |  | Fixed/Worth | .4 | .3 |
|  | 1.0 | .8 | .4 |  |  |  | .8 | .5 |
|  | 3.1 | .9 | .8 |  |  |  | 1.9 | .9 |
|  | .4 | .1 | .1 |  |  | Debt/Worth | .3 | .2 |
|  | .7 | .4 | .2 |  |  |  | .8 | .4 |
|  | 4.1 | 1.0 | .6 |  |  |  | 2.5 | 1.7 |
|  |  | 19.7 | 18.1 |  |  | % Profit Before Taxes/Tangible Net Worth | 46.8 | 35.5 |
|  |  | (10) 6.9 | 6.0 |  |  |  | (32) 15.5 | (48) 4.1 |
|  |  | -5.6 | .5 |  |  |  | 2.4 | -6.5 |
|  | 25.3 | 12.9 | 13.5 |  |  | % Profit Before Taxes/Total Assets | 18.0 | 16.9 |
|  | 9.8 | 8.3 | 5.0 |  |  |  | 6.5 | 2.9 |
|  | 3.9 | -4.9 | .0 |  |  |  | .8 | -3.7 |
|  | 46.5 | 4.9 | 4.5 |  |  | Sales/Net Fixed Assets | 10.7 | 13.9 |
|  | 2.7 | 2.5 | 2.5 |  |  |  | 3.4 | 4.5 |
|  | 1.4 | .8 | 1.7 |  |  |  | 2.0 | 2.2 |
|  | 3.2 | 1.6 | 1.2 |  |  | Sales/Total Assets | 2.6 | 2.3 |
|  | 1.6 | 1.2 | .9 |  |  |  | 1.7 | 1.4 |
|  | 1.1 | .6 | .7 |  |  |  | 1.0 | .8 |
|  |  |  | 2.1 |  |  | % Depr., Dep., Amort./Sales | (31) 1.4 | (43) 1.5 |
|  |  |  | 3.0 |  |  |  | 2.7 | 2.5 |
|  |  |  | 3.5 |  |  |  | 3.5 | 3.4 |
|  |  |  |  |  |  | % Officers', Directors' Owners' Comp/Sales |  |  |
| 25392M | 28293M | 91914M | 385877M | 185528M | 273582M | Net Sales ($) | 517104M | 1201654M |
| 1952M | 10872M | 58583M | 396299M | 311381M | 157504M | Total Assets ($) | 456982M | 1008015M |

M = $ thousand    MM = $ million
See Pages 9 through 22 for Explanation of Ratios and Data

## Comparative Historical Data  —  Current Data Sorted by Sales

| | | | Type of Statement | | | | | | |
|---|---|---|---|---|---|---|---|---|---|
| 33 | 33 | 28 | Unqualified | 2 | 2 | 3 | 2 | 8 | 11 |
| 1 | 1 | 2 | Reviewed | 2 | 1 | | 1 | | |
| | 1 | 2 | Compiled | | 2 | | | | |
| 4 | 2 | 1 | Tax Returns | 1 | | | | | |
| 17 | 14 | 15 | Other | 4 | 2 | 3 | 1 | 2 | 3 |
| 4/1/09- | 4/1/10- | 4/1/11- | | | 19 (4/1-9/30/11) | | | 29 (10/1/11-3/31/12) | |
| 3/31/10 | 3/31/11 | 3/31/12 | | | | | | | |
| ALL | ALL | ALL | | 0-1MM | 1-3MM | 3-5MM | 5-10MM | 10-25MM | 25MM & OVER |
| 55 | 51 | 48 | **NUMBER OF STATEMENTS** | 7 | 7 | 6 | 4 | 10 | 14 |
| % | % | % | **ASSETS** | % | % | % | % | % | % |
| 18.2 | 22.8 | 24.4 | Cash & Equivalents | | | | | 24.7 | 21.0 |
| 11.0 | 12.1 | 11.3 | Trade Receivables (net) | | | | | 14.7 | 14.7 |
| 1.5 | 1.5 | 1.3 | Inventory | | | | | 1.6 | 2.3 |
| 2.3 | 2.4 | 1.7 | All Other Current | | | | | 2.5 | 1.9 |
| 33.0 | 38.9 | 38.6 | Total Current | | | | | 43.5 | 39.9 |
| 49.8 | 43.2 | 44.2 | Fixed Assets (net) | | | | | 37.8 | 36.0 |
| 4.5 | 2.0 | 2.9 | Intangibles (net) | | | | | .1 | 3.2 |
| 12.7 | 16.0 | 14.2 | All Other Non-Current | | | | | 18.6 | 20.9 |
| 100.0 | 100.0 | 100.0 | Total | | | | | 100.0 | 100.0 |
| | | | **LIABILITIES** | | | | | | |
| 1.9 | 4.9 | 3.1 | Notes Payable-Short Term | | | | | 6.8 | 1.2 |
| 1.8 | 2.0 | 2.9 | Cur. Mat.-L.T.D. | | | | | 2.3 | .6 |
| 4.6 | 4.7 | 3.8 | Trade Payables | | | | | 8.3 | 4.1 |
| .1 | .0 | .0 | Income Taxes Payable | | | | | .0 | .0 |
| 5.6 | 8.3 | 10.4 | All Other Current | | | | | 22.5 | 8.2 |
| 14.0 | 19.8 | 20.2 | Total Current | | | | | 39.9 | 14.1 |
| 26.2 | 15.9 | 23.8 | Long-Term Debt | | | | | 34.5 | 11.6 |
| .0 | .1 | .1 | Deferred Taxes | | | | | .0 | .2 |
| 3.7 | 2.1 | 2.2 | All Other Non-Current | | | | | 1.2 | .3 |
| 56.0 | 62.1 | 53.8 | Net Worth | | | | | 24.3 | 73.7 |
| 100.0 | 100.0 | 100.0 | Total Liabilities & Net Worth | | | | | 100.0 | 100.0 |
| | | | **INCOME DATA** | | | | | | |
| 100.0 | 100.0 | 100.0 | Net Sales | | | | | 100.0 | 100.0 |
| | | | Gross Profit | | | | | | |
| 92.3 | 90.4 | 92.2 | Operating Expenses | | | | | 97.0 | 95.1 |
| 7.7 | 9.6 | 7.8 | Operating Profit | | | | | 3.0 | 4.9 |
| 2.1 | .7 | .9 | All Other Expenses (net) | | | | | -1.4 | -.3 |
| 5.7 | 8.9 | 6.9 | Profit Before Taxes | | | | | 4.4 | 5.2 |
| | | | **RATIOS** | | | | | | |
| 4.5 | 5.1 | 5.9 | | | | | | 9.1 | 4.9 |
| 2.5 | 2.4 | 2.7 | Current | | | | | 2.7 | 3.0 |
| 1.2 | 1.2 | 1.0 | | | | | | .8 | 2.0 |
| 3.7 | 4.7 | 5.0 | | | | | | 7.6 | 4.3 |
| 2.2 | 2.1 | 2.5 | Quick | | | | | 2.5 | 2.3 |
| .9 | .8 | 1.0 | | | | | | .6 | 1.6 |
| 5  71.5 | 8  44.1 | 1  729.3 | | | | | | 11  33.2 | 20  18.0 |
| 22  16.6 | 27  13.6 | 19  19.4 | Sales/Receivables | | | | | 30  12.2 | 33  10.9 |
| 38  9.6 | 41  8.8 | 39  9.3 | | | | | | 48  7.6 | 58  6.3 |
| | | | Cost of Sales/Inventory | | | | | | |
| | | | Cost of Sales/Payables | | | | | | |
| 3.4 | 3.3 | 2.8 | | | | | | 1.7 | 4.0 |
| 6.5 | 6.6 | 6.2 | Sales/Working Capital | | | | | 8.2 | 5.5 |
| 33.7 | 34.4 | 198.3 | | | | | | -24.4 | 8.6 |
| 14.5 | 21.2 | 18.1 | | | | | | 17.7 | 57.2 |
| (41)  2.7 | (34)  6.5 | (39)  7.3 | EBIT/Interest | | | | | 1.2 | (10)  13.8 |
| .2 | 1.6 | -2.0 | | | | | | -3.8 | -5.0 |
| | | | Net Profit + Depr., Dep., Amort./Cur. Mat. L/T/D | | | | | | |
| .4 | .3 | .3 | | | | | | .3 | .3 |
| 1.0 | .7 | .7 | Fixed/Worth | | | | | .6 | .5 |
| 2.4 | 1.3 | 1.2 | | | | | | NM | .8 |
| .2 | .1 | .1 | | | | | | .1 | .1 |
| .7 | .4 | .5 | Debt/Worth | | | | | .4 | .3 |
| 2.2 | 1.4 | 1.5 | | | | | | NM | .8 |
| 13.8 | 19.4 | 19.7 | % Profit Before Taxes/Tangible Net Worth | | | | | | 19.8 |
| (48)  6.6 | (46)  9.0 | (42)  10.0 | | | | | | | 10.9 |
| -5.9 | 2.7 | 1.6 | | | | | | | 1.9 |
| 10.0 | 12.3 | 13.7 | % Profit Before Taxes/Total Assets | | | | | 12.6 | 11.2 |
| 3.5 | 6.7 | 7.5 | | | | | | -.6 | 6.7 |
| -3.1 | 1.9 | .9 | | | | | | -5.8 | 1.9 |
| 5.8 | 6.2 | 10.2 | | | | | | 25.8 | 5.4 |
| 2.5 | 2.8 | 2.7 | Sales/Net Fixed Assets | | | | | 2.9 | 2.7 |
| 1.4 | 1.9 | 1.7 | | | | | | 1.6 | 1.8 |
| 1.7 | 1.7 | 2.0 | | | | | | 5.2 | 1.7 |
| 1.2 | 1.1 | 1.3 | Sales/Total Assets | | | | | 1.0 | 1.0 |
| .7 | .7 | .7 | | | | | | .6 | .8 |
| 1.9 | 1.9 | 1.5 | | | | | | 1.0 | 2.8 |
| (45)  2.9 | (46)  2.9 | (43)  3.4 | % Depr., Dep., Amort./Sales | | | | | 2.4 | (13)  3.2 |
| 4.6 | 4.3 | 4.7 | | | | | | 3.7 | 4.3 |
| | | | % Officers', Directors' Owners' Comp/Sales | | | | | | |
| 1099743M | 923497M | 990586M | Net Sales ($) | 3829M | 12272M | 23438M | 28359M | 152455M | 770233M |
| 1024244M | 1060838M | 936591M | Total Assets ($) | 10832M | 6062M | 19029M | 16725M | 186072M | 697871M |

M = $ thousand    MM = $ million
See Pages 9 through 22 for Explanation of Ratios and Data

## Current Data Sorted by Assets        Comparative Historical Data

| | | | | | | Type of Statement | | |
|---|---|---|---|---|---|---|---|---|
| 2 | 15 | 47 | 60 | 3 | 1 | Unqualified | 84 | 77 |
| | | 3 | 1 | | | Reviewed | | 1 |
| 1 | 3 | 2 | 2 | | | Compiled | 5 | 6 |
| 8 | 3 | 5 | | | | Tax Returns | 6 | 11 |
| 3 | 4 | 24 | 9 | 2 | | Other | 23 | 37 |
| | 141 (4/1-9/30/11) | | 57 (10/1/11-3/31/12) | | | | 4/1/07-3/31/08 | 4/1/08-3/31/09 |
| 0-500M | 500M-2MM | 2-10MM | 10-50MM | 50-100MM | 100-250MM | | ALL | ALL |
| 14 | 25 | 81 | 72 | 5 | 1 | NUMBER OF STATEMENTS | 118 | 132 |
| % | % | % | % | % | % | ASSETS | % | % |
| 40.1 | 18.0 | 21.5 | 23.2 | | | Cash & Equivalents | 20.7 | 21.2 |
| 11.8 | 31.0 | 20.5 | 12.2 | | | Trade Receivables (net) | 20.2 | 19.9 |
| .4 | .1 | .2 | .1 | | | Inventory | .5 | .2 |
| .6 | 4.1 | 2.6 | 2.9 | | | All Other Current | 4.6 | 5.3 |
| 53.0 | 53.3 | 44.8 | 38.4 | | | Total Current | 46.0 | 46.6 |
| 31.3 | 42.0 | 44.9 | 50.0 | | | Fixed Assets (net) | 40.5 | 41.8 |
| .0 | .9 | .5 | 4.4 | | | Intangibles (net) | 2.4 | 2.6 |
| 15.8 | 3.9 | 9.7 | 7.1 | | | All Other Non-Current | 11.2 | 9.0 |
| 100.0 | 100.0 | 100.0 | 100.0 | | | Total | 100.0 | 100.0 |
| | | | | | | LIABILITIES | | |
| 30.5 | 8.7 | 3.0 | .9 | | | Notes Payable-Short Term | 3.2 | 3.1 |
| 1.8 | 1.8 | 1.9 | 1.7 | | | Cur. Mat.-L.T.D. | 2.2 | 2.6 |
| 8.5 | 8.5 | 6.4 | 4.7 | | | Trade Payables | 8.9 | 6.2 |
| .0 | .0 | .0 | .0 | | | Income Taxes Payable | .1 | .1 |
| 24.4 | 16.6 | 14.1 | 10.9 | | | All Other Current | 12.0 | 11.7 |
| 65.2 | 35.7 | 25.5 | 18.1 | | | Total Current | 26.4 | 23.6 |
| 28.5 | 18.1 | 21.0 | 26.5 | | | Long-Term Debt | 22.9 | 21.6 |
| .0 | .0 | .1 | .2 | | | Deferred Taxes | .1 | .0 |
| 24.3 | 4.2 | 1.6 | 2.5 | | | All Other Non-Current | 3.0 | 2.3 |
| -17.4 | 41.9 | 51.8 | 52.7 | | | Net Worth | 47.6 | 52.4 |
| 100.0 | 100.0 | 100.0 | 100.0 | | | Total Liabilities & Net Worth | 100.0 | 100.0 |
| | | | | | | INCOME DATA | | |
| 100.0 | 100.0 | 100.0 | 100.0 | | | Net Sales | 100.0 | 100.0 |
| | | | | | | Gross Profit | | |
| 88.6 | 94.2 | 96.5 | 96.3 | | | Operating Expenses | 94.5 | 94.8 |
| 11.4 | 5.8 | 3.5 | 3.7 | | | Operating Profit | 5.5 | 5.2 |
| -.3 | 2.9 | 2.0 | .8 | | | All Other Expenses (net) | .3 | .7 |
| 11.8 | 2.8 | 1.6 | 2.9 | | | Profit Before Taxes | 5.2 | 4.5 |
| | | | | | | RATIOS | | |
| 27.1 | 4.0 | 3.5 | 3.5 | | | | 3.1 | 3.2 |
| .8 | 1.7 | 2.3 | 2.2 | | | Current | 2.0 | 2.1 |
| .1 | .6 | 1.5 | 1.7 | | | | 1.2 | 1.3 |
| 27.1 | 3.6 | 3.3 | 3.3 | | | | 2.8 | 3.1 |
| .8 | 1.4 | 2.1 | 2.1 | | | Quick | 1.7 | 1.9 |
| .1 | .6 | 1.3 | 1.5 | | | | 1.1 | 1.0 |
| 0   UND | 2   178.7 | 16   22.8 | 15   24.6 | | | | 17   22.1 | 14   25.7 |
| 0   UND | 30   12.2 | 30   12.0 | 27   13.4 | | | Sales/Receivables | 32   11.3 | 32   11.4 |
| 9   39.3 | 38   9.5 | 53   6.9 | 44   8.3 | | | | 46   8.0 | 47   7.8 |
| | | | | | | Cost of Sales/Inventory | | |
| | | | | | | Cost of Sales/Payables | | |
| 16.0 | 6.3 | 4.9 | 4.1 | | | | 5.4 | 5.1 |
| NM | 13.7 | 7.0 | 6.7 | | | Sales/Working Capital | 9.8 | 9.4 |
| -9.7 | -33.8 | 20.8 | 14.7 | | | | 33.2 | 28.5 |
| | 23.4 | 9.2 | 10.7 | | | | 9.5 | 10.2 |
| (22) 11.5 | (62) 2.3 | (66) 2.9 | | | | EBIT/Interest | (95) 2.9 | (100) 3.0 |
| .8 | .0 | .9 | | | | | 1.0 | .9 |
| | | | | | | Net Profit + Depr., Dep., Amort./Cur. Mat. L/T/D | | |
| .0 | .2 | .5 | .6 | | | | .5 | .4 |
| 1.9 | .9 | .9 | 1.0 | | | Fixed/Worth | .9 | .9 |
| UND | 2.5 | 1.5 | 1.7 | | | | 1.8 | 1.6 |
| .9 | .6 | .3 | .5 | | | | .5 | .4 |
| 11.7 | .9 | .9 | .8 | | | Debt/Worth | 1.0 | .9 |
| -2.5 | 5.1 | 1.6 | 1.8 | | | | 2.3 | 1.8 |
| 882.1 | 24.7 | 17.5 | 13.2 | | | | 25.7 | 24.2 |
| (10) 110.2 | (21) 13.2 | (78) 4.2 | (68) 6.2 | | | % Profit Before Taxes/Tangible Net Worth | (108) 7.1 | (125) 8.2 |
| 5.8 | .1 | -3.6 | .2 | | | | .1 | .9 |
| 123.6 | 16.0 | 8.5 | 6.8 | | | | 12.3 | 14.0 |
| 25.0 | 8.9 | 1.7 | 3.6 | | | % Profit Before Taxes/Total Assets | 3.3 | 4.3 |
| .5 | .1 | -2.7 | .1 | | | | .1 | .1 |
| UND | 71.1 | 10.6 | 5.2 | | | | 15.5 | 18.9 |
| 26.2 | 6.0 | 4.2 | 2.6 | | | Sales/Net Fixed Assets | 4.2 | 4.6 |
| 9.4 | 3.0 | 2.1 | 1.5 | | | | 2.2 | 2.1 |
| 9.5 | 5.7 | 2.4 | 1.8 | | | | 3.2 | 3.6 |
| 7.7 | 3.1 | 1.6 | 1.2 | | | Sales/Total Assets | 1.8 | 1.7 |
| 2.7 | 1.9 | 1.0 | .9 | | | | 1.1 | 1.2 |
| | .3 | 1.2 | 1.7 | | | | 1.3 | 1.1 |
| | (22) 1.4 | (70) 2.1 | (71) 2.7 | | | % Depr., Dep., Amort./Sales | (108) 2.3 | (111) 2.1 |
| | 3.2 | 3.3 | 3.6 | | | | 3.3 | 3.2 |
| | | | | | | | | 2.9 |
| | | | | | | % Officers', Directors' Owners' Comp/Sales | | (17) 8.9 |
| | | | | | | | | 14.6 |
| 21259M | 106564M | 784839M | 2392092M | 358312M | 103109M | Net Sales ($) | 2658130M | 2397367M |
| 2993M | 30667M | 423357M | 1492656M | 351215M | 102830M | Total Assets ($) | 1545424M | 1413395M |

M = $ thousand     MM = $ million
See Pages 9 through 22 for Explanation of Ratios and Data

## Comparative Historical Data | Current Data Sorted by Sales

| | | | Type of Statement | | | | | | |
|---|---|---|---|---|---|---|---|---|---|
| 91 | 124 | 128 | Unqualified | 3 | 12 | 9 | 29 | 41 | 34 |
| | 2 | 4 | Reviewed | 1 | | | 2 | | 1 |
| 3 | 4 | 8 | Compiled | | 2 | | 3 | 2 | 1 |
| 12 | 16 | 16 | Tax Returns | 7 | 2 | 2 | 4 | 1 | |
| 33 | 49 | 42 | Other | 3 | 3 | 4 | 8 | 18 | 6 |
| 4/1/09-<br>3/31/10<br>ALL | 4/1/10-<br>3/31/11<br>ALL | 4/1/11-<br>3/31/12<br>ALL | | 0-1MM | 141 (4/1-9/30/11)<br>1-3MM | 3-5MM | 5-10MM | 57 (10/1/11-3/31/12)<br>10-25MM | 25MM & OVER |
| 139 | 195 | 198 | **NUMBER OF STATEMENTS** | 14 | 19 | 15 | 46 | 62 | 42 |
| % | % | % | **ASSETS** | % | % | % | % | % | % |
| 22.1 | 22.4 | 22.9 | Cash & Equivalents | 23.4 | 22.7 | 28.3 | 20.3 | 21.6 | 25.7 |
| 20.4 | 18.7 | 17.9 | Trade Receivables (net) | 2.5 | 13.4 | 20.2 | 23.2 | 20.3 | 15.1 |
| .1 | .2 | .2 | Inventory | .6 | .0 | .0 | .1 | .1 | .4 |
| 5.3 | 4.1 | 2.7 | All Other Current | .9 | 1.9 | 2.9 | 2.3 | 3.6 | 2.9 |
| 47.9 | 45.4 | 43.7 | Total Current | 27.3 | 38.0 | 51.3 | 45.9 | 45.6 | 44.0 |
| 40.4 | 44.2 | 45.3 | Fixed Assets (net) | 62.3 | 53.1 | 41.1 | 43.6 | 44.4 | 40.6 |
| 4.4 | 3.0 | 2.6 | Intangibles (net) | .1 | .0 | 1.5 | 1.0 | 1.3 | 8.8 |
| 7.3 | 7.5 | 8.4 | All Other Non-Current | 10.4 | 8.9 | 6.1 | 9.5 | 8.7 | 6.6 |
| 100.0 | 100.0 | 100.0 | Total | 100.0 | 100.0 | 100.0 | 100.0 | 100.0 | 100.0 |
| | | | **LIABILITIES** | | | | | | |
| 5.6 | 4.5 | 4.9 | Notes Payable-Short Term | 17.8 | 7.8 | 7.4 | 3.7 | 3.9 | 1.1 |
| 3.1 | 2.8 | 1.8 | Cur. Mat.-L.T.D. | 2.1 | 1.5 | 1.8 | 1.3 | 2.2 | 1.9 |
| 7.1 | 7.2 | 6.1 | Trade Payables | 6.9 | 5.3 | 5.1 | 5.6 | 6.4 | 6.6 |
| .1 | .1 | .0 | Income Taxes Payable | .0 | .0 | .0 | .0 | .0 | .0 |
| 16.0 | 15.1 | 13.8 | All Other Current | 9.6 | 9.6 | 9.6 | 15.0 | 17.8 | 11.4 |
| 32.0 | 29.6 | 26.6 | Total Current | 36.4 | 24.2 | 23.9 | 25.5 | 30.4 | 20.9 |
| 21.0 | 21.0 | 23.7 | Long-Term Debt | 37.7 | 27.1 | 22.4 | 19.2 | 23.2 | 23.6 |
| .0 | .0 | .1 | Deferred Taxes | .0 | .0 | .0 | .0 | .1 | .4 |
| 3.0 | 3.4 | 4.1 | All Other Non-Current | .6 | 20.3 | 2.1 | 2.7 | 1.5 | 4.0 |
| 44.1 | 45.9 | 45.6 | Net Worth | 25.8 | 28.4 | 51.6 | 52.6 | 44.9 | 51.1 |
| 100.0 | 100.0 | 100.0 | Total Liabilities & Net Worth | 100.0 | 100.0 | 100.0 | 100.0 | 100.0 | 100.0 |
| | | | **INCOME DATA** | | | | | | |
| 100.0 | 100.0 | 100.0 | Net Sales | 100.0 | 100.0 | 100.0 | 100.0 | 100.0 | 100.0 |
| | | | Gross Profit | | | | | | |
| 95.9 | 93.9 | 95.4 | Operating Expenses | 81.2 | 97.4 | 98.6 | 94.7 | 97.5 | 95.5 |
| 4.1 | 6.1 | 4.6 | Operating Profit | 18.8 | 2.6 | 1.4 | 5.3 | 2.5 | 4.5 |
| .4 | 2.0 | 1.5 | All Other Expenses (net) | 13.1 | 3.8 | -.3 | .5 | .3 | .1 |
| 3.7 | 4.1 | 3.2 | Profit Before Taxes | 5.6 | -1.2 | 1.7 | 4.8 | 2.2 | 4.4 |
| | | | **RATIOS** | | | | | | |
| 2.8 | 2.9 | 3.5 | | 4.3 | 7.8 | 6.3 | 4.0 | 3.1 | 3.0 |
| 1.9 | 1.9 | 2.1 | Current | 1.3 | 2.0 | 2.3 | 2.3 | 2.1 | 2.0 |
| 1.2 | 1.2 | 1.4 | | .1 | .7 | 1.6 | 1.4 | 1.4 | 1.6 |
| 2.6 | 2.8 | 3.3 | | 3.8 | 7.4 | 6.3 | 3.9 | 3.0 | 2.8 |
| 1.7 | 1.7 | 1.9 | Quick | 1.3 | 1.7 | 2.1 | 2.2 | 2.1 | 1.8 |
| 1.0 | 1.0 | 1.2 | | .1 | .3 | 1.1 | 1.2 | 1.2 | 1.4 |

| | | | | | | | | | | | | | | | | | |
|---|---|---|---|---|---|---|---|---|---|---|---|---|---|---|---|---|---|
| 14 | 25.9 | 12 | 31.2 | 9 | 40.8 | Sales/Receivables | 0 | UND | 4 | 93.2 | 19 | 19.7 | 6 | 58.5 | 21 | 17.4 | 14 | 25.8 |
| 30 | 12.0 | 30 | 12.0 | 28 | 13.2 | | 0 | UND | 22 | 16.3 | 51 | 7.1 | 29 | 12.7 | 33 | 11.2 | 26 | 13.8 |
| 46 | 7.9 | 48 | 7.6 | 49 | 7.5 | | 0 | UND | 39 | 9.4 | 76 | 4.8 | 49 | 7.5 | 49 | 7.5 | 54 | 6.7 |

| | | | | | | | | | | | |
|---|---|---|---|---|---|---|---|---|---|---|---|
| | | | Cost of Sales/Inventory | | | | | | | | |
| | | | Cost of Sales/Payables | | | | | | | | |
| 5.8 | 5.6 | 4.9 | Sales/Working Capital | 2.3 | 3.3 | 3.1 | 4.8 | 5.2 | 5.3 |
| 10.9 | 10.2 | 7.6 | | NM | 7.6 | 5.9 | 7.5 | 7.3 | 8.9 |
| 39.1 | 46.6 | 23.5 | | -5.9 | -18.4 | 38.0 | 27.2 | 21.6 | 16.6 |

| | | | | | | | | | | | | | | | |
|---|---|---|---|---|---|---|---|---|---|---|---|---|---|---|---|
| | 8.3 | | 9.9 | | 11.2 | EBIT/Interest | | 2.3 | | 20.3 | | 3.1 | | 16.5 | | 12.0 | | 11.1 |
| (107) | 3.4 | (157) | 3.1 | (165) | 2.9 | | (13) | 1.9 | (14) | 2.4 | (37) | 2.7 | (54) | 2.6 | (39) | 4.3 |
| | 1.0 | | 1.3 | | .7 | | | -11.5 | | -.4 | | .5 | | .5 | | 2.2 |

| | | | | | | | | | | | | | | |
|---|---|---|---|---|---|---|---|---|---|---|---|---|---|---|
| | | | 22.7 | | 31.8 | Net Profit + Depr., Dep.,<br>Amort./Cur. Mat. L/T/D | | | | | | | | | | | | |
| | | (10) | 5.7 | (10) | 4.6 | | | | | | | | | | |
| | | | 2.4 | | 1.3 | | | | | | | | | | |

| | | | | | | | | | | | |
|---|---|---|---|---|---|---|---|---|---|---|---|
| .4 | .5 | .5 | Fixed/Worth | .6 | .5 | .5 | .1 | .5 | .5 |
| 1.0 | .9 | .9 | | 3.1 | 1.2 | .8 | .8 | .9 | .9 |
| 1.9 | 2.0 | 1.8 | | UND | 3.6 | 1.1 | 1.8 | 1.6 | 1.4 |
| .5 | .5 | .4 | Debt/Worth | .5 | .4 | .5 | .3 | .5 | .5 |
| 1.1 | 1.0 | .9 | | 2.8 | .8 | 1.0 | .7 | .9 | .8 |
| 2.9 | 2.4 | 2.0 | | UND | 4.8 | 2.0 | 1.9 | 1.9 | 2.1 |

| | | | | | | | | | | | | | | | |
|---|---|---|---|---|---|---|---|---|---|---|---|---|---|---|---|
| | 21.4 | | 19.4 | | 16.8 | % Profit Before Taxes/Tangible<br>Net Worth | | 115.3 | | 16.3 | | 7.4 | | 18.4 | | 18.9 | | 12.1 |
| (123) | 6.6 | (177) | 5.9 | (181) | 6.1 | | (12) | 20.1 | (17) | 4.0 | | 2.6 | (41) | 3.3 | (58) | 7.2 | (38) | 7.2 |
| | -.3 | | .5 | | -.5 | | | -3.3 | | -7.7 | | -2.3 | | -3.7 | | -1.4 | | 4.7 |

| | | | | | | | | | | | |
|---|---|---|---|---|---|---|---|---|---|---|---|
| 9.7 | 10.4 | 9.0 | % Profit Before Taxes/Total<br>Assets | 44.7 | 9.4 | 3.5 | 15.5 | 8.7 | 7.6 |
| 3.1 | 2.8 | 3.3 | | 4.1 | .0 | 1.8 | 1.7 | 4.3 | 4.9 |
| -.2 | .1 | -.7 | | -.5 | -7.2 | -.7 | -1.9 | -1.0 | 2.7 |
| 25.5 | 12.6 | 11.1 | Sales/Net Fixed Assets | 14.2 | 22.7 | 11.0 | 42.8 | 7.5 | 9.3 |
| 4.3 | 3.9 | 3.5 | | .5 | 3.7 | 3.3 | 3.8 | 3.8 | 3.8 |
| 2.2 | 2.1 | 1.7 | | .2 | 1.1 | 1.6 | 1.4 | 2.4 | 2.1 |
| 3.9 | 3.1 | 2.5 | Sales/Total Assets | 5.0 | 3.0 | 2.0 | 3.1 | 2.4 | 2.5 |
| 1.8 | 1.8 | 1.6 | | .3 | 1.9 | 1.7 | 1.5 | 1.6 | 1.6 |
| 1.2 | 1.1 | 1.0 | | .2 | .5 | 1.0 | .9 | 1.2 | 1.1 |

| | | | | | | | | | | | | | | | |
|---|---|---|---|---|---|---|---|---|---|---|---|---|---|---|---|
| | .9 | | 1.3 | | 1.2 | % Depr., Dep., Amort./Sales | | | | 1.5 | | 1.4 | | .9 | | 1.3 | | 1.0 |
| (122) | 1.8 | (174) | 2.1 | (174) | 2.3 | | | | (15) | 3.0 | (14) | 2.4 | (41) | 2.5 | (55) | 2.0 | (40) | 2.1 |
| | 2.5 | | 3.3 | | 3.4 | | | | | 4.8 | | 3.5 | | 3.8 | | 3.0 | | 3.0 |

| | | | | | | | |
|---|---|---|---|---|---|---|---|
| | 5.9 | | 2.1 | | 7.6 | % Officers', Directors'<br>Owners' Comp/Sales | |
| (24) | 11.6 | (26) | 6.1 | (22) | 10.8 | | |
| | 25.0 | | 11.6 | | 27.0 | | |

| | | | | | | | | | |
|---|---|---|---|---|---|---|---|---|---|
| 2296461M | 3730706M | 3766175M | Net Sales ($) | 6215M | 35444M | 58096M | 334219M | 980577M | 2351624M |
| 1333839M | 2212061M | 2403718M | Total Assets ($) | 18675M | 55077M | 59593M | 257319M | 642683M | 1370371M |

**M = $ thousand     MM = $ million**
See Pages 9 through 22 for Explanation of Ratios and Data

## Current Data Sorted by Assets / Comparative Historical Data

| Type of Statement | 0-500M | 500M-2MM | 2-10MM | 10-50MM | 50-100MM | 100-250MM | 4/1/07-3/31/08 ALL | 4/1/08-3/31/09 ALL |
|---|---|---|---|---|---|---|---|---|
| Unqualified | | 3 | 4 | 3 | 2 | 2 | 8 | 10 |
| Reviewed | | 1 | 2 | 2 | | | 3 | 4 |
| Compiled | 1 | 2 | 2 | | | | 3 | 3 |
| Tax Returns | 5 | 5 | 5 | | | | 11 | 9 |
| Other | 3 | 14 | 14 | 9 | 4 | 1 | 24 | 31 |
| | | 16 (4/1-9/30/11) | | 66 (10/1/11-3/31/12) | | | | |
| **NUMBER OF STATEMENTS** | 9 | 25 | 27 | 12 | 6 | 3 | 49 | 57 |
| | % | % | % | % | % | % | % | % |
| **ASSETS** | | | | | | | | |
| Cash & Equivalents | | 13.3 | 13.3 | 11.5 | | | 17.5 | 17.7 |
| Trade Receivables (net) | | 30.4 | 24.8 | 20.0 | | | 26.0 | 25.0 |
| Inventory | | 2.0 | 1.4 | 1.3 | | | 2.5 | 2.2 |
| All Other Current | | .7 | 2.0 | 8.4 | | | 5.5 | 3.9 |
| Total Current | | 46.3 | 41.5 | 41.2 | | | 51.6 | 48.9 |
| Fixed Assets (net) | | 34.8 | 43.5 | 31.4 | | | 32.2 | 35.1 |
| Intangibles (net) | | 10.1 | 10.3 | 6.1 | | | 7.0 | 10.6 |
| All Other Non-Current | | 8.7 | 4.7 | 21.3 | | | 9.1 | 5.4 |
| Total | | 100.0 | 100.0 | 100.0 | | | 100.0 | 100.0 |
| **LIABILITIES** | | | | | | | | |
| Notes Payable-Short Term | | 9.7 | 3.9 | 5.8 | | | 8.7 | 5.5 |
| Cur. Mat.-L.T.D. | | 5.1 | 6.0 | 2.4 | | | 5.1 | 4.4 |
| Trade Payables | | 9.4 | 7.3 | 4.9 | | | 7.4 | 8.0 |
| Income Taxes Payable | | .0 | .9 | .1 | | | .1 | .0 |
| All Other Current | | 16.7 | 13.7 | 13.8 | | | 21.0 | 17.6 |
| Total Current | | 41.0 | 31.7 | 27.0 | | | 42.2 | 35.5 |
| Long-Term Debt | | 25.9 | 24.5 | 18.4 | | | 23.8 | 30.0 |
| Deferred Taxes | | .0 | .1 | .0 | | | .0 | .1 |
| All Other Non-Current | | 1.1 | 4.8 | 1.2 | | | 3.9 | 5.1 |
| Net Worth | | 32.0 | 38.8 | 53.4 | | | 30.0 | 29.3 |
| Total Liabilities & Net Worth | | 100.0 | 100.0 | 100.0 | | | 100.0 | 100.0 |
| **INCOME DATA** | | | | | | | | |
| Net Sales | | 100.0 | 100.0 | 100.0 | | | 100.0 | 100.0 |
| Gross Profit | | | | | | | | |
| Operating Expenses | | 88.3 | 83.8 | 80.2 | | | 86.1 | 90.6 |
| Operating Profit | | 11.7 | 16.2 | 19.8 | | | 13.9 | 9.4 |
| All Other Expenses (net) | | 1.2 | 2.5 | 1.4 | | | 3.0 | 1.9 |
| Profit Before Taxes | | 10.5 | 13.7 | 18.4 | | | 10.9 | 7.5 |
| **RATIOS** | | | | | | | | |
| Current | | 3.0 | 4.0 | 3.0 | | | 3.2 | 2.9 |
| | | 1.2 | 1.9 | 1.5 | | | 1.5 | 1.8 |
| | | .5 | .7 | 1.3 | | | .9 | .9 |
| Quick | | 2.5 | 3.9 | 2.5 | | | 2.9 | 2.7 |
| | | 1.2 | 1.8 | 1.2 | | | 1.1 | 1.4 |
| | | .4 | .5 | .9 | | | .7 | .7 |
| Sales/Receivables | 0 | UND | 11 | 32.3 | 25 | 14.7 | 18 | 20.2 | 8 | 47.8 |
| | 17 | 21.8 | 46 | 7.9 | 50 | 7.3 | 48 | 7.5 | 53 | 6.9 |
| | 62 | 5.9 | 70 | 5.2 | 107 | 3.4 | 68 | 5.3 | 65 | 5.6 |
| Cost of Sales/Inventory | | | | | | | | |
| Cost of Sales/Payables | | | | | | | | |
| Sales/Working Capital | | 12.1 | 4.2 | 5.1 | | | 5.2 | 5.7 |
| | | 34.5 | 7.6 | 7.3 | | | 14.4 | 11.6 |
| | | -15.3 | -23.2 | 13.7 | | | -265.5 | -83.4 |
| EBIT/Interest | | 58.2 | 28.3 | 33.1 | | | 19.1 | 14.2 |
| | (23) | 9.2 | (21) 17.4 | (10) 15.2 | | | (38) 7.8 | (51) 4.5 |
| | | -1.6 | 2.9 | 4.5 | | | 2.4 | 1.6 |
| Net Profit + Depr., Dep., Amort./Cur. Mat. L/T/D | | | | | | | | |
| Fixed/Worth | | .1 | .6 | .3 | | | .3 | .5 |
| | | 1.0 | 1.5 | .5 | | | .9 | 1.1 |
| | | -4.4 | -3.8 | 1.0 | | | UND | -6.8 |
| Debt/Worth | | .4 | .5 | .5 | | | .4 | .7 |
| | | 1.9 | 2.0 | 1.0 | | | 2.0 | 1.9 |
| | | -9.0 | -9.9 | 1.7 | | | -11.5 | -16.2 |
| % Profit Before Taxes/Tangible Net Worth | | 196.3 | 113.6 | 47.4 | | | 127.5 | 115.5 |
| | (17) | 68.5 | (19) 57.6 | 26.6 | | | (35) 47.3 | (39) 32.7 |
| | | 44.3 | 15.3 | 7.3 | | | 7.4 | 4.7 |
| % Profit Before Taxes/Total Assets | | 48.9 | 41.5 | 21.2 | | | 38.2 | 32.3 |
| | | 18.7 | 14.6 | 11.2 | | | 14.4 | 10.6 |
| | | -7.7 | 1.4 | 5.0 | | | 3.4 | 1.3 |
| Sales/Net Fixed Assets | | 37.3 | 17.3 | 9.3 | | | 32.9 | 16.4 |
| | | 19.6 | 5.9 | 3.8 | | | 6.6 | 6.7 |
| | | 8.1 | 1.8 | 2.6 | | | 3.9 | 3.7 |
| Sales/Total Assets | | 6.8 | 3.0 | 1.6 | | | 3.7 | 3.8 |
| | | 4.5 | 1.9 | 1.0 | | | 2.1 | 1.7 |
| | | 2.4 | 1.1 | .6 | | | 1.3 | 1.2 |
| % Depr., Dep., Amort./Sales | | .7 | 1.2 | 2.0 | | | 1.7 | 1.7 |
| | (20) | 1.3 | 2.3 | (10) 2.2 | | | (42) 2.9 | (53) 3.1 |
| | | 3.1 | 5.0 | 3.2 | | | 4.6 | 4.7 |
| % Officers', Directors' Owners' Comp/Sales | | | | | | | 4.7 | 2.6 |
| | | | | | | | (10) 31.9 | (12) 7.7 |
| | | | | | | | 41.3 | 34.1 |
| Net Sales ($) | 20973M | 151591M | 272471M | 274810M | 508112M | 471758M | 1195225M | 1725392M |
| Total Assets ($) | 2442M | 32997M | 120812M | 257486M | 438731M | 349271M | 843566M | 1229370M |

M = $ thousand    MM = $ million
See Pages 9 through 22 for Explanation of Ratios and Data

## Comparative Historical Data          Current Data Sorted by Sales

| | 11 | 9 | 14 | | 0-1MM | 1-3MM | 3-5MM | 5-10MM | 10-25MM | 25MM & OVER |
|---|---|---|---|---|---|---|---|---|---|---|
| **Type of Statement** | | | | | | | | | | |
| Unqualified | 11 | 9 | 14 | | | 3 | | 2 | 4 | 5 |
| Reviewed | 7 | 3 | 3 | | 1 | | | 1 | 1 | |
| Compiled | 2 | 8 | 5 | | 2 | 2 | 1 | | | |
| Tax Returns | 8 | 9 | 15 | | 1 | 3 | 3 | 4 | 4 | |
| Other | 41 | 35 | 45 | | 1 | 6 | 10 | 9 | 10 | 9 |
| | 4/1/09-3/31/10 ALL | 4/1/10-3/31/11 ALL | 4/1/11-3/31/12 ALL | | | 16 (4/1-9/30/11) | | 66 (10/1/11-3/31/12) | | |
| **NUMBER OF STATEMENTS** | 69 | 64 | 82 | | 5 | 14 | 14 | 16 | 19 | 14 |
| **ASSETS** | % | % | % | | % | % | % | % | % | % |
| Cash & Equivalents | 13.0 | 13.6 | 16.2 | | | 20.1 | 21.3 | 18.0 | 14.7 | 8.7 |
| Trade Receivables (net) | 25.9 | 22.4 | 23.4 | | | 27.7 | 21.4 | 25.8 | 25.1 | 19.4 |
| Inventory | 2.6 | 1.5 | 1.9 | | | .7 | .9 | 2.5 | 2.1 | 1.6 |
| All Other Current | 6.0 | 5.7 | 3.4 | | | 2.7 | .9 | 2.6 | 3.2 | 2.9 |
| Total Current | 47.5 | 43.2 | 45.0 | | | 51.2 | 44.5 | 48.8 | 45.1 | 32.6 |
| Fixed Assets (net) | 34.2 | 38.5 | 35.7 | | | 35.5 | 24.8 | 34.1 | 40.4 | 37.5 |
| Intangibles (net) | 8.8 | 9.2 | 9.5 | | | 4.0 | 11.2 | 13.2 | 6.9 | 16.2 |
| All Other Non-Current | 9.5 | 9.1 | 9.8 | | | 9.2 | 19.5 | 3.9 | 7.6 | 13.7 |
| Total | 100.0 | 100.0 | 100.0 | | | 100.0 | 100.0 | 100.0 | 100.0 | 100.0 |
| **LIABILITIES** | | | | | | | | | | |
| Notes Payable-Short Term | 1.5 | 11.2 | 5.7 | | | 7.5 | 10.0 | 3.2 | 5.4 | 2.6 |
| Cur. Mat.-L.T.D. | 7.2 | 8.9 | 6.7 | | | 4.5 | 18.5 | 2.5 | 8.1 | 1.7 |
| Trade Payables | 11.4 | 6.8 | 6.7 | | | 7.2 | 6.0 | 6.7 | 9.8 | 3.3 |
| Income Taxes Payable | .3 | .3 | .3 | | | .0 | .0 | .0 | 1.3 | .0 |
| All Other Current | 22.8 | 17.7 | 18.5 | | | 13.5 | 19.4 | 27.1 | 20.2 | 10.1 |
| Total Current | 43.1 | 45.0 | 37.9 | | | 32.8 | 53.9 | 39.5 | 44.8 | 17.6 |
| Long-Term Debt | 21.1 | 21.7 | 21.0 | | | 17.6 | 22.5 | 18.3 | 23.5 | 14.8 |
| Deferred Taxes | .1 | .0 | .0 | | | .0 | .0 | .0 | .2 | .0 |
| All Other Non-Current | 8.9 | 8.6 | 4.6 | | | 4.7 | .1 | 5.2 | 3.0 | 12.2 |
| Net Worth | 26.8 | 24.6 | 36.4 | | | 45.0 | 23.5 | 37.0 | 28.6 | 55.4 |
| Total Liabilities & Net Worth | 100.0 | 100.0 | 100.0 | | | 100.0 | 100.0 | 100.0 | 100.0 | 100.0 |
| **INCOME DATA** | | | | | | | | | | |
| Net Sales | 100.0 | 100.0 | 100.0 | | | 100.0 | 100.0 | 100.0 | 100.0 | 100.0 |
| Gross Profit | | | | | | | | | | |
| Operating Expenses | 88.4 | 86.1 | 86.5 | | | 92.4 | 77.3 | 87.5 | 90.7 | 91.1 |
| Operating Profit | 11.6 | 13.9 | 13.5 | | | 7.6 | 22.7 | 12.5 | 9.3 | 8.9 |
| All Other Expenses (net) | 2.7 | 1.5 | 1.5 | | | .8 | 1.6 | -.1 | .5 | .8 |
| Profit Before Taxes | 9.0 | 12.4 | 12.0 | | | 6.8 | 21.1 | 12.6 | 8.7 | 8.1 |
| **RATIOS** | | | | | | | | | | |
| Current | 3.5 | 2.7 | 3.3 | | | 2.6 | 2.5 | 4.3 | 3.9 | 3.3 |
| | 1.8 | 1.6 | 1.7 | | | 1.7 | 1.4 | 2.2 | 1.4 | 2.2 |
| | .7 | .6 | .8 | | | 1.0 | .5 | .6 | .5 | 1.6 |
| Quick | 3.1 | 2.4 | 2.7 | | | 2.6 | 2.5 | 4.2 | 3.8 | 2.9 |
| | 1.5 | 1.2 | 1.5 | | | 1.6 | 1.4 | 1.9 | 1.3 | 1.8 |
| | .5 | .4 | .7 | | | .9 | .5 | .5 | .5 | 1.2 |
| Sales/Receivables | 10   35.1 | 1   307.0 | 0   UND | | | 0   UND | 0   UND | 3   133.7 | 10   38.3 | 31   11.6 |
| | 51   7.2 | 46   7.9 | 44   8.3 | | | 65   5.6 | 0   UND | 30   12.2 | 44   8.3 | 55   6.6 |
| | 69   5.3 | 65   5.7 | 63   5.8 | | | 101   3.6 | 54   6.7 | 68   5.4 | 52   7.0 | 66   5.5 |
| Cost of Sales/Inventory | | | | | | | | | | |
| Cost of Sales/Payables | | | | | | | | | | |
| Sales/Working Capital | 4.9 | 5.4 | 5.9 | | | 4.9 | 10.2 | 4.1 | 4.8 | 5.5 |
| | 8.7 | 20.3 | 12.1 | | | 8.7 | 25.4 | 19.7 | 9.2 | 7.0 |
| | -35.3 | -11.9 | -45.2 | | | -398.0 | -8.9 | -58.9 | -21.6 | 10.9 |
| EBIT/Interest | 35.4 | 16.2 | 29.7 | | | 15.1 | 136.1 | 67.2 | 29.6 | 17.7 |
| | (50) 8.8 | (55) 6.7 | (67) 9.2 | | | (11) 6.7 | (12) 14.2 | (12) 36.7 | (17) 17.6 | (11) 7.1 |
| | 1.2 | 1.5 | 2.4 | | | .6 | 5.0 | 3.5 | -.5 | 1.8 |
| Net Profit + Depr., Dep., Amort./Cur. Mat. L/T/D | 47.0 | | | | | | | | | |
| | (13) 9.3 | | | | | | | | | |
| | 1.0 | | | | | | | | | |
| Fixed/Worth | .4 | .4 | .4 | | | .1 | .0 | .3 | .5 | .5 |
| | 1.0 | 1.6 | .8 | | | .8 | 1.2 | 1.1 | .8 | .6 |
| | -6.0 | -4.3 | -18.2 | | | 6.1 | -1.3 | -2.7 | -3.8 | NM |
| Debt/Worth | .5 | .5 | .4 | | | .3 | .4 | .3 | .5 | .3 |
| | 1.8 | 2.9 | 1.5 | | | .9 | 6.2 | 1.0 | 1.7 | .8 |
| | -6.6 | -6.3 | -48.3 | | | NM | -8.1 | -20.7 | -9.9 | NM |
| % Profit Before Taxes/Tangible Net Worth | 96.9 | 167.6 | 121.2 | | | 68.5 | | 180.3 | 90.7 | 49.5 |
| | (49) 30.3 | (46) 57.1 | (60) 52.4 | | | (11) 12.6 | | (11) 109.5 | (13) 47.6 | (11) 24.4 |
| | 6.0 | 6.7 | 16.0 | | | -1.2 | | 57.9 | 23.9 | 2.8 |
| % Profit Before Taxes/Total Assets | 31.0 | 38.2 | 35.5 | | | 20.7 | 57.3 | 63.9 | 22.2 | 17.6 |
| | 10.0 | 10.7 | 11.4 | | | 9.5 | 24.7 | 27.2 | 10.8 | 9.7 |
| | .9 | 1.2 | 2.7 | | | -2.5 | 10.3 | 4.4 | -4.0 | 2.0 |
| Sales/Net Fixed Assets | 19.4 | 13.3 | 28.7 | | | 29.9 | UND | 41.9 | 16.3 | 5.6 |
| | 8.8 | 5.6 | 6.7 | | | 8.1 | 36.3 | 16.7 | 5.9 | 4.2 |
| | 3.7 | 3.6 | 3.4 | | | 1.7 | 5.5 | 3.3 | 3.8 | 3.0 |
| Sales/Total Assets | 3.5 | 3.7 | 4.6 | | | 2.9 | 5.5 | 5.7 | 4.8 | 1.7 |
| | 2.0 | 2.0 | 2.0 | | | 1.9 | 2.5 | 3.7 | 3.0 | 1.3 |
| | 1.3 | 1.3 | 1.2 | | | .7 | 1.7 | 1.9 | 1.3 | 1.0 |
| % Depr., Dep., Amort./Sales | 1.3 | 1.8 | 1.2 | | | 2.1 | | .9 | 1.0 | 2.2 |
| | (61) 2.4 | (55) 3.0 | (69) 2.1 | | | (11) 3.2 | | (14) 1.3 | (18) 2.1 | (13) 4.0 |
| | 3.8 | 4.7 | 4.0 | | | 6.4 | | 2.3 | 2.6 | 4.8 |
| % Officers', Directors' Owners' Comp/Sales | 4.4 | 2.9 | 6.3 | | | | | | | |
| | (17) 8.0 | (12) 7.3 | (14) 8.7 | | | | | | | |
| | 33.2 | 32.0 | 23.9 | | | | | | | |
| Net Sales ($) | 1384215M | 1451181M | 1699715M | | 2693M | 30732M | 54592M | 116854M | 306405M | 1188439M |
| Total Assets ($) | 923818M | 1067345M | 1201739M | | 5223M | 35830M | 30500M | 50037M | 186587M | 893562M |

M = $ thousand    MM = $ million
See Pages 9 through 22 for Explanation of Ratios and Data

**Current Data Sorted by Assets**  |  **Comparative Historical Data**

| Type of Statement | 0-500M | 500M-2MM | 2-10MM | 10-50MM | 50-100MM | 100-250MM | | 4/1/07-3/31/08 ALL | 4/1/08-3/31/09 ALL |
|---|---|---|---|---|---|---|---|---|---|
| Unqualified | | 2 | 21 | 9 | 5 | 4 | | 25 | 27 |
| Reviewed | 1 | 3 | 10 | 6 | | | | 12 | 22 |
| Compiled | 13 | 17 | 22 | 2 | | | | 41 | 59 |
| Tax Returns | 41 | 43 | 27 | 6 | | 1 | | 54 | 62 |
| Other | 19 | 37 | 99 | 18 | 2 | | | 97 | 104 |
| | | 27 (4/1-9/30/11) | | 381 (10/1/11-3/31/12) | | | | | |
| NUMBER OF STATEMENTS | 74 | 102 | 179 | 41 | 7 | 5 | | 229 | 274 |
| **ASSETS** | % | % | % | % | % | % | | % | % |
| Cash & Equivalents | 32.6 | 25.7 | 14.7 | 11.5 | | | | 19.0 | 19.0 |
| Trade Receivables (net) | 7.2 | 8.8 | 18.3 | 23.8 | | | | 14.1 | 14.7 |
| Inventory | 1.2 | 2.8 | 3.4 | 2.0 | | | | 2.8 | 2.7 |
| All Other Current | 3.9 | 4.5 | 1.5 | 5.4 | | | | 1.9 | 2.8 |
| Total Current | 44.7 | 41.7 | 37.9 | 42.7 | | | | 37.7 | 39.2 |
| Fixed Assets (net) | 43.2 | 43.4 | 48.2 | 42.5 | | | | 49.9 | 46.6 |
| Intangibles (net) | 5.5 | 5.9 | 8.0 | 10.2 | | | | 4.9 | 6.1 |
| All Other Non-Current | 6.5 | 9.0 | 6.0 | 4.6 | | | | 7.5 | 8.0 |
| Total | 100.0 | 100.0 | 100.0 | 100.0 | | | | 100.0 | 100.0 |
| **LIABILITIES** | | | | | | | | | |
| Notes Payable-Short Term | 21.5 | 8.5 | 4.0 | 2.7 | | | | 13.5 | 12.1 |
| Cur. Mat.-L.T.D. | 13.2 | 9.7 | 7.5 | 4.7 | | | | 9.0 | 10.7 |
| Trade Payables | 3.1 | 6.9 | 5.4 | 6.0 | | | | 4.6 | 4.4 |
| Income Taxes Payable | .0 | .0 | .0 | .4 | | | | .0 | .2 |
| All Other Current | 29.6 | 11.0 | 8.5 | 8.2 | | | | 13.3 | 16.4 |
| Total Current | 67.3 | 36.1 | 25.6 | 22.1 | | | | 40.4 | 43.8 |
| Long-Term Debt | 37.1 | 43.8 | 34.0 | 32.2 | | | | 36.8 | 34.1 |
| Deferred Taxes | .0 | .0 | .0 | .0 | | | | .0 | .1 |
| All Other Non-Current | 6.0 | 3.7 | 3.4 | 5.2 | | | | 3.7 | 6.6 |
| Net Worth | -10.5 | 16.4 | 37.0 | 40.5 | | | | 19.0 | 15.4 |
| Total Liabilities & Net Worth | 100.0 | 100.0 | 100.0 | 100.0 | | | | 100.0 | 100.0 |
| **INCOME DATA** | | | | | | | | | |
| Net Sales | 100.0 | 100.0 | 100.0 | 100.0 | | | | 100.0 | 100.0 |
| Gross Profit | | | | | | | | | |
| Operating Expenses | 86.0 | 77.1 | 74.6 | 72.6 | | | | 78.8 | 80.6 |
| Operating Profit | 14.0 | 22.9 | 25.4 | 27.4 | | | | 21.2 | 19.4 |
| All Other Expenses (net) | .9 | 2.4 | 3.8 | 4.5 | | | | 2.5 | 3.4 |
| Profit Before Taxes | 13.1 | 20.5 | 21.5 | 22.9 | | | | 18.7 | 16.0 |
| **RATIOS** | | | | | | | | | |
| Current | 2.6 | 3.3 | 3.5 | 3.6 | | | | 2.8 | 2.8 |
| | .8 | 1.3 | 1.6 | 1.6 | | | | 1.4 | 1.3 |
| | .2 | .5 | .7 | 1.0 | | | | .5 | .5 |
| Quick | 2.3 | 2.6 | 3.2 | 2.6 | | | | 2.5 | 2.5 |
| | .7 | 1.1 | 1.4 | 1.3 | | | | 1.2 | 1.1 |
| | .2 | .3 | .6 | .8 | | | | .4 | .3 |
| Sales/Receivables | 0 UND | 0 UND | 0 UND | 27 13.4 | | | | 0 UND | 0 UND |
| | 0 UND | 0 UND | 36 10.1 | 45 8.2 | | | | 23 16.0 | 17 21.7 |
| | 0 UND | 25 14.5 | 49 7.5 | 68 5.4 | | | | 46 8.0 | 45 8.2 |
| Cost of Sales/Inventory | | | | | | | | | |
| Cost of Sales/Payables | | | | | | | | | |
| Sales/Working Capital | 53.3 | 10.2 | 6.1 | 4.4 | | | | 8.4 | 8.7 |
| | -301.6 | 49.2 | 14.3 | 10.9 | | | | 34.5 | 33.5 |
| | -21.6 | -21.2 | -18.7 | NM | | | | -22.0 | -22.5 |
| EBIT/Interest | 43.7 | 50.6 | 97.6 | 41.5 | | | | 37.9 | 34.1 |
| | (47) 6.8 | (82) 16.4 | (157) 14.4 | (31) 8.8 | | | | (200) 10.2 | (232) 8.8 |
| | .6 | 3.8 | 3.6 | 4.5 | | | | 1.9 | 1.8 |
| Net Profit + Depr., Dep., Amort./Cur. Mat. L/T/D | | | 18.1 | | | | | 18.3 | 7.7 |
| | | (12) 7.0 | | | | | | (13) 4.0 | (15) 3.3 |
| | | | 3.1 | | | | | .8 | 1.8 |
| Fixed/Worth | .6 | .5 | .5 | .4 | | | | .7 | .7 |
| | -17.6 | 1.7 | 1.5 | 1.2 | | | | 1.8 | 1.9 |
| | -.7 | -2.1 | 9.2 | 5.4 | | | | -16.3 | -10.3 |
| Debt/Worth | .6 | .6 | .5 | .4 | | | | .7 | .7 |
| | -36.6 | 2.0 | 1.7 | 1.8 | | | | 2.7 | 2.6 |
| | -2.6 | -4.6 | 9.7 | 7.4 | | | | -15.3 | -16.9 |
| % Profit Before Taxes/Tangible Net Worth | 414.1 | 308.6 | 181.2 | 151.0 | | | | 279.1 | 192.9 |
| | (36) 196.6 | (68) 143.1 | (143) 93.1 | (34) 92.5 | | | | (167) 95.1 | (195) 75.4 |
| | 24.4 | 63.3 | 43.5 | 33.0 | | | | 28.3 | 22.7 |
| % Profit Before Taxes/Total Assets | 246.0 | 133.8 | 68.8 | 47.2 | | | | 70.6 | 65.0 |
| | 45.0 | 45.5 | 26.8 | 23.7 | | | | 27.0 | 20.7 |
| | .3 | 10.9 | 6.8 | 4.9 | | | | 2.9 | 3.1 |
| Sales/Net Fixed Assets | 124.0 | 31.3 | 9.1 | 8.5 | | | | 19.3 | 22.2 |
| | 37.9 | 9.5 | 4.0 | 4.9 | | | | 5.2 | 6.9 |
| | 12.4 | 4.2 | 1.9 | 1.9 | | | | 2.5 | 2.5 |
| Sales/Total Assets | 25.3 | 6.8 | 2.7 | 1.8 | | | | 4.7 | 5.8 |
| | 10.1 | 3.3 | 1.8 | 1.3 | | | | 2.2 | 2.3 |
| | 5.6 | 2.1 | 1.0 | .9 | | | | 1.4 | 1.3 |
| % Depr., Dep., Amort./Sales | .7 | 1.6 | 2.4 | 2.8 | | | | 2.1 | 2.1 |
| | (39) 1.4 | (68) 3.2 | (159) 4.7 | (39) 4.0 | | | | (196) 4.1 | (222) 4.0 |
| | 2.8 | 6.4 | 9.4 | 5.8 | | | | 7.6 | 8.2 |
| % Officers', Directors' Owners' Comp/Sales | 4.7 | 4.0 | 3.6 | | | | | 5.9 | 3.6 |
| | (32) 10.4 | (18) 17.6 | (24) 14.3 | | | | | (63) 14.3 | (77) 8.2 |
| | 34.2 | 24.7 | 27.3 | | | | | 26.2 | 26.7 |
| Net Sales ($) | 240552M | 563510M | 1613920M | 1312410M | 804139M | 357812M | | 2565124M | 3585593M |
| Total Assets ($) | 18181M | 114447M | 817746M | 877890M | 563578M | 778976M | | 1457460M | 1904892M |

M = $ thousand    MM = $ million
See Pages 9 through 22 for Explanation of Ratios and Data

## Comparative Historical Data / Current Data Sorted by Sales

| | | | Type of Statement | | | | | | |
|---|---|---|---|---|---|---|---|---|---|
| 30 | 36 | 41 | Unqualified | | 1 | 2 | 10 | 10 | 18 |
| 23 | 30 | 20 | Reviewed | | 1 | 4 | 6 | 5 | 4 |
| 44 | 37 | 54 | Compiled | 9 | 17 | 7 | 10 | 9 | 2 |
| 81 | 67 | 117 | Tax Returns | 14 | 32 | 27 | 28 | 10 | 6 |
| 127 | 146 | 176 | Other | 11 | 31 | 33 | 46 | 10 | 17 |
| 4/1/09-3/31/10 ALL | 4/1/10-3/31/11 ALL | 4/1/11-3/31/12 ALL | | 27 (4/1-9/30/11) | 381 (10/1/11-3/31/12) | | | | |
| | | | | 0-1MM | 1-3MM | 3-5MM | 5-10MM | 10-25MM | 25MM & OVER |
| 305 | 316 | 408 | NUMBER OF STATEMENTS | 34 | 82 | 73 | 100 | 72 | 47 |
| % | % | % | **ASSETS** | % | % | % | % | % | % |
| 17.3 | 19.8 | 20.1 | Cash & Equivalents | 15.6 | 22.1 | 20.7 | 24.0 | 17.8 | 14.2 |
| 16.0 | 15.6 | 14.3 | Trade Receivables (net) | 8.9 | 8.1 | 9.1 | 13.6 | 25.3 | 22.0 |
| 2.3 | 2.9 | 2.6 | Inventory | .0 | 2.1 | 2.9 | 3.7 | 2.8 | 2.6 |
| 2.7 | 2.9 | 3.1 | All Other Current | 5.9 | 2.0 | 4.2 | 1.6 | 3.6 | 3.8 |
| 38.4 | 41.2 | 40.2 | Total Current | 30.5 | 34.3 | 36.9 | 42.8 | 49.4 | 42.6 |
| 45.6 | 45.7 | 45.1 | Fixed Assets (net) | 53.2 | 50.5 | 47.4 | 46.7 | 37.3 | 35.0 |
| 8.3 | 7.7 | 8.0 | Intangibles (net) | 2.4 | 8.9 | 9.7 | 5.5 | 8.2 | 12.2 |
| 7.7 | 5.4 | 6.7 | All Other Non-Current | 13.9 | 6.3 | 6.0 | 4.9 | 5.1 | 10.1 |
| 100.0 | 100.0 | 100.0 | Total | 100.0 | 100.0 | 100.0 | 100.0 | 100.0 | 100.0 |
| | | | **LIABILITIES** | | | | | | |
| 13.3 | 10.0 | 8.1 | Notes Payable-Short Term | 6.9 | 15.6 | 8.1 | 5.8 | 6.3 | 3.5 |
| 7.4 | 9.2 | 8.7 | Cur. Mat.-L.T.D. | 4.5 | 10.9 | 8.3 | 12.2 | 5.9 | 5.0 |
| 5.2 | 5.3 | 5.4 | Trade Payables | 2.1 | 6.0 | 6.7 | 5.0 | 5.2 | 5.7 |
| .4 | .4 | .1 | Income Taxes Payable | .0 | .0 | .0 | .0 | .1 | .6 |
| 14.0 | 14.2 | 12.9 | All Other Current | 22.0 | 10.0 | 13.8 | 9.4 | 14.6 | 14.6 |
| 40.4 | 39.0 | 35.1 | Total Current | 35.5 | 42.4 | 36.9 | 32.4 | 32.1 | 29.5 |
| 35.7 | 36.7 | 36.7 | Long-Term Debt | 47.4 | 47.2 | 43.5 | 35.6 | 19.4 | 28.6 |
| .1 | .1 | .0 | Deferred Taxes | .0 | .0 | .0 | .0 | .0 | .2 |
| 4.4 | 5.2 | 4.2 | All Other Non-Current | 5.0 | 7.9 | 1.0 | 3.4 | 3.2 | 5.3 |
| 19.4 | 19.1 | 24.0 | Net Worth | 12.0 | 2.5 | 18.6 | 28.6 | 45.3 | 36.4 |
| 100.0 | 100.0 | 100.0 | Total Liabilities & Net Worth | 100.0 | 100.0 | 100.0 | 100.0 | 100.0 | 100.0 |
| | | | **INCOME DATA** | | | | | | |
| 100.0 | 100.0 | 100.0 | Net Sales | 100.0 | 100.0 | 100.0 | 100.0 | 100.0 | 100.0 |
| | | | Gross Profit | | | | | | |
| 80.1 | 80.1 | 77.5 | Operating Expenses | 59.8 | 85.2 | 82.5 | 75.3 | 72.5 | 81.5 |
| 19.9 | 19.9 | 22.5 | Operating Profit | 40.2 | 14.8 | 17.5 | 24.7 | 27.5 | 18.5 |
| 3.4 | 2.8 | 3.0 | All Other Expenses (net) | 15.7 | 3.5 | 1.9 | 1.2 | .9 | 2.0 |
| 16.5 | 17.1 | 19.4 | Profit Before Taxes | 24.5 | 11.2 | 15.6 | 23.5 | 26.6 | 16.5 |
| | | | **RATIOS** | | | | | | |
| 2.8 / 1.5 / .5 | 2.9 / 1.5 / .6 | 3.3 / 1.5 / .6 | Current | 2.4 / .7 / .2 | 3.4 / 1.1 / .3 | 2.2 / 1.1 / .5 | 3.7 / 1.8 / .8 | 4.3 / 1.8 / 1.0 | 2.8 / 1.8 / 1.0 |
| 2.4 / 1.1 / .4 | 2.6 / 1.2 / .5 | 2.8 / 1.2 / .5 | Quick | 2.3 / .6 / .1 | 3.2 / 1.0 / .2 | 1.8 / .7 / .4 | 3.3 / 1.4 / .7 | 3.7 / 1.7 / .7 | 2.5 / 1.5 / .9 |
| 0 UND / 24 15.2 / 47 7.7 | 0 UND / 26 13.8 / 46 7.9 | 0 UND / 19 19.3 / 45 8.2 | Sales/Receivables | 0 UND / 0 UND / 0 UND | 0 UND / 0 UND / 39 9.3 | 0 UND / 0 UND / 36 10.0 | 0 UND / 28 12.9 / 42 8.6 | 0 UND / 40 9.2 / 55 6.6 | 21 17.8 / 39 9.4 / 54 6.8 |
| | | | Cost of Sales/Inventory | | | | | | |
| | | | Cost of Sales/Payables | | | | | | |
| 7.8 / 29.2 / -25.6 | 7.7 / 24.7 / -28.5 | 7.3 / 31.2 / -31.3 | Sales/Working Capital | 9.6 / -113.3 / -3.0 | 9.2 / 280.7 / -7.3 | 11.0 / 116.2 / -16.3 | 7.0 / 21.1 / -68.2 | 5.6 / 11.2 / NM | 6.8 / 17.3 / 262.2 |
| 39.8 / (261) 11.0 / 2.7 | 42.8 / (270) 13.0 / 3.1 | 64.7 / (329) 11.9 / 3.3 | EBIT/Interest | | 16.5 / (63) 4.6 / -1.5 | 91.1 / (67) 11.7 / 2.9 | 92.6 / (88) 22.4 / 4.7 | 145.4 / (63) 40.9 / 6.4 | 30.2 / (39) 8.0 / 3.4 |
| 6.6 / (19) 2.3 / 1.4 | 10.9 / (22) 4.3 / 1.5 | 16.4 / (26) 5.1 / 2.1 | Net Profit + Depr., Dep., Amort./Cur. Mat. L/T/D | | | | | | 18.6 / (10) 6.0 / 1.5 |
| .5 / 1.6 / 13.5 | .6 / 1.7 / -9.4 | .5 / 1.6 / -8.4 | Fixed/Worth | .1 / 2.6 / -64.5 | .9 / 7.0 / -1.6 | .8 / 2.1 / -10.9 | .6 / 1.3 / -7.0 | .3 / .8 / 1.9 | .5 / 1.6 / 9.5 |
| .7 / 2.6 / 64.1 | .7 / 2.5 / -10.9 | .6 / 2.0 / -13.7 | Debt/Worth | .7 / 4.5 / -66.4 | 1.1 / 9.5 / -3.0 | .9 / 3.7 / -24.4 | .5 / 1.4 / -10.6 | .4 / .8 / 2.5 | .5 / 2.2 / 16.2 |
| 183.3 / (234) 79.2 / 20.0 | 188.4 / (226) 91.3 / 33.1 | 212.6 / (289) 98.4 / 40.2 | % Profit Before Taxes/Tangible Net Worth | 71.7 / (25) 23.2 / 10.7 | 206.1 / (45) 74.1 / 13.2 | 306.2 / (51) 87.3 / 39.5 | 221.9 / (72) 130.2 / 62.6 | 207.6 / (59) 128.6 / 60.6 | 200.2 / (37) 91.9 / 31.2 |
| 69.1 / 24.6 / 4.7 | 67.3 / 29.0 / 6.1 | 89.0 / 29.4 / 6.3 | % Profit Before Taxes/Total Assets | 18.6 / 6.7 / 2.7 | 58.7 / 19.4 / -5.7 | 129.6 / 27.9 / 7.0 | 109.5 / 55.0 / 19.8 | 102.0 / 50.7 / 18.7 | 58.8 / 23.7 / 4.3 |
| 24.5 / 6.6 / 2.6 | 18.6 / 6.2 / 2.9 | 22.5 / 7.0 / 2.8 | Sales/Net Fixed Assets | 72.3 / 8.8 / .2 | 15.2 / 5.9 / 2.4 | 21.2 / 5.2 / 2.3 | 21.2 / 6.1 / 2.9 | 23.6 / 10.3 / 5.6 | 19.6 / 7.9 / 3.7 |
| 5.1 / 2.2 / 1.2 | 4.3 / 2.4 / 1.4 | 5.2 / 2.4 / 1.3 | Sales/Total Assets | 5.5 / .6 / .1 | 5.3 / 2.5 / 1.1 | 5.4 / 2.5 / 1.2 | 5.6 / 2.4 / 1.5 | 4.4 / 2.6 / 1.7 | 4.9 / 2.2 / 1.2 |
| 2.2 / (248) 3.8 / 7.5 | 2.5 / (261) 4.4 / 7.7 | 1.9 / (317) 3.6 / 7.4 | % Depr., Dep., Amort./Sales | 1.5 / (21) 17.4 / 24.2 | 2.3 / (59) 5.2 / 8.4 | 2.1 / (57) 3.4 / 9.6 | 2.1 / (81) 3.8 / 7.9 | 1.6 / (55) 2.6 / 4.3 | 1.9 / (44) 3.4 / 5.4 |
| 5.8 / (80) 14.6 / 33.0 | 4.3 / (60) 13.2 / 31.3 | 4.5 / (77) 12.2 / 27.9 | % Officers', Directors' Owners' Comp/Sales | | 6.9 / (17) 14.8 / 24.0 | 4.4 / (15) 16.5 / 28.8 | .7 / (20) 5.2 / 30.3 | 6.5 / (13) 18.4 / 30.4 | |
| 4286828M | 3845529M | 4892343M | Net Sales ($) | 18092M | 162091M | 288096M | 716107M | 1029847M | 2678110M |
| 2908497M | 2423440M | 3170818M | Total Assets ($) | 58793M | 138340M | 187305M | 339384M | 469626M | 1977370M |

M = $ thousand    MM = $ million
See Pages 9 through 22 for Explanation of Ratios and Data

## Current Data Sorted by Assets | Comparative Historical Data

| | | | | | | Type of Statement | | | | |
|---|---|---|---|---|---|---|---|---|---|---|
| 1 | 4 | 39 | 44 | 6 | 1 | Unqualified | | 95 | 115 | |
| 1 | 1 | 10 | 3 | | | Reviewed | | 14 | 12 | |
| 6 | 9 | 12 | | | 1 | Compiled | | 29 | 22 | |
| 34 | 27 | 12 | 4 | 1 | | Tax Returns | | 38 | 48 | |
| 12 | 27 | 57 | 28 | 3 | 4 | Other | | 101 | 106 | |
| | 97 (4/1-9/30/11) | | 250 (10/1/11-3/31/12) | | | | | 4/1/07-3/31/08 | 4/1/08-3/31/09 | |
| 0-500M | 500M-2MM | 2-10MM | 10-50MM | 50-100MM | 100-250MM | | | ALL | ALL | |
| 54 | 68 | 130 | 79 | 10 | 6 | NUMBER OF STATEMENTS | | 277 | 303 | |
| % | % | % | % | % | % | ASSETS | | % | % | |
| 37.7 | 21.7 | 14.8 | 21.4 | 14.9 | | Cash & Equivalents | | 17.7 | 19.7 | |
| 9.0 | 15.4 | 20.9 | 16.7 | 13.7 | | Trade Receivables (net) | | 20.0 | 18.8 | |
| 1.4 | 1.4 | 1.4 | .8 | 1.3 | | Inventory | | 1.5 | 1.6 | |
| 4.3 | 3.0 | 4.6 | 4.3 | 5.3 | | All Other Current | | 5.0 | 5.3 | |
| 52.3 | 41.6 | 41.7 | 43.2 | 35.2 | | Total Current | | 44.2 | 45.4 | |
| 27.6 | 37.3 | 48.0 | 44.2 | 48.6 | | Fixed Assets (net) | | 43.2 | 41.1 | |
| 7.8 | 7.6 | 2.8 | 5.9 | 5.1 | | Intangibles (net) | | 3.9 | 5.2 | |
| 12.3 | 13.5 | 7.6 | 6.7 | 11.1 | | All Other Non-Current | | 8.7 | 8.2 | |
| 100.0 | 100.0 | 100.0 | 100.0 | 100.0 | | Total | | 100.0 | 100.0 | |
| | | | | | | LIABILITIES | | | | |
| 23.2 | 11.4 | 3.2 | 2.0 | 1.7 | | Notes Payable-Short Term | | 7.4 | 8.8 | |
| 7.5 | 4.3 | 5.7 | 3.0 | 4.1 | | Cur. Mat.-L.T.D. | | 5.4 | 6.1 | |
| 4.6 | 3.8 | 6.3 | 6.4 | 6.9 | | Trade Payables | | 6.8 | 6.3 | |
| .0 | .0 | .1 | .3 | 1.1 | | Income Taxes Payable | | .3 | .2 | |
| 15.3 | 12.6 | 14.3 | 10.6 | 5.1 | | All Other Current | | 13.2 | 14.0 | |
| 50.6 | 32.1 | 29.5 | 22.3 | 18.9 | | Total Current | | 33.1 | 35.5 | |
| 38.8 | 34.7 | 27.6 | 22.0 | 25.8 | | Long-Term Debt | | 28.7 | 27.4 | |
| .0 | .4 | .1 | .2 | .0 | | Deferred Taxes | | .2 | .4 | |
| 9.4 | 10.4 | 8.5 | 2.8 | 2.4 | | All Other Non-Current | | 3.9 | 6.3 | |
| 1.3 | 22.5 | 34.3 | 52.7 | 52.8 | | Net Worth | | 34.1 | 30.5 | |
| 100.0 | 100.0 | 100.0 | 100.0 | 100.0 | | Total Liabilties & Net Worth | | 100.0 | 100.0 | |
| | | | | | | INCOME DATA | | | | |
| 100.0 | 100.0 | 100.0 | 100.0 | 100.0 | | Net Sales | | 100.0 | 100.0 | |
| | | | | | | Gross Profit | | | | |
| 85.7 | 82.2 | 87.9 | 91.7 | 88.8 | | Operating Expenses | | 87.8 | 90.5 | |
| 14.3 | 17.8 | 12.1 | 8.3 | 11.2 | | Operating Profit | | 12.2 | 9.5 | |
| .9 | 1.7 | 3.8 | -.2 | .7 | | All Other Expenses (net) | | 2.6 | 2.2 | |
| 13.4 | 16.0 | 8.4 | 8.5 | 10.5 | | Profit Before Taxes | | 9.6 | 7.3 | |
| | | | | | | RATIOS | | | | |
| 6.0 | 4.0 | 3.2 | 3.4 | 3.2 | | | | 3.5 | 3.7 | |
| 1.4 | 1.7 | 2.0 | 2.0 | 2.2 | | Current | | 1.6 | 1.8 | |
| .5 | .5 | 1.0 | 1.2 | 1.0 | | | | .8 | .9 | |
| 5.9 | 3.7 | 2.7 | 3.4 | 2.5 | | | | 2.8 | 2.8 | |
| 1.2 | 1.6 | 1.7 | 1.9 | 1.8 | | Quick | | 1.3 | 1.5 | |
| .3 | .5 | 1.0 | 1.0 | .7 | | | | .6 | .7 | |
| 0 UND | 0 UND | 20 18.4 | 19 19.5 | 24 15.4 | | | | 0 813.5 | 0 UND | |
| 0 UND | 0 UND | 34 10.7 | 38 9.7 | 39 9.4 | | Sales/Receivables | | 33 11.2 | 31 11.9 | |
| 0 UND | 37 9.9 | 54 6.7 | 54 6.7 | 74 4.9 | | | | 56 6.5 | 52 7.1 | |
| | | | | | | Cost of Sales/Inventory | | | | |
| | | | | | | Cost of Sales/Payables | | | | |
| 14.6 | 8.2 | 5.5 | 4.3 | 4.0 | | | | 5.1 | 5.0 | |
| 82.0 | 35.6 | 9.5 | 7.2 | 6.5 | | Sales/Working Capital | | 14.5 | 13.1 | |
| -27.8 | -25.2 | 999.8 | 32.8 | NM | | | | -54.4 | -84.0 | |
| 60.3 | 91.4 | 14.4 | 16.2 | 20.7 | | | | 19.4 | 16.6 | |
| (36) 10.0 | (51) 8.7 | (104) 4.9 | (65) 4.9 | 8.6 | | EBIT/Interest | | (217) 5.2 | (230) 3.3 | |
| 1.0 | 3.2 | 1.1 | 1.6 | 3.4 | | | | 1.2 | .8 | |
| | | 11.5 | | | | | | 9.0 | 18.0 | |
| | | (10) 3.4 | | | | Net Profit + Depr., Dep., Amort./Cur. Mat. L/T/D | | (14) 6.5 | (14) 6.6 | |
| | | 1.9 | | | | | | 2.3 | .5 | |
| .1 | .2 | .5 | .6 | .6 | | | | .5 | .4 | |
| .9 | .9 | 1.1 | 1.0 | 1.0 | | Fixed/Worth | | 1.1 | 1.0 | |
| -2.2 | 5.0 | 3.4 | 1.5 | 1.7 | | | | 4.8 | 4.3 | |
| .5 | .4 | .4 | .5 | .4 | | | | .6 | .6 | |
| 3.0 | 2.0 | 1.2 | 1.0 | 1.1 | | Debt/Worth | | 1.3 | 1.3 | |
| -3.4 | 24.9 | 5.3 | 1.8 | 1.6 | | | | 7.2 | 9.9 | |
| 425.4 | 202.2 | 73.7 | 30.4 | | | | | 80.7 | 60.2 | |
| (33) 126.7 | (54) 83.2 | (112) 23.8 | (74) 13.6 | | | % Profit Before Taxes/Tangible Net Worth | | (229) 19.7 | (243) 12.6 | |
| 38.2 | 34.2 | 3.3 | 3.4 | | | | | 3.2 | .8 | |
| 164.5 | 70.2 | 26.0 | 16.9 | 14.9 | | | | 30.2 | 26.1 | |
| 35.2 | 25.2 | 8.1 | 7.3 | 8.3 | | % Profit Before Taxes/Total Assets | | 7.5 | 5.5 | |
| 7.7 | 6.0 | .3 | 1.4 | 7.0 | | | | .5 | -.1 | |
| 273.2 | 37.3 | 10.8 | 6.6 | 5.2 | | | | 16.9 | 16.2 | |
| 62.6 | 14.5 | 4.1 | 2.7 | 2.3 | | Sales/Net Fixed Assets | | 4.6 | 5.6 | |
| 14.9 | 3.6 | 1.7 | 1.6 | 1.4 | | | | 2.1 | 2.6 | |
| 12.9 | 5.1 | 2.9 | 2.0 | 1.4 | | | | 3.4 | 3.8 | |
| 7.2 | 2.7 | 1.7 | 1.3 | 1.1 | | Sales/Total Assets | | 1.9 | 2.0 | |
| 4.0 | 1.6 | .9 | .9 | .8 | | | | 1.1 | 1.1 | |
| .7 | 1.5 | 1.8 | 1.8 | | | | | 1.3 | 1.6 | |
| (30) 1.8 | (44) 3.1 | (117) 3.7 | (75) 2.8 | | | % Depr., Dep., Amort./Sales | | (236) 2.7 | (248) 3.0 | |
| 3.7 | 6.0 | 8.8 | 4.1 | | | | | 5.1 | 5.5 | |
| 3.3 | 2.2 | 3.0 | 1.0 | | | | | 4.2 | 3.4 | |
| (21) 8.0 | (17) 8.0 | (14) 6.0 | (11) 6.0 | | | % Officers', Directors' Owners' Comp/Sales | | (52) 7.1 | (48) 6.8 | |
| 28.0 | 15.6 | 9.4 | 16.0 | | | | | 18.2 | 17.3 | |
| 109675M | 302555M | 1319700M | 2499851M | 817578M | 1247858M | Net Sales ($) | | 5320406M | 7537356M | |
| 13984M | 78084M | 659314M | 1607828M | 678383M | 930100M | Total Assets ($) | | 3371779M | 5170930M | |

© RMA 2012

M = $ thousand   MM = $ million
See Pages 9 through 22 for Explanation of Ratios and Data

## Comparative Historical Data | Current Data Sorted by Sales

| | | | Type of Statement | | | | | | |
|---|---|---|---|---|---|---|---|---|---|
| 110 | 102 | 95 | Unqualified | | 4 | 9 | 18 | 33 | 31 |
| 19 | 16 | 15 | Reviewed | | 4 | 2 | 2 | 4 | 3 |
| 29 | 18 | 28 | Compiled | 3 | 6 | 8 | 6 | 4 | 1 |
| 59 | 57 | 78 | Tax Returns | 18 | 27 | 17 | 5 | 7 | 4 |
| 119 | 126 | 131 | Other | 4 | 23 | 17 | 28 | 37 | 22 |
| 4/1/09-3/31/10 ALL | 4/1/10-3/31/11 ALL | 4/1/11-3/31/12 ALL | | 97 (4/1-9/30/11) | | | 250 (10/1/11-3/31/12) | | |
| | | | | 0-1MM | 1-3MM | 3-5MM | 5-10MM | 10-25MM | 25MM & OVER |
| 336 | 319 | 347 | NUMBER OF STATEMENTS | 25 | 64 | 53 | 59 | 85 | 61 |
| % | % | % | ASSETS | % | % | % | % | % | % |
| 20.1 | 17.9 | 21.3 | Cash & Equivalents | 17.2 | 27.4 | 22.6 | 23.1 | 16.2 | 20.8 |
| 18.4 | 16.2 | 16.6 | Trade Receivables (net) | 9.4 | 10.6 | 13.9 | 16.5 | 23.2 | 19.1 |
| 1.9 | 2.0 | 1.3 | Inventory | .8 | 1.7 | .8 | 1.2 | 1.3 | 1.3 |
| 4.7 | 4.6 | 4.2 | All Other Current | 1.1 | 3.5 | 3.6 | 4.6 | 5.4 | 4.7 |
| 45.1 | 40.7 | 43.4 | Total Current | 28.5 | 43.3 | 41.0 | 45.4 | 46.0 | 45.9 |
| 40.6 | 44.1 | 41.6 | Fixed Assets (net) | 43.0 | 39.8 | 44.0 | 44.1 | 40.1 | 40.6 |
| 4.8 | 5.6 | 5.5 | Intangibles (net) | 11.1 | 6.7 | 4.8 | 5.2 | 3.4 | 5.8 |
| 9.5 | 9.6 | 9.5 | All Other Non-Current | 17.4 | 10.2 | 10.2 | 5.3 | 10.5 | 7.6 |
| 100.0 | 100.0 | 100.0 | Total | 100.0 | 100.0 | 100.0 | 100.0 | 100.0 | 100.0 |
| | | | LIABILITIES | | | | | | |
| 6.2 | 5.8 | 7.5 | Notes Payable-Short Term | 8.0 | 16.6 | 8.9 | 4.1 | 3.0 | 6.4 |
| 4.9 | 4.8 | 4.9 | Cur. Mat.-L.T.D. | 5.6 | 4.5 | 9.7 | 5.4 | 3.0 | 3.3 |
| 6.8 | 7.2 | 5.6 | Trade Payables | .9 | 3.3 | 5.9 | 5.3 | 7.1 | 7.6 |
| .1 | .2 | .1 | Income Taxes Payable | .0 | .0 | .1 | .2 | .1 | .5 |
| 13.5 | 11.3 | 12.9 | All Other Current | 9.5 | 11.5 | 9.5 | 9.5 | 20.4 | 11.7 |
| 31.5 | 29.3 | 31.1 | Total Current | 24.1 | 35.9 | 34.0 | 24.4 | 33.6 | 29.6 |
| 27.6 | 28.6 | 29.2 | Long-Term Debt | 44.0 | 37.9 | 41.2 | 26.5 | 19.0 | 20.5 |
| .3 | .3 | .2 | Deferred Taxes | .0 | .0 | .5 | .4 | .0 | .1 |
| 5.5 | 8.4 | 7.4 | All Other Non-Current | 5.7 | 7.4 | 10.2 | 9.0 | 8.0 | 3.4 |
| 35.1 | 33.4 | 32.1 | Net Worth | 26.2 | 18.8 | 14.1 | 39.6 | 39.5 | 46.4 |
| 100.0 | 100.0 | 100.0 | Total Liabilities & Net Worth | 100.0 | 100.0 | 100.0 | 100.0 | 100.0 | 100.0 |
| | | | INCOME DATA | | | | | | |
| 100.0 | 100.0 | 100.0 | Net Sales | 100.0 | 100.0 | 100.0 | 100.0 | 100.0 | 100.0 |
| | | | Gross Profit | | | | | | |
| 87.8 | 89.4 | 87.4 | Operating Expenses | 76.4 | 84.2 | 86.0 | 84.5 | 93.0 | 91.3 |
| 12.2 | 10.6 | 12.6 | Operating Profit | 23.6 | 15.8 | 14.0 | 15.5 | 7.0 | 8.7 |
| 2.6 | 1.9 | 1.9 | All Other Expenses (net) | 9.8 | 3.4 | 1.5 | 1.0 | .6 | .1 |
| 9.6 | 8.7 | 10.7 | Profit Before Taxes | 13.8 | 12.5 | 12.4 | 14.5 | 6.5 | 8.6 |
| | | | RATIOS | | | | | | |
| 3.5 | 3.2 | 3.4 | | 8.4 | 4.5 | 3.5 | 5.0 | 3.0 | 2.5 |
| 1.7 | 1.7 | 1.9 | Current | 1.3 | 2.0 | 1.6 | 2.6 | 2.0 | 1.9 |
| .9 | 1.0 | 1.0 | | .4 | .6 | .5 | 1.1 | 1.0 | 1.2 |
| 3.1 | 2.6 | 3.0 | | 8.4 | 4.0 | 3.4 | 4.8 | 2.6 | 2.3 |
| (335) 1.4 | (318) 1.5 | 1.7 | Quick | 1.0 | 1.7 | 1.5 | 2.1 | 1.7 | 1.7 |
| .7 | .8 | .7 | | .3 | .5 | .4 | .9 | .8 | 1.0 |
| 0 UND | 0 UND | 0 UND | | 0 UND | 0 UND | 0 UND | 0 UND | 20 18.2 | 19 19.7 |
| 28 12.9 | 29 12.7 | 26 13.9 | Sales/Receivables | 0 UND | 0 UND | 19 19.1 | 27 13.6 | 34 10.6 | 34 10.6 |
| 50 7.3 | 49 7.4 | 50 7.3 | | 32 11.4 | 36 10.1 | 42 8.7 | 52 7.0 | 55 6.6 | 53 6.9 |
| | | | Cost of Sales/Inventory | | | | | | |
| | | | Cost of Sales/Payables | | | | | | |
| 5.8 | 6.5 | 5.6 | | 4.3 | 6.8 | 6.5 | 5.4 | 5.5 | 5.2 |
| 16.5 | 15.4 | 11.8 | Sales/Working Capital | 42.5 | 24.8 | 14.0 | 9.3 | 10.8 | 9.8 |
| -87.3 | -818.9 | -274.2 | | -9.0 | -32.5 | -24.6 | 284.6 | 558.4 | 39.9 |
| 28.5 | 23.3 | 22.4 | | 11.7 | 11.0 | 58.0 | 24.1 | 29.9 | 23.2 |
| (257) 6.0 | (247) 5.5 | (271) 6.0 | EBIT/Interest | (17) 6.5 | (44) 4.5 | (43) 6.7 | (46) 10.1 | (68) 4.1 | (53) 7.8 |
| 1.3 | 1.6 | 2.0 | | 2.7 | .3 | 1.3 | 4.8 | 1.0 | 3.6 |
| 12.9 | 4.1 | 10.0 | | | | | | | 9.5 |
| (27) 5.2 | (22) 1.8 | (24) 3.2 | Net Profit + Depr., Dep., Amort./Cur. Mat. L/T/D | | | | | (11) 3.6 |
| 1.1 | 1.1 | 1.8 | | | | | | | 1.9 |
| .4 | .6 | .4 | | .1 | .1 | .3 | .5 | .3 | .5 |
| 1.0 | 1.1 | 1.0 | Fixed/Worth | 1.9 | 1.2 | 1.0 | 1.0 | .9 | .9 |
| 3.7 | 4.0 | 2.9 | | -6.8 | UND | 10.3 | 3.4 | 1.6 | 1.4 |
| .6 | .6 | .5 | | 1.0 | .5 | .4 | .4 | .4 | .5 |
| 1.4 | 1.3 | 1.2 | Debt/Worth | 4.7 | 2.0 | 2.3 | 1.1 | 1.0 | 1.0 |
| 7.1 | 6.2 | 5.9 | | -12.8 | -10.1 | UND | 6.9 | 2.0 | 1.7 |
| 100.8 | 78.6 | 90.2 | | 312.4 | 154.4 | 181.7 | 120.6 | 36.8 | 53.1 |
| (277) 24.3 | (270) 19.7 | (288) 30.1 | % Profit Before Taxes/Tangible Net Worth | (17) 69.4 | (46) 77.3 | (41) 54.6 | (50) 47.2 | (77) 15.5 | (57) 19.2 |
| 3.4 | 5.5 | 8.0 | | 18.5 | 23.1 | 16.0 | 11.0 | 1.9 | 7.7 |
| 37.0 | 28.4 | 34.3 | | 29.4 | 58.4 | 61.6 | 55.2 | 13.3 | 22.5 |
| 9.3 | 7.7 | 11.9 | % Profit Before Taxes/Total Assets | 11.3 | 19.2 | 18.1 | 18.7 | 7.3 | 9.4 |
| .3 | 1.2 | 1.4 | | 1.5 | -.3 | 1.3 | 5.8 | .2 | 3.5 |
| 17.4 | 15.5 | 22.7 | | 106.8 | 96.8 | 32.1 | 14.1 | 15.0 | 12.2 |
| 6.3 | 4.8 | 5.2 | Sales/Net Fixed Assets | 3.8 | 13.2 | 6.0 | 5.2 | 5.0 | 5.1 |
| 2.4 | 2.2 | 2.2 | | .4 | 1.7 | 2.3 | 2.3 | 2.4 | 2.5 |
| 3.9 | 3.5 | 3.9 | | 3.1 | 5.9 | 6.8 | 3.9 | 3.2 | 3.1 |
| 1.9 | 1.8 | 2.0 | Sales/Total Assets | 1.7 | 2.2 | 2.4 | 2.1 | 1.8 | 1.8 |
| 1.1 | 1.0 | 1.1 | | .3 | .8 | 1.3 | 1.2 | 1.2 | 1.2 |
| 1.6 | 1.6 | 1.6 | | 3.7 | .8 | 1.6 | 1.7 | 1.5 | 1.4 |
| (271) 3.0 | (270) 2.8 | (281) 3.0 | % Depr., Dep., Amort./Sales | (15) 8.5 | (43) 3.7 | (42) 3.8 | (46) 4.3 | (76) 2.4 | (59) 2.6 |
| 5.5 | 4.9 | 5.5 | | 21.6 | 15.3 | 8.1 | 7.4 | 3.9 | 3.5 |
| 3.2 | 3.2 | 2.6 | | | 5.2 | 2.2 | 5.0 | .4 | |
| (60) 9.8 | (55) 7.2 | (64) 6.8 | % Officers', Directors' Owners' Comp/Sales | (15) 7.4 | (13) 4.1 | (10) 9.4 | (13) 1.7 | |
| 20.8 | 17.4 | 15.7 | | | 15.7 | 9.2 | 19.6 | 3.9 | |
| 7138527M | 6803997M | 6297217M | Net Sales ($) | 13635M | 123921M | 204796M | 422692M | 1322968M | 4209205M |
| 3979168M | 4663866M | 3967693M | Total Assets ($) | 25953M | 125733M | 116939M | 279736M | 887800M | 2531532M |

M = $ thousand    MM = $ million
See Pages 9 through 22 for Explanation of Ratios and Data

## Current Data Sorted by Assets | Comparative Historical Data

| Type of Statement | 0-500M | 500M-2MM | 2-10MM | 10-50MM | 50-100MM | 100-250MM | 4/1/07-3/31/08 ALL | 4/1/08-3/31/09 ALL |
|---|---|---|---|---|---|---|---|---|
| Unqualified | | | 8 | 17 | 4 | 7 | 35 | 50 |
| Reviewed | 2 | 3 | 17 | 3 | 1 | | 19 | 16 |
| Compiled | 10 | 10 | 15 | 2 | | | 21 | 23 |
| Tax Returns | 25 | 22 | 13 | | | | 24 | 40 |
| Other | 21 | 26 | 34 | 28 | 13 | 10 | 107 | 108 |
| | 42 (4/1-9/30/11) | | | 249 (10/1/11-3/31/12) | | | | |
| NUMBER OF STATEMENTS | 58 | 61 | 87 | 50 | 18 | 17 | 206 | 237 |
| **ASSETS** | % | % | % | % | % | % | % | % |
| Cash & Equivalents | 36.9 | 18.7 | 14.8 | 14.1 | 10.1 | 12.2 | 15.8 | 13.4 |
| Trade Receivables (net) | 8.8 | 15.7 | 26.9 | 26.1 | 18.1 | 13.5 | 21.8 | 24.0 |
| Inventory | .4 | 1.9 | 2.0 | 3.4 | 2.3 | 3.5 | 3.0 | 2.8 |
| All Other Current | 2.8 | 4.1 | 4.1 | 3.2 | 5.2 | 4.3 | 3.6 | 5.2 |
| Total Current | 49.0 | 40.5 | 47.7 | 46.8 | 35.8 | 33.5 | 44.2 | 45.3 |
| Fixed Assets (net) | 37.7 | 36.9 | 38.7 | 37.0 | 30.8 | 23.0 | 40.2 | 38.1 |
| Intangibles (net) | 5.7 | 6.1 | 6.0 | 7.8 | 28.3 | 30.6 | 8.4 | 9.3 |
| All Other Non-Current | 7.8 | 16.5 | 7.6 | 8.5 | 5.1 | 13.0 | 7.1 | 7.2 |
| Total | 100.0 | 100.0 | 100.0 | 100.0 | 100.0 | 100.0 | 100.0 | 100.0 |
| **LIABILITIES** | | | | | | | | |
| Notes Payable-Short Term | 42.6 | 7.2 | 5.8 | 3.1 | .8 | .9 | 9.0 | 6.9 |
| Cur. Mat.-L.T.D. | 8.2 | 8.8 | 7.0 | 7.5 | 3.0 | 4.4 | 7.4 | 8.0 |
| Trade Payables | 12.4 | 5.8 | 8.2 | 8.4 | 4.7 | 4.7 | 7.9 | 9.5 |
| Income Taxes Payable | .3 | .4 | .3 | .1 | .1 | .5 | .5 | .8 |
| All Other Current | 24.1 | 10.9 | 11.4 | 14.0 | 11.7 | 8.6 | 12.6 | 12.9 |
| Total Current | 87.6 | 33.1 | 32.7 | 33.1 | 20.4 | 19.2 | 37.4 | 38.1 |
| Long-Term Debt | 16.7 | 34.6 | 22.0 | 17.4 | 15.5 | 27.0 | 31.8 | 25.1 |
| Deferred Taxes | .0 | .0 | .3 | .4 | 1.9 | 2.2 | 1.0 | .3 |
| All Other Non-Current | 10.8 | 6.1 | 7.0 | 3.7 | 5.0 | 28.8 | 8.8 | 3.3 |
| Net Worth | -15.1 | 26.2 | 38.1 | 45.5 | 57.3 | 22.9 | 21.0 | 33.2 |
| Total Liabilties & Net Worth | 100.0 | 100.0 | 100.0 | 100.0 | 100.0 | 100.0 | 100.0 | 100.0 |
| **INCOME DATA** | | | | | | | | |
| Net Sales | 100.0 | 100.0 | 100.0 | 100.0 | 100.0 | 100.0 | 100.0 | 100.0 |
| Gross Profit | | | | | | | | |
| Operating Expenses | 89.2 | 88.1 | 85.8 | 91.1 | 87.7 | 88.8 | 89.7 | 89.7 |
| Operating Profit | 10.8 | 11.9 | 14.2 | 8.9 | 12.3 | 11.2 | 10.3 | 10.3 |
| All Other Expenses (net) | .4 | 1.6 | 3.2 | 1.4 | 1.5 | 7.2 | 2.1 | 1.7 |
| Profit Before Taxes | 10.4 | 10.3 | 11.0 | 7.5 | 10.8 | 4.0 | 8.2 | 8.6 |
| **RATIOS** | | | | | | | | |
| Current | 2.7 | 2.5 | 2.8 | 2.9 | 2.7 | 2.7 | 2.5 | 2.6 |
| | .7 | 1.3 | 1.5 | 1.7 | 1.7 | 1.5 | 1.6 | 1.4 |
| | .1 | .6 | .7 | 1.0 | 1.2 | .9 | .8 | .9 |
| Quick | 2.7 | 2.2 | 2.4 | 2.3 | 2.2 | 2.3 | 2.2 | 2.2 |
| | .6 | 1.0 | 1.3 | 1.4 | 1.5 | 1.0 | 1.3 (236) | 1.2 |
| | .1 | .2 | .6 | .8 | 1.0 | .7 | .6 | .7 |
| Sales/Receivables | 0 UND | 0 UND | 9 40.2 | 35 10.3 | 42 8.7 | 40 9.2 | 5 72.5 | 21 17.8 |
| | 0 UND | 0 UND | 41 9.0 | 47 7.7 | 54 6.7 | 47 7.8 | 41 8.8 | 44 8.3 |
| | 0 UND | 39 9.4 | 62 5.9 | 68 5.4 | 68 5.4 | 64 5.7 | 58 6.3 | 59 6.2 |
| Cost of Sales/Inventory | | | | | | | | |
| Cost of Sales/Payables | | | | | | | | |
| Sales/Working Capital | 21.3 | 10.4 | 6.1 | 5.2 | 4.6 | 2.9 | 6.7 | 6.2 |
| | -91.0 | 125.5 | 16.4 | 15.7 | 8.0 | 9.7 | 17.3 | 17.5 |
| | -19.5 | -18.0 | -22.8 | -442.5 | 48.1 | -33.6 | -35.7 | -46.3 |
| EBIT/Interest | 52.1 | 31.8 | 29.2 | 12.0 | 91.3 | 6.6 | 13.6 | 21.4 |
| | (42) 2.3 | (53) 6.8 | (74) 7.9 | (43) 4.6 | (15) 16.2 | (15) 2.9 | (171) 4.3 | (208) 5.0 |
| | -4.8 | 1.0 | 2.3 | 1.3 | .7 | .6 | 1.2 | 1.4 |
| Net Profit + Depr., Dep., Amort./Cur. Mat. L/T/D | | | 22.0 | 4.8 | | | 9.0 | 7.6 |
| | | | (10) 2.9 | (10) 3.0 | | | (30) 3.7 | (44) 4.2 |
| | | | .8 | 1.4 | | | 1.3 | 1.5 |
| Fixed/Worth | .0 | .3 | .5 | .4 | .5 | .4 | .5 | .5 |
| | .9 | 1.3 | 1.2 | 1.0 | .8 | -3.3 | 1.2 | 1.1 |
| | -2.2 | 23.5 | 5.6 | 2.5 | 2.3 | -.3 | UND | 6.6 |
| Debt/Worth | .5 | .8 | .7 | .6 | .6 | .5 | .8 | .7 |
| | 7.2 | 5.2 | 1.7 | 1.2 | 1.0 | -27.4 | 1.9 | 2.1 |
| | -2.6 | -379.0 | 12.1 | 3.5 | 2.7 | -1.8 | -147.7 | 18.2 |
| % Profit Before Taxes/Tangible Net Worth | 507.8 | 174.4 | 69.5 | 49.3 | 48.9 | | 71.8 | 97.2 |
| | (32) 111.2 | (45) 79.8 | (75) 43.9 | (43) 22.9 | (15) 23.7 | | (153) 28.2 | (187) 36.9 |
| | 24.5 | 16.5 | 2.3 | 4.2 | 8.7 | | 7.5 | 7.3 |
| % Profit Before Taxes/Total Assets | 135.4 | 47.0 | 29.7 | 20.3 | 20.8 | 6.7 | 26.4 | 29.9 |
| | 19.3 | 15.1 | 15.8 | 9.7 | 6.5 | 4.3 | 8.0 | 11.1 |
| | -10.9 | .4 | 1.8 | .6 | 2.7 | -2.0 | .7 | 1.2 |
| Sales/Net Fixed Assets | 473.6 | 61.2 | 20.8 | 13.6 | 7.5 | 9.7 | 21.7 | 20.0 |
| | 45.8 | 10.7 | 5.6 | 6.5 | 4.5 | 5.2 | 7.5 | 7.1 |
| | 9.0 | 4.9 | 2.1 | 2.7 | 2.9 | 2.7 | 2.6 | 2.9 |
| Sales/Total Assets | 20.9 | 6.6 | 3.1 | 2.4 | 1.9 | 1.1 | 3.8 | 3.5 |
| | 8.2 | 3.2 | 1.9 | 1.7 | 1.1 | .7 | 2.1 | 2.0 |
| | 4.2 | 2.2 | 1.0 | 1.1 | .7 | .6 | 1.1 | 1.2 |
| % Depr., Dep., Amort./Sales | .9 | 1.1 | 1.9 | 1.7 | 2.2 | 2.5 | 1.6 | 1.8 |
| | (24) 2.7 | (40) 3.7 | (78) 3.5 | (46) 3.5 | (13) 6.2 | (14) 3.2 | (164) 3.7 | (189) 3.8 |
| | 6.1 | 8.3 | 8.4 | 6.3 | 9.0 | 5.2 | 7.8 | 7.8 |
| % Officers', Directors' Owners' Comp/Sales | 6.8 | 4.3 | 3.1 | | | | 2.7 | 2.9 |
| | (20) 11.0 | (22) 6.5 | (31) 7.5 | | | | (53) 11.3 | (53) 8.5 |
| | 20.0 | 13.0 | 17.5 | | | | 20.3 | 15.2 |
| Net Sales ($) | 173750M | 269599M | 993207M | 1955130M | 1656407M | 2353338M | 6480955M | 7977926M |
| Total Assets ($) | 12875M | 64349M | 431385M | 1064237M | 1294480M | 2709746M | 4658427M | 5707933M |

© RMA 2012

M = $ thousand    MM = $ million
See Pages 9 through 22 for Explanation of Ratios and Data

## Comparative Historical Data — Current Data Sorted by Sales

| | 4/1/09-3/31/10 ALL | 4/1/10-3/31/11 ALL | 4/1/11-3/31/12 ALL | 0-1MM | 1-3MM | 3-5MM | 5-10MM | 10-25MM | 25MM & OVER |
|---|---|---|---|---|---|---|---|---|---|
| | | | | 42 (4/1-9/30/11) | | | 249 (10/1/11-3/31/12) | | |
| **Type of Statement** | | | | | | | | | |
| Unqualified | 50 | 32 | 36 | | 2 | 2 | 2 | 5 | 25 |
| Reviewed | 25 | 19 | 26 | | 4 | 3 | 5 | 10 | 4 |
| Compiled | 24 | 43 | 37 | 4 | 5 | 5 | 9 | 12 | 2 |
| Tax Returns | 51 | 49 | 60 | 13 | 14 | 14 | 15 | 3 | 1 |
| Other | 124 | 106 | 132 | 8 | 31 | 12 | 13 | 25 | 43 |
| **NUMBER OF STATEMENTS** | 274 | 249 | 291 | 25 | 56 | 36 | 44 | 55 | 75 |
| **ASSETS** | % | % | % | % | % | % | % | % | % |
| Cash & Equivalents | 16.7 | 18.7 | 19.5 | 25.0 | 23.0 | 15.7 | 22.7 | 19.3 | 15.0 |
| Trade Receivables (net) | 23.9 | 22.0 | 19.5 | 8.1 | 13.6 | 15.4 | 22.1 | 28.5 | 21.4 |
| Inventory | 2.2 | 2.4 | 2.0 | .1 | 1.3 | 2.7 | 2.4 | 1.5 | 3.0 |
| All Other Current | 3.0 | 4.0 | 3.8 | 2.1 | 3.2 | 6.0 | 4.7 | 1.9 | 4.5 |
| Total Current | 45.8 | 47.1 | 44.7 | 35.4 | 41.1 | 39.9 | 51.9 | 51.1 | 43.9 |
| Fixed Assets (net) | 36.6 | 36.2 | 36.4 | 51.8 | 44.2 | 39.1 | 31.8 | 32.7 | 29.6 |
| Intangibles (net) | 8.7 | 8.5 | 9.1 | 5.7 | 5.0 | 7.8 | 5.5 | 7.7 | 17.0 |
| All Other Non-Current | 9.0 | 8.2 | 9.8 | 7.3 | 9.7 | 13.2 | 10.7 | 8.4 | 9.5 |
| Total | 100.0 | 100.0 | 100.0 | 100.0 | 100.0 | 100.0 | 100.0 | 100.0 | 100.0 |
| **LIABILITIES** | | | | | | | | | |
| Notes Payable-Short Term | 7.3 | 10.5 | 12.3 | 13.2 | 17.8 | 18.6 | 22.5 | 5.4 | 4.1 |
| Cur. Mat.-L.T.D. | 7.7 | 9.2 | 7.3 | 16.0 | 5.8 | 7.8 | 7.1 | 6.3 | 6.1 |
| Trade Payables | 8.5 | 7.8 | 8.2 | 20.7 | 5.1 | 7.7 | 7.7 | 8.9 | 6.2 |
| Income Taxes Payable | .6 | .5 | .3 | .0 | .3 | .2 | .0 | .8 | .2 |
| All Other Current | 17.5 | 19.2 | 14.1 | 9.6 | 12.0 | 13.4 | 16.4 | 13.0 | 17.1 |
| Total Current | 41.5 | 47.2 | 42.2 | 59.6 | 40.9 | 47.7 | 53.7 | 34.4 | 33.8 |
| Long-Term Debt | 26.1 | 26.7 | 22.7 | 35.7 | 30.2 | 18.8 | 24.8 | 19.0 | 16.1 |
| Deferred Taxes | .3 | .4 | .4 | .0 | .0 | .0 | .2 | .3 | 1.2 |
| All Other Non-Current | 8.0 | 6.2 | 8.1 | 4.8 | 14.5 | 8.5 | .4 | 6.2 | 10.3 |
| Net Worth | 24.0 | 19.5 | 26.6 | .0 | 14.3 | 25.0 | 21.0 | 40.1 | 38.7 |
| Total Liabilties & Net Worth | 100.0 | 100.0 | 100.0 | 100.0 | 100.0 | 100.0 | 100.0 | 100.0 | 100.0 |
| **INCOME DATA** | | | | | | | | | |
| Net Sales | 100.0 | 100.0 | 100.0 | 100.0 | 100.0 | 100.0 | 100.0 | 100.0 | 100.0 |
| Gross Profit | | | | | | | | | |
| Operating Expenses | 88.4 | 89.6 | 88.2 | 83.2 | 82.2 | 89.1 | 93.2 | 89.5 | 90.0 |
| Operating Profit | 11.6 | 10.4 | 11.8 | 16.8 | 17.8 | 10.9 | 6.8 | 10.5 | 10.0 |
| All Other Expenses (net) | 1.7 | 2.0 | 2.1 | 6.8 | 2.9 | .8 | .7 | .6 | 2.6 |
| Profit Before Taxes | 9.9 | 8.3 | 9.7 | 10.0 | 15.0 | 10.1 | 6.1 | 9.9 | 7.4 |
| **RATIOS** | | | | | | | | | |
| Current | 2.6 | 2.4 | 2.7 | 2.7 | 3.7 | 1.8 | 2.5 | 3.1 | 2.7 |
| | 1.5 | 1.4 | 1.4 | .5 | 1.3 | .9 | 1.5 | 1.5 | 1.7 |
| | .9 | .7 | .6 | .1 | .3 | .5 | .8 | .8 | 1.0 |
| Quick | 2.2 | 2.0 | 2.3 | 2.7 | 3.5 | 1.5 | 2.3 | 2.4 | 2.2 |
| | 1.2 | 1.1 | 1.2 | .4 | .9 | .7 | 1.2 | 1.3 | 1.4 |
| | .7 | .5 | .6 | .1 | .3 | .3 | .7 | .8 | .8 |
| Sales/Receivables | 13   29.1 | 0   UND | 0   UND | 0   UND | 0   UND | 0   UND | 0   UND | 12   31.3 | 32   11.3 |
| | 39   9.4 | 33   10.9 | 32   11.3 | 0   UND | 0   UND | 12   29.8 | 32   11.5 | 39   9.3 | 47   7.8 |
| | 61   6.0 | 56   6.5 | 54   6.8 | 9   41.7 | 37   9.9 | 49   7.5 | 57   6.4 | 57   6.4 | 61   6.0 |
| Cost of Sales/Inventory | | | | | | | | | |
| Cost of Sales/Payables | | | | | | | | | |
| Sales/Working Capital | 7.0 | 7.7 | 7.4 | 17.7 | 9.3 | 10.5 | 7.2 | 6.8 | 5.1 |
| | 17.6 | 27.6 | 24.4 | -6.7 | 45.5 | -106.0 | 45.2 | 18.5 | 10.9 |
| | -60.9 | -28.4 | -24.1 | -3.3 | -19.9 | -11.9 | -23.2 | -114.5 | 999.8 |
| EBIT/Interest | 28.3 | 26.5 | 23.9 | 6.4 | 15.8 | 39.8 | 18.8 | 58.9 | 23.1 |
| | (227) 6.8 | (201) 4.5 | (242) 5.2 | (17) 1.3 | (43) 2.8 | (35) 11.7 | (38) 6.8 | (45) 8.5 | (64) 5.1 |
| | 2.3 | 1.2 | .9 | -2.4 | .9 | 2.0 | -1.0 | 1.6 | 1.4 |
| Net Profit + Depr., Dep., Amort./Cur. Mat. L/T/D | 9.9 | 5.0 | 7.8 | | | | | | 5.2 |
| | (46) 2.4 | (41) 2.5 | (32) 3.2 | | | | | | (18) 2.9 |
| | 1.3 | 1.0 | 1.3 | | | | | | 1.4 |
| Fixed/Worth | .4 | .5 | .4 | .5 | .5 | .2 | .3 | .2 | .5 |
| | 1.1 | 1.3 | 1.1 | 3.8 | 2.0 | 1.2 | 1.0 | 1.0 | .9 |
| | 8.2 | 11.3 | 11.0 | -4.7 | -10.8 | 6.0 | 9.2 | 3.8 | 11.0 |
| Debt/Worth | .6 | .7 | .6 | .4 | .8 | .7 | .7 | .6 | .6 |
| | 1.8 | 2.6 | 2.0 | 5.9 | 3.9 | 2.2 | 2.4 | 1.6 | 1.3 |
| | 31.2 | 52.8 | -679.0 | -4.3 | -6.1 | 85.8 | 28.8 | 16.8 | 15.2 |
| % Profit Before Taxes/Tangible Net Worth | 101.3 | 110.0 | 81.3 | 141.3 | 215.5 | 111.2 | 110.9 | 72.6 | 53.0 |
| | (213) 39.2 | (190) 37.0 | (218) 39.9 | (15) 36.4 | (38) 67.2 | (29) 36.4 | (35) 53.1 | (44) 46.9 | (57) 23.7 |
| | 10.4 | 4.4 | 5.3 | -9.5 | 1.9 | 17.3 | -9.6 | 4.5 | 6.6 |
| % Profit Before Taxes/Total Assets | 35.5 | 34.9 | 33.9 | 31.9 | 77.3 | 33.3 | 40.5 | 38.8 | 20.4 |
| | 12.7 | 11.2 | 10.4 | 2.0 | 16.7 | 14.3 | 8.8 | 18.3 | 7.2 |
| | 2.9 | 1.0 | .0 | -6.7 | .0 | 3.9 | -4.4 | .7 | 1.2 |
| Sales/Net Fixed Assets | 24.7 | 26.3 | 32.1 | 43.2 | 39.6 | 61.8 | 81.7 | 43.2 | 14.5 |
| | 7.5 | 9.6 | 9.0 | 7.1 | 9.3 | 6.1 | 12.1 | 13.4 | 6.5 |
| | 3.2 | 3.5 | 3.4 | 1.2 | 2.8 | 2.1 | 4.7 | 5.0 | 3.8 |
| Sales/Total Assets | 3.9 | 5.0 | 4.7 | 5.3 | 5.8 | 5.9 | 6.8 | 5.4 | 2.8 |
| | 2.2 | 2.5 | 2.4 | 2.8 | 2.8 | 2.4 | 2.9 | 2.9 | 1.7 |
| | 1.3 | 1.5 | 1.3 | .6 | 1.6 | 1.1 | 1.5 | 1.5 | 1.0 |
| % Depr., Dep., Amort./Sales | 1.9 | 1.7 | 1.7 | 3.7 | 1.4 | 2.1 | 1.7 | 1.0 | 1.7 |
| | (212) 3.8 | (191) 3.6 | (215) 3.5 | (16) 7.2 | (35) 5.1 | (25) 6.2 | (30) 3.2 | (44) 2.5 | (65) 3.1 |
| | 6.3 | 6.3 | 7.6 | 15.1 | 9.3 | 13.8 | 6.3 | 6.1 | 6.0 |
| % Officers', Directors' Owners' Comp/Sales | 2.8 | 3.4 | 3.7 | | 5.8 | 10.8 | 1.8 | 2.7 | 1.6 |
| | (65) 8.5 | (69) 8.2 | (84) 7.3 | | (14) 6.9 | (12) 15.0 | (21) 5.1 | (21) 7.7 | (10) 7.3 |
| | 16.7 | 17.6 | 17.5 | | 13.1 | 20.2 | 10.9 | 26.6 | 26.4 |
| Net Sales ($) | 8613558M | 7664890M | 7401431M | 11656M | 103573M | 139606M | 312309M | 901592M | 5932695M |
| Total Assets ($) | 6193601M | 4652708M | 5577072M | 17471M | 74149M | 84308M | 152568M | 441357M | 4807219M |

M = $ thousand    MM = $ million
See Pages 9 through 22 for Explanation of Ratios and Data

## Current Data Sorted by Assets      Comparative Historical Data

| 0-500M | 500M-2MM | 2-10MM | 10-50MM | 50-100MM | 100-250MM | Type of Statement | 4/1/07-3/31/08 ALL | 4/1/08-3/31/09 ALL |
|---|---|---|---|---|---|---|---|---|
|  | 1 | 9 | 8 |  | 1 | Unqualified | 16 | 19 |
| 2 | 3 | 15 | 8 |  |  | Reviewed | 26 | 29 |
| 1 | 16 | 14 | 1 |  |  | Compiled | 25 | 33 |
| 17 | 13 | 16 | 4 |  | 1 | Tax Returns | 31 | 36 |
| 20 | 46 | 42 | 23 | 4 |  | Other | 107 | 113 |
|  | 15 (4/1-9/30/11) |  | 250 (10/1/11-3/31/12) |  |  |  |  |  |
| 40 | 79 | 96 | 44 | 4 | 2 | NUMBER OF STATEMENTS | 205 | 230 |
| % | % | % | % | % | % | ASSETS | % | % |
| 28.0 | 19.1 | 14.6 | 11.5 |  |  | Cash & Equivalents | 12.4 | 13.2 |
| 4.7 | 20.8 | 18.3 | 19.8 |  |  | Trade Receivables (net) | 17.7 | 14.2 |
| .0 | .1 | .5 | 1.0 |  |  | Inventory | .4 | .3 |
| .9 | 3.2 | 2.8 | 4.3 |  |  | All Other Current | 4.3 | 4.0 |
| 33.6 | 43.3 | 36.1 | 36.6 |  |  | Total Current | 34.8 | 31.7 |
| 55.7 | 44.1 | 48.4 | 40.4 |  |  | Fixed Assets (net) | 49.6 | 54.6 |
| 1.7 | 6.0 | 6.0 | 15.2 |  |  | Intangibles (net) | 6.8 | 6.5 |
| 9.1 | 6.6 | 9.5 | 7.8 |  |  | All Other Non-Current | 8.8 | 7.1 |
| 100.0 | 100.0 | 100.0 | 100.0 |  |  | Total | 100.0 | 100.0 |
|  |  |  |  |  |  | LIABILITIES |  |  |
| 23.6 | 13.8 | 7.8 | 3.3 |  |  | Notes Payable-Short Term | 7.8 | 7.5 |
| 21.4 | 14.2 | 10.7 | 11.3 |  |  | Cur. Mat.-L.T.D. | 10.7 | 12.6 |
| 12.7 | 6.3 | 4.7 | 4.4 |  |  | Trade Payables | 5.3 | 5.8 |
| .0 | .0 | .5 | .3 |  |  | Income Taxes Payable | .4 | .2 |
| 27.1 | 13.0 | 9.6 | 11.2 |  |  | All Other Current | 13.2 | 10.8 |
| 84.9 | 47.3 | 33.3 | 30.6 |  |  | Total Current | 37.4 | 36.9 |
| 37.3 | 43.9 | 30.0 | 25.7 |  |  | Long-Term Debt | 36.5 | 44.7 |
| .0 | .0 | .0 | .1 |  |  | Deferred Taxes | .1 | .0 |
| 5.1 | 4.8 | 6.0 | 5.4 |  |  | All Other Non-Current | 6.2 | 5.9 |
| -27.3 | 4.0 | 30.8 | 38.2 |  |  | Net Worth | 19.8 | 12.5 |
| 100.0 | 100.0 | 100.0 | 100.0 |  |  | Total Liabilities & Net Worth | 100.0 | 100.0 |
|  |  |  |  |  |  | INCOME DATA |  |  |
| 100.0 | 100.0 | 100.0 | 100.0 |  |  | Net Sales | 100.0 | 100.0 |
|  |  |  |  |  |  | Gross Profit |  |  |
| 89.4 | 91.3 | 85.1 | 83.3 |  |  | Operating Expenses | 86.6 | 85.7 |
| 10.6 | 8.7 | 14.9 | 16.7 |  |  | Operating Profit | 13.4 | 14.3 |
| 1.1 | 1.3 | 3.3 | 1.1 |  |  | All Other Expenses (net) | 2.6 | 3.5 |
| 9.4 | 7.4 | 11.6 | 15.6 |  |  | Profit Before Taxes | 10.7 | 10.8 |
|  |  |  |  |  |  | RATIOS |  |  |
| 1.6 | 2.6 | 2.5 | 2.0 |  |  | Current | 2.1 | 1.8 |
| .5 | 1.2 | 1.1 | 1.2 |  |  | | 1.0 | .9 |
| .1 | .5 | .6 | .7 |  |  | | .6 | .4 |
| 1.6 | 2.6 | 2.4 | 1.7 |  |  | Quick | 1.9 | 1.6 |
| .5 | .9 | 1.0 | 1.0 |  |  | | .9 (229) | .8 |
| .1 | .4 | .5 | .6 |  |  | | .4 | .3 |
| 0 UND | 0 UND | 0 UND | 29 12.6 |  |  | Sales/Receivables | 0 UND | 0 UND |
| 0 UND | 14 26.9 | 29 12.5 | 41 8.9 |  |  | | 37 9.7 | 26 14.0 |
| 0 UND | 51 7.2 | 45 8.1 | 61 6.0 |  |  | | 55 6.6 | 47 7.8 |
|  |  |  |  |  |  | Cost of Sales/Inventory |  |  |
|  |  |  |  |  |  | Cost of Sales/Payables |  |  |
| 35.0 | 9.3 | 8.0 | 6.7 |  |  | Sales/Working Capital | 9.7 | 12.8 |
| -25.4 | 79.3 | 43.6 | 26.1 |  |  | | 999.8 | -70.7 |
| -6.4 | -12.9 | -15.1 | -18.1 |  |  | | -12.0 | -10.8 |
| 13.4 | 17.4 | 29.3 | 28.6 |  |  | EBIT/Interest | 14.0 | 12.4 |
| (28) 5.2 | (67) 8.3 | (83) 10.2 | (41) 9.3 |  |  | | (174) 4.1 | (196) 4.1 |
| 2.3 | .5 | 3.2 | 5.1 |  |  | | 1.0 | .9 |
|  |  |  |  |  |  | Net Profit + Depr., Dep., Amort./Cur. Mat. L/T/D | 2.5 | 3.1 |
|  |  |  |  |  |  | | (14) 1.4 (17) | 1.2 |
|  |  |  |  |  |  | | .5 | .8 |
| .9 | .5 | .7 | .8 |  |  | Fixed/Worth | .9 | 1.1 |
| 3.0 | 2.2 | 1.4 | 1.3 |  |  | | 2.5 | 3.7 |
| -.7 | -1.5 | 3.8 | 4.6 |  |  | | -15.0 | -5.0 |
| .8 | .9 | .7 | .9 |  |  | Debt/Worth | 1.1 | 1.3 |
| 6.9 | 3.2 | 1.5 | 2.3 |  |  | | 3.1 | 5.8 |
| -2.2 | -4.2 | 5.8 | 7.1 |  |  | | -32.3 | -9.6 |
| 173.2 | 103.3 | 85.8 | 133.8 |  |  | % Profit Before Taxes/Tangible Net Worth | 118.7 | 132.9 |
| (22) 79.3 | (52) 36.5 | (76) 42.6 | (37) 77.4 |  |  | | (149) 46.5 | (156) 60.0 |
| 8.3 | 3.0 | 14.5 | 24.7 |  |  | | 9.4 | 8.1 |
| 91.8 | 37.7 | 32.3 | 37.5 |  |  | % Profit Before Taxes/Total Assets | 40.4 | 33.2 |
| 33.8 | 10.1 | 15.8 | 19.4 |  |  | | 10.8 | 11.0 |
| 2.2 | -2.6 | 3.0 | 5.3 |  |  | | -.2 | -1.5 |
| 78.3 | 24.8 | 12.0 | 7.6 |  |  | Sales/Net Fixed Assets | 9.8 | 8.3 |
| 9.4 | 7.8 | 4.1 | 4.9 |  |  | | 4.2 | 3.6 |
| 3.7 | 2.6 | 2.1 | 3.0 |  |  | | 2.2 | 1.8 |
| 9.5 | 4.7 | 3.1 | 2.6 |  |  | Sales/Total Assets | 3.5 | 3.7 |
| 4.5 | 2.8 | 1.9 | 1.8 |  |  | | 1.9 | 1.9 |
| 2.4 | 1.4 | 1.2 | 1.1 |  |  | | 1.1 | 1.1 |
| .6 | 1.7 | 3.8 | 3.9 |  |  | % Depr., Dep., Amort./Sales | 4.4 | 4.7 |
| (24) 1.2 | (61) 4.7 | (78) 7.5 | 5.2 |  |  | | (174) 8.1 | (191) 8.4 |
| 3.4 | 10.9 | 12.9 | 8.0 |  |  | | 13.6 | 14.5 |
| 7.1 | 7.4 | 3.2 | 1.1 |  |  | % Officers', Directors' Owners' Comp/Sales | 4.3 | 7.1 |
| (12) 15.5 | (20) 10.2 | (17) 14.6 | (14) 18.9 |  |  | | (45) 10.9 | (58) 13.6 |
| 31.1 | 28.7 | 32.9 | 27.7 |  |  | | 25.8 | 23.5 |
| 92630M | 438075M | 1170296M | 1631396M | 538241M | 646812M | Net Sales ($) | 3381016M | 3659940M |
| 11140M | 95812M | 434173M | 838763M | 277496M | 298557M | Total Assets ($) | 1886849M | 2198651M |

M = $ thousand     MM = $ million
See Pages 9 through 22 for Explanation of Ratios and Data

## Comparative Historical Data | | | | Current Data Sorted by Sales

| Hist 1 | Hist 2 | Hist 3 | Type of Statement | 0-1MM | 1-3MM | 3-5MM | 5-10MM | 10-25MM | 25MM & OVER |
|---|---|---|---|---|---|---|---|---|---|
| 18 | 28 | 19 | Unqualified | | 2 | 1 | 2 | 3 | 11 |
| 23 | 21 | 28 | Reviewed | | 2 | 6 | 4 | 10 | 6 |
| 35 | 42 | 32 | Compiled | 1 | 9 | 6 | 8 | 6 | 2 |
| 39 | 50 | 51 | Tax Returns | 12 | 12 | 12 | 9 | 3 | 3 |
| 122 | 127 | 135 | Other | 20 | 29 | 20 | 17 | 26 | 23 |
| 4/1/09-3/31/10 ALL | 4/1/10-3/31/11 ALL | 4/1/11-3/31/12 ALL | | 15 (4/1-9/30/11) | | | 250 (10/1/11-3/31/12) | | |
| 237 | 268 | 265 | NUMBER OF STATEMENTS | 33 | 54 | 45 | 40 | 48 | 45 |
| % | % | % | ASSETS | % | % | % | % | % | % |
| 14.9 | 14.9 | 17.5 | Cash & Equivalents | 15.1 | 17.2 | 15.3 | 23.4 | 19.2 | 14.7 |
| 16.8 | 14.8 | 17.2 | Trade Receivables (net) | 7.1 | 13.2 | 14.1 | 28.7 | 20.4 | 18.6 |
| .6 | .3 | .4 | Inventory | .0 | .2 | .0 | 1.4 | .3 | .5 |
| 3.6 | 4.6 | 2.9 | All Other Current | .7 | .3 | 3.7 | 2.9 | 5.1 | 4.5 |
| 35.8 | 34.7 | 37.9 | Total Current | 23.0 | 30.9 | 33.1 | 56.3 | 45.0 | 38.2 |
| 49.8 | 47.8 | 46.9 | Fixed Assets (net) | 60.8 | 51.0 | 55.7 | 28.4 | 42.7 | 43.7 |
| 7.1 | 7.4 | 7.0 | Intangibles (net) | 2.9 | 8.1 | 6.5 | 9.7 | 4.2 | 10.0 |
| 7.3 | 10.2 | 8.2 | All Other Non-Current | 13.4 | 10.0 | 4.7 | 5.6 | 8.1 | 8.1 |
| 100.0 | 100.0 | 100.0 | Total | 100.0 | 100.0 | 100.0 | 100.0 | 100.0 | 100.0 |
| | | | LIABILITIES | | | | | | |
| 9.9 | 9.2 | 11.0 | Notes Payable-Short Term | 14.5 | 10.4 | 13.9 | 10.8 | 5.9 | 12.1 |
| 12.5 | 13.0 | 13.5 | Cur. Mat.-L.T.D. | 17.2 | 9.9 | 18.5 | 16.8 | 9.5 | 11.4 |
| 7.0 | 4.7 | 6.4 | Trade Payables | 12.6 | 5.8 | 5.6 | 5.8 | 6.4 | 3.9 |
| .3 | .2 | .3 | Income Taxes Payable | .0 | .0 | .0 | .6 | .2 | .9 |
| 11.7 | 12.0 | 13.5 | All Other Current | 12.6 | 7.3 | 7.2 | 11.5 | 24.2 | 18.1 |
| 41.5 | 39.1 | 44.6 | Total Current | 56.9 | 33.4 | 45.1 | 45.5 | 46.1 | 46.3 |
| 36.5 | 37.4 | 34.4 | Long-Term Debt | 38.0 | 47.6 | 37.2 | 30.5 | 25.4 | 26.4 |
| .1 | .1 | .1 | Deferred Taxes | .0 | .0 | .0 | .0 | .0 | .5 |
| 4.7 | 6.8 | 5.3 | All Other Non-Current | .5 | 8.3 | 5.8 | 3.0 | 8.0 | 3.9 |
| 17.2 | 16.6 | 15.5* | Net Worth | 4.5 | 10.7 | 11.9 | 21.0 | 20.5 | 22.9 |
| 100.0 | 100.0 | 100.0 | Total Liabilities & Net Worth | 100.0 | 100.0 | 100.0 | 100.0 | 100.0 | 100.0 |
| | | | INCOME DATA | | | | | | |
| 100.0 | 100.0 | 100.0 | Net Sales | 100.0 | 100.0 | 100.0 | 100.0 | 100.0 | 100.0 |
| | | | Gross Profit | | | | | | |
| 87.6 | 85.3 | 87.5 | Operating Expenses | 88.4 | 84.6 | 86.0 | 91.0 | 88.5 | 87.6 |
| 12.4 | 14.7 | 12.5 | Operating Profit | 11.6 | 15.4 | 14.0 | 9.0 | 11.5 | 12.4 |
| 2.5 | 2.1 | 1.9 | All Other Expenses (net) | 7.0 | 2.9 | 2.7 | .1 | .5 | -.6 |
| 9.9 | 12.6 | 10.6 | Profit Before Taxes | 4.6 | 12.5 | 11.3 | 8.9 | 11.0 | 13.0 |
| | | | RATIOS | | | | | | |
| 1.9 / 1.0 / .4 | 2.4 / 1.1 / .4 | 2.2 / 1.1 / .5 | Current | 1.2 / .6 / .2 | 4.6 / 1.1 / .3 | 2.4 / .9 / .4 | 3.0 / 1.5 / .9 | 2.1 / 1.2 / .7 | 1.6 / 1.1 / .5 |
| 1.8 / .8 / .3 | 2.0 / 1.0 / .3 | 2.1 / 1.0 / .4 | Quick | 1.2 / .5 / .2 | 4.6 / 1.1 / .3 | 2.1 / .9 / .3 | 2.5 / 1.4 / .8 | 1.7 / .9 / .6 | 1.5 / 1.0 / .5 |
| 0 UND / 26 14.0 / 46 7.9 | 0 UND / 24 15.3 / 42 8.8 | 0 UND / 24 15.0 / 46 8.0 | Sales/Receivables | 0 UND / 0 UND / 39 9.4 | 0 UND / 0 UND / 49 7.4 | 0 UND / 18 20.7 / 42 8.6 | 18 20.4 / 41 8.8 / 64 5.7 | 0 UND / 26 13.8 / 40 9.2 | 0 UND / 32 11.4 / 47 7.8 |
| | | | Cost of Sales/Inventory | | | | | | |
| | | | Cost of Sales/Payables | | | | | | |
| 12.2 / -327.6 / -10.6 | 11.1 / 63.1 / -14.5 | 10.2 / 79.3 / -13.5 | Sales/Working Capital | 19.3 / -10.5 / -2.1 | 7.1 / 46.8 / -10.9 | 11.3 / -199.1 / -7.9 | 6.6 / 15.3 / -175.0 | 10.8 / 63.0 / -28.8 | 12.6 / 51.1 / -24.7 |
| 14.7 / (208) 4.6 / 1.2 | 23.4 / (233) 6.4 / 2.0 | 22.7 / (225) 8.2 / 2.1 | EBIT/Interest | 8.5 / (22) 2.2 / -.1 | 13.9 / (42) 6.5 / 1.5 | 14.5 / (41) 7.6 / 3.2 | 34.6 / (33) 9.9 / 2.4 | 48.2 / (44) 11.9 / 2.0 | 29.7 / (43) 9.3 / 4.9 |
| 3.2 / (15) 2.0 / 1.0 | 6.6 / (16) 2.2 / 1.4 | 3.2 / (15) 1.7 / 1.2 | Net Profit + Depr., Dep., Amort./Cur. Mat. L/T/D | | | | | | |
| 1.0 / 2.6 / -6.8 | .8 / 2.1 / -3.9 | .7 / 1.5 / -81.8 | Fixed/Worth | .9 / 3.4 / -5.5 | .6 / 1.9 / -3.1 | .9 / 2.6 / -49.7 | .2 / 1.0 / -3.3 | .6 / 1.2 / 2.4 | 1.0 / 1.5 / 8.1 |
| 1.1 / 3.7 / -8.6 | .8 / 2.9 / -8.8 | .8 / 2.0 / -22.3 | Debt/Worth | 1.6 / 15.1 / -5.9 | .5 / 2.4 / -4.3 | 1.1 / 3.0 / -20.2 | .9 / 1.3 / -7.6 | .8 / 1.4 / 5.0 | 1.3 / 2.6 / 10.0 |
| 115.2 / (166) 53.9 / 15.6 | 129.1 / (188) 56.2 / 18.8 | 104.6 / (192) 48.9 / 11.4 | % Profit Before Taxes/Tangible Net Worth | 63.2 / (20) 12.9 / -5.6 | 113.1 / (39) 51.5 / 7.4 | 79.7 / (31) 53.3 / 24.1 | 81.3 / (29) 33.1 / 6.8 | 139.4 / (38) 49.7 / 12.5 | 134.5 / (35) 77.7 / 12.9 |
| 42.2 / 14.0 / 1.6 | 43.8 / 18.5 / 1.7 | 39.9 / 16.0 / 1.9 | % Profit Before Taxes/Total Assets | 28.6 / 2.5 / -2.8 | 46.1 / 16.4 / 1.6 | 40.6 / 18.1 / 8.8 | 29.5 / 12.5 / 2.3 | 58.7 / 22.4 / .0 | 47.3 / 21.7 / 6.1 |
| 10.8 / 4.6 / 2.3 | 12.0 / 5.2 / 2.7 | 17.9 / 5.1 / 2.8 | Sales/Net Fixed Assets | 5.8 / 2.6 / .9 | 11.5 / 4.8 / 1.8 | 7.7 / 3.7 / 1.9 | 39.7 / 16.3 / 4.0 | 34.4 / 5.5 / 4.0 | 10.1 / 6.6 / 4.4 |
| 3.7 / 2.0 / 1.2 | 3.8 / 2.2 / 1.3 | 4.1 / 2.3 / 1.3 | Sales/Total Assets | 2.6 / 1.3 / .5 | 3.5 / 2.0 / .9 | 3.6 / 1.9 / 1.2 | 4.9 / 2.7 / 1.8 | 4.6 / 2.6 / 1.9 | 4.5 / 2.6 / 1.8 |
| 3.8 / (202) 6.9 / 12.5 | 3.8 / (215) 6.7 / 13.8 | 2.7 / (208) 5.6 / 10.4 | % Depr., Dep., Amort./Sales | 2.0 / (22) 15.6 / 36.8 | 1.9 / (43) 4.7 / 11.7 | 3.4 / (38) 8.6 / 11.1 | (28) 4.9 / 12.1 | 3.3 / (41) 4.8 / 7.8 | 2.9 / (36) 4.6 / 6.6 |
| 5.0 / (56) 13.7 / 23.5 | 4.1 / (67) 9.8 / 22.5 | 6.0 / (64) 14.0 / 30.0 | % Officers', Directors' Owners' Comp/Sales | | 3.4 / (10) 7.6 / 19.9 | | 3.5 / (16) 10.3 / 28.7 | 10.0 / (10) 16.6 / 28.3 | 9.4 / (13) 20.8 / 38.5 |
| 4073446M | 4450823M | 4517450M | Net Sales ($) | 20876M | 102895M | 171605M | 300746M | 778367M | 3142961M |
| 2150317M | 2216101M | 1955941M | Total Assets ($) | 32984M | 98354M | 99600M | 151153M | 295953M | 1277897M |

M = $ thousand    MM = $ million
See Pages 9 through 22 for Explanation of Ratios and Data

## Current Data Sorted by Assets

## Comparative Historical Data

| Type of Statement | 0-500M | 500M-2MM | 2-10MM | 10-50MM | 50-100MM | 100-250MM | | | 4/1/07-3/31/08 ALL | 4/1/08-3/31/09 ALL |
|---|---|---|---|---|---|---|---|---|---|---|
| Unqualified | 3 | 11 | 36 | 62 | 14 | 9 | | | 99 | 123 |
| Reviewed | 1 | 3 | 23 | 10 | | | | | 21 | 31 |
| Compiled | 11 | 22 | 27 | 3 | | 2 | | | 24 | 35 |
| Tax Returns | 66 | 55 | 21 | 4 | | | | | 85 | 85 |
| Other | 51 | 80 | 86 | 43 | 10 | 6 | | | 161 | 182 |
| | 117 (4/1-9/30/11) | | | 542 (10/1/11-3/31/12) | | | | | | |
| NUMBER OF STATEMENTS | 132 | 171 | 193 | 122 | 24 | 17 | | | 390 | 456 |
| **ASSETS** | % | % | % | % | % | % | | | % | % |
| Cash & Equivalents | 30.8 | 20.1 | 17.2 | 24.2 | 18.0 | 9.2 | | | 19.9 | 18.8 |
| Trade Receivables (net) | 22.5 | 37.4 | 41.2 | 25.4 | 19.5 | 15.1 | | | 35.7 | 35.9 |
| Inventory | 1.1 | .9 | 2.7 | 1.0 | .9 | .9 | | | 1.5 | 1.3 |
| All Other Current | 4.1 | 2.3 | 2.6 | 2.2 | 3.9 | 1.6 | | | 4.9 | 4.5 |
| Total Current | 58.5 | 60.7 | 63.8 | 52.9 | 42.2 | 26.9 | | | 61.9 | 60.5 |
| Fixed Assets (net) | 16.0 | 16.9 | 19.1 | 20.7 | 20.5 | 11.0 | | | 19.9 | 21.1 |
| Intangibles (net) | 8.1 | 9.4 | 5.2 | 9.7 | 22.7 | 57.4 | | | 6.5 | 7.4 |
| All Other Non-Current | 17.4 | 13.0 | 11.9 | 16.7 | 14.6 | 4.8 | | | 11.7 | 11.0 |
| Total | 100.0 | 100.0 | 100.0 | 100.0 | 100.0 | 100.0 | | | 100.0 | 100.0 |
| **LIABILITIES** | | | | | | | | | | |
| Notes Payable-Short Term | 21.6 | 10.1 | 6.5 | 3.4 | 1.6 | 1.2 | | | 10.2 | 11.0 |
| Cur. Mat.-L.T.D. | 5.6 | 1.9 | 3.4 | 2.2 | 4.8 | 2.2 | | | 2.8 | 3.7 |
| Trade Payables | 8.4 | 8.7 | 10.4 | 8.6 | 10.7 | 3.3 | | | 7.3 | 8.4 |
| Income Taxes Payable | .4 | .3 | .2 | .3 | .0 | .4 | | | .4 | .4 |
| All Other Current | 33.0 | 17.2 | 15.3 | 14.9 | 13.0 | 8.3 | | | 18.0 | 18.1 |
| Total Current | 69.0 | 38.1 | 35.8 | 29.3 | 30.2 | 15.4 | | | 38.7 | 41.6 |
| Long-Term Debt | 25.6 | 13.2 | 12.1 | 13.4 | 25.2 | 35.6 | | | 15.4 | 15.9 |
| Deferred Taxes | .2 | .1 | .4 | .2 | 2.1 | 3.5 | | | .1 | .2 |
| All Other Non-Current | 17.9 | 7.2 | 5.3 | 5.9 | 3.4 | 5.5 | | | 7.6 | 9.8 |
| Net Worth | -12.8 | 41.3 | 46.4 | 51.2 | 39.1 | 40.0 | | | 38.1 | 32.5 |
| Total Liabilities & Net Worth | 100.0 | 100.0 | 100.0 | 100.0 | 100.0 | 100.0 | | | 100.0 | 100.0 |
| **INCOME DATA** | | | | | | | | | | |
| Net Sales | 100.0 | 100.0 | 100.0 | 100.0 | 100.0 | 100.0 | | | 100.0 | 100.0 |
| Gross Profit | | | | | | | | | | |
| Operating Expenses | 92.7 | 90.4 | 94.8 | 95.0 | 93.1 | 92.3 | | | 93.0 | 93.3 |
| Operating Profit | 7.3 | 9.6 | 5.2 | 5.0 | 6.9 | 7.7 | | | 7.0 | 6.7 |
| All Other Expenses (net) | .8 | 1.9 | 1.4 | .0 | 1.4 | 4.5 | | | .6 | 1.6 |
| Profit Before Taxes | 6.5 | 7.7 | 3.8 | 5.0 | 5.5 | 3.2 | | | 6.4 | 5.1 |
| **RATIOS** | | | | | | | | | | |
| Current | 2.8 | 4.0 | 3.5 | 3.9 | 2.4 | 1.9 | | | 3.5 | 3.5 |
| | 1.1 | 1.7 | 1.8 | 2.0 | 1.6 | 1.6 | | | 1.8 | 1.9 |
| | .4 | .9 | 1.2 | 1.2 | 1.0 | 1.4 | | | 1.1 | 1.1 |
| Quick | 2.4 | 4.0 | 3.3 | 3.5 | 2.1 | 1.8 | | | 3.3 | 3.2 |
| | (131) 1.1 | 1.6 | 1.7 | 1.9 | 1.3 | 1.6 | | | 1.6 | 1.7 |
| | .3 | .8 | 1.0 | 1.1 | .9 | 1.1 | | | .9 | .9 |
| Sales/Receivables | 0 UND | 0 UND | 33 11.2 | 33 10.9 | 33 11.1 | 38 9.7 | | | 21 17.5 | 24 15.5 |
| | 0 UND | 34 10.7 | 47 7.8 | 46 7.9 | 44 8.3 | 47 7.7 | | | 43 8.4 | 44 8.2 |
| | 28 13.0 | 58 6.3 | 65 5.6 | 58 6.3 | 54 6.8 | 62 5.9 | | | 61 6.0 | 64 5.7 |
| Cost of Sales/Inventory | | | | | | | | | | |
| Cost of Sales/Payables | | | | | | | | | | |
| Sales/Working Capital | 19.1 | 7.5 | 5.9 | 3.6 | 5.0 | 8.5 | | | 6.2 | 5.7 |
| | 213.5 | 17.5 | 11.0 | 9.1 | 13.6 | 11.9 | | | 12.7 | 12.6 |
| | -23.6 | -108.2 | 43.2 | 28.3 | 133.1 | 23.7 | | | 104.2 | 89.8 |
| EBIT/Interest | 29.9 | 63.4 | 29.9 | 33.0 | 10.3 | 3.3 | | | 23.7 | 26.6 |
| | (66) 9.7 | (114) 14.3 | (139) 7.9 | (87) 9.1 | (19) 5.2 | (16) 2.1 | | | (289) 7.2 | (331) 7.8 |
| | .8 | 1.8 | 1.3 | 1.1 | 3.0 | .8 | | | 1.8 | 1.3 |
| Net Profit + Depr., Dep., Amort./Cur. Mat. L/T/D | | | 4.6 | 11.0 | | | | | 16.8 | 6.7 |
| | | (20) 1.6 | (10) 5.0 | | | | | | (28) 3.8 | (35) 2.4 |
| | | 1.0 | .8 | | | | | | 1.7 | 1.1 |
| Fixed/Worth | .0 | .1 | .1 | .1 | .5 | NM | | | .1 | .1 |
| | .5 | .3 | .3 | .4 | 1.9 | -.1 | | | .4 | .4 |
| | -.3 | 2.4 | 1.0 | 1.3 | -.2 | -.1 | | | 1.4 | 2.0 |
| Debt/Worth | .5 | .4 | .5 | .3 | .7 | NM | | | .5 | .5 |
| | 14.7 | 1.3 | 1.1 | .8 | 4.5 | -1.6 | | | 1.3 | 1.2 |
| | -2.4 | 10.8 | 3.5 | 4.2 | -3.4 | -1.5 | | | 6.1 | 11.7 |
| % Profit Before Taxes/Tangible Net Worth | 295.3 | 115.1 | 61.4 | 38.3 | 19.9 | | | | 84.3 | 75.5 |
| | (72) 83.7 | (137) 39.4 | (175) 23.1 | (103) 11.1 | (14) 5.8 | | | | (327) 28.5 | (363) 25.4 |
| | 24.6 | 12.8 | 2.6 | 2.1 | 1.8 | | | | 6.6 | 3.2 |
| % Profit Before Taxes/Total Assets | 78.7 | 39.2 | 22.6 | 13.6 | 12.4 | 6.4 | | | 33.3 | 30.5 |
| | 22.4 | 15.6 | 9.2 | 6.3 | 5.6 | 3.3 | | | 11.5 | 9.5 |
| | -1.7 | 2.6 | .2 | .4 | 2.4 | -.6 | | | 2.4 | .5 |
| Sales/Net Fixed Assets | 999.8 | 240.2 | 156.8 | 91.7 | 60.8 | 60.1 | | | 155.6 | 139.6 |
| | 100.8 | 66.4 | 36.4 | 12.3 | 10.9 | 28.3 | | | 37.5 | 35.6 |
| | 36.9 | 18.4 | 8.7 | 3.9 | 3.5 | 8.4 | | | 9.4 | 7.4 |
| Sales/Total Assets | 19.0 | 6.0 | 4.1 | 2.4 | 2.2 | 1.2 | | | 5.0 | 4.7 |
| | 8.7 | 4.1 | 2.9 | 1.6 | 1.3 | .9 | | | 3.2 | 3.0 |
| | 4.5 | 2.5 | 2.0 | 1.1 | .8 | .8 | | | 1.7 | 1.6 |
| % Depr., Dep., Amort./Sales | .2 | .2 | .4 | .8 | .5 | 1.7 | | | .4 | .4 |
| | (59) .5 | (102) .6 | (142) .8 | (97) 1.6 | (18) 1.3 | (10) 1.9 | | | (282) 1.0 | (337) 1.0 |
| | 1.1 | 1.9 | 2.0 | 2.8 | 2.3 | 2.4 | | | 2.2 | 2.2 |
| % Officers', Directors' Owners' Comp/Sales | 4.2 | 2.3 | 2.4 | 1.8 | | | | | 3.1 | 2.3 |
| | (64) 7.3 | (60) 4.0 | (54) 4.1 | (13) 3.9 | | | | | (100) 5.2 | (108) 5.7 |
| | 11.7 | 7.7 | 9.9 | 17.7 | | | | | 8.9 | 10.2 |
| Net Sales ($) | 304336M | 793198M | 2708935M | 5196322M | 3049269M | 2988085M | | | 8583959M | 12201616M |
| Total Assets ($) | 30071M | 184917M | 871106M | 2800936M | 1769350M | 2889359M | | | 4186073M | 6648118M |

M = $ thousand　　MM = $ million
See Pages 9 through 22 for Explanation of Ratios and Data

## Comparative Historical Data | Current Data Sorted by Sales

| | | | Type of Statement | | | | | | |
|---|---|---|---|---|---|---|---|---|---|
| 128 | 147 | 135 | Unqualified | 3 | 6 | 5 | 16 | 33 | 72 |
| 36 | 28 | 37 | Reviewed | 1 | 1 | 5 | 6 | 12 | 12 |
| 40 | 58 | 65 | Compiled | 3 | 14 | 8 | 15 | 18 | 7 |
| 83 | 107 | 146 | Tax Returns | 32 | 39 | 25 | 32 | 13 | 5 |
| 216 | 256 | 276 | Other | 22 | 43 | 39 | 61 | 53 | 58 |
| 4/1/09-3/31/10 ALL | 4/1/10-3/31/11 ALL | 4/1/11-3/31/12 ALL | | 117 (4/1-9/30/11) | | | 542 (10/1/11-3/31/12) | | |
| | | | | 0-1MM | 1-3MM | 3-5MM | 5-10MM | 10-25MM | 25MM & OVER |
| 503 | 596 | 659 | NUMBER OF STATEMENTS | 61 | 103 | 82 | 130 | 129 | 154 |
| % | % | % | ASSETS | % | % | % | % | % | % |
| 21.5 | 20.8 | 21.8 | Cash & Equivalents | 22.2 | 21.7 | 18.3 | 25.1 | 20.8 | 21.6 |
| 34.0 | 29.2 | 32.1 | Trade Receivables (net) | 20.0 | 26.8 | 36.8 | 35.2 | 37.5 | 30.9 |
| 1.1 | 1.7 | 1.5 | Inventory | 1.0 | 1.0 | 2.0 | 2.0 | 1.8 | 1.1 |
| 3.4 | 3.9 | 2.8 | All Other Current | 4.2 | 3.4 | 2.1 | 1.8 | 3.1 | 2.7 |
| 60.0 | 55.6 | 58.2 | Total Current | 47.5 | 52.9 | 59.1 | 64.1 | 63.2 | 56.2 |
| 18.9 | 21.5 | 18.0 | Fixed Assets (net) | 32.0 | 15.9 | 15.4 | 18.9 | 17.5 | 15.0 |
| 9.1 | 10.6 | 9.7 | Intangibles (net) | 8.1 | 11.1 | 10.2 | 5.2 | 5.5 | 16.4 |
| 12.0 | 12.4 | 14.1 | All Other Non-Current | 12.4 | 20.1 | 15.3 | 11.8 | 13.8 | 12.3 |
| 100.0 | 100.0 | 100.0 | Total | 100.0 | 100.0 | 100.0 | 100.0 | 100.0 | 100.0 |
| | | | LIABILITIES | | | | | | |
| 10.0 | 10.4 | 9.6 | Notes Payable-Short Term | 18.4 | 14.3 | 12.9 | 9.9 | 6.5 | 3.4 |
| 2.9 | 4.5 | 3.2 | Cur. Mat.-L.T.D. | 4.9 | 4.0 | 2.3 | 3.8 | 2.4 | 2.7 |
| 8.6 | 8.4 | 9.1 | Trade Payables | 5.2 | 7.1 | 12.3 | 8.1 | 9.9 | 10.2 |
| .3 | .2 | .3 | Income Taxes Payable | .1 | .1 | .1 | .6 | .4 | .1 |
| 21.2 | 18.0 | 19.0 | All Other Current | 29.7 | 20.5 | 20.8 | 17.7 | 15.3 | 17.1 |
| 43.0 | 41.4 | 41.1 | Total Current | 58.4 | 46.0 | 48.3 | 40.1 | 34.6 | 33.6 |
| 13.7 | 16.1 | 16.4 | Long-Term Debt | 28.8 | 25.7 | 15.1 | 11.3 | 8.5 | 17.0 |
| .7 | .3 | .4 | Deferred Taxes | .0 | .0 | .4 | .5 | .2 | .9 |
| 6.6 | 8.2 | 8.4 | All Other Non-Current | 15.1 | 17.2 | 12.4 | 2.9 | 4.8 | 5.3 |
| 36.0 | 34.0 | 33.7 | Net Worth | -2.4 | 11.1 | 23.8 | 45.2 | 51.9 | 43.3 |
| 100.0 | 100.0 | 100.0 | Total Liabilities & Net Worth | 100.0 | 100.0 | 100.0 | 100.0 | 100.0 | 100.0 |
| | | | INCOME DATA | | | | | | |
| 100.0 | 100.0 | 100.0 | Net Sales | 100.0 | 100.0 | 100.0 | 100.0 | 100.0 | 100.0 |
| | | | Gross Profit | | | | | | |
| 93.2 | 91.8 | 93.2 | Operating Expenses | 81.2 | 93.8 | 93.4 | 94.7 | 95.0 | 94.5 |
| 6.8 | 8.2 | 6.8 | Operating Profit | 18.8 | 6.2 | 6.6 | 5.3 | 5.0 | 5.5 |
| 1.0 | 1.2 | 1.2 | All Other Expenses (net) | 7.8 | .8 | .1 | .3 | .6 | .8 |
| 5.8 | 7.1 | 5.6 | Profit Before Taxes | 11.0 | 5.5 | 6.4 | 5.1 | 4.4 | 4.7 |
| | | | RATIOS | | | | | | |
| 3.3 | 3.1 | 3.5 | | 3.1 | 4.5 | 2.8 | 3.8 | 4.0 | 3.0 |
| 1.8 | 1.7 | 1.7 | Current | 1.0 | 1.6 | 1.5 | 1.8 | 2.1 | 1.8 |
| 1.0 | 1.0 | 1.0 | | .3 | .5 | .7 | 1.1 | 1.3 | 1.1 |
| 3.1 | 2.8 | 3.3 | | 2.9 | 3.9 | 2.8 | 3.7 | 3.5 | 2.7 |
| 1.6 | 1.5 (658) | 1.6 | Quick | (60) .9 | 1.6 | 1.3 | 1.6 | 1.8 | 1.6 |
| .8 | .8 | .9 | | .2 | .3 | .7 | 1.0 | 1.1 | 1.0 |
| 19 18.9 | 10 35.0 | 12 30.2 | | 0 UND | 0 UND | 3 107.6 | 1 609.3 | 31 11.8 | 34 10.8 |
| 38 9.5 | 37 9.8 | 38 9.7 | Sales/Receivables | 0 UND | 18 20.2 | 34 10.8 | 37 9.8 | 46 8.0 | 47 7.8 |
| 56 6.5 | 55 6.6 | 56 6.5 | | 36 10.1 | 48 7.6 | 61 6.0 | 51 7.1 | 62 5.9 | 59 6.2 |
| | | | Cost of Sales/Inventory | | | | | | |
| | | | Cost of Sales/Payables | | | | | | |
| 6.3 | 6.2 | 6.7 | | 11.0 | 7.8 | 8.2 | 7.6 | 4.9 | 5.2 |
| 15.4 | 15.4 | 15.8 | Sales/Working Capital | UND | 29.9 | 27.5 | 19.2 | 9.6 | 11.8 |
| -999.8 | -936.2 | -385.1 | | -5.2 | -31.8 | -33.5 | 219.1 | 38.7 | 37.5 |
| 26.7 | 37.4 | 32.1 | | 17.3 | 36.5 | 41.4 | 83.4 | 42.8 | 25.7 |
| (362) 7.1 | (443) 9.6 | (441) 8.3 | EBIT/Interest | (23) 3.3 | (62) 8.8 | (58) 10.1 | (91) 9.2 | (94) 9.2 | (113) 5.9 |
| 1.7 | 2.9 | 1.4 | | .4 | 1.0 | 1.7 | 1.3 | 1.7 | 1.7 |
| 23.0 | 12.5 | 5.5 | | | | | 2.3 | 5.9 | 5.5 |
| (39) 3.7 | (41) 3.0 | (53) 1.7 | Net Profit + Depr., Dep., Amort./Cur. Mat. L/T/D | | | (11) 2.0 | (12) 1.5 | (25) 1.4 | |
| 1.8 | 1.6 | .8 | | | | | .9 | 1.0 | .1 |
| .1 | .1 | .1 | | .0 | .0 | .1 | .1 | .1 | .1 |
| .4 | .5 | .4 | Fixed/Worth | 2.8 | .4 | .5 | .3 | .2 | .5 |
| 2.7 | 4.5 | 3.6 | | -.7 | -1.6 | -2.8 | 1.2 | .8 | -18.1 |
| .4 | .5 | .4 | | .7 | .3 | .5 | .3 | .3 | .5 |
| 1.4 | 1.5 | 1.3 | Debt/Worth | 3.8 | 2.5 | 2.9 | 1.1 | .8 | 1.4 |
| 12.8 | 21.3 | 81.0 | | -4.0 | -2.9 | -9.3 | 5.3 | 2.6 | -82.4 |
| 91.7 | 94.9 | 73.4 | | 162.9 | 137.8 | 137.4 | 81.5 | 53.0 | 46.3 |
| (398) 29.7 | (461) 34.3 | (505) 27.5 | % Profit Before Taxes/Tangible Net Worth | (36) 37.6 | (68) 49.6 | (56) 45.0 | (113) 30.3 | (119) 20.0 | (113) 17.2 |
| 5.9 | 8.8 | 5.5 | | 11.1 | 7.9 | 6.2 | 8.8 | 3.3 | 3.6 |
| 33.6 | 35.3 | 29.4 | | 38.0 | 56.4 | 48.3 | 35.4 | 20.2 | 15.8 |
| 11.4 | 12.4 | 9.8 | % Profit Before Taxes/Total Assets | 5.8 | 19.0 | 17.7 | 12.0 | 9.0 | 6.9 |
| 2.2 | 3.5 | .6 | | -2.6 | .0 | 1.0 | 2.4 | 1.4 | .6 |
| 159.4 | 135.9 | 194.4 | | 249.0 | 431.0 | 400.3 | 198.1 | 176.5 | 130.2 |
| 44.3 | 31.7 | 48.1 | Sales/Net Fixed Assets | 34.7 | 60.0 | 63.7 | 62.8 | 41.5 | 34.2 |
| 11.2 | 7.2 | 10.7 | | 2.5 | 17.7 | 15.9 | 15.7 | 6.8 | 7.4 |
| 5.5 | 5.0 | 5.5 | | 6.7 | 9.5 | 6.8 | 6.8 | 5.0 | 3.4 |
| 3.2 | 2.9 | 3.1 | Sales/Total Assets | 2.2 | 3.8 | 4.3 | 4.1 | 2.8 | 2.0 |
| 1.7 | 1.5 | 1.6 | | .8 | 2.0 | 2.4 | 2.7 | 1.4 | 1.2 |
| .4 | .5 | .3 | | .4 | .3 | .3 | .2 | .5 | .5 |
| (350) 1.0 | (402) 1.2 | (428) .9 | % Depr., Dep., Amort./Sales | (35) 1.3 | (50) .9 | (52) .7 | (85) .7 | (94) 1.0 | (112) 1.4 |
| 2.2 | 2.4 | 2.2 | | 15.3 | 2.2 | 1.6 | 1.5 | 2.2 | 2.1 |
| 2.3 | 2.6 | 2.7 | | 7.7 | 4.0 | 2.3 | 2.8 | 2.4 | .9 |
| (125) 5.0 | (155) 4.8 | (192) 5.2 | % Officers', Directors' Owners' Comp/Sales | (18) 11.4 | (44) 6.7 | (38) 4.2 | (42) 4.9 | (33) 3.9 | (17) 2.3 |
| 10.2 | 8.8 | 10.3 | | 19.0 | 11.6 | 7.4 | 8.0 | 5.9 | 14.2 |
| 12583706M | 16392439M | 15040145M | Net Sales ($) | 29823M | 197055M | 319927M | 920189M | 1947173M | 11625978M |
| 6372925M | 8834946M | 8545739M | Total Assets ($) | 32316M | 84216M | 114070M | 274539M | 984667M | 7055931M |

© RMA 2012

M = $ thousand    MM = $ million
See Pages 9 through 22 for Explanation of Ratios and Data

## Current Data Sorted by Assets | Comparative Historical Data

| Type of Statement | 0-500M | 500M-2MM | 2-10MM | 10-50MM | 50-100MM | 100-250MM | | 4/1/07-3/31/08 ALL | 4/1/08-3/31/09 ALL |
|---|---|---|---|---|---|---|---|---|---|
| Unqualified | | | 7 | 12 | | 2 | | 14 | 21 |
| Reviewed | | | 10 | 3 | | | | 9 | 17 |
| Compiled | 3 | 8 | 9 | 1 | 1 | | | 10 | 11 |
| Tax Returns | 9 | 9 | 7 | | | 1 | | 9 | 12 |
| Other | 5 | 17 | 20 | 11 | 5 | | | 30 | 35 |
| | | 32 (4/1-9/30/11) | | 108 (10/1/11-3/31/12) | | | | | |
| NUMBER OF STATEMENTS | 17 | 34 | 53 | 27 | 6 | 3 | | 72 | 96 |
| **ASSETS** | % | % | % | % | % | % | | % | % |
| Cash & Equivalents | 25.6 | 23.0 | 13.1 | 10.4 | | | | 18.7 | 15.6 |
| Trade Receivables (net) | 18.8 | 18.6 | 29.2 | 32.5 | | | | 29.3 | 31.7 |
| Inventory | 3.2 | .4 | .9 | 2.2 | | | | 1.0 | 1.3 |
| All Other Current | 1.1 | 3.1 | 1.8 | 4.2 | | | | 3.3 | 2.3 |
| Total Current | 48.8 | 45.1 | 45.1 | 49.4 | | | | 52.3 | 50.9 |
| Fixed Assets (net) | 39.5 | 37.0 | 46.2 | 39.9 | | | | 35.9 | 36.6 |
| Intangibles (net) | 1.4 | 7.1 | 2.8 | 4.3 | | | | 4.5 | 3.4 |
| All Other Non-Current | 10.0 | 10.8 | 5.9 | 6.4 | | | | 7.4 | 9.1 |
| Total | 100.0 | 100.0 | 100.0 | 100.0 | | | | 100.0 | 100.0 |
| **LIABILITIES** | | | | | | | | | |
| Notes Payable-Short Term | 20.6 | 14.4 | 6.7 | 5.2 | | | | 8.7 | 10.7 |
| Cur. Mat.-L.T.D. | 9.2 | 5.0 | 5.1 | 5.0 | | | | 5.7 | 8.2 |
| Trade Payables | 16.6 | 7.1 | 3.4 | 4.6 | | | | 4.3 | 5.8 |
| Income Taxes Payable | .0 | .0 | .1 | 1.5 | | | | .4 | .2 |
| All Other Current | 4.6 | 9.6 | 8.3 | 8.7 | | | | 7.1 | 13.8 |
| Total Current | 51.0 | 36.0 | 23.7 | 25.0 | | | | 26.2 | 38.7 |
| Long-Term Debt | 27.2 | 28.4 | 23.9 | 27.0 | | | | 29.0 | 22.7 |
| Deferred Taxes | .0 | .0 | .5 | .8 | | | | .0 | .4 |
| All Other Non-Current | 4.7 | 8.4 | 8.5 | 3.9 | | | | 5.1 | 3.9 |
| Net Worth | 16.8 | 27.1 | 43.4 | 43.3 | | | | 39.7 | 34.3 |
| Total Liabilties & Net Worth | 100.0 | 100.0 | 100.0 | 100.0 | | | | 100.0 | 100.0 |
| **INCOME DATA** | | | | | | | | | |
| Net Sales | 100.0 | 100.0 | 100.0 | 100.0 | | | | 100.0 | 100.0 |
| Gross Profit | | | | | | | | | |
| Operating Expenses | 89.4 | 91.5 | 88.6 | 93.9 | | | | 91.7 | 94.0 |
| Operating Profit | 10.6 | 8.5 | 11.4 | 6.1 | | | | 8.3 | 6.0 |
| All Other Expenses (net) | .3 | 1.7 | 3.1 | .5 | | | | 2.2 | 1.4 |
| Profit Before Taxes | 10.3 | 6.8 | 8.3 | 5.5 | | | | 6.1 | 4.6 |
| **RATIOS** | | | | | | | | | |
| Current | 7.6 | 3.6 | 4.8 | 3.0 | | | | 3.8 | 3.4 |
| | 1.5 | 1.7 | 2.0 | 2.2 | | | | 2.2 | 1.6 |
| | .2 | .5 | 1.2 | 1.5 | | | | 1.4 | .9 |
| Quick | 7.6 | 3.6 | 4.6 | 2.9 | | | | 3.4 | 3.3 |
| | 1.5 | 1.4 | 2.0 | 1.8 | | | | 2.1 | 1.5 |
| | .2 | .5 | 1.0 | 1.2 | | | | 1.3 | .7 |
| Sales/Receivables | 0 UND | 0 UND | 24 15.0 | 42 8.7 | | | | 21 17.1 | 26 14.0 |
| | 0 UND | 0 UND | 49 7.4 | 79 4.6 | | | | 51 7.2 | 50 7.3 |
| | 53 6.9 | 62 5.9 | 78 4.7 | 107 3.4 | | | | 78 4.7 | 81 4.5 |
| Cost of Sales/Inventory | | | | | | | | | |
| Cost of Sales/Payables | | | | | | | | | |
| Sales/Working Capital | 5.9 | 6.8 | 3.7 | 2.7 | | | | 3.9 | 5.4 |
| | 37.3 | 19.7 | 10.6 | 7.4 | | | | 8.4 | 11.8 |
| | -107.7 | -30.5 | 32.5 | 12.2 | | | | 32.1 | -46.5 |
| EBIT/Interest | 21.7 | | 13.3 | 7.2 | | | | 14.1 | 13.9 |
| | | (29) 9.5 | (46) 3.3 | (24) 3.4 | | | | (63) 5.5 | (84) 3.6 |
| | | 3.0 | -.1 | 2.3 | | | | 1.2 | 1.2 |
| Net Profit + Depr., Dep., Amort./Cur. Mat. L/T/D | | | | 2.3 | | | | 5.0 | 4.4 |
| | | | | (11) 1.3 | | | | (11) 2.5 | (16) 2.8 |
| | | | | .5 | | | | 1.8 | 2.0 |
| Fixed/Worth | .4 | .4 | .6 | .5 | | | | .4 | .4 |
| | 1.3 | 1.0 | 1.2 | 1.0 | | | | .8 | 1.0 |
| | 24.8 | 3.5 | 2.0 | 6.7 | | | | 2.7 | 2.5 |
| Debt/Worth | .4 | .8 | .5 | .5 | | | | .5 | .6 |
| | 1.7 | 2.1 | 1.2 | 1.4 | | | | 1.2 | 1.4 |
| | 92.1 | 4.3 | 3.3 | 12.9 | | | | 4.2 | 5.7 |
| % Profit Before Taxes/Tangible Net Worth | 566.9 | 112.2 | 39.8 | 37.2 | | | | 50.3 | 58.3 |
| | (14) 57.6 | (28) 36.8 | (49) 16.7 | (23) 12.8 | | | | (61) 26.8 | (79) 21.9 |
| | 28.9 | 9.2 | -2.8 | 4.9 | | | | 7.7 | 4.3 |
| % Profit Before Taxes/Total Assets | 100.6 | 33.1 | 19.2 | 8.2 | | | | 22.2 | 16.4 |
| | 29.2 | 13.9 | 6.4 | 4.2 | | | | 9.9 | 8.8 |
| | -6.4 | 2.6 | -.9 | 1.2 | | | | 1.1 | .8 |
| Sales/Net Fixed Assets | 111.7 | 39.6 | 8.2 | 6.6 | | | | 14.8 | 16.7 |
| | 27.1 | 12.5 | 5.5 | 3.8 | | | | 6.8 | 7.2 |
| | 8.6 | 3.9 | 1.5 | 1.9 | | | | 3.7 | 4.0 |
| Sales/Total Assets | 19.1 | 5.6 | 2.8 | 2.0 | | | | 2.9 | 4.0 |
| | 6.9 | 3.2 | 1.8 | 1.6 | | | | 2.0 | 2.4 |
| | 2.4 | 1.6 | 1.0 | 1.0 | | | | 1.4 | 1.3 |
| % Depr., Dep., Amort./Sales | .8 | 1.3 | 2.7 | 2.6 | | | | 2.4 | 2.9 |
| | (10) 3.1 | (20) 2.9 | (46) 4.8 | (26) 4.6 | | | | (62) 4.2 | (78) 4.1 |
| | 5.1 | 5.0 | 6.8 | 7.2 | | | | 6.6 | 6.2 |
| % Officers', Directors' Owners' Comp/Sales | | 3.8 | 1.8 | | | | | 1.8 | 2.6 |
| | | (12) 5.6 | (16) 3.6 | | | | | (21) 2.8 | (23) 4.7 |
| | | 13.9 | 6.1 | | | | | 6.9 | 7.2 |
| Net Sales ($) | 40207M | 140702M | 468716M | 800583M | 457096M | 762654M | | 998848M | 1809580M |
| Total Assets ($) | 4007M | 40444M | 245931M | 626896M | 398781M | 580134M | | 660008M | 992716M |

M = $ thousand   MM = $ million
See Pages 9 through 22 for Explanation of Ratios and Data

## Comparative Historical Data | Current Data Sorted by Sales

| | | | Type of Statement | 0-1MM | 1-3MM | 3-5MM | 5-10MM | 10-25MM | 25MM & OVER |
|---|---|---|---|---|---|---|---|---|---|
| 20 | 27 | 21 | Unqualified | 1 | | | 6 | 2 | 12 |
| 11 | 14 | 13 | Reviewed | | | | 4 | 7 | 2 |
| 13 | 16 | 22 | Compiled | 4 | | 5 | 7 | 5 | 1 |
| 24 | 25 | 25 | Tax Returns | 3 | 5 | 7 | 6 | 4 | |
| 41 | 47 | 59 | Other | 9 | 13 | 8 | 9 | 6 | 14 |
| 4/1/09-3/31/10 ALL | 4/1/10-3/31/11 ALL | 4/1/11-3/31/12 ALL | | 32 (4/1-9/30/11) | | | 108 (10/1/11-3/31/12) | | |
| 109 | 129 | 140 | NUMBER OF STATEMENTS | 17 | 18 | 20 | 32 | 24 | 29 |
| % | % | % | ASSETS | % | % | % | % | % | % |
| 16.1 | 18.0 | 16.0 | Cash & Equivalents | 12.4 | 20.2 | 12.2 | 23.7 | 16.8 | 9.1 |
| 26.3 | 23.9 | 25.6 | Trade Receivables (net) | 15.2 | 22.4 | 16.7 | 21.0 | 38.1 | 34.7 |
| .8 | 1.0 | 1.4 | Inventory | .6 | 2.5 | 2.1 | .2 | .6 | 2.5 |
| 5.3 | 3.6 | 2.6 | All Other Current | .7 | 3.4 | 4.2 | 3.1 | 1.2 | 2.6 |
| 48.5 | 46.5 | 45.6 | Total Current | 28.9 | 48.4 | 35.1 | 48.0 | 56.7 | 48.9 |
| 37.9 | 39.2 | 41.5 | Fixed Assets (net) | 67.7 | 34.1 | 38.6 | 40.8 | 34.1 | 39.8 |
| .6 | 3.4 | 4.2 | Intangibles (net) | .1 | 2.0 | 8.6 | 6.2 | 4.5 | 2.7 |
| 6.8 | 10.9 | 8.6 | All Other Non-Current | 2.9 | 15.5 | 17.7 | 5.0 | 4.7 | 8.6 |
| 100.0 | 100.0 | 100.0 | Total | 100.0 | 100.0 | 100.0 | 100.0 | 100.0 | 100.0 |
| | | | LIABILITIES | | | | | | |
| 9.6 | 6.2 | 10.1 | Notes Payable-Short Term | 3.0 | 16.5 | 16.7 | 7.5 | 11.5 | 7.3 |
| 5.8 | 5.8 | 5.5 | Cur. Mat.-L.T.D. | 2.0 | 1.2 | 9.1 | 7.4 | 6.2 | 5.0 |
| 4.5 | 7.1 | 6.2 | Trade Payables | 2.5 | 24.5 | 2.0 | 2.1 | 5.2 | 5.5 |
| .5 | .4 | .3 | Income Taxes Payable | .0 | .0 | .0 | .2 | .0 | 1.4 |
| 11.3 | 10.6 | 9.8 | All Other Current | 1.4 | 19.1 | 8.4 | 8.5 | 10.0 | 11.1 |
| 31.5 | 30.1 | 31.9 | Total Current | 8.9 | 61.2 | 36.2 | 25.6 | 33.0 | 30.2 |
| 28.3 | 21.5 | 25.7 | Long-Term Debt | 36.6 | 15.5 | 29.4 | 29.2 | 21.8 | 22.5 |
| .6 | .6 | .4 | Deferred Taxes | .0 | .0 | .1 | .4 | 1.0 | .5 |
| 4.3 | 3.3 | 7.0 | All Other Non-Current | 7.5 | 4.9 | 18.2 | 6.9 | 1.0 | 5.4 |
| 35.3 | 44.5 | 35.0 | Net Worth | 46.8 | 18.3 | 16.2 | 37.9 | 43.3 | 41.4 |
| 100.0 | 100.0 | 100.0 | Total Liabilities & Net Worth | 100.0 | 100.0 | 100.0 | 100.0 | 100.0 | 100.0 |
| | | | INCOME DATA | | | | | | |
| 100.0 | 100.0 | 100.0 | Net Sales | 100.0 | 100.0 | 100.0 | 100.0 | 100.0 | 100.0 |
| | | | Gross Profit | | | | | | |
| 91.2 | 91.6 | 90.2 | Operating Expenses | 69.7 | 90.3 | 90.0 | 94.8 | 94.6 | 93.8 |
| 8.8 | 8.4 | 9.8 | Operating Profit | 30.3 | 9.7 | 10.0 | 5.2 | 5.4 | 6.2 |
| 1.6 | 1.7 | 1.8 | All Other Expenses (net) | 10.1 | .1 | 1.4 | .3 | .9 | .8 |
| 7.3 | 6.7 | 7.9 | Profit Before Taxes | 20.2 | 9.6 | 8.6 | 4.8 | 4.5 | 5.4 |
| | | | RATIOS | | | | | | |
| 3.8 | 3.7 | 4.3 | | 13.1 | 3.2 | 4.7 | 5.2 | 3.4 | 2.9 |
| 1.7 | 1.8 | 1.9 | Current | 4.7 | 1.3 | 2.1 | 1.9 | 2.0 | 1.7 |
| .9 | 1.0 | 1.0 | | .8 | .2 | .4 | 1.3 | 1.2 | 1.2 |
| 3.3 | 3.4 | 3.7 | | 11.7 | 2.7 | 4.2 | 4.6 | 3.0 | 2.5 |
| 1.4 | 1.5 | 1.7 | Quick | 4.7 | 1.1 | 1.2 | 1.8 | 1.9 | 1.6 |
| .8 | .8 | .8 | | .3 | .2 | .2 | 1.3 | 1.2 | .8 |
| 0 UND | 0 UND | 0 UND | | 0 UND | 0 UND | 0 UND | 0 UND | 27 13.3 | 42 8.6 |
| 41 8.9 | 43 8.5 | 46 7.9 | Sales/Receivables | 24 15.0 | 12 31.0 | 0 UND | 35 10.3 | 56 6.5 | 72 5.1 |
| 66 5.5 | 69 5.3 | 81 4.5 | | 91 4.0 | 94 3.9 | 59 6.2 | 69 5.3 | 83 4.4 | 91 4.0 |
| | | | Cost of Sales/Inventory | | | | | | |
| | | | Cost of Sales/Payables | | | | | | |
| 5.8 | 4.7 | 4.0 | | 1.7 | 3.6 | 4.2 | 3.7 | 7.3 | 4.5 |
| 16.0 | 14.5 | 10.9 | Sales/Working Capital | 4.9 | 14.2 | 32.1 | 12.9 | 11.1 | 8.1 |
| -65.7 | 629.4 | 271.8 | | NM | -109.0 | -17.4 | -59.4 | 37.2 | 28.0 |
| 17.0 | 15.5 | 15.8 | | | 19.6 | 35.9 | 12.5 | 12.0 | 16.0 |
| (93) 5.6 | (103) 5.6 | (115) 4.7 | EBIT/Interest | | (10) 11.9 | (19) 6.1 | (28) 5.3 | (23) 3.8 | (26) 3.4 |
| 2.9 | 1.7 | 1.4 | | | 3.2 | .1 | .4 | 1.1 | 1.9 |
| 4.7 | 2.6 | 2.8 | | | | | | | 2.3 |
| (24) 2.8 | (25) 1.6 | (21) 1.6 | Net Profit + Depr., Dep., Amort./Cur. Mat. L/T/D | | | | | (12) | 1.5 |
| 1.9 | 1.1 | 1.2 | | | | | | | 1.0 |
| .5 | .5 | .5 | | .9 | .2 | .7 | .4 | .5 | .6 |
| 1.1 | 1.0 | 1.2 | Fixed/Worth | 1.7 | 1.0 | 1.4 | .9 | 1.1 | 1.0 |
| 5.1 | 2.9 | 3.3 | | 2.9 | 5.3 | -7.1 | 4.3 | 1.6 | 4.9 |
| .4 | .3 | .5 | | .4 | .5 | .5 | .6 | .7 | .5 |
| 1.9 | 1.2 | 1.6 | Debt/Worth | 1.3 | 1.6 | 4.0 | 1.4 | 1.6 | 1.4 |
| 7.7 | 4.6 | 5.2 | | 2.3 | 14.0 | -25.1 | 4.4 | 3.0 | 9.3 |
| 68.6 | 48.2 | 60.7 | | 36.2 | 71.4 | 166.2 | 55.6 | 39.0 | 54.8 |
| (87) 33.8 | (114) 19.4 | (121) 24.6 | % Profit Before Taxes/Tangible Net Worth | 10.8 | (15) 47.3 | (14) 45.3 | (27) 28.7 | (23) 26.9 | (25) 12.8 |
| 9.4 | 3.6 | 3.5 | | 2.2 | 2.8 | -2.2 | 1.5 | 4.5 | 4.3 |
| 27.0 | 19.5 | 22.0 | | 15.3 | 36.9 | 54.3 | 21.7 | 21.9 | 10.6 |
| 11.5 | 7.8 | 7.7 | % Profit Before Taxes/Total Assets | 6.2 | 9.2 | 17.8 | 12.2 | 7.9 | 4.5 |
| 3.2 | .5 | .9 | | 1.2 | -1.0 | -2.3 | -1.1 | 1.3 | .7 |
| 13.8 | 15.0 | 13.3 | | 2.3 | 38.9 | 23.4 | 22.9 | 19.7 | 6.6 |
| 7.3 | 6.3 | 5.9 | Sales/Net Fixed Assets | .5 | 11.2 | 9.5 | 6.0 | 6.9 | 4.3 |
| 4.3 | 3.1 | 2.2 | | .2 | 3.2 | 3.6 | 2.9 | 5.0 | 2.8 |
| 3.5 | 3.6 | 3.1 | | 1.1 | 5.3 | 6.2 | 5.1 | 3.1 | 1.9 |
| 2.2 | 2.1 | 1.9 | Sales/Total Assets | .3 | 1.9 | 2.1 | 2.5 | 2.7 | 1.8 |
| 1.6 | 1.1 | 1.0 | | .2 | 1.2 | 1.4 | 1.4 | 1.7 | 1.1 |
| 2.1 | 2.6 | 2.4 | | 3.7 | 1.0 | 2.3 | 3.8 | 2.0 | 2.2 |
| (90) 3.5 | (108) 4.3 | (108) 3.9 | % Depr., Dep., Amort./Sales | (11) 10.3 | (10) 2.8 | (13) 2.6 | (26) 5.4 | (22) 4.6 | (26) 3.5 |
| 5.6 | 6.5 | 6.2 | | 15.4 | 5.1 | 4.2 | 6.8 | 6.1 | 4.8 |
| 1.9 | 2.1 | 2.8 | | | | | 3.6 | | |
| (33) 4.0 | (29) 3.4 | (40) 4.7 | % Officers', Directors' Owners' Comp/Sales | | | | (10) 4.1 | | |
| 7.8 | 5.1 | 7.5 | | | | | 5.2 | | |
| 7892524M | 2478212M | 2669958M | Net Sales ($) | 7475M | 34979M | 81867M | 223485M | 363238M | 1958914M |
| 2343736M | 1452786M | 1896193M | Total Assets ($) | 27188M | 205336M | 58698M | 137778M | 186199M | 1280994M |

© RMA 2012

M = $ thousand     MM = $ million
See Pages 9 through 22 for Explanation of Ratios and Data

**Current Data Sorted by Assets**       **Comparative Historical Data**

| 0-500M | 500M-2MM | 2-10MM | 10-50MM | 50-100MM | 100-250MM | Type of Statement | 4/1/07-3/31/08 ALL | 4/1/08-3/31/09 ALL |
|---|---|---|---|---|---|---|---|---|
| | 1 | 9 | 24 | 5 | 2 | Unqualified | 22 | 31 |
| | 1 | | | | | Reviewed | | 1 |
| | 1 | | | | | Compiled | 1 | 1 |
| | 1 | | | | | Tax Returns | / | 3 |
| | 2 | 2 | 6 | 1 | 3 | Other | 16 | 13 |
| | 2 | 31 (4/1-9/30/11) | 27 (10/1/11-3/31/12) | 1 | 3 | | 16<br>4/1/07-3/31/08 ALL | 13<br>4/1/08-3/31/09 ALL |
| | 3 | 14 | 30 | 6 | 5 | **NUMBER OF STATEMENTS** | 39 | 49 |
| % | % | % | % | % | % | **ASSETS** | % | % |
| | | 18.3 | 20.0 | | | Cash & Equivalents | 19.4 | 18.1 |
| | | 28.6 | 17.7 | | | Trade Receivables (net) | 23.6 | 17.3 |
| | | 8.0 | 4.1 | | | Inventory | 6.3 | 7.8 |
| | | 1.7 | 5.3 | | | All Other Current | 3.0 | 2.6 |
| | | 56.6 | 47.1 | | | Total Current | 52.3 | 45.9 |
| | | 31.3 | 38.1 | | | Fixed Assets (net) | 35.2 | 36.4 |
| | | 5.6 | .3 | | | Intangibles (net) | .5 | 2.5 |
| | | 6.5 | 14.4 | | | All Other Non-Current | 12.2 | 15.2 |
| | | 100.0 | 100.0 | | | Total | 100.0 | 100.0 |
| | | | | | | **LIABILITIES** | | |
| | | 2.1 | 1.6 | | | Notes Payable-Short Term | 5.5 | 1.5 |
| | | 2.5 | 1.9 | | | Cur. Mat.-L.T.D. | 1.6 | 1.8 |
| | | 21.4 | 9.4 | | | Trade Payables | 12.3 | 8.5 |
| | | .0 | .0 | | | Income Taxes Payable | .1 | .1 |
| | | 8.1 | 7.5 | | | All Other Current | 8.5 | 8.1 |
| | | 34.0 | 20.3 | | | Total Current | 28.0 | 20.0 |
| | | 10.5 | 8.4 | | | Long-Term Debt | 15.7 | 16.8 |
| | | .4 | .0 | | | Deferred Taxes | .0 | .0 |
| | | 4.7 | 3.2 | | | All Other Non-Current | 1.2 | .9 |
| | | 50.4 | 68.1 | | | Net Worth | 55.0 | 62.4 |
| | | 100.0 | 100.0 | | | Total Liabilities & Net Worth | 100.0 | 100.0 |
| | | | | | | **INCOME DATA** | | |
| | | 100.0 | 100.0 | | | Net Sales | 100.0 | 100.0 |
| | | | | | | Gross Profit | | |
| | | 93.7 | 97.2 | | | Operating Expenses | 96.1 | 95.1 |
| | | 6.3 | 2.8 | | | Operating Profit | 3.9 | 4.9 |
| | | .6 | -.9 | | | All Other Expenses (net) | -1.5 | .8 |
| | | 5.7 | 3.7 | | | Profit Before Taxes | 5.5 | 4.1 |
| | | | | | | **RATIOS** | | |
| | | 5.7 | 5.1 | | | | 4.3 | 3.4 |
| | | 3.1 | 2.6 | | | Current | 2.6 | 2.5 |
| | | 1.2 | 1.8 | | | | 1.8 | 1.8 |
| | | 5.0 | 3.8 | | | | 3.8 | 2.8 |
| | | 2.8 | 2.1 | | | Quick | 2.2 | 2.1 |
| | | 1.2 | 1.3 | | | | 1.1 | 1.1 |
| | | 23   15.8 | 39   9.4 | | | | 37   9.9 | 34   10.7 |
| | | 41   8.9 | 45   8.1 | | | Sales/Receivables | 49   7.4 | 46   7.9 |
| | | 53   6.9 | 59   6.2 | | | | 60   6.0 | 57   6.4 |
| | | | | | | | | |
| | | | | | | Cost of Sales/Inventory | | |
| | | | | | | | | |
| | | | | | | Cost of Sales/Payables | | |
| | | 4.0 | 2.5 | | | | 3.1 | 3.3 |
| | | 7.6 | 5.0 | | | Sales/Working Capital | 5.2 | 5.8 |
| | | NM | 10.6 | | | | 11.4 | 12.5 |
| | | 27.4 | 28.6 | | | | 20.5 | 13.8 |
| | | (10) 8.9 | (21) 6.3 | | | EBIT/Interest | (28) 8.6 | (36) 5.9 |
| | | -.4 | 1.3 | | | | 3.4 | 1.5 |
| | | | | | | Net Profit + Depr., Dep., Amort./Cur. Mat. L/T/D | | |
| | | .3 | .4 | | | | .3 | .4 |
| | | .7 | .5 | | | Fixed/Worth | .5 | .6 |
| | | NM | .9 | | | | 1.1 | .9 |
| | | .1 | .2 | | | | .3 | .4 |
| | | .7 | .4 | | | Debt/Worth | .6 | .6 |
| | | NM | .8 | | | | 1.1 | 1.0 |
| | | 13.2 | 11.7 | | | | 17.3 | 17.7 |
| | | (11) 8.1 | 6.4 | | | % Profit Before Taxes/Tangible Net Worth | (37) 10.5 | (48) 7.4 |
| | | 2.7 | .2 | | | | 6.2 | .4 |
| | | 22.9 | 9.5 | | | | 9.8 | 10.8 |
| | | 6.1 | 4.5 | | | % Profit Before Taxes/Total Assets | 6.4 | 4.7 |
| | | 3.2 | .2 | | | | 2.8 | .0 |
| | | 21.1 | 6.0 | | | | 13.0 | 9.3 |
| | | 8.7 | 3.3 | | | Sales/Net Fixed Assets | 4.4 | 3.4 |
| | | 4.9 | 1.8 | | | | 2.2 | 2.6 |
| | | 5.1 | 1.6 | | | | 2.1 | 1.9 |
| | | 2.1 | 1.2 | | | Sales/Total Assets | 1.4 | 1.3 |
| | | 1.4 | .9 | | | | 1.1 | 1.0 |
| | | 1.1 | 2.3 | | | | 1.8 | 1.8 |
| | | (29) 2.6 | 2.8 | | | % Depr., Dep., Amort./Sales | (35) 2.6 | (48) 2.6 |
| | | 5.0 | 4.3 | | | | 3.7 | 3.5 |
| | | | | | | % Officers', Directors' Owners' Comp/Sales | | |
| | 18801M | 237048M | 1099788M | 427295M | 933104M | Net Sales ($) | 1931827M | 2586112M |
| | 3611M | 86077M | 865299M | 423005M | 763296M | Total Assets ($) | 1336918M | 1945086M |

*(The 0-500M column is marked vertically: DATA NOT AVAILABLE)*

## Comparative Historical Data / Current Data Sorted by Sales

| | 4/1/09-3/31/10 ALL | 4/1/10-3/31/11 ALL | 4/1/11-3/31/12 ALL | Type of Statement | 0-1MM | 1-3MM | 3-5MM | 5-10MM | 10-25MM | 25MM & over |
|---|---|---|---|---|---|---|---|---|---|---|
| | 38 | 33 | 41 | Unqualified | | | 1 | 2 | 9 | 29 |
| | 1 | 1 | 1 | Reviewed | | | | | 1 | |
| | | 1 | 1 | Compiled | | | | 1 | | |
| | | 3 | 1 | Tax Returns | | | | | 1 | |
| | 13 | 13 | 14 | Other | 1 | 1 | | | 6 | 6 |
| | | | | | | 31 (4/1-9/30/11) | | | 27 (10/1/11-3/31/12) | |
| | 52 | 51 | 58 | NUMBER OF STATEMENTS | 1 | 1 | 2 | 3 | 17 | 35 |
| | % | % | % | ASSETS | % | % | % | % | % | % |
| | 15.8 | 18.6 | 18.5 | Cash & Equivalents | | | | | 26.4 | 15.7 |
| | 20.8 | 17.7 | 19.6 | Trade Receivables (net) | | | | | 18.9 | 18.0 |
| | 6.7 | 9.8 | 6.8 | Inventory | | | | | 6.1 | 7.1 |
| | 2.1 | 1.6 | 3.9 | All Other Current | | | | | 4.2 | 3.8 |
| | 45.3 | 47.7 | 48.7 | Total Current | | | | | 55.6 | 44.6 |
| | 39.2 | 38.4 | 35.2 | Fixed Assets (net) | | | | | 32.9 | 37.3 |
| | 1.8 | 1.4 | 3.1 | Intangibles (net) | | | | | .1 | 2.2 |
| | 13.7 | 12.6 | 13.1 | All Other Non-Current | | | | | 11.4 | 16.0 |
| | 100.0 | 100.0 | 100.0 | Total | | | | | 100.0 | 100.0 |
| | | | | LIABILITIES | | | | | | |
| | 2.1 | 3.3 | 1.6 | Notes Payable-Short Term | | | | | 1.4 | 1.4 |
| | 1.5 | 2.4 | 1.8 | Cur. Mat.-L.T.D. | | | | | .6 | 1.9 |
| | 10.0 | 12.2 | 12.6 | Trade Payables | | | | | 19.9 | 10.4 |
| | .1 | .0 | .0 | Income Taxes Payable | | | | | .0 | .0 |
| | 9.3 | 8.4 | 7.4 | All Other Current | | | | | 10.0 | 6.9 |
| | 23.1 | 26.3 | 23.4 | Total Current | | | | | 31.9 | 20.6 |
| | 17.0 | 17.0 | 10.6 | Long-Term Debt | | | | | 5.2 | 12.1 |
| | .0 | .0 | .4 | Deferred Taxes | | | | | .0 | .4 |
| | 2.5 | 1.9 | 3.8 | All Other Non-Current | | | | | 5.1 | 2.6 |
| | 57.3 | 54.8 | 61.8 | Net Worth | | | | | 57.8 | 64.2 |
| | 100.0 | 100.0 | 100.0 | Total Liabilities & Net Worth | | | | | 100.0 | 100.0 |
| | | | | INCOME DATA | | | | | | |
| | 100.0 | 100.0 | 100.0 | Net Sales | | | | | 100.0 | 100.0 |
| | | | | Gross Profit | | | | | | |
| | 94.5 | 92.0 | 95.3 | Operating Expenses | | | | | 97.2 | 95.7 |
| | 5.5 | 8.0 | 4.7 | Operating Profit | | | | | 2.8 | 4.3 |
| | -.1 | .2 | -.4 | All Other Expenses (net) | | | | | -.4 | -.8 |
| | 5.6 | 7.8 | 5.1 | Profit Before Taxes | | | | | 3.2 | 5.1 |
| | | | | RATIOS | | | | | | |
| | 3.7 | 4.4 | 4.5 | Current | | | | | 6.8 | 3.1 |
| | 2.1 | 2.5 | 2.6 | | | | | | 2.7 | 2.2 |
| | 1.4 | 1.6 | 1.6 | | | | | | 1.2 | 1.5 |
| | 3.3 | 3.6 | 3.4 | Quick | | | | | 4.7 | 2.7 |
| | 1.5 | 1.9 | 2.0 | | | | | | 2.4 | 1.8 |
| | .9 | 1.0 | 1.2 | | | | | | 1.1 | 1.1 |
| | 34  10.7 | 34  10.8 | 36  10.2 | Sales/Receivables | | | | | 20  18.3 | 39  9.4 |
| | 42  8.7 | 42  8.7 | 44  8.3 | | | | | | 35  10.4 | 49  7.5 |
| | 51  7.1 | 48  7.5 | 58  6.3 | | | | | | 44  8.3 | 63  5.8 |
| | | | | Cost of Sales/Inventory | | | | | | |
| | | | | Cost of Sales/Payables | | | | | | |
| | 4.0 | 2.9 | 3.0 | Sales/Working Capital | | | | | 2.4 | 3.0 |
| | 7.0 | 6.2 | 5.3 | | | | | | 5.1 | 6.1 |
| | 16.7 | 13.5 | 11.6 | | | | | | 67.3 | 12.9 |
| | 31.6 | 65.4 | 33.5 | EBIT/Interest | | | | | | 35.2 |
| | (42) 14.7 | (37) 12.3 | (45) 8.7 | | | | | | | (30) 8.6 |
| | 4.1 | 5.3 | 3.1 | | | | | | | 2.4 |
| | | | | Net Profit + Depr., Dep., Amort./Cur. Mat. L/T/D | | | | | | |
| | .5 | .4 | .4 | Fixed/Worth | | | | | .4 | .4 |
| | .6 | .6 | .5 | | | | | | .5 | .5 |
| | .9 | 1.2 | 1.1 | | | | | | 1.5 | 1.1 |
| | .3 | .3 | .3 | Debt/Worth | | | | | .1 | .3 |
| | .6 | .6 | .5 | | | | | | .4 | .5 |
| | 1.3 | 1.1 | 1.2 | | | | | | 9.4 | .9 |
| | 18.4 | 24.5 | 12.9 | % Profit Before Taxes/Tangible Net Worth | | | | | 11.3 | 12.3 |
| | (50) 12.2 | (48) 10.2 | (54) 8.1 | | | | | | (14) 8.1 | (34) 6.4 |
| | 4.3 | 6.5 | 2.3 | | | | | | 4.6 | 1.0 |
| | 10.0 | 12.6 | 10.4 | % Profit Before Taxes/Total Assets | | | | | 11.6 | 10.1 |
| | 7.7 | 7.0 | 5.6 | | | | | | 7.9 | 4.6 |
| | 1.3 | 4.0 | 1.8 | | | | | | 4.3 | .4 |
| | 8.2 | 9.8 | 10.0 | Sales/Net Fixed Assets | | | | | 20.6 | 8.0 |
| | 3.5 | 3.2 | 4.0 | | | | | | 4.7 | 3.3 |
| | 2.3 | 2.4 | 2.3 | | | | | | 2.5 | 2.2 |
| | 2.2 | 1.9 | 2.0 | Sales/Total Assets | | | | | 4.1 | 1.7 |
| | 1.5 | 1.4 | 1.3 | | | | | | 1.8 | 1.2 |
| | 1.0 | 1.0 | 1.0 | | | | | | .9 | .9 |
| | 1.9 | 2.1 | 1.9 | % Depr., Dep., Amort./Sales | | | | | 1.1 | 2.0 |
| | (49) 2.8 | (46) 3.0 | (55) 2.7 | | | | | | (16) 2.5 | (33) 2.8 |
| | 3.3 | 4.1 | 4.3 | | | | | | 4.8 | 4.0 |
| | | | | % Officers', Directors' Owners' Comp/Sales | | | | | | |
| | 3010679M | 2447852M | 2716036M | Net Sales ($) | | 2314M | 8839M | 23117M | 298945M | 2382821M |
| | 1996571M | 1827449M | 2141288M | Total Assets ($) | | 653M | 7551M | 15661M | 212329M | 1905094M |

*(Columns 0-1MM, 1-3MM, 3-5MM, and 5-10MM are marked "DATA NOT AVAILABLE" for the asset, liability, income and ratio sections.)*

| Current Data Sorted by Assets | | | | | | | Comparative Historical Data | |
|---|---|---|---|---|---|---|---|---|
| | | | | | | **Type of Statement** | | |
| 2 | 4 | 31 | 33 | 4 | 6 | Unqualified | 113 | 108 |
| | 1 | 7 | 4 | | | Reviewed | 20 | 18 |
| 5 | 7 | 5 | 1 | | | Compiled | 17 | 21 |
| 24 | 21 | 7 | 1 | | | Tax Returns | 39 | 45 |
| 22 | 20 | 37 | 16 | 2 | 6 | Other | 109 | 124 |
| | 58 (4/1-9/30/11) | | 208 (10/1/11-3/31/12) | | | | 4/1/07-3/31/08 | 4/1/08-3/31/09 |
| 0-500M | 500M-2MM | 2-10MM | 10-50MM | 50-100MM | 100-250MM | | ALL | ALL |
| 53 | 53 | 87 | 55 | 6 | 12 | **NUMBER OF STATEMENTS** | 298 | 316 |
| % | % | % | % | % | % | **ASSETS** | % | % |
| 35.8 | 21.1 | 20.3 | 23.8 | | 5.0 | Cash & Equivalents | 15.0 | 17.6 |
| 11.4 | 19.4 | 25.8 | 22.4 | | 25.9 | Trade Receivables (net) | 26.8 | 24.7 |
| 4.4 | 1.5 | 2.0 | 1.5 | | 8.7 | Inventory | 3.1 | 2.8 |
| 4.7 | 4.6 | 4.6 | 5.6 | | 3.5 | All Other Current | 3.9 | 4.1 |
| 56.4 | 46.5 | 52.7 | 53.2 | | 43.1 | Total Current | 48.8 | 49.2 |
| 27.5 | 37.6 | 35.0 | 26.6 | | 18.0 | Fixed Assets (net) | 34.5 | 34.2 |
| 3.4 | 6.9 | 4.6 | 5.6 | | 24.6 | Intangibles (net) | 7.6 | 6.8 |
| 12.6 | 9.0 | 7.8 | 14.6 | | 14.2 | All Other Non-Current | 9.1 | 9.9 |
| 100.0 | 100.0 | 100.0 | 100.0 | | 100.0 | Total | 100.0 | 100.0 |
| | | | | | | **LIABILITIES** | | |
| 23.0 | 12.6 | 3.7 | 3.3 | | 2.0 | Notes Payable-Short Term | 8.8 | 8.7 |
| 5.4 | 5.6 | 3.9 | 3.9 | | 1.6 | Cur. Mat.-L.T.D. | 5.5 | 5.9 |
| 5.2 | 5.5 | 9.5 | 6.9 | | 9.1 | Trade Payables | 9.4 | 8.8 |
| .0 | .0 | .0 | .3 | | .2 | Income Taxes Payable | .4 | .1 |
| 22.3 | 14.4 | 13.3 | 16.3 | | 14.1 | All Other Current | 15.9 | 14.9 |
| 56.1 | 38.1 | 30.3 | 30.8 | | 27.1 | Total Current | 40.0 | 38.4 |
| 24.3 | 22.1 | 23.7 | 13.6 | | 25.4 | Long-Term Debt | 23.6 | 25.8 |
| .0 | .0 | .2 | .3 | | 1.0 | Deferred Taxes | .2 | .2 |
| 12.6 | 6.4 | 5.5 | 4.8 | | 1.3 | All Other Non-Current | 4.6 | 7.5 |
| 7.0 | 33.5 | 40.1 | 50.6 | | 45.3 | Net Worth | 31.6 | 28.1 |
| 100.0 | 100.0 | 100.0 | 100.0 | | 100.0 | Total Liabilties & Net Worth | 100.0 | 100.0 |
| | | | | | | **INCOME DATA** | | |
| 100.0 | 100.0 | 100.0 | 100.0 | | 100.0 | Net Sales | 100.0 | 100.0 |
| | | | | | | Gross Profit | | |
| 89.6 | 85.3 | 92.6 | 91.8 | | 98.6 | Operating Expenses | 89.6 | 90.0 |
| 10.4 | 14.7 | 7.4 | 8.2 | | 1.4 | Operating Profit | 10.4 | 10.0 |
| 1.5 | 4.5 | 2.7 | .6 | | -.3 | All Other Expenses (net) | 2.4 | 3.0 |
| 8.9 | 10.2 | 4.7 | 7.6 | | 1.8 | Profit Before Taxes | 7.9 | 7.0 |
| | | | | | | **RATIOS** | | |
| 5.5 | 3.8 | 3.8 | 3.8 | | 2.1 | | 2.7 | 2.8 |
| 1.5 | 1.4 | 1.7 | 2.0 | | 1.4 | Current | 1.4 | 1.5 |
| .6 | .7 | 1.1 | 1.2 | | .9 | | .8 | .9 |
| 5.1 | 3.4 | 2.8 | 3.3 | | 1.8 | | 2.3 | 2.6 |
| 1.3 | 1.4 | 1.4 | 1.5 | | 1.0 | Quick | 1.2 | 1.4 |
| .4 | .5 | .9 | 1.1 | | .7 | | .7 | .7 |
| 0 UND | 0 UND | 8 48.2 | 19 19.4 | | 29 12.7 | | 11 32.0 | 5 69.3 |
| 0 UND | 1 255.3 | 39 9.4 | 38 9.6 | | 43 8.4 | Sales/Receivables | 39 9.3 | 35 10.6 |
| 10 36.3 | 41 8.9 | 60 6.1 | 69 5.3 | | 73 5.0 | | 62 5.9 | 61 5.9 |
| | | | | | | Cost of Sales/Inventory | | |
| | | | | | | Cost of Sales/Payables | | |
| 13.5 | 11.0 | 5.0 | 3.0 | | 7.9 | | 6.3 | 6.0 |
| 71.3 | 34.6 | 15.2 | 6.6 | | 13.8 | Sales/Working Capital | 20.2 | 16.0 |
| -41.9 | -18.3 | 46.3 | 25.6 | | NM | | -63.4 | -107.4 |
| 35.6 | 31.0 | 20.2 | 24.6 | | 342.9 | | 17.1 | 17.6 |
| (33) 11.6 | (38) 8.1 | (64) 7.1 | (41) 7.4 | | (10) 5.1 | EBIT/Interest | (233) 4.0 | (244) 5.2 |
| -.5 | 2.4 | 2.5 | 1.0 | | 1.8 | | 1.2 | 1.0 |
| | | | | | | Net Profit + Depr., Dep., Amort./Cur. Mat. L/T/D | 5.7 | 8.7 |
| | | | | | | | (34) 1.2 | (38) 2.1 |
| | | | | | | | .3 | 1.2 |
| .0 | .3 | .2 | .2 | | .4 | | .4 | .3 |
| .6 | 1.0 | .6 | .4 | | .9 | Fixed/Worth | 1.1 | 1.1 |
| -8.6 | 5.2 | 2.3 | 1.3 | | NM | | 10.7 | 5.0 |
| .5 | .7 | .4 | .4 | | .6 | | .6 | .6 |
| 5.9 | 1.6 | 1.3 | 1.0 | | 3.3 | Debt/Worth | 2.0 | 1.8 |
| -5.7 | 9.6 | 5.2 | 2.3 | | NM | | 31.8 | 16.4 |
| 623.3 | 113.9 | 71.6 | 38.9 | | | | 55.1 | 69.9 |
| (35) 97.4 | (41) 50.4 | (75) 20.7 | (49) 16.6 | | | % Profit Before Taxes/Tangible Net Worth | (229) 21.7 | (248) 20.2 |
| 6.3 | 10.1 | 4.8 | 3.4 | | | | 5.3 | 3.2 |
| 105.1 | 43.3 | 22.2 | 16.1 | | 8.3 | | 22.9 | 25.8 |
| 24.0 | 15.5 | 6.8 | 6.4 | | 3.3 | % Profit Before Taxes/Total Assets | 7.6 | 7.2 |
| .0 | 2.9 | 1.9 | .2 | | 1.4 | | 1.5 | .0 |
| UND | 39.7 | 48.7 | 27.2 | | 58.5 | | 36.7 | 42.5 |
| 62.6 | 13.4 | 8.3 | 10.9 | | 20.7 | Sales/Net Fixed Assets | 9.7 | 11.7 |
| 11.7 | 3.7 | 3.0 | 2.7 | | 2.3 | | 3.3 | 2.8 |
| 16.1 | 5.2 | 3.4 | 2.6 | | 2.3 | | 4.0 | 4.2 |
| 6.9 | 2.9 | 2.0 | 1.5 | | 1.6 | Sales/Total Assets | 2.1 | 2.2 |
| 3.2 | 1.4 | 1.3 | .9 | | 1.0 | | 1.2 | 1.1 |
| .7 | .9 | .9 | 1.2 | | .9 | | .9 | 1.1 |
| (27) 1.5 | (40) 2.5 | (74) 2.3 | (50) 2.3 | | (10) 1.2 | % Depr., Dep., Amort./Sales | (243) 2.4 | (245) 2.6 |
| 5.0 | 8.7 | 4.6 | 3.4 | | 5.1 | | 4.4 | 4.8 |
| 3.5 | 4.6 | | | | | | 4.3 | 5.3 |
| (23) 11.1 | (14) 8.3 | | | | | % Officers', Directors' Owners' Comp/Sales | (45) 7.3 | (50) 9.8 |
| 28.8 | 16.9 | | | | | | 24.5 | 25.6 |
| 128786M | 198377M | 1063090M | 2301373M | 977793M | 3373939M | Net Sales ($) | 12419348M | 11332833M |
| 12901M | 61023M | 402332M | 1347838M | 397904M | 1693854M | Total Assets ($) | 6109414M | 5820088M |

M = $ thousand    MM = $ million
See Pages 9 through 22 for Explanation of Ratios and Data

## Comparative Historical Data | Current Data Sorted by Sales

| | | | Type of Statement | | | | | | |
|---|---|---|---|---|---|---|---|---|---|
| 98 | 88 | 80 | Unqualified | 2 | 4 | 5 | 15 | 21 | 33 |
| 15 | 13 | 12 | Reviewed | | 1 | 2 | 2 | 4 | 3 |
| 30 | 21 | 18 | Compiled | 6 | 3 | 2 | 2 | 3 | 2 |
| 46 | 30 | 53 | Tax Returns | 16 | 15 | 8 | 11 | 2 | 1 |
| 109 | 120 | 103 | Other | 11 | 21 | 13 | 18 | 14 | 26 |
| 4/1/09-3/31/10 ALL | 4/1/10-3/31/11 ALL | 4/1/11-3/31/12 ALL | | 58 (4/1-9/30/11) | | | 208 (10/1/11-3/31/12) | | |
| | | | | 0-1MM | 1-3MM | 3-5MM | 5-10MM | 10-25MM | 25MM & OVER |
| 298 | 272 | 266 | NUMBER OF STATEMENTS | 35 | 44 | 30 | 48 | 44 | 65 |
| % | % | % | ASSETS | % | % | % | % | % | % |
| 19.4 | 20.6 | 23.4 | Cash & Equivalents | 17.8 | 28.9 | 24.2 | 23.9 | 26.8 | 19.8 |
| 22.3 | 22.5 | 21.0 | Trade Receivables (net) | 8.3 | 12.0 | 24.8 | 22.4 | 25.5 | 28.0 |
| 3.5 | 3.4 | 2.5 | Inventory | 1.4 | 3.6 | 1.9 | 2.6 | 1.2 | 3.6 |
| 4.1 | 4.8 | 4.8 | All Other Current | 2.3 | 6.0 | 2.2 | 4.5 | 8.1 | 4.3 |
| 49.3 | 51.3 | 51.7 | Total Current | 29.8 | 50.5 | 52.9 | 53.4 | 61.7 | 55.7 |
| 33.7 | 31.2 | 31.2 | Fixed Assets (net) | 58.9 | 29.4 | 33.6 | 31.4 | 23.2 | 21.8 |
| 7.3 | 6.1 | 6.3 | Intangibles (net) | 1.2 | 7.6 | 7.4 | 4.5 | 4.3 | 10.3 |
| 9.8 | 11.4 | 10.8 | All Other Non-Current | 9.8 | 12.5 | 6.1 | 10.7 | 10.7 | 12.3 |
| 100.0 | 100.0 | 100.0 | Total | 100.0 | 100.0 | 100.0 | 100.0 | 100.0 | 100.0 |
| | | | LIABILITIES | | | | | | |
| 7.8 | 8.3 | 9.1 | Notes Payable-Short Term | 21.9 | 8.3 | 8.3 | 12.7 | 1.9 | 5.3 |
| 4.0 | 4.8 | 4.4 | Cur. Mat.-L.T.D. | 7.2 | 3.7 | 6.5 | 4.8 | 4.1 | 2.4 |
| 8.5 | 7.9 | 7.4 | Trade Payables | 1.3 | 7.1 | 5.5 | 9.2 | 7.9 | 9.9 |
| .1 | .1 | .1 | Income Taxes Payable | .0 | .0 | .0 | .1 | .2 | .2 |
| 13.5 | 16.4 | 15.9 | All Other Current | 8.8 | 20.5 | 16.4 | 10.8 | 18.7 | 18.4 |
| 34.0 | 37.5 | 36.9 | Total Current | 39.3 | 39.7 | 36.7 | 37.6 | 32.8 | 36.1 |
| 21.7 | 21.2 | 22.0 | Long-Term Debt | 41.5 | 23.7 | 21.2 | 21.9 | 14.9 | 15.7 |
| .3 | .2 | .2 | Deferred Taxes | .0 | .0 | .0 | .1 | .4 | .4 |
| 7.5 | 10.2 | 7.2 | All Other Non-Current | 7.7 | 12.1 | 3.2 | 10.2 | 4.8 | 4.7 |
| 36.5 | 31.0 | 33.7 | Net Worth | 11.6 | 24.6 | 38.9 | 30.2 | 47.1 | 43.1 |
| 100.0 | 100.0 | 100.0 | Total Liabilties & Net Worth | 100.0 | 100.0 | 100.0 | 100.0 | 100.0 | 100.0 |
| | | | INCOME DATA | | | | | | |
| 100.0 | 100.0 | 100.0 | Net Sales | 100.0 | 100.0 | 100.0 | 100.0 | 100.0 | 100.0 |
| | | | Gross Profit | | | | | | |
| 90.8 | 90.7 | 90.6 | Operating Expenses | 82.7 | 89.3 | 87.6 | 94.6 | 91.0 | 94.0 |
| 9.2 | 9.3 | 9.4 | Operating Profit | 17.3 | 10.7 | 12.4 | 5.4 | 9.0 | 6.0 |
| 2.8 | 2.2 | 2.3 | All Other Expenses (net) | 12.9 | 1.6 | .6 | .7 | .7 | .0 |
| 6.5 | 7.1 | 7.1 | Profit Before Taxes | 4.4 | 9.0 | 11.8 | 4.7 | 8.3 | 6.0 |
| | | | RATIOS | | | | | | |
| 2.9 | 3.0 | 3.8 | | 4.8 | 3.7 | 4.0 | 4.3 | 4.6 | 2.5 |
| 1.6 | 1.6 | 1.7 | Current | .8 | 1.4 | 1.5 | 2.1 | 2.4 | 1.7 |
| 1.0 | .9 | 1.0 | | .2 | .8 | .8 | 1.1 | 1.4 | 1.2 |
| 2.3 | 2.4 | 3.2 | | 4.8 | 3.4 | 3.6 | 3.9 | 4.4 | 2.0 |
| 1.4 | 1.3 | 1.4 | Quick | .7 | 1.2 | 1.3 | 1.5 | 2.2 | 1.4 |
| .8 | .6 | .8 | | .0 | .5 | .7 | .9 | 1.1 | 1.0 |
| 3 105.3 | 2 219.0 | 0 UND | | 0 UND | 0 UND | 0 UND | 0 UND | 20 18.5 | 16 23.1 |
| 33 11.0 | 33 10.9 | 27 13.7 | Sales/Receivables | 0 UND | 0 UND | 31 11.6 | 25 14.4 | 45 8.2 | 38 9.6 |
| 54 6.8 | 53 6.9 | 53 6.9 | | 32 11.4 | 24 15.0 | 60 6.1 | 54 6.8 | 59 6.2 | 64 5.7 |
| | | | Cost of Sales/Inventory | | | | | | |
| | | | Cost of Sales/Payables | | | | | | |
| 6.1 | 5.9 | 6.0 | | 5.4 | 11.9 | 10.5 | 6.0 | 3.4 | 6.8 |
| 14.4 | 14.7 | 18.4 | Sales/Working Capital | -43.0 | 43.1 | 24.6 | 12.9 | 6.7 | 13.7 |
| 680.1 | -143.4 | 601.0 | | -5.6 | -51.3 | -45.0 | 125.1 | 39.6 | 43.6 |
| 21.2 | 18.9 | 23.7 | | 4.6 | 37.8 | 19.8 | 33.8 | 43.8 | 24.9 |
| (219) 5.2 | (202) 4.8 | (192) 7.1 | EBIT/Interest | (18) 2.0 | (31) 8.3 | (20) 8.0 | (41) 9.2 | (34) 8.8 | (48) 7.2 |
| 1.4 | 1.5 | 1.7 | | .6 | .6 | 3.5 | 3.2 | 1.1 | 2.0 |
| 10.1 | 5.9 | 11.7 | | | | | | | 12.1 |
| (29) 2.6 | (30) 3.2 | (22) 2.7 | Net Profit + Depr., Dep., Amort./Cur. Mat. L/T/D | | | | | (13) 2.8 | |
| 1.6 | 1.7 | 1.5 | | | | | | | 1.7 |
| .2 | .2 | .2 | | .7 | .0 | .4 | .2 | .1 | .2 |
| .9 | .8 | .7 | Fixed/Worth | 4.8 | .6 | .9 | .5 | .4 | .6 |
| 3.3 | 4.8 | 4.3 | | -15.8 | NM | 3.4 | 5.0 | 1.3 | 1.7 |
| .6 | .7 | .5 | | .8 | .7 | .3 | .6 | .3 | .7 |
| 1.6 | 1.6 | 1.5 | Debt/Worth | 9.0 | 1.3 | 1.2 | 1.8 | 1.1 | 1.2 |
| 6.2 | 10.6 | 13.1 | | -15.0 | -7.1 | 8.4 | 8.2 | 2.4 | 4.4 |
| 64.6 | 69.4 | 94.4 | | 100.3 | 168.6 | 141.3 | 82.1 | 70.5 | 59.2 |
| (251) 14.4 | (220) 18.3 | (212) 24.3 | % Profit Before Taxes/Tangible Net Worth | (22) 11.3 | (30) 81.1 | (25) 45.9 | (40) 32.1 | (41) 17.4 | (54) 20.3 |
| 2.1 | 4.3 | 5.4 | | -5.5 | 5.1 | 2.0 | 7.6 | 4.2 | 5.4 |
| 21.5 | 20.0 | 32.5 | | 16.7 | 55.5 | 54.0 | 25.6 | 35.8 | 17.2 |
| 6.4 | 6.9 | 9.0 | % Profit Before Taxes/Total Assets | 2.5 | 13.7 | 19.2 | 10.4 | 8.8 | 6.3 |
| .3 | .6 | 1.2 | | -1.7 | .1 | 2.5 | 2.9 | 1.0 | 1.4 |
| 42.9 | 57.0 | 59.5 | | 12.6 | 952.0 | 43.0 | 47.4 | 63.6 | 50.6 |
| 10.4 | 12.9 | 13.6 | Sales/Net Fixed Assets | 3.0 | 49.8 | 14.6 | 19.7 | 11.4 | 17.8 |
| 3.0 | 3.2 | 3.4 | | .2 | 2.4 | 5.0 | 5.2 | 5.2 | 6.3 |
| 4.1 | 4.3 | 4.9 | | 3.3 | 6.6 | 5.7 | 6.1 | 3.4 | 4.1 |
| 2.1 | 2.2 | 2.4 | Sales/Total Assets | 1.2 | 2.8 | 2.9 | 3.2 | 2.0 | 2.3 |
| 1.1 | 1.2 | 1.3 | | .2 | 1.3 | 1.5 | 1.6 | 1.3 | 1.2 |
| 1.1 | 1.0 | 1.0 | | 3.3 | .7 | 1.2 | 1.0 | .8 | .7 |
| (230) 2.3 | (207) 2.3 | (205) 2.2 | % Depr., Dep., Amort./Sales | (28) 10.1 | (22) 2.5 | (23) 3.1 | (41) 1.5 | (37) 1.7 | (54) 1.4 |
| 4.1 | 4.4 | 4.7 | | 30.3 | 8.3 | 5.9 | 3.6 | 3.3 | 3.1 |
| 4.2 | 3.7 | 4.1 | | | | 5.5 | | | |
| (60) 7.9 | (48) 10.3 | (54) 7.8 | % Officers', Directors' Owners' Comp/Sales | | (16) 10.3 | | | | |
| 16.7 | 24.3 | 17.4 | | | | 26.7 | | | |
| 12693628M | 13357263M | 8043358M | Net Sales ($) | 15009M | 89225M | 124813M | 356657M | 683997M | 6773657M |
| 6726600M | 6273289M | 3915852M | Total Assets ($) | 32914M | 64914M | 56757M | 181192M | 408504M | 3171571M |

M = $ thousand     MM = $ million
See Pages 9 through 22 for Explanation of Ratios and Data

## Current Data Sorted by Assets      Comparative Historical Data

| 0-500M | 500M-2MM | 2-10MM | 10-50MM | 50-100MM | 100-250MM | Type of Statement | 4/1/07-3/31/08 ALL | 4/1/08-3/31/09 ALL |
|---|---|---|---|---|---|---|---|---|
|  | 3 | 25 | 111 | 79 | 91 | Unqualified | 317 | 321 |
|  |  | 9 | 5 |  |  | Reviewed | 8 | 10 |
| 5 | 7 | 16 | 6 | 6 | 1 | Compiled | 20 | 22 |
| 9 | 2 | 6 | 2 |  |  | Tax Returns | 20 | 22 |
| 6 | 16 | 46 | 103 | 43 | 48 | Other | 237 | 233 |
|  | 288 (4/1-9/30/11) |  | 351 (10/1/11-3/31/12) |  |  |  |  |  |
| 20 | 28 | 102 | 227 | 122 | 140 | NUMBER OF STATEMENTS | 602 | 608 |
| % | % | % | % | % | % | ASSETS | % | % |
| 47.7 | 34.1 | 13.4 | 14.3 | 12.8 | 13.2 | Cash & Equivalents | 11.8 | 11.9 |
| 5.4 | 7.6 | 19.7 | 18.2 | 13.8 | 12.1 | Trade Receivables (net) | 18.3 | 17.0 |
| 1.8 | 3.2 | 3.8 | 2.3 | 1.9 | 1.8 | Inventory | 2.3 | 2.1 |
| 6.4 | 1.5 | 3.0 | 3.0 | 2.7 | 2.6 | All Other Current | 3.4 | 3.7 |
| 61.3 | 46.4 | 39.8 | 37.8 | 31.2 | 29.8 | Total Current | 35.8 | 34.7 |
| 24.2 | 32.8 | 48.1 | 49.0 | 45.4 | 42.2 | Fixed Assets (net) | 44.0 | 46.2 |
| 6.1 | 5.9 | 2.5 | 2.1 | 2.1 | 3.2 | Intangibles (net) | 2.4 | 2.6 |
| 8.5 | 14.9 | 9.6 | 11.1 | 21.3 | 24.8 | All Other Non-Current | 17.8 | 16.5 |
| 100.0 | 100.0 | 100.0 | 100.0 | 100.0 | 100.0 | Total | 100.0 | 100.0 |
|  |  |  |  |  |  | LIABILITIES |  |  |
| 32.2 | 12.0 | 4.7 | 2.3 | 1.8 | .7 | Notes Payable-Short Term | 2.5 | 2.6 |
| 2.8 | 4.5 | 5.2 | 3.5 | 2.8 | 2.0 | Cur. Mat.-L.T.D. | 3.4 | 3.4 |
| 2.9 | 6.7 | 9.1 | 6.4 | 5.6 | 4.4 | Trade Payables | 7.4 | 5.5 |
| .1 | .2 | .0 | .1 | .1 | .0 | Income Taxes Payable | .1 | .1 |
| 48.0 | 16.5 | 17.7 | 10.5 | 9.9 | 7.4 | All Other Current | 10.4 | 10.6 |
| 86.0 | 40.0 | 36.8 | 22.8 | 20.3 | 14.5 | Total Current | 23.8 | 22.2 |
| 12.7 | 23.5 | 28.4 | 34.4 | 25.8 | 28.1 | Long-Term Debt | 27.9 | 30.2 |
| .0 | .2 | .0 | .1 | .0 | .1 | Deferred Taxes | .1 | .0 |
| 2.2 | 4.1 | 4.6 | 2.6 | 4.4 | 5.6 | All Other Non-Current | 4.7 | 5.4 |
| -.8 | 32.2 | 30.2 | 40.1 | 49.4 | 51.8 | Net Worth | 43.6 | 42.1 |
| 100.0 | 100.0 | 100.0 | 100.0 | 100.0 | 100.0 | Total Liabilities & Net Worth | 100.0 | 100.0 |
|  |  |  |  |  |  | INCOME DATA |  |  |
| 100.0 | 100.0 | 100.0 | 100.0 | 100.0 | 100.0 | Net Sales | 100.0 | 100.0 |
|  |  |  |  |  |  | Gross Profit |  |  |
| 95.6 | 81.9 | 87.4 | 91.4 | 97.0 | 95.2 | Operating Expenses | 94.1 | 94.2 |
| 4.4 | 18.1 | 12.6 | 8.6 | 3.0 | 4.8 | Operating Profit | 5.9 | 5.8 |
| -.7 | 2.3 | 4.6 | 2.2 | .0 | .0 | All Other Expenses (net) | .5 | 2.0 |
| 5.1 | 15.8 | 8.0 | 6.4 | 3.0 | 4.7 | Profit Before Taxes | 5.4 | 3.8 |
|  |  |  |  |  |  | RATIOS |  |  |
| 12.1 | 4.1 | 2.6 | 2.9 | 2.6 | 2.8 |  | 2.7 | 2.6 |
| 1.8 | 1.1 | 1.6 | 1.9 | 1.7 | 2.1 | Current | 1.8 | 1.8 |
| .6 | .4 | .6 | 1.2 | 1.1 | 1.5 |  | 1.2 | 1.3 |
| 12.1 | 3.5 | 2.2 | 2.4 | 2.3 | 2.5 |  | 2.3 | 2.3 |
| 1.2 | .9 | 1.2 | 1.6 | 1.5 | 1.7 | Quick | (601) 1.5 | 1.5 |
| .3 | .3 | .6 | .9 | .9 | 1.2 |  | 1.0 | 1.0 |
| 0 UND | 0 UND | 1 640.0 | 36 10.1 | 37 9.9 | 40 9.2 |  | 37 10.0 | 37 9.8 |
| 0 UND | 0 UND | 33 11.0 | 47 7.8 | 45 8.2 | 47 7.8 | Sales/Receivables | 48 7.5 | 48 7.5 |
| 0 UND | 17 21.6 | 51 7.1 | 59 6.2 | 54 6.7 | 54 6.7 |  | 61 6.0 | 60 6.1 |
|  |  |  |  |  |  | Cost of Sales/Inventory |  |  |
|  |  |  |  |  |  | Cost of Sales/Payables |  |  |
| 11.3 | 6.9 | 5.8 | 4.4 | 5.1 | 3.7 |  | 5.2 | 5.3 |
| 41.9 | NM | 16.2 | 8.1 | 9.3 | 7.3 | Sales/Working Capital | 9.3 | 9.4 |
| -22.3 | -13.9 | -10.6 | 39.8 | 98.1 | 13.7 |  | 40.1 | 24.9 |
| 54.8 | 40.1 | 34.2 | 9.9 | 7.3 | 7.9 |  | 8.9 | 6.5 |
| (10) 2.9 | (21) 9.1 | (82) 6.5 | (197) 3.1 | (113) 3.0 | 3.3 | EBIT/Interest | (542) 3.5 | (549) 2.1 |
| -10.8 | 2.5 | .8 | .8 | .4 | .8 |  | 1.1 | -.4 |
|  |  |  | 11.6 |  |  | Net Profit + Depr., Dep., | 6.7 | 9.2 |
|  |  |  | (11) 3.5 |  |  | Amort./Cur. Mat. L/T/D | (38) 3.6 | (31) 4.8 |
|  |  |  | 2.8 |  |  |  | 1.6 | 1.8 |
| .0 | .1 | .5 | .6 | .7 | .6 |  | .6 | .7 |
| .6 | .9 | 1.1 | 1.1 | 1.0 | .9 | Fixed/Worth | .9 | 1.0 |
| -.5 | NM | 19.3 | 2.9 | 1.4 | 1.3 |  | 1.9 | 1.9 |
| .2 | .5 | .5 | .5 | .5 | .5 |  | .5 | .6 |
| 1.8 | 2.2 | 1.4 | 1.1 | 1.0 | .9 | Debt/Worth | 1.0 | 1.1 |
| -3.9 | -22.9 | 36.7 | 3.9 | 2.1 | 1.6 |  | 3.1 | 2.7 |
| 196.4 | 224.5 | 65.6 | 24.8 | 14.3 | 10.9 | % Profit Before Taxes/Tangible | 21.5 | 15.3 |
| (11) 138.4 | (20) 86.5 | (79) 27.2 | (200) 7.7 | (116) 5.2 | (134) 5.4 | Net Worth | (542) 9.0 | (543) 4.8 |
| 58.4 | 7.2 | .4 | 1.0 | .0 | -.4 |  | 2.5 | -4.2 |
| 117.1 | 78.5 | 23.1 | 8.8 | 6.9 | 6.2 | % Profit Before Taxes/Total | 8.3 | 7.2 |
| 18.9 | 24.0 | 6.1 | 3.1 | 2.9 | 2.7 | Assets | 4.1 | 2.2 |
| -8.7 | 1.2 | -1.1 | -.2 | -.3 | -.4 |  | .2 | -2.2 |
| UND | 125.3 | 8.7 | 4.7 | 3.5 | 2.7 |  | 5.3 | 4.5 |
| 67.1 | 35.0 | 4.6 | 2.5 | 2.5 | 2.1 | Sales/Net Fixed Assets | 2.6 | 2.4 |
| 25.3 | 3.9 | 2.2 | 1.4 | 1.6 | 1.5 |  | 1.8 | 1.7 |
| 20.5 | 9.5 | 2.8 | 1.7 | 1.4 | 1.1 |  | 1.9 | 1.7 |
| 8.9 | 3.5 | 1.8 | 1.2 | 1.1 | .9 | Sales/Total Assets | 1.2 | 1.1 |
| 5.5 | 1.5 | .9 | .8 | .8 | .7 |  | .8 | .8 |
| .2 | .9 | 2.2 | 2.8 | 3.7 | 4.3 |  | 3.1 | 3.2 |
| (10) .8 | (17) 3.5 | (96) 3.7 | (223) 4.4 | (119) 4.7 | (100) 5.4 | % Depr., Dep., Amort./Sales | (530) 4.6 | (540) 4.6 |
| 3.3 | -10.3 | 7.2 | 6.6 | 6.4 | 6.8 |  | 6.1 | 6.1 |
| 25.7 |  |  | 1.6 | 5.0 | 9.2 |  | 6.7 | 5.1 |
| (13) 32.8 |  |  | (21) 9.2 | (10) | (10) 28.8 | % Officers', Directors' | (69) 17.6 | (64) 13.5 |
| 37.1 |  |  | 40.1 | 35.4 | 42.2 | Owners' Comp/Sales | 37.4 | 37.0 |
| 61816M | 188415M | 1080814M | 8660079M | 10178603M | 21667670M | Net Sales ($) | 44328410M | 45792607M |
| 4529M | 34116M | 559931M | 6116278M | 8756671M | 23476667M | Total Assets ($) | 39495844M | 42589129M |

M = $ thousand     MM = $ million
See Pages 9 through 22 for Explanation of Ratios and Data

## Comparative Historical Data | | | | Current Data Sorted by Sales

| Hist 1 | Hist 2 | Hist 3 | Type of Statement | 0-1MM | 1-3MM | 3-5MM | 5-10MM | 10-25MM | 25MM & OVER |
|---|---|---|---|---|---|---|---|---|---|
| 284 | 320 | 309 | Unqualified | 5 | 4 | 3 | 15 | 47 | 235 |
| 13 | 23 | 14 | Reviewed | | 3 | | 3 | 5 | 3 |
| 21 | 21 | 35 | Compiled | 6 | 2 | 2 | 11 | 8 | 6 |
| 13 | 18 | 19 | Tax Returns | 4 | 5 | 1 | 3 | 5 | 1 |
| 237 | 251 | 262 | Other | 7 | 22 | 10 | 19 | 47 | 157 |
| 4/1/09-3/31/10 ALL | 4/1/10-3/31/11 ALL | 4/1/11-3/31/12 ALL | | 288 (4/1-9/30/11) | | | 351 (10/1/11-3/31/12) | | |
| 568 | 633 | 639 | **NUMBER OF STATEMENTS** | 22 | 36 | 16 | 51 | 112 | 402 |
| % | % | % | **ASSETS** | % | % | % | % | % | % |
| 14.4 | 14.8 | 15.6 | Cash & Equivalents | 16.2 | 17.5 | 25.6 | 21.7 | 18.0 | 13.5 |
| 17.6 | 17.6 | 15.4 | Trade Receivables (net) | 4.1 | 4.1 | 11.9 | 12.3 | 19.0 | 16.5 |
| 2.2 | 2.2 | 2.4 | Inventory | .0 | 1.5 | 1.7 | 2.6 | 3.8 | 2.2 |
| 3.5 | 3.3 | 2.9 | All Other Current | 1.6 | 3.0 | 7.1 | 2.6 | 2.9 | 2.8 |
| 37.6 | 37.9 | 36.2 | Total Current | 21.9 | 26.0 | 46.3 | 39.2 | 43.7 | 35.0 |
| 44.7 | 45.1 | 45.2 | Fixed Assets (net) | 70.7 | 59.1 | 35.6 | 41.9 | 45.7 | 43.2 |
| 2.6 | 3.1 | 2.7 | Intangibles (net) | .7 | 2.9 | 1.6 | 3.9 | 2.3 | 2.8 |
| 15.1 | 13.8 | 15.9 | All Other Non-Current | 6.8 | 12.0 | 16.6 | 15.0 | 8.3 | 19.0 |
| 100.0 | 100.0 | 100.0 | Total | 100.0 | 100.0 | 100.0 | 100.0 | 100.0 | 100.0 |
| | | | **LIABILITIES** | | | | | | |
| 3.1 | 3.7 | 3.6 | Notes Payable-Short Term | 34.7 | 1.8 | 7.8 | 4.5 | 3.6 | 1.8 |
| 3.9 | 3.6 | 3.3 | Cur. Mat.-L.T.D. | 4.8 | 4.6 | 2.5 | 3.8 | 3.6 | 3.0 |
| 6.0 | 6.8 | 6.1 | Trade Payables | 4.4 | 2.3 | 1.9 | 4.2 | 9.3 | 6.1 |
| .0 | .1 | .1 | Income Taxes Payable | .2 | .0 | .0 | .1 | .0 | .1 |
| 11.7 | 11.3 | 12.3 | All Other Current | 10.0 | 6.4 | 19.3 | 27.8 | 14.8 | 10.0 |
| 24.7 | 25.5 | 25.5 | Total Current | 54.1 | 15.1 | 31.4 | 40.5 | 31.3 | 21.1 |
| 29.3 | 29.2 | 29.3 | Long-Term Debt | 44.8 | 46.5 | 25.1 | 25.0 | 31.5 | 27.0 |
| .1 | .1 | .1 | Deferred Taxes | .0 | .0 | .4 | .0 | .0 | .1 |
| 5.1 | 5.5 | 3.9 | All Other Non-Current | 5.6 | 3.0 | .6 | 2.8 | 4.1 | 4.2 |
| 40.8 | 39.7 | 41.3 | Net Worth | -4.4 | 35.5 | 42.4 | 31.7 | 33.1 | 47.7 |
| 100.0 | 100.0 | 100.0 | Total Liabilties & Net Worth | 100.0 | 100.0 | 100.0 | 100.0 | 100.0 | 100.0 |
| | | | **INCOME DATA** | | | | | | |
| 100.0 | 100.0 | 100.0 | Net Sales | 100.0 | 100.0 | 100.0 | 100.0 | 100.0 | 100.0 |
| | | | Gross Profit | | | | | | |
| 93.3 | 91.9 | 92.4 | Operating Expenses | 75.7 | 71.7 | 78.6 | 93.1 | 93.2 | 95.4 |
| 6.7 | 8.1 | 7.6 | Operating Profit | 24.3 | 28.3 | 21.4 | 6.9 | 6.8 | 4.6 |
| 1.5 | 1.4 | 1.6 | All Other Expenses (net) | 14.8 | 14.9 | 3.9 | .2 | .5 | .1 |
| 5.2 | 6.7 | 6.0 | Profit Before Taxes | 9.5 | 13.4 | 17.5 | 6.7 | 6.3 | 4.5 |
| | | | **RATIOS** | | | | | | |
| 3.0 | 2.8 | 2.8 | Current | 4.1 | 3.7 | 12.4 | 2.6 | 3.3 | 2.7 |
| 1.9 | 1.8 | 1.8 | | .4 | 1.4 | 3.2 | 1.5 | 1.9 | 1.8 |
| 1.3 | 1.2 | 1.1 | | .1 | .6 | .6 | .7 | 1.1 | 1.2 |
| 2.4 | 2.5 | 2.5 | Quick | 4.0 | 3.1 | 11.5 | 2.2 | 2.9 | 2.3 |
| 1.6 | 1.5 | 1.5 | | .4 | 1.2 | 2.7 | 1.2 | 1.6 | 1.6 |
| 1.1 | .9 | .9 | | .0 | .5 | .5 | .6 | .9 | 1.0 |
| 36  10.2 | 34  10.8 | 33  11.2 | Sales/Receivables | 0  UND | 0  UND | 0  UND | 0  UND | 31  11.6 | 38  9.5 |
| 45  8.1 | 44  8.4 | 45  8.2 | | 0  UND | 0  UND | 0  UND | 33  11.2 | 42  8.7 | 47  7.8 |
| 55  6.7 | 55  6.7 | 54  6.7 | | 1  595.8 | 31  11.7 | 69  5.3 | 51  7.1 | 57  6.4 | 55  6.6 |
| | | | Cost of Sales/Inventory | | | | | | |
| | | | Cost of Sales/Payables | | | | | | |
| 4.7 | 5.0 | 4.8 | Sales/Working Capital | 9.9 | 5.2 | 4.4 | 5.2 | 4.3 | 4.8 |
| 8.6 | 9.5 | 9.0 | | -3.6 | 22.3 | 6.5 | 16.3 | 8.6 | 8.5 |
| 24.0 | 37.4 | 63.7 | | -1.1 | -10.6 | -14.4 | -67.9 | 104.1 | 30.1 |
| 8.3 | 11.5 | 10.7 | EBIT/Interest | 6.2 | 11.4 | 43.8 | 21.3 | 19.6 | 8.9 |
| (517) 2.9 | (569) 3.6 | (563) 3.5 | | (11) .2 | (20) 5.2 | (11) 16.0 | (42) 3.4 | (98) 3.1 | (381) 3.4 |
| .9 | 1.4 | .8 | | -1.5 | 1.6 | 2.9 | -.1 | .7 | .9 |
| 5.6 | 5.2 | 7.9 | Net Profit + Depr., Dep., | | | | | | 6.1 |
| (23) 2.9 | (36) 2.8 | (32) 2.9 | Amort./Cur. Mat. L/T/D | | | | | | (21) 2.2 |
| 1.6 | .9 | 1.6 | | | | | | | 1.2 |
| .7 | .6 | .6 | Fixed/Worth | 1.5 | .4 | .1 | .4 | .6 | .6 |
| 1.0 | 1.0 | 1.0 | | 8.6 | 4.3 | .5 | .9 | 1.1 | 1.0 |
| 2.0 | 2.1 | 2.2 | | -2.8 | 33.6 | 2.3 | 7.8 | 3.1 | 1.5 |
| .6 | .5 | .5 | Debt/Worth | 1.8 | .5 | .1 | .5 | .5 | .5 |
| 1.1 | 1.1 | 1.1 | | 7.9 | 4.6 | 1.2 | 1.3 | 1.2 | 1.0 |
| 2.9 | 3.4 | 3.2 | | -61.9 | 34.4 | NM | 26.1 | 5.0 | 2.3 |
| 17.2 | 29.2 | 26.7 | % Profit Before Taxes/Tangible | 128.8 | 98.5 | 103.7 | 60.7 | 37.1 | 15.1 |
| (500) 6.6 | (551) 8.1 | (560) 7.6 | Net Worth | (16) 35.7 | (29) 26.9 | (12) 46.1 | (39) 13.8 | (93) 8.8 | (371) 6.5 |
| .0 | 1.6 | .6 | | -.4 | 3.4 | 1.0 | 2.9 | -1.9 | .7 |
| 9.0 | 10.8 | 9.3 | % Profit Before Taxes/Total | 9.3 | 23.1 | 78.5 | 18.3 | 15.0 | 7.7 |
| 3.1 | 4.3 | 3.4 | Assets | 1.6 | 5.9 | 10.7 | 3.9 | 4.2 | 3.3 |
| -.5 | .5 | -.4 | | -1.3 | 1.5 | .5 | -2.4 | -1.3 | .0 |
| 4.7 | 5.3 | 5.2 | Sales/Net Fixed Assets | 6.8 | 17.6 | 38.2 | 12.4 | 8.4 | 4.3 |
| 2.6 | 2.8 | 2.5 | | .2 | .5 | 3.6 | 4.0 | 3.1 | 2.5 |
| 1.8 | 1.8 | 1.6 | | .1 | .2 | .9 | 1.9 | 1.7 | 1.8 |
| 1.7 | 1.8 | 1.8 | Sales/Total Assets | 2.8 | 1.5 | 3.6 | 3.0 | 2.5 | 1.6 |
| 1.2 | 1.2 | 1.1 | | .2 | .3 | 1.7 | 1.6 | 1.5 | 1.1 |
| .8 | .8 | .8 | | .1 | .1 | .4 | .7 | .9 | .8 |
| 3.3 | 2.9 | 3.0 | % Depr., Dep., Amort./Sales | 10.2 | 6.3 | 1.0 | 2.4 | 2.3 | 3.1 |
| (481) 4.7 | (558) 4.5 | (565) 4.6 | | (17) 18.8 | (30) 17.3 | (13) 6.2 | (45) 4.2 | (106) 4.1 | (354) 4.5 |
| 6.1 | 6.3 | 6.6 | | 32.6 | 26.3 | 16.7 | 6.7 | 6.0 | 5.9 |
| 6.2 | 7.9 | 5.0 | % Officers', Directors' | | | | 6.0 | 1.2 | 5.6 |
| (66) 13.8 | (65) 15.3 | (68) 23.9 | Owners' Comp/Sales | | | (10) 23.4 | (12) 37.1 | (35) 14.9 | |
| 36.5 | 39.8 | 39.1 | | | | | 37.5 | 40.4 | 40.3 |
| 39889287M | 43915672M | 41837397M | Net Sales ($) | 12160M | 71192M | 62297M | 376890M | 1841624M | 39473234M |
| 36954669M | 38810551M | 38948192M | Total Assets ($) | 68946M | 292159M | 157894M | 433507M | 1657146M | 36338540M |

M = $ thousand     MM = $ million
See Pages 9 through 22 for Explanation of Ratios and Data

## Current Data Sorted by Assets

## Comparative Historical Data

| | | | | | | Type of Statement | | |
|---|---|---|---|---|---|---|---|---|
| 3 | 1 | 7 | 36 | 31 | 36 | Unqualified | 229 | 245 |
| | | | | | | Reviewed | 1 | |
| | | | | | 1 | Compiled | 2 | 1 |
| | | | | | | Tax Returns | 1 | |
| 1 | 1 | 5 | 9 | 7 | 18 | Other | 113 | 134 |
| | 113 (4/1-9/30/11) | | | 43 (10/1/11-3/31/12) | | | 4/1/07- | 4/1/08- |
| | | | | | | | 3/31/08 | 3/31/09 |
| 0-500M | 500M-2MM | 2-10MM | 10-50MM | 50-100MM | 100-250MM | | ALL | ALL |
| 4 | 2 | 12 | 45 | 38 | 55 | NUMBER OF STATEMENTS | 346 | 380 |
| % | % | % | % | % | % | ASSETS | % | % |
| | | 11.1 | 12.2 | 14.6 | 12.4 | Cash & Equivalents | 11.2 | 11.5 |
| | | 32.4 | 14.9 | 14.1 | 11.2 | Trade Receivables (net) | 15.6 | 15.2 |
| | | 2.9 | 2.5 | 2.2 | 1.6 | Inventory | 1.8 | 1.8 |
| | | 2.1 | 3.1 | 2.1 | 5.1 | All Other Current | 2.8 | 3.0 |
| | | 48.6 | 32.7 | 33.0 | 30.3 | Total Current | 31.5 | 31.5 |
| | | 43.6 | 48.5 | 44.7 | 45.8 | Fixed Assets (net) | 43.6 | 46.2 |
| | | .0 | .6 | .6 | 1.1 | Intangibles (net) | .9 | .7 |
| | | 7.8 | 18.3 | 21.6 | 22.8 | All Other Non-Current | 23.9 | 21.5 |
| | | 100.0 | 100.0 | 100.0 | 100.0 | Total | 100.0 | 100.0 |
| | | | | | | LIABILITIES | | |
| | | 2.1 | .3 | .6 | 1.5 | Notes Payable-Short Term | .8 | .7 |
| | | 2.9 | 2.0 | 1.8 | 1.8 | Cur. Mat.-L.T.D. | 2.4 | 2.1 |
| | | 15.8 | 5.9 | 5.5 | 4.8 | Trade Payables | 6.6 | 6.0 |
| | | .0 | .0 | .1 | .0 | Income Taxes Payable | .0 | .0 |
| | | 14.9 | 7.8 | 9.9 | 7.4 | All Other Current | 9.4 | 10.6 |
| | | 35.7 | 16.0 | 17.9 | 15.6 | Total Current | 19.1 | 19.4 |
| | | 16.0 | 30.0 | 24.6 | 28.9 | Long-Term Debt | 27.1 | 27.6 |
| | | .0 | .0 | .0 | .2 | Deferred Taxes | .0 | .0 |
| | | 6.0 | 6.2 | 6.7 | 9.3 | All Other Non-Current | 4.5 | 6.9 |
| | | 42.3 | 47.8 | 50.8 | 46.1 | Net Worth | 49.3 | 46.2 |
| | | 100.0 | 100.0 | 100.0 | 100.0 | Total Liabilities & Net Worth | 100.0 | 100.0 |
| | | | | | | INCOME DATA | | |
| | | 100.0 | 100.0 | 100.0 | 100.0 | Net Sales | 100.0 | 100.0 |
| | | | | | | Gross Profit | | |
| | | 101.4 | 98.4 | 97.2 | 94.8 | Operating Expenses | 96.7 | 97.5 |
| | | -1.4 | 1.6 | 2.8 | 5.2 | Operating Profit | 3.3 | 2.5 |
| | | -2.0 | -.5 | .3 | 2.4 | All Other Expenses (net) | -.1 | 2.1 |
| | | .7 | 2.1 | 2.5 | 2.8 | Profit Before Taxes | 3.5 | .4 |
| | | | | | | RATIOS | | |
| | | 2.1 | 3.2 | 3.2 | 2.8 | | 2.5 | 2.5 |
| | | 1.3 | 2.3 | 2.1 | 1.8 | Current | 1.8 | 1.7 |
| | | .9 | 1.3 | 1.3 | 1.4 | | 1.3 | 1.3 |
| | | 2.0 | 2.9 | 3.0 | 2.3 | | 2.2 | 2.3 |
| | | 1.2 | 1.9 | 1.8 | 1.6 | Quick | 1.6 | 1.5 |
| | | .8 | 1.0 | 1.1 | 1.0 | | 1.0 | 1.0 |
| | 38 | 9.6 | 37   9.9 | 34   10.7 | 35   10.5 | | 42   8.8 | 39   9.3 |
| | 47 | 7.8 | 47   7.8 | 45   8.2 | 41   8.8 | Sales/Receivables | 50   7.3 | 49   7.5 |
| | 68 | 5.4 | 54   6.8 | 54   6.7 | 51   7.1 | | 58   6.2 | 57   6.4 |
| | | | | | | Cost of Sales/Inventory | | |
| | | | | | | Cost of Sales/Payables | | |
| | | 6.9 | 3.5 | 3.7 | 3.7 | | 5.0 | 5.1 |
| | | 23.1 | 7.8 | 6.4 | 8.9 | Sales/Working Capital | 8.3 | 9.6 |
| | | -107.6 | 28.1 | 18.5 | 18.2 | | 25.6 | 24.4 |
| | | 6.1 | 8.6 | 6.0 | | | 6.3 | 4.4 |
| | | (41)   1.9 | (36)   2.1 | (53)   3.7 | | EBIT/Interest | (329)   3.0 | (354)   1.8 |
| | | .1 | .6 | 1.2 | | | 1.2 | -.5 |
| | | | | | | Net Profit + Depr., Dep., Amort./Cur. Mat. L/T/D | | |
| | | .6 | .6 | .6 | .8 | | .6 | .7 |
| | | 1.3 | 1.0 | .9 | 1.0 | Fixed/Worth | .9 | 1.0 |
| | | 1.8 | 2.2 | 1.3 | 1.3 | | 1.2 | 1.5 |
| | | .5 | .6 | .4 | .6 | | .6 | .6 |
| | | 1.3 | .9 | 1.0 | 1.1 | Debt/Worth | .9 | 1.1 |
| | | 2.6 | 3.0 | 1.7 | 1.8 | | 1.5 | 1.9 |
| | | 16.2 | 11.5 | 8.3 | 12.2 | | 10.4 | 9.0 |
| | | (10)   5.0 | (43)   3.2 | (37)   3.4 | (51)   4.7 | % Profit Before Taxes/Tangible Net Worth | (331)   6.4 | (365)   2.4 |
| | | -16.2 | -2.4 | -.4 | 1.0 | | .6 | -6.6 |
| | | 9.1 | 5.6 | 4.8 | 6.0 | | 5.5 | 4.3 |
| | | 1.9 | 1.5 | 1.4 | 2.5 | % Profit Before Taxes/Total Assets | 2.7 | 1.0 |
| | | -10.7 | -1.6 | -.7 | .3 | | .1 | -3.0 |
| | | 11.4 | 4.0 | 3.3 | 2.8 | | 3.4 | 3.0 |
| | | 4.1 | 2.4 | 2.2 | 2.1 | Sales/Net Fixed Assets | 2.4 | 2.3 |
| | | 3.0 | 1.6 | 1.5 | 1.6 | | 1.9 | 1.8 |
| | | 2.4 | 1.6 | 1.4 | 1.1 | | 1.4 | 1.3 |
| | | 1.9 | 1.1 | 1.0 | .9 | Sales/Total Assets | 1.1 | 1.0 |
| | | 1.6 | .9 | .8 | .8 | | .8 | .8 |
| | | 1.3 | 3.2 | 4.0 | 4.1 | | 3.8 | 3.7 |
| | | 3.1 | 4.6   (37) | 5.2   (45) | 5.4 | % Depr., Dep., Amort./Sales | (298)   4.6 | (322)   4.9 |
| | | 4.7 | 6.5 | 6.4 | 6.2 | | 5.7 | 5.9 |
| | | | | | | | 2.0 | 4.0 |
| | | | | | | % Officers', Directors' Owners' Comp/Sales | (16)   10.6 | (17)   11.2 |
| | | | | | | | 17.2 | 17.7 |
| 727M | 15604M | 151902M | 1616629M | 2894047M | 8708403M | Net Sales ($) | 34155607M | 40264786M |
| 748M | 3887M | 70324M | 1374119M | 2492346M | 9085288M | Total Assets ($) | 33396848M | 38525970M |

M = $ thousand    MM = $ million
See Pages 9 through 22 for Explanation of Ratios and Data

## Comparative Historical Data / Current Data Sorted by Sales

| | 207 | 231 | 114 | Type of Statement | 3 | 1 | | 10 | 12 | 88 |
|---|---|---|---|---|---|---|---|---|---|---|
| | | | | Unqualified | | | | | | |
| | | | | Reviewed | | | | | | |
| | | | 1 | Compiled | | | | | | 1 |
| | | | | Tax Returns | | | | | | |
| | 116 | 134 | 41 | Other | 1 | | | 2 | 7 | 31 |
| | 4/1/09-3/31/10 ALL | 4/1/10-3/31/11 ALL | 4/1/11-3/31/12 ALL | | 113 (4/1-9/30/11) | | | 43 (10/1/11-3/31/12) | | |
| | | | | | 0-1MM | 1-3MM | 3-5MM | 5-10MM | 10-25MM | 25MM & OVER |
| | 323 | 365 | 156 | NUMBER OF STATEMENTS | 4 | 1 | | 12 | 19 | 120 |
| | % | % | % | | % | % | | % | % | % |
| | | | | **ASSETS** | | | | | | |
| | 11.0 | 12.9 | 12.9 | Cash & Equivalents | | | | 12.8 | 12.9 | 13.1 |
| | 14.7 | 15.1 | 14.9 | Trade Receivables (net) | | | | 24.9 | 14.2 | 14.1 |
| | 2.1 | 2.0 | 2.4 | Inventory | | | | 4.7 | 2.5 | 2.2 |
| | 2.9 | 3.7 | 3.4 | All Other Current | | | | 3.0 | 6.8 | 3.0 |
| | 30.7 | 33.7 | 33.6 | Total Current | | | | 45.5 | 36.3 | 32.3 |
| | 47.1 | 46.5 | 45.7 | Fixed Assets (net) | | | | 38.6 | 49.9 | 46.1 |
| | .8 | .8 | .7 | Intangibles (net) | | | | .1 | .6 | .8 |
| | 21.4 | 19.0 | 20.0 | All Other Non-Current | | | | 15.8 | 13.3 | 20.7 |
| | 100.0 | 100.0 | 100.0 | Total | | | | 100.0 | 100.0 | 100.0 |
| | | | | **LIABILITIES** | | | | | | |
| | .5 | .8 | 1.0 | Notes Payable-Short Term | | | | 2.6 | .3 | 1.0 |
| | 2.2 | 2.4 | 2.0 | Cur. Mat.-L.T.D. | | | | .9 | 2.5 | 2.0 |
| | 5.9 | 6.7 | 6.2 | Trade Payables | | | | 10.3 | 6.5 | 5.9 |
| | .0 | .0 | .0 | Income Taxes Payable | | | | .0 | .0 | .0 |
| | 9.6 | 11.1 | 8.8 | All Other Current | | | | 9.8 | 8.2 | 8.8 |
| | 18.2 | 21.0 | 18.0 | Total Current | | | | 23.5 | 17.4 | 17.7 |
| | 26.2 | 28.7 | 26.7 | Long-Term Debt | | | | 22.7 | 35.0 | 26.0 |
| | .0 | .0 | .1 | Deferred Taxes | | | | .0 | .0 | .1 |
| | 6.1 | 7.1 | 7.3 | All Other Non-Current | | | | .9 | 7.0 | 8.1 |
| | 49.5 | 43.2 | 47.9 | Net Worth | | | | 52.9 | 40.5 | 48.2 |
| | 100.0 | 100.0 | 100.0 | Total Liabilities & Net Worth | | | | 100.0 | 100.0 | 100.0 |
| | | | | **INCOME DATA** | | | | | | |
| | 100.0 | 100.0 | 100.0 | Net Sales | | | | 100.0 | 100.0 | 100.0 |
| | | | | Gross Profit | | | | | | |
| | 97.5 | 97.3 | 97.1 | Operating Expenses | | | | 97.5 | 97.0 | 97.4 |
| | 2.5 | 2.7 | 2.9 | Operating Profit | | | | 2.5 | 3.0 | 2.6 |
| | .8 | .8 | .6 | All Other Expenses (net) | | | | -.6 | 5.0 | .2 |
| | 1.6 | 1.8 | 2.3 | Profit Before Taxes | | | | 3.1 | -2.0 | 2.4 |
| | | | | **RATIOS** | | | | | | |
| | 2.5 | 2.8 | 3.1 | Current | | | | 2.4 | 4.6 | 3.0 |
| | 1.8 | 1.8 | 2.0 | | | | | 1.7 | 2.8 | 2.0 |
| | 1.3 | 1.2 | 1.3 | | | | | 1.2 | 1.3 | 1.3 |
| | 2.1 | 2.3 | 2.6 | Quick | | | | 2.2 | 3.2 | 2.5 |
| | 1.5 | 1.5 | 1.6 | | | | | 1.2 | 1.9 | 1.6 |
| | 1.0 | .9 | 1.0 | | | | | .9 | 1.1 | 1.0 |
| | 38  9.6 | 38  9.6 | 35  10.3 | Sales/Receivables | | | | 30  12.1 | 40  9.2 | 35  10.3 |
| | 46  7.9 | 46  8.0 | 44  8.3 | | | | | 42  8.6 | 47  7.7 | 43  8.4 |
| | 54  6.7 | 54  6.8 | 53  6.9 | | | | | 79  4.6 | 60  6.1 | 52  7.0 |
| | | | | Cost of Sales/Inventory | | | | | | |
| | | | | Cost of Sales/Payables | | | | | | |
| | 5.5 | 4.6 | 3.8 | Sales/Working Capital | | | | 5.1 | 2.7 | 4.1 |
| | 9.1 | 9.0 | 8.4 | | | | | 9.7 | 5.6 | 8.7 |
| | 21.2 | 29.1 | 20.6 | | | | | 50.6 | 23.9 | 17.8 |
| | 4.9 | 5.1 | 6.1 | EBIT/Interest | | | | | 3.0 | 6.2 |
| | (308) 2.6 | (340) 2.5 | (143) 2.5 | | | | | | (18) .8 | (112) 2.9 |
| | .4 | .7 | .8 | | | | | | -4.2 | 1.0 |
| | | | | Net Profit + Depr., Dep., Amort./Cur. Mat. L/T/D | | | | | | |
| | .7 | .7 | .7 | Fixed/Worth | | | | .3 | .7 | .7 |
| | 1.0 | 1.0 | 1.0 | | | | | .8 | 1.5 | 1.0 |
| | 1.4 | 1.5 | 1.3 | | | | | 1.2 | 4.5 | 1.3 |
| | .6 | .6 | .6 | Debt/Worth | | | | .4 | .5 | .6 |
| | .9 | 1.1 | 1.0 | | | | | .7 | 1.3 | 1.0 |
| | 1.7 | 2.0 | 1.9 | | | | | 1.7 | 5.3 | 1.7 |
| | 9.2 | 9.6 | 10.3 | % Profit Before Taxes/Tangible Net Worth | | | | 16.7 | 8.9 | 10.3 |
| | (317) 3.6 | (344) 4.4 | (147) 4.0 | | | | | (11) 5.2 | (16) -.2 | (115) 4.0 |
| | -.9 | -1.2 | -.7 | | | | | -10.6 | -6.5 | .3 |
| | 4.8 | 4.6 | 5.0 | % Profit Before Taxes/Total Assets | | | | 9.1 | 2.6 | 5.3 |
| | 1.8 | 2.1 | 1.8 | | | | | 2.9 | -.4 | 2.2 |
| | -.6 | -.6 | -.6 | | | | | -5.8 | -3.7 | .0 |
| | 3.1 | 3.4 | 3.3 | Sales/Net Fixed Assets | | | | 20.3 | 3.6 | 3.1 |
| | 2.3 | 2.4 | 2.2 | | | | | 3.7 | 1.7 | 2.3 |
| | 1.7 | 1.8 | 1.6 | | | | | 1.8 | 1.0 | 1.7 |
| | 1.4 | 1.5 | 1.5 | Sales/Total Assets | | | | 2.7 | 1.2 | 1.4 |
| | 1.0 | 1.1 | 1.0 | | | | | 1.7 | 1.0 | 1.0 |
| | .8 | .9 | .8 | | | | | .9 | .5 | .8 |
| | 4.0 | 3.8 | 3.7 | % Depr., Dep., Amort./Sales | | | | 1.2 | 4.6 | 3.7 |
| | (274) 5.0 | (324) 4.8 | (145) 5.1 | | | | | 3.1 | (18) 6.7 | (110) 5.1 |
| | 6.0 | 6.0 | 6.2 | | | | | 4.9 | 9.2 | 5.9 |
| | 10.1 | | | % Officers', Directors', Owners' Comp/Sales | | | | | | |
| | (10) 21.1 | | | | | | | | | |
| | 41.6 | | | | | | | | | |
| | 33447591M | 36209025M | 13387312M | Net Sales ($) | 727M | 1392M | | 97859M | 334781M | 12952553M |
| | 31586656M | 33016109M | 13026712M | Total Assets ($) | 748M | 39028M | | 114353M | 661063M | 12211520M |

*(Current data columns 0-1MM, 1-3MM, and 3-5MM: DATA NOT AVAILABLE)*

© RMA 2012

M = $ thousand    MM = $ million
See Pages 9 through 22 for Explanation of Ratios and Data

## Current Data Sorted by Assets      Comparative Historical Data

| 0-500M | 500M-2MM | 2-10MM | 10-50MM | 50-100MM | 100-250MM | Type of Statement | 4/1/07-3/31/08 ALL | 4/1/08-3/31/09 ALL |
|---|---|---|---|---|---|---|---|---|
| 1 | 3 | 14 | 20 | 8 | | Unqualified | 57 | 56 |
| | | 1 | | | | Reviewed | 1 | 3 |
| 1 | 3 | 1 | | | | Compiled | 2 | 4 |
| 3 | | | | | | Tax Returns | | 1 |
| | 4 | 7 | 9 | 1 | 1 | Other | 25 | 28 |
| | 45 (4/1-9/30/11) | | 32 (10/1/11-3/31/12) | | | | | |
| 5 | 10 | 23 | 29 | 9 | 1 | NUMBER OF STATEMENTS | 85 | 92 |
| % | % | % | % | % | % | **ASSETS** | % | % |
| | 22.0 | 20.2 | 16.8 | | | Cash & Equivalents | 18.6 | 19.1 |
| | 16.9 | 22.1 | 14.7 | | | Trade Receivables (net) | 19.0 | 18.0 |
| | .2 | .4 | .4 | | | Inventory | .5 | .6 |
| | 7.0 | 4.1 | 5.0 | | | All Other Current | 4.9 | 3.5 |
| | 46.1 | 46.7 | 36.9 | | | Total Current | 43.0 | 41.2 |
| | 26.9 | 39.1 | 45.2 | | | Fixed Assets (net) | 43.2 | 42.9 |
| | 4.5 | .8 | 4.8 | | | Intangibles (net) | 3.1 | 4.7 |
| | 22.5 | 13.5 | 13.1 | | | All Other Non-Current | 10.8 | 11.3 |
| | 100.0 | 100.0 | 100.0 | | | Total | 100.0 | 100.0 |
| | | | | | | **LIABILITIES** | | |
| | 10.2 | 1.0 | .7 | | | Notes Payable-Short Term | 3.3 | 3.8 |
| | 15.1 | 1.9 | 2.3 | | | Cur. Mat.-L.T.D. | 2.3 | 2.4 |
| | 3.7 | 5.7 | 5.8 | | | Trade Payables | 5.7 | 5.9 |
| | .0 | .0 | .0 | | | Income Taxes Payable | .3 | .1 |
| | 22.3 | 11.2 | 12.9 | | | All Other Current | 14.2 | 13.3 |
| | 51.3 | 19.8 | 21.6 | | | Total Current | 25.8 | 25.6 |
| | 21.1 | 10.5 | 25.3 | | | Long-Term Debt | 21.5 | 27.8 |
| | .0 | .0 | .0 | | | Deferred Taxes | .0 | .1 |
| | 2.3 | 8.8 | 3.4 | | | All Other Non-Current | 3.6 | 9.4 |
| | 25.2 | 60.9 | 49.6 | | | Net Worth | 49.1 | 37.1 |
| | 100.0 | 100.0 | 100.0 | | | Total Liabilities & Net Worth | 100.0 | 100.0 |
| | | | | | | **INCOME DATA** | | |
| | 100.0 | 100.0 | 100.0 | | | Net Sales | 100.0 | 100.0 |
| | | | | | | Gross Profit | | |
| | 86.6 | 96.7 | 96.9 | | | Operating Expenses | 95.9 | 95.2 |
| | 13.4 | 3.3 | 3.1 | | | Operating Profit | 4.1 | 4.8 |
| | -.4 | -.8 | .5 | | | All Other Expenses (net) | .5 | 3.2 |
| | 13.9 | 4.0 | 2.6 | | | Profit Before Taxes | 3.7 | 1.6 |
| | | | | | | **RATIOS** | | |
| | 3.6 | 3.5 | 2.9 | | | | 2.8 | 3.1 |
| | 1.7 | 2.7 | 1.9 | | | Current | 1.9 | 2.0 |
| | .2 | 1.7 | 1.3 | | | | 1.1 | 1.2 |
| | 3.5 | 3.5 | 2.7 | | | | 2.7 | 2.8 |
| | 1.7 | 2.6 | 1.8 | | | Quick | 1.6 | 1.7 |
| | .1 | 1.3 | 1.1 | | | | 1.0 | .9 |
| | 0 UND | 16 22.8 | 16 22.5 | | | | 17 20.9 | 16 23.2 |
| | 16 22.2 | 31 11.6 | 36 10.0 | | | Sales/Receivables | 37 9.9 | 39 9.3 |
| | 38 9.6 | 60 6.1 | 51 7.2 | | | | 59 6.2 | 54 6.7 |
| | | | | | | Cost of Sales/Inventory | | |
| | | | | | | Cost of Sales/Payables | | |
| | 11.2 | 3.7 | 5.1 | | | | 4.7 | 5.1 |
| | 28.1 | 6.6 | 12.3 | | | Sales/Working Capital | 10.5 | 8.9 |
| | -12.2 | 12.5 | 30.7 | | | | 49.0 | 39.5 |
| | | 10.8 | 12.1 | | | | 12.2 | 10.5 |
| | | (18) 5.6 | (25) 4.6 | | | EBIT/Interest | (68) 3.0 | (76) 2.0 |
| | | -.4 | 1.4 | | | | 1.4 | -.9 |
| | | | | | | Net Profit + Depr., Dep., Amort./Cur. Mat. L/T/D | | |
| | .2 | .3 | .6 | | | | .5 | .6 |
| | .4 | .7 | .9 | | | Fixed/Worth | .9 | 1.0 |
| | 1.0 | 1.1 | 1.9 | | | | 1.4 | 2.4 |
| | .2 | .2 | .5 | | | | .5 | .5 |
| | 1.1 | .5 | .8 | | | Debt/Worth | .9 | 1.0 |
| | 2.8 | .8 | 2.7 | | | | 2.2 | 3.7 |
| | | 18.6 | 19.9 | | | | 22.4 | 18.4 |
| | | (22) 9.1 | (26) 9.1 | | | % Profit Before Taxes/Tangible Net Worth | (79) 6.6 | (79) 6.0 |
| | | -1.5 | 4.2 | | | | 1.6 | -5.9 |
| | 53.5 | 11.0 | 7.8 | | | | 11.8 | 9.6 |
| | 10.8 | 7.1 | 4.1 | | | % Profit Before Taxes/Total Assets | 3.2 | 2.5 |
| | -5.0 | -.9 | .6 | | | | .6 | -2.6 |
| | 53.9 | 17.4 | 6.5 | | | | 7.6 | 8.6 |
| | 15.5 | 5.2 | 3.1 | | | Sales/Net Fixed Assets | 3.3 | 3.4 |
| | 4.9 | 2.1 | 1.9 | | | | 1.9 | 2.0 |
| | 5.2 | 2.6 | 2.0 | | | | 2.5 | 2.3 |
| | 3.1 | 1.4 | 1.6 | | | Sales/Total Assets | 1.5 | 1.5 |
| | 1.4 | 1.1 | 1.1 | | | | 1.1 | 1.0 |
| | | 1.2 | 1.6 | | | | 1.5 | 1.5 |
| | | (22) 2.0 | (27) 2.5 | | | % Depr., Dep., Amort./Sales | (81) 2.7 | (81) 2.5 |
| | | 3.9 | 3.4 | | | | 3.7 | 3.7 |
| | | | | | | % Officers', Directors' Owners' Comp/Sales | | |
| 3386M | 35395M | 242853M | 1197517M | 862220M | 298293M | Net Sales ($) | 2036852M | 2987261M |
| 393M | 10007M | 129860M | 713958M | 611876M | 131056M | Total Assets ($) | 1526606M | 2272749M |

M = $ thousand   MM = $ million
See Pages 9 through 22 for Explanation of Ratios and Data

## Comparative Historical Data

## Current Data Sorted by Sales

| 4/1/09-3/31/10 ALL | 4/1/10-3/31/11 ALL | 4/1/11-3/31/12 ALL | Type of Statement | 0-1MM | 1-3MM | 3-5MM | 5-10MM | 10-25MM | 25MM & OVER |
|---|---|---|---|---|---|---|---|---|---|
| 46 | 49 | 46 | Unqualified | 2 | 3 | 1 | 7 | 11 | 22 |
| 5 | 11 | 1 | Reviewed | | | | 1 | | |
| 2 | 3 | 5 | Compiled | 1 | 3 | | 1 | | |
| 5 | 9 | 3 | Tax Returns | 2 | 1 | | | | |
| 27 | 22 | 22 | Other | 1 | 2 | | 5 | 4 | 10 |
| | | | | 45 (4/1-9/30/11) | | | 32 (10/1/11-3/31/12) | | |
| 85 | 94 | 77 | **NUMBER OF STATEMENTS** | 6 | 9 | 1 | 14 | 15 | 32 |
| % | % | % | **ASSETS** | % | % | % | % | % | % |
| 17.9 | 21.1 | 20.0 | Cash & Equivalents | | | | 22.1 | 15.6 | 18.0 |
| 18.9 | 14.9 | 17.1 | Trade Receivables (net) | | | | 18.3 | 22.3 | 18.3 |
| .5 | .3 | .4 | Inventory | | | | .2 | .4 | .7 |
| 4.0 | 3.5 | 5.0 | All Other Current | | | | 5.0 | 3.0 | 5.0 |
| 41.3 | 39.8 | 42.6 | Total Current | | | | 45.5 | 41.2 | 42.0 |
| 42.6 | 40.3 | 38.2 | Fixed Assets (net) | | | | 27.4 | 45.8 | 41.4 |
| 5.3 | 4.2 | 2.9 | Intangibles (net) | | | | 2.1 | .3 | 4.3 |
| 10.8 | 15.8 | 16.4 | All Other Non-Current | | | | 25.1 | 12.7 | 12.3 |
| 100.0 | 100.0 | 100.0 | Total | | | | 100.0 | 100.0 | 100.0 |
| | | | **LIABILITIES** | | | | | | |
| 12.6 | 8.6 | 9.6 | Notes Payable-Short Term | | | | 5.3 | 1.7 | .9 |
| 3.7 | 2.5 | 4.2 | Cur. Mat.-L.T.D. | | | | .9 | 1.5 | 3.0 |
| 8.6 | 5.9 | 5.4 | Trade Payables | | | | 3.3 | 8.0 | 7.0 |
| .1 | .1 | .0 | Income Taxes Payable | | | | .0 | .0 | .0 |
| 13.5 | 25.5 | 12.4 | All Other Current | | | | 11.2 | 10.1 | 13.9 |
| 38.4 | 42.7 | 31.6 | Total Current | | | | 20.7 | 21.3 | 24.8 |
| 27.7 | 22.9 | 18.0 | Long-Term Debt | | | | 6.8 | 20.1 | 21.9 |
| .0 | .0 | .0 | Deferred Taxes | | | | .0 | .0 | .0 |
| 4.5 | 7.0 | 8.7 | All Other Non-Current | | | | 2.3 | 12.4 | 7.1 |
| 29.4 | 27.3 | 41.7 | Net Worth | | | | 70.2 | 46.3 | 46.2 |
| 100.0 | 100.0 | 100.0 | Total Liabilities & Net Worth | | | | 100.0 | 100.0 | 100.0 |
| | | | **INCOME DATA** | | | | | | |
| 100.0 | 100.0 | 100.0 | Net Sales | | | | 100.0 | 100.0 | 100.0 |
| | | | Gross Profit | | | | | | |
| 93.6 | 91.6 | 94.4 | Operating Expenses | | | | 93.3 | 96.3 | 95.9 |
| 6.4 | 8.4 | 5.6 | Operating Profit | | | | 6.7 | 3.7 | 4.1 |
| 2.4 | 1.6 | -.3 | All Other Expenses (net) | | | | -.4 | -.6 | .2 |
| 4.0 | 6.8 | 5.8 | Profit Before Taxes | | | | 7.1 | 4.3 | 3.9 |
| | | | **RATIOS** | | | | | | |
| 2.8 | 3.0 | 3.3 | Current | | | | 4.7 | 3.0 | 2.9 |
| 1.8 | 1.8 | 2.0 | | | | | 3.0 | 2.0 | 1.7 |
| 1.0 | .7 | 1.3 | | | | | 1.9 | 1.4 | 1.3 |
| 2.5 | 2.8 | 3.1 | Quick | | | | 4.6 | 3.0 | 2.7 |
| 1.6 | 1.6 | 1.8 | | | | | 3.0 | 1.8 | 1.6 |
| .8 | .6 | 1.1 | | | | | 1.3 | 1.0 | 1.1 |
| (18) 20.0 | (7) 48.8 | (13) 29.0 | Sales/Receivables | (0) UND | | (29) 12.5 | | (17) 21.2 | |
| (37) 9.8 | (28) 13.0 | (30) 12.0 | | (31) 11.9 | | (43) 8.4 | | (36) 10.0 | |
| (55) 6.7 | (41) 9.0 | (49) 7.4 | | (68) 5.4 | | (56) 6.5 | | (50) 7.3 | |
| | | | Cost of Sales/Inventory | | | | | | |
| | | | Cost of Sales/Payables | | | | | | |
| 4.6 | 5.7 | 4.9 | Sales/Working Capital | | | | 3.6 | 5.8 | 4.9 |
| 11.4 | 13.0 | 10.8 | | | | | 6.4 | 10.3 | 12.8 |
| -365.2 | -42.0 | 27.6 | | | | | 12.4 | 17.1 | 31.5 |
| 8.8 | 14.6 | 14.2 | EBIT/Interest | | | | | 15.1 | 13.0 |
| (71) 3.1 | (77) 6.4 | (60) 6.0 | | | | | | (14) 5.4 | (27) 6.3 |
| .4 | 1.6 | 1.5 | | | | | | .9 | 1.5 |
| 16.2 | 39.9 | | Net Profit + Depr., Dep., | | | | | | |
| (10) 3.1 | (11) 16.3 | | Amort./Cur. Mat. L/T/D | | | | | | |
| .2 | 2.8 | | | | | | | | |
| .7 | .5 | .4 | Fixed/Worth | | | | .1 | .5 | .5 |
| 1.1 | 1.0 | .7 | | | | | .5 | .9 | .9 |
| 3.1 | 2.0 | 1.1 | | | | | .7 | 1.9 | 1.7 |
| .6 | .6 | .3 | Debt/Worth | | | | .1 | .5 | .6 |
| 1.3 | 1.1 | .7 | | | | | .3 | .8 | .8 |
| 6.5 | 4.7 | 2.1 | | | | | .8 | 2.1 | 2.7 |
| 28.3 | 43.5 | 24.4 | % Profit Before Taxes/Tangible | | | | 31.6 | 17.8 | 33.0 |
| (68) 6.6 | (78) 11.0 | (69) 11.2 | Net Worth | | | | 14.2 | (14) 10.5 | (28) 10.5 |
| -1.7 | 1.4 | 3.9 | | | | | 3.7 | .3 | 3.8 |
| 12.4 | 25.9 | 12.5 | % Profit Before Taxes/Total | | | | 14.9 | 10.0 | 11.0 |
| 4.1 | 7.5 | 6.1 | Assets | | | | 9.9 | 5.3 | 6.0 |
| -1.3 | .6 | .9 | | | | | 3.2 | .2 | 1.0 |
| 10.0 | 17.7 | 16.9 | Sales/Net Fixed Assets | | | | 35.8 | 7.3 | 7.5 |
| 3.5 | 4.3 | 4.6 | | | | | 15.5 | 3.5 | 4.1 |
| 2.2 | 2.6 | 2.1 | | | | | 2.6 | 1.7 | 2.3 |
| 2.7 | 3.3 | 2.6 | Sales/Total Assets | | | | 2.9 | 2.8 | 2.4 |
| 1.8 | 2.0 | 1.6 | | | | | 1.6 | 1.5 | 1.7 |
| 1.1 | 1.3 | 1.1 | | | | | 1.1 | 1.0 | 1.1 |
| 1.5 | 1.1 | 1.3 | % Depr., Dep., Amort./Sales | | | | 1.2 | 1.3 | 1.5 |
| (79) 2.4 | (81) 2.0 | (63) 2.3 | | | | | (10) 1.9 | 2.1 | (29) 2.4 |
| 3.6 | 3.5 | 3.4 | | | | | 3.6 | 3.3 | 3.4 |
| | | .7 | % Officers', Directors' | | | | | | |
| | (10) 2.5 | | Owners' Comp/Sales | | | | | | |
| | | 26.0 | | | | | | | |
| 2603123M | 2701356M | 2639664M | Net Sales ($) | 3128M | 17671M | 3731M | 99154M | 271131M | 2244849M |
| 1937680M | 1578541M | 1597150M | Total Assets ($) | 4766M | 12355M | 3281M | 90414M | 239337M | 1246997M |

© RMA 2012

M = $ thousand    MM = $ million
See Pages 9 through 22 for Explanation of Ratios and Data

## Current Data Sorted by Assets | Comparative Historical Data

| Type of Statement | | | | | | | | |
|---|---|---|---|---|---|---|---|---|
| 0-500M | 500M-2MM 39 (4/1-9/30/11) | 2-10MM | 10-50MM 84 (10/1/11-3/31/12) | 50-100MM | 100-250MM | | 4/1/07-3/31/08 ALL | 4/1/08-3/31/09 ALL |

| 0-500M | 500M-2MM | 2-10MM | 10-50MM | 50-100MM | 100-250MM | Type of Statement | 4/1/07-3/31/08 ALL | 4/1/08-3/31/09 ALL |
|---|---|---|---|---|---|---|---|---|
| | | 6 | 24 | 10 | 9 | Unqualified | 58 | 54 |
| | 1 | 1 | | | | Reviewed | 4 | 2 |
| | 2 | 4 | 2 | | | Compiled | 7 | 9 |
| 6 | 3 | 1 | | | | Tax Returns | 8 | 8 |
| 5 | 7 | 16 | 18 | 4 | 4 | Other | 50 | 51 |
| 11 | 13 | 28 | 44 | 14 | 13 | **NUMBER OF STATEMENTS** | 127 | 124 |
| % | % | % | % | % | % | **ASSETS** | % | % |
| 35.9 | 14.7 | 20.8 | 13.2 | 16.9 | 12.9 | Cash & Equivalents | 18.7 | 15.6 |
| .1 | 21.5 | 32.3 | 21.4 | 9.2 | 9.7 | Trade Receivables (net) | 18.9 | 20.2 |
| .2 | 1.2 | 2.4 | 2.6 | .8 | 5.5 | Inventory | 2.0 | 1.3 |
| 1.0 | .2 | 1.6 | 2.1 | 1.8 | 1.4 | All Other Current | 5.6 | 6.0 |
| 37.2 | 37.6 | 57.0 | 39.4 | 28.8 | 29.4 | Total Current | 45.1 | 43.2 |
| 45.9 | 40.7 | 35.5 | 48.1 | 33.6 | 37.8 | Fixed Assets (net) | 38.2 | 37.5 |
| 1.0 | 10.8 | .8 | 6.2 | 7.7 | 16.3 | Intangibles (net) | 3.6 | 2.1 |
| 15.9 | 11.0 | 6.8 | 6.3 | 29.9 | 16.4 | All Other Non-Current | 13.0 | 17.1 |
| 100.0 | 100.0 | 100.0 | 100.0 | 100.0 | 100.0 | Total | 100.0 | 100.0 |
| | | | | | | **LIABILITIES** | | |
| 94.8 | 5.3 | 3.9 | 3.3 | 1.4 | .1 | Notes Payable-Short Term | 8.1 | 10.8 |
| 2.1 | 4.8 | 5.1 | 6.1 | 2.3 | 4.8 | Cur. Mat.-L.T.D. | 4.8 | 3.6 |
| 7.7 | 4.7 | 11.6 | 7.7 | 2.8 | 2.1 | Trade Payables | 7.8 | 8.1 |
| .0 | .0 | .1 | .0 | .0 | .0 | Income Taxes Payable | .0 | .2 |
| 65.2 | 18.0 | 12.2 | 11.6 | 4.6 | 5.1 | All Other Current | 12.8 | 12.1 |
| 169.9 | 32.8 | 32.9 | 28.8 | 11.0 | 12.1 | Total Current | 33.5 | 34.8 |
| 41.3 | 36.7 | 16.6 | 33.0 | 18.0 | 33.2 | Long-Term Debt | 26.9 | 23.4 |
| .0 | .0 | .0 | .2 | .0 | .2 | Deferred Taxes | .1 | .1 |
| .0 | 5.4 | 1.1 | 2.9 | 10.0 | 6.1 | All Other Non-Current | 4.2 | 4.6 |
| -111.2 | 25.2 | 49.4 | 35.0 | 60.9 | 48.4 | Net Worth | 35.3 | 37.0 |
| 100.0 | 100.0 | 100.0 | 100.0 | 100.0 | 100.0 | Total Liabilities & Net Worth | 100.0 | 100.0 |
| | | | | | | **INCOME DATA** | | |
| 100.0 | 100.0 | 100.0 | 100.0 | 100.0 | 100.0 | Net Sales | 100.0 | 100.0 |
| | | | | | | Gross Profit | | |
| 100.8 | 88.0 | 87.5 | 88.6 | 92.3 | 89.4 | Operating Expenses | 90.9 | 91.9 |
| -.8 | 12.0 | 12.5 | 11.4 | 7.7 | 10.6 | Operating Profit | 9.1 | 8.1 |
| .2 | 1.7 | -.7 | 2.0 | .9 | 2.1 | All Other Expenses (net) | 1.6 | 3.6 |
| -.9 | 10.3 | 13.2 | 9.5 | 6.8 | 8.4 | Profit Before Taxes | 7.5 | 4.5 |
| | | | | | | **RATIOS** | | |
| 2.0 | 2.7 | 5.6 | 2.4 | 4.1 | 4.5 | | 3.0 | 3.0 |
| .2 | 1.5 | 1.6 | 1.6 | 2.1 | 2.2 | Current | 1.7 | 1.8 |
| .0 | .3 | 1.2 | .9 | 1.1 | 1.5 | | .9 | 1.1 |
| 2.0 | 2.7 | 4.9 | 2.2 | 3.9 | 4.0 | | 2.5 | 2.5 |
| .2 | 1.5 | 1.5 | 1.4 | 1.7 | 2.0 | Quick | 1.4 | 1.5 |
| .0 | .3 | 1.1 | .7 | .9 | 1.2 | | .7 | .8 |
| 0 UND | 0 UND | 16 22.3 | 39 9.4 | 30 12.0 | 45 8.2 | | 11 33.3 | 14 26.0 |
| 0 UND | 0 UND | 43 8.5 | 45 8.2 | 45 8.1 | 53 6.9 | Sales/Receivables | 46 8.0 | 47 7.7 |
| 0 UND | 62 5.9 | 58 6.3 | 61 6.0 | 57 6.4 | 57 6.4 | | 67 5.5 | 64 5.7 |
| | | | | | | Cost of Sales/Inventory | | |
| | | | | | | Cost of Sales/Payables | | |
| 58.6 | 6.6 | 2.8 | 7.3 | 2.8 | 2.6 | | 4.8 | 5.2 |
| -42.6 | 27.5 | 14.5 | 13.1 | 5.8 | 5.6 | Sales/Working Capital | 11.0 | 11.4 |
| -7.7 | -12.6 | 100.3 | NM | NM | 9.7 | | -148.5 | 175.6 |
| | 14.8 | 43.2 | 27.8 | 15.5 | 9.5 | | 15.3 | 16.4 |
| | (11) 6.0 | (20) 11.2 | (41) 7.0 | (12) 3.3 | (12) 3.5 | EBIT/Interest | (100) 3.5 | (100) 4.0 |
| | 1.1 | 1.0 | 1.8 | .6 | 1.3 | | 1.3 | .5 |
| | | | | | | Net Profit + Depr., Dep., Amort./Cur. Mat. L/T/D | | |
| 2.0 | .4 | .2 | .7 | .3 | .5 | | .4 | .4 |
| -.4 | 2.2 | .7 | 2.1 | .6 | .8 | Fixed/Worth | 1.0 | .8 |
| -.1 | NM | 1.1 | 9.5 | 2.5 | 22.7 | | 8.0 | 3.1 |
| 2.9 | 1.8 | .3 | .9 | .2 | .5 | | .5 | .4 |
| -2.1 | 3.9 | .8 | 2.3 | .5 | .9 | Debt/Worth | 1.6 | 1.0 |
| -1.4 | NM | 1.8 | 22.3 | 2.9 | 32.4 | | 17.5 | 7.2 |
| | 403.4 | 72.2 | 125.1 | 14.5 | 50.3 | | 69.9 | 48.7 |
| | (10) 220.1 | (24) 25.5 | (36) 72.3 | (13) 9.8 | (11) 14.0 | % Profit Before Taxes/Tangible Net Worth | (101) 10.8 | (101) 9.3 |
| | -30.7 | 7.3 | 5.6 | -.8 | 5.5 | | 3.5 | .3 |
| 72.5 | 61.6 | 47.6 | 29.7 | 7.7 | 8.5 | | 26.4 | 15.4 |
| 12.1 | 17.8 | 22.2 | 10.3 | 4.8 | 5.2 | % Profit Before Taxes/Total Assets | 5.4 | 3.8 |
| -19.3 | -6.1 | 3.4 | 2.7 | -.1 | 1.9 | | .8 | -1.0 |
| 120.4 | 24.7 | 29.9 | 7.6 | 2.7 | 3.0 | | 16.8 | 15.9 |
| 62.0 | 9.7 | 7.1 | 2.9 | 2.1 | 1.9 | Sales/Net Fixed Assets | 4.5 | 3.9 |
| 20.4 | 3.3 | 3.0 | 1.9 | 1.5 | 1.0 | | 2.1 | 1.8 |
| 39.8 | 4.1 | 3.9 | 2.5 | 1.0 | .9 | | 2.9 | 2.8 |
| 31.5 | 2.5 | 2.5 | 1.6 | .7 | .6 | Sales/Total Assets | 1.6 | 1.5 |
| 4.4 | 1.8 | 1.1 | 1.1 | .3 | .4 | | .7 | .7 |
| | 1.0 | 1.1 | 1.6 | 3.6 | 3.8 | | 1.6 | 1.8 |
| | (12) 2.1 | (22) 3.5 | (43) 2.9 | 5.7 | (12) 4.9 | % Depr., Dep., Amort./Sales | (109) 3.2 | (106) 3.7 |
| | 8.1 | 5.6 | 6.1 | 6.8 | 6.6 | | 5.0 | 5.1 |
| | | | | | | | 4.6 | 3.5 |
| | | | | | | % Officers', Directors' Owners' Comp/Sales | (18) 8.0 | (19) 9.7 |
| | | | | | | | 19.8 | 24.8 |
| 44081M | 54490M | 468380M | 1859344M | 754375M | 1353194M | Net Sales ($) | 5234318M | 5144051M |
| 1729M | 18213M | 150629M | 1094314M | 1038973M | 2057828M | Total Assets ($) | 5137682M | 5074935M |

M = $ thousand   MM = $ million
See Pages 9 through 22 for Explanation of Ratios and Data

## Comparative Historical Data | | Type of Statement | Current Data Sorted by Sales

| | | | Type of Statement | 0-1MM | 1-3MM | 3-5MM | 5-10MM | 10-25MM | 25MM & OVER |
|---|---|---|---|---|---|---|---|---|---|
| 68 | 58 | 49 | Unqualified | | 4 | 1 | 3 | 9 | 32 |
| 12 | 5 | 2 | Reviewed | | | 1 | | 1 | |
| 8 | 5 | 8 | Compiled | 1 | 1 | 1 | 1 | 3 | 1 |
| 8 | 13 | 10 | Tax Returns | 3 | 3 | 1 | 2 | 1 | |
| 75 | 58 | 54 | Other | 2 | 3 | 5 | 6 | 12 | 26 |
| 4/1/09-3/31/10 ALL | 4/1/10-3/31/11 ALL | 4/1/11-3/31/12 ALL | | | 39 (4/1-9/30/11) | | 84 (10/1/11-3/31/12) | | |
| 171 | 139 | 123 | **NUMBER OF STATEMENTS** | 6 | 11 | 9 | 12 | 26 | 59 |
| % | % | % | **ASSETS** | % | % | % | % | % | % |
| 15.3 | 16.8 | 17.5 | Cash & Equivalents | | 29.6 | | 30.3 | 11.7 | 16.1 |
| 19.0 | 19.9 | 19.3 | Trade Receivables (net) | | 12.2 | | 11.9 | 26.9 | 19.9 |
| 1.9 | 2.2 | 2.3 | Inventory | | .0 | | 1.1 | 1.6 | 3.5 |
| 5.4 | 2.6 | 1.6 | All Other Current | | .4 | | 1.8 | 1.6 | 1.9 |
| 41.5 | 41.5 | 40.7 | Total Current | | 42.2 | | 45.1 | 41.8 | 41.4 |
| 40.6 | 40.9 | 41.5 | Fixed Assets (net) | | 46.6 | | 35.1 | 47.9 | 38.4 |
| 5.2 | 5.5 | 6.2 | Intangibles (net) | | 2.2 | | 6.1 | 6.2 | 8.1 |
| 12.7 | 11.9 | 11.5 | All Other Non-Current | | 8.9 | | 13.8 | 4.2 | 12.2 |
| 100.0 | 100.0 | 100.0 | Total | | 100.0 | | 100.0 | 100.0 | 100.0 |
| | | | **LIABILITIES** | | | | | | |
| 3.2 | 12.1 | 11.3 | Notes Payable-Short Term | | 44.7 | | 9.8 | 8.9 | 2.2 |
| 3.3 | 4.1 | 4.8 | Cur. Mat.-L.T.D. | | 2.0 | | 2.1 | 7.8 | 5.1 |
| 7.3 | 7.5 | 7.1 | Trade Payables | | 3.8 | | 5.8 | 10.3 | 7.0 |
| .2 | .1 | .0 | Income Taxes Payable | | .0 | | .0 | .0 | .1 |
| 18.0 | 14.9 | 15.7 | All Other Current | | 3.0 | | 18.3 | 17.1 | 11.6 |
| 32.0 | 38.6 | 39.0 | Total Current | | 53.4 | | 36.1 | 44.1 | 26.0 |
| 30.3 | 27.0 | 28.7 | Long-Term Debt | | 67.1 | | 18.4 | 28.5 | 27.7 |
| .1 | .2 | .1 | Deferred Taxes | | .6 | | .0 | .0 | .1 |
| 3.8 | 5.1 | 3.6 | All Other Non-Current | | 6.8 | | .1 | 4.3 | 4.2 |
| 33.8 | 28.9 | 28.5 | Net Worth | | -27.9 | | 45.4 | 23.0 | 42.1 |
| 100.0 | 100.0 | 100.0 | Total Liabilities & Net Worth | | 100.0 | | 100.0 | 100.0 | 100.0 |
| | | | **INCOME DATA** | | | | | | |
| 100.0 | 100.0 | 100.0 | Net Sales | | 100.0 | | 100.0 | 100.0 | 100.0 |
| | | | Gross Profit | | | | | | |
| 88.9 | 89.6 | 89.9 | Operating Expenses | | 97.6 | | 87.0 | 88.4 | 89.3 |
| 11.1 | 10.4 | 10.1 | Operating Profit | | 2.4 | | 13.0 | 11.6 | 10.7 |
| 3.3 | 1.3 | 1.1 | All Other Expenses (net) | | 2.1 | | .8 | 1.4 | .5 |
| 7.8 | 9.0 | 9.1 | Profit Before Taxes | | .4 | | 12.2 | 10.2 | 10.3 |
| | | | **RATIOS** | | | | | | |
| 2.7 | 2.5 | 3.2 | | | 7.5 | | 4.1 | 3.2 | 2.5 |
| 1.7 | 1.6 | 1.7 | Current | | 3.2 | | 1.6 | 1.5 | 1.8 |
| 1.0 | .8 | .9 | | | 1.1 | | .4 | .8 | 1.2 |
| 2.3 | 2.4 | 3.0 | | | 7.4 | | 3.7 | 2.4 | 2.3 |
| 1.4 | 1.5 | 1.5 | Quick | | 3.1 | | 1.3 | 1.3 | 1.6 |
| .8 | .7 | .8 | | | .5 | | .4 | .6 | 1.0 |

### Sales/Receivables and below

| | | | | | | | | | | | | | | | | |
|---|---|---|---|---|---|---|---|---|---|---|---|---|---|---|---|---|
| 8 | 48.5 | 7 | 51.4 | 15 | 24.4 | Sales/Receivables | 0 | UND | 0 | UND | 30 | 12.3 | 39 | 9.3 |
| 38 | 9.5 | 39 | 9.4 | 43 | 8.4 | | 0 | UND | 23 | 15.7 | 44 | 8.3 | 46 | 7.9 |
| 55 | 6.7 | 53 | 6.8 | 55 | 6.6 | | 49 | 7.5 | 56 | 6.5 | 62 | 5.9 | 55 | 6.6 |

Cost of Sales/Inventory

Cost of Sales/Payables

| 6.4 | 6.1 | 5.3 | Sales/Working Capital | 5.7 | 2.7 | 5.4 | 5.6 |
|---|---|---|---|---|---|---|---|
| 13.4 | 14.3 | 13.4 | | 24.7 | 18.3 | 15.5 | 10.3 |
| 155.5 | -50.4 | -125.4 | | 40.8 | -50.5 | -30.1 | 38.0 |

| | | | | | | | EBIT/Interest | | | | | | | | |
|---|---|---|---|---|---|---|---|---|---|---|---|---|---|---|---|
| | 19.6 | | 20.8 | | 17.9 | | | | | | | | 17.4 | | 20.2 |
| (128) | 3.4 | (116) | 6.8 | (103) | 5.6 | | | | | | (24) | 5.5 | (52) | 5.4 |
| | 1.0 | | 1.4 | | 1.2 | | | | | | | -1.0 | | 2.3 |

| | | | | | Net Profit + Depr., Dep., Amort./Cur. Mat. L/T/D | | | |
|---|---|---|---|---|---|---|---|---|
| | 4.3 | | | | | | | |
| (14) | 2.5 | | | | | | | |
| | -.9 | | | | | | | |

| .4 | .5 | .5 | Fixed/Worth | .4 | .1 | .7 | .5 |
|---|---|---|---|---|---|---|---|
| .9 | 1.3 | 1.1 | | 2.8 | .8 | 1.9 | .8 |
| 10.1 | 10.5 | 15.8 | | -16.8 | 2.2 | -11.3 | 9.2 |

| .5 | .5 | .5 | Debt/Worth | .6 | .1 | .9 | .5 |
|---|---|---|---|---|---|---|---|
| 1.5 | 1.7 | 1.7 | | 2.0 | 1.0 | 2.7 | 1.4 |
| 14.8 | 26.9 | 27.0 | | -19.9 | 3.5 | -15.1 | 26.0 |

| | | | | | | | % Profit Before Taxes/Tangible Net Worth | | | | | | | | |
|---|---|---|---|---|---|---|---|---|---|---|---|---|---|---|---|
| | 82.4 | | 112.8 | | 98.5 | | | | | | | 143.8 | | 126.1 | 95.0 |
| (138) | 21.8 | (109) | 28.9 | (97) | 21.9 | | | (10) | 16.3 | (19) | 54.0 | (49) | 28.0 |
| | .9 | | 6.4 | | 2.9 | | | | | | 3.4 | | -1.2 | 8.9 |

| 24.0 | 33.5 | 30.2 | % Profit Before Taxes/Total Assets | 17.8 | 50.9 | 48.0 | 23.5 |
|---|---|---|---|---|---|---|---|
| 6.7 | 8.7 | 8.2 | | -.6 | 19.4 | 10.8 | 8.2 |
| .0 | 2.1 | .7 | | -6.2 | 3.5 | -4.2 | 4.2 |

| 21.4 | 17.5 | 15.9 | Sales/Net Fixed Assets | 70.8 | 56.3 | 18.7 | 8.7 |
|---|---|---|---|---|---|---|---|
| 4.7 | 5.7 | 3.5 | | 2.9 | 8.6 | 3.5 | 3.0 |
| 1.6 | 2.0 | 1.9 | | 1.5 | 2.7 | 1.6 | 2.0 |

| 3.1 | 3.2 | 3.0 | Sales/Total Assets | 15.0 | 4.2 | 3.8 | 2.5 |
|---|---|---|---|---|---|---|---|
| 1.5 | 1.8 | 1.6 | | 1.9 | 3.0 | 1.7 | 1.3 |
| .8 | 1.0 | .8 | | .9 | .7 | .9 | .9 |

| | | | | | | | % Depr., Dep., Amort./Sales | | | | | | | | |
|---|---|---|---|---|---|---|---|---|---|---|---|---|---|---|---|
| | 1.2 | | 1.5 | | 1.7 | | | | | | | .8 | | 1.7 | 1.8 |
| (155) | 2.7 | (120) | 3.2 | (107) | 3.9 | | | | (10) | 2.5 | (22) | 5.7 | (56) | 3.6 |
| | 5.5 | | 5.5 | | 6.1 | | | | | | 5.5 | | 9.2 | 5.7 |

| | | | | | | % Officers', Directors' Owners' Comp/Sales | | | |
|---|---|---|---|---|---|---|---|---|
| | 5.0 | | 3.8 | | 8.6 | | | |
| (29) | 11.4 | (28) | 10.0 | (22) | 22.6 | | | |
| | 28.4 | | 30.8 | | 40.6 | | | |

| 8339835M | 6989521M | 4533864M | Net Sales ($) | 3453M | 22691M | 34045M | 83374M | 439373M | 3950928M |
|---|---|---|---|---|---|---|---|---|---|
| 6187651M | 5399983M | 4361686M | Total Assets ($) | 8444M | 30866M | 77425M | 127876M | 398717M | 3718358M |

© RMA 2012

**M = $ thousand    MM = $ million**
See Pages 9 through 22 for Explanation of Ratios and Data

## Current Data Sorted by Assets      Comparative Historical Data

| | | | | | | Type of Statement | | |
|---|---|---|---|---|---|---|---|---|
| 2 | 23 | 115 | 155 | 46 | 45 | Unqualified | 508 | 449 |
| 3 | 23 | 105 | 35 | 2 | 3 | Reviewed | 125 | 129 |
| 13 | 44 | 68 | 16 | 3 | 3 | Compiled | 137 | 130 |
| 37 | 55 | 58 | 5 | | | Tax Returns | 120 | 155 |
| 45 | 150 | 331 | 170 | 36 | 40 | Other | 574 | 644 |
| | 390 (4/1-9/30/11) | | 1,241 (10/1/11-3/31/12) | | | | 4/1/07-3/31/08 | 4/1/08-3/31/09 |
| 0-500M | 500M-2MM | 2-10MM | 10-50MM | 50-100MM | 100-250MM | | ALL | ALL |
| 100 | 295 | 677 | 381 | 87 | 91 | NUMBER OF STATEMENTS | 1464 | 1507 |
| % | % | % | % | % | % | ASSETS | % | % |
| 28.5 | 15.8 | 11.0 | 12.2 | 11.0 | 9.6 | Cash & Equivalents | 11.7 | 11.5 |
| 17.8 | 30.8 | 22.0 | 15.4 | 12.2 | 12.7 | Trade Receivables (net) | 21.4 | 21.7 |
| .3 | .3 | .2 | .3 | .2 | .2 | Inventory | .4 | .2 |
| 2.0 | 3.5 | 3.4 | 3.3 | 4.3 | 3.9 | All Other Current | 5.4 | 4.0 |
| 48.6 | 50.5 | 36.6 | 31.2 | 27.8 | 26.4 | Total Current | 38.8 | 37.4 |
| 28.4 | 35.6 | 47.1 | 50.7 | 49.0 | 48.6 | Fixed Assets (net) | 44.4 | 44.9 |
| 8.2 | 3.9 | 6.1 | 6.3 | 5.2 | 7.3 | Intangibles (net) | 3.8 | 3.7 |
| 14.8 | 10.0 | 10.2 | 11.7 | 18.0 | 17.6 | All Other Non-Current | 13.0 | 14.0 |
| 100.0 | 100.0 | 100.0 | 100.0 | 100.0 | 100.0 | Total | 100.0 | 100.0 |
| | | | | | | LIABILITIES | | |
| 11.5 | 5.6 | 4.0 | 2.2 | 1.6 | 1.8 | Notes Payable-Short Term | 5.8 | 4.7 |
| 2.4 | 2.1 | 4.1 | 5.0 | 2.8 | 3.7 | Cur. Mat.-L.T.D. | 3.2 | 3.1 |
| 15.1 | 13.4 | 9.8 | 5.9 | 5.5 | 5.0 | Trade Payables | 10.8 | 10.4 |
| .0 | .0 | .1 | .0 | .0 | .0 | Income Taxes Payable | .1 | .1 |
| 59.7 | 29.5 | 13.9 | 11.0 | 9.9 | 11.5 | All Other Current | 17.3 | 19.6 |
| 88.7 | 50.5 | 31.9 | 24.1 | 19.9 | 22.1 | Total Current | 37.1 | 37.9 |
| 23.0 | 28.4 | 42.9 | 41.4 | 43.5 | 45.7 | Long-Term Debt | 40.5 | 41.7 |
| .0 | .0 | .1 | .0 | .2 | .1 | Deferred Taxes | .1 | .1 |
| 9.9 | 8.3 | 5.7 | 7.3 | 9.7 | 13.8 | All Other Non-Current | 8.5 | 7.4 |
| -21.8 | 12.8 | 19.4 | 27.1 | 26.6 | 18.4 | Net Worth | 13.8 | 12.9 |
| 100.0 | 100.0 | 100.0 | 100.0 | 100.0 | 100.0 | Total Liabilities & Net Worth | 100.0 | 100.0 |
| | | | | | | INCOME DATA | | |
| 100.0 | 100.0 | 100.0 | 100.0 | 100.0 | 100.0 | Net Sales | 100.0 | 100.0 |
| | | | | | | Gross Profit | | |
| 92.1 | 89.3 | 86.1 | 89.1 | 90.2 | 90.9 | Operating Expenses | 89.4 | 88.6 |
| 7.9 | 10.7 | 13.9 | 10.9 | 9.8 | 9.1 | Operating Profit | 10.6 | 11.4 |
| 2.2 | 2.4 | 6.4 | 4.8 | 4.8 | 4.5 | All Other Expenses (net) | 5.1 | 6.3 |
| 5.8 | 8.2 | 7.5 | 6.1 | 4.9 | 4.6 | Profit Before Taxes | 5.5 | 5.1 |
| | | | | | | RATIOS | | |
| 2.0 | 2.1 | 2.2 | 2.7 | 2.4 | 1.7 | | 2.2 | 2.1 |
| .7 | 1.1 | 1.3 | 1.4 | 1.3 | 1.3 | Current | 1.3 | 1.2 |
| .3 | .6 | .7 | .8 | .9 | .9 | | .8 | .7 |
| 1.9 | 1.9 | 2.0 | 2.4 | 2.1 | 1.4 | | 1.9 | 1.9 |
| .7 | 1.0 | (676) 1.1 | 1.3 | 1.1 | 1.0 | Quick | 1.1 (1506) 1.1 |
| .2 | .5 | .6 | .7 | .8 | .8 | | .6 | .6 |

| | | | | | | | | | | | | Sales/Receivables | | | | |
|---|---|---|---|---|---|---|---|---|---|---|---|---|---|---|---|---|
| 0 | UND | 3 | 134.1 | 10 | 34.8 | 23 | 15.6 | 28 | 13.0 | 25 | 14.6 | | 13 | 27.5 | 14 | 26.8 |
| 1 | 348.7 | 28 | 13.0 | 32 | 11.3 | 35 | 10.4 | 33 | 10.9 | 34 | 10.8 | | 34 | 10.7 | 34 | 10.7 |
| 17 | 21.4 | 38 | 9.5 | 47 | 7.8 | 47 | 7.8 | 46 | 7.9 | 45 | 8.1 | | 47 | 7.8 | 48 | 7.6 |

| | | | | | | Cost of Sales/Inventory | | |
|---|---|---|---|---|---|---|---|---|

| | | | | | | Cost of Sales/Payables | | |
|---|---|---|---|---|---|---|---|---|

| | | | | | | | | |
|---|---|---|---|---|---|---|---|---|
| 24.2 | 14.4 | 8.2 | 5.5 | 5.4 | 6.2 | Sales/Working Capital | 8.2 | 9.4 |
| -35.7 | 110.8 | 28.5 | 15.7 | 15.3 | 26.3 | | 27.3 | 34.0 |
| -9.7 | -14.7 | -19.3 | -28.6 | -101.5 | -34.4 | | -22.8 | -15.5 |
| 33.0 | 48.5 | 12.0 | 7.2 | 6.4 | 5.5 | | 4.9 | 6.3 |
| (43) 6.7 | (198) 8.8 | (537) 3.7 | (333) 2.9 | (77) 2.7 | (84) 2.2 | EBIT/Interest | (1126) 2.2 | (1173) 2.3 |
| 1.7 | 1.4 | 1.5 | 1.3 | 1.1 | 1.3 | | .9 | .7 |
| | | 12.0 | 6.0 | | 5.9 | | 6.5 | 7.1 |
| | | (42) 3.9 | (34) 3.7 | | (13) 3.0 | Net Profit + Depr., Dep., Amort./Cur. Mat. L/T/D | (103) 3.0 | (94) 3.6 |
| | | 1.6 | 2.1 | | .7 | | 1.5 | 1.0 |
| .2 | .3 | .6 | .9 | .8 | 1.4 | | .7 | .7 |
| 2.0 | 1.2 | 2.9 | 2.7 | 2.5 | 4.9 | Fixed/Worth | 2.5 | 3.0 |
| -.5 | -4.3 | -8.6 | NM | -22.2 | -7.4 | | -9.0 | -6.4 |
| 1.1 | .7 | 1.3 | 1.0 | .7 | 2.2 | | 1.2 | 1.3 |
| 9.1 | 2.9 | 4.5 | 3.5 | 3.7 | 7.0 | Debt/Worth | 4.3 | 5.2 |
| -2.4 | -8.7 | -14.2 | -148.6 | -36.3 | -14.0 | | -14.3 | -11.8 |
| 168.3 | 91.7 | 87.2 | 42.9 | 20.7 | 44.4 | % Profit Before Taxes/Tangible Net Worth | 54.3 | 71.7 |
| (58) 84.3 | (202) 49.1 | (458) 36.4 | (284) 14.7 | (60) 9.1 | (58) 18.3 | | (1024) 18.2 | (1011) 22.2 |
| 36.2 | 16.6 | 12.0 | 3.3 | 1.7 | 2.4 | | 3.9 | 2.2 |
| 55.8 | 32.4 | 18.2 | 11.0 | 7.9 | 6.3 | % Profit Before Taxes/Total Assets | 12.8 | 13.7 |
| 26.0 | 13.9 | 6.5 | 4.4 | 3.7 | 3.0 | | 4.2 | 4.3 |
| 2.0 | 1.7 | 1.4 | .6 | .2 | 1.0 | | -.1 | -.9 |
| 153.5 | 66.3 | 17.2 | 5.7 | 3.8 | 4.2 | Sales/Net Fixed Assets | 19.8 | 22.7 |
| 33.4 | 18.7 | 3.6 | 1.8 | 1.5 | 1.6 | | 3.1 | 3.3 |
| 12.6 | 2.9 | 1.0 | .9 | .7 | .8 | | 1.2 | 1.1 |
| 9.8 | 5.6 | 3.0 | 1.7 | 1.5 | 1.8 | Sales/Total Assets | 3.1 | 3.4 |
| 6.1 | 3.7 | 1.5 | .9 | .8 | .8 | | 1.4 | 1.4 |
| 2.9 | 1.5 | .7 | .5 | .4 | .4 | | .7 | .6 |
| .3 | .5 | 1.1 | 1.9 | 2.6 | 2.2 | % Depr., Dep., Amort./Sales | 1.1 | 1.0 |
| (62) 1.3 | (239) 1.1 | (639) 2.6 | (366) 3.7 | (84) 4.2 | (82) 4.0 | | (1307) 2.7 | (1371) 2.8 |
| 2.7 | 3.7 | 6.3 | 6.6 | 9.1 | 8.2 | | 5.9 | 5.9 |
| 2.3 | 2.2 | 1.5 | 2.3 | | | % Officers', Directors' Owners' Comp/Sales | 2.1 | 1.6 |
| (29) 5.3 | (40) 3.9 | (78) 3.5 | (42) 5.4 | | | | (230) 4.3 | (181) 3.5 |
| 9.7 | 6.1 | 7.9 | 14.4 | | | | 9.5 | 7.2 |
| 137769M | 1368455M | 5994433M | 11050117M | 7354024M | 16068217M | Net Sales ($) | 32100782M | 31076987M |
| 24200M | 371342M | 3388763M | 8176093M | 6154121M | 13760407M | Total Assets ($) | 28882403M | 27822741M |

M = $ thousand   MM = $ million
See Pages 9 through 22 for Explanation of Ratios and Data

## Comparative Historical Data | | | Current Data Sorted by Sales

| Comp Hist 1 | Comp Hist 2 | Comp Hist 3 | Type of Statement | 0-1MM | 1-3MM | 3-5MM | 5-10MM | 10-25MM | 25MM & OVER |
|---|---|---|---|---|---|---|---|---|---|
| 513 | 487 | 386 | Unqualified | 9 | 21 | 23 | 70 | 133 | 130 |
| 174 | 158 | 171 | Reviewed | 6 | 14 | 16 | 47 | 68 | 20 |
| 117 | 121 | 147 | Compiled | 23 | 21 | 17 | 47 | 28 | 11 |
| 149 | 145 | 155 | Tax Returns | 36 | 57 | 18 | 27 | 15 | 2 |
| 685 | 822 | 772 | Other | 86 | 107 | 78 | 186 | 181 | 134 |
| 4/1/09-3/31/10 ALL | 4/1/10-3/31/11 ALL | 4/1/11-3/31/12 ALL | | 390 (4/1-9/30/11) | | | 1,241 (10/1/11-3/31/12) | | |
| 1638 | 1733 | 1631 | NUMBER OF STATEMENTS | 160 | 220 | 152 | 377 | 425 | 297 |
| % | % | % | ASSETS | % | % | % | % | % | % |
| 12.2 | 13.2 | 13.2 | Cash & Equivalents | 11.4 | 15.6 | 11.1 | 14.3 | 13.2 | 11.9 |
| 20.2 | 19.9 | 20.7 | Trade Receivables (net) | 4.1 | 10.3 | 18.4 | 26.2 | 26.7 | 23.3 |
| .3 | .3 | .3 | Inventory | .1 | .2 | .5 | .4 | .2 | .3 |
| 3.5 | 3.7 | 3.4 | All Other Current | 1.0 | 2.7 | 2.3 | 3.0 | 4.2 | 5.1 |
| 36.1 | 37.2 | 37.6 | Total Current | 16.5 | 28.7 | 32.3 | 43.8 | 44.3 | 40.6 |
| 46.2 | 46.2 | 44.9 | Fixed Assets (net) | 65.3 | 55.4 | 48.0 | 39.4 | 39.2 | 39.7 |
| 5.3 | 4.8 | 5.9 | Intangibles (net) | 7.0 | 5.6 | 7.0 | 5.5 | 5.3 | 6.4 |
| 12.4 | 11.9 | 11.6 | All Other Non-Current | 11.1 | 10.2 | 12.7 | 11.3 | 11.3 | 13.3 |
| 100.0 | 100.0 | 100.0 | Total | 100.0 | 100.0 | 100.0 | 100.0 | 100.0 | 100.0 |
| | | | LIABILITIES | | | | | | |
| 3.8 | 4.4 | 4.1 | Notes Payable-Short Term | 4.0 | 4.4 | 5.7 | 4.0 | 4.1 | 3.2 |
| 3.7 | 3.6 | 3.8 | Cur. Mat.-L.T.D. | 4.8 | 4.0 | 3.8 | 3.8 | 3.6 | 3.2 |
| 9.5 | 9.9 | 9.4 | Trade Payables | 2.2 | 8.4 | 8.8 | 10.1 | 12.2 | 9.2 |
| .0 | .1 | .0 | Income Taxes Payable | .0 | .0 | .0 | .1 | .0 | .1 |
| 17.9 | 16.9 | 18.5 | All Other Current | 19.3 | 23.7 | 20.0 | 21.7 | 14.3 | 15.6 |
| 34.9 | 35.1 | 35.7 | Total Current | 30.3 | 40.4 | 38.2 | 39.7 | 34.2 | 31.2 |
| 41.4 | 40.7 | 38.9 | Long-Term Debt | 60.4 | 57.8 | 42.7 | 32.4 | 28.4 | 34.7 |
| .1 | .1 | .1 | Deferred Taxes | .0 | .0 | .0 | .2 | .0 | .0 |
| 7.8 | 8.1 | 7.5 | All Other Non-Current | 6.9 | 8.5 | 6.5 | 7.1 | 6.9 | 8.7 |
| 15.8 | 16.1 | 17.8 | Net Worth | 2.3 | -6.7 | 12.6 | 20.7 | 30.4 | 25.3 |
| 100.0 | 100.0 | 100.0 | Total Liabilities & Net Worth | 100.0 | 100.0 | 100.0 | 100.0 | 100.0 | 100.0 |
| | | | INCOME DATA | | | | | | |
| 100.0 | 100.0 | 100.0 | Net Sales | 100.0 | 100.0 | 100.0 | 100.0 | 100.0 | 100.0 |
| | | | Gross Profit | | | | | | |
| 87.7 | 87.6 | 88.2 | Operating Expenses | 63.2 | 84.0 | 90.1 | 92.5 | 92.1 | 93.1 |
| 12.3 | 12.4 | 11.8 | Operating Profit | 36.8 | 16.0 | 9.9 | 7.5 | 7.9 | 6.9 |
| 5.1 | 5.0 | 4.8 | All Other Expenses (net) | 20.0 | 7.4 | 4.0 | 2.5 | 2.2 | 2.0 |
| 7.2 | 7.4 | 6.9 | Profit Before Taxes | 16.8 | 8.6 | 6.0 | 5.0 | 5.8 | 4.9 |
| | | | RATIOS | | | | | | |
| 2.1 | 2.2 | 2.3 | | 1.9 | 2.2 | 2.2 | 2.3 | 2.5 | 2.1 |
| 1.2 | 1.3 | 1.3 | Current | .8 | .8 | .9 | 1.4 | 1.4 | 1.3 |
| .7 | .7 | .7 | | .1 | .3 | .5 | .8 | .9 | .9 |
| 2.0 | 2.0 | 2.1 | | 1.8 | 2.2 | 2.0 | 2.2 | 2.3 | 1.9 |
| 1.1 | 1.1 (1630) | 1.1 | Quick | .5 (219) | .7 | .8 | 1.3 | 1.3 | 1.2 |
| .6 | .6 | .6 | | .1 | .3 | .4 | .7 | .9 | .8 |
| 11 32.2 | 11 34.5 | 12 30.9 | | 0 UND | 0 UND | 2 157.9 | 24 15.3 | 28 12.9 | 30 12.0 |
| 32 11.3 | 32 11.5 | 31 11.7 | Sales/Receivables | 0 UND | 3 145.2 | 25 14.4 | 34 10.7 | 37 9.9 | 37 9.9 |
| 44 8.3 | 44 8.3 | 45 8.2 | | 5 80.8 | 18 20.6 | 38 9.6 | 45 8.1 | 49 7.4 | 48 7.6 |
| | | | Cost of Sales/Inventory | | | | | | |
| | | | Cost of Sales/Payables | | | | | | |
| 8.9 | 8.4 | 8.2 | | 10.3 | 9.3 | 10.0 | 8.6 | 6.8 | 7.5 |
| 34.2 | 28.7 | 29.1 | Sales/Working Capital | -21.9 | -35.0 | -130.3 | 23.4 | 19.6 | 21.3 |
| -19.5 | -21.3 | -19.1 | | -3.4 | -7.9 | -13.3 | -28.7 | -132.3 | -71.9 |
| 9.5 | 11.0 | 12.5 | | 10.5 | 5.0 | 5.5 | 16.8 | 21.6 | 10.2 |
| (1268) 3.1 | (1339) 3.1 | (1272) 3.4 | EBIT/Interest | (65) 4.7 | (149) 2.1 | (112) 2.4 | (296) 3.9 | (370) 4.4 | (280) 3.7 |
| 1.3 | 1.3 | 1.4 | | 1.8 | .9 | 1.2 | 1.3 | 1.5 | 1.6 |
| 7.3 | 6.7 | 7.9 | | | | | 5.2 | 44.4 | 8.0 |
| (118) 3.6 | (124) 3.3 | (101) 3.8 | Net Profit + Depr., Dep., Amort./Cur. Mat. L/T/D | | | (15) 2.7 | (34) 4.6 | (42) 4.0 | |
| 1.6 | 1.5 | 1.8 | | | | | 1.4 | 2.5 | 1.7 |
| .7 | .7 | .6 | | 2.1 | 1.0 | .8 | .4 | .5 | .8 |
| 3.0 | 2.7 | 2.5 | Fixed/Worth | 20.0 | 9.5 | 4.6 | 2.0 | 1.2 | 2.5 |
| -8.9 | -13.4 | -8.8 | | -3.5 | -1.6 | -3.3 | -13.4 | 7.9 | -13.6 |
| 1.3 | 1.2 | 1.1 | | 2.4 | 1.7 | 1.4 | .9 | .8 | 1.1 |
| 4.9 | 4.1 | 4.0 | Debt/Worth | 21.8 | 18.6 | 7.4 | 3.5 | 2.4 | 3.9 |
| -13.0 | -17.5 | -14.9 | | -5.0 | -3.6 | -6.7 | -21.3 | 14.7 | -25.3 |
| 74.8 | 71.0 | 76.6 | | 92.8 | 89.7 | 62.8 | 67.6 | 89.6 | 62.5 |
| (1128) 28.7 | (1206) 26.0 | (1120) 29.5 | % Profit Before Taxes/Tangible Net Worth | (94) 25.2 | (115) 33.0 | (95) 26.0 | (260) 33.4 | (342) 33.3 | (214) 22.0 |
| 6.1 | 6.7 | 7.0 | | 9.0 | 7.2 | 6.3 | 7.1 | 6.0 | 7.3 |
| 16.7 | 18.0 | 17.9 | | 13.5 | 17.6 | 14.7 | 21.0 | 21.2 | 13.0 |
| 5.9 | 6.0 | 6.2 | % Profit Before Taxes/Total Assets | 4.3 | 4.9 | 5.1 | 7.4 | 8.2 | 6.2 |
| .6 | .9 | 1.0 | | .3 | -.3 | .6 | 1.3 | 1.3 | 1.8 |
| 19.6 | 17.6 | 20.6 | | 3.9 | 16.5 | 25.0 | 33.4 | 24.4 | 15.4 |
| 3.1 | 3.0 | 3.6 | Sales/Net Fixed Assets | .4 | 1.4 | 3.3 | 5.3 | 5.2 | 4.2 |
| 1.1 | 1.0 | 1.1 | | .1 | .5 | 1.1 | 1.6 | 1.6 | 1.6 |
| 3.3 | 3.4 | 3.4 | | 1.0 | 3.0 | 3.6 | 4.0 | 3.6 | 2.9 |
| 1.4 | 1.4 | 1.5 | Sales/Total Assets | .3 | 1.0 | 1.4 | 1.9 | 1.8 | 1.7 |
| .7 | .6 | .7 | | .1 | .4 | .8 | .9 | .9 | .8 |
| 1.2 | 1.2 | 1.1 | | 5.3 | 1.7 | 1.2 | .6 | 1.0 | 1.2 |
| (1482) 2.9 | (1554) 3.1 | (1472) 2.7 | % Depr., Dep., Amort./Sales | (136) 18.0 | (184) 6.0 | (129) 3.2 | (346) 2.1 | (400) 2.0 | (277) 2.3 |
| 5.9 | 6.2 | 6.0 | | 36.7 | 12.0 | 6.7 | 4.2 | 4.3 | 4.1 |
| 1.7 | 1.7 | 1.8 | | 4.1 | 2.1 | 2.2 | 2.3 | 1.4 | 1.4 |
| (217) 3.9 | (247) 4.2 | (202) 4.3 | % Officers', Directors' Owners' Comp/Sales | (20) 6.3 | (33) 5.1 | (24) 4.2 | (41) 3.8 | (57) 3.5 | (27) 4.7 |
| 7.8 | 7.8 | 8.9 | | 11.0 | 8.2 | 6.4 | 9.9 | 8.9 | 9.5 |
| 36304439M | 37746672M | 41973015M | Net Sales ($) | 88609M | 415597M | 603467M | 2822308M | 6425050M | 31617984M |
| 30224820M | 31360308M | 31874926M | Total Assets ($) | 424592M | 703996M | 776038M | 2678738M | 6481958M | 20809604M |

© RMA 2012

M = $ thousand    MM = $ million
See Pages 9 through 22 for Explanation of Ratios and Data

**Current Data Sorted by Assets**      **Comparative Historical Data**

| | | | | | | Type of Statement | | |
|---|---|---|---|---|---|---|---|---|
| 1 | 14 | 55 | 46 | 11 | 7 | Unqualified | 86 | 85 |
| 2 | | 1 | 1 | | | Reviewed | 1 | 2 |
| | 2 | 2 | | | 5 | Compiled | 4 | 5 |
| 2 | 3 | 2 | | | | Tax Returns | 5 | 9 |
| 5 | 14 | 24 | 10 | 3 | 3 | Other | 24 | 37 |
| | 127 (4/1-9/30/11) | | 81 (10/1/11-3/31/12) | | | | 4/1/07-3/31/08 ALL | 4/1/08-3/31/09 ALL |
| 0-500M | 500M-2MM | 2-10MM | 10-50MM | 50-100MM | 100-250MM | | | |
| 10 | 33 | 84 | 57 | 14 | 10 | **NUMBER OF STATEMENTS** | 120 | 138 |
| % | % | % | % | % | % | **ASSETS** | % | % |
| 32.7 | 24.2 | 16.0 | 18.3 | 18.6 | 6.0 | Cash & Equivalents | 17.1 | 17.1 |
| 16.1 | 20.1 | 17.2 | 13.9 | 15.5 | 9.5 | Trade Receivables (net) | 19.6 | 19.3 |
| .1 | .0 | .2 | .5 | .0 | .1 | Inventory | .1 | .2 |
| 11.8 | 11.5 | 1.7 | 3.6 | 4.9 | 2.9 | All Other Current | 4.3 | 3.5 |
| 60.7 | 55.7 | 35.1 | 36.2 | 39.1 | 18.5 | Total Current | 41.2 | 40.1 |
| 26.4 | 38.7 | 53.7 | 50.0 | 48.9 | 62.0 | Fixed Assets (net) | 47.7 | 47.6 |
| 7.4 | 2.4 | 2.4 | 2.8 | 1.7 | 1.8 | Intangibles (net) | 1.1 | 3.1 |
| 5.5 | 3.1 | 8.8 | 11.0 | 10.4 | 17.7 | All Other Non-Current | 10.0 | 9.2 |
| 100.0 | 100.0 | 100.0 | 100.0 | 100.0 | 100.0 | Total | 100.0 | 100.0 |
| | | | | | | **LIABILITIES** | | |
| 1.4 | 4.5 | 4.5 | 1.8 | 1.3 | 2.1 | Notes Payable-Short Term | 4.4 | 5.4 |
| 3.3 | 2.9 | 2.9 | 3.5 | 2.8 | 1.9 | Cur. Mat.-L.T.D. | 2.7 | 3.4 |
| 8.1 | 5.9 | 5.1 | 4.5 | 7.1 | 6.1 | Trade Payables | 7.9 | 7.1 |
| .1 | .4 | .2 | .1 | .2 | .0 | Income Taxes Payable | .2 | .2 |
| 59.3 | 15.4 | 12.3 | 10.6 | 14.2 | 3.5 | All Other Current | 13.4 | 13.6 |
| 72.2 | 29.1 | 25.1 | 20.4 | 25.6 | 13.6 | Total Current | 28.7 | 29.6 |
| 12.4 | 30.5 | 31.4 | 28.4 | 32.8 | 39.1 | Long-Term Debt | 31.3 | 29.0 |
| .3 | .0 | .1 | .1 | .0 | .0 | Deferred Taxes | .0 | .0 |
| .0 | 3.5 | 2.2 | 2.9 | 3.8 | 18.8 | All Other Non-Current | 2.6 | 3.7 |
| 15.1 | 37.0 | 41.2 | 48.2 | 37.7 | 28.5 | Net Worth | 37.5 | 37.6 |
| 100.0 | 100.0 | 100.0 | 100.0 | 100.0 | 100.0 | Total Liabilities & Net Worth | 100.0 | 100.0 |
| | | | | | | **INCOME DATA** | | |
| 100.0 | 100.0 | 100.0 | 100.0 | 100.0 | 100.0 | Net Sales | 100.0 | 100.0 |
| | | | | | | Gross Profit | | |
| 89.3 | 91.3 | 94.8 | 96.3 | 95.8 | 87.7 | Operating Expenses | 94.1 | 94.3 |
| 10.7 | 8.7 | 5.2 | 3.7 | 4.2 | 12.3 | Operating Profit | 5.9 | 5.7 |
| 3.3 | 4.1 | 1.4 | .2 | 2.5 | 2.2 | All Other Expenses (net) | 1.4 | 2.4 |
| 7.4 | 4.5 | 3.7 | 3.5 | 1.6 | 10.1 | Profit Before Taxes | 4.5 | 3.2 |
| | | | | | | **RATIOS** | | |
| 3.2 | 4.3 | 2.4 | 2.9 | 1.9 | 2.2 | | 3.0 | 2.2 |
| 1.2 | 2.2 | 1.6 | 2.0 | 1.4 | 1.5 | Current | 1.4 | 1.3 |
| .6 | 1.0 | .9 | 1.2 | 1.1 | .5 | | .9 | .9 |
| 2.8 | 3.0 | 2.3 | 2.5 | 1.6 | 1.7 | | 2.8 | 2.0 |
| 1.0 | 1.9 | 1.4 | 1.9 | 1.3 | 1.0 | Quick | 1.1 | 1.1 |
| .1 | .8 | .8 | 1.2 | 1.0 | .3 | | .7 | .7 |
| 0   UND | 1   514.6 | 19   19.4 | 26   13.9 | 15   24.5 | 6   62.7 | | 23   15.6 | 17   22.0 |
| 1   301.6 | 23   15.7 | 32   11.5 | 33   11.1 | 37   9.8 | 11   32.6 | Sales/Receivables | 34   10.7 | 33   11.1 |
| 33   10.9 | 33   11.0 | 37   9.8 | 41   8.8 | 46   8.0 | 50   7.3 | | 48   7.5 | 46   8.0 |
| | | | | | | Cost of Sales/Inventory | | |
| | | | | | | Cost of Sales/Payables | | |
| 9.1 | 3.8 | 6.3 | 4.1 | 6.6 | 4.1 | | 5.2 | 6.6 |
| 87.5 | 11.2 | 15.2 | 10.4 | 16.9 | 25.7 | Sales/Working Capital | 15.9 | 25.1 |
| -23.7 | -404.1 | -59.3 | 30.4 | 56.9 | -130.0 | | -89.2 | -50.2 |
| | 11.5 | 6.6 | 6.3 | 4.2 | | | 4.7 | 4.4 |
| | (21) 1.8 | (74) 2.5 | (53) 3.4 | (10) 3.5 | | EBIT/Interest | (89) 2.5 | (113) 2.0 |
| | .7 | 1.0 | 1.7 | 2.0 | | | 1.1 | .9 |
| | | 4.0 | | | | Net Profit + Depr., Dep., | | |
| | | (12) 3.0 | | | | Amort./Cur. Mat. L/T/D | | |
| | | 2.0 | | | | | | |
| .2 | .4 | .8 | .7 | 1.0 | 1.7 | | .7 | .6 |
| 1.2 | .9 | 1.2 | 1.0 | 1.3 | 3.9 | Fixed/Worth | 1.4 | 1.4 |
| -2.4 | 4.3 | 2.1 | 2.5 | 1.8 | 7.4 | | 3.3 | 2.9 |
| .5 | .5 | .6 | .4 | 1.3 | 1.6 | | .6 | .7 |
| 4.9 | 1.1 | 1.4 | .9 | 1.8 | 4.6 | Debt/Worth | 1.7 | 1.8 |
| -8.2 | 7.2 | 3.0 | 3.1 | 3.0 | 16.9 | | 4.5 | 4.1 |
| | 26.4 | 20.0 | 15.2 | 11.7 | 50.1 | % Profit Before Taxes/Tangible | 20.9 | 19.1 |
| | (27) 16.4 | (76) 7.3 | (53) 7.1 | 7.5 | 24.4 | Net Worth | (106) 9.9 | (129) 5.3 |
| | 1.0 | .4 | 2.9 | 4.1 | -1.1 | | 3.8 | -.8 |
| 87.8 | 15.4 | 9.7 | 6.1 | 4.6 | 7.1 | % Profit Before Taxes/Total | 7.9 | 5.4 |
| 36.7 | 5.8 | 2.9 | 3.6 | 3.0 | 2.1 | Assets | 3.6 | 1.5 |
| 3.6 | .3 | .0 | 1.4 | 1.2 | .1 | | .5 | -.3 |
| UND | 37.8 | 5.5 | 5.0 | 5.1 | 3.3 | | 5.8 | 8.4 |
| 28.6 | 9.5 | 2.5 | 2.7 | 3.9 | .9 | Sales/Net Fixed Assets | 3.1 | 3.6 |
| 18.8 | 1.6 | 1.7 | 1.8 | 2.1 | .3 | | 2.0 | 2.1 |
| 9.1 | 4.3 | 2.2 | 1.7 | 2.2 | 1.7 | | 2.4 | 2.7 |
| 5.8 | 2.6 | 1.5 | 1.3 | 1.8 | .4 | Sales/Total Assets | 1.6 | 1.6 |
| 4.4 | 1.0 | 1.0 | 1.0 | 1.2 | .2 | | 1.2 | 1.2 |
| | .8 | 1.7 | 1.9 | 2.0 | | | 1.5 | 1.5 |
| | (28) 1.4 | (80) 2.8 | (55) 2.6 | (12) 2.2 | | % Depr., Dep., Amort./Sales | (108) 2.5 | (122) 2.3 |
| | 3.5 | 3.7 | 3.8 | 3.4 | | | 3.5 | 3.6 |
| | | | | | | % Officers', Directors' | 2.6 | 2.8 |
| | | | | | | Owners' Comp/Sales | (13) 4.4   (15) 6.0 | |
| | | | | | | | 24.7 | 12.5 |
| 16565M | 124559M | 872221M | 1811695M | 1648778M | 1036964M | Net Sales ($) | 3662286M | 4121118M |
| 2446M | 40779M | 501037M | 1240866M | 994708M | 1411357M | Total Assets ($) | 2800442M | 2857567M |

| Comparative Historical Data | | | Type of Statement | Current Data Sorted by Sales | | | | | |
|---|---|---|---|---|---|---|---|---|---|
| 108 | 126 | 134 | Unqualified | 3 | 10 | 7 | 28 | 43 | 43 |
| 2 | 3 | 4 | Reviewed | | 2 | 1 | 1 | | |
| 3 | 4 | 4 | Compiled | 1 | | 1 | 1 | 1 | |
| 4 | 10 | 7 | Tax Returns | 1 | 3 | 2 | | 1 | |
| 53 | 40 | 59 | Other | 9 | 3 | 9 | 11 | 15 | 12 |
| 4/1/09-<br>3/31/10 | 4/1/10-<br>3/31/11 | 4/1/11-<br>3/31/12 | | 127 (4/1-9/30/11) | | | 81 (10/1/11-3/31/12) | | |
| ALL | ALL | ALL | | 0-1MM | 1-3MM | 3-5MM | 5-10MM | 10-25MM | 25MM & OVER |
| 170 | 183 | 208 | NUMBER OF STATEMENTS | 14 | 18 | 20 | 41 | 60 | 55 |
| % | % | % | ASSETS | % | % | % | % | % | % |
| 16.1 | 17.3 | 18.4 | Cash & Equivalents | 21.7 | 18.0 | 19.8 | 20.3 | 18.9 | 15.2 |
| 20.4 | 18.0 | 16.2 | Trade Receivables (net) | 4.8 | 11.5 | 18.8 | 18.0 | 15.1 | 19.6 |
| .2 | .2 | .2 | Inventory | .0 | .1 | .1 | .2 | .4 | .2 |
| 4.0 | 2.8 | 4.6 | All Other Current | 6.8 | 17.5 | 1.7 | 1.8 | 3.8 | 3.6 |
| 40.7 | 38.3 | 39.4 | Total Current | 33.4 | 47.2 | 40.3 | 40.3 | 38.2 | 38.7 |
| 48.1 | 48.3 | 49.1 | Fixed Assets (net) | 54.0 | 45.2 | 51.1 | 50.5 | 50.4 | 45.8 |
| 1.9 | 3.4 | 2.7 | Intangibles (net) | 7.4 | .8 | .9 | 1.6 | 2.3 | 3.5 |
| 9.2 | 9.9 | 8.9 | All Other Non-Current | 5.3 | 6.8 | 6.7 | 7.7 | 9.1 | 12.0 |
| 100.0 | 100.0 | 100.0 | Total | 100.0 | 100.0 | 100.0 | 100.0 | 100.0 | 100.0 |
| | | | LIABILITIES | | | | | | |
| 4.3 | 3.3 | 3.3 | Notes Payable-Short Term | 1.8 | 1.7 | 3.0 | 4.2 | 2.7 | 4.2 |
| 3.2 | 3.3 | 3.0 | Cur. Mat.-L.T.D. | 3.3 | 4.3 | 2.3 | 2.3 | 2.8 | 3.7 |
| 6.4 | 7.1 | 5.4 | Trade Payables | 2.5 | 6.0 | 4.8 | 4.9 | 3.7 | 8.4 |
| .1 | .2 | .2 | Income Taxes Payable | .1 | .1 | .8 | .0 | .0 | .4 |
| 13.3 | 13.1 | 14.3 | All Other Current | 14.7 | 30.7 | 10.8 | 12.3 | 12.8 | 13.3 |
| 27.3 | 27.1 | 26.2 | Total Current | 22.4 | 42.7 | 21.7 | 23.7 | 21.9 | 30.0 |
| 30.0 | 32.5 | 30.0 | Long-Term Debt | 53.6 | 26.7 | 27.2 | 35.1 | 24.0 | 28.8 |
| .1 | .1 | .1 | Deferred Taxes | .0 | .2 | .1 | .0 | .0 | .2 |
| 4.0 | 4.2 | 3.4 | All Other Non-Current | 4.6 | 1.5 | 1.2 | 1.9 | 4.7 | 4.1 |
| 38.7 | 36.0 | 40.3 | Net Worth | 19.4 | 28.9 | 49.7 | 39.2 | 49.4 | 36.9 |
| 100.0 | 100.0 | 100.0 | Total Liabilties & Net Worth | 100.0 | 100.0 | 100.0 | 100.0 | 100.0 | 100.0 |
| | | | INCOME DATA | | | | | | |
| 100.0 | 100.0 | 100.0 | Net Sales | 100.0 | 100.0 | 100.0 | 100.0 | 100.0 | 100.0 |
| | | | Gross Profit | | | | | | |
| 94.5 | 93.3 | 94.1 | Operating Expenses | 86.0 | 92.6 | 89.2 | 94.0 | 97.7 | 94.7 |
| 5.5 | 6.7 | 5.9 | Operating Profit | 14.0 | 7.4 | 10.8 | 6.0 | 2.3 | 5.3 |
| 2.8 | 2.5 | 1.7 | All Other Expenses (net) | 11.3 | 1.6 | 3.9 | 1.5 | -.1 | .7 |
| 2.7 | 4.1 | 4.1 | Profit Before Taxes | 2.6 | 5.8 | 6.9 | 4.5 | 2.4 | 4.6 |
| | | | RATIOS | | | | | | |
| 2.7 | 2.5 | 2.7 | | 3.7 | 4.2 | 3.6 | 2.6 | 2.9 | 2.0 |
| 1.4 | 1.5 | 1.8 | Current | 1.1 | 2.0 | 1.8 | 1.9 | 1.9 | 1.3 |
| 1.0 | .9 | 1.0 | | .2 | .7 | 1.0 | 1.2 | 1.2 | 1.0 |
| 2.6 | 2.4 | 2.3 | | 3.0 | 2.8 | 3.6 | 2.5 | 2.6 | 1.7 |
| 1.3 | 1.4 | 1.5 | Quick | 1.1 | 1.0 | 1.8 | 1.7 | 1.7 | 1.2 |
| .8 | .9 | .9 | | .2 | .2 | 1.0 | 1.1 | 1.1 | .9 |
| 20 18.4 | 23 16.1 | 17 21.6 | | 0 UND | 0 UND | 9 38.7 | 21 17.4 | 23 15.6 | 26 13.8 |
| 34 10.6 | 32 11.4 | 31 11.7 | Sales/Receivables | 0 UND | 15 24.5 | 27 13.6 | 32 11.5 | 31 11.8 | 34 10.6 |
| 51 7.2 | 41 8.8 | 38 9.6 | | 28 12.9 | 35 10.5 | 33 11.0 | 40 9.2 | 37 9.8 | 42 8.6 |
| | | | Cost of Sales/Inventory | | | | | | |
| | | | Cost of Sales/Payables | | | | | | |
| 6.5 | 5.9 | 5.8 | | 2.8 | 4.8 | 7.1 | 5.0 | 4.6 | 8.0 |
| 17.2 | 17.1 | 13.4 | Sales/Working Capital | NM | 8.5 | 12.1 | 13.2 | 11.0 | 18.4 |
| -401.7 | -97.3 | 193.8 | | -8.3 | -17.7 | NM | 39.7 | 40.0 | 249.6 |
| 5.2 | 5.5 | 6.4 | | 2.8 | 24.7 | 13.3 | 6.0 | 7.3 | 5.4 |
| (140) 2.3 | (156) 2.9 | (173) 2.9 | EBIT/Interest | (13) 5.4 | (17) 3.4 | (34) 2.3 | (55) 3.0 | (48) 3.4 | |
| .8 | 1.6 | 1.3 | | 1.5 | 1.0 | .9 | 1.1 | 1.7 | |
| | 2.0 | 4.1 | Net Profit + Depr., Dep., | | | | | | |
| (12) | 1.2 (21) | 2.7 | Amort./Cur. Mat. L/T/D | | | | | | |
| | .3 | 1.3 | | | | | | | |
| .7 | .7 | .7 | | .3 | .5 | .4 | .8 | .7 | .8 |
| 1.2 | 1.3 | 1.2 | Fixed/Worth | 2.6 | .9 | 1.1 | 1.1 | 1.1 | 1.3 |
| 2.7 | 2.5 | 2.7 | | -4.0 | NM | 1.8 | 3.0 | 2.0 | 2.9 |
| .7 | .6 | .6 | | .3 | .5 | .4 | .5 | .5 | .7 |
| 1.5 | 1.6 | 1.5 | Debt/Worth | 5.4 | 1.5 | .9 | 1.1 | 1.2 | 1.9 |
| 4.3 | 4.5 | 3.4 | | -5.6 | NM | 1.7 | 11.1 | 2.2 | 3.9 |
| 21.2 | 19.4 | 21.2 | % Profit Before Taxes/Tangible | 20.6 | 172.0 | 22.3 | 20.6 | 18.4 | |
| (161) 8.3 | (171) 10.1 | (187) 7.9 | Net Worth | (14) 8.2 | (18) 17.1 | (36) 8.8 | (59) 6.9 | (51) 8.4 | |
| .7 | 3.4 | 2.3 | | 2.2 | 2.6 | .1 | .3 | 3.8 | |
| 7.8 | 7.0 | 10.1 | % Profit Before Taxes/Total | 16.0 | 13.6 | 18.7 | 10.7 | 10.5 | 5.9 |
| 2.6 | 3.2 | 3.3 | Assets | 1.1 | 3.9 | 8.8 | 2.9 | 3.3 | 2.9 |
| -.2 | .8 | .5 | | -2.3 | .9 | .1 | -.1 | .1 | 1.6 |
| 7.9 | 6.1 | 7.1 | | 16.2 | 25.3 | 19.8 | 7.2 | 5.8 | 5.6 |
| 3.4 | 3.1 | 3.0 | Sales/Net Fixed Assets | 1.0 | 4.3 | 3.0 | 2.3 | 3.1 | 3.8 |
| 2.0 | 1.8 | 1.7 | | .2 | 1.6 | 1.1 | 1.5 | 1.9 | 2.2 |
| 2.5 | 2.2 | 2.5 | | 1.4 | 4.8 | 4.4 | 2.8 | 2.2 | 2.3 |
| 1.7 | 1.5 | 1.5 | Sales/Total Assets | .5 | 1.6 | 1.5 | 1.3 | 1.5 | 1.7 |
| 1.2 | 1.1 | 1.0 | | .1 | .9 | .8 | 1.0 | 1.1 | 1.2 |
| 1.6 | 1.7 | 1.5 | | 2.9 | .8 | 1.1 | 1.4 | 1.7 | 1.6 |
| (156) 2.4 | (173) 2.4 | (192) 2.6 | % Depr., Dep., Amort./Sales | (12) 13.3 | (17) 2.3 | (17) 3.6 | (39) 3.2 | (58) 2.5 | (49) 2.3 |
| 3.4 | 3.6 | 3.8 | | 35.6 | 3.5 | 4.3 | 3.6 | 3.5 | 3.6 |
| 1.2 | 1.5 | 1.8 | % Officers', Directors' | | | | | | |
| (23) 2.7 | (26) 3.9 | (17) 2.7 | Owners' Comp/Sales | | | | | | |
| 4.6 | 8.1 | 5.2 | | | | | | | |
| 5064276M | 5308052M | 5510782M | Net Sales ($) | 7708M | 33519M | 79432M | 290995M | 930509M | 4168619M |
| 3487884M | 4073645M | 4191193M | Total Assets ($) | 20336M | 31989M | 64738M | 285036M | 950299M | 2838795M |

M = $ thousand    MM = $ million
See Pages 9 through 22 for Explanation of Ratios and Data

## Current Data Sorted by Assets      Comparative Historical Data

| 0-500M | 500M-2MM | 2-10MM | 10-50MM | 50-100MM | 100-250MM | Type of Statement | 4/1/07-3/31/08 ALL | 4/1/08-3/31/09 ALL |
|---|---|---|---|---|---|---|---|---|
| 1 | 15 | 75 | 74 | 5 | 4 | Unqualified | 171 | 86 |
| 1 | | 3 | 3 | | | Reviewed | 4 | 5 |
| 8 | 4 | 3 | | | | Compiled | 6 | 7 |
| 4 | 5 | 2 | | | | Tax Returns | 10 | 10 |
| 4 | 8 | 22 | 20 | 6 | 4 | Other | 70 | 53 |
| | 186 (4/1-9/30/11) | | | 85 (10/1/11-3/31/12) | | | | |
| 18 | 32 | 105 | 97 | 11 | 8 | **NUMBER OF STATEMENTS** | 261 | 161 |
| % | % | % | % | % | % | **ASSETS** | % | % |
| 20.4 | 15.0 | 16.2 | 15.9 | 16.7 | | Cash & Equivalents | 14.7 | 16.1 |
| 8.1 | 20.2 | 16.7 | 14.8 | 16.5 | | Trade Receivables (net) | 16.3 | 19.9 |
| .0 | .0 | .1 | .2 | .0 | | Inventory | .2 | .2 |
| 5.0 | 3.1 | 3.7 | 2.1 | 2.4 | | All Other Current | 3.8 | 3.4 |
| 33.5 | 38.4 | 36.7 | 33.1 | 35.7 | | Total Current | 35.0 | 39.5 |
| 53.1 | 54.0 | 57.1 | 55.8 | 55.3 | | Fixed Assets (net) | 52.5 | 49.3 |
| .6 | 1.2 | .9 | 1.5 | .4 | | Intangibles (net) | 1.5 | 1.5 |
| 12.8 | 6.4 | 5.3 | 9.6 | 8.6 | | All Other Non-Current | 11.0 | 9.7 |
| 100.0 | 100.0 | 100.0 | 100.0 | 100.0 | | Total | 100.0 | 100.0 |
| | | | | | | **LIABILITIES** | | |
| 12.6 | 2.4 | 2.1 | 2.0 | .6 | | Notes Payable-Short Term | 4.2 | 4.2 |
| 2.1 | 2.4 | 3.2 | 2.2 | 1.1 | | Cur. Mat.-L.T.D. | 2.9 | 2.7 |
| 8.7 | 5.9 | 5.2 | 5.6 | 6.0 | | Trade Payables | 5.3 | 6.3 |
| .8 | .1 | .0 | .0 | .0 | | Income Taxes Payable | .0 | .0 |
| 21.5 | 15.3 | 12.0 | 12.7 | 6.9 | | All Other Current | 12.8 | 13.4 |
| 45.6 | 26.0 | 22.6 | 22.4 | 14.6 | | Total Current | 25.3 | 26.6 |
| 75.8 | 32.7 | 28.8 | 30.6 | 33.2 | | Long-Term Debt | 32.9 | 28.9 |
| .0 | .0 | .1 | .1 | .0 | | Deferred Taxes | .0 | .1 |
| 24.7 | 4.5 | 2.7 | 4.7 | 7.0 | | All Other Non-Current | 4.7 | 1.9 |
| -46.1 | 36.7 | 45.9 | 42.3 | 45.2 | | Net Worth | 37.1 | 42.5 |
| 100.0 | 100.0 | 100.0 | 100.0 | 100.0 | | Total Liabilities & Net Worth | 100.0 | 100.0 |
| | | | | | | **INCOME DATA** | | |
| 100.0 | 100.0 | 100.0 | 100.0 | 100.0 | | Net Sales | 100.0 | 100.0 |
| | | | | | | Gross Profit | | |
| 91.7 | 90.4 | 95.3 | 97.2 | 95.7 | | Operating Expenses | 94.8 | 97.2 |
| 8.3 | 9.6 | 4.7 | 2.8 | 4.3 | | Operating Profit | 5.2 | 2.8 |
| 14.6 | 6.4 | 1.2 | -.1 | -1.9 | | All Other Expenses (net) | 2.1 | 1.4 |
| -6.2 | 3.2 | 3.6 | 2.9 | 6.2 | | Profit Before Taxes | 3.1 | 1.3 |
| | | | | | | **RATIOS** | | |
| 2.0 | 2.9 | 3.4 | 2.6 | 4.6 | | | 2.5 | 2.7 |
| .5 | 1.7 | 1.7 | 1.7 | 2.8 | | Current | 1.6 | 1.7 |
| .0 | .6 | 1.1 | 1.1 | 1.1 | | | 1.0 | 1.0 |
| 1.8 | 2.9 | 3.0 | 2.4 | 4.3 | | | 2.3 | 2.7 |
| .4 | 1.3 | 1.5 | 1.5 | 2.5 | | Quick | 1.4 | 1.4 |
| .0 | .5 | 1.0 | 1.0 | 1.0 | | | .9 | .9 |
| 0 UND | 0 UND | 19   19.3 | 22   16.7 | 26   13.8 | | | 15   24.9 | 19   19.4 |
| 0 UND | 19   19.3 | 33   11.2 | 36   10.1 | 51   7.1 | | Sales/Receivables | 34   10.8 | 37   9.9 |
| 10   36.8 | 33   11.1 | 49   7.4 | 48   7.6 | 79   4.6 | | | 48   7.6 | 52   7.0 |
| | | | | | | Cost of Sales/Inventory | | |
| | | | | | | Cost of Sales/Payables | | |
| 16.8 | 6.7 | 5.3 | 5.0 | 2.5 | | | 5.7 | 6.0 |
| -93.0 | 25.1 | 11.9 | 10.1 | 4.4 | | Sales/Working Capital | 14.0 | 13.7 |
| -1.3 | -36.0 | 90.3 | 67.3 | 47.2 | | | 196.5 | 351.5 |
| | 6.2 | 6.1 | 7.3 | | | | 5.1 | 5.7 |
| | (20) 4.3 | (96) 2.1 | (90) 2.6 | | | EBIT/Interest | (213) 2.3 | (130) 2.6 |
| | 1.1 | .0 | .6 | | | | .9 | .4 |
| | | | | | | Net Profit + Depr., Dep., Amort./Cur. Mat. L/T/D | | |
| .4 | .7 | .8 | .8 | .8 | | | .7 | .6 |
| NM | 1.5 | 1.3 | 1.4 | 1.2 | | Fixed/Worth | 1.5 | 1.2 |
| -.7 | 5.6 | 2.1 | 2.2 | 1.9 | | | 2.8 | 2.4 |
| 1.9 | .6 | .5 | .7 | .6 | | | .6 | .6 |
| NM | 2.1 | 1.1 | 1.4 | 1.0 | | Debt/Worth | 1.6 | 1.1 |
| -1.9 | 8.5 | 2.9 | 3.0 | 2.0 | | | 3.7 | 3.1 |
| | 44.3 | 19.4 | 13.6 | 26.1 | | | 19.3 | 19.7 |
| | (27) 9.9 | (101) 4.6 | (90) 6.1 | 8.6 | | % Profit Before Taxes/Tangible Net Worth | (233) 7.8 | (148) 7.6 |
| | -8.9 | -4.3 | -1.2 | 3.1 | | | .6 | -4.1 |
| 34.3 | 14.4 | 8.7 | 6.1 | 6.5 | | | 6.9 | 8.9 |
| -1.1 | 2.5 | 2.9 | 2.6 | 4.4 | | % Profit Before Taxes/Total Assets | 2.5 | 3.2 |
| -8.2 | -2.6 | -1.8 | -.8 | 1.9 | | | -.7 | -2.4 |
| 47.9 | 16.1 | 5.6 | 4.1 | 3.3 | | | 6.1 | 7.1 |
| 3.2 | 3.9 | 2.4 | 2.1 | 2.3 | | Sales/Net Fixed Assets | 2.4 | 3.5 |
| .7 | 1.6 | 1.4 | 1.3 | .9 | | | 1.3 | 2.0 |
| 6.9 | 3.7 | 2.2 | 1.7 | 1.4 | | | 2.2 | 2.7 |
| 1.5 | 2.2 | 1.6 | 1.2 | 1.0 | | Sales/Total Assets | 1.3 | 1.8 |
| .5 | 1.0 | .9 | .7 | .6 | | | .7 | 1.1 |
| 6.8 | 1.1 | 1.6 | 1.8 | 2.6 | | | 1.8 | 1.5 |
| (12) 12.8 | (28) 1.9 | (103) 2.7 | (94) 2.7 | (10) 3.4 | | % Depr., Dep., Amort./Sales | (242) 2.8 | (151) 2.1 |
| 18.5 | 4.7 | 4.4 | 4.1 | 5.6 | | | 5.1 | 3.4 |
| | | | | 2.6 | | | 4.1 | 4.2 |
| | | | (10) 6.7 | | | % Officers', Directors' Owners' Comp/Sales | (22) 7.5 | (23) 8.3 |
| | | | 10.7 | | | | 21.5 | 11.1 |
| 13615M | 114734M | 948364M | 2780833M | 750036M | 651129M | Net Sales ($) | 4742171M | 2506062M |
| 3577M | 35620M | 575403M | 2082677M | 730959M | 1249359M | Total Assets ($) | 4549380M | 1780799M |

## Comparative Historical Data | | | Type of Statement | ## Current Data Sorted by Sales

| | | | Type of Statement | | | | | | |
|---|---|---|---|---|---|---|---|---|---|
| 150 | 161 | 174 | Unqualified | 6 | 17 | 13 | 40 | 55 | 43 |
| 2 | 3 | 7 | Reviewed | 1 | | | 1 | 2 | 3 |
| 4 | 8 | 15 | Compiled | 8 | 2 | 2 | 3 | | |
| 12 | 13 | 11 | Tax Returns | 3 | 7 | | 1 | | |
| 87 | 83 | 64 | Other | 2 | 10 | 5 | 15 | 13 | 19 |
| 4/1/09-3/31/10 ALL | 4/1/10-3/31/11 ALL | 4/1/11-3/31/12 ALL | | | 186 (4/1-9/30/11) | | | 85 (10/1/11-3/31/12) | |
| | | | | 0-1MM | 1-3MM | 3-5MM | 5-10MM | 10-25MM | 25MM & OVER |
| 255 | 268 | 271 | NUMBER OF STATEMENTS | 20 | 36 | 20 | 60 | 70 | 65 |
| % | % | % | ASSETS | % | % | % | % | % | % |
| 15.7 | 18.8 | 16.0 | Cash & Equivalents | 8.4 | 17.0 | 17.6 | 17.6 | 17.3 | 14.2 |
| 15.7 | 15.8 | 15.6 | Trade Receivables (net) | .6 | 11.7 | 15.2 | 18.9 | 14.6 | 20.4 |
| .1 | .1 | .1 | Inventory | .0 | .1 | .0 | .1 | .1 | .3 |
| 2.7 | 3.0 | 3.1 | All Other Current | 3.0 | 3.1 | 5.4 | 2.2 | 3.3 | 2.8 |
| 34.3 | 37.7 | 34.7 | Total Current | 12.0 | 31.9 | 38.2 | 38.9 | 35.4 | 37.7 |
| 53.2 | 51.5 | 56.1 | Fixed Assets (net) | 76.6 | 63.7 | 53.8 | 53.3 | 55.3 | 49.5 |
| 1.9 | 1.6 | 1.1 | Intangibles (net) | 1.2 | .9 | .3 | 1.1 | 1.2 | 1.4 |
| 10.6 | 9.2 | 8.1 | All Other Non-Current | 10.2 | 3.5 | 7.6 | 6.8 | 8.1 | 11.4 |
| 100.0 | 100.0 | 100.0 | Total | 100.0 | 100.0 | 100.0 | 100.0 | 100.0 | 100.0 |
| | | | LIABILITIES | | | | | | |
| 2.8 | 2.6 | 2.7 | Notes Payable-Short Term | 7.3 | 4.5 | 1.2 | 1.8 | 1.8 | 2.6 |
| 5.1 | 2.8 | 2.6 | Cur. Mat.-L.T.D. | 3.8 | 2.8 | 1.8 | 3.2 | 2.0 | 2.3 |
| 5.1 | 5.1 | 5.6 | Trade Payables | 7.0 | 2.5 | 6.3 | 5.5 | 5.1 | 7.4 |
| .1 | .1 | .1 | Income Taxes Payable | .0 | .4 | .1 | .0 | .1 | .0 |
| 13.3 | 12.4 | 12.8 | All Other Current | 16.3 | 9.3 | 15.6 | 15.2 | 11.1 | 12.4 |
| 26.4 | 23.0 | 23.8 | Total Current | 34.3 | 19.5 | 24.9 | 25.8 | 20.0 | 24.7 |
| 31.3 | 29.4 | 34.1 | Long-Term Debt | 86.9 | 36.9 | 23.9 | 26.6 | 29.3 | 31.4 |
| .0 | .1 | .1 | Deferred Taxes | .0 | .0 | .0 | .1 | .1 | .1 |
| 5.9 | 4.5 | 5.8 | All Other Non-Current | 2.8 | 3.4 | 21.2 | 3.0 | 3.1 | 8.8 |
| 36.4 | 43.0 | 36.3 | Net Worth | -24.1 | 40.2 | 29.9 | 44.5 | 47.5 | 34.9 |
| 100.0 | 100.0 | 100.0 | Total Liabilities & Net Worth | 100.0 | 100.0 | 100.0 | 100.0 | 100.0 | 100.0 |
| | | | INCOME DATA | | | | | | |
| 100.0 | 100.0 | 100.0 | Net Sales | 100.0 | 100.0 | 100.0 | 100.0 | 100.0 | 100.0 |
| | | | Gross Profit | | | | | | |
| 95.3 | 95.4 | 95.1 | Operating Expenses | 83.1 | 89.7 | 100.1 | 97.0 | 98.1 | 95.2 |
| 4.7 | 4.6 | 4.9 | Operating Profit | 16.9 | 10.3 | -.1 | 3.0 | 1.9 | 4.8 |
| 2.5 | 1.3 | 2.3 | All Other Expenses (net) | 23.0 | 2.0 | 1.3 | .6 | .0 | .3 |
| 2.2 | 3.3 | 2.7 | Profit Before Taxes | -6.2 | 8.3 | -1.4 | 2.3 | 2.0 | 4.5 |
| | | | RATIOS | | | | | | |
| 2.8 | 2.9 | 3.0 | | 1.1 | 3.6 | 5.8 | 3.6 | 2.8 | 2.6 |
| 1.6 | 1.7 | 1.6 | Current | .2 | 2.0 | 2.1 | 1.6 | 1.8 | 1.6 |
| 1.0 | 1.1 | 1.0 | | .1 | 1.1 | 1.3 | 1.0 | 1.3 | 1.1 |
| 2.5 | 2.7 | 2.7 | | .5 | 3.3 | 4.4 | 3.6 | 2.5 | 2.1 |
| 1.4 | 1.6 | 1.5 | Quick | .2 | 2.0 | 1.7 | 1.5 | 1.6 | 1.5 |
| .8 | 1.0 | 1.0 | | .1 | .9 | .9 | 1.0 | 1.1 | 1.0 |
| 13 27.8 | 13 28.7 | 13 27.7 | | 0 UND | 0 UND | 9 42.1 | 23 15.8 | 16 22.5 | 24 15.1 |
| 33 10.9 | 34 10.9 | 31 11.8 | Sales/Receivables | 0 UND | 19 19.3 | 29 12.7 | 33 11.1 | 35 10.4 | 39 9.4 |
| 50 7.3 | 47 7.7 | 47 7.7 | | 8 46.8 | 45 8.1 | 62 5.9 | 50 7.3 | 46 7.9 | 51 7.1 |
| | | | Cost of Sales/Inventory | | | | | | |
| | | | Cost of Sales/Payables | | | | | | |
| 6.6 | 5.7 | 5.4 | | NM | 6.1 | 3.2 | 4.9 | 5.1 | 6.9 |
| 15.0 | 11.3 | 13.1 | Sales/Working Capital | -3.3 | 10.7 | 7.3 | 12.5 | 10.1 | 13.1 |
| 999.8 | 56.2 | 507.4 | | -1.6 | 132.5 | 39.8 | -244.1 | 29.8 | 160.0 |
| 5.1 | 7.6 | 6.3 | | | 6.1 | 6.7 | 5.1 | 6.1 | 9.8 |
| (205) 1.8 | (231) 2.4 | (229) 2.5 | EBIT/Interest | (30) 3.2 | (16) .0 | (55) 2.0 | (65) 2.1 | (58) 3.8 | |
| .2 | 1.0 | .4 | | | 1.2 | -4.2 | .0 | -.5 | 1.4 |
| | | | Net Profit + Depr., Dep., Amort./Cur. Mat. L/T/D | | | | | | |
| .8 | .7 | .8 | | 1.5 | 1.1 | .7 | .8 | .8 | .8 |
| 1.4 | 1.2 | 1.4 | Fixed/Worth | NM | 1.6 | 1.1 | 1.2 | 1.2 | 1.4 |
| 2.9 | 2.4 | 2.9 | | -.9 | 3.8 | 2.7 | 2.0 | 2.1 | 3.0 |
| .7 | .6 | .6 | | 2.0 | .6 | .2 | .5 | .6 | .9 |
| 1.4 | 1.2 | 1.4 | Debt/Worth | NM | 1.8 | 1.4 | 1.1 | 1.1 | 1.6 |
| 3.9 | 2.7 | 3.6 | | -2.3 | 4.6 | 5.1 | 3.6 | 2.2 | 3.7 |
| 18.8 | 20.2 | 20.1 | | 20.7 | 52.9 | 19.0 | 13.9 | 13.2 | 32.7 |
| (228) 6.7 | (249) 7.1 | (242) 6.3 | % Profit Before Taxes/Tangible Net Worth | (10) 1.8 | 12.8 | (18) -1.8 | (53) 3.0 | (68) 4.5 | (57) 9.4 |
| -1.3 | .5 | -2.6 | | -18.3 | .9 | -13.5 | -2.1 | -5.0 | 3.1 |
| 6.6 | 8.3 | 8.1 | | 4.1 | 18.4 | 10.7 | 6.1 | 5.9 | 9.6 |
| 2.0 | 2.7 | 2.6 | % Profit Before Taxes/Total Assets | -2.5 | 3.6 | -1.2 | 1.8 | 1.9 | 3.8 |
| -.9 | .0 | -1.6 | | -7.3 | .6 | -6.3 | -1.3 | -2.3 | .9 |
| 6.0 | 6.2 | 5.3 | | 1.1 | 5.2 | 7.4 | 5.7 | 4.5 | 6.0 |
| 2.6 | 2.7 | 2.3 | Sales/Net Fixed Assets | .6 | 1.5 | 3.4 | 2.3 | 2.4 | 2.9 |
| 1.5 | 1.4 | 1.2 | | .2 | .6 | .7 | 1.6 | 1.5 | 1.8 |
| 2.2 | 2.2 | 2.2 | | .7 | 2.3 | 2.1 | 2.3 | 2.0 | 2.5 |
| 1.4 | 1.4 | 1.3 | Sales/Total Assets | .5 | 1.0 | 1.6 | 1.2 | 1.4 | 1.5 |
| .9 | .8 | .8 | | .1 | .5 | .5 | .9 | .9 | 1.0 |
| 1.7 | 1.7 | 1.7 | | 11.8 | 1.8 | 1.1 | 1.5 | 1.8 | 1.4 |
| (232) 2.8 | (243) 2.7 | (254) 2.8 | % Depr., Dep., Amort./Sales | (19) 15.7 | (30) 4.2 | (18) 2.7 | (57) 3.7 | (67) 2.5 | (63) 2.2 |
| 4.3 | 4.2 | 4.7 | | 34.0 | 7.0 | 6.0 | 4.5 | 3.8 | 3.8 |
| 3.9 | 2.3 | 1.5 | | | 5.5 | | | | |
| (27) 8.1 | (33) 6.9 | (31) 6.0 | % Officers', Directors' Owners' Comp/Sales | (10) 10.1 | | | | | |
| 11.3 | 10.4 | 10.9 | | 13.0 | | | | | |
| 4977347M | 5560151M | 5258711M | Net Sales ($) | 4011M | 73836M | 77595M | 426707M | 1165630M | 3510932M |
| 4375838M | 4932760M | 4677595M | Total Assets ($) | 10404M | 112688M | 98907M | 388025M | 976471M | 3091100M |

© RMA 2012

M = $ thousand     MM = $ million
See Pages 9 through 22 for Explanation of Ratios and Data

## Current Data Sorted by Assets      Comparative Historical Data

| | | | | | | Type of Statement | | |
|---|---|---|---|---|---|---|---|---|
| 2 | 17 | 39 | 67 | 49 | 59 | Unqualified | 174 | 232 |
| | 8 | 14 | 6 | | | Reviewed | 26 | 33 |
| 3 | 10 | 11 | 5 | | 1 | Compiled | 34 | 26 |
| 24 | 8 | 12 | 2 | | | Tax Returns | 19 | 48 |
| 14 | 20 | 60 | 54 | 30 | 22 | Other | 125 | 166 |
| | 143 (4/1-9/30/11) | | 394 (10/1/11-3/31/12) | | | | 4/1/07-3/31/08 | 4/1/08-3/31/09 |
| 0-500M | 500M-2MM | 2-10MM | 10-50MM | 50-100MM | 100-250MM | | ALL | ALL |
| 43 | 63 | 136 | 134 | 79 | 82 | NUMBER OF STATEMENTS | 378 | 505 |
| % | % | % | % | % | % | ASSETS | % | % |
| 27.1 | 12.1 | 10.1 | 8.5 | 11.4 | 10.8 | Cash & Equivalents | 10.1 | 11.1 |
| 13.2 | 15.9 | 7.9 | 4.6 | 3.2 | 2.8 | Trade Receivables (net) | 9.9 | 11.3 |
| .3 | .3 | .2 | .6 | .2 | .1 | Inventory | .2 | .4 |
| 6.6 | 3.5 | 1.4 | 2.6 | 1.2 | 2.9 | All Other Current | 2.9 | 3.2 |
| 47.2 | 31.9 | 19.7 | 16.2 | 16.0 | 16.5 | Total Current | 23.1 | 26.0 |
| 29.8 | 54.3 | 67.0 | 66.2 | 62.3 | 61.2 | Fixed Assets (net) | 59.5 | 56.2 |
| 9.1 | 4.0 | 3.3 | 2.7 | 2.3 | 3.2 | Intangibles (net) | 2.6 | 2.8 |
| 13.9 | 9.7 | 10.0 | 14.9 | 19.4 | 19.0 | All Other Non-Current | 14.8 | 15.0 |
| 100.0 | 100.0 | 100.0 | 100.0 | 100.0 | 100.0 | Total | 100.0 | 100.0 |
| | | | | | | LIABILITIES | | |
| 21.7 | 3.9 | 2.8 | 1.5 | 1.1 | .4 | Notes Payable-Short Term | 2.7 | 2.7 |
| 3.4 | 6.5 | 4.1 | 4.3 | 2.4 | 4.2 | Cur. Mat.-L.T.D. | 2.9 | 4.3 |
| 21.3 | 6.5 | 3.0 | 2.2 | 2.3 | 1.6 | Trade Payables | 4.4 | 5.2 |
| .0 | .0 | .1 | .0 | .0 | .0 | Income Taxes Payable | .0 | .0 |
| 45.9 | 21.1 | 9.0 | 6.7 | 6.6 | 8.0 | All Other Current | 13.2 | 13.4 |
| 92.3 | 38.0 | 19.0 | 14.7 | 12.4 | 14.2 | Total Current | 23.2 | 25.7 |
| 27.7 | 40.3 | 56.7 | 53.3 | 51.1 | 46.1 | Long-Term Debt | 49.2 | 46.5 |
| .0 | .0 | .0 | .1 | .3 | .0 | Deferred Taxes | .4 | .3 |
| 18.1 | 9.1 | 5.4 | 16.5 | 32.9 | 32.1 | All Other Non-Current | 13.5 | 14.8 |
| -38.2 | 12.6 | 18.9 | 15.4 | 3.3 | 7.6 | Net Worth | 13.7 | 12.7 |
| 100.0 | 100.0 | 100.0 | 100.0 | 100.0 | 100.0 | Total Liabilities & Net Worth | 100.0 | 100.0 |
| | | | | | | INCOME DATA | | |
| 100.0 | 100.0 | 100.0 | 100.0 | 100.0 | 100.0 | Net Sales | 100.0 | 100.0 |
| | | | | | | Gross Profit | | |
| 97.9 | 87.5 | 82.0 | 90.9 | 93.8 | 93.4 | Operating Expenses | 91.1 | 92.6 |
| 2.1 | 12.5 | 18.0 | 9.1 | 6.2 | 6.6 | Operating Profit | 8.9 | 7.4 |
| 2.0 | 2.0 | 9.9 | 7.2 | 5.6 | 8.3 | All Other Expenses (net) | 5.6 | 7.0 |
| .1 | 10.5 | 8.1 | 1.9 | .6 | -1.7 | Profit Before Taxes | 3.2 | .4 |
| | | | | | | RATIOS | | |
| 1.3 | 1.9 | 1.7 | 2.1 | 3.3 | 2.6 | | 2.4 | 2.4 |
| .7 | .9 | .9 | 1.3 | 1.7 | 1.4 | Current | 1.3 | 1.3 |
| .2 | .5 | .4 | .6 | .8 | .8 | | .7 | .7 |
| 1.2 | 1.8 | 1.6 | 1.9 | 2.9 | 2.2 | | 2.1 | 2.1 |
| .6 | .9 | (133) .8 | 1.2 | 1.5 | 1.3 | Quick | 1.0 | 1.0 |
| .1 | .5 | .3 | .4 | .7 | .5 | | .5 | .5 |
| 0 UND | 1 510.2 | 0 UND | 7 53.0 | 11 32.0 | 10 36.7 | | 3 108.3 | 4 82.4 |
| 1 609.6 | 15 24.9 | 7 54.3 | 23 15.7 | 19 19.2 | 19 19.3 | Sales/Receivables | 20 18.2 | 22 17.0 |
| 10 35.4 | 32 11.5 | 32 11.3 | 35 10.4 | 34 10.7 | 34 10.7 | | 38 9.7 | 38 9.5 |
| | | | | | | Cost of Sales/Inventory | | |
| | | | | | | Cost of Sales/Payables | | |
| 69.5 | 15.7 | 13.4 | 5.5 | 2.3 | 2.1 | | 5.9 | 6.1 |
| -60.5 | -95.2 | -52.6 | 22.9 | 10.8 | 11.4 | Sales/Working Capital | 24.0 | 23.3 |
| -10.4 | -21.7 | -6.3 | -11.3 | -23.3 | -25.8 | | -15.6 | -14.8 |
| 16.9 | 20.3 | 7.2 | 3.0 | 3.1 | 2.5 | | 3.7 | 3.8 |
| (24) .5 | (40) 5.4 | (100) 2.5 | (122) 1.6 | (74) 1.5 | (71) 1.2 | EBIT/Interest | (306) 1.9 | (408) 1.3 |
| -14.0 | 1.1 | .9 | .3 | .5 | .4 | | .9 | .1 |
| | | | | | | Net Profit + Depr., Dep., | 6.3 | 8.1 |
| | | | | | | Amort./Cur. Mat. L/T/D | (11) 2.0    (23) 2.9 | |
| | | | | | | | 1.2 | 2.1 |
| .2 | .6 | 1.2 | 1.7 | 1.8 | 3.0 | | 1.3 | 1.2 |
| 7.9 | 2.6 | 5.4 | 3.9 | 30.3 | 7.3 | Fixed/Worth | 3.8 | 3.9 |
| -.5 | -5.0 | -5.7 | -13.6 | -3.6 | -4.2 | | -12.4 | -6.4 |
| 1.0 | .6 | 1.3 | 1.7 | 2.5 | 4.2 | | 1.5 | 1.3 |
| -13.0 | 3.0 | 5.5 | 5.2 | 37.6 | 11.0 | Debt/Worth | 5.6 | 5.5 |
| -1.9 | -10.8 | -8.2 | -16.3 | -5.7 | -6.8 | | -19.9 | -11.0 |
| 171.6 | 72.2 | 46.8 | 20.8 | 18.2 | 19.7 | % Profit Before Taxes/Tangible | 42.5 | 36.6 |
| (20) 54.8 | (43) 33.5 | (80) 17.3 | (94) 6.3 | (45) 6.2 | (49) 4.8 | Net Worth | (260) 10.4 | (341) 8.0 |
| 9.9 | 12.1 | 3.4 | -1.2 | -7.8 | -4.0 | | 1.2 | -3.7 |
| 54.3 | 26.0 | 11.1 | 3.9 | 2.8 | 2.1 | % Profit Before Taxes/Total | 7.1 | 7.5 |
| 7.6 | 11.9 | 4.2 | 1.1 | .8 | -.3 | Assets | 1.9 | 1.1 |
| -15.4 | .1 | -.3 | -1.3 | -1.3 | -2.0 | | -.6 | -2.2 |
| 309.0 | 23.3 | 2.8 | 1.1 | .7 | .7 | | 3.0 | 4.6 |
| 64.2 | 4.8 | .9 | .7 | .5 | .4 | Sales/Net Fixed Assets | .9 | 1.0 |
| 13.1 | .9 | .4 | .4 | .4 | .3 | | .4 | .4 |
| 12.8 | 4.4 | 1.3 | .6 | .4 | .4 | | 1.4 | 1.7 |
| 6.9 | 2.0 | .6 | .5 | .3 | .3 | Sales/Total Assets | .6 | .6 |
| 5.1 | .8 | .3 | .3 | .2 | .2 | | .3 | .3 |
| .2 | 1.0 | 3.3 | 5.4 | 9.7 | 7.9 | | 2.8 | 2.3 |
| (28) .6 | (56) 4.4 | (121) 7.2 | (133) 8.5 | (78) 12.0 | (81) 12.8 | % Depr., Dep., Amort./Sales | (359) 6.4 | (463) 6.2 |
| 1.5 | 8.1 | 14.4 | 13.3 | 14.9 | 17.9 | | 11.8 | 11.7 |
| 1.8 | | 3.0 | 1.9 | | | % Officers', Directors' | 2.7 | 2.5 |
| (12) 5.4 | | (18) 6.0 | (17) 5.5 | | | Owners' Comp/Sales | (49) 4.8 | (64) 5.2 |
| 13.1 | | 13.0 | 8.1 | | | | 10.9 | 9.2 |
| 72700M | 190354M | 706202M | 1688035M | 2448154M | 4865127M | Net Sales ($) | 7682723M | 10028324M |
| 8738M | 77099M | 708447M | 3309578M | 5801371M | 12568625M | Total Assets ($) | 13127485M | 17241637M |

© RMA 2012

M = $ thousand    MM = $ million
See Pages 9 through 22 for Explanation of Ratios and Data

| Comparative Historical Data | | | Type of Statement | Current Data Sorted by Sales | | | | | |
|---|---|---|---|---|---|---|---|---|---|
| 234 | 245 | 233 | Unqualified | 11 | 23 | 13 | 29 | 90 | 67 |
| 32 | 36 | 28 | Reviewed | 4 | 13 | 3 | 6 | 2 | |
| 24 | 23 | 30 | Compiled | 7 | 10 | 4 | 5 | 3 | 1 |
| 31 | 36 | 46 | Tax Returns | 12 | 22 | 5 | 4 | 3 | |
| 174 | 197 | 200 | Other | 17 | 41 | 22 | 30 | 63 | 27 |
| 4/1/09-3/31/10 | 4/1/10-3/31/11 | 4/1/11-3/31/12 | | 143 (4/1-9/30/11) | | | 394 (10/1/11-3/31/12) | | |
| ALL | ALL | ALL | | 0-1MM | 1-3MM | 3-5MM | 5-10MM | 10-25MM | 25MM & OVER |
| 495 | 537 | 537 | NUMBER OF STATEMENTS | 51 | 109 | 47 | 74 | 161 | 95 |
| % | % | % | ASSETS | % | % | % | % | % | % |
| 10.9 | 10.8 | 11.6 | Cash & Equivalents | 8.7 | 13.3 | 10.8 | 9.5 | 12.0 | 12.5 |
| 9.5 | 7.9 | 7.0 | Trade Receivables (net) | 2.0 | 8.0 | 8.1 | 12.1 | 6.0 | 5.7 |
| .2 | .5 | .3 | Inventory | .9 | .1 | .4 | .3 | .3 | .2 |
| 3.0 | 2.1 | 2.5 | All Other Current | .8 | 3.1 | 5.6 | 2.2 | 2.1 | 2.3 |
| 23.7 | 21.3 | 21.4 | Total Current | 12.4 | 24.5 | 24.9 | 24.0 | 20.5 | 20.6 |
| 57.9 | 61.9 | 60.8 | Fixed Assets (net) | 71.2 | 59.8 | 62.5 | 58.2 | 60.5 | 57.8 |
| 3.0 | 2.9 | 3.6 | Intangibles (net) | 5.0 | 5.0 | 2.1 | 2.3 | 2.7 | 4.2 |
| 15.5 | 13.9 | 14.3 | All Other Non-Current | 11.4 | 10.7 | 10.5 | 15.4 | 16.2 | 17.4 |
| 100.0 | 100.0 | 100.0 | Total | 100.0 | 100.0 | 100.0 | 100.0 | 100.0 | 100.0 |
| | | | LIABILITIES | | | | | | |
| 4.2 | 2.3 | 3.5 | Notes Payable-Short Term | 10.1 | 7.3 | 3.0 | 1.8 | 1.1 | 1.2 |
| 4.0 | 3.3 | 4.2 | Cur. Mat.-L.T.D. | 7.0 | 5.1 | 4.9 | 3.4 | 2.5 | 4.7 |
| 4.9 | 4.4 | 4.4 | Trade Payables | 4.4 | 5.7 | 8.1 | 5.4 | 2.6 | 3.1 |
| .1 | .1 | .0 | Income Taxes Payable | .0 | .0 | .0 | .1 | .0 | .0 |
| 12.8 | 12.8 | 12.3 | All Other Current | 8.8 | 16.6 | 26.4 | 13.9 | 8.0 | 8.3 |
| 26.0 | 23.0 | 24.3 | Total Current | 30.3 | 34.7 | 42.5 | 24.6 | 14.2 | 17.2 |
| 49.5 | 52.9 | 49.2 | Long-Term Debt | 66.4 | 51.9 | 49.9 | 41.2 | 48.9 | 42.9 |
| .5 | .2 | .1 | Deferred Taxes | .0 | .0 | .0 | .0 | .1 | .3 |
| 18.1 | 16.7 | 17.8 | All Other Non-Current | 11.2 | 9.5 | 9.3 | 12.4 | 25.2 | 26.6 |
| 6.0 | 7.2 | 8.7 | Net Worth | -7.9 | 3.9 | -1.7 | 21.8 | 11.6 | 13.0 |
| 100.0 | 100.0 | 100.0 | Total Liabilties & Net Worth | 100.0 | 100.0 | 100.0 | 100.0 | 100.0 | 100.0 |
| | | | INCOME DATA | | | | | | |
| 100.0 | 100.0 | 100.0 | Net Sales | 100.0 | 100.0 | 100.0 | 100.0 | 100.0 | 100.0 |
| | | | Gross Profit | | | | | | |
| 91.9 | 90.2 | 89.6 | Operating Expenses | 73.2 | 86.0 | 89.0 | 94.0 | 93.6 | 92.7 |
| 8.1 | 9.8 | 10.4 | Operating Profit | 26.8 | 14.0 | 11.0 | 6.0 | 6.4 | 7.3 |
| 5.9 | 7.0 | 6.8 | All Other Expenses (net) | 14.6 | 6.8 | 9.7 | 4.4 | 5.3 | 5.5 |
| 2.2 | 2.8 | 3.6 | Profit Before Taxes | 12.2 | 7.2 | 1.3 | 1.6 | 1.1 | 1.8 |
| | | | RATIOS | | | | | | |
| 2.5 | 2.4 | 2.0 | | 1.0 | 1.7 | 1.8 | 1.8 | 3.1 | 2.1 |
| 1.3 | 1.2 | 1.1 | Current | .5 | .8 | .7 | 1.1 | 1.5 | 1.4 |
| .6 | .6 | .5 | | .1 | .4 | .2 | .6 | .8 | 1.0 |
| 2.0 | 2.1 | 1.9 | | 1.0 | 1.7 | 1.8 | 1.8 | 2.6 | 1.8 |
| 1.1 | 1.0 (534) | 1.0 | Quick | (50) .4 (107) .8 | | .7 | 1.0 | 1.4 | 1.3 |
| .5 | .5 | .4 | | .1 | .3 | .2 | .4 | .7 | .7 |
| 5 74.0 | 4 99.1 | 3 136.8 | | 0 UND | 0 UND | 1 418.2 | 4 81.3 | 13 27.3 | 13 27.5 |
| 19 18.9 | 16 22.8 | 16 23.5 | Sales/Receivables | 0 UND | 3 107.9 | 6 63.9 | 24 15.4 | 25 14.7 | 24 15.0 |
| 34 10.7 | 32 11.6 | 33 11.2 | | 4 91.4 | 17 21.6 | 18 19.8 | 35 10.5 | 36 10.0 | 38 9.6 |
| | | | Cost of Sales/Inventory | | | | | | |
| | | | Cost of Sales/Payables | | | | | | |
| 6.1 | 5.9 | 6.7 | | 907.0 | 13.5 | 17.5 | 11.4 | 3.3 | 4.5 |
| 31.7 | 41.5 | 65.6 | Sales/Working Capital | -10.2 | -54.1 | -28.5 | 162.5 | 10.9 | 13.4 |
| -11.7 | -11.7 | -10.5 | | -2.0 | -8.3 | -5.3 | -13.2 | -23.6 | -122.8 |
| 3.9 | 3.8 | 4.2 | | 15.1 | 5.5 | 3.8 | 4.7 | 3.6 | 3.5 |
| (383) 1.5 | (438) 1.6 | (431) 1.8 | EBIT/Interest | (24) 6.0 | (80) 1.8 | (34) 1.7 | (61) 1.7 | (142) 2.0 | (90) 1.5 |
| .5 | .7 | .6 | | 1.4 | .2 | .9 | .7 | .5 | .5 |
| 6.3 | 5.2 | 4.0 | Net Profit + Depr., Dep., | | | | | | |
| (12) 2.7 | (18) 2.3 | (11) 1.7 | Amort./Cur. Mat. L/T/D | | | | | | |
| .8 | .6 | .2 | | | | | | | |
| 1.4 | 1.7 | 1.4 | | 1.9 | 1.1 | .8 | 1.0 | 1.6 | 1.5 |
| 5.7 | 7.2 | 5.7 | Fixed/Worth | -10.6 | 5.3 | -40.8 | 2.6 | 5.8 | 5.7 |
| -5.0 | -5.2 | -5.0 | | -3.5 | -4.2 | -4.0 | -8.3 | -4.9 | -7.4 |
| 1.7 | 1.9 | 1.6 | | 1.8 | 1.1 | .9 | 1.2 | 1.9 | 2.4 |
| 8.0 | 9.7 | 8.0 | Debt/Worth | -13.0 | 6.2 | -49.6 | 2.9 | 8.4 | 7.2 |
| -7.5 | -7.5 | -7.7 | | -5.0 | -6.6 | -6.5 | -16.0 | -7.3 | -23.9 |
| 36.8 | 35.3 | 37.2 | % Profit Before Taxes/Tangible | 93.1 | 41.6 | 50.5 | 47.1 | 39.7 | 18.8 |
| (302) 11.0 | (324) 11.2 | (331) 11.4 | Net Worth | (24) 14.9 | (65) 15.3 | (23) 14.6 | (50) 16.3 | (105) 8.4 | (64) 4.7 |
| -1.8 | 1.7 | .3 | | 2.3 | .3 | -2.2 | 3.3 | -.5 | -3.7 |
| 7.8 | 5.8 | 6.9 | % Profit Before Taxes/Total | 15.6 | 13.0 | 9.7 | 11.3 | 5.2 | 3.7 |
| 1.7 | 1.7 | 1.8 | Assets | 3.1 | 2.8 | 2.3 | 2.3 | 1.6 | 1.1 |
| -1.5 | -1.0 | -1.2 | | -.2 | -1.6 | -1.4 | -1.0 | -1.5 | -1.0 |
| 3.7 | 2.4 | 2.4 | | 5.9 | 11.0 | 9.2 | 4.1 | 1.1 | 1.5 |
| .8 | .6 | .7 | Sales/Net Fixed Assets | .6 | 1.0 | .9 | 1.2 | .6 | .6 |
| .4 | .3 | .4 | | .2 | .5 | .4 | .5 | .4 | .4 |
| 1.5 | 1.2 | 1.2 | | 2.5 | 2.3 | 3.0 | 1.9 | .7 | .7 |
| .5 | .5 | .5 | Sales/Total Assets | .5 | .7 | .6 | .8 | .4 | .4 |
| .3 | .2 | .3 | | .1 | .4 | .3 | .3 | .2 | .3 |
| 2.8 | 4.0 | 4.0 | | 6.3 | 4.1 | 2.5 | 2.2 | 5.6 | 4.6 |
| (466) 7.2 | (499) 9.2 | (497) 8.8 | % Depr., Dep., Amort./Sales | (43) 12.7 | (87) 8.2 | (45) 6.9 | (72) 5.4 | (158) 10.4 | (92) 9.7 |
| 13.0 | 14.9 | 14.6 | | 30.7 | 14.8 | 14.8 | 12.4 | 14.5 | 13.1 |
| 2.6 | 2.4 | 2.5 | % Officers', Directors' | | 1.9 | | 2.0 | 2.3 | 2.1 |
| (54) 5.3 | (69) 4.9 | (59) 5.8 | Owners' Comp/Sales | (10) 3.9 | | (12) 4.6 | (14) 7.8 | (10) 5.7 | |
| 11.9 | 9.6 | 12.4 | | | 5.2 | | 12.1 | 25.3 | 11.7 |
| 8994926M | 9725456M | 9970572M | Net Sales ($) | 29875M | 201117M | 186942M | 560182M | 2703716M | 6288740M |
| 17805355M | 21219813M | 22473858M | Total Assets ($) | 105349M | 397598M | 404516M | 1148270M | 8550343M | 11867782M |

M = $ thousand    MM = $ million
See Pages 9 through 22 for Explanation of Ratios and Data

## Current Data Sorted by Assets      Comparative Historical Data

| 0-500M | 500M-2MM | 2-10MM | 10-50MM | 50-100MM | 100-250MM | Type of Statement | 4/1/07-3/31/08 ALL | 4/1/08-3/31/09 ALL |
|---|---|---|---|---|---|---|---|---|
| 1 | 6 | 19 | 20 | 13 | 3 | Unqualified | 38 | 112 |
| 1 | 1 | 5 | | 1 | | Reviewed | 12 | 10 |
| 8 | 2 | 4 | 1 | | | Compiled | 8 | 10 |
| 16 | 7 | 7 | 7 | | | Tax Returns | 15 | 26 |
| 9 | 19 | 21 | 19 | | 4 | Other | 56 | 89 |
| | 46 (4/1-9/30/11) | | 141 (10/1/11-3/31/12) | | | | | |
| 35 | 35 | 56 | 40 | 14 | 7 | **NUMBER OF STATEMENTS** | 129 | 247 |
| % | % | % | % | % | % | **ASSETS** | % | % |
| 28.8 | 15.3 | 9.1 | 9.6 | 7.9 | | Cash & Equivalents | 12.4 | 15.1 |
| 8.5 | 11.7 | 7.4 | 2.2 | 7.1 | | Trade Receivables (net) | 7.6 | 11.1 |
| .2 | .1 | .1 | .1 | .1 | | Inventory | .7 | .2 |
| 11.3 | 3.9 | 1.8 | 1.4 | 3.5 | | All Other Current | 5.0 | 2.6 |
| 48.8 | 31.0 | 18.4 | 13.3 | 18.6 | | Total Current | 25.8 | 29.0 |
| 31.5 | 50.8 | 70.1 | 75.4 | 65.5 | | Fixed Assets (net) | 61.4 | 55.8 |
| 6.9 | 6.8 | 2.6 | 4.2 | 4.9 | | Intangibles (net) | 2.1 | 2.4 |
| 12.9 | 11.4 | 8.9 | 7.2 | 11.0 | | All Other Non-Current | 10.6 | 12.9 |
| 100.0 | 100.0 | 100.0 | 100.0 | 100.0 | | Total | 100.0 | 100.0 |
| | | | | | | **LIABILITIES** | | |
| 23.0 | 2.0 | .8 | 2.9 | 1.9 | | Notes Payable-Short Term | 3.4 | 4.8 |
| 5.5 | 3.6 | 2.9 | 4.5 | 6.9 | | Cur. Mat.-L.T.D. | 4.4 | 4.8 |
| 8.9 | 8.3 | 6.0 | 1.1 | 4.9 | | Trade Payables | 5.3 | 5.5 |
| .6 | .0 | .0 | .0 | .0 | | Income Taxes Payable | .1 | .0 |
| 55.5 | 25.9 | 6.2 | 5.7 | 9.4 | | All Other Current | 19.5 | 19.8 |
| 93.5 | 39.7 | 15.9 | 14.2 | 23.1 | | Total Current | 32.7 | 34.9 |
| 31.2 | 43.9 | 64.7 | 62.4 | 47.6 | | Long-Term Debt | 51.9 | 43.1 |
| .0 | .0 | .0 | .2 | .1 | | Deferred Taxes | .0 | .0 |
| 10.9 | 9.3 | 6.8 | 21.0 | 25.4 | | All Other Non-Current | 10.1 | 7.1 |
| -35.5 | 7.1 | 12.7 | 2.2 | 3.9 | | Net Worth | 5.2 | 14.8 |
| 100.0 | 100.0 | 100.0 | 100.0 | 100.0 | | Total Liabilities & Net Worth | 100.0 | 100.0 |
| | | | | | | **INCOME DATA** | | |
| 100.0 | 100.0 | 100.0 | 100.0 | 100.0 | | Net Sales | 100.0 | 100.0 |
| | | | | | | Gross Profit | | |
| 96.7 | 89.0 | 83.7 | 91.0 | 100.2 | | Operating Expenses | 88.6 | 91.9 |
| 3.3 | 11.0 | 16.3 | 9.0 | -.2 | | Operating Profit | 11.4 | 8.1 |
| .2 | 4.6 | 9.8 | 10.0 | 4.7 | | All Other Expenses (net) | 9.1 | 6.5 |
| 3.1 | 6.4 | 6.4 | -1.0 | -4.9 | | Profit Before Taxes | 2.4 | 1.6 |
| | | | | | | **RATIOS** | | |
| 1.6 | 1.6 | 2.1 | 2.7 | 2.4 | | | 2.5 | 2.2 |
| .8 | .6 | 1.3 | .9 | 1.1 | | Current | 1.0 | 1.2 |
| .4 | .3 | .5 | .3 | .5 | | | .4 | .6 |
| 1.6 | 1.0 | 1.7 | 2.1 | 2.1 | | | 2.3 | 2.0 |
| .7 | .5 | 1.1 | .7 | .9 | | Quick | (128) .9 | 1.0 |
| .1 | .2 | .5 | .3 | .4 | | | .3 | .5 |
| 0 UND | 0 UND | 0 UND | 1 434.8 | 21 17.3 | | | 0 UND | 2 173.6 |
| 0 999.8 | 2 187.0 | 4 92.3 | 9 42.0 | 38 9.7 | | Sales/Receivables | 6 57.8 | 18 20.0 |
| 6 62.4 | 17 21.5 | 24 15.3 | 24 15.5 | 52 7.0 | | | 30 12.0 | 42 8.8 |
| | | | | | | Cost of Sales/Inventory | | |
| | | | | | | Cost of Sales/Payables | | |
| 29.1 | 20.6 | 8.9 | 3.8 | 3.6 | | | 7.4 | 6.8 |
| -38.4 | -16.8 | 23.1 | -143.0 | NM | | Sales/Working Capital | 171.7 | 39.2 |
| -18.0 | -7.5 | -13.7 | -5.0 | -8.6 | | | -8.5 | -14.4 |
| 35.4 | 26.1 | 7.0 | 5.1 | 2.0 | | | 3.6 | 4.7 |
| (22) 17.4 | (25) 1.9 | (43) 2.3 | (29) 1.2 | (13) .9 | | EBIT/Interest | (90) 1.3 | (185) 1.6 |
| -.1 | 1.4 | 1.0 | .4 | -.3 | | | .6 | .4 |
| | | | | | | Net Profit + Depr., Dep., Amort./Cur. Mat. L/T/D | | |
| .7 | .7 | 1.5 | 2.2 | 2.8 | | | 1.2 | 1.0 |
| 2.1 | 4.7 | 4.7 | -16.3 | 16.6 | | Fixed/Worth | 5.5 | 2.6 |
| -.1 | -1.5 | -5.6 | -2.3 | -4.8 | | | -8.6 | -12.4 |
| .9 | .6 | 1.8 | 1.8 | 3.8 | | | 1.5 | 1.1 |
| 11.8 | 42.2 | 5.1 | -17.8 | 20.5 | | Debt/Worth | 10.7 | 3.6 |
| -2.9 | -3.1 | -7.2 | -3.5 | -7.8 | | | -10.7 | -15.0 |
| 161.6 | 82.7 | 43.5 | 11.9 | | | | 45.4 | 22.7 |
| (18) 88.9 | (18) 29.4 | (38) 13.3 | (18) 4.8 | | | % Profit Before Taxes/Tangible Net Worth | (74) 10.2 | (174) 7.4 |
| 53.8 | 8.8 | 1.5 | -7.9 | | | | .5 | -3.9 |
| 57.0 | 24.1 | 9.4 | 3.7 | 2.0 | | | 9.3 | 6.8 |
| 27.8 | 7.7 | 3.4 | .1 | -.7 | | % Profit Before Taxes/Total Assets | .8 | 1.2 |
| -17.3 | -.7 | .1 | -3.5 | -3.3 | | | -1.2 | -2.3 |
| 85.4 | 23.7 | 1.5 | .8 | 1.1 | | | 5.9 | 5.8 |
| 35.7 | 4.6 | .7 | .5 | .5 | | Sales/Net Fixed Assets | 1.0 | 1.7 |
| 11.4 | .9 | .3 | .3 | .4 | | | .4 | .6 |
| 9.3 | 4.1 | 1.1 | .6 | .7 | | | 2.0 | 2.1 |
| 6.0 | 1.2 | .5 | .3 | .4 | | Sales/Total Assets | .7 | .9 |
| 3.9 | .6 | .3 | .2 | .3 | | | .3 | .4 |
| .6 | .6 | 4.0 | 5.9 | 4.1 | | | 2.8 | 1.8 |
| (23) 1.2 | (31) 5.0 | (51) 8.5 | (37) 12.9 | 10.5 | | % Depr., Dep., Amort./Sales | (117) 6.0 | (220) 4.0 |
| 2.3 | 6.7 | 12.5 | 18.1 | 15.3 | | | 12.6 | 10.3 |
| | | | | | | | 6.0 | 5.1 |
| | | | | | | % Officers', Directors' Owners' Comp/Sales | (24) 9.1 | (21) 6.4 |
| | | | | | | | 16.8 | 15.9 |
| 44105M | 98670M | 298865M | 544608M | 707135M | 800164M | Net Sales ($) | 1200256M | 4537967M |
| 7261M | 42902M | 281029M | 883242M | 1057320M | 1168863M | Total Assets ($) | 1979682M | 5756804M |

M = $ thousand    MM = $ million
See Pages 9 through 22 for Explanation of Ratios and Data

| Comparative Historical Data | | | Type of Statement | Current Data Sorted by Sales | | | | | |
|---|---|---|---|---|---|---|---|---|---|
| 61 | 53 | 62 | Unqualified | 8 | 9 | 10 | 11 | 12 | 12 |
| 10 | 19 | 8 | Reviewed | 1 | 2 | 2 | 1 | 1 | 1 |
| 16 | 18 | 15 | Compiled | 4 | 8 | 2 | 1 | | |
| 44 | 38 | 30 | Tax Returns | 13 | 16 | | | 1 | |
| 53 | 72 | 72 | Other | 10 | 27 | 11 | 11 | 5 | 8 |
| 4/1/09-3/31/10 ALL | 4/1/10-3/31/11 ALL | 4/1/11-3/31/12 ALL | | 0-1MM | 46 (4/1-9/30/11) 1-3MM | 3-5MM | 141 (10/1/11-3/31/12) 5-10MM | 10-25MM | 25MM & OVER |
| 184 | 200 | 187 | NUMBER OF STATEMENTS | 36 | 62 | 25 | 24 | 19 | 21 |
| % | % | % | ASSETS | % | % | % | % | % | % |
| 15.1 | 16.4 | 13.9 | Cash & Equivalents | 13.6 | 17.4 | 10.1 | 9.5 | 12.4 | 14.4 |
| 6.4 | 7.4 | 7.3 | Trade Receivables (net) | 1.3 | 3.5 | 7.1 | 17.9 | 10.7 | 13.7 |
| .2 | .3 | .1 | Inventory | .1 | .1 | .1 | .1 | .1 | .2 |
| 3.1 | 2.6 | 4.1 | All Other Current | 10.0 | 2.8 | 2.8 | 1.3 | 2.4 | 3.8 |
| 24.7 | 26.7 | 25.3 | Total Current | 25.0 | 23.8 | 20.2 | 28.8 | 25.7 | 32.2 |
| 59.3 | 60.5 | 59.5 | Fixed Assets (net) | 61.6 | 60.3 | 69.0 | 55.5 | 56.9 | 49.6 |
| 2.7 | 4.2 | 4.7 | Intangibles (net) | 7.7 | 3.8 | 5.8 | 3.4 | 3.0 | 3.7 |
| 13.3 | 8.6 | 10.5 | All Other Non-Current | 5.8 | 12.2 | 4.9 | 12.2 | 14.5 | 14.5 |
| 100.0 | 100.0 | 100.0 | Total | 100.0 | 100.0 | 100.0 | 100.0 | 100.0 | 100.0 |
| | | | LIABILITIES | | | | | | |
| 4.0 | 4.1 | 5.7 | Notes Payable-Short Term | 7.9 | 9.9 | 4.2 | .2 | .3 | 2.3 |
| 4.1 | 4.9 | 4.2 | Cur. Mat.-L.T.D. | 2.4 | 3.9 | 8.1 | 3.5 | 1.6 | 6.2 |
| 7.3 | 5.9 | 5.7 | Trade Payables | 1.9 | 4.6 | 5.1 | 14.3 | 5.2 | 6.5 |
| .0 | .4 | .1 | Income Taxes Payable | .6 | .0 | .0 | .0 | .0 | .0 |
| 18.6 | 15.7 | 19.3 | All Other Current | 12.2 | 32.7 | 15.7 | 11.9 | 9.9 | 13.0 |
| 34.0 | 31.0 | 34.9 | Total Current | 25.0 | 51.1 | 33.1 | 30.0 | 17.0 | 28.0 |
| 51.6 | 55.1 | 52.2 | Long-Term Debt | 44.8 | 57.8 | 61.8 | 50.8 | 47.8 | 42.8 |
| .0 | .0 | .0 | Deferred Taxes | .0 | .0 | .0 | .0 | .5 | .0 |
| 9.0 | 9.4 | 12.4 | All Other Non-Current | 6.2 | 12.5 | 9.4 | 16.1 | 27.1 | 9.0 |
| 5.4 | 4.5 | .4 | Net Worth | 24.0 | -21.3 | -4.3 | 3.1 | 7.7 | 20.3 |
| 100.0 | 100.0 | 100.0 | Total Liabilties & Net Worth | 100.0 | 100.0 | 100.0 | 100.0 | 100.0 | 100.0 |
| | | | INCOME DATA | | | | | | |
| 100.0 | 100.0 | 100.0 | Net Sales | 100.0 | 100.0 | 100.0 | 100.0 | 100.0 | 100.0 |
| | | | Gross Profit | | | | | | |
| 87.3 | 88.5 | 90.0 | Operating Expenses | 86.3 | 88.6 | 90.9 | 92.7 | 94.7 | 92.0 |
| 12.7 | 11.5 | 10.0 | Operating Profit | 13.7 | 11.4 | 9.1 | 7.3 | 5.3 | 8.0 |
| 9.9 | 7.7 | 6.7 | All Other Expenses (net) | 6.9 | 7.7 | 6.5 | 6.4 | 5.8 | 4.7 |
| 2.8 | 3.8 | 3.3 | Profit Before Taxes | 6.8 | 3.7 | 2.6 | .9 | -.5 | 3.3 |
| | | | RATIOS | | | | | | |
| 2.2 | 2.5 | 2.0 | Current | 1.9 | 1.7 | 2.0 | 1.8 | 2.3 | 2.9 |
| 1.0 | 1.2 | 1.0 | | 1.0 | .8 | 1.0 | 1.0 | 1.3 | 1.3 |
| .4 | .5 | .4 | | .4 | .3 | .3 | .5 | .9 | .6 |
| 1.7 | 2.3 | 1.6 | Quick | 1.6 | 1.6 | 1.7 | 1.5 | 1.6 | 2.0 |
| .8 | (199) 1.1 | .7 | | .6 | .6 | .7 | .9 | 1.2 | 1.0 |
| .2 | .4 | .3 | | .1 | .2 | .2 | .4 | .8 | .6 |
| 0 UND | 0 UND | 0 UND | Sales/Receivables | 0 UND | 0 UND | 1 631.0 | 6 65.0 | 15 24.2 | 16 23.2 |
| 4 89.7 | 4 91.0 | 4 81.8 | | 0 UND | 0 987.9 | 7 50.2 | 21 17.5 | 30 12.2 | 26 14.1 |
| 20 18.2 | 23 15.7 | 25 14.8 | | 5 79.0 | 4 95.9 | 12 31.5 | 37 9.8 | 47 7.8 | 38 9.5 |
| | | | Cost of Sales/Inventory | | | | | | |
| | | | Cost of Sales/Payables | | | | | | |
| 9.0 | 7.2 | 9.8 | Sales/Working Capital | 13.1 | 11.0 | 9.3 | 12.7 | 8.9 | 4.9 |
| NM | 63.3 | 577.3 | | NM | -38.2 | -916.8 | -501.5 | 17.0 | 28.0 |
| -6.8 | -10.0 | -8.8 | | -7.0 | -8.9 | -6.9 | -18.4 | -10.6 | -12.8 |
| 6.7 | 4.7 | 8.1 | EBIT/Interest | 18.6 | 4.8 | 6.7 | 10.3 | 2.5 | 8.7 |
| (126) 1.8 | (144) 2.0 | (139) 1.8 | | (26) 1.8 | (42) 1.7 | (16) 2.4 | (19) 2.5 | (15) 1.1 | 2.4 |
| 1.0 | .9 | .9 | | 1.0 | .3 | 1.5 | .9 | .2 | 1.2 |
| | | | Net Profit + Depr., Dep., Amort./Cur. Mat. L/T/D | | | | | | |
| 1.1 | 1.1 | 1.2 | Fixed/Worth | 1.0 | 1.8 | 1.9 | .4 | .8 | .6 |
| 7.7 | 11.4 | 10.3 | | 4.1 | 16.5 | -7.9 | 3.0 | 10.8 | 2.5 |
| -4.3 | -3.9 | -2.8 | | -3.0 | -1.7 | -1.5 | -13.9 | -1.9 | -19.6 |
| 1.7 | 1.7 | 1.7 | Debt/Worth | .4 | 1.6 | 1.9 | 1.9 | 1.8 | 1.2 |
| 12.4 | 17.6 | 13.3 | | 5.7 | 17.6 | -9.6 | 17.8 | 14.2 | 3.7 |
| -5.9 | -5.9 | -4.5 | | -4.7 | -3.1 | -3.2 | -15.6 | -3.3 | -33.3 |
| 68.9 | 68.9 | 59.0 | % Profit Before Taxes/Tangible Net Worth | 143.2 | 77.3 | 25.0 | 29.2 | 113.6 | 23.0 |
| (106) 11.7 | (113) 16.4 | (105) 13.7 | | (20) 28.5 | (33) 34.6 | (10) 14.4 | (15) 13.7 | (12) 4.2 | (15) 11.3 |
| 1.9 | .9 | 1.1 | | 3.9 | .4 | 6.5 | -28.4 | -11.6 | 2.4 |
| 8.1 | 9.6 | 14.6 | % Profit Before Taxes/Total Assets | 31.0 | 18.3 | 9.8 | 13.2 | 7.0 | 9.1 |
| 2.2 | 2.9 | 2.2 | | 3.4 | 2.1 | 3.4 | 2.4 | .4 | 3.1 |
| -.6 | -1.0 | -1.3 | | -.1 | -3.1 | -1.7 | -3.0 | -2.9 | .6 |
| 8.7 | 11.9 | 14.7 | Sales/Net Fixed Assets | 11.2 | 25.8 | 1.9 | 34.4 | 3.0 | 13.8 |
| .9 | .9 | 1.0 | | 1.0 | 1.1 | .7 | 1.3 | .6 | 1.7 |
| .4 | .4 | .4 | | .4 | .4 | .3 | .5 | .5 | .9 |
| 2.5 | 2.9 | 3.3 | Sales/Total Assets | 2.8 | 4.9 | 1.3 | 3.3 | 1.1 | 3.2 |
| .7 | .7 | .7 | | .8 | .8 | .5 | 1.1 | .5 | .9 |
| .3 | .4 | .3 | | .3 | .3 | .3 | .4 | .3 | .5 |
| 2.6 | 2.6 | 2.8 | % Depr., Dep., Amort./Sales | 3.2 | .9 | 4.0 | 1.7 | 5.8 | 2.0 |
| (159) 6.9 | (175) 6.6 | (163) 6.0 | | (30) 6.9 | (52) 5.5 | (22) 7.6 | (21) 4.6 | (17) 11.2 | 3.9 |
| 14.3 | 12.2 | 12.5 | | 13.1 | 13.8 | 16.2 | 10.8 | 14.1 | 6.8 |
| 5.0 | 2.7 | 2.4 | % Officers', Directors' Owners' Comp/Sales | 2.4 | | | | | |
| (31) 6.5 | (38) 5.9 | (27) 5.0 | | (11) 5.0 | | | | | |
| 11.4 | 11.0 | 8.0 | | 9.3 | | | | | |
| 2004492M | 1877574M | 2493547M | Net Sales ($) | 21130M | 109817M | 99766M | 165397M | 311762M | 1785675M |
| 2843097M | 2883463M | 3440617M | Total Assets ($) | 59609M | 245127M | 282419M | 264309M | 708088M | 1881065M |

© RMA 2012

M = $ thousand    MM = $ million
See Pages 9 through 22 for Explanation of Ratios and Data

## Current Data Sorted by Assets       Comparative Historical Data

| | 0-500M | 500M-2MM | 2-10MM | 10-50MM | 50-100MM | 100-250MM | | 4/1/07-3/31/08 ALL | 4/1/08-3/31/09 ALL |
|---|---|---|---|---|---|---|---|---|---|
| **Type of Statement** | | | | | | | | | |
| Unqualified | 2 | 15 | 50 | 44 | 10 | 4 | | 85 | 118 |
| Reviewed | 2 | | 1 | 1 | | | | 6 | 6 |
| Compiled | | 3 | 4 | 1 | | | | 7 | 11 |
| Tax Returns | 17 | 14 | 5 | | | | | 14 | 14 |
| Other | 14 | 12 | 32 | 18 | 2 | 2 | | 46 | 58 |
| | | 119 (4/1-9/30/11) | | 134 (10/1/11-3/31/12) | | | | | |
| **NUMBER OF STATEMENTS** | 35 | 44 | 92 | 64 | 12 | 6 | | 158 | 207 |
| | % | % | % | % | % | % | | % | % |
| **ASSETS** | | | | | | | | | |
| Cash & Equivalents | 30.9 | 15.2 | 16.6 | 14.9 | 17.4 | | | 16.6 | 16.5 |
| Trade Receivables (net) | 13.0 | 15.9 | 15.0 | 11.2 | 12.5 | | | 15.5 | 15.3 |
| Inventory | .6 | .4 | .3 | .1 | .3 | | | .3 | .1 |
| All Other Current | 7.5 | 4.9 | 2.9 | 2.2 | 4.4 | | | 2.4 | 2.6 |
| Total Current | 52.0 | 36.4 | 34.8 | 28.5 | 34.6 | | | 34.7 | 34.6 |
| Fixed Assets (net) | 35.3 | 52.6 | 52.0 | 54.5 | 47.9 | | | 51.9 | 49.1 |
| Intangibles (net) | 3.4 | 3.7 | 2.6 | 1.9 | 1.4 | | | 3.4 | 2.8 |
| All Other Non-Current | 9.3 | 7.3 | 10.6 | 15.1 | 16.0 | | | 10.1 | 13.5 |
| Total | 100.0 | 100.0 | 100.0 | 100.0 | 100.0 | | | 100.0 | 100.0 |
| **LIABILITIES** | | | | | | | | | |
| Notes Payable-Short Term | 16.5 | 2.1 | 1.7 | 1.9 | 1.0 | | | 6.0 | 5.1 |
| Cur. Mat.-L.T.D. | 4.3 | 2.6 | 3.4 | 2.4 | 2.0 | | | 2.4 | 3.5 |
| Trade Payables | 6.3 | 5.7 | 4.9 | 3.7 | 7.0 | | | 5.3 | 5.0 |
| Income Taxes Payable | .0 | .0 | .0 | .0 | .0 | | | .0 | .0 |
| All Other Current | 33.5 | 12.6 | 16.8 | 8.6 | 9.3 | | | 11.0 | 11.6 |
| Total Current | 60.5 | 23.0 | 26.8 | 16.7 | 19.4 | | | 24.6 | 25.2 |
| Long-Term Debt | 19.8 | 36.4 | 33.1 | 33.2 | 34.2 | | | 29.7 | 29.7 |
| Deferred Taxes | .0 | .0 | .0 | .4 | .0 | | | .0 | .1 |
| All Other Non-Current | 21.1 | 4.0 | 4.1 | 5.6 | 5.7 | | | 5.8 | 7.3 |
| Net Worth | -1.3 | 36.6 | 35.9 | 44.1 | 40.7 | | | 39.9 | 37.6 |
| Total Liabilities & Net Worth | 100.0 | 100.0 | 100.0 | 100.0 | 100.0 | | | 100.0 | 100.0 |
| **INCOME DATA** | | | | | | | | | |
| Net Sales | 100.0 | 100.0 | 100.0 | 100.0 | 100.0 | | | 100.0 | 100.0 |
| Gross Profit | | | | | | | | | |
| Operating Expenses | 97.7 | 89.5 | 90.1 | 94.8 | 92.3 | | | 93.1 | 93.2 |
| Operating Profit | 2.3 | 10.5 | 9.9 | 5.2 | 7.7 | | | 6.9 | 6.8 |
| All Other Expenses (net) | 1.3 | 4.7 | 3.9 | 3.1 | .3 | | | 2.5 | 4.0 |
| Profit Before Taxes | 1.0 | 5.8 | 6.0 | 2.1 | 7.4 | | | 4.4 | 2.8 |
| **RATIOS** | | | | | | | | | |
| Current | 5.2 | 4.1 | 3.1 | 3.5 | 2.2 | | | 3.0 | 3.0 |
| | 1.9 | 1.5 | 1.4 | 1.8 | 1.9 | | | 1.6 | 1.5 |
| | .5 | .8 | .6 | 1.0 | 1.1 | | | .9 | .8 |
| Quick | 4.4 | 4.0 | 2.8 | 3.1 | 2.1 | | | 2.6 | 2.8 |
| | 1.0 | 1.1 | 1.3 | 1.7 | 1.4 | | | 1.5 | 1.4 |
| | .3 | .6 | .5 | .8 | .9 | | | .9 | .7 |
| Sales/Receivables | 0 UND | 0 UND | 1 343.7 | 11 32.3 | 20 18.0 | | | 5 79.7 | 4 89.6 |
| | 0 UND | 13 27.9 | 27 13.5 | 32 11.3 | 38 9.6 | | | 30 12.1 | 29 12.4 |
| | 22 16.6 | 30 12.2 | 40 9.2 | 45 8.2 | 47 7.7 | | | 48 7.6 | 46 7.9 |
| Cost of Sales/Inventory | | | | | | | | | |
| Cost of Sales/Payables | | | | | | | | | |
| Sales/Working Capital | 8.9 | 9.2 | 4.6 | 3.2 | 4.3 | | | 4.6 | 5.9 |
| | 39.0 | 21.9 | 16.6 | 9.9 | 8.1 | | | 14.5 | 16.2 |
| | -28.0 | -73.7 | -12.4 | -295.4 | 109.2 | | | -111.6 | -45.0 |
| EBIT/Interest | 9.1 | 6.5 | 7.9 | 3.9 | 5.6 | | | 9.7 | 6.1 |
| | (16) 1.3 | (31) 2.3 | (72) 2.3 | (54) 1.5 | (10) 2.4 | | | (122) 2.8 | (169) 1.8 |
| | -13.0 | .2 | .7 | .6 | 1.2 | | | 1.5 | .3 |
| Net Profit + Depr., Dep., Amort./Cur. Mat. L/T/D | | | | | | | | | |
| Fixed/Worth | .1 | .6 | .5 | .6 | .4 | | | .6 | .5 |
| | .7 | 1.2 | 1.4 | 1.4 | 1.6 | | | 1.3 | 1.2 |
| | -1.0 | 5.0 | 3.4 | 2.8 | 2.5 | | | 4.9 | 4.6 |
| Debt/Worth | .4 | .5 | .6 | .4 | .7 | | | .5 | .5 |
| | 1.2 | 1.9 | 1.5 | 1.4 | 1.8 | | | 1.3 | 1.3 |
| | -3.6 | 10.0 | 4.7 | 3.3 | 2.5 | | | 6.3 | 6.6 |
| % Profit Before Taxes/Tangible Net Worth | 33.6 | 51.5 | 22.0 | 11.8 | 28.0 | | | 24.4 | 26.0 |
| | (24) 9.6 | (36) 14.4 | (80) 10.1 | (58) 2.6 | (10) 11.0 | | | (138) 11.3 | (183) 6.0 |
| | .1 | -2.9 | -.1 | -2.8 | 6.2 | | | 2.6 | -2.3 |
| % Profit Before Taxes/Total Assets | 20.1 | 19.7 | 8.7 | 5.4 | 8.8 | | | 10.0 | 7.7 |
| | 4.0 | 4.8 | 3.7 | .8 | 4.3 | | | 4.4 | 2.5 |
| | -4.6 | -.7 | -.6 | -1.3 | .9 | | | .8 | -1.0 |
| Sales/Net Fixed Assets | 180.5 | 21.7 | 9.5 | 3.4 | 5.6 | | | 7.0 | 7.2 |
| | 20.6 | 3.3 | 2.8 | 1.5 | 1.7 | | | 2.6 | 2.7 |
| | 7.5 | .9 | .5 | .6 | 1.0 | | | 1.1 | 1.1 |
| Sales/Total Assets | 8.7 | 3.8 | 2.2 | 1.6 | 1.8 | | | 2.3 | 2.3 |
| | 5.2 | 1.9 | 1.3 | .8 | 1.1 | | | 1.3 | 1.3 |
| | 3.3 | .8 | .5 | .4 | .4 | | | .7 | .6 |
| % Depr., Dep., Amort./Sales | .6 | 1.2 | 1.7 | 2.2 | 1.8 | | | 1.8 | 2.0 |
| | (21) 1.6 | (34) 2.8 | (77) 3.0 | (60) 3.5 | 4.3 | | | (145) 2.8 | (189) 2.9 |
| | 5.5 | 6.1 | 9.7 | 9.0 | 6.5 | | | 5.3 | 6.5 |
| % Officers', Directors' Owners' Comp/Sales | | | 1.5 | | | | | 1.7 | 3.1 |
| | | | (11) 6.5 | | | | | (28) 5.4 | (33) 5.9 |
| | | | 10.9 | | | | | 9.6 | 10.9 |
| Net Sales ($) | 48843M | 130931M | 703702M | 1416202M | 1158376M | 987503M | | 2361502M | 4425843M |
| Total Assets ($) | 8156M | 55796M | 486766M | 1372913M | 778849M | 890401M | | 2167072M | 4101974M |

M = $ thousand    MM = $ million
See Pages 9 through 22 for Explanation of Ratios and Data

| | Comparative Historical Data | | | Type of Statement | Current Data Sorted by Sales | | | | | |
|---|---|---|---|---|---|---|---|---|---|---|
| | 106 | 120 | 125 | Unqualified | 11 | 14 | 11 | 27 | 36 | 26 |
| | 8 | 5 | 4 | Reviewed | 2 | 1 | | 1 | | |
| | 8 | 8 | 8 | Compiled | 3 | 3 | | 2 | | |
| | 22 | 26 | 36 | Tax Returns | 18 | 11 | 5 | 1 | 1 | |
| | 60 | 62 | 80 | Other | 11 | 21 | 9 | 16 | 14 | 9 |
| | 4/1/09-3/31/10 ALL | 4/1/10-3/31/11 ALL | 4/1/11-3/31/12 ALL | | 119 (4/1-9/30/11) | | | 134 (10/1/11-3/31/12) | | |
| | | | | | 0-1MM | 1-3MM | 3-5MM | 5-10MM | 10-25MM | 25MM & OVER |
| NUMBER OF STATEMENTS | 204 | 221 | 253 | | 45 | 49 | 26 | 47 | 51 | 35 |
| | % | % | % | ASSETS | % | % | % | % | % | % |
| | 15.4 | 17.8 | 18.0 | Cash & Equivalents | 14.7 | 19.6 | 18.0 | 21.1 | 16.6 | 18.2 |
| | 16.3 | 13.9 | 13.8 | Trade Receivables (net) | 4.6 | 7.6 | 15.5 | 18.4 | 16.7 | 22.5 |
| | .4 | .2 | .3 | Inventory | .0 | .5 | .1 | .4 | .4 | .4 |
| | 3.1 | 3.5 | 3.7 | All Other Current | 2.4 | 4.7 | 4.1 | 5.7 | 2.6 | 2.9 |
| | 35.2 | 35.4 | 35.8 | Total Current | 21.6 | 32.4 | 37.7 | 45.6 | 36.3 | 44.0 |
| | 50.8 | 50.3 | 50.2 | Fixed Assets (net) | 67.1 | 57.0 | 48.6 | 38.8 | 46.9 | 40.5 |
| | 2.6 | 2.6 | 2.7 | Intangibles (net) | 3.8 | 3.7 | 1.6 | 2.2 | 1.1 | 3.6 |
| | 11.4 | 11.7 | 11.2 | All Other Non-Current | 7.5 | 6.8 | 12.2 | 13.4 | 15.7 | 12.0 |
| | 100.0 | 100.0 | 100.0 | Total | 100.0 | 100.0 | 100.0 | 100.0 | 100.0 | 100.0 |
| | | | | LIABILITIES | | | | | | |
| | 6.1 | 4.6 | 3.9 | Notes Payable-Short Term | 7.2 | 6.0 | 3.7 | .9 | 2.3 | 2.9 |
| | 2.7 | 3.3 | 3.0 | Cur. Mat.-L.T.D. | 3.0 | 3.3 | 6.0 | 1.5 | 2.4 | 3.3 |
| | 5.4 | 6.8 | 5.0 | Trade Payables | 1.7 | 3.6 | 5.0 | 6.9 | 5.6 | 7.8 |
| | .0 | .0 | .0 | Income Taxes Payable | .0 | .0 | .0 | .0 | .0 | .0 |
| | 13.1 | 15.4 | 15.7 | All Other Current | 9.2 | 23.9 | 10.8 | 19.0 | 12.4 | 16.6 |
| | 27.3 | 30.2 | 27.6 | Total Current | 21.2 | 36.8 | 25.5 | 28.3 | 22.7 | 30.6 |
| | 34.7 | 31.2 | 32.1 | Long-Term Debt | 50.7 | 36.4 | 30.1 | 19.2 | 23.9 | 32.7 |
| | .1 | .0 | .1 | Deferred Taxes | .0 | .5 | .0 | .1 | .0 | .0 |
| | 6.5 | 8.4 | 6.9 | All Other Non-Current | 5.9 | 11.7 | 12.8 | 3.1 | 4.7 | 5.4 |
| | 31.3 | 30.2 | 33.3 | Net Worth | 22.2 | 14.5 | 31.6 | 49.3 | 48.7 | 31.3 |
| | 100.0 | 100.0 | 100.0 | Total Liabilities & Net Worth | 100.0 | 100.0 | 100.0 | 100.0 | 100.0 | 100.0 |
| | | | | INCOME DATA | | | | | | |
| | 100.0 | 100.0 | 100.0 | Net Sales | 100.0 | 100.0 | 100.0 | 100.0 | 100.0 | 100.0 |
| | | | | Gross Profit | | | | | | |
| | 93.8 | 92.8 | 92.4 | Operating Expenses | 83.8 | 89.1 | 93.7 | 95.9 | 98.0 | 94.6 |
| | 6.2 | 7.2 | 7.6 | Operating Profit | 16.2 | 10.9 | 6.3 | 4.1 | 2.0 | 5.4 |
| | 3.5 | 3.3 | 3.4 | All Other Expenses (net) | 8.7 | 5.1 | 2.5 | 1.2 | .4 | 2.2 |
| | 2.8 | 4.0 | 4.2 | Profit Before Taxes | 7.5 | 5.8 | 3.9 | 2.9 | 1.6 | 3.2 |
| | | | | RATIOS | | | | | | |
| | 3.0 | 3.1 | 3.5 | Current | 4.1 | 5.6 | 4.2 | 3.9 | 3.4 | 2.2 |
| | 1.5 | 1.6 | 1.6 | | .8 | 1.4 | 1.8 | 2.0 | 1.6 | 1.7 |
| | .8 | .8 | .7 | | .3 | .4 | .9 | 1.2 | 1.1 | 1.0 |
| | 2.7 | 2.9 | 3.0 | Quick | 3.1 | 4.5 | 4.2 | 3.3 | 2.8 | 2.2 |
| | 1.4 | 1.4 | 1.3 | | .5 | 1.2 | 1.7 | 1.5 | 1.4 | 1.4 |
| | .7 | .6 | .6 | | .3 | .4 | .8 | .9 | .8 | .9 |
| | 3 108.8 | 5 71.1 | 1 491.8 | Sales/Receivables | 0 UND | 0 UND | 11 32.9 | 7 50.2 | 26 13.9 | 25 14.5 |
| | 29 12.7 | 27 13.6 | 25 14.5 | | 0 UND | 1 393.0 | 27 13.7 | 31 11.9 | 31 11.9 | 40 9.1 |
| | 48 7.6 | 42 8.7 | 40 9.2 | | 5 78.6 | 23 15.6 | 42 8.7 | 51 7.2 | 41 8.8 | 55 6.6 |
| | | | | Cost of Sales/Inventory | | | | | | |
| | | | | Cost of Sales/Payables | | | | | | |
| | 5.5 | 5.1 | 5.1 | Sales/Working Capital | 9.0 | 5.6 | 4.9 | 3.5 | 5.2 | 4.6 |
| | 21.1 | 15.6 | 15.5 | | -48.8 | 18.1 | 15.9 | 10.8 | 17.2 | 11.1 |
| | -43.1 | -31.8 | -32.7 | | -5.0 | -7.9 | -342.1 | 30.6 | 85.1 | -285.8 |
| | (160) 6.1 | (166) 5.8 | (189) 5.8 | EBIT/Interest | (29) 3.2 | (33) 5.6 | (20) 5.9 | (35) 8.1 | (44) 7.7 | (28) 5.0 |
| | 2.1 | 2.1 | 2.1 | | 2.0 | 2.6 | 2.0 | 1.4 | 1.9 | 2.2 |
| | .6 | .8 | .6 | | .4 | -.2 | 1.0 | -2.2 | .4 | 1.2 |
| | | | (15) 3.1 | Net Profit + Depr., Dep., Amort./Cur. Mat. L/T/D | | | | | | |
| | | | 1.8 | | | | | | | |
| | | | .3 | | | | | | | |
| | .6 | .6 | .5 | Fixed/Worth | .8 | .7 | .5 | .4 | .5 | .4 |
| | 1.3 | 1.4 | 1.3 | | 3.3 | 1.5 | 1.6 | .7 | .9 | 1.4 |
| | 6.4 | 4.5 | 3.4 | | -27.1 | 13.0 | 3.2 | 1.5 | 1.9 | 2.8 |
| | .5 | .6 | .5 | Debt/Worth | .6 | .5 | .8 | .3 | .4 | 1.0 |
| | 1.5 | 1.5 | 1.5 | | 2.4 | 1.5 | 2.0 | .9 | .9 | 2.1 |
| | 10.7 | 10.4 | 4.8 | | -32.5 | 12.8 | 6.0 | 1.8 | 2.6 | 4.8 |
| | (170) 28.4 | (179) 27.1 | (214) 25.1 | % Profit Before Taxes/Tangible Net Worth | (31) 80.0 | (40) 43.4 | (22) 31.6 | (43) 13.6 | (46) 13.2 | (32) 29.4 |
| | 8.0 | 8.5 | 8.7 | | 5.6 | 13.2 | 10.4 | 3.3 | 3.6 | 13.9 |
| | -1.1 | .8 | -1.4 | | -6.0 | .4 | 3.3 | -1.9 | -2.4 | 2.7 |
| | 9.3 | 8.6 | 9.1 | % Profit Before Taxes/Total Assets | 10.7 | 11.4 | 8.8 | 9.9 | 5.5 | 10.2 |
| | 3.4 | 3.3 | 3.2 | | 3.0 | 5.2 | 3.5 | 2.5 | 1.8 | 3.7 |
| | -.7 | -.2 | -.7 | | -.8 | -.6 | -.3 | -1.3 | -1.4 | .6 |
| | 9.0 | 9.5 | 11.9 | Sales/Net Fixed Assets | 9.4 | 13.1 | 15.9 | 26.1 | 5.2 | 14.5 |
| | 2.8 | 2.7 | 2.8 | | .8 | 2.6 | 3.2 | 3.5 | 2.8 | 4.7 |
| | 1.1 | 1.0 | .8 | | .2 | .5 | 1.2 | 1.3 | 1.3 | 2.1 |
| | 2.6 | 2.5 | 2.6 | Sales/Total Assets | 4.0 | 3.5 | 4.0 | 2.7 | 2.3 | 2.6 |
| | 1.4 | 1.3 | 1.4 | | .6 | 1.3 | 1.5 | 1.4 | 1.5 | 1.9 |
| | .6 | .6 | .5 | | .2 | .4 | .7 | .6 | .8 | 1.2 |
| | (180) 1.8 | (195) 1.6 | (210) 1.6 | % Depr., Dep., Amort./Sales | (34) 5.2 | (36) 1.7 | (21) 1.7 | (38) 1.3 | (49) 1.5 | (32) 1.4 |
| | 3.0 | 3.0 | 3.1 | | 12.7 | 5.1 | 2.8 | 2.7 | 2.5 | 2.1 |
| | 5.5 | 6.0 | 8.1 | | 23.9 | 13.8 | 6.6 | 5.3 | 4.2 | 3.8 |
| | (25) 4.1 | (35) 2.1 | (31) 2.9 | % Officers', Directors' Owners' Comp/Sales | (13) 5.6 | | | | | |
| | 6.4 | 6.3 | 6.5 | | 7.7 | | | | | |
| | 12.1 | 11.3 | 10.9 | | 11.3 | | | | | |
| | 3726694M | 5141275M | 4445557M | Net Sales ($) | 25766M | 92498M | 101058M | 337163M | 796643M | 3092429M |
| | 3261640M | 3736392M | 3592881M | Total Assets ($) | 129939M | 169625M | 116349M | 355022M | 842333M | 1979613M |

M = $ thousand     MM = $ million
See Pages 9 through 22 for Explanation of Ratios and Data

## Current Data Sorted by Assets      Comparative Historical Data

| | 0-500M | 500M-2MM | 2-10MM | 10-50MM | 50-100MM | 100-250MM | Type of Statement | 4/1/07-3/31/08 ALL | 4/1/08-3/31/09 ALL |
|---|---|---|---|---|---|---|---|---|---|
| | 14 | 44 | 108 | 92 | 22 | 7 | Unqualified | 243 | 246 |
| | 2 | | 2 | 3 | | | Reviewed | 7 | 6 |
| | 3 | 2 | 1 | | | | Compiled | 7 | 7 |
| | 13 | 11 | 5 | 1 | | | Tax Returns | 15 | 16 |
| | 17 | 24 | 47 | 41 | 5 | 2 | Other | 76 | 76 |
| | | 332 (4/1-9/30/11) | | 134 (10/1/11-3/31/12) | | | | | |
| NUMBER OF STATEMENTS | 49 | 81 | 163 | 137 | 27 | 9 | | 348 | 351 |
| | % | % | % | % | % | % | **ASSETS** | % | % |
| | 30.6 | 25.8 | 17.7 | 18.1 | 10.5 | | Cash & Equivalents | 22.2 | 20.6 |
| | 20.3 | 22.5 | 16.9 | 12.7 | 9.1 | | Trade Receivables (net) | 15.7 | 18.1 |
| | .4 | .4 | .2 | .3 | .3 | | Inventory | .5 | .5 |
| | 3.9 | 3.9 | 4.3 | 2.1 | 2.1 | | All Other Current | 4.2 | 3.4 |
| | 55.2 | 52.6 | 39.1 | 33.2 | 22.0 | | Total Current | 42.7 | 42.6 |
| | 29.7 | 39.5 | 48.4 | 45.8 | 48.1 | | Fixed Assets (net) | 44.0 | 42.8 |
| | 4.4 | 1.9 | .6 | 2.1 | 1.7 | | Intangibles (net) | .8 | .8 |
| | 10.4 | 6.1 | 12.0 | 18.9 | 28.3 | | All Other Non-Current | 12.6 | 13.8 |
| | 100.0 | 100.0 | 100.0 | 100.0 | 100.0 | | Total | 100.0 | 100.0 |
| | | | | | | | **LIABILITIES** | | |
| | 16.9 | 7.0 | 3.1 | 1.6 | 1.3 | | Notes Payable-Short Term | 3.4 | 3.4 |
| | 1.7 | 2.0 | 1.6 | 1.2 | 1.0 | | Cur. Mat.-L.T.D. | 2.0 | 1.1 |
| | 9.3 | 10.8 | 7.9 | 4.3 | 3.6 | | Trade Payables | 6.7 | 7.3 |
| | .0 | .0 | .0 | .0 | .0 | | Income Taxes Payable | .0 | .0 |
| | 38.0 | 14.0 | 11.2 | 9.1 | 5.9 | | All Other Current | 8.7 | 9.9 |
| | 66.0 | 33.9 | 23.8 | 16.2 | 11.8 | | Total Current | 20.8 | 21.6 |
| | 12.4 | 13.4 | 17.9 | 18.5 | 22.6 | | Long-Term Debt | 18.6 | 17.2 |
| | .0 | .0 | .0 | .0 | .0 | | Deferred Taxes | .0 | .0 |
| | 6.4 | 5.9 | 3.5 | 2.3 | 9.0 | | All Other Non-Current | 3.4 | 3.0 |
| | 15.1 | 46.9 | 54.8 | 63.1 | 56.6 | | Net Worth | 57.2 | 58.1 |
| | 100.0 | 100.0 | 100.0 | 100.0 | 100.0 | | Total Liabilities & Net Worth | 100.0 | 100.0 |
| | | | | | | | **INCOME DATA** | | |
| | 100.0 | 100.0 | 100.0 | 100.0 | 100.0 | | Net Sales | 100.0 | 100.0 |
| | | | | | | | Gross Profit | | |
| | 95.3 | 97.3 | 96.6 | 99.2 | 99.8 | | Operating Expenses | 93.9 | 97.6 |
| | 4.7 | 2.7 | 3.4 | .8 | .2 | | Operating Profit | 6.1 | 2.4 |
| | 1.5 | 1.2 | 1.5 | -.1 | .4 | | All Other Expenses (net) | .9 | 1.8 |
| | 3.2 | 1.6 | 1.9 | .9 | -.2 | | Profit Before Taxes | 5.2 | .6 |
| | | | | | | | **RATIOS** | | |
| | 4.7 | 3.9 | 3.2 | 3.7 | 3.0 | | | 4.4 | 3.9 |
| | 2.5 | 1.5 | 1.8 | 2.2 | 2.0 | | Current | 2.3 | 2.1 |
| | .4 | .9 | .9 | 1.2 | .9 | | | 1.3 | 1.3 |
| | 4.5 | 3.8 | 2.9 | 3.4 | 2.7 | | | 4.0 | 3.6 |
| | 2.0 | 1.5 | 1.6 | 1.9 | 1.6 | | Quick | 2.0 | 1.8 |
| | .3 | .7 | .8 | 1.1 | .8 | | | 1.0 | 1.0 |
| | 0   UND | 7   55.0 | 3   142.2 | 14   25.4 | 21   17.4 | | | 4   95.8 | 11   32.7 |
| | 5   76.5 | 24   14.9 | 30   12.3 | 34   10.6 | 40   9.2 | | Sales/Receivables | 29   12.8 | 33   11.0 |
| | 28   12.9 | 39   9.4 | 47   7.7 | 50   7.3 | 49   7.5 | | | 49   7.5 | 54   6.7 |
| | | | | | | | Cost of Sales/Inventory | | |
| | | | | | | | Cost of Sales/Payables | | |
| | 5.9 | 4.9 | 5.6 | 3.5 | 4.9 | | | 3.6 | 3.8 |
| | 15.5 | 20.6 | 12.7 | 6.4 | 10.2 | | Sales/Working Capital | 7.8 | 9.0 |
| | -18.4 | -90.9 | -322.5 | 40.9 | -99.5 | | | 36.8 | 37.4 |
| | 13.7 | 5.7 | 5.4 | 10.0 | 6.4 | | | 10.2 | 6.7 |
| | (26) 6.0 | (48) 1.9 | (113) 1.5 | (105) 3.5 | (21) 1.6 | | EBIT/Interest | (236) 3.0 | (247) 1.4 |
| | -3.6 | -1.4 | -2.5 | -.6 | -1.1 | | | .4 | -1.9 |
| | | | | | | | Net Profit + Depr., Dep., Amort./Cur. Mat. L/T/D | | |
| | .0 | .3 | .4 | .4 | .4 | | | .3 | .3 |
| | .6 | .8 | .9 | .7 | .9 | | Fixed/Worth | .7 | .7 |
| | 7.0 | 1.9 | 1.5 | 1.2 | 1.8 | | | 1.3 | 1.2 |
| | .2 | .3 | .3 | .3 | .3 | | | .2 | .2 |
| | .9 | .9 | .7 | .5 | .6 | | Debt/Worth | .6 | .6 |
| | -30.2 | 4.3 | 1.5 | 1.2 | 2.0 | | | 1.6 | 1.3 |
| | 59.4 | 21.4 | 9.8 | 9.0 | 6.5 | | | 14.2 | 11.5 |
| | (36) 6.6 | (70) 3.8 | (155) 1.9 | (135) 3.0 | (26) .3 | | % Profit Before Taxes/Tangible Net Worth | (335) 5.8 | (338) 1.7 |
| | -21.2 | -6.9 | -5.3 | -2.7 | -2.6 | | | -1.5 | -6.0 |
| | 37.6 | 7.6 | 4.6 | 5.1 | 3.4 | | | 9.3 | 5.8 |
| | 5.7 | 1.7 | .9 | 1.7 | .5 | | % Profit Before Taxes/Total Assets | 2.9 | .6 |
| | -15.7 | -3.4 | -3.3 | -1.5 | -1.7 | | | -1.0 | -3.2 |
| | 174.0 | 31.5 | 9.6 | 5.0 | 3.0 | | | 14.0 | 13.0 |
| | 34.5 | 11.0 | 3.4 | 2.0 | 2.0 | | Sales/Net Fixed Assets | 3.3 | 3.1 |
| | 8.0 | 1.9 | 1.3 | .9 | 1.3 | | | 1.3 | 1.2 |
| | 8.1 | 4.8 | 2.8 | 1.5 | 1.3 | | | 2.3 | 2.5 |
| | 4.1 | 2.2 | 1.5 | 1.0 | .7 | | Sales/Total Assets | 1.3 | 1.3 |
| | 2.1 | 1.0 | .7 | .5 | .5 | | | .7 | .7 |
| | .5 | .7 | 1.1 | 1.7 | 2.1 | | | 1.2 | 1.2 |
| | (33) 1.5 | (63) 1.6 | (139) 2.1 | (129) 2.9 | 3.2 | | % Depr., Dep., Amort./Sales | (306) 2.3 | (319) 2.2 |
| | 2.8 | 2.9 | 4.1 | 4.8 | 7.5 | | | 3.9 | 4.0 |
| | 4.0 | 5.3 | 1.4 | | | | | 2.9 | 2.5 |
| | (12) 6.7 | (12) 9.2 | (11) 2.8 | | | | % Officers', Directors' Owners' Comp/Sales | (35) 6.4 | (41) 5.5 |
| | 19.9 | 13.5 | 5.5 | | | | | 11.9 | 15.7 |
| | 51272M | 342605M | 1638503M | 3360233M | 1667226M | 1459854M | Net Sales ($) | 6049248M | 8469766M |
| | 11031M | 100534M | 859186M | 2891510M | 1955658M | 1161255M | Total Assets ($) | 5209319M | 6040500M |

M = $ thousand    MM = $ million
See Pages 9 through 22 for Explanation of Ratios and Data

## Comparative Historical Data | Current Data Sorted by Sales

| Type of Statement | | | | | | | | | |
|---|---|---|---|---|---|---|---|---|---|
| Unqualified | 262 | 292 | 287 | 16 | 41 | 35 | 45 | 80 | 70 |
| Reviewed | 5 | 7 | 7 | 3 | | | | 3 | 1 |
| Compiled | 3 | 4 | 6 | 4 | 1 | 1 | | | |
| Tax Returns | 23 | 29 | 30 | 9 | 9 | 5 | 3 | 3 | 1 |
| Other | 94 | 105 | 136 | 21 | 31 | 16 | 21 | 3 | 19 |
| | 4/1/09-3/31/10 ALL | 4/1/10-3/31/11 ALL | 4/1/11-3/31/12 ALL | 332 (4/1-9/30/11) | | | 134 (10/1/11-3/31/12) | | |
| | | | | 0-1MM | 1-3MM | 3-5MM | 5-10MM | 10-25MM | 25MM & OVER |
| **NUMBER OF STATEMENTS** | 387 | 437 | 466 | 53 | 82 | 57 | 69 | 114 | 91 |

| ASSETS | % | % | % | % | % | % | % | % | % |
|---|---|---|---|---|---|---|---|---|---|
| Cash & Equivalents | 20.5 | 20.5 | 20.3 | 21.5 | 23.3 | 17.2 | 16.9 | 17.6 | 24.9 |
| Trade Receivables (net) | 15.1 | 16.9 | 16.4 | 13.3 | 12.0 | 17.3 | 16.3 | 19.0 | 18.2 |
| Inventory | .4 | .5 | .3 | .1 | .4 | .3 | .2 | .2 | .5 |
| All Other Current | 3.5 | 3.6 | 3.4 | .9 | 3.4 | 3.3 | 3.9 | 4.7 | 2.9 |
| Total Current | 39.5 | 41.5 | 40.3 | 35.8 | 39.0 | 38.1 | 37.3 | 41.4 | 46.5 |
| Fixed Assets (net) | 47.7 | 44.3 | 43.9 | 53.0 | 45.8 | 48.5 | 46.1 | 41.7 | 35.0 |
| Intangibles (net) | .8 | 1.6 | 1.7 | 2.0 | 1.5 | 1.5 | 2.0 | 1.5 | 2.1 |
| All Other Non-Current | 12.0 | 12.6 | 14.0 | 9.0 | 13.7 | 12.0 | 14.5 | 15.4 | 16.4 |
| Total | 100.0 | 100.0 | 100.0 | 100.0 | 100.0 | 100.0 | 100.0 | 100.0 | 100.0 |

| LIABILITIES | | | | | | | | | |
|---|---|---|---|---|---|---|---|---|---|
| Notes Payable-Short Term | 4.3 | 3.8 | 4.6 | 13.0 | 4.0 | 4.2 | 5.1 | 3.3 | 1.8 |
| Cur. Mat.-L.T.D. | 1.5 | 1.7 | 1.5 | 1.5 | 1.6 | 1.5 | 2.5 | 1.4 | 1.0 |
| Trade Payables | 7.8 | 8.2 | 7.3 | 5.7 | 5.0 | 7.0 | 6.6 | 6.9 | 11.3 |
| Income Taxes Payable | .0 | .0 | .0 | .0 | .0 | .0 | .0 | .0 | .0 |
| All Other Current | 10.4 | 11.0 | 13.4 | 18.5 | 13.6 | 11.1 | 10.8 | 12.9 | 14.5 |
| Total Current | 24.0 | 24.6 | 26.9 | 38.7 | 24.3 | 23.9 | 25.1 | 24.5 | 28.6 |
| Long-Term Debt | 20.5 | 20.2 | 17.0 | 20.9 | 14.5 | 18.8 | 20.7 | 14.5 | 16.2 |
| Deferred Taxes | .0 | .0 | .0 | .0 | .0 | .0 | .0 | .0 | .0 |
| All Other Non-Current | 4.6 | 3.8 | 4.4 | 4.2 | 4.3 | 3.0 | 3.9 | 4.0 | 6.1 |
| Net Worth | 50.9 | 51.3 | 51.8 | 36.2 | 56.9 | 54.3 | 50.4 | 57.0 | 49.1 |
| Total Liabilities & Net Worth | 100.0 | 100.0 | 100.0 | 100.0 | 100.0 | 100.0 | 100.0 | 100.0 | 100.0 |

| INCOME DATA | | | | | | | | | |
|---|---|---|---|---|---|---|---|---|---|
| Net Sales | 100.0 | 100.0 | 100.0 | 100.0 | 100.0 | 100.0 | 100.0 | 100.0 | 100.0 |
| Gross Profit | | | | | | | | | |
| Operating Expenses | 99.0 | 96.3 | 97.6 | 92.5 | 94.2 | 98.2 | 101.0 | 98.9 | 98.8 |
| Operating Profit | 1.0 | 3.7 | 2.4 | 7.5 | 5.8 | 1.8 | -1.0 | 1.1 | 1.2 |
| All Other Expenses (net) | 1.6 | .3 | .9 | 5.2 | 1.4 | 1.6 | -.3 | -.4 | -.1 |
| Profit Before Taxes | -.6 | 3.4 | 1.6 | 2.3 | 4.5 | .2 | -.7 | 1.5 | 1.3 |

| RATIOS | | | | | | | | | |
|---|---|---|---|---|---|---|---|---|---|
| Current | 3.7 | 3.7 | 3.6 | 5.2 | 5.4 | 4.5 | 3.6 | 3.2 | 3.0 |
| | 2.0 | 2.0 | 2.0 | 2.1 | 2.5 | 2.1 | 1.8 | 1.9 | 1.9 |
| | 1.0 | 1.1 | 1.0 | .6 | .9 | 1.0 | .9 | 1.0 | 1.2 |
| Quick | 3.5 | 3.2 | 3.2 | 4.8 | 5.3 | 3.4 | 2.9 | 2.8 | 2.7 |
| | 1.8 | 1.7 | 1.7 | 2.0 | 2.0 | 2.0 | 1.6 | 1.7 | 1.7 |
| | .9 | 1.0 | .9 | .6 | .8 | .8 | .8 | .9 | 1.0 |
| Sales/Receivables | 6  66.1 | 7  53.4 | 6  60.2 | 0  UND | 0  UND | 1  246.3 | 15  23.8 | 16  22.2 | 16  22.2 |
| | 26  14.0 | 30  12.2 | 29  12.7 | 10  36.0 | 11  34.1 | 25  14.5 | 27  13.7 | 36  10.2 | 34  10.7 |
| | 44  8.2 | 50  7.3 | 45  8.1 | 35  10.3 | 39  9.3 | 42  8.7 | 43  8.5 | 51  7.1 | 48  7.6 |
| Cost of Sales/Inventory | | | | | | | | | |
| Cost of Sales/Payables | | | | | | | | | |
| Sales/Working Capital | 4.5 | 4.5 | 4.6 | 3.3 | 3.1 | 4.2 | 4.7 | 5.2 | 4.9 |
| | 10.5 | 10.5 | 10.5 | 8.5 | 9.5 | 12.9 | 12.1 | 10.5 | 11.1 |
| | 754.0 | 166.7 | NM | -34.5 | -130.7 | NM | -199.2 | 164.1 | 49.7 |
| EBIT/Interest | 4.7 | 10.6 | 7.4 | 9.5 | 9.9 | 7.3 | 4.3 | 8.0 | 11.5 |
| | (269)  1.2 | (314)  2.7 | (318)  2.3 | (30)  2.7 | (48)  1.5 | (41)  2.0 | (53)  1.5 | (82)  2.9 | (64)  2.4 |
| | -3.0 | .1 | -1.4 | -1.6 | -1.4 | -2.5 | -1.5 | -3.0 | .2 |
| Net Profit + Depr., Dep., Amort./Cur. Mat. L/T/D | | | | | | | | | |
| Fixed/Worth | .5 | .4 | .4 | .4 | .3 | .4 | .5 | .4 | .3 |
| | .9 | .8 | .8 | 1.1 | .7 | .9 | 1.0 | .7 | .7 |
| | 1.6 | 1.6 | 1.5 | 2.8 | 1.3 | 1.5 | 1.6 | 1.3 | 1.4 |
| Debt/Worth | .3 | .3 | .3 | .2 | .2 | .2 | .3 | .3 | .5 |
| | .7 | .7 | .6 | .6 | .4 | .6 | .9 | .6 | .8 |
| | 1.9 | 2.0 | 1.8 | 3.4 | 1.3 | 1.3 | 2.4 | 1.3 | 2.3 |
| % Profit Before Taxes/Tangible Net Worth | 8.6 | 13.3 | 10.9 | 14.9 | 11.7 | 10.6 | 9.0 | 10.7 | 11.8 |
| | (365)  .6 | (409)  4.1 | (430)  2.9 | (44)  .9 | (75)  2.2 | (55)  1.9 | (64)  2.4 | (105)  4.4 | (87)  2.9 |
| | -5.9 | -1.9 | -4.4 | -10.3 | -4.4 | -7.0 | -4.4 | -3.1 | -2.7 |
| % Profit Before Taxes/Total Assets | 4.2 | 7.4 | 6.0 | 8.3 | 9.6 | 5.2 | 3.7 | 6.6 | 5.8 |
| | .3 | 2.1 | 1.5 | 1.1 | 1.7 | 1.0 | 1.1 | 2.6 | 1.0 |
| | -4.0 | -1.2 | -2.9 | -6.9 | -2.6 | -4.4 | -2.0 | -2.0 | -1.8 |
| Sales/Net Fixed Assets | 10.2 | 14.1 | 13.8 | 39.6 | 20.5 | 12.2 | 11.4 | 8.6 | 15.3 |
| | 2.9 | 3.2 | 3.4 | 1.7 | 3.0 | 2.4 | 2.5 | 3.7 | 5.1 |
| | 1.1 | 1.3 | 1.4 | .5 | .7 | 1.1 | 1.0 | 1.9 | 2.2 |
| Sales/Total Assets | 2.9 | 2.9 | 2.9 | 2.9 | 2.8 | 2.0 | 2.8 | 2.9 | 3.1 |
| | 1.3 | 1.4 | 1.4 | .9 | 1.1 | 1.4 | 1.1 | 1.5 | 1.6 |
| | .7 | .7 | .7 | .4 | .5 | .6 | .6 | .9 | 1.0 |
| % Depr., Dep., Amort./Sales | 1.3 | 1.3 | 1.2 | 1.5 | 1.2 | 1.1 | 1.6 | 1.3 | .9 |
| | (339)  2.3 | (384)  2.4 | (400)  2.2 | (37)  4.6 | (65)  2.4 | (47)  2.5 | (60)  2.8 | (104)  2.0 | (87)  1.9 |
| | 4.5 | 4.4 | 4.2 | 9.7 | 7.5 | 5.3 | 4.9 | 3.0 | 2.9 |
| % Officers', Directors' Owners' Comp/Sales | 2.2 | 2.4 | 3.2 | | 5.3 | | | | |
| | (37)  6.2 | (54)  4.6 | (41)  6.0 | | (13)  8.9 | | | | |
| | 12.3 | 14.0 | 11.4 | | 16.0 | | | | |
| Net Sales ($) | 6406904M | 7981294M | 8519693M | 28528M | 151042M | 226857M | 524927M | 1752011M | 5836328M |
| Total Assets ($) | 4908119M | 6832681M | 6979174M | 78755M | 283800M | 258279M | 699277M | 1502790M | 4156273M |

M = $ thousand    MM = $ million
See Pages 9 through 22 for Explanation of Ratios and Data

## Current Data Sorted by Assets  |  Comparative Historical Data

| | | | | | | Type of Statement | | |
|---|---|---|---|---|---|---|---|---|
| 3 | 26 | 85 | 60 | 11 | 5 | Unqualified | 109 | 122 |
| | 1 | 5 | 1 | | | Reviewed | 5 | 6 |
| 4 | | 1 | | | | Compiled | 5 | 5 |
| 6 | 2 | 3 | | | | Tax Returns | 9 | 9 |
| 9 | 17 | 24 | 12 | 2 | 1 | Other | 43 | 58 |
| | 182 (4/1-9/30/11) | | 96 (10/1/11-3/31/12) | | | | 4/1/07-3/31/08 | 4/1/08-3/31/09 |
| 0-500M | 500M-2MM | 2-10MM | 10-50MM | 50-100MM | 100-250MM | | ALL | ALL |
| 22 | 46 | 118 | 73 | 13 | 6 | **NUMBER OF STATEMENTS** | 171 | 200 |
| % | % | % | % | % | % | **ASSETS** | % | % |
| 39.1 | 27.0 | 18.7 | 23.2 | 19.3 | | Cash & Equivalents | 20.5 | 22.9 |
| 15.4 | 20.4 | 19.1 | 17.1 | 19.0 | | Trade Receivables (net) | 18.3 | 19.9 |
| .2 | .3 | .5 | .4 | .9 | | Inventory | .8 | .6 |
| 4.4 | 5.6 | 3.3 | 2.9 | 4.8 | | All Other Current | 3.0 | 4.4 |
| 59.1 | 53.4 | 41.7 | 43.6 | 44.0 | | Total Current | 42.7 | 47.8 |
| 26.6 | 30.4 | 47.3 | 43.8 | 42.7 | | Fixed Assets (net) | 45.0 | 41.5 |
| 3.8 | .2 | .7 | 2.1 | .8 | | Intangibles (net) | 2.5 | 1.6 |
| 10.6 | 16.0 | 10.4 | 10.5 | 12.4 | | All Other Non-Current | 9.8 | 9.2 |
| 100.0 | 100.0 | 100.0 | 100.0 | 100.0 | | Total | 100.0 | 100.0 |
| | | | | | | **LIABILITIES** | | |
| 12.7 | 6.0 | 4.2 | 2.9 | 4.5 | | Notes Payable-Short Term | 3.2 | 6.5 |
| 5.9 | 3.5 | 1.5 | 1.6 | 5.6 | | Cur. Mat.-L.T.D. | 2.3 | 2.7 |
| 6.7 | 8.2 | 6.7 | 7.2 | 7.9 | | Trade Payables | 8.0 | 7.7 |
| .0 | .0 | .0 | .4 | .0 | | Income Taxes Payable | .0 | .0 |
| 23.0 | 20.5 | 14.0 | 9.4 | 13.2 | | All Other Current | 14.8 | 15.6 |
| 48.3 | 38.3 | 26.4 | 21.5 | 31.2 | | Total Current | 28.4 | 32.5 |
| 14.3 | 17.2 | 23.2 | 23.5 | 25.6 | | Long-Term Debt | 25.6 | 20.2 |
| .0 | .0 | .1 | .0 | .0 | | Deferred Taxes | .1 | .1 |
| 1.0 | 1.8 | 1.9 | 3.4 | 9.0 | | All Other Non-Current | 3.6 | 5.2 |
| 36.4 | 42.7 | 48.4 | 51.6 | 34.2 | | Net Worth | 42.3 | 42.0 |
| 100.0 | 100.0 | 100.0 | 100.0 | 100.0 | | Total Liabilties & Net Worth | 100.0 | 100.0 |
| | | | | | | **INCOME DATA** | | |
| 100.0 | 100.0 | 100.0 | 100.0 | 100.0 | | Net Sales | 100.0 | 100.0 |
| | | | | | | Gross Profit | | |
| 92.6 | 100.1 | 96.9 | 96.8 | 97.2 | | Operating Expenses | 95.8 | 96.2 |
| 7.4 | -.1 | 3.1 | 3.2 | 2.8 | | Operating Profit | 4.2 | 3.8 |
| .4 | .9 | 1.0 | .4 | .2 | | All Other Expenses (net) | 1.0 | 1.1 |
| 7.0 | -.9 | 2.1 | 2.8 | 2.6 | | Profit Before Taxes | 3.2 | 2.7 |
| | | | | | | **RATIOS** | | |
| 3.7 | 5.2 | 3.7 | 3.9 | 3.2 | | | 3.3 | 3.5 |
| 1.2 | 2.1 | 1.9 | 2.2 | 1.3 | | Current | 1.7 | 2.1 |
| .7 | .6 | 1.1 | 1.2 | 1.0 | | | 1.0 | 1.1 |
| 3.1 | 4.7 | 3.6 | 3.6 | 3.0 | | | 3.0 | 3.2 |
| 1.2 | 1.7 | 1.8 | 2.0 | 1.1 | | Quick | 1.5 | 1.7 |
| .5 | .5 | .9 | 1.2 | .9 | | | .9 | .9 |

| | | | | | | | | | | | | | | |
|---|---|---|---|---|---|---|---|---|---|---|---|---|---|---|
| 0 | UND | 2 | 158.5 | 13 | 27.3 | 23 | 16.1 | 27 | 13.3 | | | Sales/Receivables | 8 | 46.2 | 14 | 25.4 |
| 0 | UND | 26 | 13.9 | 30 | 12.2 | 39 | 9.4 | 47 | 7.7 | | | | 27 | 13.6 | 31 | 11.8 |
| 23 | 15.9 | 42 | 8.7 | 48 | 7.6 | 58 | 6.3 | 62 | 5.9 | | | | 45 | 8.2 | 47 | 7.8 |

| 0-500M | 500M-2MM | 2-10MM | 10-50MM | 50-100MM | 100-250MM | | ALL | ALL |
|---|---|---|---|---|---|---|---|---|
| | | | | | | Cost of Sales/Inventory | | |
| | | | | | | Cost of Sales/Payables | | |
| 17.8 | 4.2 | 5.1 | 3.1 | 2.3 | | Sales/Working Capital | 5.3 | 4.4 |
| 47.1 | 10.2 | 10.8 | 6.7 | 19.6 | | | 13.4 | 10.9 |
| -63.6 | -20.9 | 118.4 | 26.5 | NM | | | 302.5 | 116.1 |

| | | | | | | | | | | | | | |
|---|---|---|---|---|---|---|---|---|---|---|---|---|---|
| | 34.8 | | 13.1 | | 8.7 | | 7.6 | | 8.3 | | EBIT/Interest | | 7.1 | | 7.2 |
| (11) | 5.0 | (27) | 1.1 | (92) | 2.6 | (64) | 3.3 | (11) | 2.3 | | | (122) | 2.7 | (153) | 2.7 |
| | -.1 | | -5.3 | | .1 | | .9 | | 1.3 | | | | .8 | | .3 |

| 0-500M | 500M-2MM | 2-10MM | 10-50MM | 50-100MM | 100-250MM | | ALL | ALL |
|---|---|---|---|---|---|---|---|---|
| | | | | | | Net Profit + Depr., Dep., Amort./Cur. Mat. L/T/D | | |
| .1 | .1 | .5 | .5 | .8 | | Fixed/Worth | .4 | .3 |
| .6 | .4 | .8 | .9 | 1.3 | | | 1.0 | .9 |
| 12.0 | 3.0 | 1.8 | 1.8 | 3.6 | | | 2.2 | 1.9 |
| .3 | .2 | .3 | .4 | .7 | | Debt/Worth | .4 | .5 |
| 2.4 | .9 | .9 | .9 | 1.8 | | | .9 | 1.0 |
| 18.1 | 3.4 | 1.9 | 2.2 | 6.5 | | | 3.2 | 2.8 |

| | | | | | | | | | | | | | |
|---|---|---|---|---|---|---|---|---|---|---|---|---|---|
| | 148.9 | | 14.3 | | 11.3 | | 13.4 | | 16.2 | % Profit Before Taxes/Tangible Net Worth | | 19.6 | | 23.3 |
| (18) | 19.6 | (40) | 5.3 | (108) | 3.9 | (70) | 6.2 | (12) | 7.9 | | (152) | 9.1 | (182) | 6.7 |
| | -10.7 | | -26.0 | | -3.3 | | -.5 | | 4.0 | | | 2.3 | | -.9 |

| 0-500M | 500M-2MM | 2-10MM | 10-50MM | 50-100MM | 100-250MM | | ALL | ALL |
|---|---|---|---|---|---|---|---|---|
| 80.3 | 8.8 | 6.9 | 7.1 | 5.6 | | % Profit Before Taxes/Total Assets | 9.9 | 10.8 |
| 24.0 | 3.0 | 2.1 | 2.3 | 4.3 | | | 3.9 | 2.9 |
| -1.0 | -10.8 | -1.9 | -.2 | .9 | | | .0 | -.7 |
| 196.7 | 61.1 | 13.9 | 5.5 | 5.3 | | Sales/Net Fixed Assets | 13.0 | 26.9 |
| 31.9 | 18.7 | 3.4 | 2.8 | 2.5 | | | 3.6 | 4.4 |
| 13.5 | 3.3 | 1.5 | 1.4 | 1.9 | | | 1.9 | 1.8 |
| 12.0 | 3.5 | 2.8 | 2.0 | 1.5 | | Sales/Total Assets | 2.9 | 3.3 |
| 5.9 | 2.4 | 1.7 | 1.3 | 1.3 | | | 1.7 | 1.8 |
| 3.3 | 1.6 | .9 | .8 | .8 | | | 1.1 | 1.0 |

| | | | | | | | | | | | | | |
|---|---|---|---|---|---|---|---|---|---|---|---|---|---|
| | .3 | | .6 | | 1.0 | | 1.5 | | 2.0 | % Depr., Dep., Amort./Sales | | 1.4 | | 1.1 |
| (13) | .9 | (39) | 1.2 | (113) | 2.3 | (72) | 2.8 | | 2.5 | | (152) | 2.6 | (179) | 2.3 |
| | 2.1 | | 2.6 | | 4.3 | | 4.2 | | 3.7 | | | 4.0 | | 4.1 |

| | | | | | | | | | | | | | |
|---|---|---|---|---|---|---|---|---|---|---|---|---|---|
| | | | | | 1.9 | | | | | % Officers', Directors' Owners' Comp/Sales | | 1.3 | | 5.1 |
| | | | | (11) | 3.7 | | | | | | (20) | 4.7 | (24) | 6.7 |
| | | | | | 9.4 | | | | | | | 6.3 | | 11.0 |

| 35243M | 160656M | 1111415M | 2433924M | 1157478M | 1598609M | Net Sales ($) | 3007958M | 3922747M |
|---|---|---|---|---|---|---|---|---|
| 5338M | 58861M | 569387M | 1574812M | 839717M | 864523M | Total Assets ($) | 1873149M | 2353122M |

M = $ thousand    MM = $ million
See Pages 9 through 22 for Explanation of Ratios and Data

## Comparative Historical Data / Current Data Sorted by Sales

| 4/1/09-3/31/10 ALL | 4/1/10-3/31/11 ALL | 4/1/11-3/31/12 ALL | | 0-1MM | 1-3MM | 3-5MM | 5-10MM | 10-25MM | 25MM & OVER |
|---|---|---|---|---|---|---|---|---|---|
| | | | **Type of Statement** | | 182 (4/1-9/30/11) | | 96 (10/1/11-3/31/12) | | |
| 144 | 167 | 190 | Unqualified | 5 | 25 | 22 | 39 | 50 | 49 |
| 6 | 6 | 7 | Reviewed | 1 | 2 | | 1 | 2 | 1 |
| 4 | 6 | 5 | Compiled | 1 | 3 | 1 | | | |
| 10 | 17 | 11 | Tax Returns | 4 | 4 | 3 | | | |
| 44 | 58 | 65 | Other | 7 | 8 | 16 | 11 | 12 | 11 |
| 208 | 254 | 278 | **NUMBER OF STATEMENTS** | 18 | 42 | 42 | 51 | 64 | 61 |
| % | % | % | **ASSETS** | % | % | % | % | % | % |
| 20.1 | 20.8 | 22.7 | Cash & Equivalents | 31.2 | 22.7 | 24.8 | 19.2 | 21.1 | 23.2 |
| 18.3 | 18.2 | 18.2 | Trade Receivables (net) | 9.4 | 11.5 | 16.1 | 17.3 | 22.6 | 23.1 |
| .6 | .5 | .4 | Inventory | .2 | .0 | .6 | .7 | .5 | .4 |
| 4.4 | 3.8 | 3.7 | All Other Current | 3.3 | 3.1 | 3.8 | 4.1 | 3.9 | 3.6 |
| 43.4 | 43.3 | 45.0 | Total Current | 44.1 | 37.3 | 45.2 | 41.3 | 48.0 | 50.4 |
| 44.9 | 43.5 | 41.5 | Fixed Assets (net) | 47.2 | 46.1 | 35.2 | 50.4 | 38.9 | 36.3 |
| 1.8 | 3.2 | 1.3 | Intangibles (net) | .0 | 1.9 | .6 | .6 | 1.4 | 2.5 |
| 9.9 | 10.0 | 12.1 | All Other Non-Current | 8.7 | 14.7 | 19.0 | 7.7 | 11.8 | 10.8 |
| 100.0 | 100.0 | 100.0 | Total | 100.0 | 100.0 | 100.0 | 100.0 | 100.0 | 100.0 |
| | | | **LIABILITIES** | | | | | | |
| 4.6 | 4.2 | 4.9 | Notes Payable-Short Term | 3.6 | 5.3 | 5.2 | 5.3 | 4.4 | 4.9 |
| 2.4 | 2.7 | 2.4 | Cur. Mat.-L.T.D. | 7.2 | 1.8 | 2.1 | 1.2 | 2.5 | 2.5 |
| 5.9 | 6.5 | 7.1 | Trade Payables | 3.5 | 2.6 | 6.3 | 5.9 | 10.3 | 9.3 |
| .0 | .1 | .1 | Income Taxes Payable | .0 | .0 | .0 | .0 | .4 | .1 |
| 14.9 | 12.8 | 14.4 | All Other Current | 6.9 | 12.0 | 18.7 | 12.8 | 16.4 | 14.6 |
| 27.7 | 26.4 | 28.8 | Total Current | 21.2 | 21.7 | 32.2 | 25.3 | 34.0 | 31.3 |
| 24.2 | 27.5 | 21.8 | Long-Term Debt | 26.7 | 31.3 | 12.0 | 26.1 | 17.2 | 21.8 |
| .0 | .1 | .1 | Deferred Taxes | .0 | .0 | .0 | .0 | .2 | .0 |
| 5.6 | 3.6 | 2.5 | All Other Non-Current | .1 | 1.4 | 1.8 | 1.0 | 3.5 | 4.8 |
| 42.5 | 42.5 | 46.8 | Net Worth | 51.9 | 45.6 | 54.0 | 47.7 | 45.1 | 42.1 |
| 100.0 | 100.0 | 100.0 | Total Liabilties & Net Worth | 100.0 | 100.0 | 100.0 | 100.0 | 100.0 | 100.0 |
| | | | **INCOME DATA** | | | | | | |
| 100.0 | 100.0 | 100.0 | Net Sales | 100.0 | 100.0 | 100.0 | 100.0 | 100.0 | 100.0 |
| | | | Gross Profit | | | | | | |
| 96.3 | 94.4 | 97.1 | Operating Expenses | 86.9 | 96.8 | 101.5 | 97.7 | 97.2 | 96.8 |
| 3.7 | 5.6 | 2.9 | Operating Profit | 13.1 | 3.2 | -1.5 | 2.3 | 2.8 | 3.2 |
| 1.9 | 1.5 | .8 | All Other Expenses (net) | 2.5 | 2.0 | .1 | .7 | .4 | .4 |
| 1.9 | 4.1 | 2.1 | Profit Before Taxes | 10.6 | 1.1 | -1.6 | 1.7 | 2.4 | 2.8 |
| | | | **RATIOS** | | | | | | |
| 3.6 | 3.5 | 3.8 | | 11.8 | 5.8 | 4.8 | 3.4 | 3.5 | 2.9 |
| 2.0 | 2.0 | 1.9 | Current | 1.9 | 2.2 | 2.4 | 1.9 | 2.1 | 1.5 |
| 1.1 | 1.1 | 1.1 | | 1.1 | .7 | 1.1 | 1.1 | 1.0 | 1.2 |
| 3.4 | 3.1 | 3.6 | | 9.3 | 5.4 | 4.4 | 3.3 | 3.0 | 2.6 |
| 1.8 | 1.6 | 1.6 | Quick | 1.8 | 2.0 | 2.0 | 1.8 | 1.9 | 1.4 |
| .9 | .9 | .9 | | 1.1 | .6 | 1.0 | .8 | .8 | 1.0 |
| 18  20.8 | 10  37.9 | 12  29.6 | | 0  UND | 1  269.1 | 15  25.0 | 10  36.1 | 20  18.2 | 26  14.1 |
| 31  11.7 | 29  12.8 | 30  12.0 | Sales/Receivables | 0  UND | 25  14.7 | 27  13.5 | 29  12.5 | 34  10.6 | 35  10.3 |
| 47  7.8 | 46  7.9 | 49  7.5 | | 37  9.9 | 36  10.0 | 41  9.0 | 53  6.9 | 51  7.2 | 57  6.4 |
| | | | Cost of Sales/Inventory | | | | | | |
| | | | Cost of Sales/Payables | | | | | | |
| 4.6 | 5.0 | 4.4 | | 2.2 | 3.7 | 4.2 | 4.9 | 4.3 | 5.7 |
| 8.9 | 11.0 | 11.3 | Sales/Working Capital | 15.7 | 11.7 | 10.8 | 11.8 | 10.0 | 14.1 |
| 74.6 | 218.4 | 204.7 | | UND | -38.3 | 296.8 | 166.6 | NM | 47.5 |
| 7.1 | 13.3 | 8.3 | | | 6.0 | 7.6 | 4.2 | 20.2 | 8.4 |
| (170)  2.3 | (201)  3.2 | (211)  2.6 | EBIT/Interest | (30)  1.0 | (29)  1.1 | (37)  2.1 | (55)  4.2 | (52)  3.4 | |
| .3 | .8 | .1 | | | -1.6 | -7.2 | .5 | .1 | 1.5 |
| | 3.3 | | | | | | | | |
| | (10)  2.1 | | Net Profit + Depr., Dep., Amort./Cur. Mat. L/T/D | | | | | | |
| | .4 | | | | | | | | |
| .5 | .4 | .4 | | .3 | .3 | .2 | .6 | .3 | .6 |
| 1.0 | .9 | .8 | Fixed/Worth | .6 | .8 | .6 | 1.2 | .7 | .9 |
| 2.1 | 2.2 | 1.9 | | 7.0 | 3.8 | 1.2 | 1.9 | 2.0 | 1.7 |
| .5 | .4 | .3 | | .1 | .1 | .2 | .4 | .3 | .6 |
| 1.2 | 1.1 | 1.0 | Debt/Worth | .5 | .8 | .6 | 1.0 | .8 | 1.6 |
| 2.8 | 4.0 | 3.0 | | 9.1 | 5.6 | 1.6 | 1.9 | 3.0 | 4.6 |
| 14.3 | 18.6 | 14.1 | | 21.1 | 10.3 | 12.1 | 13.2 | 13.1 | 18.4 |
| (189)  5.6 | (223)  6.6 | (254)  5.0 | % Profit Before Taxes/Tangible Net Worth | (15)  3.9 | (36)  2.9 | (39)  1.0 | (48)  4.1 | (57)  6.5 | (59)  8.2 |
| -2.3 | -.5 | -2.1 | | -3.8 | -10.7 | -9.6 | -1.3 | -1.2 | 3.8 |
| 8.0 | 10.8 | 8.3 | % Profit Before Taxes/Total Assets | 50.9 | 6.5 | 8.9 | 6.6 | 8.6 | 8.3 |
| 2.6 | 3.6 | 2.3 | | 3.3 | 1.3 | .4 | 1.8 | 3.1 | 4.3 |
| -1.1 | -.4 | -1.5 | | -.5 | -4.3 | -8.3 | -1.1 | -.8 | 1.1 |
| 9.9 | 15.7 | 20.2 | | 16.9 | 22.9 | 61.1 | 8.4 | 21.9 | 16.5 |
| 3.4 | 4.0 | 3.9 | Sales/Net Fixed Assets | 4.6 | 2.4 | 5.9 | 3.2 | 4.6 | 4.6 |
| 1.8 | 1.7 | 1.7 | | .2 | 1.2 | 1.6 | 1.3 | 1.9 | 2.6 |
| 2.6 | 2.9 | 3.2 | | 4.3 | 2.7 | 3.3 | 2.8 | 3.5 | 3.1 |
| 1.6 | 1.7 | 1.7 | Sales/Total Assets | 1.5 | 1.5 | 2.0 | 1.8 | 1.8 | 1.8 |
| 1.0 | .9 | .9 | | .2 | .7 | .9 | .9 | 1.0 | 1.3 |
| 1.3 | 1.2 | 1.0 | | 1.2 | 1.4 | .6 | 1.0 | .9 | .7 |
| (191)  2.4 | (230)  2.4 | (256)  2.4 | % Depr., Dep., Amort./Sales | (12)  3.3 | (35)  3.4 | (39)  1.9 | (47)  2.4 | 2.2 | (59)  2.3 |
| 3.9 | 4.0 | 4.0 | | 22.9 | 5.9 | 3.9 | 4.0 | 3.5 | 3.3 |
| 1.2 | 2.3 | 2.3 | | | | | | | |
| (29)  4.3 | (30)  4.6 | (27)  3.8 | % Officers', Directors' Owners' Comp/Sales | | | | | | |
| 7.3 | 9.0 | 7.9 | | | | | | | |
| 3688218M | 4896281M | 6497325M | Net Sales ($) | 11138M | 88276M | 161288M | 356112M | 1008628M | 4871883M |
| 2402714M | 3230895M | 3912638M | Total Assets ($) | 25445M | 113707M | 138003M | 261434M | 822053M | 2551996M |

M = $ thousand    MM = $ million
See Pages 9 through 22 for Explanation of Ratios and Data

## Current Data Sorted by Assets | Comparative Historical Data

| | | | | | | Type of Statement | | |
|---|---|---|---|---|---|---|---|---|
| 10 | 59 | 241 | 205 | 30 | 11 | Unqualified | 526 | 577 |
| | 2 | 4 | 1 | | | Reviewed | 3 | 6 |
| 6 | 4 | 3 | 2 | | | Compiled | 10 | 10 |
| 8 | 13 | 7 | 1 | 1 | | Tax Returns | 23 | 26 |
| 19 | 29 | 75 | 61 | 4 | 4 | Other | 168 | 192 |
| | 587 (4/1-9/30/11) | | 213 (10/1/11-3/31/12) | | | | 4/1/07-3/31/08 ALL | 4/1/08-3/31/09 ALL |
| 0-500M | 500M-2MM | 2-10MM | 10-50MM | 50-100MM | 100-250MM | | | |
| 43 | 107 | 330 | 270 | 35 | 15 | NUMBER OF STATEMENTS | 730 | 811 |
| % | % | % | % | % | % | ASSETS | % | % |
| 38.1 | 28.1 | 20.2 | 18.6 | 13.7 | 18.6 | Cash & Equivalents | 20.5 | 19.5 |
| 20.2 | 19.6 | 18.3 | 13.9 | 10.3 | 7.2 | Trade Receivables (net) | 17.9 | 16.5 |
| 3.4 | .7 | 1.2 | 1.4 | 1.5 | 5.9 | Inventory | 1.3 | 1.2 |
| 6.5 | 4.3 | 4.0 | 2.7 | 2.2 | 1.7 | All Other Current | 5.3 | 5.3 |
| 68.2 | 52.6 | 43.6 | 36.6 | 27.6 | 33.4 | Total Current | 45.0 | 42.4 |
| 24.5 | 40.6 | 44.0 | 46.9 | 45.4 | 39.5 | Fixed Assets (net) | 41.9 | 43.7 |
| .8 | .5 | 1.1 | 1.0 | .8 | .5 | Intangibles (net) | .8 | 1.0 |
| 6.4 | 6.3 | 11.4 | 15.6 | 26.2 | 26.6 | All Other Non-Current | 12.2 | 12.8 |
| 100.0 | 100.0 | 100.0 | 100.0 | 100.0 | 100.0 | Total | 100.0 | 100.0 |
| | | | | | | **LIABILITIES** | | |
| 22.1 | 3.7 | 3.3 | 1.9 | 2.4 | .9 | Notes Payable-Short Term | 4.2 | 3.8 |
| 1.7 | 2.1 | 2.1 | 2.2 | 1.3 | .8 | Cur. Mat.-L.T.D. | 1.7 | 1.8 |
| 11.5 | 4.9 | 7.6 | 6.1 | 5.1 | 4.0 | Trade Payables | 7.3 | 6.6 |
| .8 | .2 | .1 | .0 | .0 | .0 | Income Taxes Payable | .1 | .1 |
| 21.4 | 11.1 | 10.6 | 9.0 | 6.7 | 5.6 | All Other Current | 11.1 | 10.3 |
| 57.4 | 22.0 | 23.6 | 19.2 | 15.5 | 11.4 | Total Current | 24.4 | 22.6 |
| 12.1 | 23.6 | 17.5 | 21.2 | 20.8 | 20.9 | Long-Term Debt | 19.0 | 19.1 |
| .0 | .0 | .0 | .0 | .2 | .0 | Deferred Taxes | .0 | .0 |
| 7.0 | 3.4 | 3.3 | 4.5 | 4.7 | 3.4 | All Other Non-Current | 3.5 | 3.0 |
| 23.3 | 51.0 | 55.6 | 55.1 | 59.0 | 64.3 | Net Worth | 53.0 | 55.3 |
| 100.0 | 100.0 | 100.0 | 100.0 | 100.0 | 100.0 | Total Liabilties & Net Worth | 100.0 | 100.0 |
| | | | | | | **INCOME DATA** | | |
| 100.0 | 100.0 | 100.0 | 100.0 | 100.0 | 100.0 | Net Sales | 100.0 | 100.0 |
| | | | | | | Gross Profit | | |
| 93.6 | 96.0 | 97.3 | 95.5 | 97.3 | 90.6 | Operating Expenses | 96.3 | 96.9 |
| 6.4 | 4.0 | 2.7 | 4.5 | 2.7 | 9.4 | Operating Profit | 3.7 | 3.1 |
| .9 | 1.0 | .5 | .5 | 2.2 | -.8 | All Other Expenses (net) | .3 | 1.7 |
| 5.5 | 2.9 | 2.2 | 4.0 | .5 | 10.2 | Profit Before Taxes | 3.4 | 1.4 |
| | | | | | | **RATIOS** | | |
| 8.3 | 6.0 | 3.8 | 3.8 | 3.3 | 4.6 | | 3.6 | 3.9 |
| 1.6 | 2.9 | 2.1 | 2.1 | 2.0 | 1.9 | Current | 1.9 | 2.0 |
| .9 | 1.4 | 1.2 | 1.3 | .9 | .8 | | 1.1 | 1.2 |
| 8.3 | 5.9 | 3.5 | 3.2 | 2.7 | 3.5 | | 3.1 | 3.2 |
| 1.5 | 2.7 | 1.7 | 1.8 | 1.5 | 1.5 | Quick | 1.6 | 1.7 |
| .5 | 1.2 | 1.0 | 1.1 | .9 | .8 | | 1.0 | 1.0 |
| 0 UND | 6 61.7 | 12 31.2 | 17 21.8 | 12 31.4 | 17 21.7 | | 13 28.7 | 12 31.5 |
| 1 287.0 | 26 13.9 | 32 11.3 | 36 10.2 | 28 12.9 | 26 14.2 | Sales/Receivables | 33 10.9 | 31 11.9 |
| 28 13.0 | 43 8.4 | 49 7.5 | 49 7.4 | 44 8.3 | 58 6.3 | | 55 6.7 | 51 7.2 |
| | | | | | | Cost of Sales/Inventory | | |
| | | | | | | Cost of Sales/Payables | | |
| 7.7 | 3.8 | 4.2 | 3.6 | 3.4 | 4.1 | | 4.3 | 4.3 |
| 20.0 | 7.4 | 9.3 | 7.7 | 9.8 | 8.1 | Sales/Working Capital | 9.5 | 9.3 |
| -62.5 | 38.5 | 38.8 | 22.2 | -106.0 | -25.8 | | 51.0 | 45.7 |
| 21.0 | 20.6 | 8.4 | 9.1 | 2.7 | 137.0 | | 8.9 | 6.4 |
| (23) 4.8 | (65) 3.4 | (235) 2.5 | (220) 2.3 | (28) 1.0 | (12) 8.3 | EBIT/Interest | (514) 2.6 | (588) 1.6 |
| -1.5 | .0 | -.1 | .1 | -1.1 | 1.6 | | .8 | -1.3 |
| | | | | | | Net Profit + Depr., Dep., Amort./Cur. Mat. L/T/D | | |
| .0 | .3 | .4 | .5 | .4 | .1 | | .3 | .4 |
| .3 | .6 | .8 | .8 | .8 | .8 | Fixed/Worth | .7 | .8 |
| 2.4 | 1.2 | 1.4 | 1.5 | 1.4 | 1.3 | | 1.4 | 1.4 |
| .2 | .2 | .3 | .3 | .2 | .1 | | .3 | .3 |
| 1.4 | .5 | .7 | .7 | .6 | .8 | Debt/Worth | .7 | .7 |
| 29.6 | 1.9 | 1.8 | 1.5 | 1.5 | 1.5 | | 1.8 | 1.7 |
| 55.9 | 19.3 | 13.2 | 11.5 | 3.7 | 11.5 | | 12.6 | 12.1 |
| (33) 17.1 | (100) 5.5 | (322) 3.6 | (262) 4.6 | (34) 1.1 | 10.1 | % Profit Before Taxes/Tangible Net Worth | (703) 4.9 | (784) 1.6 |
| 1.1 | -1.9 | -1.9 | -.6 | -1.5 | 4.0 | | -.7 | -5.7 |
| 43.8 | 12.7 | 6.8 | 6.4 | 2.2 | 9.5 | | 7.3 | 6.6 |
| 6.3 | 2.6 | 1.9 | 2.1 | .3 | 4.7 | % Profit Before Taxes/Total Assets | 2.7 | .8 |
| -1.3 | -2.9 | -1.2 | -.6 | -.9 | 2.1 | | -.6 | -3.2 |
| 652.3 | 22.9 | 13.4 | 5.2 | 3.9 | 7.0 | | 13.5 | 11.4 |
| 44.3 | 5.3 | 4.1 | 2.5 | 1.5 | 1.7 | Sales/Net Fixed Assets | 3.6 | 3.4 |
| 14.1 | 1.6 | 1.7 | 1.2 | .7 | 1.3 | | 1.7 | 1.4 |
| 8.3 | 3.4 | 2.6 | 1.8 | 1.5 | 1.0 | | 2.5 | 2.5 |
| 4.9 | 1.9 | 1.7 | 1.1 | .7 | .8 | Sales/Total Assets | 1.5 | 1.4 |
| 3.2 | 1.0 | .9 | .6 | .4 | .4 | | .8 | .7 |
| .5 | .7 | 1.0 | 1.5 | 2.4 | .6 | | 1.2 | 1.2 |
| (23) .8 | (86) 1.3 | (291) 2.0 | (247) 2.7 | (14) 6.2 | 3.1 | % Depr., Dep., Amort./Sales | (644) 2.2 | (731) 2.4 |
| 1.6 | 2.3 | 3.5 | 4.3 | 8.7 | 5.0 | | 3.7 | 3.8 |
| 5.1 | 2.9 | 1.3 | 1.7 | | | | 2.7 | 2.9 |
| (11) 8.3 | (19) 5.0 | (18) 6.7 | (14) 4.3 | | | % Officers', Directors' Owners' Comp/Sales | (71) 6.6 | (84) 6.6 |
| 19.5 | 8.8 | 16.4 | 13.2 | | | | 13.7 | 14.3 |
| 49329M | 312735M | 3424243M | 7339984M | 2150148M | 2457781M | Net Sales ($) | 13826589M | 15732387M |
| 9708M | 129543M | 1759115M | 5949866M | 2216132M | 2288962M | Total Assets ($) | 10743927M | 12381963M |

© RMA 2012

M = $ thousand    MM = $ million
See Pages 9 through 22 for Explanation of Ratios and Data

**Comparative Historical Data**                                    **Current Data Sorted by Sales**

| | | | Type of Statement | | | | | | |
|---|---|---|---|---|---|---|---|---|---|
| 480 | 579 | 556 | Unqualified | 18 | 65 | 57 | 111 | 173 | 132 |
| 8 | 12 | 7 | Reviewed | 1 | 3 | | 2 | 2 | 1 |
| 14 | 9 | 15 | Compiled | 5 | 1 | 3 | 3 | 1 | 2 |
| 28 | 23 | 30 | Tax Returns | 8 | 11 | 3 | 4 | 4 | |
| 194 | 210 | 192 | Other | 21 | 42 | 18 | 26 | 43 | 42 |
| 4/1/09-3/31/10 ALL | 4/1/10-3/31/11 ALL | 4/1/11-3/31/12 ALL | | 0-1MM | 587 (4/1-9/30/11) 1-3MM | 3-5MM | 5-10MM | 213 (10/1/11-3/31/12) 10-25MM | 25MM & OVER |
| 724 | 833 | 800 | **NUMBER OF STATEMENTS** | 53 | 122 | 81 | 144 | 223 | 177 |
| % | % | % | **ASSETS** | % | % | % | % | % | % |
| 20.7 | 21.0 | 21.4 | Cash & Equivalents | 23.5 | 25.7 | 20.1 | 23.9 | 19.1 | 19.1 |
| 17.6 | 17.2 | 16.5 | Trade Receivables (net) | 10.8 | 13.3 | 14.5 | 18.0 | 18.3 | 17.9 |
| 1.4 | 1.3 | 1.4 | Inventory | 2.5 | .6 | .4 | .8 | 1.2 | 2.9 |
| 4.8 | 4.3 | 3.6 | All Other Current | 4.6 | 3.7 | 2.5 | 4.0 | 3.7 | 3.2 |
| 44.4 | 43.8 | 42.9 | Total Current | 41.3 | 43.2 | 37.4 | 46.7 | 42.4 | 43.0 |
| 42.2 | 42.6 | 43.4 | Fixed Assets (net) | 50.8 | 43.5 | 49.5 | 39.3 | 45.1 | 39.6 |
| 1.0 | 1.1 | .9 | Intangibles (net) | .5 | .8 | .5 | .6 | 1.3 | 1.1 |
| 12.3 | 12.6 | 12.8 | All Other Non-Current | 7.3 | 12.4 | 12.6 | 13.4 | 11.2 | 16.3 |
| 100.0 | 100.0 | 100.0 | Total | 100.0 | 100.0 | 100.0 | 100.0 | 100.0 | 100.0 |
| | | | **LIABILITIES** | | | | | | |
| 3.9 | 2.7 | 3.8 | Notes Payable-Short Term | 11.5 | 3.1 | 2.9 | 5.6 | 2.7 | 2.2 |
| 1.8 | 1.9 | 2.0 | Cur. Mat.-L.T.D. | 2.0 | 1.9 | 1.6 | 2.2 | 2.0 | 2.2 |
| 6.5 | 6.5 | 6.8 | Trade Payables | 5.3 | 4.9 | 4.0 | 6.0 | 7.6 | 9.3 |
| .1 | .1 | .1 | Income Taxes Payable | .3 | .3 | .0 | .1 | .0 | .0 |
| 12.6 | 12.1 | 10.4 | All Other Current | 11.0 | 8.4 | 6.2 | 10.8 | 10.9 | 12.7 |
| 24.9 | 23.3 | 23.1 | Total Current | 30.0 | 18.7 | 14.8 | 24.7 | 23.2 | 26.5 |
| 17.7 | 19.1 | 19.5 | Long-Term Debt | 27.4 | 20.2 | 23.9 | 15.4 | 19.0 | 18.6 |
| .0 | .0 | .0 | Deferred Taxes | .0 | .0 | .0 | .0 | .0 | .1 |
| 4.4 | 3.8 | 4.0 | All Other Non-Current | 8.4 | 2.4 | 2.3 | 2.8 | 4.4 | 4.9 |
| 53.0 | 53.7 | 53.4 | Net Worth | 34.0 | 58.6 | 59.0 | 57.1 | 53.4 | 49.9 |
| 100.0 | 100.0 | 100.0 | Total Liabilities & Net Worth | 100.0 | 100.0 | 100.0 | 100.0 | 100.0 | 100.0 |
| | | | **INCOME DATA** | | | | | | |
| 100.0 | 100.0 | 100.0 | Net Sales | 100.0 | 100.0 | 100.0 | 100.0 | 100.0 | 100.0 |
| | | | Gross Profit | | | | | | |
| 97.9 | 96.7 | 96.2 | Operating Expenses | 92.8 | 94.0 | 96.2 | 97.1 | 96.1 | 97.9 |
| 2.1 | 3.3 | 3.8 | Operating Profit | 7.2 | 6.0 | 3.8 | 2.9 | 3.9 | 2.1 |
| 1.4 | .5 | .7 | All Other Expenses (net) | 3.4 | 1.3 | .1 | .2 | .5 | .2 |
| .6 | 2.8 | 3.2 | Profit Before Taxes | 3.7 | 4.6 | 3.7 | 2.6 | 3.4 | 1.9 |
| | | | **RATIOS** | | | | | | |
| 3.6 | 3.9 | 4.1 | Current | 11.0 | 7.2 | 6.5 | 4.5 | 3.3 | 2.7 |
| 1.9 | 2.1 | 2.1 | | 1.7 | 2.9 | 3.0 | 2.3 | 2.1 | 1.7 |
| 1.2 | 1.2 | 1.2 | | .8 | 1.3 | 1.5 | 1.3 | 1.3 | 1.1 |
| 3.2 | 3.4 | 3.6 | Quick | 10.4 | 6.7 | 5.6 | 4.2 | 3.0 | 2.2 |
| 1.7 | 1.8 | 1.8 | | 1.6 | 2.7 | 2.7 | 1.8 | 1.8 | 1.4 |
| 1.0 | 1.0 | 1.0 | | .4 | 1.3 | 1.3 | 1.3 | 1.1 | .9 |
| 13 29.2 | 13 28.7 | 11 33.0 | Sales/Receivables | 0 UND | 2 181.0 | 8 48.5 | 16 22.4 | 17 21.6 | 16 22.3 |
| 31 11.6 | 33 11.1 | 31 11.7 | | 5 68.7 | 24 15.5 | 31 11.8 | 33 11.1 | 36 10.2 | 33 11.0 |
| 49 7.4 | 51 7.2 | 47 7.7 | | 24 15.4 | 43 8.5 | 56 6.5 | 48 7.6 | 54 6.7 | 46 7.9 |
| | | | Cost of Sales/Inventory | | | | | | |
| | | | Cost of Sales/Payables | | | | | | |
| 4.7 | 4.0 | 3.9 | Sales/Working Capital | 2.9 | 3.3 | 3.0 | 3.7 | 4.2 | 5.9 |
| 9.9 | 8.5 | 8.7 | | 20.0 | 6.1 | 6.1 | 8.3 | 8.5 | 14.3 |
| 44.3 | 33.7 | 37.6 | | -30.7 | 29.8 | 16.3 | 28.2 | 24.5 | 66.5 |
| 6.7 | 10.3 | 9.1 | EBIT/Interest | 5.3 | 13.1 | 9.0 | 11.7 | 9.1 | 8.4 |
| (516) 1.6 | (612) 2.9 | (583) 2.5 | | (27) 1.8 | (78) 2.7 | (56) 2.8 | (102) 2.1 | (176) 3.0 | (144) 2.2 |
| -1.6 | .5 | .0 | | -2.8 | -.5 | -.4 | -1.4 | .4 | .7 |
| | | | Net Profit + Depr., Dep., Amort./Cur. Mat. L/T/D | | | | | | |
| .4 | .3 | .4 | Fixed/Worth | .3 | .1 | .4 | .3 | .5 | .4 |
| .8 | .8 | .8 | | 1.0 | .6 | .7 | .7 | .9 | .8 |
| 1.4 | 1.4 | 1.4 | | 2.7 | 1.4 | 1.2 | 1.3 | 1.4 | 1.6 |
| .3 | .3 | .3 | Debt/Worth | .3 | .2 | .1 | .2 | .4 | .4 |
| .8 | .7 | .7 | | 1.3 | .5 | .4 | .6 | .8 | .9 |
| 1.8 | 1.7 | 1.7 | | 4.7 | 1.9 | .9 | 1.7 | 1.5 | 1.7 |
| 14.9 | 13.2 | 13.2 | % Profit Before Taxes/Tangible Net Worth | 30.7 | 12.8 | 13.2 | 13.8 | 14.0 | 10.0 |
| (694) 2.8 | (805) 3.8 | (766) 4.3 | | (45) 6.3 | (119) 3.0 | (77) 3.0 | (140) 3.4 | (215) 5.3 | (170) 4.4 |
| -4.7 | -1.9 | -1.3 | | -1.0 | -1.5 | -2.6 | -3.4 | -.4 | -.3 |
| 7.0 | 7.1 | 7.3 | % Profit Before Taxes/Total Assets | 10.7 | 8.8 | 7.6 | 7.9 | 7.6 | 4.8 |
| 1.4 | 1.9 | 2.1 | | 1.9 | 1.7 | 2.8 | 2.0 | 2.6 | 1.6 |
| -3.0 | -1.1 | -1.0 | | -2.6 | -1.2 | -2.1 | -2.3 | -.2 | -.6 |
| 13.2 | 11.8 | 11.8 | Sales/Net Fixed Assets | 29.9 | 19.6 | 4.9 | 20.9 | 7.1 | 11.1 |
| 4.0 | 3.8 | 3.6 | | 1.9 | 3.3 | 1.9 | 4.6 | 2.9 | 4.8 |
| 1.7 | 1.6 | 1.4 | | .4 | .9 | .9 | 1.7 | 1.6 | 2.4 |
| 2.8 | 2.5 | 2.5 | Sales/Total Assets | 3.8 | 2.3 | 1.8 | 2.7 | 2.3 | 2.9 |
| 1.5 | 1.5 | 1.4 | | 1.0 | 1.1 | 1.0 | 1.6 | 1.4 | 1.8 |
| .8 | .8 | .7 | | .2 | .5 | .5 | .8 | .8 | 1.0 |
| 1.1 | 1.1 | 1.1 | % Depr., Dep., Amort./Sales | 1.2 | 1.0 | 1.6 | .8 | 1.4 | 1.0 |
| (625) 2.2 | (744) 2.1 | (696) 2.2 | | (30) 2.4 | (96) 2.1 | (76) 3.2 | (130) 2.0 | (199) 2.4 | (165) 1.7 |
| 3.9 | 3.7 | 3.8 | | 11.8 | 4.8 | 4.9 | 3.4 | 3.9 | 3.2 |
| 2.5 | 2.4 | 2.8 | % Officers', Directors' Owners' Comp/Sales | 6.1 | 4.3 | | | 1.3 | |
| (74) 6.1 | (68) 4.6 | (66) 6.0 | | (10) 9.9 | (16) 8.1 | | | (18) 5.4 | |
| 13.8 | 14.5 | 12.4 | | 20.2 | 9.9 | | | 12.5 | |
| 15874106M | 20043330M | 15734220M | Net Sales ($) | 27734M | 242969M | 318872M | 1065191M | 3601664M | 10477790M |
| 11473874M | 13797065M | 12353326M | Total Assets ($) | 61112M | 329994M | 510082M | 1098009M | 3495503M | 6858626M |

M = $ thousand    MM = $ million
See Pages 9 through 22 for Explanation of Ratios and Data

## Current Data Sorted by Assets      Comparative Historical Data

| 0-500M | 500M-2MM | 2-10MM | 10-50MM | 50-100MM | 100-250MM | Type of Statement | 4/1/07-3/31/08 ALL | 4/1/08-3/31/09 ALL |
|---|---|---|---|---|---|---|---|---|
| | 1 | 11 | 14 | | 1 | Unqualified | 9 | 10 |
| | | | | | | Reviewed | | |
| 1 | 1 | | 1 | | | Compiled | 1 | 2 |
| 5 | 3 | 1 | 1 | 1 | | Tax Returns | 7 | 8 |
| | 3 | 3 | 1 | 1 | | Other | 1 | 3 |
| 25 (4/1-9/30/11) | | | 22 (10/1/11-3/31/12) | | | | | |
| 6 | 8 | 15 | 16 | 2 | | NUMBER OF STATEMENTS | 18 | 23 |
| % | % | % | % | % | % | | % | % |
| | | | | | | **ASSETS** | | |
| | | 18.9 | 18.0 | | | Cash & Equivalents | 16.3 | 17.6 |
| | | 4.1 | 3.5 | | | Trade Receivables (net) | 10.1 | 8.0 |
| | | 15.5 | 20.1 | | | Inventory | 7.9 | 10.8 |
| | | 4.8 | 3.0 | | | All Other Current | 11.5 | 14.5 |
| | | 43.3 | 44.6 | | | Total Current | 45.8 | 50.9 |
| | | 39.3 | 35.3 | | | Fixed Assets (net) | 41.6 | 37.2 |
| | | .3 | .3 | | | Intangibles (net) | 2.3 | 2.0 |
| | | 17.0 | 19.7 | | | All Other Non-Current | 10.3 | 9.9 |
| | | 100.0 | 100.0 | | | Total | 100.0 | 100.0 |
| | | | | | | **LIABILITIES** | | |
| | | 1.5 | .7 | | | Notes Payable-Short Term | .7 | 4.6 |
| | | 2.4 | .4 | | | Cur. Mat.-L.T.D. | 2.0 | 5.3 |
| | | 3.9 | 3.1 | | | Trade Payables | 4.0 | 3.8 |
| | | .0 | .0 | | | Income Taxes Payable | .0 | .0 |
| | | 3.6 | 1.8 | | | All Other Current | 24.8 | 22.7 |
| | | 11.5 | 6.0 | | | Total Current | 31.4 | 36.5 |
| | | 7.0 | 9.1 | | | Long-Term Debt | 16.8 | 8.3 |
| | | .0 | .0 | | | Deferred Taxes | .0 | .0 |
| | | 1.0 | 2.6 | | | All Other Non-Current | 1.0 | 2.3 |
| | | 80.5 | 82.4 | | | Net Worth | 50.8 | 52.8 |
| | | 100.0 | 100.0 | | | Total Liabilities & Net Worth | 100.0 | 100.0 |
| | | | | | | **INCOME DATA** | | |
| | | 100.0 | 100.0 | | | Net Sales | 100.0 | 100.0 |
| | | | | | | Gross Profit | | |
| | | 89.9 | 92.6 | | | Operating Expenses | 98.9 | 96.8 |
| | | 10.1 | 7.4 | | | Operating Profit | 1.1 | 3.2 |
| | | 4.2 | -1.4 | | | All Other Expenses (net) | -.6 | .4 |
| | | 5.9 | 8.8 | | | Profit Before Taxes | 1.6 | 2.8 |
| | | | | | | **RATIOS** | | |
| | | 11.7 | 22.5 | | | | 8.6 | 9.7 |
| | | 5.7 | 7.7 | | | Current | 3.1 | 4.5 |
| | | 1.6 | 4.4 | | | | .9 | 1.0 |
| | | 6.9 | 10.6 | | | | 4.8 | 6.0 |
| | | 2.7 | 4.1 | | | Quick | 2.7 | 2.4 |
| | | .6 | 1.7 | | | | .2 | .2 |
| | 0   804.1 | | 0   UND | | | | 0   UND | 0   UND |
| | 13   27.4 | | 3   105.1 | | | Sales/Receivables | 2   160.4 | 2   148.4 |
| | 23   16.0 | | 11   32.9 | | | | 19   19.4 | 15   24.8 |
| | | | | | | Cost of Sales/Inventory | | |
| | | | | | | Cost of Sales/Payables | | |
| | | 3.3 | 2.7 | | | | 6.6 | 4.0 |
| | | 9.0 | 5.8 | | | Sales/Working Capital | 8.9 | 9.1 |
| | | 17.8 | 11.1 | | | | -125.7 | -676.7 |
| | | | 521.4 | | | | 28.1 | 56.3 |
| | | (13) | 15.9 | | | EBIT/Interest | (14) 5.1 | (16) 8.7 |
| | | | 1.6 | | | | -1.5 | -1.1 |
| | | | | | | Net Profit + Depr., Dep., Amort./Cur. Mat. L/T/D | | |
| | | .3 | .2 | | | | .4 | .1 |
| | | .3 | .4 | | | Fixed/Worth | .6 | .6 |
| | | .6 | .7 | | | | 1.5 | 1.6 |
| | | .1 | .1 | | | | .1 | .1 |
| | | .1 | .2 | | | Debt/Worth | .8 | .4 |
| | | .5 | .4 | | | | 2.3 | 3.4 |
| | | 8.2 | 10.5 | | | | 14.8 | 31.9 |
| | | -1.1 | 4.6 | | | % Profit Before Taxes/Tangible Net Worth | (15) 5.3 | (20) 14.1 |
| | | -5.5 | .9 | | | | -8.8 | 1.7 |
| | | 7.9 | 8.3 | | | | 11.9 | 17.4 |
| | | -.6 | 3.7 | | | % Profit Before Taxes/Total Assets | 3.4 | 6.0 |
| | | -4.8 | .6 | | | | -6.2 | -1.0 |
| | | 14.4 | 19.8 | | | | 15.5 | 23.1 |
| | | 6.1 | 7.7 | | | Sales/Net Fixed Assets | 8.0 | 7.3 |
| | | 2.2 | 1.9 | | | | 2.0 | 2.5 |
| | | 3.0 | 3.3 | | | | 4.7 | 3.4 |
| | | 1.5 | 2.2 | | | Sales/Total Assets | 2.5 | 2.5 |
| | | .7 | .6 | | | | 1.1 | 1.3 |
| | | .9 | .5 | | | | .9 | .6 |
| | (14) | 1.9 | 1.2 | | | % Depr., Dep., Amort./Sales | (16) 1.2 | (22) 1.7 |
| | | 4.4 | 4.2 | | | | 2.7 | 3.1 |
| | | | | | | % Officers', Directors' Owners' Comp/Sales | | |
| 6324M | 25540M | 251029M | 683196M | 171134M | | Net Sales ($) | 176941M | 945922M |
| 1528M | 9465M | 102800M | 334420M | 120435M | | Total Assets ($) | 70381M | 201839M |

*Columns 0-500M and 500M-2MM (asset/liability/income sections), 50-100MM and 100-250MM marked:* **DATA NOT AVAILABLE**

## Comparative Historical Data | Current Data Sorted by Sales

| Type of Statement | 4/1/09-3/31/10 ALL | 4/1/10-3/31/11 ALL | 4/1/11-3/31/12 ALL | 0-1MM | 1-3MM | 3-5MM | 5-10MM | 10-25MM | 25MM & OVER |
|---|---|---|---|---|---|---|---|---|---|
| | | | | | 25 (4/1-9/30/11) | | | 22 (10/1/11-3/31/12) | |
| Unqualified | 21 | 20 | 27 | 1 | 1 | 2 | 4 | 6 | 13 |
| Reviewed | 1 | | | | | | | | |
| Compiled | 3 | 1 | 3 | 1 | 1 | | 1 | | |
| Tax Returns | | 1 | 9 | 3 | 4 | | 1 | 1 | |
| Other | 8 | 11 | 8 | 1 | 1 | 2 | 2 | 1 | 1 |
| **NUMBER OF STATEMENTS** | 33 | 33 | 47 | 6 | 7 | 4 | 8 | 8 | 14 |
| **ASSETS** | % | % | % | % | % | % | % | % | % |
| Cash & Equivalents | 21.6 | 22.3 | 15.9 | | | | | | 24.4 |
| Trade Receivables (net) | 5.9 | 10.4 | 4.2 | | | | | | 5.7 |
| Inventory | 14.4 | 10.6 | 13.3 | | | | | | 20.4 |
| All Other Current | 2.2 | 3.3 | 7.8 | | | | | | 3.8 |
| Total Current | 44.1 | 46.5 | 41.3 | | | | | | 54.3 |
| Fixed Assets (net) | 45.0 | 43.6 | 42.9 | | | | | | 31.6 |
| Intangibles (net) | .4 | .1 | 1.5 | | | | | | .4 |
| All Other Non-Current | 10.4 | 9.9 | 14.3 | | | | | | 13.6 |
| Total | 100.0 | 100.0 | 100.0 | | | | | | 100.0 |
| **LIABILITIES** | | | | | | | | | |
| Notes Payable-Short Term | 2.8 | 2.3 | 1.9 | | | | | | .8 |
| Cur. Mat.-L.T.D. | .9 | 2.9 | 1.4 | | | | | | .6 |
| Trade Payables | 6.1 | 6.4 | 4.6 | | | | | | 3.8 |
| Income Taxes Payable | .0 | .0 | .0 | | | | | | .0 |
| All Other Current | 3.7 | 4.1 | 9.1 | | | | | | 3.3 |
| Total Current | 13.5 | 15.7 | 17.0 | | | | | | 8.6 |
| Long-Term Debt | 9.8 | 9.1 | 9.8 | | | | | | 7.1 |
| Deferred Taxes | .0 | .0 | .0 | | | | | | .0 |
| All Other Non-Current | 5.2 | 4.8 | 5.8 | | | | | | 1.0 |
| Net Worth | 71.5 | 70.4 | 67.4 | | | | | | 83.3 |
| Total Liabilities & Net Worth | 100.0 | 100.0 | 100.0 | | | | | | 100.0 |
| **INCOME DATA** | | | | | | | | | |
| Net Sales | 100.0 | 100.0 | 100.0 | | | | | | 100.0 |
| Gross Profit | | | | | | | | | |
| Operating Expenses | 91.7 | 92.0 | 94.2 | | | | | | 100.5 |
| Operating Profit | 8.3 | 8.0 | 5.8 | | | | | | -.5 |
| All Other Expenses (net) | .4 | .2 | 1.0 | | | | | | -.1 |
| Profit Before Taxes | 7.9 | 7.7 | 4.8 | | | | | | -.4 |
| **RATIOS** | | | | | | | | | |
| Current | 14.1 | 13.7 | 11.6 | | | | | | 17.0 |
| | 6.9 | 6.1 | 4.3 | | | | | | 6.9 |
| | 1.8 | 1.8 | 1.5 | | | | | | 4.3 |
| Quick | 6.1 | 7.2 | 5.8 | | | | | | 8.2 |
| | 3.5 | 3.0 | 2.0 | | | | | | 3.7 |
| | 1.3 | 1.3 | .4 | | | | | | 1.8 |
| Sales/Receivables | 0  999.8 | 0  839.7 | 0  UND | | | | | | 0  853.0 |
| | 3  118.9 | 7  53.8 | 3  116.5 | | | | | | 3  123.0 |
| | 10  37.2 | 36  10.0 | 18  20.5 | | | | | | 4  81.3 |
| Cost of Sales/Inventory | | | | | | | | | |
| Cost of Sales/Payables | | | | | | | | | |
| Sales/Working Capital | 5.0 | 3.5 | 4.6 | | | | | | 5.4 |
| | 7.0 | 6.1 | 9.2 | | | | | | 9.0 |
| | 13.2 | 13.0 | 24.4 | | | | | | 12.1 |
| EBIT/Interest | 21.6 | 49.1 | 116.8 | | | | | | |
| | (17)  6.1 | (17)  6.0 | (28)  6.3 | | | | | | |
| | -4.0 | 2.4 | -1.4 | | | | | | |
| Net Profit + Depr., Dep., Amort./Cur. Mat. L/T/D | | | | | | | | | |
| Fixed/Worth | .3 | .3 | .3 | | | | | | .2 |
| | .6 | .6 | .5 | | | | | | .3 |
| | .9 | .9 | 1.0 | | | | | | .6 |
| Debt/Worth | .1 | .1 | .1 | | | | | | .1 |
| | .3 | .3 | .2 | | | | | | .2 |
| | .5 | .8 | .6 | | | | | | .4 |
| % Profit Before Taxes/Tangible Net Worth | 35.7 | 14.9 | 10.7 | | | | | | 8.6 |
| | (32)  16.9 | (32)  6.8 | (43)  2.4 | | | | | | 3.4 |
| | -1.9 | -1.4 | -4.8 | | | | | | -4.9 |
| % Profit Before Taxes/Total Assets | 22.8 | 10.6 | 8.2 | | | | | | 7.5 |
| | 11.4 | 6.2 | 1.2 | | | | | | 2.5 |
| | -2.7 | -.6 | -3.5 | | | | | | -3.7 |
| Sales/Net Fixed Assets | 14.9 | 20.7 | 21.0 | | | | | | 26.7 |
| | 5.7 | 4.1 | 6.1 | | | | | | 15.4 |
| | 2.4 | 1.8 | 2.0 | | | | | | 7.4 |
| Sales/Total Assets | 3.8 | 3.4 | 3.4 | | | | | | 5.3 |
| | 2.2 | 1.4 | 1.9 | | | | | | 3.3 |
| | 1.3 | 1.0 | .7 | | | | | | 2.6 |
| % Depr., Dep., Amort./Sales | .7 | .9 | .6 | | | | | | .4 |
| | (28)  1.3 | (29)  1.4 | (42)  1.5 | | | | | | .7 |
| | 2.1 | 3.4 | 4.4 | | | | | | 1.0 |
| % Officers', Directors' Owners' Comp/Sales | | | | | | | | | |
| Net Sales ($) | 1705237M | 792611M | 1137223M | 3783M | 11635M | 16158M | 54019M | 137414M | 914214M |
| Total Assets ($) | 449949M | 364549M | 568648M | 4391M | 11008M | 16993M | 105186M | 141041M | 290029M |

## Current Data Sorted by Assets      Comparative Historical Data

| | | | | | | Type of Statement | | |
|---|---|---|---|---|---|---|---|---|
| | 4 | 14 | 9 | 2 | 2 | Unqualified | 16 | 18 |
| 1 | | | | | | Reviewed | 1 | 1 |
| 1 | | | | | | Compiled | 1 | 1 |
| | | 1 | | | | Tax Returns | | |
| 1 | 3 | 1 | 2 | | | Other | 7 | 8 |
| | 35 (4/1-9/30/11) | | 6 (10/1/11-3/31/12) | | | | 4/1/07- | 4/1/08- |
| | | | | | | | 3/31/08 | 3/31/09 |
| 0-500M | 500M-2MM | 2-10MM | 10-50MM | 50-100MM | 100-250MM | | ALL | ALL |
| 3 | 7 | 16 | 11 | 2 | 2 | NUMBER OF STATEMENTS | 25 | 28 |
| % | % | % | % | % | % | ASSETS | % | % |
| | | 23.2 | 10.6 | | | Cash & Equivalents | 17.7 | 17.9 |
| | | 7.4 | 11.1 | | | Trade Receivables (net) | 4.5 | 11.3 |
| | | .3 | .2 | | | Inventory | .3 | .3 |
| | | 4.6 | 3.0 | | | All Other Current | 6.5 | 5.8 |
| | | 35.3 | 24.9 | | | Total Current | 29.0 | 35.2 |
| | | 55.2 | 67.2 | | | Fixed Assets (net) | 55.3 | 51.6 |
| | | .0 | 2.0 | | | Intangibles (net) | .0 | 1.0 |
| | | 9.4 | 5.9 | | | All Other Non-Current | 15.7 | 12.2 |
| | | 100.0 | 100.0 | | | Total | 100.0 | 100.0 |
| | | | | | | LIABILITIES | | |
| | | 2.1 | 2.3 | | | Notes Payable-Short Term | 1.0 | 3.5 |
| | | .3 | 1.4 | | | Cur. Mat.-L.T.D. | 1.0 | .4 |
| | | 3.2 | 4.1 | | | Trade Payables | 2.4 | 3.7 |
| | | .0 | .0 | | | Income Taxes Payable | .0 | .0 |
| | | 4.5 | 1.7 | | | All Other Current | 8.2 | 3.6 |
| | | 10.1 | 9.5 | | | Total Current | 12.5 | 11.3 |
| | | 19.8 | 24.6 | | | Long-Term Debt | 14.6 | 11.3 |
| | | .0 | .0 | | | Deferred Taxes | .0 | .0 |
| | | 2.1 | 4.9 | | | All Other Non-Current | .5 | 1.0 |
| | | 67.9 | 60.9 | | | Net Worth | 72.4 | 76.5 |
| | | 100.0 | 100.0 | | | Total Liabilities & Net Worth | 100.0 | 100.0 |
| | | | | | | INCOME DATA | | |
| | | 100.0 | 100.0 | | | Net Sales | 100.0 | 100.0 |
| | | | | | | Gross Profit | | |
| | | 98.3 | 93.8 | | | Operating Expenses | 92.4 | 96.3 |
| | | 1.7 | 6.2 | | | Operating Profit | 7.6 | 3.7 |
| | | -1.6 | 2.5 | | | All Other Expenses (net) | -.4 | -.6 |
| | | 3.3 | 3.7 | | | Profit Before Taxes | 8.0 | 4.3 |
| | | | | | | RATIOS | | |
| | | 7.2 | 5.1 | | | | 5.3 | 8.8 |
| | | 4.8 | 3.1 | | | Current | 3.1 | 3.7 |
| | | 2.1 | 1.8 | | | | 1.5 | 1.1 |
| | | 6.7 | 4.4 | | | | 4.6 | 6.4 |
| | | 2.7 | 2.9 | | | Quick | 1.6 | 2.7 |
| | | 1.8 | 1.3 | | | | 1.0 | .8 |
| | | 6   65.3 | 12   31.6 | | | | 0 UND | 1 469.3 |
| | | 16   22.8 | 21   17.6 | | | Sales/Receivables | 7   54.1 | 22   16.3 |
| | | 44   8.3 | 79   4.6 | | | | 30   12.0 | 56   6.5 |
| | | | | | | Cost of Sales/Inventory | | |
| | | | | | | Cost of Sales/Payables | | |
| | | 2.3 | 2.7 | | | | 3.1 | 2.8 |
| | | 4.5 | 4.8 | | | Sales/Working Capital | 7.6 | 4.7 |
| | | 8.7 | 11.3 | | | | 15.3 | 55.2 |
| | | 30.3 | | | | | 13.7 | 29.8 |
| | | (11) 2.4 | | | | EBIT/Interest | (15) 7.8 | (19) 1.3 |
| | | -.2 | | | | | 2.2 | -3.2 |
| | | | | | | Net Profit + Depr., Dep., Amort./Cur. Mat. L/T/D | | |
| | | .4 | .7 | | | | .4 | .4 |
| | | 1.0 | 1.2 | | | Fixed/Worth | .8 | .7 |
| | | 1.2 | 2.3 | | | | 1.1 | 1.0 |
| | | .2 | .3 | | | | .1 | .1 |
| | | .4 | .7 | | | Debt/Worth | .3 | .2 |
| | | 1.1 | 1.6 | | | | .7 | .6 |
| | | 8.5 | 6.3 | | | | 14.6 | 4.8 |
| | | .2 | 4.5 | | | % Profit Before Taxes/Tangible Net Worth | 6.2 | .5 |
| | | -5.2 | -4.9 | | | | 1.6 | -3.6 |
| | | 5.9 | 5.8 | | | | 11.6 | 3.9 |
| | | .1 | 1.7 | | | % Profit Before Taxes/Total Assets | 3.8 | .4 |
| | | -4.6 | -3.2 | | | | 1.3 | -2.6 |
| | | 2.8 | 1.0 | | | | 2.8 | 3.6 |
| | | 1.4 | .8 | | | Sales/Net Fixed Assets | 1.2 | 1.7 |
| | | .9 | .6 | | | | .7 | .7 |
| | | 1.5 | .7 | | | | 1.2 | 1.4 |
| | | .8 | .5 | | | Sales/Total Assets | .7 | .8 |
| | | .6 | .4 | | | | .5 | .4 |
| | | 1.6 | 3.2 | | | | 2.2 | 2.0 |
| | | 3.4 | 6.2 | | | % Depr., Dep., Amort./Sales | (21) 3.1 | (24) 2.9 |
| | | 5.2 | 7.7 | | | | 5.6 | 5.3 |
| | | | | | | % Officers', Directors' Owners' Comp/Sales | | |
| 2437M | 14722M | 88796M | 121460M | 43730M | 219435M | Net Sales ($) | 274588M | 204468M |
| 936M | 8069M | 88333M | 186643M | 120860M | 393289M | Total Assets ($) | 329150M | 298961M |

M = $ thousand     MM = $ million
See Pages 9 through 22 for Explanation of Ratios and Data

## Comparative Historical Data | Current Data Sorted by Sales

| | | | Type of Statement | | | | | | |
|---|---|---|---|---|---|---|---|---|---|
| 23 | 27 | 31 | Unqualified | 1 | 5 | 6 | 11 | 5 | 3 |
| 1 | 1 | 1 | Reviewed | 1 | | | | | |
| 1 | 1 | 1 | Compiled | 1 | | | | | |
| | | 1 | Tax Returns | | 1 | | | | |
| 9 | 8 | 7 | Other | 1 | 3 | 1. | 2 | | |
| 4/1/09- | 4/1/10- | 4/1/11- | | | 35 (4/1-9/30/11) | | 6 (10/1/11-3/31/12) | | |
| 3/31/10 | 3/31/11 | 3/31/12 | | 0-1MM | 1-3MM | 3-5MM | 5-10MM | 10-25MM | 25MM & OVER |
| ALL | ALL | ALL | | | | | | | |
| 34 | 38 | 41 | NUMBER OF STATEMENTS | 4 | 9 | 7 | 13 | 5 | 3 |
| % | % | % | ASSETS | % | % | % | % | % | % |
| 16.9 | 17.8 | 19.3 | Cash & Equivalents | | | | 15.6 | | |
| 8.9 | 7.7 | 9.2 | Trade Receivables (net) | | | | 9.9 | | |
| .2 | .3 | .5 | Inventory | | | | .3 | | |
| 3.1 | 2.6 | 4.6 | All Other Current | | | | 2.8 | | |
| 29.1 | 28.4 | 33.6 | Total Current | | | | 28.7 | | |
| 56.6 | 62.0 | 57.4 | Fixed Assets (net) | | | | 61.8 | | |
| .0 | .7 | .6 | Intangibles (net) | | | | 1.7 | | |
| 14.2 | 8.9 | 8.4 | All Other Non-Current | | | | 7.8 | | |
| 100.0 | 100.0 | 100.0 | Total | | | | 100.0 | | |
| | | | LIABILITIES | | | | | | |
| 4.0 | 2.4 | 2.3 | Notes Payable-Short Term | | | | 1.8 | | |
| 1.1 | .8 | .6 | Cur. Mat.-L.T.D. | | | | 1.1 | | |
| 2.5 | 1.8 | 3.7 | Trade Payables | | | | 2.1 | | |
| .0 | .0 | .0 | Income Taxes Payable | | | | .0 | | |
| 4.3 | 3.8 | 3.8 | All Other Current | | | | 3.6 | | |
| 11.8 | 8.8 | 10.3 | Total Current | | | | 8.7 | | |
| 21.1 | 15.9 | 18.6 | Long-Term Debt | | | | 27.5 | | |
| .0 | .0 | .0 | Deferred Taxes | | | | .0 | | |
| 1.2 | 3.1 | 4.7 | All Other Non-Current | | | | 4.5 | | |
| 65.8 | 72.1 | 66.3 | Net Worth | | | | 59.3 | | |
| 100.0 | 100.0 | 100.0 | Total Liabilities & Net Worth | | | | 100.0 | | |
| | | | INCOME DATA | | | | | | |
| 100.0 | 100.0 | 100.0 | Net Sales | | | | 100.0 | | |
| | | | Gross Profit | | | | | | |
| 98.8 | 95.0 | 96.9 | Operating Expenses | | | | 97.7 | | |
| 1.2 | 5.0 | 3.1 | Operating Profit | | | | 2.3 | | |
| 2.2 | -.1 | -.4 | All Other Expenses (net) | | | | .5 | | |
| -1.0 | 5.1 | 3.5 | Profit Before Taxes | | | | 1.8 | | |
| | | | RATIOS | | | | | | |
| 5.4 | 7.4 | 6.2 | | | | | 5.5 | | |
| 3.1 | 3.4 | 4.0 | Current | | | | 3.9 | | |
| 1.4 | 1.7 | 1.9 | | | | | 1.9 | | |
| 4.0 | 7.2 | 5.3 | | | | | 4.7 | | |
| 2.3 | 2.9 | 2.8 | Quick | | | | 2.9 | | |
| 1.3 | 1.6 | 1.7 | | | | | 1.2 | | |
| 2 204.1 | 8 44.5 | 6 59.9 | | | | | 9 40:1 | | |
| 22 16.8 | 20 18.6 | 20 18.7 | Sales/Receivables | | | | 20 18.7 | | |
| 48 7.6 | 32 11.4 | 41 8.8 | | | | | 62 5.9 | | |
| | | | Cost of Sales/Inventory | | | | | | |
| | | | Cost of Sales/Payables | | | | | | |
| 3.2 | 2.7 | 2.9 | | | | | 2.7 | | |
| 4.8 | 5.6 | 4.8 | Sales/Working Capital | | | | 4.7 | | |
| 14.2 | 10.5 | 9.0 | | | | | 7.7 | | |
| 14.8 | 11.0 | 10.4 | | | | | 13.5 | | |
| (23) 1.9 | (24) 1.7 | (30) 1.9 | EBIT/Interest | | | | (10) 2.5 | | |
| -2.2 | .6 | -1.6 | | | | | -2.8 | | |
| | | | Net Profit + Depr., Dep., Amort./Cur. Mat. L/T/D | | | | | | |
| .5 | .6 | .6 | | | | | .8 | | |
| .9 | .9 | .9 | Fixed/Worth | | | | 1.2 | | |
| 1.3 | 1.3 | 1.3 | | | | | 1.6 | | |
| .2 | .1 | .2 | | | | | .2 | | |
| .4 | .2 | .4 | Debt/Worth | | | | 1.0 | | |
| 1.2 | .9 | 1.1 | | | | | 1.5 | | |
| 6.9 | 13.3 | 14.0 | % Profit Before Taxes/Tangible Net Worth | | | | 12.6 | | |
| -.6 | 2.1 | 1.5 | | | | | -.7 | | |
| -7.7 | -1.7 | -5.9 | | | | | -5.3 | | |
| 4.0 | 10.4 | 8.4 | % Profit Before Taxes/Total Assets | | | | 5.9 | | |
| -.4 | 1.5 | 1.2 | | | | | -.3 | | |
| -5.0 | -.9 | -3.6 | | | | | -4.2 | | |
| 3.0 | 2.3 | 3.4 | Sales/Net Fixed Assets | | | | 2.0 | | |
| 1.3 | .9 | 1.3 | | | | | .9 | | |
| .7 | .7 | .7 | | | | | .6 | | |
| 1.2 | 1.1 | 1.7 | Sales/Total Assets | | | | 1.0 | | |
| .8 | .7 | .8 | | | | | .5 | | |
| .5 | .5 | .5 | | | | | .4 | | |
| 1.9 | 2.8 | 2.2 | % Depr., Dep., Amort./Sales | | | | 3.1 | | |
| (29) 3.1 | (35) 4.3 | (39) 3.5 | | | | | 4.7 | | |
| 5.7 | 6.3 | 5.7 | | | | | 7.5 | | |
| | | | % Officers', Directors' Owners' Comp/Sales | | | | | | |
| 797560M | 360305M | 490580M | Net Sales ($) | 3014M | 18016M | 29656M | 93685M | 92150M | 254059M |
| 684050M | 567340M | 798130M | Total Assets ($) | 1502M | 24395M | 32769M | 170170M | 164452M | 404842M |

M = $ thousand    MM = $ million
See Pages 9 through 22 for Explanation of Ratios and Data

## Current Data Sorted by Assets      Comparative Historical Data

| 3 | 10 | 40 | 24 | 9 | 4 | Type of Statement | | |
|---|---|---|---|---|---|---|---|---|
| | 1 | | | | | Unqualified | 30 | 44 |
| | 3 | 1 | | | | Reviewed | 2 | 1 |
| 2 | 2 | | 1 | | | Compiled | | 2 |
| 1 | 5 | 16 | 8 | 4 | 1 | Tax Returns | 2 | 2 |
| | | | | | | Other | 14 | 19 |
| | 94 (4/1-9/30/11) | | 41 (10/1/11-3/31/12) | | | | 4/1/07-3/31/08 | 4/1/08-3/31/09 |
| 0-500M | 500M-2MM | 2-10MM | 10-50MM | 50-100MM | 100-250MM | | ALL | ALL |
| 6 | 21 | 57 | 33 | 13 | 5 | NUMBER OF STATEMENTS | 48 | 68 |
| % | % | % | % | % | % | ASSETS | % | % |
| | 18.2 | 12.2 | 11.1 | 13.0 | | Cash & Equivalents | 18.5 | 9.7 |
| | 9.5 | 11.8 | 9.1 | 2.7 | | Trade Receivables (net) | 7.7 | 8.2 |
| | 10.3 | 3.0 | 3.0 | 1.1 | | Inventory | 3.6 | 4.5 |
| | 2.1 | 3.7 | 3.6 | 5.0 | | All Other Current | 6.6 | 3.5 |
| | 40.1 | 30.7 | 26.9 | 21.7 | | Total Current | 36.4 | 25.9 |
| | 43.0 | 54.6 | 43.5 | 54.9 | | Fixed Assets (net) | 43.5 | 45.1 |
| | .2 | 1.1 | .3 | .5 | | Intangibles (net) | 1.5 | 2.6 |
| | 16.7 | 13.5 | 29.4 | 22.9 | | All Other Non-Current | 18.7 | 26.4 |
| | 100.0 | 100.0 | 100.0 | 100.0 | | Total | 100.0 | 100.0 |
| | | | | | | LIABILITIES | | |
| | 2.5 | 2.2 | 2.6 | 1.3 | | Notes Payable-Short Term | 2.8 | 2.7 |
| | 1.0 | 1.6 | 2.4 | 1.5 | | Cur. Mat.-L.T.D. | 2.0 | 2.7 |
| | 3.8 | 2.8 | 2.5 | 2.3 | | Trade Payables | 2.6 | 4.4 |
| | .0 | .0 | .0 | .1 | | Income Taxes Payable | .0 | .0 |
| | 5.5 | 7.9 | 5.8 | 5.7 | | All Other Current | 4.0 | 4.2 |
| | 12.8 | 14.5 | 13.2 | 11.0 | | Total Current | 11.5 | 14.0 |
| | 36.3 | 32.1 | 28.2 | 37.4 | | Long-Term Debt | 29.7 | 25.9 |
| | .0 | .0 | .0 | .0 | | Deferred Taxes | .0 | .0 |
| | 2.5 | 3.3 | 3.8 | 6.4 | | All Other Non-Current | 3.4 | 3.8 |
| | 48.4 | 50.1 | 54.7 | 45.2 | | Net Worth | 55.4 | 56.3 |
| | 100.0 | 100.0 | 100.0 | 100.0 | | Total Liabilties & Net Worth | 100.0 | 100.0 |
| | | | | | | INCOME DATA | | |
| | 100.0 | 100.0 | 100.0 | 100.0 | | Net Sales | 100.0 | 100.0 |
| | | | | | | Gross Profit | | |
| | 87.4 | 90.0 | 90.9 | 91.4 | | Operating Expenses | 92.2 | 89.3 |
| | 12.6 | 10.0 | 9.1 | 8.6 | | Operating Profit | 7.8 | 10.7 |
| | 3.0 | 4.3 | 5.1 | -2.9 | | All Other Expenses (net) | 2.3 | 3.1 |
| | 9.6 | 5.7 | 4.0 | 11.5 | | Profit Before Taxes | 5.6 | 7.6 |
| | | | | | | RATIOS | | |
| | 8.9 | 6.6 | 4.7 | 4.1 | | | 6.8 | 5.4 |
| | 3.4 | 2.8 | 2.8 | 1.8 | | Current | 4.7 | 2.4 |
| | 1.2 | 1.1 | .9 | .9 | | | 1.5 | 1.0 |
| | 6.7 | 5.1 | 3.4 | 3.0 | | | 5.3 | 3.0 |
| | 1.7 | 1.7 | 1.3 | 1.6 | | Quick | 2.6 | 1.7 |
| | .6 | .7 | .4 | .7 | | | 1.0 | .7 |
| 0 UND | 7 53.8 | 4 98.6 | 0 UND | | | | 2 185.5 | 1 677.5 |
| 5 80.2 | 31 11.7 | 22 16.4 | 9 41.3 | | | Sales/Receivables | 22 16.9 | 21 17.8 |
| 22 16.3 | 55 6.6 | 61 6.0 | 22 16.4 | | | | 60 6.0 | 65 5.6 |
| | | | | | | Cost of Sales/Inventory | | |
| | | | | | | Cost of Sales/Payables | | |
| | .9 | 2.3 | 2.1 | 2.2 | | | 1.5 | 1.7 |
| | 5.8 | 5.6 | 3.8 | 6.9 | | Sales/Working Capital | 3.0 | 6.0 |
| | 224.0 | 56.5 | -17.2 | -171.9 | | | 12.1 | 116.9 |
| | 5.1 | 13.2 | 20.6 | 19.9 | | | 13.4 | 8.1 |
| (13) 2.3 | (44) 3.0 | (29) 2.9 | (10) 4.8 | | | EBIT/Interest | (33) 1.8 | (41) 1.2 |
| | .3 | .1 | -.1 | 1.6 | | | -.6 | -1.1 |
| | | | | | | Net Profit + Depr., Dep., Amort./Cur. Mat. L/T/D | | |
| | .0 | .7 | .2 | .7 | | | .2 | .2 |
| | 1.0 | 1.1 | .7 | 1.2 | | Fixed/Worth | .7 | .7 |
| | 2.4 | 2.8 | 1.3 | 4.2 | | | 1.3 | 1.4 |
| | .4 | .3 | .3 | .3 | | | .2 | .3 |
| | 1.1 | .9 | .6 | 1.5 | | Debt/Worth | .6 | .7 |
| | 3.6 | 3.0 | 2.2 | 4.2 | | | 1.7 | 1.8 |
| | 36.6 | 12.7 | 18.1 | 15.3 | | | 18.3 | 8.9 |
| (19) 5.4 | (53) 5.9 | (32) 4.2 | 7.7 | | | % Profit Before Taxes/Tangible Net Worth | (44) 4.1 | (65) 3.0 |
| | 1.7 | -2.2 | -3.7 | 3.9 | | | -.3 | -3.4 |
| | 11.7 | 7.1 | 9.9 | 6.4 | | | 8.2 | 5.6 |
| | 5.1 | 2.4 | 1.7 | 3.6 | | % Profit Before Taxes/Total Assets | 2.5 | 1.1 |
| | 1.2 | -1.1 | -1.7 | 1.3 | | | -1.0 | -2.0 |
| | 20.3 | 3.7 | 4.7 | 2.4 | | | 3.5 | 5.4 |
| | 1.6 | 1.0 | 1.2 | 1.0 | | Sales/Net Fixed Assets | 1.4 | 1.5 |
| | .4 | .5 | .4 | .3 | | | .4 | .5 |
| | 1.7 | 1.2 | .7 | .8 | | | 1.2 | .7 |
| | .4 | .5 | .4 | .4 | | Sales/Total Assets | .6 | .4 |
| | .2 | .3 | .2 | .2 | | | .2 | .3 |
| | 1.5 | 1.7 | 1.2 | 2.6 | | | 1.7 | 1.4 |
| (16) 6.2 | (54) 3.4 | (32) 2.2 | 8.4 | | | % Depr., Dep., Amort./Sales | (40) 3.1 | (52) 2.8 |
| | 14.2 | 7.4 | 11.3 | 11.0 | | | 12.0 | 7.4 |
| | | | | | | % Officers', Directors' Owners' Comp/Sales | | |
| 6353M | 34893M | 280188M | 371494M | 460558M | 236404M | Net Sales ($) | 299894M | 621131M |
| 876M | 25568M | 335082M | 646557M | 877508M | 632693M | Total Assets ($) | 553679M | 1288066M |

M = $ thousand     MM = $ million
See Pages 9 through 22 for Explanation of Ratios and Data

## Comparative Historical Data | Current Data Sorted by Sales

| 64 | 75 | 90 | Type of Statement | 15 | 18 | 13 | 19 | 14 | 11 |
|---|---|---|---|---|---|---|---|---|---|
| 1 | 2 | 1 | Unqualified | 1 | | | | | |
| | | 4 | Reviewed | 1 | | | | | |
| 2 | 3 | 5 | Compiled | 2 | 1 | 1 | | | |
| 32 | 36 | 35 | Tax Returns | 2 | 1 | | 2 | | |
| | | | Other | 8 | 9 | 2 | 7 | 5 | 4 |
| 4/1/09- | 4/1/10- | 4/1/11- | | | 94 (4/1-9/30/11) | | 41 (10/1/11-3/31/12) | | |
| 3/31/10 | 3/31/11 | 3/31/12 | | | | | | | |
| ALL | ALL | ALL | | 0-1MM | 1-3MM | 3-5MM | 5-10MM | 10-25MM | 25MM & OVER |
| 99 | 116 | 135 | **NUMBER OF STATEMENTS** | 28 | 29 | 16 | 28 | 19 | 15 |
| % | % | % | **ASSETS** | % | % | % | % | % | % |
| 11.1 | 15.6 | 14.3 | Cash & Equivalents | 11.6 | 14.9 | 11.1 | 17.9 | 6.7 | 24.4 |
| 9.0 | 10.1 | 9.6 | Trade Receivables (net) | 5.4 | 10.2 | 10.8 | 9.9 | 13.8 | 9.5 |
| 4.2 | 3.2 | 3.7 | Inventory | 8.0 | 2.1 | .8 | 5.6 | 1.8 | .9 |
| 4.8 | 3.5 | 3.5 | All Other Current | 4.0 | 1.6 | 5.0 | 2.7 | 4.6 | 5.0 |
| 29.1 | 32.4 | 31.2 | Total Current | 29.0 | 28.8 | 27.7 | 36.0 | 26.8 | 39.8 |
| 45.6 | 43.3 | 49.4 | Fixed Assets (net) | 55.9 | 59.0 | 41.8 | 39.4 | 52.4 | 41.7 |
| .6 | .9 | .6 | Intangibles (net) | .4 | .1 | 2.5 | .2 | 1.0 | .4 |
| 24.6 | 23.3 | 18.9 | All Other Non-Current | 15.0 | 12.1 | 27.9 | 24.3 | 19.8 | 18.0 |
| 100.0 | 100.0 | 100.0 | Total | 100.0 | 100.0 | 100.0 | 100.0 | 100.0 | 100.0 |
| | | | **LIABILITIES** | | | | | | |
| 3.2 | 2.2 | 2.5 | Notes Payable-Short Term | 3.2 | 3.3 | 2.2 | 1.6 | 2.5 | 1.4 |
| 2.3 | 3.1 | 1.7 | Cur. Mat.-L.T.D. | 1.2 | 2.1 | 1.4 | 2.1 | 1.7 | 1.6 |
| 4.0 | 3.5 | 3.2 | Trade Payables | 2.9 | 2.2 | 1.3 | 5.0 | 3.2 | 4.3 |
| .0 | .0 | .0 | Income Taxes Payable | .0 | .0 | .0 | .0 | .0 | .1 |
| 5.5 | 9.7 | 6.6 | All Other Current | 7.8 | 3.8 | 5.7 | 6.1 | 8.9 | 8.6 |
| 15.0 | 18.5 | 14.0 | Total Current | 15.1 | 11.5 | 10.6 | 14.8 | 16.3 | 16.0 |
| 33.7 | 26.5 | 33.1 | Long-Term Debt | 42.8 | 37.9 | 28.7 | 26.1 | 31.8 | 25.0 |
| .0 | .0 | .0 | Deferred Taxes | .0 | .0 | .0 | .0 | .0 | .0 |
| 3.1 | 5.0 | 5.2 | All Other Non-Current | 2.1 | 7.9 | 3.6 | 5.4 | 3.8 | 8.8 |
| 48.2 | 50.0 | 47.7 | Net Worth | 39.9 | 42.6 | 57.0 | 53.6 | 48.0 | 50.2 |
| 100.0 | 100.0 | 100.0 | Total Liabilities & Net Worth | 100.0 | 100.0 | 100.0 | 100.0 | 100.0 | 100.0 |
| | | | **INCOME DATA** | | | | | | |
| 100.0 | 100.0 | 100.0 | Net Sales | 100.0 | 100.0 | 100.0 | 100.0 | 100.0 | 100.0 |
| | | | Gross Profit | | | | | | |
| 90.2 | 89.6 | 90.5 | Operating Expenses | 83.8 | 89.8 | 95.5 | 89.1 | 98.0 | 91.8 |
| 9.8 | 10.4 | 9.5 | Operating Profit | 16.2 | 10.2 | 4.5 | 10.9 | 2.0 | 8.2 |
| 5.9 | 2.8 | 3.2 | All Other Expenses (net) | 8.3 | 2.6 | 6.2 | 1.2 | -.2 | -.1 |
| 4.0 | 7.6 | 6.3 | Profit Before Taxes | 7.9 | 7.6 | -1.7 | 9.7 | 2.2 | 8.3 |
| | | | **RATIOS** | | | | | | |
| 4.2 | 5.2 | 5.4 | | 5.2 | 6.8 | 6.7 | 6.1 | 3.4 | 5.4 |
| 2.2 | 2.1 | 2.6 | Current | 2.1 | 2.3 | 3.0 | 3.7 | 1.6 | 2.6 |
| 1.1 | 1.0 | 1.0 | | .5 | .9 | 1.2 | 1.1 | 1.0 | 1.8 |
| 2.8 | 3.9 | 4.2 | | 4.0 | 5.5 | 4.4 | 4.4 | 1.7 | 4.2 |
| 1.3 | 1.6 | 1.6 | Quick | .9 | 2.3 | 2.4 | 1.6 | 1.2 | 2.4 |
| .6 | .6 | .7 | | .3 | .7 | .9 | .9 | .6 | 1.2 |
| 3  123.8 | 3  117.7 | 2  197.0 | | 0  UND | 0  UND | 4  87.3 | 6  58.9 | 4  85.8 | 4  98.4 |
| 21  17.0 | 23  15.7 | 20  18.7 | Sales/Receivables | 7  53.0 | 23  16.2 | 41  8.8 | 20  17.9 | 31  11.8 | 11  33.7 |
| 49  7.4 | 50  7.3 | 49  7.4 | | 27  13.5 | 63  5.8 | 61  6.0 | 50  7.3 | 43  8.5 | 54  6.8 |
| | | | Cost of Sales/Inventory | | | | | | |
| | | | Cost of Sales/Payables | | | | | | |
| 1.9 | 1.8 | 1.9 | | 1.1 | 2.1 | 1.6 | 2.3 | 4.2 | 1.6 |
| 6.3 | 5.7 | 5.6 | Sales/Working Capital | 6.0 | 5.6 | 3.3 | 4.2 | 21.7 | 3.8 |
| 56.9 | UND | -482.8 | | -9.6 | -253.4 | 16.7 | 320.8 | -294.8 | 7.0 |
| 14.9 | 11.4 | 11.2 | | 5.3 | 18.2 | 5.0 | 41.1 | 6.0 | 26.2 |
| (62)  1.9 | (88)  2.9 | (105)  2.9 | EBIT/Interest | (18)  2.3 | (23)  6.8 | (15)  2.4 | (19)  3.2 | (16)  3.1 | (14)  7.0 |
| .0 | -.4 | .3 | | .4 | -.7 | -11.1 | .1 | -.3 | 1.6 |
| | | | Net Profit + Depr., Dep., Amort./Cur. Mat. L/T/D | | | | | | |
| .3 | .3 | .5 | | .5 | .7 | .2 | .1 | .8 | .3 |
| .9 | .8 | 1.0 | Fixed/Worth | 1.4 | 1.1 | .6 | .7 | 1.2 | .8 |
| 2.1 | 1.6 | 2.6 | | 3.7 | 4.2 | 2.9 | 1.5 | 2.4 | 1.4 |
| .3 | .3 | .4 | | .5 | .3 | .3 | .2 | .7 | .5 |
| 1.0 | .9 | .9 | Debt/Worth | 1.5 | .6 | .5 | 1.0 | 1.5 | .8 |
| 2.4 | 2.5 | 2.9 | | 4.3 | 4.5 | 3.5 | 2.5 | 2.2 | 3.1 |
| 9.7 | 15.1 | 17.2 | % Profit Before Taxes/Tangible Net Worth | 19.9 | 13.6 | 9.4 | 22.2 | 13.0 | 23.0 |
| (91)  3.4 | (109)  6.1 | (126)  5.8 | | (24)  4.2 | (26)  6.4 | (15)  5.9 | (27)  10.5 | 2.4 | 9.7 |
| -1.6 | -1.8 | -1.2 | | -3.0 | -1.9 | -6.8 | -.7 | -2.9 | 4.3 |
| 5.8 | 8.4 | 7.8 | % Profit Before Taxes/Total Assets | 7.4 | 9.0 | 6.6 | 12.8 | 5.3 | 8.4 |
| 1.6 | 2.6 | 3.6 | | 3.3 | 3.6 | 2.2 | 6.4 | 1.2 | 5.2 |
| -.8 | -1.5 | -.6 | | -1.0 | -1.1 | -5.9 | -.3 | -1.7 | 2.0 |
| 4.4 | 5.2 | 5.6 | | 4.7 | 1.5 | 10.6 | 11.6 | 5.2 | 7.3 |
| 1.4 | 1.8 | 1.2 | Sales/Net Fixed Assets | .6 | .7 | .9 | 2.4 | 2.5 | 2.2 |
| .6 | .5 | .4 | | .2 | .4 | .4 | 1.0 | .5 | 1.4 |
| .9 | 1.1 | 1.1 | | .6 | .6 | .6 | 1.3 | 1.9 | 1.3 |
| .5 | .5 | .5 | Sales/Total Assets | .3 | .3 | .4 | .8 | 1.2 | 1.0 |
| .2 | .3 | .3 | | .2 | .2 | .2 | .4 | .3 | .5 |
| 1.4 | 1.0 | 1.5 | | 2.6 | 1.6 | 1.5 | .8 | 1.2 | 1.5 |
| (84)  3.6 | (106)  3.1 | (124)  3.6 | % Depr., Dep., Amort./Sales | (23)  6.9 | (27)  4.4 | (14)  3.5 | (26)  2.3 | 2.4 | 3.7 |
| 8.6 | 7.8 | 9.5 | | 21.1 | 9.7 | 9.3 | 3.9 | 9.0 | 9.2 |
| | 3.9 | 6.5 | % Officers', Directors' Owners' Comp/Sales | | | | | | |
| | (12)  6.6 | (15)  14.2 | | | | | | | |
| | 13.6 | 31.2 | | | | | | | |
| 1015670M | 1003842M | 1389890M | Net Sales ($) | 14706M | 53480M | 64683M | 195955M | 286274M | 774792M |
| 1967712M | 1993183M | 2518284M | Total Assets ($) | 58160M | 176197M | 252281M | 389860M | 627911M | 1013875M |

© RMA 2012

**M = $ thousand    MM = $ million**
See Pages 9 through 22 for Explanation of Ratios and Data

## Current Data Sorted by Assets | Comparative Historical Data

| 0-500M | 500M-2MM | 2-10MM | 10-50MM | 50-100MM | 100-250MM | | 4/1/07-3/31/08 ALL | 4/1/08-3/31/09 ALL |
|---|---|---|---|---|---|---|---|---|
| | | | | | | **Type of Statement** | | |
| 3 | 17 | 83 | 72 | 11 | 6 | Unqualified | 188 | 199 |
| | 3 | 2 | 1 | | | Reviewed | 9 | 6 |
| | 5 | 5 | 1 | | | Compiled | 5 | 2 |
| 2 | 4 | 2 | | | | Tax Returns | 11 | 10 |
| 9 | 7 | 31 | 24 | 2 | 1 | Other | 50 | 81 |
| | 173 (4/1-9/30/11) | | 118 (10/1/11-3/31/12) | | | | | |
| 14 | 36 | 123 | 98 | 13 | 7 | **NUMBER OF STATEMENTS** | 263 | 298 |
| % | % | % | % | % | % | **ASSETS** | % | % |
| 32.9 | 23.6 | 20.4 | 18.6 | 12.3 | | Cash & Equivalents | 18.1 | 19.1 |
| 18.1 | 25.1 | 21.7 | 16.5 | 12.8 | | Trade Receivables (net) | 19.3 | 18.6 |
| .0 | 2.8 | 3.5 | 3.2 | 4.9 | | Inventory | 3.3 | 3.1 |
| 4.4 | 1.9 | 3.2 | 2.5 | 5.5 | | All Other Current | 2.8 | 3.5 |
| 55.4 | 53.5 | 48.8 | 40.7 | 35.5 | | Total Current | 43.6 | 44.1 |
| 21.1 | 36.9 | 42.7 | 48.4 | 47.8 | | Fixed Assets (net) | 45.1 | 44.8 |
| 11.0 | 3.4 | 1.2 | .9 | .6 | | Intangibles (net) | 1.5 | 1.4 |
| 12.0 | 6.2 | 7.3 | 9.9 | 16.1 | | All Other Non-Current | 9.8 | 9.7 |
| 100.0 | 100.0 | 100.0 | 100.0 | 100.0 | | Total | 100.0 | 100.0 |
| | | | | | | **LIABILITIES** | | |
| 9.7 | 10.7 | 4.6 | 1.7 | 2.2 | | Notes Payable-Short Term | 4.2 | 4.8 |
| .7 | 4.9 | 2.1 | 1.8 | 1.7 | | Cur. Mat.-L.T.D. | 2.3 | 1.8 |
| 13.5 | 5.1 | 6.2 | 6.7 | 8.7 | | Trade Payables | 6.6 | 6.5 |
| .7 | .0 | .0 | .0 | .0 | | Income Taxes Payable | .1 | .2 |
| 33.7 | 16.7 | 11.8 | 10.4 | 7.5 | | All Other Current | 12.5 | 12.8 |
| 58.2 | 37.4 | 24.7 | 20.6 | 20.1 | | Total Current | 25.7 | 26.1 |
| 31.4 | 16.6 | 18.6 | 19.4 | 23.2 | | Long-Term Debt | 19.3 | 17.3 |
| .0 | .0 | .0 | .0 | .0 | | Deferred Taxes | .0 | .1 |
| 6.5 | 6.2 | 4.9 | 2.5 | 5.1 | | All Other Non-Current | 3.4 | 3.2 |
| 3.9 | 39.8 | 51.9 | 57.5 | 51.6 | | Net Worth | 51.5 | 53.4 |
| 100.0 | 100.0 | 100.0 | 100.0 | 100.0 | | Total Liabilities & Net Worth | 100.0 | 100.0 |
| | | | | | | **INCOME DATA** | | |
| 100.0 | 100.0 | 100.0 | 100.0 | 100.0 | | Net Sales | 100.0 | 100.0 |
| | | | | | | Gross Profit | | |
| 98.6 | 94.6 | 95.5 | 95.4 | 96.8 | | Operating Expenses | 96.2 | 96.8 |
| 1.4 | 5.4 | 4.5 | 4.6 | 3.2 | | Operating Profit | 3.8 | 3.2 |
| .7 | 1.7 | .8 | .2 | .2 | | All Other Expenses (net) | .6 | 1.1 |
| .7 | 3.7 | 3.8 | 4.4 | 3.0 | | Profit Before Taxes | 3.2 | 2.1 |
| | | | | | | **RATIOS** | | |
| 5.7 | 3.9 | 3.7 | 3.6 | 3.3 | | | 3.2 | 3.6 |
| 1.0 | 1.7 | 2.4 | 2.6 | 1.9 | | Current | 1.9 | 2.0 |
| .5 | .9 | 1.4 | 1.5 | 1.3 | | | 1.1 | 1.3 |
| 5.7 | 3.5 | 3.4 | 3.1 | 2.0 | | | 2.7 | 3.1 |
| .9 | 1.7 | 2.0 | 2.1 | 1.4 | | Quick | 1.6 | 1.6 |
| .4 | .9 | 1.0 | 1.3 | .8 | | | 1.0 | 1.0 |
| 0  UND | 20  18.3 | 12  31.3 | 12  30.2 | 10  37.3 | | | 15  24.1 | 15  24.2 |
| 18  20.6 | 31  11.6 | 34  10.6 | 32  11.4 | 22  16.8 | | Sales/Receivables | 33  11.1 | 32  11.3 |
| 38  9.7 | 47  7.8 | 48  7.6 | 48  7.6 | 52  7.0 | | | 47  7.7 | 45  8.1 |
| | | | | | | Cost of Sales/Inventory | | |
| | | | | | | Cost of Sales/Payables | | |
| 11.3 | 4.5 | 4.2 | 3.8 | 4.2 | | | 4.8 | 4.6 |
| NM | 14.0 | 8.7 | 6.9 | 7.7 | | Sales/Working Capital | 10.7 | 9.7 |
| -9.5 | -70.2 | 20.9 | 17.9 | 23.7 | | | 53.7 | 32.1 |
| | 8.2 | 8.6 | 10.2 | 29.0 | | | 10.1 | 7.4 |
| | (23)  2.5 | (101)  3.8 | (82)  4.3 | (11)  5.5 | | EBIT/Interest | (208)  3.7 | (244)  2.2 |
| | -1.2 | 1.0 | 1.8 | 3.2 | | | 1.2 | -.7 |
| | | | | | | Net Profit + Depr., Dep., Amort./Cur. Mat. L/T/D | | |
| .0 | .4 | .3 | .6 | .7 | | | .5 | .5 |
| .4 | 1.2 | .9 | .9 | 1.1 | | Fixed/Worth | .9 | .9 |
| NM | 18.0 | 1.3 | 1.2 | 1.5 | | | 1.5 | 1.3 |
| 1.0 | .3 | .5 | .4 | .5 | | | .4 | .4 |
| 8.0 | 2.0 | .8 | .7 | .9 | | Debt/Worth | .9 | .7 |
| -4.1 | 81.2 | 1.8 | 1.2 | 1.6 | | | 1.7 | 1.5 |
| | 70.6 | 17.3 | 15.3 | 19.1 | | | 14.7 | 12.6 |
| | (29)  7.9 | (118)  7.2 | (97)  6.8 | 10.4 | | % Profit Before Taxes/Tangible Net Worth | (251)  6.5 | (289)  3.7 |
| | -6.4 | -1.5 | 2.0 | 4.9 | | | .5 | -3.2 |
| 12.8 | 16.1 | 9.3 | 8.8 | 8.2 | | | 7.6 | 7.4 |
| -5.1 | 3.0 | 4.1 | 4.0 | 4.7 | | % Profit Before Taxes/Total Assets | 3.2 | 1.8 |
| -20.3 | -4.2 | -.7 | .9 | 1.6 | | | .2 | -2.0 |
| UND | 65.0 | 22.7 | 4.8 | 6.5 | | | 10.6 | 10.0 |
| 38.5 | 7.9 | 4.3 | 2.7 | 2.6 | | Sales/Net Fixed Assets | 3.3 | 3.2 |
| 14.5 | 2.7 | 1.8 | 1.8 | 1.5 | | | 1.9 | 1.9 |
| 11.1 | 3.7 | 2.9 | 2.0 | 1.8 | | | 2.5 | 2.5 |
| 4.2 | 2.1 | 1.7 | 1.4 | 1.3 | | Sales/Total Assets | 1.6 | 1.6 |
| 2.1 | 1.5 | 1.0 | .9 | .8 | | | 1.1 | 1.0 |
| | .4 | 1.2 | 1.9 | 1.9 | | | 1.6 | 1.4 |
| | (33)  2.0 | (108)  2.6 | (94)  2.9 | 4.1 | | % Depr., Dep., Amort./Sales | (242)  2.9 | (270)  2.7 |
| | 3.8 | 4.1 | 4.0 | 5.0 | | | 4.2 | 4.1 |
| | | | | | | | 3.9 | 5.3 |
| | | | | | | % Officers', Directors' Owners' Comp/Sales | (28)  9.1 | (33)  7.7 |
| | | | | | | | 34.4 | 31.9 |
| 15866M | 125585M | 1454021M | 3613417M | 1056824M | 4448400M | Net Sales ($) | 6328351M | 6757440M |
| 2851M | 44537M | 656811M | 2100586M | 793680M | 1131551M | Total Assets ($) | 3845222M | 4322266M |

M = $ thousand    MM = $ million
See Pages 9 through 22 for Explanation of Ratios and Data

## Comparative Historical Data | | Type of Statement | Current Data Sorted by Sales

| Comp 1 | Comp 2 | Comp 3 | Type of Statement | 0-1MM | 1-3MM | 3-5MM | 5-10MM | 10-25MM | 25MM & OVER |
|---|---|---|---|---|---|---|---|---|---|
| 159 | 190 | 192 | Unqualified | 6 | 20 | 18 | 29 | 56 | 63 |
| 3 | 4 | 6 | Reviewed | | 1 | 2 | | 2 | 1 |
| 8 | 4 | 11 | Compiled | | | 4 | 4 | 2 | 1 |
| 11 | 7 | 8 | Tax Returns | 2 | 3 | 1 | 1 | 1 | |
| 80 | 77 | 74 | Other | 7 | 12 | 3 | 12 | 19 | 21 |
| 4/1/09-3/31/10 ALL | 4/1/10-3/31/11 ALL | 4/1/11-3/31/12 ALL | | 173 (4/1-9/30/11) | | | 118 (10/1/11-3/31/12) | | |
| 261 | 282 | 291 | NUMBER OF STATEMENTS | 15 | 40 | 28 | 44 | 78 | 86 |
| % | % | % | ASSETS | % | % | % | % | % | % |
| 19.0 | 19.9 | 20.2 | Cash & Equivalents | 20.7 | 25.8 | 22.5 | 18.0 | 21.2 | 16.9 |
| 20.3 | 19.4 | 19.8 | Trade Receivables (net) | 7.1 | 14.5 | 17.7 | 22.8 | 18.0 | 25.4 |
| 4.1 | 3.1 | 3.2 | Inventory | .0 | 2.9 | 1.9 | 3.0 | 4.7 | 3.0 |
| 3.4 | 2.7 | 2.4 | All Other Current | .5 | 3.9 | 1.5 | 1.5 | 2.7 | 4.9 |
| 46.8 | 45.1 | 46.3 | Total Current | 28.2 | 47.1 | 43.5 | 45.4 | 46.7 | 50.2 |
| 42.1 | 43.8 | 42.9 | Fixed Assets (net) | 49.1 | 43.7 | 48.1 | 41.8 | 44.8 | 38.6 |
| 1.2 | 1.5 | 1.8 | Intangibles (net) | 5.8 | 2.1 | .4 | 4.7 | .6 | 1.1 |
| 9.9 | 9.6 | 8.9 | All Other Non-Current | 16.4 | 7.1 | 8.0 | 8.0 | 7.9 | 10.2 |
| 100.0 | 100.0 | 100.0 | Total | 100.0 | 100.0 | 100.0 | 100.0 | 100.0 | 100.0 |
| | | | LIABILITIES | | | | | | |
| 5.6 | 3.5 | 4.4 | Notes Payable-Short Term | 6.7 | 6.7 | 2.6 | 8.4 | 2.4 | 3.4 |
| 2.2 | 2.1 | 2.2 | Cur. Mat.-L.T.D. | 1.4 | 3.9 | 3.6 | 2.1 | 1.8 | 1.6 |
| 7.8 | 6.7 | 6.8 | Trade Payables | 12.2 | 3.2 | 1.9 | 5.8 | 6.0 | 10.4 |
| .1 | .1 | .1 | Income Taxes Payable | .0 | .2 | .1 | .1 | .0 | .0 |
| 13.0 | 11.9 | 13.3 | All Other Current | 7.7 | 14.5 | 11.4 | 9.9 | 13.2 | 16.1 |
| 28.7 | 24.3 | 26.8 | Total Current | 28.0 | 28.6 | 19.7 | 26.3 | 23.4 | 31.6 |
| 17.4 | 19.0 | 19.3 | Long-Term Debt | 47.5 | 21.4 | 19.9 | 17.9 | 16.6 | 16.2 |
| .0 | .0 | .0 | Deferred Taxes | .0 | .0 | .0 | .0 | .0 | .0 |
| 3.7 | 3.7 | 4.4 | All Other Non-Current | .9 | 4.1 | 6.4 | 6.2 | 4.7 | 3.3 |
| 50.2 | 53.0 | 49.5 | Net Worth | 23.7 | 46.0 | 54.0 | 49.6 | 55.3 | 48.8 |
| 100.0 | 100.0 | 100.0 | Total Liabilities & Net Worth | 100.0 | 100.0 | 100.0 | 100.0 | 100.0 | 100.0 |
| | | | INCOME DATA | | | | | | |
| 100.0 | 100.0 | 100.0 | Net Sales | 100.0 | 100.0 | 100.0 | 100.0 | 100.0 | 100.0 |
| | | | Gross Profit | | | | | | |
| 96.6 | 95.8 | 95.6 | Operating Expenses | 88.2 | 93.5 | 95.9 | 96.2 | 96.5 | 96.7 |
| 3.4 | 4.2 | 4.4 | Operating Profit | 11.8 | 6.5 | 4.1 | 3.8 | 3.5 | 3.3 |
| 1.0 | .9 | .6 | All Other Expenses (net) | 4.6 | 1.6 | .9 | -.1 | .3 | .1 |
| 2.4 | 3.3 | 3.8 | Profit Before Taxes | 7.2 | 5.0 | 3.2 | 3.9 | 3.2 | 3.2 |
| | | | RATIOS | | | | | | |
| 3.3 | 3.6 | 3.6 | | 7.7 | 6.7 | 4.9 | 4.1 | 3.7 | 3.0 |
| 1.9 | 2.2 | 2.2 | Current | 1.7 | 2.5 | 2.8 | 2.4 | 2.4 | 1.8 |
| 1.2 | 1.4 | 1.3 | | .6 | 1.0 | 1.6 | 1.2 | 1.4 | 1.2 |
| 2.7 | 3.2 | 3.2 | | 7.6 | 5.3 | 4.5 | 3.3 | 3.2 | 2.4 |
| 1.5 | 1.8 | 1.8 | Quick | 1.6 | 2.1 | 2.6 | 2.0 | 1.9 | 1.5 |
| 1.0 | 1.2 | 1.0 | | .5 | .4 | 1.4 | 1.0 | 1.0 | 1.1 |
| 14  26.2 | 15  24.0 | 11  33.1 | | 0  UND | 7  53.1 | 7  54.8 | 24  15.2 | 10  35.2 | 13  27.8 |
| 31  11.6 | 33  11.0 | 32  11.3 | Sales/Receivables | 11  33.2 | 29  12.8 | 33  10.9 | 36  10.0 | 33  11.1 | 33  10.9 |
| 53  6.9 | 50  7.3 | 48  7.6 | | 29  12.7 | 37  9.8 | 64  5.7 | 52  7.0 | 46  8.0 | 52  7.0 |
| | | | Cost of Sales/Inventory | | | | | | |
| | | | Cost of Sales/Payables | | | | | | |
| 5.0 | 4.7 | 4.2 | | 3.5 | 2.8 | 2.6 | 4.5 | 4.1 | 6.3 |
| 11.6 | 8.7 | 8.9 | Sales/Working Capital | 12.1 | 8.3 | 6.4 | 8.9 | 7.8 | 11.2 |
| 30.1 | 19.8 | 31.4 | | -16.9 | -137.6 | 14.0 | 23.9 | 19.8 | 31.8 |
| 13.2 | 10.3 | 9.8 | | | 6.7 | 5.4 | 15.2 | 13.7 | 11.4 |
| (216)  3.5 | (227)  4.1 | (229)  3.9 | EBIT/Interest | (30)  2.1 | (20)  3.0 | (39)  3.9 | (63)  5.0 | (72)  5.0 | |
| -.5 | 1.0 | 1.3 | | | -.4 | -4.1 | 1.0 | 1.9 | 2.2 |
| | | | Net Profit + Depr., Dep., Amort./Cur. Mat. L/T/D | | | | | | |
| .4 | .4 | .4 | | .3 | .1 | .6 | .5 | .4 | .4 |
| .8 | .9 | .9 | Fixed/Worth | 1.5 | 1.0 | .9 | 1.0 | .8 | .8 |
| 1.4 | 1.4 | 1.4 | | 5.7 | 2.2 | 1.6 | 1.5 | 1.2 | 1.2 |
| .4 | .4 | .4 | | .3 | .2 | .5 | .5 | .3 | .5 |
| .9 | .8 | .8 | Debt/Worth | 2.7 | 1.0 | .7 | .8 | .6 | 1.0 |
| 2.4 | 1.7 | 1.9 | | 38.0 | 3.7 | 1.6 | 1.7 | 1.4 | 1.7 |
| 17.9 | 16.9 | 17.1 | | 57.1 | 16.3 | 14.4 | 18.7 | 16.1 | 17.4 |
| (249)  6.6 | (269)  7.2 | (272)  7.5 | % Profit Before Taxes/Tangible Net Worth | (12)  .9 | (35)  5.8 | (27)  6.9 | (40)  7.0 | (74)  7.0 | (84)  10.5 |
| -3.5 | .2 | .0 | | -10.8 | -4.9 | -2.8 | .0 | 1.7 | 1.6 |
| 9.4 | 9.0 | 9.5 | | 7.3 | 9.9 | 8.6 | 11.8 | 9.4 | 8.7 |
| 3.1 | 3.9 | 3.9 | % Profit Before Taxes/Total Assets | .0 | 1.3 | 3.2 | 4.6 | 4.7 | 4.8 |
| -2.2 | .1 | -.1 | | -5.8 | -3.9 | -2.1 | .1 | 1.0 | .5 |
| 16.5 | 10.8 | 13.7 | | 40.7 | 55.5 | 8.0 | 15.2 | 7.6 | 16.4 |
| 3.6 | 3.5 | 3.9 | Sales/Net Fixed Assets | 2.1 | 2.7 | 2.5 | 3.5 | 3.8 | 4.0 |
| 2.0 | 1.8 | 1.9 | | .2 | .9 | 1.6 | 1.8 | 2.2 | 2.5 |
| 2.6 | 2.5 | 2.7 | | 3.5 | 2.4 | 2.3 | 2.4 | 2.6 | 3.5 |
| 1.6 | 1.6 | 1.6 | Sales/Total Assets | .8 | 1.3 | 1.3 | 1.5 | 1.7 | 1.9 |
| 1.1 | 1.0 | 1.0 | | .2 | .6 | .9 | 1.1 | 1.1 | 1.3 |
| 1.4 | 1.6 | 1.4 | | .4 | 1.0 | 1.5 | 1.8 | 1.5 | 1.3 |
| (228)  2.6 | (254)  2.8 | (260)  2.7 | % Depr., Dep., Amort./Sales | (11)  14.0 | (33)  3.5 | (25)  3.3 | (39)  2.9 | (73)  2.6 | (79)  2.4 |
| 4.0 | 4.0 | 4.1 | | 25.8 | 6.1 | 4.7 | 3.9 | 3.8 | 3.4 |
| 2.2 | 5.0 | 3.3 | % Officers', Directors' Owners' Comp/Sales | | | | | | |
| (34)  3.8 | (26)  9.3 | (24)  9.7 | | | | | | | |
| 8.8 | 19.3 | 29.6 | | | | | | | |
| 8433012M | 8532590M | 10714113M | Net Sales ($) | 8048M | 80605M | 111058M | 333512M | 1306631M | 8874259M |
| 4405106M | 4727261M | 4730016M | Total Assets ($) | 17752M | 99393M | 105690M | 226211M | 899886M | 3381084M |

## Current Data Sorted by Assets     Comparative Historical Data

| 0-500M | 500M-2MM | 2-10MM | 10-50MM | 50-100MM | 100-250MM | Type of Statement | | 4/1/07-3/31/08 ALL | 4/1/08-3/31/09 ALL |
|---|---|---|---|---|---|---|---|---|---|
| 2 | 19 | 47 | 23 | 2 | | Unqualified | | 78 | 76 |
| 4 | 4 | 9 | 3 | | | Reviewed | | 8 | 9 |
| 37 | 15 | 15 | 1 | 1 | | Compiled | | 44 | 42 |
| 184 | 81 | 28 | | | 1 | Tax Returns | | 177 | 173 |
| 112 | 71 | 50 | 5 | 1 | 1 | Other | | 111 | 139 |
| | 142 (4/1-9/30/11) | | 574 (10/1/11-3/31/12) | | | | | | |
| 339 | 190 | 149 | 32 | 4 | 2 | NUMBER OF STATEMENTS | | 418 | 439 |
| % | % | % | % | % | % | ASSETS | | % | % |
| 29.7 | 14.3 | 11.7 | 14.3 | | | Cash & Equivalents | | 19.5 | 22.8 |
| 4.6 | 4.6 | 10.0 | 9.0 | | | Trade Receivables (net) | | 8.8 | 7.9 |
| .3 | .1 | .4 | .1 | | | Inventory | | .5 | .3 |
| 2.5 | 3.4 | 2.0 | 2.9 | | | All Other Current | | 3.8 | 3.4 |
| 37.2 | 22.4 | 24.1 | 26.3 | | | Total Current | | 32.6 | 34.3 |
| 39.8 | 62.6 | 64.6 | 59.1 | | | Fixed Assets (net) | | 50.0 | 49.0 |
| 9.3 | 6.6 | 3.5 | 2.7 | | | Intangibles (net) | | 7.4 | 6.7 |
| 13.7 | 8.5 | 7.7 | 11.9 | | | All Other Non-Current | | 10.0 | 10.0 |
| 100.0 | 100.0 | 100.0 | 100.0 | | | Total | | 100.0 | 100.0 |
| | | | | | | LIABILITIES | | | |
| 13.0 | 4.5 | 2.5 | .9 | | | Notes Payable-Short Term | | 5.9 | 8.4 |
| 5.4 | 3.4 | 3.9 | 3.4 | | | Cur. Mat.-L.T.D. | | 5.1 | 5.0 |
| 4.3 | 3.0 | 4.8 | 6.2 | | | Trade Payables | | 6.0 | 5.9 |
| .1 | .1 | .0 | .2 | | | Income Taxes Payable | | .1 | .2 |
| 30.4 | 7.7 | 6.8 | 9.5 | | | All Other Current | | 16.6 | 15.9 |
| 53.3 | 18.7 | 18.0 | 20.4 | | | Total Current | | 33.7 | 35.4 |
| 28.7 | 53.5 | 42.3 | 31.1 | | | Long-Term Debt | | 40.1 | 37.9 |
| .0 | .0 | .2 | .2 | | | Deferred Taxes | | .1 | .0 |
| 25.0 | 7.9 | 4.2 | 8.2 | | | All Other Non-Current | | 8.4 | 9.1 |
| -6.9 | 19.8 | 35.3 | 40.1 | | | Net Worth | | 17.8 | 17.6 |
| 100.0 | 100.0 | 100.0 | 100.0 | | | Total Liabilties & Net Worth | | 100.0 | 100.0 |
| | | | | | | INCOME DATA | | | |
| 100.0 | 100.0 | 100.0 | 100.0 | | | Net Sales | | 100.0 | 100.0 |
| | | | | | | Gross Profit | | | |
| 93.6 | 82.3 | 84.5 | 93.6 | | | Operating Expenses | | 89.4 | 90.7 |
| 6.4 | 17.7 | 15.5 | 6.4 | | | Operating Profit | | 10.6 | 9.3 |
| 1.1 | 8.9 | 9.2 | 1.7 | | | All Other Expenses (net) | | 3.7 | 4.4 |
| 5.3 | 8.8 | 6.4 | 4.7 | | | Profit Before Taxes | | 7.0 | 4.9 |
| | | | | | | RATIOS | | | |
| 3.9 | 2.6 | 2.5 | 1.9 | | | | | 2.9 | 3.4 |
| 1.0 | 1.1 | 1.2 | 1.3 | | | Current | | 1.2 | 1.3 |
| .3 | .4 | .4 | .7 | | | | | .5 | .4 |
| 3.3 | 2.3 | 2.3 | 1.8 | | | | | 2.5 | 3.1 |
| (338) .9 | (188) .8 | 1.1 | 1.1 | | | Quick | | 1.1 | 1.1 |
| .3 | .3 | .3 | .6 | | | | | .3 | .3 |
| 0 UND | 0 UND | 0 UND | 4 86.6 | | | | | 0 UND | 0 UND |
| 0 UND | 0 UND | 5 74.5 | 17 21.9 | | | Sales/Receivables | | 0 UND | 0 UND |
| 0 UND | 8 47.2 | 22 16.6 | 32 11.5 | | | | | 16 22.5 | 10 35.5 |
| | | | | | | Cost of Sales/Inventory | | | |
| | | | | | | Cost of Sales/Payables | | | |
| 23.7 | 12.6 | 9.0 | 9.4 | | | | | 12.6 | 12.1 |
| 956.0 | 245.0 | 48.5 | 38.9 | | | Sales/Working Capital | | 87.5 | 78.0 |
| -23.8 | -18.5 | -13.5 | -26.6 | | | | | -18.7 | -25.6 |
| 27.8 | 6.7 | 7.3 | 7.6 | | | | | 11.5 | 10.0 |
| (208) 8.0 | (140) 2.2 | (103) 2.4 | (28) 4.4 | | | EBIT/Interest | | (286) 3.7 | (300) 3.1 |
| 1.0 | .9 | 1.0 | 1.1 | | | | | 1.2 | 1.1 |
| | | | | | | Net Profit + Depr., Dep., | | 11.8 | 7.9 |
| | | | | | | Amort./Cur. Mat. L/T/D | | (16) 4.5 | (20) 1.9 |
| | | | | | | | | 2.1 | .5 |
| .4 | 1.3 | .8 | 1.1 | | | | | .6 | .5 |
| 1.7 | 4.7 | 2.0 | 1.5 | | | Fixed/Worth | | 1.6 | 1.7 |
| -.9 | -6.1 | 32.7 | 2.4 | | | | | -10.3 | -22.7 |
| .4 | 1.3 | .7 | .9 | | | | | .6 | .7 |
| 3.4 | 6.4 | 2.1 | 1.6 | | | Debt/Worth | | 2.6 | 2.6 |
| -2.8 | -9.1 | 35.4 | 2.9 | | | | | -11.9 | -11.4 |
| 218.7 | 76.1 | 28.8 | 24.8 | | | % Profit Before Taxes/Tangible | | 108.0 | 93.4 |
| (203) 68.1 | (121) 22.6 | (120) 9.0 | (30) 9.9 | | | Net Worth | | (296) 29.0 | (314) 23.9 |
| 15.3 | 1.8 | .3 | -.9 | | | | | 6.0 | 3.9 |
| 65.4 | 13.0 | 8.0 | 8.5 | | | % Profit Before Taxes/Total | | 37.0 | 26.7 |
| 22.2 | 5.5 | 2.7 | 4.7 | | | Assets | | 8.8 | 5.9 |
| 2.1 | .0 | -.4 | .0 | | | | | .9 | -.3 |
| 67.3 | 12.0 | 6.4 | 4.5 | | | | | 28.1 | 34.3 |
| 23.2 | 1.9 | 1.3 | 2.5 | | | Sales/Net Fixed Assets | | 8.7 | 9.0 |
| 9.9 | .8 | .5 | 1.5 | | | | | 1.7 | 1.7 |
| 11.3 | 2.3 | 2.3 | 2.7 | | | | | 6.0 | 6.8 |
| 6.7 | 1.3 | .9 | 1.5 | | | Sales/Total Assets | | 3.2 | 3.2 |
| 4.0 | .7 | .4 | .8 | | | | | 1.2 | 1.0 |
| .7 | 1.4 | 1.6 | 1.7 | | | | | 1.0 | 1.1 |
| (203) 1.5 | (150) 3.0 | (125) 3.8 | 2.7 | | | % Depr., Dep., Amort./Sales | | (316) 2.2 | (333) 2.2 |
| 2.7 | 7.2 | 8.8 | 4.4 | | | | | 4.1 | 4.5 |
| 2.6 | 3.9 | 2.9 | | | | % Officers', Directors' | | 2.6 | 2.7 |
| (177) 5.2 | (66) 5.9 | (21) 4.1 | | | | Owners' Comp/Sales | | (163) 5.9 | (179) 4.8 |
| 8.6 | 10.7 | 10.2 | | | | | | 10.6 | 8.3 |
| 373561M | 383892M | 1143444M | 974003M | 287932M | 404701M | Net Sales ($) | | 2896137M | 2981409M |
| 61112M | 204075M | 624221M | 603472M | 314253M | 229001M | Total Assets ($) | | 1401519M | 1721672M |

M = $ thousand    MM = $ million
See Pages 9 through 22 for Explanation of Ratios and Data

| | **Comparative Historical Data** | | | **Type of Statement** | **Current Data Sorted by Sales** | | | | | |
|---|---|---|---|---|---|---|---|---|---|---|
| | 92 | 96 | 93 | Unqualified | 4 | 16 | 12 | 15 | 25 | 21 |
| | 27 | 10 | 20 | Reviewed | 3 | 4 | 1 | 6 | 4 | 2 |
| | 55 | 59 | 69 | Compiled | 27 | 31 | 3 | 6 | 2 | |
| | 201 | 236 | 294 | Tax Returns | 140 | 134 | 11 | 8 | | 1 |
| | 171 | 223 | 240 | Other | 108 | 87 | 17 | | 9 | 5 |
| | 4/1/09-3/31/10 ALL | 4/1/10-3/31/11 ALL | 4/1/11-3/31/12 ALL | | 142 (4/1-9/30/11) | | | 574 (10/1/11-3/31/12) | | |
| | | | | | 0-1MM | 1-3MM | 3-5MM | 5-10MM | 10-25MM | 25MM & OVER |
| **NUMBER OF STATEMENTS** | 546 | 624 | 716 | | 282 | 272 | 44 | 49 | 40 | 29 |
| | % | % | % | **ASSETS** | % | % | % | % | % | % |
| Cash & Equivalents | 20.9 | 22.3 | 21.1 | | 18.9 | 23.8 | 23.1 | 17.6 | 20.0 | 21.1 |
| Trade Receivables (net) | 8.0 | 7.5 | 5.9 | | 3.7 | 3.3 | 11.3 | 11.4 | 17.8 | 18.8 |
| Inventory | .3 | .3 | .2 | | .2 | .2 | .1 | .2 | .6 | .1 |
| All Other Current | 2.5 | 2.7 | 2.7 | | 2.4 | 2.2 | 4.8 | 2.7 | 4.5 | 2.9 |
| Total Current | 31.7 | 32.7 | 29.9 | | 25.3 | 29.5 | 39.2 | 31.9 | 42.9 | 42.9 |
| Fixed Assets (net) | 50.8 | 49.8 | 51.8 | | 56.8 | 50.2 | 46.1 | 55.5 | 43.2 | 32.9 |
| Intangibles (net) | 7.0 | 7.1 | 7.4 | | 7.4 | 8.7 | 4.8 | 1.2 | 7.3 | 9.1 |
| All Other Non-Current | 10.5 | 10.5 | 10.9 | | 10.5 | 11.6 | 9.9 | 11.4 | 6.6 | 15.1 |
| Total | 100.0 | 100.0 | 100.0 | | 100.0 | 100.0 | 100.0 | 100.0 | 100.0 | 100.0 |
| | | | | **LIABILITIES** | | | | | | |
| Notes Payable-Short Term | 6.2 | 7.7 | 8.0 | | 9.3 | 8.7 | 3.8 | 3.3 | 7.6 | 2.2 |
| Cur. Mat.-L.T.D. | 5.3 | 2.7 | 4.5 | | 5.3 | 4.4 | 2.6 | 4.5 | 1.9 | 3.1 |
| Trade Payables | 4.9 | 5.1 | 4.1 | | 2.2 | 4.0 | 4.5 | 5.3 | 9.0 | 14.3 |
| Income Taxes Payable | .0 | .1 | .1 | | .0 | .1 | .0 | .4 | .0 | .3 |
| All Other Current | 22.4 | 15.9 | 18.3 | | 21.0 | 19.1 | 13.6 | 12.6 | 11.0 | 11.6 |
| Total Current | 38.8 | 31.5 | 35.0 | | 37.9 | 36.4 | 24.6 | 26.0 | 29.6 | 31.6 |
| Long-Term Debt | 37.4 | 38.8 | 38.2 | | 47.4 | 37.9 | 31.7 | 22.9 | 19.2 | 13.6 |
| Deferred Taxes | .1 | .1 | .1 | | .0 | .0 | .0 | .5 | .1 | .3 |
| All Other Non-Current | 9.8 | 13.1 | 15.4 | | 21.4 | 13.1 | 6.6 | 9.0 | 5.6 | 15.7 |
| Net Worth | 14.0 | 16.5 | 11.4 | | -6.7 | 12.7 | 37.1 | 41.6 | 45.6 | 38.8 |
| Total Liabilities & Net Worth | 100.0 | 100.0 | 100.0 | | 100.0 | 100.0 | 100.0 | 100.0 | 100.0 | 100.0 |
| | | | | **INCOME DATA** | | | | | | |
| Net Sales | 100.0 | 100.0 | 100.0 | | 100.0 | 100.0 | 100.0 | 100.0 | 100.0 | 100.0 |
| Gross Profit | | | | | | | | | | |
| Operating Expenses | 90.5 | 89.6 | 88.6 | | 82.2 | 91.6 | 92.2 | 96.3 | 94.8 | 95.8 |
| Operating Profit | 9.5 | 10.4 | 11.4 | | 17.8 | 8.4 | 7.8 | 3.7 | 5.2 | 4.2 |
| All Other Expenses (net) | 4.4 | 4.4 | 4.9 | | 10.0 | 1.9 | 2.2 | .4 | 1.3 | .5 |
| Profit Before Taxes | 5.1 | 6.0 | 6.5 | | 7.8 | 6.6 | 5.5 | 3.3 | 3.8 | 3.7 |
| | | | | **RATIOS** | | | | | | |
| Current | 2.8 | 3.8 | 2.8 | | 2.7 | 3.5 | 3.4 | 2.1 | 2.5 | 2.1 |
| | 1.0 | 1.4 | 1.1 | | .9 | 1.1 | 1.9 | 1.3 | 1.4 | 1.3 |
| | .3 | .5 | .3 | | .2 | .3 | .9 | .7 | 1.1 | .8 |
| Quick | 2.5 | 3.2 | 2.5 | | 2.4 | 2.9 | 3.3 | 2.1 | 2.5 | 2.0 |
| | 1.0 | 1.3 | (713) .9 | | (279) .6 | .9 | 1.3 | 1.1 | 1.3 | 1.3 |
| | .3 | .4 | .3 | | .2 | .3 | .4 | .5 | 1.3 | .5 |
| Sales/Receivables | 0 UND | 0 UND | 0 UND | | 0 UND | 0 UND | 0 UND | 0 UND | 4 88.0 | 9 40.0 |
| | 0 UND | 0 UND | 0 UND | | 0 UND | 0 UND | 1 250.5 | 11 33.2 | 19 18.9 | 17 21.6 |
| | 11 32.2 | 11 32.9 | 7 53.3 | | 0 UND | 1 533.5 | 33 11.1 | 21 17.2 | 29 12.5 | 32 11.4 |
| Cost of Sales/Inventory | | | | | | | | | | |
| Cost of Sales/Payables | | | | | | | | | | |
| Sales/Working Capital | 14.4 | 11.4 | 15.6 | | 17.5 | 18.0 | 7.1 | 13.6 | 9.2 | 13.5 |
| | 999.8 | 84.6 | 218.8 | | -461.0 | 342.7 | 26.2 | 51.2 | 31.6 | 38.6 |
| | -15.3 | -25.0 | -21.2 | | -9.0 | -24.2 | -113.0 | -38.1 | 125.6 | -49.0 |
| EBIT/Interest | 9.4 | 9.9 | 13.0 | | 8.0 | 21.0 | 13.6 | 14.7 | 16.2 | 8.8 |
| | (361) 2.7 | (397) 3.1 | (483) 3.5 | | (163) 2.4 | (195) 5.7 | (34) 3.2 | (40) 3.3 | (32) 5.5 | (19) 5.0 |
| | .7 | 1.0 | 1.0 | | .6 | 1.3 | .3 | 1.2 | .6 | 1.2 |
| Net Profit + Depr., Dep., Amort./Cur. Mat. L/T/D | 8.6 | 11.7 | 6.8 | | | | | | | |
| | (18) 2.4 | (18) 5.0 | (23) 2.4 | | | | | | | |
| | 1.3 | 1.8 | .9 | | | | | | | |
| Fixed/Worth | .7 | .5 | .6 | | .8 | .6 | .6 | .5 | .5 | .2 |
| | 2.0 | 2.1 | 2.4 | | 8.4 | 3.0 | 1.2 | 1.2 | 1.2 | 1.1 |
| | -6.2 | -16.0 | -6.5 | | -2.5 | -5.0 | 2.2 | 3.0 | 2.1 | 2.0 |
| Debt/Worth | .7 | .6 | .7 | | 1.0 | .6 | .4 | .5 | .5 | .7 |
| | 3.5 | 3.1 | 3.4 | | 12.7 | 4.3 | 1.3 | 1.0 | 1.3 | 1.5 |
| | -8.7 | -13.0 | -9.1 | | -3.7 | -8.1 | 5.5 | 3.6 | 6.0 | 5.1 |
| % Profit Before Taxes/Tangible Net Worth | 73.8 | 84.3 | 99.4 | | 84.1 | 213.3 | 41.6 | 31.2 | 22.2 | 28.5 |
| | (366) 20.9 | (433) 24.1 | (478) 24.9 | | (163) 29.7 | (174) 62.1 | (37) 9.3 | (42) 10.3 | (37) 10.6 | (25) 13.6 |
| | 1.4 | 4.5 | 4.0 | | 5.6 | 8.0 | -2.0 | -2.0 | -1.4 | 2.8 |
| % Profit Before Taxes/Total Assets | 26.5 | 22.8 | 27.9 | | 22.5 | 56.3 | 18.0 | 9.3 | 9.5 | 15.5 |
| | 5.9 | 6.4 | 7.4 | | 5.4 | 14.6 | 7.2 | 4.8 | 1.8 | 5.4 |
| | -.4 | .4 | .2 | | -.4 | 2.0 | -.2 | -.7 | -1.9 | .6 |
| Sales/Net Fixed Assets | 28.1 | 30.2 | 33.7 | | 26.8 | 44.5 | 27.5 | 12.1 | 31.1 | 49.9 |
| | 8.2 | 8.7 | 9.0 | | 6.5 | 13.6 | 9.7 | 5.7 | 7.9 | 9.1 |
| | 1.6 | 1.2 | 1.5 | | .7 | 1.8 | 1.6 | 1.7 | 2.3 | 3.9 |
| Sales/Total Assets | 6.4 | 6.8 | 6.9 | | 6.1 | 9.5 | 5.6 | 3.9 | 4.1 | 5.3 |
| | 3.1 | 2.7 | 3.0 | | 2.1 | 4.3 | 2.0 | 2.3 | 2.5 | 2.9 |
| | 1.0 | .9 | 1.0 | | .6 | 1.2 | 1.1 | 1.1 | 1.5 | 1.6 |
| % Depr., Dep., Amort./Sales | 1.0 | 1.1 | 1.0 | | 1.5 | .8 | 1.0 | 1.1 | .7 | .6 |
| | (412) 2.3 | (459) 2.6 | (514) 2.4 | | (189) 3.3 | (188) 2.0 | (34) 2.0 | (41) 2.0 | (35) 1.9 | (27) 1.6 |
| | 4.7 | 5.1 | 4.9 | | 12.1 | 4.1 | 3.6 | 3.3 | 3.6 | 3.4 |
| % Officers', Directors' Owners' Comp/Sales | 2.7 | 2.9 | 2.9 | | 3.2 | 2.6 | 3.7 | 1.9 | | |
| | (175) 5.5 | (238) 5.2 | (270) 5.3 | | (105) 4.8 | (130) 4.8 | (14) 5.1 | (12) 5.9 | | |
| | 11.0 | 9.9 | 9.6 | | 11.7 | 8.1 | 7.4 | 6.3 | | |
| Net Sales ($) | 5317596M | 5708220M | 3567533M | | 152038M | 452591M | 168029M | 348503M | 656948M | 1789424M |
| Total Assets ($) | 2295982M | 2184653M | 2036134M | | 183273M | 267889M | 113447M | 200420M | 506290M | 764815M |

M = $ thousand    MM = $ million
See Pages 9 through 22 for Explanation of Ratios and Data

# ARTS, ENTERTAINMENT, AND RECREATION

## Current Data Sorted by Assets | Comparative Historical Data

| 0-500M | 500M-2MM | 2-10MM | 10-50MM | 50-100MM | 100-250MM | Type of Statement | 4/1/07-3/31/08 ALL | 4/1/08-3/31/09 ALL |
|---|---|---|---|---|---|---|---|---|
| 3 | 7 | 25 | 25 | 9 | 9 | Unqualified | 58 | 85 |
| 2 | 1 | 3 | | | | Reviewed | 9 | 8 |
| 3 | 4 | 2 | 1 | | | Compiled | 6 | 11 |
| 6 | 12 | 4 | | | | Tax Returns | 32 | 24 |
| 3 | 8 | 21 | 11 | 1 | 1 | Other | 47 | 60 |
| | 95 (4/1-9/30/11) | | 66 (10/1/11-3/31/12) | | | | | |
| 17 | 32 | 55 | 37 | 10 | 10 | NUMBER OF STATEMENTS | 152 | 188 |
| % | % | % | % | % | % | ASSETS | % | % |
| 33.1 | 23.7 | 12.1 | 13.9 | 7.6 | 7.4 | Cash & Equivalents | 18.5 | 17.1 |
| 6.8 | 2.5 | 6.0 | 3.8 | 4.1 | 1.0 | Trade Receivables (net) | 6.2 | 7.0 |
| 4.5 | 1.6 | 2.9 | .2 | .3 | .3 | Inventory | 3.4 | 2.6 |
| 5.8 | 4.8 | 4.0 | 4.6 | 1.2 | 3.7 | All Other Current | 4.9 | 5.2 |
| 50.1 | 32.6 | 25.1 | 22.6 | 13.2 | 12.4 | Total Current | 33.0 | 31.8 |
| 34.2 | 54.3 | 48.7 | 47.7 | 60.1 | 53.4 | Fixed Assets (net) | 46.2 | 45.5 |
| 5.3 | 3.4 | 5.2 | 1.5 | 5.1 | .8 | Intangibles (net) | 5.7 | 3.8 |
| 10.4 | 9.8 | 21.0 | 28.2 | 21.6 | 33.4 | All Other Non-Current | 15.1 | 18.8 |
| 100.0 | 100.0 | 100.0 | 100.0 | 100.0 | 100.0 | Total | 100.0 | 100.0 |
| | | | | | | LIABILITIES | | |
| 14.5 | 8.1 | 4.0 | 2.0 | .7 | .0 | Notes Payable-Short Term | 5.4 | 9.3 |
| 1.1 | 1.6 | 2.1 | 1.8 | 1.9 | .6 | Cur. Mat.-L.T.D. | 2.4 | 2.8 |
| 23.3 | 6.3 | 4.2 | 3.7 | 3.0 | 3.0 | Trade Payables | 7.0 | 7.3 |
| .0 | .0 | .0 | .1 | .0 | .0 | Income Taxes Payable | .1 | .2 |
| 52.8 | 16.8 | 9.9 | 13.2 | 4.8 | 2.5 | All Other Current | 11.6 | 12.1 |
| 91.7 | 32.8 | 20.2 | 20.7 | 10.4 | 6.1 | Total Current | 26.4 | 31.8 |
| 23.0 | 17.7 | 15.2 | 18.7 | 33.5 | 43.7 | Long-Term Debt | 22.1 | 22.6 |
| .0 | .0 | .0 | .1 | .0 | .0 | Deferred Taxes | .4 | .4 |
| 3.6 | 6.8 | 6.5 | 9.7 | 11.6 | 4.9 | All Other Non-Current | 12.4 | 9.9 |
| -18.2 | 42.8 | 58.1 | 50.9 | 44.5 | 45.3 | Net Worth | 38.7 | 35.3 |
| 100.0 | 100.0 | 100.0 | 100.0 | 100.0 | 100.0 | Total Liabilties & Net Worth | 100.0 | 100.0 |
| | | | | | | INCOME DATA | | |
| 100.0 | 100.0 | 100.0 | 100.0 | 100.0 | 100.0 | Net Sales | 100.0 | 100.0 |
| | | | | | | Gross Profit | | |
| 100.7 | 92.2 | 93.5 | 99.3 | 108.5 | 93.7 | Operating Expenses | 92.7 | 96.6 |
| -.7 | 7.8 | 6.5 | .7 | -8.5 | 6.3 | Operating Profit | 7.3 | 3.4 |
| .9 | 1.6 | 1.8 | -.9 | 2.6 | 1.2 | All Other Expenses (net) | .9 | 2.0 |
| -1.6 | 6.2 | 4.7 | 1.6 | -11.1 | 5.1 | Profit Before Taxes | 6.5 | 1.4 |
| | | | | | | RATIOS | | |
| 2.3 | 3.3 | 3.1 | 2.3 | 4.0 | 3.8 | | 3.4 | 2.9 |
| 1.0 | 1.2 | 1.1 | 1.2 | 1.1 | 1.5 | Current | 1.3 | 1.2 |
| .2 | .2 | .6 | .6 | .7 | .7 | | .6 | .5 |
| 1.7 | 2.7 | 2.3 | 1.8 | 3.0 | 3.2 | | 2.6 | 2.2 |
| .5 | .8 | .9 | .8 | .9 | .9 | Quick | 1.0 (187) | .9 |
| .2 | .2 | .3 | .4 | .5 | .2 | | .3 | .3 |
| 0 UND | 0 UND | 1 587.3 | 2 191.8 | 5 67.7 | 2 208.1 | | 0 UND | 0 999.8 |
| 0 UND | 0 UND | 9 40.0 | 11 33.6 | 24 15.3 | 5 66.9 | Sales/Receivables | 3 128.1 | 5 74.5 |
| 7 52.0 | 4 83.3 | 24 15.4 | 33 11.2 | 41 9.0 | 31 11.7 | | 14 25.7 | 24 15.3 |
| | | | | | | Cost of Sales/Inventory | | |
| | | | | | | Cost of Sales/Payables | | |
| 21.2 | 7.2 | 4.2 | 3.8 | 2.7 | 4.8 | | 5.3 | 5.4 |
| UND | 184.2 | 56.4 | 26.0 | 66.4 | 7.4 | Sales/Working Capital | 36.2 | 44.8 |
| -14.5 | -5.9 | -10.3 | -8.4 | -13.6 | -15.9 | | -18.1 | -13.6 |
| | 11.5 | 10.9 | 34.2 | | | | 17.5 | 9.8 |
| (23) 1.8 | (45) 1.8 | (27) 1.8 | | | | EBIT/Interest | (112) 3.5 | (138) 1.9 |
| | -2.1 | -1.9 | -2.2 | | | | .5 | -1.1 |
| | | | | | | Net Profit + Depr., Dep., Amort./Cur. Mat. L/T/D | | 11.6 |
| | | | | | | | (12) 2.4 | |
| | | | | | | | | 1.1 |
| .2 | .7 | .2 | .4 | .9 | .7 | | .4 | .4 |
| 1.6 | 1.2 | .9 | .8 | 1.1 | 1.5 | Fixed/Worth | 1.2 | 1.0 |
| -8.3 | 9.0 | 1.4 | 1.7 | NM | 2.8 | | 5.6 | 3.6 |
| 1.3 | .3 | .2 | .1 | .3 | .2 | | .3 | .3 |
| 12.8 | .7 | .6 | .3 | .7 | 1.5 | Debt/Worth | 1.1 | .8 |
| -5.9 | 8.2 | 2.4 | 1.7 | NM | 2.7 | | 7.0 | 4.2 |
| 227.6 | 40.3 | 25.3 | 9.3 | | | % Profit Before Taxes/Tangible Net Worth | 47.6 | 31.6 |
| (11) 4.5 | (25) 3.2 | (48) 3.3 | (33) 2.3 | | | | (124) 10.9 | (158) 6.2 |
| -11.1 | -7.0 | -1.6 | -4.1 | | | | -3.8 | -4.9 |
| 29.0 | 16.1 | 10.2 | 4.4 | .1 | 12.8 | % Profit Before Taxes/Total Assets | 18.8 | 12.8 |
| .3 | 1.6 | 1.7 | .9 | -2.0 | -.9 | | 5.3 | 1.7 |
| -26.2 | -6.0 | -1.4 | -4.1 | -4.5 | -3.9 | | -1.8 | -4.1 |
| 222.6 | 17.6 | 8.2 | 3.6 | 2.4 | 1.3 | | 11.7 | 10.4 |
| 18.5 | 4.7 | 2.1 | 1.5 | .6 | .4 | Sales/Net Fixed Assets | 4.0 | 3.4 |
| 7.0 | .6 | .8 | .7 | .2 | .2 | | 1.3 | 1.2 |
| 7.2 | 3.4 | 1.4 | .7 | .8 | .4 | | 3.3 | 2.9 |
| 3.9 | 1.6 | .8 | .5 | .4 | .2 | Sales/Total Assets | 1.5 | 1.3 |
| 2.8 | .5 | .4 | .3 | .1 | .1 | | .6 | .5 |
| .6 | 1.2 | 2.3 | 3.5 | 6.6 | | | 1.5 | 1.9 |
| (13) 2.0 | (22) 2.4 | (51) 3.7 | (34) 5.3 | 8.3 | | % Depr., Dep., Amort./Sales | (128) 3.0 | (159) 3.5 |
| 3.0 | 10.5 | 6.2 | 7.8 | 22.6 | | | 5.6 | 6.2 |
| | | | | | | % Officers', Directors' Owners' Comp/Sales | 3.7 | 2.6 |
| | | | | | | | (39) 5.3 | (33) 6.6 |
| | | | | | | | 12.8 | 11.3 |
| 14390M | 79936M | 334708M | 591634M | 346125M | 525586M | Net Sales ($) | 1377246M | 2500801M |
| 3515M | 35409M | 259199M | 775238M | 679439M | 1863736M | Total Assets ($) | 1784877M | 3800914M |

© RMA 2012

M = $ thousand   MM = $ million
See Pages 9 through 22 for Explanation of Ratios and Data

## Comparative Historical Data | Current Data Sorted by Sales

| | | | Type of Statement | | | | | | |
|---|---|---|---|---|---|---|---|---|---|
| 71 | 71 | 78 | Unqualified | 7 | 13 | 12 | 20 | 13 | 13 |
| 5 | 7 | 6 | Reviewed | 2 | | | 2 | 1 | 1 |
| 18 | 12 | 10 | Compiled | 2 | 4 | 1 | 3 | | |
| 30 | 24 | 22 | Tax Returns | 11 | 7 | 3 | 1 | | |
| 42 | 49 | 45 | Other | 9 | 10 | 3 | 8 | 11 | 4 |
| 4/1/09-3/31/10 | 4/1/10-3/31/11 | 4/1/11-3/31/12 | | | 95 (4/1-9/30/11) | | 66 (10/1/11-3/31/12) | | |
| ALL | ALL | ALL | | 0-1MM | 1-3MM | 3-5MM | 5-10MM | 10-25MM | 25MM & OVER |
| 166 | 163 | 161 | NUMBER OF STATEMENTS | 31 | 34 | 19 | 34 | 25 | 18 |
| % | % | % | ASSETS | % | % | % | % | % | % |
| 16.0 | 16.7 | 16.5 | Cash & Equivalents | 20.5 | 15.0 | 16.1 | 18.6 | 14.4 | 11.6 |
| 3.9 | 6.1 | 4.5 | Trade Receivables (net) | 2.0 | 3.7 | 6.1 | 6.2 | 4.3 | 5.5 |
| 1.7 | 2.1 | 1.9 | Inventory | 3.8 | 2.6 | .4 | .8 | 1.6 | 1.2 |
| 4.2 | 5.1 | 4.3 | All Other Current | 1.8 | 5.8 | 6.9 | 3.4 | 5.8 | 2.6 |
| 25.8 | 30.0 | 27.1 | Total Current | 28.1 | 27.1 | 29.5 | 29.0 | 26.0 | 20.9 |
| 51.0 | 47.5 | 49.1 | Fixed Assets (net) | 61.0 | 48.2 | 52.6 | 37.3 | 49.0 | 48.7 |
| 6.3 | 3.8 | 3.7 | Intangibles (net) | 3.3 | 3.2 | 2.5 | 2.2 | 4.9 | 7.9 |
| 16.9 | 18.7 | 20.1 | All Other Non-Current | 7.5 | 21.5 | 15.5 | 31.5 | 20.0 | 22.5 |
| 100.0 | 100.0 | 100.0 | Total | 100.0 | 100.0 | 100.0 | 100.0 | 100.0 | 100.0 |
| | | | LIABILITIES | | | | | | |
| 5.9 | 7.4 | 5.0 | Notes Payable-Short Term | 7.0 | 6.5 | 9.0 | 2.4 | 1.4 | 4.4 |
| 2.4 | 2.1 | 1.7 | Cur. Mat.-L.T.D. | 1.2 | 2.2 | 1.8 | 1.1 | 1.9 | 2.6 |
| 6.4 | 9.1 | 6.3 | Trade Payables | 11.3 | 4.8 | 5.6 | 5.0 | 3.5 | 8.0 |
| .1 | .1 | .0 | Income Taxes Payable | .0 | .0 | .0 | .0 | .0 | .1 |
| 9.9 | 13.4 | 15.8 | All Other Current | 33.8 | 8.9 | 11.4 | 13.6 | 8.6 | 16.6 |
| 24.7 | 32.1 | 28.9 | Total Current | 53.3 | 22.3 | 27.8 | 22.2 | 15.3 | 31.7 |
| 25.6 | 18.3 | 20.2 | Long-Term Debt | 19.8 | 19.0 | 21.2 | 8.8 | 27.6 | 33.6 |
| .0 | .0 | .0 | Deferred Taxes | .0 | .0 | .0 | .0 | .0 | .2 |
| 7.9 | 8.4 | 7.2 | All Other Non-Current | 6.7 | 3.6 | 6.4 | 10.9 | 7.4 | 8.1 |
| 41.8 | 41.1 | 43.7 | Net Worth | 20.2 | 55.0 | 44.6 | 58.1 | 49.7 | 26.4 |
| 100.0 | 100.0 | 100.0 | Total Liabilties & Net Worth | 100.0 | 100.0 | 100.0 | 100.0 | 100.0 | 100.0 |
| | | | INCOME DATA | | | | | | |
| 100.0 | 100.0 | 100.0 | Net Sales | 100.0 | 100.0 | 100.0 | 100.0 | 100.0 | 100.0 |
| | | | Gross Profit | | | | | | |
| 99.3 | 98.0 | 96.3 | Operating Expenses | 91.8 | 95.4 | 102.5 | 97.0 | 97.9 | 95.4 |
| .7 | 2.0 | 3.7 | Operating Profit | 8.2 | 4.6 | -2.5 | 3.0 | 2.1 | 4.6 |
| 2.8 | 1.4 | 1.0 | All Other Expenses (net) | 4.3 | .7 | .9 | -.2 | -.5 | .9 |
| -2.0 | .6 | 2.7 | Profit Before Taxes | 3.9 | 3.9 | -3.4 | 3.2 | 2.5 | 3.7 |
| | | | RATIOS | | | | | | |
| 2.5 | 2.4 | 2.7 | | 4.3 | 2.4 | 3.7 | 3.3 | 3.8 | 1.7 |
| 1.0 | 1.1 | 1.1 | Current | .9 | 1.1 | 1.4 | 1.2 | 1.2 | .8 |
| .6 | .5 | .5 | | .2 | .4 | .5 | .8 | .8 | .3 |
| 2.0 | 2.1 | 2.1 | | 4.3 | 1.4 | 3.1 | 2.7 | 2.4 | 1.3 |
| (165) .8 | (162) .8 | .8 | Quick | .6 | .8 | 1.1 | .9 | .9 | .5 |
| .3 | .3 | .3 | | .2 | .3 | .4 | .5 | .5 | .2 |
| 0 UND | 0 UND | 0 UND | | 0 UND | 0 UND | 2 228.6 | 0 UND | 1 383.7 | 4 93.5 |
| 3 106.4 | 6 65.8 | 4 81.3 | Sales/Receivables | 0 UND | 3 133.6 | 5 80.4 | 11 34.1 | 18 20.5 | 6 58.1 |
| 20 18.2 | 23 15.7 | 22 16.6 | | 7 55.4 | 17 21.1 | 30 12.3 | 24 15.0 | 44 8.3 | 14 25.2 |
| | | | Cost of Sales/Inventory | | | | | | |
| | | | Cost of Sales/Payables | | | | | | |
| 6.2 | 7.9 | 5.4 | | 5.1 | 6.1 | 4.2 | 6.2 | 2.8 | 7.5 |
| 228.2 | 88.1 | 59.5 | Sales/Working Capital | -36.5 | 224.6 | 10.4 | 80.0 | 24.2 | -41.8 |
| -12.9 | -10.9 | -9.6 | | -3.8 | -8.3 | -9.8 | -12.8 | -34.3 | -7.7 |
| 4.7 | 9.4 | 9.2 | | 12.2 | 6.6 | 3.0 | 51.1 | 15.0 | 21.5 |
| (116) 1.0 | (122) 1.6 | (119) 1.7 | EBIT/Interest | (24) 1.7 | (23) 1.8 | (15) -.5 | (22) 3.1 | (17) 1.6 | 1.7 |
| -4.5 | -1.9 | -2.2 | | -2.1 | -1.2 | -2.1 | -3.5 | -2.3 | -12.3 |
| 18.1 | | | Net Profit + Depr., Dep., | | | | | | |
| (13) 4.5 | | | Amort./Cur. Mat. L/T/D | | | | | | |
| 1.5 | | | | | | | | | |
| .5 | .4 | .5 | | .9 | .3 | .6 | .2 | .7 | .6 |
| 1.1 | 1.0 | 1.0 | Fixed/Worth | 1.5 | .9 | .9 | .7 | 1.0 | 1.5 |
| 5.9 | 5.8 | 3.2 | | 4.9 | 5.0 | 5.7 | 1.0 | 1.7 | -3.0 |
| .2 | .3 | .2 | | .4 | .2 | .2 | .2 | .2 | 1.0 |
| .8 | .9 | .8 | Debt/Worth | 1.3 | .5 | 1.1 | .4 | .8 | 2.8 |
| 5.5 | 6.2 | 5.0 | | 8.2 | 15.9 | 4.9 | .9 | 1.5 | -6.0 |
| 10.0 | 20.7 | 18.6 | % Profit Before Taxes/Tangible | 17.2 | 15.5 | 11.8 | 27.0 | 8.3 | 53.0 |
| (132) -.2 | (137) 1.4 | (134) 2.1 | Net Worth | (26) 2.1 | (27) 1.9 | (15) -.1 | (31) 1.7 | (22) 1.8 | (13) 21.3 |
| -10.2 | -5.4 | -4.3 | | -5.7 | -1.5 | -5.5 | -6.6 | -2.9 | -7.3 |
| 5.3 | 8.8 | 9.2 | % Profit Before Taxes/Total | 10.2 | 9.0 | 3.9 | 14.9 | 4.6 | 15.2 |
| .0 | .7 | 1.0 | Assets | .8 | 1.5 | -1.5 | 2.0 | .9 | 3.5 |
| -6.5 | -4.4 | -3.8 | | -4.0 | -1.3 | -6.5 | -2.9 | -2.8 | -4.9 |
| 7.7 | 11.9 | 8.3 | | 8.4 | 10.0 | 11.9 | 18.6 | 4.2 | 7.2 |
| 2.8 | 2.7 | 1.8 | Sales/Net Fixed Assets | .9 | 2.7 | 1.5 | 2.1 | 1.5 | 2.0 |
| .7 | .9 | .6 | | .3 | .8 | .4 | 1.0 | .6 | .6 |
| 2.3 | 2.7 | 2.3 | | 2.8 | 2.8 | 2.4 | 2.0 | 1.7 | 2.8 |
| 1.0 | 1.3 | .8 | Sales/Total Assets | .5 | .8 | 1.0 | .7 | .6 | 1.2 |
| .4 | .5 | .3 | | .2 | .5 | .4 | .5 | .3 | .3 |
| 2.2 | 1.8 | 2.1 | | 2.2 | 1.0 | 2.7 | 1.2 | 2.7 | 2.5 |
| (142) 4.1 | (138) 4.1 | (138) 4.0 | % Depr., Dep., Amort./Sales | (21) 5.2 | (30) 3.0 | (18) 5.4 | (29) 4.0 | (23) 3.8 | (17) 4.7 |
| 8.1 | 8.7 | 7.4 | | 14.6 | 5.2 | 9.5 | 6.4 | 7.5 | 8.2 |
| 2.9 | 3.7 | 4.0 | % Officers', Directors' | | | | | | |
| (27) 4.4 | (21) 7.9 | (24) 7.0 | Owners' Comp/Sales | | | | | | |
| 12.5 | 13.2 | 16.5 | | | | | | | |
| 2717815M | 3865112M | 1892379M | Net Sales ($) | 15442M | 66840M | 73774M | 248977M | 400392M | 1086954M |
| 4212677M | 3250419M | 3616536M | Total Assets ($) | 35237M | 104852M | 186313M | 419146M | 1137773M | 1733215M |

© RMA 2012

M = $ thousand　MM = $ million
See Pages 9 through 22 for Explanation of Ratios and Data

## Current Data Sorted by Assets     Comparative Historical Data

| 0-500M | 500M-2MM | 2-10MM | 10-50MM | 50-100MM | 100-250MM | Type of Statement | 4/1/07-3/31/08 ALL | 4/1/08-3/31/09 ALL |
|---|---|---|---|---|---|---|---|---|
| 3 | 2 | 3 | 7 | | 2 | Unqualified | 32 | 36 |
| | | | | | | Reviewed | 1 | 1 |
| 2 | 1 | | 1 | | | Compiled | 2 | 1 |
| 4 | | | | | | Tax Returns | 5 | 3 |
| 7 | 4 | 4 | 3 | | 1 | Other | 17 | 19 |
| 26 (4/1-9/30/11) | | | 18 (10/1/11-3/31/12) | | | | | |
| 16 | 7 | 7 | 11 | | 3 | NUMBER OF STATEMENTS | 57 | 60 |
| % | % | % | % | % | % | **ASSETS** | % | % |
| 32.0 | | | 14.0 | | | Cash & Equivalents | 18.5 | 24.4 |
| 14.9 | | | 6.5 | | | Trade Receivables (net) | 11.0 | 8.3 |
| 2.4 | | | 4.6 | | | Inventory | 2.3 | .9 |
| 20.8 | | | 6.5 | | | All Other Current | 3.5 | 5.1 |
| 70.1 | | | 31.6 | | | Total Current | 35.3 | 38.6 |
| 20.7 | | | 22.9 | | | Fixed Assets (net) | 25.8 | 23.1 |
| .7 | | | 2.0 | | | Intangibles (net) | 1.6 | 1.0 |
| 8.6 | | | 43.5 | | | All Other Non-Current | 37.3 | 37.2 |
| 100.0 | | | 100.0 | | | Total | 100.0 | 100.0 |
| | | | | | | **LIABILITIES** | | |
| 19.1 | | | 4.4 | | | Notes Payable-Short Term | 10.0 | 8.3 |
| .3 | | | .6 | | | Cur. Mat.-L.T.D. | 2.3 | 1.6 |
| 10.6 | | | 3.3 | | | Trade Payables | 8.7 | 5.5 |
| .0 | | | .0 | | | Income Taxes Payable | .0 | .2 |
| 12.6 | | | 8.7 | | | All Other Current | 8.5 | 9.4 |
| 42.5 | | | 17.1 | | | Total Current | 29.4 | 25.0 |
| 15.7 | | | 13.0 | | | Long-Term Debt | 11.1 | 13.3 |
| .0 | | | .1 | | | Deferred Taxes | .0 | .3 |
| 2.8 | | | 14.9 | | | All Other Non-Current | 11.7 | 15.8 |
| 39.0 | | | 54.9 | | | Net Worth | 47.7 | 45.6 |
| 100.0 | | | 100.0 | | | Total Liabilities & Net Worth | 100.0 | 100.0 |
| | | | | | | **INCOME DATA** | | |
| 100.0 | | | 100.0 | | | Net Sales | 100.0 | 100.0 |
| | | | | | | Gross Profit | | |
| 89.7 | | | 93.2 | | | Operating Expenses | 92.3 | 96.5 |
| 10.3 | | | 6.8 | | | Operating Profit | 7.7 | 3.5 |
| .1 | | | -1.4 | | | All Other Expenses (net) | 1.5 | 4.2 |
| 10.1 | | | 8.3 | | | Profit Before Taxes | 6.2 | -.7 |
| | | | | | | **RATIOS** | | |
| 33.9 | | | 5.5 | | | | 3.8 | 5.2 |
| 4.3 | | | 2.9 | | | Current | 1.1 | 1.5 |
| .8 | | | .6 | | | | .5 | .5 |
| 24.9 | | | 3.0 | | | | 3.5 | 4.6 |
| 1.9 | | | 1.7 | | | Quick | .8 | 1.1 |
| .3 | | | .3 | | | | .2 | .2 |
| 0 UND | | | 0 UND | | | | 2 238.0 | 2 235.1 |
| 0 UND | | | 45 8.2 | | | Sales/Receivables | 11 33.3 | 11 34.5 |
| 10 35.5 | | | 72 5.1 | | | | 57 6.4 | 39 9.3 |
| | | | | | | Cost of Sales/Inventory | | |
| | | | | | | Cost of Sales/Payables | | |
| 2.8 | | | 2.1 | | | | 4.4 | 2.8 |
| 4.2 | | | 6.6 | | | Sales/Working Capital | 45.5 | 11.7 |
| -59.1 | | | -21.7 | | | | -8.0 | -7.8 |
| | | | | | | | 30.7 | 8.3 |
| | | | | | | EBIT/Interest | (42) 2.8 | (43) .2 |
| | | | | | | | -1.7 | -6.4 |
| | | | | | | Net Profit + Depr., Dep., Amort./Cur. Mat. L/T/D | | |
| .0 | | | .0 | | | | .0 | .0 |
| .1 | | | .1 | | | Fixed/Worth | .2 | .2 |
| .9 | | | 2.6 | | | | 1.3 | 1.2 |
| .1 | | | .1 | | | | .2 | .2 |
| .4 | | | .4 | | | Debt/Worth | .5 | .5 |
| NM | | | 2.0 | | | | 1.4 | 1.7 |
| 77.3 | | | 22.8 | | | | 19.2 | 9.1 |
| (12) 20.9 | | | (10) 7.7 | | | % Profit Before Taxes/Tangible Net Worth | (51) 5.9 | (53) -2.4 |
| -7.7 | | | 2.7 | | | | -6.3 | -10.3 |
| 37.0 | | | 8.1 | | | | 9.2 | 5.7 |
| 11.5 | | | 3.7 | | | % Profit Before Taxes/Total Assets | 3.0 | -1.0 |
| -5.2 | | | .4 | | | | -4.9 | -5.8 |
| UND | | | 51.8 | | | | 35.9 | 54.6 |
| 77.8 | | | 18.8 | | | Sales/Net Fixed Assets | 11.7 | 19.4 |
| 7.9 | | | 2.4 | | | | 2.3 | 2.1 |
| 4.7 | | | 1.3 | | | | 1.6 | 1.7 |
| 2.9 | | | .5 | | | Sales/Total Assets | .8 | .8 |
| 1.5 | | | .2 | | | | .4 | .4 |
| | | | | | | | .6 | .7 |
| | | | | | | % Depr., Dep., Amort./Sales | (47) 1.3 | (49) 1.0 |
| | | | | | | | 3.4 | 4.2 |
| | | | | | | % Officers', Directors' Owners' Comp/Sales | | |
| 8698M | 16727M | 66035M | 229774M | | 72436M | Net Sales ($) | 746836M | 1463696M |
| 2940M | 7567M | 35361M | 289920M | | 519238M | Total Assets ($) | 1505080M | 1793422M |

Note: columns 500M-2MM, 2-10MM, 50-100MM, and 100-250MM display "DATA NOT AVAILABLE" for the percentage and ratio sections.

© RMA 2012    M = $ thousand    MM = $ million
See Pages 9 through 22 for Explanation of Ratios and Data

## Comparative Historical Data     Current Data Sorted by Sales

| | | | Type of Statement | | | | | | |
|---|---|---|---|---|---|---|---|---|---|
| 22 | 21 | 17 | Unqualified | 3 | 3 | 2 | 1 | 6 | 2 |
| 3 | 1 | | Reviewed | | | | | | |
| 2 | 6 | 4 | Compiled | 1 | 1 | 1 | | | 1 |
| 3 | 4 | 4 | Tax Returns | 3 | 1 | | | | |
| 12 | 17 | 19 | Other | 6 | 5 | 3 | | 4 | 1 |
| 4/1/09-<br>3/31/10<br>ALL | 4/1/10-<br>3/31/11<br>ALL | 4/1/11-<br>3/31/12<br>ALL | | 0-1MM | 26 (4/1-9/30/11)<br>1-3MM | 3-5MM | 5-10MM | 18 (10/1/11-3/31/12)<br>10-25MM | 25MM & OVER |
| 42 | 49 | 44 | **NUMBER OF STATEMENTS** | 13 | 10 | 6 | 1 | 10 | 4 |
| % | % | % | **ASSETS** | % | % | % | % | % | % |
| 17.4 | 20.8 | 26.0 | Cash & Equivalents | 41.6 | 22.8 | | | 14.4 | |
| 8.3 | 4.8 | 9.9 | Trade Receivables (net) | 6.5 | 24.0 | | | 4.9 | |
| 1.0 | 2.8 | 2.3 | Inventory | .8 | 2.8 | | | 1.1 | |
| 4.4 | 4.6 | 11.7 | All Other Current | 25.6 | 3.7 | | | 1.1 | |
| 31.1 | 33.0 | 50.0 | Total Current | 74.5 | 53.3 | | | 21.4 | |
| 30.0 | 33.1 | 19.4 | Fixed Assets (net) | 17.0 | 14.3 | | | 18.6 | |
| 5.5 | 1.6 | 1.7 | Intangibles (net) | .8 | 3.5 | | | .6 | |
| 33.5 | 32.3 | 29.0 | All Other Non-Current | 7.8 | 29.0 | | | 59.4 | |
| 100.0 | 100.0 | 100.0 | Total | 100.0 | 100.0 | | | 100.0 | |
| | | | **LIABILITIES** | | | | | | |
| 8.9 | 10.0 | 11.1 | Notes Payable-Short Term | 20.0 | 15.0 | | | 6.8 | |
| 1.0 | 2.6 | 1.4 | Cur. Mat.-L.T.D. | .2 | .2 | | | 5.0 | |
| 6.2 | 6.1 | 6.2 | Trade Payables | 11.8 | 3.9 | | | 3.3 | |
| .0 | .0 | .0 | Income Taxes Payable | .0 | .0 | | | .0 | |
| 6.8 | 5.8 | 12.0 | All Other Current | 12.4 | 20.7 | | | 7.8 | |
| 23.0 | 24.5 | 30.6 | Total Current | 44.4 | 39.8 | | | 22.9 | |
| 22.5 | 19.9 | 11.9 | Long-Term Debt | 7.0 | 19.9 | | | 6.0 | |
| .3 | .1 | .0 | Deferred Taxes | .0 | .0 | | | .0 | |
| 11.3 | 5.9 | 6.3 | All Other Non-Current | 3.4 | 2.2 | | | 6.0 | |
| 42.9 | 49.6 | 51.2 | Net Worth | 45.1 | 38.2 | | | 65.1 | |
| 100.0 | 100.0 | 100.0 | Total Liabilities & Net Worth | 100.0 | 100.0 | | | 100.0 | |
| | | | **INCOME DATA** | | | | | | |
| 100.0 | 100.0 | 100.0 | Net Sales | 100.0 | 100.0 | | | 100.0 | |
| | | | Gross Profit | | | | | | |
| 97.8 | 96.7 | 94.0 | Operating Expenses | 87.3 | 96.0 | | | 108.5 | |
| 2.2 | 3.3 | 6.0 | Operating Profit | 12.7 | 4.0 | | | -8.5 | |
| 5.9 | .8 | -1.2 | All Other Expenses (net) | -.2 | -2.0 | | | -3.1 | |
| -3.7 | 2.5 | 7.2 | Profit Before Taxes | 12.8 | 6.0 | | | -5.4 | |
| | | | **RATIOS** | | | | | | |
| 4.3 | 3.8 | 9.2 | | 27.4 | 10.0 | | | 3.6 | |
| 1.8 | 2.0 | 3.0 | Current | 4.3 | 1.0 | | | 1.4 | |
| .3 | .7 | .8 | | 1.0 | .7 | | | .3 | |
| 4.0 | 2.9 | 6.6 | | 19.5 | 9.9 | | | 3.4 | |
| 1.3 | 1.0 | 1.3 | Quick | 2.5 | .9 | | | .9 | |
| .1 | .3 | .4 | | .2 | .5 | | | .2 | |
| 1   499.3 | 0   UND | 0   UND | | 0   UND | 2   213.6 | | | 0   UND | |
| 10   36.5 | 6   64.4 | 6   56.9 | Sales/Receivables | 0   UND | 27   13.5 | | | 17   21.0 | |
| 40   9.2 | 33   11.0 | 65   5.6 | | 3   129.0 | 107   3.4 | | | 68   5.4 | |
| | | | Cost of Sales/Inventory | | | | | | |
| | | | Cost of Sales/Payables | | | | | | |
| 4.6 | 4.4 | 2.8 | | 1.8 | 4.0 | | | 3.9 | |
| 24.1 | 13.3 | 6.5 | Sales/Working Capital | 4.1 | NM | | | 110.8 | |
| -4.9 | -7.8 | -46.8 | | NM | -8.6 | | | -3.1 | |
| 3.3 | 8.3 | 38.5 | | | | | | | |
| (32) -2.9 | (32) 1.4 | (22) 5.7 | EBIT/Interest | | | | | | |
| -25.7 | -4.8 | 1.4 | | | | | | | |
| | | | Net Profit + Depr., Dep.,<br>Amort./Cur. Mat. L/T/D | | | | | | |
| .1 | .0 | .0 | | .0 | .0 | | | .0 | |
| .5 | .4 | .1 | Fixed/Worth | .0 | .1 | | | .0 | |
| 1.3 | 1.3 | .7 | | .4 | NM | | | .8 | |
| .3 | .2 | .2 | | .1 | .5 | | | .1 | |
| .8 | .7 | .5 | Debt/Worth | .4 | .9 | | | .4 | |
| 3.0 | 2.1 | 1.9 | | NM | NM | | | 1.4 | |
| 9.2 | 15.4 | 39.2 | % Profit Before Taxes/Tangible<br>Net Worth | 91.8 | | | | 3.8 | |
| (36) -7.2 | (45) 3.4 | (38) 8.2 | | (10) 20.9 | | | | 1.9 | |
| -42.4 | -7.2 | .3 | | 3.8 | | | | -10.3 | |
| 3.8 | 8.8 | 18.1 | % Profit Before Taxes/Total<br>Assets | 49.3 | 16.7 | | | 3.1 | |
| -4.3 | 2.2 | 5.1 | | 15.5 | 5.5 | | | .9 | |
| -16.8 | -4.7 | .1 | | .9 | -4.4 | | | -2.6 | |
| 45.2 | 57.2 | 888.8 | | UND | 309.0 | | | 300.5 | |
| 9.1 | 7.2 | 20.9 | Sales/Net Fixed Assets | 277.7 | 20.9 | | | 25.0 | |
| 1.8 | 1.6 | 5.6 | | 8.1 | 7.3 | | | .7 | |
| 2.2 | 1.8 | 2.9 | | 5.1 | 3.6 | | | 1.8 | |
| 1.0 | .9 | 1.5 | Sales/Total Assets | 1.7 | 2.2 | | | .6 | |
| .4 | .4 | .6 | | 1.3 | 1.1 | | | .2 | |
| 1.0 | .8 | .7 | | | | | | | |
| (28) 1.9 | (36) 2.2 | (22) 2.5 | % Depr., Dep., Amort./Sales | | | | | | |
| 4.1 | 5.0 | 4.3 | | | | | | | |
| | | | % Officers', Directors'<br>Owners' Comp/Sales | | | | | | |
| 572572M | 565531M | 393670M | Net Sales ($) | 4665M | 16478M | 24675M | 7743M | 160877M | 179232M |
| 958838M | 1112079M | 855026M | Total Assets ($) | 2864M | 18767M | 36768M | 23300M | 491828M | 281499M |

M = $ thousand   MM = $ million
See Pages 9 through 22 for Explanation of Ratios and Data

## Current Data Sorted by Assets     Comparative Historical Data

| | | | | | | Type of Statement | | |
|---|---|---|---|---|---|---|---|---|
| 2 | 2 | 6 | 12 | 7 | 24 | Unqualified | 51 | 56 |
| | 1 | 3 | 3 | | | Reviewed | 10 | 9 |
| | 3 | 3 | | | 1 | Compiled | 5 | 2 |
| 21 | 10 | 4 | | | | Tax Returns | 13 | 9 |
| 4 | 17 | 13 | 6 | 12 | 24 | Other | 54 | 54 |
| | 76 (4/1-9/30/11) | | | 104 (10/1/11-3/31/12) | | | 4/1/07-3/31/08 ALL | 4/1/08-3/31/09 ALL |
| 0-500M | 500M-2MM | 2-10MM | 10-50MM | 50-100MM | 100-250MM | | | |
| 29 | 33 | 29 | 21 | 19 | 49 | NUMBER OF STATEMENTS | 133 | 130 |
| % | % | % | % | % | % | ASSETS | % | % |
| 29.4 | 16.2 | 17.8 | 13.6 | 10.7 | 7.4 | Cash & Equivalents | 15.4 | 15.4 |
| 7.0 | 12.6 | 7.0 | 6.9 | 15.0 | 8.5 | Trade Receivables (net) | 9.8 | 8.8 |
| 2.0 | 3.8 | 1.6 | 1.2 | .8 | .4 | Inventory | 1.3 | 1.0 |
| 1.1 | 4.0 | 2.9 | 2.9 | 4.5 | 7.5 | All Other Current | 6.8 | 5.7 |
| 39.5 | 36.6 | 29.3 | 24.7 | 31.0 | 23.8 | Total Current | 33.3 | 31.0 |
| 29.3 | 29.7 | 32.9 | 39.5 | 14.2 | 24.0 | Fixed Assets (net) | 29.2 | 31.0 |
| 15.9 | 18.2 | 17.4 | 29.5 | 27.3 | 23.5 | Intangibles (net) | 22.4 | 19.4 |
| 15.4 | 15.5 | 20.4 | 6.3 | 27.5 | 28.6 | All Other Non-Current | 15.2 | 18.6 |
| 100.0 | 100.0 | 100.0 | 100.0 | 100.0 | 100.0 | Total | 100.0 | 100.0 |
| | | | | | | LIABILITIES | | |
| 24.7 | 24.7 | 3.2 | 28.4 | 8.8 | 9.5 | Notes Payable-Short Term | 14.3 | 11.2 |
| 7.4 | .8 | 3.4 | 9.6 | 6.3 | 8.2 | Cur. Mat.-L.T.D. | 4.6 | 3.1 |
| 7.7 | 8.4 | 5.4 | 5.0 | 5.0 | 6.7 | Trade Payables | 6.9 | 7.2 |
| .0 | .0 | .2 | .2 | .2 | .3 | Income Taxes Payable | .1 | .0 |
| 25.4 | 43.4 | 16.1 | 27.5 | 52.2 | 16.6 | All Other Current | 28.1 | 19.0 |
| 65.3 | 77.2 | 28.4 | 70.7 | 72.4 | 41.3 | Total Current | 54.0 | 40.5 |
| 28.9 | 16.9 | 16.1 | 25.5 | 78.7 | 53.5 | Long-Term Debt | 33.5 | 36.5 |
| .0 | .2 | .0 | .2 | .5 | .9 | Deferred Taxes | .2 | .2 |
| 31.3 | 33.3 | 11.0 | 35.5 | 30.2 | 36.2 | All Other Non-Current | 19.5 | 18.2 |
| -25.5 | -27.6 | 44.5 | -31.8 | -81.8 | -32.0 | Net Worth | -7.2 | 4.5 |
| 100.0 | 100.0 | 100.0 | 100.0 | 100.0 | 100.0 | Total Liabilties & Net Worth | 100.0 | 100.0 |
| | | | | | | INCOME DATA | | |
| 100.0 | 100.0 | 100.0 | 100.0 | 100.0 | 100.0 | Net Sales | 100.0 | 100.0 |
| | | | | | | Gross Profit | | |
| 90.3 | 98.8 | 95.8 | 97.5 | 94.8 | 96.2 | Operating Expenses | 93.1 | 95.8 |
| 9.7 | 1.2 | 4.2 | 2.5 | 5.2 | 3.8 | Operating Profit | 6.9 | 4.2 |
| 3.1 | 2.5 | 1.4 | 6.2 | 5.8 | 6.5 | All Other Expenses (net) | 3.8 | 5.4 |
| 6.6 | -1.2 | 2.7 | -3.7 | -.6 | -2.7 | Profit Before Taxes | 3.0 | -1.2 |
| | | | | | | RATIOS | | |
| 9.8 | 2.5 | 1.8 | 1.1 | 1.4 | 1.3 | | 1.6 | 1.6 |
| 1.2 | 1.1 | .9 | .5 | .6 | .6 | Current | .8 | .8 |
| .4 | .5 | .6 | .1 | .1 | .4 | | .3 | .5 |
| 7.0 | 1.8 | 1.4 | .8 | 1.1 | .8 | | 1.3 | 1.2 |
| 1.2 | (32) .7 | .7 | .3 | .5 | .4 | Quick | .5 | .6 |
| .4 | .4 | .4 | .1 | .1 | .2 | | .2 | .3 |
| 0 UND | 0 UND | 4 99.8 | 10 38.2 | 11 32.2 | 10 36.7 | | 6 66.0 | 7 54.9 |
| 0 UND | 7 48.7 | 15 23.9 | 15 25.1 | 34 10.8 | 17 21.2 | Sales/Receivables | 20 18.2 | 23 16.0 |
| 8 47.5 | 32 11.4 | 39 9.3 | 25 14.5 | 54 6.8 | 34 10.6 | | 41 8.8 | 44 8.3 |
| | | | | | | Cost of Sales/Inventory | | |
| | | | | | | Cost of Sales/Payables | | |
| 9.8 | 13.2 | 7.6 | 56.5 | 12.1 | 24.8 | | 9.3 | 13.0 |
| 102.0 | 110.0 | -35.7 | -4.5 | -3.6 | -11.6 | Sales/Working Capital | -17.8 | -28.4 |
| -43.5 | -6.8 | -6.4 | -1.0 | -.9 | -3.3 | | -3.5 | -5.3 |
| 19.5 | 3.6 | 18.4 | 2.4 | 2.1 | 2.1 | | 3.9 | 2.7 |
| (13) 2.8 | (26) 1.0 | (18) 3.5 | (18) -.2 | (17) -.7 | (42) .7 | EBIT/Interest | (110) .7 | (100) .7 |
| -5.9 | -4.0 | .6 | -1.0 | -3.3 | -1.4 | | -2.1 | -2.2 |
| | | | | | | Net Profit + Depr., Dep., Amort./Cur. Mat. L/T/D | | |
| .2 | .4 | .3 | .6 | 1.6 | 8.0 | | .9 | .7 |
| .9 | 2.3 | 1.1 | 2.3 | .0 | -.5 | Fixed/Worth | -10.6 | 9.4 |
| -1.1 | -.5 | 3.6 | -.6 | .0 | -.1 | | -.1 | -.3 |
| .1 | 1.7 | .6 | 1.1 | 4.7 | -92.8 | | 1.9 | 1.2 |
| 2.3 | 34.2 | 1.5 | -6.8 | -1.8 | -3.2 | Debt/Worth | -12.8 | -188.7 |
| -1.6 | -2.8 | 6.6 | -1.6 | -1.3 | -1.7 | | -1.7 | -2.3 |
| 194.8 | 25.8 | 27.7 | 30.4 | | 64.6 | | 57.8 | 21.0 |
| (17) 43.3 | (17) 4.8 | (23) 8.1 | (10) 7.0 | | (11) 3.7 | % Profit Before Taxes/Tangible Net Worth | (62) 14.3 | (64) 3.9 |
| 9.8 | -19.6 | .7 | -4.2 | | -.2 | | -5.4 | -16.0 |
| 53.1 | 8.4 | 8.7 | 3.9 | 7.2 | 6.7 | | 10.1 | 5.1 |
| 7.6 | .1 | 3.1 | -2.0 | -2.8 | -.1 | % Profit Before Taxes/Total Assets | -.4 | .2 |
| -9.0 | -9.4 | -4.3 | -10.4 | -14.8 | -8.1 | | -13.7 | -8.8 |
| 123.3 | 85.0 | 14.9 | 16.6 | 83.1 | 25.2 | | 45.3 | 52.0 |
| 29.0 | 11.2 | 5.0 | 3.0 | 47.1 | 7.1 | Sales/Net Fixed Assets | 11.2 | 8.7 |
| 4.6 | 3.8 | 1.8 | .6 | 6.9 | 2.8 | | 1.9 | 1.6 |
| 8.5 | 3.4 | 1.3 | 1.4 | 2.1 | 1.2 | | 1.8 | 1.5 |
| 4.1 | 1.9 | 1.0 | .6 | 1.3 | .8 | Sales/Total Assets | 1.0 | .9 |
| 1.2 | 1.2 | .5 | .3 | .6 | .6 | | .6 | .5 |
| 1.1 | .7 | 2.1 | 4.0 | .5 | 1.1 | | 1.2 | 1.0 |
| (15) 3.9 | (23) 2.1 | (23) 4.3 | (17) 7.2 | (12) 1.0 | (23) 2.7 | % Depr., Dep., Amort./Sales | (100) 3.6 | (88) 3.2 |
| 6.7 | 4.0 | 8.5 | 11.4 | 5.2 | 5.2 | | 8.3 | 8.7 |
| 4.2 | 3.6 | | | | | | 3.6 | 5.1 |
| (10) 6.8 | (12) 6.1 | | | | | % Officers', Directors' Owners' Comp/Sales | (23) 8.3 | (16) 9.6 |
| 16.5 | 10.8 | | | | | | 17.7 | 14.9 |
| 19152M | 82017M | 131055M | 597593M | 1909918M | 7188255M | Net Sales ($) | 7215850M | 8185833M |
| 5726M | 38653M | 143035M | 517708M | 1441293M | 8503867M | Total Assets ($) | 7445233M | 10223798M |

M = $ thousand     MM = $ million
See Pages 9 through 22 for Explanation of Ratios and Data

## Comparative Historical Data | Current Data Sorted by Sales

| | | | | | | Type of Statement | | | | | | |
|---|---|---|---|---|---|---|---|---|---|---|---|---|
| | 47 | | 46 | | 53 | Unqualified | 2 | 3 | 1 | 7 | 7 | 33 |
| | 7 | | 8 | | 7 | Reviewed | | 2 | 2 | 2 | 1 | |
| | 4 | | 5 | | 9 | Compiled | 4 | 3 | 1 | | | 1 |
| | 19 | | 22 | | 35 | Tax Returns | 21 | 9 | 4 | 1 | | |
| | 61 | | 60 | | 76 | Other | 4 | 13 | 15 | 5 | 2 | 37 |
| | 4/1/09- | | 4/1/10- | | 4/1/11- | | | 76 (4/1-9/30/11) | | | 104 (10/1/11-3/31/12) | |
| | 3/31/10 | | 3/31/11 | | 3/31/12 | | | | | | | |
| | ALL | | ALL | | ALL | | 0-1MM | 1-3MM | 3-5MM | 5-10MM | 10-25MM | 25MM & OVER |
| | 138 | | 141 | | 180 | NUMBER OF STATEMENTS | 31 | 30 | 23 | 15 | 10 | 71 |
| | % | | % | | % | ASSETS | % | % | % | % | % | % |
| | 14.3 | | 13.7 | | 15.3 | Cash & Equivalents | 26.1 | 17.2 | 9.4 | 14.4 | 37.5 | 8.8 |
| | 8.4 | | 7.1 | | 9.3 | Trade Receivables (net) | 7.6 | 6.5 | 7.3 | 23.0 | 2.2 | 9.9 |
| | 1.2 | | 1.2 | | 1.6 | Inventory | 2.9 | 2.1 | 2.6 | 1.6 | .5 | .7 |
| | 5.0 | | 5.2 | | 4.2 | All Other Current | 1.0 | 2.6 | 4.4 | 1.0 | 4.5 | 6.9 |
| | 29.0 | | 27.2 | | 30.4 | Total Current | 37.5 | 28.4 | 23.8 | 39.9 | 44.7 | 26.3 |
| | 32.1 | | 30.3 | | 28.1 | Fixed Assets (net) | 32.1 | 30.6 | 42.2 | 30.1 | 25.6 | 20.7 |
| | 20.8 | | 23.1 | | 21.4 | Intangibles (net) | 16.2 | 19.9 | 18.7 | 18.6 | 18.0 | 26.3 |
| | 18.1 | | 19.3 | | 20.1 | All Other Non-Current | 14.2 | 21.1 | 15.4 | 11.4 | 11.8 | 26.6 |
| | 100.0 | | 100.0 | | 100.0 | Total | 100.0 | 100.0 | 100.0 | 100.0 | 100.0 | 100.0 |
| | | | | | | LIABILITIES | | | | | | |
| | 6.4 | | 13.3 | | 15.8 | Notes Payable-Short Term | 25.4 | 3.2 | 28.0 | 12.0 | 4.7 | 15.5 |
| | 4.1 | | 4.2 | | 5.9 | Cur. Mat.-L.T.D. | 6.7 | 3.2 | 3.1 | 6.8 | 4.7 | 7.5 |
| | 5.8 | | 7.0 | | 6.6 | Trade Payables | 4.7 | 6.2 | 10.4 | 6.0 | 4.5 | 6.8 |
| | .1 | | .1 | | .2 | Income Taxes Payable | .0 | .0 | .3 | .3 | .0 | .2 |
| | 20.5 | | 24.8 | | 27.9 | All Other Current | 22.7 | 12.5 | 34.4 | 45.4 | 17.4 | 32.3 |
| | 36.8 | | 49.4 | | 56.4 | Total Current | 59.5 | 25.1 | 76.1 | 70.5 | 31.3 | 62.4 |
| | 40.4 | | 39.8 | | 36.2 | Long-Term Debt | 25.0 | 24.8 | 23.1 | 9.1 | 4.4 | 60.4 |
| | .3 | | .4 | | .4 | Deferred Taxes | .0 | .0 | .2 | .0 | .4 | .8 |
| | 23.4 | | 19.8 | | 30.1 | All Other Non-Current | 22.3 | 29.3 | 32.5 | 8.3 | 15.3 | 39.8 |
| | -.9 | | -9.4 | | -23.0 | Net Worth | -6.8 | 20.8 | -31.9 | 12.1 | 48.7 | -63.3 |
| | 100.0 | | 100.0 | | 100.0 | Total Liabilities & Net Worth | 100.0 | 100.0 | 100.0 | 100.0 | 100.0 | 100.0 |
| | | | | | | INCOME DATA | | | | | | |
| | 100.0 | | 100.0 | | 100.0 | Net Sales | 100.0 | 100.0 | 100.0 | 100.0 | 100.0 | 100.0 |
| | | | | | | Gross Profit | | | | | | |
| | 97.0 | | 97.8 | | 95.7 | Operating Expenses | 89.1 | 96.9 | 97.0 | 90.3 | 94.5 | 98.9 |
| | 3.0 | | 2.2 | | 4.3 | Operating Profit | 10.9 | 3.1 | 3.0 | 9.7 | 5.5 | 1.1 |
| | 4.8 | | 4.5 | | 4.3 | All Other Expenses (net) | 4.7 | 1.0 | 3.9 | 7.8 | 2.3 | 5.2 |
| | -1.8 | | -2.3 | | .0 | Profit Before Taxes | 6.2 | 2.0 | -.9 | 1.9 | 3.2 | -4.0 |
| | | | | | | RATIOS | | | | | | |
| | 1.7 | | 1.7 | | 1.7 | | 10.0 | 3.0 | .9 | 1.7 | 5.9 | 1.1 |
| | .8 | | .7 | | .8 | Current | 1.2 | 1.2 | .5 | 1.0 | 1.5 | .6 |
| | .4 | | .4 | | .4 | | .6 | .7 | .4 | .2 | .6 | .3 |
| | 1.2 | | 1.4 | | 1.4 | | 7.4 | 2.8 | .7 | 1.5 | 5.6 | .8 |
| | .6 | | .5 | (179) | .6 | Quick | 1.2 | 1.1 | (22) .4 | 1.0 | 1.3 | .4 |
| | .3 | | .2 | | .3 | | .4 | .3 | .3 | .1 | .3 | .2 |
| 6 | 58.6 | 4 | 90.3 | 3 | 104.5 | | 0 UND | 0 UND | 6 61.5 | 10 36.0 | 3 115.9 | 11 34.6 |
| 18 | 20.5 | 16 | 22.7 | 12 | 29.3 | Sales/Receivables | 0 UND | 7 54.9 | 16 22.8 | 14 25.6 | 8 48.2 | 18 20.6 |
| 42 | 8.6 | 40 | 9.1 | 33 | 11.0 | | 18 19.9 | 23 15.7 | 36 10.0 | 70 5.2 | 19 19.3 | 38 9.7 |
| | | | | | | Cost of Sales/Inventory | | | | | | |
| | | | | | | Cost of Sales/Payables | | | | | | |
| | 10.6 | | 11.2 | | 12.6 | | 8.1 | 13.6 | -33.7 | 5.8 | 1.9 | 36.3 |
| | -16.4 | | -14.2 | | -27.7 | Sales/Working Capital | 102.0 | 42.3 | -9.4 | 101.5 | 8.5 | -6.9 |
| | -4.4 | | -3.6 | | -3.6 | | -64.8 | -21.7 | -3.2 | -2.4 | -5.5 | -2.6 |
| | 2.9 | | 2.7 | | 3.6 | | 14.4 | 9.5 | 5.9 | | | 1.7 |
| (108) | .4 | (113) | .3 | (134) | 1.0 | EBIT/Interest | (18) 1.9 | (21) 1.5 | (19) 1.3 | | (63) | .3 |
| | -1.9 | | -2.6 | | -1.4 | | -.6 | -.4 | -1.3 | | | -1.7 |
| | | | | | | Net Profit + Depr., Dep., Amort./Cur. Mat. L/T/D | | | | | | |
| | .8 | | .7 | | .5 | | .0 | .5 | .5 | .2 | .2 | -27.3 |
| | 19.0 | | 18.6 | | 10.3 | Fixed/Worth | 1.0 | 2.8 | 2.2 | .9 | .6 | -.3 |
| | -.3 | | -.2 | | -.2 | | UND | -.5 | -.1 | -4.4 | NM | .0 |
| | 1.6 | | 1.4 | | 1.2 | | .1 | .7 | .8 | 1.2 | .5 | -6.7 |
| | -7.5 | | -6.1 | | -8.9 | Debt/Worth | 2.6 | 6.5 | 2.0 | 3.8 | 1.0 | -2.3 |
| | -2.2 | | -2.0 | | -1.9 | | -3.7 | -4.7 | -2.1 | -5.8 | NM | -1.4 |
| | 26.8 | | 24.9 | | 41.7 | | 113.4 | 37.7 | 16.7 | | | 100.0 |
| (64) | 2.5 | (64) | 6.4 | (83) | 11.6 | % Profit Before Taxes/Tangible Net Worth | (20) 20.0 | (19) 8.1 | (14) 2.6 | | (13) | 22.1 |
| | -27.6 | | -9.5 | | -.2 | | -2.3 | .7 | -11.3 | | | -17.8 |
| | 6.4 | | 5.9 | | 8.7 | | 26.2 | 12.6 | 7.3 | 11.1 | 10.0 | 6.4 |
| | -.5 | | -.6 | | .7 | % Profit Before Taxes/Total Assets | 3.8 | 3.3 | .1 | 2.3 | 3.3 | -2.0 |
| | -9.0 | | -9.9 | | -8.1 | | -1.9 | -3.5 | -11.7 | -3.9 | -1.7 | -14.3 |
| | 28.4 | | 24.5 | | 47.2 | | 391.5 | 43.3 | 19.6 | 21.4 | 13.9 | 60.6 |
| | 5.7 | | 6.6 | | 8.6 | Sales/Net Fixed Assets | 17.1 | 12.3 | 3.8 | 6.4 | 7.4 | 12.3 |
| | 1.6 | | 2.2 | | 2.8 | | 2.8 | 3.5 | 1.9 | 2.4 | 1.1 | 3.8 |
| | 1.7 | | 1.6 | | 2.0 | | 6.7 | 3.6 | 1.9 | 1.9 | 1.1 | 1.4 |
| | .9 | | 1.0 | | 1.1 | Sales/Total Assets | 1.3 | 1.5 | 1.2 | 1.0 | .9 | 1.0 |
| | .5 | | .5 | | .6 | | .6 | .6 | .5 | .6 | .5 | .6 |
| | 1.7 | | 1.6 | | 1.1 | | 1.6 | .6 | 3.0 | 2.5 | 1.0 | .7 |
| (93) | 3.7 | (94) | 3.3 | (113) | 3.3 | % Depr., Dep., Amort./Sales | (16) 5.6 | (21) 1.7 | (17) 6.6 | (13) 3.5 | 4.4 | (36) 1.9 |
| | 9.3 | | 8.0 | | 7.1 | | 9.0 | 4.7 | 12.2 | 7.5 | 7.2 | 5.1 |
| | 5.0 | | 4.8 | | 4.6 | | | 3.6 | | | | |
| (14) | 6.6 | (16) | 7.1 | (29) | 7.8 | % Officers', Directors' Owners' Comp/Sales | | (12) 7.0 | | | | |
| | 13.9 | | 21.8 | | 18.1 | | | 19.1 | | | | |
| | 8089347M | | 8408501M | | 9927990M | Net Sales ($) | 14843M | 56728M | 85029M | 109564M | 139909M | 9521917M |
| | 9698000M | | 8872931M | | 10650282M | Total Assets ($) | 10617M | 59805M | 192006M | 386408M | 298538M | 9702908M |

M = $ thousand    MM = $ million
See Pages 9 through 22 for Explanation of Ratios and Data

## Current Data Sorted by Assets

## Comparative Historical Data

|  |  |  |  |  |  | Type of Statement |  |  |
|---|---|---|---|---|---|---|---|---|
|  |  | 1 | 9 | 3 |  | Unqualified | 13 | 8 |
|  | 1 | 1 |  |  |  | Reviewed | 7 | 7 |
| 1 |  |  |  |  |  | Compiled | 5 | 3 |
| 3 | 2 | 2 |  |  |  | Tax Returns | 9 | 3 |
| 1 | 4 | 5 |  | 1 | 1 | Other | 14 | 23 |
|  | 3 (4/1-9/30/11) |  | 31 (10/1/11-3/31/12) |  |  |  | 4/1/07-3/31/08 | 4/1/08-3/31/09 |
| 0-500M | 500M-2MM | 2-10MM | 10-50MM | 50-100MM | 100-250MM |  | ALL | ALL |
| 5 | 6 | 9 | 9 | 4 | 1 | NUMBER OF STATEMENTS | 48 | 44 |

| % | % | % | % | % | % |  | % | % |
|---|---|---|---|---|---|---|---|---|
|  |  |  |  |  |  | **ASSETS** |  |  |
|  |  |  |  |  |  | Cash & Equivalents | 16.0 | 18.4 |
|  |  |  |  |  |  | Trade Receivables (net) | 5.2 | 7.2 |
|  |  |  |  |  |  | Inventory | 1.8 | 3.2 |
|  |  |  |  |  |  | All Other Current | 2.1 | 1.9 |
|  |  |  |  |  |  | Total Current | 25.1 | 30.8 |
|  |  |  |  |  |  | Fixed Assets (net) | 65.6 | 55.1 |
|  |  |  |  |  |  | Intangibles (net) | 4.1 | 4.9 |
|  |  |  |  |  |  | All Other Non-Current | 5.2 | 9.3 |
|  |  |  |  |  |  | Total | 100.0 | 100.0 |
|  |  |  |  |  |  | **LIABILITIES** |  |  |
|  |  |  |  |  |  | Notes Payable-Short Term | 12.9 | 5.9 |
|  |  |  |  |  |  | Cur. Mat.-L.T.D. | 8.4 | 10.2 |
|  |  |  |  |  |  | Trade Payables | 8.6 | 6.3 |
|  |  |  |  |  |  | Income Taxes Payable | .1 | .0 |
|  |  |  |  |  |  | All Other Current | 16.9 | 17.9 |
|  |  |  |  |  |  | Total Current | 46.9 | 40.2 |
|  |  |  |  |  |  | Long-Term Debt | 39.8 | 27.9 |
|  |  |  |  |  |  | Deferred Taxes | .7 | .0 |
|  |  |  |  |  |  | All Other Non-Current | 10.1 | 5.2 |
|  |  |  |  |  |  | Net Worth | 2.5 | 26.7 |
|  |  |  |  |  |  | Total Liabilities & Net Worth | 100.0 | 100.0 |
|  |  |  |  |  |  | **INCOME DATA** |  |  |
|  |  |  |  |  |  | Net Sales | 100.0 | 100.0 |
|  |  |  |  |  |  | Gross Profit |  |  |
|  |  |  |  |  |  | Operating Expenses | 90.3 | 95.5 |
|  |  |  |  |  |  | Operating Profit | 9.7 | 4.5 |
|  |  |  |  |  |  | All Other Expenses (net) | 3.4 | 3.2 |
|  |  |  |  |  |  | Profit Before Taxes | 6.3 | 1.4 |
|  |  |  |  |  |  | **RATIOS** |  |  |
|  |  |  |  |  |  | Current | 1.5 / .7 / .2 | 2.3 / .8 / .3 |
|  |  |  |  |  |  | Quick | 1.3 / .5 / .2 | 1.6 / .6 / .3 |
|  |  |  |  |  |  | Sales/Receivables | 2 182.3 / 7 49.3 / 23 15.8 | 5 70.3 / 12 31.1 / 31 11.7 |
|  |  |  |  |  |  | Cost of Sales/Inventory |  |  |
|  |  |  |  |  |  | Cost of Sales/Payables |  |  |
|  |  |  |  |  |  | Sales/Working Capital | 13.6 / -13.8 / -5.4 | 12.2 / -21.9 / -5.5 |
|  |  |  |  |  |  | EBIT/Interest | (43) 10.8 / 3.6 / .9 | (36) 11.0 / 2.4 / -.2 |
|  |  |  |  |  |  | Net Profit + Depr., Dep., Amort./Cur. Mat. L/T/D |  |  |
|  |  |  |  |  |  | Fixed/Worth | 1.1 / 3.1 / NM | .8 / 1.8 / UND |
|  |  |  |  |  |  | Debt/Worth | .9 / 3.4 / -9.0 | .4 / 2.3 / UND |
|  |  |  |  |  |  | % Profit Before Taxes/Tangible Net Worth | (35) 47.4 / 16.0 / 6.7 | (33) 29.1 / 10.9 / -2.7 |
|  |  |  |  |  |  | % Profit Before Taxes/Total Assets | 19.1 / 5.5 / -.4 | 15.1 / 4.4 / -2.4 |
|  |  |  |  |  |  | Sales/Net Fixed Assets | 3.4 / 1.7 / 1.0 | 4.5 / 2.2 / 1.1 |
|  |  |  |  |  |  | Sales/Total Assets | 2.1 / 1.2 / .6 | 2.0 / 1.2 / .8 |
|  |  |  |  |  |  | % Depr., Dep., Amort./Sales | (45) 3.0 / 5.4 / 7.9 | (40) 2.9 / 4.9 / 7.2 |
|  |  |  |  |  |  | % Officers', Directors' Owners' Comp/Sales |  |  |
| 4574M | 15757M | 57596M | 436461M | 204681M | 78536M | Net Sales ($) | 1393790M | 1377109M |
| 1212M | 7233M | 45372M | 312411M | 357864M | 181661M | Total Assets ($) | 1413981M | 1295253M |

M = $ thousand    MM = $ million
See Pages 9 through 22 for Explanation of Ratios and Data

| Comparative Historical Data | | | | Current Data Sorted by Sales | | | | | |
|---|---|---|---|---|---|---|---|---|---|
| | | | **Type of Statement** | 0-1MM | 1-3MM | 3-5MM | 5-10MM | 10-25MM | 25MM & OVER |
| 11 | 13 | 13 | Unqualified | | | | 1 | 2 | 10 |
| 2 | 2 | 1 | Reviewed | | | | | 1 | |
| 2 | 1 | 1 | Compiled | 1 | | | | | |
| 15 | 4 | 7 | Tax Returns | 3 | | 1 | 2 | | |
| 31 | 19 | 12 | Other | 3 | 1 | 4 | 3 | 1 | 1 |
| 4/1/09-3/31/10 ALL | 4/1/10-3/31/11 ALL | 4/1/11-3/31/12 ALL | | | 3 (4/1-9/30/11) | | 31 (10/1/11-3/31/12) | | |
| 61 | 39 | 34 | **NUMBER OF STATEMENTS** | 7 | 1 | 5 | 6 | 4 | 11 |
| % | % | % | **ASSETS** | % | % | % | % | % | % |
| 13.5 | 16.8 | 15.3 | Cash & Equivalents | | | | | | 14.5 |
| 6.5 | 7.0 | 5.6 | Trade Receivables (net) | | | | | | 5.9 |
| 2.8 | 3.8 | 2.2 | Inventory | | | | | | 3.4 |
| 2.0 | 3.3 | 1.8 | All Other Current | | | | | | .9 |
| 24.9 | 31.0 | 25.0 | Total Current | | | | | | 24.6 |
| 61.6 | 54.9 | 59.1 | Fixed Assets (net) | | | | | | 65.2 |
| 4.3 | 3.2 | 6.6 | Intangibles (net) | | | | | | 5.9 |
| 9.3 | 10.9 | 9.3 | All Other Non-Current | | | | | | 4.2 |
| 100.0 | 100.0 | 100.0 | Total | | | | | | 100.0 |
| | | | **LIABILITIES** | | | | | | |
| 6.9 | 5.3 | 4.8 | Notes Payable-Short Term | | | | | | 7.9 |
| 9.4 | 2.5 | 3.8 | Cur. Mat.-L.T.D. | | | | | | 1.5 |
| 5.1 | 5.7 | 8.8 | Trade Payables | | | | | | 7.3 |
| .0 | .1 | .2 | Income Taxes Payable | | | | | | .1 |
| 22.7 | 21.1 | 37.9 | All Other Current | | | | | | 14.9 |
| 44.2 | 34.7 | 55.6 | Total Current | | | | | | 31.7 |
| 39.5 | 24.6 | 27.9 | Long-Term Debt | | | | | | 12.1 |
| 1.0 | .9 | 1.4 | Deferred Taxes | | | | | | 1.3 |
| 6.5 | 9.4 | 9.4 | All Other Non-Current | | | | | | 4.8 |
| 8.8 | 30.5 | 5.6 | Net Worth | | | | | | 50.0 |
| 100.0 | 100.0 | 100.0 | Total Liabilties & Net Worth | | | | | | 100.0 |
| | | | **INCOME DATA** | | | | | | |
| 100.0 | 100.0 | 100.0 | Net Sales | | | | | | 100.0 |
| | | | Gross Profit | | | | | | |
| 94.1 | 91.5 | 90.5 | Operating Expenses | | | | | | 92.9 |
| 5.9 | 8.5 | 9.5 | Operating Profit | | | | | | 7.1 |
| 5.5 | 2.9 | 3.7 | All Other Expenses (net) | | | | | | 4.5 |
| .4 | 5.6 | 5.8 | Profit Before Taxes | | | | | | 2.6 |
| | | | **RATIOS** | | | | | | |
| 2.0 | 2.9 | 2.0 | | | | | | | .8 |
| .6 | 1.0 | .7 | Current | | | | | | .7 |
| .2 | .4 | .3 | | | | | | | .3 |
| 1.9 | 2.0 | 1.9 | | | | | | | .8 |
| .4 | .8 | .6 | Quick | | | | | | .3 |
| .1 | .2 | .2 | | | | | | | .2 |
| 1 423.6 | 4 101.3 | 0 UND | | | | | | | 5 75.3 |
| 10 36.4 | 11 32.3 | 10 36.3 | Sales/Receivables | | | | | | 10 36.0 |
| 24 15.1 | 26 14.0 | 25 14.8 | | | | | | | 25 14.7 |
| | | | Cost of Sales/Inventory | | | | | | |
| | | | Cost of Sales/Payables | | | | | | |
| 8.5 | 5.2 | 11.1 | | | | | | | -28.3 |
| -19.5 | 405.4 | -24.4 | Sales/Working Capital | | | | | | -10.2 |
| -3.8 | -6.5 | -4.7 | | | | | | | -5.3 |
| 7.0 | 12.5 | 13.4 | | | | | | | 11.7 |
| (47) 1.0 | (28) 2.3 | (27) 2.5 | EBIT/Interest | | | | | (10) -.4 | |
| -1.3 | -2.9 | -.9 | | | | | | | -7.1 |
| | | | Net Profit + Depr., Dep., Amort./Cur. Mat. L/T/D | | | | | | |
| .8 | .4 | 1.1 | | | | | | | 1.1 |
| 2.1 | 1.2 | 1.8 | Fixed/Worth | | | | | | 1.5 |
| -3.9 | 10.6 | -2.3 | | | | | | | 2.8 |
| .6 | .3 | .6 | | | | | | | .6 |
| 1.4 | .9 | 2.0 | Debt/Worth | | | | | | 1.0 |
| -5.4 | 9.8 | -3.3 | | | | | | | 1.9 |
| 36.6 | 33.1 | 27.5 | % Profit Before Taxes/Tangible Net Worth | | | | | | |
| (43) 12.4 | (31) 12.4 | (20) 12.2 | | | | | | | |
| -4.0 | -9.7 | -4.3 | | | | | | | |
| 11.5 | 16.5 | 14.5 | % Profit Before Taxes/Total Assets | | | | | | 14.3 |
| 1.1 | 3.6 | 3.2 | | | | | | | -1.1 |
| -5.9 | -7.6 | -3.8 | | | | | | | -2.9 |
| 5.0 | 5.6 | 5.2 | | | | | | | 4.4 |
| 2.1 | 1.9 | 2.6 | Sales/Net Fixed Assets | | | | | | 1.6 |
| .7 | 1.0 | .8 | | | | | | | .7 |
| 2.0 | 1.7 | 2.3 | | | | | | | 1.7 |
| 1.0 | 1.2 | 1.4 | Sales/Total Assets | | | | | | 1.1 |
| .5 | .7 | .6 | | | | | | | .6 |
| 3.4 | 3.0 | 2.6 | | | | | | | 2.8 |
| (53) 7.0 | (33) 5.0 | (29) 4.5 | % Depr., Dep., Amort./Sales | | | | | | 3.9 |
| 13.8 | 11.4 | 10.1 | | | | | | | 8.8 |
| 1.8 | | | % Officers', Directors' Owners' Comp/Sales | | | | | | |
| (10) 7.0 | | | | | | | | | |
| 9.4 | | | | | | | | | |
| 1715339M | 1375738M | 797605M | Net Sales ($) | 2899M | 1288M | 19243M | 41114M | 82506M | 650555M |
| 1862385M | 1129113M | 905753M | Total Assets ($) | 5289M | 569M | 10997M | 27273M | 153380M | 708245M |

© RMA 2012                    M = $ thousand    MM = $ million
See Pages 9 through 22 for Explanation of Ratios and Data

**Current Data Sorted by Assets**      **Comparative Historical Data**

| | | | | | | Type of Statement | | |
|---|---|---|---|---|---|---|---|---|
| | 3 | 9 | 16 | 8 | 4 | Unqualified | 38 | 58 |
| | 2 | 3 | 2 | 1 | | Reviewed | 8 | 10 |
| 3 | 2 | 8 | 2 | | | Compiled | 10 | 21 |
| 13 | 7 | 7 | 1 | | 1 | Tax Returns | 33 | 21 |
| 7 | 15 | 28 | 14 | 5 | 4 | Other | 34 | 32 |
| | 47 (4/1-9/30/11) | | 118 (10/1/11-3/31/12) | | | | 4/1/07-3/31/08 | 4/1/08-3/31/09 |
| 0-500M | 500M-2MM | 2-10MM | 10-50MM | 50-100MM | 100-250MM | | ALL | ALL |
| 23 | 29 | 55 | 35 | 14 | 9 | **NUMBER OF STATEMENTS** | 123 | 142 |
| % | % | % | % | % | % | **ASSETS** | % | % |
| 35.2 | 25.4 | 15.9 | 13.8 | 17.5 | | Cash & Equivalents | 14.3 | 16.9 |
| 3.5 | 6.0 | 10.1 | 7.0 | 5.6 | | Trade Receivables (net) | 8.5 | 8.3 |
| 7.4 | 2.9 | .6 | 2.9 | .4 | | Inventory | 2.4 | 1.7 |
| 2.6 | 5.9 | 5.5 | 1.0 | 6.5 | | All Other Current | 3.7 | 5.0 |
| 48.7 | 40.2 | 32.1 | 24.7 | 30.0 | | Total Current | 29.0 | 31.8 |
| 30.3 | 44.0 | 56.5 | 57.9 | 49.0 | | Fixed Assets (net) | 51.8 | 49.3 |
| 7.8 | .4 | 4.5 | 7.9 | 7.7 | | Intangibles (net) | 3.6 | 6.2 |
| 13.1 | 15.3 | 6.9 | 9.5 | 13.3 | | All Other Non-Current | 15.6 | 12.6 |
| 100.0 | 100.0 | 100.0 | 100.0 | 100.0 | | Total | 100.0 | 100.0 |
| | | | | | | **LIABILITIES** | | |
| 43.7 | 5.3 | 4.5 | 2.9 | 1.3 | | Notes Payable-Short Term | 6.9 | 3.4 |
| 2.9 | 1.3 | 2.9 | 4.0 | 8.4 | | Cur. Mat.-L.T.D. | 3.5 | 4.4 |
| 28.3 | 8.8 | 7.5 | 3.0 | 4.2 | | Trade Payables | 5.2 | 6.1 |
| .0 | .0 | .1 | .0 | .2 | | Income Taxes Payable | .8 | .0 |
| 31.3 | 16.0 | 12.9 | 13.1 | 10.0 | | All Other Current | 10.7 | 12.9 |
| 106.2 | 31.4 | 27.8 | 23.1 | 24.1 | | Total Current | 27.2 | 26.9 |
| 19.7 | 10.3 | 25.4 | 22.9 | 17.3 | | Long-Term Debt | 23.5 | 29.2 |
| .0 | .0 | .5 | .1 | .1 | | Deferred Taxes | .1 | .3 |
| 19.8 | 8.3 | 5.3 | 7.7 | 12.1 | | All Other Non-Current | 13.0 | 7.6 |
| -45.4 | 50.0 | 41.1 | 46.3 | 46.4 | | Net Worth | 36.3 | 36.1 |
| 100.0 | 100.0 | 100.0 | 100.0 | 100.0 | | Total Liabilities & Net Worth | 100.0 | 100.0 |
| | | | | | | **INCOME DATA** | | |
| 100.0 | 100.0 | 100.0 | 100.0 | 100.0 | | Net Sales | 100.0 | 100.0 |
| | | | | | | Gross Profit | | |
| 90.3 | 86.7 | 86.2 | 92.7 | 80.4 | | Operating Expenses | 84.3 | 84.3 |
| 9.7 | 13.3 | 13.8 | 7.3 | 19.6 | | Operating Profit | 15.7 | 15.7 |
| 3.2 | 2.1 | 6.9 | 6.9 | 4.4 | | All Other Expenses (net) | 5.3 | 6.1 |
| 6.5 | 11.2 | 7.0 | .4 | 15.2 | | Profit Before Taxes | 10.4 | 9.7 |
| | | | | | | **RATIOS** | | |
| 1.7 | 4.7 | 3.0 | 2.3 | 7.0 | | | 3.6 | 4.0 |
| .6 | 1.5 | 1.4 | 1.1 | 1.2 | | Current | 1.1 | 1.3 |
| .3 | .5 | .7 | .3 | .9 | | | .4 | .5 |
| 1.6 | 3.8 | 2.5 | 2.1 | 3.0 | | | 2.6 | 2.9 |
| .5 | 1.2 | 1.1 | 1.0 | 1.1 | | Quick | .8 | 1.1 |
| .1 | .4 | .4 | .3 | .5 | | | .3 | .4 |
| 0 UND | 0 UND | 0 999.8 | 3 120.6 | 7 53.0 | | | 0 UND | 0 UND |
| 0 UND | 4 97.5 | 5 80.5 | 18 20.2 | 33 11.0 | | Sales/Receivables | 6 59.1 | 7 49.2 |
| 0 999.8 | 16 23.0 | 28 12.9 | 39 9.4 | 59 6.2 | | | 34 10.6 | 26 14.2 |
| | | | | | | Cost of Sales/Inventory | | |
| | | | | | | Cost of Sales/Payables | | |
| 68.5 | 6.2 | 6.2 | 2.8 | 2.8 | | | 3.7 | 3.6 |
| -43.8 | 21.6 | 23.7 | 39.0 | 22.3 | | Sales/Working Capital | 79.3 | 25.3 |
| -13.6 | -17.5 | -11.3 | -3.0 | -23.5 | | | -10.0 | -12.5 |
| 24.3 | 36.8 | 13.4 | 17.7 | 24.1 | | | 18.6 | 6.7 |
| (18) 5.6 | (16) 13.2 | (38) 3.9 | (22) 2.1 | (11) 3.1 | | EBIT/Interest | (85) 4.1 | (95) 3.1 |
| -.5 | .2 | .9 | -3.8 | 1.2 | | | 1.2 | .6 |
| | | | | | | Net Profit + Depr., Dep., Amort./Cur. Mat. L/T/D | | |
| .1 | .2 | .8 | .5 | .5 | | | .5 | .5 |
| 1.5 | .9 | 1.8 | 1.2 | 1.3 | | Fixed/Worth | 1.1 | 1.2 |
| -1.0 | 1.5 | 4.3 | 7.9 | 2.8 | | | 4.4 | 10.2 |
| 1.2 | .2 | .5 | .3 | .3 | | | .3 | .3 |
| 18.0 | .4 | 2.0 | 1.4 | 1.4 | | Debt/Worth | 1.1 | 1.2 |
| -2.3 | 3.7 | 7.9 | 8.8 | 10.3 | | | 5.3 | 28.4 |
| 367.9 | 34.7 | 51.6 | 11.0 | 33.3 | | | 32.5 | 42.8 |
| (14) 72.3 | (26) 14.5 | (46) 7.1 | (32) 1.5 | (12) 11.2 | | % Profit Before Taxes/Tangible Net Worth | (100) 12.8 | (114) 9.6 |
| -.3 | 5.8 | .4 | -5.4 | 1.4 | | | 2.1 | -.1 |
| 56.1 | 17.3 | 14.6 | 5.1 | 9.1 | | | 15.3 | 13.8 |
| 25.8 | 6.8 | 3.1 | .8 | 3.4 | | % Profit Before Taxes/Total Assets | 4.9 | 2.7 |
| -7.0 | 1.9 | -.2 | -2.4 | .6 | | | -.7 | -1.3 |
| 999.8 | 39.2 | 33.3 | 2.7 | 13.1 | | | 22.0 | 17.9 |
| 32.8 | 8.5 | 1.3 | .6 | 1.1 | | Sales/Net Fixed Assets | 1.8 | 1.7 |
| 5.3 | 1.1 | .3 | .3 | .4 | | | .3 | .5 |
| 16.2 | 3.5 | 2.8 | 1.0 | .7 | | | 2.0 | 1.8 |
| 6.1 | 1.9 | 1.0 | .4 | .4 | | Sales/Total Assets | .7 | .7 |
| 2.1 | .9 | .2 | .2 | .3 | | | .3 | .3 |
| .7 | .6 | 2.5 | 5.8 | 3.9 | | | 1.9 | 2.2 |
| (10) 3.3 | (17) 2.8 | (42) 6.3 | (28) 9.7 | (12) 8.0 | | % Depr., Dep., Amort./Sales | (101) 6.1 | (115) 5.0 |
| 8.2 | 8.4 | 15.0 | 18.6 | 12.9 | | | 12.3 | 10.9 |
| 4.7 | | 1.6 | | | | | 3.7 | 3.6 |
| (13) 7.7 | | (10) 2.7 | | | | % Officers', Directors' Owners' Comp/Sales | (19) 6.4 | (22) 5.6 |
| 10.0 | | 5.4 | | | | | 13.3 | 10.4 |
| 40609M | 82332M | 392803M | 534202M | 648985M | 7601170M | Net Sales ($) | 2025691M | 3201839M |
| 5121M | 33504M | 220244M | 776939M | 1026589M | 1559500M | Total Assets ($) | 2386156M | 4208974M |

© RMA 2012

M = $ thousand    MM = $ million
See Pages 9 through 22 for Explanation of Ratios and Data

## Comparative Historical Data | Current Data Sorted by Sales

| | | | Type of Statement | | | | | | |
|---|---|---|---|---|---|---|---|---|---|
| 61 | 39 | 40 | Unqualified | 2 | 7 | 5 | 7 | 10 | 9 |
| 9 | 9 | 8 | Reviewed | | 1 | 2 | 2 | 1 | 2 |
| 15 | 8 | 15 | Compiled | 6 | 6 | | 1 | 2 | |
| 34 | 27 | 29 | Tax Returns | 12 | 9 | 3 | 1 | 1 | 3 |
| 43 | 46 | 73 | Other | 14 | 18 | 5 | 15 | 15 | 12 |
| 4/1/09-3/31/10 ALL | 4/1/10-3/31/11 ALL | 4/1/11-3/31/12 ALL | | 47 (4/1-9/30/11) | | 118 (10/1/11-3/31/12) | | | |
| | | | | 0-1MM | 1-3MM | 3-5MM | 5-10MM | 10-25MM | 25MM & OVER |
| 162 | 129 | 165 | **NUMBER OF STATEMENTS** | 34 | 41 | 15 | 20 | 29 | 26 |
| % | % | % | **ASSETS** | % | % | % | % | % | % |
| 16.1 | 15.4 | 20.5 | Cash & Equivalents | 10.0 | 24.1 | 27.8 | 12.5 | 26.7 | 23.4 |
| 7.8 | 8.3 | 7.2 | Trade Receivables (net) | .4 | 6.3 | 5.3 | 6.3 | 13.5 | 12.1 |
| 1.1 | 1.8 | 2.4 | Inventory | 1.9 | 3.5 | 1.2 | .2 | 2.2 | 4.0 |
| 4.2 | 7.3 | 4.3 | All Other Current | .5 | 6.2 | 1.6 | 8.0 | 5.0 | 4.0 |
| 29.2 | 32.8 | 34.3 | Total Current | 12.8 | 40.1 | 35.9 | 27.0 | 47.5 | 43.3 |
| 47.8 | 45.1 | 49.0 | Fixed Assets (net) | 78.5 | 47.8 | 44.0 | 50.7 | 36.2 | 28.4 |
| 8.9 | 7.6 | 5.6 | Intangibles (net) | 5.2 | 2.1 | .8 | 7.3 | 4.7 | 14.3 |
| 14.2 | 14.6 | 11.0 | All Other Non-Current | 3.5 | 10.0 | 19.4 | 15.0 | 11.7 | 14.0 |
| 100.0 | 100.0 | 100.0 | Total | 100.0 | 100.0 | 100.0 | 100.0 | 100.0 | 100.0 |
| | | | **LIABILITIES** | | | | | | |
| 4.7 | 7.9 | 9.3 | Notes Payable-Short Term | 5.9 | 15.2 | 34.3 | 2.1 | 2.0 | 3.4 |
| 5.5 | 3.5 | 3.4 | Cur. Mat.-L.T.D. | 3.2 | 2.7 | .1 | 4.5 | 3.2 | 5.7 |
| 6.6 | 5.9 | 11.6 | Trade Payables | 1.4 | 16.9 | 8.6 | 7.4 | 9.2 | 24.0 |
| .3 | .6 | .0 | Income Taxes Payable | .0 | .0 | .0 | .2 | .0 | .1 |
| 14.1 | 14.0 | 16.3 | All Other Current | 5.0 | 13.1 | 32.6 | 14.1 | 22.7 | 21.5 |
| 31.2 | 31.9 | 40.6 | Total Current | 15.5 | 47.9 | 75.7 | 28.1 | 37.2 | 54.8 |
| 29.7 | 19.8 | 22.8 | Long-Term Debt | 40.4 | 19.2 | 8.0 | 23.6 | 13.4 | 23.9 |
| .3 | .3 | .2 | Deferred Taxes | .0 | .0 | 1.7 | .0 | .0 | .1 |
| 10.2 | 13.3 | 9.5 | All Other Non-Current | 4.6 | 11.1 | 18.6 | 11.9 | 9.6 | 6.3 |
| 28.6 | 34.7 | 27.0 | Net Worth | 39.5 | 22.0 | -4.0 | 36.4 | 39.8 | 14.8 |
| 100.0 | 100.0 | 100.0 | Total Liabilities & Net Worth | 100.0 | 100.0 | 100.0 | 100.0 | 100.0 | 100.0 |
| | | | **INCOME DATA** | | | | | | |
| 100.0 | 100.0 | 100.0 | Net Sales | 100.0 | 100.0 | 100.0 | 100.0 | 100.0 | 100.0 |
| | | | Gross Profit | | | | | | |
| 90.2 | 90.6 | 87.4 | Operating Expenses | 71.8 | 89.0 | 94.7 | 92.8 | 96.0 | 87.6 |
| 9.8 | 9.4 | 12.6 | Operating Profit | 28.2 | 11.0 | 5.3 | 7.2 | 4.0 | 12.4 |
| 5.7 | 3.6 | 5.4 | All Other Expenses (net) | 13.8 | 4.0 | 5.3 | 3.3 | .8 | 3.4 |
| 4.2 | 5.7 | 7.2 | Profit Before Taxes | 14.4 | 7.1 | .0 | 3.9 | 3.2 | 8.9 |
| | | | **RATIOS** | | | | | | |
| 3.1 | 2.5 | 2.6 | | 2.3 | 2.7 | 6.3 | 2.5 | 2.5 | 2.8 |
| 1.1 | 1.0 | 1.2 | Current | .7 | 1.1 | 2.2 | 1.0 | 1.4 | 1.3 |
| .4 | .5 | .5 | | .4 | .5 | .3 | .3 | .9 | .8 |
| 2.7 | 1.8 | 2.3 | | 1.9 | 2.3 | 4.6 | 1.3 | 2.5 | 2.0 |
| .9 | .8 | 1.0 | Quick | .6 | .9 | 2.1 | .6 | 1.1 | 1.1 |
| .3 | .3 | .3 | | .3 | .3 | .3 | .3 | .7 | .4 |
| 0 UND | 0 UND | 0 UND | | 0 UND | 0 UND | 2 158.0 | 1 479.1 | 3 142.7 | 4 92.7 |
| 9 40.8 | 5 73.3 | 5 73.7 | Sales/Receivables | 0 UND | 1 350.5 | 8 46.7 | 9 39.6 | 14 25.5 | 21 17.6 |
| 23 15.6 | 21 17.0 | 27 13.7 | | 5 73.8 | 9 42.4 | 28 12.9 | 26 13.9 | 45 8.1 | 40 9.1 |
| | | | Cost of Sales/Inventory | | | | | | |
| | | | Cost of Sales/Payables | | | | | | |
| 5.6 | 6.9 | 5.5 | | 3.8 | 5.3 | 4.4 | 11.6 | 4.2 | 6.6 |
| 51.8 | 200.5 | 33.8 | Sales/Working Capital | -39.7 | 149.4 | 8.0 | NM | 20.2 | 26.5 |
| -9.7 | -17.0 | -10.1 | | -5.1 | -12.6 | -3.5 | -7.1 | -334.3 | -23.9 |
| 12.7 | 15.9 | 21.4 | | 13.8 | 26.0 | | 8.3 | 26.0 | 35.2 |
| (110) 2.2 | (89) 3.6 | (110) 3.9 | EBIT/Interest | (20) 4.9 | (25) 4.0 | | (15) 1.4 | (24) 6.1 | (19) 4.0 |
| -1.4 | -.6 | .8 | | 1.2 | -.3 | | -.5 | 1.3 | 2.3 |
| | | | Net Profit + Depr., Dep., Amort./Cur. Mat. L/T/D | | | | | | |
| .7 | .5 | .4 | | 1.3 | .3 | .2 | .2 | .4 | .1 |
| 1.6 | 1.4 | 1.4 | Fixed/Worth | 2.3 | 1.1 | .8 | 2.1 | 1.0 | .9 |
| -17.0 | 10.6 | 5.3 | | 6.3 | 9.2 | 1.1 | 5.7 | 5.1 | 3.5 |
| .4 | .3 | .4 | | .6 | .4 | .1 | 1.1 | .4 | .4 |
| 2.1 | 1.6 | 2.0 | Debt/Worth | 2.0 | 2.2 | .3 | 2.7 | 1.2 | 2.3 |
| -16.9 | 17.3 | 10.1 | | 7.7 | 16.4 | 8.9 | 44.8 | 9.0 | NM |
| 29.5 | 60.0 | 43.3 | | 38.6 | 41.6 | 27.6 | 23.0 | 60.4 | 93.7 |
| (117) 6.3 | (100) 8.4 | (135) 8.7 | % Profit Before Taxes/Tangible Net Worth | (29) 8.9 | (33) 7.3 | (12) 6.0 | (16) 3.4 | (25) 9.3 | (20) 24.5 |
| -5.6 | -2.3 | -.5 | | 2.0 | -7.8 | -2.0 | -7.0 | 1.5 | 1.5 |
| 9.8 | 19.4 | 15.0 | | 11.4 | 14.8 | 23.5 | 8.0 | 24.7 | 20.3 |
| 2.1 | 3.6 | 3.4 | % Profit Before Taxes/Total Assets | 3.0 | 3.4 | 4.0 | 1.8 | 2.7 | 6.6 |
| -4.2 | -1.7 | -.6 | | -.1 | -3.3 | -2.4 | -2.0 | .5 | .3 |
| 22.1 | 38.9 | 33.1 | | 1.4 | 83.3 | 31.0 | 29.5 | 62.3 | 153.6 |
| 2.6 | 2.9 | 2.2 | Sales/Net Fixed Assets | .2 | 2.6 | 1.5 | 3.4 | 5.4 | 14.1 |
| .6 | .6 | .5 | | .1 | 1.1 | .6 | .6 | .6 | 1.2 |
| 2.6 | 3.4 | 2.9 | | 1.2 | 4.3 | 3.2 | 3.4 | 3.8 | 2.9 |
| .8 | 1.0 | 1.0 | Sales/Total Assets | .2 | 1.2 | 1.0 | 1.2 | 1.3 | 1.2 |
| .3 | .4 | .3 | | .1 | .5 | .3 | .4 | .4 | .4 |
| 1.9 | 1.3 | 2.4 | | 9.5 | 1.6 | | 2.9 | 1.4 | .2 |
| (119) 5.3 | (99) 5.8 | (115) 6.3 | % Depr., Dep., Amort./Sales | (24) 18.7 | (26) 5.3 | | (15) 5.9 | (22) 5.7 | (19) 2.9 |
| 11.6 | 10.6 | 13.3 | | 29.5 | 9.0 | | 12.0 | 11.2 | 8.3 |
| 3.9 | 2.6 | 2.4 | | | 2.4 | | | | |
| (24) 6.9 | (25) 5.5 | (32) 5.5 | % Officers', Directors' Owners' Comp/Sales | | (10) 5.1 | | | | |
| 11.2 | 11.3 | 9.2 | | | 8.9 | | | | |
| 4469713M | 2629640M | 9300101M | Net Sales ($) | 19238M | 78804M | 58365M | 140237M | 462799M | 8540658M |
| 5393117M | 3057610M | 3621897M | Total Assets ($) | 102060M | 176636M | 108344M | 239807M | 839644M | 2155406M |

M = $ thousand    MM = $ million
See Pages 9 through 22 for Explanation of Ratios and Data

## Current Data Sorted by Assets

## Comparative Historical Data

| | | | | | | Type of Statement | | |
|---|---|---|---|---|---|---|---|---|
| | 1 | 2 | 1 | | 1 | Unqualified | 2 | 5 |
| | 1 | 1 | 2 | | | Reviewed | 1 | |
| | 1 | 1 | 1 | | | Compiled | 2 | 4 |
| 5 | 1 | 2 | | | | Tax Returns | 2 | 1 |
| 2 | 5 | 2 | | | | Other | 6 | 5 |
| | 3 (4/1-9/30/11) | | 29 (10/1/11-3/31/12) | | | | 4/1/07-3/31/08 | 4/1/08-3/31/09 |
| 0-500M | 500M-2MM | 2-10MM | 10-50MM | 50-100MM | 100-250MM | | ALL | ALL |
| 7 | 8 | 8 | 7 | 1 | 1 | NUMBER OF STATEMENTS | 13 | 15 |
| % | % | % | % | % | % | | % | % |
| | | | | | | **ASSETS** | | |
| | | | | | | Cash & Equivalents | 23.1 | 10.6 |
| | | | | | | Trade Receivables (net) | 14.9 | 21.1 |
| | | | | | | Inventory | 7.0 | 3.1 |
| | | | | | | All Other Current | 2.3 | 15.3 |
| | | | | | | Total Current | 47.2 | 50.1 |
| | | | | | | Fixed Assets (net) | 30.7 | 26.3 |
| | | | | | | Intangibles (net) | 10.0 | 9.2 |
| | | | | | | All Other Non-Current | 12.0 | 14.5 |
| | | | | | | Total | 100.0 | 100.0 |
| | | | | | | **LIABILITIES** | | |
| | | | | | | Notes Payable-Short Term | 16.5 | 9.3 |
| | | | | | | Cur. Mat.-L.T.D. | 2.3 | 7.1 |
| | | | | | | Trade Payables | 11.9 | 20.3 |
| | | | | | | Income Taxes Payable | .1 | .6 |
| | | | | | | All Other Current | 20.9 | 19.0 |
| | | | | | | Total Current | 51.7 | 56.3 |
| | | | | | | Long-Term Debt | 17.5 | 23.2 |
| | | | | | | Deferred Taxes | .4 | .5 |
| | | | | | | All Other Non-Current | 30.7 | 7.1 |
| | | | | | | Net Worth | -1.0 | 12.8 |
| | | | | | | Total Liabilties & Net Worth | 100.0 | 100.0 |
| | | | | | | **INCOME DATA** | | |
| | | | | | | Net Sales | 100.0 | 100.0 |
| | | | | | | Gross Profit | | |
| | | | | | | Operating Expenses | 94.1 | 94.2 |
| | | | | | | Operating Profit | 5.9 | 5.8 |
| | | | | | | All Other Expenses (net) | .6 | 1.0 |
| | | | | | | Profit Before Taxes | 5.3 | 4.8 |
| | | | | | | **RATIOS** | | |
| | | | | | | | 1.6 | 2.2 |
| | | | | | | Current | 1.3 | 1.4 |
| | | | | | | | .7 | .6 |
| | | | | | | | 1.4 | 1.8 |
| | | | | | | Quick | .9 | .8 |
| | | | | | | | .7 | .4 |
| | | | | | | | 1   519.5 | 17   21.0 |
| | | | | | | Sales/Receivables | 14   26.3 | 31   11.9 |
| | | | | | | | 42   8.6 | 40   9.2 |
| | | | | | | Cost of Sales/Inventory | | |
| | | | | | | Cost of Sales/Payables | | |
| | | | | | | | 9.7 | 10.2 |
| | | | | | | Sales/Working Capital | 62.3 | 28.2 |
| | | | | | | | -39.1 | -14.3 |
| | | | | | | | 113.6 | 18.3 |
| | | | | | | EBIT/Interest | (10)   16.9 | (12)   2.1 |
| | | | | | | | -1.8 | -3.5 |
| | | | | | | Net Profit + Depr., Dep., Amort./Cur. Mat. L/T/D | | |
| | | | | | | | .3 | .4 |
| | | | | | | Fixed/Worth | .9 | 2.1 |
| | | | | | | | -2.3 | -1.0 |
| | | | | | | | 1.0 | .8 |
| | | | | | | Debt/Worth | 3.6 | 35.7 |
| | | | | | | | -6.5 | -3.6 |
| | | | | | | | | 149.1 |
| | | | | | | % Profit Before Taxes/Tangible Net Worth | | (10)   33.4 |
| | | | | | | | | 4.7 |
| | | | | | | | 27.6 | 22.0 |
| | | | | | | % Profit Before Taxes/Total Assets | 4.9 | 2.6 |
| | | | | | | | 2.3 | -7.9 |
| | | | | | | | 84.7 | 46.8 |
| | | | | | | Sales/Net Fixed Assets | 10.9 | 16.2 |
| | | | | | | | 3.5 | 2.3 |
| | | | | | | | 2.8 | 4.2 |
| | | | | | | Sales/Total Assets | 2.2 | 2.4 |
| | | | | | | | 1.0 | 1.1 |
| | | | | | | | .7 | .4 |
| | | | | | | % Depr., Dep., Amort./Sales | (11)   1.6 | (11)   1.1 |
| | | | | | | | 12.2 | 2.3 |
| | | | | | | % Officers', Directors' Owners' Comp/Sales | | |
| 25708M | 34468M | 84853M | 511774M | 81996M | 97196M | Net Sales ($) | 892873M | 840751M |
| 1944M | 7821M | 32026M | 143366M | 57153M | 138005M | Total Assets ($) | 529048M | 485075M |

M = $ thousand MM = $ million
See Pages 9 through 22 for Explanation of Ratios and Data

| | Comparative Historical Data | | | | Current Data Sorted by Sales | | | | | |
|---|---|---|---|---|---|---|---|---|---|---|
| **Type of Statement** | | | | | | 3 (4/1-9/30/11) | | | 29 (10/1/11-3/31/12) | |
| | | | | | 0-1MM | 1-3MM | 3-5MM | 5-10MM | 10-25MM | 25MM & OVER |
| Unqualified | 7 | 5 | 5 | | | 1 | | 1 | 1 | 2 |
| Reviewed | | 1 | 3 | | | | | 1 | | 2 |
| Compiled | 3 | 4 | 3 | | | 1 | 1 | | | 1 |
| Tax Returns | 4 | 3 | 8 | | | 4 | 1 | 2 | | 1 |
| Other | 5 | 3 | 13 | | 2 | 2 | 1 | 2 | 2 | 4 |
| | 4/1/09-3/31/10 ALL | 4/1/10-3/31/11 ALL | 4/1/11-3/31/12 ALL | | | | | | | |
| **NUMBER OF STATEMENTS** | 19 | 16 | 32 | | 2 | 8 | 3 | 6 | 3 | 10 |
| | % | % | % | | % | % | % | % | % | % |
| **ASSETS** | | | | | | | | | | |
| Cash & Equivalents | 27.3 | 22.3 | 25.2 | | | | | | | 11.7 |
| Trade Receivables (net) | 15.0 | 16.2 | 12.7 | | | | | | | 15.9 |
| Inventory | 1.8 | 1.1 | 4.7 | | | | | | | 9.8 |
| All Other Current | 6.3 | 10.7 | 6.6 | | | | | | | 7.6 |
| Total Current | 50.5 | 50.3 | 49.1 | | | | | | | 45.1 |
| Fixed Assets (net) | 22.7 | 22.8 | 24.5 | | | | | | | 23.5 |
| Intangibles (net) | 10.9 | 10.7 | 13.5 | | | | | | | 23.8 |
| All Other Non-Current | 15.8 | 16.1 | 12.9 | | | | | | | 7.5 |
| Total | 100.0 | 100.0 | 100.0 | | | | | | | 100.0 |
| **LIABILITIES** | | | | | | | | | | |
| Notes Payable-Short Term | 7.5 | 13.5 | 11.7 | | | | | | | 2.0 |
| Cur. Mat.-L.T.D. | 5.3 | 22.0 | 1.5 | | | | | | | 1.9 |
| Trade Payables | 11.6 | 12.4 | 9.3 | | | | | | | 9.8 |
| Income Taxes Payable | .2 | .7 | .2 | | | | | | | .5 |
| All Other Current | 13.0 | 25.8 | 17.7 | | | | | | | 18.7 |
| Total Current | 37.6 | 74.5 | 40.4 | | | | | | | 33.0 |
| Long-Term Debt | 10.3 | 47.2 | 17.9 | | | | | | | 26.5 |
| Deferred Taxes | .5 | .7 | .3 | | | | | | | 1.1 |
| All Other Non-Current | 8.7 | 7.2 | 12.3 | | | | | | | 12.4 |
| Net Worth | 42.9 | -29.6 | 29.1 | | | | | | | 27.0 |
| Total Liabilities & Net Worth | 100.0 | 100.0 | 100.0 | | | | | | | 100.0 |
| **INCOME DATA** | | | | | | | | | | |
| Net Sales | 100.0 | 100.0 | 100.0 | | | | | | | 100.0 |
| Gross Profit | | | | | | | | | | |
| Operating Expenses | 98.4 | 92.7 | 94.6 | | | | | | | 93.7 |
| Operating Profit | 1.6 | 7.3 | 5.4 | | | | | | | 6.3 |
| All Other Expenses (net) | 3.8 | .7 | -.2 | | | | | | | 1.5 |
| Profit Before Taxes | -2.2 | 6.6 | 5.6 | | | | | | | 4.9 |
| **RATIOS** | | | | | | | | | | |
| Current | 2.6 | 1.7 | 3.7 | | | | | | | 4.1 |
| | 1.6 | 1.0 | 1.4 | | | | | | | 1.8 |
| | .6 | .6 | .8 | | | | | | | .7 |
| Quick | 2.2 | 1.2 | 1.9 | | | | | | | 2.3 |
| | 1.1 | .7 | 1.1 | | | | | | | 1.2 |
| | .5 | .3 | .7 | | | | | | | .3 |
| Sales/Receivables | 0 UND | 0 UND | 0 UND | | | | | | 3 | 117.0 |
| | 14 26.3 | 13 28.1 | 3 108.1 | | | | | | 22 | 16.8 |
| | 37 9.9 | 36 10.0 | 25 14.6 | | | | | | 28 | 13.0 |
| Cost of Sales/Inventory | | | | | | | | | | |
| Cost of Sales/Payables | | | | | | | | | | |
| Sales/Working Capital | 4.6 | 21.0 | 12.8 | | | | | | | 11.5 |
| | 12.6 | NM | 40.6 | | | | | | | 15.2 |
| | -33.1 | -16.2 | -25.2 | | | | | | | -11.4 |
| EBIT/Interest | 45.9 | 37.6 | 46.0 | | | | | | | |
| | (13) 3.3 | (13) 7.1 | (19) 13.8 | | | | | | | |
| | -.5 | 3.6 | .7 | | | | | | | |
| Net Profit + Depr., Dep., Amort./Cur. Mat. L/T/D | | | | | | | | | | |
| Fixed/Worth | .0 | .4 | .3 | | | | | | | .2 |
| | .3 | -2.3 | 1.2 | | | | | | | 12.0 |
| | 8.2 | -.1 | -.6 | | | | | | | -2.0 |
| Debt/Worth | .2 | 3.1 | .5 | | | | | | | 3.5 |
| | 1.4 | -13.2 | 6.1 | | | | | | | 24.5 |
| | 38.8 | -1.7 | -4.6 | | | | | | | -4.5 |
| % Profit Before Taxes/Tangible Net Worth | 364.2 | | 133.4 | | | | | | | |
| | (16) 15.3 | | (20) 51.9 | | | | | | | |
| | -3.2 | | 5.1 | | | | | | | |
| % Profit Before Taxes/Total Assets | 41.8 | 66.5 | 32.4 | | | | | | | 29.7 |
| | 3.5 | 19.5 | 11.6 | | | | | | | 11.6 |
| | -7.0 | 2.4 | .2 | | | | | | | 3.7 |
| Sales/Net Fixed Assets | 110.0 | 525.6 | 148.5 | | | | | | | 68.1 |
| | 44.1 | 22.0 | 23.5 | | | | | | | 23.5 |
| | 3.5 | 4.0 | 9.9 | | | | | | | 11.2 |
| Sales/Total Assets | 6.9 | 7.8 | 6.3 | | | | | | | 4.9 |
| | 2.1 | 3.6 | 3.2 | | | | | | | 3.2 |
| | .5 | 1.2 | 1.7 | | | | | | | 1.6 |
| % Depr., Dep., Amort./Sales | .2 | .8 | .2 | | | | | | | |
| | (10) .7 | (11) 1.2 | (20) .7 | | | | | | | |
| | 2.4 | 1.9 | 3.5 | | | | | | | |
| % Officers', Directors' Owners' Comp/Sales | | | | | | | | | | |
| Net Sales ($) | 601414M | 997202M | 835995M | | 1235M | 13192M | 11912M | 40425M | 46542M | 722689M |
| Total Assets ($) | 435431M | 493086M | 380315M | | 3016M | 4080M | 9013M | 14668M | 4061M | 345477M |

© RMA 2012

M = $ thousand    MM = $ million
See Pages 9 through 22 for Explanation of Ratios and Data

## Current Data Sorted by Assets | Comparative Historical Data

| | | | | | | Type of Statement | | |
|---|---|---|---|---|---|---|---|---|
| | 5 | 22 | 45 | 26 | 21 | Unqualified | 115 | 126 |
| | | 3 | | | | Reviewed | 5 | 5 |
| | 3 | 1 | | | | Compiled | 7 | 3 |
| 1 | 1 | 3 | | | | Tax Returns | 3 | 9 |
| 4 | 9 | 24 | 15 | 9 | 6 | Other | 45 | 52 |
| | 110 (4/1-9/30/11) | | 88 (10/1/11-3/31/12) | | | | 4/1/07-3/31/08 | 4/1/08-3/31/09 |
| 0-500M | 500M-2MM | 2-10MM | 10-50MM | 50-100MM | 100-250MM | | ALL | ALL |
| 5 | 18 | 53 | 60 | 35 | 27 | NUMBER OF STATEMENTS | 175 | 195 |
| % | % | % | % | % | % | ASSETS | % | % |
| | 14.0 | 12.8 | 10.8 | 8.2 | 8.4 | Cash & Equivalents | 13.8 | 13.3 |
| | 3.3 | 4.9 | 2.8 | 2.2 | 2.0 | Trade Receivables (net) | 5.4 | 3.7 |
| | 8.1 | 4.5 | 1.0 | .5 | 2.0 | Inventory | 2.9 | 2.8 |
| | 3.2 | 3.8 | 3.1 | 2.5 | 2.3 | All Other Current | 3.8 | 3.4 |
| | 28.6 | 26.0 | 17.6 | 13.5 | 14.7 | Total Current | 25.8 | 23.2 |
| | 54.5 | 55.2 | 55.5 | 61.4 | 39.1 | Fixed Assets (net) | 48.2 | 52.9 |
| | .0 | 2.2 | 1.1 | 1.6 | .1 | Intangibles (net) | .5 | .6 |
| | 17.0 | 16.6 | 25.8 | 23.6 | 46.1 | All Other Non-Current | 25.5 | 23.3 |
| | 100.0 | 100.0 | 100.0 | 100.0 | 100.0 | Total | 100.0 | 100.0 |
| | | | | | | LIABILITIES | | |
| | 4.1 | 2.5 | 1.3 | 1.3 | .3 | Notes Payable-Short Term | 3.6 | 4.2 |
| | 1.4 | 1.4 | 1.0 | .6 | .8 | Cur. Mat.-L.T.D. | 1.0 | .8 |
| | 3.2 | 4.3 | 2.8 | 1.4 | 2.0 | Trade Payables | 3.6 | 3.2 |
| | .0 | .0 | .1 | .0 | .0 | Income Taxes Payable | .0 | .0 |
| | 2.4 | 6.1 | 2.5 | 1.8 | 2.3 | All Other Current | 4.8 | 4.2 |
| | 11.0 | 14.4 | 7.7 | 5.2 | 5.3 | Total Current | 13.0 | 12.5 |
| | 21.2 | 11.7 | 12.6 | 16.0 | 7.2 | Long-Term Debt | 16.3 | 12.9 |
| | .0 | .0 | .0 | .0 | .0 | Deferred Taxes | .0 | .1 |
| | 17.9 | 3.7 | 2.3 | 3.0 | 1.9 | All Other Non-Current | 3.5 | 3.2 |
| | 50.0 | 70.2 | 77.5 | 75.8 | 85.5 | Net Worth | 67.3 | 71.3 |
| | 100.0 | 100.0 | 100.0 | 100.0 | 100.0 | Total Liabilties & Net Worth | 100.0 | 100.0 |
| | | | | | | INCOME DATA | | |
| | 100.0 | 100.0 | 100.0 | 100.0 | 100.0 | Net Sales | 100.0 | 100.0 |
| | | | | | | Gross Profit | | |
| | 87.9 | 93.1 | 96.4 | 94.3 | 93.0 | Operating Expenses | 83.9 | 93.6 |
| | 12.1 | 6.9 | 3.6 | 5.7 | 7.0 | Operating Profit | 16.1 | 6.4 |
| | 2.3 | 3.4 | 3.8 | 4.9 | .1 | All Other Expenses (net) | 2.6 | 5.0 |
| | 9.8 | 3.6 | -.3 | .8 | 6.9 | Profit Before Taxes | 13.4 | 1.4 |
| | | | | | | RATIOS | | |
| | 12.1 | 6.9 | 5.4 | 6.5 | 5.1 | | 7.7 | 6.0 |
| | 3.6 | 2.2 | 2.3 | 2.9 | 2.9 | Current | 2.9 | 2.3 |
| | .7 | 1.1 | .9 | 1.5 | 1.7 | | 1.1 | 1.0 |
| | 7.9 | 5.0 | 3.7 | 5.1 | 4.8 | | 5.4 | 4.4 |
| | 1.7 | 1.6 | 1.5 | 1.5 | 1.9 | Quick | 1.6 | 1.4 |
| | .5 | .6 | .6 | .4 | .8 | | .7 | .5 |
| 0 UND | 0 842.8 | 2 155.3 | 3 127.7 | 7 53.8 | | Sales/Receivables | 2 146.0 | 1 274.5 |
| 3 123.4 | 6 56.8 | 11 34.4 | 11 33.5 | 11 32.4 | | | 18 20.0 | 11 34.8 |
| 11 33.1 | 42 8.7 | 33 10.9 | 78 4.7 | 35 10.4 | | | 54 6.8 | 41 9.0 |
| | | | | | | Cost of Sales/Inventory | | |
| | | | | | | Cost of Sales/Payables | | |
| | 3.0 | 2.5 | 2.0 | 1.4 | 1.7 | | 1.6 | 1.8 |
| | 12.4 | 7.2 | 4.6 | 3.2 | 3.3 | Sales/Working Capital | 4.7 | 6.5 |
| | -35.8 | 114.8 | -67.0 | 10.1 | 6.9 | | 35.7 | -126.0 |
| | 35.4 | 5.4 | 14.6 | 4.1 | 31.2 | | 14.5 | 8.9 |
| (15) 5.1 | (27) -.1 | (38) 2.5 | (30) .9 | (19) 4.3 | | EBIT/Interest | (115) 3.6 | (132) .8 |
| -.3 | -5.9 | -.6 | -7.3 | -.3 | | | -.2 | -7.2 |
| | | | | | | Net Profit + Depr., Dep., Amort./Cur. Mat. L/T/D | | |
| | .4 | .5 | .4 | .6 | .1 | | .3 | .4 |
| | 1.0 | .9 | .7 | .9 | .4 | Fixed/Worth | .7 | .7 |
| | 2.8 | 1.1 | .9 | 1.1 | .8 | | 1.0 | 1.1 |
| | .1 | .1 | .1 | .1 | .0 | | .1 | .1 |
| | .5 | .3 | .2 | .2 | .1 | Debt/Worth | .2 | .2 |
| | 4.1 | .7 | .5 | .6 | .3 | | .8 | .7 |
| | 27.8 | 7.5 | 8.1 | 3.9 | 4.4 | % Profit Before Taxes/Tangible Net Worth | 16.2 | 9.6 |
| (17) 7.9 | (50) 1.1 | (58) .2 | .0 | 1.2 | | (165) 3.3 | (189) -.5 |
| -7.4 | -3.3 | -4.0 | -3.0 | -.6 | | -1.9 | -6.5 |
| | 15.9 | 4.7 | 5.9 | 2.6 | 3.7 | % Profit Before Taxes/Total Assets | 11.1 | 6.5 |
| | 3.5 | .9 | -.2 | .0 | .7 | | 2.4 | -.5 |
| | -3.9 | -3.0 | -3.6 | -2.1 | -.6 | | -1.2 | -4.8 |
| | 6.0 | 2.5 | 1.0 | .5 | 1.1 | | 2.3 | 1.6 |
| | 1.6 | .7 | .5 | .3 | .6 | Sales/Net Fixed Assets | .7 | .6 |
| | .4 | .3 | .3 | .2 | .3 | | .4 | .3 |
| | 1.4 | .8 | .4 | .2 | .3 | | .6 | .6 |
| | .7 | .4 | .3 | .1 | .2 | Sales/Total Assets | .3 | .3 |
| | .3 | .2 | .2 | .1 | .1 | | .2 | .2 |
| | 1.6 | 2.3 | 7.2 | 8.9 | 5.0 | | 2.7 | 4.0 |
| (11) 3.0 | (40) 8.1 | (58) 12.0 | (34) 13.1 | (25) 8.7 | % Depr., Dep., Amort./Sales | (147) 7.1 | (163) 8.5 |
| 5.4 | 15.4 | 17.4 | 20.9 | 12.3 | | 13.2 | 14.3 |
| | | | | | | % Officers', Directors' Owners' Comp/Sales | 4.4 | 1.6 |
| | | | | | | | (22) 6.6 | (20) 6.7 |
| | | | | | | | 12.7 | 14.6 |
| 1756M | 34590M | 167246M | 539404M | 587807M | 1161911M | Net Sales ($) | 2323268M | 2391781M |
| 1274M | 22752M | 284441M | 1496396M | 2519246M | 4192928M | Total Assets ($) | 7220773M | 7730159M |

M = $ thousand　　MM = $ million
See Pages 9 through 22 for Explanation of Ratios and Data

## Comparative Historical Data | Current Data Sorted by Sales

| | | | Type of Statement | | | | | | |
|---|---|---|---|---|---|---|---|---|---|
| 120 | 123 | 119 | Unqualified | 8 | 15 | 18 | 29 | 31 | 18 |
| 6 | 3 | 3 | Reviewed | | 2 | | 1 | | |
| 6 | 2 | 4 | Compiled | 2 | 1 | | | 1 | |
| 9 | 5 | 5 | Tax Returns | 2 | 1 | 1 | | 1 | |
| 43 | 55 | 67 | Other | 18 | 11 | 6 | 15 | 11 | 6 |
| 4/1/09-3/31/10 ALL | 4/1/10-3/31/11 ALL | 4/1/11-3/31/12 ALL | | 110 (4/1-9/30/11) | | | 88 (10/1/11-3/31/12) | | |
| | | | | 0-1MM | 1-3MM | 3-5MM | 5-10MM | 10-25MM | 25MM & OVER |
| 184 | 188 | 198 | **NUMBER OF STATEMENTS** | 30 | 30 | 25 | 45 | 44 | 24 |
| % | % | % | **ASSETS** | % | % | % | % | % | % |
| 12.0 | 11.5 | 11.3 | Cash & Equivalents | 14.2 | 8.7 | 9.7 | 8.7 | 14.4 | 12.1 |
| 4.3 | 4.0 | 3.2 | Trade Receivables (net) | 3.7 | 1.6 | 4.5 | 2.0 | 4.2 | 3.3 |
| 3.9 | 3.1 | 3.5 | Inventory | 7.0 | 3.4 | 3.2 | 2.4 | 3.0 | 2.8 |
| 3.1 | 3.3 | 3.0 | All Other Current | .6 | 4.0 | 3.8 | 5.1 | 1.5 | 2.7 |
| 23.3 | 21.9 | 21.1 | Total Current | 25.6 | 17.6 | 21.2 | 18.3 | 23.1 | 21.0 |
| 52.5 | 53.4 | 53.3 | Fixed Assets (net) | 59.8 | 60.6 | 59.1 | 48.7 | 46.5 | 50.9 |
| .3 | .8 | 1.4 | Intangibles (net) | 1.3 | .1 | .3 | 4.0 | .2 | 1.4 |
| 23.9 | 23.9 | 24.3 | All Other Non-Current | 13.3 | 21.8 | 19.3 | 29.0 | 30.2 | 26.7 |
| 100.0 | 100.0 | 100.0 | Total | 100.0 | 100.0 | 100.0 | 100.0 | 100.0 | 100.0 |
| | | | **LIABILITIES** | | | | | | |
| 5.5 | 4.2 | 2.0 | Notes Payable-Short Term | 4.2 | 1.2 | 1.4 | 2.8 | .9 | 1.5 |
| 1.0 | 1.1 | 1.9 | Cur. Mat.-L.T.D. | 7.9 | .6 | 2.1 | .5 | .5 | .9 |
| 3.6 | 3.2 | 2.9 | Trade Payables | 1.7 | 1.3 | 1.7 | 3.4 | 4.4 | 4.3 |
| .0 | .1 | .0 | Income Taxes Payable | .0 | .0 | .0 | .0 | .1 | .0 |
| 4.1 | 4.2 | 3.6 | All Other Current | 3.5 | 4.9 | 5.3 | 2.2 | 2.3 | 5.2 |
| 14.2 | 12.7 | 10.5 | Total Current | 17.3 | 8.0 | 10.5 | 9.0 | 8.2 | 12.0 |
| 14.3 | 12.0 | 13.1 | Long-Term Debt | 13.9 | 15.7 | 14.2 | 16.6 | 9.0 | 8.9 |
| .0 | .0 | .0 | Deferred Taxes | .0 | .0 | .0 | .0 | .0 | .0 |
| 3.9 | 3.4 | 4.1 | All Other Non-Current | 1.3 | 9.0 | .6 | 3.9 | 4.6 | 4.6 |
| 67.6 | 71.9 | 72.3 | Net Worth | 67.5 | 67.3 | 74.8 | 70.5 | 78.2 | 74.5 |
| 100.0 | 100.0 | 100.0 | Total Liabilities & Net Worth | 100.0 | 100.0 | 100.0 | 100.0 | 100.0 | 100.0 |
| | | | **INCOME DATA** | | | | | | |
| 100.0 | 100.0 | 100.0 | Net Sales | 100.0 | 100.0 | 100.0 | 100.0 | 100.0 | 100.0 |
| | | | Gross Profit | | | | | | |
| 97.2 | 92.6 | 93.9 | Operating Expenses | 94.2 | 96.7 | 95.6 | 90.0 | 98.1 | 87.8 |
| 2.8 | 7.4 | 6.1 | Operating Profit | 5.8 | 3.3 | 4.4 | 10.0 | 1.9 | 12.2 |
| 5.4 | 2.0 | 3.2 | All Other Expenses (net) | 4.2 | 6.5 | 2.5 | 3.4 | 2.0 | .4 |
| -2.6 | 5.4 | 2.9 | Profit Before Taxes | 1.6 | -3.2 | 2.0 | 6.5 | -.1 | 11.8 |
| | | | **RATIOS** | | | | | | |
| 7.2 | 6.8 | 5.9 | | 12.1 | 7.2 | 9.7 | 5.4 | 6.2 | 4.7 |
| 2.2 | 2.7 | 2.5 | Current | 1.8 | 3.4 | 3.1 | 2.4 | 2.3 | 2.0 |
| 1.0 | 1.1 | 1.2 | | .6 | 1.2 | 1.2 | 1.2 | 1.3 | 1.0 |
| 5.1 | 5.1 | 4.6 | | 10.6 | 5.8 | 3.3 | 3.8 | 5.1 | 4.1 |
| 1.5 | 1.7 | 1.5 | Quick | 1.1 | 2.9 | 1.6 | 1.5 | 1.5 | 1.4 |
| .5 | .6 | .6 | | .5 | .7 | .9 | .4 | .6 | .6 |
| 1   725.5 | 1   421.8 | 1   245.6 | | 0   UND | 0   999.8 | 1   494.8 | 1   547.6 | 3   110.9 | 8   46.1 |
| 11   33.4 | 8   48.5 | 8   43.6 | Sales/Receivables | 5   81.1 | 6   65.9 | 7   51.1 | 7   49.9 | 12   31.2 | 16   23.3 |
| 50   7.3 | 41   8.8 | 39   9.4 | | 54   6.8 | 13   28.2 | 41   8.8 | 35   10.5 | 54   6.7 | 37   9.8 |
| | | | Cost of Sales/Inventory | | | | | | |
| | | | Cost of Sales/Payables | | | | | | |
| 1.8 | 1.8 | 2.0 | | .8 | 3.0 | 1.1 | 2.0 | 1.8 | 2.1 |
| 4.3 | 4.6 | 4.8 | Sales/Working Capital | 6.4 | 4.5 | 3.9 | 5.1 | 4.8 | 6.3 |
| NM | 83.2 | 49.7 | | -8.7 | NM | 20.2 | 114.8 | 26.2 | 79.9 |
| 6.7 | 17.7 | 7.3 | | 5.0 | 8.0 | 8.7 | 6.5 | 10.1 | 42.7 |
| (119) -.6 | (123) 3.3 | (132) -1.9 | EBIT/Interest | (21) 1.9 | (16) 2.8 | (13) .7 | (32) .6 | (33) 2.9 | (17) 4.3 |
| -7.5 | -2.5 | -3.6 | | -.6 | -1.9 | -4.7 | -6.6 | -5.0 | 1.3 |
| | | | Net Profit + Depr., Dep., Amort./Cur. Mat. L/T/D | | | | | | |
| .4 | .4 | .4 | | .5 | .6 | .5 | .4 | .2 | .4 |
| .8 | .7 | .8 | Fixed/Worth | .9 | .9 | .9 | .7 | .6 | .8 |
| 1.1 | 1.1 | 1.0 | | 1.4 | 1.1 | 1.2 | 1.1 | 1.0 | 1.0 |
| .1 | .1 | .1 | | .1 | .0 | .1 | .1 | .1 | .1 |
| .3 | .2 | .2 | Debt/Worth | .2 | .2 | .2 | .3 | .2 | .3 |
| .8 | .6 | .6 | | .9 | .4 | .5 | .7 | .6 | .7 |
| 7.8 | 7.8 | 7.5 | | 7.7 | 4.8 | 9.3 | 7.1 | 8.0 | 5.3 |
| (178) -1.5 | (184) 1.3 | (190) .9 | % Profit Before Taxes/Tangible Net Worth | (28) .5 | (28) -.6 | (41) -.5 | 1.5 | .6 | 2.8 |
| -5.3 | -2.4 | -2.9 | | -3.7 | -4.5 | -4.0 | -2.9 | -2.5 | .4 |
| 5.2 | 5.1 | 4.8 | | 5.1 | 4.1 | 5.7 | 5.0 | 5.5 | 5.1 |
| .9 | .9 | .6 | % Profit Before Taxes/Total Assets | .4 | -1.2 | -.5 | .3 | .5 | 2.1 |
| -4.5 | -2.1 | -2.4 | | -3.0 | -4.1 | -3.3 | -3.2 | -2.2 | .1 |
| 1.4 | 1.4 | 1.6 | | 3.9 | .9 | 1.5 | 1.4 | 1.7 | 2.5 |
| .6 | .5 | .5 | Sales/Net Fixed Assets | .3 | .5 | .4 | .6 | .4 | .9 |
| .3 | .3 | .3 | | .2 | .3 | .2 | .3 | .3 | .5 |
| .5 | .5 | .5 | | .7 | .5 | .7 | .6 | .4 | .7 |
| .3 | .3 | .3 | Sales/Total Assets | .2 | .3 | .3 | .3 | .2 | .3 |
| .2 | .1 | .2 | | .1 | .2 | .1 | .1 | .2 | .3 |
| 4.4 | 4.0 | 4.7 | | 2.1 | 4.1 | 4.9 | 6.4 | 6.2 | 4.0 |
| (160) 9.5 | (167) 9.6 | (171) 10.2 | % Depr., Dep., Amort./Sales | (21) 7.5 | (22) 12.3 | (24) 10.4 | (40) 11.0 | (41) 11.8 | (23) 7.8 |
| 17.2 | 19.6 | 17.2 | | 23.4 | 20.8 | 17.0 | 17.5 | 17.6 | 11.4 |
| 2.9 | 1.7 | 4.4 | | | | | | | |
| (23) 6.0 | (17) 4.3 | (24) 6.7 | % Officers', Directors' Owners' Comp/Sales | | | | | | |
| 14.9 | 10.0 | 13.8 | | | | | | | |
| 2145985M | 2414793M | 2492714M | Net Sales ($) | 16885M | 53438M | 97247M | 316124M | 659273M | 1349747M |
| 7482266M | 8347309M | 8517037M | Total Assets ($) | 93277M | 223808M | 604377M | 1482893M | 2861302M | 3251380M |

M = $ thousand    MM = $ million
See Pages 9 through 22 for Explanation of Ratios and Data

## Current Data Sorted by Assets

## Comparative Historical Data

| 0-500M | 500M-2MM | 2-10MM | 10-50MM | 50-100MM | 100-250MM | Type of Statement | | 4/1/07-3/31/08 ALL | 4/1/08-3/31/09 ALL |
|---|---|---|---|---|---|---|---|---|---|
| 1 | 2 | 2 | 7 1 16 | 5 2 | 5 1 | Unqualified | 10 | | 24 |
| | | | | | | Reviewed | 2 | | 1 |
| | | | | | | Compiled | | | |
| | | | | | | Tax Returns | 1 | | |
| | 14 (4/1-9/30/11) | | 16 (10/1/11-3/31/12) | | | Other | 5 | | 6 |
| | 3 | 2 | 12 | 7 | 6 | NUMBER OF STATEMENTS | 18 | | 31 |
| % | % | % | % | % | % | **ASSETS** | % | | % |
| | | | 12.5 | | | Cash & Equivalents | 13.1 | | 15.0 |
| | | | 3.3 | | | Trade Receivables (net) | 4.1 | | 4.3 |
| | | | .6 | | | Inventory | 1.1 | | 1.0 |
| | | | 1.6 | | | All Other Current | 1.7 | | 4.8 |
| | | | 18.0 | | | Total Current | 20.1 | | 25.1 |
| | | | 65.9 | | | Fixed Assets (net) | 58.3 | | 54.2 |
| | | | .2 | | | Intangibles (net) | .0 | | .0 |
| | | | 15.8 | | | All Other Non-Current | 21.2 | | 20.7 |
| | | | 100.0 | | | Total | 100.0 | | 100.0 |
| | | | | | | **LIABILITIES** | | | |
| | | | .8 | | | Notes Payable-Short Term | .7 | | 2.0 |
| | | | 5.4 | | | Cur. Mat.-L.T.D. | 1.3 | | 1.4 |
| | | | 2.0 | | | Trade Payables | 3.3 | | 3.0 |
| | | | .0 | | | Income Taxes Payable | .0 | | .0 |
| | | | 2.9 | | | All Other Current | 4.1 | | 5.2 |
| | | | 11.2 | | | Total Current | 9.4 | | 11.5 |
| | | | 11.7 | | | Long-Term Debt | 23.4 | | 20.5 |
| | | | .0 | | | Deferred Taxes | .4 | | .2 |
| | | | 1.4 | | | All Other Non-Current | .3 | | 2.6 |
| | | | 75.7 | | | Net Worth | 66.2 | | 65.3 |
| | | | 100.0 | | | Total Liabilities & Net Worth | 100.0 | | 100.0 |
| | | | | | | **INCOME DATA** | | | |
| | | | 100.0 | | | Net Sales | 100.0 | | 100.0 |
| | | | | | | Gross Profit | | | |
| | | | 93.5 | | | Operating Expenses | 87.8 | | 97.1 |
| | | | 6.5 | | | Operating Profit | 12.2 | | 2.9 |
| | | | 4.2 | | | All Other Expenses (net) | .7 | | 2.2 |
| | | | 2.3 | | | Profit Before Taxes | 11.5 | | .7 |
| | | | | | | **RATIOS** | | | |
| | | | 7.1 | | | | 4.3 | | 3.6 |
| | | | 1.1 | | | Current | 2.3 | | 1.5 |
| | | | .6 | | | | .9 | | .9 |
| | | | 6.8 | | | | 3.4 | | 3.1 |
| | | | .7 | | | Quick | 1.5 | | 1.2 |
| | | | .4 | | | | .7 | | .5 |
| | | | 2 190.0 | | | | 0 UND | 0 | UND |
| | | | 10 38.4 | | | Sales/Receivables | 10 36.5 | 8 | 48.2 |
| | | | 28 13.1 | | | | 19 18.7 | 22 | 16.5 |
| | | | | | | Cost of Sales/Inventory | | | |
| | | | | | | Cost of Sales/Payables | | | |
| | | | 1.4 | | | | 2.2 | | 2.3 |
| | | | 100.6 | | | Sales/Working Capital | 9.0 | | 12.6 |
| | | | -12.9 | | | | -90.9 | | -38.1 |
| | | | | | | | 11.5 | | 6.9 |
| | | | | | | EBIT/Interest | (13) 6.0 | (23) | .3 |
| | | | | | | | .0 | | -9.4 |
| | | | | | | Net Profit + Depr., Dep., Amort./Cur. Mat. L/T/D | | | |
| | | | .7 | | | | .4 | | .1 |
| | | | 1.0 | | | Fixed/Worth | 1.0 | | 1.0 |
| | | | 1.1 | | | | 1.6 | | 1.3 |
| | | | .1 | | | | .1 | | .2 |
| | | | .2 | | | Debt/Worth | .2 | | .4 |
| | | | .4 | | | | 1.2 | | .8 |
| | | | 9.1 | | | | 10.3 | | 7.7 |
| | | | -.4 | | | % Profit Before Taxes/Tangible Net Worth | (17) 4.5 | | 2.2 |
| | | | -4.5 | | | | 1.5 | | -10.5 |
| | | | 4.6 | | | | 9.8 | | 6.5 |
| | | | -.1 | | | % Profit Before Taxes/Total Assets | 5.0 | | 1.5 |
| | | | -3.7 | | | | .8 | | -7.0 |
| | | | .8 | | | | 6.7 | | 12.9 |
| | | | .5 | | | Sales/Net Fixed Assets | .5 | | .8 |
| | | | .3 | | | | .4 | | .4 |
| | | | .5 | | | | 1.1 | | 1.1 |
| | | | .3 | | | Sales/Total Assets | .3 | | .4 |
| | | | .2 | | | | .3 | | .3 |
| | | | 10.9 | | | | 5.1 | | 2.7 |
| | | (10) | 13.1 | | | % Depr., Dep., Amort./Sales | (16) 11.5 | (29) | 9.6 |
| | | | 16.1 | | | | 15.2 | | 13.3 |
| | | | | | | % Officers', Directors' Owners' Comp/Sales | | | |
| | 11423M | 12994M | 142227M | 170030M | 274150M | Net Sales ($) | 325099M | | 480805M |
| | 5027M | 9673M | 419433M | 462719M | 938864M | Total Assets ($) | 927661M | | 1287812M |

© RMA 2012

M = $ thousand    MM = $ million

See Pages 9 through 22 for Explanation of Ratios and Data

Note: In the leftmost data column the notation "DATA NOT AVAILABLE" is printed vertically.

## Comparative Historical Data | Current Data Sorted by Sales

| | | | Type of Statement | | | | | | |
|---|---|---|---|---|---|---|---|---|---|
| 11 | 10 | 18 | Unqualified | | | | 1 | 3 | 8 |
| 1 | 1 | 1 | Reviewed | | | | | | |
| | | | Compiled | | | | | | |
| | | | Tax Returns | | | | | | |
| | 2 | | Other | | | | | | |
| 5 | 6 | 11 | | | | | | | 6 |
| 4/1/09-3/31/10 ALL | 4/1/10-3/31/11 ALL | 4/1/11-3/31/12 ALL | | 0-1MM | 14 (4/1-9/30/11) 1-3MM | 3-5MM | 5-10MM | 16 (10/1/11-3/31/12) 10-25MM | 25MM & OVER |
| 17 | 19 | 30 | **NUMBER OF STATEMENTS** | | 1 | 2 | 7 | 12 | 8 |
| % | % | % | **ASSETS** | % | % | % | % | % | % |
| 20.2 | 11.7 | 13.4 | Cash & Equivalents | | | | | 10.1 | |
| 4.3 | 2.1 | 2.6 | Trade Receivables (net) | | | | | 2.6 | |
| 1.1 | 3.8 | 1.1 | Inventory | | | | | .6 | |
| 2.0 | 1.5 | 3.1 | All Other Current | | | | | 3.0 | |
| 27.7 | 19.2 | 20.3 | Total Current | | | | | 16.4 | |
| 52.6 | 52.6 | 61.2 | Fixed Assets (net) | | | | | 68.1 | |
| .0 | 3.3 | .2 | Intangibles (net) | | | | | .1 | |
| 19.7 | 25.0 | 18.4 | All Other Non-Current | | | | | 15.3 | |
| 100.0 | 100.0 | 100.0 | Total | | | | | 100.0 | |
| | | | **LIABILITIES** | | | | | | |
| 1.6 | 1.1 | 2.0 | Notes Payable-Short Term | | | | | .6 | |
| 9.2 | 1.8 | 2.6 | Cur. Mat.-L.T.D. | | | | | .9 | |
| 2.2 | 2.1 | 1.8 | Trade Payables | | | | | 2.3 | |
| .0 | .0 | .0 | Income Taxes Payable | | | | | .0 | |
| 4.8 | 7.4 | 4.1 | All Other Current | | | | | 2.2 | |
| 17.9 | 12.3 | 10.4 | Total Current | | | | | 6.0 | |
| 43.7 | 19.0 | 17.5 | Long-Term Debt | | | | | 10.4 | |
| .0 | .0 | .0 | Deferred Taxes | | | | | .0 | |
| 3.9 | 1.1 | 1.6 | All Other Non-Current | | | | | 1.4 | |
| 34.6 | 67.6 | 70.5 | Net Worth | | | | | 82.3 | |
| 100.0 | 100.0 | 100.0 | Total Liabilities & Net Worth | | | | | 100.0 | |
| | | | **INCOME DATA** | | | | | | |
| 100.0 | 100.0 | 100.0 | Net Sales | | | | | 100.0 | |
| | | | Gross Profit | | | | | | |
| 94.8 | 82.3 | 88.9 | Operating Expenses | | | | | 91.2 | |
| 5.2 | 17.7 | 11.1 | Operating Profit | | | | | 8.8 | |
| 2.1 | 3.4 | 3.9 | All Other Expenses (net) | | | | | 4.5 | |
| 3.0 | 14.3 | 7.2 | Profit Before Taxes | | | | | 4.3 | |
| | | | **RATIOS** | | | | | | |
| 3.4 | 6.8 | 6.4 | | | | | | 5.1 | |
| 1.6 | 2.0 | 1.2 | Current | | | | | 1.1 | |
| .8 | 1.0 | .8 | | | | | | .7 | |
| 3.3 | 5.9 | 4.8 | | | | | | 3.9 | |
| 1.5 | 1.6 | 1.0 | Quick | | | | | .8 | |
| .8 | .8 | .6 | | | | | | .4 | |
| 2 · 218.8 | 2 · 229.0 | 0 · UND | | | | | | 0 · UND | |
| 9 · 40.9 | 7 · 55.4 | 7 · 53.8 | Sales/Receivables | | | | | 2 · 179.5 | |
| 44 · 8.3 | 29 · 12.7 | 19 · 19.0 | | | | | | 16 · 22.4 | |
| | | | Cost of Sales/Inventory | | | | | | |
| | | | Cost of Sales/Payables | | | | | | |
| 3.3 | 2.1 | 2.3 | | | | | | 3.3 | |
| 8.1 | 7.5 | 23.2 | Sales/Working Capital | | | | | 114.4 | |
| -35.2 | 71.0 | -22.4 | | | | | | -25.3 | |
| 17.3 | 34.0 | 7.4 | | | | | | | |
| (12) 1.8 | (14) 2.4 | (23) 2.2 | EBIT/Interest | | | | | | |
| -1.3 | -.1 | -2.6 | | | | | | | |
| | | | Net Profit + Depr., Dep., Amort./Cur. Mat. L/T/D | | | | | | |
| .0 | .2 | .6 | | | | | | .7 | |
| .8 | .9 | .9 | Fixed/Worth | | | | | .9 | |
| 1.2 | 1.4 | 1.1 | | | | | | 1.1 | |
| .1 | .1 | .1 | | | | | | .1 | |
| .3 | .2 | .2 | Debt/Worth | | | | | .2 | |
| 1.4 | 1.3 | .6 | | | | | | .3 | |
| 7.4 | 14.1 | 10.6 | % Profit Before Taxes/Tangible Net Worth | | | | | 9.1 | |
| (16) 1.0 | (17) 5.8 | (29) .8 | | | | | | .4 | |
| -2.4 | -.6 | -3.5 | | | | | | -3.7 | |
| 6.3 | 6.9 | 9.1 | % Profit Before Taxes/Total Assets | | | | | 4.6 | |
| .5 | 5.3 | .8 | | | | | | .3 | |
| -1.9 | .3 | -1.9 | | | | | | -3.3 | |
| 84.2 | 4.5 | 1.7 | | | | | | .8 | |
| .5 | .9 | .5 | Sales/Net Fixed Assets | | | | | .5 | |
| .3 | .3 | .4 | | | | | | .4 | |
| 1.4 | .9 | .6 | | | | | | .5 | |
| .4 | .5 | .3 | Sales/Total Assets | | | | | .3 | |
| .2 | .3 | .3 | | | | | | .3 | |
| .7 | 2.0 | 6.8 | | | | | | 6.9 | |
| (15) 9.6 | (17) 5.4 | (27) 12.2 | % Depr., Dep., Amort./Sales | | | | | (11) 12.7 | |
| 14.2 | 14.0 | 13.7 | | | | | | 13.7 | |
| | | | % Officers', Directors' Owners' Comp/Sales | | | | | | |
| 222640M | 311812M | 610824M | Net Sales ($) | | 1767M | 8835M | 52452M | 198726M | 349044M |
| 664948M | 887020M | 1835716M | Total Assets ($) | | 1957M | 5076M | 191836M | 554565M | 1082282M |

Note: Columns 0-1MM through 5-10MM (and 25MM & OVER) for the Assets/Liabilities/Income/Ratios sections are marked **DATA NOT AVAILABLE**.

M = $ thousand    MM = $ million
See Pages 9 through 22 for Explanation of Ratios and Data

## Current Data Sorted by Assets       Comparative Historical Data

| Type of Statement | 0-500M | 500M-2MM | 2-10MM | 10-50MM | 50-100MM | 100-250MM | 4/1/07-3/31/08 ALL | 4/1/08-3/31/09 ALL |
|---|---|---|---|---|---|---|---|---|
| Unqualified | | | | 7 | 2 | 2 | 11 | 13 |
| Reviewed | | | 7 | 8 | | | 19 | 16 |
| Compiled | | 4 | 10 | 3 | | | 13 | 19 |
| Tax Returns | 12 | 8 | 3 | | | | 21 | 19 |
| Other | 7 | 12 | 15 | 9 | 2 | 3 | 20 | 44 |
| | 13 (4/1-9/30/11) | | 101 (10/1/11-3/31/12) | | | | | |
| **NUMBER OF STATEMENTS** | 19 | 24 | 35 | 27 | 4 | 5 | 84 | 111 |
| | % | % | % | % | % | % | % | % |
| **ASSETS** | | | | | | | | |
| Cash & Equivalents | 20.4 | 15.3 | 14.9 | 5.6 | | | 12.6 | 11.0 |
| Trade Receivables (net) | 3.3 | .8 | 1.4 | 1.2 | | | 1.3 | 1.6 |
| Inventory | 4.5 | 3.9 | 1.3 | 1.3 | | | 4.2 | 3.3 |
| All Other Current | 2.7 | 3.7 | 1.3 | 4.0 | | | 1.5 | 3.6 |
| Total Current | 30.9 | 23.8 | 18.9 | 12.1 | | | 19.6 | 19.6 |
| Fixed Assets (net) | 56.9 | 52.7 | 71.7 | 80.8 | | | 70.3 | 66.4 |
| Intangibles (net) | 3.7 | 15.5 | .9 | 2.4 | | | 1.8 | 2.8 |
| All Other Non-Current | 8.5 | 8.0 | 8.5 | 4.7 | | | 8.2 | 11.2 |
| Total | 100.0 | 100.0 | 100.0 | 100.0 | | | 100.0 | 100.0 |
| **LIABILITIES** | | | | | | | | |
| Notes Payable-Short Term | 14.0 | 8.8 | 1.3 | 3.9 | | | 6.5 | 4.0 |
| Cur. Mat.-L.T.D. | 3.5 | 3.1 | 4.8 | 5.3 | | | 4.6 | 6.3 |
| Trade Payables | 1.5 | 3.8 | 3.3 | 2.0 | | | 4.6 | 4.4 |
| Income Taxes Payable | .0 | .0 | .0 | .0 | | | .1 | .3 |
| All Other Current | 26.6 | 19.6 | 8.5 | 10.7 | | | 12.1 | 12.5 |
| Total Current | 45.6 | 35.3 | 17.8 | 21.9 | | | 27.9 | 27.5 |
| Long-Term Debt | 58.3 | 37.2 | 46.8 | 35.2 | | | 49.8 | 39.8 |
| Deferred Taxes | .0 | .0 | .2 | .0 | | | .7 | .7 |
| All Other Non-Current | 25.5 | 10.3 | 9.1 | 22.7 | | | 5.8 | 10.3 |
| Net Worth | -29.4 | 17.3 | 26.1 | 20.1 | | | 15.8 | 21.7 |
| Total Liabilties & Net Worth | 100.0 | 100.0 | 100.0 | 100.0 | | | 100.0 | 100.0 |
| **INCOME DATA** | | | | | | | | |
| Net Sales | 100.0 | 100.0 | 100.0 | 100.0 | | | 100.0 | 100.0 |
| Gross Profit | | | | | | | | |
| Operating Expenses | 92.8 | 90.3 | 91.1 | 88.9 | | | 88.7 | 90.2 |
| Operating Profit | 7.2 | 9.7 | 8.9 | 11.1 | | | 11.3 | 9.8 |
| All Other Expenses (net) | 2.7 | 4.6 | 5.2 | 5.8 | | | 4.5 | 4.4 |
| Profit Before Taxes | 4.5 | 5.0 | 3.7 | 5.3 | | | 6.7 | 5.4 |
| **RATIOS** | | | | | | | | |
| Current | 1.5 | 2.6 | 3.0 | 1.3 | | | 2.1 | 2.0 |
| | .8 | .7 | .8 | .4 | | | .9 | .7 |
| | .1 | .2 | .4 | .2 | | | .3 | .2 |
| Quick | 1.1 | 1.2 | 1.7 | 1.0 | | | 1.8 | 1.6 |
| | .4 | .6 | .7 | .3 | | | .4 (110) | .5 |
| | .0 | .1 | .3 | .1 | | | .1 | .1 |
| Sales/Receivables | 0 UND | 0 UND | 0 UND | 0 999.8 | | | 0 UND | 0 UND |
| | 0 UND | 0 UND | 0 783.1 | 2 181.4 | | | 0 999.8 | 1 714.0 |
| | 0 UND | 0 UND | 3 116.4 | 8 47.9 | | | 4 100.6 | 4 90.9 |
| Cost of Sales/Inventory | | | | | | | | |
| Cost of Sales/Payables | | | | | | | | |
| Sales/Working Capital | 21.0 | 12.1 | 7.5 | 18.3 | | | 11.9 | 12.6 |
| | -49.3 | -66.9 | -45.4 | -6.9 | | | -46.0 | -33.2 |
| | -6.3 | -5.0 | -7.0 | -4.4 | | | -6.1 | -5.4 |
| EBIT/Interest | 10.1 | 15.5 | 6.8 | 4.6 | | | 4.6 | 3.9 |
| | (14) 2.2 | (17) 1.4 | (32) 2.2 | (25) 2.2 | | | (71) 2.2 | (88) 1.8 |
| | .2 | -.2 | .6 | 1.2 | | | 1.2 | .0 |
| Net Profit + Depr., Dep., Amort./Cur. Mat. L/T/D | | | | | | | 16.6 | 4.6 |
| | | | | | | | (15) 2.6 | (14) 2.9 |
| | | | | | | | 1.3 | 1.5 |
| Fixed/Worth | 1.5 | .9 | 1.1 | 1.4 | | | 1.2 | 1.0 |
| | -1.9 | 2.6 | 3.9 | 3.3 | | | 2.8 | 2.6 |
| | -.7 | -1.2 | 12.5 | 7.8 | | | 23.7 | 18.2 |
| Debt/Worth | 3.0 | 1.3 | 1.0 | .6 | | | .8 | .6 |
| | -6.2 | 4.7 | 3.7 | 2.9 | | | 2.6 | 2.6 |
| | -2.7 | -2.8 | 12.4 | 7.6 | | | 24.2 | 575.3 |
| % Profit Before Taxes/Tangible Net Worth | | 142.4 | 33.9 | 22.8 | | | 34.4 | 37.4 |
| | | (15) 19.6 | (27) 6.6 | (23) 13.6 | | | (64) 17.0 | (86) 13.7 |
| | | -3.5 | -3.9 | 8.6 | | | 4.3 | -.4 |
| % Profit Before Taxes/Total Assets | 47.3 | 15.6 | 10.0 | 8.4 | | | 14.0 | 11.2 |
| | 5.7 | 4.2 | 1.3 | 2.4 | | | 4.5 | 4.0 |
| | -4.5 | -4.0 | -2.1 | .4 | | | .5 | -2.9 |
| Sales/Net Fixed Assets | 16.4 | 10.5 | 3.6 | .9 | | | 2.8 | 3.7 |
| | 6.8 | 3.5 | 1.1 | .6 | | | 1.6 | 1.3 |
| | 2.5 | .7 | .6 | .4 | | | .7 | .6 |
| Sales/Total Assets | 4.7 | 2.9 | 1.6 | .8 | | | 2.1 | 1.9 |
| | 3.0 | 1.6 | .9 | .5 | | | .9 | .8 |
| | 2.2 | .6 | .5 | .3 | | | .6 | .5 |
| % Depr., Dep., Amort./Sales | 3.2 | 4.3 | 4.9 | 9.9 | | | 4.1 | 4.6 |
| | (13) 4.6 | (21) 9.9 | 8.2 | 13.3 | | | (83) 8.5 | (98) 9.6 |
| | 9.5 | 14.0 | 15.7 | 17.0 | | | 12.4 | 13.8 |
| % Officers', Directors' Owners' Comp/Sales | 5.4 | | | | | | 2.7 | 1.5 |
| | (10) 7.1 | | | | | | (23) 6.9 | (22) 5.2 |
| | 10.2 | | | | | | 13.6 | 8.6 |
| Net Sales ($) | 13580M | 43582M | 203666M | 359338M | 222405M | 407153M | 999623M | 1362861M |
| Total Assets ($) | 4572M | 26174M | 185918M | 590022M | 274476M | 900501M | 1158862M | 2022629M |

© RMA 2012

M = $ thousand     MM = $ million
See Pages 9 through 22 for Explanation of Ratios and Data

## Comparative Historical Data

## Current Data Sorted by Sales

| Type of Statement | | | | | | | | | |
|---|---|---|---|---|---|---|---|---|---|
| | | | | **Unqualified** | | | | 3 | 3 | 5 |

| Item | 4/1/09-3/31/10 ALL | 4/1/10-3/31/11 ALL | 4/1/11-3/31/12 ALL | 0-1MM | 1-3MM | 3-5MM | 5-10MM | 10-25MM | 25MM & OVER |
|---|---|---|---|---|---|---|---|---|---|
| **Type of Statement** | | | | | 13 (4/1-9/30/11) | | 101 (10/1/11-3/31/12) | | |
| Unqualified | 6 | 7 | 11 | | | | 3 | 3 | 5 |
| Reviewed | 14 | 16 | 15 | | 1 | 2 | 6 | 5 | 1 |
| Compiled | 24 | 10 | 17 | 3 | 2 | 4 | 6 | 2 | |
| Tax Returns | 25 | 23 | 23 | 10 | 10 | 1 | 1 | 1 | |
| Other | 40 | 58 | 48 | 16 | 8 | 4 | 7 | 6 | 7 |
| **NUMBER OF STATEMENTS** | 109 | 114 | 114 | 29 | 21 | 11 | 23 | 17 | 13 |
| **ASSETS** | % | % | % | % | % | % | % | % | % |
| Cash & Equivalents | 8.9 | 10.4 | 13.2 | 12.8 | 16.1 | 27.0 | 11.1 | 8.1 | 8.2 |
| Trade Receivables (net) | 1.4 | 1.6 | 1.5 | 2.5 | .6 | .3 | 1.8 | 1.7 | 1.1 |
| Inventory | 4.6 | 1.6 | 2.4 | 3.2 | 1.7 | 4.6 | 2.0 | 1.5 | 2.0 |
| All Other Current | 1.2 | 4.3 | 3.1 | 3.2 | 2.4 | 2.8 | .4 | 6.0 | 5.0 |
| Total Current | 16.1 | 17.9 | 20.2 | 21.7 | 20.7 | 34.7 | 15.3 | 17.4 | 16.4 |
| Fixed Assets (net) | 72.2 | 69.9 | 67.6 | 63.8 | 59.8 | 55.6 | 76.2 | 72.2 | 77.6 |
| Intangibles (net) | 2.0 | 3.3 | 4.9 | 4.6 | 14.5 | 1.4 | 2.1 | 2.1 | 1.3 |
| All Other Non-Current | 9.7 | 8.9 | 7.3 | 9.9 | 5.0 | 8.3 | 6.3 | 8.4 | 4.7 |
| Total | 100.0 | 100.0 | 100.0 | 100.0 | 100.0 | 100.0 | 100.0 | 100.0 | 100.0 |
| **LIABILITIES** | | | | | | | | | |
| Notes Payable-Short Term | 5.9 | 6.4 | 6.1 | 7.6 | 5.9 | 12.2 | 1.4 | 3.6 | 9.8 |
| Cur. Mat.-L.T.D. | 6.7 | 5.1 | 4.0 | 3.7 | 3.9 | 1.6 | 4.5 | 8.1 | 1.0 |
| Trade Payables | 3.6 | 3.6 | 2.6 | 1.5 | 2.3 | 3.5 | 3.2 | 4.2 | 1.9 |
| Income Taxes Payable | .1 | .0 | .0 | .0 | .0 | .0 | .0 | .0 | .0 |
| All Other Current | 12.8 | 10.8 | 14.2 | 27.2 | 11.7 | 7.5 | 7.6 | 12.2 | 9.4 |
| Total Current | 29.1 | 25.8 | 27.0 | 40.0 | 23.7 | 24.8 | 16.8 | 28.2 | 22.1 |
| Long-Term Debt | 45.9 | 40.4 | 42.2 | 63.3 | 46.9 | 37.3 | 39.5 | 23.7 | 20.9 |
| Deferred Taxes | .8 | 1.0 | .4 | .0 | .0 | .0 | .0 | .4 | 2.6 |
| All Other Non-Current | 11.6 | 15.0 | 14.8 | 17.1 | 12.1 | 7.2 | 11.0 | 10.8 | 32.9 |
| Net Worth | 12.6 | 17.8 | 15.5 | -20.3 | 17.4 | 30.7 | 32.7 | 36.8 | 21.5 |
| Total Liabilities & Net Worth | 100.0 | 100.0 | 100.0 | 100.0 | 100.0 | 100.0 | 100.0 | 100.0 | 100.0 |
| **INCOME DATA** | | | | | | | | | |
| Net Sales | 100.0 | 100.0 | 100.0 | 100.0 | 100.0 | 100.0 | 100.0 | 100.0 | 100.0 |
| Gross Profit | | | | | | | | | |
| Operating Expenses | 90.7 | 85.0 | 90.0 | 87.1 | 94.1 | 92.3 | 91.0 | 91.9 | 83.6 |
| Operating Profit | 9.3 | 15.0 | 10.0 | 12.9 | 5.9 | 7.7 | 9.0 | 8.1 | 16.4 |
| All Other Expenses (net) | 4.1 | 6.0 | 4.8 | 9.1 | 2.6 | 5.0 | 2.6 | 3.3 | 4.2 |
| Profit Before Taxes | 5.2 | 9.0 | 5.2 | 3.8 | 3.2 | 2.7 | 6.4 | 4.9 | 12.2 |
| **RATIOS** | | | | | | | | | |
| Current | 1.5 | 2.6 | 1.8 | 1.4 | 2.3 | 4.9 | 1.7 | 1.2 | 3.5 |
| | .6 | .7 | .7 | .4 | .7 | 1.4 | 1.0 | .7 | .6 |
| | .2 | .2 | .2 | .1 | .2 | .4 | .4 | .2 | .2 |
| Quick | 1.2 | 1.8 | 1.4 | .7 | 2.0 | 4.9 | 1.7 | 1.1 | 2.9 |
| | .3 | .4 | .4 | .3 | .6 | 1.0 | .8 | .3 | .3 |
| | .1 | .1 | .1 | .1 | .1 | .2 | .3 | .1 | .1 |
| Sales/Receivables | 0 UND | 0 UND | 0 UND | 0 UND | 0 UND | 0 UND | 0 976.6 | 0 UND | 2 178.6 |
| | 0 999.8 | 0 959.3 | 0 999.8 | 0 UND | 0 UND | 0 UND | 2 154.0 | 1 255.4 | 3 112.5 |
| | 3 114.2 | 7 49.3 | 3 112.6 | 1 624.5 | 0 UND | 1 316.0 | 9 40.6 | 4 85.2 | 8 48.0 |
| Cost of Sales/Inventory | | | | | | | | | |
| Cost of Sales/Payables | | | | | | | | | |
| Sales/Working Capital | 24.0 | 12.6 | 13.3 | 24.2 | 17.6 | 2.4 | 12.4 | 38.6 | 3.5 |
| | -23.0 | -28.4 | -36.1 | -8.9 | -58.1 | 72.7 | -214.2 | -39.0 | -6.1 |
| | -4.5 | -4.9 | -4.9 | -2.3 | -6.7 | -5.4 | -6.9 | -5.8 | -4.5 |
| EBIT/Interest | 4.6 | 7.4 | 5.7 | 18.0 | 3.3 | 8.9 | 7.1 | 8.4 | 5.8 |
| | (88) 1.6 | (94) 2.8 | (97) 2.3 | (19) 2.6 | (17) 1.4 | (10) .6 | 2.7 | (16) 3.4 | (12) 4.2 |
| | .2 | 1.0 | .7 | .6 | .0 | -9.5 | .5 | 1.3 | 2.2 |
| Net Profit + Depr., Dep., Amort./Cur. Mat. L/T/D | 3.4 | 3.9 | 5.1 | | | | | | |
| | (16) 2.3 | (20) 2.4 | (13) 1.3 | | | | | | |
| | 1.5 | 1.3 | -.1 | | | | | | |
| Fixed/Worth | 1.3 | .9 | 1.1 | 2.1 | .8 | .3 | 1.1 | 1.1 | .9 |
| | 3.8 | 2.9 | 3.6 | -9.5 | 6.7 | 2.2 | 3.5 | 1.5 | 1.3 |
| | -10.0 | 23.8 | -9.5 | -1.2 | -5.7 | -11.8 | 5.1 | 5.6 | 13.5 |
| Debt/Worth | .8 | .7 | .8 | 2.8 | 1.8 | .2 | .5 | .5 | .3 |
| | 3.7 | 2.7 | 3.6 | -12.6 | 9.8 | 2.6 | 3.1 | 2.4 | .8 |
| | -13.3 | 42.8 | -10.7 | -2.8 | -3.0 | -13.6 | 7.1 | 5.3 | 13.8 |
| % Profit Before Taxes/Tangible Net Worth | 40.7 | 54.9 | 37.3 | 143.8 | 65.3 | | 25.8 | 21.1 | 45.5 |
| | (72) 13.3 | (87) 21.2 | (81) 13.1 | (13) 16.1 | (14) 9.4 | | (20) 12.3 | (15) 11.9 | (11) 13.2 |
| | .8 | 2.5 | -1.6 | -13.7 | -15.5 | | -2.4 | 1.5 | 1.9 |
| % Profit Before Taxes/Total Assets | 8.3 | 15.2 | 13.7 | 18.0 | 12.9 | 13.6 | 10.0 | 7.6 | 20.4 |
| | 1.9 | 5.6 | 3.4 | 3.3 | 4.3 | -1.4 | 2.2 | 2.3 | 8.6 |
| | -2.9 | .3 | -1.9 | -3.4 | -3.1 | -12.2 | -1.4 | .3 | 1.9 |
| Sales/Net Fixed Assets | 3.5 | 3.8 | 4.2 | 8.0 | 12.6 | 9.7 | 1.7 | 4.0 | 1.3 |
| | 1.3 | 1.3 | 1.2 | 2.5 | 3.3 | 2.4 | .9 | 1.2 | .9 |
| | .5 | .6 | .5 | .4 | .9 | .5 | .4 | .7 | .6 |
| Sales/Total Assets | 2.1 | 1.6 | 2.2 | 3.2 | 2.9 | 2.2 | 1.2 | 1.7 | .9 |
| | .8 | .9 | .8 | .8 | 2.2 | .9 | .7 | .9 | .7 |
| | .4 | .5 | .5 | .4 | .7 | .5 | .3 | .6 | .5 |
| % Depr., Dep., Amort./Sales | 5.4 | 5.9 | 5.3 | 3.9 | 5.6 | 2.6 | 5.9 | 5.4 | 7.9 |
| | (99) 10.0 | (99) 9.0 | (104) 10.1 | (23) 8.5 | (18) 8.3 | 8.4 | 10.2 | 10.2 | (12) 10.9 |
| | 14.3 | 13.6 | 13.9 | 19.7 | 16.1 | 14.0 | 15.9 | 13.2 | 13.1 |
| % Officers', Directors' Owners' Comp/Sales | 3.8 | 1.7 | 4.5 | 4.9 | | | | | |
| | (30) 5.5 | (25) 4.8 | (28) 6.1 | (11) 8.5 | | | | | |
| | 10.9 | 6.7 | 9.3 | 9.9 | | | | | |
| Net Sales ($) | 1061394M | 1209600M | 1249724M | 16969M | 41653M | 42936M | 162772M | 246200M | 739194M |
| Total Assets ($) | 1720020M | 1714907M | 1981663M | 27763M | 41026M | 64546M | 293245M | 274769M | 1280314M |

© RMA 2012

M = $ thousand    MM = $ million
See Pages 9 through 22 for Explanation of Ratios and Data

## Current Data Sorted by Assets　　　　　Comparative Historical Data

Type of Statement (stacked counts as printed per column):

```
                        2       3     1     9
                1       4
                1       5
        1       4       5
        2       5       3
        2       5       7     8     3     7
```

| | 0-500M | 500M-2MM | 2-10MM | 10-50MM | 50-100MM | 100-250MM | Type of Statement | 4/1/07-3/31/08 ALL | 4/1/08-3/31/09 ALL |
|---|---|---|---|---|---|---|---|---|---|
| | | | | | | | Unqualified | 13 | 12 |
| | | | | | | | Reviewed | 6 | 2 |
| | | | | | | | Compiled | 6 | 4 |
| | | | | | | | Tax Returns | 12 | 3 |
| | | | | | | | Other | 45 | 46 |
| | | 10 (4/1-9/30/11) | | 58 (10/1/11-3/31/12) | | | | | |
| | 0-500M | 500M-2MM | 2-10MM | 10-50MM | 50-100MM | 100-250MM | | | |
| | 5 | 11 | 21 | 11 | 4 | 16 | NUMBER OF STATEMENTS | 82 | 67 |
| | % | % | % | % | % | % | ASSETS | % | % |
| | | 7.9 | 11.0 | 10.9 | | 19.5 | Cash & Equivalents | 20.2 | 14.6 |
| | | 5.0 | 2.9 | 2.9 | | 1.1 | Trade Receivables (net) | 5.0 | 2.9 |
| | | 3.6 | 9.1 | 2.6 | | .5 | Inventory | 3.5 | 4.9 |
| | | 5.3 | 7.7 | 1.6 | | .9 | All Other Current | 2.0 | 2.3 |
| | | 21.8 | 30.7 | 18.0 | | 21.9 | Total Current | 30.7 | 24.7 |
| | | 45.6 | 48.5 | 57.1 | | 75.7 | Fixed Assets (net) | 59.3 | 63.3 |
| | | 17.2 | 9.1 | 12.4 | | .9 | Intangibles (net) | 5.9 | 5.1 |
| | | 15.5 | 11.7 | 12.5 | | 1.4 | All Other Non-Current | 4.1 | 6.9 |
| | | 100.0 | 100.0 | 100.0 | | 100.0 | Total | 100.0 | 100.0 |
| | | | | | | | LIABILITIES | | |
| | | .7 | 4.0 | 7.2 | | .0 | Notes Payable-Short Term | 5.1 | 6.5 |
| | | 7.8 | 7.3 | 5.3 | | 7.4 | Cur. Mat.-L.T.D. | 5.3 | 8.0 |
| | | 12.2 | 3.3 | 5.1 | | 2.1 | Trade Payables | 5.2 | 7.5 |
| | | .0 | .0 | .0 | | .0 | Income Taxes Payable | .0 | .1 |
| | | 8.8 | 14.2 | 10.5 | | 7.6 | All Other Current | 12.2 | 9.2 |
| | | 29.5 | 28.8 | 28.0 | | 17.2 | Total Current | 27.7 | 31.3 |
| | | 43.3 | 28.9 | 33.4 | | 37.4 | Long-Term Debt | 31.6 | 26.6 |
| | | .0 | .1 | .0 | | .0 | Deferred Taxes | .1 | .1 |
| | | 4.7 | 5.9 | 3.9 | | .6 | All Other Non-Current | 5.1 | 6.1 |
| | | 22.4 | 36.2 | 34.6 | | 44.8 | Net Worth | 35.6 | 35.9 |
| | | 100.0 | 100.0 | 100.0 | | 100.0 | Total Liabilities & Net Worth | 100.0 | 100.0 |
| | | | | | | | INCOME DATA | | |
| | | 100.0 | 100.0 | 100.0 | | 100.0 | Net Sales | 100.0 | 100.0 |
| | | | | | | | Gross Profit | | |
| | | 85.4 | 89.4 | 84.0 | | 68.6 | Operating Expenses | 79.8 | 83.6 |
| | | 14.6 | 10.6 | 16.0 | | 31.4 | Operating Profit | 20.2 | 16.4 |
| | | 3.9 | 2.9 | 2.0 | | 3.3 | All Other Expenses (net) | 3.9 | 3.5 |
| | | 10.6 | 7.7 | 14.0 | | 28.2 | Profit Before Taxes | 16.3 | 12.9 |
| | | | | | | | RATIOS | | |
| | | 3.3 | 3.5 | 1.6 | | 1.7 | | 3.4 | 1.6 |
| | | 1.1 | 1.2 | .5 | | 1.3 | Current | 1.6 | .9 |
| | | .4 | .1 | .4 | | .9 | | .8 | .5 |
| | | 2.7 | 1.3 | .6 | | 1.7 | | 3.0 | 1.0 |
| | | .6 | .4 | .4 | | 1.2 | Quick | 1.2 | .7 |
| | | .2 | .0 | .4 | | | | .5 | .3 |
| | 0 UND | 0 UND | 1 266.0 | | | 2 201.2 | | 0 UND | 0 999.8 |
| | 0 UND | 0 UND | 5 70.5 | | | 2 160.3 | Sales/Receivables | 2 199.8 | 2 206.0 |
| | 9 41.3 | 1 510.2 | 20 17.9 | | | 3 111.2 | | 6 56.6 | 6 64.2 |
| | | | | | | | Cost of Sales/Inventory | | |
| | | | | | | | Cost of Sales/Payables | | |
| | 8.1 | 3.5 | 13.2 | | | 9.8 | | 6.8 | 15.5 |
| | 67.9 | 24.6 | -10.0 | | | 24.7 | Sales/Working Capital | 26.3 | -40.4 |
| | -4.3 | -4.3 | -5.0 | | | NM | | -24.9 | -7.6 |
| | | | 8.2 | 16.0 | | 26.8 | | 29.5 | 18.8 |
| | | (20) | 5.0 | 3.0 | (15) | 16.5 | EBIT/Interest | (67) 6.4 | (57) 5.5 |
| | | | 1.2 | 2.1 | | 5.9 | | .9 | .4 |
| | | | | | | | Net Profit + Depr., Dep., Amort./Cur. Mat. L/T/D | | |
| | | .9 | .3 | 1.6 | | 1.2 | | .8 | .9 |
| | | 18.3 | 1.6 | 3.3 | | 1.6 | Fixed/Worth | 1.4 | 1.6 |
| | | -1.4 | 6.1 | -17.5 | | 2.9 | | 8.1 | 7.7 |
| | | 1.6 | .7 | 1.4 | | .4 | | .4 | .5 |
| | | 20.2 | 1.9 | 2.7 | | 1.1 | Debt/Worth | 1.4 | 1.3 |
| | | -4.7 | 7.5 | -30.1 | | 2.5 | | 7.9 | 7.9 |
| | | | 79.3 | | | 86.4 | | 90.0 | 84.7 |
| | | (17) | 13.5 | | (14) | 51.2 | % Profit Before Taxes/Tangible Net Worth | (64) 47.8 | (54) 36.3 |
| | | | 3.9 | | | 36.1 | | 14.6 | 5.3 |
| | | 11.7 | 21.0 | 29.7 | | 45.3 | | 42.7 | 36.9 |
| | | 6.7 | 4.4 | 8.1 | | 30.4 | % Profit Before Taxes/Total Assets | 15.3 | 14.7 |
| | | 1.3 | .5 | 1.1 | | 16.3 | | .2 | -1.1 |
| | | 14.4 | 18.2 | 2.7 | | 1.8 | | 4.4 | 4.1 |
| | | 3.4 | 1.7 | 1.9 | | 1.3 | Sales/Net Fixed Assets | 2.3 | 2.0 |
| | | 1.1 | 1.2 | 1.4 | | .9 | | 1.1 | 1.2 |
| | | 2.0 | 1.1 | 1.3 | | 1.1 | | 2.2 | 1.9 |
| | | .9 | .9 | 1.0 | | 1.0 | Sales/Total Assets | 1.3 | 1.3 |
| | | .7 | .7 | .6 | | .7 | | .8 | .8 |
| | | | 1.9 | 3.4 | | | | 3.7 | 4.5 |
| | | (16) | 8.9 | 6.6 | | | % Depr., Dep., Amort./Sales | (66) 7.3 | (50) 7.2 |
| | | | 10.9 | 8.8 | | | | 11.7 | 9.9 |
| | | | | | | | | 1.9 | 1.9 |
| | | | | | | | % Officers', Directors' Owners' Comp/Sales | (15) 4.6 | (15) 4.2 |
| | | | | | | | | 7.7 | 10.9 |
| | 5345M | 21699M | 137172M | 366604M | 332090M | 2693146M | Net Sales ($) | 6218450M | 4243140M |
| | 1025M | 14336M | 95575M | 334078M | 352386M | 2597683M | Total Assets ($) | 4056349M | 3748134M |

M = $ thousand　　MM = $ million
See Pages 9 through 22 for Explanation of Ratios and Data

## Comparative Historical Data | Current Data Sorted by Sales

| | | | Type of Statement | | | | | | |
|---|---|---|---|---|---|---|---|---|---|
| 13 | 13 | 15 | Unqualified | | 1 | | 1 | 2 | 11 |
| 2 | 6 | 5 | Reviewed | 1 | 2 | 1 | 1 | | |
| 6 | 4 | 7 | Compiled | | 3 | 1 | 3 | | |
| 8 | 6 | 9 | Tax Returns | | 4 | | 1 | | 1 |
| 35 | 38 | 32 | Other | 3 | 7 | 2 | 2 | 3 | 15 |
| 4/1/09- | 4/1/10- | 4/1/11- | | 3 | | | | | |
| 3/31/10 | 3/31/11 | 3/31/12 | | | 10 (4/1-9/30/11) | | 58 (10/1/11-3/31/12) | | |
| ALL | ALL | ALL | | 0-1MM | 1-3MM | 3-5MM | 5-10MM | 10-25MM | 25MM & OVER |
| 64 | 67 | 68 | **NUMBER OF STATEMENTS** | 7 | 17 | 4 | 8 | 5 | 27 |
| % | % | % | **ASSETS** | % | % | % | % | % | % |
| 14.5 | 16.9 | 13.8 | Cash & Equivalents | | 8.0 | | | | 17.8 |
| 2.7 | 3.5 | 2.5 | Trade Receivables (net) | | .8 | | | | 3.3 |
| 5.7 | 3.6 | 4.2 | Inventory | | 5.7 | | | | 2.5 |
| 4.8 | 1.6 | 4.5 | All Other Current | | 10.8 | | | | 1.4 |
| 27.6 | 25.6 | 25.0 | Total Current | | 25.3 | | | | 25.0 |
| 61.7 | 60.5 | 57.1 | Fixed Assets (net) | | 51.4 | | | | 69.0 |
| 4.5 | 7.3 | 8.6 | Intangibles (net) | | 12.7 | | | | 4.1 |
| 6.3 | 6.6 | 9.3 | All Other Non-Current | | 10.7 | | | | 1.9 |
| 100.0 | 100.0 | 100.0 | Total | | 100.0 | | | | 100.0 |
| | | | **LIABILITIES** | | | | | | |
| 5.4 | 6.2 | 2.8 | Notes Payable-Short Term | | 3.4 | | | | .6 |
| 6.3 | 6.7 | 6.5 | Cur. Mat.-L.T.D. | | 7.0 | | | | 6.6 |
| 7.2 | 4.1 | 6.4 | Trade Payables | | 4.2 | | | | 2.9 |
| .0 | .0 | .0 | Income Taxes Payable | | .0 | | | | .1 |
| 10.5 | 8.5 | 10.0 | All Other Current | | 11.9 | | | | 8.4 |
| 29.4 | 25.6 | 25.8 | Total Current | | 26.5 | | | | 18.6 |
| 36.1 | 37.0 | 33.5 | Long-Term Debt | | 33.8 | | | | 33.5 |
| .1 | .4 | .0 | Deferred Taxes | | .1 | | | | .0 |
| 4.3 | 12.2 | 8.0 | All Other Non-Current | | 15.1 | | | | .7 |
| 30.1 | 24.7 | 32.7 | Net Worth | | 24.5 | | | | 47.2 |
| 100.0 | 100.0 | 100.0 | Total Liabilties & Net Worth | | 100.0 | | | | 100.0 |
| | | | **INCOME DATA** | | | | | | |
| 100.0 | 100.0 | 100.0 | Net Sales | | 100.0 | | | | 100.0 |
| | | | Gross Profit | | | | | | |
| 88.5 | 84.2 | 81.9 | Operating Expenses | | 92.5 | | | | 71.9 |
| 11.5 | 15.8 | 18.1 | Operating Profit | | 7.5 | | | | 28.1 |
| 2.4 | 4.4 | 3.1 | All Other Expenses (net) | | 2.4 | | | | 3.7 |
| 9.0 | 11.4 | 15.1 | Profit Before Taxes | | 5.1 | | | | 24.4 |
| | | | **RATIOS** | | | | | | |
| 2.3 | 1.9 | 1.8 | | | 3.4 | | | | 1.8 |
| 1.0 | 1.1 | 1.2 | Current | | 1.2 | | | | 1.4 |
| .4 | .7 | .5 | | | .5 | | | | .9 |
| 1.6 | 1.7 | 1.5 | | | 1.5 | | | | 1.7 |
| .6 | .9 | .7 | Quick | | .4 | | | | 1.1 |
| .1 | .4 | .2 | | | .1 | | | | .7 |
| 0 UND | 0 UND | 0 UND | | 0 UND | | | | 1 247.7 | |
| 1 372.9 | 1 259.7 | 1 288.4 | Sales/Receivables | 0 UND | | | | 3 138.8 | |
| 5 74.8 | 5 73.7 | 3 108.0 | | 1 689.9 | | | | 5 70.5 | |
| | | | Cost of Sales/Inventory | | | | | | |
| | | | Cost of Sales/Payables | | | | | | |
| 8.4 | 9.7 | 9.1 | | | 6.4 | | | | 9.1 |
| 646.5 | 39.8 | 68.5 | Sales/Working Capital | | 75.9 | | | | 19.8 |
| -7.8 | -16.6 | -10.0 | | | -17.6 | | | | -49.9 |
| 17.8 | 15.2 | 16.8 | | | 31.3 | | | | 23.1 |
| (58) 3.5 | (60) 5.1 | (62) 6.2 | EBIT/Interest | (15) 2.2 | | | | (26) 15.4 | |
| -.3 | 1.2 | 2.1 | | | .1 | | | | 3.5 |
| | | | Net Profit + Depr., Dep., Amort./Cur. Mat. L/T/D | | | | | | |
| .8 | .9 | 1.0 | | | .8 | | | | 1.2 |
| 1.4 | 1.5 | 1.7 | Fixed/Worth | | 1.5 | | | | 1.6 |
| NM | -197.8 | 17.5 | | | -4.0 | | | | 2.9 |
| .5 | .6 | .9 | | | .6 | | | | .5 |
| 1.0 | 1.3 | 1.9 | Debt/Worth | | 1.7 | | | | 1.1 |
| NM | -246.9 | 55.1 | | | -7.8 | | | | 2.2 |
| 56.8 | 69.6 | 92.4 | | | 55.1 | | | | 111.1 |
| (48) 17.9 | (50) 31.1 | (52) 44.1 | % Profit Before Taxes/Tangible Net Worth | (11) 7.5 | | | | (25) 65.6 | |
| .2 | 4.8 | 10.7 | | | 2.2 | | | | 25.0 |
| 23.1 | 24.3 | 28.0 | | | 19.0 | | | | 44.7 |
| 4.9 | 11.5 | 11.7 | % Profit Before Taxes/Total Assets | | 4.4 | | | | 25.9 |
| -1.6 | .8 | 3.1 | | | -.8 | | | | 12.0 |
| 4.2 | 3.4 | 4.1 | | | 23.1 | | | | 2.5 |
| 2.1 | 1.7 | 1.7 | Sales/Net Fixed Assets | | 3.4 | | | | 1.3 |
| 1.3 | 1.1 | 1.1 | | | 1.2 | | | | .9 |
| 2.0 | 1.5 | 1.3 | | | 2.6 | | | | 1.3 |
| 1.3 | 1.0 | 1.0 | Sales/Total Assets | | .9 | | | | 1.0 |
| .8 | .8 | .7 | | | .6 | | | | .8 |
| 5.6 | 6.7 | 5.8 | | | 6.9 | | | | 6.2 |
| (52) 7.6 | (43) 9.5 | (47) 7.8 | % Depr., Dep., Amort./Sales | (11) 8.8 | | | | (16) 7.5 | |
| 10.6 | 12.7 | 10.6 | | | 11.3 | | | | 8.8 |
| 2.3 | 2.3 | 1.7 | | | | | | | |
| (18) 4.4 | (15) 5.2 | (11) 5.1 | % Officers', Directors' Owners' Comp/Sales | | | | | | |
| 6.9 | 7.4 | 11.5 | | | | | | | |
| 2556439M | 3750231M | 3556056M | Net Sales ($) | 4236M | 32582M | 15898M | 57938M | 96844M | 3348558M |
| 2501070M | 3540487M | 3395083M | Total Assets ($) | 5301M | 34680M | 12630M | 51911M | 131365M | 3159196M |

M = $ thousand    MM = $ million
See Pages 9 through 22 for Explanation of Ratios and Data

**Current Data Sorted by Assets**      **Comparative Historical Data**

| Type of Statement | 0-500M | 500M-2MM | 2-10MM | 10-50MM | 50-100MM | 100-250MM | 4/1/07-3/31/08 ALL | 4/1/08-3/31/09 ALL |
|---|---|---|---|---|---|---|---|---|
| Unqualified | 1 | | 3 | 4 | 7 | 12 | 40 | 36 |
| Reviewed | | | 3 | | | | | 1 |
| Compiled | | | 2 | | | 1 | 2 | 3 |
| Tax Returns | 1 | 2 | 5 | | | | 11 | 7 |
| Other | 13 | 5 | 14 | 11 | 11 | 12 | 51 | 62 |
| | 18 (4/1-9/30/11) | | 93 (10/1/11-3/31/12) | | | | | |
| **NUMBER OF STATEMENTS** | 17 | 9 | 27 | 15 | 19 | 24 | 104 | 109 |
| **ASSETS** | % | % | % | % | % | % | % | % |
| Cash & Equivalents | 29.4 | | 18.3 | 26.7 | 18.3 | 15.9 | 20.4 | 19.7 |
| Trade Receivables (net) | 1.0 | | 3.0 | 3.0 | 1.6 | 1.1 | 1.3 | 1.9 |
| Inventory | 1.2 | | 4.2 | 1.8 | .8 | .6 | .5 | .6 |
| All Other Current | 2.5 | | 3.3 | 3.8 | 1.7 | 2.1 | 3.0 | 2.2 |
| Total Current | 34.0 | | 28.8 | 35.3 | 22.5 | 19.7 | 25.2 | 24.4 |
| Fixed Assets (net) | 34.9 | | 52.1 | 49.7 | 64.1 | 65.8 | 66.4 | 65.6 |
| Intangibles (net) | 16.8 | | 6.7 | 2.2 | 10.1 | 7.7 | 4.0 | 3.2 |
| All Other Non-Current | 13.9 | | 12.4 | 12.9 | 3.3 | 6.8 | 4.4 | 6.8 |
| Total | 100.0 | | 100.0 | 100.0 | 100.0 | 100.0 | 100.0 | 100.0 |
| **LIABILITIES** | | | | | | | | |
| Notes Payable-Short Term | 6.3 | | 4.2 | 11.2 | 6.0 | 1.6 | 3.2 | 2.3 |
| Cur. Mat.-L.T.D. | 3.8 | | 11.9 | 10.3 | 11.6 | 12.1 | 4.8 | 3.7 |
| Trade Payables | 3.7 | | 9.2 | 4.4 | 2.4 | 3.0 | 3.9 | 4.5 |
| Income Taxes Payable | .0 | | .7 | .0 | .1 | .0 | .0 | .1 |
| All Other Current | 9.9 | | 7.6 | 23.1 | 7.9 | 8.2 | 10.4 | 10.6 |
| Total Current | 23.7 | | 33.5 | 49.0 | 28.0 | 24.9 | 22.3 | 21.3 |
| Long-Term Debt | 41.1 | | 42.3 | 28.1 | 18.9 | 26.2 | 34.9 | 32.7 |
| Deferred Taxes | .0 | | .0 | .0 | .1 | .2 | .1 | .1 |
| All Other Non-Current | 27.7 | | 1.9 | 6.4 | 19.4 | 2.0 | 4.0 | 5.5 |
| Net Worth | 7.6 | | 22.2 | 16.5 | 33.7 | 46.6 | 38.7 | 40.4 |
| Total Liabilities & Net Worth | 100.0 | | 100.0 | 100.0 | 100.0 | 100.0 | 100.0 | 100.0 |
| **INCOME DATA** | | | | | | | | |
| Net Sales | 100.0 | | 100.0 | 100.0 | 100.0 | 100.0 | 100.0 | 100.0 |
| Gross Profit | | | | | | | | |
| Operating Expenses | 100.2 | | 92.2 | 80.4 | 81.8 | 77.0 | 74.2 | 78.6 |
| Operating Profit | -.2 | | 7.8 | 19.6 | 18.2 | 23.0 | 25.8 | 21.4 |
| All Other Expenses (net) | 3.1 | | 2.8 | 4.0 | 5.2 | 5.7 | 4.0 | 4.3 |
| Profit Before Taxes | -3.3 | | 5.0 | 15.6 | 13.0 | 17.4 | 21.8 | 17.2 |
| **RATIOS** | | | | | | | | |
| Current | 3.3 | | 4.2 | 1.9 | 1.9 | 1.7 | 2.2 | 2.1 |
| | 1.8 | | 1.6 | 1.1 | 1.3 | 1.0 | 1.2 | 1.3 |
| | 1.1 | | .5 | .5 | .8 | .5 | .7 | .8 |
| Quick | 2.9 | | 1.8 | 1.3 | 1.6 | 1.3 | 2.0 | 1.9 |
| | 1.5 | | 1.0 | .9 | 1.1 | .7 | 1.1 | 1.1 |
| | .7 | | .4 | .4 | .9 | .4 | .6 | .6 |
| Sales/Receivables | 0 UND | | 0 999.8 | 1 482.0 | 1 532.2 | 1 303.5 | 0 999.8 | 0 768.4 |
| | 0 UND | | 1 634.0 | 2 211.7 | 3 125.2 | 3 137.9 | 1 372.5 | 1 260.8 |
| | 0 UND | | 5 76.7 | 10 37.2 | 10 37.1 | 4 91.7 | 3 112.1 | 4 82.2 |
| Cost of Sales/Inventory | | | | | | | | |
| Cost of Sales/Payables | | | | | | | | |
| Sales/Working Capital | 22.5 | | 9.5 | 9.8 | 12.8 | 9.0 | 11.4 | 10.6 |
| | 60.6 | | 19.7 | 61.4 | 23.3 | NM | 69.8 | 39.0 |
| | NM | | -20.2 | -7.9 | -31.7 | -7.1 | -19.0 | -23.3 |
| EBIT/Interest | | | 4.6 | 14.7 | 10.8 | 21.6 | 27.2 | 28.4 |
| | | | (21) 2.6 | (12) 7.0 | (16) 5.8 | (20) 10.1 | (78) 9.7 | (82) 10.9 |
| | | | -1.7 | .9 | 2.2 | 3.2 | 3.0 | 2.5 |
| Net Profit + Depr., Dep., Amort./Cur. Mat. L/T/D | | | | | | | | |
| Fixed/Worth | .4 | | .9 | .8 | 1.0 | 1.1 | .9 | .9 |
| | 3.8 | | 1.7 | 1.8 | 1.4 | 1.6 | 1.6 | 1.4 |
| | -1.1 | | 12.3 | -2.3 | -6.9 | 3.3 | 5.3 | 7.4 |
| Debt/Worth | .3 | | .9 | .5 | .4 | .5 | .4 | .4 |
| | 11.3 | | 3.1 | 1.9 | .9 | 1.2 | 1.4 | 1.1 |
| | -5.0 | | -24.9 | -11.6 | -10.9 | 2.6 | 6.9 | 7.8 |
| % Profit Before Taxes/Tangible Net Worth | 100.7 | | 121.4 | 128.0 | 65.5 | 63.0 | 148.3 | 107.8 |
| | (10) 46.0 | | (20) 30.2 | (11) 40.6 | (14) 39.0 | (20) 41.3 | (84) 72.8 | (91) 58.6 |
| | -21.4 | | -5.6 | 14.1 | 21.6 | 18.1 | 29.2 | 19.9 |
| % Profit Before Taxes/Total Assets | 43.9 | | 15.3 | 50.9 | 26.9 | 32.5 | 59.8 | 49.2 |
| | 5.7 | | 7.4 | 22.6 | 14.3 | 15.2 | 31.2 | 20.3 |
| | -29.9 | | -7.7 | 4.6 | 4.8 | 4.5 | 5.7 | 5.0 |
| Sales/Net Fixed Assets | 80.6 | | 13.6 | 11.2 | 3.3 | 1.8 | 4.0 | 3.4 |
| | 27.1 | | 3.1 | 2.4 | 1.8 | 1.3 | 1.9 | 1.6 |
| | 3.3 | | 1.5 | 1.2 | 1.2 | .8 | 1.1 | 1.0 |
| Sales/Total Assets | 15.8 | | 3.3 | 2.7 | 1.6 | 1.0 | 2.2 | 1.9 |
| | 4.0 | | 1.7 | 1.3 | 1.1 | .8 | 1.4 | 1.2 |
| | 1.6 | | .9 | .8 | .9 | .6 | .8 | .8 |
| % Depr., Dep., Amort./Sales | .7 | | 2.8 | 3.3 | 5.5 | 5.7 | 3.8 | 4.2 |
| | (13) 2.2 | | (24) 5.0 | 4.7 | (16) 6.9 | (11) 6.4 | (83) 6.2 | (86) 6.3 |
| | 4.9 | | 8.6 | 8.6 | 10.0 | 7.6 | 8.9 | 8.7 |
| % Officers', Directors' Owners' Comp/Sales | | | | | | | 2.1 | 2.4 |
| | | | | | | | (14) 3.1 | (11) 3.8 |
| | | | | | | | 7.4 | 5.0 |
| Net Sales ($) | 30222M | 25279M | 290744M | 664743M | 1756945M | 3316521M | 9620075M | 7904068M |
| Total Assets ($) | 4138M | 9672M | 131369M | 407860M | 1303510M | 4031737M | 6691547M | 7057498M |

M = $ thousand    MM = $ million
See Pages 9 through 22 for Explanation of Ratios and Data

## Comparative Historical Data / Current Data Sorted by Sales

| | | | Type of Statement | | | | | | |
|---|---|---|---|---|---|---|---|---|---|
| 38 | 35 | 27 | Unqualified | | 1 | 2 | 2 | 22 |
| 2 | 3 | 3 | Reviewed | | 1 | 2 | | |
| 8 | 4 | 5 | Compiled | 1 | 2 | 1 | | 1 |
| 14 | 16 | 20 | Tax Returns | 5 | 6 | 2 | 4 | 3 | |
| 72 | 53 | 56 | Other | 5 | 5 | 2 | 3 | 8 | 33 |
| 4/1/09-3/31/10 ALL | 4/1/10-3/31/11 ALL | 4/1/11-3/31/12 ALL | | 0-1MM | 18 (4/1-9/30/11) 1-3MM | 3-5MM | 93 (10/1/11-3/31/12) 5-10MM | 10-25MM | 25MM & OVER |
| 134 | 111 | 111 | NUMBER OF STATEMENTS | 11 | 11 | 8 | 12 | 13 | 56 |
| % | % | % | ASSETS | % | % | % | % | % | % |
| 19.0 | 17.5 | 21.1 | Cash & Equivalents | 18.7 | 31.5 | | 21.2 | 23.7 | 19.3 |
| 2.3 | 1.6 | 1.8 | Trade Receivables (net) | .0 | .7 | | 4.2 | 1.9 | 1.8 |
| .9 | 1.9 | 2.2 | Inventory | 1.6 | 5.5 | | 1.2 | 3.7 | .8 |
| 2.9 | 2.9 | 2.6 | All Other Current | 2.3 | 2.7 | | 2.0 | 8.1 | 1.8 |
| 25.1 | 24.0 | 27.7 | Total Current | 22.6 | 40.4 | | 28.6 | 37.5 | 23.7 |
| 62.7 | 60.4 | 53.4 | Fixed Assets (net) | 40.2 | 38.9 | | 41.1 | 53.0 | 60.6 |
| 5.9 | 8.5 | 9.9 | Intangibles (net) | 24.4 | 9.2 | | 13.6 | 3.8 | 8.4 |
| 6.3 | 7.1 | 9.0 | All Other Non-Current | 12.2 | 11.4 | | 16.7 | 5.8 | 7.3 |
| 100.0 | 100.0 | 100.0 | Total | 100.0 | 100.0 | | 100.0 | 100.0 | 100.0 |
| | | | LIABILITIES | | | | | | |
| 2.5 | 4.6 | 4.9 | Notes Payable-Short Term | 2.0 | 8.2 | | 8.7 | .4 | 5.7 |
| 9.0 | 12.1 | 9.7 | Cur. Mat.-L.T.D. | 4.7 | 2.4 | | 3.7 | 16.6 | 12.6 |
| 3.7 | 4.3 | 5.0 | Trade Payables | 3.5 | 2.1 | | 11.0 | 7.5 | 3.5 |
| .1 | .3 | .2 | Income Taxes Payable | .0 | .0 | | .8 | .0 | .2 |
| 10.9 | 9.4 | 10.4 | All Other Current | 7.3 | 7.8 | | 6.4 | 12.3 | 12.3 |
| 26.2 | 30.6 | 30.2 | Total Current | 17.6 | 20.4 | | 30.5 | 36.9 | 34.2 |
| 34.2 | 32.8 | 32.5 | Long-Term Debt | 59.7 | 41.5 | | 25.5 | 32.3 | 25.3 |
| .0 | .0 | .1 | Deferred Taxes | .0 | .0 | | .0 | .0 | .1 |
| 7.1 | 10.6 | 9.3 | All Other Non-Current | 39.9 | 2.9 | | 1.6 | 2.3 | 9.2 |
| 32.5 | 25.9 | 27.8 | Net Worth | -17.0 | 35.2 | | 42.4 | 28.5 | 31.2 |
| 100.0 | 100.0 | 100.0 | Total Liabilities & Net Worth | 100.0 | 100.0 | | 100.0 | 100.0 | 100.0 |
| | | | INCOME DATA | | | | | | |
| 100.0 | 100.0 | 100.0 | Net Sales | 100.0 | 100.0 | | 100.0 | 100.0 | 100.0 |
| | | | Gross Profit | | | | | | |
| 79.6 | 84.2 | 87.1 | Operating Expenses | 95.6 | 98.0 | | 92.5 | 92.7 | 79.1 |
| 20.4 | 15.8 | 12.9 | Operating Profit | 4.4 | 2.0 | | 7.5 | 7.3 | 20.9 |
| 4.5 | 5.5 | 4.0 | All Other Expenses (net) | 6.8 | 1.4 | | 2.1 | 2.7 | 5.0 |
| 15.9 | 10.3 | 8.9 | Profit Before Taxes | -2.5 | .6 | | 5.5 | 4.6 | 15.9 |
| | | | RATIOS | | | | | | |
| 2.1 | 1.9 | 2.1 | | 2.2 | 9.1 | | 3.8 | 4.4 | 1.6 |
| 1.1 | 1.2 | 1.2 | Current | 1.2 | 1.8 | | 1.7 | 1.2 | 1.1 |
| .5 | .6 | .6 | | .8 | 1.4 | | .6 | .6 | .5 |
| 1.8 | 1.6 | 1.7 | | 1.9 | 2.4 | | 3.4 | 2.4 | 1.4 |
| (132) .9 | (110) 1.0 | 1.0 | Quick | 1.0 | 1.4 | | 1.5 | .8 | .9 |
| .4 | .5 | .5 | | .5 | 1.0 | | .4 | .5 | .4 |
| 0 999.8 | 0 999.8 | 0 UND | | 0 UND | 0 UND | | 0 UND | 0 999.8 | 1 377.6 |
| 1 315.3 | 1 295.2 | 1 332.1 | Sales/Receivables | 0 UND | 0 UND | | 0 UND | 3 104.6 | 3 143.3 |
| 3 120.5 | 4 95.3 | 4 90.3 | | 0 UND | 0 UND | | 7 53.4 | 5 69.2 | 6 60.5 |
| | | | Cost of Sales/Inventory | | | | | | |
| | | | Cost of Sales/Payables | | | | | | |
| 12.0 | 11.1 | 10.4 | | 20.3 | 2.6 | | 8.1 | 9.6 | 12.2 |
| 116.2 | 63.0 | 60.2 | Sales/Working Capital | 52.8 | 28.4 | | 54.7 | 19.7 | 145.5 |
| -15.0 | -15.3 | -19.6 | | -47.6 | 608.5 | | -27.1 | -18.0 | -10.6 |
| 31.0 | 14.3 | 10.4 | | | | | | | 19.4 |
| (109) 5.8 | (93) 4.2 | (84) 4.0 | EBIT/Interest | | | | | (48) | 7.0 |
| 1.7 | .7 | .6 | | | | | | | 2.3 |
| | | | Net Profit + Depr., Dep., Amort./Cur. Mat. L/T/D | | | | | | |
| 1.0 | 1.0 | .9 | | 1.1 | .3 | | .4 | .4 | 1.1 |
| 1.9 | 2.0 | 1.7 | Fixed/Worth | 6.4 | 1.1 | | 1.5 | 1.1 | 1.7 |
| 37.7 | -5.8 | -7.0 | | -.6 | -1.2 | | 6.1 | NM | NM |
| .5 | .6 | .5 | | .7 | .4 | | .4 | .3 | .5 |
| 1.5 | 1.9 | 1.5 | Debt/Worth | 98.1 | 1.5 | | 2.5 | .9 | 1.3 |
| -139.1 | -8.4 | -20.0 | | -2.1 | -6.7 | | NM | NM | NM |
| 96.1 | 71.0 | 66.0 | | | | | | 156.7 | 67.0 |
| (100) 45.7 | (81) 35.6 | (81) 39.4 | % Profit Before Taxes/Tangible Net Worth | | | | (10) | 30.9 | (42) 45.8 |
| 16.9 | 10.6 | 13.5 | | | | | | 14.6 | 20.8 |
| 38.9 | 27.6 | 26.8 | | 8.1 | 14.1 | | 24.5 | 33.4 | 36.3 |
| 13.9 | 10.0 | 10.1 | % Profit Before Taxes/Total Assets | 1.6 | .9 | | 8.6 | 10.1 | 15.5 |
| .5 | -.7 | -1.4 | | -36.1 | -10.5 | | 1.6 | -2.4 | 4.8 |
| 4.0 | 4.8 | 10.6 | | 34.1 | 47.8 | | 79.2 | 18.9 | 4.2 |
| 1.7 | 1.8 | 2.4 | Sales/Net Fixed Assets | 6.5 | 6.9 | | 4.8 | 3.7 | 1.6 |
| 1.1 | 1.1 | 1.2 | | 2.0 | 1.9 | | 1.7 | 1.6 | 1.1 |
| 2.1 | 2.3 | 2.7 | | 3.7 | 16.0 | | 3.4 | 4.0 | 1.5 |
| 1.1 | 1.1 | 1.3 | Sales/Total Assets | 1.5 | 3.3 | | 1.5 | 2.3 | 1.0 |
| .8 | .7 | .8 | | 1.0 | 1.5 | | .9 | 1.4 | .8 |
| 4.8 | 3.8 | 2.9 | | | | | .9 | 1.6 | 4.0 |
| (103) 6.8 | (92) 6.4 | (82) 5.7 | % Depr., Dep., Amort./Sales | | | | (10) 6.4 | 5.0 | (40) 6.1 |
| 9.8 | 9.1 | 8.3 | | | | | 8.8 | 8.3 | 8.2 |
| 1.7 | 1.0 | 2.2 | | | | | | | |
| (19) 3.8 | (14) 2.9 | (14) 3.0 | % Officers', Directors' Owners' Comp/Sales | | | | | | |
| 5.2 | 5.8 | 4.8 | | | | | | | |
| 7792600M | 6449335M | 6084454M | Net Sales ($) | 4509M | 21363M | 30955M | 81063M | 197292M | 5749272M |
| 7413417M | 6158384M | 5888286M | Total Assets ($) | 6133M | 11159M | 16795M | 61206M | 113607M | 5679386M |

M = $ thousand    MM = $ million
See Pages 9 through 22 for Explanation of Ratios and Data

| | Current Data Sorted by Assets | | | | | | Comparative Historical Data | |
|---|---|---|---|---|---|---|---|---|

| 0-500M | 500M-2MM | 2-10MM | 10-50MM | 50-100MM | 100-250MM | Type of Statement | 4/1/07-3/31/08 ALL | 4/1/08-3/31/09 ALL |
|---|---|---|---|---|---|---|---|---|
| | | 2 | 7 | 2 | 7 | Unqualified | 6 | 6 |
| | 1 | | | | | Reviewed | 1 | 2 |
| | 2 | 1 | | | | Compiled | 3 | 3 |
| | | 4 | | | | Tax Returns | 4 | 5 |
| | | | 11 | 7 | 13 | Other | 15 | 10 |
| | 9 (4/1-9/30/11) | | 48 (10/1/11-3/31/12) | | | | | |
| | 3 | 7 | 18 | 9 | 20 | NUMBER OF STATEMENTS | 29 | 26 |
| % | % | % | % | % | % | **ASSETS** | % | % |
| | | | 18.7 | | 17.0 | Cash & Equivalents | 14.1 | 17.2 |
| | | | 3.5 | | 1.9 | Trade Receivables (net) | 5.3 | 2.4 |
| | | | .6 | | .8 | Inventory | 1.5 | 7.0 |
| | | | 7.1 | | 3.5 | All Other Current | 7.8 | 4.9 |
| | | | 29.8 | | 23.2 | Total Current | 28.7 | 31.5 |
| | | | 56.1 | | 67.1 | Fixed Assets (net) | 56.1 | 52.9 |
| | | | 4.2 | | 5.0 | Intangibles (net) | 11.5 | 11.5 |
| | | | 9.9 | | 4.7 | All Other Non-Current | 3.8 | 4.2 |
| | | | 100.0 | | 100.0 | Total | 100.0 | 100.0 |
| | | | | | | **LIABILITIES** | | |
| | | | .7 | | 1.2 | Notes Payable-Short Term | .5 | 6.0 |
| | | | 3.8 | | 11.0 | Cur. Mat.-L.T.D. | 5.2 | 3.6 |
| | | | 4.3 | | 2.2 | Trade Payables | 5.8 | 6.5 |
| | | | .1 | | .0 | Income Taxes Payable | .0 | .8 |
| | | | 17.1 | | 10.0 | All Other Current | 13.7 | 12.8 |
| | | | 25.9 | | 24.4 | Total Current | 25.3 | 29.7 |
| | | | 24.1 | | 37.3 | Long-Term Debt | 40.5 | 35.8 |
| | | | .5 | | .1 | Deferred Taxes | .2 | .1 |
| | | | 6.3 | | .9 | All Other Non-Current | 7.1 | 6.9 |
| | | | 43.1 | | 37.3 | Net Worth | 27.0 | 27.5 |
| | | | 100.0 | | 100.0 | Total Liabilities & Net Worth | 100.0 | 100.0 |
| | | | | | | **INCOME DATA** | | |
| | | | 100.0 | | 100.0 | Net Sales | 100.0 | 100.0 |
| | | | | | | Gross Profit | | |
| | | | 75.7 | | 76.0 | Operating Expenses | 85.2 | 89.7 |
| | | | 24.3 | | 24.0 | Operating Profit | 14.8 | 10.3 |
| | | | 1.9 | | 9.5 | All Other Expenses (net) | 4.1 | 4.3 |
| | | | 22.4 | | 14.5 | Profit Before Taxes | 10.8 | 6.0 |
| | | | | | | **RATIOS** | | |
| | | | 2.4 | | 1.7 | | 2.0 | 2.4 |
| | | | 1.2 | | 1.0 | Current | 1.3 | 1.3 |
| | | | .8 | | .7 | | .7 | .6 |
| | | | 2.1 | | 1.3 | | 1.6 | 1.5 |
| | | | 1.0 | | .9 | Quick | .9 | .9 |
| | | | .7 | | .7 | | .5 | .4 |
| | | | 2 161.9 | | 1 294.3 | | 0 UND | 0 UND |
| | | | 7 49.0 | | 2 151.6 | Sales/Receivables | 6 58.5 | 1 253.7 |
| | | | 34 10.8 | | 6 61.2 | | 19 18.9 | 13 27.3 |
| | | | | | | Cost of Sales/Inventory | | |
| | | | | | | Cost of Sales/Payables | | |
| | | | 5.2 | | 14.3 | | 8.0 | 5.9 |
| | | | 21.7 | | 99.0 | Sales/Working Capital | 56.3 | 79.4 |
| | | | -25.9 | | -9.4 | | -33.1 | -11.1 |
| | | | 51.3 | | 22.7 | | 12.1 | 22.2 |
| | | | (17) 9.9 | | 5.9 | EBIT/Interest | (27) 3.1 | (25) 5.9 |
| | | | 4.5 | | 1.6 | | .8 | .7 |
| | | | | | | Net Profit + Depr., Dep., Amort./Cur. Mat. L/T/D | | |
| | | | .7 | | 1.2 | | 1.3 | 1.1 |
| | | | 1.2 | | 1.6 | Fixed/Worth | 2.7 | 3.1 |
| | | | 2.1 | | 12.4 | | -12.5 | -4.8 |
| | | | .3 | | .6 | | .9 | .8 |
| | | | 1.0 | | 1.4 | Debt/Worth | 3.5 | 4.0 |
| | | | 2.6 | | 13.3 | | -17.0 | -7.4 |
| | | | 134.1 | | 79.7 | % Profit Before Taxes/Tangible | 71.9 | 60.0 |
| | | | (17) 17.6 | | (16) 43.9 | Net Worth | (20) 23.0 | (17) 19.2 |
| | | | 6.7 | | 10.3 | | -2.9 | 1.3 |
| | | | 53.9 | | 23.1 | % Profit Before Taxes/Total | 22.9 | 15.6 |
| | | | 13.7 | | 16.5 | Assets | 6.7 | 10.0 |
| | | | 1.9 | | -2.4 | | -.9 | -.9 |
| | | | 2.9 | | 1.9 | | 5.3 | 5.1 |
| | | | 2.0 | | 1.3 | Sales/Net Fixed Assets | 3.3 | 2.9 |
| | | | 1.1 | | .8 | | 1.1 | 1.3 |
| | | | 1.7 | | 1.1 | | 2.5 | 2.3 |
| | | | 1.0 | | .8 | Sales/Total Assets | 1.1 | 1.2 |
| | | | .5 | | .6 | | .7 | .6 |
| | | | 3.6 | | | | 2.7 | 3.0 |
| | | | (17) 7.0 | | | % Depr., Dep., Amort./Sales | (21) 3.5 | (20) 6.1 |
| | | | 15.1 | | | | 10.2 | 10.5 |
| | | | | | | % Officers', Directors' Owners' Comp/Sales | | |
| | 64520M | 74347M | 624372M | 738925M | 3149451M | Net Sales ($) | 1430518M | 1316200M |
| | 3998M | 23264M | 557123M | 656444M | 3479012M | Total Assets ($) | 1296171M | 1271681M |

M = $ thousand    MM = $ million
See Pages 9 through 22 for Explanation of Ratios and Data

## Comparative Historical Data                                                                 ## Current Data Sorted by Sales

| | | | Type of Statement | | | | | | |
|---|---|---|---|---|---|---|---|---|---|
| 5 | 10 | 18 | Unqualified | | | | | 5 | 13 |
| 2 | 2 | 1 | Reviewed | | | | | 1 | |
| | | | Compiled | | | | | | |
| 2 | 2 | 3 | Tax Returns | | | | | 1 | 1 |
| 17 | 22 | 35 | Other | 1 | 3 | | 4 | 2 | 26 |
| 4/1/09- | 4/1/10- | 4/1/11- | | 3 | | | 48 (10/1/11-3/31/12) | | |
| 3/31/10 | 3/31/11 | 3/31/12 | | 9 (4/1-9/30/11) | | | | | |
| ALL | ALL | ALL | | 0-1MM | 1-3MM | 3-5MM | 5-10MM | 10-25MM | 25MM & OVER |
| 26 | 36 | 57 | NUMBER OF STATEMENTS | | 4 | | 4 | 9 | 40 |
| % | % | % | ASSETS | % | % | % | % | % | % |
| 24.4 | 20.9 | 20.2 | Cash & Equivalents | D | | D | | | 21.6 |
| 4.4 | 4.3 | 4.6 | Trade Receivables (net) | A | | A | | | 2.3 |
| 3.9 | 1.2 | 1.8 | Inventory | T | | T | | | 1.0 |
| 6.8 | 4.2 | 4.2 | All Other Current | A | | A | | | 2.6 |
| 39.5 | 30.5 | 30.8 | Total Current | | | | | | 27.6 |
| 48.5 | 48.0 | 57.7 | Fixed Assets (net) | N | | N | | | 64.7 |
| 6.7 | 15.5 | 3.7 | Intangibles (net) | O | | O | | | 3.5 |
| 5.2 | 5.9 | 7.8 | All Other Non-Current | T | | T | | | 4.2 |
| 100.0 | 100.0 | 100.0 | Total | | | | | | 100.0 |
| | | | LIABILITIES | A | | A | | | |
| 4.4 | 2.3 | 2.8 | Notes Payable-Short Term | V | | V | | | 1.8 |
| 12.1 | 7.3 | 8.3 | Cur. Mat.-L.T.D. | A | | A | | | 10.9 |
| 8.9 | 5.1 | 5.9 | Trade Payables | I | | I | | | 3.4 |
| 1.0 | .0 | .1 | Income Taxes Payable | L | | L | | | .1 |
| 13.6 | 11.2 | 11.6 | All Other Current | A | | A | | | 11.3 |
| 40.1 | 26.0 | 28.6 | Total Current | B | | B | | | 27.6 |
| 32.6 | 29.9 | 30.9 | Long-Term Debt | L | | L | | | 28.4 |
| .1 | .6 | .2 | Deferred Taxes | E | | E | | | .0 |
| 11.3 | 11.7 | 5.5 | All Other Non-Current | | | | | | 5.9 |
| 15.9 | 31.8 | 34.8 | Net Worth | | | | | | 38.2 |
| 100.0 | 100.0 | 100.0 | Total Liabilties & Net Worth | | | | | | 100.0 |
| | | | INCOME DATA | | | | | | |
| 100.0 | 100.0 | 100.0 | Net Sales | | | | | | 100.0 |
| | | | Gross Profit | | | | | | |
| 95.2 | 84.5 | 76.9 | Operating Expenses | | | | | | 75.9 |
| 4.8 | 15.5 | 23.1 | Operating Profit | | | | | | 24.1 |
| 4.6 | 4.6 | 5.5 | All Other Expenses (net) | | | | | | 6.3 |
| .2 | 10.9 | 17.7 | Profit Before Taxes | | | | | | 17.7 |
| | | | RATIOS | | | | | | |
| 2.3 | 1.6 | 2.0 | | | | | | | 1.7 |
| 1.1 | .8 | 1.1 | Current | | | | | | 1.0 |
| .7 | .5 | .8 | | | | | | | .7 |
| 2.1 | 1.6 | 1.5 | | | | | | | 1.5 |
| 1.0 | .7 | .9 | Quick | | | | | | .9 |
| .4 | .4 | .7 | | | | | | | .6 |
| 0 UND | 0 816.5 | 1 305.2 | | | | | | 1 | 255.6 |
| 1 331.8 | 5 70.4 | 4 99.2 | Sales/Receivables | | | | | 3 | 115.6 |
| 22 16.9 | 35 10.5 | 22 16.9 | | | | | | 6 | 60.8 |
| | | | Cost of Sales/Inventory | | | | | | |
| | | | Cost of Sales/Payables | | | | | | |
| 11.1 | 13.9 | 10.2 | | | | | | | 16.0 |
| 42.0 | -21.4 | 69.9 | Sales/Working Capital | | | | | | 119.4 |
| -14.6 | -9.5 | -20.5 | | | | | | | -11.1 |
| 12.0 | 7.6 | 25.8 | | | | | | | 27.4 |
| (23) 3.6 | (32) 4.5 | (49) 7.4 | EBIT/Interest | | | | | (34) | 8.5 |
| -.3 | .2 | 1.6 | | | | | | | 2.8 |
| | | | Net Profit + Depr., Dep., Amort./Cur. Mat. L/T/D | | | | | | |
| 1.0 | 1.2 | .7 | | | | | | | 1.0 |
| 3.0 | 2.6 | 1.4 | Fixed/Worth | | | | | | 1.6 |
| -4.7 | NM | 4.1 | | | | | | | 3.6 |
| .5 | 1.2 | .4 | | | | | | | .4 |
| 3.9 | 4.6 | 1.2 | Debt/Worth | | | | | | 1.1 |
| -12.6 | NM | 9.9 | | | | | | | 3.9 |
| 61.0 | 124.5 | 93.8 | | | | | | | 100.2 |
| (18) 23.0 | (27) 64.3 | (45) 33.6 | % Profit Before Taxes/Tangible Net Worth | | | | | (33) | 45.1 |
| 1.7 | -4.0 | 8.8 | | | | | | | 15.1 |
| 14.9 | 25.6 | 37.9 | | | | | | | 38.8 |
| 4.7 | 9.4 | 16.6 | % Profit Before Taxes/Total Assets | | | | | | 19.7 |
| -2.7 | -.6 | 1.4 | | | | | | | 3.7 |
| 8.8 | 6.3 | 3.4 | | | | | | | 3.1 |
| 3.2 | 1.9 | 1.8 | Sales/Net Fixed Assets | | | | | | 1.8 |
| 1.3 | 1.0 | 1.0 | | | | | | | .9 |
| 2.6 | 2.0 | 1.6 | | | | | | | 1.6 |
| 1.3 | 1.0 | 1.0 | Sales/Total Assets | | | | | | 1.0 |
| .7 | .6 | .7 | | | | | | | .7 |
| 3.0 | 3.7 | 3.3 | | | | | | | 3.6 |
| (21) 5.5 | (26) 9.0 | (36) 6.3 | % Depr., Dep., Amort./Sales | | | | | (22) | 5.9 |
| 12.9 | 19.9 | 10.0 | | | | | | | 8.3 |
| | | | % Officers', Directors' Owners' Comp/Sales | | | | | | |
| 860405M | 1469393M | 4651615M | Net Sales ($) | | 7098M | | 28417M | 171221M | 4444879M |
| 908813M | 1932743M | 4719841M | Total Assets ($) | | 35577M | | 78009M | 160400M | 4445855M |

**M = $ thousand    MM = $ million**
See Pages 9 through 22 for Explanation of Ratios and Data

## Current Data Sorted by Assets     Comparative Historical Data

| Type of Statement | 0-500M | 500M-2MM | 2-10MM | 10-50MM | 50-100MM | 100-250MM | | 4/1/07-3/31/08 ALL | 4/1/08-3/31/09 ALL |
|---|---|---|---|---|---|---|---|---|---|
| Unqualified | 1 | 8 | 120 | 152 | 10 | 4 | | 268 | 249 |
| Reviewed | 14 | 16 | 83 | 19 | | | | 106 | 103 |
| Compiled | 45 | 41 | 52 | 4 | | | | 141 | 98 |
| Tax Returns | 22 | 66 | 56 | 11 | | | | 87 | 107 |
| Other | | 62 | 170 | 101 | 8 | 4 | | 306 | 283 |
| | 184 (4/1-9/30/11) | | | 885 (10/1/11-3/31/12) | | | | | |
| **NUMBER OF STATEMENTS** | 82 | 193 | 481 | 287 | 18 | 8 | | 908 | 840 |
| **ASSETS** | % | % | % | % | % | % | | % | % |
| Cash & Equivalents | 25.6 | 9.7 | 6.3 | 6.8 | 8.8 | | | 6.8 | 7.5 |
| Trade Receivables (net) | 4.5 | 3.7 | 4.7 | 4.3 | 5.3 | | | 4.8 | 4.7 |
| Inventory | 10.1 | 3.6 | 2.1 | 1.3 | 1.7 | | | 2.0 | 2.6 |
| All Other Current | 1.3 | 2.6 | .8 | 1.4 | .4 | | | 1.4 | 1.2 |
| Total Current | 41.4 | 19.7 | 14.0 | 13.8 | 16.1 | | | 14.9 | 16.0 |
| Fixed Assets (net) | 45.2 | 69.6 | 79.9 | 80.1 | 74.8 | | | 78.8 | 77.3 |
| Intangibles (net) | 5.7 | 4.1 | 1.5 | .8 | 3.9 | | | 1.4 | 1.3 |
| All Other Non-Current | 7.7 | 6.6 | 4.5 | 5.3 | 5.1 | | | 4.9 | 5.5 |
| Total | 100.0 | 100.0 | 100.0 | 100.0 | 100.0 | | | 100.0 | 100.0 |
| **LIABILITIES** | | | | | | | | | |
| Notes Payable-Short Term | 15.3 | 8.8 | 3.2 | 1.2 | .0 | | | 4.1 | 4.2 |
| Cur. Mat.-L.T.D. | 10.5 | 5.8 | 4.4 | 2.2 | 2.1 | | | 4.4 | 3.8 |
| Trade Payables | 13.5 | 4.4 | 2.6 | 2.3 | 2.2 | | | 3.0 | 3.4 |
| Income Taxes Payable | .1 | .1 | .0 | .1 | .0 | | | .1 | .1 |
| All Other Current | 37.3 | 22.2 | 10.4 | 6.5 | 9.2 | | | 10.4 | 11.0 |
| Total Current | 76.7 | 41.4 | 20.5 | 12.2 | 13.6 | | | 22.0 | 22.4 |
| Long-Term Debt | 42.1 | 51.5 | 46.6 | 24.5 | 19.2 | | | 40.5 | 40.2 |
| Deferred Taxes | .0 | .1 | .1 | .0 | .8 | | | .1 | .1 |
| All Other Non-Current | 24.7 | 13.7 | 7.8 | 9.2 | 17.9 | | | 9.7 | 10.0 |
| Net Worth | -43.6 | -6.6 | 25.0 | 54.1 | 48.6 | | | 27.7 | 27.3 |
| Total Liabilities & Net Worth | 100.0 | 100.0 | 100.0 | 100.0 | 100.0 | | | 100.0 | 100.0 |
| **INCOME DATA** | | | | | | | | | |
| Net Sales | 100.0 | 100.0 | 100.0 | 100.0 | 100.0 | | | 100.0 | 100.0 |
| Gross Profit | | | | | | | | | |
| Operating Expenses | 98.2 | 97.6 | 98.8 | 102.8 | 101.4 | | | 97.2 | 99.8 |
| Operating Profit | 1.8 | 2.4 | 1.2 | -2.8 | -1.4 | | | 2.8 | .2 |
| All Other Expenses (net) | 1.4 | 4.6 | 4.4 | .2 | 3.7 | | | 4.3 | 3.6 |
| Profit Before Taxes | .4 | -2.2 | -3.2 | -3.0 | -5.1 | | | -1.4 | -3.3 |
| **RATIOS** | | | | | | | | | |
| Current | 2.0 | 1.5 | 1.7 | 2.1 | 3.4 | | | 1.7 | 1.7 |
| | .7 | .6 | .9 | 1.3 | 1.3 | | | .9 | 1.0 |
| | .3 | .2 | .4 | .8 | .8 | | | .4 | .5 |
| Quick | 1.5 | 1.1 | 1.3 | 1.6 | 2.7 | | | 1.3 | 1.4 |
| | .5 | .4 | .7 | 1.0 | 1.2 | | (907) | .7 | (839) .7 |
| | .3 | .1 | .2 | .6 | .8 | | | .3 | .3 |
| Sales/Receivables | 0 UND | 0 UND | 3 142.3 | 17 21.4 | 11 32.5 | | 1 | 257.5 | 2 186.5 |
| | 0 UND | 1 446.5 | 22 16.6 | 30 12.1 | 24 15.2 | | 19 | 18.9 | 19 19.0 |
| | 1 295.9 | 11 32.9 | 37 9.8 | 43 8.4 | 49 7.4 | | 37 | 9.9 | 35 10.4 |
| Cost of Sales/Inventory | | | | | | | | | |
| Cost of Sales/Payables | | | | | | | | | |
| Sales/Working Capital | 28.1 | 18.8 | 11.4 | 5.6 | 3.4 | | | 11.8 | 11.2 |
| | -35.5 | -19.5 | -113.7 | 17.7 | 11.6 | | | -52.4 | -160.8 |
| | -6.7 | -3.3 | -6.8 | -22.8 | -22.6 | | | -6.9 | -7.4 |
| EBIT/Interest | 6.3 | 2.4 | 1.6 | 2.3 | 4.8 | | | 2.1 | 1.7 |
| | (51) 1.0 | (170) .9 | (431) .6 | (248) .5 | (15) -.2 | | (763) | .9 | (700) .5 |
| | -1.0 | -.8 | -.8 | -1.3 | -8.2 | | | -.4 | -.9 |
| Net Profit + Depr., Dep., Amort./Cur. Mat. L/T/D | | | 3.1 | 2.6 | | | | 3.9 | 3.9 |
| | | (33) 2.1 | (18) 1.5 | | | | (67) | 2.4 | (66) 2.2 |
| | | | .9 | .3 | | | | .7 | .4 |
| Fixed/Worth | .7 | 1.9 | 1.4 | 1.0 | 1.0 | | | 1.3 | 1.2 |
| | 3.5 | 7.7 | 2.8 | 1.4 | 1.2 | | | 2.1 | 2.1 |
| | -.9 | -2.1 | -73.8 | 2.2 | 1.8 | | | 9.4 | 9.7 |
| Debt/Worth | 1.1 | 1.5 | .8 | .3 | .3 | | | .6 | .6 |
| | UND | 10.1 | 2.4 | .7 | .5 | | | 1.6 | 1.6 |
| | -2.0 | -4.4 | -91.5 | 1.6 | 1.7 | | | 11.3 | 12.6 |
| % Profit Before Taxes/Tangible Net Worth | 99.2 | 18.5 | 4.9 | 3.0 | 2.6 | | | 6.6 | 4.8 |
| | (41) 18.9 | (116) 2.3 | (356) -3.1 | (267) -1.2 | (15) -.4 | | (729) | .0 | (670) -1.4 |
| | -35.3 | -11.2 | -12.3 | -5.5 | -2.3 | | | -7.7 | -10.5 |
| % Profit Before Taxes/Total Assets | 19.7 | 4.2 | 1.9 | 1.5 | 2.3 | | | 2.7 | 2.1 |
| | -.2 | -.2 | -1.4 | -.8 | -.5 | | | -.5 | -1.2 |
| | -22.0 | -7.6 | -4.7 | -3.0 | -3.4 | | | -4.1 | -5.2 |
| Sales/Net Fixed Assets | 72.6 | 2.8 | 1.1 | .8 | .8 | | | 1.2 | 1.2 |
| | 7.7 | 1.3 | .7 | .6 | .6 | | | .7 | .7 |
| | 3.1 | .8 | .5 | .4 | .4 | | | .5 | .5 |
| Sales/Total Assets | 7.1 | 1.6 | .8 | .6 | .6 | | | .9 | .9 |
| | 3.7 | .9 | .6 | .4 | .4 | | | .6 | .6 |
| | 2.2 | .7 | .4 | .3 | .3 | | | .4 | .4 |
| % Depr., Dep., Amort./Sales | 1.7 | 4.2 | 7.7 | 9.3 | 6.7 | | | 6.9 | 6.6 |
| | (52) 4.7 | (166) 7.5 | (445) 10.1 | (271) 10.2 | (16) 10.8 | | (823) | 9.6 | (772) 9.6 |
| | 9.0 | 11.4 | 13.3 | 15.5 | 14.3 | | | 12.8 | 12.6 |
| % Officers', Directors' Owners' Comp/Sales | 3.5 | 3.0 | 3.3 | 3.2 | | | | 3.1 | 3.3 |
| | (28) 6.9 | (52) 7.2 | (64) 6.2 | (20) 5.5 | | | (138) | 6.7 | (134) 7.4 |
| | 13.9 | 14.4 | 25.6 | 25.5 | | | | 14.5 | 17.0 |
| Net Sales ($) | 69955M | 283382M | 1602305M | 2570389M | 672052M | 922719M | | 5113414M | 4689497M |
| Total Assets ($) | 18200M | 228185M | 2546395M | 5714609M | 1175504M | 1109653M | | 7928848M | 8729475M |

## Comparative Historical Data      Current Data Sorted by Sales

| | | | Type of Statement | | | | | | |
|---|---|---|---|---|---|---|---|---|---|
| 257 | 263 | 295 | Unqualified | 3 | 33 | 71 | 125 | 47 | 16 |
| 112 | 99 | 118 | Reviewed | 11 | 37 | 44 | 20 | 4 | 2 |
| 113 | 107 | 111 | Compiled | 34 | 66 | 7 | 4 | | |
| 130 | 138 | 178 | Tax Returns | 75 | 78 | 14 | 7 | 4 | |
| 280 | 330 | 367 | Other | 52 | 126 | 73 | 80 | 27 | 9 |
| 4/1/09- | 4/1/10- | 4/1/11- | | | 184 (4/1-9/30/11) | | | 885 (10/1/11-3/31/12) | |
| 3/31/10 | 3/31/11 | 3/31/12 | | | | | | | |
| ALL | ALL | ALL | | 0-1MM | 1-3MM | 3-5MM | 5-10MM | 10-25MM | 25MM & OVER |
| 892 | 937 | 1069 | **NUMBER OF STATEMENTS** | 175 | 340 | 209 | 236 | 82 | 27 |
| % | % | % | **ASSETS** | % | % | % | % | % | % |
| 7.9 | 8.2 | 8.6 | Cash & Equivalents | 10.7 | 8.3 | 8.3 | 7.5 | 9.5 | 8.1 |
| 4.3 | 4.4 | 4.4 | Trade Receivables (net) | 1.0 | 4.2 | 6.2 | 5.4 | 4.7 | 6.4 |
| 2.3 | 2.4 | 2.8 | Inventory | 4.3 | 2.8 | 2.1 | 2.3 | 3.0 | 3.4 |
| 1.3 | 1.8 | 1.3 | All Other Current | 1.1 | 1.4 | 1.4 | 1.3 | 1.8 | .7 |
| 15.9 | 16.9 | 17.2 | Total Current | 17.1 | 16.7 | 18.0 | 16.5 | 19.0 | 18.5 |
| 76.1 | 75.1 | 75.3 | Fixed Assets (net) | 73.4 | 74.3 | 76.8 | 78.4 | 71.3 | 72.7 |
| 2.0 | 2.1 | 2.2 | Intangibles (net) | 3.5 | 3.6 | .8 | .4 | 2.5 | 2.6 |
| 6.0 | 5.9 | 5.3 | All Other Non-Current | 6.0 | 5.4 | 4.5 | 4.7 | 7.1 | 6.3 |
| 100.0 | 100.0 | 100.0 | Total | 100.0 | 100.0 | 100.0 | 100.0 | 100.0 | 100.0 |
| | | | **LIABILITIES** | | | | | | |
| 3.7 | 4.2 | 4.6 | Notes Payable-Short Term | 13.3 | 5.0 | 1.5 | 1.2 | 2.2 | 2.4 |
| 4.3 | 3.5 | 4.4 | Cur. Mat.-L.T.D. | 4.9 | 6.6 | 3.5 | 3.0 | 1.8 | 2.1 |
| 3.6 | 3.1 | 3.7 | Trade Payables | 3.6 | 4.9 | 2.6 | 2.6 | 4.6 | 3.6 |
| .1 | .1 | .1 | Income Taxes Payable | .1 | .1 | .1 | .0 | .1 | .0 |
| 13.7 | 13.2 | 13.5 | All Other Current | 21.7 | 17.7 | 10.2 | 6.8 | 7.2 | 10.5 |
| 25.5 | 24.2 | 26.2 | Total Current | 43.6 | 34.3 | 18.0 | 13.6 | 15.9 | 18.7 |
| 40.0 | 41.5 | 40.6 | Long-Term Debt | 50.5 | 53.0 | 35.8 | 26.5 | 25.8 | 24.9 |
| .1 | .2 | .1 | Deferred Taxes | .0 | .1 | .0 | .0 | .2 | .0 |
| 10.3 | 11.6 | 10.7 | All Other Non-Current | 15.2 | 10.6 | 9.6 | 7.6 | 12.5 | 14.4 |
| 24.2 | 22.5 | 22.4 | Net Worth | -9.4 | 2.1 | 36.6 | 52.3 | 45.6 | 42.0 |
| 100.0 | 100.0 | 100.0 | Total Liabilties & Net Worth | 100.0 | 100.0 | 100.0 | 100.0 | 100.0 | 100.0 |
| | | | **INCOME DATA** | | | | | | |
| 100.0 | 100.0 | 100.0 | Net Sales | 100.0 | 100.0 | 100.0 | 100.0 | 100.0 | 100.0 |
| | | | Gross Profit | | | | | | |
| 99.8 | 99.0 | 99.7 | Operating Expenses | 96.3 | 98.8 | 101.4 | 101.8 | 100.4 | 98.5 |
| .2 | 1.0 | .3 | Operating Profit | 3.7 | 1.2 | -1.4 | -1.8 | -.4 | 1.5 |
| 3.3 | 3.1 | 3.0 | All Other Expenses (net) | 7.6 | 4.7 | 1.6 | -.8 | 1.5 | .8 |
| -3.0 | -2.1 | -2.7 | Profit Before Taxes | -3.9 | -3.4 | -3.0 | -1.0 | -1.9 | .7 |
| | | | **RATIOS** | | | | | | |
| 1.7 | 1.7 | 1.8 | | 1.9 | 1.5 | 1.7 | 1.9 | 2.5 | 2.0 |
| .9 | 1.0 | 1.0 | Current | .5 | .7 | 1.1 | 1.3 | 1.3 | 1.1 |
| .4 | .5 | .4 | | .1 | .2 | .7 | .8 | .9 | .6 |
| 1.4 | 1.4 | 1.4 | | 1.4 | 1.2 | 1.4 | 1.5 | 1.9 | 1.6 |
| (890) .7 | (936) .7 | .8 | Quick | .3 | .5 | .9 | 1.0 | 1.0 | .9 |
| .2 | .3 | .3 | | .1 | .1 | .6 | .6 | .6 | .3 |
| 1 391.6 | 1 351.7 | 1 413.7 | | 0 UND | 0 UND | 15 24.7 | 19 19.3 | 10 37.1 | 17 20.9 |
| 17 21.1 | 17 21.0 | 18 20.7 | Sales/Receivables | 0 UND | 8 48.5 | 32 11.5 | 31 11.7 | 24 15.5 | 24 15.5 |
| 35 10.4 | 35 10.3 | 35 10.4 | | 2 174.6 | 30 12.3 | 42 8.6 | 42 8.6 | 36 10.1 | 33 11.1 |
| | | | Cost of Sales/Inventory | | | | | | |
| | | | Cost of Sales/Payables | | | | | | |
| 11.6 | 10.5 | 9.9 | | 18.8 | 16.6 | 8.8 | 6.9 | 4.7 | 7.6 |
| -59.3 | -127.3 | 999.8 | Sales/Working Capital | -12.7 | -23.5 | 42.6 | 19.8 | 16.8 | 197.6 |
| -6.9 | -7.8 | -7.5 | | -2.8 | -4.8 | -16.6 | -20.6 | -30.2 | -7.8 |
| 1.9 | 1.8 | 1.9 | | 1.9 | 1.5 | 1.5 | 2.4 | 3.8 | 6.6 |
| (752) .5 | (807) .5 | (923) .6 | EBIT/Interest | (127) .4 | (306) .6 | (184) .4 | (209) .7 | (71) .7 | (26) 1.6 |
| -1.2 | -.9 | -1.0 | | -1.2 | -.8 | -1.3 | -.9 | -1.2 | -2.2 |
| 3.5 | 3.9 | 3.0 | Net Profit + Depr., Dep., | | 2.8 | 2.9 | 2.9 | | 15.6 |
| (69) 1.5 | (60) 1.8 | (62) 1.9 | Amort./Cur. Mat. L/T/D | | (17) 1.5 | (14) 1.4 | (11) 2.3 | (10) 3.3 | |
| .6 | .6 | .8 | | | .6 | .1 | 1.8 | | 1.2 |
| 1.2 | 1.2 | 1.2 | | 1.7 | 1.7 | 1.1 | 1.0 | 1.0 | 1.1 |
| 2.2 | 2.2 | 2.2 | Fixed/Worth | 5.7 | 6.2 | 1.8 | 1.4 | 1.5 | 1.4 |
| 28.6 | 13.4 | 72.0 | | -2.5 | -4.6 | 4.3 | 2.3 | 2.2 | 2.9 |
| .5 | .6 | .6 | | 1.2 | 1.3 | .5 | .3 | .4 | .3 |
| 1.8 | 1.7 | 1.8 | Debt/Worth | 5.9 | 9.1 | 1.2 | .8 | 1.0 | .8 |
| 54.5 | 16.6 | UND | | -4.0 | -5.6 | 4.4 | 1.8 | 1.9 | 2.7 |
| 4.5 | 4.8 | 5.9 | % Profit Before Taxes/Tangible | 15.5 | 10.4 | 1.6 | 5.0 | 4.1 | 7.0 |
| (688) -1.5 | (734) -1.5 | (802) -1.4 | Net Worth | (106) -1.6 | (207) -2.5 | (173) -2.4 | (220) -.7 | (73) -.5 | (23) 2.3 |
| -10.9 | -8.8 | -8.9 | | -11.4 | -14.8 | -10.0 | -5.0 | -7.2 | -2.9 |
| 2.0 | 2.2 | 2.3 | % Profit Before Taxes/Total | 2.7 | 2.3 | 1.4 | 2.7 | 2.7 | 3.4 |
| -1.2 | -1.1 | -1.0 | Assets | -1.6 | -1.5 | -1.4 | -.3 | -.3 | 1.2 |
| -4.9 | -4.5 | -4.7 | | -9.2 | -5.9 | -4.6 | -3.1 | -3.0 | -1.9 |
| 1.3 | 1.3 | 1.3 | | 2.9 | 1.7 | 1.2 | 1.0 | 1.1 | 1.9 |
| .7 | .7 | .7 | Sales/Net Fixed Assets | .9 | .8 | .7 | .7 | .7 | .8 |
| .5 | .5 | .5 | | .4 | .5 | .5 | .5 | .5 | .5 |
| .9 | .9 | .9 | | 1.7 | 1.1 | .8 | .7 | .7 | 1.2 |
| .6 | .6 | .6 | Sales/Total Assets | .7 | .7 | .6 | .6 | .5 | .6 |
| .4 | .4 | .4 | | .4 | .5 | .4 | .4 | .4 | .4 |
| 6.9 | 7.0 | 7.1 | | 5.5 | 6.0 | 8.1 | 8.6 | 8.1 | 5.6 |
| (822) 10.3 | (843) 10.2 | (955) 10.2 | % Depr., Dep., Amort./Sales | (138) 10.0 | (303) 9.0 | (192) 10.1 | (221) 11.3 | (77) 10.2 | (24) 10.1 |
| 13.9 | 13.6 | 13.5 | | 15.0 | 12.8 | 13.5 | 13.9 | 12.7 | 12.4 |
| 2.8 | 3.3 | 3.4 | % Officers', Directors' | 5.0 | 3.3 | 4.2 | 2.5 | | |
| (139) 6.7 | (161) 6.3 | (170) 6.4 | Owners' Comp/Sales | (43) 10.0 | (69) 5.1 | (28) 7.6 | (19) 4.5 | | |
| 16.0 | 17.2 | 16.5 | | 19.5 | 8.7 | 23.8 | 27.7 | | |
| 4809586M | 6111780M | 6120802M | Net Sales ($) | 104797M | 651259M | 833156M | 1649870M | 1126123M | 1755597M |
| 8880453M | 9818942M | 10792546M | Total Assets ($) | 237812M | 1115722M | 1690246M | 3379656M | 2279289M | 2089821M |

M = $ thousand    MM = $ million
See Pages 9 through 22 for Explanation of Ratios and Data

## Current Data Sorted by Assets      Comparative Historical Data

### Type of Statement

| Type of Statement | 0-500M | 500M-2MM | 2-10MM | 10-50MM | 50-100MM | 100-250MM | 4/1/07-3/31/08 ALL | 4/1/08-3/31/09 ALL |
|---|---|---|---|---|---|---|---|---|
| Unqualified | | 1 | 2 | 12 | 3 | 3 | 20 | 16 |
| Reviewed | | 1 | 5 | 5 | 1 | | 5 | 9 |
| Compiled | 1 | 2 | 3 | | | | 5 | 4 |
| Tax Returns | | 3 | 2 | | | | 1 | 1 |
| Other | | 1 | 4 | 12 | 1 | 2 | 18 | 23 |
| | 46 (4/1-9/30/11) | | | 18 (10/1/11-3/31/12) | | | | |
| NUMBER OF STATEMENTS | 1 | 8 | 16 | 29 | 5 | 5 | 49 | 53 |

### Data

| | 0-500M % | 500M-2MM % | 2-10MM % | 10-50MM % | 50-100MM % | 100-250MM % | | 4/1/07-3/31/08 ALL % | 4/1/08-3/31/09 ALL % |
|---|---|---|---|---|---|---|---|---|---|
| **ASSETS** | | | | | | | | | |
| Cash & Equivalents | | | 12.2 | 9.6 | | | | 7.8 | 7.2 |
| Trade Receivables (net) | | | .6 | 2.1 | | | | 1.6 | 1.9 |
| Inventory | | | 2.8 | 3.0 | | | | 2.9 | 4.1 |
| All Other Current | | | 2.0 | 1.2 | | | | 3.8 | 2.4 |
| Total Current | | | 17.7 | 15.9 | | | | 16.2 | 15.6 |
| Fixed Assets (net) | | | 69.9 | 66.8 | | | | 69.7 | 73.4 |
| Intangibles (net) | | | 2.6 | 2.8 | | | | 1.8 | 2.8 |
| All Other Non-Current | | | 9.8 | 14.5 | | | | 12.3 | 8.2 |
| Total | | | 100.0 | 100.0 | | | | 100.0 | 100.0 |
| **LIABILITIES** | | | | | | | | | |
| Notes Payable-Short Term | | | 3.4 | 2.9 | | | | 4.3 | 3.1 |
| Cur. Mat.-L.T.D. | | | 7.3 | 2.0 | | | | 3.7 | 3.1 |
| Trade Payables | | | 5.3 | 4.4 | | | | 5.8 | 4.9 |
| Income Taxes Payable | | | .1 | .0 | | | | .2 | .4 |
| All Other Current | | | 11.2 | 11.3 | | | | 12.5 | 11.7 |
| Total Current | | | 27.3 | 20.8 | | | | 26.5 | 23.2 |
| Long-Term Debt | | | 36.3 | 33.3 | | | | 25.0 | 26.0 |
| Deferred Taxes | | | .4 | 2.0 | | | | 1.3 | 1.9 |
| All Other Non-Current | | | 9.6 | 10.6 | | | | 9.1 | 8.0 |
| Net Worth | | | 26.5 | 33.3 | | | | 38.2 | 40.8 |
| Total Liabilities & Net Worth | | | 100.0 | 100.0 | | | | 100.0 | 100.0 |
| **INCOME DATA** | | | | | | | | | |
| Net Sales | | | 100.0 | 100.0 | | | | 100.0 | 100.0 |
| Gross Profit | | | | | | | | | |
| Operating Expenses | | | 92.5 | 92.4 | | | | 91.9 | 89.2 |
| Operating Profit | | | 7.5 | 7.6 | | | | 8.1 | 10.8 |
| All Other Expenses (net) | | | 2.9 | 4.4 | | | | 1.7 | 3.5 |
| Profit Before Taxes | | | 4.6 | 3.3 | | | | 6.3 | 7.3 |

### RATIOS

| | 2-10MM | 10-50MM | | 4/1/07-3/31/08 ALL | 4/1/08-3/31/09 ALL |
|---|---|---|---|---|---|
| Current | 1.4 | 1.6 | | 1.0 | 1.0 |
| | .4 | .5 | | .4 | .6 |
| | .2 | .3 | | .2 | .2 |
| Quick | .7 | 1.0 | | .5 | .7 |
| | .2 | .3 | | .2 | .3 |
| | .1 | .1 | | .1 | .1 |
| Sales/Receivables | 0   UND | 1   282.3 | | 1   583.1 | 0   761.2 |
| | 0   766.9 | 4   83.7 | | 4   103.4 | 5   71.4 |
| | 4   92.8 | 9   41.2 | | 11   33.3 | 10   36.3 |
| Cost of Sales/Inventory | | | | | |
| Cost of Sales/Payables | | | | | |
| Sales/Working Capital | NM | 17.3 | | 120.7 | NM |
| | -9.5 | -11.9 | | -7.9 | -9.7 |
| | -4.9 | -5.4 | | -4.3 | -4.9 |
| EBIT/Interest | 6.9 | 5.3 | | 5.8 | 22.8 |
| | 1.9 | (25) 2.4 | | (47) 1.8 | (50) 4.2 |
| | 1.2 | .8 | | .1 | 1.0 |
| Net Profit + Depr., Dep., Amort./Cur. Mat. L/T/D | | 6.0 | | 6.3 | 6.4 |
| | | (10) 4.2 | | (21) 2.8 | (18) 2.9 |
| | | 2.9 | | 1.4 | 1.5 |
| Fixed/Worth | 1.0 | 1.1 | | 1.2 | 1.2 |
| | 3.1 | 1.4 | | 1.8 | 1.8 |
| | -2.9 | 2.7 | | 3.4 | 3.1 |
| Debt/Worth | .8 | .5 | | .6 | .8 |
| | 2.5 | 1.1 | | 1.4 | 1.3 |
| | -4.4 | 2.8 | | 5.2 | 3.3 |
| % Profit Before Taxes/Tangible Net Worth | 53.9 | 16.3 | | 22.1 | 31.8 |
| | (11) 8.7 | (28) 5.4 | | (43) 9.4 | (46) 18.6 |
| | 1.3 | .1 | | -1.5 | 4.9 |
| % Profit Before Taxes/Total Assets | 13.9 | 6.7 | | 10.6 | 14.8 |
| | 5.6 | 2.6 | | 3.6 | 6.0 |
| | .7 | -.5 | | -1.4 | -.2 |
| Sales/Net Fixed Assets | 2.9 | 1.7 | | 1.9 | 1.8 |
| | 1.3 | 1.0 | | 1.3 | 1.3 |
| | 1.1 | .5 | | .9 | .8 |
| Sales/Total Assets | 1.6 | 1.1 | | 1.3 | 1.3 |
| | 1.1 | .7 | | .9 | .9 |
| | .9 | .4 | | .7 | .6 |
| % Depr., Dep., Amort./Sales | 6.1 | 6.8 | | 5.5 | 6.3 |
| | (13) 7.9 | (27) 11.7 | | (46) 10.1 | (48) 9.6 |
| | 12.0 | 17.0 | | 12.3 | 13.1 |
| % Officers', Directors' Owners' Comp/Sales | | | | | |

| | 0-500M | 500M-2MM | 2-10MM | 10-50MM | 50-100MM | 100-250MM | | 4/1/07-3/31/08 ALL | 4/1/08-3/31/09 ALL |
|---|---|---|---|---|---|---|---|---|---|
| Net Sales ($) | 2534M | 17180M | 126437M | 605037M | 378933M | 538262M | | 1381878M | 1762040M |
| Total Assets ($) | 403M | 11058M | 71679M | 803147M | 344497M | 1016903M | | 1508627M | 2187596M |

M = $ thousand    MM = $ million
See Pages 9 through 22 for Explanation of Ratios and Data

## Comparative Historical Data | Current Data Sorted by Sales

| 4/1/09-3/31/10 ALL | 4/1/10-3/31/11 ALL | 4/1/11-3/31/12 ALL | Type of Statement | 0-1MM | 1-3MM | 3-5MM | 5-10MM | 10-25MM | 25MM & OVER |
|---|---|---|---|---|---|---|---|---|---|
| 22 | 22 | 21 | Unqualified | | | | 4 | 9 | 8 |
| 12 | 10 | 12 | Reviewed | | 2 | 2 | 3 | 3 | 2 |
| 7 | 4 | 6 | Compiled | | 3 | 1 | 1 | 1 | |
| | 5 | 5 | Tax Returns | | 3 | | 1 | | |
| 16 | 23 | 20 | Other | 1 | 3 | | 3 | 8 | 6 |
| | | | | | 46 (4/1-9/30/11) | | | 18 (10/1/11-3/31/12) | |
| 57 | 64 | 64 | **NUMBER OF STATEMENTS** | 1 | 11 | 3 | 12 | 21 | 16 |
| % | % | % | **ASSETS** | % | % | % | % | % | % |
| 8.8 | 10.7 | 9.5 | Cash & Equivalents | | 6.2 | | 4.4 | 17.4 | 5.7 |
| 1.4 | 1.4 | 1.7 | Trade Receivables (net) | | 1.0 | | .8 | 1.3 | 3.8 |
| 1.7 | 3.2 | 3.1 | Inventory | | 3.7 | | 1.5 | 4.3 | 2.9 |
| 3.2 | 1.6 | 3.1 | All Other Current | | 8.3 | | 1.0 | 2.1 | 2.4 |
| 15.1 | 17.0 | 17.4 | Total Current | | 19.2 | | 7.7 | 25.0 | 14.7 |
| 72.1 | 67.5 | 66.3 | Fixed Assets (net) | | 71.7 | | 71.6 | 64.0 | 61.4 |
| 3.2 | 3.5 | 3.9 | Intangibles (net) | | .3 | | 4.2 | 2.4 | 7.8 |
| 9.6 | 12.0 | 12.3 | All Other Non-Current | | 8.8 | | 16.5 | 8.5 | 16.1 |
| 100.0 | 100.0 | 100.0 | Total | | 100.0 | | 100.0 | 100.0 | 100.0 |
| | | | **LIABILITIES** | | | | | | |
| 4.8 | 8.7 | 3.6 | Notes Payable-Short Term | | 9.7 | | 1.9 | 3.8 | 1.1 |
| 4.5 | 4.5 | 3.6 | Cur. Mat.-L.T.D. | | 7.4 | | 5.2 | 1.8 | 2.0 |
| 4.3 | 5.8 | 5.0 | Trade Payables | | 6.2 | | 4.1 | 3.9 | 6.1 |
| .2 | .2 | .1 | Income Taxes Payable | | .0 | | .1 | .1 | .4 |
| 13.6 | 13.9 | 12.1 | All Other Current | | 13.7 | | 6.2 | 13.2 | 16.2 |
| 27.4 | 33.1 | 24.4 | Total Current | | 36.9 | | 17.5 | 22.9 | 25.8 |
| 20.6 | 29.4 | 34.6 | Long-Term Debt | | 42.3 | | 33.0 | 21.8 | 37.2 |
| 1.9 | 1.4 | 1.2 | Deferred Taxes | | .1 | | .5 | 2.2 | 1.2 |
| 7.1 | 9.1 | 9.4 | All Other Non-Current | | 5.7 | | 3.9 | 3.7 | 21.4 |
| 42.9 | 27.1 | 30.3 | Net Worth | | 15.0 | | 45.1 | 49.4 | 14.4 |
| 100.0 | 100.0 | 100.0 | Total Liabilities & Net Worth | | 100.0 | | 100.0 | 100.0 | 100.0 |
| | | | **INCOME DATA** | | | | | | |
| 100.0 | 100.0 | 100.0 | Net Sales | | 100.0 | | 100.0 | 100.0 | 100.0 |
| | | | Gross Profit | | | | | | |
| 92.1 | 93.2 | 93.7 | Operating Expenses | | 93.2 | | 84.5 | 93.0 | 97.9 |
| 7.9 | 6.8 | 6.3 | Operating Profit | | 6.8 | | 15.5 | 7.0 | 2.1 |
| 3.0 | 4.1 | 3.4 | All Other Expenses (net) | | 1.8 | | 6.4 | 3.1 | 2.5 |
| 4.9 | 2.7 | 2.9 | Profit Before Taxes | | 5.0 | | 9.2 | 3.9 | -.4 |
| | | | **RATIOS** | | | | | | |
| 1.2 | 1.1 | 1.2 | Current | | .8 | | 1.4 | 1.9 | .8 |
| .6 | .6 | .5 | | | .3 | | .4 | .9 | .6 |
| .2 | .3 | .3 | | | .0 | | .2 | .4 | .3 |
| .8 | .8 | .7 | Quick | | .3 | | 1.2 | 1.3 | .5 |
| .3 | .4 | .3 | | | .2 | | .2 | .5 | .3 |
| .1 | .1 | .1 | | | .0 | | .1 | .2 | .1 |
| 0   915.5 | 0   994.6 | 0   999.8 | Sales/Receivables | | 0   UND | | 0   999.8 | 1   696.4 | 4   92.1 |
| 4   87.6 | 4   92.0 | 3   117.8 | | | 0   999.8 | | 2   209.6 | 3   120.9 | 11   32.7 |
| 8   44.0 | 7   50.4 | 9   39.0 | | | 5   77.8 | | 5   68.5 | 7   52.3 | 17   21.5 |
| | | | Cost of Sales/Inventory | | | | | | |
| | | | Cost of Sales/Payables | | | | | | |
| 50.1 | 313.9 | UND | Sales/Working Capital | | -9.8 | | NM | 16.5 | -50.3 |
| -11.0 | -12.8 | -9.5 | | | -7.8 | | -10.4 | -13.7 | -7.7 |
| -3.8 | -5.4 | -5.1 | | | -1.9 | | -4.9 | -4.6 | -6.0 |
| 11.2 | 7.1 | 6.2 | EBIT/Interest | | 5.7 | | 21.8 | 7.2 | 5.5 |
| (54) 2.2 | (54) 2.8 | (59) 2.5 | | | 2.5 | | (10) 4.9 | (19) 3.2 | 1.6 |
| .6 | 1.2 | 1.1 | | | 1.2 | | 1.9 | 1.1 | -.1 |
| 9.1 | 4.3 | 6.2 | Net Profit + Depr., Dep., Amort./Cur. Mat. L/T/D | | | | | | |
| (19) 4.4 | (13) 2.3 | (17) 3.7 | | | | | | | |
| 2.0 | .4 | 2.1 | | | | | | | |
| 1.1 | 1.0 | 1.1 | Fixed/Worth | | 1.8 | | .9 | 1.0 | 1.2 |
| 1.7 | 1.8 | 1.9 | | | 2.7 | | 1.4 | 1.4 | 2.3 |
| 3.8 | 8.7 | 11.3 | | | -2.6 | | 531.7 | 2.2 | 25.0 |
| .6 | .6 | .7 | Debt/Worth | | 1.0 | | .3 | .6 | .6 |
| 1.3 | 1.3 | 1.3 | | | 2.8 | | 1.1 | 1.2 | 1.8 |
| 4.3 | 11.0 | 15.7 | | | -3.9 | | 687.3 | 1.9 | 29.2 |
| 22.1 | 24.6 | 27.1 | % Profit Before Taxes/Tangible Net Worth | | | | 53.1 | 18.3 | 33.6 |
| (47) 6.6 | (51) 11.6 | (54) 10.6 | | | | | (10) 9.1 | 11.6 | (13) 6.6 |
| -1.2 | .3 | 1.1 | | | | | 5.5 | -.9 | -2.6 |
| 9.3 | 11.9 | 9.2 | % Profit Before Taxes/Total Assets | | 14.3 | | 17.3 | 8.9 | 6.1 |
| 3.3 | 3.6 | 4.4 | | | 7.6 | | 6.1 | 5.3 | 2.1 |
| -1.1 | -2.3 | .3 | | | 1.2 | | 2.3 | -.4 | -2.8 |
| 2.0 | 2.2 | 2.0 | Sales/Net Fixed Assets | | 2.8 | | 1.8 | 2.4 | 1.7 |
| 1.2 | 1.2 | 1.3 | | | 1.2 | | 1.2 | 1.3 | 1.4 |
| .8 | .9 | .8 | | | 1.1 | | .4 | .7 | .7 |
| 1.3 | 1.4 | 1.4 | Sales/Total Assets | | 1.4 | | 1.5 | 1.3 | 1.2 |
| .9 | .9 | .9 | | | 1.0 | | 1.0 | .8 | .9 |
| .7 | .5 | .5 | | | .9 | | .4 | .5 | .5 |
| 6.7 | 6.4 | 6.7 | % Depr., Dep., Amort./Sales | | | | 7.9 | 6.7 | 6.6 |
| (53) 10.0 | (56) 9.6 | (54) 10.2 | | | | | (11) 12.5 | (19) 10.8 | (12) 7.9 |
| 13.4 | 12.8 | 13.8 | | | | | 14.1 | 15.6 | 11.3 |
| | | 2.1 | % Officers', Directors' Owners' Comp/Sales | | | | | | |
| | (10) 5.0 | | | | | | | | |
| | | 10.3 | | | | | | | |
| 1415453M | 1346756M | 1668383M | Net Sales ($) | 299M | 21607M | 12454M | 82181M | 366053M | 1185789M |
| 1895868M | 1788306M | 2247687M | Total Assets ($) | 1567M | 19525M | 17858M | 161123M | 482795M | 1564819M |

M = $ thousand    MM = $ million
See Pages 9 through 22 for Explanation of Ratios and Data

## Current Data Sorted by Assets      Comparative Historical Data

| Type of Statement | 0-500M | 500M-2MM | 2-10MM | 10-50MM | 50-100MM | 100-250MM | 4/1/07-3/31/08 ALL | 4/1/08-3/31/09 ALL |
|---|---|---|---|---|---|---|---|---|
| Unqualified | | 1 | 5 | 3 | | | 13 | 10 |
| Reviewed | | 2 | 18 | 8 | | | 19 | 14 |
| Compiled | 4 | 13 | 19 | 3 | | | 24 | 25 |
| Tax Returns | 13 | 20 | 20 | 1 | | | 46 | 47 |
| Other | 3 | 14 | 36 | 16 | 1 | 1 | 58 | 74 |
| | | 18 (4/1-9/30/11) | | 183 (10/1/11-3/31/12) | | | | |
| **NUMBER OF STATEMENTS** | 20 | 50 | 98 | 31 | 1 | 1 | 160 | 170 |
| **ASSETS** | % | % | % | % | % | % | % | % |
| Cash & Equivalents | 19.9 | 9.0 | 7.9 | 4.8 | | | 9.4 | 8.8 |
| Trade Receivables (net) | 10.6 | 7.9 | 5.6 | 4.0 | | | 6.1 | 6.2 |
| Inventory | 17.0 | 13.7 | 11.8 | 6.4 | | | 12.4 | 13.8 |
| All Other Current | 2.7 | 2.1 | .8 | 1.5 | | | 2.1 | 2.4 |
| Total Current | 50.3 | 32.6 | 26.1 | 16.8 | | | 29.9 | 31.2 |
| Fixed Assets (net) | 30.5 | 55.2 | 59.8 | 67.5 | | | 55.7 | 55.9 |
| Intangibles (net) | 7.4 | 5.1 | 7.8 | 7.0 | | | 5.5 | 4.7 |
| All Other Non-Current | 11.9 | 7.1 | 6.3 | 8.7 | | | 8.8 | 8.2 |
| Total | 100.0 | 100.0 | 100.0 | 100.0 | | | 100.0 | 100.0 |
| **LIABILITIES** | | | | | | | | |
| Notes Payable-Short Term | 11.9 | 10.4 | 6.5 | 4.5 | | | 8.1 | 7.1 |
| Cur. Mat.-L.T.D. | 21.6 | 4.5 | 2.6 | 5.7 | | | 5.8 | 5.3 |
| Trade Payables | 8.5 | 7.0 | 1.9 | 2.0 | | | 3.3 | 3.3 |
| Income Taxes Payable | 4.0 | .0 | .1 | .0 | | | .1 | .1 |
| All Other Current | 39.1 | 19.3 | 10.8 | 6.5 | | | 10.6 | 8.6 |
| Total Current | 85.1 | 41.1 | 21.8 | 18.7 | | | 27.9 | 24.4 |
| Long-Term Debt | 26.5 | 49.9 | 48.4 | 52.8 | | | 50.4 | 50.3 |
| Deferred Taxes | .0 | .0 | .1 | .4 | | | .1 | .1 |
| All Other Non-Current | 15.5 | 9.7 | 8.5 | 3.9 | | | 7.0 | 8.6 |
| Net Worth | -27.1 | -.8 | 21.2 | 24.2 | | | 14.6 | 16.6 |
| Total Liabilities & Net Worth | 100.0 | 100.0 | 100.0 | 100.0 | | | 100.0 | 100.0 |
| **INCOME DATA** | | | | | | | | |
| Net Sales | 100.0 | 100.0 | 100.0 | 100.0 | | | 100.0 | 100.0 |
| Gross Profit | | | | | | | | |
| Operating Expenses | 96.1 | 88.2 | 89.9 | 85.6 | | | 86.4 | 86.3 |
| Operating Profit | 3.9 | 11.8 | 10.1 | 14.4 | | | 13.6 | 13.7 |
| All Other Expenses (net) | 2.4 | 7.8 | 7.1 | 10.0 | | | 8.4 | 7.7 |
| Profit Before Taxes | 1.6 | 4.0 | 2.9 | 4.5 | | | 5.3 | 6.0 |
| **RATIOS** | | | | | | | | |
| Current | 2.6 | 3.8 | 2.5 | 1.6 | | | 2.4 | 3.7 |
| | 1.5 | 1.6 | 1.2 | .8 | | | 1.1 | 1.4 |
| | .2 | .7 | .6 | .5 | | | .6 | .7 |
| Quick | 2.3 | 2.4 | 1.5 | 1.3 | | | 1.7 | 2.6 |
| | .5 | .9 (97) | .7 | .3 | | | .6 | .7 |
| | .1 | .2 | .2 | .2 | | | .2 | .2 |
| Sales/Receivables | 0 UND | 3 115.4 | 5 75.2 | 6 59.4 | | | 3 113.5 | 3 132.4 |
| | 3 122.6 | 19 19.5 | 16 23.0 | 14 27.0 | | | 13 28.7 | 19 19.2 |
| | 25 14.8 | 46 8.0 | 42 8.6 | 39 9.4 | | | 28 12.9 | 33 11.1 |
| Cost of Sales/Inventory | | | | | | | | |
| Cost of Sales/Payables | | | | | | | | |
| Sales/Working Capital | 6.5 | 4.1 | 5.1 | 11.0 | | | 6.2 | 4.8 |
| | 67.6 | 13.3 | 35.3 | -21.1 | | | 38.6 | 16.8 |
| | -2.5 | -20.2 | -8.1 | -5.9 | | | -9.3 | -16.2 |
| EBIT/Interest | 8.1 | 3.2 | 4.0 | 4.5 | | | 5.3 | 3.7 |
| | (16) 1.9 | (40) 2.0 | (82) 1.7 | (23) 1.9 | | | (125) 1.7 | (143) 1.8 |
| | -.6 | 1.2 | .8 | 1.2 | | | 1.0 | .8 |
| Net Profit + Depr., Dep., Amort./Cur. Mat. L/T/D | | | | | | | | |
| Fixed/Worth | .3 | .7 | 1.1 | 1.7 | | | 1.2 | .9 |
| | 2.1 | 5.6 | 2.8 | 3.8 | | | 5.9 | 3.2 |
| | -.5 | -2.2 | -4.9 | -10.0 | | | -6.4 | -5.4 |
| Debt/Worth | .7 | 1.4 | .9 | 1.6 | | | 1.4 | 1.0 |
| | 3.9 | 10.8 | 5.6 | 3.7 | | | 8.3 | 4.9 |
| | -2.4 | -3.2 | -7.4 | -18.0 | | | -9.9 | -10.2 |
| % Profit Before Taxes/Tangible Net Worth | 35.4 | 45.4 | 19.2 | 21.2 | | | 36.2 | 33.0 |
| | (12) 10.8 | (30) 9.0 | (64) 5.4 | (21) 8.6 | | | (105) 13.3 | (119) 12.9 |
| | -.2 | 1.6 | -2.1 | 1.4 | | | -2.3 | 1.9 |
| % Profit Before Taxes/Total Assets | 22.7 | 6.6 | 4.7 | 5.4 | | | 8.8 | 7.6 |
| | 4.1 | 2.4 | .7 | 2.0 | | | 2.2 | 2.7 |
| | -8.2 | .0 | -2.6 | .2 | | | -.8 | -.7 |
| Sales/Net Fixed Assets | 28.3 | 5.6 | 2.3 | 1.3 | | | 6.1 | 4.3 |
| | 11.0 | 1.6 | .8 | .8 | | | 1.6 | 1.4 |
| | 4.2 | .7 | .5 | .3 | | | .5 | .6 |
| Sales/Total Assets | 4.7 | 1.5 | 1.0 | .7 | | | 1.5 | 1.3 |
| | 2.6 | 1.0 | .6 | .5 | | | .8 | .7 |
| | 1.1 | .4 | .3 | .2 | | | .3 | .4 |
| % Depr., Dep., Amort./Sales | 1.1 | 2.7 | 3.8 | 6.2 | | | 2.7 | 3.1 |
| | (16) 1.9 | (43) 7.6 | (88) 7.6 | (29) 10.6 | | | (137) 6.3 | (143) 6.3 |
| | 9.1 | 14.4 | 14.8 | 18.9 | | | 12.2 | 11.3 |
| % Officers', Directors' Owners' Comp/Sales | | 2.1 | 1.6 | | | | 2.0 | 2.4 |
| | | (18) 3.3 | (27) 3.7 | | | | (52) 3.6 | (51) 4.9 |
| | | 8.0 | 8.1 | | | | 8.2 | 8.9 |
| Net Sales ($) | 14009M | 65403M | 300542M | 324539M | 32102M | 568189M | 1721111M | 735460M |
| Total Assets ($) | 5613M | 58769M | 429621M | 646121M | 51837M | 236664M | 1251357M | 897491M |

© RMA 2012

M = $ thousand    MM = $ million
See Pages 9 through 22 for Explanation of Ratios and Data

## Comparative Historical Data | Current Data Sorted by Sales

| | | | Type of Statement | 0-1MM | 1-3MM | 3-5MM | 5-10MM | 10-25MM | 25MM & OVER |
|---|---|---|---|---|---|---|---|---|---|
| 9 | 7 | 9 | Unqualified | | 3 | 1 | 4 | | 1 |
| 33 | 20 | 28 | Reviewed | 3 | 9 | 5 | 8 | 3 | |
| 25 | 24 | 39 | Compiled | 12 | 18 | 2 | 5 | 2 | |
| 39 | 41 | 55 | Tax Returns | 21 | 25 | 6 | 1 | 1 | 1 |
| 69 | 75 | 70 | Other | 18 | 23 | 8 | 13 | 6 | 2 |
| 4/1/09-3/31/10 | 4/1/10-3/31/11 | 4/1/11-3/31/12 | | 18 (4/1-9/30/11) | | | 183 (10/1/11-3/31/12) | | |
| ALL | ALL | ALL | | | | | | | |
| 175 | 167 | 201 | **NUMBER OF STATEMENTS** | 54 | 78 | 22 | 31 | 12 | 4 |
| % | % | % | **ASSETS** | % | % | % | % | % | % |
| 8.9 | 11.7 | 9.0 | Cash & Equivalents | 11.6 | 7.0 | 10.0 | 9.9 | 5.8 | |
| 5.2 | 6.7 | 6.4 | Trade Receivables (net) | 5.1 | 7.6 | 7.7 | 6.1 | 4.1 | |
| 12.9 | 9.9 | 11.9 | Inventory | 7.0 | 12.1 | 11.7 | 19.0 | 11.0 | |
| 2.5 | 1.8 | 1.4 | All Other Current | .4 | 2.1 | .9 | 1.2 | 3.1 | |
| 29.4 | 30.1 | 28.7 | Total Current | 24.1 | 28.8 | 30.4 | 36.2 | 24.1 | |
| 57.2 | 55.3 | 56.6 | Fixed Assets (net) | 62.4 | 54.9 | 55.5 | 53.0 | 61.9 | |
| 5.5 | 5.7 | 7.3 | Intangibles (net) | 6.9 | 8.2 | 5.9 | 6.0 | 2.4 | |
| 7.9 | 8.9 | 7.4 | All Other Non-Current | 6.6 | 8.1 | 8.2 | 4.9 | 11.7 | |
| 100.0 | 100.0 | 100.0 | Total | 100.0 | 100.0 | 100.0 | 100.0 | 100.0 | |
| | | | **LIABILITIES** | | | | | | |
| 6.6 | 5.8 | 7.6 | Notes Payable-Short Term | 8.1 | 6.8 | 5.7 | 10.3 | 4.9 | |
| 4.9 | 3.5 | 5.6 | Cur. Mat.-L.T.D. | 11.6 | 2.6 | 3.8 | 3.7 | 3.4 | |
| 3.4 | 3.1 | 3.8 | Trade Payables | 5.9 | 3.6 | 1.5 | 2.4 | 4.2 | |
| .1 | .0 | .5 | Income Taxes Payable | 1.5 | .0 | .0 | .0 | .5 | |
| 11.2 | 12.2 | 15.2 | All Other Current | 21.8 | 15.1 | 11.5 | 9.5 | 6.6 | |
| 26.2 | 24.7 | 32.7 | Total Current | 48.9 | 28.2 | 22.5 | 25.9 | 19.5 | |
| 51.4 | 49.9 | 47.2 | Long-Term Debt | 51.4 | 52.3 | 39.1 | 33.6 | 46.4 | |
| .2 | .1 | .1 | Deferred Taxes | .0 | .1 | .0 | .3 | .2 | |
| 15.4 | 13.4 | 8.7 | All Other Non-Current | 8.1 | 9.9 | 2.0 | 10.8 | 12.6 | |
| 6.8 | 11.9 | 11.2 | Net Worth | -8.4 | 9.5 | 36.3 | 29.4 | 21.2 | |
| 100.0 | 100.0 | 100.0 | Total Liabilities & Net Worth | 100.0 | 100.0 | 100.0 | 100.0 | 100.0 | |
| | | | **INCOME DATA** | | | | | | |
| 100.0 | 100.0 | 100.0 | Net Sales | 100.0 | 100.0 | 100.0 | 100.0 | 100.0 | |
| | | | Gross Profit | | | | | | |
| 88.9 | 87.6 | 89.5 | Operating Expenses | 84.4 | 90.9 | 90.3 | 94.0 | 88.4 | |
| 11.1 | 12.4 | 10.5 | Operating Profit | 15.6 | 9.1 | 9.7 | 6.0 | 11.6 | |
| 8.2 | 6.5 | 7.2 | All Other Expenses (net) | 12.1 | 6.5 | 4.7 | 2.5 | 8.7 | |
| 3.0 | 6.0 | 3.3 | Profit Before Taxes | 3.5 | 2.7 | 5.0 | 3.6 | 2.9 | |
| | | | **RATIOS** | | | | | | |
| 2.8 | 3.2 | 2.7 | | 2.7 | 2.2 | 3.3 | 2.9 | 2.4 | |
| 1.2 | 1.4 | 1.3 | Current | .9 | 1.1 | 1.6 | 1.4 | 1.4 | |
| .5 | .7 | .5 | | .2 | .4 | .7 | .9 | .6 | |
| 1.7 | 2.2 | 1.7 | | 2.5 | 1.5 | 2.6 | 1.5 | 1.6 | |
| (174) .5 | .9 (200) | .6 | Quick | .5 | .7 | .7 (30) | .7 | .4 | |
| .2 | .3 | .2 | | .1 | .3 | .2 | .3 | .2 | |
| 4 83.2 | 2 225.8 | 4 88.1 | | 0 UND | 7 53.2 | 10 35.7 | 5 73.3 | 6 56.3 | |
| 16 22.8 | 13 28.7 | 15 24.4 | Sales/Receivables | 6 64.8 | 16 23.4 | 26 14.3 | 14 26.9 | 14 26.6 | |
| 32 11.3 | 37 9.7 | 41 8.8 | | 49 7.5 | 38 9.7 | 47 7.7 | 34 10.6 | 31 11.8 | |
| | | | Cost of Sales/Inventory | | | | | | |
| | | | Cost of Sales/Payables | | | | | | |
| 5.4 | 4.3 | 5.2 | | 4.0 | 6.5 | 3.6 | 4.0 | 4.6 | |
| 28.5 | 17.5 | 23.7 | Sales/Working Capital | -50.4 | 27.8 | 12.6 | 13.0 | 14.8 | |
| -6.9 | -12.5 | -6.6 | | -1.6 | -9.7 | -10.7 | -21.4 | -8.4 | |
| 3.6 | 5.2 | 3.9 | | 4.1 | 3.3 | 7.1 | 4.1 | | |
| (132) 1.5 | (135) 2.3 | (163) 1.8 | EBIT/Interest | (34) 1.6 | (66) 1.8 | (19) 2.2 | 1.4 | | |
| .5 | .8 | .9 | | -.1 | 1.0 | .8 | .8 | | |
| | 4.0 | | Net Profit + Depr., Dep., | | | | | | |
| | (12) 2.4 | | Amort./Cur. Mat. L/T/D | | | | | | |
| | .6 | | | | | | | | |
| 1.2 | .8 | 1.0 | | 1.4 | 1.1 | .8 | .7 | 1.2 | |
| 4.8 | 2.9 | 3.6 | Fixed/Worth | 7.6 | 16.5 | 1.6 | 1.6 | 3.4 | |
| -3.9 | -4.9 | -3.2 | | -2.1 | -2.7 | -5.8 | -10.0 | 26.6 | |
| .9 | .8 | 1.0 | | 2.0 | 1.3 | .3 | .5 | 1.7 | |
| 8.0 | 4.3 | 5.7 | Debt/Worth | 12.8 | 28.5 | 2.6 | 1.2 | 5.3 | |
| -6.5 | -6.4 | -5.3 | | -3.0 | -4.4 | -7.8 | -18.0 | 30.0 | |
| 25.6 | 30.7 | 21.9 | % Profit Before Taxes/Tangible | 27.0 | 30.0 | 17.8 | 20.4 | 43.1 | |
| (106) 6.5 | (110) 10.9 | (127) 7.1 | Net Worth | (34) 7.7 | (43) 7.8 | (16) 5.3 | (23) 2.5 | (10) 14.5 | |
| -3.9 | -.9 | .4 | | -1.2 | .9 | -1.0 | .2 | 6.2 | |
| 6.2 | 9.6 | 5.6 | % Profit Before Taxes/Total | 5.7 | 5.8 | 11.2 | 5.4 | 5.9 | |
| 1.8 | 2.8 | 1.2 | Assets | .5 | 1.8 | 2.8 | .7 | 1.9 | |
| -2.0 | -.8 | -1.0 | | -3.4 | -.3 | -.7 | -.9 | .9 | |
| 3.1 | 5.7 | 3.3 | | 3.3 | 3.3 | 2.7 | 7.3 | 2.8 | |
| 1.1 | 1.4 | 1.2 | Sales/Net Fixed Assets | .5 | 1.4 | 1.2 | 1.3 | 1.4 | |
| .5 | .6 | .5 | | .2 | .6 | .7 | .8 | .5 | |
| 1.2 | 1.4 | 1.3 | | 1.1 | 1.3 | 1.2 | 1.7 | 1.1 | |
| .7 | .8 | .7 | Sales/Total Assets | .3 | .7 | .7 | .8 | .9 | |
| .4 | .4 | .3 | | .2 | .4 | .5 | .5 | .4 | |
| 3.8 | 3.1 | 3.4 | | 7.2 | 3.3 | 2.3 | 2.2 | 3.2 | |
| (148) 7.7 | (136) 7.2 | (177) 7.7 | % Depr., Dep., Amort./Sales | (44) 13.0 | (68) 7.4 | 5.9 | (30) 6.0 | (10) 6.3 | |
| 14.9 | 12.5 | 14.5 | | 27.5 | 14.8 | 8.7 | 11.5 | 7.4 | |
| 2.2 | 2.1 | 2.1 | % Officers', Directors' | 3.2 | 2.0 | | 1.1 | | |
| (50) 5.2 | (45) 6.5 | (58) 4.4 | Owners' Comp/Sales | (10) 7.4 | (26) 3.9 | | (11) 3.1 | | |
| 9.2 | 9.2 | 8.9 | | 13.3 | 11.2 | | 7.7 | | |
| 764936M | 994848M | 1304784M | Net Sales ($) | 28306M | 134479M | 82979M | 214962M | 156633M | 687425M |
| 1255846M | 1115751M | 1428625M | Total Assets ($) | 89479M | 253784M | 163834M | 298779M | 255042M | 367707M |

© RMA 2012

**M = $ thousand    MM = $ million**
See Pages 9 through 22 for Explanation of Ratios and Data

## Current Data Sorted by Assets        Comparative Historical Data

| | | | | | | Type of Statement | | |
|---|---|---|---|---|---|---|---|---|
| 1 | 3 | 29 | 40 | 14 | 6 | Unqualified | 70 | 75 |
| 2 | 5 | 29 | 23 | | | Reviewed | 43 | 39 |
| 19 | 28 | 22 | 2 | | | Compiled | 60 | 63 |
| 81 | 60 | 28 | 3 | | 1 | Tax Returns | 114 | 136 |
| 51 | 62 | 75 | 41 | 10 | 6 | Other | 159 | 193 |
| | 86 (4/1-9/30/11) | | 555 (10/1/11-3/31/12) | | | | 4/1/07-3/31/08 | 4/1/08-3/31/09 |
| 0-500M | 500M-2MM | 2-10MM | 10-50MM | 50-100MM | 100-250MM | | ALL | ALL |
| 154 | 158 | 183 | 109 | 24 | 13 | NUMBER OF STATEMENTS | 446 | 506 |
| % | % | % | % | % | % | ASSETS | % | % |
| 22.8 | 11.3 | 8.8 | 9.4 | 10.0 | 8.9 | Cash & Equivalents | 11.4 | 9.5 |
| 3.3 | 2.3 | 3.6 | 3.6 | 3.6 | 2.5 | Trade Receivables (net) | 3.6 | 4.2 |
| 3.3 | .7 | 1.3 | .7 | 1.0 | .5 | Inventory | 1.7 | 1.3 |
| 2.9 | 2.9 | 1.9 | 1.6 | 2.6 | 2.7 | All Other Current | 2.8 | 3.2 |
| 32.3 | 17.3 | 15.7 | 15.4 | 17.2 | 14.5 | Total Current | 19.6 | 18.3 |
| 51.2 | 68.7 | 74.2 | 73.2 | 71.8 | 66.6 | Fixed Assets (net) | 66.4 | 67.6 |
| 8.9 | 6.4 | 3.4 | 4.8 | 4.1 | 14.5 | Intangibles (net) | 5.4 | 6.0 |
| 7.6 | 7.6 | 6.7 | 6.6 | 7.0 | 4.4 | All Other Non-Current | 8.7 | 8.2 |
| 100.0 | 100.0 | 100.0 | 100.0 | 100.0 | 100.0 | Total | 100.0 | 100.0 |
| | | | | | | LIABILITIES | | |
| 14.3 | 4.8 | 2.7 | 1.6 | .7 | .0 | Notes Payable-Short Term | 5.3 | 6.3 |
| 6.6 | 5.5 | 4.9 | 3.8 | 3.1 | 7.8 | Cur. Mat.-L.T.D. | 5.3 | 5.4 |
| 9.3 | 3.7 | 3.8 | 2.8 | 3.6 | 2.5 | Trade Payables | 3.9 | 4.8 |
| .1 | .1 | .1 | .2 | .4 | .0 | Income Taxes Payable | .0 | .1 |
| 20.2 | 11.1 | 8.3 | 9.0 | 8.3 | 10.4 | All Other Current | 12.6 | 13.4 |
| 50.5 | 25.1 | 19.7 | 17.5 | 16.2 | 20.8 | Total Current | 27.1 | 30.0 |
| 42.4 | 46.3 | 44.7 | 47.5 | 31.8 | 32.7 | Long-Term Debt | 38.3 | 42.2 |
| .0 | .0 | .1 | .0 | .0 | .9 | Deferred Taxes | .1 | .1 |
| 26.3 | 7.9 | 6.5 | 9.3 | 10.0 | 15.1 | All Other Non-Current | 13.0 | 11.2 |
| -19.2 | 20.7 | 29.1 | 25.7 | 42.0 | 30.5 | Net Worth | 21.5 | 16.5 |
| 100.0 | 100.0 | 100.0 | 100.0 | 100.0 | 100.0 | Total Liabilties & Net Worth | 100.0 | 100.0 |
| | | | | | | INCOME DATA | | |
| 100.0 | 100.0 | 100.0 | 100.0 | 100.0 | 100.0 | Net Sales | 100.0 | 100.0 |
| | | | | | | Gross Profit | | |
| 93.3 | 86.7 | 89.3 | 89.6 | 90.4 | 91.1 | Operating Expenses | 90.4 | 92.9 |
| 6.7 | 13.3 | 10.7 | 10.4 | 9.6 | 8.9 | Operating Profit | 9.6 | 7.1 |
| 1.7 | 5.4 | 6.4 | 5.1 | 3.5 | 7.0 | All Other Expenses (net) | 5.2 | 5.1 |
| 4.9 | 7.9 | 4.3 | 5.3 | 6.0 | 1.9 | Profit Before Taxes | 4.5 | 1.9 |
| | | | | | | RATIOS | | |
| 2.4 | 2.0 | 2.5 | 2.5 | 2.9 | 1.3 | | 2.4 | 2.0 |
| .7 | .9 | 1.0 | 1.0 | 1.0 | .6 | Current | .9 | .8 |
| .2 | .2 | .3 | .4 | .5 | .2 | | .3 | .3 |
| 2.0 | 1.5 | 2.0 | 1.9 | 1.4 | 1.1 | | 1.8 | 1.3 |
| .5 | .6 | .8 | .8 | .8 | .4 | Quick | (444) .7 | .6 |
| .1 | .2 | .2 | .3 | .4 | .2 | | .2 | .2 |
| 0 UND | 0 UND | 0 UND | 1 333.8 | 3 114.7 | 0 UND | | 0 UND | 0 UND |
| 0 UND | 0 UND | 5 69.8 | 10 35.9 | 10 35.3 | 4 88.5 | Sales/Receivables | 2 196.9 | 3 140.8 |
| 0 UND | 5 80.0 | 21 17.2 | 22 16.7 | 24 15.4 | 15 24.8 | | 16 23.1 | 17 21.3 |
| | | | | | | Cost of Sales/Inventory | | |
| | | | | | | Cost of Sales/Payables | | |
| 22.2 | 19.6 | 8.7 | 7.1 | 4.5 | 15.9 | | 11.3 | 16.6 |
| -100.2 | -78.8 | 999.8 | -239.2 | NM | -6.2 | Sales/Working Capital | -94.3 | -36.5 |
| -8.8 | -7.4 | -8.2 | -6.4 | -9.9 | -2.8 | | -8.7 | -6.8 |
| 11.4 | 8.4 | 4.1 | 4.3 | 8.0 | 3.8 | | 5.9 | 4.3 |
| (106) 2.6 | (131) 3.1 | (152) 1.5 | (97) 2.2 | (21) 2.2 | (12) .8 | EBIT/Interest | (366) 1.6 | (418) 1.4 |
| -.3 | .9 | .2 | .3 | 1.0 | -.5 | | .4 | -.4 |
| | | 2.8 | 3.9 | | | | 5.5 | 3.8 |
| | | (16) 1.6 | (20) 2.3 | | | Net Profit + Depr., Dep., Amort./Cur. Mat. L/T/D | (37) 2.7 | (46) 1.7 |
| | | .9 | 1.6 | | | | 1.1 | .4 |
| .7 | 1.4 | 1.2 | 1.4 | 1.3 | 1.4 | | 1.2 | 1.3 |
| 5.7 | 3.0 | 2.6 | 3.0 | 2.4 | 10.7 | Fixed/Worth | 2.8 | 3.1 |
| -1.0 | -15.7 | 48.7 | 10.2 | 5.2 | -17.5 | | -19.1 | -14.9 |
| 1.0 | .8 | .6 | .9 | .7 | .8 | | .7 | .9 |
| 33.9 | 2.9 | 2.3 | 2.5 | 1.8 | 12.0 | Debt/Worth | 2.7 | 3.3 |
| -2.2 | -20.4 | 62.2 | 10.4 | 5.5 | -22.7 | | -21.9 | -17.3 |
| 154.4 | 69.0 | 29.5 | 41.3 | 18.9 | | % Profit Before Taxes/Tangible Net Worth | 48.9 | 52.4 |
| (81) 49.8 | (112) 24.6 | (141) 5.6 | (90) 8.5 | (22) 6.9 | | | (323) 12.2 | (360) 7.9 |
| 8.5 | .8 | -3.8 | -1.4 | 2.8 | | | -1.2 | -5.3 |
| 41.8 | 21.4 | 8.2 | 9.2 | 5.3 | 5.8 | % Profit Before Taxes/Total Assets | 13.8 | 10.2 |
| 8.3 | 5.4 | 2.0 | 2.9 | 3.3 | -.2 | | 2.7 | 1.4 |
| -7.0 | -.4 | -2.0 | -1.4 | .1 | -2.8 | | -1.9 | -4.0 |
| 31.8 | 4.4 | 1.7 | 1.7 | 1.4 | 1.8 | | 4.6 | 4.9 |
| 8.4 | 1.8 | .8 | .7 | .9 | .9 | Sales/Net Fixed Assets | 1.5 | 1.4 |
| 3.4 | 1.0 | .4 | .5 | .6 | .6 | | .7 | .6 |
| 6.8 | 2.4 | 1.0 | 1.0 | .8 | .8 | | 2.2 | 2.1 |
| 3.9 | 1.3 | .6 | .6 | .6 | .7 | Sales/Total Assets | .9 | .9 |
| 1.9 | .8 | .4 | .4 | .5 | .5 | | .6 | .5 |
| 1.8 | 3.4 | 5.2 | 5.4 | 5.8 | | | 4.0 | 4.5 |
| (105) 4.1 | (137) 6.7 | (167) 8.0 | (104) 7.7 | (19) 7.9 | | % Depr., Dep., Amort./Sales | (372) 6.7 | (416) 7.1 |
| 7.7 | 11.0 | 11.8 | 12.6 | 10.8 | | | 10.0 | 11.0 |
| 4.7 | 2.5 | 2.8 | 2.1 | | | | 3.2 | 3.2 |
| (55) 8.7 | (45) 5.0 | (44) 5.0 | (13) 5.1 | | | % Officers', Directors' Owners' Comp/Sales | (115) 5.5 | (131) 6.3 |
| 12.8 | 12.4 | 7.7 | 8.9 | | | | 10.8 | 13.2 |
| 143976M | 284356M | 802171M | 1886012M | 1189025M | 1338918M | Net Sales ($) | 4371789M | 5113917M |
| 36719M | 179271M | 902431M | 2082105M | 1630459M | 1895410M | Total Assets ($) | 5993886M | 5563009M |

© RMA 2012

M = $ thousand     MM = $ million
See Pages 9 through 22 for Explanation of Ratios and Data

| Comparative Historical Data | | | Type of Statement | Current Data Sorted by Sales | | | | | |
|---|---|---|---|---|---|---|---|---|---|
| 75 | 92 | 93 | Unqualified | 5 | 15 | 18 | 12 | 18 | 25 |
| 49 | 55 | 59 | Reviewed | 3 | 11 | 14 | 14 | 16 | 1 |
| 65 | 55 | 71 | Compiled | 22 | 27 | 8 | 11 | 3 | |
| 136 | 142 | 173 | Tax Returns | 84 | 77 | 4 | 5 | 1 | 2 |
| 193 | 229 | 245 | Other | 62 | 79 | 29 | 21 | 29 | 25 |
| 4/1/09-3/31/10 | 4/1/10-3/31/11 | 4/1/11-3/31/12 | | | 86 (4/1-9/30/11) | | 555 (10/1/11-3/31/12) | | |
| ALL | ALL | ALL | | 0-1MM | 1-3MM | 3-5MM | 5-10MM | 10-25MM | 25MM & OVER |
| 518 | 573 | 641 | **NUMBER OF STATEMENTS** | 176 | 209 | 73 | 63 | 67 | 53 |
| % | % | % | **ASSETS** | % | % | % | % | % | % |
| 11.0 | 12.4 | 12.9 | Cash & Equivalents | 14.8 | 13.1 | 12.8 | 10.1 | 10.0 | 13.4 |
| 3.2 | 3.0 | 3.2 | Trade Receivables (net) | 1.8 | 3.1 | 3.6 | 2.7 | 5.9 | 5.3 |
| 1.8 | 2.1 | 1.5 | Inventory | 2.2 | 1.3 | 1.1 | .9 | 1.4 | 1.3 |
| 3.1 | 2.5 | 2.4 | All Other Current | 1.9 | 2.1 | 3.8 | 1.3 | 3.9 | 2.9 |
| 19.0 | 20.0 | 20.1 | Total Current | 20.6 | 19.6 | 21.3 | 15.0 | 21.1 | 22.9 |
| 66.8 | 68.1 | 66.9 | Fixed Assets (net) | 64.5 | 67.0 | 68.9 | 75.8 | 67.1 | 61.3 |
| 5.8 | 4.5 | 6.0 | Intangibles (net) | 7.8 | 5.7 | 3.0 | 2.5 | 6.0 | 8.7 |
| 8.4 | 7.4 | 7.1 | All Other Non-Current | 7.1 | 7.7 | 6.8 | 6.6 | 5.9 | 7.1 |
| 100.0 | 100.0 | 100.0 | Total | 100.0 | 100.0 | 100.0 | 100.0 | 100.0 | 100.0 |
| | | | **LIABILITIES** | | | | | | |
| 6.6 | 6.3 | 5.7 | Notes Payable-Short Term | 11.4 | 4.7 | 3.3 | 2.3 | 2.7 | 1.3 |
| 5.3 | 5.8 | 5.2 | Cur. Mat.-L.T.D. | 6.1 | 5.8 | 4.3 | 3.4 | 4.2 | 5.2 |
| 4.1 | 5.0 | 4.9 | Trade Payables | 5.9 | 4.5 | 3.5 | 3.8 | 6.1 | 4.8 |
| .1 | .2 | .1 | Income Taxes Payable | .0 | .2 | .2 | .0 | .3 | .3 |
| 10.0 | 11.6 | 12.0 | All Other Current | 15.5 | 11.4 | 8.9 | 6.7 | 11.7 | 13.9 |
| 26.2 | 28.9 | 27.9 | Total Current | 38.9 | 26.5 | 20.2 | 16.2 | 25.0 | 25.5 |
| 42.4 | 46.2 | 44.3 | Long-Term Debt | 54.8 | 42.2 | 35.9 | 44.7 | 34.5 | 40.8 |
| .1 | .1 | .0 | Deferred Taxes | .0 | .0 | .2 | .0 | .0 | .3 |
| 11.4 | 11.6 | 12.4 | All Other Non-Current | 14.5 | 13.1 | 9.3 | 9.7 | 8.9 | 13.8 |
| 20.0 | 13.2 | 15.4 | Net Worth | -8.2 | 18.1 | 34.4 | 29.3 | 31.5 | 19.6 |
| 100.0 | 100.0 | 100.0 | Total Liabilities & Net Worth | 100.0 | 100.0 | 100.0 | 100.0 | 100.0 | 100.0 |
| | | | **INCOME DATA** | | | | | | |
| 100.0 | 100.0 | 100.0 | Net Sales | 100.0 | 100.0 | 100.0 | 100.0 | 100.0 | 100.0 |
| | | | Gross Profit | | | | | | |
| 91.5 | 91.4 | 89.8 | Operating Expenses | 86.2 | 90.6 | 94.2 | 91.7 | 88.9 | 91.0 |
| 8.5 | 8.6 | 10.2 | Operating Profit | 13.8 | 9.4 | 5.8 | 8.3 | 11.1 | 9.0 |
| 4.3 | 4.3 | 4.7 | All Other Expenses (net) | 8.5 | 3.4 | 2.3 | 3.4 | 2.8 | 4.3 |
| 4.2 | 4.3 | 5.5 | Profit Before Taxes | 5.3 | 6.0 | 3.5 | 4.9 | 8.3 | 4.8 |
| | | | **RATIOS** | | | | | | |
| 2.0 | 2.2 | 2.2 | | 1.9 | 2.5 | 2.9 | 2.4 | 2.3 | 1.6 |
| .8 | .8 | .9 | Current | .6 | .9 | 1.2 | .9 | 1.0 | .8 |
| .3 | .3 | .3 | | .2 | .3 | .4 | .4 | .4 | .4 |
| 1.6 | 1.8 | 1.9 | | 1.8 | 2.0 | 2.1 | 1.9 | 1.9 | 1.2 |
| (515) .6 | (571) .6 | .7 | Quick | .5 | .7 | 1.0 | .8 | .8 | .6 |
| .2 | .2 | .2 | | .1 | .2 | .3 | .3 | .2 | .3 |
| 0 UND | 0 UND | 0 UND | | 0 UND | 0 UND | 0 UND | 0 999.8 | 1 548.6 | 2 222.4 |
| 1 271.3 | 1 277.0 | 1 655.8 | Sales/Receivables | 0 UND | 0 999.8 | 6 59.9 | 6 57.0 | 7 55.0 | 10 36.0 |
| 16 23.2 | 12 30.1 | 13 27.8 | | 0 UND | 11 32.2 | 24 15.5 | 18 20.7 | 16 22.8 | 17 21.2 |
| | | | Cost of Sales/Inventory | | | | | | |
| | | | Cost of Sales/Payables | | | | | | |
| 13.1 | 11.7 | 12.7 | | 17.4 | 15.8 | 8.2 | 11.5 | 8.4 | 15.5 |
| -55.4 | -59.8 | -118.3 | Sales/Working Capital | -25.2 | -118.3 | 42.0 | -77.3 | -478.5 | -31.3 |
| -6.8 | -7.0 | -7.8 | | -4.7 | -9.4 | -13.1 | -10.4 | -7.0 | -6.1 |
| 4.9 | 5.1 | 6.2 | | 4.7 | 7.6 | 7.1 | 5.4 | 8.2 | 5.5 |
| (431) 1.8 | (460) 2.0 | (519) 2.2 | EBIT/Interest | (116) 1.5 | (179) 2.6 | (64) 1.7 | (57) 2.5 | (58) 3.4 | (45) 2.2 |
| .3 | .3 | .4 | | -.1 | .7 | -.5 | .5 | 1.2 | .8 |
| 4.9 | 5.3 | 4.7 | Net Profit + Depr., Dep., Amort./Cur. Mat. L/T/D | | 3.9 | | | 4.2 | 9.1 |
| (39) 2.6 | (53) 2.5 | (46) 2.3 | | | (10) 2.2 | | | (11) 1.9 | (13) 3.1 |
| .8 | 1.5 | 1.4 | | | 1.2 | | | 1.4 | 2.1 |
| 1.2 | 1.2 | 1.2 | | 1.3 | 1.2 | 1.1 | 1.4 | 1.1 | 1.3 |
| 3.1 | 3.3 | 3.0 | Fixed/Worth | 6.5 | 2.8 | 2.1 | 2.2 | 2.7 | 3.4 |
| -24.6 | -7.2 | -11.8 | | -2.6 | -8.5 | 9.6 | 10.0 | 6.5 | -24.5 |
| .8 | .8 | .8 | | 1.2 | .7 | .6 | .8 | .9 | .9 |
| 3.0 | 3.2 | 3.0 | Debt/Worth | 11.7 | 2.7 | 1.9 | 1.8 | 2.5 | 2.8 |
| -24.7 | -10.4 | -13.1 | | -3.4 | -12.6 | 15.5 | 11.8 | 9.3 | -29.9 |
| 56.6 | 61.5 | 55.2 | % Profit Before Taxes/Tangible Net Worth | 51.7 | 62.6 | 23.2 | 55.0 | 77.9 | 41.6 |
| (372) 14.0 | (392) 12.0 | (455) 14.1 | | (100) 15.0 | (148) 14.6 | (59) 3.4 | (51) 9.3 | (58) 23.0 | (39) 16.1 |
| -1.3 | .0 | -.4 | | .6 | -2.9 | -6.6 | 1.0 | 4.2 | 3.6 |
| 12.2 | 13.7 | 15.2 | % Profit Before Taxes/Total Assets | 11.9 | 19.9 | 8.9 | 14.3 | 14.9 | 14.3 |
| 2.8 | 3.3 | 3.9 | | 2.6 | 5.4 | 2.6 | 3.5 | 5.3 | 4.4 |
| -2.7 | -1.9 | -1.4 | | -2.8 | -1.0 | -3.3 | -.5 | 1.4 | -.1 |
| 4.7 | 4.4 | 4.9 | | 8.3 | 7.4 | 3.4 | 2.1 | 3.5 | 4.7 |
| 1.4 | 1.5 | 1.5 | Sales/Net Fixed Assets | 2.0 | 1.8 | 1.2 | 1.0 | 1.3 | 1.6 |
| .7 | .7 | .6 | | .5 | .8 | .6 | .6 | .7 | .8 |
| 2.1 | 2.5 | 2.5 | | 3.4 | 3.0 | 1.9 | 1.2 | 1.9 | 1.9 |
| 1.0 | 1.0 | 1.0 | Sales/Total Assets | 1.2 | 1.3 | .9 | .8 | 1.0 | .9 |
| .5 | .5 | .5 | | .3 | .6 | .5 | .5 | .5 | .6 |
| 4.8 | 4.5 | 4.0 | | 4.5 | 3.6 | 3.5 | 5.3 | 4.5 | 4.1 |
| (436) 7.6 | (480) 7.2 | (539) 7.2 | % Depr., Dep., Amort./Sales | (128) 9.5 | (183) 6.7 | (67) 7.6 | (59) 7.0 | (60) 5.9 | (42) 6.1 |
| 11.4 | 11.1 | 10.9 | | 18.4 | 10.2 | 10.3 | 8.9 | 8.4 | 8.8 |
| 3.3 | 3.6 | 3.4 | % Officers', Directors' Owners' Comp/Sales | 5.0 | 3.0 | 3.1 | 2.4 | 1.9 | |
| (138) 6.3 | (149) 6.2 | (160) 6.6 | | (43) 9.6 | (69) 6.3 | (18) 6.2 | (13) 3.3 | (10) 6.0 | |
| 12.2 | 12.9 | 10.6 | | 16.2 | 9.6 | 12.7 | 5.0 | 9.2 | |
| 4890502M | 6855852M | 5644458M | Net Sales ($) | 89719M | 379410M | 281790M | 440639M | 1031881M | 3421019M |
| 5961467M | 6827826M | 6726395M | Total Assets ($) | 159146M | 479634M | 417348M | 610857M | 1450783M | 3608627M |

© RMA 2012

M = $ thousand    MM = $ million
See Pages 9 through 22 for Explanation of Ratios and Data

## Current Data Sorted by Assets      Comparative Historical Data

| Type of Statement | 0-500M | 500M-2MM | 2-10MM | 10-50MM | 50-100MM | 100-250MM | | 4/1/07-3/31/08 ALL | 4/1/08-3/31/09 ALL |
|---|---|---|---|---|---|---|---|---|---|
| Unqualified | | 1 | 1 | 1 | 1 | | | 5 | 6 |
| Reviewed | 1 | 4 | 6 | 1 | | | | 13 | 11 |
| Compiled | 9 | 19 | 1 | | | | | 39 | 44 |
| Tax Returns | 32 | 28 | 11 | 1 | | | | 56 | 60 |
| Other | 10 | 19 | 16 | 6 | | | | 38 | 24 |
| | 36 (4/1-9/30/11) | | | 132 (10/1/11-3/31/12) | | | | | |
| NUMBER OF STATEMENTS | 52 | 71 | 35 | 9 | 1 | | | 151 | 145 |
| | % | % | % | % | % | % | | % | % |
| **ASSETS** | | | | | | | | | |
| Cash & Equivalents | 21.2 | 9.6 | 6.2 | | | | D | 15.1 | 13.6 |
| Trade Receivables (net) | 1.6 | .6 | .6 | | | | A | 1.3 | .6 |
| Inventory | 8.6 | 2.6 | 1.3 | | | | T | 3.9 | 3.8 |
| All Other Current | 3.7 | 3.3 | 1.1 | | | | A | 3.1 | 2.4 |
| Total Current | 35.1 | 16.1 | 9.3 | | | | | 23.5 | 20.3 |
| Fixed Assets (net) | 43.4 | 73.6 | 76.2 | | | | N | 62.8 | 65.9 |
| Intangibles (net) | 8.4 | 3.8 | 5.4 | | | | O | 4.9 | 3.8 |
| All Other Non-Current | 13.2 | 6.6 | 9.1 | | | | T | 8.8 | 10.0 |
| Total | 100.0 | 100.0 | 100.0 | | | | | 100.0 | 100.0 |
| **LIABILITIES** | | | | | | | A | | |
| Notes Payable-Short Term | 10.8 | 4.6 | 1.9 | | | | V | 4.9 | 8.5 |
| Cur. Mat.-L.T.D. | 4.1 | 7.5 | 4.4 | | | | A | 7.3 | 5.1 |
| Trade Payables | 6.3 | 5.0 | 2.7 | | | | I | 4.8 | 3.8 |
| Income Taxes Payable | .4 | .1 | .0 | | | | L | .0 | .0 |
| All Other Current | 43.9 | 10.6 | 10.1 | | | | A | 18.9 | 11.5 |
| Total Current | 65.6 | 27.9 | 19.1 | | | | B | 35.9 | 28.9 |
| Long-Term Debt | 32.8 | 53.5 | 61.9 | | | | L | 60.0 | 59.2 |
| Deferred Taxes | .0 | .2 | .3 | | | | E | .2 | .2 |
| All Other Non-Current | 50.2 | 25.5 | 7.5 | | | | | 19.2 | 15.9 |
| Net Worth | -48.5 | -7.1 | 11.3 | | | | | -15.2 | -4.2 |
| Total Liabilities & Net Worth | 100.0 | 100.0 | 100.0 | | | | | 100.0 | 100.0 |
| **INCOME DATA** | | | | | | | | | |
| Net Sales | 100.0 | 100.0 | 100.0 | | | | | 100.0 | 100.0 |
| Gross Profit | | | | | | | | | |
| Operating Expenses | 101.1 | 93.4 | 85.2 | | | | | 91.3 | 92.8 |
| Operating Profit | -1.1 | 6.6 | 14.8 | | | | | 8.7 | 7.2 |
| All Other Expenses (net) | .7 | 4.0 | 12.8 | | | | | 5.7 | 5.7 |
| Profit Before Taxes | -1.8 | 2.6 | 1.9 | | | | | 2.9 | 1.5 |
| **RATIOS** | | | | | | | | | |
| Current | 2.8 | 1.7 | 1.2 | | | | | 1.7 | 1.9 |
| | .7 | .7 | .7 | | | | | .8 | .7 |
| | .2 | .2 | .1 | | | | | .3 | .3 |
| Quick | 1.5 | 1.4 | .9 | | | | | 1.1 | 1.1 |
| | (51) .5 | .3 | .5 | | | | | (150) .5 | .4 |
| | .1 | .1 | .1 | | | | | .1 | .2 |
| Sales/Receivables | 0 UND | 0 UND | 0 UND | | | | | 0 UND | 0 UND |
| | 0 UND | 0 UND | 1 476.7 | | | | | 0 UND | 0 UND |
| | 0 891.2 | 2 242.0 | 3 113.5 | | | | | 2 229.3 | 0 999.8 |
| Cost of Sales/Inventory | | | | | | | | | |
| Cost of Sales/Payables | | | | | | | | | |
| Sales/Working Capital | 25.3 | 16.2 | 32.1 | | | | | 22.8 | 19.4 |
| | -48.9 | -19.6 | -22.0 | | | | | -36.7 | -34.5 |
| | -6.9 | -5.7 | -3.0 | | | | | -8.8 | -7.4 |
| EBIT/Interest | 1.4 | 4.4 | 2.1 | | | | | 3.1 | 2.1 |
| | (34) .1 | (68) 1.5 | (27) 1.1 | | | | | (120) 1.2 | (119) 1.1 |
| | -1.8 | .1 | .3 | | | | | .3 | .1 |
| Net Profit + Depr., Dep., Amort./Cur. Mat. L/T/D | | | | | | | | 2.0 | 3.0 |
| | | | | | | | | (12) 1.3 | (12) 1.2 |
| | | | | | | | | .5 | .7 |
| Fixed/Worth | .9 | 3.2 | 2.8 | | | | | 2.5 | 1.7 |
| | -2.0 | -8.6 | 44.3 | | | | | -148.3 | 14.2 |
| | -.3 | -2.1 | -3.5 | | | | | -1.7 | -1.9 |
| Debt/Worth | 1.9 | 3.3 | 2.0 | | | | | 2.5 | 1.9 |
| | -4.5 | -17.4 | 44.3 | | | | | -64.0 | 51.8 |
| | -1.6 | -3.4 | -4.6 | | | | | -3.5 | -4.1 |
| % Profit Before Taxes/Tangible Net Worth | 36.6 | 33.3 | 30.8 | | | | | 58.2 | 37.2 |
| | (22) 2.1 | (33) 15.9 | (20) 11.3 | | | | | (73) 20.7 | (75) 14.2 |
| | -19.0 | -6.1 | -1.9 | | | | | .9 | -6.2 |
| % Profit Before Taxes/Total Assets | 8.4 | 9.7 | 4.0 | | | | | 12.7 | 7.8 |
| | -3.1 | 3.2 | .4 | | | | | 1.8 | 1.3 |
| | -12.4 | -4.1 | -2.4 | | | | | -4.3 | -4.0 |
| Sales/Net Fixed Assets | 32.7 | 2.4 | 1.5 | | | | | 6.9 | 5.0 |
| | 9.9 | 1.4 | .7 | | | | | 1.9 | 1.8 |
| | 4.3 | .9 | .4 | | | | | 1.0 | 1.0 |
| Sales/Total Assets | 6.2 | 1.6 | .9 | | | | | 3.2 | 2.4 |
| | 3.7 | 1.1 | .5 | | | | | 1.1 | 1.2 |
| | 1.8 | .8 | .4 | | | | | .8 | .7 |
| % Depr., Dep., Amort./Sales | .9 | 4.3 | 6.1 | | | | | 2.9 | 4.4 |
| | (44) 2.8 | (66) 6.5 | (34) 9.3 | | | | | (136) 5.8 | (134) 7.0 |
| | 5.2 | 9.1 | 13.1 | | | | | 9.4 | 10.5 |
| % Officers', Directors' Owners' Comp/Sales | 2.9 | 3.1 | | | | | | 2.9 | 4.0 |
| | (29) 8.1 | (30) 6.2 | | | | | | (66) 5.6 | (65) 7.7 |
| | 14.5 | 18.3 | | | | | | 11.2 | 11.5 |
| Net Sales ($) | 47328M | 93624M | 90448M | 220925M | 94314M | | | 1324514M | 398267M |
| Total Assets ($) | 12733M | 76637M | 141592M | 243122M | 79353M | | | 604673M | 446536M |

M = $ thousand     MM = $ million
See Pages 9 through 22 for Explanation of Ratios and Data

## Comparative Historical Data / Current Data Sorted by Sales

| | | | Type of Statement | | | | | | |
|---|---|---|---|---|---|---|---|---|---|
| 3 | 3 | 4 | Unqualified | 1 | 1 | | | | 2 |
| 15 | 15 | 12 | Reviewed | 2 | 7 | 1 | 1 | 1 | |
| 49 | 52 | 29 | Compiled | 15 | 13 | 1 | 1 | | |
| 75 | 55 | 72 | Tax Returns | 37 | 28 | 6 | 1 | | |
| 37 | 53 | 51 | Other | 18 | 20 | 5 | 1 | 3 | 4 |
| 4/1/09-3/31/10 | 4/1/10-3/31/11 | 4/1/11-3/31/12 | | | 36 (4/1-9/30/11) | | 132 (10/1/11-3/31/12) | | |
| ALL | ALL | ALL | | 0-1MM | 1-3MM | 3-5MM | 5-10MM | 10-25MM | 25MM & OVER |
| 179 | 178 | 168 | NUMBER OF STATEMENTS | 73 | 69 | 12 | 4 | 4 | 6 |
| % | % | % | **ASSETS** | % | % | % | % | % | % |
| 12.2 | 12.5 | 12.3 | Cash & Equivalents | 13.7 | 12.0 | 9.8 | | | |
| .6 | 1.7 | 1.1 | Trade Receivables (net) | .4 | 1.3 | 1.0 | | | |
| 4.6 | 3.5 | 4.3 | Inventory | 4.7 | 4.2 | 2.8 | | | |
| 2.6 | 3.6 | 2.9 | All Other Current | 4.5 | 1.8 | 1.1 | | | |
| 20.0 | 21.2 | 20.5 | Total Current | 23.3 | 19.3 | 14.6 | | | |
| 66.4 | 65.2 | 64.1 | Fixed Assets (net) | 60.9 | 68.1 | 61.7 | | | |
| 4.1 | 5.4 | 5.7 | Intangibles (net) | 6.1 | 5.2 | 6.0 | | | |
| 9.5 | 8.2 | 9.7 | All Other Non-Current | 9.8 | 7.5 | 17.7 | | | |
| 100.0 | 100.0 | 100.0 | Total | 100.0 | 100.0 | 100.0 | | | |
| | | | **LIABILITIES** | | | | | | |
| 4.9 | 9.2 | 5.9 | Notes Payable-Short Term | 3.4 | 6.9 | 16.6 | | | |
| 5.7 | 6.4 | 5.7 | Cur. Mat.-L.T.D. | 4.4 | 7.3 | 5.3 | | | |
| 5.0 | 5.5 | 4.9 | Trade Payables | 3.8 | 5.0 | 11.0 | | | |
| .0 | .1 | .2 | Income Taxes Payable | .3 | .1 | .0 | | | |
| 17.4 | 14.0 | 20.7 | All Other Current | 22.3 | 21.3 | 20.7 | | | |
| 33.0 | 35.2 | 37.4 | Total Current | 34.2 | 40.6 | 53.6 | | | |
| 59.7 | 58.4 | 48.1 | Long-Term Debt | 48.9 | 49.7 | 47.2 | | | |
| .1 | .1 | .2 | Deferred Taxes | .0 | .3 | .0 | | | |
| 17.1 | 23.2 | 28.5 | All Other Non-Current | 39.7 | 22.0 | 6.5 | | | |
| -9.9 | -16.8 | -14.2 | Net Worth | -22.8 | -12.6 | -7.2 | | | |
| 100.0 | 100.0 | 100.0 | Total Liabilties & Net Worth | 100.0 | 100.0 | 100.0 | | | |
| | | | **INCOME DATA** | | | | | | |
| 100.0 | 100.0 | 100.0 | Net Sales | 100.0 | 100.0 | 100.0 | | | |
| | | | Gross Profit | | | | | | |
| 96.3 | 94.4 | 94.1 | Operating Expenses | 94.1 | 93.4 | 96.8 | | | |
| 3.7 | 5.6 | 5.9 | Operating Profit | 5.9 | 6.6 | 3.2 | | | |
| 3.9 | 4.9 | 4.8 | All Other Expenses (net) | 6.3 | 3.8 | 3.2 | | | |
| -.3 | .8 | 1.1 | Profit Before Taxes | -.4 | 2.8 | -.1 | | | |
| | | | **RATIOS** | | | | | | |
| 1.3 | 1.5 | 1.6 | | 2.2 | 1.6 | .8 | | | |
| .7 | .7 | .7 | Current | .6 | .7 | .3 | | | |
| .3 | .3 | .2 | | .2 | .2 | .1 | | | |
| .9 | 1.0 | 1.1 | | 1.6 | 1.1 | .5 | | | |
| (178) .4 | (177) .4 | (167) .4 | Quick | (72) .3 | .5 | .2 | | | |
| .1 | .1 | .1 | | .1 | .1 | .0 | | | |
| 0 UND | 0 UND | 0 UND | | 0 UND | 0 UND | 0 UND | | | |
| 0 UND | 0 UND | 0 UND | Sales/Receivables | 0 UND | 0 UND | 0 UND | | | |
| 1 435.2 | 1 443.2 | 2 240.4 | | 1 604.0 | 2 240.9 | 2 219.2 | | | |
| | | | Cost of Sales/Inventory | | | | | | |
| | | | Cost of Sales/Payables | | | | | | |
| 34.5 | 24.8 | 24.8 | | 20.1 | 23.5 | -50.2 | | | |
| -28.8 | -33.5 | -25.9 | Sales/Working Capital | -19.7 | -28.5 | -7.8 | | | |
| -7.5 | -6.8 | -5.7 | | -5.5 | -9.8 | -2.9 | | | |
| 2.1 | 2.7 | 2.6 | | 2.1 | 2.7 | 17.1 | | | |
| (150) 1.0 | (141) .9 | (138) 1.0 | EBIT/Interest | (55) .4 | (58) 1.8 | 1.0 | | | |
| -.1 | -.1 | -.2 | | -1.1 | .6 | .3 | | | |
| 3.1 | 2.5 | 3.0 | Net Profit + Depr., Dep., | | | | | | |
| (13) 1.1 | (16) 1.4 | (13) 2.0 | Amort./Cur. Mat. L/T/D | | | | | | |
| .1 | .3 | .8 | | | | | | | |
| 1.9 | 2.0 | 2.7 | | 2.7 | 2.3 | 3.1 | | | |
| 22.1 | 32.7 | -503.8 | Fixed/Worth | -12.0 | -49.6 | 17.7 | | | |
| -2.0 | -1.5 | -1.4 | | -1.0 | -1.5 | -1.5 | | | |
| 2.1 | 2.1 | 2.8 | | 2.8 | 2.3 | 2.4 | | | |
| 32.0 | 39.0 | -79.6 | Debt/Worth | -13.2 | -57.6 | 30.4 | | | |
| -3.5 | -2.9 | -3.3 | | -2.7 | -3.5 | -2.8 | | | |
| 31.5 | 47.6 | 29.8 | % Profit Before Taxes/Tangible | 28.5 | 31.2 | | | | |
| (93) 6.0 | (94) 13.6 | (82) 10.9 | Net Worth | (33) 5.1 | (34) 16.1 | | | | |
| -13.1 | -11.9 | -5.8 | | -19.1 | -.8 | | | | |
| 6.0 | 8.9 | 7.6 | % Profit Before Taxes/Total | 4.3 | 8.8 | 6.2 | | | |
| .0 | .5 | .0 | Assets | -2.0 | 3.6 | -.3 | | | |
| -6.4 | -7.2 | -5.7 | | -9.1 | -2.8 | -1.5 | | | |
| 5.8 | 5.6 | 4.9 | | 9.9 | 4.3 | 4.5 | | | |
| 1.9 | 1.9 | 1.9 | Sales/Net Fixed Assets | 1.7 | 1.8 | 2.9 | | | |
| 1.0 | 1.0 | .9 | | .7 | 1.1 | .7 | | | |
| 2.6 | 2.5 | 2.5 | | 2.8 | 2.4 | 2.9 | | | |
| 1.2 | 1.2 | 1.1 | Sales/Total Assets | 1.1 | 1.2 | 2.0 | | | |
| .8 | .8 | .7 | | .6 | .8 | .5 | | | |
| 3.5 | 3.1 | 3.3 | | 2.8 | 3.4 | 2.7 | | | |
| (170) 6.4 | (161) 5.8 | (154) 6.0 | % Depr., Dep., Amort./Sales | (62) 6.0 | (66) 5.8 | 5.5 | | | |
| 10.2 | 9.6 | 9.0 | | 8.9 | 9.2 | 11.2 | | | |
| 2.7 | 3.2 | 2.6 | % Officers', Directors' | 5.8 | 2.4 | | | | |
| (78) 6.3 | (65) 7.0 | (71) 6.1 | Owners' Comp/Sales | (31) 11.4 | (29) 4.0 | | | | |
| 9.8 | 12.7 | 14.4 | | 19.0 | 7.6 | | | | |
| 576261M | 464012M | 546639M | Net Sales ($) | 43679M | 115693M | 41725M | 29306M | 56458M | 259778M |
| 610333M | 452489M | 553437M | Total Assets ($) | 53649M | 114422M | 46746M | 31395M | 69041M | 238184M |

© RMA 2012

M = $ thousand    MM = $ million
See Pages 9 through 22 for Explanation of Ratios and Data

## Current Data Sorted by Assets | Comparative Historical Data

| | | | | | | Type of Statement | | |
|---|---|---|---|---|---|---|---|---|
| 1 | 2 | 19 | 21 | 2 | 5 | Unqualified | 58 | 59 |
| 1 | 1 | 17 | 2 | 1 | | Reviewed | 24 | 21 |
| 8 | 24 | 12 | 6 | | | Compiled | 44 | 44 |
| 65 | 46 | 21 | 2 | | | Tax Returns | 70 | 71 |
| 41 | 34 | 61 | 19 | 6 | 6 | Other | 127 | 105 |
| | 79 (4/1-9/30/11) | | 344 (10/1/11-3/31/12) | | | | 4/1/07-3/31/08 | 4/1/08-3/31/09 |
| 0-500M | 500M-2MM | 2-10MM | 10-50MM | 50-100MM | 100-250MM | | ALL | ALL |
| 116 | 107 | 130 | 50 | 9 | 11 | NUMBER OF STATEMENTS | 323 | 300 |
| % | % | % | % | % | % | ASSETS | % | % |
| 25.1 | 10.5 | 12.4 | 7.9 | | 13.6 | Cash & Equivalents | 16.3 | 16.4 |
| 8.1 | 5.2 | 4.7 | 3.9 | | 4.5 | Trade Receivables (net) | 4.2 | 4.8 |
| 6.2 | 5.4 | 4.8 | 4.9 | | 3.7 | Inventory | 4.6 | 3.8 |
| 3.2 | 1.1 | 2.3 | 1.8 | | 2.8 | All Other Current | 4.3 | 3.0 |
| 42.5 | 22.3 | 24.2 | 18.5 | | 24.6 | Total Current | 29.5 | 28.0 |
| 40.2 | 63.4 | 60.9 | 59.9 | | 46.7 | Fixed Assets (net) | 54.7 | 56.4 |
| 5.6 | 6.7 | 6.4 | 9.9 | | 12.6 | Intangibles (net) | 5.7 | 6.2 |
| 11.7 | 7.6 | 8.6 | 11.8 | | 16.1 | All Other Non-Current | 10.1 | 9.4 |
| 100.0 | 100.0 | 100.0 | 100.0 | | 100.0 | Total | 100.0 | 100.0 |
| | | | | | | LIABILITIES | | |
| 26.6 | 4.0 | 4.1 | 2.5 | | .4 | Notes Payable-Short Term | 6.6 | 13.4 |
| 3.6 | 4.3 | 4.4 | 3.0 | | 2.4 | Cur. Mat.-L.T.D. | 4.4 | 4.4 |
| 10.4 | 5.6 | 6.2 | 3.1 | | 3.3 | Trade Payables | 6.7 | 5.1 |
| .1 | .3 | .1 | .1 | | .0 | Income Taxes Payable | .1 | .3 |
| 18.6 | 9.2 | 12.2 | 10.5 | | 5.2 | All Other Current | 16.9 | 12.3 |
| 59.3 | 23.5 | 26.9 | 19.1 | | 11.4 | Total Current | 34.8 | 35.5 |
| 23.8 | 43.9 | 33.9 | 26.2 | | 35.2 | Long-Term Debt | 32.1 | 34.5 |
| .0 | .1 | .3 | 1.3 | | 1.8 | Deferred Taxes | .2 | .2 |
| 21.6 | 9.9 | 8.3 | 7.3 | | 10.9 | All Other Non-Current | 9.4 | 7.2 |
| -4.8 | 22.7 | 30.6 | 46.1 | | 40.7 | Net Worth | 23.4 | 22.6 |
| 100.0 | 100.0 | 100.0 | 100.0 | | 100.0 | Total Liabilities & Net Worth | 100.0 | 100.0 |
| | | | | | | INCOME DATA | | |
| 100.0 | 100.0 | 100.0 | 100.0 | | 100.0 | Net Sales | 100.0 | 100.0 |
| | | | | | | Gross Profit | | |
| 94.5 | 85.8 | 92.7 | 95.7 | | 81.3 | Operating Expenses | 89.9 | 91.1 |
| 5.5 | 14.2 | 7.3 | 4.3 | | 18.7 | Operating Profit | 10.1 | 8.9 |
| 1.3 | 5.9 | 4.2 | 1.7 | | 5.3 | All Other Expenses (net) | 4.2 | 4.1 |
| 4.1 | 8.3 | 3.1 | 2.6 | | 13.4 | Profit Before Taxes | 5.9 | 4.8 |
| | | | | | | RATIOS | | |
| 3.3 | 2.2 | 1.9 | 2.3 | | 3.3 | | 2.3 | 3.0 |
| 1.1 | .9 | 1.0 | 1.0 | | 1.8 | Current | 1.0 | 1.2 |
| .4 | .3 | .4 | .5 | | .7 | | .5 | .5 |
| 3.0 | 1.8 | 1.7 | 1.7 | | 2.9 | | 1.8 | 2.4 |
| .6 | .6 | .7 | .8 | | 1.4 | Quick | .7 | .8 |
| .2 | .3 | .2 | .4 | | .6 | | .2 | .3 |
| 0 UND | 0 UND | 0 UND | 3 107.1 | | 2 156.2 | | 0 UND | 0 UND |
| 0 UND | 0 UND | 4 83.5 | 13 28.1 | | 7 53.8 | Sales/Receivables | 0 832.8 | 1 591.3 |
| 2 150.0 | 4 88.0 | 16 22.9 | 31 11.6 | | 23 15.8 | | 8 48.5 | 12 29.7 |
| | | | | | | Cost of Sales/Inventory | | |
| | | | | | | Cost of Sales/Payables | | |
| 10.4 | 12.3 | 10.8 | 6.0 | | 5.8 | | 10.3 | 6.5 |
| 285.6 | -102.4 | 268.8 | -287.9 | | 7.3 | Sales/Working Capital | -999.8 | 59.5 |
| -11.1 | -7.1 | -7.0 | -9.2 | | -10.6 | | -11.1 | -11.8 |
| 10.7 | 17.0 | 5.5 | 12.4 | | 14.3 | | 8.9 | 8.5 |
| (70) 2.1 | (82) 2.9 | (106) 1.5 | (44) 2.2 | | (10) 5.2 | EBIT/Interest | (233) 2.5 | (228) 2.7 |
| -.8 | 1.1 | -.5 | .4 | | 2.1 | | .6 | .5 |
| | | 4.4 | | | | | 15.1 | 4.5 |
| | (10) 1.5 | | | | | Net Profit + Depr., Dep., Amort./Cur. Mat. L/T/D | (22) 2.8 | (24) 3.0 |
| | | 1.2 | | | | | 1.2 | .8 |
| .3 | 1.0 | .9 | .8 | | .7 | | .8 | .9 |
| 1.9 | 2.9 | 2.4 | 2.0 | | 1.2 | Fixed/Worth | 1.9 | 1.7 |
| -.9 | -5.3 | -12.0 | 5.0 | | -3.0 | | -25.2 | 55.3 |
| .3 | .5 | .8 | .4 | | .5 | | .5 | .5 |
| 3.6 | 2.9 | 2.8 | 2.0 | | .9 | Debt/Worth | 2.3 | 1.6 |
| -2.7 | -8.2 | -18.5 | 7.6 | | -5.0 | | -26.4 | UND |
| 88.4 | 64.1 | 31.3 | 24.7 | | | % Profit Before Taxes/Tangible Net Worth | 62.0 | 43.1 |
| (70) 49.2 | (73) 20.1 | (92) 5.7 | (43) 7.3 | | | | (238) 15.8 | (227) 12.5 |
| 1.9 | .4 | -3.6 | -3.6 | | | | .7 | -.2 |
| 37.5 | 18.4 | 9.0 | 9.1 | | 33.1 | % Profit Before Taxes/Total Assets | 19.5 | 15.8 |
| 10.9 | 6.2 | 1.5 | 1.9 | | 7.6 | | 5.4 | 4.2 |
| -6.6 | -.1 | -2.6 | -2.7 | | 1.0 | | -1.2 | -2.2 |
| 61.0 | 6.7 | 4.8 | 3.1 | | 2.7 | | 9.9 | 9.0 |
| 9.2 | 1.4 | 1.5 | 1.1 | | 1.4 | Sales/Net Fixed Assets | 2.6 | 2.2 |
| 5.0 | .5 | .6 | .6 | | .7 | | 1.0 | .8 |
| 6.3 | 1.9 | 1.6 | 1.1 | | 1.1 | | 2.9 | 2.7 |
| 3.9 | .9 | .9 | .7 | | .7 | Sales/Total Assets | 1.3 | 1.1 |
| 2.2 | .5 | .5 | .5 | | .3 | | .7 | .5 |
| 1.4 | 2.3 | 3.5 | 5.3 | | | | 2.5 | 3.1 |
| (73) 3.3 | (82) 5.6 | (114) 7.5 | (47) 7.4 | | | % Depr., Dep., Amort./Sales | (258) 5.8 | (234) 6.1 |
| 7.4 | 15.0 | 13.3 | 12.4 | | | | 9.4 | 11.1 |
| 4.3 | 3.4 | 1.7 | | | | | 1.9 | 4.0 |
| (52) 7.7 | (28) 5.7 | (28) 4.3 | | | | % Officers', Directors' Owners' Comp/Sales | (85) 4.9 | (74) 6.1 |
| 11.0 | 8.2 | 6.7 | | | | | 9.9 | 13.2 |
| 122957M | 184719M | 890911M | 1074320M | 589482M | 2454928M | Net Sales ($) | 7839425M | 4029350M |
| 28148M | 118402M | 592434M | 1220409M | 642400M | 2047381M | Total Assets ($) | 5157534M | 4325135M |

M = $ thousand　　MM = $ million
See Pages 9 through 22 for Explanation of Ratios and Data

## Comparative Historical Data

## Current Data Sorted by Sales

| | | | Type of Statement | | | | | | |
|---|---|---|---|---|---|---|---|---|---|
| 48 | 55 | 50 | Unqualified | 1 | 8 | 8 | 12 | 8 | 13 |
| 22 | 25 | 22 | Reviewed | 1 | 4 | 3 | 6 | 7 | 1 |
| 37 | 48 | 50 | Compiled | 24 | 11 | 4 | 6 | 4 | 1 |
| 96 | 90 | 134 | Tax Returns | 73 | 48 | 7 | 3 | 2 | 1 |
| 125 | 128 | 167 | Other | 43 | 49 | 21 | 9 | 22 | 23 |
| 4/1/09-3/31/10 ALL | 4/1/10-3/31/11 ALL | 4/1/11-3/31/12 ALL | | 79 (4/1-9/30/11) | | | 344 (10/1/11-3/31/12) | | |
| | | | | 0-1MM | 1-3MM | 3-5MM | 5-10MM | 10-25MM | 25MM & OVER |
| 328 | 346 | 423 | NUMBER OF STATEMENTS | 142 | 120 | 43 | 36 | 43 | 39 |
| % | % | % | ASSETS | % | % | % | % | % | % |
| 15.0 | 15.9 | 14.8 | Cash & Equivalents | 13.8 | 18.6 | 12.1 | 9.6 | 17.7 | 11.6 |
| 4.2 | 5.2 | 5.6 | Trade Receivables (net) | 5.8 | 4.9 | 3.5 | 7.1 | 7.6 | 6.4 |
| 5.4 | 6.3 | 5.3 | Inventory | 3.8 | 4.1 | 4.3 | 4.8 | 10.9 | 10.3 |
| 4.6 | 3.9 | 2.2 | All Other Current | 1.9 | 1.1 | 3.3 | 1.5 | 2.8 | 5.9 |
| 29.1 | 31.3 | 28.1 | Total Current | 25.3 | 28.7 | 23.1 | 23.0 | 39.0 | 34.3 |
| 55.3 | 54.9 | 55.2 | Fixed Assets (net) | 60.7 | 54.2 | 62.9 | 59.4 | 42.7 | 39.4 |
| 7.3 | 5.2 | 7.0 | Intangibles (net) | 5.5 | 7.3 | 5.4 | 6.5 | 5.7 | 15.4 |
| 8.3 | 8.7 | 9.8 | All Other Non-Current | 8.6 | 9.8 | 8.6 | 11.1 | 12.7 | 11.0 |
| 100.0 | 100.0 | 100.0 | Total | 100.0 | 100.0 | 100.0 | 100.0 | 100.0 | 100.0 |
| | | | LIABILITIES | | | | | | |
| 10.6 | 9.4 | 9.9 | Notes Payable-Short Term | 16.9 | 7.5 | 4.7 | 5.9 | 6.1 | 5.0 |
| 3.6 | 3.5 | 3.9 | Cur. Mat.-L.T.D. | 4.2 | 3.7 | 5.4 | 4.2 | 3.0 | 2.2 |
| 6.5 | 6.5 | 6.7 | Trade Payables | 6.0 | 7.0 | 5.0 | 5.5 | 9.5 | 8.4 |
| .5 | .1 | .1 | Income Taxes Payable | .0 | .3 | .0 | .2 | .1 | .2 |
| 17.3 | 15.1 | 12.7 | All Other Current | 8.3 | 16.4 | 10.2 | 12.9 | 19.1 | 13.1 |
| 38.4 | 34.5 | 33.3 | Total Current | 35.5 | 35.0 | 25.3 | 28.8 | 37.8 | 28.9 |
| 34.0 | 28.3 | 32.5 | Long-Term Debt | 38.4 | 36.4 | 29.3 | 29.6 | 16.5 | 23.4 |
| .2 | .4 | .3 | Deferred Taxes | .0 | .1 | .3 | .8 | .6 | 1.4 |
| 13.2 | 15.1 | 12.4 | All Other Non-Current | 18.0 | 11.8 | 5.7 | 11.1 | 5.7 | 9.7 |
| 14.2 | 21.7 | 21.4 | Net Worth | 8.1 | 16.7 | 39.4 | 29.6 | 39.5 | 36.6 |
| 100.0 | 100.0 | 100.0 | Total Liabilities & Net Worth | 100.0 | 100.0 | 100.0 | 100.0 | 100.0 | 100.0 |
| | | | INCOME DATA | | | | | | |
| 100.0 | 100.0 | 100.0 | Net Sales | 100.0 | 100.0 | 100.0 | 100.0 | 100.0 | 100.0 |
| | | | Gross Profit | | | | | | |
| 92.4 | 91.6 | 91.5 | Operating Expenses | 87.0 | 93.5 | 96.5 | 93.8 | 95.6 | 89.5 |
| 7.6 | 8.4 | 8.5 | Operating Profit | 13.0 | 6.5 | 3.5 | 6.2 | 4.4 | 10.5 |
| 4.3 | 3.7 | 3.5 | All Other Expenses (net) | 6.4 | 2.4 | 2.3 | 1.6 | .6 | 2.8 |
| 3.3 | 4.7 | 5.0 | Profit Before Taxes | 6.7 | 4.1 | 1.2 | 4.7 | 3.8 | 7.7 |
| | | | RATIOS | | | | | | |
| 2.6 | 2.8 | 2.3 | | 4.4 | 2.0 | 2.0 | 1.9 | 2.6 | 2.1 |
| 1.0 | 1.2 | 1.0 | Current | 1.0 | .9 | 1.0 | 1.0 | 1.7 | 1.2 |
| .4 | .4 | .4 | | .3 | .4 | .6 | .3 | .6 | .6 |
| 1.9 | 2.2 | 1.9 | | 3.8 | 1.7 | 1.9 | 1.4 | 2.2 | 1.5 |
| .6 (343) | .7 | .7 | Quick | .6 | .7 | .5 | .8 | 1.1 | .7 |
| .2 | .2 | .2 | | .2 | .3 | .2 | .3 | .2 | .3 |
| 0 UND | 0 UND | 0 UND | | 0 UND | 0 UND | 1 664.7 | 2 227.2 | 1 404.8 | 2 153.0 |
| 1 607.4 | 2 234.4 | 1 404.8 | Sales/Receivables | 0 UND | 0 UND | 5 75.2 | 11 32.7 | 8 45.4 | 8 48.4 |
| 9 41.8 | 13 27.3 | 14 25.7 | | 2 227.4 | 5 69.0 | 17 21.6 | 26 13.8 | 28 13.1 | 23 15.8 |
| | | | Cost of Sales/Inventory | | | | | | |
| | | | Cost of Sales/Payables | | | | | | |
| 8.3 | 7.8 | 9.7 | | 8.9 | 17.3 | 10.6 | 12.4 | 5.1 | 6.4 |
| 722.7 | 67.2 | 322.0 | Sales/Working Capital | NM | -146.1 | 339.9 | NM | 13.8 | 35.5 |
| -7.6 | -9.2 | -9.2 | | -5.3 | -11.2 | -10.2 | -8.4 | -9.0 | -11.4 |
| 7.0 | 8.4 | 9.7 | | 5.5 | 12.4 | 3.8 | 6.0 | 25.8 | 13.6 |
| (253) 2.3 | (246) 1.8 | (320) 2.2 | EBIT/Interest | (93) 1.4 | (93) 2.9 | (38) 1.5 | (28) 1.7 | (35) 6.2 | (33) 3.1 |
| .3 | -.1 | .3 | | -.1 | .6 | -1.2 | .1 | -.5 | 1.6 |
| 4.1 | 5.7 | 3.3 | | | | | | | 2.6 |
| (24) 2.9 | (32) 2.6 | (28) 1.5 | Net Profit + Depr., Dep., Amort./Cur. Mat. L/T/D | | | | | (10) | 1.7 |
| 1.0 | 1.5 | 1.1 | | | | | | | 1.2 |
| .8 | .6 | .8 | | .8 | .9 | .9 | .8 | .3 | 1.0 |
| 1.9 | 1.5 | 2.1 | Fixed/Worth | 3.0 | 2.0 | 1.6 | 2.7 | 1.0 | 2.2 |
| -6.5 | UND | -6.4 | | -3.8 | -5.5 | -172.8 | -3.9 | 3.4 | -2.4 |
| .5 | .4 | .5 | | .3 | .8 | .3 | .4 | .4 | .9 |
| 2.3 | 1.6 | 2.7 | Debt/Worth | 3.1 | 3.4 | 1.3 | 2.2 | 1.0 | 3.4 |
| -7.8 | -43.5 | -8.2 | | -4.0 | -7.9 | -196.7 | -6.4 | 5.4 | -7.1 |
| 36.6 | 47.6 | 53.0 | | 52.6 | 100.0 | 25.2 | 67.5 | 32.0 | 41.0 |
| (226) 7.8 | (255) 11.5 | (291) 13.9 | % Profit Before Taxes/Tangible Net Worth | (89) 15.3 | (83) 25.7 | (32) -.7 | (25) 11.1 | (35) 9.5 | (27) 18.0 |
| -2.9 | -2.5 | -.9 | | -.9 | 1.2 | -9.6 | -1.4 | -.2 | 7.3 |
| 13.1 | 16.5 | 17.4 | | 19.2 | 19.9 | 8.2 | 21.1 | 11.6 | 15.3 |
| 2.9 | 3.4 | 4.2 | % Profit Before Taxes/Total Assets | 3.0 | 5.1 | .9 | 2.8 | 3.5 | 5.8 |
| -3.8 | -2.8 | -1.7 | | -1.8 | -.6 | -3.9 | -2.7 | -4.0 | 1.4 |
| 12.9 | 13.4 | 11.3 | | 8.7 | 17.7 | 3.6 | 5.1 | 22.0 | 19.4 |
| 2.5 | 2.5 | 2.3 | Sales/Net Fixed Assets | 1.4 | 4.6 | 1.5 | 1.7 | 4.9 | 2.7 |
| .9 | .8 | .7 | | .5 | .8 | .9 | .7 | 1.2 | 1.3 |
| 2.9 | 3.3 | 3.2 | | 2.6 | 4.2 | 1.5 | 2.2 | 2.6 | 3.0 |
| 1.3 | 1.2 | 1.2 | Sales/Total Assets | 1.0 | 1.8 | 1.0 | 1.1 | 1.6 | 1.1 |
| .6 | .6 | .5 | | .4 | .7 | .6 | .5 | .7 | .7 |
| 2.1 | 2.4 | 2.8 | | 3.1 | 2.2 | 5.4 | 3.1 | 2.7 | 1.9 |
| (262) 5.3 | (266) 6.2 | (329) 6.3 | % Depr., Dep., Amort./Sales | (102) 7.0 | (91) 4.4 | (38) 9.5 | (31) 6.4 | (37) 5.2 | (30) 6.6 |
| 10.6 | 11.2 | 11.6 | | 16.7 | 11.1 | 14.0 | 8.2 | 7.3 | 10.7 |
| 2.4 | 3.5 | 3.1 | | 5.4 | 3.1 | 2.2 | 1.6 | | |
| (94) 5.1 | (104) 6.6 | (115) 6.3 | % Officers', Directors' Owners' Comp/Sales | (40) 8.5 | (43) 6.3 | (15) 3.8 | (12) 2.6 | | |
| 9.5 | 11.3 | 9.2 | | 14.4 | 8.4 | 4.8 | | | |
| 4646323M | 5009671M | 5317317M | Net Sales ($) | 73311M | 215573M | 167938M | 258606M | 648921M | 3952968M |
| 3951271M | 4783281M | 4649174M | Total Assets ($) | 116279M | 205433M | 211413M | 363436M | 649990M | 3102623M |

M = $ thousand    MM = $ million
See Pages 9 through 22 for Explanation of Ratios and Data

# ACCOMMODATION AND
# FOOD SERVICES

## Current Data Sorted by Assets            Comparative Historical Data

| 0-500M | 500M-2MM | 2-10MM | 10-50MM | 50-100MM | 100-250MM | Type of Statement | 4/1/07-3/31/08 ALL | 4/1/08-3/31/09 ALL |
|---|---|---|---|---|---|---|---|---|
| 1 | 9 | 15 | 40 | 16 | 18 | Unqualified | 139 | 135 |
| 4 | 9 | 54 | 33 | 3 | 3 | Reviewed | 94 | 110 |
| 31 | 76 | 160 | 40 |  |  | Compiled | 275 | 268 |
| 150 | 356 | 523 | 54 | 2 | 5 | Tax Returns | 930 | 893 |
| 62 | 142 | 406 | 124 | 28 | 16 | Other | 545 | 641 |
|  | 120 (4/1-9/30/11) |  | 2,260 (10/1/11-3/31/12) |  |  |  |  |  |
| 248 | 592 | 1158 | 291 | 49 | 42 | **NUMBER OF STATEMENTS** | 1983 | 2047 |
| % | % | % | % | % | % | **ASSETS** | % | % |
| 30.5 | 8.4 | 6.1 | 5.9 | 7.5 | 10.0 | Cash & Equivalents | 9.5 | 8.7 |
| 4.9 | 2.2 | 1.5 | 2.1 | 3.3 | 2.2 | Trade Receivables (net) | 2.3 | 2.4 |
| 2.7 | .8 | .7 | .9 | .5 | .8 | Inventory | 1.0 | .9 |
| 3.7 | 1.6 | 1.3 | 1.4 | 2.3 | 3.2 | All Other Current | 2.2 | 2.0 |
| 41.8 | 13.0 | 9.5 | 10.2 | 13.6 | 16.1 | Total Current | 15.0 | 14.1 |
| 41.2 | 76.2 | 81.7 | 77.6 | 76.4 | 71.4 | Fixed Assets (net) | 74.4 | 74.3 |
| 5.4 | 3.2 | 3.1 | 3.4 | 3.0 | 4.2 | Intangibles (net) | 3.4 | 3.8 |
| 11.6 | 7.6 | 5.7 | 8.8 | 7.0 | 8.3 | All Other Non-Current | 7.2 | 7.8 |
| 100.0 | 100.0 | 100.0 | 100.0 | 100.0 | 100.0 | Total | 100.0 | 100.0 |
|  |  |  |  |  |  | **LIABILITIES** |  |  |
| 9.7 | 2.5 | 1.4 | 3.0 | 1.5 | 3.6 | Notes Payable-Short Term | 2.5 | 3.4 |
| 2.7 | 4.2 | 3.7 | 3.5 | 2.5 | 4.9 | Cur. Mat.-L.T.D. | 3.8 | 4.0 |
| 7.2 | 2.5 | 1.4 | 2.0 | 3.2 | 2.5 | Trade Payables | 2.9 | 2.7 |
| .5 | .0 | .0 | .1 | .0 | .1 | Income Taxes Payable | .1 | .1 |
| 37.6 | 11.8 | 6.8 | 6.8 | 9.5 | 12.5 | All Other Current | 9.2 | 10.7 |
| 57.6 | 21.0 | 13.4 | 15.4 | 16.8 | 23.6 | Total Current | 18.4 | 20.9 |
| 31.1 | 68.4 | 72.0 | 63.8 | 58.8 | 52.8 | Long-Term Debt | 64.4 | 65.4 |
| .0 | .0 | .0 | .4 | .5 | .2 | Deferred Taxes | .0 | .0 |
| 14.5 | 6.7 | 5.0 | 4.4 | 2.3 | 11.5 | All Other Non-Current | 5.8 | 5.6 |
| -3.3 | 3.8 | 9.6 | 15.9 | 21.7 | 11.9 | Net Worth | 11.3 | 8.0 |
| 100.0 | 100.0 | 100.0 | 100.0 | 100.0 | 100.0 | Total Liabilities & Net Worth | 100.0 | 100.0 |
|  |  |  |  |  |  | **INCOME DATA** |  |  |
| 100.0 | 100.0 | 100.0 | 100.0 | 100.0 | 100.0 | Net Sales | 100.0 | 100.0 |
|  |  |  |  |  |  | Gross Profit |  |  |
| 92.4 | 85.3 | 82.3 | 86.8 | 91.8 | 92.6 | Operating Expenses | 81.4 | 84.8 |
| 7.6 | 14.7 | 17.7 | 13.2 | 8.2 | 7.4 | Operating Profit | 18.6 | 15.2 |
| 2.4 | 9.3 | 12.6 | 10.3 | 10.1 | 6.1 | All Other Expenses (net) | 11.4 | 11.0 |
| 5.3 | 5.4 | 5.1 | 2.9 | -2.0 | 1.3 | Profit Before Taxes | 7.2 | 4.2 |
|  |  |  |  |  |  | **RATIOS** |  |  |
| 3.5 | 1.6 | 2.2 | 1.4 | 1.8 | 1.5 | Current | 2.4 | 2.0 |
| 1.1 | .6 | .8 | .7 | 1.0 | .8 |  | 1.0 | .8 |
| .3 | .2 | .2 | .3 | .5 | .1 |  | .3 | .3 |
| 2.8 | 1.4 | 1.8 | 1.2 | 1.4 | 1.1 | Quick | 2.0 | 1.6 |
| (245) .9 | .5 | (1152) .6 | .6 | .6 | .7 | .6 | (1976) .7 | (2044) .6 |
| .2 | .1 | .2 | .2 | .3 | .1 |  | .2 | .2 |
| 0 UND | 0 UND | 0 UND | 2 161.0 | 5 70.9 | 4 91.0 | Sales/Receivables | 0 UND | 0 UND |
| 0 UND | 0 UND | 3 127.4 | 6 58.3 | 10 38.0 | 8 47.4 |  | 3 125.7 | 2 149.4 |
| 3 118.1 | 5 81.0 | 7 50.2 | 12 30.6 | 20 18.7 | 17 21.5 |  | 9 40.1 | 8 45.4 |
|  |  |  |  |  |  | Cost of Sales/Inventory |  |  |
|  |  |  |  |  |  | Cost of Sales/Payables |  |  |
| 14.6 | 21.2 | 10.2 | 18.0 | 5.1 | 13.1 | Sales/Working Capital | 11.4 | 14.9 |
| 270.6 | -19.0 | -35.4 | -21.1 | 999.8 | -36.3 |  | -283.5 | -44.9 |
| -13.6 | -5.2 | -6.1 | -4.8 | -9.1 | -3.0 |  | -8.3 | -6.2 |
| 9.4 | 3.0 | 2.9 | 2.5 | 3.6 | 2.1 | EBIT/Interest | 3.1 | 2.9 |
| (113) 2.2 | (458) 1.7 | (918) 1.6 | (234) 1.5 | (40) 1.6 | (37) 1.1 |  | (1486) 1.8 | (1515) 1.6 |
| .0 | .8 | .9 | .7 | .3 | -.7 |  | 1.1 | .7 |
|  |  | 4.8 | 3.5 |  |  | Net Profit + Depr., Dep., | 6.7 | 6.0 |
|  | (34) 1.9 | (36) 2.3 |  |  |  | Amort./Cur. Mat. L/T/D | (81) 3.2 | (93) 2.8 |
|  | .8 | 1.1 |  |  |  |  | 1.2 | 1.1 |
| .2 | 2.3 | 3.3 | 2.3 | 1.9 | 1.8 | Fixed/Worth | 2.4 | 2.6 |
| 1.5 | 9.8 | 10.6 | 6.6 | 3.3 | 4.1 |  | 7.2 | 8.7 |
| -4.5 | -5.3 | -8.6 | -15.1 | 8.5 | -16.1 |  | -12.9 | -9.1 |
| .4 | 2.0 | 2.9 | 2.1 | 1.5 | 1.3 | Debt/Worth | 2.1 | 2.5 |
| 3.3 | 11.2 | 11.3 | 6.8 | 3.6 | 5.1 |  | 7.7 | 10.3 |
| -3.6 | -7.0 | -10.9 | -19.0 | 10.5 | -13.1 |  | -15.2 | -10.7 |
| 83.7 | 43.8 | 40.9 | 25.4 | 12.1 | 12.1 | % Profit Before Taxes/Tangible | 62.0 | 50.3 |
| (160) 26.1 | (352) 16.0 | (727) 14.8 | (198) 7.0 | (40) 3.4 | (30) 3.6 | Net Worth | (1315) 22.0 | (1293) 15.3 |
| -6.2 | 2.1 | .3 | -4.7 | -9.8 | -9.8 |  | 3.2 | -1.4 |
| 32.7 | 9.0 | 6.2 | 4.6 | 5.2 | 4.7 | % Profit Before Taxes/Total | 9.7 | 7.6 |
| 8.6 | 2.9 | 1.9 | .9 | 1.0 | .0 | Assets | 3.5 | 2.2 |
| -9.2 | -.7 | -1.3 | -1.9 | -2.8 | -3.6 |  | -.5 | -2.2 |
| 161.8 | 1.5 | .7 | .9 | .8 | 1.4 | Sales/Net Fixed Assets | 1.2 | 1.3 |
| 16.8 | .7 | .5 | .5 | .5 | .7 |  | .6 | .6 |
| 3.4 | .4 | .3 | .3 | .3 | .4 |  | .4 | .4 |
| 8.0 | 1.0 | .6 | .6 | .6 | 1.0 | Sales/Total Assets | .8 | .8 |
| 4.0 | .6 | .4 | .4 | .5 | .4 |  | .5 | .5 |
| 1.6 | .4 | .3 | .3 | .3 | .3 |  | .4 | .3 |
| 1.0 | 5.1 | 7.9 | 8.3 | 8.6 | 5.5 | % Depr., Dep., Amort./Sales | 5.7 | 6.2 |
| (153) 3.0 | (516) 9.1 | (1037) 11.7 | (267) 11.6 | (48) 12.1 | (28) 11.4 |  | (1764) 8.7 | (1791) 9.6 |
| 6.0 | 13.6 | 17.0 | 18.6 | 16.3 | 14.1 |  | 12.6 | 14.7 |
| 1.9 | 2.4 | 1.7 | 1.7 |  |  | % Officers', Directors' | 2.2 | 2.2 |
| (97) 4.8 | (193) 4.7 | (252) 3.8 | (42) 3.2 |  |  | Owners' Comp/Sales | (545) 4.2 | (530) 4.4 |
| 8.6 | 8.0 | 6.0 | 5.9 |  |  |  | 7.8 | 7.3 |
| 272803M | 676807M | 2652439M | 3701861M | 1704404M | 4940182M | Net Sales ($) | 12990211M | 11054434M |
| 59021M | 749663M | 5344861M | 5860307M | 3350423M | 6454805M | Total Assets ($) | 18862413M | 18413725M |

M = $ thousand     MM = $ million
See Pages 9 through 22 for Explanation of Ratios and Data

| Comparative Historical Data | | | | Current Data Sorted by Sales | | | | | |
|---|---|---|---|---|---|---|---|---|---|

**Type of Statement**

| | | | Type of Statement | | | | | | |
|---|---|---|---|---|---|---|---|---|---|
| 115 | 107 | 99 | Unqualified | 3 | 11 | 12 | 15 | 19 | 39 |
| 124 | 102 | 106 | Reviewed | 9 | 41 | 16 | 15 | 18 | 7 |
| 316 | 275 | 307 | Compiled | 110 | 127 | 36 | 20 | 11 | 3 |
| 1009 | 889 | 1090 | Tax Returns | 486 | 478 | 75 | 31 | 9 | 11 |
| 683 | 718 | 778 | Other | 203 | 324 | 73 | 83 | 50 | 45 |
| 4/1/09-3/31/10 ALL | 4/1/10-3/31/11 ALL | 4/1/11-3/31/12 ALL | | 120 (4/1-9/30/11) | | | 2,260 (10/1/11-3/31/12) | | |
| | | | | 0-1MM | 1-3MM | 3-5MM | 5-10MM | 10-25MM | 25MM & OVER |
| 2247 | 2091 | 2380 | NUMBER OF STATEMENTS | 811 | 981 | 212 | 164 | 107 | 105 |
| % | % | % | **ASSETS** | % | % | % | % | % | % |
| 8.4 | 8.5 | 9.3 | Cash & Equivalents | 8.8 | 8.9 | 10.7 | 11.2 | 9.6 | 10.5 |
| 2.5 | 2.1 | 2.1 | Trade Receivables (net) | 1.1 | 1.9 | 3.3 | 3.9 | 4.0 | 5.5 |
| .8 | .7 | .9 | Inventory | .4 | .8 | 2.0 | 1.9 | 2.1 | 1.5 |
| 1.8 | 1.6 | 1.7 | All Other Current | 1.4 | 1.5 | 2.0 | 2.3 | 3.6 | 2.6 |
| 13.5 | 12.9 | 14.0 | Total Current | 11.7 | 13.0 | 18.0 | 19.3 | 19.2 | 20.0 |
| 74.9 | 75.9 | 75.3 | Fixed Assets (net) | 77.6 | 77.0 | 70.9 | 69.2 | 67.5 | 68.4 |
| 3.5 | 3.8 | 3.4 | Intangibles (net) | 3.2 | 3.6 | 2.8 | 4.2 | 2.9 | 3.7 |
| 8.0 | 7.5 | 7.3 | All Other Non-Current | 7.5 | 6.4 | 8.3 | 7.3 | 10.4 | 7.9 |
| 100.0 | 100.0 | 100.0 | Total | 100.0 | 100.0 | 100.0 | 100.0 | 100.0 | 100.0 |
| | | | **LIABILITIES** | | | | | | |
| 2.7 | 2.7 | 2.8 | Notes Payable-Short Term | 3.6 | 1.9 | 3.2 | 2.6 | 3.4 | 3.0 |
| 3.9 | 3.6 | 3.7 | Cur. Mat.-L.T.D. | 3.4 | 3.9 | 3.0 | 4.7 | 3.8 | 4.3 |
| 3.1 | 2.4 | 2.4 | Trade Payables | 1.6 | 2.3 | 2.9 | 4.4 | 4.6 | 3.8 |
| .1 | .1 | .1 | Income Taxes Payable | .0 | .1 | .0 | .2 | .0 | .1 |
| 11.2 | 10.3 | 11.4 | All Other Current | 12.9 | 9.3 | 12.7 | 12.0 | 12.5 | 15.3 |
| 21.1 | 19.1 | 20.4 | Total Current | 21.5 | 17.5 | 21.9 | 23.9 | 24.3 | 26.4 |
| 66.5 | 65.9 | 65.2 | Long-Term Debt | 65.9 | 67.6 | 69.5 | 56.0 | 52.9 | 57.0 |
| .0 | .1 | .1 | Deferred Taxes | .0 | .0 | .0 | .4 | .3 | .3 |
| 6.8 | 6.8 | 6.4 | All Other Non-Current | 7.1 | 5.7 | 6.9 | 6.8 | 5.1 | 7.3 |
| 5.7 | 8.2 | 7.9 | Net Worth | 5.5 | 9.2 | 1.7 | 12.8 | 17.3 | 9.0 |
| 100.0 | 100.0 | 100.0 | Total Liabilities & Net Worth | 100.0 | 100.0 | 100.0 | 100.0 | 100.0 | 100.0 |
| | | | **INCOME DATA** | | | | | | |
| 100.0 | 100.0 | 100.0 | Net Sales | 100.0 | 100.0 | 100.0 | 100.0 | 100.0 | 100.0 |
| | | | Gross Profit | | | | | | |
| 88.4 | 86.1 | 85.0 | Operating Expenses | 82.8 | 84.6 | 86.1 | 89.3 | 90.0 | 91.9 |
| 11.6 | 13.9 | 15.0 | Operating Profit | 17.2 | 15.4 | 13.9 | 10.7 | 10.0 | 8.1 |
| 12.4 | 11.2 | 10.3 | All Other Expenses (net) | 13.4 | 9.7 | 8.4 | 6.1 | 6.8 | 5.3 |
| -.8 | 2.7 | 4.7 | Profit Before Taxes | 3.9 | 5.6 | 5.5 | 4.6 | 3.3 | 2.7 |
| | | | **RATIOS** | | | | | | |
| 1.7 | 1.9 | 2.0 | Current | 1.7 | 2.3 | 2.3 | 1.9 | 1.9 | 1.5 |
| .6 | .7 | .7 | | .5 | .8 | 1.0 | .9 | .8 | .9 |
| .2 | .2 | .2 | | .2 | .3 | .4 | .4 | .4 | .4 |
| 1.5 | 1.6 | 1.7 | Quick | 1.4 | 2.0 | 1.7 | 1.6 | 1.1 | 1.1 |
| (2245) .5 | (2086) .6 | (2371) .6 | | (806) .4 | (979) .7 | (210) .7 | .6 | .6 | .7 |
| .2 | .2 | .2 | | .1 | .2 | .2 | .2 | .3 | .2 |
| 0 UND | 0 UND | 0 UND | Sales/Receivables | 0 UND | 0 UND | 2 215.5 | 2 181.7 | 4 94.8 | 5 67.7 |
| 2 146.9 | 3 143.0 | 2 155.1 | | 0 UND | 3 127.4 | 5 79.8 | 6 58.7 | 8 46.4 | 10 37.3 |
| 8 45.7 | 8 46.1 | 7 49.1 | | 3 127.7 | 7 51.7 | 8 44.0 | 11 31.9 | 15 23.7 | 18 20.0 |
| | | | Cost of Sales/Inventory | | | | | | |
| | | | Cost of Sales/Payables | | | | | | |
| 18.0 | 15.2 | 13.4 | Sales/Working Capital | 21.6 | 10.8 | 10.7 | 12.8 | 12.8 | 12.6 |
| -22.4 | -30.3 | -33.1 | | -15.3 | -64.6 | NM | -53.6 | -23.8 | -68.7 |
| -4.9 | -5.8 | -6.0 | | -4.3 | -7.0 | -7.4 | -6.9 | -8.5 | -7.0 |
| 2.4 | 2.8 | 3.0 | EBIT/Interest | 2.4 | 3.2 | 3.2 | 3.6 | 3.9 | 3.7 |
| (1555) 1.2 | (1460) 1.5 | (1800) 1.6 | | (509) 1.4 | (793) 1.7 | (169) 1.6 | (141) 1.6 | (96) 1.9 | (92) 1.4 |
| .2 | .6 | .7 | | .6 | .9 | .7 | .7 | .8 | .1 |
| 2.4 | 4.0 | 4.5 | Net Profit + Depr., Dep., Amort./Cur. Mat. L/T/D | | 4.6 | | 2.6 | 17.1 | 3.6 |
| (73) 1.5 | (74) 2.0 | (96) 2.4 | | | (32) 1.7 | | (12) 1.6 | (21) 3.5 | (18) 2.6 |
| .6 | .7 | 1.1 | | | .9 | | .9 | 1.7 | 1.3 |
| 2.7 | 2.5 | 2.3 | Fixed/Worth | 2.3 | 2.7 | 2.3 | 1.8 | 1.2 | 1.7 |
| 10.8 | 8.8 | 7.8 | | 8.1 | 9.0 | 15.1 | 7.2 | 3.4 | 3.2 |
| -7.0 | -8.2 | -7.7 | | -10.2 | -7.7 | -5.3 | -5.4 | -18.5 | -48.9 |
| 2.5 | 2.3 | 2.1 | Debt/Worth | 2.1 | 2.4 | 2.3 | 1.7 | 1.1 | 1.5 |
| 13.0 | 10.5 | 8.8 | | 8.7 | 10.6 | 19.6 | 7.6 | 4.1 | 4.6 |
| -8.5 | -10.0 | -9.5 | | -10.5 | -9.7 | -6.7 | -7.9 | -26.0 | -14.1 |
| 26.6 | 37.7 | 40.9 | % Profit Before Taxes/Tangible Net Worth | 33.3 | 49.7 | 46.9 | 47.0 | 30.9 | 25.1 |
| (1363) 4.9 | (1314) 9.6 | (1507) 12.9 | | (515) 9.5 | (614) 17.2 | (120) 17.4 | (104) 20.4 | (78) 11.7 | (76) 7.1 |
| -12.2 | -5.2 | -.9 | | -3.0 | 1.1 | -1.1 | 1.2 | -1.4 | -8.4 |
| 4.5 | 6.3 | 7.7 | % Profit Before Taxes/Total Assets | 5.8 | 8.4 | 9.8 | 9.4 | 10.9 | 7.3 |
| .0 | 1.3 | 2.1 | | 1.4 | 2.8 | 2.4 | 2.4 | 2.5 | 1.6 |
| -4.2 | -2.5 | -1.6 | | -1.8 | -1.2 | -1.6 | -1.3 | -1.3 | -2.8 |
| 1.2 | 1.1 | 1.2 | Sales/Net Fixed Assets | .9 | 1.0 | 1.9 | 1.8 | 2.5 | 2.0 |
| .5 | .5 | .6 | | .5 | .6 | .7 | .9 | .9 | 1.0 |
| .3 | .3 | .4 | | .3 | .4 | .4 | .5 | .6 | .5 |
| .8 | .8 | .8 | Sales/Total Assets | .6 | .8 | 1.1 | 1.1 | 1.4 | 1.1 |
| .4 | .4 | .5 | | .4 | .5 | .6 | .6 | .7 | .7 |
| .3 | .3 | .3 | | .2 | .3 | .4 | .4 | .4 | .4 |
| 6.9 | 6.6 | 6.4 | % Depr., Dep., Amort./Sales | 7.7 | 6.5 | 5.2 | 4.7 | 4.8 | 6.5 |
| (1991) 11.2 | (1827) 10.6 | (2049) 10.5 | | (695) 11.4 | (841) 10.8 | (180) 9.5 | (150) 8.5 | (98) 8.3 | (85) 9.0 |
| 16.8 | 15.9 | 15.8 | | 17.5 | 16.0 | 15.0 | 12.3 | 12.1 | 12.1 |
| 2.3 | 2.1 | 2.0 | % Officers', Directors' Owners' Comp/Sales | 2.6 | 1.8 | 1.3 | 1.4 | 1.7 | 1.8 |
| (576) 4.4 | (523) 4.2 | (592) 4.0 | | (254) 4.9 | (239) 3.8 | (43) 3.1 | (29) 2.4 | (16) 2.7 | (11) 4.0 |
| 7.9 | 7.7 | 7.2 | | 8.7 | 6.3 | 5.2 | 4.6 | 4.9 | 12.0 |
| 11528331M | 11010263M | 13948496M | Net Sales ($) | 465584M | 1745688M | 798051M | 1151950M | 1608047M | 8179176M |
| 19491656M | 18957806M | 21819080M | Total Assets ($) | 1406240M | 4339140M | 1512597M | 2103236M | 2770408M | 9687459M |

M = $ thousand    MM = $ million
See Pages 9 through 22 for Explanation of Ratios and Data

## Current Data Sorted by Assets     Comparative Historical Data

| 0-500M | 500M-2MM | 2-10MM | 10-50MM | 50-100MM | 100-250MM | Type of Statement | ALL 4/1/07-3/31/08 | ALL 4/1/08-3/31/09 |
|---|---|---|---|---|---|---|---|---|
| | 1 | 1 | 8 | 12 | 12 | Unqualified | 26 | 13 |
| | | 4 | 2 | | | Reviewed | 2 | 1 |
| 1 | 3 | 2 | 3 | | | Compiled | 2 | |
| 3 | 3 | 2 | 13 | 11 | 17 | Tax Returns | | 3 |
| | 22 (4/1-9/30/11) | | 76 (10/1/11-3/31/12) | | | Other | 30 | 43 |
| 0-500M | 500M-2MM | 2-10MM | 10-50MM | 50-100MM | 100-250MM | | | |
| 4 | 7 | 9 | 26 | 23 | 29 | NUMBER OF STATEMENTS | 60 | 60 |
| % | % | % | % | % | % | **ASSETS** | % | % |
| | | | 12.0 | 14.5 | 13.4 | Cash & Equivalents | 17.4 | 12.5 |
| | | | .9 | 2.1 | .6 | Trade Receivables (net) | 1.0 | 3.6 |
| | | | .6 | .6 | .4 | Inventory | .8 | .7 |
| | | | 5.4 | 1.2 | 1.8 | All Other Current | 1.8 | 4.0 |
| | | | 18.9 | 18.4 | 16.2 | Total Current | 21.0 | 20.8 |
| | | | 75.3 | 71.0 | 74.9 | Fixed Assets (net) | 73.5 | 71.8 |
| | | | 2.8 | 8.5 | 3.3 | Intangibles (net) | 2.7 | 2.1 |
| | | | 3.1 | 2.2 | 5.7 | All Other Non-Current | 2.8 | 5.3 |
| | | | 100.0 | 100.0 | 100.0 | Total | 100.0 | 100.0 |
| | | | | | | **LIABILITIES** | | |
| | | | .9 | 1.7 | 3.2 | Notes Payable-Short Term | 1.2 | 1.3 |
| | | | 5.5 | 4.2 | 16.5 | Cur. Mat.-L.T.D. | 3.6 | 14.9 |
| | | | 2.3 | 3.0 | 1.4 | Trade Payables | 3.7 | 4.7 |
| | | | .0 | .0 | .6 | Income Taxes Payable | .0 | .1 |
| | | | 8.3 | 8.2 | 7.4 | All Other Current | 11.2 | 11.9 |
| | | | 17.1 | 17.0 | 29.1 | Total Current | 19.7 | 33.0 |
| | | | 36.8 | 35.9 | 36.6 | Long-Term Debt | 36.3 | 30.2 |
| | | | .1 | .0 | .8 | Deferred Taxes | .1 | .1 |
| | | | 8.0 | 3.8 | 8.5 | All Other Non-Current | 3.3 | 5.9 |
| | | | 38.0 | 43.3 | 25.0 | Net Worth | 40.6 | 30.8 |
| | | | 100.0 | 100.0 | 100.0 | Total Liabilties & Net Worth | 100.0 | 100.0 |
| | | | | | | **INCOME DATA** | | |
| | | | 100.0 | 100.0 | 100.0 | Net Sales | 100.0 | 100.0 |
| | | | | | | Gross Profit | | |
| | | | 82.9 | 79.1 | 79.0 | Operating Expenses | 74.2 | 82.2 |
| | | | 17.1 | 20.9 | 21.0 | Operating Profit | 25.8 | 17.8 |
| | | | 2.7 | 4.1 | 10.5 | All Other Expenses (net) | 4.4 | 5.2 |
| | | | 14.4 | 16.8 | 10.6 | Profit Before Taxes | 21.4 | 12.6 |
| | | | | | | **RATIOS** | | |
| | | | 1.6 | 1.6 | 1.5 | | 1.8 | 1.6 |
| | | | 1.0 | 1.1 | 1.1 | Current | 1.2 | .8 |
| | | | .6 | .6 | .8 | | .7 | .5 |
| | | | 1.2 | 1.5 | 1.3 | | 1.7 | 1.5 |
| | | | .8 | 1.1 | .9 | Quick | 1.1 | .7 |
| | | | .4 | .5 | .7 | | .5 | .3 |
| | | | 1 362.6 | 1 330.2 | 1 287.2 | | 1 726.6 | 1 483.6 |
| | | | 2 224.2 | 2 154.6 | 3 138.8 | Sales/Receivables | 2 217.5 | 2 182.2 |
| | | | 5 79.2 | 5 80.6 | 3 108.0 | | 4 82.7 | 5 74.0 |
| | | | | | | Cost of Sales/Inventory | | |
| | | | | | | Cost of Sales/Payables | | |
| | | | 17.3 | 10.5 | 10.0 | | 12.1 | 15.2 |
| | | | 319.4 | 61.3 | 70.9 | Sales/Working Capital | 38.9 | -50.3 |
| | | | -23.6 | -15.9 | -39.8 | | -18.6 | -10.0 |
| | | | 9.8 | 14.3 | 21.3 | | 37.9 | 14.4 |
| | | | (24) 2.7 | (21) 6.6 | (22) 10.8 | EBIT/Interest | (51) 7.9 | (52) 6.0 |
| | | | .0 | 1.8 | 3.3 | | 1.7 | 1.1 |
| | | | | | | Net Profit + Depr., Dep., Amort./Cur. Mat. L/T/D | | |
| | | | 1.2 | 1.2 | 1.4 | | 1.1 | 1.2 |
| | | | 2.5 | 1.9 | 2.7 | Fixed/Worth | 1.6 | 1.9 |
| | | | 4.3 | 10.0 | 337.8 | | 4.3 | 8.7 |
| | | | .6 | .6 | .7 | | .5 | .7 |
| | | | 2.5 | 1.4 | 2.2 | Debt/Worth | 1.1 | 1.4 |
| | | | 4.1 | 10.6 | 453.9 | | 4.6 | 9.8 |
| | | | 70.6 | 69.1 | 66.9 | % Profit Before Taxes/Tangible | 134.1 | 89.2 |
| | | | (23) 26.5 | (19) 65.7 | (23) 47.4 | Net Worth | (49) 60.0 | (48) 38.2 |
| | | | -11.4 | 13.4 | 6.8 | | 26.9 | 17.9 |
| | | | 27.4 | 27.2 | 35.6 | % Profit Before Taxes/Total | 72.1 | 35.1 |
| | | | 10.2 | 16.7 | 16.3 | Assets | 22.5 | 13.0 |
| | | | -3.4 | 3.6 | -2.2 | | 3.5 | -.4 |
| | | | 1.9 | 2.1 | 1.3 | | 2.5 | 1.9 |
| | | | 1.6 | 1.2 | 1.1 | Sales/Net Fixed Assets | 1.8 | 1.3 |
| | | | .8 | 1.0 | .7 | | 1.1 | .9 |
| | | | 1.4 | 1.6 | 1.0 | | 1.8 | 1.4 |
| | | | 1.1 | 1.0 | .8 | Sales/Total Assets | 1.3 | 1.0 |
| | | | .6 | .7 | .6 | | .8 | .7 |
| | | | 5.8 | 5.7 | 6.9 | | 4.2 | 5.8 |
| | | | 7.3 | (21) 7.3 | (11) 7.5 | % Depr., Dep., Amort./Sales | (41) 6.5 | (28) 7.5 |
| | | | 9.6 | 10.6 | 13.4 | | 9.8 | 11.2 |
| | | | | | | % Officers', Directors' Owners' Comp/Sales | | |
| 2663M | 9373M | 30236M | 897894M | 2035617M | 4203858M | Net Sales ($) | 8495224M | 6417783M |
| 752M | 7836M | 51970M | 707425M | 1764532M | 5206961M | Total Assets ($) | 6337226M | 6611135M |

© RMA 2012

M = $ thousand    MM = $ million
See Pages 9 through 22 for Explanation of Ratios and Data

## Comparative Historical Data                                    Current Data Sorted by Sales

| 4/1/09-3/31/10 ALL | 4/1/10-3/31/11 ALL | 4/1/11-3/31/12 ALL | Type of Statement | 0-1MM | 1-3MM | 3-5MM | 5-10MM | 10-25MM | 25MM & OVER |
|---|---|---|---|---|---|---|---|---|---|
| 24 | 28 | 32 | Unqualified | | 1 | | 1 | 4 | 26 |
| 3 | 4 | 4 | Reviewed | | 1 | | 1 | 1 | 1 |
| 2 | 2 | 4 | Compiled | 1 | 1 | | 1 | | |
| 4 | 2 | 9 | Tax Returns | | | 1 | 1 | | |
| 46 | 57 | 49 | Other | 3 | 3 | 1 | | 2 | 37 |
| | | | | 3 | 4 | | 1 | 4 | |
| | | | | | 22 (4/1-9/30/11) | | | 76 (10/1/11-3/31/12) | |
| 79 | 93 | 98 | **NUMBER OF STATEMENTS** | 7 | 10 | 3 | 3 | 11 | 64 |
| % | % | % | **ASSETS** | % | % | % | % | % | % |
| 16.0 | 16.0 | 13.6 | Cash & Equivalents | | 12.6 | | | 9.2 | 14.3 |
| 2.4 | 1.5 | 1.4 | Trade Receivables (net) | | 4.2 | | | .8 | 1.2 |
| .7 | 1.2 | .6 | Inventory | | .7 | | | .9 | .5 |
| 2.9 | 1.9 | 3.1 | All Other Current | | 6.8 | | | 2.9 | 2.1 |
| 22.1 | 20.6 | 18.7 | Total Current | | 24.3 | | | 13.8 | 18.2 |
| 68.0 | 70.8 | 71.5 | Fixed Assets (net) | | 58.8 | | | 77.7 | 73.1 |
| 3.9 | 4.0 | 4.7 | Intangibles (net) | | 6.0 | | | 2.7 | 5.2 |
| 6.1 | 4.6 | 5.2 | All Other Non-Current | | 10.9 | | | 5.8 | 3.6 |
| 100.0 | 100.0 | 100.0 | Total | | 100.0 | | | 100.0 | 100.0 |
| | | | **LIABILITIES** | | | | | | |
| 1.8 | 2.6 | 1.8 | Notes Payable-Short Term | | 1.5 | | | 1.3 | 2.2 |
| 17.3 | 6.4 | 8.2 | Cur. Mat.-L.T.D. | | 3.9 | | | 2.2 | 10.7 |
| 3.3 | 2.5 | 2.2 | Trade Payables | | 1.7 | | | 4.1 | 1.9 |
| .2 | .1 | .2 | Income Taxes Payable | | .0 | | | .0 | .3 |
| 10.0 | 10.0 | 7.5 | All Other Current | | 7.0 | | | 7.2 | 8.3 |
| 32.6 | 21.4 | 19.9 | Total Current | | 14.1 | | | 14.8 | 23.4 |
| 34.6 | 34.1 | 43.1 | Long-Term Debt | | 63.5 | | | 58.8 | 33.5 |
| .3 | .4 | .3 | Deferred Taxes | | .0 | | | 1.1 | .3 |
| 9.1 | 7.3 | 7.2 | All Other Non-Current | | 11.7 | | | 8.6 | 6.1 |
| 23.4 | 36.7 | 29.6 | Net Worth | | 10.8 | | | 16.7 | 36.8 |
| 100.0 | 100.0 | 100.0 | Total Liabilities & Net Worth | | 100.0 | | | 100.0 | 100.0 |
| | | | **INCOME DATA** | | | | | | |
| 100.0 | 100.0 | 100.0 | Net Sales | | 100.0 | | | 100.0 | 100.0 |
| | | | Gross Profit | | | | | | |
| 83.6 | 83.0 | 81.0 | Operating Expenses | | 86.1 | | | 93.5 | 77.8 |
| 16.4 | 17.0 | 19.0 | Operating Profit | | 13.9 | | | 6.5 | 22.2 |
| 5.6 | 4.8 | 6.7 | All Other Expenses (net) | | 3.4 | | | 8.7 | 5.9 |
| 10.8 | 12.2 | 12.3 | Profit Before Taxes | | 10.5 | | | -2.1 | 16.3 |
| | | | **RATIOS** | | | | | | |
| 2.1 | 1.9 | 1.7 | Current | | 4.3 | | | 1.5 | 1.6 |
| 1.1 | 1.1 | 1.1 | | | .7 | | | 1.1 | 1.1 |
| .5 | .6 | .6 | | | .2 | | | .6 | .8 |
| 1.8 | 1.7 | 1.5 | Quick | | 4.1 | | | 1.1 | 1.4 |
| (77) 1.0 | 1.0 | (97) .8 | | | .4 | | | .8 | .9 |
| .4 | .4 | .4 | | | .1 | | | .4 | .6 |
| 1  451.2 | 1  379.2 | 1  349.9 | Sales/Receivables | | 0  UND | | | 1  267.6 | 1  324.5 |
| 2  217.2 | 2  202.0 | 2  154.4 | | | 4  81.7 | | | 3  105.8 | 2  153.8 |
| 4  91.7 | 4  94.2 | 4  93.4 | | | 9  38.6 | | | 8  44.4 | 3  107.4 |
| | | | Cost of Sales/Inventory | | | | | | |
| | | | Cost of Sales/Payables | | | | | | |
| 11.4 | 10.3 | 10.5 | Sales/Working Capital | | 8.0 | | | 14.3 | 11.1 |
| 83.4 | 59.5 | 148.1 | | | -40.5 | | | 34.6 | 107.7 |
| -16.9 | -14.5 | -13.3 | | | -6.6 | | | -9.2 | -30.9 |
| 14.6 | 16.1 | 16.5 | EBIT/Interest | | | | | 3.9 | 21.3 |
| (67) 6.4 | (82) 3.7 | (82) 3.9 | | | | | (10) | .6 | (54) 8.4 |
| 1.0 | .3 | 1.1 | | | | | | -.1 | 2.2 |
| | | 3.2 | Net Profit + Depr., Dep., | | | | | | |
| | (10) 2.0 | | Amort./Cur. Mat. L/T/D | | | | | | |
| | | .5 | | | | | | | |
| 1.0 | 1.1 | 1.3 | Fixed/Worth | | 1.0 | | | 2.9 | 1.2 |
| 1.8 | 1.9 | 2.8 | | | NM | | | 3.6 | 2.0 |
| -30.2 | 5.3 | 34.8 | | | -1.4 | | | 11.0 | 8.9 |
| .5 | .6 | .7 | Debt/Worth | | .2 | | | 2.7 | .6 |
| 1.7 | 1.4 | 2.6 | | | NM | | | 3.1 | 1.5 |
| -50.6 | 5.1 | 42.8 | | | -2.7 | | | 13.6 | 9.7 |
| 70.3 | 72.5 | 70.1 | % Profit Before Taxes/Tangible | | | | | | 69.7 |
| (57) 39.5 | (75) 32.8 | (76) 50.1 | Net Worth | | | | | (53) | 53.4 |
| 8.4 | 1.7 | 4.2 | | | | | | | 13.1 |
| 28.6 | 29.0 | 25.9 | % Profit Before Taxes/Total | | 23.2 | | | 8.1 | 35.8 |
| 9.4 | 8.3 | 9.4 | Assets | | 6.9 | | | -1.4 | 17.7 |
| -1.6 | -1.5 | -1.0 | | | .9 | | | -3.6 | 2.7 |
| 2.8 | 2.4 | 2.0 | Sales/Net Fixed Assets | | 12.2 | | | 1.5 | 2.1 |
| 1.6 | 1.3 | 1.2 | | | 1.7 | | | .9 | 1.2 |
| .9 | .9 | .7 | | | .5 | | | .7 | .9 |
| 1.7 | 1.4 | 1.4 | Sales/Total Assets | | 2.1 | | | 1.1 | 1.3 |
| 1.0 | .9 | .9 | | | 1.3 | | | .7 | 1.0 |
| .7 | .6 | .6 | | | .3 | | | .5 | .7 |
| 4.9 | 5.5 | 5.9 | % Depr., Dep., Amort./Sales | | | | | 7.4 | 5.9 |
| (53) 6.6 | (61) 7.2 | (74) 7.3 | | | | | | 9.5 | (44) 7.0 |
| 9.1 | 9.9 | 10.2 | | | | | | 12.5 | 8.8 |
| 2.5 | | 2.9 | % Officers', Directors' | | | | | | |
| (11) 6.7 | (14) 6.0 | | Owners' Comp/Sales | | | | | | |
| 13.8 | | 12.5 | | | | | | | |
| 6496012M | 8126110M | 7179641M | Net Sales ($) | 3472M | 18518M | 12231M | 21762M | 187406M | 6936252M |
| 6625493M | 7751044M | 7739476M | Total Assets ($) | 10708M | 36326M | 28125M | 28837M | 424472M | 7211008M |

M = $ thousand     MM = $ million
See Pages 9 through 22 for Explanation of Ratios and Data

## Current Data Sorted by Assets

## Comparative Historical Data

| | | | | | | | Type of Statement | | |
|---|---|---|---|---|---|---|---|---|---|
| | | 1 | 2 | 2 | | 1 | Unqualified | 4 | 2 |
| | | 1 | 3 | 1 | | | Reviewed | 3 | 6 |
| 2 | | 16 | 9 | 1 | | | Compiled | 18 | 13 |
| 12 | | 27 | 10 | 1 | | | Tax Returns | 36 | 34 |
| 3 | | 12 | 25 | 4 | | | Other | 26 | 22 |
| | | 7 (4/1-9/30/11) | | 126 (10/1/11-3/31/12) | | | | 4/1/07- 3/31/08 | 4/1/08- 3/31/09 |
| 0-500M | | 500M-2MM | 2-10MM | 10-50MM | 50-100MM | 100-250MM | | ALL | ALL |
| 17 | | 57 | 49 | 9 | | 1 | NUMBER OF STATEMENTS | 87 | 77 |
| % | | % | % | % | % | % | ASSETS | % | % |
| 15.8 | | 7.4 | 9.2 | | | | Cash & Equivalents | 8.8 | 11.5 |
| 3.4 | | .9 | 1.7 | | | | Trade Receivables (net) | 2.0 | 2.3 |
| 3.0 | | 1.8 | .8 | | | | Inventory | 3.4 | 5.4 |
| 4.4 | | .6 | 2.0 | | | | All Other Current | 2.2 | 1.4 |
| 26.6 | | 10.8 | 13.7 | | | | Total Current | 16.4 | 20.5 |
| 63.4 | | 76.1 | 67.0 | | | | Fixed Assets (net) | 70.0 | 69.1 |
| 9.0 | | 6.6 | 7.3 | | | | Intangibles (net) | 5.7 | 3.4 |
| 1.0 | | 6.6 | 11.9 | | | | All Other Non-Current | 7.9 | 7.0 |
| 100.0 | | 100.0 | 100.0 | | | | Total | 100.0 | 100.0 |
| | | | | | | | LIABILITIES | | |
| 3.2 | | 4.8 | 2.4 | | | | Notes Payable-Short Term | 5.1 | 4.0 |
| 2.7 | | 4.6 | 2.0 | | | | Cur. Mat.-L.T.D. | 3.4 | 3.2 |
| 1.0 | | 2.4 | 1.0 | | | | Trade Payables | 1.9 | 1.5 |
| .0 | | .0 | .0 | | | | Income Taxes Payable | .0 | .0 |
| 20.7 | | 7.3 | 13.0 | | | | All Other Current | 8.3 | 9.3 |
| 27.5 | | 19.1 | 18.5 | | | | Total Current | 18.8 | 18.0 |
| 64.2 | | 65.4 | 55.3 | | | | Long-Term Debt | 59.3 | 52.1 |
| .0 | | .1 | .0 | | | | Deferred Taxes | .1 | .0 |
| 29.7 | | 12.1 | 5.0 | | | | All Other Non-Current | 12.2 | 10.9 |
| -21.5 | | 3.4 | 21.2 | | | | Net Worth | 9.6 | 19.0 |
| 100.0 | | 100.0 | 100.0 | | | | Total Liabilities & Net Worth | 100.0 | 100.0 |
| | | | | | | | INCOME DATA | | |
| 100.0 | | 100.0 | 100.0 | | | | Net Sales | 100.0 | 100.0 |
| | | | | | | | Gross Profit | | |
| 85.7 | | 82.9 | 85.3 | | | | Operating Expenses | 82.2 | 85.8 |
| 14.3 | | 17.1 | 14.7 | | | | Operating Profit | 17.8 | 14.2 |
| 4.0 | | 8.7 | 12.7 | | | | All Other Expenses (net) | 10.1 | 7.9 |
| 10.4 | | 8.3 | 2.0 | | | | Profit Before Taxes | 7.8 | 6.3 |
| | | | | | | | RATIOS | | |
| 13.0 | | 1.9 | 2.7 | | | | | 2.1 | 4.1 |
| 2.2 | | .7 | 1.1 | | | | Current | .7 | 1.3 |
| .4 | | .2 | .3 | | | | | .3 | .4 |
| 11.0 | | 1.5 | 1.6 | | | | | 1.4 | 3.2 |
| (16) 1.8 | | (56) .6 | .8 | | | | Quick | .5 (76) | .7 |
| .2 | | .1 | .2 | | | | | .1 | .2 |
| 0 UND | | 0 UND | 0 UND | | | | | 0 UND | 0 UND |
| 0 UND | | 0 UND | 0 UND | | | | Sales/Receivables | 0 UND | 0 UND |
| 0 UND | | 0 UND | 5 76.5 | | | | | 3 111.8 | 2 231.2 |
| | | | | | | | Cost of Sales/Inventory | | |
| | | | | | | | Cost of Sales/Payables | | |
| 5.3 | | 44.2 | 10.3 | | | | | 14.5 | 6.6 |
| 20.6 | | -21.1 | 65.8 | | | | Sales/Working Capital | -19.9 | 90.5 |
| -25.1 | | -5.9 | -3.9 | | | | | -7.0 | -9.0 |
| 36.4 | | 2.8 | 5.0 | | | | | 3.6 | 6.2 |
| (10) 4.0 | | (45) 1.5 | (33) 1.8 | | | | EBIT/Interest | (59) 2.1 | (55) 2.3 |
| 1.1 | | .8 | .7 | | | | | .8 | 1.2 |
| | | | | | | | Net Profit + Depr., Dep., Amort./Cur. Mat. L/T/D | | |
| 1.6 | | 4.2 | 1.4 | | | | | 1.8 | 1.1 |
| 8.5 | | 89.7 | 4.3 | | | | Fixed/Worth | 7.0 | 3.6 |
| -.3 | | -3.2 | -5.5 | | | | | -3.3 | -5.0 |
| .8 | | 3.7 | 1.3 | | | | | 1.7 | .7 |
| 11.8 | | 89.9 | 7.9 | | | | Debt/Worth | 6.8 | 3.9 |
| -1.9 | | -4.5 | -7.2 | | | | | -5.8 | -7.0 |
| | | 128.6 | 47.9 | | | | | 59.0 | 46.3 |
| | | (31) 13.2 | (30) 7.1 | | | | % Profit Before Taxes/Tangible Net Worth | (55) 27.9 | (51) 19.6 |
| | | 3.9 | -.6 | | | | | 3.5 | .7 |
| 23.1 | | 10.9 | 8.0 | | | | | 12.2 | 12.7 |
| 11.9 | | 2.8 | .7 | | | | % Profit Before Taxes/Total Assets | 4.6 | 4.3 |
| -7.3 | | -.7 | -1.8 | | | | | -.7 | -1.0 |
| 6.1 | | 1.7 | 1.2 | | | | | 3.1 | 2.8 |
| 2.1 | | .7 | .7 | | | | Sales/Net Fixed Assets | .9 | 1.0 |
| 1.6 | | .4 | .4 | | | | | .5 | .5 |
| 3.4 | | 1.1 | .8 | | | | | 1.5 | 1.6 |
| 1.6 | | .5 | .5 | | | | Sales/Total Assets | .7 | .8 |
| .7 | | .3 | .3 | | | | | .4 | .4 |
| 3.4 | | 6.3 | 6.8 | | | | | 4.7 | 3.7 |
| (16) 8.2 | | (48) 11.6 | (45) 12.2 | | | | % Depr., Dep., Amort./Sales | (71) 8.7 | (69) 8.8 |
| 15.4 | | 16.9 | 25.1 | | | | | 13.1 | 15.3 |
| | | 4.4 | | | | | | 3.8 | 2.6 |
| | | (24) 6.8 | | | | | % Officers', Directors' Owners' Comp/Sales | (36) 7.5 | (28) 5.5 |
| | | 12.2 | | | | | | 11.0 | 9.2 |
| 7269M | | 64225M | 134630M | 125040M | | 57112M | Net Sales ($) | 507058M | 356328M |
| 4494M | | 70500M | 230052M | 171234M | | 106353M | Total Assets ($) | 661868M | 570055M |

M = $ thousand　　MM = $ million
See Pages 9 through 22 for Explanation of Ratios and Data

| Comparative Historical Data | | | | Current Data Sorted by Sales | | | | | |
|---|---|---|---|---|---|---|---|---|---|
| | | | **Type of Statement** | | | | | | |
| | 4 | 6 | Unqualified | | | | 3 | 2 | 1 |
| 5 | 4 | 5 | Reviewed | 1 | 2 | | 1 | 1 | |
| 21 | 16 | 28 | Compiled | 13 | 9 | 5 | 1 | | |
| 47 | 49 | 50 | Tax Returns | 36 | 10 | 3 | 1 | | |
| 31 | 31 | 44 | Other | 18 | 17 | 3 | 2 | 3 | 1 |
| 4/1/09-3/31/10 | 4/1/10-3/31/11 | 4/1/11-3/31/12 | | 7 (4/1-9/30/11) | | | 126 (10/1/11-3/31/12) | | |
| ALL | ALL | ALL | | 0-1MM | 1-3MM | 3-5MM | 5-10MM | 10-25MM | 25MM & OVER |
| 104 | 104 | 133 | **NUMBER OF STATEMENTS** | 68 | 38 | 11 | 8 | 6 | 2 |
| % | % | % | **ASSETS** | % | % | % | % | % | % |
| 8.6 | 12.0 | 9.3 | Cash & Equivalents | 6.3 | 10.4 | 19.2 | | | |
| 1.2 | 1.6 | 1.7 | Trade Receivables (net) | .3 | 3.4 | 3.2 | | | |
| 3.8 | 3.1 | 1.5 | Inventory | 1.2 | 1.5 | 3.7 | | | |
| 1.1 | 2.0 | 1.7 | All Other Current | 1.7 | 1.5 | 1.9 | | | |
| 14.7 | 18.7 | 14.3 | Total Current | 9.6 | 16.8 | 27.9 | | | |
| 72.1 | 64.2 | 70.1 | Fixed Assets (net) | 78.9 | 65.5 | 58.1 | | | |
| 5.7 | 6.5 | 7.4 | Intangibles (net) | 7.1 | 9.2 | 6.4 | | | |
| 7.5 | 10.6 | 8.2 | All Other Non-Current | 4.3 | 8.5 | 7.5 | | | |
| 100.0 | 100.0 | 100.0 | Total | 100.0 | 100.0 | 100.0 | | | |
| | | | **LIABILITIES** | | | | | | |
| 2.9 | 2.2 | 3.3 | Notes Payable-Short Term | 4.5 | 1.9 | 5.8 | | | |
| 4.4 | 3.0 | 3.3 | Cur. Mat.-L.T.D. | 3.8 | 3.0 | 2.9 | | | |
| 1.5 | 1.5 | 1.7 | Trade Payables | .6 | 1.5 | 8.3 | | | |
| 1.0 | .1 | .1 | Income Taxes Payable | .0 | .0 | .8 | | | |
| 8.4 | 11.5 | 11.6 | All Other Current | 9.3 | 14.9 | 6.7 | | | |
| 18.2 | 18.4 | 20.1 | Total Current | 18.1 | 21.4 | 24.4 | | | |
| 63.0 | 55.4 | 60.7 | Long-Term Debt | 65.1 | 67.3 | 50.0 | | | |
| .0 | .0 | .1 | Deferred Taxes | .0 | .1 | .3 | | | |
| 7.3 | 7.9 | 11.3 | All Other Non-Current | 18.5 | 1.1 | 5.8 | | | |
| 11.4 | 18.4 | 7.9 | Net Worth | -1.7 | 10.1 | 19.5 | | | |
| 100.0 | 100.0 | 100.0 | Total Liabilities & Net Worth | 100.0 | 100.0 | 100.0 | | | |
| | | | **INCOME DATA** | | | | | | |
| 100.0 | 100.0 | 100.0 | Net Sales | 100.0 | 100.0 | 100.0 | | | |
| | | | Gross Profit | | | | | | |
| 79.7 | 83.5 | 84.6 | Operating Expenses | 83.7 | 84.9 | 82.7 | | | |
| 20.3 | 16.5 | 15.4 | Operating Profit | 16.3 | 15.1 | 17.3 | | | |
| 10.1 | 8.5 | 9.7 | All Other Expenses (net) | 11.2 | 11.6 | 5.8 | | | |
| 10.1 | 8.1 | 5.7 | Profit Before Taxes | 5.1 | 3.4 | 11.5 | | | |
| | | | **RATIOS** | | | | | | |
| 2.6 | 3.0 | 2.2 | Current | 2.2 | 2.4 | 5.6 | | | |
| .8 | 1.2 | .8 | | .7 | .8 | 1.2 | | | |
| .3 | .4 | .3 | | .2 | .2 | .8 | | | |
| 2.2 | 2.1 | 1.7 | Quick | 1.8 | 1.6 | 5.0 | | | |
| .6 | .9 | (131) .7 | | (66) .6 | .5 | 1.0 | | | |
| .1 | .2 | .2 | | .1 | .2 | .6 | | | |
| 0 UND | 0 UND | 0 UND | Sales/Receivables | 0 UND | 0 UND | 0 UND | | | |
| 0 UND | 0 UND | 0 UND | | 0 UND | 0 UND | 0 UND | | | |
| 2 183.3 | 2 231.9 | 2 149.2 | | 0 UND | 6 59.4 | 0 UND | | | |
| | | | Cost of Sales/Inventory | | | | | | |
| | | | Cost of Sales/Payables | | | | | | |
| 9.3 | 11.1 | 11.6 | Sales/Working Capital | 15.0 | 9.7 | 4.4 | | | |
| -114.3 | 64.3 | -37.4 | | -33.0 | -54.4 | 82.2 | | | |
| -7.0 | -10.8 | -5.4 | | -4.8 | -3.9 | -21.1 | | | |
| 5.7 | 5.5 | 5.0 | EBIT/Interest | 2.1 | 3.9 | | | | |
| (66) 2.4 | (69) 2.5 | (95) 1.7 | | (43) 1.5 | (31) 1.6 | | | | |
| 1.2 | 1.0 | .9 | | .8 | .6 | | | | |
| | | | Net Profit + Depr., Dep., Amort./Cur. Mat. L/T/D | | | | | | |
| 1.4 | 1.0 | 1.9 | Fixed/Worth | 4.2 | 1.6 | 2.1 | | | |
| 6.4 | 4.8 | 16.6 | | 107.4 | 130.8 | 3.1 | | | |
| -3.7 | -7.1 | -3.0 | | -3.0 | -1.4 | -3.0 | | | |
| .9 | .8 | 1.6 | Debt/Worth | 3.4 | 1.0 | 1.4 | | | |
| 7.7 | 5.1 | 21.4 | | 111.5 | 383.4 | 2.9 | | | |
| -6.2 | -11.0 | -4.7 | | -4.4 | -3.1 | -9.5 | | | |
| 67.4 | 48.5 | 84.1 | % Profit Before Taxes/Tangible Net Worth | 85.3 | 66.2 | | | | |
| (66) 17.9 | (67) 13.0 | (76) 12.7 | | (35) 12.6 | (20) 8.6 | | | | |
| 3.6 | 2.6 | 1.6 | | -3.1 | -.4 | | | | |
| 13.5 | 13.6 | 11.0 | % Profit Before Taxes/Total Assets | 8.5 | 9.8 | 40.9 | | | |
| 4.3 | 4.7 | 2.7 | | 1.9 | .7 | 7.9 | | | |
| -.1 | -1.0 | -1.3 | | -1.5 | -3.7 | .7 | | | |
| 2.3 | 3.2 | 1.9 | Sales/Net Fixed Assets | 1.1 | 1.8 | 7.1 | | | |
| .8 | 1.0 | .8 | | .5 | .8 | 1.3 | | | |
| .4 | .5 | .4 | | .3 | .6 | .8 | | | |
| 1.3 | 1.2 | 1.1 | Sales/Total Assets | .7 | 1.1 | 2.3 | | | |
| .6 | .7 | .6 | | .4 | .7 | .8 | | | |
| .3 | .4 | .3 | | .3 | .4 | .4 | | | |
| 5.2 | 5.2 | 4.8 | % Depr., Dep., Amort./Sales | 9.0 | 5.9 | 3.2 | | | |
| (87) 10.4 | (88) 11.2 | (119) 11.8 | | (58) 15.0 | (35) 11.3 | 8.6 | | | |
| 18.1 | 16.5 | 18.5 | | 18.7 | 27.0 | 12.0 | | | |
| 2.7 | 3.4 | 3.3 | % Officers', Directors' Owners' Comp/Sales | 2.9 | 4.9 | | | | |
| (35) 5.8 | (35) 6.3 | (43) 6.2 | | (25) 5.8 | (11) 7.4 | | | | |
| 10.8 | 8.6 | 10.6 | | 11.8 | 10.6 | | | | |
| 1183808M | 454006M | 388276M | Net Sales ($) | 36418M | 64734M | 41215M | 55173M | 80718M | 110018M |
| 1033571M | 702323M | 582633M | Total Assets ($) | 104955M | 119644M | 57540M | 89612M | 81991M | 128891M |

M = $ thousand    MM = $ million
See Pages 9 through 22 for Explanation of Ratios and Data

## Current Data Sorted by Assets      Comparative Historical Data

| Type of Statement | | | | | | | | 7 | 8 |
|---|---|---|---|---|---|---|---|---|---|
| | | | | | | | Unqualified | 7 | 8 |
| | | | | | | | Reviewed | 4 | 2 |
| | | | | | | | Compiled | 5 | 8 |
| | | | | | | | Tax Returns | 22 | 13 |
| | | | | | | | Other | 17 | 9 |

| 0-500M | 500M-2MM | 2-10MM | 10-50MM | 50-100MM | 100-250MM | | 4/1/07-3/31/08 ALL | 4/1/08-3/31/09 ALL |
|---|---|---|---|---|---|---|---|---|
| 5 1 | 2 9 5 14 (4/1-9/30/11) | 2 3 3 3 5 | 8 1 4 37 (10/1/11-3/31/12) | | | | | |
| 6 | 16 | 16 | 13 | | | NUMBER OF STATEMENTS | 55 | 40 |
| % | % | % | % | % | % | ASSETS | % | % |
| | 18.5 | 5.1 | 19.7 | | | Cash & Equivalents | 8.4 | 12.8 |
| | 3.6 | 2.6 | 1.1 | | | Trade Receivables (net) | 3.3 | 3.5 |
| | .4 | .2 | .6 | | | Inventory | 1.7 | 2.0 |
| | .2 | .9 | 2.2 | | | All Other Current | 4.6 | 2.1 |
| | 22.6 | 8.9 | 23.5 | DATA | DATA | Total Current | 17.8 | 20.3 |
| | 71.9 | 67.8 | 53.4 | NOT | NOT | Fixed Assets (net) | 65.5 | 67.3 |
| | .5 | 13.1 | 10.7 | AVAILABLE | AVAILABLE | Intangibles (net) | 4.4 | 2.3 |
| | 5.0 | 10.2 | 12.5 | | | All Other Non-Current | 12.2 | 10.1 |
| | 100.0 | 100.0 | 100.0 | | | Total | 100.0 | 100.0 |
| | | | | | | LIABILITIES | | |
| | 3.4 | 3.3 | 1.4 | | | Notes Payable-Short Term | 5.1 | 5.6 |
| | 2.7 | 6.8 | 3.2 | | | Cur. Mat.-L.T.D. | 4.0 | 4.8 |
| | 1.9 | 1.5 | 1.7 | | | Trade Payables | 3.4 | 1.6 |
| | .0 | .1 | .0 | | | Income Taxes Payable | .0 | .0 |
| | 13.5 | 6.3 | 3.3 | | | All Other Current | 14.5 | 12.7 |
| | 21.6 | 17.9 | 9.6 | | | Total Current | 27.1 | 24.7 |
| | 55.5 | 31.2 | 40.0 | | | Long-Term Debt | 41.8 | 37.6 |
| | .0 | .0 | .0 | | | Deferred Taxes | .1 | .0 |
| | 4.5 | 15.1 | 4.5 | | | All Other Non-Current | 13.2 | 6.0 |
| | 18.4 | 35.8 | 45.9 | | | Net Worth | 17.8 | 31.7 |
| | 100.0 | 100.0 | 100.0 | | | Total Liabilities & Net Worth | 100.0 | 100.0 |
| | | | | | | INCOME DATA | | |
| | 100.0 | 100.0 | 100.0 | | | Net Sales | 100.0 | 100.0 |
| | | | | | | Gross Profit | | |
| | 83.6 | 92.7 | 83.7 | | | Operating Expenses | 87.4 | 93.0 |
| | 16.4 | 7.3 | 16.3 | | | Operating Profit | 12.6 | 7.0 |
| | 6.2 | 4.5 | 3.0 | | | All Other Expenses (net) | 7.5 | 2.9 |
| | 10.2 | 2.9 | 13.3 | | | Profit Before Taxes | 5.1 | 4.1 |
| | | | | | | RATIOS | | |
| | 2.4 | 1.2 | 10.5 | | | | 1.8 | 2.6 |
| | .5 | .9 | 1.1 | | | Current | .5 | 1.1 |
| | .3 | .1 | .5 | | | | .2 | .2 |
| | 2.2 | 1.2 | 10.4 | | | | 1.2 | 1.4 |
| | .5 | .7 | .8 | | | Quick | .3 | .8 |
| | .3 | .1 | .2 | | | | .0 | .1 |
| | 0 UND | 0 UND | 0 UND | | | | 0 UND | 0 UND |
| | 0 UND | 1 326.0 | 2 238.6 | | | Sales/Receivables | 0 UND | 1 293.0 |
| | 5 74.0 | 13 28.7 | 11 31.8 | | | | 3 112.4 | 9 41.8 |
| | | | | | | Cost of Sales/Inventory | | |
| | | | | | | Cost of Sales/Payables | | |
| | 11.8 | 37.5 | 2.1 | | | | 9.0 | 9.3 |
| | -12.6 | -67.3 | 73.6 | | | Sales/Working Capital | -11.5 | 91.1 |
| | -5.6 | -4.0 | -20.1 | | | | -4.6 | -7.5 |
| | 10.0 | 2.9 | 10.3 | | | | 6.9 | 6.5 |
| | (10) 2.8 | (14) 1.9 | (12) 3.9 | | | EBIT/Interest | (41) 1.5 | (34) 2.3 |
| | 1.4 | -.2 | 1.7 | | | | .1 | .3 |
| | | | | | | Net Profit + Depr., Dep., Amort./Cur. Mat. L/T/D | | |
| | 1.2 | 1.1 | .8 | | | | 1.2 | .9 |
| | 3.0 | 2.7 | 1.3 | | | Fixed/Worth | 3.7 | 1.8 |
| | 5.6 | -3.5 | NM | | | | -5.9 | NM |
| | .4 | .3 | .4 | | | | .7 | .4 |
| | 3.0 | 3.2 | .6 | | | Debt/Worth | 3.6 | 1.4 |
| | 7.6 | -4.8 | NM | | | | -6.9 | NM |
| | 30.2 | 19.4 | 121.7 | | | | 51.8 | 23.3 |
| | (13) 14.4 | (10) 5.0 | (10) 13.8 | | | % Profit Before Taxes/Tangible Net Worth | (37) 12.8 | (30) 7.7 |
| | 3.2 | -1.5 | -.4 | | | | -2.6 | -3.4 |
| | 8.0 | 5.7 | 8.9 | | | | 14.0 | 10.7 |
| | 4.0 | 2.5 | 3.8 | | | % Profit Before Taxes/Total Assets | 1.3 | 2.1 |
| | 1.0 | -1.2 | .7 | | | | -2.3 | -3.7 |
| | 2.7 | 1.4 | 1.8 | | | | 4.1 | 2.6 |
| | 1.6 | .8 | 1.1 | | | Sales/Net Fixed Assets | 1.1 | 1.6 |
| | .3 | .4 | .5 | | | | .6 | .7 |
| | 1.9 | .9 | .7 | | | | 1.5 | 1.7 |
| | 1.1 | .6 | .5 | | | Sales/Total Assets | .7 | .8 |
| | .2 | .4 | .3 | | | | .4 | .4 |
| | 4.1 | 5.8 | 4.6 | | | | 4.5 | 4.3 |
| | (12) 6.1 | (13) 8.0 | 5.8 | | | % Depr., Dep., Amort./Sales | (50) 6.7 | (35) 5.3 |
| | 14.6 | 15.8 | 9.5 | | | | 12.2 | 8.5 |
| | | | | | | | 5.1 | 1.7 |
| | | | | | | % Officers', Directors' Owners' Comp/Sales | (16) 8.0 | (16) 4.5 |
| | | | | | | | 13.4 | 9.9 |
| 7448M | 22683M | 64978M | 137679M | | | Net Sales ($) | 357066M | 155074M |
| 1871M | 18531M | 71842M | 259295M | | | Total Assets ($) | 386880M | 303604M |

M = $ thousand    MM = $ million
See Pages 9 through 22 for Explanation of Ratios and Data

## Comparative Historical Data                    ## Current Data Sorted by Sales

| | | | Type of Statement | | | | | | |
|---|---|---|---|---|---|---|---|---|---|
| 7 | 7 | 10 | Unqualified | | 3 | 2 | 1 | 4 | |
| 9 | 7 | 3 | Reviewed | 1 | | 1 | | 1 | |
| 7 | 6 | 6 | Compiled | 1 | 2 | 1 | 1 | 1 | |
| 15 | 16 | 17 | Tax Returns | 5 | 11 | 1 | | | |
| 14 | 12 | 15 | Other | 6 | 5 | | 1 | 3 | |
| 4/1/09-3/31/10 ALL | 4/1/10-3/31/11 ALL | 4/1/11-3/31/12 ALL | | 0-1MM | 14 (4/1-9/30/11) 1-3MM | 3-5MM | 37 (10/1/11-3/31/12) 5-10MM | 10-25MM | 25MM & OVER |
| 52 | 48 | 51 | **NUMBER OF STATEMENTS** | 13 | 21 | 5 | 3 | 9 | |
| % | % | % | **ASSETS** | % | % | % | % | % | % |
| 9.7 | 6.3 | 13.4 | Cash & Equivalents | 6.5 | 16.4 | | | | D |
| 1.7 | 1.8 | 2.2 | Trade Receivables (net) | .6 | 4.4 | | | | A |
| 2.0 | 2.2 | .6 | Inventory | 1.1 | .2 | | | | T |
| 2.3 | 1.6 | 3.7 | All Other Current | 10.9 | .6 | | | | A |
| 15.7 | 11.9 | 19.8 | Total Current | 19.1 | 21.7 | | | | |
| 64.7 | 66.7 | 63.7 | Fixed Assets (net) | 79.7 | 62.1 | | | | N |
| 4.8 | 5.3 | 7.4 | Intangibles (net) | .6 | 5.4 | | | | O |
| 14.8 | 16.2 | 9.1 | All Other Non-Current | .6 | 10.8 | | | | T |
| 100.0 | 100.0 | 100.0 | Total | 100.0 | 100.0 | | | | |
| | | | **LIABILITIES** | | | | | | A |
| 7.7 | 6.9 | 4.6 | Notes Payable-Short Term | 9.9 | 2.0 | | | | V |
| 4.3 | 5.3 | 4.0 | Cur. Mat.-L.T.D. | 1.7 | 4.0 | | | | A |
| 2.5 | 1.8 | 1.5 | Trade Payables | .8 | 1.7 | | | | I |
| .0 | .0 | .0 | Income Taxes Payable | .0 | .0 | | | | L |
| 7.1 | 19.1 | 13.1 | All Other Current | 15.8 | 13.7 | | | | A |
| 21.5 | 33.0 | 23.2 | Total Current | 28.1 | 21.3 | | | | B |
| 34.2 | 41.7 | 40.7 | Long-Term Debt | 47.1 | 40.8 | | | | L |
| .0 | .0 | .0 | Deferred Taxes | .0 | .0 | | | | E |
| 19.1 | 20.8 | 8.3 | All Other Non-Current | 6.5 | 7.4 | | | | |
| 25.1 | 4.5 | 27.8 | Net Worth | 18.3 | 30.5 | | | | |
| 100.0 | 100.0 | 100.0 | Total Liabilties & Net Worth | 100.0 | 100.0 | | | | |
| | | | **INCOME DATA** | | | | | | |
| 100.0 | 100.0 | 100.0 | Net Sales | 100.0 | 100.0 | | | | |
| | | | Gross Profit | | | | | | |
| 91.9 | 90.8 | 87.5 | Operating Expenses | 86.7 | 89.3 | | | | |
| 8.1 | 9.2 | 12.5 | Operating Profit | 13.3 | 10.7 | | | | |
| 3.6 | 3.7 | 4.1 | All Other Expenses (net) | 8.9 | 2.0 | | | | |
| 4.5 | 5.5 | 8.3 | Profit Before Taxes | 4.4 | 8.7 | | | | |
| | | | **RATIOS** | | | | | | |
| 1.6 | 1.0 | 2.5 | | 2.5 | 1.7 | | | | |
| .5 | .3 | .8 | Current | .5 | .8 | | | | |
| .1 | .1 | .2 | | .1 | .4 | | | | |
| 1.2 | .6 | 2.2 | | 2.3 | 1.7 | | | | |
| .3 | .1 | .5 | Quick | .2 | .7 | | | | |
| .1 | .0 | .2 | | .0 | .3 | | | | |
| 0 UND | 0 UND | 0 UND | | 0 UND | 0 UND | | | | |
| 0 UND | 0 UND | 0 999.8 | Sales/Receivables | 0 UND | 2 220.8 | | | | |
| 3 104.5 | 5 76.2 | 8 45.2 | | 0 UND | 17 21.5 | | | | |
| | | | Cost of Sales/Inventory | | | | | | |
| | | | Cost of Sales/Payables | | | | | | |
| 12.9 | NM | 12.3 | | 11.5 | 24.3 | | | | |
| -21.0 | -13.6 | -34.8 | Sales/Working Capital | -3.3 | -79.8 | | | | |
| -8.0 | -4.0 | -6.3 | | -2.5 | -13.5 | | | | |
| 9.1 | 4.1 | 6.5 | | | 7.4 | | | | |
| (39) 2.9 | (39) 1.8 | (39) 2.6 | EBIT/Interest | | (17) 2.7 | | | | |
| 1.2 | .7 | 1.2 | | | 2.0 | | | | |
| | | | Net Profit + Depr., Dep., Amort./Cur. Mat. L/T/D | | | | | | |
| 1.1 | 1.5 | 1.1 | | 1.1 | 1.0 | | | | |
| 2.6 | 5.4 | 2.9 | Fixed/Worth | 3.8 | 2.2 | | | | |
| -12.8 | -6.7 | -4.0 | | -4.7 | NM | | | | |
| .8 | 1.0 | .4 | | .2 | .3 | | | | |
| 2.9 | 8.7 | 3.0 | Debt/Worth | 3.0 | 2.8 | | | | |
| -15.1 | -8.1 | -6.1 | | -5.9 | NM | | | | |
| 25.2 | 29.7 | 25.9 | | | 34.8 | | | | |
| (36) 10.8 | (30) 5.9 | (35) 10.5 | % Profit Before Taxes/Tangible Net Worth | | (16) 14.5 | | | | |
| .0 | -1.9 | .7 | | | 2.2 | | | | |
| 12.4 | 5.0 | 7.2 | | 5.5 | 10.5 | | | | |
| 3.0 | 2.3 | 3.8 | % Profit Before Taxes/Total Assets | 4.6 | 3.7 | | | | |
| -.6 | -1.5 | .6 | | -1.0 | 1.5 | | | | |
| 4.3 | 3.5 | 3.2 | | 2.0 | 6.0 | | | | |
| 1.4 | 1.4 | 1.3 | Sales/Net Fixed Assets | .3 | 1.6 | | | | |
| .7 | .6 | .6 | | .2 | .8 | | | | |
| 1.4 | 1.8 | 1.4 | | 1.0 | 2.2 | | | | |
| .9 | .8 | .7 | Sales/Total Assets | .2 | .9 | | | | |
| .5 | .5 | .4 | | .2 | .5 | | | | |
| 3.4 | 4.3 | 3.7 | | 3.4 | 3.0 | | | | |
| (47) 5.1 | (42) 5.9 | (44) 6.0 | % Depr., Dep., Amort./Sales | (10) 12.5 | (18) 5.3 | | | | |
| 7.9 | 9.1 | 9.1 | | 28.1 | 8.2 | | | | |
| 2.7 | 2.0 | 3.1 | | | 2.8 | | | | |
| (20) 7.7 | (16) 4.0 | (15) 4.8 | % Officers', Directors' Owners' Comp/Sales | | (10) 6.6 | | | | |
| 12.5 | 8.9 | 13.0 | | | 16.9 | | | | |
| 175470M | 164136M | 232788M | Net Sales ($) | 6157M | 42001M | 18422M | 22436M | 143772M | |
| 206861M | 198926M | 351539M | Total Assets ($) | 20964M | 63416M | 29082M | 47452M | 190625M | |

M = $ thousand    MM = $ million
See Pages 9 through 22 for Explanation of Ratios and Data

<table>
<tr><td colspan="6">Current Data Sorted by Assets</td><td></td><td colspan="2">Comparative Historical Data</td></tr>
</table>

| 0-500M | 500M-2MM | 2-10MM | 10-50MM | 50-100MM | 100-250MM | Type of Statement | 4/1/07-3/31/08 ALL | 4/1/08-3/31/09 ALL |
|---|---|---|---|---|---|---|---|---|
|  | 1 | 1 | 2 | 1 |  | Unqualified | 7 | 4 |
|  |  |  | 1 |  |  | Reviewed |  | 1 |
|  |  |  |  |  |  | Compiled | 1 |  |
| 2 | 2 | 2 |  |  |  | Tax Returns | 5 | 4 |
| 3 | 3 | 4 | 1 |  |  | Other | 3 | 6 |
|  |  | 5 | 1 | 1 |  |  |  |  |
| | 17 (4/1-9/30/11) | | 13 (10/1/11-3/31/12) | | | | | |
| 5 | 11 | 8 | 5 | 1 |  | NUMBER OF STATEMENTS | 16 | 15 |
| % | % | % | % | % | % | **ASSETS** | % | % |
|  | 28.4 |  |  |  |  | Cash & Equivalents | 25.5 | 15.5 |
|  | 1.4 |  |  |  |  | Trade Receivables (net) | 6.3 | 1.1 |
|  | .1 |  |  |  |  | Inventory | .3 | .4 |
|  | .4 |  |  |  |  | All Other Current | 5.0 | .4 |
|  | 30.3 |  |  |  |  | Total Current | 37.2 | 17.4 |
|  | 49.6 |  |  |  |  | Fixed Assets (net) | 56.1 | 74.8 |
|  | .0 |  |  |  |  | Intangibles (net) | 4.1 | 3.9 |
|  | 20.1 |  |  |  |  | All Other Non-Current | 2.6 | 3.9 |
|  | 100.0 |  |  |  |  | Total | 100.0 | 100.0 |
|  |  |  |  |  |  | **LIABILITIES** |  |  |
|  | 1.0 |  |  |  |  | Notes Payable-Short Term | 3.7 | 1.8 |
|  | .8 |  |  |  |  | Cur. Mat.-L.T.D. | 3.4 | 2.7 |
|  | .2 |  |  |  |  | Trade Payables | 3.0 | 1.9 |
|  | .0 |  |  |  |  | Income Taxes Payable | .0 | .0 |
|  | 45.7 |  |  |  |  | All Other Current | 7.7 | 2.0 |
|  | 47.7 |  |  |  |  | Total Current | 17.8 | 8.4 |
|  | 47.9 |  |  |  |  | Long-Term Debt | 28.3 | 47.9 |
|  | .0 |  |  |  |  | Deferred Taxes | .0 | .0 |
|  | .0 |  |  |  |  | All Other Non-Current | 3.1 | 2.2 |
|  | 4.4 |  |  |  |  | Net Worth | 50.8 | 41.4 |
|  | 100.0 |  |  |  |  | Total Liabilities & Net Worth | 100.0 | 100.0 |
|  |  |  |  |  |  | **INCOME DATA** |  |  |
|  | 100.0 |  |  |  |  | Net Sales | 100.0 | 100.0 |
|  |  |  |  |  |  | Gross Profit |  |  |
|  | 92.8 |  |  |  |  | Operating Expenses | 83.9 | 91.6 |
|  | 7.2 |  |  |  |  | Operating Profit | 16.1 | 8.4 |
|  | 2.6 |  |  |  |  | All Other Expenses (net) | 4.4 | 8.9 |
|  | 4.6 |  |  |  |  | Profit Before Taxes | 11.8 | -.5 |
|  |  |  |  |  |  | **RATIOS** |  |  |
|  | 33.5 |  |  |  |  | Current | 8.3 | 4.2 |
|  | 1.7 |  |  |  |  |  | 2.1 | 2.1 |
|  | .2 |  |  |  |  |  | 1.2 | .7 |
|  | 32.9 |  |  |  |  | Quick | 8.1 | 4.2 |
|  | 1.7 |  |  |  |  |  | 1.6 | 2.1 |
|  | .2 |  |  |  |  |  | .5 | .1 |
| 0 UND |  |  |  |  |  | Sales/Receivables | 0 UND | 0 UND |
| 0 UND |  |  |  |  |  |  | 8 47.8 | 0 UND |
| 2 180.8 |  |  |  |  |  |  | 27 13.3 | 15 -24.9 |
|  |  |  |  |  |  | Cost of Sales/Inventory |  |  |
|  |  |  |  |  |  | Cost of Sales/Payables |  |  |
|  | 1.3 |  |  |  |  | Sales/Working Capital | 1.4 | 1.5 |
|  | 5.4 |  |  |  |  |  | 13.0 | 4.9 |
|  | -2.8 |  |  |  |  |  | 39.7 | -19.2 |
|  |  |  |  |  |  | EBIT/Interest |  | 3.6 |
|  |  |  |  |  |  |  | (11) | .9 |
|  |  |  |  |  |  |  |  | -2.8 |
|  |  |  |  |  |  | Net Profit + Depr., Dep., Amort./Cur. Mat. L/T/D |  |  |
|  | .5 |  |  |  |  | Fixed/Worth | .4 | .9 |
|  | 3.4 |  |  |  |  |  | 1.7 | 2.4 |
|  | -1.9 |  |  |  |  |  | 6.4 | 5.5 |
|  | .7 |  |  |  |  | Debt/Worth | .1 | .5 |
|  | 3.2 |  |  |  |  |  | 1.1 | 2.0 |
|  | -3.2 |  |  |  |  |  | 6.7 | 5.2 |
|  |  |  |  |  |  | % Profit Before Taxes/Tangible Net Worth | 40.1 | 11.9 |
|  |  |  |  |  |  |  | (15) 10.9 | (13) .4 |
|  |  |  |  |  |  |  | -1.2 | -11.5 |
|  | 16.0 |  |  |  |  | % Profit Before Taxes/Total Assets | 11.2 | 2.4 |
|  | 3.0 |  |  |  |  |  | 4.6 | -.3 |
|  | -9.2 |  |  |  |  |  | -.6 | -8.5 |
|  | 7.8 |  |  |  |  | Sales/Net Fixed Assets | 26.8 | 1.2 |
|  | 2.7 |  |  |  |  |  | 1.0 | .3 |
|  | .4 |  |  |  |  |  | .4 | .2 |
|  | .9 |  |  |  |  | Sales/Total Assets | 1.5 | .6 |
|  | .4 |  |  |  |  |  | .4 | .3 |
|  | .3 |  |  |  |  |  | .3 | .2 |
|  |  |  |  |  |  | % Depr., Dep., Amort./Sales | 8.0 | 8.6 |
|  |  |  |  |  |  |  | (11) 10.0 | (13) 14.3 |
|  |  |  |  |  |  |  | 13.1 | 23.9 |
|  |  |  |  |  |  | % Officers', Directors', Owners' Comp/Sales |  |  |
| 1099M | 8700M | 8904M | 17684M | 10705M |  | Net Sales ($) | 65424M | 36359M |
| 920M | 10615M | 29172M | 108335M | 96697M |  | Total Assets ($) | 102581M | 104662M |

(Middle current-data columns indicated: **DATA NOT AVAILABLE**)

M = $ thousand    MM = $ million
See Pages 9 through 22 for Explanation of Ratios and Data

## Comparative Historical Data

## Current Data Sorted by Sales

| | | | Type of Statement | | | | | | |
|---|---|---|---|---|---|---|---|---|---|
| 7 | 4 | 5 | Unqualified | 1 | | 3 | | 1 | |
| | 1 | 1 | Reviewed | | | | 1 | | |
| 3 | 2 | 4 | Compiled | 3 | 1 | | | | |
| 3 | 12 | 10 | Tax Returns | 9 | 1 | | | | |
| 2 | 3 | 10 | Other | 8 | 1 | | 1 | | |
| 4/1/09- | 4/1/10- | 4/1/11- | | | 17 (4/1-9/30/11) | | 13 (10/1/11-3/31/12) | | |
| 3/31/10 | 3/31/11 | 3/31/12 | | | | | | | |
| ALL | ALL | ALL | | 0-1MM | 1-3MM | 3-5MM | 5-10MM | 10-25MM | 25MM & OVER |
| 15 | 22 | 30 | **NUMBER OF STATEMENTS** | 21 | 3 | 4 | 1 | 1 | |
| % | % | % | **ASSETS** | % | % | % | % | % | % |
| 17.3 | 15.9 | 20.1 | Cash & Equivalents | 19.0 | | | | | D |
| 1.9 | .7 | .8 | Trade Receivables (net) | 1.1 | | | | | A |
| .4 | 1.6 | 1.2 | Inventory | .0 | | | | | T |
| .8 | .5 | .7 | All Other Current | .8 | | | | | A |
| 20.5 | 18.7 | 22.8 | Total Current | 20.9 | | | | | |
| 65.4 | 71.1 | 67.6 | Fixed Assets (net) | 69.5 | | | | | N |
| 3.1 | 3.2 | .9 | Intangibles (net) | .9 | | | | | O |
| 11.0 | 7.0 | 8.7 | All Other Non-Current | 8.7 | | | | | T |
| 100.0 | 100.0 | 100.0 | Total | 100.0 | | | | | |
| | | | **LIABILITIES** | | | | | | A |
| .9 | 3.3 | 2.2 | Notes Payable-Short Term | 2.4 | | | | | V |
| 3.2 | 1.9 | 1.6 | Cur. Mat.-L.T.D. | 1.6 | | | | | A |
| 3.6 | 2.8 | 1.4 | Trade Payables | 1.6 | | | | | I |
| .0 | .0 | .0 | Income Taxes Payable | .0 | | | | | L |
| 3.8 | 2.9 | 25.2 | All Other Current | 14.9 | | | | | A |
| 11.5 | 11.0 | 30.4 | Total Current | 20.5 | | | | | B |
| 43.2 | 49.1 | 51.6 | Long-Term Debt | 55.3 | | | | | L |
| .0 | .0 | .0 | Deferred Taxes | .0 | | | | | E |
| 1.4 | 4.5 | 3.4 | All Other Non-Current | 3.3 | | | | | |
| 43.9 | 35.4 | 14.7 | Net Worth | 20.9 | | | | | |
| 100.0 | 100.0 | 100.0 | Total Liabilities & Net Worth | 100.0 | | | | | |
| | | | **INCOME DATA** | | | | | | |
| 100.0 | 100.0 | 100.0 | Net Sales | 100.0 | | | | | |
| | | | Gross Profit | | | | | | |
| 95.3 | 84.4 | 86.2 | Operating Expenses | 78.6 | | | | | |
| 4.7 | 15.6 | 13.8 | Operating Profit | 21.4 | | | | | |
| 8.7 | 10.4 | 9.6 | All Other Expenses (net) | 12.0 | | | | | |
| -4.0 | 5.2 | 4.2 | Profit Before Taxes | 9.4 | | | | | |
| | | | **RATIOS** | | | | | | |
| 3.4 | 4.7 | 5.4 | | 5.6 | | | | | |
| 2.7 | 1.9 | 1.5 | Current | 1.4 | | | | | |
| .9 | .6 | .2 | | .2 | | | | | |
| 3.4 | 3.5 | 5.3 | | 5.6 | | | | | |
| 2.0 | 1.4 | 1.1 | Quick | .8 | | | | | |
| .7 | .5 | .2 | | .2 | | | | | |
| 0 UND | 0 UND | 0 UND | | 0 UND | | | | | |
| 0 UND | 0 UND | 0 UND | Sales/Receivables | 0 UND | | | | | |
| 18 20.5 | 7 50.0 | 5 75.7 | | 9 41.6 | | | | | |
| | | | Cost of Sales/Inventory | | | | | | |
| | | | Cost of Sales/Payables | | | | | | |
| 2.0 | 4.7 | 3.2 | | 3.8 | | | | | |
| 12.9 | 11.8 | 17.8 | Sales/Working Capital | 34.9 | | | | | |
| -316.0 | -8.0 | -2.9 | | -2.9 | | | | | |
| | 6.5 | 2.9 | | | | | | | |
| | (14) 1.9 | (15) 1.7 | EBIT/Interest | | | | | | |
| | .2 | .5 | | | | | | | |
| | | | Net Profit + Depr., Dep., Amort./Cur. Mat. L/T/D | | | | | | |
| .9 | .9 | 1.8 | | 1.7 | | | | | |
| 1.7 | 2.0 | 4.6 | Fixed/Worth | 3.4 | | | | | |
| 6.1 | NM | -50.2 | | NM | | | | | |
| .2 | .4 | 1.6 | | 1.4 | | | | | |
| .8 | 1.2 | 4.1 | Debt/Worth | 3.2 | | | | | |
| 5.6 | NM | -64.8 | | NM | | | | | |
| 3.5 | 24.4 | 21.1 | | 27.0 | | | | | |
| (12) -4.0 | (17) 3.6 | (22) 11.7 | % Profit Before Taxes/Tangible Net Worth | (16) 17.0 | | | | | |
| -12.6 | -2.3 | -3.2 | | -.3 | | | | | |
| 3.6 | 10.5 | 6.3 | | 10.0 | | | | | |
| -2.0 | 2.0 | 1.2 | % Profit Before Taxes/Total Assets | 3.0 | | | | | |
| -8.9 | -1.8 | -2.4 | | -1.0 | | | | | |
| 1.2 | .8 | 3.0 | | 3.2 | | | | | |
| .8 | .4 | .5 | Sales/Net Fixed Assets | .4 | | | | | |
| .2 | .2 | .3 | | .2 | | | | | |
| .6 | .7 | .8 | | .8 | | | | | |
| .3 | .3 | .3 | Sales/Total Assets | .3 | | | | | |
| .2 | .2 | .1 | | .1 | | | | | |
| 7.3 | 7.3 | 4.0 | | 3.2 | | | | | |
| (11) 10.4 | (16) 13.2 | (24) 9.3 | % Depr., Dep., Amort./Sales | (17) 9.1 | | | | | |
| 17.9 | 20.2 | 19.2 | | 23.8 | | | | | |
| | | | % Officers', Directors' Owners' Comp/Sales | | | | | | |
| 45404M | 41919M | 47092M | Net Sales ($) | 8541M | 6896M | 13939M | 7011M | 10705M | |
| 136878M | 150366M | 245739M | Total Assets ($) | 51247M | 16036M | 71073M | 10686M | 96697M | |

© RMA 2012

**M = $ thousand   MM = $ million**
See Pages 9 through 22 for Explanation of Ratios and Data

## Current Data Sorted by Assets — Comparative Historical Data

| | | | | | | Type of Statement | | |
|---|---|---|---|---|---|---|---|---|
| 3 | 7 | 27 | 53 | 20 | 19 | Unqualified | 129 | 141 |
| 11 | 39 | 84 | 45 | 1 | | Reviewed | 130 | 126 |
| 193 | 234 | 136 | 25 | | 1 | Compiled | 499 | 502 |
| 916 | 558 | 167 | 3 | 3 | 9 | Tax Returns | 1083 | 1102 |
| 434 | 423 | 303 | 140 | 28 | 44 | Other | 951 | 1086 |
| | 271 (4/1-9/30/11) | | 3,655 (10/1/11-3/31/12) | | | | 4/1/07-3/31/08 ALL | 4/1/08-3/31/09 ALL |
| 0-500M | 500M-2MM | 2-10MM | 10-50MM | 50-100MM | 100-250MM | | | |
| 1557 | 1261 | 717 | 266 | 52 | 73 | NUMBER OF STATEMENTS | 2792 | 2957 |
| % | % | % | % | % | % | ASSETS | % | % |
| 21.4 | 13.5 | 13.2 | 12.0 | 8.6 | 9.2 | Cash & Equivalents | 13.7 | 13.9 |
| 2.4 | 1.9 | 2.3 | 2.3 | 3.6 | 3.2 | Trade Receivables (net) | 2.6 | 2.1 |
| 9.7 | 4.5 | 3.8 | 3.4 | 4.1 | 4.8 | Inventory | 6.2 | 6.4 |
| 2.6 | 2.7 | 2.8 | 1.7 | 1.3 | 2.3 | All Other Current | 3.2 | 3.2 |
| 36.1 | 22.6 | 22.1 | 19.4 | 17.7 | 19.5 | Total Current | 25.6 | 25.6 |
| 42.6 | 54.1 | 57.1 | 56.9 | 58.3 | 52.0 | Fixed Assets (net) | 53.1 | 52.6 |
| 10.2 | 10.0 | 10.0 | 16.1 | 17.6 | 19.9 | Intangibles (net) | 11.4 | 10.9 |
| 11.1 | 13.3 | 10.8 | 7.6 | 6.4 | 8.6 | All Other Non-Current | 9.9 | 11.0 |
| 100.0 | 100.0 | 100.0 | 100.0 | 100.0 | 100.0 | Total | 100.0 | 100.0 |
| | | | | | | LIABILITIES | | |
| 9.1 | 4.0 | 2.8 | 2.3 | 1.7 | 1.6 | Notes Payable-Short Term | 5.2 | 6.2 |
| 3.6 | 3.8 | 5.3 | 7.2 | 6.8 | 6.0 | Cur. Mat.-L.T.D. | 4.8 | 4.7 |
| 15.7 | 7.9 | 7.8 | 8.3 | 8.8 | 9.0 | Trade Payables | 10.1 | 10.1 |
| .2 | .1 | .1 | .1 | .2 | .1 | Income Taxes Payable | .2 | .2 |
| 30.7 | 17.0 | 14.3 | 11.4 | 16.8 | 15.1 | All Other Current | 19.8 | 20.6 |
| 59.3 | 32.8 | 30.3 | 29.2 | 34.2 | 31.8 | Total Current | 40.1 | 41.8 |
| 27.3 | 34.6 | 39.5 | 36.4 | 46.5 | 31.5 | Long-Term Debt | 36.5 | 35.9 |
| .0 | .0 | .1 | .4 | .7 | 1.2 | Deferred Taxes | .1 | .1 |
| 21.4 | 11.8 | 8.4 | 7.9 | 11.3 | 15.5 | All Other Non-Current | 11.3 | 11.7 |
| -8.1 | 20.8 | 21.7 | 26.0 | 7.3 | 20.0 | Net Worth | 12.0 | 10.6 |
| 100.0 | 100.0 | 100.0 | 100.0 | 100.0 | 100.0 | Total Liabilities & Net Worth | 100.0 | 100.0 |
| | | | | | | INCOME DATA | | |
| 100.0 | 100.0 | 100.0 | 100.0 | 100.0 | 100.0 | Net Sales | 100.0 | 100.0 |
| 60.2 | 60.8 | 60.3 | 59.7 | 55.3 | 59.0 | Gross Profit | 60.1 | 60.3 |
| 57.0 | 56.3 | 55.2 | 54.1 | 51.1 | 54.9 | Operating Expenses | 56.0 | 56.9 |
| 3.2 | 4.5 | 5.0 | 5.6 | 4.3 | 4.1 | Operating Profit | 4.1 | 3.3 |
| .3 | .9 | 1.5 | 1.3 | 2.9 | 2.0 | All Other Expenses (net) | 1.5 | 1.4 |
| 2.8 | 3.5 | 3.5 | 4.2 | 1.4 | 2.1 | Profit Before Taxes | 2.6 | 1.9 |
| | | | | | | RATIOS | | |
| 2.0 | 1.8 | 1.4 | 1.1 | .9 | .9 | | 1.5 | 1.5 |
| .8 | .8 | .7 | .6 | .6 | .6 | Current | .7 | .7 |
| .3 | .3 | .3 | .4 | .4 | .3 | | .3 | .3 |
| 1.4 | 1.2 | 1.0 | .8 | .7 | .6 | | 1.0 | 1.0 |
| (1542) .5 | (1255) .4 | (715) .5 | .4 | .4 | .3 | Quick | (2769) .4 | (2937) .4 |
| .1 | .1 | .1 | .2 | .2 | .2 | | .1 | .1 |
| 0 UND | 0 UND | 0 UND | 0 999.8 | 0 UND | 0 889.8 | | 0 UND | 0 UND |
| 0 UND | 0 UND | 0 969.4 | 1 287.1 | 1 251.5 | 3 141.9 | Sales/Receivables | 0 UND | 0 UND |
| 0 UND | 1 475.0 | 2 153.8 | 5 79.9 | 6 59.9 | 7 54.6 | | 2 182.5 | 1 255.3 |
| 5 75.1 | 6 64.9 | 7 53.8 | 7 55.6 | 5 69.2 | 9 41.5 | | 6 64.4 | 6 62.8 |
| 9 41.3 | 10 38.4 | 11 34.7 | 10 35.3 | 9 41.7 | 11 32.8 | Cost of Sales/Inventory | 10 36.8 | 10 36.4 |
| 16 22.9 | 16 22.6 | 18 20.8 | 15 24.2 | 20 18.5 | 17 21.5 | | 17 21.0 | 17 21.3 |
| 0 UND | 2 229.7 | 11 32.0 | 15 24.3 | 13 27.7 | 14 25.2 | | 2 156.5 | 2 233.7 |
| 7 50.2 | 15 23.8 | 23 15.9 | 29 12.8 | 24 15.0 | 28 13.2 | Cost of Sales/Payables | 17 21.1 | 16 22.4 |
| 26 14.1 | 33 11.1 | 43 8.5 | 47 7.7 | 47 7.7 | 43 8.4 | | 37 9.8 | 35 10.4 |
| 36.6 | 30.7 | 40.0 | 261.7 | -136.9 | -114.9 | | 49.1 | 49.7 |
| -138.7 | -74.0 | -44.7 | -27.5 | -24.5 | -22.8 | Sales/Working Capital | -49.6 | -45.2 |
| -18.4 | -15.4 | -12.6 | -12.3 | -12.9 | -11.8 | | -13.4 | -12.3 |
| 14.6 | 10.3 | 10.2 | 9.3 | 3.1 | 6.4 | | 7.5 | 7.5 |
| (865) 4.0 | (969) 3.2 | (650) 3.5 | (255) 3.7 | (50) 2.2 | (63) 2.4 | EBIT/Interest | (2180) 2.5 | (2277) 2.3 |
| -.5 | .7 | 1.2 | 1.6 | 1.2 | 1.2 | | .5 | .0 |
| 3.6 | 6.6 | 5.5 | 3.4 | 6.0 | | Net Profit + Depr., Dep., | 5.4 | 4.4 |
| (11) 2.2 | (33) 4.1 | (57) 2.3 | (69) 2.1 | (24) 2.7 | | Amort./Cur. Mat. L/T/D | (183) 2.2 | (188) 1.8 |
| 1.4 | 1.4 | 1.5 | 1.2 | 2.1 | | | 1.0 | .8 |
| .6 | .9 | 1.4 | 1.5 | 2.3 | 1.9 | | 1.1 | 1.0 |
| 2.3 | 3.3 | 4.4 | 6.1 | 32.0 | -63.6 | Fixed/Worth | 4.0 | 4.3 |
| -.9 | -4.5 | -7.5 | -2.9 | -2.3 | -1.6 | | -3.0 | -2.5 |
| .6 | .9 | 1.4 | 1.1 | 3.8 | 2.1 | | 1.1 | 1.1 |
| 4.8 | 4.6 | 5.7 | 7.3 | 40.3 | -106.8 | Debt/Worth | 5.7 | 6.3 |
| -2.6 | -6.9 | -11.2 | -5.0 | -4.0 | -3.2 | | -4.6 | -4.4 |
| 138.8 | 84.4 | 70.0 | 53.5 | 79.8 | 65.1 | % Profit Before Taxes/Tangible | 99.2 | 99.1 |
| (908) 55.1 | (841) 34.4 | (467) 30.2 | (162) 23.6 | (27) 29.9 | (36) 19.0 | Net Worth | (1724) 37.2 | (1782) 34.1 |
| 11.4 | 8.1 | 7.6 | 8.9 | 4.3 | 3.4 | | 7.5 | 4.3 |
| 46.2 | 22.1 | 16.7 | 15.0 | 7.8 | 9.4 | % Profit Before Taxes/Total | 24.8 | 22.9 |
| 14.4 | 8.8 | 6.6 | 6.7 | 4.6 | 4.5 | Assets | 7.6 | 5.9 |
| -4.1 | -.3 | .7 | 2.3 | 1.2 | .4 | | -2.3 | -3.7 |
| 55.7 | 13.6 | 9.0 | 6.2 | 7.4 | 6.7 | | 16.6 | 18.4 |
| 18.8 | 5.7 | 4.4 | 3.8 | 3.2 | 4.3 | Sales/Net Fixed Assets | 6.8 | 6.8 |
| 7.9 | 2.8 | 2.0 | 2.4 | 2.0 | 2.7 | | 3.0 | 3.1 |
| 10.6 | 4.3 | 3.5 | 2.8 | 2.6 | 3.3 | | 5.7 | 5.9 |
| 6.2 | 2.8 | 2.3 | 2.0 | 1.9 | 2.0 | Sales/Total Assets | 3.2 | 3.3 |
| 4.0 | 1.7 | 1.3 | 1.4 | 1.4 | 1.5 | | 1.9 | 1.9 |
| .8 | 1.3 | 1.8 | 2.4 | 3.1 | .8 | | 1.3 | 1.3 |
| (1114) 1.5 | (1041) 2.3 | (652) 2.9 | (250) 3.5 | (46) 3.8 | (19) 3.1 | % Depr., Dep., Amort./Sales | (2357) 2.5 | (2461) 2.6 |
| 2.7 | 4.1 | 4.6 | 4.6 | 4.8 | 4.3 | | 4.2 | 4.3 |
| 2.8 | 2.0 | 1.3 | 1.0 | | .4 | % Officers', Directors' | 2.2 | 2.0 |
| (766) 4.6 | (500) 3.5 | (252) 2.5 | (47) 2.8 | | (14) 2.4 | Owners' Comp/Sales | (1158) 4.2 | (1176) 3.8 |
| 7.4 | 6.1 | 4.6 | 6.1 | | | | 7.4 | 7.1 |
| 2267855M | 4243838M | 8463339M | 13122699M | 10698818M | 38498886M | Net Sales ($) | 46442489M | 56407256M |
| 357715M | 1295950M | 3153133M | 5672355M | 3722879M | 11520309M | Total Assets ($) | 22147813M | 21935029M |

M = $ thousand    MM = $ million
See Pages 9 through 22 for Explanation of Ratios and Data

## Comparative Historical Data | | | | Current Data Sorted by Sales

| Hist 1 | Hist 2 | Hist 3 | Type of Statement | 0-1MM | 1-3MM | 3-5MM | 5-10MM | 10-25MM | 25MM & OVER |
|---|---|---|---|---|---|---|---|---|---|
| 135 | 130 | 129 | Unqualified | 1 | 10 | 1 | 6 | 17 | 94 |
| 172 | 156 | 180 | Reviewed | 2 | 21 | 17 | 33 | 58 | 49 |
| 498 | 511 | 589 | Compiled | 88 | 227 | 105 | 74 | 69 | 26 |
| 1309 | 1271 | 1656 | Tax Returns | 428 | 835 | 214 | 127 | 33 | 19 |
| 1073 | 1215 | 1372 | Other | 186 | 499 | 178 | 148 | 159 | 202 |
| 4/1/09-3/31/10 ALL | 4/1/10-3/31/11 ALL | 4/1/11-3/31/12 ALL | | 271 (4/1-9/30/11) | | | 3,655 (10/1/11-3/31/12) | | |
| 3187 | 3283 | 3926 | **NUMBER OF STATEMENTS** | 705 | 1592 | 515 | 388 | 336 | 390 |
| % | % | % | **ASSETS** | % | % | % | % | % | % |
| 14.7 | 14.8 | 16.3 | Cash & Equivalents | 17.5 | 16.3 | 17.1 | 16.3 | 17.3 | 12.6 |
| 2.0 | 1.9 | 2.2 | Trade Receivables (net) | 1.5 | 2.1 | 2.4 | 2.7 | 2.9 | 2.9 |
| 6.2 | 6.1 | 6.4 | Inventory | 7.7 | 6.9 | 5.9 | 5.1 | 5.2 | 4.3 |
| 2.8 | 2.9 | 2.6 | All Other Current | 2.3 | 2.3 | 3.9 | 3.8 | 1.9 | 1.9 |
| 25.7 | 25.7 | 27.5 | Total Current | 29.0 | 27.6 | 29.3 | 27.8 | 27.4 | 21.8 |
| 52.8 | 51.5 | 50.3 | Fixed Assets (net) | 50.1 | 49.6 | 49.0 | 48.9 | 51.7 | 55.5 |
| 11.4 | 11.3 | 10.8 | Intangibles (net) | 10.1 | 10.0 | 10.1 | 11.1 | 10.6 | 16.1 |
| 10.2 | 11.5 | 11.4 | All Other Non-Current | 10.8 | 12.8 | 11.5 | 12.2 | 10.3 | 6.6 |
| 100.0 | 100.0 | 100.0 | Total | 100.0 | 100.0 | 100.0 | 100.0 | 100.0 | 100.0 |
| | | | **LIABILITIES** | | | | | | |
| 5.4 | 5.5 | 5.6 | Notes Payable-Short Term | 9.6 | 6.3 | 4.7 | 2.8 | 3.0 | 1.9 |
| 5.0 | 4.2 | 4.3 | Cur. Mat.-L.T.D. | 3.5 | 3.2 | 4.2 | 5.7 | 6.3 | 7.1 |
| 9.7 | 10.1 | 11.0 | Trade Payables | 11.1 | 11.2 | 11.8 | 10.4 | 10.9 | 10.2 |
| .1 | .1 | .1 | Income Taxes Payable | .1 | .1 | .2 | .1 | .1 | .1 |
| 21.5 | 19.6 | 21.5 | All Other Current | 26.6 | 23.7 | 18.1 | 17.4 | 16.7 | 16.1 |
| 41.7 | 39.6 | 42.6 | Total Current | 51.0 | 44.6 | 39.0 | 36.4 | 37.0 | 35.5 |
| 36.3 | 34.6 | 32.8 | Long-Term Debt | 31.8 | 32.8 | 32.6 | 34.1 | 29.9 | 36.2 |
| .1 | .1 | .1 | Deferred Taxes | .0 | .0 | .0 | .1 | .3 | .5 |
| 13.2 | 13.4 | 14.8 | All Other Non-Current | 22.8 | 16.0 | 11.8 | 10.4 | 6.8 | 10.5 |
| 8.7 | 12.2 | 9.7 | Net Worth | -5.6 | 6.6 | 16.6 | 19.0 | 26.0 | 17.3 |
| 100.0 | 100.0 | 100.0 | Total Liabilties & Net Worth | 100.0 | 100.0 | 100.0 | 100.0 | 100.0 | 100.0 |
| | | | **INCOME DATA** | | | | | | |
| 100.0 | 100.0 | 100.0 | Net Sales | 100.0 | 100.0 | 100.0 | 100.0 | 100.0 | 100.0 |
| 61.3 | 60.9 | 60.3 | Gross Profit | 60.0 | 60.6 | 61.5 | 60.2 | 59.7 | 58.3 |
| 57.5 | 56.9 | 56.1 | Operating Expenses | 57.4 | 56.5 | 56.5 | 55.6 | 54.6 | 53.7 |
| 3.8 | 4.0 | 4.1 | Operating Profit | 2.6 | 4.1 | 5.0 | 4.6 | 5.0 | 4.6 |
| 1.3 | 1.1 | .9 | All Other Expenses (net) | 1.0 | .8 | .8 | .6 | .9 | 1.4 |
| 2.5 | 2.9 | 3.2 | Profit Before Taxes | 1.6 | 3.3 | 4.3 | 3.9 | 4.1 | 3.2 |
| | | | **RATIOS** | | | | | | |
| 1.6 | 1.6 | 1.7 | Current | 2.6 | 1.8 | 1.7 | 1.5 | 1.3 | 1.0 |
| .7 | .7 | .8 | | .9 | .8 | .8 | .8 | .7 | .6 |
| .3 | .3 | .3 | | .3 | .3 | .4 | .3 | .4 | .3 |
| 1.0 | 1.1 | 1.2 | Quick | 1.6 | 1.3 | 1.2 | 1.1 | 1.0 | .7 |
| (3160) .4 | (3258) .4 | (3903) .4 | | (697) .4 | (1579) .4 | .5 | (387) .5 | (335) .5 | .4 |
| .1 | .1 | .1 | | .1 | .1 | .1 | .2 | .2 | .2 |
| 0 UND | 0 UND | 0 UND | Sales/Receivables | 0 UND | 0 UND | 0 UND | 0 UND | 0 UND | 0 999.8 |
| 0 UND | 0 UND | 0 UND | | 0 UND | 0 UND | 0 UND | 0 999.8 | 1 484.9 | 1 287.1 |
| 1 276.1 | 1 289.7 | 1 303.3 | | 0 UND | 0 999.8 | 1 247.5 | 2 178.1 | 3 120.6 | 5 78.7 |
| 6 64.4 | 6 60.5 | 6 65.4 | Cost of Sales/Inventory | 4 84.0 | 5 67.7 | 6 61.7 | 7 55.7 | 6 57.9 | 7 55.9 |
| 10 35.1 | 10 35.6 | 10 37.6 | | 10 38.3 | 9 38.9 | 10 38.2 | 10 37.8 | 10 36.9 | 10 35.8 |
| 18 20.2 | 17 21.1 | 16 22.3 | | 18 19.8 | 17 21.8 | 15 24.2 | 16 23.5 | 14 25.2 | 15 24.5 |
| 1 424.0 | 2 170.0 | 0 UND | Cost of Sales/Payables | 0 UND | 0 UND | 5 68.5 | 9 39.4 | 12 29.7 | 14 26.4 |
| 16 22.5 | 17 21.7 | 16 23.5 | | 0 UND | 12 29.4 | 18 20.5 | 21 17.2 | 23 16.0 | 27 13.5 |
| 36 10.2 | 36 10.1 | 34 10.7 | | 21 17.0 | 31 11.6 | 38 9.7 | 39 9.4 | 43 8.4 | 45 8.1 |
| 42.6 | 43.7 | 38.4 | Sales/Working Capital | 26.5 | 36.9 | 34.1 | 31.9 | 49.6 | -465.3 |
| -51.2 | -60.6 | -67.4 | | -184.0 | -84.0 | -95.5 | -71.6 | -46.2 | -23.7 |
| -12.4 | -13.4 | -15.3 | | -13.5 | -16.9 | -17.6 | -15.7 | -16.0 | -12.7 |
| 9.1 | 10.3 | 10.8 | EBIT/Interest | 7.0 | 11.3 | 12.2 | 12.0 | 13.8 | 8.3 |
| (2407) 2.8 | (2459) 2.9 | (2852) 3.3 | | (387) 1.7 | (1091) 3.3 | (378) 4.5 | (328) 3.4 | (302) 4.7 | (366) 3.3 |
| .4 | .5 | .8 | | -1.5 | .5 | 1.3 | 1.1 | 1.9 | 1.6 |
| 4.9 | 5.8 | 5.1 | Net Profit + Depr., Dep., Amort./Cur. Mat. L/T/D | | 5.2 | 5.8 | 6.6 | 4.8 | 5.1 |
| (218) 2.4 | (181) 2.3 | (201) 2.3 | | (22) 2.2 | (17) 2.6 | (26) 3.8 | (37) 2.2 | (98) 2.2 | |
| 1.2 | 1.4 | 1.4 | | 1.6 | 1.1 | 1.3 | 1.5 | 1.4 | |
| 1.0 | .9 | .9 | Fixed/Worth | .7 | .8 | .8 | 1.0 | 1.1 | 1.8 |
| 4.3 | 3.7 | 3.5 | | 3.0 | 3.5 | 2.6 | 3.2 | 2.6 | 9.6 |
| -2.3 | -2.4 | -2.3 | | -1.3 | -2.2 | -2.5 | -4.2 | -12.0 | -2.0 |
| 1.0 | .9 | .9 | Debt/Worth | .6 | .8 | .8 | 1.1 | 1.5 | 1.5 |
| 6.1 | 5.4 | 5.5 | | 4.8 | 5.9 | 3.8 | 5.1 | 3.7 | 12.4 |
| -4.3 | -4.4 | -4.7 | | -2.7 | -4.6 | -5.6 | -7.5 | -17.4 | -3.7 |
| 94.1 | 95.3 | 100.5 | % Profit Before Taxes/Tangible Net Worth | 78.0 | 117.0 | 107.9 | 109.1 | 93.3 | 68.4 |
| (1924) 36.5 | (1989) 35.1 | (2441) 36.7 | | (422) 28.3 | (988) 41.5 | (325) 42.2 | (258) 38.2 | (232) 38.4 | (216) 30.1 |
| 7.2 | 7.6 | 9.0 | | .7 | 9.5 | 13.1 | 10.0 | 10.6 | 10.9 |
| 23.9 | 24.8 | 26.0 | % Profit Before Taxes/Total Assets | 26.6 | 29.1 | 31.9 | 22.4 | 22.0 | 15.9 |
| 7.3 | 7.7 | 9.0 | | 4.7 | 9.8 | 13.1 | 8.6 | 10.2 | 7.2 |
| -2.0 | -1.1 | -.2 | | -7.7 | -.9 | 2.0 | .8 | 2.9 | 2.2 |
| 17.6 | 18.7 | 21.2 | Sales/Net Fixed Assets | 32.9 | 28.0 | 22.0 | 15.9 | 13.2 | 8.2 |
| 6.7 | 6.9 | 7.7 | | 8.4 | 9.7 | 8.2 | 6.8 | 6.1 | 5.0 |
| 3.0 | 3.1 | 3.4 | | 3.2 | 3.8 | 3.7 | 3.4 | 3.4 | 3.1 |
| 5.7 | 5.7 | 6.2 | Sales/Total Assets | 6.9 | 7.3 | 5.9 | 5.2 | 4.8 | 3.8 |
| 3.2 | 3.2 | 3.4 | | 3.5 | 4.1 | 3.7 | 3.0 | 3.2 | 2.5 |
| 1.8 | 1.9 | 2.0 | | 1.8 | 2.2 | 2.2 | 2.0 | 2.0 | 1.7 |
| 1.3 | 1.3 | 1.2 | % Depr., Dep., Amort./Sales | .9 | 1.0 | 1.1 | 1.3 | 1.7 | 2.2 |
| (2652) 2.7 | (2652) 2.6 | (3122) 2.3 | | (516) 2.2 | (1226) 2.0 | (424) 2.0 | (337) 2.5 | (306) 2.5 | (313) 3.3 |
| 4.5 | 4.3 | 3.9 | | 4.2 | 3.7 | 3.4 | 4.0 | 3.7 | 4.3 |
| 2.0 | 1.8 | 2.1 | % Officers', Directors' Owners' Comp/Sales | 2.9 | 2.4 | 1.8 | 1.3 | 1.2 | 1.0 |
| (1297) 4.0 | (1340) 3.7 | (1586) 3.8 | | (336) 5.1 | (724) 4.2 | (199) 3.0 | (154) 2.5 | (98) 1.8 | (75) 2.4 |
| 7.0 | 6.7 | 6.5 | | 8.2 | 6.7 | 5.5 | 4.5 | 3.4 | 7.4 |
| 56991284M | 60039762M | 77295435M | Net Sales ($) | 457836M | 2929730M | 1979086M | 2762133M | 5402167M | 63764483M |
| 25318175M | 24590828M | 25722341M | Total Assets ($) | 218144M | 1100789M | 711927M | 1175724M | 2146961M | 20368796M |

© RMA 2012

M = $ thousand    MM = $ million
See Pages 9 through 22 for Explanation of Ratios and Data

## Current Data Sorted by Assets      Comparative Historical Data

| | 0-500M | 500M-2MM | 2-10MM | 10-50MM | 50-100MM | 100-250MM | | 4/1/07-3/31/08 ALL | 4/1/08-3/31/09 ALL |
|---|---|---|---|---|---|---|---|---|---|
| **Type of Statement** | | | | | | | | | |
| Unqualified | 7 | 6 | 19 | 53 | 17 | 17 | | 82 | 95 |
| Reviewed | 1 | 22 | 56 | 28 | 3 | | | 64 | 78 |
| Compiled | 108 | 177 | 204 | 39 | 1 | 1 | | 260 | 373 |
| Tax Returns | 371 | 166 | 75 | 3 | 1 | 1 | | 316 | 481 |
| Other | 228 | 209 | 215 | 126 | 26 | 24 | | 374 | 474 |
| | 176 (4/1-9/30/11) | | | 2,028 (10/1/11-3/31/12) | | | | | |
| NUMBER OF STATEMENTS | 715 | 580 | 569 | 249 | 48 | 43 | | 1096 | 1501 |
| **ASSETS** | % | % | % | % | % | % | | % | % |
| Cash & Equivalents | 20.2 | 16.2 | 15.6 | 10.9 | 8.1 | 6.3 | | 13.9 | 12.7 |
| Trade Receivables (net) | 2.3 | 1.5 | 1.7 | 1.4 | 1.1 | 1.8 | | 1.2 | 1.2 |
| Inventory | 6.4 | 3.4 | 2.5 | 2.1 | 1.6 | 1.6 | | 3.9 | 4.0 |
| All Other Current | 3.2 | 1.9 | 2.3 | 2.5 | 2.1 | 2.4 | | 2.3 | 2.7 |
| Total Current | 32.1 | 23.0 | 22.1 | 17.0 | 12.9 | 12.1 | | 21.4 | 20.5 |
| Fixed Assets (net) | 44.9 | 49.8 | 50.8 | 55.0 | 50.8 | 48.3 | | 52.7 | 51.5 |
| Intangibles (net) | 14.8 | 17.7 | 19.5 | 20.5 | 30.3 | 32.3 | | 16.3 | 18.7 |
| All Other Non-Current | 8.3 | 9.5 | 7.7 | 7.5 | 6.0 | 7.3 | | 9.6 | 9.3 |
| Total | 100.0 | 100.0 | 100.0 | 100.0 | 100.0 | 100.0 | | 100.0 | 100.0 |
| **LIABILITIES** | | | | | | | | | |
| Notes Payable-Short Term | 7.0 | 2.8 | 1.9 | 1.0 | .5 | .9 | | 4.3 | 5.3 |
| Cur. Mat.-L.T.D. | 6.8 | 7.4 | 8.5 | 7.3 | 6.2 | 7.0 | | 6.9 | 6.3 |
| Trade Payables | 9.9 | 7.6 | 6.6 | 5.4 | 4.4 | 5.1 | | 7.8 | 7.7 |
| Income Taxes Payable | .1 | .1 | .1 | .0 | .1 | .2 | | .1 | .1 |
| All Other Current | 25.8 | 16.4 | 11.6 | 11.0 | 9.6 | 9.6 | | 19.4 | 15.9 |
| Total Current | 49.5 | 34.2 | 28.6 | 24.6 | 20.8 | 22.8 | | 38.5 | 35.3 |
| Long-Term Debt | 37.9 | 43.0 | 43.5 | 44.7 | 51.6 | 46.5 | | 45.4 | 46.7 |
| Deferred Taxes | .0 | .0 | .0 | .3 | .6 | 2.8 | | .2 | .1 |
| All Other Non-Current | 17.5 | 7.9 | 4.6 | 6.6 | 6.2 | 13.7 | | 10.5 | 9.5 |
| Net Worth | -4.9 | 14.8 | 23.2 | 23.7 | 20.8 | 14.4 | | 5.5 | 8.4 |
| Total Liabilities & Net Worth | 100.0 | 100.0 | 100.0 | 100.0 | 100.0 | 100.0 | | 100.0 | 100.0 |
| **INCOME DATA** | | | | | | | | | |
| Net Sales | 100.0 | 100.0 | 100.0 | 100.0 | 100.0 | 100.0 | | 100.0 | 100.0 |
| Gross Profit | 61.6 | 61.7 | 61.9 | 60.6 | 59.5 | 56.8 | | 61.4 | 60.9 |
| Operating Expenses | 57.2 | 57.4 | 57.1 | 55.5 | 53.0 | 50.7 | | 56.8 | 57.3 |
| Operating Profit | 4.4 | 4.3 | 4.8 | 5.1 | 6.6 | 6.1 | | 4.6 | 3.6 |
| All Other Expenses (net) | .6 | 1.0 | .9 | 1.1 | 2.6 | 2.3 | | 1.7 | 1.4 |
| Profit Before Taxes | 3.8 | 3.3 | 3.9 | 3.9 | 4.0 | 3.8 | | 2.9 | 2.2 |
| **RATIOS** | | | | | | | | | |
| Current | 2.3 | 1.3 | 1.3 | 1.1 | 1.1 | .8 | | 1.2 | 1.2 |
| | .9 | .6 | .7 | .6 | .6 | .5 | | .6 | .6 |
| | .4 | .3 | .3 | .4 | .2 | .2 | | .3 | .3 |
| Quick | 1.6 | 1.1 | 1.0 | .8 | .9 | .5 | | .9 | .9 |
| | (713) .5 | (578) .5 | (568) .5 | (248) .4 | .4 | .3 | | (1088) .4 | (1495) .4 |
| | .2 | .1 | .2 | .2 | .1 | .1 | | .1 | .1 |
| Sales/Receivables | 0 UND | 0 UND | 0 UND | 0 UND | 0 UND | 1 403.9 | | 0 UND | 0 UND |
| | 0 UND | 0 UND | 0 999.8 | 0 768.3 | 1 314.8 | 2 163.5 | | 0 UND | 0 UND |
| | 0 UND | 0 942.6 | 1 275.9 | 2 172.0 | 3 131.9 | 7 55.3 | | 1 414.3 | 1 450.8 |
| Cost of Sales/Inventory | 4 86.8 | 5 66.4 | 6 60.7 | 6 62.2 | 5 75.6 | 4 90.1 | | 5 72.0 | 5 68.5 |
| | 7 49.2 | 8 45.1 | 8 43.7 | 9 42.3 | 7 50.5 | 8 47.5 | | 8 43.2 | 9 42.2 |
| | 11 33.5 | 11 33.8 | 10 35.0 | 11 34.3 | 11 33.5 | 10 38.1 | | 12 30.4 | 12 30.1 |
| Cost of Sales/Payables | 0 UND | 4 102.9 | 8 43.4 | 10 35.7 | 13 28.4 | 14 26.7 | | 4 99.7 | 3 122.9 |
| | 4 102.6 | 15 23.8 | 17 21.1 | 21 17.8 | 25 14.8 | 27 13.5 | | 14 25.5 | 15 24.2 |
| | 19 19.0 | 29 12.5 | 31 11.8 | 33 11.0 | 40 9.1 | 41 9.0 | | 31 11.9 | 30 12.1 |
| Sales/Working Capital | 39.8 | 56.4 | 51.2 | 108.8 | 185.8 | -33.4 | | 95.2 | 104.1 |
| | -242.9 | -42.1 | -38.3 | -33.3 | -29.2 | -17.0 | | -39.5 | -36.0 |
| | -21.8 | -14.8 | -14.7 | -14.2 | -11.9 | -9.8 | | -13.1 | -12.7 |
| EBIT/Interest | 15.6 | 9.8 | 9.3 | 7.0 | 5.1 | 5.8 | | 7.4 | 6.6 |
| | (477) 4.8 | (521) 3.5 | (537) 4.0 | (245) 3.2 | (46) 2.6 | 2.0 | | (965) 2.7 | (1304) 2.3 |
| | .5 | 1.0 | 1.5 | 1.5 | 1.7 | .8 | | .8 | .6 |
| Net Profit + Depr., Dep., Amort./Cur. Mat. L/T/D | | 3.7 | 6.3 | 3.7 | 2.8 | 6.8 | | 7.0 | 4.7 |
| | | (15) 1.4 | (57) 2.1 | (53) 2.1 | (16) 2.3 | (12) 1.6 | | (95) 2.7 | (107) 2.1 |
| | | .9 | 1.3 | 1.0 | 1.9 | 1.0 | | 1.3 | 1.1 |
| Fixed/Worth | .8 | 1.4 | 1.5 | 1.7 | 3.1 | 5.0 | | 1.7 | 1.8 |
| | 4.9 | 13.5 | 11.3 | 11.5 | -3.7 | -9.8 | | 86.3 | -102.3 |
| | -.9 | -1.3 | -2.3 | -2.3 | -1.0 | -.6 | | -1.7 | -1.3 |
| Debt/Worth | .9 | 1.5 | 1.6 | 1.4 | 3.5 | 4.5 | | 1.9 | 2.2 |
| | 17.2 | 19.0 | 16.0 | 16.1 | -6.0 | -17.3 | | -110.3 | -47.8 |
| | -2.4 | -3.1 | -4.4 | -3.8 | -2.8 | -1.8 | | -3.3 | -2.9 |
| % Profit Before Taxes/Tangible Net Worth | 209.2 | 108.0 | 99.1 | 62.9 | 59.4 | 67.6 | | 114.8 | 103.1 |
| | (381) 91.0 | (319) 41.3 | (323) 40.9 | (139) 27.5 | (20) 30.6 | (19) 14.3 | | (542) 45.6 | (731) 38.0 |
| | 28.5 | 12.5 | 10.3 | 13.6 | 16.2 | -6.4 | | 12.8 | 7.9 |
| % Profit Before Taxes/Total Assets | 52.6 | 23.1 | 18.4 | 12.5 | 9.4 | 8.3 | | 22.5 | 18.3 |
| | 21.3 | 9.9 | 9.1 | 6.3 | 5.0 | 3.3 | | 7.7 | 6.1 |
| | -2.1 | .5 | 1.7 | 1.8 | 2.9 | -1.1 | | -.9 | -1.4 |
| Sales/Net Fixed Assets | 49.9 | 17.0 | 11.0 | 6.6 | 6.5 | 7.0 | | 13.2 | 13.6 |
| | 15.0 | 7.4 | 6.2 | 4.0 | 2.9 | 3.7 | | 6.7 | 6.3 |
| | 6.0 | 3.5 | 3.5 | 2.5 | 1.9 | 2.6 | | 3.2 | 3.1 |
| Sales/Total Assets | 10.2 | 5.0 | 3.9 | 2.8 | 2.0 | 2.1 | | 5.1 | 4.7 |
| | 5.8 | 3.3 | 2.7 | 2.1 | 1.4 | 1.7 | | 3.2 | 2.9 |
| | 3.3 | 1.9 | 1.9 | 1.6 | 1.0 | 1.2 | | 1.9 | 1.7 |
| % Depr., Dep., Amort./Sales | 1.1 | 1.8 | 2.2 | 2.6 | 2.7 | 2.2 | | 1.8 | 1.9 |
| | (474) 2.4 | (465) 2.9 | (508) 3.4 | (236) 3.5 | (42) 3.6 | (15) 3.2 | | (956) 2.8 | (1274) 3.2 |
| | 3.9 | 4.8 | 4.9 | 4.6 | 4.6 | 4.5 | | 4.4 | 4.9 |
| % Officers', Directors' Owners' Comp/Sales | 2.2 | 1.4 | .8 | .7 | | | | 1.6 | 1.4 |
| | (315) 4.0 | (219) 2.7 | (185) 1.4 | (45) 1.3 | | | | (424) 3.2 | (562) 3.0 |
| | 6.6 | 4.6 | 3.4 | 2.7 | | | | 5.4 | 5.7 |
| Net Sales ($) | 884362M | 2323227M | 7701511M | 12312431M | 5301618M | 10977120M | | 21518858M | 30224552M |
| Total Assets ($) | 153159M | 621222M | 2621521M | 5577662M | 3292021M | 6779686M | | 10292280M | 13390780M |

## Comparative Historical Data | | | | Current Data Sorted by Sales

| | | | Type of Statement | | | | | | |
|---|---|---|---|---|---|---|---|---|---|
| 118 | 74 | 119 | Unqualified | 4 | 4 | 3 | 7 | 12 | 89 |
| 112 | 110 | 110 | Reviewed | | 6 | 12 | 27 | 37 | 28 |
| 452 | 554 | 530 | Compiled | 49 | 110 | 82 | 105 | 132 | 52 |
| 591 | 548 | 617 | Tax Returns | 238 | 234 | 52 | 49 | 39 | 5 |
| 617 | 702 | 828 | Other | 131 | 220 | 74 | 106 | 123 | 174 |
| 4/1/09-3/31/10 ALL | 4/1/10-3/31/11 ALL | 4/1/11-3/31/12 ALL | | 176 (4/1-9/30/11) | | 2,028 (10/1/11-3/31/12) | | | |
| | | | | 0-1MM | 1-3MM | 3-5MM | 5-10MM | 10-25MM | 25MM & OVER |
| 1890 | 1988 | 2204 | **NUMBER OF STATEMENTS** | 422 | 574 | 223 | 294 | 343 | 348 |
| % | % | % | **ASSETS** | % | % | % | % | % | % |
| 13.6 | 16.0 | 16.4 | Cash & Equivalents | 16.9 | 18.3 | 18.6 | 16.2 | 16.3 | 11.3 |
| 1.6 | 1.6 | 1.8 | Trade Receivables (net) | 2.3 | 1.6 | 1.2 | 1.7 | 2.2 | 1.5 |
| 4.2 | 4.2 | 3.9 | Inventory | 5.2 | 4.6 | 4.1 | 3.6 | 3.1 | 2.3 |
| 3.0 | 1.8 | 2.5 | All Other Current | 3.4 | 2.0 | 1.7 | 3.2 | 2.5 | 2.1 |
| 22.4 | 23.6 | 24.6 | Total Current | 27.8 | 26.5 | 25.6 | 24.8 | 24.2 | 17.2 |
| 50.8 | 49.5 | 49.0 | Fixed Assets (net) | 50.7 | 47.9 | 46.1 | 46.2 | 50.1 | 52.0 |
| 18.0 | 18.0 | 18.1 | Intangibles (net) | 13.9 | 15.8 | 20.4 | 19.6 | 18.7 | 23.5 |
| 8.8 | 8.9 | 8.3 | All Other Non-Current | 7.5 | 9.8 | 8.0 | 9.4 | 7.1 | 7.2 |
| 100.0 | 100.0 | 100.0 | Total | 100.0 | 100.0 | 100.0 | 100.0 | 100.0 | 100.0 |
| | | | **LIABILITIES** | | | | | | |
| 3.9 | 4.8 | 3.6 | Notes Payable-Short Term | 6.8 | 4.2 | 4.4 | 1.6 | 2.2 | 1.3 |
| 7.2 | 7.5 | 7.4 | Cur. Mat.-L.T.D. | 6.5 | 6.1 | 8.6 | 9.0 | 8.4 | 7.9 |
| 7.5 | 8.1 | 7.7 | Trade Payables | 6.3 | 8.6 | 8.6 | 9.1 | 7.6 | 6.5 |
| .1 | .1 | .1 | Income Taxes Payable | .1 | .1 | .0 | .1 | .1 | .1 |
| 17.6 | 15.6 | 17.3 | All Other Current | 17.8 | 23.5 | 16.8 | 15.8 | 13.1 | 12.4 |
| 36.3 | 36.1 | 36.1 | Total Current | 37.4 | 42.4 | 38.5 | 35.5 | 31.4 | 28.2 |
| 47.2 | 41.6 | 41.9 | Long-Term Debt | 41.1 | 40.8 | 42.8 | 42.2 | 40.8 | 45.2 |
| .1 | .1 | .1 | Deferred Taxes | .0 | .0 | .0 | .0 | .1 | .6 |
| 8.7 | 9.8 | 10.1 | All Other Non-Current | 18.8 | 11.9 | 4.9 | 7.1 | 5.1 | 7.3 |
| 7.8 | 12.3 | 11.7 | Net Worth | 2.8 | 4.9 | 13.8 | 15.2 | 22.7 | 18.7 |
| 100.0 | 100.0 | 100.0 | Total Liabilities & Net Worth | 100.0 | 100.0 | 100.0 | 100.0 | 100.0 | 100.0 |
| | | | **INCOME DATA** | | | | | | |
| 100.0 | 100.0 | 100.0 | Net Sales | 100.0 | 100.0 | 100.0 | 100.0 | 100.0 | 100.0 |
| 62.0 | 62.3 | 61.4 | Gross Profit | 60.7 | 61.9 | 62.8 | 61.4 | 61.4 | 60.8 |
| 57.3 | 57.2 | 56.8 | Operating Expenses | 56.7 | 56.7 | 57.8 | 57.1 | 57.1 | 55.9 |
| 4.7 | 5.1 | 4.6 | Operating Profit | 4.1 | 5.1 | 4.9 | 4.3 | 4.3 | 4.9 |
| 1.1 | 1.1 | .9 | All Other Expenses (net) | 1.2 | 1.0 | .6 | .6 | .5 | 1.3 |
| 3.6 | 4.0 | 3.7 | Profit Before Taxes | 2.8 | 4.1 | 4.4 | 3.7 | 3.8 | 3.6 |
| | | | **RATIOS** | | | | | | |
| 1.4 | 1.5 | 1.5 | | 2.9 | 1.8 | 1.3 | 1.4 | 1.3 | 1.0 |
| .7 | .7 | .7 | Current | 1.0 | .7 | .6 | .6 | .7 | .6 |
| .3 | .3 | .3 | | .4 | .3 | .4 | .3 | .4 | .3 |
| 1.0 | 1.2 | 1.1 | | 2.1 | 1.3 | 1.0 | 1.0 | 1.0 | .7 |
| (1877) .4 | (1984) .5 | (2198) .5 | Quick | (420) .6 | (573) .5 | (293) .5 | (342) .4 | (347) .6 | .4 |
| .1 | .2 | .2 | | .2 | .3 | .2 | .2 | .3 | .2 |
| 0 UND | 0 UND | 0 UND | | 0 UND | 0 UND | 0 UND | 0 UND | 0 UND | 0 UND |
| 0 UND | 0 UND | 0 UND | Sales/Receivables | 0 UND | 0 UND | 0 UND | 0 999.8 | 0 999.8 | 1 451.8 |
| 1 453.8 | 1 495.2 | 1 380.0 | | 0 UND | 0 999.8 | 0 999.8 | 1 273.1 | 1 245.1 | 2 157.5 |
| 5 69.1 | 5 68.8 | 5 72.2 | | 4 87.5 | 4 85.1 | 6 59.9 | 6 62.4 | 6 58.9 | 6 65.1 |
| 9 42.3 | 8 43.6 | 8 45.6 | Cost of Sales/Inventory | 8 45.3 | 7 44.9 | 8 44.3 | 8 45.8 | 8 44.3 | |
| 12 31.5 | 11 32.0 | 11 34.3 | | 14 26.0 | 11 34.7 | 11 34.0 | 10 36.4 | 10 35.5 | 10 35.5 |
| 3 138.3 | 4 97.6 | 2 187.6 | | 0 UND | 1 662.0 | 4 86.4 | 8 47.7 | 8 44.2 | 12 31.6 |
| 15 24.0 | 15 24.1 | 14 25.7 | Cost of Sales/Payables | 0 UND | 11 31.8 | 15 25.0 | 17 22.0 | 18 20.8 | 22 16.8 |
| 28 13.2 | 29 12.4 | 28 12.9 | | 16 23.5 | 26 13.8 | 30 12.2 | 30 12.3 | 30 12.2 | 36 10.1 |
| 59.9 | 44.0 | 49.8 | | 29.2 | 44.3 | 69.0 | 52.1 | 65.9 | -213.2 |
| -44.5 | -48.9 | -51.6 | Sales/Working Capital | -817.5 | -73.4 | -46.1 | -36.0 | -52.2 | -27.0 |
| -14.7 | -14.6 | -15.3 | | -16.5 | -15.3 | -15.4 | -14.6 | -18.8 | -13.8 |
| 9.1 | 10.4 | 10.0 | | 8.4 | 12.5 | 12.6 | 9.0 | 11.7 | 7.0 |
| (1622) 3.4 | (1664) 3.8 | (1869) 3.8 | EBIT/Interest | (267) 2.8 | (462) 3.8 | (203) 5.3 | (272) 3.9 | (324) 4.3 | (341) 3.3 |
| 1.2 | 1.3 | 1.2 | | -.3 | 1.0 | 1.3 | 1.3 | 1.8 | 1.5 |
| 3.9 | 5.2 | 4.6 | | | | 8.6 | 2.6 | 11.0 | 4.1 |
| (151) 2.1 | (116) 2.5 | (154) 2.1 | Net Profit + Depr., Dep., Amort./Cur. Mat. L/T/D | | | (12) 2.0 | (22) 1.6 | (31) 2.9 | (82) 2.1 |
| 1.1 | 1.3 | 1.3 | | | | .6 | .8 | 1.6 | 1.4 |
| 1.5 | 1.2 | 1.2 | | .9 | .9 | 1.5 | 1.3 | 1.5 | 2.2 |
| 22.5 | 11.9 | 10.9 | Fixed/Worth | 5.6 | 6.0 | 60.7 | 89.1 | 8.0 | 133.5 |
| -1.3 | -1.5 | -1.4 | | -1.5 | -1.2 | -1.1 | -1.2 | -2.6 | -1.4 |
| 1.8 | 1.3 | 1.4 | | .9 | 1.2 | 1.6 | 1.4 | 1.5 | 2.3 |
| 42.1 | 22.7 | 19.0 | Debt/Worth | 15.4 | 13.9 | 135.1 | 136.5 | 11.8 | 181.8 |
| -2.8 | -3.2 | -3.1 | | -3.0 | -2.7 | -3.1 | -2.9 | -4.7 | -3.1 |
| 130.6 | 118.1 | 127.2 | | 148.7 | 171.7 | 136.8 | 98.1 | 117.2 | 75.9 |
| (978) 50.9 | (1052) 46.7 | (1201) 47.8 | % Profit Before Taxes/Tangible Net Worth | (233) 57.1 | (324) 60.8 | (113) 50.7 | (150) 39.6 | (202) 44.7 | (179) 32.6 |
| 16.9 | 14.6 | 14.4 | | 10.2 | 18.6 | 14.8 | 10.8 | 16.4 | 10.7 |
| 23.6 | 25.6 | 25.3 | | 37.2 | 39.0 | 27.5 | 21.1 | 19.9 | 13.2 |
| 9.4 | 10.3 | 9.7 | % Profit Before Taxes/Total Assets | 10.3 | 12.8 | 12.7 | 10.5 | 9.7 | 6.3 |
| 1.0 | 1.3 | .7 | | -6.3 | .3 | 1.5 | 1.3 | 2.9 | 1.7 |
| 14.4 | 15.6 | 17.0 | | 29.3 | 26.1 | 19.8 | 18.0 | 12.7 | 8.6 |
| 6.4 | 7.1 | 7.4 | Sales/Net Fixed Assets | 7.5 | 9.5 | 9.2 | 8.0 | 6.9 | 4.9 |
| 3.4 | 3.6 | 3.7 | | 3.1 | 4.1 | 4.4 | 4.2 | 4.0 | 3.0 |
| 5.0 | 5.3 | 5.4 | | 6.9 | 7.3 | 5.4 | 5.0 | 4.5 | 3.4 |
| 3.0 | 3.1 | 3.2 | Sales/Total Assets | 3.4 | 3.9 | 3.7 | 3.3 | 3.1 | 2.3 |
| 1.8 | 1.8 | 1.9 | | 1.7 | 2.1 | 2.1 | 2.2 | 2.2 | 1.6 |
| 1.8 | 1.8 | 1.8 | | 1.5 | 1.4 | 1.4 | 1.4 | 1.7 | 2.4 |
| (1591) 3.2 | (1621) 3.2 | (1740) 3.0 | % Depr., Dep., Amort./Sales | (279) 3.1 | (427) 2.7 | (177) 2.7 | (247) 3.0 | (312) 3.2 | (298) 3.3 |
| 4.9 | 4.8 | 4.6 | | 5.7 | 4.4 | 4.2 | 4.7 | 4.6 | 4.5 |
| 1.5 | 1.4 | 1.3 | | 2.7 | 1.9 | 1.4 | .9 | .8 | .5 |
| (660) 3.1 | (695) 3.0 | (778) 2.7 | % Officers', Directors' Owners' Comp/Sales | (176) 4.8 | (245) 3.4 | (74) 2.6 | (87) 1.6 | (130) 1.4 | (66) 1.0 |
| 5.6 | 5.1 | 5.2 | | 7.1 | 5.6 | 4.3 | 3.2 | 3.2 | 2.0 |
| 34025855M | 34366617M | 39500269M | Net Sales ($) | 261903M | 1052132M | 875053M | 2126275M | 5474583M | 29710323M |
| 16878193M | 15838135M | 19045271M | Total Assets ($) | 113309M | 401901M | 313778M | 813484M | 2012485M | 15390314M |

© RMA 2012

M = $ thousand    MM = $ million
See Pages 9 through 22 for Explanation of Ratios and Data

**Current Data Sorted by Assets**      **Comparative Historical Data**

| | 0-500M | 500M-2MM | 2-10MM | 10-50MM | 50-100MM | 100-250MM | | 4/1/07-3/31/08 ALL | 4/1/08-3/31/09 ALL |
|---|---|---|---|---|---|---|---|---|---|
| Type of Statement | | | | | | | | | |
| Unqualified | 10 | 11 | 6 | 6 | | | | 5 | 4 |
| Reviewed | 7 | 3 | 3 | 1 | | | | 9 | 2 |
| Compiled | 5 | | | | | | | 5 | 9 |
| Tax Returns | 24 | 14 | 5 | | 1 | | | 67 | 31 |
| Other | 23 | 16 | 16 | 4 | 1 | 2 | | 39 | 58 |
| | 10 (4/1-9/30/11) | | | 144 (10/1/11-3/31/12) | | | | | |
| **NUMBER OF STATEMENTS** | 64 | 44 | 30 | 11 | 2 | 3 | | 125 | 104 |
| | % | % | % | % | % | % | | % | % |
| **ASSETS** | | | | | | | | | |
| Cash & Equivalents | 13.0 | 8.8 | 10.8 | 4.9 | | | | 10.3 | 8.3 |
| Trade Receivables (net) | 1.4 | 4.7 | 2.3 | 3.8 | | | | 1.2 | 3.3 |
| Inventory | 4.6 | 4.9 | 3.0 | 4.5 | | | | 3.6 | 6.7 |
| All Other Current | 2.6 | 2.2 | 6.1 | 1.4 | | | | 1.3 | 2.9 |
| Total Current | 21.6 | 20.5 | 22.2 | 14.6 | | | | 16.4 | 21.2 |
| Fixed Assets (net) | 54.0 | 45.4 | 46.4 | 50.4 | | | | 55.4 | 50.0 |
| Intangibles (net) | 18.6 | 30.3 | 24.3 | 28.9 | | | | 15.8 | 19.3 |
| All Other Non-Current | 5.8 | 3.8 | 7.1 | 6.0 | | | | 12.5 | 9.5 |
| Total | 100.0 | 100.0 | 100.0 | 100.0 | | | | 100.0 | 100.0 |
| **LIABILITIES** | | | | | | | | | |
| Notes Payable-Short Term | 12.5 | 5.4 | 4.0 | 9.4 | | | | 6.1 | 4.7 |
| Cur. Mat.-L.T.D. | 5.5 | 9.8 | 7.7 | 6.7 | | | | 4.9 | 5.1 |
| Trade Payables | 7.0 | 7.1 | 3.6 | 7.3 | | | | 5.6 | 7.7 |
| Income Taxes Payable | .0 | .0 | .1 | .0 | | | | .0 | .1 |
| All Other Current | 15.8 | 8.7 | 6.7 | 7.0 | | | | 12.3 | 16.3 |
| Total Current | 40.8 | 31.0 | 22.1 | 30.3 | | | | 28.9 | 33.9 |
| Long-Term Debt | 43.0 | 46.2 | 43.6 | 41.3 | | | | 47.5 | 44.9 |
| Deferred Taxes | .0 | .0 | .0 | .6 | | | | .0 | .0 |
| All Other Non-Current | 11.1 | 3.6 | 5.4 | 3.5 | | | | 13.9 | 18.0 |
| Net Worth | 5.1 | 19.2 | 28.9 | 24.3 | | | | 9.7 | 3.1 |
| Total Liabilities & Net Worth | 100.0 | 100.0 | 100.0 | 100.0 | | | | 100.0 | 100.0 |
| **INCOME DATA** | | | | | | | | | |
| Net Sales | 100.0 | 100.0 | 100.0 | 100.0 | | | | 100.0 | 100.0 |
| Gross Profit | | | | | | | | | |
| Operating Expenses | 95.7 | 93.3 | 91.5 | 93.4 | | | | 94.9 | 99.4 |
| Operating Profit | 4.3 | 6.7 | 8.5 | 6.6 | | | | 5.1 | .6 |
| All Other Expenses (net) | 1.5 | 1.4 | 2.9 | 1.6 | | | | 3.0 | 2.2 |
| Profit Before Taxes | 2.7 | 5.3 | 5.5 | 5.0 | | | | 2.1 | -1.6 |
| **RATIOS** | | | | | | | | | |
| Current | 1.5 | 1.4 | 1.4 | .9 | | | | 1.4 | 1.1 |
| | .6 | .6 | .9 | .5 | | | | .7 | .6 |
| | .3 | .2 | .5 | .4 | | | | .2 | .2 |
| Quick | .9 | .9 | 1.0 | .4 | | | | 1.0 | .7 |
| | (63) .3 | (43) .4 | (29) .5 | .3 | | | | (102) .4 | .4 |
| | .1 | .1 | .3 | .1 | | | | .1 | .1 |
| Sales/Receivables | 0 UND | 0 UND | 0 999.8 | 2 192.4 | | | | 0 UND | 0 UND |
| | 0 UND | 0 999.8 | 1 681.2 | 3 110.6 | | | | 0 UND | 0 UND |
| | 0 999.8 | 3 144.0 | 2 151.1 | 7 53.3 | | | | 0 UND | 4 89.6 |
| Cost of Sales/Inventory | | | | | | | | | |
| Cost of Sales/Payables | | | | | | | | | |
| Sales/Working Capital | 58.0 | 48.8 | 25.6 | -41.7 | | | | 86.4 | 118.1 |
| | -31.3 | -24.7 | -50.3 | -21.7 | | | | -37.5 | -36.4 |
| | -12.3 | -8.3 | -13.2 | -7.9 | | | | -11.4 | -10.3 |
| EBIT/Interest | 10.8 | 10.8 | 12.7 | 3.9 | | | | 6.8 | 4.0 |
| | (54) 3.3 | (41) 3.8 | (28) 3.6 | 3.3 | | | | (103) 2.6 | (82) 1.6 |
| | .0 | .6 | 1.5 | 2.1 | | | | .3 | -2.3 |
| Net Profit + Depr., Dep., Amort./Cur. Mat. L/T/D | | | | | | | | | |
| Fixed/Worth | 1.7 | 2.2 | 1.2 | 2.5 | | | | 1.3 | 1.7 |
| | NM | -7.3 | 2.2 | -6.2 | | | | -129.3 | -8.6 |
| | -.9 | -.8 | -1.0 | -2.2 | | | | -1.4 | -.8 |
| Debt/Worth | 1.9 | 3.1 | 1.3 | 2.2 | | | | 1.3 | 2.5 |
| | NM | -11.2 | 2.9 | -15.8 | | | | -92.8 | -15.0 |
| | -2.6 | -2.0 | -2.3 | -4.5 | | | | -2.8 | -2.6 |
| % Profit Before Taxes/Tangible Net Worth | 167.3 | 230.9 | 70.2 | | | | | 129.3 | 127.3 |
| | (32) 65.7 | (18) 76.8 | (19) 33.2 | | | | | (60) 67.2 | (46) 51.3 |
| | 22.1 | 45.6 | 2.0 | | | | | 17.2 | 4.9 |
| % Profit Before Taxes/Total Assets | 28.3 | 22.3 | 16.6 | 11.4 | | | | 23.3 | 18.1 |
| | 12.3 | 11.0 | 7.8 | 7.2 | | | | 6.2 | 4.0 |
| | -5.2 | -1.5 | 2.1 | 5.3 | | | | -1.3 | -7.3 |
| Sales/Net Fixed Assets | 12.9 | 11.6 | 7.3 | 5.4 | | | | 9.4 | 11.5 |
| | 7.3 | 6.4 | 5.0 | 4.0 | | | | 5.0 | 5.0 |
| | 3.4 | 3.2 | 3.1 | 3.0 | | | | 2.5 | 2.4 |
| Sales/Total Assets | 4.8 | 3.5 | 2.5 | 2.5 | | | | 3.8 | 3.8 |
| | 2.8 | 2.3 | 2.0 | 1.9 | | | | 2.4 | 2.3 |
| | 2.2 | 1.3 | 1.0 | 1.6 | | | | 1.4 | 1.4 |
| % Depr., Dep., Amort./Sales | 2.3 | 2.3 | 2.9 | 2.2 | | | | 2.4 | 2.1 |
| | (53) 4.6 | (37) 4.0 | (25) 4.8 | (10) 4.4 | | | | (111) 4.1 | (85) 3.8 |
| | 6.7 | 7.7 | 7.7 | 6.0 | | | | 6.6 | 7.0 |
| % Officers', Directors' Owners' Comp/Sales | 3.8 | 2.7 | | | | | | 2.9 | 2.6 |
| | (17) 7.2 | (18) 4.2 | | | | | | (42) 4.6 | (28) 5.2 |
| | 9.7 | 6.8 | | | | | | 8.0 | 8.9 |
| Net Sales ($) | 50973M | 113444M | 248736M | 490809M | 367010M | 907489M | | 2007215M | 1543136M |
| Total Assets ($) | 16716M | 42275M | 126744M | 219817M | 173450M | 353561M | | 694303M | 721248M |

M = $ thousand    MM = $ million
See Pages 9 through 22 for Explanation of Ratios and Data

| | Comparative Historical Data | | | | Current Data Sorted by Sales | | | | | |
|---|---|---|---|---|---|---|---|---|---|---|
| **Type of Statement** | | | | | | | | | | |
| Unqualified | 7 | 5 | 1 | | 9 | 13 | 2 | 2 | 4 | 1 |
| Reviewed | 16 | 11 | 33 | | | | | | | 3 |
| Compiled | 24 | 13 | 14 | | 3 | 6 | | 3 | 1 | 1 |
| Tax Returns | 52 | 44 | 44 | | 21 | 15 | 3 | 2 | 2 | 1 |
| Other | 31 | 31 | 62 | | 22 | 13 | 4 | 9 | 9 | 5 |
| | 4/1/09-3/31/10 ALL | 4/1/10-3/31/11 ALL | 4/1/11-3/31/12 ALL | | 10 (4/1-9/30/11) | | | 144 (10/1/11-3/31/12) | | |
| | | | | | 0-1MM | 1-3MM | 3-5MM | 5-10MM | 10-25MM | 25MM & OVER |
| **NUMBER OF STATEMENTS** | 130 | 104 | 154 | | 55 | 47 | 9 | 16 | 16 | 11 |
| | % | % | % | | % | % | % | % | % | % |
| **ASSETS** | | | | | | | | | | |
| Cash & Equivalents | 12.7 | 13.3 | 10.7 | | 13.0 | 6.2 | | 13.4 | 13.5 | 7.3 |
| Trade Receivables (net) | 3.2 | 2.9 | 2.8 | | 1.4 | 3.8 | | 5.1 | 2.5 | 3.9 |
| Inventory | 4.9 | 4.4 | 4.4 | | 3.5 | 4.4 | | 7.8 | 4.4 | 3.6 |
| All Other Current | 2.9 | 2.6 | 3.3 | | 2.4 | 3.6 | | 1.7 | 1.8 | 4.0 |
| Total Current | 23.6 | 23.1 | 21.1 | | 20.3 | 18.0 | | 28.0 | 22.3 | 18.8 |
| Fixed Assets (net) | 45.7 | 51.1 | 49.9 | | 52.6 | 47.0 | | 41.9 | 54.5 | 53.3 |
| Intangibles (net) | 20.1 | 15.1 | 23.2 | | 23.5 | 28.8 | | 21.4 | 17.4 | 17.3 |
| All Other Non-Current | 10.6 | 10.8 | 5.8 | | 3.6 | 6.2 | | 8.7 | 5.9 | 10.7 |
| Total | 100.0 | 100.0 | 100.0 | | 100.0 | 100.0 | | 100.0 | 100.0 | 100.0 |
| **LIABILITIES** | | | | | | | | | | |
| Notes Payable-Short Term | 3.7 | 7.9 | 8.2 | | 12.0 | 8.2 | | 3.9 | 6.0 | 2.3 |
| Cur. Mat.-L.T.D. | 6.2 | 7.7 | 7.2 | | 5.1 | 10.4 | | 8.6 | 6.5 | 4.9 |
| Trade Payables | 4.8 | 8.8 | 6.5 | | 6.1 | 5.9 | | 7.2 | 5.3 | 8.4 |
| Income Taxes Payable | .0 | .1 | .0 | | .0 | .0 | | .0 | .1 | .1 |
| All Other Current | 10.2 | 15.0 | 11.7 | | 13.0 | 11.9 | | 10.6 | 5.7 | 17.0 |
| Total Current | 24.8 | 39.6 | 33.5 | | 36.3 | 36.4 | | 30.3 | 23.6 | 32.7 |
| Long-Term Debt | 41.4 | 47.8 | 43.1 | | 49.9 | 42.1 | | 51.4 | 34.7 | 27.9 |
| Deferred Taxes | .0 | .1 | .0 | | .0 | .0 | | .0 | .0 | .6 |
| All Other Non-Current | 13.4 | 20.5 | 7.1 | | 11.5 | 4.9 | | 7.0 | 3.1 | 5.3 |
| Net Worth | 20.4 | -7.9 | 16.2 | | 2.3 | 16.6 | | 11.3 | 38.6 | 33.5 |
| Total Liabilities & Net Worth | 100.0 | 100.0 | 100.0 | | 100.0 | 100.0 | | 100.0 | 100.0 | 100.0 |
| **INCOME DATA** | | | | | | | | | | |
| Net Sales | 100.0 | 100.0 | 100.0 | | 100.0 | 100.0 | | 100.0 | 100.0 | 100.0 |
| Gross Profit | | | | | | | | | | |
| Operating Expenses | 94.4 | 94.7 | 94.2 | | 94.4 | 94.0 | | 93.3 | 93.3 | 95.7 |
| Operating Profit | 5.6 | 5.3 | 5.8 | | 5.6 | 6.0 | | 6.7 | 6.7 | 4.3 |
| All Other Expenses (net) | 1.9 | 2.0 | 1.8 | | 2.4 | 1.7 | | 1.6 | 1.3 | .8 |
| Profit Before Taxes | 3.7 | 3.3 | 4.1 | | 3.2 | 4.4 | | 5.1 | 5.4 | 3.6 |
| **RATIOS** | | | | | | | | | | |
| Current | 2.0 | 1.3 | 1.3 | | 2.0 | .8 | | 1.3 | 1.3 | .7 |
| | .9 | .6 | .6 | | .7 | .5 | | .9 | .9 | .5 |
| | .4 | .3 | .3 | | .2 | .2 | | .5 | .5 | .4 |
| Quick | 1.2 | 1.0 | .9 | | 1.2 | .6 | | .9 | 1.2 | .6 |
| | (128) .6 | (103) .4 | (151) .4 | | (54) .4 | (46) .2 | | .6 | .6 | .3 |
| | .2 | .2 | .1 | | .1 | .1 | | .3 | .3 | .1 |
| Sales/Receivables | 0 UND | 0 UND | 0 UND | | 0 UND | 0 UND | | 0 999.8 | 0 UND | 3 116.4 |
| | 0 UND | 0 UND | 0 999.8 | | 0 UND | 0 999.8 | | 2 233.3 | 1 520.7 | 4 94.4 |
| | 1 366.1 | 3 108.6 | 2 175.7 | | 0 UND | 2 217.5 | | 7 51.8 | 2 149.9 | 13 28.7 |
| Cost of Sales/Inventory | | | | | | | | | | |
| Cost of Sales/Payables | | | | | | | | | | |
| Sales/Working Capital | 26.1 | 56.4 | 56.3 | | 30.9 | -88.4 | | 43.4 | 33.5 | -22.0 |
| | -153.3 | -40.6 | -30.7 | | -54.5 | -16.4 | | -164.3 | -234.8 | -16.2 |
| | -18.9 | -9.6 | -11.5 | | -11.6 | -8.3 | | -18.6 | -27.1 | -7.9 |
| EBIT/Interest | 8.2 | 6.2 | 9.7 | | 8.6 | 8.6 | | 14.1 | 12.7 | 8.4 |
| | (110) 3.1 | (94) 2.1 | (139) 3.4 | | (47) 3.0 | (41) 4.1 | | 5.7 | 3.1 | 3.5 |
| | .9 | -.3 | 1.0 | | .0 | .9 | | 1.6 | 2.0 | 1.5 |
| Net Profit + Depr., Dep., Amort./Cur. Mat. L/T/D | | | 3.4 | | | | | | | |
| | | (10) 2.6 | | | | | | | | |
| | | | .9 | | | | | | | |
| Fixed/Worth | 1.1 | 1.6 | 1.7 | | 2.8 | 2.0 | | 1.4 | 1.2 | 1.6 |
| | 10.1 | UND | 16.8 | | -10.5 | -3.2 | | 19.4 | 1.9 | 2.5 |
| | -1.3 | -.9 | -1.0 | | -.7 | -.7 | | -.9 | NM | -5.4 |
| Debt/Worth | 1.2 | 1.6 | 1.7 | | 1.9 | 2.5 | | 2.6 | 1.0 | 1.3 |
| | 27.3 | UND | 20.2 | | -16.7 | -5.2 | | 30.6 | 1.8 | 3.8 |
| | -3.3 | -2.5 | -2.5 | | -2.2 | -2.3 | | -2.1 | NM | -8.5 |
| % Profit Before Taxes/Tangible Net Worth | 105.9 | 97.6 | 113.6 | | 182.2 | 134.2 | | | 97.1 | |
| | (70) 34.8 | (52) 37.4 | (79) 52.9 | | (25) 67.1 | (17) 67.5 | | | (12) 34.5 | |
| | 4.7 | -1.0 | 14.3 | | 13.9 | 27.3 | | | 9.8 | |
| % Profit Before Taxes/Total Assets | 21.9 | 17.3 | 22.0 | | 19.1 | 22.3 | | 28.5 | 19.2 | 11.4 |
| | 8.5 | 6.4 | 9.4 | | 8.1 | 10.3 | | 15.9 | 8.0 | 9.4 |
| | -.4 | -3.4 | .0 | | -6.5 | 2.4 | | 3.0 | 3.4 | 2.0 |
| Sales/Net Fixed Assets | 14.5 | 12.5 | 9.7 | | 12.9 | 10.4 | | 12.3 | 7.0 | 5.9 |
| | 5.4 | 6.3 | 5.9 | | 5.1 | 6.6 | | 7.9 | 4.6 | 5.1 |
| | 2.8 | 3.3 | 3.4 | | 2.1 | 4.1 | | 4.5 | 3.1 | 3.6 |
| Sales/Total Assets | 3.7 | 4.4 | 3.5 | | 3.2 | 3.5 | | 4.7 | 3.2 | 2.6 |
| | 2.1 | 2.4 | 2.4 | | 2.2 | 2.7 | | 2.3 | 2.2 | 2.3 |
| | 1.2 | 1.5 | 1.6 | | 1.3 | 1.7 | | 1.9 | 1.8 | 1.7 |
| % Depr., Dep., Amort./Sales | 2.5 | 2.4 | 2.4 | | 3.6 | 2.1 | | 2.7 | 2.8 | |
| | (104) 4.5 | (83) 3.7 | (128) 4.6 | | (45) 5.6 | (41) 4.0 | | (13) 4.8 | (11) 3.8 | |
| | 7.3 | 6.7 | 6.9 | | 10.0 | 5.8 | | 6.8 | 5.4 | |
| % Officers', Directors' Owners' Comp/Sales | 1.9 | 3.0 | 2.7 | | 3.7 | 2.8 | | | | |
| | (31) 5.1 | (40) 6.8 | (46) 4.9 | | (13) 7.2 | (15) 5.3 | | | | |
| | 9.4 | 10.7 | 9.1 | | 9.7 | 9.2 | | | | |
| Net Sales ($) | 1243686M | 1432167M | 2178461M | | 31430M | 78892M | 35684M | 114711M | 240166M | 1677578M |
| Total Assets ($) | 565537M | 827106M | 932563M | | 20174M | 45748M | 17877M | 44683M | 115058M | 689023M |

M = $ thousand   MM = $ million
See Pages 9 through 22 for Explanation of Ratios and Data

## Current Data Sorted by Assets      Comparative Historical Data

### Type of Statement

| | | | | | | | 4/1/07-3/31/08 ALL | 4/1/08-3/31/09 ALL |
|---|---|---|---|---|---|---|---|---|
| | 2 | 4 | 5 | 3 | 5 | Unqualified | 13 | 18 |
| | 2 | 13 | 4 | 1 | 1 | Reviewed | 5 | 10 |
| 7 | 10 | 7 | 1 | 1 | | Compiled | 10 | 18 |
| 28 | 13 | 10 | 1 | | | Tax Returns | 17 | 22 |
| 19 | 9 | 19 | 11 | 1 | 2 | Other | 23 | 27 |
| | 28 (4/1-9/30/11) | | 150 (10/1/11-3/31/12) | | | | | |
| 0-500M | 500M-2MM | 2-10MM | 10-50MM | 50-100MM | 100-250MM | NUMBER OF STATEMENTS | 68 | 95 |
| 54 | 36 | 53 | 22 | 5 | 8 | | | |
| % | % | % | % | % | % | **ASSETS** | % | % |
| 18.4 | 7.4 | 13.5 | 5.4 | | | Cash & Equivalents | 11.9 | 10.2 |
| 6.2 | 17.8 | 29.0 | 30.6 | | | Trade Receivables (net) | 21.5 | 19.8 |
| 4.7 | 6.1 | 10.6 | 14.5 | | | Inventory | 7.9 | 10.5 |
| 2.8 | 7.2 | 3.9 | 1.5 | | | All Other Current | 4.8 | 2.4 |
| 32.1 | 38.5 | 57.1 | 52.0 | | | Total Current | 46.1 | 43.0 |
| 43.2 | 37.9 | 23.1 | 31.2 | | | Fixed Assets (net) | 33.4 | 34.8 |
| 9.9 | 9.3 | 6.8 | 9.9 | | | Intangibles (net) | 10.2 | 12.9 |
| 14.7 | 14.4 | 12.9 | 6.9 | | | All Other Non-Current | 10.3 | 9.4 |
| 100.0 | 100.0 | 100.0 | 100.0 | | | Total | 100.0 | 100.0 |
| | | | | | | **LIABILITIES** | | |
| 11.2 | 11.2 | 5.2 | 16.6 | | | Notes Payable-Short Term | 6.3 | 10.4 |
| 8.3 | 3.9 | 1.9 | 4.5 | | | Cur. Mat.-L.T.D. | 4.0 | 3.3 |
| 13.8 | 10.5 | 18.6 | 18.8 | | | Trade Payables | 15.2 | 17.7 |
| .2 | .2 | .0 | .1 | | | Income Taxes Payable | .1 | .2 |
| 23.6 | 11.7 | 13.8 | 9.6 | | | All Other Current | 17.2 | 19.0 |
| 57.1 | 37.4 | 39.5 | 49.6 | | | Total Current | 42.9 | 50.6 |
| 28.4 | 22.5 | 15.0 | 18.2 | | | Long-Term Debt | 27.2 | 29.0 |
| .0 | .0 | .0 | .5 | | | Deferred Taxes | .2 | .2 |
| 13.4 | 8.4 | 11.4 | 4.4 | | | All Other Non-Current | 7.0 | 6.1 |
| 1.1 | 31.7 | 34.0 | 27.4 | | | Net Worth | 22.7 | 14.0 |
| 100.0 | 100.0 | 100.0 | 100.0 | | | Total Liabilities & Net Worth | 100.0 | 100.0 |
| | | | | | | **INCOME DATA** | | |
| 100.0 | 100.0 | 100.0 | 100.0 | | | Net Sales | 100.0 | 100.0 |
| | | | | | | Gross Profit | | |
| 95.8 | 92.7 | 95.7 | 96.5 | | | Operating Expenses | 91.8 | 94.9 |
| 4.2 | 7.3 | 4.3 | 3.5 | | | Operating Profit | 8.2 | 5.1 |
| .4 | 4.2 | 1.7 | 1.6 | | | All Other Expenses (net) | 3.7 | 2.6 |
| 3.8 | 3.2 | 2.6 | 1.9 | | | Profit Before Taxes | 4.5 | 2.5 |
| | | | | | | **RATIOS** | | |
| 1.6 | 1.7 | 2.4 | 1.5 | | | | 2.1 | 1.7 |
| .6 | 1.0 | 1.4 | 1.1 | | | Current | 1.1 | 1.1 |
| .2 | .3 | .8 | .5 | | | | .4 | .4 |
| 1.1 | 1.2 | 1.8 | 1.0 | | | | 1.4 | 1.1 |
| .4 | .5 | 1.1 | .8 | | | Quick | .8 | .8 |
| .1 | .2 | .5 | .3 | | | | .3 | .3 |
| 0 UND | 0 UND | 9   42.7 | 6   61.7 | | | | 1   305.1 | 0 UND |
| 0 UND | 0 UND | 19   18.9 | 29   12.4 | | | Sales/Receivables | 16   22.5 | 14   25.2 |
| 2   160.9 | 17   21.0 | 32   11.3 | 45   8.2 | | | | 37   10.0 | 32   11.4 |
| | | | | | | Cost of Sales/Inventory | | |
| | | | | | | Cost of Sales/Payables | | |
| 56.2 | 18.8 | 13.3 | 22.4 | | | | 14.8 | 19.3 |
| -28.7 | NM | 37.7 | 129.5 | | | Sales/Working Capital | 77.4 | 121.9 |
| -9.9 | -17.2 | -26.5 | -16.9 | | | | -16.8 | -21.6 |
| 8.9 | 12.7 | 63.8 | 8.4 | | | | 20.0 | 10.9 |
| (35) 4.0 | (25) 2.3 | (46) 10.1 | (21) 3.6 | | | EBIT/Interest | (60) 5.6 | (80) 3.1 |
| -.3 | 1.2 | 1.3 | 1.0 | | | | 1.6 | .7 |
| | | | | | | | 7.6 | 7.0 |
| | | | | | | Net Profit + Depr., Dep., Amort./Cur. Mat. L/T/D | (11) 3.3 | (17) 3.1 |
| | | | | | | | 1.5 | 1.4 |
| .8 | .6 | .2 | .4 | | | | .4 | .5 |
| 4.8 | 1.0 | .8 | 1.3 | | | Fixed/Worth | 1.7 | 2.1 |
| -.8 | NM | 7.3 | 83.8 | | | | -7.4 | -2.5 |
| 1.1 | .6 | .8 | 1.6 | | | | 1.2 | 1.7 |
| 6.4 | 3.0 | 2.6 | 4.0 | | | Debt/Worth | 3.9 | 6.7 |
| -2.7 | NM | 51.6 | 115.5 | | | | -29.6 | -4.1 |
| 120.0 | 70.4 | 62.9 | 29.9 | | | | 111.6 | 77.8 |
| (30) 68.2 | (27) 10.8 | (41) 36.1 | (18) 11.7 | | | % Profit Before Taxes/Tangible Net Worth | (49) 46.3 | (63) 38.0 |
| 4.6 | -1.6 | 6.5 | -21.0 | | | | 18.0 | 14.3 |
| 32.5 | 18.3 | 26.3 | 10.8 | | | | 20.4 | 17.9 |
| 14.2 | 4.2 | 9.2 | 6.3 | | | % Profit Before Taxes/Total Assets | 10.1 | 5.5 |
| -5.7 | .6 | .4 | .4 | | | | 1.6 | -1.2 |
| 35.9 | 128.7 | 159.0 | 39.5 | | | | 45.4 | 41.3 |
| 9.1 | 9.8 | 33.8 | 13.3 | | | Sales/Net Fixed Assets | 11.4 | 12.6 |
| 6.7 | 2.9 | 7.5 | 5.4 | | | | 5.6 | 4.6 |
| 6.9 | 4.5 | 6.2 | 4.5 | | | | 5.4 | 5.4 |
| 4.7 | 2.9 | 4.3 | 3.3 | | | Sales/Total Assets | 3.3 | 3.2 |
| 3.6 | 1.0 | 2.5 | 1.8 | | | | 2.1 | 2.0 |
| 1.0 | .8 | .2 | .9 | | | | 1.0 | .6 |
| (38) 1.7 | (27) 2.7 | (44) .7 | (21) 1.9 | | | % Depr., Dep., Amort./Sales | (54) 2.1 | (79) 1.9 |
| 3.4 | 5.9 | 3.3 | 2.9 | | | | 4.0 | 3.9 |
| 2.8 | 1.5 | 1.4 | | | | | 1.7 | 1.9 |
| (20) 7.3 | (14) 3.7 | (21) 3.7 | | | | % Officers', Directors' Owners' Comp/Sales | (26) 2.8 | (31) 5.3 |
| 12.6 | 4.6 | 7.4 | | | | | 12.6 | 8.8 |
| 62379M | 122979M | 1071697M | 1652731M | 773233M | 3409966M | Net Sales ($) | 3494590M | 3341136M |
| 12891M | 33033M | 250476M | 477163M | 333718M | 1015251M | Total Assets ($) | 1086235M | 1160919M |

## Comparative Historical Data

## Current Data Sorted by Sales

| Type of Statement | 4/1/09-3/31/10 | 4/1/10-3/31/11 | 4/1/11-3/31/12 | 0-1MM | 1-3MM | 3-5MM | 5-10MM | 10-25MM | 25MM & OVER |
|---|---|---|---|---|---|---|---|---|---|
| Unqualified | 12 | 13 | 19 | | 1 | | | 3 | 15 |
| Reviewed | 10 | 22 | 21 | | | 1 | 3 | 6 | 11 |
| Compiled | 16 | 17 | 25 | 11 | 7 | 1 | 1 | 3 | 2 |
| Tax Returns | 30 | 33 | 52 | 18 | 17 | 7 | 4 | 3 | 3 |
| Other | 36 | 40 | 61 | 11 | 13 | 4 | 4 | 8 | 21 |
| | **ALL** | **ALL** | **ALL** | **28 (4/1-9/30/11)** | | | **150 (10/1/11-3/31/12)** | | |
| **NUMBER OF STATEMENTS** | 104 | 125 | 178 | 40 | 38 | 13 | 12 | 23 | 52 |
| | % | % | % | % | % | % | % | % | % |
| **ASSETS** | | | | | | | | | |
| Cash & Equivalents | 12.6 | 13.6 | 12.2 | 8.6 | 18.5 | 17.8 | 6.8 | 9.0 | 11.6 |
| Trade Receivables (net) | 20.3 | 22.9 | 19.2 | 2.7 | 10.9 | 16.1 | 20.7 | 31.4 | 32.9 |
| Inventory | 8.1 | 8.7 | 8.3 | 2.8 | 4.9 | 8.4 | 5.5 | 15.3 | 12.5 |
| All Other Current | 4.5 | 4.8 | 4.2 | 2.4 | 4.7 | 7.9 | 10.5 | 3.2 | 3.2 |
| Total Current | 45.5 | 50.1 | 43.8 | 16.4 | 39.0 | 50.2 | 43.5 | 58.9 | 60.2 |
| Fixed Assets (net) | 35.7 | 31.4 | 33.8 | 53.0 | 38.1 | 25.9 | 34.1 | 24.6 | 21.9 |
| Intangibles (net) | 7.9 | 8.2 | 9.7 | 9.7 | 8.4 | 14.9 | 2.2 | 11.9 | 10.4 |
| All Other Non-Current | 10.9 | 10.3 | 12.6 | 20.9 | 14.5 | 9.0 | 20.2 | 4.7 | 7.5 |
| Total | 100.0 | 100.0 | 100.0 | 100.0 | 100.0 | 100.0 | 100.0 | 100.0 | 100.0 |
| **LIABILITIES** | | | | | | | | | |
| Notes Payable-Short Term | 12.3 | 13.2 | 9.3 | 8.0 | 9.8 | 20.5 | 1.3 | 11.6 | 7.9 |
| Cur. Mat.-L.T.D. | 3.9 | 3.6 | 4.7 | 2.7 | 9.9 | 5.4 | 4.4 | 3.8 | 2.7 |
| Trade Payables | 14.5 | 16.5 | 15.3 | 6.7 | 15.4 | 5.7 | 17.3 | 22.8 | 20.6 |
| Income Taxes Payable | .1 | 1.3 | .2 | .1 | .2 | .0 | .6 | .0 | .3 |
| All Other Current | 18.8 | 17.2 | 15.8 | 17.1 | 18.8 | 18.4 | 15.5 | 9.4 | 14.9 |
| Total Current | 49.6 | 51.8 | 45.3 | 34.6 | 54.1 | 49.9 | 39.1 | 47.6 | 46.4 |
| Long-Term Debt | 28.9 | 20.7 | 22.4 | 35.2 | 25.2 | 20.8 | 14.4 | 16.4 | 15.4 |
| Deferred Taxes | .3 | .1 | .2 | .0 | .0 | .0 | .0 | .0 | .6 |
| All Other Non-Current | 11.0 | 14.7 | 10.3 | 14.3 | 7.0 | 15.6 | 11.1 | 8.6 | 8.9 |
| Net Worth | 10.1 | 12.7 | 21.8 | 15.8 | 13.7 | 13.7 | 35.3 | 27.3 | 28.7 |
| Total Liabilities & Net Worth | 100.0 | 100.0 | 100.0 | 100.0 | 100.0 | 100.0 | 100.0 | 100.0 | 100.0 |
| **INCOME DATA** | | | | | | | | | |
| Net Sales | 100.0 | 100.0 | 100.0 | 100.0 | 100.0 | 100.0 | 100.0 | 100.0 | 100.0 |
| Gross Profit | | | | | | | | | |
| Operating Expenses | 92.8 | 95.7 | 95.1 | 92.1 | 94.5 | 100.0 | 96.7 | 95.8 | 95.8 |
| Operating Profit | 7.2 | 4.3 | 4.9 | 7.9 | 5.5 | .0 | 3.3 | 4.2 | 4.2 |
| All Other Expenses (net) | 2.4 | 1.7 | 1.9 | 4.7 | .4 | .6 | .3 | 2.0 | 1.4 |
| Profit Before Taxes | 4.7 | 2.7 | 3.1 | 3.2 | 5.1 | -.5 | 3.0 | 2.3 | 2.8 |
| **RATIOS** | | | | | | | | | |
| Current | 1.8 | 2.0 | 1.8 | 1.6 | 1.4 | 2.0 | 3.4 | 1.7 | 1.9 |
| | 1.1 | 1.2 | 1.1 | .4 | .6 | 1.4 | 1.0 | 1.1 | 1.2 |
| | .6 | .7 | .4 | .1 | .2 | .8 | .3 | .7 | 1.0 |
| Quick | 1.2 | 1.5 | 1.2 | 1.0 | 1.1 | 1.6 | 1.8 | 1.3 | 1.4 |
| | .8 | (124) .8 | .7 | .2 | .3 | .8 | .7 | .7 | 1.0 |
| | .4 | .4 | .4 | .0 | .1 | .3 | .2 | .4 | .5 |
| Sales/Receivables | 0 999.8 | 0 UND | 0 UND | 0 UND | 0 UND | 0 UND | 2 160.0 | 10 36.4 | 13 27.6 |
| | 16 22.4 | 15 24.2 | 8 48.3 | 0 UND | 0 UND | 0 UND | 15 24.2 | 16 22.2 | 28 13.1 |
| | 32 11.5 | 30 12.0 | 29 12.7 | 0 UND | 9 39.8 | 25 14.8 | 33 11.0 | 29 12.5 | 39 9.4 |
| Cost of Sales/Inventory | | | | | | | | | |
| Cost of Sales/Payables | | | | | | | | | |
| Sales/Working Capital | 17.0 | 15.2 | 19.1 | 83.6 | 24.1 | 20.6 | 6.5 | 20.1 | 14.8 |
| | 125.5 | 90.8 | 136.7 | -27.0 | -26.9 | 62.3 | NM | 139.3 | 41.0 |
| | -14.3 | -20.5 | -17.5 | -5.4 | -10.6 | -37.3 | -10.9 | -25.2 | 620.0 |
| EBIT/Interest | 15.8 | 13.1 | 14.9 | 7.7 | 11.5 | 11.0 | 21.8 | 11.6 | 47.9 |
| | (88) 3.7 | (110) 4.6 | (139) 4.0 | (21) 2.9 | (26) 5.5 | 2.0 | (10) 5.5 | (22) 2.6 | (47) 7.9 |
| | .5 | .7 | 1.1 | .5 | 1.0 | -.8 | 1.2 | 1.1 | 1.7 |
| Net Profit + Depr., Dep., Amort./Cur. Mat. L/T/D | 7.0 | 4.4 | 7.0 | | | | | | 6.0 |
| | (14) 2.8 | (20) 3.2 | (28) 2.4 | | | | | (16) | 2.4 |
| | .3 | .8 | 1.4 | | | | | | 1.5 |
| Fixed/Worth | .3 | .5 | .4 | .8 | .6 | .4 | .4 | .2 | .2 |
| | 2.6 | 1.6 | 1.6 | 3.6 | 1.6 | 5.4 | 1.0 | 1.9 | .8 |
| | -2.0 | -2.0 | -6.0 | -1.8 | NM | -.3 | 4.3 | -1.2 | 225.1 |
| Debt/Worth | 1.6 | 1.3 | 1.2 | .4 | 1.2 | .8 | .8 | 1.3 | 1.5 |
| | 7.0 | 5.9 | 4.0 | 7.2 | 4.5 | 372.0 | 2.9 | 3.5 | 3.5 |
| | -4.7 | -5.5 | -18.1 | -4.6 | NM | -3.3 | 23.3 | -6.5 | 322.1 |
| % Profit Before Taxes/Tangible Net Worth | 98.7 | 65.7 | 69.7 | 74.5 | 122.0 | | 99.7 | 64.7 | 44.3 |
| | (67) 40.9 | (80) 20.1 | (124) 25.7 | (23) 10.8 | (29) 62.0 | | (10) 32.2 | (15) 25.5 | (40) 24.4 |
| | 6.1 | -3.9 | 1.7 | -1.7 | 6.5 | | -1.7 | 2.1 | -.2 |
| % Profit Before Taxes/Total Assets | 22.3 | 18.2 | 22.6 | 21.7 | 28.6 | 10.6 | 27.4 | 13.2 | 21.5 |
| | 6.9 | 6.9 | 8.3 | 4.0 | 17.0 | 2.6 | 9.0 | 4.1 | 9.5 |
| | .3 | -.7 | .2 | -2.9 | .8 | -12.8 | .3 | .2 | 1.8 |
| Sales/Net Fixed Assets | 36.4 | 71.1 | 76.1 | 9.0 | 61.3 | 425.4 | 75.7 | 152.0 | 122.4 |
| | 12.4 | 19.4 | 15.2 | 6.4 | 19.4 | 18.2 | 14.1 | 28.6 | 30.0 |
| | 4.5 | 6.2 | 5.0 | 1.2 | 4.6 | 7.2 | 5.9 | 10.9 | 9.9 |
| Sales/Total Assets | 5.9 | 6.3 | 6.0 | 4.7 | 6.8 | 5.4 | 5.7 | 6.3 | 6.2 |
| | 3.2 | 4.1 | 3.9 | 2.2 | 4.4 | 4.0 | 2.9 | 4.2 | 4.3 |
| | 2.0 | 2.2 | 2.0 | .9 | 2.6 | 2.7 | 2.0 | 2.6 | 2.5 |
| % Depr., Dep., Amort./Sales | .8 | .5 | .6 | 2.2 | 1.0 | | .7 | .2 | .3 |
| | (88) 1.8 | (101) 1.6 | (140) 1.7 | (31) 3.4 | (26) 1.5 | (10) 1.0 | (19) 2.0 | (45) .9 | |
| | 3.2 | 3.5 | 3.5 | 5.9 | 3.0 | | 5.3 | 3.5 | 1.8 |
| % Officers', Directors' Owners' Comp/Sales | 1.8 | 1.2 | 1.5 | 6.2 | 2.4 | | | | .4 |
| | (33) 3.4 | (51) 2.9 | (61) 3.7 | (10) 10.2 | (15) 3.6 | | | (15) | 1.4 |
| | 7.6 | 9.2 | 7.9 | 16.0 | 6.1 | | | | 6.5 |
| Net Sales ($) | 3030712M | 4451659M | 7092985M | 22601M | 67451M | 47236M | 83332M | 399958M | 6472407M |
| Total Assets ($) | 1438213M | 1117949M | 2122532M | 23448M | 25607M | 15739M | 30265M | 113191M | 1914282M |

© RMA 2012

M = $ thousand    MM = $ million

See Pages 9 through 22 for Explanation of Ratios and Data

## Current Data Sorted by Assets

## Comparative Historical Data

| | | | | | | Type of Statement | | |
|---|---|---|---|---|---|---|---|---|
| | | | | | | Unqualified | 5 | 3 |
| | 1 | | 1 | | | Reviewed | 3 | 7 |
| 1 | 4 | 7 | 1 | 2 | 1 | Compiled | 14 | 25 |
| 5 | 8 | 13 | 1 | | | Tax Returns | 33 | 49 |
| 21 | 18 | 18 | 1 | | | Other | 31 | 36 |
| 13 | 12 | 8 | 2 | | | | 4/1/07- | 4/1/08- |
| | 19 (4/1-9/30/11) | | 118 (10/1/11-3/31/12) | | | | 3/31/08 | 3/31/09 |
| | | | | | | | ALL | ALL |
| 0-500M | 500M-2MM | 2-10MM | 10-50MM | 50-100MM | 100-250MM | NUMBER OF STATEMENTS | 86 | 120 |
| 40 | 43 | 46 | 5 | 2 | 1 | | | |
| % | % | % | % | % | % | ASSETS | % | % |
| 29.0 | 16.2 | 14.3 | | | | Cash & Equivalents | 18.4 | 15.1 |
| 12.9 | 8.9 | 11.6 | | | | Trade Receivables (net) | 17.3 | 13.4 |
| 5.8 | 3.6 | 2.9 | | | | Inventory | 5.9 | 5.4 |
| 3.0 | 5.8 | 3.6 | | | | All Other Current | 2.7 | 4.2 |
| 50.7 | 34.4 | 32.4 | | | | Total Current | 44.3 | 38.2 |
| 30.1 | 43.3 | 43.1 | | | | Fixed Assets (net) | 37.6 | 44.0 |
| 8.7 | 9.0 | 11.7 | | | | Intangibles (net) | 8.1 | 6.3 |
| 10.6 | 13.3 | 12.9 | | | | All Other Non-Current | 10.0 | 11.5 |
| 100.0 | 100.0 | 100.0 | | | | Total | 100.0 | 100.0 |
| | | | | | | LIABILITIES | | |
| 11.8 | 10.0 | 2.2 | | | | Notes Payable-Short Term | 6.8 | 7.9 |
| 2.7 | 3.9 | 2.6 | | | | Cur. Mat.-L.T.D. | 2.9 | 5.3 |
| 10.5 | 8.0 | 9.4 | | | | Trade Payables | 11.9 | 12.8 |
| .1 | .2 | .3 | | | | Income Taxes Payable | .2 | .1 |
| 32.3 | 15.2 | 18.4 | | | | All Other Current | 19.9 | 26.4 |
| 57.5 | 37.4 | 32.9 | | | | Total Current | 41.7 | 52.5 |
| 32.4 | 28.4 | 31.1 | | | | Long-Term Debt | 35.2 | 30.7 |
| .0 | .0 | .1 | | | | Deferred Taxes | .1 | .0 |
| 13.1 | 15.5 | 9.5 | | | | All Other Non-Current | 15.7 | 7.2 |
| -3.1 | 18.7 | 26.4 | | | | Net Worth | 7.4 | 9.6 |
| 100.0 | 100.0 | 100.0 | | | | Total Liabilities & Net Worth | 100.0 | 100.0 |
| | | | | | | INCOME DATA | | |
| 100.0 | 100.0 | 100.0 | | | | Net Sales | 100.0 | 100.0 |
| | | | | | | Gross Profit | | |
| 91.4 | 92.8 | 91.4 | | | | Operating Expenses | 93.5 | 93.3 |
| 8.6 | 7.2 | 8.6 | | | | Operating Profit | 6.5 | 6.7 |
| 2.0 | 1.5 | 2.7 | | | | All Other Expenses (net) | 1.9 | 2.6 |
| 6.6 | 5.7 | 5.9 | | | | Profit Before Taxes | 4.6 | 4.1 |
| | | | | | | RATIOS | | |
| 1.7 | 2.0 | 1.7 | | | | | 1.9 | 1.6 |
| 1.0 | .9 | .4 | | | | Current | 1.2 | 1.0 |
| .5 | .4 | .2 | | | | | .5 | .4 |
| 1.3 | 1.2 | 1.5 | | | | | 1.7 | 1.3 |
| .6 | .6 | .4 | | | | Quick | 1.0 | .6 |
| .2 | .2 | .1 | | | | | .3 | .2 |
| 0   UND | 0   UND | 0   UND | | | | | 0   UND | 0   UND |
| 2   199.9 | 1   696.0 | 3   139.0 | | | | Sales/Receivables | 11   34.6 | 6   66.2 |
| 16   23.1 | 15   24.2 | 14   26.0 | | | | | 27   13.5 | 22   16.8 |
| | | | | | | Cost of Sales/Inventory | | |
| | | | | | | Cost of Sales/Payables | | |
| 26.7 | 20.1 | 19.3 | | | | | 17.3 | 22.9 |
| UND | -53.0 | -13.0 | | | | Sales/Working Capital | 69.5 | -458.3 |
| -12.3 | -10.6 | -4.4 | | | | | -11.8 | -10.4 |
| 18.5 | 20.1 | 16.8 | | | | | 11.6 | 13.3 |
| (26)   4.9 | (28)   3.5 | (38)   3.2 | | | | EBIT/Interest | (61)   3.0 | (96)   3.0 |
| 1.7 | 1.3 | .7 | | | | | -.1 | .6 |
| | | | | | | Net Profit + Depr., Dep., | 7.0 | 12.9 |
| | | | | | | Amort./Cur. Mat. L/T/D | (10)   1.5 | (11)   2.1 |
| | | | | | | | -.1 | 1.1 |
| .5 | .5 | .6 | | | | | .3 | .7 |
| UND | 3.1 | 3.0 | | | | Fixed/Worth | 2.0 | 2.5 |
| -.4 | -7.3 | -6.2 | | | | | -8.3 | -5.2 |
| 1.2 | .6 | 1.4 | | | | | 1.2 | 1.6 |
| UND | 4.4 | 4.5 | | | | Debt/Worth | 5.3 | 4.5 |
| -2.9 | -19.9 | -8.3 | | | | | -13.7 | -9.7 |
| 504.4 | 147.4 | 74.1 | | | | % Profit Before Taxes/Tangible | 98.6 | 105.8 |
| (23)   73.7 | (30)   50.4 | (31)   26.2 | | | | Net Worth | (59)   46.3 | (80)   42.2 |
| 17.6 | 10.0 | 13.4 | | | | | 17.5 | 8.3 |
| 35.0 | 22.6 | 15.8 | | | | % Profit Before Taxes/Total | 23.8 | 25.0 |
| 12.8 | 5.9 | 6.9 | | | | Assets | 10.2 | 7.7 |
| .5 | 1.7 | .4 | | | | | -1.3 | -1.0 |
| 141.5 | 22.7 | 30.3 | | | | | 38.7 | 38.4 |
| 27.5 | 9.0 | 5.1 | | | | Sales/Net Fixed Assets | 14.3 | 11.1 |
| 10.5 | 3.8 | .8 | | | | | 3.5 | 3.1 |
| 9.7 | 4.5 | 3.3 | | | | | 5.3 | 6.4 |
| 4.9 | 3.1 | 1.7 | | | | Sales/Total Assets | 3.6 | 3.5 |
| 2.8 | 1.8 | .6 | | | | | 1.6 | 1.7 |
| .8 | .9 | 1.4 | | | | | .7 | .8 |
| (27)   1.4 | (31)   1.8 | (36)   2.8 | | | | % Depr., Dep., Amort./Sales | (62)   2.0 | (97)   1.9 |
| 3.9 | 2.6 | 7.9 | | | | | 3.9 | 4.2 |
| 2.7 | 2.5 | 1.4 | | | | | 2.6 | 2.4 |
| (16)   4.4 | (23)   4.3 | (22)   3.0 | | | | % Officers', Directors' | (43)   4.0 | (52)   4.4 |
| 8.6 | 7.7 | 5.6 | | | | Owners' Comp/Sales | 6.1 | 7.0 |
| 49795M | 129874M | 465439M | 126801M | 604485M | 301441M | Net Sales ($) | 1550099M | 1990905M |
| 9075M | 42161M | 194843M | 81727M | 143665M | 172788M | Total Assets ($) | 467131M | 688297M |

M = $ thousand    MM = $ million
See Pages 9 through 22 for Explanation of Ratios and Data

## Comparative Historical Data / Current Data Sorted by Sales

| 7 | 3 | 4 | Type of Statement | 1MM | | | | | |
|---|---|---|---|---|---|---|---|---|---|
| 13 | 12 | 13 | Unqualified | | 1 | | | | 3 |
| 31 | 26 | 27 | Reviewed | 1 | 3 | 2 | 4 | 3 | |
| 70 | 62 | 58 | Compiled | 6 | 7 | 7 | 4 | 2 | 1 |
| 37 | 40 | 35 | Tax Returns | 11 | 22 | 11 | 9 | 4 | 1 |
| 4/1/09-3/31/10 ALL | 4/1/10-3/31/11 ALL | 4/1/11-3/31/12 ALL | Other | 12 | 10 | 5 | 4 | 1 | 3 |
| | | | | 19 (4/1-9/30/11) | | | 118 (10/1/11-3/31/12) | | |
| | | | | 0-1MM | 1-3MM | 3-5MM | 5-10MM | 10-25MM | 25MM & OVER |
| 158 | 143 | 137 | NUMBER OF STATEMENTS | 30 | 43 | 25 | 21 | 10 | 8 |
| % | % | % | **ASSETS** | % | % | % | % | % | % |
| 15.1 | 16.6 | 19.1 | Cash & Equivalents | 26.4 | 13.9 | 18.4 | 17.0 | 19.6 | |
| 8.5 | 14.0 | 12.0 | Trade Receivables (net) | 7.5 | 10.9 | 9.7 | 9.3 | 23.4 | |
| 6.3 | 5.8 | 3.9 | Inventory | 3.4 | 4.1 | 4.2 | 3.1 | 5.9 | |
| 2.6 | 2.5 | 4.0 | All Other Current | .1 | 4.8 | 6.3 | 5.7 | 4.1 | |
| 32.5 | 38.9 | 39.0 | Total Current | 37.4 | 33.7 | 38.6 | 35.1 | 53.0 | |
| 46.2 | 41.2 | 39.5 | Fixed Assets (net) | 38.6 | 45.6 | 46.4 | 36.1 | 25.3 | |
| 8.8 | 7.5 | 9.6 | Intangibles (net) | 13.4 | 6.5 | 4.9 | 17.6 | 10.0 | |
| 12.5 | 12.4 | 11.8 | All Other Non-Current | 10.5 | 14.2 | 10.2 | 11.3 | 11.7 | |
| 100.0 | 100.0 | 100.0 | Total | 100.0 | 100.0 | 100.0 | 100.0 | 100.0 | |
| | | | **LIABILITIES** | | | | | | |
| 9.3 | 6.9 | 7.5 | Notes Payable-Short Term | 12.4 | 8.9 | 7.1 | 1.9 | 2.5 | |
| 5.0 | 5.2 | 3.2 | Cur. Mat.-L.T.D. | 1.6 | 2.5 | 6.5 | 2.8 | 3.0 | |
| 10.6 | 13.8 | 9.0 | Trade Payables | 3.0 | 9.5 | 9.2 | 11.6 | 18.5 | |
| .1 | .2 | .2 | Income Taxes Payable | .2 | .2 | .1 | .1 | 1.0 | |
| 29.9 | 22.3 | 21.2 | All Other Current | 21.1 | 25.0 | 16.1 | 20.3 | 20.5 | |
| 55.0 | 48.4 | 41.2 | Total Current | 38.3 | 46.0 | 39.0 | 36.6 | 45.4 | |
| 33.0 | 30.8 | 30.8 | Long-Term Debt | 31.3 | 43.6 | 32.0 | 18.7 | 15.1 | |
| .0 | .0 | .0 | Deferred Taxes | .0 | .0 | .0 | .0 | .4 | |
| 14.2 | 10.8 | 12.2 | All Other Non-Current | 14.2 | 13.5 | 17.3 | 7.7 | 2.4 | |
| -2.2 | 10.1 | 15.8 | Net Worth | 16.2 | -3.1 | 11.7 | 37.0 | 36.7 | |
| 100.0 | 100.0 | 100.0 | Total Liabilities & Net Worth | 100.0 | 100.0 | 100.0 | 100.0 | 100.0 | |
| | | | **INCOME DATA** | | | | | | |
| 100.0 | 100.0 | 100.0 | Net Sales | 100.0 | 100.0 | 100.0 | 100.0 | 100.0 | |
| | | | Gross Profit | | | | | | |
| 92.9 | 93.0 | 91.9 | Operating Expenses | 82.2 | 94.4 | 96.3 | 91.5 | 98.9 | |
| 7.1 | 7.0 | 8.1 | Operating Profit | 17.8 | 5.6 | 3.7 | 8.5 | 1.1 | |
| 3.3 | 2.6 | 2.0 | All Other Expenses (net) | 6.5 | 1.2 | .7 | 1.5 | -1.3 | |
| 3.8 | 4.4 | 6.0 | Profit Before Taxes | 11.2 | 4.4 | 3.0 | 7.0 | 2.4 | |
| | | | **RATIOS** | | | | | | |
| 1.3 | 1.6 | 1.7 | | 1.5 | 1.7 | 1.8 | 2.4 | 1.8 | |
| .6 | .9 | .8 | Current | .8 | .5 | .8 | .5 | 1.4 | |
| .2 | .3 | .3 | | .4 | .3 | .4 | .3 | .5 | |
| .9 | 1.4 | 1.3 | | 1.4 | .8 | 1.2 | 1.8 | 1.7 | |
| .5 | (142) .6 | .5 | Quick | .6 | .3 | .6 | .4 | 1.0 | |
| .1 | .2 | .2 | | .2 | .2 | .2 | .2 | .4 | |
| 0 UND | 0 UND | 0 UND | | 0 UND | 0 UND | 0 UND | 2 190.5 | 11 33.2 | |
| 2 225.5 | 2 155.0 | 3 141.8 | Sales/Receivables | 0 UND | 1 637.7 | 1 393.4 | 6 58.1 | 15 24.2 | |
| 15 24.3 | 18 19.7 | 17 21.7 | | 11 32.2 | 13 27.5 | 11 31.9 | 17 20.9 | 21 17.4 | |
| | | | Cost of Sales/Inventory | | | | | | |
| | | | Cost of Sales/Payables | | | | | | |
| 60.1 | 21.0 | 22.1 | | 26.0 | 61.3 | 28.1 | 9.2 | 13.2 | |
| -35.6 | -107.2 | -45.3 | Sales/Working Capital | -51.3 | -22.4 | -200.5 | -13.2 | 34.0 | |
| -7.0 | -10.3 | -6.9 | | -4.6 | -5.7 | -9.6 | -4.4 | -15.5 | |
| 8.5 | 13.4 | 17.9 | | 9.6 | 13.5 | 16.5 | 43.5 | 94.8 | |
| (115) 2.4 | (100) 3.6 | (98) 3.5 | EBIT/Interest | (14) 2.4 | (33) 2.8 | (20) 3.5 | (16) 4.4 | -11.0 | |
| .1 | .9 | 1.3 | | 1.4 | .8 | .0 | 1.4 | 2.8 | |
| 4.5 | 5.6 | 5.1 | | | | | | | |
| (16) 2.3 | (12) 1.8 | (11) 1.7 | Net Profit + Depr., Dep., Amort./Cur. Mat. L/T/D | | | | | | |
| 1.3 | 1.1 | .7 | | | | | | | |
| .9 | .5 | .5 | | .4 | .8 | .6 | .5 | .2 | |
| 3.5 | 2.4 | 3.2 | Fixed/Worth | 70.3 | UND | 1.7 | 2.2 | .8 | |
| -3.4 | -3.8 | -3.1 | | -1.1 | -1.4 | 101.4 | NM | -4.6 | |
| 1.8 | 1.1 | 1.3 | | 1.5 | 1.8 | 1.5 | 1.4 | .5 | |
| 8.3 | 4.3 | 6.3 | Debt/Worth | 111.3 | UND | 7.1 | 2.7 | 2.0 | |
| -5.4 | -5.2 | -6.6 | | -4.0 | -4.1 | 220.6 | NM | -10.7 | |
| 92.2 | 79.0 | 117.7 | | 432.5 | 102.4 | 159.4 | 120.3 | | |
| (95) 34.4 | (94) 33.7 | (90) 46.0 | % Profit Before Taxes/Tangible Net Worth | (17) 41.3 | (23) 27.2 | (20) 47.3 | (16) 51.7 | | |
| 5.1 | 10.0 | 13.5 | | 10.7 | 6.4 | 15.6 | 15.2 | | |
| 19.5 | 23.1 | 22.6 | | 12.5 | 31.0 | 41.5 | 19.7 | 14.8 | |
| 3.9 | 7.1 | 8.1 | % Profit Before Taxes/Total Assets | 4.8 | 5.8 | 5.9 | 9.6 | 9.8 | |
| -2.3 | .2 | 1.3 | | .0 | .7 | -.9 | 2.6 | 3.8 | |
| 30.2 | 38.4 | 33.8 | | 193.4 | 28.1 | 22.8 | 31.1 | 47.0 | |
| 7.9 | 12.2 | 11.7 | Sales/Net Fixed Assets | 9.2 | 9.2 | 11.7 | 8.2 | 29.0 | |
| 2.5 | 3.7 | 3.0 | | .8 | 3.1 | 3.3 | 3.1 | 12.3 | |
| 6.3 | 6.7 | 5.3 | | 4.1 | 6.5 | 6.3 | 3.2 | 5.5 | |
| 2.8 | 3.7 | 3.0 | Sales/Total Assets | 1.9 | 3.3 | 3.2 | 2.0 | 3.9 | |
| 1.4 | 1.7 | 1.4 | | .3 | 1.2 | 2.1 | 1.3 | 3.4 | |
| 1.5 | 1.1 | 1.1 | | 2.2 | 1.0 | .8 | 1.2 | | |
| (130) 2.1 | (122) 2.2 | (101) 2.0 | % Depr., Dep., Amort./Sales | (16) 4.0 | (36) 1.8 | (19) 2.0 | (17) 2.0 | | |
| 4.4 | 5.4 | 4.8 | | 23.8 | 4.0 | 5.9 | 4.5 | | |
| 2.4 | 2.7 | 2.2 | | | 2.6 | 1.2 | | | |
| (73) 4.8 | (60) 4.4 | (64) 3.7 | % Officers', Directors' Owners' Comp/Sales | | (27) 5.2 | (15) 3.1 | | | |
| 8.7 | 7.4 | 7.6 | | | 9.3 | 6.6 | | | |
| 3364442M | 1763016M | 1677835M | Net Sales ($) | 16178M | 87551M | 96903M | 153600M | 149051M | 1174552M |
| 1120677M | 615116M | 644259M | Total Assets ($) | 23696M | 53794M | 56244M | 110062M | 41413M | 359050M |

© RMA 2012

M = $ thousand   MM = $ million
See Pages 9 through 22 for Explanation of Ratios and Data

## Current Data Sorted by Assets        Comparative Historical Data

| 0-500M | 500M-2MM | 2-10MM | 10-50MM | 50-100MM | 100-250MM | Type of Statement | 4/1/07-3/31/08 ALL | 4/1/08-3/31/09 ALL |
|---|---|---|---|---|---|---|---|---|
| | 1 | 2 | 2 | | | Unqualified | 2 | 3 |
| | | | 1 | | | Reviewed | 5 | 2 |
| 21 | 9 | 4 | | | | Compiled | 25 | 33 |
| 103 | 38 | 11 | 2 | | | Tax Returns | 102 | 128 |
| 43 | 29 | 18 | 3 | | | Other | 55 | 42 |
| | 14 (4/1-9/30/11) | | 273 (10/1/11-3/31/12) | | | | | |
| 167 | 77 | 35 | 8 | | | **NUMBER OF STATEMENTS** | 189 | 208 |
| % | % | % | % | % | % | **ASSETS** | % | % |
| 17.7 | 13.8 | 8.7 | | | | Cash & Equivalents | 16.9 | 13.5 |
| .8 | 1.3 | 1.0 | | | | Trade Receivables (net) | 1.2 | 1.2 |
| 11.7 | 4.4 | 5.3 | D | D | | Inventory | 8.7 | 8.4 |
| 2.7 | 2.5 | 6.8 | A | A | | All Other Current | 3.0 | 4.8 |
| 32.9 | 21.9 | 21.7 | T | T | | Total Current | 29.8 | 27.8 |
| 41.3 | 56.6 | 55.6 | A | A | | Fixed Assets (net) | 47.4 | 48.9 |
| 13.2 | 9.0 | 9.3 | | | | Intangibles (net) | 14.4 | 14.6 |
| 12.7 | 12.5 | 13.4 | N | N | | All Other Non-Current | 8.4 | 8.6 |
| 100.0 | 100.0 | 100.0 | O | O | | Total | 100.0 | 100.0 |
| | | | T | T | | **LIABILITIES** | | |
| 10.8 | 5.7 | 3.1 | | | | Notes Payable-Short Term | 7.2 | 6.4 |
| 4.1 | 2.1 | 3.4 | A | A | | Cur. Mat.-L.T.D. | 3.8 | 3.1 |
| 9.0 | 5.1 | 5.6 | V | V | | Trade Payables | 8.5 | 8.1 |
| .1 | .0 | .2 | A | A | | Income Taxes Payable | .1 | .1 |
| 18.7 | 13.8 | 12.6 | I | I | | All Other Current | 17.4 | 19.9 |
| 42.7 | 26.6 | 24.9 | L | L | | Total Current | 37.0 | 37.4 |
| 28.0 | 31.9 | 27.6 | A | A | | Long-Term Debt | 32.6 | 33.1 |
| .0 | .0 | .0 | B | B | | Deferred Taxes | .1 | .2 |
| 27.8 | 14.6 | 3.4 | L | L | | All Other Non-Current | 18.6 | 15.9 |
| 1.5 | 26.8 | 44.2 | E | E | | Net Worth | 11.7 | 13.4 |
| 100.0 | 100.0 | 100.0 | | | | Total Liabilities & Net Worth | 100.0 | 100.0 |
| | | | | | | **INCOME DATA** | | |
| 100.0 | 100.0 | 100.0 | | | | Net Sales | 100.0 | 100.0 |
| 60.5 | 62.7 | 70.3 | | | | Gross Profit | 60.3 | 59.7 |
| 56.8 | 57.4 | 58.9 | | | | Operating Expenses | 56.5 | 55.1 |
| 3.7 | 5.4 | 11.3 | | | | Operating Profit | 3.7 | 4.6 |
| .1 | .9 | 1.5 | | | | All Other Expenses (net) | .9 | 1.1 |
| 3.6 | 4.4 | 9.9 | | | | Profit Before Taxes | 2.8 | 3.6 |
| | | | | | | **RATIOS** | | |
| 3.3 | 2.5 | 2.8 | | | | | 2.8 | 2.0 |
| 1.1 | 1.3 | .8 | | | | Current | 1.3 | .9 |
| .4 | .4 | .3 | | | | | .4 | .4 |
| 1.9 | 2.0 | 1.7 | | | | | 1.7 | 1.2 |
| .6 | (76) .8 | .3 | | | | Quick | (186) .7 | (205) .4 |
| .1 | .2 | .1 | | | | | .1 | .1 |
| 0 UND | 0 UND | 0 UND | | | | | 0 UND | 0 UND |
| 0 UND | 0 UND | 0 999.8 | | | | Sales/Receivables | 0 UND | 0 UND |
| 0 UND | 0 998.9 | 2 156.9 | | | | | 0 999.8 | 0 UND |
| 6 59.8 | 6 58.3 | 14 26.9 | | | | | 8 45.5 | 9 42.5 |
| 13 27.3 | 16 22.7 | 24 14.9 | | | | Cost of Sales/Inventory | 15 25.0 | 15 24.0 |
| 30 12.3 | 27 13.3 | 38 9.6 | | | | | 25 14.9 | 29 12.6 |
| 0 UND | 0 UND | 8 48.1 | | | | | 0 UND | 0 UND |
| 0 UND | 13 27.1 | 29 12.6 | | | | Cost of Sales/Payables | 8 46.4 | 9 42.4 |
| 18 20.6 | 33 11.2 | 47 7.7 | | | | | 27 13.5 | 30 12.3 |
| 23.0 | 19.0 | 11.8 | | | | | 17.5 | 27.0 |
| 159.0 | 49.2 | -42.6 | | | | Sales/Working Capital | 68.5 | -157.2 |
| -23.9 | -14.6 | -8.8 | | | | | -17.1 | -15.0 |
| 15.8 | 14.0 | 34.6 | | | | | 9.9 | 8.8 |
| (100) 3.9 | (56) 3.1 | (30) 5.6 | | | | EBIT/Interest | (134) 2.1 | (153) 2.7 |
| -.5 | .3 | 1.8 | | | | | .2 | .2 |
| | | | | | | | 5.9 | |
| | | | | | | Net Profit + Depr., Dep., Amort./Cur. Mat. L/T/D | (10) 2.1 | |
| | | | | | | | -.4 | |
| .5 | .9 | .6 | | | | | .7 | 1.1 |
| 2.9 | 4.1 | 2.0 | | | | Fixed/Worth | 4.1 | 4.0 |
| -.9 | -8.5 | 131.7 | | | | | -1.2 | -1.3 |
| .4 | .7 | .3 | | | | | .8 | 1.0 |
| 8.6 | 5.3 | 1.4 | | | | Debt/Worth | 8.3 | 6.1 |
| -2.8 | -10.6 | 143.1 | | | | | -2.8 | -3.7 |
| 134.1 | 92.2 | 56.9 | | | | | 78.9 | 77.4 |
| (95) 47.1 | (53) 41.7 | (27) 37.2 | | | | % Profit Before Taxes/Tangible Net Worth | (107) 40.5 | (122) 38.2 |
| 1.5 | 8.7 | 17.0 | | | | | 1.8 | 4.3 |
| 45.8 | 27.2 | 20.9 | | | | | 25.1 | 25.2 |
| 12.7 | 8.0 | 10.7 | | | | % Profit Before Taxes/Total Assets | 5.7 | 6.7 |
| -4.8 | -.2 | 2.9 | | | | | -5.3 | -4.1 |
| 38.5 | 9.1 | 7.9 | | | | | 25.3 | 18.3 |
| 14.1 | 3.1 | 2.8 | | | | Sales/Net Fixed Assets | 7.6 | 7.7 |
| 6.0 | 2.0 | 1.5 | | | | | 3.7 | 3.5 |
| 7.9 | 2.8 | 2.4 | | | | | 5.6 | 5.5 |
| 4.4 | 1.9 | 1.4 | | | | Sales/Total Assets | 3.1 | 3.2 |
| 3.0 | 1.2 | .9 | | | | | 1.8 | 1.8 |
| 1.0 | 2.0 | 1.5 | | | | | 1.2 | 1.6 |
| (114) 2.0 | (59) 3.3 | (26) 2.8 | | | | % Depr., Dep., Amort./Sales | (160) 2.2 | (170) 2.8 |
| 3.9 | 6.4 | 6.2 | | | | | 4.3 | 4.6 |
| 3.1 | 2.5 | 2.3 | | | | | 2.6 | 2.2 |
| (71) 5.7 | (34) 3.9 | (21) 3.0 | | | | % Officers', Directors' Owners' Comp/Sales | (88) 4.8 | (88) 3.9 |
| 10.0 | 5.5 | 4.4 | | | | | 8.9 | 7.3 |
| 169836M | 156321M | 249536M | 652686M | | | Net Sales ($) | 5080841M | 3295620M |
| 36199M | 72495M | 138763M | 178577M | | | Total Assets ($) | 838565M | 989206M |

## Comparative Historical Data | Current Data Sorted by Sales

| 2 / 1 / 28 / 118 / 55 | 1 / 27 / 129 / 66 | 2 / 4 / 34 / 154 / 93 | Type of Statement | 0-1MM | 1-3MM | 3-5MM | 5-10MM | 10-25MM | 25MM & OVER |
|---|---|---|---|---|---|---|---|---|---|
| 2 | 1 | 2 | Unqualified |  |  |  |  |  | 2 |
| 1 |  | 4 | Reviewed |  | 1 |  |  | 2 | 1 |
| 28 | 27 | 34 | Compiled | 12 | 16 | 3 | 2 | 1 |  |
| 118 | 129 | 154 | Tax Returns | 68 | 67 | 11 | 7 |  | 1 |
| 55 | 66 | 93 | Other | 35 | 33 | 12 | 6 | 6 | 1 |
| 4/1/09-3/31/10 ALL | 4/1/10-3/31/11 ALL | 4/1/11-3/31/12 ALL |  | 14 (4/1-9/30/11) | | | 273 (10/1/11-3/31/12) | | |
| 204 | 223 | 287 | **NUMBER OF STATEMENTS** | 115 | 117 | 26 | 15 | 9 | 5 |
| % | % | % | **ASSETS** | % | % | % | % | % | % |
| 16.4 | 15.4 | 15.4 | Cash & Equivalents | 15.9 | 15.1 | 15.1 | 15.9 |  |  |
| 1.4 | 1.0 | 1.0 | Trade Receivables (net) | .6 | 1.4 | .6 | 1.2 |  |  |
| 7.6 | 8.8 | 8.8 | Inventory | 10.1 | 8.8 | 4.8 | 3.0 |  |  |
| 2.5 | 1.9 | 3.1 | All Other Current | 2.2 | 2.4 | 10.0 | 5.1 |  |  |
| 27.9 | 27.2 | 28.4 | Total Current | 28.9 | 27.6 | 30.6 | 25.2 |  |  |
| 46.9 | 51.6 | 47.3 | Fixed Assets (net) | 46.8 | 48.1 | 43.7 | 50.7 |  |  |
| 17.1 | 12.2 | 11.6 | Intangibles (net) | 11.4 | 13.0 | 5.8 | 10.3 |  |  |
| 8.1 | 9.1 | 12.8 | All Other Non-Current | 13.0 | 11.3 | 20.0 | 13.7 |  |  |
| 100.0 | 100.0 | 100.0 | Total | 100.0 | 100.0 | 100.0 | 100.0 |  |  |
|  |  |  | **LIABILITIES** |  |  |  |  |  |  |
| 5.9 | 5.7 | 8.2 | Notes Payable-Short Term | 9.5 | 9.1 | 4.7 | 3.8 |  |  |
| 2.0 | 2.4 | 3.4 | Cur. Mat.-L.T.D. | 4.3 | 2.7 | 2.3 | 1.7 |  |  |
| 5.9 | 6.1 | 7.5 | Trade Payables | 6.8 | 8.1 | 6.8 | 7.8 |  |  |
| .1 | .0 | .1 | Income Taxes Payable | .0 | .2 | .0 | .0 |  |  |
| 17.8 | 16.5 | 16.8 | All Other Current | 17.5 | 16.8 | 17.5 | 9.5 |  |  |
| 31.7 | 30.8 | 36.0 | Total Current | 38.1 | 36.9 | 31.4 | 22.9 |  |  |
| 29.6 | 28.3 | 29.3 | Long-Term Debt | 31.2 | 31.6 | 20.6 | 7.4 |  |  |
| .1 | .1 | .0 | Deferred Taxes | .0 | .0 | .0 | .0 |  |  |
| 20.9 | 21.9 | 21.6 | All Other Non-Current | 28.1 | 18.0 | 15.5 | 10.3 |  |  |
| 17.7 | 19.0 | 13.1 | Net Worth | 2.6 | 13.5 | 32.4 | 59.5 |  |  |
| 100.0 | 100.0 | 100.0 | Total Liabilties & Net Worth | 100.0 | 100.0 | 100.0 | 100.0 |  |  |
|  |  |  | **INCOME DATA** |  |  |  |  |  |  |
| 100.0 | 100.0 | 100.0 | Net Sales | 100.0 | 100.0 | 100.0 | 100.0 |  |  |
| 60.0 | 61.2 | 62.5 | Gross Profit | 59.2 | 63.1 | 66.4 | 72.8 |  |  |
| 56.1 | 56.1 | 57.3 | Operating Expenses | 56.9 | 57.6 | 55.7 | 60.9 |  |  |
| 4.0 | 5.1 | 5.1 | Operating Profit | 2.3 | 5.5 | 10.7 | 11.9 |  |  |
| .9 | .9 | .6 | All Other Expenses (net) | .5 | .4 | 1.2 | .5 |  |  |
| 3.0 | 4.3 | 4.6 | Profit Before Taxes | 1.7 | 5.2 | 9.5 | 11.3 |  |  |
|  |  |  | **RATIOS** |  |  |  |  |  |  |
| 3.2 | 2.8 | 2.8 | Current | 3.3 | 2.7 | 4.6 | 2.5 |  |  |
| 1.0 | 1.2 | 1.1 |  | 1.0 | 1.3 | 1.5 | 1.6 |  |  |
| .4 | .4 | .4 |  | .4 | .5 | .3 | .3 |  |  |
| 2.2 | 1.8 | 1.9 | Quick | 1.6 | 1.9 | 3.0 | 1.8 |  |  |
| (202) .5 | (221) .6 | (286) .6 |  | .5 | .6 | (25) .5 | 1.2 |  |  |
| .1 | .1 | .1 |  | .1 | .2 | .1 | .2 |  |  |
| 0 UND | 0 UND | 0 UND | Sales/Receivables | 0 UND | 0 UND | 0 UND | 0 UND |  |  |
| 0 UND | 0 UND | 0 UND |  | 0 UND | 0 UND | 0 UND | 1 422.2 |  |  |
| 0 UND | 0 UND | 0 UND |  | 0 UND | 0 UND | 0 910.7 | 4 91.7 |  |  |
| 7 52.7 | 9 39.8 | 7 53.8 | Cost of Sales/Inventory | 4 91.0 | 8 47.5 | 8 43.7 | 10 37.0 |  |  |
| 15 24.5 | 19 19.5 | 15 23.8 |  | 15 23.7 | 14 25.6 | 15 25.0 | 16 25.0 |  |  |
| 26 14.2 | 34 10.8 | 30 12.3 |  | 36 10.1 | 26 13.8 | 37 9.8 | 36 10.0 |  |  |
| 0 UND | 0 UND | 0 UND | Cost of Sales/Payables | 0 UND | 0 UND | 0 UND | 15 24.4 |  |  |
| 4 90.2 | 5 74.0 | 6 57.5 |  | 0 UND | 8 47.8 | 8 43.9 | 25 14.6 |  |  |
| 24 15.0 | 26 14.3 | 31 11.6 |  | 22 16.3 | 25 14.4 | 34 10.7 | 46 7.9 |  |  |
| 19.0 | 21.8 | 21.1 | Sales/Working Capital | 20.2 | 22.9 | 13.8 | 17.9 |  |  |
| UND | 121.4 | 148.2 |  | UND | 92.4 | NM | 37.8 |  |  |
| -24.9 | -19.4 | -17.5 |  | -17.5 | -23.7 | -9.5 | -11.9 |  |  |
| 8.7 | 13.6 | 15.9 | EBIT/Interest | 10.3 | 15.5 | 29.3 | 266.7 |  |  |
| (140) 2.3 | (138) 2.7 | (194) 3.8 |  | (67) 2.1 | (86) 4.3 | (16) 2.9 | (11) 37.0 |  |  |
| .4 | 1.0 | .2 |  | -1.0 | .7 | 1.1 | 2.9 |  |  |
|  |  |  | Net Profit + Depr., Dep., Amort./Cur. Mat. L/T/D |  |  |  |  |  |  |
| .8 | .8 | .6 | Fixed/Worth | .5 | .8 | .3 | .6 |  |  |
| 3.2 | 2.2 | 2.6 |  | 5.2 | 4.4 | .7 | 1.2 |  |  |
| -1.8 | -3.2 | -2.2 |  | -1.4 | -1.8 | 9.8 | 2.7 |  |  |
| .8 | .5 | .4 | Debt/Worth | .5 | .7 | .2 | .2 |  |  |
| 6.2 | 2.4 | 5.2 |  | 17.1 | 6.4 | .7 | .6 |  |  |
| -3.4 | -4.6 | -3.8 |  | -3.0 | -3.6 | 27.8 | 5.3 |  |  |
| 97.8 | 87.7 | 101.9 | % Profit Before Taxes/Tangible Net Worth | 81.3 | 139.0 | 95.8 | 112.6 |  |  |
| (127) 40.6 | (151) 34.9 | (181) 41.7 |  | (64) 29.3 | (72) 47.7 | (21) 57.0 | (13) 50.4 |  |  |
| 3.1 | .8 | 7.2 |  | -10.8 | 7.2 | 39.1 | 18.3 |  |  |
| 28.1 | 31.9 | 34.0 | % Profit Before Taxes/Total Assets | 26.5 | 36.3 | 49.2 | 46.5 |  |  |
| 7.7 | 8.3 | 10.7 |  | 5.7 | 10.5 | 18.8 | 27.2 |  |  |
| -1.6 | -1.6 | -2.3 |  | -8.3 | -1.2 | 2.8 | 7.9 |  |  |
| 27.1 | 25.1 | 21.8 | Sales/Net Fixed Assets | 25.0 | 20.1 | 25.6 | 16.4 |  |  |
| 8.6 | 6.4 | 8.0 |  | 8.9 | 9.1 | 10.0 | 7.9 |  |  |
| 3.4 | 2.5 | 3.0 |  | 3.4 | 3.0 | 2.9 | 1.9 |  |  |
| 5.8 | 6.1 | 5.1 | Sales/Total Assets | 5.1 | 6.1 | 5.2 | 3.8 |  |  |
| 3.1 | 3.2 | 3.1 |  | 3.3 | 3.5 | 2.2 | 2.3 |  |  |
| 1.6 | 1.6 | 1.5 |  | 1.4 | 1.9 | 1.3 | 1.4 |  |  |
| 1.6 | 1.2 | 1.2 | % Depr., Dep., Amort./Sales | 1.2 | 1.0 | 1.4 | 1.4 |  |  |
| (162) 2.8 | (170) 2.5 | (205) 2.7 |  | (76) 2.7 | (87) 2.7 | (19) 2.5 | (13) 2.6 |  |  |
| 5.0 | 4.7 | 5.6 |  | 6.2 | 5.4 | 5.6 | 4.4 |  |  |
| 2.4 | 2.3 | 2.5 | % Officers', Directors' Owners' Comp/Sales | 3.1 | 2.5 | 2.5 |  |  |  |
| (104) 4.6 | (98) 4.9 | (129) 4.7 |  | (43) 5.7 | (57) 4.8 | (15) 3.4 |  |  |  |
| 9.1 | 8.9 | 7.5 |  | 10.5 | 6.8 | 4.7 |  |  |  |
| 2407176M | 3761890M | 1228379M | Net Sales ($) | 62259M | 195478M | 97799M | 108667M | 137887M | 626289M |
| 780191M | 1119727M | 426034M | Total Assets ($) | 28597M | 78202M | 53775M | 58584M | 67675M | 139201M |

© RMA 2012

M = $ thousand    MM = $ million
See Pages 9 through 22 for Explanation of Ratios and Data

# OTHER SERVICES (EXCEPT PUBLIC ADMINISTRATION)

## Current Data Sorted by Assets     Comparative Historical Data

| Type of Statement | 0-500M | 500M-2MM | 2-10MM | 10-50MM | 50-100MM | 100-250MM | 443 (4/1/07-3/31/08 ALL) | 469 (4/1/08-3/31/09 ALL) |
|---|---|---|---|---|---|---|---|---|
| Unqualified | | 1 | | 2 | | 2 | 5 | 8 |
| Reviewed | 1 | 4 | 9 | 3 | | | 28 | 20 |
| Compiled | 41 | 32 | 14 | 2 | | | 77 | 64 |
| Tax Returns | 268 | 82 | 14 | 1 | 1 | 1 | 217 | 238 |
| Other | 100 | 63 | 27 | 14 | 3 | 3 | 116 | 139 |
| | | | 66 (4/1-9/30/11) | 622 (10/1/11-3/31/12) | | | | |
| **NUMBER OF STATEMENTS** | 410 | 182 | 64 | 22 | 4 | 6 | 443 | 469 |
| **ASSETS** | % | % | % | % | % | % | % | % |
| Cash & Equivalents | 21.7 | 13.3 | 11.3 | 11.1 | | | 14.3 | 15.4 |
| Trade Receivables (net) | 10.9 | 11.5 | 11.3 | 9.5 | | | 11.7 | 12.0 |
| Inventory | 17.3 | 14.2 | 21.9 | 15.9 | | | 18.4 | 19.7 |
| All Other Current | 2.6 | 2.2 | 3.0 | 2.6 | | | 3.1 | 2.7 |
| Total Current | 52.6 | 41.2 | 47.4 | 39.0 | | | 47.4 | 49.9 |
| Fixed Assets (net) | 31.5 | 42.9 | 36.3 | 41.5 | | | 36.2 | 33.5 |
| Intangibles (net) | 4.4 | 6.6 | 6.5 | 10.3 | | | 6.5 | 6.9 |
| All Other Non-Current | 11.6 | 9.3 | 9.7 | 9.3 | | | 9.9 | 9.6 |
| Total | 100.0 | 100.0 | 100.0 | 100.0 | | | 100.0 | 100.0 |
| **LIABILITIES** | | | | | | | | |
| Notes Payable-Short Term | 17.4 | 5.3 | 6.6 | 5.6 | | | 9.9 | 13.9 |
| Cur. Mat.-L.T.D. | 5.6 | 3.5 | 2.9 | 6.0 | | | 5.1 | 6.4 |
| Trade Payables | 16.4 | 11.4 | 15.1 | 8.6 | | | 15.9 | 15.5 |
| Income Taxes Payable | .1 | .0 | .0 | .3 | | | .1 | .1 |
| All Other Current | 23.9 | 9.6 | 12.8 | 11.8 | | | 14.9 | 17.7 |
| Total Current | 63.4 | 29.8 | 37.4 | 32.3 | | | 45.9 | 53.6 |
| Long-Term Debt | 32.1 | 36.1 | 32.5 | 25.3 | | | 31.3 | 32.0 |
| Deferred Taxes | .0 | .1 | .3 | .1 | | | .0 | .1 |
| All Other Non-Current | 24.2 | 9.3 | 4.5 | 15.7 | | | 10.2 | 13.7 |
| Net Worth | -19.7 | 24.7 | 25.3 | 26.6 | | | 12.6 | .8 |
| Total Liabilities & Net Worth | 100.0 | 100.0 | 100.0 | 100.0 | | | 100.0 | 100.0 |
| **INCOME DATA** | | | | | | | | |
| Net Sales | 100.0 | 100.0 | 100.0 | 100.0 | | | 100.0 | 100.0 |
| Gross Profit | | | | | | | | |
| Operating Expenses | 95.0 | 89.6 | 93.8 | 82.8 | | | 94.2 | 95.7 |
| Operating Profit | 5.0 | 10.4 | 6.2 | 17.2 | | | 5.8 | 4.3 |
| All Other Expenses (net) | 1.1 | 4.2 | 1.8 | 4.9 | | | 1.7 | 1.5 |
| Profit Before Taxes | 3.9 | 6.2 | 4.4 | 12.3 | | | 4.1 | 2.9 |
| **RATIOS** | | | | | | | | |
| Current | 2.5 | 2.8 | 2.4 | 1.5 | | | 2.4 | 2.3 |
| | 1.2 | 1.4 | 1.3 | .8 | | | 1.2 | 1.2 |
| | .5 | .6 | .9 | .4 | | | .7 | .6 |
| Quick | 1.8 | 1.7 | 1.3 | .8 | | | 1.6 | 1.5 |
| | (407) .8 | (181) .8 | .8 | .6 | .4 | | (440) .6 | (467) .6 |
| | .2 | .3 | .3 | .2 | | | .2 | .2 |
| Sales/Receivables | 0 UND | 0 UND | 2 148.3 | 0 UND | | | 0 UND | 0 UND |
| | 2 229.5 | 7 56.0 | 10 38.1 | 8 47.7 | | | 5 72.6 | 5 70.3 |
| | 9 41.4 | 23 16.0 | 24 15.0 | 39 9.4 | | | 18 19.9 | 17 21.0 |
| Cost of Sales/Inventory | | | | | | | | |
| Cost of Sales/Payables | | | | | | | | |
| Sales/Working Capital | 18.8 | 8.5 | 7.7 | 17.2 | | | 13.2 | 12.3 |
| | 115.3 | 32.4 | 24.8 | -31.5 | | | 51.5 | 88.3 |
| | -25.3 | -18.9 | -121.4 | -7.0 | | | -34.2 | -24.6 |
| EBIT/Interest | 11.2 | 13.3 | 10.0 | 31.5 | | | 8.2 | 8.4 |
| | (267) 4.3 | (140) 4.0 | (53) 3.6 | (19) 2.9 | | | (326) 3.0 | (374) 2.9 |
| | 1.0 | 1.2 | 1.5 | 1.5 | | | 1.2 | .9 |
| Net Profit + Depr., Dep., Amort./Cur. Mat. L/T/D | | | 6.0 | | | | 6.3 | 4.6 |
| | | (12) 3.6 | | | | | (36) 2.1 | (29) 2.2 |
| | | | 1.4 | | | | 1.2 | .8 |
| Fixed/Worth | .3 | .4 | .5 | .6 | | | .4 | .4 |
| | 2.4 | 2.0 | 1.2 | 6.0 | | | 1.7 | 2.6 |
| | -.8 | -12.9 | 3.1 | -751.6 | | | -5.4 | -1.6 |
| Debt/Worth | 1.0 | 1.0 | 1.3 | 1.3 | | | .8 | 1.2 |
| | 8.2 | 3.2 | 2.7 | 7.1 | | | 3.5 | 5.6 |
| | -2.8 | -24.0 | 6.1 | -760.0 | | | -11.3 | -4.2 |
| % Profit Before Taxes/Tangible Net Worth | 174.6 | 48.9 | 58.0 | 56.1 | | | 97.8 | 92.4 |
| | (240) 55.1 | (132) 23.7 | (52) 22.6 | (16) 33.7 | | | (305) 38.0 | (296) 30.1 |
| | 10.2 | 9.5 | 9.7 | 17.7 | | | 10.1 | 6.7 |
| % Profit Before Taxes/Total Assets | 35.8 | 17.2 | 15.4 | 13.0 | | | 28.9 | 24.0 |
| | 13.2 | 6.2 | 6.0 | 4.5 | | | 9.1 | 7.3 |
| | .4 | .9 | 2.1 | 1.6 | | | 1.3 | -.9 |
| Sales/Net Fixed Assets | 105.0 | 36.5 | 30.1 | 17.6 | | | 43.0 | 60.9 |
| | 29.1 | 9.7 | 12.5 | 5.8 | | | 16.2 | 19.7 |
| | 11.7 | 2.2 | 4.7 | 1.1 | | | 6.1 | 6.3 |
| Sales/Total Assets | 11.7 | 4.1 | 4.1 | 3.3 | | | 6.7 | 6.9 |
| | 6.3 | 2.6 | 2.6 | 1.4 | | | 3.9 | 3.9 |
| | 3.8 | 1.3 | 1.8 | .5 | | | 2.4 | 2.3 |
| % Depr., Dep., Amort./Sales | .5 | .8 | 1.0 | 1.9 | | | .8 | .7 |
| | (259) 1.4 | (131) 1.8 | (58) 1.5 | (18) 2.4 | | | (335) 1.7 | (347) 1.5 |
| | 2.6 | 4.8 | 2.8 | 4.5 | | | 3.9 | 3.3 |
| % Officers', Directors' Owners' Comp/Sales | 3.8 | 2.3 | 1.5 | | | | 3.9 | 3.1 |
| | (259) 6.7 | (102) 4.2 | (28) 2.2 | | | | (260) 5.9 | (290) 5.5 |
| | 9.4 | 6.8 | 5.3 | | | | 9.7 | 9.1 |
| Net Sales ($) | 442435M | 512309M | 933302M | 2481703M | 1275061M | 2563129M | 7841371M | 6939033M |
| Total Assets ($) | 73890M | 174955M | 266507M | 460994M | 252846M | 1092598M | 2249921M | 2328782M |

M = $ thousand    MM = $ million

See Pages 9 through 22 for Explanation of Ratios and Data

## Comparative Historical Data | Current Data Sorted by Sales

| 7 | 9 | 5 | Type of Statement | | | | | | |
|---|---|---|---|---|---|---|---|---|---|
| 16 | 20 | 17 | Unqualified | | | 1 | | | 4 |
| 54 | 88 | 89 | Reviewed | 4 | | 2 | 1 | 4 | 6 |
| 282 | 289 | 367 | Compiled | 23 | 35 | 8 | 15 | 7 | 1 |
| 158 | 190 | 210 | Tax Returns | 202 | 113 | 29 | 15 | 5 | 3 |
|  |  |  | Other | 69 | 71 | 23 | 18 | 15 | 14 |
| 4/1/09-3/31/10 | 4/1/10-3/31/11 | 4/1/11-3/31/12 | | | 66 (4/1-9/30/11) | | 622 (10/1/11-3/31/12) | | |
| ALL | ALL | ALL | | 0-1MM | 1-3MM | 3-5MM | 5-10MM | 10-25MM | 25MM & OVER |
| 517 | 596 | 688 | **NUMBER OF STATEMENTS** | 294 | 223 | 63 | 49 | 31 | 28 |
| % | % | % | **ASSETS** | % | % | % | % | % | % |
| 15.8 | 17.8 | 18.3 | Cash & Equivalents | 19.6 | 17.7 | 15.2 | 18.8 | 12.0 | 21.1 |
| 11.3 | 11.2 | 11.0 | Trade Receivables (net) | 9.0 | 12.1 | 15.2 | 10.1 | 15.1 | 10.9 |
| 18.0 | 16.4 | 16.8 | Inventory | 14.1 | 17.2 | 21.8 | 20.8 | 20.3 | 19.7 |
| 3.2 | 3.2 | 2.7 | All Other Current | 1.8 | 3.4 | 2.2 | 4.0 | 1.8 | 5.6 |
| 48.2 | 48.5 | 48.7 | Total Current | 44.5 | 50.4 | 54.4 | 53.7 | 49.2 | 57.3 |
| 35.0 | 34.3 | 35.2 | Fixed Assets (net) | 38.8 | 34.5 | 30.4 | 32.5 | 28.2 | 26.4 |
| 7.0 | 6.6 | 5.5 | Intangibles (net) | 5.2 | 4.8 | 5.3 | 5.9 | 8.8 | 9.6 |
| 9.9 | 10.6 | 10.6 | All Other Non-Current | 11.5 | 10.3 | 10.0 | 8.0 | 13.7 | 6.7 |
| 100.0 | 100.0 | 100.0 | Total | 100.0 | 100.0 | 100.0 | 100.0 | 100.0 | 100.0 |
|  |  |  | **LIABILITIES** | | | | | | |
| 14.0 | 12.1 | 12.7 | Notes Payable-Short Term | 11.7 | 18.5 | 6.8 | 7.6 | 7.4 | 4.6 |
| 6.0 | 4.8 | 4.7 | Cur. Mat.-L.T.D. | 4.8 | 5.2 | 4.3 | 3.9 | 2.8 | 4.7 |
| 15.4 | 14.9 | 14.6 | Trade Payables | 12.9 | 15.6 | 15.9 | 16.4 | 16.2 | 17.4 |
| .1 | .2 | .1 | Income Taxes Payable | .1 | .2 | .0 | .1 | .2 | .3 |
| 17.9 | 15.3 | 18.6 | All Other Current | 22.3 | 18.1 | 10.8 | 9.6 | 11.4 | 24.8 |
| 53.3 | 47.3 | 50.7 | Total Current | 51.7 | 57.5 | 37.8 | 37.5 | 37.9 | 51.8 |
| 35.2 | 29.8 | 32.7 | Long-Term Debt | 39.2 | 29.8 | 24.3 | 30.9 | 32.7 | 9.9 |
| .1 | .1 | .1 | Deferred Taxes | .0 | .0 | .1 | .2 | .4 | .3 |
| 9.2 | 12.6 | 17.9 | All Other Non-Current | 23.8 | 16.4 | 14.7 | 2.5 | 7.3 | 14.9 |
| 2.1 | 10.2 | -1.4 | Net Worth | -14.6 | -3.7 | 23.1 | 29.0 | 21.7 | 23.1 |
| 100.0 | 100.0 | 100.0 | Total Liabilities & Net Worth | 100.0 | 100.0 | 100.0 | 100.0 | 100.0 | 100.0 |
|  |  |  | **INCOME DATA** | | | | | | |
| 100.0 | 100.0 | 100.0 | Net Sales | 100.0 | 100.0 | 100.0 | 100.0 | 100.0 | 100.0 |
|  |  |  | Gross Profit | | | | | | |
| 94.5 | 93.5 | 93.0 | Operating Expenses | 89.6 | 95.4 | 96.2 | 94.6 | 97.0 | 95.8 |
| 5.5 | 6.5 | 7.0 | Operating Profit | 10.4 | 4.6 | 3.8 | 5.4 | 3.0 | 4.2 |
| 2.3 | 2.1 | 2.1 | All Other Expenses (net) | 4.0 | .8 | .7 | .5 | .0 | .7 |
| 3.2 | 4.4 | 4.9 | Profit Before Taxes | 6.4 | 3.8 | 3.1 | 4.9 | 3.0 | 3.5 |
|  |  |  | **RATIOS** | | | | | | |
| 2.3 | 2.7 | 2.6 |  | 2.7 | 2.4 | 2.9 | 3.1 | 1.9 | 1.6 |
| 1.1 | 1.2 | 1.3 | Current | 1.1 | 1.2 | 1.6 | 1.5 | 1.3 | 1.0 |
| .5 | .6 | .6 |  | .5 | .5 | .9 | 1.0 | .8 | .8 |
| 1.3 | 1.7 | 1.7 |  | 1.9 | 1.4 | 1.7 | 1.7 | 1.4 | 1.1 |
| (516) .5 | (593) .7 | (684) .7 | Quick | (292) .8 | (221) .6 | .9 | .8 | .6 | .5 |
| .2 | .2 | .2 |  | .2 | .2 | .4 | .3 | .2 |  |
| 0 UND | 0 UND | 0 UND |  | 0 UND | 0 UND | 1 277.0 | 2 174.7 | 2 217.6 | 0 858.8 |
| 4 91.0 | 4 86.5 | 3 118.4 | Sales/Receivables | 1 503.5 | 4 100.1 | 11 33.8 | 8 48.0 | 8 44.3 | 8 46.9 |
| 15 24.9 | 16 23.4 | 13 27.3 |  | 9 42.5 | 15 25.1 | 29 12.5 | 15 24.3 | 28 13.1 | 33 11.1 |
|  |  |  | Cost of Sales/Inventory | | | | | | |
|  |  |  | Cost of Sales/Payables | | | | | | |
| 13.3 | 11.5 | 14.1 |  | 12.9 | 19.2 | 10.0 | 8.2 | 17.8 | 11.1 |
| 126.7 | 75.7 | 66.0 | Sales/Working Capital | 130.0 | 110.0 | 25.9 | 25.5 | 40.0 | 546.3 |
| -19.8 | -25.3 | -23.5 |  | -18.6 | -24.0 | -199.6 | NM | -20.0 | -45.3 |
| 9.7 | 10.3 | 11.2 |  | 7.7 | 12.5 | 15.8 | 18.1 | 11.1 | 31.5 |
| (392) 2.5 | (424) 3.6 | (486) 4.0 | EBIT/Interest | (180) 2.4 | (169) 5.3 | (49) 5.1 | (37) 4.6 | (28) 6.0 | (23) 9.6 |
| .6 | 1.1 | 1.3 |  | .8 | 1.5 | 1.0 | 1.5 | 2.0 | 1.9 |
| 5.8 | 5.5 | 6.4 | Net Profit + Depr., Dep., |  |  |  |  | 5.8 |  |
| (23) 1.4 | (28) 2.7 | (29) 2.5 | Amort./Cur. Mat. L/T/D |  |  |  |  | (10) 2.8 |  |
| .7 | 1.0 | 1.2 |  |  |  |  |  | 1.2 |  |
| .4 | .3 | .4 |  | .4 | .3 | .3 | .3 | .5 | .5 |
| 2.6 | 1.7 | 1.8 | Fixed/Worth | 3.4 | 1.7 | 1.3 | 1.0 | 1.0 | 1.3 |
| -1.4 | -2.5 | -2.2 |  | -1.0 | -1.8 | -6.0 | 3.1 | 8.9 | NM |
| 1.1 | .9 | 1.0 |  | 1.3 | .8 | .6 | 1.0 | 1.3 | 1.4 |
| 7.7 | 4.3 | 4.6 | Debt/Worth | 7.9 | 4.7 | 3.0 | 1.7 | 3.0 | 2.3 |
| -4.4 | -5.8 | -4.7 |  | -2.8 | -4.7 | -13.7 | 5.6 | 10.8 | -17.9 |
| 100.0 | 90.9 | 98.0 | % Profit Before Taxes/Tangible | 173.8 | 97.3 | 56.7 | 59.3 | 53.1 | 133.5 |
| (308) 30.8 | (393) 31.1 | (448) 33.1 | Net Worth | (174) 32.3 | (144) 36.4 | (45) 33.1 | (40) 19.6 | (25) 41.7 | (20) 45.9 |
| 4.5 | 5.5 | 10.2 |  | 10.3 | 7.9 | 3.1 | 12.5 | 22.1 | 22.0 |
| 27.2 | 28.0 | 27.5 | % Profit Before Taxes/Total | 29.0 | 30.9 | 24.6 | 20.3 | 16.9 | 27.6 |
| 7.5 | 9.6 | 9.2 | Assets | 7.7 | 11.5 | 11.9 | 8.4 | 6.1 | 10.7 |
| -.4 | .5 | 1.1 |  | .0 | .9 | .2 | 3.1 | 3.2 | 2.2 |
| 48.5 | 58.7 | 64.8 |  | 89.1 | 68.0 | 54.8 | 58.7 | 40.9 | 34.2 |
| 18.3 | 19.2 | 18.2 | Sales/Net Fixed Assets | 15.7 | 22.8 | 24.6 | 14.9 | 15.4 | 15.7 |
| 5.9 | 6.9 | 6.8 |  | 4.2 | 8.8 | 8.5 | 5.8 | 8.4 | 8.5 |
| 6.8 | 7.3 | 7.8 |  | 8.3 | 8.6 | 5.9 | 6.0 | 4.6 | 5.7 |
| 3.9 | 4.2 | 4.3 | Sales/Total Assets | 4.4 | 5.3 | 4.1 | 3.6 | 3.9 | 3.8 |
| 2.1 | 2.3 | 2.3 |  | 1.5 | 2.7 | 2.6 | 2.1 | 2.3 | 1.8 |
| .8 | .7 | .7 |  | .8 | .6 | .4 | .6 | .8 | 1.0 |
| (390) 1.7 | (416) 1.5 | (472) 1.5 | % Depr., Dep., Amort./Sales | (188) 2.2 | (152) 1.4 | (44) 1.1 | (38) 1.2 | (30) 1.4 | (20) 1.4 |
| 3.0 | 2.9 | 3.1 |  | 5.0 | 2.6 | 2.3 | 2.0 | 2.5 | 2.3 |
| 2.9 | 3.3 | 3.0 | % Officers', Directors' | 4.2 | 3.0 | 3.0 | 1.6 | .9 |  |
| (326) 5.2 | (364) 5.7 | (395) 5.6 | Owners' Comp/Sales | (161) 7.3 | (146) 5.8 | (38) 4.2 | (28) 2.6 | (15) 1.6 |  |
| 9.1 | 8.7 | 8.6 |  | 10.5 | 8.1 | 6.2 | 5.6 | 2.5 |  |
| 6205688M | 8134657M | 8207939M | Net Sales ($) | 163796M | 376526M | 240827M | 336088M | 491931M | 6598771M |
| 1686598M | 2508894M | 2321790M | Total Assets ($) | 84221M | 156654M | 78869M | 134385M | 196775M | 1670886M |

© RMA 2012

M = $ thousand     MM = $ million
See Pages 9 through 22 for Explanation of Ratios and Data

**Current Data Sorted by Assets**          **Comparative Historical Data**

| 0-500M | 500M-2MM | 2-10MM | 10-50MM | 50-100MM | 100-250MM | Type of Statement | 4/1/07-3/31/08 ALL | 4/1/08-3/31/09 ALL |
|---|---|---|---|---|---|---|---|---|
| | | | | | | Unqualified | 1 | 1 |
| | | 1 | | | | Reviewed | 2 | 2 |
| | | 2 | | | | Compiled | 1 | 4 |
| 9 | 2 | | 1 | | | Tax Returns | 8 | 10 |
| 3 | 1 | | 1 | | | Other | 4 | 8 |
| | 1 (4/1-9/30/11) | | 19 (10/1/11-3/31/12) | | | | | |
| 12 | 3 | 3 | 2 | | | NUMBER OF STATEMENTS | 16 | 25 |
| % | % | % | % | % | % | **ASSETS** | % | % |
| 9.9 | | | | D | D | Cash & Equivalents | 13.5 | 7.9 |
| 9.5 | | | | A | A | Trade Receivables (net) | 6.3 | 7.4 |
| 24.1 | | | | T | T | Inventory | 21.2 | 16.8 |
| 7.4 | | | | A | A | All Other Current | 3.4 | 4.8 |
| 50.9 | | | | | | Total Current | 44.4 | 36.9 |
| 39.2 | | | | N | N | Fixed Assets (net) | 34.8 | 39.4 |
| 3.3 | | | | O | O | Intangibles (net) | 15.9 | 13.2 |
| 6.6 | | | | T | T | All Other Non-Current | 4.9 | 10.6 |
| 100.0 | | | | | | Total | 100.0 | 100.0 |
| | | | | A | A | **LIABILITIES** | | |
| 8.0 | | | | V | V | Notes Payable-Short Term | 4.7 | 11.6 |
| .9 | | | | A | A | Cur. Mat.-L.T.D. | 4.4 | 2.5 |
| 9.9 | | | | I | I | Trade Payables | 13.2 | 20.0 |
| .0 | | | | L | L | Income Taxes Payable | .0 | .0 |
| 8.8 | | | | A | A | All Other Current | 5.7 | 19.2 |
| 27.7 | | | | B | B | Total Current | 28.0 | 53.3 |
| 17.3 | | | | L | L | Long-Term Debt | 27.1 | 27.2 |
| .0 | | | | E | E | Deferred Taxes | .9 | .3 |
| 30.0 | | | | | | All Other Non-Current | 21.4 | 4.4 |
| 25.2 | | | | | | Net Worth | 22.6 | 14.8 |
| 100.0 | | | | | | Total Liabilities & Net Worth | 100.0 | 100.0 |
| | | | | | | **INCOME DATA** | | |
| 100.0 | | | | | | Net Sales | 100.0 | 100.0 |
| | | | | | | Gross Profit | | |
| 93.3 | | | | | | Operating Expenses | 96.0 | 93.5 |
| 6.7 | | | | | | Operating Profit | 4.0 | 6.5 |
| .2 | | | | | | All Other Expenses (net) | .8 | 3.5 |
| 6.5 | | | | | | Profit Before Taxes | 3.1 | 2.9 |
| | | | | | | **RATIOS** | | |
| 4.3 | | | | | | | 4.3 | 1.6 |
| 2.7 | | | | | | Current | 1.8 | .8 |
| 1.2 | | | | | | | 1.0 | .3 |
| 2.1 | | | | | | | 1.5 | .7 |
| .6 | | | | | | Quick | 1.0 | .2 |
| .2 | | | | | | | .4 | .1 |
| 0   880.4 | | | | | | | 0   UND | 1   621.9 |
| 5   75.2 | | | | | | Sales/Receivables | 3   104.7 | 4   97.7 |
| 12   31.2 | | | | | | | 10   35.3 | 8   46.8 |
| | | | | | | Cost of Sales/Inventory | | |
| | | | | | | Cost of Sales/Payables | | |
| 9.9 | | | | | | | 8.6 | 38.8 |
| 29.5 | | | | | | Sales/Working Capital | 23.5 | -38.3 |
| NM | | | | | | | NM | -8.4 |
| | | | | | | | 17.1 | 8.0 |
| | | | | | | EBIT/Interest | (13) 2.0 | (17) 1.4 |
| | | | | | | | 1.4 | -5.4 |
| | | | | | | Net Profit + Depr., Dep., Amort./Cur. Mat. L/T/D | | |
| .3 | | | | | | | .7 | .6 |
| 1.0 | | | | | | Fixed/Worth | 8.4 | 2.2 |
| NM | | | | | | | -.6 | -3.7 |
| .2 | | | | | | | .9 | 1.1 |
| .6 | | | | | | Debt/Worth | 13.3 | 4.0 |
| NM | | | | | | | -3.3 | -8.1 |
| | | | | | | | 82.2 | |
| | | | | | | % Profit Before Taxes/Tangible Net Worth | (16) 17.9 | |
| | | | | | | | -8.5 | |
| 77.7 | | | | | | | 33.4 | 14.8 |
| 38.8 | | | | | | % Profit Before Taxes/Total Assets | 5.2 | 1.6 |
| 4.6 | | | | | | | 2.8 | -9.5 |
| 44.9 | | | | | | | 55.0 | 32.6 |
| 15.3 | | | | | | Sales/Net Fixed Assets | 17.6 | 18.7 |
| 6.2 | | | | | | | 6.3 | 5.7 |
| 7.6 | | | | | | | 4.9 | 9.2 |
| 6.6 | | | | | | Sales/Total Assets | 3.6 | 5.0 |
| 3.4 | | | | | | | 3.1 | 1.6 |
| | | | | | | | 1.1 | .9 |
| | | | | | | % Depr., Dep., Amort./Sales | (12) 2.6 | (22) 1.6 |
| | | | | | | | 3.2 | 2.9 |
| | | | | | | | 2.9 | |
| | | | | | | % Officers', Directors' Owners' Comp/Sales | (12) 5.4 | |
| | | | | | | | 8.3 | |
| 8105M | 13511M | 35194M | 75318M | | | Net Sales ($) | 111430M | 98377M |
| 1662M | 3555M | 11202M | 63405M | | | Total Assets ($) | 122770M | 50824M |

© RMA 2012

M = $ thousand    MM = $ million
See Pages 9 through 22 for Explanation of Ratios and Data

## Comparative Historical Data | Current Data Sorted by Sales

| | | | Type of Statement | | | | | | |
|---|---|---|---|---|---|---|---|---|---|
| 2 | 1 | 1 | Unqualified | | | | | 1 | |
| 3 | 3 | 2 | Reviewed | | | | 1 | 1 | |
| 12 | 16 | 12 | Compiled | | | | | 1 | |
| 9 | 7 | 5 | Tax Returns | | | | | 1 | |
| | | | Other | 9 | 1 | | 1 | 1 | 1 |
| 4/1/09- | 4/1/10- | 4/1/11- | | 4 | 1 | | | | |
| 3/31/10 | 3/31/11 | 3/31/12 | | | 1 (4/1-9/30/11) | | 19 (10/1/11-3/31/12) | | |
| ALL | ALL | ALL | | 0-1MM | 1-3MM | 3-5MM | 5-10MM | 10-25MM | 25MM & OVER |
| 26 | 27 | 20 | NUMBER OF STATEMENTS | 13 | 2 | | 1 | 3 | 1 |
| % | % | % | ASSETS | % | % | % | % | % | % |
| 12.3 | 9.8 | 12.2 | Cash & Equivalents | 9.2 | | | | | |
| 6.2 | 8.9 | 7.5 | Trade Receivables (net) | 8.8 | | | | | |
| 13.9 | 18.0 | 17.9 | Inventory | 17.6 | | | | | |
| 2.6 | 2.6 | 5.9 | All Other Current | 8.2 | | | | | |
| 35.0 | 39.3 | 43.4 | Total Current | 43.8 | | | | | |
| 36.6 | 25.2 | 38.3 | Fixed Assets (net) | 39.5 | | | | | |
| 11.7 | 18.5 | 7.0 | Intangibles (net) | 9.4 | | | | | |
| 16.6 | 17.1 | 11.2 | All Other Non-Current | 7.3 | | | | | |
| 100.0 | 100.0 | 100.0 | Total | 100.0 | | | | | |
| | | | LIABILITIES | | | | | | |
| 3.4 | 11.2 | 5.8 | Notes Payable-Short Term | 8.2 | | | | | |
| 1.4 | 3.4 | 1.8 | Cur. Mat.-L.T.D. | .9 | | | | | |
| 12.8 | 17.1 | 10.5 | Trade Payables | 8.5 | | | | | |
| .1 | .1 | .0 | Income Taxes Payable | .0 | | | | | |
| 22.5 | 13.5 | 8.8 | All Other Current | 8.5 | | | | | |
| 40.2 | 45.2 | 26.9 | Total Current | 26.1 | | | | | |
| 32.2 | 39.6 | 19.7 | Long-Term Debt | 23.1 | | | | | |
| .1 | .6 | .1 | Deferred Taxes | .0 | | | | | |
| 15.3 | 14.8 | 19.0 | All Other Non-Current | 27.8 | | | | | |
| 12.1 | -.2 | 34.4 | Net Worth | 23.2 | | | | | |
| 100.0 | 100.0 | 100.0 | Total Liabilities & Net Worth | 100.0 | | | | | |
| | | | INCOME DATA | | | | | | |
| 100.0 | 100.0 | 100.0 | Net Sales | 100.0 | | | | | |
| | | | Gross Profit | | | | | | |
| 95.9 | 91.0 | 85.4 | Operating Expenses | 82.3 | | | | | |
| 4.1 | 9.0 | 14.6 | Operating Profit | 17.7 | | | | | |
| 4.1 | 5.2 | 2.6 | All Other Expenses (net) | 4.7 | | | | | |
| .0 | 3.8 | 12.0 | Profit Before Taxes | 13.0 | | | | | |
| | | | RATIOS | | | | | | |
| 3.0 | 2.2 | 3.2 | | 3.9 | | | | | |
| 1.0 | 1.1 | 1.9 | Current | 2.6 | | | | | |
| .3 | .4 | .8 | | .9 | | | | | |
| 1.5 | .9 | 1.9 | | 2.0 | | | | | |
| .3 | .5 | .6 | Quick | .5 | | | | | |
| .2 | .1 | .2 | | .2 | | | | | |
| 1  675.1 | 1  295.6 | 1  493.0 | | 0  UND | | | | | |
| 2  190.2 | 3  126.0 | 5  75.2 | Sales/Receivables | 5  68.4 | | | | | |
| 8  46.8 | 13  27.3 | 12  30.5 | | 12  29.3 | | | | | |
| | | | Cost of Sales/Inventory | | | | | | |
| | | | Cost of Sales/Payables | | | | | | |
| 14.6 | 16.1 | 9.9 | | 11.2 | | | | | |
| NM | 51.9 | 26.9 | Sales/Working Capital | 31.5 | | | | | |
| -13.7 | -9.8 | -65.3 | | -69.9 | | | | | |
| 5.7 | 8.4 | 32.2 | | | | | | | |
| (18) 1.6 | (22) 3.1 | (12) 21.3 | EBIT/Interest | | | | | | |
| -4.2 | .9 | 3.2 | | | | | | | |
| | | | Net Profit + Depr., Dep., Amort./Cur. Mat. L/T/D | | | | | | |
| .5 | .6 | .2 | | .1 | | | | | |
| 3.0 | 10.0 | 1.0 | Fixed/Worth | 1.0 | | | | | |
| 18.9 | -.5 | 6.9 | | -8.0 | | | | | |
| 1.1 | 1.9 | .2 | | .2 | | | | | |
| 6.2 | 28.5 | 1.2 | Debt/Worth | 3.3 | | | | | |
| NM | -2.2 | 95.5 | | -11.0 | | | | | |
| 45.2 | 234.5 | 122.2 | % Profit Before Taxes/Tangible Net Worth | | | | | | |
| (20) 17.5 | (15) 40.0 | (16) 48.2 | | | | | | | |
| .9 | 10.2 | 8.2 | | | | | | | |
| 10.8 | 17.5 | 49.7 | % Profit Before Taxes/Total Assets | 58.8 | | | | | |
| 2.9 | 6.0 | 12.4 | | 16.5 | | | | | |
| -13.8 | -1.4 | 4.5 | | 2.8 | | | | | |
| 22.6 | 69.8 | 45.6 | Sales/Net Fixed Assets | 271.2 | | | | | |
| 13.5 | 21.8 | 16.7 | | 14.4 | | | | | |
| 5.4 | 8.4 | 5.4 | | 5.4 | | | | | |
| 5.2 | 6.5 | 7.1 | Sales/Total Assets | 7.2 | | | | | |
| 3.2 | 3.3 | 4.5 | | 4.8 | | | | | |
| 1.6 | 1.6 | 2.1 | | 2.5 | | | | | |
| 1.0 | .6 | .8 | | | | | | | |
| (22) 1.8 | (22) 1.9 | (15) 1.7 | % Depr., Dep., Amort./Sales | | | | | | |
| 2.5 | 2.7 | 2.6 | | | | | | | |
| 2.2 | 2.7 | | % Officers', Directors' Owners' Comp/Sales | | | | | | |
| (10) 4.8 | (13) 5.3 | | | | | | | | |
| 14.3 | 9.6 | | | | | | | | |
| 174607M | 208182M | 132128M | Net Sales ($) | 7203M | 3680M | | 9727M | 38750M | 72768M |
| 189902M | 302463M | 79824M | Total Assets ($) | 3212M | 16535M | | 3306M | 9797M | 46974M |

Note: In the "3-5MM" column the source prints vertically: D A T A  N O T  A V A I L A B L E

© RMA 2012    M = $ thousand    MM = $ million
See Pages 9 through 22 for Explanation of Ratios and Data

## Current Data Sorted by Assets      Comparative Historical Data

### Type of Statement

| 0-500M | 500M-2MM | 2-10MM | 10-50MM | 50-100MM | 100-250MM | Type of Statement | 4/1/07-3/31/08 ALL | 4/1/08-3/31/09 ALL |
|---|---|---|---|---|---|---|---|---|
| | | | | 1 | | Unqualified | 2 | 1 |
| | | 3 | | | | Reviewed | 1 | 3 |
| 5 | 10 | 4 | 1 | | | Compiled | 23 | 15 |
| 17 | 5 | 1 | | | | Tax Returns | 25 | 40 |
| 8 | 3 | 4 | 5 | 1 | | Other | 17 | 24 |
| | 8 (4/1-9/30/11) | | 60 (10/1/11-3/31/12) | | | | | |
| **30** | **18** | **12** | **6** | **2** | | **NUMBER OF STATEMENTS** | **68** | **83** |

### ASSETS

| 0-500M % | 500M-2MM % | 2-10MM % | 10-50MM % | 50-100MM % | 100-250MM % | | 4/1/07-3/31/08 % | 4/1/08-3/31/09 % |
|---|---|---|---|---|---|---|---|---|
| 22.3 | 13.7 | 10.3 | | | | Cash & Equivalents | 12.8 | 15.7 |
| 18.6 | 19.7 | 18.8 | | | | Trade Receivables (net) | 18.0 | 15.5 |
| 22.4 | 11.6 | 19.5 | | | | Inventory | 21.1 | 18.8 |
| .4 | .5 | 1.9 | | | | All Other Current | 1.9 | 3.1 |
| 63.7 | 45.6 | 50.4 | | DATA | | Total Current | 53.8 | 53.1 |
| 23.6 | 37.9 | 43.6 | | NOT | | Fixed Assets (net) | 35.0 | 33.7 |
| 3.2 | 5.1 | 4.8 | | AVAILABLE | | Intangibles (net) | 4.2 | 4.6 |
| 9.5 | 11.4 | 1.2 | | | | All Other Non-Current | 7.0 | 8.6 |
| 100.0 | 100.0 | 100.0 | | | | Total | 100.0 | 100.0 |

### LIABILITIES

| 0-500M | 500M-2MM | 2-10MM | | | | | 4/1/07-3/31/08 | 4/1/08-3/31/09 |
|---|---|---|---|---|---|---|---|---|
| 10.7 | 9.0 | 6.9 | | | | Notes Payable-Short Term | 10.9 | 9.2 |
| 2.8 | 2.4 | 4.8 | | | | Cur. Mat.-L.T.D. | 2.8 | 6.4 |
| 18.7 | 15.6 | 13.7 | | | | Trade Payables | 12.9 | 13.1 |
| .0 | .0 | .7 | | | | Income Taxes Payable | .0 | .1 |
| 15.7 | 5.7 | 6.4 | | DATA NOT AVAILABLE | | All Other Current | 14.2 | 12.5 |
| 47.9 | 32.7 | 32.5 | | | | Total Current | 40.9 | 41.3 |
| 15.7 | 35.2 | 32.5 | | | | Long-Term Debt | 30.6 | 22.7 |
| .0 | .0 | .0 | | | | Deferred Taxes | .1 | .1 |
| 21.1 | 7.9 | 4.6 | | | | All Other Non-Current | 11.0 | 11.7 |
| 15.3 | 24.3 | 30.4 | | | | Net Worth | 17.5 | 24.2 |
| 100.0 | 100.0 | 100.0 | | | | Total Liabilities & Net Worth | 100.0 | 100.0 |

### INCOME DATA

| 0-500M | 500M-2MM | 2-10MM | | | | | 4/1/07-3/31/08 | 4/1/08-3/31/09 |
|---|---|---|---|---|---|---|---|---|
| 100.0 | 100.0 | 100.0 | | | | Net Sales | 100.0 | 100.0 |
| | | | | | | Gross Profit | | |
| 93.1 | 86.9 | 84.4 | | | | Operating Expenses | 94.0 | 93.0 |
| 6.9 | 13.1 | 15.6 | | | | Operating Profit | 6.0 | 7.0 |
| .1 | 6.3 | 8.0 | | | | All Other Expenses (net) | 2.6 | 2.1 |
| 6.8 | 6.8 | 7.7 | | | | Profit Before Taxes | 3.4 | 5.0 |

### RATIOS

| 0-500M | 500M-2MM | 2-10MM | | | | | 4/1/07-3/31/08 | 4/1/08-3/31/09 |
|---|---|---|---|---|---|---|---|---|
| 3.5 | 2.7 | 1.9 | | | | Current | 2.9 | 2.6 |
| 1.8 | 1.2 | 1.4 | | | | | 1.7 | 1.5 |
| 1.0 | .5 | .8 | | | | | 1.1 | .7 |
| 1.8 | 1.8 | 1.3 | | | | Quick | 2.0 | 1.5 |
| 1.0 | 1.0 | .9 | | | | | .8 (82) | .7 |
| .4 | .4 | .5 | | | | | .3 | .3 |
| 0 UND | 2 174.0 | 2 153.8 | | | | Sales/Receivables | 2 161.7 | 1 427.7 |
| 8 46.6 | 21 17.5 | 19 19.6 | | | | | 17 21.3 | 13 27.9 |
| 24 15.4 | 32 11.5 | 50 7.3 | | | | | 31 11.7 | 33 11.2 |
| | | | | | | Cost of Sales/Inventory | | |
| | | | | | | Cost of Sales/Payables | | |
| 10.3 | 5.8 | 6.0 | | | | Sales/Working Capital | 7.7 | 8.3 |
| 16.9 | 58.4 | 26.9 | | | | | 17.2 | 33.7 |
| UND | -9.3 | -30.3 | | | | | 148.0 | -24.8 |
| 20.7 | 6.7 | 14.9 | | | | EBIT/Interest | 7.5 | 6.4 |
| (20) 3.7 | (15) 3.8 | (10) 6.6 | | | | | (55) 2.6 | (67) 2.6 |
| -.8 | .9 | 2.5 | | | | | .4 | 1.0 |
| | | | | | | Net Profit + Depr., Dep., Amort./Cur. Mat. L/T/D | 14.7 | |
| | | | | | | | (10) 7.3 | |
| | | | | | | | .6 | |
| .2 | .4 | .3 | | | | Fixed/Worth | .3 | .2 |
| 1.2 | 1.4 | 1.7 | | | | | 1.1 | 1.0 |
| -.3 | NM | 5.0 | | | | | 5.4 | 40.7 |
| .6 | 1.3 | 1.4 | | | | Debt/Worth | .6 | .5 |
| 4.2 | 3.1 | 2.2 | | | | | 2.1 | 2.1 |
| -3.9 | NM | 4.6 | | | | | 19.6 | 77.1 |
| 84.7 | 31.7 | 44.6 | | | | % Profit Before Taxes/Tangible Net Worth | 48.6 | 89.3 |
| (18) 35.4 | (14) 6.0 | (10) 21.0 | | | | | (52) 23.4 | (63) 26.8 |
| 23.2 | -2.1 | 8.7 | | | | | -1.4 | .0 |
| 32.0 | 10.3 | 17.6 | | | | % Profit Before Taxes/Total Assets | 17.8 | 22.6 |
| 17.7 | 3.0 | 7.6 | | | | | 6.2 | 4.5 |
| .2 | -.2 | 1.5 | | | | | -2.0 | .0 |
| 157.3 | 52.7 | 19.8 | | | | Sales/Net Fixed Assets | 41.0 | 34.1 |
| 45.8 | 17.3 | 8.1 | | | | | 16.9 | 16.6 |
| 11.3 | 1.5 | 1.9 | | | | | 6.0 | 7.7 |
| 10.2 | 3.8 | 3.3 | | | | Sales/Total Assets | 4.9 | 5.4 |
| 4.5 | 2.8 | 1.9 | | | | | 3.0 | 3.5 |
| 2.7 | .7 | 1.3 | | | | | 2.1 | 2.2 |
| .2 | .9 | 1.2 | | | | % Depr., Dep., Amort./Sales | .9 | .8 |
| (16) .9 | (11) 2.1 | (10) 2.1 | | | | | (51) 1.6 | (69) 1.4 |
| 2.4 | 4.1 | 11.4 | | | | | 2.6 | 2.4 |
| 3.1 | | | | | | % Officers', Directors' Owners' Comp/Sales | 2.0 | 1.9 |
| (20) 6.3 | | | | | | | (40) 4.9 | (41) 5.2 |
| 12.1 | | | | | | | 9.0 | 8.8 |

| 0-500M | 500M-2MM | 2-10MM | 10-50MM | 50-100MM | 100-250MM | | 4/1/07-3/31/08 | 4/1/08-3/31/09 |
|---|---|---|---|---|---|---|---|---|
| 40857M | 45607M | 111903M | 412136M | 209390M | | Net Sales ($) | 577315M | 701879M |
| 7171M | 20255M | 46917M | 187868M | 174764M | | Total Assets ($) | 207040M | 282945M |

M = $ thousand     MM = $ million

See Pages 9 through 22 for Explanation of Ratios and Data

## Comparative Historical Data | Current Data Sorted by Sales

**Type of Statement**

| | 4/1/09-3/31/10 ALL | 4/1/10-3/31/11 ALL | 4/1/11-3/31/12 ALL | 0-1MM | 1-3MM | 3-5MM | 5-10MM | 10-25MM | 25MM & OVER |
|---|---|---|---|---|---|---|---|---|---|
| Unqualified | 2 | 5 | 1 | | | | 1 | 1 | 1 |
| Reviewed | 3 | 2 | 3 | | | | 4 | 1 | 1 |
| Compiled | 20 | 18 | 20 | 10 | 5 | | 4 | | 1 |
| Tax Returns | 23 | 26 | 23 | 6 | 12 | 3 | 2 | | |
| Other | 23 | 38 | 21 | 5 | 4 | 1 | 3 | 3 | 5 |
| | | | | 8 (4/1-9/30/11) | | | 60 (10/1/11-3/31/12) | | |
| **NUMBER OF STATEMENTS** | 71 | 89 | 68 | 21 | 21 | 4 | 10 | 4 | 8 |
| **ASSETS** | % | % | % | % | % | % | % | % | % |
| Cash & Equivalents | 13.9 | 14.1 | 15.7 | 17.1 | 15.4 | | 17.6 | | |
| Trade Receivables (net) | 14.8 | 15.1 | 19.0 | 12.5 | 19.7 | | 25.4 | | |
| Inventory | 19.4 | 15.1 | 18.1 | 8.3 | 27.9 | | 19.0 | | |
| All Other Current | 4.5 | 2.9 | 1.1 | .2 | .8 | | 2.0 | | |
| Total Current | 52.6 | 47.2 | 53.9 | 38.0 | 63.8 | | 64.0 | | |
| Fixed Assets (net) | 35.5 | 38.3 | 32.8 | 48.4 | 22.8 | | 24.0 | | |
| Intangibles (net) | 6.8 | 6.9 | 4.7 | 3.7 | 4.5 | | 7.0 | | |
| All Other Non-Current | 5.1 | 7.6 | 8.6 | 9.9 | 8.9 | | 5.1 | | |
| Total | 100.0 | 100.0 | 100.0 | 100.0 | 100.0 | | 100.0 | | |
| **LIABILITIES** | | | | | | | | | |
| Notes Payable-Short Term | 12.5 | 10.4 | 9.0 | 3.4 | 17.1 | | 4.4 | | |
| Cur. Mat.-L.T.D. | 2.6 | 4.0 | 3.2 | 4.2 | 1.7 | | 3.1 | | |
| Trade Payables | 12.0 | 15.9 | 16.4 | 9.4 | 14.3 | | 32.1 | | |
| Income Taxes Payable | .2 | .0 | .1 | .0 | .0 | | .3 | | |
| All Other Current | 13.1 | 11.6 | 10.8 | 5.5 | 13.6 | | 17.8 | | |
| Total Current | 40.4 | 41.9 | 39.5 | 22.6 | 46.6 | | 57.7 | | |
| Long-Term Debt | 25.1 | 30.9 | 25.4 | 32.8 | 23.9 | | 17.2 | | |
| Deferred Taxes | .3 | .0 | .3 | .0 | .0 | | .0 | | |
| All Other Non-Current | 9.0 | 12.2 | 14.1 | 13.3 | 22.4 | | 5.2 | | |
| Net Worth | 25.2 | 15.1 | 20.7 | 31.3 | 7.0 | | 19.9 | | |
| Total Liabilities & Net Worth | 100.0 | 100.0 | 100.0 | 100.0 | 100.0 | | 100.0 | | |
| **INCOME DATA** | | | | | | | | | |
| Net Sales | 100.0 | 100.0 | 100.0 | 100.0 | 100.0 | | 100.0 | | |
| Gross Profit | | | | | | | | | |
| Operating Expenses | 93.5 | 91.7 | 90.5 | 77.9 | 95.9 | | 94.4 | | |
| Operating Profit | 6.5 | 8.3 | 9.5 | 22.1 | 4.1 | | 5.6 | | |
| All Other Expenses (net) | 2.2 | 4.0 | 3.4 | 9.4 | .4 | | .5 | | |
| Profit Before Taxes | 4.3 | 4.2 | 6.1 | 12.7 | 3.7 | | 5.1 | | |
| **RATIOS** | | | | | | | | | |
| Current | 3.1 | 2.3 | 2.5 | 3.4 | 3.5 | | 2.0 | | |
| | 1.5 | 1.2 | 1.4 | 1.3 | 1.4 | | 1.4 | | |
| | .9 | .6 | .8 | .6 | .9 | | 1.1 | | |
| Quick | 2.5 | 1.5 | 1.6 | 2.6 | 1.7 | | 2.0 | | |
| | .8 | .7 | .9 | .9 | .8 | | 1.2 | | |
| | .3 | .3 | .4 | .5 | .3 | | .6 | | |
| Sales/Receivables | (1) 381.5 | (1) 403.0 | (2) 200.0 | (0) UND | (2) 204.6 | | (6) 66.0 | | |
| | (14) 26.2 | (9) 39.3 | (16) 23.3 | (3) 130.5 | (8) 44.2 | | (17) 21.0 | | |
| | (37) 9.8 | (22) 16.7 | (38) 9.7 | (24) 15.1 | (31) 11.9 | | (47) 7.8 | | |
| Cost of Sales/Inventory | | | | | | | | | |
| Cost of Sales/Payables | | | | | | | | | |
| Sales/Working Capital | 7.5 | 10.5 | 7.8 | 7.9 | 9.7 | | 6.5 | | |
| | 21.0 | 95.1 | 26.1 | 21.0 | 31.7 | | 26.1 | | |
| | -156.9 | -24.4 | -28.6 | -8.7 | -78.7 | | NM | | |
| EBIT/Interest | 6.1 | 12.2 | 10.6 | 7.1 | 10.6 | | 14.9 | | |
| | (58) 2.1 | (64) 3.4 | (53) 4.0 | (10) 2.1 | (17) 4.5 | | 5.3 | | |
| | .6 | .2 | .3 | -5.8 | .1 | | 2.1 | | |
| Net Profit + Depr., Dep., Amort./Cur. Mat. L/T/D | | | | | | | | | |
| Fixed/Worth | .3 | .4 | .3 | .6 | .2 | | .5 | | |
| | 1.3 | 1.7 | 1.6 | 2.5 | .9 | | 1.8 | | |
| | 12.5 | -2.7 | -2.8 | NM | -.9 | | -.2 | | |
| Debt/Worth | .6 | .9 | .9 | .6 | 1.2 | | 1.4 | | |
| | 2.3 | 2.6 | 2.9 | 1.8 | 5.8 | | 2.2 | | |
| | -55.3 | -4.6 | -5.0 | NM | -3.5 | | -3.5 | | |
| % Profit Before Taxes/Tangible Net Worth | 60.7 | 54.0 | 51.5 | 33.2 | 82.0 | | | | |
| | (53) 12.5 | (62) 21.0 | (48) 23.3 | (16) 16.0 | (12) 23.9 | | | | |
| | -1.4 | -5.8 | 4.1 | 4.4 | -5.2 | | | | |
| % Profit Before Taxes/Total Assets | 15.0 | 24.9 | 24.2 | 23.9 | 34.9 | | 23.7 | | |
| | 3.4 | 5.2 | 6.4 | 4.0 | 13.2 | | 7.8 | | |
| | -1.1 | -2.1 | -.7 | -.2 | .2 | | 2.0 | | |
| Sales/Net Fixed Assets | 35.5 | 37.7 | 61.4 | 34.2 | 109.4 | | 92.5 | | |
| | 19.1 | 16.0 | 18.6 | 9.7 | 44.0 | | 31.9 | | |
| | 4.6 | 5.5 | 4.2 | .4 | 11.3 | | 7.5 | | |
| Sales/Total Assets | 4.5 | 6.1 | 4.7 | 4.2 | 8.2 | | 8.3 | | |
| | 2.9 | 3.6 | 3.0 | 2.2 | 4.0 | | 3.6 | | |
| | 1.9 | 1.8 | 1.7 | .3 | 2.8 | | 1.8 | | |
| % Depr., Dep., Amort./Sales | .7 | .6 | .4 | 1.1 | .2 | | | | |
| | (55) 1.9 | (66) 1.5 | (43) 1.8 | (14) 3.3 | (12) 1.0 | | | | |
| | 3.0 | 2.8 | 3.3 | 23.2 | 2.1 | | | | |
| % Officers', Directors' Owners' Comp/Sales | 2.1 | 2.6 | 3.0 | | 3.0 | | | | |
| | (35) 4.8 | (46) 6.1 | (29) 10.8 | | (15) 6.5 | | | | |
| | 8.2 | 9.1 | 10.8 | | 7.9 | | | | |
| Net Sales ($) | 1769501M | 624669M | 819893M | 9443M | 36118M | 15355M | 67067M | 65693M | 626217M |
| Total Assets ($) | 602897M | 307627M | 436975M | 16310M | 10273M | 5690M | 23511M | 32751M | 348440M |

M = $ thousand   MM = $ million
See Pages 9 through 22 for Explanation of Ratios and Data

| Current Data Sorted by Assets | | | | | | | Comparative Historical Data | |
|---|---|---|---|---|---|---|---|---|

| 0-500M | 500M-2MM | 2-10MM | 10-50MM | 50-100MM | 100-250MM | Type of Statement | 10 | 7 |
|---|---|---|---|---|---|---|---|---|
| | | 1 | | | | Unqualified | 10 | 7 |
| | 14 | 12 | 4 | | | Reviewed | 16 | 20 |
| 27 | 24 | 6 | 2 | | 1 | Compiled | 41 | 45 |
| 119 | 105 | 16 | 2 | 1 | 1 | Tax Returns | 137 | 143 |
| 45 | 62 | 27 | 5 | | 2 | Other | 95 | 85 |
| | 64 (4/1-9/30/11) | | 412 (10/1/11-3/31/12) | | | | 4/1/07- 3/31/08 ALL | 4/1/08- 3/31/09 ALL |
| 191 | 205 | 62 | 13 | 1 | 4 | NUMBER OF STATEMENTS | 299 | 300 |
| % | % | % | % | % | % | ASSETS | % | % |
| 21.9 | 18.1 | 14.1 | 7.5 | | | Cash & Equivalents | 15.0 | 17.8 |
| 13.3 | 13.4 | 12.2 | 17.7 | | | Trade Receivables (net) | 13.4 | 13.2 |
| 10.7 | 9.2 | 8.1 | 11.1 | | | Inventory | 11.9 | 11.3 |
| 3.7 | 3.1 | 3.4 | 4.4 | | | All Other Current | 3.2 | 2.7 |
| 49.6 | 43.8 | 37.8 | 40.8 | | | Total Current | 43.5 | 44.9 |
| 32.7 | 35.9 | 40.8 | 41.6 | | | Fixed Assets (net) | 39.5 | 37.3 |
| 5.4 | 7.7 | 9.3 | 12.9 | | | Intangibles (net) | 8.5 | 6.0 |
| 12.3 | 12.6 | 12.2 | 4.7 | | | All Other Non-Current | 8.6 | 11.8 |
| 100.0 | 100.0 | 100.0 | 100.0 | | | Total | 100.0 | 100.0 |
| | | | | | | LIABILITIES | | |
| 25.9 | 7.6 | 2.4 | 6.9 | | | Notes Payable-Short Term | 14.7 | 11.1 |
| 3.7 | 3.0 | 3.2 | 3.7 | | | Cur. Mat.-L.T.D. | 4.4 | 5.0 |
| 17.5 | 13.9 | 13.2 | 17.4 | | | Trade Payables | 16.2 | 17.6 |
| .1 | .2 | .1 | .0 | | | Income Taxes Payable | .1 | .2 |
| 20.6 | 10.5 | 13.2 | 8.1 | | | All Other Current | 12.1 | 19.7 |
| 67.8 | 35.2 | 32.2 | 36.1 | | | Total Current | 47.4 | 53.6 |
| 28.3 | 24.3 | 34.6 | 52.3 | | | Long-Term Debt | 30.2 | 29.1 |
| .0 | .1 | .1 | 1.3 | | | Deferred Taxes | .2 | .2 |
| 18.4 | 10.5 | 9.2 | 6.0 | | | All Other Non-Current | 12.8 | 12.8 |
| -14.6 | 29.9 | 23.9 | 4.3 | | | Net Worth | 9.4 | 4.3 |
| 100.0 | 100.0 | 100.0 | 100.0 | | | Total Liabilities & Net Worth | 100.0 | 100.0 |
| | | | | | | INCOME DATA | | |
| 100.0 | 100.0 | 100.0 | 100.0 | | | Net Sales | 100.0 | 100.0 |
| | | | | | | Gross Profit | | |
| 97.2 | 92.7 | 88.0 | 87.5 | | | Operating Expenses | 93.8 | 95.2 |
| 2.8 | 7.3 | 12.0 | 12.5 | | | Operating Profit | 6.2 | 4.8 |
| .6 | 1.3 | 4.7 | 3.2 | | | All Other Expenses (net) | 1.4 | 2.0 |
| 2.2 | 6.0 | 7.3 | 9.2 | | | Profit Before Taxes | 4.7 | 2.8 |
| | | | | | | RATIOS | | |
| 1.9 | 2.8 | 2.1 | 1.5 | | | Current | 2.1 | 2.1 |
| .8 | 1.4 | 1.3 | 1.2 | | | | 1.0 | 1.0 |
| .5 | .7 | .6 | .8 | | | | .6 | .6 |
| 1.4 | 2.1 | 1.6 | .8 | | | Quick | 1.5 | 1.5 |
| (190) .5 | .9 | 1.0 | .6 | | | | (298) .7 | .7 |
| .3 | .4 | .4 | .4 | | | | .3 | .3 |
| 0 UND | 4 99.1 | 1 342.5 | 4 87.3 | | | Sales/Receivables | 0 UND | 0 UND |
| 4 100.5 | 10 37.6 | 9 39.1 | 21 17.6 | | | | 8 44.5 | 8 43.7 |
| 11 34.3 | 19 19.5 | 17 21.2 | 32 11.3 | | | | 19 18.8 | 15 24.0 |
| | | | | | | Cost of Sales/Inventory | | |
| | | | | | | Cost of Sales/Payables | | |
| 30.1 | 12.4 | 8.8 | 7.9 | | | Sales/Working Capital | 17.9 | 19.4 |
| -99.0 | 39.1 | 34.8 | 57.9 | | | | 267.0 | -999.8 |
| -24.2 | -33.0 | -18.9 | -34.0 | | | | -28.1 | -18.5 |
| 15.0 | 16.9 | 12.9 | 12.6 | | | EBIT/Interest | 8.5 | 7.2 |
| (135) 3.8 | (145) 4.6 | (47) 6.9 | (11) 4.9 | | | | (250) 2.6 | (236) 2.3 |
| .6 | 1.7 | 1.5 | 2.2 | | | | .9 | .4 |
| | | | | | | Net Profit + Depr., Dep., Amort./Cur. Mat. L/T/D | 3.3 | 4.4 |
| | | | | | | | (24) 2.4 | (19) 1.4 |
| | | | | | | | .8 | .6 |
| .4 | .3 | .6 | .6 | | | Fixed/Worth | .7 | .6 |
| 1.7 | 1.3 | 1.7 | 5.7 | | | | 2.9 | 2.7 |
| -1.1 | 11.2 | NM | -.5 | | | | -2.1 | -1.9 |
| 1.0 | .8 | 1.3 | 2.4 | | | Debt/Worth | 1.3 | 1.4 |
| 7.2 | 2.4 | 3.9 | 6.8 | | | | 4.8 | 7.0 |
| -3.1 | 70.1 | NM | -10.1 | | | | -6.7 | -5.9 |
| 124.1 | 70.3 | 90.9 | | | | % Profit Before Taxes/Tangible Net Worth | 124.8 | 104.8 |
| (113) 43.2 | (156) 29.9 | (47) 39.1 | | | | | (197) 42.0 | (199) 30.8 |
| 1.9 | 8.0 | 13.1 | | | | | 6.4 | 6.3 |
| 36.3 | 22.7 | 20.6 | 22.1 | | | % Profit Before Taxes/Total Assets | 24.1 | 19.1 |
| 11.6 | 9.7 | 11.9 | 8.4 | | | | 8.1 | 5.2 |
| -2.3 | 1.1 | 1.8 | 4.0 | | | | .0 | -1.4 |
| 80.6 | 46.6 | 24.2 | 32.5 | | | Sales/Net Fixed Assets | 35.5 | 41.2 |
| 30.2 | 14.9 | 11.9 | 9.2 | | | | 14.5 | 18.0 |
| 10.9 | 5.0 | 2.5 | 2.3 | | | | 5.5 | 7.1 |
| 11.6 | 5.2 | 3.8 | 2.5 | | | Sales/Total Assets | 7.2 | 7.6 |
| 6.9 | 3.5 | 2.5 | 1.7 | | | | 4.3 | 4.5 |
| 4.3 | 2.1 | 1.8 | 1.3 | | | | 2.5 | 2.5 |
| .5 | .7 | 1.1 | 1.0 | | | % Depr., Dep., Amort./Sales | .7 | .8 |
| (120) 1.0 | (150) 1.4 | (48) 1.7 | (12) 2.6 | | | | (232) 1.5 | (238) 1.7 |
| 2.3 | 2.9 | 3.2 | 4.3 | | | | 2.6 | 3.0 |
| 2.8 | 2.5 | 1.0 | | | | % Officers', Directors' Owners' Comp/Sales | 2.4 | 3.0 |
| (121) 5.2 | (116) 4.5 | (26) 2.2 | | | | | (188) 4.3 | (179) 5.1 |
| 9.4 | 7.0 | 4.4 | | | | | 8.1 | 7.8 |
| 295498M | 760840M | 709771M | 1090624M | 1112642M | 2764949M | Net Sales ($) | 7658377M | 2449796M |
| 41322M | 206045M | 237681M | 236507M | 75601M | 611919M | Total Assets ($) | 1298484M | 947951M |

M = $ thousand    MM = $ million
See Pages 9 through 22 for Explanation of Ratios and Data

## Comparative Historical Data  /  Current Data Sorted by Sales

| Hist 1 | Hist 2 | Hist 3 | Type of Statement | 0-1MM | 1-3MM | 3-5MM | 5-10MM | 10-25MM | 25MM & OVER |
|---|---|---|---|---|---|---|---|---|---|
| 8 | 6 | 1 | Unqualified | | | | | 1 | |
| 18 | 21 | 30 | Reviewed | | 6 | 5 | 6 | 8 | 5 |
| 43 | 51 | 60 | Compiled | 11 | 26 | 9 | 9 | 3 | 2 |
| 165 | 187 | 244 | Tax Returns | 64 | 100 | 34 | 34 | 7 | 5 |
| 105 | 121 | 141 | Other | 22 | 58 | 19 | 22 | 12 | 8 |
| 4/1/09-3/31/10 ALL | 4/1/10-3/31/11 ALL | 4/1/11-3/31/12 ALL | | 64 (4/1-9/30/11) | | | 412 (10/1/11-3/31/12) | | |
| 339 | 386 | 476 | NUMBER OF STATEMENTS | 97 | 190 | 67 | 71 | 31 | 20 |
| % | % | % | **ASSETS** | % | % | % | % | % | % |
| 19.2 | 20.1 | 18.7 | Cash & Equivalents | 15.9 | 19.6 | 21.3 | 22.3 | 12.7 | 10.8 |
| 13.4 | 12.2 | 13.5 | Trade Receivables (net) | 9.0 | 12.7 | 13.9 | 17.1 | 19.4 | 18.6 |
| 9.5 | 9.7 | 9.6 | Inventory | 9.7 | 9.1 | 7.2 | 11.0 | 14.2 | 10.5 |
| 3.1 | 3.6 | 3.4 | All Other Current | 2.7 | 3.8 | 3.0 | 4.1 | 2.9 | 3.4 |
| 45.1 | 45.5 | 45.2 | Total Current | 37.3 | 45.2 | 45.4 | 54.5 | 49.3 | 43.3 |
| 36.0 | 37.9 | 35.3 | Fixed Assets (net) | 45.5 | 34.6 | 33.5 | 28.7 | 30.8 | 30.2 |
| 8.4 | 5.5 | 7.4 | Intangibles (net) | 6.0 | 6.0 | 9.8 | 6.1 | 9.5 | 20.0 |
| 10.5 | 11.1 | 12.1 | All Other Non-Current | 11.2 | 14.3 | 11.3 | 10.7 | 10.4 | 6.4 |
| 100.0 | 100.0 | 100.0 | Total | 100.0 | 100.0 | 100.0 | 100.0 | 100.0 | 100.0 |
| | | | **LIABILITIES** | | | | | | |
| 9.8 | 13.1 | 14.2 | Notes Payable-Short Term | 27.4 | 13.1 | 11.7 | 7.7 | 6.0 | 3.7 |
| 3.8 | 3.8 | 3.4 | Cur. Mat.-L.T.D. | 3.9 | 2.9 | 2.5 | 4.0 | 4.2 | 5.2 |
| 15.9 | 14.6 | 15.6 | Trade Payables | 11.3 | 15.1 | 14.9 | 17.5 | 20.4 | 28.4 |
| .1 | .2 | .1 | Income Taxes Payable | .0 | .1 | .0 | .2 | .5 | .1 |
| 16.9 | 15.5 | 15.1 | All Other Current | 14.8 | 15.0 | 12.9 | 14.1 | 22.9 | 15.8 |
| 46.6 | 47.2 | 48.3 | Total Current | 57.3 | 46.3 | 42.0 | 43.5 | 54.0 | 53.2 |
| 31.8 | 27.7 | 28.3 | Long-Term Debt | 40.0 | 26.9 | 23.9 | 19.7 | 23.9 | 37.6 |
| .2 | .2 | .1 | Deferred Taxes | .0 | .0 | .1 | .3 | .5 | .8 |
| 9.0 | 16.7 | 13.4 | All Other Non-Current | 25.8 | 10.2 | 9.9 | 9.3 | 12.6 | 11.2 |
| 12.6 | 8.2 | 9.8 | Net Worth | -23.1 | 16.5 | 24.1 | 27.3 | 9.0 | -2.9 |
| 100.0 | 100.0 | 100.0 | Total Liabilties & Net Worth | 100.0 | 100.0 | 100.0 | 100.0 | 100.0 | 100.0 |
| | | | **INCOME DATA** | | | | | | |
| 100.0 | 100.0 | 100.0 | Net Sales | 100.0 | 100.0 | 100.0 | 100.0 | 100.0 | 100.0 |
| | | | Gross Profit | | | | | | |
| 95.3 | 93.2 | 93.8 | Operating Expenses | 88.2 | 95.5 | 93.6 | 96.0 | 94.5 | 95.8 |
| 4.7 | 6.8 | 6.2 | Operating Profit | 11.8 | 4.5 | 6.4 | 4.0 | 5.5 | 4.2 |
| 2.0 | 1.8 | 1.5 | All Other Expenses (net) | 5.6 | .7 | .4 | -.1 | 1.1 | .4 |
| 2.7 | 5.0 | 4.7 | Profit Before Taxes | 6.3 | 3.8 | 6.0 | 4.1 | 4.4 | 3.8 |
| | | | **RATIOS** | | | | | | |
| 2.0 | 2.2 | 2.3 | Current | 2.6 | 2.9 | 2.3 | 2.4 | 1.7 | 1.2 |
| 1.1 | 1.1 | 1.1 | | .7 | 1.1 | 1.4 | 1.4 | 1.0 | .8 |
| .6 | .6 | .6 | | .4 | .6 | .6 | .7 | .5 | .5 |
| 1.6 | 1.6 | 1.7 | Quick | 1.5 | 2.0 | 1.8 | 1.8 | 1.4 | .7 |
| .7 (385) | .7 (475) | .7 | | .5 (189) | .8 | 1.1 | .9 | .6 | .6 |
| .3 | .4 | .3 | | .2 | .3 | .5 | .4 | .4 | .4 |
| 1  541.0 | 0  UND | 0  UND | Sales/Receivables | 0  UND | 0  UND | 0  UND | 5  74.8 | 8  44.0 | 9  41.7 |
| 7  49.1 | 8  47.6 | 8  44.0 | | 0  UND | 8  44.1 | 9  41.6 | 9  40.3 | 11  31.8 | 16  23.2 |
| 14  25.7 | 15  24.8 | 16  22.3 | | 12  29.7 | 16  22.7 | 13  28.5 | 18  20.4 | 16  23.3 | 21  17.3 |
| | | | Cost of Sales/Inventory | | | | | | |
| | | | Cost of Sales/Payables | | | | | | |
| 16.3 | 18.2 | 16.1 | Sales/Working Capital | 17.2 | 16.5 | 16.9 | 13.7 | 16.3 | 30.3 |
| 149.3 | 188.6 | 132.2 | | -57.8 | 107.9 | 40.0 | 43.0 | 610.1 | -65.3 |
| -26.8 | -20.2 | -28.2 | | -8.3 | -35.0 | -33.4 | -48.7 | -19.6 | -28.2 |
| 9.6 | 11.7 | 14.2 | EBIT/Interest | 8.0 | 13.5 | 21.7 | 33.5 | 15.4 | 24.6 |
| (258) 3.0 | (284) 3.7 | (342) 4.9 | | (69) 2.5 | (127) 4.2 | (50) 5.8 | (54) 8.3 | (25) 5.9 | (17) 8.4 |
| .8 | 1.1 | 1.4 | | 1.0 | .8 | 2.2 | 1.5 | 1.5 | 2.7 |
| 6.6 | 5.2 | 4.5 | Net Profit + Depr., Dep., Amort./Cur. Mat. L/T/D | | | | | | |
| (27) 2.3 | (23) 1.5 | (21) 2.7 | | | | | | | |
| 1.2 | .5 | .7 | | | | | | | |
| .5 | .5 | .4 | Fixed/Worth | .7 | .3 | .4 | .5 | .5 | .7 |
| 2.3 | 2.3 | 1.6 | | 6.2 | 1.3 | .9 | 1.2 | 3.4 | NM |
| -2.4 | -2.7 | -4.7 | | -1.6 | -116.6 | -2.9 | -9.0 | -2.3 | -.3 |
| 1.0 | 1.1 | 1.0 | Debt/Worth | 1.8 | .7 | .7 | 1.0 | 2.5 | 1.4 |
| 5.4 | 5.7 | 3.5 | | 11.5 | 2.3 | 2.8 | 2.4 | 5.4 | NM |
| -6.3 | -6.5 | -6.8 | | -3.1 | -15.4 | -5.2 | -61.5 | -9.2 | -2.1 |
| 106.1 | 89.2 | 86.2 | % Profit Before Taxes/Tangible Net Worth | 67.8 | 84.5 | 91.7 | 73.2 | 134.0 | 155.7 |
| (229) 39.7 | (252) 35.4 | (326) 36.5 | | (58) 20.6 | (137) 36.0 | (46) 34.5 | (52) 39.0 | (23) 57.0 | (10) 88.2 |
| 5.0 | 8.1 | 6.6 | | -.9 | 1.9 | 16.0 | 10.7 | 20.7 | 48.9 |
| 22.0 | 23.7 | 25.7 | % Profit Before Taxes/Total Assets | 15.6 | 27.8 | 26.7 | 25.9 | 22.5 | 28.1 |
| 7.7 | 8.4 | 10.9 | | 5.0 | 10.4 | 16.2 | 17.1 | 14.5 | 9.2 |
| -.5 | .5 | .8 | | -2.4 | -.1 | 5.3 | 2.1 | 1.0 | 3.9 |
| 43.9 | 44.5 | 54.1 | Sales/Net Fixed Assets | 50.9 | 63.9 | 52.2 | 61.7 | 44.4 | 35.5 |
| 19.5 | 16.4 | 19.6 | | 9.0 | 20.8 | 19.9 | 21.7 | 22.7 | 16.8 |
| 8.0 | 5.8 | 6.7 | | 1.6 | 7.4 | 8.8 | 10.6 | 6.6 | 10.5 |
| 7.4 | 6.6 | 7.1 | Sales/Total Assets | 6.2 | 8.2 | 6.7 | 6.0 | 7.3 | 7.5 |
| 4.5 | 4.2 | 4.3 | | 3.0 | 4.4 | 5.0 | 4.6 | 4.2 | 3.9 |
| 2.6 | 2.3 | 2.4 | | 1.0 | 2.6 | 3.2 | 3.2 | 2.6 | 1.8 |
| .7 | .6 | .7 | % Depr., Dep., Amort./Sales | .8 | .5 | .7 | .7 | 1.0 | .6 |
| (264) 1.4 | (277) 1.4 | (332) 1.4 | | (68) 2.7 | (136) 1.2 | (42) 1.2 | (49) 1.3 | (23) 1.6 | (14) 1.0 |
| 2.6 | 2.7 | 2.9 | | 7.7 | 2.3 | 2.3 | 1.8 | 3.2 | 2.9 |
| 2.6 | 2.7 | 2.4 | % Officers', Directors' Owners' Comp/Sales | 4.6 | 3.0 | 2.3 | 1.9 | 1.0 | .6 |
| (219) 4.8 | (221) 5.0 | (271) 4.4 | | (41) 9.3 | (119) 5.0 | (39) 3.6 | (50) 2.8 | (12) 2.9 | (10) 1.3 |
| 7.7 | 7.5 | 7.7 | | 13.4 | 7.7 | 5.2 | 5.2 | 7.9 | 7.5 |
| 6030364M | 5217576M | 6734324M | Net Sales ($) | 53352M | 356769M | 260675M | 464855M | 489299M | 5109374M |
| 1464296M | 1224165M | 1409075M | Total Assets ($) | 48486M | 115181M | 70650M | 114064M | 157949M | 902745M |

M = $ thousand   MM = $ million
See Pages 9 through 22 for Explanation of Ratios and Data

## Current Data Sorted by Assets | Comparative Historical Data

| | | | | | | | Type of Statement | | |
|---|---|---|---|---|---|---|---|---|---|
| | | 1 | 1 | | 1 | | Unqualified | 4 | 2 |
| | 1 | | 1 | | | | Reviewed | 6 | 3 |
| | | 2 | 2 | | | | Compiled | 3 | 4 |
| 10 | 2 | 1 | 1 | | | | Tax Returns | 16 | 14 |
| | 1 | | | 1 | | | Other | 7 | 8 |
| | 4 (4/1-9/30/11) | | | 17 (10/1/11-3/31/12) | | | | 4/1/07-3/31/08 | 4/1/08-3/31/09 |
| 0-500M | 500M-2MM | 2-10MM | 10-50MM | 50-100MM | 100-250MM | | | ALL | ALL |
| 10 | 4 | 5 | 1 | 1 | | NUMBER OF STATEMENTS | | 36 | 31 |
| % | % | % | % | % | % | | ASSETS | % | % |
| 18.6 | | | | | | | Cash & Equivalents | 11.6 | 9.0 |
| 33.6 | | | | | | | Trade Receivables (net) | 19.5 | 26.8 |
| 7.6 | | | | | | | Inventory | 12.8 | 13.0 |
| 2.4 | | | | | | | All Other Current | 4.7 | 3.9 |
| 62.2 | | | | | | | Total Current | 48.7 | 52.6 |
| 23.4 | | | | | | | Fixed Assets (net) | 34.5 | 27.4 |
| 4.2 | | | | | | | Intangibles (net) | 8.6 | 9.8 |
| 10.3 | | | | | | | All Other Non-Current | 8.2 | 10.1 |
| 100.0 | | | | | | | Total | 100.0 | 100.0 |
| | | | | | | | LIABILITIES | | |
| 17.1 | | | | | | | Notes Payable-Short Term | 16.0 | 9.4 |
| 5.6 | | | | | | | Cur. Mat.-L.T.D. | 5.8 | 13.5 |
| 27.7 | | | | | | | Trade Payables | 13.6 | 14.9 |
| 3.2 | | | | | | | Income Taxes Payable | .1 | .0 |
| 27.4 | | | | | | | All Other Current | 9.8 | 13.3 |
| 81.0 | | | | | | | Total Current | 45.3 | 51.0 |
| 33.9 | | | | | | | Long-Term Debt | 22.7 | 23.3 |
| .0 | | | | | | | Deferred Taxes | .0 | .0 |
| 1.3 | | | | | | | All Other Non-Current | 6.5 | 2.6 |
| -16.2 | | | | | | | Net Worth | 25.5 | 23.1 |
| 100.0 | | | | | | | Total Liabilities & Net Worth | 100.0 | 100.0 |
| | | | | | | | INCOME DATA | | |
| 100.0 | | | | | | | Net Sales | 100.0 | 100.0 |
| | | | | | | | Gross Profit | | |
| 95.1 | | | | | | | Operating Expenses | 93.1 | 92.8 |
| 4.9 | | | | | | | Operating Profit | 6.9 | 7.2 |
| .4 | | | | | | | All Other Expenses (net) | 1.5 | 1.6 |
| 4.5 | | | | | | | Profit Before Taxes | 5.4 | 5.6 |
| | | | | | | | RATIOS | | |
| 1.4 | | | | | | | | 2.5 | 2.8 |
| 1.1 | | | | | | | Current | 1.4 | 1.4 |
| .2 | | | | | | | | .5 | 1.0 |
| 1.2 | | | | | | | | 1.4 | 1.5 |
| .9 | | | | | | | Quick | .8 | 1.0 |
| .2 | | | | | | | | .3 | .3 |
| 0 UND | | | | | | | | 0 UND 10 35.8 | |
| 16 22.5 | | | | | | | Sales/Receivables | 20 18.7 20 18.4 | |
| 24 15.4 | | | | | | | | 39 9.4 44 8.3 | |
| | | | | | | | Cost of Sales/Inventory | | |
| | | | | | | | Cost of Sales/Payables | | |
| 51.6 | | | | | | | | 9.3 | 11.8 |
| NM | | | | | | | Sales/Working Capital | 27.0 | 31.4 |
| -20.7 | | | | | | | | -23.3 | -823.3 |
| | | | | | | | | 15.9 | 8.3 |
| | | | | | | | EBIT/Interest | (33) 4.7 (25) 2.0 | |
| | | | | | | | | .9 | -.1 |
| | | | | | | | Net Profit + Depr., Dep., Amort./Cur. Mat. L/T/D | | |
| .5 | | | | | | | | .3 | .3 |
| NM | | | | | | | Fixed/Worth | .7 | .7 |
| -.6 | | | | | | | | -13.3 | -4.9 |
| 1.9 | | | | | | | | .6 | .6 |
| NM | | | | | | | Debt/Worth | 2.5 | 2.5 |
| -3.0 | | | | | | | | -9.2 | -15.2 |
| | | | | | | | % Profit Before Taxes/Tangible Net Worth | 99.1 | 29.3 |
| | | | | | | | | (25) 13.4 (21) 12.0 | |
| | | | | | | | | 6.2 | -.2 |
| 113.0 | | | | | | | % Profit Before Taxes/Total Assets | 18.8 | 14.8 |
| 22.9 | | | | | | | | 4.6 | 4.9 |
| -23.0 | | | | | | | | -.3 | -2.6 |
| 118.7 | | | | | | | Sales/Net Fixed Assets | 43.2 | 50.2 |
| 47.9 | | | | | | | | 12.2 | 16.0 |
| 24.1 | | | | | | | | 3.6 | 6.1 |
| 11.1 | | | | | | | Sales/Total Assets | 5.4 | 5.5 |
| 7.0 | | | | | | | | 3.4 | 3.1 |
| 6.0 | | | | | | | | 1.4 | 2.2 |
| | | | | | | | % Depr., Dep., Amort./Sales | 1.2 | .8 |
| | | | | | | | | (28) 2.0 (20) 1.5 | |
| | | | | | | | | 3.2 | 3.4 |
| | | | | | | | % Officers', Directors' Owners' Comp/Sales | 3.8 | 3.2 |
| | | | | | | | | (19) 5.4 (18) 4.9 | |
| | | | | | | | | 12.9 | 7.3 |
| 10157M | 29989M | 43092M | 15437M | 28971M | | Net Sales ($) | | 298823M | 193173M |
| 1501M | 5688M | 16738M | 10417M | 50275M | | Total Assets ($) | | 309238M | 62022M |

© RMA 2012

**M = $ thousand   MM = $ million**
See Pages 9 through 22 for Explanation of Ratios and Data

## Comparative Historical Data

## Current Data Sorted by Sales

| | | | | Type of Statement | | | | | | |
|---|---|---|---|---|---|---|---|---|---|---|
| 3 | 1 | 1 | | Unqualified | | | | | | 1 |
| 2 | 3 | 2 | | Reviewed | | | 2 | | | |
| 3 | 1 | 1 | | Compiled | | | 1 | | | |
| 16 | 12 | 14 | | Tax Returns | | | 2 | | 1 | |
| 7 | 6 | 3 | | Other | 8 | 3 | 2 | 1 | 2 | |
| 4/1/09-3/31/10 ALL | 4/1/10-3/31/11 ALL | 4/1/11-3/31/12 ALL | | | | 4 (4/1-9/30/11) | | 17 (10/1/11-3/31/12) | | |
| | | | | | 0-1MM | 1-3MM | 3-5MM | 5-10MM | 10-25MM | 25MM & OVER |
| 31 | 23 | 21 | | **NUMBER OF STATEMENTS** | 8 | 3 | | 6 | 3 | 1 |
| % | % | % | | **ASSETS** | % | % | % | % | % | % |
| 12.5 | 12.8 | 13.0 | | Cash & Equivalents | | | D | | | |
| 26.3 | 21.5 | 27.3 | | Trade Receivables (net) | | | A | | | |
| 24.0 | 29.2 | 13.6 | | Inventory | | | T | | | |
| 2.0 | 1.1 | 1.7 | | All Other Current | | | A | | | |
| 64.8 | 64.7 | 55.6 | | Total Current | | | | | | |
| 21.9 | 27.0 | 29.7 | | Fixed Assets (net) | | | N | | | |
| 3.1 | 2.2 | 3.6 | | Intangibles (net) | | | O | | | |
| 10.1 | 6.1 | 11.2 | | All Other Non-Current | | | T | | | |
| 100.0 | 100.0 | 100.0 | | Total | | | | | | |
| | | | | **LIABILITIES** | | | A | | | |
| 10.5 | 16.4 | 15.6 | | Notes Payable-Short Term | | | V | | | |
| 7.6 | 2.2 | 4.3 | | Cur. Mat.-L.T.D. | | | A | | | |
| 17.8 | 16.3 | 21.9 | | Trade Payables | | | I | | | |
| .0 | .3 | 1.5 | | Income Taxes Payable | | | L | | | |
| 9.0 | 10.7 | 27.8 | | All Other Current | | | A | | | |
| 44.9 | 45.9 | 71.1 | | Total Current | | | B | | | |
| 25.5 | 20.5 | 25.6 | | Long-Term Debt | | | L | | | |
| .9 | .3 | .2 | | Deferred Taxes | | | E | | | |
| 9.3 | 5.2 | 2.3 | | All Other Non-Current | | | | | | |
| 19.4 | 28.1 | .7 | | Net Worth | | | | | | |
| 100.0 | 100.0 | 100.0 | | Total Liabilties & Net Worth | | | | | | |
| | | | | **INCOME DATA** | | | | | | |
| 100.0 | 100.0 | 100.0 | | Net Sales | | | | | | |
| | | | | Gross Profit | | | | | | |
| 95.9 | 94.3 | 93.5 | | Operating Expenses | | | | | | |
| 4.1 | 5.7 | 6.5 | | Operating Profit | | | | | | |
| 1.9 | .9 | 1.5 | | All Other Expenses (net) | | | | | | |
| 2.2 | 4.8 | 5.0 | | Profit Before Taxes | | | | | | |
| | | | | **RATIOS** | | | | | | |
| 2.8 | 3.4 | 1.5 | | | | | | | | |
| 1.4 | 1.3 | 1.0 | | Current | | | | | | |
| .9 | .8 | .4 | | | | | | | | |
| 2.0 | 1.8 | 1.1 | | | | | | | | |
| .8 | .8 | .6 | | Quick | | | | | | |
| .4 | .3 | .2 | | | | | | | | |
| 14  25.5 | 6  59.0 | 13  27.4 | | | | | | | | |
| 18  19.7 | 18  20.3 | 19  19.2 | | Sales/Receivables | | | | | | |
| 31  11.7 | 28  13.2 | 30  12.2 | | | | | | | | |
| | | | | Cost of Sales/Inventory | | | | | | |
| | | | | Cost of Sales/Payables | | | | | | |
| 10.3 | 8.7 | 34.3 | | | | | | | | |
| 18.3 | 34.8 | 999.8 | | Sales/Working Capital | | | | | | |
| -40.5 | -37.8 | -10.6 | | | | | | | | |
| 3.8 | 14.4 | 5.1 | | | | | | | | |
| (24)  .3 | (19)  4.9 | (16)  1.8 | | EBIT/Interest | | | | | | |
| -3.5 | .3 | -3.9 | | | | | | | | |
| | | | | Net Profit + Depr., Dep., Amort./Cur. Mat. L/T/D | | | | | | |
| .2 | .2 | .3 | | | | | | | | |
| .9 | .5 | 1.9 | | Fixed/Worth | | | | | | |
| -7.4 | 1.9 | -2.1 | | | | | | | | |
| .7 | .6 | 1.7 | | | | | | | | |
| 2.8 | 2.3 | 4.0 | | Debt/Worth | | | | | | |
| -40.7 | 7.7 | -6.5 | | | | | | | | |
| 22.2 | 106.5 | 123.0 | | % Profit Before Taxes/Tangible Net Worth | | | | | | |
| (22)  1.9 | (21)  21.1 | (14)  30.8 | | | | | | | | |
| -40.5 | -.1 | -8.6 | | | | | | | | |
| 8.1 | 14.9 | 30.8 | | % Profit Before Taxes/Total Assets | | | | | | |
| .9 | 6.2 | 5.4 | | | | | | | | |
| -10.2 | -2.0 | -12.8 | | | | | | | | |
| 84.9 | 73.3 | 96.6 | | Sales/Net Fixed Assets | | | | | | |
| 29.3 | 24.3 | 27.8 | | | | | | | | |
| 6.5 | 9.2 | 5.4 | | | | | | | | |
| 6.2 | 5.7 | 7.4 | | Sales/Total Assets | | | | | | |
| 3.3 | 4.0 | 5.1 | | | | | | | | |
| 1.5 | 2.5 | 2.4 | | | | | | | | |
| .7 | .5 | .7 | | % Depr., Dep., Amort./Sales | | | | | | |
| (24)  1.1 | (17)  1.3 | (17)  1.4 | | | | | | | | |
| 2.7 | 3.7 | 2.8 | | | | | | | | |
| 2.0 | 2.4 | 2.3 | | % Officers', Directors' Owners' Comp/Sales | | | | | | |
| (18)  4.1 | (15)  4.0 | (13)  5.9 | | | | | | | | |
| 8.6 | 9.7 | 10.8 | | | | | | | | |
| 2281002M | 558171M | 127646M | | Net Sales ($) | 3844M | 6481M | | 42540M | 45810M | 28971M |
| 346680M | 94383M | 84619M | | Total Assets ($) | 1556M | 983M | | 12288M | 19517M | 50275M |

© RMA 2012

**M = $ thousand     MM = $ million**
See Pages 9 through 22 for Explanation of Ratios and Data

**Current Data Sorted by Assets**          **Comparative Historical Data**

| 0-500M | 500M-2MM | 2-10MM | 10-50MM | 50-100MM | 100-250MM | Type of Statement | 4/1/07-3/31/08 ALL | 4/1/08-3/31/09 ALL |
|---|---|---|---|---|---|---|---|---|
| | | | 2 | | | Unqualified | 1 | 1 |
| | | 3 | 2 | 1 | | Reviewed | 4 | 3 |
| 4 | 1 | 6 | | | | Compiled | 6 | 2 |
| 27 | 16 | 9 | 1 | | | Tax Returns | 10 | 19 |
| 12 | 8 | 10 | 3 | | 1 | Other | 8 | 12 |
| | 8 (4/1-9/30/11) | | 98 (10/1/11-3/31/12) | | | | | |
| **43** | **25** | **28** | **8** | **1** | **1** | **NUMBER OF STATEMENTS** | **29** | **37** |
| % | % | % | % | % | % | **ASSETS** | % | % |
| 22.8 | 9.0 | 10.6 | | | | Cash & Equivalents | 18.1 | 11.6 |
| 3.7 | 4.6 | 1.8 | | | | Trade Receivables (net) | 2.7 | 1.5 |
| 14.3 | 9.4 | 7.5 | | | | Inventory | 9.0 | 9.3 |
| 4.3 | 1.1 | 2.7 | | | | All Other Current | 3.0 | 3.6 |
| 45.0 | 24.2 | 22.6 | | | | Total Current | 32.8 | 25.9 |
| 31.6 | 61.1 | 60.9 | | | | Fixed Assets (net) | 50.9 | 55.2 |
| 15.5 | 4.5 | 14.0 | | | | Intangibles (net) | 8.6 | 12.8 |
| 7.9 | 10.3 | 2.5 | | | | All Other Non-Current | 7.7 | 6.1 |
| 100.0 | 100.0 | 100.0 | | | | Total | 100.0 | 100.0 |
| | | | | | | **LIABILITIES** | | |
| 7.4 | 6.7 | 4.8 | | | | Notes Payable-Short Term | 1.2 | 2.2 |
| 5.1 | 1.5 | 4.2 | | | | Cur. Mat.-L.T.D. | 3.7 | 6.4 |
| 14.9 | 10.7 | 4.7 | | | | Trade Payables | 8.0 | 8.6 |
| .5 | .0 | .0 | | | | Income Taxes Payable | .0 | .0 |
| 12.9 | 10.4 | 5.2 | | | | All Other Current | 7.1 | 21.9 |
| 40.8 | 29.3 | 18.9 | | | | Total Current | 20.0 | 39.1 |
| 39.8 | 45.7 | 48.7 | | | | Long-Term Debt | 39.0 | 50.7 |
| .0 | .0 | .3 | | | | Deferred Taxes | .0 | .2 |
| 25.9 | 15.8 | 2.4 | | | | All Other Non-Current | 30.3 | 17.4 |
| -6.3 | 9.3 | 29.7 | | | | Net Worth | 10.7 | -7.3 |
| 100.0 | 100.0 | 100.0 | | | | Total Liabilities & Net Worth | 100.0 | 100.0 |
| | | | | | | **INCOME DATA** | | |
| 100.0 | 100.0 | 100.0 | | | | Net Sales | 100.0 | 100.0 |
| | | | | | | Gross Profit | | |
| 96.2 | 84.8 | 86.9 | | | | Operating Expenses | 90.0 | 84.5 |
| 3.8 | 15.2 | 13.1 | | | | Operating Profit | 10.0 | 15.5 |
| .6 | 6.5 | 7.4 | | | | All Other Expenses (net) | 4.4 | 7.2 |
| 3.2 | 8.8 | 5.6 | | | | Profit Before Taxes | 5.7 | 8.2 |
| | | | | | | **RATIOS** | | |
| 6.8 | 1.7 | 2.2 | | | | | 4.4 | 1.5 |
| 1.6 | 1.0 | 1.1 | | | | Current | 1.6 | .9 |
| .6 | .5 | .5 | | | | | .8 | .3 |
| 3.8 | 1.1 | 1.3 | | | | | 3.3 | 1.0 |
| (42) .5 | .6 | .5 | | | | Quick (36) | 1.1 | .3 |
| .2 | .2 | .2 | | | | | .3 | .2 |
| 0 UND | 0 UND | 0 872.0 | | | | | 0 UND | 0 UND |
| 0 UND | 2 231.0 | 2 208.7 | | | | Sales/Receivables | 1 323.6 | 2 180.9 |
| 2 158.0 | 5 68.1 | 4 91.4 | | | | | 3 116.0 | 4 98.8 |
| | | | | | | Cost of Sales/Inventory | | |
| | | | | | | Cost of Sales/Payables | | |
| 14.9 | 20.7 | 16.0 | | | | | 8.1 | 26.8 |
| 125.7 | -267.6 | 70.9 | | | | Sales/Working Capital | 28.0 | -116.5 |
| -20.4 | -10.1 | -8.7 | | | | | -56.9 | -7.4 |
| 14.2 | 5.7 | 10.1 | | | | | 11.6 | 4.9 |
| (24) 2.3 | (21) 1.7 | (24) 4.9 | | | | EBIT/Interest (25) | 2.4 | (25) 2.0 |
| -1.3 | .9 | 1.8 | | | | | 1.4 | .0 |
| | | | | | | Net Profit + Depr., Dep., Amort./Cur. Mat. L/T/D | | |
| .2 | 2.4 | 1.1 | | | | | .7 | 1.1 |
| 1.4 | 146.8 | 4.7 | | | | Fixed/Worth | 2.0 | 8.8 |
| -1.5 | -4.4 | -15.4 | | | | | -3.1 | -1.0 |
| .4 | 3.0 | 1.4 | | | | | 1.2 | 2.6 |
| 4.3 | -57.0 | 5.8 | | | | Debt/Worth | 5.4 | 11.9 |
| -2.8 | -6.8 | -19.9 | | | | | -4.9 | -2.6 |
| 155.5 | 74.2 | 72.4 | | | | % Profit Before Taxes/Tangible | 67.4 | 68.7 |
| (25) 52.9 | (12) 32.4 | (20) 31.2 | | | | Net Worth (18) | 34.0 | (21) 26.2 |
| 7.7 | 9.7 | 8.5 | | | | | 12.7 | 3.6 |
| 42.1 | 11.2 | 15.5 | | | | % Profit Before Taxes/Total | 24.4 | 8.8 |
| 10.4 | 4.2 | 9.0 | | | | Assets | 6.9 | 4.4 |
| -3.4 | .0 | 2.1 | | | | | -2.8 | -3.2 |
| 94.2 | 31.1 | 10.3 | | | | | 15.4 | 12.7 |
| 27.4 | 1.8 | 1.8 | | | | Sales/Net Fixed Assets | 5.5 | 5.7 |
| 4.3 | .5 | .7 | | | | | 1.4 | .7 |
| 8.1 | 3.1 | 2.6 | | | | | 4.4 | 3.6 |
| 5.8 | 1.1 | 1.2 | | | | Sales/Total Assets | 2.3 | 1.7 |
| 2.5 | .5 | .5 | | | | | 1.0 | .6 |
| 1.1 | 1.8 | 1.8 | | | | | 1.5 | 2.3 |
| (26) 2.2 | (20) 4.6 | (24) 3.8 | | | | % Depr., Dep., Amort./Sales (27) | 2.6 | (30) 3.8 |
| 5.9 | 7.4 | 9.1 | | | | | 6.4 | 12.9 |
| 4.5 | | .9 | | | | | 1.9 | 2.6 |
| (19) 7.6 | | (10) 2.4 | | | | % Officers', Directors' Owners' Comp/Sales (10) | 4.1 | (12) 3.6 |
| 8.8 | | 5.9 | | | | | 7.9 | 8.5 |
| 36848M | 73586M | 223676M | 268574M | 6086M | 179823M | Net Sales ($) | 711304M | 242826M |
| 8485M | 27768M | 124894M | 161940M | 60504M | 162356M | Total Assets ($) | 578172M | 186853M |

M = $ thousand    MM = $ million
See Pages 9 through 22 for Explanation of Ratios and Data

| Comparative Historical Data | | | Type of Statement | Current Data Sorted by Sales | | | | | |
|---|---|---|---|---|---|---|---|---|---|
| 2 | 4 | 2 | Unqualified | | | | | 1 | 1 |
| 1 | 4 | 6 | Reviewed | | 1 | | 2 | 1 | 2 |
| 6 | 9 | 11 | Compiled | 5 | 1 | 2 | 1 | 2 | |
| 23 | 38 | 53 | Tax Returns | 30 | 13 | 3 | 3 | 4 | 4 |
| 22 | 38 | 34 | Other | 13 | 6 | 4 | 3 | 4 | |
| 4/1/09-3/31/10 | 4/1/10-3/31/11 | 4/1/11-3/31/12 | | 8 (4/1-9/30/11) | | 98 (10/1/11-3/31/12) | | | |
| ALL | ALL | ALL | | 0-1MM | 1-3MM | 3-5MM | 5-10MM | 10-25MM | 25MM & OVER |
| 54 | 93 | 106 | **NUMBER OF STATEMENTS** | 48 | 21 | 9 | 9 | 12 | 7 |
| % | % | % | **ASSETS** | % | % | % | % | % | % |
| 8.9 | 13.6 | 15.0 | Cash & Equivalents | 18.2 | 14.0 | | | 16.3 | |
| 3.1 | 4.7 | 3.2 | Trade Receivables (net) | 2.2 | 4.5 | | | 3.4 | |
| 10.7 | 11.6 | 10.8 | Inventory | 8.5 | 12.3 | | | 16.0 | |
| 2.5 | 4.2 | 2.8 | All Other Current | 3.0 | 2.1 | | | 1.9 | |
| 25.3 | 34.0 | 31.8 | Total Current | 31.9 | 32.9 | | | 37.6 | |
| 58.8 | 44.4 | 47.0 | Fixed Assets (net) | 51.1 | 43.0 | | | 48.1 | |
| 12.0 | 13.9 | 13.9 | Intangibles (net) | 10.6 | 12.9 | | | 11.4 | |
| 3.9 | 7.7 | 7.3 | All Other Non-Current | 6.5 | 11.2 | | | 2.9 | |
| 100.0 | 100.0 | 100.0 | Total | 100.0 | 100.0 | | | 100.0 | |
| | | | **LIABILITIES** | | | | | | |
| 4.6 | 3.0 | 6.1 | Notes Payable-Short Term | 6.8 | 6.9 | | | 4.3 | |
| 4.0 | 3.9 | 3.8 | Cur. Mat.-L.T.D. | 3.8 | 4.6 | | | 1.7 | |
| 11.0 | 14.9 | 10.5 | Trade Payables | 3.8 | 14.6 | | | 11.4 | |
| .0 | .0 | .2 | Income Taxes Payable | .4 | .0 | | | .0 | |
| 11.7 | 10.0 | 9.5 | All Other Current | 12.5 | 9.4 | | | 6.0 | |
| 31.3 | 31.9 | 30.2 | Total Current | 27.3 | 35.5 | | | 23.4 | |
| 56.3 | 53.7 | 43.7 | Long-Term Debt | 47.8 | 43.4 | | | 31.3 | |
| .1 | .2 | .2 | Deferred Taxes | .0 | .0 | | | .3 | |
| 23.6 | 12.4 | 15.4 | All Other Non-Current | 16.1 | 21.5 | | | 7.7 | |
| -11.4 | 1.8 | 10.6 | Net Worth | 8.9 | -.3 | | | 37.4 | |
| 100.0 | 100.0 | 100.0 | Total Liabilities & Net Worth | 100.0 | 100.0 | | | 100.0 | |
| | | | **INCOME DATA** | | | | | | |
| 100.0 | 100.0 | 100.0 | Net Sales | 100.0 | 100.0 | | | 100.0 | |
| | | | Gross Profit | | | | | | |
| 91.4 | 91.0 | 90.3 | Operating Expenses | 86.9 | 92.4 | | | 96.1 | |
| 8.6 | 9.0 | 9.7 | Operating Profit | 13.1 | 7.6 | | | 3.9 | |
| 4.5 | 3.6 | 3.7 | All Other Expenses (net) | 6.9 | 2.8 | | | -.4 | |
| 4.1 | 5.4 | 6.0 | Profit Before Taxes | 6.2 | 4.8 | | | 4.3 | |
| | | | **RATIOS** | | | | | | |
| 1.6 | 2.1 | 3.4 | | 8.4 | 2.9 | | | 3.6 | |
| .8 | 1.2 | 1.1 | Current | 1.3 | .9 | | | 1.6 | |
| .3 | .6 | .6 | | .3 | .7 | | | .6 | |
| .9 | 1.6 | 1.6 | | 5.3 | 1.6 | | | 2.3 | |
| .4 (92) | .6 (105) | .5 | Quick | (47) .7 | .5 | | | .4 | |
| .2 | .2 | .2 | | .2 | .2 | | | .2 | |
| 0 UND | 0 UND | 0 UND | | 0 UND | 0 UND | | | 1 654.4 | |
| 0 759.3 | 1 244.0 | 1 321.1 | Sales/Receivables | 0 UND | 1 488.6 | | | 2 174.5 | |
| 4 85.9 | 7 53.4 | 3 106.7 | | 2 169.8 | 4 90.6 | | | 4 84.4 | |
| | | | Cost of Sales/Inventory | | | | | | |
| | | | Cost of Sales/Payables | | | | | | |
| 43.2 | 11.2 | 17.8 | | 14.6 | 17.5 | | | 11.5 | |
| -44.4 | 75.7 | 162.0 | Sales/Working Capital | 121.2 | -361.3 | | | 45.3 | |
| -8.1 | -17.7 | -14.8 | | -11.8 | -17.4 | | | -74.2 | |
| 5.3 | 6.9 | 9.3 | | 6.6 | 4.1 | | | 14.6 | |
| (42) 2.3 | (66) 2.4 | (79) 3.1 | EBIT/Interest | (29) 1.9 | (15) 1.6 | | | 3.8 | |
| 1.3 | 1.2 | 1.0 | | -.1 | .7 | | | 2.1 | |
| | | | Net Profit + Depr., Dep., Amort./Cur. Mat. L/T/D | | | | | | |
| 1.2 | .7 | .9 | | .6 | .1 | | | .9 | |
| 102.8 | 7.4 | 5.6 | Fixed/Worth | 4.9 | 2.7 | | | 3.3 | |
| -1.9 | -1.8 | -3.7 | | -7.4 | -4.7 | | | NM | |
| 2.6 | 2.6 | 1.4 | | 1.2 | 1.2 | | | .7 | |
| -45.1 | -66.2 | 15.8 | Debt/Worth | 6.2 | 16.6 | | | 4.9 | |
| -3.6 | -2.8 | -5.5 | | -15.6 | -4.1 | | | NM | |
| 56.8 | 90.1 | 88.1 | | 128.6 | 71.6 | | | | |
| (26) 25.5 | (45) 34.2 | (61) 34.5 | % Profit Before Taxes/Tangible Net Worth | (31) 39.0 | (11) 25.0 | | | | |
| 3.8 | 9.6 | 9.1 | | 5.4 | 7.0 | | | | |
| 12.9 | 18.7 | 17.5 | | 23.3 | 19.3 | | | 16.9 | |
| 6.4 | 6.9 | 7.8 | % Profit Before Taxes/Total Assets | 4.5 | 12.0 | | | 9.1 | |
| -1.0 | -.2 | .0 | | -.8 | -.8 | | | 3.8 | |
| 9.1 | 45.3 | 34.6 | | 46.8 | 353.0 | | | 25.7 | |
| 2.5 | 5.3 | 4.8 | Sales/Net Fixed Assets | 3.8 | 25.8 | | | 8.1 | |
| .8 | 1.4 | 1.3 | | .7 | 1.5 | | | 2.3 | |
| 3.7 | 3.3 | 5.4 | | 6.1 | 8.0 | | | 4.7 | |
| 1.5 | 1.8 | 2.3 | Sales/Total Assets | 2.0 | 3.3 | | | 2.5 | |
| .6 | .9 | .9 | | .5 | 1.3 | | | 1.2 | |
| 2.5 | 1.3 | 1.5 | | 1.5 | 1.5 | | | .5 | |
| (42) 3.8 | (68) 3.1 | (80) 2.8 | % Depr., Dep., Amort./Sales | (38) 3.3 | (10) 4.5 | | | (10) 2.1 | |
| 13.4 | 6.8 | 7.4 | | 14.5 | 10.3 | | | 5.5 | |
| 1.9 | 3.3 | 2.8 | | 4.6 | 3.7 | | | | |
| (18) 4.1 | (31) 4.2 | (41) 5.1 | % Officers', Directors' Owners' Comp/Sales | (16) 4.1 | (12) 5.9 | | | | |
| 8.4 | 7.2 | 8.2 | | 10.7 | 8.0 | | | | |
| 213435M | 788649M | 788593M | Net Sales ($) | 25884M | 36431M | 33980M | 64694M | 204920M | 422684M |
| 165325M | 573907M | 545947M | Total Assets ($) | 26962M | 24388M | 32805M | 83360M | 125510M | 252922M |

M = $ thousand    MM = $ million
See Pages 9 through 22 for Explanation of Ratios and Data

## Current Data Sorted by Assets

## Comparative Historical Data

| | | | | | | Type of Statement | | |
|---|---|---|---|---|---|---|---|---|
| 1 | 1 | 2 | 2 | | | Unqualified | 6 | 5 |
| | 2 | 7 | 11 | | 1 | Reviewed | 8 | 14 |
| 18 | 30 | 14 | 2 | | | Compiled | 53 | 54 |
| 71 | 93 | 28 | 2 | | | Tax Returns | 117 | 141 |
| 21 | 53 | 41 | 4 | 2 | 1 | Other | 100 | 116 |
| | 18 (4/1-9/30/11) | | | 389 (10/1/11-3/31/12) | | | 4/1/07-3/31/08 | 4/1/08-3/31/09 |
| 0-500M | 500M-2MM | 2-10MM | 10-50MM | 50-100MM | 100-250MM | | ALL | ALL |
| 111 | 179 | 92 | 21 | 2 | 2 | NUMBER OF STATEMENTS | 284 | 330 |
| % | % | % | % | % | % | ASSETS | % | % |
| 22.8 | 7.4 | 5.5 | 9.7 | | | Cash & Equivalents | 8.5 | 10.1 |
| 1.6 | 2.5 | 2.5 | 1.0 | | | Trade Receivables (net) | 2.2 | 2.4 |
| 4.7 | 3.1 | 2.6 | 4.8 | | | Inventory | 3.3 | 3.7 |
| 4.4 | 1.2 | 1.3 | .7 | | | All Other Current | 2.8 | 2.9 |
| 33.4 | 14.2 | 11.9 | 16.4 | | | Total Current | 16.8 | 19.0 |
| 47.1 | 71.8 | 69.3 | 69.6 | | | Fixed Assets (net) | 67.5 | 63.2 |
| 7.1 | 7.7 | 10.1 | 5.3 | | | Intangibles (net) | 9.1 | 8.5 |
| 12.4 | 6.2 | 8.7 | 8.7 | | | All Other Non-Current | 6.6 | 9.2 |
| 100.0 | 100.0 | 100.0 | 100.0 | | | Total | 100.0 | 100.0 |
| | | | | | | LIABILITIES | | |
| 7.7 | 5.5 | 3.2 | 7.1 | | | Notes Payable-Short Term | 6.0 | 6.1 |
| 9.4 | 5.8 | 3.6 | 3.4 | | | Cur. Mat.-L.T.D. | 4.0 | 4.6 |
| 4.9 | 2.3 | 2.5 | 3.5 | | | Trade Payables | 5.5 | 4.3 |
| .4 | .0 | .0 | .0 | | | Income Taxes Payable | .2 | .2 |
| 19.9 | 10.5 | 3.6 | 8.5 | | | All Other Current | 10.9 | 15.8 |
| 42.2 | 24.1 | 12.9 | 22.5 | | | Total Current | 26.7 | 30.9 |
| 49.3 | 72.3 | 61.3 | 41.2 | | | Long-Term Debt | 63.5 | 57.2 |
| .0 | .0 | .0 | .0 | | | Deferred Taxes | .0 | .0 |
| 15.4 | 11.6 | 6.1 | 4.9 | | | All Other Non-Current | 11.1 | 10.7 |
| -6.9 | -8.0 | 19.7 | 31.5 | | | Net Worth | -1.3 | 1.2 |
| 100.0 | 100.0 | 100.0 | 100.0 | | | Total Liabilties & Net Worth | 100.0 | 100.0 |
| | | | | | | INCOME DATA | | |
| 100.0 | 100.0 | 100.0 | 100.0 | | | Net Sales | 100.0 | 100.0 |
| | | | | | | Gross Profit | | |
| 92.5 | 89.0 | 79.6 | 82.4 | | | Operating Expenses | 87.3 | 90.7 |
| 7.5 | 11.0 | 20.4 | 17.6 | | | Operating Profit | 12.7 | 9.3 |
| 4.2 | 12.4 | 13.5 | 5.1 | | | All Other Expenses (net) | 9.7 | 8.7 |
| 3.3 | -1.3 | 6.9 | 12.5 | | | Profit Before Taxes | 3.0 | .7 |
| | | | | | | RATIOS | | |
| 2.5 | 2.3 | 2.5 | 1.6 | | | | 2.2 | 2.2 |
| 1.0 | .6 | .8 | .7 | | | Current | .8 | .7 |
| .4 | .1 | .2 | .3 | | | | .2 | .2 |
| 1.8 | 1.7 | 1.6 | 1.6 | | | | 1.4 | 1.6 |
| (110) .8 | .4 | .5 | .4 | | | Quick | (282) .5 | .4 |
| .2 | .1 | .1 | .1 | | | | .1 | .1 |
| 0 UND | 0 UND | 0 UND | 0 999.8 | | | | 0 UND | 0 UND |
| 0 UND | 0 UND | 0 999.8 | 0 768.9 | | | Sales/Receivables | 0 UND | 0 UND |
| 0 999.8 | 2 219.0 | 2 229.2 | 4 86.8 | | | | 2 212.1 | 2 182.1 |
| | | | | | | Cost of Sales/Inventory | | |
| | | | | | | Cost of Sales/Payables | | |
| 31.0 | 15.2 | 18.0 | 18.4 | | | | 20.7 | 19.6 |
| -512.0 | -19.2 | -40.7 | -36.6 | | | Sales/Working Capital | -31.9 | -48.8 |
| -17.9 | -4.3 | -4.4 | -7.6 | | | | -4.8 | -5.4 |
| 12.8 | 3.2 | 3.7 | 9.6 | | | | 4.2 | 3.5 |
| (73) 4.0 | (120) 1.5 | (73) 1.8 | (19) 2.5 | | | EBIT/Interest | (202) 1.6 | (219) 1.7 |
| 1.0 | .4 | 1.0 | .9 | | | | .9 | .5 |
| | | | | | | | 4.2 | 3.9 |
| | | | | | | Net Profit + Depr., Dep., Amort./Cur. Mat. L/T/D | (14) 1.3 | (22) 1.7 |
| | | | | | | | .5 | 1.0 |
| .6 | 4.3 | 2.4 | 1.4 | | | | 2.2 | 1.8 |
| 4.2 | -14.0 | 6.1 | 2.2 | | | Fixed/Worth | 23.9 | 11.8 |
| -1.9 | -1.9 | -12.3 | 6.3 | | | | -2.3 | -2.3 |
| .9 | 5.3 | 2.7 | .8 | | | | 2.2 | 1.7 |
| 27.4 | -16.7 | 5.7 | 2.0 | | | Debt/Worth | 40.7 | 23.3 |
| -3.4 | -3.1 | -14.0 | 7.9 | | | | -3.7 | -3.7 |
| 164.6 | 58.4 | 50.8 | 30.8 | | | | 62.7 | 44.0 |
| (62) 51.3 | (68) 23.2 | (64) 20.9 | (17) 20.3 | | | % Profit Before Taxes/Tangible Net Worth | (154) 24.7 | (179) 15.6 |
| 15.6 | .0 | .2 | 3.5 | | | | 1.0 | -1.5 |
| 45.2 | 7.9 | 7.9 | 12.2 | | | | 11.1 | 8.4 |
| 12.4 | 1.0 | 3.2 | 6.4 | | | % Profit Before Taxes/Total Assets | 2.1 | 1.6 |
| -1.3 | -3.9 | .0 | -.1 | | | | -3.4 | -5.1 |
| 81.8 | 2.9 | 1.4 | 3.8 | | | | 5.1 | 9.4 |
| 9.4 | .8 | .7 | 1.3 | | | Sales/Net Fixed Assets | 1.2 | 1.5 |
| 1.9 | .4 | .4 | .5 | | | | .4 | .5 |
| 7.4 | 1.3 | .9 | 2.3 | | | | 2.2 | 2.8 |
| 3.5 | .5 | .5 | .9 | | | Sales/Total Assets | .7 | .9 |
| 1.3 | .3 | .3 | .4 | | | | .4 | .4 |
| 1.7 | 4.6 | 4.8 | 2.6 | | | | 3.8 | 3.0 |
| (72) 4.1 | (149) 13.4 | (80) 10.7 | (20) 6.5 | | | % Depr., Dep., Amort./Sales | (225) 9.7 | (262) 8.4 |
| 10.6 | 24.9 | 17.4 | 9.6 | | | | 20.9 | 18.9 |
| 5.1 | 4.5 | 2.4 | | | | | 2.8 | 2.4 |
| (50) 7.5 | (51) 6.9 | (17) 4.9 | | | | % Officers', Directors' Owners' Comp/Sales | (89) 6.2 | (116) 5.1 |
| 14.5 | 10.5 | 9.1 | | | | | 11.7 | 9.2 |
| 86399M | 203446M | 294663M | 916332M | 248289M | 321369M | Net Sales ($) | 1793632M | 4436632M |
| 25934M | 189579M | 391359M | 463375M | 108038M | 302060M | Total Assets ($) | 1327240M | 1585779M |

© RMA 2012

M = $ thousand    MM = $ million
See Pages 9 through 22 for Explanation of Ratios and Data

## Comparative Historical Data / Current Data Sorted by Sales

| | | | Type of Statement | | | | | | |
|---|---|---|---|---|---|---|---|---|---|
| 5 | 7 | 6 | Unqualified | 2 | | | 2 | 1 | 1 |
| 16 | 16 | 21 | Reviewed | | 3 | | 6 | 6 | 6 |
| 59 | 75 | 64 | Compiled | 43 | 17 | 1 | 3 | | |
| 170 | 171 | 194 | Tax Returns | 119 | 60 | 7 | 6 | 1 | 1 |
| 110 | 136 | 122 | Other | 62 | 35 | 7 | 10 | 3 | 5 |
| 4/1/09-3/31/10 | 4/1/10-3/31/11 | 4/1/11-3/31/12 | | 18 (4/1-9/30/11) | | | 389 (10/1/11-3/31/12) | | |
| ALL | ALL | ALL | | 0-1MM | 1-3MM | 3-5MM | 5-10MM | 10-25MM | 25MM & OVER |
| 360 | 405 | 407 | **NUMBER OF STATEMENTS** | 226 | 115 | 15 | 27 | 11 | 13 |
| % | % | % | **ASSETS** | % | % | % | % | % | % |
| 10.7 | 11.7 | 11.2 | Cash & Equivalents | 10.5 | 12.9 | 14.2 | 9.5 | 9.9 | 10.0 |
| 1.7 | 2.3 | 2.2 | Trade Receivables (net) | .4 | 3.6 | 3.9 | 6.7 | 9.9 | 2.3 |
| 3.8 | 4.1 | 3.5 | Inventory | 1.3 | 6.0 | 4.2 | 8.2 | 6.4 | 7.5 |
| 2.9 | 2.6 | 2.1 | All Other Current | 2.7 | 1.2 | .5 | 1.1 | 2.2 | 1.2 |
| 19.1 | 20.7 | 19.0 | Total Current | 14.9 | 23.8 | 22.9 | 25.5 | 28.3 | 21.1 |
| 63.3 | 61.0 | 64.4 | Fixed Assets (net) | 72.3 | 52.2 | 63.8 | 61.3 | 37.9 | 63.1 |
| 9.6 | 9.0 | 8.1 | Intangibles (net) | 5.9 | 11.8 | 2.0 | 8.3 | 21.7 | 8.2 |
| 8.0 | 9.3 | 8.6 | All Other Non-Current | 6.9 | 12.2 | 11.3 | 4.9 | 12.0 | 7.7 |
| 100.0 | 100.0 | 100.0 | Total | 100.0 | 100.0 | 100.0 | 100.0 | 100.0 | 100.0 |
| | | | **LIABILITIES** | | | | | | |
| 4.9 | 6.4 | 5.6 | Notes Payable-Short Term | 5.5 | 6.0 | 3.7 | 4.6 | 5.7 | 8.8 |
| 5.4 | 4.4 | 6.1 | Cur. Mat.-L.T.D. | 7.2 | 5.2 | 5.0 | 5.1 | 3.0 | 1.9 |
| 4.0 | 7.3 | 3.1 | Trade Payables | 1.8 | 4.7 | 4.4 | 5.5 | 3.5 | 5.0 |
| .1 | .2 | .1 | Income Taxes Payable | .2 | .0 | .0 | .0 | .0 | .0 |
| 15.9 | 14.7 | 11.3 | All Other Current | 13.0 | 8.1 | 11.5 | 10.9 | 8.7 | 14.0 |
| 30.3 | 32.9 | 26.3 | Total Current | 27.7 | 24.0 | 24.6 | 26.2 | 20.9 | 29.7 |
| 59.2 | 55.9 | 61.4 | Long-Term Debt | 72.0 | 50.3 | 56.3 | 52.6 | 26.9 | 29.8 |
| .1 | .1 | .0 | Deferred Taxes | .0 | .0 | .0 | .0 | .0 | 1.1 |
| 12.7 | 13.4 | 11.1 | All Other Non-Current | 12.4 | 11.2 | 2.7 | 7.2 | 8.9 | 6.2 |
| -2.3 | -2.3 | 1.1 | Net Worth | -12.1 | 14.5 | 16.4 | 14.0 | 43.2 | 33.2 |
| 100.0 | 100.0 | 100.0 | Total Liabilties & Net Worth | 100.0 | 100.0 | 100.0 | 100.0 | 100.0 | 100.0 |
| | | | **INCOME DATA** | | | | | | |
| 100.0 | 100.0 | 100.0 | Net Sales | 100.0 | 100.0 | 100.0 | 100.0 | 100.0 | 100.0 |
| | | | Gross Profit | | | | | | |
| 89.3 | 86.9 | 87.5 | Operating Expenses | 86.8 | 88.0 | 86.2 | 87.1 | 92.5 | 93.5 |
| 10.7 | 13.1 | 12.5 | Operating Profit | 13.2 | 12.0 | 13.8 | 12.9 | 7.5 | 6.5 |
| 9.4 | 8.1 | 9.9 | All Other Expenses (net) | 14.7 | 4.7 | 3.5 | 3.6 | .7 | 1.1 |
| 1.3 | 5.0 | 2.6 | Profit Before Taxes | -1.5 | 7.4 | 10.2 | 9.2 | 6.8 | 5.4 |
| | | | **RATIOS** | | | | | | |
| 2.0 | 2.0 | 2.3 | | 2.0 | 2.6 | 4.0 | 1.6 | 3.3 | 1.8 |
| .7 | .7 | .7 | Current | .6 | 1.0 | .9 | .9 | 1.3 | .6 |
| .2 | .2 | .2 | | .1 | .5 | .4 | .6 | .7 | .5 |
| 1.2 | 1.4 | 1.6 | | 1.9 | 1.6 | 3.3 | 1.1 | 1.6 | 1.6 |
| (359) .4 | .4 | (406) .5 | Quick | (225) .4 | .6 | .8 | .6 | .7 | .4 |
| .1 | .1 | .1 | | .1 | .2 | .2 | .3 | .3 | .2 |
| 0 UND | 0 UND | 0 UND | | 0 UND | 0 UND | 0 UND | 1 489.7 | 0 768.9 | 0 999.8 |
| 0 UND | 0 UND | 0 UND | Sales/Receivables | 0 UND | 0 999.8 | 0 999.8 | 1 291.3 | 3 136.1 | 4 97.4 |
| 1 271.2 | 1 269.7 | 2 219.0 | | 0 UND | 4 97.7 | 3 119.4 | 7 49.6 | 26 13.9 | 7 55.8 |
| | | | Cost of Sales/Inventory | | | | | | |
| | | | Cost of Sales/Payables | | | | | | |
| 25.5 | 26.8 | 20.8 | | 30.1 | 19.0 | 8.5 | 19.9 | 10.6 | 22.9 |
| -41.9 | -43.3 | -36.6 | Sales/Working Capital | -17.4 | UND | -51.3 | -182.5 | 22.0 | -50.7 |
| -5.1 | -6.2 | -5.5 | | -3.5 | -13.3 | -10.1 | -19.2 | -47.0 | -16.6 |
| 4.7 | 6.4 | 5.0 | | 3.1 | 10.0 | 6.6 | 5.6 | 10.5 | 99.8 |
| (238) 1.6 | (273) 2.3 | (289) 2.0 | EBIT/Interest | (132) 1.4 | (98) 2.6 | (13) 5.8 | (23) 3.0 | (10) 6.1 | 3.1 |
| .6 | 1.2 | .9 | | .2 | 1.1 | 1.4 | 1.8 | 2.4 | 1.0 |
| 2.9 | 2.3 | 2.5 | | | | | | | |
| (21) 2.5 | (18) 1.8 | (14) 1.8 | Net Profit + Depr., Dep., Amort./Cur. Mat. L/T/D | | | | | | |
| 1.7 | 1.2 | 1.5 | | | | | | | |
| 2.0 | 1.5 | 1.8 | | 2.8 | 1.6 | 1.4 | 1.3 | .6 | 1.1 |
| 28.5 | 13.4 | 20.3 | Fixed/Worth | -21.3 | 11.3 | 4.8 | 3.6 | 1.3 | 1.7 |
| -1.9 | -1.7 | -3.0 | | -2.1 | -3.8 | 57.0 | 27.1 | -5.1 | NM |
| 2.3 | 1.8 | 2.1 | | 3.7 | 2.0 | 1.1 | 1.7 | .9 | .4 |
| 120.3 | 21.5 | 50.3 | Debt/Worth | -23.8 | 15.5 | 6.0 | 3.9 | 2.9 | 1.7 |
| -3.1 | -3.2 | -4.2 | | -3.2 | -6.5 | 448.5 | 30.1 | -6.3 | NM |
| 38.4 | 86.0 | 66.7 | | 52.2 | 91.1 | 70.7 | 74.4 | | 34.0 |
| (182) 16.1 | (226) 29.2 | (214) 25.3 | % Profit Before Taxes/Tangible Net Worth | (96) 16.3 | (66) 44.8 | (12) 24.8 | (22) 31.1 | (10) 25.2 | |
| -2.1 | 3.9 | 1.0 | | -.1 | 6.5 | 10.6 | 15.3 | | -.3 |
| 9.6 | 15.4 | 12.4 | | 6.9 | 26.1 | 22.7 | 13.2 | 20.3 | 18.3 |
| 1.8 | 4.5 | 3.2 | % Profit Before Taxes/Total Assets | .6 | 7.9 | 10.2 | 6.0 | 7.8 | 6.8 |
| -4.0 | -.2 | -2.0 | | -3.9 | .4 | 2.6 | 2.9 | 6.4 | -.1 |
| 8.2 | 9.3 | 6.1 | | 3.2 | 23.5 | 5.9 | 10.0 | 36.8 | 5.7 |
| 1.3 | 1.7 | 1.1 | Sales/Net Fixed Assets | .5 | 2.4 | 2.0 | 2.0 | 7.1 | 3.1 |
| .5 | .5 | .4 | | .3 | .8 | 1.2 | .8 | 1.2 | 2.5 |
| 2.6 | 3.1 | 2.6 | | 1.3 | 3.6 | 3.5 | 4.2 | 3.5 | 3.8 |
| .8 | 1.0 | .7 | Sales/Total Assets | .4 | 1.2 | 1.7 | 1.7 | 1.2 | 2.2 |
| .4 | .4 | .4 | | .3 | .6 | .6 | .6 | .9 | 1.4 |
| 2.9 | 3.0 | 3.4 | | 6.8 | 3.0 | .8 | 2.3 | .4 | 1.6 |
| (298) 8.0 | (319) 7.8 | (324) 8.9 | % Depr., Dep., Amort./Sales | (183) 16.2 | (84) 5.8 | (13) 4.6 | (22) 3.9 | (10) 5.1 | (12) 2.3 |
| 22.3 | 18.9 | 19.7 | | 25.8 | 11.9 | 9.6 | 8.3 | 8.9 | 4.2 |
| 2.7 | 2.8 | 3.9 | | 6.3 | 3.8 | | | | |
| (124) 5.3 | (132) 4.9 | (125) 6.7 | % Officers', Directors' Owners' Comp/Sales | (55) 9.6 | (49) 5.6 | | | | |
| 9.2 | 9.3 | 10.5 | | 14.3 | 8.6 | | | | |
| 1001842M | 5365202M | 2070498M | Net Sales ($) | 98204M | 200582M | 52957M | 180804M | 157612M | 1380339M |
| 1032971M | 2221084M | 1480345M | Total Assets ($) | 232908M | 224217M | 45422M | 228300M | 112630M | 636868M |

M = $ thousand    MM = $ million
See Pages 9 through 22 for Explanation of Ratios and Data

## Current Data Sorted by Assets

## Comparative Historical Data

| | | | | | | Type of Statement | | |
|---|---|---|---|---|---|---|---|---|
| | | 2 | | 2 | | Unqualified | 5 | 3 |
| 1 | 2 | 6 | 4 | | | Reviewed | 6 | 9 |
| 4 | 9 | 6 | 2 | | | Compiled | 18 | 25 |
| 41 | 24 | 8 | | | | Tax Returns | 34 | 63 |
| 19 | 18 | 11 | | | 1 | Other | 34 | 47 |
| | 17 (4/1-9/30/11) | | 146 (10/1/11-3/31/12) | | | | 4/1/07-3/31/08 | 4/1/08-3/31/09 |
| 0-500M | 500M-2MM | 2-10MM | 10-50MM | 50-100MM | 100-250MM | | ALL | ALL |
| 65 | 53 | 33 | 9 | 2 | 1 | NUMBER OF STATEMENTS | 97 | 147 |
| % | % | % | % | % | % | ASSETS | % | % |
| 21.4 | 14.8 | 10.3 | | | | Cash & Equivalents | 13.9 | 12.0 |
| 13.3 | 16.7 | 17.2 | | | | Trade Receivables (net) | 16.2 | 11.0 |
| 21.8 | 16.8 | 18.5 | | | | Inventory | 18.6 | 15.8 |
| .9 | 5.5 | 2.9 | | | | All Other Current | 2.4 | 1.9 |
| 57.5 | 53.8 | 49.0 | | | | Total Current | 51.1 | 40.7 |
| 28.2 | 33.7 | 35.2 | | | | Fixed Assets (net) | 35.5 | 43.7 |
| 4.2 | 3.0 | 7.5 | | | | Intangibles (net) | 5.9 | 8.8 |
| 10.0 | 9.6 | 8.4 | | | | All Other Non-Current | 7.5 | 6.9 |
| 100.0 | 100.0 | 100.0 | | | | Total | 100.0 | 100.0 |
| | | | | | | LIABILITIES | | |
| 9.1 | 7.0 | 3.4 | | | | Notes Payable-Short Term | 8.0 | 9.5 |
| 1.6 | 2.7 | 2.5 | | | | Cur. Mat.-L.T.D. | 5.1 | 6.4 |
| 17.3 | 13.1 | 15.9 | | | | Trade Payables | 14.2 | 9.6 |
| .2 | .1 | .1 | | | | Income Taxes Payable | .7 | .2 |
| 20.2 | 11.0 | 9.4 | | | | All Other Current | 10.7 | 7.0 |
| 48.4 | 34.0 | 31.4 | | | | Total Current | 38.8 | 32.8 |
| 24.0 | 30.9 | 21.7 | | | | Long-Term Debt | 24.0 | 37.1 |
| .0 | .0 | .4 | | | | Deferred Taxes | .1 | .1 |
| 34.7 | 7.8 | 13.6 | | | | All Other Non-Current | 11.3 | 10.4 |
| -7.1 | 27.3 | 32.9 | | | | Net Worth | 25.7 | 19.5 |
| 100.0 | 100.0 | 100.0 | | | | Total Liabilities & Net Worth | 100.0 | 100.0 |
| | | | | | | INCOME DATA | | |
| 100.0 | 100.0 | 100.0 | | | | Net Sales | 100.0 | 100.0 |
| | | | | | | Gross Profit | | |
| 96.2 | 92.3 | 93.1 | | | | Operating Expenses | 95.5 | 91.1 |
| 3.8 | 7.7 | 6.9 | | | | Operating Profit | 4.5 | 8.9 |
| .3 | 2.8 | 2.5 | | | | All Other Expenses (net) | 1.1 | 4.2 |
| 3.5 | 4.9 | 4.5 | | | | Profit Before Taxes | 3.4 | 4.7 |
| | | | | | | RATIOS | | |
| 3.1 | 4.1 | 2.5 | | | | | 2.6 | 2.0 |
| 1.5 | 2.3 | 1.6 | | | | Current | 1.4 | 1.1 |
| .6 | .6 | .9 | | | | | .9 | .6 |
| 1.9 | 2.5 | 1.3 | | | | | 1.6 | 1.4 |
| .7 | 1.3 | .8 | | | | Quick | .7 | .6 |
| .2 | .3 | .3 | | | | | .4 | .2 |
| 0 UND | 1 673.4 | 2 159.4 | | | | | 2 147.2 | 0 UND |
| 2 156.3 | 10 38.3 | 18 20.1 | | | | Sales/Receivables | 14 26.5 | 6 57.8 |
| 14 27.0 | 32 11.4 | 37 9.9 | | | | | 23 15.6 | 22 16.5 |
| | | | | | | Cost of Sales/Inventory | | |
| | | | | | | Cost of Sales/Payables | | |
| 13.3 | 6.2 | 7.0 | | | | | 9.9 | 12.0 |
| 53.4 | 11.4 | 18.5 | | | | Sales/Working Capital | 31.5 | 88.6 |
| -35.3 | -10.7 | -162.8 | | | | | -116.0 | -18.6 |
| 35.1 | 14.2 | 19.5 | | | | | 10.5 | 6.4 |
| (30) 3.4 | (42) 3.5 | (29) 6.5 | | | | EBIT/Interest | (81) 3.6 | (118) 2.5 |
| .7 | 1.1 | 2.5 | | | | | .8 | .9 |
| | | | | | | Net Profit + Depr., Dep., | | 5.5 |
| | | | | | | Amort./Cur. Mat. L/T/D | (16) 1.8 | |
| | | | | | | | | 1.0 |
| .1 | .2 | .2 | | | | | .4 | .6 |
| .8 | 1.4 | 1.1 | | | | Fixed/Worth | 1.2 | 2.8 |
| -1.6 | -84.7 | 5.2 | | | | | 43.6 | -2.6 |
| .8 | .6 | 1.0 | | | | | .8 | 1.1 |
| 4.1 | 3.8 | 2.2 | | | | Debt/Worth | 2.2 | 4.1 |
| -3.6 | -111.3 | 10.3 | | | | | 74.2 | -5.0 |
| 121.0 | 56.9 | 41.9 | | | | | 74.6 | 93.3 |
| (42) 40.2 | (39) 30.1 | (27) 26.5 | | | | % Profit Before Taxes/Tangible Net Worth | (76) 32.1 | (99) 35.2 |
| 12.9 | 7.2 | 7.2 | | | | | 9.1 | 10.1 |
| 41.2 | 20.6 | 11.0 | | | | | 21.8 | 19.3 |
| 13.1 | 7.8 | 6.4 | | | | % Profit Before Taxes/Total Assets | 8.0 | 5.6 |
| -1.3 | .4 | 3.1 | | | | | 1.1 | -.1 |
| 127.9 | 34.4 | 33.3 | | | | | 43.6 | 29.1 |
| 32.3 | 17.8 | 8.5 | | | | Sales/Net Fixed Assets | 12.0 | 8.0 |
| 12.5 | 5.4 | 2.9 | | | | | 5.3 | 2.2 |
| 9.0 | 4.8 | 4.0 | | | | | 5.8 | 4.4 |
| 5.9 | 2.4 | 2.1 | | | | Sales/Total Assets | 3.2 | 2.5 |
| 3.5 | 1.5 | 1.6 | | | | | 2.0 | 1.3 |
| .4 | .6 | 1.1 | | | | | .8 | 1.0 |
| (39) 1.5 | (42) 1.4 | (27) 1.9 | | | | % Depr., Dep., Amort./Sales | (76) 2.0 | (116) 2.1 |
| 3.1 | 3.6 | 5.7 | | | | | 3.8 | 6.4 |
| 2.3 | 2.7 | .6 | | | | | 2.9 | 2.4 |
| (31) 5.0 | (30) 3.9 | (13) 1.8 | | | | % Officers', Directors' Owners' Comp/Sales | (46) 6.7 | (67) 4.5 |
| 7.8 | 7.1 | 4.8 | | | | | 13.8 | 10.8 |
| 79190M | 182257M | 411582M | 335621M | 135203M | 180539M | Net Sales ($) | 1433640M | 2918220M |
| 13054M | 56681M | 151000M | 187215M | 146973M | 240154M | Total Assets ($) | 630974M | 929883M |

© RMA 2012

M = $ thousand    MM = $ million
See Pages 9 through 22 for Explanation of Ratios and Data

## Comparative Historical Data

## Current Data Sorted by Sales

| | | | Type of Statement | | | | | | |
|---|---|---|---|---|---|---|---|---|---|
| 3 | 1 | 4 | Unqualified | | | 2 | 2 | 4 | 2 |
| 7 | 6 | 13 | Reviewed | 1 | 2 | 2 | 3 | 3 | 4 |
| 16 | 19 | 21 | Compiled | 3 | 3 | 6 | 3 | 3 | 3 |
| 68 | 57 | 73 | Tax Returns | 33 | 24 | 11 | 3 | 2 | 2 |
| 52 | 41 | 52 | Other | 10 | 16 | 8 | 7 | 9 | 2 |
| 4/1/09-3/31/10 ALL | 4/1/10-3/31/11 ALL | 4/1/11-3/31/12 ALL | | 17 (4/1-9/30/11) | | | 146 (10/1/11-3/31/12) | | |
| | | | | 0-1MM | 1-3MM | 3-5MM | 5-10MM | 10-25MM | 25MM & OVER |
| 146 | 124 | 163 | NUMBER OF STATEMENTS | 47 | 43 | 27 | 17 | 18 | 11 |
| % | % | % | ASSETS | % | % | % | % | % | % |
| 15.2 | 14.5 | 15.8 | Cash & Equivalents | 17.1 | 17.3 | 21.7 | 13.1 | 9.0 | 5.2 |
| 16.3 | 12.8 | 15.4 | Trade Receivables (net) | 9.9 | 12.8 | 22.5 | 14.3 | 23.7 | 19.2 |
| 16.3 | 18.5 | 18.9 | Inventory | 18.5 | 19.1 | 17.2 | 15.3 | 26.6 | 16.3 |
| 2.0 | 2.1 | 2.8 | All Other Current | .4 | 2.2 | 7.4 | 5.9 | 1.9 | .8 |
| 49.9 | 47.9 | 52.8 | Total Current | 45.9 | 51.4 | 68.8 | 48.7 | 61.2 | 41.5 |
| 33.8 | 35.2 | 31.8 | Fixed Assets (net) | 39.5 | 32.1 | 21.8 | 31.4 | 25.8 | 32.6 |
| 9.0 | 6.9 | 5.7 | Intangibles (net) | 4.4 | 4.8 | 1.4 | 12.2 | 1.2 | 23.1 |
| 7.4 | 10.1 | 9.6 | All Other Non-Current | 10.0 | 11.6 | 8.0 | 7.7 | 11.7 | 2.8 |
| 100.0 | 100.0 | 100.0 | Total | 100.0 | 100.0 | 100.0 | 100.0 | 100.0 | 100.0 |
| | | | LIABILITIES | | | | | | |
| 7.0 | 11.4 | 6.8 | Notes Payable-Short Term | 5.7 | 9.1 | 8.7 | 6.8 | 3.5 | 3.5 |
| 3.6 | 4.1 | 2.3 | Cur. Mat.-L.T.D. | 3.3 | 2.1 | .4 | 2.5 | 2.2 | 3.2 |
| 20.1 | 19.1 | 15.4 | Trade Payables | 13.0 | 13.6 | 23.8 | 12.5 | 14.6 | 18.3 |
| .0 | .1 | .1 | Income Taxes Payable | .1 | .1 | .3 | .1 | .1 | .1 |
| 22.3 | 11.6 | 14.2 | All Other Current | 22.1 | 6.2 | 12.9 | 21.0 | 14.1 | 5.5 |
| 53.1 | 46.2 | 38.9 | Total Current | 44.2 | 31.1 | 46.1 | 42.8 | 34.6 | 30.7 |
| 32.1 | 28.7 | 25.7 | Long-Term Debt | 33.4 | 30.5 | 18.6 | 16.1 | 17.0 | 20.0 |
| .0 | .0 | .2 | Deferred Taxes | .0 | .0 | .4 | .2 | .2 | 1.2 |
| 8.4 | 14.8 | 20.7 | All Other Non-Current | 42.5 | 6.3 | 10.3 | 22.5 | 13.0 | 19.2 |
| 6.5 | 10.3 | 14.5 | Net Worth | -20.1 | 32.1 | 24.6 | 18.4 | 35.2 | 28.9 |
| 100.0 | 100.0 | 100.0 | Total Liabilities & Net Worth | 100.0 | 100.0 | 100.0 | 100.0 | 100.0 | 100.0 |
| | | | INCOME DATA | | | | | | |
| 100.0 | 100.0 | 100.0 | Net Sales | 100.0 | 100.0 | 100.0 | 100.0 | 100.0 | 100.0 |
| | | | Gross Profit | | | | | | |
| 94.7 | 94.6 | 94.1 | Operating Expenses | 92.2 | 92.2 | 97.6 | 96.3 | 96.4 | 94.0 |
| 5.3 | 5.4 | 5.9 | Operating Profit | 7.8 | 7.8 | 2.4 | 3.7 | 3.6 | 6.0 |
| 2.0 | 1.3 | 1.7 | All Other Expenses (net) | 3.3 | 1.5 | .4 | .9 | .6 | 1.6 |
| 3.3 | 4.1 | 4.2 | Profit Before Taxes | 4.4 | 6.3 | 2.0 | 2.8 | 3.1 | 4.4 |
| | | | RATIOS | | | | | | |
| 2.3 | 2.3 | 3.2 | | 2.3 | 4.7 | 3.7 | 2.0 | 2.9 | 2.6 |
| 1.1 | 1.2 | 1.6 | Current | 1.4 | 2.3 | 2.0 | 1.2 | 1.8 | 1.1 |
| .6 | .6 | .7 | | .3 | .5 | 1.1 | .8 | 1.2 | .5 |
| 1.6 | 1.4 | 2.0 | | 1.5 | 2.7 | 2.2 | 1.3 | 1.6 | 1.5 |
| .6 | .6 | .8 | Quick | .4 | .8 | 1.2 | .4 | 1.0 | .6 |
| .2 | .2 | .3 | | .1 | .3 | .5 | .2 | .6 | .1 |
| 1 628.0 | 0 989.8 | 0 955.0 | | 0 UND | 0 999.8 | 2 158.0 | 1 283.1 | 16 23.2 | 2 197.0 |
| 7 52.2 | 7 52.4 | 7 54.5 | Sales/Receivables | 1 647.0 | 4 89.8 | 20 18.6 | 10 38.3 | 24 14.9 | 7 49.2 |
| 25 14.6 | 24 15.2 | 28 13.0 | | 14 26.6 | 20 18.5 | 29 12.7 | 36 10.0 | 36 10.0 | 51 7.1 |
| | | | Cost of Sales/Inventory | | | | | | |
| | | | Cost of Sales/Payables | | | | | | |
| 10.6 | 10.5 | 7.8 | | 13.5 | 6.5 | 7.8 | 8.6 | 7.3 | 5.6 |
| 64.5 | 52.0 | 23.8 | Sales/Working Capital | 96.3 | 12.2 | 21.6 | 39.4 | 12.5 | 31.2 |
| -15.3 | -21.2 | -32.3 | | -8.0 | -18.0 | 193.1 | -35.9 | 57.3 | -19.2 |
| 10.5 | 12.0 | 17.1 | | 37.3 | 16.1 | 47.0 | 8.2 | 16.0 | |
| (107) 2.8 | (86) 4.6 | (112) 3.7 | EBIT/Interest | (20) 4.3 | (32) 4.0 | (19) 3.4 | (16) 3.3 | (16) 6.6 | |
| .9 | 2.1 | 1.6 | | 1.0 | 1.7 | 1.0 | .9 | 2.7 | |
| | | | Net Profit + Depr., Dep., Amort./Cur. Mat. L/T/D | | | | | | |
| .3 | .4 | .2 | | .5 | .1 | .2 | .4 | .2 | .3 |
| 2.1 | 1.7 | 1.2 | Fixed/Worth | 2.9 | 1.2 | .7 | 2.5 | .6 | 3.7 |
| -1.3 | -2.5 | -8.9 | | -1.5 | 13.5 | 238.0 | -.9 | 1.9 | -1.8 |
| .9 | .9 | .8 | | 1.0 | .4 | .5 | 1.6 | 1.0 | 2.0 |
| 4.5 | 4.2 | 3.8 | Debt/Worth | 47.3 | 2.3 | 1.2 | 7.2 | 2.1 | 8.2 |
| -4.9 | -6.7 | -10.6 | | -2.4 | 13.4 | 626.0 | -4.8 | 3.9 | -4.4 |
| 85.5 | 71.9 | 63.6 | | 128.1 | 71.8 | 43.6 | 35.7 | 44.2 | |
| (91) 23.7 | (81) 29.0 | (115) 30.1 | % Profit Before Taxes/Tangible Net Worth | (26) 40.2 | (33) 23.3 | (21) 30.1 | (11) 32.3 | (17) 27.1 | |
| 8.1 | 13.5 | 7.2 | | .8 | 15.6 | 1.0 | -16.4 | 7.2 | |
| 19.6 | 17.4 | 19.8 | | 27.7 | 22.9 | 21.8 | 13.5 | 15.0 | 9.1 |
| 5.3 | 9.3 | 7.1 | % Profit Before Taxes/Total Assets | 4.9 | 14.0 | 9.3 | 5.6 | 8.2 | 5.9 |
| -.5 | 1.5 | .7 | | -1.7 | 3.6 | .3 | -4.3 | 3.6 | 3.4 |
| 91.6 | 38.5 | 58.2 | | 43.1 | 78.2 | 62.9 | 33.3 | 116.6 | 47.1 |
| 21.0 | 16.0 | 21.7 | Sales/Net Fixed Assets | 15.4 | 17.5 | 34.2 | 10.9 | 25.8 | 31.0 |
| 4.8 | 4.8 | 5.7 | | 5.7 | 2.9 | 15.3 | 6.5 | 4.6 | 4.2 |
| 5.5 | 5.8 | 5.9 | | 7.2 | 4.9 | 7.6 | 4.3 | 4.8 | 3.7 |
| 3.1 | 2.5 | 3.2 | Sales/Total Assets | 4.1 | 2.3 | 5.3 | 2.4 | 2.8 | 2.0 |
| 1.3 | 1.8 | 1.8 | | 1.9 | 1.5 | 3.2 | 1.8 | 1.8 | 1.0 |
| .6 | 1.0 | .7 | | 1.1 | .9 | .4 | .4 | .7 | |
| (105) 1.9 | (94) 1.7 | (117) 1.5 | % Depr., Dep., Amort./Sales | (34) 2.4 | (29) 2.3 | (19) .8 | (12) 1.3 | (16) 1.2 | |
| 3.9 | 3.4 | 3.6 | | 4.4 | 3.8 | 2.1 | 2.3 | 1.8 | |
| 2.2 | 2.8 | 1.9 | | 7.0 | 2.0 | 2.4 | | | |
| (67) 4.5 | (57) 5.5 | (76) 3.7 | % Officers', Directors' Owners' Comp/Sales | (15) 7.8 | (24) 3.7 | (20) 3.9 | | | |
| 8.8 | 8.6 | 7.2 | | 10.5 | 5.5 | 6.9 | | | |
| 1020588M | 1344374M | 1324392M | Net Sales ($) | 24926M | 71605M | 102639M | 126135M | 274003M | 725084M |
| 524975M | 435874M | 795077M | Total Assets ($) | 14611M | 45825M | 24964M | 54843M | 115663M | 539171M |

M = $ thousand    MM = $ million
See Pages 9 through 22 for Explanation of Ratios and Data

## Current Data Sorted by Assets  |  Comparative Historical Data

| Type of Statement | 0-500M | 500M-2MM | 2-10MM | 10-50MM | 50-100MM | 100-250MM | | 4/1/07-3/31/08 ALL | 4/1/08-3/31/09 ALL |
|---|---|---|---|---|---|---|---|---|---|
| Unqualified | | | 1 | 2 | | 1 | | 5 | 3 |
| Reviewed | | 1 | 1 | 2 | | | | 8 | 5 |
| Compiled | 2 | 2 | 6 | | | | | 7 | 8 |
| Tax Returns | 6 | 2 | 3 | | | | | 11 | 9 |
| Other | 1 | 7 | 15 | | | | | 12 | 19 |
| | 6 (4/1-9/30/11) | | | 52 (10/1/11-3/31/12) | | | | | |
| **NUMBER OF STATEMENTS** | 9 | 12 | 26 | 9 | 1 | 1 | | 43 | 44 |
| **ASSETS** | % | % | % | % | % | % | | % | % |
| Cash & Equivalents | | 13.5 | 9.7 | | | | | 12.3 | 11.7 |
| Trade Receivables (net) | | 42.1 | 42.2 | | | | | 39.2 | 33.8 |
| Inventory | | 24.6 | 16.3 | | | | | 13.2 | 22.1 |
| All Other Current | | .6 | 5.0 | | | | | 4.9 | 3.2 |
| Total Current | | 80.8 | 73.2 | | | | | 69.6 | 70.7 |
| Fixed Assets (net) | | 11.1 | 14.0 | | | | | 22.8 | 21.3 |
| Intangibles (net) | | 1.5 | 7.5 | | | | | 2.8 | 3.8 |
| All Other Non-Current | | 6.6 | 5.4 | | | | | 4.8 | 4.1 |
| Total | | 100.0 | 100.0 | | | | | 100.0 | 100.0 |
| **LIABILITIES** | | | | | | | | | |
| Notes Payable-Short Term | | 14.7 | 14.6 | | | | | 17.9 | 16.0 |
| Cur. Mat.-L.T.D. | | 6.4 | 2.2 | | | | | 6.8 | 4.0 |
| Trade Payables | | 22.3 | 19.8 | | | | | 16.8 | 18.7 |
| Income Taxes Payable | | .0 | .0 | | | | | .3 | .3 |
| All Other Current | | 7.0 | 15.6 | | | | | 15.8 | 17.4 |
| Total Current | | 50.4 | 52.2 | | | | | 57.6 | 56.4 |
| Long-Term Debt | | 13.7 | 9.7 | | | | | 24.4 | 21.5 |
| Deferred Taxes | | .0 | .0 | | | | | .0 | .1 |
| All Other Non-Current | | 16.4 | 9.2 | | | | | 9.2 | 9.4 |
| Net Worth | | 19.4 | 28.9 | | | | | 8.8 | 12.6 |
| Total Liabilties & Net Worth | | 100.0 | 100.0 | | | | | 100.0 | 100.0 |
| **INCOME DATA** | | | | | | | | | |
| Net Sales | | 100.0 | 100.0 | | | | | 100.0 | 100.0 |
| Gross Profit | | | | | | | | | |
| Operating Expenses | | 99.9 | 94.1 | | | | | 95.5 | 95.8 |
| Operating Profit | | .1 | 5.9 | | | | | 4.5 | 4.2 |
| All Other Expenses (net) | | .8 | .7 | | | | | 1.0 | 1.2 |
| Profit Before Taxes | | -.7 | 5.3 | | | | | 3.6 | 3.0 |
| **RATIOS** | | | | | | | | | |
| Current | | 3.3 | 2.2 | | | | | 2.0 | 3.1 |
| | | 1.8 | 1.4 | | | | | 1.3 | 1.3 |
| | | 1.3 | 1.1 | | | | | 1.0 | .9 |
| Quick | | 2.5 | 1.8 | | | | | 1.8 | 1.7 |
| | | 1.3 | .9 | | | | | 1.0 | .9 |
| | | .6 | .6 | | | | | .6 | .5 |
| Sales/Receivables | 31 | 11.6 | 32 11.4 | | | | | 24 15.0 | 24 15.0 |
| | 40 | 9.1 | 41 8.8 | | | | | 43 8.5 | 36 10.2 |
| | 50 | 7.3 | 54 6.7 | | | | | 60 6.1 | 56 6.6 |
| Cost of Sales/Inventory | | | | | | | | | |
| Cost of Sales/Payables | | | | | | | | | |
| Sales/Working Capital | | 6.4 | 6.9 | | | | | 9.7 | 8.0 |
| | | 11.7 | 16.2 | | | | | 17.7 | 23.3 |
| | | 37.0 | 270.1 | | | | | UND | -55.9 |
| EBIT/Interest | | 20.2 | 55.5 | | | | | 9.2 | 13.2 |
| | (10) | 4.4 | (23) 9.3 | | | | | (35) 2.3 | (35) 2.1 |
| | | -4.0 | 2.9 | | | | | .0 | -.7 |
| Net Profit + Depr., Dep., Amort./Cur. Mat. L/T/D | | | | | | | | 12.3 | |
| | | | | | | | | (10) 4.7 | |
| | | | | | | | | 1.1 | |
| Fixed/Worth | | .1 | .2 | | | | | .2 | .3 |
| | | .4 | .7 | | | | | .8 | 1.1 |
| | | 7.8 | 1.1 | | | | | UND | -15.3 |
| Debt/Worth | | .8 | 1.1 | | | | | 1.0 | 1.4 |
| | | 2.0 | 2.4 | | | | | 3.1 | 3.5 |
| | | 141.4 | 33.6 | | | | | -15.2 | -91.2 |
| % Profit Before Taxes/Tangible Net Worth | | 68.4 | 98.6 | | | | | 62.8 | 91.3 |
| | (10) | 25.8 | (21) 46.0 | | | | | (32) 33.8 | (32) 19.9 |
| | | 12.9 | 24.9 | | | | | 12.7 | .6 |
| % Profit Before Taxes/Total Assets | | 18.6 | 25.7 | | | | | 22.5 | 17.9 |
| | | 7.6 | 16.0 | | | | | 6.9 | 4.2 |
| | | -14.0 | 3.1 | | | | | -2.2 | -1.8 |
| Sales/Net Fixed Assets | | 343.0 | 54.3 | | | | | 69.5 | 45.9 |
| | | 43.5 | 32.3 | | | | | 32.3 | 25.9 |
| | | 15.7 | 16.4 | | | | | 9.8 | 10.9 |
| Sales/Total Assets | | 5.7 | 4.1 | | | | | 5.3 | 4.2 |
| | | 3.8 | 3.4 | | | | | 3.5 | 3.1 |
| | | 2.7 | 2.5 | | | | | 2.6 | 2.4 |
| % Depr., Dep., Amort./Sales | | | .6 | | | | | .4 | .4 |
| | | (18) | 1.2 | | | | | (36) .7 | (31) .8 |
| | | | 1.9 | | | | | 1.7 | 2.2 |
| % Officers', Directors' Owners' Comp/Sales | | | | | | | | 3.0 | 3.0 |
| | | | | | | | | (17) 7.0 | (17) 4.9 |
| | | | | | | | | 10.4 | 9.6 |
| Net Sales ($) | 13349M | 61369M | 440916M | 528840M | 72795M | 253274M | | 751406M | 790059M |
| Total Assets ($) | 2663M | 12823M | 135742M | 216536M | 77505M | 168528M | | 219863M | 266755M |

M = $ thousand    MM = $ million
See Pages 9 through 22 for Explanation of Ratios and Data

## Comparative Historical Data / Current Data Sorted by Sales

**Type of Statement**

| 4/1/09-3/31/10 ALL | 4/1/10-3/31/11 ALL | 4/1/11-3/31/12 ALL | | 0-1MM | 1-3MM | 3-5MM | 5-10MM | 10-25MM | 25MM & OVER |
|---|---|---|---|---|---|---|---|---|---|
| 7 | 4 | 4 | Unqualified | | | | | 1 | 3 |
| 4 | 4 | 4 | Reviewed | | | | 1 | 2 | 1 |
| 5 | 5 | 10 | Compiled | | 2 | | 4 | 3 | |
| 15 | 14 | 11 | Tax Returns | | 4 | 1 | 1 | 3 | |
| 20 | 17 | 29 | Other | 3 | 4 | 3 | 2 | 11 | 9 |
| | | | | | 6 (4/1-9/30/11) | | | 52 (10/1/11-3/31/12) | |
| 51 | 44 | 58 | **NUMBER OF STATEMENTS** | 3 | 10 | 4 | 8 | 20 | 13 |

| % | % | % | | % | % | % | % | % | % |
|---|---|---|---|---|---|---|---|---|---|
| | | | **ASSETS** | | | | | | |
| 10.7 | 12.4 | 11.3 | Cash & Equivalents | | 20.0 | | | 12.8 | 6.4 |
| 32.1 | 32.4 | 39.6 | Trade Receivables (net) | | 29.1 | | | 42.6 | 39.9 |
| 16.8 | 17.6 | 19.6 | Inventory | | 33.8 | | | 12.0 | 14.5 |
| 4.2 | 3.0 | 4.1 | All Other Current | | 3.9 | | | 2.9 | 10.3 |
| 63.8 | 65.4 | 74.5 | Total Current | | 86.8 | | | 70.3 | 71.1 |
| 21.2 | 19.4 | 12.9 | Fixed Assets (net) | | 8.5 | | | 13.4 | 13.6 |
| 10.8 | 6.4 | 7.2 | Intangibles (net) | | .4 | | | 9.0 | 11.9 |
| 4.2 | 8.7 | 5.4 | All Other Non-Current | | 4.2 | | | 7.3 | 3.4 |
| 100.0 | 100.0 | 100.0 | Total | | 100.0 | | | 100.0 | 100.0 |
| | | | **LIABILITIES** | | | | | | |
| 13.6 | 13.8 | 15.1 | Notes Payable-Short Term | | 8.3 | | | 13.5 | 17.7 |
| 6.2 | 3.0 | 3.2 | Cur. Mat.-L.T.D. | | 2.1 | | | 2.1 | 3.4 |
| 19.9 | 13.7 | 20.6 | Trade Payables | | 15.7 | | | 21.5 | 26.6 |
| .4 | .2 | .1 | Income Taxes Payable | | .0 | | | .0 | .4 |
| 18.4 | 12.3 | 19.7 | All Other Current | | 44.2 | | | 15.6 | 12.3 |
| 58.4 | 43.0 | 58.7 | Total Current | | 70.3 | | | 52.8 | 60.4 |
| 31.5 | 15.9 | 12.3 | Long-Term Debt | | 5.8 | | | 8.6 | 15.6 |
| .5 | .4 | .3 | Deferred Taxes | | .0 | | | .1 | 1.3 |
| 7.8 | 6.3 | 11.8 | All Other Non-Current | | 29.2 | | | 8.9 | 11.1 |
| 1.8 | 34.4 | 16.9 | Net Worth | | -5.3 | | | 29.6 | 11.5 |
| 100.0 | 100.0 | 100.0 | Total Liabilities & Net Worth | | 100.0 | | | 100.0 | 100.0 |
| | | | **INCOME DATA** | | | | | | |
| 100.0 | 100.0 | 100.0 | Net Sales | | 100.0 | | | 100.0 | 100.0 |
| | | | Gross Profit | | | | | | |
| 95.5 | 93.5 | 94.9 | Operating Expenses | | 97.9 | | | 94.4 | 95.6 |
| 4.5 | 6.5 | 5.1 | Operating Profit | | 2.1 | | | 5.6 | 4.4 |
| .8 | 1.2 | 1.0 | All Other Expenses (net) | | 1.5 | | | .7 | .9 |
| 3.6 | 5.3 | 4.1 | Profit Before Taxes | | .5 | | | 4.9 | 3.5 |
| | | | **RATIOS** | | | | | | |
| 1.6 | 2.6 | 2.5 | Current | | 4.4 | | | 2.3 | 1.7 |
| 1.2 | 1.7 | 1.5 | | | 2.7 | | | 1.3 | 1.2 |
| .9 | 1.1 | 1.0 | | | 1.0 | | | .9 | 1.0 |
| 1.4 | 2.2 | 1.7 | Quick | | 3.1 | | | 2.1 | 1.2 |
| .8 | 1.1 | .9 | | | 1.3 | | | .9 | .8 |
| .5 | .8 | .6 | | | .4 | | | .4 | .5 |
| 23  15.6 | 27  13.4 | 31  11.6 | Sales/Receivables | | 19  18.9 | | | 34  10.8 | 43  8.5 |
| 37  10.0 | 41  9.0 | 41  8.8 | | | 24  15.2 | | | 41  8.8 | 54  6.7 |
| 58  6.3 | 58  6.3 | 55  6.6 | | | 43  8.5 | | | 66  5.5 | 72  5.1 |
| | | | Cost of Sales/Inventory | | | | | | |
| | | | Cost of Sales/Payables | | | | | | |
| 10.9 | 7.6 | 7.2 | Sales/Working Capital | | 4.9 | | | 7.1 | 13.5 |
| 38.3 | 12.0 | 17.1 | | | 8.0 | | | 26.5 | 22.6 |
| -53.4 | 36.1 | -107.3 | | | NM | | | NM | -87.1 |
| 12.7 | 14.1 | 16.6 | EBIT/Interest | | | | | 117.8 | 15.1 |
| (46) 3.2 | (37) 5.9 | (52) 6.8 | | | | | | (17) 6.8 | (12) 6.6 |
| .9 | 2.4 | 1.4 | | | | | | 2.1 | 2.5 |
| 3.2 | | 4.7 | Net Profit + Depr., Dep., | | | | | | |
| (10) 1.3 | | (12) 2.0 | Amort./Cur. Mat. L/T/D | | | | | | |
| .3 | | .1 | | | | | | | |
| .4 | .2 | .2 | Fixed/Worth | | .1 | | | .1 | .4 |
| 1.7 | .7 | .6 | | | .4 | | | .9 | 1.0 |
| -.6 | 2.4 | NM | | | -.3 | | | NM | NM |
| 1.4 | .8 | 1.0 | Debt/Worth | | .5 | | | 1.0 | 2.2 |
| 4.5 | 1.7 | 2.7 | | | 94.0 | | | 2.5 | 7.4 |
| -2.9 | 10.3 | -12.5 | | | -4.6 | | | NM | -8.8 |
| 79.3 | 75.8 | 87.3 | % Profit Before Taxes/Tangible | | | | | 95.8 | |
| (30) 38.6 | (36) 34.7 | (42) 40.1 | Net Worth | | | | | (15) 44.1 | |
| 7.5 | 14.8 | 19.2 | | | | | | 18.0 | |
| 18.3 | 18.3 | 20.7 | % Profit Before Taxes/Total | | 11.9 | | | 22.4 | 22.0 |
| 5.6 | 11.9 | 9.1 | Assets | | 1.1 | | | 14.2 | 7.0 |
| -.5 | 2.5 | .9 | | | -19.0 | | | 3.2 | 3.8 |
| 60.8 | 59.4 | 70.9 | Sales/Net Fixed Assets | | 127.5 | | | 68.7 | 56.6 |
| 25.6 | 24.1 | 28.9 | | | 45.5 | | | 33.6 | 21.0 |
| 13.1 | 12.5 | 15.5 | | | 18.7 | | | 17.7 | 15.5 |
| 4.5 | 4.1 | 4.1 | Sales/Total Assets | | 5.7 | | | 4.7 | 4.1 |
| 3.2 | 3.1 | 3.3 | | | 3.4 | | | 3.4 | 3.0 |
| 2.1 | 2.2 | 2.4 | | | 2.5 | | | 2.5 | 1.8 |
| .9 | .6 | .6 | % Depr., Dep., Amort./Sales | | | | | .6 | .2 |
| (39) 1.5 | (32) 1.0 | (43) 1.1 | | | | | | (14) 1.3 | (11) 1.4 |
| 2.5 | 1.8 | 1.7 | | | | | | 1.9 | 1.8 |
| 2.3 | 2.9 | 2.2 | % Officers', Directors' | | | | | | |
| (20) 4.9 | (15) 4.3 | (20) 4.6 | Owners' Comp/Sales | | | | | | |
| 9.3 | 11.0 | 7.0 | | | | | | | |
| 1132518M | 862245M | 1370543M | Net Sales ($) | 1972M | 18279M | 17834M | 55568M | 332775M | 944115M |
| 432341M | 556497M | 613797M | Total Assets ($) | 505M | 5277M | 4184M | 23971M | 112941M | 466919M |

M = $ thousand    MM = $ million
See Pages 9 through 22 for Explanation of Ratios and Data

## Current Data Sorted by Assets        Comparative Historical Data

| | | | | | | Type of Statement | | |
|---|---|---|---|---|---|---|---|---|
| | 1 | 2<br>16 | 5<br>5 | | | Unqualified<br>Reviewed | 13<br>24 | 9<br>18 |
| 2<br>19<br>10 | 10<br>13<br>12 | 5<br>1<br>18 | 1<br>1<br>8 | 1 | 1 | Compiled<br>Tax Returns<br>Other | 20<br>26<br>47 | 10<br>20<br>27 |
| | 23 (4/1-9/30/11) | | 109 (10/1/11-3/31/12) | | | | 4/1/07-<br>3/31/08 | 4/1/08-<br>3/31/09 |
| 0-500M | 500M-2MM | 2-10MM | 10-50MM | 50-100MM | 100-250MM | | ALL | ALL |
| 31 | 36 | 42 | 20 | 1 | 2 | **NUMBER OF STATEMENTS** | 130 | 84 |
| % | % | % | % | % | % | **ASSETS** | % | % |
| 23.5 | 14.9 | 11.1 | 7.9 | | | Cash & Equivalents | 12.8 | 11.0 |
| 23.8 | 27.9 | 41.7 | 32.3 | | | Trade Receivables (net) | 32.5 | 39.4 |
| 11.7 | 18.1 | 15.2 | 14.6 | | | Inventory | 19.6 | 17.1 |
| 2.4 | 2.1 | 3.1 | 3.8 | | | All Other Current | 3.2 | 2.7 |
| 61.4 | 62.9 | 71.1 | 58.7 | | | Total Current | 68.1 | 70.2 |
| 23.1 | 21.3 | 18.3 | 20.4 | | | Fixed Assets (net) | 21.0 | 21.1 |
| 4.9 | 8.2 | 2.6 | 17.6 | | | Intangibles (net) | 5.3 | 3.4 |
| 10.6 | 7.5 | 8.1 | 3.3 | | | All Other Non-Current | 5.6 | 5.4 |
| 100.0 | 100.0 | 100.0 | 100.0 | | | Total | 100.0 | 100.0 |
| | | | | | | **LIABILITIES** | | |
| 28.2 | 8.9 | 6.0 | 8.6 | | | Notes Payable-Short Term | 11.3 | 10.7 |
| 2.1 | 2.7 | 3.9 | 3.6 | | | Cur. Mat.-L.T.D. | 5.3 | 4.9 |
| 8.1 | 15.8 | 14.4 | 12.1 | | | Trade Payables | 14.5 | 15.2 |
| .0 | .2 | .2 | .8 | | | Income Taxes Payable | .3 | .2 |
| 17.4 | 9.8 | 13.2 | 11.1 | | | All Other Current | 11.0 | 11.7 |
| 55.7 | 37.4 | 37.8 | 36.2 | | | Total Current | 42.4 | 42.7 |
| 12.4 | 24.8 | 9.2 | 13.4 | | | Long-Term Debt | 16.6 | 16.1 |
| 1.1 | .0 | 1.4 | .9 | | | Deferred Taxes | .2 | .2 |
| 13.6 | 6.1 | 5.1 | 6.3 | | | All Other Non-Current | 3.8 | 3.0 |
| 17.2 | 31.6 | 46.5 | 43.2 | | | Net Worth | 37.0 | 38.0 |
| 100.0 | 100.0 | 100.0 | 100.0 | | | Total Liabilties & Net Worth | 100.0 | 100.0 |
| | | | | | | **INCOME DATA** | | |
| 100.0 | 100.0 | 100.0 | 100.0 | | | Net Sales | 100.0 | 100.0 |
| | | | | | | Gross Profit | | |
| 95.1 | 91.0 | 94.0 | 93.0 | | | Operating Expenses | 91.5 | 91.0 |
| 4.9 | 9.0 | 6.0 | 7.0 | | | Operating Profit | 8.5 | 9.0 |
| .6 | 1.9 | .2 | 2.1 | | | All Other Expenses (net) | 1.3 | 1.2 |
| 4.4 | 7.1 | 5.8 | 4.9 | | | Profit Before Taxes | 7.2 | 7.8 |
| | | | | | | **RATIOS** | | |
| 3.8 | 3.1 | 2.7 | 2.1 | | | | 3.0 | 2.9 |
| 1.3 | 1.7 | 2.2 | 1.5 | | | Current | 1.8 | 1.7 |
| .8 | .9 | 1.3 | 1.3 | | | | 1.1 | 1.1 |
| 2.8 | 2.4 | 2.0 | 1.4 | | | | 2.1 | 2.2 |
| .9 | 1.3 | 1.4 | 1.0 | | | Quick | (129) 1.1 | 1.2 |
| .6 | .4 | 1.0 | .7 | | | | .7 | .8 |
| 0 UND | 6 61.0 | 41 9.0 | 46 8.0 | | | | 27 13.3 | 33 11.0 |
| 13 27.6 | 36 10.0 | 50 7.3 | 56 6.5 | | | Sales/Receivables | 43 8.5 | 46 8.0 |
| 50 7.3 | 57 6.4 | 64 5.7 | 73 5.0 | | | | 58 6.3 | 59 6.2 |
| | | | | | | Cost of Sales/Inventory | | |
| | | | | | | Cost of Sales/Payables | | |
| 8.3 | 5.1 | 5.0 | 6.3 | | | | 5.1 | 6.7 |
| 33.5 | 12.2 | 8.4 | 9.0 | | | Sales/Working Capital | 10.5 | 10.0 |
| -37.6 | NM | 19.0 | 14.6 | | | | 86.1 | 34.8 |
| 15.9 | 10.9 | 33.4 | 13.5 | | | | 14.5 | 25.0 |
| (22) 4.8 | (30) 3.6 | (37) 6.2 | (19) 5.9 | | | EBIT/Interest | (110) 5.6 | (75) 6.9 |
| -1.0 | .9 | 2.3 | 2.0 | | | | 1.6 | 3.0 |
| | | | | | | Net Profit + Depr., Dep., | 4.9 | 13.1 |
| | | | | | | Amort./Cur. Mat. L/T/D | (24) 2.8 | (15) 4.1 |
| | | | | | | | 1.0 | 1.6 |
| .0 | .2 | .1 | .3 | | | | .2 | .2 |
| .5 | .6 | .4 | .7 | | | Fixed/Worth | .5 | .5 |
| -1.0 | -32.9 | .7 | 1.3 | | | | 1.7 | 1.3 |
| .5 | .7 | .6 | .9 | | | | .7 | .6 |
| 2.0 | 4.3 | 1.0 | 2.2 | | | Debt/Worth | 1.7 | 1.3 |
| -5.2 | -32.4 | 2.4 | 3.8 | | | | 8.6 | 3.4 |
| 75.4 | 58.0 | 58.5 | 55.7 | | | | 75.5 | 67.5 |
| (19) 44.9 | (23) 32.3 | (39) 20.0 | (17) 30.4 | | | % Profit Before Taxes/Tangible<br>Net Worth | (112) 41.0 | (76) 34.9 |
| 7.4 | 16.5 | 6.3 | 12.6 | | | | 7.4 | 14.3 |
| 32.0 | 22.3 | 22.5 | 13.6 | | | | 27.4 | 25.8 |
| 22.0 | 9.3 | 10.3 | 8.2 | | | % Profit Before Taxes/Total<br>Assets | 13.1 | 11.6 |
| 1.8 | 1.0 | 3.0 | 5.3 | | | | 1.6 | 5.4 |
| 392.1 | 87.7 | 43.2 | 27.5 | | | | 48.2 | 48.3 |
| 38.0 | 18.1 | 23.4 | 16.0 | | | Sales/Net Fixed Assets | 16.0 | 18.6 |
| 14.8 | 11.2 | 10.8 | 8.2 | | | | 8.7 | 8.5 |
| 9.9 | 4.3 | 3.6 | 2.6 | | | | 3.7 | 4.0 |
| 4.5 | 3.2 | 2.8 | 1.9 | | | Sales/Total Assets | 2.5 | 2.8 |
| 2.9 | 1.6 | 2.1 | 1.2 | | | | 1.8 | 2.0 |
| .4 | .9 | 1.0 | .8 | | | | .8 | .8 |
| (14) .9 | (22) 1.1 | (33) 1.5 | (18) 1.2 | | | % Depr., Dep., Amort./Sales | (100) 1.6 | (61) 1.6 |
| 1.6 | 2.5 | 2.6 | 4.0 | | | | 2.9 | 3.3 |
| 4.4 | .9 | 1.7 | 3.2 | | | | 3.5 | 2.7 |
| (22) 9.3 | (19) 5.1 | (11) 4.6 | | | | % Officers', Directors'<br>Owners' Comp/Sales | (57) 5.5 | (33) 6.3 |
| 14.9 | 12.1 | 11.3 | | | | | 9.0 | 10.3 |
| 44641M | 114429M | 491256M | 775363M | 193322M | 562676M | Net Sales ($) | 1952568M | 1349720M |
| 7554M | 37502M | 178596M | 402242M | 87597M | 266710M | Total Assets ($) | 997001M | 722090M |

M = $ thousand     MM = $ million
See Pages 9 through 22 for Explanation of Ratios and Data

## Comparative Historical Data | Current Data Sorted by Sales

| Hist 4/1/09-3/31/10 ALL | Hist 4/1/10-3/31/11 ALL | Hist 4/1/11-3/31/12 ALL | Type of Statement | 0-1MM | 1-3MM | 3-5MM | 5-10MM | 10-25MM | 25MM & OVER |
|---|---|---|---|---|---|---|---|---|---|
| 12 | 12 | 7 | Unqualified | | | | 1 | 3 | 3 |
| 24 | 20 | 22 | Reviewed | | | | 7 | 11 | 4 |
| 26 | 14 | 18 | Compiled | 3 | 6 | 4 | 3 | 1 | 1 |
| 22 | 20 | 35 | Tax Returns | 9 | 13 | 9 | 1 | 1 | 2 |
| 45 | 50 | 50 | Other | 6 | 9 | 6 | 9 | 13 | 7 |
| | | | | | | 23 (4/1-9/30/11) | | 109 (10/1/11-3/31/12) | |
| 129 | 116 | 132 | NUMBER OF STATEMENTS | 18 | 28 | 19 | 21 | 29 | 17 |
| % | % | % | ASSETS | % | % | % | % | % | % |
| 13.0 | 12.0 | 14.4 | Cash & Equivalents | 25.9 | 15.6 | 15.2 | 17.4 | 7.5 | 7.5 |
| 31.2 | 33.3 | 32.0 | Trade Receivables (net) | 22.7 | 25.9 | 27.5 | 38.2 | 38.6 | 38.3 |
| 17.4 | 17.1 | 15.0 | Inventory | 11.2 | 17.5 | 13.3 | 8.7 | 20.3 | 15.7 |
| 4.7 | 4.2 | 2.7 | All Other Current | 2.4 | 1.8 | 4.5 | 2.0 | 2.4 | 4.1 |
| 66.2 | 66.6 | 64.2 | Total Current | 62.2 | 60.7 | 60.5 | 66.4 | 68.8 | 65.5 |
| 23.7 | 20.4 | 20.4 | Fixed Assets (net) | 19.5 | 22.5 | 26.1 | 23.0 | 16.5 | 15.3 |
| 4.0 | 6.7 | 7.7 | Intangibles (net) | 10.1 | 7.1 | 3.6 | 3.9 | 7.5 | 15.6 |
| 6.1 | 6.3 | 7.7 | All Other Non-Current | 8.3 | 9.7 | 9.8 | 6.7 | 7.3 | 3.6 |
| 100.0 | 100.0 | 100.0 | Total | 100.0 | 100.0 | 100.0 | 100.0 | 100.0 | 100.0 |
| | | | LIABILITIES | | | | | | |
| 12.3 | 8.8 | 12.9 | Notes Payable-Short Term | 17.3 | 18.3 | 15.1 | 6.8 | 7.7 | 13.7 |
| 3.7 | 3.7 | 3.0 | Cur. Mat.-L.T.D. | 2.4 | 2.5 | 2.1 | 4.5 | 4.1 | 2.1 |
| 11.9 | 12.0 | 12.9 | Trade Payables | 3.1 | 11.0 | 16.8 | 12.3 | 17.6 | 15.3 |
| .5 | .1 | .3 | Income Taxes Payable | .1 | .1 | .3 | .8 | .2 | .1 |
| 13.9 | 12.2 | 12.8 | All Other Current | 9.4 | 17.3 | 12.4 | 5.2 | 16.3 | 12.7 |
| 42.3 | 36.7 | 42.0 | Total Current | 32.3 | 49.2 | 46.7 | 29.5 | 45.8 | 43.8 |
| 17.3 | 14.7 | 14.9 | Long-Term Debt | 11.7 | 19.7 | 25.4 | 12.3 | 9.8 | 10.8 |
| .5 | .7 | .8 | Deferred Taxes | 1.9 | .0 | .4 | .9 | 1.1 | 1.0 |
| 3.4 | 9.3 | 7.6 | All Other Non-Current | 15.4 | 7.3 | 3.9 | 6.2 | 6.9 | 6.8 |
| 36.5 | 38.6 | 34.7 | Net Worth | 38.7 | 23.7 | 23.6 | 51.1 | 36.4 | 37.6 |
| 100.0 | 100.0 | 100.0 | Total Liabilities & Net Worth | 100.0 | 100.0 | 100.0 | 100.0 | 100.0 | 100.0 |
| | | | INCOME DATA | | | | | | |
| 100.0 | 100.0 | 100.0 | Net Sales | 100.0 | 100.0 | 100.0 | 100.0 | 100.0 | 100.0 |
| | | | Gross Profit | | | | | | |
| 94.0 | 91.7 | 93.2 | Operating Expenses | 86.3 | 95.0 | 94.4 | 93.4 | 94.2 | 94.8 |
| 6.0 | 8.3 | 6.8 | Operating Profit | 13.7 | 5.0 | 5.6 | 6.6 | 5.8 | 5.2 |
| 1.5 | 1.0 | 1.1 | All Other Expenses (net) | 2.9 | .5 | 1.0 | 1.2 | .5 | 1.2 |
| 4.5 | 7.3 | 5.7 | Profit Before Taxes | 10.9 | 4.6 | 4.6 | 5.4 | 5.3 | 4.0 |
| | | | RATIOS | | | | | | |
| 3.1 | 3.5 | 2.7 | Current | 11.6 | 3.5 | 2.5 | 4.0 | 2.2 | 2.3 |
| 1.5 | 1.9 | 1.6 | | 1.6 | 2.1 | 1.2 | 2.5 | 1.6 | 1.5 |
| 1.1 | 1.2 | 1.1 | | .9 | .9 | .8 | 1.3 | 1.2 | 1.3 |
| 2.1 | 2.2 | 2.0 | Quick | 8.2 | 2.5 | 1.4 | 3.7 | 1.4 | 1.5 |
| 1.0 | 1.4 | 1.2 | | 1.0 | 1.3 | .9 | 1.9 | 1.0 | 1.0 |
| .6 | .7 | .7 | | .6 | .4 | .6 | 1.1 | .7 | .7 |
| 29  12.8 | 29  12.6 | 23  15.9 | Sales/Receivables | 0  UND | 0  UND | 0  UND | 35  10.3 | 36  10.0 | 46  8.0 |
| 42  8.8 | 48  7.6 | 45  8.1 | | 20  17.9 | 31  11.7 | 37  9.8 | 57  6.4 | 49  7.5 | 64  5.7 |
| 58  6.3 | 68  5.4 | 62  5.9 | | 60  6.1 | 46  7.9 | 52  7.0 | 62  5.9 | 64  5.7 | 74  4.9 |
| | | | Cost of Sales/Inventory | | | | | | |
| | | | Cost of Sales/Payables | | | | | | |
| 5.9 | 5.3 | 5.3 | Sales/Working Capital | 2.8 | 5.6 | 5.2 | 4.7 | 6.7 | 6.3 |
| 11.7 | 8.7 | 11.6 | | 9.3 | 13.8 | 46.7 | 6.6 | 12.6 | 8.7 |
| 67.0 | 26.1 | 62.7 | | UND | NM | -62.0 | 14.0 | 39.3 | 15.9 |
| 12.2 | 20.4 | 15.0 | EBIT/Interest | 22.0 | 13.9 | 18.4 | 16.1 | 17.9 | 16.8 |
| (112) 4.1 | (94) 5.3 | (111) 5.4 | | (10) 3.1 | (22) 4.4 | (18) 6.3 | (19) 4.0 | (26) 5.6 | (16) 10.3 |
| .9 | 1.7 | 2.0 | | -2.5 | .9 | 1.5 | 1.7 | 2.1 | 2.7 |
| 3.6 | 11.8 | 6.0 | Net Profit + Depr., Dep., Amort./Cur. Mat. L/T/D | | | | | | |
| (27) 2.6 | (24) 3.9 | (22) 3.4 | | | | | | | |
| 1.2 | 1.2 | 1.3 | | | | | | | |
| .2 | .2 | .1 | Fixed/Worth | .0 | .2 | .4 | .1 | .3 | .3 |
| .6 | .4 | .5 | | .2 | .4 | 1.4 | .2 | .5 | .5 |
| 1.6 | 2.3 | 16.3 | | 10.1 | -1.9 | -2.7 | 1.2 | 1.7 | NM |
| .7 | .5 | .6 | Debt/Worth | .2 | .5 | .7 | .4 | .9 | .9 |
| 2.1 | 1.8 | 1.8 | | 1.7 | 3.4 | 2.4 | .9 | 1.8 | 2.4 |
| 4.7 | 7.6 | NM | | NM | -6.1 | -8.2 | 2.6 | 10.2 | NM |
| 45.9 | 62.2 | 60.7 | % Profit Before Taxes/Tangible Net Worth | 77.5 | 66.1 | 73.5 | 69.7 | 57.2 | 55.7 |
| (114) 22.0 | (98) 26.7 | (99) 30.1 | | (14) 43.4 | (17) 40.4 | (13) 28.7 | (18) 14.4 | (24) 28.4 | (13) 30.4 |
| 2.9 | 6.9 | 9.2 | | 4.8 | 16.9 | 14.3 | 5.6 | 6.6 | 15.5 |
| 17.3 | 22.2 | 22.7 | % Profit Before Taxes/Total Assets | 28.5 | 29.7 | 25.6 | 17.8 | 19.0 | 15.7 |
| 6.9 | 9.9 | 10.3 | | 16.7 | 12.7 | 15.8 | 5.7 | 8.8 | 8.3 |
| .2 | 1.3 | 2.8 | | -1.8 | 3.9 | 2.0 | 2.7 | 3.0 | 7.7 |
| 44.0 | 48.4 | 65.0 | Sales/Net Fixed Assets | UND | 82.9 | 92.4 | 51.2 | 54.8 | 25.7 |
| 14.9 | 17.3 | 23.6 | | 35.9 | 29.0 | 18.2 | 24.6 | 23.7 | 14.3 |
| 6.1 | 7.9 | 11.2 | | 11.1 | 14.4 | 7.2 | 8.4 | 10.9 | 9.3 |
| 3.7 | 3.5 | 4.0 | Sales/Total Assets | 3.8 | 6.9 | 5.6 | 3.4 | 4.0 | 2.8 |
| 2.4 | 2.2 | 2.9 | | 2.6 | 3.7 | 3.3 | 2.8 | 3.0 | 2.2 |
| 1.7 | 1.6 | 1.9 | | 1.3 | 2.0 | 2.3 | 1.8 | 2.0 | 1.8 |
| .8 | .9 | .8 | % Depr., Dep., Amort./Sales | .5 | .5 | 1.0 | .3 | .9 | .8 |
| (106) 1.8 | (85) 1.8 | (90) 1.3 | | (10) 1.1 | (13) 1.3 | (13) 1.4 | (14) 1.5 | (24) 1.2 | (16) 1.1 |
| 3.8 | 3.0 | 2.5 | | 3.4 | 1.9 | 3.4 | 4.7 | 2.0 | 2.7 |
| 3.1 | 2.4 | 3.0 | % Officers', Directors' Owners' Comp/Sales | 7.7 | 4.2 | 1.7 | | | |
| (49) 6.3 | (45) 5.0 | (56) 5.6 | | (11) 12.1 | (18) 7.2 | (11) 3.2 | | | |
| 9.7 | 7.4 | 11.9 | | 19.6 | 13.2 | 5.1 | | | |
| 2267479M | 1998201M | 2181687M | Net Sales ($) | 9162M | 55430M | 73492M | 154830M | 437258M | 1451515M |
| 1175752M | 1230546M | 980201M | Total Assets ($) | 5888M | 17905M | 21176M | 86844M | 175484M | 672904M |

M = $ thousand     MM = $ million
See Pages 9 through 22 for Explanation of Ratios and Data

## Current Data Sorted by Assets — Comparative Historical Data

| Type of Statement | 0-500M | 500M-2MM | 2-10MM | 10-50MM | 50-100MM | 100-250MM | 4/1/07-3/31/08 ALL | 4/1/08-3/31/09 ALL |
|---|---|---|---|---|---|---|---|---|
| Unqualified | 1 | 1 | 11 | 7 | 3 | 2 | 28 | 21 |
| Reviewed | | 13 | 33 | 13 | 2 | | 49 | 42 |
| Compiled | 11 | 33 | 28 | | | | 56 | 57 |
| Tax Returns | 64 | 61 | 31 | | 1 | 1 | 97 | 121 |
| Other | 31 | 56 | 42 | 12 | 3 | 3 | 99 | 115 |
| | | 84 (4/1-9/30/11) | | 379 (10/1/11-3/31/12) | | | | |
| **NUMBER OF STATEMENTS** | 107 | 164 | 145 | 32 | 9 | 6 | 329 | 356 |
| **ASSETS** | % | % | % | % | % | % | % | % |
| Cash & Equivalents | 16.8 | 9.6 | 7.3 | 10.5 | | | 10.1 | 12.4 |
| Trade Receivables (net) | 30.2 | 34.5 | 31.7 | 25.9 | | | 31.4 | 27.9 |
| Inventory | 14.0 | 18.4 | 21.1 | 16.5 | | | 18.6 | 17.3 |
| All Other Current | 2.6 | 2.5 | 2.7 | 4.1 | | | 3.2 | 2.9 |
| Total Current | 63.5 | 64.9 | 62.9 | 57.0 | | | 63.2 | 60.5 |
| Fixed Assets (net) | 24.6 | 26.0 | 28.4 | 23.6 | | | 27.1 | 29.2 |
| Intangibles (net) | 4.2 | 3.5 | 4.3 | 13.7 | | | 3.8 | 3.7 |
| All Other Non-Current | 7.7 | 5.6 | 4.4 | 5.6 | | | 5.9 | 6.6 |
| Total | 100.0 | 100.0 | 100.0 | 100.0 | | | 100.0 | 100.0 |
| **LIABILITIES** | | | | | | | | |
| Notes Payable-Short Term | 18.5 | 9.6 | 11.3 | 11.9 | | | 11.4 | 11.1 |
| Cur. Mat.-L.T.D. | 5.0 | 4.0 | 3.9 | 3.3 | | | 5.4 | 5.0 |
| Trade Payables | 16.1 | 15.5 | 13.4 | 11.0 | | | 17.0 | 14.3 |
| Income Taxes Payable | .1 | .4 | .2 | .5 | | | .3 | .2 |
| All Other Current | 16.8 | 10.4 | 10.8 | 12.1 | | | 10.9 | 9.8 |
| Total Current | 56.4 | 40.0 | 39.6 | 38.9 | | | 44.9 | 40.3 |
| Long-Term Debt | 35.2 | 20.9 | 15.3 | 12.7 | | | 22.6 | 23.9 |
| Deferred Taxes | .0 | .3 | .2 | .8 | | | .3 | 1.0 |
| All Other Non-Current | 16.3 | 6.0 | 3.5 | 6.3 | | | 5.7 | 6.4 |
| Net Worth | -7.9 | 32.9 | 41.4 | 41.3 | | | 26.6 | 28.4 |
| Total Liabilties & Net Worth | 100.0 | 100.0 | 100.0 | 100.0 | | | 100.0 | 100.0 |
| **INCOME DATA** | | | | | | | | |
| Net Sales | 100.0 | 100.0 | 100.0 | 100.0 | | | 100.0 | 100.0 |
| Gross Profit | | | | | | | | |
| Operating Expenses | 94.4 | 93.6 | 92.0 | 94.9 | | | 93.0 | 93.4 |
| Operating Profit | 5.6 | 6.4 | 8.0 | 5.1 | | | 7.0 | 6.6 |
| All Other Expenses (net) | 1.0 | 1.5 | 1.5 | .7 | | | 1.2 | 1.6 |
| Profit Before Taxes | 4.6 | 4.8 | 6.5 | 4.4 | | | 5.8 | 5.1 |
| **RATIOS** | | | | | | | | |
| Current | 3.2 | 2.8 | 2.7 | 2.0 | | | 2.6 | 3.0 |
| | 1.5 | 1.8 | 1.7 | 1.4 | | | 1.5 | 1.7 |
| | .8 | 1.1 | 1.1 | 1.2 | | | 1.0 | 1.1 |
| Quick | 2.3 | 2.0 | 1.7 | 1.4 | | | 1.7 | 1.9 |
| | 1.0 | 1.0 | .9 | 1.0 | | | 1.0 (355) | 1.1 |
| | .4 | .7 | .6 | .5 | | | .6 | .6 |
| Sales/Receivables | 0 UND | 27 13.3 | 34 10.8 | 37 9.9 | | | 26 14.1 | 17 21.9 |
| | 25 14.7 | 43 8.5 | 47 7.8 | 55 6.6 | | | 41 8.9 | 37 9.8 |
| | 45 8.1 | 56 6.5 | 66 5.5 | 70 5.2 | | | 59 6.2 | 56 6.6 |
| Cost of Sales/Inventory | | | | | | | | |
| | | | | | | | | |
| | | | | | | | | |
| Cost of Sales/Payables | | | | | | | | |
| | | | | | | | | |
| | | | | | | | | |
| Sales/Working Capital | 8.3 | 6.2 | 4.8 | 7.7 | | | 6.6 | 6.2 |
| | 26.6 | 12.0 | 8.9 | 10.6 | | | 13.7 | 12.8 |
| | -68.5 | 65.1 | 39.5 | 20.9 | | | 422.4 | 152.4 |
| EBIT/Interest | 16.8 | 15.3 | 20.0 | 21.7 | | | 13.3 | 10.8 |
| | (81) 5.3 | (141) 4.4 | (134) 5.4 | (28) 5.2 | | | (302) 4.0 | (318) 4.2 |
| | 1.5 | 1.1 | 2.4 | .7 | | | 1.5 | 1.2 |
| Net Profit + Depr., Dep., Amort./Cur. Mat. L/T/D | | 3.3 | 8.6 | 2.0 | | | 4.4 | 6.7 |
| | (12) | 2.2 | (26) 3.8 | (10) 1.4 | | | (48) 2.1 | (56) 2.3 |
| | | 1.0 | 1.7 | -2.3 | | | 1.0 | .6 |
| Fixed/Worth | .2 | .3 | .2 | .3 | | | .3 | .3 |
| | .9 | .7 | .6 | .9 | | | .9 | .8 |
| | -2.0 | 5.5 | 1.7 | 2.0 | | | 3.5 | 3.3 |
| Debt/Worth | 1.0 | .7 | .7 | 1.3 | | | .9 | .9 |
| | 4.6 | 2.3 | 1.7 | 2.1 | | | 2.5 | 2.2 |
| | -2.9 | 19.7 | 4.9 | 9.4 | | | 11.9 | 10.1 |
| % Profit Before Taxes/Tangible Net Worth | 135.5 | 59.6 | 51.0 | 52.5 | | | 73.8 | 68.4 |
| | (70) 50.0 | (132) 21.0 | (135) 31.9 | (26) 22.7 | | | (271) 34.2 | (291) 25.2 |
| | 15.1 | 3.2 | 7.1 | -1.3 | | | 9.6 | 9.2 |
| % Profit Before Taxes/Total Assets | 39.2 | 22.7 | 19.9 | 14.8 | | | 24.5 | 21.2 |
| | 17.8 | 6.7 | 8.4 | 8.4 | | | 9.1 | 7.5 |
| | 1.3 | .3 | 2.6 | 4.0 | | | 1.8 | .5 |
| Sales/Net Fixed Assets | 112.4 | 41.5 | 30.7 | 31.5 | | | 31.1 | 31.5 |
| | 34.8 | 17.0 | 10.9 | 11.1 | | | 14.4 | 14.9 |
| | 13.0 | 7.8 | 4.7 | 3.9 | | | 6.7 | 5.3 |
| Sales/Total Assets | 6.8 | 3.6 | 3.1 | 2.0 | | | 3.9 | 3.9 |
| | 4.0 | 2.8 | 2.2 | 1.6 | | | 2.8 | 2.6 |
| | 2.8 | 1.8 | 1.5 | 1.3 | | | 1.9 | 1.7 |
| % Depr., Dep., Amort./Sales | .8 | 1.0 | 1.1 | .8 | | | .9 | 1.0 |
| | (56) 1.5 | (115) 1.9 | (121) 1.9 | (31) 2.0 | | | (264) 1.8 | (273) 2.0 |
| | 5.2 | 3.2 | 3.5 | 3.8 | | | 3.7 | 3.7 |
| % Officers', Directors' Owners' Comp/Sales | 4.2 | 3.2 | 1.9 | | | | 2.6 | 2.8 |
| | (62) 7.6 | (84) 5.2 | (68) 3.4 | | | | (172) 4.8 | (182) 4.6 |
| | 12.6 | 8.9 | 4.9 | | | | 7.6 | 7.7 |
| Net Sales ($) | 127087M | 519012M | 1449945M | 1125622M | 1514548M | 1703648M | 11022140M | 5425792M |
| Total Assets ($) | 25029M | 181131M | 640933M | 644630M | 662967M | 935178M | 3375811M | 2913165M |

M = $ thousand    MM = $ million
See Pages 9 through 22 for Explanation of Ratios and Data

## Comparative Historical Data — Current Data Sorted by Sales

| Type of Statement | | | | | | | | | |
|---|---|---|---|---|---|---|---|---|---|
| Unqualified | 17 | 29 | 25 | 1 | 1 | 1 | 2 | 7 | 13 |
| Reviewed | 59 | 54 | 61 | 1 | 2 | 9 | 19 | 18 | 13 |
| Compiled | 62 | 55 | 72 | 8 | 19 | 12 | 24 | 9 | |
| Tax Returns | 130 | 125 | 158 | 38 | 60 | 27 | 26 | 5 | 2 |
| Other | 110 | 127 | 147 | 31 | 47 | 14 | 20 | 21 | 14 |
| | 4/1/09-3/31/10 ALL | 4/1/10-3/31/11 ALL | 4/1/11-3/31/12 ALL | 84 (4/1-9/30/11) 0-1MM | 1-3MM | 3-5MM | 379 (10/1/11-3/31/12) 5-10MM | 10-25MM | 25MM & OVER |
| **NUMBER OF STATEMENTS** | 378 | 390 | 463 | 78 | 129 | 63 | 91 | 60 | 42 |
| **ASSETS** | % | % | % | % | % | % | % | % | % |
| Cash & Equivalents | 9.9 | 10.3 | 10.4 | 11.2 | 12.7 | 8.4 | 10.5 | 8.3 | 7.8 |
| Trade Receivables (net) | 26.8 | 29.6 | 31.7 | 23.2 | 32.2 | 31.6 | 36.6 | 35.6 | 29.5 |
| Inventory | 18.9 | 17.2 | 18.1 | 14.1 | 16.2 | 20.7 | 21.8 | 21.3 | 14.7 |
| All Other Current | 3.1 | 3.9 | 2.7 | 2.0 | 1.5 | 5.4 | 1.6 | 2.6 | 5.7 |
| Total Current | 58.7 | 61.1 | 62.8 | 50.6 | 62.6 | 66.2 | 70.4 | 67.8 | 57.6 |
| Fixed Assets (net) | 30.5 | 27.1 | 26.3 | 35.6 | 26.5 | 25.2 | 23.1 | 21.8 | 23.0 |
| Intangibles (net) | 4.1 | 5.6 | 5.2 | 6.5 | 4.3 | 2.0 | 2.5 | 7.2 | 13.2 |
| All Other Non-Current | 6.7 | 6.2 | 5.7 | 7.3 | 6.6 | 6.5 | 4.0 | 3.2 | 6.2 |
| Total | 100.0 | 100.0 | 100.0 | 100.0 | 100.0 | 100.0 | 100.0 | 100.0 | 100.0 |
| **LIABILITIES** | | | | | | | | | |
| Notes Payable-Short Term | 10.9 | 12.1 | 12.5 | 16.1 | 12.0 | 11.4 | 9.8 | 13.5 | 13.2 |
| Cur. Mat.-L.T.D. | 4.6 | 4.5 | 4.1 | 5.9 | 4.5 | 3.7 | 3.2 | 3.4 | 3.0 |
| Trade Payables | 14.0 | 14.6 | 14.5 | 11.0 | 16.2 | 15.7 | 14.4 | 14.9 | 13.1 |
| Income Taxes Payable | .2 | .3 | .3 | .5 | .0 | .2 | .3 | .3 | .3 |
| All Other Current | 10.8 | 11.0 | 12.1 | 16.2 | 11.5 | 11.0 | 10.8 | 11.5 | 11.6 |
| Total Current | 40.5 | 42.6 | 43.4 | 49.8 | 44.1 | 42.0 | 38.7 | 43.6 | 41.1 |
| Long-Term Debt | 23.8 | 21.3 | 21.9 | 41.7 | 24.7 | 17.3 | 14.0 | 11.1 | 16.7 |
| Deferred Taxes | .4 | .5 | .3 | .0 | .1 | .3 | .3 | .6 | 1.0 |
| All Other Non-Current | 5.3 | 7.3 | 7.7 | 15.9 | 7.9 | 5.8 | 4.9 | 4.2 | 6.3 |
| Net Worth | 30.1 | 28.3 | 26.7 | -7.3 | 23.2 | 34.6 | 42.1 | 40.5 | 34.9 |
| Total Liabilities & Net Worth | 100.0 | 100.0 | 100.0 | 100.0 | 100.0 | 100.0 | 100.0 | 100.0 | 100.0 |
| **INCOME DATA** | | | | | | | | | |
| Net Sales | 100.0 | 100.0 | 100.0 | 100.0 | 100.0 | 100.0 | 100.0 | 100.0 | 100.0 |
| Gross Profit | | | | | | | | | |
| Operating Expenses | 95.2 | 93.5 | 93.3 | 88.2 | 94.3 | 95.2 | 93.3 | 95.3 | 94.4 |
| Operating Profit | 4.8 | 6.5 | 6.7 | 11.8 | 5.7 | 4.8 | 6.7 | 4.7 | 5.6 |
| All Other Expenses (net) | 1.5 | 1.7 | 1.4 | 4.7 | 1.0 | .3 | .4 | .6 | 1.1 |
| Profit Before Taxes | 3.4 | 4.8 | 5.3 | 7.2 | 4.7 | 4.6 | 6.3 | 4.1 | 4.6 |
| **RATIOS** | | | | | | | | | |
| Current | 2.8 | 2.6 | 2.8 | 4.1 | 2.6 | 2.6 | 3.4 | 2.2 | 2.0 |
| | 1.6 | 1.5 | 1.6 | 1.5 | 1.4 | 1.9 | 1.9 | 1.5 | 1.5 |
| | 1.0 | 1.1 | 1.1 | .5 | 1.0 | 1.1 | 1.2 | 1.1 | 1.2 |
| Quick | 1.9 | 1.8 | 2.0 | 2.2 | 2.0 | 1.5 | 2.5 | 1.6 | 1.4 |
| | (377) 1.0 | (389) 1.1 | 1.0 | .9 | 1.1 | 1.0 | 1.0 | 1.0 | 1.0 |
| | .5 | .5 | .6 | .2 | .6 | .6 | .7 | .7 | .6 |
| Sales/Receivables | 22 16.8 | 25 14.6 | 25 14.4 | 0 UND | 24 14.9 | 22 16.8 | 34 10.7 | 36 10.1 | 35 10.4 |
| | 39 9.3 | 44 8.4 | 42 8.7 | 24 15.1 | 38 9.5 | 42 8.7 | 45 8.1 | 49 7.5 | 54 6.7 |
| | 56 6.5 | 60 6.1 | 59 6.2 | 53 6.9 | 54 6.7 | 55 6.6 | 58 6.3 | 72 5.1 | 69 5.3 |
| Cost of Sales/Inventory | | | | | | | | | |
| Cost of Sales/Payables | | | | | | | | | |
| Sales/Working Capital | 5.8 | 5.7 | 6.1 | 5.7 | 8.2 | 5.8 | 4.5 | 6.8 | 8.1 |
| | 13.6 | 13.4 | 12.3 | 19.2 | 17.2 | 11.0 | 8.6 | 11.2 | 13.2 |
| | -874.3 | 104.9 | 117.9 | -9.0 | -774.0 | 78.2 | 27.1 | 34.1 | 38.8 |
| EBIT/Interest | 9.9 | 13.4 | 17.1 | 9.9 | 14.8 | 19.6 | 23.6 | 20.1 | 19.8 |
| | (330) 2.5 | (346) 4.7 | (399) 5.1 | (50) 2.1 | (113) 5.3 | (57) 5.6 | (84) 6.9 | (55) 5.2 | (40) 5.2 |
| | .0 | 1.1 | 1.6 | .7 | 1.2 | 1.4 | 2.6 | 2.0 | 2.4 |
| Net Profit + Depr., Dep., Amort./Cur. Mat. L/T/D | 8.1 | 5.2 | 7.4 | | | | 4.9 | 8.6 | 8.7 |
| | (59) 2.2 | (65) 2.1 | (55) 2.2 | | | | (14) 2.1 | (18) 3.3 | (13) 1.7 |
| | 1.1 | 1.2 | 1.4 | | | | 1.6 | .9 | .0 |
| Fixed/Worth | .3 | .3 | .2 | .2 | .3 | .2 | .2 | .3 | .3 |
| | .8 | .7 | .7 | 1.5 | .9 | .7 | .6 | .6 | .6 |
| | 4.2 | 3.5 | 3.4 | -2.6 | 175.3 | 2.9 | 1.2 | 1.8 | -27.0 |
| Debt/Worth | .7 | .8 | .8 | .9 | 1.0 | .6 | .5 | .9 | 1.2 |
| | 2.1 | 2.2 | 2.1 | 4.8 | 2.9 | 2.2 | 1.3 | 2.1 | 2.9 |
| | 16.1 | 11.6 | 12.4 | -2.8 | UND | 14.4 | 3.4 | 5.4 | -45.8 |
| % Profit Before Taxes/Tangible Net Worth | 40.4 | 58.8 | 62.0 | 56.2 | 94.2 | 59.3 | 58.5 | 51.4 | 88.8 |
| | (309) 14.0 | (315) 22.6 | (371) 29.8 | (50) 21.1 | (97) 29.1 | (53) 35.2 | (84) 32.1 | (56) 24.7 | (31) 35.7 |
| | -1.1 | 4.5 | 6.6 | 3.3 | 4.4 | 4.4 | 10.2 | 4.0 | 17.1 |
| % Profit Before Taxes/Total Assets | 16.4 | 18.9 | 23.2 | 26.6 | 25.8 | 25.9 | 27.8 | 16.1 | 16.2 |
| | 3.3 | 7.3 | 9.2 | 7.3 | 8.8 | 10.2 | 12.7 | 7.3 | 9.1 |
| | -2.7 | .4 | 1.6 | -.4 | .7 | 1.1 | 3.3 | 1.4 | 5.0 |
| Sales/Net Fixed Assets | 32.8 | 38.2 | 44.2 | 65.4 | 81.7 | 73.8 | 33.2 | 34.4 | 27.2 |
| | 12.6 | 13.8 | 16.5 | 16.9 | 16.1 | 19.5 | 16.3 | 15.2 | 13.5 |
| | 4.7 | 5.3 | 6.5 | 2.3 | 7.7 | 8.6 | 6.8 | 6.3 | 5.6 |
| Sales/Total Assets | 3.6 | 3.6 | 3.6 | 3.4 | 4.4 | 4.1 | 3.5 | 3.3 | 3.2 |
| | 2.4 | 2.4 | 2.7 | 2.4 | 3.0 | 3.0 | 2.5 | 2.5 | 1.8 |
| | 1.6 | 1.5 | 1.7 | 1.2 | 1.8 | 1.9 | 1.9 | 2.0 | 1.4 |
| % Depr., Dep., Amort./Sales | .9 | .9 | 1.0 | 1.1 | 1.0 | .4 | 1.0 | .8 | .8 |
| | (302) 2.0 | (292) 1.9 | (335) 1.9 | (46) 3.4 | (81) 2.3 | (48) 1.4 | (75) 1.8 | (48) 1.6 | (37) 1.9 |
| | 4.2 | 4.3 | 3.5 | 11.2 | 3.9 | 2.6 | 2.9 | 2.8 | 3.6 |
| % Officers', Directors' Owners' Comp/Sales | 2.9 | 2.5 | 2.7 | 4.6 | 3.8 | 2.5 | 2.6 | 1.3 | |
| | (182) 5.5 | (173) 5.3 | (222) 4.7 | (35) 9.2 | (75) 5.9 | (35) 4.3 | (43) 4.0 | (26) 2.6 | |
| | 9.0 | 8.9 | 8.8 | 14.0 | 10.7 | 6.1 | 5.6 | 5.3 | |
| Net Sales ($) | 5600415M | 7933671M | 6439862M | 42265M | 246574M | 247520M | 648913M | 921456M | 4333134M |
| Total Assets ($) | 2763258M | 3403862M | 3089868M | 42613M | 105686M | 100394M | 277039M | 447851M | 2116285M |

M = $ thousand    MM = $ million
See Pages 9 through 22 for Explanation of Ratios and Data

## Current Data Sorted by Assets | Comparative Historical Data

| Type of Statement | 0-500M | 500M-2MM | 2-10MM | 10-50MM | 50-100MM | 100-250MM | | 4/1/07-3/31/08 ALL | 4/1/08-3/31/09 ALL |
|---|---|---|---|---|---|---|---|---|---|
| Unqualified | | | 1 | 1 | | | | | |
| Reviewed | | 1 | 7 | | | | | 5 | 11 |
| Compiled | | 1 | 3 | | | | | 4 | 5 |
| Tax Returns | 3 | 2 | 10 | | | | | 10 | 12 |
| Other | 4 | 3 | | 2 | | | | 8 | 26 |
| | 4 (4/1-9/30/11) | | | 34 (10/1/11-3/31/12) | | | | 28 | 56 |
| **NUMBER OF STATEMENTS** | 7 | 7 | 21 | 3 | | | | 28 | 56 |
| | % | % | % | % | % | % | | % | % |
| **ASSETS** | | | | | | | | | |
| Cash & Equivalents | | | 11.2 | | D | D | | 15.2 | 10.0 |
| Trade Receivables (net) | | | 25.0 | | A | A | | 31.1 | 24.9 |
| Inventory | | | 16.5 | | T | T | | 20.9 | 16.6 |
| All Other Current | | | 6.5 | | A | A | | 1.8 | 3.7 |
| Total Current | | | 59.1 | | | | | 69.0 | 55.2 |
| Fixed Assets (net) | | | 26.5 | | N | N | | 22.8 | 26.0 |
| Intangibles (net) | | | 6.2 | | O | O | | 5.0 | 4.2 |
| All Other Non-Current | | | 8.1 | | T | T | | 3.2 | 14.6 |
| Total | | | 100.0 | | | | | 100.0 | 100.0 |
| **LIABILITIES** | | | | | A | A | | | |
| Notes Payable-Short Term | | | 8.1 | | V | V | | 8.5 | 7.4 |
| Cur. Mat.-L.T.D. | | | 2.9 | | A | A | | 5.6 | 3.5 |
| Trade Payables | | | 12.5 | | I | I | | 11.6 | 16.6 |
| Income Taxes Payable | | | .4 | | L | L | | 1.2 | .3 |
| All Other Current | | | 14.0 | | A | A | | 10.5 | 21.7 |
| Total Current | | | 38.0 | | B | B | | 37.4 | 49.7 |
| Long-Term Debt | | | 15.8 | | L | L | | 24.1 | 19.7 |
| Deferred Taxes | | | 1.1 | | E | E | | .5 | .4 |
| All Other Non-Current | | | 4.3 | | | | | 5.4 | 6.9 |
| Net Worth | | | 40.8 | | | | | 32.6 | 23.4 |
| Total Liabilities & Net Worth | | | 100.0 | | | | | 100.0 | 100.0 |
| **INCOME DATA** | | | | | | | | | |
| Net Sales | | | 100.0 | | | | | 100.0 | 100.0 |
| Gross Profit | | | | | | | | | |
| Operating Expenses | | | 92.1 | | | | | 94.7 | 92.7 |
| Operating Profit | | | 7.9 | | | | | 5.3 | 7.3 |
| All Other Expenses (net) | | | 3.0 | | | | | 2.0 | 1.5 |
| Profit Before Taxes | | | 4.9 | | | | | 3.4 | 5.8 |
| **RATIOS** | | | | | | | | | |
| Current | | | 1.9 | | | | | 3.7 | 2.6 |
| | | | 1.5 | | | | | 1.7 | 1.4 |
| | | | 1.2 | | | | | 1.1 | .6 |
| Quick | | | 1.5 | | | | | 2.4 | 1.7 |
| | | | .9 | | | | | 1.0 | .7 |
| | | | .5 | | | | | .5 | .2 |
| Sales/Receivables | | | 20  18.6 | | | | | 23  15.9 | 4  95.3 |
| | | | 42  8.7 | | | | | 36  10.1 | 35  10.6 |
| | | | 58  6.3 | | | | | 61  5.9 | 58  6.3 |
| Cost of Sales/Inventory | | | | | | | | | |
| Cost of Sales/Payables | | | | | | | | | |
| Sales/Working Capital | | | 5.9 | | | | | 6.4 | 7.8 |
| | | | 13.0 | | | | | 10.2 | 26.2 |
| | | | 36.3 | | | | | 73.1 | -10.2 |
| EBIT/Interest | | | 20.3 | | | | | 18.1 | 17.1 |
| | | (18) | 4.9 | | | | (24) | 4.2  (44) | 3.4 |
| | | | 3.1 | | | | | 1.8 | 1.6 |
| Net Profit + Depr., Dep., Amort./Cur. Mat. L/T/D | | | | | | | | | |
| Fixed/Worth | | | .2 | | | | | .2 | .3 |
| | | | .4 | | | | | .5 | .8 |
| | | | 2.5 | | | | | 3.7 | 4.3 |
| Debt/Worth | | | 1.0 | | | | | .9 | 1.1 |
| | | | 1.5 | | | | | 2.3 | 3.4 |
| | | | 3.8 | | | | | 38.9 | 9.9 |
| % Profit Before Taxes/Tangible Net Worth | | | 42.7 | | | | | 81.2 | 103.8 |
| | | (19) | 12.6 | | | | (23) | 44.9  (46) | 34.6 |
| | | | 6.3 | | | | | 23.0 | 12.5 |
| % Profit Before Taxes/Total Assets | | | 18.7 | | | | | 25.3 | 24.4 |
| | | | 5.4 | | | | | 12.1 | 8.4 |
| | | | 2.5 | | | | | 1.7 | 3.4 |
| Sales/Net Fixed Assets | | | 36.2 | | | | | 63.3 | 42.4 |
| | | | 17.7 | | | | | 20.7 | 17.9 |
| | | | 8.3 | | | | | 11.3 | 6.5 |
| Sales/Total Assets | | | 3.6 | | | | | 3.5 | 4.1 |
| | | | 2.4 | | | | | 2.9 | 2.6 |
| | | | 1.4 | | | | | 2.0 | 1.9 |
| % Depr., Dep., Amort./Sales | | | .7 | | | | | 1.2 | .7 |
| | | (17) | 1.3 | | | | (21) | 1.8  (45) | 1.9 |
| | | | 1.7 | | | | | 3.2 | 4.2 |
| % Officers', Directors', Owners' Comp/Sales | | | | | | | | 2.0 | 3.4 |
| | | | | | | | (12) | 4.5  (18) | 4.3 |
| | | | | | | | | 11.0 | 6.5 |
| Net Sales ($) | 9491M | 25467M | 248634M | 113811M | | | | 1393837M | 898772M |
| Total Assets ($) | 1060M | 8118M | 108095M | 87658M | | | | 482737M | 446292M |

M = $ thousand    MM = $ million
See Pages 9 through 22 for Explanation of Ratios and Data

## Comparative Historical Data | Current Data Sorted by Sales

Type of Statement / current data groupings: **4 (4/1-9/30/11)** covers 0-1MM through 3-5MM; **34 (10/1/11-3/31/12)** covers 5-10MM through 25MM & OVER.

| 4/1/09-3/31/10 ALL | 4/1/10-3/31/11 ALL | 4/1/11-3/31/12 ALL | Type of Statement | 0-1MM | 1-3MM | 3-5MM | 5-10MM | 10-25MM | 25MM & OVER |
|---|---|---|---|---|---|---|---|---|---|
| 1 | 1 | 2 | Unqualified | | | | | 1 | |
| 12 | 11 | 8 | Reviewed | | 1 | 1 | 3 | 4 | 1 |
| 7 | 4 | 1 | Compiled | | | 1 | | | |
| 13 | 19 | 8 | Tax Returns | 3 | | 1 | 2 | 1 | |
| 22 | 23 | 19 | Other | 4 | | 2 | 5 | 5 | 3 |
| 55 | 58 | 38 | **NUMBER OF STATEMENTS** | 7 | 1 | 5 | 10 | 11 | 4 |
| % | % | % | **ASSETS** | % | % | % | % | % | % |
| 15.1 | 15.6 | 15.1 | Cash & Equivalents | | | | 13.1 | 11.2 | |
| 26.2 | 25.8 | 22.1 | Trade Receivables (net) | | | | 26.0 | 30.1 | |
| 19.2 | 16.8 | 17.9 | Inventory | | | | 16.6 | 17.3 | |
| 5.8 | 2.7 | 3.8 | All Other Current | | | | 8.7 | 1.6 | |
| 66.3 | 60.9 | 58.8 | Total Current | | | | 64.4 | 60.2 | |
| 22.4 | 24.7 | 28.1 | Fixed Assets (net) | | | | 21.5 | 24.6 | |
| 3.5 | 4.5 | 3.8 | Intangibles (net) | | | | 7.0 | 5.4 | |
| 7.8 | 9.9 | 9.3 | All Other Non-Current | | | | 7.0 | 9.7 | |
| 100.0 | 100.0 | 100.0 | Total | | | | 100.0 | 100.0 | |
| | | | **LIABILITIES** | | | | | | |
| 23.5 | 15.7 | 17.0 | Notes Payable-Short Term | | | | 9.4 | 7.0 | |
| 10.1 | 4.3 | 3.0 | Cur. Mat.-L.T.D. | | | | 1.5 | 3.7 | |
| 18.0 | 16.0 | 17.8 | Trade Payables | | | | 25.5 | 12.4 | |
| .2 | .2 | .3 | Income Taxes Payable | | | | .5 | .4 | |
| 18.0 | 21.9 | 16.1 | All Other Current | | | | 12.1 | 16.5 | |
| 69.8 | 58.1 | 54.3 | Total Current | | | | 48.9 | 39.8 | |
| 18.6 | 18.3 | 19.0 | Long-Term Debt | | | | 15.5 | 9.2 | |
| .6 | .5 | .6 | Deferred Taxes | | | | .2 | 2.0 | |
| 4.5 | 4.0 | 8.8 | All Other Non-Current | | | | 1.9 | 7.3 | |
| 6.5 | 19.1 | 17.4 | Net Worth | | | | 33.5 | 41.6 | |
| 100.0 | 100.0 | 100.0 | Total Liabilities & Net Worth | | | | 100.0 | 100.0 | |
| | | | **INCOME DATA** | | | | | | |
| 100.0 | 100.0 | 100.0 | Net Sales | | | | 100.0 | 100.0 | |
| | | | Gross Profit | | | | | | |
| 95.8 | 93.4 | 92.9 | Operating Expenses | | | | 97.8 | 95.3 | |
| 4.2 | 6.6 | 7.1 | Operating Profit | | | | 2.2 | 4.7 | |
| .8 | 1.1 | 2.8 | All Other Expenses (net) | | | | 1.2 | .2 | |
| 3.4 | 5.5 | 4.3 | Profit Before Taxes | | | | 1.0 | 4.5 | |
| | | | **RATIOS** | | | | | | |
| 2.5 | 2.6 | 2.0 |  | | | | 2.5 | 1.9 | |
| 1.6 | 1.5 | 1.6 | Current | | | | 1.5 | 1.5 | |
| .9 | 1.0 | .6 |  | | | | .6 | 1.4 | |
| 1.4 | 1.6 | 1.5 |  | | | | 1.6 | 1.5 | |
| .9 | .9 | .8 | Quick | | | | .7 | 1.1 | |
| .4 | .5 | .4 |  | | | | .4 | .8 | |
| 2  186.1 | 5  79.7 | 8  45.5 |  | | | | 18  20.5 | 19  19.2 | |
| 34  10.9 | 30  12.2 | 35  10.4 | Sales/Receivables | | | | 35  10.4 | 44  8.3 | |
| 51  7.1 | 53  6.9 | 54  6.8 |  | | | | 55  6.6 | 64  5.7 | |
| | | | Cost of Sales/Inventory | | | | | | |
| | | | Cost of Sales/Payables | | | | | | |
| 5.9 | 5.9 | 5.4 |  | | | | 4.5 | 11.6 | |
| 13.6 | 18.2 | 13.1 | Sales/Working Capital | | | | 16.3 | 13.0 | |
| -48.1 | NM | -26.1 |  | | | | -14.6 | 17.0 | |
| 24.2 | 34.2 | 10.3 |  | | | | | 36.1 | |
| (47) 6.4 | (49) 7.2 | (31) 4.1 | EBIT/Interest | | | | | (10) 8.1 | |
| .4 | 2.9 | 1.6 |  | | | | | 3.9 | |
| | | | Net Profit + Depr., Dep., Amort./Cur. Mat. L/T/D | | | | | | |
| .1 | .2 | .1 |  | | | | .0 | .3 | |
| .5 | .8 | .5 | Fixed/Worth | | | | .6 | .4 | |
| 2.4 | NM | 3.2 |  | | | | NM | 1.4 | |
| .7 | .7 | .9 |  | | | | .9 | 1.2 | |
| 2.3 | 2.2 | 1.5 | Debt/Worth | | | | 1.6 | 1.3 | |
| 24.6 | -248.1 | 11.0 |  | | | | NM | 2.7 | |
| 70.3 | 63.8 | 37.4 |  | | | | | 54.9 | |
| (44) 25.7 | (43) 21.1 | (30) 11.8 | % Profit Before Taxes/Tangible Net Worth | | | | | (10) 26.5 | |
| 10.0 | 6.6 | 3.1 |  | | | | | 12.4 | |
| 20.7 | 22.0 | 13.2 |  | | | | 8.7 | 22.3 | |
| 6.9 | 11.3 | 4.8 | % Profit Before Taxes/Total Assets | | | | 3.5 | 17.7 | |
| .2 | 4.0 | .8 |  | | | | -7.2 | 4.7 | |
| 66.0 | 47.1 | 43.0 |  | | | | 154.9 | 23.0 | |
| 20.9 | 19.4 | 20.0 | Sales/Net Fixed Assets | | | | 33.2 | 17.7 | |
| 9.4 | 7.5 | 6.6 |  | | | | 12.6 | 9.5 | |
| 4.6 | 4.7 | 3.8 |  | | | | 4.6 | 3.9 | |
| 3.3 | 3.0 | 2.5 | Sales/Total Assets | | | | 2.0 | 3.0 | |
| 2.1 | 2.0 | 1.4 |  | | | | 1.4 | 1.7 | |
| .4 | .9 | .6 |  | | | | | .7 | |
| (40) 1.3 | (39) 1.7 | (28) 1.2 | % Depr., Dep., Amort./Sales | | | | | (10) 1.3 | |
| 2.1 | 2.7 | 2.5 |  | | | | | 2.3 | |
| 2.6 | 2.9 | 2.9 |  | | | | | | |
| (26) 4.7 | (26) 5.5 | (14) 4.9 | % Officers', Directors' Owners' Comp/Sales | | | | | | |
| 8.4 | 6.8 | 6.4 |  | | | | | | |
| 711707M | 568593M | 397403M | Net Sales ($) | 2201M | 1487M | 20466M | 73705M | 160301M | 139243M |
| 280035M | 234832M | 204931M | Total Assets ($) | 7074M | 506M | 5740M | 34855M | 59423M | 97333M |

M = $ thousand     MM = $ million
See Pages 9 through 22 for Explanation of Ratios and Data

## Current Data Sorted by Assets      Comparative Historical Data

| 0-500M | 500M-2MM | 2-10MM | 10-50MM | 50-100MM | 100-250MM | Type of Statement | 4/1/07-3/31/08 ALL | 4/1/08-3/31/09 ALL |
|---|---|---|---|---|---|---|---|---|
| 1 | 2 | 2 | 2 | | | Unqualified | 2 | 12 |
| | 2 | 2 | | | | Reviewed | 4 | 14 |
| 2 | 5 | 2 | | 2 | 1 | Compiled | 8 | 19 |
| 31 | 12 | 2 | | 2 | 1 | Tax Returns | 20 | 37 |
| 14 | 15 | 5 | 2 | 1 | 1 | Other | 14 | 42 |
| | 9 (4/1-9/30/11) | | | 97 (10/1/11-3/31/12) | | | | |
| 48 | 36 | 14 | 4 | 2 | 2 | NUMBER OF STATEMENTS | 48 | 124 |
| % | % | % | % | % | % | ASSETS | % | % |
| 26.0 | 13.9 | 16.6 | | | | Cash & Equivalents | 15.3 | 12.7 |
| 14.5 | 25.6 | 26.7 | | | | Trade Receivables (net) | 28.8 | 25.0 |
| 9.2 | 13.9 | 6.1 | | | | Inventory | 15.6 | 16.0 |
| 1.5 | 1.1 | .2 | | | | All Other Current | 1.9 | 4.0 |
| 51.2 | 54.5 | 49.6 | | | | Total Current | 61.6 | 57.7 |
| 25.5 | 29.0 | 43.3 | | | | Fixed Assets (net) | 27.4 | 29.6 |
| 12.4 | 6.6 | .8 | | | | Intangibles (net) | 4.8 | 7.2 |
| 10.7 | 9.9 | 6.4 | | | | All Other Non-Current | 6.2 | 5.4 |
| 100.0 | 100.0 | 100.0 | | | | Total | 100.0 | 100.0 |
| | | | | | | LIABILITIES | | |
| 24.5 | 9.5 | 3.4 | | | | Notes Payable-Short Term | 12.9 | 10.0 |
| 5.8 | 1.8 | 4.1 | | | | Cur. Mat.-L.T.D. | 3.0 | 6.0 |
| 7.7 | 13.8 | 5.7 | | | | Trade Payables | 10.3 | 11.8 |
| .0 | .1 | .0 | | | | Income Taxes Payable | .1 | .4 |
| 18.6 | 7.6 | 5.9 | | | | All Other Current | 10.1 | 11.9 |
| 56.6 | 32.8 | 19.2 | | | | Total Current | 36.4 | 40.0 |
| 32.7 | 23.9 | 23.3 | | | | Long-Term Debt | 27.0 | 26.2 |
| .0 | .1 | .7 | | | | Deferred Taxes | .0 | .5 |
| 8.4 | 5.1 | 9.6 | | | | All Other Non-Current | 5.7 | 6.0 |
| 2.2 | 38.1 | 47.2 | | | | Net Worth | 30.9 | 27.3 |
| 100.0 | 100.0 | 100.0 | | | | Total Liabilities & Net Worth | 100.0 | 100.0 |
| | | | | | | INCOME DATA | | |
| 100.0 | 100.0 | 100.0 | | | | Net Sales | 100.0 | 100.0 |
| | | | | | | Gross Profit | | |
| 93.7 | 95.0 | 86.6 | | | | Operating Expenses | 90.2 | 92.7 |
| 6.3 | 5.0 | 13.4 | | | | Operating Profit | 9.8 | 7.3 |
| .7 | 4.7 | 1.8 | | | | All Other Expenses (net) | .7 | 1.8 |
| 5.6 | .3 | 11.5 | | | | Profit Before Taxes | 9.1 | 5.5 |
| | | | | | | RATIOS | | |
| 4.9 | 5.1 | 14.2 | | | | | 3.8 | 2.7 |
| 1.1 | 1.3 | 2.0 | | | | Current | 1.9 | 1.6 |
| .4 | .9 | 1.7 | | | | | 1.1 | 1.1 |
| 4.3 | 3.3 | 13.6 | | | | | 2.9 | 2.0 |
| (47) .9 | 1.2 | 1.9 | | | | Quick | 1.1 (123) | 1.1 |
| .3 | .6 | 1.2 | | | | | .6 | .6 |
| 0 UND | 0 UND | 20 18.6 | | | | | 3 106.8 | 11 32.4 |
| 0 UND | 27 13.7 | 40 9.2 | | | | Sales/Receivables | 33 11.2 | 31 11.9 |
| 20 18.2 | 65 5.6 | 53 6.9 | | | | | 50 7.4 | 47 7.8 |
| | | | | | | Cost of Sales/Inventory | | |
| | | | | | | Cost of Sales/Payables | | |
| 7.8 | 6.3 | 5.1 | | | | | 5.7 | 7.0 |
| UND | 22.1 | 10.3 | | | | Sales/Working Capital | 13.1 | 16.5 |
| -17.0 | -169.8 | 15.6 | | | | | 178.5 | 56.3 |
| 22.8 | 6.1 | 10.8 | | | | | 20.5 | 13.0 |
| (31) 4.4 | (29) 2.3 | (11) 4.4 | | | | EBIT/Interest | (40) 7.7 | (103) 4.2 |
| -1.5 | -5.0 | 2.1 | | | | | 2.7 | 1.2 |
| | | | | | | Net Profit + Depr., Dep., Amort./Cur. Mat. L/T/D | | 10.1 |
| | | | | | | | (18) | 2.8 |
| | | | | | | | | 1.3 |
| .1 | .1 | .5 | | | | | .2 | .3 |
| .9 | .6 | .9 | | | | Fixed/Worth | .7 | 1.0 |
| -.4 | 3.1 | 2.5 | | | | | 2.3 | 5.7 |
| .3 | .8 | .4 | | | | | .5 | .7 |
| 3.2 | 2.2 | .9 | | | | Debt/Worth | 1.4 | 2.6 |
| -2.1 | 9.2 | 4.6 | | | | | 5.6 | 43.0 |
| 132.1 | 47.7 | 54.0 | | | | | 94.1 | 76.3 |
| (31) 33.3 | (29) 7.1 | (13) 38.0 | | | | % Profit Before Taxes/Tangible Net Worth | (40) 46.6 | (98) 30.0 |
| 10.7 | -13.3 | 5.7 | | | | | 20.4 | 5.7 |
| 56.4 | 14.9 | 18.9 | | | | | 42.6 | 26.2 |
| 15.3 | 3.8 | 7.6 | | | | % Profit Before Taxes/Total Assets | 19.9 | 9.5 |
| -4.8 | -8.5 | 3.5 | | | | | 4.8 | 1.2 |
| 344.1 | 50.3 | 12.1 | | | | | 36.0 | 46.9 |
| 50.7 | 18.7 | 6.8 | | | | Sales/Net Fixed Assets | 19.6 | 15.7 |
| 19.0 | 5.5 | 2.3 | | | | | 5.9 | 5.4 |
| 9.1 | 4.5 | 3.4 | | | | | 4.8 | 4.5 |
| 4.9 | 2.7 | 2.6 | | | | Sales/Total Assets | 3.4 | 2.8 |
| 3.5 | 1.5 | 1.6 | | | | | 2.5 | 1.8 |
| .7 | .6 | 1.2 | | | | | 1.0 | .9 |
| (24) 1.1 | (25) 1.9 | (13) 3.2 | | | | % Depr., Dep., Amort./Sales | (36) 1.7 | (97) 1.9 |
| 3.9 | 4.5 | 10.6 | | | | | 3.8 | 4.0 |
| 6.1 | 1.9 | | | | | | 3.4 | 3.2 |
| (30) 9.6 | (18) 4.9 | | | | | % Officers', Directors', Owners' Comp/Sales | (26) 5.3 | (52) 5.3 |
| 16.6 | 8.1 | | | | | | 11.5 | 8.1 |
| 49659M | 123142M | 157298M | 55575M | 672198M | 66292M | Net Sales ($) | 2847364M | 3154841M |
| 8494M | 38215M | 59492M | 58650M | 164302M | 203355M | Total Assets ($) | 407570M | 1380170M |

M = $ thousand    MM = $ million
See Pages 9 through 22 for Explanation of Ratios and Data

## Comparative Historical Data      Current Data Sorted by Sales

| Hist 1 | Hist 2 | Hist 3 | Type of Statement | 0-1MM | 1-3MM | 3-5MM | 5-10MM | 10-25MM | 25MM & OVER |
|---|---|---|---|---|---|---|---|---|---|
| 3 | 2 | 5 | Unqualified | | 4 | | | 1 | |
| 6 | 6 | 4 | Reviewed | | 1 | 1 | 2 | | |
| 13 | 9 | 12 | Compiled | 2 | 3 | 1 | 2 | 3 | 1 |
| 42 | 43 | 48 | Tax Returns | 25 | 12 | 5 | 2 | 1 | 3 |
| 22 | 33 | 37 | Other | 7 | 14 | 7 | 5 | 4 | |
| 4/1/09-3/31/10 ALL | 4/1/10-3/31/11 ALL | 4/1/11-3/31/12 ALL | | 9 (4/1-9/30/11) | | | 97 (10/1/11-3/31/12) | | |
| 86 | 93 | 106 | **NUMBER OF STATEMENTS** | 34 | 34 | 14 | 11 | 9 | 4 |
| % | % | % | **ASSETS** | % | % | % | % | % | % |
| 13.9 | 16.3 | 20.3 | Cash & Equivalents | 22.2 | 22.6 | 12.9 | 18.4 | | |
| 20.6 | 20.2 | 19.2 | Trade Receivables (net) | 11.5 | 23.2 | 19.2 | 26.5 | | |
| 18.9 | 15.1 | 10.7 | Inventory | 10.4 | 7.7 | 15.3 | 11.3 | | |
| 4.7 | 4.0 | 1.6 | All Other Current | 1.1 | 2.9 | 1.5 | .5 | | |
| 58.1 | 55.5 | 51.9 | Total Current | 45.2 | 56.4 | 49.0 | 56.8 | | |
| 29.5 | 27.4 | 29.4 | Fixed Assets (net) | 33.8 | 23.0 | 32.7 | 33.4 | | |
| 4.8 | 7.6 | 8.8 | Intangibles (net) | 11.0 | 10.9 | 6.3 | 1.4 | | |
| 7.5 | 9.5 | 9.9 | All Other Non-Current | 10.1 | 9.7 | 12.1 | 8.5 | | |
| 100.0 | 100.0 | 100.0 | Total | 100.0 | 100.0 | 100.0 | 100.0 | | |
| | | | **LIABILITIES** | | | | | | |
| 13.4 | 9.8 | 15.4 | Notes Payable-Short Term | 19.9 | 16.6 | 14.3 | 9.7 | | |
| 6.1 | 3.8 | 3.9 | Cur. Mat.-L.T.D. | 3.8 | 5.9 | 1.9 | 2.1 | | |
| 11.4 | 12.4 | 9.2 | Trade Payables | 6.6 | 11.3 | 15.8 | 3.5 | | |
| .2 | .1 | .0 | Income Taxes Payable | .0 | .0 | .1 | .0 | | |
| 13.7 | 10.6 | 12.3 | All Other Current | 15.4 | 13.7 | 9.2 | 8.9 | | |
| 44.8 | 36.8 | 40.8 | Total Current | 45.7 | 47.5 | 41.2 | 24.2 | | |
| 27.8 | 16.8 | 29.6 | Long-Term Debt | 41.6 | 25.0 | 25.6 | 9.1 | | |
| .1 | .1 | .1 | Deferred Taxes | .0 | .0 | .1 | .0 | | |
| 5.8 | 11.9 | 7.0 | All Other Non-Current | 8.7 | 7.0 | 4.7 | 10.1 | | |
| 21.5 | 34.5 | 22.4 | Net Worth | 3.9 | 20.5 | 28.3 | 56.6 | | |
| 100.0 | 100.0 | 100.0 | Total Liabilities & Net Worth | 100.0 | 100.0 | 100.0 | 100.0 | | |
| | | | **INCOME DATA** | | | | | | |
| 100.0 | 100.0 | 100.0 | Net Sales | 100.0 | 100.0 | 100.0 | 100.0 | | |
| | | | Gross Profit | | | | | | |
| 92.4 | 93.9 | 92.3 | Operating Expenses | 88.1 | 92.9 | 98.6 | 92.8 | | |
| 7.6 | 6.1 | 7.7 | Operating Profit | 11.9 | 7.1 | 1.4 | 7.2 | | |
| 1.7 | 1.1 | 2.5 | All Other Expenses (net) | 5.8 | 1.1 | 1.0 | .1 | | |
| 5.9 | 5.1 | 5.3 | Profit Before Taxes | 6.1 | 6.0 | .4 | 7.1 | | |
| | | | **RATIOS** | | | | | | |
| 3.4 | 4.5 | 5.3 | Current | 2.5 | 5.2 | 7.4 | 7.0 | | |
| 1.5 | 1.7 | 1.4 | | 1.1 | 1.7 | 1.1 | 2.1 | | |
| .7 | .9 | .8 | | .3 | .9 | .8 | 1.1 | | |
| 2.1 | 3.3 | 3.8 | Quick | 1.9 | 4.8 | 2.3 | 7.0 | | |
| .8 | 1.0 (105) | 1.2 | | (33) .9 | 1.5 | .9 | 2.0 | | |
| .3 | .3 | .5 | | .2 | .6 | .3 | .6 | | |
| 0 UND | 0 UND | 0 UND | Sales/Receivables | 0 UND | 0 UND | 0 UND | 10 36.7 | | |
| 22 16.5 | 15 23.6 | 10 36.5 | | 0 UND | 24 15.0 | 8 46.9 | 25 14.4 | | |
| 46 7.9 | 47 7.7 | 40 9.2 | | 10 34.8 | 53 6.9 | 35 10.3 | 39 9.4 | | |
| | | | Cost of Sales/Inventory | | | | | | |
| | | | Cost of Sales/Payables | | | | | | |
| 6.1 | 5.6 | 6.7 | Sales/Working Capital | 7.2 | 6.2 | 18.1 | 4.9 | | |
| 17.7 | 13.2 | 21.9 | | UND | 11.4 | 71.9 | 9.8 | | |
| -28.5 | -74.8 | -96.4 | | -14.2 | -201.7 | -47.4 | 124.2 | | |
| 19.3 | 18.5 | 10.9 | EBIT/Interest | 7.9 | 28.0 | 4.2 | | | |
| (67) 3.0 | (73) 4.4 | (76) 3.3 | | (19) 1.3 | (27) 5.0 | (13) 2.0 | | | |
| .4 | 1.4 | -1.7 | | -4.5 | -2.0 | -8.4 | | | |
| | | | Net Profit + Depr., Dep., Amort./Cur. Mat. L/T/D | | | | | | |
| .2 | .2 | .1 | Fixed/Worth | .1 | .1 | .4 | .2 | | |
| 1.3 | .7 | .7 | | 1.2 | .6 | 1.2 | .5 | | |
| -2.1 | 3.8 | UND | | -.5 | -.9 | -6.4 | 1.2 | | |
| .7 | .5 | .5 | Debt/Worth | .6 | .5 | .9 | .1 | | |
| 2.5 | 1.6 | 2.3 | | 4.2 | 2.4 | 4.5 | .9 | | |
| -10.9 | 10.3 | -19.0 | | -2.7 | -4.1 | -11.5 | 2.3 | | |
| 61.2 | 70.8 | 66.1 | % Profit Before Taxes/Tangible Net Worth | 126.7 | 62.4 | | 60.6 | | |
| (61) 22.3 | (74) 25.7 | (79) 15.7 | | (24) 18.5 | (25) 17.6 | | 38.1 | | |
| -2.2 | 7.7 | -2.6 | | -21.0 | 4.5 | | 15.7 | | |
| 29.3 | 29.4 | 24.2 | % Profit Before Taxes/Total Assets | 43.7 | 21.0 | 11.9 | 37.7 | | |
| 8.3 | 9.3 | 7.1 | | 7.2 | 9.2 | 2.5 | 14.9 | | |
| -2.0 | 1.9 | -4.6 | | -10.3 | -3.9 | -11.7 | 5.7 | | |
| 59.2 | 59.0 | 82.3 | Sales/Net Fixed Assets | UND | 164.5 | 35.4 | 44.7 | | |
| 17.1 | 19.3 | 24.0 | | 25.2 | 45.9 | 25.7 | 15.0 | | |
| 5.8 | 6.1 | 6.4 | | 4.5 | 8.2 | 7.4 | 7.7 | | |
| 5.3 | 4.5 | 6.1 | Sales/Total Assets | 7.9 | 5.5 | 5.6 | 8.1 | | |
| 2.8 | 2.7 | 3.6 | | 4.0 | 3.9 | 4.1 | 3.5 | | |
| 1.8 | 1.8 | 1.7 | | 1.1 | 1.6 | 2.5 | 2.6 | | |
| .8 | .5 | .8 | % Depr., Dep., Amort./Sales | 1.9 | .3 | .7 | | | |
| (59) 1.7 | (65) 1.2 | (68) 2.1 | | (19) 3.9 | (18) .8 | (10) 1.7 | | | |
| 4.5 | 3.5 | 4.4 | | 16.4 | 4.4 | 2.9 | | | |
| 2.8 | 2.7 | 4.9 | % Officers', Directors' Owners' Comp/Sales | 6.6 | 4.0 | | | | |
| (47) 5.1 | (48) 6.1 | (53) 7.7 | | (20) 9.6 | (18) 7.0 | | | | |
| 9.2 | 9.3 | 12.4 | | 16.2 | 13.0 | | | | |
| 834639M | 1583453M | 1124164M | Net Sales ($) | 14988M | 62436M | 51746M | 73212M | 149477M | 772305M |
| 349237M | 294281M | 532508M | Total Assets ($) | 12492M | 133212M | 15013M | 19011M | 80223M | 272557M |

M = $ thousand    MM = $ million
See Pages 9 through 22 for Explanation of Ratios and Data

## Current Data Sorted by Assets         Comparative Historical Data

| | | | | | | Type of Statement | | |
|---|---|---|---|---|---|---|---|---|
| | 2 | 1 | 1 | 1 | 1 | Unqualified | 7 | 8 |
| | 1 | 1 | 1 | | | Reviewed | 2 | 4 |
| 14 | 9 | 4 | | | | Compiled | 15 | 18 |
| 75 | 26 | 7 | | 1 | 1 | Tax Returns | 61 | 106 |
| 51 | 24 | 14 | 2 | 4 | 1 | Other | 60 | 67 |
| | 23 (4/1-9/30/11) | | 219 (10/1/11-3/31/12) | | | | 4/1/07-3/31/08 | 4/1/08-3/31/09 |
| 0-500M | 500M-2MM | 2-10MM | 10-50MM | 50-100MM | 100-250MM | | ALL | ALL |
| 140 | 62 | 27 | 4 | 6 | 3 | NUMBER OF STATEMENTS | 145 | 203 |
| % | % | % | % | % | % | ASSETS | % | % |
| 24.3 | 23.5 | 13.1 | | | | Cash & Equivalents | 17.8 | 17.4 |
| 1.4 | 4.8 | 8.8 | | | | Trade Receivables (net) | 1.9 | 3.4 |
| 12.7 | 6.8 | 9.0 | | | | Inventory | 13.9 | 12.2 |
| .7 | 1.9 | 1.6 | | | | All Other Current | 2.3 | 2.4 |
| 39.1 | 37.0 | 32.5 | | | | Total Current | 35.9 | 35.5 |
| 46.7 | 48.1 | 40.0 | | | | Fixed Assets (net) | 46.7 | 48.3 |
| 5.4 | 5.2 | 8.3 | | | | Intangibles (net) | 8.3 | 5.9 |
| 8.8 | 9.7 | 19.2 | | | | All Other Non-Current | 9.0 | 10.3 |
| 100.0 | 100.0 | 100.0 | | | | Total | 100.0 | 100.0 |
| | | | | | | LIABILITIES | | |
| 14.6 | 7.7 | 2.7 | | | | Notes Payable-Short Term | 10.7 | 13.7 |
| 3.4 | 1.8 | 3.1 | | | | Cur. Mat.-L.T.D. | 3.2 | 4.5 |
| 4.7 | 7.5 | 7.2 | | | | Trade Payables | 6.6 | 7.0 |
| .1 | .0 | .2 | | | | Income Taxes Payable | .2 | .1 |
| 27.6 | 15.7 | 19.4 | | | | All Other Current | 21.5 | 24.2 |
| 50.3 | 32.8 | 32.6 | | | | Total Current | 42.3 | 49.4 |
| 32.7 | 24.3 | 25.9 | | | | Long-Term Debt | 30.3 | 37.2 |
| .0 | .0 | .0 | | | | Deferred Taxes | .1 | .0 |
| 25.1 | 7.9 | 3.8 | | | | All Other Non-Current | 14.0 | 14.8 |
| -8.1 | 35.0 | 37.6 | | | | Net Worth | 13.4 | -1.4 |
| 100.0 | 100.0 | 100.0 | | | | Total Liabilties & Net Worth | 100.0 | 100.0 |
| | | | | | | INCOME DATA | | |
| 100.0 | 100.0 | 100.0 | | | | Net Sales | 100.0 | 100.0 |
| | | | | | | Gross Profit | | |
| 93.5 | 91.3 | 87.4 | | | | Operating Expenses | 94.8 | 96.0 |
| 6.5 | 8.7 | 12.6 | | | | Operating Profit | 5.2 | 4.0 |
| 1.8 | 1.5 | 3.9 | | | | All Other Expenses (net) | 1.3 | 2.1 |
| 4.7 | 7.2 | 8.7 | | | | Profit Before Taxes | 3.9 | 1.9 |
| | | | | | | RATIOS | | |
| 2.8 | 2.7 | 1.8 | | | | | 2.1 | 1.7 |
| 1.0 | 1.3 | .9 | | | | Current | 1.0 | .8 |
| .4 | .5 | .4 | | | | | .5 | .3 |
| 1.8 | 2.1 | .8 | | | | | 1.2 | 1.0 |
| .6 | .9 | .6 | | | | Quick (144) | .5 | .4 |
| .2 | .2 | .2 | | | | | .2 | .1 |
| 0 UND | 0 UND | 0 UND | | | | | 0 UND | 0 UND |
| 0 UND | 0 UND | 0 UND | | | | Sales/Receivables | 0 UND | 0 UND |
| 0 UND | 1 333.1 | 11 33.6 | | | | | 0 999.8 | 0 UND |
| | | | | | | Cost of Sales/Inventory | | |
| | | | | | | Cost of Sales/Payables | | |
| 25.6 | 11.4 | 22.5 | | | | | 22.8 | 32.3 |
| UND | 47.0 | -56.9 | | | | Sales/Working Capital | UND | -70.9 |
| -15.7 | -22.0 | -9.2 | | | | | -16.1 | -10.6 |
| 9.9 | 40.5 | 45.6 | | | | | 11.3 | 6.1 |
| (78) 2.8 | (50) 5.7 | (23) 18.0 | | | | EBIT/Interest (107) | 3.7 (153) | 1.6 |
| -.1 | 1.9 | 6.3 | | | | | .8 | -.3 |
| | | | | | | Net Profit + Depr., Dep., Amort./Cur. Mat. L/T/D | | |
| .7 | .5 | .3 | | | | | .6 | .8 |
| 5.3 | 1.3 | 1.3 | | | | Fixed/Worth | 2.2 | 5.3 |
| -1.3 | NM | 4.3 | | | | | -4.1 | -2.1 |
| .8 | .8 | .8 | | | | | .8 | 1.6 |
| 9.3 | 1.5 | 1.8 | | | | Debt/Worth | 3.2 | 8.9 |
| -3.5 | NM | 4.5 | | | | | -6.4 | -3.8 |
| 131.3 | 79.1 | 121.7 | | | | | 116.1 | 95.7 |
| (80) 68.4 | (47) 35.2 | (24) 64.2 | | | | % Profit Before Taxes/Tangible Net Worth (98) | 47.8 (121) | 46.6 |
| 14.1 | 7.0 | 17.0 | | | | | 16.3 | 6.7 |
| 48.7 | 22.7 | 34.1 | | | | | 28.2 | 23.2 |
| 15.8 | 11.4 | 16.3 | | | | % Profit Before Taxes/Total Assets | 10.5 | 5.1 |
| -.9 | 3.7 | 3.7 | | | | | .0 | -5.3 |
| 49.2 | 17.7 | 20.6 | | | | | 23.7 | 22.4 |
| 12.7 | 8.4 | 8.4 | | | | Sales/Net Fixed Assets | 9.9 | 9.3 |
| 4.5 | 1.9 | 4.6 | | | | | 4.6 | 3.8 |
| 9.6 | 4.6 | 3.8 | | | | | 6.8 | 6.8 |
| 5.4 | 2.3 | 2.9 | | | | Sales/Total Assets | 4.0 | 3.9 |
| 2.5 | 1.3 | 1.6 | | | | | 1.9 | 2.2 |
| .9 | .9 | 1.1 | | | | | 1.1 | .9 |
| (88) 2.0 | (42) 1.6 | (23) 1.9 | | | | % Depr., Dep., Amort./Sales (111) | 2.2 (152) | 2.1 |
| 4.2 | 4.0 | 3.0 | | | | | 3.6 | 3.8 |
| 2.8 | 2.8 | | | | | | 2.7 | 3.8 |
| (61) 7.8 | (28) 3.8 | | | | | % Officers', Directors' Owners' Comp/Sales (69) | 4.6 (98) | 6.0 |
| 14.5 | 7.7 | | | | | | 10.0 | 10.5 |
| 116884M | 231002M | 296213M | 101914M | 1257511M | 1590227M | Net Sales ($) | 2112820M | 1604397M |
| 23432M | 65212M | 103294M | 66110M | 465109M | 439639M | Total Assets ($) | 816099M | 651221M |

M = $ thousand     MM = $ million
See Pages 9 through 22 for Explanation of Ratios and Data

## Comparative Historical Data | Current Data Sorted by Sales

© RMA 2012    M = $ thousand    MM = $ million
See Pages 9 through 22 for Explanation of Ratios and Data

| | | | Type of Statement | | | | | | |
|---|---|---|---|---|---|---|---|---|---|
| 5 | 11 | 6 | Unqualified | | | 1 | 1 | 1 | 3 |
| 5 | 6 | 3 | Reviewed | | | | | 3 | |
| 24 | 32 | 27 | Compiled | 10 | 8 | 4 | 1 | 4 | |
| 102 | 89 | 110 | Tax Returns | 62 | 28 | 9 | 5 | 4 | 2 |
| 61 | 51 | 96 | Other | 41 | 24 | 6 | 10 | 9 | 6 |
| 4/1/09-3/31/10 ALL | 4/1/10-3/31/11 ALL | 4/1/11-3/31/12 ALL | | 23 (4/1-9/30/11) | | | 219 (10/1/11-3/31/12) | | |
| | | | | 0-1MM | 1-3MM | 3-5MM | 5-10MM | 10-25MM | 25MM & OVER |
| 197 | 189 | 242 | **NUMBER OF STATEMENTS** | 113 | 60 | 20 | 17 | 21 | 11 |
| % | % | % | **ASSETS** | % | % | % | % | % | % |
| 18.3 | 21.3 | 22.0 | Cash & Equivalents | 20.6 | 27.6 | 22.6 | 17.5 | 23.3 | 9.9 |
| 3.7 | 4.0 | 3.2 | Trade Receivables (net) | 1.2 | 1.8 | 9.5 | 7.6 | 8.4 | 2.8 |
| 10.4 | 9.6 | 10.6 | Inventory | 11.8 | 9.5 | 9.3 | 7.1 | 12.9 | 7.4 |
| 2.5 | 2.8 | 1.3 | All Other Current | .4 | 1.2 | .6 | 5.3 | 1.7 | 4.9 |
| 34.9 | 37.6 | 37.1 | Total Current | 34.0 | 40.0 | 42.0 | 37.5 | 46.4 | 25.1 |
| 46.5 | 43.8 | 46.2 | Fixed Assets (net) | 51.7 | 43.7 | 36.7 | 45.0 | 34.8 | 44.0 |
| 10.3 | 7.8 | 6.5 | Intangibles (net) | 4.9 | 6.7 | 8.5 | 3.0 | 6.7 | 22.7 |
| 8.3 | 10.8 | 10.3 | All Other Non-Current | 9.5 | 9.6 | 12.8 | 14.5 | 12.1 | 8.3 |
| 100.0 | 100.0 | 100.0 | Total | 100.0 | 100.0 | 100.0 | 100.0 | 100.0 | 100.0 |
| | | | **LIABILITIES** | | | | | | |
| 8.8 | 8.2 | 10.9 | Notes Payable-Short Term | 13.4 | 12.2 | 6.9 | 8.9 | 2.6 | 3.4 |
| 3.9 | 4.3 | 3.0 | Cur. Mat.-L.T.D. | 2.1 | 4.3 | 4.5 | 2.0 | 2.7 | 3.9 |
| 7.5 | 6.4 | 5.9 | Trade Payables | 3.3 | 5.7 | 9.4 | 14.1 | 9.0 | 9.6 |
| .1 | .1 | .1 | Income Taxes Payable | .0 | .0 | .5 | .1 | .0 | .2 |
| 25.6 | 24.9 | 22.7 | All Other Current | 25.9 | 20.0 | 22.5 | 23.8 | 17.9 | 11.7 |
| 45.9 | 43.9 | 42.5 | Total Current | 44.8 | 42.3 | 43.7 | 49.0 | 32.2 | 28.8 |
| 30.8 | 32.8 | 29.6 | Long-Term Debt | 38.5 | 23.0 | 25.2 | 18.2 | 15.5 | 26.7 |
| .0 | .0 | .0 | Deferred Taxes | .0 | .0 | .0 | .0 | .0 | .8 |
| 15.2 | 16.4 | 18.3 | All Other Non-Current | 25.6 | 14.7 | 10.4 | 1.5 | 5.0 | 27.5 |
| 8.1 | 6.9 | 9.5 | Net Worth | -9.0 | 20.0 | 20.7 | 31.3 | 47.3 | 16.2 |
| 100.0 | 100.0 | 100.0 | Total Liabilties & Net Worth | 100.0 | 100.0 | 100.0 | 100.0 | 100.0 | 100.0 |
| | | | **INCOME DATA** | | | | | | |
| 100.0 | 100.0 | 100.0 | Net Sales | 100.0 | 100.0 | 100.0 | 100.0 | 100.0 | 100.0 |
| | | | Gross Profit | | | | | | |
| 92.7 | 91.6 | 92.3 | Operating Expenses | 91.1 | 93.8 | 92.8 | 92.5 | 92.9 | 94.2 |
| 7.3 | 8.4 | 7.7 | Operating Profit | 8.9 | 6.2 | 7.2 | 7.5 | 7.1 | 5.8 |
| 2.0 | 2.9 | 1.9 | All Other Expenses (net) | 3.4 | .6 | .6 | .3 | .5 | 1.3 |
| 5.3 | 5.5 | 5.8 | Profit Before Taxes | 5.5 | 5.6 | 6.6 | 7.2 | 6.6 | 4.5 |
| | | | **RATIOS** | | | | | | |
| 2.0 | 2.6 | 2.4 | Current | 3.4 | 2.5 | 1.8 | 1.3 | 2.4 | 1.9 |
| .9 | 1.1 | 1.0 | | 1.0 | 1.0 | 1.0 | .9 | 1.9 | .6 |
| .3 | .4 | .4 | | .4 | .5 | .3 | .5 | .7 | .4 |
| 1.1 | 1.8 | 1.7 | Quick | 2.0 | 1.9 | 1.4 | .9 | 2.0 | .9 |
| (196) .4 | .7 | .6 | | .6 | .7 | .7 | .6 | .8 | .3 |
| .1 | .2 | .2 | | .2 | .3 | .2 | .1 | .4 | .2 |
| 0 UND | 0 UND | 0 UND | Sales/Receivables | 0 UND | 0 UND | 0 UND | 0 UND | 0 UND | 0 UND |
| 0 UND | 0 UND | 0 UND | | 0 UND | 0 UND | 0 UND | 0 UND | 1 651.4 | 4 87.6 |
| 0 UND | 1 300.5 | 0 UND | | 0 UND | 0 UND | 16 23.3 | 2 174.9 | 13 28.6 | 14 25.4 |
| | | | Cost of Sales/Inventory | | | | | | |
| | | | Cost of Sales/Payables | | | | | | |
| 21.6 | 18.2 | 19.0 | Sales/Working Capital | 23.8 | 16.2 | 9.1 | 33.0 | 14.3 | 33.6 |
| -195.5 | 225.0 | UND | | UND | NM | -425.6 | -107.9 | 35.6 | -19.3 |
| -14.5 | -14.4 | -14.6 | | -11.3 | -28.2 | -11.6 | -22.5 | -38.6 | -11.9 |
| 12.1 | 13.6 | 19.9 | EBIT/Interest | 6.0 | 21.3 | 58.7 | 39.5 | 91.8 | 21.1 |
| (147) 4.3 | (145) 3.9 | (163) 5.2 | | (61) 2.0 | (40) 5.6 | (18) 8.2 | (13) 21.5 | 19.9 | (10) 2.9 |
| 1.3 | .9 | 1.2 | | -.5 | 1.6 | 3.0 | 5.2 | 7.5 | -.5 |
| | 14.9 | 9.2 | Net Profit + Depr., Dep., Amort./Cur. Mat. L/T/D | | | | | | |
| | (13) 4.9 | (10) 3.6 | | | | | | | |
| | 2.8 | 2.0 | | | | | | | |
| .6 | .5 | .6 | Fixed/Worth | .8 | .3 | .5 | .5 | .3 | .6 |
| 3.1 | 3.2 | 2.0 | | 7.4 | 1.6 | 1.2 | 1.4 | .9 | 16.0 |
| -1.7 | -2.0 | -2.9 | | -1.3 | -3.5 | -47.2 | NM | 1.8 | -.8 |
| .8 | .7 | .8 | Debt/Worth | .8 | .4 | .9 | .9 | .5 | 1.0 |
| 5.0 | 5.2 | 3.7 | | 9.2 | 1.7 | 2.5 | 1.5 | 1.0 | 22.4 |
| -3.6 | -3.8 | -5.6 | | -3.5 | -6.9 | -68.0 | NM | 3.4 | -2.1 |
| 92.7 | 98.8 | 102.1 | % Profit Before Taxes/Tangible Net Worth | 97.5 | 110.7 | 116.6 | 97.1 | 154.7 | |
| (123) 50.4 | (112) 41.0 | (159) 53.5 | | (65) 35.6 | (41) 61.3 | (14) 55.3 | (13) 43.7 | (20) 65.4 | |
| 14.0 | 13.7 | 13.6 | | 5.4 | 17.6 | 26.8 | 13.3 | 17.4 | |
| 30.1 | 32.2 | 34.4 | % Profit Before Taxes/Total Assets | 43.3 | 32.7 | 30.2 | 38.9 | 49.3 | 29.5 |
| 11.3 | 9.4 | 13.6 | | 7.5 | 15.9 | 15.2 | 16.4 | 21.3 | 3.1 |
| .5 | .0 | 1.4 | | -3.3 | 3.7 | 8.2 | 6.9 | 6.3 | -4.4 |
| 25.3 | 24.9 | 28.7 | Sales/Net Fixed Assets | 32.1 | 58.8 | 21.9 | 22.1 | 38.7 | 13.4 |
| 10.1 | 10.9 | 9.4 | | 8.0 | 12.7 | 11.1 | 10.9 | 14.0 | 6.7 |
| 4.7 | 4.1 | 3.8 | | 2.0 | 5.5 | 5.9 | 6.0 | 6.6 | 3.1 |
| 6.0 | 6.2 | 7.0 | Sales/Total Assets | 6.9 | 8.7 | 7.0 | 5.5 | 6.9 | 4.4 |
| 3.6 | 3.5 | 3.5 | | 3.4 | 4.3 | 3.5 | 4.1 | 4.8 | 2.0 |
| 1.7 | 1.7 | 1.7 | | 1.2 | 2.3 | 2.1 | 2.8 | 3.1 | 1.2 |
| 1.0 | 1.1 | 1.0 | % Depr., Dep., Amort./Sales | 1.4 | .9 | .7 | .8 | 1.1 | |
| (158) 1.8 | (142) 2.4 | (160) 1.9 | | (71) 3.1 | (35) 1.6 | (18) 1.0 | (13) .9 | (18) 1.9 | |
| 3.5 | 4.1 | 4.0 | | 6.7 | 3.1 | 1.9 | 2.6 | 2.6 | |
| 2.3 | 2.9 | 2.8 | % Officers', Directors' Owners' Comp/Sales | 4.6 | 2.5 | | | | |
| (86) 4.6 | (89) 6.2 | (99) 5.6 | | (45) 8.9 | (27) 4.2 | | | | |
| 11.2 | 10.1 | 10.0 | | 17.8 | 8.6 | | | | |
| 2788639M | 3440500M | 3593751M | Net Sales ($) | 47470M | 98711M | 79628M | 120826M | 342396M | 2904720M |
| 711407M | 1053557M | 1162796M | Total Assets ($) | 30572M | 28178M | 27757M | 35384M | 108069M | 932836M |

## Current Data Sorted by Assets     Comparative Historical Data

| | | | | | | Type of Statement | | |
|---|---|---|---|---|---|---|---|---|
| 1 | | | 2 | | 1 | Unqualified | 4 | 3 |
| | 1 | | | | | Reviewed | 1 | |
| 1 | | | | | | Compiled | 2 | 2 |
| 13 | 5 | 1 | 3 | | | Tax Returns | 6 | 14 |
| 10 | 6 | 3 | 3 | 1 | 2 | Other | 4 | 5 |
| | 4 (4/1-9/30/11) | | 46 (10/1/11-3/31/12) | | | | 4/1/07- 3/31/08 | 4/1/08- 3/31/09 |
| 0-500M | 500M-2MM | 2-10MM | 10-50MM | 50-100MM | 100-250MM | | ALL | ALL |
| 25 | 12 | 4 | 5 | 1 | 3 | NUMBER OF STATEMENTS | 17 | 24 |
| % | % | % | % | % | % | ASSETS | % | % |
| 21.7 | 17.8 | | | | | Cash & Equivalents | 19.7 | 14.0 |
| .3 | .1 | | | | | Trade Receivables (net) | 11.2 | 4.6 |
| 3.0 | 2.8 | | | | | Inventory | 10.5 | 10.7 |
| 3.1 | 3.1 | | | | | All Other Current | 2.6 | 6.0 |
| 28.0 | 23.8 | | | | | Total Current | 44.0 | 35.4 |
| 48.2 | 62.4 | | | | | Fixed Assets (net) | 46.6 | 54.2 |
| 15.7 | 8.9 | | | | | Intangibles (net) | 4.9 | 7.4 |
| 8.1 | 4.9 | | | | | All Other Non-Current | 4.5 | 3.0 |
| 100.0 | 100.0 | | | | | Total | 100.0 | 100.0 |
| | | | | | | LIABILITIES | | |
| 4.7 | 10.6 | | | | | Notes Payable-Short Term | 49.3 | 15.6 |
| 2.8 | 6.0 | | | | | Cur. Mat.-L.T.D. | 4.5 | 6.9 |
| 6.6 | 6.2 | | | | | Trade Payables | 6.7 | 6.8 |
| .0 | .0 | | | | | Income Taxes Payable | .0 | .0 |
| 25.0 | 8.4 | | | | | All Other Current | 25.2 | 28.4 |
| 39.2 | 31.1 | | | | | Total Current | 85.7 | 57.7 |
| 34.1 | 41.4 | | | | | Long-Term Debt | 37.6 | 32.4 |
| .0 | .0 | | | | | Deferred Taxes | .1 | .0 |
| 23.9 | 21.0 | | | | | All Other Non-Current | 25.7 | 13.6 |
| 2.8 | 6.5 | | | | | Net Worth | -49.1 | -3.7 |
| 100.0 | 100.0 | | | | | Total Liabilities & Net Worth | 100.0 | 100.0 |
| | | | | | | INCOME DATA | | |
| 100.0 | 100.0 | | | | | Net Sales | 100.0 | 100.0 |
| | | | | | | Gross Profit | | |
| 98.3 | 92.6 | | | | | Operating Expenses | 96.6 | 87.7 |
| 1.7 | 7.4 | | | | | Operating Profit | 3.4 | 12.3 |
| .7 | 2.4 | | | | | All Other Expenses (net) | 1.6 | 3.9 |
| 1.0 | 5.0 | | | | | Profit Before Taxes | 1.8 | 8.4 |
| | | | | | | RATIOS | | |
| 3.1 | 4.0 | | | | | | 1.6 | 2.8 |
| 1.1 | .8 | | | | | Current | .9 | .5 |
| .3 | .3 | | | | | | .5 | .2 |
| 2.5 | 3.2 | | | | | | 1.2 | 1.4 |
| .8 | .5 | | | | | Quick | .5 | .3 |
| .3 | .2 | | | | | | .1 | .1 |
| 0 UND | 0 UND | | | | | | 0 UND | 0 UND |
| 0 UND | 0 UND | | | | | Sales/Receivables | 0 UND | 0 UND |
| 0 UND | 0 UND | | | | | | 7 49.3 | 15 24.3 |
| | | | | | | Cost of Sales/Inventory | | |
| | | | | | | Cost of Sales/Payables | | |
| 14.4 | 17.6 | | | | | | 9.0 | 26.2 |
| 386.5 | NM | | | | | Sales/Working Capital | -57.3 | -13.9 |
| -8.6 | -9.8 | | | | | | -6.1 | -3.9 |
| 11.1 | 8.8 | | | | | | 10.7 | 15.3 |
| (13) 4.9 | 3.7 | | | | | EBIT/Interest | (16) 3.3 | (20) 4.1 |
| -10.0 | 1.4 | | | | | | -3.2 | .2 |
| | | | | | | Net Profit + Depr., Dep., Amort./Cur. Mat. L/T/D | | |
| .9 | 2.4 | | | | | | .4 | .9 |
| 2.6 | 18.1 | | | | | Fixed/Worth | 1.9 | UND |
| -.9 | -2.1 | | | | | | -3.6 | -1.2 |
| .9 | 2.7 | | | | | | .8 | 1.2 |
| 3.6 | 26.7 | | | | | Debt/Worth | 2.5 | UND |
| -2.2 | -4.4 | | | | | | -2.4 | -3.5 |
| 120.3 | | | | | | % Profit Before Taxes/Tangible Net Worth | 131.8 | 93.6 |
| (14) 28.0 | | | | | | | (10) 44.1 | (13) 21.5 |
| -42.6 | | | | | | | 7.2 | -5.4 |
| 42.9 | 32.0 | | | | | % Profit Before Taxes/Total Assets | 29.9 | 30.3 |
| 7.4 | 11.9 | | | | | | 11.5 | 10.2 |
| -15.3 | 2.5 | | | | | | -21.8 | -3.7 |
| 19.5 | 12.8 | | | | | | 20.9 | 14.7 |
| 7.3 | 5.4 | | | | | Sales/Net Fixed Assets | 9.0 | 5.1 |
| 2.2 | 1.5 | | | | | | 2.8 | 1.5 |
| 4.9 | 4.8 | | | | | | 7.0 | 3.9 |
| 2.9 | 2.7 | | | | | Sales/Total Assets | 2.2 | 2.4 |
| 1.3 | 1.2 | | | | | | 1.5 | .9 |
| 1.3 | 1.4 | | | | | | 2.0 | 1.6 |
| (15) 3.3 | (10) 3.5 | | | | | % Depr., Dep., Amort./Sales | (14) 4.6 | (18) 4.6 |
| 22.0 | 9.0 | | | | | | 8.7 | 10.4 |
| 4.9 | | | | | | % Officers', Directors' Owners' Comp/Sales | | |
| (12) 9.7 | | | | | | | | |
| 13.8 | | | | | | | | |
| 16673M | 45407M | 29303M | 169864M | 98645M | 253789M | Net Sales ($) | 79416M | 84282M |
| 5602M | 12891M | 15708M | 106241M | 82985M | 481249M | Total Assets ($) | 55632M | 35752M |

M = $ thousand     MM = $ million
See Pages 9 through 22 for Explanation of Ratios and Data

## Comparative Historical Data | Current Data Sorted by Sales

| Type of Statement | 4/1/09-3/31/10 ALL | 4/1/10-3/31/11 ALL | 4/1/11-3/31/12 ALL | 0-1MM | 1-3MM | 3-5MM | 5-10MM | 10-25MM | 25MM & OVER |
|---|---|---|---|---|---|---|---|---|---|
| Unqualified | 1 | 1 | 4 | | 1 | | | 1 | 2 |
| Reviewed | 3 | 2 | 1 | 1 | | | | | |
| Compiled | 4 | 1 | 1 | 1 | | | | | |
| Tax Returns | 8 | 19 | 19 | 12 | 5 | 1 | 2 | 1 | 4 |
| Other | 10 | 20 | 25 | 8 | | | 1 | 4 | 4 |
| | | | | 4 (4/1-9/30/11) | | 46 (10/1/11-3/31/12) | | | |
| **NUMBER OF STATEMENTS** | 26 | 43 | 50 | 22 | 12 | 1 | 3 | 6 | 6 |
| | % | % | % | % | % | % | % | % | % |
| **ASSETS** | | | | | | | | | |
| Cash & Equivalents | 15.5 | 18.9 | 18.4 | 16.8 | 24.8 | | | | |
| Trade Receivables (net) | 4.0 | 7.3 | .8 | .2 | .2 | | | | |
| Inventory | 14.3 | 6.5 | 3.3 | 2.1 | 3.6 | | | | |
| All Other Current | 1.5 | 2.0 | 2.8 | 3.3 | .5 | | | | |
| Total Current | 35.2 | 34.7 | 25.3 | 22.4 | 29.1 | | | | |
| Fixed Assets (net) | 49.4 | 41.2 | 48.2 | 54.7 | 54.4 | | | | |
| Intangibles (net) | 10.5 | 13.4 | 19.0 | 15.6 | 9.4 | | | | |
| All Other Non-Current | 4.9 | 10.7 | 7.6 | 7.3 | 7.1 | | | | |
| Total | 100.0 | 100.0 | 100.0 | 100.0 | 100.0 | | | | |
| **LIABILITIES** | | | | | | | | | |
| Notes Payable-Short Term | 17.4 | 11.2 | 5.8 | 5.2 | 3.3 | | | | |
| Cur. Mat.-L.T.D. | 2.9 | 4.5 | 3.3 | 2.2 | 5.2 | | | | |
| Trade Payables | 6.4 | 3.9 | 6.2 | 2.4 | 10.0 | | | | |
| Income Taxes Payable | .0 | .0 | .0 | .0 | .0 | | | | |
| All Other Current | 18.2 | 17.8 | 17.1 | 22.3 | 13.5 | | | | |
| Total Current | 45.0 | 37.4 | 32.5 | 32.1 | 32.0 | | | | |
| Long-Term Debt | 31.2 | 31.3 | 34.3 | 36.9 | 44.3 | | | | |
| Deferred Taxes | .0 | .1 | .0 | .0 | .0 | | | | |
| All Other Non-Current | 20.1 | 14.6 | 20.6 | 24.8 | 26.5 | | | | |
| Net Worth | 3.7 | 16.6 | 12.6 | 6.3 | -2.8 | | | | |
| Total Liabilities & Net Worth | 100.0 | 100.0 | 100.0 | 100.0 | 100.0 | | | | |
| **INCOME DATA** | | | | | | | | | |
| Net Sales | 100.0 | 100.0 | 100.0 | 100.0 | 100.0 | | | | |
| Gross Profit | | | | | | | | | |
| Operating Expenses | 92.9 | 91.5 | 94.1 | 102.8 | 84.7 | | | | |
| Operating Profit | 7.1 | 8.5 | 5.9 | -2.8 | 15.3 | | | | |
| All Other Expenses (net) | 3.8 | 4.0 | 2.2 | 1.5 | 3.2 | | | | |
| Profit Before Taxes | 3.3 | 4.5 | 3.7 | -4.3 | 12.1 | | | | |
| **RATIOS** | | | | | | | | | |
| Current | 3.9 | 3.7 | 2.3 | 3.4 | 2.3 | | | | |
| | 1.5 | 1.2 | 1.1 | 1.1 | 1.4 | | | | |
| | .3 | .4 | .4 | .3 | .3 | | | | |
| Quick | 2.6 | 3.2 | 1.9 | 3.1 | 2.0 | | | | |
| | .6 | .9 | .7 | .8 | 1.1 | | | | |
| | .1 | .1 | .2 | .3 | .2 | | | | |
| Sales/Receivables | 0 UND | 0 UND | 0 UND | 0 UND | 0 UND | | | | |
| | 0 UND | 0 UND | 0 UND | 0 UND | 0 UND | | | | |
| | 6 57.7 | 10 35.5 | 0 999.8 | 0 UND | 0 UND | | | | |
| Cost of Sales/Inventory | | | | | | | | | |
| Cost of Sales/Payables | | | | | | | | | |
| Sales/Working Capital | 7.7 | 11.4 | 12.0 | 10.6 | 18.3 | | | | |
| | 47.1 | 64.8 | 504.3 | 504.3 | 215.7 | | | | |
| | -6.4 | -8.0 | -10.6 | -4.2 | -14.8 | | | | |
| EBIT/Interest | 6.2 | 12.8 | 11.0 | 4.7 | | | | | |
| | (22) 2.4 | (35) 3.7 | (35) 4.9 | (12) -.1 | | | | | |
| | .1 | .9 | 1.6 | -10.5 | | | | | |
| Net Profit + Depr., Dep., Amort./Cur. Mat. L/T/D | | | | | | | | | |
| Fixed/Worth | .5 | .6 | 1.3 | 1.3 | 1.0 | | | | |
| | 10.9 | 1.4 | 5.8 | 4.6 | 6.1 | | | | |
| | -1.4 | -1.8 | -1.1 | -1.0 | -1.2 | | | | |
| Debt/Worth | .8 | .7 | 1.6 | 1.6 | .9 | | | | |
| | 24.6 | 6.9 | 12.0 | 11.5 | 9.6 | | | | |
| | -2.6 | -6.0 | -4.1 | -2.2 | -3.5 | | | | |
| % Profit Before Taxes/Tangible Net Worth | 103.7 | 139.6 | 184.1 | 133.0 | | | | | |
| | (14) 42.0 | (28) 40.7 | (29) 74.0 | (13) 56.1 | | | | | |
| | 2.4 | -.2 | .9 | -55.5 | | | | | |
| % Profit Before Taxes/Total Assets | 18.4 | 42.2 | 32.4 | 14.4 | 103.8 | | | | |
| | 7.3 | 13.2 | 8.1 | .2 | 39.0 | | | | |
| | -1.6 | -.1 | -1.8 | -17.7 | 8.9 | | | | |
| Sales/Net Fixed Assets | 16.4 | 27.2 | 17.8 | 8.1 | 19.7 | | | | |
| | 9.8 | 7.6 | 5.9 | 3.2 | 7.4 | | | | |
| | 2.8 | 2.7 | 2.3 | 1.5 | 2.9 | | | | |
| Sales/Total Assets | 4.8 | 3.9 | 4.0 | 3.4 | 6.7 | | | | |
| | 2.7 | 2.2 | 2.1 | 1.6 | 3.6 | | | | |
| | 1.2 | 1.2 | 1.0 | .9 | 2.2 | | | | |
| % Depr., Dep., Amort./Sales | 2.4 | 2.1 | 1.3 | 3.2 | .9 | | | | |
| | (21) 3.8 | (32) 4.6 | (32) 3.5 | (13) 10.8 | (10) 1.4 | | | | |
| | 9.3 | 10.4 | 12.0 | 27.6 | 9.0 | | | | |
| % Officers', Directors' Owners' Comp/Sales | 2.5 | 1.4 | 3.2 | 4.4 | | | | | |
| | (13) 4.7 | (11) 7.2 | (19) 5.7 | (10) 9.7 | | | | | |
| | 19.8 | 11.2 | 12.2 | 14.3 | | | | | |
| Net Sales ($) | 1049139M | 425261M | 613681M | 8580M | 20496M | 3501M | 16084M | 81462M | 483558M |
| Total Assets ($) | 568420M | 505591M | 704676M | 7097M | 9539M | 2037M | 3735M | 59319M | 622949M |

M = $ thousand    MM = $ million
See Pages 9 through 22 for Explanation of Ratios and Data

## Current Data Sorted by Assets     Comparative Historical Data

| 0-500M | 500M-2MM | 2-10MM | 10-50MM | 50-100MM | 100-250MM | Type of Statement | 4/1/07-3/31/08 ALL | 4/1/08-3/31/09 ALL |
|---|---|---|---|---|---|---|---|---|
| 3 | 1 | 2 | 2 | 3 | 1 | Unqualified | 5 | 11 |
| 2 | 7 | 13 | 2 | | | Reviewed | 26 | 32 |
| 15 | 34 | 20 | 3 | | | Compiled | 77 | 85 |
| 67 | 91 | 25 | | 4 | | Tax Returns | 123 | 133 |
| 21 | 42 | 22 | 6 | 4 | 2 | Other | 74 | 81 |
| | 65 (4/1-9/30/11) | | 327 (10/1/11-3/31/12) | 4 | 2 | | | |
| 108 | 175 | 82 | 13 | 7 | 7 | **NUMBER OF STATEMENTS** | 305 | 342 |
| % | % | % | % | % | % | **ASSETS** | % | % |
| 15.1 | 12.1 | 11.5 | 9.2 | | | Cash & Equivalents | 10.7 | 11.0 |
| 18.1 | 14.9 | 8.2 | 5.6 | | | Trade Receivables (net) | 15.2 | 13.6 |
| 6.9 | 3.6 | 3.6 | 5.7 | | | Inventory | 4.9 | 5.4 |
| 3.6 | 2.0 | 2.0 | 5.5 | | | All Other Current | 2.4 | 3.4 |
| 43.7 | 32.6 | 25.3 | 26.1 | | | Total Current | 33.2 | 33.5 |
| 39.8 | 44.6 | 48.1 | 40.8 | | | Fixed Assets (net) | 41.3 | 43.6 |
| 7.5 | 10.1 | 8.5 | 4.0 | | | Intangibles (net) | 9.6 | 7.4 |
| 9.0 | 12.6 | 18.1 | 29.1 | | | All Other Non-Current | 15.9 | 15.5 |
| 100.0 | 100.0 | 100.0 | 100.0 | | | Total | 100.0 | 100.0 |
| | | | | | | **LIABILITIES** | | |
| 14.2 | 2.6 | 2.5 | 3.4 | | | Notes Payable-Short Term | 5.8 | 6.1 |
| 6.0 | 2.5 | 2.9 | 1.4 | | | Cur. Mat.-L.T.D. | 4.0 | 4.8 |
| 8.1 | 5.5 | 3.6 | .9 | | | Trade Payables | 7.3 | 6.5 |
| .4 | .0 | .3 | .2 | | | Income Taxes Payable | .2 | .2 |
| 15.9 | 9.2 | 5.7 | 4.3 | | | All Other Current | 11.4 | 10.7 |
| 44.6 | 19.8 | 15.0 | 10.3 | | | Total Current | 28.7 | 28.3 |
| 33.5 | 44.8 | 40.9 | 19.5 | | | Long-Term Debt | 39.4 | 40.4 |
| .0 | .1 | 1.6 | .0 | | | Deferred Taxes | .1 | .1 |
| 12.5 | 6.5 | 9.0 | 26.1 | | | All Other Non-Current | 12.6 | 12.3 |
| 9.3 | 28.8 | 33.5 | 44.1 | | | Net Worth | 19.1 | 19.0 |
| 100.0 | 100.0 | 100.0 | 100.0 | | | Total Liabilities & Net Worth | 100.0 | 100.0 |
| | | | | | | **INCOME DATA** | | |
| 100.0 | 100.0 | 100.0 | 100.0 | | | Net Sales | 100.0 | 100.0 |
| | | | | | | Gross Profit | | |
| 94.5 | 89.6 | 86.9 | 84.4 | | | Operating Expenses | 92.4 | 91.5 |
| 5.5 | 10.4 | 13.1 | 15.6 | | | Operating Profit | 7.6 | 8.5 |
| 1.3 | 3.3 | 6.3 | 1.3 | | | All Other Expenses (net) | 2.8 | 2.7 |
| 4.2 | 7.0 | 6.8 | 14.3 | | | Profit Before Taxes | 4.8 | 5.8 |
| | | | | | | **RATIOS** | | |
| 3.5 | 5.0 | 3.2 | 7.1 | | | | 3.3 | 3.1 |
| 1.2 | 2.1 | 1.5 | 2.1 | | | Current | 1.7 | 1.5 |
| .4 | 1.0 | .7 | .9 | | | | .8 | .7 |
| 3.0 | 4.6 | 2.5 | 3.8 | | | | 2.6 | 2.3 |
| .8 | 1.6 | 1.2 | 1.5 | | | Quick | 1.2 | 1.1 |
| .3 | .7 | .6 | .7 | | | | .5 | .5 |
| 0 UND | 13   28.4 | 18   20.8 | 16   22.9 | | | | 12   29.6 | 10   37.5 |
| 16   22.8 | 25   14.4 | 30   12.0 | 34   10.8 | | | Sales/Receivables | 30   12.2 | 26   13.9 |
| 33   11.2 | 42   8.7 | 41   9.0 | 44   8.3 | | | | 44   8.3 | 43   8.4 |
| | | | | | | Cost of Sales/Inventory | | |
| | | | | | | Cost of Sales/Payables | | |
| 9.2 | 6.1 | 5.8 | 1.7 | | | | 5.9 | 6.2 |
| 70.0 | 11.1 | 18.1 | 6.6 | | | Sales/Working Capital | 16.8 | 20.3 |
| -16.9 | -264.3 | -16.4 | NM | | | | -35.9 | -20.5 |
| 9.2 | 11.0 | 7.0 | 10.2 | | | | 6.1 | 8.5 |
| (84) 3.4 | (147) 3.3 | (73) 2.6 | (10) 7.2 | | | EBIT/Interest | (245) 2.2 | (281) 2.6 |
| .8 | 1.2 | 1.5 | 2.2 | | | | 1.0 | 1.3 |
| | 8.4 | 6.0 | | | | | 3.5 | 2.5 |
| | (13) 3.3 | (20) 1.6 | | | | Net Profit + Depr., Dep., Amort./Cur. Mat. L/T/D | (43) 1.4 | (45) 1.3 |
| | 2.0 | 1.0 | | | | | .7 | .9 |
| .4 | .5 | .9 | .5 | | | | .6 | .5 |
| 2.1 | 2.3 | 2.2 | 1.1 | | | Fixed/Worth | 1.8 | 1.8 |
| -1.2 | -22.8 | NM | 1.9 | | | | -8.7 | -5.6 |
| .4 | .6 | .8 | .7 | | | | .8 | .7 |
| 3.4 | 2.9 | 2.6 | 1.9 | | | Debt/Worth | 2.8 | 2.6 |
| -4.0 | -30.5 | NM | 4.4 | | | | -13.9 | -16.0 |
| 80.0 | 36.7 | 33.0 | 26.2 | | | | 43.7 | 43.3 |
| (70) 25.4 | (123) 21.4 | (62) 14.7 | 20.8 | | | % Profit Before Taxes/Tangible Net Worth | (214) 13.8 | (239) 15.9 |
| 2.3 | 6.1 | 4.7 | 7.2 | | | | 1.1 | 3.8 |
| 27.5 | 14.7 | 8.8 | 9.2 | | | | 13.1 | 14.4 |
| 9.1 | 5.3 | 4.2 | 4.4 | | | % Profit Before Taxes/Total Assets | 4.7 | 5.3 |
| -1.7 | 1.3 | 1.3 | 1.9 | | | | -.4 | 1.0 |
| 27.3 | 10.7 | 3.8 | 2.0 | | | | 10.8 | 10.3 |
| 12.9 | 4.5 | 2.1 | 1.3 | | | Sales/Net Fixed Assets | 5.2 | 4.5 |
| 7.1 | 1.5 | 1.2 | .8 | | | | 1.8 | 1.6 |
| 6.5 | 2.5 | 1.3 | .7 | | | | 2.7 | 2.7 |
| 3.6 | 1.5 | .9 | .4 | | | Sales/Total Assets | 1.6 | 1.6 |
| 2.5 | .8 | .5 | .2 | | | | .7 | .7 |
| 1.3 | 1.9 | 2.7 | 2.4 | | | | 1.8 | 2.0 |
| (82) 2.1 | (157) 3.2 | (77) 4.1 | 4.9 | | | % Depr., Dep., Amort./Sales | (274) 3.2 | (301) 3.3 |
| 3.8 | 6.8 | 6.6 | 5.9 | | | | 5.6 | 6.0 |
| 6.0 | 6.9 | 4.4 | | | | | 7.1 | 6.9 |
| (69) 8.4 | (117) 9.5 | (47) 8.3 | | | | % Officers', Directors' Owners' Comp/Sales | (200) 10.5 | (192) 9.5 |
| 12.6 | 15.3 | 12.6 | | | | | 14.5 | 14.0 |
| 97411M | 286740M | 316627M | 149008M | 158375M | 1746632M | Net Sales ($) | 1738157M | 1288233M |
| 24790M | 181885M | 334814M | 263203M | 495245M | 1032250M | Total Assets ($) | 1169469M | 1332939M |

© RMA 2012

M = $ thousand    MM = $ million
See Pages 9 through 22 for Explanation of Ratios and Data

## Comparative Historical Data | Current Data Sorted by Sales

| Comparative Historical Data | | | Type of Statement | Current Data Sorted by Sales | | | | | |
|---|---|---|---|---|---|---|---|---|---|
| 14 | 2 | 12 | Unqualified | 3 | 2 | 1 | | 3 | 3 |
| 29 | 17 | 24 | Reviewed | 4 | 9 | 7 | 3 | 1 | |
| 77 | 69 | 72 | Compiled | 18 | 37 | 10 | 6 | 1 | |
| 162 | 171 | 187 | Tax Returns | 82 | 81 | 14 | 6 | | 4 |
| 80 | 89 | 97 | Other | 33 | 34 | 10 | 10 | 7 | 3 |
| 4/1/09-3/31/10 ALL | 4/1/10-3/31/11 ALL | 4/1/11-3/31/12 ALL | | 65 (4/1-9/30/11) | | | 327 (10/1/11-3/31/12) | | |
| | | | | 0-1MM | 1-3MM | 3-5MM | 5-10MM | 10-25MM | 25MM & OVER |
| 362 | 348 | 392 | NUMBER OF STATEMENTS | 140 | 163 | 42 | 25 | 12 | 10 |
| % | % | % | ASSETS | % | % | % | % | % | % |
| 11.8 | 14.0 | 12.6 | Cash & Equivalents | 12.0 | 13.6 | 12.8 | 12.1 | 5.0 | 14.9 |
| 13.8 | 13.9 | 13.9 | Trade Receivables (net) | 11.6 | 15.5 | 16.2 | 14.3 | 12.6 | 11.8 |
| 4.7 | 5.3 | 4.7 | Inventory | 4.6 | 4.4 | 3.5 | 6.8 | 6.0 | 10.8 |
| 2.2 | 2.4 | 2.6 | All Other Current | 3.1 | 1.5 | 5.1 | 2.7 | 3.2 | 2.9 |
| 32.5 | 35.6 | 33.9 | Total Current | 31.3 | 34.9 | 37.7 | 35.9 | 26.9 | 40.4 |
| 42.2 | 41.8 | 43.4 | Fixed Assets (net) | 51.9 | 38.0 | 38.7 | 42.4 | 41.3 | 38.8 |
| 10.0 | 8.5 | 8.9 | Intangibles (net) | 7.9 | 9.6 | 10.2 | 7.3 | 11.0 | 9.8 |
| 15.3 | 14.2 | 13.7 | All Other Non-Current | 8.9 | 17.5 | 13.4 | 14.4 | 20.8 | 11.0 |
| 100.0 | 100.0 | 100.0 | Total | 100.0 | 100.0 | 100.0 | 100.0 | 100.0 | 100.0 |
| | | | LIABILITIES | | | | | | |
| 5.2 | 6.6 | 5.7 | Notes Payable-Short Term | 9.5 | 3.8 | 4.4 | 2.9 | 2.8 | .1 |
| 4.9 | 5.2 | 3.5 | Cur. Mat.-L.T.D. | 3.7 | 3.5 | 5.0 | 1.9 | 1.4 | .6 |
| 5.7 | 5.4 | 5.5 | Trade Payables | 5.8 | 4.9 | 9.6 | 4.1 | 2.3 | 2.1 |
| .2 | .1 | .2 | Income Taxes Payable | .3 | .1 | .5 | .2 | .1 | .0 |
| 7.7 | 14.5 | 10.0 | All Other Current | 11.6 | 11.0 | 5.8 | 6.2 | 3.5 | 7.4 |
| 23.7 | 31.9 | 24.9 | Total Current | 30.8 | 23.2 | 25.3 | 15.3 | 10.2 | -10.2 |
| 39.9 | 39.6 | 39.5 | Long-Term Debt | 45.1 | 37.4 | 39.0 | 34.6 | 25.2 | 25.2 |
| .1 | .1 | .4 | Deferred Taxes | .0 | .8 | .5 | .3 | .3 | .0 |
| 10.9 | 12.7 | 10.4 | All Other Non-Current | 11.9 | 7.8 | 10.3 | 6.0 | 22.8 | 27.0 |
| 25.4 | 15.6 | 24.9 | Net Worth | 12.2 | 30.9 | 24.9 | 43.8 | 41.6 | 37.6 |
| 100.0 | 100.0 | 100.0 | Total Liabilities & Net Worth | 100.0 | 100.0 | 100.0 | 100.0 | 100.0 | 100.0 |
| | | | INCOME DATA | | | | | | |
| 100.0 | 100.0 | 100.0 | Net Sales | 100.0 | 100.0 | 100.0 | 100.0 | 100.0 | 100.0 |
| | | | Gross Profit | | | | | | |
| 91.5 | 90.6 | 90.2 | Operating Expenses | 85.6 | 93.2 | 92.5 | 92.0 | 88.4 | 91.9 |
| 8.5 | 9.4 | 9.8 | Operating Profit | 14.4 | 6.8 | 7.5 | 8.0 | 11.6 | 8.1 |
| 2.6 | 3.0 | 3.5 | All Other Expenses (net) | 7.3 | 1.1 | 2.4 | .8 | 1.6 | 2.2 |
| 6.0 | 6.4 | 6.4 | Profit Before Taxes | 7.1 | 5.7 | 5.1 | 7.3 | 10.0 | 5.9 |
| | | | RATIOS | | | | | | |
| 3.9 | 4.2 | 4.4 | | 4.1 | 4.4 | 3.1 | 4.1 | 11.4 | 10.7 |
| 1.7 | 1.7 | 1.8 | Current | 1.2 | 2.0 | 1.8 | 1.8 | 2.4 | 5.3 |
| .8 | .7 | .7 | | .4 | .9 | .9 | 1.1 | 1.6 | 2.4 |
| 3.2 | 3.2 | 3.3 | | 3.0 | 3.4 | 2.8 | 3.0 | 5.6 | 7.2 |
| 1.4 | 1.3 | 1.3 | Quick | .8 | 1.6 | 1.5 | 1.2 | 1.5 | 4.1 |
| .6 | .5 | .5 | | .3 | .7 | .6 | .8 | 1.2 | .8 |
| 15 24.3 | 8 43.4 | 9 39.3 | | 0 UND | 17 21.9 | 17 21.8 | 22 16.4 | 20 18.6 | 0 UND |
| 29 12.8 | 25 14.7 | 25 14.5 | Sales/Receivables | 14 26.3 | 27 13.4 | 26 13.8 | 33 11.1 | 41 8.8 | 19 19.3 |
| 44 8.2 | 43 8.4 | 39 9.4 | | 34 10.7 | 40 9.1 | 38 9.5 | 43 8.4 | 51 7.1 | 89 4.1 |
| | | | Cost of Sales/Inventory | | | | | | |
| | | | Cost of Sales/Payables | | | | | | |
| 5.8 | 5.9 | 6.1 | | 7.3 | 6.4 | 5.9 | 4.8 | 1.0 | 1.5 |
| 15.7 | 18.2 | 16.5 | Sales/Working Capital | 54.9 | 13.5 | 14.7 | 10.9 | 7.8 | 7.8 |
| -40.7 | -34.5 | -30.9 | | -14.3 | -67.8 | -72.6 | NM | 15.3 | NM |
| 7.1 | 8.6 | 9.5 | | 7.7 | 13.0 | 10.4 | 6.2 | 10.4 | |
| (299) 2.7 | (277) 2.8 | (327) 3.0 | EBIT/Interest | (106) 2.7 | (143) 2.9 | (36) 3.3 | (22) 3.1 | (11) 3.8 | |
| 1.3 | 1.3 | 1.2 | | 1.0 | 1.2 | 1.8 | 2.0 | 1.1 | |
| 2.9 | 5.5 | 5.7 | | | 6.3 | 6.1 | | | |
| (33) 1.2 | (39) 2.8 | (40) 2.5 | Net Profit + Depr., Dep., Amort./Cur. Mat. L/T/D | | (17) 1.9 | (13) 2.7 | | | |
| .7 | 1.1 | 1.2 | | | 1.3 | 1.1 | | | |
| .6 | .6 | .5 | | 1.0 | .5 | .5 | .4 | .8 | .2 |
| 1.9 | 2.1 | 2.2 | Fixed/Worth | 6.2 | 1.3 | 1.1 | 1.4 | 1.4 | 3.1 |
| -6.4 | -6.6 | -11.6 | | -2.2 | 311.7 | -12.3 | 3.5 | 2.5 | -2.2 |
| .8 | .9 | .6 | | 1.2 | .5 | .6 | .5 | .8 | .2 |
| 3.4 | 3.6 | 2.9 | Debt/Worth | 7.8 | 1.6 | 2.7 | 1.4 | 1.9 | 2.8 |
| -14.8 | -11.0 | -20.9 | | -7.4 | 369.7 | -18.9 | 5.1 | 11.3 | -5.5 |
| 43.8 | 47.5 | 43.1 | | 48.2 | 47.6 | 33.4 | 24.6 | 40.5 | |
| (253) 17.6 | (241) 21.5 | (275) 20.8 | % Profit Before Taxes/Tangible Net Worth | (86) 20.4 | (123) 22.1 | (29) 14.2 | (21) 12.9 | (10) 25.4 | |
| 5.3 | 4.6 | 4.8 | | 3.8 | 3.3 | 4.5 | 6.0 | 15.0 | |
| 12.9 | 17.3 | 15.3 | | 14.9 | 18.3 | 13.1 | 11.4 | 10.4 | 28.6 |
| 5.4 | 6.3 | 5.3 | % Profit Before Taxes/Total Assets | 4.6 | 6.5 | 6.0 | 4.7 | 4.5 | 2.1 |
| .7 | .9 | .9 | | .0 | 1.1 | 1.0 | 2.1 | 1.3 | -.5 |
| 11.0 | 14.1 | 12.3 | | 14.3 | 12.7 | 13.4 | 9.2 | 3.2 | 7.9 |
| 4.6 | 4.9 | 4.8 | Sales/Net Fixed Assets | 4.6 | 5.8 | 6.1 | 3.2 | 1.6 | 4.6 |
| 1.5 | 1.8 | 1.7 | | 1.0 | 2.2 | 2.6 | 1.8 | 1.2 | 1.2 |
| 2.4 | 3.0 | 3.0 | | 3.4 | 2.7 | 3.6 | 2.1 | 1.2 | 2.6 |
| 1.4 | 1.6 | 1.5 | Sales/Total Assets | 1.4 | 1.7 | 1.9 | 1.3 | .6 | 1.0 |
| .7 | .9 | .8 | | .5 | 1.0 | .9 | .8 | .3 | .4 |
| 1.7 | 1.8 | 1.9 | | 1.8 | 1.8 | 2.0 | 1.9 | 2.9 | |
| (320) 3.4 | (298) 3.0 | (340) 3.2 | % Depr., Dep., Amort./Sales | (115) 4.3 | (143) 3.0 | (38) 2.9 | (24) 3.3 | 5.0 | |
| 6.2 | 5.2 | 5.8 | | 9.9 | 5.1 | 4.1 | 4.9 | 6.6 | |
| 6.2 | 5.6 | 5.6 | | 6.1 | 5.9 | 6.0 | 4.2 | | |
| (214) 9.6 | (208) 8.7 | (240) 8.7 | % Officers', Directors' Owners' Comp/Sales | (73) 9.5 | (117) 8.5 | (30) 8.1 | (14) 7.0 | | |
| 14.7 | 14.0 | 13.7 | | 14.8 | 14.5 | 10.5 | 12.5 | | |
| 1767784M | 2183384M | 2754793M | Net Sales ($) | 79249M | 288582M | 164153M | 164492M | 188049M | 1870268M |
| 1591710M | 1979947M | 2332187M | Total Assets ($) | 92951M | 259327M | 185447M | 172129M | 447327M | 1175006M |

© RMA 2012

M = $ thousand     MM = $ million
See Pages 9 through 22 for Explanation of Ratios and Data

## Current Data Sorted by Assets

## Comparative Historical Data

| | | | | | | | Type of Statement | | |
|---|---|---|---|---|---|---|---|---|---|
| | | | | | | 1 | Unqualified | 7 | 7 |
| 1 | | 1 | 1 | | | | Reviewed | 7 | 10 |
| 2 | 4 | 1 | | | | | Compiled | 9 | 8 |
| 9 | 5 | 1 | | | | | Tax Returns | 11 | 10 |
| 5 | 5 | 6 | | 5 | 1 | 1 | Other | 20 | 18 |
| | 3 (4/1-9/30/11) | | | 46 (10/1/11-3/31/12) | | | | 4/1/07-3/31/08 | 4/1/08-3/31/09 |
| 0-500M | 500M-2MM | 2-10MM | 10-50MM | 50-100MM | 100-250MM | | | ALL | ALL |
| 17 | 14 | 9 | 6 | 1 | 2 | NUMBER OF STATEMENTS | 54 | 53 |
| % | % | % | % | % | % | ASSETS | % | % |
| 11.4 | 5.8 | | | | | Cash & Equivalents | 10.6 | 9.5 |
| 12.1 | 14.2 | | | | | Trade Receivables (net) | 13.4 | 15.3 |
| 10.7 | 24.0 | | | | | Inventory | 7.4 | 11.3 |
| 4.2 | 1.1 | | | | | All Other Current | 2.0 | 1.2 |
| 38.4 | 45.0 | | | | | Total Current | 33.4 | 37.3 |
| 34.7 | 38.3 | | | | | Fixed Assets (net) | 30.4 | 36.6 |
| 4.1 | 3.6 | | | | | Intangibles (net) | 3.3 | 5.3 |
| 22.7 | 13.1 | | | | | All Other Non-Current | 32.9 | 20.9 |
| 100.0 | 100.0 | | | | | Total | 100.0 | 100.0 |
| | | | | | | LIABILITIES | | |
| 11.5 | 7.2 | | | | | Notes Payable-Short Term | 3.4 | 10.3 |
| 6.3 | 9.2 | | | | | Cur. Mat.-L.T.D. | 1.6 | 2.2 |
| 1.7 | 9.0 | | | | | Trade Payables | 5.2 | 6.5 |
| .9 | .0 | | | | | Income Taxes Payable | .1 | .0 |
| 27.6 | 9.0 | | | | | All Other Current | 10.0 | 9.5 |
| 48.0 | 34.3 | | | | | Total Current | 20.2 | 28.5 |
| 46.3 | 23.1 | | | | | Long-Term Debt | 26.3 | 23.7 |
| .0 | .0 | | | | | Deferred Taxes | .6 | .7 |
| 15.4 | 15.8 | | | | | All Other Non-Current | 25.3 | 18.1 |
| -9.7 | 26.7 | | | | | Net Worth | 27.6 | 29.1 |
| 100.0 | 100.0 | | | | | Total Liabilties & Net Worth | 100.0 | 100.0 |
| | | | | | | INCOME DATA | | |
| 100.0 | 100.0 | | | | | Net Sales | 100.0 | 100.0 |
| | | | | | | Gross Profit | | |
| 88.0 | 89.0 | | | | | Operating Expenses | 90.7 | 95.0 |
| 12.0 | 11.0 | | | | | Operating Profit | 9.3 | 5.0 |
| 3.6 | 1.3 | | | | | All Other Expenses (net) | 2.1 | 1.8 |
| 8.4 | 9.6 | | | | | Profit Before Taxes | 7.2 | 3.2 |
| | | | | | | RATIOS | | |
| 3.5 | 9.8 | | | | | | 6.0 | 6.0 |
| .8 | 1.5 | | | | | Current | 2.7 | 2.4 |
| .4 | .7 | | | | | | 1.5 | .9 |
| 1.7 | 5.7 | | | | | | 4.9 | 3.1 |
| .5 | .6 | | | | | Quick | 1.6 | 1.4 |
| .1 | .2 | | | | | | .8 | .6 |
| 0 UND | 12 30.4 | | | | | | 24 15.5 | 13 27.5 |
| 0 UND | 33 10.9 | | | | | Sales/Receivables | 58 6.3 | 55 6.7 |
| 24 15.4 | 99 3.7 | | | | | | 127 2.9 | 164 2.2 |
| | | | | | | Cost of Sales/Inventory | | |
| | | | | | | Cost of Sales/Payables | | |
| 6.0 | 1.2 | | | | | | 1.6 | 1.7 |
| -35.5 | 5.9 | | | | | Sales/Working Capital | 4.5 | 6.3 |
| -6.5 | -6.6 | | | | | | 11.1 | -76.0 |
| 8.6 | 9.9 | | | | | | 6.0 | 4.9 |
| (14) 1.9 | (12) 3.1 | | | | | EBIT/Interest | (46) 2.7 | (43) 1.9 |
| .8 | .7 | | | | | | 1.2 | .3 |
| | | | | | | Net Profit + Depr., Dep., | 6.0 | |
| | | | | | | Amort./Cur. Mat. L/T/D | (11) 4.9 | |
| | | | | | | | 1.7 | |
| .4 | .8 | | | | | | .4 | .6 |
| 1.8 | 1.6 | | | | | Fixed/Worth | 1.1 | 1.0 |
| -1.5 | 4.0 | | | | | | 6.5 | 13.2 |
| 1.3 | 1.3 | | | | | | .5 | .7 |
| 7.5 | 2.6 | | | | | Debt/Worth | 3.7 | 4.4 |
| -3.6 | 10.8 | | | | | | 26.7 | 23.4 |
| 194.4 | 36.7 | | | | | % Profit Before Taxes/Tangible | 27.9 | 24.3 |
| (10) 54.1 | (12) 4.7 | | | | | Net Worth | (46) 12.7 | (42) 4.4 |
| 4.5 | -7.8 | | | | | | 2.9 | -2.2 |
| 46.9 | 11.0 | | | | | % Profit Before Taxes/Total | 7.0 | 5.8 |
| 4.4 | 1.6 | | | | | Assets | 3.4 | 1.9 |
| .0 | -1.9 | | | | | | 1.1 | -.9 |
| 28.4 | 4.2 | | | | | | 4.9 | 6.1 |
| 11.2 | 2.2 | | | | | Sales/Net Fixed Assets | 2.5 | 2.4 |
| 1.9 | .9 | | | | | | 1.0 | 1.2 |
| 4.4 | 1.2 | | | | | | 1.3 | 1.7 |
| 1.9 | .5 | | | | | Sales/Total Assets | .4 | .6 |
| .6 | .3 | | | | | | .3 | .3 |
| 1.4 | 1.7 | | | | | | 2.2 | 2.5 |
| (13) 3.4 | (12) 3.2 | | | | | % Depr., Dep., Amort./Sales | (47) 3.3 | (42) 4.6 |
| 12.5 | 8.2 | | | | | | 7.8 | 7.5 |
| | | | | | | % Officers', Directors' | 5.9 | 2.4 |
| | | | | | | Owners' Comp/Sales | (13) 13.4 | (16) 5.6 |
| | | | | | | | 20.0 | 11.3 |
| 6292M | 14902M | 17988M | 29542M | 13736M | 56907M | Net Sales ($) | 616609M | 381292M |
| 3736M | 14570M | 52124M | 91474M | 79371M | 335199M | Total Assets ($) | 1179193M | 914359M |

M = $ thousand    MM = $ million
See Pages 9 through 22 for Explanation of Ratios and Data

## Comparative Historical Data

## Current Data Sorted by Sales

| Comparative Historical Data | | | Type of Statement | 0-1MM | 1-3MM | 3-5MM | 5-10MM | 10-25MM | 25MM & OVER |
|---|---|---|---|---|---|---|---|---|---|
| 7 | 6 | 1 | Unqualified | | | | | | 1 |
| 6 | 2 | 3 | Reviewed | 1 | | 1 | 1 | | |
| 10 | 8 | 7 | Compiled | 5 | 1 | 1 | | | |
| 9 | 21 | 15 | Tax Returns | 12 | 2 | | 1 | | |
| 21 | 25 | 23 | Other | 12 | 5 | 3 | | 2 | 1 |
| 4/1/09-3/31/10 ALL | 4/1/10-3/31/11 ALL | 4/1/11-3/31/12 ALL | | | 3 (4/1-9/30/11) | | 46 (10/1/11-3/31/12) | | |
| 53 | 62 | 49 | **NUMBER OF STATEMENTS** | 30 | 8 | 3 | 2 | 2 | 2 |
| % | % | % | **ASSETS** | % | % | % | % | % | % |
| 9.4 | 8.2 | 8.1 | Cash & Equivalents | 8.9 | | | | | |
| 12.3 | 11.6 | 11.5 | Trade Receivables (net) | 10.2 | | | | | |
| 7.5 | 12.5 | 14.0 | Inventory | 18.3 | | | | | |
| 1.9 | 2.2 | 4.7 | All Other Current | 2.9 | | | | | |
| 31.1 | 34.6 | 38.2 | Total Current | 40.3 | | | | | |
| 39.1 | 34.1 | 30.6 | Fixed Assets (net) | 34.8 | | | | | |
| 4.7 | 4.6 | 2.9 | Intangibles (net) | 2.8 | | | | | |
| 25.1 | 26.7 | 28.4 | All Other Non-Current | 22.2 | | | | | |
| 100.0 | 100.0 | 100.0 | Total | 100.0 | | | | | |
| | | | **LIABILITIES** | | | | | | |
| 4.5 | 4.0 | 6.5 | Notes Payable-Short Term | 8.7 | | | | | |
| 2.6 | 4.0 | 5.1 | Cur. Mat.-L.T.D. | 6.3 | | | | | |
| 3.4 | 2.6 | 3.6 | Trade Payables | 3.1 | | | | | |
| .0 | .0 | .3 | Income Taxes Payable | .5 | | | | | |
| 16.9 | 19.1 | 16.8 | All Other Current | 18.9 | | | | | |
| 27.3 | 29.7 | 32.3 | Total Current | 37.5 | | | | | |
| 21.3 | 25.0 | 26.0 | Long-Term Debt | 36.4 | | | | | |
| .7 | .6 | .0 | Deferred Taxes | .0 | | | | | |
| 20.0 | 22.2 | 25.2 | All Other Non-Current | 20.5 | | | | | |
| 30.7 | 22.6 | 16.5 | Net Worth | 5.5 | | | | | |
| 100.0 | 100.0 | 100.0 | Total Liabilities & Net Worth | 100.0 | | | | | |
| | | | **INCOME DATA** | | | | | | |
| 100.0 | 100.0 | 100.0 | Net Sales | 100.0 | | | | | |
| | | | Gross Profit | | | | | | |
| 90.3 | 92.2 | 91.0 | Operating Expenses | 89.2 | | | | | |
| 9.7 | 7.8 | 9.0 | Operating Profit | 10.8 | | | | | |
| 2.1 | .7 | 1.4 | All Other Expenses (net) | 3.1 | | | | | |
| 7.6 | 7.1 | 7.6 | Profit Before Taxes | 7.7 | | | | | |
| | | | **RATIOS** | | | | | | |
| 4.9 | 4.7 | 4.6 | Current | 3.8 | | | | | |
| 2.4 | 2.7 | 2.5 | | 1.9 | | | | | |
| .7 | .7 | .7 | | .5 | | | | | |
| 3.3 | 2.5 | 3.1 | Quick | 2.5 | | | | | |
| 1.4 | 1.0 | 1.2 | | .7 | | | | | |
| .6 | .3 | .3 | | .2 | | | | | |
| 24  15.1 | 10  36.1 | 0  UND | Sales/Receivables | 0  UND | | | | | |
| 59  6.2 | 40  9.2 | 48  7.6 | | 18  20.4 | | | | | |
| 133  2.8 | 85  4.3 | 107  3.4 | | 83  4.4 | | | | | |
| | | | Cost of Sales/Inventory | | | | | | |
| | | | Cost of Sales/Payables | | | | | | |
| 1.9 | 1.8 | 1.5 | Sales/Working Capital | 1.5 | | | | | |
| 6.6 | 4.5 | 5.0 | | 14.7 | | | | | |
| -5.6 | -14.3 | -10.5 | | -7.3 | | | | | |
| 5.7 | 8.0 | 7.8 | EBIT/Interest | 7.9 | | | | | |
| (44)  3.3 | (50)  2.4 | (43)  2.7 | | (26)  2.0 | | | | | |
| .9 | .5 | 1.1 | | .9 | | | | | |
| | | | Net Profit + Depr., Dep., Amort./Cur. Mat. L/T/D | | | | | | |
| .6 | .5 | .5 | Fixed/Worth | .4 | | | | | |
| 1.2 | 1.0 | 1.3 | | 1.7 | | | | | |
| 6.1 | 4.1 | 6.2 | | -23.6 | | | | | |
| .4 | .8 | 1.1 | Debt/Worth | 1.2 | | | | | |
| 2.9 | 3.0 | 4.9 | | 4.2 | | | | | |
| 11.1 | 13.8 | 30.4 | | -7.1 | | | | | |
| 29.7 | 24.4 | 21.5 | % Profit Before Taxes/Tangible Net Worth | 76.6 | | | | | |
| (43)  13.1 | (49)  11.0 | (39)  8.3 | | (21)  8.3 | | | | | |
| 1.1 | 3.8 | .6 | | .5 | | | | | |
| 11.4 | 7.7 | 9.3 | % Profit Before Taxes/Total Assets | 15.1 | | | | | |
| 3.7 | 3.2 | 1.7 | | 1.7 | | | | | |
| .4 | .1 | .1 | | -.2 | | | | | |
| 3.9 | 4.5 | 11.5 | Sales/Net Fixed Assets | 15.9 | | | | | |
| 1.8 | 2.5 | 2.4 | | 2.5 | | | | | |
| .8 | 1.0 | .9 | | .9 | | | | | |
| 1.1 | 1.5 | 1.6 | Sales/Total Assets | 2.0 | | | | | |
| .5 | .4 | .5 | | .6 | | | | | |
| .3 | .3 | .2 | | .2 | | | | | |
| 3.3 | 3.2 | 2.0 | % Depr., Dep., Amort./Sales | 1.8 | | | | | |
| (45)  4.7 | (56)  4.1 | (43)  3.2 | | (24)  3.4 | | | | | |
| 8.3 | 7.4 | 7.9 | | 11.1 | | | | | |
| 4.0 | 3.3 | 5.1 | % Officers', Directors' Owners' Comp/Sales | | | | | | |
| (12)  11.1 | (11)  7.5 | (13)  11.9 | | | | | | | |
| 16.5 | 22.8 | 28.9 | | | | | | | |
| 305415M | 288959M | 139367M | Net Sales ($) | 12745M | 12688M | 18671M | 12478M | 25878M | 56907M |
| 809576M | 715980M | 576474M | Total Assets ($) | 27134M | 48475M | 43793M | 22123M | 99750M | 335199M |

M = $ thousand    MM = $ million
See Pages 9 through 22 for Explanation of Ratios and Data

## Current Data Sorted by Assets

## Comparative Historical Data

| | | | | | | Type of Statement | | |
|---|---|---|---|---|---|---|---|---|
| 1 | | | 2 | | | Unqualified | 3 | 1 |
| | | 3 | 3 | | | Reviewed | 4 | 4 |
| 3 | 11 | 2 | 1 | | | Compiled | 13 | 18 |
| 26 | 13 | 1 | | | | Tax Returns | 18 | 32 |
| 7 | 7 | 6 | 2 | | | Other | 29 | 14 |
| | 8 (4/1-9/30/11) | | 80 (10/1/11-3/31/12) | | | | 4/1/07- 3/31/08 ALL | 4/1/08- 3/31/09 ALL |
| 0-500M | 500M-2MM | 2-10MM | 10-50MM | 50-100MM | 100-250MM | NUMBER OF STATEMENTS | 67 | 69 |
| 37 | 31 | 12 | 8 | | | | | |
| % | % | % | % | % | % | ASSETS | % | % |
| 15.8 | 14.3 | 7.6 | | | | Cash & Equivalents | 14.4 | 11.6 |
| .3 | 3.0 | 3.4 | D | D | | Trade Receivables (net) | 4.0 | 2.7 |
| .7 | 3.3 | 1.1 | A | A | | Inventory | 2.9 | 3.3 |
| 2.4 | 6.4 | 2.3 | T | T | | All Other Current | 1.0 | 2.4 |
| 19.2 | 27.0 | 14.4 | A | A | | Total Current | 22.3 | 19.9 |
| 62.5 | 59.8 | 72.4 | | | | Fixed Assets (net) | 59.8 | 62.6 |
| 7.7 | 6.2 | 4.9 | N | N | | Intangibles (net) | 10.2 | 7.5 |
| 10.5 | 7.0 | 8.3 | O | O | | All Other Non-Current | 7.6 | 10.0 |
| 100.0 | 100.0 | 100.0 | T | T | | Total | 100.0 | 100.0 |
| | | | A | A | | LIABILITIES | | |
| 6.5 | 4.8 | 2.4 | V | V | | Notes Payable-Short Term | 5.9 | 7.5 |
| 3.9 | 6.3 | 5.1 | A | A | | Cur. Mat.-L.T.D. | 8.3 | 9.2 |
| 1.2 | 2.9 | 2.6 | I | I | | Trade Payables | 3.4 | 3.7 |
| .0 | .0 | .8 | L | L | | Income Taxes Payable | .1 | .1 |
| 13.1 | 15.7 | 7.3 | A | A | | All Other Current | 18.9 | 11.4 |
| 24.8 | 29.7 | 18.2 | B | B | | Total Current | 36.6 | 32.0 |
| 40.0 | 44.0 | 36.5 | L | L | | Long-Term Debt | 51.1 | 45.5 |
| .0 | .0 | .0 | E | E | | Deferred Taxes | .1 | .1 |
| 15.9 | 3.4 | 12.4 | | | | All Other Non-Current | 8.3 | 6.7 |
| 19.4 | 22.9 | 32.9 | | | | Net Worth | 3.9 | 15.8 |
| 100.0 | 100.0 | 100.0 | | | | Total Liabilities & Net Worth | 100.0 | 100.0 |
| | | | | | | INCOME DATA | | |
| 100.0 | 100.0 | 100.0 | | | | Net Sales | 100.0 | 100.0 |
| | | | | | | Gross Profit | | |
| 88.7 | 83.4 | 87.7 | | | | Operating Expenses | 92.0 | 90.4 |
| 11.3 | 16.6 | 12.3 | | | | Operating Profit | 8.0 | 9.6 |
| 4.5 | 4.7 | 10.7 | | | | All Other Expenses (net) | 4.3 | 4.2 |
| 6.8 | 11.9 | 1.7 | | | | Profit Before Taxes | 3.6 | 5.3 |
| | | | | | | RATIOS | | |
| 4.8 | 2.4 | 1.6 | | | | | 2.2 | 2.3 |
| 1.1 | .8 | .7 | | | | Current | .9 | .6 |
| .2 | .4 | .2 | | | | | .3 | .2 |
| 3.8 | 1.7 | 1.3 | | | | | 1.9 | 1.8 |
| .7 | .5 | .6 | | | | Quick | .6 | .4 |
| .2 | .3 | .2 | | | | | .1 | .1 |
| 0 UND | 0 UND | 0 UND | | | | | 0 UND | 0 UND |
| 0 UND | 0 UND | 0 UND | | | | Sales/Receivables | 0 UND | 0 UND |
| 0 UND | 2 181.9 | 6 59.2 | | | | | 4 94.1 | 2 157.5 |
| | | | | | | Cost of Sales/Inventory | | |
| | | | | | | Cost of Sales/Payables | | |
| 12.8 | 7.0 | 13.9 | | | | | 23.3 | 23.2 |
| 65.0 | -82.0 | -26.4 | | | | Sales/Working Capital | -148.8 | -22.6 |
| -9.2 | -7.8 | -5.4 | | | | | -7.0 | -4.6 |
| 7.3 | 7.2 | | | | | | 5.2 | 5.9 |
| (24) 3.1 | (26) 3.2 | | | | | EBIT/Interest | (60) 2.1 | (55) 1.9 |
| .8 | .4 | | | | | | .7 | 1.0 |
| | | | | | | Net Profit + Depr., Dep., Amort./Cur. Mat. L/T/D | | |
| 1.0 | 1.0 | 1.0 | | | | | 1.4 | .9 |
| 3.1 | 2.6 | 2.8 | | | | Fixed/Worth | 6.1 | 10.4 |
| -1.6 | -5.0 | NM | | | | | -4.8 | -4.1 |
| .3 | .8 | .6 | | | | | .9 | .7 |
| 5.5 | 4.9 | 2.4 | | | | Debt/Worth | 6.5 | 11.0 |
| -3.0 | -9.1 | NM | | | | | -6.7 | -6.0 |
| 61.8 | 97.8 | | | | | % Profit Before Taxes/Tangible Net Worth | 86.4 | 49.8 |
| (23) 25.2 | (22) 46.3 | | | | | | (40) 19.2 | (37) 17.4 |
| 1.6 | 5.0 | | | | | | 6.4 | 2.5 |
| 23.4 | 16.7 | 6.1 | | | | % Profit Before Taxes/Total Assets | 22.5 | 16.0 |
| 7.5 | 8.3 | 2.4 | | | | | 6.7 | 3.6 |
| -4.7 | -1.2 | -2.3 | | | | | -1.9 | -.8 |
| 4.1 | 6.6 | 2.3 | | | | Sales/Net Fixed Assets | 7.3 | 5.7 |
| 2.1 | 1.8 | 1.4 | | | | | 3.0 | 2.4 |
| 1.3 | .5 | .3 | | | | | 1.2 | 1.4 |
| 2.6 | 2.3 | 1.7 | | | | Sales/Total Assets | 3.9 | 2.4 |
| 1.6 | .9 | 1.1 | | | | | 1.7 | 1.4 |
| .7 | .3 | .2 | | | | | .8 | .8 |
| 3.0 | 4.1 | 8.2 | | | | % Depr., Dep., Amort./Sales | 6.5 | 4.6 |
| (28) 10.8 | (21) 8.0 | 15.1 | | | | | (53) 10.5 | (65) 9.1 |
| 17.8 | 19.4 | 30.2 | | | | | 18.0 | 16.6 |
| 3.4 | 4.5 | | | | | % Officers', Directors' Owners' Comp/Sales | 2.7 | 3.1 |
| (15) 6.5 | (10) 8.6 | | | | | | (34) 4.8 | (22) 6.5 |
| 10.9 | 13.9 | | | | | | 8.3 | 9.3 |
| 11487M | 54611M | 50359M | 215675M | | | Net Sales ($) | 310700M | 482924M |
| 8418M | 34954M | 48287M | 165989M | | | Total Assets ($) | 201196M | 329551M |

M = $ thousand    MM = $ million
See Pages 9 through 22 for Explanation of Ratios and Data

## Comparative Historical Data | | Current Data Sorted by Sales

| | | | Type of Statement | 0-1MM | 1-3MM | 3-5MM | 5-10MM | 10-25MM | 25MM & OVER |
|---|---|---|---|---|---|---|---|---|---|
| 2 | 2 | 3 | Unqualified | 1 | | | | 1 | 1 |
| 7 | 7 | 6 | Reviewed | | 1 | | 2 | 3 | |
| 6 | 8 | 17 | Compiled | 7 | 6 | 2 | 1 | 1 | |
| 35 | 36 | 40 | Tax Returns | 36 | 4 | | | | |
| 21 | 18 | 22 | Other | 11 | 3 | 4 | 1 | 2 | 1 |
| 4/1/09-3/31/10 ALL | 4/1/10-3/31/11 ALL | 4/1/11-3/31/12 ALL | | 8 (4/1-9/30/11) | | | 80 (10/1/11-3/31/12) | | |
| 71 | 71 | 88 | **NUMBER OF STATEMENTS** | 55 | 14 | 6 | 4 | 7 | 2 |
| % | % | % | **ASSETS** | % | % | % | % | % | % |
| 11.7 | 9.1 | 13.3 | Cash & Equivalents | 12.2 | 25.7 | | | | |
| 3.9 | 3.1 | 1.9 | Trade Receivables (net) | .3 | 1.9 | | | | |
| 1.7 | 2.5 | 1.9 | Inventory | .5 | 3.3 | | | | |
| 3.9 | 2.4 | 4.0 | All Other Current | 3.2 | 1.2 | | | | |
| 21.2 | 17.0 | 21.2 | Total Current | 16.2 | 32.2 | | | | |
| 61.0 | 61.4 | 63.3 | Fixed Assets (net) | 65.4 | 61.4 | | | | |
| 8.0 | 11.4 | 6.2 | Intangibles (net) | 8.9 | 1.7 | | | | |
| 9.7 | 10.2 | 9.3 | All Other Non-Current | 9.4 | 4.7 | | | | |
| 100.0 | 100.0 | 100.0 | Total | 100.0 | 100.0 | | | | |
| | | | **LIABILITIES** | | | | | | |
| 6.7 | 6.4 | 5.9 | Notes Payable-Short Term | 5.0 | 6.9 | | | | |
| 7.5 | 6.6 | 5.2 | Cur. Mat.-L.T.D. | 3.7 | 2.7 | | | | |
| 4.0 | 4.3 | 2.4 | Trade Payables | .9 | 1.3 | | | | |
| .2 | .2 | .1 | Income Taxes Payable | .0 | .7 | | | | |
| 6.1 | 11.4 | 12.6 | All Other Current | 11.1 | 23.6 | | | | |
| 24.5 | 29.0 | 26.3 | Total Current | 20.7 | 35.2 | | | | |
| 60.2 | 57.5 | 40.1 | Long-Term Debt | 47.1 | 23.5 | | | | |
| .2 | .1 | .1 | Deferred Taxes | .0 | .0 | | | | |
| 8.2 | 6.5 | 9.7 | All Other Non-Current | 11.4 | 12.2 | | | | |
| 6.9 | 6.8 | 23.8 | Net Worth | 20.9 | 29.2 | | | | |
| 100.0 | 100.0 | 100.0 | Total Liabilities & Net Worth | 100.0 | 100.0 | | | | |
| | | | **INCOME DATA** | | | | | | |
| 100.0 | 100.0 | 100.0 | Net Sales | 100.0 | 100.0 | | | | |
| | | | Gross Profit | | | | | | |
| 93.4 | 94.9 | 86.9 | Operating Expenses | 83.2 | 91.4 | | | | |
| 6.6 | 5.1 | 13.1 | Operating Profit | 16.8 | 8.6 | | | | |
| 4.1 | 3.9 | 5.2 | All Other Expenses (net) | 7.8 | .4 | | | | |
| 2.5 | 1.3 | 7.9 | Profit Before Taxes | 9.0 | 8.1 | | | | |
| | | | **RATIOS** | | | | | | |
| 2.8 | 1.7 | 2.2 | | 3.5 | 2.4 | | | | |
| .8 | .4 | .9 | Current | .9 | .9 | | | | |
| .2 | .2 | .4 | | .2 | .4 | | | | |
| 1.5 | 1.0 | 1.6 | | 2.0 | 2.3 | | | | |
| .4 | .4 | .5 | Quick | .5 | .7 | | | | |
| .2 | .2 | .2 | | .2 | .3 | | | | |
| 0 UND | 0 UND | 0 UND | | 0 UND | 0 UND | | | | |
| 0 UND | 0 UND | 0 UND | Sales/Receivables | 0 UND | 0 UND | | | | |
| 7 51.8 | 2 217.3 | 2 220.5 | | 0 UND | 4 83.2 | | | | |
| | | | Cost of Sales/Inventory | | | | | | |
| | | | Cost of Sales/Payables | | | | | | |
| 8.9 | 36.4 | 10.8 | | 11.5 | 9.6 | | | | |
| -71.0 | -15.0 | -72.6 | Sales/Working Capital | -82.0 | NM | | | | |
| -6.7 | -5.7 | -8.0 | | -7.8 | -5.8 | | | | |
| 4.6 | 6.2 | 7.1 | | 7.2 | 9.2 | | | | |
| (53) 1.6 | (54) 1.5 | (66) 3.2 | EBIT/Interest | (37) 3.1 | (11) 3.3 | | | | |
| .6 | .0 | .9 | | .7 | -.3 | | | | |
| | | | Net Profit + Depr., Dep., Amort./Cur. Mat. L/T/D | | | | | | |
| .8 | 1.1 | 1.0 | | 1.0 | .8 | | | | |
| 6.3 | 5.5 | 2.5 | Fixed/Worth | 3.4 | 1.5 | | | | |
| -2.5 | -2.0 | -3.8 | | -2.1 | NM | | | | |
| .7 | .9 | .6 | | .5 | .5 | | | | |
| 8.5 | 5.5 | 3.6 | Debt/Worth | 5.0 | 1.3 | | | | |
| -4.2 | -3.2 | -5.5 | | -3.8 | NM | | | | |
| 53.9 | 58.3 | 60.5 | % Profit Before Taxes/Tangible Net Worth | 71.0 | 96.4 | | | | |
| (41) 19.6 | (42) 12.0 | (61) 23.7 | | (34) 27.3 | (11) 16.1 | | | | |
| -7.2 | -1.3 | 6.5 | | 4.3 | -3.1 | | | | |
| 12.8 | 11.7 | 17.5 | % Profit Before Taxes/Total Assets | 17.9 | 24.0 | | | | |
| 3.6 | 1.0 | 6.7 | | 5.9 | 9.9 | | | | |
| -3.3 | -6.7 | -1.8 | | -3.4 | -2.8 | | | | |
| 6.5 | 6.2 | 3.9 | | 3.4 | 6.6 | | | | |
| 2.4 | 2.2 | 1.9 | Sales/Net Fixed Assets | 1.8 | 2.0 | | | | |
| 1.1 | 1.2 | .9 | | .4 | 1.1 | | | | |
| 2.2 | 2.1 | 2.0 | | 1.8 | 3.0 | | | | |
| 1.4 | 1.5 | 1.4 | Sales/Total Assets | .9 | 1.5 | | | | |
| .7 | .8 | .7 | | .3 | .9 | | | | |
| 4.5 | 4.7 | 4.7 | | 4.9 | | | | | |
| (62) 8.0 | (61) 13.4 | (69) 10.6 | % Depr., Dep., Amort./Sales | (43) 13.5 | | | | | |
| 15.8 | 19.3 | 18.1 | | 25.2 | | | | | |
| 2.6 | 2.0 | 3.3 | | 3.5 | | | | | |
| (29) 4.4 | (34) 4.6 | (34) 5.1 | % Officers', Directors' Owners' Comp/Sales | (19) 6.6 | | | | | |
| 7.7 | 6.9 | 11.7 | | 13.2 | | | | | |
| 572930M | 303207M | 332132M | Net Sales ($) | 19969M | 26291M | 22860M | 31425M | 115363M | 116224M |
| 501316M | 180341M | 257648M | Total Assets ($) | 40781M | 17556M | 15319M | 21779M | 92942M | 69271M |

© RMA 2012

M = $ thousand    MM = $ million
See Pages 9 through 22 for Explanation of Ratios and Data

## Current Data Sorted by Assets    Comparative Historical Data

| 0-500M | 500M-2MM | 2-10MM | 10-50MM | 50-100MM | 100-250MM | Type of Statement | 4/1/07-3/31/08 ALL | 4/1/08-3/31/09 ALL |
|---|---|---|---|---|---|---|---|---|
| | | 4 | 1 | | | Unqualified | 7 | 13 |
| | | 10 | 1 | | | Reviewed | 17 | 17 |
| 2 | 11 | 8 | | | | Compiled | 22 | 28 |
| 50 | 29 | 11 | 2 | | 2 | Tax Returns | 55 | 63 |
| 19 | 10 | 10 | 5 | | | Other | 35 | 37 |
| 26 (4/1-9/30/11) | | | 149 (10/1/11-3/31/12) | | | | | |
| 71 | 50 | 43 | 9 | | 2 | **NUMBER OF STATEMENTS** | 136 | 158 |
| % | % | % | % | % | % | **ASSETS** | % | % |
| 16.2 | 12.4 | 6.6 | | | | Cash & Equivalents | 11.8 | 9.4 |
| 7.8 | 10.4 | 14.6 | | | | Trade Receivables (net) | 10.2 | 10.1 |
| 1.7 | 2.0 | 6.0 | | | | Inventory | 2.4 | 3.1 |
| 1.0 | .9 | 2.7 | | | | All Other Current | 2.3 | 2.0 |
| 26.8 | 25.7 | 30.0 | | | | Total Current | 26.7 | 24.6 |
| 46.9 | 55.7 | 47.6 | | | | Fixed Assets (net) | 53.4 | 51.3 |
| 17.4 | 12.0 | 9.2 | | | | Intangibles (net) | 10.2 | 11.5 |
| 9.0 | 6.6 | 13.1 | | | | All Other Non-Current | 9.6 | 12.6 |
| 100.0 | 100.0 | 100.0 | | | | Total | 100.0 | 100.0 |
| | | | | | | **LIABILITIES** | | |
| 8.2 | 8.2 | 5.6 | | | | Notes Payable-Short Term | 5.8 | 5.6 |
| 7.0 | 6.9 | 7.9 | | | | Cur. Mat.-L.T.D. | 9.4 | 8.1 |
| 5.9 | 5.6 | 8.2 | | | | Trade Payables | 5.0 | 5.5 |
| .0 | .1 | .1 | | | | Income Taxes Payable | .2 | .2 |
| 13.3 | 6.5 | 9.2 | | | | All Other Current | 9.8 | 9.8 |
| 34.4 | 27.3 | 30.9 | | | | Total Current | 30.1 | 29.2 |
| 48.8 | 41.3 | 31.6 | | | | Long-Term Debt | 42.7 | 41.5 |
| .0 | .0 | .3 | | | | Deferred Taxes | .2 | .2 |
| 20.6 | 7.0 | 6.3 | | | | All Other Non-Current | 5.8 | 5.6 |
| -3.8 | 24.3 | 30.8 | | | | Net Worth | 21.2 | 23.5 |
| 100.0 | 100.0 | 100.0 | | | | Total Liabilities & Net Worth | 100.0 | 100.0 |
| | | | | | | **INCOME DATA** | | |
| 100.0 | 100.0 | 100.0 | | | | Net Sales | 100.0 | 100.0 |
| | | | | | | Gross Profit | | |
| 94.0 | 90.9 | 94.4 | | | | Operating Expenses | 91.1 | 92.5 |
| 6.0 | 9.1 | 5.6 | | | | Operating Profit | 8.9 | 7.5 |
| 1.6 | 4.5 | 2.1 | | | | All Other Expenses (net) | 3.9 | 3.8 |
| 4.4 | 4.6 | 3.4 | | | | Profit Before Taxes | 5.1 | 3.7 |
| | | | | | | **RATIOS** | | |
| 4.4 | 3.6 | 1.5 | | | | | 2.1 | 2.1 |
| 1.0 | 1.0 | .9 | | | | Current | 1.0 | 1.0 |
| .3 | .4 | .6 | | | | | .4 | .4 |
| 3.5 | 2.9 | 1.1 | | | | | 1.7 | 1.6 |
| .8 | .8 | .7 | | | | Quick | .7 | .8 |
| .2 | .4 | .3 | | | | | .2 | .3 |
| 0 UND | 0 UND | 7 50.9 | | | | | 0 UND | 0 UND |
| 0 UND | 4 89.8 | 26 14.3 | | | | Sales/Receivables | 6 60.8 | 9 38.6 |
| 8 44.8 | 31 11.6 | 32 11.3 | | | | | 29 12.4 | 32 11.5 |
| | | | | | | Cost of Sales/Inventory | | |
| | | | | | | Cost of Sales/Payables | | |
| 21.5 | 9.5 | 18.0 | | | | | 14.3 | 17.5 |
| UND | NM | -157.6 | | | | Sales/Working Capital | -301.3 | -299.2 |
| -18.1 | -10.0 | -17.1 | | | | | -12.6 | -11.6 |
| 8.3 | 5.7 | 6.8 | | | | | 6.4 | 5.0 |
| (50) 2.1 | (42) 2.1 | (39) 3.0 | | | | EBIT/Interest | (111) 2.8 | (132) 2.3 |
| -.2 | .7 | 1.2 | | | | | .8 | .7 |
| | | | | | | Net Profit + Depr., Dep., | 3.5 | 3.2 |
| | | | | | | Amort./Cur. Mat. L/T/D | (20) 2.3 (20) 1.6 | |
| | | | | | | | 1.2 | 1.0 |
| .9 | 1.0 | .9 | | | | | .9 | .9 |
| 42.0 | 4.5 | 2.2 | | | | Fixed/Worth | 3.2 | 3.0 |
| -.7 | -6.1 | -22.8 | | | | | -9.1 | -6.9 |
| .5 | 1.1 | .8 | | | | | 1.0 | .9 |
| 104.0 | 6.1 | 3.9 | | | | Debt/Worth | 4.7 | 4.4 |
| -2.1 | -8.6 | -26.3 | | | | | -11.5 | -9.0 |
| 85.3 | 53.3 | 83.4 | | | | % Profit Before Taxes/Tangible | 67.9 | 42.2 |
| (37) 16.7 | (33) 18.3 | (31) 10.5 | | | | Net Worth | (93) 22.4 | (101) 19.3 |
| 2.4 | -1.6 | 3.7 | | | | | 6.6 | 3.8 |
| 25.8 | 10.7 | 14.3 | | | | % Profit Before Taxes/Total | 16.8 | 12.3 |
| 7.4 | 2.7 | 5.8 | | | | Assets | 5.9 | 4.1 |
| -.4 | -1.5 | 1.2 | | | | | -.4 | -1.1 |
| 20.4 | 10.6 | 7.0 | | | | | 9.8 | 7.8 |
| 11.1 | 4.1 | 5.5 | | | | Sales/Net Fixed Assets | 5.1 | 4.3 |
| 5.2 | 1.2 | 2.7 | | | | | 2.0 | 2.0 |
| 7.4 | 3.3 | 2.8 | | | | | 3.6 | 3.1 |
| 4.5 | 1.9 | 1.9 | | | | Sales/Total Assets | 2.2 | 1.8 |
| 1.9 | .8 | 1.2 | | | | | 1.1 | 1.0 |
| 1.7 | 2.4 | 3.0 | | | | | 2.8 | 3.1 |
| (43) 3.3 | (43) 4.6 | (38) 4.1 | | | | % Depr., Dep., Amort./Sales | (117) 4.3 | (139) 5.0 |
| 6.7 | 10.5 | 7.9 | | | | | 8.2 | 8.0 |
| 3.9 | 2.3 | 2.6 | | | | % Officers', Directors' | 2.9 | 3.6 |
| (45) 7.9 | (33) 5.7 | (19) 5.3 | | | | Owners' Comp/Sales | (63) 6.4 | (73) 5.6 |
| 12.3 | 7.6 | 8.6 | | | | | 9.0 | 9.9 |
| 65899M | 124466M | 334752M | 237470M | | 1570345M | Net Sales ($) | 1659676M | 845715M |
| 15360M | 59342M | 174228M | 142495M | | 216737M | Total Assets ($) | 557969M | 571698M |

*(Columns 10-50MM, 50-100MM, 100-250MM in the ratios section marked "DATA NOT AVAILABLE")*

M = $ thousand    MM = $ million
See Pages 9 through 22 for Explanation of Ratios and Data

## Comparative Historical Data / Current Data Sorted by Sales

| Type of Statement | | | | 0-1MM | 1-3MM | 3-5MM | 5-10MM | 10-25MM | 25MM & OVER |
|---|---|---|---|---|---|---|---|---|---|
| 12 | 8 | 5 | Unqualified | | | | 4 | | 1 |
| 11 | 14 | 11 | Reviewed | | | 1 | 4 | 6 | |
| 31 | 15 | 21 | Compiled | 1 | 5 | 4 | 9 | 2 | |
| 58 | 62 | 94 | Tax Returns | 48 | 28 | 8 | 4 | 4 | 2 |
| 39 | 56 | 44 | Other | 19 | 7 | 6 | 5 | 5 | 2 |
| 4/1/09-3/31/10 ALL | 4/1/10-3/31/11 ALL | 4/1/11-3/31/12 ALL | | 26 (4/1-9/30/11) | | 149 (10/1/11-3/31/12) | | | |
| 151 | 155 | 175 | **NUMBER OF STATEMENTS** | 68 | 40 | 19 | 26 | 17 | 5 |
| % | % | % | **ASSETS** | % | % | % | % | % | % |
| 10.3 | 10.3 | 12.2 | Cash & Equivalents | 13.6 | 14.4 | 12.6 | 9.2 | 6.7 | |
| 10.6 | 10.9 | 10.7 | Trade Receivables (net) | 4.9 | 10.3 | 12.9 | 19.2 | 15.4 | |
| 3.1 | 2.9 | 2.9 | Inventory | 1.6 | 1.2 | 2.2 | 7.6 | 6.1 | |
| 2.4 | 3.5 | 1.6 | All Other Current | .7 | 1.5 | 4.3 | .3 | 2.8 | |
| 26.4 | 27.6 | 27.4 | Total Current | 20.8 | 27.4 | 32.0 | 36.4 | 30.9 | |
| 52.8 | 51.7 | 49.8 | Fixed Assets (net) | 54.8 | 50.6 | 46.0 | 41.2 | 50.3 | |
| 11.0 | 10.7 | 13.3 | Intangibles (net) | 18.2 | 13.6 | 6.4 | 8.0 | 9.2 | |
| 9.8 | 10.0 | 9.5 | All Other Non-Current | 6.2 | 8.5 | 15.7 | 14.4 | 9.5 | |
| 100.0 | 100.0 | 100.0 | Total | 100.0 | 100.0 | 100.0 | 100.0 | 100.0 | |
| | | | **LIABILITIES** | | | | | | |
| 8.4 | 7.7 | 7.3 | Notes Payable-Short Term | 4.4 | 10.5 | 8.0 | 11.5 | 3.8 | |
| 8.8 | 7.8 | 7.0 | Cur. Mat.-L.T.D. | 7.2 | 6.2 | 7.2 | 6.0 | 9.5 | |
| 4.7 | 6.5 | 6.4 | Trade Payables | 4.0 | 7.1 | 8.0 | 9.9 | 6.4 | |
| .1 | .1 | .1 | Income Taxes Payable | .0 | .0 | .2 | .1 | .2 | |
| 15.2 | 12.8 | 10.1 | All Other Current | 11.2 | 9.8 | 6.4 | 9.6 | 9.8 | |
| 37.2 | 35.0 | 30.9 | Total Current | 26.7 | 33.6 | 29.7 | 37.1 | 29.7 | |
| 43.6 | 42.8 | 40.8 | Long-Term Debt | 52.8 | 44.7 | 36.9 | 23.1 | 25.3 | |
| .2 | .2 | .2 | Deferred Taxes | .0 | .0 | .0 | .2 | 1.4 | |
| 10.8 | 10.1 | 12.1 | All Other Non-Current | 19.1 | 11.1 | 9.3 | 2.2 | 6.8 | |
| 8.2 | 11.9 | 16.0 | Net Worth | 1.3 | 10.6 | 24.1 | 37.4 | 36.8 | |
| 100.0 | 100.0 | 100.0 | Total Liabilities & Net Worth | 100.0 | 100.0 | 100.0 | 100.0 | 100.0 | |
| | | | **INCOME DATA** | | | | | | |
| 100.0 | 100.0 | 100.0 | Net Sales | 100.0 | 100.0 | 100.0 | 100.0 | 100.0 | |
| | | | Gross Profit | | | | | | |
| 92.6 | 90.9 | 92.8 | Operating Expenses | 89.5 | 94.3 | 95.2 | 96.0 | 95.6 | |
| 7.4 | 9.1 | 7.2 | Operating Profit | 10.5 | 5.7 | 4.8 | 4.0 | 4.4 | |
| 3.1 | 3.3 | 2.6 | All Other Expenses (net) | 4.7 | 2.2 | 1.1 | .6 | .2 | |
| 4.3 | 5.8 | 4.7 | Profit Before Taxes | 5.8 | 3.5 | 3.7 | 3.5 | 4.3 | |
| | | | **RATIOS** | | | | | | |
| 2.1 | 2.0 | 3.0 | Current | 5.2 | 2.4 | 1.9 | 2.2 | 2.4 | |
| .9 | .9 | 1.0 | | 1.0 | .8 | .8 | 1.2 | 1.1 | |
| .4 | .3 | .4 | | .3 | .3 | .4 | .7 | .7 | |
| 1.8 | 1.8 | 2.5 | Quick | 4.3 | 2.4 | 1.5 | 1.8 | 1.6 | |
| .7 | .7 | .8 | | .9 | .6 | .5 | .9 | .8 | |
| .3 | .3 | .3 | | .2 | .3 | .3 | .5 | .5 | |
| 0  UND | 0  UND | 0  UND | Sales/Receivables | 0  UND | 0  UND | 7  50.9 | 6  58.3 | 9  41.9 | |
| 10  36.8 | 10  35.8 | 7  56.1 | | 0  UND | 1  245.0 | 22  16.9 | 30  12.1 | 27  13.3 | |
| 29  12.5 | 30  12.2 | 27  13.3 | | 6  56.9 | 16  22.4 | 32  11.3 | 45  8.1 | 33  11.0 | |
| | | | Cost of Sales/Inventory | | | | | | |
| | | | Cost of Sales/Payables | | | | | | |
| 15.9 | 18.7 | 17.1 | Sales/Working Capital | 19.7 | 15.4 | 19.9 | 14.1 | 11.7 | |
| -151.7 | -75.7 | UND | | UND | -319.1 | -36.9 | 83.0 | 92.7 | |
| -11.9 | -10.4 | -15.0 | | -13.0 | -7.4 | -13.5 | -23.3 | -35.3 | |
| (129)  5.2 | (132)  7.9 | (142)  7.7 | EBIT/Interest | (46)  4.5 | (35)  6.8 | (17)  5.9 | (23)  5.2 | (16)  17.8 | |
| 2.3 | 2.7 | 2.6 | | 2.0 | 2.3 | 1.9 | 2.8 | 5.7 | |
| .7 | 1.3 | .8 | | -.2 | 1.0 | .5 | -1.6 | 3.2 | |
| (12)  4.8 | (16)  2.9 | (15)  3.6 | Net Profit + Depr., Dep., Amort./Cur. Mat. L/T/D | | | | | | |
| 1.2 | 1.2 | 1.9 | | | | | | | |
| .9 | .3 | 1.5 | | | | | | | |
| 1.1 | 1.0 | .9 | Fixed/Worth | 1.0 | 1.0 | .9 | .4 | .9 | |
| 3.8 | 6.1 | 3.5 | | 9.3 | 11.2 | 1.9 | 1.4 | 1.4 | |
| -1.6 | -1.9 | -2.8 | | -1.1 | -1.1 | -7.1 | 5.5 | 7.3 | |
| 1.0 | 1.0 | .8 | Debt/Worth | .9 | .9 | .9 | .6 | .7 | |
| 5.2 | 10.5 | 5.0 | | 13.7 | 15.6 | 5.3 | 1.6 | 2.5 | |
| -3.5 | -4.6 | -4.6 | | -2.0 | -2.6 | -9.6 | 6.4 | 11.6 | |
| 53.2 | 64.7 | 72.6 | % Profit Before Taxes/Tangible Net Worth | 76.8 | 67.1 | 83.4 | 29.5 | 115.6 | |
| (88)  20.5 | (89)  25.9 | (112)  17.4 | | (38)  17.4 | (22)  15.4 | (11)  23.5 | (21)  6.3 | (15)  14.7 | |
| -.1 | 8.4 | 4.0 | | 3.6 | 4.0 | 7.8 | -7.0 | 8.1 | |
| 17.0 | 18.4 | 17.5 | % Profit Before Taxes/Total Assets | 15.3 | 14.7 | 23.9 | 15.7 | 20.4 | |
| 4.3 | 6.8 | 5.8 | | 6.5 | 3.5 | 4.4 | 5.7 | 8.5 | |
| -1.2 | 2.0 | .0 | | -.4 | -.4 | -2.1 | -2.2 | 4.3 | |
| 9.5 | 11.0 | 14.0 | Sales/Net Fixed Assets | 14.8 | 21.3 | 9.6 | 14.0 | 8.1 | |
| 5.2 | 5.3 | 6.0 | | 5.7 | 8.8 | 4.3 | 6.8 | 5.5 | |
| 2.2 | 2.3 | 2.7 | | 1.2 | 3.2 | 2.7 | 5.5 | 2.8 | |
| 3.8 | 3.6 | 4.5 | Sales/Total Assets | 5.0 | 5.8 | 2.4 | 3.9 | 3.2 | |
| 1.9 | 2.1 | 2.4 | | 1.9 | 3.2 | 2.0 | 2.8 | 2.2 | |
| 1.1 | 1.1 | 1.3 | | .8 | 1.6 | 1.3 | 1.8 | 1.7 | |
| 2.8 | 2.9 | 2.4 | % Depr., Dep., Amort./Sales | 2.5 | 2.1 | 2.4 | 2.3 | 3.3 | |
| (135)  4.8 | (128)  4.8 | (133)  4.0 | | (45)  5.8 | (32)  3.4 | (15)  5.2 | (23)  3.5 | (15)  4.1 | |
| 8.6 | 9.5 | 8.5 | | 11.8 | 6.7 | 9.2 | 4.1 | 7.6 | |
| 2.5 | 3.0 | 2.7 | % Officers', Directors' Owners' Comp/Sales | 4.3 | 2.7 | 1.5 | 3.2 | | |
| (77)  4.7 | (76)  5.4 | (99)  5.7 | | (36)  8.0 | (31)  5.4 | (15)  3.3 | (11)  5.3 | | |
| 9.4 | 8.9 | 9.9 | | 12.7 | 8.5 | 8.6 | | | |
| 979536M | 986909M | 2332932M | Net Sales ($) | 34480M | 73416M | 77878M | 175011M | 243032M | 1729115M |
| 561249M | 568218M | 608162M | Total Assets ($) | 28962M | 43131M | 46697M | 82583M | 125091M | 281698M |

M = $ thousand    MM = $ million
See Pages 9 through 22 for Explanation of Ratios and Data

## Current Data Sorted by Assets

## Comparative Historical Data

| | | | | | | Type of Statement | | |
|---|---|---|---|---|---|---|---|---|
| | 1 | 1 | 7 | | 1 | Unqualified | 16 | 13 |
| | 5 | 13 | 6 | 1 | | Reviewed | 15 | 15 |
| 2 | 7 | 5 | 1 | | | Compiled | 14 | 11 |
| 4 | 7 | 7 | | | | Tax Returns | 9 | 10 |
| | 7 | 10 | 6 | 1 | | Other | 26 | 32 |
| | 17 (4/1-9/30/11) | | 68 (10/1/11-3/31/12) | | | | 4/1/07-3/31/08 | 4/1/08-3/31/09 |
| 0-500M | 500M-2MM | 2-10MM | 10-50MM | 50-100MM | 100-250MM | | ALL | ALL |
| 6 | 20 | 36 | 20 | 2 | 1 | NUMBER OF STATEMENTS | 80 | 81 |
| % | % | % | % | % | % | ASSETS | % | % |
| | 9.5 | 8.8 | 11.1 | | | Cash & Equivalents | 11.4 | 8.9 |
| | 24.6 | 20.4 | 19.0 | | | Trade Receivables (net) | 19.3 | 20.0 |
| | 14.0 | 13.4 | 13.6 | | | Inventory | 6.9 | 10.5 |
| | 1.0 | 3.3 | 4.1 | | | All Other Current | 1.9 | 1.8 |
| | 49.1 | 46.0 | 47.9 | | | Total Current | 39.4 | 41.2 |
| | 41.3 | 40.6 | 37.0 | | | Fixed Assets (net) | 48.2 | 47.5 |
| | 6.0 | 8.2 | 8.4 | | | Intangibles (net) | 5.0 | 5.2 |
| | 3.7 | 5.2 | 6.6 | | | All Other Non-Current | 7.4 | 6.1 |
| | 100.0 | 100.0 | 100.0 | | | Total | 100.0 | 100.0 |
| | | | | | | LIABILITIES | | |
| | 14.1 | 9.6 | 8.6 | | | Notes Payable-Short Term | 5.8 | 10.5 |
| | 3.5 | 5.9 | 4.6 | | | Cur. Mat.-L.T.D. | 6.1 | 3.9 |
| | 6.0 | 12.4 | 11.6 | | | Trade Payables | 8.6 | 8.8 |
| | .0 | .5 | .1 | | | Income Taxes Payable | .2 | .1 |
| | 5.3 | 7.8 | 7.8 | | | All Other Current | 7.4 | 10.3 |
| | 28.9 | 36.2 | 32.7 | | | Total Current | 28.1 | 33.5 |
| | 34.2 | 21.8 | 16.1 | | | Long-Term Debt | 28.3 | 27.0 |
| | .8 | .0 | .3 | | | Deferred Taxes | .5 | .4 |
| | 8.7 | 7.3 | 5.2 | | | All Other Non-Current | 6.0 | 3.8 |
| | 27.5 | 34.7 | 45.7 | | | Net Worth | 37.1 | 35.3 |
| | 100.0 | 100.0 | 100.0 | | | Total Liabilities & Net Worth | 100.0 | 100.0 |
| | | | | | | INCOME DATA | | |
| | 100.0 | 100.0 | 100.0 | | | Net Sales | 100.0 | 100.0 |
| | | | | | | Gross Profit | | |
| | 87.4 | 97.3 | 94.3 | | | Operating Expenses | 93.2 | 92.7 |
| | 12.6 | 2.7 | 5.7 | | | Operating Profit | 6.8 | 7.3 |
| | 3.5 | .8 | .5 | | | All Other Expenses (net) | 1.7 | 2.8 |
| | 9.1 | 1.9 | 5.3 | | | Profit Before Taxes | 5.0 | 4.5 |
| | | | | | | RATIOS | | |
| | 4.3 | 2.4 | 2.6 | | | | 2.6 | 2.6 |
| | 1.8 | 1.5 | 1.6 | | | Current | 1.6 | 1.4 |
| | 1.1 | .9 | 1.1 | | | | .9 | .8 |
| | 3.4 | 1.8 | 1.9 | | | | 2.1 | 1.8 |
| | 1.5 | .8 | 1.1 | | | Quick | 1.1 | .9 |
| | .6 | .4 | .4 | | | | .7 | .5 |
| 21 | 17.8 | 28   13.0 | 29   12.8 | | | | 29   12.5 | 27   13.4 |
| 34 | 10.8 | 32   11.3 | 37   9.8 | | | Sales/Receivables | 34   10.8 | 35   10.6 |
| 41 | 8.8 | 40   9.2 | 42   8.7 | | | | 39   9.4 | 41   9.0 |
| | | | | | | Cost of Sales/Inventory | | |
| | | | | | | Cost of Sales/Payables | | |
| | 6.3 | 7.3 | 5.4 | | | | 7.6 | 7.5 |
| | 9.1 | 16.0 | 13.2 | | | Sales/Working Capital | 15.5 | 22.2 |
| | 43.4 | -55.3 | 66.3 | | | | -68.1 | -25.6 |
| | 8.7 | 9.8 | 13.0 | | | | 12.1 | 9.0 |
| (17) | 2.1 | (35)   3.0 | (18)   6.3 | | | EBIT/Interest | (73)   4.1 | (66)   3.9 |
| | -.3 | .7 | 2.9 | | | | 1.4 | .7 |
| | | | | | | Net Profit + Depr., Dep., | 8.4 | 5.8 |
| | | | | | | Amort./Cur. Mat. L/T/D | (22)   3.9 | (17)   3.4 |
| | | | | | | | 1.4 | 1.8 |
| | .3 | .6 | .4 | | | | .7 | .7 |
| | .9 | 1.2 | 1.0 | | | Fixed/Worth | 1.4 | 1.4 |
| | 6.2 | 3.7 | 2.6 | | | | 4.3 | 4.6 |
| | .7 | .6 | .7 | | | | .7 | .6 |
| | 2.3 | 1.9 | 1.8 | | | Debt/Worth | 1.5 | 2.1 |
| | 6.6 | 7.1 | 5.0 | | | | 5.3 | 8.5 |
| | 26.9 | 45.5 | 69.1 | | | % Profit Before Taxes/Tangible | 47.0 | 55.5 |
| (16) | 8.2 | (30)   12.8 | 25.2 | | | Net Worth | (71)   16.4 | (75)   18.3 |
| | -5.1 | -3.3 | 8.5 | | | | 6.0 | 3.5 |
| | 16.1 | 10.9 | 14.1 | | | % Profit Before Taxes/Total | 15.8 | 13.7 |
| | 3.0 | 4.4 | 6.7 | | | Assets | 7.5 | 3.8 |
| | -4.5 | -1.7 | 3.8 | | | | 1.9 | .3 |
| | 21.3 | 10.0 | 9.5 | | | | 7.7 | 8.5 |
| | 10.4 | 5.8 | 5.0 | | | Sales/Net Fixed Assets | 4.3 | 4.3 |
| | 4.1 | 3.3 | 2.7 | | | | 2.4 | 2.5 |
| | 3.9 | 2.7 | 2.3 | | | | 2.7 | 2.6 |
| | 2.5 | 2.0 | 1.8 | | | Sales/Total Assets | 2.0 | 2.0 |
| | 1.9 | 1.4 | 1.4 | | | | 1.5 | 1.3 |
| | 1.5 | 2.5 | 2.0 | | | | 3.0 | 2.2 |
| (18) | 2.8 | (29)   4.8 | (18)   4.2 | | | % Depr., Dep., Amort./Sales | (73)   4.2 | (71)   4.4 |
| | 6.4 | 7.1 | 11.0 | | | | 7.0 | 7.1 |
| | 2.6 | 1.7 | | | | | 2.8 | 1.8 |
| (11) | 3.6 | (18)   3.0 | | | | % Officers', Directors' Owners' Comp/Sales | (33)   4.9 | (29)   4.0 |
| | 7.2 | 6.0 | | | | | 7.0 | 6.8 |
| 7842M | 67071M | 407930M | 827640M | 322303M | 212913M | Net Sales ($) | 1994170M | 1814865M |
| 1814M | 24642M | 195521M | 473615M | 138415M | 102505M | Total Assets ($) | 1027568M | 950594M |

M = $ thousand    MM = $ million
See Pages 9 through 22 for Explanation of Ratios and Data

## Comparative Historical Data — Current Data Sorted by Sales

| | 4/1/09-3/31/10 ALL | 4/1/10-3/31/11 ALL | 4/1/11-3/31/12 ALL | 0-1MM | 1-3MM 17 (4/1-9/30/11) | 3-5MM | 5-10MM 68 (10/1/11-3/31/12) | 10-25MM | 25MM & OVER |
|---|---|---|---|---|---|---|---|---|---|
| **Type of Statement** | | | | | | | | | |
| Unqualified | 11 | 11 | 9 | | | | 1 | 3 | 5 |
| Reviewed | 14 | 19 | 21 | | 1 | | 2 | 10 | 8 |
| Compiled | 8 | 9 | 13 | 2 | 3 | 1 | 3 | 4 | |
| Tax Returns | 9 | 9 | 18 | 2 | 4 | 6 | 5 | 1 | |
| Other | 33 | 27 | 24 | 1 | 3 | 4 | 5 | 5 | 6 |
| **NUMBER OF STATEMENTS** | 75 | 75 | 85 | 5 | 11 | 11 | 16 | 23 | 19 |
| | % | % | % | % | % | % | % | % | % |
| **ASSETS** | | | | | | | | | |
| Cash & Equivalents | 11.5 | 11.8 | 9.5 | | 8.3 | 14.6 | 9.4 | 8.9 | 9.3 |
| Trade Receivables (net) | 22.7 | 20.2 | 21.1 | | 25.0 | 20.3 | 25.4 | 18.8 | 23.7 |
| Inventory | 6.7 | 10.0 | 14.5 | | 15.0 | 11.8 | 8.1 | 16.9 | 17.0 |
| All Other Current | 2.8 | 2.5 | 2.7 | | 1.2 | 2.8 | 3.2 | 2.4 | 3.9 |
| Total Current | 43.7 | 44.5 | 47.8 | | 49.5 | 49.5 | 46.1 | 47.1 | 53.9 |
| Fixed Assets (net) | 45.3 | 41.5 | 39.6 | | 31.6 | 46.9 | 40.0 | 37.2 | 33.3 |
| Intangibles (net) | 6.0 | 6.1 | 7.0 | | 7.8 | .3 | 7.2 | 12.8 | 5.0 |
| All Other Non-Current | 5.0 | 7.9 | 5.7 | | 11.0 | 3.3 | 6.7 | 2.9 | 7.9 |
| Total | 100.0 | 100.0 | 100.0 | | 100.0 | 100.0 | 100.0 | 100.0 | 100.0 |
| **LIABILITIES** | | | | | | | | | |
| Notes Payable-Short Term | 8.0 | 5.9 | 11.3 | | 31.8 | 5.7 | 4.7 | 12.8 | 8.8 |
| Cur. Mat.-L.T.D. | 4.9 | 4.0 | 5.8 | | 3.2 | 1.5 | 7.7 | 5.1 | 3.8 |
| Trade Payables | 8.6 | 10.1 | 10.4 | | 7.6 | 5.5 | 7.3 | 11.5 | 18.4 |
| Income Taxes Payable | .2 | .2 | .3 | | .0 | .1 | 1.0 | .2 | .1 |
| All Other Current | 9.6 | 5.9 | 7.5 | | 3.5 | 4.3 | 8.1 | 8.3 | 9.9 |
| Total Current | 31.2 | 26.1 | 35.3 | | 46.1 | 17.0 | 28.7 | 37.9 | 41.0 |
| Long-Term Debt | 22.4 | 26.1 | 22.8 | | 40.7 | 29.0 | 20.2 | 17.6 | 9.4 |
| Deferred Taxes | .4 | .5 | .3 | | .0 | 1.4 | .0 | .2 | .2 |
| All Other Non-Current | 4.9 | 5.4 | 7.6 | | 8.2 | 7.2 | 9.8 | 9.0 | 5.7 |
| Net Worth | 41.1 | 41.9 | 34.1 | | 5.0 | 45.4 | 41.3 | 35.3 | 43.7 |
| Total Liabilities & Net Worth | 100.0 | 100.0 | 100.0 | | 100.0 | 100.0 | 100.0 | 100.0 | 100.0 |
| **INCOME DATA** | | | | | | | | | |
| Net Sales | 100.0 | 100.0 | 100.0 | | 100.0 | 100.0 | 100.0 | 100.0 | 100.0 |
| Gross Profit | | | | | | | | | |
| Operating Expenses | 94.7 | 93.5 | 93.8 | | 94.8 | 97.5 | 97.3 | 95.3 | 95.0 |
| Operating Profit | 5.3 | 6.5 | 6.2 | | 5.2 | 2.5 | 2.7 | 4.7 | 5.0 |
| All Other Expenses (net) | 1.6 | 1.4 | 1.4 | | 1.1 | 2.8 | .1 | .8 | -.1 |
| Profit Before Taxes | 3.8 | 5.1 | 4.8 | | 4.0 | -.4 | 2.6 | 3.9 | 5.1 |
| **RATIOS** | | | | | | | | | |
| Current | 2.6 | 3.1 | 2.6 | | 5.2 | 4.7 | 2.5 | 2.7 | 2.0 |
| | 1.9 | 1.7 | 1.7 | | 2.0 | 2.4 | 1.8 | 1.5 | 1.5 |
| | .9 | 1.1 | 1.0 | | .5 | 1.7 | 1.1 | .8 | 1.0 |
| Quick | 2.2 | 2.2 | 2.2 | | 4.0 | 4.2 | 2.2 | 2.1 | 1.7 |
| | 1.2 | 1.2 | 1.1 | | .7 | 2.4 | 1.5 | .8 | .8 |
| | .5 | .8 | .4 | | .3 | .7 | .6 | .4 | .5 |
| Sales/Receivables | 30  12.0 | 31  12.0 | 28  13.2 | | 12  30.4 | 19  18.9 | 29  12.7 | 28  13.1 | 30  12.3 |
| | 36  10.2 | 35  10.4 | 33  11.1 | | 32  11.5 | 30  12.1 | 35  10.3 | 34  10.8 | 35  10.4 |
| | 42  8.8 | 41  9.0 | 41  9.0 | | 36  10.2 | 42  8.6 | 41  8.8 | 39  9.4 | 42  8.6 |
| Cost of Sales/Inventory | | | | | | | | | |
| Cost of Sales/Payables | | | | | | | | | |
| Sales/Working Capital | 7.1 | 6.4 | 7.1 | | 7.2 | 5.4 | 7.9 | 5.4 | 7.0 |
| | 12.2 | 10.9 | 12.8 | | 12.8 | 7.3 | 13.6 | 7.3 | 17.4 |
| | -63.7 | 62.9 | -133.5 | | -12.9 | 15.0 | 76.9 | -32.1 | -238.5 |
| EBIT/Interest | 12.8 | 16.0 | 10.6 | | 8.4 | | 5.6 | 13.6 | 25.9 |
| | (63) 3.8 | (71) 6.7 | (78) 3.8 | | (10) 2.6 | | (15) 2.8 | 4.7 | (17) 10.6 |
| | 1.1 | 1.8 | 1.0 | | .6 | | -1.5 | 1.5 | 3.4 |
| Net Profit + Depr., Dep., Amort./Cur. Mat. L/T/D | 9.3 | 6.3 | 5.8 | | | | | | |
| | (15) 5.0 | (12) 2.6 | (14) 2.6 | | | | | | |
| | 1.0 | .8 | .6 | | | | | | |
| Fixed/Worth | .7 | .5 | .4 | | .4 | .3 | .7 | .5 | .4 |
| | 1.2 | .9 | 1.0 | | 4.6 | .8 | 1.1 | 1.3 | .6 |
| | 2.6 | 2.9 | 3.9 | | -1.7 | 6.8 | 2.3 | 5.5 | 2.0 |
| Debt/Worth | .5 | .5 | .6 | | 1.1 | .3 | .9 | .6 | .5 |
| | 1.9 | 1.5 | 2.1 | | 6.7 | .8 | 1.3 | 2.0 | 1.5 |
| | 3.6 | 4.9 | 6.5 | | -3.7 | 6.2 | 3.8 | 9.1 | 5.1 |
| % Profit Before Taxes/Tangible Net Worth | 38.5 | 41.0 | 54.4 | | 44.2 | | 49.5 | 57.0 | 70.5 |
| | (66) 21.4 | (66) 14.7 | (72) 17.1 | | (10) .8 | | (14) 17.1 | (19) 18.6 | 26.6 |
| | 5.2 | 4.7 | 1.9 | | -32.8 | | -3.6 | 4.0 | 6.4 |
| % Profit Before Taxes/Total Assets | 15.5 | 16.7 | 15.4 | | 21.0 | 3.2 | 14.4 | 10.5 | 19.1 |
| | 6.6 | 6.7 | 5.0 | | 10.4 | 1.4 | 4.3 | 5.4 | 8.0 |
| | .5 | .7 | -.2 | | -1.4 | -10.2 | -4.3 | .6 | 3.4 |
| Sales/Net Fixed Assets | 7.7 | 9.6 | 12.9 | | 22.2 | 18.8 | 11.9 | 10.0 | 32.5 |
| | 4.3 | 5.5 | 6.0 | | 13.8 | 5.2 | 5.8 | 6.1 | 5.3 |
| | 2.6 | 2.9 | 3.4 | | 8.1 | 2.9 | 3.3 | 3.2 | 3.7 |
| Sales/Total Assets | 2.6 | 2.5 | 3.0 | | 4.3 | 3.6 | 3.3 | 2.7 | 2.6 |
| | 1.8 | 1.8 | 2.0 | | 3.9 | 2.1 | 2.0 | 1.8 | 2.0 |
| | 1.4 | 1.5 | 1.6 | | 2.2 | 1.5 | 1.7 | 1.4 | 1.6 |
| % Depr., Dep., Amort./Sales | 2.5 | 2.3 | 1.9 | | .6 | | 1.7 | 2.8 | 1.6 |
| | (67) 4.4 | (66) 4.4 | (72) 3.9 | | 2.7 | | (13) 2.8 | (19) 5.5 | (16) 4.1 |
| | 6.9 | 7.4 | 6.4 | | 3.4 | | 6.2 | 8.8 | 5.5 |
| % Officers', Directors' Owners' Comp/Sales | 1.7 | 2.9 | 2.0 | | | | 2.1 | | |
| | (24) 3.7 | (30) 3.9 | (38) 3.6 | | | | (10) 4.4 | | |
| | 9.1 | 5.9 | 7.1 | | | | 7.6 | | |
| Net Sales ($) | 1507996M | 2021614M | 1845699M | 1646M | 22837M | 44880M | 114769M | 329454M | 1332113M |
| Total Assets ($) | 848317M | 1192470M | 936512M | 3379M | 7665M | 28970M | 55968M | 213054M | 627476M |

M = $ thousand   MM = $ million
See Pages 9 through 22 for Explanation of Ratios and Data

## Current Data Sorted by Assets

## Comparative Historical Data

| 0-500M | 500M-2MM | 2-10MM | 10-50MM | 50-100MM | 100-250MM | | 4/1/07-3/31/08 ALL | 4/1/08-3/31/09 ALL |
|---|---|---|---|---|---|---|---|---|
| | | | | | | **Type of Statement** | | |
| | | | 5 | | | Unqualified | 2 | 4 |
| | | 3 | 3 | | | Reviewed | 2 | 2 |
| | | 2 | | | | Compiled | 2 | 4 |
| 2 | 1 | 1 | | | | Tax Returns | 3 | |
| 1 | | 1 | | | | Other | 7 | 9 |
| | | 6 | 5 | | | | | |
| | 6 (4/1-9/30/11) | | 24 (10/1/11-3/31/12) | | | | | |
| 3 | 1 | 13 | 13 | | | **NUMBER OF STATEMENTS** | 16 | 19 |
| % | % | % | % | % | % | **ASSETS** | % | % |
| | | 3.1 | 3.2 | | | Cash & Equivalents | 12.1 | 11.7 |
| | | 14.6 | 20.2 | D | D | Trade Receivables (net) | 18.2 | 17.0 |
| | | 6.5 | 9.0 | A | A | Inventory | 13.5 | 6.4 |
| | | 1.8 | 10.7 | T | T | All Other Current | 1.6 | 2.6 |
| | | 26.0 | 43.1 | A | A | Total Current | 45.4 | 37.7 |
| | | 42.5 | 40.8 | | | Fixed Assets (net) | 46.1 | 48.9 |
| | | 22.3 | 6.5 | N | N | Intangibles (net) | 1.1 | 5.9 |
| | | 9.1 | 9.6 | O | O | All Other Non-Current | 7.4 | 7.6 |
| | | 100.0 | 100.0 | T | T | Total | 100.0 | 100.0 |
| | | | | | | **LIABILITIES** | | |
| | | 6.6 | 4.4 | A | A | Notes Payable-Short Term | 1.6 | 3.3 |
| | | 7.2 | 12.0 | V | V | Cur. Mat.-L.T.D. | 6.3 | 6.3 |
| | | 9.3 | 11.8 | A | A | Trade Payables | 10.1 | 8.0 |
| | | .2 | .2 | I | I | Income Taxes Payable | .2 | .1 |
| | | 2.5 | 16.1 | L | L | All Other Current | 7.1 | 6.4 |
| | | 25.7 | 44.5 | A | A | Total Current | 25.3 | 24.0 |
| | | 33.7 | 18.8 | B | B | Long-Term Debt | 30.8 | 34.9 |
| | | .3 | .0 | L | L | Deferred Taxes | .9 | .6 |
| | | 8.6 | 10.2 | E | E | All Other Non-Current | 7.4 | 6.3 |
| | | 31.7 | 26.5 | | | Net Worth | 35.7 | 34.2 |
| | | 100.0 | 100.0 | | | Total Liabilties & Net Worth | 100.0 | 100.0 |
| | | | | | | **INCOME DATA** | | |
| | | 100.0 | 100.0 | | | Net Sales | 100.0 | 100.0 |
| | | | | | | Gross Profit | | |
| | | 90.4 | 97.9 | | | Operating Expenses | 94.9 | 94.1 |
| | | 9.6 | 2.1 | | | Operating Profit | 5.1 | 5.9 |
| | | 6.4 | .7 | | | All Other Expenses (net) | 3.4 | 2.1 |
| | | 3.2 | 1.4 | | | Profit Before Taxes | 1.7 | 3.8 |
| | | | | | | **RATIOS** | | |
| | | 1.7 | 1.7 | | | | 2.8 | 2.5 |
| | | .9 | 1.0 | | | Current | 1.8 | 1.4 |
| | | .7 | .7 | | | | 1.1 | .9 |
| | | 1.1 | .9 | | | | 1.9 | 1.9 |
| | | .8 | .6 | | | Quick | 1.1 | 1.0 |
| | | .4 | .5 | | | | .8 | .8 |
| 27 | | 13.3 | 27   13.5 | | | | 33   11.1 | 32   11.3 |
| 31 | | 11.9 | 45   8.1 | | | Sales/Receivables | 40   9.0 | 41   8.9 |
| 42 | | 8.6 | 89   4.1 | | | | 48   7.6 | 51   7.2 |
| | | | | | | Cost of Sales/Inventory | | |
| | | | | | | Cost of Sales/Payables | | |
| | | 12.7 | 11.3 | | | | 3.8 | 5.8 |
| | | -90.8 | -584.2 | | | Sales/Working Capital | 9.1 | 13.0 |
| | | -12.9 | -15.5 | | | | NM | -41.8 |
| | | 8.4 | 9.3 | | | | 6.0 | 5.9 |
| | | (12) 4.1 | (12) 1.0 | | | EBIT/Interest | (14) 3.1 | (18) 2.5 |
| | | 1.4 | -1.6 | | | | 1.0 | 1.2 |
| | | | | | | Net Profit + Depr., Dep., Amort./Cur. Mat. L/T/D | | |
| | | 1.1 | .6 | | | | .6 | .6 |
| | | 3.1 | 2.4 | | | Fixed/Worth | 1.4 | 1.5 |
| | | -1.0 | -10.3 | | | | 3.3 | -29.0 |
| | | 1.0 | 1.0 | | | | .6 | .6 |
| | | 5.1 | 2.1 | | | Debt/Worth | 1.8 | 2.8 |
| | | -2.7 | -18.4 | | | | 6.6 | -43.8 |
| | | | | | | | 34.2 | 32.6 |
| | | | | | | % Profit Before Taxes/Tangible Net Worth | (14) 17.6 | (14) 18.9 |
| | | | | | | | 8.5 | 7.3 |
| | | 12.8 | 8.7 | | | | 10.6 | 9.1 |
| | | 4.9 | 1.2 | | | % Profit Before Taxes/Total Assets | 4.1 | 5.8 |
| | | -.5 | -5.6 | | | | 1.5 | 1.3 |
| | | 8.2 | 8.1 | | | | 6.6 | 6.2 |
| | | 4.5 | 2.9 | | | Sales/Net Fixed Assets | 3.9 | 3.6 |
| | | 1.8 | 2.2 | | | | 2.4 | 2.7 |
| | | 1.9 | 1.8 | | | | 2.4 | 2.4 |
| | | 1.2 | 1.2 | | | Sales/Total Assets | 1.7 | 1.6 |
| | | 1.0 | .9 | | | | 1.2 | 1.2 |
| | | 2.7 | 3.2 | | | | 2.1 | 2.3 |
| | | 4.3 | (11) 3.7 | | | % Depr., Dep., Amort./Sales | (15) 4.8 | 4.0 |
| | | 12.7 | 6.0 | | | | 6.9 | 6.8 |
| | | | | | | % Officers', Directors' Owners' Comp/Sales | | |
| 2102M | 153M | 118125M | 419257M | | | Net Sales ($) | 409736M | 495427M |
| 473M | 1969M | 79409M | 319545M | | | Total Assets ($) | 278287M | 347377M |

M = $ thousand    MM = $ million
See Pages 9 through 22 for Explanation of Ratios and Data

## Comparative Historical Data      Current Data Sorted by Sales

| | | | Type of Statement | | | | | | |
|---|---|---|---|---|---|---|---|---|---|
| 5 | 5 | 8 | Unqualified | | | 1 | 2 | 1 | 4 |
| 2 | 8 | 6 | Reviewed | 2 | | | | 4 | |
| 1 | 1 | 1 | Compiled | | | | | 1 | |
| | 1 | 3 | Tax Returns | 1 | 1 | | 1 | | |
| 6 | 11 | 12 | Other | 1 | | | 5 | 3 | 3 |
| 4/1/09- | 4/1/10- | 4/1/11- | | | 6 (4/1-9/30/11) | | 24 (10/1/11-3/31/12) | | |
| 3/31/10 | 3/31/11 | 3/31/12 | | | | | | | |
| ALL | ALL | ALL | | 0-1MM | 1-3MM | 3-5MM | 5-10MM | 10-25MM | 25MM & OVER |
| 14 | 26 | 30 | **NUMBER OF STATEMENTS** | 4 | 1 | 1 | 8 | 9 | 7 |
| % | % | % | **ASSETS** | % | % | % | % | % | % |
| 11.9 | 8.6 | 6.7 | Cash & Equivalents | | | | | | |
| 19.6 | 23.2 | 18.7 | Trade Receivables (net) | | | | | | |
| 11.8 | 9.7 | 7.4 | Inventory | | | | | | |
| 1.8 | 1.4 | 7.3 | All Other Current | | | | | | |
| 45.0 | 42.9 | 40.1 | Total Current | | | | | | |
| 39.1 | 41.9 | 39.2 | Fixed Assets (net) | | | | | | |
| 6.5 | 7.3 | 12.5 | Intangibles (net) | | | | | | |
| 9.4 | 7.9 | 8.2 | All Other Non-Current | | | | | | |
| 100.0 | 100.0 | 100.0 | Total | | | | | | |
| | | | **LIABILITIES** | | | | | | |
| 3.3 | 6.8 | 4.8 | Notes Payable-Short Term | | | | | | |
| 11.4 | 10.0 | 11.4 | Cur. Mat.-L.T.D. | | | | | | |
| 8.7 | 11.9 | 10.5 | Trade Payables | | | | | | |
| .0 | .1 | .2 | Income Taxes Payable | | | | | | |
| 4.9 | 7.5 | 9.5 | All Other Current | | | | | | |
| 28.3 | 36.3 | 36.3 | Total Current | | | | | | |
| 19.6 | 26.3 | 26.8 | Long-Term Debt | | | | | | |
| .1 | .1 | .2 | Deferred Taxes | | | | | | |
| 4.0 | 4.9 | 9.5 | All Other Non-Current | | | | | | |
| 48.0 | 32.4 | 27.3 | Net Worth | | | | | | |
| 100.0 | 100.0 | 100.0 | Total Liabilties & Net Worth | | | | | | |
| | | | **INCOME DATA** | | | | | | |
| 100.0 | 100.0 | 100.0 | Net Sales | | | | | | |
| | | | Gross Profit | | | | | | |
| 92.6 | 95.5 | 93.9 | Operating Expenses | | | | | | |
| 7.4 | 4.5 | 6.1 | Operating Profit | | | | | | |
| 2.1 | 2.2 | 3.5 | All Other Expenses (net) | | | | | | |
| 5.3 | 2.3 | 2.7 | Profit Before Taxes | | | | | | |
| | | | **RATIOS** | | | | | | |
| 3.6 | 2.2 | 1.8 | | | | | | | |
| 2.0 | 1.3 | 1.0 | Current | | | | | | |
| 1.1 | .9 | .7 | | | | | | | |
| 2.5 | 1.3 | 1.1 | | | | | | | |
| 1.5 | 1.0 | .6 | Quick | | | | | | |
| .8 | .6 | .4 | | | | | | | |
| 32   11.3 | 30   12.1 | 27   13.5 | | | | | | | |
| 43   8.5 | 44   8.3 | 38   9.6 | Sales/Receivables | | | | | | |
| 52   7.1 | 64   5.7 | 56   6.5 | | | | | | | |
| | | | Cost of Sales/Inventory | | | | | | |
| | | | Cost of Sales/Payables | | | | | | |
| 6.1 | 6.8 | 13.8 | | | | | | | |
| 7.0 | 26.6 | UND | Sales/Working Capital | | | | | | |
| 50.4 | -38.6 | -14.6 | | | | | | | |
| 14.7 | 6.3 | 7.5 | | | | | | | |
| (13)   4.0 | 2.6 | (26)   3.0 | EBIT/Interest | | | | | | |
| 1.3 | 1.2 | .6 | | | | | | | |
| | | | Net Profit + Depr., Dep., Amort./Cur. Mat. L/T/D | | | | | | |
| .4 | .9 | 1.0 | | | | | | | |
| 1.1 | 1.4 | 2.5 | Fixed/Worth | | | | | | |
| 2.7 | NM | -2.9 | | | | | | | |
| .3 | 1.0 | 1.0 | | | | | | | |
| 1.0 | 2.1 | -4.9 | Debt/Worth | | | | | | |
| 4.2 | NM | -6.3 | | | | | | | |
| 29.6 | 31.0 | 106.1 | | | | | | | |
| (12)   15.5 | (20)   15.3 | (20)   19.9 | % Profit Before Taxes/Tangible Net Worth | | | | | | |
| 4.7 | 3.5 | -.1 | | | | | | | |
| 16.3 | 8.5 | 12.2 | | | | | | | |
| 4.1 | 3.5 | 4.8 | % Profit Before Taxes/Total Assets | | | | | | |
| .6 | .9 | -1.7 | | | | | | | |
| 7.0 | 7.0 | 10.3 | | | | | | | |
| 3.1 | 5.1 | 3.9 | Sales/Net Fixed Assets | | | | | | |
| 2.2 | 2.9 | 2.1 | | | | | | | |
| 2.3 | 2.2 | 1.9 | | | | | | | |
| 1.6 | 1.6 | 1.3 | Sales/Total Assets | | | | | | |
| 1.0 | 1.2 | .9 | | | | | | | |
| 2.9 | 2.5 | 3.2 | | | | | | | |
| (13)   4.2 | (25)   4.3 | (25)   4.3 | % Depr., Dep., Amort./Sales | | | | | | |
| 7.0 | 6.1 | 10.2 | | | | | | | |
| | | | % Officers', Directors' Owners' Comp/Sales | | | | | | |
| 312641M | 648620M | 539637M | Net Sales ($) | 455M | 1870M | 4741M | 59951M | 152226M | 320394M |
| 223406M | 410072M | 401396M | Total Assets ($) | 4075M | 456M | 6081M | 47395M | 120197M | 223192M |

M = $ thousand    MM = $ million
See Pages 9 through 22 for Explanation of Ratios and Data

**Current Data Sorted by Assets**  |  **Comparative Historical Data**

| Type of Statement | 0-500M | 500M-2MM | 2-10MM | 10-50MM | 50-100MM | 100-250MM | | 4/1/07-3/31/08 ALL | 4/1/08-3/31/09 ALL |
|---|---|---|---|---|---|---|---|---|---|
| Unqualified | | | 6 | 2 | 1 | 2 | | 1 | 2 |
| Reviewed | | 1 | 4 | | | 1 | | 1 | 1 |
| Compiled | 3 | 4 | 2 | 1 | 1 | | | 2 | 3 |
| Tax Returns | 31 | 10 | 3 | | | | | 15 | 15 |
| Other | 15 | 16 | 11 | 4 | 1 | | | 4 | 9 |
| | 19 (4/1-9/30/11) | | | 100 (10/1/11-3/31/12) | | | | ALL | ALL |
| **NUMBER OF STATEMENTS** | 49 | 31 | 26 | 7 | 3 | 3 | | 23 | 30 |

| | 0-500M % | 500M-2MM % | 2-10MM % | 10-50MM % | 50-100MM % | 100-250MM % | | % | % |
|---|---|---|---|---|---|---|---|---|---|
| **ASSETS** | | | | | | | | | |
| Cash & Equivalents | 24.5 | 14.0 | 13.3 | | | | | 21.3 | 12.5 |
| Trade Receivables (net) | 3.7 | 7.2 | 10.0 | | | | | 3.3 | 4.2 |
| Inventory | 11.1 | 4.4 | 6.1 | | | | | 4.0 | 5.6 |
| All Other Current | .8 | .1 | 1.1 | | | | | 2.9 | .8 |
| Total Current | 40.1 | 25.7 | 30.5 | | | | | 31.5 | 23.1 |
| Fixed Assets (net) | 39.1 | 55.0 | 51.8 | | | | | 62.2 | 60.5 |
| Intangibles (net) | 8.1 | 6.5 | 5.3 | | | | | 3.4 | 4.6 |
| All Other Non-Current | 12.6 | 12.8 | 12.4 | | | | | 2.8 | 11.8 |
| Total | 100.0 | 100.0 | 100.0 | | | | | 100.0 | 100.0 |
| **LIABILITIES** | | | | | | | | | |
| Notes Payable-Short Term | 9.0 | 3.0 | 4.7 | | | | | 12.6 | 16.9 |
| Cur. Mat.-L.T.D. | 4.9 | 3.8 | 6.7 | | | | | 1.6 | 1.1 |
| Trade Payables | 6.0 | 2.4 | 6.2 | | | | | 2.1 | 4.7 |
| Income Taxes Payable | .1 | .1 | .4 | | | | | .0 | .0 |
| All Other Current | 32.8 | 8.0 | 17.4 | | | | | 28.7 | 6.0 |
| Total Current | 52.8 | 17.3 | 35.5 | | | | | 45.0 | 28.7 |
| Long-Term Debt | 42.8 | 43.2 | 30.5 | | | | | 35.3 | 36.2 |
| Deferred Taxes | .0 | .0 | .1 | | | | | .0 | .0 |
| All Other Non-Current | 16.5 | 3.6 | 2.1 | | | | | 29.8 | 9.4 |
| Net Worth | -12.1 | 35.9 | 31.9 | | | | | -10.1 | 25.7 |
| Total Liabilities & Net Worth | 100.0 | 100.0 | 100.0 | | | | | 100.0 | 100.0 |
| **INCOME DATA** | | | | | | | | | |
| Net Sales | 100.0 | 100.0 | 100.0 | | | | | 100.0 | 100.0 |
| Gross Profit | | | | | | | | | |
| Operating Expenses | 91.2 | 84.1 | 89.2 | | | | | 85.9 | 89.7 |
| Operating Profit | 8.8 | 15.9 | 10.8 | | | | | 14.1 | 10.3 |
| All Other Expenses (net) | 1.9 | 9.6 | 5.6 | | | | | 5.5 | 5.5 |
| Profit Before Taxes | 6.9 | 6.3 | 5.3 | | | | | 8.5 | 4.8 |

| **RATIOS** | 0-500M | 500M-2MM | 2-10MM | 10-50MM | 50-100MM | 100-250MM | | | |
|---|---|---|---|---|---|---|---|---|---|
| Current | 4.7 | 3.2 | 2.3 | | | | | 4.5 | 4.3 |
| | 1.4 | 1.3 | 1.1 | | | | | 1.0 | .9 |
| | .3 | .2 | .6 | | | | | .4 | .4 |
| Quick | 3.8 | 3.2 | 1.4 | | | | | 3.0 | 3.1 |
| | 1.0 | .8 | .8 | | | | | .8 | .7 |
| | .1 | .2 | .4 | | | | | .3 | .2 |
| Sales/Receivables | 0 UND | 0 UND | 0 UND | | | | | 0 UND | 0 UND |
| | 0 UND | 0 UND | 9 38.5 | | | | | 0 UND | 0 UND |
| | 0 UND | 9 41.7 | 37 9.8 | | | | | 1 411.3 | 5 67.8 |
| Cost of Sales/Inventory | | | | | | | | | |
| Cost of Sales/Payables | | | | | | | | | |
| Sales/Working Capital | 16.0 | 8.5 | 4.3 | | | | | 9.9 | 11.8 |
| | 52.4 | 47.2 | 47.2 | | | | | UND | -135.0 |
| | -11.7 | -3.7 | -8.6 | | | | | -16.5 | -14.2 |
| EBIT/Interest | 11.6 | 5.6 | 31.7 | | | | | 13.8 | 25.4 |
| | (32) 3.4 | (22) 1.8 | (22) 4.4 | | | | | (15) 4.4 | (24) 3.7 |
| | 1.1 | .5 | -.2 | | | | | 1.5 | .2 |
| Net Profit + Depr., Dep., Amort./Cur. Mat. L/T/D | | | | | | | | | |
| Fixed/Worth | .5 | .1 | .5 | | | | | 1.8 | .6 |
| | 3.7 | 2.7 | 2.2 | | | | | 12.3 | 2.5 |
| | -.6 | -13.9 | NM | | | | | -1.8 | -32.4 |
| Debt/Worth | .8 | .3 | .7 | | | | | 1.4 | .8 |
| | 40.5 | 2.2 | 3.9 | | | | | 13.0 | 2.8 |
| | -1.9 | -13.1 | NM | | | | | -3.8 | -43.4 |
| % Profit Before Taxes/Tangible Net Worth | 226.4 | 41.4 | 35.4 | | | | | 179.4 | 66.3 |
| | (27) 88.0 | (21) 11.7 | (20) 10.0 | | | | | (14) 57.7 | (22) 23.2 |
| | 30.8 | -1.3 | -3.0 | | | | | 17.2 | -5.3 |
| % Profit Before Taxes/Total Assets | 48.4 | 14.9 | 8.5 | | | | | 50.1 | 20.3 |
| | 13.8 | 4.5 | 3.2 | | | | | 19.1 | 3.3 |
| | .0 | -1.4 | -3.7 | | | | | 1.7 | -4.8 |
| Sales/Net Fixed Assets | 75.2 | 97.8 | 5.0 | | | | | 24.0 | 12.3 |
| | 12.9 | 2.4 | 1.3 | | | | | 4.7 | 1.8 |
| | 4.8 | .6 | .5 | | | | | 1.5 | .8 |
| Sales/Total Assets | 7.3 | 2.9 | 1.8 | | | | | 7.3 | 4.6 |
| | 4.3 | 1.5 | .8 | | | | | 2.6 | 1.3 |
| | 2.0 | .4 | .3 | | | | | 1.0 | .5 |
| % Depr., Dep., Amort./Sales | 1.1 | 1.9 | 2.8 | | | | | 1.4 | 2.3 |
| | (28) 2.0 | (18) 3.7 | (21) 5.5 | | | | | (14) 3.5 | (27) 3.3 |
| | 3.9 | 6.1 | 10.6 | | | | | 7.6 | 7.5 |
| % Officers', Directors' Owners' Comp/Sales | 8.0 | 3.6 | | | | | | 2.7 | 4.8 |
| | (29) 10.4 | (12) 5.0 | | | | | | (12) 6.9 | (13) 8.9 |
| | 17.9 | 10.7 | | | | | | 13.9 | 13.1 |
| Net Sales ($) | 52098M | 63310M | 157647M | 93143M | 65509M | 1103955M | | 30611M | 97112M |
| Total Assets ($) | 10128M | 36063M | 120026M | 161447M | 180526M | 467249M | | 22673M | 143290M |

M = $ thousand   MM = $ million
See Pages 9 through 22 for Explanation of Ratios and Data

## Comparative Historical Data | | | | Current Data Sorted by Sales

| | | | Type of Statement | 0-1MM | 1-3MM | 3-5MM | 5-10MM | 10-25MM | 25MM & OVER |
|---|---|---|---|---|---|---|---|---|---|
| 11 | 7 | 11 | Unqualified | | 3 | 1 | 2 | 3 | 2 |
| 2 | 1 | 6 | Reviewed | | | 2 | 2 | 1 | 1 |
| 5 | 5 | 10 | Compiled | 5 | 3 | 1 | 1 | | |
| 20 | 27 | 45 | Tax Returns | 22 | 15 | 4 | 1 | 1 | 2 |
| 20 | 36 | 47 | Other | 24 | 11 | 2 | 7 | | 3 |
| 4/1/09-3/31/10 ALL | 4/1/10-3/31/11 ALL | 4/1/11-3/31/12 ALL | | 19 (4/1-9/30/11) | | | 100 (10/1/11-3/31/12) | | |
| 58 | 76 | 119 | **NUMBER OF STATEMENTS** | 51 | 32 | 10 | 13 | 5 | 8 |
| % | % | % | **ASSETS** | % | % | % | % | % | % |
| 18.1 | 18.5 | 18.6 | Cash & Equivalents | 19.2 | 18.2 | 26.2 | 14.5 | | |
| 5.4 | 5.2 | 5.8 | Trade Receivables (net) | 1.1 | 3.6 | 19.7 | 17.8 | | |
| 3.3 | 3.1 | 7.1 | Inventory | 3.7 | 11.5 | 12.8 | 3.2 | | |
| 1.2 | 2.5 | .6 | All Other Current | .6 | 1.2 | .2 | .4 | | |
| 28.0 | 29.3 | 32.1 | Total Current | 24.6 | 34.4 | 59.0 | 35.9 | | |
| 59.5 | 52.2 | 46.8 | Fixed Assets (net) | 53.9 | 53.2 | 28.5 | 20.8 | | |
| 2.0 | 9.3 | 6.3 | Intangibles (net) | 7.6 | 5.9 | 1.1 | 6.4 | | |
| 10.6 | 9.2 | 14.8 | All Other Non-Current | 13.8 | 6.4 | 11.4 | 36.9 | | |
| 100.0 | 100.0 | 100.0 | Total | 100.0 | 100.0 | 100.0 | 100.0 | | |
| | | | **LIABILITIES** | | | | | | |
| 12.4 | 8.2 | 5.7 | Notes Payable-Short Term | 5.8 | 6.6 | 5.3 | 5.9 | | |
| 4.2 | 2.7 | 5.0 | Cur. Mat.-L.T.D. | 7.6 | 3.5 | .3 | .9 | | |
| 6.2 | 1.6 | 4.6 | Trade Payables | 4.0 | 4.2 | 4.9 | 7.9 | | |
| .9 | .0 | .2 | Income Taxes Payable | .1 | .0 | .3 | .9 | | |
| 9.8 | 11.9 | 20.9 | All Other Current | 21.0 | 23.8 | 21.5 | 13.2 | | |
| 33.5 | 24.4 | 36.4 | Total Current | 38.5 | 38.0 | 32.2 | 28.7 | | |
| 32.3 | 47.8 | 38.4 | Long-Term Debt | 55.1 | 34.6 | 4.7 | 14.5 | | |
| .1 | .0 | .0 | Deferred Taxes | .0 | .0 | .0 | .1 | | |
| 5.0 | 8.2 | 8.7 | All Other Non-Current | 9.3 | 13.5 | 4.4 | 1.7 | | |
| 29.1 | 19.6 | 16.5 | Net Worth | -2.9 | 13.9 | 58.6 | 55.0 | | |
| 100.0 | 100.0 | 100.0 | Total Liabilities & Net Worth | 100.0 | 100.0 | 100.0 | 100.0 | | |
| | | | **INCOME DATA** | | | | | | |
| 100.0 | 100.0 | 100.0 | Net Sales | 100.0 | 100.0 | 100.0 | 100.0 | | |
| | | | Gross Profit | | | | | | |
| 88.3 | 86.5 | 87.8 | Operating Expenses | 85.7 | 88.1 | 95.7 | 86.4 | | |
| 11.7 | 13.5 | 12.2 | Operating Profit | 14.3 | 11.9 | 4.3 | 13.6 | | |
| 7.6 | 6.5 | 4.8 | All Other Expenses (net) | 7.4 | 3.6 | .5 | 2.5 | | |
| 4.0 | 7.0 | 7.4 | Profit Before Taxes | 6.9 | 8.3 | 3.8 | 11.0 | | |
| | | | **RATIOS** | | | | | | |
| 2.6 | 4.7 | 3.5 | | 4.6 | 3.9 | 4.2 | 2.7 | | |
| 1.3 | 1.6 | 1.3 | Current | .5 | 1.7 | 2.5 | 1.5 | | |
| .3 | .7 | .3 | | .1 | .5 | 1.3 | .7 | | |
| 2.2 | 4.0 | 3.0 | | 3.5 | 3.6 | 4.2 | 2.7 | | |
| 1.1 | 1.1 | 1.0 | Quick | .4 | .9 | 2.1 | 1.0 | | |
| .3 | .2 | .2 | | .1 | .3 | 1.0 | .6 | | |
| 0 UND | 0 UND | 0 UND | | 0 UND | 0 UND | 0 UND | 6 58.5 | | |
| 2 209.0 | 0 UND | 0 UND | Sales/Receivables | 0 UND | 0 UND | 5 76.8 | 25 14.4 | | |
| 20 18.1 | 6 63.9 | 7 50.0 | | 0 UND | 2 212.2 | 29 12.8 | 64 5.7 | | |
| | | | Cost of Sales/Inventory | | | | | | |
| | | | Cost of Sales/Payables | | | | | | |
| 7.2 | 7.8 | 12.0 | | 14.2 | 12.8 | 4.5 | 4.2 | | |
| 71.1 | 34.7 | 47.2 | Sales/Working Capital | -18.3 | 39.2 | 12.9 | 20.9 | | |
| -4.8 | -19.7 | -9.4 | | -3.0 | -15.1 | 70.9 | -27.6 | | |
| 9.6 | 7.2 | 11.6 | | 3.8 | 9.0 | | 25.9 | | |
| (39) 2.3 | (51) 2.2 | (88) 3.2 | EBIT/Interest | (32) 2.5 | (24) 2.6 | | (12) 1.7 | | |
| .8 | .8 | .8 | | .6 | 1.3 | | -2.4 | | |
| | | | Net Profit + Depr., Dep., Amort./Cur. Mat. L/T/D | | | | | | |
| .6 | .5 | .4 | | .6 | .7 | .0 | .0 | | |
| 1.5 | 2.3 | 2.0 | Fixed/Worth | 6.3 | 2.7 | .4 | .6 | | |
| 7.9 | -4.0 | -6.4 | | -1.7 | -10.3 | .7 | 3.1 | | |
| .5 | .5 | .4 | | .9 | .5 | .2 | .2 | | |
| 1.6 | 2.6 | 4.1 | Debt/Worth | 42.3 | 4.9 | .3 | .9 | | |
| 21.7 | -5.7 | -7.8 | | -3.0 | -11.9 | 2.3 | 10.7 | | |
| 32.6 | 87.4 | 84.5 | | 163.6 | 98.8 | | 13.2 | | |
| (46) 10.3 | (50) 15.1 | (79) 15.2 | % Profit Before Taxes/Tangible Net Worth | (27) 34.6 | (22) 60.7 | | (11) -4.2 | | |
| -1.0 | .1 | 2.2 | | .0 | 9.9 | | -12.9 | | |
| 14.1 | 19.4 | 23.4 | | 31.7 | 47.2 | 18.1 | 10.8 | | |
| 2.1 | 3.9 | 5.4 | % Profit Before Taxes/Total Assets | 4.5 | 8.5 | 10.6 | 4.4 | | |
| -1.8 | -.5 | -1.3 | | -1.4 | .9 | 3.5 | -4.1 | | |
| 10.1 | 23.9 | 31.5 | | 17.6 | 28.0 | 347.1 | 932.6 | | |
| 1.4 | 4.1 | 5.0 | Sales/Net Fixed Assets | 3.5 | 6.1 | 7.1 | 28.3 | | |
| .4 | .8 | .9 | | .6 | .9 | 4.6 | 4.0 | | |
| 3.2 | 3.6 | 4.1 | | 3.6 | 5.0 | 9.4 | 3.6 | | |
| .7 | 1.3 | 1.6 | Sales/Total Assets | 1.4 | 2.2 | 3.4 | 2.2 | | |
| .3 | .5 | .6 | | .4 | .8 | 1.3 | .5 | | |
| 1.7 | 2.0 | 1.4 | | 1.9 | 1.3 | | | | |
| (50) 4.0 | (54) 4.7 | (77) 3.9 | % Depr., Dep., Amort./Sales | (31) 3.9 | (21) 4.2 | | | | |
| 8.6 | 7.9 | 7.2 | | 7.2 | 6.5 | | | | |
| 3.1 | 4.5 | 3.6 | | 8.5 | 4.4 | | | | |
| (19) 6.0 | (32) 7.1 | (50) 8.2 | % Officers', Directors' Owners' Comp/Sales | (20) 13.9 | (16) 7.6 | | | | |
| 11.2 | 12.1 | 14.3 | | 19.1 | 10.3 | | | | |
| 533298M | 210774M | 1535662M | Net Sales ($) | 21387M | 56524M | 40124M | 88873M | 67362M | 1261392M |
| 582657M | 269803M | 975439M | Total Assets ($) | 41715M | 50246M | 26305M | 143087M | 100722M | 613364M |

M = $ thousand    MM = $ million
See Pages 9 through 22 for Explanation of Ratios and Data

## Current Data Sorted by Assets      Comparative Historical Data

**Type of Statement**

| 0-500M | 500M-2MM | 2-10MM | 10-50MM | 50-100MM | 100-250MM | Type of Statement | 4/1/07-3/31/08 ALL | 4/1/08-3/31/09 ALL |
|---|---|---|---|---|---|---|---|---|
|  |  | 1 | 1 |  |  | Unqualified | 3 | 4 |
|  |  | 3 |  |  |  | Reviewed | 5 | 3 |
|  |  | 1 |  |  |  | Compiled | 1 | 5 |
| 5 | 2 | 1 |  |  |  | Tax Returns | 7 | 8 |
|  | 9 | 3 | 2 |  |  | Other | 13 | 16 |
|  | 6 (4/1-9/30/11) |  | 22 (10/1/11-3/31/12) |  |  |  |  |  |
| 5 | 11 | 9 | 3 |  |  | NUMBER OF STATEMENTS | 29 | 36 |
| % | % | % | % | % | % | | % | % |

**ASSETS**

| 0-500M | 500M-2MM | 2-10MM | 10-50MM | 50-100MM | 100-250MM | | 07-08 ALL | 08-09 ALL |
|---|---|---|---|---|---|---|---|---|
|  | 17.4 |  |  | D A T A | D A T A | Cash & Equivalents | 14.1 | 10.2 |
|  | 13.8 |  |  |  |  | Trade Receivables (net) | 21.5 | 21.6 |
|  | 5.3 |  |  |  |  | Inventory | 13.6 | 9.6 |
|  | .3 |  |  |  |  | All Other Current | 2.0 | 1.8 |
|  | 36.8 |  |  | N O T | N O T | Total Current | 51.1 | 43.3 |
|  | 50.0 |  |  |  |  | Fixed Assets (net) | 39.7 | 35.0 |
|  | 8.0 |  |  |  |  | Intangibles (net) | 4.4 | 10.9 |
|  | 5.3 |  |  | A V A I L A B L E | A V A I L A B L E | All Other Non-Current | 4.7 | 10.9 |
|  | 100.0 |  |  |  |  | Total | 100.0 | 100.0 |

**LIABILITIES**

| 0-500M | 500M-2MM | 2-10MM | 10-50MM | 50-100MM | 100-250MM | | 07-08 ALL | 08-09 ALL |
|---|---|---|---|---|---|---|---|---|
|  | 9.8 |  |  |  |  | Notes Payable-Short Term | 5.9 | 15.4 |
|  | 3.3 |  |  |  |  | Cur. Mat.-L.T.D. | 7.8 | 11.3 |
|  | 9.0 |  |  |  |  | Trade Payables | 10.9 | 10.9 |
|  | .0 |  |  |  |  | Income Taxes Payable | .2 | .0 |
|  | 21.1 |  |  |  |  | All Other Current | 12.7 | 20.0 |
|  | 43.2 |  |  |  |  | Total Current | 37.4 | 57.6 |
|  | 30.6 |  |  |  |  | Long-Term Debt | 27.6 | 21.6 |
|  | .1 |  |  |  |  | Deferred Taxes | .4 | .2 |
|  | 4.0 |  |  |  |  | All Other Non-Current | 4.4 | 4.4 |
|  | 22.1 |  |  |  |  | Net Worth | 30.2 | 16.2 |
|  | 100.0 |  |  |  |  | Total Liabilities & Net Worth | 100.0 | 100.0 |

**INCOME DATA**

| 0-500M | 500M-2MM | 2-10MM | 10-50MM | 50-100MM | 100-250MM | | 07-08 ALL | 08-09 ALL |
|---|---|---|---|---|---|---|---|---|
|  | 100.0 |  |  |  |  | Net Sales | 100.0 | 100.0 |
|  |  |  |  |  |  | Gross Profit |  |  |
|  | 91.5 |  |  |  |  | Operating Expenses | 92.2 | 94.8 |
|  | 8.5 |  |  |  |  | Operating Profit | 7.8 | 5.2 |
|  | 5.7 |  |  |  |  | All Other Expenses (net) | 2.9 | 2.9 |
|  | 2.8 |  |  |  |  | Profit Before Taxes | 4.8 | 2.3 |

**RATIOS**

| 0-500M | 500M-2MM | 2-10MM | 10-50MM | 50-100MM | 100-250MM | | 07-08 ALL | 08-09 ALL |
|---|---|---|---|---|---|---|---|---|
|  | 1.4 |  |  |  |  | Current | 2.6 | 1.8 |
|  | .7 |  |  |  |  |  | 1.5 | 1.1 |
|  | .1 |  |  |  |  |  | .8 | .5 |
|  | 1.2 |  |  |  |  | Quick | 1.7 | 1.2 |
|  | .5 |  |  |  |  |  | .9 | .8 |
|  | .1 |  |  |  |  |  | .4 | .3 |
|  | 0   UND |  |  |  |  | Sales/Receivables | 13   29.1 | 11   32.1 |
|  | 5   74.2 |  |  |  |  |  | 32   11.5 | 28   13.0 |
|  | 25   14.7 |  |  |  |  |  | 44   8.4 | 51   7.1 |
|  |  |  |  |  |  | Cost of Sales/Inventory |  |  |
|  |  |  |  |  |  | Cost of Sales/Payables |  |  |
|  | 19.9 |  |  |  |  | Sales/Working Capital | 7.1 | 9.1 |
|  | -20.7 |  |  |  |  |  | 27.4 | 58.6 |
|  | -2.7 |  |  |  |  |  | -65.9 | -10.2 |
|  |  |  |  |  |  | EBIT/Interest | 21.1 | 6.0 |
|  |  |  |  |  |  |  | (26) 2.9 | (35) 1.8 |
|  |  |  |  |  |  |  | .3 | -.3 |
|  |  |  |  |  |  | Net Profit + Depr., Dep., Amort./Cur. Mat. L/T/D |  |  |
|  | .9 |  |  |  |  | Fixed/Worth | .4 | .3 |
|  | 2.0 |  |  |  |  |  | 1.2 | 1.4 |
|  | 5.0 |  |  |  |  |  | 3.7 | -39.6 |
|  | 1.6 |  |  |  |  | Debt/Worth | .9 | 1.0 |
|  | 2.0 |  |  |  |  |  | 1.9 | 2.6 |
|  | 4.2 |  |  |  |  |  | 6.0 | -9.8 |
|  |  |  |  |  |  | % Profit Before Taxes/Tangible Net Worth | 75.2 | 44.1 |
|  |  |  |  |  |  |  | (25) 23.4 | (25) 12.0 |
|  |  |  |  |  |  |  | 6.2 | -8.4 |
|  | 12.3 |  |  |  |  | % Profit Before Taxes/Total Assets | 26.9 | 10.2 |
|  | 4.3 |  |  |  |  |  | 5.8 | 2.5 |
|  | -2.9 |  |  |  |  |  | -1.0 | -3.8 |
|  | 32.6 |  |  |  |  | Sales/Net Fixed Assets | 18.7 | 55.0 |
|  | 8.9 |  |  |  |  |  | 7.8 | 9.1 |
|  | 1.4 |  |  |  |  |  | 3.6 | 3.9 |
|  | 4.8 |  |  |  |  | Sales/Total Assets | 4.2 | 4.1 |
|  | 3.1 |  |  |  |  |  | 2.7 | 2.4 |
|  | .9 |  |  |  |  |  | 1.8 | 1.0 |
|  |  |  |  |  |  | % Depr., Dep., Amort./Sales | 2.2 | 1.3 |
|  |  |  |  |  |  |  | (25) 3.9 | (24) 2.9 |
|  |  |  |  |  |  |  | 6.9 | 7.4 |
|  |  |  |  |  |  | % Officers', Directors' Owners' Comp/Sales | 5.3 | 2.1 |
|  |  |  |  |  |  |  | (13) 7.0 | (15) 4.7 |
|  |  |  |  |  |  |  | 10.4 | 9.5 |

| 0-500M | 500M-2MM | 2-10MM | 10-50MM | | 07-08 ALL | 08-09 ALL |
|---|---|---|---|---|---|---|
| 5121M | 48249M | 109073M | 154444M | Net Sales ($) | 563776M | 285416M |
| 963M | 11824M | 45150M | 70493M | Total Assets ($) | 146564M | 173421M |

M = $ thousand    MM = $ million
See Pages 9 through 22 for Explanation of Ratios and Data

## Comparative Historical Data                     Current Data Sorted by Sales

| | | | Type of Statement | | | | | | |
|---|---|---|---|---|---|---|---|---|---|
| 5 | 6 | 2 | Unqualified | | | | | | 2 |
| 2 | 4 | 3 | Reviewed | | 1 | | 2 | | |
| 3 | 2 | 1 | Compiled | | | | | 1 | |
| 9 | 10 | 8 | Tax Returns | 3 | 2 | 1 | 2 | | |
| 15 | 25 | 14 | Other | 3 | 3 | 2 | 1 | 3 | 2 |
| 4/1/09-3/31/10 ALL | 4/1/10-3/31/11 ALL | 4/1/11-3/31/12 ALL | | | 6 (4/1-9/30/11) | | 22 (10/1/11-3/31/12) | | |
| | | | | 0-1MM | 1-3MM | 3-5MM | 5-10MM | 10-25MM | 25MM & OVER |
| 34 | 47 | 28 | NUMBER OF STATEMENTS | 6 | 5 | 4 | 5 | 4 | 4 |
| % | % | % | ASSETS | % | % | % | % | % | % |
| 13.6 | 14.9 | 16.4 | Cash & Equivalents | | | | | | |
| 14.8 | 13.6 | 14.7 | Trade Receivables (net) | | | | | | |
| 8.2 | 5.9 | 8.9 | Inventory | | | | | | |
| 2.7 | 5.9 | 2.6 | All Other Current | | | | | | |
| 39.2 | 40.2 | 42.6 | Total Current | | | | | | |
| 45.4 | 46.3 | 40.8 | Fixed Assets (net) | | | | | | |
| 7.7 | 5.4 | 7.0 | Intangibles (net) | | | | | | |
| 7.7 | 8.2 | 9.6 | All Other Non-Current | | | | | | |
| 100.0 | 100.0 | 100.0 | Total | | | | | | |
| | | | LIABILITIES | | | | | | |
| 6.5 | 4.9 | 12.3 | Notes Payable-Short Term | | | | | | |
| 7.7 | 7.9 | 5.1 | Cur. Mat.-L.T.D. | | | | | | |
| 8.3 | 8.9 | 9.4 | Trade Payables | | | | | | |
| .1 | .0 | .1 | Income Taxes Payable | | | | | | |
| 14.2 | 19.3 | 12.8 | All Other Current | | | | | | |
| 36.8 | 41.1 | 39.6 | Total Current | | | | | | |
| 31.4 | 24.7 | 24.4 | Long-Term Debt | | | | | | |
| .3 | .2 | .2 | Deferred Taxes | | | | | | |
| 2.1 | 7.8 | 5.5 | All Other Non-Current | | | | | | |
| 29.3 | 26.3 | 30.3 | Net Worth | | | | | | |
| 100.0 | 100.0 | 100.0 | Total Liabilities & Net Worth | | | | | | |
| | | | INCOME DATA | | | | | | |
| 100.0 | 100.0 | 100.0 | Net Sales | | | | | | |
| | | | Gross Profit | | | | | | |
| 91.5 | 90.5 | 92.6 | Operating Expenses | | | | | | |
| 8.5 | 9.5 | 7.4 | Operating Profit | | | | | | |
| 3.7 | 4.1 | 2.3 | All Other Expenses (net) | | | | | | |
| 4.8 | 5.4 | 5.0 | Profit Before Taxes | | | | | | |
| | | | RATIOS | | | | | | |
| 1.9 | 3.6 | 1.8 | | | | | | | |
| 1.1 | 1.0 | 1.2 | Current | | | | | | |
| .5 | .4 | .6 | | | | | | | |
| 1.3 | 2.1 | 1.2 | | | | | | | |
| .9 | .9 | .7 | Quick | | | | | | |
| .4 | .3 | .5 | | | | | | | |
| 0  UND | 0  UND | 0  UND | | | | | | | |
| 21  17.4 | 15  24.4 | 13  28.3 | Sales/Receivables | | | | | | |
| 34  10.8 | 32  11.3 | 38  9.7 | | | | | | | |
| | | | Cost of Sales/Inventory | | | | | | |
| | | | Cost of Sales/Payables | | | | | | |
| 10.3 | 8.0 | 16.2 | | | | | | | |
| 54.5 | 192.7 | 44.6 | Sales/Working Capital | | | | | | |
| -12.2 | -8.3 | -13.8 | | | | | | | |
| 2.3 | 7.1 | 7.3 | | | | | | | |
| (25)  .7 | (37)  3.6 | (23)  2.7 | EBIT/Interest | | | | | | |
| -2.2 | 1.0 | 1.0 | | | | | | | |
| | | | Net Profit + Depr., Dep., Amort./Cur. Mat. L/T/D | | | | | | |
| .5 | .5 | .5 | | | | | | | |
| 1.4 | 1.9 | 1.5 | Fixed/Worth | | | | | | |
| 3.7 | 11.2 | 4.8 | | | | | | | |
| 1.0 | .7 | .8 | | | | | | | |
| 1.9 | 2.4 | 2.0 | Debt/Worth | | | | | | |
| 5.3 | 11.9 | 4.1 | | | | | | | |
| 15.3 | 28.8 | 39.3 | | | | | | | |
| (28)  6.0 | (37)  13.7 | (24)  15.0 | % Profit Before Taxes/Tangible Net Worth | | | | | | |
| -13.1 | 3.5 | 1.1 | | | | | | | |
| 9.7 | 14.7 | 23.6 | | | | | | | |
| 1.5 | 6.6 | 6.5 | % Profit Before Taxes/Total Assets | | | | | | |
| -7.6 | .4 | .6 | | | | | | | |
| 16.6 | 16.2 | 31.8 | | | | | | | |
| 7.9 | 7.6 | 9.2 | Sales/Net Fixed Assets | | | | | | |
| 2.5 | 2.2 | 3.6 | | | | | | | |
| 3.6 | 4.4 | 4.3 | | | | | | | |
| 2.2 | 2.3 | 2.5 | Sales/Total Assets | | | | | | |
| 1.4 | 1.1 | 1.3 | | | | | | | |
| 1.2 | 2.6 | 1.9 | | | | | | | |
| (28)  3.7 | (34)  3.7 | (23)  3.5 | % Depr., Dep., Amort./Sales | | | | | | |
| 7.2 | 7.2 | 6.7 | | | | | | | |
| 4.2 | 5.1 | 4.2 | | | | | | | |
| (12)  5.5 | (14)  8.0 | (10)  6.8 | % Officers', Directors' Owners' Comp/Sales | | | | | | |
| 7.7 | 11.9 | 13.9 | | | | | | | |
| 328013M | 912020M | 316887M | Net Sales ($) | 2218M | 11216M | 16084M | 35212M | 58360M | 193797M |
| 166665M | 467754M | 128430M | Total Assets ($) | 2859M | 3793M | 6887M | 18345M | 16648M | 79898M |

**M = $ thousand     MM = $ million**
See Pages 9 through 22 for Explanation of Ratios and Data

## Current Data Sorted by Assets     Comparative Historical Data

| Type of Statement | 0-500M | 500M-2MM | 2-10MM | 10-50MM | 50-100MM | 100-250MM | 4/1/07-3/31/08 ALL | 4/1/08-3/31/09 ALL |
|---|---|---|---|---|---|---|---|---|
| | | 12 (4/1-9/30/11) | | 76 (10/1/11-3/31/12) | | | | |
| Unqualified | | | 1 | 6 | | 1 | 9 | 15 |
| Reviewed | 1 | 1 | 4 | 3 | | | 3 | 5 |
| Compiled | | 2 | 4 | 1 | | | 7 | 2 |
| Tax Returns | 9 | 7 | 9 | 1 | | | 9 | 15 |
| Other | 3 | 5 | 11 | 15 | 2 | 2 | 27 | 27 |
| **NUMBER OF STATEMENTS** | 13 | 15 | 29 | 26 | 2 | 3 | 55 | 64 |
| **ASSETS** | % | % | % | % | % | % | % | % |
| Cash & Equivalents | 36.0 | 15.5 | 7.1 | 13.0 | | | 11.9 | 15.6 |
| Trade Receivables (net) | 13.1 | 14.0 | 17.8 | 9.9 | | | 12.8 | 15.5 |
| Inventory | .5 | 2.4 | .7 | .6 | | | .0 | .1 |
| All Other Current | .4 | 1.2 | 7.8 | 6.6 | | | 4.2 | 3.3 |
| Total Current | 50.0 | 33.0 | 33.4 | 30.0 | | | 29.0 | 34.4 |
| Fixed Assets (net) | 30.7 | 54.0 | 42.8 | 54.4 | | | 47.9 | 40.0 |
| Intangibles (net) | 6.4 | 2.5 | 7.3 | 1.4 | | | 6.1 | 7.8 |
| All Other Non-Current | 12.8 | 10.5 | 16.6 | 14.1 | | | 17.0 | 17.7 |
| Total | 100.0 | 100.0 | 100.0 | 100.0 | | | 100.0 | 100.0 |
| **LIABILITIES** | | | | | | | | |
| Notes Payable-Short Term | 15.9 | 3.7 | 5.6 | .8 | | | 4.7 | 6.5 |
| Cur. Mat.-L.T.D. | 10.8 | 4.3 | 2.4 | 2.7 | | | 3.5 | 5.7 |
| Trade Payables | 3.9 | 3.9 | 5.8 | 9.1 | | | 9.9 | 9.4 |
| Income Taxes Payable | .0 | .0 | .0 | .1 | | | .0 | .1 |
| All Other Current | 16.1 | 9.9 | 13.7 | 16.9 | | | 12.4 | 17.1 |
| Total Current | 46.7 | 21.8 | 27.5 | 29.6 | | | 30.5 | 38.8 |
| Long-Term Debt | 65.6 | 34.8 | 39.5 | 48.3 | | | 43.8 | 43.8 |
| Deferred Taxes | .0 | .4 | .0 | .0 | | | .2 | .6 |
| All Other Non-Current | 10.8 | 9.9 | 6.0 | 2.9 | | | 10.2 | 5.6 |
| Net Worth | -23.1 | 33.1 | 26.9 | 19.1 | | | 15.3 | 11.2 |
| Total Liabilities & Net Worth | 100.0 | 100.0 | 100.0 | 100.0 | | | 100.0 | 100.0 |
| **INCOME DATA** | | | | | | | | |
| Net Sales | 100.0 | 100.0 | 100.0 | 100.0 | | | 100.0 | 100.0 |
| Gross Profit | | | | | | | | |
| Operating Expenses | 89.3 | 71.1 | 77.9 | 81.1 | | | 81.5 | 84.8 |
| Operating Profit | 10.7 | 28.9 | 22.1 | 18.9 | | | 18.5 | 15.2 |
| All Other Expenses (net) | 1.0 | 12.7 | 8.4 | 9.1 | | | 7.5 | 5.0 |
| Profit Before Taxes | 9.7 | 16.2 | 13.7 | 9.7 | | | 11.0 | 10.2 |
| **RATIOS** | | | | | | | | |
| Current | 3.3 | 5.3 | 3.0 | 1.4 | | | 1.9 | 2.0 |
| | 1.6 | 2.5 | 1.3 | 1.0 | | | 1.0 | 1.0 |
| | .4 | .9 | .6 | .6 | | | .6 | .6 |
| Quick | 3.1 | 4.5 | 2.3 | 1.2 | | | 1.7 | 2.0 |
| | 1.6 | 2.3 | .9 | .7 | | | (54) .9 | .9 |
| | .4 | .9 | .4 | .3 | | | .6 | .5 |
| Sales/Receivables | 0 UND | 0 UND | 0 UND | 1 388.1 | | | 0 999.8 | 0 999.8 |
| | 0 UND | 2 215.5 | 5 73.8 | 13 27.3 | | | 4 100.9 | 12 29.2 |
| | 20 18.3 | 31 11.9 | 41 8.9 | 27 13.3 | | | 20 18.2 | 30 12.4 |
| Cost of Sales/Inventory | | | | | | | | |
| Cost of Sales/Payables | | | | | | | | |
| Sales/Working Capital | 16.2 | 3.4 | 6.7 | 17.0 | | | 14.0 | 11.7 |
| | 50.8 | 12.8 | 14.9 | -257.9 | | | -371.7 | NM |
| | -16.3 | -51.0 | -18.5 | -10.2 | | | -8.6 | -15.5 |
| EBIT/Interest | | 29.0 | 14.6 | 15.5 | | | 15.8 | 7.3 |
| | | (10) 8.3 | (23) 3.4 | (17) 9.1 | | | (39) 5.6 | (48) 3.6 |
| | | 3.1 | 1.1 | 1.9 | | | 2.0 | 1.3 |
| Net Profit + Depr., Dep., Amort./Cur. Mat. L/T/D | | | | | | | | |
| Fixed/Worth | .1 | .5 | .7 | .8 | | | 1.0 | .8 |
| | .3 | 1.4 | 2.2 | 2.0 | | | 2.8 | 3.0 |
| | -.8 | 4.1 | -35.6 | -3.5 | | | -2.6 | -18.5 |
| Debt/Worth | .2 | .8 | 1.0 | 1.4 | | | 1.0 | 2.0 |
| | 1.4 | 2.7 | 5.2 | 3.2 | | | 6.9 | 7.9 |
| | -3.1 | 7.7 | -46.2 | -12.1 | | | -6.4 | -16.2 |
| % Profit Before Taxes/Tangible Net Worth | | 38.4 | 67.5 | 58.5 | | | 146.1 | 118.2 |
| | | (12) 19.6 | (21) 24.7 | (18) 26.2 | | | (36) 42.0 | (44) 37.2 |
| | | 10.2 | 5.4 | 1.4 | | | 10.9 | 7.5 |
| % Profit Before Taxes/Total Assets | 70.7 | 12.7 | 12.8 | 13.1 | | | 26.8 | 18.8 |
| | 15.2 | 8.7 | 5.5 | 6.7 | | | 10.0 | 6.0 |
| | 6.0 | 3.5 | .6 | -1.1 | | | 1.3 | .0 |
| Sales/Net Fixed Assets | 77.8 | 9.0 | 55.3 | 28.2 | | | 28.3 | 26.8 |
| | 39.0 | 1.0 | 5.4 | 1.2 | | | 6.6 | 10.2 |
| | 18.7 | .2 | .4 | .3 | | | .5 | .8 |
| Sales/Total Assets | 12.1 | 2.9 | 3.7 | 2.4 | | | 3.6 | 5.5 |
| | 8.5 | .8 | 1.0 | .5 | | | 1.2 | 1.6 |
| | 4.3 | .2 | .3 | .2 | | | .3 | .4 |
| % Depr., Dep., Amort./Sales | | .7 | 1.0 | .5 | | | 1.5 | .8 |
| | | (13) 2.5 | (24) 4.3 | (24) 3.6 | | | (42) 3.5 | (47) 3.3 |
| | | 6.5 | 9.8 | 19.5 | | | 9.2 | 8.6 |
| % Officers', Directors' Owners' Comp/Sales | | .7 | | | | | 2.0 | 1.4 |
| | | (12) 1.3 | | | | | (12) 8.7 | (15) 2.7 |
| | | 6.3 | | | | | 26.3 | 12.6 |
| Net Sales ($) | 18885M | 29839M | 248645M | 803969M | 177671M | 156685M | 1762276M | 2637924M |
| Total Assets ($) | 2867M | 17508M | 139359M | 589627M | 154163M | 425057M | 1197352M | 1736064M |

M = $ thousand    MM = $ million
See Pages 9 through 22 for Explanation of Ratios and Data

## Comparative Historical Data | | | | Current Data Sorted by Sales

| | | | Type of Statement | | | | | | |
|---|---|---|---|---|---|---|---|---|---|
| 20 | 17 | 8 | Unqualified | | 2 | | 1 | 2 | 3 |
| 11 | 9 | 9 | Reviewed | | 1 | | 1 | 3 | 2 |
| 9 | 5 | 7 | Compiled | | 2 | 1 | 1 | 3 | |
| 14 | 18 | 26 | Tax Returns | 11 | 9 | 3 | 1 | 2 | |
| 33 | 27 | 38 | Other | 7 | 5 | 6 | 7 | 6 | 7 |
| 4/1/09-3/31/10 ALL | 4/1/10-3/31/11 ALL | 4/1/11-3/31/12 ALL | | 0-1MM | 1-3MM 12 (4/1-9/30/11) | 3-5MM | 5-10MM | 10-25MM 76 (10/1/11-3/31/12) | 25MM & OVER |
| 87 | 76 | 88 | NUMBER OF STATEMENTS | 18 | 19 | 12 | 11 | 16 | 12 |
| % | % | % | ASSETS | % | % | % | % | % | % |
| 13.3 | 14.7 | 14.3 | Cash & Equivalents | 20.2 | 11.5 | 17.8 | 8.7 | 7.7 | 20.6 |
| 12.7 | 9.9 | 13.3 | Trade Receivables (net) | 2.8 | 9.7 | 4.2 | 18.1 | 29.3 | 18.4 |
| 1.7 | .7 | .9 | Inventory | .9 | 2.0 | .0 | .4 | 1.0 | .2 |
| 4.1 | 2.9 | 5.0 | All Other Current | 4.4 | 1.2 | .1 | 8.0 | 12.5 | 4.0 |
| 31.9 | 28.2 | 33.5 | Total Current | 28.3 | 24.4 | 22.1 | 35.1 | 50.5 | 43.2 |
| 51.7 | 53.5 | 47.4 | Fixed Assets (net) | 59.0 | 53.0 | 63.1 | 41.7 | 31.5 | 31.6 |
| 7.8 | 7.5 | 5.1 | Intangibles (net) | .5 | 6.1 | .9 | 11.7 | 5.4 | 8.4 |
| 8.6 | 10.8 | 14.0 | All Other Non-Current | 12.2 | 16.5 | 13.9 | 11.5 | 12.6 | 16.8 |
| 100.0 | 100.0 | 100.0 | Total | 100.0 | 100.0 | 100.0 | 100.0 | 100.0 | 100.0 |
| | | | LIABILITIES | | | | | | |
| 8.4 | 4.5 | 5.1 | Notes Payable-Short Term | 5.4 | 7.3 | .3 | 2.6 | 10.9 | .5 |
| 6.9 | 7.4 | 4.1 | Cur. Mat.-L.T.D. | .8 | 10.1 | 2.9 | 3.8 | 2.5 | 3.1 |
| 6.8 | 4.1 | 6.0 | Trade Payables | 1.2 | 2.4 | 1.4 | 7.7 | 12.5 | 13.1 |
| .1 | .0 | .0 | Income Taxes Payable | .0 | .0 | .0 | .0 | .0 | .2 |
| 15.2 | 10.6 | 13.9 | All Other Current | 8.0 | 9.3 | 7.2 | 17.1 | 22.0 | 22.6 |
| 37.4 | 26.7 | 29.1 | Total Current | 15.4 | 29.1 | 11.8 | 31.2 | 47.9 | 39.6 |
| 43.5 | 46.0 | 47.7 | Long-Term Debt | 64.3 | 56.3 | 55.8 | 38.4 | 31.4 | 31.5 |
| .3 | .3 | .1 | Deferred Taxes | .0 | .0 | .0 | .6 | .0 | .3 |
| 5.5 | 6.1 | 6.4 | All Other Non-Current | 10.7 | 7.8 | 8.0 | 1.8 | 3.3 | 4.7 |
| 13.3 | 20.9 | 16.7 | Net Worth | 9.5 | 6.7 | 24.4 | 28.0 | 17.4 | 23.9 |
| 100.0 | 100.0 | 100.0 | Total Liabilities & Net Worth | 100.0 | 100.0 | 100.0 | 100.0 | 100.0 | 100.0 |
| | | | INCOME DATA | | | | | | |
| 100.0 | 100.0 | 100.0 | Net Sales | 100.0 | 100.0 | 100.0 | 100.0 | 100.0 | 100.0 |
| | | | Gross Profit | | | | | | |
| 82.4 | 83.0 | 79.4 | Operating Expenses | 54.5 | 83.5 | 80.8 | 84.1 | 87.0 | 94.0 |
| 17.6 | 17.0 | 20.6 | Operating Profit | 45.5 | 16.5 | 19.2 | 15.9 | 13.0 | 6.0 |
| 10.1 | 10.3 | 8.8 | All Other Expenses (net) | 20.3 | 8.3 | 9.7 | 2.3 | 5.7 | 1.5 |
| 7.5 | 6.7 | 11.9 | Profit Before Taxes | 25.2 | 8.2 | 9.5 | 13.6 | 7.3 | 4.5 |
| | | | RATIOS | | | | | | |
| 2.0 | 2.8 | 3.2 | | 9.1 | 3.3 | 2.7 | 1.4 | 2.0 | 1.4 |
| .9 | 1.1 | 1.2 | Current | 3.3 | 1.1 | 1.4 | .9 | 1.2 | .9 |
| .5 | .6 | .6 | | .2 | .3 | .5 | .5 | .8 | .7 |
| 1.6 | 2.0 | 2.5 | | 4.7 | 2.8 | 2.7 | 1.0 | 1.6 | 1.2 |
| .7 | 1.0 | 1.0 | Quick | 2.8 | 1.0 | 1.4 | .5 | .7 | .8 |
| .4 | .4 | .4 | | .1 | .3 | .4 | .2 | .4 | .6 |
| 0 UND | 0 UND | 0 UND | | 0 UND | 0 UND | 0 UND | 0 999.8 | 6 59.4 | 9 42.7 |
| 8 45.7 | 5 68.9 | 8 45.1 | Sales/Receivables | 0 UND | 2 215.5 | 1 491.1 | 17 22.1 | 28 13.1 | 26 14.3 |
| 37 10.0 | 29 12.5 | 30 12.3 | | 5 69.7 | 28 13.2 | 9 42.0 | 42 8.7 | 47 7.8 | 30 12.2 |
| | | | Cost of Sales/Inventory | | | | | | |
| | | | Cost of Sales/Payables | | | | | | |
| 12.5 | 7.5 | 7.4 | | .3 | 9.7 | 10.0 | 7.2 | 6.8 | 33.9 |
| -166.7 | 41.9 | 52.8 | Sales/Working Capital | 7.9 | 52.6 | 37.3 | -45.2 | 19.8 | -107.6 |
| -7.8 | -10.1 | -14.9 | | -20.3 | -10.3 | -22.1 | -5.2 | -33.2 | -17.0 |
| 10.2 | 8.8 | 15.3 | | | 30.8 | | 22.1 | 16.0 | 16.0 |
| (58) 3.2 | (54) 3.4 | (60) 5.1 | EBIT/Interest | (13) 1.8 | | (10) 8.0 | (14) 10.7 | (10) 6.9 | |
| 1.4 | 1.5 | 1.3 | | | 1.2 | | 1.7 | .7 | 2.1 |
| 17.1 | | 4.0 | | | | | | | |
| (10) 3.5 | | (14) 2.5 | Net Profit + Depr., Dep., Amort./Cur. Mat. L/T/D | | | | | | |
| .1 | | 1.0 | | | | | | | |
| 1.3 | .8 | .5 | | .8 | .3 | .5 | .5 | .6 | .4 |
| 4.0 | 3.2 | 2.1 | Fixed/Worth | 2.3 | 3.1 | 2.5 | 1.8 | 2.2 | 1.7 |
| -5.6 | -44.8 | -5.2 | | -18.2 | -3.5 | -9.2 | -52.1 | -.8 | NM |
| 1.7 | 1.4 | 1.0 | | .8 | .4 | .9 | 1.4 | 1.1 | 1.5 |
| 5.6 | 5.0 | 3.0 | Debt/Worth | 2.3 | 2.5 | 2.7 | 3.0 | 6.8 | 4.2 |
| -9.2 | -34.4 | -12.0 | | -19.7 | -4.9 | -12.4 | -71.1 | -7.2 | NM |
| 104.7 | 51.7 | 50.4 | | 30.3 | 36.8 | | | 47.3 | |
| (61) 31.1 | (55) 25.9 | (60) 24.9 | % Profit Before Taxes/Tangible Net Worth | (13) 11.4 | (12) 21.6 | | | (10) 21.6 | |
| 1.3 | 1.4 | 7.3 | | 5.7 | 7.6 | | | -1.4 | |
| 13.4 | 12.7 | 13.2 | | 16.2 | 12.7 | 11.5 | 26.1 | 13.2 | 14.8 |
| 4.1 | 4.1 | 6.9 | % Profit Before Taxes/Total Assets | 3.8 | 4.7 | 9.7 | 12.4 | 7.4 | 9.7 |
| -.2 | .1 | .9 | | 1.2 | .4 | .5 | .9 | -.9 | 2.2 |
| 25.9 | 19.7 | 42.1 | | 19.9 | 39.0 | 46.9 | 43.9 | 60.4 | 63.3 |
| 1.6 | 1.4 | 4.0 | Sales/Net Fixed Assets | .3 | 1.6 | 1.1 | 8.6 | 25.3 | 20.4 |
| .3 | .3 | .4 | | .2 | .4 | .2 | .4 | 1.3 | 2.1 |
| 3.7 | 3.4 | 4.1 | | 2.6 | 5.7 | 2.8 | 2.4 | 4.6 | 4.3 |
| 1.2 | .8 | 1.1 | Sales/Total Assets | .2 | 1.0 | .4 | 1.1 | 3.3 | 2.5 |
| .2 | .2 | .3 | | .1 | .3 | .2 | .4 | .8 | 1.2 |
| .9 | 1.9 | .8 | | 2.7 | 1.8 | .6 | | .6 | .4 |
| (74) 5.8 | (65) 6.2 | (73) 3.8 | % Depr., Dep., Amort./Sales | (14) 5.8 | (15) 4.9 | (10) 3.3 | | (15) 1.1 | (11) .7 |
| 13.0 | 14.4 | 10.1 | | 14.9 | 13.4 | 13.2 | | 6.4 | 3.8 |
| 1.7 | 1.4 | .9 | | | | | | | |
| (21) 4.2 | (15) 3.4 | (27) 3.2 | % Officers', Directors' Owners' Comp/Sales | | | | | | |
| 11.3 | 12.3 | 7.9 | | | | | | | |
| 2325808M | 1446154M | 1435694M | Net Sales ($) | 7555M | 38632M | 44647M | 76658M | 313863M | 954339M |
| 1955832M | 1667018M | 1328581M | Total Assets ($) | 30504M | 94385M | 160434M | 103009M | 320351M | 619898M |

M = $ thousand    MM = $ million
See Pages 9 through 22 for Explanation of Ratios and Data

## Current Data Sorted by Assets            Comparative Historical Data

| | | | | | | Type of Statement | | |
|---|---|---|---|---|---|---|---|---|
| 3 | 6 | 11 | 10 | 2 | 3 | Unqualified | 30 | 37 |
| | 4 | 8 | 3 | | | Reviewed | 18 | 39 |
| 19 | 17 | 13 | 1 | | 1 | Compiled | 30 | 53 |
| 141 | 60 | 18 | 4 | | 1 | Tax Returns | 173 | 214 |
| 64 | 69 | 40 | 21 | 3 | 1 | Other | 123 | 151 |
| | 48 (4/1-9/30/11) | | 475 (10/1/11-3/31/12) | | | | 4/1/07-3/31/08 | 4/1/08-3/31/09 |
| 0-500M | 500M-2MM | 2-10MM | 10-50MM | 50-100MM | 100-250MM | | ALL | ALL |
| 227 | 156 | 90 | 39 | 5 | 6 | NUMBER OF STATEMENTS | 374 | 494 |
| % | % | % | % | % | % | ASSETS | % | % |
| 29.3 | 17.9 | 15.3 | 20.2 | | | Cash & Equivalents | 18.6 | 18.1 |
| 9.2 | 18.6 | 22.4 | 15.7 | | | Trade Receivables (net) | 16.8 | 18.0 |
| 3.1 | 3.6 | 9.9 | 8.7 | | | Inventory | 6.5 | 7.6 |
| 3.1 | 3.5 | 4.1 | 1.8 | | | All Other Current | 4.4 | 4.1 |
| 44.7 | 43.5 | 51.6 | 46.4 | | | Total Current | 46.3 | 47.8 |
| 37.0 | 37.5 | 31.9 | 39.5 | | | Fixed Assets (net) | 38.5 | 36.8 |
| 4.4 | 5.4 | 4.7 | 5.8 | | | Intangibles (net) | 6.7 | 6.0 |
| 13.9 | 13.5 | 11.8 | 8.2 | | | All Other Non-Current | 8.4 | 9.4 |
| 100.0 | 100.0 | 100.0 | 100.0 | | | Total | 100.0 | 100.0 |
| | | | | | | LIABILITIES | | |
| 17.7 | 9.3 | 7.4 | 1.9 | | | Notes Payable-Short Term | 10.8 | 9.9 |
| 3.6 | 3.6 | 2.8 | 4.0 | | | Cur. Mat.-L.T.D. | 4.0 | 4.6 |
| 6.6 | 6.6 | 10.7 | 18.5 | | | Trade Payables | 8.7 | 10.1 |
| .0 | .0 | .0 | .0 | | | Income Taxes Payable | .1 | .6 |
| 21.0 | 10.9 | 12.8 | 6.9 | | | All Other Current | 17.6 | 17.0 |
| 48.9 | 30.5 | 33.8 | 31.3 | | | Total Current | 41.2 | 42.1 |
| 25.0 | 24.5 | 22.5 | 33.4 | | | Long-Term Debt | 29.6 | 30.0 |
| .0 | .0 | .3 | .4 | | | Deferred Taxes | .2 | .1 |
| 16.4 | 11.7 | 5.9 | 2.9 | | | All Other Non-Current | 7.9 | 6.7 |
| 9.7 | 33.3 | 37.5 | 31.9 | | | Net Worth | 21.2 | 21.1 |
| 100.0 | 100.0 | 100.0 | 100.0 | | | Total Liabilities & Net Worth | 100.0 | 100.0 |
| | | | | | | INCOME DATA | | |
| 100.0 | 100.0 | 100.0 | 100.0 | | | Net Sales | 100.0 | 100.0 |
| | | | | | | Gross Profit | | |
| 92.3 | 88.3 | 86.8 | 94.0 | | | Operating Expenses | 91.3 | 91.7 |
| 7.7 | 11.7 | 13.2 | 6.0 | | | Operating Profit | 8.7 | 8.3 |
| 1.3 | 4.0 | 3.6 | 4.0 | | | All Other Expenses (net) | 2.5 | 3.6 |
| 6.3 | 7.7 | 9.6 | 2.0 | | | Profit Before Taxes | 6.3 | 4.7 |
| | | | | | | RATIOS | | |
| 3.6 | 3.0 | 3.3 | 3.8 | | | | 3.1 | 2.7 |
| 1.2 | 1.5 | 1.4 | 1.2 | | | Current | 1.2 | 1.2 |
| .4 | .7 | .7 | .9 | | | | .6 | .6 |
| 2.9 | 2.6 | 2.5 | 2.5 | | | | 2.0 | 2.1 |
| 1.0 | 1.1 | .9 | 1.1 | | | Quick | .8 | .9 |
| .3 | .4 | .4 | .5 | | | | .4 | .3 |
| 0 UND | 0 UND | 2 188.5 | 3 121.8 | | | | 0 UND | 0 UND |
| 0 UND | 3 129.2 | 20 18.7 | 25 14.5 | | | Sales/Receivables | 5 78.9 | 6 58.0 |
| 4 84.1 | 33 11.0 | 42 8.6 | 47 7.7 | | | | 34 10.9 | 34 10.7 |
| | | | | | | Cost of Sales/Inventory | | |
| | | | | | | Cost of Sales/Payables | | |
| 13.3 | 8.0 | 5.5 | 5.6 | | | | 9.5 | 8.7 |
| 170.2 | 21.7 | 21.3 | 22.4 | | | Sales/Working Capital | 65.1 | 47.2 |
| -19.8 | -29.6 | -23.8 | -71.9 | | | | -19.6 | -20.7 |
| 11.1 | 14.8 | 44.9 | 7.4 | | | | 11.6 | 12.9 |
| (122) 3.6 | (106) 4.9 | (64) 7.9 | (30) 2.1 | | | EBIT/Interest | (285) 3.5 | (378) 3.3 |
| .6 | 1.4 | 1.8 | -6.5 | | | | 1.0 | .6 |
| | | | | | | Net Profit + Depr., Dep., | 20.3 | 14.0 |
| | | | | | | Amort./Cur. Mat. L/T/D | (22) 2.4 | (33) 5.5 |
| | | | | | | | 1.0 | .8 |
| .1 | .2 | .1 | .2 | | | | .2 | .2 |
| 1.2 | 1.1 | .7 | 1.1 | | | Fixed/Worth | 1.4 | 1.2 |
| -4.1 | 8.2 | 3.1 | 3.4 | | | | -27.2 | -38.6 |
| .4 | .7 | .7 | .7 | | | | .8 | .8 |
| 2.5 | 1.6 | 2.0 | 1.8 | | | Debt/Worth | 3.2 | 3.5 |
| -5.2 | 13.3 | 8.8 | 7.2 | | | | -26.2 | -30.7 |
| 156.1 | 91.0 | 79.7 | 31.1 | | | | 108.2 | 84.0 |
| (150) 54.6 | (125) 35.6 | (76) 33.5 | (34) 8.2 | | | % Profit Before Taxes/Tangible Net Worth | (268) 50.2 | (358) 28.9 |
| 4.9 | 5.3 | 5.2 | -7.8 | | | | 14.8 | 1.8 |
| 53.8 | 29.6 | 31.0 | 11.5 | | | | 33.5 | 24.0 |
| 12.8 | 11.8 | 8.5 | 1.7 | | | % Profit Before Taxes/Total Assets | 12.0 | 6.7 |
| -.9 | .5 | 1.9 | -3.4 | | | | .8 | -1.2 |
| 177.3 | 56.0 | 53.7 | 33.6 | | | | 51.3 | 60.1 |
| 22.9 | 10.4 | 14.4 | 6.2 | | | Sales/Net Fixed Assets | 11.2 | 14.2 |
| 6.2 | 2.6 | 3.1 | 1.3 | | | | 2.7 | 3.2 |
| 8.6 | 4.0 | 3.4 | 2.1 | | | | 4.7 | 4.9 |
| 5.1 | 2.3 | 2.1 | 1.0 | | | Sales/Total Assets | 2.7 | 2.6 |
| 2.8 | .8 | .8 | .7 | | | | 1.4 | 1.2 |
| 1.0 | 1.0 | .6 | .9 | | | | 1.0 | .9 |
| (120) 2.4 | (103) 3.1 | (59) 1.7 | (30) 3.7 | | | % Depr., Dep., Amort./Sales | (277) 2.4 | (356) 2.1 |
| 4.9 | 8.6 | 6.2 | 7.3 | | | | 7.1 | 5.8 |
| 3.0 | 3.3 | 2.0 | | | | | 3.1 | 2.8 |
| (118) 6.5 | (65) 5.5 | (25) 2.7 | | | | % Officers', Directors' Owners' Comp/Sales | (166) 6.4 | (231) 5.1 |
| 14.8 | 10.8 | 4.4 | | | | | 12.4 | 9.7 |
| 281580M | 515498M | 946129M | 1676647M | 1701852M | 2522931M | Net Sales ($) | 5474001M | 5045837M |
| 47818M | 167009M | 356881M | 948569M | 328204M | 1153079M | Total Assets ($) | 2283191M | 2486263M |

M = $ thousand     MM = $ million
See Pages 9 through 22 for Explanation of Ratios and Data

## Comparative Historical Data                    Current Data Sorted by Sales

| Hist 1 | Hist 2 | Hist 3 | Type of Statement | 0-1MM | 1-3MM | 3-5MM | 5-10MM | 10-25MM | 25MM & OVER |
|---|---|---|---|---|---|---|---|---|---|
| 37 | 28 | 35 | Unqualified | 1 | 5 | 3 | 8 | 9 | 9 |
| 34 | 21 | 15 | Reviewed | 1 | 2 | 2 | 2 | 5 | 3 |
| 103 | 58 | 51 | Compiled | 14 | 19 | 6 | 6 | 5 | 1 |
| 280 | 210 | 224 | Tax Returns | 110 | 74 | 18 | 10 | 6 | 6 |
| 218 | 156 | 198 | Other | 58 | 47 | 30 | 23 | 18 | 22 |
| 4/1/09-3/31/10 ALL | 4/1/10-3/31/11 ALL | 4/1/11-3/31/12 ALL | | 48 (4/1-9/30/11) | | | 475 (10/1/11-3/31/12) | | |
| 672 | 473 | 523 | **NUMBER OF STATEMENTS** | 184 | 147 | 59 | 49 | 43 | 41 |
| % | % | % | **ASSETS** | % | % | % | % | % | % |
| 19.0 | 19.3 | 22.7 | Cash & Equivalents | 23.3 | 23.5 | 25.0 | 15.8 | 17.4 | 27.8 |
| 15.8 | 14.0 | 14.8 | Trade Receivables (net) | 7.7 | 10.9 | 23.2 | 27.0 | 26.6 | 21.0 |
| 8.2 | 5.8 | 4.8 | Inventory | 2.5 | 4.9 | 3.1 | 11.0 | 7.1 | 7.0 |
| 2.8 | 3.3 | 3.4 | All Other Current | 3.2 | 3.4 | 3.1 | 2.0 | 4.1 | 6.0 |
| 45.9 | 42.4 | 45.7 | Total Current | 36.6 | 42.7 | 54.4 | 55.9 | 55.2 | 61.9 |
| 37.0 | 38.7 | 36.1 | Fixed Assets (net) | 45.0 | 36.7 | 30.3 | 28.6 | 26.5 | 21.7 |
| 5.8 | 7.8 | 5.2 | Intangibles (net) | 4.4 | 6.5 | 2.9 | 3.0 | 6.6 | 9.2 |
| 11.3 | 11.0 | 13.0 | All Other Non-Current | 14.0 | 14.1 | 12.4 | 12.5 | 11.7 | 7.2 |
| 100.0 | 100.0 | 100.0 | Total | 100.0 | 100.0 | 100.0 | 100.0 | 100.0 | 100.0 |
| | | | **LIABILITIES** | | | | | | |
| 12.1 | 8.9 | 11.9 | Notes Payable-Short Term | 14.3 | 12.2 | 14.3 | 10.0 | 8.4 | 2.2 |
| 4.6 | 4.7 | 3.6 | Cur. Mat.-L.T.D. | 2.7 | 4.2 | 4.4 | 4.6 | 2.0 | 4.0 |
| 9.1 | 7.6 | 8.3 | Trade Payables | 4.5 | 7.0 | 6.7 | 13.8 | 12.5 | 21.1 |
| .2 | .1 | .0 | Income Taxes Payable | .0 | .0 | .1 | .0 | .1 | .1 |
| 17.7 | 16.9 | 15.6 | All Other Current | 15.6 | 16.7 | 15.4 | 12.2 | 14.6 | 17.2 |
| 43.6 | 38.3 | 39.3 | Total Current | 37.1 | 40.1 | 40.8 | 40.7 | 37.7 | 44.6 |
| 29.0 | 31.1 | 25.3 | Long-Term Debt | 30.3 | 27.0 | 19.2 | 17.2 | 11.9 | 28.4 |
| .1 | .1 | .1 | Deferred Taxes | .0 | .0 | .1 | .1 | .4 | .5 |
| 9.6 | 13.4 | 12.0 | All Other Non-Current | 17.2 | 13.2 | 7.6 | 5.8 | 5.4 | 4.4 |
| 17.6 | 17.1 | 23.3 | Net Worth | 15.3 | 19.6 | 32.3 | 36.1 | 44.7 | 22.2 |
| 100.0 | 100.0 | 100.0 | Total Liabilities & Net Worth | 100.0 | 100.0 | 100.0 | 100.0 | 100.0 | 100.0 |
| | | | **INCOME DATA** | | | | | | |
| 100.0 | 100.0 | 100.0 | Net Sales | 100.0 | 100.0 | 100.0 | 100.0 | 100.0 | 100.0 |
| | | | Gross Profit | | | | | | |
| 91.7 | 89.7 | 90.4 | Operating Expenses | 86.7 | 91.3 | 91.9 | 92.7 | 94.7 | 93.8 |
| 8.3 | 10.3 | 9.6 | Operating Profit | 13.3 | 8.7 | 8.1 | 7.3 | 5.3 | 6.2 |
| 3.0 | 2.9 | 2.7 | All Other Expenses (net) | 5.4 | 1.1 | .8 | 1.1 | 2.0 | 1.7 |
| 5.3 | 7.4 | 6.9 | Profit Before Taxes | 7.9 | 7.5 | 7.2 | 6.1 | 3.4 | 4.5 |
| | | | **RATIOS** | | | | | | |
| 3.7 / 1.3 / .5 | 3.1 / 1.3 / .6 | 3.3 / 1.3 / .5 | Current | 4.7 / 1.1 / .3 | 2.9 / 1.2 / .5 | 4.4 / 1.4 / .8 | 2.7 / 1.7 / .7 | 2.6 / 1.6 / .8 | 2.3 / 1.4 / 1.0 |
| 2.7 / (671) 1.0 / .3 | 2.4 / (471) 1.0 / .3 | 2.6 / 1.1 / .4 | Quick | 3.0 / .9 / .2 | 2.6 / 1.1 / .3 | 3.3 / 1.2 / .6 | 2.2 / 1.0 / .5 | 2.4 / 1.0 / .6 | 1.8 / 1.1 / .6 |
| 0 UND / 5 77.0 / 37 9.9 | 0 UND / 0 999.8 / 31 11.8 | 0 UND / 1 277.2 / 28 13.0 | Sales/Receivables | 0 UND / 0 UND / 3 125.1 | 0 UND / 0 UND / 24 15.4 | 0 UND / 12 29.8 / 45 8.2 | 7 55.2 / 25 14.6 / 39 9.4 | 2 156.0 / 23 15.7 / 50 7.3 | 1 549.2 / 18 20.0 / 45 8.1 |
| | | | Cost of Sales/Inventory | | | | | | |
| | | | Cost of Sales/Payables | | | | | | |
| 7.2 / 38.2 / -17.0 | 9.7 / 65.6 / -17.8 | 9.1 / 45.0 / -24.3 | Sales/Working Capital | 7.9 / 154.7 / -8.7 | 10.6 / 49.9 / -25.6 | 7.3 / 28.2 / -36.6 | 9.3 / 20.0 / -24.2 | 7.7 / 24.7 / -30.2 | 7.7 / 25.9 / -497.8 |
| 14.1 / (499) 3.0 / .4 | 18.5 / (343) 4.5 / 1.4 | 14.7 / (332) 4.1 / 1.1 | EBIT/Interest | 9.0 / (93) 2.7 / .3 | 10.3 / (100) 4.8 / 1.1 | 56.8 / (40) 6.0 / 1.9 | 29.9 / (34) 5.5 / 2.0 | 72.8 / (36) 6.3 / 1.5 | 16.4 / (29) 4.3 / 1.0 |
| 25.3 / (40) 2.3 / .7 | 12.7 / (20) 3.3 / 1.5 | 7.3 / (18) 2.6 / .7 | Net Profit + Depr., Dep., Amort./Cur. Mat. L/T/D | | | | | | |
| .2 / 1.4 / -21.4 | .2 / 1.5 / -6.6 | .1 / 1.0 / 18.9 | Fixed/Worth | .1 / 1.8 / -13.4 | .3 / 1.2 / -42.4 | .1 / .8 / 8.4 | .1 / .6 / 2.5 | .1 / .6 / 2.1 | .1 / .5 / 4.2 |
| .7 / 3.1 / -17.6 | .8 / 2.7 / -12.6 | .6 / 1.9 / UND | Debt/Worth | .4 / 2.7 / -9.9 | .6 / 2.3 / -17.7 | .4 / 1.4 / 32.1 | .7 / 1.5 / 8.0 | .7 / 1.4 / 4.3 | .9 / 2.4 / 25.3 |
| 71.2 / (485) 24.4 / 2.6 | 96.9 / (330) 37.2 / 6.1 | 104.0 / (393) 35.6 / 4.2 | % Profit Before Taxes/Tangible Net Worth | 107.8 / (128) 30.0 / 2.5 | 130.9 / (107) 49.6 / 4.2 | 106.6 / (45) 27.3 / 7.9 | 98.6 / (41) 36.9 / 5.3 | 77.3 / (39) 32.1 / 5.1 | 100.6 / (33) 37.1 / 9.9 |
| 22.6 / 6.7 / -1.1 | 35.1 / 10.0 / .8 | 36.4 / 10.7 / -.1 | % Profit Before Taxes/Total Assets | 31.1 / 6.5 / -1.5 | 37.8 / 12.1 / .3 | 48.3 / 13.5 / 2.3 | 33.6 / 12.2 / 3.8 | 32.3 / 7.7 / 1.7 | 39.3 / 11.5 / 1.0 |
| 59.9 / 12.8 / 3.2 | 55.8 / 12.9 / 3.1 | 71.3 / 15.2 / 4.3 | Sales/Net Fixed Assets | 70.6 / 10.0 / 1.4 | 67.3 / 13.8 / 4.8 | 56.4 / 20.5 / 6.7 | 51.5 / 25.4 / 6.9 | 169.1 / 36.2 / 6.0 | 111.2 / 33.6 / 7.5 |
| 4.4 / 2.5 / 1.3 | 5.1 / 2.7 / 1.3 | 6.0 / 3.0 / 1.3 | Sales/Total Assets | 5.1 / 2.0 / .6 | 6.9 / 3.5 / 1.6 | 6.5 / 3.6 / 2.0 | 4.8 / 3.6 / 2.1 | 7.0 / 3.0 / 1.8 | 6.6 / 2.3 / 1.4 |
| .8 / (474) 2.6 / 7.1 | .9 / (319) 2.9 / 7.2 | .9 / (316) 2.6 / 6.0 | % Depr., Dep., Amort./Sales | 1.9 / (92) 5.7 / 12.6 | 1.0 / (98) 2.9 / 5.4 | .5 / (37) 1.2 / 3.0 | .8 / (33) 1.5 / 4.1 | .5 / (28) 1.6 / 4.3 | .3 / (28) 1.0 / 3.3 |
| 3.0 / (285) 5.7 / 10.8 | 2.7 / (212) 5.8 / 11.1 | 2.8 / (214) 5.3 / 11.0 | % Officers', Directors' Owners' Comp/Sales | 3.3 / (72) 8.9 / 16.2 | 2.7 / (80) 5.0 / 16.5 | 2.8 / (26) 4.1 / 16.3 | 2.7 / (16) 3.9 / 5.2 | 2.0 / (15) 2.6 / 5.9 | |
| 7583258M | 6472785M | 7644637M | Net Sales ($) | 86488M | 256271M | 229058M | 345092M | 659056M | 6068672M |
| 3520629M | 3500846M | 3001560M | Total Assets ($) | 85044M | 147423M | 99544M | 240411M | 325557M | 2103581M |

M = $ thousand     MM = $ million
See Pages 9 through 22 for Explanation of Ratios and Data

## Current Data Sorted by Assets | Comparative Historical Data

| | | | | | | Type of Statement | | |
|---|---|---|---|---|---|---|---|---|
| 7 | 22 | 140 | 290 | 56 | 43 | Unqualified | 351 | 483 |
| 3 | 18 | 175 | 96 | 4 | 2 | Reviewed | 133 | 213 |
| 12 | 100 | 234 | 46 | 2 | 1 | Compiled | 208 | 259 |
| 1 | 6 | 3 | 2 | | | Tax Returns | 17 | 16 |
| 126 | 372 | 948 | 305 | 21 | 17 | Other | 1198 | 1422 |
| | 976 (4/1-9/30/11) | | 2,076 (10/1/11-3/31/12) | | | | 4/1/07-3/31/08 ALL | 4/1/08-3/31/09 ALL |
| 0-500M | 500M-2MM | 2-10MM | 10-50MM | 50-100MM | 100-250MM | | | |
| 149 | 518 | 1500 | 739 | 83 | 63 | NUMBER OF STATEMENTS | 1907 | 2393 |
| % | % | % | % | % | % | ASSETS | % | % |
| 59.7 | 16.5 | 9.0 | 10.6 | 21.8 | 31.1 | Cash & Equivalents | 16.6 | 15.2 |
| 2.0 | .9 | .7 | 1.2 | 4.5 | 4.1 | Trade Receivables (net) | 1.8 | 1.5 |
| .6 | .2 | .2 | .2 | .3 | .6 | Inventory | .4 | .4 |
| .9 | 1.2 | .5 | .9 | 3.7 | 1.8 | All Other Current | 1.5 | 1.3 |
| 63.2 | 18.8 | 10.4 | 13.0 | 30.4 | 37.6 | Total Current | 20.3 | 18.4 |
| 29.3 | 76.6 | 86.4 | 79.5 | 45.4 | 28.4 | Fixed Assets (net) | 72.6 | 74.6 |
| .5 | .5 | .3 | .3 | .3 | 1.2 | Intangibles (net) | .2 | .2 |
| 7.0 | 4.1 | 2.9 | 7.2 | 24.0 | 32.9 | All Other Non-Current | 6.9 | 6.7 |
| 100.0 | 100.0 | 100.0 | 100.0 | 100.0 | 100.0 | Total | 100.0 | 100.0 |
| | | | | | | LIABILITIES | | |
| 8.1 | 2.5 | 1.3 | 1.3 | 4.1 | 1.5 | Notes Payable-Short Term | 2.5 | 2.7 |
| 1.9 | 1.7 | 1.8 | 2.3 | 1.3 | .6 | Cur. Mat.-L.T.D. | 1.7 | 2.2 |
| 6.6 | 1.2 | .5 | .9 | 1.7 | 2.2 | Trade Payables | 1.4 | 1.2 |
| .0 | .0 | .0 | .0 | .0 | .0 | Income Taxes Payable | .0 | .0 |
| 17.6 | 2.7 | 1.8 | 2.7 | 6.7 | 12.9 | All Other Current | 3.8 | 4.2 |
| 34.2 | 8.0 | 5.4 | 7.3 | 13.8 | 17.1 | Total Current | 9.5 | 10.3 |
| 35.8 | 41.9 | 33.3 | 29.0 | 15.4 | 9.7 | Long-Term Debt | 29.0 | 30.8 |
| .0 | .0 | .0 | .0 | .0 | .1 | Deferred Taxes | .0 | .0 |
| 1.4 | 1.3 | .9 | 2.3 | 8.8 | 16.1 | All Other Non-Current | 2.1 | 2.2 |
| 28.6 | 48.8 | 60.4 | 61.3 | 62.0 | 57.0 | Net Worth | 59.4 | 56.7 |
| 100.0 | 100.0 | 100.0 | 100.0 | 100.0 | 100.0 | Total Liabilities & Net Worth | 100.0 | 100.0 |
| | | | | | | INCOME DATA | | |
| 100.0 | 100.0 | 100.0 | 100.0 | 100.0 | 100.0 | Net Sales | 100.0 | 100.0 |
| | | | | | | Gross Profit | | |
| 89.4 | 85.9 | 86.2 | 88.5 | 91.7 | 90.0 | Operating Expenses | 85.9 | 89.1 |
| 10.6 | 14.1 | 13.8 | 11.5 | 8.3 | 10.0 | Operating Profit | 14.1 | 10.9 |
| 4.3 | 7.6 | 7.8 | 6.3 | 2.4 | .2 | All Other Expenses (net) | 5.8 | 6.8 |
| 6.2 | 6.5 | 6.0 | 5.2 | 5.9 | 9.8 | Profit Before Taxes | 8.3 | 4.0 |
| | | | | | | RATIOS | | |
| 19.8 | 13.0 | 7.3 | 6.4 | 7.4 | 7.6 | | 9.9 | 8.4 |
| 2.9 | 2.8 | 2.6 | 2.6 | 2.4 | 3.0 | Current | 2.9 | 2.5 |
| 1.0 | .7 | .9 | 1.0 | 1.1 | 1.0 | | 1.0 | .9 |
| 19.8 | 11.5 | 7.0 | 6.2 | 6.4 | 7.6 | | 9.0 | 7.8 |
| 2.9 | (517) 2.7 | 2.5 | 2.4 | 1.9 | 3.0 | Quick | 2.6 (2392) | 2.2 |
| 1.0 | .6 | .9 | .9 | .9 | .8 | | .8 | .7 |
| 0 UND | 0 UND | 0 UND | 0 UND | 0 UND | 7 49.9 | | 0 UND | 0 UND |
| 0 UND | 0 UND | 0 UND | 0 UND | 7 55.6 | 21 17.8 | Sales/Receivables | 0 UND | 0 UND |
| 0 UND | 0 UND | 0 UND | 4 93.2 | 33 11.2 | 58 6.3 | | 2 215.3 | 1 267.1 |
| | | | | | | Cost of Sales/Inventory | | |
| | | | | | | Cost of Sales/Payables | | |
| 4.3 | 3.4 | 3.5 | 2.8 | 1.1 | .9 | | 2.9 | 3.3 |
| 8.6 | 9.9 | 8.8 | 7.4 | 4.9 | 3.6 | Sales/Working Capital | 7.8 | 9.6 |
| UND | -29.1 | -174.8 | -446.8 | 171.6 | 143.8 | | UND | -77.9 |
| 5.0 | 3.0 | 3.1 | 3.6 | 11.8 | 12.9 | | 4.5 | 3.2 |
| (63) 2.0 | (313) 1.7 | (1058) 1.6 | (551) 1.6 | (59) 3.3 | (41) 2.3 | EBIT/Interest | (1117) 2.1 | (1502) 1.5 |
| 1.0 | 1.0 | .8 | .5 | 1.1 | .8 | | .9 | .4 |
| | | | | | | Net Profit + Depr., Dep., Amort./Cur. Mat. L/T/D | | |
| .0 | 1.0 | 1.1 | 1.0 | .3 | .2 | | .9 | .9 |
| .1 | 1.5 | 1.4 | 1.3 | .7 | .3 | Fixed/Worth | 1.3 | 1.3 |
| 1.8 | 2.5 | 2.0 | 1.9 | 1.2 | .9 | | 1.8 | 2.0 |
| .1 | .3 | .3 | .3 | .2 | .4 | | .2 | .2 |
| .6 | .8 | .6 | .6 | .5 | .6 | Debt/Worth | .6 | .6 |
| 6.4 | 2.0 | 1.2 | 1.2 | 1.5 | 1.8 | | 1.3 | 1.4 |
| 39.3 | 10.6 | 5.5 | 5.5 | 8.5 | 10.1 | % Profit Before Taxes/Tangible | 10.6 | 6.9 |
| (126) 11.7 | (488) 2.8 | (1485) 1.5 | (731) 1.5 | (61) 1.9 | 4.4 | Net Worth | (1857) 3.1 | (2322) 1.1 |
| .2 | -.3 | -.5 | -1.4 | -.3 | -1.2 | | -.3 | -2.2 |
| 21.6 | 5.2 | 3.0 | 3.3 | 3.5 | 5.7 | % Profit Before Taxes/Total | 5.9 | 3.8 |
| 5.4 | 1.5 | .9 | .8 | 1.1 | 2.0 | Assets | 1.8 | .6 |
| .0 | -.3 | -.3 | -.7 | -.2 | -.4 | | -.2 | -1.3 |
| UND | .9 | .5 | .6 | 2.4 | 4.0 | | .9 | .8 |
| UND | .4 | .3 | .3 | .7 | 2.0 | Sales/Net Fixed Assets | .4 | .4 |
| 1.9 | .3 | .2 | .2 | .4 | .9 | | .2 | .2 |
| 5.1 | .7 | .4 | .4 | .5 | .4 | | .5 | .5 |
| 2.4 | .4 | .3 | .3 | .3 | .3 | Sales/Total Assets | .3 | .3 |
| .8 | .2 | .2 | .2 | .2 | .2 | | .2 | .2 |
| 2.0 | 3.0 | 5.4 | 5.6 | 1.9 | 1.5 | | 3.4 | 3.9 |
| (23) 7.3 | (176) 7.9 | (665) 8.9 | (501) 8.8 | (70) 5.1 | (52) 2.9 | % Depr., Dep., Amort./Sales | (817) 6.7 | (1116) 7.2 |
| 12.5 | 13.4 | 13.0 | 13.2 | 10.2 | 5.3 | | 10.6 | 10.7 |
| 9.9 | 6.3 | 5.8 | 4.3 | | | % Officers', Directors' | 5.6 | 5.9 |
| (20) 22.0 | (69) 15.2 | (173) 12.3 | (70) 10.7 | | | Owners' Comp/Sales | (309) 13.0 | (318) 13.3 |
| 29.5 | 23.5 | 22.0 | 24.1 | | | | 22.7 | 23.5 |
| 88275M | 426488M | 2621834M | 5143785M | 2164360M | 4698237M | Net Sales ($) | 10126196M | 14375459M |
| 36001M | 664987M | 7578369M | 14448184M | 5479916M | 9470048M | Total Assets ($) | 25694391M | 34857681M |

M = $ thousand    MM = $ million
See Pages 9 through 22 for Explanation of Ratios and Data

| Comparative Historical Data | | | | Current Data Sorted by Sales | | | | | |
|---|---|---|---|---|---|---|---|---|---|
| | | | **Type of Statement** | | | | | | |
| 507 | 526 | 558 | Unqualified | 30 | 94 | 117 | 124 | 123 | 70 |
| 264 | 261 | 298 | Reviewed | 45 | 151 | 51 | 40 | 10 | 1 |
| 291 | 329 | 395 | Compiled | 198 | 150 | 33 | 11 | 2 | 1 |
| 10 | 13 | 12 | Tax Returns | 8 | 1 | | | 3 | |
| 1324 | 1537 | 1789 | Other | 893 | 595 | 140 | 98 | 38 | 25 |
| 4/1/09-3/31/10 | 4/1/10-3/31/11 | 4/1/11-3/31/12 | | 976 (4/1-9/30/11) | | 2,076 (10/1/11-3/31/12) | | | |
| ALL | ALL | ALL | | 0-1MM | 1-3MM | 3-5MM | 5-10MM | 10-25MM | 25MM & OVER |
| 2396 | 2666 | 3052 | **NUMBER OF STATEMENTS** | 1174 | 991 | 341 | 273 | 176 | 97 |
| % | % | % | **ASSETS** | % | % | % | % | % | % |
| 13.9 | 14.1 | 14.0 | Cash & Equivalents | 12.7 | 12.6 | 13.1 | 15.6 | 20.7 | 29.2 |
| 1.4 | 1.2 | 1.1 | Trade Receivables (net) | .5 | .7 | 1.4 | 1.7 | 3.2 | 5.1 |
| .3 | .3 | .2 | Inventory | .1 | .2 | .2 | .4 | .6 | .8 |
| 1.0 | 1.2 | .9 | All Other Current | .5 | .6 | .6 | 1.0 | 3.1 | 4.5 |
| 16.7 | 16.8 | 16.1 | Total Current | 13.9 | 14.0 | 15.4 | 18.8 | 27.6 | 39.6 |
| 76.5 | 76.5 | 78.0 | Fixed Assets (net) | 82.7 | 81.8 | 78.2 | 71.4 | 59.8 | 31.4 |
| .2 | .3 | .3 | Intangibles (net) | .3 | .3 | .3 | .3 | .3 | .9 |
| 6.6 | 6.4 | 5.6 | All Other Non-Current | 3.0 | 3.9 | 6.1 | 9.5 | 12.3 | 28.1 |
| 100.0 | 100.0 | 100.0 | Total | 100.0 | 100.0 | 100.0 | 100.0 | 100.0 | 100.0 |
| | | | **LIABILITIES** | | | | | | |
| 2.7 | 1.9 | 1.9 | Notes Payable-Short Term | 2.3 | 1.8 | .8 | 1.3 | 2.8 | 2.3 |
| 2.0 | 2.0 | 1.9 | Cur. Mat.-L.T.D. | 1.6 | 1.9 | 2.1 | 2.7 | 2.6 | .8 |
| 1.1 | 1.1 | 1.1 | Trade Payables | 1.0 | .7 | .8 | 1.1 | 2.7 | 3.6 |
| .0 | .0 | .0 | Income Taxes Payable | .0 | .0 | .0 | .1 | .0 | .0 |
| 3.5 | 3.7 | 3.3 | All Other Current | 2.9 | 2.4 | 2.7 | 4.1 | 6.1 | 11.1 |
| 9.4 | 8.6 | 8.2 | Total Current | 7.9 | 6.8 | 6.4 | 9.3 | 14.2 | 17.8 |
| 33.8 | 32.8 | 32.9 | Long-Term Debt | 35.8 | 35.0 | 34.3 | 25.8 | 21.6 | 10.5 |
| .0 | .0 | .0 | Deferred Taxes | .0 | .0 | .0 | .0 | .0 | .1 |
| 2.0 | 2.1 | 1.9 | All Other Non-Current | .7 | 1.0 | 2.2 | 3.5 | 5.7 | 12.1 |
| 54.9 | 56.4 | 57.1 | Net Worth | 55.6 | 57.2 | 57.1 | 61.3 | 58.5 | 59.5 |
| 100.0 | 100.0 | 100.0 | Total Liabilities & Net Worth | 100.0 | 100.0 | 100.0 | 100.0 | 100.0 | 100.0 |
| | | | **INCOME DATA** | | | | | | |
| 100.0 | 100.0 | 100.0 | Net Sales | 100.0 | 100.0 | 100.0 | 100.0 | 100.0 | 100.0 |
| | | | Gross Profit | | | | | | |
| 88.7 | 87.9 | 87.1 | Operating Expenses | 83.0 | 88.1 | 90.7 | 89.5 | 93.3 | 95.3 |
| 11.3 | 12.1 | 12.9 | Operating Profit | 17.0 | 11.9 | 9.3 | 10.5 | 6.7 | 4.7 |
| 7.2 | 6.7 | 6.9 | All Other Expenses (net) | 9.8 | 6.3 | 5.9 | 4.2 | 2.0 | -.3 |
| 4.1 | 5.4 | 6.0 | Profit Before Taxes | 7.2 | 5.6 | 3.4 | 6.3 | 4.8 | 5.0 |
| | | | **RATIOS** | | | | | | |
| 8.0 | 8.2 | 7.9 | | 9.3 | 8.1 | 7.7 | 7.6 | 5.2 | 7.3 |
| 2.6 | 2.6 | 2.7 | Current | 2.3 | 3.0 | 2.8 | 3.1 | 2.1 | 2.7 |
| .9 | .9 | .9 | | .7 | 1.2 | 1.2 | 1.0 | .9 | 1.1 |
| 7.4 | 7.5 | 7.6 | | 8.8 | 7.8 | 7.5 | 6.6 | 4.3 | 6.7 |
| 2.3 | 2.3 (3051) | 2.5 | Quick | 2.2 (990) | 2.9 | 2.7 | 2.9 | 1.8 | 2.2 |
| .8 | .8 | .8 | | .6 | 1.1 | 1.1 | .9 | .7 | .9 |
| 0 UND | 0 UND | 0 UND | | 0 UND | 0 UND | 0 UND | 0 UND | 0 UND | 1 585.5 |
| 0 UND | 0 UND | 0 UND | Sales/Receivables | 0 UND | 0 UND | 0 UND | 0 UND | 3 138.4 | 16 22.5 |
| 1 294.2 | 1 577.5 | 1 572.9 | | 0 UND | 0 UND | 2 175.9 | 7 54.5 | 19 19.0 | 34 10.7 |
| | | | Cost of Sales/Inventory | | | | | | |
| | | | Cost of Sales/Payables | | | | | | |
| 3.2 | 3.0 | 3.2 | | 3.4 | 3.5 | 2.8 | 3.1 | 2.5 | 1.9 |
| 9.2 | 8.6 | 8.3 | Sales/Working Capital | 10.7 | 8.1 | 7.5 | 6.7 | 9.3 | 5.5 |
| -81.0 | -95.7 | -144.9 | | -25.3 | 73.8 | 55.4 | 714.9 | -33.2 | 120.8 |
| 3.1 | 3.2 | 3.3 | | 2.8 | 3.2 | 3.3 | 4.3 | 6.2 | 16.3 |
| (1558) 1.4 | (1732) 1.5 | (2085) 1.6 | EBIT/Interest | (699) 1.6 | (713) 1.6 | (262) 1.4 | (207) 1.8 | (136) 1.6 | (68) 4.2 |
| .5 | .6 | .8 | | 1.0 | .7 | .4 | .7 | .1 | 1.0 |
| | | | Net Profit + Depr., Dep., Amort./Cur. Mat. L/T/D | | | | | | |
| 1.0 | 1.0 | 1.0 | | 1.1 | 1.0 | 1.0 | .8 | .5 | .3 |
| 1.4 | 1.3 | 1.4 | Fixed/Worth | 1.5 | 1.4 | 1.4 | 1.2 | 1.1 | .4 |
| 2.1 | 2.0 | 2.0 | | 2.1 | 2.0 | 2.0 | 1.8 | 1.8 | .9 |
| .3 | .3 | .3 | | .3 | .3 | .3 | .2 | .2 | .3 |
| .7 | .6 | .6 | Debt/Worth | .7 | .6 | .7 | .6 | .6 | .6 |
| 1.5 | 1.4 | 1.4 | | 1.5 | 1.3 | 1.5 | 1.2 | 1.4 | 1.2 |
| 6.2 | 6.5 | 6.8 | | 6.3 | 6.0 | 6.1 | 8.7 | 9.0 | 10.2 |
| (2333) 1.2 | (2587) 1.6 | (2974) 1.8 | % Profit Before Taxes/Tangible Net Worth | (1136) 1.6 | (964) 1.7 | (334) 1.3 | (271) 3.4 | (174) 2.0 | (95) 4.5 |
| -2.1 | -1.0 | -.7 | | .0 | -.9 | -2.4 | -1.1 | -2.9 | -2.0 |
| 3.5 | 3.7 | 3.7 | | 3.4 | 3.6 | 3.3 | 5.1 | 4.5 | 5.7 |
| .7 | .9 | 1.1 | % Profit Before Taxes/Total Assets | 1.0 | 1.0 | .7 | 1.9 | 1.1 | 2.7 |
| -1.2 | -.7 | -.4 | | -.1 | -.5 | -1.3 | -.6 | -1.5 | -.5 |
| .7 | .7 | .6 | | .4 | .6 | .7 | .9 | 1.9 | 6.1 |
| .4 | .4 | .3 | Sales/Net Fixed Assets | .2 | .3 | .4 | .5 | .8 | 2.4 |
| .2 | .2 | .2 | | .2 | .2 | .3 | .3 | .5 | 1.3 |
| .5 | .5 | .5 | | .4 | .5 | .5 | .6 | .8 | 1.1 |
| .3 | .3 | .3 | Sales/Total Assets | .2 | .3 | .3 | .4 | .4 | .5 |
| .2 | .2 | .2 | | .1 | .2 | .2 | .3 | .3 | .3 |
| 4.5 | 4.1 | 4.6 | | 5.9 | 5.7 | 5.7 | 4.5 | 2.8 | 1.1 |
| (1187) 8.1 | (1346) 8.4 | (1487) 8.5 | % Depr., Dep., Amort./Sales | (321) 10.7 | (466) 9.2 | (240) 9.1 | (217) 7.6 | (161) 6.6 | (82) 2.0 |
| 12.3 | 12.3 | 12.8 | | 16.3 | 13.2 | 12.9 | 10.6 | 9.6 | 4.0 |
| 5.1 | 4.4 | 5.5 | | 7.7 | 4.7 | 4.1 | 3.8 | 1.3 | |
| (312) 12.8 | (301) 12.2 | (341) 12.5 | % Officers', Directors' Owners' Comp/Sales | (166) 15.1 | (105) 10.9 | (26) 8.9 | (22) 10.9 | (13) 4.6 | |
| 24.7 | 22.7 | 23.7 | | 24.1 | 22.2 | 23.9 | 26.5 | 18.9 | |
| 14053686M | 13993502M | 15142979M | Net Sales ($) | 620594M | 1783211M | 1333203M | 1924536M | 2679864M | 6801571M |
| 33925080M | 35798224M | 37677505M | Total Assets ($) | 3232303M | 6998376M | 4553439M | 5694244M | 7434422M | 9764721M |

M = $ thousand    MM = $ million
See Pages 9 through 22 for Explanation of Ratios and Data

**Current Data Sorted by Assets**  |  **Comparative Historical Data**

| 0-500M | 500M-2MM | 2-10MM | 10-50MM | 50-100MM | 100-250MM | Type of Statement | 4/1/07-3/31/08 ALL | 4/1/08-3/31/09 ALL |
|---|---|---|---|---|---|---|---|---|
| 4 | | 10 | 30 | 9 | 14 | Unqualified | 33 | 47 |
| | | | | | | Reviewed | | |
| 1 | 1 | 1 | | | | Compiled | 1 | |
| 3 | | | | | | Tax Returns | | |
| | 3 | 6 | 7 | 2 | 2 | Other | 14 | 10 |
| | 70 (4/1-9/30/11) | | 23 (10/1/11-3/31/12) | | | | | |
| 8 | 4 | 17 | 37 | 11 | 16 | NUMBER OF STATEMENTS | 48 | 57 |
| % | % | % | % | % | % | **ASSETS** | % | % |
| | | 34.5 | 28.6 | 28.0 | 39.0 | Cash & Equivalents | 34.0 | 32.1 |
| | | 14.4 | 6.6 | 4.1 | 4.3 | Trade Receivables (net) | 5.2 | 7.2 |
| | | .2 | .1 | .4 | .0 | Inventory | 1.0 | .7 |
| | | .5 | 3.6 | 2.2 | 2.2 | All Other Current | 3.2 | 4.4 |
| | | 49.7 | 38.9 | 34.7 | 45.5 | Total Current | 43.3 | 44.4 |
| | | 36.1 | 29.4 | 30.6 | 13.0 | Fixed Assets (net) | 25.6 | 26.1 |
| | | .2 | .3 | .7 | .4 | Intangibles (net) | .2 | 1.6 |
| | | 14.0 | 31.4 | 34.1 | 41.1 | All Other Non-Current | 29.6 | 27.9 |
| | | 100.0 | 100.0 | 100.0 | 100.0 | Total | 100.0 | 100.0 |
| | | | | | | **LIABILITIES** | | |
| | | 6.3 | .3 | .2 | .3 | Notes Payable-Short Term | 3.3 | 1.2 |
| | | 1.7 | .8 | .9 | .3 | Cur. Mat.-L.T.D. | .3 | .4 |
| | | 1.8 | 4.2 | 1.5 | 1.9 | Trade Payables | 2.5 | 2.6 |
| | | .0 | .0 | .0 | .0 | Income Taxes Payable | .0 | .0 |
| | | 7.4 | 5.4 | 11.6 | 10.5 | All Other Current | 5.2 | 8.3 |
| | | 17.1 | 10.8 | 14.3 | 13.0 | Total Current | 11.3 | 12.6 |
| | | 23.0 | 20.1 | 29.1 | 18.0 | Long-Term Debt | 18.7 | 15.1 |
| | | .0 | .0 | .0 | .0 | Deferred Taxes | .0 | .0 |
| | | 2.4 | 3.3 | 2.8 | 8.3 | All Other Non-Current | 2.2 | 3.8 |
| | | 57.4 | 65.8 | 53.9 | 60.6 | Net Worth | 67.8 | 68.6 |
| | | 100.0 | 100.0 | 100.0 | 100.0 | Total Liabilities & Net Worth | 100.0 | 100.0 |
| | | | | | | **INCOME DATA** | | |
| | | 100.0 | 100.0 | 100.0 | 100.0 | Net Sales | 100.0 | 100.0 |
| | | | | | | Gross Profit | | |
| | | 83.7 | 71.0 | 66.9 | 77.2 | Operating Expenses | 71.4 | 89.5 |
| | | 16.3 | 29.0 | 33.1 | 22.8 | Operating Profit | 28.6 | 10.5 |
| | | 7.5 | 9.7 | 6.1 | 1.2 | All Other Expenses (net) | 4.0 | 10.1 |
| | | 8.8 | 19.3 | 27.1 | 21.7 | Profit Before Taxes | 24.7 | .3 |
| | | | | | | **RATIOS** | | |
| | | 22.2 | 22.0 | 13.8 | 10.9 | | 26.4 | 23.5 |
| | | 4.4 | 6.2 | 1.0 | 4.9 | Current | 6.5 | 4.6 |
| | | 1.6 | 1.7 | .4 | 1.8 | | 1.5 | 2.3 |
| | | 22.2 | 22.0 | 10.5 | 10.3 | | 24.5 | 23.5 |
| | | 4.3 | 4.6 | 1.0 | 4.5 | Quick | 4.6 | 4.6 |
| | | 1.6 | 1.7 | .4 | 1.3 | | 1.4 | 1.6 |
| | | 1  296.0 | 5  73.8 | 0  UND | 2  154.3 | | 0  UND | 0  UND |
| | | 13  27.5 | 27  13.4 | 5  77.2 | 9  39.8 | Sales/Receivables | 1  271.8 | 9  42.5 |
| | | 72  5.1 | 52  7.0 | 37  9.8 | 41  9.0 | | 19  18.9 | 39  9.4 |
| | | | | | | Cost of Sales/Inventory | | |
| | | | | | | Cost of Sales/Payables | | |
| | | 1.0 | .6 | .2 | .4 | | .4 | .4 |
| | | 1.9 | 1.3 | -10.5 | 2.0 | Sales/Working Capital | 1.5 | 1.5 |
| | | 15.2 | 7.2 | -9.0 | 4.7 | | 11.3 | 5.5 |
| | | 4.3 | 13.8 | | | | 17.9 | 5.2 |
| | | (11) 1.5 | (18) 3.9 | | | EBIT/Interest | (19) 3.8 | (26) .2 |
| | | .0 | 1.4 | | | | 1.2 | -4.9 |
| | | | | | | Net Profit + Depr., Dep., Amort./Cur. Mat. L/T/D | | |
| | | .1 | .0 | .0 | .0 | | .0 | .0 |
| | | .6 | .4 | .1 | .1 | Fixed/Worth | .2 | .2 |
| | | 3.0 | 1.1 | 2.5 | .6 | | .9 | .8 |
| | | .1 | .0 | .1 | .1 | | .0 | .0 |
| | | .5 | .4 | 1.0 | .3 | Debt/Worth | .3 | .3 |
| | | 3.2 | 1.5 | 3.5 | 2.8 | | 1.4 | 1.0 |
| | | 13.8 | 13.4 | 16.4 | 16.3 | | 17.3 | 4.4 |
| | | (16) 8.1 | (35) 5.5 | (10) 6.4 | (15) 8.2 | % Profit Before Taxes/Tangible Net Worth | (46) 5.9 | (55) -1.1 |
| | | 1.7 | 1.0 | 1.9 | -.1 | | 1.4 | -5.4 |
| | | 8.2 | 7.7 | 8.2 | 6.6 | | 9.8 | 3.4 |
| | | 3.6 | 2.3 | 2.6 | 3.7 | % Profit Before Taxes/Total Assets | 3.6 | -1.4 |
| | | -.5 | .6 | .2 | .2 | | .3 | -3.6 |
| | | 100.9 | 79.7 | 46.9 | 63.0 | | 88.4 | 55.5 |
| | | 3.2 | 3.0 | 6.1 | 6.8 | Sales/Net Fixed Assets | 2.7 | 3.7 |
| | | .7 | .4 | .2 | 2.1 | | .5 | .6 |
| | | 1.2 | .4 | .3 | .6 | | .6 | .6 |
| | | .6 | .2 | .1 | .2 | Sales/Total Assets | .2 | .3 |
| | | .2 | .1 | .1 | .1 | | .1 | .1 |
| | | 1.5 | 1.5 | .3 | .2 | | .6 | .7 |
| | | (12) 2.9 | (29) 5.1 | (10) 3.0 | (12) 1.3 | % Depr., Dep., Amort./Sales | (39) 2.8 | (44) 2.8 |
| | | 6.7 | 9.4 | 11.6 | 3.0 | | 9.1 | 7.7 |
| | | | | | | % Officers', Directors' Owners' Comp/Sales | | |
| 4809M | 5443M | 83674M | 433031M | 288598M | 837468M | Net Sales ($) | 602274M | 1188089M |
| 1768M | 4028M | 97133M | 918661M | 800101M | 2210542M | Total Assets ($) | 2655653M | 3385999M |

M = $ thousand    MM = $ million
See Pages 9 through 22 for Explanation of Ratios and Data

## Comparative Historical Data | Current Data Sorted by Sales

| | | Comparative Historical Data | | Type of Statement | 0-1MM | 1-3MM | 3-5MM | 5-10MM | 10-25MM | 25MM & OVER |
|---|---|---|---|---|---|---|---|---|---|---|
| | 52 | 66 | 67 | Unqualified | 5 | 17 | 9 | 14 | 9 | 13 |
| | 2 | | | Reviewed | | | | | | |
| | | | 3 | Compiled | 1 | 1 | | 1 | | |
| | 19 | 1 | 3 | Tax Returns | 3 | | | | | |
| | | 14 | 20 | Other | 2 | 5 | 3 | 3 | 5 | 2 |
| | 4/1/09-3/31/10 | 4/1/10-3/31/11 | 4/1/11-3/31/12 | | 70 (4/1-9/30/11) | | | 23 (10/1/11-3/31/12) | | |
| | ALL | ALL | ALL | | | | | | | |
| | 73 | 81 | 93 | **NUMBER OF STATEMENTS** | 11 | 23 | 12 | 18 | 14 | 15 |
| | % | % | % | **ASSETS** | % | % | % | % | % | % |
| | 32.6 | 27.0 | 34.5 | Cash & Equivalents | 46.6 | 28.3 | 35.1 | 35.4 | 34.4 | 33.8 |
| | 8.4 | 9.8 | 7.5 | Trade Receivables (net) | 8.2 | 6.4 | 5.7 | 3.5 | 6.7 | 15.4 |
| | .7 | .3 | .3 | Inventory | .0 | .1 | 1.5 | .1 | .0 | .4 |
| | 2.7 | 4.8 | 2.8 | All Other Current | 1.3 | 3.3 | 2.2 | 1.9 | 1.0 | 6.3 |
| | 44.3 | 42.0 | 45.1 | Total Current | 56.0 | 38.0 | 44.6 | 41.0 | 42.2 | 55.9 |
| | 30.4 | 28.3 | 26.6 | Fixed Assets (net) | 34.8 | 25.3 | 28.0 | 30.3 | 22.8 | 20.4 |
| | .4 | .5 | .6 | Intangibles (net) | .7 | 1.0 | 1.0 | .1 | .4 | .4 |
| | 24.9 | 29.3 | 27.8 | All Other Non-Current | 8.5 | 35.7 | 26.4 | 28.6 | 34.6 | 23.3 |
| | 100.0 | 100.0 | 100.0 | Total | 100.0 | 100.0 | 100.0 | 100.0 | 100.0 | 100.0 |
| | | | | **LIABILITIES** | | | | | | |
| | 2.8 | 4.8 | 2.9 | Notes Payable-Short Term | 13.0 | 4.7 | .0 | .1 | .1 | 1.0 |
| | .6 | 1.4 | .8 | Cur. Mat.-L.T.D. | 1.0 | .9 | .6 | 1.0 | .4 | .9 |
| | 3.9 | 6.2 | 5.0 | Trade Payables | 17.8 | 2.0 | 2.0 | .4 | 3.4 | 9.6 |
| | .1 | .0 | .0 | Income Taxes Payable | .0 | .0 | .0 | .0 | .0 | .0 |
| | 10.7 | 7.6 | 7.6 | All Other Current | 2.4 | 5.1 | 2.2 | 8.0 | 9.9 | 17.1 |
| | 18.2 | 20.0 | 16.4 | Total Current | 34.3 | 12.7 | 4.9 | 9.5 | 13.8 | 28.6 |
| | 15.5 | 17.1 | 19.6 | Long-Term Debt | 15.9 | 17.7 | 17.0 | 25.9 | 25.6 | 13.8 |
| | .0 | .0 | .0 | Deferred Taxes | .0 | .0 | .0 | .0 | .0 | .0 |
| | 2.8 | 3.1 | 4.6 | All Other Non-Current | 7.9 | 2.5 | 4.6 | 3.7 | 3.3 | 7.8 |
| | 63.5 | 59.8 | 59.4 | Net Worth | 42.0 | 67.0 | 73.5 | 60.8 | 57.2 | 49.7 |
| | 100.0 | 100.0 | 100.0 | Total Liabilities & Net Worth | 100.0 | 100.0 | 100.0 | 100.0 | 100.0 | 100.0 |
| | | | | **INCOME DATA** | | | | | | |
| | 100.0 | 100.0 | 100.0 | Net Sales | 100.0 | 100.0 | 100.0 | 100.0 | 100.0 | 100.0 |
| | | | | Gross Profit | | | | | | |
| | 83.0 | 82.0 | 76.7 | Operating Expenses | 82.6 | 77.9 | 69.1 | 72.9 | 70.2 | 87.5 |
| | 17.0 | 18.0 | 23.3 | Operating Profit | 17.4 | 22.1 | 30.9 | 27.1 | 29.8 | 12.5 |
| | 10.7 | 3.8 | 6.3 | All Other Expenses (net) | 5.7 | 15.3 | 6.1 | 4.1 | 1.0 | .6 |
| | 6.3 | 14.2 | 17.0 | Profit Before Taxes | 11.6 | 6.8 | 24.8 | 23.0 | 28.8 | 12.0 |
| | | | | **RATIOS** | | | | | | |
| | 12.9 | 9.0 | 16.3 | | 12.4 | 36.4 | 20.1 | 19.3 | 6.1 | 7.5 |
| | 2.5 | 2.5 | 5.1 | Current | 4.5 | 7.3 | 8.9 | 7.9 | 2.6 | 1.9 |
| | 1.3 | 1.2 | 1.7 | | 2.1 | 1.3 | 2.9 | 1.4 | 1.6 | 1.3 |
| | 11.9 | 9.0 | 16.0 | | 12.4 | 36.1 | 20.1 | 19.3 | 6.1 | 7.2 |
| | 2.3 | 2.3 | 4.4 | Quick | 4.5 | 4.9 | 8.0 | 7.8 | 2.6 | 1.9 |
| | 1.1 | 1.1 | 1.3 | | 1.9 | 1.3 | 2.3 | 1.2 | 1.5 | 1.1 |
| | 0 UND | 0 UND | 0 UND | | 0 UND | 0 UND | 0 UND | 4 100.2 | 5 80.4 | 5 71.7 |
| | 8 44.0 | 22 16.5 | 14 26.4 | Sales/Receivables | 0 UND | 12 31.6 | 3 122.7 | 18 20.0 | 26 14.0 | 23 16.2 |
| | 61 6.0 | 103 3.5 | 43 8.4 | | 29 12.7 | 43 8.5 | 89 4.1 | 46 8.0 | 69 5.3 | 43 8.4 |
| | | | | Cost of Sales/Inventory | | | | | | |
| | | | | Cost of Sales/Payables | | | | | | |
| | .7 | .8 | .7 | | 2.0 | .7 | .3 | .2 | .6 | 1.8 |
| | 2.8 | 3.4 | 1.9 | Sales/Working Capital | 2.6 | 1.2 | 1.1 | 1.8 | 3.3 | 4.7 |
| | 13.6 | 12.7 | 12.4 | | 16.7 | 2.2 | 4.6 | 21.0 | 13.3 | 14.5 |
| | 10.1 | 11.6 | 11.4 | | | | | 6.0 | | 35.1 |
| | (31) 2.8 | (42) 4.2 | (47) 4.0 | EBIT/Interest | | | | (11) 2.0 | | (10) 6.6 |
| | -1.2 | 1.0 | 1.3 | | | | | 1.3 | | -1.3 |
| | | | | Net Profit + Depr., Dep., Amort./Cur. Mat. L/T/D | | | | | | |
| | .0 | .0 | .0 | | .2 | .0 | .0 | .0 | .0 | .1 |
| | .3 | .4 | .3 | Fixed/Worth | .3 | .2 | .1 | .1 | .3 | .5 |
| | .8 | 1.3 | 1.1 | | 1.2 | 1.0 | 1.0 | 1.7 | 1.1 | 1.2 |
| | .1 | .1 | .1 | | .1 | .0 | .1 | .1 | .2 | .2 |
| | .5 | .5 | .5 | Debt/Worth | .6 | .2 | .3 | .4 | .5 | 1.5 |
| | 1.5 | 1.7 | 1.8 | | 1.1 | 2.4 | .9 | 1.6 | 7.0 | 3.1 |
| | 11.1 | 13.1 | 14.6 | | 55.0 | 8.0 | 17.0 | 13.5 | 18.3 | 18.9 |
| | (69) 2.5 | (76) 4.6 | (87) 7.3 | % Profit Before Taxes/Tangible Net Worth | (10) 12.7 | (21) 1.6 | 6.0 | (16) 7.6 | (13) 9.8 | 11.2 |
| | -2.6 | -.1 | 1.1 | | -.9 | -1.4 | 1.4 | 1.5 | 5.1 | -7.7 |
| | 6.3 | 7.9 | 8.5 | | 35.2 | 3.4 | 14.6 | 9.2 | 8.9 | 11.1 |
| | 1.2 | 1.9 | 2.9 | % Profit Before Taxes/Total Assets | 9.2 | 1.3 | 4.5 | 2.8 | 6.2 | 4.6 |
| | -2.0 | -.9 | .2 | | -7.8 | -.9 | .8 | .1 | 2.6 | -2.3 |
| | 55.2 | 66.0 | 55.8 | | 12.0 | 351.0 | 54.9 | 128.8 | UND | 21.0 |
| | 2.5 | 4.1 | 5.4 | Sales/Net Fixed Assets | 5.3 | 3.0 | 2.5 | 5.8 | 5.8 | 8.0 |
| | .4 | .5 | .8 | | .8 | .5 | .3 | .5 | 1.3 | 4.4 |
| | .7 | .8 | .9 | | 1.9 | .3 | .4 | .5 | .5 | 2.3 |
| | .3 | .3 | .2 | Sales/Total Assets | 1.5 | .2 | .2 | .2 | .3 | 1.1 |
| | .1 | .1 | .1 | | .2 | .1 | .1 | .1 | .1 | .3 |
| | .5 | .6 | .8 | | 1.4 | 1.6 | .8 | .1 | .4 | 1.0 |
| | (58) 2.0 | (60) 2.4 | (74) 2.8 | % Depr., Dep., Amort./Sales | (10) 2.5 | (17) 5.1 | (11) 3.0 | (12) 3.4 | (10) 1.7 | (14) 2.0 |
| | 7.7 | 10.4 | 6.5 | | 5.7 | 7.6 | 9.7 | 14.1 | 6.4 | 3.3 |
| | | | | % Officers', Directors' Owners' Comp/Sales | | | | | | |
| | 1064506M | 1086093M | 1653023M | Net Sales ($) | 5726M | 40256M | 46908M | 126622M | 257342M | 1176169M |
| | 3154483M | 3359153M | 4032233M | Total Assets ($) | 14978M | 289584M | 343776M | 948618M | 1069577M | 1365700M |

M = $ thousand    MM = $ million
See Pages 9 through 22 for Explanation of Ratios and Data

## Current Data Sorted by Assets      Comparative Historical Data

| 0-500M | 500M-2MM | 2-10MM | 10-50MM | 50-100MM | 100-250MM | | ALL 4/1/07-3/31/08 | ALL 4/1/08-3/31/09 |
|---|---|---|---|---|---|---|---|---|
| 3 | 6 | 28 | 23 | 2 | 4 | Type of Statement — Unqualified | 65 | 77 |
| | | 1 | | | | Reviewed | | 1 |
| | | | | | | Compiled | 2 | |
| 1 | 1 | | | | | Tax Returns | 1 | 2 |
| 2 | 3 | 6 | 4 | 2 | | Other | 23 | 21 |
| 0-500M | 60 (4/1-9/30/11) 500M-2MM | 2-10MM | 26 (10/1/11-3/31/12) 10-50MM | 50-100MM | 100-250MM | | 4/1/07-3/31/08 ALL | 4/1/08-3/31/09 ALL |
| 6 | 10 | 35 | 27 | 4 | 4 | NUMBER OF STATEMENTS | 91 | 101 |
| % | % | % | % | % | % | | % | % |
| | 24.1 | 28.1 | 34.3 | | | ASSETS — Cash & Equivalents | 24.5 | 26.8 |
| | 43.9 | 15.7 | 13.9 | | | Trade Receivables (net) | 16.8 | 16.6 |
| | 3.5 | 1.0 | 1.6 | | | Inventory | .8 | .5 |
| | 2.0 | 6.2 | 3.0 | | | All Other Current | 5.2 | 3.3 |
| | 73.5 | 51.0 | 52.8 | | | Total Current | 47.3 | 47.2 |
| | 19.5 | 32.3 | 30.2 | | | Fixed Assets (net) | 34.9 | 35.1 |
| | .0 | .6 | .0 | | | Intangibles (net) | 1.3 | 2.3 |
| | 7.1 | 16.1 | 16.9 | | | All Other Non-Current | 16.5 | 15.4 |
| | 100.0 | 100.0 | 100.0 | | | Total | 100.0 | 100.0 |
| | 3.9 | 2.7 | .9 | | | LIABILITIES — Notes Payable-Short Term | 5.4 | 2.5 |
| | .4 | .8 | 1.1 | | | Cur. Mat.-L.T.D. | 1.3 | 1.0 |
| | 35.2 | 7.5 | 8.9 | | | Trade Payables | 6.2 | 9.1 |
| | .0 | .0 | .3 | | | Income Taxes Payable | .1 | .1 |
| | 9.7 | 9.8 | 13.7 | | | All Other Current | 11.5 | 11.1 |
| | 49.1 | 20.8 | 24.8 | | | Total Current | 24.6 | 23.8 |
| | 8.0 | 10.3 | 10.1 | | | Long-Term Debt | 18.3 | 18.2 |
| | .0 | .1 | .0 | | | Deferred Taxes | .1 | .0 |
| | .9 | 3.7 | 3.2 | | | All Other Non-Current | 4.0 | 3.8 |
| | 42.0 | 65.1 | 62.0 | | | Net Worth | 53.0 | 54.2 |
| | 100.0 | 100.0 | 100.0 | | | Total Liabilities & Net Worth | 100.0 | 100.0 |
| | 100.0 | 100.0 | 100.0 | | | INCOME DATA — Net Sales | 100.0 | 100.0 |
| | | | | | | Gross Profit | | |
| | 100.3 | 95.3 | 97.4 | | | Operating Expenses | 94.3 | 95.0 |
| | -.3 | 4.7 | 2.6 | | | Operating Profit | 5.7 | 5.0 |
| | 1.0 | .5 | -1.9 | | | All Other Expenses (net) | 1.0 | 3.4 |
| | -1.2 | 4.2 | 4.5 | | | Profit Before Taxes | 4.7 | 1.6 |
| | 4.3 | 4.8 | 3.9 | | | RATIOS — Current | 5.4 | 4.5 |
| | 2.5 | 2.8 | 2.2 | | | Current | 2.0 | 2.0 |
| | .9 | 1.1 | 1.5 | | | Current | 1.2 | 1.2 |
| | 3.4 | 4.5 | 3.3 | | | Quick | 4.1 | 3.9 |
| | 1.6 | 2.0 | 1.8 | | | Quick | 1.8 | 1.8 |
| | .9 | 1.1 | 1.2 | | | Quick | 1.0 | 1.1 |
| | 0   UND | 5   71.3 | 9   38.5 | | | Sales/Receivables | 7   55.8 | 4   85.3 |
| | 43   8.5 | 39   9.3 | 35   10.5 | | | Sales/Receivables | 28   13.0 | 30   12.1 |
| | 73   5.0 | 52   7.0 | 51   7.1 | | | Sales/Receivables | 53   6.9 | 53   6.9 |
| | | | | | | Cost of Sales/Inventory | | |
| | | | | | | Cost of Sales/Payables | | |
| | 5.6 | 3.1 | 3.3 | | | Sales/Working Capital | 2.2 | 2.5 |
| | 9.3 | 6.2 | 6.9 | | | Sales/Working Capital | 10.1 | 6.5 |
| | -176.4 | 16.6 | 17.2 | | | Sales/Working Capital | 29.6 | 30.8 |
| | | 6.3 | 35.1 | | | EBIT/Interest | 10.4 | 4.5 |
| | | (22) 2.2 | (19) 4.1 | | | EBIT/Interest | (56) 3.4 | (59) 1.2 |
| | | -3.4 | 1.3 | | | EBIT/Interest | 1.0 | -2.0 |
| | | | | | | Net Profit + Depr., Dep., Amort./Cur. Mat. L/T/D | | |
| | .1 | .1 | .2 | | | Fixed/Worth | .2 | .2 |
| | .4 | .4 | .4 | | | Fixed/Worth | .6 | .4 |
| | NM | .9 | 1.0 | | | Fixed/Worth | 1.4 | 1.4 |
| | .3 | .2 | .2 | | | Debt/Worth | .3 | .3 |
| | 1.6 | .4 | .5 | | | Debt/Worth | .8 | .9 |
| | NM | 1.1 | 1.2 | | | Debt/Worth | 2.1 | 1.8 |
| | | 11.5 | 17.8 | | | % Profit Before Taxes/Tangible Net Worth | 19.0 | 13.3 |
| | | 3.7 | 7.4 | | | % Profit Before Taxes/Tangible Net Worth | (86) 7.9 | (98) 1.7 |
| | | -1.9 | 1.2 | | | % Profit Before Taxes/Tangible Net Worth | .3 | -9.1 |
| | 7.3 | 9.2 | 7.8 | | | % Profit Before Taxes/Total Assets | 6.9 | 5.3 |
| | -.9 | 2.1 | 3.7 | | | % Profit Before Taxes/Total Assets | 3.4 | .4 |
| | -8.9 | -.8 | .4 | | | % Profit Before Taxes/Total Assets | .0 | -3.5 |
| | 346.3 | 46.7 | 50.1 | | | Sales/Net Fixed Assets | 33.4 | 18.8 |
| | 42.3 | 5.2 | 4.8 | | | Sales/Net Fixed Assets | 4.2 | 4.5 |
| | 10.7 | 2.7 | 1.9 | | | Sales/Net Fixed Assets | 2.0 | 1.9 |
| | 6.5 | 2.0 | 1.9 | | | Sales/Total Assets | 2.0 | 2.1 |
| | 3.1 | 1.4 | 1.3 | | | Sales/Total Assets | 1.2 | 1.2 |
| | 2.2 | .9 | .8 | | | Sales/Total Assets | .7 | .7 |
| | | .6 | .9 | | | % Depr., Dep., Amort./Sales | 1.2 | 1.0 |
| | | (32) 1.8 | (25) 1.9 | | | % Depr., Dep., Amort./Sales | (77) 2.3 | (88) 2.0 |
| | | 3.0 | 3.1 | | | % Depr., Dep., Amort./Sales | 3.5 | 3.9 |
| | | | | | | % Officers', Directors' Owners' Comp/Sales | 3.2 | 2.6 |
| | | | | | | % Officers', Directors' Owners' Comp/Sales | (16) 9.0 | (11) 8.1 |
| | | | | | | % Officers', Directors' Owners' Comp/Sales | 22.1 | 13.5 |
| 9515M | 35787M | 298451M | 1088845M | 184841M | 325775M | Net Sales ($) | 2843963M | 2660877M |
| 1695M | 9834M | 196186M | 630199M | 271868M | 594394M | Total Assets ($) | 2428628M | 2569269M |

M = $ thousand    MM = $ million
See Pages 9 through 22 for Explanation of Ratios and Data

| Comparative Historical Data | | | Type of Statement | Current Data Sorted by Sales | | | | | |
|---|---|---|---|---|---|---|---|---|---|
| 73 | 53 | 66 | Unqualified | 2 | 5 | 6 | 14 | 19 | 20 |
| 1 | 1 | 1 | Reviewed | 1 | | | | | |
| | 1 | | Compiled | | | | | | |
| 1 | | 2 | Tax Returns | 2 | | | | | |
| 12 | 28 | 17 | Other | 1 | | | | | |
| 4/1/09-3/31/10 ALL | 4/1/10-3/31/11 ALL | 4/1/11-3/31/12 ALL | | 0-1MM | 1-3MM | 3-5MM | 5-10MM | 10-25MM | 25MM & OVER |
| | | | | | 60 (4/1-9/30/11) | | 26 (10/1/11-3/31/12) | | |
| 87 | 83 | 86 | **NUMBER OF STATEMENTS** | 6 | 7 | 11 | 17 | 22 | 23 |
| % | % | % | **ASSETS** | % | % | % | % | % | % |
| 25.8 | 25.4 | 28.9 | Cash & Equivalents | | | 23.2 | 34.6 | 27.7 | 32.3 |
| 17.9 | 15.3 | 19.8 | Trade Receivables (net) | | | 40.6 | 16.8 | 14.5 | 12.7 |
| 1.5 | .8 | 1.3 | Inventory | | | .2 | .0 | 1.6 | 1.7 |
| 4.2 | 6.6 | 4.8 | All Other Current | | | 2.1 | 9.7 | 3.0 | 3.4 |
| 49.5 | 48.0 | 54.8 | Total Current | | | 66.1 | 61.0 | 46.8 | 50.1 |
| 32.4 | 38.6 | 28.2 | Fixed Assets (net) | | | 19.8 | 22.9 | 38.3 | 25.3 |
| .8 | 1.0 | .3 | Intangibles (net) | | | .0 | .4 | .7 | .0 |
| 17.3 | 12.4 | 16.7 | All Other Non-Current | | | 14.0 | 15.7 | 14.1 | 24.5 |
| 100.0 | 100.0 | 100.0 | Total | | | 100.0 | 100.0 | 100.0 | 100.0 |
| | | | **LIABILITIES** | | | | | | |
| 2.8 | 3.4 | 2.6 | Notes Payable-Short Term | | | 3.9 | 2.2 | 2.7 | .8 |
| 1.9 | 1.3 | .8 | Cur. Mat.-L.T.D. | | | .3 | .7 | .9 | 1.0 |
| 10.2 | 9.7 | 11.1 | Trade Payables | | | 12.0 | 11.0 | 8.8 | 8.6 |
| .1 | .2 | .1 | Income Taxes Payable | | | .0 | .5 | .0 | .0 |
| 14.6 | 10.8 | 12.2 | All Other Current | | | 9.3 | 7.0 | 10.1 | 20.0 |
| 29.6 | 25.5 | 26.8 | Total Current | | | 25.4 | 21.4 | 22.5 | 30.3 |
| 15.6 | 17.2 | 10.1 | Long-Term Debt | | | 1.2 | 7.4 | 14.7 | 11.2 |
| .0 | .1 | .0 | Deferred Taxes | | | .0 | .1 | .0 | .0 |
| 2.7 | 2.3 | 4.1 | All Other Non-Current | | | 10.8 | 3.3 | 1.9 | 5.9 |
| 52.1 | 54.9 | 59.0 | Net Worth | | | 62.5 | 67.8 | 60.9 | 52.5 |
| 100.0 | 100.0 | 100.0 | Total Liabilities & Net Worth | | | 100.0 | 100.0 | 100.0 | 100.0 |
| | | | **INCOME DATA** | | | | | | |
| 100.0 | 100.0 | 100.0 | Net Sales | | | 100.0 | 100.0 | 100.0 | 100.0 |
| | | | Gross Profit | | | | | | |
| 94.9 | 92.9 | 97.2 | Operating Expenses | | | 107.5 | 93.3 | 98.8 | 98.5 |
| 5.1 | 7.1 | 2.8 | Operating Profit | | | -7.5 | 6.7 | 1.2 | 1.5 |
| 2.2 | 1.6 | -.4 | All Other Expenses (net) | | | -1.5 | -2.4 | -.4 | -1.3 |
| 2.8 | 5.6 | 3.2 | Profit Before Taxes | | | -6.1 | 9.1 | 1.6 | 2.8 |
| | | | **RATIOS** | | | | | | |
| 4.3 | 3.9 | 3.9 | Current | | | 20.8 | 5.5 | 3.4 | 3.3 |
| 2.0 | 2.0 | 2.3 | | | | 3.3 | 3.1 | 2.3 | 1.6 |
| 1.3 | 1.1 | 1.3 | | | | 1.0 | 2.2 | 1.7 | 1.1 |
| 3.5 | 3.4 | 3.3 | Quick | | | 20.8 | 5.4 | 3.2 | 2.8 |
| 1.8 | 1.7 | 1.9 | | | | 3.3 | 2.8 | 1.9 | 1.5 |
| 1.0 | .9 | 1.0 | | | | .9 | 1.8 | 1.6 | 1.0 |
| 4  85.3 | 4  84.2 | 7  52.0 | Sales/Receivables | | | 42  8.7 | 8  47.5 | 21  17.7 | 0  UND |
| 35  10.5 | 28  13.1 | 36  10.1 | | | | 61  6.0 | 22  16.7 | 42  8.6 | 21  17.3 |
| 54  6.8 | 49  7.4 | 53  6.9 | | | | 68  5.4 | 42  8.6 | 53  6.9 | 46  7.9 |
| | | | Cost of Sales/Inventory | | | | | | |
| | | | Cost of Sales/Payables | | | | | | |
| 3.1 | 3.9 | 3.6 | Sales/Working Capital | | | 1.2 | 2.9 | 3.8 | 4.3 |
| 6.5 | 7.8 | 7.1 | | | | 4.4 | 4.8 | 6.4 | 7.4 |
| 29.7 | 55.0 | 19.0 | | | | -227.6 | 10.2 | 7.9 | 60.5 |
| 8.9 | 19.5 | 9.7 | EBIT/Interest | | | | | 6.4 | 36.9 |
| (60)  2.3 | (58)  4.8 | (57)  2.6 | | | | | (17)  | 1.8 | (18)  3.5 |
| .5 | 2.0 | -3.3 | | | | | | -3.6 | .3 |
| | | | Net Profit + Depr., Dep., Amort./Cur. Mat. L/T/D | | | | | | |
| .1 | .2 | .1 | Fixed/Worth | | | .1 | .1 | .2 | .1 |
| .5 | .7 | .4 | | | | .2 | .4 | .7 | .4 |
| 1.4 | 1.3 | .9 | | | | .5 | .6 | 1.1 | .8 |
| .3 | .3 | .3 | Debt/Worth | | | .2 | .2 | .3 | .4 |
| .7 | .8 | .6 | | | | .3 | .3 | .5 | .8 |
| 2.6 | 2.0 | 1.2 | | | | 3.9 | .9 | 1.1 | 1.8 |
| 13.7 | 18.2 | 11.9 | % Profit Before Taxes/Tangible Net Worth | | | 2.4 | 27.9 | 8.9 | 16.2 |
| (84)  2.5 | (81)  7.6 | (84)  5.3 | | | (10) | -4.2 | 13.8 | 2.5 | 6.9 |
| -5.8 | 1.3 | -1.7 | | | | -24.1 | 1.5 | -3.7 | 1.2 |
| 7.6 | 8.2 | 7.5 | % Profit Before Taxes/Total Assets | | | .6 | 21.6 | 5.7 | 7.5 |
| .9 | 3.8 | 1.9 | | | | -2.3 | 10.3 | 1.4 | 3.2 |
| -2.8 | .8 | -.8 | | | | -16.4 | 1.1 | -2.3 | .0 |
| 58.1 | 22.6 | 82.0 | Sales/Net Fixed Assets | | | 46.7 | 79.1 | 11.8 | 81.2 |
| 5.3 | 4.1 | 5.5 | | | | 11.2 | 6.2 | 4.0 | 5.5 |
| 2.3 | 2.0 | 2.3 | | | | 2.7 | 3.4 | 2.0 | 2.3 |
| 2.6 | 2.3 | 2.5 | Sales/Total Assets | | | 3.2 | 3.1 | 1.9 | 2.4 |
| 1.4 | 1.5 | 1.4 | | | | 1.1 | 1.4 | 1.4 | 1.3 |
| .7 | .8 | .8 | | | | .7 | 1.0 | 1.0 | .7 |
| .8 | 1.2 | .5 | % Depr., Dep., Amort./Sales | | | | .6 | 1.3 | .5 |
| (76)  1.9 | (70)  2.1 | (74)  1.8 | | | | (16) | 1.3  (20) | 2.4  (22) | 1.5 |
| 3.3 | 3.6 | 3.3 | | | | | 2.1 | 3.3 | 2.6 |
| 2.3 | | | % Officers', Directors' Owners' Comp/Sales | | | | | | |
| (11)  4.8 | | | | | | | | | |
| 7.6 | | | | | | | | | |
| 2756757M | 1949190M | 1943214M | Net Sales ($) | 2786M | 13625M | 45422M | 123284M | 319472M | 1438625M |
| 1827531M | 1689121M | 1704176M | Total Assets ($) | 9666M | 13727M | 44351M | 90710M | 286718M | 1259004M |

© RMA 2012

M = $ thousand    MM = $ million
See Pages 9 through 22 for Explanation of Ratios and Data

## Current Data Sorted by Assets | Comparative Historical Data

| | 0-500M | 500M-2MM | 2-10MM | 10-50MM | 50-100MM | 100-250MM | Type of Statement | 4/1/07-3/31/08 ALL | 4/1/08-3/31/09 ALL |
|---|---|---|---|---|---|---|---|---|---|
| | 5 | 2 | 18 | 18 | 9 | 9 | Unqualified | 17 | 30 |
| | | | | | | | Reviewed | | 1 |
| | 1 | 1 | | | | | Compiled | 1 | 1 |
| | 1 | 1 | 2 | | | | Tax Returns | 1 | 1 |
| | 2 | 1 | 8 | 6 | | 2 | Other | 4 | 8 |
| | | 58 (4/1-9/30/11) | | 27 (10/1/11-3/31/12) | | | | | |
| **NUMBER OF STATEMENTS** | 8 | 5 | 28 | 24 | 9 | 11 | | 23 | 41 |
| | % | % | % | % | % | % | **ASSETS** | % | % |
| | | | 21.0 | 26.6 | | 36.9 | Cash & Equivalents | 18.8 | 23.2 |
| | | | 15.4 | 14.4 | | 5.9 | Trade Receivables (net) | 14.8 | 9.4 |
| | | | 3.4 | 7.6 | | .3 | Inventory | 6.9 | 8.9 |
| | | | 1.7 | 3.1 | | 2.9 | All Other Current | 6.5 | 3.3 |
| | | | 41.5 | 51.7 | | 46.0 | Total Current | 47.1 | 44.8 |
| | | | 37.9 | 18.5 | | 25.4 | Fixed Assets (net) | 29.8 | 36.0 |
| | | | 2.3 | 1.6 | | .0 | Intangibles (net) | .5 | 1.2 |
| | | | 18.2 | 28.2 | | 28.7 | All Other Non-Current | 22.6 | 18.1 |
| | | | 100.0 | 100.0 | | 100.0 | Total | 100.0 | 100.0 |
| | | | | | | | **LIABILITIES** | | |
| | | | 1.1 | 1.6 | | 1.3 | Notes Payable-Short Term | 6.5 | 2.7 |
| | | | .3 | .7 | | 1.4 | Cur. Mat.-L.T.D. | 1.0 | .8 |
| | | | 3.6 | 9.2 | | 3.2 | Trade Payables | 4.2 | 3.0 |
| | | | .0 | .0 | | .0 | Income Taxes Payable | .0 | .0 |
| | | | 10.7 | 10.7 | | 10.8 | All Other Current | 14.0 | 9.3 |
| | | | 15.7 | 22.2 | | 16.7 | Total Current | 25.8 | 15.7 |
| | | | 13.7 | 9.3 | | 2.9 | Long-Term Debt | 10.4 | 17.6 |
| | | | .0 | .0 | | .0 | Deferred Taxes | .0 | .0 |
| | | | 5.6 | 7.2 | | 4.7 | All Other Non-Current | 3.1 | 1.5 |
| | | | 65.0 | 61.3 | | 75.8 | Net Worth | 60.7 | 65.2 |
| | | | 100.0 | 100.0 | | 100.0 | Total Liabilities & Net Worth | 100.0 | 100.0 |
| | | | | | | | **INCOME DATA** | | |
| | | | 100.0 | 100.0 | | 100.0 | Net Sales | 100.0 | 100.0 |
| | | | | | | | Gross Profit | | |
| | | | 94.7 | 92.0 | | 80.3 | Operating Expenses | 95.4 | 96.6 |
| | | | 5.3 | 8.0 | | 19.7 | Operating Profit | 4.6 | 3.4 |
| | | | -1.1 | 1.4 | | 2.0 | All Other Expenses (net) | -1.6 | .2 |
| | | | 6.4 | 6.6 | | 17.8 | Profit Before Taxes | 6.1 | 3.1 |
| | | | | | | | **RATIOS** | | |
| | | | 7.1 | 6.6 | | 4.2 | Current | 3.3 | 9.0 |
| | | | 3.4 | 2.4 | | 2.5 | | 2.0 | 3.7 |
| | | | 1.3 | 1.6 | | 2.0 | | 1.2 | 1.5 |
| | | | 7.0 | 6.1 | | 4.2 | Quick | 2.3 | 6.0 |
| | | | 2.9 | 1.8 | | 2.0 | | 1.4 | 2.8 |
| | | | .8 | .9 | | 1.7 | | .7 | 1.1 |
| | | | 0 UND | 10 36.8 | | 0 UND | Sales/Receivables | 0 UND | 0 UND |
| | | | 10 36.2 | 27 13.3 | | 0 999.8 | | 21 17.4 | 10 34.9 |
| | | | 54 6.7 | 78 4.7 | | 8 46.1 | | 62 5.9 | 61 6.0 |
| | | | | | | | Cost of Sales/Inventory | | |
| | | | | | | | Cost of Sales/Payables | | |
| | | | 2.1 | 1.8 | | .8 | Sales/Working Capital | 4.5 | 1.8 |
| | | | 4.7 | 2.8 | | 3.1 | | 8.6 | 4.1 |
| | | | 40.7 | 12.2 | | 4.3 | | 39.8 | 13.5 |
| | | | 17.5 | 25.5 | | | EBIT/Interest | 14.2 | 9.8 |
| | | | (18) 3.6 | (12) 9.2 | | | | (12) 3.9 | (20) 1.0 |
| | | | .7 | -1.4 | | | | -.3 | -1.0 |
| | | | | | | | Net Profit + Depr., Dep., Amort./Cur. Mat. L/T/D | | |
| | | | .1 | .0 | | .0 | Fixed/Worth | .1 | .0 |
| | | | .6 | .2 | | .5 | | .5 | .4 |
| | | | .9 | .6 | | .6 | | .7 | .9 |
| | | | .1 | .1 | | .1 | Debt/Worth | .2 | .1 |
| | | | .3 | .6 | | .2 | | .7 | .6 |
| | | | 1.0 | 2.5 | | .6 | | 1.6 | 1.0 |
| | | | 9.7 | 18.2 | | 12.3 | % Profit Before Taxes/Tangible Net Worth | 12.4 | 14.8 |
| | | | (27) 4.6 | 4.8 | | 3.2 | | 4.3 | (40) 2.6 |
| | | | 2.0 | -2.8 | | -.7 | | -2.2 | -4.8 |
| | | | 5.6 | 7.7 | | 10.5 | % Profit Before Taxes/Total Assets | 10.5 | 6.6 |
| | | | 3.1 | 1.9 | | 3.2 | | 3.2 | 1.6 |
| | | | .0 | -2.3 | | -.4 | | -.6 | -2.7 |
| | | | 16.7 | 147.2 | | 9.7 | Sales/Net Fixed Assets | 65.3 | 27.3 |
| | | | 6.7 | 24.5 | | 4.9 | | 8.1 | 3.9 |
| | | | .6 | 1.5 | | .5 | | 2.1 | 1.4 |
| | | | 2.1 | 1.2 | | 1.1 | Sales/Total Assets | 2.5 | 1.8 |
| | | | 1.0 | .7 | | .3 | | 1.5 | .9 |
| | | | .4 | .4 | | .2 | | .6 | .4 |
| | | | 1.0 | .3 | | | % Depr., Dep., Amort./Sales | .4 | .7 |
| | | | (23) 2.3 | (22) 1.3 | | | | (20) 1.7 | (33) 2.4 |
| | | | 4.6 | 4.2 | | | | 3.8 | 4.6 |
| | | | | | | | % Officers', Directors' Owners' Comp/Sales | | |
| 7951M | 11118M | 221491M | 679304M | 426322M | 1560431M | | Net Sales ($) | 463137M | 850400M |
| 2079M | 5761M | 184025M | 643329M | 686396M | 1903853M | | Total Assets ($) | 395208M | 693456M |

M = $ thousand   MM = $ million
See Pages 9 through 22 for Explanation of Ratios and Data

## Comparative Historical Data / Current Data Sorted by Sales

| 32 | 41 | 61 | Type of Statement | 6 | 5 | 8 | 10 | 15 | 17 |
|---|---|---|---|---|---|---|---|---|---|
| 1 | | | Unqualified |  |  |  |  |  |  |
| | 1 | 2 | Reviewed |  |  |  |  |  |  |
| 2 | 2 | 3 | Compiled | 1 | 1 |  |  |  |  |
| 11 | 9 | 19 | Tax Returns |  | 1 | 1 |  | 1 |  |
| | | | Other | 3 | 4 | 1 | 4 | 4 | 3 |
| 4/1/09- | 4/1/10- | 4/1/11- | | | 58 (4/1-9/30/11) | | 27 (10/1/11-3/31/12) | | |
| 3/31/10 | 3/31/11 | 3/31/12 | | | | | | | |
| ALL | ALL | ALL | | 0-1MM | 1-3MM | 3-5MM | 5-10MM | 10-25MM | 25MM & OVER |
| 46 | 53 | 85 | **NUMBER OF STATEMENTS** | 10 | 11 | 10 | 14 | 20 | 20 |
| % | % | % | **ASSETS** | % | % | % | % | % | % |
| 27.5 | 27.3 | 28.5 | Cash & Equivalents | 42.8 | 18.4 | 23.4 | 24.7 | 20.0 | 40.7 |
| 17.1 | 14.9 | 14.2 | Trade Receivables (net) | 6.9 | 11.8 | 18.0 | 4.7 | 22.1 | 15.9 |
| 2.3 | 4.9 | 4.1 | Inventory | .0 | 6.5 | .1 | 13.7 | 1.4 | 2.8 |
| 1.6 | 4.8 | 2.9 | All Other Current | 3.1 | 1.2 | 1.7 | 2.7 | 3.7 | 3.9 |
| 48.5 | 51.9 | 49.8 | Total Current | 52.8 | 37.9 | 43.3 | 45.8 | 47.2 | 63.4 |
| 36.3 | 26.1 | 25.8 | Fixed Assets (net) | 27.1 | 49.7 | 18.1 | 29.6 | 22.6 | 16.3 |
| 2.4 | 1.4 | 1.3 | Intangibles (net) | .0 | .0 | 1.6 | .0 | 4.3 | .3 |
| 12.8 | 20.6 | 23.2 | All Other Non-Current | 20.2 | 12.4 | 37.0 | 24.6 | 25.9 | 20.1 |
| 100.0 | 100.0 | 100.0 | Total | 100.0 | 100.0 | 100.0 | 100.0 | 100.0 | 100.0 |
| | | | **LIABILITIES** | | | | | | |
| 2.7 | 2.7 | 2.7 | Notes Payable-Short Term | 10.7 | .5 | 3.5 | 1.0 | 2.9 | .5 |
| 1.3 | .8 | .8 | Cur. Mat.-L.T.D. | .4 | .8 | .6 | 1.4 | 1.0 | .6 |
| 5.8 | 6.4 | 5.4 | Trade Payables | 2.3 | 2.5 | 4.0 | 1.8 | 5.6 | 11.5 |
| .0 | .0 | .0 | Income Taxes Payable | .0 | .0 | .0 | .0 | .0 | .0 |
| 15.2 | 13.9 | 10.9 | All Other Current | 10.8 | 12.5 | 5.5 | 5.8 | 7.5 | 19.7 |
| 25.0 | 23.7 | 19.8 | Total Current | 24.3 | 16.3 | 13.6 | 10.0 | 16.9 | 32.2 |
| 16.3 | 10.2 | 11.0 | Long-Term Debt | 11.1 | 14.2 | 18.4 | 8.8 | 11.3 | 6.9 |
| .0 | .0 | .0 | Deferred Taxes | .0 | .0 | .0 | .0 | .0 | .0 |
| 4.1 | 3.5 | 5.4 | All Other Non-Current | .4 | 13.1 | .9 | 3.4 | 4.8 | 7.9 |
| 54.7 | 62.6 | 63.8 | Net Worth | 64.2 | 56.3 | 67.1 | 77.9 | 67.1 | 53.0 |
| 100.0 | 100.0 | 100.0 | Total Liabilties & Net Worth | 100.0 | 100.0 | 100.0 | 100.0 | 100.0 | 100.0 |
| | | | **INCOME DATA** | | | | | | |
| 100.0 | 100.0 | 100.0 | Net Sales | 100.0 | 100.0 | 100.0 | 100.0 | 100.0 | 100.0 |
| | | | Gross Profit | | | | | | |
| 96.9 | 94.6 | 92.0 | Operating Expenses | 93.9 | 101.6 | 82.3 | 89.1 | 95.3 | 89.1 |
| 3.1 | 5.4 | 8.0 | Operating Profit | 6.1 | -1.6 | 17.7 | 10.9 | 4.7 | 10.9 |
| 1.8 | -.6 | 1.8 | All Other Expenses (net) | 1.9 | .1 | 8.5 | 1.6 | -.7 | 1.9 |
| 1.3 | 6.0 | 6.3 | Profit Before Taxes | 4.2 | -1.7 | 9.2 | 9.3 | 5.4 | 9.0 |
| | | | **RATIOS** | | | | | | |
| 8.5 | 7.3 | 7.1 | | 23.7 | 13.9 | 6.2 | 7.6 | 12.1 | 3.1 |
| 2.5 | 2.8 | 3.1 | Current | 10.0 | 5.4 | 3.9 | 2.6 | 3.6 | 1.9 |
| 1.1 | 1.3 | 1.5 | | 1.0 | .6 | 1.4 | 1.7 | 1.8 | 1.2 |
| 5.7 | 5.6 | 6.5 | | 23.5 | 13.9 | 6.0 | 4.8 | 8.4 | 3.0 |
| 2.4 | 1.9 | 2.0 | Quick | 8.5 | 1.5 | 3.2 | 1.9 | 2.9 | 1.8 |
| 1.0 | 1.0 | 1.0 | | 1.0 | .6 | .9 | .6 | 1.5 | 1.1 |
| 1 287.6 | 1 305.1 | 0 780.8 | | 0 UND | 1 640.8 | 1 498.0 | 0 UND | 5 72.2 | 0 UND |
| 20 17.9 | 17 21.2 | 12 30.0 | Sales/Receivables | 2 169.5 | 5 75.0 | 17 21.8 | 8 46.1 | 47 7.8 | 0 34.8 |
| 59 6.2 | 53 6.9 | 65 5.6 | | 68 5.4 | 31 11.8 | 73 5.0 | 25 14.7 | 140 2.6 | 96 3.8 |
| | | | Cost of Sales/Inventory | | | | | | |
| | | | Cost of Sales/Payables | | | | | | |
| 3.0 | 2.0 | 1.9 | | 1.9 | 1.8 | 1.1 | .5 | 1.6 | 2.9 |
| 6.1 | 5.8 | 3.6 | Sales/Working Capital | 4.0 | 2.8 | 2.9 | 2.3 | 2.8 | 4.6 |
| 41.1 | 23.2 | 13.2 | | UND | -17.4 | 24.7 | 13.7 | 5.8 | 12.1 |
| 5.0 | 12.4 | 17.5 | | | | 7.3 | | 49.0 | |
| (21) .7 | (23) 1.5 | (46) 2.0 | EBIT/Interest | (10) 1.0 | | | (11) 9.1 | |
| -4.6 | -.2 | .2 | | | -9.4 | | | .4 | |
| | | | Net Profit + Depr., Dep., Amort./Cur. Mat. L/T/D | | | | | | |
| .1 | .0 | .0 | | .0 | .3 | .0 | .0 | .0 | .0 |
| .6 | .2 | .2 | Fixed/Worth | .1 | .8 | .1 | .3 | .2 | .2 |
| 1.9 | .8 | .7 | | 1.4 | 1.2 | .7 | .7 | .7 | .5 |
| .3 | .1 | .1 | | .0 | .1 | .1 | .1 | .1 | .2 |
| .7 | .4 | .4 | Debt/Worth | .2 | .7 | .3 | .2 | .4 | .8 |
| 2.6 | 1.3 | 1.2 | | 9.3 | 3.0 | 1.8 | .7 | 1.0 | 4.1 |
| 11.4 | 9.4 | 10.6 | | 26.6 | 5.3 | 5.5 | 11.2 | 14.0 | 18.7 |
| (45) 3.5 | (51) 3.1 | (83) 3.5 | % Profit Before Taxes/Tangible Net Worth | 2.7 | 2.6 | 1.0 | (19) 6.1 | 4.8 | (19) 5.1 |
| -13.9 | -2.3 | -1.4 | | .8 | -3.0 | -12.2 | -.1 | -3.6 | -2.1 |
| 5.9 | 4.5 | 5.7 | | 2.2 | 4.5 | 3.9 | 9.1 | 7.4 | 10.1 |
| .3 | 1.3 | 1.6 | % Profit Before Taxes/Total Assets | .9 | .0 | .2 | 4.6 | 3.6 | 1.9 |
| -5.3 | -1.0 | -1.3 | | .3 | -2.8 | -6.4 | -.1 | -3.3 | -1.5 |
| 94.2 | 67.6 | 62.5 | | UND | 8.7 | 160.3 | 74.2 | 26.8 | 132.4 |
| 4.7 | 9.1 | 8.9 | Sales/Net Fixed Assets | 101.0 | .6 | 10.0 | 4.5 | 7.0 | 16.8 |
| 1.2 | 1.5 | 1.3 | | 1.1 | .5 | 1.8 | 1.0 | 1.8 | 6.3 |
| 2.6 | 2.4 | 1.7 | | 1.9 | 2.0 | 1.9 | 1.1 | 2.3 | 2.1 |
| 1.1 | .9 | .7 | Sales/Total Assets | .8 | .4 | .4 | .6 | .7 | 1.3 |
| .5 | .3 | .3 | | .4 | .2 | .3 | .2 | .3 | .5 |
| .4 | .3 | .4 | | | | | 1.2 | .9 | .2 |
| (36) 1.3 | (41) 1.1 | (71) 1.4 | % Depr., Dep., Amort./Sales | | | (11) | 3.0 | (19) 1.1 | (18) .6 |
| 3.7 | 3.3 | 4.0 | | | | | 4.6 | 3.8 | 1.7 |
| | | | % Officers', Directors' Owners' Comp/Sales | | | | | | |
| 661033M | 1790694M | 2906617M | Net Sales ($) | 5503M | 20830M | 38612M | 94858M | 350350M | 2396464M |
| 752584M | 1392840M | 3425443M | Total Assets ($) | 20072M | 54996M | 147709M | 424926M | 856376M | 1921364M |

M = $ thousand    MM = $ million
See Pages 9 through 22 for Explanation of Ratios and Data

**Current Data Sorted by Assets** | **Comparative Historical Data**

| | | | | | | Type of Statement | | |
|---|---|---|---|---|---|---|---|---|
| 1 | 2 | 10 | 5 | 2 | | Unqualified | 5 | 5 |
| | | | 1 | | | Reviewed | | |
| | | | | | | Compiled | | |
| | 1 | | | | | Tax Returns | | |
| 2 | 1 | 6 | 3 | 1 | | Other | 3 | 3 |
| | 21 (4/1-9/30/11) | | 14 (10/1/11-3/31/12) | | | | 4/1/07-3/31/08 ALL | 4/1/08-3/31/09 ALL |
| 0-500M | 500M-2MM | 2-10MM | 10-50MM | 50-100MM | 100-250MM | NUMBER OF STATEMENTS | | |
| 3 | 4 | 16 | 9 | 3 | | | 8 | 8 |
| % | % | % | % | % | % | ASSETS | % | % |
| | | 10.6 | | | | Cash & Equivalents | | |
| | | 8.8 | | | | Trade Receivables (net) | | |
| | | 5.8 | | | | Inventory | | |
| | | .9 | | | | All Other Current | | |
| | | 26.1 | | | | Total Current | | |
| | | 59.6 | | | | Fixed Assets (net) | | |
| | | .1 | | | | Intangibles (net) | | |
| | | 14.2 | | | | All Other Non-Current | | |
| | | 100.0 | | | | Total | | |
| | | | | | | LIABILITIES | | |
| | | 1.6 | | | | Notes Payable-Short Term | | |
| | | 2.0 | | | | Cur. Mat.-L.T.D. | | |
| | | 3.8 | | | | Trade Payables | | |
| | | .0 | | | | Income Taxes Payable | | |
| | | 3.0 | | | | All Other Current | | |
| | | 10.5 | | | | Total Current | | |
| | | 28.4 | | | | Long-Term Debt | | |
| | | .0 | | | | Deferred Taxes | | |
| | | 1.3 | | | | All Other Non-Current | | |
| | | 59.8 | | | | Net Worth | | |
| | | 100.0 | | | | Total Liabilities & Net Worth | | |
| | | | | | | INCOME DATA | | |
| | | 100.0 | | | | Net Sales | | |
| | | | | | | Gross Profit | | |
| | | 95.5 | | | | Operating Expenses | | |
| | | 4.5 | | | | Operating Profit | | |
| | | 3.8 | | | | All Other Expenses (net) | | |
| | | .7 | | | | Profit Before Taxes | | |
| | | | | | | RATIOS | | |
| | | 9.0 | | | | | | |
| | | 2.4 | | | | Current | | |
| | | .9 | | | | | | |
| | | 2.9 | | | | | | |
| | | 2.0 | | | | Quick | | |
| | | .8 | | | | | | |
| | | 0   UND | | | | | | |
| | | 20   18.3 | | | | Sales/Receivables | | |
| | | 68   5.4 | | | | | | |
| | | | | | | Cost of Sales/Inventory | | |
| | | | | | | Cost of Sales/Payables | | |
| | | 3.3 | | | | | | |
| | | 7.0 | | | | Sales/Working Capital | | |
| | | NM | | | | | | |
| | | | | | | EBIT/Interest | | |
| | | | | | | Net Profit + Depr., Dep., Amort./Cur. Mat. L/T/D | | |
| | | .5 | | | | | | |
| | | 1.2 | | | | Fixed/Worth | | |
| | | 1.6 | | | | | | |
| | | .4 | | | | | | |
| | | .7 | | | | Debt/Worth | | |
| | | 1.2 | | | | | | |
| | | 13.8 | | | | % Profit Before Taxes/Tangible Net Worth | | |
| | | .7 | | | | | | |
| | | -2.0 | | | | | | |
| | | 6.0 | | | | % Profit Before Taxes/Total Assets | | |
| | | .3 | | | | | | |
| | | -.9 | | | | | | |
| | | 3.3 | | | | | | |
| | | .8 | | | | Sales/Net Fixed Assets | | |
| | | .5 | | | | | | |
| | | 1.6 | | | | | | |
| | | .5 | | | | Sales/Total Assets | | |
| | | .3 | | | | | | |
| | | 1.5 | | | | | | |
| | (13) | 3.1 | | | | % Depr., Dep., Amort./Sales | | |
| | | 9.3 | | | | | | |
| | | | | | | % Officers', Directors' Owners' Comp/Sales | | |
| 910M | 14489M | 93110M | 145858M | 241042M | | Net Sales ($) | 37081M | 177074M |
| 751M | 4366M | 82688M | 184840M | 203991M | | Total Assets ($) | 42730M | 81114M |

*Note: Columns 10-50MM, 50-100MM, and 100-250MM marked "DATA NOT AVAILABLE" across the ratio/asset rows.*

M = $ thousand    MM = $ million
See Pages 9 through 22 for Explanation of Ratios and Data

## Comparative Historical Data

## Current Data Sorted by Sales

| | | | | Type of Statement | | | | | | |
|---|---|---|---|---|---|---|---|---|---|---|
| | | | | Unqualified | 1 | 5 | 1 | 3 | 6 | 3 |
| | | | | Reviewed | 1 | | | 1 | | |
| | | | | Compiled | | | | | | |
| | | | | Tax Returns | 1 | | | | | |
| | 15 | 20 | 19 | Other | 5 | 2 | 2 | 1 | 1 | 2 |
| | | | 2 | | | 21 (4/1-9/30/11) | | 14 (10/1/11-3/31/12) | | |
| | 2 | | 1 | | | | | | | |
| | 9 | 8 | 13 | | 0-1MM | 1-3MM | 3-5MM | 5-10MM | 10-25MM | 25MM & OVER |
| | 4/1/09- | 4/1/10- | 4/1/11- | | | | | | | |
| | 3/31/10 | 3/31/11 | 3/31/12 | | | | | | | |
| | ALL | ALL | ALL | | | | | | | |
| | 26 | 28 | 35 | NUMBER OF STATEMENTS | 8 | 7 | 3 | 5 | 7 | 5 |
| | % | % | % | ASSETS | % | % | % | % | % | % |
| | 17.8 | 31.5 | 20.2 | Cash & Equivalents | | | | | | |
| | 14.7 | 11.4 | 7.8 | Trade Receivables (net) | | | | | | |
| | .8 | 2.9 | 2.9 | Inventory | | | | | | |
| | 5.6 | 5.7 | 4.5 | All Other Current | | | | | | |
| | 38.9 | 51.5 | 35.3 | Total Current | | | | | | |
| | 50.5 | 39.5 | 45.5 | Fixed Assets (net) | | | | | | |
| | .1 | .1 | 1.1 | Intangibles (net) | | | | | | |
| | 10.4 | 8.9 | 18.1 | All Other Non-Current | | | | | | |
| | 100.0 | 100.0 | 100.0 | Total | | | | | | |
| | | | | LIABILITIES | | | | | | |
| | 10.0 | 2.5 | 1.6 | Notes Payable-Short Term | | | | | | |
| | 2.2 | 1.0 | 1.4 | Cur. Mat.-L.T.D. | | | | | | |
| | 5.1 | 4.5 | 3.3 | Trade Payables | | | | | | |
| | .7 | .0 | .0 | Income Taxes Payable | | | | | | |
| | 9.3 | 28.2 | 10.8 | All Other Current | | | | | | |
| | 27.3 | 36.2 | 17.2 | Total Current | | | | | | |
| | 24.5 | 18.9 | 17.3 | Long-Term Debt | | | | | | |
| | .0 | .0 | .0 | Deferred Taxes | | | | | | |
| | 2.3 | 2.2 | 1.1 | All Other Non-Current | | | | | | |
| | 46.0 | 42.7 | 64.4 | Net Worth | | | | | | |
| | 100.0 | 100.0 | 100.0 | Total Liabilities & Net Worth | | | | | | |
| | | | | INCOME DATA | | | | | | |
| | 100.0 | 100.0 | 100.0 | Net Sales | | | | | | |
| | | | | Gross Profit | | | | | | |
| | 94.3 | 98.5 | 95.5 | Operating Expenses | | | | | | |
| | 5.7 | 1.5 | 4.5 | Operating Profit | | | | | | |
| | 2.2 | 3.1 | 1.5 | All Other Expenses (net) | | | | | | |
| | 3.4 | -1.7 | 3.1 | Profit Before Taxes | | | | | | |
| | | | | RATIOS | | | | | | |
| | 5.9 | 8.9 | 7.2 | | | | | | | |
| | 2.4 | 2.8 | 2.6 | Current | | | | | | |
| | 1.1 | 1.2 | .9 | | | | | | | |
| | 4.4 | 5.8 | 6.2 | | | | | | | |
| | 1.4 | 1.9 | 1.6 | Quick | | | | | | |
| | 1.0 | .7 | .8 | | | | | | | |
| 0 UND | 4 88.1 | 0 UND | Sales/Receivables | | | | | | | |
| 22 17.0 | 18 20.1 | 10 35.8 | Sales/Receivables | | | | | | | |
| 46 8.0 | 50 7.2 | 53 6.9 | | | | | | | | |
| | | | | Cost of Sales/Inventory | | | | | | |
| | | | | Cost of Sales/Payables | | | | | | |
| | 3.8 | 1.7 | 2.6 | | | | | | | |
| | 10.9 | 5.6 | 6.7 | Sales/Working Capital | | | | | | |
| | 288.8 | 60.6 | -36.4 | | | | | | | |
| | 7.9 | 13.4 | 9.0 | | | | | | | |
| (17) | 1.9 | (17) 4.0 | (18) 3.2 | EBIT/Interest | | | | | | |
| | -3.8 | -.2 | .0 | | | | | | | |
| | | | | Net Profit + Depr., Dep., Amort./Cur. Mat. L/T/D | | | | | | |
| | .7 | .1 | .0 | | | | | | | |
| | 1.2 | .6 | .7 | Fixed/Worth | | | | | | |
| | 1.4 | 1.1 | 1.5 | | | | | | | |
| | .4 | .1 | .1 | | | | | | | |
| | .8 | .6 | .6 | Debt/Worth | | | | | | |
| | 1.6 | 1.8 | .8 | | | | | | | |
| | 15.3 | 15.2 | 16.1 | | | | | | | |
| (24) | 5.1 | (26) 3.2 | (34) .6 | % Profit Before Taxes/Tangible Net Worth | | | | | | |
| | -2.7 | -3.5 | -1.9 | | | | | | | |
| | 7.1 | 5.8 | 7.6 | | | | | | | |
| | 1.4 | 1.3 | .1 | % Profit Before Taxes/Total Assets | | | | | | |
| | -3.0 | -2.4 | -1.2 | | | | | | | |
| | 28.9 | 39.8 | 28.6 | | | | | | | |
| | 2.1 | 2.9 | 1.4 | Sales/Net Fixed Assets | | | | | | |
| | .6 | 1.1 | .7 | | | | | | | |
| | 2.8 | 2.4 | 1.2 | | | | | | | |
| | 1.2 | 1.1 | .7 | Sales/Total Assets | | | | | | |
| | .4 | .5 | .4 | | | | | | | |
| | 1.0 | 1.3 | 1.8 | | | | | | | |
| (19) | 1.7 | (22) 2.7 | (28) 2.9 | % Depr., Dep., Amort./Sales | | | | | | |
| | 4.8 | 5.5 | 6.0 | | | | | | | |
| | | | | % Officers', Directors' Owners' Comp/Sales | | | | | | |
| | 388592M | 649745M | 495409M | Net Sales ($) | 3390M | 13972M | 11426M | 34542M | 108190M | 323889M |
| | 266704M | 412875M | 476636M | Total Assets ($) | 16345M | 29631M | 18249M | 46461M | 112470M | 253480M |

M = $ thousand   MM = $ million
See Pages 9 through 22 for Explanation of Ratios and Data

## Current Data Sorted by Assets

## Comparative Historical Data

| | | | | | | Type of Statement | | |
|---|---|---|---|---|---|---|---|---|
| | 2 | 7 | 10 | 5 | 3 | Unqualified | 17 | 18 |
| | | 1 | | | | Reviewed | 2 | 1 |
| | 1 | | | | | Compiled | 1 | |
| | 1 | 1 | 1 | | | Tax Returns | 2 | |
| 1 | 1 | 2 | 3 | | 1 | Other | 8 | 10 |
| | 25 (4/1-9/30/11) | | 14 (10/1/11-3/31/12) | | | | 4/1/07-3/31/08 | 4/1/08-3/31/09 |
| 0-500M | 500M-2MM | 2-10MM | 10-50MM | 50-100MM | 100-250MM | | ALL | ALL |
| 1 | 5 | 11 | 13 | 5 | 4 | NUMBER OF STATEMENTS | 30 | 29 |
| % | % | % | % | % | % | ASSETS | % | % |
| | | 17.8 | 19.5 | | | Cash & Equivalents | 26.4 | 28.4 |
| | | 16.8 | 9.6 | | | Trade Receivables (net) | 16.3 | 8.5 |
| | | 3.4 | 1.1 | | | Inventory | 1.3 | 1.4 |
| | | .0 | 16.2 | | | All Other Current | 2.5 | 6.5 |
| | | 38.0 | 46.5 | | | Total Current | 46.6 | 44.8 |
| | | 48.5 | 24.7 | | | Fixed Assets (net) | 29.9 | 31.8 |
| | | .1 | .2 | | | Intangibles (net) | .1 | .5 |
| | | 13.4 | 28.6 | | | All Other Non-Current | 23.4 | 22.9 |
| | | 100.0 | 100.0 | | | Total | 100.0 | 100.0 |
| | | | | | | LIABILITIES | | |
| | | 1.0 | 2.6 | | | Notes Payable-Short Term | 2.3 | 4.0 |
| | | 1.4 | .4 | | | Cur. Mat.-L.T.D. | 1.3 | 2.7 |
| | | 12.8 | 9.0 | | | Trade Payables | 5.1 | 3.6 |
| | | .0 | .0 | | | Income Taxes Payable | .1 | .0 |
| | | 2.9 | 8.0 | | | All Other Current | 12.0 | 9.2 |
| | | 18.2 | 19.9 | | | Total Current | 20.8 | 19.4 |
| | | 10.1 | 6.7 | | | Long-Term Debt | 9.9 | 9.5 |
| | | .0 | .0 | | | Deferred Taxes | .0 | .0 |
| | | 8.4 | 2.4 | | | All Other Non-Current | 7.2 | 5.0 |
| | | 63.4 | 71.1 | | | Net Worth | 62.1 | 66.1 |
| | | 100.0 | 100.0 | | | Total Liabilities & Net Worth | 100.0 | 100.0 |
| | | | | | | INCOME DATA | | |
| | | 100.0 | 100.0 | | | Net Sales | 100.0 | 100.0 |
| | | | | | | Gross Profit | | |
| | | 89.9 | 95.3 | | | Operating Expenses | 89.9 | 91.7 |
| | | 10.1 | 4.7 | | | Operating Profit | 10.1 | 8.3 |
| | | 1.6 | -2.9 | | | All Other Expenses (net) | -1.7 | 2.2 |
| | | 8.5 | 7.6 | | | Profit Before Taxes | 11.8 | 6.1 |
| | | | | | | RATIOS | | |
| | | 5.5 | 7.6 | | | | 8.1 | 9.1 |
| | | 3.5 | 2.9 | | | Current | 2.9 | 4.2 |
| | | 1.2 | 1.4 | | | | 1.4 | 1.5 |
| | | 5.5 | 5.0 | | | | 8.1 | 8.1 |
| | | 3.5 | 2.9 | | | Quick | 2.9 | 2.2 |
| | | 1.0 | 1.2 | | | | .8 | .9 |
| | | 1  640.5 | 9  41.8 | | | | 0  UND | 0  UND |
| | | 26  13.8 | 27  13.7 | | | Sales/Receivables | 8  46.5 | 8  48.2 |
| | | 36  10.0 | 62  5.9 | | | | 46  8.0 | 42  8.7 |
| | | | | | | Cost of Sales/Inventory | | |
| | | | | | | Cost of Sales/Payables | | |
| | | 3.7 | 1.8 | | | | 2.3 | 1.6 |
| | | 7.0 | 4.3 | | | Sales/Working Capital | 6.1 | 2.9 |
| | | 26.1 | 9.2 | | | | 21.3 | 11.9 |
| | | | | | | | 35.9 | 10.2 |
| | | | | | | EBIT/Interest | (20)  7.0 | (18)  2.9 |
| | | | | | | | 4.6 | -4.1 |
| | | | | | | Net Profit + Depr., Dep., Amort./Cur. Mat. L/T/D | | |
| | | .5 | .0 | | | | .1 | .1 |
| | | .8 | .5 | | | Fixed/Worth | .4 | .4 |
| | | .9 | .5 | | | | .9 | .8 |
| | | .1 | .1 | | | | .2 | .1 |
| | | .5 | .3 | | | Debt/Worth | .6 | .6 |
| | | 1.3 | .9 | | | | 1.0 | 1.2 |
| | | 11.6 | 14.9 | | | | 21.8 | 22.7 |
| | | 6.8 | 2.5 | | | % Profit Before Taxes/Tangible Net Worth | 12.7 | 1.5 |
| | | -3.9 | .2 | | | | 2.8 | -5.7 |
| | | 7.6 | 5.0 | | | | 13.7 | 6.4 |
| | | 1.3 | 2.4 | | | % Profit Before Taxes/Total Assets | 6.5 | 1.3 |
| | | -2.7 | .1 | | | | .7 | -3.6 |
| | | 8.8 | 31.2 | | | | 47.8 | 15.8 |
| | | 1.4 | 4.5 | | | Sales/Net Fixed Assets | 3.7 | 2.7 |
| | | .5 | 1.5 | | | | 1.1 | 1.0 |
| | | 1.8 | 1.4 | | | | 1.9 | .9 |
| | | 1.1 | .9 | | | Sales/Total Assets | .8 | .6 |
| | | .4 | .4 | | | | .5 | .4 |
| | | 1.0 | 1.1 | | | | .6 | 1.2 |
| | | 4.4 | (12)  2.3 | | | % Depr., Dep., Amort./Sales | (25)  1.4 | (25)  1.8 |
| | | 6.7 | 4.5 | | | | 3.7 | 4.1 |
| | | | | | | % Officers', Directors' Owners' Comp/Sales | | |
| 322M | 9852M | 59385M | 288241M | 187540M | 403006M | Net Sales ($) | 637414M | 732885M |
| 165M | 7094M | 55006M | 302486M | 326929M | 516809M | Total Assets ($) | 1015215M | 1323056M |

© RMA 2012

M = $ thousand   MM = $ million
See Pages 9 through 22 for Explanation of Ratios and Data

## Comparative Historical Data       Current Data Sorted by Sales

| | | | Type of Statement | 0-1MM | 1-3MM | 3-5MM | 5-10MM | 10-25MM | 25MM & OVER |
|---|---|---|---|---|---|---|---|---|---|
| 14 | 26 | 27 | Unqualified | 1 | 5 | 2 | 3 | 5 | 11 |
| 1 | | 1 | Reviewed | | | | 1 | | |
| | 2 | 1 | Compiled | 1 | | | | | |
| 1 | | 2 | Tax Returns | | 1 | | 1 | | |
| 8 | 14 | 8 | Other | 1 | 2 | 2 | | | 3 |
| 4/1/09-3/31/10 | 4/1/10-3/31/11 | 4/1/11-3/31/12 | | | 25 (4/1-9/30/11) | | | 14 (10/1/11-3/31/12) | |
| ALL | ALL | ALL | | | | | | | |
| 24 | 42 | 39 | NUMBER OF STATEMENTS | 3 | 8 | 4 | 5 | 5 | 14 |
| % | % | % | ASSETS | % | % | % | % | % | % |
| 20.7 | 23.0 | 18.2 | Cash & Equivalents | | | | | | 16.8 |
| 9.4 | 10.7 | 14.7 | Trade Receivables (net) | | | | | | 14.3 |
| 1.8 | 1.3 | 1.6 | Inventory | | | | | | 1.5 |
| 3.6 | 3.7 | 7.1 | All Other Current | | | | | | 9.9 |
| 35.4 | 38.7 | 41.6 | Total Current | | | | | | 42.5 |
| 40.1 | 38.8 | 32.8 | Fixed Assets (net) | | | | | | 26.8 |
| .1 | .0 | .1 | Intangibles (net) | | | | | | .1 |
| 24.5 | 22.5 | 25.6 | All Other Non-Current | | | | | | 30.6 |
| 100.0 | 100.0 | 100.0 | Total | | | | | | 100.0 |
| | | | LIABILITIES | | | | | | |
| .8 | 1.0 | 1.2 | Notes Payable-Short Term | | | | | | 2.4 |
| 1.5 | .5 | .8 | Cur. Mat.-L.T.D. | | | | | | .6 |
| 5.8 | 5.0 | 11.7 | Trade Payables | | | | | | 9.5 |
| .0 | .0 | .0 | Income Taxes Payable | | | | | | .0 |
| 7.1 | 4.4 | 5.0 | All Other Current | | | | | | 3.5 |
| 15.1 | 11.0 | 18.6 | Total Current | | | | | | 16.1 |
| 8.0 | 8.5 | 7.8 | Long-Term Debt | | | | | | 8.9 |
| .0 | .0 | .0 | Deferred Taxes | | | | | | .0 |
| 8.1 | 3.6 | 6.7 | All Other Non-Current | | | | | | 7.2 |
| 68.8 | 76.9 | 66.9 | Net Worth | | | | | | 67.9 |
| 100.0 | 100.0 | 100.0 | Total Liabilities & Net Worth | | | | | | 100.0 |
| | | | INCOME DATA | | | | | | |
| 100.0 | 100.0 | 100.0 | Net Sales | | | | | | 100.0 |
| | | | Gross Profit | | | | | | |
| 96.8 | 94.9 | 95.5 | Operating Expenses | | | | | | 96.0 |
| 3.2 | 5.1 | 4.5 | Operating Profit | | | | | | 4.0 |
| 2.9 | .2 | .4 | All Other Expenses (net) | | | | | | -.9 |
| .3 | 4.9 | 4.1 | Profit Before Taxes | | | | | | 4.9 |
| | | | RATIOS | | | | | | |
| 9.6 | 9.6 | 7.1 | Current | | | | | | 7.3 |
| 3.0 | 4.8 | 3.6 | | | | | | | 3.7 |
| 1.7 | 1.6 | 1.2 | | | | | | | 1.2 |
| 6.2 | 9.3 | 5.5 | Quick | | | | | | 5.4 |
| 2.7 | 4.0 | 3.3 | | | | | | | 2.8 |
| 1.3 | 1.4 | 1.0 | | | | | | | .8 |
| 0 UND | 5 77.3 | 7 54.5 | Sales/Receivables | | | | | | 4 103.8 |
| 7 51.9 | 25 14.4 | 30 12.3 | | | | | | | 28 13.0 |
| 37 9.7 | 62 5.9 | 73 5.0 | | | | | | | 85 4.3 |
| | | | Cost of Sales/Inventory | | | | | | |
| | | | Cost of Sales/Payables | | | | | | |
| 2.5 | 2.0 | 1.9 | Sales/Working Capital | | | | | | 2.0 |
| 4.8 | 3.3 | 6.4 | | | | | | | 6.1 |
| 23.2 | 9.1 | 19.2 | | | | | | | 25.7 |
| 17.1 | 17.3 | 19.3 | EBIT/Interest | | | | | | |
| (17) 1.0 | (23) 3.3 | (22) 4.0 | | | | | | | |
| -9.9 | -.6 | -1.5 | | | | | | | |
| | | | Net Profit + Depr., Dep., Amort./Cur. Mat. L/T/D | | | | | | |
| .2 | .1 | .1 | Fixed/Worth | | | | | | .1 |
| .6 | .5 | .5 | | | | | | | .5 |
| 1.0 | .8 | .9 | | | | | | | .6 |
| .1 | .1 | .1 | Debt/Worth | | | | | | .1 |
| .3 | .2 | .3 | | | | | | | .3 |
| .8 | .5 | 1.1 | | | | | | | 1.2 |
| 4.6 | 8.8 | 11.6 | % Profit Before Taxes/Tangible Net Worth | | | | | | 16.7 |
| (23) -.2 | 2.9 (38) | 2.0 | | | | | | | 2.7 |
| -4.3 | -1.1 | -3.4 | | | | | | | .4 |
| 4.5 | 7.7 | 6.2 | % Profit Before Taxes/Total Assets | | | | | | 11.6 |
| -.7 | 2.1 | 1.1 | | | | | | | 1.6 |
| -3.5 | -.9 | -2.5 | | | | | | | .4 |
| 19.0 | 20.8 | 19.1 | Sales/Net Fixed Assets | | | | | | 20.8 |
| 3.2 | 3.2 | 3.3 | | | | | | | 4.6 |
| .9 | .6 | 1.1 | | | | | | | 1.9 |
| 2.1 | 1.4 | 1.5 | Sales/Total Assets | | | | | | 1.4 |
| .8 | .7 | .9 | | | | | | | .9 |
| .5 | .4 | .4 | | | | | | | .7 |
| 1.2 | 1.1 | 1.1 | % Depr., Dep., Amort./Sales | | | | | | 1.1 |
| (20) 2.2 | (38) 2.3 | (35) 2.2 | | | | | | (13) | 1.4 |
| 4.3 | 5.0 | 5.1 | | | | | | | 2.3 |
| | | | % Officers', Directors' Owners' Comp/Sales | | | | | | |
| 762525M | 945170M | 948346M | Net Sales ($) | 1516M | 15586M | 14030M | 35356M | 83165M | 798693M |
| 861462M | 1363738M | 1208489M | Total Assets ($) | 5168M | 74915M | 22218M | 74364M | 80037M | 951787M |

© RMA 2012     M = $ thousand    MM = $ million
See Pages 9 through 22 for Explanation of Ratios and Data

## Current Data Sorted by Assets

## Comparative Historical Data

| | | | | | | Type of Statement | | |
|---|---|---|---|---|---|---|---|---|
| 9 | 43 | 142 | 116 | 22 | 26 | Unqualified | 329 | 357 |
| 2 | 1 | 2 | | | | Reviewed | 5 | 7 |
| 1 | | 2 | 1 | | | Compiled | 12 | 10 |
| 7 | 8 | 7 | 1 | | | Tax Returns | 7 | 9 |
| 22 | 22 | 50 | 41 | 11 | 7 | Other | 123 | 124 |
| | 359 (4/1-9/30/11) | | 184 (10/1/11-3/31/12) | | | | 4/1/07-3/31/08 | 4/1/08-3/31/09 |
| 0-500M | 500M-2MM | 2-10MM | 10-50MM | 50-100MM | 100-250MM | | ALL | ALL |
| 41 | 74 | 203 | 159 | 33 | 33 | NUMBER OF STATEMENTS | 476 | 507 |
| % | % | % | % | % | % | ASSETS | % | % |
| 38.0 | 27.6 | 25.5 | 19.6 | 18.6 | 19.6 | Cash & Equivalents | 22.3 | 20.0 |
| 23.2 | 19.4 | 14.2 | 10.1 | 10.2 | 2.7 | Trade Receivables (net) | 14.4 | 13.1 |
| 1.6 | 1.8 | 2.5 | 2.4 | .5 | .5 | Inventory | 1.5 | 1.8 |
| 5.1 | 3.7 | 3.4 | 5.5 | 2.0 | 4.6 | All Other Current | 5.1 | 4.8 |
| 67.8 | 52.5 | 45.5 | 37.6 | 31.3 | 27.4 | Total Current | 43.3 | 39.7 |
| 23.0 | 35.8 | 41.1 | 40.9 | 38.4 | 27.1 | Fixed Assets (net) | 38.4 | 42.3 |
| .1 | 2.2 | .1 | 1.0 | 1.9 | 1.0 | Intangibles (net) | .8 | .8 |
| 9.1 | 9.5 | 13.3 | 20.6 | 28.4 | 44.5 | All Other Non-Current | 17.5 | 17.2 |
| 100.0 | 100.0 | 100.0 | 100.0 | 100.0 | 100.0 | Total | 100.0 | 100.0 |
| | | | | | | LIABILITIES | | |
| 7.7 | 3.6 | 2.6 | 1.6 | 1.9 | .7 | Notes Payable-Short Term | 2.9 | 2.6 |
| .4 | .9 | 1.9 | 2.3 | 2.5 | 1.1 | Cur. Mat.-L.T.D. | 2.3 | 1.9 |
| 6.8 | 8.9 | 5.5 | 4.8 | 4.6 | 4.4 | Trade Payables | 6.0 | 6.7 |
| .0 | .1 | .0 | .0 | .0 | .0 | Income Taxes Payable | .1 | .0 |
| 18.2 | 12.8 | 10.7 | 8.6 | 9.2 | 7.3 | All Other Current | 9.4 | 9.8 |
| 33.1 | 26.3 | 20.9 | 17.3 | 18.2 | 13.5 | Total Current | 20.6 | 21.1 |
| 6.9 | 19.0 | 17.3 | 21.4 | 21.5 | 18.5 | Long-Term Debt | 18.4 | 20.6 |
| .0 | .0 | .0 | .0 | .0 | .0 | Deferred Taxes | .0 | .0 |
| 2.1 | 4.4 | 3.4 | 4.5 | 2.7 | 9.1 | All Other Non-Current | 3.2 | 3.9 |
| 58.1 | 50.3 | 58.4 | 56.8 | 57.5 | 59.0 | Net Worth | 57.8 | 54.4 |
| 100.0 | 100.0 | 100.0 | 100.0 | 100.0 | 100.0 | Total Liabilities & Net Worth | 100.0 | 100.0 |
| | | | | | | INCOME DATA | | |
| 100.0 | 100.0 | 100.0 | 100.0 | 100.0 | 100.0 | Net Sales | 100.0 | 100.0 |
| | | | | | | Gross Profit | | |
| 94.0 | 94.5 | 94.5 | 92.5 | 94.7 | 90.0 | Operating Expenses | 93.4 | 96.1 |
| 6.0 | 5.5 | 5.5 | 7.5 | 5.3 | 10.0 | Operating Profit | 6.6 | 3.9 |
| .4 | 1.7 | 1.2 | 2.5 | .7 | 3.8 | All Other Expenses (net) | 1.1 | 2.2 |
| 5.6 | 3.8 | 4.2 | 5.0 | 4.6 | 6.2 | Profit Before Taxes | 5.6 | 1.6 |
| | | | | | | RATIOS | | |
| 6.9 | 6.6 | 5.6 | 4.4 | 3.5 | 4.3 | | 4.7 | 4.7 |
| 3.4 | 2.5 | 2.1 | 2.2 | 1.8 | 1.9 | Current | 2.1 | 2.1 |
| 1.1 | 1.5 | 1.3 | 1.2 | 1.3 | .9 | | 1.2 | 1.1 |
| 6.2 | 5.6 | 4.8 | 3.7 | 3.1 | 3.4 | | 4.0 | 4.0 |
| 2.9 | 2.2 | 1.8 | 1.8 | 1.7 | 1.4 | Quick | 1.8 (506) | 1.8 |
| .9 | 1.0 | 1.1 | .9 | 1.1 | .6 | | 1.0 | .9 |
| 0 UND | 1 350.7 | 6 63.5 | 2 201.4 | 13 28.8 | 0 UND | | 5 77.3 | 4 93.0 |
| 21 17.7 | 17 21.6 | 25 14.7 | 22 16.6 | 43 8.5 | 14 26.1 | Sales/Receivables | 26 13.9 | 23 16.0 |
| 35 10.4 | 50 7.3 | 51 7.2 | 53 6.9 | 166 2.2 | 30 12.1 | | 48 7.5 | 47 7.8 |
| | | | | | | Cost of Sales/Inventory | | |
| | | | | | | Cost of Sales/Payables | | |
| 5.0 | 3.3 | 2.4 | 2.7 | 1.6 | 1.9 | | 3.4 | 2.9 |
| 8.2 | 7.8 | 7.9 | 6.1 | 7.8 | 4.9 | Sales/Working Capital | 7.4 | 8.3 |
| 49.3 | 31.0 | 24.7 | 26.9 | 29.2 | NM | | 28.4 | 69.6 |
| 34.4 | 9.3 | 7.3 | 8.9 | 13.1 | 24.2 | | 9.3 | 6.8 |
| (15) 6.5 | (39) 2.6 | (133) 2.2 | (100) 2.9 | (22) 2.6 | (23) 1.2 | EBIT/Interest | (297) 2.6 | (326) 1.7 |
| 1.8 | -.5 | -.4 | .2 | 1.0 | -.2 | | .5 | -.8 |
| | | | | | | Net Profit + Depr., Dep., Amort./Cur. Mat. L/T/D | | |
| .1 | .1 | .2 | .2 | .1 | .1 | | .2 | .3 |
| .3 | .6 | .7 | .7 | .6 | .4 | Fixed/Worth | .6 | .7 |
| .9 | 1.7 | 1.2 | 1.4 | 1.2 | .8 | | 1.2 | 1.4 |
| .2 | .3 | .3 | .3 | .3 | .3 | | .2 | .3 |
| .4 | .7 | .6 | .7 | 1.0 | .7 | Debt/Worth | .7 | .7 |
| 2.0 | 2.7 | 1.5 | 1.8 | 1.5 | 1.1 | | 1.6 | 1.8 |
| 56.4 | 19.6 | 15.0 | 12.0 | 9.6 | 7.8 | % Profit Before Taxes/Tangible Net Worth | 17.0 | 11.0 |
| (39) 7.2 | (67) 3.5 | (201) 4.9 | (155) 4.4 | 3.4 | 1.6 | | (464) 6.4 | (481) 1.8 |
| -3.9 | -5.3 | -2.8 | -1.7 | -.5 | -.8 | | -1.0 | -5.5 |
| 25.1 | 11.3 | 9.2 | 5.8 | 4.7 | 4.8 | % Profit Before Taxes/Total Assets | 9.0 | 5.4 |
| 6.1 | 1.8 | 2.5 | 2.1 | 1.6 | 1.0 | | 3.2 | .8 |
| -4.4 | -2.8 | -1.5 | -1.1 | -.3 | -.5 | | -.8 | -3.4 |
| 82.9 | 82.6 | 23.6 | 9.0 | 5.9 | 11.9 | Sales/Net Fixed Assets | 20.3 | 16.1 |
| 33.5 | 13.5 | 3.4 | 2.5 | 1.3 | 1.8 | | 4.0 | 3.1 |
| 9.2 | 1.4 | 1.1 | 1.0 | .9 | .9 | | 1.3 | 1.1 |
| 5.3 | 3.8 | 2.2 | 1.5 | 1.2 | .6 | | 2.3 | 2.0 |
| 3.0 | 2.1 | 1.2 | .8 | .6 | .4 | Sales/Total Assets | 1.1 | 1.1 |
| 1.4 | .8 | .5 | .3 | .2 | .2 | | .5 | .5 |
| .5 | .6 | .9 | 1.2 | 1.7 | 1.4 | | .9 | 1.0 |
| (22) 1.4 | (51) 1.2 | (176) 2.0 | (142) 2.4 | (32) 4.2 | (31) 3.3 | % Depr., Dep., Amort./Sales | (401) 2.0 | (431) 2.2 |
| 2.7 | 2.2 | 4.8 | 5.7 | 5.9 | 6.7 | | 3.9 | 4.6 |
| | | 1.8 | | | | | 3.0 | 2.1 |
| | (18) | 8.5 | | | | % Officers', Directors' Owners' Comp/Sales | (29) 9.9 | (34) 8.5 |
| | | 18.0 | | | | | 24.1 | 18.8 |
| 36419M | 220110M | 1766241M | 3604368M | 1830461M | 2973637M | Net Sales ($) | 9052605M | 10038971M |
| 10665M | 88656M | 1076582M | 3594877M | 2402311M | 5102979M | Total Assets ($) | 8527616M | 8473172M |

M = $ thousand    MM = $ million
See Pages 9 through 22 for Explanation of Ratios and Data

## Comparative Historical Data | Current Data Sorted by Sales

| | | | Type of Statement | | | | | | |
|---|---|---|---|---|---|---|---|---|---|
| 347 | 333 | 358 | Unqualified | 18 | 57 | 46 | 64 | 88 | 85 |
| 8 | 3 | 5 | Reviewed | 3 | 1 | | 1 | | |
| 5 | 4 | 4 | Compiled | | 3 | | 1 | | |
| 8 | 11 | 23 | Tax Returns | 7 | 8 | 4 | 4 | | |
| 133 | 147 | 153 | Other | 28 | 36 | 17 | 19 | 26 | 27 |
| 4/1/09-3/31/10 ALL | 4/1/10-3/31/11 ALL | 4/1/11-3/31/12 ALL | | 359 (4/1-9/30/11) 0-1MM | 1-3MM | 3-5MM | 184 (10/1/11-3/31/12) 5-10MM | 10-25MM | 25MM & OVER |
| 501 | 498 | 543 | NUMBER OF STATEMENTS | 56 | 104 | 68 | 89 | 114 | 112 |
| % | % | % | ASSETS | % | % | % | % | % | % |
| 22.3 | 24.5 | 24.2 | Cash & Equivalents | 26.9 | 23.7 | 21.3 | 23.6 | 26.0 | 23.7 |
| 14.8 | 14.9 | 13.4 | Trade Receivables (net) | 13.1 | 13.1 | 16.2 | 12.2 | 15.5 | 11.1 |
| 1.3 | 1.8 | 2.0 | Inventory | 1.6 | 1.0 | 1.3 | 2.4 | .8 | 4.7 |
| 4.8 | 5.1 | 4.2 | All Other Current | 4.6 | 2.8 | 2.9 | 4.3 | 5.6 | 4.4 |
| 43.3 | 46.3 | 43.9 | Total Current | 46.2 | 40.7 | 41.7 | 42.5 | 47.9 | 43.9 |
| 39.3 | 36.9 | 37.9 | Fixed Assets (net) | 43.9 | 44.2 | 39.3 | 35.6 | 34.5 | 33.7 |
| .6 | .5 | .8 | Intangibles (net) | .1 | 1.1 | 1.0 | .9 | .1 | 1.3 |
| 16.8 | 16.2 | 17.4 | All Other Non-Current | 9.8 | 14.0 | 17.9 | 21.0 | 17.5 | 21.1 |
| 100.0 | 100.0 | 100.0 | Total | 100.0 | 100.0 | 100.0 | 100.0 | 100.0 | 100.0 |
| | | | LIABILITIES | | | | | | |
| 2.7 | 2.9 | 2.7 | Notes Payable-Short Term | 6.1 | 2.8 | 2.9 | 1.8 | 3.0 | 1.1 |
| 1.7 | 1.8 | 1.8 | Cur. Mat.-L.T.D. | 1.2 | 1.3 | 2.2 | 2.0 | 2.3 | 1.5 |
| 6.2 | 7.0 | 5.8 | Trade Payables | 2.9 | 4.3 | 4.4 | 6.0 | 7.7 | 7.3 |
| .2 | .0 | .0 | Income Taxes Payable | .0 | .1 | .0 | .0 | .0 | .0 |
| 10.5 | 10.7 | 10.7 | All Other Current | 15.0 | 6.6 | 9.3 | 9.5 | 12.4 | 12.1 |
| 21.2 | 22.4 | 20.9 | Total Current | 25.2 | 15.2 | 18.9 | 19.3 | 25.3 | 21.9 |
| 18.5 | 16.1 | 18.3 | Long-Term Debt | 24.0 | 20.7 | 21.1 | 17.0 | 15.9 | 14.9 |
| .0 | .0 | .0 | Deferred Taxes | .0 | .0 | .0 | .0 | .0 | .0 |
| 4.0 | 4.3 | 4.0 | All Other Non-Current | 2.0 | 3.5 | 5.5 | 5.6 | 3.3 | 4.3 |
| 56.3 | 57.2 | 56.8 | Net Worth | 49.0 | 60.6 | 54.4 | 58.1 | 55.5 | 58.9 |
| 100.0 | 100.0 | 100.0 | Total Liabilities & Net Worth | 100.0 | 100.0 | 100.0 | 100.0 | 100.0 | 100.0 |
| | | | INCOME DATA | | | | | | |
| 100.0 | 100.0 | 100.0 | Net Sales | 100.0 | 100.0 | 100.0 | 100.0 | 100.0 | 100.0 |
| | | | Gross Profit | | | | | | |
| 97.0 | 94.7 | 93.6 | Operating Expenses | 89.7 | 92.7 | 90.6 | 93.7 | 96.4 | 95.5 |
| 3.0 | 5.3 | 6.4 | Operating Profit | 10.3 | 7.3 | 9.4 | 6.3 | 3.6 | 4.5 |
| 2.2 | 1.0 | 1.7 | All Other Expenses (net) | 5.2 | 1.3 | 2.5 | 1.9 | .5 | 1.0 |
| .8 | 4.3 | 4.7 | Profit Before Taxes | 5.2 | 6.1 | 6.9 | 4.4 | 3.0 | 3.5 |
| | | | RATIOS | | | | | | |
| 4.8 | 5.7 | 5.4 | Current | 7.9 | 6.7 | 7.3 | 4.9 | 3.9 | 4.2 |
| 2.3 | 2.3 | 2.2 | | 3.2 | 2.9 | 2.1 | 2.2 | 1.9 | 2.0 |
| 1.2 | 1.3 | 1.3 | | 1.4 | 1.1 | 1.2 | 1.5 | 1.3 | 1.2 |
| 3.7 | 4.8 | 4.3 | Quick | 6.5 | 6.2 | 6.4 | 3.8 | 3.4 | 3.4 |
| 1.9 | 1.9 | 1.8 | | 2.5 | 2.5 | 2.0 | 1.7 | 1.7 | 1.7 |
| 1.0 | 1.0 | 1.0 | | .8 | 1.0 | .8 | 1.0 | 1.0 | 1.0 |
| 7 55.1 | 6 64.2 | 2 200.7 | Sales/Receivables | 0 UND | 0 855.3 | 8 45.7 | 3 140.6 | 7 49.8 | 3 138.6 |
| 27 13.4 | 25 14.5 | 22 16.4 | | 8 44.8 | 20 18.1 | 31 11.6 | 22 16.7 | 29 12.8 | 19 19.2 |
| 54 6.8 | 49 7.5 | 50 7.3 | | 40 9.2 | 57 6.4 | 57 6.4 | 43 8.4 | 52 7.0 | 41 9.0 |
| | | | Cost of Sales/Inventory | | | | | | |
| | | | Cost of Sales/Payables | | | | | | |
| 2.8 | 2.6 | 2.6 | Sales/Working Capital | 1.5 | 2.3 | 2.5 | 2.3 | 2.7 | 4.5 |
| 7.2 | 6.7 | 7.1 | | 5.2 | 6.2 | 6.8 | 7.1 | 6.6 | 9.7 |
| 30.8 | 22.7 | 26.9 | | 14.7 | 133.4 | 17.0 | 20.8 | 23.3 | 38.4 |
| 8.8 | 13.0 | 9.9 | EBIT/Interest | 6.5 | 5.8 | 7.9 | 11.7 | 8.5 | 14.7 |
| (322) 2.3 | (314) 3.1 | (332) 2.4 | | (27) 2.7 | (61) 1.4 | (45) 2.6 | (52) 3.5 | (78) 2.2 | (69) 3.5 |
| -1.1 | .3 | .2 | | -1.5 | -4.2 | .6 | .7 | .3 | .5 |
| | | | Net Profit + Depr., Dep., Amort./Cur. Mat. L/T/D | | | | | | |
| .2 | .1 | .1 | Fixed/Worth | .1 | .2 | .2 | .1 | .2 | .1 |
| .6 | .6 | .6 | | .9 | .7 | .6 | .5 | .5 | .6 |
| 1.2 | 1.2 | 1.2 | | 2.1 | 1.4 | 1.2 | 1.1 | 1.3 | 1.0 |
| .3 | .2 | .3 | Debt/Worth | .3 | .2 | .3 | .2 | .3 | .3 |
| .7 | .6 | .7 | | .8 | .5 | .6 | .7 | .7 | .7 |
| 1.8 | 1.6 | 1.7 | | 2.1 | 1.5 | 1.9 | 1.8 | 1.7 | 1.3 |
| 11.7 | 14.1 | 14.3 | % Profit Before Taxes/Tangible Net Worth | 15.8 | 19.9 | 12.4 | 16.5 | 12.6 | 13.5 |
| (483) 3.4 | (477) 5.0 | (528) 4.4 | | (51) 3.9 | (100) 4.5 | (63) 5.1 | (113) 4.0 | 4.3 | 5.0 |
| -4.5 | -1.2 | -2.1 | | -3.9 | -3.7 | .5 | -3.0 | -2.2 | -.9 |
| 6.0 | 7.7 | 7.3 | % Profit Before Taxes/Total Assets | 10.8 | 10.9 | 7.0 | 8.6 | 5.5 | 7.2 |
| 1.2 | 2.5 | 2.3 | | 2.1 | 1.7 | 2.6 | 2.1 | 2.4 | 2.4 |
| -3.0 | -.9 | -1.1 | | -3.3 | -2.5 | .3 | -1.4 | -1.1 | -.7 |
| 20.5 | 30.2 | 25.9 | Sales/Net Fixed Assets | 42.4 | 29.9 | 22.0 | 52.9 | 23.2 | 17.3 |
| 3.8 | 4.5 | 3.8 | | 3.3 | 1.7 | 2.1 | 4.8 | 4.1 | 5.3 |
| 1.3 | 1.3 | 1.1 | | .4 | .6 | .8 | 1.4 | 1.6 | 2.0 |
| 2.2 | 2.2 | 2.1 | Sales/Total Assets | 1.9 | 1.8 | 1.7 | 2.2 | 2.3 | 2.5 |
| 1.1 | 1.1 | 1.0 | | .7 | .7 | .9 | 1.0 | 1.2 | 1.4 |
| .5 | .5 | .5 | | .2 | .4 | .2 | .6 | .7 | .7 |
| .9 | .8 | .9 | % Depr., Dep., Amort./Sales | 1.6 | .9 | 1.1 | .9 | .8 | .9 |
| (431) 2.2 | (420) 1.9 | (454) 2.1 | | (34) 3.2 | (82) 2.7 | (59) 2.4 | (71) 2.3 | (104) 1.6 | (104) 1.8 |
| 4.4 | 4.2 | 5.1 | | 14.9 | 7.4 | 5.3 | 5.4 | 3.2 | 3.8 |
| 2.9 | 2.3 | 2.1 | % Officers', Directors' Owners' Comp/Sales | | 4.0 | | | | |
| (44) 5.5 | (28) 10.2 | (40) 8.4 | | | (12) 10.5 | | | | |
| 16.1 | 29.2 | 11.8 | | | 21.4 | | | | |
| 10562276M | 11523689M | 10431236M | Net Sales ($) | 27870M | 199760M | 262793M | 639386M | 1792356M | 7509071M |
| 9515603M | 9883561M | 12276070M | Total Assets ($) | 86399M | 425592M | 699499M | 1062620M | 2507012M | 7494948M |

M = $ thousand    MM = $ million
See Pages 9 through 22 for Explanation of Ratios and Data

## Current Data Sorted by Assets     Comparative Historical Data

| | | | | | | Type of Statement | | | | |
|---|---|---|---|---|---|---|---|---|---|---|
| 11 | 52 | 167 | 168 | 29 | 18 | Unqualified | | | 280 | 304 |
| 1 | 5 | 19 | 4 | | | Reviewed | | | 8 | 10 |
| 5 | 11 | 16 | 4 | 1 | 1 | Compiled | | | 18 | 30 |
| 19 | 32 | 14 | | | | Tax Returns | | | 41 | 40 |
| 25 | 42 | 114 | 73 | 10 | 6 | Other | | | 118 | 151 |
| | 505 (4/1-9/30/11) | | 342 (10/1/11-3/31/12) | | | | | | 4/1/07-3/31/08 | 4/1/08-3/31/09 |
| 0-500M | 500M-2MM | 2-10MM | 10-50MM | 50-100MM | 100-250MM | | | | ALL | ALL |
| 61 | 142 | 330 | 249 | 40 | 25 | NUMBER OF STATEMENTS | | | 465 | 535 |
| % | % | % | % | % | % | ASSETS | | | % | % |
| 46.1 | 23.7 | 19.8 | 18.7 | 17.0 | 13.5 | Cash & Equivalents | | | 23.3 | 22.7 |
| 14.9 | 7.7 | 7.4 | 5.9 | 3.0 | 5.3 | Trade Receivables (net) | | | 8.2 | 7.4 |
| 1.7 | 1.2 | 1.1 | 1.0 | 1.0 | 1.3 | Inventory | | | 1.1 | 1.0 |
| 3.4 | 2.7 | 1.5 | 2.4 | 2.9 | 3.2 | All Other Current | | | 3.0 | 3.4 |
| 66.0 | 35.2 | 29.8 | 28.0 | 23.8 | 23.4 | Total Current | | | 35.6 | 34.5 |
| 24.5 | 52.8 | 56.1 | 51.9 | 55.8 | 32.5 | Fixed Assets (net) | | | 49.1 | 49.6 |
| .2 | 1.2 | .3 | .4 | .6 | .5 | Intangibles (net) | | | .5 | .7 |
| 9.3 | 10.8 | 13.8 | 19.7 | 19.7 | 43.6 | All Other Non-Current | | | 14.7 | 15.1 |
| 100.0 | 100.0 | 100.0 | 100.0 | 100.0 | 100.0 | Total | | | 100.0 | 100.0 |
| | | | | | | LIABILITIES | | | | |
| 10.8 | 1.7 | 1.8 | 1.3 | .6 | 1.5 | Notes Payable-Short Term | | | 3.2 | 2.6 |
| 1.0 | 1.3 | 1.6 | 1.5 | 1.9 | .5 | Cur. Mat.-L.T.D. | | | 1.9 | 1.7 |
| 12.8 | 4.3 | 3.6 | 2.7 | 3.0 | 3.2 | Trade Payables | | | 4.2 | 4.0 |
| .0 | .0 | .0 | .0 | .0 | .0 | Income Taxes Payable | | | .0 | .0 |
| 18.1 | 8.3 | 7.6 | 6.6 | 5.3 | 4.5 | All Other Current | | | 8.0 | 7.0 |
| 42.7 | 15.6 | 14.6 | 12.2 | 10.8 | 9.8 | Total Current | | | 17.4 | 15.3 |
| 17.9 | 27.8 | 22.0 | 18.5 | 27.8 | 17.6 | Long-Term Debt | | | 20.2 | 20.6 |
| .0 | .0 | .0 | .0 | .0 | .0 | Deferred Taxes | | | .0 | .0 |
| 3.4 | 3.2 | 4.0 | 3.5 | 4.2 | 4.8 | All Other Non-Current | | | 3.8 | 4.1 |
| 36.0 | 53.4 | 59.4 | 65.9 | 57.3 | 67.7 | Net Worth | | | 58.6 | 60.0 |
| 100.0 | 100.0 | 100.0 | 100.0 | 100.0 | 100.0 | Total Liabilities & Net Worth | | | 100.0 | 100.0 |
| | | | | | | INCOME DATA | | | | |
| 100.0 | 100.0 | 100.0 | 100.0 | 100.0 | 100.0 | Net Sales | | | 100.0 | 100.0 |
| | | | | | | Gross Profit | | | | |
| 95.0 | 95.8 | 93.7 | 95.8 | 95.6 | 84.1 | Operating Expenses | | | 92.6 | 95.1 |
| 5.0 | 4.2 | 6.3 | 4.2 | 4.4 | 15.9 | Operating Profit | | | 7.4 | 4.9 |
| 1.2 | 3.2 | 2.0 | 1.3 | 1.5 | 4.4 | All Other Expenses (net) | | | 1.4 | 3.9 |
| 3.8 | 1.0 | 4.3 | 2.8 | 2.9 | 11.5 | Profit Before Taxes | | | 6.1 | 1.0 |
| | | | | | | RATIOS | | | | |
| 12.2 | 10.5 | 5.6 | 5.2 | 3.4 | 4.1 | | | | 6.5 | 6.1 |
| 4.1 | 3.4 | 2.2 | 2.4 | 1.6 | 1.9 | Current | | | 2.5 | 2.4 |
| 1.2 | 1.3 | 1.0 | 1.2 | .9 | 1.0 | | | | 1.1 | 1.1 |
| 12.2 | 8.7 | 5.3 | 4.3 | 3.1 | 4.1 | | | | 5.5 | 5.7 |
| 2.7 | 2.6 | 2.0 | 2.2 | 1.2 | 1.4 | Quick | (464) | | 2.1 | (534) 1.9 |
| .9 | 1.1 | .8 | .9 | .7 | .5 | | | | .8 | .8 |
| 0 UND | 0 UND | 0 999.8 | 2 157.2 | 3 114.3 | 0 UND | | 1 | | 557.4 | 1 658.9 |
| 2 165.0 | 1 650.6 | 12 30.2 | 13 28.5 | 13 28.9 | 30 12.2 | Sales/Receivables | 12 | | 29.6 | 11 34.6 |
| 20 17.9 | 28 13.2 | 35 10.4 | 41 9.0 | 33 11.1 | 81 4.5 | | 36 | | 10.1 | 36 10.0 |
| | | | | | | Cost of Sales/Inventory | | | | |
| | | | | | | Cost of Sales/Payables | | | | |
| 2.6 | 2.7 | 2.6 | 2.3 | 3.6 | 1.5 | | | | 2.2 | 2.3 |
| 7.9 | 6.4 | 7.3 | 5.4 | 7.6 | 5.0 | Sales/Working Capital | | | 6.8 | 6.5 |
| 65.6 | 38.3 | -524.8 | 29.6 | -43.5 | NM | | | | 66.7 | 103.7 |
| 6.3 | 4.1 | 5.0 | 6.7 | 3.1 | 11.3 | | | | 7.9 | 4.2 |
| (22) 1.3 | (63) 1.3 | (224) 1.7 | (171) 1.6 | (32) .7 | (13) 2.5 | EBIT/Interest | (301) | | 2.3 | (362) 1.1 |
| -.7 | -.9 | -.6 | -1.5 | -1.2 | -2.0 | | | | .6 | -2.7 |
| | | | | | | Net Profit + Depr., Dep., Amort./Cur. Mat. L/T/D | | | | |
| .0 | .2 | .5 | .4 | .4 | .0 | | | | .3 | .3 |
| .1 | .9 | 1.0 | .8 | 1.1 | .4 | Fixed/Worth | | | .8 | .8 |
| 1.0 | 1.8 | 1.6 | 1.3 | 2.0 | 1.0 | | | | 1.4 | 1.4 |
| .1 | .2 | .2 | .1 | .2 | .1 | | | | .2 | .2 |
| .6 | .6 | .6 | .5 | .7 | .4 | Debt/Worth | | | .5 | .5 |
| 3.5 | 2.2 | 1.3 | .9 | 1.4 | .8 | | | | 1.2 | 1.2 |
| 34.3 | 14.3 | 10.4 | 7.5 | 6.6 | 10.3 | | | | 13.5 | 7.7 |
| (50) 10.4 | (125) 1.1 | (321) 2.0 | (244) 1.8 | (38) .0 | (24) 3.1 | % Profit Before Taxes/Tangible Net Worth | (445) | | 4.7 | (515) .8 |
| -2.8 | -5.2 | -3.1 | -3.1 | -4.4 | -.6 | | | | -1.1 | -5.7 |
| 20.3 | 6.0 | 5.7 | 4.3 | 3.0 | 5.3 | | | | 8.3 | 4.8 |
| 3.9 | .2 | 1.0 | 1.0 | -.3 | 2.2 | % Profit Before Taxes/Total Assets | | | 2.3 | .5 |
| -3.1 | -3.8 | -1.9 | -1.9 | -2.6 | -.4 | | | | -.9 | -3.6 |
| UND | 15.1 | 4.2 | 2.8 | 1.9 | 11.2 | | | | 6.8 | 5.4 |
| 57.0 | 1.7 | 1.2 | 1.0 | .7 | 1.2 | Sales/Net Fixed Assets | | | 1.5 | 1.2 |
| 4.5 | .5 | .5 | .5 | .6 | .6 | | | | .7 | .6 |
| 5.4 | 1.8 | 1.3 | .7 | .7 | .5 | | | | 1.3 | 1.2 |
| 2.3 | .8 | .6 | .5 | .5 | .2 | Sales/Total Assets | | | .7 | .6 |
| 1.2 | .4 | .3 | .3 | .3 | .1 | | | | .4 | .4 |
| .7 | 1.6 | 1.8 | 2.8 | 5.5 | .7 | | | | 2.0 | 1.9 |
| (29) 1.1 | (100) 4.6 | (255) 4.4 | (219) 5.5 | (35) 7.1 | (18) 5.2 | % Depr., Dep., Amort./Sales | (359) | | 4.5 | (418) 4.5 |
| 3.7 | 11.2 | 8.3 | 9.3 | 10.5 | 10.4 | | | | 7.8 | 8.4 |
| 3.8 | 4.9 | 3.3 | 2.4 | | | | | | 4.5 | 3.5 |
| (10) 9.7 | (14) 8.8 | (32) 8.5 | (16) 7.4 | | | % Officers', Directors' Owners' Comp/Sales | (50) | | 10.6 | (49) 7.1 |
| 29.6 | 19.2 | 16.7 | 10.7 | | | | | | 21.2 | 25.8 |
| 44265M | 266171M | 1528186M | 3853721M | 1605064M | 1649302M | Net Sales ($) | | | 4692191M | 5749889M |
| 15359M | 162499M | 1704431M | 5172240M | 2597362M | 4155034M | Total Assets ($) | | | 8233753M | 9980617M |

M = $ thousand  MM = $ million
See Pages 9 through 22 for Explanation of Ratios and Data

## Comparative Historical Data | Current Data Sorted by Sales

| Hist 1 | Hist 2 | Hist 3 | Type of Statement | 0-1MM | 1-3MM | 3-5MM | 5-10MM | 10-25MM | 25MM & OVER |
|---|---|---|---|---|---|---|---|---|---|
| 331 | 393 | 445 | Unqualified | 40 | 73 | 69 | 116 | 95 | 52 |
| 21 | 24 | 29 | Reviewed | 7 | 15 | 1 | 4 | 2 | |
| 38 | 44 | 38 | Compiled | 18 | 11 | 5 | 2 | 1 | 1 |
| 40 | 58 | 65 | Tax Returns | 43 | 17 | 5 | | | |
| 216 | 240 | 270 | Other | 71 | 65 | 34 | 42 | 32 | 26 |
| 4/1/09-3/31/10 | 4/1/10-3/31/11 | 4/1/11-3/31/12 | | 505 (4/1-9/30/11) | | | 342 (10/1/11-3/31/12) | | |
| ALL | ALL | ALL | | 0-1MM | 1-3MM | 3-5MM | 5-10MM | 10-25MM | 25MM & OVER |
| 646 | 759 | 847 | **NUMBER OF STATEMENTS** | 179 | 181 | 114 | 164 | 130 | 79 |
| % | % | % | **ASSETS** | % | % | % | % | % | % |
| 21.5 | 20.4 | 21.7 | Cash & Equivalents | 22.7 | 20.1 | 22.9 | 21.3 | 21.5 | 22.3 |
| 8.1 | 7.9 | 7.3 | Trade Receivables (net) | 4.1 | 7.1 | 8.6 | 7.6 | 9.0 | 9.5 |
| 1.2 | 1.2 | 1.1 | Inventory | .6 | 1.1 | .8 | 1.2 | 1.8 | 1.8 |
| 3.0 | 2.2 | 2.2 | All Other Current | 2.0 | 2.3 | 1.3 | 1.6 | 3.2 | 3.7 |
| 33.8 | 31.6 | 32.3 | Total Current | 29.5 | 30.6 | 33.6 | 31.6 | 35.5 | 37.2 |
| 52.5 | 51.7 | 51.3 | Fixed Assets (net) | 61.4 | 54.4 | 46.8 | 50.3 | 44.5 | 41.3 |
| .6 | .7 | .5 | Intangibles (net) | .3 | .9 | .9 | .2 | .3 | .6 |
| 13.1 | 15.9 | 15.8 | All Other Non-Current | 8.8 | 14.2 | 18.7 | 17.8 | 19.7 | 20.9 |
| 100.0 | 100.0 | 100.0 | Total | 100.0 | 100.0 | 100.0 | 100.0 | 100.0 | 100.0 |
| | | | **LIABILITIES** | | | | | | |
| 2.9 | 2.7 | 2.2 | Notes Payable-Short Term | 3.9 | 2.3 | 1.4 | 1.5 | 1.4 | 2.0 |
| 2.2 | 1.7 | 1.5 | Cur. Mat.-L.T.D. | 1.6 | 1.5 | 1.5 | 1.2 | 1.4 | 2.1 |
| 4.1 | 5.1 | 4.1 | Trade Payables | 3.8 | 2.8 | 4.0 | 4.1 | 5.6 | 5.4 |
| .1 | .0 | .0 | Income Taxes Payable | .0 | .0 | .0 | .0 | .0 | .0 |
| 8.5 | 7.7 | 8.0 | All Other Current | 6.7 | 8.0 | 6.5 | 8.0 | 10.1 | 9.2 |
| 17.8 | 17.2 | 15.8 | Total Current | 15.9 | 14.6 | 13.4 | 14.9 | 18.5 | 18.6 |
| 23.5 | 22.3 | 21.8 | Long-Term Debt | 31.9 | 22.1 | 17.3 | 20.4 | 16.1 | 16.8 |
| .0 | .0 | .0 | Deferred Taxes | .0 | .0 | .0 | .0 | .0 | .0 |
| 4.8 | 3.7 | 3.7 | All Other Non-Current | 1.6 | 3.1 | 3.2 | 3.8 | 6.7 | 5.2 |
| 53.9 | 56.8 | 58.7 | Net Worth | 50.5 | 60.1 | 66.0 | 60.9 | 58.7 | 59.4 |
| 100.0 | 100.0 | 100.0 | Total Liabilities & Net Worth | 100.0 | 100.0 | 100.0 | 100.0 | 100.0 | 100.0 |
| | | | **INCOME DATA** | | | | | | |
| 100.0 | 100.0 | 100.0 | Net Sales | 100.0 | 100.0 | 100.0 | 100.0 | 100.0 | 100.0 |
| | | | Gross Profit | | | | | | |
| 96.5 | 94.8 | 94.6 | Operating Expenses | 92.2 | 93.0 | 98.2 | 95.5 | 96.4 | 93.6 |
| 3.5 | 5.2 | 5.4 | Operating Profit | 7.8 | 7.0 | 1.8 | 4.5 | 3.6 | 6.4 |
| 2.7 | 1.8 | 2.0 | All Other Expenses (net) | 4.6 | 2.9 | .6 | .5 | .6 | 1.5 |
| .7 | 3.4 | 3.4 | Profit Before Taxes | 3.2 | 4.2 | 1.2 | 4.0 | 3.0 | 4.9 |
| | | | **RATIOS** | | | | | | |
| 5.6 | 5.6 | 5.9 | | 9.9 | 8.2 | 7.2 | 5.2 | 4.4 | 3.1 |
| 2.3 | 2.5 | 2.4 | Current | 3.1 | 2.6 | 2.6 | 2.3 | 2.2 | 1.9 |
| 1.0 | 1.1 | 1.1 | | 1.1 | 1.0 | 1.1 | 1.3 | 1.2 | .9 |
| 5.1 | 5.0 | 5.3 | | 8.7 | 6.9 | 7.1 | 4.8 | 4.1 | 2.8 |
| 2.0 | 2.1 | 2.1 | Quick | 2.7 | 2.3 | 2.4 | 2.1 | 1.8 | 1.4 |
| .8 | .9 | .9 | | .9 | .9 | .9 | 1.1 | .9 | .7 |
| 0 UND | 0 999.8 | 0 UND | | 0 UND | 0 UND | 2 215.1 | 3 140.3 | 5 74.5 | 3 131.3 |
| 9 42.4 | 10 35.3 | 10 36.1 | Sales/Receivables | 0 UND | 8 43.4 | 19 18.8 | 15 24.0 | 15 24.9 | 16 22.6 |
| 36 10.2 | 35 10.4 | 35 10.4 | | 10 35.6 | 41 9.0 | 37 9.9 | 39 9.3 | 44 8.3 | 40 9.1 |
| | | | Cost of Sales/Inventory | | | | | | |
| | | | Cost of Sales/Payables | | | | | | |
| 2.4 | 2.7 | 2.5 | | 2.3 | 2.6 | 2.2 | 2.4 | 3.1 | 4.3 |
| 6.4 | 6.3 | 6.3 | Sales/Working Capital | 5.8 | 6.5 | 5.7 | 6.0 | 5.6 | 10.7 |
| 436.0 | 114.9 | 75.8 | | 65.5 | -738.0 | NM | 28.8 | 25.0 | -56.7 |
| 4.3 | 5.6 | 5.1 | | 3.5 | 4.8 | 3.5 | 5.5 | 7.6 | 12.5 |
| (422) 1.1 | (503) 1.8 | (525) 1.5 | EBIT/Interest | (94) 1.4 | (111) 1.4 | (72) 1.0 | (111) 2.0 | (83) 1.3 | (54) 2.3 |
| -2.4 | -.3 | -.9 | | -.7 | -.6 | -2.7 | -.2 | -1.5 | -.7 |
| | | | Net Profit + Depr., Dep., Amort./Cur. Mat. L/T/D | | | | | | |
| .4 | .4 | .3 | | .4 | .4 | .1 | .4 | .4 | .2 |
| .9 | .9 | .9 | Fixed/Worth | 1.1 | 1.0 | .7 | .8 | .8 | .5 |
| 1.6 | 1.5 | 1.5 | | 1.8 | 1.8 | 1.2 | 1.3 | 1.4 | 1.2 |
| .2 | .2 | .2 | | .2 | .2 | .1 | .2 | .2 | .4 |
| .6 | .5 | .5 | Debt/Worth | .7 | .5 | .3 | .5 | .5 | .6 |
| 1.5 | 1.3 | 1.3 | | 1.6 | 1.3 | .9 | 1.1 | 1.5 | 1.2 |
| 7.0 | 10.4 | 10.1 | | 12.1 | 12.4 | 4.9 | 10.1 | 9.4 | 11.8 |
| (608) .8 | (720) 2.3 | (802) 2.1 | % Profit Before Taxes/Tangible Net Worth | (160) 1.9 | (172) 2.2 | (110) .0 | (158) 2.5 | (126) 1.5 | (76) 4.4 |
| -5.3 | -2.2 | -3.2 | | -2.1 | -3.0 | -4.6 | -3.5 | -3.0 | -1.8 |
| 4.1 | 5.3 | 5.6 | | 5.9 | 6.5 | 3.3 | 6.2 | 4.4 | 7.0 |
| .3 | 1.4 | 1.1 | % Profit Before Taxes/Total Assets | .8 | 1.1 | -.1 | 1.7 | .7 | 2.3 |
| -3.6 | -1.6 | -2.0 | | -1.9 | -1.6 | -3.1 | -1.9 | -2.1 | -1.3 |
| 5.9 | 5.5 | 5.8 | | 4.5 | 5.6 | 10.4 | 3.8 | 7.1 | 11.1 |
| 1.2 | 1.3 | 1.2 | Sales/Net Fixed Assets | .5 | .9 | 1.3 | 1.5 | 1.8 | 3.1 |
| .6 | .5 | .5 | | .2 | .5 | .7 | .7 | .8 | .9 |
| 1.2 | 1.2 | 1.3 | | .9 | 1.3 | 1.1 | 1.3 | 1.6 | 1.9 |
| .6 | .6 | .6 | Sales/Total Assets | .4 | .5 | .6 | .6 | .7 | .9 |
| .3 | .4 | .3 | | .2 | .3 | .3 | .5 | .5 | .5 |
| 2.0 | 2.0 | 1.9 | | 3.7 | 1.7 | 1.8 | 1.8 | 2.0 | 1.5 |
| (510) 4.7 | (602) 4.6 | (656) 5.0 | % Depr., Dep., Amort./Sales | (107) 8.4 | (126) 5.1 | (92) 5.4 | (150) 4.3 | (115) 4.3 | (66) 3.3 |
| 8.9 | 9.1 | 8.9 | | 18.5 | 9.8 | 8.3 | 7.7 | 7.4 | 7.0 |
| 2.6 | 1.9 | 3.8 | | 7.7 | 3.8 | | 2.3 | | |
| (54) 7.0 | (57) 5.9 | (74) 8.7 | % Officers', Directors' Owners' Comp/Sales | (21) 10.9 | (23) 7.5 | | (14) 4.5 | | |
| 14.6 | 17.3 | 17.0 | | 24.6 | 13.1 | | 9.2 | | |
| 7539462M | 8036057M | 8946709M | Net Sales ($) | 93478M | 335961M | 445682M | 1187779M | 2026459M | 4857350M |
| 11373463M | 12459294M | 13806925M | Total Assets ($) | 338020M | 821631M | 1127665M | 2010421M | 3924207M | 5584981M |

M = $ thousand    MM = $ million
See Pages 9 through 22 for Explanation of Ratios and Data

## Current Data Sorted by Assets     Comparative Historical Data

| | | | | | | Type of Statement | | |
|---|---|---|---|---|---|---|---|---|
| 10 | 20 | 73 | 65 | 10 | 10 | Unqualified | 134 | 154 |
| 7 | 6 | 11 | 2 | | | Reviewed | 10 | 16 |
| 10 | 4 | 4 | | | | Compiled | 11 | 9 |
| 7 | 6 | 3 | | | | Tax Returns | 14 | 14 |
| 19 | 30 | 34 | 17 | 5 | 1 | Other | 65 | 77 |
| | 151 (4/1-9/30/11) | | 203 (10/1/11-3/31/12) | | | | 4/1/07-3/31/08 | 4/1/08-3/31/09 |
| 0-500M | 500M-2MM | 2-10MM | 10-50MM | 50-100MM | 100-250MM | | ALL | ALL |
| 53 | 66 | 125 | 84 | 15 | 11 | NUMBER OF STATEMENTS | 234 | 270 |
| % | % | % | % | % | % | ASSETS | % | % |
| 43.8 | 37.6 | 38.7 | 43.7 | 30.2 | 45.7 | Cash & Equivalents | 39.4 | 36.6 |
| 11.4 | 14.2 | 8.1 | 9.4 | 8.3 | 14.2 | Trade Receivables (net) | 10.6 | 11.2 |
| .4 | 3.6 | 1.0 | 1.2 | .1 | 3.2 | Inventory | 1.9 | 2.8 |
| 5.7 | 1.8 | 3.8 | 3.4 | 3.0 | 1.6 | All Other Current | 4.0 | 3.8 |
| 61.3 | 57.1 | 51.6 | 57.8 | 41.6 | 64.7 | Total Current | 55.9 | 54.3 |
| 25.9 | 30.1 | 31.9 | 21.0 | 20.9 | 22.7 | Fixed Assets (net) | 27.2 | 28.8 |
| 2.5 | 1.1 | .9 | 3.0 | 1.1 | 2.2 | Intangibles (net) | 1.2 | 1.9 |
| 10.3 | 11.7 | 15.7 | 18.2 | 36.4 | 10.4 | All Other Non-Current | 15.7 | 14.9 |
| 100.0 | 100.0 | 100.0 | 100.0 | 100.0 | 100.0 | Total | 100.0 | 100.0 |
| | | | | | | LIABILITIES | | |
| 17.7 | 4.9 | 2.3 | 1.6 | .1 | 6.4 | Notes Payable-Short Term | 3.3 | 3.8 |
| 3.4 | 1.2 | 2.6 | 1.6 | .6 | 1.4 | Cur. Mat.-L.T.D. | 2.3 | 2.4 |
| 10.5 | 5.2 | 7.1 | 9.0 | 5.9 | 6.6 | Trade Payables | 9.3 | 9.0 |
| 1.4 | .0 | .2 | .2 | .6 | .0 | Income Taxes Payable | .1 | .1 |
| 19.2 | 13.5 | 15.6 | 14.0 | 17.9 | 6.1 | All Other Current | 13.8 | 14.1 |
| 52.4 | 24.9 | 27.8 | 26.4 | 25.1 | 20.5 | Total Current | 28.9 | 29.4 |
| 16.0 | 15.4 | 11.2 | 8.8 | 6.9 | 17.8 | Long-Term Debt | 12.5 | 10.9 |
| .0 | .0 | .1 | .3 | .7 | .2 | Deferred Taxes | .1 | .2 |
| 3.9 | 5.6 | 10.2 | 15.0 | 14.0 | 13.3 | All Other Non-Current | 9.4 | 10.3 |
| 27.8 | 54.1 | 50.7 | 49.5 | 53.3 | 48.2 | Net Worth | 49.1 | 49.3 |
| 100.0 | 100.0 | 100.0 | 100.0 | 100.0 | 100.0 | Total Liabilities & Net Worth | 100.0 | 100.0 |
| | | | | | | INCOME DATA | | |
| 100.0 | 100.0 | 100.0 | 100.0 | 100.0 | 100.0 | Net Sales | 100.0 | 100.0 |
| | | | | | | Gross Profit | | |
| 93.2 | 95.3 | 96.1 | 96.3 | 96.3 | 95.9 | Operating Expenses | 95.6 | 97.8 |
| 6.8 | 4.7 | 3.9 | 3.7 | 3.7 | 4.1 | Operating Profit | 4.4 | 2.2 |
| 1.2 | 1.0 | .3 | 1.1 | 1.9 | 4.3 | All Other Expenses (net) | .3 | 3.6 |
| 5.6 | 3.6 | 3.6 | 2.7 | 1.8 | -.2 | Profit Before Taxes | 4.1 | -1.3 |
| | | | | | | RATIOS | | |
| 8.0 | 15.8 | 5.5 | 5.1 | 2.3 | 7.8 | | 5.1 | 5.4 |
| 1.6 | 2.8 | 2.1 | 2.4 | 2.0 | 4.2 | Current | 2.1 | 2.0 |
| .7 | 1.1 | 1.2 | 1.2 | 1.0 | 1.5 | | 1.3 | 1.2 |
| 7.0 | 15.8 | 4.9 | 4.8 | 2.2 | 7.5 | | 5.0 | 4.7 |
| 1.4 | 2.6 | 1.9 | 2.1 | 1.3 | 4.2 | Quick | 1.9 | 1.8 |
| .4 | 1.0 | 1.0 | 1.1 | 1.0 | 1.4 | | 1.1 | .9 |
| 0   UND | 0   UND | 3   130.4 | 4   93.3 | 11   32.3 | 9   40.4 | | 5   78.1 | 5   75.2 |
| 5   75.0 | 15   24.3 | 14   27.0 | 15   23.9 | 30   12.0 | 24   15.0 | Sales/Receivables | 16   23.4 | 16   22.3 |
| 21   17.2 | 61   6.0 | 36   10.2 | 43   8.5 | 54   6.8 | 87   4.2 | | 36   10.2 | 35   10.4 |
| | | | | | | Cost of Sales/Inventory | | |
| | | | | | | Cost of Sales/Payables | | |
| 3.6 | 1.6 | 2.3 | 1.6 | 2.3 | .4 | | 2.2 | 2.3 |
| 10.0 | 3.7 | 4.7 | 3.1 | 6.3 | 1.0 | Sales/Working Capital | 4.7 | 5.6 |
| -61.1 | 57.9 | 20.8 | 11.6 | 17.2 | 6.4 | | 22.7 | 27.5 |
| 8.7 | 16.9 | 9.8 | 18.2 | | | | 12.6 | 4.6 |
| (24) 3.0 | (36) 2.2 | (65) 3.5 | (34) 3.5 | | | EBIT/Interest | (113) 4.0 | (131) .7 |
| -1.5 | .2 | .1 | -.2 | | | | 1.2 | -4.1 |
| | | | | | | Net Profit + Depr., Dep., | 14.6 | 4.7 |
| | | | | | | Amort./Cur. Mat. L/T/D | (13) 8.6 | (18) 2.3 |
| | | | | | | | 2.3 | -.3 |
| .0 | .0 | .1 | .1 | .1 | .1 | | .1 | .1 |
| .2 | .3 | .5 | .3 | .3 | .4 | Fixed/Worth | .4 | .5 |
| 1.9 | 1.6 | 1.4 | .9 | 1.1 | 1.0 | | 1.0 | 1.2 |
| .2 | .2 | .5 | .4 | .4 | .3 | | .4 | .4 |
| 1.0 | .8 | 1.0 | .9 | .6 | 1.6 | Debt/Worth | .9 | 1.0 |
| -8.9 | 1.8 | 1.9 | 2.0 | 1.8 | 2.7 | | 2.1 | 2.6 |
| 41.1 | 20.5 | 15.1 | 14.2 | 5.6 | 11.4 | % Profit Before Taxes/Tangible | 20.8 | 13.4 |
| (37) 14.6 | (61) 3.2 | (123) 5.0 | (78) 3.6 | (14) 1.6 | 3.8 | Net Worth | (219) 8.4 | (257) -.4 |
| .2 | -4.1 | -2.8 | -3.5 | -3.4 | -4.8 | | -.2 | -14.6 |
| 20.4 | 9.1 | 7.7 | 7.3 | 4.3 | 2.9 | % Profit Before Taxes/Total | 9.9 | 4.9 |
| 7.7 | 1.8 | 2.2 | 1.8 | 1.2 | 1.8 | Assets | 3.7 | -.3 |
| -5.9 | -2.3 | -.9 | -2.3 | -.9 | -4.2 | | -.6 | -7.5 |
| UND | 177.5 | 23.2 | 19.6 | 14.9 | 16.5 | | 38.7 | 41.4 |
| 65.9 | 15.0 | 5.0 | 10.1 | 5.9 | 8.9 | Sales/Net Fixed Assets | 7.0 | 6.7 |
| 3.9 | 1.3 | 1.3 | 2.7 | 1.1 | 1.4 | | 2.3 | 1.8 |
| 6.6 | 2.3 | 1.7 | 1.3 | .8 | .8 | | 1.9 | 1.8 |
| 2.5 | 1.1 | 1.0 | .8 | .5 | .4 | Sales/Total Assets | 1.1 | 1.1 |
| 1.0 | .6 | .6 | .5 | .4 | .3 | | .6 | .6 |
| 1.1 | .8 | 1.1 | 1.4 | 1.1 | | | 1.1 | .9 |
| (23) 2.2 | (45) 2.2 | (111) 2.6 | (73) 2.1 | (12) 4.6 | | % Depr., Dep., Amort./Sales | (181) 1.9 | (207) 2.2 |
| 5.1 | 4.2 | 4.3 | 3.7 | 5.7 | | | 3.5 | 4.1 |
| | | | | | | % Officers', Directors' | 4.9 | 4.4 |
| | | | | | | Owners' Comp/Sales | (24) 10.0 | (25) 8.7 |
| | | | | | | | 27.9 | 19.9 |
| 56965M | 149405M | 851128M | 1867567M | 729870M | 1449617M | Net Sales ($) | 6155217M | 6481515M |
| 13718M | 82847M | 635840M | 1895102M | 1089249M | 1758869M | Total Assets ($) | 4518702M | 4929000M |

© RMA 2012

M = $ thousand    MM = $ million
See Pages 9 through 22 for Explanation of Ratios and Data

## Comparative Historical Data | Current Data Sorted by Sales

| | | | Type of Statement | | | | | | |
|---|---|---|---|---|---|---|---|---|---|
| 160 | 182 | 188 | Unqualified | 10 | 37 | 22 | 36 | 45 | 38 |
| 14 | 14 | 26 | Reviewed | 9 | 10 | 2 | 2 | 2 | 1 |
| 14 | 9 | 18 | Compiled | 10 | 4 | | 2 | 2 | |
| 12 | 14 | 16 | Tax Returns | 10 | 5 | | | 1 | |
| 103 | 115 | 106 | Other | 29 | 31 | 8 | 12 | 14 | 12 |
| 4/1/09-3/31/10 ALL | 4/1/10-3/31/11 ALL | 4/1/11-3/31/12 ALL | | 151 (4/1-9/30/11) 0-1MM | 1-3MM | 3-5MM | 203 (10/1/11-3/31/12) 5-10MM | 10-25MM | 25MM & OVER |
| 303 | 334 | 354 | **NUMBER OF STATEMENTS** | 68 | 87 | 32 | 52 | 64 | 51 |
| % | % | % | **ASSETS** | % | % | % | % | % | % |
| 37.7 | 39.3 | 40.3 | Cash & Equivalents | 39.5 | 35.5 | 38.2 | 39.3 | 47.3 | 43.2 |
| 12.8 | 10.7 | 10.2 | Trade Receivables (net) | 10.2 | 7.8 | 9.6 | 10.3 | 12.0 | 12.3 |
| 2.0 | 1.2 | 1.4 | Inventory | .2 | 3.0 | .2 | 1.1 | 1.3 | 1.9 |
| 3.1 | 3.5 | 3.5 | All Other Current | 3.0 | 2.8 | 4.5 | 3.3 | 5.4 | 2.8 |
| 55.6 | 54.6 | 55.5 | Total Current | 52.9 | 49.1 | 52.4 | 54.1 | 65.9 | 60.2 |
| 28.2 | 27.7 | 27.3 | Fixed Assets (net) | 36.3 | 35.7 | 30.3 | 24.9 | 13.1 | 19.6 |
| 1.4 | 1.9 | 1.7 | Intangibles (net) | 1.8 | 1.1 | .0 | 1.9 | 2.7 | 2.3 |
| 14.8 | 15.8 | 15.5 | All Other Non-Current | 9.0 | 14.1 | 17.3 | 19.1 | 18.3 | 17.8 |
| 100.0 | 100.0 | 100.0 | Total | 100.0 | 100.0 | 100.0 | 100.0 | 100.0 | 100.0 |
| | | | **LIABILITIES** | | | | | | |
| 4.1 | 3.8 | 5.0 | Notes Payable-Short Term | 6.3 | 9.7 | 2.4 | 3.4 | 2.9 | .8 |
| 2.8 | 1.9 | 2.1 | Cur. Mat.-L.T.D. | 2.3 | 3.2 | 2.7 | 2.5 | .5 | 1.0 |
| 10.9 | 8.1 | 7.7 | Trade Payables | 4.2 | 6.6 | 11.3 | 7.0 | 8.2 | 11.8 |
| .2 | .1 | .4 | Income Taxes Payable | .0 | .8 | .5 | .0 | .5 | .2 |
| 16.0 | 15.2 | 15.2 | All Other Current | 9.2 | 15.3 | 13.3 | 18.9 | 17.1 | 18.0 |
| 34.1 | 29.1 | 30.3 | Total Current | 22.0 | 35.6 | 30.2 | 31.9 | 29.2 | 31.8 |
| 12.7 | 13.3 | 12.2 | Long-Term Debt | 23.0 | 13.7 | 11.6 | 9.0 | 3.8 | 9.1 |
| .1 | .1 | .1 | Deferred Taxes | .0 | .1 | .0 | .1 | .2 | .4 |
| 9.7 | 9.8 | 9.8 | All Other Non-Current | 5.0 | 6.2 | 5.3 | 12.4 | 14.5 | 16.4 |
| 43.5 | 47.8 | 47.7 | Net Worth | 50.0 | 44.3 | 52.8 | 46.5 | 52.3 | 42.4 |
| 100.0 | 100.0 | 100.0 | Total Liabilties & Net Worth | 100.0 | 100.0 | 100.0 | 100.0 | 100.0 | 100.0 |
| | | | **INCOME DATA** | | | | | | |
| 100.0 | 100.0 | 100.0 | Net Sales | 100.0 | 100.0 | 100.0 | 100.0 | 100.0 | 100.0 |
| | | | Gross Profit | | | | | | |
| 96.6 | 95.3 | 95.6 | Operating Expenses | 92.3 | 95.8 | 94.3 | 96.7 | 97.0 | 97.3 |
| 3.4 | 4.7 | 4.4 | Operating Profit | 7.7 | 4.2 | 5.7 | 3.3 | 3.0 | 2.7 |
| 2.0 | .7 | .9 | All Other Expenses (net) | 1.2 | .3 | 1.2 | 1.4 | .7 | 1.5 |
| 1.4 | 3.9 | 3.5 | Profit Before Taxes | 6.5 | 3.9 | 4.6 | 1.9 | 2.3 | 1.2 |
| | | | **RATIOS** | | | | | | |
| 5.6 | 6.7 | 6.2 | | 11.8 | 6.0 | 9.2 | 5.5 | 4.4 | 4.9 |
| 2.2 | 2.2 | 2.2 | Current | 3.2 | 1.9 | 2.2 | 2.0 | 2.4 | 2.0 |
| 1.1 | 1.1 | 1.1 | | 1.3 | .8 | 1.0 | 1.0 | 1.6 | 1.1 |
| 5.1 | 5.9 | 6.1 | | 11.7 | 5.9 | 9.2 | 4.9 | 4.0 | 4.5 |
| 2.1 | 2.1 | 2.0 | Quick | 2.8 | 1.7 | 1.7 | 1.8 | 2.1 | 1.8 |
| .9 | .9 | 1.0 | | 1.1 | .7 | 1.0 | .8 | 1.3 | 1.1 |
| 3 114.5 | 3 115.8 | 3 129.9 | | 0 UND | 1 504.8 | 2 223.1 | 3 106.9 | 4 91.9 | 10 38.4 |
| 15 24.6 | 14 26.6 | 14 26.8 | Sales/Receivables | 10 34.8 | 12 30.7 | 10 36.7 | 12 30.3 | 13 27.5 | 28 13.1 |
| 39 9.3 | 37 9.9 | 41 9.0 | | 47 7.7 | 43 8.4 | 22 16.9 | 38 9.7 | 38 9.6 | 47 7.8 |
| | | | Cost of Sales/Inventory | | | | | | |
| | | | Cost of Sales/Payables | | | | | | |
| 2.0 | 1.9 | 1.9 | | 1.5 | 2.3 | 1.4 | 2.5 | 1.8 | 2.0 |
| 4.9 | 4.7 | 4.5 | Sales/Working Capital | 3.7 | 4.5 | 3.6 | 5.6 | 4.5 | 4.8 |
| 61.9 | 37.5 | 30.1 | | 18.2 | -14.0 | 62.4 | NM | 11.6 | 27.0 |
| 9.2 | 12.2 | 12.6 | | 6.2 | 9.0 | 10.8 | 13.6 | 28.6 | 42.3 |
| (145) 2.3 | (146) 2.7 | (174) 3.2 | EBIT/Interest | (32) 2.0 | (51) 2.7 | (20) 1.9 | (23) 2.3 | (22) 5.2 | (26) 6.1 |
| -1.1 | .4 | -.2 | | -.6 | .3 | -.3 | -.6 | -.5 | .9 |
| 19.0 | 16.0 | 10.7 | Net Profit + Depr., Dep., | | | | | | |
| (17) 3.2 | (17) 7.9 | (19) 3.7 | Amort./Cur. Mat. L/T/D | | | | | | |
| .2 | 1.0 | .4 | | | | | | | |
| .1 | .1 | .1 | | .0 | .1 | .1 | .1 | .1 | .1 |
| .4 | .4 | .3 | Fixed/Worth | .5 | .7 | .4 | .5 | .2 | .4 |
| 1.3 | 1.1 | 1.3 | | 1.7 | 1.7 | 1.0 | 1.1 | .3 | 1.0 |
| .4 | .3 | .3 | | .2 | .3 | .2 | .5 | .5 | .6 |
| .9 | .8 | .9 | Debt/Worth | .7 | 1.1 | .8 | 1.0 | .9 | 1.5 |
| 2.5 | 2.5 | 2.1 | | 2.1 | 3.1 | 1.8 | 2.8 | 1.5 | 2.7 |
| 15.1 | 16.6 | 15.8 | % Profit Before Taxes/Tangible | 24.9 | 20.9 | 12.3 | 12.0 | 15.1 | 17.1 |
| (274) 2.9 | (303) 6.5 | (324) 4.5 | Net Worth | (59) 4.7 | (79) 4.6 | (30) 2.6 | (48) 4.3 | (61) 5.1 | (47) 3.8 |
| -10.1 | -1.9 | -3.3 | | -4.2 | -1.5 | -2.3 | -4.0 | -4.4 | -3.2 |
| 8.3 | 8.1 | 8.4 | % Profit Before Taxes/Total | 15.5 | 7.5 | 10.0 | 7.5 | 8.4 | 6.1 |
| 1.3 | 3.0 | 2.2 | Assets | 3.3 | 1.7 | 1.3 | 2.5 | 2.8 | 2.4 |
| -5.4 | -1.0 | -1.9 | | -2.8 | -1.7 | -1.5 | -1.6 | -2.2 | -2.1 |
| 32.1 | 45.5 | 43.2 | | UND | 20.7 | 15.5 | 35.1 | 55.7 | 17.0 |
| 6.8 | 8.5 | 9.7 | Sales/Net Fixed Assets | 9.4 | 3.2 | 4.9 | 9.0 | 17.8 | 9.7 |
| 1.9 | 1.6 | 1.6 | | .8 | 1.1 | 1.4 | 2.3 | 10.0 | 3.6 |
| 2.0 | 1.6 | 1.9 | | 2.0 | 1.4 | 1.7 | 2.0 | 2.2 | 1.6 |
| 1.0 | 1.0 | 1.0 | Sales/Total Assets | .9 | .9 | .8 | 1.1 | 1.3 | 1.0 |
| .6 | .6 | .6 | | .4 | .5 | .4 | .8 | .6 | .6 |
| 1.1 | 1.2 | 1.1 | | 2.1 | 1.6 | 1.1 | 1.1 | .7 | .9 |
| (241) 2.0 | (244) 2.3 | (272) 2.3 | % Depr., Dep., Amort./Sales | (34) 4.2 | (68) 2.9 | (29) 2.9 | (44) 1.9 | (55) 1.7 | (42) 2.4 |
| 3.9 | 4.2 | 4.3 | | 7.9 | 4.5 | 5.6 | 3.8 | 2.7 | 3.3 |
| 2.7 | 1.7 | 2.6 | % Officers', Directors' | | | | | | |
| (26) 6.0 | (27) 8.2 | (27) 11.5 | Owners' Comp/Sales | | | | | | |
| 10.8 | 18.6 | 31.8 | | | | | | | |
| 6595203M | 7318614M | 5104552M | Net Sales ($) | 30689M | 163617M | 122684M | 383199M | 1054723M | 3349640M |
| 5254040M | 6963737M | 5475625M | Total Assets ($) | 54465M | 250431M | 244004M | 411693M | 1305716M | 3209316M |

© RMA 2012

M = $ thousand    MM = $ million
See Pages 9 through 22 for Explanation of Ratios and Data

## Current Data Sorted by Assets     Comparative Historical Data

| | | | | | | Type of Statement | | |
|---|---|---|---|---|---|---|---|---|
| 5 | 10 | 60 | 79 | 13 | 22 | Unqualified | 140 | 160 |
| 1 | 3 | | 2 | | | Reviewed | 3 | 5 |
| | 3 | 2 | | | | Compiled | 2 | 11 |
| 1 | 3 | 1 | | | | Tax Returns | 5 | 4 |
| 6 | 4 | 23 | 22 | 3 | 3 | Other | 42 | 44 |
| | 130 (4/1-9/30/11) | | | 136 (10/1/11-3/31/12) | | | 4/1/07-3/31/08 ALL | 4/1/08-3/31/09 ALL |
| 0-500M | 500M-2MM | 2-10MM | 10-50MM | 50-100MM | 100-250MM | | | |
| 13 | 23 | 86 | 103 | 16 | 25 | NUMBER OF STATEMENTS | 192 | 224 |
| % | % | % | % | % | % | ASSETS | % | % |
| 58.4 | 43.6 | 38.3 | 39.1 | 44.2 | 28.2 | Cash & Equivalents | 39.4 | 37.9 |
| 4.2 | 11.6 | 10.5 | 7.5 | 5.8 | 4.8 | Trade Receivables (net) | 10.3 | 10.3 |
| 3.5 | .2 | .4 | 2.0 | .5 | .4 | Inventory | 1.1 | 1.3 |
| 10.0 | 4.3 | 5.1 | 3.5 | 2.2 | 1.7 | All Other Current | 3.9 | 4.2 |
| 76.0 | 59.7 | 54.2 | 52.0 | 52.6 | 35.1 | Total Current | 54.7 | 53.7 |
| 12.4 | 29.5 | 31.1 | 22.6 | 21.0 | 25.4 | Fixed Assets (net) | 27.1 | 25.4 |
| 5.3 | 1.4 | .8 | 2.5 | 5.1 | 1.1 | Intangibles (net) | .7 | 1.8 |
| 6.3 | 9.5 | 13.9 | 22.9 | 21.3 | 38.4 | All Other Non-Current | 17.4 | 19.1 |
| 100.0 | 100.0 | 100.0 | 100.0 | 100.0 | 100.0 | Total | 100.0 | 100.0 |
| | | | | | | LIABILITIES | | |
| 26.1 | 3.3 | .8 | .7 | .6 | .1 | Notes Payable-Short Term | 2.9 | 2.2 |
| 1.2 | 4.1 | 1.1 | 1.0 | 1.1 | 1.2 | Cur. Mat.-L.T.D. | 1.0 | .9 |
| 10.9 | 10.9 | 5.7 | 7.2 | 11.1 | 4.6 | Trade Payables | 8.9 | 8.1 |
| .0 | 2.5 | .2 | .5 | .0 | .1 | Income Taxes Payable | .4 | .7 |
| 16.6 | 21.3 | 15.3 | 12.8 | 13.8 | 15.0 | All Other Current | 12.9 | 14.2 |
| 54.7 | 42.0 | 23.0 | 22.2 | 26.6 | 20.9 | Total Current | 26.1 | 26.0 |
| 8.9 | 9.3 | 12.6 | 10.1 | 5.3 | 15.8 | Long-Term Debt | 12.3 | 13.7 |
| .0 | .0 | .2 | .2 | .9 | .1 | Deferred Taxes | .2 | .1 |
| 18.0 | 7.1 | 12.2 | 12.3 | 14.1 | 15.5 | All Other Non-Current | 11.7 | 11.6 |
| 18.5 | 41.7 | 52.0 | 55.3 | 53.2 | 47.7 | Net Worth | 49.8 | 48.6 |
| 100.0 | 100.0 | 100.0 | 100.0 | 100.0 | 100.0 | Total Liabilities & Net Worth | 100.0 | 100.0 |
| | | | | | | INCOME DATA | | |
| 100.0 | 100.0 | 100.0 | 100.0 | 100.0 | 100.0 | Net Sales | 100.0 | 100.0 |
| | | | | | | Gross Profit | | |
| 91.8 | 92.9 | 95.6 | 96.2 | 97.1 | 91.9 | Operating Expenses | 93.2 | 96.6 |
| 8.2 | 7.1 | 4.4 | 3.8 | 2.9 | 8.1 | Operating Profit | 6.8 | 3.4 |
| 2.0 | 4.2 | -.3 | -.1 | -1.3 | 3.3 | All Other Expenses (net) | -1.0 | 3.8 |
| 6.3 | 2.9 | 4.8 | 3.9 | 4.2 | 4.8 | Profit Before Taxes | 7.8 | -.4 |
| | | | | | | RATIOS | | |
| 12.0 | 8.4 | 7.9 | 5.8 | 4.3 | 2.7 | | 5.3 | 5.2 |
| 9.0 | 2.4 | 2.6 | 2.2 | 2.2 | 1.5 | Current | 2.6 | 2.3 |
| .8 | 1.0 | 1.2 | 1.4 | 1.2 | .8 | | 1.3 | 1.3 |
| 10.1 | 8.3 | 7.3 | 5.4 | 4.0 | 2.6 | | 5.0 | 4.9 |
| 2.8 | 2.3 | 2.3 | 2.0 | 2.1 | 1.4 | Quick | 2.3 | 2.1 |
| .6 | 1.0 | 1.1 | 1.1 | 1.0 | .7 | | 1.2 | 1.1 |
| 0 UND | 0 UND | 5 78.6 | 4 84.1 | 7 50.7 | 5 78.8 | | 5 75.3 | 6 57.9 |
| 0 UND | 4 86.9 | 14 26.9 | 12 31.5 | 17 21.0 | 26 14.1 | Sales/Receivables | 15 24.4 | 16 23.3 |
| 11 34.6 | 8 43.0 | 39 9.4 | 23 16.0 | 29 12.5 | 38 9.6 | | 37 9.7 | 37 9.9 |
| | | | | | | Cost of Sales/Inventory | | |
| | | | | | | Cost of Sales/Payables | | |
| .8 | 2.0 | 1.6 | 1.5 | 1.4 | 3.1 | | 2.0 | 1.8 |
| 3.8 | 3.4 | 4.2 | 3.8 | 3.0 | 10.7 | Sales/Working Capital | 4.0 | 4.3 |
| NM | 67.1 | 13.7 | 13.0 | 27.8 | -31.0 | | 14.3 | 14.4 |
| | | 10.0 | 17.9 | | 30.6 | | 21.7 | 9.0 |
| | (44) 3.2 | (47) 5.1 | | (17) 2.3 | | EBIT/Interest | (86) 6.1 | (108) 1.8 |
| | | -1.8 | 1.9 | | .0 | | 1.2 | -2.8 |
| | | | | | | | 15.3 | 3.1 |
| | | | | | | Net Profit + Depr., Dep., Amort./Cur. Mat. L/T/D | (12) 11.7 | (14) 1.3 |
| | | | | | | | 3.8 | -17.0 |
| .0 | .1 | .1 | .1 | .1 | .1 | | .1 | .1 |
| .0 | .7 | .7 | .4 | .3 | .3 | Fixed/Worth | .4 | .4 |
| .8 | 1.7 | .9 | .7 | .6 | 1.8 | | 1.1 | 1.2 |
| .1 | .2 | .3 | .4 | .4 | .4 | | .4 | .4 |
| .7 | 1.0 | .9 | .8 | .7 | 1.0 | Debt/Worth | .8 | 1.0 |
| 77.1 | 3.9 | 1.9 | 1.5 | 2.3 | 3.6 | | 2.0 | 1.7 |
| 45.3 | 33.0 | 15.7 | 14.0 | 9.4 | 14.8 | | 17.9 | 11.6 |
| (11) 12.9 | (21) 9.8 | (82) 6.7 | (99) 6.9 | (15) 4.7 | (24) 3.7 | % Profit Before Taxes/Tangible Net Worth | (182) 10.7 | (208) .5 |
| .0 | -6.0 | -3.0 | 1.5 | -.5 | -2.9 | | 2.3 | -14.8 |
| 14.7 | 10.9 | 7.6 | 7.1 | 5.9 | 5.6 | | 11.4 | 5.6 |
| 10.7 | 7.0 | 4.1 | 3.3 | 2.8 | 2.1 | % Profit Before Taxes/Total Assets | 5.1 | .1 |
| -5.1 | -3.7 | -1.5 | .3 | -.1 | -.5 | | .9 | -7.2 |
| UND | 64.0 | 17.7 | 20.6 | 9.0 | 9.3 | | 21.5 | 23.1 |
| UND | 6.7 | 3.9 | 5.9 | 4.4 | 3.1 | Sales/Net Fixed Assets | 5.9 | 6.5 |
| 41.8 | 2.3 | 1.3 | 2.0 | 3.1 | 1.4 | | 2.1 | 2.1 |
| 4.7 | 2.5 | 1.5 | 1.1 | 1.0 | .9 | | 1.5 | 1.4 |
| 1.9 | 1.1 | .8 | .8 | .7 | .6 | Sales/Total Assets | .9 | .9 |
| .6 | .5 | .5 | .6 | .6 | .4 | | .6 | .6 |
| | 1.3 | 1.3 | 1.3 | 2.2 | 1.4 | | 1.3 | 1.3 |
| (17) | 2.2 | (66) 2.5 | (94) 2.2 | (15) 3.6 | (24) 2.8 | % Depr., Dep., Amort./Sales | (166) 2.2 | (193) 2.3 |
| | 4.7 | 4.8 | 3.5 | 5.2 | 5.3 | | 3.5 | 3.5 |
| | | | | | | | 2.8 | 2.7 |
| | | | | | | % Officers', Directors' Owners' Comp/Sales | (11) 6.8 | (14) 8.0 |
| | | | | | | | 27.9 | 25.8 |
| 7134M | 57283M | 604683M | 2907634M | 1339309M | 3751039M | Net Sales ($) | 4651308M | 6792129M |
| 2413M | 30158M | 476203M | 2414709M | 1115321M | 4307689M | Total Assets ($) | 5170141M | 7229900M |

© RMA 2012

M = $ thousand    MM = $ million
See Pages 9 through 22 for Explanation of Ratios and Data

## Comparative Historical Data      Current Data Sorted by Sales

| | | | | Type of Statement | 0-1MM | 1-3MM | 3-5MM | 5-10MM | 10-25MM | 25MM & OVER |
|---|---|---|---|---|---|---|---|---|---|---|
| | 146 | 167 | 189 | Unqualified | 10 | 28 | 17 | 29 | 49 | 56 |
| | 4 | 8 | 6 | Reviewed | 2 | 2 | | | 1 | 1 |
| | 7 | 5 | 5 | Compiled | 1 | 3 | 1 | | | |
| | 10 | 13 | 5 | Tax Returns | 3 | 1 | | | 1 | |
| | 59 | 62 | 61 | Other | 8 | 10 | 4 | 7 | 14 | 18 |
| | 4/1/09-3/31/10 ALL | 4/1/10-3/31/11 ALL | 4/1/11-3/31/12 ALL | | 130 (4/1-9/30/11) | | | 136 (10/1/11-3/31/12) | | |
| | 226 | 255 | 266 | **NUMBER OF STATEMENTS** | 24 | 44 | 22 | 36 | 65 | 75 |
| | % | % | % | **ASSETS** | % | % | % | % | % | % |
| | 38.3 | 40.2 | 39.4 | Cash & Equivalents | 45.5 | 41.7 | 40.1 | 40.9 | 36.4 | 37.8 |
| | 9.8 | 8.5 | 8.3 | Trade Receivables (net) | 1.2 | 8.1 | 4.7 | 9.7 | 6.4 | 12.7 |
| | 1.6 | 1.1 | 1.1 | Inventory | 1.2 | 1.1 | .0 | .2 | 1.1 | 2.0 |
| | 3.2 | 4.6 | 4.1 | All Other Current | 5.2 | 5.0 | 4.6 | 2.6 | 5.9 | 2.4 |
| | 52.9 | 54.4 | 53.0 | Total Current | 53.2 | 55.9 | 49.4 | 53.4 | 49.8 | 55.0 |
| | 28.9 | 25.2 | 25.6 | Fixed Assets (net) | 35.7 | 31.2 | 28.1 | 23.1 | 26.1 | 19.1 |
| | 1.4 | 1.3 | 2.0 | Intangibles (net) | 2.9 | 3.1 | .6 | .7 | 1.6 | 2.4 |
| | 16.9 | 19.1 | 19.4 | All Other Non-Current | 8.1 | 9.8 | 21.9 | 22.8 | 22.5 | 23.5 |
| | 100.0 | 100.0 | 100.0 | Total | 100.0 | 100.0 | 100.0 | 100.0 | 100.0 | 100.0 |
| | | | | **LIABILITIES** | | | | | | |
| | 2.8 | 1.8 | 2.1 | Notes Payable-Short Term | .7 | 8.6 | 2.3 | 1.1 | .3 | .8 |
| | 1.5 | 1.0 | 1.3 | Cur. Mat.-L.T.D. | 4.4 | .9 | 1.1 | .9 | .7 | 1.4 |
| | 7.4 | 7.2 | 7.2 | Trade Payables | 2.1 | 5.9 | 6.6 | 7.0 | 7.9 | 9.2 |
| | .6 | .4 | .5 | Income Taxes Payable | .0 | .3 | 2.6 | .0 | .7 | .1 |
| | 14.6 | 15.6 | 14.8 | All Other Current | 10.4 | 16.0 | 8.2 | 17.3 | 14.5 | 16.4 |
| | 26.8 | 26.1 | 25.9 | Total Current | 17.5 | 31.6 | 20.8 | 26.4 | 24.2 | 27.9 |
| | 15.6 | 12.6 | 11.0 | Long-Term Debt | 12.2 | 14.6 | 13.2 | 9.4 | 10.6 | 8.9 |
| | .3 | .2 | .2 | Deferred Taxes | .0 | .4 | .0 | .0 | .2 | .3 |
| | 11.3 | 11.5 | 12.5 | All Other Non-Current | 9.9 | 8.9 | 17.5 | 9.0 | 12.7 | 15.4 |
| | 46.1 | 49.6 | 50.4 | Net Worth | 60.4 | 44.4 | 48.4 | 55.2 | 52.3 | 47.4 |
| | 100.0 | 100.0 | 100.0 | Total Liabilities & Net Worth | 100.0 | 100.0 | 100.0 | 100.0 | 100.0 | 100.0 |
| | | | | **INCOME DATA** | | | | | | |
| | 100.0 | 100.0 | 100.0 | Net Sales | 100.0 | 100.0 | 100.0 | 100.0 | 100.0 | 100.0 |
| | | | | Gross Profit | | | | | | |
| | 97.5 | 95.3 | 95.2 | Operating Expenses | 86.3 | 94.4 | 98.7 | 98.3 | 97.1 | 94.2 |
| | 2.5 | 4.7 | 4.8 | Operating Profit | 13.7 | 5.6 | 1.3 | 1.7 | 2.9 | 5.8 |
| | 1.9 | -.4 | .5 | All Other Expenses (net) | 6.7 | .4 | -.9 | -.5 | -1.2 | 1.1 |
| | .6 | 5.0 | 4.3 | Profit Before Taxes | 7.0 | 5.2 | 2.2 | 2.2 | 4.2 | 4.6 |
| | | | | **RATIOS** | | | | | | |
| | 5.3 | 6.7 | 6.2 | | 13.0 | 8.5 | 9.7 | 6.0 | 4.8 | 3.6 |
| | 2.2 | 2.1 | 2.3 | Current | 5.6 | 3.6 | 3.5 | 1.8 | 2.2 | 2.0 |
| | 1.3 | 1.1 | 1.2 | | 1.8 | 1.1 | 1.3 | 1.1 | 1.5 | 1.1 |
| | 4.5 | 6.5 | 5.9 | | 10.5 | 8.5 | 9.7 | 5.9 | 4.5 | 3.6 |
| | 1.9 | 1.8 | 2.1 | Quick | 3.7 | 3.4 | 3.0 | 1.7 | 1.8 | 1.8 |
| | 1.0 | 1.0 | 1.0 | | 1.3 | 1.1 | .7 | 1.0 | 1.1 | 1.0 |
| | 3  106.6 | 4  93.2 | 4  100.7 | | 0  UND | 0  UND | 5  68.2 | 9  41.2 | 4  84.2 | 8  45.0 |
| | 14  26.2 | 14  26.7 | 11  33.0 | Sales/Receivables | 0  UND | 5  69.4 | 8  46.3 | 15  24.6 | 10  35.0 | 23  16.0 |
| | 32  11.5 | 28  13.1 | 27  13.6 | | 4  91.6 | 25  14.7 | 25  14.8 | 28  12.9 | 18  20.1 | 39  9.4 |
| | | | | Cost of Sales/Inventory | | | | | | |
| | | | | Cost of Sales/Payables | | | | | | |
| | 1.8 | 1.6 | 1.7 | | 1.1 | 1.3 | 1.0 | 1.5 | 2.6 | 2.1 |
| | 4.6 | 4.4 | 4.3 | Sales/Working Capital | 1.9 | 3.2 | 3.2 | 4.7 | 4.9 | 7.0 |
| | 20.1 | 30.9 | 19.7 | | 10.5 | 15.4 | 16.7 | 41.6 | 10.7 | 51.2 |
| | 6.7 | 13.5 | 11.4 | | | | 5.3 | 6.7 | 21.9 | 35.6 |
| | (115)  2.1 | (126)  3.4 | (127)  4.4 | EBIT/Interest | (19)  1.1 | (12)  2.8 | (18)  4.4 | (33)  5.4 | (38)  5.7 | |
| | -1.7 | 1.2 | .6 | | | -2.5 | -2.4 | -2.8 | 2.6 | 1.4 |
| | 9.7 | | 4.3 | | | | | | | |
| | (15)  2.7 | (13)  1.9 | | Net Profit + Depr., Dep., Amort./Cur. Mat. L/T/D | | | | | | |
| | 1.1 | | 1.0 | | | | | | | |
| | .2 | .1 | .1 | | .0 | .1 | .2 | .1 | .1 | .1 |
| | .5 | .4 | .4 | Fixed/Worth | .7 | .7 | .6 | .4 | .4 | .3 |
| | 1.2 | 1.0 | .9 | | .9 | 1.3 | 1.2 | .8 | .9 | .7 |
| | .4 | .4 | .4 | | .1 | .3 | .3 | .3 | .4 | .5 |
| | 1.0 | .8 | .9 | Debt/Worth | .4 | .9 | 1.0 | .7 | .9 | 1.0 |
| | 2.5 | 2.2 | 1.8 | | 1.6 | 2.7 | 3.0 | 2.0 | 1.5 | 2.5 |
| | 11.4 | 13.4 | 15.4 | | 22.9 | 12.2 | 16.6 | 15.3 | 14.2 | 19.1 |
| | (210)  .8 | (241)  5.8 | (252)  6.9 | % Profit Before Taxes/Tangible Net Worth | (23)  10.8 | (41)  5.7 | (21)  5.4 | (35)  6.6 | (62)  7.5 | (70)  7.0 |
| | -9.8 | -.4 | -1.8 | | -3.7 | -3.1 | -9.6 | -2.1 | .2 | .6 |
| | 5.0 | 7.0 | 8.0 | | 10.9 | 7.4 | 9.0 | 7.1 | 7.5 | 9.8 |
| | .3 | 2.8 | 3.8 | % Profit Before Taxes/Total Assets | 6.2 | 3.1 | 3.5 | 3.8 | 4.5 | 3.1 |
| | -6.3 | -.2 | -.7 | | -3.1 | -1.8 | -6.3 | -1.3 | .4 | .5 |
| | 18.4 | 30.0 | 24.7 | | 830.3 | 18.0 | 15.7 | 22.0 | 18.1 | 32.9 |
| | 5.0 | 5.6 | 5.0 | Sales/Net Fixed Assets | 6.3 | 2.5 | 2.3 | 4.6 | 4.9 | 8.4 |
| | 1.9 | 1.8 | 1.7 | | .4 | .8 | 1.2 | 1.8 | 2.4 | 3.6 |
| | 1.5 | 1.4 | 1.3 | | 1.5 | 1.1 | 1.3 | 1.5 | 1.3 | 2.4 |
| | .9 | .8 | .8 | Sales/Total Assets | .6 | .6 | .6 | .9 | .9 | .9 |
| | .5 | .5 | .5 | | .2 | .4 | .4 | .6 | .6 | .6 |
| | 1.5 | 1.3 | 1.3 | | 1.3 | 2.2 | 1.6 | 1.1 | 1.2 | 1.2 |
| | (191)  2.5 | (211)  2.5 | (219)  2.4 | % Depr., Dep., Amort./Sales | (14)  4.2 | (30)  3.3 | (19)  3.4 | (30)  2.4 | (62)  2.1 | (64)  2.1 |
| | 4.7 | 4.4 | 4.1 | | 12.4 | 5.9 | 5.3 | 3.6 | 3.2 | 3.8 |
| | 3.3 | 2.1 | 5.7 | | | | | | | |
| | (17)  8.3 | (15)  7.5 | (12)  14.7 | % Officers', Directors' Owners' Comp/Sales | | | | | | |
| | 29.9 | 23.1 | 32.2 | | | | | | | |
| | 7507235M | 7250987M | 8667082M | Net Sales ($) | 11194M | 89262M | 81163M | 283694M | 1021231M | 7180538M |
| | 7176157M | 8047759M | 8346493M | Total Assets ($) | 28869M | 211124M | 153307M | 490866M | 1223378M | 6238949M |

© RMA 2012       M = $ thousand    MM = $ million

See Pages 9 through 22 for Explanation of Ratios and Data

## Current Data Sorted by Assets      Comparative Historical Data

| Type of Statement | 0-500M | 500M-2MM | 2-10MM | 10-50MM | 50-100MM | 100-250MM | | 4/1/07-3/31/08 ALL | 4/1/08-3/31/09 ALL |
|---|---|---|---|---|---|---|---|---|---|
| Unqualified | 1 | 5 | 34 | 20 | 6 | 7 | | 49 | 54 |
| Reviewed | | 1 | 2 | | | | | 3 | 3 |
| Compiled | | | 1 | 1 | | | | 5 | 1 |
| Tax Returns | 2 | 2 | 1 | | | | | 7 | 6 |
| Other | 2 | 7 | 15 | 7 | 2 | 2 | | 14 | 22 |
| | | 59 (4/1-9/30/11) | | 59 (10/1/11-3/31/12) | | | | | |
| **NUMBER OF STATEMENTS** | 5 | 15 | 53 | 28 | 8 | 9 | | 78 | 86 |
| **ASSETS** | % | % | % | % | % | % | | % | % |
| Cash & Equivalents | | 48.1 | 35.4 | 52.0 | | | | 41.8 | 48.4 |
| Trade Receivables (net) | | 5.3 | 2.2 | 5.2 | | | | 4.0 | 4.7 |
| Inventory | | 1.6 | .0 | .2 | | | | .4 | .4 |
| All Other Current | | 4.7 | 1.7 | 3.8 | | | | 5.9 | 3.5 |
| Total Current | | 59.7 | 39.3 | 61.2 | | | | 52.0 | 57.0 |
| Fixed Assets (net) | | 30.8 | 49.7 | 24.2 | | | | 35.8 | 30.9 |
| Intangibles (net) | | .9 | .4 | .0 | | | | .1 | .1 |
| All Other Non-Current | | 8.5 | 10.7 | 14.6 | | | | 12.1 | 12.1 |
| Total | | 100.0 | 100.0 | 100.0 | | | | 100.0 | 100.0 |
| **LIABILITIES** | | | | | | | | | |
| Notes Payable-Short Term | | .5 | .8 | .6 | | | | 1.3 | .8 |
| Cur. Mat.-L.T.D. | | .8 | 2.5 | .5 | | | | .9 | 1.0 |
| Trade Payables | | 2.9 | 1.1 | 2.4 | | | | 4.1 | 4.4 |
| Income Taxes Payable | | .0 | .0 | .0 | | | | .0 | .0 |
| All Other Current | | 1.7 | 4.8 | 13.6 | | | | 7.1 | 6.8 |
| Total Current | | 5.8 | 9.2 | 17.2 | | | | 13.5 | 13.0 |
| Long-Term Debt | | 11.3 | 16.5 | 8.7 | | | | 17.3 | 14.2 |
| Deferred Taxes | | .0 | .0 | .2 | | | | .0 | .0 |
| All Other Non-Current | | 8.0 | 2.8 | 12.9 | | | | 7.8 | 8.7 |
| Net Worth | | 75.0 | 71.5 | 60.9 | | | | 61.4 | 64.0 |
| Total Liabilties & Net Worth | | 100.0 | 100.0 | 100.0 | | | | 100.0 | 100.0 |
| **INCOME DATA** | | | | | | | | | |
| Net Sales | | 100.0 | 100.0 | 100.0 | | | | 100.0 | 100.0 |
| Gross Profit | | | | | | | | | |
| Operating Expenses | | 96.1 | 94.5 | 93.6 | | | | 93.4 | 93.7 |
| Operating Profit | | 3.9 | 5.5 | 6.4 | | | | 6.6 | 6.3 |
| All Other Expenses (net) | | 1.7 | .8 | .5 | | | | .6 | 1.9 |
| Profit Before Taxes | | 2.3 | 4.7 | 5.9 | | | | 6.0 | 4.3 |
| **RATIOS** | | | | | | | | | |
| Current | | 143.0 | 20.9 | 35.6 | | | | 40.5 | 42.5 |
| | | 9.7 | 6.2 | 7.5 | | | | 5.6 | 6.1 |
| | | 3.9 | 2.3 | 2.6 | | | | 2.4 | 2.4 |
| Quick | | 143.0 | 20.9 | 35.6 | | | | 40.3 | 42.4 |
| | | 6.9 | 6.1 | 6.8 | | | | 5.2 | 5.9 |
| | | 3.9 | 2.1 | 2.5 | | | | 1.8 | 2.2 |
| Sales/Receivables | 0 UND | 0 UND | 0 UND | 0 UND | | | | 0 UND | 0 UND |
| | 0 UND | 0 UND | 0 UND | 5 66.4 | | | | 0 999.8 | 1 688.7 |
| | 12 31.1 | 24 15.1 | 29 12.7 | | | | | 20 18.3 | 26 14.2 |
| Cost of Sales/Inventory | | | | | | | | | |
| Cost of Sales/Payables | | | | | | | | | |
| Sales/Working Capital | | 1.7 | 1.3 | 1.2 | | | | 1.6 | 1.1 |
| | | 3.2 | 3.2 | 1.7 | | | | 3.0 | 2.5 |
| | | 5.5 | 12.5 | 3.8 | | | | 7.7 | 6.5 |
| EBIT/Interest | | | 6.8 | 14.2 | | | | 15.2 | 14.6 |
| | | (27) | 2.7 (14) | 3.4 | | | | (43) 2.5 | (44) 2.2 |
| | | | .9 | .0 | | | | -2.0 | -.1 |
| Net Profit + Depr., Dep., Amort./Cur. Mat. L/T/D | | | | | | | | | |
| Fixed/Worth | | .0 | .2 | .0 | | | | .0 | .0 |
| | | .2 | .8 | .3 | | | | .5 | .3 |
| | | 1.5 | 1.2 | .8 | | | | 1.3 | .9 |
| Debt/Worth | | .0 | .0 | .1 | | | | .0 | .0 |
| | | .1 | .3 | .3 | | | | .4 | .3 |
| | | .5 | .9 | 1.0 | | | | 1.3 | .9 |
| % Profit Before Taxes/Tangible Net Worth | | 19.7 | 9.9 | 9.6 | | | | 17.7 | 15.1 |
| | | 2.3 (52) | 4.6 (25) | 2.5 | | | | (72) 6.1 | (83) 4.9 |
| | | -7.7 | -2.1 | -.8 | | | | -4.3 | -4.0 |
| % Profit Before Taxes/Total Assets | | 7.0 | 7.4 | 5.0 | | | | 12.9 | 10.1 |
| | | 2.3 | 2.7 | 1.0 | | | | 2.8 | 3.0 |
| | | -7.7 | -1.2 | -1.3 | | | | -3.0 | -2.8 |
| Sales/Net Fixed Assets | | 343.6 | 6.7 | 328.9 | | | | 33.5 | 60.6 |
| | | 26.7 | 1.6 | 6.0 | | | | 4.1 | 4.4 |
| | | 1.2 | .8 | 1.8 | | | | 1.1 | 1.5 |
| Sales/Total Assets | | 2.6 | 1.3 | 1.4 | | | | 1.6 | 1.5 |
| | | 1.0 | .7 | .8 | | | | .9 | .8 |
| | | .5 | .4 | .5 | | | | .5 | .5 |
| % Depr., Dep., Amort./Sales | | | 1.6 | .6 | | | | .9 | .9 |
| | | (44) | 3.2 (21) | 1.7 | | | | (63) 1.9 | (69) 2.2 |
| | | | 7.6 | 2.8 | | | | 4.6 | 4.3 |
| % Officers', Directors' Owners' Comp/Sales | | | | | | | | 7.1 | 5.2 |
| | | | (21) 13.6 | (16) 11.1 | | | | | |
| | | | 27.1 | 26.6 | | | | | |
| Net Sales ($) | 1324M | 22691M | 241536M | 696272M | 219193M | 1257878M | | 1495172M | 2042583M |
| Total Assets ($) | 1850M | 16286M | 273562M | 722725M | 503492M | 1490226M | | 1527054M | 1998866M |

M = $ thousand    MM = $ million
See Pages 9 through 22 for Explanation of Ratios and Data

| Comparative Historical Data | | | | Current Data Sorted by Sales | | | | | |
|---|---|---|---|---|---|---|---|---|---|
| 60 | 67 | 73 | **Type of Statement** Unqualified | 4 | 16 | 5 | 15 | 16 | 17 |
| 3 | 2 | 3 | Reviewed | 1 | 2 | | | | |
| 5 | 6 | 2 | Compiled | | | | 2 | | |
| 7 | 5 | 5 | Tax Returns | 4 | 1 | | | | |
| 31 | 22 | 35 | Other | 8 | 9 | 2 | 8 | 3 | 5 |
| 4/1/09- 3/31/10 ALL | 4/1/10- 3/31/11 ALL | 4/1/11- 3/31/12 ALL | | 59 (4/1-9/30/11) | | | 59 (10/1/11-3/31/12) | | |
| | | | | 0-1MM | 1-3MM | 3-5MM | 5-10MM | 10-25MM | 25MM & OVER |
| 106 | 102 | 118 | **NUMBER OF STATEMENTS** | 17 | 28 | 7 | 25 | 19 | 22 |
| % | % | % | **ASSETS** | % | % | % | % | % | % |
| 48.2 | 45.7 | 41.4 | Cash & Equivalents | 32.1 | 40.2 | | 42.4 | 40.5 | 45.1 |
| 4.0 | 3.8 | 3.7 | Trade Receivables (net) | 2.4 | 1.5 | | 2.4 | 2.0 | 9.0 |
| .2 | .5 | .3 | Inventory | .0 | .1 | | .0 | .0 | .2 |
| 3.5 | 2.5 | 2.4 | All Other Current | .5 | 3.6 | | 2.3 | 2.1 | 3.7 |
| 55.9 | 52.5 | 47.9 | Total Current | 35.0 | 45.4 | | 47.1 | 44.6 | 58.1 |
| 33.7 | 35.2 | 35.2 | Fixed Assets (net) | 58.5 | 43.8 | | 39.7 | 23.7 | 16.7 |
| .1 | .4 | .3 | Intangibles (net) | .0 | .1 | | .7 | .0 | .1 |
| 10.3 | 11.9 | 16.7 | All Other Non-Current | 6.5 | 10.7 | | 12.5 | 31.7 | 25.1 |
| 100.0 | 100.0 | 100.0 | Total | 100.0 | 100.0 | | 100.0 | 100.0 | 100.0 |
| | | | **LIABILITIES** | | | | | | |
| 1.9 | .8 | .7 | Notes Payable-Short Term | .0 | .7 | | 1.3 | .1 | .6 |
| 1.5 | 1.0 | 1.4 | Cur. Mat.-L.T.D. | 3.9 | 1.5 | | 1.4 | .7 | .3 |
| 2.5 | 3.2 | 2.0 | Trade Payables | 1.1 | 1.2 | | 1.3 | 1.5 | 4.6 |
| .0 | .0 | .0 | Income Taxes Payable | .0 | .0 | | .0 | .0 | .0 |
| 10.4 | 9.5 | 6.2 | All Other Current | .6 | 2.0 | | 9.6 | 2.6 | 16.8 |
| 16.3 | 14.5 | 10.2 | Total Current | 5.6 | 5.5 | | 13.6 | 4.8 | 22.3 |
| 11.6 | 14.8 | 12.1 | Long-Term Debt | 13.8 | 19.7 | | 13.8 | 9.8 | 4.8 |
| .0 | .0 | .1 | Deferred Taxes | .0 | .0 | | .0 | .0 | .3 |
| 3.9 | 4.5 | 6.0 | All Other Non-Current | .3 | 4.2 | | 7.3 | 6.6 | 12.1 |
| 68.2 | 66.2 | 71.7 | Net Worth | 80.3 | 70.6 | | 65.4 | 78.8 | 60.5 |
| 100.0 | 100.0 | 100.0 | Total Liabilities & Net Worth | 100.0 | 100.0 | | 100.0 | 100.0 | 100.0 |
| | | | **INCOME DATA** | | | | | | |
| 100.0 | 100.0 | 100.0 | Net Sales | 100.0 | 100.0 | | 100.0 | 100.0 | 100.0 |
| | | | Gross Profit | | | | | | |
| 95.0 | 94.3 | 91.7 | Operating Expenses | 96.1 | 91.2 | | 93.7 | 86.0 | 92.8 |
| 5.0 | 5.7 | 8.3 | Operating Profit | 3.9 | 8.8 | | 6.3 | 14.0 | 7.2 |
| 2.9 | .4 | .8 | All Other Expenses (net) | 2.6 | 2.0 | | -.9 | 1.2 | -.1 |
| 2.0 | 5.3 | 7.5 | Profit Before Taxes | 1.3 | 6.9 | | 7.2 | 12.7 | 7.3 |
| | | | **RATIOS** | | | | | | |
| 64.5 | 49.2 | 29.0 | | 29.0 | 37.4 | | 8.0 | 54.8 | 32.0 |
| 6.8 | 5.5 | 7.5 | Current | 13.9 | 9.5 | | 5.3 | 15.4 | 3.9 |
| 2.1 | 2.2 | 2.4 | | 2.6 | 3.6 | | 2.3 | 5.5 | 2.2 |
| 63.5 | 46.6 | 28.2 | | 29.0 | 34.2 | | 8.0 | 54.8 | 30.9 |
| 6.1 | 5.0 | 6.7 | Quick | 12.8 | 8.7 | | 5.3 | 14.0 | 3.8 |
| 1.8 | 2.0 | 2.4 | | 2.6 | 3.6 | | 2.2 | 5.5 | 2.1 |
| 0  UND | 0  UND | 0  UND | | 0  UND | 0  UND | | 0  UND | 0  UND | 0  UND |
| 1  299.4 | 3  118.7 | 0  UND | Sales/Receivables | 0  UND | 0  UND | | 0  UND | 4  94.5 | 25  14.6 |
| 22  16.4 | 26  13.8 | 27  13.7 | | 7  52.1 | 21  17.2 | | 18  20.6 | 27  13.3 | 37  9.8 |
| | | | Cost of Sales/Inventory | | | | | | |
| | | | Cost of Sales/Payables | | | | | | |
| 1.3 | 1.0 | 1.3 | | 1.1 | 1.1 | | 1.5 | 1.3 | 1.7 |
| 2.9 | 2.5 | 2.4 | Sales/Working Capital | 2.2 | 1.9 | | 3.3 | 2.5 | 3.1 |
| 7.8 | 6.4 | 5.6 | | 63.1 | 3.8 | | 11.3 | 9.5 | 5.3 |
| 6.6 | 9.9 | 7.3 | | | 3.7 | | 30.1 | | |
| (46)  .5 | (46)  1.4 | (52)  2.6 | EBIT/Interest | (12)  2.2 | | (14)  10.7 | | | |
| -4.0 | -1.0 | .6 | | | 1.2 | | 2.1 | | |
| | | | Net Profit + Depr., Dep., Amort./Cur. Mat. L/T/D | | | | | | |
| .1 | .0 | .0 | | .3 | .1 | | .0 | .0 | .0 |
| .4 | .5 | .5 | Fixed/Worth | .8 | .6 | | .6 | .2 | .1 |
| 1.0 | 1.2 | 1.1 | | 1.4 | 1.4 | | 1.2 | .6 | .6 |
| .0 | .0 | .0 | | .0 | .0 | | .2 | .0 | .0 |
| .3 | .3 | .2 | Debt/Worth | .1 | .3 | | .4 | .1 | .3 |
| 1.0 | 1.0 | .9 | | .5 | .8 | | 1.1 | .2 | 2.2 |
| 12.9 | 9.6 | 10.0 | | 7.0 | 10.8 | | 13.4 | 9.6 | 9.9 |
| (102)  .7 | (97)  2.6 | (114)  4.7 | % Profit Before Taxes/Tangible Net Worth | 2.3 | 5.3 | | 7.0 | (17)  1.1 | (20)  5.7 |
| -8.5 | -5.1 | -.9 | | -8.2 | -.9 | | .5 | -.8 | -6.7 |
| 9.3 | 7.0 | 7.8 | | 3.9 | 6.4 | | 8.4 | 8.5 | 7.9 |
| .1 | 1.9 | 2.9 | % Profit Before Taxes/Total Assets | 2.3 | 2.7 | | 5.5 | 1.0 | 4.1 |
| -6.0 | -3.3 | -1.0 | | -5.8 | -.8 | | .3 | -.7 | -3.5 |
| 28.2 | 45.0 | 72.3 | | 2.3 | 19.5 | | 15.1 | 114.9 | 886.9 |
| 4.4 | 4.2 | 4.0 | Sales/Net Fixed Assets | .5 | 1.1 | | 4.3 | 4.3 | 12.7 |
| 1.3 | 1.1 | 1.1 | | .3 | .6 | | 1.5 | 2.2 | 6.1 |
| 1.4 | 1.3 | 1.3 | | .7 | .9 | | 1.7 | 1.2 | 1.7 |
| .9 | .7 | .7 | Sales/Total Assets | .4 | .6 | | 1.1 | .8 | 1.3 |
| .5 | .4 | .4 | | .2 | .3 | | .6 | .3 | .6 |
| 1.0 | .7 | .7 | | 3.8 | 1.8 | | 1.2 | .4 | .0 |
| (80)  2.1 | (79)  2.0 | (88)  2.1 | % Depr., Dep., Amort./Sales | (12)  7.3 | (21)  4.4 | | (20)  2.2 | (15)  .9 | (16)  1.0 |
| 4.4 | 4.4 | 5.8 | | 16.0 | 7.6 | | 4.6 | 1.9 | 1.9 |
| 6.3 | 6.5 | 4.7 | % Officers', Directors' Owners' Comp/Sales | | | | | | |
| (18)  16.1 | (11)  12.8 | (17)  9.7 | | | | | | | |
| 32.2 | 19.3 | 20.7 | | | | | | | |
| 2569269M | 2301826M | 2438894M | Net Sales ($) | 7308M | 53021M | 26014M | 175712M | 294355M | 1882484M |
| 2802757M | 3508218M | 3008141M | Total Assets ($) | 30081M | 108026M | 49012M | 219117M | 639568M | 1962337M |

© RMA 2012

M = $ thousand    MM = $ million
See Pages 9 through 22 for Explanation of Ratios and Data

## Current Data Sorted by Assets | Comparative Historical Data

| | | | | | | Type of Statement | | |
|---|---|---|---|---|---|---|---|---|
| 16 | 54 | 67 | 65 | 9 | 8 | Unqualified | 140 | 195 |
| 10 | 8 | 6 | 2 | | | Reviewed | 18 | 15 |
| 4 | 10 | 6 | | 1 | | Compiled | 16 | 23 |
| 4 | 10 | 1 | | | | Tax Returns | 12 | 13 |
| 66 | 60 | 31 | 23 | 3 | 2 | Other | 113 | 143 |
| | 156 (4/1-9/30/11) | | 310 (10/1/11-3/31/12) | | | | 4/1/07-3/31/08 ALL | 4/1/08-3/31/09 ALL |
| 0-500M | 500M-2MM | 2-10MM | 10-50MM | 50-100MM | 100-250MM | | | |
| 100 | 142 | 111 | 90 | 13 | 10 | NUMBER OF STATEMENTS | 299 | 389 |
| % | % | % | % | % | % | ASSETS | % | % |
| 68.5 | 46.8 | 29.0 | 19.3 | 32.3 | 42.4 | Cash & Equivalents | 37.5 | 35.8 |
| 5.1 | 10.1 | 8.3 | 5.8 | 6.8 | 4.3 | Trade Receivables (net) | 8.4 | 8.8 |
| .1 | .7 | 1.0 | 1.0 | .2 | .2 | Inventory | 1.2 | 1.1 |
| 4.6 | 3.2 | 3.4 | 3.1 | 3.9 | 1.2 | All Other Current | 4.5 | 4.7 |
| 78.3 | 60.8 | 41.7 | 29.2 | 43.2 | 48.2 | Total Current | 51.5 | 50.4 |
| 6.5 | 19.8 | 46.5 | 53.4 | 35.1 | 24.0 | Fixed Assets (net) | 34.6 | 33.1 |
| 1.1 | 2.0 | 1.0 | 1.2 | .3 | 7.1 | Intangibles (net) | 1.1 | .7 |
| 14.1 | 17.4 | 10.8 | 16.2 | 21.4 | 20.8 | All Other Non-Current | 12.8 | 15.8 |
| 100.0 | 100.0 | 100.0 | 100.0 | 100.0 | 100.0 | Total | 100.0 | 100.0 |
| | | | | | | LIABILITIES | | |
| 4.3 | 4.1 | 1.6 | 2.4 | 3.6 | .4 | Notes Payable-Short Term | 2.3 | 6.0 |
| 2.2 | 2.8 | 1.7 | 1.1 | .9 | 1.5 | Cur. Mat.-L.T.D. | 3.0 | 2.6 |
| 8.9 | 6.4 | 4.5 | 4.0 | 2.8 | 1.6 | Trade Payables | 6.6 | 7.2 |
| .0 | .2 | .1 | .0 | .4 | .1 | Income Taxes Payable | .2 | .1 |
| 22.6 | 15.2 | 11.3 | 9.6 | 8.2 | 15.2 | All Other Current | 11.9 | 12.3 |
| 38.0 | 28.8 | 19.3 | 17.1 | 15.9 | 18.7 | Total Current | 24.0 | 28.1 |
| 40.5 | 32.1 | 26.3 | 15.2 | 15.5 | 18.3 | Long-Term Debt | 21.9 | 21.8 |
| .0 | .0 | .1 | .0 | .0 | .5 | Deferred Taxes | .1 | .0 |
| 1.9 | 3.2 | 4.7 | 3.6 | 3.6 | 3.1 | All Other Non-Current | 4.5 | 6.3 |
| 19.6 | 35.9 | 49.7 | 64.1 | 64.9 | 59.4 | Net Worth | 49.5 | 43.8 |
| 100.0 | 100.0 | 100.0 | 100.0 | 100.0 | 100.0 | Total Liabilites & Net Worth | 100.0 | 100.0 |
| | | | | | | INCOME DATA | | |
| 100.0 | 100.0 | 100.0 | 100.0 | 100.0 | 100.0 | Net Sales | 100.0 | 100.0 |
| | | | | | | Gross Profit | | |
| 89.3 | 85.1 | 92.1 | 96.4 | 89.7 | 89.8 | Operating Expenses | 89.7 | 92.7 |
| 10.7 | 14.9 | 7.9 | 3.6 | 10.3 | 10.2 | Operating Profit | 10.3 | 7.3 |
| 2.0 | 4.6 | 3.8 | 1.2 | .4 | 2.7 | All Other Expenses (net) | 2.3 | 3.7 |
| 8.7 | 10.3 | 4.0 | 2.3 | 10.0 | 7.5 | Profit Before Taxes | 8.0 | 3.6 |
| | | | | | | RATIOS | | |
| 11.5 | 7.9 | 4.8 | 4.9 | 3.6 | 6.0 | | 7.0 | 5.8 |
| 3.9 | 3.1 | 2.0 | 1.9 | 2.6 | 3.0 | Current | 2.7 | 2.5 |
| 1.3 | 1.2 | 1.1 | .9 | 1.7 | 1.0 | | 1.1 | 1.0 |
| 11.0 | 7.5 | 3.8 | 3.6 | 3.1 | 5.9 | | 6.7 | 5.4 |
| 3.6 | 2.8 | 1.9 | 1.4 | 2.5 | 2.8 | Quick | 2.2 | 2.1 |
| 1.1 | 1.1 | 1.0 | .7 | 1.3 | .9 | | .9 | .8 |
| 0 UND | 0 UND | 3 105.7 | 3 118.0 | 6 59.2 | 1 308.8 | | 1 711.0 | 2 163.6 |
| 2 179.9 | 7 49.0 | 7 50.5 | 11 32.6 | 8 44.4 | 20 18.7 | Sales/Receivables | 8 43.4 | 11 32.5 |
| 13 27.6 | 24 15.0 | 34 10.7 | 39 9.3 | 24 15.1 | 53 6.9 | | 26 14.3 | 32 11.3 |
| | | | | | | Cost of Sales/Inventory | | |
| | | | | | | Cost of Sales/Payables | | |
| 1.5 | 1.6 | 2.1 | 2.9 | 1.4 | .6 | | 1.9 | 2.0 |
| 4.6 | 4.3 | 5.8 | 9.6 | 5.3 | 3.5 | Sales/Working Capital | 4.1 | 4.9 |
| 16.8 | 33.7 | 35.7 | -69.6 | 7.2 | NM | | 32.8 | 256.8 |
| 9.0 | 12.4 | 3.7 | 12.6 | 19.0 | | | 10.2 | 7.6 |
| (23) 4.3 | (63) 3.6 | (64) 1.2 | (56) 2.3 | (10) 8.5 | | EBIT/Interest | (155) 3.3 | (225) 1.6 |
| 1.7 | .8 | -.3 | .0 | .6 | | | .8 | -1.3 |
| | | | | | | Net Profit + Depr., Dep., Amort./Cur. Mat. L/T/D | 6.8 | 6.5 |
| | | | | | | | (13) 3.0 | (16) 2.6 |
| | | | | | | | 1.3 | .0 |
| .0 | .0 | .2 | .4 | .2 | .0 | | .0 | .0 |
| .0 | .0 | .8 | .9 | .5 | .2 | Fixed/Worth | .5 | .5 |
| .0 | .7 | 2.3 | 1.3 | .9 | 2.2 | | 1.1 | 1.3 |
| .1 | .3 | .3 | .2 | .2 | .2 | | .2 | .2 |
| .6 | 1.3 | 1.0 | .5 | .4 | .5 | Debt/Worth | .6 | .8 |
| 19.1 | 5.2 | 2.9 | 1.2 | 1.4 | 4.5 | | 2.0 | 3.6 |
| 38.8 | 34.7 | 15.2 | 8.0 | 11.4 | | % Profit Before Taxes/Tangible Net Worth | 20.7 | 16.1 |
| (78) 11.7 | (120) 12.9 | (106) 4.0 | (88) 2.7 | 5.0 | | | (272) 6.6 | (348) 3.9 |
| -1.7 | .2 | -3.7 | -2.3 | .2 | | | -1.1 | -5.8 |
| 29.6 | 16.6 | 7.2 | 4.9 | 5.6 | 6.0 | % Profit Before Taxes/Total Assets | 12.2 | 9.6 |
| 8.5 | 7.2 | 1.8 | 1.7 | 3.7 | 2.0 | | 3.3 | 1.6 |
| -.5 | -.1 | -2.2 | -1.6 | .2 | .6 | | -.6 | -3.4 |
| UND | UND | 24.3 | 3.6 | 4.9 | UND | | 547.3 | 335.6 |
| UND | 442.9 | 1.6 | 1.0 | 1.1 | 7.3 | Sales/Net Fixed Assets | 4.1 | 5.5 |
| UND | 3.9 | .6 | .5 | .6 | .7 | | .9 | 1.1 |
| 3.3 | 2.1 | 1.3 | 1.1 | .8 | .7 | | 1.5 | 1.8 |
| 1.6 | 1.3 | .7 | .6 | .5 | .3 | Sales/Total Assets | .9 | 1.0 |
| 1.0 | .6 | .4 | .4 | .3 | .3 | | .5 | .5 |
| .3 | .3 | 1.9 | 2.5 | 2.2 | | | 1.6 | 1.3 |
| (14) 1.7 | (58) 1.5 | (80) 4.3 | (79) 5.8 | (12) 4.7 | | % Depr., Dep., Amort./Sales | (184) 3.9 | (240) 3.3 |
| 5.7 | 7.0 | 9.0 | 10.0 | 9.4 | | | 7.9 | 7.8 |
| 3.5 | 3.8 | 2.7 | | | | % Officers', Directors' Owners' Comp/Sales | 1.9 | 4.6 |
| (12) 5.3 | (25) 6.8 | (14) 10.2 | | | | | (19) 6.2 | (36) 9.0 |
| 9.4 | 10.7 | 32.4 | | | | | 14.0 | 15.5 |
| 47431M | 247824M | 532834M | 1767592M | 632848M | 1037019M | Net Sales ($) | 3576179M | 5037478M |
| 21722M | 157168M | 535562M | 2036509M | 884794M | 1457471M | Total Assets ($) | 4899800M | 6152411M |

© RMA 2012

**M = $ thousand    MM = $ million**
See Pages 9 through 22 for Explanation of Ratios and Data

| Comparative Historical Data | | | | Current Data Sorted by Sales | | | | | |
|---|---|---|---|---|---|---|---|---|---|
| | | | **Type of Statement** | | | | | | |
| 174 | 198 | 219 | Unqualified | 29 | 56 | 37 | 26 | 45 | 26 |
| 11 | 19 | 26 | Reviewed | 17 | 6 | 2 | 1 | | |
| 15 | 15 | 21 | Compiled | 10 | 7 | 1 | 2 | | 1 |
| 16 | 18 | 15 | Tax Returns | 10 | 3 | 2 | | | |
| 132 | 135 | 185 | Other | 88 | 47 | 16 | 13 | 13 | 8 |
| 4/1/09-3/31/10 ALL | 4/1/10-3/31/11 ALL | 4/1/11-3/31/12 ALL | | 156 (4/1-9/30/11) 0-1MM | 1-3MM | 3-5MM | 310 (10/1/11-3/31/12) 5-10MM | 10-25MM | 25MM & OVER |
| 348 | 385 | 466 | **NUMBER OF STATEMENTS** | 154 | 119 | 58 | 42 | 58 | 35 |
| % | % | % | **ASSETS** | % | % | % | % | % | % |
| 35.2 | 39.3 | 41.4 | Cash & Equivalents | 54.3 | 43.2 | 38.1 | 23.8 | 24.1 | 33.7 |
| 9.0 | 8.0 | 7.6 | Trade Receivables (net) | 6.1 | 6.4 | 7.2 | 12.6 | 9.6 | 9.3 |
| 1.2 | 1.6 | .7 | Inventory | .2 | .4 | 1.4 | .4 | 1.6 | 1.4 |
| 4.7 | 5.0 | 3.5 | All Other Current | 4.0 | 3.6 | 2.0 | 3.1 | 4.4 | 2.8 |
| 50.0 | 53.8 | 53.2 | Total Current | 64.6 | 53.5 | 48.8 | 39.9 | 39.7 | 47.1 |
| 36.7 | 30.4 | 30.3 | Fixed Assets (net) | 20.8 | 30.5 | 28.5 | 50.1 | 43.0 | 29.9 |
| .9 | .9 | 1.5 | Intangibles (net) | .8 | .9 | 2.9 | .1 | 2.3 | 4.6 |
| 12.4 | 14.8 | 15.0 | All Other Non-Current | 13.8 | 15.1 | 19.9 | 9.9 | 15.0 | 18.4 |
| 100.0 | 100.0 | 100.0 | Total | 100.0 | 100.0 | 100.0 | 100.0 | 100.0 | 100.0 |
| | | | **LIABILITIES** | | | | | | |
| 4.7 | 3.5 | 3.1 | Notes Payable-Short Term | 4.1 | 3.2 | 2.1 | 4.0 | 1.2 | 2.7 |
| 2.8 | 2.2 | 2.0 | Cur. Mat.-L.T.D. | 2.4 | 2.5 | 2.1 | .8 | 1.3 | .9 |
| 6.1 | 6.1 | 5.8 | Trade Payables | 6.6 | 4.7 | 7.4 | 4.5 | 5.7 | 5.6 |
| .1 | .1 | .1 | Income Taxes Payable | .0 | .1 | .6 | .0 | .1 | .1 |
| 12.2 | 11.4 | 14.6 | All Other Current | 17.7 | 11.6 | 13.5 | 12.2 | 14.4 | 16.1 |
| 25.8 | 23.3 | 25.7 | Total Current | 30.7 | 22.2 | 25.7 | 21.5 | 22.6 | 25.3 |
| 25.7 | 25.8 | 28.5 | Long-Term Debt | 38.1 | 36.4 | 21.3 | 13.5 | 13.6 | 14.0 |
| .0 | .0 | .0 | Deferred Taxes | .0 | .0 | .1 | .0 | .0 | .2 |
| 4.3 | 6.0 | 3.4 | All Other Non-Current | 1.7 | 1.8 | 3.7 | 10.2 | 4.9 | 4.6 |
| 44.2 | 44.8 | 42.5 | Net Worth | 29.5 | 39.6 | 49.3 | 54.9 | 58.9 | 55.8 |
| 100.0 | 100.0 | 100.0 | Total Liabilities & Net Worth | 100.0 | 100.0 | 100.0 | 100.0 | 100.0 | 100.0 |
| | | | **INCOME DATA** | | | | | | |
| 100.0 | 100.0 | 100.0 | Net Sales | 100.0 | 100.0 | 100.0 | 100.0 | 100.0 | 100.0 |
| | | | Gross Profit | | | | | | |
| 91.8 | 90.8 | 90.1 | Operating Expenses | 84.6 | 89.7 | 91.6 | 97.9 | 96.5 | 93.4 |
| 8.2 | 9.2 | 9.9 | Operating Profit | 15.4 | 10.3 | 8.4 | 2.1 | 3.5 | 6.6 |
| 4.5 | 1.9 | 3.0 | All Other Expenses (net) | 5.1 | 3.8 | 2.8 | -.5 | .6 | .4 |
| 3.7 | 7.3 | 6.8 | Profit Before Taxes | 10.4 | 6.5 | 5.6 | 2.6 | 2.9 | 6.2 |
| | | | **RATIOS** | | | | | | |
| 6.0 | 6.7 | 6.8 | | 11.2 | 8.7 | 4.6 | 3.9 | 3.3 | 4.7 |
| 2.4 | 3.0 | 2.6 | Current | 3.5 | 3.2 | 2.6 | 1.7 | 1.9 | 1.9 |
| 1.2 | 1.3 | 1.1 | | 1.1 | 1.6 | 1.2 | 1.0 | 1.0 | .9 |
| 5.7 | 6.5 | 6.3 | | 10.8 | 7.4 | 4.2 | 3.4 | 2.6 | 4.6 |
| (347) 2.1 | 2.3 | 2.3 | Quick | 3.0 | 2.8 | 2.3 | 1.4 | 1.6 | 1.9 |
| 1.0 | 1.0 | .9 | | 1.0 | 1.2 | 1.1 | 1.0 | .8 | .7 |
| 1 473.4 | 2 233.3 | 1 419.9 | | 0 UND | 1 404.6 | 2 163.2 | 4 93.6 | 3 139.1 | 7 49.2 |
| 10 35.0 | 9 41.2 | 7 51.2 | Sales/Receivables | 4 92.0 | 7 55.5 | 6 61.2 | 11 32.7 | 12 30.5 | 17 22.0 |
| 36 10.2 | 32 11.5 | 24 15.5 | | 15 24.7 | 23 15.8 | 26 14.0 | 22 16.4 | 43 8.5 | 45 8.2 |
| | | | Cost of Sales/Inventory | | | | | | |
| | | | Cost of Sales/Payables | | | | | | |
| 2.1 | 1.9 | 1.8 | | 1.1 | 1.9 | 2.8 | 3.5 | 3.5 | 2.3 |
| 4.9 | 4.9 | 5.3 | Sales/Working Capital | 3.1 | 4.0 | 5.7 | 9.6 | 8.8 | 10.3 |
| 30.5 | 25.4 | 34.5 | | 33.4 | 14.1 | 45.3 | 112.1 | -127.4 | -78.4 |
| 9.6 | 8.4 | 9.5 | | 6.0 | 9.0 | 8.6 | 11.1 | 14.3 | 17.0 |
| (204) 2.7 | (214) 2.5 | (223) 2.1 | EBIT/Interest | (53) 2.6 | (58) 1.7 | (32) 1.6 | (21) 1.2 | (36) 3.9 | (23) 3.6 |
| .2 | .2 | .3 | | .9 | .3 | .5 | -1.4 | .2 | .5 |
| 45.8 | | 5.5 | Net Profit + Depr., Dep., | | | | | | |
| (14) 8.1 | | (11) 3.2 | Amort./Cur. Mat. L/T/D | | | | | | |
| 2.1 | | .3 | | | | | | | |
| .0 | .0 | .0 | | .0 | .0 | .0 | .4 | .3 | .1 |
| .5 | .3 | .2 | Fixed/Worth | .0 | .1 | .3 | .9 | .8 | .3 |
| 1.3 | 1.2 | 1.1 | | .7 | 1.2 | 1.1 | 1.4 | 1.3 | 1.1 |
| .2 | .2 | .2 | | .2 | .2 | .3 | .2 | .3 | .3 |
| .8 | .6 | .7 | Debt/Worth | 1.0 | .7 | .8 | .6 | .7 | .6 |
| 2.7 | 2.3 | 2.9 | | 9.0 | 4.1 | 3.1 | 2.3 | 1.5 | 2.7 |
| 17.3 | 21.4 | 21.8 | % Profit Before Taxes/Tangible | 33.4 | 33.4 | 14.9 | 13.6 | 10.5 | 23.2 |
| (311) 4.2 | (345) 6.6 | (414) 6.6 | Net Worth | (126) 9.2 | (105) 12.0 | (55) 5.5 | (40) 3.7 | (56) 3.4 | (32) 7.1 |
| -4.4 | -.6 | -1.7 | | -1.5 | -2.5 | .0 | -2.3 | -3.3 | 1.2 |
| 9.2 | 14.3 | 12.5 | % Profit Before Taxes/Total | 19.9 | 17.2 | 9.6 | 4.8 | 6.4 | 11.2 |
| 2.0 | 3.8 | 3.4 | Assets | 4.9 | 5.7 | 2.7 | 2.1 | 2.9 | 2.5 |
| -2.8 | -.6 | -1.1 | | -.6 | -2.8 | .2 | -1.5 | -1.6 | .7 |
| 351.2 | UND | UND | | UND | UND | UND | 16.7 | 10.2 | 18.9 |
| 5.6 | 10.8 | 15.4 | Sales/Net Fixed Assets | UND | 31.6 | 20.8 | 1.7 | 2.2 | 5.4 |
| .8 | 1.0 | 1.0 | | 1.7 | 1.0 | .9 | .6 | .8 | 2.1 |
| 1.7 | 1.9 | 1.9 | | 1.7 | 1.9 | 2.6 | 1.9 | 1.7 | 1.7 |
| .8 | 1.0 | 1.0 | Sales/Total Assets | .9 | 1.1 | 1.0 | .8 | .9 | 1.1 |
| .4 | .5 | .5 | | .5 | .6 | .4 | .4 | .5 | .6 |
| 1.2 | 1.0 | 1.4 | | 3.2 | .6 | 1.0 | 2.0 | 1.6 | 1.0 |
| (220) 4.0 | (220) 2.9 | (250) 4.0 | % Depr., Dep., Amort./Sales | (38) 10.6 | (58) 2.9 | (36) 3.8 | (37) 6.0 | (52) 3.3 | (29) 2.4 |
| 9.4 | 8.5 | 9.3 | | 16.8 | 8.5 | 9.9 | 9.5 | 6.3 | 4.3 |
| 5.3 | 5.1 | 3.2 | % Officers', Directors' | 4.6 | 3.8 | | | | |
| (43) 8.1 | (53) 11.3 | (55) 5.5 | Owners' Comp/Sales | (19) 6.9 | (23) 7.2 | | | | |
| 23.1 | 24.1 | 11.0 | | 10.8 | 13.0 | | | | |
| 4896269M | 5335122M | 4265548M | Net Sales ($) | 60837M | 212025M | 228148M | 297780M | 943177M | 2523581M |
| 5458144M | 6875674M | 5093226M | Total Assets ($) | 123548M | 302065M | 454382M | 477575M | 1262710M | 2472946M |

M = $ thousand    MM = $ million
See Pages 9 through 22 for Explanation of Ratios and Data

## Current Data Sorted by Assets | Comparative Historical Data

| Type of Statement | 0-500M | 500M-2MM | 2-10MM | 10-50MM | 50-100MM | 100-250MM | | 4/1/07-3/31/08 ALL | 4/1/08-3/31/09 ALL |
|---|---|---|---|---|---|---|---|---|---|
| Unqualified | | 1 | 2 | 6 | | 1 | | 12 | 11 |
| Reviewed | | 4 | 3 | 2 | | | | 11 | 16 |
| Compiled | 3 | 2 | 3 | 1 | | | | 16 | 13 |
| Tax Returns | 8 | 7 | 5 | 2 | | | | 25 | 23 |
| Other | 7 | 10 | 15 | 6 | 1 | | | 41 | 44 |
| | 13 (4/1-9/30/11) | | | 76 (10/1/11-3/31/12) | | | | | |
| **NUMBER OF STATEMENTS** | 18 | 24 | 28 | 17 | 1 | 1 | | 105 | 107 |
| **ASSETS** | % | % | % | % | % | % | | % | % |
| Cash & Equivalents | 27.7 | 19.7 | 8.0 | 22.4 | | | | 15.4 | 16.8 |
| Trade Receivables (net) | 9.6 | 15.9 | 18.1 | 8.2 | | | | 14.7 | 14.2 |
| Inventory | 19.0 | 5.4 | 15.7 | 2.7 | | | | 10.4 | 15.3 |
| All Other Current | 6.2 | 6.6 | 2.0 | .4 | | | | 3.0 | 5.4 |
| Total Current | 62.4 | 47.6 | 43.8 | 33.8 | | | | 43.5 | 51.7 |
| Fixed Assets (net) | 29.3 | 42.7 | 43.3 | 39.5 | | | | 42.0 | 34.7 |
| Intangibles (net) | 3.1 | 4.0 | 4.5 | .7 | | | | 4.3 | 2.6 |
| All Other Non-Current | 5.2 | 5.7 | 8.4 | 26.1 | | | | 10.2 | 11.0 |
| Total | 100.0 | 100.0 | 100.0 | 100.0 | | | | 100.0 | 100.0 |
| **LIABILITIES** | | | | | | | | | |
| Notes Payable-Short Term | 30.6 | 6.4 | 5.9 | 5.2 | | | | 13.2 | 13.1 |
| Cur. Mat.-L.T.D. | 2.9 | 3.7 | 1.4 | 2.7 | | | | 5.5 | 3.6 |
| Trade Payables | 19.2 | 5.4 | 13.4 | 6.6 | | | | 9.3 | 10.1 |
| Income Taxes Payable | .0 | .0 | .1 | 1.3 | | | | .3 | .2 |
| All Other Current | 14.9 | 12.2 | 4.3 | 4.0 | | | | 11.1 | 16.8 |
| Total Current | 67.5 | 27.7 | 25.1 | 19.7 | | | | 39.4 | 43.8 |
| Long-Term Debt | 19.2 | 58.9 | 28.0 | 30.3 | | | | 31.6 | 29.7 |
| Deferred Taxes | .0 | .0 | .2 | .0 | | | | .1 | .1 |
| All Other Non-Current | 9.2 | 4.4 | 4.7 | 14.1 | | | | 3.5 | 8.7 |
| Net Worth | 4.1 | 9.0 | 42.1 | 36.0 | | | | 25.4 | 17.8 |
| Total Liabilities & Net Worth | 100.0 | 100.0 | 100.0 | 100.0 | | | | 100.0 | 100.0 |
| **INCOME DATA** | | | | | | | | | |
| Net Sales | 100.0 | 100.0 | 100.0 | 100.0 | | | | 100.0 | 100.0 |
| Gross Profit | | | | | | | | | |
| Operating Expenses | 86.6 | 83.8 | 78.2 | 83.0 | | | | 82.0 | 85.8 |
| Operating Profit | 13.4 | 16.2 | 21.8 | 17.0 | | | | 18.0 | 14.2 |
| All Other Expenses (net) | 1.0 | 5.1 | 5.2 | 1.3 | | | | 7.2 | 5.2 |
| Profit Before Taxes | 12.4 | 11.1 | 16.5 | 15.7 | | | | 10.8 | 9.0 |
| **RATIOS** | | | | | | | | | |
| Current | 3.3 | 4.5 | 3.0 | 8.1 | | | | 2.2 | 2.6 |
| | 1.3 | 2.0 | 1.8 | 2.0 | | | | 1.2 | 1.5 |
| | .7 | 1.0 | .6 | .7 | | | | .6 | .8 |
| Quick | 2.7 | 3.9 | 2.5 | 8.1 | | | | 1.7 | 1.8 |
| | .8 | 1.2 | 1.0 | 2.0 | | | | .8 | .7 |
| | .3 | .6 | .4 | .6 | | | | .2 | .2 |
| Sales/Receivables | 0 UND | 0 UND | 0 UND | 5 68.2 | | | | 0 UND | 0 UND |
| | 0 UND | 0 UND | 23 15.8 | 23 15.9 | | | | 5 80.3 | 7 49.4 |
| | 4 84.8 | 51 7.1 | 60 6.1 | 42 8.6 | | | | 39 9.3 | 33 10.9 |
| Cost of Sales/Inventory | | | | | | | | | |
| Cost of Sales/Payables | | | | | | | | | |
| Sales/Working Capital | 10.9 | 4.5 | 4.4 | 1.6 | | | | 8.4 | 6.0 |
| | 111.9 | 8.3 | 8.4 | 16.6 | | | | 40.2 | 29.4 |
| | -19.7 | 564.1 | NM | -10.3 | | | | -22.0 | -26.8 |
| EBIT/Interest | | 7.3 | 7.7 | 421.0 | | | | 9.1 | 14.7 |
| | | (19) 3.3 | (21) 4.1 | (11) 3.0 | | | | (72) 5.1 | (76) 4.1 |
| | | -4.0 | 2.6 | .5 | | | | 1.1 | .8 |
| Net Profit + Depr., Dep., Amort./Cur. Mat. L/T/D | | | | | | | | 5.1 | 5.7 |
| | | | | | | | | (11) 2.5 | (12) 3.9 |
| | | | | | | | | 1.1 | .7 |
| Fixed/Worth | .2 | .5 | .1 | .0 | | | | .3 | .2 |
| | 1.4 | 1.0 | 1.1 | 1.1 | | | | 1.2 | .9 |
| | -1.8 | 6.6 | 1.9 | 13.9 | | | | 5.6 | 9.6 |
| Debt/Worth | .4 | .6 | .5 | .4 | | | | .6 | .8 |
| | 5.4 | 1.6 | 1.3 | 1.4 | | | | 2.1 | 1.9 |
| | -3.5 | 19.2 | 6.4 | 16.0 | | | | 12.9 | 84.5 |
| % Profit Before Taxes/Tangible Net Worth | 390.8 | 58.2 | 60.9 | 12.3 | | | | 47.9 | 42.7 |
| | (12) 52.0 | (20) 9.5 | (25) 23.7 | (14) 7.5 | | | | (83) 21.0 | (81) 15.9 |
| | 13.0 | -15.3 | 4.3 | 1.1 | | | | 4.5 | 2.8 |
| % Profit Before Taxes/Total Assets | 98.8 | 19.1 | 15.6 | 5.2 | | | | 17.2 | 18.9 |
| | 31.2 | 5.2 | 6.4 | 2.6 | | | | 6.5 | 5.4 |
| | -2.3 | -4.1 | 2.0 | -1.8 | | | | .4 | .0 |
| Sales/Net Fixed Assets | 350.4 | 39.0 | 35.1 | 137.5 | | | | 36.4 | 80.3 |
| | 57.1 | 7.5 | 3.7 | 2.4 | | | | 7.2 | 14.1 |
| | 4.8 | .8 | .4 | .5 | | | | 1.1 | 1.7 |
| Sales/Total Assets | 9.5 | 3.7 | 2.9 | 1.4 | | | | 4.7 | 6.2 |
| | 4.3 | 1.1 | 1.4 | .4 | | | | 1.6 | 2.3 |
| | 2.0 | .5 | .2 | .1 | | | | .5 | .6 |
| % Depr., Dep., Amort./Sales | .1 | .7 | .8 | 1.8 | | | | 1.0 | .6 |
| | (10) .8 | (19) 3.2 | (22) 3.0 | (11) 5.7 | | | | (84) 2.3 | (82) 1.5 |
| | 4.6 | 6.4 | 12.8 | 10.1 | | | | 7.2 | 6.4 |
| % Officers', Directors' Owners' Comp/Sales | | | 1.0 | | | | | 1.5 | 1.8 |
| | | | (10) 5.1 | | | | | (30) 2.3 | (31) 4.1 |
| | | | 21.9 | | | | | 6.6 | 9.5 |
| Net Sales ($) | 36228M | 67126M | 179915M | 329389M | 177500M | 820286M | | 2427861M | 5667577M |
| Total Assets ($) | 5072M | 26226M | 122785M | 297480M | 60896M | 215560M | | 1328845M | 1874564M |

© RMA 2012

M = $ thousand   MM = $ million
See Pages 9 through 22 for Explanation of Ratios and Data

## Comparative Historical Data | Current Data Sorted by Sales

| Type of Statement | 4/1/09-3/31/10 ALL | 4/1/10-3/31/11 ALL | 4/1/11-3/31/12 ALL | 0-1MM | 1-3MM | 3-5MM | 5-10MM | 10-25MM | 25MM & OVER |
|---|---|---|---|---|---|---|---|---|---|
| Unqualified | 12 | 14 | 10 | 1 | 1 | 1 | 1 | 5 | 1 |
| Reviewed | 15 | 15 | 9 | 1 | 2 | | 2 | 2 | 2 |
| Compiled | 14 | 13 | 9 | | 3 | 3 | 2 | 1 | |
| Tax Returns | 15 | 16 | 22 | 6 | 10 | 3 | 2 | 1 | |
| Other | 40 | 42 | 39 | 16 | 10 | 2 | 3 | 4 | 4 |
| | 96 | 100 | 89 | 13 (4/1-9/30/11) | | | 76 (10/1/11-3/31/12) | | |
| **NUMBER OF STATEMENTS** | 96 | 100 | 89 | 26 | 25 | 8 | 10 | 13 | 7 |
| **ASSETS** | % | % | % | % | % | % | % | % | % |
| Cash & Equivalents | 13.4 | 17.5 | 17.8 | 9.5 | 22.0 | | 15.7 | 28.0 | |
| Trade Receivables (net) | 16.0 | 15.4 | 13.6 | 6.3 | 11.2 | | 19.5 | 26.0 | |
| Inventory | 10.7 | 11.2 | 12.1 | .7 | 16.0 | | 16.1 | 15.9 | |
| All Other Current | 2.9 | 3.1 | 3.8 | 3.9 | 3.3 | | 8.6 | 4.2 | |
| Total Current | 43.1 | 47.2 | 47.4 | 20.4 | 52.5 | | 59.9 | 74.1 | |
| Fixed Assets (net) | 39.4 | 35.5 | 39.1 | 67.0 | 23.9 | | 33.9 | 18.6 | |
| Intangibles (net) | 6.8 | 4.6 | 3.3 | 5.0 | 3.5 | | .8 | 3.0 | |
| All Other Non-Current | 10.7 | 12.6 | 10.2 | 7.6 | 20.1 | | 5.4 | 4.3 | |
| Total | 100.0 | 100.0 | 100.0 | 100.0 | 100.0 | | 100.0 | 100.0 | |
| **LIABILITIES** | | | | | | | | | |
| Notes Payable-Short Term | 10.2 | 17.9 | 10.8 | 1.0 | 9.0 | | 46.9 | 10.9 | |
| Cur. Mat.-L.T.D. | 3.2 | 3.0 | 2.9 | 1.4 | 3.6 | | 1.6 | 3.6 | |
| Trade Payables | 7.0 | 11.2 | 11.2 | 5.2 | 8.0 | | 12.8 | 17.2 | |
| Income Taxes Payable | .2 | .1 | .3 | .2 | .0 | | .2 | 1.3 | |
| All Other Current | 6.6 | 8.4 | 9.0 | 9.1 | 8.0 | | 10.1 | 10.5 | |
| Total Current | 27.2 | 40.7 | 34.1 | 16.9 | 28.6 | | 71.6 | 43.5 | |
| Long-Term Debt | 32.3 | 26.9 | 34.3 | 39.2 | 34.7 | | 28.5 | 47.2 | |
| Deferred Taxes | .7 | .2 | .1 | .0 | .0 | | .5 | .0 | |
| All Other Non-Current | 5.2 | 5.0 | 7.2 | 8.7 | 5.7 | | 3.2 | 2.0 | |
| Net Worth | 34.6 | 27.3 | 24.2 | 35.2 | 31.0 | | -3.7 | 7.3 | |
| Total Liabilities & Net Worth | 100.0 | 100.0 | 100.0 | 100.0 | 100.0 | | 100.0 | 100.0 | |
| **INCOME DATA** | | | | | | | | | |
| Net Sales | 100.0 | 100.0 | 100.0 | 100.0 | 100.0 | | 100.0 | 100.0 | |
| Gross Profit | | | | | | | | | |
| Operating Expenses | 81.4 | 83.3 | 82.8 | 69.9 | 76.9 | | 95.0 | 96.0 | |
| Operating Profit | 18.6 | 16.7 | 17.2 | 30.1 | 23.1 | | 5.0 | 4.0 | |
| All Other Expenses (net) | 5.8 | 3.2 | 3.5 | 10.1 | 1.1 | | 1.7 | -.1 | |
| Profit Before Taxes | 12.9 | 13.5 | 13.8 | 20.1 | 22.0 | | 3.3 | 4.1 | |
| **RATIOS** | | | | | | | | | |
| Current | 3.4 | 3.1 | 4.0 | 4.0 | 6.8 | | 2.5 | 9.5 | |
| | 1.8 | 1.4 | 1.8 | 1.6 | 1.6 | | 1.6 | 2.3 | |
| | .8 | .8 | .8 | .7 | 1.1 | | .6 | 1.1 | |
| Quick | 2.6 | 2.4 | 3.4 | 3.5 | 4.3 | | 1.7 | 7.1 | |
| | 1.0 | 1.0 | 1.1 | 1.6 | 1.1 | | .7 | 1.9 | |
| | .4 | .4 | .4 | .7 | .7 | | .4 | .4 | |
| Sales/Receivables | 0 UND | 0 UND | 0 UND | 0 UND | 0 UND | | 0 UND | 4 85.6 | |
| | 9 42.8 | 3 115.2 | 8 44.1 | 0 UND | 2 241.0 | | 33 10.9 | 22 16.8 | |
| | 47 7.8 | 40 9.2 | 42 8.7 | 4 82.8 | 61 6.0 | | 49 7.5 | 51 7.2 | |
| Cost of Sales/Inventory | | | | | | | | | |
| Cost of Sales/Payables | | | | | | | | | |
| Sales/Working Capital | 4.6 | 6.6 | 4.7 | 3.5 | 3.3 | | 7.7 | 4.6 | |
| | 22.9 | 26.4 | 12.8 | 40.1 | 9.4 | | 11.9 | 8.0 | |
| | -45.4 | -34.0 | -35.1 | -10.0 | 64.7 | | -18.9 | 450.8 | |
| EBIT/Interest | 14.2 | 22.8 | 15.5 | 5.6 | 57.2 | | | 41.1 | |
| | (69) 3.7 | (65) 6.6 | (61) 3.5 | (16) 3.1 | (14) 14.1 | | (10) 3.1 | | |
| | .5 | 1.6 | .7 | -.8 | 2.1 | | | .5 | |
| Net Profit + Depr., Dep., Amort./Cur. Mat. L/T/D | 5.3 | | | | | | | | |
| | (13) 1.4 | | | | | | | | |
| | .9 | | | | | | | | |
| Fixed/Worth | .3 | .2 | .2 | 1.1 | .1 | | .5 | .0 | |
| | .9 | .7 | 1.1 | 1.9 | .6 | | .9 | .2 | |
| | 5.5 | 2.9 | 8.5 | UND | 1.5 | | 6.1 | 1.4 | |
| Debt/Worth | .6 | .4 | .5 | .5 | .4 | | 1.6 | .2 | |
| | 1.6 | 1.1 | 1.6 | 1.4 | 1.6 | | 3.2 | .9 | |
| | 8.9 | 6.4 | 15.0 | UND | 16.3 | | 12.7 | 4.9 | |
| % Profit Before Taxes/Tangible Net Worth | 34.4 | 53.5 | 57.5 | 58.5 | 54.8 | | | 54.5 | |
| | (77) 14.0 | (82) 17.9 | (73) 11.4 | (21) 8.5 | (20) 13.1 | | (12) 13.0 | | |
| | .7 | 4.9 | 3.9 | -1.4 | 6.6 | | | 2.6 | |
| % Profit Before Taxes/Total Assets | 19.0 | 28.3 | 17.2 | 12.4 | 26.2 | | 28.7 | 45.3 | |
| | 4.5 | 7.5 | 4.8 | 2.4 | 6.6 | | 5.9 | 6.7 | |
| | -1.0 | 2.0 | -.1 | -1.7 | 1.5 | | -5.2 | 1.7 | |
| Sales/Net Fixed Assets | 32.1 | 62.5 | 67.2 | 2.8 | 115.3 | | 45.6 | 264.5 | |
| | 5.8 | 10.9 | 8.6 | .3 | 16.0 | | 18.6 | 47.0 | |
| | .6 | 1.4 | .9 | .1 | 3.5 | | 1.7 | 16.2 | |
| Sales/Total Assets | 3.2 | 4.5 | 3.7 | .9 | 3.9 | | 5.8 | 6.2 | |
| | 1.7 | 2.2 | 1.5 | .2 | 1.3 | | 2.7 | 3.5 | |
| | .4 | .6 | .3 | .1 | .2 | | 1.3 | 1.9 | |
| % Depr., Dep., Amort./Sales | .9 | .6 | .7 | 5.0 | .7 | | | .5 | |
| | (72) 3.0 | (71) 1.9 | (64) 2.0 | (16) 15.3 | (15) 1.1 | | (10) 1.1 | | |
| | 8.2 | 7.0 | 10.5 | 22.6 | 6.3 | | | 2.0 | |
| % Officers', Directors' Owners' Comp/Sales | 2.1 | 2.3 | 2.9 | | 5.2 | | | | |
| | (18) 5.8 | (31) 5.7 | (27) 6.5 | | (12) 7.5 | | | | |
| | 9.0 | 19.4 | 19.7 | | 16.4 | | | | |
| Net Sales ($) | 2703065M | 1980590M | 1610444M | 11135M | 42434M | 28538M | 72613M | 199896M | 1255828M |
| Total Assets ($) | 1588287M | 1206599M | 728019M | 70876M | 103387M | 27997M | 47263M | 83998M | 394498M |

© RMA 2012

M = $ thousand      MM = $ million
See Pages 9 through 22 for Explanation of Ratios and Data

# PUBLIC ADMINISTRATION

## Current Data Sorted by Assets            Comparative Historical Data

| | | | | | | Type of Statement | | |
|---|---|---|---|---|---|---|---|---|
| 2 | 6 | 25 | 55 | 33 | 43 | Unqualified | 63 | 72 |
| | | | 1 | | | Reviewed | 1 | 1 |
| | | | | | | Compiled | 3 | 1 |
| | | | | | | Tax Returns | 5 | 3 |
| 1 | 1 | 7 | 4 | 1 | 2 | Other | 8 | 17 |
| | 163 (4/1-9/30/11) | | 18 (10/1/11-3/31/12) | | | | 4/1/07-3/31/08 | 4/1/08-3/31/09 |
| 0-500M | 500M-2MM | 2-10MM | 10-50MM | 50-100MM | 100-250MM | | ALL | ALL |
| 3 | 7 | 32 | 60 | 34 | 45 | NUMBER OF STATEMENTS | 80 | 94 |
| % | % | % | % | % | % | ASSETS | % | % |
| | | 23.5 | 22.8 | 16.2 | 20.6 | Cash & Equivalents | 23.7 | 25.6 |
| | | 14.2 | 7.9 | 3.6 | 4.6 | Trade Receivables (net) | 5.1 | 5.5 |
| | | 1.9 | .5 | .3 | .1 | Inventory | .7 | .9 |
| | | 2.9 | 5.1 | 2.8 | 2.7 | All Other Current | 4.7 | 5.6 |
| | | 42.5 | 36.3 | 22.9 | 28.0 | Total Current | 34.2 | 37.6 |
| | | 44.6 | 53.2 | 66.6 | 65.6 | Fixed Assets (net) | 56.6 | 53.7 |
| | | .4 | .6 | .2 | .5 | Intangibles (net) | .7 | .3 |
| | | 12.6 | 9.9 | 10.3 | 5.9 | All Other Non-Current | 8.5 | 8.4 |
| | | 100.0 | 100.0 | 100.0 | 100.0 | Total | 100.0 | 100.0 |
| | | | | | | LIABILITIES | | |
| | | 2.1 | .5 | .0 | .2 | Notes Payable-Short Term | 2.0 | 3.5 |
| | | 1.4 | 3.5 | 2.5 | 1.7 | Cur. Mat.-L.T.D. | 1.6 | 1.6 |
| | | 5.0 | 3.3 | 1.3 | 1.7 | Trade Payables | 3.0 | 4.1 |
| | | .0 | .1 | .0 | .0 | Income Taxes Payable | .1 | .5 |
| | | 20.0 | 9.2 | 2.8 | 3.3 | All Other Current | 5.8 | 6.3 |
| | | 28.5 | 16.6 | 6.6 | 6.9 | Total Current | 12.5 | 16.0 |
| | | 15.5 | 33.0 | 38.1 | 25.2 | Long-Term Debt | 23.3 | 20.7 |
| | | .0 | .0 | .0 | .0 | Deferred Taxes | .0 | .0 |
| | | 1.5 | 4.4 | 1.4 | 1.1 | All Other Non-Current | 4.3 | 6.9 |
| | | 54.4 | 46.0 | 53.9 | 66.8 | Net Worth | 59.9 | 56.2 |
| | | 100.0 | 100.0 | 100.0 | 100.0 | Total Liabilties & Net Worth | 100.0 | 100.0 |
| | | | | | | INCOME DATA | | |
| | | 100.0 | 100.0 | 100.0 | 100.0 | Net Sales | 100.0 | 100.0 |
| | | | | | | Gross Profit | | |
| | | 88.4 | 89.0 | 88.4 | 88.6 | Operating Expenses | 80.4 | 86.9 |
| | | 11.6 | 11.0 | 11.6 | 11.4 | Operating Profit | 19.6 | 13.1 |
| | | 3.3 | 7.6 | 4.2 | 2.5 | All Other Expenses (net) | 5.3 | 4.3 |
| | | 8.3 | 3.5 | 7.4 | 8.9 | Profit Before Taxes | 14.3 | 8.8 |
| | | | | | | RATIOS | | |
| | | 4.7 | 4.7 | 4.8 | 6.2 | | 7.2 | 6.2 |
| | | 2.2 | 2.7 | 3.0 | 3.7 | Current | 3.3 | 3.0 |
| | | .9 | 1.5 | 2.2 | 2.5 | | 1.8 | 1.5 |
| | | 4.4 | 3.8 | 4.3 | 6.0 | | 6.8 | 5.6 |
| | | 1.9 | 2.3 | 2.7 | 3.7 | Quick | 2.7 | 2.8 |
| | | .9 | 1.4 | 1.9 | 2.2 | | 1.3 | 1.2 |
| | (2) | 196.3 (8) | 46.2 (12) | 30.1 (14) | 26.1 | | (0) 972.5 | (2) 171.9 |
| | 23 | 16.0 31 | 11.6 29 | 12.8 30 | 12.0 | Sales/Receivables | 18 20.1 | 13 27.2 |
| | 46 | 8.0 60 | 6.1 43 | 8.5 57 | 6.4 | | 41 8.8 | 37 10.0 |
| | | | | | | Cost of Sales/Inventory | | |
| | | | | | | Cost of Sales/Payables | | |
| | | 1.4 | 1.9 | 1.2 | 1.2 | | 1.5 | 1.4 |
| | | 3.6 | 3.4 | 2.4 | 2.0 | Sales/Working Capital | 2.7 | 3.3 |
| | | -164.9 | 8.2 | 4.6 | 3.4 | | 9.0 | 13.2 |
| | | 13.0 | 8.1 | 8.1 | 7.6 | | 17.0 | 8.6 |
| | | (24) 3.6 | (47) 2.3 | (31) 2.3 | (41) 4.1 | EBIT/Interest | (52) 5.9 | (67) 3.7 |
| | | -2.1 | .9 | .7 | 1.1 | | 2.0 | .1 |
| | | | | | | Net Profit + Depr., Dep., Amort./Cur. Mat. L/T/D | | |
| | | .4 | .5 | 1.0 | .9 | | .6 | .5 |
| | | .8 | 1.1 | 1.2 | 1.0 | Fixed/Worth | 1.0 | 1.0 |
| | | 1.3 | 1.7 | 1.9 | 1.4 | | 1.5 | 1.5 |
| | | .2 | .4 | .4 | .3 | | .2 | .2 |
| | | .5 | .7 | .6 | .4 | Debt/Worth | .6 | .5 |
| | | 2.6 | 1.6 | 2.0 | .8 | | 1.3 | 1.2 |
| | | 16.5 | 8.6 | 6.1 | 5.8 | | 14.2 | 15.3 |
| | | (28) 5.7 | (56) 3.6 | (32) 2.1 | (44) 2.6 | % Profit Before Taxes/Tangible Net Worth | (77) 5.5 | (91) 5.2 |
| | | -3.1 | -.1 | .0 | .0 | | 1.4 | .8 |
| | | 8.6 | 4.6 | 3.9 | 4.8 | | 7.6 | 8.1 |
| | | 2.7 | 1.7 | 1.4 | 1.6 | % Profit Before Taxes/Total Assets | 3.3 | 2.8 |
| | | -3.4 | -.1 | -.1 | .2 | | 1.1 | .0 |
| | | 296.3 | 2.7 | .8 | .6 | | 1.5 | 8.9 |
| | | 1.2 | .7 | .5 | .4 | Sales/Net Fixed Assets | .6 | .6 |
| | | .3 | .3 | .3 | .3 | | .3 | .4 |
| | | 2.0 | 1.2 | .5 | .4 | | .6 | .8 |
| | | .7 | .4 | .3 | .3 | Sales/Total Assets | .4 | .4 |
| | | .2 | .2 | .2 | .2 | | .2 | .2 |
| | | 1.8 | 4.9 | 5.4 | 5.3 | | 4.7 | 4.5 |
| | | (21) 6.0 | (44) 7.5 | (33) 9.7 | (32) 12.4 | % Depr., Dep., Amort./Sales | (49) 8.9 | (55) 10.2 |
| | | 16.4 | 11.9 | 15.9 | 17.2 | | 14.9 | 16.7 |
| | | | | | | % Officers', Directors' Owners' Comp/Sales | 4.5 | 1.3 |
| | | | | | | | (10) 6.8 | (14) 8.6 |
| | | | | | | | 16.7 | 20.9 |
| 1861M | 22836M | 212881M | 1631724M | 845494M | 3415874M | Net Sales ($) | 2174528M | 2897555M |
| 806M | 9408M | 198924M | 1646884M | 2502283M | 7014877M | Total Assets ($) | 4021140M | 4917901M |

M = $ thousand      MM = $ million
See Pages 9 through 22 for Explanation of Ratios and Data

## Comparative Historical Data / Current Data Sorted by Sales

| 103 | 109 | 164 | | 0-1MM | 1-3MM | 3-5MM | 5-10MM | 10-25MM | 25MM & OVER |
|---|---|---|---|---|---|---|---|---|---|
| | | | **Type of Statement** | | | | | | |
| 103 | 109 | 164 | Unqualified | 6 | 15 | 16 | 16 | 53 | 58 |
| 5 | 2 | 1 | Reviewed | | | | | | |
| 5 | 1 | | Compiled | | | 1 | | | |
| | | | Tax Returns | | | | | | |
| 21 | 35 | 16 | Other | 1 | 3 | 2 | 2 | 5 | 3 |
| 4/1/09-3/31/10 ALL | 4/1/10-3/31/11 ALL | 4/1/11-3/31/12 ALL | | | 163 (4/1-9/30/11) | | 18 (10/1/11-3/31/12) | | |
| 134 | 147 | 181 | **NUMBER OF STATEMENTS** | 7 | 18 | 19 | 18 | 58 | 61 |
| % | % | % | **ASSETS** | % | % | % | % | % | % |
| 21.4 | 23.3 | 22.6 | Cash & Equivalents | | 26.5 | 12.5 | 22.5 | 19.7 | 26.3 |
| 7.6 | 7.7 | 7.6 | Trade Receivables (net) | | 5.9 | 3.0 | 4.0 | 8.1 | 10.8 |
| 1.0 | 1.4 | .7 | Inventory | | .3 | .9 | .2 | .4 | .3 |
| 3.8 | 3.3 | 3.4 | All Other Current | | .6 | 2.9 | 3.5 | 1.7 | 6.4 |
| 33.8 | 35.7 | 34.3 | Total Current | | 33.3 | 19.3 | 30.2 | 30.0 | 43.9 |
| 55.6 | 53.1 | 56.0 | Fixed Assets (net) | | 55.9 | 67.4 | 59.2 | 60.7 | 48.3 |
| .2 | .5 | .4 | Intangibles (net) | | .2 | 1.0 | .0 | .3 | .6 |
| 10.4 | 10.7 | 9.2 | All Other Non-Current | | 10.6 | 12.3 | 10.6 | 9.0 | 7.2 |
| 100.0 | 100.0 | 100.0 | Total | | 100.0 | 100.0 | 100.0 | 100.0 | 100.0 |
| | | | **LIABILITIES** | | | | | | |
| 1.7 | 2.1 | .9 | Notes Payable-Short Term | | 3.6 | 1.2 | .0 | 1.1 | .2 |
| 2.2 | 2.9 | 2.4 | Cur. Mat.-L.T.D. | | 1.7 | 1.9 | 1.9 | 1.9 | 3.5 |
| 4.0 | 3.5 | 3.3 | Trade Payables | | 2.5 | 1.3 | 2.7 | 4.4 | 3.5 |
| .3 | .5 | .0 | Income Taxes Payable | | .0 | .0 | .3 | .0 | .0 |
| 9.1 | 10.9 | 8.3 | All Other Current | | 4.4 | 3.0 | 4.4 | 11.6 | 9.9 |
| 17.3 | 19.9 | 14.9 | Total Current | | 12.2 | 7.3 | 9.3 | 19.1 | 17.1 |
| 24.7 | 25.6 | 27.6 | Long-Term Debt | | 17.4 | 38.1 | 21.8 | 29.3 | 27.2 |
| .1 | .0 | .0 | Deferred Taxes | | .0 | .0 | .0 | .0 | .0 |
| 4.0 | 4.3 | 2.5 | All Other Non-Current | | 2.0 | 2.8 | 1.9 | 1.5 | 3.8 |
| 53.8 | 50.2 | 55.0 | Net Worth | | 68.4 | 51.9 | 67.0 | *50.2 | 52.0 |
| 100.0 | 100.0 | 100.0 | Total Liabilities & Net Worth | | 100.0 | 100.0 | 100.0 | 100.0 | 100.0 |
| | | | **INCOME DATA** | | | | | | |
| 100.0 | 100.0 | 100.0 | Net Sales | | 100.0 | 100.0 | 100.0 | 100.0 | 100.0 |
| | | | Gross Profit | | | | | | |
| 90.0 | 88.0 | 88.8 | Operating Expenses | | 84.8 | 87.6 | 87.4 | 89.3 | 91.8 |
| 10.0 | 12.0 | 11.2 | Operating Profit | | 15.2 | 12.4 | 12.6 | 10.7 | 8.2 |
| 4.9 | 5.5 | 4.7 | All Other Expenses (net) | | 5.9 | 10.8 | 4.7 | 3.8 | 3.1 |
| 5.2 | 6.5 | 6.5 | Profit Before Taxes | | 9.4 | 1.5 | 7.9 | 6.9 | 5.1 |
| | | | **RATIOS** | | | | | | |
| 5.1 | 4.6 | 5.1 | | | 7.3 | 4.2 | 4.8 | 4.7 | 6.1 |
| 2.5 | 2.7 | 3.1 | Current | | 3.6 | 1.9 | 3.0 | 2.8 | 3.1 |
| 1.1 | 1.2 | 1.8 | | | 1.3 | .9 | 1.8 | 2.0 | 2.1 |
| 4.8 | 4.1 | 4.5 | | | 7.2 | 2.7 | 4.5 | 4.3 | 5.5 |
| 2.1 | 2.2 | 2.7 | Quick | | 3.6 | 1.4 | 2.9 | 2.6 | 2.8 |
| .9 | 1.1 | 1.5 | | | 1.3 | .7 | 1.8 | 1.5 | 1.9 |
| 5  76.0 | 1  376.2 | 9  39.5 | | 0  UND | 8  48.3 | 8  46.7 | 17  21.5 | 11  34.5 | |
| 23  15.7 | 20  18.5 | 28  13.1 | Sales/Receivables | 25  14.6 | 23  15.9 | 37  9.8 | 33  11.0 | 24  15.0 | |
| 46  7.9 | 48  7.5 | 49  7.4 | | 61  6.0 | 63  5.8 | 60  6.1 | 51  7.1 | 41  8.8 | |
| | | | Cost of Sales/Inventory | | | | | | |
| | | | Cost of Sales/Payables | | | | | | |
| 1.8 | 1.9 | 1.5 | | | 1.3 | 1.4 | 1.3 | 1.4 | 1.7 |
| 3.9 | 4.5 | 2.7 | Sales/Working Capital | | 2.1 | 3.8 | 2.6 | 2.7 | 3.0 |
| 99.6 | 18.9 | 5.7 | | | 17.2 | -164.3 | 4.4 | 5.3 | 5.4 |
| 5.9 | 11.1 | 8.2 | | | 27.5 | 4.1 | 9.4 | 9.7 | 7.0 |
| (101) 2.0 | (106) 2.6 | (146) 2.6 | EBIT/Interest | | (12) 1.1 | (15) 1.1 | (16) 3.9 | (51) 2.9 | (49) 3.0 |
| -1.1 | .4 | .7 | | | -2.1 | -3.4 | 1.0 | 1.2 | .6 |
| | | | Net Profit + Depr., Dep., Amort./Cur. Mat. L/T/D | | | | | | |
| .7 | .5 | .7 | | | .5 | .8 | .4 | .9 | .0 |
| 1.0 | 1.0 | 1.0 | Fixed/Worth | | .9 | 1.3 | 1.1 | 1.1 | 1.0 |
| 1.5 | 1.6 | 1.5 | | | 1.1 | 1.8 | 1.2 | 1.8 | 1.3 |
| .3 | .3 | .3 | | | .1 | .3 | .2 | .3 | .3 |
| .7 | .6 | .6 | Debt/Worth | | .5 | .8 | .4 | .6 | .5 |
| 1.7 | 2.0 | 1.3 | | | .9 | 1.5 | .7 | 1.9 | 1.5 |
| 8.6 | 9.4 | 7.4 | | | 16.1 | 6.5 | 8.3 | 5.8 | 8.0 |
| (128) 2.1 | (138) 2.5 | (169) 3.2 | % Profit Before Taxes/Tangible Net Worth | | .2 | (17) .3 | 5.8 | (51) 2.1 | (58) 3.7 |
| -3.1 | -2.3 | -.4 | | | -3.2 | -4.5 | -.2 | .7 | -.7 |
| 4.2 | 4.8 | 4.7 | | | 7.0 | 2.5 | 6.0 | 4.1 | 5.2 |
| 1.1 | 1.3 | 1.6 | % Profit Before Taxes/Total Assets | | .1 | .2 | 2.4 | 1.4 | 1.9 |
| -1.4 | -1.8 | -.6 | | | -1.9 | -2.8 | -.2 | .2 | -.5 |
| 3.9 | 4.2 | 2.2 | | | 2.8 | .7 | 2.3 | 1.5 | 674.5 |
| .6 | .7 | .6 | Sales/Net Fixed Assets | | .8 | .4 | .4 | .4 | .7 |
| .3 | .4 | .3 | | | .2 | .2 | .3 | .3 | .5 |
| 1.0 | 1.3 | .8 | | | 1.0 | .4 | .9 | .5 | 1.4 |
| .4 | .4 | .4 | Sales/Total Assets | | .4 | .2 | .3 | .3 | .5 |
| .2 | .2 | .2 | | | .2 | .1 | .2 | .2 | .3 |
| 5.0 | 4.5 | 5.0 | | | 4.2 | 7.8 | 5.2 | 5.3 | 3.5 |
| (88) 8.9 | (95) 8.4 | (134) 8.0 | % Depr., Dep., Amort./Sales | | (14) 6.8 | (15) 10.7 | (14) 9.7 | (50) 7.5 | (38) 6.0 |
| 15.7 | 13.8 | 14.5 | | | 15.3 | 15.5 | 15.1 | 15.7 | 10.6 |
| 3.0 | 1.2 | 3.3 | | | | | | | |
| (15) 8.9 | (10) 7.7 | (13) 6.6 | % Officers', Directors' Owners' Comp/Sales | | | | | | |
| 26.1 | 21.5 | 13.0 | | | | | | | |
| 4631603M | 5727994M | 6130670M | Net Sales ($) | 3470M | 32041M | 72308M | 122132M | 951043M | 4949676M |
| 7884151M | 8907485M | 11373182M | Total Assets ($) | 20448M | 114766M | 349756M | 592872M | 3448963M | 6846377M |

M = $ thousand    MM = $ million
See Pages 9 through 22 for Explanation of Ratios and Data

## Current Data Sorted by Assets                    ## Comparative Historical Data

| 0-500M | 500M-2MM | 2-10MM | 10-50MM | 50-100MM | 100-250MM | Type of Statement | 6  4/1/07-3/31/08 ALL | 7  4/1/08-3/31/09 ALL |
|---|---|---|---|---|---|---|---|---|
| 3 | 1 | 28 | 33 | 26 | 22 | Unqualified | 28 | 28 |
|  | 1 | 4 | 2 | 1 | 2 | Reviewed |  |  |
|  |  |  |  |  |  | Compiled |  |  |
|  |  |  |  |  |  | Tax Returns |  |  |
|  |  |  |  |  |  | Other |  |  |
| 109 (4/1-9/30/11) | | | 14 (10/1/11-3/31/12) | | | | | |
| 3 | 2 | 32 | 35 | 27 | 24 | **NUMBER OF STATEMENTS** | 34 | 35 |
| % | % | % | % | % | % | **ASSETS** | % | % |
|  |  | 22.4 | 16.5 | 19.7 | 21.5 | Cash & Equivalents | 24.4 | 26.6 |
|  |  | 5.7 | 6.4 | 8.1 | 6.6 | Trade Receivables (net) | 4.8 | 10.0 |
|  |  | .5 | .1 | .4 | .4 | Inventory | .1 | .1 |
|  |  | 1.9 | 2.9 | 3.3 | 2.2 | All Other Current | 2.1 | 2.4 |
|  |  | 30.6 | 25.9 | 31.5 | 30.6 | Total Current | 31.4 | 39.2 |
|  |  | 64.4 | 68.4 | 62.3 | 64.2 | Fixed Assets (net) | 59.5 | 53.8 |
|  |  | .8 | .4 | 1.0 | .6 | Intangibles (net) | .3 | .4 |
|  |  | 4.2 | 5.4 | 5.2 | 4.6 | All Other Non-Current | 8.8 | 6.6 |
|  |  | 100.0 | 100.0 | 100.0 | 100.0 | Total | 100.0 | 100.0 |
|  |  |  |  |  |  | **LIABILITIES** |  |  |
|  |  | .6 | .5 | .3 | 3.5 | Notes Payable-Short Term | .8 | .8 |
|  |  | 2.2 | 2.4 | 2.5 | 2.6 | Cur. Mat.-L.T.D. | 2.7 | 2.0 |
|  |  | 3.2 | 1.4 | 2.3 | 2.5 | Trade Payables | 3.9 | 3.9 |
|  |  | .0 | .0 | .0 | .0 | Income Taxes Payable | .0 | .9 |
|  |  | 7.3 | 4.4 | 5.6 | 4.3 | All Other Current | 2.9 | 4.8 |
|  |  | 13.3 | 8.7 | 10.6 | 13.0 | Total Current | 10.3 | 12.4 |
|  |  | 21.1 | 26.9 | 32.4 | 37.7 | Long-Term Debt | 26.9 | 20.5 |
|  |  | .0 | .0 | .0 | .0 | Deferred Taxes | .0 | .0 |
|  |  | 4.7 | 2.2 | 3.4 | 3.1 | All Other Non-Current | 2.8 | 2.4 |
|  |  | 60.9 | 62.1 | 53.6 | 46.2 | Net Worth | 59.9 | 64.8 |
|  |  | 100.0 | 100.0 | 100.0 | 100.0 | Total Liabilities & Net Worth | 100.0 | 100.0 |
|  |  |  |  |  |  | **INCOME DATA** |  |  |
|  |  | 100.0 | 100.0 | 100.0 | 100.0 | Net Sales | 100.0 | 100.0 |
|  |  |  |  |  |  | Gross Profit |  |  |
|  |  | 88.9 | 87.8 | 86.3 | 89.9 | Operating Expenses | 88.3 | 89.8 |
|  |  | 11.1 | 12.2 | 13.7 | 10.1 | Operating Profit | 11.7 | 10.2 |
|  |  | 5.7 | 3.6 | 3.9 | 3.7 | All Other Expenses (net) | -1.5 | 3.3 |
|  |  | 5.4 | 8.6 | 9.8 | 6.4 | Profit Before Taxes | 13.2 | 6.9 |
|  |  |  |  |  |  | **RATIOS** |  |  |
|  |  | 6.9 | 4.3 | 5.5 | 5.4 |  | 8.9 | 5.0 |
|  |  | 3.3 | 2.0 | 2.8 | 3.5 | Current | 4.7 | 3.4 |
|  |  | .7 | 1.4 | 1.3 | 2.0 |  | 2.3 | 1.5 |
|  |  | 6.6 | 3.5 | 5.0 | 5.0 |  | 7.4 | 4.9 |
|  |  | 2.9 | 1.8 | 2.8 | 2.9 | Quick | 4.6 | 3.4 |
|  |  | .7 | 1.4 | 1.1 | 1.9 |  | 1.5 | 1.3 |
|  | 5 | 79.4   15 | 24.8   27 | 13.3   21 | 17.4 |  | 5   68.0   9 | 40.2 |
|  | 29 | 12.8   41 | 9.0   55 | 6.6   50 | 7.3 | Sales/Receivables | 19   19.7   38 | 9.6 |
|  | 79 | 4.6   74 | 4.9   140 | 2.6   104 | 3.5 |  | 40   9.1   65 | 5.6 |
|  |  |  |  |  |  | Cost of Sales/Inventory |  |  |
|  |  |  |  |  |  | Cost of Sales/Payables |  |  |
|  |  | 1.4 | 1.6 | 1.0 | .8 |  | 1.2 | 1.4 |
|  |  | 3.1 | 4.4 | 1.6 | 1.8 | Sales/Working Capital | 2.5 | 3.0 |
|  |  | -12.8 | 7.0 | 3.5 | 4.3 |  | 5.5 | 7.9 |
|  |  | 10.7 | 7.0 | 9.7 | 11.3 |  | 11.1 | 6.8 |
|  | (23) | 3.6   (31) | 3.1   (22) | 3.0   (22) | 2.2 | EBIT/Interest | (26)   4.1   (30) | 2.9 |
|  |  | -.6 | 1.2 | 1.3 | -.2 |  | 2.3 | -.4 |
|  |  |  |  |  |  | Net Profit + Depr., Dep., Amort./Cur. Mat. L/T/D |  |  |
|  |  | .8 | 1.0 | .8 | .9 |  | .8 | .2 |
|  |  | 1.2 | 1.1 | 1.1 | 1.0 | Fixed/Worth | .9 | 1.0 |
|  |  | 1.4 | 1.7 | 1.6 | 1.5 |  | 1.2 | 1.3 |
|  |  | .3 | .3 | .3 | .2 |  | .3 | .3 |
|  |  | .4 | .6 | .7 | .4 | Debt/Worth | .4 | .5 |
|  |  | 1.1 | 1.1 | 1.4 | 1.0 |  | 1.4 | .8 |
|  |  | 13.2 | 9.7 | 7.6 | 5.4 |  | 10.5 | 9.0 |
|  | (30) | 3.9 | 5.0   (26) | 4.9   (20) | 1.3 | % Profit Before Taxes/Tangible Net Worth | (32)   4.8 | 3.3 |
|  |  | -3.2 | .3 | .4 | -.9 |  | 1.1 | -4.5 |
|  |  | 7.2 | 5.3 | 5.3 | 4.9 |  | 6.3 | 5.0 |
|  |  | 1.5 | 2.4 | 3.0 | .9 | % Profit Before Taxes/Total Assets | 3.0 | 2.3 |
|  |  | -3.4 | .2 | .4 | -.7 |  | .4 | -3.5 |
|  |  | 1.0 | .7 | .7 | .7 |  | 1.4 | 4.9 |
|  |  | .6 | .3 | .5 | .5 | Sales/Net Fixed Assets | .5 | .5 |
|  |  | .2 | .2 | .2 | .3 |  | .4 | .3 |
|  |  | .7 | .6 | .4 | .4 |  | .9 | .8 |
|  |  | .4 | .2 | .3 | .3 | Sales/Total Assets | .4 | .3 |
|  |  | .2 | .2 | .2 | .2 |  | .2 | .2 |
|  |  | 7.7 | 6.9 | 9.5 | 6.5 |  | 5.5 | 6.8 |
|  | (26) | 16.5   (32) | 14.9   (25) | 14.1   (22) | 8.9 | % Depr., Dep., Amort./Sales | (25)   11.1   (21) | 11.0 |
|  |  | 20.8 | 26.1 | 20.2 | 13.0 |  | 17.3 | 14.2 |
|  |  |  |  |  |  | % Officers', Directors' Owners' Comp/Sales |  |  |
| 926M | 13110M | 136067M | 607229M | 955543M | 1549006M | Net Sales ($) | 768813M | 772788M |
| 532M | 3365M | 188837M | 956864M | 2047482M | 3836181M | Total Assets ($) | 1662860M | 1743110M |

M = $ thousand    MM = $ million
See Pages 9 through 22 for Explanation of Ratios and Data

## Comparative Historical Data       Current Data Sorted by Sales

| Comparative Historical Data | | | Type of Statement | Current Data Sorted by Sales | | | | | |
|---|---|---|---|---|---|---|---|---|---|
| 56 | 54 | 113 | Unqualified | 11 | 20 | 9 | 19 | 23 | 31 |
| | 1 | | Reviewed | | | | | | |
| 1 | 1 | | Compiled | | | | | | |
| | | | Tax Returns | | | | | | |
| 6 | 8 | 10 | Other | 1 | 2 | 1 | 2 | 1 | 3 |
| 4/1/09- | 4/1/10- | 4/1/11- | | | 109 (4/1-9/30/11) | | 14 (10/1/11-3/31/12) | | |
| 3/31/10 | 3/31/11 | 3/31/12 | | | | | | | |
| ALL | ALL | ALL | | 0-1MM | 1-3MM | 3-5MM | 5-10MM | 10-25MM | 25MM & OVER |
| 63 | 64 | 123 | **NUMBER OF STATEMENTS** | 12 | 22 | 10 | 21 | 24 | 34 |
| % | % | % | **ASSETS** | % | % | % | % | % | % |
| 22.3 | 14.9 | 19.9 | Cash & Equivalents | 12.5 | 19.4 | 21.1 | 18.2 | 16.4 | 26.0 |
| 4.9 | 5.2 | 6.8 | Trade Receivables (net) | 1.2 | 5.1 | 7.0 | 6.7 | 5.3 | 11.0 |
| .2 | .3 | .3 | Inventory | .1 | .3 | .9 | .2 | .2 | .4 |
| 5.0 | 1.6 | 3.1 | All Other Current | 6.7 | 2.4 | 2.4 | 3.5 | 1.2 | 3.5 |
| 32.5 | 22.1 | 30.1 | Total Current | 20.6 | 27.2 | 31.4 | 28.5 | 23.1 | 40.9 |
| 60.5 | 68.7 | 63.8 | Fixed Assets (net) | 76.7 | 64.9 | 62.1 | 61.5 | 72.7 | 54.0 |
| .5 | .9 | .7 | Intangibles (net) | .1 | 1.5 | .0 | .2 | .3 | 1.1 |
| 6.4 | 8.3 | 5.5 | All Other Non-Current | 2.7 | 6.3 | 6.5 | 9.8 | 4.0 | 4.0 |
| 100.0 | 100.0 | 100.0 | Total | 100.0 | 100.0 | 100.0 | 100.0 | 100.0 | 100.0 |
| | | | **LIABILITIES** | | | | | | |
| .7 | .7 | 1.0 | Notes Payable-Short Term | .4 | .5 | .0 | 1.3 | .0 | 2.5 |
| 2.1 | 2.4 | 2.4 | Cur. Mat.-L.T.D. | 2.1 | 1.8 | 2.2 | 2.3 | 2.2 | 3.1 |
| 2.6 | 1.5 | 2.3 | Trade Payables | 1.4 | 1.8 | 2.7 | 1.7 | 1.4 | 4.0 |
| .5 | .0 | .0 | Income Taxes Payable | .0 | .0 | .0 | .0 | .0 | .0 |
| 5.2 | 4.0 | 5.4 | All Other Current | .9 | 4.2 | 4.3 | 11.1 | 3.4 | 5.9 |
| 11.2 | 8.5 | 11.1 | Total Current | 4.8 | 8.2 | 9.2 | 16.4 | 7.1 | 15.5 |
| 29.1 | 30.8 | 28.2 | Long-Term Debt | 25.4 | 27.2 | 17.4 | 21.8 | 24.9 | 39.4 |
| .0 | .1 | .0 | Deferred Taxes | .0 | .0 | .0 | .0 | .0 | .0 |
| 2.7 | 2.9 | 4.0 | All Other Non-Current | .2 | 1.1 | 13.3 | 6.1 | 3.3 | 3.8 |
| 57.1 | 57.7 | 56.6 | Net Worth | 69.6 | 63.5 | 60.1 | 55.7 | 64.7 | 41.2 |
| 100.0 | 100.0 | 100.0 | Total Liabilties & Net Worth | 100.0 | 100.0 | 100.0 | 100.0 | 100.0 | 100.0 |
| | | | **INCOME DATA** | | | | | | |
| 100.0 | 100.0 | 100.0 | Net Sales | 100.0 | 100.0 | 100.0 | 100.0 | 100.0 | 100.0 |
| | | | Gross Profit | | | | | | |
| 89.0 | 87.9 | 87.8 | Operating Expenses | 78.5 | 87.3 | 91.7 | 89.6 | 85.6 | 90.6 |
| 11.0 | 12.1 | 12.2 | Operating Profit | 21.5 | 12.7 | 8.3 | 10.4 | 14.4 | 9.4 |
| 3.4 | 5.0 | 4.3 | All Other Expenses (net) | 11.1 | 4.5 | 2.0 | 4.7 | 2.2 | 3.6 |
| 7.5 | 7.1 | 8.0 | Profit Before Taxes | 10.4 | 8.2 | 6.4 | 5.7 | 12.2 | 5.8 |
| | | | **RATIOS** | | | | | | |
| 4.7 | 4.2 | 5.5 | | 17.6 | 6.4 | 6.4 | 3.2 | 5.5 | 5.3 |
| 2.5 | 2.7 | 2.8 | Current | 2.2 | 3.2 | 3.5 | 1.9 | 3.7 | 3.1 |
| 1.7 | 1.3 | 1.4 | | .7 | 1.2 | 1.6 | 1.1 | 2.1 | 1.9 |
| 4.6 | 3.9 | 5.0 | | 12.3 | 5.1 | 5.6 | 2.5 | 5.0 | 5.1 |
| 2.3 | 2.5 | 2.5 | Quick | 2.0 | 2.9 | 3.3 | 1.6 | 3.5 | 2.8 |
| 1.5 | 1.3 | 1.4 | | .7 | 1.2 | 1.6 | .9 | 2.0 | 1.6 |
| 10   36.6 | 11   33.8 | 16   22.9 | | 0   UND | 14   25.4 | 6   64.9 | 6   57.9 | 19   19.7 | 21   17.8 |
| 28   13.1 | 32   11.4 | 41   9.0 | Sales/Receivables | 7   49.4 | 42   8.7 | 34   10.6 | 39   9.3 | 56   6.5 | 39   9.4 |
| 50   7.3 | 69   5.3 | 96   3.8 | | 94   3.9 | 81   4.5 | 54   6.8 | 104   3.5 | 122   3.0 | 91   4.0 |
| | | | Cost of Sales/Inventory | | | | | | |
| | | | Cost of Sales/Payables | | | | | | |
| 1.6 | 1.7 | 1.2 | | .8 | 1.0 | 1.9 | 1.4 | .8 | 1.5 |
| 3.4 | 3.8 | 2.3 | Sales/Working Capital | 3.0 | 2.3 | 4.3 | 4.4 | 1.4 | 2.8 |
| 6.5 | 10.0 | 7.0 | | -11.0 | 22.2 | 6.2 | 55.1 | 3.6 | 5.5 |
| 5.1 | 5.3 | 9.1 | | 10.9 | 9.2 | | 5.2 | 16.4 | 6.9 |
| (52)   2.4 | (54)   2.4 | (102)   3.2 | EBIT/Interest | (10)   2.9 | (19)   3.6 | (15)   2.6 | (21)   4.6 | (30)   2.8 | |
| .8 | .9 | .8 | | -.6 | .2 | | .3 | 1.3 | .9 |
| | | | Net Profit + Depr., Dep., Amort./Cur. Mat. L/T/D | | | | | | |
| .9 | .9 | .9 | | 1.0 | .8 | .7 | .9 | .9 | .8 |
| 1.1 | 1.3 | 1.1 | Fixed/Worth | 1.2 | 1.1 | 1.1 | 1.2 | 1.0 | 1.1 |
| 1.6 | 1.7 | 1.6 | | 1.6 | 1.6 | 1.4 | 2.1 | 1.6 | 1.7 |
| .3 | .3 | .3 | | .2 | .2 | .3 | .3 | .2 | .3 |
| .7 | .8 | .5 | Debt/Worth | .5 | .5 | .4 | .5 | .4 | .9 |
| 1.1 | 1.1 | 1.1 | | .8 | 1.2 | .9 | 1.5 | .9 | 1.9 |
| 7.6 | 8.8 | 8.7 | | 10.4 | 14.5 | | 11.2 | 9.4 | 7.8 |
| (62)   1.9 | (62)   2.6 | (115)   4.0 | % Profit Before Taxes/Tangible Net Worth | 1.8 | (21)   4.0 | (20)   4.3 | (23)   5.7 | (30)   3.4 | |
| -3.8 | -.4 | -.2 | | -1.5 | -2.0 | | -.5 | .1 | -.2 |
| 4.8 | 4.3 | 5.4 | | 7.7 | 6.7 | 5.5 | 4.5 | 6.1 | 5.7 |
| 1.0 | 1.5 | 2.4 | % Profit Before Taxes/Total Assets | 1.5 | 2.0 | 1.7 | 2.4 | 3.2 | 2.5 |
| -.8 | -.4 | -.3 | | -1.0 | -2.4 | -4.9 | -1.1 | .1 | -.1 |
| 1.4 | .8 | .8 | | .3 | .6 | 1.2 | 1.4 | .6 | 1.9 |
| .5 | .3 | .5 | Sales/Net Fixed Assets | .1 | .3 | .7 | .3 | .3 | .7 |
| .3 | .2 | .2 | | .1 | .2 | .4 | .2 | .2 | .5 |
| .8 | .4 | .6 | | .2 | .4 | .7 | .7 | .4 | 1.0 |
| .4 | .2 | .3 | Sales/Total Assets | .1 | .2 | .5 | .3 | .2 | .4 |
| .2 | .1 | .2 | | .1 | .2 | .3 | | | |
| 4.5 | 7.0 | 7.1 | | 15.8 | 16.4 | | 6.8 | 7.1 | 4.3 |
| (48)   8.8 | (52)   14.2 | (108)   12.9 | % Depr., Dep., Amort./Sales | (11)   35.5 | (19)   18.8 | (18)   14.8 | (23)   13.0 | (29)   7.9 | |
| 18.2 | 20.7 | 20.4 | | 55.0 | 25.2 | | 26.1 | 16.9 | 11.7 |
| | | | % Officers', Directors' Owners' Comp/Sales | | | | | | |
| 2310105M | 1010607M | 3261881M | Net Sales ($) | 6099M | 44214M | 42303M | 152481M | 385345M | 2631439M |
| 3308378M | 3303039M | 7033261M | Total Assets ($) | 64744M | 234886M | 126801M | 648412M | 1930551M | 4027867M |

© RMA 2012     **M = $ thousand    MM = $ million**
See Pages 9 through 22 for Explanation of Ratios and Data

## Current Data Sorted by Assets | Comparative Historical Data

| | | | | | | Type of Statement | | |
|---|---|---|---|---|---|---|---|---|
| | | 6 | 19 | 13 | 17 | Unqualified | 30 | 52 |
| | | | 1 | | | Reviewed | | |
| | | 1 | | | | Compiled | | 1 |
| | | 2 | 2 | 3 | | Tax Returns | | |
| | 55 (4/1-9/30/11) | | 9 (10/1/11-3/31/12) | | | Other | 13 | 13 |
| | | | | | | | 4/1/07- | 4/1/08- |
| | | | | | | | 3/31/08 | 3/31/09 |
| 0-500M | 500M-2MM | 2-10MM | 10-50MM | 50-100MM | 100-250MM | | ALL | ALL |
| | | 9 | 22 | 16 | 17 | NUMBER OF STATEMENTS | 43 | 66 |
| % | % | % | % | % | % | ASSETS | % | % |
| D | D | | 17.0 | 13.1 | 14.7 | Cash & Equivalents | 31.8 | 30.9 |
| A | A | | 5.0 | 3.4 | 6.4 | Trade Receivables (net) | 11.6 | 7.9 |
| T | T | | .4 | .3 | .3 | Inventory | .3 | .8 |
| A | A | | 3.4 | 1.1 | 1.1 | All Other Current | 2.8 | 3.6 |
| | | | 25.8 | 17.9 | 22.6 | Total Current | 46.5 | 43.2 |
| N | N | | 63.3 | 75.2 | 65.6 | Fixed Assets (net) | 41.2 | 49.5 |
| O | O | | .3 | .1 | 1.3 | Intangibles (net) | .3 | .2 |
| T | T | | 10.6 | 6.9 | 10.5 | All Other Non-Current | 12.1 | 7.1 |
| | | | 100.0 | 100.0 | 100.0 | Total | 100.0 | 100.0 |
| A | A | | | | | LIABILITIES | | |
| V | V | | .1 | .3 | .0 | Notes Payable-Short Term | 1.0 | 1.9 |
| A | A | | 1.9 | 1.8 | 2.1 | Cur. Mat.-L.T.D. | 1.2 | 1.3 |
| I | I | | 1.4 | 1.5 | 1.4 | Trade Payables | 4.0 | 3.9 |
| L | L | | .0 | .0 | .0 | Income Taxes Payable | .6 | .5 |
| A | A | | 6.5 | 2.8 | 11.1 | All Other Current | 8.8 | 9.4 |
| B | B | | 9.9 | 6.4 | 14.6 | Total Current | 15.6 | 16.8 |
| L | L | | 21.0 | 25.2 | 29.0 | Long-Term Debt | 19.5 | 19.3 |
| E | E | | .0 | .0 | .0 | Deferred Taxes | .0 | .0 |
| | | | 2.0 | 1.6 | 3.1 | All Other Non-Current | 4.0 | 2.7 |
| | | | 67.1 | 66.7 | 53.3 | Net Worth | 60.8 | 61.2 |
| | | | 100.0 | 100.0 | 100.0 | Total Liabilities & Net Worth | 100.0 | 100.0 |
| | | | | | | INCOME DATA | | |
| | | | 100.0 | 100.0 | 100.0 | Net Sales | 100.0 | 100.0 |
| | | | | | | Gross Profit | | |
| | | | 83.2 | 90.1 | 85.3 | Operating Expenses | 90.5 | 92.0 |
| | | | 16.8 | 9.9 | 14.7 | Operating Profit | 9.5 | 8.0 |
| | | | 2.7 | 1.9 | 4.8 | All Other Expenses (net) | 2.6 | -.4 |
| | | | 14.1 | 8.0 | 9.9 | Profit Before Taxes | 6.8 | 8.4 |
| | | | | | | RATIOS | | |
| | | | 8.6 | 5.0 | 7.5 | | 5.6 | 5.9 |
| | | | 3.6 | 3.2 | 3.0 | Current | 3.3 | 3.8 |
| | | | 1.6 | 1.7 | 1.1 | | 2.0 | 1.9 |
| | | | 6.3 | 4.7 | 7.3 | | 4.9 | 5.6 |
| | | | 3.1 | 2.9 | 2.7 | Quick | 3.1 | 3.4 |
| | | | 1.4 | 1.4 | 1.0 | | 1.9 | 1.7 |
| | | 0 UND | 25 14.6 | 9 40.5 | | | 8 43.8 | 9 39.1 |
| | | 28 13.1 | 41 8.9 | 34 10.6 | | Sales/Receivables | 27 13.3 | 27 13.3 |
| | | 45 8.2 | 61 6.0 | 89 4.1 | | | 62 5.9 | 55 6.6 |
| | | | | | | Cost of Sales/Inventory | | |
| | | | | | | Cost of Sales/Payables | | |
| | | | .8 | 1.7 | 1.2 | | 1.8 | 1.5 |
| | | | 4.3 | 2.1 | 2.2 | Sales/Working Capital | 2.8 | 3.0 |
| | | | 14.4 | 8.2 | 157.7 | | 5.4 | 6.2 |
| | | | 16.7 | 7.7 | 10.6 | | 17.9 | 10.6 |
| | | (17) 5.2 | (15) 2.1 | (16) 3.1 | | EBIT/Interest | (29) 4.6 | (54) 3.4 |
| | | 1.1 | .7 | .5 | | | 1.8 | .6 |
| | | | | | | Net Profit + Depr., Dep., Amort./Cur. Mat. L/T/D | | |
| | | | .7 | 1.0 | 1.1 | | .0 | .0 |
| | | | 1.0 | 1.1 | 1.3 | Fixed/Worth | .8 | .9 |
| | | | 1.4 | 1.4 | 1.4 | | 1.2 | 1.2 |
| | | | .1 | .3 | .5 | | .2 | .2 |
| | | | .4 | .5 | .7 | Debt/Worth | .5 | .5 |
| | | | .9 | .8 | 1.5 | | 1.0 | 1.0 |
| | | | 9.5 | 5.9 | 9.2 | | 18.4 | 11.5 |
| | | | 6.3 | 2.7 (16) | 3.5 | % Profit Before Taxes/Tangible Net Worth | (41) 4.7 | (65) 5.2 |
| | | | .4 | -.1 | -.7 | | 1.7 | -.4 |
| | | | 5.6 | 3.9 | 5.6 | | 9.4 | 7.6 |
| | | | 4.1 | 1.6 | 2.2 | % Profit Before Taxes/Total Assets | 2.8 | 3.3 |
| | | | .2 | .0 | -1.9 | | .7 | -.3 |
| | | | 1.1 | .5 | .5 | | UND | UND |
| | | | .4 | .4 | .4 | Sales/Net Fixed Assets | 1.0 | .6 |
| | | | .3 | .3 | .2 | | .4 | .3 |
| | | | .8 | .4 | .4 | | 1.9 | 1.4 |
| | | | .3 | .3 | .3 | Sales/Total Assets | .6 | .4 |
| | | | .2 | .2 | .1 | | .3 | .2 |
| | | | 5.0 | 4.6 | 6.3 | | 2.9 | 4.0 |
| | | (18) 9.8 | (14) 11.3 | (14) 10.4 | % Depr., Dep., Amort./Sales | (19) 7.5 | (41) 9.6 |
| | | 16.2 | 21.8 | 14.8 | | 16.1 | 15.7 |
| | | | | | | % Officers', Directors' Owners' Comp/Sales | | 3.7 |
| | | | | | | | | (12) 13.2 |
| | | | | | | | | 27.1 |
| | | 59327M | 255535M | 369987M | 1066618M | Net Sales ($) | 1552865M | 2414053M |
| | | 57582M | 509894M | 1090642M | 2447959M | Total Assets ($) | 2159845M | 3935444M |

M = $ thousand    MM = $ million
See Pages 9 through 22 for Explanation of Ratios and Data

## Comparative Historical Data

## Current Data Sorted by Sales

| 70 | 48 | 55 | Type of Statement | 1 | 6 | 3 | 12 | 13 | 20 |
|---|---|---|---|---|---|---|---|---|---|
| 1 | 1 | 1 | Unqualified | | | | | | |
| | 1 | 1 | Reviewed | | | | | | |
| | | | Compiled | 1 | | | 1 | | |
| | | | Tax Returns | | | | | | |
| 14 | 7 | 7 | Other | | | 2 | | 4 | 1 |
| | | | | | | | | | |
| 4/1/09-3/31/10 | 4/1/10-3/31/11 | 4/1/11-3/31/12 | | 55 (4/1-9/30/11) | | | 9 (10/1/11-3/31/12) | | |
| ALL | ALL | ALL | | 0-1MM | 1-3MM | 3-5MM | 5-10MM | 10-25MM | 25MM & OVER |
| 85 | 57 | 64 | **NUMBER OF STATEMENTS** | 2 | 6 | 5 | 13 | 17 | 21 |
| % | % | % | **ASSETS** | % | % | % | % | % | % |
| 22.9 | 16.8 | 16.4 | Cash & Equivalents | | | | 12.7 | 15.4 | 16.5 |
| 8.3 | 8.2 | 6.3 | Trade Receivables (net) | | | | 4.6 | 5.2 | 9.5 |
| 1.0 | 1.1 | .9 | Inventory | | | | 3.0 | .6 | .5 |
| 3.9 | 1.8 | 2.7 | All Other Current | | | | 2.6 | 4.0 | 2.8 |
| 36.1 | 27.8 | 26.4 | Total Current | | | | 22.9 | 25.2 | 29.3 |
| 56.2 | 62.5 | 62.0 | Fixed Assets (net) | | | | 70.9 | 65.5 | 54.1 |
| .7 | .5 | .6 | Intangibles (net) | | | | .2 | .1 | 1.0 |
| 7.0 | 9.1 | 11.0 | All Other Non-Current | | | | 6.1 | 9.2 | 15.6 |
| 100.0 | 100.0 | 100.0 | Total | | | | 100.0 | 100.0 | 100.0 |
| | | | **LIABILITIES** | | | | | | |
| 1.6 | .2 | .2 | Notes Payable-Short Term | | | | .7 | .3 | .1 |
| 1.9 | 1.8 | 2.0 | Cur. Mat.-L.T.D. | | | | 2.1 | 1.3 | 2.1 |
| 3.2 | 2.1 | 2.1 | Trade Payables | | | | 2.7 | 1.6 | 2.4 |
| .4 | .1 | .0 | Income Taxes Payable | | | | .0 | .0 | .0 |
| 6.7 | 5.2 | 7.6 | All Other Current | | | | 2.0 | 6.0 | 13.9 |
| 13.8 | 9.5 | 12.0 | Total Current | | | | 7.6 | 9.2 | 18.5 |
| 21.8 | 22.4 | 30.5 | Long-Term Debt | | | | 30.9 | 21.2 | 25.2 |
| .0 | .2 | .1 | Deferred Taxes | | | | .0 | .0 | .0 |
| 5.4 | 3.5 | 2.2 | All Other Non-Current | | | | 1.4 | 1.1 | 4.2 |
| 59.1 | 64.5 | 55.3 | Net Worth | | | | 60.2 | 68.5 | 52.2 |
| 100.0 | 100.0 | 100.0 | Total Liabilities & Net Worth | | | | 100.0 | 100.0 | 100.0 |
| | | | **INCOME DATA** | | | | | | |
| 100.0 | 100.0 | 100.0 | Net Sales | | | | 100.0 | 100.0 | 100.0 |
| | | | Gross Profit | | | | | | |
| 92.4 | 92.2 | 85.4 | Operating Expenses | | | | 85.3 | 86.2 | 92.1 |
| 7.6 | 7.8 | 14.6 | Operating Profit | | | | 14.7 | 13.8 | 7.9 |
| 1.8 | 2.1 | 4.0 | All Other Expenses (net) | | | | 4.1 | .4 | 3.1 |
| 5.9 | 5.7 | 10.6 | Profit Before Taxes | | | | 10.7 | 13.4 | 4.9 |
| | | | **RATIOS** | | | | | | |
| 6.8 | 7.9 | 6.2 | Current | | | | 5.7 | 5.0 | 6.1 |
| 2.6 | 3.4 | 3.2 | | | | | 3.1 | 3.4 | 2.9 |
| 1.6 | 1.4 | 1.6 | | | | | 1.7 | 1.8 | 1.0 |
| 6.5 | 7.1 | 5.6 | Quick | | | | 5.6 | 4.6 | 5.4 |
| 2.3 | 2.9 | 2.8 | | | | | 2.2 | 2.9 | 2.4 |
| 1.3 | 1.2 | 1.1 | | | | | 1.4 | 1.3 | 1.0 |
| 8  46.6 | 14  25.6 | 14  25.9 | Sales/Receivables | | | | 8  43.8 | 29  12.8 | 15  25.1 |
| 25  14.7 | 34  10.7 | 33  11.0 | | | | | 25  14.4 | 41  8.8 | 33  11.1 |
| 55  6.7 | 79  4.6 | 56  6.5 | | | | | 54  6.8 | 54  6.7 | 72  5.1 |
| | | | Cost of Sales/Inventory | | | | | | |
| | | | Cost of Sales/Payables | | | | | | |
| 1.3 | 1.3 | 1.5 | Sales/Working Capital | | | | .8 | 1.5 | 1.8 |
| 2.3 | 2.4 | 2.9 | | | | | 3.1 | 2.3 | 4.4 |
| 10.3 | 12.4 | 12.1 | | | | | 9.6 | 5.6 | 281.9 |
| 6.5 | 6.8 | 11.6 | EBIT/Interest | | | | 9.9 | 12.0 | 11.0 |
| (72)  2.0 | (50)  2.0 | (54)  3.0 | | (10)  3.9 | | | | (15)  2.8 | (19)  1.7 |
| -.2 | -1.2 | .7 | | | | | 1.2 | .4 | .6 |
| | | | Net Profit + Depr., Dep., Amort./Cur. Mat. L/T/D | | | | | | |
| .6 | .7 | .8 | Fixed/Worth | | | | 1.0 | .8 | .5 |
| 1.0 | 1.0 | 1.1 | | | | | 1.2 | 1.1 | 1.2 |
| 1.5 | 1.4 | 1.4 | | | | | 1.6 | 1.3 | 1.5 |
| .3 | .2 | .3 | Debt/Worth | | | | .4 | .2 | .4 |
| .7 | .4 | .5 | | | | | .6 | .5 | .7 |
| 1.3 | .9 | 1.0 | | | | | .9 | .7 | 1.9 |
| 7.4 | 5.8 | 8.4 | % Profit Before Taxes/Tangible Net Worth | | | | 7.9 | 10.3 | 7.6 |
| (83)  1.9 | (56)  1.9 | (61)  4.1 | | (12)  6.2 | | | | 2.8 | (20)  3.9 |
| -2.3 | -1.9 | -.1 | | | | | .8 | -.4 | -.1 |
| 4.7 | 4.2 | 5.3 | % Profit Before Taxes/Total Assets | | | | 5.0 | 5.6 | 4.6 |
| .9 | 1.1 | 2.5 | | | | | 3.7 | 2.0 | 1.7 |
| -1.4 | -1.6 | .0 | | | | | .8 | -.4 | -.7 |
| 1.8 | 1.1 | .8 | Sales/Net Fixed Assets | | | | .6 | .9 | 3.2 |
| .7 | .4 | .5 | | | | | .4 | .4 | .5 |
| .3 | .3 | .3 | | | | | .2 | .2 | .4 |
| .9 | .6 | .5 | Sales/Total Assets | | | | .4 | .4 | 1.0 |
| .4 | .3 | .3 | | | | | .3 | .3 | .4 |
| .2 | .2 | .2 | | | | | .1 | .2 | .3 |
| 4.4 | 4.9 | 5.1 | % Depr., Dep., Amort./Sales | | | | 4.9 | 4.6 | 4.6 |
| (51)  9.7 | (41)  9.8 | (50)  10.0 | | (11)  10.0 | | | | (13)  12.6 | (17)  8.2 |
| 13.1 | 14.6 | 15.5 | | | | | 22.2 | 20.9 | 12.9 |
| | | | % Officers', Directors' Owners' Comp/Sales | | | | | | |
| 3146493M | 1498350M | 1751467M | Net Sales ($) | 1954M | 15290M | 18715M | 103884M | 269983M | 1341641M |
| 5146232M | 3544996M | 4106077M | Total Assets ($) | 33628M | 63432M | 81820M | 506488M | 1062395M | 2358314M |

M = $ thousand    MM = $ million
See Pages 9 through 22 for Explanation of Ratios and Data

| Current Data Sorted by Assets | | | | | | | Comparative Historical Data | |
|---|---|---|---|---|---|---|---|---|

| | | | 8 | 2 | 4 | Type of Statement | 15 | 16 |
|---|---|---|---|---|---|---|---|---|
| | | | | | | Unqualified | | |
| | | | | | | Reviewed | | |
| | | | | | | Compiled | | |
| | | | | | | Tax Returns | | |
| | | | | | | Other | | |
| | 1 | | 5 | 4 | 10 | | 15 4/1/07-3/31/08 ALL | 16 4/1/08-3/31/09 ALL |
| | 16 (4/1-9/30/11) | | 18 (10/1/11-3/31/12) | | | | | |
| 0-500M | 500M-2MM | 2-10MM | 10-50MM | 50-100MM | 100-250MM | | | |
| 1 | | | 13 | 6 | 14 | NUMBER OF STATEMENTS | 30 | 32 |
| % | % | % | % | % | % | ASSETS | % | % |
| | | | 28.7 | | 16.0 | Cash & Equivalents | 20.2 | 22.0 |
| D | D | | 1.8 | | 1.5 | Trade Receivables (net) | 3.3 | 1.9 |
| A | A | | 1.5 | | .1 | Inventory | 1.3 | .4 |
| T | T | | 8.1 | | 3.3 | All Other Current | 2.2 | 2.8 |
| A | A | | 40.2 | | 21.0 | Total Current | 27.0 | 27.2 |
| | | | 58.1 | | 70.3 | Fixed Assets (net) | 70.9 | 70.4 |
| N | N | | .1 | | .5 | Intangibles (net) | .2 | .1 |
| O | O | | 1.7 | | 8.3 | All Other Non-Current | 1.8 | 2.3 |
| T | T | | 100.0 | | 100.0 | Total | 100.0 | 100.0 |
| | | | | | | LIABILITIES | | |
| A | A | | .7 | | .0 | Notes Payable-Short Term | 1.5 | 1.1 |
| V | V | | 2.3 | | 3.6 | Cur. Mat.-L.T.D. | 8.5 | 4.0 |
| A | A | | 2.7 | | 1.2 | Trade Payables | 2.1 | 3.6 |
| I | I | | .0 | | .0 | Income Taxes Payable | .0 | .0 |
| L | L | | 15.7 | | 8.2 | All Other Current | 17.9 | 20.9 |
| A | A | | 21.6 | | 12.9 | Total Current | 30.1 | 29.7 |
| B | B | | 37.0 | | 37.0 | Long-Term Debt | 18.6 | 21.7 |
| L | L | | .3 | | .0 | Deferred Taxes | .0 | .0 |
| E | E | | 6.3 | | 1.8 | All Other Non-Current | .7 | 2.9 |
| | | | 34.8 | | 48.3 | Net Worth | 50.6 | 45.7 |
| | | | 100.0 | | 100.0 | Total Liabilities & Net Worth | 100.0 | 100.0 |
| | | | | | | INCOME DATA | | |
| | | | 100.0 | | 100.0 | Net Sales | 100.0 | 100.0 |
| | | | | | | Gross Profit | | |
| | | | 81.7 | | 72.7 | Operating Expenses | 70.3 | 72.6 |
| | | | 18.3 | | 27.3 | Operating Profit | 29.7 | 27.4 |
| | | | 3.6 | | 5.4 | All Other Expenses (net) | .5 | 4.1 |
| | | | 14.7 | | 21.9 | Profit Before Taxes | 29.2 | 23.3 |
| | | | | | | RATIOS | | |
| | | | 4.2 | | 2.6 | | 2.4 | 2.1 |
| | | | 2.5 | | 1.6 | Current | 1.2 | 1.5 |
| | | | 1.0 | | 1.1 | | .6 | .7 |
| | | | 3.1 | | 2.2 | | 2.0 | 1.9 |
| | | | 1.7 | | 1.2 | Quick | 1.0 | 1.0 |
| | | | .6 | | .9 | | .5 | .5 |
| | | | 1 561.7 | | 1 287.8 | | 1 288.0 | 1 307.8 |
| | | | 2 227.5 | | 3 122.6 | Sales/Receivables | 3 134.8 | 2 179.1 |
| | | | 8 46.3 | | 11 32.9 | | 6 57.0 | 7 54.7 |
| | | | | | | Cost of Sales/Inventory | | |
| | | | | | | Cost of Sales/Payables | | |
| | | | 2.2 | | 5.0 | | 9.7 | 10.6 |
| | | | 6.4 | | 16.2 | Sales/Working Capital | 38.3 | 26.0 |
| | | | NM | | 59.1 | | -15.6 | -22.0 |
| | | | 13.7 | | 29.4 | | 53.1 | 38.4 |
| | | | (11) 5.7 | | (11) 17.3 | EBIT/Interest | (22) 22.8 | (19) 9.9 |
| | | | 2.5 | | 6.4 | | 8.2 | 1.2 |
| | | | | | | Net Profit + Depr., Dep., Amort./Cur. Mat. L/T/D | | |
| | | | .7 | | .9 | | .9 | .9 |
| | | | .9 | | 1.5 | Fixed/Worth | 1.3 | 1.3 |
| | | | 2.5 | | 5.3 | | 3.0 | 3.0 |
| | | | .4 | | .4 | | .2 | .2 |
| | | | .7 | | .9 | Debt/Worth | .7 | .8 |
| | | | 2.7 | | 6.8 | | 3.0 | 2.8 |
| | | | 80.7 | | 140.1 | % Profit Before Taxes/Tangible Net Worth | 168.9 | 114.4 |
| | | | (12) 11.6 | | 46.1 | | (29) 87.5 | (29) 58.6 |
| | | | 4.4 | | 7.3 | | 15.7 | 6.2 |
| | | | 30.4 | | 44.1 | % Profit Before Taxes/Total Assets | 96.9 | 62.1 |
| | | | 6.2 | | 19.9 | | 44.1 | 38.6 |
| | | | 2.5 | | 2.5 | | 13.6 | 4.3 |
| | | | 3.7 | | 1.9 | | 3.1 | 3.2 |
| | | | 1.7 | | 1.2 | Sales/Net Fixed Assets | 2.3 | 2.1 |
| | | | 1.2 | | .9 | | 1.2 | 1.2 |
| | | | 1.8 | | 1.1 | | 2.4 | 2.2 |
| | | | .9 | | .8 | Sales/Total Assets | 1.6 | 1.5 |
| | | | .7 | | .7 | | .9 | .7 |
| | | | 2.6 | | | | 3.0 | 2.4 |
| | | | (11) 6.4 | | | % Depr., Dep., Amort./Sales | (20) 4.9 | (20) 4.4 |
| | | | 8.3 | | | | 8.2 | 5.7 |
| | | | | | | % Officers', Directors' Owners' Comp/Sales | | |
| 3479M | | | 501600M | 265422M | 2463361M | Net Sales ($) | 4515377M | 3400775M |
| 1183M | | | 420241M | 449154M | 2534207M | Total Assets ($) | 2905409M | 2684449M |

© RMA 2012

M = $ thousand    MM = $ million
See Pages 9 through 22 for Explanation of Ratios and Data

## Comparative Historical Data | Current Data Sorted by Sales

| 7 | 12 | 14 | Type of Statement | | | 1 | | 2 | 11 |
|---|---|---|---|---|---|---|---|---|---|
| | 1 | | Unqualified | | | | | | |
| | | | Reviewed | | | | | | |
| | | | Compiled | | | | | | |
| | | | Tax Returns | | | | | | |
| 1 | | | Other | | | 1 | 2 | 1 | 16 |
| 17 | 24 | 20 | | | 16 (4/1-9/30/11) | | 18 (10/1/11-3/31/12) | | |
| 4/1/09-3/31/10 | 4/1/10-3/31/11 | 4/1/11-3/31/12 | | | | | | | |
| ALL | ALL | ALL | | 0-1MM | 1-3MM | 3-5MM | 5-10MM | 10-25MM | 25MM & OVER |
| 25 | 37 | 34 | **NUMBER OF STATEMENTS** | | | 2 | 2 | 3 | 27 |
| % | % | % | **ASSETS** | % | % | % | % | % | % |
| 19.6 | 28.0 | 21.2 | Cash & Equivalents | D | D | | | | 19.1 |
| 7.5 | 3.6 | 1.8 | Trade Receivables (net) | A | A | | | | 1.6 |
| .3 | .7 | 1.0 | Inventory | T | T | | | | .4 |
| 3.0 | 6.4 | 5.1 | All Other Current | A | A | | | | 5.4 |
| 30.4 | 38.7 | 29.1 | Total Current | | | | | | 26.4 |
| 66.4 | 56.1 | 66.1 | Fixed Assets (net) | N | N | | | | 68.3 |
| .1 | .2 | .5 | Intangibles (net) | O | O | | | | .5 |
| 3.1 | 5.0 | 4.3 | All Other Non-Current | T | T | | | | 4.7 |
| 100.0 | 100.0 | 100.0 | Total | | | | | | 100.0 |
| | | | **LIABILITIES** | A | A | | | | |
| 2.9 | .7 | .3 | Notes Payable-Short Term | V | V | | | | .3 |
| 2.6 | 2.3 | 3.1 | Cur. Mat.-L.T.D. | A | A | | | | 3.6 |
| 2.0 | 2.5 | 2.1 | Trade Payables | I | I | | | | 1.4 |
| .0 | .4 | .0 | Income Taxes Payable | L | L | | | | .0 |
| 9.7 | 13.0 | 10.5 | All Other Current | A | A | | | | 9.6 |
| 17.2 | 18.8 | 16.0 | Total Current | B | B | | | | 14.9 |
| 26.3 | 25.5 | 36.2 | Long-Term Debt | L | L | | | | 41.3 |
| .0 | .1 | .1 | Deferred Taxes | E | E | | | | .1 |
| 3.3 | 4.5 | 3.2 | All Other Non-Current | | | | | | 3.8 |
| 53.3 | 51.1 | 44.5 | Net Worth | | | | | | 39.8 |
| 100.0 | 100.0 | 100.0 | Total Liabilties & Net Worth | | | | | | 100.0 |
| | | | **INCOME DATA** | | | | | | |
| 100.0 | 100.0 | 100.0 | Net Sales | | | | | | 100.0 |
| | | | Gross Profit | | | | | | |
| 77.1 | 83.1 | 75.2 | Operating Expenses | | | | | | 73.4 |
| 22.9 | 16.9 | 24.8 | Operating Profit | | | | | | 26.6 |
| 3.5 | 2.0 | 4.9 | All Other Expenses (net) | | | | | | 6.4 |
| 19.4 | 14.9 | 19.8 | Profit Before Taxes | | | | | | 20.2 |
| | | | **RATIOS** | | | | | | |
| 2.3 | 3.1 | 3.3 | | | | | | | 2.7 |
| 1.6 | 1.8 | 2.0 | Current | | | | | | 1.4 |
| 1.2 | 1.2 | 1.1 | | | | | | | .9 |
| 2.1 | 2.6 | 2.6 | | | | | | | 2.6 |
| 1.4 | 1.3 | 1.6 | Quick | | | | | | 1.3 |
| 1.0 | 1.0 | .8 | | | | | | | .7 |
| 1  381.7 | 1  294.9 | 1  355.1 | | | | | | | 1  362.6 |
| 3  122.6 | 3  113.7 | 3  125.7 | Sales/Receivables | | | | | | 3  139.1 |
| 13  27.3 | 24  15.5 | 12  30.7 | | | | | | | 8  45.1 |
| | | | Cost of Sales/Inventory | | | | | | |
| | | | Cost of Sales/Payables | | | | | | |
| 9.4 | 3.3 | 3.0 | | | | | | | 3.9 |
| 11.9 | 8.8 | 10.0 | Sales/Working Capital | | | | | | 14.2 |
| 37.0 | 27.9 | 59.1 | | | | | | | -70.3 |
| 69.9 | 29.8 | 27.1 | | | | | | | 24.7 |
| (20) 11.1 | (30) 10.0 | (29) 10.1 | EBIT/Interest | | | | | (23) | 10.1 |
| 3.5 | 2.5 | 3.0 | | | | | | | 3.0 |
| | | | Net Profit + Depr., Dep., Amort./Cur. Mat. L/T/D | | | | | | |
| .8 | .5 | .8 | | | | | | | .9 |
| 1.1 | 1.0 | 1.1 | Fixed/Worth | | | | | | 1.4 |
| 1.9 | 1.7 | 2.9 | | | | | | | 9.1 |
| .3 | .2 | .4 | | | | | | | .4 |
| .6 | .7 | .7 | Debt/Worth | | | | | | .9 |
| 1.3 | 1.9 | 3.3 | | | | | | | 9.2 |
| 90.7 | 47.3 | 77.8 | | | | | | | 92.4 |
| (24) 34.2 | (35) 13.3 | (31) 21.4 | % Profit Before Taxes/Tangible Net Worth | | | | | (24) | 31.4 |
| 7.6 | 7.8 | 5.0 | | | | | | | 5.3 |
| 53.5 | 21.0 | 36.6 | | | | | | | 39.8 |
| 19.7 | 9.4 | 14.6 | % Profit Before Taxes/Total Assets | | | | | | 19.9 |
| 4.8 | 3.8 | 3.2 | | | | | | | 3.2 |
| 3.1 | 4.3 | 2.0 | | | | | | | 1.8 |
| 1.3 | 1.2 | 1.3 | Sales/Net Fixed Assets | | | | | | 1.3 |
| .9 | .8 | .9 | | | | | | | .9 |
| 2.0 | 1.4 | 1.2 | | | | | | | 1.4 |
| 1.0 | .8 | .8 | Sales/Total Assets | | | | | | .9 |
| .6 | .6 | .7 | | | | | | | .7 |
| 2.9 | 1.6 | 2.5 | | | | | | | 3.5 |
| (11) 6.8 | (22) 5.0 | (22) 5.6 | % Depr., Dep., Amort./Sales | | | | | (16) | 6.9 |
| 8.3 | 7.0 | 8.0 | | | | | | | 8.2 |
| | | | % Officers', Directors' Owners' Comp/Sales | | | | | | |
| 2544736M | 2939202M | 3233862M | Net Sales ($) | | | 7844M | 14956M | 49979M | 3161083M |
| 2377743M | 3294884M | 3404785M | Total Assets ($) | | | 17798M | 149134M | 73491M | 3164362M |

M = $ thousand    MM = $ million
See Pages 9 through 22 for Explanation of Ratios and Data

## Current Data Sorted by Assets

## Comparative Historical Data

| | | | | | | Type of Statement | | |
|---|---|---|---|---|---|---|---|---|
| 5 | 15 | 56 | 76 | 39 | 38 | Unqualified | 183 | 220 |
| | | 1 | | | | Reviewed | 5 | 1 |
| | 1 | 3 | | | | Compiled | 2 | 6 |
| 3 | | | | | | Tax Returns | 2 | 3 |
| 3 | 15 | 10 | 16 | 9 | 4 | Other | 40 | 47 |
| | 220 (4/1-9/30/11) | | 74 (10/1/11-3/31/12) | | | | 4/1/07-3/31/08 | 4/1/08-3/31/09 |
| 0-500M | 500M-2MM | 2-10MM | 10-50MM | 50-100MM | 100-250MM | | ALL | ALL |
| 11 | 31 | 70 | 92 | 48 | 42 | NUMBER OF STATEMENTS | 232 | 277 |
| % | % | % | % | % | % | ASSETS | % | % |
| 49.9 | 49.1 | 28.8 | 27.6 | 18.7 | 18.8 | Cash & Equivalents | 29.2 | 31.7 |
| 12.2 | 13.1 | 11.0 | 7.0 | 4.8 | 4.3 | Trade Receivables (net) | 7.3 | 7.4 |
| .0 | .6 | 2.6 | 1.3 | .3 | .3 | Inventory | 1.1 | .6 |
| 6.0 | 12.1 | 5.8 | 5.1 | 2.3 | 1.9 | All Other Current | 4.7 | 5.0 |
| 68.1 | 75.0 | 48.3 | 41.0 | 26.1 | 25.3 | Total Current | 42.3 | 44.8 |
| 18.0 | 16.2 | 42.2 | 51.9 | 66.0 | 63.9 | Fixed Assets (net) | 51.0 | 46.7 |
| 5.1 | .0 | .6 | .7 | 1.0 | .3 | Intangibles (net) | .2 | .3 |
| 8.8 | 8.8 | 8.9 | 6.4 | 6.9 | 10.5 | All Other Non-Current | 6.6 | 8.2 |
| 100.0 | 100.0 | 100.0 | 100.0 | 100.0 | 100.0 | Total | 100.0 | 100.0 |
| | | | | | | LIABILITIES | | |
| 6.6 | 2.4 | .9 | .1 | .5 | .6 | Notes Payable-Short Term | 1.8 | .9 |
| .6 | .6 | 1.8 | 1.6 | 1.6 | 2.3 | Cur. Mat.-L.T.D. | 1.7 | 1.7 |
| 10.0 | 13.2 | 7.0 | 4.6 | 1.8 | 3.0 | Trade Payables | 4.3 | 5.1 |
| 4.6 | .2 | .1 | .4 | .0 | .1 | Income Taxes Payable | .3 | .1 |
| 12.8 | 13.4 | 12.5 | 8.1 | 4.1 | 4.0 | All Other Current | 6.7 | 8.6 |
| 34.5 | 29.9 | 22.2 | 14.9 | 8.1 | 10.0 | Total Current | 14.8 | 16.3 |
| 1.8 | 4.5 | 27.2 | 24.5 | 22.3 | 25.3 | Long-Term Debt | 23.3 | 20.1 |
| .0 | .0 | .0 | .0 | .0 | .2 | Deferred Taxes | .0 | .0 |
| 1.1 | 3.9 | 4.4 | 5.0 | 4.2 | 2.6 | All Other Non-Current | 3.8 | 3.6 |
| 62.6 | 61.7 | 46.2 | 55.6 | 65.4 | 61.9 | Net Worth | 58.1 | 59.9 |
| 100.0 | 100.0 | 100.0 | 100.0 | 100.0 | 100.0 | Total Liabilities & Net Worth | 100.0 | 100.0 |
| | | | | | | INCOME DATA | | |
| 100.0 | 100.0 | 100.0 | 100.0 | 100.0 | 100.0 | Net Sales | 100.0 | 100.0 |
| | | | | | | Gross Profit | | |
| 98.3 | 95.6 | 86.9 | 91.6 | 92.1 | 87.8 | Operating Expenses | 87.8 | 88.2 |
| 1.7 | 4.4 | 13.1 | 8.4 | 7.9 | 12.2 | Operating Profit | 12.2 | 11.8 |
| .8 | 2.8 | 4.2 | 4.3 | 1.5 | 3.9 | All Other Expenses (net) | 1.9 | 2.6 |
| .9 | 1.6 | 8.9 | 4.1 | 6.3 | 8.3 | Profit Before Taxes | 10.3 | 9.2 |
| | | | | | | RATIOS | | |
| 3.9 | 7.6 | 5.7 | 7.0 | 7.0 | 4.1 | | 6.4 | 7.1 |
| 2.7 | 4.3 | 2.0 | 3.3 | 3.2 | 2.4 | Current | 3.2 | 3.5 |
| 1.5 | 1.2 | 1.3 | 1.9 | 1.4 | 1.6 | | 1.8 | 1.9 |
| 3.9 | 7.3 | 5.3 | 6.3 | 6.6 | 3.9 | | 6.0 | 6.7 |
| 2.7 | 3.9 | 1.7 | 3.0 | 2.9 | 2.4 | Quick | 2.8 | 3.1 |
| 1.2 | 1.2 | .9 | 1.6 | 1.2 | 1.5 | | 1.4 | 1.6 |
| 0 UND | 0 UND | 1 627.9 | 9 40.3 | 16 22.2 | 12 29.9 | | 6 65.4 | 2 148.8 |
| 6 57.8 | 3 121.0 | 20 18.7 | 30 12.0 | 36 10.1 | 32 11.5 | Sales/Receivables | 20 17.9 | 17 21.4 |
| 18 20.3 | 20 18.3 | 46 8.0 | 49 7.5 | 72 5.1 | 43 8.4 | | 41 9.0 | 42 8.7 |
| | | | | | | Cost of Sales/Inventory | | |
| | | | | | | Cost of Sales/Payables | | |
| 5.4 | 1.7 | 2.0 | 1.2 | 1.2 | 1.9 | | 1.4 | 1.3 |
| 9.4 | 3.6 | 5.4 | 2.7 | 2.2 | 3.2 | Sales/Working Capital | 2.8 | 3.0 |
| 482.8 | 33.1 | 15.0 | 6.1 | 10.5 | 6.2 | | 7.4 | 7.3 |
| | 5.3 | 20.6 | 7.1 | 8.2 | 9.9 | | 10.2 | 10.6 |
| (14) .6 | (49) 2.9 | (64) 2.1 | (42) 3.4 | (35) 4.4 | | EBIT/Interest | (152) 4.2 | (187) 4.0 |
| | -12.1 | 1.0 | .5 | .8 | 2.3 | | 1.5 | 1.1 |
| | | | | | | Net Profit + Depr., Dep., Amort./Cur. Mat. L/T/D | | |
| .0 | .0 | .0 | .3 | .8 | .8 | | .4 | .1 |
| .1 | .0 | .7 | .9 | 1.1 | 1.1 | Fixed/Worth | 1.0 | .9 |
| .7 | .6 | 1.3 | 1.4 | 1.3 | 1.4 | | 1.3 | 1.2 |
| .2 | .2 | .3 | .2 | .2 | .3 | | .3 | .2 |
| .5 | .3 | .9 | .5 | .4 | .4 | Debt/Worth | .6 | .5 |
| .6 | 1.2 | 1.9 | 1.2 | .8 | 1.1 | | 1.4 | 1.2 |
| 30.0 | 19.2 | 18.1 | 5.9 | 6.8 | 8.0 | | 15.1 | 12.8 |
| (10) -.1 | (29) 5.5 | (67) 5.6 | (86) 2.2 | (44) 2.8 | (41) 4.3 | % Profit Before Taxes/Tangible Net Worth | (225) 5.9 | (267) 5.0 |
| -11.7 | -2.2 | -.7 | -.7 | -.4 | 2.0 | | 1.3 | .0 |
| 11.3 | 15.0 | 10.5 | 3.3 | 4.0 | 4.6 | | 7.5 | 7.3 |
| .8 | 1.9 | 3.2 | 1.2 | 2.0 | 2.6 | % Profit Before Taxes/Total Assets | 3.2 | 2.9 |
| -4.2 | -3.0 | -.5 | -1.0 | -.3 | 1.5 | | .4 | -.1 |
| UND | UND | UND | 7.3 | .9 | .8 | | 13.5 | 118.3 |
| 58.5 | UND | 2.2 | .7 | .4 | .5 | Sales/Net Fixed Assets | .8 | .8 |
| 13.9 | 27.8 | .5 | .3 | .2 | .3 | | .4 | .4 |
| 6.9 | 3.9 | 2.2 | 1.0 | .4 | .5 | | 1.2 | 1.4 |
| 3.6 | 2.2 | .7 | .4 | .3 | .3 | Sales/Total Assets | .5 | .4 |
| 2.3 | .9 | .3 | .2 | .2 | .2 | | .2 | .3 |
| | | .8 | 4.6 | 5.9 | 6.2 | | 2.4 | 4.0 |
| | (47) 6.2 | (60) 10.0 | (39) 12.4 | (35) 11.2 | | % Depr., Dep., Amort./Sales | (135) 7.1 | (166) 8.0 |
| | | 17.1 | 21.3 | 18.0 | 16.6 | | 11.0 | 13.4 |
| | | | | | | % Officers', Directors' Owners' Comp/Sales | 2.3 | 3.9 |
| | | | | | | | (19) 8.5 | (19) 11.0 |
| | | | | | | | 15.6 | 18.2 |
| 13300M | 96808M | 584922M | 1848912M | 1327931M | 3382058M | Net Sales ($) | 6970509M | 8477845M |
| 3234M | 35270M | 398267M | 2318523M | 3340644M | 6573736M | Total Assets ($) | 10604440M | 13993055M |

M = $ thousand    MM = $ million
See Pages 9 through 22 for Explanation of Ratios and Data

## Comparative Historical Data / Current Data Sorted by Sales

| | | | Type of Statement | | | | | | |
|---|---|---|---|---|---|---|---|---|---|
| 196 | 200 | 229 | Unqualified | 15 | 33 | 21 | 41 | 59 | 60 |
| 7 | 2 | 1 | Reviewed | | | | 1 | | |
| 9 | 4 | 4 | Compiled | | 1 | 1 | | 1 | 1 |
| 2 | | 3 | Tax Returns | | 3 | | | | |
| 65 | 38 | 57 | Other | 12 | 10 | 8 | 6 | 9 | 12 |
| 4/1/09- | 4/1/10- | 4/1/11- | | | 220 (4/1-9/30/11) | | 74 (10/1/11-3/31/12) | | |
| 3/31/10 | 3/31/11 | 3/31/12 | | | | | | | |
| ALL | ALL | ALL | | 0-1MM | 1-3MM | 3-5MM | 5-10MM | 10-25MM | 25MM & OVER |
| 279 | 244 | 294 | **NUMBER OF STATEMENTS** | 27 | 47 | 30 | 48 | 69 | 73 |
| % | % | % | **ASSETS** | % | % | % | % | % | % |
| 28.3 | 30.0 | 28.3 | Cash & Equivalents | 33.5 | 28.0 | 30.9 | 23.4 | 25.3 | 31.5 |
| 8.2 | 8.0 | 8.0 | Trade Receivables (net) | 4.9 | 9.2 | 4.4 | 6.1 | 8.2 | 11.1 |
| .7 | .5 | 1.2 | Inventory | .1 | 2.1 | .3 | .9 | 1.0 | 1.8 |
| 4.7 | 5.5 | 5.1 | All Other Current | 2.3 | 6.1 | 3.1 | 7.8 | 3.1 | 6.5 |
| 41.9 | 44.0 | 42.7 | Total Current | 40.8 | 45.4 | 38.8 | 38.1 | 37.5 | 51.0 |
| 49.5 | 47.6 | 48.6 | Fixed Assets (net) | 47.3 | 43.2 | 57.5 | 50.7 | 53.9 | 42.4 |
| .9 | .4 | .7 | Intangibles (net) | .2 | 1.2 | .1 | .2 | .7 | 1.3 |
| 7.8 | 8.0 | 8.0 | All Other Non-Current | 11.6 | 10.2 | 3.6 | 11.0 | 7.8 | 5.3 |
| 100.0 | 100.0 | 100.0 | Total | 100.0 | 100.0 | 100.0 | 100.0 | 100.0 | 100.0 |
| | | | **LIABILITIES** | | | | | | |
| 2.4 | .9 | .9 | Notes Payable-Short Term | 1.2 | 2.2 | .0 | 1.1 | .4 | .7 |
| 2.0 | 1.8 | 1.6 | Cur. Mat.-L.T.D. | 2.0 | 1.0 | 1.6 | 1.6 | 1.9 | 1.7 |
| 4.0 | 4.8 | 5.6 | Trade Payables | 4.2 | 4.8 | 2.3 | 4.7 | 6.0 | 8.2 |
| .3 | .8 | .4 | Income Taxes Payable | .0 | 1.1 | .0 | .1 | .3 | .4 |
| 7.3 | 8.2 | 8.7 | All Other Current | 4.1 | 5.8 | 5.2 | 11.8 | 9.4 | 10.8 |
| 16.0 | 16.4 | 17.1 | Total Current | 11.6 | 14.9 | 9.1 | 19.3 | 18.0 | 21.8 |
| 23.7 | 22.9 | 21.9 | Long-Term Debt | 26.7 | 18.4 | 18.4 | 21.7 | 27.0 | 19.4 |
| .0 | .0 | .0 | Deferred Taxes | .0 | .0 | .0 | .0 | .0 | .1 |
| 4.2 | 4.4 | 4.1 | All Other Non-Current | 3.3 | 5.7 | 1.7 | 2.8 | 2.6 | 6.7 |
| 56.0 | 56.2 | 56.8 | Net Worth | 58.5 | 61.1 | 70.8 | 56.2 | 52.4 | 52.0 |
| 100.0 | 100.0 | 100.0 | Total Liabilties & Net Worth | 100.0 | 100.0 | 100.0 | 100.0 | 100.0 | 100.0 |
| | | | **INCOME DATA** | | | | | | |
| 100.0 | 100.0 | 100.0 | Net Sales | 100.0 | 100.0 | 100.0 | 100.0 | 100.0 | 100.0 |
| | | | Gross Profit | | | | | | |
| 92.4 | 90.6 | 90.7 | Operating Expenses | 84.2 | 92.2 | 90.2 | 89.8 | 91.8 | 92.0 |
| 7.6 | 9.4 | 9.3 | Operating Profit | 15.8 | 7.8 | 9.8 | 10.2 | 8.2 | 8.0 |
| 3.8 | 2.8 | 3.5 | All Other Expenses (net) | 9.9 | 3.9 | 2.3 | 2.9 | 1.6 | 3.3 |
| 3.8 | 6.6 | 5.8 | Profit Before Taxes | 5.9 | 3.9 | 7.5 | 7.2 | 6.6 | 4.7 |
| | | | **RATIOS** | | | | | | |
| 7.4 | 6.4 | 6.2 | | 5.7 | 10.1 | 8.2 | 5.2 | 5.1 | 6.0 |
| 3.1 | 3.3 | 2.9 | Current | 3.8 | 4.4 | 5.2 | 2.0 | 2.9 | 3.1 |
| 1.6 | 1.7 | 1.5 | | 1.5 | 1.8 | 1.6 | 1.2 | 1.5 | 1.9 |
| 6.4 | 5.6 | 5.4 | | 5.7 | 9.4 | 7.4 | 4.8 | 4.9 | 4.9 |
| 2.9 (243) | 3.1 | 2.6 | Quick | 3.7 | 3.6 | 5.0 | 1.7 | 2.5 | 2.5 |
| 1.3 | 1.5 | 1.4 | | 1.2 | 1.8 | 1.6 | .8 | 1.3 | 1.4 |
| 0 999.8 | 3 115.8 | 6 58.0 | | 0 UND | 0 UND | 4 95.4 | 5 72.8 | 12 29.3 | 11 33.4 |
| 19 19.2 | 25 14.3 | 25 14.6 | Sales/Receivables | 6 57.8 | 9 42.3 | 35 10.5 | 29 12.8 | 25 14.4 | 29 12.8 |
| 52 7.1 | 49 7.5 | 47 7.8 | | 47 7.7 | 45 8.2 | 89 4.1 | 53 6.9 | 47 7.8 | 42 8.6 |
| | | | Cost of Sales/Inventory | | | | | | |
| | | | Cost of Sales/Payables | | | | | | |
| 1.5 | 1.5 | 1.6 | | 1.3 | .9 | 1.6 | 1.4 | 1.7 | 1.9 |
| 2.8 | 3.2 | 3.3 | Sales/Working Capital | 3.5 | 2.5 | 2.5 | 4.2 | 3.2 | 4.1 |
| 8.9 | 9.0 | 10.0 | | 9.1 | 10.5 | 6.0 | 47.7 | 8.1 | 9.5 |
| 8.0 | 9.7 | 8.3 | | 3.9 | 3.7 | 25.9 | 8.2 | 8.5 | 11.8 |
| (180) 2.2 | (173) 2.4 | (207) 2.8 | EBIT/Interest | (10) 1.6 | (30) 1.0 | (21) 6.9 | (33) 1.9 | (58) 3.2 | (55) 4.3 |
| -.3 | .6 | .8 | | .4 | -.7 | .6 | .5 | 1.1 | 2.0 |
| | | | Net Profit + Depr., Dep., Amort./Cur. Mat. L/T/D | | | | | | |
| .2 | .0 | .1 | | .0 | .0 | .5 | .3 | .6 | .0 |
| .9 | .9 | .9 | Fixed/Worth | .8 | .7 | .9 | 1.0 | .9 | .8 |
| 1.4 | 1.2 | 1.3 | | 2.0 | 1.3 | 1.4 | 1.2 | 1.2 | 1.2 |
| .2 | .2 | .3 | | .2 | .2 | .2 | .3 | .3 | .3 |
| .6 | .5 | .5 | Debt/Worth | .5 | .5 | .4 | .6 | .5 | .5 |
| 1.6 | 1.3 | 1.2 | | 1.7 | 1.5 | .8 | 1.5 | 1.1 | 2.0 |
| 7.5 | 9.0 | 10.0 | % Profit Before Taxes/Tangible Net Worth | 15.8 | 6.2 | 14.2 | 8.3 | 8.2 | 11.0 |
| (267) 1.1 | (234) 2.4 | (277) 3.0 | | (25) 3.3 | (46) 1.2 | 1.7 | (44) 2.0 | (66) 3.1 | (66) 6.1 |
| -3.2 | -1.7 | -.5 | | -1.2 | -3.3 | -.7 | -1.1 | .0 | 2.3 |
| 4.1 | 6.2 | 5.2 | % Profit Before Taxes/Total Assets | 6.6 | 4.4 | 12.3 | 3.6 | 4.0 | 6.6 |
| .8 | 1.5 | 1.9 | | 1.5 | .9 | 1.3 | 1.2 | 2.2 | 3.9 |
| -1.8 | -.9 | -.7 | | -1.0 | -1.5 | -.5 | -.8 | .0 | .9 |
| 34.1 | 173.0 | 67.3 | Sales/Net Fixed Assets | UND | UND | 2.6 | 27.1 | 8.8 | UND |
| .8 | .8 | .8 | | 1.0 | 1.5 | .7 | .9 | .5 | 1.5 |
| .3 | .3 | .3 | | .2 | .2 | .2 | .3 | .3 | .6 |
| 1.5 | 1.8 | 1.4 | | 1.3 | 2.1 | 1.1 | 1.0 | 1.1 | 2.3 |
| .5 | .5 | .5 | Sales/Total Assets | .5 | .4 | .5 | .4 | .3 | .7 |
| .2 | .2 | .2 | | .1 | .2 | .2 | .2 | .2 | .4 |
| 3.8 | 4.7 | 4.4 | | 13.5 | 4.4 | 5.2 | 4.5 | 4.8 | 2.5 |
| (160) 8.2 | (157) 9.7 | (192) 9.6 | % Depr., Dep., Amort./Sales | (12) 24.3 | (31) 8.5 | (21) 10.2 | (31) 11.7 | (54) 11.3 | (43) 5.4 |
| 15.9 | 16.4 | 17.2 | | 29.3 | 24.0 | 19.7 | 19.9 | 16.3 | 9.9 |
| 5.3 | 2.6 | 2.3 | % Officers', Directors' Owners' Comp/Sales | | | | | | |
| (30) 8.9 | (22) 5.8 | (25) 7.4 | | | | | | | |
| 18.1 | 13.1 | 14.5 | | | | | | | |
| 6180462M | 6260311M | 7253931M | Net Sales ($) | 19278M | 87596M | 117278M | 342363M | 1128617M | 5558799M |
| 11715031M | 11560135M | 12669674M | Total Assets ($) | 75794M | 414262M | 506548M | 1447705M | 3521057M | 6704308M |

© RMA 2012

M = $ thousand    MM = $ million
See Pages 9 through 22 for Explanation of Ratios and Data

## Current Data Sorted by Assets | Comparative Historical Data

| 0-500M | 500M-2MM | 2-10MM | 10-50MM | 50-100MM | 100-250MM | Type of Statement | 4/1/07-3/31/08 ALL | 4/1/08-3/31/09 ALL |
|---|---|---|---|---|---|---|---|---|
| | 17 | 27 | 21 | 3 | 2 | Unqualified | 36 | 44 |
| | 4 | 7 | | | | Reviewed | 13 | 15 |
| 1 | 1 | 2 | 1 | | | Compiled | 11 | 5 |
| 1 | 4 | 1 | | | | Tax Returns | 7 | 8 |
| 3 | 4 | 18 | 2 | | | Other | 10 | 22 |
| | 82 (4/1-9/30/11) | | 37 (10/1/11-3/31/12) | | | | | |
| 5 | 30 | 55 | 24 | 3 | 2 | NUMBER OF STATEMENTS | 77 | 94 |
| % | % | % | % | % | % | **ASSETS** | % | % |
| | 27.1 | 28.3 | 25.6 | | | Cash & Equivalents | 20.7 | 23.3 |
| | 4.1 | 9.8 | 13.3 | | | Trade Receivables (net) | 12.6 | 11.6 |
| | .0 | .5 | 1.0 | | | Inventory | 2.2 | 1.7 |
| | .3 | 2.4 | 2.8 | | | All Other Current | 2.8 | 3.7 |
| | 31.5 | 40.9 | 42.6 | | | Total Current | 38.2 | 40.3 |
| | 67.4 | 55.8 | 49.2 | | | Fixed Assets (net) | 56.6 | 52.7 |
| | .0 | .3 | 3.7 | | | Intangibles (net) | .8 | .8 |
| | 1.1 | 3.0 | 4.4 | | | All Other Non-Current | 4.3 | 6.2 |
| | 100.0 | 100.0 | 100.0 | | | Total | 100.0 | 100.0 |
| | | | | | | **LIABILITIES** | | |
| | .9 | 1.9 | 1.4 | | | Notes Payable-Short Term | 4.0 | 3.8 |
| | 2.7 | 2.2 | 4.4 | | | Cur. Mat.-L.T.D. | 2.9 | 3.2 |
| | 1.0 | 3.1 | 3.5 | | | Trade Payables | 5.2 | 3.2 |
| | .0 | .0 | 2.3 | | | Income Taxes Payable | .0 | .0 |
| | 2.5 | 5.3 | 7.0 | | | All Other Current | 5.2 | 5.5 |
| | 7.2 | 12.5 | 18.5 | | | Total Current | 17.4 | 15.6 |
| | 30.2 | 28.3 | 23.3 | | | Long-Term Debt | 20.9 | 22.7 |
| | .2 | .2 | .2 | | | Deferred Taxes | .2 | .1 |
| | .8 | 1.2 | 6.1 | | | All Other Non-Current | 1.0 | 3.6 |
| | 61.7 | 57.8 | 52.0 | | | Net Worth | 60.6 | 58.0 |
| | 100.0 | 100.0 | 100.0 | | | Total Liabilities & Net Worth | 100.0 | 100.0 |
| | | | | | | **INCOME DATA** | | |
| | 100.0 | 100.0 | 100.0 | | | Net Sales | 100.0 | 100.0 |
| | | | | | | Gross Profit | | |
| | 94.2 | 89.9 | 95.0 | | | Operating Expenses | 87.3 | 92.0 |
| | 5.8 | 10.1 | 5.0 | | | Operating Profit | 12.7 | 8.0 |
| | 5.4 | 2.8 | 2.6 | | | All Other Expenses (net) | 4.1 | 2.2 |
| | .4 | 7.3 | 2.4 | | | Profit Before Taxes | 8.6 | 5.8 |
| | | | | | | **RATIOS** | | |
| | 8.6 | 15.4 | 8.3 | | | | 8.2 | 8.5 |
| | 4.8 | 5.0 | 2.6 | | | Current | 3.3 | 3.1 |
| | 2.2 | 1.8 | 1.4 | | | | 1.5 | 1.5 |
| | 8.6 | 15.4 | 8.3 | | | | 7.6 | 8.4 |
| | 4.8 | 4.7 | 2.4 | | | Quick | 3.0 | 2.8 |
| | 2.2 | 1.7 | 1.2 | | | | 1.2 | 1.3 |
| | 0 UND | 0 UND | 1 275.1 | | | | 0 UND | 0 UND |
| | 0 UND | 3 135.1 | 15 24.9 | | | Sales/Receivables | 1 520.3 | 7 48.8 |
| | 27 13.6 | 36 10.2 | 61 6.0 | | | | 37 9.8 | 29 12.7 |
| | | | | | | Cost of Sales/Inventory | | |
| | | | | | | Cost of Sales/Payables | | |
| | 1.2 | 1.4 | 1.5 | | | | 1.5 | 1.8 |
| | 2.4 | 2.3 | 2.3 | | | Sales/Working Capital | 3.3 | 4.4 |
| | 44.1 | 10.2 | 9.3 | | | | 14.6 | 13.6 |
| | 1.1 | 12.3 | 5.6 | | | | 11.3 | 6.4 |
| | (22) .1 | (42) 4.7 | (21) 2.0 | | | EBIT/Interest | (54) 4.0 | (73) 3.5 |
| | -1.1 | 1.9 | -.6 | | | | .5 | 1.4 |
| | | | | | | Net Profit + Depr., Dep., Amort./Cur. Mat. L/T/D | | |
| | .7 | .5 | .7 | | | | .5 | .4 |
| | 1.0 | .9 | 1.2 | | | Fixed/Worth | .8 | .9 |
| | 2.0 | 1.5 | 2.0 | | | | 1.4 | 1.4 |
| | .2 | .2 | .3 | | | | .2 | .3 |
| | .5 | .6 | 1.1 | | | Debt/Worth | .5 | .6 |
| | 1.4 | 1.2 | 2.8 | | | | 1.8 | 1.5 |
| | 6.6 | 16.3 | 10.0 | | | | 23.3 | 18.0 |
| | (29) -1.0 | (54) 6.4 | (23) 3.8 | | | % Profit Before Taxes/Tangible Net Worth | (75) 7.7 | (91) 6.9 |
| | -8.0 | 1.2 | -4.2 | | | | .3 | .1 |
| | 3.6 | 8.5 | 4.8 | | | | 9.8 | 9.6 |
| | -.5 | 4.2 | 1.9 | | | % Profit Before Taxes/Total Assets | 3.4 | 3.5 |
| | -3.3 | .5 | -2.4 | | | | -.3 | -.2 |
| | 1.7 | 2.2 | 2.3 | | | | 7.8 | 8.8 |
| | .7 | 1.0 | .9 | | | Sales/Net Fixed Assets | .9 | 1.1 |
| | .3 | .4 | .6 | | | | .3 | .4 |
| | 1.0 | 1.0 | .9 | | | | 1.8 | 2.0 |
| | .5 | .6 | .4 | | | Sales/Total Assets | .5 | .7 |
| | .3 | .3 | .4 | | | | .2 | .3 |
| | 8.0 | 4.1 | 4.7 | | | | 1.6 | 2.3 |
| | (24) 13.9 | (32) 9.9 | (20) 7.4 | | | % Depr., Dep., Amort./Sales | (59) 10.4 | (67) 7.8 |
| | 24.0 | 20.3 | 10.4 | | | | 18.8 | 18.8 |
| | | | | | | | 2.1 | 2.4 |
| | | | | | | % Officers', Directors' Owners' Comp/Sales | (12) 5.1 | (15) 3.9 |
| | | | | | | | 11.6 | 8.1 |
| 3661M | 26066M | 193854M | 412111M | 139375M | 241328M | Net Sales ($) | 375306M | 746514M |
| 1479M | 36916M | 227103M | 430146M | 236580M | 449192M | Total Assets ($) | 329150M | 893732M |

M = $ thousand   MM = $ million
See Pages 9 through 22 for Explanation of Ratios and Data

## Comparative Historical Data

## Current Data Sorted by Sales

| | | | Type of Statement | | | | | | |
|---|---|---|---|---|---|---|---|---|---|
| 38 | 48 | 70 | Unqualified | 11 | 17 | 14 | 13 | 7 | 8 |
| 6 | 5 | 11 | Reviewed | 5 | 2 | | 2 | 2 | |
| 7 | 7 | 5 | Compiled | 3 | 1 | | 1 | | |
| 8 | 8 | 6 | Tax Returns | 5 | | 1 | | | |
| 27 | 25 | 27 | Other | 12 | 10 | 2 | 1 | 1 | 1 |
| 4/1/09-3/31/10 | 4/1/10-3/31/11 | 4/1/11-3/31/12 | | | 82 (4/1-9/30/11) | | | 37 (10/1/11-3/31/12) | |
| ALL | ALL | ALL | | 0-1MM | 1-3MM | 3-5MM | 5-10MM | 10-25MM | 25MM & OVER |
| 86 | 93 | 119 | NUMBER OF STATEMENTS | 36 | 30 | 17 | 17 | 10 | 9 |
| % | % | % | ASSETS | % | % | % | % | % | % |
| 23.5 | 27.6 | 29.4 | Cash & Equivalents | 30.5 | 27.6 | 22.6 | 37.2 | 29.1 | |
| 10.8 | 10.8 | 8.4 | Trade Receivables (net) | .7 | 5.1 | 10.7 | 16.0 | 24.2 | |
| 2.0 | 1.5 | .5 | Inventory | .0 | .2 | .1 | .4 | 1.8 | |
| 3.1 | 3.7 | 1.8 | All Other Current | .1 | .4 | 2.5 | 2.9 | 7.7 | |
| 39.3 | 43.7 | 40.1 | Total Current | 31.3 | 33.3 | 35.9 | 56.5 | 62.8 | |
| 52.7 | 49.2 | 55.8 | Fixed Assets (net) | 68.0 | 64.9 | 61.0 | 33.4 | 29.8 | |
| 2.2 | 1.8 | 1.0 | Intangibles (net) | .0 | .3 | .2 | 3.2 | 1.6 | |
| 5.8 | 5.3 | 3.1 | All Other Non-Current | .7 | 1.4 | 2.9 | 6.9 | 5.8 | |
| 100.0 | 100.0 | 100.0 | Total | 100.0 | 100.0 | 100.0 | 100.0 | 100.0 | |
| | | | LIABILITIES | | | | | | |
| 3.5 | 4.1 | 1.4 | Notes Payable-Short Term | .7 | .5 | .2 | 4.3 | 1.6 | |
| 3.3 | 3.3 | 3.1 | Cur. Mat.-L.T.D. | 3.2 | 3.4 | 2.0 | 1.8 | 5.8 | |
| 4.0 | 4.1 | 2.7 | Trade Payables | 1.0 | 1.0 | 2.4 | 3.1 | 8.8 | |
| .2 | .1 | .5 | Income Taxes Payable | .0 | .0 | .0 | 3.0 | .0 | |
| 5.2 | 5.3 | 4.8 | All Other Current | .5 | 3.7 | 8.3 | 6.6 | 10.7 | |
| 16.2 | 16.8 | 12.4 | Total Current | 5.4 | 8.6 | 13.0 | 18.8 | 26.9 | |
| 21.8 | 27.1 | 33.4 | Long-Term Debt | 50.0 | 29.6 | 40.5 | 17.8 | 13.7 | |
| .4 | .4 | .2 | Deferred Taxes | .0 | .2 | .6 | .0 | .0 | |
| 2.0 | 1.5 | 2.7 | All Other Non-Current | .0 | 2.9 | 1.4 | 2.5 | 9.2 | |
| 59.6 | 54.2 | 51.2 | Net Worth | 44.5 | 58.7 | 44.5 | 60.8 | 50.3 | |
| 100.0 | 100.0 | 100.0 | Total Liabilties & Net Worth | 100.0 | 100.0 | 100.0 | 100.0 | 100.0 | |
| | | | INCOME DATA | | | | | | |
| 100.0 | 100.0 | 100.0 | Net Sales | 100.0 | 100.0 | 100.0 | 100.0 | 100.0 | |
| | | | Gross Profit | | | | | | |
| 92.0 | 94.3 | 92.4 | Operating Expenses | 87.5 | 93.2 | 92.1 | 93.1 | 99.0 | |
| 8.0 | 5.7 | 7.6 | Operating Profit | 12.5 | 6.8 | 7.9 | 6.9 | 1.0 | |
| 2.2 | 2.5 | 3.4 | All Other Expenses (net) | 6.2 | 2.1 | 4.1 | .8 | 3.1 | |
| 5.9 | 3.2 | 4.2 | Profit Before Taxes | 6.4 | 4.7 | 3.8 | 6.1 | -2.2 | |
| | | | RATIOS | | | | | | |
| 6.6 | 9.4 | 9.9 | | 13.5 | 8.4 | 6.0 | 15.0 | 6.9 | |
| 3.5 | 3.7 | 4.5 | Current | 7.7 | 4.5 | 4.2 | 4.0 | 1.7 | |
| 1.5 | 1.4 | 1.8 | | 2.8 | 2.5 | 1.9 | 1.6 | 1.5 | |
| 6.4 | 9.1 | 9.9 | | 13.4 | 8.4 | 6.0 | 14.4 | 6.1 | |
| 3.1 | 3.5 | 4.4 | Quick | 7.7 | 4.2 | 3.9 | 4.0 | 1.7 | |
| 1.3 | 1.2 | 1.3 | | 2.8 | 2.4 | 1.3 | 1.3 | 1.3 | |
| 0 UND | 0 UND | 0 UND | | 0 UND | 0 UND | 0 UND | 1 611.6 | 9 41.3 | |
| 5 67.6 | 8 45.7 | 4 97.0 | Sales/Receivables | 0 UND | 1 585.5 | 6 60.5 | 28 13.1 | 30 12.2 | |
| 29 12.7 | 35 10.4 | 32 11.3 | | 5 68.9 | 35 10.5 | 33 11.2 | 69 5.3 | 87 4.2 | |
| | | | Cost of Sales/Inventory | | | | | | |
| | | | Cost of Sales/Payables | | | | | | |
| 1.9 | 1.6 | 1.4 | | .7 | 1.4 | 2.2 | 1.6 | 1.6 | |
| 4.4 | 4.1 | 2.3 | Sales/Working Capital | 1.5 | 3.6 | 2.3 | 2.3 | 4.9 | |
| 10.4 | 10.8 | 9.0 | | 5.3 | 12.4 | 7.5 | 6.7 | 8.1 | |
| 8.1 | 8.2 | 5.9 | | 5.7 | 5.9 | 5.1 | 6.2 | | |
| (60) 2.9 | (69) 2.8 | (93) 2.2 | EBIT/Interest | (26) 1.3 | (20) 3.1 | (15) 2.0 | (16) 2.9 | | |
| .7 | .4 | -.1 | | .0 | .1 | -.3 | 2.0 | | |
| | | | Net Profit + Depr., Dep., Amort./Cur. Mat. L/T/D | | | | | | |
| .5 | .3 | .6 | | .7 | .7 | .7 | .1 | .0 | |
| .9 | .9 | 1.0 | Fixed/Worth | 1.1 | 1.0 | 1.1 | .8 | .7 | |
| 1.7 | 1.5 | 1.6 | | 1.9 | 1.8 | 1.5 | 1.3 | 2.2 | |
| .2 | .2 | .3 | | .2 | .3 | .3 | .2 | .3 | |
| .5 | .6 | .7 | Debt/Worth | .7 | .5 | .8 | 1.0 | .8 | |
| 1.9 | 2.0 | 1.6 | | 1.4 | 1.2 | 1.7 | 1.6 | 5.1 | |
| 17.4 | 17.5 | 13.0 | | 7.9 | 15.3 | 13.1 | 17.7 | | |
| (83) 5.6 | (89) 5.8 | (114) 3.4 | % Profit Before Taxes/Tangible Net Worth | (34) 1.5 | (29) 6.0 | (16) 5.1 | 6.7 | | |
| -.5 | -5.1 | -3.2 | | -2.3 | -3.5 | -.3 | 2.6 | | |
| 9.1 | 8.2 | 6.5 | | 6.2 | 7.5 | 6.6 | 11.2 | 8.9 | |
| 3.3 | 3.6 | 2.0 | % Profit Before Taxes/Total Assets | 1.0 | 3.4 | 2.4 | 3.6 | 2.3 | |
| -.4 | -4.1 | -1.9 | | -.9 | -2.6 | -1.6 | 1.5 | -5.4 | |
| 10.6 | 17.9 | 2.2 | | .7 | 1.7 | 1.6 | UND | 152.7 | |
| 1.1 | 1.4 | 1.0 | Sales/Net Fixed Assets | .4 | 1.1 | 1.0 | 2.2 | 2.1 | |
| .4 | .6 | .5 | | .2 | .6 | .5 | .9 | 1.4 | |
| 1.9 | 1.8 | 1.0 | | .5 | 1.0 | .9 | 2.0 | 2.2 | |
| .7 | .8 | .5 | Sales/Total Assets | .3 | .7 | .6 | .7 | .9 | |
| .3 | .4 | .3 | | .2 | .4 | .4 | .5 | .5 | |
| 3.9 | 3.3 | 5.2 | | 14.6 | 5.1 | 6.7 | 1.1 | | |
| (61) 8.5 | (62) 7.2 | (82) 9.5 | % Depr., Dep., Amort./Sales | (24) 20.8 | (19) 9.2 | (13) 9.7 | (12) 5.7 | | |
| 19.1 | 14.9 | 19.3 | | 35.0 | 12.7 | 13.0 | 7.6 | | |
| 2.5 | 1.2 | | | | | | | | |
| (13) 4.4 | (13) 3.4 | | % Officers', Directors' Owners' Comp/Sales | | | | | | |
| 11.3 | 6.4 | | | | | | | | |
| 1024833M | 1296465M | 1016395M | Net Sales ($) | 17378M | 49622M | 64408M | 114963M | 139820M | 630204M |
| 666735M | 853510M | 1381416M | Total Assets ($) | 65782M | 84435M | 117892M | 145165M | 178473M | 789669M |

© RMA 2012

M = $ thousand     MM = $ million
See Pages 9 through 22 for Explanation of Ratios and Data

**Current Data Sorted by Assets**          **Comparative Historical Data**

| Type of Statement | 0-500M | 500M-2MM | 2-10MM | 10-50MM | 50-100MM | 100-250MM | 4/1/07-3/31/08 ALL | 4/1/08-3/31/09 ALL |
|---|---|---|---|---|---|---|---|---|
| Unqualified | 2 | 10 | 22 | 44 | 23 | 29 | 102 | 125 |
| Reviewed | | 1 | | | | | | 3 |
| Compiled | | | | | | | 2 | 1 |
| Tax Returns | | | | | | | 3 | 1 |
| Other | | 2 | 6 | 6 | 2 | 4 | 18 | 26 |
| (date ranges) | | 138 (4/1-9/30/11) | | | 13 (10/1/11-3/31/12) | | | |
| **NUMBER OF STATEMENTS** | 2 | 13 | 28 | 50 | 25 | 33 | 125 | 156 |
| **ASSETS** | % | % | % | % | % | % | % | % |
| Cash & Equivalents | | 33.7 | 29.8 | 17.5 | 21.2 | 16.0 | 30.8 | 25.5 |
| Trade Receivables (net) | | 18.4 | 15.2 | 8.6 | 8.1 | 8.4 | 8.0 | 9.9 |
| Inventory | | 1.4 | .1 | 1.3 | .1 | .5 | .9 | .5 |
| All Other Current | | 7.8 | 2.9 | 2.8 | 3.5 | 1.0 | 4.6 | 4.4 |
| Total Current | | 61.2 | 47.9 | 30.3 | 33.0 | 25.9 | 44.3 | 40.4 |
| Fixed Assets (net) | | 22.1 | 42.2 | 56.7 | 57.5 | 62.1 | 45.9 | 47.3 |
| Intangibles (net) | | .0 | .7 | 3.0 | 3.0 | 3.4 | 1.1 | 1.1 |
| All Other Non-Current | | 16.6 | 9.2 | 10.1 | 6.5 | 8.6 | 8.7 | 11.2 |
| Total | | 100.0 | 100.0 | 100.0 | 100.0 | 100.0 | 100.0 | 100.0 |
| **LIABILITIES** | | | | | | | | |
| Notes Payable-Short Term | | 4.0 | 2.3 | 1.4 | .0 | .9 | 1.4 | 2.1 |
| Cur. Mat.-L.T.D. | | 4.7 | 2.3 | 2.0 | 2.2 | 1.6 | 3.3 | 2.8 |
| Trade Payables | | 17.5 | 8.1 | 4.5 | 2.7 | 1.6 | 6.9 | 5.2 |
| Income Taxes Payable | | .0 | .0 | .0 | .0 | .0 | .2 | .0 |
| All Other Current | | 13.8 | 8.5 | 6.9 | 8.0 | 9.7 | 9.3 | 10.6 |
| Total Current | | 40.0 | 21.2 | 14.8 | 12.9 | 13.8 | 21.0 | 20.8 |
| Long-Term Debt | | 4.5 | 19.5 | 25.4 | 25.7 | 27.5 | 28.8 | 26.0 |
| Deferred Taxes | | .0 | .3 | .1 | .0 | .4 | .1 | .1 |
| All Other Non-Current | | 10.0 | 13.5 | 6.3 | 1.9 | 3.0 | 7.4 | 3.5 |
| Net Worth | | 45.5 | 45.5 | 53.4 | 59.6 | 55.3 | 42.6 | 49.5 |
| Total Liabilities & Net Worth | | 100.0 | 100.0 | 100.0 | 100.0 | 100.0 | 100.0 | 100.0 |
| **INCOME DATA** | | | | | | | | |
| Net Sales | | 100.0 | 100.0 | 100.0 | 100.0 | 100.0 | 100.0 | 100.0 |
| Gross Profit | | | | | | | | |
| Operating Expenses | | 90.7 | 92.5 | 97.2 | 98.3 | 95.4 | 93.3 | 93.9 |
| Operating Profit | | 9.3 | 7.5 | 2.8 | 1.7 | 4.6 | 6.7 | 6.1 |
| All Other Expenses (net) | | 6.2 | .9 | .3 | -1.9 | .5 | 1.3 | 2.7 |
| Profit Before Taxes | | 3.0 | 6.6 | 2.6 | 3.6 | 4.1 | 5.3 | 3.4 |
| **RATIOS** | | | | | | | | |
| Current | | 4.9 | 8.5 | 3.6 | 4.2 | 3.4 | 4.7 | 4.6 |
| | | 1.5 | 2.9 | 1.8 | 2.3 | 1.6 | 2.5 | 2.2 |
| | | 1.1 | 1.7 | 1.2 | 1.3 | 1.2 | 1.5 | 1.2 |
| Quick | | 4.3 | 8.2 | 2.9 | 3.6 | 3.3 | 4.1 | 4.4 |
| | | 1.5 | 2.7 | 1.7 | 1.5 | 1.4 | 2.2 | 1.7 |
| | | .6 | 1.3 | 1.0 | 1.2 | 1.1 | 1.2 | 1.0 |
| Sales/Receivables | | 0 UND | 0 UND | 2 169.5 | 11 34.2 | 9 42.1 | 0 UND | 2 216.3 |
| | | 3 113.5 | 18 20.2 | 14 26.0 | 27 13.7 | 25 14.4 | 7 50.7 | 14 26.4 |
| | | 33 11.1 | 56 6.5 | 38 9.7 | 70 5.2 | 46 7.9 | 33 11.1 | 42 8.7 |
| Cost of Sales/Inventory | | | | | | | | |
| Cost of Sales/Payables | | | | | | | | |
| Sales/Working Capital | | 6.1 | 2.2 | 4.8 | 2.6 | 3.8 | 3.3 | 2.9 |
| | | 10.4 | 5.4 | 9.2 | 6.5 | 8.0 | 6.6 | 7.6 |
| | | 74.3 | 10.5 | 34.8 | 20.4 | 24.2 | 24.1 | 40.5 |
| EBIT/Interest | | | 5.7 | 6.5 | 6.3 | 5.9 | 8.4 | 6.4 |
| | | (17) 2.0 | (40) 1.5 | (23) 1.9 | (28) 2.1 | | (75) 4.0 | (109) 2.1 |
| | | | -.3 | .0 | -.2 | .7 | 1.5 | .8 |
| Net Profit + Depr., Dep., Amort./Cur. Mat. L/T/D | | | | | | | | |
| Fixed/Worth | | .1 | .4 | .7 | .8 | .9 | .4 | .4 |
| | | .3 | .8 | 1.2 | 1.1 | 1.1 | 1.0 | 1.0 |
| | | .8 | 1.7 | 2.2 | 1.7 | 2.0 | 2.0 | 1.9 |
| Debt/Worth | | .2 | .3 | .3 | .2 | .3 | .4 | .4 |
| | | .8 | .9 | .9 | .8 | .9 | 1.2 | 1.0 |
| | | 6.0 | 2.4 | 2.1 | 2.0 | 1.8 | 3.0 | 2.1 |
| % Profit Before Taxes/Tangible Net Worth | | 30.4 | 22.3 | 9.2 | 8.2 | 8.2 | 21.0 | 14.7 |
| | (12) | 7.1 | (25) 6.7 | (48) 4.4 | 5.6 | (32) 2.6 | (114) 9.0 | (148) 4.3 |
| | | -17.1 | -5.0 | -3.8 | -.7 | -1.4 | 3.3 | -.3 |
| % Profit Before Taxes/Total Assets | | 22.6 | 8.8 | 4.9 | 4.2 | 3.9 | 8.5 | 6.5 |
| | | 2.7 | 2.9 | 1.7 | 2.4 | 1.2 | 4.0 | 2.0 |
| | | -1.0 | -2.0 | -1.4 | -.6 | -.5 | 1.0 | -.5 |
| Sales/Net Fixed Assets | | 135.3 | 14.5 | 3.5 | 4.0 | 1.4 | 12.2 | 8.3 |
| | | 31.4 | 2.9 | 1.7 | 1.1 | .8 | 2.2 | 2.0 |
| | | 9.4 | 1.2 | .8 | .8 | .6 | 1.1 | 1.0 |
| Sales/Total Assets | | 6.3 | 2.3 | 1.6 | 1.0 | .9 | 2.3 | 1.7 |
| | | 3.4 | 1.1 | 1.0 | .7 | .5 | 1.1 | 1.0 |
| | | 1.9 | .6 | .6 | .5 | .4 | .7 | .6 |
| % Depr., Dep., Amort./Sales | | | 1.9 | 1.3 | 1.5 | 2.8 | .9 | 1.6 |
| | (22) | 3.0 | (39) 3.6 | (21) 2.2 | (29) 4.6 | | (86) 2.3 | (120) 3.0 |
| | | 4.3 | 6.6 | 6.2 | 6.2 | | 4.0 | 4.8 |
| % Officers', Directors' Owners' Comp/Sales | | | | | | | 1.6 | 2.3 |
| | (16) | | | | | | 5.9 | (18) 7.7 |
| | | | | | | | 15.1 | 19.2 |
| Net Sales ($) | 3540M | 75938M | 218497M | 1443759M | 1369548M | 3424375M | 6674942M | 5605142M |
| Total Assets ($) | 785M | 16488M | 144906M | 1306411M | 1717058M | 5048906M | 4918226M | 5939363M |

© RMA 2012

M = $ thousand   MM = $ million
See Pages 9 through 22 for Explanation of Ratios and Data

| Comparative Historical Data | | | | | Current Data Sorted by Sales | | | | | |
|---|---|---|---|---|---|---|---|---|---|---|

| | | | | Type of Statement | | | | | | |
|---|---|---|---|---|---|---|---|---|---|---|
| 124 | 136 | 130 | | Unqualified | 3 | 10 | 12 | 9 | 33 | 63 |
| 2 | 1 | 1 | | Reviewed | | 1 | | | | |
| 2 | | | | Compiled | | | | | | |
| | | | | Tax Returns | | | | | | |
| 28 | 22 | 20 | | Other | 1 | | 2 | 2 | 4 | 11 |
| 4/1/09- | 4/1/10- | 4/1/11- | | | | 138 (4/1-9/30/11) | | 13 (10/1/11-3/31/12) | | |
| 3/31/10 | 3/31/11 | 3/31/12 | | | 0-1MM | 1-3MM | 3-5MM | 5-10MM | 10-25MM | 25MM & OVER |
| ALL | ALL | ALL | | | | | | | | |
| 156 | 159 | 151 | | **NUMBER OF STATEMENTS** | 4 | 10 | 15 | 11 | 37 | 74 |
| % | % | % | | **ASSETS** | % | % | % | % | % | % |
| 24.1 | 22.4 | 21.5 | | Cash & Equivalents | | 17.6 | 31.4 | 23.6 | 19.5 | 20.3 |
| 8.2 | 12.7 | 10.9 | | Trade Receivables (net) | | 21.7 | 5.7 | 8.7 | 16.1 | 8.7 |
| .8 | .8 | .7 | | Inventory | | .0 | .3 | .5 | 1.1 | .7 |
| 3.1 | 4.0 | 2.9 | | All Other Current | | 2.5 | 3.0 | 4.0 | 2.6 | 2.6 |
| 36.2 | 39.9 | 36.0 | | Total Current | | 41.8 | 40.5 | 36.8 | 39.3 | 32.4 |
| 51.0 | 50.3 | 52.1 | | Fixed Assets (net) | | 51.7 | 39.2 | 45.0 | 52.5 | 55.9 |
| .7 | 1.1 | 2.4 | | Intangibles (net) | | .1 | .1 | 1.7 | .3 | 4.4 |
| 12.2 | 8.7 | 9.5 | | All Other Non-Current | | 6.4 | 20.2 | 16.5 | 8.0 | 7.3 |
| 100.0 | 100.0 | 100.0 | | Total | | 100.0 | 100.0 | 100.0 | 100.0 | 100.0 |
| | | | | **LIABILITIES** | | | | | | |
| 1.7 | 3.3 | 1.4 | | Notes Payable-Short Term | | .5 | .5 | 1.1 | 3.1 | 1.0 |
| 2.7 | 2.7 | 2.2 | | Cur. Mat.-L.T.D. | | 1.5 | 2.0 | 1.4 | 2.3 | 1.7 |
| 5.2 | 5.1 | 5.4 | | Trade Payables | | 5.8 | 5.3 | 4.7 | 10.0 | 3.4 |
| .0 | .0 | .0 | | Income Taxes Payable | | .0 | .0 | .0 | .0 | .0 |
| 9.7 | 11.2 | 8.8 | | All Other Current | | 6.3 | 8.3 | 8.0 | 10.0 | 9.1 |
| 19.2 | 22.4 | 17.8 | | Total Current | | 14.1 | 16.1 | 15.2 | 25.4 | 15.3 |
| 25.4 | 23.8 | 22.7 | | Long-Term Debt | | 10.6 | 24.0 | 20.1 | 22.3 | 25.2 |
| .1 | .0 | .2 | | Deferred Taxes | | .0 | .0 | .0 | .2 | .2 |
| 5.1 | 6.4 | 6.4 | | All Other Non-Current | | 7.0 | 1.7 | 11.6 | 8.8 | 4.3 |
| 50.2 | 47.4 | 53.0 | | Net Worth | | 68.3 | 58.2 | 53.1 | 43.3 | 55.0 |
| 100.0 | 100.0 | 100.0 | | Total Liabilities & Net Worth | | 100.0 | 100.0 | 100.0 | 100.0 | 100.0 |
| | | | | **INCOME DATA** | | | | | | |
| 100.0 | 100.0 | 100.0 | | Net Sales | | 100.0 | 100.0 | 100.0 | 100.0 | 100.0 |
| | | | | Gross Profit | | | | | | |
| 96.7 | 95.2 | 95.6 | | Operating Expenses | | 102.2 | 94.0 | 94.7 | 95.1 | 96.9 |
| 3.3 | 4.8 | 4.4 | | Operating Profit | | -2.2 | 6.0 | 5.3 | 4.9 | 3.1 |
| 2.5 | .9 | .6 | | All Other Expenses (net) | | 1.0 | -1.8 | .4 | -.7 | .5 |
| .8 | 3.9 | 3.8 | | Profit Before Taxes | | -3.2 | 7.9 | 4.9 | 5.6 | 2.6 |
| | | | | **RATIOS** | | | | | | |
| 4.0 | 3.0 | 4.2 | | | | 8.7 | 6.7 | 4.5 | 2.9 | 3.6 |
| 2.0 | 1.8 | 1.9 | | Current | | 3.1 | 3.0 | 2.6 | 1.7 | 1.8 |
| 1.3 | 1.1 | 1.2 | | | | 1.8 | 1.5 | 1.7 | 1.0 | 1.2 |
| 3.9 | 2.8 | 3.7 | | | | 8.3 | 5.9 | 3.9 | 2.5 | 3.4 |
| 1.8 | 1.5 | 1.7 | | Quick | | 3.1 | 2.9 | 2.1 | 1.7 | 1.5 |
| 1.1 | .9 | 1.1 | | | | 1.7 | 1.3 | 1.1 | .9 | 1.1 |
| 2 | 195.3 | 4 | 96.4 | 3 | 120.1 | Sales/Receivables | 9 | 38.6 | 0 | UND | 0 | UND | 6 | 61.9 | 5 | 72.9 |

| 2 | 195.3 | 4 | 96.4 | 3 | 120.1 | | Sales/Receivables | 9 | 38.6 | 0 | UND | 0 | UND | 6 | 61.9 | 5 | 72.9 |
|---|---|---|---|---|---|---|---|---|---|---|---|---|---|---|---|---|---|
| 14 | 25.9 | 22 | 16.9 | 17 | 21.1 | | | 40 | 9.2 | 11 | 32.6 | 13 | 27.1 | 23 | 15.9 | 17 | 21.4 |
| 33 | 11.2 | 44 | 8.4 | 45 | 8.2 | | | 60 | 6.1 | 58 | 6.3 | 41 | 8.9 | 68 | 5.4 | 43 | 8.4 |

| | | | | Cost of Sales/Inventory | | | | | | |
|---|---|---|---|---|---|---|---|---|---|---|
| | | | | Cost of Sales/Payables | | | | | | |
| 3.4 | 4.7 | 3.7 | | | | 1.4 | 1.8 | 3.3 | 5.0 | 4.0 |
| 7.3 | 8.6 | 7.9 | | Sales/Working Capital | | 7.5 | 5.9 | 6.0 | 10.7 | 8.8 |
| 26.6 | 76.8 | 24.4 | | | | 11.0 | 13.0 | 10.4 | NM | 24.4 |

| 4.3 | 4.8 | 6.4 | | EBIT/Interest | | | | | 18.0 | 5.1 |
|---|---|---|---|---|---|---|---|---|---|---|
| (112) 1.2 | (113) 2.0 | (113) 2.0 | | | | | | (33) 1.8 | (62) 2.0 | |
| -.7 | .6 | .4 | | | | | | .7 | .3 | |

| | | | | Net Profit + Depr., Dep., Amort./Cur. Mat. L/T/D | | | | | | |
|---|---|---|---|---|---|---|---|---|---|---|
| .5 | .3 | .6 | | | | .6 | .1 | .4 | .8 | .8 |
| 1.0 | 1.1 | 1.0 | | Fixed/Worth | | .8 | .7 | .9 | 1.1 | 1.1 |
| 1.9 | 2.2 | 1.8 | | | | .9 | 1.2 | 2.3 | 2.0 | 2.0 |
| .3 | .4 | .3 | | | | .1 | .3 | .2 | .3 | .3 |
| .8 | 1.1 | .8 | | Debt/Worth | | .6 | .4 | .8 | 1.2 | .9 |
| 2.2 | 2.2 | 2.0 | | | | .9 | 1.2 | 1.9 | 3.2 | 2.0 |
| 7.6 | 11.5 | 10.5 | | % Profit Before Taxes/Tangible Net Worth | | 10.7 | 44.4 | | 8.1 | 9.1 |
| (149) 1.7 | (148) 3.8 | (144) 4.2 | | | | -5.1 | (14) 12.0 | (35) 4.9 | (72) 3.4 | |
| -5.8 | -1.8 | -2.3 | | | | -21.7 | 1.3 | | -2.4 | -2.4 |
| 4.6 | 6.4 | 5.2 | | % Profit Before Taxes/Total Assets | | 7.4 | 19.6 | 4.8 | 5.6 | 4.7 |
| .8 | 2.0 | 2.2 | | | | -4.7 | 5.6 | 2.1 | 2.1 | 2.2 |
| -2.8 | -.8 | -1.0 | | | | -12.7 | 1.4 | .8 | -.7 | -1.1 |
| 5.6 | 13.0 | 6.7 | | Sales/Net Fixed Assets | | 6.0 | 23.6 | 10.7 | 23.5 | 3.8 |
| 1.5 | 2.0 | 1.6 | | | | 1.9 | 2.5 | 2.1 | 2.0 | 1.3 |
| .8 | .8 | .8 | | | | 1.1 | 1.0 | .8 | .7 | .8 |
| 1.5 | 2.0 | 1.6 | | Sales/Total Assets | | 3.2 | 2.5 | 2.1 | 2.1 | 1.5 |
| .8 | 1.0 | .9 | | | | 1.0 | .7 | .9 | 1.2 | .9 |
| .5 | .6 | .5 | | | | .6 | .3 | .5 | .4 | .5 |
| 2.0 | 1.6 | 1.6 | | % Depr., Dep., Amort./Sales | | | 1.8 | | 1.1 | 1.6 |
| (123) 3.3 | (132) 3.0 | (121) 3.4 | | | | (11) 3.7 | (30) 3.6 | (60) 3.1 | |
| 5.1 | 4.9 | 5.8 | | | | | 13.6 | | 6.8 | 5.0 |
| 2.3 | 3.2 | 3.2 | | % Officers', Directors' Owners' Comp/Sales | | | | | | 4.8 |
| (23) 7.3 | (16) 6.5 | (12) 5.3 | | | | | | | (10) 6.8 | |
| 14.3 | 15.0 | 10.6 | | | | | | | | 17.1 |
| 6098055M | 7325453M | 6535657M | | Net Sales ($) | 1407M | 20992M | 58740M | 77384M | 665055M | 5712079M |
| 7529500M | 8087131M | 8234554M | | Total Assets ($) | 13647M | 24340M | 117838M | 106845M | 984040M | 6987844M |

© RMA 2012

M = $ thousand    MM = $ million
See Pages 9 through 22 for Explanation of Ratios and Data

## Current Data Sorted by Assets         Comparative Historical Data

| 0-500M | 500M-2MM | 2-10MM | 10-50MM | 50-100MM | 100-250MM | | 4/1/07-3/31/08 ALL | 4/1/08-3/31/09 ALL |
|---|---|---|---|---|---|---|---|---|
| | | | | | | **Type of Statement** | | |
| 3 | 3 | 9 | 11 | 6 | | Unqualified | 20 | 18 |
| | | 1 | | | | Reviewed | | 1 |
| | | | 1 | | | Compiled | 1 | |
| | | | | | | Tax Returns | | 1 |
| | | 2 | 4 | | | Other | 8 | 3 |
| | 28 (4/1-9/30/11) | | 9 (10/1/11-3/31/12) | | | | | |
| | 3 | 12 | 16 | 6 | | **NUMBER OF STATEMENTS** | 29 | 23 |
| % | % | % | % | % | % | **ASSETS** | % | % |
| | | 21.3 | 31.7 | | | Cash & Equivalents | 35.5 | 33.7 |
| | | 19.6 | 20.5 | | | Trade Receivables (net) | 16.7 | 20.3 |
| | | .8 | .9 | | | Inventory | 1.5 | 1.1 |
| | | 10.9 | 3.4 | | | All Other Current | 2.6 | 5.4 |
| | | 52.5 | 56.5 | | | Total Current | 56.3 | 60.5 |
| | | 34.6 | 30.5 | | | Fixed Assets (net) | 29.4 | 25.8 |
| | | 3.8 | .3 | | | Intangibles (net) | 2.1 | 2.2 |
| | | 9.0 | 12.8 | | | All Other Non-Current | 12.3 | 11.5 |
| | | 100.0 | 100.0 | | | Total | 100.0 | 100.0 |
| | | | | | | **LIABILITIES** | | |
| | | 2.8 | 2.3 | | | Notes Payable-Short Term | 4.0 | 3.2 |
| | | 1.8 | 1.1 | | | Cur. Mat.-L.T.D. | 1.0 | 1.1 |
| | | 6.8 | 6.2 | | | Trade Payables | 6.1 | 11.2 |
| | | .0 | .0 | | | Income Taxes Payable | .2 | .0 |
| | | 19.4 | 18.0 | | | All Other Current | 15.4 | 18.1 |
| | | 30.9 | 27.6 | | | Total Current | 26.7 | 33.6 |
| | | 16.0 | 16.8 | | | Long-Term Debt | 15.3 | 8.7 |
| | | .0 | .0 | | | Deferred Taxes | .0 | .0 |
| | | 2.1 | 6.0 | | | All Other Non-Current | 4.1 | 6.2 |
| | | 51.0 | 49.6 | | | Net Worth | 53.9 | 51.5 |
| | | 100.0 | 100.0 | | | Total Liabilities & Net Worth | 100.0 | 100.0 |
| | | | | | | **INCOME DATA** | | |
| | | 100.0 | 100.0 | | | Net Sales | 100.0 | 100.0 |
| | | | | | | Gross Profit | | |
| | | 96.6 | 95.4 | | | Operating Expenses | 89.0 | 96.0 |
| | | 3.4 | 4.6 | | | Operating Profit | 11.0 | 4.0 |
| | | 2.6 | -.4 | | | All Other Expenses (net) | 1.9 | .4 |
| | | .8 | 5.0 | | | Profit Before Taxes | 9.1 | 3.6 |
| | | | | | | **RATIOS** | | |
| | | 3.1 | 2.8 | | | | 4.9 | 3.1 |
| | | 2.1 | 1.9 | | | Current | 2.5 | 1.9 |
| | | 1.2 | 1.4 | | | | 1.2 | 1.3 |
| | | 3.1 | 2.2 | | | | 4.4 | 2.9 |
| | | 1.3 | 1.6 | | | Quick | 2.4 | 1.6 |
| | | 1.0 | 1.2 | | | | 1.2 | .8 |
| | | 4  97.1 | 4  95.3 | | | | 6  65.9 | 3  132.6 |
| | | 31  11.6 | 29  12.6 | | | Sales/Receivables | 38  9.5 | 34  10.7 |
| | | 45  8.1 | 64  5.7 | | | | 54  6.8 | 57  6.5 |
| | | | | | | Cost of Sales/Inventory | | |
| | | | | | | Cost of Sales/Payables | | |
| | | 3.3 | 4.5 | | | | 2.4 | 4.1 |
| | | 9.2 | 15.0 | | | Sales/Working Capital | 5.7 | 11.8 |
| | | 48.3 | 22.2 | | | | 16.3 | 25.0 |
| | | | 15.7 | | | | 14.7 | 36.1 |
| | | (12) 5.9 | | | | EBIT/Interest | (17) 4.8 | (12) 9.6 |
| | | | 1.9 | | | | 2.5 | -4.2 |
| | | | | | | Net Profit + Depr., Dep., Amort./Cur. Mat. L/T/D | | |
| | | .1 | .1 | | | | .0 | .1 |
| | | .6 | .4 | | | Fixed/Worth | .5 | .3 |
| | | 1.5 | 1.1 | | | | 1.4 | .8 |
| | | .5 | .6 | | | | .3 | .6 |
| | | 1.0 | 1.0 | | | Debt/Worth | .9 | .9 |
| | | 2.7 | 2.1 | | | | 2.2 | 2.1 |
| | | 10.9 | 29.1 | | | | 22.6 | 47.8 |
| | | 4.8 | 10.3 | | | % Profit Before Taxes/Tangible Net Worth | 9.6 | (22) 6.8 |
| | | -3.7 | 2.7 | | | | 3.5 | -2.5 |
| | | 9.6 | 13.6 | | | | 9.2 | 16.2 |
| | | 1.1 | 4.4 | | | % Profit Before Taxes/Total Assets | 3.4 | 3.6 |
| | | -2.7 | 1.4 | | | | 1.5 | -1.9 |
| | | 46.3 | 73.6 | | | | 63.3 | 70.3 |
| | | 6.0 | 15.1 | | | Sales/Net Fixed Assets | 6.3 | 10.4 |
| | | 2.1 | 1.9 | | | | 3.9 | 5.5 |
| | | 3.9 | 4.0 | | | | 3.1 | 4.4 |
| | | 1.8 | 1.6 | | | Sales/Total Assets | 1.8 | 3.0 |
| | | 1.0 | 1.1 | | | | .5 | 1.1 |
| | | | .3 | | | | .5 | .4 |
| | | (15) | .9 | | | % Depr., Dep., Amort./Sales | (21) 1.7 | (16) 1.0 |
| | | | 4.4 | | | | 3.6 | 1.4 |
| | | | | | | % Officers', Directors' Owners' Comp/Sales | | |
| | 12944M | 121830M | 980615M | 977615M | | Net Sales ($) | 1904918M | 870688M |
| | 4591M | 48844M | 467292M | 409237M | | Total Assets ($) | 1130792M | 678620M |

*Columns 0-500M (and 500M-2MM) on the left and 50-100MM (and 100-250MM) on the right are marked "DATA NOT AVAILABLE".*

M = $ thousand    MM = $ million
See Pages 9 through 22 for Explanation of Ratios and Data

| | Comparative Historical Data | | | Type of Statement | Current Data Sorted by Sales | | | | | |
|---|---|---|---|---|---|---|---|---|---|---|
| | 28 | 24 | 29 | Unqualified | 1 | 2 | 3 | 3 | 7 | 14 |
| | 1 | | 1 | Reviewed | | | | | | |
| | 1 | 1 | | Compiled | 1 | | | | | |
| | 2 | 1 | 1 | Tax Returns | | | | | 1 | |
| | 6 | 8 | 6 | Other | | | | | 1 | 4 |
| | 4/1/09-3/31/10 ALL | 4/1/10-3/31/11 ALL | 4/1/11-3/31/12 ALL | | 28 (4/1-9/30/11) | | | 9 (10/1/11-3/31/12) | | |
| | | | | | 0-1MM | 1-3MM | 3-5MM | 5-10MM | 10-25MM | 25MM & OVER |
| | 38 | 34 | 37 | NUMBER OF STATEMENTS | 1 | 2 | 3 | 4 | 9 | 18 |
| | % | % | % | ASSETS | % | % | % | % | % | % |
| | 29.3 | 27.3 | 31.2 | Cash & Equivalents | | | | | | 33.2 |
| | 20.4 | 22.2 | 21.6 | Trade Receivables (net) | | | | | | 28.2 |
| | 1.9 | .3 | .6 | Inventory | | | | | | .7 |
| | 4.4 | 6.3 | 5.6 | All Other Current | | | | | | 3.5 |
| | 56.0 | 56.2 | 59.1 | Total Current | | | | | | 65.6 |
| | 30.8 | 24.1 | 29.3 | Fixed Assets (net) | | | | | | 24.8 |
| | 2.1 | .2 | 1.4 | Intangibles (net) | | | | | | .2 |
| | 11.1 | 19.5 | 10.3 | All Other Non-Current | | | | | | 9.4 |
| | 100.0 | 100.0 | 100.0 | Total | | | | | | 100.0 |
| | | | | LIABILITIES | | | | | | |
| | 4.6 | 2.7 | 3.0 | Notes Payable-Short Term | | | | | | 3.2 |
| | 2.2 | .5 | 2.5 | Cur. Mat.-L.T.D. | | | | | | 3.6 |
| | 6.8 | 6.9 | 7.6 | Trade Payables | | | | | | 9.0 |
| | .0 | 1.8 | .0 | Income Taxes Payable | | | | | | .0 |
| | 13.2 | 22.9 | 21.4 | All Other Current | | | | | | 24.9 |
| | 26.8 | 34.8 | 34.6 | Total Current | | | | | | 40.7 |
| | 8.5 | 10.2 | 12.9 | Long-Term Debt | | | | | | 10.9 |
| | .0 | .0 | .0 | Deferred Taxes | | | | | | .0 |
| | 7.6 | 7.7 | 7.6 | All Other Non-Current | | | | | | 4.3 |
| | 57.1 | 47.3 | 44.9 | Net Worth | | | | | | 44.1 |
| | 100.0 | 100.0 | 100.0 | Total Liabilities & Net Worth | | | | | | 100.0 |
| | | | | INCOME DATA | | | | | | |
| | 100.0 | 100.0 | 100.0 | Net Sales | | | | | | 100.0 |
| | | | | Gross Profit | | | | | | |
| | 94.8 | 96.8 | 97.4 | Operating Expenses | | | | | | 98.2 |
| | 5.2 | 3.2 | 2.6 | Operating Profit | | | | | | 1.8 |
| | .9 | -.6 | .3 | All Other Expenses (net) | | | | | | -.7 |
| | 4.3 | 3.8 | 2.4 | Profit Before Taxes | | | | | | 2.6 |
| | | | | RATIOS | | | | | | |
| | 5.1 | 3.8 | 2.7 | Current | | | | | | 2.6 |
| | 2.1 | 1.6 | 2.1 | | | | | | | 1.9 |
| | 1.2 | 1.1 | 1.2 | | | | | | | 1.3 |
| | 4.2 | 3.3 | 2.4 | Quick | | | | | | 2.3 |
| | 1.9 | 1.4 | 1.4 | | | | | | | 1.6 |
| | 1.1 | .9 | 1.1 | | | | | | | 1.1 |
| | 2  161.6 | 7  52.1 | 4  99.1 | Sales/Receivables | | | | | | 9  42.7 |
| | 23  15.9 | 34  10.7 | 29  12.5 | | | | | | | 34  10.6 |
| | 51  7.2 | 53  6.9 | 62  5.9 | | | | | | | 69  5.3 |
| | | | | Cost of Sales/Inventory | | | | | | |
| | | | | Cost of Sales/Payables | | | | | | |
| | 3.2 | 3.7 | 4.3 | Sales/Working Capital | | | | | | 5.1 |
| | 6.7 | 12.3 | 11.7 | | | | | | | 15.0 |
| | 23.5 | 40.1 | 42.8 | | | | | | | 267.2 |
| | 18.6 | 30.1 | 15.7 | EBIT/Interest | | | | | | 15.7 |
| | (16)  6.1 | (14)  1.6 | (21)  4.4 | | | | | | | (12)  5.9 |
| | -1.6 | .2 | 1.7 | | | | | | | 2.0 |
| | | | | Net Profit + Depr., Dep., Amort./Cur. Mat. L/T/D | | | | | | |
| | .1 | .1 | .1 | Fixed/Worth | | | | | | .1 |
| | .5 | .4 | .5 | | | | | | | .2 |
| | 1.1 | .8 | 1.1 | | | | | | | 1.0 |
| | .2 | .4 | .6 | Debt/Worth | | | | | | .6 |
| | .6 | 1.0 | 1.0 | | | | | | | 1.1 |
| | 2.2 | 4.7 | 2.6 | | | | | | | 2.3 |
| | 19.8 | 30.1 | 24.3 | % Profit Before Taxes/Tangible Net Worth | | | | | | 29.6 |
| | (37)  7.0 | (33)  4.7 | 6.4 | | | | | | | 10.1 |
| | -3.6 | -4.7 | .0 | | | | | | | 2.0 |
| | 11.2 | 14.0 | 7.3 | % Profit Before Taxes/Total Assets | | | | | | 9.5 |
| | 3.4 | .8 | 2.2 | | | | | | | 4.2 |
| | -1.5 | -1.3 | .0 | | | | | | | .2 |
| | 35.2 | 79.2 | 72.8 | Sales/Net Fixed Assets | | | | | | 87.0 |
| | 9.6 | 23.1 | 21.7 | | | | | | | 40.7 |
| | 2.6 | 2.5 | 2.3 | | | | | | | 2.3 |
| | 3.2 | 4.0 | 3.8 | Sales/Total Assets | | | | | | 4.0 |
| | 1.6 | 2.0 | 2.0 | | | | | | | 2.8 |
| | .9 | .6 | 1.2 | | | | | | | 1.3 |
| | .9 | .4 | .5 | % Depr., Dep., Amort./Sales | | | | | | .3 |
| | (30)  1.9 | (29)  1.1 | (28)  .9 | | | | | | | (13)  .5 |
| | 3.3 | 3.5 | 3.3 | | | | | | | 3.9 |
| | | | | % Officers', Directors' Owners' Comp/Sales | | | | | | |
| | 990210M | 3503871M | 2093004M | Net Sales ($) | 132M | 4083M | 11756M | 26035M | 153495M | 1897503M |
| | 788975M | 1351328M | 929964M | Total Assets ($) | 3732M | 2934M | 83522M | 16009M | 95781M | 727986M |

© RMA 2012

M = $ thousand    MM = $ million

See Pages 9 through 22 for Explanation of Ratios and Data

## Current Data Sorted by Assets

## Comparative Historical Data

| | | | | | | Type of Statement | | |
|---|---|---|---|---|---|---|---|---|
| 1 | 4 | 11 | 30 | 14 | 17 | Unqualified | 45 | 45 |
| | 1 | 1 | | | | Reviewed | 7 | 5 |
| | | | 2 | 1 | | Compiled | 5 | 6 |
| | 1 | | | | | Tax Returns | 5 | 9 |
| 1 | 2 | 4 | 6 | | 2 | Other | 18 | 31 |
| | 66 (4/1-9/30/11) | | 32 (10/1/11-3/31/12) | | | | 4/1/07-3/31/08 | 4/1/08-3/31/09 |
| 0-500M | 500M-2MM | 2-10MM | 10-50MM | 50-100MM | 100-250MM | | ALL | ALL |
| 2 | 8 | 16 | 38 | 15 | 19 | NUMBER OF STATEMENTS | 80 | 96 |
| % | % | % | % | % | % | ASSETS | % | % |
| | | 9.4 | 13.7 | 13.6 | 13.6 | Cash & Equivalents | 13.7 | 11.4 |
| | | 6.5 | 4.3 | 2.3 | 2.8 | Trade Receivables (net) | 9.3 | 10.1 |
| | | 1.4 | .2 | .1 | .3 | Inventory | 2.9 | 1.7 |
| | | 1.6 | 1.8 | .4 | 1.8 | All Other Current | 2.5 | 1.8 |
| | | 18.9 | 20.0 | 16.4 | 18.4 | Total Current | 28.4 | 25.0 |
| | | 68.4 | 67.4 | 77.6 | 68.4 | Fixed Assets (net) | 59.2 | 63.8 |
| | | .3 | .4 | .2 | .5 | Intangibles (net) | 2.0 | 1.3 |
| | | 12.5 | 12.3 | 5.8 | 12.6 | All Other Non-Current | 10.5 | 9.9 |
| | | 100.0 | 100.0 | 100.0 | 100.0 | Total | 100.0 | 100.0 |
| | | | | | | LIABILITIES | | |
| | | .3 | .2 | .0 | .0 | Notes Payable-Short Term | 2.3 | 3.1 |
| | | 4.0 | 3.4 | 1.7 | 2.0 | Cur. Mat.-L.T.D. | 3.6 | 4.1 |
| | | 2.0 | 1.7 | 1.6 | 2.1 | Trade Payables | 5.3 | 5.0 |
| | | .0 | .0 | .1 | .0 | Income Taxes Payable | .0 | .0 |
| | | 1.4 | 3.3 | 1.0 | 1.7 | All Other Current | 4.5 | 3.4 |
| | | 7.6 | 8.6 | 4.4 | 5.8 | Total Current | 15.8 | 15.7 |
| | | 26.4 | 37.4 | 34.1 | 33.3 | Long-Term Debt | 29.4 | 31.2 |
| | | .0 | .0 | .0 | .0 | Deferred Taxes | .3 | .1 |
| | | 5.0 | 4.0 | .9 | 1.2 | All Other Non-Current | 2.5 | 2.9 |
| | | 61.0 | 50.0 | 60.6 | 59.7 | Net Worth | 52.1 | 50.1 |
| | | 100.0 | 100.0 | 100.0 | 100.0 | Total Liabilities & Net Worth | 100.0 | 100.0 |
| | | | | | | INCOME DATA | | |
| | | 100.0 | 100.0 | 100.0 | 100.0 | Net Sales | 100.0 | 100.0 |
| | | | | | | Gross Profit | | |
| | | 88.3 | 81.6 | 85.4 | 81.9 | Operating Expenses | 83.7 | 86.1 |
| | | 11.7 | 18.4 | 14.6 | 18.1 | Operating Profit | 16.3 | 13.9 |
| | | 4.5 | 10.5 | 9.4 | 3.4 | All Other Expenses (net) | 3.4 | 5.1 |
| | | 7.2 | 8.0 | 5.2 | 14.7 | Profit Before Taxes | 12.8 | 8.8 |
| | | | | | | RATIOS | | |
| | | 6.3 | 4.9 | 9.0 | 5.1 | | 4.0 | 4.9 |
| | | 2.6 | 2.3 | 2.4 | 3.1 | Current | 2.0 | 1.8 |
| | | 1.3 | 1.4 | 1.5 | 1.6 | | 1.1 | .9 |
| | | 5.2 | 4.9 | 8.6 | 5.1 | | 3.3 | 4.8 |
| | | 2.2 | 1.8 | 2.2 | 3.1 | Quick | 1.6 | 1.6 |
| | | 1.2 | .9 | 1.4 | 1.1 | | .8 | .8 |
| 27 | 13.3 | 11 | 34.7 | 17 | 22.0 | 30 | 12.2 | Sales/Receivables | 23 | 16.0 | 20 | 18.0 |
| 35 | 10.5 | 38 | 9.6 | 30 | 12.1 | 41 | 9.0 | | 36 | 10.2 | 38 | 9.5 |
| 53 | 6.9 | 56 | 6.5 | 66 | 5.5 | 62 | 5.9 | | 55 | 6.6 | 61 | 6.0 |
| | | | | | | Cost of Sales/Inventory | | |
| | | | | | | Cost of Sales/Payables | | |
| | | 2.0 | 1.4 | .6 | 1.1 | | 1.6 | 1.9 |
| | | 2.7 | 2.7 | 2.3 | 1.9 | Sales/Working Capital | 6.5 | 6.7 |
| | | 13.4 | 19.4 | 9.2 | 7.5 | | 60.6 | -36.6 |
| | | 14.2 | 6.1 | 4.9 | 4.6 | | 6.2 | 9.3 |
| | (13) | 6.0 | (30) | 2.9 | (10) | 2.3 | (16) | 3.1 | EBIT/Interest | (64) | 3.6 | (73) | 3.1 |
| | | .9 | 1.2 | -1.3 | 1.4 | | 2.2 | 1.3 |
| | | | | | | Net Profit + Depr., Dep., Amort./Cur. Mat. L/T/D | | |
| | | .8 | 1.0 | 1.0 | .9 | | .8 | .9 |
| | | 1.0 | 1.2 | 1.2 | 1.2 | Fixed/Worth | 1.3 | 1.2 |
| | | 1.6 | 1.7 | 1.7 | 1.4 | | 2.0 | 2.2 |
| | | .3 | .4 | .3 | .4 | | .4 | .4 |
| | | .6 | .8 | .5 | .6 | Debt/Worth | .8 | 1.0 |
| | | .9 | 1.6 | 1.1 | 1.2 | | 1.8 | 2.1 |
| | | 16.2 | 7.5 | 4.1 | 8.0 | | 11.8 | 8.1 |
| | (15) | 5.1 | (35) | 3.0 | (14) | 2.5 | 3.8 | % Profit Before Taxes/Tangible Net Worth | (74) | 5.2 | (87) | 3.4 |
| | | .1 | -.2 | -1.9 | .6 | | 1.9 | .4 |
| | | 9.3 | 4.2 | 2.9 | 4.5 | | 6.5 | 5.3 |
| | | 3.3 | 1.7 | 1.1 | 1.7 | % Profit Before Taxes/Total Assets | 3.3 | 2.0 |
| | | -.3 | -.2 | -1.2 | .4 | | .9 | .1 |
| | | 1.6 | .6 | .3 | .5 | | 4.0 | 2.6 |
| | | .3 | .2 | .2 | .3 | Sales/Net Fixed Assets | .5 | .3 |
| | | .2 | .1 | .1 | .2 | | .2 | .1 |
| | | .5 | .2 | .2 | .3 | | 1.6 | 1.0 |
| | | .2 | .1 | .1 | .2 | Sales/Total Assets | .2 | .2 |
| | | .2 | .1 | .1 | .1 | | .1 | .1 |
| | | 14.7 | 11.6 | 11.4 | 10.2 | | 4.5 | 3.6 |
| | (15) | 16.6 | (33) | 16.5 | 17.8 | (18) | 14.2 | % Depr., Dep., Amort./Sales | (77) | 11.5 | (87) | 14.9 |
| | | 22.2 | 26.1 | 32.1 | 16.6 | | 19.9 | 23.1 |
| | | | | | | | 3.1 | 3.2 |
| | | | | | | % Officers', Directors' Owners' Comp/Sales | (17) | 4.3 | (20) | 6.1 |
| | | | | | | | 8.5 | 7.8 |
| 393M | 10805M | 36272M | 339063M | 184564M | 668724M | Net Sales ($) | 1233432M | 1525014M |
| 635M | 9937M | 92103M | 1006785M | 1095418M | 2952791M | Total Assets ($) | 3446738M | 4556536M |

M = $ thousand    MM = $ million
See Pages 9 through 22 for Explanation of Ratios and Data

## Comparative Historical Data            Current Data Sorted by Sales

Current data date spans: **66 (4/1-9/30/11)** covers 0-1MM, 1-3MM, 3-5MM · **32 (10/1/11-3/31/12)** covers 5-10MM, 10-25MM, 25MM & OVER

| 4/1/09-3/31/10 ALL | 4/1/10-3/31/11 ALL | 4/1/11-3/31/12 ALL | | 0-1MM | 1-3MM | 3-5MM | 5-10MM | 10-25MM | 25MM & OVER |
|---|---|---|---|---|---|---|---|---|---|
| | | | **Type of Statement** | | | | | | |
| 61 | 63 | 77 | Unqualified | 11 | 18 | 5 | 17 | 12 | 14 |
| 7 | 3 | 2 | Reviewed | | | | 1 | | |
| 6 | 4 | 3 | Compiled | | | | 1 | | |
| | 1 | 2 | Tax Returns | 2 | | | | | |
| 19 | 23 | 14 | Other | 4 | 4 | 1 | 2 | 4 | 2 |
| 93 | 94 | 98 | **NUMBER OF STATEMENTS** | 17 | 22 | 6 | 21 | 16 | 16 |
| % | % | % | **ASSETS** | % | % | % | % | % | % |
| 12.9 | 13.8 | 14.5 | Cash & Equivalents | 13.6 | 11.7 | | 14.4 | 18.1 | 15.5 |
| 6.6 | 6.6 | 4.5 | Trade Receivables (net) | 3.9 | 1.3 | | 6.5 | 2.6 | 8.6 |
| 1.5 | 1.9 | 1.2 | Inventory | 4.6 | .2 | | .3 | .3 | .4 |
| 2.1 | 1.6 | 1.5 | All Other Current | 1.4 | 2.0 | | .2 | .5 | 4.3 |
| 23.1 | 23.9 | 21.7 | Total Current | 23.5 | 15.1 | | 21.4 | 21.4 | 28.8 |
| 66.1 | 66.9 | 67.6 | Fixed Assets (net) | 62.5 | 75.6 | | 66.9 | 69.3 | 59.5 |
| 2.7 | .7 | .3 | Intangibles (net) | .1 | .1 | | .4 | .8 | .3 |
| 8.1 | 8.5 | 10.4 | All Other Non-Current | 13.9 | 9.1 | | 11.4 | 8.5 | 11.4 |
| 100.0 | 100.0 | 100.0 | Total | 100.0 | 100.0 | | 100.0 | 100.0 | 100.0 |
| | | | **LIABILITIES** | | | | | | |
| 2.6 | 1.4 | .5 | Notes Payable-Short Term | .3 | .8 | | 1.0 | .0 | .1 |
| 4.6 | 3.1 | 3.0 | Cur. Mat.-L.T.D. | 5.7 | 2.2 | | 3.1 | 1.4 | 2.7 |
| 3.0 | 3.4 | 1.9 | Trade Payables | 1.2 | .9 | | 2.6 | 1.6 | 3.8 |
| .0 | .1 | .0 | Income Taxes Payable | .0 | .0 | | .1 | .0 | .0 |
| 3.7 | 3.3 | 3.1 | All Other Current | 7.2 | 2.5 | | 1.1 | 1.3 | 4.1 |
| 13.9 | 11.2 | 8.6 | Total Current | 14.4 | 6.4 | | 7.9 | 4.3 | 10.7 |
| 30.1 | 32.3 | 35.8 | Long-Term Debt | 56.0 | 31.2 | | 30.2 | 44.2 | 24.8 |
| .1 | .2 | .0 | Deferred Taxes | .0 | .0 | | .0 | .0 | .0 |
| 1.6 | 2.9 | 2.8 | All Other Non-Current | 3.4 | 4.5 | | 1.4 | 4.1 | 1.2 |
| 54.2 | 53.3 | 52.9 | Net Worth | 26.1 | 57.9 | | 60.5 | 47.3 | 63.3 |
| 100.0 | 100.0 | 100.0 | Total Liabilities & Net Worth | 100.0 | 100.0 | | 100.0 | 100.0 | 100.0 |
| | | | **INCOME DATA** | | | | | | |
| 100.0 | 100.0 | 100.0 | Net Sales | 100.0 | 100.0 | | 100.0 | 100.0 | 100.0 |
| | | | Gross Profit | | | | | | |
| 85.2 | 87.9 | 83.3 | Operating Expenses | 80.8 | 81.0 | | 90.0 | 76.6 | 87.0 |
| 14.8 | 12.1 | 16.7 | Operating Profit | 19.2 | 19.0 | | 10.0 | 23.4 | 13.0 |
| 7.3 | 5.7 | 8.0 | All Other Expenses (net) | 19.7 | 9.6 | | 3.3 | 11.9 | .7 |
| 7.4 | 6.4 | 8.7 | Profit Before Taxes | -.5 | 9.4 | | 6.7 | 11.6 | 12.3 |
| | | | **RATIOS** | | | | | | |
| 4.9 | 4.9 | 6.3 | | 9.0 | 4.8 | | 6.5 | 8.8 | 4.1 |
| 1.9 | 2.2 | 2.6 | Current | 2.1 | 2.3 | | 3.0 | 3.7 | 2.4 |
| .9 | 1.3 | 1.5 | | .4 | 1.4 | | 1.5 | 2.3 | 1.4 |
| 4.6 | 4.6 | 5.5 | | 6.6 | 3.8 | | 6.5 | 8.2 | 3.6 |
| 1.7 | 1.9 | 2.3 | Quick | 2.0 | 1.6 | | 3.0 | 3.3 | 1.9 |
| .6 | 1.0 | 1.1 | | 1.3 | .9 | | 1.3 | 2.1 | 1.1 |
| 13 · 27.7 | 19 · 18.7 | 15 · 24.1 | | 0 · UND | 5 · 68.9 | | 32 · 11.3 | 18 · 20.0 | 29 · 12.6 |
| 33 · 11.1 | 35 · 10.4 | 36 · 10.0 | Sales/Receivables | 41 · 8.8 | 31 · 11.7 | | 45 · 8.2 | 37 · 9.8 | 39 · 9.3 |
| 48 · 7.6 | 51 · 7.2 | 57 · 6.4 | | 73 · 5.0 | 37 · 9.8 | | 57 · 6.4 | 65 · 5.6 | 59 · 6.2 |
| | | | Cost of Sales/Inventory | | | | | | |
| | | | Cost of Sales/Payables | | | | | | |
| 1.4 | 1.4 | 1.3 | | 1.3 | 1.6 | | 1.2 | .8 | 1.9 |
| 6.0 | 3.9 | 2.4 | Sales/Working Capital | 3.7 | 2.3 | | 2.6 | 1.6 | 4.6 |
| -14.3 | 15.7 | 9.7 | | -1.2 | 22.2 | | 9.0 | 2.9 | 14.3 |
| 6.6 | 6.2 | 6.1 | | | 13.2 | | 6.1 | 4.0 | 16.7 |
| (69) 2.6 | (70) 2.3 | (75) 2.7 | EBIT/Interest | (17) 2.5 | | | (18) 2.5 | (14) 2.3 | (13) 4.4 |
| .8 | 1.2 | 1.0 | | | .5 | | .7 | 1.0 | 1.7 |
| | | | Net Profit + Depr., Dep., Amort./Cur. Mat. L/T/D | | | | | | |
| .9 | 1.0 | .9 | | .4 | 1.0 | | 1.0 | 1.1 | .6 |
| 1.2 | 1.3 | 1.2 | Fixed/Worth | 1.1 | 1.2 | | 1.2 | 1.3 | 1.0 |
| 2.2 | 1.9 | 1.6 | | 2.0 | 2.0 | | 1.5 | 2.0 | 1.4 |
| .3 | .4 | .3 | | .3 | .2 | | .4 | .4 | .2 |
| .8 | .8 | .6 | Debt/Worth | .8 | .5 | | .8 | .7 | .4 |
| 1.9 | 2.0 | 1.2 | | NM | 1.6 | | .9 | 1.7 | 1.1 |
| 7.8 | 6.9 | 7.5 | | 3.4 | 5.2 | | 10.4 | 5.6 | 16.2 |
| (83) 2.3 | (88) 2.6 | (91) 3.1 | % Profit Before Taxes/Tangible Net Worth | (13) 2.0 | (21) 2.6 | | 3.2 | (14) 3.1 | 5.1 |
| -.5 | -.1 | -.2 | | -.5 | -1.2 | | -.5 | 1.8 | 1.0 |
| 5.6 | 3.6 | 4.3 | | 1.5 | 4.2 | | 5.6 | 3.6 | 12.0 |
| 1.3 | 1.5 | 1.7 | % Profit Before Taxes/Total Assets | .1 | .6 | | 2.3 | 1.7 | 3.8 |
| -.3 | -.2 | -.2 | | -.8 | -1.1 | | -.3 | 1.1 | .7 |
| 1.1 | .9 | .7 | | UND | .4 | | .6 | .3 | 2.2 |
| .3 | .2 | .2 | Sales/Net Fixed Assets | .3 | .2 | | .3 | .2 | .5 |
| .1 | .1 | .2 | | .1 | .1 | | .2 | .2 | .3 |
| .6 | .5 | .3 | | .4 | .3 | | .3 | .2 | .9 |
| .2 | .2 | .2 | Sales/Total Assets | .1 | .1 | | .2 | .2 | .3 |
| .1 | .1 | .1 | | .1 | .1 | | .1 | .1 | .2 |
| 7.1 | 8.5 | 11.0 | | 12.2 | 14.8 | | 10.2 | 11.0 | 5.8 |
| (83) 18.2 | (83) 16.7 | (87) 15.2 | % Depr., Dep., Amort./Sales | (12) 21.6 | (20) 18.5 | | (20) 14.0 | (15) 16.4 | (14) 11.1 |
| 27.4 | 28.2 | 22.5 | | 31.5 | 31.7 | | 28.4 | 17.8 | 14.1 |
| | | 1.1 | | | | | | | |
| | (12) | 3.2 | % Officers', Directors' Owners' Comp/Sales | | | | | | |
| | | 6.3 | | | | | | | |
| 1549335M | 1656233M | 1239821M | Net Sales ($) | 10811M | 42516M | 23601M | 144930M | 252973M | 764990M |
| 3912737M | 5155685M | 5157669M | Total Assets ($) | 108120M | 379997M | 183766M | 845333M | 1627470M | 2012983M |

M = $ thousand    MM = $ million
See Pages 9 through 22 for Explanation of Ratios and Data

## Current Data Sorted by Assets     Comparative Historical Data

| | | | | | | Type of Statement | | |
|---|---|---|---|---|---|---|---|---|
| 1 | 4 | 20 | 33 | 13 | 8 | Unqualified | 90 | 72 |
| | | 1 | | | | Reviewed | 3 | 1 |
| | | 1 | | | | Compiled | | 7 |
| 1 | | | 1 | | | Tax Returns | 2 | 1 |
| 2 | 4 | 11 | 13 | 3 | | Other | 35 | 26 |
| | 78 (4/1-9/30/11) | | 38 (10/1/11-3/31/12) | | | | 4/1/07-3/31/08 | 4/1/08-3/31/09 |
| 0-500M | 500M-2MM | 2-10MM | 10-50MM | 50-100MM | 100-250MM | | ALL | ALL |
| 4 | 8 | 33 | 47 | 16 | 8 | NUMBER OF STATEMENTS | 130 | 107 |
| % | % | % | % | % | % | ASSETS | % | % |
| | | 15.4 | 19.2 | 17.2 | | Cash & Equivalents | 16.1 | 15.1 |
| | | 4.4 | 3.4 | 1.5 | | Trade Receivables (net) | 7.7 | 5.9 |
| | | 1.7 | 2.0 | .1 | | Inventory | 5.5 | 4.7 |
| | | 3.6 | 2.3 | 1.0 | | All Other Current | 4.2 | 3.7 |
| | | 25.2 | 26.8 | 19.8 | | Total Current | 33.6 | 29.4 |
| | | 47.5 | 54.4 | 68.1 | | Fixed Assets (net) | 44.3 | 46.9 |
| | | 2.4 | .5 | .1 | | Intangibles (net) | .3 | 1.0 |
| | | 25.0 | 18.3 | 12.0 | | All Other Non-Current | 21.8 | 22.7 |
| | | 100.0 | 100.0 | 100.0 | | Total | 100.0 | 100.0 |
| | | | | | | LIABILITIES | | |
| | | 2.7 | .6 | .1 | | Notes Payable-Short Term | 4.1 | 3.4 |
| | | 3.1 | 1.4 | .8 | | Cur. Mat.-L.T.D. | 2.6 | 2.4 |
| | | 1.9 | 1.6 | 1.7 | | Trade Payables | 3.0 | 3.5 |
| | | .0 | .1 | .0 | | Income Taxes Payable | .4 | .0 |
| | | 6.1 | 3.8 | 2.3 | | All Other Current | 5.0 | 4.7 |
| | | 13.9 | 7.5 | 4.9 | | Total Current | 15.1 | 13.9 |
| | | 26.7 | 29.8 | 24.8 | | Long-Term Debt | 33.7 | 33.0 |
| | | .0 | .0 | .0 | | Deferred Taxes | .0 | .0 |
| | | 6.6 | 4.7 | 9.6 | | All Other Non-Current | 3.4 | 3.7 |
| | | 52.8 | 58.0 | 60.8 | | Net Worth | 47.8 | 49.4 |
| | | 100.0 | 100.0 | 100.0 | | Total Liabilties & Net Worth | 100.0 | 100.0 |
| | | | | | | INCOME DATA | | |
| | | 100.0 | 100.0 | 100.0 | | Net Sales | 100.0 | 100.0 |
| | | | | | | Gross Profit | | |
| | | 94.0 | 88.0 | 96.2 | | Operating Expenses | 90.6 | 92.4 |
| | | 6.0 | 12.0 | 3.8 | | Operating Profit | 9.4 | 7.6 |
| | | 3.6 | 5.4 | 3.4 | | All Other Expenses (net) | 4.4 | 4.2 |
| | | 2.3 | 6.6 | .4 | | Profit Before Taxes | 5.0 | 3.4 |
| | | | | | | RATIOS | | |
| | | 4.3 | 8.0 | 5.5 | | | 6.2 | 5.6 |
| | | 1.8 | 3.7 | 3.4 | | Current | 2.4 | 2.3 |
| | | 1.0 | 1.2 | 2.1 | | | 1.3 | 1.0 |
| | | 3.5 | 6.7 | 5.3 | | | 4.9 | 4.0 |
| | | 1.3 | 3.2 | 3.1 | | Quick | 1.6 | 1.3 |
| | | .7 | 1.1 | 1.9 | | | .6 | .7 |
| | 0   UND | 2   182.3 | 3   130.4 | | | | 1   336.0 | 1   510.0 |
| | 12   29.6 | 5   76.2 | 7   51.2 | | | Sales/Receivables | 8   44.4 | 9   42.0 |
| | 29   12.5 | 22   16.4 | 19   19.6 | | | | 36   10.1 | 31   11.6 |
| | | | | | | Cost of Sales/Inventory | | |
| | | | | | | Cost of Sales/Payables | | |
| | | 1.2 | 1.3 | 3.3 | | | 1.5 | 2.2 |
| | | 13.1 | 3.6 | 4.6 | | Sales/Working Capital | 3.6 | 5.9 |
| | | 85.1 | 18.0 | 9.0 | | | 24.7 | -944.5 |
| | | 7.9 | 9.0 | 5.0 | | | 10.5 | 12.4 |
| | (25)   2.7 | (34)   4.0 | (15)   3.4 | | | EBIT/Interest | (95)   2.3 | (74)   2.4 |
| | | -.6 | .1 | -1.8 | | | .3 | -.2 |
| | | | | | | Net Profit + Depr., Dep., Amort./Cur. Mat. L/T/D | | |
| | | .2 | .4 | .8 | | | .2 | .2 |
| | | 1.0 | 1.0 | .9 | | Fixed/Worth | .8 | .8 |
| | | 2.4 | 1.7 | 1.8 | | | 1.8 | 1.8 |
| | | .4 | .2 | .3 | | | .3 | .2 |
| | | .6 | .5 | .4 | | Debt/Worth | 1.0 | .8 |
| | | 2.3 | 1.8 | 2.1 | | | 3.7 | 3.3 |
| | | 11.6 | 9.1 | 3.8 | | | 10.6 | 12.2 |
| | (31)   2.6 | (45)   4.1 | 1.8 | | | % Profit Before Taxes/Tangible Net Worth | (123)   3.7 | (99)   4.5 |
| | | -1.1 | -2.0 | -5.7 | | | -1.7 | -1.6 |
| | | 4.7 | 6.1 | 3.1 | | | 5.5 | 4.6 |
| | | 1.3 | 2.0 | 1.5 | | % Profit Before Taxes/Total Assets | 1.0 | 1.9 |
| | | -1.8 | -.7 | -2.1 | | | -1.1 | -1.0 |
| | | 3.7 | 2.0 | 1.2 | | | 6.8 | 5.2 |
| | | 1.5 | .8 | .7 | | Sales/Net Fixed Assets | 1.4 | 1.1 |
| | | .4 | .3 | .4 | | | .6 | .4 |
| | | .6 | .7 | .8 | | | .7 | .7 |
| | | .4 | .4 | .4 | | Sales/Total Assets | .4 | .5 |
| | | .2 | .2 | .3 | | | .2 | .2 |
| | | 1.5 | 4.0 | 4.7 | | | 1.3 | 1.9 |
| | (29)   6.4 | (42)   7.0 | 7.1 | | % Depr., Dep., Amort./Sales | (108)   4.4 | (94)   5.4 |
| | | 11.1 | 13.3 | 14.2 | | | 10.5 | 12.7 |
| | | | | | | % Officers', Directors' Owners' Comp/Sales | | 4.8 |
| | | | | | | | (11) | 16.7 |
| | | | | | | | | 23.0 |
| 1393M | 7251M | 127431M | 638743M | 605505M | 394334M | Net Sales ($) | 1651244M | 2500828M |
| 1336M | 10503M | 174265M | 1204060M | 1210819M | 1241407M | Total Assets ($) | 3837946M | 3455466M |

© RMA 2012

M = $ thousand     MM = $ million
See Pages 9 through 22 for Explanation of Ratios and Data

## Comparative Historical Data | | Current Data Sorted by Sales

| | | | Type of Statement | | | | | | |
|---|---|---|---|---|---|---|---|---|---|
| 84 | 77 | 79 | Unqualified | 6 | 16 | 7 | 14 | 15 | 21 |
| 1 | 2 | 1 | Reviewed | | 1 | | | | |
| 2 | 1 | 1 | Compiled | 1 | | | | | |
| 1 | | 2 | Tax Returns | 1 | | | | 1 | |
| 21 | 39 | 33 | Other | 6 | 8 | 3 | 9 | 5 | 2 |
| 4/1/09-3/31/10 ALL | 4/1/10-3/31/11 ALL | 4/1/11-3/31/12 ALL | | 78 (4/1-9/30/11) 0-1MM | 1-3MM | 3-5MM | 38 (10/1/11-3/31/12) 5-10MM | 10-25MM | 25MM & OVER |
| 109 | 119 | 116 | **NUMBER OF STATEMENTS** | 14 | 25 | 10 | 23 | 21 | 23 |
| % | % | % | **ASSETS** | % | % | % | % | % | % |
| 15.7 | 15.3 | 17.2 | Cash & Equivalents | 17.1 | 14.4 | 14.8 | 17.1 | 18.7 | 20.0 |
| 6.1 | 4.2 | 3.5 | Trade Receivables (net) | .1 | 6.2 | 1.9 | 2.0 | 2.1 | 5.9 |
| 2.7 | 2.7 | 2.0 | Inventory | 3.2 | 2.7 | 3.0 | 3.4 | .2 | .1 |
| 3.4 | 2.8 | 3.1 | All Other Current | 1.3 | 6.7 | .4 | 2.0 | 4.0 | 1.9 |
| 27.9 | 25.0 | 25.7 | Total Current | 21.6 | 30.0 | 20.0 | 24.6 | 25.0 | 27.9 |
| 52.7 | 54.0 | 52.8 | Fixed Assets (net) | 50.5 | 46.0 | 61.7 | 52.5 | 54.2 | 56.8 |
| 1.2 | 1.7 | 1.2 | Intangibles (net) | .2 | 1.2 | .3 | 3.6 | .3 | .5 |
| 18.2 | 19.3 | 20.3 | All Other Non-Current | 27.6 | 22.8 | 18.1 | 19.3 | 20.5 | 14.9 |
| 100.0 | 100.0 | 100.0 | Total | 100.0 | 100.0 | 100.0 | 100.0 | 100.0 | 100.0 |
| | | | **LIABILITIES** | | | | | | |
| 2.4 | 3.8 | 1.5 | Notes Payable-Short Term | 1.4 | 4.9 | .0 | .8 | .7 | .1 |
| 2.8 | 1.9 | 1.9 | Cur. Mat.-L.T.D. | 1.7 | 3.7 | 1.1 | 1.1 | 1.1 | 2.0 |
| 3.3 | 2.4 | 1.6 | Trade Payables | .6 | 2.0 | 1.2 | 1.2 | 1.5 | 2.5 |
| .0 | .0 | .0 | Income Taxes Payable | .0 | .0 | .4 | .0 | .0 | .0 |
| 5.4 | 6.6 | 4.2 | All Other Current | 4.1 | 3.8 | 5.0 | 3.7 | 3.5 | 5.4 |
| 13.9 | 14.8 | 9.3 | Total Current | 7.9 | 14.4 | 7.7 | 6.7 | 6.9 | 9.9 |
| 34.6 | 30.2 | 29.6 | Long-Term Debt | 34.9 | 26.5 | 51.9 | 30.3 | 25.4 | 23.3 |
| .3 | .3 | .0 | Deferred Taxes | .0 | .0 | .0 | .0 | .0 | .0 |
| 3.2 | 2.2 | 6.7 | All Other Non-Current | 7.3 | 7.3 | 1.7 | 3.2 | 9.6 | 8.5 |
| 48.0 | 52.5 | 54.4 | Net Worth | 49.9 | 51.8 | 38.7 | 59.8 | 58.2 | 58.3 |
| 100.0 | 100.0 | 100.0 | Total Liabilities & Net Worth | 100.0 | 100.0 | 100.0 | 100.0 | 100.0 | 100.0 |
| | | | **INCOME DATA** | | | | | | |
| 100.0 | 100.0 | 100.0 | Net Sales | 100.0 | 100.0 | 100.0 | 100.0 | 100.0 | 100.0 |
| | | | Gross Profit | | | | | | |
| 94.1 | 90.2 | 91.0 | Operating Expenses | 88.2 | 94.7 | 74.8 | 88.1 | 94.1 | 95.7 |
| 5.9 | 9.8 | 9.0 | Operating Profit | 11.8 | 5.3 | 25.2 | 11.9 | 5.9 | 4.3 |
| 4.8 | 5.2 | 5.1 | All Other Expenses (net) | 5.8 | 3.3 | 18.1 | 8.3 | 4.0 | -1.1 |
| 1.1 | 4.5 | 3.9 | Profit Before Taxes | 6.0 | 1.9 | 7.2 | 3.6 | 2.0 | 5.4 |
| | | | **RATIOS** | | | | | | |
| 5.2 | 4.9 | 5.8 | Current | 4.7 | 5.5 | 8.5 | 11.0 | 6.2 | 5.2 |
| 2.3 | 2.1 | 3.2 | | 3.0 | 1.8 | 1.6 | 4.1 | 3.5 | 3.0 |
| 1.1 | .9 | 1.3 | | .8 | 1.1 | .7 | 1.4 | 1.9 | 1.8 |
| 4.2 | 3.9 | 5.1 | Quick | 4.0 | 4.9 | 7.4 | 7.4 | 5.2 | 4.7 |
| 1.5 | 1.5 | 2.4 | | 1.9 | 1.3 | 1.6 | 3.6 | 3.3 | 2.7 |
| .7 | .7 | 1.0 | | .8 | .4 | .6 | 1.1 | 1.6 | 1.3 |
| 2  157.9 | 1  422.3 | 1  437.1 | Sales/Receivables | 0  UND | 1  390.0 | 4  103.6 | 1  428.5 | 1  267.1 | 5  79.8 |
| 8  44.6 | 7  54.6 | 6  62.0 | | 0  UND | 24  15.2 | 8  47.5 | 5  76.9 | 7  53.2 | 7  49.1 |
| 32  11.5 | 26  14.0 | 25  14.5 | | 1  305.4 | 47  7.7 | 29  12.6 | 15  23.6 | 26  14.2 | 22  16.4 |
| | | | Cost of Sales/Inventory | | | | | | |
| | | | Cost of Sales/Payables | | | | | | |
| 1.6 | 2.1 | 1.8 | Sales/Working Capital | .8 | 1.2 | 1.1 | 1.3 | 1.9 | 2.7 |
| 4.8 | 6.2 | 4.2 | | 5.9 | 6.2 | 11.5 | 3.7 | 3.5 | 5.7 |
| 43.2 | -80.2 | 18.0 | | -56.2 | 49.0 | -21.4 | 17.7 | 8.8 | 13.5 |
| 6.7 | 7.8 | 8.3 | EBIT/Interest | | | 6.1 | 9.2 | 9.0 | 8.0 |
| (74)  1.3 | (83)  3.3 | (84)  2.8 | | | (20)  1.0 | | (16)  4.7 | (18)  1.5 | (21)  4.8 |
| -.5 | .6 | -.5 | | | -3.3 | | .1 | -1.9 | 1.5 |
| | | | Net Profit + Depr., Dep., Amort./Cur. Mat. L/T/D | | | | | | |
| .5 | .4 | .5 | Fixed/Worth | .1 | .2 | .3 | .5 | .6 | .8 |
| 1.0 | 1.0 | 1.0 | | 1.0 | 1.3 | 1.9 | 1.0 | .8 | .9 |
| 2.0 | 1.9 | 2.3 | | 11.4 | 2.3 | NM | 1.5 | 3.0 | 1.2 |
| .4 | .2 | .3 | Debt/Worth | .2 | .2 | .5 | .2 | .1 | .3 |
| .8 | .7 | .5 | | .4 | .7 | 1.2 | .5 | .5 | .5 |
| 2.4 | 2.2 | 2.6 | | 21.4 | 2.6 | NM | 1.8 | 2.9 | 1.5 |
| 9.2 | 11.1 | 9.1 | % Profit Before Taxes/Tangible Net Worth | 17.5 | 7.9 | | 9.1 | 7.8 | 12.2 |
| (101)  1.5 | (112)  4.1 | (109)  3.0 | | (13)  .9 | (22)  1.4 | | 3.0 | 2.0 | (22)  4.4 |
| -3.9 | -3.6 | -2.6 | | -5.1 | -15.1 | | -1.4 | -5.5 | 1.0 |
| 3.0 | 5.5 | 4.9 | % Profit Before Taxes/Total Assets | 3.4 | 4.2 | 4.2 | 6.1 | 4.9 | 6.2 |
| .3 | 1.9 | 1.5 | | .5 | .6 | .8 | 1.7 | 1.8 | 2.6 |
| -2.0 | -1.8 | -1.8 | | -1.9 | -5.9 | -.4 | -.7 | -2.4 | .1 |
| 3.0 | 2.8 | 2.9 | Sales/Net Fixed Assets | 28.8 | 3.8 | 24.5 | 2.5 | 3.1 | 1.9 |
| .9 | 1.0 | .8 | | .4 | 1.5 | .2 | .8 | .8 | .9 |
| .4 | .4 | .4 | | .1 | .4 | .1 | .4 | .4 | .6 |
| .8 | .9 | .7 | Sales/Total Assets | .4 | .6 | .5 | .6 | .8 | 1.0 |
| .4 | .5 | .4 | | .2 | .4 | .2 | .5 | .5 | .7 |
| .2 | .2 | .2 | | .1 | .3 | .1 | .2 | .3 | .4 |
| 2.4 | 1.9 | 3.0 | % Depr., Dep., Amort./Sales | 6.4 | 1.5 | | 2.8 | 3.5 | 3.2 |
| (92)  6.6 | (104)  5.7 | (102)  6.6 | | (11)  14.3 | (21)  6.8 | | (20)  6.7 | (20)  6.0 | 5.4 |
| 13.0 | 12.6 | 13.4 | | 16.8 | 10.7 | | 12.7 | 14.8 | 9.1 |
| 2.7 | 3.8 | 3.2 | % Officers', Directors', Owners' Comp/Sales | | | | | | |
| (12)  7.3 | (12)  7.2 | (12)  5.3 | | | | | | | |
| 18.8 | 16.9 | 13.8 | | | | | | | |
| 1440944M | 1576651M | 1774657M | Net Sales ($) | 6051M | 46585M | 37805M | 159230M | 365721M | 1159265M |
| 3818664M | 3203606M | 3842390M | Total Assets ($) | 34612M | 151238M | 226120M | 554922M | 1000734M | 1874764M |

© RMA 2012

M = $ thousand   MM = $ million

See Pages 9 through 22 for Explanation of Ratios and Data

## Current Data Sorted by Assets | Comparative Historical Data

| 1 | 4 | 16 | 21 | 8 | 10 | Type of Statement | | |
|---|---|---|---|---|---|---|---|---|
| 1 | | | | | | Unqualified | 65 | 60 |
| | | | | | | Reviewed | 1 | |
| | 2 | 2 | 2 | 1 | 1 | Compiled | 6 | 5 |
| | | 1 | | | | Tax Returns | 2 | |
| 1 | | 8 | 9 | 2 | | Other | 22 | 26 |
| | 58 (4/1-9/30/11) | | 32 (10/1/11-3/31/12) | | | | 4/1/07-3/31/08 | 4/1/08-3/31/09 |
| 0-500M | 500M-2MM | 2-10MM | 10-50MM | 50-100MM | 100-250MM | | ALL | ALL |
| 3 | 6 | 27 | 32 | 11 | 11 | NUMBER OF STATEMENTS | 96 | 91 |
| % | % | % | % | % | % | ASSETS | % | % |
| | | 24.2 | 28.2 | 12.7 | 10.1 | Cash & Equivalents | 16.3 | 21.2 |
| | | 5.2 | 8.7 | 7.9 | 12.3 | Trade Receivables (net) | 16.1 | 15.1 |
| | | 7.2 | 1.3 | .1 | .2 | Inventory | 3.0 | 1.9 |
| | | 1.3 | 5.4 | 4.5 | .4 | All Other Current | 5.1 | 4.6 |
| | | 37.8 | 43.6 | 25.1 | 23.0 | Total Current | 40.6 | 42.8 |
| | | 43.5 | 31.3 | 53.2 | 41.8 | Fixed Assets (net) | 35.9 | 30.6 |
| | | .3 | .2 | .3 | .7 | Intangibles (net) | .5 | .7 |
| | | 18.3 | 24.9 | 21.3 | 34.5 | All Other Non-Current | 23.0 | 25.9 |
| | | 100.0 | 100.0 | 100.0 | 100.0 | Total | 100.0 | 100.0 |
| | | | | | | LIABILITIES | | |
| | | 6.1 | 1.1 | .1 | 2.2 | Notes Payable-Short Term | 7.0 | 6.0 |
| | | 2.5 | 3.7 | 4.5 | 2.9 | Cur. Mat.-L.T.D. | 3.2 | 3.9 |
| | | 2.9 | 3.1 | 1.1 | 1.4 | Trade Payables | 3.5 | 3.1 |
| | | .0 | .0 | .0 | .0 | Income Taxes Payable | .0 | .0 |
| | | 8.0 | 6.9 | 1.2 | 5.8 | All Other Current | 8.8 | 6.5 |
| | | 19.4 | 14.9 | 6.9 | 12.3 | Total Current | 22.5 | 19.6 |
| | | 37.3 | 50.5 | 49.3 | 65.8 | Long-Term Debt | 35.5 | 36.9 |
| | | .0 | .0 | .0 | .0 | Deferred Taxes | .0 | .0 |
| | | 5.5 | 3.1 | 6.3 | 7.4 | All Other Non-Current | 3.4 | 4.1 |
| | | 37.8 | 31.5 | 37.5 | 14.4 | Net Worth | 38.6 | 39.4 |
| | | 100.0 | 100.0 | 100.0 | 100.0 | Total Liabilities & Net Worth | 100.0 | 100.0 |
| | | | | | | INCOME DATA | | |
| | | 100.0 | 100.0 | 100.0 | 100.0 | Net Sales | 100.0 | 100.0 |
| | | | | | | Gross Profit | | |
| | | 69.5 | 79.9 | 80.8 | 80.3 | Operating Expenses | 78.3 | 75.1 |
| | | 30.5 | 20.1 | 19.2 | 19.7 | Operating Profit | 21.7 | 24.9 |
| | | 14.1 | 15.1 | 14.8 | 16.8 | All Other Expenses (net) | 11.3 | 13.7 |
| | | 16.4 | 5.0 | 4.4 | 2.9 | Profit Before Taxes | 10.4 | 11.1 |
| | | | | | | RATIOS | | |
| | | 10.7 | 6.9 | 11.0 | 6.3 | | 5.3 | 7.4 |
| | | 2.5 | 3.4 | 2.6 | 2.0 | Current | 2.0 | 3.4 |
| | | 1.1 | 1.5 | 1.1 | .4 | | 1.2 | 1.3 |
| | | 9.5 | 6.2 | 5.0 | 5.7 | | 4.2 | 5.0 |
| | | 2.3 | 2.3 | 2.6 | 1.9 | Quick | 1.6 | 2.4 |
| | | .7 | 1.1 | .7 | .4 | | .6 | 1.1 |
| 0 | UND | 0 | UND | 5 | 76.6 | 1 | 276.7 | 0 | UND | 0 | UND |
| 11 | 32.2 | 8 | 46.0 | 45 | 8.1 | 22 | 16.4 | Sales/Receivables | 20 | 18.5 | 25 | 14.4 |
| 62 | 5.9 | 73 | 5.0 | 107 | 3.4 | 203 | 1.8 | | 128 | 2.9 | 194 | 1.9 |
| | | | | | | Cost of Sales/Inventory | | |
| | | | | | | Cost of Sales/Payables | | |
| | | .8 | .5 | .6 | .8 | | .6 | .5 |
| | | 2.3 | 1.7 | 2.0 | 2.9 | Sales/Working Capital | 4.5 | 1.8 |
| | | 42.1 | 4.8 | 95.3 | -1.0 | | 19.8 | 14.4 |
| | | 9.9 | 10.1 | | | | 6.6 | 6.5 |
| | (18) | 2.7 | (21) 2.4 | | | EBIT/Interest | (57) 1.7 | (62) 2.7 |
| | | .9 | -2.6 | | | | -.2 | .5 |
| | | | | | | Net Profit + Depr., Dep., Amort./Cur. Mat. L/T/D | | |
| | | .1 | .0 | .2 | .0 | | .0 | .0 |
| | | .9 | .5 | 1.0 | .9 | Fixed/Worth | .5 | .4 |
| | | 2.6 | 1.4 | 2.1 | 2.3 | | 1.5 | 1.7 |
| | | .6 | .5 | .6 | .6 | | .5 | .6 |
| | | 1.3 | 1.6 | 1.7 | 3.8 | Debt/Worth | 1.4 | 1.6 |
| | | 7.3 | 19.4 | 3.3 | -22.6 | | 3.4 | 3.6 |
| | | 15.2 | 9.2 | 16.8 | | % Profit Before Taxes/Tangible Net Worth | 16.1 | 10.7 |
| | (23) | 5.4 | (26) 4.0 | (10) 2.3 | | | (90) 4.8 | (84) 3.6 |
| | | -.8 | -3.5 | .4 | | | -2.0 | -1.9 |
| | | 5.2 | 3.5 | 1.7 | 1.8 | % Profit Before Taxes/Total Assets | 5.3 | 5.5 |
| | | 2.0 | 1.0 | .5 | -.2 | | 2.0 | 2.0 |
| | | -.3 | -1.1 | -.3 | -1.3 | | -1.0 | -.9 |
| | | 11.0 | 142.8 | 1.5 | 999.8 | | 87.4 | 92.8 |
| | | 1.6 | 1.3 | .4 | .3 | Sales/Net Fixed Assets | 2.5 | 3.3 |
| | | .3 | .7 | .1 | .2 | | .5 | .5 |
| | | .7 | .5 | .3 | .4 | | .8 | .5 |
| | | .3 | .2 | .1 | .1 | Sales/Total Assets | .3 | .2 |
| | | .2 | .1 | .1 | .1 | | .1 | .1 |
| | | .7 | 1.3 | | | | .6 | .8 |
| | (19) | 7.7 | (24) 3.6 | | | % Depr., Dep., Amort./Sales | (65) 1.6 | (63) 3.1 |
| | | 18.2 | 10.5 | | | | 6.2 | 6.6 |
| | | | | | | % Officers', Directors' Owners' Comp/Sales | | |
| 1498M | 9526M | 54360M | 285213M | 134113M | 315001M | Net Sales ($) | 808275M | 839530M |
| 364M | 7424M | 138342M | 703639M | 732094M | 1609617M | Total Assets ($) | 2932143M | 3404604M |

M = $ thousand    MM = $ million
See Pages 9 through 22 for Explanation of Ratios and Data

## Comparative Historical Data | Current Data Sorted by Sales

| | | | Type of Statement | | | | | | |
|---|---|---|---|---|---|---|---|---|---|
| 57 | 54 | 60 | Unqualified | 8 | 13 | 6 | 12 | 13 | 8 |
| 3 | 1 | 1 | Reviewed | 1 | | | | | |
| 5 | 9 | 8 | Compiled | 2 | 4 | 1 | 1 | | |
| 1 | | 1 | Tax Returns | 1 | | | | | |
| 25 | 25 | 20 | Other | 7 | 5 | 3 | 2 | 3 | |
| 4/1/09- | 4/1/10- | 4/1/11- | | | 58 (4/1-9/30/11) | | | 32 (10/1/11-3/31/12) | |
| 3/31/10 | 3/31/11 | 3/31/12 | | | | | | | |
| ALL | ALL | ALL | | 0-1MM | 1-3MM | 3-5MM | 5-10MM | 10-25MM | 25MM & OVER |
| 91 | 89 | 90 | **NUMBER OF STATEMENTS** | 19 | 22 | 10 | 15 | 16 | 8 |
| % | % | % | **ASSETS** | % | % | % | % | % | % |
| 19.7 | 23.1 | 24.0 | Cash & Equivalents | 25.7 | 18.5 | 19.6 | 32.8 | 26.1 | |
| 14.9 | 10.2 | 8.4 | Trade Receivables (net) | 9.4 | 5.7 | 8.7 | 5.9 | 10.8 | |
| 2.7 | 1.6 | 2.7 | Inventory | 5.5 | 4.1 | 3.8 | .0 | .1 | |
| 3.5 | 5.0 | 4.5 | All Other Current | 1.9 | 7.6 | 4.0 | 4.1 | 5.1 | |
| 40.9 | 39.9 | 39.6 | Total Current | 42.5 | 35.9 | 36.1 | 42.8 | 42.1 | |
| 33.1 | 38.6 | 36.9 | Fixed Assets (net) | 31.8 | 45.9 | 27.1 | 28.3 | 39.5 | |
| .3 | .4 | .3 | Intangibles (net) | .5 | .1 | .1 | .4 | .3 | |
| 25.7 | 21.1 | 23.3 | All Other Non-Current | 25.2 | 18.1 | 36.7 | 28.6 | 18.1 | |
| 100.0 | 100.0 | 100.0 | Total | 100.0 | 100.0 | 100.0 | 100.0 | 100.0 | |
| | | | **LIABILITIES** | | | | | | |
| 4.9 | 6.1 | 2.6 | Notes Payable-Short Term | 3.5 | 4.9 | 1.0 | .8 | 2.4 | |
| 4.8 | 3.0 | 3.5 | Cur. Mat.-L.T.D. | 5.4 | 2.6 | 3.9 | 2.9 | 3.2 | |
| 4.0 | 3.2 | 3.0 | Trade Payables | 2.7 | 2.5 | 2.3 | 2.8 | 2.9 | |
| .0 | .0 | .0 | Income Taxes Payable | .0 | .0 | .0 | .0 | .0 | |
| 9.6 | 6.7 | 8.8 | All Other Current | 11.8 | 6.7 | 4.3 | 11.7 | 7.2 | |
| 23.3 | 19.0 | 17.9 | Total Current | 23.5 | 16.7 | 11.5 | 18.2 | 15.7 | |
| 33.9 | 28.9 | 46.7 | Long-Term Debt | 55.8 | 37.9 | 34.8 | 59.4 | 43.1 | |
| .0 | .0 | .0 | Deferred Taxes | .0 | .0 | .0 | .0 | .0 | |
| 4.1 | 6.7 | 6.3 | All Other Non-Current | 7.5 | 9.6 | 5.5 | 1.3 | 3.4 | |
| 38.8 | 45.4 | 29.2 | Net Worth | 13.3 | 35.8 | 48.2 | 21.1 | 37.8 | |
| 100.0 | 100.0 | 100.0 | Total Liabilities & Net Worth | 100.0 | 100.0 | 100.0 | 100.0 | 100.0 | |
| | | | **INCOME DATA** | | | | | | |
| 100.0 | 100.0 | 100.0 | Net Sales | 100.0 | 100.0 | 100.0 | 100.0 | 100.0 | |
| | | | Gross Profit | | | | | | |
| 81.2 | 77.4 | 78.3 | Operating Expenses | 72.1 | 73.6 | 71.2 | 77.6 | 89.4 | |
| 18.8 | 22.6 | 21.7 | Operating Profit | 27.9 | 26.4 | 28.8 | 22.4 | 10.6 | |
| 10.9 | 11.6 | 13.6 | All Other Expenses (net) | 16.1 | 15.9 | 11.2 | 20.7 | 7.5 | |
| 7.9 | 11.0 | 8.1 | Profit Before Taxes | 11.8 | 10.5 | 17.5 | 1.7 | 3.0 | |
| | | | **RATIOS** | | | | | | |
| 5.4 | 5.6 | 6.9 | | 9.0 | 9.8 | 6.8 | 14.3 | 6.2 | |
| 2.5 | 2.4 | 2.6 | Current | 3.1 | 2.0 | 2.8 | 3.0 | 2.6 | |
| 1.4 | 1.2 | 1.2 | | 1.1 | 1.1 | 1.2 | 1.2 | .6 | |
| 4.6 | 4.6 | 6.3 | | 9.0 | 7.4 | 5.1 | 14.3 | 5.9 | |
| 2.0 | 2.0 | 2.1 | Quick | 3.0 | 1.9 | 1.6 | 2.3 | 2.1 | |
| 1.2 | .8 | .8 | | .8 | .7 | .6 | 1.1 | .5 | |

| | | | | | | | Sales/Receivables | | | | | |
|---|---|---|---|---|---|---|---|---|---|---|---|---|
| 5 | 66.8 | 0 | UND | 0 | UND | | 0 | UND | 1 | 266.8 | 0 | UND |
| 45 | 8.2 | 26 | 13.8 | 16 | 23.0 | | 18 | 20.3 | 30 | 12.1 | 5 | 68.0 |
| 123 | 3.0 | 69 | 5.3 | 72 | 5.1 | | 203 | 1.8 | 79 | 4.6 | 26 | 14.0 |

(continued columns for Sales/Receivables 5-10MM, 10-25MM): 0 UND / 4 101.9 / 54 6.7 ; 0 813.7 / 12 31.7 / 89 4.1

| | | | Cost of Sales/Inventory | | | | | | |
|---|---|---|---|---|---|---|---|---|---|
| | | | Cost of Sales/Payables | | | | | | |
| .6 | .7 | .6 | Sales/Working Capital | .5 | .8 | .7 | .5 | .8 | |
| 1.7 | 2.0 | 2.3 | | .8 | 2.6 | 2.4 | 1.7 | 2.2 | |
| 9.0 | 34.4 | 16.1 | | 31.8 | NM | 16.2 | 15.1 | NM | |

| | | | | | | EBIT/Interest | | | | | |
|---|---|---|---|---|---|---|---|---|---|---|---|
| | 7.5 | | 9.6 | | 9.9 | | | | 15.8 | | 3.2 |
| (65) | 2.4 | (59) | 1.9 | (54) | 2.4 | (15) | 3.0 | (11) | 2.1 | | |
| | .6 | | .3 | | .2 | | .3 | | .2 | | |

| | | | Net Profit + Depr., Dep., Amort./Cur. Mat. L/T/D | | | | | | |
|---|---|---|---|---|---|---|---|---|---|
| .0 | .0 | .0 | Fixed/Worth | .0 | .1 | .2 | .0 | .2 | |
| .7 | .9 | .9 | | .1 | .9 | .3 | .6 | 1.0 | |
| 1.6 | 1.2 | 1.8 | | 2.6 | 4.8 | 1.5 | 1.4 | 1.2 | |
| .6 | .4 | .6 | Debt/Worth | .9 | .4 | .3 | .8 | .6 | |
| 1.5 | 1.1 | 1.6 | | 11.7 | 1.4 | .9 | 2.0 | 1.2 | |
| 3.8 | 4.4 | 14.3 | | -10.0 | 7.4 | 20.2 | 12.7 | 2.4 | |

| | | | | | | % Profit Before Taxes/Tangible Net Worth | | | | | |
|---|---|---|---|---|---|---|---|---|---|---|---|
| | 8.4 | | 16.7 | | 10.4 | | 29.9 | | 17.8 | | 8.6 / 8.8 |
| (83) | 2.1 | (85) | 3.1 | (72) | 3.9 | (12) 8.3 | (19) 5.4 | (12) 1.0 | (14) 2.3 | | |
| | -2.6 | | -1.5 | | -.8 | 1.1 | -.8 | -4.5 | -3.1 | | |

| 4.1 | 8.2 | 3.8 | % Profit Before Taxes/Total Assets | 4.4 | 5.8 | 6.9 | 3.3 | 3.5 | |
|---|---|---|---|---|---|---|---|---|---|
| .9 | 1.3 | 1.1 | | 1.0 | 2.2 | .7 | .1 | 1.4 | |
| -.9 | -.8 | -.5 | | -.3 | -.4 | -4.2 | -1.9 | -1.0 | |
| 43.2 | 44.4 | 53.5 | Sales/Net Fixed Assets | UND | 40.8 | 12.4 | 36.3 | 5.1 | |
| 2.5 | 1.8 | 1.3 | | 53.0 | .4 | 1.8 | 1.5 | .9 | |
| .4 | .3 | .3 | | .2 | .2 | .9 | .6 | .3 | |
| .8 | .6 | .5 | Sales/Total Assets | .3 | .4 | 1.0 | .4 | .6 | |
| .2 | .3 | .2 | | .1 | .2 | .3 | .2 | .3 | |
| .1 | .1 | .1 | | .1 | .1 | .1 | .1 | .1 | |

| | | | | | | % Depr., Dep., Amort./Sales | | | | | |
|---|---|---|---|---|---|---|---|---|---|---|---|
| | .6 | | .6 | | .9 | | 3.1 | | .7 | | .9 |
| (68) | 2.9 | (65) | 2.7 | (62) | 4.8 | (11) 17.4 | (15) 5.0 | (14) 5.1 | | | |
| | 9.8 | | 10.4 | | 17.0 | 21.3 | 15.4 | 11.1 | | | |

| | | | % Officers', Directors' Owners' Comp/Sales | | | | | | |
|---|---|---|---|---|---|---|---|---|---|

| 715852M | 751325M | 799711M | Net Sales ($) | 10714M | 40272M | 38089M | 93458M | 265728M | 351450M |
|---|---|---|---|---|---|---|---|---|---|
| 3089947M | 2591769M | 3191480M | Total Assets ($) | 89621M | 249078M | 288331M | 558858M | 1191833M | 813759M |

M = $ thousand    MM = $ million
See Pages 9 through 22 for Explanation of Ratios and Data

## Current Data Sorted by Assets      Comparative Historical Data

| | | | | | | Type of Statement | | |
|---|---|---|---|---|---|---|---|---|
| 2 | 9 | 24 | 46 | 10 | 16 | Unqualified | 66 | 80 |
| | 1 | 1 | | | | Reviewed | 4 | 3 |
| 1 | 1 | 4 | 1 | 1 | | Compiled | 6 | 5 |
| | 1 | 1 | | | | Tax Returns | 2 | 1 |
| 3 | 5 | 12 | 3 | 2 | 2 | Other | 32 | 28 |
| | 115 (4/1-9/30/11) | | 31 (10/1/11-3/31/12) | | | | 4/1/07-<br>3/31/08 | 4/1/08-<br>3/31/09 |
| 0-500M | 500M-2MM | 2-10MM | 10-50MM | 50-100MM | 100-250MM | | ALL | ALL |
| 6 | 17 | 42 | 50 | 13 | 18 | NUMBER OF STATEMENTS | 110 | 117 |
| % | % | % | % | % | % | ASSETS | % | % |
| | 24.6 | 26.8 | 30.4 | 12.6 | 23.8 | Cash & Equivalents | 24.1 | 25.2 |
| | 13.4 | 10.8 | 6.4 | 3.3 | 14.0 | Trade Receivables (net) | 11.8 | 13.6 |
| | 2.6 | 5.2 | .1 | .2 | .1 | Inventory | 1.4 | 2.1 |
| | 5.2 | 6.9 | 4.1 | 2.2 | 1.5 | All Other Current | 5.4 | 5.0 |
| | 45.8 | 49.8 | 41.0 | 18.2 | 39.4 | Total Current | 42.6 | 46.0 |
| | 30.2 | 33.0 | 33.4 | 66.8 | 37.5 | Fixed Assets (net) | 34.5 | 36.9 |
| | 6.3 | .1 | 1.3 | .2 | .9 | Intangibles (net) | 1.2 | .4 |
| | 17.6 | 17.1 | 24.3 | 14.8 | 22.2 | All Other Non-Current | 21.7 | 16.7 |
| | 100.0 | 100.0 | 100.0 | 100.0 | 100.0 | Total | 100.0 | 100.0 |
| | | | | | | LIABILITIES | | |
| | 16.5 | 2.8 | 1.4 | .1 | 4.2 | Notes Payable-Short Term | 5.8 | 4.6 |
| | 1.5 | 1.1 | 2.3 | 4.0 | 1.1 | Cur. Mat.-L.T.D. | 1.7 | 1.6 |
| | 7.0 | 4.8 | 4.7 | 1.1 | 5.0 | Trade Payables | 6.4 | 6.3 |
| | .0 | .0 | .0 | .0 | .0 | Income Taxes Payable | .4 | .0 |
| | 9.3 | 7.2 | 9.0 | 2.4 | 8.2 | All Other Current | 8.5 | 10.7 |
| | 34.3 | 15.8 | 17.5 | 7.6 | 18.5 | Total Current | 22.8 | 23.1 |
| | 21.4 | 27.0 | 36.3 | 34.8 | 15.8 | Long-Term Debt | 27.5 | 23.0 |
| | .0 | .0 | .0 | .0 | .0 | Deferred Taxes | .1 | .0 |
| | 14.8 | 3.3 | 3.9 | 5.0 | 6.4 | All Other Non-Current | 4.2 | 4.5 |
| | 29.6 | 53.9 | 42.4 | 52.6 | 59.3 | Net Worth | 45.3 | 49.4 |
| | 100.0 | 100.0 | 100.0 | 100.0 | 100.0 | Total Liabilities & Net Worth | 100.0 | 100.0 |
| | | | | | | INCOME DATA | | |
| | 100.0 | 100.0 | 100.0 | 100.0 | 100.0 | Net Sales | 100.0 | 100.0 |
| | | | | | | Gross Profit | | |
| | 87.8 | 84.9 | 77.6 | 78.4 | 81.3 | Operating Expenses | 81.0 | 88.5 |
| | 12.2 | 15.1 | 22.4 | 21.6 | 18.7 | Operating Profit | 19.0 | 11.5 |
| | 8.3 | 5.5 | 12.0 | 12.2 | 2.1 | All Other Expenses (net) | 8.0 | 6.6 |
| | 4.0 | 9.5 | 10.4 | 9.4 | 16.6 | Profit Before Taxes | 11.0 | 4.9 |
| | | | | | | RATIOS | | |
| | 3.5 | 10.5 | 5.6 | 3.8 | 5.1 | | 5.5 | 5.4 |
| | 1.2 | 4.4 | 2.7 | 2.2 | 3.2 | Current | 2.3 | 2.5 |
| | .5 | 1.9 | 1.3 | 1.6 | 1.3 | | 1.1 | 1.0 |
| | 3.2 | 7.5 | 4.7 | 3.2 | 4.5 | | 5.4 | 5.0 |
| | 1.1 | 2.6 | 2.5 | 2.2 | 2.8 | Quick | 1.9 | 2.2 |
| | .3 | 1.1 | .9 | 1.3 | 1.3 | | .8 | .8 |
| 0 UND | 1 436.1 | 2 218.9 | 0 UND | 16 23.4 | | | 2 183.3 | 4 99.8 |
| 2 205.7 | 23 16.0 | 15 24.9 | 16 22.7 | 47 7.7 | | Sales/Receivables | 18 20.3 | 19 19.1 |
| 24 15.5 | 51 7.2 | 37 9.9 | 81 4.5 | 152 2.4 | | | 55 6.7 | 49 7.4 |
| | | | | | | Cost of Sales/Inventory | | |
| | | | | | | Cost of Sales/Payables | | |
| | 4.0 | .7 | 1.5 | 1.2 | .8 | | 1.2 | 1.8 |
| | 31.1 | 2.3 | 3.7 | 3.1 | 2.0 | Sales/Working Capital | 4.7 | 4.4 |
| | -9.1 | 14.0 | 15.0 | 6.6 | 7.6 | | 62.7 | 225.0 |
| | | 4.6 | 6.2 | | 6.5 | | 5.5 | 11.8 |
| | (21) 1.8 | (26) 2.1 | | (15) 3.9 | | EBIT/Interest | (59) 2.2 | (65) 2.0 |
| | | -.7 | .3 | | 1.9 | | .5 | -.8 |
| | | | | | | Net Profit + Depr., Dep.,<br>Amort./Cur. Mat. L/T/D | | |
| | .0 | .0 | .0 | .9 | .0 | | .1 | .1 |
| | .4 | .4 | .6 | 1.2 | .7 | Fixed/Worth | .7 | .7 |
| | 4.1 | 1.6 | 1.8 | 1.5 | .9 | | 1.3 | 1.7 |
| | .8 | .4 | .3 | .4 | .2 | | .5 | .3 |
| | 2.2 | .6 | 1.0 | .5 | .6 | Debt/Worth | 1.2 | 1.0 |
| | NM | 1.6 | 3.1 | 3.9 | 1.7 | | 3.6 | 2.5 |
| | 29.4 | 8.7 | 16.4 | 6.8 | 10.1 | % Profit Before Taxes/Tangible<br>Net Worth | 14.8 | 12.7 |
| (13) 12.6 | (41) 2.1 | (44) 5.8 | 3.1 | 3.9 | | (104) 4.8 | (109) 2.8 |
| | -15.1 | -4.0 | -1.8 | .0 | 1.6 | | -1.1 | -5.2 |
| | 15.3 | 5.0 | 8.5 | 3.2 | 3.5 | % Profit Before Taxes/Total<br>Assets | 5.1 | 5.9 |
| | 3.6 | 1.0 | 2.1 | 1.5 | 2.2 | | 2.2 | .9 |
| | -1.7 | -2.5 | .0 | -.7 | 1.0 | | -.7 | -2.2 |
| | UND | 47.7 | UND | .5 | 31.3 | | 26.3 | 42.6 |
| | 19.2 | 4.9 | 3.2 | .3 | .8 | Sales/Net Fixed Assets | 4.4 | 4.3 |
| | 2.0 | .5 | .3 | .2 | .3 | | .4 | .5 |
| | 3.8 | 1.4 | 1.3 | .3 | .5 | | 1.6 | 1.8 |
| | 2.0 | .5 | .4 | .2 | .2 | Sales/Total Assets | .4 | .6 |
| | .3 | .1 | .1 | .1 | .1 | | .1 | .2 |
| | | 1.4 | 1.5 | 4.2 | 1.2 | | 1.3 | 1.0 |
| | (29) 2.6 | (34) 6.2 | (10) 16.1 | (15) 5.5 | | % Depr., Dep., Amort./Sales | (79) 2.8 | (87) 2.0 |
| | | 9.8 | 13.2 | 25.8 | 18.4 | | 7.7 | 5.8 |
| | | | | | | % Officers', Directors' | | 4.4 |
| | | | | | | Owners' Comp/Sales | (11) 11.9 | |
| | | | | | | | 27.5 | |
| 6808M | 37223M | 337854M | 900185M | 203127M | 1113818M | Net Sales ($) | 1202402M | 2364355M |
| 1655M | 17195M | 224496M | 1123440M | 898302M | 2605493M | Total Assets ($) | 2570260M | 2440742M |

M = $ thousand     MM = $ million
See Pages 9 through 22 for Explanation of Ratios and Data

## Comparative Historical Data      Current Data Sorted by Sales

| | | | Type of Statement | | | | | | |
|---|---|---|---|---|---|---|---|---|---|
| 62 | 82 | 107 | Unqualified | 15 | 18 | 16 | 8 | 24 | 26 |
| 3 | 3 | 2 | Reviewed | 2 | | | | | |
| 3 | 5 | 8 | Compiled | 4 | 2 | | | | 2 |
| 3 | 1 | 2 | Tax Returns | | 2 | | | | |
| 33 | 29 | 27 | Other | 5 | 6 | 6 | 2 | 4 | 4 |
| 4/1/09-3/31/10 ALL | 4/1/10-3/31/11 ALL | 4/1/11-3/31/12 ALL | | 115 (4/1-9/30/11) | | | 31 (10/1/11-3/31/12) | | |
| | | | | 0-1MM | 1-3MM | 3-5MM | 5-10MM | 10-25MM | 25MM & OVER |
| 104 | 120 | 146 | NUMBER OF STATEMENTS | 26 | 28 | 22 | 10 | 28 | 32 |
| % | % | % | ASSETS | % | % | % | % | % | % |
| 24.6 | 23.8 | 28.2 | Cash & Equivalents | 22.2 | 27.6 | 34.1 | 16.4 | 27.6 | 33.6 |
| 8.4 | 10.3 | 9.0 | Trade Receivables (net) | 5.6 | 6.9 | 8.6 | 11.1 | 12.0 | 10.7 |
| .9 | 3.2 | 1.9 | Inventory | 4.7 | 1.6 | 4.4 | .1 | .1 | .3 |
| 4.4 | 7.0 | 4.5 | All Other Current | 4.2 | 5.8 | 3.5 | 4.2 | 4.5 | .5 |
| 38.3 | 44.3 | 43.5 | Total Current | 36.7 | 41.8 | 50.6 | 31.9 | 44.2 | 48.7 |
| 42.0 | 36.3 | 35.4 | Fixed Assets (net) | 37.6 | 38.0 | 38.6 | 37.7 | 35.1 | 28.8 |
| .4 | .8 | 1.3 | Intangibles (net) | .1 | .4 | .6 | .7 | 5.1 | .5 |
| 19.2 | 18.6 | 19.7 | All Other Non-Current | 25.6 | 19.8 | 10.1 | 29.8 | 15.5 | 21.9 |
| 100.0 | 100.0 | 100.0 | Total | 100.0 | 100.0 | 100.0 | 100.0 | 100.0 | 100.0 |
| | | | LIABILITIES | | | | | | |
| 3.4 | 1.6 | 3.7 | Notes Payable-Short Term | 8.1 | 6.3 | .8 | 2.6 | 3.0 | .9 |
| 1.9 | 2.7 | 1.8 | Cur. Mat.-L.T.D. | 1.5 | 2.8 | 1.1 | 2.1 | 1.9 | 1.3 |
| 5.3 | 4.5 | 5.0 | Trade Payables | 1.4 | 3.1 | 6.3 | 4.6 | 5.4 | 8.6 |
| .0 | .0 | .0 | Income Taxes Payable | .0 | .0 | .0 | .0 | .0 | .0 |
| 9.4 | 8.7 | 7.8 | All Other Current | 3.6 | 3.9 | 7.9 | 3.4 | 8.4 | 15.5 |
| 20.0 | 17.5 | 18.3 | Total Current | 14.6 | 16.1 | 16.1 | 12.7 | 18.6 | 26.3 |
| 28.6 | 27.8 | 27.7 | Long-Term Debt | 26.2 | 35.9 | 38.5 | 27.6 | 29.2 | 13.2 |
| .0 | .0 | .0 | Deferred Taxes | .0 | .0 | .0 | .0 | .0 | .0 |
| 4.1 | 3.5 | 5.7 | All Other Non-Current | 4.8 | 12.7 | .9 | 5.5 | 5.6 | 3.8 |
| 47.3 | 51.2 | 48.3 | Net Worth | 54.4 | 35.4 | 44.5 | 54.2 | 46.5 | 56.8 |
| 100.0 | 100.0 | 100.0 | Total Liabilties & Net Worth | 100.0 | 100.0 | 100.0 | 100.0 | 100.0 | 100.0 |
| | | | INCOME DATA | | | | | | |
| 100.0 | 100.0 | 100.0 | Net Sales | 100.0 | 100.0 | 100.0 | 100.0 | 100.0 | 100.0 |
| | | | Gross Profit | | | | | | |
| 86.1 | 85.3 | 82.2 | Operating Expenses | 70.0 | 82.1 | 85.4 | 90.1 | 78.2 | 90.8 |
| 13.9 | 14.7 | 17.8 | Operating Profit | 30.0 | 17.9 | 14.6 | 9.9 | 21.8 | 9.2 |
| 11.2 | 7.2 | 8.2 | All Other Expenses (net) | 15.7 | 10.2 | 12.2 | 3.5 | 5.3 | 1.4 |
| 2.8 | 7.5 | 9.7 | Profit Before Taxes | 14.3 | 7.6 | 2.4 | 6.4 | 16.5 | 7.8 |
| | | | RATIOS | | | | | | |
| 4.9 | 7.7 | 6.5 | | 10.1 | 7.6 | 10.1 | 9.3 | 4.0 | 4.4 |
| 2.0 | 2.5 | 2.7 | Current | 3.0 | 3.4 | 5.3 | 2.3 | 2.4 | 2.3 |
| 1.2 | 1.2 | 1.3 | | .7 | 1.1 | 1.9 | 1.1 | 1.4 | 1.2 |
| 4.7 | 5.4 | 5.3 | | 6.9 | 5.6 | 9.7 | 8.8 | 3.2 | 4.0 |
| 1.6 | 1.8 | 2.4 | Quick | 2.5 | 2.3 | 4.2 | 1.9 | 2.2 | 2.2 |
| .8 | .7 | 1.1 | | .6 | .6 | 1.6 | 1.1 | 1.3 | 1.0 |
| 0 UND | 0 906.4 | 2 236.4 | | 0 UND | 0 UND | 2 214.4 | 17 21.2 | 4 87.3 | 5 67.1 |
| 9 41.2 | 13 27.4 | 18 20.4 | Sales/Receivables | 0 UND | 11 34.3 | 17 21.1 | 43 8.4 | 29 12.8 | 22 16.4 |
| 43 8.5 | 45 8.0 | 48 7.6 | | 10 36.8 | 26 14.2 | 41 8.9 | 73 5.0 | 63 5.8 | 48 7.6 |
| | | | Cost of Sales/Inventory | | | | | | |
| | | | Cost of Sales/Payables | | | | | | |
| 1.3 | .9 | 1.2 | | .6 | .9 | .9 | 1.8 | 1.1 | 2.1 |
| 5.1 | 3.8 | 3.2 | Sales/Working Capital | 3.3 | 3.1 | 2.4 | 5.3 | 2.9 | 5.0 |
| 23.7 | 22.8 | 14.3 | | -7.2 | 41.3 | 5.1 | NM | 7.1 | 14.0 |
| 11.8 | 5.1 | 5.9 | | 4.6 | 3.1 | | | 5.1 | 12.2 |
| (54) 2.6 | (69) 2.0 | (82) 2.4 | EBIT/Interest | (13) 2.3 | (16) 1.8 | | (16) | 2.8 (22) | 4.3 |
| -.1 | .5 | .3 | | -.4 | 1.1 | | | 1.4 | -5.2 |
| | | | Net Profit + Depr., Dep., Amort./Cur. Mat. L/T/D | | | | | | |
| .1 | .1 | .0 | | .0 | .1 | .0 | .2 | .0 | .0 |
| .8 | .6 | .7 | Fixed/Worth | .6 | 1.0 | .7 | .6 | .7 | .1 |
| 1.5 | 1.4 | 1.3 | | 1.6 | 2.1 | 2.7 | 2.2 | 1.2 | 1.0 |
| .4 | .4 | .3 | | .4 | .4 | .1 | .3 | .5 | .2 |
| .9 | 1.0 | .8 | Debt/Worth | .8 | 1.5 | 1.1 | .6 | .9 | .5 |
| 2.7 | 1.9 | 2.1 | | 1.6 | 22.4 | 10.9 | 6.1 | 2.1 | 1.3 |
| 12.9 | 12.8 | 13.3 | % Profit Before Taxes/Tangible | 9.9 | 7.6 | 20.8 | 20.0 | 13.7 | 10.1 |
| (98) 2.7 | (118) 3.2 | (135) 3.6 | Net Worth | 2.7 | (24) 3.3 | (19) 6.4 | 8.0 | (25) 3.1 | (31) 4.2 |
| -4.2 | -2.2 | -1.8 | | -4.6 | -4.2 | -5.0 | -.3 | .2 | -1.1 |
| 4.7 | 6.6 | 6.0 | % Profit Before Taxes/Total | 4.7 | 3.1 | 8.0 | 4.2 | 13.1 | 7.6 |
| .8 | 1.6 | 1.8 | Assets | 1.7 | .6 | 2.5 | 2.1 | 2.3 | 3.0 |
| -1.6 | -.8 | -.6 | | -2.3 | -1.9 | -2.4 | -.2 | .6 | -.7 |
| 34.9 | 43.3 | 108.1 | | 164.1 | 17.6 | UND | 46.0 | 48.6 | UND |
| 2.2 | 2.6 | 3.8 | Sales/Net Fixed Assets | .9 | 2.5 | 1.8 | 3.7 | 3.1 | 76.1 |
| .2 | .4 | .3 | | .2 | .2 | .2 | .5 | .4 | .8 |
| 1.4 | 1.4 | 1.5 | | .3 | 1.4 | 1.6 | 1.6 | 1.3 | 3.0 |
| .3 | .4 | .4 | Sales/Total Assets | .1 | .3 | .6 | .4 | .4 | 1.3 |
| .1 | .1 | .1 | | .1 | .1 | .1 | .2 | .2 | .4 |
| .9 | 1.2 | 1.4 | | 1.4 | 1.5 | 5.4 | | .9 | .7 |
| (82) 3.7 | (92) 3.9 | (99) 4.9 | % Depr., Dep., Amort./Sales | (17) 9.9 | (25) 2.8 | (12) 10.8 | | (22) 2.6 | (17) 4.9 |
| 16.0 | 14.3 | 13.8 | | 24.1 | 12.0 | 30.8 | | 10.1 | 9.2 |
| 3.0 | 3.1 | 2.7 | % Officers', Directors' | | | | | | |
| (17) 7.5 | (10) 6.7 | (12) 6.3 | Owners' Comp/Sales | | | | | | |
| 17.8 | 28.1 | 22.2 | | | | | | | |
| 1057916M | 1591763M | 2599015M | Net Sales ($) | 12689M | 50840M | 86426M | 71816M | 449101M | 1928143M |
| 2158283M | 3060193M | 4870581M | Total Assets ($) | 103415M | 286878M | 402128M | 193120M | 1597748M | 2287292M |

M = $ thousand    MM = $ million
See Pages 9 through 22 for Explanation of Ratios and Data

# CONSTRUCTION—
# PERCENTAGE OF
# COMPLETION BASIS OF
# ACCOUNTING*

## Current Data Sorted by Revenue      Comparative Historical Data

| | | | | | Type of Statement | | | | | |
|---|---|---|---|---|---|---|---|---|---|---|
| | | 1 | 7 | 8 | Unqualified | 26 | 25 | 18 | 10 | 8 |
| | | 1 | | 1 | Reviewed | 3 | 6 | 3 | 1 | 1 |
| 1 | 1 | | | 2 | Compiled | 17 | 22 | 19 | 2 | 2 |
| 2 | 2 | 1 | | 5 | Tax Returns | 2 | 7 | 9 | 4 | 5 |
| 1 | 3 | 1 | 8 | 13 | Other | 28 | 24 | 31 | 10 | 13 |
| | | | | | | 4/1/07- | 4/1/08- | 4/1/09- | 4/1/10- | 4/1/11- |
| | 1 (4/1-9/30/11) | | 28 (10/1/11-3/31/12) | | | 3/31/08 | 3/31/09 | 3/31/10 | 3/31/11 | 3/31/12 |
| 0-1MM | 1-10MM | 10-50MM | 50 & OVER | ALL | | ALL | ALL | ALL | ALL | ALL |
| 4 | 6 | 3 | 16 | 29 | NUMBER OF STATEMENTS | 76 | 84 | 80 | 27 | 29 |
| % | % | % | % | % | ASSETS | % | % | % | % | % |
| | | | 14.9 | 14.4 | Cash & Equivalents | 9.9 | 11.7 | 13.1 | 9.6 | 14.4 |
| | | | 17.2 | 18.8 | A/R - Progress Billings | 32.5 | 29.5 | 22.6 | 16.6 | 18.8 |
| | | | .5 | .3 | A/R - Current Retention | .0 | .8 | .1 | .7 | .3 |
| | | | 6.8 | 8.4 | Inventory | 6.8 | 5.0 | 5.7 | 9.4 | 8.4 |
| | | | .5 | 1.9 | Cost & Est. Earnings In Excess Billings | .1 | .1 | .2 | .2 | 1.9 |
| | | | 1.9 | 1.7 | All Other Current | 3.0 | 1.6 | 3.2 | 2.7 | 1.7 |
| | | | 41.8 | 45.5 | Total Current | 52.3 | 48.8 | 44.9 | 39.2 | 45.5 |
| | | | 42.0 | 39.5 | Fixed Assets (net) | 33.6 | 37.5 | 40.6 | 44.3 | 39.5 |
| | | | 1.3 | .8 | Joint Ventures & Investments | .8 | .9 | 1.2 | 1.4 | .8 |
| | | | 6.7 | 4.3 | Intangibles (net) | 5.9 | 4.8 | 4.0 | 6.7 | 4.3 |
| | | | 8.2 | 9.9 | All Other Non-Current | 7.4 | 8.0 | 9.3 | 8.4 | 9.9 |
| | | | 100.0 | 100.0 | Total | 100.0 | 100.0 | 100.0 | 100.0 | 100.0 |
| | | | | | LIABILITIES | | | | | |
| | | | 2.2 | 4.3 | Notes Payable-Short Term | 6.8 | 6.5 | 6.9 | 7.2 | 4.3 |
| | | | 4.3 | 9.0 | A/P - Trade | 9.2 | 8.8 | 7.2 | 8.1 | 9.0 |
| | | | .7 | .5 | A/P - Retention | .0 | .1 | .0 | .0 | .5 |
| | | | 1.0 | .5 | Billings in Excess of Costs & Est. Earnings | .3 | .1 | .2 | 1.4 | .5 |
| | | | .3 | .3 | Income Taxes Payable | .5 | .1 | .3 | .3 | .3 |
| | | | .8 | 2.7 | Cur. Mat.-L/T/D | 3.8 | 2.5 | 3.7 | 2.7 | 2.7 |
| | | | 8.5 | 8.7 | All Other Current | 6.5 | 6.3 | 5.2 | 4.0 | 8.7 |
| | | | 17.8 | 26.1 | Total Current | 27.0 | 24.4 | 23.6 | 23.6 | 26.1 |
| | | | 19.9 | 25.1 | Long-Term Debt | 16.8 | 20.6 | 22.4 | 26.5 | 25.1 |
| | | | 5.1 | 2.9 | Deferred Taxes | 1.8 | 1.7 | 1.7 | 2.8 | 2.9 |
| | | | 4.8 | 5.7 | All Other Non-Current | 5.5 | 5.0 | 5.0 | 5.1 | 5.7 |
| | | | 52.4 | 40.2 | Net Worth | 48.9 | 48.3 | 47.3 | 42.0 | 40.2 |
| | | | 100.0 | 100.0 | Total Liabilities & Net Worth | 100.0 | 100.0 | 100.0 | 100.0 | 100.0 |
| | | | | | INCOME DATA | | | | | |
| | | | 100.0 | 100.0 | Contract Revenues | 100.0 | 100.0 | 100.0 | 100.0 | 100.0 |
| | | | 89.3 | 89.4 | Gross Profit Operating Expenses | 85.0 | 83.0 | 91.7 | 89.8 | 89.4 |
| | | | 10.7 | 10.6 | Operating Profit | 15.0 | 17.0 | 8.3 | 10.2 | 10.6 |
| | | | 2.6 | 2.8 | All Other Expenses (net) | 1.7 | 2.2 | 1.8 | 3.3 | 2.8 |
| | | | 8.1 | 7.9 | Profit Before Taxes | 13.4 | 14.8 | 6.6 | 6.8 | 7.9 |
| | | | | | RATIOS | | | | | |
| | | | 3.5 | 3.2 | | 3.0 | 4.2 | 3.5 | 2.7 | 3.2 |
| | | | 2.5 | 1.9 | Current | 1.8 | 2.0 | 2.2 | 1.7 | 1.9 |
| | | | 1.8 | 1.3 | | 1.1 | 1.2 | 1.1 | 1.3 | 1.3 |
| | | | 5.3 | UND | | 10.3 | 10.1 | 10.0 | 31.5 | UND |
| | | (15) | 3.0 | (25) 3.0 | Receivables/Payables | (81) 3.3 | (72) 4.3 | (24) 3.3 | (25) 3.3 | 3.0 |
| | | | 2.0 | 1.9 | | 1.9 | 2.4 | 1.7 | 1.3 | 1.9 |
| | | 63 | 5.8 | 14 25.8 | | 50 7.3 | 44 8.3 | 35 10.4 | 26 14.1 | 14 25.8 |
| | | 76 | 4.8 | 70 5.2 | Revenues/Receivables | 70 5.2 | 70 5.2 | 53 6.8 | 55 6.6 | 70 5.2 |
| | | 94 | 3.9 | 85 4.3 | | 90 4.1 | 86 4.3 | 69 5.3 | 87 4.2 | 85 4.3 |
| | | | | | Cost of Revenues/Payables | | | | | |
| | | | 2.6 | 3.0 | | 4.2 | 4.5 | 3.4 | 4.1 | 3.0 |
| | | | 4.2 | 5.4 | Revenues/Working Capital | 7.3 | 7.3 | 7.3 | 7.7 | 5.4 |
| | | | 5.8 | 24.1 | | 40.5 | 19.8 | 45.4 | 20.0 | 24.1 |
| | | | 28.4 | 14.5 | | 18.2 | 24.9 | 8.4 | 8.7 | 14.5 |
| | | (15) | 4.7 | (25) 4.0 | EBIT/Interest | (66) 8.2 | (81) 10.2 | (70) 2.8 | (24) 3.3 | (25) 4.0 |
| | | | 2.5 | 1.0 | | 3.8 | 2.9 | -1.0 | .5 | 1.0 |
| | | | | | Net Profit + Depr., Dep., Amort./Cur. Mat. L/T/D | 73.4 | | | | |
| | | | | | | (11) 6.0 | | | | |
| | | | | | | 1.1 | | | | |
| | | | .4 | .3 | | .2 | .3 | .4 | .5 | .3 |
| | | | 1.1 | 1.2 | Fixed/Worth | .7 | 1.0 | .9 | 1.8 | 1.2 |
| | | | 1.8 | 3.3 | | 1.9 | 2.1 | 2.6 | 2.6 | 3.3 |
| | | | .4 | .5 | | .4 | .4 | .3 | .7 | .5 |
| | | | 1.2 | 1.4 | Debt/Worth | 1.2 | 1.2 | .9 | 1.8 | 1.4 |
| | | | 2.4 | 4.3 | | 2.6 | 3.6 | 3.6 | 5.9 | 4.3 |
| | | | 31.0 | 40.6 | | 54.6 | 75.9 | 23.1 | 25.5 | 40.6 |
| | | | 22.3 | (25) 27.4 | % Profit Before Taxes/ Tangible Net Worth | (70) 29.6 | (77) 35.3 | (70) 7.9 | (23) 10.5 | (25) 27.4 |
| | | | 3.7 | 4.7 | | 15.9 | 19.5 | -8.2 | -13.9 | 4.7 |
| | | | 14.4 | 16.3 | | 22.1 | 27.4 | 12.7 | 19.7 | 16.3 |
| | | | 5.8 | 6.1 | % Profit Before Taxes/ Total Assets | 13.4 | 14.5 | 4.2 | 5.3 | 6.1 |
| | | | 1.4 | .0 | | 6.0 | 7.2 | -3.7 | .5 | .0 |
| | | | | .7 | | 1.4 | 2.0 | 2.3 | 2.2 | .7 |
| | | | (12) | 6.3 | % Depr., Dep., Amort./ Revenues | (41) 3.7 | (49) 4.2 | (49) 4.7 | (12) 7.5 | (12) 6.3 |
| | | | | 11.9 | | 7.4 | 9.7 | 11.4 | 19.9 | 11.9 |
| | | | | | % Officers', Directors' Owners' Comp/Revenues | 3.9 | 4.3 | 4.2 | | |
| | | | | | | (18) 7.3 | (26) 6.9 | (22) 7.1 | | |
| | | | | | | 10.0 | 13.0 | 9.6 | | |
| 2114M | 14165M | 56517M | 14270773M | 14343569M | Contract Revenues ($) | 23858274M | 31950373M | 20941799M | 9709508M | 14343569M |
| 1280M | 13439M | 26706M | 21715843M | 21757268M | Total Assets ($) | 33013528M | 39179109M | 33995654M | 18022787M | 21757268M |

M = $ thousand     MM = $ million
See Pages 9 through 22 for Explanation of Ratios and Data

**Current Data Sorted by Revenue** | **Comparative Historical Data**

| | | | | | Type of Statement | | | | | |
|---|---|---|---|---|---|---|---|---|---|---|
| | | | 1 | 1 | Unqualified | 28 | 8 | 9 | 4 | 1 |
| 1 | 18 | 23 | 4 | 46 | Reviewed | 71 | 33 | 37 | 36 | 46 |
| 4 | 20 | 4 | 2 | 30 | Compiled | 84 | 61 | 65 | 52 | 30 |
| 23 | 56 | 5 | 3 | 87 | Tax Returns | 171 | 151 | 128 | 117 | 87 |
| 11 | 20 | 10 | 12 | 53 | Other | 145 | 102 | 93 | 62 | 53 |
| 25 (4/1-9/30/11) | | 192 (10/1/11-3/31/12) | | | | 4/1/07-3/31/08 | 4/1/08-3/31/09 | 4/1/09-3/31/10 | 4/1/10-3/31/11 | 4/1/11-3/31/12 |
| 0-1MM | 1-10MM | 10-50MM | 50 & OVER | ALL | | ALL | ALL | ALL | ALL | ALL |
| 39 | 114 | 42 | 22 | 217 | **NUMBER OF STATEMENTS** | 499 | 355 | 332 | 271 | 217 |
| % | % | % | % | % | **ASSETS** | % | % | % | % | % |
| 9.7 | 10.2 | 12.6 | 7.8 | 10.3 | Cash & Equivalents | 7.4 | 7.0 | 9.2 | 8.7 | 10.3 |
| 8.7 | 7.2 | 20.4 | 6.4 | 9.9 | A/R - Progress Billings | 6.5 | 6.6 | 6.9 | 6.2 | 9.9 |
| .3 | 2.3 | 1.4 | 1.6 | 1.7 | A/R - Current Retention | .2 | .5 | .5 | 1.8 | 1.7 |
| 41.1 | 47.2 | 32.7 | 63.4 | 44.9 | Inventory | 55.3 | 53.9 | 50.9 | 49.9 | 44.9 |
| .0 | 1.2 | 4.0 | 1.8 | 1.6 | Cost & Est. Earnings In Excess Billings | 2.5 | 1.9 | 2.2 | 1.5 | 1.6 |
| 7.9 | 4.0 | 4.5 | 1.8 | 4.6 | All Other Current | 6.7 | 6.3 | 6.1 | 5.6 | 4.6 |
| 67.6 | 72.0 | 75.7 | 82.7 | 73.0 | Total Current | 78.6 | 76.1 | 75.7 | 73.7 | 73.0 |
| 23.5 | 14.9 | 7.0 | 4.0 | 13.8 | Fixed Assets (net) | 11.0 | 13.3 | 12.4 | 12.0 | 13.8 |
| 1.4 | 3.2 | .6 | 7.0 | 2.8 | Joint Ventures & Investments | 2.6 | 2.2 | 2.7 | 2.9 | 2.8 |
| 2.6 | .7 | .7 | .1 | 1.0 | Intangibles (net) | .7 | .9 | .7 | 1.0 | 1.0 |
| 4.9 | 9.2 | 16.0 | 6.1 | 9.4 | All Other Non-Current | 7.1 | 7.4 | 8.4 | 10.4 | 9.4 |
| 100.0 | 100.0 | 100.0 | 100.0 | 100.0 | Total | 100.0 | 100.0 | 100.0 | 100.0 | 100.0 |
| | | | | | **LIABILITIES** | | | | | |
| 33.4 | 31.0 | 18.1 | 22.3 | 28.0 | Notes Payable-Short Term | 37.6 | 38.4 | 35.4 | 32.0 | 28.0 |
| 8.0 | 9.0 | 16.7 | 6.7 | 10.1 | A/P - Trade | 7.8 | 8.2 | 8.0 | 8.0 | 10.1 |
| .1 | 1.6 | .9 | .0 | 1.0 | A/P - Retention | .3 | .2 | .2 | .2 | 1.0 |
| 1.8 | 2.6 | 2.2 | 1.6 | 2.3 | Billings in Excess of Costs & Est. Earnings | 1.0 | 1.6 | 2.0 | 1.5 | 2.3 |
| .4 | .1 | .2 | .2 | .2 | Income Taxes Payable | .1 | .2 | .1 | .1 | .2 |
| 7.3 | 3.4 | 5.7 | 5.7 | 4.8 | Cur. Mat.-L/T/D | 4.9 | 3.8 | 2.9 | 4.3 | 4.8 |
| 7.3 | 10.2 | 8.4 | 4.6 | 8.8 | All Other Current | 8.2 | 6.9 | 8.9 | 9.4 | 8.8 |
| 58.3 | 58.0 | 52.3 | 41.1 | 55.2 | Total Current | 59.8 | 59.3 | 57.4 | 55.4 | 55.2 |
| 18.8 | 14.3 | 11.3 | 13.4 | 14.4 | Long-Term Debt | 15.7 | 16.5 | 17.4 | 16.8 | 14.4 |
| .0 | .0 | .2 | .0 | .0 | Deferred Taxes | .1 | .1 | .1 | .0 | .0 |
| 5.1 | 7.5 | 7.4 | 4.6 | 6.8 | All Other Non-Current | 7.7 | 7.4 | 7.6 | 7.9 | 6.8 |
| 17.9 | 20.1 | 28.8 | 40.9 | 23.5 | Net Worth | 16.6 | 16.7 | 17.5 | 19.9 | 23.5 |
| 100.0 | 100.0 | 100.0 | 100.0 | 100.0 | Total Liabilities & Net Worth | 100.0 | 100.0 | 100.0 | 100.0 | 100.0 |
| | | | | | **INCOME DATA** | | | | | |
| 100.0 | 100.0 | 100.0 | 100.0 | 100.0 | Contract Revenues | 100.0 | 100.0 | 100.0 | 100.0 | 100.0 |
| 27.7 | 16.6 | 14.2 | 20.0 | 18.5 | Gross Profit | 17.7 | 18.0 | 18.3 | 17.8 | 18.5 |
| 22.6 | 15.8 | 12.2 | 13.7 | 16.1 | Operating Expenses | 14.9 | 15.3 | 16.4 | 15.7 | 16.1 |
| 5.1 | .8 | 1.9 | 6.3 | 2.4 | Operating Profit | 2.8 | 2.7 | 1.9 | 2.0 | 2.4 |
| 2.4 | .9 | 1.5 | 1.2 | 1.3 | All Other Expenses (net) | 1.9 | 2.2 | 1.7 | 2.1 | 1.3 |
| 2.7 | -.1 | .5 | 5.1 | 1.0 | Profit Before Taxes | 1.0 | .5 | .2 | -.1 | 1.0 |
| | | | | | **RATIOS** | | | | | |
| 2.3 | 2.6 | 2.0 | 4.4 | 2.3 | Current | 2.2 | 2.2 | 2.6 | 2.4 | 2.3 |
| 1.2 | 1.4 | 1.5 | 2.0 | 1.4 | | 1.2 | 1.3 | 1.3 | 1.4 | 1.4 |
| .7 | .9 | 1.2 | 1.5 | 1.0 | | 1.0 | 1.0 | .9 | .9 | 1.0 |
| 17.2 | 1.4 | 1.8 | 1.3 | 1.7 | Receivables/Payables | 1.0 | 1.4 | 1.2 | 1.5 | 1.7 |
| (23) 1.6 | (92) .2 | (40) 1.0 | (17) .5 | (172) .5 | | (394) .1 | (260) .1 | (245) .1 | (191) .3 | (172) .5 |
| .0 | .0 | .1 | .0 | .0 | | .0 | .0 | .0 | .0 | .0 |
| 0 UND | 0 UND | 1 600.4 | 0 UND | 0 UND | Revenues/Receivables | 0 UND | 0 UND | 0 UND | 0 UND | 0 UND |
| 0 UND | 0 UND | 22 16.9 | 2 149.3 | 1 428.1 | | 0 UND | 0 UND | 0 UND | 0 UND | 1 428.1 |
| 29 12.6 | 17 21.6 | 45 8.2 | 19 19.7 | 27 13.4 | | 7 54.0 | 8 47.0 | 8 43.3 | 14 26.1 | 27 13.4 |
| 0 UND | 0 UND | 7 51.0 | 0 UND | 0 UND | Cost of Revenues/Payables | 0 UND | 0 UND | 0 UND | 0 UND | 0 UND |
| 0 UND | 11 33.6 | 25 14.7 | 17 21.0 | 14 26.5 | | 10 36.3 | 7 48.7 | 8 43.3 | 10 36.9 | 14 26.5 |
| 35 10.3 | 32 11.3 | 49 7.5 | 46 8.0 | 38 9.5 | | 26 13.8 | 26 14.0 | 28 13.0 | 27 13.6 | 38 9.5 |
| 2.0 | 3.9 | 4.9 | 1.5 | 3.5 | Revenues/Working Capital | 3.3 | 2.9 | 2.4 | 2.5 | 3.5 |
| 10.5 | 12.3 | 9.6 | 3.0 | 9.3 | | 10.4 | 9.0 | 9.8 | 8.7 | 9.3 |
| -10.2 | -19.5 | 24.9 | 5.8 | 168.9 | | 159.7 | -428.5 | -43.5 | -71.0 | 168.9 |
| 6.7 | 5.6 | 14.9 | 17.3 | 9.0 | EBIT/Interest | 8.1 | 6.0 | 8.8 | 6.9 | 9.0 |
| (26) 1.6 | (87) 1.6 | (34) 2.6 | (21) 6.5 | (168) 2.0 | | (407) 2.0 | (284) 1.4 | (270) 1.3 | (210) 2.0 | (168) 2.0 |
| -1.0 | -.1 | .0 | 1.9 | .4 | | .4 | -.4 | -.8 | -.1 | .4 |
| | | | | 5.5 | Net Profit + Depr., Dep., Amort./Cur. Mat. L/T/D | 18.2 | 23.1 | 3.5 | 25.3 | 5.5 |
| | | | (11) 1.1 | 1.1 | | (28) 3.9 | (17) 1.9 | (17) .5 | (10) 13.1 | (11) 1.1 |
| | | | | .1 | | 1.1 | .2 | -1.8 | 1.1 | .1 |
| .0 | .0 | .0 | .0 | .0 | Fixed/Worth | .0 | .0 | .0 | .0 | .0 |
| .9 | .3 | .1 | .0 | .2 | | .2 | .2 | .2 | .1 | .2 |
| 29.8 | 2.8 | .5 | .1 | 1.4 | | 2.1 | 2.6 | 3.4 | 1.9 | 1.4 |
| 1.6 | 1.6 | 1.1 | .8 | 1.2 | Debt/Worth | 2.0 | 1.7 | 1.4 | 1.5 | 1.2 |
| 5.9 | 4.7 | 2.7 | 1.2 | 3.4 | | 5.6 | 5.4 | 4.6 | 3.9 | 3.4 |
| 174.2 | 18.7 | 5.5 | 3.6 | 16.7 | | 39.8 | 86.8 | 44.9 | 34.1 | 16.7 |
| 50.0 | 42.8 | 32.2 | 19.2 | 34.7 | % Profit Before Taxes/Tangible Net Worth | 52.4 | 38.2 | 38.2 | 41.5 | 34.7 |
| (30) 5.6 | (93) 8.0 | (40) 7.1 | 12.3 | (185) 8.0 | | (404) 17.8 | (279) 6.9 | (263) 7.8 | (222) 10.5 | (185) 8.0 |
| -3.7 | -2.9 | -4.0 | 4.8 | -2.4 | | .3 | -10.2 | -7.9 | -8.0 | -2.4 |
| 7.9 | 8.3 | 8.7 | 8.3 | 8.1 | % Profit Before Taxes/Total Assets | 9.0 | 6.2 | 8.1 | 9.1 | 8.1 |
| 1.0 | 1.7 | 2.0 | 4.0 | 2.0 | | 2.3 | .7 | .7 | 1.8 | 2.0 |
| -.8 | -1.8 | -.3 | 1.4 | -.9 | | -1.4 | -3.2 | -3.4 | -2.6 | -.9 |
| .8 | .3 | .1 | | .2 | % Depr., Dep., Amort./Revenues | .2 | .2 | .3 | .2 | .2 |
| (24) 1.7 | (80) .5 | (31) .3 | | (144) .4 | | (309) .5 | (217) .6 | (197) .7 | (170) .6 | (144) .4 |
| 3.3 | 1.1 | .8 | | 1.4 | | 1.2 | 1.2 | 1.6 | 1.3 | 1.4 |
| 4.0 | 1.3 | .8 | | 1.2 | % Officers', Directors' Owners' Comp/Revenues | 1.5 | 1.6 | 1.7 | 1.7 | 1.2 |
| (15) 8.0 | (67) 3.1 | (17) 1.2 | | (107) 2.9 | | (253) 2.8 | (173) 3.2 | (164) 3.1 | (131) 3.0 | (107) 2.9 |
| 11.0 | 5.5 | 1.9 | | 6.5 | | 5.5 | 6.6 | 5.7 | 5.5 | 6.5 |
| 21612M | 402036M | 950660M | 87995588M | 89369896M | Contract Revenues ($) | 57759246M | 28436314M | 79940276M | 72988581M | 89369896M |
| 49097M | 419826M | 744894M | 66789416M | 68003233M | Total Assets ($) | 50831635M | 33542288M | 53992673M | 50223707M | 68003233M |

M = $ thousand    MM = $ million
See Pages 9 through 22 for Explanation of Ratios and Data

**Current Data Sorted by Revenue**               **Comparative Historical Data**

| 0-1MM | 1-10MM | 10-50MM | 50 & OVER | ALL | Type of Statement | 4/1/07-3/31/08 ALL | 4/1/08-3/31/09 ALL | 4/1/09-3/31/10 ALL | 4/1/10-3/31/11 ALL | 4/1/11-3/31/12 ALL |
|---|---|---|---|---|---|---|---|---|---|---|
| | | 2 | 2 | 4 | Unqualified | 1 | 3 | 3 | 1 | 4 |
| | 4 | 3 | 1 | 8 | Reviewed | 12 | 6 | 8 | 7 | 8 |
| | | 1 | 1 | 2 | Compiled | 3 | 6 | 6 | 1 | 2 |
| 2 | 1 | 1 | | 4 | Tax Returns | 16 | 6 | 13 | 7 | 4 |
| 1 | 2 | 4 | 2 | 9 | Other | 8 | 8 | 10 | 12 | 9 |
| | | | | | | 4/1/07-3/31/08 | 4/1/08-3/31/09 | 4/1/09-3/31/10 | 4/1/10-3/31/11 | 4/1/11-3/31/12 |
| 3 (4/1-9/30/11) | | 24 (10/1/11-3/31/12) | | | | ALL | ALL | ALL | ALL | ALL |
| 3 | 8 | 11 | 5 | 27 | **NUMBER OF STATEMENTS** | 40 | 29 | 40 | 28 | 27 |
| % | % | % | % | % | **ASSETS** | % | % | % | % | % |
| | | 23.7 | | 17.1 | Cash & Equivalents | 11.9 | 10.5 | 14.9 | 18.7 | 17.1 |
| | | 26.1 | | 22.7 | A/R - Progress Billings | 18.9 | 11.9 | 13.7 | 11.4 | 22.7 |
| | | 5.0 | | 3.7 | A/R - Current Retention | .1 | 1.5 | 1.3 | 16.9 | 3.7 |
| | | 20.9 | | 16.5 | Inventory | 15.7 | 39.4 | 25.8 | 24.2 | 16.5 |
| | | 7.8 | | 4.6 | Cost & Est. Earnings In Excess Billings | 2.1 | 1.1 | 2.2 | 2.0 | 4.6 |
| | | 9.3 | | 8.2 | All Other Current | 8.1 | 12.6 | 11.3 | 9.9 | 8.2 |
| | | 92.9 | | 72.8 | Total Current | 56.8 | 76.9 | 69.1 | 83.0 | 72.8 |
| | | 4.8 | | 19.2 | Fixed Assets (net) | 25.5 | 16.0 | 20.6 | 10.1 | 19.2 |
| | | .1 | | .1 | Joint Ventures & Investments | 2.8 | 1.1 | 1.7 | .4 | .1 |
| | | .0 | | .1 | Intangibles (net) | 2.7 | .0 | .4 | 1.8 | .1 |
| | | 2.1 | | 7.8 | All Other Non-Current | 12.2 | 6.0 | 8.2 | 4.7 | 7.8 |
| | | 100.0 | | 100.0 | Total | 100.0 | 100.0 | 100.0 | 100.0 | 100.0 |
| | | | | | **LIABILITIES** | | | | | |
| | | 3.8 | | 11.5 | Notes Payable-Short Term | 14.1 | 17.1 | 21.5 | 19.3 | 11.5 |
| | | 22.3 | | 18.6 | A/P - Trade | 10.8 | 15.3 | 11.6 | 18.2 | 18.6 |
| | | 10.3 | | 5.8 | A/P - Retention | 1.4 | .9 | .4 | 4.1 | 5.8 |
| | | 8.4 | | 6.1 | Billings in Excess of Costs & Est. Earnings | 4.0 | 2.2 | 1.9 | 4.6 | 6.1 |
| | | .0 | | .1 | Income Taxes Payable | .0 | .1 | .1 | .0 | .1 |
| | | 3.8 | | 2.5 | Cur. Mat.-L/T/D | 5.2 | 3.3 | 10.8 | 7.1 | 2.5 |
| | | 8.1 | | 5.4 | All Other Current | 12.4 | 7.5 | 6.9 | 4.9 | 5.4 |
| | | 56.8 | | 50.0 | Total Current | 47.9 | 46.3 | 53.2 | 58.2 | 50.0 |
| | | 7.0 | | 14.8 | Long-Term Debt | 26.0 | 26.0 | 30.6 | 11.0 | 14.8 |
| | | .2 | | .4 | Deferred Taxes | .1 | .1 | .3 | .0 | .4 |
| | | 3.3 | | 6.5 | All Other Non-Current | 7.6 | 2.4 | 4.7 | 5.7 | 6.5 |
| | | 32.6 | | 28.4 | Net Worth | 18.4 | 25.2 | 11.2 | 25.1 | 28.4 |
| | | 100.0 | | 100.0 | Total Liabilties & Net Worth | 100.0 | 100.0 | 100.0 | 100.0 | 100.0 |
| | | | | | **INCOME DATA** | | | | | |
| | | 100.0 | | 100.0 | Contract Revenues | 100.0 | 100.0 | 100.0 | 100.0 | 100.0 |
| | | 8.8 | | 11.8 | Gross Profit | 24.8 | 13.6 | 23.4 | 16.0 | 11.8 |
| | | 8.3 | | 12.5 | Operating Expenses | 21.0 | 14.9 | 23.3 | 12.1 | 12.5 |
| | | .5 | | -.8 | Operating Profit | 3.7 | -1.2 | .1 | 3.9 | -.8 |
| | | -.6 | | 1.3 | All Other Expenses (net) | 1.8 | 2.7 | 2.8 | 2.0 | 1.3 |
| | | 1.1 | | -2.0 | Profit Before Taxes | 1.9 | -3.9 | -2.7 | 2.0 | -2.0 |
| | | | | | **RATIOS** | | | | | |
| | | 2.0 | | 2.0 | | 3.0 | 3.1 | 3.9 | 2.2 | 2.0 |
| | | 1.4 | | 1.3 | Current | 1.3 | 1.5 | 1.6 | 1.4 | 1.3 |
| | | 1.3 | | 1.1 | | .5 | 1.0 | 1.1 | 1.2 | 1.1 |
| | | 1.7 | | 2.0 | | 3.6 | 1.1 | 2.3 | 3.0 | 2.0 |
| | | .8 | | (24) 1.1 | Receivables/Payables | (31) 1.3 | (27) .3 | (33) .6 | (25) 1.3 | (24) 1.1 |
| | | .2 | | .4 | | .0 | .0 | .0 | .5 | .4 |
| | 7 | 51.4 | 0 | 999.8 | | 0 UND | 0 UND | 0 UND | 0 818.5 | 0 999.8 |
| | 61 | 6.0 | 49 | 7.4 | Revenues/Receivables | 2 159.0 | 4 96.5 | 4 82.0 | 45 8.1 | 49 7.4 |
| | 66 | 5.5 | 66 | 5.5 | | 54 6.8 | 44 8.3 | 49 7.4 | 75 4.9 | 66 5.5 |
| | 19 | 19.2 | 10 | 36.0 | | 0 UND | 15 24.4 | 1 333.9 | 9 38.5 | 10 36.0 |
| | 73 | 5.0 | 34 | 10.7 | Cost of Revenues/Payables | 11 31.9 | 31 11.6 | 28 12.9 | 35 10.4 | 34 10.7 |
| | 104 | 3.5 | 73 | 5.0 | | 41 8.8 | 63 5.8 | 58 6.2 | 78 4.7 | 73 5.0 |
| | | 2.2 | | 3.9 | | 6.6 | 1.7 | 1.4 | 4.7 | 3.9 |
| | | 7.5 | | 11.5 | Revenues/Working Capital | 18.4 | 11.2 | 6.4 | 8.9 | 11.5 |
| | | 15.5 | | 45.9 | | -7.9 | 37.8 | 157.5 | 21.3 | 45.9 |
| | | 42.7 | | 42.7 | | 21.2 | 21.0 | 7.3 | 63.5 | 42.7 |
| | | | | (19) 1.8 | EBIT/Interest | (33) 2.3 | (20) 3.5 | (29) 1.5 | (15) 7.6 | (19) 1.8 |
| | | | | -.6 | | .4 | 1.1 | -2.9 | 2.2 | -.6 |
| | | | | | Net Profit + Depr., Dep., Amort./Cur. Mat. L/T/D | | | | | |
| | | .0 | | .0 | | .1 | .0 | .0 | .0 | .0 |
| | | .1 | | .3 | Fixed/Worth | .4 | .2 | .3 | .1 | .3 |
| | | .3 | | .9 | | 9.1 | 1.0 | 7.7 | 1.0 | .9 |
| | | 1.3 | | 1.3 | | 1.5 | 1.3 | 1.1 | 1.4 | 1.3 |
| | | 2.3 | | 2.8 | Debt/Worth | 5.1 | 4.3 | 2.4 | 3.1 | 2.8 |
| | | 4.9 | | 9.1 | | 117.8 | 15.7 | 10.4 | 8.8 | 9.1 |
| | | 14.5 | | 20.2 | | 74.1 | 32.8 | 28.6 | 68.3 | 20.2 |
| | | 10.1 | | (24) 8.8 | % Profit Before Taxes/Tangible Net Worth | (31) 21.4 | (25) 9.5 | (33) 1.5 | (24) 17.2 | (24) 8.8 |
| | | 4.9 | | -.7 | | -.3 | -5.2 | -21.8 | 3.9 | -.7 |
| | | 5.4 | | 5.4 | | 13.7 | 6.8 | 9.7 | 12.2 | 5.4 |
| | | 2.8 | | 2.4 | % Profit Before Taxes/Total Assets | 3.4 | 3.2 | .7 | 4.4 | 2.4 |
| | | .8 | | -1.5 | | -.9 | -2.5 | -6.0 | .8 | -1.5 |
| | | .2 | | .2 | | .3 | .2 | .4 | .1 | .2 |
| | (10) | .3 | (19) | .3 | % Depr., Dep., Amort./Revenues | (24) 1.5 | (16) .8 | (24) .7 | (17) .2 | (19) .3 |
| | | .6 | | .9 | | 2.7 | 2.2 | 1.8 | .7 | .9 |
| | | | | .4 | | 1.5 | 1.0 | 1.4 | .8 | .4 |
| | | | | (12) 1.0 | % Officers', Directors' Owners' Comp/Revenues | (20) 2.1 | (10) 2.7 | (17) 4.1 | (12) 1.8 | (12) 1.0 |
| | | | | 1.9 | | 7.9 | 11.6 | 11.5 | 2.2 | 1.9 |
| 1237M | 53007M | 305076M | 749973M | 1109293M | Contract Revenues ($) | 10557982M | 6008892M | 5589802M | 1616638M | 1109293M |
| 15466M | 45224M | 248713M | 3471116M | 3780519M | Total Assets ($) | 14682719M | 7603974M | 8343364M | 6445379M | 3780519M |

M = $ thousand     MM = $ million
See Pages 9 through 22 for Explanation of Ratios and Data

## Current Data Sorted by Revenue      Comparative Historical Data

| | | | | | Type of Statement | | | | | |
|---|---|---|---|---|---|---|---|---|---|---|
| | 1 | | 2 | 3 | Unqualified | 13 | 3 | 2 | 4 | 3 |
| | 1 | 2 | | 3 | Reviewed | 19 | 2 | 6 | 3 | 3 |
| 2 | 3 | 2 | | 7 | Compiled | 21 | 9 | 10 | 3 | 7 |
| 2 | 2 | | 2 | 4 | Tax Returns | 31 | 19 | 6 | 9 | 4 |
| 2 | 6 | 3 | 2 | 13 | Other | 32 | 16 | 15 | 8 | 13 |
| | 3 (4/1-9/30/11) | | 27 (10/1/11-3/31/12) | | | 4/1/07-3/31/08 | 4/1/08-3/31/09 | 4/1/09-3/31/10 | 4/1/10-3/31/11 | 4/1/11-3/31/12 |
| 0-1MM | 1-10MM | 10-50MM | 50 & OVER | ALL | | ALL | ALL | ALL | ALL | ALL |
| 6 | 13 | 7 | 4 | 30 | NUMBER OF STATEMENTS | 116 | 49 | 39 | 27 | 30 |
| % | % | % | % | % | ASSETS | % | % | % | % | % |
| | 10.1 | | | 12.1 | Cash & Equivalents | 6.9 | 6.9 | 6.8 | 11.0 | 12.1 |
| | 22.8 | | | 12.4 | A/R - Progress Billings | 3.8 | 3.4 | 4.7 | 9.7 | 12.4 |
| | .9 | | | .4 | A/R - Current Retention | .1 | .4 | 1.0 | 3.3 | .4 |
| | 35.1 | | | 38.5 | Inventory | 57.5 | 58.1 | 53.6 | 30.2 | 38.5 |
| | 4.0 | | | 2.1 | Cost & Est. Earnings In Excess Billings | 4.0 | .6 | .7 | 2.5 | 2.1 |
| | 10.8 | | | 6.4 | All Other Current | 5.5 | 4.6 | 8.5 | 8.1 | 6.4 |
| | 83.7 | | | 72.0 | Total Current | 77.8 | 73.9 | 75.3 | 65.0 | 72.0 |
| | 11.0 | | | 20.5 | Fixed Assets (net) | 13.6 | 15.1 | 15.5 | 18.7 | 20.5 |
| | .6 | | | .7 | Joint Ventures & Investments | 1.3 | 1.1 | 2.9 | .5 | .7 |
| | .0 | | | .0 | Intangibles (net) | .3 | .0 | .0 | .0 | .0 |
| | 4.8 | | | 6.8 | All Other Non-Current | 6.9 | 9.8 | 6.3 | 15.8 | 6.8 |
| | 100.0 | | | 100.0 | Total | 100.0 | 100.0 | 100.0 | 100.0 | 100.0 |
| | | | | | LIABILITIES | | | | | |
| | 15.6 | | | 18.0 | Notes Payable-Short Term | 39.5 | 31.2 | 20.0 | 18.1 | 18.0 |
| | 12.9 | | | 10.6 | A/P - Trade | 6.5 | 7.5 | 4.4 | 10.1 | 10.6 |
| | .0 | | | .0 | A/P - Retention | .3 | .0 | .0 | .3 | .0 |
| | 3.5 | | | 1.9 | Billings in Excess of Costs & Est. Earnings | .7 | .3 | .6 | 1.5 | 1.9 |
| | .0 | | | .0 | Income Taxes Payable | .0 | .1 | .0 | .0 | .0 |
| | 2.0 | | | 4.8 | Cur. Mat.-L/T/D | 2.6 | 3.6 | 5.0 | 2.0 | 4.8 |
| | 14.4 | | | 11.2 | All Other Current | 8.6 | 5.1 | 9.0 | 8.3 | 11.2 |
| | 48.4 | | | 46.5 | Total Current | 58.3 | 47.9 | 39.0 | 40.3 | 46.5 |
| | 14.7 | | | 11.4 | Long-Term Debt | 14.2 | 20.5 | 17.6 | 20.6 | 11.4 |
| | .7 | | | .3 | Deferred Taxes | .4 | .2 | .2 | .0 | .3 |
| | 7.4 | | | 5.3 | All Other Non-Current | 6.8 | 14.6 | 12.5 | 12.5 | 5.3 |
| | 28.9 | | | 36.4 | Net Worth | 20.2 | 16.7 | 30.7 | 26.7 | 36.4 |
| | 100.0 | | | 100.0 | Total Liabilties & Net Worth | 100.0 | 100.0 | 100.0 | 100.0 | 100.0 |
| | | | | | INCOME DATA | | | | | |
| | 100.0 | | | 100.0 | Contract Revenues | 100.0 | 100.0 | 100.0 | 100.0 | 100.0 |
| | 14.9 | | | 16.1 | Gross Profit | 18.1 | 17.4 | 17.1 | 27.2 | 16.1 |
| | 15.9 | | | 12.5 | Operating Expenses | 14.2 | 16.3 | 19.3 | 22.8 | 12.5 |
| | -1.0 | | | 3.6 | Operating Profit | 3.9 | 1.0 | -2.2 | 4.4 | 3.6 |
| | .5 | | | 1.4 | All Other Expenses (net) | 3.1 | 3.7 | 4.4 | 4.0 | 1.4 |
| | -1.5 | | | 2.2 | Profit Before Taxes | .9 | -2.7 | -6.6 | .4 | 2.2 |
| | | | | | RATIOS | | | | | |
| | 3.7 | | | 2.5 | | 1.9 | 2.9 | 4.3 | 3.9 | 2.5 |
| | 1.5 | | | 1.5 | Current | 1.2 | 1.5 | 1.7 | 1.4 | 1.5 |
| | 1.2 | | | 1.1 | | 1.0 | 1.1 | 1.0 | 1.1 | 1.1 |
| | 3.2 | | | 1.1 | | .9 | .4 | 2.0 | 1.6 | 1.1 |
| | (12) 1.1 | | (27) | .3 | Receivables/Payables | (97) .1 | (41) .0 | (35) .1 | (25) .1 | (27) .3 |
| | .0 | | | .0 | | .0 | .0 | .0 | .0 | .0 |
| 0 | UND | | 0 | UND | | 0 UND | 0 UND | 0 UND | 0 UND | 0 UND |
| 17 | 21.4 | | 2 | 180.0 | Revenues/Receivables | 0 999.8 | 0 UND | 0 479.0 | 0 999.8 | 2 180.0 |
| 47 | 7.7 | | 23 | 16.2 | | 7 55.7 | 2 158.3 | 9 41.3 | 27 13.6 | 23 16.2 |
| 5 | 79.9 | | 5 | 69.3 | | 1 422.7 | 1 258.2 | 0 797.0 | 1 411.9 | 5 69.3 |
| 15 | 24.4 | | 18 | 19.8 | Cost of Revenues/Payables | 12 30.0 | 16 22.2 | 12 30.9 | 17 21.4 | 18 19.8 |
| 43 | 8.4 | | 34 | 10.6 | | 34 10.7 | 51 7.1 | 29 12.8 | 41 8.8 | 34 10.6 |
| | 2.1 | | | 2.2 | | 3.4 | 1.6 | .8 | 2.6 | 2.2 |
| | 13.4 | | | 7.6 | Revenues/Working Capital | 9.2 | 4.3 | 6.1 | 16.5 | 7.6 |
| | 25.3 | | | 33.3 | | -140.5 | 42.9 | 50.0 | 493.5 | 33.3 |
| | 5.2 | | | 5.2 | | 5.5 | 4.2 | 2.2 | 5.2 | 5.2 |
| | (21) 1.7 | | | 1.7 | EBIT/Interest | (83) 1.8 | (41) .8 | (23) 1.1 | (17) 2.1 | (21) 1.7 |
| | .0 | | | .0 | | .9 | -.8 | -3.1 | 1.3 | .0 |
| | | | | | Net Profit + Depr., Dep., Amort./Cur. Mat. L/T/D | | | | | |
| | .1 | | | .0 | | .0 | .0 | .0 | .0 | .0 |
| | .5 | | | .3 | Fixed/Worth | .1 | .2 | .2 | .1 | .3 |
| | NM | | | 1.4 | | 1.0 | 1.4 | .8 | 1.1 | 1.4 |
| | 1.1 | | | .9 | | 2.0 | 1.5 | 1.1 | 1.8 | .9 |
| | 2.2 | | | 1.7 | Debt/Worth | 5.7 | 2.9 | 2.4 | 4.1 | 1.7 |
| | NM | | | 5.3 | | 24.3 | 23.0 | 6.3 | 9.9 | 5.3 |
| | 10.4 | | | 20.5 | | 60.2 | 30.2 | 9.0 | 34.7 | 20.5 |
| | (10) -2.9 | | (27) | 2.5 | % Profit Before Taxes/Tangible Net Worth | (101) 16.4 | (41) 5.3 | (33) -2.5 | (24) 13.2 | (27) 2.5 |
| | -60.4 | | | -4.5 | | 1.4 | -6.6 | -22.8 | .4 | -4.5 |
| | 3.5 | | | 7.3 | | 7.6 | 3.0 | 3.2 | 6.0 | 7.3 |
| | -1.1 | | | .7 | % Profit Before Taxes/Total Assets | 1.7 | .1 | -2.0 | 2.4 | .7 |
| | -10.0 | | | -1.9 | | -1.3 | -2.9 | -8.1 | .1 | -1.9 |
| | | | | .3 | | .1 | .3 | .2 | .1 | .3 |
| | | | (15) | .8 | % Depr., Dep., Amort./Revenues | (63) .4 | (26) .5 | (24) .5 | (20) .4 | (15) .8 |
| | | | | 1.1 | | 1.3 | 1.4 | 1.5 | 1.6 | 1.1 |
| | | | | | | 1.0 | .8 | 1.3 | | |
| | | | | | % Officers', Directors' Owners' Comp/Revenues | (44) 2.7 | (20) 1.8 | (10) 1.8 | | |
| | | | | | | 5.3 | 4.0 | 5.2 | | |
| 2011M | 44546M | 165064M | 2269956M | 2481577M | Contract Revenues ($) | 16442642M | 1697106M | 514409M | 621815M | 2481577M |
| 5807M | 36502M | 136723M | 2402176M | 2581208M | Total Assets ($) | 15806132M | 2773168M | 1224331M | 681761M | 2581208M |

M = $ thousand     MM = $ million
See Pages 9 through 22 for Explanation of Ratios and Data

**Current Data Sorted by Revenue**      **Comparative Historical Data**

| 0-1MM | 1-10MM | 10-50MM | 50 & OVER | ALL | Type of Statement | 4/1/07-3/31/08 | 4/1/08-3/31/09 | 4/1/09-3/31/10 | 4/1/10-3/31/11 | 4/1/11-3/31/12 |
|---|---|---|---|---|---|---|---|---|---|---|
| | | | | | | | | | | |
| | | | | | Unqualified | 1 | | | | |
| | 5 | 1 | | 6 | Reviewed | 4 | 3 | 3 | 3 | 6 |
| | 4 | 1 | | 5 | Compiled | 3 | 4 | 6 | 7 | 5 |
| 5 | 10 | 1 | | 16 | Tax Returns | 20 | 14 | 14 | 12 | 16 |
| 3 | 8 | 4 | 2 | 17 | Other | 9 | 8 | 4 | 13 | 17 |
| | 5 (4/1-9/30/11) | | 39 (10/1/11-3/31/12) | | | ALL | ALL | ALL | ALL | ALL |
| 8 | 27 | 7 | 2 | 44 | **NUMBER OF STATEMENTS** | 37 | 29 | 27 | 35 | 44 |
| % | % | % | % | % | **ASSETS** | % | % | % | % | % |
| | 20.5 | | | 21.0 | Cash & Equivalents | 15.3 | 21.3 | 24.1 | 18.0 | 21.0 |
| | 23.9 | | | 25.6 | A/R - Progress Billings | 14.3 | 18.2 | 12.5 | 21.2 | 25.6 |
| | .0 | | | .0 | A/R - Current Retention | 1.0 | .0 | .0 | 5.2 | .0 |
| | 5.4 | | | 8.7 | Inventory | 13.5 | 14.7 | 11.6 | 10.8 | 8.7 |
| | 6.2 | | | 5.4 | Cost & Est. Earnings In Excess Billings | 3.3 | 1.0 | 1.7 | 5.7 | 5.4 |
| | 3.7 | | | 3.2 | All Other Current | 10.3 | 7.4 | 2.4 | 3.2 | 3.2 |
| | 59.8 | | | 63.8 | Total Current | 57.7 | 62.6 | 52.3 | 64.2 | 63.8 |
| | 27.5 | | | 25.3 | Fixed Assets (net) | 27.2 | 22.1 | 33.8 | 24.9 | 25.3 |
| | .8 | | | .5 | Joint Ventures & Investments | .0 | .4 | 2.0 | .0 | .5 |
| | 2.4 | | | 2.8 | Intangibles (net) | 2.5 | 2.7 | .0 | 3.1 | 2.8 |
| | 9.6 | | | 7.6 | All Other Non-Current | 12.5 | 12.1 | 11.8 | 7.8 | 7.6 |
| | 100.0 | | | 100.0 | Total | 100.0 | 100.0 | 100.0 | 100.0 | 100.0 |
| | | | | | **LIABILITIES** | | | | | |
| | 17.4 | | | 14.7 | Notes Payable-Short Term | 25.6 | 21.2 | 15.0 | 24.0 | 14.7 |
| | 19.1 | | | 22.1 | A/P - Trade | 20.1 | 10.2 | 17.9 | 14.0 | 22.1 |
| | .0 | | | .0 | A/P - Retention | .0 | .0 | .0 | .0 | .0 |
| | 5.6 | | | 4.7 | Billings in Excess of Costs & Est. Earnings | 4.7 | 3.3 | 1.1 | 4.5 | 4.7 |
| | .0 | | | .0 | Income Taxes Payable | .0 | .0 | .0 | .1 | .0 |
| | 5.6 | | | 12.2 | Cur. Mat.-L/T/D | 4.0 | 4.5 | 8.2 | 2.3 | 12.2 |
| | 11.8 | | | 18.9 | All Other Current | 12.6 | 14.0 | 18.2 | 16.4 | 18.9 |
| | 59.5 | | | 72.5 | Total Current | 67.1 | 53.1 | 60.4 | 61.3 | 72.5 |
| | 14.7 | | | 12.8 | Long-Term Debt | 20.6 | 15.9 | 27.1 | 9.5 | 12.8 |
| | .3 | | | .3 | Deferred Taxes | .0 | 1.1 | .0 | .3 | .3 |
| | 2.6 | | | 7.2 | All Other Non-Current | 13.5 | 6.4 | 10.6 | 5.0 | 7.2 |
| | 22.9 | | | 7.2 | Net Worth | -1.2 | 23.6 | 1.8 | 23.9 | 7.2 |
| | 100.0 | | | 100.0 | Total Liabilities & Net Worth | 100.0 | 100.0 | 100.0 | 100.0 | 100.0 |
| | | | | | **INCOME DATA** | | | | | |
| | 100.0 | | | 100.0 | Contract Revenues | 100.0 | 100.0 | 100.0 | 100.0 | 100.0 |
| | 33.9 | | | 33.0 | Gross Profit | 30.2 | 36.3 | 33.1 | 35.4 | 33.0 |
| | 30.8 | | | 31.5 | Operating Expenses | 30.2 | 31.6 | 28.2 | 30.5 | 31.5 |
| | 3.2 | | | 1.6 | Operating Profit | .0 | 4.7 | 4.8 | 5.0 | 1.6 |
| | .6 | | | .6 | All Other Expenses (net) | .9 | .7 | .5 | .4 | .6 |
| | 2.6 | | | 1.0 | Profit Before Taxes | -.9 | 4.0 | 4.3 | 4.5 | 1.0 |
| | | | | | **RATIOS** | | | | | |
| | 1.6 | | | 1.6 | Current | 1.7 | 3.8 | 4.0 | 2.5 | 1.6 |
| | 1.1 | | | 1.1 | | .9 | 1.3 | .9 | 1.2 | 1.1 |
| | .8 | | | .8 | | .4 | .6 | .5 | .7 | .8 |
| | 3.3 | | | 2.4 | Receivables/Payables | 3.6 | 8.8 | 1.6 | 6.1 | 2.4 |
| | (24) 1.4 | | (38) | 1.3 | | (22) .6 | (19) 2.7 | (20) .8 | (27) 1.7 | (38) 1.3 |
| | .7 | | | .7 | | .2 | 1.0 | .2 | 1.2 | .7 |
| 0 | 921.0 | | 2 | 190.2 | Revenues/Receivables | 0 UND | 0 UND | 0 UND | 0 862.8 | 2 190.2 |
| 19 | 18.9 | | 19 | 19.3 | | 0 UND | 6 58.3 | 4 82.1 | 31 11.8 | 19 19.3 |
| 40 | 9.2 | | 48 | 7.6 | | 18 20.0 | 40 9.2 | 14 25.3 | 50 7.3 | 48 7.6 |
| 3 | 126.8 | | 4 | 89.3 | Cost of Revenues/Payables | 0 UND | 0 UND | 0 UND | 0 UND | 4 89.3 |
| 26 | 14.0 | | 25 | 14.6 | | 15 24.5 | 5 68.8 | 9 40.1 | 20 18.5 | 25 14.6 |
| 36 | 10.1 | | 46 | 7.9 | | 33 10.9 | 20 18.5 | 19 19.2 | 38 9.7 | 46 7.9 |
| | 17.5 | | | 15.3 | Revenues/Working Capital | 9.0 | 7.8 | 5.5 | 6.6 | 15.3 |
| | 118.6 | | | 84.9 | | -259.2 | 28.6 | -260.1 | 61.4 | 84.9 |
| | -18.3 | | | -14.0 | | -11.2 | -21.2 | -25.6 | -25.8 | -14.0 |
| | 21.8 | | | 16.2 | EBIT/Interest | (26) 6.5 | (22) 28.8 | (23) 37.0 | (29) 27.6 | (37) 16.2 |
| | (24) 5.5 | | (37) | 4.3 | | 1.8 | 5.7 | 14.0 | 7.1 | 4.3 |
| | 2.4 | | | -1.9 | | -1.6 | 1.3 | -.6 | -3.1 | -1.9 |
| | | | | | Net Profit + Depr., Dep., Amort./Cur. Mat. L/T/D | | | | | |
| | .4 | | | .4 | Fixed/Worth | .2 | .1 | .3 | .1 | .4 |
| | 1.1 | | | 1.0 | | 1.8 | .4 | 1.5 | .6 | 1.0 |
| | 81.0 | | | -3.5 | | -2.7 | 4.4 | UND | 3.8 | -3.5 |
| | 1.1 | | | 1.3 | Debt/Worth | 1.2 | 1.2 | .7 | .5 | 1.3 |
| | 3.4 | | | 3.9 | | 6.3 | 2.4 | 5.6 | 2.6 | 3.9 |
| | 272.0 | | | -23.6 | | -7.9 | 15.0 | UND | 13.3 | -23.6 |
| | 78.4 | | | 64.2 | % Profit Before Taxes/Tangible Net Worth | 99.1 | 115.3 | 102.3 | 93.4 | 64.2 |
| | (21) 39.6 | | (30) | 34.9 | | (24) 28.5 | (24) 64.2 | (21) 53.3 | (28) 32.4 | (30) 34.9 |
| | 12.7 | | | -5.9 | | 3.3 | 15.5 | 2.1 | -7.7 | -5.9 |
| | 21.1 | | | 20.9 | % Profit Before Taxes/Total Assets | 19.3 | 37.5 | 44.3 | 25.3 | 20.9 |
| | 9.1 | | | 8.7 | | 1.6 | 17.2 | 20.0 | 8.6 | 8.7 |
| | 1.9 | | | -3.7 | | -9.2 | .9 | -4.8 | -4.8 | -3.7 |
| | .5 | | | .6 | % Depr., Dep., Amort./Revenues | .4 | .5 | .4 | .6 | .6 |
| | (22) .9 | | (37) | 1.0 | | (23) 1.1 | (18) 1.0 | (23) .9 | (23) .9 | (37) 1.0 |
| | 1.6 | | | 1.7 | | 1.9 | 2.1 | 2.2 | 2.0 | 1.7 |
| | 4.5 | | | 2.8 | % Officers', Directors' Owners' Comp/Revenues | 2.3 | 3.4 | 3.5 | 2.8 | 2.8 |
| | (15) 5.0 | | (22) | 4.9 | | (20) 5.3 | (18) 5.6 | (22) 5.1 | (22) 4.9 | 4.9 |
| | 7.6 | | | 7.8 | | 9.5 | 11.3 | 7.8 | 8.7 | 7.8 |
| 4739M | 114028M | 192067M | 163124M | 473958M | Contract Revenues ($) | 4824907M | 289684M | 86698M | 4281227M | 473958M |
| 2543M | 29399M | 53291M | 116457M | 201690M | Total Assets ($) | 1154223M | 72207M | 23180M | 886693M | 201690M |

M = $ thousand    MM = $ million
See Pages 9 through 22 for Explanation of Ratios and Data

## Current Data Sorted by Revenue | | | | Comparative Historical Data

| 0-1MM | 1-10MM | 10-50MM | 50 & OVER | ALL | Type of Statement | 4/1/07-3/31/08 ALL | 4/1/08-3/31/09 ALL | 4/1/09-3/31/10 ALL | 4/1/10-3/31/11 ALL | 4/1/11-3/31/12 ALL |
|---|---|---|---|---|---|---|---|---|---|---|
| | | 7 | 4 | 11 | Unqualified | 23 | 20 | 19 | 8 | 11 |
| | 10 | 18 | 3 | 31 | Reviewed | 42 | 34 | 35 | 45 | 31 |
| | 3 | 3 | 1 | 7 | Compiled | 15 | 11 | 8 | 7 | 7 |
| | 4 | 2 | | 6 | Tax Returns | 18 | 10 | 6 | 11 | 6 |
| 2 | 9 | 12 | 8 | 31 | Other | 35 | 17 | 20 | 34 | 31 |
| **11 (4/1-9/30/11)** | | **75 (10/1/11-3/31/12)** | | | | | | | | |
| 2 | 26 | 42 | 16 | 86 | **NUMBER OF STATEMENTS** | 133 | 92 | 88 | 105 | 86 |
| % | % | % | % | % | **ASSETS** | % | % | % | % | % |
| | 21.3 | 23.3 | 27.8 | 23.1 | Cash & Equivalents | 18.6 | 21.2 | 23.0 | 18.2 | 23.1 |
| | 39.7 | 40.6 | 34.9 | 38.8 | A/R - Progress Billings | 38.1 | 35.6 | 33.9 | 25.9 | 38.8 |
| | 1.4 | 2.5 | 3.9 | 2.4 | A/R - Current Retention | 2.9 | 2.6 | 2.6 | 19.0 | 2.4 |
| | 4.1 | 1.0 | 3.0 | 2.3 | Inventory | 2.7 | 2.2 | 2.4 | 3.0 | 2.3 |
| | 5.5 | 6.9 | 6.5 | 7.0 | Cost & Est. Earnings In Excess Billings | 4.0 | 4.5 | 4.1 | 6.1 | 7.0 |
| | 6.6 | 6.3 | 4.4 | 6.2 | All Other Current | 6.3 | 6.5 | 6.4 | 5.0 | 6.2 |
| | 78.7 | 80.7 | 80.4 | 79.9 | Total Current | 72.6 | 72.6 | 72.4 | 77.2 | 79.9 |
| | 10.3 | 14.2 | 11.6 | 12.3 | Fixed Assets (net) | 18.2 | 19.0 | 18.6 | 14.8 | 12.3 |
| | .6 | .4 | .0 | .4 | Joint Ventures & Investments | .5 | .4 | .7 | .4 | .4 |
| | 1.2 | .7 | 2.0 | 1.1 | Intangibles (net) | 1.1 | 1.5 | 1.8 | 1.6 | 1.1 |
| | 9.2 | 4.0 | 6.0 | 6.4 | All Other Non-Current | 7.7 | 6.4 | 6.5 | 5.9 | 6.4 |
| | 100.0 | 100.0 | 100.0 | 100.0 | Total | 100.0 | 100.0 | 100.0 | 100.0 | 100.0 |
| | | | | | **LIABILITIES** | | | | | |
| | 12.5 | 2.6 | 1.1 | 5.2 | Notes Payable-Short Term | 7.6 | 3.6 | 5.3 | 4.1 | 5.2 |
| | 29.0 | 31.4 | 25.8 | 30.0 | A/P - Trade | 25.6 | 25.2 | 25.8 | 32.9 | 30.0 |
| | 1.0 | 1.4 | 1.8 | 1.3 | A/P - Retention | 1.7 | 1.7 | 1.2 | 2.0 | 1.3 |
| | 3.0 | 9.9 | 13.1 | 8.4 | Billings in Excess of Costs & Est. Earnings | 7.8 | 9.2 | 7.9 | 8.8 | 8.4 |
| | .4 | .0 | .2 | .2 | Income Taxes Payable | .4 | .3 | .5 | .4 | .2 |
| | 1.0 | 2.8 | 1.3 | 1.9 | Cur. Mat.-L/T/D | 3.2 | 2.9 | 2.3 | 2.3 | 1.9 |
| | 8.4 | 7.2 | 8.5 | 8.1 | All Other Current | 6.8 | 6.4 | 7.7 | 6.7 | 8.1 |
| | 55.4 | 55.3 | 51.7 | 55.1 | Total Current | 52.9 | 49.3 | 50.7 | 57.1 | 55.1 |
| | 5.2 | 5.8 | 10.2 | 6.3 | Long-Term Debt | 10.7 | 9.1 | 7.5 | 6.7 | 6.3 |
| | .6 | .5 | .2 | .5 | Deferred Taxes | .7 | .9 | .7 | .5 | .5 |
| | 5.1 | 1.9 | 1.0 | 2.7 | All Other Non-Current | 3.8 | 5.0 | 4.5 | 5.4 | 2.7 |
| | 33.7 | 36.5 | 36.9 | 35.5 | Net Worth | 31.9 | 35.8 | 36.5 | 30.2 | 35.5 |
| | 100.0 | 100.0 | 100.0 | 100.0 | Total Liabilities & Net Worth | 100.0 | 100.0 | 100.0 | 100.0 | 100.0 |
| | | | | | **INCOME DATA** | | | | | |
| | 100.0 | 100.0 | 100.0 | 100.0 | Contract Revenues | 100.0 | 100.0 | 100.0 | 100.0 | 100.0 |
| | 20.4 | 14.7 | 11.3 | 16.4 | Gross Profit | 19.4 | 17.1 | 19.2 | 16.4 | 16.4 |
| | 19.5 | 12.9 | 8.1 | 14.3 | Operating Expenses | 14.7 | 12.8 | 16.6 | 14.3 | 14.3 |
| | .9 | 1.8 | 3.2 | 2.1 | Operating Profit | 4.7 | 4.3 | 2.6 | 2.1 | 2.1 |
| | -.1 | -.1 | -.6 | -.2 | All Other Expenses (net) | .0 | .1 | .5 | .0 | -.2 |
| | 1.1 | 2.0 | 3.9 | 2.3 | Profit Before Taxes | 4.7 | 4.2 | 2.2 | 2.1 | 2.3 |
| | | | | | **RATIOS** | | | | | |
| | 2.9 | 2.0 | 1.9 | 2.1 | Current | 1.9 | 2.0 | 1.8 | 1.8 | 2.1 |
| | 1.8 | 1.4 | 1.5 | 1.5 | | 1.3 | 1.4 | 1.4 | 1.4 | 1.5 |
| | 1.2 | 1.2 | 1.2 | 1.2 | | 1.1 | 1.2 | 1.2 | 1.2 | 1.2 |
| | 2.8 | 2.5 | 2.1 | 2.5 | Receivables/Payables | 2.8 | 2.6 | 2.3 | 2.0 | 2.5 |
| | (25) 1.5 | (41) 1.3 | 1.5 | (84) 1.3 | | (122) 1.5 | (88) 1.4 | (86) 1.4 | (104) 1.3 | (84) 1.3 |
| | .9 | 1.0 | 1.1 | 1.0 | | 1.0 | .9 | 1.0 | .9 | 1.0 |
| 25  14.5 | 34  10.6 | 42  8.7 | 33  10.9 | | Revenues/Receivables | 33  11.2 | 23  15.9 | 30  12.1 | 34  10.9 | 33  10.9 |
| 47  7.7 | 58  6.3 | 54  6.7 | 51  7.1 | | | 48  7.6 | 39  9.4 | 50  7.3 | 55  6.7 | 51  7.1 |
| 65  5.6 | 73  5.0 | 73  5.0 | 72  5.1 | | | 73  5.0 | 60  6.0 | 67  5.4 | 75  4.9 | 72  5.1 |
| 21  17.7 | 26  14.3 | 29  12.4 | 26  14.3 | | Cost of Revenues/Payables | 15  23.7 | 18  20.5 | 18  19.8 | 26  14.3 | 26  14.3 |
| 34  10.6 | 45  8.1 | 45  8.2 | 42  8.6 | | | 38  9.7 | 30  12.1 | 39  9.4 | 44  8.2 | 42  8.6 |
| 68  5.4 | 58  6.3 | 51  7.1 | 58  6.3 | | | 60  6.0 | 52  7.0 | 59  6.2 | 62  5.9 | 58  6.3 |
| | 3.9 | 6.9 | 5.6 | 5.6 | Revenues/Working Capital | 8.7 | 7.8 | 7.1 | 7.4 | 5.6 |
| | 10.7 | 14.6 | 11.1 | 12.0 | | 16.7 | 14.8 | 12.8 | 13.7 | 12.0 |
| | 19.4 | 25.7 | 20.4 | 24.5 | | 49.6 | 38.3 | 32.5 | 32.8 | 24.5 |
| | 12.8 | 80.7 | 51.0 | 59.6 | EBIT/Interest | 32.2 | 69.6 | 67.8 | 31.8 | 59.6 |
| | (19) 2.1 | (34) 29.7 | (12) 13.3 | (65) 11.2 | | (112) 9.0 | (74) 15.4 | (66) 6.3 | (82) 4.5 | (65) 11.2 |
| | -2.1 | 1.9 | 3.0 | 1.1 | | 3.6 | 2.2 | -.4 | -1.1 | 1.1 |
| | | | | 12.8 | Net Profit + Depr., Dep., Amort./Cur. Mat. L/T/D | 10.9 | 12.9 | 6.1 | 7.9 | 12.8 |
| | | | (15) 5.4 | | | (37) 3.4 | (24) 5.4 | (17) 3.2 | (27) 5.4 | (15) 5.4 |
| | | | -5.1 | | | 1.5 | 2.3 | .2 | .3 | -5.1 |
| | .1 | .1 | .0 | .1 | Fixed/Worth | .2 | .2 | .1 | .1 | .1 |
| | .2 | .2 | .2 | .2 | | .4 | .4 | .4 | .3 | .2 |
| | .6 | .6 | .7 | .6 | | .9 | .8 | 1.0 | .8 | .6 |
| | .6 | .8 | 1.3 | .8 | Debt/Worth | 1.0 | .9 | .8 | 1.1 | .8 |
| | 1.2 | 1.7 | 2.0 | 1.7 | | 1.9 | 2.0 | 1.8 | 2.2 | 1.7 |
| | 4.7 | 4.3 | 2.6 | 4.3 | | 4.4 | 3.6 | 3.2 | 3.8 | 4.3 |
| | 34.7 | 42.9 | 59.1 | 44.5 | % Profit Before Taxes/Tangible Net Worth | 52.2 | 51.9 | 49.9 | 35.4 | 44.5 |
| | (21) 12.2 | (40) 19.5 | 19.1 | (78) 17.4 | | (123) 33.7 | (90) 30.8 | (82) 20.7 | (96) 12.3 | (78) 17.4 |
| | -5.8 | 4.8 | 6.2 | 4.7 | | 12.3 | 14.4 | .6 | .1 | 4.7 |
| | 11.5 | 12.8 | 13.2 | 12.2 | % Profit Before Taxes/Total Assets | 23.1 | 20.4 | 16.4 | 11.2 | 12.2 |
| | 4.3 | 6.4 | 6.4 | 5.7 | | 9.8 | 9.9 | 5.3 | 3.3 | 5.7 |
| | -6.2 | .6 | 2.2 | .1 | | 3.9 | 2.7 | -1.2 | -1.8 | .1 |
| | .4 | .2 | .3 | .3 | % Depr., Dep., Amort./Revenues | .3 | .3 | .4 | .3 | .3 |
| | (24) .7 | (39) .6 | (12) .4 | (75) .7 | | (115) .8 | (82) .9 | (69) .8 | (88) .7 | (75) .7 |
| | 1.3 | 1.6 | 1.7 | 1.6 | | 1.8 | 1.6 | 1.9 | 1.9 | 1.6 |
| | 1.7 | .8 | | 1.0 | % Officers', Directors' Owners' Comp/Revenues | 1.0 | .9 | 1.1 | 1.2 | 1.0 |
| | (11) 4.0 | (17) 1.9 | | (33) 2.0 | | (57) 2.1 | (37) 2.3 | (36) 3.3 | (45) 2.2 | (33) 2.0 |
| | 7.9 | 2.7 | | 4.0 | | 5.0 | 4.1 | 6.9 | 3.8 | 4.0 |
| 870M | 138569M | 1082510M | 5870555M | 7092504M | Contract Revenues ($) | 8516638M | 31034859M | 10494772M | 6377258M | 7092504M |
| 344M | 70214M | 435416M | 2658041M | 3164015M | Total Assets ($) | 2949634M | 9777481M | 6040337M | 3232821M | 3164015M |

M = $ thousand     MM = $ million

See Pages 9 through 22 for Explanation of Ratios and Data

## Current Data Sorted by Revenue      Comparative Historical Data

### Type of Statement

| 0-1MM | 1-10MM | 10-50MM | 50 & OVER | ALL | Type of Statement | 4/1/07-3/31/08 | 4/1/08-3/31/09 | 4/1/09-3/31/10 | 4/1/10-3/31/11 | 4/1/11-3/31/12 |
|---|---|---|---|---|---|---|---|---|---|---|
| | 3 | 15 | 23 | 41 | Unqualified | 98 | 86 | 66 | 50 | 41 |
| 2 | 94 | 71 | 11 | 178 | Reviewed | 159 | 159 | 127 | 167 | 178 |
| 8 | 14 | 2 | 1 | 17 | Compiled | 26 | 23 | 18 | 20 | 17 |
| | 16 | 5 | | 29 | Tax Returns | 34 | 16 | 18 | 30 | 29 |
| 3 | 24 | 41 | 36 | 104 | Other | 57 | 46 | 49 | 91 | 104 |

66 (4/1-9/30/11)    303 (10/1/11-3/31/12) — ALL periods ALL

| 0-1MM | 1-10MM | 10-50MM | 50 & OVER | ALL | NUMBER OF STATEMENTS | ALL | ALL | ALL | ALL | ALL |
|---|---|---|---|---|---|---|---|---|---|---|
| 13 | 151 | 134 | 71 | 369 | | 374 | 330 | 278 | 358 | 369 |
| % | % | % | % | % | **ASSETS** | % | % | % | % | % |
| 24.5 | 22.9 | 28.3 | 25.2 | 25.4 | Cash & Equivalents | 21.8 | 24.6 | 28.5 | 25.1 | 25.4 |
| 17.6 | 40.1 | 39.7 | 39.9 | 39.1 | A/R - Progress Billings | 39.2 | 38.1 | 32.5 | 27.2 | 39.1 |
| .3 | 2.4 | 5.2 | 7.4 | 4.3 | A/R - Current Retention | 3.0 | 3.1 | 3.0 | 14.9 | 4.3 |
| 10.8 | 1.7 | .6 | 3.5 | 1.9 | Inventory | 3.1 | 3.1 | 2.3 | 2.0 | 1.9 |
| .5 | 5.8 | 6.3 | 4.2 | 5.5 | Cost & Est. Earnings In Excess Billings | 4.8 | 3.9 | 3.7 | 5.0 | 5.5 |
| 5.1 | 5.0 | 6.1 | 7.2 | 5.8 | All Other Current | 6.6 | 5.8 | 6.6 | 5.0 | 5.8 |
| 58.8 | 77.9 | 86.1 | 87.4 | 82.0 | Total Current | 78.5 | 78.6 | 76.6 | 79.2 | 82.0 |
| 33.9 | 13.7 | 8.3 | 5.9 | 11.0 | Fixed Assets (net) | 13.8 | 13.6 | 15.1 | 12.7 | 11.0 |
| .4 | .4 | .8 | 1.2 | .7 | Joint Ventures & Investments | 2.3 | 1.7 | 1.2 | 1.1 | .7 |
| 3.6 | 1.6 | .1 | 1.7 | 1.2 | Intangibles (net) | .8 | 1.0 | 1.1 | .9 | 1.2 |
| 3.2 | 6.4 | 4.6 | 3.7 | 5.1 | All Other Non-Current | 4.6 | 5.0 | 6.1 | 6.0 | 5.1 |
| 100.0 | 100.0 | 100.0 | 100.0 | 100.0 | Total | 100.0 | 100.0 | 100.0 | 100.0 | 100.0 |
| | | | | | **LIABILITIES** | | | | | |
| 4.0 | 8.9 | 3.8 | .9 | 5.3 | Notes Payable-Short Term | 6.8 | 4.7 | 7.4 | 5.8 | 5.3 |
| 9.0 | 26.8 | 34.1 | 35.4 | 30.5 | A/P - Trade | 31.1 | 29.2 | 26.3 | 29.6 | 30.5 |
| .0 | 1.0 | 3.9 | 6.0 | 3.0 | A/P - Retention | 1.8 | 2.4 | 2.1 | 2.6 | 3.0 |
| 1.9 | 6.8 | 9.2 | 10.1 | 8.1 | Billings in Excess of Costs & Est. Earnings | 7.5 | 8.8 | 6.9 | 8.5 | 8.1 |
| 1.5 | .1 | .2 | .3 | .2 | Income Taxes Payable | .3 | .4 | .3 | .4 | .2 |
| 19.6 | 2.6 | .7 | .7 | 2.2 | Cur. Mat.-L/T/D | 2.1 | 2.0 | 2.0 | 2.1 | 2.2 |
| 13.3 | 8.4 | 6.1 | 9.6 | 8.0 | All Other Current | 8.5 | 7.4 | 9.4 | 7.2 | 8.0 |
| 49.4 | 54.6 | 58.1 | 62.8 | 57.3 | Total Current | 58.2 | 54.9 | 54.4 | 56.2 | 57.3 |
| 28.2 | 6.9 | 3.3 | 3.8 | 5.8 | Long-Term Debt | 7.3 | 6.6 | 7.0 | 6.7 | 5.8 |
| .0 | .5 | .4 | .3 | .4 | Deferred Taxes | .5 | .5 | .6 | .3 | .4 |
| 27.9 | 3.5 | 2.5 | 3.0 | 3.9 | All Other Non-Current | 2.2 | 2.2 | 2.9 | 4.5 | 3.9 |
| -5.4 | 34.6 | 35.6 | 30.1 | 32.7 | Net Worth | 31.8 | 35.9 | 35.1 | 32.2 | 32.7 |
| 100.0 | 100.0 | 100.0 | 100.0 | 100.0 | Total Liabilities & Net Worth | 100.0 | 100.0 | 100.0 | 100.0 | 100.0 |
| | | | | | **INCOME DATA** | | | | | |
| 100.0 | 100.0 | 100.0 | 100.0 | 100.0 | Contract Revenues | 100.0 | 100.0 | 100.0 | 100.0 | 100.0 |
| 35.3 | 17.4 | 11.4 | 9.6 | 14.4 | Gross Profit | 16.4 | 15.4 | 17.4 | 15.8 | 14.4 |
| 35.9 | 16.9 | 9.3 | 7.8 | 13.1 | Operating Expenses | 12.8 | 12.2 | 15.8 | 14.7 | 13.1 |
| -.6 | .5 | 2.1 | 1.8 | 1.3 | Operating Profit | 3.6 | 3.2 | 1.6 | 1.1 | 1.3 |
| -.3 | .5 | -.2 | .0 | .1 | All Other Expenses (net) | .3 | .2 | .4 | .2 | .1 |
| -.3 | .0 | 2.3 | 1.8 | 1.2 | Profit Before Taxes | 3.3 | 3.0 | 1.3 | .9 | 1.2 |
| | | | | | **RATIOS** | | | | | |
| 6.1 | 2.3 | 1.8 | 1.7 | 2.0 | Current | 1.8 | 1.9 | 2.1 | 2.0 | 2.0 |
| 3.0 | 1.6 | 1.5 | 1.3 | 1.4 | | 1.4 | 1.4 | 1.5 | 1.4 | 1.4 |
| .3 | 1.2 | 1.2 | 1.2 | 1.2 | | 1.2 | 1.2 | 1.2 | 1.1 | 1.2 |
| | 2.7 | 1.7 | 1.5 | 2.1 | Receivables/Payables | 1.9 | 2.1 | 1.9 | 2.2 | 2.1 |
| (148) 1.5 | 1.2 | 1.1 | (362) 1.3 | | (356) 1.3 | (319) 1.3 | (266) 1.3 | (346) 1.3 | (362) 1.3 |
| | 1.0 | .8 | .9 | .9 | | .9 | .9 | .9 | .9 | .9 |
| 0 UND | 30 12.0 | 33 11.0 | 46 8.0 | 31 11.8 | Revenues/Receivables | 27 13.7 | 29 12.8 | 23 15.5 | 33 11.0 | 31 11.8 |
| 0 UND | 53 6.9 | 54 6.8 | 62 5.9 | 55 6.6 | | 48 7.6 | 48 7.7 | 44 8.3 | 54 6.8 | 55 6.6 |
| 73 5.0 | 81 4.5 | 74 4.9 | 73 5.0 | 76 4.8 | | 69 5.3 | 66 5.6 | 64 5.7 | 76 4.8 | 76 4.8 |
| 0 UND | 18 20.1 | 30 12.3 | 34 10.6 | 25 14.7 | Cost of Revenues/Payables | 21 17.1 | 20 18.5 | 20 18.4 | 25 14.6 | 25 14.7 |
| 21 17.8 | 37 9.8 | 52 7.0 | 59 6.2 | 47 7.8 | | 43 8.5 | 39 9.4 | 40 9.0 | 46 7.9 | 47 7.8 |
| 49 7.4 | 64 5.7 | 69 5.3 | 76 4.8 | 69 5.3 | | 61 6.0 | 60 6.1 | 58 6.3 | 70 5.2 | 69 5.3 |
| 1.8 | 5.3 | 7.7 | 8.4 | 6.5 | Revenues/Working Capital | 8.2 | 8.0 | 6.5 | 6.2 | 6.5 |
| 5.2 | 11.0 | 11.9 | 15.6 | 11.7 | | 14.7 | 13.6 | 12.0 | 11.8 | 11.7 |
| -7.4 | 31.2 | 22.8 | 24.2 | 26.9 | | 37.2 | 25.7 | 27.8 | 30.4 | 26.9 |
| | 14.7 | 40.2 | 153.0 | 30.7 | EBIT/Interest | 54.1 | 48.5 | 35.6 | 37.9 | 30.7 |
| (110) 2.4 | (96) 9.4 | (46) 13.7 | (261) 6.9 | | (297) 12.1 | (248) 10.0 | (202) 5.3 | (266) 6.2 | (261) 6.9 |
| | -1.8 | 1.7 | 3.5 | .5 | | 2.5 | 2.5 | -4.9 | -.5 | .5 |
| | 4.5 | 14.2 | | 7.4 | Net Profit + Depr., Dep., Amort./Cur. Mat. L/T/D | 10.8 | 11.9 | 13.0 | 8.3 | 7.4 |
| (28) 1.7 | (20) 4.4 | | (58) 2.7 | | (84) 4.5 | (83) 3.8 | (57) 4.6 | (53) 2.7 | (58) 2.7 |
| | -3.1 | 1.7 | | -.1 | | 1.3 | 1.4 | .2 | .8 | -.1 |
| .0 | .1 | .1 | .1 | .1 | Fixed/Worth | .1 | .1 | .1 | .1 | .1 |
| .6 | .2 | .2 | .1 | .2 | | .2 | .2 | .2 | .2 | .2 |
| -1.2 | .7 | .4 | .4 | .5 | | .6 | .5 | .6 | .5 | .5 |
| .4 | .8 | 1.1 | 1.7 | 1.0 | Debt/Worth | 1.1 | 1.0 | .8 | .9 | 1.0 |
| .6 | 1.5 | 2.0 | 3.1 | 2.0 | | 2.2 | 1.8 | 1.7 | 2.0 | 2.0 |
| -2.5 | 3.8 | 3.2 | 4.3 | 4.0 | | 4.4 | 3.6 | 3.5 | 3.9 | 4.0 |
| | 23.1 | 45.8 | 29.3 | 30.1 | % Profit Before Taxes/Tangible Net Worth | 50.1 | 48.1 | 36.6 | 31.0 | 30.1 |
| (137) 6.4 | (132) 14.6 | (70) 15.8 | (348) 10.1 | | (354) 26.1 | (314) 22.4 | (260) 11.9 | (331) 12.0 | (348) 10.1 |
| | -9.4 | 2.5 | 2.2 | .0 | | 9.0 | 5.6 | -6.4 | .3 | .0 |
| 43.2 | 9.4 | 12.7 | 7.6 | 10.3 | % Profit Before Taxes/Total Assets | 16.3 | 15.2 | 13.7 | 9.2 | 10.3 |
| 2.6 | 1.7 | 4.4 | 3.8 | 3.7 | | 7.6 | 7.0 | 4.0 | 3.4 | 3.7 |
| -6.3 | -3.7 | .9 | .6 | -.4 | | 2.0 | 1.4 | -3.7 | -.8 | -.4 |
| | .4 | .2 | .1 | .2 | % Depr., Dep., Amort./Revenues | .3 | .2 | .2 | .3 | .2 |
| (129) .7 | (121) .4 | (57) .3 | (315) .5 | | (311) .5 | (286) .5 | (231) .6 | (303) .5 | (315) .5 |
| | 1.8 | .7 | .4 | 1.1 | | 1.2 | 1.2 | 1.7 | 1.2 | 1.1 |
| | 2.0 | .9 | .3 | 1.5 | % Officers', Directors' Owners' Comp/Revenues | 1.1 | 1.3 | 1.4 | 1.5 | 1.5 |
| (66) 3.1 | (50) 1.8 | (11) 1.0 | (134) 2.6 | | (187) 2.4 | (148) 3.1 | (133) 3.4 | (154) 2.6 | (134) 2.6 |
| | 5.9 | 3.5 | 3.9 | 4.9 | | 4.5 | 6.0 | 6.7 | 5.3 | 4.9 |
| 8610M | 773385M | 2852548M | 37548375M | 41182918M | Contract Revenues ($) | 66762127M | 74343772M | 106919533M | 57172335M | 41182918M |
| 6367M | 328523M | 1027930M | 23567386M | 24930206M | Total Assets ($) | 38690253M | 36047329M | 50228561M | 38866333M | 24930206M |

M = $ thousand    MM = $ million
See Pages 9 through 22 for Explanation of Ratios and Data

## Current Data Sorted by Revenue | | | Comparative Historical Data

| 0-1MM | 1-10MM | 10-50MM | 50 & OVER | ALL | Type of Statement | ALL | ALL | ALL | ALL | ALL |
|---|---|---|---|---|---|---|---|---|---|---|
| | 2 | 3 | 4 | 9 | Unqualified | 19 | 20 | 14 | 11 | 9 |
| | 25 | 8 | 1 | 34 | Reviewed | 34 | 32 | 26 | 31 | 34 |
| 2 | 3 | | 1 | 6 | Compiled | 11 | 15 | 12 | 9 | 6 |
| 1 | 3 | | 1 | 5 | Tax Returns | 6 | 5 | 5 | 4 | 5 |
| | 9 | 13 | 6 | 28 | Other | 18 | 12 | 5 | 36 | 28 |
| 16 (4/1-9/30/11) | | 66 (10/1/11-3/31/12) | | | | 4/1/07-3/31/08 | 4/1/08-3/31/09 | 4/1/09-3/31/10 | 4/1/10-3/31/11 | 4/1/11-3/31/12 |
| 3 | 42 | 24 | 13 | 82 | **NUMBER OF STATEMENTS** | 88 | 84 | 62 | 91 | 82 |
| % | % | % | % | % | **ASSETS** | % | % | % | % | % |
| | 19.9 | 20.9 | 10.6 | 18.2 | Cash & Equivalents | 15.4 | 16.3 | 17.8 | 17.8 | 18.2 |
| | 28.9 | 33.3 | 27.3 | 30.1 | A/R - Progress Billings | 30.6 | 31.6 | 29.2 | 20.3 | 30.1 |
| | 2.3 | 4.1 | 1.5 | 2.6 | A/R - Current Retention | 1.9 | 2.1 | .9 | 12.8 | 2.6 |
| | 2.4 | 2.0 | 3.8 | 2.7 | Inventory | 2.2 | 2.5 | 4.3 | 2.9 | 2.7 |
| | 3.5 | 12.0 | 6.8 | 7.0 | Cost & Est. Earnings In Excess Billings | 3.4 | 3.1 | 4.0 | 5.7 | 7.0 |
| | 3.8 | 2.9 | 7.0 | 3.9 | All Other Current | 6.4 | 5.4 | 4.2 | 3.3 | 3.9 |
| | 60.8 | 75.3 | 57.0 | 64.6 | Total Current | 59.9 | 60.9 | 60.3 | 62.8 | 64.6 |
| | 28.0 | 21.7 | 34.5 | 27.4 | Fixed Assets (net) | 33.3 | 32.2 | 30.8 | 28.2 | 27.4 |
| | .2 | .0 | 1.3 | .3 | Joint Ventures & Investments | .7 | .6 | .4 | .6 | .3 |
| | .6 | .0 | 1.8 | .6 | Intangibles (net) | .9 | 1.2 | 2.4 | 3.4 | .6 |
| | 10.4 | 3.0 | 5.4 | 7.1 | All Other Non-Current | 5.3 | 5.0 | 6.1 | 5.0 | 7.1 |
| | 100.0 | 100.0 | 100.0 | 100.0 | Total | 100.0 | 100.0 | 100.0 | 100.0 | 100.0 |
| | | | | | **LIABILITIES** | | | | | |
| | 8.7 | 3.8 | 6.9 | 7.5 | Notes Payable-Short Term | 8.1 | 6.3 | 7.3 | 5.1 | 7.5 |
| | 15.9 | 23.8 | 16.6 | 18.1 | A/P - Trade | 15.0 | 14.1 | 16.4 | 20.9 | 18.1 |
| | .3 | .8 | .3 | .4 | A/P - Retention | .7 | .9 | .2 | .5 | .4 |
| | 2.2 | 7.1 | 3.0 | 4.6 | Billings in Excess of Costs & Est. Earnings | 4.4 | 4.3 | 3.1 | 5.0 | 4.6 |
| | .9 | .1 | .2 | .5 | Income Taxes Payable | .1 | .2 | .1 | .3 | .5 |
| | 5.2 | 2.6 | 4.2 | 5.2 | Cur. Mat.-L/T/D | 5.8 | 5.9 | 4.6 | 4.8 | 5.2 |
| | 3.5 | 5.5 | 8.5 | 4.9 | All Other Current | 6.7 | 6.0 | 6.5 | 4.0 | 4.9 |
| | 36.8 | 43.6 | 39.6 | 41.3 | Total Current | 40.9 | 37.7 | 38.2 | 40.5 | 41.3 |
| | 11.0 | 9.1 | 11.4 | 11.2 | Long-Term Debt | 16.5 | 15.0 | 15.0 | 12.9 | 11.2 |
| | 1.4 | .8 | .1 | 1.0 | Deferred Taxes | 1.8 | 1.4 | 2.3 | .9 | 1.0 |
| | 4.2 | 1.8 | 1.3 | 2.9 | All Other Non-Current | 3.2 | 3.9 | 3.3 | 3.7 | 2.9 |
| | 46.6 | 44.6 | 47.5 | 43.6 | Net Worth | 37.7 | 42.0 | 41.1 | 42.0 | 43.6 |
| | 100.0 | 100.0 | 100.0 | 100.0 | Total Liabilities & Net Worth | 100.0 | 100.0 | 100.0 | 100.0 | 100.0 |
| | | | | | **INCOME DATA** | | | | | |
| | 100.0 | 100.0 | 100.0 | 100.0 | Contract Revenues | 100.0 | 100.0 | 100.0 | 100.0 | 100.0 |
| | 20.8 | 18.1 | 14.2 | 20.4 | Gross Profit | 27.4 | 24.6 | 23.7 | 19.0 | 20.4 |
| | 21.0 | 14.4 | 13.5 | 18.9 | Operating Expenses | 22.2 | 22.3 | 22.5 | 18.0 | 18.9 |
| | -.2 | 3.8 | .7 | 1.5 | Operating Profit | 5.2 | 2.3 | 1.2 | 1.1 | 1.5 |
| | .1 | -.2 | -.3 | .0 | All Other Expenses (net) | .0 | .4 | .0 | -.3 | .0 |
| | -.4 | 4.0 | 1.1 | 1.5 | Profit Before Taxes | 5.1 | 1.9 | 1.2 | 1.4 | 1.5 |
| | | | | | **RATIOS** | | | | | |
| | 2.6 | 2.6 | 1.9 | 2.2 | Current | 2.1 | 2.3 | 2.5 | 2.4 | 2.2 |
| | 1.6 | 1.6 | 1.5 | 1.6 | | 1.5 | 1.5 | 1.5 | 1.6 | 1.6 |
| | 1.2 | 1.3 | 1.2 | 1.2 | | 1.1 | 1.3 | 1.1 | 1.2 | 1.2 |
| | 3.7 | 2.7 | 3.5 | 3.6 | Receivables/Payables | 5.5 | 3.7 | 3.0 | 3.2 | 3.6 |
| (41) | 2.4 | 1.5 | 1.4 | (81) 1.7 | | (85) 2.3 | (83) 2.4 | (60) 1.9 | 1.7 | (81) 1.7 |
| | 1.2 | 1.1 | .7 | 1.1 | | 1.2 | 1.6 | 1.2 | 1.0 | 1.1 |
| 28 13.1 | 38 9.7 | 27 13.3 | 36 10.0 | | Revenues/Receivables | 27 13.5 | 36 10.2 | 29 12.5 | 38 9.5 | 36 10.0 |
| 56 6.5 | 58 6.3 | 50 7.3 | 55 6.6 | | | 57 6.5 | 52 7.0 | 48 7.6 | 57 7.1 | 55 6.6 |
| 83 4.4 | 74 4.9 | 60 6.1 | 74 4.9 | | | 80 4.5 | 74 4.9 | 72 5.0 | 67 5.5 | 74 4.9 |
| 13 27.5 | 24 15.5 | 21 17.6 | 18 20.2 | | Cost of Revenues/Payables | 10 36.6 | 14 26.3 | 15 23.8 | 22 16.8 | 18 20.2 |
| 36 10.1 | 45 8.2 | 36 10.1 | 38 9.6 | | | 26 13.9 | 30 12.2 | 31 11.8 | 38 9.6 | 38 9.6 |
| 55 6.2 | 59 6.2 | 51 7.1 | 55 6.6 | | | 54 8.5 | 43 8.5 | 60 6.1 | 52 7.0 | 55 6.6 |
| | 5.6 | 5.2 | 7.0 | 5.7 | Revenues/Working Capital | 6.2 | 5.7 | 5.3 | 6.1 | 5.7 |
| | 10.5 | 8.2 | 11.6 | 9.9 | | 11.4 | 9.6 | 10.9 | 10.9 | 9.9 |
| | 30.2 | 11.7 | 25.8 | 25.1 | | 30.8 | 20.1 | 56.2 | 25.7 | 25.1 |
| | 11.0 | 23.5 | 8.8 | 12.0 | EBIT/Interest | 12.8 | 19.1 | 10.2 | 12.4 | 12.0 |
| (36) | .1 | (20) 9.6 | (12) 6.1 | (70) 5.9 | | (77) 4.4 | (72) 4.0 | (51) 2.6 | (78) 3.2 | (70) 5.9 |
| | -6.2 | 6.3 | 1.5 | -2.9 | | 1.3 | -.1 | -3.0 | -1.4 | -2.9 |
| | | | | 4.1 | Net Profit + Depr., Dep., Amort./Cur. Mat. L/T/D | 4.6 | 4.9 | 6.3 | 5.7 | 4.1 |
| | | | (13) | 3.3 | | (27) 1.7 | (18) 2.5 | (18) 2.8 | (22) 2.6 | (13) 3.3 |
| | | | | -.1 | | 1.2 | 1.0 | 1.5 | .5 | -.1 |
| | .3 | .2 | .5 | .3 | Fixed/Worth | .3 | .3 | .3 | .3 | .3 |
| | .6 | .5 | .8 | .6 | | .8 | .7 | .6 | .6 | .6 |
| | 1.3 | .8 | 1.2 | 1.2 | | 1.3 | 1.4 | 1.4 | 1.2 | 1.2 |
| | .4 | .9 | .6 | .7 | Debt/Worth | .8 | .7 | .6 | .6 | .7 |
| | 1.4 | 1.4 | .9 | 1.4 | | 1.5 | 1.5 | 1.1 | 1.5 | 1.4 |
| | 2.7 | 1.8 | 1.8 | 2.6 | | 3.1 | 2.9 | 2.9 | 3.1 | 2.6 |
| | 20.1 | 42.9 | 15.6 | 24.7 | % Profit Before Taxes/Tangible Net Worth | 41.8 | 34.2 | 34.1 | 27.7 | 24.7 |
| (40) | 4.4 | 19.5 | 9.9 | (78) 10.3 | | (80) 15.7 | (79) 11.5 | (56) 8.8 | (86) 9.8 | (78) 10.3 |
| | -18.6 | 7.6 | 2.6 | -6.3 | | 5.6 | -3.5 | .6 | -.4 | -6.3 |
| | 9.3 | 14.6 | 6.6 | 11.1 | % Profit Before Taxes/Total Assets | 17.7 | 12.1 | 14.2 | 9.9 | 11.1 |
| | 1.1 | 9.1 | 5.2 | 5.3 | | 5.7 | 4.4 | 3.3 | 4.7 | 5.3 |
| | -8.0 | 3.5 | .4 | -3.5 | | 1.1 | -3.9 | -1.7 | -1.5 | -3.5 |
| | 2.8 | .6 | | 1.7 | % Depr., Dep., Amort./Revenues | 1.7 | 2.2 | 2.1 | 1.2 | 1.7 |
| (39) | 4.4 | (22) 2.4 | | (70) 3.3 | | (81) 3.5 | (69) 4.1 | (50) 3.6 | (79) 3.0 | (70) 3.3 |
| | 5.8 | 3.5 | | 5.3 | | 6.0 | 6.8 | 6.6 | 4.8 | 5.3 |
| | 2.2 | | | 1.5 | % Officers', Directors' Owners' Comp/Revenues | 1.5 | 1.9 | 1.3 | 1.4 | 1.5 |
| (19) | 3.7 | | | (29) 3.6 | | (47) 3.2 | (47) 3.4 | (25) 2.5 | (40) 2.7 | (29) 3.6 |
| | 9.0 | | | 6.6 | | 5.4 | 6.0 | 5.9 | 4.9 | 6.6 |
| 1640M | 203346M | 390659M | 6562116M | 7157761M | Contract Revenues ($) | 2097834M | 3604883M | 4498342M | 9545546M | 7157761M |
| 842M | 113291M | 179952M | 3227681M | 3521766M | Total Assets ($) | 1174683M | 1983786M | 3264021M | 8374601M | 3521766M |

M = $ thousand    MM = $ million
See Pages 9 through 22 for Explanation of Ratios and Data

**Current Data Sorted by Revenue**      **Comparative Historical Data**

| 0-1MM | 1-10MM | 10-50MM | 50 & OVER | ALL | Type of Statement | 4/1/07-3/31/08 | 4/1/08-3/31/09 | 4/1/09-3/31/10 | 4/1/10-3/31/11 | 4/1/11-3/31/12 |
|---|---|---|---|---|---|---|---|---|---|---|
| 4 | 7 | 1 | 1 | 2 | Unqualified | 8 | 3 | 4 | 4 | 2 |
|  |  | 1 |  | 12 | Reviewed | 22 | 14 | 17 | 11 | 12 |
|  | 5 |  |  | 5 | Compiled | 26 | 18 | 16 | 11 | 5 |
| 18 | 10 | 5 |  | 28 | Tax Returns | 79 | 44 | 42 | 36 | 28 |
| 3 | 5 |  | 2 | 15 | Other | 52 | 39 | 33 | 27 | 15 |
|  | 5 (4/1-9/30/11) | | 57 (10/1/11-3/31/12) | | | ALL | ALL | ALL | ALL | ALL |
| 25 | 27 | 7 | 3 | 62 | **NUMBER OF STATEMENTS** | 187 | 118 | 112 | 89 | 62 |
| % | % | % | % | % | **ASSETS** | % | % | % | % | % |
| 2.9 | 5.6 |  |  | 6.1 | Cash & Equivalents | 5.4 | 3.8 | 4.4 | 3.7 | 6.1 |
| .7 | 14.4 |  |  | 9.2 | A/R - Progress Billings | 4.6 | 4.5 | 4.2 | 3.2 | 9.2 |
| .0 | .9 |  |  | .7 | A/R - Current Retention | .5 | .0 | .2 | .4 | .7 |
| 23.0 | 34.2 |  |  | 25.1 | Inventory | 38.8 | 34.4 | 29.4 | 28.1 | 25.1 |
| .2 | 1.2 |  |  | .9 | Cost & Est. Earnings In Excess Billings | 1.1 | .7 | .9 | .5 | .9 |
| 9.6 | 8.6 |  |  | 8.0 | All Other Current | 6.4 | 5.6 | 7.6 | 5.3 | 8.0 |
| 36.4 | 64.9 |  |  | 49.9 | Total Current | 56.7 | 49.1 | 46.6 | 41.2 | 49.9 |
| 41.3 | 20.4 |  |  | 30.0 | Fixed Assets (net) | 27.6 | 33.3 | 39.4 | 45.2 | 30.0 |
| 1.9 | 5.7 |  |  | 6.9 | Joint Ventures & Investments | 3.4 | 4.4 | 3.6 | 5.4 | 6.9 |
| .5 | .0 |  |  | .3 | Intangibles (net) | 1.3 | 1.5 | 1.8 | .3 | .3 |
| 19.9 | 9.0 |  |  | 12.9 | All Other Non-Current | 11.0 | 11.7 | 8.7 | 7.9 | 12.9 |
| 100.0 | 100.0 |  |  | 100.0 | Total | 100.0 | 100.0 | 100.0 | 100.0 | 100.0 |
|  |  |  |  |  | **LIABILITIES** |  |  |  |  |  |
| 13.5 | 17.0 |  |  | 13.7 | Notes Payable-Short Term | 20.4 | 17.1 | 13.7 | 22.6 | 13.7 |
| 1.7 | 6.0 |  |  | 5.1 | A/P - Trade | 3.3 | 3.7 | 2.9 | 2.1 | 5.1 |
| .0 | 1.8 |  |  | 1.2 | A/P - Retention | .8 | .1 | .0 | .0 | 1.2 |
| .3 | .3 |  |  | .8 | Billings in Excess of Costs & Est. Earnings | .6 | 1.1 | .5 | .6 | .8 |
| .0 | .0 |  |  | .0 | Income Taxes Payable | .0 | .0 | .0 | .0 | .0 |
| .7 | 4.0 |  |  | 2.1 | Cur. Mat.-L/T/D | 4.4 | 4.2 | 7.5 | 2.1 | 2.1 |
| 2.4 | 4.9 |  |  | 4.0 | All Other Current | 6.0 | 5.1 | 4.9 | 3.9 | 4.0 |
| 18.5 | 33.9 |  |  | 26.8 | Total Current | 35.6 | 31.2 | 29.5 | 31.3 | 26.8 |
| 48.2 | 18.5 |  |  | 31.6 | Long-Term Debt | 31.5 | 37.4 | 37.0 | 42.0 | 31.6 |
| .0 | .0 |  |  | .0 | Deferred Taxes | .2 | .0 | .3 | .4 | .0 |
| 5.5 | 9.3 |  |  | 6.4 | All Other Non-Current | 11.0 | 8.5 | 7.2 | 12.3 | 6.4 |
| 27.8 | 38.3 |  |  | 35.1 | Net Worth | 21.7 | 22.8 | 25.9 | 14.0 | 35.1 |
| 100.0 | 100.0 |  |  | 100.0 | Total Liabilities & Net Worth | 100.0 | 100.0 | 100.0 | 100.0 | 100.0 |
|  |  |  |  |  | **INCOME DATA** |  |  |  |  |  |
| 100.0 | 100.0 |  |  | 100.0 | Contract Revenues | 100.0 | 100.0 | 100.0 | 100.0 | 100.0 |
|  |  |  |  |  | Gross Profit |  |  |  |  |  |
| 78.3 | 93.4 |  |  | 85.5 | Operating Expenses | 83.8 | 88.6 | 85.0 | 79.6 | 85.5 |
| 21.7 | 6.6 |  |  | 14.5 | Operating Profit | 16.2 | 11.4 | 15.0 | 20.4 | 14.5 |
| 16.7 | 6.0 |  |  | 10.8 | All Other Expenses (net) | 9.9 | 10.0 | 17.1 | 20.5 | 10.8 |
| 5.0 | .7 |  |  | 3.7 | Profit Before Taxes | 6.3 | 1.4 | -2.2 | -.1 | 3.7 |
|  |  |  |  |  | **RATIOS** |  |  |  |  |  |
| 13.0 | 4.2 |  |  | 4.6 | | 4.7 | 4.7 | 5.5 | 4.9 | 4.6 |
| 2.0 | 2.0 |  |  | 1.8 | Current | 1.6 | 1.3 | 1.4 | 1.5 | 1.8 |
| .2 | 1.2 |  |  | .9 | | .8 | .6 | .6 | .5 | .9 |
| .0 | 4.9 |  |  | 3.6 | | 2.2 | 2.3 | 4.6 | 5.1 | 3.6 |
| (15) .0 | (24) .5 |  | (48) .1 | | Receivables/Payables | (129) .1 | (84) .1 | (68) .5 | (57) .2 | (48) .1 |
| .0 | .0 |  |  | .0 | | .0 | .0 | .0 | .0 | .0 |
| 0 UND | 0 UND |  | 0 UND | | | 0 UND | 0 UND | 0 UND | 0 UND | 0 UND |
| 0 UND | 2 160.5 |  | 0 UND | | Revenues/Receivables | 0 UND | 0 UND | 0 UND | 0 UND | 0 UND |
| 0 UND | 43 8.4 |  | 33 11.2 | | | 6 57.0 | 10 36.7 | 8 48.5 | 5 77.3 | 33 11.2 |
|  |  |  |  |  | Cost of Revenues/Payables |  |  |  |  |  |
| .3 | .9 |  |  | .7 | | .8 | 1.3 | .7 | .7 | .7 |
| 1.6 | 4.2 |  |  | 4.2 | Revenues/Working Capital | 4.1 | 7.7 | 5.3 | 4.2 | 4.2 |
| -15.2 | 11.2 |  |  | -74.4 | | -13.9 | -8.3 | -5.8 | -5.6 | -74.4 |
| 5.6 | 8.2 |  |  | 7.4 | | 5.5 | 3.3 | 4.1 | 5.4 | 7.4 |
| (13) 2.3 | (18) 1.2 |  | (38) 1.5 | | EBIT/Interest | (111) 1.5 | (77) 1.2 | (51) 1.5 | (39) 1.4 | (38) 1.5 |
| .6 | -2.8 |  |  | -.7 | | .5 | -.4 | -.5 | .8 | -.7 |
|  |  |  |  |  | Net Profit + Depr., Dep., Amort./Cur. Mat. L/T/D |  |  |  |  |  |
| .0 | .0 |  |  | .0 | | .0 | .0 | .0 | .0 | .0 |
| 1.1 | .1 |  |  | .2 | Fixed/Worth | .5 | .8 | 1.1 | 1.9 | .2 |
| 7.0 | .7 |  |  | 2.3 | | 5.8 | 7.6 | 11.1 | 8.9 | 2.3 |
| 1.0 | .8 |  |  | .9 | | 1.4 | 1.5 | 1.2 | 1.7 | .9 |
| 2.2 | 2.1 |  |  | 2.0 | Debt/Worth | 6.5 | 4.8 | 3.4 | 4.9 | 2.0 |
| 40.2 | 3.4 |  |  | 4.5 | | 70.9 | 34.8 | 26.4 | -210.9 | 4.5 |
| 20.3 | 17.5 |  |  | 16.7 | | 37.3 | 22.1 | 10.3 | 17.2 | 16.7 |
| (22) 1.8 | (25) 6.9 |  | (57) 3.3 | | % Profit Before Taxes/ Tangible Net Worth | (147) 8.7 | (96) 4.8 | (91) .0 | (65) 4.2 | (57) 3.3 |
| -7.5 | -2.9 |  |  | -5.8 | | -3.6 | -10.4 | -7.5 | -7.1 | -5.8 |
| 3.3 | 5.2 |  |  | 4.3 | | 7.7 | 4.9 | 3.1 | 3.5 | 4.3 |
| .6 | 2.2 |  |  | 1.4 | % Profit Before Taxes/ Total Assets | 1.4 | .5 | .0 | .3 | 1.4 |
| -1.3 | -2.6 |  |  | -1.2 | | -1.1 | -3.2 | -2.7 | -1.6 | -1.2 |
| 2.6 | .4 |  |  | 1.0 | | .8 | .9 | 1.3 | 1.7 | 1.0 |
| (12) 9.8 | (18) 1.1 |  | (38) 2.2 | | % Depr., Dep., Amort./ Revenues | (102) 2.4 | (71) 3.0 | (68) 7.5 | (58) 12.0 | (38) 2.2 |
| 24.5 | 5.2 |  |  | 10.8 | | 11.8 | 16.9 | 19.9 | 18.8 | 10.8 |
|  |  |  |  | .6 | | 2.3 | 1.8 | .8 | .4 | .6 |
|  |  |  | (15) 3.0 | | % Officers', Directors' Owners' Comp/Revenues | (38) 4.8 | (26) 3.2 | (24) 3.3 | (15) 2.9 | (15) 3.0 |
|  |  |  |  | 5.8 | | 7.1 | 6.8 | 6.4 | 5.3 | 5.8 |
| 11304M | 90214M | 148097M | 297955M | 547570M | Contract Revenues ($) | 1888207M | 2259339M | 849933M | 709997M | 547570M |
| 85070M | 257380M | 751581M | 660569M | 1754600M | Total Assets ($) | 6105175M | 4099390M | 5824551M | 5213510M | 1754600M |

© RMA 2012

M = $ thousand     MM = $ million
See Pages 9 through 22 for Explanation of Ratios and Data

**Current Data Sorted by Revenue**  |  **Comparative Historical Data**

| 0-1MM | 1-10MM | 10-50MM | 50 & OVER | ALL | Type of Statement | 4/1/07-3/31/08 ALL | 4/1/08-3/31/09 ALL | 4/1/09-3/31/10 ALL | 4/1/10-3/31/11 ALL | 4/1/11-3/31/12 ALL |
|---|---|---|---|---|---|---|---|---|---|---|
| | 10 | 21 | 10 | 41 | Unqualified | 85 | 49 | 47 | 44 | 41 |
| 1 | 22 | 22 | 2 | 47 | Reviewed | 54 | 40 | 37 | 43 | 47 |
| | 4 | | | 4 | Compiled | 10 | 5 | 8 | 5 | 4 |
| | 4 | 2 | | 6 | Tax Returns | 5 | 5 | 9 | 8 | 6 |
| 1 | 17 | 50 | 47 | 115 | Other | 28 | 21 | 19 | 95 | 115 |
| | 30 (4/1-9/30/11) | | 183 (10/1/11-3/31/12) | | | | | | | |
| 2 | 57 | 95 | 59 | 213 | **NUMBER OF STATEMENTS** | 182 | 120 | 120 | 195 | 213 |
| % | % | % | % | % | **ASSETS** | % | % | % | % | % |
| | 17.2 | 18.2 | 18.7 | 18.1 | Cash & Equivalents | 15.1 | 15.7 | 17.9 | 20.3 | 18.1 |
| | 34.9 | 30.0 | 24.9 | 29.9 | A/R - Progress Billings | 28.7 | 26.2 | 27.4 | 15.6 | 29.9 |
| | 1.9 | 2.7 | 4.6 | 3.0 | A/R - Current Retention | 3.4 | 2.8 | 2.1 | 13.9 | 3.0 |
| | 2.9 | 4.4 | 4.7 | 4.0 | Inventory | 3.0 | 3.9 | 3.2 | 3.9 | 4.0 |
| | 3.5 | 4.7 | 4.6 | 4.4 | Cost & Est. Earnings In Excess Billings | 3.5 | 2.5 | 2.3 | 4.2 | 4.4 |
| | 3.7 | 2.9 | 3.7 | 3.3 | All Other Current | 3.8 | 4.9 | 4.2 | 4.2 | 3.3 |
| | 64.2 | 62.9 | 61.3 | 62.8 | Total Current | 57.4 | 55.9 | 57.1 | 62.1 | 62.8 |
| | 28.0 | 30.7 | 28.3 | 29.2 | Fixed Assets (net) | 34.9 | 36.0 | 34.0 | 30.8 | 29.2 |
| | 1.2 | .2 | .4 | .5 | Joint Ventures & Investments | 1.1 | 1.5 | .9 | .4 | .5 |
| | .2 | 1.4 | 2.1 | 1.2 | Intangibles (net) | .8 | .8 | 1.4 | .9 | 1.2 |
| | 6.5 | 4.8 | 7.8 | 6.2 | All Other Non-Current | 5.8 | 5.7 | 6.7 | 5.7 | 6.2 |
| | 100.0 | 100.0 | 100.0 | 100.0 | Total | 100.0 | 100.0 | 100.0 | 100.0 | 100.0 |
| | | | | | **LIABILITIES** | | | | | |
| | 12.4 | 3.8 | 1.7 | 5.6 | Notes Payable-Short Term | 5.1 | 4.6 | 5.6 | 3.6 | 5.6 |
| | 16.5 | 16.6 | 16.6 | 16.5 | A/P - Trade | 15.6 | 15.5 | 16.1 | 15.1 | 16.5 |
| | .1 | .4 | 1.9 | .7 | A/P - Retention | .8 | .5 | .6 | .5 | .7 |
| | 3.1 | 4.2 | 6.6 | 4.5 | Billings in Excess of Costs & Est. Earnings | 4.4 | 3.3 | 3.9 | 4.2 | 4.5 |
| | .2 | .3 | .0 | .2 | Income Taxes Payable | .4 | .4 | .2 | .3 | .2 |
| | 4.1 | 4.0 | 2.9 | 3.7 | Cur. Mat.-L/T/D | 5.5 | 6.5 | 5.1 | 4.1 | 3.7 |
| | 3.5 | 5.7 | 6.4 | 5.3 | All Other Current | 8.7 | 5.7 | 6.5 | 5.5 | 5.3 |
| | 39.9 | 35.0 | 36.1 | 36.5 | Total Current | 40.5 | 36.6 | 37.9 | 33.2 | 36.5 |
| | 9.6 | 11.4 | 12.7 | 11.1 | Long-Term Debt | 15.1 | 14.9 | 14.1 | 12.4 | 11.1 |
| | 2.0 | 1.1 | 1.0 | 1.3 | Deferred Taxes | 1.4 | 1.6 | 1.1 | 1.0 | 1.3 |
| | 2.6 | 2.1 | 3.9 | 2.7 | All Other Non-Current | 3.2 | 5.3 | 1.6 | 2.7 | 2.7 |
| | 45.9 | 50.4 | 46.3 | 48.3 | Net Worth | 39.8 | 41.7 | 45.4 | 50.7 | 48.3 |
| | 100.0 | 100.0 | 100.0 | 100.0 | Total Liabilities & Net Worth | 100.0 | 100.0 | 100.0 | 100.0 | 100.0 |
| | | | | | **INCOME DATA** | | | | | |
| | 100.0 | 100.0 | 100.0 | 100.0 | Contract Revenues | 100.0 | 100.0 | 100.0 | 100.0 | 100.0 |
| | 22.8 | 14.3 | 9.9 | 15.4 | Gross Profit | 21.2 | 19.9 | 21.3 | 18.6 | 15.4 |
| | 20.7 | 11.1 | 8.7 | 13.2 | Operating Expenses | 16.0 | 16.4 | 18.8 | 15.5 | 13.2 |
| | 2.1 | 3.2 | 1.2 | 2.2 | Operating Profit | 5.2 | 3.5 | 2.5 | 3.2 | 2.2 |
| | -.2 | .0 | -.1 | -.1 | All Other Expenses (net) | .3 | .4 | .5 | -.1 | -.1 |
| | 2.3 | 3.2 | 1.3 | 2.3 | Profit Before Taxes | 4.9 | 3.1 | 2.0 | 3.2 | 2.3 |
| | | | | | **RATIOS** | | | | | |
| | 2.7 | 2.6 | 2.3 | 2.4 | Current | 2.2 | 2.2 | 2.2 | 2.8 | 2.4 |
| | 1.6 | 1.9 | 1.6 | 1.7 | | 1.5 | 1.6 | 1.6 | 1.8 | 1.7 |
| | 1.2 | 1.4 | 1.4 | 1.3 | | 1.2 | 1.2 | 1.1 | 1.4 | 1.3 |
| | 5.3 | 3.5 | 2.0 | 3.5 | Receivables/Payables | 3.7 | 3.8 | 4.0 | 3.5 | 3.5 |
| (56) | 2.7 | 2.0 | 1.6 | (212) 1.8 | | (181) 2.0 | (118) 2.0 | (117) 1.8 | (193) 2.0 | (212) 1.8 |
| | 1.4 | 1.3 | 1.2 | 1.3 | | 1.3 | 1.3 | 1.3 | 1.2 | 1.3 |
| 31 11.8 | 33 11.0 | 35 10.3 | 33 10.9 | | Revenues/Receivables | 29 12.6 | 30 12.0 | 27 13.7 | 25 14.8 | 33 10.9 |
| 64 5.7 | 49 7.5 | 46 7.9 | 51 7.2 | | | 47 7.7 | 45 7.5 | 45 8.1 | 47 7.8 | 51 7.2 |
| 81 4.5 | 74 4.9 | 66 5.5 | 73 5.0 | | | 67 5.5 | 66 5.5 | 67 5.4 | 71 5.2 | 73 5.0 |
| 11 31.9 | 13 28.7 | 23 16.1 | 14 25.6 | | Cost of Revenues/Payables | 15 24.5 | 11 33.1 | 13 29.1 | 13 28.2 | 14 25.6 |
| 25 14.5 | 29 12.5 | 35 10.4 | 32 11.5 | | | 28 13.0 | 26 14.1 | 27 13.4 | 25 14.7 | 32 11.5 |
| 52 7.0 | 48 7.6 | 46 7.9 | 48 7.6 | | | 42 8.7 | 46 8.0 | 52 7.1 | 43 8.5 | 48 7.6 |
| | 5.0 | 5.2 | 5.8 | 5.2 | Revenues/Working Capital | 7.5 | 6.5 | 6.0 | 4.8 | 5.2 |
| | 11.6 | 8.9 | 8.6 | 9.1 | | 11.8 | 12.3 | 12.1 | 8.3 | 9.1 |
| | 30.4 | 15.4 | 14.3 | 16.6 | | 28.2 | 26.2 | 32.4 | 15.0 | 16.6 |
| | 8.7 | 24.1 | 17.3 | 17.8 | EBIT/Interest | 14.8 | 13.1 | 15.1 | 19.7 | 17.8 |
| (52) | 2.4 | (86) 6.4 | (52) 3.5 | (190) 3.9 | | (165) 5.9 | (106) 4.6 | (108) 4.5 | (173) 5.8 | (190) 3.9 |
| | -3.5 | 1.9 | -2.6 | .5 | | 2.4 | 1.5 | -.8 | 1.5 | .5 |
| | 9.1 | 5.6 | 3.4 | 5.4 | Net Profit + Depr., Dep., Amort./Cur. Mat. L/T/D | 4.2 | 3.1 | 4.6 | 4.0 | 5.4 |
| (15) | 1.6 | (21) 2.4 | (11) 2.7 | (47) 2.4 | | (59) 2.1 | (40) 2.0 | (26) 2.1 | (43) 2.5 | (47) 2.4 |
| | .6 | 1.4 | 1.7 | 1.1 | | 1.4 | .9 | .7 | 1.3 | 1.1 |
| | .2 | .4 | .4 | .4 | Fixed/Worth | .5 | .5 | .4 | .3 | .4 |
| | .6 | .6 | .6 | .6 | | .8 | .8 | .7 | .7 | .6 |
| | 1.1 | .9 | .9 | .9 | | 1.4 | 1.4 | 1.4 | 1.0 | .9 |
| | .4 | .6 | .7 | .6 | Debt/Worth | .8 | .6 | .5 | .5 | .6 |
| | 1.3 | 1.0 | 1.5 | 1.2 | | 1.3 | 1.3 | 1.3 | 1.0 | 1.2 |
| | 2.5 | 1.8 | 2.0 | 1.9 | | 2.7 | 2.5 | 2.5 | 2.0 | 1.9 |
| | 25.0 | 26.2 | 18.8 | 21.4 | % Profit Before Taxes/Tangible Net Worth | 47.6 | 31.4 | 32.4 | 27.9 | 21.4 |
| (56) | 5.1 | 11.1 | 6.2 | (212) 9.3 | | (174) 24.4 | (114) 12.3 | (114) 12.0 | (192) 11.1 | (212) 9.3 |
| | -2.2 | 3.5 | -4.3 | -.8 | | 9.0 | 3.3 | -1.8 | 2.4 | -.8 |
| | 11.5 | 12.1 | 7.2 | 9.7 | % Profit Before Taxes/Total Assets | 17.0 | 13.0 | 13.0 | 12.8 | 9.7 |
| | 2.1 | 5.0 | 3.5 | 4.2 | | 9.2 | 5.4 | 5.7 | 5.5 | 4.2 |
| | -1.7 | 1.6 | -2.9 | -.3 | | 2.7 | 1.1 | -1.7 | .9 | -.3 |
| | 1.7 | 1.8 | 2.0 | 1.9 | % Depr., Dep., Amort./Revenues | 2.1 | 2.4 | 1.7 | 1.9 | 1.9 |
| (54) | 3.0 | (87) 3.1 | (45) 2.4 | (186) 2.9 | | (166) 3.1 | (110) 3.3 | (108) 3.5 | (177) 3.1 | (186) 2.9 |
| | 4.7 | 4.3 | 4.0 | 4.3 | | 4.6 | 4.9 | 5.5 | 4.7 | 4.3 |
| | 1.7 | 1.0 | | 1.1 | % Officers', Directors' Owners' Comp/Revenues | 1.3 | 1.4 | 1.2 | 1.3 | 1.1 |
| (31) | 2.9 | (39) 1.4 | | (73) 1.9 | | (78) 2.7 | (61) 2.2 | (62) 2.2 | (74) 2.9 | (73) 1.9 |
| | 4.1 | 2.7 | | 3.4 | | 5.3 | 4.0 | 5.9 | 4.8 | 3.4 |
| 368M | 307505M | 2350098M | 22910977M | 25568948M | Contract Revenues ($) | 15109325M | 13593931M | 24664202M | 29688922M | 25568948M |
| 354M | 148865M | 1186891M | 12931033M | 14267143M | Total Assets ($) | 8348429M | 7028336M | 22560228M | 14849751M | 14267143M |

M = $ thousand    MM = $ million
See Pages 9 through 22 for Explanation of Ratios and Data

**Current Data Sorted by Revenue**  |  **Comparative Historical Data**

| 0-1MM | 1-10MM | 10-50MM | 50 & OVER | ALL | Type of Statement | 4/1/07-3/31/08 ALL | 4/1/08-3/31/09 ALL | 4/1/09-3/31/10 ALL | 4/1/10-3/31/11 ALL | 4/1/11-3/31/12 ALL |
|---|---|---|---|---|---|---|---|---|---|---|
|  | 1 | 5 | 5 | 11 | Unqualified | 16 | 11 | 12 | 4 | 11 |
| 1 | 10 | 12 | 2 | 25 | Reviewed | 24 | 16 | 20 | 21 | 25 |
|  | 4 | 1 |  | 5 | Compiled | 7 | 3 | 2 | 3 | 5 |
| 1 | 5 | 1 |  | 7 | Tax Returns | 3 | 2 | 7 | 6 | 7 |
| 1 | 6 | 9 | 18 | 34 | Other | 9 | 12 | 14 | 34 | 34 |
| 14 (4/1-9/30/11) | | 68 (10/1/11-3/31/12) | | | | | | | | |
| 3 | 26 | 28 | 25 | 82 | **NUMBER OF STATEMENTS** | 59 | 44 | 55 | 68 | 82 |
| % | % | % | % | % | **ASSETS** | % | % | % | % | % |
|  | 14.9 | 18.7 | 20.7 | 18.1 | Cash & Equivalents | 16.3 | 20.7 | 19.2 | 20.9 | 18.1 |
|  | 37.5 | 39.1 | 28.5 | 34.3 | A/R - Progress Billings | 33.2 | 35.2 | 30.8 | 17.0 | 34.3 |
|  | 1.0 | 1.6 | 5.2 | 2.4 | A/R - Current Retention | 1.4 | 1.0 | 1.6 | 17.3 | 2.4 |
|  | 1.7 | .8 | 2.0 | 2.3 | Inventory | 3.7 | 1.0 | 1.8 | 2.0 | 2.3 |
|  | 4.2 | 6.3 | 5.6 | 5.4 | Cost & Est. Earnings In Excess Billings | 3.1 | 3.6 | 3.3 | 4.4 | 5.4 |
|  | 7.8 | 8.5 | 3.0 | 6.3 | All Other Current | 6.2 | 4.8 | 3.7 | 5.4 | 6.3 |
|  | 67.3 | 75.0 | 64.9 | 68.9 | Total Current | 63.9 | 66.4 | 60.4 | 67.0 | 68.9 |
|  | 22.8 | 17.5 | 23.8 | 21.1 | Fixed Assets (net) | 27.4 | 26.7 | 32.6 | 24.5 | 21.1 |
|  | .0 | .1 | .8 | .3 | Joint Ventures & Investments | .3 | 1.1 | 1.1 | .0 | .3 |
|  | .9 | .5 | 4.5 | 1.8 | Intangibles (net) | 1.7 | .5 | .8 | 1.2 | 1.8 |
|  | 9.0 | 7.0 | 6.0 | 7.9 | All Other Non-Current | 6.8 | 5.3 | 5.1 | 7.3 | 7.9 |
|  | 100.0 | 100.0 | 100.0 | 100.0 | Total | 100.0 | 100.0 | 100.0 | 100.0 | 100.0 |
| | | | | | **LIABILITIES** | | | | | |
|  | 20.2 | 6.1 | 1.3 | 14.6 | Notes Payable-Short Term | 5.3 | 9.9 | 7.0 | 10.4 | 14.6 |
|  | 17.7 | 27.3 | 18.0 | 21.6 | A/P - Trade | 17.5 | 20.8 | 15.8 | 19.5 | 21.6 |
|  | .0 | 1.0 | 1.5 | .8 | A/P - Retention | .3 | .3 | .3 | 1.1 | .8 |
|  | 2.4 | 6.9 | 11.2 | 6.5 | Billings in Excess of Costs & Est. Earnings | 5.5 | 4.8 | 4.7 | 6.8 | 6.5 |
|  | 1.6 | .1 | .4 | .7 | Income Taxes Payable | .3 | .1 | .2 | .2 | .7 |
|  | 5.6 | 2.7 | 2.2 | 3.6 | Cur. Mat.-L/T/D | 5.9 | 4.8 | 5.1 | 5.7 | 3.6 |
|  | 4.8 | 7.3 | 9.1 | 8.5 | All Other Current | 9.0 | 5.9 | 6.0 | 8.5 | 8.5 |
|  | 52.4 | 51.4 | 43.7 | 56.3 | Total Current | 43.7 | 46.6 | 39.1 | 52.2 | 56.3 |
|  | 11.6 | 7.1 | 11.2 | 9.9 | Long-Term Debt | 14.3 | 12.2 | 14.2 | 14.1 | 9.9 |
|  | .6 | .9 | 1.1 | .8 | Deferred Taxes | 1.1 | 1.3 | .9 | .8 | .8 |
|  | 19.9 | 1.2 | 6.0 | 8.8 | All Other Non-Current | 4.4 | 4.4 | 4.6 | 5.7 | 8.8 |
|  | 15.6 | 39.4 | 38.0 | 24.2 | Net Worth | 36.4 | 35.5 | 41.0 | 27.1 | 24.2 |
|  | 100.0 | 100.0 | 100.0 | 100.0 | Total Liabilities & Net Worth | 100.0 | 100.0 | 100.0 | 100.0 | 100.0 |
| | | | | | **INCOME DATA** | | | | | |
|  | 100.0 | 100.0 | 100.0 | 100.0 | Contract Revenues | 100.0 | 100.0 | 100.0 | 100.0 | 100.0 |
|  | 26.1 | 13.2 | 15.2 | 19.0 | Gross Profit | 25.7 | 21.2 | 26.9 | 19.9 | 19.0 |
|  | 25.2 | 12.3 | 10.2 | 16.6 | Operating Expenses | 19.4 | 18.5 | 22.7 | 16.8 | 16.6 |
|  | .9 | .9 | 4.9 | 2.4 | Operating Profit | 6.3 | 2.7 | 4.2 | 3.1 | 2.4 |
|  | .1 | -.2 | -.3 | -.1 | All Other Expenses (net) | .3 | .5 | .8 | .3 | -.1 |
|  | .9 | 1.1 | 5.2 | 2.5 | Profit Before Taxes | 6.0 | 2.2 | 3.4 | 2.8 | 2.5 |
| | | | | | **RATIOS** | | | | | |
|  | 2.7 | 2.0 | 1.9 | 2.0 | Current | 2.2 | 2.2 | 2.2 | 2.6 | 2.0 |
|  | 1.5 | 1.5 | 1.4 | 1.5 | | 1.5 | 1.5 | 1.6 | 1.5 | 1.5 |
|  | 1.2 | 1.2 | 1.2 | 1.2 | | 1.1 | 1.2 | 1.1 | 1.2 | 1.2 |
|  | 6.0 | 3.6 | 3.1 | 3.9 | Receivables/Payables | 4.1 | 3.9 | 5.3 | 4.0 | 3.9 |
|  | (25) 2.9 | 1.5 | 1.7 (81) | 1.8 | | 2.0 | (52) 2.2 | (65) 2.2 | (81) 1.6 | 1.8 |
|  | 1.5 | .9 | 1.2 | 1.1 | | 1.3 | 1.1 | 1.2 | 1.0 | 1.1 |
| 35 10.4 | 43 8.4 | 39 9.4 | 38 9.7 | | Revenues/Receivables | 31 11.9 | 37 9.8 | 29 12.5 | 39 9.4 | 38 9.7 |
| 63 5.8 | 59 6.2 | 69 5.3 | 63 5.8 | | | 55 6.7 | 54 6.6 | 55 6.6 | 63 6.6 | 63 5.8 |
| 99 3.7 | 76 4.8 | 89 4.1 | 89 4.1 | | | 91 4.0 | 90 4.1 | 86 4.3 | 87 4.2 | 89 4.1 |
| 12 30.0 | 21 17.0 | 29 12.6 | 22 16.4 | | Cost of Revenues/Payables | 18 20.1 | 19 19.4 | 7 54.4 | 20 18.5 | 22 16.4 |
| 27 13.3 | 40 9.1 | 41 8.8 | 38 9.6 | | | 31 11.7 | 31 11.6 | 29 12.6 | 38 9.5 | 38 9.6 |
| 65 5.6 | 68 5.4 | 68 5.4 | 68 5.4 | | | 60 6.0 | 53 6.8 | 52 7.0 | 63 5.8 | 68 5.4 |
|  | 5.4 | 5.3 | | 5.6 | Revenues/Working Capital | 5.9 | 5.7 | 4.7 | 4.5 | 5.6 |
|  | 9.3 | 9.2 | 10.0 | 9.3 | | 12.6 | 11.1 | 9.8 | 9.3 | 9.3 |
|  | 23.2 | 31.5 | 16.6 | 24.4 | | 38.6 | 35.6 | 90.4 | 28.4 | 24.4 |
|  | 21.8 | 17.4 | 58.0 | 21.8 | EBIT/Interest | 17.2 | 29.5 | 24.1 | 30.4 | 21.8 |
|  | (24) 1.8 | (20) 6.2 | (24) 8.9 | (70) 5.7 | | (56) 5.4 | (39) 7.0 | (52) 6.1 | (63) 5.6 | (70) 5.7 |
|  | -2.3 | 1.2 | 2.9 | 1.1 | | 2.6 | 1.1 | -.3 | .4 | 1.1 |
|  |  | 8.9 |  | 14.3 | Net Profit + Depr., Dep., Amort./Cur. Mat. L/T/D | 14.9 | 18.6 | 8.9 | 18.9 | 14.3 |
|  |  | (11) 4.9 |  | (20) 4.5 | | (25) 4.1 | (16) 3.4 | (13) 3.1 | (14) 4.2 | (20) 4.5 |
|  |  | 2.6 |  | 2.6 | | 1.6 | 1.0 | .3 | .4 | 2.6 |
|  | .2 | .1 | .3 | .2 | Fixed/Worth | .3 | .2 | .3 | .3 | .2 |
|  | .4 | .4 | .7 | .5 | | .8 | .6 | .5 | .5 | .5 |
|  | 1.0 | .8 | 1.3 | 1.0 | | 1.5 | 1.6 | 1.6 | 1.2 | 1.0 |
|  | .6 | .8 | 1.2 | .9 | Debt/Worth | .7 | .7 | .6 | .9 | .9 |
|  | 1.4 | 1.8 | 2.1 | 1.9 | | 1.9 | 1.7 | 1.3 | 1.7 | 1.9 |
|  | 2.9 | 3.0 | 4.0 | 3.3 | | 4.0 | 5.1 | 2.8 | 4.1 | 3.3 |
|  | 46.0 | 22.5 | 41.2 | 29.2 | % Profit Before Taxes/ Tangible Net Worth | 51.5 | 42.0 | 35.0 | 37.5 | 29.2 |
|  | (23) 1.6 | (26) 7.3 | (24) 21.5 | (75) 13.8 | | (53) 22.3 | (41) 17.1 | (51) 16.3 | (61) 18.2 | (75) 13.8 |
|  | -9.6 | -6.5 | 13.2 | -1.7 | | 6.8 | 2.5 | .1 | .6 | -1.7 |
|  | 24.5 | 9.0 | 9.5 | 11.2 | % Profit Before Taxes/ Total Assets | 17.1 | 16.1 | 16.8 | 12.7 | 11.2 |
|  | .5 | 2.9 | 6.4 | 4.0 | | 8.0 | 6.8 | 5.3 | 4.6 | 4.0 |
|  | -8.3 | -1.5 | 3.2 | -.5 | | 2.2 | -.4 | -.6 | -1.3 | -.5 |
|  | 1.9 | .4 | 1.2 | .8 | % Depr., Dep., Amort./ Revenues | .9 | .7 | 1.0 | 1.0 | .8 |
|  | (24) 3.4 | (26) 1.3 | (11) 2.7 | (62) 2.2 | | (55) 2.5 | (37) 2.0 | (48) 2.7 | (56) 2.4 | (62) 2.2 |
|  | 6.4 | 3.0 | 3.1 | 3.7 | | 4.8 | 4.7 | 4.9 | 3.8 | 3.7 |
|  | 3.0 | 1.4 |  | 1.9 | % Officers', Directors' Owners' Comp/Revenues | 1.3 | 1.5 | 1.7 | 1.8 | 1.9 |
|  | (15) 4.0 | (14) 2.1 |  | (32) 3.0 | | (30) 3.0 | (18) 2.6 | (21) 4.7 | (29) 2.8 | (32) 3.0 |
|  | 4.7 | 2.9 |  | 4.4 | | 4.6 | 6.6 | 6.2 | 4.8 | 4.4 |
| 1559M | 123631M | 581164M | 53278941M | 53985295M | Contract Revenues ($) | 1045430M | 6369802M | 1846474M | 12648638M | 53985295M |
| 914M | 88059M | 292621M | 36264738M | 36646332M | Total Assets ($) | 538704M | 5377672M | 1677847M | 8882264M | 36646332M |

M = $ thousand    MM = $ million
See Pages 9 through 22 for Explanation of Ratios and Data

## Current Data Sorted by Revenue | | | | | | Comparative Historical Data

| | | | | | Type of Statement | | | | | |
|---|---|---|---|---|---|---|---|---|---|---|
| | 1 | 1 | 1 | 3 | Unqualified | 8 | 7 | 3 | 2 | 3 |
| | 15 | 9 | 1 | 25 | Reviewed | 27 | 26 | 25 | 24 | 25 |
| 2 | 3 | 2 | | 7 | Compiled | 13 | 9 | 14 | 9 | 7 |
| 5 | 6 | 1 | | 12 | Tax Returns | 15 | 12 | 8 | 11 | 12 |
| 9 | 9 | 8 | 5 | 22 | Other | 21 | 9 | 31 | | 22 |
| 6 (4/1-9/30/11) | | 63 (10/1/11-3/31/12) | | | | 4/1/07- | 4/1/08- | 4/1/09- | 4/1/10- | 4/1/11- |
| | | | | | | 3/31/08 | 3/31/09 | 3/31/10 | 3/31/11 | 3/31/12 |
| 0-1MM | 1-10MM | 10-50MM | 50 & OVER | ALL | NUMBER OF STATEMENTS | ALL | ALL | ALL | ALL | ALL |
| 7 | 34 | 21 | 7 | 69 | | 84 | 63 | 65 | 77 | 69 |
| % | % | % | % | % | ASSETS | % | % | % | % | % |
| | 15.4 | 13.3 | | 14.6 | Cash & Equivalents | 13.9 | 13.3 | 12.7 | 9.7 | 14.6 |
| | 36.5 | 44.2 | | 38.4 | A/R - Progress Billings | 34.3 | 33.8 | 38.5 | 27.5 | 38.4 |
| | 2.3 | 4.3 | | 2.9 | A/R - Current Retention | 2.1 | 2.4 | 1.5 | 10.8 | 2.9 |
| | 3.9 | 3.4 | | 3.2 | Inventory | 3.1 | 3.0 | 2.6 | 3.1 | 3.2 |
| | 3.0 | 5.5 | | 3.7 | Cost & Est. Earnings In Excess Billings | 1.4 | 1.8 | 1.8 | 3.7 | 3.7 |
| | 4.7 | 4.2 | | 5.6 | All Other Current | 4.3 | 4.1 | 4.9 | 4.3 | 5.6 |
| | 65.9 | 74.8 | | 68.4 | Total Current | 59.0 | 58.3 | 62.0 | 59.0 | 68.4 |
| | 26.7 | 15.3 | | 23.0 | Fixed Assets (net) | 32.2 | 33.3 | 27.5 | 32.0 | 23.0 |
| | .3 | .0 | | .5 | Joint Ventures & Investments | .3 | .9 | .1 | .1 | .5 |
| | 1.6 | 5.9 | | 3.1 | Intangibles (net) | 2.3 | 2.6 | 2.5 | 1.5 | 3.1 |
| | 5.4 | 3.9 | | 5.0 | All Other Non-Current | 6.1 | 5.0 | 8.0 | 7.4 | 5.0 |
| | 100.0 | 100.0 | | 100.0 | Total | 100.0 | 100.0 | 100.0 | 100.0 | 100.0 |
| | | | | | LIABILITIES | | | | | |
| | 12.6 | 11.3 | | 15.4 | Notes Payable-Short Term | 11.8 | 11.6 | 12.0 | 14.9 | 15.4 |
| | 18.3 | 25.9 | | 21.2 | A/P - Trade | 17.5 | 14.5 | 16.3 | 16.2 | 21.2 |
| | .0 | 1.0 | | .6 | A/P - Retention | .3 | .0 | .1 | .2 | .6 |
| | 2.0 | 4.4 | | 3.1 | Billings in Excess of Costs & Est. Earnings | 2.4 | 2.7 | 3.1 | 3.3 | 3.1 |
| | .3 | .0 | | .2 | Income Taxes Payable | .5 | .3 | .5 | .0 | .2 |
| | 4.8 | 3.3 | | 3.6 | Cur. Mat.-L/T/D | 4.7 | 5.0 | 4.4 | 5.5 | 3.6 |
| | 8.4 | 9.3 | | 8.5 | All Other Current | 6.9 | 6.6 | 6.6 | 7.1 | 8.5 |
| | 46.3 | 55.3 | | 52.5 | Total Current | 44.2 | 40.7 | 42.8 | 47.3 | 52.5 |
| | 11.9 | 7.3 | | 12.1 | Long-Term Debt | 18.8 | 18.0 | 14.1 | 13.5 | 12.1 |
| | .8 | .3 | | .6 | Deferred Taxes | .8 | .7 | .7 | 1.3 | .6 |
| | 2.0 | 5.8 | | 4.6 | All Other Non-Current | 2.0 | 8.3 | 5.7 | 8.1 | 4.6 |
| | 39.0 | 31.2 | | 30.2 | Net Worth | 34.2 | 32.4 | 36.7 | 29.8 | 30.2 |
| | 100.0 | 100.0 | | 100.0 | Total Liabilities & Net Worth | 100.0 | 100.0 | 100.0 | 100.0 | 100.0 |
| | | | | | INCOME DATA | | | | | |
| | 100.0 | 100.0 | | 100.0 | Contract Revenues | 100.0 | 100.0 | 100.0 | 100.0 | 100.0 |
| | 22.3 | 13.2 | | 20.9 | Gross Profit | 29.5 | 24.2 | 25.0 | 23.2 | 20.9 |
| | 23.3 | 12.2 | | 20.1 | Operating Expenses | 25.1 | 21.6 | 24.6 | 23.7 | 20.1 |
| | -1.1 | 1.0 | | .7 | Operating Profit | 4.4 | 2.7 | .4 | -.5 | .7 |
| | .0 | .4 | | .5 | All Other Expenses (net) | 1.0 | .6 | .3 | 1.0 | .5 |
| | -1.0 | .6 | | .2 | Profit Before Taxes | 3.4 | 2.0 | .1 | -1.5 | .2 |
| | | | | | RATIOS | | | | | |
| | 3.3 | 1.7 | | 2.3 | | 2.4 | 2.4 | 2.9 | 2.4 | 2.3 |
| | 1.4 | 1.4 | | 1.4 | Current | 1.3 | 1.5 | 1.7 | 1.5 | 1.4 |
| | 1.0 | 1.2 | | 1.0 | | 1.0 | 1.0 | 1.0 | 1.0 | 1.0 |
| | 3.7 | 2.7 | | 2.9 | | 3.9 | 6.1 | 7.8 | 5.5 | 2.9 |
| (30) | 2.3 | 2.1 | (64) | 2.0 | Receivables/Payables | (79) 2.4 | (59) 3.3 | (64) 3.2 | (72) 2.6 | (64) 2.0 |
| | 1.3 | 1.2 | | 1.2 | | 1.7 | 1.7 | 1.8 | 1.6 | 1.2 |
| 34 10.7 | 48 7.6 | | 34 10.7 | | 21 17.4 | 29 12.7 | 31 11.7 | 31 11.9 | 34 10.7 | |
| 64 5.7 | 64 5.7 | | 64 5.7 | Revenues/Receivables | 49 7.5 | 52 7.0 | 60 6.1 | 54 6.8 | 64 5.7 | |
| 89 4.1 | 101 3.6 | | 99 3.7 | | 80 4.6 | 72 5.1 | 83 4.4 | 85 4.3 | 99 3.7 | |
| 5 68.3 | 21 17.8 | | 9 40.2 | | 12 31.2 | 6 62.9 | 10 35.0 | 10 37.0 | 9 40.2 | |
| 31 11.7 | 31 11.9 | | 33 11.1 | Cost of Revenues/Payables | 23 16.2 | 20 18.3 | 24 14.9 | 26 14.2 | 33 11.1 | |
| 55 6.6 | 56 6.6 | | 62 5.9 | | 51 7.2 | 42 8.6 | 48 7.6 | 49 7.5 | 62 5.9 | |
| | 6.6 | 6.5 | | 6.5 | | 8.3 | 6.8 | 5.9 | 6.6 | 6.5 |
| | 12.2 | 14.7 | | 13.9 | Revenues/Working Capital | 18.9 | 14.3 | 10.6 | 12.5 | 13.9 |
| | -194.5 | 30.1 | | UND | | NM | 125.2 | 237.7 | -188.4 | UND |
| | 13.2 | 17.0 | | 15.5 | | 10.9 | 15.9 | 13.2 | 6.6 | 15.5 |
| (32) | 1.8 | (20) 3.1 | (65) | 2.6 | EBIT/Interest | (82) 4.7 | (60) 2.5 | (57) 2.3 | (72) 1.8 | (65) 2.6 |
| | -12.2 | -1.7 | | -2.5 | | .7 | .6 | -5.6 | -4.7 | -2.5 |
| | | | | | Net Profit + Depr., Dep., Amort./Cur. Mat. L/T/D | 10.7 | 7.1 | 4.6 | 7.4 | |
| | | | | | | (23) 2.8 | (11) 4.3 | (16) 2.7 | (14) 3.4 | |
| | | | | | | 1.0 | 2.0 | .6 | 1.2 | |
| | .3 | .2 | | .2 | | .3 | .4 | .3 | .4 | .2 |
| | .6 | .4 | | .5 | Fixed/Worth | .8 | .8 | .6 | 1.0 | .5 |
| | 4.5 | 2.4 | | 2.1 | | 2.1 | 3.9 | 1.3 | 2.2 | 2.1 |
| | .6 | .9 | | .7 | | .8 | .9 | .6 | .6 | .7 |
| | 1.4 | 2.6 | | 1.6 | Debt/Worth | 2.2 | 2.4 | 1.3 | 1.8 | 1.6 |
| | 7.3 | 8.4 | | 6.2 | | 5.2 | 7.6 | 3.3 | 4.4 | 6.2 |
| | 27.1 | 32.1 | | 29.3 | | 69.3 | 54.3 | 37.1 | 28.3 | 29.3 |
| (28) | 7.6 | (17) 3.6 | (57) | 7.1 | % Profit Before Taxes/ Tangible Net Worth | (75) 23.1 | (53) 13.4 | (57) 12.4 | (64) 3.6 | (57) 7.1 |
| | -5.9 | -6.0 | | -3.8 | | 5.0 | 2.3 | -17.6 | -9.4 | -3.8 |
| | 14.3 | 9.5 | | 12.5 | | 19.5 | 15.7 | 16.8 | 7.8 | 12.5 |
| | 2.6 | 2.3 | | 2.2 | % Profit Before Taxes/ Total Assets | 6.8 | 3.9 | 4.0 | 2.0 | 2.2 |
| | -3.9 | -2.9 | | -3.0 | | -.1 | -1.5 | -8.5 | -6.9 | -3.0 |
| | 1.8 | .5 | | .8 | | .9 | 1.5 | 1.4 | 1.8 | .8 |
| (29) | 3.0 | (19) .8 | (58) | 2.3 | % Depr., Dep., Amort./ Revenues | (71) 2.4 | (53) 2.6 | (60) 2.8 | (66) 2.5 | (58) 2.3 |
| | 4.3 | 2.7 | | 4.3 | | 4.9 | 4.7 | 4.9 | 4.3 | 4.3 |
| | 1.9 | | | 1.9 | | 1.8 | 1.9 | 1.9 | 1.9 | 1.9 |
| (21) | 3.5 | | (36) | 3.6 | % Officers', Directors' Owners' Comp/Revenues | (48) 3.7 | (35) 4.1 | (38) 4.2 | (39) 3.2 | (36) 3.6 |
| | 6.8 | | | 8.6 | | 8.1 | 9.2 | 8.4 | 7.7 | 8.6 |
| 4594M | 161780M | 451216M | 26282236M | 26899826M | Contract Revenues ($) | 12336218M | 5251846M | 24751762M | 32191425M | 26899826M |
| 1840M | 68323M | 216636M | 9308997M | 9595796M | Total Assets ($) | 7968552M | 2859822M | 22364101M | 12864213M | 9595796M |

M = $ thousand    MM = $ million
See Pages 9 through 22 for Explanation of Ratios and Data

## Current Data Sorted by Revenue        Comparative Historical Data

| | | | | | | Type of Statement | | | | | |
|---|---|---|---|---|---|---|---|---|---|---|---|
| | 1 | | 2 | 3 | | Unqualified | 6 | 6 | 6 | 3 | 3 |
| | 6 | 9 | | 15 | | Reviewed | 16 | 15 | 15 | 23 | 15 |
| 1 | 2 | 2 | | 5 | | Compiled | 6 | 6 | 4 | 5 | 5 |
| 1 | 1 | 1 | | 2 | | Tax Returns | 6 | 2 | 3 | 1 | 2 |
| | 5 | 6 | 5 | 16 | | Other | 5 | 9 | 8 | 18 | 16 |
| | 8 (4/1-9/30/11) | | 33 (10/1/11-3/31/12) | | | | 4/1/07-3/31/08 | 4/1/08-3/31/09 | 4/1/09-3/31/10 | 4/1/10-3/31/11 | 4/1/11-3/31/12 |
| 0-1MM | 1-10MM | 10-50MM | 50 & OVER | ALL | | | ALL | ALL | ALL | ALL | ALL |
| 2 | 15 | 17 | 7 | 41 | | NUMBER OF STATEMENTS | 39 | 38 | 36 | 50 | 41 |
| % | % | % | % | % | | ASSETS | % | % | % | % | % |
| | 10.0 | 6.7 | | 9.8 | | Cash & Equivalents | 14.2 | 16.5 | 25.3 | 16.7 | 9.8 |
| | 40.0 | 40.4 | | 37.2 | | A/R - Progress Billings | 49.1 | 43.5 | 35.8 | 25.2 | 37.2 |
| | 4.2 | 7.8 | | 7.0 | | A/R - Current Retention | 1.8 | 3.6 | 2.7 | 19.6 | 7.0 |
| | 1.8 | 4.1 | | 3.4 | | Inventory | 3.6 | 2.8 | 1.7 | 2.9 | 3.4 |
| | 6.5 | 4.1 | | 5.2 | | Cost & Est. Earnings In Excess of Billings | 2.6 | 3.9 | 2.4 | 3.5 | 5.2 |
| | 7.4 | 8.8 | | 9.0 | | All Other Current | 3.1 | 5.1 | 4.6 | 3.4 | 9.0 |
| | 70.1 | 71.8 | | 71.6 | | Total Current | 74.4 | 75.5 | 72.5 | 71.4 | 71.6 |
| | 24.8 | 15.2 | | 18.2 | | Fixed Assets (net) | 21.0 | 19.9 | 19.4 | 18.2 | 18.2 |
| | .0 | .1 | | .1 | | Joint Ventures & Investments | .0 | .1 | .3 | .2 | .1 |
| | .6 | 2.9 | | 1.5 | | Intangibles (net) | .4 | .2 | .1 | 1.3 | 1.5 |
| | 4.6 | 10.0 | | 8.7 | | All Other Non-Current | 4.2 | 4.4 | 7.7 | 9.0 | 8.7 |
| | 100.0 | 100.0 | | 100.0 | | Total | 100.0 | 100.0 | 100.0 | 100.0 | 100.0 |
| | | | | | | LIABILITIES | | | | | |
| | 13.4 | 9.8 | | 13.1 | | Notes Payable-Short Term | 16.6 | 5.7 | 10.3 | 11.2 | 13.1 |
| | 15.8 | 20.8 | | 17.5 | | A/P - Trade | 22.0 | 15.0 | 11.4 | 14.9 | 17.5 |
| | .2 | .7 | | .8 | | A/P - Retention | .0 | 1.3 | 1.0 | .3 | .8 |
| | 4.0 | 4.5 | | 5.8 | | Billings in Excess of Costs & Est. Earnings | 5.9 | 6.4 | 4.1 | 6.9 | 5.8 |
| | .0 | .0 | | .0 | | Income Taxes Payable | .3 | .6 | .0 | .2 | .0 |
| | 6.8 | 2.8 | | 3.8 | | Cur. Mat.-L/T/D | 2.0 | 2.4 | 3.0 | 2.1 | 3.8 |
| | 5.3 | 5.6 | | 7.4 | | All Other Current | 7.2 | 8.8 | 5.9 | 6.3 | 7.4 |
| | 45.5 | 44.2 | | 48.4 | | Total Current | 53.9 | 40.1 | 35.8 | 41.9 | 48.4 |
| | 29.9 | 7.2 | | 16.7 | | Long-Term Debt | 9.9 | 10.3 | 11.5 | 11.9 | 16.7 |
| | .0 | .5 | | .3 | | Deferred Taxes | .6 | .7 | 1.1 | .4 | .3 |
| | 3.9 | 10.6 | | 5.9 | | All Other Non-Current | 3.9 | 1.5 | 3.8 | 11.1 | 5.9 |
| | 20.7 | 37.5 | | 28.6 | | Net Worth | 31.7 | 47.4 | 47.7 | 34.7 | 28.6 |
| | 100.0 | 100.0 | | 100.0 | | Total Liabilities & Net Worth | 100.0 | 100.0 | 100.0 | 100.0 | 100.0 |
| | | | | | | INCOME DATA | | | | | |
| | 100.0 | 100.0 | | 100.0 | | Contract Revenues | 100.0 | 100.0 | 100.0 | 100.0 | 100.0 |
| | 21.1 | 12.0 | | 15.7 | | Gross Profit | 23.5 | 24.0 | 26.2 | 17.8 | 15.7 |
| | 24.6 | 11.6 | | 16.5 | | Operating Expenses | 21.1 | 17.5 | 22.9 | 18.9 | 16.5 |
| | -3.4 | .5 | | -.9 | | Operating Profit | 2.4 | 6.4 | 3.2 | -1.1 | -.9 |
| | .2 | -.2 | | .2 | | All Other Expenses (net) | -.1 | .1 | .1 | .1 | .2 |
| | -3.7 | .7 | | -1.0 | | Profit Before Taxes | 2.4 | 6.3 | 3.1 | -1.3 | -1.0 |
| | | | | | | RATIOS | | | | | |
| | 2.2 | 2.6 | | 2.0 | | | 2.3 | 2.9 | 4.1 | 2.5 | 2.0 |
| | 1.6 | 1.5 | | 1.5 | | Current | 1.8 | 1.9 | 2.3 | 1.6 | 1.5 |
| | 1.1 | 1.2 | | 1.1 | | | 1.0 | 1.3 | 1.4 | 1.3 | 1.1 |
| | 25.3 | 3.8 | | 4.1 | | | 5.7 | 5.3 | 6.6 | 5.7 | 4.1 |
| | 2.3 | 2.9 | (40) 2.8 | | | Receivables/Payables | (36) 2.3 | (35) 3.0 | (34) 4.1 | (48) 3.4 | (40) 2.8 |
| | 1.6 | 1.7 | | 1.6 | | | 1.5 | 2.2 | 1.7 | 2.5 | 1.6 |
| 48 | 7.6 | 51 7.1 | 47 | 7.7 | | | 41 8.9 | 47 7.7 | 32 11.6 | 58 6.2 | 47 7.7 |
| 70 | 5.2 | 81 4.5 | 74 | 4.9 | | Revenues/Receivables | 66 5.5 | 56 6.5 | 57 6.4 | 85 4.3 | 74 4.9 |
| 81 | 4.5 | 101 3.6 | 101 | 3.6 | | | 85 4.3 | 75 4.9 | 73 5.0 | 108 3.4 | 101 3.6 |
| 4 | 101.8 | 21 17.3 | 15 | 24.1 | | | 8 47.5 | 9 39.2 | 10 38.1 | 17 21.5 | 15 24.1 |
| 40 | 9.2 | 32 11.5 | 30 | 12.2 | | Cost of Revenues/Payables | 26 14.1 | 21 17.2 | 21 17.5 | 28 12.8 | 30 12.2 |
| 58 | 6.3 | 54 6.8 | 58 | 6.3 | | | 58 6.3 | 36 10.0 | 26 14.1 | 46 8.0 | 58 6.3 |
| | 6.6 | 5.3 | | 5.2 | | | 6.4 | 4.9 | 3.8 | 4.3 | 5.2 |
| | 8.4 | 8.0 | | 8.0 | | Revenues/Working Capital | 10.8 | 7.6 | 5.8 | 7.2 | 8.0 |
| | 52.3 | 23.3 | | 34.0 | | | 152.1 | 22.2 | 13.6 | 15.7 | 34.0 |
| | 1.4 | 16.0 | | 6.5 | | | 21.1 | 63.2 | 35.4 | 8.7 | 6.5 |
| (13) | -4.0 | 6.4 | (39) 1.0 | | | EBIT/Interest | (34) 5.6 | (35) 10.8 | (28) 4.4 | (42) 2.5 | (39) 1.0 |
| | -30.3 | -1.2 | | -13.2 | | | 1.3 | 6.0 | 1.1 | -5.0 | -13.2 |
| | | | | | | Net Profit + Depr., Dep., Amort./Cur. Mat. L/T/D | | 53.2 | | 3.3 | |
| | | | | | | | | (10) 14.5 | | (12) 3.1 | |
| | | | | | | | | 2.5 | | -.1 | |
| | .3 | .2 | | .2 | | | .1 | .1 | .1 | .1 | .2 |
| | .8 | .3 | | .4 | | Fixed/Worth | .5 | .4 | .5 | .4 | .4 |
| | 2.0 | .8 | | .9 | | | 2.2 | .6 | .7 | 1.0 | .9 |
| | .7 | .8 | | .9 | | | .8 | .4 | .4 | .7 | .9 |
| | 1.6 | 1.4 | | 1.4 | | Debt/Worth | 1.5 | 1.2 | .7 | 1.3 | 1.4 |
| | 9.3 | 4.1 | | 3.6 | | | 6.0 | 2.3 | 1.8 | 2.2 | 3.6 |
| | 10.9 | 21.2 | | 18.7 | | | 50.8 | 62.6 | 42.2 | 21.8 | 18.7 |
| (13) | -1.5 | (16) 13.5 | (37) 4.6 | | | % Profit Before Taxes/ Tangible Net Worth | (33) 26.7 | (36) 33.0 | (34) 12.4 | (45) 5.5 | (37) 4.6 |
| | -37.3 | -1.8 | | -20.8 | | | 11.2 | 11.4 | .8 | -11.1 | -20.8 |
| | 5.5 | 9.6 | | 8.1 | | | 21.2 | 28.9 | 28.2 | 8.5 | 8.1 |
| | -.5 | 5.2 | | .6 | | % Profit Before Taxes/ Total Assets | 8.0 | 14.5 | 5.0 | 1.9 | .6 |
| | -25.5 | -5.5 | | -9.9 | | | 1.1 | 6.4 | .1 | -8.7 | -9.9 |
| | 1.4 | 1.0 | | .9 | | | .5 | .3 | .5 | 1.1 | .9 |
| (13) | 2.4 | (15) 1.1 | (35) 1.6 | | | % Depr., Dep., Amort./ Revenues | (33) 1.0 | (32) .9 | (28) 1.6 | (42) 1.6 | (35) 1.6 |
| | 4.0 | 1.8 | | 2.4 | | | 2.3 | 2.1 | 2.7 | 3.2 | 2.4 |
| | | | | 1.2 | | | 1.5 | .8 | 1.0 | 2.6 | 1.2 |
| | | | (18) 1.8 | | | % Officers', Directors' Owners' Comp/Revenues | (23) 5.7 | (17) 3.9 | (19) 4.2 | (18) 5.7 | (18) 1.8 |
| | | | | 4.0 | | | 9.5 | 7.2 | 13.5 | 8.8 | 4.0 |
| 1427M | 84225M | 331188M | 1204976M | 1621816M | | Contract Revenues ($) | 7791812M | 761765M | 35222235M | 8630796M | 1621816M |
| 225M | 36825M | 163936M | 901347M | 1102333M | | Total Assets ($) | 4430386M | 295147M | 21872885M | 6164336M | 1102333M |

M = $ thousand     MM = $ million
See Pages 9 through 22 for Explanation of Ratios and Data

**Current Data Sorted by Revenue**  |  **Comparative Historical Data**

Type of Statement

| 0-1MM | 1-10MM | 10-50MM | 50 & OVER | ALL | Type of Statement | 4/1/07-3/31/08 ALL | 4/1/08-3/31/09 ALL | 4/1/09-3/31/10 ALL | 4/1/10-3/31/11 ALL | 4/1/11-3/31/12 ALL |
|---|---|---|---|---|---|---|---|---|---|---|
|  |  | 2 |  | 2 | Unqualified | 2 | 3 |  | 2 | 2 |
| 2 | 15 | 9 |  | 26 | Reviewed | 20 | 15 | 14 | 30 | 26 |
|  | 4 |  |  | 4 | Compiled | 7 | 6 | 7 | 2 | 4 |
| 1 | 6 | 1 |  | 8 | Tax Returns | 12 | 10 | 7 | 4 | 8 |
|  | 4 | 1 |  | 5 | Other | 7 | 3 | 4 | 10 | 5 |

_Current Data groupings: 8 (4/1-9/30/11) and 37 (10/1/11-3/31/12). 50 & OVER column: DATA NOT AVAILABLE._

| 0-1MM | 1-10MM | 10-50MM | 50 & OVER | ALL | | '08 ALL | '09 ALL | '10 ALL | '11 ALL | '12 ALL |
|---|---|---|---|---|---|---|---|---|---|---|
| 3 | 29 | 13 |  | 45 | **NUMBER OF STATEMENTS** | 48 | 37 | 32 | 48 | 45 |
| % | % | % | % | % | **ASSETS** | % | % | % | % | % |
|  | 14.1 | 16.2 |  | 16.0 | Cash & Equivalents | 12.9 | 12.9 | 15.0 | 16.0 | 16.0 |
|  | 41.5 | 39.6 |  | 40.4 | A/R - Progress Billings | 42.1 | 36.0 | 40.3 | 19.8 | 40.4 |
|  | 5.6 | 10.3 |  | 6.7 | A/R - Current Retention | 1.7 | 5.6 | 1.9 | 26.6 | 6.7 |
|  | 3.3 | 1.9 |  | 2.6 | Inventory | 4.9 | 2.5 | 1.2 | 1.6 | 2.6 |
|  | 4.0 | 7.3 |  | 4.7 | Cost & Est. Earnings In Excess Billings | 2.7 | 2.4 | 1.4 | 3.5 | 4.7 |
|  | 5.2 | 5.6 |  | 5.5 | All Other Current | 4.4 | 8.5 | 3.7 | 5.6 | 5.5 |
|  | 73.8 | 80.7 |  | 75.9 | Total Current | 68.7 | 67.8 | 63.5 | 73.1 | 75.9 |
|  | 20.5 | 12.5 |  | 17.8 | Fixed Assets (net) | 22.1 | 24.7 | 25.6 | 16.1 | 17.8 |
|  | .4 | .2 |  | .3 | Joint Ventures & Investments | 1.3 | .5 | 2.3 | 2.6 | .3 |
|  | 1.3 | .0 |  | .9 | Intangibles (net) | .7 | 1.2 | 1.7 | .4 | .9 |
|  | 4.0 | 6.6 |  | 5.1 | All Other Non-Current | 7.2 | 5.8 | 6.9 | 7.8 | 5.1 |
|  | 100.0 | 100.0 |  | 100.0 | Total | 100.0 | 100.0 | 100.0 | 100.0 | 100.0 |
|  |  |  |  |  | **LIABILITIES** |  |  |  |  |  |
|  | 10.9 | 15.4 |  | 13.2 | Notes Payable-Short Term | 10.5 | 12.8 | 23.9 | 17.6 | 13.2 |
|  | 16.3 | 15.7 |  | 15.6 | A/P - Trade | 20.7 | 15.1 | 12.3 | 13.0 | 15.6 |
|  | .1 | .9 |  | .3 | A/P - Retention | .1 | .0 | .0 | .3 | .3 |
|  | 5.7 | 8.6 |  | 6.2 | Billings in Excess of Costs & Est. Earnings | 5.7 | 6.3 | 2.5 | 5.6 | 6.2 |
|  | 1.2 | .0 |  | .8 | Income Taxes Payable | .3 | .2 | .1 | .3 | .8 |
|  | 3.9 | 1.8 |  | 3.3 | Cur. Mat.-L/T/D | 3.1 | 2.7 | 2.8 | 2.3 | 3.3 |
|  | 6.7 | 6.6 |  | 7.2 | All Other Current | 8.1 | 9.0 | 6.9 | 6.0 | 7.2 |
|  | 44.9 | 49.1 |  | 46.5 | Total Current | 48.4 | 46.2 | 48.5 | 45.2 | 46.5 |
|  | 12.0 | 4.2 |  | 9.5 | Long-Term Debt | 15.3 | 16.0 | 14.3 | 5.5 | 9.5 |
|  | .3 | .2 |  | .3 | Deferred Taxes | .7 | .5 | .3 | .4 | .3 |
|  | .7 | .5 |  | .6 | All Other Non-Current | 5.0 | 7.2 | 9.8 | 3.6 | .6 |
|  | 42.1 | 46.0 |  | 43.1 | Net Worth | 30.6 | 30.2 | 27.1 | 45.4 | 43.1 |
|  | 100.0 | 100.0 |  | 100.0 | Total Liabilities & Net Worth | 100.0 | 100.0 | 100.0 | 100.0 | 100.0 |
|  |  |  |  |  | **INCOME DATA** |  |  |  |  |  |
|  | 100.0 | 100.0 |  | 100.0 | Contract Revenues | 100.0 | 100.0 | 100.0 | 100.0 | 100.0 |
|  | 22.1 | 15.7 |  | 20.2 | Gross Profit | 26.8 | 24.2 | 25.2 | 19.0 | 20.2 |
|  | 22.5 | 14.4 |  | 21.1 | Operating Expenses | 24.8 | 20.7 | 24.4 | 22.9 | 21.1 |
|  | -.4 | 1.3 |  | -.9 | Operating Profit | 2.0 | 3.6 | .8 | -3.9 | -.9 |
|  | .1 | .3 |  | .2 | All Other Expenses (net) | .1 | .4 | -.1 | .6 | .2 |
|  | -.5 | 1.0 |  | -1.1 | Profit Before Taxes | 1.9 | 3.1 | .8 | -4.5 | -1.1 |
|  |  |  |  |  | **RATIOS** |  |  |  |  |  |
|  | 3.3 | 2.9 |  | 3.2 | Current | 1.9 | 2.2 | 3.7 | 3.5 | 3.2 |
|  | 1.9 | 2.4 |  | 1.9 |  | 1.6 | 1.5 | 1.8 | 1.9 | 1.9 |
|  | 1.1 | 1.1 |  | 1.1 |  | 1.2 | 1.1 | 1.0 | 1.0 | 1.1 |
|  | 10.6 | 6.0 |  | 10.6 | Receivables/Payables | 4.5 | 6.0 | 7.7 | 12.4 | 10.6 |
|  | 5.1 | 2.7 |  | 4.5 |  | (46) 2.8 | (32) 3.6 | (28) 5.5 | 3.9 | 4.5 |
|  | 1.6 | 1.9 |  | 1.9 |  | 1.7 | 2.2 | 3.2 | 2.2 | 1.9 |
|  | (38) 9.7 | (58) 6.3 |  | (41) 8.8 | Revenues/Receivables | (36) 10.2 | (13) 29.0 | (33) 11.2 | (55) 6.6 | (41) 8.8 |
|  | (62) 5.9 | (79) 4.6 |  | (69) 5.3 |  | (57) 6.4 | (48) 7.6 | (57) 6.5 | (80) 4.6 | (69) 5.3 |
|  | (96) 3.8 | (101) 3.6 |  | (99) 3.7 |  | (83) 4.4 | (84) 4.3 | (85) 4.3 | (104) 3.5 | (99) 3.7 |
|  | (7) 51.3 | (16) 23.1 |  | (7) 51.3 | Cost of Revenues/Payables | (10) 38.1 | (4) 87.6 | (4) 88.0 | (6) 56.5 | (7) 51.3 |
|  | (14) 25.4 | (26) 14.1 |  | (21) 17.4 |  | (26) 14.2 | (21) 17.3 | (15) 25.2 | (26) 13.9 | (21) 17.4 |
|  | (39) 9.4 | (52) 7.0 |  | (44) 8.3 |  | (53) 6.9 | (33) 11.0 | (33) 11.1 | (40) 9.0 | (44) 8.3 |
|  | 4.8 | 4.3 |  | 4.5 | Revenues/Working Capital | 6.7 | 7.3 | 4.9 | 4.0 | 4.5 |
|  | 6.8 | 6.0 |  | 6.4 |  | 12.2 | 14.6 | 9.1 | 7.5 | 6.4 |
|  | NM | 36.0 |  | 36.0 |  | 53.4 | 100.8 | -185.6 | 81.7 | 36.0 |
|  | 15.9 | 7.5 |  | 8.9 | EBIT/Interest | 17.7 | 12.0 | 17.2 | 6.0 | 8.9 |
|  | (23) 2.2 | (12) 2.4 |  | (35) 2.2 |  | (44) 3.4 | (32) 2.9 | (28) 6.6 | (37) 2.2 | (35) 2.2 |
|  | -14.7 | -1.3 |  | -8.0 |  | .6 | -.6 | -8.5 | -10.6 | -8.0 |
|  |  |  |  |  | Net Profit + Depr., Dep., Amort./Cur. Mat. L/T/D |  |  |  |  |  |
|  | .1 | .2 |  | .1 | Fixed/Worth | .2 | .2 | .2 | .1 | .1 |
|  | .3 | .3 |  | .3 |  | .4 | .5 | .4 | .4 | .3 |
|  | .7 | .6 |  | .7 |  | 1.3 | 1.6 | 2.3 | .7 | .7 |
|  | .4 | .5 |  | .4 | Debt/Worth | .9 | .7 | .3 | .4 | .4 |
|  | 1.0 | .6 |  | 1.0 |  | 1.8 | 1.5 | .9 | 1.1 | 1.0 |
|  | 2.0 | 5.8 |  | 2.9 |  | 10.3 | 5.4 | 3.7 | 4.1 | 2.9 |
|  | 26.8 | 21.8 |  | 22.9 | % Profit Before Taxes/Tangible Net Worth | 45.9 | 80.1 | 54.8 | 22.6 | 22.9 |
|  | (24) 4.0 | (12) 3.9 |  | (38) 3.2 |  | (42) 18.4 | (33) 30.6 | (25) 9.3 | (45) .4 | (38) 3.2 |
|  | -21.0 | -9.4 |  | -13.2 |  | 5.1 | -6.0 | -19.8 | -37.8 | -13.2 |
|  | 12.6 | 5.8 |  | 11.3 | % Profit Before Taxes/Total Assets | 15.1 | 35.5 | 25.1 | 6.6 | 11.3 |
|  | .6 | .6 |  | 1.2 |  | 4.2 | 5.9 | 3.0 | -.1 | 1.2 |
|  | -13.4 | -4.3 |  | -9.5 |  | .3 | -2.7 | -15.2 | -22.2 | -9.5 |
|  | .6 | .8 |  | .8 | % Depr., Dep., Amort./Revenues | .8 | 1.0 | 1.0 | 1.3 | .8 |
|  | (23) 1.7 | 1.0 |  | (37) 1.4 |  | (38) 1.7 | (31) 1.3 | (27) 1.6 | (43) 2.1 | (37) 1.4 |
|  | 2.3 | 1.5 |  | 2.2 |  | 2.7 | 2.2 | 3.4 | 3.3 | 2.2 |
|  | 2.9 |  |  | 2.3 | % Officers', Directors' Owners' Comp/Revenues | 2.8 | 1.9 | 2.7 | 2.7 | 2.3 |
|  | (14) 4.6 |  |  | (25) 3.8 |  | (30) 4.6 | (23) 3.3 | (20) 3.1 | (22) 4.7 | (25) 3.8 |
|  | 6.9 |  |  | 6.4 |  | 6.2 | 6.2 | 6.2 | 6.2 | 6.4 |
| 993M | 119298M | 245950M |  | 366241M | Contract Revenues ($) | 11599329M | 252020M | 4596064M | 328675M | 366241M |
| 726M | 50046M | 113133M |  | 163905M | Total Assets ($) | 3908385M | 85772M | 1651203M | 164541M | 163905M |

M = $ thousand    MM = $ million
See Pages 9 through 22 for Explanation of Ratios and Data

## Current Data Sorted by Revenue      Comparative Historical Data

| | 0-1MM | 1-10MM | 10-50MM | 50 & OVER | ALL | Type of Statement | 4/1/07-3/31/08 ALL | 4/1/08-3/31/09 ALL | 4/1/09-3/31/10 ALL | 4/1/10-3/31/11 ALL | 4/1/11-3/31/12 ALL |
|---|---|---|---|---|---|---|---|---|---|---|---|
| | | | 1 | 1 | 2 | Unqualified | 2 | 1 | 1 | 1 | 2 |
| | | 13 | 5 | | 18 | Reviewed | 12 | 13 | 12 | 15 | 18 |
| | | | 1 | | 1 | Compiled | 7 | 7 | 3 | | 1 |
| | 2 | 1 | | | 3 | Tax Returns | 2 | 4 | 2 | 2 | 3 |
| | 2 | 3 | | | 5 | Other | 3 | 3 | 2 | 5 | 5 |
| | | | 13 (4/1-9/30/11) | 16 (10/1/11-3/31/12) | | | | | | | |
| | 4 | 17 | 6 | 2 | 29 | **NUMBER OF STATEMENTS** | 26 | 28 | 20 | 23 | 29 |
| | % | % | % | % | % | **ASSETS** | % | % | % | % | % |
| | | 20.1 | | | 23.4 | Cash & Equivalents | 9.8 | 20.5 | 25.7 | 19.7 | 23.4 |
| | | 38.5 | | | 37.4 | A/R - Progress Billings | 56.8 | 49.6 | 42.8 | 26.6 | 37.4 |
| | | 3.7 | | | 2.8 | A/R - Current Retention | 1.8 | 1.1 | 3.1 | 19.4 | 2.8 |
| | | 2.8 | | | 4.3 | Inventory | 7.9 | 7.7 | 3.2 | 6.6 | 4.3 |
| | | 5.9 | | | 5.1 | Cost & Est. Earnings In Excess Billings | 2.8 | 2.4 | 4.3 | 4.0 | 5.1 |
| | | 10.5 | | | 6.3 | All Other Current | 3.4 | 2.9 | 7.9 | 3.8 | 6.3 |
| | | 81.5 | | | 79.4 | Total Current | 82.5 | 84.2 | 87.0 | 80.0 | 79.4 |
| | | 12.4 | | | 13.0 | Fixed Assets (net) | 13.4 | 11.9 | 6.9 | 12.9 | 13.0 |
| | | .0 | | | .0 | Joint Ventures & Investments | .1 | .9 | 1.2 | 1.4 | .0 |
| | | .4 | | | .6 | Intangibles (net) | 1.0 | .1 | .2 | .8 | .6 |
| | | 5.7 | | | 7.0 | All Other Non-Current | 3.0 | 2.9 | 4.7 | 4.8 | 7.0 |
| | | 100.0 | | | 100.0 | Total | 100.0 | 100.0 | 100.0 | 100.0 | 100.0 |
| | | | | | | **LIABILITIES** | | | | | |
| | | 13.2 | | | 9.3 | Notes Payable-Short Term | 15.5 | 18.0 | 7.6 | 5.2 | 9.3 |
| | | 14.0 | | | 12.9 | A/P - Trade | 25.0 | 23.1 | 13.3 | 14.8 | 12.9 |
| | | .0 | | | .1 | A/P - Retention | .0 | .7 | .1 | .2 | .1 |
| | | 3.9 | | | 4.6 | Billings in Excess of Costs & Est. Earnings | 8.9 | 4.9 | 7.5 | 5.6 | 4.6 |
| | | 1.3 | | | .7 | Income Taxes Payable | .4 | .4 | .7 | 1.6 | .7 |
| | | 1.1 | | | 1.0 | Cur. Mat.-L/T/D | 3.5 | 2.5 | 1.1 | 3.5 | 1.0 |
| | | 4.8 | | | 6.4 | All Other Current | 7.3 | 6.2 | 7.5 | 7.7 | 6.4 |
| | | 38.2 | | | 34.9 | Total Current | 60.6 | 55.8 | 37.9 | 38.5 | 34.9 |
| | | 5.0 | | | 5.8 | Long-Term Debt | 8.6 | 6.5 | 3.1 | 6.2 | 5.8 |
| | | 1.8 | | | 1.1 | Deferred Taxes | .3 | .3 | .2 | .3 | 1.1 |
| | | .2 | | | 1.0 | All Other Non-Current | 5.0 | 5.2 | 5.2 | 2.4 | 1.0 |
| | | 54.8 | | | 57.2 | Net Worth | 25.5 | 32.2 | 53.6 | 52.5 | 57.2 |
| | | 100.0 | | | 100.0 | Total Liabilities & Net Worth | 100.0 | 100.0 | 100.0 | 100.0 | 100.0 |
| | | | | | | **INCOME DATA** | | | | | |
| | | 100.0 | | | 100.0 | Contract Revenues | 100.0 | 100.0 | 100.0 | 100.0 | 100.0 |
| | | 29.3 | | | 32.9 | Gross Profit | 27.0 | 33.7 | 30.0 | 28.9 | 32.9 |
| | | 29.9 | | | 31.1 | Operating Expenses | 24.0 | 29.7 | 22.7 | 25.6 | 31.1 |
| | | -.6 | | | 1.8 | Operating Profit | 3.0 | 3.9 | 7.3 | 3.3 | 1.8 |
| | | .1 | | | .1 | All Other Expenses (net) | .8 | .1 | .1 | .6 | .1 |
| | | -.7 | | | 1.7 | Profit Before Taxes | 2.2 | 3.8 | 7.3 | 2.7 | 1.7 |
| | | | | | | **RATIOS** | | | | | |
| | | 5.3 | | | 4.2 | Current | 1.9 | 2.8 | 3.9 | 4.2 | 4.2 |
| | | 2.8 | | | 3.1 | | 1.5 | 1.8 | 2.2 | 2.3 | 3.1 |
| | | 1.4 | | | 1.6 | | 1.1 | 1.2 | 1.7 | 1.2 | 1.6 |
| | | 8.3 | | | 6.6 | Receivables/Payables | 4.3 | 4.4 | 4.3 | 4.6 | 6.6 |
| | | 3.3 | | (28) | 3.4 | | 2.5 | 2.1 | 3.5 | 3.4 | (28) 3.4 |
| | | 1.6 | | | 1.9 | | 1.8 | 1.4 | 2.0 | 2.1 | 1.9 |
| | 49 | 7.5 | 41 | | 8.8 | Revenues/Receivables | 53 6.9 | 38 9.6 | 31 11.7 | 62 5.9 | 41 8.8 |
| | 69 | 5.3 | 72 | | 5.1 | | 74 4.9 | 59 6.1 | 56 6.5 | 78 4.7 | 72 5.1 |
| | 101 | 3.6 | 104 | | 3.5 | | 101 3.6 | 90 4.1 | 74 4.9 | 89 4.1 | 104 3.5 |
| | 12 | 30.5 | 13 | | 28.9 | Cost of Revenues/Payables | 26 13.8 | 20 18.1 | 17 21.4 | 16 22.2 | 13 28.9 |
| | 24 | 15.3 | 26 | | 14.2 | | 41 8.9 | 39 9.4 | 24 15.3 | 28 13.1 | 26 14.2 |
| | 49 | 7.5 | 49 | | 7.5 | | 64 5.7 | 58 6.3 | 28 13.2 | 40 9.1 | 49 7.5 |
| | | 3.3 | | | 2.9 | Revenues/Working Capital | 7.4 | 6.2 | 4.2 | 4.0 | 2.9 |
| | | 5.0 | | | 4.4 | | 10.8 | 10.4 | 8.0 | 6.0 | 4.4 |
| | | 10.5 | | | 7.5 | | 30.6 | 29.4 | 9.9 | 14.1 | 7.5 |
| | | 24.3 | | | 33.8 | EBIT/Interest | (23) 17.0 | (23) 22.0 | (17) 95.1 | (17) 21.3 | (22) 33.8 |
| | (14) | -.8 | (22) | | 3.1 | | 4.8 | 9.8 | 25.2 | 1.7 | 3.1 |
| | | -21.6 | | | -9.2 | | 1.6 | 2.8 | 6.4 | -11.6 | -9.2 |
| | | | | | | Net Profit + Depr., Dep., Amort./Cur. Mat. L/T/D | | | | | |
| | | .1 | | | .1 | Fixed/Worth | .2 | .0 | .0 | .1 | .1 |
| | | .2 | | | .2 | | .4 | .3 | .1 | .2 | .2 |
| | | .2 | | | .4 | | 1.1 | .6 | .2 | .5 | .4 |
| | | .3 | | | .3 | Debt/Worth | 1.3 | .5 | .4 | .3 | .3 |
| | | .8 | | | .7 | | 1.9 | 1.5 | 1.0 | .7 | .7 |
| | | 2.0 | | | 1.6 | | 4.4 | 2.7 | 1.1 | 1.7 | 1.6 |
| | | 15.4 | | | 18.7 | % Profit Before Taxes/Tangible Net Worth | 43.9 | 78.5 | 69.7 | 41.7 | 18.7 |
| | | -2.4 | | | 6.9 | | (22) 26.3 | (26) 29.7 | 30.4 | (22) 10.4 | 6.9 |
| | | -28.9 | | | -12.4 | | 7.5 | 8.2 | 11.4 | -14.5 | -12.4 |
| | | 7.5 | | | 10.6 | % Profit Before Taxes/Total Assets | 18.0 | 38.5 | 28.9 | 15.1 | 10.6 |
| | | -1.9 | | | 3.9 | | 5.9 | 7.7 | 13.8 | 6.1 | 3.9 |
| | | -11.0 | | | -5.2 | | 1.3 | 4.1 | 5.8 | -8.3 | -5.2 |
| | | .7 | | | .7 | % Depr., Dep., Amort./Revenues | .5 | .3 | .4 | .5 | .7 |
| | (13) | .9 | (24) | | 1.2 | | (24) .9 | (24) .6 | (16) .6 | (20) 1.2 | (24) 1.2 |
| | | 1.5 | | | 1.8 | | 1.5 | 1.8 | 1.2 | 1.9 | 1.8 |
| | | | | | 1.6 | % Officers', Directors' Owners' Comp/Revenues | 3.0 | 2.0 | 1.7 | 2.1 | 1.6 |
| | | | (16) | | 3.5 | | (14) 7.5 | (15) 5.4 | (12) 5.0 | (10) 3.5 | (16) 3.5 |
| | | | | | 7.4 | | 9.9 | 9.6 | 12.1 | 7.3 | 7.4 |
| 2176M | 871M | 94678M | 109552M | 640749M | 847155M | Contract Revenues ($) | 814614M | 938669M | 361448M | 350593M | 847155M |
| 871M | | 48534M | 65338M | 285567M | 400310M | Total Assets ($) | 274050M | 347489M | 194199M | 186308M | 400310M |

M = $ thousand    MM = $ million
See Pages 9 through 22 for Explanation of Ratios and Data

## Current Data Sorted by Revenue      Comparative Historical Data

Type of Statement — current sample composition: 9 (4/1-9/30/11); 70 (10/1/11-3/31/12)

| 0-1MM | 1-10MM | 10-50MM | 50 & OVER | ALL | | 4/1/07-3/31/08 ALL | 4/1/08-3/31/09 ALL | 4/1/09-3/31/10 ALL | 4/1/10-3/31/11 ALL | 4/1/11-3/31/12 ALL |
|---|---|---|---|---|---|---|---|---|---|---|
| | | | 1 | 1 | Unqualified | 7 | 3 | 2 | 1 | 1 |
| | 21 | 15 | 1 | 37 | Reviewed | 40 | 29 | 27 | 31 | 37 |
| 1 | 5 | 1 | | 7 | Compiled | 16 | 8 | 9 | 11 | 7 |
| 5 | 6 | | | 11 | Tax Returns | 5 | 8 | 7 | 9 | 11 |
| 2 | 12 | 6 | 3 | 23 | Other | 10 | 8 | 11 | 15 | 23 |
| 8 | 44 | 22 | 5 | 79 | **NUMBER OF STATEMENTS** | 78 | 56 | 56 | 67 | 79 |
| % | % | % | % | % | **ASSETS** | % | % | % | % | % |
| | 15.4 | 13.8 | | 14.9 | Cash & Equivalents | 16.3 | 16.1 | 13.9 | 16.6 | 14.9 |
| | 41.1 | 48.5 | | 40.4 | A/R - Progress Billings | 40.0 | 42.6 | 41.4 | 27.7 | 40.4 |
| | 1.6 | 6.2 | | 2.7 | A/R - Current Retention | 1.8 | 1.8 | 1.7 | 19.6 | 2.7 |
| | 6.4 | 4.9 | | 7.8 | Inventory | 4.6 | 4.5 | 8.5 | 6.7 | 7.8 |
| | 6.0 | 6.7 | | 5.7 | Cost & Est. Earnings In Excess Billings | 4.6 | 4.3 | 3.2 | 3.9 | 5.7 |
| | 5.1 | 4.4 | | 4.2 | All Other Current | 5.9 | 4.0 | 3.5 | 4.0 | 4.2 |
| | 75.5 | 84.4 | | 75.7 | Total Current | 73.2 | 73.2 | 72.2 | 78.5 | 75.7 |
| | 19.9 | 11.4 | | 18.3 | Fixed Assets (net) | 18.2 | 18.9 | 20.7 | 15.8 | 18.3 |
| | .0 | .5 | | .2 | Joint Ventures & Investments | .4 | .6 | .1 | .0 | .2 |
| | .4 | .0 | | .5 | Intangibles (net) | 1.5 | 1.2 | 1.7 | .7 | .5 |
| | 4.2 | 3.6 | | 5.2 | All Other Non-Current | 6.8 | 6.1 | 5.3 | 5.0 | 5.2 |
| | 100.0 | 100.0 | | 100.0 | Total | 100.0 | 100.0 | 100.0 | 100.0 | 100.0 |
| | | | | | **LIABILITIES** | | | | | |
| | 10.6 | 3.6 | | 10.4 | Notes Payable-Short Term | 6.5 | 10.2 | 10.1 | 14.0 | 10.4 |
| | 21.8 | 22.0 | | 21.4 | A/P - Trade | 20.4 | 20.2 | 19.1 | 24.6 | 21.4 |
| | .0 | .9 | | .3 | A/P - Retention | .3 | .6 | .2 | .0 | .3 |
| | 4.6 | 9.2 | | 5.4 | Billings in Excess of Costs & Est. Earnings | 4.7 | 4.1 | 4.0 | 5.6 | 5.4 |
| | .2 | .1 | | .1 | Income Taxes Payable | .5 | .3 | .1 | .2 | .1 |
| | 3.0 | 3.1 | | 3.4 | Cur. Mat.-L/T/D | 3.1 | 3.0 | 3.0 | 7.2 | 3.4 |
| | 7.2 | 8.0 | | 7.7 | All Other Current | 8.4 | 8.5 | 6.6 | 10.3 | 7.7 |
| | 47.5 | 46.8 | | 48.8 | Total Current | 43.7 | 46.7 | 43.0 | 62.0 | 48.8 |
| | 9.5 | 1.8 | | 10.0 | Long-Term Debt | 8.9 | 10.3 | 10.2 | 10.8 | 10.0 |
| | .5 | .4 | | .4 | Deferred Taxes | .7 | .7 | 1.4 | .4 | .4 |
| | 6.9 | 2.6 | | 9.2 | All Other Non-Current | 2.2 | 3.4 | 4.0 | 4.4 | 9.2 |
| | 35.6 | 48.4 | | 31.5 | Net Worth | 44.5 | 38.8 | 41.5 | 22.5 | 31.5 |
| | 100.0 | 100.0 | | 100.0 | Total Liabilties & Net Worth | 100.0 | 100.0 | 100.0 | 100.0 | 100.0 |
| | | | | | **INCOME DATA** | | | | | |
| | 100.0 | 100.0 | | 100.0 | Contract Revenues | 100.0 | 100.0 | 100.0 | 100.0 | 100.0 |
| | 25.5 | 22.8 | | 26.1 | Gross Profit | 29.3 | 29.6 | 26.9 | 25.7 | 26.1 |
| | 23.3 | 17.8 | | 23.1 | Operating Expenses | 23.3 | 24.4 | 25.3 | 23.2 | 23.1 |
| | 2.2 | 5.0 | | 3.1 | Operating Profit | 6.0 | 5.3 | 1.5 | 2.5 | 3.1 |
| | .2 | .3 | | .3 | All Other Expenses (net) | .4 | .2 | .0 | .0 | .3 |
| | 2.0 | 4.7 | | 2.8 | Profit Before Taxes | 5.6 | 5.1 | 1.5 | 2.5 | 2.8 |
| | | | | | **RATIOS** | | | | | |
| | 2.6 | 2.9 | | 2.7 | | 2.7 | 2.8 | 2.4 | 2.9 | 2.7 |
| | 1.9 | 1.7 | | 1.7 | Current | 1.7 | 1.6 | 1.7 | 1.7 | 1.7 |
| | 1.1 | 1.5 | | 1.1 | | 1.3 | 1.1 | 1.3 | 1.1 | 1.1 |
| | 3.5 | 4.0 | | 3.5 | | 4.5 | 6.0 | 4.6 | 3.7 | 3.5 |
| | (41) 2.0 | 2.5 | | (73) 2.2 | Receivables/Payables | (76) 2.3 | (53) 2.6 | (55) 2.2 | (64) 2.3 | (73) 2.2 |
| | 1.5 | 1.9 | | 1.5 | | 1.4 | 1.4 | 1.4 | 1.7 | 1.5 |
| | 36 10.0 | 49 7.5 | | 38 9.6 | | 32 11.5 | 27 13.3 | 33 11.1 | 30 12.2 | 38 9.6 |
| | 56 6.5 | 58 6.3 | | 55 6.6 | Revenues/Receivables | 48 6.9 | 53 6.9 | 54 6.7 | 53 6.9 | 55 6.6 |
| | 72 5.1 | 79 4.6 | | 73 5.0 | | 71 5.1 | 73 5.0 | 77 4.8 | 83 4.4 | 73 5.0 |
| | 19 19.1 | 19 18.8 | | 17 21.4 | | 15 24.7 | 11 33.5 | 15 25.0 | 17 21.3 | 17 21.4 |
| | 32 11.5 | 29 12.4 | | 31 11.6 | Cost of Revenues/Payables | 32 11.6 | 26 14.3 | 29 12.6 | 33 11.1 | 31 11.6 |
| | 45 8.1 | 45 8.1 | | 49 7.5 | | 49 7.4 | 50 7.3 | 52 7.0 | 50 7.3 | 49 7.5 |
| | 5.4 | 6.0 | | 6.0 | | 5.5 | 6.9 | 7.1 | 6.1 | 6.0 |
| | 12.2 | 8.1 | | 11.9 | Revenues/Working Capital | 11.2 | 15.4 | 11.5 | 12.6 | 11.9 |
| | 55.0 | 13.3 | | 31.2 | | 22.3 | 64.4 | 20.5 | 32.7 | 31.2 |
| | 8.2 | 45.1 | | 13.2 | | 30.8 | 34.8 | 18.3 | 47.4 | 13.2 |
| | (38) 4.6 | (19) 13.5 | | (69) 5.1 | EBIT/Interest | (67) 9.4 | (47) 8.0 | (48) 4.6 | (62) 3.7 | (69) 5.1 |
| | .3 | 3.8 | | 1.1 | | 2.7 | 1.2 | -.7 | -3.4 | 1.1 |
| | | | | 4.0 | | 13.8 | | 10.3 | 2.4 | 4.0 |
| | | | | (15) 2.3 | Net Profit + Depr., Dep., Amort./Cur. Mat. L/T/D | (16) 5.3 | | (14) 2.4 | (10) 1.1 | (15) 2.3 |
| | | | | 1.0 | | 2.2 | | .7 | -5.5 | 1.0 |
| | .2 | .1 | | .2 | | .1 | .1 | .2 | .1 | .2 |
| | .5 | .2 | | .4 | Fixed/Worth | .3 | .4 | .4 | .5 | .4 |
| | 1.1 | .4 | | 1.0 | | .8 | .9 | 1.2 | .9 | 1.0 |
| | .6 | .5 | | .7 | | .6 | .5 | .5 | .6 | .7 |
| | 1.8 | 1.1 | | 1.8 | Debt/Worth | 1.2 | 1.5 | 1.6 | 1.5 | 1.8 |
| | 3.7 | 2.2 | | 4.6 | | 2.2 | 3.5 | 3.4 | 3.9 | 4.6 |
| | 39.4 | 45.7 | | 45.2 | | 70.7 | 67.6 | 37.6 | 34.0 | 45.2 |
| | (38) 13.8 | 16.1 | | (70) 14.9 | % Profit Before Taxes/Tangible Net Worth | (73) 35.3 | (49) 35.5 | (53) 6.3 | (56) 12.3 | (70) 14.9 |
| | 2.8 | 4.0 | | 3.4 | | 10.8 | 5.8 | -11.0 | -3.7 | 3.4 |
| | 12.7 | 27.5 | | 18.6 | | 28.5 | 28.5 | 22.8 | 22.3 | 18.6 |
| | 3.3 | 9.8 | | 4.1 | % Profit Before Taxes/Total Assets | 12.0 | 12.1 | 3.5 | 5.3 | 4.1 |
| | .0 | 1.3 | | .5 | | 3.4 | .8 | -5.6 | -3.6 | .5 |
| | .7 | .7 | | .7 | | .8 | 1.0 | .6 | .7 | .7 |
| | (36) 1.1 | (21) 1.1 | | (67) 1.1 | % Depr., Dep., Amort./Revenues | (67) 1.3 | (46) 1.5 | (50) 1.6 | (58) 1.3 | (67) 1.1 |
| | 2.0 | 1.6 | | 1.8 | | 2.1 | 2.0 | 2.4 | 2.3 | 1.8 |
| | 2.4 | 2.1 | | 2.4 | | 2.1 | 1.9 | 1.9 | 2.5 | 2.4 |
| | (23) 4.1 | (10) 4.0 | | (40) 4.2 | % Officers', Directors' Owners' Comp/Revenues | (52) 4.7 | (35) 3.1 | (37) 3.6 | (39) 3.5 | (40) 4.2 |
| | 6.0 | 7.1 | | 6.4 | | 7.8 | 6.3 | 5.2 | 6.2 | 6.4 |
| 4981M | 237560M | 394216M | 3886593M | 4523350M | Contract Revenues ($) | 596818M | 446313M | 631640M | 1261427M | 4523350M |
| 2361M | 88281M | 130874M | 1631884M | 1853400M | Total Assets ($) | 225859M | 144742M | 208200M | 533265M | 1853400M |

© RMA 2012

M = $ thousand    MM = $ million

See Pages 9 through 22 for Explanation of Ratios and Data

**Current Data Sorted by Revenue**      **Comparative Historical Data**

| 0-1MM | 1-10MM | 10-50MM | 50 & OVER | ALL | Type of Statement | 4/1/07-3/31/08 ALL | 4/1/08-3/31/09 ALL | 4/1/09-3/31/10 ALL | 4/1/10-3/31/11 ALL | 4/1/11-3/31/12 ALL |
|---|---|---|---|---|---|---|---|---|---|---|
| | 2 | 6 | 5 | 13 | Unqualified | 24 | 15 | 17 | 14 | 13 |
| | 49 | 61 | 3 | 113 | Reviewed | 100 | 80 | 80 | 130 | 113 |
| 2 | 23 | 2 | 3 | 30 | Compiled | 27 | 21 | 29 | 28 | 30 |
| 8 | 15 | | 3 | 23 | Tax Returns | 41 | 34 | 30 | 23 | 23 |
| 1 | 29 | 20 | 16 | 66 | Other | 55 | 31 | 35 | 63 | 66 |

50 (4/1-9/30/11)    195 (10/1/11-3/31/12)

| 0-1MM | 1-10MM | 10-50MM | 50 & OVER | ALL | | 4/1/07-3/31/08 ALL | 4/1/08-3/31/09 ALL | 4/1/09-3/31/10 ALL | 4/1/10-3/31/11 ALL | 4/1/11-3/31/12 ALL |
|---|---|---|---|---|---|---|---|---|---|---|
| 11 | 118 | 89 | 27 | 245 | **NUMBER OF STATEMENTS** | 247 | 181 | 191 | 258 | 245 |
| % | % | % | % | % | **ASSETS** | % | % | % | % | % |
| 14.1 | 16.9 | 11.9 | 9.2 | 14.1 | Cash & Equivalents | 14.0 | 14.6 | 17.3 | 16.2 | 14.1 |
| 20.6 | 46.0 | 50.4 | 43.9 | 46.2 | A/R - Progress Billings | 46.4 | 41.2 | 40.2 | 28.3 | 46.2 |
| .0 | 1.9 | 4.3 | 4.6 | 3.0 | A/R - Current Retention | 1.9 | 2.5 | 1.3 | 16.5 | 3.0 |
| 16.5 | 6.8 | 3.6 | 4.0 | 5.7 | Inventory | 6.9 | 6.3 | 5.8 | 6.0 | 5.7 |
| .0 | 4.7 | 9.8 | 7.7 | 6.7 | Cost & Est. Earnings In Excess Billings | 4.7 | 4.4 | 4.8 | 6.3 | 6.7 |
| 4.5 | 4.5 | 4.5 | 8.8 | 4.9 | All Other Current | 5.1 | 5.9 | 5.7 | 3.7 | 4.9 |
| 55.8 | 80.7 | 84.6 | 78.3 | 80.7 | Total Current | 79.0 | 74.9 | 75.0 | 77.0 | 80.7 |
| 34.2 | 13.0 | 11.4 | 11.6 | 13.2 | Fixed Assets (net) | 13.9 | 17.4 | 17.2 | 15.6 | 13.2 |
| 2.7 | .2 | .2 | .6 | .3 | Joint Ventures & Investments | .4 | .4 | .7 | .5 | .3 |
| .1 | 1.2 | .3 | 6.5 | 1.4 | Intangibles (net) | 1.5 | 1.4 | .7 | 1.0 | 1.4 |
| 7.3 | 4.9 | 3.5 | 3.1 | 4.3 | All Other Non-Current | 5.2 | 5.9 | 6.4 | 5.8 | 4.3 |
| 100.0 | 100.0 | 100.0 | 100.0 | 100.0 | Total | 100.0 | 100.0 | 100.0 | 100.0 | 100.0 |
| | | | | | **LIABILITIES** | | | | | |
| 37.8 | 12.0 | 12.0 | 7.3 | 12.6 | Notes Payable-Short Term | 9.9 | 10.4 | 12.0 | 11.5 | 12.6 |
| 11.1 | 19.9 | 21.0 | 19.3 | 19.8 | A/P - Trade | 20.0 | 16.5 | 17.5 | 18.7 | 19.8 |
| .0 | .0 | .1 | .0 | .1 | A/P - Retention | .2 | .1 | .1 | .3 | .1 |
| .0 | 6.7 | 10.0 | 11.6 | 8.1 | Billings in Excess of Costs & Est. Earnings | 7.1 | 7.7 | 6.5 | 6.7 | 8.1 |
| .0 | .5 | .3 | .2 | .4 | Income Taxes Payable | .2 | .5 | .3 | .7 | .4 |
| 10.4 | 2.5 | 1.8 | 3.6 | 2.7 | Cur. Mat.-L/T/D | 2.7 | 3.3 | 3.7 | 3.6 | 2.7 |
| 4.2 | 6.6 | 7.6 | 8.7 | 7.1 | All Other Current | 8.2 | 8.8 | 8.9 | 8.4 | 7.1 |
| 63.6 | 48.1 | 52.8 | 50.8 | 50.8 | Total Current | 48.2 | 47.3 | 48.9 | 50.0 | 50.8 |
| 13.2 | 7.2 | 4.4 | 4.1 | 6.1 | Long-Term Debt | 11.7 | 10.2 | 11.0 | 8.1 | 6.1 |
| .0 | .4 | .4 | .4 | .4 | Deferred Taxes | .5 | .7 | .6 | .5 | .4 |
| 4.5 | 2.4 | 2.3 | 2.6 | 2.4 | All Other Non-Current | 3.9 | 4.0 | 4.6 | 4.1 | 2.4 |
| 18.7 | 41.9 | 40.2 | 42.2 | 40.3 | Net Worth | 35.6 | 37.7 | 34.8 | 37.4 | 40.3 |
| 100.0 | 100.0 | 100.0 | 100.0 | 100.0 | Total Liabilities & Net Worth | 100.0 | 100.0 | 100.0 | 100.0 | 100.0 |
| | | | | | **INCOME DATA** | | | | | |
| 100.0 | 100.0 | 100.0 | 100.0 | 100.0 | Contract Revenues | 100.0 | 100.0 | 100.0 | 100.0 | 100.0 |
| 41.3 | 24.3 | 15.7 | 15.7 | 21.0 | Gross Profit | 27.4 | 28.9 | 30.1 | 24.8 | 21.0 |
| 40.6 | 22.0 | 13.3 | 12.2 | 18.6 | Operating Expenses | 21.8 | 24.4 | 28.3 | 23.9 | 18.6 |
| .7 | 2.3 | 2.4 | 3.5 | 2.4 | Operating Profit | 5.5 | 4.4 | 1.8 | .9 | 2.4 |
| -.3 | .0 | .1 | .2 | .1 | All Other Expenses (net) | .4 | .5 | .4 | .2 | .1 |
| 1.0 | 2.3 | 2.3 | 3.4 | 2.4 | Profit Before Taxes | 5.1 | 3.9 | 1.4 | .7 | 2.4 |
| | | | | | **RATIOS** | | | | | |
| 1.3 | 2.8 | 2.2 | 1.9 | 2.3 | Current | 2.6 | 2.7 | 2.6 | 2.5 | 2.3 |
| .9 | 1.7 | 1.5 | 1.7 | 1.7 | | 1.7 | 1.7 | 1.7 | 1.6 | 1.7 |
| .4 | 1.3 | 1.3 | 1.4 | 1.3 | | 1.2 | 1.3 | 1.1 | 1.2 | 1.3 |
| | 5.0 | 4.7 | 4.1 | 4.6 | Receivables/Payables | 4.8 | 5.3 | 4.7 | 4.4 | 4.6 |
| (115) 2.8 | 2.8 | 2.8 | 2.7 (240) | 2.8 | | (240) 2.6 | (171) 3.0 | (183) 2.7 | (248) 2.6 | (240) 2.8 |
| 1.7 | 2.0 | 1.7 | 1.8 | | | 1.5 | 1.7 | 1.7 | 1.6 | 1.8 |
| 2 162.0 | 41 8.9 | 53 6.9 | 59 6.2 | 47 7.8 | Revenues/Receivables | 40 9.1 | 35 10.4 | 34 10.7 | 43 8.6 | 47 7.8 |
| 34 10.7 | 65 5.6 | 72 5.1 | 74 4.9 | 68 5.4 | | 59 6.2 | 52 7.0 | 49 7.4 | 60 6.0 | 68 5.4 |
| 47 7.8 | 87 4.2 | 91 4.0 | 87 4.2 | 87 4.2 | | 78 4.7 | 72 5.1 | 72 5.0 | 82 4.5 | 87 4.2 |
| 0 UND | 16 22.3 | 17 21.1 | 24 14.9 | 17 21.9 | Cost of Revenues/Payables | 15 25.0 | 11 33.2 | 11 32.5 | 16 22.3 | 17 21.9 |
| 27 13.3 | 31 11.6 | 29 12.5 | 33 10.9 | 30 12.0 | | 28 12.9 | 23 16.1 | 25 14.7 | 27 13.5 | 30 12.0 |
| 63 5.8 | 49 7.5 | 43 8.5 | 42 8.7 | 46 8.0 | | 48 7.7 | 41 9.0 | 42 8.8 | 45 8.2 | 46 8.0 |
| 25.6 | 4.7 | 5.8 | 6.7 | 5.5 | Revenues/Working Capital | 5.8 | 6.4 | 5.2 | 5.1 | 5.5 |
| -77.1 | 8.6 | 9.1 | 8.2 | 8.9 | | 9.5 | 10.0 | 10.2 | 9.5 | 8.9 |
| -3.7 | 18.7 | 16.5 | 13.2 | 19.3 | | 22.0 | 21.2 | 48.5 | 27.9 | 19.3 |
| | 24.0 | 19.2 | 20.6 | 19.3 | EBIT/Interest | 25.0 | 32.3 | 13.6 | 11.4 | 19.3 |
| (96) 5.6 | 5.6 | (77) 7.5 | (21) 5.9 | (203) 5.9 | | (217) 6.9 | (160) 9.2 | (165) 4.3 | (211) 4.3 | (203) 5.9 |
| 1.3 | 1.7 | 3.1 | 1.6 | | | 2.2 | 1.6 | -1.2 | -2.4 | 1.6 |
| | 4.5 | 8.4 | | 4.8 | Net Profit + Depr., Dep., Amort./Cur. Mat. L/T/D | 10.9 | 9.8 | 9.6 | 7.8 | 4.8 |
| (17) 1.2 | 1.2 | (18) 2.6 | (40) 2.6 | 2.6 | | (38) 4.2 | (32) 3.9 | (35) 2.9 | (54) 2.0 | (40) 2.6 |
| -2.2 | 1.9 | 1.0 | | | | .9 | 1.2 | 1.4 | .8 | 1.0 |
| .9 | .1 | .1 | .1 | .1 | Fixed/Worth | .1 | .2 | .1 | .1 | .1 |
| 1.2 | .3 | .3 | .2 | .3 | | .3 | .3 | .4 | .3 | .3 |
| -1.4 | .8 | .5 | .7 | .7 | | .8 | 1.0 | 1.1 | .8 | .7 |
| 1.3 | .6 | .8 | 1.0 | .8 | Debt/Worth | .8 | .7 | .7 | .7 | .8 |
| 3.2 | 1.2 | 1.7 | 1.5 | 1.4 | | 1.7 | 1.6 | 1.6 | 1.5 | 1.4 |
| -4.8 | 3.3 | 2.8 | 2.5 | 3.2 | | 4.8 | 3.6 | 4.4 | 3.8 | 3.2 |
| | 40.5 | 35.5 | 30.1 | 37.8 | % Profit Before Taxes/ Tangible Net Worth | 63.8 | 54.8 | 44.2 | 26.8 | 37.8 |
| (108) 13.5 | 13.5 | (86) 15.3 | (24) 14.5 | (226) 14.8 | | (219) 31.2 | (159) 27.8 | (168) 18.2 | (233) 8.9 | (226) 14.8 |
| .9 | 3.2 | 5.0 | 2.2 | | | 10.1 | 4.8 | -1.9 | -6.4 | 2.2 |
| 11.8 | 17.5 | 12.4 | 12.3 | 14.4 | % Profit Before Taxes/ Total Assets | 24.8 | 23.6 | 17.2 | 11.4 | 14.4 |
| 8.2 | 4.9 | 5.4 | 6.1 | 5.3 | | 11.0 | 7.9 | 5.0 | 3.7 | 5.3 |
| -16.3 | .4 | .7 | 2.6 | .8 | | 2.8 | 1.5 | -2.4 | -4.6 | .8 |
| | .4 | .4 | .4 | .4 | % Depr., Dep., Amort./ Revenues | .4 | .5 | .5 | .6 | .4 |
| (101) .9 | .9 | (85) .7 | (20) .7 | (214) .8 | | (194) .9 | (148) 1.0 | (164) 1.1 | (225) 1.1 | (214) .8 |
| 1.5 | 1.1 | 1.3 | 1.4 | | | 1.5 | 2.1 | 2.0 | 1.8 | 1.4 |
| | 2.3 | 1.1 | | 1.8 | % Officers', Directors' Owners' Comp/Revenues | 2.3 | 2.4 | 3.4 | 2.4 | 1.8 |
| (70) 4.4 | 4.4 | (42) 1.8 | (129) 3.3 | 3.3 | | (141) 4.1 | (109) 5.4 | (118) 4.5 | (128) 4.5 | (129) 3.3 |
| 7.1 | 3.8 | 6.2 | | | | 7.8 | 8.4 | 9.1 | 7.7 | 6.2 |
| 6321M | 551459M | 1729534M | 16299392M | 18586706M | Contract Revenues ($) | 8309209M | 48104221M | 26630772M | 19686913M | 18586706M |
| 3335M | 232949M | 660501M | 6555482M | 7452267M | Total Assets ($) | 2438338M | 24767710M | 10442463M | 7456585M | 7452267M |

M = $ thousand     MM = $ million
See Pages 9 through 22 for Explanation of Ratios and Data

## Current Data Sorted by Revenue

## Comparative Historical Data

| | | | | | Type of Statement | | | | | |
|---|---|---|---|---|---|---|---|---|---|---|
| 1 | 1 | 1 | 1 | 3 | Unqualified | 18 | 6 | 14 | 4 | 3 |
| 1 | 53 | 54 | 10 | 118 | Reviewed | 101 | 76 | 81 | 122 | 118 |
| 1 | 28 | 1 | 1 | 31 | Compiled | 51 | 37 | 29 | 37 | 31 |
| 10 | 30 | 2 | 3 | 45 | Tax Returns | 62 | 54 | 44 | 51 | 45 |
| 3 | 30 | 34 | 11 | 78 | Other | 35 | 36 | 38 | 58 | 78 |
| 44 (4/1-9/30/11) | | 231 (10/1/11-3/31/12) | | | | 4/1/07-3/31/08 | 4/1/08-3/31/09 | 4/1/09-3/31/10 | 4/1/10-3/31/11 | 4/1/11-3/31/12 |
| 0-1MM | 1-10MM | 10-50MM | 50 & OVER | ALL | | ALL | ALL | ALL | ALL | ALL |
| 15 | 142 | 92 | 26 | 275 | NUMBER OF STATEMENTS | 267 | 209 | 206 | 272 | 275 |
| % | % | % | % | % | ASSETS | % | % | % | % | % |
| 21.4 | 15.2 | 11.7 | 11.7 | 14.0 | Cash & Equivalents | 14.7 | 14.5 | 17.6 | 16.5 | 14.0 |
| 24.8 | 38.8 | 52.1 | 44.8 | 43.0 | A/R - Progress Billings | 40.4 | 38.7 | 37.5 | 25.3 | 43.0 |
| .0 | 2.1 | 4.8 | 3.1 | 3.0 | A/R - Current Retention | 1.5 | 1.9 | 1.4 | 17.4 | 3.0 |
| 7.4 | 10.7 | 4.4 | 4.8 | 7.9 | Inventory | 7.8 | 9.8 | 8.7 | 7.6 | 7.9 |
| .5 | 3.4 | 5.5 | 6.1 | 4.2 | Cost & Est. Earnings In Excess Billings | 2.9 | 2.5 | 2.6 | 4.7 | 4.2 |
| 4.6 | 3.8 | 4.3 | 2.8 | 3.9 | All Other Current | 5.5 | 5.1 | 5.0 | 5.2 | 3.9 |
| 58.8 | 74.0 | 82.8 | 73.3 | 76.0 | Total Current | 72.8 | 72.4 | 72.8 | 76.6 | 76.0 |
| 25.7 | 15.2 | 11.0 | 12.5 | 14.1 | Fixed Assets (net) | 17.3 | 18.8 | 17.9 | 14.8 | 14.1 |
| .0 | .4 | .4 | .3 | .3 | Joint Ventures & Investments | .7 | .9 | .8 | .1 | .3 |
| 6.4 | 1.7 | .8 | 4.5 | 2.0 | Intangibles (net) | 2.2 | 2.0 | 2.1 | 2.0 | 2.0 |
| 9.2 | 8.7 | 5.0 | 9.3 | 7.5 | All Other Non-Current | 7.0 | 5.9 | 6.5 | 6.4 | 7.5 |
| 100.0 | 100.0 | 100.0 | 100.0 | 100.0 | Total | 100.0 | 100.0 | 100.0 | 100.0 | 100.0 |
| | | | | | LIABILITIES | | | | | |
| 10.8 | 12.6 | 6.8 | 9.9 | 10.3 | Notes Payable-Short Term | 8.9 | 12.9 | 12.7 | 10.2 | 10.3 |
| 29.6 | 19.9 | 26.4 | 24.3 | 23.0 | A/P - Trade | 21.5 | 21.9 | 22.8 | 23.5 | 23.0 |
| .0 | .3 | 1.0 | 2.5 | .7 | A/P - Retention | .2 | .2 | .4 | .7 | .7 |
| .0 | 4.0 | 10.6 | 8.3 | 6.4 | Billings in Excess of Costs & Est. Earnings | 6.6 | 5.9 | 5.1 | 6.7 | 6.4 |
| .0 | .1 | .1 | .0 | .1 | Income Taxes Payable | .4 | .3 | .2 | .2 | .1 |
| 2.9 | 3.1 | 1.7 | 1.6 | 2.5 | Cur. Mat.-L/T/D | 4.2 | 3.7 | 5.0 | 3.1 | 2.5 |
| 7.5 | 10.8 | 10.2 | 9.5 | 10.3 | All Other Current | 11.1 | 10.0 | 10.5 | 9.7 | 10.3 |
| 50.8 | 50.9 | 56.8 | 56.1 | 53.4 | Total Current | 52.9 | 54.9 | 56.7 | 54.2 | 53.4 |
| 26.1 | 13.5 | 5.7 | 6.7 | 10.9 | Long-Term Debt | 12.5 | 17.0 | 17.0 | 10.0 | 10.9 |
| .2 | .2 | .2 | .6 | .2 | Deferred Taxes | .4 | .3 | .4 | .5 | .2 |
| 2.3 | 4.2 | 2.5 | 4.7 | 3.6 | All Other Non-Current | 5.7 | 6.5 | 4.6 | 3.3 | 3.6 |
| 20.7 | 31.2 | 34.8 | 32.0 | 31.9 | Net Worth | 28.4 | 21.3 | 21.3 | 32.1 | 31.9 |
| 100.0 | 100.0 | 100.0 | 100.0 | 100.0 | Total Liabilties & Net Worth | 100.0 | 100.0 | 100.0 | 100.0 | 100.0 |
| | | | | | INCOME DATA | | | | | |
| 100.0 | 100.0 | 100.0 | 100.0 | 100.0 | Contract Revenues | 100.0 | 100.0 | 100.0 | 100.0 | 100.0 |
| 48.3 | 28.1 | 18.6 | 21.1 | 25.4 | Gross Profit | 30.7 | 30.0 | 29.4 | 25.2 | 25.4 |
| 44.4 | 26.0 | 16.1 | 18.2 | 23.0 | Operating Expenses | 26.1 | 26.7 | 26.5 | 23.6 | 23.0 |
| 3.9 | 2.1 | 2.4 | 2.8 | 2.4 | Operating Profit | 4.6 | 3.4 | 2.9 | 1.7 | 2.4 |
| -.1 | .1 | .0 | 1.0 | .2 | All Other Expenses (net) | .3 | .8 | .5 | .2 | .2 |
| 3.9 | 2.0 | 2.4 | 1.9 | 2.2 | Profit Before Taxes | 4.3 | 2.6 | 2.4 | 1.5 | 2.2 |
| | | | | | RATIOS | | | | | |
| 6.0 | 2.6 | 1.7 | 1.6 | 2.3 | | 2.0 | 2.4 | 2.3 | 2.2 | 2.3 |
| 2.5 | 1.7 | 1.4 | 1.4 | 1.5 | Current | 1.4 | 1.5 | 1.5 | 1.4 | 1.5 |
| .7 | 1.2 | 1.2 | 1.2 | 1.2 | | 1.1 | 1.1 | 1.0 | 1.1 | 1.2 |
| 7.8 | 4.2 | 3.5 | 3.3 | 3.6 | | 4.0 | 3.8 | 3.3 | 3.3 | 3.6 |
| (12) 1.1 | (137) 2.3 | 2.3 | 2.1 | (267) 2.2 | Receivables/Payables | (245) 2.1 | (194) 1.9 | (197) 1.9 | (261) 1.9 | (267) 2.2 |
| .7 | 1.2 | 1.6 | 1.3 | 1.4 | | 1.2 | 1.4 | 1.0 | 1.2 | 1.4 |
| 0 UND 27 | 13.5 52 | 7.0 51 | 7.2 38 | 9.6 | Revenues/Receivables | 24 15.5 18 | 20.0 20 | 18.6 32 | 11.4 38 | 9.6 |
| 24 15.1 52 | 7.0 72 | 5.1 64 | 5.7 61 | 6.0 | | 47 7.8 47 | 7.7 40 | 9.0 53 | 6.9 61 | 6.0 |
| 74 4.9 72 | 5.1 87 | 4.2 74 | 4.9 78 | 4.7 | | 70 5.2 71 | 5.1 67 | 5.4 78 | 4.7 78 | 4.7 |
| 0 UND 14 | 25.2 23 | 15.9 24 | 15.0 19 | 19.2 | Cost of Revenues/Payables | 15 24.7 15 | 25.2 18 | 20.7 19 | 19.5 19 | 19.2 |
| 24 15.0 27 | 13.3 37 | 9.9 43 | 8.5 31 | 11.7 | | 28 13.3 26 | 13.8 27 | 13.3 33 | 11.1 31 | 11.7 |
| 87 4.2 42 | 8.6 53 | 6.9 58 | 6.3 51 | 7.1 | | 47 7.8 49 | 7.5 45 | 8.1 53 | 6.9 51 | 7.1 |
| 5.3 | 5.6 | 7.2 | 9.9 | 6.7 | | 8.2 | 7.3 | 6.8 | 6.7 | 6.7 |
| 30.5 | 11.7 | 12.2 | 13.8 | 12.1 | Revenues/Working Capital | 16.0 | 13.6 | 15.3 | 12.4 | 12.1 |
| -8.1 | 42.3 | 23.4 | 30.0 | 35.6 | | 85.8 | 94.0 | 521.3 | 43.9 | 35.6 |
| 20.0 | 21.2 | 40.7 | 48.5 | 27.6 | | 23.8 | 17.6 | 15.2 | 20.5 | 27.6 |
| (11) 2.1 | (129) 4.8 | (83) 8.5 | (25) 7.8 | (248) 6.5 | EBIT/Interest | (234) 5.5 | (178) 4.5 | (177) 5.4 | (236) 4.6 | (248) 6.5 |
| .1 | .9 | 1.4 | .8 | 1.0 | | 1.6 | 1.0 | .8 | -.5 | 1.0 |
| | 5.7 | 4.0 | | 4.0 | | 15.8 | 5.3 | 7.7 | 6.0 | 4.0 |
| (20) | 2.9 (19) | 2.6 | (43) | 2.6 | Net Profit + Depr., Dep., Amort./Cur. Mat. L/T/D | (53) 3.2 | (32) 2.6 | (38) 2.6 | (46) 2.1 | (43) 2.6 |
| | .5 | .5 | | .5 | | 1.2 | 1.4 | -.1 | -.4 | .5 |
| .2 | .1 | .1 | .1 | .1 | | .2 | .2 | .1 | .1 | .1 |
| 27.0 | .4 | .2 | .3 | .3 | Fixed/Worth | .4 | .5 | .4 | .3 | .3 |
| -6.2 | 1.2 | .8 | .9 | 1.0 | | 1.9 | 2.9 | 2.6 | 1.2 | 1.0 |
| .7 | .7 | 1.3 | 1.1 | .9 | | 1.0 | 1.0 | .9 | .8 | .9 |
| 214.0 | 1.6 | 2.0 | 2.0 | 1.9 | Debt/Worth | 2.3 | 2.4 | 2.0 | 1.9 | 1.9 |
| -7.7 | 6.2 | 3.4 | 4.1 | 4.5 | | 9.2 | 18.2 | 10.5 | 5.8 | 4.5 |
| | 35.1 | 39.6 | 26.2 | 39.1 | | 69.3 | 66.7 | 46.6 | 35.5 | 39.1 |
| (123) | 14.0 (89) | 15.9 (22) | 13.4 (243) | 14.9 | % Profit Before Taxes/ Tangible Net Worth | (222) 32.5 | (164) 26.8 | (162) 20.0 | (232) 11.7 | (243) 14.9 |
| | 1.2 | 3.5 | 7.7 | 2.6 | | 10.0 | 7.6 | 2.4 | .5 | 2.6 |
| 51.4 | 16.0 | 14.5 | 11.7 | 14.9 | | 23.7 | 19.4 | 17.6 | 13.2 | 14.9 |
| 5.6 | 4.4 | 6.1 | 5.6 | 5.4 | % Profit Before Taxes/ Total Assets | 9.2 | 7.4 | 6.5 | 4.4 | 5.4 |
| .2 | .0 | .8 | -.1 | .4 | | 2.0 | .6 | -.8 | -1.6 | .4 |
| .6 | .7 | .4 | .4 | .6 | | .6 | .5 | .7 | .6 | .6 |
| (10) 1.7 | (109) 1.1 | (88) .7 | (17) .7 | (224) .9 | % Depr., Dep., Amort./ Revenues | (217) 1.0 | (170) 1.1 | (171) 1.1 | (219) 1.0 | (224) .9 |
| 3.0 | 1.7 | 1.7 | 1.0 | 1.4 | | 1.7 | 1.9 | 1.9 | 1.7 | 1.4 |
| 3.4 | 1.6 | 1.2 | | 1.5 | | 2.0 | 2.5 | 2.8 | 2.0 | 1.5 |
| (12) 11.0 | (83) 3.2 | (40) 2.2 | | (142) 3.0 | % Officers', Directors' Owners' Comp/Revenues | (169) 4.4 | (125) 4.4 | (125) 5.0 | (149) 3.6 | (142) 3.0 |
| 17.5 | 5.7 | 3.6 | | 5.3 | | 7.7 | 8.2 | 8.2 | 6.4 | 5.3 |
| 7878M | 684552M | 1954768M | 23799037M | 26446235M | Contract Revenues ($) | 30337111M | 24041075M | 58656308M | 29407531M | 26446235M |
| 4011M | 233725M | 676710M | 7969909M | 8884355M | Total Assets ($) | 8293981M | 6055177M | 13672430M | 9245807M | 8884355M |

© RMA 2012

M = $ thousand     MM = $ million
See Pages 9 through 22 for Explanation of Ratios and Data

**Current Data Sorted by Revenue**       **Comparative Historical Data**

| 0-1MM | 1-10MM | 10-50MM | 50 & OVER | ALL | Type of Statement | 4/1/07-3/31/08 ALL | 4/1/08-3/31/09 ALL | 4/1/09-3/31/10 ALL | 4/1/10-3/31/11 ALL | 4/1/11-3/31/12 ALL |
|---|---|---|---|---|---|---|---|---|---|---|
| | 1 | 3 | | 4 | Unqualified | 9 | 8 | 8 | 4 | 4 |
| | 15 | 13 | 1 | 29 | Reviewed | 40 | 29 | 25 | 39 | 29 |
| | 8 | 2 | | 10 | Compiled | 11 | 10 | 7 | 12 | 10 |
| 2 | 15 | | 1 | 18 | Tax Returns | 13 | 9 | 8 | 8 | 18 |
| 1 | 9 | 6 | 1 | 17 | Other | 14 | 9 | 13 | 20 | 17 |
| | 11 (4/1-9/30/11) | | 67 (10/1/11-3/31/12) | | | | | | | |
| 3 | 48 | 24 | 3 | 78 | **NUMBER OF STATEMENTS** | 87 | 65 | 61 | 83 | 78 |
| % | % | % | % | % | **ASSETS** | % | % | % | % | % |
| | 13.4 | 10.9 | | 12.8 | Cash & Equivalents | 16.4 | 11.7 | 17.6 | 13.1 | 12.8 |
| | 52.8 | 53.5 | | 51.9 | A/R - Progress Billings | 50.0 | 54.6 | 47.5 | 35.6 | 51.9 |
| | 1.6 | 7.1 | | 3.8 | A/R - Current Retention | 2.5 | 2.3 | 1.4 | 18.8 | 3.8 |
| | 7.1 | 1.3 | | 5.2 | Inventory | 4.9 | 6.1 | 4.9 | 2.8 | 5.2 |
| | 4.5 | 6.7 | | 5.1 | Cost & Est. Earnings In Excess Billings | 3.6 | 2.9 | 2.2 | 5.1 | 5.1 |
| | 2.1 | 4.5 | | 3.3 | All Other Current | 3.6 | 6.3 | 4.9 | 4.8 | 3.3 |
| | 81.5 | 83.9 | | 82.1 | Total Current | 81.0 | 83.9 | 78.5 | 80.2 | 82.1 |
| | 10.3 | 6.9 | | 9.4 | Fixed Assets (net) | 11.2 | 10.7 | 12.0 | 10.5 | 9.4 |
| | .0 | .1 | | .1 | Joint Ventures & Investments | 1.1 | .1 | .3 | .1 | .1 |
| | 1.4 | 2.4 | | 1.7 | Intangibles (net) | .3 | .5 | .7 | 1.6 | 1.7 |
| | 6.8 | 6.7 | | 6.8 | All Other Non-Current | 6.5 | 5.0 | 8.5 | 7.6 | 6.8 |
| | 100.0 | 100.0 | | 100.0 | Total | 100.0 | 100.0 | 100.0 | 100.0 | 100.0 |
| | | | | | **LIABILITIES** | | | | | |
| | 16.5 | 11.6 | | 15.1 | Notes Payable-Short Term | 11.9 | 12.6 | 9.9 | 17.7 | 15.1 |
| | 15.7 | 13.9 | | 15.4 | A/P - Trade | 12.5 | 14.2 | 16.6 | 13.1 | 15.4 |
| | .2 | .2 | | .3 | A/P - Retention | .3 | .1 | .0 | .2 | .3 |
| | 5.5 | 9.1 | | 6.5 | Billings in Excess of Costs & Est. Earnings | 10.1 | 7.9 | 6.8 | 5.0 | 6.5 |
| | .6 | .2 | | .4 | Income Taxes Payable | .1 | .1 | .0 | .3 | .4 |
| | 2.4 | .9 | | 2.1 | Cur. Mat.-L/T/D | 2.3 | 1.4 | 1.4 | 2.6 | 2.1 |
| | 6.1 | 7.8 | | 8.5 | All Other Current | 10.3 | 9.8 | 10.8 | 9.5 | 8.5 |
| | 46.9 | 43.8 | | 48.4 | Total Current | 47.5 | 46.1 | 45.6 | 48.3 | 48.4 |
| | 4.7 | 2.3 | | 5.7 | Long-Term Debt | 9.3 | 7.3 | 5.5 | 8.0 | 5.7 |
| | .3 | .2 | | .3 | Deferred Taxes | .4 | .5 | .5 | .4 | .3 |
| | 7.7 | 3.2 | | 5.7 | All Other Non-Current | 7.7 | 3.8 | 8.8 | 6.3 | 5.7 |
| | 40.4 | 50.5 | | 39.9 | Net Worth | 35.1 | 42.4 | 39.5 | 37.1 | 39.9 |
| | 100.0 | 100.0 | | 100.0 | Total Liabilities & Net Worth | 100.0 | 100.0 | 100.0 | 100.0 | 100.0 |
| | | | | | **INCOME DATA** | | | | | |
| | 100.0 | 100.0 | | 100.0 | Contract Revenues | 100.0 | 100.0 | 100.0 | 100.0 | 100.0 |
| | 20.9 | 15.3 | | 19.7 | Gross Profit | 24.3 | 25.4 | 24.8 | 19.0 | 19.7 |
| | 20.8 | 12.8 | | 18.6 | Operating Expenses | 19.5 | 20.6 | 23.4 | 18.8 | 18.6 |
| | .2 | 2.5 | | 1.1 | Operating Profit | 4.9 | 4.8 | 1.4 | .3 | 1.1 |
| | .0 | .0 | | .1 | All Other Expenses (net) | .5 | .1 | .3 | .1 | .1 |
| | .1 | 2.6 | | 1.0 | Profit Before Taxes | 4.4 | 4.7 | 1.1 | .1 | 1.0 |
| | | | | | **RATIOS** | | | | | |
| | 2.8 | 2.8 | | 2.8 | | 2.9 | 3.6 | 3.6 | 3.2 | 2.8 |
| | 1.8 | 2.0 | | 1.8 | Current | 1.8 | 1.9 | 2.0 | 1.8 | 1.8 |
| | 1.2 | 1.5 | | 1.3 | | 1.4 | 1.3 | 1.3 | 1.3 | 1.3 |
| | 7.2 | 6.7 | | 6.5 | | 7.3 | 7.7 | 9.6 | 8.4 | 6.5 |
| | (45) 4.8 | (74) 4.2 | | 4.0 | Receivables/Payables | (79) 4.8 | (64) 4.9 | (60) 4.8 | (77) 4.5 | (74) 4.0 |
| | 2.4 | 2.9 | | 2.6 | | 3.3 | 2.9 | 2.7 | 3.2 | 2.6 |
| 54 6.7 | 63 5.8 | | 55 6.6 | | | 37 9.7 | 50 7.3 | 44 8.3 | 60 6.1 | 55 6.6 |
| 70 5.2 | 87 4.2 | | 76 4.8 | | Revenues/Receivables | 67 5.5 | 63 5.8 | 54 6.8 | 78 4.7 | 76 4.8 |
| 87 4.2 | 107 3.4 | | 94 3.9 | | | 81 4.5 | 87 4.2 | 69 5.3 | 101 3.6 | 94 3.9 |
| 11 33.9 | 14 26.8 | | 11 32.2 | | | 7 50.3 | 9 40.9 | 8 46.1 | 9 41.8 | 11 32.2 |
| 20 18.7 | 21 17.8 | | 21 17.6 | | Cost of Revenues/Payables | 17 21.0 | 17 21.6 | 15 24.9 | 18 19.8 | 21 17.6 |
| 34 10.6 | 33 11.2 | | 35 10.5 | | | 24 15.1 | 30 12.0 | 28 13.1 | 30 12.1 | 35 10.5 |
| | 5.4 | 5.2 | | 5.4 | | 6.4 | 5.5 | 4.7 | 5.1 | 5.4 |
| | 10.7 | 7.6 | | 9.1 | Revenues/Working Capital | 9.6 | 8.4 | 8.5 | 8.2 | 9.1 |
| | 29.1 | 11.3 | | 18.8 | | 16.3 | 16.4 | 18.6 | 15.9 | 18.8 |
| | 13.6 | 29.1 | | 20.5 | | 44.4 | 35.4 | 24.2 | 13.8 | 20.5 |
| | (43) 2.0 | (19) 6.7 | | (68) 2.4 | EBIT/Interest | (72) 9.2 | (55) 8.6 | (49) 3.8 | (76) 2.6 | (68) 2.4 |
| | -6.4 | 1.6 | | -.5 | | 2.3 | 1.5 | -6.7 | -.5 | -.5 |
| | | | | 20.3 | | 12.8 | 42.3 | | | 20.3 |
| | | | | (12) 3.4 | Net Profit + Depr., Dep., Amort./Cur. Mat. L/T/D | (17) 4.3 | (11) 4.6 | | | (12) 3.4 |
| | | | | .8 | | 2.7 | 2.1 | | | .8 |
| | .1 | .0 | | .1 | | .1 | .1 | .1 | .1 | .1 |
| | .2 | .1 | | .2 | Fixed/Worth | .2 | .2 | .1 | .2 | .2 |
| | .7 | .2 | | .5 | | .4 | .4 | .5 | .4 | .5 |
| | .7 | .5 | | .7 | | .6 | .6 | .4 | .4 | .7 |
| | 1.8 | 1.1 | | 1.4 | Debt/Worth | 1.5 | 1.5 | 1.0 | 1.4 | 1.4 |
| | 3.8 | 1.7 | | 3.7 | | 2.6 | 3.0 | 2.5 | 2.8 | 3.7 |
| | 30.4 | 28.0 | | 29.4 | | 58.0 | 53.9 | 32.9 | 19.7 | 29.4 |
| | (46) 6.9 | 11.0 | | (74) 8.3 | % Profit Before Taxes/Tangible Net Worth | (80) 33.3 | (61) 33.3 | (55) 16.1 | (75) 5.2 | (74) 8.3 |
| | -14.9 | 2.9 | | -4.1 | | 9.3 | 8.9 | -10.1 | -2.9 | -4.1 |
| | 10.9 | 11.2 | | 11.1 | | 30.7 | 26.2 | 16.9 | 7.0 | 11.1 |
| | 1.7 | 4.3 | | 2.5 | % Profit Before Taxes/Total Assets | 11.0 | 10.3 | 4.7 | 1.7 | 2.5 |
| | -9.4 | 1.5 | | -1.7 | | 3.1 | 1.3 | -6.8 | -1.5 | -1.7 |
| | .4 | .4 | | .4 | | .3 | .3 | .5 | .5 | .4 |
| | (40) .7 | (23) .5 | | (67) .6 | % Depr., Dep., Amort./Revenues | (70) .6 | (51) .6 | (51) .7 | (66) .8 | (67) .6 |
| | 1.5 | .8 | | 1.0 | | 1.0 | 1.1 | 1.6 | 1.1 | 1.0 |
| | 2.4 | 1.1 | | 1.7 | | 1.7 | 1.8 | 2.0 | 1.9 | 1.7 |
| | (33) 4.3 | (16) 2.6 | | (53) 3.4 | % Officers', Directors' Owners' Comp/Revenues | (57) 2.6 | (37) 3.3 | (30) 4.0 | (44) 4.4 | (53) 3.4 |
| | 7.6 | 5.4 | | 6.4 | | 7.6 | 6.8 | 11.1 | 7.4 | 6.4 |
| 1920M | 239482M | 517127M | 3482194M | 4240723M | Contract Revenues ($) | 11179995M | 8423309M | 779420M | 5314392M | 4240723M |
| 693M | 93104M | 215568M | 1312095M | 1621460M | Total Assets ($) | 2968525M | 2531323M | 297755M | 1804340M | 1621460M |

M = $ thousand    MM = $ million
See Pages 9 through 22 for Explanation of Ratios and Data

**Current Data Sorted by Revenue**                                    **Comparative Historical Data**

| | | | | | Type of Statement | | | | | |
|---|---|---|---|---|---|---|---|---|---|---|
| | | | | | Unqualified | 2 | 1 | 2 | 4 | |
| 1 | 7 | 4 | | 12 | Reviewed | 20 | 14 | 18 | 17 | 12 |
| | 4 | | | 4 | Compiled | 15 | 9 | 6 | 7 | 4 |
| 2 | 7 | | | 9 | Tax Returns | 12 | 5 | 5 | 3 | 9 |
| 2 | 7 | 2 | 1 | 12 | Other | 7 | 5 | 14 | 6 | 12 |
| | | | | | | 4/1/07- | 4/1/08- | 4/1/09- | 4/1/10- | 4/1/11- |
| | | | | | | 3/31/08 | 3/31/09 | 3/31/10 | 3/31/11 | 3/31/12 |
| 8 (4/1-9/30/11) | | 29 (10/1/11-3/31/12) | | | | ALL | ALL | ALL | ALL | ALL |
| 0-1MM | 1-10MM | 10-50MM | 50 & OVER | ALL | NUMBER OF STATEMENTS | 56 | 34 | 45 | 37 | 37 |
| 5 | 25 | 6 | 1 | 37 | | | | | | |
| % | % | % | % | % | ASSETS | % | % | % | % | % |
| | 13.0 | | | 15.2 | Cash & Equivalents | 19.4 | 19.2 | 17.2 | 17.3 | 15.2 |
| | 42.7 | | | 41.0 | A/R - Progress Billings | 43.7 | 39.2 | 44.4 | 34.5 | 41.0 |
| | .4 | | | .7 | A/R - Current Retention | 2.0 | .3 | .3 | 9.8 | .7 |
| | 4.2 | | | 3.4 | Inventory | 2.5 | 2.4 | 2.3 | 2.8 | 3.4 |
| | 5.7 | | | 5.5 | Cost & Est. Earnings In Excess Billings | 2.8 | 3.2 | 5.4 | 6.9 | 5.5 |
| | 3.8 | | | 3.1 | All Other Current | 4.7 | 3.4 | 5.2 | 3.5 | 3.1 |
| | 69.9 | | | 68.9 | Total Current | 75.1 | 67.5 | 74.8 | 74.8 | 68.9 |
| | 18.3 | | | 17.2 | Fixed Assets (net) | 16.4 | 17.3 | 16.1 | 15.9 | 17.2 |
| | 3.9 | | | 2.6 | Joint Ventures & Investments | 1.1 | .8 | .6 | .0 | 2.6 |
| | 3.9 | | | 3.4 | Intangibles (net) | 1.3 | 2.2 | 1.1 | 1.7 | 3.4 |
| | 4.1 | | | 7.9 | All Other Non-Current | 6.2 | 12.1 | 7.4 | 7.6 | 7.9 |
| | 100.0 | | | 100.0 | Total | 100.0 | 100.0 | 100.0 | 100.0 | 100.0 |
| | | | | | LIABILITIES | | | | | |
| | 18.9 | | | 14.2 | Notes Payable-Short Term | 13.2 | 12.4 | 13.4 | 13.7 | 14.2 |
| | 12.1 | | | 13.2 | A/P - Trade | 15.5 | 15.7 | 13.4 | 12.2 | 13.2 |
| | .0 | | | .0 | A/P - Retention | .1 | .0 | .0 | .0 | .0 |
| | 2.8 | | | 2.9 | Billings in Excess of Costs & Est. Earnings | 2.1 | 2.6 | 3.0 | 2.1 | 2.9 |
| | 1.0 | | | .7 | Income Taxes Payable | .2 | .1 | .2 | 1.2 | .7 |
| | 2.4 | | | 1.7 | Cur. Mat.-L/T/D | 2.8 | 3.0 | 2.2 | 1.9 | 1.7 |
| | 7.3 | | | 13.1 | All Other Current | 12.0 | 7.6 | 10.0 | 10.1 | 13.1 |
| | 44.4 | | | 45.8 | Total Current | 45.9 | 41.4 | 42.2 | 41.1 | 45.8 |
| | 10.2 | | | 10.0 | Long-Term Debt | 12.7 | 8.9 | 10.1 | 6.2 | 10.0 |
| | .5 | | | .4 | Deferred Taxes | .6 | .9 | .6 | 1.5 | .4 |
| | 7.0 | | | 8.0 | All Other Non-Current | 6.9 | 7.5 | 6.8 | 7.3 | 8.0 |
| | 37.8 | | | 35.8 | Net Worth | 33.8 | 41.3 | 40.4 | 44.0 | 35.8 |
| | 100.0 | | | 100.0 | Total Liabilties & Net Worth | 100.0 | 100.0 | 100.0 | 100.0 | 100.0 |
| | | | | | INCOME DATA | | | | | |
| | 100.0 | | | 100.0 | Contract Revenues | 100.0 | 100.0 | 100.0 | 100.0 | 100.0 |
| | 32.4 | | | 32.5 | Gross Profit | 32.6 | 36.5 | 28.6 | 30.1 | 32.5 |
| | 29.9 | | | 29.5 | Operating Expenses | 26.8 | 31.2 | 27.6 | 29.1 | 29.5 |
| | 2.5 | | | 3.0 | Operating Profit | 5.8 | 5.3 | 1.0 | .9 | 3.0 |
| | .3 | | | -.1 | All Other Expenses (net) | .4 | -.5 | .1 | -.1 | -.1 |
| | 2.2 | | | 3.1 | Profit Before Taxes | 5.5 | 5.8 | .9 | 1.0 | 3.1 |
| | | | | | RATIOS | | | | | |
| | 2.9 | | | 3.0 | | 3.3 | 4.7 | 3.2 | 3.6 | 3.0 |
| | 1.9 | | | 2.0 | Current | 1.9 | 1.8 | 2.0 | 2.0 | 2.0 |
| | 1.2 | | | 1.2 | | 1.1 | 1.1 | 1.3 | 1.3 | 1.2 |
| | 7.3 | | | 6.4 | | 8.7 | 11.5 | 9.4 | 7.8 | 6.4 |
| (23) | 3.5 | | (33) | 4.3 | Receivables/Payables | (50) 3.8 | (30) 4.1 | (43) 4.2 | (36) 4.1 | (33) 4.3 |
| | 1.9 | | | 2.1 | | 2.3 | 2.1 | 1.9 | 2.5 | 2.1 |
| 13 | 28.6 | | 31 | 11.7 | | 29 12.7 | 27 13.7 | 29 12.4 | 41 8.9 | 31 11.7 |
| 49 | 7.4 | | 49 | 7.4 | Revenues/Receivables | 54 6.8 | 47 7.7 | 56 6.6 | 62 5.9 | 49 7.4 |
| 79 | 4.6 | | 85 | 4.3 | | 77 4.8 | 79 4.6 | 72 5.1 | 86 4.2 | 85 4.3 |
| 8 | 43.6 | | 8 | 44.2 | | 6 57.7 | 0 UND | 8 43.8 | 11 31.9 | 8 44.2 |
| 19 | 19.4 | | 19 | 19.5 | Cost of Revenues/Payables | 16 22.6 | 14 26.7 | 14 26.0 | 24 15.0 | 19 19.5 |
| 27 | 13.5 | | 29 | 12.8 | | 34 10.8 | 34 10.9 | 37 9.7 | 34 10.6 | 29 12.8 |
| | 4.8 | | | 4.8 | | 6.1 | 7.0 | 5.0 | 4.0 | 4.8 |
| | 11.2 | | | 9.0 | Revenues/Working Capital | 12.3 | 9.9 | 8.7 | 8.1 | 9.0 |
| | 102.6 | | | 83.9 | | 42.7 | 152.8 | 22.6 | 17.8 | 83.9 |
| | 11.1 | | | 14.9 | | 18.5 | 21.2 | 21.7 | 19.4 | 14.9 |
| (22) | 5.5 | | (29) | 7.3 | EBIT/Interest | (46) 5.4 | (28) 6.8 | (38) 3.8 | (31) 7.9 | (29) 7.3 |
| | 3.1 | | | 3.3 | | 1.8 | 1.3 | -3.2 | -2.5 | 3.3 |
| | | | | | Net Profit + Depr., Dep., Amort./Cur. Mat. L/T/D | 9.1 | | | | |
| | | | | | | (14) 2.7 | | | | |
| | | | | | | 1.4 | | | | |
| | .2 | | | .2 | | .1 | .1 | .1 | .1 | .2 |
| | .4 | | | .4 | Fixed/Worth | .3 | .3 | .3 | .3 | .4 |
| | 1.5 | | | 1.5 | | 1.5 | .9 | .8 | .9 | 1.5 |
| | .6 | | | .6 | | .5 | .3 | .5 | .4 | .6 |
| | 1.2 | | | 1.2 | Debt/Worth | 1.3 | 1.0 | 1.0 | 1.3 | 1.2 |
| | 6.0 | | | 4.7 | | 5.8 | 3.2 | 3.0 | 2.5 | 4.7 |
| | 29.8 | | | 28.9 | | 55.0 | 74.5 | 26.0 | 31.9 | 28.9 |
| (22) | 14.7 | | (32) | 13.0 | % Profit Before Taxes/ Tangible Net Worth | (47) 26.3 | (31) 28.2 | (39) 12.0 | (34) 8.6 | (32) 13.0 |
| | -1.7 | | | 3.8 | | 6.0 | 1.6 | -6.0 | -14.2 | 3.8 |
| | 17.2 | | | 17.2 | | 29.6 | 41.5 | 14.5 | 13.1 | 17.2 |
| | 6.8 | | | 6.8 | % Profit Before Taxes/ Total Assets | 12.8 | 13.1 | 3.6 | 6.8 | 6.8 |
| | .3 | | | 1.0 | | 3.1 | .4 | -9.4 | -6.1 | 1.0 |
| | .5 | | | .6 | | .6 | .7 | .7 | .7 | .6 |
| (19) | 1.1 | | (28) | 1.0 | % Depr., Dep., Amort./ Revenues | (43) 1.0 | (28) 1.4 | (37) 1.1 | (31) 1.2 | (28) 1.0 |
| | 2.4 | | | 2.2 | | 2.0 | 2.1 | 2.0 | 2.3 | 2.2 |
| | 2.6 | | | 2.4 | | 2.2 | 2.6 | 2.1 | 2.6 | 2.4 |
| (16) | 5.7 | | (24) | 5.7 | % Officers', Directors' Owners' Comp/Revenues | (33) 5.4 | (23) 5.5 | (21) 3.5 | (23) 4.0 | (24) 5.7 |
| | 9.3 | | | 10.8 | | 8.8 | 8.1 | 6.3 | 7.0 | 10.8 |
| 1723M | 94922M | 144184M | 7321000M | 7561829M | Contract Revenues ($) | 2049461M | 522849M | 282326M | 235156M | 7561829M |
| 815M | 38788M | 57808M | 7084000M | 7181411M | Total Assets ($) | 521621M | 228821M | 104809M | 90129M | 7181411M |

© RMA 2012

M = $ thousand     MM = $ million
See Pages 9 through 22 for Explanation of Ratios and Data

**Current Data Sorted by Revenue**        **Comparative Historical Data**

| 0-1MM | 1-10MM | 10-50MM | 50 & OVER | ALL | | 4/1/07-3/31/08 ALL | 4/1/08-3/31/09 ALL | 4/1/09-3/31/10 ALL | 4/1/10-3/31/11 ALL | 4/1/11-3/31/12 ALL |
|---|---|---|---|---|---|---|---|---|---|---|
| | | | | | **Type of Statement** | | | | | |
| | 6 | 8 | | 14 | Unqualified | 2 | | 1 | 1 | |
| | | 1 | | 1 | Reviewed | 10 | 6 | 7 | 12 | 14 |
| | 2 | | | 2 | Compiled | 9 | 4 | 2 | 3 | 1 |
| 1 | 6 | 1 | | 8 | Tax Returns | 6 | 7 | 2 | 1 | 2 |
| | | | | | Other | 5 | 4 | 4 | 4 | 8 |
| | 2 (4/1-9/30/11) | | 23 (10/1/11-3/31/12) | | | | | | | |
| 1 | 14 | 10 | | 25 | **NUMBER OF STATEMENTS** | 32 | 21 | 16 | 21 | 25 |
| % | % | % | % | % | | % | % | % | % | % |
| | | | | | **ASSETS** | | | | | |
| | 9.0 | 8.0 | | 8.4 | Cash & Equivalents | 6.4 | 12.9 | 11.9 | 8.1 | 8.4 |
| | 49.0 | 54.8 | | 51.0 | A/R - Progress Billings | 47.3 | 41.6 | 41.6 | 26.6 | 51.0 |
| | 1.7 | 3.9 | | 2.5 | A/R - Current Retention | .1 | .0 | .0 | 20.6 | 2.5 |
| | 9.0 | 1.7 | | 5.9 | Inventory | 17.1 | 9.8 | 11.8 | 13.0 | 5.9 |
| | 6.3 | 6.0 | | 6.0 | Cost & Est. Earnings In Excess Billings | 2.3 | 2.3 | 5.2 | 8.3 | 6.0 |
| | 1.7 | 4.6 | | 3.4 | All Other Current | 3.4 | 7.3 | 4.3 | 2.2 | 3.4 |
| | 76.7 | 79.0 | | 77.3 | Total Current | 76.6 | 73.8 | 74.8 | 78.8 | 77.3 |
| | 19.8 | 5.4 | | 13.5 | Fixed Assets (net) | 14.9 | 19.4 | 16.5 | 12.2 | 13.5 |
| | .0 | .0 | | .0 | Joint Ventures & Investments | .1 | 1.4 | 1.0 | .0 | .0 |
| | 1.2 | 8.7 | | 4.1 | Intangibles (net) | 2.0 | 2.1 | .7 | 2.7 | 4.1 |
| | 2.3 | 6.9 | | 5.1 | All Other Non-Current | 6.4 | 3.2 | 7.0 | 6.4 | 5.1 |
| | 100.0 | 100.0 | | 100.0 | Total | 100.0 | 100.0 | 100.0 | 100.0 | 100.0 |
| | | | | | **LIABILITIES** | | | | | |
| | 14.4 | 17.2 | | 15.4 | Notes Payable-Short Term | 22.9 | 18.6 | 48.5 | 12.5 | 15.4 |
| | 13.9 | 16.6 | | 15.0 | A/P - Trade | 20.1 | 13.4 | 17.3 | 15.2 | 15.0 |
| | .1 | .4 | | .2 | A/P - Retention | .0 | .0 | .0 | .2 | .2 |
| | 4.5 | 6.7 | | 5.2 | Billings in Excess of Costs & Est. Earnings | 4.0 | 2.4 | 3.3 | 8.1 | 5.2 |
| | .3 | .0 | | .2 | Income Taxes Payable | .2 | .1 | .0 | .4 | .2 |
| | 2.5 | 1.0 | | 1.8 | Cur. Mat.-L/T/D | 2.2 | 2.3 | 2.5 | 1.0 | 1.8 |
| | 5.2 | 6.5 | | 5.8 | All Other Current | 20.8 | 20.2 | 5.9 | 9.9 | 5.8 |
| | 40.9 | 48.3 | | 43.6 | Total Current | 70.2 | 57.0 | 77.5 | 47.2 | 43.6 |
| | 5.9 | 8.4 | | 6.7 | Long-Term Debt | 11.9 | 18.4 | 4.7 | 11.1 | 6.7 |
| | .1 | .0 | | .1 | Deferred Taxes | .0 | .0 | .0 | .1 | .1 |
| | 5.9 | 4.0 | | 5.9 | All Other Non-Current | 2.5 | 13.0 | 8.5 | 9.4 | 5.9 |
| | 47.2 | 39.2 | | 43.8 | Net Worth | 15.4 | 11.6 | 9.2 | 32.2 | 43.8 |
| | 100.0 | 100.0 | | 100.0 | Total Liabilities & Net Worth | 100.0 | 100.0 | 100.0 | 100.0 | 100.0 |
| | | | | | **INCOME DATA** | | | | | |
| | 100.0 | 100.0 | | 100.0 | Contract Revenues | 100.0 | 100.0 | 100.0 | 100.0 | 100.0 |
| | 28.3 | 20.3 | | 25.6 | Gross Profit | 26.0 | 27.1 | 27.3 | 24.5 | 25.6 |
| | 25.9 | 17.1 | | 22.8 | Operating Expenses | 23.6 | 24.8 | 25.3 | 21.8 | 22.8 |
| | 2.5 | 3.2 | | 2.8 | Operating Profit | 2.4 | 2.3 | 2.0 | 2.7 | 2.8 |
| | .1 | .7 | | .3 | All Other Expenses (net) | .7 | .4 | .3 | .9 | .3 |
| | 2.3 | 2.6 | | 2.5 | Profit Before Taxes | 1.7 | 2.0 | 1.7 | 1.8 | 2.5 |
| | | | | | **RATIOS** | | | | | |
| | 2.9 | 2.0 | | 2.4 | | 2.3 | 3.9 | 3.5 | 2.5 | 2.4 |
| | 1.8 | 1.9 | | 1.8 | Current | 1.1 | 2.1 | 1.6 | 1.8 | 1.8 |
| | 1.4 | 1.3 | | 1.4 | | .9 | 1.2 | 1.0 | 1.3 | 1.4 |
| | 9.8 | 6.0 | | 7.2 | | 4.6 | 7.0 | 5.7 | 6.0 | 7.2 |
| | (13) 2.7 | 2.8 | | (24) 2.8 | Receivables/Payables | (31) 2.1 | (20) 4.8 | 2.2 | (20) 3.0 | (24) 2.8 |
| | 2.5 | 2.2 | | 2.4 | | 1.4 | 1.4 | 1.8 | 2.2 | 2.4 |
| | 48   7.6 | 51   7.2 | | 52   7.0 | | 21   17.4 | 12   29.3 | 30   12.2 | 38   9.7 | 52   7.0 |
| | 59   6.2 | 79   4.6 | | 61   6.0 | Revenues/Receivables | 58   6.3 | 43   8.5 | 59   6.2 | 70   5.2 | 61   6.0 |
| | 72   5.1 | 91   4.0 | | 87   4.2 | | 71   5.1 | 63   5.8 | 75   4.9 | 77   4.7 | 87   4.2 |
| | 7   48.9 | 19   19.3 | | 17   21.5 | | 19   19.7 | 2   167.4 | 12   31.2 | 9   39.5 | 17   21.5 |
| | 26   14.3 | 24   15.1 | | 25   14.6 | Cost of Revenues/Payables | 26   14.1 | 14   25.6 | 25   14.8 | 25   14.5 | 25   14.6 |
| | 31   11.6 | 35   10.4 | | 32   11.3 | | 44   8.2 | 36   10.3 | 45   8.2 | 45   8.1 | 32   11.3 |
| | 6.9 | 6.8 | | 6.8 | | 8.4 | 6.6 | 5.3 | 6.8 | 6.8 |
| | 9.9 | 8.2 | | 8.7 | Revenues/Working Capital | 41.4 | 11.6 | 17.0 | 8.6 | 8.7 |
| | 16.1 | 17.8 | | 15.3 | | -28.4 | 41.9 | NM | 15.0 | 15.3 |
| | 18.2 | 21.2 | | 17.0 | | 8.1 | 17.8 | 8.8 | 6.6 | 17.0 |
| | (12) 4.7 | 5.0 | | (23) 5.4 | EBIT/Interest | (31) 4.1 | 5.9 | (14) 2.1 | (19) 4.9 | (23) 5.4 |
| | -2.1 | 1.7 | | .7 | | 1.2 | 1.1 | .3 | 1.5 | .7 |
| | | | | | | 24.3 | | | | |
| | | | | | Net Profit + Depr., Dep., Amort./Cur. Mat. L/T/D | (10) 3.3 | | | | |
| | | | | | | .7 | | | | |
| | .2 | .0 | | .1 | | .1 | .1 | .1 | .1 | .1 |
| | .4 | .2 | | .3 | Fixed/Worth | .4 | .4 | .2 | .3 | .3 |
| | .7 | .3 | | .6 | | NM | 6.0 | 2.2 | .5 | .6 |
| | .5 | 1.1 | | .7 | | 1.1 | .9 | 1.2 | 1.2 | .7 |
| | 1.1 | 1.8 | | 1.4 | Debt/Worth | 3.4 | 2.3 | 1.6 | 2.8 | 1.4 |
| | 3.1 | 3.4 | | 2.9 | | NM | NM | 3.4 | 4.1 | 2.9 |
| | 38.7 | | | 37.6 | | 66.6 | 40.6 | 48.1 | 33.9 | 37.6 |
| | (13) 14.8 | | | (23) 14.8 | % Profit Before Taxes/ Tangible Net Worth | (24) 22.3 | (16) 20.0 | (14) 10.5 | (20) 11.0 | (23) 14.8 |
| | -7.9 | | | -1.4 | | 3.4 | 3.1 | -2.0 | 3.9 | -1.4 |
| | 21.1 | 14.8 | | 15.7 | | 19.4 | 18.3 | 16.0 | 9.0 | 15.7 |
| | 7.3 | 3.2 | | 4.7 | % Profit Before Taxes/ Total Assets | 5.6 | 5.9 | 2.6 | 5.0 | 4.7 |
| | -4.6 | .3 | | -.8 | | .1 | .3 | -5.7 | 1.0 | -.8 |
| | | | | .2 | | .3 | .2 | .5 | .4 | .2 |
| | | | (17) | .6 | % Depr., Dep., Amort./ Revenues | (25) .8 | (14) .8 | (10) .9 | (19) .8 | (17) .6 |
| | | | | 1.1 | | 1.7 | 1.1 | 1.8 | 1.5 | 1.1 |
| | | | | 2.1 | | 2.2 | 1.7 | 1.6 | 1.3 | 2.1 |
| | | | (15) | 3.4 | % Officers', Directors' Owners' Comp/Revenues | (18) 3.1 | (13) 4.3 | (11) 8.1 | (13) 2.2 | (15) 3.4 |
| | | | | 3.6 | | 6.8 | 9.2 | 10.1 | 6.6 | 3.6 |
| 471M | 71769M | 222665M | | 294905M | Contract Revenues ($) | 301998M | 162817M | 155709M | 293406M | 294905M |
| 341M | 24598M | 84094M | | 109033M | Total Assets ($) | 90728M | 50787M | 63051M | 112311M | 109033M |

*(Left columns "DATA NOT AVAILABLE" for the 0-1MM and 50 & OVER groups.)*

M = $ thousand     MM = $ million
See Pages 9 through 22 for Explanation of Ratios and Data

## Current Data Sorted by Revenue | Comparative Historical Data

| | | | | | Type of Statement | | | | | |
|---|---|---|---|---|---|---|---|---|---|---|
| | 1 | 7 | 2 | 10 | Unqualified | 35 | 28 | 19 | 19 | 10 |
| 3 | 37 | 20 | | 60 | Reviewed | 82 | 46 | 61 | 63 | 60 |
| 1 | 14 | | | 15 | Compiled | 26 | 25 | 12 | 19 | 15 |
| 3 | 10 | | 2 | 15 | Tax Returns | 22 | 27 | 18 | 22 | 15 |
| 11 | | 17 | 4 | 32 | Other | 33 | 34 | 28 | 41 | 32 |
| | 18 (4/1-9/30/11) | 114 (10/1/11-3/31/12) | | | | 4/1/07-3/31/08 | 4/1/08-3/31/09 | 4/1/09-3/31/10 | 4/1/10-3/31/11 | 4/1/11-3/31/12 |
| 0-1MM | 1-10MM | 10-50MM | 50 & OVER | ALL | | ALL | ALL | ALL | ALL | ALL |
| 7 | 73 | 44 | 8 | 132 | NUMBER OF STATEMENTS | 198 | 160 | 138 | 164 | 132 |
| % | % | % | % | % | ASSETS | % | % | % | % | % |
| | 8.9 | 9.7 | | 9.5 | Cash & Equivalents | 9.4 | 9.7 | 11.3 | 12.1 | 9.5 |
| | 36.4 | 37.2 | | 35.1 | A/R - Progress Billings | 29.9 | 26.7 | 24.8 | 23.6 | 35.1 |
| | 2.1 | 6.3 | | 3.3 | A/R - Current Retention | 1.4 | 2.1 | 1.5 | 8.4 | 3.3 |
| | 1.8 | 1.4 | | 1.6 | Inventory | 3.0 | 2.8 | 2.8 | 3.0 | 1.6 |
| | 2.9 | 4.6 | | 3.7 | Cost & Est. Earnings In Excess Billings | 2.2 | 3.0 | 3.0 | 3.0 | 3.7 |
| | 6.2 | 5.3 | | 5.5 | All Other Current | 4.3 | 5.4 | 4.1 | 5.2 | 5.5 |
| | 58.2 | 64.5 | | 58.8 | Total Current | 50.2 | 49.7 | 47.5 | 55.3 | 58.8 |
| | 34.1 | 29.2 | | 33.1 | Fixed Assets (net) | 41.8 | 43.0 | 45.0 | 35.2 | 33.1 |
| | .6 | .8 | | .8 | Joint Ventures & Investments | .7 | .6 | .8 | 1.1 | .8 |
| | .6 | 1.2 | | .8 | Intangibles (net) | 1.4 | 1.2 | .9 | 1.6 | .8 |
| | 6.5 | 4.4 | | 6.4 | All Other Non-Current | 5.8 | 5.6 | 5.8 | 6.7 | 6.4 |
| | 100.0 | 100.0 | | 100.0 | Total | 100.0 | 100.0 | 100.0 | 100.0 | 100.0 |
| | | | | | LIABILITIES | | | | | |
| | 13.2 | 6.4 | | 10.0 | Notes Payable-Short Term | 7.5 | 9.8 | 8.6 | 12.2 | 10.0 |
| | 17.4 | 21.9 | | 18.3 | A/P - Trade | 12.6 | 13.1 | 12.6 | 16.7 | 18.3 |
| | .3 | .4 | | .5 | A/P - Retention | .2 | .2 | .1 | .2 | .5 |
| | 2.7 | 6.0 | | 4.2 | Billings in Excess of Costs & Est. Earnings | 4.1 | 3.3 | 2.5 | 4.0 | 4.2 |
| | .2 | .1 | | .1 | Income Taxes Payable | .2 | .3 | .0 | .1 | .1 |
| | 8.0 | 4.9 | | 7.1 | Cur. Mat.-L/T/D | 8.8 | 7.9 | 8.9 | 6.8 | 7.1 |
| | 4.9 | 6.5 | | 6.3 | All Other Current | 4.6 | 5.5 | 5.9 | 6.1 | 6.3 |
| | 46.7 | 46.3 | | 46.5 | Total Current | 38.1 | 40.0 | 38.6 | 46.1 | 46.5 |
| | 17.4 | 11.1 | | 15.5 | Long-Term Debt | 22.9 | 20.8 | 24.6 | 16.4 | 15.5 |
| | 1.1 | 1.1 | | 1.0 | Deferred Taxes | 1.4 | 1.1 | 1.3 | .7 | 1.0 |
| | 5.4 | 1.4 | | 3.9 | All Other Non-Current | 5.8 | 3.0 | 3.8 | 6.8 | 3.9 |
| | 29.3 | 40.2 | | 33.1 | Net Worth | 31.8 | 35.1 | 31.6 | 30.0 | 33.1 |
| | 100.0 | 100.0 | | 100.0 | Total Liabilties & Net Worth | 100.0 | 100.0 | 100.0 | 100.0 | 100.0 |
| | | | | | INCOME DATA | | | | | |
| | 100.0 | 100.0 | | 100.0 | Contract Revenues | 100.0 | 100.0 | 100.0 | 100.0 | 100.0 |
| | 25.6 | 16.1 | | 23.0 | Gross Profit | 29.7 | 30.6 | 31.9 | 26.2 | 23.0 |
| | 24.2 | 13.2 | | 20.4 | Operating Expenses | 24.7 | 28.7 | 31.4 | 25.9 | 20.4 |
| | 1.4 | 2.9 | | 2.5 | Operating Profit | 5.0 | 2.0 | .6 | .4 | 2.5 |
| | .1 | .3 | | .4 | All Other Expenses (net) | 1.1 | .6 | 1.5 | .2 | .4 |
| | 1.2 | 2.6 | | 2.2 | Profit Before Taxes | 3.9 | 1.3 | -.9 | .1 | 2.2 |
| | | | | | RATIOS | | | | | |
| | 2.1 | 1.9 | | 1.9 | | 2.0 | 2.1 | 2.1 | 2.0 | 1.9 |
| | 1.3 | 1.4 | | 1.3 | Current | 1.3 | 1.3 | 1.3 | 1.4 | 1.3 |
| | .9 | 1.1 | | 1.0 | | 1.0 | .9 | .8 | .9 | 1.0 |
| | 5.4 | 3.1 | | 4.1 | | 5.1 | 5.7 | 7.2 | 4.7 | 4.1 |
| (68) | 3.2 | 2.0 | (123) | 2.3 | Receivables/Payables | (182) 2.6 | (149) 2.8 | (125) 2.7 | (151) 2.4 | (123) 2.3 |
| | 1.4 | 1.3 | | 1.4 | | 1.5 | 1.5 | 1.5 | 1.3 | 1.4 |
| 36 10.0 | 48 7.6 | 36 10.1 | | | Revenues/Receivables | 31 11.8 | 31 11.9 | 28 13.2 | 25 14.6 | 36 10.1 |
| 62 5.9 | 69 5.3 | 64 5.7 | | | | 56 6.5 | 48 7.6 | 49 7.5 | 55 6.7 | 64 5.7 |
| 85 4.3 | 85 4.3 | 85 4.3 | | | | 81 4.5 | 72 5.1 | 72 5.1 | 80 4.6 | 85 4.3 |
| 12 30.3 | 24 15.3 | 15 23.6 | | | Cost of Revenues/Payables | 10 35.0 | 9 38.8 | 5 73.0 | 11 34.5 | 15 23.6 |
| 24 15.2 | 39 9.3 | 31 11.8 | | | | 28 13.0 | 26 14.0 | 24 15.4 | 28 13.2 | 31 11.8 |
| 50 7.3 | 57 6.4 | 53 6.9 | | | | 47 7.8 | 47 7.8 | 52 7.0 | 57 6.4 | 53 6.9 |
| | 6.0 | 7.0 | | 6.9 | Revenues/Working Capital | 8.0 | 6.6 | 6.7 | 7.3 | 6.9 |
| | 18.4 | 13.7 | | 17.6 | | 18.2 | 18.0 | 19.2 | 16.8 | 17.6 |
| | -35.2 | 32.0 | | NM | | -158.5 | -59.8 | -36.0 | -32.5 | NM |
| | 7.6 | 14.7 | | 12.4 | | 8.5 | 8.3 | 4.3 | 7.1 | 12.4 |
| (67) | 2.0 | (43) 6.0 | (124) | 3.2 | EBIT/Interest | (188) 2.8 | (143) 1.9 | (123) 1.2 | (147) 2.1 | (124) 3.2 |
| | -3.1 | -.5 | | -.4 | | 1.1 | -1.2 | -3.4 | -1.2 | -.4 |
| | 3.3 | 4.1 | | 3.7 | Net Profit + Depr., Dep., Amort./Cur. Mat. L/T/D | 2.4 | 2.9 | 2.9 | 2.6 | 3.7 |
| (11) | 2.2 | (11) 2.4 | (25) | 2.3 | | (61) 1.5 | (36) 2.0 | (34) 1.4 | (30) 1.5 | (25) 2.3 |
| | 1.2 | 1.9 | | 1.5 | | 1.1 | 1.0 | .7 | -.2 | 1.5 |
| | .5 | .5 | | .5 | | .6 | .6 | .6 | .5 | .5 |
| | 1.0 | .7 | | .8 | Fixed/Worth | 1.2 | 1.1 | 1.2 | 1.0 | .8 |
| | 2.1 | 1.2 | | 1.7 | | 2.0 | 2.6 | 2.8 | 2.5 | 1.7 |
| | 1.0 | .9 | | .9 | | 1.0 | .8 | .8 | .8 | .9 |
| | 1.5 | 1.7 | | 1.6 | Debt/Worth | 1.8 | 1.7 | 1.6 | 1.8 | 1.6 |
| | 5.4 | 3.2 | | 3.7 | | 4.3 | 4.3 | 4.6 | 6.3 | 3.7 |
| | 45.7 | 27.5 | | 39.3 | % Profit Before Taxes/ Tangible Net Worth | 41.9 | 31.5 | 20.9 | 27.2 | 39.3 |
| (62) | 5.7 | (43) 13.0 | (118) | 11.2 | | (180) 17.5 | (142) 7.6 | (114) 3.2 | (142) 8.1 | (118) 11.2 |
| | -5.4 | -3.8 | | -4.0 | | 2.1 | -7.3 | -19.8 | -7.9 | -4.0 |
| | 15.0 | 12.0 | | 14.6 | % Profit Before Taxes/ Total Assets | 14.3 | 14.6 | 8.0 | 9.3 | 14.6 |
| | 3.4 | 4.6 | | 4.3 | | 5.5 | 3.1 | .8 | 2.9 | 4.3 |
| | -2.3 | -.3 | | -1.9 | | .5 | -4.9 | -11.4 | -4.1 | -1.9 |
| | 2.5 | 2.1 | | 2.4 | % Depr., Dep., Amort./ Revenues | 3.1 | 4.0 | 4.2 | 3.1 | 2.4 |
| (66) | 4.8 | (43) 3.5 | (119) | 4.1 | | (177) 5.6 | (141) 6.5 | (118) 7.4 | (145) 5.1 | (119) 4.1 |
| | 8.1 | 4.5 | | 6.9 | | 8.4 | 9.1 | 11.7 | 7.7 | 6.9 |
| | 2.4 | 1.1 | | 1.8 | % Officers', Directors' Owners' Comp/Revenues | 2.0 | 2.4 | 2.2 | 2.0 | 1.8 |
| (38) | 4.7 | (19) 2.2 | (65) | 3.7 | | (100) 4.1 | (70) 4.6 | (53) 4.8 | (73) 4.0 | (65) 3.7 |
| | 8.7 | 2.5 | | 6.6 | | 6.2 | 7.8 | 9.5 | 7.5 | 6.6 |
| 4314M | 302909M | 861305M | 6327313M | 7495841M | Contract Revenues ($) | 66001098M | 42605534M | 4950012M | 8150918M | 7495841M |
| 2174M | 154448M | 408814M | 2966188M | 3531624M | Total Assets ($) | 26833564M | 17114825M | 4055686M | 4808902M | 3531624M |

© RMA 2012

M = $ thousand      MM = $ million
See Pages 9 through 22 for Explanation of Ratios and Data

**Current Data Sorted by Revenue**      **Comparative Historical Data**

Type of Statement

| | 0-1MM | 1-10MM | 10-50MM | 50 & OVER | ALL | | 4/1/07-3/31/08 ALL | 4/1/08-3/31/09 ALL | 4/1/09-3/31/10 ALL | 4/1/10-3/31/11 ALL | 4/1/11-3/31/12 ALL |
|---|---|---|---|---|---|---|---|---|---|---|---|
| Unqualified | | 2 | 2 | 3 | 7 | | 8 | 10 | 5 | 6 | 7 |
| Reviewed | | 32 | 16 | 1 | 49 | | 37 | 31 | 36 | 57 | 49 |
| Compiled | | 15 | 3 | | 18 | | 26 | 23 | 20 | 19 | 18 |
| Tax Returns | 7 | 10 | 4 | | 21 | | 36 | 36 | 33 | 28 | 21 |
| Other | 3 | 18 | 6 | 5 | 32 | | 26 | 23 | 29 | 43 | 32 |
| | 17 (4/1-9/30/11) | | 110 (10/1/11-3/31/12) | | | | | | | | |
| **NUMBER OF STATEMENTS** | 10 | 77 | 31 | 9 | 127 | | 133 | 123 | 123 | 153 | 127 |
| | % | % | % | % | % | **ASSETS** | % | % | % | % | % |
| | 32.3 | 13.7 | 19.9 | | 16.1 | Cash & Equivalents | 14.0 | 11.3 | 14.8 | 13.9 | 16.1 |
| | 23.3 | 41.6 | 40.2 | | 39.3 | A/R - Progress Billings | 35.9 | 33.5 | 34.1 | 24.7 | 39.3 |
| | .0 | 1.2 | 2.4 | | 1.3 | A/R - Current Retention | 1.6 | 1.1 | .8 | 13.5 | 1.3 |
| | 1.2 | 9.5 | 5.5 | | 7.6 | Inventory | 8.0 | 8.8 | 9.2 | 6.4 | 7.6 |
| | .0 | 4.1 | 6.6 | | 4.5 | Cost & Est. Earnings In Excess Billings | 2.2 | 3.1 | 2.9 | 4.5 | 4.5 |
| | 3.8 | 2.0 | 3.0 | | 2.4 | All Other Current | 4.4 | 6.3 | 2.9 | 3.1 | 2.4 |
| | 60.7 | 72.1 | 77.6 | | 71.3 | Total Current | 65.9 | 64.1 | 64.7 | 66.0 | 71.3 |
| | 33.5 | 19.0 | 15.6 | | 20.5 | Fixed Assets (net) | 24.5 | 25.7 | 21.2 | 23.2 | 20.5 |
| | .0 | .2 | .3 | | .2 | Joint Ventures & Investments | .6 | .1 | .5 | .3 | .2 |
| | 3.8 | 1.7 | 1.2 | | 2.0 | Intangibles (net) | 2.8 | 3.4 | 2.9 | 3.3 | 2.0 |
| | 2.0 | 7.0 | 5.3 | | 5.9 | All Other Non-Current | 6.2 | 6.7 | 10.7 | 7.1 | 5.9 |
| | 100.0 | 100.0 | 100.0 | | 100.0 | Total | 100.0 | 100.0 | 100.0 | 100.0 | 100.0 |
| | | | | | | **LIABILITIES** | | | | | |
| | 24.5 | 12.8 | 7.5 | | 12.9 | Notes Payable-Short Term | 14.2 | 13.9 | 14.6 | 10.5 | 12.9 |
| | 13.9 | 19.1 | 24.2 | | 20.0 | A/P - Trade | 19.6 | 18.4 | 17.8 | 16.7 | 20.0 |
| | 3.0 | .0 | .3 | | .3 | A/P - Retention | .2 | .2 | .1 | .3 | .3 |
| | 3.2 | 5.3 | 6.2 | | 5.3 | Billings in Excess of Costs & Est. Earnings | 2.8 | 2.7 | 2.4 | 4.6 | 5.3 |
| | .0 | .4 | .3 | | .3 | Income Taxes Payable | .2 | .1 | .1 | .2 | .3 |
| | 1.0 | 4.2 | 3.5 | | 3.8 | Cur. Mat.-L/T/D | 5.0 | 10.0 | 5.3 | 5.6 | 3.8 |
| | 67.1 | 10.5 | 8.6 | | 14.2 | All Other Current | 7.9 | 9.8 | 8.8 | 7.4 | 14.2 |
| | 112.6 | 52.4 | 50.7 | | 56.9 | Total Current | 50.0 | 55.1 | 49.1 | 45.4 | 56.9 |
| | 17.4 | 14.9 | 6.9 | | 13.8 | Long-Term Debt | 20.6 | 21.0 | 23.8 | 16.3 | 13.8 |
| | .0 | .7 | .2 | | .7 | Deferred Taxes | .1 | 1.4 | .5 | .4 | .7 |
| | 10.1 | 7.0 | .8 | | 5.4 | All Other Non-Current | 3.4 | 4.6 | 3.3 | 5.1 | 5.4 |
| | -40.1 | 24.9 | 41.5 | | 23.2 | Net Worth | 25.8 | 17.9 | 23.4 | 32.8 | 23.2 |
| | 100.0 | 100.0 | 100.0 | | 100.0 | Total Liabilities & Net Worth | 100.0 | 100.0 | 100.0 | 100.0 | 100.0 |
| | | | | | | **INCOME DATA** | | | | | |
| | 100.0 | 100.0 | 100.0 | | 100.0 | Contract Revenues | 100.0 | 100.0 | 100.0 | 100.0 | 100.0 |
| | 56.6 | 29.1 | 19.5 | | 28.9 | Gross Profit | 32.6 | 31.9 | 33.9 | 28.4 | 28.9 |
| | 47.3 | 25.3 | 16.2 | | 24.5 | Operating Expenses | 27.3 | 29.6 | 29.5 | 25.5 | 24.5 |
| | 9.3 | 3.8 | 3.3 | | 4.4 | Operating Profit | 5.3 | 2.3 | 4.4 | 3.0 | 4.4 |
| | 1.0 | 1.0 | .0 | | .9 | All Other Expenses (net) | .7 | .6 | .7 | .5 | .9 |
| | 8.3 | 2.8 | 3.2 | | 3.5 | Profit Before Taxes | 4.7 | 1.6 | 3.7 | 2.5 | 3.5 |
| | | | | | | **RATIOS** | | | | | |
| | 2.5 | 2.7 | 2.4 | | 2.5 | Current | 2.4 | 2.6 | 2.5 | 2.6 | 2.5 |
| | 1.2 | 1.5 | 1.6 | | 1.5 | | 1.5 | 1.5 | 1.4 | 1.5 | 1.5 |
| | .2 | 1.1 | 1.2 | | 1.1 | | 1.0 | .9 | .9 | 1.0 | 1.1 |
| | | 5.9 | 3.8 | | 5.7 | Receivables/Payables | 4.7 | 5.6 | 5.8 | 5.4 | 5.7 |
| | (76) 2.6 | 1.6 | (123) 2.4 | | 2.4 | | (126) 2.4 | (114) 2.2 | (108) 2.4 | (144) 2.6 | (123) 2.4 |
| | 1.6 | 1.1 | | 1.3 | | | 1.1 | 1.0 | 1.2 | 1.3 | 1.3 |
| | 0 UND | 31 11.7 | 30 12.1 | | 30 12.1 | Revenues/Receivables | 22 16.3 | 19 19.4 | 14 25.4 | 24 14.9 | 30 12.1 |
| | 19 19.7 | 58 6.3 | 52 7.0 | | 54 6.7 | | 43 8.5 | 42 8.8 | 39 9.4 | 52 7.0 | 54 6.7 |
| | 45 8.1 | 85 4.3 | 68 5.4 | | 78 4.7 | | 69 5.3 | 64 5.7 | 66 5.5 | 74 4.9 | 78 4.7 |
| | 0 UND | 13 27.5 | 16 22.7 | | 13 28.6 | Cost of Revenues/Payables | 9 40.5 | 7 53.4 | 8 48.6 | 9 40.3 | 13 28.6 |
| | 0 UND | 23 16.1 | 33 11.0 | | 24 15.3 | | 25 14.8 | 22 16.4 | 22 16.5 | 23 15.8 | 24 15.3 |
| | 61 6.0 | 51 7.2 | 51 7.2 | | 51 7.2 | | 49 7.4 | 47 7.8 | 46 8.0 | 53 6.9 | 51 7.2 |
| | 10.3 | 4.7 | 6.2 | | 5.3 | Revenues/Working Capital | 8.3 | 6.8 | 6.3 | 6.5 | 5.3 |
| | 37.4 | 12.4 | 9.6 | | 13.1 | | 15.3 | 15.5 | 18.5 | 11.3 | 13.1 |
| | -7.8 | 37.7 | 29.9 | | 41.0 | | UND | -74.3 | -65.7 | 936.5 | 41.0 |
| | | 11.6 | 64.8 | | 17.2 | EBIT/Interest | 14.8 | 12.3 | 20.2 | 15.3 | 17.2 |
| | (66) 4.1 | (25) 15.0 | (109) 4.9 | | 4.9 | | (123) 5.2 | (109) 2.8 | (108) 5.6 | (134) 4.1 | (109) 4.9 |
| | .1 | 3.2 | | 1.1 | | | 1.7 | -.2 | 1.2 | .8 | 1.1 |
| | | 4.3 | | 8.1 | | Net Profit + Depr., Dep., Amort./Cur. Mat. L/T/D | 14.8 | 5.2 | 8.8 | 8.0 | 8.1 |
| | (18) 1.7 | (24) 3.3 | | 3.3 | | | (21) 7.0 | (19) 2.6 | (18) 3.4 | (24) 2.1 | (24) 3.3 |
| | .1 | | .9 | | | | 1.8 | 1.3 | .3 | .8 | .9 |
| | .3 | .2 | .1 | | .2 | Fixed/Worth | .3 | .2 | .1 | .2 | .2 |
| | 6.2 | .5 | .2 | | .5 | | .6 | .6 | .7 | .5 | .5 |
| | -1.6 | 2.0 | .9 | | 2.0 | | 2.7 | 8.1 | 2.8 | 1.8 | 2.0 |
| | .6 | .6 | .6 | | .6 | Debt/Worth | .9 | .7 | .8 | .6 | .6 |
| | NM | 2.6 | 1.5 | | 2.4 | | 2.7 | 2.1 | 2.3 | 1.8 | 2.4 |
| | -2.7 | 5.3 | 3.2 | | 5.6 | | 10.6 | 38.5 | 18.4 | 6.0 | 5.6 |
| | | 53.7 | 47.2 | | 57.8 | % Profit Before Taxes/Tangible Net Worth | 79.1 | 49.1 | 73.8 | 51.5 | 57.8 |
| | (63) 16.5 | (28) 22.5 | (103) 19.6 | | 19.6 | | (110) 38.9 | (96) 19.7 | (99) 26.7 | (129) 20.0 | (103) 19.6 |
| | .9 | 12.1 | | 4.8 | | | 9.1 | 3.8 | 3.5 | .4 | 4.8 |
| | 57.3 | 17.2 | 21.0 | | 17.9 | % Profit Before Taxes/Total Assets | 25.5 | 18.3 | 25.6 | 16.7 | 17.9 |
| | 10.0 | 6.3 | 11.3 | | 7.3 | | 10.1 | 5.3 | 10.0 | 5.6 | 7.3 |
| | -7.3 | -1.3 | 3.1 | | .3 | | 1.4 | -2.2 | .0 | -.9 | .3 |
| | | .9 | .4 | | .8 | % Depr., Dep., Amort./Revenues | .8 | 1.0 | .7 | .8 | .8 |
| | (58) 2.0 | (27) 1.3 | (96) 1.8 | | 1.8 | | (108) 1.8 | (92) 2.0 | (94) 1.6 | (119) 1.8 | (96) 1.8 |
| | 3.6 | 2.4 | | 3.2 | | | 3.3 | 3.7 | 3.2 | 3.2 | 3.2 |
| | | 2.8 | 1.3 | | 2.7 | % Officers', Directors' Owners' Comp/Revenues | 1.7 | 2.4 | 2.6 | 2.5 | 2.7 |
| | (39) 3.9 | (10) 2.6 | (57) 3.9 | | 3.9 | | (84) 3.9 | (78) 4.2 | (76) 4.7 | (70) 4.1 | (57) 3.9 |
| | 6.1 | 4.3 | | 6.3 | | | 6.6 | 6.9 | 8.5 | 7.4 | 6.3 |
| | 6549M | 356894M | 601214M | 3560410M | 4525067M | Contract Revenues ($) | 25225136M | 22991743M | 926661M | 5669988M | 4525067M |
| | 2501M | 158609M | 203461M | 1709201M | 2073772M | Total Assets ($) | 8639005M | 8446341M | 346370M | 4781974M | 2073772M |

M = $ thousand    MM = $ million
See Pages 9 through 22 for Explanation of Ratios and Data

# CONSTRUCTION
# FINANCIAL MANAGEMENT
# ASSOCIATION DATA

In the following section, we are unable to provide the 2012 CFMA reports due to scheduling. Please contact RMA directly to receive copies of the reports, studies@rmahq.org. eStatement Studies users will be able to access the reports starting on December 1, 2012. We apologize for the inconvenience.

# About the Construction Financial Management Association (CFMA) Data
## Web site: www.cfma.org

Once again, we are delighted to include excerpts from *CFMA's 2012 Construction Industry Annual Financial Survey.* CFMA is **The Source and Resource for Construction Financial Professionals** and has nearly 6,500 members in 89 chapters throughout the U.S. and Canada.

The data presented are based on an online survey to which nearly 4,000 general members employed within U.S. and Canadian construction firms were invited to respond. Additionally, this data was augmented by several hundred firms outside of CFMA member ranks. The data submitted were compiled and analyzed by Real Measures, Inc. (RMi) in cooperation with CFMA. RMi was not engaged to and did not audit or review this information and, accordingly, does not express an opinion or any other form of assurance on it.

Almost all companies **(97.3%)** included in the survey recognize contract revenue and profit in accordance with the percentage of completion method of accounting. Likewise, our Statement Studies contractor data primarily reflects only this method of accounting. It is entirely possible that some of the same contractor companies are included in both the CFMA and Statement Studies data presentations. The inclusion of the CFMA data has not affected our Statement Studies contractor composite data.

Fiscal year-end closing dates reflected in the CFMA survey range from 3/31/11 through 3/31/12. The CFMA data are most comparable to the RMA contractor data from 4/1/1 through 3/31/12 appearing in this edition.

The survey respondents were classified into four categories of construction based on the type of work performed. Classification was based on the level of contract volume reported for various NAICS codes. A contractor was included in a classification if at least one half of its annual contract revenue was attributable to that classification. CFMA categorized certain NAICS codes together. The classifications and NAICS codes included in each are as follows:

## NAICS Codes

**INDUSTRIAL AND NONRESIDENTIAL CONTRACTORS:**
236210  Industrial Building Construction
236220  Commercial and Institutional Building Construction

**HEAVY AND HIGHWAY CONTRACTORS:**
237110  Water and Sewer Line and Related Structures Construction
237120  Oil and Gas Pipeline and Related Structures Construction
237130  Power and Communication Line and Related Structures Construction
237210  Land Subdivision
237310  Highway, Street, and Bridge Construction
237990  Other Heavy and Civil Engineering Construction

**SPECIALTY TRADES CONTRACTORS:**
238110  Poured Concrete Foundation and Structure Contractors
238120  Structural Steel and Precast Concrete Contractors
238130  Framing Contractors
238140  Masonry Contractors
238150  Glass and Glazing Contractors
238160  Roofing Contractors
238170  Siding Contractors
238190  Other Foundation, Structure, and Building Exterior Contractors
238210  Electrical Contractors
238220  Plumbing, Heating, and Air-Conditioning Contractors
238290  Other Building Equipment Contractors
238310  Drywall and Insulation Contractors
238320  Painting and Wall Covering Contractors
238330  Flooring Contractors
238340  Tile and Terrazzo Contractors
238350  Finish Carpentry Contractors
238390  Other Building Finishing Contractors
238910  Site Preparation Contractors
238990  All Other Specialty Trade Contractors
561621  Security Systems Services (except Locksmiths)
562910  Environmental Remediation Services

The CFMA financial data includes balance sheets, statements of earnings, and financial ratios. The balance sheets and statements of earnings represent a weighted average of all companies included in each classification. Percentages are presented for each dollar amount in the financial statements. Due to rounding, the totals may not agree to the sum of various accounts. Such variations are few and insignificant.

The financial ratios are calculated from the composite balance sheets and statements of earnings data. They are not averages of ratios for all companies included in the classification.

If you wish to purchase *CFMA's 2012 Construction Industry Annual Financial Survey* or have questions regarding the data, contact Fern Oram, Associate Director of Product Management; Construction Financial Management Association, 100 Village Blvd, Suite 200, Princeton, NJ 08540; Phone 609-452-8000; Fax 609-452-0474; E-mail foram@cfma.org.

## Interpretation of the
## Construction Financial Management Association (CFMA) Data

CFMA's data should only be regarded as general information. It cannot be used to establish industry norms for a number of reasons, including the following:

(1) The financial statements used in the composite are not selected by any random or statistically reliable method. CFMA members voluntarily submitted their financial data. Note that contractors' statements have no upper asset/sales limit.
(2) Many companies provide varied services; CFMA includes a contractor in a classification if at least one-half (1/2) of its annual contract revenue was completed within that classification.
(3) Some of the NAICS group samples may be rather small in relation to the total number of firms in a given industry category. A relatively small sample can increase the chances that some of our composites do not fully represent an industry group.
(4) There is the chance that an extreme statement can be present in a sample, causing a disproportionate influence on the industry composite. This is particularly true in a relatively small sample.
(5) Companies within the same industry may differ in their method of operations, which in turn can directly influence their financial statements. Since such differences affect financial data included in our sample, our composite calculations could be significantly affected.
(6) Other considerations that can result in variation among different companies engaged in the same general line of business are: different labor markets; geographical location; different accounting methods; quality of service rendered; sources and methods of financing; and terms of sale.

The use of CFMA data may be helpful when considered with other methods of financial analysis. Nevertheless, RMA and CFMA do not recommend the use of CFMA's data to establish norms or parameters for a given industry or grouping, or the industry as a whole. Although CFMA believes that its data is accurate and representative within the confines of the aforementioned reasons, RMA and CFMA specifically make no representations regarding the accuracy of representativeness of the figures printed in this supplement of the RMA Annual Statement Studies.

**PLEASE NOTE:** If you wish to receive the 2012 CFMA data reports, please send your request to studies@rmahq.org. We apologize for any inconvenience.

# TEXT—KEY WORD INDEX
# OF INDUSTRIES APPEARING
# IN THE STATEMENT
# STUDIES

# STATEMENT STUDIES KEY WORD INDEX

*A complete description of each industry category listed below begins on page 35.*

## STATEMENT STUDIES KEY WORD INDEX

*A complete description of each industry category listed below begins on page 35.*

# STATEMENT STUDIES KEY WORD INDEX

*A complete description of each industry category listed below begins on page 35.*

# STATEMENT STUDIES KEY WORD INDEX

*A complete description of each industry category listed below begins on page 35.*

# STATEMENT STUDIES KEY WORD INDEX

*A complete description of each industry category listed below begins on page 35.*

# STATEMENT STUDIES KEY WORD INDEX

*A complete description of each industry category listed below begins on page 35.*

# RMA'S CREDIT & LENDING DICTIONARY

# A

**Absentee Owner:** landlord who does not reside in his or her rental property.

**Abstract of Title:** condensed history of title to land and real property, consisting of ownership transfers and any conveyances or liens that may affect future ownership.

**Acceleration Clause:** provision in note or contract that allows holder to declare remaining balance due and payable immediately upon default in an obligation. Usual causes of default are failure to pay interest or principal installments in a timely manner, an adverse change in financing conditions, or failure to meet loan covenants.

**Acceptance:** drawee's signed agreement to honor draft as presented, which consists of signature alone, but will frequently be evidenced by drawee writing word "accepted," date it is payable, and signature. Sometimes called Trade Acceptance or Banker's Acceptance, depending upon function of acceptor.

**Accommodation:** 1. lending or extending credit to borrower. 2. loan or commitment to lend money.

**Accord and Satisfaction:** agreement between two or more persons or entities that satisfies or discharges obligation or settles claim or lawsuit. Generally involves disputed matter in which one party agrees to give and other party agrees to accept something in satisfaction different from, and usually less than, that originally asked for.

**Account:** 1. statement showing balance along with detailed explanation covering debits and credits. 2. right of payment for goods sold or leased or for services rendered on open account basis. 3. summarized record of financial transaction. 4. customer.

**Accountant:** person in charge of and skilled in the recording of financial transactions and maintenance of financial records.

**Accounting:** 1. theory and system of classifying, recording, summarizing, and auditing books of firm. 2. art of analyzing, interpreting, and reporting financial position and operating results of business.

**Account Manager:** 1. sometimes called Relationship Manager or Account Officer. 2. person responsible for overseeing all matters relating to a specific client or group of customers.

**Account Number:** unique identification number used to designate specific customer.

**Accounts Payable:** short-term liability representing amounts due trade creditors.

**Accounts Payable Department:** section of business office responsible for processing open account balances and paying amounts owed for goods and services purchased.

**Accounts Receivable:** money due to a business by its customers for goods sold or services performed on open account (or credit). Usually refers to short-term receivables.

**Accounts Receivable Aging Report:** report by customer that lists age of accounts receivable generally by 30-day intervals from invoice or due date. See also Aging of Accounts Receivable.

**Accounts Receivable Financing:** form of secured lending in which borrowings are typically limited to percentage of receivables pledged as collateral.

**Accrual Accounting:** basis of accounting in which expenses are recorded when incurred and revenues are recognized when earned, regardless of when cash is actually paid or received.

**Accrue:** 1. something gained, added, or accumulated, such as profit from a business transaction. 2. right to sue has become exercisable.

**Accrued Expenses:** short-term liabilities that represent expenses for goods used but not yet paid.

**Accrued Income:** income earned but not yet collected.

**Accrued Interest:** interest accumulated since last interest payment due date.

**Accrued Liabilities:** expenses or obligations for goods or services incurred but not yet paid.

**ACH:** see Automated Clearinghouse.

**Acid Test:** ratio between company's most liquid assets (generally, cash and accounts receivable) and current liabilities that represents the degree to which current liabilities can be paid with those assets.

**Acknowledgment:** 1. declaration making known receipt of something done or to be done; confirmation of receipt of order or of terms of contract. 2. statement of notary or other competent officer certifying that signature on document was personally signed by individual whose signature is affixed to instrument.

**Acquisition:** merger or taking over of controlling interest of one business by another.

**Acquisition and Development Loan:** loan made for the purpose of purchasing a property and completing all on-site improvements such as street layout, utility installation, and community area grading necessary to bring the site to a buildable state.

**Acquittal:** 1. release from obligation or contract. 2. to have accusation of crime dismissed by some formal legal procedure.

**Active Account:** 1. customer who makes frequent purchases. 2. bank account in which regular deposits or withdrawals are made.

**Activity Charge:** service charge imposed for check or deposit activity or any other maintenance charge.

**Act of God:** event that could not be prevented by reasonable foresight, is caused exclusively by forces and violence of nature, and is uninfluenced by human power (storm, flood, earthquake, or lightning).

**Additional Dating:** means of extending credit beyond normal sales terms, granted to induce buyers to place orders in advance of season or for other special reasons. See also Advance Dating and Dating.

**Adjudication:** judgment rendered by court, primarily used in bankruptcy proceedings.

**Adjustable Interest Rate:** interest rate on loan that may be adjusted up or down at specific intervals. Index used in determining adjusted interest rate and potential frequency of adjustments must be stated in loan documents.

**Adjustable Rate Mortgage:** loan is pursuant to an agreement executed at the inception of the loan that permits creditor to adjust interest rate from time to time based on a specific interest rate index.

**Adjuster:** person who deals with insured party to settle amount of loss, claim, or debt.

**Adjustment:** 1. settlement of disputed account. 2. change or concession in price or terms. 3. determining amount one is to receive in settlement of claim. 4. in accounting, entry made to correct or compensate for error or difference in account.

**Adjustment Bureau:** organization that supervises debt extensions and compromise arrangements or oversees orderly liquidation of troubled businesses for benefit of creditors.

**Advance:** 1. payment made before it is due. 2. disbursement of loan proceeds.

**Advance Dating:** additional time granted customers to pay for goods received and to earn available discounts. See also Additional Dating and Dating.

**Advancement of Costs:** prepayment of necessary legal expenses. Such charges, set by law, may be for commencement of suit and vary in different courts and states. Some items for which prepaid costs may be requested are filing fees, process serving, premiums on court bonds, trial fees, posting security for costs, entering judgment, recording abstract of judgment, issue execution, and discovery actions after judgment.

**Advertising Allowance:** promotional discount in price or payment given customers who share expense of advertising supplier's product.

**Affidavit:** voluntary written statement of facts pertaining to a transaction or event, signed under oath and witnessed by an authorized person.

**Affiliate:** business entity connected with another through common ownership or management, usually responsible for payment of its own obligations.

**After-Acquired Property:** security interest by which secured creditor automatically obtains interest in assets that debtor acquires after lien had been filed.

**Agency:** legal relationship between two parties in which one is authorized to act for another.

**Agent:** person legally authorized to act for another.

**Agent Bank:** formal designation that applies to a bank responsible for negotiating, structuring, and overseeing a loan or commitment to a borrower in which more than one bank is involved. See also Lead Bank.

**Aggregate Balances:** combined total of two or more demand deposit accounts, money markets, or time certificates of deposit. Term can also be applied to credit facility totals.

**Aging of Accounts Receivable:** accounting record of customer's receivables showing how long receivables have remained unpaid beyond regular terms of sale. Used as basis for advancing credit.

**Agreement:** a contract involving an offer and an acceptance between two or more parties, governing the terms of the contract and binding on the parties to the agreement (e.g., a loan agreement, security agreement, or guaranty).

**AKA:** see Also Known As.

**Alert Action:** a series of information services provided by credit reporting agencies; provides subscribers with listing of specific accounts on which unfavorable payment condition has recently been reported.

**Allegation:** statement of party to action, setting out what he or she intends to prove or contend.

**ALLL:** see Allowance for Loan and Lease Losses.

**Allocation:** sub-limit within a total credit facility that is to be used for a specific purpose.

**Allonge:** paper attached to a negotiable instrument for additional endorsements or other terms and conditions.

**Allowance:** accounting provision used to set aside amounts for depreciation, returns, or bad debts.

**Allowance for Bad Debts:** contra account against which uncollectible receivables are charged. See also Bad Debt Reserve.

**Allowance for Loan and Lease Losses (ALLL):** contra account, generally found on asset side of balance sheet as deduction from total loans outstanding; amount is intended to cover future losses of loans currently in the financial institution's portfolio. The ALLL should be adjusted monthly, concurrently with the generation of current financial statements.

**Also Known As (AKA):** sometimes used to designate a fictitious trade style or name.

**ALTA Policy:** an extended coverage title insurance policy that protects the lender against losses resulting from any defects in the title or claims against the property. The policy's coverage includes encroachments, mechanic's liens, and other matters that a physical inspection or inquiry of the parties would disclose.

**Altered Check:** check on which original entries have been changed (date, payee, or amount); financial institutions generally refuse to honor or pay checks that have been altered.

**Amend:** to correct, add to, or alter legal document.

**Amicus Curiae:** friend of court; uninvolved third party who intervenes in lawsuit, with court's permission, to introduce information or arguments in respect to the issue or principle of law to be decided.

**Amortization:** 1. reduction of loan by periodic principal payments. 2. decline in the book value of an intangible asset over the period owned.

**Amortization Tables:** calculation charts showing amounts required periodically to discharge debts over various periods of time and at different interest rates.

**Amortize:** 1. to write off the value of an intangible asset over the period owned. 2. to reduce or pay off debt or obligation by making periodic payments of principal.

**Annual Percentage Rate (APR):** annual cost of credit expressed as percentage; creditors are required under Federal Truth in Lending Act to disclose true annual interest on consumer loans, as well as the total dollar cost and other terms of loan.

**Annual Report:** yearly report detailing a company's comparative financial and organizational conditions.

**Annuity:** series of fixed periodic payments made at regular intervals.

**Antecedent Credit Information:** historical record of significant business information concerning individuals who are involved in ownership or management of business enterprise.

**Anticipation:** bridge loan made to a municipal or government borrower to cover expenses until revenue or tax proceeds are collected.

**Appeal:** complaint made to higher court by either plaintiff or defendant for court's review, correction, or reversal of lower court's decision.

**Appearance:** coming into court formally as plaintiff or defendant in lawsuit.

**Appraisal:** opinion of current value of real or personal property based upon cost of replacement, market, income, or fair value analysis.

**Appreciation:** increase in value of asset over its cost due to economic and other conditions. Property that increases in value as result of improvements or additions is not considered to have appreciated.

**Appropriation:** sum of money designated for a special purpose only.

**APR:** See *Annual Percentage Rate.*

**Arbitration:** submission for settlement of disputed matter, by nonjudicial means, to one or more impartial or disinterested third persons selected by disputants.

**Arm's Length:** business transaction between two or more parties that is open, sincere, and without personal influence, favoritism, or close relations.

**Arrangement:** plan for corporate reorganization for rescheduling or extension of time for payment of unsecured debts, such as an arrangement under Chapter 11 or 13 of the U. S. Bankruptcy Code.

**Arrears:** total or partial debt amounts that remain unpaid and past due.

**Articles of Agreement:** any written statement or contract, terms to which all parties consent.

**Articles of Incorporation:** formal papers that set forth pertinent data for formation of corporation and are filed with appropriate state agency.

**Assess:** 1. to fix rate or amount. 2. to set value of real and personal property, as for tax purposes.

**Assessed Value:** in the case of real property, value set by government agency for purpose of levying taxes.

**Asset:** 1. anything owned having monetary value. 2. item listed on left-hand side of balance sheet representing cash, or property, real or personal, belonging to an individual or company and convertible to cash.

**Assigned Account:** 1. account receivable pledged by borrower to factor or lender as security. 2. past-due customer whose account has been placed with collection agency.

**Assigned Risk:** insurance plan that provides coverage for risks rejected by regular markets and in which all licensed insurers are made to participate by various state laws.

**Assignee:** person to whom some rights, authority, or property is assigned.

**Assignment:** 1. written contract for transfer of one's title, legal rights, or property from one person to another. 2. in some states, form used to transfer claim to agency that undertakes collection of account for benefit of assigning creditor.

**Assignment for the Benefit of Creditors:** A liquidation technique in which an insolvent debtor goes out of business and an assignee facilitates the transfer of the insolvent debtor's estate for administration and payment of debts. Property transferred to assignee places such assets beyond control of debtor or reach of creditors.

**Assignment of Claim:** claim assigned to third party for collection.

**Assignor:** 1. one who transfers claim, right, or property. 2. individual, partnership, or corporation making assignment.

**Assumed Liability:** acknowledgment of responsibility for payment of obligation by third party.

**At Sight:** words used in negotiable instrument directing that payment be made upon presentation or demand.

**Attached Account:** legally frozen account on which payments have been suspended; release or disbursement of funds can be made only after court order.

**Attachment:** 1. legal writ or process by which debtor's property (or any interest therein) is seized and placed in custody of law. 2. Supplemental data provided as clarifying information to a document.

**Attorney-in-Fact:** private attorney who has written authorization to act for another. This authority is given by an instrument called power of attorney.

**Attorney of Record:** lawyer whose name must appear in permanent court records as person acting on behalf of party in legal matter.

**Auction:** public sale of property that is sold to highest bidder.

**Audit:** to examine a firm's records, accounts, or procedures for purpose of substantiating or verifying individual transactions or to confirm if assets and liabilities are properly accounted for, including income and expense items.

**Audited Financial Statements:** financial statements that have been examined by an independent certified public accountant to determine if the financial statements present fairly the financial position, results of operations, and cash flows in conformity with generally accepted accounting principles.

**Auditor:** person who deals with examination and verification of financial accounts and with making financial reports.

**Auditor's Report:** part of complete set of financial statements that explains degree of responsibility that independent accountant assumed for expressing an opinion on management's financial statements and assurance that is provided by said opinion.

**Automated Cash Application:** computerized procedures enabling payments to be quickly and automatically applied to accounts receivable.

**Automated Clearinghouse (ACH):** computer-based clearing and settlement facility for interchange of electronic debits and credits among financial institutions. ACH entries can be substituted for checks in recurring payments such as mortgages or in direct deposit distribution of federal and corporate benefits payments. Federal Reserve Banks furnish data processing services for most ACHs, although some are privately operated. Final settlement, or net settlement, of ACH transfers is made against reserve accounts at Federal Reserve Banks.

**Available Balance:** checking account balance that the customer actually may use; that is, current balance less deposits not yet cleared through the account.

**Average Collected Balances:** average dollar amount on deposit in checking accounts defined as the difference between ledger balance and deposit float, or those deposits posted to the account but having not yet cleared the financial institution upon which they are drawn. See also Uncollected Funds.

**Average Collection Period:** average number of days required to convert accounts receivable to cash.

**Average Daily Balance:** average amount of money that depositor keeps on deposit when calculated on a daily basis.

## B

**Backdating:** predating document prior to date on which it was drawn.

**Backlog:** amount of revenue expected to be realized from work to be performed on uncompleted contracts, including new contractual agreements on which work has not begun.

**Bad Check Laws:** laws enacted in various states to encourage and facilitate lawful use of checks; statutes differ in various jurisdictions and are generally enforced according to state laws as well as local custom and usage.

**Bad Debt:** account receivable that proves uncollectible in normal course of business; full payment is doubtful.

**Bad Debt Ratio:** ratio of bad debt expense to sales, used as measure of quality of accounts receivable.

**Bad Debt Reserve:** reserve or provision for accounts receivables to be charged off company's books based on historical levels of bad debts or industry averages.

**Balance:** amount owed or unpaid on loan or credit transaction. Also called outstanding or unpaid balance.

**Balance Due:** total amount owed after applying debits and credits of account.

**Balance Sheet:** A financial statement listing the assets, liabilities, and owner's equity of a business entity or individual as of a specific date.

**Balloon Payment:** lump-sum payment of principal and sometimes accrued interest, usually due at end of term of installment loan in which periodic installments of principal and interest did not fully amortize loan.

**Bank:** financial institution chartered by state or federal government to transact financial business that includes receiving deposits, lending money, exchanging currencies, providing safekeeping, and investing money.

**Bank Draft:** sight or demand draft (order to pay) drawn by a bank (drawer) on its account at another bank (drawee).

**Banker's Acceptance:** draft or order to pay specified amount at specified time not to exceed 270 days, drawn on individuals, business firms, or financial institutions; draft becomes accepted when a financial institution formally acknowledges its obligation to honor such draft, usually by writing or stamping "Accepted" on face of instrument. When accepted in this manner, draft becomes liability of bank. See also *Draft* and *Time Draft.*

**Bank Overdraft:** check presented for collection for which there are not sufficient funds on deposit to make normal payment. Financial institution may honor such check, considering payment as loan to depositor for which the institution will usually collect interest or service charge.

**Bankrupt:** debtor who is unable to meet debt obligations as they become due or is insolvent and whose assets are administered for benefit of creditors.

**Bankruptcy:** Legal action taken under the U.S. Bankruptcy Code by or against an insolvent debtor who is unable to meet obligations as they become due. The bankrupt, if given discharge, is released from further liability of most debts listed as of the date of the bankruptcy filing.

• *Voluntary Bankruptcy:* any individual, partnership, corporation, estate, trust, or governmental unit may be afforded protection of debtor under U.S. Bankruptcy Code by filing petition. Exceptions: railroads, insurance or banking corporations, building and loan associations.

• *Involuntary Bankruptcy:* involuntary petition can be filed in bankruptcy court by three or more creditors or, if there are fewer than 12 creditors, by any one creditor. Petitioning creditors' claims must aggregate at least $5,000 in excess of value of any collateral of debtor. Involuntary cases may be filed against individuals, partnerships, or corporations other than farmers and nonprofit corporations and may be instituted under either Chapter 7 or Chapter 11 of the U.S. Bankruptcy Code. Involuntary petition must allege one of two grounds for relief: either that the debtor is generally not paying debts as they become due, or that the non-bankruptcy custodian, other than one appointed to enforce lien on less than substantially all of debtor's property, was appointed for, or took possession of, substantially all of debtor's property within 120 days of filing.

• *Chapter 7 Cases:* liquidation proceedings, formerly referred to as "straight bankruptcy," wherein nonexempt assets of debtor are converted to cash and proceeds distributed pro rata among creditors.

• *Chapter 9 Cases:* reorganization proceedings wherein municipality that is insolvent or unable to meet debts as they mature effects plan to adjust such debts.

• *Chapter 11 Cases:* reorganization proceedings available to all business enterprises; may be instituted either by debtor or creditor(s). For plan to be confirmed by court under Chapter 11, each class of creditors, as set forth in such plan, must accept plan or each class must receive at least that which it would receive on liquidation. Class of creditors has accepted plan when majority in number and two-thirds in dollar amount of those creditors actually voting approve it.

• *Chapter 12 Cases:* reorganization proceedings for agricultural concerns and small family-owned farms having debts under $1.5 million.

• *Chapter 13 Cases:* reorganization cases that may be instituted only by individuals with regular income who owe unsecured debts of less than $100,000 and secured debts of less than $350,000, other than stockbroker or commodity broker. For plan to be confirmed, it must provide for submission to trustee of all or any portion of debtor's future earnings as necessary for execution of plan, payment in full of all priority claims, and equal treatment of each member of class of creditors. While consent of unsecured creditors is not required, value of what they receive under plan may not be less than if debtor were liquidated.

**Bankruptcy Judge:** presiding judge of court in which bankruptcy cases are heard. (Formerly called Referee in Bankruptcy.) Duties of judge include supervising administrative details of bankrupt estates and ruling on all matters involving debtor-creditor problems.

**Basis:** 1. number of days used in calculating interest earned in investment or interest payable on bank loan. Also called accrual base. 2. original cost of asset plus capital improvements from which any taxable gains (or losses) are determined after deducting depreciation expenses.

**Basis Point:** 1/100th of a percent; 100 basis points equal 1%.

**Bearer:** negotiable item (check, note, bill, or draft) in which no payee is indicated or payee is shown as "cash" or "bearer." Item is payable to person in possession of it or to person who presents it for payment.

**Bearer Paper:** instrument that is made "payable to bearer." When negotiable instrument is endorsed in blank, it becomes bearer paper and can be transferred by delivery since it does not require endorsement.

**Beneficiary:** 1. person or organization named in will to inherit or receive property. 2. person or organization to whom insurance policy is payable. 3. person or organization for whose benefit trust is created.

**Bid Bond:** bond issued by surety on behalf of contractor that provides assurance to recipient of contractor's bid that if bid is accepted, contractor will execute contract and provide performance bond. Under bond, surety is obligated to pay recipient difference between contractor's bid and bid of next lowest responsible bidder if bid is accepted and contractor fails to execute contract or to provide performance bond.

**Billing Cycle:** number of days between payment due dates.

**Bill of Costs:** certified itemization of costs associated with lawsuit.

**Bill of Lading:** written instrument signed by common carrier or agent identifying freight and representing both receipt and contract for shipment. It must show name of consignee, description of goods, terms of carrier's contract, and directions for assigning to specific person at specific place. In form of negotiable instrument, it is evidence of holding title to goods being shipped.

**Bill of Sale:** written instrument evidencing transfer of title of specific personal property to buyer.

**Binder:** 1. written agreement that provides temporary legal protection pending issuance of final contract or policy. 2. temporary insurance contract; may be oral or written; also called cover note.

**Blank Endorsement:** endorser's writing on check, promissory note, or bill of exchange without indicating party to whom it is payable. Endorser merely signs his or her name, making the instrument "payable to bearer." Also called endorsement in blank.

**Blanket Coverage:** property coverage applicable to group of exposures (buildings, inventory, equipment, etc., combined or individually, at one or more locations), in single total amount of insurance; contrasts with Specific Coverage.

**Blanket Mortgage:** mortgage secured by two or more parcels of real property, frequently used by developers who acquire large tract of land for subdivision and resale to individual homeowners. Also called blanket trust deed.

**Bond:** contract issued by insurance or bonding company in support of principal's obligation to obligee. See also *Fidelity Bond* and *Surety Bond.*

**Bonded Warehouse:** federally approved warehouse under bond for strict observance of revenue laws; used for storing goods until duties are paid or property is otherwise released. Bonded warehouse assures owner of property that operators of warehouse are insured against loss by fraud and will keep proper inventory and accounting of goods in transit.

**Bonding Company:** company authorized to issue bid bonds, performance bonds, labor and materials bonds, or other types of surety bonds.

**Book Value:** 1. company's net worth calculated by adding total assets minus total liabilities. 2. value of asset (cost plus additions, less depreciation) shown on books or financial report of an entity.

**Borrower's Certificate:** A document required under a loan or other agreement to be submitted by the borrower or another designated party to certify the value of collateral and compliance with the terms of the agreement.

**Bottom Line:** (colloq.) final price, net profit, or end results.

**Branch Banking:** multioffice banking. Branch is any banking facility away from bank's main office that accepts deposits or makes loans. State laws strictly control opening of new banking offices by state-chartered banks, national banks, and thrift institutions.

**Breach of Contract:** failure to fulfill terms of contract, in part or whole.

**Breach of Warranty:** 1. failure to fully disclose information about condition of property or insured party. 2. failure to perform as promised.

**Break-Even Analysis:** A method of determining the number of units that must be sold at a given price to recover all fixed and variable costs.

**Break-even Point:** 1. point at which total sales are equal to total expenses. May be expressed in units or dollars. 2. amount received from sale that exactly equals amount of expense or cost.

**Bridge Loan:** loan that provides liquidity until defined event occurs that will generate cash, such as sale of noncurrent asset, replacement financing, or equity infusion.

**Bulk Sales Acts:** statutes designed to prevent defrauding of creditors through secret sale in bulk of merchant's goods. Most states require notice of proposed sale to all creditors.

**Burden of Proof:** 1. duty of producing sufficient evidence to prove position taken in lawsuit. 2. necessity of proving fact or facts as to truth of claim.

**Business:** 1. commercial, industrial, or mercantile activity engaged in by individual, partnership, corporation, or other form of organization for purpose of making, buying, or selling goods or services at profit. 2. occupation, profession, or trade.

**Business Failure:** 1. suspension of business resulting from insolvency or bankruptcy. 2. inability to fulfill normal business obligations.

**Business Interruption Insurance:** property insurance written to cover loss of profits and continuing expenses as result of shutdown by insured peril; exposure is classified as consequential loss. Also called earnings insurance.

**Buyer's Market:** market condition in which supply exceeds demand, which causes prices to decline.

**Buy Out:** to purchase at least a controlling percentage of a company's stock to take over its assets.

**Bylaws:** set of rules or regulations adopted to control internal affairs of organization.

## C

**C's of Credit:** the "Five C's" of credit. A longstanding means of evaluating a customer by investigating Character, Collateral, Capacity, Conditions, and Capital.

**Calendar Year:** 12-month accounting period ending December 31.

**Callable Loan:** loan payable on demand.

**Canceled Check:** check that has been paid by a financial institution and on which the financial institution has imprinted evidence of payment so that it cannot be presented again.

**Cancellation Clause:** provision in contract or agreement allowing parties to rescind agreement under certain conditions.

**Capacity:** one of the "Five C's" of credit; a customer's ability to successfully absorb merchandise and to pay for the merchandise. Refers to customer's ability to produce sufficient cash so as to meet obligations when due.

**Capital:** 1. one of the "Five Cs" of credit; refers to financial resources the customer has at the time order is placed and those that he or she is likely to have when payment is due. 2. amount invested in business by owners or stockholders. 3. owner's equity in the business.

**Cash:** 1. money readily available for current expenditures; usually consists of cash on hand or money in a financial institution. 2. money equivalent, such as a check, paid at time of purchase. 3. any medium of exchange that the financial institution will accept at face value upon deposit.

**Cash Basis Accounting:** basis of accounting in which revenues and expenses are reported in the income statement when cash is received or paid out for the time period in which the revenues and expenses occur.

**Cash Basis Loan:** loan on which interest payments are recorded when collected from borrower. This is a loan in which the borrower has fallen behind on interest payments and is classified as a nonaccrual asset.

**Cash Concentration and Disbursement (CCD):** corporate electronic payment used in business-to-business and intracompany transfers of funds. Funds are cleared on overnight basis through nationwide automated clearinghouse network.

**Cash Equivalents:** accounting term for actual cash on hand and total of bank deposits.

**Cash Flow:** is based on an activity format, which classifies cash inflows and outflows in terms of operating, investing, and financing activities.

**Cashier's Check:** check drawn on financial institution's account, becoming direct obligation of the financial institution.

**Cash Management Account:** special type of deposit service that permits corporate customers to invest cash in demand deposit account until needed for operations.

**Cash Surrender Value:** in life insurance, amount payable under whole life policy when terminated by insured.

**Casualty Insurance:** coverage for automobile, liability, crime, boiler and machinery, health, bonds, aviation, workers' compensation, and other miscellaneous lines; contrasts with Property Insurance.

**Certificate of Insurance:** written statement issued by insurer indicating that insurance policy has been issued and showing details of coverage at time certificate was written; used as evidence of insurance.

**Certified Check:** depositor's check confirmed on its face as good by a financial institution and stamped "certified." It is then dated and signed by an authorized officer of the institution. Such check becomes an obligation of the financial institution, which guarantees that it is holding sufficient funds to cover payment of check on demand.

**Certified Copy of Policy:** document that provides evidence of insurance as of certain date; coverage may be terminated or changed after certification.

**Certified Public Accountant (CPA):** one who has been trained to do accounting and who has passed state test and received title of CPA; title certifies holder's qualification to practice accounting, audit, prepare reports, and analyze accounting information.

**CGL:** see *Comprehensive General Liability.*

**Character:** one of the "Five Cs" of credit; refers to evaluating qualities that would impel debtor to meet his or her obligations. Generally identified as customer's reputation, responsibility, integrity, and honesty.

**Charge-Off:** portion of principal balance of a loan or account receivable that an entity considers uncollectible; this amount may be partially or fully recovered in future. Also called a *Write-Off.*

**Chart of Accounts:** listing of all financial accounts or categories (usually numbered) into which business transactions are classified and recorded.

**Chattel:** item of tangible personal property, animate or inanimate, as distinguished from real property.

**Chattel Mortgage:** instrument of sale in which debtor transfers title in property to creditor as security for debt. Failure by debtor to comply with terms of contract may cause creditor's title in property to become absolute.

**Check:** order on a financial institution for payment of funds from depositor's account and payable on demand.

**Claim:** 1. action to recover payment, reimbursement, or compensation from entity legally liable for damage or injury.

**Claimant:** one who makes claim or asserts right.

**Cleanup:** period during which particular loan or entire borrowing has been paid off; out-of-debt period required under line of credit.

**Clearinghouse:** association of financial institutions or security dealers created to permit daily settlement and exchange of checks or delivery of stocks and other items between members in local geographic area.

**Closed-End Credit:** consumer installment loan made for predetermined amount, calling for periodic payments of principal and interest over specified period or term. Finance charge may be fixed or variable rate. Borrower does not have option of obtaining extra funds under original loan agreement. Contrasts with Open-End Credit.

**Cloud on Title:** outstanding claim or encumbrance on property that may impair owner's title.

**Cognovit Note:** form of promissory note or statement that allows creditor, in case of default by debtor, to enter judgment without trial. (Not recognized in all jurisdictions.)

**Collateral:** 1. one of the "Five C's" of credit; refers to real or personal property that may be available as security. 2. asset pledged by borrower in support of loan. See also *Secured Loan.*

**Collateral Note:** form of promissory note given for loan, pledging real or personal property as security for payment of debt.

**Collectible:** account capable of being collected.

**Collection Agency:** professional business service employed as agent to collect creditors' unpaid (past-due) accounts. Collection agency is usually compensated by receiving agreed upon contingent percentage of amount collected.

**Collection Agency Report:** report from collection agency that informs client of results of collection efforts, investigations, or recommendations.

**Collection Charges:** 1. fees charged by bank for collecting drafts, notes, coupons, or other instruments. 2. compensation paid to collection agency or attorney for collecting delinquent accounts.

**Collection Item:** 1. term for item received for collection that is to be credited to depositor's account after payment. Most financial institutions charge special (collection) fees for handling such items. 2. past due account assigned for collection.

**Collection Period:** number of days required for company's receivables to be collected and converted to cash.

**Comaker:** person who signs (and guarantees) note of another and by so doing promises to pay in full. See also *Cosigner.*

**Commensurate:** describes deposit balances that are in acceptable proportion to size of loan or commitment.

**Commercial Debt:** loan or obligation incurred for business purposes.

**Commercial Law League of America (C.L.L.A.):** national membership organization of commercial attorneys, commercial credit and collection agencies, credit insurance companies, and law list publishers. Objectives include setting standards for honorable dealings among members, improving the practice of commercial law, and promoting uniformity of legislation affecting commercial law.

**Commercial Paper:** short-term securities such as notes, drafts, bills of exchange, and other negotiable paper that arise out of commercial activity and become due on a definite maturity date.

**Commercial Property:** real estate used for business purposes or managed so as to produce income from rents and leases.

**Commitment:** agreement between a financial institution and borrower to make funds available under certain conditions for a specified period of time.

**Commitment Fee:** lender's charge for holding credit available, usually replaced with interest when funds are advanced, as in revolving credit. In business credit, a commitment fee is often charged for unused portion of line of credit.

**Commitment Letter:** letter from lender stating willingness to advance funds to named borrower, repayable at specified rate and time period, subject to escape clause(s) allowing lender to rescind agreement in event of materially adverse changes in borrower's financial condition.

**Committee Approval:** credit is approved by several people acting as group.

**Common Law:** body of law that was originated, developed, and administered in England.

**Community Property:** property shared by husband and wife, each having one-half interest in earnings of other; form of joint property ownership in some states.

**Community Reinvestment Act of 1977 (CRA):** federal law that requires mortgage lenders to demonstrate their commitment to home mortgage financing in economically disadvantaged areas. Prohibits redlining or credit allocation based on geographic region and requires lenders to file annual compliance statements.

**Compensating Balance:** demand deposit balance that must be maintained by borrower to compensate financial institution for loan accommodations and other services.

**Compound Interest:** interest calculated by adding accumulated interest to date to original principal. New balance becomes principal for additional interest calculations.

**Comprehensive General Liability (CGL):** policy form providing automatic coverage for all insured's business operations; may include auto exposures; newer form of CGL is called commercial general liability.

**Concession:** 1. granting of special privilege to digress from regular terms or previous conditions. 2. allowance or rebate from established price. 3. business enterprise operated under special permission.

**Conditional Sales Contract:** contract for sale of goods under which possession is delivered to buyer but title retained by seller until goods are paid for in full or until other conditions are met. In most states, conditional sales contracts have been replaced by security agreements having substantially the same definition under Uniform Commercial Code.

**Conditions:** one of the "Five C's" of credit; refers to general business environment and status of borrower's industry.

**Confession of Judgment Note:** note in which (after maturity) debtor permits attorney to appear in court and have judgment entered if payment is not made as agreed. Acceptance of note varies by state. See also *Cognovit Note.*

**Confirmation:** 1. supplier's written acknowledgment that he or she has accepted buyer's order. 2. customer's written verification of order previously placed. 3. proof verifying agreement or existence of assets and liabilities or claims against assets and liabilities.

**Consent Judgment:** judgment that debtor allows to be entered against him or her by motion filed with court.

**Consideration:** 1. element in contract without which contract is not binding. Contract is generally not valid without consideration. 2. reason for contracting parties to enter into contract. Act, promise, price, or motive for which agreement is entered into. 3. value given in exchange for benefit that is to be derived from contract. 4. compensation. Exchange of consideration is usually mutual, each party giving something up to other.

**Consign:** to send or forward goods to merchant, factor, or agent for sale with title retained by seller and with payment delayed, generally until sale is made.

**Consignee:** person or entity to which goods or property is consigned or shipped; ultimate recipient of shipment.

**Consignment:** arrangement under which consignor (seller) remains owner of property until such time as consignee (buyer) pays for goods; usually consignee pays consignor when goods are sold or holds proceeds of sale in trust for benefit of consignor.

**Consignor:** 1. one who delivers shipment or turns it over to carrier for transportation and delivery. 2. one who consigns goods to be sold without giving up title.

**Consolidated Financial Statement:** combined statement showing financial condition of parent corporation and its subsidiaries.

**Consolidating Financial Statement:** combined statement of subsidiary and parent companies that shows complete statement for each entity without netting intercompany transactions.

**Construction Loan:** interim financing for development and construction of real property, generally converted to long-term financing upon completion of construction.

**Consumer Credit:** debt incurred for personal, family, or household use.

**Consumer Credit Protection Act (Truth in Lending Act of 1968):** law that requires most lenders and those who extend consumer credit to disclose true credit costs. Act provides for limits on garnishment of wages, prohibits excessive interest, and makes available contents of consumer credit reports.

**Consumer Sale Disclosure Statement:** form required to be provided by creditor to customer, disclosing finance charge details as required under Consumer Credit Protection Act.

**Contingent Fee:** fee to be paid only in event of specific occurrence, usually successful results. Arrangement, for example, in which collection agency will receive stated percentage of any amounts recovered or in which lawyer will receive payment only if successful in prosecuting lawsuit.

**Contingent Liability:** liability in which a person(s) or business(es) is indirectly responsible for obligations of a third party. Such indirect liability is usually established by guaranty or endorsement, and the liability holder may turn to guarantors or endorsers for satisfaction of debt. See also Endorsement and Guaranty.

**Contra Account:** account that partially or wholly offsets another account or balance.

**Contract:** agreement between two or more entities or legally competent persons that creates, modifies, or destroys legal arrangement.

**Controlled Disbursement:** funds management technique in corporate cash management designed to maximize funds available for temporary investment in money market or for payment to trade creditors. Controls flow of checks through banking system to meet corporate investment and funds management requirements. Contrasts with delayed disbursement. See also *Federal Reserve Float* and *Treasury Workstation.*

**Controller:** person in business organization responsible for finances, internal auditing, and accounting systems in use in company's operations.

**Conversion:** process of consolidating or transferring data from one system to another.

**Conveyance:** 1. transfer of right, generally instrument transferring interest in real estate in form of deed. 2. transfer of property ownership (sometimes includes leases and mortgages) from one person or organization to another.

**Copyright:** intangible right granted to author or originator by federal government to solely and exclusively reproduce or publish specific literary, musical, or artistic work for certain number of years.

**Corporate Reorganization:** see *Bankruptcy.*

**Corporate Veil:** convention that corporate organization insulates organization's owners from liability for corporate activities.

**Corporation:** artificial person or legal entity organized under and treated by state laws, legally distinct from its shareholders and vested with capacity of continuous succession irrespective of changes in its ownership either in perpetuity or for limited term. It may be set up to contract, own, and discharge business within boundaries of powers granted it by its corporate charter.

**Correspondent:** organization or individual that carries on business relations or acts as agent with others in different cities or countries.

**Cosigner:** one of joint signers of loan documents. One who signs note of another as support for credit of the principal maker.

**Cost of Funds:** dollar cost of interest paid or accrued on funds acquired from various sources within bank and borrowed funds acquired from other financial institutions, including time deposits, advances at Federal Reserve discount window, federal funds purchased, and Eurodollar deposits. Financial institution may use internal cost of funds in pricing loans it makes.

**Covenant:** written agreement, convention, or promise between parties who pledge to do or not to do certain things or that stipulates truth of certain facts.

**CPA:** see *Certified Public Accountant.*

**CRA:** see *Community Reinvestment Act of 1977.*

**Crash:** sudden sharp decrease in business activity that can negatively affect stock market volumes and prices.

**Credit:** 1. privilege of buying goods and services, or for borrowing money in return for promise of future payment. 2. in bookkeeping, entry on ledger signifying cash payment, merchandise returned, or allowance to reduce debt. 3. accounting entry on right side of ledger sheet.

**Credit Advisory Board (CAB):** agency established by Financial Institutions Reform, Recovery, and Enforcement Act of 1989 "to monitor the credit standards and lending practices of insured depository institutions and the supervision of such standards and practices by the federal financial regulators" as well as to "ensure that insured depository institutions can meet the demands of a modern and globally competitive world." This board was granted permanent authorization by the Federal Deposit Insurance Corporation Improvement Act of 1991. Formerly known as Credit Standards Advisory Committee (CSAC).

**Credit Analyst:** person who evaluates the financial history and financial statements of credit applicants to assess creditworthiness. Analysts are trained to evaluate applicant's financial strength and to opine on the probability of full repayment, collateral adequacy, or whether a credit enhancement through a cosigner or guarantor is needed.

**Credit Application:** form completed by potential borrower and used by creditor to determine applicant's creditworthiness.

**Credit Approval:** decision to extend credit.

**Credit Approval System:** internal methods by which credit decisions are made.

**Credit Bureau:** agency that gathers information and provides its subscribers with credit reports on consumers.

**Credit Checking:** examining and analyzing creditworthiness of customer by contacting references, reviewing credit reports, etc.

**Credit Department:** department within a financial institution that performs operations and credit support functions for underwriting activities. May include maintenance of credit files, credit investigations, financial statement analysis and spreading, customers' accounts receivable audits, lender training, portfolio reporting, facilitation of credit meetings, etc.

**Credit Enhancement:** enhancement to creditworthiness of loans underlying asset-backed security or municipal bond, generally to get investment-grade rating from bond rating agency and to improve marketability of debt securities to investors. There are two general classifications of credit enhancements:

- third-party enhancement, in which third party pledges its own creditworthiness and guarantees repayment in form of standby letter of credit or commercial letter of credit issued by a financial institution, surety bond from insurance company, or special reserve fund managed by financial guaranty firm in exchange for fee.
- self-enhancement, which is generally done by issuer through over-collateralization—that is, pledging loans with book value greater than face value of bonds offered for sale.

**Credit File:** creditor's file that compiles information about customer, including correspondence, credit memorandums and analyses, credit ratings, a credit history, payment patterns, and credit inquiries.

**Credit Granting:** approval and extension of credit to a customer.

**Credit Inquiry:** request made by a financial institution or trade creditor concerning the responding bank's own customer.

**Credit Insurance:** life and health insurance issued in conjunction with borrowing by individuals; covers payments or unpaid balance when borrower is disabled or dies; in business, covers loss of receivables when debtor becomes insolvent.

**Credit Interchange:** exchange of credit information between individuals or groups.

**Credit Interchange Bureau (CIB):** 1. local bureaus offering members or subscribers credit reports usually based on recent ledger experiences. Generally refers to organized system of cooperating bureaus operated by regional credit associations. 2. credit agency that may limit its reporting to a particular trade.

**Credit Investigation:** inquiry made by a financial institution or trade creditor concerning subject that is not the responding financial institution's customer.

**Credit Limit:** maximum amount of credit made available to customer by specific creditor.

**Credit Line:** commitment by a financial institution to lend funds to a borrower up to a given amount over a specified future period under certain pre-established conditions. Normally reviewed annually.

**Credit Management:** function of planning, organizing, implementing, and supervising credit policies of a company.

**Creditor:** 1. one to whom debt is owed by another as a result of a financial transaction. 2. one who extends credit and to whom money is due.

**Creditors' Committee:** voluntary representative group of creditors that may examine affairs of insolvent debtor. Group will usually advise as to continuation of business, study accountant's and appraiser's reports, act as watchdog over operating business, make recommendations to appropriate groups or legal body so that creditors will realize largest settlement possible, and advise as to acceptability of settlement.

**Creditors' Remedies:** legal rights enabling creditors to collect delinquent debts owed them.

**Credit Policy:** company's written procedures for making credit decisions. Used to aid company in meeting its overall risk management objectives.

**Credit Process Review:** assessment of entire credit-granting process concerning specific financial institution loan portfolio(s).

**Credit Rating:** appraisal made by a financial institution or credit agency as to creditworthiness of a person or company. Such a report will include background on owners, estimate of financial strength and ability to pay when due, and company's payment record.

**Credit Record:** written history of how well a customer has handled debt repayment.

**Credit Report:** 1. report to aid management in reaching credit, sales, and financial decisions. 2. confidential report containing information obtained by mercantile agency that has investigated a company's background, credit history, financial strength, and payment record.

**Credit Reporting Agency:** company or trade interchange group that confidentially supplies subscribers or members with credit information and other relevant data as to a company's ability or likelihood to pay for goods and services purchased on credit.

**Credit Research Foundation (CRF):** education and research affiliate of National Association of Credit Management.

**Credit Review:** follow-up monitoring of loan or extension of credit by credit review officer or department, senior loan committee, auditor, or regulatory agency intended to determine whether loan was made in accordance with lender's written credit standards and policies and in compliance with banking regulations. Errors, omissions, concentrations, etc., if detected by credit review process, can then be corrected by lending officers, thus preventing deterioration in credit quality and possible loan losses. Also called loan review.

**Credit Risk:** 1. evaluation of a customer's ability or willingness to pay debts on time. 2. risk that a financial institution assumes when it makes an irrevocable payment on behalf of its customer against insufficient funds.

**Credit Scoring:** statistical model used to predict the creditworthiness of credit applicants. Credit scoring estimates repayment probability based on information in credit application and credit bureau report. The two main types of credit scoring are application scoring for new accounts and behavior scoring for accounts that have been activated and are carrying balances.

**Credit Terms:** stated and agreed on terms for debt repayment.

**Credit Union:** nonprofit cooperative financial organization chartered by state or federal government to provide financial services such as deposit and loan activities to a specific and limited group of people.

**Creditworthy:** term used to describe individual or entity deemed worthy of extension of credit.

**CSAC:** see *Credit Advisory Board.*

**Current Assets:** short-term assets of company, including cash, accounts receivable, temporary investments, and goods and materials in inventory.

**Current Liabilities:** short-term obligations due within one year, including current maturities of long-term debts.

**Current Open Account:** sale of goods or services for which customer does not pay for each purchase but rather is required to settle in full periodically or within specified time period after each transaction.

**Current Ratio:** total of current assets divided by total current liabilities; used as indication of a company's liquidity and ability to service current obligations.

## D

**D&B:** see *Dun & Bradstreet, Inc.*

**Dating (Terms):** extension of credit terms beyond normal terms because of industry's seasonality or unusual circumstance.

**Days Sales Outstanding (DSO):** a calculation that expresses the average time in days that receivables are outstanding.

**DBA:** see *Doing Business As.*

**DDA:** see *Demand Deposit Account.*

**Dealer Loan:** see *Floor Plan.*

**Debenture:** unsecured, long-term indebtedness or corporate obligation.

**Debit:** entry on left side of accounting ledger.

**Debit Card:** magnetized plastic card that permits customers to withdraw cash from automatic teller machines and make purchases with charges deducted from funds on deposit at a predesignated account.

**Debt:** 1. specified amount of money, goods, or services that is owed from one to another, including not only obligation of debtor to pay but also right of creditor to receive and enforce payment. 2. financial obligation of debtor.

**Debtor:** person or entity indebted to or owing money to another.

**Debtor in Possession (DIP):** In a Chapter 11 bankruptcy, a debtor may continue to maintain possession of its assets and use them in normal business operations.

**Debtor-in-Possession Financing:** credit facilities extended to borrower who is reorganizing under Chapter 11 bankruptcy.

**Debt Ratio:** measure of firm's leverage position derived by dividing total debts by equity.

**Debt Service:** total interest and scheduled principal payments on debt due within given time frame.

**Decision:** judgment, decree, or verdict pronounced by court in determination of case.

**Declarations Page:** policy form containing data regarding insured, policy term, premium, type and amount of coverage, designation of forms and endorsements incorporated at time policy is issued, name of insurer, and countersignature of agent.

**Deductible:** portion of loss that is not insured; may be stated amount deducted from loss or percentage of loss or of value of property at time of loss.

**Deduction:** partial amount of payment that is withheld.

**Deed:** legal, written document used to transfer ownership of real property from one party to another.

**Deed of Trust:** legal document used in some states in lieu of mortgage. Title to real property passes from seller to trustee, who holds mortgaged property until mortgage has been fully paid and then releases title to borrower. Trustee is authorized to sell property if borrower defaults, paying amount of mortgage loan to lender and any remaining balance to former owner.

**Defalcation:** misappropriation of funds held in trust for another.

**Defamation:** injury to person's or entity's character, reputation, or good name by false and malicious statements (includes both libel and slander).

**Default:** to fail to meet obligation or terms of loan agreement such as payment of principal or interest.

**Default Charge:** legally agreed upon charge or penalty added to account when payment of debt is late or another event of default occurs under a loan agreement.

**Defendant:** person or entity defending or denying claim; party against which suit or charge has been filed in court of law. See also Plaintiff.

**Defer:** to postpone or delay action.

**Deferred Payment Sale:** selling on installment plan with payments delayed or postponed until future date.

**Deficiency Judgment:** decree requiring debtor to pay amount remaining due under defaulted contract after secured property has been liquidated.

**Deficit:** difference between receipts and expenses when expenses are greater.

**Defraud:** to deprive person of property by fraud, deceit, or artifice.

**Defunct:** business that has ceased to exist and is without assets; concern that has failed.

**Delayed Disbursement:** practice in cash management whereby a firm pays vendors and other corporations by disbursing payments from a financial institution in a remote city. Also called remote disbursement. Contrasts with controlled disbursement. See also Federal Reserve Float.

**Delinquent:** 1. past-due obligation; overdue and unpaid account. 2. to be in arrears in payment of debts, loans, taxes. 3. to have failed in duty or responsibility.

**Demand Deposit Account (DDA):** funds on deposit in checking account that are payable by a financial institution upon demand of depositor. See also *Time Deposit.*

**Demand Draft:** written order directing that payment be made, on sight, to a third party.

**Demand Letter:** correspondence sent by creditor, collection agency, or lawyer to debtor requesting payment of obligation by specific date.

**Demand Loan:** loan with no fixed due date and payable on demand by maker of loan; loan that can be "called" by lender at any time.

**Demurrage:** charge that is fixed by contract and payable by recipient of goods for detaining freight car or ship longer than agreed in order to load or unload. Purpose is remuneration to owner of vessel for earnings he or she was improperly caused to lose.

**Deposit:** 1. amount of money given as down payment for goods or as consideration for contract. 2. funds retained in customer's bank account.

**Depreciation:** decline in value of fixed assets, allocating purchase cost of an asset plus additions to value over its useful economic life as outlined by the Federal Tax Code.

**Derivatives:** broad family of financial instruments with characteristics of forward or option contracts.

**Derogatory Account Information:** adverse information on customers who have not paid accounts with other creditors according to payment terms, as reported to a credit bureau.

**Directors and Officers Liability Insurance:** legal liability coverage for wrongful acts including breach of duty but not fraud or dishonesty. Often known as E & O, or Errors and Omissions Insurance.

**Disbursement:** full or partial advancement of funds.

**Discharge:** 1. to cancel or release obligation. 2. to release debtor from all or most debts in bankruptcy.

**Disclaimer Statement:** notice disclaiming responsibility for accuracy, completeness, or timeliness of credit information. Most disclaimer statements urge recipients of the information not to rely unduly on it and stress the confidential nature of information being disclosed.

**Discontinued Operations:** operations of a segment of a company, usually a subsidiary whose activities represent a separate line of business that, although still operating, is the subject of a formal plan of disposal approved by management.

**Discount:** 1. interest deducted from face amount of note at time loan is made. 2. trade term used for reduction of invoice amount when payment has been made within specified terms.

**Discounted Note:** 1. borrowing arrangement in which interest is deducted from face amount of note before proceeds are advanced (see also Note). 2. term used when customer endorses note received from another party and presents it to a financial institution to obtain funds.

**Dishonor:** to fail to make payment of negotiable instrument on its due date.

**Disintermediation:** withdrawal of funds from interest-bearing deposit accounts when rates on competing financial instruments, such as money market mutual funds, stocks, and bonds, offer better returns.

**Dismissal:** court order or judgment disposing action, suit, or motion without trial.

**Dispossess:** legal action taken by landlord to put individual or business tenant out of his or her property.

**Dissolution of Corporation:** termination of entity's existence by law, expiration of charter, loss of all members, or failure to meet statutory level of members.

**Distribution:** one or more payments made to creditors who have approved claims filed in a bankruptcy proceeding, assignment for the benefit of creditors, or receivership.

**Distributor:** business engaged in the distribution or marketing of manufacturer's goods to customers or dealers. See also Wholesaler.

**Dividend:** 1. periodic distribution of cash or property to shareholders of corporation as return on their investment.

**Document:** any written instrument that records letters with figures or marks that may be used as evidence.

**Documentary Evidence:** any written record or inanimate object, as distinguished from oral evidence.

**Documents of Title:** Include bill of lading, dock warrant, dock receipt, warehouse receipt, order for the delivery of goods, and any other document that in the regular course of business or financing is treated as adequately evidencing that the person in possession of it is entitled to receive, hold, and dispose of the document and the goods it covers. To be a document of title, a document must purport to be issued by, or addressed to, a bailee and purport to cover goods in the bailee's possession that are either identified or are fungible portions of an identified mass.

**Doing Business As (DBA):** reference term placed before trade name under which business operates. Sometimes used as fictitious trade style acknowledging that name is not part of corporation title or registered trademark.

**Domestic Corporation:** company doing business in state in which it is incorporated.

**Dormant Account:** inactive deposit account in which there have been no deposits or withdrawals for a long period of time.

**Doubtful Assets:** assets that have all weaknesses inherent in substandard assets with added characteristic that weaknesses make collection or liquidation in full, on basis of currently existing facts, conditions, and values, highly questionable and improbable. Possibility of loss is extremely high. Because of certain important and reasonably specific pending factors that may strengthen assets, classification as estimated loss is deferred until more exact status may be determined. Pending factors include proposed merger, acquisition, or liquidation procedures, capital injection, perfecting liens on additional collateral, and refinancing plans.

**Downgrading:** 1. lowering of assessment of customer's creditworthiness. 2. worsening the internally assigned credit quality rating of a loan or relationship in order to appropriately report risk.

**Down Payment:** up-front partial payment made to secure right to purchase goods.

**Downstream Funding:** funds borrowed by holding company for a subsidiary's use, generally to obtain more favorable rate; contrasts with Upstream Funding.

**Draft:** written order by one party (drawer) directing second party (drawee) to pay sum of money to third party (payee). See also *Banker's Acceptance, Letter of Credit, Sight Draft,* and *Time Draft.*

**Drawee:** person or entity that is expected to pay check or draft when instrument is presented for payment.

**Drawer:** party instructing drawee to pay someone else by writing or drawing check or draft. Also called maker or writer.

**Drop Shipment:** shipment of goods delivered directly from manufacturer to customer.

**DSO:** see *Days Sales Outstanding.*

**Dual Banking:** banking system in U.S., consisting of state banks, chartered and supervised by state banking departments, and national banks, chartered and regulated by Office of the Comptroller of the Currency.

**Due Date:** stated maturity date for debt obligation.

**Due Diligence:** 1. responsibility of an entity's directors and officers to act in a prudent manner in evaluating credit applications; in essence, using same degree of care that an ordinary person would use in making same analysis. 2. review that is made of a loan portfolio of a potential merger candidate by an acquiring institution.

**Due Process of Law:** law in its regular course of administration through courts as guaranteed by U.S. Constitution.

**Dun:** to repeatedly demand payment of debt; to be insistent in following debtor for payment.

**Dun & Bradstreet, Inc. (D&B):** international mercantile agency supplying information and credit ratings on all types of businesses.

**Dun Letter:** letter or notice sent by creditor requesting payment of past-due debt.

**D-U-N-S Number:** (Data Universal Numbering System) code developed by Dun & Bradstreet that identifies specific business name and location.

**Durable Goods:** goods that provide long-lasting qualities and continuing services.

**Duress:** unlawful constraint that forces person to do what he or she would not have done by choice.

**Duty:** 1. legal, moral, or ethical obligation. 2. tax collected on import or export of goods.

## E

**Earnest Money:** money that one contracting party gives to another at the time of entering into the contract in order to bind the contract in good faith, and which will be forfeited if the purchaser fails to carry out the contract.

**Earnings Report:** 1. income statement showing a business's or individual's revenues and expenses for stated period of time.

**Easement:** right of owner of one parcel of land to use land of another for special purpose. Usually easement rights pass with land when it is sold.

**Edge Act:** banking legislation, passed in 1919, that allows national banks to conduct foreign lending operations through federal or state-chartered subsidiaries called Edge Act corporations. Such corporations can be chartered by other states and are allowed to own banks in foreign countries and to invest in foreign commercial and industrial firms.

**EFT:** see *Electronic Funds Transfer.*

**Electronic Funds Transfer (EFT):** computerized system enabling funds to be debited, credited, or transferred between financial institution accounts and vendors.

**Embezzlement:** fraudulent appropriation of one's property by person to whom it was entrusted.

**Encumbrance:** any right or interest in real or other property that diminishes the property's value and alters control of disposition.

**Endorsement:** 1. act of writing one's name on back of note, bill, check, or similar written instrument for payment of money; required on negotiable instrument to pass title properly to another. By signing such instrument, endorser becomes party to it and thereby liable, under certain conditions, for its payment. 2. change or addition to insurance policy, informally called rider.

**Entrepreneur:** person who plans, organizes, and runs operation of new business.

**EOM Terms:** Shipments during a month are invoiced in a single statement dated as of the last day of that month or the first day of the following month.

**Equal Credit Opportunity Act of 1974:** Federal Reserve Regulation B that prohibits creditors from discriminating against credit applicants on basis of age, race, color, religion, national origin, sex, marital status, age, or receipt of public assistance.

**Equitable Subordination:** principles in section 510 (c) of U.S. Bankruptcy Code that permit bankruptcy court to subordinate, for purposes of distribution, all or part of creditor's claim against debtor's estate to claims of another creditor of that debtor after court has determined that first creditor has engaged in some form of wrongful conduct that has improved position relative to other creditors.

**Equity:** value of ownership, calculated by subtracting total liabilities from total assets.

**Escheat:** right of state to claim property or money if there is no legal claim made to it.

**Escrow Account:** deposit account to which access is restricted or limited by terms of written agreement entered into by three parties, including a financial institution.

**Estate:** any right, title, or interest that a person may have in lands or other personal property.

**Estimate:** amount of labor, materials, and other costs that a contractor anticipates for a project, as summarized in contractor's bid proposal for project.

**Event of Default:** a breach of an agreement between parties to a contract; a violation of one or more of the loan covenants as set forth in either the loan agreement, commitment letter, or promissory note.

**Evergreen Revolving Credit:** commitment to lend money that remains in effect unless lender takes specific action to terminate agreement; agreement may provide that, in event of termination, any outstanding amount will convert to term loan.

**Exchange Rate:** value of one country's currency to that of another country at a particular point in time.

**Exclusive Sales Agreement:** contractual arrangement, generally between a retailer and a manufacturer or wholesaler, giving retailer exclusive rights for sale of articles or services within a defined geographic area or through a defined distribution channel.

**Execute:** to complete and give validity to a legal document by signing, sealing, and delivering it.

**Exempt:** 1. to release, discharge, or waive from a liability to which others in the same general class are subject. 2. property not available for seizure.

**Exemption:** 1. immunity from general burden, tax, or charge. 2. legal right of debtor to hold portion of property free from claims or judgments.

**Expense:** cost or outlay of money used in business operating cycle.

**Export-Import Bank:** also called Ex-Im Bank. Provides guarantees of working capital loans for U.S. exporters; guarantees the repayment of loans or makes loans to foreign purchasers of U.S. goods and services. Ex-Im Bank also provides credit insurance that protects U.S. exporters against the risks of nonpayment by foreign buyers for political or commercial reasons. Ex-Im Bank does not compete with commercial lenders, but assumes the risks they cannot accept.

## F

**Face Amount:** indicated value of a financial instrument, as shown on its front.

**Facility Fee:** lender's charge for making a line of credit or other credit facility available to borrower (for example, a commitment fee).

**Facsimile:** exact copy of an original.

**Factor:** entity that purchases borrower's accounts receivable and may extend funds to borrower prior to collection of receivables.

**Factoring:** short-term financing from nonrecourse sale of accounts receivable to third party or factor. Factor assumes full risk of collection, including credit losses. Factoring is most common in the garment industry, but has been used in other industries as well. There are two basic types of factoring:

- discount factoring, in which factor pays discounted price for receivables before maturity date.
- maturity factoring, in which factor pays the client purchase price of factored accounts at maturity.

**Fair Credit Billing Act of 1974 (FCBA):** Federal Reserve Regulation Z details the provisions of this act by prescribing uniform methods of computing the cost of consumer credit, disclosure of credit terms, and procedures for resolving billing errors on certain kinds of credit accounts.

**Fair Credit Reporting Act:** federal legislation that regulates consumer credit reporting activities and gives consumer right to learn contents of his or her credit bureau file.

**Fair Market Value:** price that property would sell for between willing buyer and willing seller, neither of whom is obligated to effect transaction.

**Fannie Mae:** see *Federal National Mortgage Association.*

**FASB:** see *Financial Accounting Standards Board.*

**FFB:** see *Federal Financing Bank.*

**FCBA:** see *Fair Credit Billing Act of 1974.*

**FDIC:** see *Federal Deposit Insurance Corporation.*

**FDICIA:** see *Federal Deposit Insurance Corporation Improvement Act of 1991.*

**Federal Deposit Insurance Corporation (FDIC):** 1. federal agency that insures bank accounts for up to $100,000 at both commercial banks and thrifts through Bank Insurance Fund and Savings Association Fund. 2. federal regulator for state-chartered banks that are not members of Federal Reserve System.

**Federal Deposit Insurance Corporation Improvement Act of 1991 (FDICIA):** legislation that provides for recapitalization of Bank Insurance Fund and restructuring of financial services industry through:

- emphasis on more capital.
- government standards for lending, operations, and asset growth.
- quicker government seizure of struggling institutions.
- reduced liquidity options for all but the strongest banks.
- incentives for uninsured depositors to use only the largest and strongest banks.
- sharply increased regulatory costs and fees.
- easier rules for acquiring banks and thrifts.

**Federal Financial Institutions Examination Council (FFIEC):** interagency group of federal banking regulators formed in 1979 to maintain uniform standards for federal examination and supervision of federally insured depository institutions, bank holding companies, and savings and loan holding companies. Also runs schools for examiners employed by banks, thrifts, and credit union agencies. Council produces Uniform Bank Performance Report.

**Federal Financing Bank (FFB):** agency in U.S. Treasury established by Congress in 1973 to centralize borrowing by federal agencies. Instead of selling securities directly to financial markets, all but largest federal agencies raise capital by borrowing from U.S. Treasury through FFB. FFB makes loans at favorable rates to agencies that do not have ready access to credit markets; its debt is direct obligation of U.S. Treasury.

**Federal Funds:** unsecured advances of immediately available funds from excess balances in reserve accounts held at Federal Reserve Banks. Technically, these funds are not borrowings but purchases of immediately available funds. Banks advancing federal funds sell excess reserves; banks receiving federal funds buy excess reserves from selling banks. Federal funds sold are credit transactions on account of selling banks. See also *Federal Funds Rate.*

Federal Funds Rate: rate charged in interbank market for purchases of excess reserve balances. Rate of interest is key money market interest rate and correlates with rates on other short-term credit arrangements. Because the federal funds rate re-prices with each transaction, it is the most sensitive of money market rates and is watched carefully by the Federal Reserve Board.

**Federal Home Loan Bank Board (FHLBB):** federal agency established by Federal Home Loan Bank Act of 1932 to supervise reserve credit system, Federal Home Loan Bank System, for savings institutions. Board also acted as chartering agency and primary regulator of federal savings and loan associations under Home Owners Loan Act of 1933. Financial Institutions Reform, Recovery, and Enforcement Act of 1989 abolished board, transferring its powers in examination and supervision of federally chartered savings institutions to new agency, Office of Thrift Supervision, bureau of U.S. Treasury Department. Regulatory oversight of district Home Loan Banks was transferred to the five-member Federal Housing Finance Board.

**Federal Home Loan Bank System:** system of 11 regional banks established by Federal Home Loan Bank Act of 1932, acting as central credit system for savings and loan institutions. District Home Loan Banks make short-term credit advances to savings institutions, much like Federal Reserve System acts as lender of last resort to commercial banks. Each Home Loan Bank operates independently and has its own board of directors.

**Federal Home Loan Mortgage Corporation (FHLMC):** corporation authorized by Congress in 1970 as secondary market conduit for residential mortgages. Corporation purchases loans from mortgage originators and sells its own obligations and mortgage-backed bonds issued by Government National Mortgage Association to private investors, namely financial institution trust funds, insurance companies, pension funds, and thrift institutions. Also called Freddie Mac.

**Federal Housing Administration (FHA):** federal agency that insures residential mortgages. Created by National Housing Act of 1934, FHA is now part of Department of Housing and Urban Development. Both FHA and Department of Veterans Affairs have single-family mortgage programs to assist homebuyers who are unable to obtain financing from conventional mortgage lenders (banks, savings and loans, and other financial institutions).

**Federal Housing Finance Board (FHFB):** independent federal agency regulating credit advance activities of 11 Federal Home Loan Banks. This board, established by Financial Institutions Reform, Recovery, and Enforcement Act of 1989, has five members, including secretary of Housing and Urban Development, and four directors appointed by the President with Senate confirmation to serve seven-year terms. At least one director must represent the interests of community groups.

**Federal National Mortgage Association (FNMA):** federally chartered, stockholder-owned corporation that purchases residential mortgages insured or guaranteed by federal agencies, as well as conventional mortgages, in secondary mortgage market. Corporation raises capital to support its operations through collection of insurance and commitment fees, issuance of stock, and sale of debentures and notes. Also called Fannie Mae.

**Federal Open Market Committee (FOMC):** policy committee in Federal Reserve System that sets short-term monetary policy objectives for Fed. Committee is made up of seven governors of Federal Reserve Board, plus the presidents of six Federal Reserve Banks. President of Federal Reserve Bank of New York is permanent FOMC member. The other five slots are filled on rotating basis by presidents of other 11 Federal Reserve Banks. Committee carries out monetary objectives by instructing Open Market Desk at Federal Reserve Bank of New York to buy or sell government securities from special account, called open market account, at New York Fed.

**Federal Reserve Board (FRB):** U.S.'s central bank responsible for conduct of monetary policy; also oversees state-chartered banks that are members of Federal Reserve System, bank holding companies, and Edge Act corporations.

**Federal Reserve Float:** total amount of funds that Federal Reserve Banks, in their role as clearing agents, have credited to depositing institutions but have not charged to paying institutions.

**Federal Reserve System:** central bank of U.S. created by Federal Reserve Act of 1913. System consists of Board of Governors, made up of seven members, and a network of 12 Federal Reserve Banks and 25 branches throughout U.S. Board of Governors is responsible for setting monetary policy and reserve requirements. Board and banks share responsibility for setting the discount rate, the interest rate that depository institutions are charged for borrowing from Federal Reserve Banks.

**Federal Trade Commission (FTC):** federal regulatory agency that administers and enforces rules to prevent unfair business practices.

**Fee Simple:** estate in which owner is entitled to entire property and has unconditional power over its disposition.

**FFIEC:** see *Federal Financial Institutions Examination Council.*

**FHA:** see *Federal Housing Administration.*

**FHLBB:** see *Federal Home Loan Bank Board.*

**FHLMC:** see *Federal Home Loan Mortgage Corporation.*

**Fictitious Name:** pretend name used by firm in business transactions. Company is usually required to register this name with local authorities, along with true names and addresses of company's owners.

**Fidelity Bond:** contract issued by insurer to employer to cover loss caused by dishonest acts of employees; form of suretyship. Also called dishonesty insurance.

**Fiduciary:** person or entity acting in capacity of trustee for another.

**Field Warehousing:** method of using company's inventory to secure business loan. In leased and separate storage area of borrower's facility, goods act as security for loan and are released by custodian only upon lender's order.

**FIFO:** see *First-In First-Out.*

**File:** 1. organized folder containing accumulation of information and items retained for preservation or reference. 2. to deposit legal document with proper authority.

**File Revision:** routine gathering of credit information by credit grantor to update files on borrowers.

**Filing Claims:** 1. depositing of formal papers with proper public office and in manner and time frame prescribed by law in order to preserve creditor's rights. 2. method used to perfect security interest accomplished by recording in proper public office.

**Finance Charges:** total costs to an individual or business of obtaining credit, including interest and any fees.

**Financial Analysis:** evaluation by credit analyst of customer's financial situation to determine whether customer has ability to meet his or her obligations as they become due. Factors such as general condition of customer's industry, organizational structure, available collateral or guarantors, and past financial performance are considered.

**Financial Accounting Standards Board (FASB):** independent board responsible for establishing and interpreting generally accepted accounting principles, formed in 1973 to succeed and continue activities of Accounting Principles Board.

**Financial Institutions Reform, Recovery, and Enforcement Act of 1989 (FIRREA):** act signed into law on August 9, 1989, to provide funding and regulatory structure necessary to close several hundred insolvent savings associations and liquidate their assets, to consolidate federal insurance of banks and savings associations under direction of the Federal Deposit Insurance Corporation, to provide regulatory agencies with sweeping new enforcement powers, and to increase substantially civil and criminal penalties for violations of federal banking statutes and regulations. Act substantially alters relationship between savings institutions and regulators and imposes new requirements that must be observed in day-to-day operations of institutions.

**Financial Position:** standing of company, combining assets and liabilities as entered on balance sheet.

**Financial Statements:** reports consisting of individual's or company's balance sheet, income statement, and statement of cash flows, footnotes, and any supplemental schedules.

**Financing Statement:** form required to be completed by creditor and filed with appropriate county and state authorities in order to perfect creditor's security interest in collateral and to give public notice of such interest.

**FIRREA:** see *Financial Institutions Reform, Recovery, and Enforcement Act of 1989.*

**First Deed of Trust:** first recorded deed of trust that acts as first lien on property it describes.

**First-In First-Out (FIFO):** method of valuing inventory in which the first goods received are the first goods used or sold. Using this method, costs of inventory used to determine cost of goods sold are related to costs that were incurred first.

**First Mortgage:** mortgage on property that is superior to any others by fact of having been filed first.

**Fiscal:** anything involving financial matters or issues.

**Fiscal Agent:** person or organization serving as another's financial agent or representative.

**Fiscal Year:** fixed accounting year used as basis for annual financial reporting by business or government.

**Five C's of Credit:** method of evaluating potential borrower's creditworthiness based on five criteria: Capacity, Capital, Character, Collateral, and Conditions.

**Fixed Assets:** property used in normal course of business that is of a long-term nature, such as land, machinery, fixtures, and equipment.

**Fixed-Rate Loan:** loan with interest rate that does not vary over term of loan.

**Fixture:** that which is permanently attached or affixed to real property.

**Flagging an Account:** temporarily identifying an account for specific purpose or reason; may involve suspending activity.

**Float:** uncollected funds represented by checks deposited in one bank but not yet cleared through bank on which they are drawn.

**Floating Interest Rate:** loan interest rate that changes whenever the stated index rate, or base rate, changes.

**Floating Lien:** loan or credit facility secured by inventory or receivables. This type of security agreement gives lender interest in assets acquired by borrower after agreement, as well as those owned when agreement was made. When agreement covers proceeds from sales, lender also has recourse against cash collected from the payment of receivables.

**Floor Plan:** loan made to dealer for purchase of inventory acquired for resale and secured by that inventory, such as automobiles or appliances.

**FNMA:** see *Federal National Mortgage Association.*

**FOB:** see *Free on Board.*

**FOB Point:** point at which responsibility for freight charges begins and title passes. See also *Free on Board.*

**FOMC:** see *Federal Open Market Committee.*

**Forbearance:** Temporarily giving up the right to enforce a valid claim, in return for a promise. It is sufficient consideration to make a promise binding (for example, protracted payment arrangements or interest rate reduction in exchange for additional collateral or guarantors).

**Forced Sale:** 1. court-ordered sale of property, usually without owner's approval. 2. voluntary sale of goods or property to raise cash or to reduce inventory.

**Foreclosure:** legal termination of all of debtor's rights in property secured by mortgage after debtor has defaulted on obligation supported by such mortgage.

**Foreign Corporation:** corporation established under laws of a state other than that in which it is doing business.

**Foreign Exchange:** conversion of money of one country into its equivalent in currency of another country.

**Foreign Item:** check drawn on any financial institution other than the financial institution where it is presented for payment. Also called transit item.

**Foreign Judgment:** judgment obtained in state or country other than the one where the debtor now lives, is doing business, or has assets.

**Forfeiture:** penalty resulting in automatic loss of cash, property, or rights for not complying with legal terms of agreement.

**Forgery:** false making or material altering of any writing with intent to defraud.

**Form 8K:** report disclosing significant events potentially affecting corporation's financial condition or market value of its shares, required by Securities and Exchange Commission. Report is filed within 30 days after event (pending merger, amendment to corporate charter, charge to earnings for credit losses) took place and summarizes information that any reasonable investor would want to know before buying or selling securities.

**Form 10K:** annual financial report filed with Securities and Exchange Commission. Issuers of registered securities are required to file 10K, as are corporations with 500 or more shareholders or assets of $2 million and exchange-listed corporations. Report, which becomes public information once filed, summarizes key financial information, including sources and uses of funds by type of business, net pretax operating income, provision for income taxes and credit losses, plus comparative financial statements for past two fiscal years. Summary of 10K report is included in annual report to stockholders.

**Form 10Q:** quarterly financial report filed by companies with listed securities and those corporations required to file annual 10K report with Securities and Exchange Commission. 10Q report, which does not have to be audited, summarizes key financial data on earnings and expenses and compares current financial information with data reported in same quarter of previous year.

**Forwarding:** referral or placement of out-of-town claims with attorney who then acts on behalf of creditor. In collection process, when authorized, agency may forward account to attorney for collection or suit.

**Franchise:** business agreement whereby one company allows another the right to conduct business under its name and/or distribute its products in exchange for royalties or another agreed upon method of payment.

**Fraud:** any act of deceit, omission, or commission used to deprive someone of right or property. Elements of fraud consist of intentional misrepresentation of fact, relied on by another to his or her detriment, that results in damages.

**Fraudulent Conveyance:** a transfer of property by a debtor, for the intent and purpose of defrauding creditors. Such property may be reached by the creditors through appropriate legal proceedings.

**FRB:** see *Federal Reserve Board.*

**Freddie Mac:** see *Federal Home Loan Mortgage Corporation.*

**Free and Clear:** 1. property with an unencumbered title. 2. title that is free of defects.

**Free and Clear Delivery Receipt:** delivery receipt signed by consignee completely absolving carrier from any claim for loss or damages.

**Free Astray:** freight shipment that has been lost. If it is carrier's fault and shipment is located, it is carrier's obligation to make delivery to original destination at no additional cost to shipper or consignee.

**Free Demand Letter Service:** pre-collection letter sent by collection agency to debtor, requesting that payment be made directly to creditor by given date. No charge is made for payments received within free demand period, but balances remaining unpaid are followed for collection by agency at its regular rates.

**Free on Board (FOB):** term identifying shipping point from which buyer assumes all responsibilities and costs for transportation.

**Free Port:** place where goods are imported or exported free of any duty.

**Freight Forwarder:** business that receives goods for transportation; services include consolidation of small freight shipments of less than carload, truckload, or container lots assembled for lower shipping rates.

**Frozen Account:** 1. account to which customer no longer has access. 2. account suspended by court order, violation of loan covenants, or checking account agreement, etc.

**Frozen Assets:** any assets that cannot be used by owner because of pending legal action.

**FTC:** see *Federal Trade Commission.*

**Fund:** cash or equivalents set aside for specific purpose.

**Fund Accounting:** fiscal and accounting entity with self-balancing set of accounts recording cash and other financial resources, together with all related liabilities and residual equities or balances, and changes therein, which are segregated for purpose of carrying on specific activities or obtaining certain objectives in accordance with special regulations, restrictions, or limitations.

**Funded Debt:** mortgages, bonds, debentures, notes, or other obligations with maturity of more than one year from statement date.

## G

**GAAP:** see *Generally Accepted Accounting Principles.*

**Garnishee:** 1. person or entity that has possession of money or property belonging to defendant and is served with writ of garnishment to hold money or property for payment of defendant's debt to plaintiff. 2. one against whom garnishment has been served.

**Garnishment:** legal warning or procedure to one in possession of another's property not to allow owner access to such property as it will be used to satisfy judgment against owner.

**General Contractor:** contractor who enters into a contract with an owner for construction of a project and who takes full responsibility for its completion. Contractor may enter into subcontracts with various subcontractors for performance of specific parts or phases of project.

**General Ledger:** bookkeeping record comprising all assets, liabilities, proprietorship, revenue, and expense accounts. Entries for each account are posted, and balances are included for each entry.

**Generally Accepted Accounting Principles (GAAP):** conventions, rules, and procedures that define accepted accounting practices, including broad guidelines as well as detailed procedures. Financial Accounting Standards Board, an independent self-regulatory organization, is responsible for promulgating these principles.

**General Obligation Debt:** long-term debt or bond repaid from all otherwise unrestricted revenues, sales taxes, property taxes, license fees, property sales, rents, and so forth of municipality.

**General Partner:** participant in a business relationship who is personally liable, without limitation, for all partnership debts.

**Ginnie Mae:** see *Government National Mortgage Association.*

**GNMA:** see *Government National Mortgage Association.*

**Going Concern:** assumes that a business entity has a reasonable expectation of continuing in business and generating a profit for an indefinite period of time.

**Goods on Approval:** goods offered by seller to buyer with option of examining goods for specific period of time before deciding to purchase them.

**Goodwill:** 1. intangible assets of business consisting of its good reputation, valuable clientele, or desirable location that results in above normal earning power. 2. value or amount for which business could be sold above book value of its physical property and receivables.

**Government National Mortgage Association (GNMA):** corporation created by Congress that administers mortgage-backed securities program that channels new sources of funds into residential mortgages through sale of securities. Also called Ginnie Mae.

**Grace Period:** specified length of time beyond payment due date during which late fee will not be assessed.

**Grantee:** person to whom title in property is made.

**Grantor:** person who transfers title to property.

**Gross Margin:** gross profit as a percentage of sales.

**Gross Profit:** net sales less cost of sales.

**Gross Sales:** sales before returns and allowances; discounts are deducted to arrive at net sales.

**Guarantor:** person who agrees by execution of a contract to repay the debt of another if that person defaults.

**Guaranty:** separate agreement by which a party (or parties) other than debtor assumes responsibility for payment of obligation if principal debtor defaults or is subsequently unable to perform under the terms of the obligation.

**Guardian:** person who is legally responsible for the care and management of a minor or individual who is not mentally or legally competent (or of such person's property).

## H

**Hard Goods:** durable consumer goods, usually including such items as major appliances and furniture, with relatively long, useful lives.

**Heavy Industry:** industry involved in manufacturing basic products such as metals, machinery, or other equipment.

**Hidden Assets:** assets not easily identified and either intentionally not disclosed or publicly reported at lower value than their true worth.

**High Credit:** largest amount of credit used by borrower during specified period of time.

**Holder in Due Course:** person who has taken negotiable instrument (check or note) for value, in good faith, and on assurance that it is complete and regular, not overdue or dishonored, and has no defect in ownership on part of previous holder or endorser.

**Holding Company:** company organized to hold and control stock in other companies.

**Homestead Exemption:** state's law allowing householder or head of family to exempt residence from attachment by creditors.

**Housing and Urban Development, Department of:** cabinet-level federal agency, founded in 1965, that promotes housing development in U.S. through direct loans, mortgage insurance, and guaranties. It houses Federal Housing Administration and Government National Mortgage Association.

**HUD:** see *Housing and Urban Development, Department of.*

**Hypothecate:** to pledge or assign property owned by one entity as security or collateral for loan to second entity.

**Hypothecation:** 1. offer of stocks, bonds, or other assets owned by party other than borrower as collateral for loan, without transferring title. Borrower retains possession but gives lender right to sell property in event of default by borrower. 2. pledging of negotiable securities to collateralize broker's margin loan. If broker pledges same securities to bank as collateral for broker's loan, process is referred to as re-hypothecation.

## I

**Immunity:** condition of being exempt from duty that others are generally required to perform.

**Import Letter of Credit:** commercial letter of credit issued to finance import of goods.

**Import Duty:** government tax on imported items.

**Impound:** to seize or take into legal custody, usually at order of court. Cash, documents, or records may be impounded.

**Inactive Account:** account that has shown little or no activity over a substantial period of time.

**Inactive Files:** 1. accounts on which collection activity has been completed or suspended (claims either collected or found to be uncollectible) and on which no further work is being done. Also called closed or dead files. 2. stored records available for reference.

**In Arrears:** amounts due but not yet paid.

**Income Property:** real property acquired as investment and managed for profit.

**Income Statement:** summary of revenue and expenses covering a specified period.

**Income Tax:** tax levied by federal, state, or local governments on personal or business earnings.

**Incorporation:** formation of legal entity, with qualities of perpetual existence and succession.

**Incumbrance:** see *Encumbrance*.

**Indebtedness:** total amount of money or liabilities owed.

**In Default:** failing to abide by terms and conditions of note or loan agreement. This can include payments on interest or principal (or both) being past due.

**Indemnity:** 1. contract or assurance to reimburse another against anticipated loss, damage, or failure to fulfill obligation. 2. type of insurance that provides coverage for losses of this nature.

**Indirect Liability:** contingent liability such as a continuing guarantee.

**Individual Signature:** credit approved by one person on his or her own authority.

**Indorsement:** see *Endorsement*.

**Industrial Consumer:** purchaser who buys goods or services for business purposes.

**Inquiry:** request for credit information on a bank's customer.

**Insider Loans:** loans to directors and officers of bank, which must be reported to bank regulators under Financial Institutions Reform Act of 1978. Banking laws require that loans to insiders be made at substantially the same rate and credit terms as loans to other borrowers.

**Insolvency:** 1. inability to meet debts as they become due in ordinary course of business. 2. financial condition in which assets are not sufficient to satisfy liabilities.

**Installment Sale:** contract sale in which merchandise is purchased with down payment and balance is made in partial payments over agreed period of time.

**Instrument:** written formal or legal document.

**In-Substance Foreclosure Assets:** loans for which borrower is perceived to have little or no equity in the asset or project and the financial institution can reasonably anticipate proceeds for repayment only from the operation or sale of collateral.

**Insufficient Funds:** see *Non-sufficient Funds*.

**Insurable Interest:** interest such that loss or damage inflicts economic loss.

**Insurable Value:** maximum possible loss to which property is exposed; actual amount depends on basis of calculation per insurance policy.

**Intangible Assets:** nonmaterial assets of business that have no value in themselves but that represent value. Examples include trademarks, goodwill, patents, and copyrights.

**Interchange:** confidential exchange of credit information between individuals and trade groups.

**Interchange Bureau:** association organized to record and exchange or furnish confidential credit information about a member's payment experience and manner in which customers meet obligations.

**Interchange Group:** trade membership group within specific industry that meets regularly to exchange credit experiences and other confidential information.

**Interchange Report:** report usually obtained through credit interchange bureau showing recent credit experience as supplied by participating members.

**Inter-creditor Agreement:** document used when there is more than one lender involved in credit transaction to spell out each lender's rights and obligations.

**Interest:** 1. legally allowed or agreed upon compensation to lender for use of borrowed money. 2. any right in property but less than title to it.

**Interest Bearing:** term describing note or contract calling for payment of agreed interest.

**Interest Only:** loan term during which no principal repayments are made.

**Interest Rate:** cost of borrowing money expressed as an annualized percentage of the loan.

**Internal Guidance Line of Credit:** credit facility similar to a line of credit, but customer may or may not be advised of it; established for internal financial institution purposes, it provides financing for recurrent requests without referring each one to credit committee or other approval source.

**International Consumer Credit Association:** professional trade association of retail credit professionals. Association keeps members informed of latest developments in consumer credit and provides educational courses, seminars, textbooks, and other published material.

**Intestate:** dying without leaving valid will or any other specific instructions as to disposition of property.

**Inventory:** current assets of business that represent goods for sale, including raw materials, work in process, and finished goods.

**Investigation:** 1. gathering of credit information on a person or entity. 2. systematic research for information necessary for a business decision.

**Investment:** use of money for purpose of earning profit or return.

**Investor:** person or entity that puts money to use for capital appreciation or profit or to receive regular dividends.

**Invoice:** seller's descriptive, itemized billing for goods or services sold, showing date, terms, cost, purchase order number, method of shipment, and other identifying information.

**Involuntary Bankruptcy:** see *Bankruptcy*.

**Itemized Statement:** detailed listing of activity on account for particular period of time.

## J

**Jobber:** see *Wholesaler*.

**Joint Account:** financial institution account shared or owned in name of two or more persons with full privileges available to each person.

**Joint and Several:** relative to liability, a term used when creditor has option of pursuing one or more signers of an agreement individually or all signers together.

**Joint Tenancy with Rights of Survivorship:** interest in property held by two or more persons that includes right of survivorship in which deceased person's interest passes to survivors. See also *Tenancy by Entirety*.

**Joint Venture:** business or undertaking entered into on one-time basis by two or more parties in which profits, losses, and control are shared.

**Journal:** account book of original entry in which all money receipts and expenses are chronologically recorded.

**Judgment:** court's determination of rights of parties to claim.

**Judgment Creditor:** one who has obtained judgment against debtor and can enforce it.

**Judgment Debtor:** one against whom judgment has been recovered but not satisfied.

**Judgment Note:** see *Cognovit Note*.

**Judgment Lien:** claim or encumbrance on property, allowed by law, usually against real estate of judgment debtor.

**Judgment-Proof:** term to describe judgment debtor from whom collection cannot be obtained or person who has no money or assets or has concealed or removed property subject to execution.

**Judicial Sale:** see *Forced Sale*.

**Junior Mortgage:** any mortgage filed after and subject to satisfaction of first mortgage.

**Jurisdiction:** 1. legal authority, power, capacity, and right of court to act. 2. geographic area within which court or government agency exercises power.

## K

**Keyperson Life Insurance:** insurance policy written on owner or principal employee in which death benefits are payable to company.

**Key Ratios:** performance measures used to determine probable ability of business to operate profitably. Results are expressed in percentages that are then weighed against average percentages in each industry.

## L

**Landlord's Waiver:** the relinquishment of a right(s) contained in a lease agreement by a lessor.

**Last-In First-Out (LIFO):** method of valuating inventory in which last goods received are the first ones sold. Using this method, inventory costs used to determine cost of goods sold are related to costs of inventory that were incurred last.

**Late Charge:** special legally agreed upon fee, charged by creditor, on any payment that is not made when due.

**Lawful Money:** legal tender for payment of all debts.

**Law List:** compiled publication of names and addresses of those in legal profession, often including court calendars, private investigators, and other information of interest to legal profession.

**Lawsuit:** suit, action, or cause instituted by one person against another in a court of law.

**Lead Bank:** financial institution that has the primary deposit or lending relationship in a multi-bank situation; usually in the context of shared credit and sometimes defined within an inter-creditor agreement. See also *Agent Bank*.

**Leaseback:** agreement by which one party sells property to another and, after completing sale, the first party rents it from second party.

**Lease Contract:** written agreement for which equipment or facilities can be obtained on rental payment basis for specified period of time.

**Leased Department:** section of department store not operated by store but by independent outside organization on contract or percentage-of-sales arrangement.

**Leasehold:** rights tenant holds in property as conferred by terms of lease.

**Leasehold Improvement:** permanent improvements made to rented property. Leasehold improvements are considered fixtures and depreciate over lease period.

**Leasehold Interest:** lessee's equity or ownership in leasehold improvements.

**Lease-Purchase Agreement:** contract providing for set amount of lease payments to be applied to purchase of property.

**Ledger:** in accounting, book of permanent records containing series of accounts to which debits and credits of transactions are posted from books of original entry.

**Ledger Experience:** trade experience reported by credit manager or interchange group. Such reports provide picture of account's paying habits, high credit, and terms of repayment.

**Legal and Sovereign Risk:** risk that government may intervene to affect bank's system or any participant of such system detrimentally.

**Legal Composition:** identification and description of lawful ownership or title to business entity.

**Legal Entity:** business organization that has capacity to make contract or agreement or assume obligation. Such organization may consist of individual proprietorship, partnership, corporation, or association.

**Legal Right:** natural right, right created by contract, and right created or recognized by law.

**Legal Tender:** any money that is recognized by law for payment of debt unless contract exists specifically calling for payment in another type of money.

**Legal Title:** document establishing right of ownership to property that is recognized and upheld by law.

**Lender:** one who extends funds to another with expectation of repayment with interest.

**Lender's Loss Payable Endorsement:** form attached to property insurance policies to cover lender's interest in what is insured; extends coverage to give lender protection beyond that in basic policy; language may be prescribed by banking industry, standard form prepared by insurance industry, or specified by lender. See also *Loss Payee Clause*.

**Lessee:** one to whom lease is given and therefore has right to use property in exchange for rental payments.

**Lessor:** owner who grants lease for use of property in return for rent.

**Letter of Agreement:** letter stating terms of agreement between addressor and addressee, usually prepared for signature by addressee as indication of acceptance of those terms as legally binding.

**Letter of Credit:** letter or document issued by bank on behalf of customer that is evidence of financial background of bank and ensures that payment will be made when proper documents confirm completion of related transaction. Such letters authorize drawing of sight or time drafts when certain terms and conditions are fulfilled. See also *Banker's Acceptance, Draft, Sight Draft, Standby Letter of Credit,* and *Time Draft*.

**Letter of Intent:** letter signifying intention to enter into formal agreement and usually setting forth general terms of such agreement.

**Liable:** duty or obligation enforceable by law.

**Liabilities:** indebtedness of an individual or entity.

**Libel:** written or published false and malicious statements about another that tend to defame or harm another's reputation.

**LIBOR:** see *London Interbank Offered Rate*.

**Lien:** legal right or encumbrance to secure payment performance on property pledged as collateral until the debt it secures is satisfied.

**LIFO:** see *Last-In First-Out*.

**Limited Liability Company:** legal entity that offers shareholders the same limitations on personal liability available to corporate shareholders. The owners of a limited liability company (LLC) have limited liability. They are not liable for the debts, liabilities, acts, or omissions of the company. Only their investment is at risk.

**Limited Liability:** legal exemption corporate stockholders or limited liability companies have from full financial responsibilities for debts of company.

**Limited Partnership:** partnership of one or more general partners who are personally, jointly, and separately responsible, with one or more special partners whose liabilities are limited to amount of investment.

**Line of Credit:** see *Credit Line*.

**Liquid Assets:** assets that can be readily converted into cash.

**Liquidate:** 1. to pay off or settle current obligation. 2. to sell off or convert assets into cash. 3. to dissolve business in order to raise cash for payment of debts.

**Liquidation:** process of dissolving a business, settling accounts, and paying off any claims or obligations; remaining cash is distributed to the owners of the business.

**Liquidation Value:** cash that can be realized from sale of assets in dissolving business, as distinct from its value as ongoing entity.

**Liquidity:** measure of quality and adequacy of current assets to meet current obligations as they come due.

**Liquidity Ratio:** company's most liquid assets (generally cash and accounts receivable) divided by current liabilities. Also called quick ratio.

**List Price:** generally advertised or posted price. Sometimes subject to trade or cash discounts.

**Litigation:** lawsuit brought to court for purpose of enforcing a right.

**LLC:** see *Limited Liability Company*.

**Loan:** money advanced to a borrower with agreement of repayment usually with interest within a specified period of time.

**Loan Agreement:** legal contract between a financial institution and a borrower that governs the terms and conditions for the life of a loan. Elements usually include description of loan, representations, and warranties reaffirming known facts about the borrower such as legal structure, affirmative and negative covenants, conditions that must be met before the loan is granted, delinquent payment penalties, and statement of remedies that the financial institution may take in event of default.

**Loan Participation:** sharing of loan(s) by a group of financial institutions that join together to make said loan(s), affording an opportunity to share the risk of a very large transaction. Arranged through correspondent banking networks in which smaller financial institutions buy a portion of an overall financing package. Participations are a convenient way for smaller financial institutions to book loans that would otherwise exceed their legal lending limits. Also called participation financing.

**Loan Policy:** principles that reflect a financial institution's credit culture, underwriting procedures, and overall approach to lending.

**Loans Past Due:** loans with interest or principal payments that are contractually past due a certain number of days.

**Loan-to-Value Ratio (LTV):** relationship, expressed as percent, between principal amount of loan and appraised value of the asset securing financing.

**Loan Value:** amount of money that can be borrowed against real or personal property.

**Lockbox:** regional financial institution depository used by corporations to obtain earlier receipt and collection of customer payments. Arrangement provides creditor with better control of accounts receivable and earlier availability of cash balances. Many large financial institutions offer lockbox processing as a cash management service to corporate customers. Lockboxes can be:
- retail, designed for remittance processing for consumer accounts.
- wholesale, in which payments from other entities are collected and submitted through depository transfer check or electronic debit into a concentration account for investment and disbursement as needed.

**London Interbank Offered Rate (LIBOR):** key rate index used in international lending. LIBOR is the rate at which major financial institutions in London are willing to lend Eurodollars to each other. This index is often used to determine interest rate charged to creditworthy borrowers.

**Long-Arm Statutes:** state statutes that allow state courts to exercise jurisdiction over nonresident persons or property outside their state's borders.

**Long-Term Capital Gain (Loss):** gain or loss realized from sale or exchange of capital asset held for longer than 12 months.

**Long-Term Liabilities:** all senior debt, including bonds, debentures, bank debt, mortgages, deferred portions of long term-debt, and capital lease obligations owed for longer than 12 months.

**Loss:** 1. circumstance in which expenses exceed revenues. 2. result if an asset is sold for less than its depreciated book value.

**Loss Assets:** assets considered uncollectible and of such little value that their continuance as realizable assets is not warranted.

**Loss Leader:** deliberate sale of product or service at or below cost in order to attract new customers.

**Loss Payee Clause:** provision in insurance policy or added by endorsement to cover lender/mortgagee's interest in property loss settlement. Provision is not as broad as lender's loss payable endorsement. Also called mortgagee clause and loss payable clause.

**LTV:** see *Loan-to-Value Ratio*.

**Lump-sum Settlement:** payment made in full with single, one-time payment.

## M

**Magnetic Ink Character Recognition (MICR):** description of numbers and symbols that are printed in magnetic ink on documents for automated processing. Fully inscribed MICR line of information may include item's serial number, routing and transit number, check digit, account number, process control number, and amount.

**Mail-Fraud Statute:** federal law against using mails to defraud creditors by mailing false financial statements. Prosecution under mail-fraud statute must prove beyond reasonable doubt that:
- statement is false.
- statement was made with intention it should be relied on.
- it was made for the purpose of securing money or property.

- statement was delivered by mail.
- money or property was obtained by means of false statement.

**Mailgram:** telegraphic message transmitted electronically by Western Union and delivered by U.S. Postal Service.

**Mail Teller:** employee of a financial institution who receives mail deposits, checks them for accuracy, and returns stamped receipts for deposits to customers.

**Majority Stockholder:** person or entity that owns more than 50% of voting stock of a corporation, thereby having controlling interest.

**Maker:** one who signs or executes negotiable instrument.

**Malpractice:** professional misconduct with negligence.

**Management:** persons responsible for administrating and carrying out policy of business or other organization.

**Management Information System (MIS):** established flow of information developed to keep managers informed of what is happening within their organization and to do it within a time frame that permits effective reaction when required. Efficient MIS helps managers make better decisions.

**Management Report:** statement in unaudited financial statements that says financials are representations of firm's management.

**Manifest:** shipping document that lists freight's origin, contents, value, destination, carrier, and other pertinent information for use at terminals or custom house.

**Manufacturers Representative (Agent):** independent, commissioned sales agent who represents several noncompeting manufacturers for sale of their products to related businesses within agreed, exclusive sales territory.

**Marginal Account:** borderline credit risk that does not have sufficient operating capital and from which payment may be delayed.

**Markdown:** price reduction of goods below normal selling price.

**Market:** 1. customer base for a company's goods or services. 2. securities exchange and its associated institutions.

**Marketability:** ease and rapidity with which product, service, or other asset can be sold or converted to cash.

**Marketing:** 1. activities necessary to facilitate the sale of goods or services through planned research, manufacturing, promotion, advertising, and distribution. 2. business promotion devoted to getting the maximum purchases of products or services by consumers.

**Market Value:** price that goods or property would bring in current market of willing buyers and sellers.

**Markup:** amount or percentage added to cost of goods to arrive at selling price.

**Maturity Date:** date when financial obligation, note, draft, bond, or instrument becomes due for payment.

**Mechanic's Lien:** enforceable claim, permitted by law in most states, securing payment to contractors, subcontractors, and suppliers of materials for work performed in constructing or repairing buildings. Lien attaches to real property, plus buildings and improvements situated on land, and remains in effect until workers have been paid in full or, in event of liquidation, gives contractor priority of lien ahead of other creditors.

**Medium of Exchange:** money or commodity accepted in payment or settlement of debt.

**Memorandum (Consignment) Sale:** sale of goods for which seller is not paid until retailer has sold merchandise. Seller retains title to such goods until retailer has sold merchandise and payment is made to retailer.

**Mercantile Agency:** organization that compiles credit and financial information and supplies subscribers or members with reports on applicants for credit; can also perform other functions such as collection of accounts or compiling of statistical trade information.

**Merchandise Shortage:** goods purchased but not included in shipment.

**Merger:** combining of two or more businesses to form a single organization.

**Mezzanine Financing:** 1. in corporate finance, leveraged buyout or restructuring financed through subordinated debt, such as preferred stock or convertible debentures. Transaction is financed by expanding equity, as opposed to debt. 2. second- or third-level financing of companies financed by venture capital. Senior to venture capital but junior to financial institution financing, it adds creditworthiness to firm. Generally used as intermediate-stage financing, preceding a company's initial public offering, it is considered less risky than start-up financing.

**MICR:** see *Magnetic Ink Character Recognition.*

**Middle-of-Month (M.O.M.) Billing Term:** billing system in which all shipments are charged on one invoice issued twice a month. For first half of month, credit period runs to the 25th and, for the second half, to the tenth of the following month.

**MIS:** see *Management Information System.*

**Modified Accrual Accounting:** basis of accounting in which expenditures are recognized when liability is incurred. Revenues are recognized when measurable and available. Exception is in debt service funds in which expenditures are recorded only when due.

**M.O.M.:** see *Middle-of-Month Billing Term.*

**Money Judgment:** court decision that adjudges payment of money rather than requiring act to be performed or property transferred.

**Monitoring:** service available through many credit reporting or interchange bureaus enabling subscribers to request that certain listed accounts be automatically monitored and reviewed and that updated reports be issued periodically.

**Moratorium:** 1. temporary extension or delay of normal period for payment of account. 2. Formal postponement during which debtor is permitted to delay payment of obligations.

**Mortgage:** debt instrument giving conditional ownership of asset to borrower, secured by the asset being financed. The instrument by which real estate is hypothecated as security for the repayment of a loan. Borrower gives lender a mortgage in exchange for the right to use property while mortgage is in effect and agrees to make regular payments of principal and interest. Mortgage lien is lender's security interest and is recorded in title documents in public land records. Lien is removed when debt is paid in full. Mortgage normally involves real estate and is considered long-term debt.

**Mortgagee:** lender who arranges mortgage financing, collects loan payments, and takes security interest in property financed.

**Mortgagee Clause:** provision in property policy, or added by endorsement, that extends protection, in limited manner, to mortgagee; not as broad as lender's loss payable endorsement.

**Mortgagee Waiver:** the relinquishment of right(s) contained in a mortgage by a mortgagee.

**Mortgage Verification:** request made by mortgagee to applicant's financial institution for information on applicant's accounts, as part of mortgagee's credit approval process.

**Mortgagor:** borrower in a mortgage contract who mortgages property in exchange for a loan.

**Multinational Corporation:** corporation whose operations are conducted on an international basis.

**Multiple Signature Credit Approval:** describes credit approval process in which credit is approved by two or more persons acting together.

**Mutual Account Revision:** routine exchange of credit information between two or more credit grantors that have extended credit to subject of inquiry.

## N

**NACM:** see *National Association of Credit Management.*

**National Association of Credit Management (NACM):** national business organization of credit and financial professionals that promotes laws for sound credit, protects businesses against fraudulent debtors, improves the interchange of commercial credit information, develops credit practices, and provides education and certification programs for its members.

**Negligence:** failure to use reasonable care that an ordinarily prudent person would in like circumstances.

**Negotiable:** anything capable of being transferred by endorsement or delivery.

**Negotiable Instrument:** any written evidence of indebtedness, transferable by endorsement and delivery or by delivery only, that contains unconditional promise to pay specified sum on demand or at some fixed date.

**Negotiate:** to discuss, bargain, or work out plan of settlement, terms, or compromise in business transaction.

**Net:** amount left after necessary deductions have been made from gross amount.

**Net Assets:** sum of individual's or entity's total assets less total liabilities.

**Net Earnings:** total sales, less total operating, administrative, and overhead expenses, but before other expenses and income such as interest and dividends.

**Net Income:** amount of income remaining after deducting all expenses from total revenues.

**Net Lease:** agreement in which tenant assumes payment of other property expenses, such as taxes, maintenance, and insurance, in addition to rental payments.

**Net Price:** actual price paid after all discounts, allowances, and other authorized deductions have been taken.

**Net Profit:** income earned by business over specific period of time. Profit from transaction or sale, after deducting all costs, expenses, and miscellaneous reserves and adjustments from gross receipts.

**Net Sales:** total sales less returns, allowances, and discounts.

**Net Working Capital:** current assets less current liabilities; used as measure of a company's liquidity and indicates its ability to finance current operations.

**Net Worth:** total assets less total liabilities; reflects owners' net interest in company.

**No Account:** notation on rejected check when check writer does not have account at the financial institution on which check is drawn.

**No Asset Case:** insolvent or bankrupt estate with no assets available for payment of creditors' claims.

**No Funds:** notation on rejected check when check writer has account but not funds to cover check.

**Nominal Balance:** an account balance of less than $100.

**Nominal Owner:** person whose name appears on title to asset, but who has no interest in it.

**Nonaccrual:** loan on which a financial institution does not accrue interest; also known as a nonperforming loan.

**Nonborrowing Account:** banking relationship in which no extension of credit is involved.

**Nonfinancial Information:** facts used to evaluate a customer's creditworthiness; focuses on background and history rather than financial measures.

**Nonpayment:** failure or neglect to pay or discharge debt in accordance with terms of agreement.

**Nonperforming Assets:** total of earning assets listed as nonaccrual; formerly, earning assets acquired in foreclosure and through in-substance foreclosures.

**Nonperforming Loans:** amount of loans not meeting original terms of agreement, including renegotiated, restructured, and nonaccrual loans. Loans included in this total vary according to bank policy and regulation.

**Nonprofit Corporation:** organization specifically classified by the IRS as generally tax exempt and whose primary purpose for existence is to provide services of a charitable, fraternal, religious, social, or civic nature.

**Nonrecource:** inability of holder in due course to demand payment from endorser of debt instrument if party(ies) primarily liable fail to make payment.

**Non-sufficient Funds (NSF):** term used when collected demand deposit balances are less than the amount of the check being presented for payment and check is returned to payee's financial institution. See also Overdraft.

**No Protest (N.P.):** instructions given by one financial institution to another not to protest check or note when presented for payment. N.P. is usually stamped on instrument to avoid protest fee.

**North American Industrial Classification System (NAICS):** the Standard Industrial Classification (SIC) code is being replaced by the NAICS code. NAICS classifies establishments by their primary type of activity within a six-digit code. NAICS provides structural enhancements over SIC and identifies over 350 new industries. See also *SIC* and *Standard Industrial Classification.*

**Notary Public:** public officer authorized to administer oaths, attest and certify certain types of documents, and to take acknowledgements of conveyances.

**Note:** unconditional written promise by borrower to pay certain amount of money to lender on demand or at specified or determinable date. This instrument should meet all requirements of laws pertaining to negotiable instruments.

**Notes Payable:** liabilities represented by promissory notes, excluding trade debts, that are payable in future.

**Notes Receivable:** assets represented by promissory notes, excluding amounts due from customers for credit sales, to be collected in future.

**Notice of Protest:** formal statement that a certain bill of exchange, check, or promissory note was presented for payment or acceptance and that such payment or acceptance was not made. Such notice will also state that because instrument has been dishonored, maker, endorsers, or other parties to document will be held responsible for payment.

**Novation:** substitution of old contract for new one between same or different parties; substitution of new debtor or creditor for previous one, by mutual agreement.

**NSF:** see *Non-sufficient Funds.*

**Nulla Bona:** report made by sheriff when no assets are found within his or her jurisdiction on which to satisfy judgment against debtor.

## O

**Obligation:** 1. law or duty binding parties to an agreement. 2. written promise to pay money or to do a specific thing.

**Obligee:** person or entity to which payment is due.

**Obligor:** person or entity required by contract to perform specific act.

**Obsolescence:** decline in perceived value of asset, frequently because of technological innovations, changes in an industry's processes, or changes required by law.

**OCC:** see *Office of the Comptroller of the Currency.*

**Offer:** proposal to make contract, usually presented by one party to another for acceptance.

**Offering Basis:** customer's loan requests considered individually on merits of each proposal.

**Office of the Comptroller of the Currency (OCC):** branch of the Treasury Department that regulates federally chartered banks.

**Office of Thrift Supervision (OTS):** branch of the Treasury Department that regulates state and federally chartered thrifts as well as those institutions in conservatorship.

**Offset:** amount allowed to be netted against another.

**On Account:** generally describes partial payment made toward settlement of unpaid balance.

**On Account Payment:** partial payment not intended as payment in full.

**On Demand:** debt instrument that is due and payable on presentation.

**Open (Book) Account:** credit extended without a formal written contract and represented on books and records of the seller as an unsecured account receivable for which payment is expected within a specified period after purchase.

**Open-End Credit:** consumer line of credit that may be added to, up to preset credit limit, or paid down at any time. Customer has option of paying off outstanding balance, without penalty, or making several installment payments. Contrasts with Closed-End Credit. Also called revolving credit or charge account credit.

**Open Terms:** selling on credit terms as opposed to having customer pay cash.

**Operating Performance Ratios:** financial measures designed to assist in evaluation of management performance.

**Operating Statement:** report of an individual's or entity's income and expenses for a specified period of time. See also Income Statement.

**Operational Risk:** risk concerning computer network failure due to system overload or other disruptions; also includes potential losses from fraud, malicious damage to data, and error.

**Oral Contract:** agreement that may or may not be written in whole or in part or signed but is legally enforceable.

**Order:** informal bill of exchange or letter or request identifying person to be paid.

**Order for Relief:** order issued by bankruptcy court judge upon filing of petition by debtor or filing of petition by creditors.

**Order to Order:** agreement for payment to be made for prior shipment before next delivery will be made.

**OREO:** see *Other Real Estate Owned.*

**Other Real Estate Owned:** real property usually taken as collateral and subsequently acquired through foreclosure, or by obtaining a deed in lieu of foreclosure, in satisfaction of the debts previously contracted. Real property formerly used as banking premises, or real property sold in a "covered transaction" as defined by banking regulations.

**OTS:** see *Office of Thrift Supervision.*

**Outlet Store:** retail operation where manufacturers' production overruns, discontinued merchandise, or irregular goods are sold at discount.

**Out-of-Court Settlement:** 1. settlement made by distressed debtor through direct negotiations with creditors or through creditors' committee; acceptance of such settlement is not obligatory to nonconsenting creditors. 2. agreement reached between opposing parties to settle pending lawsuit before matter has been decided by court.

**Out-of-Pocket Expense:** business expenses for which individual pays.

**Out-of-Trust:** an event occurring in floor plan financing where a borrower sells inventory securing the financial institution's loan and fails to promptly remit the proceeds to the financial institution in accordance with the loan agreement.

**Outstanding:** 1. amount of credit facility that is being used versus total amount made available. 2. unpaid or uncollected account.

**Overdraft:** negative account balance created when a check is paid when collected demand deposit balances are less than amount of check being presented for payment. See also Non-sufficient Funds.

**Overdue:** debt obligation on which payments are past due.

**Overhead:** selling and administrative business costs as contrasted with costs of goods sold.

**Oversold:** condition in which manufacturer or wholesaler finds itself after taking more orders than it can deliver within an agreed period of time.

**Owed:** debt that is due and payable.

**Own:** to have legal title to property.

**Owner:** person or entity that owns or has title to property.

**Owner's Equity:** mathematical difference between total assets and total liabilities that represents shareholders' equity or an individual's net worth.

**Ownership:** exclusive rights that one has to property, to exclusion of all others; having complete title to property.

**Owner's Risk:** term used in transportation contracts to exempt carrier from responsibility for loss or damage to goods.

## P

**Packing List:** detailed listing of information on shipment's contents (enclosed for inspection with package).

**Paid Direct:** payment made by debtor directly to original creditor instead of to collection agency or attorney handling account for collection.

**Paper Profit:** unrealized income or gain on asset.

**Paralegal:** trained aide to attorney who handles various legal tasks.

**Parent Company:** an entity that holds controlling majority interest in subsidiaries.

**Partial Payment:** payment not in full for amount owed.

**Participation:** purchase or sale of a loan or credit facility among two or more financial institutions in which the acquiring institution(s) has no formal or direct role in establishing the terms and conditions binding the borrower. Participants do not participate in the document negotiation between the originating financial institution and the borrower.

**Partnership:** business arrangement in which two or more persons agree to engage, upon terms of mutual participation, in profits and losses.

**Party:** person concerned or taking part in a transaction or proceeding.

**Past Due:** payment or account that remains outstanding and unpaid after its agreed-upon payment or maturity date.

**Pay:** to satisfy, or make partial payments on, a debt obligation.

**Payable:** obligation that is due now or in future.

**Payables:** liabilities owed to trade creditors for purchase of supplies. Also called accounts payable.

**Payee:** person or entity named on a negotiable instrument as the one to whom the obligation is due.

**Payer:** party responsible for making payment as shown on check, note, or other type of negotiable instrument; also called maker or writer.

**Payment:** discharge, in whole or in part, of debt or performance of agreement.

**Payment for Honor:** payment of past-due obligation by someone else to save credit or reputation of person responsible for payment.

**Payoff:** receipt of payment in full on an obligation.

**Penalty:** 1. legal fine, forfeiture, or payment imposed for defaulting or violating terms of contract. 2. interest charge imposed for late payments that is permissible by law and imposed with customer's prior agreement or knowledge of seller's terms of sale.

**Percentage Lease:** lease of real property in which rental payments are based on percentage of retailer's sales.

**Percentage of Completion:** method of accounting commonly used by contractors and developers in which costs are related to percentage of job completion.

**Perfection:** with respect to security interests in personal property under Article 9 of the UCC, the action required to give the secured party rights in the collateral as against third parties with competing claims. In general, a security interest is not perfected until a properly executed financing statement has been recorded or the secured party is in the possession of the collateral, whichever applies as to that specific collateral type.

**Performance:** fulfillment of promise or agreement according to terms of contract or obligation.

**Performance Bond:** guaranty to project owner that the contractor will perform the work called for by the contract in accordance with the plans and specifications. Customarily issued by bonding and insurance companies, although financial institution letters of credit may be used.

**Perjury:** willfully and knowingly giving false testimony under oath.

**Person:** individual (natural person) or incorporated enterprise (artificial person) having certain legal rights and responsibilities.

**Personal Check:** check drawn by individual on his or her own bank account.

**Personality:** legal term for personal property or possessions that are not real estate.

**Personally Liable:** individual's responsibility for payment of obligation, generally used to refer to owner's or guarantor's responsibility.

**Personal Property:** movable or chattel property of any kind.

Petition: written application, made in contradiction to motion. Also used in some states in place of complaint.

**Petition in Bankruptcy:** document filed in court to declare bankruptcy. Petition can be either voluntary (filed by debtor) or involuntary (filed by creditors), depending on bankruptcy chapter rules.

**Petty Cash:** cash on hand or in designated bank account that is available for small, miscellaneous purchases.

**Physical Inventory:** inventory verification obtained by visual observation of items and itemization of quantities of goods on hand.

**Piercing the Corporate Veil:** legal action taken by creditor, when fraud or unjust enrichment may be involved, to hold principals of corporation (or other entities) liable for debts of corporation.

**Plaintiff:** person or entity that initiates legal action against another.

**Plan of Arrangement:** procedure in bankruptcy under Chapter 11 for debtor to restructure debts or rehabilitate by arriving at arrangement with creditors. See also Bankruptcy, Chapter 11 Cases.

**Pledge:** promise of personal property as security for performance of act, payment of debt, or satisfaction of obligation.

**Points:** 1. percentage fee charged to obtain a mortgage loan. 2. in shares of stock, one point equals $1.00.

**Policy:** 1. written statement by management that explains an organization's philosophy and approach to doing business. 2. written contract of insurance between insured and the insurance company.

**Pooling Accounts:** arrangement by a debtor listing all his or her debts with a debt management or pro-rating service with the understanding that the service will receive, as its fee, a portion of debtor's payments to his or her creditors and proportionately distribute the balance of payments to each creditor on a scheduled basis. Activities of such services may be covered by individual state statutes.

**Postdated Check:** check written for payment, effective at future date.

**Power of Attorney:** written document that authorizes one person to act as another's agent.

**Preference:** 1. right of a creditor to be paid before other creditors by virtue of having lien or collateral. 2. improperly paying or securing of one or more creditors, in whole or part, by an insolvent debtor to the exclusion of other creditors.

**Preference Period:** in bankruptcy, the 90-day period immediately preceding debtor entering into bankruptcy. If a creditor files new or additional liens against a debtor during this time, such claims may be disallowed by bankruptcy court.

**Preferred Creditor:** creditor whose account takes legal preference for payment over claims of others.

**Prepaid Expenses:** payment for goods or services not yet received.

**Prepayment:** payment of loan or debt before it actually becomes due.

**Prime Contractor:** contractor who enters into contract with the owner of the project for completion of all or portion of the project and takes full responsibility for its completion. See also General Contractor.

**Prime Rate:** an index or base rate published or publicly announced by a financial institution from time to time as the rate it is generally willing to give its most creditworthy customers.

**Principal:** 1. amount of money loaned or borrowed. 2. key decision maker or management of entity.

**Priority:** legal preferences that secured creditors have over general creditors in bankruptcy.

**Priority Lien:** lien recorded before other secured claims and payable ahead of other liens if liquidation of pledged collateral occurs. First mortgage has priority over second and third mortgages, known as junior liens. Secured creditor holding perfected security interest has priority over liens filed afterward.

**Private Enterprise:** business established to take economic risks for purpose of making profit.

**Privilege:** right that nature of debt gives to one debt holder over others.

**Proceeds:** actual amount of money given to or received from creditor after any deductions are made.

**Profit:** 1. amount of net income made by an entity in course of doing business. 2. increase in value of an asset over its depreciated book value at the time of sale.

**Profit and Loss Statement (P & L):** financial report of an individual's or entity's revenue and expenses for a given period of time. See also Income Statement and Operating Statement.

**Pro Forma:** projected financial statements.

**Progress Payments:** partial payments made on a long-term contract as it progresses. Required when a manufacturer or contractor cannot afford, or does not wish, to finance a project.

**Projection:** borrower's estimate of future performance over designated time period.

**Promissory Note:** written promise to make unconditional payment of specified amount on designated date, signed by maker.

**Proof of Claim:** creditor's formal document filed with court against estate of debtor if creditor is owed funds.

**Proof of Loss:** sworn statement filed by insured when making claim.

**Property:** something of value that is legally owned and in which person has exclusive and unrestricted right or interest.

**Property Insurance:** coverage that applies to loss caused by physical damage to property (buildings, contents, earnings, etc.) owned by insured.

**Proposal:** oral or written offer that, if accepted, constitutes a contract.

**Proprietorship:** single and exclusive ownership of a business by one person.

**Pro Rata:** share calculated in proportion to total amount.

**Pro Rata Distribution:** payment proportionate to uniform percentage of obligations to all creditors.

**Protest:** formal, written, notarized notice stating credit instrument has not been honored and that makers or endorsers will be held responsible for payment.

**Prox.:** see Proximo.

**Proximo (Prox.):** sales term used in invoices to mean next month after month of invoice. This term is sometimes used instead of EOM terms.

**Proxy:** written statement or power of attorney, authorizing an individual to act or speak for another.

**Public Credit:** debt incurred by government, federal and local, for a use that meet the needs of its citizens.

**Purchase Money Lien:** manufacturer's legal right to goods and products until the buyer makes payment. Under the Uniform Commercial Code, manufacturer's rights can take priority over lender's lien rights if both claim interest in same inventory. Lender may receive such priority if funds were provided to purchase asset, provided liens are filed within 20 days of borrower taking possession of collateral and noticing requirements have been met.

**Purchase Money Mortgage:** mortgage given by buyer to seller in lieu of cash, as partial payment on property.

**Purchasing Power:** value of money and its ability to buy goods and services in a given period.

# Q

**Qualified Acceptance:** agreement to terms of contract only if certain conditions are meet. This constitutes counteroffer and rejection of original offer.

**Qualified Endorsement:** transfer of debt instrument to endorsee without recourse or liability to endorser.

**Qualified Financial Statement:** audit report issued by independent accountants that indicates restrictions on scope of audit performed, uncertainties, or disagreements with management.

**Qualified Prospect:** potential customer whose background and credit have been checked and approved.

**Quantity Discount:** price reduction extended to purchaser of a large volume of goods.

**Quarterly Accounts Receivable Survey:** index, compiled by Credit Research Foundation in affiliation with the National Association of Credit Management and published quarterly, that shows average days' sales outstanding for manufacturers and wholesalers.

**Quick Assets:** current assets that can be readily converted into cash (generally, accounts receivable).

**Quick Assets Ratio:** cash and cash equivalents plus trade receivables (net) divided by total current liabilities; used as measure of liquidity.

**Quid Pro Quo:** 1. giving of one valuable thing for another. 2. mutual consideration between parties to contract.

**Quitclaim:** to release or relinquish claim or title.

# R

**Rack Jobber:** wholesale distributor who sells housewares and other convenience-type merchandise through retail stores and assumes responsibility for stocking and maintaining store's inventory.

**Rate of Exchange:** amount of one country's currency that can be bought with another country's currency at a particular point in time.

**Rate of Interest:** cost of borrowing money, usually expressed as annual percentage charge.

**Rating:** 1. assessment of borrower's financial strength and creditworthiness. 2. symbol used to denote borrower's creditworthiness.

**Ratios:** mathematical relationship between two or more things, used as indication of a company's financial strength relative to other companies of comparable size or in same industry.

**Real Property:** land and anything erected or growing on it or affixed to it.

**Receivables:** money due or collectible for goods sold, services performed, or money loaned. Also called accounts receivable.

**Receivables Turnover:** measurement of how effective a company is in collecting on its trade receivables.

**Receiver:** person appointed by the court to receive, take charge, and hold in trust a property in litigation or bankruptcy until a legal decision is made as to its disposition.

**Receivership:** 1. court action whereby money or property is placed under control, and administration of receiver is to be preserved for benefit of persons or creditors ultimately entitled to it. 2. procedure used to help a distressed debtor or to resolve a dispute.

**Reclamation:** 1. legal action by titleholder to recover property from another's possession. 2. process used to restore land to usable state.

**Record:** written account of act, transaction, or instrument drawn by proper legal authority that remains as permanent evidence.

**Recourse:** right of holder in due course to demand payment from anyone who endorsed instrument if original signer fails to pay.

**Recovery:** amount finally collected; amount of judgment.

**Reference Check:** contacting and interviewing business or professional associates of credit applicant to gain information about his or her creditworthiness.

**References:** names of trade suppliers or creditors provided by a customer to be used as a source of information about that customer.

**Refer to Maker:** term stamped by financial institution on a check to indicate its rejection.

**Refinance:** to reorganize existing debts by obtaining new debt that incorporates or pays off existing debts.

**Register:** book of factual public information, kept by a public official.

**Regulation 9:** regulation issued by the Comptroller of Currency allowing national banks to operate trust departments and act as fiduciaries. Under Regulation 9, a national bank is permitted to act as trustee, administrator, and registrar of stocks and bonds and engage in related activities, such as management of a collective investment fund, as long as these activities do not violate state legislation.

**Regulation A:** Federal Reserve Board regulation governing advances by Federal Reserve Banks to depository institutions at a Federal Reserve discount window. Credit advances are available to any bank or savings institution maintaining transaction accounts or non-personal time deposits. The Fed has two different programs for handling discount window borrowings:

• adjustment credit to meet temporary needs for funds when other sources are not available.

• extended credit, designed to assist financial institutions with longer-term needs for funds. This includes seasonal credit privileges extended to smaller financial institutions that do not have ready access to money market funds. Federal Reserve Banks may also extend emergency credit to financial institutions other than depository institutions in which failure to obtain credit would affect the economy adversely.

**Regulation B:** Federal Reserve regulation prohibiting discrimination against consumer credit applicants and establishing guidelines for collecting and evaluating credit information. Regulation B prohibits creditors from discriminating on the basis of age, sex, race, color, religion, national origin, marital status, or receipt of public assistance. Regulation B also requires creditors to give written notification of rejection, statement of applicant's rights under Equal Credit Opportunity Act of 1974, and statement listing reasons for rejection, or applicant has right to request reasons. If applicant is denied credit because of adverse information in credit bureau report, applicant is entitled to receive copy of bureau report at no cost. Creditors who furnish credit information when reporting information on married borrowers must report information in name of each spouse.

**Regulation C:** Federal Reserve regulation implementing Home Mortgage Disclosure Act of 1975, requiring depository institutions to make annual disclosure of location of certain residential loans to determine whether depository institutions are meeting credit needs of their local communities. Specifically exempted are institutions with assets of $10 million or less. Regulation C requires lenders of mortgages that are insured or guaranteed by a federal agency to disclose number and total dollar amount of mortgage loans originated or purchased in recent calendar year, itemized by census tract where property is located.

**Regulation D:** Federal Reserve regulation that sets uniform reserve requirements for depository financial institutions holding transaction accounts or non-personal time deposits. Reserves are maintained in form of vault cash or non-interest-bearing balance at a Federal Reserve Bank or at a correspondent bank.

**Regulation E:** Federal Reserve regulation that sets rules, liabilities, and procedures for electronic funds transfers (EFT) and establishes consumer protections using EFT systems. This regulation prescribes rules for solicitation and issuance of EFT debit cards, governs consumer liability for unauthorized transfers, and requires financial institutions to disclose annually terms and conditions of EFT services.

**Regulation F:** Federal Reserve regulation requiring state-chartered banks with 500 or more stockholders and at least $1 million in assets to file financial statements with the Board of Governors of the Federal Reserve System. In general, these state-chartered member banks must file registration statements, periodic financial statements, proxy statements, and various other disclosures of interest to investors. These regulations are substantially similar to those issued by Securities and Exchange Commission.

**Regulation G:** Federal Reserve regulation governing credit secured by margin securities extended or arranged by parties other than banks or broker/dealers. It requires lenders to register credit extensions of $200,000, secured by margin stock, or $500,000 in total credit, within 30 days after end of quarter.

**Regulation H:** Federal Reserve regulation defining membership requirements for state-chartered banks that become members of the Federal Reserve System. The regulation sets forth procedures as well as privileges and requirements for membership. The regulation also requires state-chartered banks acting as securities transfer agents to register with board.

**Regulation I:** Federal Reserve regulation requiring each member bank joining the Federal Reserve System to purchase stock in its Federal Reserve Bank equal to 6% of its capital and surplus. Federal Reserve Bank stock, which pays interest semiannually, is nontransferable and cannot be used as collateral. When bank increases or decreases its capital base, it must adjust its ownership of Federal Reserve stock accordingly.

**Regulation J:** Federal Reserve regulation providing legal framework for collection of checks and other cash items and net settlement of balances through Federal Reserve System. It specifies terms and conditions under which Federal Reserve Banks will receive checks for collection from depository institutions, presentment to paying banks, and return of unpaid items. It is supplemented by operating circulars issued by Federal Reserve Banks.

**Regulation K:** Federal Reserve regulation governing international banking operations by bank holding companies and foreign banks in the U.S. The regulation permits Edge Act corporations to engage in range of international banking and financial activities. It also permits U.S. banks to own up to 100% of non-financial companies located outside the U.S. Regulation K also imposes reserve requirements on Edge Act corporations, as specified in Regulation D, and limits interstate activities of foreign banks in the U.S.

**Regulation L:** Federal Reserve regulation prohibiting interlocking director arrangements in member banks or bank holding companies. Management official of state member bank or bank holding company may not act simultaneously as management official of another depository institution if both are not affiliated, are very large banks, or are located in same local area. Regulation L provides 10-year grandfather period for certain interlocks and allows some on exception basis, such as organizations owned by women or minority groups, newly chartered organizations, and in situations in which implementing regulation would endanger safety and soundness.

**Regulation M:** Federal Reserve regulation implementing consumer leasing provisions of Truth in Lending Act of 1968. It covers leases on personal property for more than four months for family, personal, or household use. It requires leasing companies to disclose in writing the cost of lease, including security deposit and monthly payments, taxes, and other payments, and in case of an open-end lease, whether a balloon payment may be applied. It also requires written disclosure of terms of lease, including insurance, guaranties, responsibility for servicing property, and whether lessor has an option to buy property at lease termination.

**Regulation N:** Federal Reserve regulation governing transactions among Federal Reserve Banks and transactions involving Federal Reserve Banks and foreign banks and governments. This regulation gives the board responsibility for approving in advance negotiations or agreements by Federal Reserve Banks and foreign banks, bankers, and governments. The Federal Reserve Bank may, under direction of the Federal Open Market Committee, undertake negotiations, agreements, or facilitate open market transactions. Reserve Banks must report quarterly to the Board of Governors on accounts they maintain with foreign banks.

**Regulation O:** Federal Reserve regulation limiting amount of credit member banks may extend to their own executive officers. Regulation O also implements reporting requirements of Financial Institutions Regulatory and Interest Rate Control Act of 1978 and Garn-St. Germain Depository Institutions Act of 1982.

**Regulation P:** Federal Reserve regulation that sets minimum standards for security devices, such as bank vaults and currency handling equipment, including automated teller machines. Member bank must appoint security officer to develop and administer program to deter thefts and file the annual compliance statement with its Federal Reserve Bank.

**Regulation Q:** Federal Reserve regulation requiring depository institutions to state clearly terms for depositing and renewing time deposits and certificates of deposit and also any penalties for early withdrawal of savings accounts.

**Regulation R:** Federal Reserve regulation prohibiting individuals who are engaged in securities underwriting, sale, and distribution from serving as directors, officers, or employees of member banks. Regulation R specifically exempts those involved in government securities trading and general obligations of states and municipalities.

**Regulation S:** Federal Reserve regulation implementing section of Right to Financial Privacy Act of 1978 requiring government authorities to pay reasonable fees to financial institutions for financial records of individuals and small partnerships available to federal agencies in connection with government loan programs or Internal Revenue Service summons.

**Regulation T:** Federal Reserve regulation governing credit extensions by securities brokers and dealers, including all members of national securities exchanges. Brokers/dealers may not extend credit to their customers unless such loans are secured by margin securities—securities listed and traded on national securities exchange, mutual funds, and over-the-counter stock designated by Securities and Exchange Commission as eligible for trading in national market system. Generally, brokers/dealers may not extend credit on margin securities in excess of percentage of current market value permitted by board.

**Regulation U:** Federal Reserve regulation governing extensions of credit by banks for purchasing and carrying margin securities. Whenever lender makes loan secured by margin securities, bank must have customer execute purpose statement regardless of use of loan.

**Regulation V:** Federal Reserve regulation dealing with financing of contractors, subcontractors, and others involved in national defense work. The regulation spells out the authority granted to Federal Reserve Banks under the Defense Production Act of 1950 to assist federal departments and agencies in making and administering loan guaranties to defense-related contractors and sets maximum interest rates, guaranty fees, and commitment fees.

**Regulation X:** Federal Reserve regulation extending provisions of other securities-related regulations—Regulations G, T, and U—to foreign persons or organizations who obtain credit outside U.S. for purchase of U.S. Treasury securities.

**Regulation Y:** Federal Reserve regulation governing banking and nonbanking activities of bank holding companies and divestiture of impermissible nonbank activities. Regulation Y spells out procedures for forming bank holding company and procedures to be followed by bank holding companies acquiring voting shares in bank or nonbank companies. Regulation Y also lists those nonbank activities that are deemed closely related to banking and therefore permissible for bank holding companies.

**Regulation Z:** Federal Reserve regulation implementing consumer credit protections in the Truth in Lending Act of 1968. Major areas of regulation require lenders to:
- give borrowers written disclosure on essential credit terms, including cost of credit expressed as finance charge and annual percentage rate.
- respond to consumer complaints of billing errors on certain credit accounts within specified period.
- identify credit transactions on periodic statements of open-end credit accounts.
- provide certain rights regarding credit cards.
- inform customers of right of rescission in certain mortgage-related loans within specified period.
- comply with special requirements when advertising credit.

**Regulation AA:** Federal Reserve regulation establishing procedures for handling consumer complaints about alleged unfair or deceptive practices by a state member bank.

**Regulation BB:** Federal Reserve regulation implementing Community Reinvestment Act of 1977 (CRA). Banks are required to make available to public a statement indicating communities served, type of credit the lender is prepared to extend, and public comments to its CRA statement.

**Regulation CC:** Federal Reserve regulation implementing Expedited Funds Availability Act of 1987, setting endorsement standards on checks collected by depository financial institutions. Endorsement standard is designed to facilitate identification of endorsing bank and prompt return of unpaid checks. The regulation specifies funds availability schedules that banks must comply with and procedures for returning dishonored checks.

**Release:** to discharge debt or give up claim against party from whom it is due by party to whom it is due.

**Remedy:** legal means by which right is enforced or violation of right is prevented or compensated.

**Rent:** periodic payments made by tenant to owner in return for leasing land, building space, or equipment.

**Reorganization:** 1. voluntary or court-ordered change in capital structure of corporation in which all assets of an old corporation are transferred to a newly formed corporation. 2. restructuring of business entity, whether in or out of bankruptcy.

**Replevin:** legal action taken to recover possession of property unlawfully taken.

**Repossess:** action taken by creditor in which he or she takes possession of goods purchased under credit agreement or pledged as collateral if debtor defaults on terms of contract.

**Rescind:** to void contract from its inception. Result is that parties are restored to relative positions before contract was made.

**Rescission:** agreement by parties to contract that effects cancellation of contract.

**Reserve:** in accounting, funds set aside for specific purpose.

**Reserve for Bad Debts:** valuation account established for accounts receivable that may prove uncollectible.

**Residence:** place where person legally lives part or full time.

**Residual Value:** the estimated recoverable amount of a depreciable asset as of the time of its removal from service.

**Resolution Trust Corporation (RTC):** federal agency established in 1989 to oversee the savings and loan bailout.

**Restraint of Trade:** any action, by agreement or by combination, that tends to eliminate competition, artificially sets up prices, or results in monopoly.

**Restrictive Endorsement:** endorsement on negotiable instrument that limits any further negotiability, for example, "for deposit only" written on back of check.

**Restructured Loan:** loan on which a bank, for economic or legal reasons related to debtor's financial difficulties, grants concession to debtor that would not be considered otherwise.

**Retailer:** company that sells its product directly to end-user.

**Retained Earnings:** cumulative earnings and losses of company that remain undistributed to shareholders.

**Retentions:** amounts withheld by customer from total billings until contractor has satisfactorily completed project.

**Retroactive:** 1. effective as of past date. 2. having reference to prior time.

**Return:** rate of profit or earnings on sales or investment.

**Return Items/Returned Checks:** checks, drafts, or notes returned unpaid to originating bank by drawee bank so that originator can correct any errors or irregularities and may present items for collection again.

**Revenue:** 1. income from sales, interest, or dividends. 2. income from investment or wages.

**Reviewed Financial Statements:** business financial statements that are reviewed by independent accountants through inquiries of management and performance of analytical procedures on financials to provide limited assurance that no material modifications are necessary for statements to conform to generally accepted accounting principles. Independent accountants do not express opinion on review statements.

**Revolving Charge:** credit type that allows borrower to become indebted up to an approved credit limit, with no fixed maturity date. Finance costs are assessed monthly on unpaid balance, and periodic payments are required.

**Revolving Credit:** commitment under which funds can be borrowed, repaid, and re-borrowed during life of credit. Such credits have stated maturity date at which time borrower may have option of converting outstanding balance into term loan. See also Evergreen Revolving Credit.

**Rider:** any schedule or amendment attached to a contract or document that becomes part of it.

**Right of Rescission:** consumer's right as prescribed by Truth in Lending Act of 1968 to rescind certain credit and mortgage contracts within three days without penalty.

**Right of Setoff:** right of financial institution to apply borrower's funds on deposit to debt owed to the financial institution in event that payment on the debt is not made as agreed.

**Risk-Based Capital:** level of capital that bank is required to maintain; level is determined by relating capital to risk by type of asset.

**RMA:** see Risk Management Association.

**RMA General Figure Ranges:** dollar amount ranges established by RMA to ensure accuracy and consistency when exchanging credit information. There are four ranges: low, 1-1.9; moderate, 2-3.9; medium, 4-6.9; and high, 7-9.9. Ranges can be applied to any figure category. Sample figure categories are: nominal = under $100; 3 figures = from $100 to $999; 4 figures = from $1,000 to $9,999; 5 figures = from $10,000 to $99,999; and 6 figures = from $100,000 to $999,999. Information is reported, using both range description and figure category; for example, "average balances are in medium 4-figure range."

**Risk Management Association (RMA):** association of lending, credit, and risk management professionals. Originally, RMA was founded to facilitate the exchange of credit information. Today, RMA works continuously to improve practices of the financial services industry and to provide members with networking opportunities, training, research publications, and seminars.

**Robinson-Patman Act:** federal legislation prohibiting firms engaged in interstate commerce from charging different buyers different prices for the same goods unless there is difference in costs or the price does not restrict competition.

**R.O.G. Dating:** payment term that uses date customer is in receipt of goods as effective sale date.

**Royalty:** compensation made to another for use of his or her work.

**RTC:** see Resolution Trust Corporation.

**Rule of 72:** method commonly used to approximate time required for sum of money to double at given rate of interest. Rule of 72 is computed by dividing interest rate by 72.

**Rule of 78s:** mathematical formula used in computing interest rebated when borrower pays off loan before maturity. Rule of 78s is applied mostly to consumer loans in which finance charges were computed using add-on interest or discounted interest method of interest calculation. Also called sum of digits method.

## S

**Sale:** agreement or contract that transfers title of goods or property from one person or entity to another for consideration.

**Sale and Lease Back:** arrangement whereby company sells goods with intent to lease those same goods from buyer.

**Sale on Approval:** purchase of goods conditioned on buyer approval of goods or retention of them beyond reasonable time.

**Salvage Value:** estimated worth of a depreciated asset at the end of its useful life.

**Satisfaction:** paying debt in full.

**Satisfaction of Judgment:** legal evidence that recorded judgment has been paid or settled and entered in court records.

**Satisfaction Piece:** legal evidence that debt has been paid in full or settled and that liens on collateral have been released.

**SBA:** see Small Business Administration.

**Schedule:** listing by account name or number of total sales, current sales, monies owing or paid, chargebacks, or credits. Also called aging schedule or trial balance.

**Scheduled Liability:** 1. in property insurance, listing of property—items or locations—covered. 2. in dishonesty insurance (fidelity bonding), listing of persons or positions covered.

**Scheduled Payment:** partial payments made at dates specified in credit agreement.

**Schedules:** in bankruptcy, lists showing debtor's property—location, quantity, and money value; names and addresses of creditors and their class; or names and addresses of stockholders of each class.

**Scrap Value:** worth of asset that is going to be destroyed or used for its components.

**Seasonal Loans:** loans used to finance cyclical buildup of current (working capital) assets until those assets can be converted to cash.

**Second Lien:** lien that can be honored only after first lien is satisfied.

**Second Mortgage:** mortgage secured by equity in property but one that cannot enforce payment until claims of first mortgage are satisfied.

**Secret Partner:** partner in business whose interest in partnership is not publicly known.

**Secured Creditor:** lender or other person whose claim is supported by taking collateral.

**Secured Loan:** loan supported by borrower's pledge of an asset such as marketable securities, accounts receivable, inventories, real estate, equipment, etc.

**Secured Note:** note that provides, upon default, certain pledged or mortgaged property that may be applied or sold in payment of debt.

**Secured Party:** 1. lender or other person to whom or in whose favor security interest has been given. Includes person to whom accounts or chattel paper have been sold. 2. trustee or agent representing holders of obligations issued under indenture of trust, equipment trust agreement, or the like.

**Securities:** 1. documents that evidence debt or property pledged in fulfillment of obligation. 2. evidence of indebtedness or right to participate in earnings and distribution of corporate, trust, and other property.

**Security:** guaranty or assets pledged that can be applied to loan or obligation.

**Security Agreement:** formally executed document that gives lender rights to property pledged by borrower in support of debt.

**Security Interest:** right that lender or lienholder obtains to debtor's goods as evidenced by security agreement.

**Seller's Market:** economic condition in which demand is greater than supply, and that typically causes prices to increase.

**Sequestered Account:** account that has been attached by court order with disbursements subject to court approval.

**Service Business:** firm that performs functions for its customers rather than sells goods.

**Setoff:** 1. defendant's counterdemand against plaintiff. 2. right of parties to contract to reduce debt owed to one party by netting it against amount owed by other. See also Right of Setoff.

**Settle:** 1. to mutually reach agreement for adjustment or liquidation of debt. 2. to negotiate payment of obligation or lawsuit for less than amount claimed.

**Settlement:** 1. adjustment or liquidation of accounts. 2. full and final payment of debt. See also Out-of-Court Settlement.

**Shared National Credit (SNC):** any loan originally $20 million or more that is shared at its inception by two or more financial institutions under a formal intercreditor or participation agreement or sold in part to one or more financial institutions with purchasing financial institution assuming its pro rata share of credit risk.

**Shareholder:** person or entity that legally owns stock in a corporation.

**Sheriff's Sale:** court-ordered sale of property to satisfy judgment, mortgage, lien, or other outstanding debt against debtor.

**Sherman Antitrust Act:** federal legislation aimed at prevention of business monopoly; act declares illegal every contract, combination, or conspiracy in restraint of normal trade.

**Short-Term Liabilities:** current debts that are due within one year.

**Short-Term Loan:** current debt obligation that matures within one year, evidenced by promissory note that spells out terms of agreement.

**SIC:** see Standard Industrial Classification.

**Sight Draft:** draft payable on demand when presented to drawee. See also Draft, Letter of Credit, and Time Draft.

**Signal Action:** notices that provide subscriber with list of accounts in which subscriber has interest and on which delinquent payments have been reported.

**Signature Loan:** unsecured loan backed only by borrower's signature on promissory note. No collateral is taken by lender. This loan is generally offered to individuals with good credit standing. Also called good faith loan or character loan.

**Signature Verification:** examination of signature on negotiable instrument to determine whether handwriting is genuine and whether person signing check is authorized to use account.

**Simple Interest:** interest calculated on outstanding principal amount of debt or investment only.

**Single Proprietorship:** ownership of company by one person.

**Skip Tracing:** process used to obtain information to locate debtor's whereabouts in order to collect payment on debts. Sources used include other creditors, friends, relatives, neighbors, directories, credit bureaus, court records, and other informants or references.

**Slander:** oral defamation of another's reputation.

**Small Business Administration (SBA):** federal agency whose function is to advise and assist small businesses; provides loan guaranties for small businesses, minorities, and veterans plus financial assistance to small businesses that have suffered catastrophes.

**SNC:** see Shared National Credit.

**Soft Goods:** nondurable consumer goods such as clothing and linen, having a short-term useful life.

**Soldier's and Sailor's Relief Act:** federal act, also passed by various states, under which right to legally enforce an obligation against a person is suspended during the period that person is in military service or for period thereafter.

**Sole Owner:** one with title to proprietorship.

**Solvency:** ability to pay one's debts in usual and ordinary course of business as they mature.

**Special Material:** made-to-order material or work done to customer's specifications that has no value to seller if order is canceled.

**Special Mention Assets:** as it relates to risk assessment of bank assets, assets that deserve management's close attention. If left uncorrected, these potential weaknesses may result in deterioration of repayment prospects for asset or in institution's credit position at some future date. Special mention assets are not adversely classified and do not expose institution to sufficient risk to warrant adverse classification.

**Specific Coverage:** property coverage on designated property or item. Contrasts with Blanket Coverage.

**Specific Performance:** court order directing party guilty of breach of contract to undertake complete performance of contractual obligation in instances in which damages would inadequately compensate injured party.

**Speculation:** investment made with hope of achieving large financial gain.

**Speculator:** one who makes risky investments for quick financial gain rather than long-term investment.

**Stale Check:** negotiable draft that has been held too long to be honored for payment; time varies from state to state.

**Standard Industrial Classification (SIC):** statistical classification standard underlying all establishment-based federal economic statistics classified by industry. SIC is used to promote comparability of establishment data describing various facets of the U.S. economy. Classification covers entire field of economic activities and defines industries in accordance with composition and structure of economy. It is revised periodically to reflect economy's changing industrial organization. See also *North American Industrial Classification System* and *NAICS*.

**Standby Letter of Credit:** type of letter of credit issued by bank that may be drawn on by payee only if party that makes letter of credit (drawer) defaults or does not perform according to terms of specific contract or agreement. See also Letter of Credit.

**Statement:** 1. itemized summary and accounting of charges, payments, and balance outstanding at close of billing period. 2. financial report.

**Statement of Cash Flows:** financial statement that shows cash receipts and disbursements for given period.

**Statement of Changes in Owner's Equity:** financial statement that reconciles changes in capital accounts (capital stock, paid in surplus, and retained earnings).

**Statute:** written law.

**Statute of Frauds:** law prohibiting filing of actions or suits against certain types of contracts unless the contracts are in writing.

**Statute of Limitations:** law that sets time frame for bringing action against another. Time frame varies according to nature of claim and jurisdiction.

**Stay:** act of arresting judicial proceeding by court order.

**Stipulation:** agreement between opposing attorneys in lawsuit, usually required to be in writing.

**Stock:** 1. merchandise or inventory on hand and available for sale. 2. certificate that indicates number of shares of ownership in corporation.

**Stock Power:** document executed in form of power of attorney by which owner of stock authorizes another party to sell or transfer stock.

**Stop Payment Order:** instructions given by depositor to a financial institution to dishonor, or not make payment on, a certain check.

**Subchapter S:** business concern chartered as corporation that is taxed as partnership. An S corporation has 35 or fewer shareholders and can use cash basis of accounting. Corporate gains (or losses) from operations are taxed to shareholders as individuals.

**Subcontract:** contract between prime contractor and another contractor or supplier to perform specified work or to supply specified materials in accordance with plans and specifications for project.

**Subject:** party on which credit information is requested.

**Sublimit:** specified, partial amount of credit facility that is designated for special use.

**Subordination:** 1. signed agreement acknowledging that one's claim or interest is inferior to another's. 2. act of agreeing to take secondary position.

**Subpoena:** process to demand person to appear in court and give testimony.

**Subrogation:** substitution of one creditor for another so that substituted creditor succeeds to rights, remedies, or proceeds of claim.

**Subsidiary:** business entity owned or controlled by another organization.

**Substandard Assets:** as it relates to risk assessment of bank assets, assets that are inadequately protected by current sound worth and paying capacity of obligor or of collateral pledged, if any. Assets so classified must have well-defined weakness or weaknesses that jeopardize liquidation of debt. They are characterized by distinct possibility that bank will sustain some loss if deficiencies are not corrected.

**Summons:** formal notice served on defendant stating that action has been instituted against him or her and requiring defendant to appear in court to answer it.

**Supplementary Proceedings:** statutory action requiring judgment debtor to appear in court to discover property against which action can be taken by creditor to enforce collection of judgment.

**Supplier:** business that sells goods, materials, or services to customers. Also called vendor.

**Surety:** one who agrees to be primarily liable with another and to fulfill another's obligations under terms of agreement.

**Surety Bond:** guaranty that payment or performance of some specific act will be completed under penalty or forfeiture of bond usually issued by a bonding company.

**Suretyship:** undertaking by person or entity to pay obligation of obligee in favor of principal when obligee defaults; such undertaking by individual is known as personal suretyship and by insurance company as corporate suretyship.

**Suspense File:** group of accounts, records, or other items held temporarily until final disposition is determined.

**Swap:** A financial derivative contract between two parties to exchange fixed-rate interest payments for floating-rate interest payments, or floating-rate interest payments on different bases (e.g., prime rate versus LIBOR), calculated on specific floating indices by reference to a notional principal amount for a specified term.

**Sweep Account:** type of cash management tool in which, when prearranged amount of cash accumulates in account, amount is automatically invested.

**Swindle:** 1. to obtain money or property by deceitful misrepresentation. 2. to cheat or fraudulently induce individual to give up his or her property willingly.

**Swing Loan:** see *Bridge Loan*.

**Syndicate:** temporary association of persons or firms formed to carry out business venture or project of mutual interest.

**Syndication:** project financing whereby commercial or investment bankers agree to advance portion of funding. Syndicator acts as investment manager, collecting loan origination fee or commitment fee from borrower and arranging for sale to other banks in group. Typically, syndicator keeps only a small portion of total financing. A syndicated loan differs from loan participation because syndicate members are known at outset to borrower. Syndication also separates lead bank from group of financial institutions that ultimately fund obligation.

## T

**Takeover:** acquisition, seizure, control, or management of one business by another.

**Tangible Assets:** assets that can be weighed, measured, or counted, including cash, property, machinery, and buildings.

**Tax:** payments imposed by legislative authority for support of government and its functions.

**Taxable Income:** portion of individual's or entity's income that is subject to taxation.

**Tax Avoidance:** act of using legal deductions, exemptions, and tax code provisions to reduce taxes payable.

**Tax Evasion:** failure to report taxable income to avoid proper payment of taxes.

**Tax Foreclosure:** legal seizure and sale of property by authorized public official to satisfy unpaid taxes.

**Tax Levy:** legislative action by which tax is imposed.

**Tax Lien:** statutory claim by state or municipality against property of person owing taxes. Property may be sold to satisfy obligation or judgment filed against it.

**Tax Sale:** sale of property seized by governmental taxing body for nonpayment of taxes.

**Tenancy by Entirety:** ownership in property by husband and wife in which each becomes whole owner of the entire estate upon the other's death. See also Joint Tenancy with Rights of Survivorship.

**Tenancy in Common:** two or more persons who hold title to land or other property in undivided ownership.

**Tender:** 1. unconditional offer of money or performance to satisfy claim. 2. offer to buy stock to take control of company.

**Term Loan:** fixed-term business loan with a maturity of more than one year and with defined periodic payments, providing borrower with working capital to acquire assets or inventory or to finance plant and equipment.

**Terms:** conditions and requirements as set forth in sales proposal, contract, or promissory note.

**Terms of Sale:** mutually agreed upon conditions for transfer of title or ownership of goods or property.

**Testimony:** written or oral evidence given in court under oath.

**Third Party:** one who is not directly related to action between two parties but who may be affected by its outcome.

**Third-Party Claim:** demand made by person who is not party to action for delivery or possession of personal property, title to which is claimed by third party.

**Time Deposit:** 1. interest-bearing funds deposited in a financial institution for a specified period of time, such as certificates of deposit and savings accounts. 2. under Regulation D, deposit in which depositor is not permitted to make withdrawals within six days after date of deposit unless deposit is subject to early withdrawal penalty.

**Time Draft:** draft payable on fixed date or certain number of days after sight or date of draft. See also *Banker's Acceptance, Draft, Letter of Credit,* and *Sight Draft.*

**Title:** document that evidences legal ownership and possession of property.

**Title Company:** business that as contracted researches specific property's history through real estate records and issues policy to purchaser or lienholder guaranteeing that there are no known defects in title.

**Title Insurance:** a guarantee by a title insurance company that it will indemnify the insured, in a specific amount, against losses resulting from defects in the title to a property. The insured may be the owner of the property, that person's heirs and devises, or the lender and future assignees.

**Title Search:** to review history of property's ownership and any judgments or liens filed against it.

**Tolling the Statute:** act of debtor to freeze statute of limitations that extends period for creditor to legally enforce payment of account. Individual state laws and statutes apply.

**Tort:** violation of legal duty that results in injury or damage to another.

**Trade Acceptance:** draft, accepted by buyer, sent with shipment of goods, requiring customer to pay amount involved at specific date and place.

**Trade Credit:** accounts payable; credit extended from one company to another.

**Trade Debts:** liabilities due from one business to another for purchase of supplies, inventory, etc.

**Trade-in:** property accepted by seller as partial down payment on purchase of new item.

**Trade Information:** confidential exchange of payment history and credit information among suppliers.

**Trademark:** distinctive identifying mark, word, or logo of product or service; protected when registered with U.S. Patent Office.

**Trade Name:** name used by a company to identify itself in the course of business. Also known as Trade Style or Fictitious Name.

**Trade Payment Record:** summary of performance of company in meeting terms of its credit obligations.

**Trade References:** names of suppliers or business creditors with whom credit information on customer can be exchanged.

**Treasury Workstation:** microcomputer-based information management system that allows corporate treasurer to automate daily balance reporting of collected balances, to invest idle funds in short-term money market, and to disburse funds to trade creditors. Overall aim is improvement in productivity and eventual integration of funds management and corporate accounting systems, such as order entry and invoicing.

**Trial Balance:** listing of all account balances from general ledger used in preparing financial statements.

**Truck Jobber:** wholesale merchant who sells and delivers products from truck inventory at time of sale. Also called *Wagon Distributor.*

**Trust:** right to real or personal property that is held by one for benefit of another.

**Trust Company:** business that acts as fiduciary and agent, handling trusts, estates, and guardianships for individuals and businesses.

**Trustee:** one who holds or is entrusted with management of property or funds for benefit of another.

**Trustee in Bankruptcy:** person appointed by court or elected by creditors to manage bankrupt property and carry out responsibilities of trust in proceedings.

**Trust Receipt:** trust agreement (in receipt form) between a financial institution and borrower. It is temporarily substituted for possessory collateral securing creditor's loan so that creditor may release instruments, documents, or other property without releasing title to property. Borrower agrees to keep property (collateral), as well as any funds received from its sale, separate and distinct from borrower's own property and subject to repossession by the financial institution in event that he or she fails to comply with conditions specified in trust agreement.

**Truth in Lending Act of 1968:** See *Regulation Z.*

**Turnkey:** something that is constructed, supplied, or installed and fully ready as intended.

# U

**UCC:** see *Uniform Commercial Code.*

**Ultra Vires:** unauthorized acts taken by corporation beyond powers conferred on it by corporate charter.

**Umbrella Policy:** in liability insurance, policy that applies excess coverage to primary or underlying contract; provides large limits and broad coverage or may cover only primary basis risks not otherwise insured.

**Unaudited Financial Statement:** financial statement or report based on figures that have not been verified by a qualified accountant.

**Uncollected Funds:** deposits not yet collected by a financial institution, such as checks that have not yet cleared.

**Uncollectible Accounts:** receivables or debts not capable of being settled or recovered.

**Underwriter:** 1. person who reviews application for insurance and decides whether or not to accept risk. 2. one who agrees to purchase entire issue of bonds or securities at end of certain period.

**Undue Influence:** improper or illegal pressure used to wrongfully take advantage of person or to influence his or her actions or decisions.

**Unearned Discount:** A term used to reflect a reduced price (from the face value of an invoice) taken by a buyer without the consent of the seller.

**Unearned Income:** income received in advance of being earned.

**Unencumbered Property:** property that has no legal defects in its title; a property free and clear of any liens or debts.

**Unenforceable Claim:** debt on which all collection efforts have failed.

**Unfair Competition:** any fraudulent or dishonest practice intended to harm or unfairly attract competitor's customers.

**Uniform Commercial Code (UCC):** comprehensive set of statutes created to provide uniformity in business laws in all states, as approved by National Conference of Commissioners on Uniform State Laws. Statutes can vary from state to state.

**Unit Banking:** banking system in several states that prohibits branching or operation of more than one full-service banking office by state-chartered or national banks. Limited branching laws encourage chartering of large numbers of small, independently owned state banks and large multi-bank holding companies that own numerous unit banks.

**Unjust Enrichment:** doctrine whereby one is not allowed to profit inequitably at another's expense.

**Unsatisfied Judgment:** recorded judgment that has not been released or discharged.

**Unsecured Creditor:** one who grants credit without taking collateral in support of it.

**Unsecured Loan:** loan made on strength of borrower's general financial condition. Contrasts with Secured Loan.

**Upstream Funding:** funds borrowed by a subsidiary of a holding company for holding company's use. Contrasts with Downstream Funding.

**Usury:** The rate of interest that exceeds the legal limit allowed to be charged for the use of another's money. Legal limit of interest for different types of loan transactions is established by state law.

# V

**Valuable Consideration:** see *Consideration.*

**Valuation:** 1. the estimated or determined worth of something. 2. process of appraising or affixing value of something.

**Value Received:** phrase used in bill of exchange or promissory note to denote that lawful consideration has been given.

**Variable Interest Rate:** interest rate that fluctuates with changes in an identified base rate or index.

**Vendor:** trade supplier or service provider.

**Venture Capital:** capital invested or available for investment in the ownership element of a new enterprise.

**Verdict:** formal decision of judge or jury on matter submitted in trial.

**Verification:** 1. affidavit or statement under oath swearing to truth or accuracy of written document. 2. in accounting, confirmation of entries in books of account.

**Verification of Deposit (VOD):** formal request by creditor to debtor's bank for account balance information.

**Vest:** 1. to give immediate transfer of title to property. 2. to obtain absolute ownership.

**VOD:** see *Verification of Deposit.*

**Void:** having no legal force.

**Voidable Contract:** contract that is nullified as to party who committed invalid act but not with respect to other party, unless he or she agrees to treat it as such.

**Voluntary Bankruptcy:** bankruptcy initiated by debtor petitioning court to be declared bankrupt.

**Voucher:** 1. statement itemizing payment or receipt of money. 2. detachable portion of check that describes purpose for which check was issued.

# W

**Wage Assignment:** agreement by borrower that permits creditor to collect certain portion of borrower's wages from employer in the event of a default.

**Wage Garnishment:** court order requiring that percentage of debtor's earnings be withheld by employer and paid directly to creditor.

**Waiver:** intentional or voluntary relinquishing of known legal right.

**Warehouse Loans:** loans made against warehouse receipts that are evidence of collateral for material stored in public warehouse.

**Warehouse Receipt:** receipt issued by person engaged in business of storing goods for hire. It is document of title that gives evidence that person in possession of warehouse receipt is entitled to receive, hold, and dispose of document and goods it covers. Warehouse receipt in turn obligates warehouser to keep goods safely and to redeliver them upon surrender of receipt, properly endorsed, and payment of storage charges.

**Wholesaler:** company whose primary function is as intermediary between manufacturer of goods and retailer or other wholesalers.

**Will:** legal declaration by person making disposition of property, effective only after death.

**Windfall Profit:** large, unexpected return or income.

**Wire Fate:** instructions to financial institution requesting confirmation by wire that out-of-town check, sent for collection, has been paid.

**Without Exception:** see *Free and Clear.*

**Without Prejudice:** legal term used in offer, motion, or suit to indicate that parties' rights or privileges involved remain intact and to allow new suit to be brought on same cause of action.

**Without Recourse:** term used in endorsing negotiable instrument excluding endorser from responsibility should obligation not be paid.

**With Prejudice:** legal term used for dismissal of lawsuit that bars any future action and that, if prosecuted to final adjudication, would have been adverse to plaintiff.

**With Recourse:** endorsement of negotiable instrument on which endorser remains responsible should obligation not be paid.

**Working Capital:** 1. current assets less current liabilities, used as measure of firm's liquidity. 2. funds available to finance company's current operations.

**Working Papers:** information or schedules used by accountant in preparing financial reports.

**Work in Process (WIP):** goods in act of being manufactured, but not yet finished and ready for sale, representing a portion of inventory.

**Workout:** problem loan on which the financial institution is working closely with borrower for repayment, restructuring, or modification because of noncompliance with loan covenants.

**Wrap-Around Mortgage:** A second or junior mortgage with a face value of both the amount it secures and the balance due under the first mortgage. Covenant contained within second mortgage used to induce sellers of commercial properties to sell to buyer who has small down payment, normally when interest rates are high.

**Writ of Execution:** 1. writ issued by court ordering sheriff to attach debtor's property to enforce payment of judgment.

**Write-down:** partial reduction in book value of asset as result of obsolescence or depreciation.

**Write-off:** see *Charge-off.*

**Writ of Attachment:** court order directing sheriff to seize property of debtor held as security for satisfaction of judgment.

## Y

**Yield:** rate of return on investment.

## Z

**Zero Balance Account:** a checking account (subordinate account) used for disbursing or collecting funds in which no balances are maintained. At the end of the processing day, funds are transferred from a master account or concentration account to cover activity in the subordinate account.

**Zoning Ordinance:** municipal regulation dividing land into districts and prescribing structural, architectural, and nature of use of buildings within these districts.

# NOTES

# NOTES

# NOTES

**NOTES**

# NOTES

# NOTES

# NOTES